THE ENCYCLOPAEDIA OF ISLAM

THE ENCYCLOPAEDIA OF ISLAM

NEW EDITION

PREPARED BY A NUMBER OF
LEADING ORIENTALISTS

EDITED BY

B. LEWIS, CH. PELLAT AND J. SCHACHT

ASSISTED BY J. BURTON-PAGE, C. DUMONT AND V. L. MÉNAGE AS
EDITORIAL SECRETARIES

UNDER THE PATRONAGE OF
THE INTERNATIONAL UNION OF ACADEMIES

VOLUME II

C—G

FOURTH IMPRESSION

TUTA SUB AEGIDE PALLAS · 1683 ·

LEIDEN
E.J. BRILL
1991

The articles in volumes one and two were published in fascicules from 1954 onwards, the dates of publication of the individual fascicules being:

1954:	fascs. 1-3,	vol. i, pp. 1-192	
1955:	fascs. 4,	vol. i, pp. 193-256	
1956:	fascs. 5-7,	vol. i, pp. 257-448	
1957:	fascs. 8-10,	vol. i, pp. 449-640	
1958:	fascs. 11-14,	vol. i, pp. 641-896	
1959:	fascs. 15-19,	vol. i, pp. 897-1216	
1960:	fascs. 20-23,	vol. i, pp. 1217-1359,	vol. ii, pp. 1-64
1961:	fascs. 24-26,	vol. ii, pp. 65-256	
1962:	fascs. 27-29,	vol. ii, pp. 257-448	
1963:	fascs. 30-34,	vol. ii, pp. 449-768	
1964:	fascs. 35-37,	vol. ii, pp. 769-960	
1965:	fascs. 38-40,	vol. ii, pp. 961-1146	

First impression 1965
Second impression 1970
Third impression 1983

ISBN 90 04 07026 5

PRINTED IN THE NETHERLANDS

AUTHORS OF ARTICLES IN VOLUMES ONE AND TWO

For the benefit of readers who may wish to follow up an individual contributor's articles, the Editors have decided to place after each contributor's name the numbers of the pages on which his signature appears. Academic but not other addresses are given (for a retired scholar, the place of his last known academic appointment). The following is a consolidated list and index of authors for the first two volumes of the *Encyclopaedia*.

In this list, names in square brackets are those of authors of articles reprinted or revised from the first edition of this Encyclopaedia or from the *Shorter Encyclopaedia of Islam*. An asterisk after the name of the author in the text denotes an article reprinted from the first edition which has been brought up to date by the Editorial Committee; where an article has been revised by a second author his name appears in the text within square brackets after the name of the original author.

M. Abdul Hai, University of Dacca. i, 1167.

H. H. Abdul Wahab, Tunis. i, 24, 207, 309, 863.

Mrs Fevziye Abdullah-Tansel, University of Istanbul. ii, 683.

A. Abel, Université Libre, Brussels. i, 923, 1055, 1277; ii, 59, 71, 77, 126, 128, 131, 199.

A. Adam, University of Aix-Marseilles. i, 506, 978; ii, 117, 727.

the late A. Adnan Adivar, Istanbul. i, 393.

Aziz Ahmad, University of Toronto. ii, 297, 421, 437, 1077.

M. Münir Aktepe, University of Istanbul. ii, 713, 714.

Ömer Faruk Akün, University of Istanbul. ii, 924.

P. Alexandre, École des Langues Orientales, Paris. ii, 10, 63.

F. R. Allchin, University of Cambridge. i, 857, 1010.

Miss Günay Alpay, University of Istanbul. ii, 997, 1043, 1138.

H. W. Alter, Dhahran. ii, 109, 569.

G. C. Anawati, Cairo. ii, 755, 837.

R. Anhegger, Istanbul. i, 175, 184, 481.

A. S. Bazmee Ansari, Central Institute of Islamic Research, Karachi. i, 431, 433, 702, 808, 809, 813, 822, 828, 856, 859, 952, 954, 957, 958, 970, 1005, 1012, 1018, 1020, 1022, 1023, 1043, 1053, 1137, 1161, 1166, 1192, 1193, 1194, 1196, 1197, 1202, 1203, 1210, 1219, 1254, 1300, 1330, 1331, 1348; ii, 29, 31, 47, 104, 132, 138, 140, 187, 189, 255, 276, 317, 337, 372, 379, 381, 392, 489, 491, 494, 501, 504, 523, 558, 598, 602, 609, 736, 797, 809, 814, 837, 869, 870, 872, 974, 1004, 1046, 1092, 1093, 1123, 1131, 1135.

W. ʿArafat, University of London. i, 1078, 1215, 1241, 1313; ii, 592.

the late R. R. Arat, University of Istanbul. i, 1038; ii, 69.

A. J. Arberry, University of Cambridge. i, 1089; ii, 600.

[C. van Arendonk, Leiden]. i, 258.

R. Arnaldez, University of Lyons. ii, 767, 775.

E. Ashtor, Hebrew University, Jerusalem. i, 1128.

M. R. al-Assouad, Paris. ii, 245.

J. Aubin, École pratique des Hautes Études, Paris. i, 148.

G. Awad, Baghdad. i, 423, 846, 866, 990, 1038.

D. Ayalon, Hebrew University, Jerusalem. i, 442, 444, 445, 446, 732, 765, 945, 947, 1061, 1325; ii, 24, 172, 357, 421, 955.

A. M. A. Azeez, Zahira College, Colombo. ii, 28.

Fr. Babinger, University of Munich. i, 97, 295, 309, 707, 739, 768, 790, 826, 993; ii, 203, 292.

F. Bajraktarević, University of Belgrade. i, 131.

J. M. S. Baljon Jr., University of Groningen. i, 288.

Ö. L. Barkan, University of Istanbul. ii, 83.

[W. Barthold, Leningrad]. i, 47, 71, 91, 102, 135, 241, 278, 312, 320, 354, 419, 421, 423, 425, 453, 508, 735, 750, 767, 839, 855, 857, 987, 993, 1002, 1010, 1011, 1028, 1033, 1106, 1130, 1134, 1135, 1139, 1188, 1296, 1311, 1312, 1338, 1343; ii, 3, 4, 19, 61, 89, 607, 622, 778, 793, 976, 978, 1043, 1118.

[H. Basset, Rabat]. i, 689.

[R. Basset, Algiers]. i, 50, 1179, 1187, 1315.

A. Bausani, Istituto Universitario Orientale, Naples. i, 304, 835, 847, 912, 918; ii, 397, 758, 784, 866, 971, 1001, 1036.

M. Cavid Baysun, University of Istanbul. i, 63, 291; ii, 210, 420, 490, 713.

L. Bazin, École des Langues Orientales, Paris. i, 1159.

S. de Beaurecueil, University of Kabul. i, 516.

[C. H. Becker, Berlin]. i, 9, 42, 52, 126, 729, 736, 788, 845, 870, 933, 938, 945, 972, 1016, 1043; ii, 103.

C. F. Beckingham, University of London. i, 95, 106, 719, 929, 933, 1038, 1043, 1280, 1283; ii, 57, 522, 788, 1121.

A. F. L. Beeston, University of Oxford. i, 103; ii, 895.

[A. Bel, Tlemcen]. i, 122, 123, 155.

N. Beldiceanu, Centre national de la Recherche scientifique, Paris. i, 1299; ii, 689.

[M. Ben Cheneb, Algiers]. i, 96, 795; ii, 216, 528, 838.

A. Bennigsen, École pratique des Hautes Études, Paris. i, 422, 460, 756, 855, 958, 967, 1000, 1002, 1005, 1028, 1084, 1189, 1190, 1297; ii, 19, 89, 697.

B. Ben Yahia, University of Tunis. ii, 60.

C. C. Berg, University of Leiden. i, 1012, 1014, 1015, 1100, 1221, 1259; ii, 19, 390, 497.

M. Berger, Princeton University. ii, 1048.

S. van den Bergh, London. i, 2, 179, 514, 785; ii, 102, 249, 494, 550.

Niyazi Berkes, McGill University, Montreal. ii, 1118.

J. Berque, Collège de France, Paris. i, 428, 661; ii, 413.

A. D. H. Bivar, University of London. ii. 978, 1096, 1139.

W. Björkman, Uppsala. i, 294; ii, 307.

R. Blachère, University of Paris. i, 10, 105, 106, 149, 316, 331, 345, 452, 522, 686, 751, 822, 845, 846, 870, 1082; ii, 246, 789, 808, 1033.

[J. F. Blumhardt, London]. i, 242.

[Tj. de Boer, Amsterdam]. i, 341, 350, 427, 736; ii, 555, 837.

D. J. Boilot, Cairo. i, 1238.

S. A. Bonebakker, Columbia University, New York. i, 145, 772; ii, 1011.

P. N. Boratav, École pratique des Hautes Études, Paris. ii, 549, 708.

C. E. Bosworth, University of St. Andrews. i, 938, 1232, 1241, 1283, 1358; ii, 365, 573, 894, 1050, 1084, 1104.

G.-H. Bousquet, University of Bordeaux. i, 170, 172, 826, 911; ii, 214, 1104.
the late H. Bowen, University of London. i, 132, 207, 212, 246, 247, 271, 286, 292, 318, 358, 388, 394, 398, 399, 658, 761, 778, 807, 855, 953, 1004, 1077, 1080, 1135, 1159.
J. A. Boyle, University of Manchester. i, 987, 1106, 1130, 1188, 1311, 1312; ii. 3, 4, 44, 393, 571, 607, 976, 1043, 1141.
H. W. Brands, Fulda. i, 332; ii, 217.
W. Braune, Free University, Berlin. i, 70.
W. C. Brice, University of Manchester. ii, 991.
[C. Brockelmann, Halle]. i, 99, 100, 108, 167, 321, 388, 393, 431, 485, 486, 516, 821, 822, 965, 966, 1132, 1296, 1333; ii, 167, 606, 886, 1106.
R. Brunschvig, University of Paris. i, 40, 340, 969, 1027, 1151.
[F. Buhl, Copenhagen]. i, 169, 194, 341, 344, 418, 630; ii, 354, 438 743, 1025.
J. Burton-Page, University of London. i, 926, 1024, 1048, 1193, 1201, 1204, 1210, 1324; ii, 11, 13, 101, 113, 121, 158, 162, 180, 183, 218, 219, 266, 274, 375, 391, 405, 438, 499, 503, 545, 628, 678, 695, 976, 981, 1130, 1131, 1135.
H. Busse, University of Hamburg. ii, 313, 804.
A. Caferoğlu, University of Istanbul. i, 194.
Cl. Cahen, University of Paris. i, 239, 256, 314, 421, 434, 437, 627, 630, 640, 659, 662, 667, 730, 732, 751, 807, 823, 844, 910, 940, 955, 983, 1053, 1147, 1161, 1191, 1292, 1309, 1337, 1357, 1358; ii, 5, 15, 66, 131, 145, 188, 231, 299, 345, 348, 349, 385, 456, 490, 509 562, 707, 749, 827, 965, 1045, 1110.
J. A. M. Caldwell, University of London. ii, 667.
the late K. Callard, McGill University, Montreal. ii, 546.
M. Canard, University of Algiers. i, 11, 449, 516, 638, 650, 688, 762, 790, 792, 825, 867, 940, 1075, 1103, 1229; ii, 39, 170, 239, 319, 345, 347, 348, 441, 454, 458, 485, 488, 491, 503, 524, 681, 862.
R. Capot-Rey, University of Algiers. i, 211, 307, 910, 1222; ii, 828.
J. Carnochan, University of London. ii, 479.
[B. Carra de Vaux, Paris]. i, 1072, 1085, 1242, 1284; ii, 133, 452, 553.
Mme H. Carrère d'Encausse, Paris. i, 422, 504, 624, 756, 855, 1190; ii, 206 397, 933.
W. Caskel, University of Cologne. i, 74, 203, 210, 341, 436, 442, 529, 684, 690, 921, 964; ii, 72.
[P. de Cénival, Rabat]. ii, 368.
E. Cerulli, Rome. i, 561.
M. Chailley, Bamako. i, 1009.
E. Chédeville, Paris. ii, 536.
Chafik Chehata, University of Cairo. i, 320; ii, 231, 390, 836.
J Chelhod, Centre national de la Recherche scientifique, Paris. ii, 248, 884.
G. L. M. Clauson, London. i, 557.
G. S. Colin, École des Langues Orientales, Paris. i, 98, 245, 503, 860, 961, 1016, 1032, 1037, 1057, 1058, 1225, 1315, 1350; ii, 18, 103, 131, 175, 308, 332, 368, 527, 874, 902, 979, 1122.
M. Colombe, École des Langues Orientales, Paris. i, 13, 46, 369.
C. S. Coon, University of Pennsylvania. i, 874.
R. Cornevin, Académie des Sciences d'Outre-mer, Paris. ii, 568, 943, 961, 970, 978, 1003, 1133.
the late Ph. de Cossé-Brissac, Paris. i, 68, 85.
N. J. Coulson, University of London. i, 1143.
[A. Cour, Constantine]. i, 167, 168; ii, 173, 511, 1139.
K. A. C. Creswell, American University, Cairo. i, 624, 832.
M. Cruz Hernández, University of Salamanca. i, 772.
Mme B. Cvetkova, Bulgarian Academy of Sciences, Sofia. ii, 914.
A. H. Dani, University of Peshawar. i, 720, 1015; ii, 32, 217, 297, 486, 751, 798.
Besim Darkot, University of Ankara. ii, 210, 689, 707.
J. David-Weill, École du Louvre, Paris. i, 349.
C. Collin Davies, University of Oxford. i, 88, 153, 239, 297, 317, 444, 628, 758, 768, 796, 864, 962, 970, 979, 1024, 1026, 1170, 1193, 1206, 1357; ii, 220, 567, 602, 610.
R. H. Davison, George Washington University, Washington D.C. ii, 936.
A. Decei University of Istanbul. i, 175, 311, 340; ii, 705.
A. Demeerseman, Tunis. ii, 437.
the late J. Deny, École des Langues Orientales, Paris. i, 65, 75, 298, 641, 836.
J. Despois, University of Paris. i, 366, 374, 460, 749, 763, 789, 809, 1050, 1169, 1197, 1232, 1247; ii, 378, 461, 464, 575, 603, 782, 877, 885, 993, 1010, 1023.
G. Deverdun, Saint-Germain-en-Laye. ii, 623, 1110, 1116.
A. Dietrich, University of Göttingen. i, 752; ii, 90, 93, 455.
B. Djurdjev, University of Sarajevo. i, 1018, 1165, 1275; ii, 682.
G. Douillet, Paris. ii, 954.
J. Dresch, University of Paris. i, 98.
C. E. Dubler, University of Zurich. i, 204, 243; ii, 350.
H. W. Duda, University of Vienna. i, 1197, 1221; ii, 720.
D. M. Dunlop, University of Columbia, New York. i, 738, 836, 837, 862, 864, 865, 921, 927, 931, 934, 936, 938, 967, 985, 1003, 1040, 1041, 1079, 1092, 1132, 1134, 1224, 1339; ii, 243, 291, 482, 522, 800, 1076.
A. A. Duri, University of Baghdad. i, 436, 439, 485, 908; ii, 166, 196, 197, 327.
A. S. Ehrenkreutz, University of Michigan. ii, 118, 214, 883.
Saleh A. El-Ali, University of Baghdad. i, 630, 760, 789, 1097; ii, 196, 197, 198.
J. Elfenbein, London. i, 1007.
C. Elgood, El-Obeid, Sudan. i, 381.
N. Elisséeff, Institut Français, Damascus. i, 194, 1030, 1102, 1138, 1281; ii, 291, 353, 541, 1106.
M. Émerit, University of Algiers. i, 282, 370.
M. Enamul Haq, Bengali Academy, Dacca. i, 1169.
Mme M. L. van Ess-Bremer, University of Frankfurt a. M. ii, 879.
R. Ettinghausen, Freer Gallery of Art, Washington. i, 1214.
T. Fahd, University of Strasbourg. ii, 242, 301, 377, 760, 917.
H. G. Farmer, Glasgow. i, 67, 1292; ii, 136, 621, 1011, 1028, 1075.
J. Faublée, École des Langues Orientales, Paris. i, 522.
A. Faure, University of Rabat. ii, 100.
L. Fekete, University of Budapest. i, 1171, 1286; ii, 716, 717, 1134.
W. J. Fischel, University of California, Berkeley. ii, 383.
H. Fleisch, Université St. Joseph, Beirut. i, 578; ii, 75, 101, 217, 233, 411, 490, 545, 725, 790, 835, 898, 927, 1027.
G. S. P. Freeman-Grenville, University of Ghana. ii, 129.
R. N. Frye, Harvard University. i, 626, 661, 680, 720, 756, 954, 1002, 1006, 1072, 1110, 1247, 1248, 1250,

1287, 1296; ii, 5, 113, 116, 142, 388, 553, 782, 806, 817, 818, 928, 975, 997, 1001, 1011, 1077, 1114.
J. W. FÜCK, University of Halle. i, 107, 453, 571, 712, 738, 827, 1082, 1089, 1241, 1348, 1358; ii, 884, 1005, 1024, 1072.
A. A. A. FYZEE, University of Jammu and Kashmir. i, 1255, 1257.
F. GABRIELI, University of Rome. i, 13, 99, 176, 196, 206, 307, 438, 681, 949, 987, 1166; ii, 428, 553.
L. GALAND, École des Langues Orientales, Paris. i, 1185.
Mme P. GALAND-PERNET, Centre national de la Recherche scientifique, Paris. i, 793.
E. GARCÍA GÓMEZ, University of Madrid. i, 130.
L. GARDET, Paris. i, 343, 352, 417, 427, 717, 1085, 1235, 1327; ii, 220, 227, 296, 382. 412, 452, 570, 606, 608, 618, 834, 892, 899, 931, 1026, 1078.
H. GÄTJE, University of Tübingen. ii, 480.
C. L. GEDDES, University of Colorado. i, 1215; ii, 441.
R. GHIRSHMAN, Institut Français, Teheran. i, 226.
M. A. GHUL, University of St. Andrews. i, 1133; ii, 730, 737, 756, 757.
H. A. R. GIBB, Harvard University. i, 43, 48, 54. 55, 66, 77, 85, 86, 119, 120, 140, 145, 150, 158, 159, 198, 209, 215, 233, 237, 241, 246, 279, 314, 327, 386, 445, 517, 599, 604, 662, 685, 714, 755, 782, 1309.
[F. GIESE, Breslau]. i, 287, 1161.
S. GLAZER, Washington. i, 126.
A. GLEDHILL, University of London. ii, 672.
H. W. GLIDDEN, Washington. i, 315, 784, 788.
N. GLUECK, Cincinnati. i, 558.
Mlle A. M. GOICHON, University of Paris. ii, 97.
S. D. GOITEIN, University of Pennsylvania. i, 1022; ii, 594, 970, 989.
M. TAYYİB GÖKBİLGİN, University of Istanbul. i, 433, 1191; ii, 184, 200, 443, 637, 686, 705.
[I. GOLDZIHER, Budapest]. i, 95, 204, 257, 258, 346, 688, 736, 772, 823, 851; ii, 97, 167, 419, 872, 887, 1099.
ABDÜLBÂKİ GÖLPINARLI, Istanbul. ii, 543, 735.
H. L. GOTTSCHALK, University of Vienna. i, 157, 766; ii, 331.
[E. GRAEFE, Hamburg]. ii, 370.
E. GRÄF, University of Cologne. i, 483.
A. GROHMANN, Academy of Sciences, Vienna. i, 527; ii, 541.
G. E. VON GRUNEBAUM, University of California, Los Angeles. i, 12, 115, 150, 405, 690, 983, 1116; ii, 827.
the late A. GUILLAUME, University of London. i, 108.
VEDAD GÜNYOL, Istanbul. ii, 476.
IRFAN HABIB, Muslim University, Aligarh. ii, 910.
MOHAMMAD HABIB, Muslim University, Aligarh. i, 769.
[A. HAFFNER, Vienna]. i, 345.
G. LANKESTER HARDING, Amman. i, 448.
P. HARDY, University of London. i, 199, 393, 426, 445, 507, 680, 686, 710, 733, 780, 848, 857, 915, 940, 1037, 1155; ii, 274, 379, 382, 567, 806, 816, 923, 1085.
J. B. HARRISON, University of London. i, 606, 625, 848; ii, 219, 322.
[R. HARTMANN, Berlin]. i, 706, 711, 737, 931, 933; ii, 251, 357, 573, 605, 609, 712, 947, 1141.
W. HARTNER, University of Frankfurt a.M. i, 133, 728; ii, 362, 502, 763.
L. P. HARVEY, University of London. i, 405.
HADI HASAN, Muslim University, Aligarh. ii, 764.
R. L. HEADLEY, Dhahran. i, 710, 759, 1098, 1141, 1313; ii, 177, 354, 569.
[J. HELL, Erlangen]. i, 3, 192, 336, 344, 921, 997.
[B. HELLER, Budapest]. i, 521.
[E. HERZFELD, Chicago]. i, 1110. 1236, 1248.
R. HERZOG, University of Freiburg i. Br. ii, 1010.
U. HEYD, Hebrew University, Jerusalem. i, 837, 1357; ii, 519, 604, 805.
R. L. HILL, University of Durham. i, 976.
the late S. HILLELSON, London. i, 2, 50, 169, 735.
HILMY AHMAD, University of Cairo. i, 150.
W. HINZ, University of Göttingen. ii, 232, 813.
P. K. HITTI, Princeton University. ii, 404, 472.
M. G. S. HODGSON, University of Chicago. i, 51, 354, 962, 1100, 1117, 1359; ii, 98, 137, 218, 362, 375, 441, 452, 485, 634, 882, 1022, 1026, 1095.
W. HOENERBACH, University of Bonn. i, 96.
P. M. HOLT, University of London. i, 765, 930, 962, 1029, 1157, 1158, 1172, 1240; ii, 109, 125, 137, 233, 292, 352, 467, 615, 697, 768, 828, 873, 875, 945, 1042, 1111, 1114.
[E. HONIGMANN, Brussels]. i, 1233.
J. F. P. HOPKINS, University of Cambridge. ii, 146, 1077.
[P. HORN, Strasbourg]. i, 1342.
[J. HOROVITZ, Frankfurt a.M.]. i, 14, 52, 113, 116, 133, 140, 955; ii, 74, 602.
A. H. HOURANI, University of Oxford. ii, 429.
F. HOURS, Université St. Joseph, Beirut. i, 1349.
[M. TH. HOUTSMA, Utrecht]. i, 84, 88, 111, 113, 120, 1309.
I. HRBEK, Oriental Institute, Prague. i, 1308.
[CL. HUART Paris]. i, 4, 60, 94, 109, 199, 241, 247, 313, 434, 939, 1012, 1013, 1073, 1139; ii, 26, 100, 179, 323, 422, 439, 542, 624, 809, 810, 882, 920, 1120.
A. HUICI MIRANDA, Valencia. i, 162, 166, 606, 634, 658, 864, 988, 991, 997, 1012, 1055, 1083, 1089, 1092, 1129, 1150, 1249, 1288, 1310, 1326, 1337, 1343; ii, 112, 353, 389, 486, 516, 525, 526, 542, 744, 915, 924, 998, 1009, 1014, 1038.
A. J. W. HUISMAN, Leiden. i, 131.
G. W. B. HUNTINGFORD, University of London. i, 992; ii, 175, 545.
H. R. IDRIS, University of Bordeaux. i, 860, 1309, 1341.
HALİL İNALCIK, University of Ankara. i, 292, 293, 658, 808, 1000, 1119, 1167, 1170, 1253, 1287, 1304, 1336; ii, 25, 32, 33, 116, 119, 148, 179, 420, 529, 531, 566, 613, 615, 712, 715, 724, 909, 915, 987, 1046, 1047, 1091, 1098, 1114, 1121.
SH. INAYATULLAH, University of the Panjab, Lahore. i, 59, 66, 69, 242, 260, 283, 298, 317, 400, 430, 431, 509, 808, 919, 1011, 1026.
[W. IRVINE]. i, 769.
FAHİR İZ, University of Istanbul. i, 299, 699, 956, 1165; ii, 99, 159, 200, 201, 206, 221, 223, 397, 440, 693, 708, 738, 758, 833, 865, 878, 885, 921, 931, 990, 1000.
[G. JACOB, Kiel]. ii, 755.
K. JAHN, University of Utrecht. ii, 14.
the late A. JEFFERY, Columbia University, New York. i, 114, 136, 680, 707, 774, 796, 810; ii, 293.
T. M. JOHNSTONE, University of London. ii, 1056.
J. JOMIER, Cairo. i, 444, 821, 1299; ii, 132, 276, 419, 438, 764, 892, 934, 959.
D. H. JONES, University of London. ii, 10, 975.
J. M. B. JONES, American University, Cairo. i, 1019.
[TH. W. JUYNBOLL, Utrecht]. i, 186, 188, 320, 337, 743, 867; ii, 441, 783, 790.
ABD AL-HAFEZ KAMAL, Dhahran. ii, 937.
ABDÜLKADİR KARAHAN, University of Istanbul. ii, 75, 702, 869, 939.
E. Z. KARAL, University of Ankara. i, 57.
A. G. KARAM, American University, Beirut. ii, 365, 796, 802.
IRFAN KAWAR [see SHAHÎD].

Mrs N. R. Keddie, University of California, Los Angeles. ii, 883.
E. Kedourie, University of London. ii, 515.
W. E. N. Kensdale, London. ii, 1146.
the late R. A. Kern, University of Leiden. i, 267 (*Ahl-i Wāris*).
M. Khadduri, Johns Hopkins University, Washington D.C. ii, 649, 660, 662, 668.
M. Khalafallah, University of Alexandria. i, 569, 858.
W. A. S. Khalidi, American University, Beirut. i, 60, 352, 1110, 1152; ii, 167.
H. Kindermann, University of Cologne. i, 683, 684.
J. S. Kirkman, Mombasa. ii, 983.
H. J. Kissling, University of Munich. i, 95, 313, 869, 1008.
M. J. Kister, Hebrew University, Jerusalem. i, 343, 345, 1248; ii, 481, 990.
Mme E. Köcher, Berlin. ii, 428.
the late L. Kopf, Jerusalem. i, 215, 239, 795, 951, 961, 1010; ii, 71, 76, 108, 223, 248, 275, 455, 497.
M. Fuad Köprülü, University of Istanbul. i, 241, 850, 862.
[T. Kowalski, Cracow]. i, 1222; ii, 203.
the late J. Kraemer, University of Erlangen. i, 1230.
[I. Kratschkowsky, Leningrad]. ii, 796.
[P. Kraus, Cairo]. ii, 359.
R. F. Kreutel, Vienna. i, 1157.
Kasim Kufrevi, Ankara. i, 1235.
E. Kühnel, Free University, Berlin. i, 561.
E. Kuran, Middle East Technical University, Ankara. i, 843; ii, 534, 694, 728, 878, 997.
F. Kussmaul, Stuttgart. i, 880.
Miss A. K. S. Lambton, University of London. i, 523, 978, 1130; ii, 153, 163, 174, 254, 336, 436, 657, 839, 906.
C. J. Lamm, Öregrund, Sweden. i, 1221.
[H. Lammens, Beirut]. i, 108, 194, 436, 920, 1283, 1344; ii, 275, 360.
J. M. Landau, Hebrew University, Jerusalem. i, 142; ii, 40.
D. M. Lang, University of London. i, 1217; ii, 1118.
H. Laoust, Collège de France, Paris. i, 277, 949, 1040; ii, 1093.
J. D. Latham, University of Manchester. i, 497.
J. Lecerf, École des Langues Orientales, Paris. i 306, 700, 1102, 1139; ii, 100, 189, 559, 835.
Mme M. Ch. LeCœur, Paris. i, 1258; ii, 368.
G. Lecomte, École des Langues Orientales, Paris. ii, 764.
R. Le Tourneau, University of Aix-Marseilles. i, 47, 56, 58, 91, 245, 679, 687, 1045, 1149, 1191, 1238, 1281, 1332; ii, 57, 134, 160, 173, 189, 373, 521, 821, 836, 945, 1009.
the late E. Lévi-Provençal, University of Paris. i, 7, 11, 12, 44, 49, 58, 70, 76, 80, 84, 85, 86, 94, 109, 121, 122, 135, 139, 141, 157, 159, 242, 251, 280, 289, 291, 315, 321, 348, 352, 390, 405, 419, 422, 496, 497, 986, 1012, 1092, 1300.
R. Levy, University of Cambridge. i, 524.
T. Lewicki, University of Cracow. i, 57, 120, 121, 125, 134, 139, 141, 167, 1288; ii, 141, 369, 441, 515.
B. Lewin, University of Gothenburg. i, 125, 214, 345, 719, 737; ii, 300.
B. Lewis, University of London. i, 23, 102, 134, 290, 389, 400, 403, 505, 679, 693, 697, 711, 712, 713, 787, 795, 796, 825, 832, 838, 843, 850, 915, 921, 975, 1032, 1042, 1082, 1091, 1148, 1156, 1157, 1171, 1214, 1229, 1236, 1280; ii, 6, 15, 26, 74, 81, 83, 165, 208, 210, 277, 301, 322, 339, 447, 466, 532, 595, 647, 678, 687, 694, 696.
G. L. Lewis, University of Oxford. i, 287, 300, 625, 792, 1137, 1207; ii, 41, 533, 840.
I. M. Lewis, University of London. i, 1173.
Y. Linant de Bellefonds, Centre national de la Recherche scientifique, Paris. ii, 164, 833.
the late E. Littmann, University of Tübingen. i, 145, 176, 281, 364, 780, 786.
L. Lockhart, University of Cambridge. i, 5, 14, 95, 247, 305, 353, 358, 393, 459, 711, 1008, 1010, 1013, 1043, 1070, 1233, 1342; ii, 181, 300, 351, 452, 486, 534, 812, 824, 926, 1136.
R. Loewenthal, Washington D.C. ii, 479.
O. Löfgren, University of Uppsala. i, 169, 182, 195, 256, 278, 355, 446, 524, 738, 763, 767, 782, 828, 830, 938, 1023, 1128, 1133, 1134; ii, 168, 218, 223, 996, 1096.
Sh. T. Lokhandwalla, University of Edinburgh. i, 173.
F. Løkkegaard, University of Copenhagen. i, 966; ii, 870, 1006, 1012.
J. Lombard, Institut français d'Afrique noire, Dakar. ii, 94.
S. H. Longrigg, Tunbridge Wells. i, 406, 424, 431, 461, 845, 871, 952, 962, 968, 1030, 1050, 1087, 1163, 1211; ii, 77, 91, 101, 103, 113, 184, 251, 253, 340, 343, 371, 402, 571, 624, 872, 1045.
[M. Longworth Dames, Guildford]. i, 223, 230, 231, 233; ii, 206, 929.
H. Louis, University of Munich. i, 465.
R. J. McCarthy, Al-Hikma University, Baghdad. i, 959.
[D. B. Macdonald, Hartford, Conn.]. i, 90; ii, 131, 165, 182, 370, 548, 756, 932, 1026, 1079.
D. N. MacKenzie, University of London. i, 863, 920, 1072; ii, 1140.
J. Mandaville, Dhahran. ii, 248, 492, 1024.
A. J. Mango, London. i, 721; ii, 476.
S. E. Mann, University of London. i, 651.
R. Mantran, University of Aix-Marseilles. i, 268, 381, 391, 394, 395, 396, 398, 630, 658, 733, 735, 790; ii, 16, 461.
S. Maqbul Ahmad, Muslim University, Aligarh. i, 991; ii, 352, 587.
the late G. Marçais, University of Algiers. i, 94, 124, 130, 138, 249, 367, 459, 512, 533, 661, 680, 685, 700, 950, 1024, 1206, 1229, 1300, 1347; ii, 115, 557, 748, 864, 957, 1008.
Ph. Marçais, École des Langues Orientales, Paris. i, 379, 515, 583, 705, 786.
the late W. Marçais, Collège de France, Paris. i, 791; ii, 175, 405, 545.
[D. S. Margoliouth, Oxford]. i, 952.
Mrs E. Marin, New York. i, 53; ii, 623.
Miss P. A. Marr, Washington D. C. ii, 160, 573, 619.
H. Massé, École des Langues Orientales, Paris. i, 60, 94, 120, 137, 152, 505, 522, 626, 686, 720, 827, 939, 955, 1011, 1012, 1013, 1073, 1342, 1359; ii, 17, 74, 100, 133, 179, 323, 406, 422, 439, 473, 548, 756, 761, 794, 798, 810, 920, 1143.
the late L. Massignon, Collège de France, Paris. i, 153, 277.
C. D. Matthews, University of Texas. i, 1091; ii, 93, 631.
R. Mauny, University of Paris. ii, 252.
F. Meier, University of Basle. i, 234, 284, 347, 961, 1246.
G. Meillon, École des Langues Orientales, Paris. ii, 9.
Mme I. Mélikoff, Centre national de la Recherche scientifique, Paris. i, 783, 1104; ii, 111, 205, 420, 600, 720, 721, 990, 1045.

701, 707, 909, 1068, 1088; ii, 68, 420, 446, 598, 783, 1135.
AYDIN SAYILI, University of Ankara. ii, 1120.
[A. SCHAADE, Hamburg]. i, 51, 107, 150, 195, 983; ii, 276, 428, 480.
J. SCHACHT, Columbia University, New York. i, 5, 124, 137, 151, 152, 155, 165, 209, 250, 255, 257, 259, 267, 310, 321, 423, 430, 692, 694, 730, 736, 773, 1020, 1113, 1242; ii, 91, 183, 373, 603, 605, 727, 887, 891.
[J. SCHLEIFER]. i, 345; ii, 218, 223.
[M. SCHMITZ]. i, 991.
M. SCHRAMM, University of Frankfurt a.M. ii, 362 (co-author of AL-DJABR WA 'L-MUKĀBALA, see Addenda *ad loc.*).
BEDİ N. ŞEHSUVAROĞLU, University of Istanbul. i, 1226.
[M. SELIGSOHN]. i, 404.
R. SELLHEIM, University of Frankfurt a.M. ii, 729.
[C. F. SEYBOLD, Tübingen]. i, 446, 1055, 1083, 1092, 1343; ii, 72, 112, 353.
F. SEZGİN, University of Frankfurt a.M. ii, 126.
the late M. SHAFI, University of the Panjab, Lahore. i, 61, 68, 72, 91, 937, 1124, 1284, 1329, 1330; ii, 49, 73, 85, 222.
IRFAN SHAHÎD, Georgetown University, Washington, D.C. i, 1250; ii, 354, 365, 1021.
S. J. SHAW, Harvard University. i, 965; ii, 128, 948.
G. E. SHAYYAL, University of Alexandria. i, 990.
H. K. SHERWANI, Hyderabad, India. i, 925, 1015, 1047, 1201; ii, 99, 180, 1119.
MUSTAFA AL-SHIHABI, Arab Academy, Damascus. ii, 901.
D. SINOR, University of Indiana. i, 913, 1249.
W. CANTWELL SMITH, Harvard University. i, 303, 443.
J. M. SMITH, Jr., University of California, Berkeley. ii, 402.
Miss MARGARET SMITH, London. i, 1248; ii, 242, 936.
[M. SOBERNHEIM, Berlin]. ii, 6.
J. DE SOMOGYI, Harvard University. ii, 216.
H. T. SORLEY, Salisbury, S. Rhodesia. i, 1195.
D. SOURDEL, University of Bordeaux. i, 208, 272, 279, 434, 447, 453, 844, 987, 1033, 1036, 1046, 1047 1093, 1141, 1209, 1287, 1293, 1298, 1312; ii, 72, 127, 195, 197, 198, 199, 354, 389, 458, 461, 462, 498, 568, 602, 624, 626, 730, 731, 732, 743, 913, 1025, 1057, 1081.
Mme J. SOURDEL-THOMINE, École pratique des Hautes Études, Paris. i, 461, 787, 953, 971, 989, 996, 998, 1017, 1025, 1073, 1139, 1140, 1141, 1149, 1214, 1292, 1293, 1318, 1345, 1358; ii, 163, 340, 347, 360, 535, 555, 556, 778, 991, 1055.
T. G. P. SPEAR, University of Cambridge. i, 914.
O. SPIES, University of Bonn. ii, 486, 1020.
B. SPULER, University of Hamburg. i, 121, 313, 314, 320, 330, 419, 423, 457, 505, 530, 531, 608, 701, 722, 750, 767, 784, 839, 894, 950, 952, 953, 984, 996, 1002, 1008, 1011, 1108, 1135, 1240, 1343; ii, 2, 15, 19, 47, 61, 67, 75, 201, 253, 366, 446, 607, 622, 737, 778, 793, 916, 928, 943, 982, 1053, 1112, 1117, 1142, 1143.
S. M. STERN, University of Oxford. i, 2, 9, 48, 60, 74, 87, 96, 104, 125, 127, 130, 149, 152, 160, 164, 216, 236, 315, 345, 348, 392, 425, 426, 435, 440, 484.
[M. STRECK, Jena]. i, 3, 133, 184, 252, 426, 427, 459, 485, 517, 603, 608, 659, 685, 711, 863 864, 871, 952, 968, 1030, 1050, 1097, 1211, 1233, 1234; ii, 107, 357, 406, 574.
G. STRENZIOK, University of Cologne. i, 813.
FARUK SÜMER, University of Ankara. i, 1117, 1133, 1159; ii, 20, 614, 724.
[K. SÜSSHEIM, Munich]. i, 287, 309, 310, 381, 777.
[H. SUTER, Zurich]. i, 159, 380, 858; ii, 357, 378, 793.
FR. TAESCHNER, University of Münster. i, 184, 200, 244, 251, 252, 312, 313, 323, 324, 325, 330, 355, 424, 432, 462, 480, 481, 511, 518, 603, 626, 667, 698, 699, 777, 778, 779, 783, 792, 794, 838, 969, 970; ii, 14, 26, 57, 62, 200, 208, 446, 590, 692, 693, 694, 695, 697, 705, 710, 712, 715, 969, 983, 987, 1138.
the late A. H. TANPINAR, University of Istanbul. i, 62.
S. H. TAQIZADEH, Teheran. ii, 400.
A. N. TARLAN, University of Istanbul. i, 1083, 1302.
M. C. ŞIHABEDDÎN TEKİNDAĞ, University of Istanbul. ii, 636.
H. TERRASSE, Casa de Velázquez, Madrid. i, 358, 1321; ii, 823, 1020.
A. TIETZE, University of California, Los Angeles. i, 245, 293, 391, 826; ii, 443.
H. R. TINKER, University of London. i, 1333.
Z. V. TOGAN, University of Istanbul. i, 1077; ii, 981, 995.
the late L. TORRES BALBÁS, University of Madrid. i, 501.
J. S. TRIMINGHAM, American University, Beirut. i, 287, 297, 764; ii, 974.
A. S. TRITTON, University of London. i, 187, 196, 258, 264, 325, 403, 660, 851, 909, 1093, 1326; ii, 442, 518, 603, 626.
the late R. TSCHUDI, University of Basle. i, 1163.
T. TYAN, Université St Joseph, Beirut. i, 210, 1114; ii, 172, 343, 540, 866, 996.
A. L. UDOVITCH, Yale University. ii, 769.
E. ULLENDORFF, University of London. i, 1220; ii, 317, 355, 710.
the late FAİK REŞİT UNAT, Ankara. ii, 630.
İ. H. UZUNÇARŞILI, University of Istanbul. i, 704, 949, 1256, 1278, 1279; ii, 62, 202.
G. VAJDA, École pratique des Hautes Études, Paris. i, 266, 404, 429, 481, 811, 984, 1230, 1298; ii, 113, 242, 293, 406, 918.
E. DE VAUMAS, Paris. ii, 948.
Mme L. VECCIA VAGLIERI, Istituto Universitario Orientale, Naples. i, 41, 54, 194, 337, 386, 696, 704, 1071, 1243, 1244; ii, 90, 162, 241, 366, 372, 416, 601, 626, 727, 745, 850, 870, 994.
J. VERNET, University of Barcelona. i, 516, 1250; ii, 378, 793, 1022.
F. S. VIDAL, Dhahran. i, 1299; ii, 868, 1001.
F. VIRÉ, Centre national de la Recherche scientifique, Paris. i, 1155; ii, 743, 775, 787, 1038.
[K. VOLLERS, Jena]. i, 281, 396.
P. VOORHOEVE, Leiden. i, 42, 88, 92, 743; ii, 183, 550.
E. WAGNER, Göttingen. i, 144.
the late J. WALKER, British Museum, London. i, 3.
J. WALSH, University of Edinburgh. i, 733; ii, 8, 20, 401, 630, 867, 879, 1141.
R. WALZER, University of Oxford. i, 236, 327, 329, 633, 1340; ii, 403, 781, 949.
J. WANSBROUGH, University of London. ii, 782.
W. MONTGOMERY WATT, University of Edinburgh. i, 5, 9, 42, 44, 53, 80, 84, 111, 115, 137, 151, 153, 169, 204, 267, 308, 314, 336, 438, 454, 515, 633, 695, 696, 713, 728, 772, 865, 868, 892; ii, 95, 365, 388, 604, 873, 1041.
H. WEHR, University of Münster. i, 573.
W. F. WEIKER, Rutgers University, N.J. ii, 597.
the late G. WEIL, Hebrew University, Jerusalem. i, 98, 186, 436, 677, 735.
[T. H. WEIR, Glasgow]. ii, 128.
[A. J. WENSINCK, Leiden]. i, 187, 445, 451, 452, 482, 604, 686, 690, 692, 693, 705, 710, 922, 958, 1230; ii, 918.
G. E. WHEELER, London. i, 418; ii, 1118.

C. E. J. Whitting, London. i, 180, 1261.
[E. Wiedemann, Erlangen]. i, 486.
G. Wiet, Collège de France, Paris. i, 14, 168, 186, 197, 198, 216, 330, 392, 418, 448, 532, 926, 1016, 1039, 1051, 1054, 1126, 1218, 1288, 1341, 1343; ii, 73, 97, 99, 106.
D. N. Wilber, Princeton, N.J. i, 426, 506, 659, 1014; ii, 107, 135.
I. Wilks, University of Ghana. ii, 1004.
H. von Wissmann, University of Tübingen. i, 880, 889.
M. E. Yapp, University of London. ii, 629, 638.
Yar Muhammad Khan, University of Sind, Hyderabad, Pakistan. i, 1069.
Tahsin Yazici, University of Istanbul. ii, 1137.
the late Mükrimin H. Yinanç, University of Istanbul. ii, 346.
Hüseyin G. Yurdaydin, University of Ankara. ii, 880.
[G. Yver, Algiers]. i, 282, 307, 460, 605, 762, 771, 1088, 1174, 1176, 1178, 1197, 1300; ii, 538, 1096.
A. Zajączkowski, University of Warsaw. ii, 203, 316, 795.
W. Zajączkowski, University of Cracow. ii, 972.
M. A. Zaki Badawi, University of Malaya. i, 980.
the late Zaky M. Hassan, Cairo. i, 279.
A. H. Zarrinkub, University of Teheran. ii, 883.
[K. V. Zetterstéen, Uppsala]. i, 3, 5, 12, 13, 43, 44, 45, 49, 50, 53, 57, 58, 78, 102, 108, 271, 381, 446, 454, 1025, 1313; ii, 391.
L. Zolondek, University of Kentucky. ii, 249.
C. K. Zurayk, American University, Beirut. ii, 427.

ABBREVIATED TITLES
OF SOME OF THE MOST OFTEN QUOTED WORKS

Abu'l-Fidā', *Taḳwīm* = *Taḳwīm al-buldān*, ed. J.-T. Reinaud and M. de Slane, Paris 1840

Abu'l-Fidā', *Taḳwīm*, tr. = *Géographie d'Aboulféda, traduite de l'arabe en français*; vol. i, ii/1 by Reinaud, Paris 1848; vol. ii/2 by St. Guyard, 1883

Aghānī[1] or [2] or [3] = Abu'l-Faradj al-Iṣfahānī, *al-Aghānī*; [1]Būlāḳ 1285; [2]Cairo 1323; [3]Cairo 1345-

Aghānī, Tables = *Tables alphabétiques du Kitāb al-aghānī*, rédigées par I. Guidi, Leiden 1900

Aghānī, Brünnow = *The XXIst vol. of the Kitāb al-Aghānī*, ed. R. E. Brünnow, Leiden 1883

ʿAlī Djewād = *Memālik-i ʿOthmāniyyeniñ taʾrīkh we djughrāfiyā lughāti*, Istanbul 1313-17/1895-9.

Anbārī, *Nuzha* = *Nuzhat al-alibbāʾ fī ṭabaḳāt al-udabāʾ*, [1]Cairo 1294; [2]Stockholm, etc. 1963.

ʿAwfī, *Lubāb* = *Lubāb al-albāb*, ed. E. G. Browne, London-Leiden 1903-6

Babinger = F. Babinger, *Die Geschichtsschreiber der Osmanen und ihre Werke*, 1st ed., Leiden 1927

Baghdādī, *Farḳ* = *al-Farḳ bayn al-firaḳ*, ed. Muḥammad Badr, Cairo 1328/1910

Balādhurī, *Futūḥ* = *Futūḥ al-buldān*, ed. M. J. de Goeje, Leiden 1866

Balādhurī, *Ansāb* = *Ansāb al-ashrāf*, i, ed. M. Hamidullah, Cairo 1960; iv B, v, ed. M. Schlössinger and S. D. F. Goitein, Jerusalem 1936-38

Barkan, *Kanunlar* = Ömer Lûtfi Barkan, *XV ve XVI inci asırlarda Osmanlı Imparatorluğunda ziraî ekonominin hukukî ve malî esasları, I. Kanunlar*, Istanbul 1943

Barthold, *Turkestan* = W. Barthold, *Turkestan down to the Mongol invasion*, London 1928 (GMS, N.S. v)

Barthold, *Turkestan*[2] = the same, 2nd edition, London 1958

Blachère, *Litt.* = R. Blachère, *Histoire de la littérature arabe*, i-ii, Paris 1952-64

Brockelmann, I, II = C. Brockelmann, *Geschichte der arabischen Literatur*, zweite den Supplementbänden angepasste Auflage, Leiden 1943-49

Brockelmann, S I, II, III = *G. d. a. L.*, Erster (zweiter, dritter) Supplementband, Leiden 1937-42

Browne, i = E. G. Browne, *A literary history of Persia, from the earliest times until Firdawsi*, London 1902

Browne, ii = *A literary history of Persia, from Firdawsi to Saʿdi*, London 1908

Browne, iii = *A history of Persian literature under Tartar Dominion*, Cambridge 1920

Browne, iv = *A history of Persian literature in modern times*, Cambridge 1924

Caetani, *Annali* = L. Caetani, *Annali dell'Islam*, Milan 1905-26

Chauvin, *Bibliographie* = V. Chauvin, *Bibliographie des ouvrages arabes et relatifs aux Arabes*, Lille 1892

Ḍabbī = *Bughyat al-multamis fī taʾrīkh ridjāl ahl al-Andalus*, ed. F. Codera and J. Ribera, Madrid 1885 (BAH III)

Damīrī = *Ḥayāt al-ḥayawān* (quoted according to titles of articles)

Dawlatshāh = *Tadhkirat al-shuʿarāʾ*, ed. E. G. Browne, London-Leiden 1901

Dhahabī, *Ḥuffāẓ* = al-Dhahabī, *Tadhkirat al-ḥuffāẓ*, 4 vols., Hyderabad 1315 H.

Djuwaynī = *Taʾrīkh-i Djihān-gushā*, ed. Muḥammad Ḳazwīnī, Leiden 1906-37 (GMS XVI)

Djuwaynī-Boyle = *The history of the World-conqueror*, by ʿAṭā-Malik Djuwaynī, trans. J. A. Boyle, 2 vols., Manchester 1958

Dozy, *Notices* = R. Dozy, *Notices sur quelques manuscrits arabes*, Leiden 1847-51

Dozy, *Recherches*[3] = *Recherches sur l'histoire et la littérature de l'Espagne pendant le moyen-âge*, third edition, Paris-Leiden 1881

Dozy, *Suppl.* = R. Dozy, *Supplément aux dictionnaires arabes*, Leiden 1881 (anastatic reprint Leiden-Paris 1927)

Fagnan, *Extraits* = E. Fagnan, *Extraits inédits relatifs au Maghreb*, Alger 1924

Farhang = Razmārā and Nawtāsh, *Farhang-i djughrāfiyā-yi Īrān*, Tehran 1949-1953

Fihrist = Ibn al-Nadīm, *K. al-Fihrist*, ed. G. Flügel, Leipzig 1871-72

Firishta = Muḥammad Ḳāsim Firishta, *Gulshan-i Ibrāhīmī*, lith. Bombay 1832

Gesch. des Qor. = Th. Nöldeke, *Geschichte des Qorāns*, new edition by F. Schwally, G. Bergsträsser and O. Pretzl, 3 vols., Leipzig 1909-38

Gibb, *Ottoman Poetry* = E. J. W. Gibb, *A history of Ottoman poetry*, London 1900-09

Gibb-Bowen = H. A. R. Gibb and Harold Bowen, *Islamic society and the West*, London 1950-1957

Goldziher, *Muh. St.* = I. Goldziher, *Muhammedanische Studien*, 2 vols., Halle 1888-90

Goldziher, *Vorlesungen* = I. Goldziher, *Vorlesungen über den Islam*, Heidelberg 1910

Goldziher, *Vorlesungen*[2] = 2nd ed., Heidelberg 1925

Goldziher, *Dogme* = *Le dogme et la loi de l'Islam*, tr. F. Arin, Paris 1920

Ḥādjdjī Khalīfa, *Djihān-nümā* = Istanbul 1145/1732

Ḥādjdjī Khalīfa = *Kashf al-ẓunūn*, ed. Ş. Yaltkaya and Kilisli Rifat Bilge, Istanbul 1941-43

Ḥādjdjī Khalīfa, ed. Flügel = *K. al-ẓ.*, Leipzig 1835-58

Ḥamd Allāh Mustawfī, *Nuzha* = *Nuzhat al-ḳulūb*, ed. G. Le Strange, Leiden 1913-19 (GMS XXIII)

Hamdānī = *Ṣifat Djazīrat al-ʿArab*, ed. D. H. Müller, Leiden 1884-91

Hammer-Purgstall, *GOR* = J. von Hammer(-Purgstall), *Geschichte des Osmanischen Reiches*, Pest 1828-35

Hammer-Purgstall, *GOR*[2] = the same, 2nd ed. Pest 1840

Hammer-Purgstall, *Histoire* = the same, trans. by J. J. Hellert, 18 vols., Bellizard [etc.], Paris [etc.], 1835-43

Hammer-Purgstall, *Staatsverfassung* = J. von Hammer, *Des Osmanischen Reichs Staatsverfassung und Staatsverwaltung*, 2 vols., Vienna 1815 (repr. 1963)

Houtsma, *Recueil* = M. Th. Houtsma, *Recueil des textes relatifs à l'histoire des Seldjoucides*, Leiden 1886-1902

Ḥudūd al-ʿālam = *The regions of the world*, translated by V. Minorsky, London 1937 (GMS, n.s. xi)
Ibn al-Abbār = *K. Takmilat al-Ṣila*, ed. F. Codera, Madrid 1887-89 (BHA V-VI)
Ibn al-Athīr = *K. al-Kāmil*, ed. C. J. Tornberg, Leiden 1851-76
Ibn al-Athīr, trad. Fagnan = *Annales du Maghreb et de l'Espagne*, tr. E. Fagnan, Algiers 1901
Ibn Bashkuwāl = *K. al-Ṣila fī akhbār aʾimmat al-Andalus*, ed. F. Codera, Madrid 1883 (BHA II)
Ibn Baṭṭūṭa = *Voyages d'Ibn Batouta*. Arabic text, ed. with Fr. tr. by C. Defrémery and B. R. Sanguinetti, 4 vols., Paris 1853-58
Ibn al-Faḳīh = *Mukhtaṣar K. al-Buldān*, ed. M. J. De Goeje, Leiden 1886 (BGA V)
Ibn Ḥawḳal = *K. Ṣūrat al-arḍ*, ed. J. H. Kramers, Leiden 1938-39 (BGA II, 2nd edition)
Ibn Ḥawḳal-Kramers-Wiet = Ibn Hauqal, *Configuration de la terre*, trans. J. H. Kramers and G. Wiet, Beirut 1964, 2 vols.
Ibn Hishām = *Sīra*, ed. F. Wüstenfeld, Göttingen 1859-60
Ibn ʿIdhārī = *K. al-Bayān al-mughrib*, ed. G. S. Colin and E. Lévi-Provençal, Leiden 1948-51; vol. iii, ed. E. Lévi-Provençal, Paris 1930
Ibn al-ʿImād, *Shadharāt* = *Shadharāt al-dhahab fī akhbār man dhahab*, Cairo 1350-51 (quoted according to years of obituaries)
Ibn Khaldūn, *ʿIbar* = *K. al-ʿIbar wa-dīwān al-mubtadaʾ wa 'l-khabar etc.*, Būlāḳ 1284
Ibn Khaldūn, *Muḳaddima* = *Prolégomènes d'Ebn Khaldoun*, ed. E. Quatremère, Paris 1858-68 (*Notices et Extraits* XVI-XVIII)
Ibn Khaldūn-Rosenthal = *The Muqaddimah*, trans. from the Arabic by Franz Rosenthal, 3 vols., London 1958
Ibn Khaldūn-de Slane = *Les prolégomènes d'Ibn Khaldoun*, traduits en français et commentés par M. de Slane, Paris 1863-68 (anastatic reprint 1934-38)
Ibn Khallikān = *Wafayāt al-aʿyān wa-anbāʾ abnāʾ al-zamān*, ed. F. Wüstenfeld, Göttingen 1835-50 (quoted after the numbers of biographies)
Ibn Khallikān, Būlāḳ = the same, ed. Būlāḳ 1275
Ibn Khallikān-de Slane = *Kitāb Wafayāt al-aʿyān*, trans. by Baron MacGuckin de Slane, 4 vols., Paris 1842-1871
Ibn Khurradādhbih = *al-Masālik wa 'l-mamālik*, ed. M. J. De Goeje, Leiden 1889 (BGA VI)
Ibn Ḳutayba, *al-Shiʿr* = Ibn Ḳutayba, *Kitāb al-Shiʿr wa'l-shuʿarā*, ed. De Goeje, Leiden 1900
Ibn Rusta = *al-Aʿlāḳ al-nafīsa*, ed. M. J. De Goeje, Leiden 1892 (BGA VII)
Ibn Rusta-Wiet = *Les Atours précieux*, traduction de G. Wiet, Cairo 1955
Ibn Saʿd = *al-Ṭabaḳāt al-kubrā*, ed. H. Sachau and others, Leiden 1905-40
Ibn Taghrībirdī = *al-Nudjūm al-zāhira fī mulūk Miṣr wa-l-Ḳāhira*, ed. W. Popper, Berkeley-Leiden 1908-1936
Ibn Taghrībirdī, Cairo = the same, ed. Cairo 1348 ff.
Idrīsī, *Maghrib* = *Description de l'Afrique et de l'Espagne*, ed. R. Dozy and M. J. De Goeje, Leiden 1866
Idrīsī-Jaubert = *Géographie d'Édrisi*, trad. de l'arabe en français par P. Amédée Jaubert, 2 vols, Paris 1836-40
Iṣṭakhrī = *al-Masālik wa 'l-mamālik*, ed. M. J. De Goeje, Leiden 1870 (BGA I) (and reprint 1927)
Juynboll, *Handbuch* = Th. W. Juynboll, *Handbuch des islāmischen Gesetzes*, Leiden 1910
Khʷāndamīr = *Ḥabīb al-siyar*, Tehran 1271
Kutubī, *Fawāt* = Ibn Shākir al-Kutubī, *Fawāt al-wafayāt*, Būlāḳ 1299
LA = *Lisān al-ʿArab* (quoted according to the root)
Lane = E. W. Lane, *An Arabic-English lexicon*, London 1863-93 (reprint New York 1955-6)
Lane-Poole, *Cat.* = S. Lane-Poole, *Catalogue of oriental coins in the British Museum*, 1877-90
Lavoix, *Cat.* = H. Lavoix, *Catalogue des monnaies musulmanes de la Bibliothèque Nationale*, Paris 1887-96
Le Strange = G. Le Strange, *The lands of the Eastern Caliphate*, 2nd ed., Cambridge 1930
Le Strange, *Baghdad*, = G. Le Strange, *Baghdad during the Abbasid Caliphate*, Oxford 1924.
Le Strange, *Palestine* = G. Le Strange, *Palestine under the Moslems*, London 1890
Lévi-Provençal, *Hist. Esp. Mus.* = E. Lévi-Provençal, *Histoire de l'Espagne musulmane*, new ed., Leiden-Paris 1950-53, 3 vols.
Lévi-Provençal, *Chorfa* = E. Lévi-Provençal, *Les historiens des Chorfa*, Paris 1922
Maḳḳarī, *Analectes* = *Nafḥ al-ṭīb fī ghuṣn al-Andalus al-raṭīb (Analectes sur l'histoire et la littérature des Arabes de l'Espagne)*, Leiden 1855-61
Maḳḳarī, Būlāḳ = the same, ed. Būlāḳ 1279/1862
Maspero-Wiet, *Matériaux* = J. Maspéro et G. Wiet, *Matériaux pour servir à la géographie de l'Egypte*, Le Caire 1914 (MIFAO XXXVI)
Masʿūdī, *Murūdj* = *Murūdj al-dhahab*, edd. C. Barbier de Meynard and Pavet de Courteille, Paris 1861-77; ed. and trans. Ch. Pellat (in press; quoted according to the paragraph)
Masʿūdī, *Tanbīh* = *K. al-Tanbīh wa 'l-ishrāf*, ed. M. J. De Goeje, Leiden 1894 (BGA VIII)
Mayer, *Architects* = L. A. Mayer, *Islamic architects and their works*, Geneva 1956
Mayer, *Astrolabists* = L. A. Mayer, *Islamic astrolabists and their works*, Geneva 1958
Mayer, *Metalworkers* = L. A. Mayer, *Islamic metalworkers and their works*, Geneva 1959
Mayer, *Woodcarvers* = L. A. Mayer, *Islamic woodcarvers and their works*, Geneva 1958
Mez, *Renaissance* = A. Mez, *Die Renaissance des Islams*, Heidelberg 1922
Mez, *Renaissance*, Eng. tr. = *The renaissance of Islam*, translated into English by Salahuddin Khuda Bukhsh and D. S. Margoliouth, London 1937
Mez, *Renaissance*, Spanish trans. = *El renacimiento del Islam*, translated into Spanish by S. Vila, Madrid-Granada 1936.
Mīrkhʷānd = *Rawḍat al-ṣafā*, Bombay 1266/1849
Muḳaddasī = *Aḥsan al-taḳāsīm fī maʿrifat al-aḳālīm*, ed. M. J. De Goeje, Leiden 1877 (BGA III)
Munadjdjim Bashī = *Ṣaḥāʾif al-akhbār*, Istanbul 1285
Nallino, *Scritti* = C. A. Nallino, *Raccolta di scritti editi e inediti*, Roma 1939-48
Zubayrī, *Nasab* = Muṣʿab al-Zubayrī, *Nasab Ḳuraysh*, ed. E. Lévi-Provençal, Cairo 1953
ʿOthmānlî Müʾellifleri = Bursalî Meḥmed Ṭāhir, *ʿOthmānlî müʾellifleri*, Istanbul 1333
Pakalın = Mehmet Zeki Pakalın, *Osmanlı tarih deyimleri ve terimleri sözlüğü*, 3 vols., Istanbul 1946 ff.
Pauly-Wissowa = *Realenzyklopaedie des klassischen Altertums*
Pearson = J. D. Pearson, *Index Islamicus*, Cambridge 1958; S I = *Supplement, 1956-60*
Pons Boigues = *Ensayo bio-bibliográfico sobre los historiadores y geógrafos arábigo-españoles*, Madrid 1898

Samʿānī = al-Samʿānī, *al-Ansāb*, ed. in facsimile by D. S. Margoliouth, Leiden 1912 (GMS XX)

Santillana, *Istituzioni* = D. Santillana, *Istituzioni di diritto musulmano malichita*, Roma 1926-38

Sarkīs = Sarkīs, *Muʿdjam al-maṭbūʿāt al-ʿarabiyya*, Cairo 1346/1928

Schwarz, *Iran* = P. Schwarz, *Iran im Mittelalter nach den arabischen Geographen*, Leipzig 1896-

Shahrastānī = *al-Milal wa 'l-niḥal*, ed. W. Cureton, London 1846

Sidjill-i ʿOthmānī = Meḥmed Thüreyyā, *Sidjill-i ʿOthmānī*, Istanbul 1308-1316

Snouck Hurgronje, *Verspr. Geschr.* = C. Snouck Hurgronje, *Verspreide Geschriften*, Bonn-Leipzig-Leiden 1923-27

Sources inédites = Comte Henry de Castries, *Les sources inédites de l'histoire du Maroc*, Première Série, Paris [etc.] 1905 —, Deuxième Série, Paris 1922 —

Spuler, *Horde* = B. Spuler, *Die Goldene Horde*, Leipzig 1943

Spuler, *Iran* = B. Spuler, *Iran in früh-islamischer Zeit*, Wiesbaden 1952

Spuler, *Mongolen*² = B. Spuler, *Die Mongolen in Iran*, 2nd ed., Berlin 1955

Storey = C. A. Storey, *Persian literature: a bio-bibliographical survey*, London 1927-

Survey of Persian Art = ed. by A. U. Pope, Oxford 1938

Suter = H. Suter, *Die Mathematiker und Astronomen der Araber und ihre Werke*, Leipzig 1900

Suyūṭī, *Bughya* = *Bughyat al-wuʿāt*, Cairo 1326

TA = Muḥammad Murtaḍā b. Muḥammad al-Zabīdī, *Tādj al-ʿarūs* (quoted according to the root)

Ṭabarī = *Taʾrīkh al-rusul wa 'l-mulūk*, ed. M. J. De Goeje and others, Leiden 1879-1901

Taeschner, *Wegenetz* = Franz Taeschner, *Die Verkehrslage und das Wegenetz Anatoliens im Wandel der Zeiten*, Gotha 1926

Taʾrīkh Baghdād = al-Khaṭīb al-Baghdādī, *Taʾrīkh Baghdād*, 14 vols., Cairo 1349/1931.

Taʾrīkh Dimashk = Ibn ʿAsākir, *Taʾrīkh Dimashk*, 7 vols., Damascus 1329-51/1911-31

Taʾrīkh-i Guzīda = Ḥamd Allāh Mustawfī al-Ḳazwīnī, *Taʾrīkh-i guzīda*, ed. in facsimile by E. G. Browne, Leiden-London 1910

Thaʿālibī, *Yatīma* = *Yatīmat al-dahr fī maḥāsin ahl al-ʿaṣr*, Damascus 1304

Tomaschek = W. Tomaschek, *Zur historischen Topographie von Kleinasien im Mittelalter*, Vienna 1891.

Weil, *Chalifen* = G. Weil, *Geschichte der Chalifen*, Mannheim-Stuttgart 1846-82

Wensinck, *Handbook* = A. J. Wensinck, *A handbook of early Muhammadan Tradition*, Leiden 1927

Yaʿḳūbī = *Taʾrīkh*, ed. M. Th. Houtsma, Leiden 1883

Yaʿḳūbī, *Buldān* = ed. M. J. De Goeje, Leiden 1892 (BGA VII)

Yaʿḳūbī-Wiet = *Yaʿḳūbī. Les pays*, trad. par Gaston Wiet, Cairo 1937

Yāḳūt = *Muʿdjam al-buldān*, ed. F. Wüstenfeld, Leipzig 1866-73 (anastatic reprint 1924)

Yāḳūt, *Udabāʾ* = *Irshād al-arīb ilā maʿrifat al-adīb*, ed. D. S. Margoliouth, Leiden 1907-31 (GMS VI)

Zambaur = E. de Zambaur, *Manuel de généalogie et de chronologie pour l'histoire de l'Islam*, Hanover 1927 (anastatic reprint Bad Pyrmont 1955)

Zinkeisen = J. Zinkeisen, *Geschichte des osmanischen Reiches in Europa*, Gotha 1840-83

ABBREVIATIONS FOR PERIODICALS ETC.

Abh. G. W. Gött. = *Abhandlungen der Gesellschaft der Wissenschaften zu Göttingen.*
Abh. K. M. = *Abhandlungen für die Kunde des Morgenlandes.*
Abh. Pr. Ak. W. = *Abhandlungen der preussischen Akademie der Wissenschaften.*
Afr. Fr. = *Bulletin du Comité de l'Afrique française.*
AIEO Alger = *Annales de l'Institut d'Études Orientales de l'Université d'Alger* (N.S. from 1964).
AIUON = *Annali dell' Istituto Universitario Orientale di Napoli.*
Anz. Wien = *Anzeiger der [kaiserlichen] Akademie der Wissenschaften, Wien. Philosophisch-historische Klasse.*
AO = *Acta Orientalia.*
AO Hung. = *Acta Orientalia (Academiae Scientiarum Hungaricae).*
ArO = *Archiv Orientální.*
ARW = *Archiv für Religionswissenschaft.*
ASI = *Archaeological Survey of India.*
ASI, NIS = *ditto*, New Imperial Series.
ASI, AR = *ditto*, Annual Reports.
AÜDTCFD = *Ankara Üniversitesi Dil ve Tarih-Coğrafya Fakültesi Dergisi.*
BAH = *Bibliotheca Arabico-Hispana.*
BASOR = *Bulletin of the American Schools of Oriental Research.*
Belleten = *Belleten* (of *Türk Tarih Kurumu*)
BFac. Ar. = *Bulletin of the Faculty of Arts of the Egyptian University.*
BÉt. Or. = *Bulletin d'Études Orientales de l'Institut Français de Damas.*
BGA = *Bibliotheca geographorum arabicorum.*
BIE = *Bulletin de l'Institut d'Égypte.*
BIFAO = *Bulletin de l'Institut Français d'Archéologie Orientale du Caire.*
BRAH = *Boletín de la Real Academia de la Historia de España.*
BSE = *Bol'shaya Sovetskaya Éntsiklopediya* (Large Soviet Encyclopaedia) 1st ed.
BSE² = the same, 2nd ed.
BSL[P] = *Bulletin de la Société de Linguistique de Paris.*
BSO[A]S = *Bulletin of the School of Oriental [and African] Studies.*
BTLV = *Bijdragen tot de Taal-, Land- en Volkenkunde [van Nederlandsch-Indië].*
BZ = *Byzantinische Zeitschrift.*
COC = *Cahiers de l'Orient contemporain.*
CT = *Cahiers de Tunisie.*
EI¹ = *Encyclopaedia of Islam*, 1st edition.
EIM = *Epigraphia Indo-Moslemica.*
ERE = *Encyclopaedia of Religions and Ethics.*
GGA = *Göttinger Gelehrte Anzeigen.*
GMS = *Gibb Memorial Series.*
Gr. I. Ph. = *Grundriss der Iranischen Philologie.*
IA = *Islâm Ansiklopedisi.*
IBLA = *Revue de l'Institut des Belles Lettres Arabes*, Tunis.
IC = *Islamic Culture.*
IFD = *Ilahiyat Fakültesi Dergisi.*
IHQ = *Indian Historical Quarterly.*
IQ = *The Islamic Quarterly.*
Isl. = *Der Islam.*
JA = *Journal Asiatique.*
JAfr. S = *Journal of the African Society.*
JAOS = *Journal of the American Oriental Society.*
JAnthr. I = *Journal of the Anthropological Institute.*
JBBRAS = *Journal of the Bombay Branch of the Royal Asiatic Society.*
JE = *Jewish Encyclopaedia.*
JESHO = *Journal of the Economic and Social History of the Orient.*
J[R]Num. S. = *Journal of the [Royal] Numismatic Society.*
JNES = *Journal of Near Eastern Studies.*
JPak.HS = *Journal of the Pakistan Historical Society.*
JPHS = *Journal of the Punjab Historical Society.*
JQR = *Jewish Quarterly Review.*
JRAS = *Journal of the Royal Asiatic Society.*
J[R]ASB = *Journal and Proceedings of the [Royal] Asiatic Society of Bengal.*
JRGeog. S. = *Journal of the Royal Geographical Society.*
JSFO = *Journal de la Société Finno-ougrienne.*
JSS = *Journal of Semitic Studies.*
KCA = *Körösi Csoma Archivum.*
KS = *Keleti Szemle* (Oriental Review).
KSIE = *Kratkie Soobshčeniya Instituta Étnografiy* (Short communications of the Institute of Ethnography).
LE = *Literaturnaya Éntsiklopediya* (Literary Encyclopaedia).
MDOG = *Mitteilungen der Deutschen Orient-Gesellschaft.*
MDPV = *Mitteilungen und Nachrichten des Deutschen Palästina-Vereins.*
MEA = *Middle Eastern Affairs.*
MEJ = *Middle East Journal.*
MFOB = *Mélanges de la Faculté Orientale de l'Université St. Joseph de Beyrouth.*
MGMN = *Mitteilungen zur Geschichte der Medizin und Naturwissenschaften.*
MGWJ = *Monatsschrift für die Geschichte und Wissenschaft des Judentums.*
MIDEO = *Mélanges de l'Institut Dominicain d'Études Orientales du Caire.*
MIE = *Mémoires de l'Institut d'Égypte.*
MIFAO = *Mémoires publiés par les membres de l'Institut Français d'Archéologie Orientale du Caire.*
MMAF = *Mémoires de la Mission Archéologique Française au Caire.*
MMIA = *Madjallat al-Madjmaʿ al-ʿIlmī al-ʿArabī*, Damascus.
MO = *Le Monde oriental.*
MOG = *Mitteilungen zur osmanischen Geschichte.*
MSE = *Malaya Sovetskaya Éntsiklopediya* (Small Soviet Encyclopaedia).
MSFO = *Mémoires de la Société Finno-ougrienne.*
MSL[P] = *Mémoires de la Société Linguistique de Paris.*
MSOS Afr. = *Mitteilungen des Seminars für Orientalische Sprachen, Afrikanische Studien.*
MSOS As. = *Mitteilungen des Seminars für Orientalische Sprachen, Westasiatische Studien.*
MTM = *Millī Tetebbüʿler Medjmūʿasī.*
MW = *The Muslim World.*
NC = *Numismatic Chronicle.*
NGW Gött. = *Nachrichten von der Gesellschaft der Wissenschaften zu Göttingen.*
OC = *Oriens Christianus.*

OLZ = *Orientalistische Literaturzeitung.*
OM = *Oriente Moderno.*
PEFQS = *Palestine Exploration Fund. Quarterly Statement.*
Pet. Mitt. = *Petermanns Mitteilungen.*
QDAP = *Quarterly Statement of the Department of Antiquities of Palestine.*
RAfr. = *Revue Africaine.*
RCEA = *Répertoire chronologique d'Épigraphie arabe.*
REJ = *Revue des Études Juives.*
Rend. Lin. = *Rendiconti della Reale Accademia dei Lincei, Classe di scienze morali, storiche e filologiche.*
REI = *Revue des Études Islamiques.*
RHR = *Revue de l'Histoire des Religions.*
RIMA = *Revue de l'Institut des Manuscrits Arabes.*
RMM = *Revue du Monde Musulman.*
RO = *Rocznik Orientalistyczny.*
ROC = *Revue de l'Orient Chrétien.*
ROL = *Revue de l'Orient Latin.*
RSO = *Rivista degli studi orientali.*
RT = *Revue Tunisienne.*
SBAk. Heid. = *Sitzungsberichte der Heidelberger Akademie der Wissenschaften.*
SBAk. Wien = *Sitzungsberichte der Akademie der Wissenschaften zu Wien.*
SBBayer. Ak. = *Sitzungsberichte der Bayerischen Akademie der Wissenschaften.*
SBPMS Erlg. = *Sitzungsberichte der Physikalisch-medizinischen Sozietät in Erlangen.*
SBPr. Ak. W. = *Sitzungsberichte der preussischen Akademie der Wissenschaften zu Berlin.*
SE = *Sovetskaya Étnografiya* (Soviet Ethnography).
SO = *Sovetskoe Vostokovedenie* (Soviet Orientalism).
Stud. Isl. = *Studia Islamica.*
S.Ya. = *Sovetskoe Yazîkoznanie* (Soviet Linguistics).
TBG = *Tijdschrift van het Bataviaasch Genootschap van Kunsten en Wetenschappen.*
TD = *Tarih Dergisi.*
TIE = *Trudî instituta Étnografiy* (Works of the Institute of Ethnography).
TM = *Türkiyat Mecmuası.*
TOEM/TTEM = *Taʾrīkh-i ʿOthmānī* (*Türk Taʾrīkhi*) *Endjümeni medjmūʿasî.*
Verh. Ak. Amst. = *Verhandelingen der Koninklijke Akademie van Wetenschappen te Amsterdam.*
Versl. Med. Ak. Amst. = *Verslagen en Mededeelingen der Koninklijke Akademie van Wetenschappen te Amsterdam.*
VI = *Voprosî Istoriy* (Historical Problems).
WI = *Die Welt des Islams.*
WI, n.s. = the same, new series.
Wiss. Veröff. DOG = *Wissenschaftliche Veröffentlichungen der Deutschen Orient-Gesellschaft.*
WZKM = *Wiener Zeitschrift für die Kunde des Morgenlandes.*
ZA = *Zeitschrift für Assyriologie.*
ZATW = *Zeitschrift für die alttestamentliche Wissenschaft.*
ZDMG = *Zeitschrift der Deutschen Morgenländischen Gesellschaft.*
ZDPV = *Zeitschrift des Deutschen Palästinavereins.*
ZGErdk. Birl. = *Zeitschrift der Gesellschaft für Erdkunde in Berlin.*
ZS = *Zeitschrift für Semitistik.*

LIST OF TRANSLITERATIONS

SYSTEM OF TRANSLITERATION OF ARABIC CHARACTERS:

Consonants

ء	ʾ (except when initial)	ز	z	ق	ḳ
ب	b	س	s	ك	k
ت	t	ش	sh	ل	l
ث	th	ص	ṣ	م	m
ج	dj	ض	ḍ	ن	n
ح	ḥ	ط	ṭ	ه	h
خ	kh	ظ	ẓ	و	w
د	d	ع	ʿ	ي	y
ذ	dh	غ	gh		
ر	r	ف	f		

Long Vowels

ا ى	ā
و	ū
ي	ī

Short Vowels

َ	a
ُ	u
ِ	i

Diphthongs

َوْ	aw
َيْ	ay
ِيّ	iyy (final form ī)
ُوّ	uww (final form ū)

ة a; at (construct state)

ال (article), al- and ʾl- (even before the antero-palatals)

PERSIAN, TURKISH AND URDU ADDITIONS TO THE ARABIC ALPHABET:

پ	p	ژ	zh	ٹ	t́	ڑ	ŕ
چ	č	ڭ or گ	g (sometimes ñ in Turkish)	ڈ	d́		

Additional vowels:

a) Turkish: e, ı, o, ö, ü. Diacritical signs proper to Arabic are, in principle, not used in words of Turkish etymology.

b) Urdu: ē, ō.

For modern Turkish, the official orthography adopted by the Turkish Republic in 1928 is used. The following letters may be noted:

c = dj	ğ = gh	j = zh	k = k and ḳ	t = t and ṭ
ç = č	h = h, ḥ and kh	ş = sh	s = s, ṣ and th	z = z, ẓ, ḍ and dh

SYSTEM OF TRANSLITERATION OF CYRILLIC CHARACTERS:

а	a	е	e	к	k	п	p	ф	f	щ	shč	ю	yu
б	b	ж	ž	л	l	р	r	х	kh	ы	ï	я	ya
в	v	з	z	м	m	с	s	ц	ts	ь	ʾ	ѣ	ě
г	g	и	i	н	n	т	t	ч	č	ъ	ʿ		
д	d	й	y	о	o	у	u	ш	sh	э	é		

ADDENDA AND CORRIGENDA

VOLUME I

P. 4ª, **ĀBĀZA,** l. 26, *read* 1036/1627.
P. 7ᵇ, **ʿABBĀS I,** l. 2, *for* second son *read* third son.
P. 60ᵇ, **ʿABD AL-ḤAḲḲ** B. **SAYF AL-DĪN,** l. 13, *for* studying *read* staying.
P. 137ª, **ABU 'L-LAYTH AL-SAMARḲANDĪ,** *add to Bibliography*: A. Zajączkowski, *Le traité arabe* Muḳaddima *d'Abou-l-Lait as-Samarḳandī en version mamelouk-kiptchak,* Warsaw 1962.
P. 173ª, l. 30, *for* Memons *read* Moplahs.
P. 207ᵇ, **ADJDĀBIYA,** l. 22, *for* Zanāna *read* Zanāta.
P. 313ª, **AḲ SHEHR** (i), last line, *read* 386/996.
P. 320ᵇ, **ĀKHĀL TEKKE,** l. 6, *after* Durūn *delete* [*q.v.*].
P. 392ª, **ʿALĪ BEY,** l. 6, *read* Abu 'l-Dhahab.
P. 430ᵇ, **AMĀN,** *add to Bibliography*: E. Nys, *Le droit des gens dans les rapports des Arabes et des Byzantins,* in *Revue de droit international et de législation comparée,* 1894, 461-87.
P. 444ᵇ, **AMĪR KHUSRAW,** l. 35, *for Ṣighār read ṣighar*; l. 40, *for Bahiyya read Baḳiyya*; l. 70, *read* 718/1318.
P. 447ª, **ʿAMMĀN,** l. 4, *insert comma after* Palestine.
P. 447ᵇ, l. 4 of *Bibliography, for Princetown read Princeton.*
P. 511ᵇ, *after* **ANḲARA** *add*: **ANMĀR** [see GHAṬAFĀN].
P. 607ᵇ, **ARAL,** l. 38, *read* 861/1456-7.
P. 608ᵇ, **ARBŪNA,** signature: *for* ED., *read* CH. PELLAT.
P. 630ᵇ, **ARISṬŪṬĀLĪS,** l. 7, *after* Nicolaus of Damascus (*saec.* I B.C. *add*: Nicolaus Damascenus, *On the philosophy of Aristotle,* ed. H. J. Drossaart Lulofs, 1965.
P. 631ᵇ, l. 25, *for* will be published by Muhsin Mahdi *read* has been published by Muhsin Mahdi (Beirut 1961).
ll. 54 f., *for* Not one . . . . library. *read* Al-Fārābī's commentary on the *De Interpretatione* (to be compared with Ammonius and Boethius) has been edited by W. Kutsch and S. Marrow, Beirut 1960, from an Istanbul manuscript [see AL-FĀRĀBĪ, iii a].
P. 632ª, l. 52 and l. 60, *for* 'Middle Commentary' *read* 'Short Commentary'.
l. 9 (*De Interpretatione*), *add*: and, together with the commentary of al-Fārābī, by W. Kutsch and S. Marrow (see above).
l. 36 (*Rhetoric*), *add*: Arabic text now edited from the Paris manuscript by A. Badawī, 1959.
l. 47 (*Poetics*), *add*: Good use of the Arabic version has been made in the new Oxford edition of the Greek text by R. Kassel, 1965.
l. 53 (*Physics*), *add*: Edition of the first book, with commentary by Abū ʿAlī b. al-Samḥ, by W. Kutsch and Kh. Georr, in *MFOB*, xxxix (1963), 268 ff.; edition of books i-iv by A. Badawī, 1964.
l. 55 (*De Caelo*), *after* al-Biṭrīq), *add* unreliable edition by A. Badawī, in *Islamica,* xxviii (1961), 123-387.
l. 65 (*Meteorology*), *add*: Unreliable edition by A. Badawī in *Islamica,* xxviii (1961), 1-121.
l. 71 (*De Naturis Animalium*), add: *De generatione animalium,* edition of the Arabic version by H. J. Drossaart Lulofs, to appear in 1965.
P. 632ᵇ, l. 16 (*De Anima*), *after* (Typescript), *add*: now published in the *Proceedings* of the Arab Academy of Damascus.
l. 27 (*De Sensu, etc.*), *add*: Critical edition by H. Gätje, *Die Epitome der* Parva Naturalia *des Averroes,* 1961.
l. 48 (*Nicomachean Ethics*), *add*: Books 1-4 have been discovered by D. M. Dunlop in the library of the Ḳarawiyyīn, Fez, see *Oriens,* xv (1962), 18-34.
l. 52 (*De Mundo*), *add*: S. M. Stern, *The Arabic translations of the Ps.-Aristotelian treatise* De mundo, in *Le Muséon,* lxxvii (1964), 187 ff.
l. 63 (*Protrepticus*), *add*: I. Düring, *Aristotle in the ancient biographical tradition,* 1957, 203.
P. 633ª, l. 3 (*De Pomo*), *add*: Edition of the Latin translation by M. Plezia, 1960.
P. 657ᵇ, **ARNAWUTLUḲ,** l. 18, *read* 29 July 1913.
P. 662ª, **ARSLAN** B. **SALDJŪḲ,** l. 34, *read* 427/1035-6.
P. 680ᵇ, **ĀRZŪ KHĀN,** ll. 12-15, *read*: He produced an enlarged and corrected edition of Hānsawī's *Gharāʾib al-lughāt* and called it *Nawādir al-alfāẓ* (ed. Saiyid Abdullah, Karachi 1951).
P. 686ª, *for* **ĀṢĀF-DJĀH** *read* **ĀṢAF-DJĀH.**
P. 697ª, *after* AL-**ASHDAḲ** *add*: **ASHDJAʿ** [see GHAṬAFĀN].
P. 822ᵇ, **ʿAẒĪM ALLĀH KHĀN,** *add to Bibliography*: Pratul Chandra Gupta, *Nana Sahib and the rising at Cawnpore,* Oxford 1963, 25-7, 63-4, 70-1, 75, 82, 84, 102-3, 115-7, 171, 177, 179, 190.
P. 825ᵇ, **ʿAZĪZ MIṢR,** ll. 25-6, *read* According to Memdūḥ Pasha, later Ottoman Minister of Internal Affairs, this . . .
P. 856ª, **BADĀʾŪN,** *add to Bibliography*: On the name Badāʾūn: A. S. Beveridge, in *JRAS,* 1925, 517; T. W. Haig, *ibid.*, 715-6; C. A. Storey, *ibid.*, 1926, 103-4; E. D. Ross, *ibid.*, 105.
P. 895ᵇ, **BAGHDĀD,** ll. 59-60, *for* S.W. *read* S.E. *and for* S.E. *read* S.W.
P. 973ᵇ, **BALADIYYA,** ll. 50 and 54, *for* Commission *read* Council.
P. 989ᵇ, **BALĀṬ AL-SHUHADĀʾ,** l. 22, *for Taʾrīkh al-Umam wa 'l-Mulūk read Taʾrīkh al-Rusul wa 'l-Mulūk.*
P. 1161ᵇ, *before* **BEIRUT** *insert* **BEING AND NON-BEING** [see WUDJŪD and ʿADAM respectively].

P. 1195ᵃ, **BHITĀ'Ī,** *add*: *Bibliography*: Annemarie Schimmel, in *Kairos* (Salzburg), iii-iv (1961), 207-16 (where additional references are given).
P. 1203ᵃ, **BĪDJĀPŪR,** *add to Bibliography*: A. Slater, *The ancient city of Bijapur*, in *Qly Journ. Mythic Soc.*, iii (1912), 45-52.
P. 1211ᵃ, **BIHZĀD,** l. 16, *for printers read painters*.
P. 1242ᵃ, **BISHR** B. **GHIYĀTH** AL-**MARĪSĪ,** last line of col., *for* S I, 340; Ritter, in *Isl.*, 16, 1927, 252 f.; *read* S I, 340 (on the spurious *K. al-Ḥayda*, allegedly the account of a disputation with Bishr by the Shāfiʿī ʿAbd al-ʿAzīz b. Yaḥyā al-Kinānī, d. 235/849; also Cairo (Maṭbaʿat al-Saʿāda) n.d); Ritter, in *Isl.*, xvii (1928), 252 f.; Massignon, in *REI*, 1938, 410 (on Bishr's name in the *isnāds* of the *al-Djāmiʿ al-ṣaḥīḥ*, attributed to the Ibāḍī authority al-Rabīʿ b. Ḥabīb);
P. 1255ᵇ, **BOHORĀS,** l. 13 of *Bibl.*, *read St. Isl.*, iii (1955).
P. 1259ᵃ, **BORNU,** l. 7, *for* were *read* where.
P. 1280ᵇ, *before* **BRUSA** *insert* **BROKER** [see DALLĀL, SIMSĀR].
P. 1348ᵇ, **BŪSTĀN** —ii, *add to Bibliography*: T. O. D. Dunn, *Kashmir and its Mughal gardens*, in *Calcutta Review*, cclxxx/8 (April 1917).

VOLUME II

P. 19ᵃ, **ČELEBI,** l. 26, *for* 'barbarian' *read* 'barber'.
P. 29ᵃ, *before* **CHINA** *insert* **CHILD** [see ṢAGHĪR and WALAD].
P. 60ᵇ, *before* **CONSUL** *insert* **CONSTITUTION** [see DUSTŪR].
P. 71ᵇ, **ḌABBA,** l. 1, *for* ṬĀBĪKHA *read* ṬĀBIKHA.
l. 14, *for* 7th/13th century *read* 7th century A.D.
l. 18, *for* 6th/12th century *read* 6th century A.D.
P. 72ᵃ, l. 41, *read* the last Amīr to lead in prayer.
P. 78ᵃ, **DAFTAR,** l. 10, *for* n. 1 *read* n. 3.
P. 79ᵇ, l. 27, *for Adab al-Kātib read Adab al-Kuttāb*.
P. 105ᵇ, **ḌAMĀN,** *add to Bibliography*: O. Spies, *Die Lehre von der Haftung für Gefahr im islamischen Recht*, in *Zeitschr. vergl. Rechtswiss.*, 1955, 79-95.
P. 107ᵃ, **DAMĀWAND,** *add to Bibliography*: M. B. Smith, *Material for a corpus of early Iranian Islamic architecture. I. Masdjid-i djumʿa, Demāwend*, in *Ars Islamica*, ii (1935), 153-73, and iv (1937), 7-41; W. Eilers, *Der Name Demawend*, in *ArO*, xxii (1954), 267-374.
P. 116ᵇ, **DĀR** AL-**ʿAHD,** *add to Bibliography*: Muḥammad ʿAbd al-Hādī Shaʿīra (Cheïra), *al-Mamālik al-ḫalīfa*, in *Bull. Fac. Arts, Farouk I Univ.*, iv (1948), Arabic section 39-81; idem, *Le statut des pays de "ʿAhd" au VIIᵉ et VIIIᵉ siècles*, in *Actes XXIᵉ Congrès intern. Oriental.*, Paris 1949, 275-7.
P. 122ᵃ, **DĀR FŪR,** ll. 39-40, *for* [see DANKALĪ] *read* [see DONGOLA].
P. 122ᵇ, l. 28, *for* 1894 *read* 1874.
P. 123ᵃ, l. 21, *for* Abu 'l-Kāsim *read* Abu 'l-Ḳāsim.
P. 137ᵇ, **DARD,** l. 36, *delete* Bahādur Shāh I.
P. 183ᵇ, **DĀWŪD PASHA,** l. 18, *for* 1021/1612 *read* 1025/1616.
Bibliography: s.v. Ḥādjdjī Khalīfa, *Fedhleke*, *read*: i, 252, 256, 268-70, 374; ii, 19 ff., . . .; s.v. Naʿīmā, *Ta'rīkh*, *read*: i, 408, 412-3, 432, 434, 436; ii, 96, 141, 224 ff., . . .; s.v. E. de Hurmuzaki, *read*: 180-1, 183, 197 ff., 200 ff.; s.v. Hammer-Purgstall, iv, *read*: 331, 356, 381-2, 407, 453, 462, 476, 549, . . . *Add to Bibliography*: M. Sertoğlu, *Tuği tarihi*, in *Belleten*, xi (1947), 489-514, *passim*.
P. 209ᵃ, **DERWĪSH MEḤMED PASHA** (V. J. Parry), *add to Bibliography*: Cl. Huart, *Histoire de Bagdad dans les temps modernes*, Paris 1901, 74-6.
Pp. 243-5 **DHŪ NUWĀS,** *passim*, *for* Yūsuf Ashʿar *read* Yūsuf As'ar.
P. 280ᵇ, **DIMASHḲ,** l. 48, *after* Marwān, *add* and nephew of the famous Ḥadjdjādj b. Yūsuf.
P. 288ᵃ, l. 27, *for* in 959/1552 *read* before 926/1520.
P. 288ᵇ, l. 21, *for* Bāb al-Ḥadīd *read* Bāb al-Naṣr.
P. 289ᵃ, l. 23, *for* Bāb al-Ḥadīd *read* Bāb al-Naṣr.
P. 290ᵇ, l. 27 *of Bibliography, to* Arabic texts *add*: Muḥammad Adīb Taḳī al-Dīn al-Ḥuṣnī, *Muntakhabāt al-tawārīkh li-Dimashḳ*, 3 vols., Damascus 1928-34.
P. 337ᵇ, **DĪWĀN-I HUMĀYŪN,** l. 13, *for* Bāyazīd II *read* Bāyazīd I.
P. 338ᵃ, l. 16, *for* every day *read* four days a week.
l. 25, *for* Four times a week a meeting was held *read* Meetings were held.
P. 339ᵃ, l. 23, *for* 1054/1654 *read* 1064/1654.
P. 362ᵇ, AL-**DJABR** WA 'L-**MUḲĀBALA,** signature: *for* W. HARTNER *read* W. HARTNER and M. SCHRAMM.
P. 372ᵃ, MĪR **DJAʿFAR,** *add to Bibliography*: M. Edwardes, *The battle of Plassey and the conquest of Bengal*, London 1963, index.
P. 392ᵇ, **DJALĀL** AL-**DĪN ḤUSAYN** AL-**BUKHĀRĪ,** *add at end of Bibliography*: A collection of 42 of his letters addressed to one Mawlānā ʿIzz al-Dīn and compiled by Tādj al-Ḥaḳḳ wa 'l-Dīn Aḥmad b. Muʿīn Siyāh-pūsh is preserved in the Subḥān Allāh collection of the Muslim University, Aligarh.
P. 404ᵇ, **DJĀLIYA,** l. 1, *for* (*al-Andalus*) *read* (*al-ʿUṣba*).
at end of article add: See further, for Muslim communities throughout the world, MUSLIM.
P. 410ᵇ, **DJAMʿ, DJAMĀʿA,** *add to first paragraph of Bibliography*: A. Murtonen, *Broken plurals. Origin and development of the system*, Leiden 1964.
P. 433ᵇ, **DJAMʿIYYA** (iii), l. 27, *for* Djīrāz *read* Shīrāz.
P. 434ᵃ, penultimate line, *for* the *read* they.
P. 435ᵇ, l. 28, *for op. cit.* (in Bibl.) *read Ta'rīkh-i mashrūṭa-i Īrān*[4].
P. 438ᵃ, **DJAMNĀ,** *at end of article add*: Djamnā is used as a name of other rivers in India, especially for part of the Brahmaputra in Bengal, called Djūn by Ibn Baṭṭūṭa. See also GANGĀ.

P. 470ᵃ, **DJARĪDA** (i) B, l. 33, *for* (1955) *read* (1956).

P. 470ᵇ, *add to Bibliography*: A. Merad, *La formation de la presse musulmane en Algérie* (*1919-1939*), in *IBLA*, 1964/1, 9-29.

P. 471ᵇ, (i) C, ll. 29-30, *delete* magazine; *for* 1928 *read* 1933; *delete* organ of.

P. 472ᵇ, (ii), ll. 10-12, *for* In 1875 .... Constantinople; *read* Newspapers in Persian appeared in India as early as 1822 and 1835 (see S. C. Sanial, *The first Persian newspapers of India: a peep into their contents*, in *IC*, vii (1934), 105-14), and in Constantinople in 1875;

P. 473ᵃ, last line, *for* Iṣfahān 1327/1949, 2 vols. *read* Iṣfahān 1327-32/1949-54, 4 vols.

P. 479ᵇ, **DJARĪMA**, l. 2, *after* ḏjereme, *add* and currently in Īrān,

P. 501ᵃ, AL-**DJAWNPŪRĪ**, *add to Bibliography*: A. S. Bazmee Ansari, *Sayyid Muḥammad Jawnpūrī and his movement*, in *Islamic Studies*, ii/2 (March 1963), 41-74.

P. 501ᵇ, AL-**DJAWWĀNĪ**, l. 40, *for* Ahmet III, 2759, *read* Ahmet III, 2799 and 2800, neither of which, however, indicates al-Djawwānī as the author, *and add* Yale, L-672 [Nemoy 1245].

at end of paragraph add: There have now appeared his *Mukhtaṣar min al-kalām fi 'l-farḳ bayn man ism abīhi Sallām wa-Salām* (ed. al-Munadjdjid, Damascus 1382/1962) and his manuscript of al-Zubayr b. Bakkār, *Djamharat nasab Ḳuraysh* (Köprülü 1141, with notes dating from the year 558/1163, see the edition by M. M. Shākir, Cairo 1381/1962, intr. 32 ff.).

P. 504ᵃ, **DJAYPUR**, l. 3, *for* craftsman *read* craftsmen.
l. 7, *for* Yād-i Ayyān *read* Yād-i Ayyām.

P. 518ᵇ, **DJAZĀʾ** (ii), l. 2, *for* ḳānūn-i djazāʾī (cezâi) *read* ḳānūn-i djazāʾ (cezâ).

P. 535ᵇ, **DJIBŪTĪ**, *after the third paragraph, ending* of the majority., *insert the following paragraph, omitted in error in the English edition*:

Djibūtī is the administrative centre of a region misleadingly called "Côte Française des Somalis", "French Somaliland": in fact more than three-quarters of its area (*ca.* 23,000 sq. km.) and of its coast belong to the ʿAfar, while less than a quarter belongs to the Somalis. It is a desert region, with practically no agriculture. Outside the capital, the population is almost entirely nomadic; all the inhabitants are Muslim. Besides the ʿAfar (numbering some 25,000), it contains the subjects of four "sultanates": the whole of Tadjoura (Tadjurra, in ʿAfar Tagorri) and Gobaʿad, the majority of Raḥayto, and a small part of Awsa. The ʿAfar (called by the Arabs Danāḳil [*q.v.*]) form a relatively organized population, with a firmly hierarchical social structure, divided into regional 'commands' ruled by hereditary chiefs and based on a family and tribal organization. Among the Somalis, the only autochthonous tribe is that of the ʿĪse, nine-tenths of whom in any case belong to Somalia or to Ethiopia. This tribe is unusually anarchical, having no true chiefs: the ugās, who lives in Ethiopia, has no effective power; a minimum of authority is exercised by councils of elders, who dispense justice. The ʿĪse groups which normally wander throughout the country during part of the year total about 6000 individuals. They belong mainly to the sub-tribes Rēr Mūse, Ūrweyne, Fūrlabe, Horrōne and Mammāsan.

P. 576ᵇ, **DJUGHRĀFIYĀ**, ll. 50, 57 and 71, *for* Āryabhaťa *read* Āryabhaṭa.

P. 587ᵃ, l. 24, *for* Siyāg̲h̲ī *read* Siyāḳī.

P. 587ᵇ, l. 18, *after* Journal *insert* of.

P. 595ᵃ, **DJUMHŪRIYYA**, l. 44, *for* Siyasat *read* Siyasal.

P. 597ᵃ, **DJŪNĀGAŔH**, l. 15, *before* thriving *insert* a.
l. 19, *for* enshines *read* enshrines.

P. 597ᵇ, l. 3, *for* Ridjāʾ *read* Radjāʾ.
l. 65, *for* Manāwādār *read* Manāwadār; *for* taʿlukas *read* taʿluḳas.
l. 67, *for* zorṭalbī *read* zōrṭalbī.

P. 598ᵃ, l. 11, *read* college.
l. 25, *read* taʿluḳas.
ll. 41-5, *for* It has .... employ of the ruler. *read* It has two large-size cannon, originally from the armament brought by Khādim Süleymān Pasha, Ottoman governor of Cairo under Süleymān I and commander of the fleet sent from Suez against the Portuguese settlement of Diu in India; they were brought to Djūnāgaŕh by Mudjāhid Khān of Pālītāna (see *Cam. Hist. India*, iii, 334, 340).

P. 598ᵇ, l. 15, *for* Zarfīn *read* zarrīn.

P. 600ᵇ, AL-**DJUNAYD** B. ʿABD ALLĀH, l. 7, *for* Djūshaba b. Dhābir *read* Djaysinh b. Dāhir; l. 12, *for* Ibn Dhābir's *read* Ibn Dāhir's [These readings, kindly communicated by Mr. A. S. Bazmee Ansari, make it possible to correct the texts of Ibn al-Athīr, iv, 465, 466, v, 40, 101, and al-Balādhurī, 441-2, which have respectively جيشبه بن داهر and حشبه (cf. *Čač-nāma*, ed. U. M. Daudpota, Delhi 1959, index; *Islamic Studies*, ii/2 (Karachi, March 1963), 139-40, n. 25).—Author's note].

P. 602ᵃ, **DJURʾAT**, l. 11, *for* Muḥabbat *read* Maḥabbat.
l. 33, *for* Yakta *read* Yaktā.

P. 602ᵇ, l. 1, *for* Mohāhī *read* Mohānī; *for* Kanpur *read* Kānpur.
add to Bibliography: Garcin de Tassy, *Histoire de la littérature hindoue* ...², Paris 1870, ii, 112-8.

P. 605ᵇ, AL-**DJUWAYNĪ**, ABU 'L-MAʿĀLĪ ʿABD AL-MALIK, l. 17, *after* century. *add* It was printed repeatedly, and was translated by L. Bercher in *Revue Tunisienne*, 1930.
ll. 33-4, *for* Unfortunately, ... published. *read* Only the first section of his great work, the *Shāmil*, has been published (ed. H. Klopfer, Cairo 1960).
l. 41, *read* 181-4.
l. 49, *after* edition. *add* There is, finally, his ʿaḳīda, which he dedicated to Niẓām al-Mulk (*al-ʿAḳīda al-Niẓāmiyya*); it was edited by Muḥammad Zāhid al-Kawtharī (Cairo 1367/1948) and translated by H. Klopfer (*Das Dogma des Imām al-Ḥaramain*, Cairo and Wiesbaden 1958).

P. 606ᵃ, l. 11, *for* Brockelmann, I, 388 *read* Brockelmann, I, 486, S I, 671 *and add to the Bibliography*: A. S.

Tritton, *Muslim theology*, London 1947, 184-90; L. Gardet and M.-M. Anawati, *Introduction à la théologie musulmane*, Paris 1948, index s.v. Juwaynī.

P. 609ᵃ, AL-**DJUZDJĀNĪ**, ABŪ ʿAMR, l. 21, *read ḥarīm*.

P. 609ᵇ, l. 7, *for* the *read* his.
l. 10, *read* Rayhān.
l. 47, *read* Nāṣirī.
l. 59, *read* Zakariyyā.
l. 63, *read* Amīr Ḥasan.

P. 640ᵇ, **DUSTŪR** (ii), l. 4, *for* 1807 *read* 1808.
l. 7, *for* and of *read* and four of.

P. 694ᵇ, **ELČI**, *add to Bibliography*: Enver Ziya Karal, *Selim III. ün hat-tı humayunları*, Ankara 1946, 163-86.

P. 694ᵇ, **ELIČPUR**, *for* [see GĀWILGAŔH] *read* [see ILIČPUR, also BERĀR, GĀWILGAŔH, ʿIMĀD SHĀHĪ].

P. 725ᵃ, **FADAK**, l. 3, *after* from Medina. *add*: C. J. Gadd has shown that the name reflects the ancient Padakku, which was occupied in 550 B.C. by the Babylonian king Nabonidus (see *Anatolian Studies*, viii (1958), 81).

P. 729ᵇ, **FAḌĪLA**, *add to Bibliography*: E. Wagner, *Die arabische Rangstreitdichtung und ihre Einordnung in die allgemeine Literaturgeschichte*, Wiesbaden 1963 (Abh. d. Ak. d. Wiss. u. Lit. in Mainz, Geistes- und Sozialwissenschaftliche Kl., Jg. 1962, Nr. 8).

P. 735ᵇ, **FAḌL ALLĀH ḤURŪFĪ**, *Bibliography*: H. Ritter, *Studien zur Geschichte der islamischen Frömmigkeit, II. Die Anfänge der Ḥurūfīsekte*, in *Oriens*, vii (1954), 1-54; Abdülbaki Gölpınarlı, *Bektaşîlik-Hurûfîlik ve Fadl Allâh'ın öldürülmesine düşürülen üç tarih*, in *Şarkiyat Mecmuası*, v (1964), 15-22.

P. 741ᵇ, **FAHD**, l. 51, *for (ḳasʿa) read (ḳaṣʿa)*.

P. 751ᵃ, **FAKHR** AL-**DĪN**, l. 13, *for* westwards *read* eastwards.

P. 852ᵇ, **FĀṬIMIDS**, l. 52, *after* bribery *add* (see also H. Monés, *Le malékisme et l'échec des Fatimides en Ifriqiya*, in *Ét. or. . . . Lévi-Provençal*, i, 197-220).

P. 853ᵃ, l. 11, *after* in the Zāb *add* (on which see L. Massiéra, *M'sila du Xᵉ au XIᵉ s.*, in *Bull. Soc. hist. et géogr. de la région de Sétif*, ii (1941), 183 ff.; M. Canard, *Une famille de partisans puis adversaires des Fatimides en Af. du N.*, in *Mél. d'hist. et d'archéol. de l'Occ. mus.*, Algiers 1957, ii, 35 ff.).

P. 862ᵇ, *add to Bibliography*: A. R. Lewis, *Naval power and trade in the Mediterranean, A.D. 500-1100*, Princeton 1951, especially 259-62 (*The disruptive role of the Fatimids*); G. Wiet, *Grandeur de l'Islam*, Paris 1961, 152-71; S. D. Goitein, *Jews and Arabs*, New York 1955, 82-4; H. Monés, *Le malékisme et l'échec des Fatimides en Ifriqiya*, in *Études d'orientalisme dédiées à la mémoire de Lévi-Provençal*, Paris 1962, i, 197 ff.

P. 864ᵃ, **FĀṬIMID ART**, l. 52, *after* traditions which they continued. *add*: On the representation of living creatures in Fāṭimid art, see al-Maḳrīzī, *Khiṭaṭ*, i, 416, 472, 477: figurines (*tamāthīl*) representing elephants, gazelles, lions, giraffes, or birds, peacocks, cocks, etc., elephants sometimes bearing warlike accoutrements. More particularly, the tents of the caliphs and the viziers were decorated with *ṣuwar adamiyya wa-waḥshiyya*: *op cit.*, i, 474; some tents bore a special name according to whether they were decorated with elephants, lions, horses, peacocks or birds: *op cit.*, i, 418. On the activity of Fāṭimid painters (*muzawwiḳūn*), see al-Maḳrīzī, *op. cit.*, ii, 318.

P. 880ᵃ, **FENER**, *add to Bibliography*: J. Gottwald, *Phanariotische Studien*, in *Vierteljahrschrift für Südosteuropa*, v/1-2 (1941), 1-58.

P. 919ᵇ, **FIRDAWSĪ**, l. 63, *for* ii, 477 *read* i, 493.

P. 965ᵃ, **FUTUWWA**, l. 36, *for Basṭ madad al-tawfīḳ read Kitāb al-Futuwwa* (*Basṭ madad al-tawfīḳ* being the title not of the *K. al-Futuwwa* but of a short treatise composed in Ottoman Egypt; see the preface of H. Thorning, *Beiträge zur Kenntnis des isl. Vereinswesen*, 1913, 9 f.).

P. 967ᵃ, l. 1, *after* documents, *add*: *e.g.* Ibn Baṭṭūṭa, selections tr. H. A. R. Gibb, London 1929, 123-41; tr. H. A. R. Gibb (Hakluyt ser.), ii, 1959, 413-68.
l. 13 *of Bibliography, add*: Irène Mélikoff, *Abū Muslim, le "Porte-hache" du Khorasan*, Paris 1962; *and at end of Bibliography, add*: M. Molé, *Kubrawiyāt II, Ali b. Şihābaddīn-i Hamadānī'nin Risāla-i futuwwatīya'sı*, in *Şarkiyat Mecmuası*, iv (1961), 33-72.

P. 969ᵃ, ll. 9-10 *of Bibliography, for* A complete copy .... Basle, *read* A complete copy, formerly in the possession of Prof. Tschudi, is now in the University Library of Basle (M. VI. 35);

P. 969ᵇ, l. 15, *after* (Rieu, 44) *add* see now the communication by R. M. Savory, in *Isl.*, xxxviii (1963), 161-5.

P. 970ᵇ, **GABAN**, *at end of article add*: In 1137 Gaban was taken by the Byzantines, but was occupied soon afterwards (1138-9) by Malik Aḥmad Dānishmand. In 613/1216 the district was attacked by Kay Kāʾūs I [*q.v.*]. In 666/1268 king Haytham was obliged to cede the fortress to Baybars. *and add to Bibl.*: Alishan, *Sissouan*, 48-9, 210; Cl. Cahen, *La Syrie . . .*, 360, 623; R. Grousset, *Hist. des Croisades*, ii, 87, 266; K. M. Setton (ed.), *History of the Crusades*, ii, 637, iii, 635; Maḳrīzī, *Sulūk*, i/2, 528-9; Ibn Iyās, *Taʾrīkh*, i, 229-30; Ramsay, *Asia Minor*, 382.

P. 996ᵇ, **GHALĀFIḲA**, l. 13, *for* L. O. Schuman *read* L. S. Schuman.

P. 1021ᵃ, **GHASSĀN**, l. 6, *after* ʿAyn Ubāgh *delete* [*q.v.*].
[Shortly before this article by Dr Shahîd was published, the editors interpolated a note communicated to them by another scholar, which introduced a newly-discovered inscription from a Ghassānid building. Dr Shahîd has now pointed out to them that this note on buildings deals with an aspect of the subject which he had discussed in articles listed in his Bibliography and which he had therefore decided not to treat in detail in the body of the article; the insertion of the note might give the impression that the editors had thought that the part allotted to Ghassānid buildings was insufficient. The editors readily express their regret if any such misunderstanding has occurred and take this opportunity of mentioning that Dr Shahîd is at present engaged on a book on Arab-Byzantine relations before the rise of Islam which will include a comprehensive chapter on Ghassanid structures.]

P. 1074ᵃ, **GHINĀʾ**, ll. 8-9, *for* Ibn Bāna [*q.v.*] or Bānata (d. 278/891) *read* ʿAmr b. Bāna or Bānata (d. 278/891) [see IBN BĀNA].

C

CABRA [see ḲABRA]

CADIZ [see ḲĀDIS]

CAESAREA [see ḲAYSARIYYA, KAYSERI, SHARSHAL]

ČAGHĀNIYĀN (Arabic rendering: Ṣaghāniyān). In the early Middle Ages this was the name given to the district of the Čaghān-Rūd [*q.v.*] valley. This river is the northernmost tributary of the river Āmū-Daryā [*q.v.*]. The district lies to the north of the town of Tirmidh [*q.v.*], the area of which, however, (including Čamangān) did not form part of Čaghāniyān either politically or administratively (Ibn Khurradādhbih, 39). Wē/aishagirt (= Fayḍābād) was regarded as the boundary with the district of Khuttalān ([*q.v.*]; between the rivers Pandj and Wakhsh). Incidentally, the area around Ḳabādiyān (Ḳuwādiyān; [*q.v.*]) to the south-east, has frequently been regarded as an independent district.

The region had a pleasant climate, good water supplies, good soil, and corresponding agriculture. Its peasants, however, were considered lazy, thus a considerable number of poor (*darwīshān*) were to be found in Čaghāniyān, and the area was sparsely populated. The capital was also called Čaghāniyān (the derivation by Markwart, Wehrot 93, from the Mongol *čaghan* 'white' is surely wrong). It was situated on the side of a hill where there was running water. The population of the town was also regarded as poor and ill-educated, and despite its greater size, it was soon overshadowed by Tirmidh (Iṣṭakhrī, 298; *Ḥudūd al-ʿĀlam*, 114, no. 25 and no. 27, also *ibid.*, 63, 119, 198; Samʿānī 352 v). Round the year 985, the taxes were 48,529 dirhams (Muḳaddasī, 283, 290). Other known places in the district were Bārangī and Dārzangī. *Maps* of the area: *Ḥudūd al-ʿĀlam*, 339, and Le Strange, map ix.

History: In the 5th and 6th centuries, Čaghāniyān was one of main Hephthalite (see HAYṬAL) areas and was under Buddhist influence. Even in the 4th/10th century it was considered a border region against the 'Kumēdjī', who are regarded as remnants of the Hephthalites (Bayhaḳī, ed. Morley, 499, 576, 611, 696; and also Markwart, *Wehrot* 93 f., with further data), though they may also have belonged to the Saks (*Ḥudūd al-ʿĀlam*, 363). In Sāsānid times, it was ruled by its own dynasty with the title Čaghān-Khudāt (Ṭabarī, ii, 1596). In 31/651, its troops took part in Yazdagird III's fight against the attacking Arabs. Some of them (prisoners ?) could be found in Baṣra around 59/678 (Balādhurī, ed. De Goeje, 419 f. = ed. Cairo 1901, 413; Spuler, *Iran*, 19). In 86/705 the Čaghān-Khudāt submitted to Ḳutayba b. Muslim [*q.v.*], who had conquered Transoxania for the Muslims. Thus Čaghāniyān became part of an Islamic region, and accepted its culture from Balkh rather than from Bukhārā and Samarḳand (*Ṭabarī*, ii, 1180; Dīnawarī, *Akhbār*, 330; Spuler, *Iran*, 29 and note 6; H. A. R. Gibb, *Arab Conquests in Central Asia*, 1923, 32 (Turkish ed., 28); Gh. H. Sadighi, *Les mouvements relig. iraniens*, 1938, 24 f.). In 119-121/737-9, the inhabitants fought on the side of the Arabs against the western Turks, their allies, and Sughd refugees (Ṭabarī, ii, 1596; Ind., p. 735; Barthold, *Turkestan*, 191; B. G. Gafurov, *Ist. Tadžikskogo Naroda*, i, 1949, 147). They took part in the civil war between the Umayyads and ʿAbbāsids (Ṭabari. ii, 1423, 1767); in 191-195/806-10, in the rising of Rāfiʿ b. Layth against the ʿAbbāsids (Yaʿḳūbī, *Hist. Isl.*, 1883, ii, 528), and in 323/934, followed for a short time a certain 'False Prophet' Mahdī (name? title?) (Gardīzī, 37 f.). Abū ʿAlī (see ILYĀSIDS), who ruled over this district as well as over Tirmidh and Shūman and Kharūn further east, had come here for purposes of defence in 337/948, after he had been deposed as governor of Khurāsān. He is described as a member of the Muḥtādj dynasty. It is not evident whether there was a link between this house and the Čaghān-Khudāt. When he became governor of Khurāsān once more in 341/952, he passed the rule of Čaghāniyān on to his son. Deposed again in 343/954, he was buried in Čaghāniyān (Radab-Shaʿbān 344/Nov. 955) (Ibn Ḥawḳal 401; Muḳaddasī 337; Gardīzī 36 f.; Yāḳūt, *Learned Men* (Gibb Mem. Ser. VI), i, 143; Barthold, *Turkestan*, 233, 247/49; Spuler, *Iran*, 97).

Towards the end of the 4th/10th century, a lengthy war broke out between the *amīr* of Čaghāniyān (who ranked as one of the *Mulūk al-aṭrāf*), the rulers of Gōzgān (Djūzdjān; [*q.v.*]), and other candidates (Narshakhī, 157; further information in Barthold, *Turkestan*, 254; Minorsky in *Ḥudūd al-ʿĀlam*, 178, with further data). It ended in 390/999, when Čaghāniyān came under Ḳarakhānid rule. In 416/1025, the district joined Maḥmūd of Ghazna, and in 426/1035, it repelled Ḳarakhānid attempts to recover it with the assistance of the Ghaznawids (Bayhaḳī, ed. Morley, 82, 98, 255, 575 f., 611, 616 [see ḲARĀKHĀNIDS]). Finally, Čaghāniyān came under Saldjūḳ rule in 451/1059. They suppressed a rising in 457/1064 (Ibn al-Athīr, ed. Tornberg, x, 22). By *ca.* 561/1165, the Ḳarakhānids (who were subject to the Ḳara Khitāy) had once again achieved a position of great influence (al-Kātib al-Samarḳandī, in Barthold, *Turk. russ.*, i, 71 f.). Around the years 570-571/1174-75, the country came under the rule of the Ghūrids (Djūzdjānī, *Ṭabaḳāt*, 423-6).

The district is not mentioned during the time of the Mongol conquests; and subsequently it is hardly found in Mongol sources. In the 7th/13th century, Čaghāniyān belonged to the Čaghatāy empire, and the Transoxanian Khān Baraḳ (generally called Burāḳ [*q.v.*] by the Muslims) had the centre of his empire here in 663-670/1264-71. In Tīmūr's time, the place-name *Dih-i naw* (now: *Dēnaw*) is mentioned (Sharaf al-Dīn Yazdī, ed. Iláhdád, 1885, i, 124), and this appears to be on the site of the ancient town of Čaghāniyān (thus Barthold, *Turkestan*, 72; Markwart, *Wehrot*, 93). There is mention of Čaghāniyān on only one further occasion, in the *Bābur-nāma* (ed. Beveridge, 1905, index), where it is probably a historical reminiscence. Apparently no mediaeval ruins have survived in Čaghāniyān, and the old settlements have vanished. Today the district belongs to the Özbek SSR, and the Özbek language has supplanted the old Iranian. The regions to the east of the Kāfirnahān river, however, together with Ḳabādiyān, belong to the Tādjīk language area and to the Tādjīk SSR.

Bibliography: W. Barthold, *Turkestan*, index; Le Strange, 435-40; J. Markwart, *Wehrot und Arang*, 1938, index; *Ḥudūd al-ʿĀlam*, index; B. Spuler, *Iran*, index. (B. SPULER)

ČAGHĀN-RŪD (ČAGHĀN-RŌDH), the seventh and last tributary on the right of the river Āmū-Daryā [*q.v.*]. It comes from the Buttam mountains, to the north of Čaghāniyān [*q.v.*], flows past that town and several smaller places, and finally into the Āmū-Daryā above Tirmidh. The river is called by this name only in the *Ḥudūd al-ʿĀlam*, (71, no. 11, p. 363), and in Sharaf al-Dīn ʿAlī Yazdī, *Ẓafar-nāma* (ed. Iláhdád), 1885, i, 196 (= translation by F. Pétis de la Croix, i, 183). Muḳaddasī, 22, calls it "river of Čaghāniyān", and distinguishes it from the Kāfirnihān, the 6th tributary (further to the east) of the Āmū-Daryā. Ibn Rusta, (*BGA* vii, 93), on the other hand, gets the two rivers, their sources, and their tributaries mixed up; he calls the Čaghān-Rūd: Zāmi/Zamul. Today, the upper part of the river is known as Ḳara Ṭagh Daryā, and from Dih-i naw (Dēnaw = Čaghāniyān) onwards: Surkhān.

Bibliography: Le Strange, 436, 440; W. Barthold, *Turkestan*, 72; J. Markwart, *Wehrot und Arang*, 1938, 89-94 (he attempts a classification of the pre-Islamic Iranian sources); B. Spuler, *Der Āmū-Darjā*, 234 (in *Jean Deny Armağanı*, Ankara 1958, 231-48); Brockhaus-Efron, *Enciklop. Slovaŕ* xxxii/1 (= 63), St. Petersburg 1901, 109; *Bol'shaya Sovetskaya Éntsiklop*². 41, (1956) 315. (B. SPULER)

ČAGHATAY KHĀN, founder of the Čaghatay Khanate [*q.v.*], the second son of Čingiz-Khān and his chief wife Börte Fudjin. Already in his father's lifetime he was regarded as the greatest authority on the *Yasa* (the tribal laws of the Mongols as codified by Čingiz-Khān). Like his brothers he took part in his father's campaigns against China (1211-1216) and against the kingdom of the Khʷārizm-Shāh (1219-1224). Urgāndj, the latter's capital, was besieged by the three princes Djoči, Čaghatay and Ögedey and taken in Ṣafar 618/27th March-24th April 1221. In the same year Čaghatay's eldest son Mö'etüken was slain before Bāmiyān. After the battle on the Indus (according to Nasawī, transl. Houdas, 83, on Wednesday 7 Shawwāl 618, probably 24 November 1221) Čaghatay was entrusted with operations against Sulṭān Djalāl al-Dīn Khʷārizm-Shāh and spent the winter of 1221-1222 in India. During Čingiz-Khān's final campaign against the Tangut (1225-1227) he remained in Mongolia in command of the forces left behind there.

After his father's death Čaghatay no longer took an active part in any of the campaigns. As the eldest surviving son of Čingiz-Khān (his brother Djoči had predeceased his father) he enjoyed enormous prestige. In the year 1229 he presided with his uncle Otčigin over the *kuriltay* at which Ögedey was elected Great Khān: owing to his position as the recognized authority on the *yasa*, he exercised an influence to which even the Great Khān Ögedey had to bow. He seems to have spent this period partly in Mongolia at his brother's court, partly in the territory allotted to him by Čingiz-Khān, where he held his own court-camp. Like all the Mongol princes Čaghatay had separate camps (*ordu*) for winter and summer. His summer residence according to Djuwaynī was at some place on the Ili whilst his winter quarters were at Ḳuyas, probably to be identified with the Equius of William of Rubruck, near Almaligh, *i.e.*, in the region of the present-day Kulja. The residence of Čaghatay's successors is called Ulugh Ef (in Turkish „Great House") by Djuwaynī and others.

Čaghatay had received from his father all the lands from the Uyghur territory in the east to Bukhārā and Samarḳand in the west: we must not however regard these lands as a single kingdom governed from the Ili valley and only indirectly subject to the Great Khān. Everywhere, even in the Ili valley itself, the local dynasties who were there before the Mongols remained. On the relationship of these dynasties to the Mongol rulers we have no accurate information; we know equally little about what sovereign rights the court on the Ili could claim from the Great Khān and his deputies. The settled lands of Central Asia were certainly not governed in the name of Čaghatay but in that of the Great Khān. In the account of the suppression of the rebellion in Bukhārā in 636/1238-1239 Čaghatay is not mentioned; the governor of Mā warāʾ al-Nahr at this period was Maḥmūd Yalavač, a Khʷārizmī by birth, who had been appointed by the Great Khān. Even the generals of the Mongol forces in Mā warāʾ al-Nahr were appointed by the Great Khān. When, soon afterwards, Maḥmūd Yalavač was arbitrarily dismissed from his office by Čaghatay the latter was called to account by his brother and had to admit the illegality of his action. Ögedey was satisfied with this apology and granted the land to his brother as a fief (*indjü*); but the legal position of this territory was not thereby altered. During the last years of Ögedey's reign, as well as under Möngke, all settled areas from the Chinese frontier to Bukhārā were governed by Masʿūd Beg, the son of Maḥmūd Yalavač, in the name of the Great Khān.

It cannot be ascertained how far Čaghatay's Muslim minister Ḳuṭb al-Dīn Ḥabash ʿAmīd had a share in the administration of the country along with the representatives of the Great Khān. According to Rashīd al-Dīn this minister came from Otrar, according to Djamāl Ḳarshī from Karmīna, and like many other Muslim dignitaries at this time had made his fortune among the Mongols as a merchant. He was on terms of such intimacy with the Khān that each of Čaghatay's sons had one of Habash ʿAmīd's sons as a companion.

In general Čaghatay was not favourably inclined towards Islam. Among the infringements of Mongol law which he rigidly punished was the observance of certain prescriptions of Islam. Among the Mongols it was forbidden to slaughter an animal by cutting its throat, which is the method prescribed by the *sharīʿa*; another law frequently broken by the Muslims at their ablutions was that which prohibited washing in running water. The cruel punishment which Čaghatay visited upon any such transgressions made his name hated among the Muslims.

According to Djuwaynī, Čaghatay survived his brother Ögedey, who died on 5 Djumādā II 639/11th December 1241 though only for a short period. On the other hand Rashīd al-Dīn states that he died seven months before Ögedey, *i.e.*, apparently in the beginning of May, 1241.

Bibliography: Djuwaynī-Boyle; Rashīd al-Dīn, *Djāmiʿ al-Tawārīkh*, ed. E. Blochet, Leiden 1911; V. V. Barthold, *Four Studies on the History of Central Asia*, Vol. i, transl. V. and T. Minorsky, Leiden 1956. (W. Barthold-[J. A. Boyle])

ČAGHATAY KHĀNATE. The Central Asian Khānate to which Čaghatay gave his name was really not founded till some decades after the Mongol prince's death. Čaghatay was succeeded by his grandson Ḳara-Hülegü, the son of Mö'etüken who fell at Bāmiyān. Ḳara-Hülegü had been designated as Čaghatay's heir both by Čingiz-Khān himself and by Ögedey; he was however deposed by the Great Khān Güyük (1241-1248) in favour of Yesü-Möngke, the fifth son of Čaghatay, with whom Güyük was on terms of personal friendship. In 1251 Yesü-Möngke was involved in the conspiracy against the Great Khān Möngke, who reinstated Kara-Hülegü and handed Yesü-Möngke over to him for execution. Ḳara-Hülegü however did not survive the homeward journey and the execution was carried out by his widow, Princess Orḳīna, who now ruled in her husband's stead, though her authority does not seem to have extended beyond the Ili valley. As appears from the narrative of William of Rubruck, the whole Empire was at this period divided between Möngke and Batu: Batu's portion was the whole area west of a line between the rivers Talas and Ču, east of which all territories were directly subject to the Great Khān. Masʿūd Beg [see the previous article], who enjoyed the confidence of both Khāns, was governor of all the settled areas between Besh-Balīgh and Khʷārizm.

With the death of the Great Khān Möngke in 1259 a different condition of things arose. During the struggle for supremacy between Ḳubilay and Arīgh Böke, the brothers of the late Khān, Alughu, a grandson of Čaghatay, agreed to take possession of Central Asia for Arīgh Böke and support him from that quarter against his enemies. He actually succeeded in bringing the whole of Central Asia under his sway, including areas such as Khʷārizm and the present-day Afghānistān which had never previously been numbered amongst the possessions of the House of Čaghatay. He had of course won these victories for himself and not for Arīgh Böke. He everywhere proclaimed himself as an independent ruler; and Arīgh Böke, who had tried to assert his rights, was finally forced to vacate this territory after some initial successes. Masʿūd Beg still remained the governor of the settled areas, now no longer in the name of the Great Khān but as the representative of Alughu.

Alughu may be regarded as the founder of an independent Mongol state in Central Asia: he enjoyed his success only for a brief period, as he died in 664/1265-1266. Mubārak-Shāh, the son of Kara-Hülegü and Orkīna, the first Čaghatay convert to Islam, was proclaimed Khān in March 1266. Already in the same year he was dethroned by his cousin Burāḳ (or rather Baraḳ) Khān [*q.v.*], the nominee of the Great Khān, who was soon however to become little more than a satellite of Ḳaydu [*q.v.*], now the real master of Central Asia. After Burāk's death in 1271 Ḳaydu appointed Nīkpāy, a grandson of Čaghatay, to succeed him; Nīkpāy was followed by Buḳa-Temür, another grandson of Čaghatay; and in 1282, Ḳaydu's choice fell upon Duʾa, the son of Burāḳ. The faithful ally of Ḳaydu in all his wars against the Great Khān, Duʾa defeated and deposed his son Čapar shortly before his own death in 1306 or 1307. The Čaghatay Khānate was from now on to remain in Duʾa's family almost to the moment of its extinction, the throne being occupied, for longer or shorter periods, by six of his sons, of whom we need mention here only Esen-Buḳa (1309-1318), Kebek (1318-1326) and Tarmashirin (1326-1334).

It was some time before the Čaghatay Khanate received an independent organisation of its own. Djamāl Karshī's work, written in the reign of Čapar shows that affairs in Central Asia were in much the same condition even at this period, when there had long been a strong Mongol central government in China and Persia, as they had been in the early years of the Mongol conquest. The Mongols were apparently less under the influence of Islam and Muslim culture than in Persia and were able to preserve their own peculiar ways of life for a much longer period of time. Except in the Uyghur country Islam was everywhere the state religion by the time of the Mongol conquest, even in the Ili valley, although these areas had been little influenced by Arabo-Persian culture. The Mongol conquest, as Rubruck pointed out, was followed in these regions by an extension of the pasture lands at the expense of the towns and cultivated areas; at a later period urban life altogether disappeared under the influence of Mongol rule, except in Mā warāʾ al-Nahr and the present-day Sinkiang. The Muslim civilisation of Mā warāʾ al-Nahr naturally exercised some influence on the Mongols, particularly the rulers; but this influence was not strong enough to induce the mass of the people to change their mode of life. When the ruling family decided to settle in Mā warāʾ al-Nahr and break with the customs of the people, their action resulted in the complete separation of the eastern provinces.

Even the brief reign of Yesü-Möngke (1246-1251) appears to have been favourable to those who professed Islam. The chief minister then was a friend of the Khān's youth and a foster-son of Ḥabash ʿAmīd, Bahāʾ al-Dīn Marghīnānī, a descendant of the *Shuyūkh al-Islām* of Farghāna. As a patron of poets and scholars he is praised by his contemporary Djuwaynī, who was personally acquainted with him. Ḥabash ʿAmid, who was hated by the Khān as an adherent of Ḳara-Hülegü, owed his life to the intercession of Bahāʾ al-Dīn. Nevertheless, when Bahāʾ al-Dīn was involved in his master's downfall, he was handed over to his foster-father, who ordered his execution in the cruellest fashion.

Under Orḳīna, Ḥabash ʿAmīd again occupied the position he had held under Čaghatay; this princess however was favourably inclined to the Muslims; she is described by Waṣṣāf as a protectress of Islam and by Djamāl Karshī was even said to be a Muslim. Her son Mubārak-Shāh, raised to the throne in Mā warāʾ al-Nahr, certainly adopted Islam, as did his rival Burāḳ Khān some years later. The rule of Alughu seems to have been less favourable to the Muslims, and the events of the following years postponed for several decades the final victory of Muslim culture. Ḳaydu and Čapar, as well as Duʾa and other princes, remained pagans and resided in the eastern provinces. In the reign of Esen-Buḳa the armies of the Great Khān penetrated deep into Central Asia and ravaged the winter and summer residences of the Khān; the continuator of Rashīd al-Dīn in his account of these happenings says that the winter residence was in the region of the Issik-Kul, while the summer residence was on the Talas.

Esen-Buḳa's successor Kebek was the first to return to the settled lands of Mā warā᾽ al-Nahr. Though he did not adopt Islam he is praised by Muslims as a just prince; he is said to have built or restored several towns; he also had built for himself a palace in the neighbourhood of Nakhshab, from which the town takes its modern name of Ḳarshî (from the Mongol word for "palace"). He introduced the silver coins afterwards called *Kebekī*, which may be considered the first independent coinage of the Čaghatay Khānate.

After two brief interregnums Kebek's brother Tarmashirin was raised to the throne. This Khān adopted Islam and took the name of ʿAlā᾽ al-Dīn; the eastern provinces were entirely neglected by him and the nomads of those provinces rose against him as a violator of the *Yasa*. This rebellion appears to have taken place about 734/1333-1334; it was headed by Buzan, a nephew of the Khān, and resulted in Tarmashirin's flight and death. Buzan can have reigned only for a few months since he was succeeded in 1334 by Čangshi, another nephew of Tarmashirin. Statements of contemporary Christian missionaries show that the centre of the Khānate was now again transferred for a brief period to the Ili valley and Christians were allowed to propagate their religion unhindered and to build churches; it is even said that a 7-year old son of Čangshi was baptised with his father's consent and received the name of Johannes.

Some years later Nakhshab is mentioned again as the residence of the Čaghatay Khān. This was Ḳazan, who was descended, not like Du᾽a and his sons from Yesün-To᾽a, but from Büri, another son of Mö᾽etüken. Ḳazan fell in battle in 747/1346-1347 in the course of a struggle against the Turkish aristocracy, and with his death the rule of his house in Mā warā᾽ al-Nahr came to an end. Till 1370, descendants of Čaghatay were placed on the throne by the Turkish amīrs as nominal rulers; in the time of Tīmūr these rulers were chosen from the family of Ögedey. Nevertheless under Tīmūr and his successors the nomad population of Mā warā᾽ al-Nahr, who as a warrior caste enjoyed many privileges, were still as before called Čaghatay.

Bibliography: As in the article on Čaghatay. For genealogical tables of the House of Čaghatay, based on both the Chinese and the Persian sources, see Louis Hambis, *Le chapitre cvii du Yuan che*, Leiden 1945.

(W. Barthold-[J. A. Boyle])

ČAGHATĀY LITERATURE [see turks]

ČAGHATĀY TURKISH [see turks]

ČAGHRÎ-BEG Dāwūd b. Mīkhā᾽īl b. Saldjūḳ was the brother of Ṭughrîl-Beg [*q.v.*], and the co-founder with him of the Saldjūḳid dynasty. The careers of both brothers were, for the most part, inextricably bound together. It is difficult to ascertain which was the elder brother. They seem to have been born about 380-385/990-995, and there is no evidence whether their family was already, or only later became, Muslim. Little is known about their life before the year 416/1025. They were orphaned at an early age, and must have been brought up, until they were about fifteen years old, by their grandfather Saldjūḳ, in the Djand region, during which time their uncle Arslan-Isrā᾽īl was fighting in the service of the last Sāmānids. After the death of the grandfather, ill-defined political reasons caused them to remove, with a section of their tribe, to the territory owned by a Ḳarakhānid who was, for a time, known under the title-name of Bughrā-Khān. Subsequently they quarrelled with him, and joined, without, however, combining their forces with his, their uncle, who was then in the service of a rival Ḳarakhānid, ʿAlī-Tegīn of Bukhārā. Tradition gives here an account of a highly improbable escapade of Čaghrî-Beg in Armenia. In 416/1025, the Saldjūḳids were involved in the defeat of ʿAlī-Tegīn by the combined forces of Maḥmūd of Ghazna and the supreme Ḳarakhānid, Ḳadir-Khān, whereupon Arslan-Isrā᾽īl, with his tribal group, had to settle in Ghazna territory. Ṭughrîl and Čaghrî, on the other hand, remained with ʿAlī-Tegīn, and then, after being involved in disagreements with him, possibly over the leadership of the tribe, transferred themselves to Khwārizm (between 421/1030 and 425/1034 ?). The threats of the Oghuz prince Shāh-Malik, the old enemy of their family, who had by then become master of Djand, forced upon them another displacement, and, as the Turcomans of the Ghazna territory had abandoned their Khurāsānian encampments as a result of disorders following the death of Mahmūd, Ṭughrîl and Čaghrî demanded, and then seized forcibly, from his successor, Masʿūd, the right to take their place. Although they had become the quasi-official concessionaries of the border plains to the north of western Khurāsān, they certainly did not show themselves to be well-behaved guests. Maʿsūd was at first unaware of the potential seriousness of what he believed to be mere local unrests, but even the town populations grew weary of paying taxes to the Ghaznawid without being safeguarded against the pillage of their countryside. The Saldjūḳids had, on the other hand, represented themselves to the Muslim aristocracy as faithful adherents of the orthodox religion, and a growing party, in Khurāsān, felt that it was advisable, by submitting to them, to divert elsewhere the depredations of their men. In 423/1036 Marw opened its gates to Čaghrî-Beg, who had the *Khuṭba* recited there in his name as autonomous prince. Soon Nishāpūr did the same for Ṭughrîl, and then, later, Čaghrî penetrated into Harāt and sent his kinsmen towards the Sīstān region. Maʿsūd reacted too late. His heavy armies wore themselves out physically and morally chasing an elusive enemy across the desert, and, in 431/1040, at Dandānḳān the Saldjūḳids defeated him beyond all hope of recovery.

The conquerors divided up their conquered territories, and, while Ṭughrîl went off to try his luck at fresh conquests in Iran, Čaghrî kept, in Khurāsān, the base of the young Saldjūḳid power. His career there has nothing to compare with the remarkable developments that followed that of his brother. During the first four years, he made complete his possession of Khurāsān by annexing, on the one hand, Balkh and then Tirmidh, and, on the other, Khwārizm, whose prince had been driven out by Shāh-Malik. In addition, a son of Čaghrî, Kavurt, acting in a more or less autonomous capacity, occupied Kirmān. But from then onwards, the chief military activity of Čaghrî's forces consisted in a difficult struggle against the Ghaznawids, who, in their mountain stronghold, and fortified with the resources found in their Indus provinces, resumed the war, sometimes with success. The intrigues of the Ghaznawids compromised, but for a very short time only, the relations of the Saldjūḳids with the neighbouring Karakhānids. On their side, the Saldjūḳids interfered in the internal quarrels of Ghazna, where Masʿūd's successor, Mawdūd, had married a daughter of Čaghrî, but where, against a successor of Mawdūd, the Saldjūḳids encouraged the usurper Farrukhzād, only to find themselves soon afterwards at war with him also. Hostilities went on intermittently in the Balkh and the Sīstān districts, and in Sīstān the danger was for a while so grave that it became necessary to recall the Turcomans temporarily from Kirmān. Čaghrî was, by that time, old, and the conduct of operations fell in fact upon his son Alp-Arslan [*q.v.*]. Saldjūḳids and Ghaznawids were forced to recognize that their power was about equal, and in 451/1060, Čaghrî and Ibrāhīm of Ghazna concluded a peace that remained virtually undisturbed by their successors. Some months later, Čaghrî died (at the beginning of 452/ end of 1060).

Practically nothing is known of Čaghrî-Beg's government. The chief of the plundering nomads became prince of a territory in which the traditional administration was continued or resumed. He gave himself the title of *Malik al-Mulūk*. A brother of the famous Ismāʿīlī writer Nāṣir-i Khusraw for a long time held a prominent position in the service of his vizir, but it would be impossible to conclude from this a heterodox orientation on the part of the sovereign. Nevertheless, the fact that neither Niẓām al-Mulk nor the authors of moral tales, nor the *dīwān*s of the poets, have preserved any noteworthy information about Čaghrî from the time that he was separated from his brother, gives the impression of a weaker personality and a rather passive political attitude, from a religious and all other points of view.

It is difficult even to obtain a clear assessment of Čaghrî's relations with his kinsfolk. After Dandāḳān, Sīstān appears to have been handed over to Mūsā Payghu (Yabghu?), the uncle of Čaghrî and Ṭughrîl, but the power of the chiefs of this family seems to have been unstable, and in 446-448/1055-1057, hostilities arose between them and Yāḳūtī, one of Čaghrî's sons, who came, it is true, from Kirmān. It appears that from then onwards Čaghrî was considered in Sīstān as the suzerain over his young cousins. A more important question is that of the relations between Čaghrî and Ṭughrîl, holding in mind the successes that made the latter the protector of the Caliphate and the legally recognized master of the entire Muslim East. The only certainty is that the good relations between them were never belied. It seems that in Sīstān Čaghrî accepted Ṭughrîl's decisions. In any case, when in 450/1058-9, the revolt of Ibrāhīm Ināl constituted a grave threat to Ṭughrîl's sultanate, Tughrîl in part owed his preservation to the help brought to him by Alp-Arslan and Yāḳūtī. Relations between Čaghrî and Ṭughrîl must have been made easier by the fact that the latter was childless. Therefore when the Caliph wanted to form a marriage alliance with him, it was a daughter of Čaghrî that became the wife of al-Ḳāʾim. Čaghrî had married a Khwārizmian princess, who had already a son, Sulaymān. When his brother died, Ṭughrîl married her. It is not certain whether Alp-Arslan, who was to unite the two inheritances, had been selected for that fortune by the two ruling brothers, or whether, as Ṭughrîl's vizir declared, Sulaymān had been intended—at all events, the latter had played no role under either Čaghrî or Ṭughrîl.

Bibliography: A. Sources. On the origins there is little information available except through the *Malik-nāma*, which is lost but utilized by Ibn al-Athīr, ʿAlī b. Nāṣir (*Akhbār al-dawla al-Saldjūḳiyya*, ed. Muḥ. Iḳbāl, Lahore 1933), Bar-Hebraeus (*Chronography*, ed. trans. Budge), and especially Mīrkhwānd. From the time of the entry into Khurāsān onwards, this source can be supplemented by the Ghazna historians, Bayhaḳī and Gardīzī (see also the analysis of the former by Kazimirski in his introduction to the *Dīwān* of Manūčihrī), and also by Ẓahīr al-Dīn Nīshāpūrī (now published by Djalāl-i Khāvar, Tehran 1953, making unnecessary the *Rāḥat al-Ṣudūr* of his embellisher Rāwandī). Sources are scanty for Čaghrî's autonomous period, the chief ones being Ibn al-Athīr and the *Akhbār*, supplemented locally by the *Taʾrīkh-i Bayhaḳ* of Ibn Funduḳ, ed. Bahmanyar, 1938, and the anonymous *Taʾrīkh-i Sīstān*, ed. Bahār 1937 (there exists, on the other hand, nothing on Čaghrî specifically in the histories of Kirmān). His relations with Ṭughrîl are treated in Ibn al-Athīr, and also in the other largely Mesopotamian chronicles, especially the *Mirʾāt al-Zamān* of Sibṭ Ibn al-Djawzī. Also to be consulted are the beginning and end of Nāṣir-i Khusraw, *Safar-nāma*.

B. Modern Studies. Barthold, *Turkestan*; Muḥ. Nāẓim, *The Life and Times of Sultan Mahmud of Ghazna*, 1931; Cl. Cahen, *Malik-nameh et l'histoire des origines saldjukides*, in *Oriens*, 1949; art. *Čaghrî-Beg*, in *IA*, by Mukr. Halil Yınanç. On the legendary escapade (?) of Čaghrî in Armenia, the article of Ibrahim Kafesoğlu, *Doğu Anadoluya ilk selcuklu akını*, in *Fuad Köprülü Armağanı*, 1953, and my discussion with him in *JA* 1954, 275 ff. and 1956, 129 ff.

(Cl. Cahen)

ČAHĀR AYMAḲ, four semi-nomadic tribes in western Afghānistān [see AYMAḲ]. There is little information and much confusion about these tribes, consequently various sources have different names, locations and even languages ascribed to them. At the present they speak Persian and are Sunnīs, unlike the Shīʿī Hazāras with whom the Čahār Aymaḳ are closely linked. Some sources erroneously identify the two. The origin of the name Čahār Aymaḳ is unknown but is at least as early as the 18th century A.D. at the time of the early Durranī empire. It may have been originally a name of a tribal confederation formed between local Persian-speakers and Mongol Hazāras against the Turkomans. The admixture of Turkic elements is also probable. The Djamshīdīs live north of Harāt with their centre at Kushk. The Taymūrī or Sunnī Hazāras are scattered with one centre at Ḳalʿa-i Naw; the Taymānī are located in Ghūr, and the Fīrūzkūhī on the upper reaches of the Murghāb River. The origins and history of the various tribes are unknown. Their number has been estimated from 400,000 to a million.

Bibliography: G. Jarring, *On the Distribution of Turk Tribes in Afghanistan*, Lunds Universitets Årsskrift, 35 (1939), 79-81, where older bibliography is given. Add. B. Dorn, *History of the Afghans*, London 1829, ii, 69; A. C. Yate, *Travels with the Afghan Boundary Commission*, London 1887, 228-234; D. Wilber, *Afghanistan* (Human Relations Area Files, New Haven 1956), 55; N. A. Kislyakov and A. Pershits, *Narodî Predney Aziy*, Moscow 1957, 23. 107, 124. (R. N. Frye)

ČAHĀR MAḲĀLA [see NIẒĀMĪ ʿARŪḌĪ SAMARḲANDĪ]

CAIN [see ḤĀBĪL WA ḲĀBĪL]

CAIRO [see AL-ḲĀHIRA].

ČAKÎRDJÎ-BASHÎ, chief falconer, a high official of the Ottoman court. In the *Ḳānūnnāme* of Meḥemmed II (*TOEM* Supp. 1330 A.H., 12) he is mentioned among the *aghas* of the stirrup, immediately before the *čashnagîr-bashî* [*q.v.*]. During the 16th century the numbers and sub-divisions of the *aghas* of the hunt (*shikār aghalarî*) increased greatly, and the *Čakîrdjî-bashî* is joined by separate officers in charge of the peregrines, lanners, and sparrow-hawks (*Shahindji-bashî*, *Doghandjî-bashî*, and *Atmadjadjî-bashî*). Until the time of Meḥemmed IV (1058/1648-1099/1687) the *Doghandjî-bashî* and his staff belonged to the Inner service (*Enderūn*); the others to the outer service (*Bîrūn*). During the 17th and 18th centuries the falconers dwindled in numbers and importance.

Bibliography: Gibb and Bowen 1/i, 347-8; Ismail Hakki Uzunçarşılı, *Osmanlı Devletinin Saray Teşkilâtı*, Ankara 1945, 420 ff.

(B. LEWIS)

ČAḲMAḲ, AL-MALIK AL-ẒĀHIR SAYF AL-DĪN, Sultan of Egypt, was in his youth enrolled among the Mamlūks of Sulṭān Barḳūḳ. He gradually rose, till under Sulṭān Barsbāy he became Chief *ḥādjib* [*q.v.*]. Chief Master of the Horse, and finally Atābeg (Commander-in-Chief). On his deathbed in 842/1438, Barsbāy appointed him regent to his infant son al-Malik al-ʿAzīz Yūsuf. The various divisions of the Mamlūks, originating in the body-guards of the Sulṭāns Barḳūḳ, Nāṣir Faradj, Muʾayyad Shaykh and Barsbāy, were at enmity with one another and their sole aim was to obtain all the wealth and influence they could. In the confusion that arose the only course open to Čaḳmaḳ was to seize the reins of government for himself. Sulṭān Yūsuf was deposed, placed in confinement in the citadel, retaken after an attempt to escape and finally taken to Alexandria and kept under a mild form of custody. Soon afterwards the resistance of the governors of Damascus and Aleppo also collapsed; they had been defending Sulṭān Yūsuf's claims to further their own interests. The Syrian rebels were defeated, the leaders executed and Čaḳmaḳ's supremacy was assured in 843/1439. Like his predecessor Barsbāy [*q.v.*] Čaḳmaḳ wished to make war on the Christians under pretence of checking piracy on the north coast and therefore sent ships via Cyprus to Rhodes but the Egyptians had to return as the resistance offered by the Knights of St. John, who were well prepared, was too strong for them. In the years 846/1442 and 848/1444 the Egyptians again made unsuccessful attempts to conquer Rhodes, and had finally to make peace with the Knights. Čaḳmaḳ's foreign policy was a successful one; he was on good terms with all Muslim rulers and did not, like Barsbāy, fall into the error of causing irritation by petty trickeries. Against the advice of his *amīrs*, he allowed Tīmūr's son Shāh Rukh to send a covering for the sacred Kaʿba, although this was a privilege of the Sultans of Egypt (see the article BAIBARS in *EI*[1]). The populace was still so strongly incensed against the Mongols that they actually attacked an embassy which included one of Tīmūr's widows. He was also on good terms with the Ottomān Sultan and the princes of Asia Minor. In his domestic policy, in Egypt itself, he was not quite able to put a stop to the mismanagement of the state monopolies [see BARSBĀY]. Jews and Christians were tormented with strictly enforced petty regulations. He could not restrain the arrogance and outrages of the Mamlūks so that the only way he could protect women from them on the occasion of festivals was to forbid them to go out. He himself was an exceedingly frugal and pious man, liberal only to the learned, and thought no price too high for a beautiful book; he left but little property behind him on his death. Through his example the morals of the court improved. When, in the year 854/1453, he felt the approach of death—he was now over 80 years old—he had homage paid to his son ʿUthmān whom the Caliph chose to be Sultan. The *amīrs* and officials of the court and a large multitude of the people attended his funeral, contrary to the usual custom sincerely grieving at his loss.

Bibliography: Weil, *Chalifen*, v, 215-248; Muir, *Mameluke or Slave Dynasty of Egypt*, 149-155; al-Sakhāwi, *al-Ḍawʾ al-Lamiʿ*, iii, 71-74; Ibn Taghribirdī, *al-Nudjūm*, ed. Popper, vol. vii, 30 ff.; *al-Manhal al-Ṣāfi*, ed. Wiet, no. 838; Ibn Iyās (Būlāḳ), *passim*. (M. SOBERNHEIM)

ÇAKMAK, MUSTAFA FEVZI, also called Kavaklı, marshal in the Turkish army. Born in Istanbul in 1876, he was the son of an artillery colonel. He entered the war academy (Harbiye, [*q.v.*]) where he became a lieutenant in 1895, joined the staff course, and was gazetted as a staff captain in 1898. After spending some time on the general staff, he was posted to Rumelia where he became successively a Colonel, divisional commander, and Army Corps Chief of Staff. He served on the staff of the army of the Vardar during the Balkan War, and during the World War saw service at the Dardanelles, in the Caucasus, and in Syria. He became a general in 1914. In December 1918 he became, for a while, Chief of the General Staff in Istanbul, and in Feb. 1920 Minister of War. He used his position to send arms and give other help to the nationalists in Anatolia, and in April 1920 left with Ismet [Inönü] to join them. In May he became minister of defence and on 21 January 1921 was elected president of the council of ministers of the Ankara government, and was sentenced to death *in absentia* in Istanbul. On 2 April 1921, after the second battle of Inönü, he was promoted full general by the Grand National Assembly, and became acting Chief of the General Staff as well as premier and defence minister. He was formally elected as Chief of Staff by the Assembly on 12 July 1922, while Raʾuf Bey became premier. In October 1922, after the victory of the Turkish forces on the Sakarya, the Assembly passed a motion of thanks to him (together with Ismet and Kâzim Karabekir Pashas), and promoted him marshal (Mushīr). He remained chief of the General Staff until his retirement, ostensibly under the age limit, in January 1944. In 1946 he was elected as an independent candidate on the Democrat Party list, and in August was nominated as opposition candidate for the Presidency, receiving 59 votes in the Assembly, as against 388 for Ismet Inönü. In 1948 he appeared as honorary president of the newly formed Party of the Nation (*Millet Partisi*). He died on 10th April 1950.

Bibliography: Ibrahim Alâettin Gövsa, *Türk Meşhurları Ansiklopedisi*, Istanbul, n.d., 90; Süleyman Külçe, *Mareşal Fevzi Çakmak*[2], Istanbul 1953; Elaine D. Smith, *Turkey: Origins of the Kemalist Movement* . . ., Washington 1959, 168-9.

(ED.)

ČALA [see BUKHĀRĀ]

CALATAYUD [see ḲALʿAT AYYŪB]

CALATRAVA]see ḲALʿAT RABĀḤ]

CALCUTTA (Kalikātā), the capital of West Bengal and the largest city in India, situated about 80 miles from the sea on the left or east bank of the Huglī, a branch of the Gangā (Ganges), which is navigable for the largest ocean vessels. A centre of rail, river and ocean traffic, and lying midway between Europe and the Far East, it is one of the busiest ports of the world. About five-sevenths of India's overseas trade is shared by Calcutta and Bombay, with Calcutta having the major share; about one-third of the country's organized factory industry is in its vicinity. It has a large international airport. Area, 32.32 sq. m.; pop. (March 1, 1951) 2,548,677, a density of 139 persons per acre. Including Howrah (pop. 433, 630) which is really a part of Calcutta, and the suburbs which are within half an hour's bus journey to the city, Calcutta has three and a half million people.

The crowded metropolis of today grew out of a cluster of three mud villages at the end of the 17th century. Calcutta is first mentioned in a Bengali poem, *Manasā-vijaya* by Vipradāsa (ASB text, 144) written in 1495, but the portion in which Calcutta is referred to is possibly a later elaboration. The first definitive mention of Calcutta then occurs in the *Āʾīn-i Akbarī* (Lucknow text, ii, 62), compiled about 1596, as a rent-paying village in the *sarkār* of Sātgāon under the Mug͟hal emperor Akbar. The foundation of the city occurred about a century later in 1690. The English merchants, who had been in Bengal for about fifty years, felt the necessity of a fortified place, and under the direction of Job Charnock and after two futile attempts after 1686 they finally settled at Sūtānuti, the northern portion of present Calcutta, on 24 August, 1690. In 1696 the English were allowed to build a fort and two years later they secured permission from Prince ʿAẓīm, grandson of the emperor Awrangzīb, to rent the three villages of Sūtānuti (north), Kalikātā (centre) and Govindapur (south), which formed the nucleus of modern Calcutta. In 1707 Calcutta was made the seat of a separate Presidency. In 1717 the English were permitted by the emperor Farruk͟hsiyar to purchase 38 villages in the vicinity of their settlement. The names of some of these 38 villages still survive in the street-names of the city today. In June, 1756 Sirād͟j al-Dawla, Nawwāb of Bengal, captured it and during his temporary occupation he named it ʿAlīnagar. Modern Calcutta dates from 1757 when, after the battle of Plassey (June), the English became virtual masters of Bengal; the old fort was abandoned and the present Fort William begun by Clive on the site of Govindapur. In 1772 the treasury of the province was transferred from Murs͟hidābād to Calcutta, which in 1773 became the official capital of British India. It remained India's capital until 1911 and that of Bengal as well until 1947.

Though Calcutta is a creation of English rule, it is an important centre of Muslim life. On 1 March 1951 Calcutta city had a Muslim population of 305,932 and including two of its immediate suburbs, Howrah and Garden Reach, Calcutta had a Muslim population almost equal to the entire population of Ḍhākā (Dacca), the capital of East Pākistān and the historic centre of Muslim activity. About 131,000 Muslims had left Calcutta on the eve of the census of 1951 in view of the unsettled conditions of the time, and the census of 1961 is likely to show a considerable increase of Muslim population. Calcutta is an important centre of Muslim culture. The Calcutta *Madrasa* was founded in 1781 by Warren Hastings for the encouragement of Islamic learning. It had among its Principals Islamic scholars of repute like H. Blochmann and Sir E. Denison Ross. The Asiatic Society, founded in 1784, possesses over 6,000 Arabic and Persian MSS. and has to its credit a large number of valued publications bearing on Muslim history and culture. The National Library has in its Būhār collection a good number of Arabic and Persian MSS. and has recently acquired the rich collection of the distinguished historian of Muslim India, Sir Jadunāth Sarkār. The Indian Museum and the Victoria Memorial exhibit some rare and beautiful examples of Indo-Islamic paintings. The University of Calcutta has two Post-Graduate Islamic departments: (i) Arabic & Persian and (ii) Islamic History & Culture. In Calcutta lived the sons of Tīpū Sulṭān, and the last king of Awadh (Oudh), Wād͟jid ʿAlī S͟hāh, who died in 1887. Of the Muslim monuments, the only one with any architectural pretensions is the mosque in Dharamtalā St., built in 1842 by Prince G͟hulām Muḥammad, son of Tīpū Sulṭān; the oldest are the Nimtalā mosque (built some time after 1784), the mosque and tomb of Bhonsri S͟hāh at Chitpur (1804) and D͟jumma S͟hāh's tomb in Netād͟jī Subhās (Clive) St. (1808).

Bibliography: G͟hulām Ḥusayn Salīm, *Riyāḍ al-Salāṭīn*, Calcutta 1890-98; C. R. Wilson, *Early Annals of the English in Bengal*, vol. i, Calcutta 1895; idem, *Old Fort William in Bengal*, 2 vols., London 1906; *List of Ancient Monuments in Bengal*, Calcutta, Bengal Secretariat Press, 1896; A. K. Ray, *A short history of Calcutta*, Calcutta 1902; H. E. A. Cotton, *Calcutta old and new*, Calcutta 1907.

(Sukumar Ray)

ČĀLDIRĀN, the plain in north-western Persian Ād͟harbayd͟jān, the western boundary forming part of the present-day frontier with Turkey (cf. *Farhang-i D͟jug͟hrāfiyāʾī-yi Īrān*, iv (Tehran, 1330 *s͟hamsī*), 154), which on the 2 Rad͟jab 920/23 August 1514 was the scene of a decisive Ottoman victory over the Ṣafawids.

The campaign was launched by Selīm I, despite the reluctance of his troops and military advisers, on the 23 Muḥarram 920/20 March 1514 as the first enterprise of his reign after he had secured his throne by the elimination of his brothers, and is properly to be regarded as the final response to those separatist tendencies which for over half a century had been manifesting themselves among the Turkish tribal elements of Anatolia in *darwīs͟h* revolts or in active support for pretenders of the Ottoman line, and which now threatened to draw the entire province into the Ṣafawid orbit. The profound disquiet of the region may be judged from the mass executions and arrests of suspected dissidents which preceded the actual military operations, and the gravity with which this situation was regarded is to be inferred from the risks which Selīm felt compelled to take in order to achieve a final settlement. Whether the Ṣafawids had inspired this dissatisfaction by their subversive missionary activities or merely benefited from the prevailing anti-Ottoman sentiments by appearing as an alternative hegemony is difficult to determine; but it is clear that the counterheretical allure which the Ottomans gave to their attack upon the S͟hīʿī Muslims of the east was but the façade to a starkly political purpose.

The campaign, which seems to have been modelled on that of Meḥmed II against Uzun Ḥasan in 1473, is described in detail in the journal preserved in Ferīdūn Beg, although the fundamental logistical problems of moving an army of the size attributed to the Ottomans across home territories where they could not live off the land are scarcely touched upon. But that these could be solved and that the fractious troops could be held under discipline throughout all the unfamiliar hardships of campaigning in these regions was certainly the most impressive display of Ottoman might that Anatolia had ever witnessed and far more overawing to Shāh Ismāʿīl and his supporters than the firearms and artillery which usually figure so prominently in the narratives as the reason for the Ottoman victory (cf. Luṭfī Pasha's highly romantic account of Ismāʿīl's astonishment as contingent after contingent of Ottoman troops took the field).

The campaign may be regarded as having succeeded in its primary object in that it neutralized for over a generation the attraction exerted on Anatolia from the east. The "scorched earth" tactics of the retreating Ṣafawids prevented any long occupation of their invaded territories, and although Tabrīz was entered by the Sulṭān on the 17th Radjab/7th Sept., within a week preparations were made for returning to winter quarters at Amasya. From here the following year operations were begun in south-eastern Anatolia which were to bring an end to the semi-independent principality of the Dhu 'l-Ḳadr-oghlī around Elbistan and add definitively to Ottoman territory Diyārbekr and northern Kurdistan.

Bibliography: Among the general histories of the Ottoman Empire, Hammer-Purgstall's is still the most circumstantial account of this campaign (ii, 392 ff.), Zinkeisen (ii, 566 ff.) and Jorga (ii, 327 ff.) affording it but casual mention; İ. H. Uzunçarşılı, *Osmanlı Tarihi*, ii, Ankara 1949, 246 ff. adds a diagram of the battle. The Ottoman historians: Kamāl Pasha-zāde, *Tawārīkh-i Āl-i ʿOthmān*, ix, Millet, Ali Emiri, no. 29, f. 35b, ff.; ʿĀlī, *Kunh al-akhbār*, Süleymaniye, Esʿad Ef., no. 2162, f. 238a, ff.; Saʿd al-Dīn, *Tādj al-Tawārīkh*, ii, Istanbul 1279, 239 ff.; Luṭfī Pasha, *Tawārīkh-i Āl-i ʿOthmān*, ed. ʿĀlī, Istanbul 1341, 206 ff.; Ṣolaḳ-zāde, *Taʾrīkh*, Istanbul 1287, 359 ff., give very much the same picture as presented by Hammer-Purgstall (who, however, did not use Kamāl Pasha-zāde and Luṭfī Pasha) which can be usefully supplemented in certain aspects by the various *Selīm-nāmes* (a fairly complete repertoire of which is to be found in A. S. Levend, *Ġazavāt-nāmeler*, etc., Ankara 1956, 22 ff.), the most important being those of Shukrī, British Museum, Or. 1039, f. 62b ff. (repeated in Djawrī, Millet, Ali Emiri, no. 1310, f. 54a ff., and Yūsuf Efendi, Süleymaniye, Esʿad Ef., no. 2146, f. 11a ff.,) Kashfī, Süleymaniye, Esʿad Ef., no. 2147, f. 31a ff.; Saʿdī b. ʿAbd al-Mutaʿāl, Topkapı, Revan, no. 1277, f. 64a ff.; Abū 'l-Faḍl b. Idrīs Bitlīsī, British Museum, Add. 24,960, f. 63b ff.; Sudjūdī, Topkapı, Revan, no. 1284/1, f. 5b ff.; Djalāl-zāde Muṣṭafā Čelebi, British Museum, Add. 7848, f. 120b ff. The documents in Ferīdūn Beğ, *Munshaʾāt al-salāṭīn*, i, Istanbul 1274, 396 ff. (correspondence, journal of the campaign, *fatḥ-nāmes*) are of exceptional importance. The Persian sources (a full discussion of which is to be found in Ghulām Sarwar, *History of Shāh Ismāʿīl Ṣafawī*, Aligarh 1939, 3-16) seek to palliate the magnitude of the defeat and their accounts are coloured by this purpose; the most important is that of Khwāndamīr, *Ḥabīb al-siyar*, iv, Tehran 1333, 543 ff., whose version underlies those of Ḥasan Rūmlū, *Aḥsan al-Tawārīkh*, ed. C. N. Seddon, Baroda 1931, 143 ff. (with various expansions) and Iskandar Beğ Munshī, *ʿĀlam-ārā-yi ʿAbbāsī*, Tehran 1341, 31 ff. (who, in addition to the above two, uses also Ghaffārī's *Djahān-ārā*). The dominant early European account is that of Paolo Giovio, *Historiae Sui Temporis*, Paris 1558, i, 133-163 ff. (an Italian translation of this section is given in F. Sansovino, *Historia Universale dell' Origine, Guerre et Imperio de Turchi*, Venice 1654, ff. 323-360); also in Sansovino are the *Vita di Sach Ismael, etc.* by Teodoro Spandugino (ff. 132-140) and the *Vita et Legge Turchesca* by G. A. Menavino (ff. 17-75), who, although claiming to have accompanied the Turks on this campaign, gives a highly distorted account of its outcome (a Latin translation in P. Lonicerus, *Chronica Turcorum*, Frankfurt 1578, i, ff. 95-97). The narrative in R. Knolles, *The Generall Historie of the Turks*, London 1621, 505-515, while noticing Menavino, follows Jovius throughout, as does also that of T. Artus in his continuation of De Vigenere's translation of Chalcocondylas, *L'Histoire de la Decadence de l'Empire Grec*, Paris 1650, i, 358-374, though this does include, too, the accounts in J. Leunclavius, *Historiae Musulmanae Turcorum*, Frankfurt 1591, cols. 691-704, 742-745. P. Bizaro, *Rerum Persicarum Historia*, Frankfurt 1601, is important only in that it contains the letter of H. Penia from Constantinople, dated 6 Nov. 1514, 275-278. The article by M. Tayyib Gökbilgin in *IA*, fasc. 24, 329-331, presents the familiar Ottoman version.

(J. R. Walsh)

CALENDAR [see ANWĀʾ, TAʾRĪKH]

CALICUT [see KALIKAT]

CALIPH [see KHALĪFA]

CALLIGRAPHY [see KHAṬṬ]

ČAM (or Cham), A people of Malayo-Polynesian origin which settled before the Christian era on the southern coasts of the Indo-Chinese peninsula. The Cham appear in history at the end of the 2nd century A.D. with their foundation, in 192, of the kingdom of Champa [see ṢANF], which occupied the coastal provinces of present-day Viet-nam, from Quang-binh in the North to Binh-thuan in the South.

Up to the 10th century Champa experienced a period of magnificence during which the Cham dynasties were able to extend their territories slightly and to develop their civilization. But during the following centuries the country came into open conflict with its Vietnamese and Khmer neighbours, and then suffered the Mongol invasions. These struggles, aggravated by internal revolts, quickly led Champa towards disintegration. In spite of a short period of victorious fighting during the reign of the famous Chê Bong Nga (1360-1390), and Chinese intervention on his side, the kingdom was nearing its end. In 1471 the Vietnamese emperor Le Thanh Ton conclusively subjected Champa and it became a dependency of Viet-nam; a part of the inhabitants took refuge on Cambodian soil, and gradually it disappears from the history of the Far East.

The Cham people, deeply affected by the culture of India, adopted its religion and writing in the second century. They practised Hinduism and Brahmanism up to the 15th century.

Although the Muslims were already established in Champa from the middle of the 4th/10th century (there is proof of the existence, from the 5th/11th century onwards, of Arab trading communities living in contact with the Cham), Islam was not seriously practised by the Cham until after the fall of their kingdom.

To-day two-thirds of the Cham living in Viet-nam still practise Brahmanism; the other third, together with the Cham who emigrated to Cambodia, are Muslims. In the absence of precise and up-to-date statistics, there are an estimated 15,000 Cham living in the south of central Viet-nam (the provinces of Phan-rang and Phan-thiet) and 20,000 living in Cambodia (on the banks of the Mekong).

Cham society, originally matriarchal and organised in clans, adopted, under influence from India, the caste system and Hindu customs. The Cham, skilful craftsmen and experienced farmers, with a reputation as courageous soldiers, lived as pirates, raiding the neigbouring provinces and trading in slaves. Nowadays they constitute racial minorities in process of assimilation. Apart from work on silk and metals and the cutting of precious stones, the Cham were outstanding builders. Cham architecture has left us numerous sites and monuments, of which most are unfortunately in extremely bad condition. Cham monuments are all identical in silhouette, a tower with diminishing stories, built in pink sandstone, terra cotta, and above all in brick. However their style is not uniform. Hindu motifs can be recognised in their decoration. These towers were religious buildings (the cult of Shiva) all of whose interior furnishings have disappeared. The scenes on the bas-reliefs again give concrete expression to the Cham's pronounced love of music, which has had a very deep influence on the music of Viet-nam.

Bibliography: Jeanne Leuba, *Les Cham d'autrefois et d'aujourd'hui*, Hanoi 1915 (re-edited with the title *Un royaume disparu, les Cham et leur art*, Paris 1923); Georges Maspéro, *Le royaume du Champa*, Paris 1928; Jean-Yves Claeys, *Introduction à l'étude de l'Annam et du Champa*, in *Bulletin des amis du Vieux Hué*, Hanoi 1934.

(G. MEILLON)

ČAMALAL [see ANDI]

CAMBAY [see KANBĀYA]

CAMEL [see DJAMAL]

CAMEROONS, a former German colony on the west coast of Africa, now consisting of (a) an independent state, formerly under French trusteeship, and (b) a territory at present (1960) under British trusteeship. It lies at the eastern end of the Gulf of Guinea, between Nigeria, Spanish Guinea, and former French Equatorial Africa. Area 503,600 sq. km., 4,000,000 inhabitants, of whom 20,000 are non-African.

Created as a result of German penetration from the Bight of Biafra towards Chad (1884-1910) and conquered by the Allied Forces between 1914 and 1916, the Cameroons was divided in 1919 into a zone under British mandate (80,000 sq. km.) and a zone under French mandate (423,000 sq. km.). The first has in practice been integrated administratively with Nigeria, while the second has developed along distinctive autonomous lines.

(a) Thanks to its geographical situation the former French Cameroons presents a remarkable assortment of climates and peoples, which make it as it were an intermediary zone between West Africa, Central Africa and Equatorial Africa. The relief map shows a narrow coastal plain separated from the forest plateau of the south by a range of fairly high mountains. North of the valley of the Sanaga the uplands and savannah country of Adamawa fall in a rugged escarpment to the Chad plain and the valley of the Benue. Along the Nigerian frontier a series of mountain ranges, including the Manengumba, Bamileke, Bamun, Alantika and Mandara massifs, culminates on the seacoast in the volcanic Mount Cameroon (4,070 m.).

The population of the forest-covered south includes pygmy hunters, Bantu and Bantu-type farmers and fishermen; in the central savannah and the Bamileke mountains, semi-Bantu farming peoples; in the uplands and the northern plains, 'Sudanese' and 'Ubangians' of various origins; in the mountains, long-established palaeonigritic peoples; in all, 3,100,000 Africans and 15,000 immigrants.

After the 1914-18 war, Cameroons was placed under a B Mandate by the League of Nations. In 1940, under Col. Leclerc, it rallied to Free France. In 1946 the system of the mandate was replaced by that of the trusteeship of the United Nations, Cameroons becoming an Associated Territory of the French Union. In 1957 it was established as a State under trusteeship, possessing some degree of internal autonomy: the Prime Minister and his government were responsible to the Legislative Assembly sitting at Yaunde. A High Commissioner dealt with the spheres reserved to France—currency, defence, and public order. The administrative structure includes 21 departments and some 60 *arrondissements*. Municipal administration is inspired by that of metropolitan France. The French government announced at the end of 1958 its intention of renouncing trusteeship and of recognising the independence of the Cameroons on 1 Jan. 1960; this decision, after arousing lively opposition in the United Nations Assembly from the Soviet block and certain Afro-Asian states, was carried through and made effective on the appointed date.

The economy is predominantly agricultural (coffee, cocoa, vegetable oils, timber, cotton, bananas) with cattle husbandry important in the north. Current industrial development: electrometallurgy at Edea, gold and diamonds in the east, tin in the west, petroleum in the south. Chief towns: the port of Duala (100,000 inhabitants), Yaunde, the capital (30,000), Garua capital of the north (15,000), Marua, Ngaundere, Edea, Nkongsamba, Fumban, Tchang, Kribi, Mbalmayo, and Ebolowa.

The south is almost entirely Christianized: 600,000 Catholics and 300,000 Protestants, with animist survivals, and a tendency toward the formation of syncretistic sects.

Islam has some 600,000 followers in the northern plain, Adamawa and the Bamun massif. It seems to have penetrated the area about the 12th century, coming from the east (Wadai, Bagirmi) and the north-west (Kanem, Bornu), but experienced its period of great expansion only at the beginning of the 19th century, under the influence of the conquering Fulani, successors of Uthmān dan Fodio: his son Mohamman Bello and particularly his lieutenant Mōdibbo Ādama (died 1847) who conquered Fumbina and gave it its present name of Adamawa. Ādama took the title of Amīru (*Amīr*) and made his capital at Yola (Nigeria) where the *lāmībe* (Fulani chiefs) went to receive the investiture until the Franco-British conquest. His work was continued up to the beginning of the 20th century by the *Amīrs* Mohammed Lawal, Sanda and Zubeiru; they were however not able to subdue the Kirdi (heathens) who took refuge in the mountains of the north.

Since the European conquest, some groups of Muslim immigrants have arisen in the towns of the south, where they are butchers, peddlers, and shoemakers. They are thought to number some 25,000. They do a little proselytising by marriage.

Fulani influence prevails in the Islam of the Cameroons, with its tendency towards Mahdism. But, in addition to the 300,000 Fulani, there are in the north some Hausa, some Kotoko, and some Shua (or black Arab) Muslims of long standing, and Islam tends to spread among the pagan farmers of the plains and the Kirdi who have come down from the mountains. The Bamun of Fumban, long at war with the Fulani, saw their aristocracy converted by agreement or by force in 1917 by the *Fon* Njoya the Great who at this time took the title of Sultan and the name of Ibrahim.

Higher Muslim education is little developed, and the *modibbe* (or *mālams*) who wish to continue their studies have to go to Nigeria, Chad, or the Sudan.

The Ḳādiriyya sect is the oldest, but not the most numerous; its principal centre is Garua. The Tidjāniyya sect has predominated since the conversion of Mohamman Bello, who received the *wird* of El Hadj Omar about 1840; its adherents probably amount to some 300,000. Mahdism comes next in importance. Local mahdīs appear every four or five years, but their influence is generally short-lived and localized. On the other hand, since the settlement of several thousand Fulani in the Sudan at the time of the British conquest of Nigeria, the Sudanese Mahdiyya has had numerous adherents in the Cameroons.

Wahhābi influence is slight, exercised chiefly through the medium of former soldiers of the negro guard of King Ibn Saʿūd, nearly all Hausas. The Muslims have long remained aloof from local political trends. Precolonial institutions and hierarchies are better preserved among them than among the peoples of the south. Nevertheless, in contrast to the confessional and political divisions of the South, the westernized *élite* of the north have been called on to play an increasingly important role as arbitrators, until, in 1958, a Fulani Muslim of modernist tendencies was appointed Premier of the newly formed State.

Bibliography: Lembezat, *Le Cameroun*, Paris 1952; Froelich, *Cameroun-Togo*, Paris 1956; Cardaire, *Contribution à l'étude de l'Islam noir: l'Islam au Cameroun*, Douala (Cameroons) 1949; Annual reports to SDN and UNO.

(P. ALEXANDRE)

British Cameroons. This territory on the West Coast of Africa, between the Cameroon Republic on the east and Nigeria on the west, is that part of the old German colony of Kamerun which passed in 1919 into British control, first under a League of Nations mandate and subsequently as a United Nations Trust territory. Following administrative practice, which is to some extent justified by real ethnic and cultural differences, it is convenient to consider it as two distinct units.

The Southern Cameroons [administrative capital Buea] has a total area of 16,581 square miles and a population of some 800,000. Until 1954 this territory was administered as an integral part of the Eastern region of Nigeria but a series of changes since that date have raised it to the status of a self-governing region within the Nigerian federation with its own regional government and a legislative assembly with a majority elected by universal adult suffrage. The political future of the region, which has not hitherto proved economically self-sufficient, is at present uncertain. The United Kingdom has undertaken to separate the administration of the region from that of the Federation of Nigeria by October 1960, the date when the Federation assumes complete independence. A plebiscite is to be held not later than March 1961 to decide between incorporation in Nigeria and reunion with the Cameroons Republic, the latter course being favoured by the present regional government.

The tribal pattern of the territory exhibits a marked degree of political fragmentation. The bulk of its population, speaking a large number of Bantu and semi-Bantu languages, have their nearest affinities with neighbouring peoples in the Cameroons republic. The Tikor and Bali peoples who are dominant in the central grasslands have migrated into this area from the north-east in the last few centuries and their traditional culture is of the pagan Sudanic type. The Christian missions have a continuous history in the area since the establishment of the Baptists at Victoria in 1858. The most reliable figures of missionary adherents show 58,000 Catholics and 65,000 Protestants but the number of those who have been strongly influenced by the missions is much greater. Islam is not numerically important.

There are no known mineral resources of commercial value within the territory and no industry beyond the processing of palm oil and rubber. The country is overwhelmingly rural in character and even the largest towns, Mamfe and Kumba, have fewer than 10,000 inhabitants. Most of the exported cash crops of bananas, palm-oil, palm kernels and rubber are produced from the plantations administered by a government subsidised agency, the Cameroons Development Corporation. The growth of cash crops, especially cocoa, by individual small farmers is increasing with official encouragement, but the mass of the people in the interior are still engaged in subsistence agriculture as are those of the Northern Cameroons.

The Northern Cameroons, an area of 17,000 square miles with a population probably slightly smaller than the Southern Cameroons, is a narrow strip of territory more than 500 miles long but nowhere more than 80 miles wide which is divided into two by a "corridor" of Nigerian territory, some 45 miles wide, on either bank of the Benue. Administratively the territory has been completely integrated with the Northern Region of Nigeria. The greater part falls within the Adamawa Province, but the Dikwa emirate in the north, formerly a part of the old "empire" of Bornu is appropriately incorporated, as a division, in Bornu province and three districts in the south belong to the Benue province. By a plebiscite held under United Nations auspices in November 1959 the people of the territory have postponed the final decision as to whether or not it is to remain with Nigeria after independence. The ruling tribes, Kanuri and Shoa Arabs in Dikwa and Fulani in Adamawa, are strongly Muslim but much of the hill country has never fallen effectively under their influence and remains entirely pagan. There are Catholic and Protestant missions in Adamawa and a few thousand converts to Christianity have been made. [For an account of the religious history see the preceding section on the French Cameroons]. (D. H. JONES)

CAMIENIEC [see KAMINČA]

ČĀMPĀNĒR, a ruined city of Gudjarat in Western India, Lat. 22° 29′ N., long. 73° 32′ E., about 78 miles south-east of Aḥmadābād, taken by the Gūdjarāt sulṭān Maḥmūd Shāh I 'Begaḍā' on his conquest (889/1484) of the adjoining stronghold of Pāwāgaṙh, which had successfully resisted Aḥmad Sh̲āh I in 821/1418. The Begadā occupied Čāmpānēr forthwith, building a city wall with bastions and gates (called D̲j̲ahānpanāh; inscription *EIM* 1929-30, 4-5), and a citadel (*bhādar*). He renamed the city Maḥmūdābād, and it was his favourite residence until his death in 917/1511; it remained the political capital of Gud̲j̲arāt until the death of Bahādur Sh̲āh in 942/1536. When Gud̲j̲arāt came under the Mug̲h̲als after 980/1572 Čāmpānēr was the head of a *sarkār* of 9 *maḥals* (Jarrett, *Āʾīn-i Akbarī*, ii, 256; of 13 divisions, according to the *Mirʾāt-i Sikandarī*); it fell to the Marāṭhās at the end of the 18th century, and came into British hands in 1853; almost deserted, it was not recolonized.

Monuments. Of Maḥmūd's seven-storeyed palace (Sāt manzil) built in steps on the cliff edge opposite Pāwāgaṙh only the lowest storey remains; the other monuments other than the walls (cf. *Bombay Gazetteer*, iii, 307-8) are all mosques and tombs, which in their similarity exhibit a local style. The D̲j̲āmiʿ Masd̲j̲id, c. 929/1523, is inspired in plan by that of Aḥmadābād [*q.v.*], 100 years older; but here there is a double clerestory in the *līwān* in the space of one dome only; the arcuate *maḳṣūra* screen and the trabeate hypostyle *līwān* are well integrated; the side wings of the *līwān* are proportioned as a double square (8.5 by 17.0 metres); a *zanāna* enclosure is formed by screening off the northernmost *miḥrāb*; and the external surfaces, as in all the Čāmpānēr buildings, are the subject of rich plastic decoration—particularly the buttresses supporting each of the 7 sumptuous *miḥrābs*. The other buildings —10 mosques, many nameless tombs—are of similar style, characterized by refinement of decoration; the niches in the *minārs* of the Naginā *masd̲j̲id* are of an exquisite marble tracery excelled only by that of Sidī Sayyid's mosque in Aḥmadābād [*q.v.*]. The tombs use the arch more freely than the mosques, and their carved decoration is of consummate delicacy, skill and craftsmanship.

Bibliography: J. Burgess, *On the Muhammadan architecture of Bharoch . . . Champanir . . .*, *ASWI* vi (= *ASI*, *NIS* xxiii), 1896 (text, measured drawings, plates); *ASI Annual Reports*, specially 1925-6, 24-5, and 1929-30, 34-5; *Bombay Gazetteer*, iii; E. B. Eastwick, *Champanir and Pawagadh* in *Indian Antiquary*, ix (1880), 221-4; J. Fergusson, *History of Indian and Eastern Architecture*, ii, 242; E. B. Havell, *Indian Architecture*, 134-43; P. Brown, *Indian Architecture* (*Islamic Period*), 58-9.

(J. Burton-Page)

CAMPIÑA [see kanbāniya]

ČANAḲ-ḲALʿE BOG̲H̲AZÎ (Çanak-kale Boğazı) is the name now given in Turkish to the Dardanelles. This narrow channel, which unites the Marmara and the Aegean Seas, has a length of about 62 km. (Gelibolu-Çardak to Seddülbahir-Kumkale) and a width ranging from 8 km. down to 1250 m. (Çanak-kale to Kilitbahir). The strait was known to the ancient Greeks as the Hellespont (ὁ Ἑλλήσποντος, in Doric ὁ Ἑλλάσποντος), a name that remained in usage amongst the Byzantines. It is called in some of the mediaeval Western sources and sea-charts Bucca Romaniae, Brachium S. Georgii (a term which denoted the entire channel separating Asia and Europe, *i.e.*, embraced the Bosphorus as well as the Dardanelles), Bocca d'Aveo (Avido, Aveo, the ancient Abydos: Ἄβυδος) and also Dardanelo (cf. Pauly-Wissowa, s.v. Hellespontos, and Tomaschek, 17). To the Ottomans it was the Aḳ Deniz Bog̲h̲azî, Ḳalʿe-i Sulṭāniyye Bog̲h̲azî and later Çanaḳ-ḳalʿe Bog̲h̲azî.

The more notable localities on or near the European shore of the Dardanelles are Bolayır, Gelibolu (*i.e.*, Gallipoli, the ancient Kallipolis), Kilya (not far from the old Sestos), Eceabad (Ed̲j̲eābād, formerly Maydos, *i.e.*, the ancient Madytos), Kilitbahir (Kilīd al-Baḥr) and Seddülbahir (Sedd al-Baḥr). Along the Asiatic shore are situated Çardak, Lapseki (the ancient Lampsakos-Lampsico, Lapsico, Lapsaco in the mediaeval Western sources), Çanak-kale (near the old Abydos), Erenköy and Kumkale (Ḳum Ḳalʿe).

Sulṭān Meḥemmed II (855-886/1451-1481), in order to establish a more effective control over the Dardanelles, built new defences on either shore of the strait, amongst them a fortress close to the ancient Abydos. This fortress received the name of Ḳalʿe-i Sulṭāniyye (according to Pīrī Reʾis (*Kitāb-i Baḥriyye*, 86), because a son of Meḥemmed II, Sulṭān Muṣṭafā, was associated with its construction. Cf. also Ibn Kemāl, 100 = *Transkripsiyon*, 101, where it is called Sulṭāniyye). The town of Ḳalʿe-i Sulṭāniyye counted amongst its inhabitants, during the 17th and 18th centuries, a considerable number of Armenians, Jews and Greeks. As a result of the establishment there (perhaps ca. 1740) of potteries, and of its subsequent reputation as a noted centre for the manufacture of earthenware, the town came to be known as Çanaḳ Ḳalʿesi (*čanaḳ* = an earthen bowl), the older name falling out of current usage. Çanaḳ Ḳalʿesi belonged, in 1876, to the Ottoman *wilāyet* of D̲j̲ezāʾir-i Baḥr-i Sefīd and thereafter to the *sand̲j̲aḳ* of Bīg̲h̲ā. It is now the centre of the present province of Çanak-kale. The town suffered much from fire in 1860 and 1865, from the earthquake of August 1912, and from naval bombardment in 1915 during the course of World War I. Çanak-kale, in recent years, has largely regained its former prosperity and was estimated, in 1940, to have 24,600 inhabitants.

The Ottoman Turks absorbed (c. 735-c. 745/c. 1335-c. 1345) into their own territories the emirate of Ḳarasī [*q.v.*] and then, after the town had been ruined in the earthquake of 755/1354, established themselves at Gallipoli [see gelibolu], which served them as a point of departure for their subsequent conquest of Thrace. It was now, for the first time, that a Muslim state held control over the lands on either side of the strait. The Ottoman Sulṭān Bāyazīd I (791-805/1389-1403) strengthened the defences of Gallipoli (792/1390), further improvements being carried out there in the reigns of Meḥemmed I (816-824/1413-1421) and Murād II (824-855/1421-1451). Ottoman control of the Dardanelles was destined, however, to remain insecure, as long as the Sulṭān had no large and efficient fleet at his command: Christian naval forces sailed into the strait in 767/1366 (the "crusade" of Amedeo of Savoy, which brought about a brief restoration of Gallipoli to Byzantine rule), in 801/1399 (expedition of the Maréchal Boucicaut to Constantinople), in 819/1416 (the Venetian defeat of the Ottoman naval forces before Gallipoli) and again in 848/1444 (Papal and Venetian squadrons sent to the Dardanelles at the time of the Varna campaign). Sulṭān Meḥemmed II (855-886/1451-1481), anxious to secure a more effective control of the Dardanelles, caused new defences to be built where the waters of the strait are at their narrowest, *i.e.*, the fortresses of Ḳalʿe-i Sulṭāniyye on the Asiatic, and of Kilīd al-Baḥr on the European shore. The manufacture and use of fire-arms had now advanced to such a degree that the Sulṭān was able to furnish these new defences with large guns capable of firing across the channel. A restoration of the two fortresses was carried out in 958/1551 during the reign of Sulṭān Sulaymān Ḳānūnī (926-974/1520-1566). At this time the region of the Dardanelles was included in the *eyālet* of Djezāʾir-i Baḥr-i Sefīd, *i.e.*, it formed, together with some of the islands and coastal areas of the Aegean Sea, the province of the Ḳapudan Pāshā or High Admiral of the Ottoman fleet.

The fortifications along the shores of the Dardanelles fell gradually into disrepair during the late 16th and early 17th centuries. It was not until the Cretan War (1055-1080/1645-1669) that the Porte, under the threat of a Venetian irruption into the strait, initiated new measures of defence. Ḳalʿe-i Sulṭāniyye and Kilīd al-Baḥr now underwent (1069-1070/1658-1660) a thorough restoration. Moreover, new forts were built at the Aegean mouth of the Dardanelles-Sedd al-Baḥr on the European, and Ḳum Ḳalʿe on the Asiatic side of the channel. The danger arising from the presence of a Russian fleet before the Dardanelles during the Ottoman-Russian war of 1182-1188/1768-1774 led to the creation of new forts along the shores of the strait, this task being carried out under the guidance of the Baron de Tott. A further effort was made to establish a more modern system of fortification in the Dardanelles towards the end of the reign of Selīm III (1203-1222/1789-1807). The fact that in 1221/1807 an English fleet under the command of Sir John Duckworth forced a passage into the strait underlined once more the urgent need for a complete modernization of the defences on the Dardanelles. Control of the strait was to become thereafter a matter of more than local concern, the status of the Dardanelles (and also of the Bosphorus) being regulated in a series of international agreements negotiated during the 19th and 20th centuries. Of more recent events associated with the Dardanelles it will be sufficient to mention here the Gallipoli campaign of 1915-1916 fought in the course of World War I.

Bibliography: Ibn Khurradādhbih, 103 ff.; Yāḳūt, i, 374; al-Idrīsī, *Nuzhat al-Mushtāḳ*, trans. Jaubert: *Géographie d'Edrisi*, ii, 135, 301 ff.; *Düstūrnāme-i Enveri*, ed. Mükrimin Halil, Istanbul 1928, 25 ff.; Ibn Kemāl (*i.e.*, Kemālpāshāzāde), *Tevārih-i Āl-i Osman*, VII Defter, ed. Şerafettin Turan (*Türk Tarih Kurumu Yayınlarından*, I. Seri, no. 5), Ankara 1954, 100 (= *Transkripsiyon*, ed. Şerafettin Turan, Ankara 1957, 101); Pīrī Reʾis, *Kitāb-i Baḥriyye*, Istanbul 1935, 86 ff.; Saʿd al-Dīn, *Tādj al-Tawārīkh*, i, Istanbul A.H. 1279, 54 ff.; Ḥādjdjī Khalīfa, *Tuḥfat al-Kibār*, Istanbul A.H. 1229, 130 ff.; Ewliyā Čelebī, *Seyāḥatnāme*, v, Istanbul A.H. 1315, 301-322; Ducas, Bonn 1834, 19; Chalkokondyles, Bonn 1843, 529 ff.; Critobulus, ed. C. Müller, *Fragmenta Historicorum Graecorum*, v, Paris 1870, 146-147, 151; N. de Nicolay, *Navigations et Pérégrinations*, Lyon 1568, 52; M. de Thevenot, *Relation d'un Voyage fait au Levant*, Paris 1664, 32 ff. and 141 ff.; P. du Fresne-Canaye, *Voyage du Levant*, ed. H. Hauser, Paris 1897, 159 ff.; G. J. Grelot, *Relation Nouvelle d'un Voyage de Constantinople*, Paris 1681, 3 ff., *passim*; J. Spon and G. Wheler, *Voyage d'Italie, de Dalmatie, de Grèce, et du Levant*, Lyon 1678, i, 203 ff.; Pitton de Tournefort, *Relation d'un Voyage du Levant*, Paris 1717, 453 ff.; R. Pococke, *A Description of the East*, ii/2, London 1745, 102 ff., 111, 143; Baron de Tott, *Mémoires sur les Turcs et les Tartares*, Amsterdam 1784, Pt. 3, 43 ff.; J. Dallaway, *Constantinople*, London 1797, 332 ff.; W. Eaton, *A Survey of the Turkish Empire*, London 1798, 88 ff.; A. Morellet, *Constantinople ancienne et moderne et Description des Côtes et Isles de l'Archipel et de la Troade*, Paris An VII, ii/8, 146 ff.; J. B. Lechevalier, *Voyage de la Troade*, i, Paris 1802, 267 ff.; A. de Juchereau de St. Denys, *Révolution de Constantinople en 1807 et 1808*, Paris 1819, ii, 53 ff.; F. de Beaujour, *Voyage militaire dans l'Empire Othoman*, Paris 1829, ii, 483 ff.; M. Michaud and M. Poujoulat, *Correspondance d'Orient* (1830-1831), Paris 1833-1834, i, 449 ff., ii, 1 ff.; H. von Moltke, *Briefe über Zustände und Begebenheiten in der Türkei aus den Jahren* 1835 *bis* 1839, Berlin 1877, 51 ff., 68 ff.; W. Ramsay, *The Historical Geography of Asia Minor*, London 1890, 152 ff.; Tomaschek, 3, 15 ff.; H. Högg, *Türkenburgen an Bosporus und Hellespont*, Dresden 1932; F. Babinger, *Beiträge zur Frühgeschichte der Türkenherrschaft in Rumelien* (14.-15. *Jahrhundert*), Munich 1944, 39 ff.; H. J. Kissling, *Beiträge zur Kenntnis Thrakiens im* 17. *Jahrhundert* (*Abh. K. M.*, xxxii/3, Wiesbaden 1956, 47 ff.; V. Cuinet, *La Turquie d'Asie*, iii, Paris 1894, 743 ff., 758 ff., 765; Pauly-Wissowa, viii, Stuttgart 1912, cols. 182-193, s.v. Hellesspontos; *İA*, s.v. Çanakkale (Besim Darkot and M. C. Şihabeddin Tekindağ). Bibliographical indications will be found in *İA*, s.v. Çanakkale on (i) the geological, geographical and hydrographical characteristics of the Dardanelles and (ii) the campaign of Gallipoli in 1915-1916. Cf. also Boghaz-içi, and Pearson, 576-577 (nos. 18440-18474), *passim*, for references relating to the international Problem of the Straits during the 18th-20th centuries. (V. J. Parry)

CANARY ISLANDS [see al-djazāʾir al-khālidāt]

ČANDĒRÎ, town and old fort in north-central India, 24° 42′ N., 78° 9′ E., on a tableland overlooking the Betwā valley on the east. Early references by al-Bīrūnī (421/1030) and Ibn Baṭṭūṭa do not mention the fort and probably relate to a site some 15 km. north-north-west known now as Būṛhī [Urdū, 'old'] Čandērī; here there are ruined Islamic fortifications among Hindū and Djayn remains, probably of the early 8th/14th century, for although the city fell in 649/1251 to Ghiyāth al-Dīn Balban, then *nāʾib* of Nāṣir al-Dīn, whose aim was the seizure of booty and captives, it did not come into Muslim hands until ʿAyn al-Mulk's defeat of the Rādjā Harānand in 705/1305. Four years later it formed the rendezvous for Malik Kāfūr's force before his march on Warangal in Telingānā. The new Čandērī seems to have been built by the Ghūrī kings of Mālwā in the early 9th/15th century (inscriptions of Dilāwar Khān and Hūshang, in *AR*, *ASI*, 1928-9, 128, and *EIM* 1943, 47), from whom it was wrested in the Mālwā interramal struggles by ʿAlāʾ al-Dīn Shāh Khaldjī I in 842/1438 (Bayley's *History of Gujarāt* [*Taʾrīkh-i Alfī*], 123), and remained under the Khaldjī's governors until the vacillating governor Bahdjat Khān revolted, supporting against Maḥmūd II his brother Ṣāḥib Khān, the puppet Muḥammad II, and appealing to Sikandar Lōdī of Dihlī for support in 919/1513. Hereafter Čandērī's position on the borders of Bundelkhand and Mālwā led to its changing hands frequently: Sikandar's forces remained in occupation until 921/1515, but after their withdrawal it was seized by the Rānā of

Čitawr who set up Medinī Rāy, Maḥmūd II's dismissed minister who had escaped the massacre at Māndū [*q.v.*], as governor; from him it was taken by Bābur in 934/1528, who restored it to Aḥmad Khān, son of Ṣāḥib Khān. Later it fell to the Pūrbīya Rādjput Pūran Mal, who lost it to Shīr Shāh c. 947/1540 but later retook it and massacred and degraded the Čandērī Muslims, an act which brought retribution from Shīr Shāh in 950/1543 (Briggs's *Ferishta*, ii, 160). After Akbar had gained the *sūba* of Mālwā, Čandērī became the headquarters of a *sarkār* (*Ā'īn-i Akbarī*, i, 122), when it was said to have been a large city with 14,000 stone houses and over 1200 mosques. Thereafter it passed frequently into Bundel hands, and after the early 12th/18th century remained in Hindū possession.

Monuments. The city is walled, with 5 gates, one of which is the Kātīghātī hewn through the rock outcrop; the fort, which stands some 70 metres higher, is dependent for its water supply on a large tank at the foot of the hill, access to which is by a covered way. (Map in Cunningham, *ASI*, ii, Plate XCIII). The Djāmiʿ Masdjid is similar to that of Māndū with its tall domes over the *līwān* stilted between springing and haunch, but with the cornice supported by a row of serpentine brackets, a contribution of Gudjarāt workmen; two tombs known as the madrasa and the Shāhzādī kā rawḍa are of excellent workmanship in a similar style; probably somewhat earlier is the Kūshk Maḥall, a large square building with intersecting passages on each of the remaining four storeys which divide the interior into four quadrants, in the suburb of Fateḥābād, 3 km. west, identified with the seven-storeyed palace (*Sāt manzil*) whose building was ordered by Maḥmūd Shāh I in 849/1445. At the western foot of the fort is an unattached gateway, the Bādal Maḥall darwāza, a triumphal arch between two tapering buttresses, somewhat over-ornamented.

Bibliography: Cunningham, *ASI*, ii, gives historical sketch with references to original sources in 404-12 (mainly Ferishta). Also C. E. Luard, *Gwalior State Gazetteer*, i, 1908, 209-12. Earliest inscr., 711/1312, in Ramsingh Saksena, *Persian Inscriptions in the Gwalior State* in *IHQ*, i, 1925, 653, there assumed to be from New Čandērī though this is not certain. On the monuments, Cunningham, *op. cit.*; M. B. Grade, *Guide to Chanderi*, Arch. Dept. Gwalior 1928; *ASI Annual Reports*, specially 1924-5, 163-4; Sir John Marshall, *The monuments of Muslim India*, in *Cambridge History of India III*, 1928, 622 ff.

(J. Burton-Page)

ČANKİRİ (earlier also known as *Kianghrī*, *Kanḳrī*, and popularly as *Čangïrï* or *Čengiri*), the ancient Gangra (in Arabic sources *Khandjara* or *Djandjara*), a town in the north of Central Anatolia, 40° 35′ north, 33° 35′ east, at the confluence of the Tatlïčay and the Acïčay, a tributary of the Kïzïl Irmak, at an altitude of 2395 ft. (730 m.); since 1933, on the Ankara-Zonguldak railway (105 m. (174 km.) from Ankara). The town was once the capital of a *sandjaḳ* (*liwā'*) of the *eyālet* of Anadolu; after the *Tanẓīmāt*, it became the capital of a *sandjaḳ* of the *wilāyet* of Kastamonu; under the Turkish Republic, it is the capital of a *wilāyet* (*il*) with 3 *kazas* (Çankırı, Çerkeš, and Ilgaz/Koçhısar).

It was known even in antiquity as a fortified place, and was occasionally used by the Byzantines as a place of exile. Later it again gained importance because of its impenetrable fortress in the battles with the Arabs and the Turks. The Umayyads repeatedly advanced as far as Khandjara in their raids against the Byzantines. They did this in 93/711-12 (al-Ṭabarī, ed. de Goeje, ii, 1236; Ibn al-Athīr, ed. Tornberg, iii, 457; al-Yaʿḳūbī, ii, 350 who calls the town *Ḥisn al-Ḥadīd*), in 109/727-28 (al-Yaʿḳūbī, ii, 395), and in 114/731-32 (Bar Hebraeus, *Keṯāḇā de Maḵṯeḇānūṯ Zaḇnē*, ed. Bruns and Kirsch, ii, 125; compare also al-Ṭabarī, ii, 1561, and Theophanes under the year 6224). When the Byzantines sacrificed the eastern border provinces as a result of their defeat near Malāzgird (Manzikert) in 1071, the Saldjūḳs and the Dānishmendids divided the loot. The former settled after a short intermission in Nicea (Iznik) and Konya, the latter spread over the northern half of Asia Minor from Amasya to Kastamonu. Čankïrï is mentioned as being among the conquests of the first Dānishmendids in 468/1075-76 (Ḥasan b. ʿAlī Tokādī (?), *Ta'rīkh-i Āl-i Dānishmand*, in Ḥusayn Ḥusam al-Dīn, *Amasya tarīkhi*, Istanbul 1322, II, 286 ff.; Hezārfenn, *Tanḳīḥ al-tawārīkh*, in *ZDMG*, 30, 470). In 1101, an army of crusaders left Constantinople for the region of the Dānishmend-oghlu, in order to rescue Bohemund of Antioch whom these had captured at Malatya and imprisoned in Nīksār. The army conquered Ankara and advanced towards Čankïrï (praesidium Gangara), but the attack failed, and shortly afterwards the army was completely routed near Amasya by the united Saldjūḳs and Dānishmendids (Albert of Aix, 1. VIII, c. 8; Ibn al-Athīr, ed. Tornberg, x, 203; cf. *ZDMG* 30, 476; Chalandon, *Les Comnènes*, i, 224 ff.). The Comnene emperor John conquered Čankïrï in 1134, with the aid of heavy siege-weapons, after he had attacked it without success in the previous year (*Chronicle of Niketas*, i, c. 6, and particularly John Prodromos; see Chalandon, *op. cit.*, ii, 84 ff.); but shortly after the emperor's departure, the fortress was recaptured by the Dānishmendids, never to return to Byzantine rule.

Subsequently we find Čankïrï in the hands of the Saldjūḳs of Konya (cf. Chalandon, *passim*). After the collapse of the Rūm Saldjūḳ empire, (Anatolia), Čankïrï became part of the region of the Čandar-oghlu of Kastamonu. For a short time the town formed part of the empire of the Ottoman Murād I (this according to ʿAzīz Astarābādī, *Bezm u rezm*), later it was taken from the Čandar-oghlu by Bāyazīd I in 795/1392-93 (according to Neshrī) or in 797/1394-95 (according to ʿĀshiḳpashazāde, and the anonymous chronicles; Saʿd al-dīn, i, 150), together with the greater part of their possessions. In 1401, Tīmūr returned them and finally, in 822/1439, they were annexed by Meḥemmed I (ʿĀshïḳpashazāde, Istanbul edition, 88 f., ed. Giese, 79; Leunclavius, *Historiae Musulmanae Turcorum*, Frankfurt 1591, col. 475; von Hammer's statements, *GOR*, i, 70, are based on a misunderstanding). During the subsequent peaceful period under Ottoman rule, Čankïrï is very much in the background. Historians hardly mention it, though Ewliyā Čelebi (*Seyāḥatnāme*, iii, 250 f.) and Kātib Čelebi (*Djihān-nümā*, 645), have left detailed descriptions of the town. The first mention by an European visitor dates from the years 1553-55, and is by Dernschwam (in his *Tagebuch einer Reise nach Konstantinopel und Kleinasien*, ed. Babinger, Munich 1923, 196). There is an eye-witness description by Ainsworth, almost 300 years later. The town has also been visited and occasionally described by Russian and German travellers in Asia Minor.

The fortress, which had been attacked by Arabs,

Dānishmendids, Byzantines and Crusaders, is now in ruins. The only surviving monument is the grave of Ḳaratekin, who conquered the town for the first Dānishmendid prince, and is now revered as a saint. The prehistoric cisterns on the castle hill, which are described in detail by both Ewliyā Čelebi and Kātib Čelebi, have not yet been closely investigated, nor has the "Medjīd Tash" (Tash Mesdjid), a monastery of the Mewlewī Dervishes. This has inscriptions, which, according to what Ainsworth was told, date from the time of the Arab Caliphs. Some of the mosques are said to date back to Byzantine times (cf. Cuinet). The main mosque was built by Suleymān I in 996/1558-59.

The extensive salt-mines near Maghāra, 2 hours south-east of Čankïrï (Cuinet, iv, 427, and Märcker), were already famous in Byzantine times. Their product was known as Γαγγρηνὸν ἅλας (Nikolaos Myrepsos, at the end of the 13th century, in Du Cange, *Glossar. ad scriptores med. et inf. Graec.*). Even today this salt is still being mined in the same way (at a rate of 3000 to 5000 tons a year.) The great earthquakes which have repeatedly shaken the town (the most recent in February 1944), were already mentioned in mediaeval times. Al-Ḳazwīnī, *Āthār al-Bilād*, ed. Wüstenfeld, 368, mentions one such catastrophe which destroyed the town in August 1050.

According to Texier, the number of inhabitants in Čankïrï in the middle of the 19th century was 16,000, predominantly Muslim. Amongst the inhabitants there were not more than 40 Greek families. In 1839, Tshihatsheff estimates about 1800 houses, 40 of them Christian. For the end of the 19th century, Cuinet gives the following figures: 15,632 inhabitants, amongst these 780 Greek and 472 Armenian. The *Sālnāme* of Kastamonu gives the number of inhabitants as 11,200, Leonhard (1903) as 25,000 in 5000 houses, J. H. Mordtmann about 30,000 in 5000 houses, amongst these 150 Greek and 50 Armenian families, who probably left after the First World War. The 1950 census gave the following figures: the town of Čankïrï 14,161, the *kaza* 73,402, and the *vilayet* 218,289 inhabitants

Bibliography: (apart from that already mentioned in the article): Ritter, *Erdkunde*, xviii, 353 ff.; Le Strange, 158; W. Ramsay, *The Historical Geography of Asia Minor*, London 1890, 258; Pauly-Wissowa, vii, 707 and 1258; W. F. Ainsworth, *Travels and Researches in Asia Minor* . . ., London 1842, i, 109 ff.; Ch. Texier, *Asie Mineure*, 617; v. Flottwell, *Aus dem Stromgebiet des Qyzyl-Yrmaq (Halys)*, in *Petermanns Mitteilungen*, Suppl. no. 114 (1895), 38 f. and 50 (with a plan of the ruins of the fortress); G. Märcker in *Zeitschrift der Ges. f. Erdkunde*, 34 (1899), 368 f. and 373; R. Leonhard, *Paphlagonia*, Berlin 1915, 66 and 120 (with illustrations); V. Cuinet, *La Turquie d'Asie*, Paris 1894, iv, 551 ff.; the yearbooks (*Sālnāmes*) of the *wilāyet* of Kastamonu since 1286/1869-70; *IA*, iii, 357-359 (Besim Darkot). (J. H. Mordtmann-[Fr. Taeschner])

CANNANORE [see kannanur]

ČAO (*čāw* Persian transcription of Chinese *ṭṣʿau*), name given to the paper currency that was in circulation in Iran for about two months in the autumn of the year 693/1294. The *Čao* was introduced at the instigation of the Chief and Finance Minister of the Ilkhān Gaykhātū (1291-95), Ṣadr al-Dīn Aḥmad b. ʿAbd al-Razzāḳ Khālidī or Zindjānī, following the example of China, and was issued for the first time, according to Rashīd al-Dīn, on the 19th Shawwāl 693/13th September 1294, according to Waṣṣāf and others somewhat later, namely in Dhu 'l-Ḳaʿda/ 23rd September—22nd October, at Tabrīz and other provincial capitals where it was manufactured and distributed by the so-called *Čao-Khānas*, specially constructed for the purpose at considerable expense.

This new currency however met with very great opposition and the result was that trade and industry came to a standstill, the towns became depopulated and the country headed towards complete ruin, so that after two months the paper money had to be withdrawn from circulation in favour of the old coins.

The *Čao*, made of the bark of the mulberry-tree, was oblong in shape and, in addition to some Chinese signs, bore the *shahāda*. Underneath this was the name "Īrīndjīn tūrčī" (transcription of "Rin-čʿen rdorje" meaning "very costly pearl") which had been given to Gaykhātū by the Tibetan Bakhshīs, and, inside a circle, the designation of the value: one (or one half) up to ten *dīnārs*. Besides this, these "bank-notes"—according to the continuator of the work of Bar Hebraeus—bore the red impression of the state seal in jade (the Altamġa), granted by the Great Khān to the Ilkhāns. As regards the method of printing, it may be assumed that this was done by means of wooden blocks.

Bibliography: K. Jahn, *Das iranische Papiergeld*, *ArO*, x (1938), 308-340; B. Spuler, *Die Mongolen in Iran*², 1955, 88-89, 301-302, and the sources and publications listed in these two works. (K. Jahn)

ČAPANOGHULLARÏ [see Supplement and derebey].

ČAPAR (Čäpär), the eldest son of Ḳaidū [*q.v.*] and great grandson of the Mongol Great Khan Ögedey (Uk/gatāy: *regn.* 1229-41), after his father's death in 700/1301 and his own succession to the throne on the Imil in the spring of 702/1303 (Djamāl Ḳarshī in W. Barthold, *Turkestan*. Russian ed. i, 1900, 138), he fought in the beginning continually against the claims of Ḳubilay's successors upon the Great Khanate, considering it his own prerogative as one of Ögedey's descendants, who were the central "protectors of the genuine Mongol tradition". In August 1303, together with Duwa, the Khan of Čaghatāy's Ulus, he submitted to the Great Khan (the emperor of China) by means of an embassy to Khānbalïgh (Peking). Thereby a plan for a Mongol federation with full freedom of movement for trade was to be realised. In September 1304 negotiations were made from China concerning it with the Īlkhān Öldjaytü [*q.v.*]. In fact, the federation did not last: with the aid of Chinese troops Duwa forced Čapar out of his Ulus in West and East Turkestan, and succeeded him there. After Duwa's death (1306-7) Čapar attempted to regain these provinces, but could not hold his own against Duwa's son Kebek (Turkish *Kepek* = "bran", cf. Ibn Baṭṭūṭa, ii, 392) and was forced in 1309 to flee to China and the court of the Great Khān. Thereupon a Ḳuriltay in the summer of 1309 confirmed the almost complete disintegration of Ögedey's Ulus, whose inheritance was for the most part taken over by the Čaghatāy line (cf. the article čingizids, II, beginning, and III). According to Rashīd al-Dīn (ed. Blochet, *Djāmiʿ al-tawārīkh*, ii, 9), Čapar looked "like a Russian or a Circassian", apparently no longer of pure Mongol stock.

Bibliography: Waṣṣāf, lith. Bombay 1269/ 1852-53, 449/56, 509/21; Ḳāshānī, *Taʾrīkh-i Sulṭān Uldjāytū*, (MS. Paris, Suppl. Persan 1419)

fo 21v-27v. — W. Barthold, 12 *Vorlesungen*..., Berlin 1935, 186 ff., 199/202; Barthold, *Four Studies in Central Asian Hist.*, Leiden 1956, 128/32; R. Grousset, *L'Empire des steppes*, Paris 1939, 362 ff.; B. Spuler, *Die Mongolen in Iran*², Berlin 1955, 107, 232, 451 (with further bibl.). — Concerning the Mongol Federation, cf. W. Kotwicz, *Les Mongols, promoteurs de l'idée de la paix universelle au début du XIIIe siècle*, in *Rocznik Orientalistyczny*, xvi (1950), 428/34. (B. Spuler)

ČAPAROGHULLARI [see čapanoghullarî, Supplement]

CAPITULATIONS [see imtiyāz].

CARACUEL [see karakay]

CARAVAN [see azalay and ķāfila]

CARAVANSERAI [see funduķ]

ČĀRDJŪY [see āmul]

CARLOWICZ [see ķarlofča]

CARMONA [see karmūna]

CARNATIC [see karnatak[

CARPETS [see ķālī]

CARTHAGENA [see ķartadjanna]

CASABLANCA [see al-dār al-bayḍā']

ČĀSHNA-GĪR, in Persian, 'taster', title of an official, generally an *amīr*, at the court of the Muslim sovereigns (including the Mamlūks) from the time of the Saldjūkids. It is not always clear in what way he is connected with the overseer of the food, *khwānsalār*; perhaps the two are often confused. The title does not appear to be found, even in Iran, under previous dynasties, although caliphs and princes did undoubtedly have overseers for their food, and even had it tasted before they eat, as the dishes were always suspected of being poisoned. The term *čāshna-gīr* is also found as the name of a kind of crystal decanter (al-Tanūkhī, *Nishwār*, viii, ed. Margoliouth, Damascus 1930, 150).

Bibliography: I. H. Uzunçarşılı, *'Osmanlı Devleti Teşkilâtına Medhal*, Istanbul 1941, index. (Cl. Cahen)

ČASHNAGĪR-BASHÎ. chief taster, a high official of the Ottoman court. Already under the Saldjūķids and other Anatolian dynasties the *čashnagīr*, *amīr čashnagīr* or *amīr-i dhawwāķ* appears among the most important officers of the Sultan. Ibn Bībī (*Al-Awāmir al-'Alā'iyya*, edd. Necati Lugal and Adnan Sadık Erzi, Ankara 1957, 164) mentions the *čashnagīr* together with the *mīr ākhūr* and the amīr *madjlis*. In the *Ķānūnnāme* of Meḥemmed II (*TOEM* Supplement 1330 A.H. 11-12) the *čashnagīr-bashî* appears as one of the *aghas* of the stirrup, in the group headed by the *agha* of the janissaries. He follows after the *Mîr-i 'Alam*, *Kapîdjî-bashî*, *Mîr ākhūr* and *Čakîrdjî-bashî*, and precedes the other *aghas* of *böluks* [*q.v.*]. A document of 883/1478-9 lists 12 *dhawwāķīn* (tasters) as subordinate to their chief Sinān Bey (Aḥmad Refīķ, *Fātiḥ dewrine 'a'id wethīķalar*, *TOEM*, no. 49/62, 1335-7, 15). Later the numbers of tasters employed rose considerably, reaching as high as 117 ('Ayn-i 'Alī, *Ķawānīn-i Āl-i 'Othmān*, 97). In the 18th century, D'Ohsson mentions only 50, and gives the *čashnagīr-bashî* a much lower rank, in the 5th class of the outside service (*bīrūn*), under the Commissioners of Kitchens. By this time he has clearly fallen in status, and has responsibilities more strictly related to the preparation of food.

Bibliography: Ismail Hakkı Uzunçarşılı, *Osmanlı Devleti Teşkilâtına Medhal*, Instabul 1941, 88; idem, *Osmanlı Devletinin Saray Teşkilâtı*, Ankara 1945, 426-7; Gibb-Bowen 1/i, 348; D'Ohsson, *Tableau*, vii, 22-3. (B. Lewis)

CASTILLE [see ķashtāla]

CASTRO GIOVANNI [see ķaṣr yānī]

ČATĀLDJA (Çatalca, ancient Metra). 1. 41° 08′ N, 28° 25′ E. Thracian capital of the most rural of the 17 *ķaḍā*'s in the *wilāyet* of Istanbul, 56 km. by asphalt road and 71.41 km. by rail (the station lies 2.3 km. NE of town) WNW of Istanbul. Çatalca borders the Kara su (ancient Athyras) stream at an altitude of 255 feet near the centre of a range of hills forming the backbone of the fortified "Çatalca Lines" extending from the Black Sea at Karaburun to the Marmara at Büyükçekmece. Çatalca was taken from the Byzantines by Murād I in 775/1373. The fortifications were built during the Russo-Turkish war of 1294-5/1877-8, but were passed without fighting by the Russians in their advance to San Stefano. The Çatalca Lines were a rallying point for Maḥmūd Shewket Pasha's forces which put down the abortive counter-revolution at Istanbul in April 1909. In November 1912 retreating Turkish troops repulsed the Bulgarians at Çatalca. The fortifications were reconditioned but saw no action in the 1914-18 and 1939-45 World Wars. Since 1950, Turkish forces have been substantially withdrawn with adverse economic consequences for the district. Some promise of producing oil wells and a proposed atomic reactor may counteract this trend. In 1955 the population was growing fast with 5,534 in town and 58,988 in the *kazas* 3 other *nahiye*'s of Büyükçekmece, Hadımköy (Boyalık) and Karacaköy, and in its 67 villages. Population pressure on the land area of 1684 sq. km. is causing litigation. The district produces beets, sunflowers, grapes, vegetables and cattle. In 1953 there were only four small industries, some 30 shops, 2 elementary and 1 middle schools in Çatalca.

2. Çatalca is also the Ottoman name of Pharsala, a town and *ķaḍā'* in Thessaly 60 km. SE of Trikala, captured in 799/1397 by Bāyazīd I (Hammer-Purgstall, i, 250). According to Shams al-Dīn Sāmī (*Ķāmūs al-A'lām*, iii, 1867) it had a population of 5,000 under Ottoman administration and boasted 6 mosques, a *medrese*, many *tekke*'s, notably that of Dürbālī Bābā, the Bektāshī and 91 villages in a fertile plain.

3. Çatalca is also the name of a village in the *ķaḍā'* of Nizip (Nisib) in the *wilāyet* of Gazi Antep (Ghāzī 'Ayntāb). The word *Çatal*, or fork (cf. *Tanıklariyye Tarama Sözlüğü*, i, Istanbul 1943, ii, 1945, 213) figures in 82 names of inhabited places in Turkey (*Türkiye'de Meskun Yerleri Kılavuzu*, i, Ankara 1946, 240-1).

Bibliography: Cuinet, *Turquie d'Asie*, iv, map between 594-5, coordinates inaccurate; I. H. Danişmend, ... *Kronoloji*, i, 54-5, ii, 343, iv, 302, *passim*; F. S. Duran, *Büyük Atlas*, Istanbul/Vienna, n.d. (1957 ed. ?), 28; *Encyclopaedia Britannica*, 1956 ed., v, 314; Great Britain, Admiralty, I.D. 1129, *A Handbook of Turkey in Europe*, London, n.d. (1919 ?), Map 1 : 800,000, *passim*; idem, B.R. 507. *Turkey*, i, London 1942, *passim*; F. F. Greene, *Report on the Russian Army and its campaigns in Turkey* 1877-1878, New York 1908, 362-3; 427-8; *Iktisat ve Ticaret Ansiklopedisi*, v, 340; *Istanbul Şehri Istatistik Yıllığı* 1948, 6; de la Jonquière, *Histoire de l'empire Ottoman*, Paris 1914, ii, 79, 408; E. Z. Karal, *Osmanlı Tarihi* vi, 127; Mehmet Ali, *Čatāldja Wilāyeti*, Istanbul 1341/1925; Muṣṭafa Reshīd Pasha, *Bir wethīķa-i ta'rīkhiyye Čatāldja mütāreke müdhākerātî*, Istanbul, 1335/1917; E. Pears, *Forty Years in Constantinople*, New York 1916, 322,

328, 342; *Türkiye Yıllıgı* 1948, 94; *Vatan Memleket Ilâveleri*, Istanbul 1953, sv., Istanbul I, 3, 9; T. C. Başvekâlet Istatistik Umum Müdürlüğü, 1955 *Genel Nüfus Sayımı, Telgrafla Alınan Neticeler*, Ankara 1955, 6. (H. A. Reed)

CATANIA [see ṢIḲILLIYA]

CATEGORIES [see MAḲŪLĀT]

ČATR [see MIẒALLA]

CAUCASUS [see ḲABḲ]

CAUSE [see ʿILLA]

ČĀʾŪSH (modern Turkish: *çavuş*). A term used by the Turks to indicate (a) officials staffing the various Palace departments, (b) low-ranking military personnel. The word is met in Uygur, where it refers to a Tou-kiu ambassador; Maḥmūd Kāshgharī defines it as 'a man who controls promotion in army ranks, and supervises the maintenance of discipline'. The word *čāʾūsh* passed from the Pečenegs and Saldjūḳids to the Turks (cf. the μέγας τζαούσιος, chief of the imperial messengers of the Lascari and Paleologi). The Persians used it as a synonym for *sarhang* and *dūrbāsh*, and under the Arabs it became variously *djāʾūsh*, *shāʾīsh*, *shāwīsh*, and *shāʾūsh*. It is still seen in the latter form in N. Africa, where it means a court usher or mace-bearer.

Under the ancient Turks, the Saldjūḳids, the Ayyūbids, and the Mamlūks, the *čāʾūsh* formed a privileged body under the direct command of the ruler, and often appointed to a special rôle. Under the Ottoman Turks, the *čāʾūshes* of the Dīwān were part of the official ceremonial escort when the Sultan left the palace, or when he was receiving viziers, foreign ambassadors etc. The Sultan or Grand Vizier also used them as ambassadors and envoys to convey or carry out their orders. The *čāʾūsh bashî*, chief of the *čāʾūshes* of the Dīwān, acted as deputy to the Grand Vizier, particularly in the administration of justice; being a court official, he was a member of the "āghās of the stirrup". The *čāʾūshes* of the Dīwān were either paid out of treasury funds or allotted *zeʿāmets* or *arpalîḳs*. Furthermore, in the *odjaḳ* of the Janissaries, the 5th Orta consisted of 330 *čāʾūshes*, men already of long service, under the command of a *bāsh-čāʾūsh*.

The ranks of *čāʾūsh* and *čāʾūsh wekīlī* were used in the cavalry and navy at the beginning of the 19th century. When the army was reorganized in 1241/1826, a *čāʾūsh* held the equivalent rank of a sergeant, and the system remains the same to this day.

In certain religious sects and orders (*e.g.*, Yazīdī and Rifāʿī), the title *čāʾūsh* corresponded to a grade in the hierarchy of the sect. There were also *čāʾūshes* in the guilds, where they were responsible for seeing that the rulings of the Guild Council were enforced.

Bibliography: Important bibliography contained in the article '*çavuş*' by M. F. Köprülü, in *İA*, iii, fasc. 25, 362-369. Additional works: Gibb-Bowen, I/1, 1950, *index*; L. Bréhier, *Les Institutions de l'Empire byzantin*, Paris 1949, 148. (R. Mantran)

ČĀWDORS (or DJĀVULDUR), a Turcoman tribe, the first settlers of which came to Khwārizm in the 16th and 17th centuries, the bulk following in the 18th century. After the wars against the Khānate of Khīwa, a proportion of them was driven off to the Mangīshlaḳ peninsula, whence some clans emigrated to the steppes of Stavropol'. Part of the tribe submitted to Khīwa and settled permanently in Khwārizm.

It is now a sedentary tribe with a population of some 25,000, in the Nukhus area (Autonomous Soviet Socialist Republic of Ḳara-Ḳalpaḳistān). [See: TÜRKMEN]. (Ed.)

ČAWGĀN (Pahlawī: *čūbikān*; other forms: *čūygān* (attested in Ibn Yamīn); *čūlgān* (cf. *čūl*, in Vullers, *Lexicon persico-latinum*; compare Arabic *sawladjan*); Greek: τζυκάνιον, French: *chicane*), stick used in polo (*bolo*: Tibetan for '*ball*', introduced into England around 1871); used in a wider sense for the game itself, (*gūy-u*) *čawgān bāzī*, "game of (ball and) *čawgān*"; also used for any stick with the end bent back, particularly those for beating drums. The *čawgān* is not the same as the mall (*malleum*), which is a hardwood sledge-hammer. According to Quatremère (*Mamluks*, i, 123), the *sawladjān*, a bent stick, was used for mall (polo), and the *djūkān* (*čawgān*), with a hollow scooped out of the end, for rackets; but Van Berchem (*C.I.A. Jerusalem-ville*, publ. *IFAO*, 1923, 269, n. I) raises the objection that al-Ḳalḳashandī does not make this distinction. The game originated in Persia, and was generally played on horseback, though sometimes on foot (*čawgān piyāda bāzī*, testified by the *Akbar-nāma*, quoted by Quatremère, 130). The earliest reference to it is in the short historical romance, *Kārnāmagh-ī Ardashēr-ī Pābhaghān* ("Deeds and exploits of Ardashīr") written in Pahlawī in the early 7th century: Ardashīr (Nöldeke, 39) and his grandson Ohrmizd (*id.*, 68) excelled at the game; the latter passage is reproduced almost word for word in al-Ṭabarī (quoted by Quatremère, 123), and put into the form of a poem by Firdawsī (*Shāhnāma*, tr. Mohl, v, 274), but in both texts Ohrmizd is replaced by his father Shāpūr. Quatremère's detailed and learned note provides many quotations: from Cinnamus, on the popularity of τζυκάνιον in Byzantium (122); from the *Aghānī* and al-Masʿūdī, on the *sawladjān* (124); from the *Ḳābūs-nāma*, on the dangers of the game (125) and the notable accidents it had caused (*ibid.*, and 127, 129); from Abū Shāma, on its suitability for keeping soldiers and horses in good physical condition; from various other writers (its popularity with the Mongols, Kurds, and rulers of Egypt) (126-28); on the metaphorical use of *gūy*, *čawgān* and *sawladjān* in prose and poetry (130-132). To these literary texts many more could be added, but it suffices to mention the references to Firdawsī (tr. Mohl, especially vii, 224; and F. Wolff, *Glossar zu Firdosis Schahname*, under *gōy* and *čōgān*), Niẓāmī (*Khusraw u Shīrīn*: description of a game between two teams of female players, led respectively by the king and his favourite), Saʿdī (cf. Massé, *Essai sur Saadi*, 228), a poem of Ḥāfiẓ (*Dīwān*, ed. Ḳazwīnī-Ghanī, no. 271, and ed. Khalkhālī, no. 268, v. 6), and above all the short mystical poem of ʿĀrifī (15th century), *Gūy u Čawgān* (see *Bibl.*). The game began by one of the players throwing the ball as high into the air as possible; another caught it and did the same thing, and thus the ball passed from team to team (there were originally four players in each team; see Firdawsī, *op. cit.*, ii, 250 ff. and 288). The *Ḳābūsnāma* (cf. R. Levy, *A Mirror for Princes*, London 1951, 86) kept the same number of players, "in order to avoid a dangerous scramble". Anthony Sherley gave a brief description of the game at the end of the 16th century, when he was at the court of the Shāh ʿAbbās (quoted by Sykes, 341); 12 players divided into two teams, and each carried a long-handled *čawgān* no thicker than the finger. Chardin (approx. 1675) described the game as follows: "the object is to get the ball through the opposing side's posts, which are at the end of the pitch and through which one can pass (*Voyages*, iii, 181); ... as the stick (*čawgān*) is short, the riders must bend below the level of the pommel .... and strike the ball on the gallop; the game is played between teams of 15 or 20 players" (440). A similar account is given in the early 19th century by Malcolm (*History of Persia*, i, 299 n.); both he and Chardin remark on the shortness of the *čawgān*, and here they are at variance with Sherley. But the information given by Sherley on the positioning of players and posts and the size and shape of the mallets agrees with the pictures on two 16th century miniatures, one in the British Museum (MS. Add. 27257, fol. 107), the other in the Imperial Persian Library (reproduced in "*Iran*", publ. by New York Soc. in conjunction with UNESCO). They illustrate the text from Niẓāmī's *Khusraw and Shīrīn* (mentioned above); one can clearly see the *čawgān*'s long thin handle and convex end (*čawgān*s of the same shape can be seen in the Victoria and Albert Museum, Salting Bequest miniature, no. 1228, 16th cent., and another miniature reproduced in René Grousset, *Civilisations de l'Orient*, i, 243, 16th century). In the British Museum miniature (Add. 27257) the mallets have circumflex-shaped heads; another 16th century miniature (H. d'Allemagne, *Du Kurdistan au pays des Bachktiaris*, i, 160) reveals both the above head and also the hammer type, with tapering handles. Others were shaped rather like a golf club; see A. Sakisian, *La miniature persane*, fig. 48 (dated 1410, Shīrāz school). An even earlier shape is mentioned by Cinnamus (quoted by Quatremère, 122: "stick with a large round end, inside which small cords are intertwined"—it was thus a sort of racket) and by the *Inshā'* (quoted by Quatremère, *ibid.*, "a stick with a bulging conical head made out of wood", *i.e.*, "convex"; *maḥdūdba* should be corrected to *maḥdūba*); this short spoon-shaped *čawgān* figures on a modern miniature of Indo-Persian style, signed and dated (Sykes, 336); another Indo-Persian miniature, more realistic, of the 18th cent., is contained Kühnel, *Miniaturmalerei in Islam. Orient.* pl. 112. The text of the *Inshā'* (and of two others, Nuwayrī and Khalīl Dhahirī, quoted by Quatremère) concerns the *djūkāndār*, an official responsible for the care of the *čawgān*s and for the conduct of the game. The coat of arms (two curved *čawgān*s placed back to back) of this officer is known from the inscriptions and coats of arms, on the one hand, of a *madrasa* in Jerusalem (built by Il-malak, *djūkāndār* to the Mamlūk sultan of Egypt, al-Malik al-Nāṣir, 1340), and of a lantern inscribed with the name of the same person, preserved in the Istanbul Museum (studied by M. van Berchem, *C.I.A. Jerusalem-ville*, 266-270, publ. *IFAO*, Cairo 1923), and on the other hand, of the tomb of a *djūkāndār* (d. at Marāgha, 1328) of the Egyptian sultan Ḳalā'ūn (A. Godard, *Āthār-è Īrān*, i, 1936, 144-149, fig. 101 & 103). According to Sykes, the political chaos following the fall of the Ṣafawids resulted in the disappearance of the game, and now it is played only in certain parts of India; Sykes claims to have reintroduced it into Tehran *ca.* 1897.

Bibliography: Maḳrīzī; *Histoire des sultans mamlouks de l'Egypte*, trans. M. Quatremère, i, 121, n. 4; *Geschichte des Artachšīr i Pāpakān*, tr. from the Pahlawī by Nöldeke, (*Beiträge z. Kunde der Indogerman. Sprachen, Festschrift Benfey*, Göttingen 1879, iv, 22 ff.); A. Christensen, *L'Iran sous les Sassanides*, 416, n. 4 (ref. to Inostrantzev); Pseudo-Djāḥiẓ, *Livre de la Couronne* (trans. by Ch. Pellat), 101-102; Ibn Ḳutayba, *'Uyūn al-Akhbār*, Cairo ed., i, 133-134; ed. Brockelmann, 166-167, unreliable and difficult text: advice to the players); J. J. Modi, *The Game of Ball-Bat-chowgangui—among the ancient Persians, as described in the Epic of Firdowsī*, in *J[R]ASB*, 1891, vol. xviii, 39 ff.; 'Ārifī, *The Ball and the Polo Stick* (*Gūy o tchūgān*) *or Book of Ecstasy* (*Hālnāme*), R. S. Greenshields ed., London 1931 (reviewed by H. Massé, with trans. of certain extracts, in *JA*, vol. ccxxiii (1933), 137-141; P. M. Sykes, *Ten Thousand Miles in Persia or eight years in Iran*, London 1902, chap. xxix; *Syria*, vol. xiii, 208, n. 3. On the *djūkāndār* and his coat of arms: Yakoub Artin Pacha, *Contribution à l'étude du blason en Orient*, London 1902, 131 ff. and reproductions of 10 *čawgāns*; L. A. Mayer, *Saracenic Heraldry*, Oxford 1933, index (s.vv. *jūkāndār* and *polo-sticks* (*jūkān*). On the present rules of the game: *Encyclopaedia Britannica* (s.v. Polo). (H. Massé)

ČAY. Tea appears to be mentioned for the first time in an Arabic text by the author of the *Akhbār al-Ṣīn wa'l-Hind* (ed. and transl. by J. Sauvaget, 18), under the form *sākh*, whereas al-Bīrūnī, *Nubadh fī Akhbār al-Ṣīn*, ed. Krenkow, in *MMIA*, xiii (1955), 388, calls it more correctly *dja'*. It was introduced into Europe towards the middle of the 16th century by the Dutch East Indies company; but it is only in the middle of 17th century that its use spread, particularly in England.

In Morocco the first mention of tea dates back to 1700. It was a French merchant, with business contacts in the Far East, who introduced it to the sultan Mawlāy Ismā'īl. For a long time this commodity remained rare and expensive. At first the use of tea was known only to the bourgeoisie, but it afterwards spread to all classes of society. In Morocco mint tea has become the national drink. Its properties, and the ceremonies of its preparation and consumption have been the subject of several poems in Arabic and Berber; at the court of the sultans of Morocco a special corps of officials, called *mwālīn ātāy*, was formed to prepare it.

In Morocco, in Mauretania, and in the departments of Oran and Algers, the name of tea is *ātāy*. Tunisia and the department of Constantine use *tāy*. In Libya *shāhī* is found; this perhaps represents the Eastern Arabic *shāy*, contaminated, by popular etymology, with the root *sh-h-w*.

The radical *tāy* certainly seems to come from the English 'tea', but with the pronunciation (*tei*) which this word had until about 1720, when it rhymed in fact with 'obey' and 'pay' (cf. Yule, *Hobson-Jobson*, 1903, 905). It is known that it was English merchants who introduced the use of tea in Morocco, and that for a long time they kept a virtual monopoly on its importation.

As for the prefix *ā-*, which figures in western Maghribī names, it must represent the Berber definite article in the masculine singular. Indeed, in Morocco and Tlemcen, its presence dispenses with the use of the Arabic definite article. Therefore the word *ātāy* was probably borrowed through Berber; it is established that in the 17th century the principal centres for importation were Agadir and then Mogador, which are situated in Berber-speaking country. [For *Čay* and *Čaykhāna* in Persia and Central Asia, see SUPPLEMENT].

Bibliography: J. L. Miège, *Origine et développement de la consommation du thé au Maroc*, in *Bulletin économique et social du Maroc*, xx (1957),

377 (includes a bibliography on the subject); W. Marçais, *Textes arabes de Tanger*, 215; L. Brunot, *Textes arabes de Rabat*, Glossary, i; P. Odinot, *Le Monde Marocain*, 158; E. Lévi-Provençal, *Les manuscrits arabes de Rabat*, 115, n° 339; Justinard, *Les Aït Ba ʿAmrān*, in *Villes et Tribus du Maroc*, viii (1936), 57).

(G. S. Colin)

ČEČENS, name given by the Russians to a Muslim people living in the valleys of the southern tributaries of the Sunja and Terek Rivers in the Central Caucasus (native name = Nakhčio or Veynakh).

The Čečens belong to the linguistic family of the Ibero-Caucasian peoples; their language forms with Ingush, Batzbi and Kistin a special group rather close to that of the Dāghistānī languages.

The Čečens are the descendants of autochthonous Ibero-Caucasian tribes which were driven back and kept in the high mountains, between the pass of Daryal and the valley of Sharo-Argun, by the Alains. Nearly all their history until the 18th century is unknown; we know only that it is in the 16th century that their tribes of shepherds began to emigrate into the piedmont which today forms the northern part of the Čečens country (in Russian "Cečnya"). At first subject to the Kabard princes [*q.v.*], they made themselves independent in the 18th century, a little before the arrival of the Russians.

Sunnī Islam of the Ḥanafī school penetrated into their country only from the 17th century, both through Dāghistān and Crimea, but until the middle of the 18th century it remained rather superficial; it was firmly implanted only at the end of the century thanks to the influence of the Naḳshbandīs. Among their western neighbours, the Ingush [*q.v.*], it was implanted still later, in the first half of the 19th century. At the beginning of the 20th century some traces of animism still persisted (cult of the patron spirit of the clan).

At the time when the first Russian detachments appeared, the Čečens were divided into clans, of which some were grouped together in tribes: Mičik, Ičkeri, Aukh, Kist, Nazran, Ḳarabulakh, Ghalghay (this latter gave birth later to the Ingush nation). The term "Čečen" was applied by the Russians to the whole of these tribes in the middle of the 18th century from the name of the "Čečen" *aul* on the river Argun where, in 1732, there occurred the first combat between a Russian detachment and the natives. The Russian advance toward the south began in the middle of the 18th century and was accelerated after the annexation of Eastern Georgia in 1801; it was slow and methodical, marked by the construction of fortresses, the establishment of Cossack colonies and the destruction of the villages of the natives, who were driven always back toward the high mountains. The Čečens offered fierce resistance to the Russian advance. A popular movement, directed by the Shaykh Manṣūr Ushurma, burst out in 1785 and was crushed only in 1791. In the first half of the 19th century the Čečen country became the principal bastion of the imāmate of Shamīl (cf. Dāghistān and Shamīl), and the Russian domination was imposed only in 1859; it was moreover marked by frequent revolts, of which the most important, that of ʿAlibek Aldamov of Simsiri in 1877, lasted a year and spread to all the Čečen country. In 1865, an important group of Čečens, nearly 40,000, emigrated to Turkey. On the eve of the revolution of 1917, the Čečen country was pacified and partially colonized by Russian colonists (especially Cossacks) in the plains of the north. Moreover, the discovery of the petroliferous strata at Grozniy attracted a growing number of Russian workers (10,000 in 1905, more than 20,000 in 1917).

Until the Revolution, Čečen society preserved a very archaic proto-feudal social structure, less developed than that of their Dāghistān and Kabard neighbours. The great patriarchal family of 40 to 50 people maintained its position almost everywhere as also the rigorously exogamous clans, *taīpa*, gathering together the descendants of a common ancestor. Finally, Čečen society did not recognize any division into social classes, all the Čečens considering themselves as *uzdens*, "nobles".

Soviet Čečnya. — After the October Revolution, the Čečen country was the last bastion of native resistance against the Soviet regime (Imāmate of Uzūn Ḥadjdjī, cf. Dāghistan); on 20 January 1921, it was included in the Mountain Republic (*Gorskaya Respublika*), and on 30 November 1922 upper Cečnya was set up as the Čečen Autonomous Region. On 7 July 1924 the Ingush country situated to the west of Čečnya was, in its turn, transformed into the Ingush Autonomous Region (cf. Ingush). On 4 November 1929 the lower country with Grozniy was included in the Čečen Autonomous Region. In January 1934, the two autonomous regions were joined into one, the Čečen-Ingush Autonomous Region, which was transformed on 5 December 1936 into the Čečen-Ingush Autonomous Soviet Socialist Republic. On 25 June 1946 a decree of the Supreme Soviet of the U.S.S.R. abolished the Republic, and Čečen and Ingush people were deported to Central Asia (the same decree affected other Caucasian peoples: Balkars, Karačays [*qq.v.*]). On 9 January 1957 a new Supreme Soviet decree rehabilitated the deportees and re-established the Čečen-Ingush Autonomous Soviet Socialist Republic, authorizing the survivors to return to their country between 1957 and 1960.

At present, the Čečen-Ingush A.S.S.R. (area 19,300 sq. km.) has a total population of 700,000 inhabitants (1958), the Čečens representing as yet only a minority.

The census of 1939 counted 407,724 Čečens, of whom roughly 30,000 were in the A.S.S.R. of Dāghistān and the rest were in their own Republic; the Ingush numbered 92,074 in the western part of the Republic (the high valleys of Asa, Sunja, and Kambileyka). The capital Grozniy, a big industrial centre (226,000 inhabitants in 1926), is an almost entirely Russian city.

The Čečen-Ingush now form a "nation", divided into two "nationalities" very closely related to one another. In fact, nothing distinguishes these two peoples except the fact that the Ingush have taken only a negligible part in the Shamīl movement. They speak very similar languages, Ingush being simply a dialect of Čečen. The Čečen language properly speaking is divided into two dialects—Upper Čečen (or Čaberloy), spoken in the nountains, and the Lower Čečen of the plains; this latter, the basis of the written language, is endowed with a Latin alphabet (after a fruitless attempt to transcribe Čečen into Arabic characters). For its part, Ingush was established as a written language in 1923 (based on the Lower Ingush dialect of the plains) and also transcribed into Latin characters. In 1934, after the fusion of the two Autonomous Regions, Čečen and and Ingush, the two written languages were unified into a single language—"Čečen-Ingush", written from 1938 in a Cyrillic alphabet. At present, they are once more officially separated. The new Čečen-Ingush literature has developed only during the Soviet period.

Bibliography: N. E. Yakovlev, *Voprosî izučeniya čečenyt zev i ingushey*, Groznîy 1927; A. R. Berge, *Čečnya i čečentzî*, Tiflis 1859; and *Shamil i Čečnya*, in *Voennîy Sbornik*, St. Petersburg 1859, ix; D. D. Mal'sagov, *Čečeno-Ingushskaya dialektologiya i puti razvitiya Čečeno-Ingushskogo literaturnogo (pis'mennogo) yazîka*, Groznîy 1941; and *Kul'turnaya rabota v Čečne i Ingushii v svyazi s unifikatziey alfavitov*, Vladikavkaz 1928; A. Dirr, *Einführung in das Studium der Kaukasischen Sprachen*, Leipzig 1928.

(A. Bennigsen)

CELEBES, one of the four larger islands in Indonesia. With the exception of the north-eastern peninsula, which was one of the areas of early Christianization, and the south-western peninsula, where Islām also started its penetration in the 16th century, the island remained inaccessible to the influence of foreign religions until the second half of the 19th century. A new Christian community then came into existence in Central Celebes, inhabited by the Jo-Radja. It is said that this community suffered a great deal from the military activity of the Dār al-Islām movement after Indonesia became a republic in 1949; reliable information is lacking, however. The Muslim community of the south-western peninsula is not very different from those elsewhere in Indonesia; some details on its history are given under Makasar. For a general discussion of Indonesian Islām cf. djāwa. (C. C. Berg)

ČELEBĪ (Turkish), "writer, poet, reader, sage, of keen common sense" (thus Moḥammad Khōʾī in *Khulāṣa-i ʿAbbāsī*, in P. Melioranskiy, *Zapiski Vostočnago Otdĕleniya*, xv, 1904, 042; similarly Aḥmed Wefīḳ Pasha in *Lehdje-i ʿUthmānī*, i, 1876, 482). It is a term applied to men of the upper classes in Turkey between the end of the 13th and the beginning of the 18th century, as a title primarily given to poets and men of letters, but also to princes (thus all the sons of Bāyazīd I (d. 805/1403) were given it). An Ādharbaydjānī poet of the 9th/15th century, Ḳāsim-i Anwār (died 835/1431-2) uses Čelebī also in the sense of the mystical term 'Beloved', *i.e.*, God (C. Salemann in *Zapiski Vost. Otd.* xvii, 1907, XXXIV). Heads of an order were also called Čelebī; it was applied to the head of the Mawlawī [*q.v.*] order from the time of Djalāl al-Dīn Rūmī's successor, Čelebī Ḥusām al-Dīn (died 1284/683 [*q.v.*]) right into the 20th century. According to its usage, the word would thus correspond roughly to the Persian Mīrzā [*q.v.*] from *amīr-zāda*. In its secular meaning the word has been replaced by *Efendi* [*q.v.*] in the Ottoman empire since ca. 1700. Occasionally, Čelebī also appears as a proper name. In Syrian and Egyptian Arabic, *shalabī/djalabī* today has the meaning of 'barbarian'.

There has been no satisfactory explanation of the origin of the word. The following have been suggested: 1) as late as the 7th/13th (!) century, borrowed by the Nestorian Mission from the Syrian *ṣĕlībhā* 'cross', which was subsequently taken to mean a worshipper of the crucifix (Aḥmed Wefīḳ Pasha, *Lehdje, loc. cit.*); the same, though taken over considerably earlier: Viktor, Baron Rosen in *Zapiski Vost. Otd.* v, 305 ff.; xi, 310 ff.; with additional source references also found in P. Melioranskiy, *Zapiski Vost. Otd.* xv, 1904, 036 ff.; cf. also Menges, as in the bibliography; the same, but taken over in Anatolia, perhaps through Kurdish intermediation (cf. below, no. 4): Nikolay N. Martinovitch, JOAS 54 (1934), 194-9 (although the Nestorians never played a role in Anatolia); 2) from the Arabic *djalab*, pl. *djulbān*, "imported slave", a separate body in the Mamlūk period in Egypt, which was specially trained in administrative work, Woldemar, Frh. von Tiessenhausen in the *Zapiski*, xi, 1898, 307 ff.; 3) from the Greek καλλίεπής "beautifully speaking, singing, writing", hence, as early as Byzantine times, "of high rank": thus Čelebī would appear to have developed in Anatolia: V. Smirnov in *Zapiski* xviii, 1908, 1 ff. (according to a private communication from F. Dölger, 3/I/1959, the meaning "of distinguished rank" is, however, not verifiable in Greek): 4) taken from the Kurdish *theleb* "God", *thelebi* "noble lord, wandering minstrel" which, in turn, had come into that language "from a non-Indo-European language": this is the explanation given by Nik. Jak. Marr in *Zapiski* xx, 1910, 99/151, and it is based on his Japhetic theory; 5) from the Anatolian Turkish *čalab/čäläb* "God" (there are examples in the 13th-15th centuries in Mansuroğlu, and in later centuries current particularly among the Yürüks [*q.v.*], a word which, according to Muḥammad Khoʾī, *Khulāsa-i ʿAbbāsī* [excerpt from Mīrzā Mahdī Khān, *Senglākh*] comes from the Greek. K. Foy, in *MSOS*, *Westasiat. Studien*, ii, 124; P. Melioranskiy in the *Zapiski*, xv, 1904, 042; W. Barthold also favours this view (in which case the development would be opposite to that of the Iranian word khvadhāi "lord" > khudā "god"); 6) Mansuroğlu (see bibliography) is undecided, but he does not believe in the foreign origin of the word. — Several of these attempts at a derivation (1, 2, and 4 in particular), seem impossible and far fetched. Though the word is apparently of Anatolian origin, there is no evidence of its Greek descent [as—on the contrary—Efendi]. It seems doubtful whether Ibn Baṭṭūṭa (ed. Defrémery and Sanguinetti, ii, 270), means "Greek" in his mention of the meaning of the word Čelebī "in the language of Rūm" (thus W. Barthold), or whether this is merely a reference to its use in Anatolia. To the Greeks (such as G. Phrantzes, *Chron.* 70), the word Čelebi appears Turkish.

Bibliography: The most recent survey of the etymology is by M. Manṣūroğlu, in the *Ural-Altaische Jahrbücher*, xxvii, 1955, 97/99; E. Rossi in *Türk Dili Araştırmaları Yıllığı*: *Belleten* 1954, 11/14; K. H. Menges in *Supplement to Word VII*, Dec. 1951, 67/70. Concerning the Greek sources of the word, G. Moravcsik, *Byzantino-Turcica*², Berlin 1958, ii, 311.

(W. Barthold-[B. Spuler])

ČELEBI EFENDI [see djalāl al-dīn, mawlānā]

ČELEBI-ZĀDE (or Küčük čelebi-zāde) Ismāʿīl ʿĀṣim Efendi, 18th century Ottoman historian, poet and *shaykh al-islām*. His familiar name (*laḳab*) derives from his father Küčük Čelebi Meḥmed Efendi (*Sidjill-i ʿOthmānī*, iv, 205) who was "foreign secretary" (*reʾīs ül-küttāb*) for about ten months in 1108-09/1699 (Rāshid, *Taʾrīkh*, ed. 1282, ii, 387, 421). He was born in Istanbul, and, from the statement of Müstaḳīm-zāde Süleymān Efendi (*Tuḥfe-i Khaṭṭāṭīn*, Istanbul 1928, 650) that he was 77 years of age at the time of his death, his birth should be fixed about 1096/1685 about 1096/1685. His contemporary, Sālim Efendi (*Tedhkire-i Shuʿarā*, Istanbul, 1315, 452) says that he was given the grade of *mülāzim* by Fayḍullāh Efendi in 1108/1696-97, but, as M. C. Baysun suggests (*İA*, fasc. xxv, 371b), this was probably an honorary degree conferred on the boy of twelve out of respect for his father's position —an action quite in character for this notoriously simonistic *shaykh al-islām*. (cf. Na^cīmā, *Ta'rīkh*, ed. 1280, vi, Supp., 6-7. It is probable that the *mustakillan* of Sēlim's text should be corrected to *mustakbilan*, "in anticipation"). His teaching career, all of which was passed in Istanbul, began in 1120/1708 at the *madrasa* of Ken^cān Pasha, from where he advanced to the Dizdāriyye (1125/1713), the Aḥmed Pasha in Demir Kapī (1130/1718), the ʿĀrifiyye (1131/1719) and finally (1135/1723) the *madrasa* founded by his father-in-law, the *kāḍī ʿasker* ʿÖmer Efendi, in Mollā Gūrānī (Sālim, *op. cit.* and Ismāʿīl ʿĀṣīm, *Ta'rīkh*, ed. 1282, 110). On 28 Ramaḍān 1135/5 April 1723, he was appointed official historiographer (*waḳāʾiʿ-nüwīs*) in succession to Rāshid Efendi, which post he filled until about 1143/1730 when his patron, the Grand Vizier Ibrāhīm Pasha, was sacrificed to the rebels and his favourites driven from office (cf. AḤMAD III). In 1145-46/1732-33, he was *kāḍī* of Yeñi Shehr (Larissa in Thessaly); in 1152-53/1738-39, of Bursa; in 1157-58/1744-45, of Medīne; and in 1161-62/1748-49, of Istanbul. His next appointment did not come until 1170/1757, when he was made *kāḍī ʿasker* of Anatolia for one year; and on the 5 Dhu 'l-Ḳaʿda 1172/30 June 1759, he attained the ultimate dignity of *shaykh al-islām*, in which office he died after eight months (28 Djumādā II 1173/16 Feb. 1760). He was buried next to his father-in-law, ʿÖmer Efendi, in the courtyard of Mollā Gūrānī (Ḥāfiẓ Ḥuseyn Efendi Ayvānsarāyī, *Ḥadīḳat al-Djewāmiʿ*, Istanbul 1291, i, 208).

His history (twice printed as a supplement to that of Rāshid: Istanbul 1153 and 1282) covers the period 1135-41/1722-29, and although, even by the standards of the official histories, notably superficial and frequently little more than a court chronicle, it has some of the virtue of its defects in being a wholly characteristic expression of the frivolity and complacency of the so-called Tulip Period of Ottoman history. In his verse he uses the poetic signature (*makhlaṣ*) ʿĀṣim; and while his stature as a poet is overshadowed by such great contemporaries as Nedīm, Seyyid Wehbī and Neylī, nevertheless, his *dīwān* (lithographed, Istanbul 1268), with its graceful language and delicate sententiousness, has always been regarded as one of the masterpieces of this period in which Ottoman *dīwān* poetry finally develops its own recognizably authentic voice. His abilities and range as a prose writer can be better appreciated from his collected letters (*Münsheʾāt*: Istanbul 1268) than from his history, where he deliberately models his style on that of Rāshid Efendi. His only other surviving work is a translation from the Persian commissioned by Dāmād Ibrāhīm Pasha of the *Sefāret-nāme-i Čīn* of Ghiyāth al-Dīn al-Naḳḳāsh (Browne, iii, 397; M. F. Köprülü, *MTM*, ii (1331), 351-68) under the title *ʿAdjāʾib al-Laṭāʾif* (ed. ʿAlī Emīrī, Istanbul 1331). A *Mawlid risālesi* attributed to him by Müstaḳīm-zāde (*op. cit.* 651) is otherwise unknown.

Bibliography: The only reliable biographical information is in the notice by M. C. Baysun already referred to (but on 372a, l. 3, for *cemāziyel-evvel* read, after Sālim, Djumādā II). Babinger, 293, is a not entirely exact translation of the *Sidjill-i ʿOthmānī*, i, 366, which itself contains errors. Both Djemāl al-Dīn, *Āyīne-i Ẓurafāʾ*, Istanbul 1314, 45 and Rifʿat Efendi, *Dawḥat al-Meshāʾikh*, Istanbul n.d., 101 derive from Wāṣif, *Taʾrīkh*, Istanbul 1219, i, 179. In addition to Sālim, *op. cit.*, Ṣafāʾī (*Tedhkire*, Millet, ʿAlī Emīrī, 771), 279 and Rāmiz (*Ādāb-i Ẓurafāʾ*, Millet, ʿAlī Emīrī, 762), 173 are contemporary opinions of his poetry. Apart from the short article of ʿAlī Djānib, *Ḥayāt*, i, no. 20 (1927), 3-5, no study has been made of his *dīwān*, which, moreover, requires re-editing from the Bāyezīd MS., no. 5644, with marginal corrections in his own hand. Sadeddin Nüzhet Ergun, *Türk Şairleri*, i, 108-111, contains extracts from some of the sources mentioned above; references to Faṭīn, von Hammer, Gibb, etc. may be found in Babinger.

(J. R. WALSH)

ČELEBI ZĀDE EFENDI [see SAʿĪD EFENDI]

ČENDERELI [see DJANDARLĪ]

ČEPNI, an Oghuz tribe, which holds an important place in the political and religious history of Turkey, and in the history of its occupation by the Turks. The most intimate *mürīd*s of Ḥādjdjī Bektāsh belonged to this tribe, an important branch of which must therefore have been living in the Ḳīrshehir region in the 13th century. In the second half of this century there was another important group of the Čepni in the Samsun region, who in 676/1277 successfully defended Samsun against the forces of the Emperor of Trebizond, and in the 14th century played the chief part in the conquest of the Djānik (Ordu-Giresun) district; the Ḥādjdjī Emīrli principality which controlled the Ordu-Giresun region in the 14th century was probably founded by this tribe. At the beginning of the 16th century the region round Trabzon, especially to the west and south-west, was in their hands and was hence called *wilāyet-i Čepni* after them. From the 16th century onwards they began to penetrate the region east of Trabzon too, where even in the 18th century the Čepni were waging fierce struggles with the local people. Thus the Čepni played a very important rôle in the conquest and turcicization of the Samsun-Rize area.

Important groups connected with this tribe are found in other parts of Turkey too in the 15th and 16th centuries. The largest lived in the Sivas region and practised agriculture. There was another important group among the Türkmens of Aleppo, one branch of which began to settle in the ʿAyntāb area in the 16th century; another, generally called the Bashīm Ḳīzdīlu, migrated to western Anatolia and settled in the districts of Izmir, Aydīn, Manisa and Balikesir.

There was another important branch of the Čepni in the Aḳ-ḳoyunlu confederation; they were led, in the time of Uzun Ḥasan and his first successors, by Il-aldī Beg, and were later in the service of the Ṣafawids. In the 16th century there were Čepni also in the Erzurum district, and some clans around Konya and Adana too.

In the 15th and 16th centuries there were many villages named, after the tribe, Čepni; in some cases the name survives to the present day. Bektāshī and Ḳīzīlbash doctrines were from of old widespread among the Čepni.

Bibliography: Faruk Sümer, *Osmanlı devrinde Anadolu'da yaşayan bazı Üçoklu Oğuz boylarına mensup teşekküller*, in *Iktisat Fakültesi Mecmuası*, x, 441-453, Istanbul 1952.

(FARUK SÜMER)

CERAMICS [see FAKHKHĀR]

ČEREMISS (native name Mari), people of the eastern Finnish group, living principally in the basin of the Middle Volga to the north-east of Ḳazan in the Autonomous Soviet Socialist Republic of the Maris as well as in the neighbouring territories: A.S.S.R. of Tātārstān and of Bas͟hkiria, regions (*oblast'*) of Gorki, of Kirov and of Sverdlovsk of the R.S.F.S.R. The total number of Čeremiss reached 481,300 in 1939; they are divided into three distinct groups by their dialects and their material culture. The Čeremiss of the plains (*lugovîe*) live on the left bank of the Volga, those of the highlands (*gornîe*) on the right bank, and the eastern Čeremiss emigrated in the 18th century into the valley of the river Belaya in Bas͟hkir country.

The Čeremiss descend from the Finnish-Ugrian tribes of the Volga, subjugated in the 8th century by the K͟hazars, then, between the 9th and the 13th century, by the Bulg͟hārs. It is through the medium of these latter that the Arabs became acquainted with the Čeremiss (under the name of Ṣarmis). After the destruction of the Kingdom of Greater Bulgaria, the Čeremiss fell under the domination of the Golden Horde, then of the K͟hānate of Ḳazan. The ancestors of the present Čeremiss were never converted to Islam, but they submitted, nevertheless, as early as the high Middle Ages, to the indirect influence which we recognise in our own day in certain ritual terms: *payrām* (the feast of spring), *ḥaram* (sacred grove), *keremet* designating the spirit of the forests (from *karāma* = miracle).

Conquered by Russia in the 16th century, the Čeremiss were from that period very strongly marked by Russian culture and, in the 19th century, the majority were officially converted to orthodox Christianity. At the end of the 19th century, only the Čeremiss of the eastern group remained Animists (the Či-maris).

From the outset of 1905 to the October Revolution and even beyond, one notes among the Čeremiss living in contact with the Tatars and the Muslim Bas͟hkirs numerous conversions to Islam. It is unfortunately impossible to judge the new influence of Islam on the Čeremiss because the converts generally adopt the language and customs of the Tatars and "Tatarize" themselves.

Bibliography: I. N. Smirnov, *Čeremisî, Istoričeskiy-Étnografičeskiy očerk*, Ḳazan 1889; and *Očerki drevney istoriy narodov Srednego Povolz'ya i Prikam'ya*, in *Materialî i Issledovaniya po Arkheologiy SSSR*, no. 28, Moscow 1952; Ya. Yalkaev, *Materialî dlya bibliografičeskogo ukazatelya po marivedeniyu*, 1762-1931, Jos͟hkar-Ola 1934.

(CH. QUELQUEJAY)

CERIGO [see ČOKA ADASÎ]

ČERKES, The name of Čerkes (in Turkish *čerkas*, perhaps from the earlier "kerkète", indigenous name: Adîg͟he) is a general designation applied to a group of peoples who form, with the Abk͟haz [*q.v.*], the Abaza (cf. BESKESEK ABAZĀ) and the Ubək͟h, the north-west or Abasgo-Adîg͟he branch of the Ibero-Caucasian peoples.

The ancestors of the Čerkes peoples were known among the ancients under the names of Σινδοί, Κερχεταί, Ζιχγοί, Ζυγοί, etc., and lived on the shores of the Sea of Azov and the Black Sea and in the plains of the Kuban to the south and the north of this river, extending perhaps to the Don.

In the 10th century, the Russians settled in the peninsula of Taman (the principality of Tmutarakan) and entered into contact with the Čerkes, whom their chronicles designate under the name of Kasog (Georgian name = Kas͟hak, Kasagi in Ossète). From the 13th to the 15th century, the north-west Caucasus was subjected to the Golden Horde and it is after the collapse of the latter that the eastern Čerkes tribes (the present Kabard) began to play a rôle in the history of the Caucasus.

The Kabard princes maintained in the 16th century friendly relations with the rulers of Moscow (the second wife of Ivan IV was a Čerkes princess). In the 17th century the Kabard tribes led the coalition of Caucasian peoples which halted and repulsed the advance of the Kalmîks and from that era, the Čerkes held supremacy which they lost only after the Russian conquest.

Distribution of the Čerkes Tribes. — Before the Russian conquest in the middle of the 19th century, the Čerkes peoples, numbering more than a million, inhabited the north-west Caucasus (country of the Kuban) and a part of the eastern coast of the Black Sea and the peninsula of Taman up to the neighbourhood of the Abk͟hazi.

The principal tribes were:

— The Natuk͟hay (Natkuad͟j) in the peninsula of Taman and near the estuary of the Kuban.

— The S͟hapsug, divided into the "Great S͟hapsug", on the left bank of the lower Kuban and along the river Afips, and the "Little S͟hapsug" on the shores of the Black Sea. These two tribes spoke the same dialect; more to the East, in the basins of the tributaries of the Kuban Belaya, Ps͟his͟h and Psekups lived the largest of the Adîg͟he tribes: the Abadzek͟h. Before 1864, these three tribes formed 9/10 of the total of the entire population of Western Adîg͟he tribes. Among the other Western tribes, the most important were the Mok͟hos͟h on the river Farsu, the Temirgoy (Kemgui, Čengui) between the Laba and the Kuban; the Bjeduk͟h at the confluence of the rivers Ps͟his͟h and Psekus͟h with the Kuban; the Khatükay between the lower Beləya and the Ps͟his͟h, and finally the most eastern of the western tribes: the Besleney to the south-east of the Mok͟hos͟h.

The eastern tribes or Kabards (Kaberdey) [cf. KABARDA] lived from the 18th century in the basin of the upper Terek and some of its tributaries. They were divided into two groups: the tribes of the Great Kabarda, between the rivers Malka and Terek (to the west of the Terek) and those of the Little Kabarda (between the Sunja and the Terek, to the east of the latter river.

To these tribes must be added two others who were of non-Adîg͟he origin but who were in point of fact assimilated by the Čerkes and whose history is indissolubly bound to that of the latter: the Ubək͟h [*q.v.*] and the Abaza (cf. BESEKESEK-ABAZA).

After the conquest of the country by the Russians, the greater part of the western Čerkes emigrated in 1864-65 to Turkey and there remained in Russia only a small fraction of them. The last Soviet census (1939) counted only 164,000 Kabards and 88,000 western Adîg͟he thus distributed:

1. — Kabard: The 152,000 in the Kabard-Balkar A.S.S.R. and 7,000 to 8,000 in the two Autonomous Regions of Adîg͟he and Karačay-Čerkes (*auls* Katzk͟habl', Blečeps and K͟hodz'). In addition, the census of 1939 counted as Kabards the 2000 Kabard-speaking Armenians of Armavir (territory of Krasnodar) of the Armenian-Gregorian religion, the 2100 "Čerkes of Mozdok" of the A.S.S.R. of North Ossetia who are Kabards converted to orthodox Christianity, and finally a little group (500 to 600) of Kabard-speaking Jews of the district of Mozdok.

2. — The Besleney: about 30,000, of whom 20,000 are in the Autonomous Region of Karačay-Čerkes (this group adopted the literary language of

the Kabards and is assimilated by the Kabard nation), and 10,000, in the Autonomous Region of Adîghe and near Armavir, who adopted the literary language of the Adîghe.

3. — The Lower Adîghe: in number about 55,000, principally in the Autonomous Region of Adîghe. After the migration of 1864-65, the tribal differences shaded off rapidly, and the scattered elements of the tribes remaining in Russia consolidated in an "Adîghe Nation" commune; only the following tribes still conserve some peculiarities of dialect and custom: the Abadzekh, about 5,000 around the *aul* Khakurinov (their dialect is on its way to disappearance); the Bjedukh, about 12,000 who populate 38 *auls* to the south of the Kuban and an *aul* near Armavir; finally, the Shapsug to the number of 10,000 on the shores of the Black Sea (14 *auls* to the north and south of Tuapse) with a little islet in the peninsula of Taman.

Language: With Abkhaz, Ubəkh and, according to some, Abaza (which others consider a simple Adîghe dialect), the Čerkes languages form the north-west branch of the Ibero-Caucasian languages. The Čerkes group is divided into several dialects of which two are now literary languages:

1. — Eastern Adîghe ("high Adîghe") or Kabard, including diverse speech characteristics a little different from one another. The speech of the Great Kabarda serves as the basis of the Kabard literary language used in the Kabardo-Balkar A.S.S.R. and in the Autonomous Republic of the Karačay-Čerkes, transcribed in the Latin alphabet since 1925 (after a trial of the Arabic alphabet in 1924). In 1938, the Latin alphabet was replaced by the Cyrillic.

2. — Lower Adîghe (or K'akh), including dialects closely related to one another: Bjedukh, Shapsug, K'emirgoy (or Temirgčy), as well as the rest of the Abadzekh and Khakuci dialects. The Bjedukh and K'emirgoy dialects serve as the basis of the Adîghe written language used in the Autonomous Republic of the Adîghe. The first attempts to give the Adîghe a written language trace back to 1855 (handbook of the Adîghe language of ʿUmar Besney). In 1865, Atakujin and in 1890 Loparinski aimed toward an Adîghe Cyrillic alphabet.

Between 1917 and 1920 there were again attempts to give Adîghe a script: Domatov worked out an Arabic alphabet and Saltokov modified Lopatinski's Cyrillic alphabet. Finally, in 1925, Adîghe received a Latin alphabet, replaced in 1935 by Cyrillic. From 1925, the linguistic unity of the Čerkes people was broken and the two written languages, Adîghe and Kabard, thereafter developed alone different lines, in spite of the vain attempt to reunite them in 1930, at the time of the conference of the Committee on the new Latin alphabet at Moscow.

Halfway between Kabard and Lower Adîghe is found the Besleney dialect, which belongs to Lower Adîghe but is full of Kabard elements.

The written Kabard and Adîghe literatures appeared after the establishment of the Soviet regime. The Čerkes had until then only an oral literature, principally of folk-lore, which included two types in particular: the legends of *Nartes* (mythological-heroic legends) which the Čerkes share in common with some other Caucasian people such as the Ossetes, and the heroic-historical songs which Shora-Bekmurzin Nogmov gathered and published (see bibliography).

Religion. — The Čerkes are Sunnī Muslims of the Ḥanafī school. Islam was brought in the 16th century by the Nogais [*q.v.*] and the Tatars of the Crimea, first to the Kabards, then, in the 17th century, to the western Adîghe. Penetration was slow and at first reached only the feudal nobility. It is only at the beginning of the 18th century, thanks to the zeal of the Khāns of the Crimea and the Turkish pashas of Anapa, that Islam was imposed on all of the people, replacing Christianity (introduced as early as the 6th century by Byzantium and, between the 10th and the 12th centuries, by Georgia) and the ancient pagan religion of which one still finds traces among the western Adîghes.

Before their conversion to Islam, the Čerkes worshipped agrarian divinities: Shible, god of storm and thunder, Sozeresh, protector of the sowings, Yemish, protector of the flocks, Khategnash, god of the gardens, etc. The cult of the god of thunder was linked to the worship of trees and sacred groves where, even recently, were offered sacrifices and prayers. A particular cult was dedicated to Tlepsh, god of the blacksmiths and doctors. The Čerkes had neither temples nor clergy; sacrifices were entrusted to the care of an old man elected for life.

Justice was rendered according to the Adîghe-Khabzə *ʿādat*, a veritable unwritten code of law which governed all Čerkes life and which was adopted by neighbouring peoples more or less subject to the influence of Kabard and Adîghe princes: Ossetes [*q.v.*], Karačays [*q.v.*], Balkars [*q.v.*] and Nogays [*q.v.*].

Social Structure and Customs. — Until the second half of the 19th century, the Čerkes people maintained a very archaic social structure different according to the tribes. The Kabards had a highly developed feudal system; their society, comprising up to thirteen classes, formed several groups clearly differentiated and not easily penetrated: 1. — at the summit of the social hierarchy, the princes (*pshə*) among whom the *wālī* was the chief of the Kabard people; 2. — under them, the nobles (*uork*, *uorkkh*, or *uzden*) subdivided into four classes according to the rights and obligations which bound them to the princes; 3. — the free peasants (*tfokhotl*) who, in certain circumstances, were kept to attend the *pshə* and the *uork*; 4. — the serfs (*og* or *pshətlə*) and finally, at the bottom of the ladder, the slaves (*unaut*).

The same feudal system, less rigorous however, existed also among the Adîghes and the lower eastern Čerkes tribes (Besleney, Bjedukh, Khatukay). On the other hand, the western Adîghe tribes (Natukhay, Shapsug, Abadzekh) did not have princes. Among them the *uork* class was weak, while that of the *tfokhotl* was the most numerous and the strongest. They are sometimes called the "democratic Adîghe tribes", as opposed to the Kabard "aristocratic tribes".

The reasons for this difference are not known. Some think that the western tribes passed the feudal stage in the 18th century after the long struggle which set the Abadzekh, Shapsug and Natukhay *tfokhotl* against the princes of Bjedukh (battle of Bziük in 1796), thanks also to the action of Ḥasan Pasha, *serʿasker* of Anapa, who abolished in 1826 the privileges which the nobles of these three tribes enjoyed.

For others, on the contrary, the social evolution toward feudalism had been retarded by several factors, notably the economic influence of the Greek colonies, then the Italian and Turkish. This last opinion seems nearer the truth, because at the beginning of the 20th century one finds among the western tribes strong survivals of the patriarchal clan system which had disappeared among the eastern Adîghe. The clan (*tleukh*) was divided into several groups of great patriarchal families (*ačikh*) which formed in their turn rural communities (*psukho*), autonomously united and independently administered by the councils of the elders.

All the Čerkes tribes maintained some customs characteristic of the patriarchal and feudal stages: 1. — blood vengeance in cases of murder, which was a right and an absolute duty for the whole of the clan; 2. — *atalikat*, which consisted of having children raised from birth in the families of strangers, often vassals (boys till 17-18 years). *Atalikat* created a sort of foster brotherhood which served to tighten the feudal bonds and unite the Čerkes tribes; 3. — diverse traditions concerning hospitality, considered sacred. The guest became, by right of protection, a veritable member of the clan of his host, who put his life and his property at the service of his guest. Hospitality was extended even to the exile (*abrek* or *khadjret*). If this latter succeeded in touching with his lips the bosom of the mistress of a strange house, he became a member of the family, and the master of the house had to provide for his safety. Among other customs of the clan stage figured the swearing of brotherhood (*kunak*) by which a man became a member of another clan; 4. — customs concerning marriage. Exogamy inside the clan or the great patriarchal family was strictly observed especially by the Kabards. The *kalym* (purchase of the fiancée) was universally practised, and could only be avoided by resorting to abduction, a frequent occurrence, in case of refusal by the parents. The pretence of forcible abduction remains an essential rite in the marriage ceremony.

The Čerkes in the Soviet Union.—It was only at the end of the civil war that the Soviet regime was established in the regions inhabited by the Čerkes—in the spring of 1920, first in the country of the Adïghe, then in that of the Kabard. Administratively, the Čerkes were divided into three territorial unities:

—The Autonomous Region of the Adïghe in the basin of the Kuban and its tributaries belonging to the territory (*kray*) of Krasnodar, formed 27 July 1922 under the name of the Autonomous Region of Adïghe-Čerkes, then, on 13 August 1928, under that of the A.R. of Adïghe. This territory has an area of 4400 sq. km. and a population of 270,000 people (in 1956), of whom the Adïghe represent only a minority. The capital Maikop is a Russian city.

—The Autonomous Region of the Karačay-Čerkes in the high valleys of the Great and Little Zelenčuk belonging to the territory (*kray*) of Stavropol', which the Čerkes share with a Turkish people (the Karačay [*q.v.*]). This territory, formed 12 January 1922, was divided, 26 April 1926, into two administrative unities: the Autonomous Region of the Karačay and the national civil district of the Čerkes, elevaled 30 March 1928 to the status of Autonomous Region. In 1944 the Karačay were deported and their Autonomous Region abolished, but after their rehabilitation, the Autonomous Region of the Karačay-Čerkes was re-established 9 January 1957. Its area is 14,200 sq. km., and the population, in 1956, was 214,000 people, in majority Russian and Ukrainian.

—The Kabard-Balkar Autonomous Soviet Socialist Republic, in the mountainous part of the Central Caucasus. It was formed 1 September 1921 as the Autonomous Region of the Kabard to which was added 16 January 1922 the national civil district of the Balkar, thus constituting the Kabard-Balkar Autonomous Region, which became on 5 December 1936 an Autonomous Republic. In 1944, following the deportation of the Balkar, the Republic, with the loss of a part of Balkar territory, was renamed the Kabard A.S.S.R. Finally, on 9 February 1957, the Balkar having been rehabilitated and authorized to return to their territory, the Republic became once more the Kabard-Balkar A.S.S.R. Its territory comprises 12,400 sq. km., and its population, in 1956, was 359,000 inhabitants. In 1939, the Kabard, Balkar and other Muslims represented 60% of the population, living mainly in the mountainous areas; Russians and Ukrainians (40% of the population) constitute the majority of the population of the capital Nalʿčik (72,000 inhabitants in 1956) and predominate in the plain of Terek.

Bibliography: A very complete bibliography appears in the article by Ramazan Traho, *Literature on Circassia and the Circassians*, in *Caucasian Review*, no. 1, 1955, Munnich, 145-162. It included more than 250 titles of works and articles in Russian, in western languages (French, English, German, Turkish, Hungarian, and Polish) and in Čerkes languages dealing directly or indirectly with the Čerkes people. It is sufficient therefore to note here a few recent works:

In French: A. Namitok, *Origines des Circassiens*, Paris 1939; G. Dumezil, *Introduction à la grammaire comparée des langues caucasiennes du Nord*, Paris 1933; and *Etudes comparatives sur les langues caucasiennes du Nord-Ouest*, Paris 1932.

In German: A. Dirr, *Einführung in das Stadium der Kaukasischen Sprachen*, Leipzig 1928; F. Hančar, *Urgeschichte Kaukasiens*, Vienna-Leipzig 1937.

In English: J. B. Baddeley, *The Russian Conquest of the Caucasus*, London 1908; W. S. Allen, *Structure and system in the Abaza Verbal complex* in *Transactions of the Philological Society*, 1956, 127-76, with extensive linguistic bibliography.

In Russian: *Adïgeïskaya Avtonomnaya Oblast'*, Maikop 1947; *Kabardinskaya ASSR*, Nal'čik 1946 Sh. B. Nogmov, *Istoriya Adïgeyskogo Naroda sostaxlennaya po predaniyam Kabardintzev*, Nal'čik 1947; K. Stal, *Étnografičeskiy očerk Čerkesskogo naroda*, in *Kavkazskiy Sbornik*, xxi, Tiflis 1900; S. A. Toharev, *Étnografiya narodov SSSR*, Moscow 1958, 246-258; D. A. Ashkhamaf, *Grammatika Adïgeiskogo yazïka*, Krasnodar 1934; T. M. Borukaev, *Grammatika Kabardino-Čerkesskogo Yazïka*, Nal'čik 1932; idem, *Yazïki severnogo Kavkaza i Dagestana*, i, Moscow-Leningrad 1935; N. F. Yakovlev and D. A Ashkhamaf, *Grammatika Adïgeyskogo literaturnogo yazïka*, Moscow-Leningrad 1941.

(Ch. Quelquejay)

ii. Mamlūk period. The Circassians are designated in Mamlūk sources as *Djarkas* or *Djarākisa* (sing. *Djarkasī*). There are also alternative spellings: *Čarkas* or *Čarākisa* (sing. *Čarkasī*); *Sharkas* or *Sharākisa* (sing. *Sharkasī*) and less frequently *Djihāraks*. Circassia is variously known as *bilād al-Djarkas*, or simply *Djarkas* and occasionally as *Djabal al-Djarkas*. According to al-Ḳalḳashandī the Circassians live in poverty and most of them are Christians (*Ṣubḥ al-Aʿshā*, v, 462, l. 5).

The Circassians, who, since the closing decades of the 8th/14th century and up to the end of the Mamlūk sultanate (922/1517), constituted the predominant element of Mamlūk military society, were quite important in that sultanate from its very inception in the middle of the 7th/13th century. They occupied a most prominent place in the *Burdjiyya* [*q.v.*] regiment founded by Sulṭān Ḳalāʾūn (678-689/1279-1290). Whether the decline of that regiment weakened their power or not, is an open question. The Ḳipčaḳ Turks, the ruling race during the first hundred and thirty years or so of the sultanate's existence, feared them very much because of their ambitious character, haughtiness and inclination to trouble and discord. As a matter of fact the Ḳipčaḳs succeeded in nipping in the bud a dangerous military coup of the Circassians during Ramaḍān-Shawwāl 748/December 1347-January 1348 (Sulṭān Ḥasan's reign). These Circassians were the favourites of Ḥasan's immediate predecessor, Sulṭān Ḥādjdjī (747-8/1346-7), who "brought them from all quarters and wanted to give them precedence over the *Atrāk*" (*Nudjūm*, v, 56, ll. 14-20). Sulṭān Ḥādjdjī's reign was apparently too short for his plan to be carried out, and thus the Circassians' rise to power had been postponed for another 35 to 45 years.

It was Sulṭān Barḳūḳ, himself a Circassian and a member of the Burdjiyya regiment, who brought about the final victory of his own race, by the systematic purchase of increasing numbers of Circassian Mamlūks and by drastically cutting at the same time the purchase of Mamlūks of other races. He is justly called "the founder of Circassian rule" (*al-Ḳāʾim bi-dawlat al-Djarākisa*) (*Nudjūm* v, 362). Though he regretted his action towards the end of his life, as a result of a Circassian attempt to assassinate him (*Nudjūm*, v, 585, 598), it was too late for him to change the situation which he himself had created. His son and successor, Sulṭān Faradj (809-815/1406-1412), paid with his life for his attempt to break the Circassians' growing power by means of large-scale massacres. As early a writer as al-Ḳalkashandī, who completed his book in 815/1412, states: "In our time most of the *amīr*s and army have become Circassians ... The *Turk* Mamlūks of Egypt have become so few in number that all that is left of them are a few survivors and their children" *Ṣubḥ al-Aʿshā*, iv, 458, ll. 16-19). Sulṭān al-Muʾayyad Shaykh (815-824/1412-1421), who is described by Ibn Taghrībirdī as resembling the former Mamlūk sultans (*mulūk al-salaf*) in that his criterion for the choice of soldiers was not race, but efficiency and courage (*al-Manhal al-Ṣāfī*, iii, fol. 168a, l. 21-168b, l. 4), had some success in curbing the power of the Circassians by strengthening the Ḳipčaḳ-Turk element in Mamlūk military society. But after his death the Circassians regained their supremacy, which they maintained without any serious challenge till the end of Mamlūk rule.

Mamlūk sources ascribe the rise of the Circassians at the expense of the Ḳipčaḳ-Turks mainly to factors existing within the Mamlūk sultanate. Equally important, however, were factors prevailing in the Mamlūks' countries of origin. The decline of the Golden Horde during the latter half of the 8th/14th century and the internal wars that broke out there must have greatly influenced the decision of Egypt's rulers to transfer the Mamluks' purchasing centre to the Caucasus.

The writers of the Circassian period held, generally speaking, a very high opinion of the Ḳipčaḳ-Turks and harshly criticized the Circassians, to whom they ascribed the sultanate's decline and misery. Typical in this respect are Ibn Taghrībirdī's following words: Referring to Ṭashtamur al-ʿAlāʾī, formerly *dawādār* and later *atābak al-ʿasākir* (commander-in-chief), who was removed by *amīr*s Berke and (later Sulṭān) Barḳūḳ, he says: "The time of Ṭashtamur was a flourishing and plentiful time for the Mamlūk sultanate under his wise direction, and that condition prevailed until he was removed from office and thrown into prison. In his place came Barḳūḳ and Berke, who did things in the sultanate from which the population suffers till this day. Then Barḳūḳ became sole ruler, and turned the affairs of the realm upside-down, and his successors have maintained his policy down to the present. For he gave precedence to the members of his own race over the others, and gave those of his own Mamlūks (*adjlāb*) who were related to him large fiefs and high offices while they were still in their minority. This is the main cause of the decline of the realm. Indeed, is there anything more grave than to set the minor over the senior? This is at variance with the practice of the former sultans; for they did not recognise the superiority of any one race. Whenever they found a man who displayed wisdom and courage, they showed him preference and favour. No-one was given office or rank who was not worthy of it" (*Manhal*, iii, f. 185b, ll. 14-23).

Though this and other statements of the same kind contain a very substantial element of truth, they certainly should not be taken at their face value. The Circassians might have accelerated the process of the realm's decline, but many of the factors that brought about that decline had already been quite visible in the closing decades of Ḳipčaḳ-Turk rule.

The predominance of the Circassian race in the later Mamlūk period was much stronger and much more comprehensive than that of the Ḳipčaḳ Turks in the early period. Unlike the Ḳipčaḳ Turks the Circassians were very hostile to the other Mamlūk races, whom they relegated to a state of political insignificance. No other Mamlūk race was so much imbued with the feeling of racial solidarity and of racial superiority as they were. Under their rule, *al-djins*, meaning the Race, denoted the Circassian race. Similarly *al-ḳawm*, the People, was applied only to the Circassians.

Of all Mamlūk races the Circassians were the only ones who claimed to trace their origin to an Arab tribe, namely, the Banū Ghassān, who entered Bilād al-Rūm with Djabala b. al-Ayham at the time of Heraclius' retreat from Syria (Ibn Khaldūn, *Kitāb al-ʿIbar*, v, 472, ll. 4-18. Ibn Iyāb, v, 193, l. 3). This legend was still alive in Egyptian Mamlūk society under the Ottomans (see bibliography).

Bibliography: D. Ayalon, *The Circassians in the Mamlūk Kingdom, in JAOS*, 1949, 135-147; idem, *Studies of the Structure of the Mamluk Army*, in *BSOAS*, 1953, 203-228, 448-476, 1954, 57-90; idem, *L'esclavage du Mamelouk*, Jerusalem 1951. P. M. Holt, *The exalted lineage of Riḍwān Bey: some observations on a seventeenth-century Mamluk genealogy*, in *BSOAS*, 1959, 221-230.

(D. AYALON)

iii. (Ottoman period) Replacing the Genoese on the Black-sea coasts the Ottomans took Anaba (Anapa) and Koba (Copa, cf. Heyd, ii, 190) in 884/1479 (cf. *Hasht Behisht*), but the Circassian tribes in the hinterland continued to be dependent on the Crimean Khāns (see KIRIM) who as under the Golden Horde sent their sons to be brought up among the Circassians (see ATALIḲ). Along with the marriages of the Crimean princes with the Circassian noblewomen this secured the attachment of the Čerkes; they gave the Khāns a yearly tribute consisting of slaves as well as auxiliary forces. The Crimean Khāns styled themselves rulers of *Tagh-ara Čerkes* or *Čergāč*. Circassia served also as a refuge for the Tatar-Noghay tribes from the *Dasht* who came often to mingle with them especially in the Kuban basin and the Taman peninsula. Later on the

Crimean K̲h̲āns built there fortresses such as Čoban-k̲al'a, Nawrūz-Kirmān. S̲h̲ād-Kirmān and settled in them Nog̲h̲ays to defend the country against the Cossacks (K̲azak̲) and the K̲almuk̲s. Not infrequently the Čerkes co-operated with the Cossacks, too. In his major efforts to subdue the rebellious Čerkes tribes Ṣāḥib Girāy K̲h̲ān made five expeditions in Circassia, the first against K̲ansāwuk̲, beg of Zhana in 946/1539, the second and the third against K̲abartāy (Kaberda). He forcibly settled on the upper Urup the tribes who had taken refuge in the high Baksan valley. Later in 956/1549 he made his last expedition against the K̲h̲atuk̲āy (Ṣāḥib Girāy Ta'rīk̲h̲i, Blochet, Cat. Man. Turc. supp., 164). But after his death the Čerkes, especially those of Zhana and P̲s̲h̲eduh (Pzheduk̲h̲) sacked the Taman peninsula, threatened Azak̲ [q.v.] and sought the protection of Ivan IV (see Belleten, no. 46, 1948, 364). At the same period the Cossacks, stationed on the Terek, also became a threat to Crimean-Ottoman influence in K̲abartāy.

The strengthening of Tatar-Circassian relations resulted in the spread of Islam among the Čerkes. But in 1076/1664-65 Ewliyā Čelebī (vii, 708-758) found that many tribes were still pagans and those professing Islam preserved their old religious beliefs and practices. Meḥmed Girāy IV induced the islamized tribes of K̲abartāy to give up pig-raising.

The Ottoman Sultans recognized Crimean sovereignty over the Čerkes, but this did not prevent their sending orders and granting titles to the Circassian chieftains as vassal begs (see Belleten, no. 46, 399). In 978/1570 Selim II wrote to the Czar not to interfere with the Čerkes, his subjects (Belleten, 400).

In 1076/1665, on his way from Taman to Albrus, Ewliyā Čelebī (vii, 698-768) found first the Nog̲h̲ays in Čoban-eli then S̲h̲k̲āg̲h̲e tribe (cf. J. Klaproth, Voyage, i, 238) on the Black Sea coast, Great and Small Zhana tribes at the foot of the Hayk̲o mountains, and further east K̲h̲atuk̲ay, Ademi, Tak̲ak̲u (?), Bolatk̲ay, Bozoduk̲ (Pzheduk̲h̲), Mams̲h̲ug̲h̲ (?), Besney (Besleney), and K̲abartāy tribes. He also reported that in this period the K̲almuk̲ raids caused the Čerkes tribes in the Kuban and K̲abartāy regions to retreat to the inaccessible parts of the mountains, while in the west the Cossacks were pressing hard the Čerkes in the lower Kuban and the Tamam peninsula.

When from the early 18th century onwards Circassia was seriously threatened by Russian expansion they became more and more co-operative with the Ottomans. In 1148/1735 they repulsed the Russian forces on the other side of the Kuban. But with the treaty of Küčük-K̲aynardja in 1188/1774 the Ottomans recognized the independence of the Crimean K̲h̲ānate with its dependencies north to the Kuban which in 1197-1783 were annexed by Russia. The K̲abartāys were already in Russian control in 1188/1774.

In order to form a defence line against the Russians on the Kuban the Ottomans were now much interested in Circassia and built or rebuilt the fortresses of Sog̲h̲udjuk̲ (Sudjuk̲), Gelendjik, Nog̲h̲ay, and Anapa in 1196/1782 and tried to reorganize the Čerkes as well as the newly arrived Tatar immigrants from the Crimea and the Nog̲h̲ays from Dobrudja. Feraḥ 'Alī Pas̲h̲a (1196/1782-1199/1785), an administrator of unusual ability, encouraged his Ottoman soldiers to establish family ties with the Čerkes which strengthened Ottoman influence and furthered the spread of Islam among the Čerkes. Anapa

rapidly developed as the chief commercial centre of the area. Meantime S̲h̲ayk̲h̲ Manṣūr, a forerunner of S̲h̲ayk̲h̲ S̲h̲āmīl [q.v.] in the Čečen area found a response among the Čerkes for his preaching of the Holy War against the Russians (for this period see the important account of Meḥmed Hās̲h̲im, the Dīwān Kātib of Feraḥ 'Alī Pas̲h̲a, MS. in Topkapi, Revān, no. 1564, cf. Djewdet, Ta'rīk̲h̲, iii, 168-272).

During the Ottoman-Russian war of 1201-1206/ 1787-1792 a K̲h̲ānate of Kuban was created with the Tatars under S̲h̲ahbāz Girāy while the Čerkes co-operated with the Ottoman army under Baṭṭāl Huseyin Pas̲h̲a and won some successes. But in the end Anapa, the main Ottoman base, fell (1205/1791). With the peace treaty the Kuban river was fixed as the border line between the Russian and Ottoman empires. After the peace, while the Ottomans neglected the area, the Russians formed a line of fortresses along the border and settled large groups of Cossacks there. At the same time they annexed Georgia and, taking control of the Daryal Pass, encircled Circassia. By the treaty of Adrianople 1245/1829 the Ottomans had to give up their rights on Circassia in favour of Russia. The Circassians, however, sustained a long and fierce struggle against the invaders until 1281/1864 and, according to an Ottoman report, 595,000 Circassians left their country for Turkey between 1272/1856 and 1281/ 1864. These were settled in Anatolia as well as in Rūmeli (see BULGARIA). According to the census of 1945 there were in Turkey 66,691 Circassians still speaking their mother-tongue. Under the Ottomans, especially from the 17th century onwards, Circassian slaves occupied an important place in the Ottoman ḳul [q.v.] system and many of them reached high positions in the state (see Ta'rīk̲h̲-i 'Aṭā, 5 vols. Istanbul 1291-1293).

Bibliography: Idrīs Bidlīsī, Has̲h̲t Behis̲h̲t (Babinger, 48), Kemāl Pas̲h̲azāde, Tawārīk̲h̲-i Āl-i 'Os̲h̲mān, facsimile ed., TTK Ankara 1954, 520; 'Ālī, Kunh al-Ak̲h̲bār, (Babinger, 129); Ewliyā Čelebī, Seyāḥatnāme, vii, Istanbul 1928, 698-767; Kātib Čelebī, Djihān-numā, Istanbul 1145, 403; Meḥmed Hās̲h̲im, Aḥwāl-i Abāzā ve Čerākise, Topkapi Sarayi, Revan kit. no. 1564; Risāla fī aḥwāl-i Kirim wa Ḳubān, Atif Ef. Kütüphanesi, no. 1886; A. Djewdet, Ta'rīk̲h̲, 12 vols. Istanbul 1271-1301; idem, Kirim we Ḳafḳas Ta'rīk̲h̲česi, Istanbul 1307; Nūh al-Matrūḳī, Nūr al-Maḳābis fī Tawārīk̲h̲ al-Čerākis, Ḳazan 1912; L. Widerszal, British Policy in the Western Caucasus, 1833-1842, Warsaw 1933; N. A. Smirnov, Rossiya i Turtsiya v XVI-XVII vv. 2 vols. Moscow 1948; E. N. Kusheva, Politika Russkogo gosudarstva na severnom Kavkaze v 1552-53 gg., in Istoričeskiye Zapiski, xxxiv (1950), 236-87; H. Inalcık, Osmanlı-Rus Rekabetinin Menşei ve Don-Volga Kanalı Teşebbüsü, in Belleten 46 (1948), 349-402; W. E. D. Allen and P. Muratoff, Caucasian Battlefields, Cambridge 1953; Mirza Bala, art. Čerkesler, in IA.

(HALIL INALCIK)

ČERKES EDHEM, Čerkes Res̲h̲īd, and Čerkes Meḥmed Tewfīḳ, Turkish guerrilla leaders, sons of a Circassian farmer in Emre near Karacabey (wilāyet of Bursa). Res̲h̲īd, the oldest, was born in 1869 (or 1877 ?—see T.B.M.M. 25ci yıldönümünü anıs [1945], 63), Edhem, the youngest, in 1883-4. Res̲h̲īd fought with the Ottoman forces in Libya and the Balkans, where he was "Deputy Commander in Chief" for the provisional government of Western Thrace (September 1913), and sat for Saruhan in the last Ottoman Chamber and the Ankara National Assembly. All three brothers took leading parts in the nationalist guerrilla movement, Edhem distinguishing himself against the Greeks at Salihli and Anzavur's *Ḳuwwa-yi Meḥmediyye* (summer 1919) and in suppressing the anti-Kemalist revolts at Düzce and Yozgad (spring 1920). As Commander of Mobile Forces (*Ḳuwwa-yi Seyyāre*, with his brother Tewfīḳ as deputy) he came into increasingly sharp conflict with the regular army command, especially after Edhem's defeat by the Greeks at Gediz (24 October 1920) and the appointment of İsmet [İnönü] as commander-in-chief of the Western front. An ad-hoc commission of the National Assembly failed to resolve the dispute. After a decisive clash with the Turkish regulars (Kütahya, 29 December), Edhem, his brothers, and several hundred Circassian guerrillas fled behind the Greek lines (5 January 1921). The Ankara Assembly denounced the brothers as traitors and expelled Reshīd; later the brothers were among the 150 persons (*yüzellilikler*) excepted from the amnesty provisions of the Lausanne Treaty of 1923. Edhem and Reshīd went to Greece, Germany, various Arab countries, and eventually to ʿAmmān. In 1935 they were briefly detained there under suspicion of plotting against Atatürk, and in 1941 Edhem was again detained in ʿAmmān because of his support of the movement of Rashīd ʿĀli in ʿIrāq. He died of throat cancer in ʿAmmān on 7 October 1949. Reshīd returned to Turkey after the Democrat Party victory of 1950 and died in Ankara in 1951. Tewfīḳ spent his exile years in Haifa as an oil refinery watchman and died soon after his return to Turkey in 1938.

Bibliography: Tevfik Bıyıklıoğlu, *Trakya'da millî mücadele*, Ankara 1955-56, i, 77 f., 87; ii, 30 f.; [Çerkes Edhem], *Çerkes Ethem hadisesi*, ed. Cemal Kutay, i-iii, İstanbul 1956; Yunus Nadi, *Çerkes Ethem kuvvetlerinin ihaneti* (Atatürk Kütüphanesi 16), İstanbul 1955; Ali Fuad Cebesoy, *Millî mücadele hatıraları*, İstanbul 1953, 403-09, 452, 466-70, 497-505; Kemal [Atatürk], *Nutuk*, 1934 edn., ii, 9, 27-85; *OM*, xv, 572; D. A. Rustow in *World Politics*, xi, 513-552 (1959); private communication from Reshīd's son Arslan in Manshiyya, Jordan, April 1960, courtesy of Messrs. Waleed and Abdel-Kader Tash.

(D. A. Rustow)

ČERKES [see MUḤAMMAD PASHA ČERKES]

ČESHME, a Persian word meaning "source, fountain" which has passed into Turkish with the same sense. It is the name of a market-town in Asia Minor with a wide and safe natural harbour on the Mediterranean coast, at the entrance to the Gulf of the same name, at the north-western extremity of the peninsula of Urla opposite the island of Chios, 26° 20′ W., 38° 23′ N. It is the chief town of a *kaza* in the *vilayet* of Izmir. The town has (1950) 3,706 inhabitants; the *kaza*, 12,337. Originally part of the principality (later *sandjaḳ*) of Aydïn, it was Ottoman from the time of Bayazīd II. There is a citadel with a mosque of Bāyazīd II, of 914/1508. The present town, which is quite modern, occupies the site of the ancient harbour of Erythrae. There are hot springs at Ilidja.

A Russian fleet of nine ships of the line and a few frigates, divided into three squadrons commanded by Spiridov, Alexis Orlov and Elphinston, which sailed from Kronstad to aid the rebel Mainots, attacked the Turkish fleet at Česhme. The Turkish fleet consisted of sixteen ships of the line besides frigates and small craft and was commanded by the Ḳapūdān-Pasha Ḥusām al-Dīn with Djezāʾirli Ḥasan Pasha and Djaʿfar Bey. The Russian and Turkish flagships both caught fire at the same moment and those of the crew who could saved themselves by swimming (11 Rabīʿ I 1183/5 July 1770). The remainder of the Turkish fleet was set on fire the following night. This defeat of the Turks at Česhme was the fore-runner of the Peace of Küčük Ḳaynardja.

Bibliography: Ewliyā Čelebi, *Seyāḥat-nāme* ix, 107 f.; ʿAlī Djewād, *Djoghrāfiyā lughātī*, 308; von Hammer, *Histoire de l'Empire Ottoman*, vol. xvi, 252 = vol. viii, 358 of German edition; Baron de Tott, *Mémoires*, iii, 35 ff.; v. Cuinet, *Turquie d'As e*, vol. iii, 488 ff.; *IA*, iii, 386-88 (by M. C. Şehabeddin Tekindağ) where further references are given; for a detailed discussion of the naval battle see R. C. Anderson, *Naval Wars in the Levant*, Princeton 1952, 286 ff.

(Cl. Huart-[Fr. Taeschner])

ČESHMĪZĀDE, Muṣṭafā Rashīd, Ottoman historian and poet, one of a family of *ʿulamāʾ* founded by the *Ḳāḍīʿasker* of Rumelia, Česhmī Meḥmed Efendi (d. 1044/1634) A grandson of the *Shaykh al-Islām* Meḥmed Ṣāliḥ Efendi, and the son of a *ḳāḍī* in the Ḥidjāz, he entered the *ʿIlmiyye* profession, and held various legal and teaching posts. After the resignation of the Imperial historiographer Meḥmed Ḥākim Efendi [*q.v.*], he was appointed to this office, which he held for a year and a half. He then returned to his teaching career, which culminated in his appointment as *müderris* at the Dār al-Ḥadith of the Sulaymāniyye. His history, which covers the period 1180-82/1766-68, was used by Wāṣif [*q.v.*]. The Turkish text was first published by Bekir Kütükoğlu in 1959; but a Swedish translation of his account of the war in Georgia in 1180-2/1766-8, with a brief account of some events in Cyprus, Egypt and Medina, was included by M. Norberg in his *Turkiska Rikets Annaler*, v, Hernösand 1822, 1416-1424. He died in Shaʿbān 1184/Nov. 1770, and was buried at Rumeli Ḥiṣārī.

Bibliographie : B. Kütükoğlu (ed.), *Çeşmizâde Tarihi*, Istanbul 1959; *Sidjill-i ʿOthmānī*, ii, 389; *ʿOthmānlī Müellifleri*, iii, 45; Babinger 302.

(B. Lewis)

CEUTA [see SABTA]

CEYLON. The Muslims constitute only 6.63% of Ceylon's population—roughly 550,000 out of a total of 8,000,000. Of this community, which is multi-racial in its composition, the Ceylon Moors form the most significant element and count 463,963. The Malays are the next in importance. They number 25,464. Nearly all of the remaining groups are of Indian origin; their ancestors first came to Ceylon after the British occupation of its Maritime Provinces during the 18th century.

As a result of the insufficiency of available evidence and the lack of sustained effort and encouragement in respect of the investigations involved, which require a good knowledge of several languages, each of them with a different background and most of them with distinctive characters, the ethnology of the Ceylon Moors has yet remained an inadequately explored field of research. A scientific and comprehensive treatment of the subject would indeed illumine some of the obscure aspects of Ceylon's history—*e.g.*, the nature and extent of the contacts the Muslims of Ceylon (Moors) had for several centuries with their brethren in faith in lands far and near; the political relations which Ceylon through these Muslims maintained with the Muslim World particularly during its period of glory; and the volume of Ceylon's external and internal trade and its geographical distribution during the early centuries.

The Muslims of Ceylon were given the appellation of 'Moors' by the Portuguese who first came to Ceylon in 1505 and encountered these Muslims as their immediate rivals to trade and influence. This name, however, has persisted, having gained currency in Ceylon through its wide use by the Colonial Powers concerned, even though this term 'Moors' had been previously unknown among the Muslims themselves. 'Sonahar' was the name familiar to them, deriving its origin from 'Yavanar', an Indian word connoting foreigners especially Greeks or Arabs.

These Moors were the descendants of Arab settlers whose numbers were later augmented by local converts and immigrant Muslims from South India. With regard to the date of the arrival of the first Arab settlers, Sir Alexander Johnstone holds that it was during the early part of the 2nd/8th century. "The first Mohammedans who settled in Ceylon were, according to the tradition which prevails amongst their descendants, a portion of those Arabs of the house of Hās͟him who were driven from Arabia in the early part of the eighth century by the tyranny of the Caliph ʿAbd al-Melek b. Merwān, and who, preceeding from the Euphrates southward, made settlements in the Concan, in the southern parts of the peninsula of India, on the island of Ceylon and at Malacca. The division of them which came to Ceylon formed eight considerable settlements along the north-east, north, and western coasts of that island; *viz*: one at Trincomalee, one at Jaffna, one at Mantotte and Mannar, one at Coodramalle, one at Putlam, one at Colombo, one at Barbareen and one at Point-de-Galle."

The presence of these settlers is strikingly corroborated by the accounts found in Muslim sources with regard to the proximate cause of the Arab conquest of Sind, during the time of Caliph al-Walīd. His governor, al-Ḥad̲j̲d̲j̲ād̲j̲ of ʿIrāḳ, initiated this conquest, under the leadership of ʿImād al-Dīn Muḥammad b. Ḳāsim, as a punishment for the plunder of the ships that carried the families of the Arabs who had died in Ceylon, together with presents from the King of Ceylon to the Caliph.

It is reasonable to suppose that during the 2nd/8th century and subsequent centuries these Arabs came in increasing numbers and settled down in Ceylon without entirely losing touch with the areas of their origin. Ceylon exercized a special fascination on these seafaring Arabs as a commercial junction of importance which afforded possibilities of profitable trade in pearls, gems, spices and other valued articles. Settlement was encouraged by the tolerant and friendly attitude of the rulers and people of the island.

After the sack of Baghdad in 1258 A.D., Arab activities in the Persian Gulf and the Indian Ocean diminished considerably. Muslim influence, however, did not thereby cease entirely. It began to emanate from India where by the 7th/13th century the Muslims had firmly established themselves along the western coast and possessed a virtual monopoly of external trade.

It may therefore be concluded that the Muslims of Ceylon began, as a result, to rely on India for their cultural leadership as well as for their commercial contacts. An Indian element was thus added into the composition of the local Muslim (Moor) community. Despite the racial admixture that took place in consequence and the new manners and customs that were acquired, the individuality of the community was preserved on account of the cherished memory of its Arab origin and the emphasis that was placed on Islam as the base of its communal structure.

These Muslims were not treated as aliens, but were favoured for the commercial and political contacts with other countries they gained for Ceylon, for the revenue they brought to the country and the foreign skills they secured, *e.g.*, medicine and weaving. Besides they encouraged local trade by the introduction of new crafts, *e.g.*, gem-cutting and of improved methods of transport, *e.g.*, *thavalam*-carriage-bullocks. They were therefore allowed to establish their local settlements, *e.g.*, Colombo, Barberyn, with a measure of autonomy and with special privileges. The important seaports of Ceylon were virtually controlled by these Muslims (Moors).

With the advent of the Portuguese in 1505 the Muslims (Moors) suffered a change in their status from which they never again recovered. The Portuguese regarded them as their rivals in trade and enemies in faith. The Dutch who superseded the former as rulers of the sea-board were not prepared to give the Muslims even a small share of their commercial gains and therefore promulgated harsh regulations to keep them down. Deprived of their traditional occupation, many of them were forced to take to agriculture. To this could be mainly attributed the concentrations of Muslim peasantry in areas like Batticaloa.

It was during the Dutch period the Malays—who form an important element of the Muslim community of Ceylon—came to Ceylon, many of them brought by the Dutch as soldiers to fight for them and some as exiles for political reasons. When the Dutch capitulated to the British, the Malay soldiers joined the British regiments specially formed. On their disbandment the Malays settled down in Ceylon. Their separate identity has been preserved by the Malay language which they still speak in their homes.

The British did not follow the undiluted policy of proselytization pursued by the Portuguese. Nor were the British so harsh as the Dutch in their economic exploitation of Ceylon. To that extent, under the new rulers, the Muslims fared better. Yet they could not gain any special favour, on account of their irreconcilable attitude towards the ways and culture of the West which they identified with Christianity. This, no doubt, handicapped the Muslims severely in the political, economic and educational spheres but ensured the preservation of their communal individuality despite the smallness of their numbers and the loss of cultural contacts with the Muslim World. As a result till about the beginning of the current century the Muslims of Ceylon remained culturally isolated, educationally backward and politically insignificant.

The Muslims, however, could not continue to ignore the trend of events taking place in Ceylon and India. Sir Sayyid Aḥmad K̲h̲ān, who founded in 1875 the Mohamedan Anglo-Oriental College, was the leader of the Aligarh Movement in India with its emphasis on educational reforms. Arumuga Navalar, who countered the efforts of the Christian Missionaries in North Ceylon, established in 1872 an English school under Hindu management. The Buddhist Theosophical Society established an English school in 1886 which finally developed into the present Ananda College, Colombo. In this year the Anagarika Dharmapala who was actively associated with the inauguration of this Society resigned his Government post to devote his entire time to Buddhist activities. During this period the Muslims of Ceylon had in M. C. Siddi Lebbe a leader of vision who understood the significance of these changes. He had for several years canvassed the opinion of his co-religionists for a new educational approach but he had not been heeded. It was at this time, in 1883, that ʿUrābī Pas̲h̲a [*q.v.*] came as an exile to Ceylon. He provided a powerful stimulus for a reappraisal on the part of the Muslims of Ceylon in regard to their attitude towards modern education and Western culture. All these together culminated in the establishment in 1892 of Al-Madrasa al-Zāhira under the patronage of ʿUrābī Pas̲h̲a which has since blossomed into Zahira College, Colombo.

The Ceylon Muslims—apart from isolated instances—belong to the S̲h̲āfiʿī school of Sunnīs. In the realm of Law the following special enactments pertaining to them may be cited—the Mohammedan Code of 1806 relating to matters of succession, inheritance etc., Mohammedan Marriage Registration Ordinance no. 8 of 1886 repealed by Ordinance no. 27 of 1929 and now superseded by the Muslim Marriage and Divorce Act no. 13 of 1951 which confers upon the Ḳāḍīs appointed by the Government exclusive jurisdiction in respect of marriages and divorces, the status and mutual rights and obligations of the parties; the Muslim Intestate Succession Ordinance no. 10 of 1931 and the Muslim Mosques and Charitable Trusts or Waḳfs Act no. 51 of 1956 which provides a separate Government Department with a purely Muslim Executive Board. Of these the Mohammedan Code of 1806 is of special value to students of Islamic Civilization, for it contains many provisions which are in conflict with the principles of Muslim law stated in standard text books on that subject. Wherever such conflict occurs the view has been taken that it is the duty of the courts in Ceylon to give effect to the provisions of the Code, which formed the statute law of this country, although they may clash with well-established principles of Muslim law."

Tamil is the home-language of the great majority of the Muslims of Ceylon. In the Tamil language as spoken and written by the Muslims of Ceylon and of South India, a number of Arabic words are used, which in many cases have displaced their pure Tamil equivalents. The term Arabic-Tamil has therefore gained currency to indicate the Tamil of the Muslims. At one time Arabic-Tamil was written in the Arabic script, ڣ ڠ ڇ ٻ being improvised to denote four Tamil sounds unknown to Arabic, and *o* being represented by 6, ō by و6, e by 6 and ā by ـيـ6. Today Arabic Tamil is being generally written in the Tamil alphabet with or without diacritical marks. The literature of the Muslims of Ceylon has to be treated as part of the Arabic-Tamil literature of South India. Although Ceylon has produced its quota of poets and writers in Arabic-Tamil none has reached the stature of their well-known South Indian counterparts.

The Muslims of Ceylon received their first political recognition when in 1889 a nominated seat was assigned to them in the Legislative Council. This representation was increased to 3 elected members in 1924. The Donoughmore Constitution of 1931 abolished communal representation but the Soulbury Constitution of 1947 envisaged a certain measure of communal representation through territorial electorates specially delimitated. In the present House of Representatives, elected in 1956, there are 7 Muslim M.P.s among 95 territorially elected members.

Bibliography: Tennent, *Ceylon. An Account of the Island-Physical, Historical and Topographical*, London 1859; Fr. S. G. Perera, *City of Colombo* 1505-1656, Ceylon Historical Association 1926; *Instuctions from Governor-General and Council of India to the Governor of Ceylon, 1656-1665*, Colombo 1908; Queyroz, *The Temporal and Spiritual Conquest of Ceylon*, Colombo 1930; I. L. M. Abdul Azeez, *A Criticism of Mr. Ramanathan's Ethnology of the Moors of Ceylon*, Colombo 1907; M. M. Uwise, *Muslim Contribution to Tamil Literature*, Ceylon 1953; M. C. Siddi Lebbe, *Muslim Neisan. An Arabic Tamil Weekly*. (1882-1889), Ceylon; *Ceylon Census Reports* 1901, 1911, 1946; *Report of the Special Commission on the Ceylon Constitution* 1928, His Majesty's Stationery Office; *Report of the Commission on Constitutional Reform*, Cmd 6677, 1945; Jennings & Tambiah, *The Dominion of Ceylon*, London 1952; *Tamil Lexicon*, University of Madras 1928; Massignon, *Annnaire du Monde Musulmon*, 155. (A. M. A. AZEEZ)

ČEYREK, a corruption of Persian *čahāryak* (1/4), has in Turkish the special meaning of a quarter of an hour, or a coin, also known as the *bes̲h̲lik*, or five piastre piece, originally the quarter of a *med̲j̲īdiyye*, introduced in 1260/1844 during the reign of ʿAbd al-Mad̲j̲īd and issued by the succeeding rulers until the end of the Ottoman Empire. The silver *čeyrek* had a fineness of 830, weighed 6.13 grams and measured 24 mm. in diameter. (G. C. MILES)

CHAM [see ČAM]

ČHAT, an ancient town, situated on the bank of the Ghaggar and 14 miles from Ambāla (India), is now practically desolate, with the exception of a few huts of Gud̲j̲d̲j̲ars (milk-sellers) and other low-caste people atop a prehistoric mound, still unexcavated. It was a *maḥāll* in the *sarkār* of Sirhind, *ṣūba* of Dihlī, during the reign of Akbar, with a cultivable area of 158,749 *bīgha*s yielding a revenue of 750,994 *dāms* annually. Its name suggests that in pre-Muslim days it was a settlement of Čhattas, *i.e.*, *Čhattarī*s (more accurately Ks̲h̲attriyas), a martial Hindū tribe. Apart from being a flourishing town peopled mainly by the Afg̲h̲āns and the Rād̲j̲pūts it was, during the early Mug̲h̲al period, a military station garrisoned by 650 cavalry and 1,100 infantry. Its history is closely connected with that of Banūr [*q.v.*] only 4 miles away. During the Sayyid and Lōdī periods, as the vast ruins, the dilapidated but very spacious D̲j̲āmiʿ Mas̲d̲j̲id of the pre-Mug̲h̲al period and the extensive grave-yard indicate, it was a town of considerable importance, and became the seat of one of the four branches of the Sayyids of Bārha, called the Čhat-Banūrī or Čhat-rāwdī Sayyids, of whom Sayyid Abu 'l-Faḍl Wāsiṭī was the first to settle in this town (see *Āʾīn-i Akbarī*, vol. i, transl. Blochmann, 430-1). In 1121/1709 it was over-run and laid almost completely waste by the Sikhs under general Banda Bayrāgī. S̲h̲ayk̲h̲ Muḥammad Dāʾim, the commandant of Ambāla, who encountered the Sikh army was defeated and fled in dismay to Lahore. The most wanton cruelties were perpetrated on the inhabitants of Čhat and Banūr and very few escaped the sword or forced apostasy. Since then Čhat has remained a dependency of Patīāla and has never regained its lost prosperity. Al-Badāʾūnī (Eng. transl. iii 47) mentions one Shaykh Dā'ūd of Čhatī, but apparently Čhatī has been misread for Djuhnī, more accurately Djuhnīwāl, once a small town in the *pargana* of Multān, and the translator has obviously confounded Čhat.

Bibliography: Abu 'l-Faḍl, *Ā'īn-i Akbarī* (Eng., transl. Blochmann and Jarrett), i 428, 430-1, ii, 70, iii, 296; al-Badā'ūnī, *Muntakhab al-Tawārīkh* (Eng. transl.) iii, 47 *n*[4]; *History of the Freedom Movement*, Karachi 1957, i, 145 (where other references are given); Gokul Chand Narang, *Transformation of Sikhism*, Lahore 1912, 174-6; James Brown, *India Tracts* (London), 9-10; S. ʿAlamdār Ḥusayn Wāsiṭī, *Ḥadīḳa-i Wāsiṭiyya* (Ms. Riḍā Library, Rāmpūr); *Settlement Report (Banūr Tehsil)*, Patiala 1904; *Patiala State Gazetteer*, s.v.; Hari Ram Gupta, *Later Mughal History of the Panjab*, Lahore 1944, 46; Khwāfī Khān, *Muntakhab al-Lubāb* (Bibliotheca Indica), ii, 652-3; *Bābur-nāma* (Eng. transl. A. S. Beveridge), ii, 645 (there it is written as *Chitr*).

(A. S. Bazmee Ansari)

ČHATR, ČHATTAR [see MIẒALLA]

CHECHAOUEN [see SHAFSHAWAN]

CHERCHELL [see SHARSHAL]

CHESS [see SHAṬRANDJ]

CHINA [see AL-ṢĪN]

CHIOS [see SAḲĪZ]

CHITRAL (Čitrāl), a princely state and a federated unit of the Republic of Pakistan, situated between 35° 15′ and 37° 8′ N. and 71° 22′ and 74° 6′ E. with an area of about 4,500 sq. miles, and a population of 105,000 in 1951, contiguous to Soviet Russia, Afghānistān and the Peoples' Republic of China. The state takes its name from the capital city, Čitrāl, also known as Ḳāshḳār or Čitrār, two ancient names still in favour with the people who call themselves Ḳāshḳārīs. The origin of Ḳāshḳār is not known; the theory that it is composed of *Ḳāsh*—a demon and *ghār*—a cave must be dismissed as absurd. The Chinese, after their conquest sometime in the first century B.C., called the area Čitar, said to mean a green garden. Bābur, in his memoirs, uses the same word for Čhat [*q.v.*], apparently struck by the large number of flower-gardens in and around the town (*Bābur-nāma*, transl. A. S. Beveridge, i, 383). The state, with an estimated annual income of 13,000,000 rupees, is now commonly known as Čitrāl; although the natives still prefer the older form Čitrār.

A mountainous country, its ice-caps and glaciers are a permanent source of water-supply for the lush green valleys of the Hindū-Kush whose off-shoots divide Čitrāl into several orographic regions. Bounded by the unnamed *kūhistāns* of Dīr and Swāt (*qq.v*), the Himalayas and the Karakoram Range there are many famous passes and peaks in Čitrāl.

The Dūrāh Pass (14,500 ft.) leads to Badakhshān [*q.v.*] and is open for only three months in the year. From ancient times it has served as an important caravan route between Čitrāl and the Central Asia. The Bārōghil pass (12,500 ft.) across the Yārkhūn valley connects China and Soviet Russia with Čitrāl and caravans from Kāshghar and Khōtan [*qq.v.*] were a common sight till recently. The other important passes are Shandūr (12,500 ft.) and Lowarā'ī (10,230 ft.) which lead to Gilgit and Dīr respectively. The Lowarā'ī pass, the only link between Čitrāl and the rest of West Pakistan, remains snow-bound for at least seven months in the year, and when open it can only be negotiated by jeep traffic. During the snow-bound period travellers cross into Čitrāl on foot and merchandise is carried on mules.

The main occupation of the people is agriculture or cattle-grazing, though the state is rich in mineral and forest wealth, which awaits large-scale exploitation. There are believed to be considerable deposits of antimony, iron-ore, lead, sulphur, mica, crystal and orpiment. The *Ta'rīkh-i Čitrāl* mentions gold, silver, lapis-lazuli, topaz and also turquoise among the rare minerals found.

Communications are a great problem; no roads worthy of the name exist. However, a good motor road, mainly for strategic purposes, is under construction across the Lowarā'ī Pass and is expected to be completed by the end of 1959. A proposal to construct an all-weather road, through a tunnel under the Lowarā'ī Pass, connecting Pēshāwar with Čitrāl, was also mooted but, in view of the huge cost involved, has been abandoned.

Since her accession to Pakistan in 1947, Čitrāl has made rapid progress in almost all spheres of life. There are now 85 regular schools including two high schools and two *dār al-ʿulūm*s for religious instruction, as compared to two middle schools and a few *maktab*s before accession. Education up to matriculation standard is free, and facilities are also provided for higher education outside the state. Two well-equipped hospitals and a number of dispensaries have been opened to provide free medical aid to the people. Small-scale and cottage industries have been set up and a fruit-crushing factory has been established at Dolomus, near Čitrāl. Other measures for raising the standard of living of the people have also been taken.

Very little is known about the early history of Čitrāl. The aborigines have been called Pishāčas and described as cannibals. They are said to have been subdued by the Chinese in the first century B. C. Nothing reliable is known thereafter till the 3rd/10th century when we have archaeological evidence to prove that Čitrāl was under the sway of king Djaypāl of Kabul in 287/900 and that the people were Buddhists. Čingīz Khān is also said to have made inroads into Čitrāl, but this lacks historical confirmation.

The founder of the present ruling dynasty was one Bābā Ayyūb, an alleged grandson of Bābur, who after the departure of his father, Mīrzā Kāmrān, to Mecca, wandered into Čitrāl and took up service with the ruling monarch, a prince of the Ra'īsīyya dynasty. His grandson Sangīn ʿAlī I is said to have found favour with the ruler, who appointed him his first subject. Gradually he assumed great power, and on his death in 978/1570 his two sons Muḥammad Riḍā' and Muḥammad Bēg succeeded to the offices he had held. On the death of the Ra'īsiyya prince, Muḥammad Riḍā' became the virtual ruler, but soon after he was murdered by his nephews for the excesses which he had perpetrated against them and their father, Muḥammad Bēg. In 993/1585 Muḥtaram Shāh I, one of the sons of Muḥammad Bēg, peacefully dethroned the last Ra'īsiyya ruler of Čitrāl, whose descendants he deported to Badakhshān, and himself assumed the reins of government. In 1024/1615 Maḥmūd b. Nāṣir Ra'īsiyya attacked Čitrāl with a large force of Badakhshānī troops, defeated Muḥtaram Shāh I, granted him pardon but expelled him from Čitrāl. In 1030/1620 Muḥtaram Shāh I returned to Čitrāl after murdering Mahmūd Ra'īsiyya, only to be attacked for the second time in 1044/1634. Subsequently Muḥtaram Shāh I had to leave the country because of the defection of his troops. He was driven from pillar to post and was ultimately killed in an encounter with the people of Gilgit [*q.v.*], who were, however, very severely punished in 1124/1712 by his son and successor Sangīn ʿAlī II, for the murder of his father. Sangīn ʿAlī II, having despaired of regaining his lost principality went to Afghānistān, then a province of the Indian Mughal empire.

On the accession of Shāh ʿĀlam Bahādur Shāh I [see BAHĀDUR SHĀH I] to the throne of Delhi, Sangīn ʿAlī II came down to India and entered in 1120/1708 the service of Shāh ʿĀlam, who appointed him custodian of the shrine of Aḥmad Sirhindī [*q.v.*]. With the monetary assistance rendered by the Mughal emperor Sangīn ʿAlī II was able to enrol Swāt levies who helped him reconquer the lost territory. Sangīn ʿAlī II was murdered in 1158/1745 by some members of the Raʾīsiyya dynasty and was followed by a number of weak and effete rulers. In 1189/1775 Frāmarz Shāh, a nephew of Muḥtaram Shāh I, came to the throne. He was a military adventurer and led a number of campaigns against the neighbouring territories of Gilgit, Nāgar and Kāfiristān. He also attacked Čaght Serai in Afghānistān and occupied it after a fierce battle. He was murdered in 1205/1790 by one of his uncles, Shāh Afḍal, who occupied the throne. On his death in 1210/1795 his brother Shāh Fāḍil succeeded him. Then follows a series of internecine battles, and the picture becomes so confused that it is difficult to follow the events with historical precision.

Shāh Fāḍil was succeeded in 1213/1798 by Shāh Nawāz Khān, his nephew, who repulsed with heavy losses an attack on Čitrāl in 1223/1808 by Khayr Allāh Khān b. ʿIṣmat Allāh Khān, one of his cousins. He was, however, forced to quit the throne but was proclaimed ruler for the third time in 1234/1818. In the meantime Muḥtaram Shāh II, one of the brothers of Shāh Nawāz, had become a prominent figure in state affairs. Čitrāl was then divided into small units each under a local chieftain, the most powerful of whom was Mulk Amān, the ruler of Čitrāl proper. On his death in 1249/1833 Muḥtaram Shah II, entitled Shāh Katōr, assumed power, brushing aside the minor sons of Mulk Amān. After a hectic and picturesque political career of 28 years Muḥtaram Shāh II, burdened with age, died in 1253/1837 and was succeeded by his son Shāh Afḍal II. In 1257/1841 Gawhar Amān, a son of Mulk Amān and ruler of Warshigūm (Yāsīn and Mastūdj) unsuccessfully invaded Gilgit whose ruler appealed for help to his over-lord, the Dōgrā Rādjā of Kashmīr. In 1265/1848 Gawhar Amān again attacked Gilgit but was forced to retire by the Kashmīr troops who occupied Gilgit. In 1269/1852 the inhabitants of Gilgit, sick of the Dōgrā excesses, secretly invited Gawhar Amān who, after a pitched battle, defeated the Sikhs and occupied Gilgit.

The Mahārādjā of Kashmīr, smarting under the blow, again invaded Gilgit in 1273/1856 but the very next year Gawhar Amān, taking advantage of the Kashmīr ruler's preoccupation with the tumult in India, drove out the Sikh garrison. A series of skirmishes then followed, neither side gaining the upper hand. Meanwhile Gawhar Amān died and the fort of Gilgit was recaptured by the Kashmīr troops in 1277/1860. Earlier in 1271/1854 Gulāb Singh, the ruler of Kashmīr was said to have entered into an alliance with Shāh Afḍal, the Mehtar of Čitrāl, against Gawhar Amān, but this statement is without foundation as Shāh Afḍal had already passed away in 1270/1853 and succeeded by his son Muḥtaram Shāh III, nick-named Ādam-Khʷur (man-eater). In spite of his valour, generosity and prowess he was disliked by the people who deposed him and placed Amān al-Mulk on the throne. In 1285/1868 Čitrāl was attacked by Maḥmūd Shāh, the ruler of Badakhshān, who suffered an ignominious defeat. In 1296/1878 the Mehtar of Čitrāl made an engagement with the Mahārādjā of Kashmīr by which the latter acknowledged the supremacy of the former, accepting in return a subsidy of 12,000 rupees (Śrīnagar coinage) annually.

In 1297/1880, after the defeat of Pahlwān Bahādur, ruler of Upper Čitrāl, the entire territory became united for the first time under one chief, Mehtar Amān al-Mulk, who also became the master of Mastūdj, Yāsīn and Ghizr. In 1303/1885-6 Čitrāl was visited by the Lockhart Mission followed in 1306/1888 by another under Captain Durand which was instrumental in getting the annual subsidy, paid by the Kashmīr Darbār, raised to 12,000 rupees in 1309/1891. In 1310/1892 Afḍal al-Mulk succeeded his father, Amān al-Mulk, who had died suddenly, but was soon afterwards murdered by his uncle, Shīr Afḍal, who was, in turn attacked and expelled by Niẓām al-Mulk, governor of Yāsīn and an elder brother of Afḍal al-Mulk, then a refugee in Gilgit. In 1312/1895 Niẓām al-Mulk was shot dead by his half-brother, Amīr al-Mulk, who seized the fort. Čitrāl was soon invaded by ʿUmrā Khān, the *wālī* of Djandōl and master at that time of Dīr [*q.v.*]. He was joined by Shīr Afḍal, an exile in Afghānistān. Both ʿUmrā Khān and Shīr Afḍal made common cause against the small British Indian force which, according to the treaty of 1307/1889, had been stationed at Čitrāl. When it was learnt that Amīr al-Mulk had made secret overtures to ʿUmrā Khān and his ally, the British Agent placed him under detention and provisionally recognized Shudjāʿ al-Mulk, a boy of 14 years, and a son of Amān al-Mulk as the Mehtar.

The British Political Agent, with a mixed force of 400 native and British troops, had occupied the fort before placing Shudjāʿ al-Mulk on the throne. The garrison attacked the forces of ʿUmrā Khān and Shīr Afḍal but met with little success. Then began the historic seige of Čitrāl by ʿUmrā Khān and his confederates which lasted from 3 March 1895 to 19 April 1895, and was finally raised by the entry into Čitrāl of the advanced guard of the main relief force on 26 April 1895 which had been despatched *via* Malākand and Dīr. Shīr Afḍal fell a prisoner into the hands of the British while ʿUmrā Khān escaped to Afghānistān. Amīr al-Mulk and his leading men were deported to India as a punishment for their complicity in the trouble which necessitated large-scale military operations. Shudjāʿ al-Mulk was confirmed as the Mehtar and since then Čitrāl has enjoyed an unbroken period of peace and progress. During the Afghān War of 1338/1919 the Čitrāl Scouts fully co-operated with the British. The Mehtar was allowed a sum of 100,000 rupees as his contribution to the expenses of the war, and the same year the title of His Highness, with a personal salute of 11 guns, was conferred on him. In 1345/1926 the Mehtar entered into an agreement with the Government of India for the prevention of smuggling of narcotics through Dīr and Swāt, into British India.

An enlightened ruler, Shudjāʿ al-Mulk introduced modern amenities like electricity, tele-communications and automobiles into the state and constructed roads, forts, grain godowns, irrigation channels and schools. He also built a Djāmiʿ Masdjid, said to be the most beautiful and the largest building between Gilgit and Pē<u>sh</u>āwar. He is known as the 'Architect' of modern Čitrāl.

On his death in 1355/1936 he was succeeded by his son Nāṣir al-Mulk. A ruler endowed with literary taste, his Persian poetic work, the *Ṣaḥīfat al-Takwīn*, a study of the theory of evolution in the light of the Ḳur'ānic teachings, has won him praise and admiration from indigenous scholars. In 1362/1943 his younger brother Muẓaffar al-Mulk succeeded him. It was he who offered the accession of Čitrāl to Pakistan in 1367/1947. He was succeeded by Sayf al-Raḥmān in 1369/1949 who, on his death in an air-crash in 1374/1954, was succeeded by his infant son, Sayf al-Mulk Nāṣir, a boy of 3 years of age. The state is now ruled by a Council of Regency presided over by the Political Agent, Malākand Agency through the *Wazīr-i Aʿẓam*, an officer appointed by the Government of Pakistan.

Bibliography: Muḥammad ʿAzīz al-Dīn, *Tā'rīkh-i Čitrāl* (in Urdu), Agra 1897; *Imp. Gazetteer of India*, Oxford 1908, 300-4; H. C. Thomson, *The Chitral Campaign*, London 1895; H. L. Nevill, *Campaigns on the North-West Frontier*, London 1912, index; G. W. Leitner, *Dardistan in* 1866, 1886 *and* 1893, London n.d., 104-6 and appendix II; C. U. Aitchison, *A Collection of Treaties, Engagements and Sanads relating to India*, Delhi 1933, xi, 414-17; *Memoranda on the Indian States* (an official publication of the late Government of India), Delhi 1940, 206-10; G. Robertson, *Chitral*, London 1898; W. R. Robertson, *The Chitral Expedition*, Calcutta 1898; Biddulph, *Tribes of the Hindoo Koosh*, Calcutta 1880; T. H. Holdich, *The Indian Borderland*, (chaps. xi, xiii), London 1901; *EI*[1], s.v. (A. S. BAZMEE ANSARI)

II. Name, languages and tribes.

Khowar Çhetrár, together with corresponding forms in neighbouring languages, goes back to *Kṣetrāt(ī ?). Sanglēčī Šām-Čatrād, etc. contains an ancient name of N. Chitral (cf. *BSOS*, vi, 441f.).

Of the 105,529 (1951) inhabitants of Chitral the great majority (90,000) speak Khowár, the language of the Kho tribe and of the state. It extends east of the <u>Sh</u>andur pass as far as <u>Gh</u>izr in Yasīn. Khowár is an Indo-Aryan language of archaic type, cf., *e.g.*, *šron* hip, *ašru* tear, *hardi* heart, *išpašur* father-in-law, etc. But it contains, apart from more recent borrowings from Pers., Ar. and Hind., also loan-words from the Pamir dialects, as well as a number of words of Middle Iranian origin. Some words are borrowed from, or shared with Buru<u>sh</u>aski and Ṣinā, and several of the most common words are of unknown origin.

Other Indo-Aryan languages are: Kalaṣa (3,000) spoken, mainly by pagans, in two dialects in the side-valleys of S. Chitral. Kalaṣa is closely related to Khowar. The Kalaṣ are said to have occupied Chitral right up to Reṣun, and to have been pushed back within the last few hundred years by the Khos, whose original home was in Torikho and Muḷikho in N. Chitral.—Phalūṛā (Ḍangarīk) (3,000) is spoken in some side valleys of S. E. Chitral by original immigrants from Cilās. It is an archaic form of Ṣinā. — Gawar-Bātī is spoken at Arandū, close to the Af<u>gh</u>ān border, and also across it. In the same neighbourhood we find Damēlī in one village.—Gu<u>dj</u>urī (2,000) is spoken by Gu<u>dj</u>ur herdsmen who have filtered through from Swāt and Dīr.

Katī, a Kāfir language, has been introduced into S. Chitral within the last few generations by settlers from Kāmdēsh and the upper Ba<u>sh</u>gal valley in Nūristān.

Iranian languages: Persian (Bada<u>kh</u><u>sh</u>ī) (1,000) at Madagla<u>sh</u>t in the <u>Sh</u>i<u>sh</u>i Kuh valley.—Pa<u>sh</u>to (at least 4,000) in the Arandū district.—Wa<u>kh</u>ī, spoken by a few settlers in upper Yār<u>kh</u>ūn. Yid<u>gh</u>ā, an offshoot of Mun<u>dj</u>ī in Mun<u>dj</u>ān, is spoken by the Yid<u>gh</u> (Idəgh, etc.) tribe, settled since long in the upper Loṭkuh valley, below the Dōrāh pass.

At a not too remote date we must suppose that Chitral was divided between Khos and Kalaṣes, and the ancestors of these languages must have been introduced from N.W. India at a very early stage of development. A couple of short Sanskrit inscriptions have been found. Khowar has no written literature, [except a translation of the Gan<u>dj</u>-i Pa<u>sh</u>tō (Calc., 1902, romanized), and a short prayer book in Urdū script (Nimež, 1958).] But the language is rich in songs and popular tales (šilo<u>gh</u> < śloka).

With the exception of most Kalaṣes the inhabitants are Muslim, mainly Maulaīs. The last pagan Katīs were converted in the 1930s. But many traces of pre-Islamic customs and festivals remain. Note also Khowar *daṣman* priest, probably < Skt. *dakṣamant.

The Khos are divided into three social classes: Ādamzādas, nobles, or at any rate free-holders; Arbābzādas, comparatively well off, being paid for their services to the Mehtar, and on that account with a higher status than the very poor Faḳīr Miskīn.

Each class contains a number of clans, some of which carry patronymical names, other such indicating foreign origin, while others are difficult to analyse. Also the Kalaṣ and Yid<u>gh</u> tribes are divided into clans.

The Khos are dolicho- to mesocephalic, of middle height, and often with eyes and hair of medium colour, a few are fair-haired and blue-eyed. Kalaṣes and Katis are more decidedly dolichocephalic, and the Katis also of greater height.

Bibliography: Biddulph, *Tribes of the Hindoo Koosh*, Calcutta 1880; D. J. T. O'Brien, *Grammar and vocabulary of the Khowar dialect*, Lahore 1895; *Linguistic Survey of India*, viii, II. G. Morgenstierne, *Report on a linguistic mission to Afghanistan*, Oslo 1926; idem, *Report on a lingu. miss. to N.W. India*, Oslo 1932; idem, *The name Munjan and some other names of places and peoples in the Hindu-Kush*, *BSOS*, vi; idem, *Iranian elements in Khowar*, in *BSOS*, viii; idem, *Some features of Khowar morphology*, *Norsk Tidsskrift for Sprogvidenskap*, xiv; idem, *Sanscritic words in Khowar*, S. K. Belvalkar Felicitation Volume, Benares 1957; A. Stein, *Serindia*, i, 26 ff., Oxford 1921.

Anthropology: T. A. Joyce, *Serindia*, iii, 1351, ff.; B. S. Guha, *Census of India* 1931, i/3, x, ff., Delhi 1935; A. Herrlich, in *Deutsche im Hindukusch* (with bibliography), 170 ff., Berlin 1937.

Kalaṣ and Kati: R. C. F. Schomberg, *Kafirs and Glaciers*, London 1938; H. Siiger, *Ethnological field-research in Chitral, Sikkim and Assam* (*Kgl. Danske Videnskabers Selskab, hist. fil. Meddelelser*, 36, 2), Copenhagen.

(G. MORGENSTIERNE)

CHITTAGONG, Tset-ta-gong, Čātigrāma, or Čātgām is the main sea-port in East Pakistan and the head-quarter of the district bordering on Arakan. The town, which has a population of 294,046 (1951 census) inhabitants, stands on the right bank of the Karnaphūli river, ten miles from the sea, and has a good natural harbour away from the flooded plains of Bengal and the silt-depositing mouths of the Ganges. Its origin is obscure. The early Arab geographers speak of only Samandar on the bank of probably the Brahmaputra as a sea-port in this region. Chittagong comes in to prominence from the 8th/14th century onward, and is referred to as the *Porto Grando* by the Portuguese. It was first conquered by the Muslims in 738/1338 possibly from the Arakanese who often disturbed the peace of the city. In 918/1512 the Bengal Sulṭān ʿAlāʾ al-Dīn Ḥusayn Shāh ousted the Arakanese and named it Fatḥābād. For about a hundred years when the Mughals were consolidating their position in Bengal, Chittagong again reverted to the Arakanese, and only in 1076/1666 it was finally conquered by the Mughal governor Shāyistā Khān, who renamed it Islāmābād and had a Djāmiʿ mosque built there.

The district of Chittagong has a large mixture of foreign populace, the men of Arab descent being in good proportion. The Arab influence is also observable in the Chittagonian dialect. Several stories about the *Māhī Sawār* (riding on fish, *i.e.*, coming by sea) saints are current here. About four miles from the town stands the locally famous *dargāh* dedicated to the memory of Bāyazīd Bisṭāmī. Within the city can be seen the tomb of Shaykh Badr al-ʿĀlam, a saint of the 14th century, and the *dargāh* of *Pāñč Pīr* [*q.v.*], a group of five saints not definitely specified but very popular in this region. Another object of great local reverence is the *Ḳadm-i Rasūl* [*q.v.*] (a stone replica of the foot-print of the Prophet), preserved in a 17th century mosque.

Bibliography: J. N. Sarkar, *The conquest of Chatgaon*, in *JASB* 1907; idem, *The Feringi pirates of Chatgaon*, in *JASB* 1907; A. H. Dani: *Early Muslim Contact with Bengal*, in *Proceedings of the First Pakistan History Conference*, Karachi 1951; Hamidullah: *Taʾrīkh-i Čātgām* (a Persian history of the 19th century). (A. H. Dani)

CHIVALRY [see FURŪSIYYA]

CHOCIM [see KHOTIN]

CHRISTIANITY, CHRISTIANS [see NAṢĀRĀ]

CHRONOLOGY [see TAʾRĪKH]

CID [see AL-SĪD]

ČIFT-RESMİ also called *čift-ḥaḳḳî* or *ḳulluḳ-aḳčasî*, in the Ottoman empire the basic *raʿiyyet* (see REʿĀYĀ) tax paid in principle by every Muslim peasant, *raʿiyyet*, possessing one *čift*. The term *čift* (original meaning = "pair") was used to denote the amount of agricultural land which could be ploughed by two oxen. It was fixed as from 60 to 150 *dönüms* according to the fertility of the soil (one *dönüm* was about 1000 sq. m. = 1196 sq. yds.). We find a *čift-aḳčasî* in Anatolia under the Saldjūḳids at the rate of one dīnār [*q.v.*]. On the other hand the Ottoman *čift-resmi* had striking similarities with the Byzantine taxes paid by the *paroikoi* to the *pronoïa*-holders. It is to be noted that, as an *ʿurfī* tax, it appeared in its original form in the lands conquered from the Byzantines in Western Anatolia and Thrace, and was applied there both to the Muslim and Christian *reʿāyā* alike, whereas in other parts of the empire the Christians were subjected to a different *raʿiyyet* tax, namely the *ispendje* or *ispenče*.

In the *Ḳānūnnāme* of Meḥemmed II it is stated that *čift-resmi* was the money equivalent of seven services such as the provision of hay, straw, wood etc., for the *tīmār*-holder. For these services, *khidmet*s or *ḳulluḳ*s, twenty-two *akča* [*q.v.*] were to be paid as *čift-resmi*. Those possessing half a *čift*, *nīm-čift*, were to pay half. Regardless of his personal condition, every *raʿiyyet* possessing a *čift* or half a *čift* had to pay this tax, and this gave it the character of a land-tax. In the 10th/16th century Abu 'l-Suʿūd and others attempted to include it among the *sharʿī* taxes as *kharādj-i muwaẓẓaf*.

Married peasants with land amounting to less than half a *čift*, or possessing no land of their own, were called *bennāk* [*q.v.*], and were subject to lower rates, for example 6 or 9 *akča*s, which were later increased to 9, 12 and 18. In the *Ḳānūn-nāme* of Meḥemmed II the *bennāk* were supposed to be subject only to three services, the money equivalent of which was 6 or 9 *akča*s. Lastly the *reʿāyā* classified as *ḳara* or *müdjerred*, the very poor or bachelors, who possessed no land of their own, paid this tax at the lowest rate of 6 *akča*s.

Thus *čift-resmi* can be regarded as the basic unit of a graduated tax system, and even *tütün-resmi* and *dönüm-resmi* can be included in the same system.

Originally the rate of *čift-resmi* was 22 *akča*s, but in 862/1458 it was raised to 33 *akča*s in the *sandjaḳ*s of the *eyālet* of Anadolu. It was further raised in some parts of Anatolia with additions made in favour of *subashi*s [*q.v.*] and *sandjaḳ-beg*s [*q.v.*], but under Süleymān I this innovation was abolished as causing confusion. Applied to Syria after its conquest with a higher rate of 40, and in Eastern Anatolia of 50 *akča*s it remained however, 22 *akča*s in Rūmeli (see the list in my *Osmanlılarda Raiyyet Rüsûmu*, in *Belleten*, no. 92, 1959). Partial or total exemptions from *čift-resmi* were granted by imperial *berāt*s in return for some public services required from the *reʿāyā*. But in the 10th/16th century many such exemptions were abolished.

As a rule *čift-resmi* was included in the *tīmār* [*q.v.*] revenue of the *sipāhī*. But it lost its importance when after 990/1582 the *akča* decreased in value and the *ʿawāriḍ* [*q.v.*] became a form of regular taxation imposed on the *reʿāyā*. (Halil Inalcik)

ČIFTLİK is the ordinary word for farm in Turkish, but in the Ottoman times it designated, at first, a certain unit of agricultural land in the land-holding system, and then, later on, a large estate. It was formed from *čift* (pair, especially a pair of oxen) from the Persian *djuft* with the Turkish suffix, *lik*. Originally, a *čiftlik* was thought of as the amount of land that could be ploughed by two oxen. *Čift* and *čiftlik* were used synonymously. In the Slav areas of the Ottoman empire the term *bashtina* was often substituted for *čiftlik*. In the Ottoman land-holding system during the period in which the *tīmār* [*q.v.*] organization prevailed, *čiftlik* was a term applied to a holding of agricultural land comprising 60 or 80 to 150 *dönüms* (one *dönüm* equals approximately 1000 sq.m.), the size varying with the fertility of the soil. The *čiftlik* was the basic land unit used in all forms of land-holding, *mīrī*, *waḳf*, and *mülk* or *mālikāne*. From the legal point of view, however, the kind of *čiftlik* varied with the type of tenure.

The *raʿiyyet čiftlik*s which the *reʿāyā*, Christian and Muslim peasants, possessed by *tapu* [*q.v.*] and for which they paid the *ʿushr* [*q.v.*] and *čift-resmi* [*q.v.*] taxes to the land-holder, made up by far the greater part of the agricultural lands. As a rule, *čiftlik*s were not to be subdivided because such a situation would, in the judgement of Abu 'l-Suʿūd, make it impossible to collect the taxes imposed on a *čiftlik* as a whole. In reality, however, during the land surveys, *taḥrīr* [*q.v.*], it was found that many *čiftlik*s had lost their original form as a result of sub-division, and the *čift-resmi* were no longer being collected. In order to preserve the *čiftlik*, which was essential to the land-holding system of the time, and which had been the basis for land and hearth taxes in the area even before the Ottomans, it was decreed that if land recorded in the *defter*s [see DAFTAR] as *čiftlik* was found divided among several persons it was to be restored to its original form, and if a *ra*ʿ*iyyet* in possession of a *čiftlik* died leaving several sons, they were to possess it collectively, *meshā*ʿ*an*.

In addition to the *ra*ʿ*iyyet čiftlik*s we also find what we can call the military *čiftlik*s which, unlike the former, were in the direct possession of the military. In this category we find the *khāṣṣa čiftlik*s of the *tīmār*-holders and the *čiftlik*s in the military organizations of the *yaya*, *müsellem* and *doghandji* etc. Their common feature was that they were not subject to the *ra*ʿ*iyyet* taxes. But, while the *khāṣṣa čiftlik*s, also known as *kilič-yeri*, were exploited by the *tīmār*-holders under a sharecropping system, *ortakdjilik* or *muḳāta*ʿ*a* [*q.v.*], the *yaya* and *müsellem čiftlik*s were cultivated, as a rule, by the *yaya*s and *müsellem*s themselves. These *čiftlik*s were never to change their original character and usually were named by their original possessors as Meḥmed-yeri, ʿAlī-yeri, etc. There were attempts by the military to add *ra*ʿ*iyyet* lands illegally to their *khāṣṣa čiftlik*s. But, in the 10th/16th century, most of the military *čiftlik*s were transformed by the government into *ra*ʿ*iyyet čiftlik*s and assigned as *tīmār*s. In the case of the *khāṣṣa čiftlik*s in Bosnia [see BOSNA], the reason given for their transformation in 936/1530 was that they lay uncultivated.

The *čiftlik*s in the *waḳf* and *mülk* or *mālikāne* lands were the same in size as other *čiftlik*s and were usually cultivated by the *ra*ʿ*iyyet*. During the reigns of Bāyazīd I, Meḥemmed II, and under the 10th/16th century Sultans, a great part of these *čiftlik*s too was converted into *tīmār*s. For example, in Erzindjan in 947/1540, each *zāwiye* [*q.v.*] under a *shaykh* was assigned a *čiftlik* while the rest of the land was distributed among the *tīmār*s.

As early as the 8th/14th and 9th/15th centuries the Ottoman Sultans granted influential men whole villages or large *tīmār*s as *čiftlik*s. In these instances we are no longer dealing with the *čiftlik* as a land measure, but as a personal estate, granted by the Sultan. For example, in the *defter* of Pasha-sandjaghī dated 859/1455 (Belediye Küt. Istanbul, Cevdet kit. no. 0.89) we find a number of people, among them the Court physician Meḥmed Shirwānī and the Sultan's tutor Seydī Ahmed, in possession of *tīmār*s as *čiftlik* (*ber wedjh-i čiftlik*). Such large lands were sometimes given as *mülk* (*ber wedjh-i mülkiyyet*). The revenues of these *čiftlik*s were farmed out by their possessors, who usually lived in the towns, for a sum of money which was called *muḳāṭa*ʿ*a*. The possessor of the *čiftlik* was usually required to equip one soldier (*eshkündji*) for the Sultan's army.

Even in this early period we find some newly opened lands or *mazra*ʿ*as* [*q.v.*] held directly as *čiftlik*s by members of the military class who, as a rule, paid the government a sum of money which was also called *muḳāṭa*ʿ*a*. Therefore, these *čiftlik*s were also known as *muḳāṭa*ʿ*alī čiftlik*s. In central and northern Anatolia the *čiftlik*s which were possessed by the pre-Ottoman aristocratic families under the names of *mālikāne* or *yurd* were given the same status with the obligation of supplying an *eshkündji*. The *čiftlik*s which were opened in the uncultivated lands by the military were subject only to the ʿ*ushr* tax. By the end of the 10th/16th century the number of such *čiftlik*s in the hands of the Janissaries increased rapidly. But, in general, the tendency in the 10th/16th century was to convert all types of military *čiftlik*s into *ra*ʿ*iyyet čiftlik*s so that the *ra*ʿ*iyyet* taxes might be included in the *tīmār*s.

With the disruption of the *tīmār* system, this course of development was reversed. During and after the period of confusion between 1003/1595-1018/1609, a great part of the *ra*ʿ*iyyet čiftlik*s found their way into the hands of the *ḳapī-ḳulu* and palace favourites, and the old practices such as possession of *tīmār*s as *čiftlik*s, *mülk* or *muḳāṭa*ʿ*alī čiftlik*s were now widespread. In the same period, moreover, when the peasantry abandoned their lands *en masse* and scattered throughout Anatolia, which is known in Ottoman history as the Great Flight, the Janissaries and others took possession of the *re*ʿ*āyā čiftlik*s by *tapu*. The accumulation of *čiftlik*s in the hands of *a*ʿ*yān* [*q.v.*], rich and influential men in the provinces, however, was mainly due to the *muḳāṭa*ʿ*a* system. This again was an old practice but now, with the disorganization of the *tīmār* system, the *tīmār* lands were increasingly rented as *muḳāṭa*ʿ*a* to private persons bidding the highest price. In reality however, through administrative abuses, the influential men managed to obtain them. *Aghas* and *a*ʿ*yān* with large *muḳāṭa*ʿ*a* holdings, *čiftlik*s, emerged everywhere in the empire, especially during the 12/18 century. Nedjātī (Süleymaniye Küt. Esad ef. no. 2278, v. 43), writing in that century, complained that many *tīmār*s had been seized by the *a*ʿ*yān* and *ahl-i* ʿ*urf*, officials, in the provinces. It was on the *muḳāṭa*ʿ*a* lands that the power of the great *a*ʿ*yān* rested in that century, and from this period on the word *čiftlik* was used to designate large personal estates. The attempts to break up these *čiftlik*s made by the *Tanẓīmāt* [*q.v.*] reformers did not meet with any great success and this became the underlying factor in the peasant uprisings in the Balkans in the 13th/19th century. Under the Turkish Republic a law passed in 1945 (modified in 1950) provided that the large estates were to be broken up and distributed to the peasants in need of land.

Bibliography: Ö. L. Barkan, *Kanunlar*; idem, *Türk Toprak Hukuku Tarihinde Tanzimat*, in *Tanzimat*, Istanbul 1940, 321-421; H. Inalcık, *Tanzimat ve Bulgar Meselesi*, Ankara 1943; idem, *Osmanlılarda Raiyyet Rüsûmu*, in *Belleten* 92 (1959), 575-608; idem, *Land Problems in Turkish History*, in *The Muslim World*, xlv (1955), 221-228; *İA*, 25. *cüz* (1945), 392-397. (HALIL INALCIK)

ČIGHĀLA-ZĀDE (DJIGHĀLA-ZĀDE) YŪSUF **SINĀN PĀSHĀ** (c. 1545-1605), also known as Čaghal (Djaghāl)-oghlu, belonged to the Genoese house of Cicala. He was born at Messina in Sicily and received the Christian name Scipione Cicala. His father, the Visconte di Cicala, was, according to Gerlach, a "corsair" in the service of Spain, while his mother is said (cf. *L'Ottomanno*, of L. Soranzo) to have been "Turca da Castelnuovo". The Visconte and his son, captured at sea by Muslim corsairs in 968/1561 (some of the sources give the year as 967/1560), were taken first to Tripoli in North Africa and then to Istanbul. The father was in due course redeemed from captivity and, after living for some time at Beyoğlu, returned to Messina, where he died in 1564. His son, Scipione, became, however, a Muslim and was trained in the Imperial Palace, rising to the rank of *silaḥdār* and later of Ḳapīdjī Bashī. Čighāla-zāde, through his marriage first to one (980-981/1573) and afterwards (983-984/1576) to another great-grand-daughter of Sulṭān Sulaymān

Ḳānūnī, found himself assured of wealth, high office and protection at the Porte.

He became Agha of the Janissaries in 982/1575 and retained this appointment until 986/1578. During the next phase of his career he saw much active service in the long Ottoman-Persian war of 986/1578-998/1590. He was *Beglerbeg* of Van in 991/1583, assumed command, in the same year, of the great fortress of Erivān—he was now raised to the rank of Vizier—and also had a prominent rôle. once more as *Beglerbeg* of Van, in the campaign of 993/1585 against Tabrīz. As *Beglerbeg* of Baghdād, an appointment which he received in 994/1586, Čighāla-zāde fought with success in western Persia during the last years of the war, reducing Nihāwand and Hamadān to Ottoman control.

After the peace of 998/1590 he was made *Beglerbeg* of Erzurum and in 999/1591 became Ḳapudān Pāshā, *i.e.*, High Admiral of the Ottoman fleet—an office that he held until 1003/1595. During the third Grand Vizierate (1001-1003/1593-1595) of Khodja Sinān Pāshā he was advanced to the rank of fourth Vizier. The Ottomans, since 1001/1593, had been at war with Austria. Čighāla-zāde, having been appointed third Vizier, accompanied Sulṭān Meḥemmed III on the Hungarian campaign of 1004-1005/1596. He tried, but in vain, to relieve the fortress of Khaṭwān (Hatvan), which fell to the Christians in Muḥarram 1005/September 1596, was present at the successful Ottoman siege of Eğri (Erlau) (Muḥarrem-Ṣafer 1005/September-October 1596) and, at the battle of Mezö-Keresztes (Ḥāç Ovasī) in Rabīʿ I 1005/October 1596, shared in the final assault that turned an imminent defeat into a notable triumph for the Ottomans. Čighāla-zāde, in reward for his service at Mezö-Keresztes, was now made Grand Vizier, but the discontent arising from the measures which he used in a effort to restore discipline amongst the Ottoman forces, the troubles which followed his intervention in the affairs of the Crimean Tatars, and the existence at court of powerful influences eager to restore Dāmād Ibrāhīm Pasha [*q.v.*] to the Grand Vizierate, brought about his deposition from this office, after he had been in control of the government for little more than a month (Rabīʿ I-Rabīʿ II 1005/October-December 1596).

Čighāla-zāde became *Beglerbeg* of Shām (Syria) in Djumādā I 1006/December 1597-January 1598 and then, in Shawwāl 1007/May 1599, was made Ḳapudān Pāshā for the second time. He assumed command, in 1013/1604, of the eastern front, where a new war between the Ottomans and the Persians had broken out in the preceding year. His campaign of 1014/1605 was unsuccessful, the forces that he led towards Tabrīz suffering defeat near the shore of Lake Urmiya. Čighāla-zāde now withdrew to the fortress of Van and thence in the direction of Diyārbekir. He died, in the course of this retreat, during the month of Radjab 1014/November-December 1605.

Bibliography: Selānīkī, *Taʾrīkh*, Istanbul 1281 A.H., 198 ff., 292, 299, 334, 342-343; Pečevī, *Taʾrīkh*, ii, Istanbul 1283 A.H., 25, 87, 97 ff., 107, 111-112, 191, 192, 197, 198, 204 ff., 261 ff., 284; Ewliyā Čelebi, *Seyāḥat-nāme*, vii, Istanbul 1928, 157, 179, 180; Naʿīmā, *Taʾrīkh*, Istanbul 1281-1283 A.H., i, 146 ff., 167 ff., 172 ff., 368, 379, 387-388 (Djighāla-zāde Sinān Pāshā oghlu Maḥmūd Pāshā), 393 ff., 425 ff.; Iskandar Beg Munshī, *Taʾrīkh-i ʿĀlam Ārā-i ʿAbbāsī*, Tehran 1955-1956, i, 311 ff., 403 ff., 470 and ii, 635, 656, 660-672 *passim*, 678-685 *passim*, 695, 702-705 *passim*, 768, 769; S. Gerlach, *Tagebuch*, Frankfurt-am-Main 1674, 27, 217, 244-245, 265-266, 269; G. T. Minadoi, *Historia della Guerra fra Turchi et Persiani*, Venice 1588, 221-222, 307, 315-317 *passim*, 324, 326, 330, 344, 345; L. Soranzo, *L'Ottomanno*, Ferrara 1599, 10-12; *The Travels of John Sanderson in the Levant* 1584-1602, ed. Sir W. Foster (Hakluyt Society), London 1931, 319 (index); C. Hughes, *Shakespeare's Europe* (*Unpublished Chapters of Fynes Moryson's Itinerary*), London 1903, 26 and 46; *Purchas His Pilgrimes*, viii, Glasgow 1905, 311, 313, 316, 320; *Ambassade en Turquie de Jean de Gontaut Biron, Baron de Salignac*, 1605-1610 (*Correspondance diplomatique et documents inédits*), in *Archives Historiques de la Gascogne*, fasc. 19, Paris 1889, 12, 19, 20, 21, 30 and also 393-397 *passim*; G. Sagredo, *Memorie Istoriche de' Monarchi Ottomani*, Venice 1673, 665, 671, 684, 749-750, 751-752, 759-761, 767-769, 773 and 830-838 *passim*; E. Alberi, *Relazioni degli Ambasciatori Veneti al Senato*, ser. 3, Florence 1840-1855, i, 380, ii, 143, 180, 249, 288-292 *passim*, 355-356 and iii, 292, 374, 424-432 *passim*; N. Barozzi and G. Berchet, *Le Relazioni degli Stati Europei lette al Senato dagli Ambasciatori Veneziani nel secolo decimosettimo*, ser. 5: Turchia, Pt. I, Venice 1866, 34, 38, 39; E. de Hurmuzaki, *Documente privitóre la Istoria Românilor*, iii/2 (1576-1600), Bucharest 1888, 215, 225; *Calendar of State Papers, Venetian*: 1581-1591, London 1894, 583 (index), 1592-1603, London 1897, 582-583 (index) and 1603-1607, London 1900, 551 (index); I. Rinieri, *Clemente VIII e Sinan Bassà Cicala. Studio storico secondo documenti inediti*, Rome 1898 (also to be found in *La Civiltà Cattolica*, ser. 16, vols. 9 (Rome 1897), 693-707 and 10 (Rome 1897), 151-161, 272-285, 671-686, and ser. 17, vol. I (Rome 1898), 165-176); G. Oliva, *Sinan-Bassà* (*Scipione Cicala*) *celebre rinnegato del secolo XVI*: *Memorie storico-critiche*, in *Archivio Storico Messinese*, Anni VIII-IX, Messina 1907-1908; Hammer-Purgstall, iii, 423 and iv, 17, 44-45, 86, 171-180 *passim*, 229-230, 245, 248, 261, 264, 268-272 *passim*, 287, 301, 321, 330, 332, 358-359, 376-379, 620, 633, 669-670; N. Jorga, *Geschichte des osmanischen Reiches*, iii, Gotha 1910, 183-185; H. Laoust, *Les Gouverneurs de Damas* .... (658-1156/1260-1744): *Traduction des Annales d'Ibn Ṭūlūn et d'Ibn Ğumʿa*, Damascus 1952, 196 (Sinān Pacha b. al-Ğaffāl); ʿOthmān-zāde Tāʾib, *Ḥadīḳat al-Wuzarāʾ*, Istanbul 1271 A.H., 47 ff.; Sāmī, *Ḳāmūs al-Aʿlām*, iii, Istanbul 1308 A.H., 1822; *Sidjill-i ʿOthmānī*, iii, 111 and iv, 319 (Djighāla-zāde Maḥmūd Pāshā); I. H. Uzunçarşılı, *Osmanlı Tarihi*, iii/2, Ankara 1954, 235, 354-357, 391; *IA*, s.v. Ciğala-zâde (M. Tayyib Gökbilgin). (V. J. Parry)

CILICIA. The name. In Assyrian writings the name Khilakku refers primarily to the western part of the region, Cilicia Trachea, but also includes a part of Cappadocia, whilst the Cilician plain is called the Ḳué. In classical times the name Cilicia covered both western and eastern parts, Cilicia Trachea and the plain of Cilicia. The name does not occur among the Arab geographers, who call Cilicia simply the region of the *thughūr* [*q.v.*], or frontier towns. The form Ḳilīḳiya (or Ḳilīḳiyā) is not met until modern times (see Ibn al-Shiḥna, *al-Durr al-muntakhab*, 180), but it is a direct derivation of the ancient name if, as is thought, the Turkish name for Cilicia Trachea, Ič-Il or Ičel [*q.v.*] (lit. 'the interior region') in fact comes from Kilikia.

Geographical outline. Cilicia is wedged

between the Anatolian plateau to the north-west and the Syrian frontier to the south-east. Its southern edge is fringed by the Mediterranean, which here reaches its most easterly extremity, and it is guarded to the north by the Taurus range, over which the Cilician Gates assure communication with the plateau. To the east are the Amanian Gates (al-Lukām), and to the west, a short distance beyond Selindi (ancient Selinonte), begins the province of Pamphylia (region of Adalia). Cilicia has at all times possessed a great strategic importance on account of the Cilician and Amanian Gates. Although the mountains and sea which isolate Cilicia have given it a marked individuality, it has rarely been able to maintain its own independance for long, even when it was the kingdom of Lesser Armenia or the Turcoman principality of the Ramaḍān-og̲h̲lus. Most of the time, from the Hittites to the Ottomans, it has been incorporated by conquest into the great empires of the eastern Mediterranean.

Cilicia falls naturally into three geographical regions, Cilicia Trachea, the Cilician Taurus, and the Plain of Cilicia. Cilicia Trachea (lit.: 'rough, rugged') is a mountainous region to the west, its coast dotted with ports where pirates took refuge when chased by Pompey's ships. It is virtually without means of communication to the Turkish interior, and has patches of cultivable land only in a few valleys, such as Gök Su (ancient Calycadnus) whose waters flow into the sea near Silifke. It is consequently a very poor region, and contains only a few small towns (Silifke, ancient Seleucia, Mut, on the road from Silifke to Karaman and Konya, and in the west Anamur on the coast and Ermenek inland).

The frontier between Cilicia Trachea and the coastal plain on the one hand and the Taurus on the other is the small river Lamos which has its spring in the Taurus. The Cilician Taurus is a strip 300 km. long by only 50 km. wide stretching in a south-west-north-east direction, and including the massifs of Dumbelek, Bulg̲h̲ar Dag̲h̲ (corruption of Bug̲h̲ā, the Turkish translation of Taurus) and the Ala Dag̲h̲, one peak of which rises to 3600 m. The Ala Dag̲h̲ continues northwards to the Ḥad̲j̲īn Dag̲h̲. The Anti-Taurus begins to the east, on the left bank of the Zamanti Su, formerly Karmalas, a tributary of the Sayḥān (Saros). Its mountains can easily be crossed, however, as the high waters have cut many valleys through them in forcing their way from the Cappadocian plateau down to the Mediterranean. The Ṭarsūs Čay, ancient Cydnus, in Arabic Baradān, rises in the Bulg̲h̲ar Dag̲h̲ massif and brings Tarsus its water. Between the Bulg̲h̲ar Dag̲h̲ and the Ala Dag̲h̲ are the valleys of the Čakīt Su and Körkün Su, the Čakīt being a tributary of the Körkün which in turn is a tributary of the Sayḥān. The road called the Cilician Gates climbs over passes and runs through these valleys. On the northern side it connects Tarsus with Ulukīs̲h̲la via Bozantī (ancient Podandos-Budandūn) where the narrowest defile, the Cilician Gates properly so called, is at Gülek Bog̲h̲az, 1160 m. high on the upper reaches of the Ṭarsūs Čay.

The most important part of Cilicia is the plain (Greek Pedias, Turkish Čukurova), a product of the alluvial deposits of its two large rivers, the Sayḥān (ancient Saros) and the D̲j̲ayḥān (ancient Pyramus). Along the left bank of the D̲j̲ayḥān's lower reaches is a less elevated outcrop of the Taurus range, the D̲j̲abal al-Nūr or D̲j̲abal Miṣṣīṣ. Sheltered from the north by the great mountain barrier, the Cilician plain is open to the southern winds, enjoys the climate and flora of Mediterranean regions, and is extremely fertile. Crops peculiar to hot countries can be grown there, and apart from sugar-cane plantations there is also intensive cultivation of cotton. The main towns of Cilicia were always situated in this area. To the north, at the foot of the Taurus but still Mediterranean in climate, lie Sīs (at the present day Kozan) and ʿAyn Zarba (ancient Anazarba), to the south Miṣṣīṣa (Mopsuestia) on the D̲j̲ayḥān, Adana on the Sayḥān, Tarsus, Ayās (ancient Aigai) on the western coast of the gulf of Alexandretta, and Alexandretta on its eastern side. Mersīn, to the west of Tarsus, is a relatively recent town, today named Ičel.

In the Islamic epoch Cilicia Trachea and Seleucia belonged to the Greeks, the frontier between the two empires being formed by the Lamos (in Arabic Lāmis).

Under the Ottomans Cilicia constituted the *wilāyet* of Adana, and was divided between the *sand̲j̲aḳs* of Ič-Il, Adana and Kozan in the north, and of D̲j̲ebel Bereket around the gulf of Alexandretta.

The main towns of Cilicia are connected by the Aleppo-Fevzipas̲h̲a-Adana-Ulukīs̲h̲la railway, with a branch line running via Tarsus to Marsīna.

Cilicia has often been stricken by earthquakes; Michael the Syrian (iii, 17) and Ṭabarī (iii, 688) record the one which occurred on 23 June 803; it blocked the river D̲j̲ayḥān and partly destroyed the walls of Miṣṣīṣa. Another one occurred in 1114 (see *EI*[1] s.v. MIṢṢIṢ). The most recent occurred in 1952.

Bibliography: K. Ritter; *Die Erdkunde von Asien. Allgemeine Erdkunde*, xviii & xix, Kleinasien, Berlin 1858-59; V. Cuinet, *La Turquie d'Asie*, Paris 1890-95, ii, 3-108; W. M. Ramsay, *The Historical Geography of Asia Minor*, London 1890, 349 ff., 361-387; Le Strange, chap. ix; Pauly-Wissowa, xi, 385 ff.; E. Banse, *Die Türkei*, 1919, 165-185; R. Blanchard, *L'Asie Occidentale*[3], vol. viii of the *Géographie Universelle* by Vidal de la Blache & Gallois, 69 ff.; Gaudefroy-Demombynes, *La Syrie à l'époque des Mamelouks*, 98-100; Cl. Cahen, *La Syrie du Nord à l'époque des Croisades*, 1938, 134-155; M. Canard, *Hist. de la dynastie des H'amdānides*, i, 278-285; see also the special monographs by Favre & Mandrot, *Voyage en Cilicie*, 1874, in *Bull. de la Soc. de Géogr.*, 1878; and V. Langlois, *Voyage dans la Cilicie et les montagnes du Taurus*, Paris 1861.

Historical outline. When the Arabs had conquered Syria, Heraclius ordered the garrisons of towns between Alexandretta and Tarsus to evacuate their positions (see MIṢṢĪṢ). It is probable that part of the civilian population had to do likewise. The Arabs did not immediately take over these towns, but restricted themselves to raids into the region or across it into Anatolia, leaving small garrisons behind them as a security measure. On his return from an expedition in 31/651-652, Muʿāwiya is said to have destroyed all the fortresses as far as Antioch. However, records exist of the Arabs' capture of Tarsus in 53/672-673, which seems to indicate that it had been reoccupied by the Greeks or defended by its inhabitants. In 65/685, furthermore, the army of Constantine Pogonatus advanced as far as Mopsuestia (Miṣṣīṣa). From 84/703 onwards the Arabs began to settle in Miṣṣīṣa, stationing a garrison there during part of the year. They realized the advantage which would accrue in permanently holding the Cilician positions, and ʿUmar b. ʿAbd al-ʿAzīz abandoned his plan to destroy all the fortresses between Miṣṣīṣa and Antioch. Sīs, at the foot of the Taurus, was captured in 103/751-732. In the first decades of the second century of the *hid̲j̲ra* it became apparent that the Arabs intended to settle in the area; Miṣṣīṣa was colonized by the Zoṭṭ [*q.v.*] with their buffaloes, and a bridge was built over the Sayḥān to the east of Adana, in order to secure communications across the country. Although the Arab armies had no difficulty in traversing the country by way of the Cilician Gates, its occupation was still precarious. There was as yet no systematic organization of the frontier strongpoints, or *t̲h̲ug̲h̲ūr*, still dependant on the *d̲j̲und* of Ḳinnasrīn, which Muʿāwiya or Yazīd b. Muʿāwiya had detached from Ḥimṣ (cf. Ibn al-S̲h̲iḥna, 9). But already the positions had been transformed into *ribāt*, that is to say posts manned by voluntary defenders of the faith, noted for both their religious and military zeal. Al-Dīnawarī, 345, points out that after his dismissal from office K̲h̲ālid al-Ḳaṣrī [*q.v.*] obtained from the caliph His̲h̲ām permission to go to Tarsus, where he remained for some time *murābit^an^*.

After the ʿAbbāsid revolution the Byzantines did not take advantage of the disturbed situation to reconquer Cilicia, but instead concentrated their attention on the regions of Malaṭya and Ḳālīḳalā. After the dynasty had become firmly established, and particularly in al-Mahdī's reign, the ʿAbbāsids undertook to fortify and populate the Cilician positions, above all at Miṣṣīṣa and Tarsus. Hārūn al-Ras̲h̲īd was the most vigorous exponent of the frontier policy. In 170/786-787 he detached the frontier strongholds from the D̲j̲azira and d̲j̲und of Ḳinnasrīn and put them under a separate government called al-ʿAwāsim [*q.v.*] (al-Tabarī, iii, 604; Ibn al-S̲h̲iḥna, 9); Cilicia now became part of the ʿAwāsim *d̲j̲und*. Its reorganization served both defensive and offensive purposes; it helped protect Muslim territory against Byzantine incursions (cf. a poem of Marwān b. Abī Ḥafṣa in Ṭabarī, iii, 742), provided a secure operational base for the Muslim armies which, by tradition, carried out one or two raids each year into Greek territory, and served as a permanent base for volunteer troops and *murābiṭūn*. The fortification of the positions went in hand with the launching of expeditions across the Cilician Gates during the reign of Hārūn al-Ras̲h̲īd and his successors. A vital step in the successful execution of these operations was the Muslim capture of Lulon (al-Luʾluʾa) in 217-832. Its fortress guarded the northern side of a pass which led over the Cilician Gates from Podandos (Budandūn, present-day Bozantı) to Tyana.

A considerable Christian population lived in the strongholds or the countryside around them. The Muslims recruited some of them as guides for their expeditions (see *AIEO Alger*, xv, 48), but they also sometimes acted as informers for the Byzantines, and it was perhaps as an act of reprisal that al-Ras̲h̲īd had all the *t̲h̲ug̲h̲ūr* churches destroyed in 191/807 (Ṭabarī, iii, 712-713; Michael the Syrian, iii, 19 ff.).

The small river Lamos, demarcation line between Cilicia Trachea and Arab Cilicia, was periodically the scene of the exchange of prisoners or their resale to the enemy; historians have left their records of these dealings, in particular al-Masʿūdī in *Tanbīh*, 189-196.

After Muʿtaṣim's famous campaign against Amorium in 223/838, which marks the end of the spectacular expeditions into Anatolia, it gradually became the custom to appoint special amīrs to Cilicia, mostly resident in Tarsus. Although nominally dependant on the ʿAwāsim governor or the ruler of Syria, they enjoyed a certain degree of autonomy and were responsible for the defence of the country and the organization of annual land and sea expeditions. Some of the amīrs of Tarsus became quite famous, *e.g.*, ʿAlī al-Armanī, the eunuch Yāzmān (Greek Esman), G̲h̲ulām Zurāfa (alias Leo of Tripoli and Ras̲h̲īk al-Wardāmī) Damyāna, T̲h̲amal, Naṣr al-T̲h̲amalī. For some time Cilicia, with its *ʿAwāṣim* and *t̲h̲ug̲h̲ūr*, passed from the control of the central government and became a dependency of Ṭūlūnid Egypt (260/873-286/891). This was a troubled chapter of its history, due to the dispute between the Ṭūlūnids and the central power, the intractability of the amīrs, and the ravages incurred through Byzantine raids. The return of Luʾluʾa (Lulon) to Byzantium in 263/876-877 constituted a serious threat to Cilicia. Nevertheless the *ribāt* of Tarsus developed during that period, and assumed greater proportions, as is shown by the sources used by Kamāl al-Dīn in the geographical introduction to his *Bug̲h̲yat al-Ṭalab* (see *AIEO Alger*, xv, 46 ff.) and the descriptions of al-Iṣṭak̲h̲rī and Ibn Ḥawḳal (see TARSŪS). In particular, the caliph al-Muʿtazz and his mother spent great sums on maintaining special units of *murābiṭūn* under military and religious leaders. At a time when the spirit of holy war gave a particular character to Cilicia, there flocked to the country a great number of scholars, traditionists, ascetics and fervent religious men, intent on fulfilling the personal obligation of *d̲j̲ihād*, teaching the old traditions and spreading a spirit of purest orthodoxy among the soldiers and the civilian population. The more well-known of them were Ibrāhīm b. Adham b. Manṣūr [*q.v.*], who died some time between 160 and 166 (776-783), and Ibrāhīm b. Muḥammad al-Fazarī (d. 188/804) (Ibn ʿAsākir, ii, 254). Several of these persons are mentioned in the obituaries of al-D̲h̲ahabī and Abu 'l-Maḥāsin, often carrying the *nisba* of *T̲h̲agrī* or *Ṭarsūsī* (see under 181, 196, 273, 297 etc.). Yāḳūt (iii, 526) also noted their arrival in great numbers (cf. i, 529). It is known that Aḥmad b. Ṭūlūn was educated at Tarsus. Muslim festivals were celebrated in great brilliance there. Abu 'l-Maḥāsin (iii, 60) considered the feast of breaking the fast in Tarsus to be one of the four wonders of Islam.

In the first part of the 4th/10th century Cilicia came under the rule of the Ik̲h̲s̲h̲īd, the governor of Egypt, who received his investiture from the caliph. After the clash between the Ik̲h̲s̲h̲īd and the Ḥāmdanīd amīr Sayf al-Dawla, who won control of northern Syria and Aleppo, the governor of the frontier province submitted to the amīr of Aleppo, and the amīrs of Tarsus henceforth participated in Sayf al-Dawla's expeditions. But the Tarsus fleet, weakened by the policy of the caliph al-Muʿtaḍid, who had had it destroyed, was only a minor factor in the struggles of the 4th/10th century. In the second half of the century the threat of Byzantium from the north caused constant disturbances and rebellions, and the operations of 352/963-354/965 resulted in the complete reconquest of Cilicia by the Greeks (or Byzantines). It remained Byzantine for more than a century, during which time the outflow of Muslims was accompanied by a considerable inflow of Armenians, stimulated by the Byzantine practice of using Armenian officers to administer the country. After the Sald̲j̲ūḳid raids had driven back those Armenians who had settled in Cappadocia after the Turkish conquest of Armenia, their number now increased once more, and, after the battle of Manzikert in 1071, a virtual Armenian principality was created, stretching from Melitene to Cilicia. Its head was the Armenian Philaretus, a former general of Romanus Diogenes, and he established his capital at Marʿas͟h (see Chalandon, *Alexis Comnène*, 95 ff.; J. Laurent, *Byzance et les Turcs Seldjoucides*, 81 ff.; idem, *Byzance et Antioche sous le curopalate Philarète*, in *Rev. des Et. arm.*, ix (1929), 61 ff.; Grousset, *Histoire des Croisades*, I, xl, ff.). The Armenian chiefs Os͟hin of Lampron (present-day Namrūn Yayla, north-west of Tarsus) and Ruben of Partzepert (north of Sīs) were perhaps his vassals. They retained their fiefs when Philaretus departed from the scene, defeated by the Turks. The Turks had ravaged Cilicia even before Manzikert, and shortly before the arrival of the Crusaders (Michael the Syrian, iii, 179) they seized the main towns, though failing to subjugate the Armenian princes in the Taurus. The latter joined forces with the Crusaders in 1097 and helped Baldwin of Boulogne and Tancred to reconquer the Cilician towns. There followed a period in which the towns continually changed hands in the struggle between Byzantium and the Frankish principality of Antioch. Alexis Comnenus recaptured them from Bohemond of Antioch, only to lose them once more to the latter's nephew Tancred, who in 1103 handed them over to his uncle upon his release from the imprisonment inposed by the Dānis͟hmandid of Malaṭya. In 1104 they were retaken by the Byzantine general Monastras (Anna Comnena, XI, xi, 6; ed. Leib iii, 49). They remained the scene of dispute until 1108, when Bohemond was forced to sign a treaty acknowledging the authority of Alexius Comnenus over the whole of Cilicia (Anne Comnena, XIII, xii, 21; ed. Leib iii, 134-135). His nephew Tancred however did not abide by the treaty.

The descendants of Ruben continued to consolidate the development of an Armenian state, and sought to bring all of Cilicia under their control. Thoros I, who had driven off the Sald̲j̲ūḳids in 1107-1108 (Tournebize, *Histoire politique et religieuse de l'Arménie*, 171; Cahen, *La Syrie du Nord à l'époque des Croisades*, 253; Matthew of Edessa, in *Hist. arm. des Croisades*, i, 84-85), captured Sīs and Anazarba from the Greeks. During the reign of his successor Leo I (1129-1137), Bohemond of Antioch attempted to re-establish his authority in Cilicia, but this brought him unto a fatal conflict with another aspirant to Cilicia, the Dānis͟hmendid of Cappadocia (Michael, iii, 227). Around 1132 Leo captured Tarsus, Adana and Miṣṣīṣa from the Greeks (Chalandon, i, 235, ii, 108-109) (or from the Franks, according to Cahen, 354). He followed this up with the seizure of Sarvantikar, on the western flank of the Amanus. This led to a rupture with Raymond of Poitiers, count of Antioch, but the quarrel was patched up shortly afterwards when Leo was faced with a new Byzantine threat from the north, and as a token of reconciliation he ceded the plain of Cilicia to Raymond. John Comnenus invaded Cilicia in 1137, and regained all the towns except Anazarba, and in the following year took Leo and his son prisoner. Leo was carried off to Constantinople, where he died in 1142. Once more Cilicia was Byzantina, and remained so until Leo's son, Thoros, who had escaped from Constantinople after accession of Manuel Comnenus in 1143, regained a foothold in upper Cilicia; Thoros II (1145-1169) retook ʿAyn Zarba and the other towns in Cilicia in 1151-52, and defended them successfully against Masʿūd, the Sald̲j̲ūḳid of Konya, who fought at the instigation of Manuel Comnenus. Thoros also aided Reynald of Châtillon, count of Antioch, in his attack on Byzantine Cyprus. Manuel Comnenus, however, was not willing to allow the situation to deteriorate any further. In 1158 he invaded Cilicia, reoccupied all the towns, and reduced the country once more to a Byzantine province. The emperor's camp was established at Mard̲j̲ al-Dībād̲j̲ (Baltolibadi, north of Miṣṣīṣa; see Honigmann, *Ostgrenze*, 121, and Cahen, 152), and Reynald of Châtillon went there to tender his submission. Thoros, who had taken refuge at Vahka, north of Sīs on the upper Sayhān, subsequently did likewise, and in return the emperor made him governor of Miṣṣīṣa, ʿAyn Zarba and Vahka, bestowing on him the title of Sebastos. But in 1162, when his brother Sdefanè perished in an ambush laid by the Byzantine governor Andronicus Comnenus, Thoros once more raised the standard of revolt, and seized ʿAyn Zarba together with other Cilician towns. Amalric, king of Jerusalem, intervened to re-establish peace. In 1164 Thoros sided with the Franks in their conflict with Nūr al-Dīn. He died in 1169. His brother Mleh, whom he (Thoros) had exiled, rallied to the side of Nūr al-Dīn, and with the aid of the latter's troops regained possession of Cilicia and obtained official recognition by Manuel Comnenus. He was assassinated in 1175, and his nephew Ruben III succeeded him. The latter was driven by betrayal into the hands of Bohemond III of Antioch, and the price of his release, negotiated by his brother Leo with Hethoum (Hetʾum, Haythūm) of Lampron, was the cession of Miṣṣīṣa, Adana and Tell Ḥamdūn to Antioch. However, he recaptured them later. In 1187 he abdicated in favour of his brother Leo (1187-1198), who in 1198 became the first king of Armenia-Cilicia when crowned in Tarsus by the Catholicos and the papal delegate. It was in Leo's reign that Frederick Barbarossa's Crusade arrived in Cilicia. Frederick was drowned in the Calycadnus (Gök Su), and part of his forces returned to Germany. The remainder were greeted by Leo upon their arrival in Tarsus. His reign was marked by a long conflict with the Sald̲j̲ūḳid of Konya, Kaykāʾūs (1210-1219); the king's troops succeeded in taking the stronghold of Laranda (present-day Ḳaraman) in 1211, but as a consequence of their defeat in 1216 he had to cede Laranda, Luʾluʾa (in the Bozantı region, north of the Cilician Gates) and a part of Cilicia Trachea to the Sald̲j̲ūḳid (Grousset, iii, 266; *Documents arméniens*, i, 644). Another feature of Leo's reign was his constant attempt, after Bohemond's death in 1201, to secure the succession to Antioch for Raymond Ruben. Although Raymond was Bohemond's grandson, he was also the son of Leo's niece Alice, and moreover had been brought up in Armenia. But Raymond had a strong competitor in Bohemond IV, count of Tripoli, who had the support of al-Malik al-Ẓāhir of Aleppo, and Bohemond IV in the end triumphed.

After Leo's death in 1219, Raymond Ruben tried in vain to win possession of Cilicia. He was taken prisoner at a battle near Tarsus by the bailiff of Constantine, of the Lampron family, and died in captivity (1222). Philip, son of Bohemond IV and his wife Isabelle (Leo's daughter), was crowned his successor. But as he was considered too 'Frankish' and not sufficiently Armenian, he was arrested by Constantine and put to death by poison. This act was one of the reasons which provoked an intervention by ʿAlāʾ al-dīn Kayḳubād (1219-37). On the instigation of Bohemond IV, he laid waste the region of Upper Cilicia in 1225 and reduced Constantine to subjection. The latter persuaded the Hospitallers to give him their stronghold at Seleucia, which they had occupied ever since Leo had handed it over to them in 1210. In 1226 Constantine obtained the succession for his son Hethoum, who married Philip's widow Isabella.

Hethoum reigned until 1270, and from the bilingual coins minted under his and Kayḳubād's name we know that in the early years of his reign he acknowledged Salḏjūḳid suzerainty (de Morgan, *Histoire du peuple arménien*, 202-3). With other Muslim and Christian princes he took part in the struggle against Čingiz Khān, but when the Mongol general Bāydjū crushed the Salḏjūḳid Kayk̲h̲usraw in 1243, he transferred his obedience to the Mongols and surrendered them Kayk̲h̲usraw's mother, wife, and daughter. In consequence the Salḏjūḳids reacted sharply against Cilicia in 1245, and Hethoum was able to avert defeat only by summoning Mongol assistance. His position as a vassal of the Mongols was formalized on several occasions; in 1247 he dispatched the High Constable Sempad to Mongolia; in 1254 he paid a personal visit to the Mongolian court; he supplied Armenian contingents for the Mongolian expedition to Syria, and co-operated in the economic blockade of Egypt by withholding exports of Cilician timber (see Mas-Latrie, *Histoire de Chypre*, i, 412; Grousset, iii, 632). From that time onwards the Armeno-Cilician kingdom, or the land of Sīs as Arab historians call it, increasingly became the object of Mamlūk attacks, as the following examples bear witness: (i) 664/1266, a retaliatory expedition under Baybars captured, pillaged, and burnt down Sīs, Miṣṣīṣa, Adana, Ayās and Tarsus; (ii) 673/1275, another expedition by Baybars seized Miṣṣīṣa, Sīs, Tarsus and Ayās, and carried out raids into the Taurus; (iii) 682/1283, a campaign under Ḳalāʾūn against Alexandretta, Ayās and Tell Ḥamdūn; (iv) 697/1297, an expedition led by Ladjīn against Alexandretta, Tell Ḥamdūn, Sīs, Adana, Miṣṣīṣa, Nudjayma, etc., during which the strongholds were occupied and a tribute of 500,000 dirhams was imposed; (v) in 703/1303, as the payments had not been made regularly, and as the strongholds were firmly held, a new expedition forced the Armenians to pay the tribute in advance and conformed the surrender of the strongholds; (vi) 705/1305, as a result of further defaults in payment, a new expedition was launched, in which the Mongols rendered assistance to the Armenians and defeated the Mamlūks; but when Egyptian reinforcements arrived, the king had to pay; (vii) 715/1315, the tribute was raised to one million dirhams; (viii) 720/1320; (ix) 722/1322, Ayās was captured, and to the tribute were added 50% of the revenues from the Ayās customs authority and the sale of salt; (x) 735/1335, a further expedition following a reprisal raid by the populace of Ayās on the merchants of Bag̲h̲dād; (xi) 737/1337, a new expedition launched by Malik Nāṣir Muḥammad because payments of the tribute had stopped. It captured Sīs (destroying its citadel in the process) and secured surrender of the forts under the name al-Futūḥāt al-Djahāniyya (from the Armenian corruption of Djayhān). They included Miṣṣīṣa, Kawarrā, Hārūniyya, Sarvantikār, Bayās, Ayās, Nudjayma, and Ḥumaysa. Further raids were carried out in 756/1355 and 760/1359. The frequency of Mamlūk incursions indicates that they did not

consolidate their occupation of the country after each expedition. Then, in 776/1375, a final expedition brought the end of Sīs as an independent kingdom. Sīs itself fell to the Mamlūks, and Leo V was captured and was not released until 1382. The Armeno-Cilician kingdom became incorporated into the Mamlūk empire (on the above events see the following under relevant dates: al-Maḳrīzī, *Sulūk*, ed. Muṣṭafā Ziyāda, and Quatremère's translation, *Hist. des sult. maml.*; Mufaḍḍal b. Abi 'l-Faḍāʾil, trans. and ed. Blochet, *Patr. Or.* xii & xiv; Abu 'l-Fidāʾ and his continuator Ibn al-Wardī, Ibn Iyās, Ibn Kathīr, *Bidāya*, Abu 'l-Maḥāsin. See also note on the expeditions in *AIEO Alger*, 1939-41, 53-54, with other references, and G. Wiet, *L'Egypte arabe*, vol. iv of the *Histoire de la Nation égyptienne*, 417, 425, 449, 466, 475, 483-484. See also Zetterstéen, *Beiträge zur Geschichte der Mamluken Sultane*, index; the articles on MIṢṢĪṢ, ADANA, AYĀS, SĪS. For the relations between the Armenians and the Ḳaramān-og̲h̲lus, see the article ḲARAMĀN and F. Taeschner, *Al-Umarī's Bericht über Anatolien*, index).

A Mamlūk governor, the Turcoman Yüregirog̲h̲lu Ramaḍān, who established himself at Adana in 1378, inaugurated the small Ramaḍān-og̲h̲ullarī [*q.v.*] dynasty, nominally vassals of the Mamlūks. In 1467 Cilicia was invaded by S̲h̲āhsuwār, of the Dhu 'l-Ḳadr [*q.v.*] dynasty. Between 1485 and 1489 the Ottomans attempted to win control of Cilicia, but it was not until 1516 that they succeeded in doing so, Sulṭān Selim I capturing it during his expedition to Egypt. The Ramaḍān-og̲h̲ullarī were not removed from power however, and they remained vassals of the Ottomans until the end of the 16th century. Cilicia was then fully integrated into the Ottoman Empire. In 1833 Ibrāhīm Pas̲h̲a, the son of Meḥmet ʿAlī who had revolted against the Porte, carried out a victorious campaign in Cilicia, and the province was ceded to his father by the treaty of Kütahya. To this day traces of the campaign can be seen in the Cilician Gates. Cilicia was returned to Turkey in 1840 and became part of the vilayet of Aleppo. In 1866 a military force was sent from Istanbul to assert the authority of the central government over the local derebeys [*q.v.*] and tribal chiefs. This prepared the way for extensive agricultural settlement, which was accomplished in part with the help of Muslim migrants and repatriates from the Crimea and from the lost Ottoman territories in Europe and North Africa. (Djewdet Pas̲h̲a, *Maʿrūḍāt*, TTEM, no. 14/91, (1926), 117 ff.; W. Eberhard, *Nomads and Farmers in south eastern Turkey*; *problems of settlement*, Oriens, vi (1953), 32-49). It was occupied by French troops from 1918 to 1922, and handed back to Turkey by the Franco-Turkish treaty of Ankara. The plain of Cukurova is now one of the most flourishing agricultural areas in Turkey.

Bibliography: Apart from the works mentioned in the text, see, for the classical period, Wellhausen, *Die Kämpfe der Araber mit den Romäern in der Zeit der Umaijiden*, in NKGW Göttingen, Phil.-Hist. Kl., 1901, 414 ff. The texts of Ṭabarī, Yaʿḳūbī, Balād̲h̲urī, *Kitāb al-ʿUyūn*, etc., are translated by Brooks, *The Arabs in Asia Minor*, 641-750, *JHS*, xviii (1898), 162-206, xix (1899), 19-33, *Byzantine and Arabs in the time of the early Abbassids*, 750-813, *EHR*, xv (1900), 728-747, xvi (1901), 84-92. For the following period, until 959, see Vasiliev, *Byzance et les Arabes*, i, French ed., ii (in Russian), ii, pt. 2 (texts translated into French). For the Ḥamdānid period, M. Canard, *Sayf al-Daula, Recueil de textes*, Algiers 1934; idem,

Histoire de la dynastie des Hamdānides, i, Algiers 1951. For the Crusades and the period immediately preceding them, see Grousset's *Histoire des Croisades*, 3 vols., 1934-36; Runciman's *History of the Crusades*, 3 vols., 1951-4; works mentioned in the text above, by Chalandon, N. Iorga. *Brève histoire de la Petite Arménie-d'Armenie Cilicienne*; L. Laurent, de Morgan, Cl. Cahen (index); Michael the Syrian, *Chronique*, translated and edited by Chabot, Bar Hebraeus, *Chronography*, translated and edited by W. Budge, and the *Recueil des Historiens des Croisades* (western, Armenian and oriental historians). See the article ARMĪNIYA, with its map, which includes Cilicia (note that Cydnus and Tarsus have been wrongly located); and K. J. Barmadjian. map of Cilicia, 1 ; 800.000.; also see the articles ADANA, AYĀS, ʿAYN ZARBA, MIṢṢĪṢ, SĪS, ṬARSŪS, and their respective bibliographies. (M. CANARD)

ČILLA [see KHALWA]

ČIMKENT, chief town of the region of South Kazakhstān of the Soviet Socialist Republic of Kazakhstān, situated on the river Badām, which flows into the river Arîs, tributary of the Sîr-Daryā.

The town is mentioned in the *Ẓafar-nāma* of Sharaf al-Dīn Yazdī as a "village" near the city of Sayrām. After its capture by the Kalmüks in 1864, Sayrām declined to the advantage of Čimkent; but at the time of the Russian conquest (1281/1864) Čimkent was still only a fortified market-town, surrounded by a clay wall and dominated by a small citadel. According to the Russian census carried out a little after the conquest, the town comprised 756 houses.

On the eve of the October Revolution, Čimkent was mainly known as a summer resort frequented by the residents of Tāshkent on account of the mildness of its climate and the excellence of its water. It had in 1897 12,500 inhabitants, of whom 800 were Russians and 150 Jews. The environs of Čimkent included at the end of the 19th century numerous prosperous Russian villages and several native villages, of which the most important were Sayrām, and the Asbīdjāb or Asfīdjāb of the Arab geographers.

The very rapid development of the city dates from the Soviet period. In 1926 it comprised 21,000 inhabitants, in 1939 74,200 and in 1956 130,000. Čimkent is an important road centre at the junction of the roads which wend their way from Russia (by way of Aktübinsk and Ḳzyl-Orda) and from Siberia (by way of Alma-Ata) towards Tāshkent, and is an important railway junction where the Djambul-Arîs, Ḳzyl-Orda and Čimkent-Lenger railways intersect.

Before the Revolution Čimkent was an agricultural centre which subsisted principally from the plantations of cotton (introduced in 1897) and from the harvesting of the medicinal plant *artemisia cinae* from which santonin is prepared.

Since the discovery in 1932 of veins of lead at Ačisay and Karamazor, and of coal at Lenger, Čimkent has become an important industrial city (factories of chemical and pharmaceutical products, combined with non-ferrous metals). The city included in 1956 35 primary and secondary schools, 19 secondary technical schools and two colleges (the Teachers' Institute and the Technological Institute of Building Materials).

The population of the city is very mixed, the Russians now constituting the majority of the inhabitants; the Muslim community includes Kazakhs and some Özbeks. (CH. QUELQUEJAY)

ČĪN [see AL-ṢĪN]

CINEMA (*sīnimā*). History. Cinema is a newly imported art into the Muslim world; as such, it is a facet of the Western impact on the inhabitants and expresses their interest in Western technical achievements and forms of entertainment. Silent films were apparently first imported into Egypt by Italians (1897), attracting considerable interest. Film shows for Allied troops, during World War I, familiarized many Near Easterners with the cinema. The influx of foreign films, the construction of entertainment halls, and the intellectual curiosity of the local intelligentsia made Egypt the centre of film shows and afterwards of local production. Most films shown then in the Near East were comedies or Westerns; in Egypt, mainly the former were emulated. Local production by foreign technicians, with Egyptians starring, started on silent films (1917); despite their mediocrity, they were warmly received. Simultaneously, cinema clubs sprang up, which eagerly discussed film-techniques and published in Arabic short-lived cinematic periodicals. Full-length Egyptian silent films were first produced (1927) by, respectively, the directors Widād ʿUrfī and Lāma Brothers, at a minimum cost. All rather resembled photographed sequences of a play, but were nonetheless welcomed by the public. This success encouraged Yūsuf Wahbī to experiment with a sound film: he took to Paris, for synchronization, an Arab silent film, *Awlād al-dhawāt* (apparently patterned after Fr. Coppée's *Le coupable*), in which he himself had starred. Its enthusiastic reception in Egypt assured the future of the Arabic-speaking film. Arabic film production has been speeded up in the last generation. In 1934, the large *Studio Miṣr* was founded near Cairo; others followed. Halls were built, chiefly in the towns. Production was encouraged, during World War II, by the lack of Italian and German competition. Commercial success led to quantity predominating over quality; the resulting lower standards were due also to inexperience in direction and photography, and to shortage of technical equipment.

Acting and actors. Most Arab filmstars are in Egypt. Some former theatre actors or singers are idolized, *e.g.*, leadingmen: the late comedians ʿAlī al-Kassār and Nadjīb al-Riḥānī, the living Yūsuf Wahbī, protagonist of the "social" film on local themes. Some leading ladies can act in character roles; most others sing well.

Characteristics and Themes. The Arabic-speaking film has been, until recently, rather imitative of its European or American counterpart, but artistic and technical standards are generally lower. While in recent years the overriding importance of music has somewhat declined, it is still customary to introduce a sub-plot that includes vocal and instrumental Arabic music and dancing. Another drawback to the plot is the somewhat faulty script-writing, due to the limited experience of local actors-authors. While scripts adapted from foreign films, plays or novels (*e.g.*, *al-Buʾasāʾ* = *Les misérables*, with ʿAbbās Fāris) were usually successful, those frequently composed at the bid of a producer-actor have often resulted in an unimaginative plot. The main types of films are: *a.* the historical (generally on themes chosen from Arab or Islamic history; in Egypt—also from Pharaonic times). *b.* the social drama or melodrama (once popular for its tear-jerking appeal, later for its social aims). *c.* the musical. *d.* the comedy or slapstick farce (usually on local background). *e.* adventure and detective films. The first two are the best, artistically. Colloquial Arabic (Egyptian dialect) is employed in most.

Attitudes. While encouraging the cinema financially, to a degree, Arab governments have supervised and censored it. Censorship has been on socio-political lines, often also on moral and religious grounds. Pressure of Muslim religious circles prevented filming a script on Muḥammad and the Four Caliphs (Egypt); on other occasions, it has opposed love films (Egypt), attendance of adolescents (Jordan) and women (Syria, Jordan). Conservative circles still regard acting as lewd. Features, documentaries and educational films have been initiated by the United Arab Republic for propaganda amongst civilians and soldiers.

The Arab countries. Outside Egypt, there is little film production. Morocco and Tunisia produce short films and occasional newsreels. Similar experiments in Syria and, more recently, in ʿIrāḳ, were short-lived. With few exceptions, most rural and lower urban audiences, in Arabic-speaking communities, prefer Egyptian films. Yemen imports very few films, while Saudi Arabia has banned their public showing on ethical grounds.

Other countries. The above applies, in varying degrees, to other Muslim countries too. In most, a part of the film production and distribution is in governmental hands, particularly documentaries and educational films. Legislation in most provides for censorship on national and political grounds (internal tranquillity, avoiding offence to friendly States), as well as religious succeptibilities and public morals. Turkey appears to have the most active film industry, although most films shown are American. Educational films are provided gratis to cinema owners (who must exhibit them). Good feature-films on local themes have been produced, with marked American influence (*e.g.*, *Ebediyete kadar*). Belly-dancing (of the Arabic-film type) and music continue, however, as an integral part of many films. Iran has started its own film production in Tehran only since 1945, on a modest scale. Most feature-films are comedies or have simple plots, often describing the rich city heir who falls in love with the peasant girl; kissing on the screen is discouraged. Sub-titling of foreign films or post-synchronizing them in Persian (the latter very efficiently done) is compulsory. In addition to other cinema halls, in Teheran a cinema club holds regular showings of good foreign films for its members and friends. In Afghanistan, the Government has established, by decree, a State monopoly of the cinema. There is no film production. Cinema halls are in Ḳābul and Ḳandahār. Women hardly ever go to the cinema, unless it is for rare private showings, specially arranged for them. Pakistan. Before partition, Indians controlled production and exhibition, as well as all technical work; their departure left Pakistan with hardly any film industry. Eventually this rallied and Pakistani companies now produce full-length and short films; their main studios are in Lahore. Urdū films are also made in India. In Indonesia, a Government-controlled company produces a few feature-films annually, as well as a weekly newsreel and some documentaries and short educational films. Private companies produce only few feature-films. Indonesia-produced films are exported to Singapore, Malaya and North Borneo.

Bibliography: Y. Fārigh, *Nigāhī bi-sīnimā-yi Īrānī*, in *Ṣadaf*, Ābān 1336 s./1957, 118-126; M. Haïrabèdian, *Les films égyptiens et ceux de Hollywood*, Paris 1950; J. M. Landau, *The Arab cinema*, in *Middle Eastern Affairs*, iv, Nov. 1953, 349-358; idem, *Studies in the Arab theater and cinema*, Philadelphia 1958; Badr Nashʾat & Fatḥī Zakī, *Muḥākamat al-film al-miṣrī ʿarḍ wa-naḳd al-sīnimā ʾl-miṣriyya mundh nashʾatihā*, n. p., 1957; J. Swanson, *Mudhakkarāt muʾassis ṣināʿat al-sīnimā fī Miṣr* (serial in *Dunyā ʾl-kawākib*, 1953-1954); *Tournée officielle de la nouvelle troupe égyptienne sous la direction de Youssef Wahbi*, n. p., n.d., [1955?]; Zakī Ṭulaymāt, *Khayṭ min al-fann al-sīnimāʾī fī Miṣr*, in *al-Kitāb*, i, Jan. 1946, 415-422; UNESCO, *Reports of the commission on technical needs. Press film radio*, ii-v & Suppl. ii, Paris 1948-1952; *Sinema Tiyatro*, Ankara (monthly). (J. M. Landau)

ČINGĀNE, one of the names applied to the gipsies in the east, which has passed into various European languages (*e.g.*, Hungarian *Czigány*, French *Tsigane*, Italian *Zingari*, German *Zigeuner*) and appears in Turkish as *Čingene*. The origin of the name is still uncertain; one suggestion is that it comes from Čangar or Zingar, said to be the name of a people formerly dwelling on the banks of the Indus. It is supposed that the Sāsānid Bahrām V Gūr (420-438 A.D.) first brought the gipsies from India to Persia, and that they spread thence over the world. In the relevant passages in Firdawsī and Ḥamza Iṣpahānī these Indians are called Lūlī or Zoṭṭ [*qq.v.*]. Other names commonly used are Nawar in Syria, Ghurbat or Ḳurbat in Syria, Persia, Egypt and elsewhere. In Egypt the name Ghadjar is also in use, while the gipsies of Egypt are fond of calling themselves Barāmika (descendants of the Barmakids).

Although the Indian origin of the gipsies is now generally accepted, various groups of them have long claimed Egypt as their earliest home; hence their English name, and hence too the Spanish *Gitano*, French *Gitane*, Turkish *Kipti* and Hungarian *Faraonépe*. The term *Bohémien*, by which they are also known in France, is due to their having first come to that country via Bohemia. Other names may be found in the works of Anastase, De Goeje and Gökbilgin cited below. Their name for themselves in their own language is Romany, the adjective of *rom*, 'man'.

As in other countries, the gipsies of the east are smiths, tinkers, pedlars, jugglers, musicians and bear-trainers; some are sedentary while others lead a wandering life. The sedentaries are generally despised by those who adhere to the old ways.

No reliable statistics about them exist, but they are certainly quite numerous in Persia and Turkey. It has been fairly conclusively shown (by G. L. Lewis; see *Bibliography*) that one tribe of 'Yürüks' in western Anatolia is in fact gipsy, and it seems likely that other Turkish gipsies are similarly hiding behind this blanket-term.

Some gipsies are nominally Christian, others nominally Muslim (thus the Geygellis are said to be ʿAlewī but not to intermarry with other ʿAlewīs); in reality they have their own religion and political organization, which need not be discussed here; a useful short account will be found in Funk and Wagnall's *Standard Dictionary of Folklore*, s.v. Romany Folklore.

Bibliography: A. G. Paspati, *Études sur les Tchingianés ou Bohémiens de l'Empire Ottoman*, Constantinople 1870; P. Bataillard, *Sur les Origines des Bohémiens ou Tsiganes*, Paris 1876; Miklosich, *Über die Mundarten und die Wanderungen der Zigeuner Europa's*, Vienna 1872-80;

P. Anastase in *Mas͟hriḳ* 1902; De Goeje, *Mémoires d'histoire et de géographie orientales*, no. 3 . . . . .; R. A. Stewart Macalister, *Language of the Nawar or Zutt, the Nomad Smiths of Palestine*, London 1914; W. R. Halliday, *The Gypsies of Turkey* (Chapter I in his *Folklore Studies Ancient and Modern*), London 1924; R. L. Turner, *The position of Romani in Indo Aryan*, Gypsy Lore Socy. Monograph iv, London 1927; Köprülü-zâde Mehmet Fuad, *Türk halk edebiyatı ansiklopedisi*, article Abdal, Istanbul 1935; G. L. Lewis, *The Secret Language of the Geygelli Yürüks*, in *Zeki Velidi Togan'a Armağan*, Istanbul 1955; *İA*, s.v. Çingeneler (by M. Tayyib Gökbilgin); articles in *Journal of the Gypsy Lore Socy., passim*. (G. L. Lewis)

In the Soviet Union Čingānes are found in the Crimea, in Ād͟harbayd͟jān and in Central Asia. The census of 1926 gave a number of 4,000 Muslims out of the 61,294 gipsies included in the census, but it is probable that the real figure is higher. S. A. Tokarev (*Étnografiya Narodov SSSR*, Moscow 1958) estimates the number of Muslim gipsies in Central Asia at 5,000, and that of Ād͟harbayd͟jān as "some thousands". According to the statistics of 1926, there were at that time 3,710 Muslim gipsies still in Özbekistān, 300 in Turkmenistān, and an indeterminate number, probably quite high, in the region of Kuliāb and in the Soviet Socialist Republic of Tād͟jīkistān.

The Čingānes of the Soviet Union comprise several groups, which are fairly distinct from each other by their language and customs. They are known either by local names: "Karačī", "Lülī", "Mazang", "D͟jugī", "Kavol", or by names of trades: Zargarān, Kāsagarān, Mard͟jān-furūs͟h. They call themselves "*lom*" or "*dom*". The Lülī and the D͟jugī live in Özbekistān and speak mainly Persian (Tād͟jīkī); a Turkish-speaking minority speak Özbek. The gipsies of Ād͟harbayd͟jān (Karačī) and Kuliāb (Kavol) speak only Persian. A group from the region of Kuliāb still uses a distinctive language of its own which has not yet been studied, and which I. M. *Oranskiy* (*Indoyazičnaya etnografičeskaya gruppa "AFGON" v Sredney Aziy*, in *Sov. Etn.*, no. 2, 1956, 117-124) considers to be an Indian dialect. Their Tād͟jīk neighbours call them 'Afg͟hāns', and wrongly confuse them with the latter, who are quite numerous in the southern part of the Kuliāb region. According to Oranskiy and Tokarev the D͟jugī, the Lülī, and the Mazang still use a 'secret language'. The gipsies of Central Asia and of the Crimea are theoretically Sunnīs and those of Ād͟harbayd͟jān S͟hīʿīs.

(Ch. Quelquejay)

ČINGIZ-K͟HĀN, the founder of the Mongol world-empire, was born in 1167 A.D. on the right bank of the Onon in the district of Deli'ün-Boldoḳ in the present-day Chita Region in eastern Siberia. The ultimate sources for the details of his early life are two Mongolian works, the *Secret History of the Mongols*, composed in 1240 (or perhaps as late as 1252), and the *Altan Debter* or "Golden Book", the official history of the Imperial family. This latter work has not survived in the original, but the greater part of it is reproduced in the *D͟jāmiʿ al-Tawārīk͟h* of Ras͟hīd al-Dīn and there is likewise an abridged Chinese translation, the *Shêng-wu chʿin-chêng lu* or "Account of the Campaigns of Čingiz-K͟hān", composed some time before 1285. There is naturally in both sources a great deal of purely legendary material. The *Secret History* begins with a long genealogy in which Čingiz-K͟hān's line of descent is traced back through many generations to the union of a grey wolf and a white doe; and in both authorities the new-born child is represented as clutching in his hand, in token as it were of his future career as a world-conqueror, a clot of blood of the size of a knuckle-bone.

Čingiz-K͟hān's father, Yesügei, was the nephew of Ḳutula, the last k͟hān or ruler of the Mongols proper, who were afterwards to give their name to all the Mongolian-speaking peoples. The Mongols had been the dominant tribe in Eastern Mongolia during the first half of the 12th century but had been forced to yield place to the Tatar, a tribe in the region of the Buir Nor, who in 1161, in alliance with the Chin rulers of Northern China, had inflicted a crushing defeat upon them. Though now leaderless and disorganized the Mongols still continued the struggle against the Tatar, for we find that at the time of Čingiz-K͟hān's birth his father had brought in two Tatar chieftains as prisoners of war. One of these was called Temüd͟jin-Üke and it was after him that Čingiz-K͟hān received his original name of Temüd͟jin. The word means "blacksmith" and this gave rise to the legend, already current at the time of William of Rubruck, that the world-conqueror had begun his career at the forge.

When Temüd͟jin was nine years old his father, following the exogamous practice of the Mongols, took the boy with him upon a journey into the extreme east of Mongolia to find him a bride amongst his mother's people, the Ḳonḳirat. According to the custom Yesügei left his son to be brought up in the tent of his future father-in-law, whose daughter, the 10-year old Börte, was destined to be the mother and grandmother of Emperors. Upon the homeward journey Yesügei fell in with a party of carousing Tatar. Unable to refuse the invitation to share in their feast he was recognized by his former enemies, who poisoned his food; and he lived only long enough to reach his own encampment and dispatch a messenger to fetch back Temüd͟jin from the Ḳonḳirat.

With Yesügei's death his family was deserted by his followers under the instigation of the Taičiʿut, a clan with aspirations to the leadership of the tribe. His widow, a woman of spirit, attempted, at first with some success, to rally the people to her; but in the end she and her young children were left to their own resources in the expectation that they would die of starvation. They survived however upon a diet of roots and berries eked out with such fish as Temüd͟jin and his brothers were able to catch in the Onon and such small prairie birds and animals as they were able to shoot with their bows and arrows. It was in a quarrel over game of this sort that Temüd͟jin is said to have been involved in the murder of one of his half-brothers.

He had grown almost into manhood when the Taiči'ut, learning of the family's survival, made a raid upon the little encampment with the object of seizing Temüd͟jin and preventing any possibility of his succeeding to his father's position. He escaped into the forests and for some days eluded his pursuers. When finally captured he was not put to death but was kept as a perpetual prisoner, the Taiči'ut taking him with them from encampment to encampment with a *cangue* or wooden collar about his neck. One evening, when they were feasting along the bank of the Onon, he made off in the dark and, to avoid detection, submerged himself in the river with only his face above water. When the pursuit started his hiding-place was discovered by a member of a kindred tribe, who however befriended the young man and saved him from immediate danger by persuading the Taiči'ut to postpone their search till the morning. In the meanwhile Temüdjin found his way to the tent of his benefactor, who concealed him once again from his enemies and then provided him with the means of escape.

It was soon after this adventure that Temüdjin bethought himself of the bride awaiting him in Eastern Mongolia and he paid a visit to the Ḳonḳirat to lay claim to her. Börte brought him as her entire dowry a black sable skin, a circumstance worthy of mention, since with this sable skin Temüdjin was to lay the foundations of his future fortune. He offered it as a present to Toghrïl, the ruler of the Kereyt, a Nestorian Christian tribe, whose territory lay along the banks of the Tula in the region of the present-day Ulan Bator. Toghrïl, better known to history as Ong-Khān (he is the Prester John of Marco Polo), had been the *anda* or blood-brother of Temüdjin's father. He expressed his pleasure at the gift and took the young man under his protection. Not long passed before Temüdjin had need of his patron's assistance. The Merkit, a forest tribe on the southern shores of Lake Baikal in what is to-day the Buryat A.S.S.R., raided Temüdjin's encampment and carried off his newly married bride. With the aid of Toghrïl and Djamuḳa, a young Mongol chieftain, who was his own *anda*, Temüdjin was able to defeat the Merkit in battle and to recover his wife. For a time, after this campaign, Temüdjin and Djamuḳa remained firm friends, pitching their tents and herding their animals side by side; but then an estrangement arose between them and they parted company. The reason for this estrangement is not clear but Barthold's theory, according to which Temüdjin represented the Mongol aristocracy whilst Djamuḳa was the champion of the common people, no longer finds acceptance.

It was immediately following the break with Djamuḳa that the Mongol princes acclaimed Temüdjin as their *khān* and conferred upon him the title by which he is known to history: Čingiz-Khān or, in its Anglicized form, Genghis Khan. The meaning of this title is not clear. The most likely interpretation is that offered by Pelliot, who sees in Čingiz a palatalised form of the Turkish *tengiz* "sea" and translates the title accordingly as "Oceanic Khān", *i.e.*, "Universal Ruler". It is not without significance in this connexion that when shortly afterwards Djamuḳa set himself at the head of a rival confederation of tribes he received the title of Gür-Khān,. which also means something like "Universal Ruler".

With his elevation to the Khānate of his tribe Čingiz-Khān was now a power to be reckoned with in the domestic wars of the Mongol peoples. In 1196 his patron Toghrïl was expelled from his throne and was for a time an exile at the court of the Ḳara-Khitay. He owed his restoration, in 1198, to the intervention of Čingiz-Khān. In the same year both rulers were the allies of the Chin in an expedition against the Tatar. For their contribution to the Chinese victory Toghrïl received the title of *wang* or "prince", whence his name of Ong-Khan, and Čingiz-Khān a much lesser title. In 1199 Čingiz-Khān and Ong-Khān launched a joint attack on the Nayman, a largely Christian tribe, apparently of Turkish origin, in Western Mongolia. The success of this campaign was nullified by the pusillanimous conduct of Ong-Khān, who first of all deserted Čingiz-Khān on the eve of a battle and then had to appeal for aid from his protégé when himself attacked by the Nayman. Despite this experience the two princes remained allies and on several occasions in 1201 and 1202 defeated the confederation of tribes headed by Čingiz-Khān's former friend Djamuḳa. In 1202 Čingiz-Khān took his final revenge upon his old enemies the Tatar in a campaign which resulted in their total extermination as a people. Meanwhile his relations with Ong-Khān had been steadily worsening and it now came to open war. The first battle was indecisive and seems in effect to have been a defeat for Čingiz-Khān, who withdrew for a while into the extreme N.E. of Mongolia to a lake or river called Baldjuna, the identity of which has not been satisfactorily established. He soon rallied however and in a second battle (1203) gained an overwhelming victory over his opponent. Ong-Khān fled westwards to meet his death at the hands of a Nayman frontier guard, and the Kereyt ceased to exist as a people, being forcibly absorbed into the Mongols.

Čingiz-Khān was now in complete control of eastern and central Mongolia. Only in the west, where the Nayman had been joined by Djamuḳa and the Merkit chieftain Toḳto'a, was his supremacy still challenged. Forestalling an attack by his enemies Čingiz-Khān defeated them in a battle in which the Nayman ruler lost his life (1204). His son, Küčlüg, fled westwards, along with the Merkit Toḳto'a, to make a last desperate stand on the upper reaches of the Irtish: Toḳto'a was killed by a stray arrow and Küčlüg, continuing his flight westwards, was granted asylum in the territory of the Ḳara-Khitay. Djamuḳa, meanwhile, deserted by his followers, had been betrayed into the hands of Čingiz-Khān, who, with the execution of his one-time *anda*, at last found himself the absolute master of Mongolia. At a *ḳuriltay* or assembly of the Mongol princes held near the sources of the Onon in the spring of 1206 he caused himself to be proclaimed supreme ruler of all the Mongol peoples. Having also at this *ḳuriltay* reorganized his military forces he was now in a position to embark upon foreign conquests.

Already in 1205 he had attacked the kingdom of the Tangut or Hsi Hsia, a people of Tibetan origin who inhabited the region of the great bend in the Yellow River, *i.e.*, what is now the province of Kansu and the Ordos Region. Two further campaigns (in 1207 and 1209) reduced the Tangut to the status of tributaries and the way lay open for an assault upon North China proper. In 1211 the Mongols invaded and overran the whole area north of the Great Wall, but the Wall itself presented a barrier to further advance. In the following year their cause was promoted by the rising of a Khitan prince in southern Manchuria; and in the summer of 1213 they finally forced their way through the Wall and spread out over the North China plain. By the spring of 1215 they controlled the whole area north of the Yellow River and were converging from three directions upon Pekin. The Chin Emperor was now offered and accepted terms of peace and secured the withdrawal of the Mongol forces by the payment of tribute which consisted, in effect, in the immense dowry of a Chin princess bestowed in marriage upon Čingiz-Khān. Circumstances however led to the Mongols' almost immediate return. Pekin was captured and sacked (summer of 1215), and the Emperor fled to Kʻai-fêng on the southern banks of the Yellow River. Though the war still continued —and, in fact, the subjugation of North China was not finally completed until 1234, seven years after Čingiz-Khān's death—Čingiz-Khān now left the command of operations in the hands of one of his generals, Muḳali of the Djalayir tribe, and, in the summer of 1216 returned to his headquarters in Mongolia, there to turn his attention to events in Central and Western Asia.

Küčlüg the Nayman, who had sought refuge with the Ḳara-Khitay, had dethroned the last of their rulers and made himself master of their territories. In 1218 a Mongol army under the famous general Djebe invaded Semirechye and Sinkiang and pursued Küčlüg from Kashghār over the Pamirs into Badakhshān, where with the co operation of the local population he was captured and put to death.

The accession of Semirechye and Sinkiang to his Empire gave Čingiz-Khan a common frontier with Sulṭān Muḥammad Khwārizm-Shāh [*q.v.*]. Relations between the two rulers had been established already in 1215, when Čingiz-Khān had received an embassy from the Sultan before Pekin. In 1216, or more probably in 1219, a battle took place to the N.E. of the Aral Sea between a force commanded by Sulṭān Muḥammad and a Mongol army led by Čingiz-Khān's eldest son Djoči which was returning from a successful campaign against the remnants of the Merkit. The encounter was indecisive and does not in any case seem to have contributed to the ultimate outbreak of hostilities. This was the result of the execution, ordered by the governor of Otrar, of an ambassador of Čingiz-Khān and a caravan of Muslim merchants accompanying him, a massacre apparently sanctioned by the Sultan himself. A second ambassador sent by Čingiz-Khān to demand satisfaction was likewise executed; and war became inevitable. Massing his forces on the Irtish in the spring of 1219, Čingiz-Khān had by the autumn of that year arrived before the walls of Otrar. He left a detachment under the command of his sons Čaghatay and Ögedey to lay siege to the town, at the same time sending Djoči upon an expedition down the Sir-Daryā, whilst he himself with the main army advanced upon Bukhārā. Abandoned by its defenders, the town surrendered after a siege of only three days (first half of February, 1220). Samarḳand, the next objective, offered as little resistance: it fell on 10 Muḥarram/19 March. Otrar had already capitulated and the besiegers of that town took part in the capture of Samarḳand.

From Samarḳand Čingiz-Khān dispatched his two best generals, Djebe and Sübetey, in pursuit of Sulṭān Muḥammad, who upon receiving news of the Mongols' rapid advance had fled panic-stricken to the West. Doubling backwards and forwards across Persia the Sultan finally found refuge in an island off the eastern shores of the Caspian, where he died, it was said, of a broken heart. The generals continued their westward drive and passing through Ādharbaydjān and over the Caucasus descended into the steppes of what is now Southern Russia to defeat an army of Russians and Ḳipčaḳ on the River Kalka in the Crimea. They then returned along the northern shores of the Caspian to rejoin Čingiz-Khān in Central Asia.

Čingiz-Khān meanwhile had passed the summer of 1220 resting his men and animals in the pastures of the Nakhshab area. In the autumn he captured Tirmidh and then proceeded up the Oxus to spend the winter of 1220-1 in the conduct of operations in the region of the present-day Stalinabad, as also in Badakhshān. Early in 1221 he crossed the Oxus and captured Balkh. Already after the capture of Samarḳand he had dispatched Čaghatay and Ögedey northwards to lay siege to Sulṭān Muḥammad's capital at Gurgandj. He now sent Toluy, his youngest son, to complete the conquest of Khurāsān, a task he accomplished with a thoroughness from which that province has never recovered. At Marw there were massacred according to Ibn al-Athīr a total of 700,000 men, women and children, whilst Djuwaynī gives the incredible figure of 1,300,000. As for Nīshāpūr, "it was commanded", says Djuwaynī, "that the town should be laid waste in such a manner that the site could be ploughed upon; and that in the exaction of vengeance [for the death of a Mongol prince] not even cats and dogs should be left alive". After the capture of Harāt Toluy rejoined his father, who was laying siege to the town of Ṭālaḳān between Balkh and Marw ar-Rūdh (not to be confused with another town of similar name, the present-day Ṭālikhān in the Afghān province of Badakhshān).

The summer of 1221 Čingiz-Khān passed in the mountains to the south of Balkh. In the meantime Djalāl al-Dīn, the son of Sulṭān Muḥammad, had made his way to Ghazna and at Parwān to the N.E. of Čārīkār had inflicted a crushing defeat upon the Mongol force dispatched against him, the only reverse suffered by the Mongols during the whole campaign. Čingiz-Khān, upon receiving news of this battle, advanced southwards at great speed in pursuit of Sulṭān Djalāl al-Dīn, whom he finally overtook on the banks of the Indus. Hemmed in on three sides by the Mongol armies and with the river behind him Djalāl al-Dīn, after offering desperate resistance, plunged into the water and swam to the farther side, surviving to conduct sporadic warfare against the Mongols for three years after Čingiz-Khān's death.

The Battle of the Indus, which took place according to Nasawī on the Shawwal 618/24th November 1221, marks the end of Čingiz-Khān's campaign in the West. He began to prepare for the homeward journey and having explored the possibility of returning though India via Assam and Tibet finally turned back along the route he had been following. He travelled by easy stages, spending the summer of 1222 in mountain pastures on the Hindū-Kush and the following winter in the neighbourhood of Samarḳand. The spring and summer of 1223 he passed in the region of the present-day Tashkent; in the summer of the following year he was on the upper reaches of the Irtish; and it was only in the spring of 1225 that he finally reached his headquarters in Mongolia.

In the autumn of the following year he was again at war with the Tangut, but did not live to see the victorious outcome of this final campaign. He died on 25 August 1227 whilst resting in his summer quarters in the district of Chʿing-shui on the Hsi River in Kansu. The authorities give no clear indication as to the cause of his death but a fall from his horse which he sustained whilst hunting during the previous winter may well have been a contributory factor.

Of his personal appearance there appears to have survived only one contemporary record, that of Djūzdjānī, who describes him as being at the time of his invasion of Khurāsān "a man of tall stature and vigorous build, robust in body, the hair on his face scanty and turned white, with cat's eyes".

Bibliography: Of the *Secret History of the Mongols* there is a Russian translation by S. A. Kozin (Leningrad 1941), a German translation by Erich Haenisch (2nd ed., Leipzig 1948), a Turkish translation by Ahmet Temir (Ankara 1948), an incomplete French translation by Paul Pelliot

(Paris 1949), and an English translation by F. W. Cleaves (Cambridge, Mass. 1960). Of a French translation of the *Shêng-wu chʿin-chêng lu* by Paul Pelliot and Louis Hambis (*Histoire des Campagnes de Genghis Khan*) only the first volume has so far appeared (Leiden 1951). See also Haenisch, *Die letzten Feldzüge Cinggis Han's und sein Tod nach der ostasiatischen Überlieferung*, in *Asia Major*, ix (1933). Djuwaynī's history is now available in the translation of J. A. Boyle (*The History of the World-Conqueror*, 2 vols., Manchester 1958) and the relevant portions of Rashīd al-Dīn in the translations of A. A. Khetagurov and O. I. Smirnova (*Sbornik letopisei*, i, 1, and i, 2, Moscow 1952). See also René Grousset, *Le Conquérant du Monde* (Paris 1944).

(J. A. Boyle)

ČINGIZIDS, the four sons of Čingiz Khān [*q.v.*] by his marriage with his favourite wife Börte, and their descendants. In contrast to them Čingiz Khān's brothers and their sons, as well as the descendents of Čingiz Khān by other marriages, were of importance only in the first decades of the Mongol Empire, after which they fell into the background.

In accordance with the will of Čingiz Khān, the empire conquered by him (including the parts whose acquisition had not yet been accomplished and which did not in fact take place until 1236/42 or 1255/59) was divided among his four sons: I) Djoči (Djöči), who may not have been a real descendent of Čingiz Khān (see further Čingiz Khān); II) Čaghatāy (Djaghatāy); III) Ögedey (Ögödäy, Ogotay, Pers. Ūk/gadāy); IV) Toluy (Tuluy, cf. these articles).

I) Djoči died before his father, in about February 1227. His legacy (Ulus), the Ḳipčaḳ Plain and West Siberia (including Khwārizm) passed to his descendants. These were in part as early as the 13th century (Berke [*q.v.*]), and certainly by the first half of the 14th century, Muslims (Sunnī), and played an extraordinary role in the spread of Islam.

A) His second son Batu (d. 1255) took over the Ḳipčāḳ Plain and founded the empire of the Golden Horde. His descendants ruled there until 1360 (for details cf. Bātūʾids, with a genealogical table).

B) After 16 years' confusion the rule of the Golden Horde 1376. passed to the descendants of Batu's older brother Orda, who had taken control of the so-called "White Horde" in Western Siberia. Little is known about him, his immediate descendants and the situation in that region. After the two year rule of his seventh generation descendants Urus Khan and two of his sons, Toḳtamïsh [*q.v.*] finally appears in the full light of history. Expelled by Tīmūr [*q.v.*] in 798/1395, four of his sons were later (815-822/1412-1419) able to assert themselves as nominal rulers of the Golden Horde (apart from the *major domus* Edigü, Russ. Yedigey, d. 1419, who exercised actual power). Since that time (and already from 1395 of 1412) the progeny of Urus Khān ruled as Khāns.

After 842/1438 the territory of the Golden Horde dissolved into several separate states in which descendants of Čingiz Khān likewise ruled:

a) The "Great Horde" in which a great-great grandson of Urus Khān, Küčük Meḥmed (Muḥammad), assumed power about 1438, and whose descendents were able to retain it until 908/1502.

b) The Khānate of Astrakhān [*q.v.*] where successors of Küčük Meḥmed ruled until 965/1557.

C) Parallel to that the descendants of a hitherto insignificant third line, that of Bātū's and Orda's brother Togha Temür (Tūḳā Tīmūr), managed to share in the dismemberment of the Ḳipčaḳ. Of these, the following succeeded:

c) Ulugh Meḥmed (murdered in 850/1446), after his expulsion from the "Great Horde", to the Khānate of Ḳazan (Russ. Kazán [*q.v.*]) which his successors (among whom were the princes of Kasimov, see "e") lost in 960/1552 to the Russians.

d) Ulugh Meḥmed's nephew, Hādjdjī Girāy ([*q.v.*]; d. 870/1466), held fast (definitively in 1449) to the Crimea (see Ḳïrïm) where his successors, under the dynastic name Girāy, ruled as the last descendants of Čingiz Khān in Europe, until the annexation of the Crimea by the Russians in 1783.

e) In the small Tatar principality of Kasimov ([*q.v.*], region of Ryazań), various princes (finally a princess) of the line of Ulugh Meḥmed (see ,'c"), of Küčük Meḥmed (see "a"), of Girāy (see "d"), and of the Siberian Shaybānids (cf. "E d") ruled between 856-861/1452-56 and about 1092/1681. Some of them (including the last ruler) became converted to Orthodox Christianity and became the forefathers of Russian noble families.

f) Descendants of the branch ruling in Astrakhān (see 'b") had fled after the Russian conquest to the Shaybānids in Bukhārā (see "E a"). One of them, Prince Djān b. Yār Muḥammad, married the daughter of the Shaybānid Khān Iskandar (968-991/1560-83). After the extinction of the male line of the Bukhārā dynasty in 1006/1598, their son Bāḳī Muḥammad assumed the rule of the land. The new dynasty was called "Astrakhānid", "Ashtarkhanid" or "Djānid" [*q.v.*], and ruled in Bukhārā [*q.v.*] until their displacement in 1200/1785 by the House of Mangit [*q.v.*].

D) Among the descendants of a further son of Djoči, Moghol (or Tewal?; P. Pelliot, Notes 52/54 considers "Boal" better), his grandson Noghay ([*q.v.*]; Mongol "Nokhay" 'dog') played a significant role as *major domus* for several rulers of the Golden Horde, until he was killed in a civil war in 699/1299. His descendants are known for a further two generations before they disappear. — Apparently the Nokhay people [*q.v.*] is called after him.

E) Finally, the descendants of Djoči's youngest son Shiban (Arabicized "Shaybān") lived originally in the region southeast of the Urals (somewhere between the source of the Tobol in the west and the Upper Irtïsh in the east, modern Ḳazakhstān) where they preserved their nomadic life. When the inhabitants of Orda's "White Horde" under Toḳtamïsh migrated far into the Ḳipcaḳ Plain, the Shaybānids [*q.v.*] occupied their territory, and the peoples under their rule came to be called Özbek (*q.v.*]; Russ. Uzbek). Of Shiban's descendents, the Shaybānids, Abu 'l-Khayr ([*q.v.*], i, 135) expelled in 851/1447 the Tīmūrids [*q.v.*] from Khwārizm [*q.v.*] and in the region north of the Sïr Dārya [*q.v.*]. He ruled the area from there to the neighbourhood of Tobol'sk, but was weakened by the devastating attacks of the Oirats ([*q.v.*]; Kalmuks) into his territory as well as by the struggles with the Ḳazakhs [*q.v.*] and died in 873/1468. His grandson Muḥammad Shaybānī [*q.v.*] conquered Transoxania in 906/1500, where he broke the rule of the Tīmūrids, penetrating finally into modern Afghānistān [*q.v.*] as well as Khurāsān [*q.v.*]. The founder of the Ṣafawid dynasty [*q.v.*], Ismāʿīl I [*q.v.*] managed to expel him from there and to defeat him near Marw in 916/1510, where Muḥammad Shaybānī was killed. With that move, the power of the Čingizids was restricted to the area north of the Amū Daryā, and of this to a frontier zone between Persian Shīʿī and Turkish Sunnī influence (not without isolated shifts in both directions in the course of time).

The reign of the Shaybānids endured in Transoxania, where they ruled:

a) until 1007/1598 in Bukhārā, where the ruling family died out with ʿAbd Allāh II ([*q.v.*], i, 46 ff.; 991-1007/1583-98). The Djānids succeeded (see "C f").

b) in Khwārizm [*q.v.*], later called for the most part Khīwa, which had fallen in 911-912/1505-6 to Muḥammed Shaybānī, the tributary line of the ʿArabshāhids succeeded in 911/1512 in the person of Ilbars I (1512-25). To this line belongs the famous historian Abu 'l-Ghāzī Bahādur Khān ([*q.v.*], i, 120 ff.; 1053-1076/1643-65), the author of the "Shadjarat al-Atrāk". The line ruled until 1106-7/1694-95, when the power passed to the erstwhile "Condottieri" (Inaḳ) of the Ḳungrat family [*q.v.*] who after 1219/1804 called themselves "Khān".

c) A further branch of the Shaybānids under Shāh Rukh I, a descendent of Abu 'l-Khayr, established himself in Farghāna [*q.v.*] in 1122/1710. He founded the Khānate of Khoḳand [*q.v.*] which was annexed in 1876 by the Russians.

d) Finally in 886/1481 the Shaybānid prince Ibak (d. 899/1493) was able to wrest the neighbourhood of the town of Tümen (Russ. Tyumeń) from the hands of the Khān of Sibir (who was not a Čingizid). In 973/1565 his grandson Ḳučum expelled the last Khān of Sibir [*q.v.*] and put down his successors, though after 1579 found himself oppressed by Russian attacks and gradually pushed out of his territory, until he had to flee to the Noghays after a defeat on the Ob′ in 1007/1598, dying there in 1009/1600. His son Ishim Khān managed to hold out on the Upper Tobol′ until about 1035/1625.

e) Kasimov (cf. "C e").

II) The descendants of the second son Čaghatāy ([*q.v.*], d. 640/1242) persisted for almost as long, managing to hold their ground against the descendents of Ögedey (see III) in the 7th/13th century, and to win out against them in 700/1309 [See ČAPAR]. After that date inner Asia belonged to their area of rule (Ulus). From then on there were various struggles with the Īlkhāns ([*q.v.*]; see also under "IV B") in Persia, and invasions into India, particularly between 697/1297 and 706/1306.

Čaghatāy's great grandson Baraḳ ([*q.v.*]; usually called by Muslims "Burāḳ") and the latter's son Duwa (about 691/1291 to 706/1306) had with Chinese aid asserted themselves against Ḳaidū (see III). Duwa's son Kebek (Köpek) was able in 709/1309 to take possession of the latter's inheritance. (d. 726/1326) His brother Termashīrīn (727-735/1326-34) was converted to Islam, taking with him the dynasty and gradually (though not without setbacks) the territory it ruled into the sphere of Islam. His death was followed by a temporary cleavage in the Ulus of Čaghatāy:

a) The branch of the house ruling in Transoxania was converted to Islam.

b) In the eastern part of the Ulus, since called Mogholistān (the land of seven rivers/Djeti suw/Semirečye; the area round Issiḳ Kul as well as the western Tarim Basin with Kāshgar) ruled a line under whom Islam only spread slowly.

A renewed unity of the two parts by Tughluḳ Temür [*q.v.*] was finally broken by Tīmūr's victory in 765/1363 by which Transoxania came to develop a separate character, where Turkish now definitely attained to leadership. Beside Tīmūr Čaghatāyids continued to rule as nominal Khāns until 805/1402. The Khāns in Mogholistān could not be eliminated, despite Tīmūr's persistent efforts.

Rather after Tīmūr's death in 808/1405, they were able gradually to regain influence in Transoxania. In particular, Esen Bogha II (833-867/1429-62) proved himself a dangerous opponent of the Tīmūrids. Between him, the Ḳara Ḳoyunlu [*q.v.*], the Aḳ Ḳoyunlu and finally, the rising Ṣafawids [*q.v.*], the Tīmūrids (with the exception of the Great Moghuls) were gradually worn down. Their territory fell finally to the Shaybānids ([*q.v.*]; see also above "I E") and to the (eastern) Čaghatāyids from Mogholistān, among whom Yūnus (874-891/1469-86), raised as a hostage in Shīrāz, took possession in 889/1484 of Tashkent [*q.v.*] and Sayrām [*q.v.*]. His successors maintained themselves there, reaching out at the same time—in opposition to China—towards Ha-mi and Turfān [*q.v.*], to whose islamization they decisively contributed. In Transoxania the Čaghatāyids were definitively eliminated in 914-15/1508-09 by the Shaybānids. Only Mogholistān east of Tʿien-shan remained in the hands of this dynasty, who were forced to share their power with the clan of Dughlat [*q.v.*], centred at Kāshghar. Living for the most part in harmony, both families took part in the struggle for Ha-mi and Turfān against China, a struggle which lasted still in the 16th century. Apparently at the end of that century a particular branch of the Čaghatāyids established itself in Turfān, and in 1057/1647 and 1068/1657 sent embassies to China. By the end of the 16th century Čaghatāyid power had split in several parts. It was fully ended in 1089/1678 when Khān Ismāʿīl of Kāshghar [*q.v.*] attempted to get rid of the control of the Khōdja [*q.v.*] which, divided in two parts, since the end of the 10th/16th century had been the real leaders in that region, which was organised in separate city states in the form of theocracies.

III) Čingiz Khān's third son Ögedey [*q.v.*], in accordance with his father's will and with the approval of his agnates, succeeded his father as the Great Khān from 627/1229 until 639/1241. His son Göyük (Pers. Güyük) too had his honour from 644/1246 to 646/1248. The widows of both, Töregene (Pers. Tūrākīnā) and Oghul Ḳaymish, conducted the regency in 639-644/1241-46 and 646-649/1248-51. Under Batu's influence however this line was unable to maintain itself in the Great Khānate, which passed to the line of Tolui (see IV). None the less, Ḳaydū, a nephew of Göyük, held his own in Ögedey's Ulus on the Imil, in the Tarbagatay Mountains and in modern Afghānistān. He conducted long wars with the princes of the House of Čaghatāy (II), especially Baraḳ, as well as with the Great Khān Ḳubilay, whose "nomadic" rival he was. He adhered to the old Mongolian religious traditions, and died in 1301 on the return march from an assault on Ḳaraḳorum [*q.v.*]. His son and successor Čäpär (Čapar; [*q.v.*]) resumed the struggle against the descendents of Čaghatāy and Ḳubilay, but had to flee from Kebek (see II) in 1309 to the court of the Mongol Emperor of China. Thereupon the Ulus of Čaghatāy ceased to exist.

IV) Čingiz Khān's youngest son Toluy had a such received as Ulus the territory of the actuals Mongolia. Since his sons Möngke (Pers. Māngū; [*q.v.*]) 1251-1259, and Ḳubilay [*q.v.*] 1259-94, were Great Khāns into whose hands until 1280 all of China had fallen, there was a dynastic connexion between Mongolia with its capital Ḳaraḳorum and the Middle Kingdom, where the Mongol dynasty was called Yüan. A third brother Ariḳ (Erik) Böge, who attempted to establish himself in Mongolia, was forced to surrender in 1264 and died in 1266 in Ḳubilay's custody. His great-grandson Arpa ruled

ČINGIZIDS

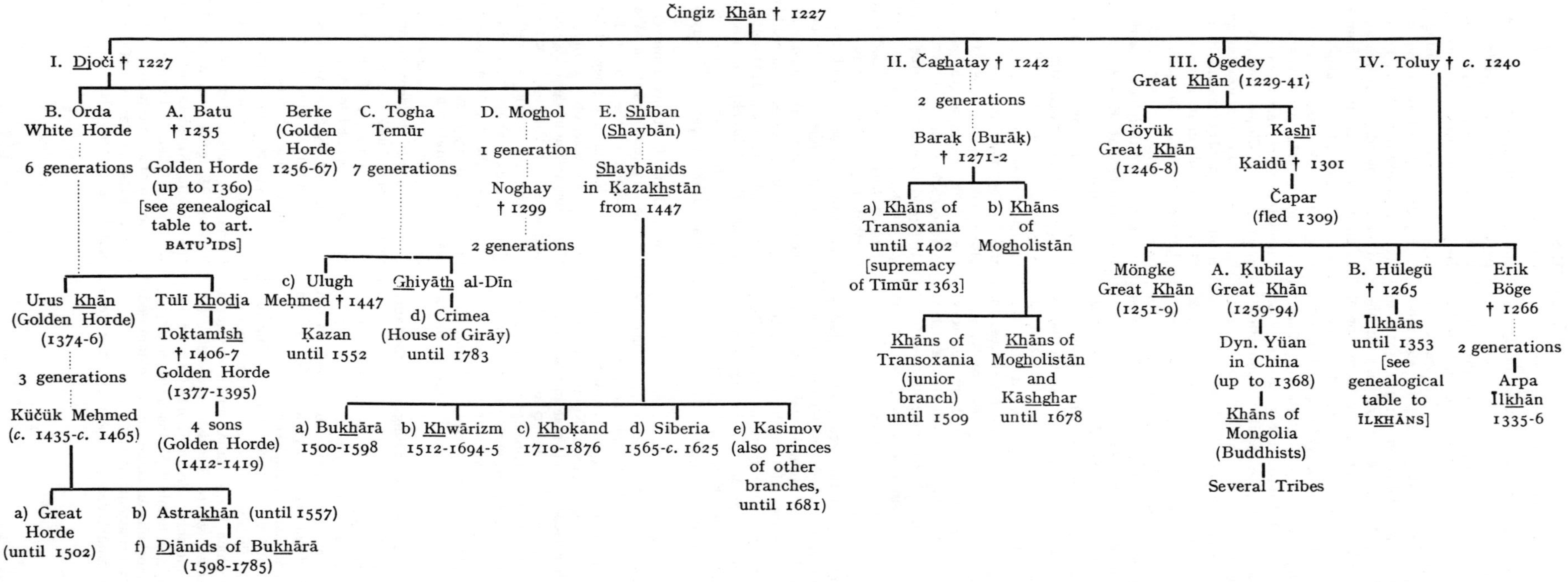

The numbers and letters of this geneological table correspond with the numbers and letters of the article "ČINGIZIDS".

for a few months in 1335/36 as Īlkhān (see "IV B").

A) Ḳubilay inclined more and more towards Buddhism, and his successors as emperors of China were completely absorbed in the indigenous culture and in the Chinese religion. The essential cause of this was that after Ḳubilay's death in 1294 the entire Mongol network collapsed, as the other branches of the house had sooner or later converted to Islam, even the Īlkhāns of Iran in 695/1295, who had hitherto particularly cultivated their relations with Khānbaligh ("Khān-city"; Peking). The Yüan dynasty, driven out of China in 1368, maintained the rule in Mongolia, where the various branches of the house drifted apart, though having nothing to do with Islam. At the end of the 16th century among the Mongols (as a linguistic community) Buddhism was established in its Tibetan form of "Lamaism" of the "Yellow Church". The Kalmuks [*q.v.*] too brought this religion to the Volga where they preserved it. After 1649 the Mongols in the Ordos region were again subject to Chinese authority.

B) A fourth brother of Ḳubilay, Hülegü (Pers. Hūlāgū; [*q.v.*] d. 1265) conquered in 653-658/1255-59 Persia, ʿIrāḳ and Mesopotamia and, temporarily, Syria. He destroyed the ʿAbbāsid caliphate and founded the empire of the Īlkhāns [*q.v.*]. He and his successors were in the beginning more or less inclined to Buddhism, but with Ghāzān [*q.v.*] in 695/1295 were converted to Islam, in which they vacillated openly between Sunnī and Shīʿī (Öldjeytü, d. 716/1316). The Īlkhān empire collapsed after 736/1335 in civil wars, and the last offspring of this line, (A)Nūshirwān disappeared from history in 754-5/1353-4. The heritage of the Īlkhāns was finally taken over by Tīmūr.

Bibliography: A. C. Mouradgea d'Ohsson, *Histoire des Mongols*[2], 4 vols., Amsterdam 1852; H. H. Howorth, *History of the Mongols*, 4 vols. and suppl., London 1876/88, 1927; R. Grousset, *L'Empire des steppes*, Paris 1939; W. Barthold, *12 Vorlesungen über die Geschichte der Türken Mittelasiens*, Berlin 1935; B. Spuler, *Die Mongolenzeit*[2], Leiden 1953 (English version, 1960).

Genealogical Tables: E. de Zambaur: *Manuel de généalogie . . .*[2], Hanover 1955, Tables 241-76 (and lists of rulers); N. I. Veselovskiy, in *Izv. otd. russk. yazîka i slovesnosti Imp. Akad. Nauk XXI*/1 (1916-17), 8-9.

Maps: A. Herrmann, *Atlas of China*, Cambridge Mass. 1935, 49-55; B. Spuler, a) *Mongolenzeit*, as above; b) in *Westermanns Atlas zur Weltgeschichte*, Braunschweig 1957, 72 ff., 99; *Hist. Atlas of the Muslim Peoples*, Amsterdam 1957, 26 ff., 31, 37; Zambaur, Map 4.

In addition, see the bibliography for the individual branches of the Čingizids, for the individual members of the family, and for the abovementioned geographical and town names.

(B. Spuler)

ČINIŌT (Činyōt), An ancient town in the district of Djhang (West Pakistan), situated in 31° 43′ N. and 73° 0′ E., on the left bank of the Čināb with a population of 39,042 in 1951. It was, in all probability, once a settlement of Chinese who not only gave their name to the town but also to the river that flows past at a distance of 2 miles only. Attempts have been made to identify it with Sākala, the capital of the White Huns, visited by the Chinese traveller Hiuen Tsiang. In 800/1398 it was captured by Tīmūr, during his Indian campaign, and remained thereafter in the possession of his dependents. In 876/1471 Sulṭān Ḥusayn b. Ḳuṭb al-Dīn Lingāh, the *wālī* of Multān, dispossessed Malik Māndjhī Khōkhar, agent of Sayyid ʿAlī Khān, the governor of Činiōt under Buhlūl Lōdī. In the meantime Buhlūl Lōdī appointed his son Bārbak Shāh as the governor of the Pandjāb. His appointment was, however, resented by Sulṭān Ḥusayn who met him in a fierce combat near Multān; defeated his troops and pursued them right upto Činiōt. The troops of Bārbak Shāh, however, succeeded in occupying the town and killed the local commandant. In 925/1519 Bābur occupied it in pursuance of a resolve to regain the territory which once was held by his ancester, Tīmūr. He ordered his troops not to indulge in plundering or over-running because he considered it to be a part of his patrimony. Prior to Bābur's occupation the town was in the possession of ʿAlī Khān b. Dawlat Khān Yūsuf-Khayl, governor of the Pandjāb.

Thereafter it remained under the Mughals and in the days of Akbar it had a brick-fort garrisoned by 5,000 infantry. During the second half of the 12th/18th century it suffered heavily from Durrānī inroads and Sikh depredations; the town was badly disturbed and the residents knew neither peace nor security. In 1264/1848 it again suffered under Narāyan Singh, the Sikh commandant. The very next year it became a British possession with the annexation of the Pandjāb in 1265/1849.

Činiōt now consists of the main town and two suburbs, one of which has grown up round the tomb of Shaykh Ismāʿīl. It is a well-built town and many of the houses, owned by the Khōdjās, are lofty and commodious. The Khōdjās are well-known for their great wealth and extensive business relations. They came to this town after its occupation by Randjīt Singh, the Sikh Mahārādjā.

Saʿd Allāh Khān ʿAllāmī al-Tamīmī the celebrated chief Minister of Shāhdjahān and the physician ʿIlm al-Dīn al-Anṣārī, better known to history as Wazīr Khān, the Mughal governor of Lahore during the reign of Shāhdjahān, were both natives of Činiōt. Saʿd Allāh Khān made a gift to his townsmen of the exceedingly handsome Djāmiʿ Masdjid built of stone obtained from the neighbouring hills; Wazīr Khān built the famous mosque of Lahore still known after him and founded the town of Wazīrābād. Some of the masons employed on the Tādj Maḥall (Agra) are said to have been drawn from Činiōt, most probably at the instance of Saʿd Allāh Khān, who knew all about their skill in masonry, and one of those who built the (Sikh) Golden Temple at Amritsar was also a resident of Činiōt. This town was also famous for wood-carving and some very fine specimens of wood-work can still be seen in the old town.

Bibliography: *Bāburnāma* (Eng. transl. A. S. Beveridge), 380-2; Sudjān Rāy, *Khulāṣat al-Tawārīkh* (ed. M. Ẓafar Ḥasan), Delhi 1918, 78, 293-4; *Punjab District Gazetteers* (*Jhang*), Lahore 1910, 163-5; D. G. Barkley in *JRAS* (1899), 132-3; ʿAbd al-Ḥayy Nadawī, *Nuzhat al-Khawāṭir*, Ḥaydarābād (Deccan) 1375/1955, 154, 279-80; *Elliot and Dowson*, iv, 232.; ʿAbd al-Ḥamīd Khān, *Pawns of Pakistan*, Karachi n.d. 129-35.

(A. S. Bazmee Ansari)

CINTRA [see shintara]

ČIRĀGH-I DIHLĪ ("Light of Dihlī"), the *laḳab* of Shaykh Naṣīr al-Dīn Maḥmūd b. Yaḥyā Yazdī, Awadhī, said to be based on a remark of his contemporary Shaykh ʿAbd Allāh b. Asʿad al-Yāfiʿī (d. 768/1367) (*Firishta*, ii, 781[7], 747[3], Djamālī, 141b). He was one of the most eminent disciples of Shaykh Niẓām al-Dīn Awliyāʾ. His father Yaḥyā was born in Lāhore. Later the family settled at Awadh (Ayōdhyā), where his father traded in woollen cloth or cotton (*pashmīna* in *Khayr al-Madjālis*, var. *panbe* in *Akhbār* 80). It was in Awadh that Maḥmūd was born, but he was not yet nine, when his father died. His widowed mother arranged for his education with a distinguished scholar of those days Mawlānā ʿAbd al-Karīm Sharwānī (*Nuzhat al-Khawāṭir*, ii, 70), with whom he studied up to al-Marghīnānī, *Hidāyat al-Fiḳh*, and Pazdawī, *Uṣūl*, (Brockelmann, I 373, S I 637). When Sharwānī died the young Maḥmūd completed his education in the usual sciences with Mawlānā Iftikhār al-Dīn Muḥammad al-Gīlānī (*Nuzha*, ii, 15). When he was about twenty-five, he renounced the world and for seven years went through a rigorous course of self-discipline and self-mortification, and fought against the passions with prayer and fasting. At forty-three he moved to Dihlī and became a disciple of Shaykh Niẓām al-Dīn Awliyāʾ, *i.e.*, Muḥammad Badāʾūnī. After this he visited Awadh only occasionally and was mostly attending on his *murshid* at the *Djamāʿat Khāna* at Kīlokhaṙī, on the bank of the Djamnā.

He resided in Dihlī in the house of his old friend and fellow-disciple Shaykh Burhān al-Dīn Gharīb [*q.v.*]. Towards the end of 724/1324, or a few months later, his Shaykh, who was then about 94, appointed him his successor in Dihlī, to carry on his life-work and passed on to him the souvenirs (*khirḳa*, rosary etc.) of his own Shaykh (Farīd al-Dīn) (Māndwī, 115, cf. Kirmānī, 220-2). He followed his Shaykh punctiliously in the path of poverty and patience, resignation (in the will of God) and acceptance (*taslīm wa riḍā*) and remained celibate like him. After the death of his Shaykh he guided the people for thirty-two years. Kirmānī (242 ff.) gives several instances of his remarkable power of thought-reading.

He and most of his *khalīfa*s lived in strict obedience to the *sharīʿa*, and engaged themselves in teaching religious sciences and the spreading of knowledge (cf. Ghulām ʿAlī Āzād, *Subḥat al-Mardjān*, 30). A contemporary *faḳīh*, Kamāl al-Dīn, the author of *Ṭurfat al-Fuḳahāʾ* (in verse), who visited his *khānaḳāh*, confirms it thus:

"On every side Jurisprudence and (its)
Principles were being taught,
On every side God, and the Apostle were
being mentioned".

Har ṭaraf dars-hā zi fiḳh u uṣūl,
Har ṭaraf dhikr az Khudāwa Rasūl.
(Panjab University MS. f. 12a)

When Sulṭān Muḥammad Tughluḳ 725-52/1324-51) adopted a hostile policy against the *ʿulamāʾ* etc. (for reasons discussed by Mahdī Ḥusayn), he created difficulties for the Shaykh too in various ways. The sultan would take him along with him on his travels and on one occasion he put him in charge of his wardrobe. The Shaykh bore all these troubles and annoyances patiently, keeping in view the injunctions of his master (Kirmānī 245 f.; Djamālī 138b; Māndwī 115; *Akhbār* 81, 91; Firishta, ii, 747; Badāʾūnī, i, 242). However his relations with the sultan's successor, Fīrūz Shāh, were much better, and the Shaykh supported the sultan's ascent to the throne (Baranī (Bib. Ind.), 535; ʿAfīf (Bib. Ind.) 29; *Mubārak Shāhī* (Bib. Ind.) 121; Badāʾūnī, i, 241f.; *Ṭabaḳāt-i Akbarī*, i, 225). True to the tradition of the great Čishtī Saints, he compiled no book (*Akhbār*, 81) but his *obiter dicta*, and anecdotes about him, were collected by Ḥamīd Ḳalandar (*Akhbār*, 109, 86). The work called *Khayr al-Madjālis*, begun in 755/1354 and completed in 756/1355, is divided into 100 *Madjālis* (Assemblies). The Shaykh himself revised this work. A *takmila* (supplement) was added to it by the author, after the death of the Shaykh. The narrative is given in simple Persian and the account is full and detailed. For quotations from it see *Akhbar*, 109-112, 82-5. An Urdū translation of it exists (*Taʾrīkh Mashayikh Čisht* 162n, 183n). A number of his sayings reveal a learned and illumined personality. For an Arabic verse of his see *Akhbār*, 97.

The enormous influence which he wielded in Dihlī and outside it (northern India and Deccan) in his own and the following generations, becomes clear from the lengthy list of his notable disciples and *khalīfa*s, who are noticed in detail in the *Akhbār*, 129-148, 141, 142-146, 147-149 and 85, (see also *Nuzhat al-Khawāṭir*, ii, 159), including as it does, among others such names as those of Ḳāḍī ʿAbd al-Muḳtadir (d. 791/1389; see also *Subḥa*, 29, *Nuzhat al-Khawāṭir*, (ii, 70), Sayyid Muḥammad b. Yūsuf, usually known as Gēsūdarāz (died in Gulbarga in 825/1422, see Firishta, ii, 748, Rieu, 347), Sayyid Djalāl Bukhārī Makhdūm-i Djahāniyan (d. 785/1384 in Sindh), Aḥmad Thānesarī (died in Kālpī; who won consideration from Amīr Tīmūr (*Akhbār*, 142), Muṭahhar of Kaṙa (for whom see the *Oriental College Magazine*, Lāhore, May 1935, 107-160, Aug. 1935, 48-216, *Akhbār*, 85 f.), and Mawlānā Khwadjagī (*Akhbār* 141). To this list may be added the names of (Akhī Sirādj Parwāna, the Shaykh's *khalīfa* in Bengāl, Ḥusām al-Dīn of Nahrawālā (Gudjarāt) (Firishta, ii, 748, 747), and Muḥammad Mudjīr Wadjīh al-Dīn Adīb, author of the *Miftāḥ al-Djinān* (Rieu, 40 f.).

The Shaykh died after a short illness on the 18th Ramaḍān 757/15 September 1356, and was buried in his own house (Kirmānī, 247), appointing no successor, and the relics he had received from his Shaykh were buried with him. This symbolised the end of the first series of the great Čishtī Saints in India. A mausoleum was built on his tomb by Sulṭān Fīrūz Shāh. A tomb close to the Shaykh's is popularly supposed to be that of Sulṭān Bahlol Lodī. For a description of it see *List of Muhammadan and Hindu Monuments, Delhi Province*, iii, *Mahrauli Zail*, Calcutta 1922,

Bibliography: Apart from the authorities quoted above, the following are important:

Muḥammad Mubārak al-Kirmānī, *Siyar al-Awliyāʾ*, Delhī 1302, 236-247; Djamālī, *Siyar al-ʿĀrifīn* no. 11, my MS., ff. 136-140, 141b; Abu 'l-Faḍl, *Āʾīn-i Akbarī* (Bib. Ind.) ii, 218; Amīn-i Aḥmad-ī Rāzī, *Haft Iḳlīm* no. 402; ʿAbd al-Ḥaḳḳ, *Akhbār al-Akhyār*, Delhi 1309, 80-6, 129 f., 134 f., 139, 141 f., 147-149, 151; Māndwī, *Adhkār-i Abrār* (Urdū version of *Gulzār-i Abrār*), Āgra 1326, 115; Dārā Shukōh, *Safīnat al-Awliyāʾ*, Lucknow 1872, 100 f.; Ḥakīm ʿAbd al-Ḥayy Lakhnawī, *Nuzhat al-Khawāṭir*, Ḥaydarābād-Deccan, 1350, ii, 158 f.; Raḥmān ʿAlī *Tadhkira ʿUlamā-i Hind*, Lucknow 1914, 238; Beale, *Oriental Biographical Dictionary*, Calcutta 1881, 205; idem, *Miftāḥ al-Tawārikh*, 89; Ghulān Sarwar, *Khazīnat al-Aṣfiyāʾ*, Lāhore 1283, 340-5; Āghā Mahdī Ḥusayn, *The Rise and fall of Muḥammad bin Tughluq*, London 1938, 209 ff., Muḥammad Ḥabīb, *Shaikh Naṣiruddīn Maḥmūd, Chirāgh-i Dehlī as a great historical personality*, in *IC*, xx/2 (1946), 129 ff.; Storey, i, 942 n. i; Khalīḳ Aḥmad

Niẓāmī, *Ta'rīkh-i Mashāyikh-i Čisht* (Urdū) Delhī n.d., 181-6. (Moḥammad Shafī)

ČIRĀGHĀN (plur. of *čirāgh*, means of illumination such as candle, torch or lamp), the name of a palace on the European side of the Bosphorus between Beshiktāsh and Ortaköy. First built by Sulṭān Murād IV for his daughter Kaya Sulṭān, it was rebuilt by Dāmād Ibrāhīm Pasha, the Grand Vizier of Sultān Aḥmad ,for his wife Faṭima Sultān. During the sultan's frequent visits, the famous *čirāghān* festivities (the illumination of tulip gardens with candles and lamps, tortoises with candles on them also wandered about in the gardens) were celebrated here. It was rebuilt of wood by Sulṭān Muṣṭafā III for this daughter Beyhan Sulṭān, with a magnificient hall 180 tr. in length, various ceremony halls, valuable floors and interior decorations. Demolished in 1859 by Sulṭān ʿAbd al-Medjīd, the reconstruction began in the time of Sulṭān ʿAbd al-ʿAzīz in 1863 and was completed in 1869. Made of stone, its architectural style was a mixture of classical styles to suit eastern taste. The building on the beach consisted of three parts, the façade with its mosaics, marble columns and stone work, the interior with its interior decorations, ceilings, wooden wall linings and doors inlaid with mother of pearl were separate works of art. After his deposition in 1876, Sulṭān ʿAbd al-ʿAzīz stayed there until his suicide. The deposed Sulṭān Murād V was forced to live there for 27 years. With small alterations, it was used as a Parliament house for the Senate and the Chamber of Deputies and was destroyed by fire three months later on 7 Muḥarram 1328/19 January 1910. The walls and the imperial doors are the only remnants.

Bibliography: C. E. Arseven, *Türk Sanatı Tarihi*, Fasc. 8; M. Z. Pakalın, *Çirağan Sarayı* in *Aylık Ansiklopedi*, Istanbul 1940; T. Öz, *Çırağan Sarayı*, in *Panoroma*, no. 1, Istanbul 1945; M. T. Gökbilgin, *Çırağan Sarayı* in *İA*, Vol. 19, Istanbul 1943); M. Z. Pakalın, *Osmanlı Tarih Deyimleri*, Istanbul 1948. (Tahsin Öz)

CIRCASSIANS [see ČERKES]

CIRCUMCISION [see KHITĀN]

ČIRMEN, located at the site of Burdipta, a fortress of the ancient Thracians (cf. Tomaschek, 325), is called Τζερνομιάνον in the chronicle of the Byzantine historian Kantakuzenos (cf. also Chalkokondyles, who mentions a Κερμιανόν χῶρον and Črŭnomêčī in the Serbian sources. It lies on the south side of the river Maritsa, not far above Adrianople (Edirne) and was, at the time of the earlier Ottoman conquests in the Balkans, a point of some strategic importance, since it commanded a ford across the river. At Čirmen, in September 1371/Rabīʿ I 773), the Ottomans inflicted a crushing defeat on the southern Serbs led by the princes Vukašin and Uglješa. As the tide of Ottoman conquest in the Balkans advanced further towards the north and west, so the significance of Čirmen as a fortress began to decline. Ewliyā Čelebī describes it as *ič il ḳalʿesi, i.e.*, a fortress of the interior, without garrison and equipment and with its walls in a state of disrepair. Čirmen was during the 14th-19th centuries the centre of a *sandjaḳ* in the *eyālet* of Rūmeli, but sank thereafter to the status of a *nāḥiye* in the *ḳaḍā'* of Muṣṭafā Pāshā Köprüsü belonging to the *wilāyet* and *sandjaḳ* of Edirne.

Bibliography: Saʿd al-Dīn, *Tādj al-Tawārīkh*, i, Istanbul A.H. 1279, 83, 518, 541; Ewliyā Čelebī, *Seyāḥatnāme*, iii, Istanbul A.H. 1314, 423; Kantakuzenos, i, (Bonn 1828), 191, ii (Bonn 1831), 526, iii (Bonn 1832), 243; Chalkokondyles, Bonn 1843, 31; J. von Hammer-Purgstall, *Rumeli und Bosna*, Vienna 1812, 49; P. A. von Tischendorf, *Das Lehnswesen in den moslemischen Staaten*, Leipzig 1872, 62, 64; C. Jireček, *Die Heerstrasse von Belgrad nach Constantinopel und die Balkanpässe*, Prague 1877, 99, 108; W. Tomaschek, *Zur Kunde der Hämus-Halbinsel*, *SBAk. Wien, Phil.-Hist. Cl.*, Bd. 113, Vienna 1886, 325; N. Jorga, *Geschichte des osmanischen Reiches*, i, Gotha 1908, 240-241; St. N. Kyriakides, βυζαντιναὶ Μελέται *II-V*, Thessalonike 1937, 189; F. Babinger, *Beiträge zur Frühgeschichte der Türkenherrschaft in Rumelien* (14.-15. *Jahrhundert*), Brünn, Munich, Vienna 1944, 29 (note 113), 50; H. J. Kissling, *Beiträge zur Kenntnis Thrakiens im 17. Jahrhundert* (*Abh.* K.M., XXXII/3), Wiesbaden, 38, 38 and 116 (index); Ö. L. Barkan, *Kanunlar*, Istanbul 1943, 257-259; M. Tayyib Gökbilgin, *XV-XVI. asırlarda Edirne ve Paşa Livâsı*, Istanbul 1952, 12 ff., 261 ff., 515 ff., and 561 (index) (cf. also, *ibid.*, Vakfiyeler, 235 ff.); Sāmī, *Ḳāmūs al-Aʿlām*, iii, Istanbul 1891, 1873 and vi, Istanbul 1898, 4309 (s.vv. Çirmen, and Muṣṭafā Pāshā Köprüsü). (V. J. Parry)

ČISHTĪ, Khwādja Muʿīn al-Dīn Ḥasan, one of the most outstanding figures in the annals of Islamic mysticism and founder of the Čishtiyya order [see the following article] in India, was born in or about 536/1141 in Sidjistān. He was in his teens when his father, Sayyid Ghiyāth al-Dīn, died leaving as legacy a grinding mill and an orchard. The sack of Sidjistān at the hands of the Ghuzz Turks turned his mind inwards and he developed strong mystic tendencies. He distributed all his assets and took to itineracy. He visited the seminaries of Samarḳand and Bukhārā and acquired religious learning at the feet of eminent scholars of his age. While on his way to ʿIrāḳ, he passed through Harvan, a *ḳaṣaba* in the district of Nīshāpūr. Here he met Khwādja ʿUthmān and joined the circle of his disciples. For twenty years he accompanied his mystic teacher on his *Wanderjahre*. Later on he undertook independent journeys and came into contact with eminent saints and scholars like Shaykh ʿAbd al-Ḳādir Gīlānī, Shaykh Nadjm al-Dīn Kubrā, Shaykh Nadjīb al-Dīn ʿAbd al-Ḳāhir Suhrawardī, Shaykh Abū Saʿīd Tabrīzī, Shaykh ʿAbd al-Waḥid Ghaznawī—all of whom were destined to exercise great influence on contemporary religious thought. He visited nearly all the great centres of Muslim culture in those days—Samarḳand, Bukhārā, Baghdād, Nīshāpūr, Tabrīz, Awsh, Iṣfahān, Sabzawār, Mihna, Khirḳān, Astarābād, Balkh and Ghaznīn—and acquainted himself with almost every important trend in Muslim religious life in the middle ages. He then turned towards India and, after a brief stay at Lahore, where he spent some time in meditation at the tomb of Shaykh ʿAlī al-Hudjwīrī, reached Adjmēr before its conquest by the Ghūrids. It was here that he married at an advanced age. According to ʿAbd al-Ḥaḳḳ Dihlawī (d. 1642) he took two wives, one of them being the daughter of a Hindu rādjā. He had three sons—Shaykh Abū Saʿīd, Shaykh Fakhr al-Dīn and Shaykh Ḥusām al-Dīn—and one daughter, Bībī Djamāl, from these wives. Bībī Djamāl had strong mystic leanings but his sons were not inclined towards mysticism. Nothing is known about Abū Saʿīd; Fakhr al-Dīn took to farming at Mandal, near Adjmēr; while Ḥusām al-Dīn disappeared mysteriously. Muʿīn al-Dīn died at Adjmēr in 633/1236. His tomb is venerated by Hindus and Muslims alike and hundreds of thousands of people from all over the Indo-Pakistan sub-continent assemble there on the occasion of his *ʿurs* (death anniversary).

The *dargāh* area contains many buildings—gates, mosques, hospices, *langars* etc.—constructed by the rulers of Malwa, the Mughal emperors, nobles, merchants and mystics during the past several centuries. Muḥammad b. Tughluḳ (626-752/1325-1351) was the first Sultan of Dihlī who visited his grave (*Futūḥ al-Salāṭīn*, Madras, 466). The Khaldjī Sultans of Malwa constructed the tomb of the saint. It was during the reign of Akbar (963-1014/1556-1605) that Adjmēr became one of the most important centres of pilgrimage in the country. The Mughal emperors displayed great reverence for the mausoleum of the saint. Akbar undertook a journey on foot to Adjmēr, and Shāh Djahān's daughter, Djahān-Ārā, cleansed and swept the tomb with her eyelids.

Khwādja Muʿīn al-Dīn laid the foundations of the Čishtī order in India and worked out its principles at Adjmēr, the seat of Čawhān power. No authentic details are available about the way he worked in the midst of a population which looked askance at every foreigner. It appears that his stay was disliked by Prithvī Rādj and the caste Hindūs but the common people flocked to him in large numbers. He visited Delhi twice during the reign of Iletmish (1210-1235), but kept himself away from the centre of political power and quietly worked for a cultural revolution in the country. His firm faith in *waḥdat al-wudjūd* (Unity of Being) provided the necessary ideological support to his mystic mission to bring about emotional integration of the people amongst whom he lived. Some of his sayings, as preserved in *Siyar al-Awliyāʾ*, reveal him as a man of wide sympathies, catholic views and deep humanism. He interpreted religion in terms of human service and exhorted his disciples "to develop river-like generosity, sun-like affection and earth-like hospitality". The highest form of devotion (*ṭāʿat*), according to him, was "to redress the misery of those in distress; to fulfil the needs of the helpless and to feed the hungry". The Čishtī order owes to him the ideology which is expounded in the conversations of Shaykh Niẓām al-Dīn Awliyāʾ (*Fawāʾid al-Fuʾād*) and other Čishtī mystic works of the 7th/13th and the 8th/14th centuries.

Bibliography: No contemporary record of the saint's life or teachings is available. The works attributed to him—*Gandj al-Asrār*, *Anīs al-Arwāḥ*, *Dalīl al-ʿĀrifīn* and *Dīwān-i Muʿīn*—are apocryphal. (See Prof. M. Ḥabīb, *Chishti Mystic Records of the Sultanate Period*, in *Medieval India Quarterly*, Vol. i, no. 2, 15-22; K. A. Niẓāmī, *Studies in Medieval Indian History*, Aligarh 1956, 40-42). The earliest notices are found in *Surūr al-Ṣudūr* (conversations of Shaykh Ḥamīd al-Dīn al-Ṣūfī, a disciple of the saint, compiled by his grandson—MSS Ḥabībgandj and personal collection) and *Siyar al-Awliyāʾ* (Delhi 1301, 45-48), but they contain very few details about his life. The first detailed account of his life is given by a sixteenth century mystic, Shaykh Djamālī (*Siyar al-ʿĀrifīn*, Delhi 1311, 4-17) who collected whatever material he could in foreign lands. All later hagiological works, with a few exceptions, have confused fact with fiction and incorporated all kinds of legends. This literature may be of value in tracing the growth of legends round the Khwādja's person; its historical value is, nevertheless, very meagre. For later authorities, Abu 'l-Faḍl, *Āʾīn-i Akbarī*, Sir Sayyid ed., 207; Ghawthī, *Gulzār-i Abrār*, As. Soc. of Bengal Ms. D. 262, f. 8v-10; *Taʾrīkh-i Firishta*, Nawal Kishore, 1281, ii, 375-378; ʿAlī Aṣghar Čishtī, *Djawāhir-i Farīdī*, Lahore 1301, 146-163; ʿAbd al-Ḥaḳḳ Dihlawī, *Akhbār al-Akhyār*, Delhi 1309, 22-24; ʿAbd al-Rahmān, *Mirʾāt al-Asrār*, MS personal collection, 408-426; *Siyar al-Aḳṭāb*, Nawal Kishore, Lucknow 1331 100-141; Ghulām Muʿīn al-Dīn, *Maʿāridj al-Walāyat*, MS personal collection, i, 3-27; Tādj al-Dīn Rūḥ Allāh, *Risāla Ḥāl Khānwāda-i Čisht*, MS. personal collection, f. 2a-5b; Bahā *alias* Radja, *Risāla Aḥwāl Pīrān-i Čisht*, MS personal collection, 77-80; Dārā Shukōh, *Safīnat al-Awliyāʾ*, Agra 1269, no. 110; Djahān-Ārā, *Munis al-Arwāḥ*, (MSS Storey, 1000); Ikrām Baraswī, *Iḳtibās al-Anwār*, Lahore 132-147; Raḥīm Bakhsh Fakhrī, *Shadjarat al-Anwār*, MS personal collection, 141b-162b; Nadjm al-Dīn, *Manāḳib al-Ḥabīb*, Delhi 1332; Muḥammad Ḥusayn, *Taḥḳīḳāt-i Awlād-i Khwādja Ṣāḥib*, Delhi; Imām al-Dīn Khān, *Muʿīn al-Awliyāʾ*, Adjmēr 1213; Bābū Lāl, *Waḳāʾ-i Shāh Muʿīn al-Dīn*, Nawal Kishore; K. A. Niẓāmī, *Taʾrīkh-i Mashāʾikh-i Čisht*, Nadwat Khādim Ḥasan, *Muʿīn al-Arwāḥ*, Agra 1953; al-Muṣannifīn, Delhi 1953, 142-147; Storey, 943.

(K. A. Nizami)

ČISHTIYYA, one of the most popular and influential mystic orders of India. It derives its name from Čisht, a village near Harat (marked as Khwādja Čisht on some maps), where the real founder of the order, Khwādja Abū Isḥāḳ of Syria (Mīr Khurd, *Siyar al-Awliyāʾ*, Delhi 1302, 39-40; Djāmī, *Nafaḥāt al-Uns*, Nawal Kishore 1915, 296) settled at the instance of his spiritual mentor, Khwādja Mamshād ʿUlw of Dinawar (a place in Ḳuhistān, between Hamadān and Baghdād). The *silsila* is traced back to the Prophet as follows: Abū Isḥāḳ, Mamshād ʿUlw Dinawarī, Amīn al-Dīn Abū Hubayrat al-Baṣrī, Sadīd al-Dīn Huzayfat al-Marʿashī, Ibrāhīm Adham al-Balkhī, Abu 'l-Fayḍ Fuḍayl b. ʿIyāḍ, Abu 'l-Faḍl ʿAbd al-Wāḥid b. Zayd, Ḥasan al-Basrī, ʿAlī b. Abī Ṭālib, the Prophet Muḥammad. Shāh Walī Allah (d. 1763) has doubted the validity of the tradition which makes Ḥasan al-Baṣrī a spiritual successor of ʿAlī (*Al-Intibāh fi Salāsil-i Awliyāʾ Allāh*, Delhi 1311, 18), but his views have been criticised by Shāh Fakhr al-Dīn Dihlawī (d. 1784) in his *Fakhr al-Ḥasan* (commentary on this, by Mawlānā Aḥsan al-Zamān, *Al-Ḳawl al-Mustaḥsin fi Fakhr al-Ḥasan*, Ḥaydarābād 1312). The pre-Indian history of the Čishtī order cannot be reconstructed on the basis of any authentic historical data. Khwādja Muʿīn al-Dīn Sidjzī Čishtī [see preceding article] brought the *silsila* to India in the 12th century and established a Čishtī mystic centre at Adjmēr, whence the order spread far and wide in India and became a force in the spiritual life of the Indian Muslims. Khwādja Muʿīn al-Dīn was connected with the founder of the *silsila* by the following chain of spiritual ancestors: Muʿīn al-Dīn Ḥasan, ʿUthmān Harvanī, Ḥādjī Sharīf Zindānī, Mawdūd Čishtī, Abī Yūsuf, Abī Muḥammad b. Aḥmad, Abī Aḥmad b. Farasnafa, Abū Isḥāḳ. (The earliest lists of the great Čishtī saints in the order of their spiritual succession are given in *Futūḥ al-Salāṭīn*, Madras, 7-8; *Khayr al-Madjālis*, Aligarh, 7-8; *Siyar al-Awliyāʾ*, Delhi, 32-45; *Aḥsan al-Aḳwāl*, MS personal collection).

A: History of the Order

The Čishtiyya order had four distinct phases of its activity in India: (i) Era of the Great

Shaykhs (circa 597/1200 to 757/1356), (ii) Era of the Provincial Khānaḳāhs (8th/14th & 9th/15th centuries), (iii) Rise of the Ṣābiriyya Branch (9th/15th century onwards), and (iv) Revival of the Niẓāmiyya Branch 12th/(18th century onwards).

The saints of the first cycle established their *khānaḳah*s mainly in Radjputāna, U.P. and the Pandjāb. Some of them, like Ḥamīd al-Dīn Ṣūfī, worked out the Čishtī mystic principles in the rural areas; others lived in *ḳaṣaba*s and towns but scrupulously avoided identification with the centre of political power. They refused to accept *djāgīr*s and government services; did not perpetuate spiritual succession in their own families and looked upon 'learning' as an essential qualification for spiritual work. Under Shaykh Farīd Gandj-i Shakar and Shaykh Niẓām al-Dīn Awliyā', the influence of the order was extended to the whole of India, and people flocked to their hospices from distant parts of the country. The *silsila* possessed during this period a highly integrated central structure which controlled and guided the activities of those associated with it. Muḥammad b. Tughluḳ's policy (1325-1351) of forcing the saints to settle in different parts of the country paralysed the central organization of the Čishtīs. Shaykh Naṣīr al-Dīn Čirāgh and a few other elder saints refused, at the risk of their lives, to co-operate with the Tughluḳ Sulṭān, but many of the younger mystics entered government service. Shaykh Naṣīr al-Dīn was also called upon to protect the mystic ideology and institutions against the attacks levelled by Ibn Taymiyya [*q.v.*]. After him the central organization of the Čishtī order broke down and provincial *khānaḳāh*s, which did not owe allegiance to any central authority, came into existence.

It was mainly through the disciples of Shaykh Niẓām al-Dīn Awliyā' that the Čishtī order spread in the various provinces of India. Some of them had taken up their residence in provincial towns at the instance of their master; others were forced by Muḥammad b. Tughluḳ to settle there. It is significant that the arrival of these saints in provincial towns coincided with the rise of provincial kingdoms. In these circumstances many of these saints could not keep themselves away from the provincial courts. The traditions of the saints of the first cycle were consequently discarded and the comfortable theory was expounded that mystics should consort with kings and high officers in order to influence them for the good. State endowments were accepted and, in return, spiritual blessings and moral support was given to the founders of the new provincial dynasties. The principle of hereditary succession was also introduced in the *silsila*.

Shaykh Sirādj al-Dīn, popularly known as Akhī Sirādj, introduced the *silsila* in Bengal. His disciple Shaykh 'Alā' al-Dīn b. As'ad was fortunate in having two eminent disciples—Sayyid Nūr Ḳuṭb-i 'Alam and Sayyid Ashraf Djahāngīr Simnānī—who played a very important role in popularising the Čishtī *silsila* in Bengal, Bihar and eastern U.P. When Rādjā Kans established his power in Bengal, Sayyid Nūr Ḳuṭb-i 'Alam organized public opinion against him and persuaded Sulṭān Ibrāhīm Sharḳī of Djawnpūr (1402-1440) to invade Bengal. Nūr Ḳuṭb-i 'Alam and his descendants had a share in creating that religious stir which ultimately led to the rise of the Bhakti movement in Bengal and Bihār.

The Čishtiyya order was introduced in the Deccan by Shaykh Burhān al-Dīn Gharīb who settled at Dawlatābād and propagated the Čishtī mystic principles. The city of Burhānpur was named after him. His disciple, Shaykh Zayn al-Dīn, was the spiritual master of 'Alā' al-Dīn Ḥasan Shāh (1347-1359), the founder of the Bahmanī kingdom. Later

(i) ERA OF THE GREAT SHAYKHS:

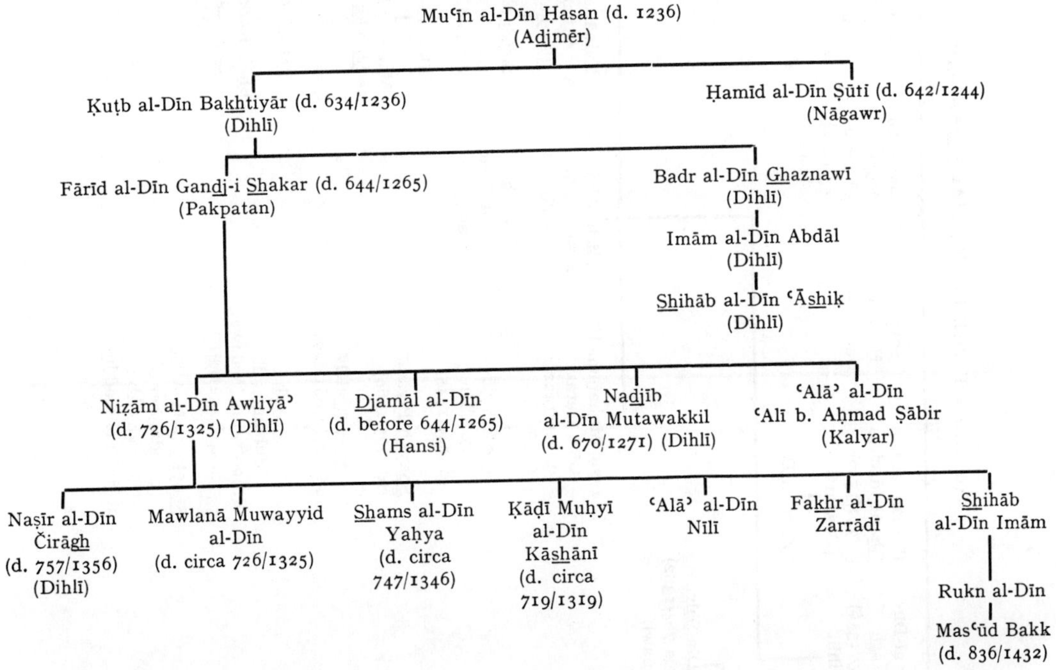

(ii) ERA OF THE PROVINCIAL KHĀNAḲĀHS:

- Sirādj al-Dīn Akhī Sirādj (d. 759/1357) (Gawŕ, Bengal)
  - ʿAlāʾ al-Dīn b. Asʿad Lāhurī Bengali (d. 801/1398) (Pandwa)
    - Nūr Ḳuṭb-i ʿAlam (d. 313/1410) (Pandwa)
      - Ḥusām al-Dīn (d.822/1477) (Mānikpur)
        - Rādjī Ḥāmid Shāh (d. 901/1495) (Mānikpur)
          - Ḥasan Ṭāhir of Djawnpur (d. 901/1503) (Dihlī)
      - Sayyid Shams al-Dīn Ṭāhir (Ranthambor)
    - Sayyid Ashraf Djāhangīr Simnānī (d. 808/1405) (Kačoča)
- Ḳuṭb al-Dīn Munawwar (d. circa 760/1358) (Hānsī)
  - Nūr al-Dīn
  - Tādj al-Dīn Shīr Suwār (d. circa 784/1382) (Narnawl)
- Naṣīr al-Dīn Čirāgh (d. 757/1356) (Dihlī)
  - Sayyid Muḥammad Gīsū Darāz (d. 826/1422) (Gulbarga)
    - Mīr Sayyid Yād Allāh (d. 849/1445)
      - Shaykh Piyāra (d. 865/1460)
        - Shāh Djalāl Gudjrātī (d. 881/1476)
          - Shaykh Muḥammad (d. 900/1494). (Malawa, near Kanawdj)
            - Shaykh Saʿd Allāh (grandfather of Shaykh ʿAbd al-Ḥaḳḳ Muḥaddith Dihlawi)
  - Ḳāḍī ʿAbd al-Muḳtadir (Dihlī)
    - Shaykh ʿAbd al-Fatḥ (Djawnpur)
  - Kamāl al-Dīn ʿAllama (Gudjarāt)
    - Sirādj al-Dīn (d. 814/1411) (Aḥmadābād)
      - ʿAlam al-Ḥaḳḳ
        - Maḥmūd known as Shaykh Rādjan
          - Ḥasan Muḥammad
            - Yaḥyā Madani
              - Shāh Kalīm Allāh Djahānābādī (Dihlī)
  - Mawlānā Khwādjgī (Nalpi)
- Burhān al-Dīn Gharīb (d. circa 741/1340) (Dawlatābād)
  - Zayn al-Dīn
- Sayyid Ḥusayn (Nahrwala)
- Ḥusām al-Dīn Multānī (d. circa 755/1354) (Nahrwala)
- Shāh Barak Allāh (Gudjarāt)
- Wadjīh al-Dīn Yūsuf (d. circa 729/1328) (Čanderī)
- Kamāl al-Dīn (Mālwa)
- Mughīth al-Dīn (Udjdjayn)

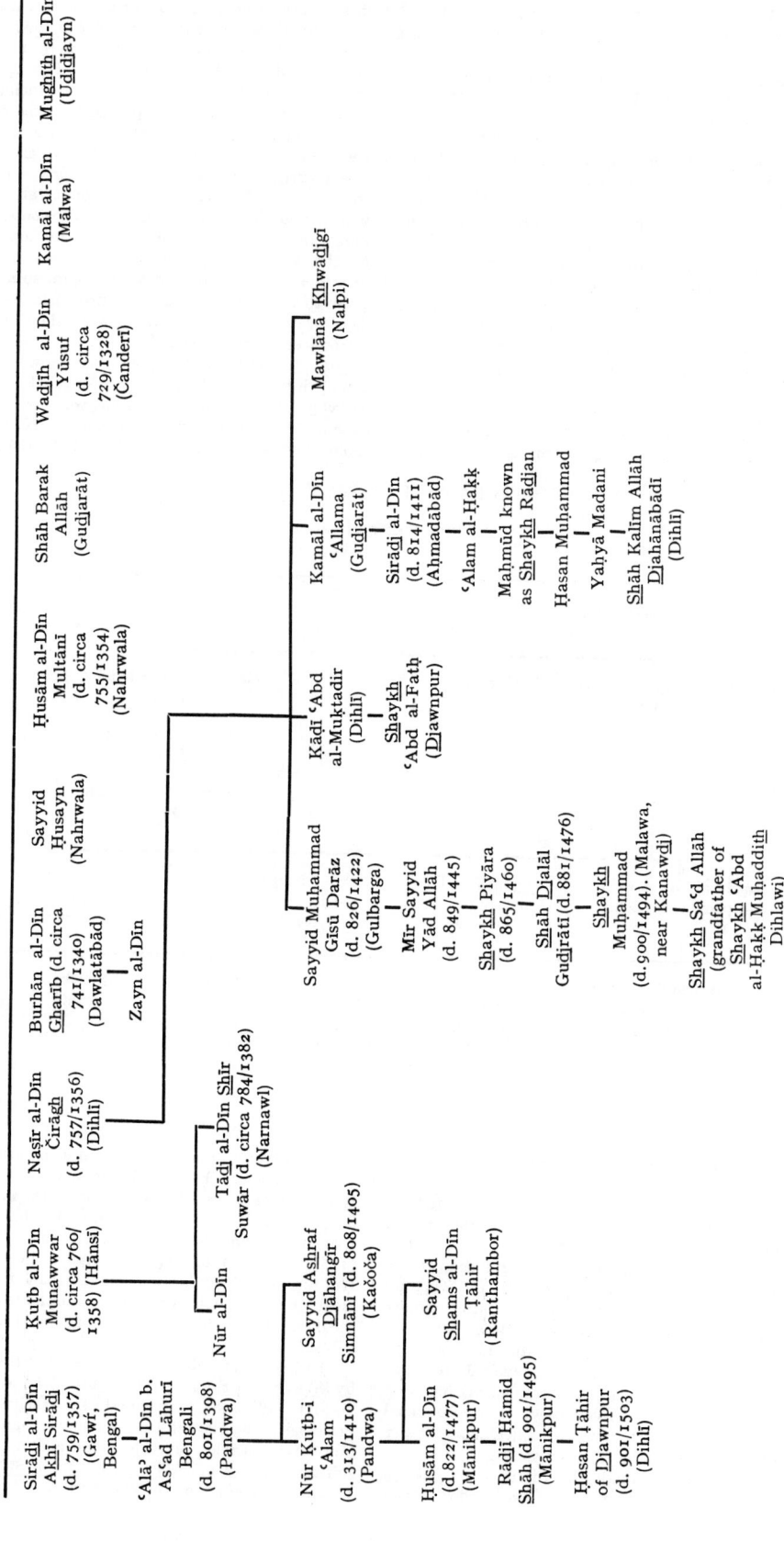

(iii) RISE OF THE ṢĀBIRIYYA BRANCH:

- Shaykh ʿAlāʾ al-Dīn ʿAlī b. Aḥmad Ṣābir (d. 691/1291) (Kalyar)
  - Shams al-Dīn Turk (Panīpat)
    - Djalāl al-Dīn Maḥmūd (Panipat)
      - Aḥmad ʿAbd al-Ḥaḳḳ (d. 838/1434) (Radawlī)
        - Shaykh ʿArif (Radawli)
          - Shaykh Muḥammad
            - ʿAbd al-Ḳuddūs (d. 944/1537) (Gangū)
              - ʿAbd al-Aḥad (father of Shaykh Aḥmad Sirhindī)
              - Djalāl al-Dīn Fārūḳī (Thanesar) (d. 990/1582)
                - Niẓām al-Dīn Fārūḳī (Balkh) (d. circa 1036/1626)
                  - Abū Saʿīd (Gangū)
                    - Muḥammad Ṣādiḳ
                      - Muḥammad Dāʾūd
                        - Shāh Abu'l-Maʿālī (d. 1112/1700)
                          - Muḥammad Saʿīd
                            - Sayyid Muḥammad Sālim (d. 1175/1761)
                              - Sayyid Muḥammad ʿAẓam (d. 1227/1812)
                                - Ḥāfiẓ Mūsā Mānikpurī (d. 1280/1863)
                                  - Sayyid Amānat ʿAli (d. 1280/1863)
                                    - Ḥāfiẓ Muḥammad Ḥusayn (author of *Anwār al-ʿĀrifīn*)
                                      - Ḥādjī Imdād Allāh of Thānā Bhawan (d. 1317/1899) (Mecca) [see below]
                        - Shaykh Saundhā (d. 1119/1707)
                          - Muḥammad Ikram (author of *Iḳtibās al-Anwār*)
                    - Muḥibb Allāh Ṣadrpurī (d. 1058/1648) (Allāhābād)
                      - Shāh Muḥammadī Fayyāḍ (d. 1107/1695) (Agra)
                        - Shāh ʿAḍd al-Dīn (d. 1172/1758)
                          - Shāh ʿAbd al-Hādī (d. 1190/1776) (Amroha)
                            - Shāh ʿAbd al-Bārī (d. 1226/1811)
                              - Sayyid ʿAbd al-Rahīm Fāṭimī (d. 1247/1831) (Balakot)
                                - Miyāndjī Nūr Muḥammad (d. 1259/1843) (Djhandjhāna)
                                  - Ḥādjī Imdād Allāh of Thānā Bhawan (d. 1317/1899) (Mecca)
            - Shaykh Budh
              - Shaykh Pīr
                - Ḳuṭb al-Dīn
                  - Shaykh Ḥāmid (d. 1033/1623)
                    - ʿAbd al-Raḥmān (author of *Mirʾāt al-Asrār*)
              - Shaykh Manṣūr
                - Shaykh ʿAlam

- Ḥādjī Imdād Allāh of Thānā Bhawan (d. 1317/1899) (Mecca)
  - Muḥammad Ḳāsim Nanawtawī (d. 1295/1878) (founder of the *madrasa* of Deoband)
  - Ashraf ʿAlī (Thāna Bhawan)
    - Sayyid Sulaymān Nadawī (d. 1953) (Karachi)
  - Rashīd Aḥmad (d. 1905) (Gangū)
    - Maḥmūd Ḥasan, *Shaykh al-Hind* (d. 1920) (Deoband)
    - Ḥusayn Aḥmad Madanī (d. 1957) (Deoband)
    - Khalīl Aḥmad Anbethawi (d. 1927) (Medina)
      - Muḥammad Ilyās Kandhlawī (d. 1944) (Dihlī)
    - ʿAbd al-Raḥmān Muḥaddith (Amroha)
  - Aḥmad Ḥasan Muḥaddith (d. 1911) (Amroha)

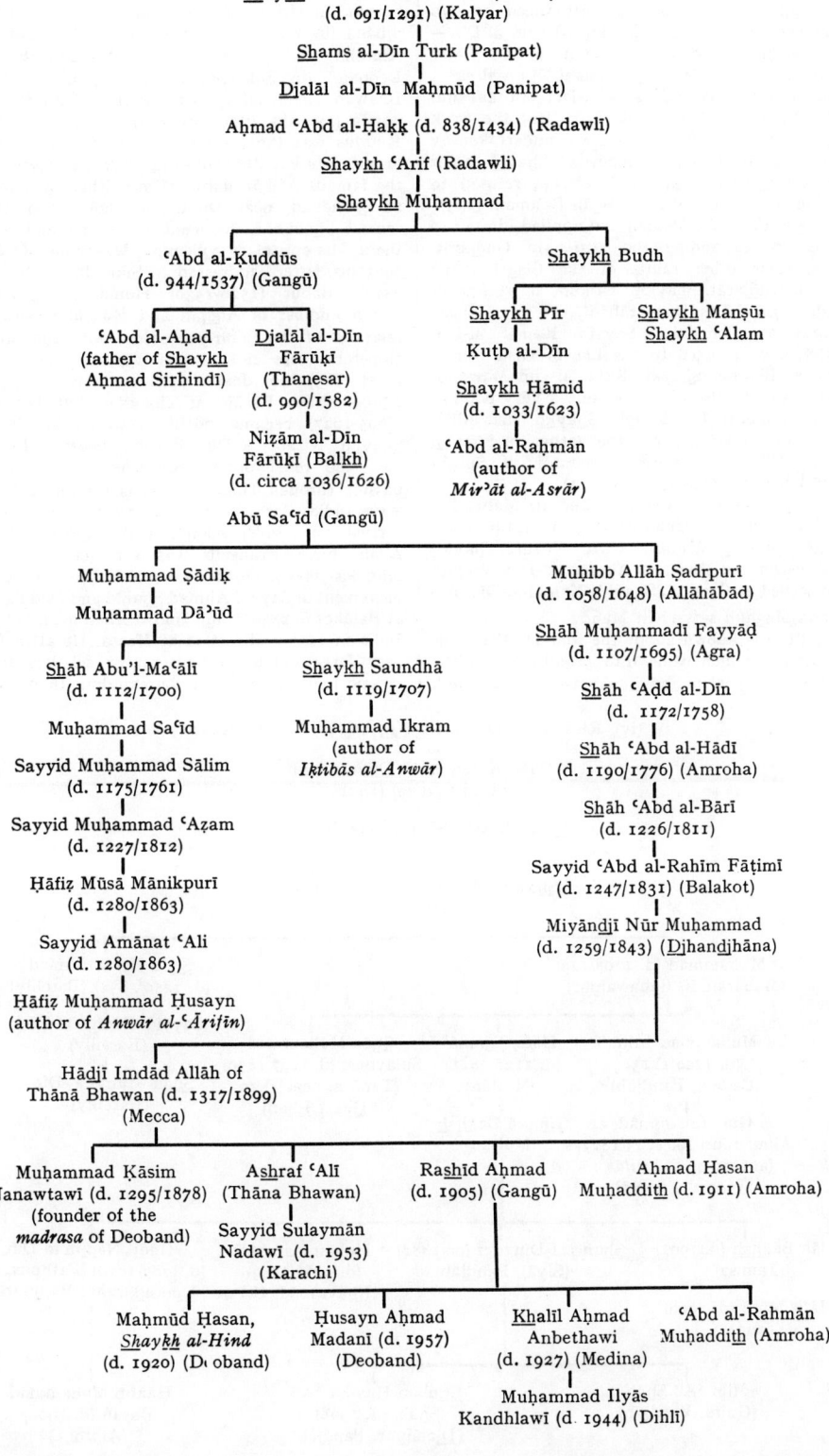

on, a disciple of Shaykh Naṣīr al-Dīn Čirāgh, Sayyid Muḥammad Gīsū Darāz, set up a Čishtī centre at Gulbarga. He was a prolific writer and a scholar of several languages. Through him the *silsila* spread in the Deccan and Gudjarāt.

In Gudjarāt, the *silsila* was introduced by two less known disciples of Khwādja Ḳuṭb al-Dīn—Shaykh Maḥmūd and Shaykh Ḥamīd al-Dīn. Later on, three disciples of Shaykh Niẓām al-Dīn Awliyā᾿—Sayyid Ḥasan, Shaykh Ḥusām al-Dīn Multānī and Shaykh Barak Allāh reached there. But the work of organizing it on effective lines was undertaken by ʿAllama Kamāl al-Dīn, a nephew of Shaykh Naṣīr al-Dīn Čirāgh. His son, Sirādj al-Dīn, refused to accede to the request of Fīrūz Shāh Bahmanī (1397-1422), to settle in the Deccan and applied himself to the task of expanding the *silsila* in Gudjarāt. Besides, some other saints of the Čishtī *silsila* settled in Gudjarāt. Shaykh Yaʿḳūb, a *khalīfa* of Shaykh Zayn al-Dīn Dawlatābādī, set up a Čishtī *khanaḳāh* at Nahrwala; Sayyid Kamāl al-Dīn Ḳazwīnī, who belonged to the line of Gīsū Darāz, settled at Bharoč. Shaykh Rukn al-Din Mawdūd, another saint of the *silsila*, became a very popular figure in Gudjarāt. His disciple, Shaykh ʿAzīz Allāh al-Muta wakkil-ila᾿llāh, was the father of Shaykh Raḥmat Allāh, the spiritual mentor of Sulṭān Maḥmūd Bēgaṙā (862-917/1458-1511).

The Čishtiyya order was organized in Mālwa by the following three disciples of Shaykh Niẓām al-Dīn Awliyā᾿: Shaykh Wadjīh al-Dīn Yūsuf, Shaykh Kamāl al-Dīn and Mawlānā Mughīth al-Dīn. Wadjīh al-Dīn settled at Čanderī, Shaykh Kamāl-al-Dīn and Mawlānā Mughīth settled in Mandū.

Very little is known about the founder the Ṣābiriyya branch, which came into prominence in the 9th/15th century when Shaykh Aḥmad ʿAbd al-Ḥaḳḳ set up a great mystic centre at Rudawli. The main centres of this branch of the Čishtī *silsila* were Kalyar (near Roorkee in the Saharanpur district of U.P.), Panīpat, Rudawli (38 miles from Bārā Bankī in Awadh), Gangu (23 miles u.c. of Saharanpur, in U.P.), Thanesar (near Panīpat), Djhandjhānā (in Muẓaffarnagar district, U.P.) Allāhābād, Amroha (in the Murādābād district of U.P.) Deoband (in Saharanpur district, U.P.); Thāna Bhawan (in Muẓaffarnagar district, U.P.) and Nānawta (in Saharanpur district). Shaykh ʿAbd al-Ḳuddus was the greatest figure of the Ṣābiriyya branch. He left Rudawli in 1491, at the suggestion of the famous Afghān noble, ʿUmar Khān, and settled at Shāhābād, near Dihlī. In 1526, when Bābur sacked Shāhābād, he went to Gangū and settled there. His epistolary collection, *Maktūbāt-i Ḳuddūsī*, contains letters addressed to Sikandar Lōdī (1488-1517), Bābur (1526-1530) Humāyūn (1530-1556) and a number of Afghān and Mughal nobles. The relations of the Ṣābiriyya saints with the Mughal emperors were not always very cordial. Akbar (1556-1605) no doubt paid a visit to Shaykh Djalāl al-Dīn Fārūḳī at Thanesar, but Djahāngīr (1605-1627) became hostile towards his disciple, Shaykh Niẓām al-Dīn Fārūḳī, because he had met the rebel prince, Khusraw, when he was passing through Thanesar. Djahāngīr forced him to leave India. Darā Shukoh had great respect for and carried on correspondence with Shaykh Muḥibb Allāh, but Awrangzīb was very critical of his religious views. Shāh ʿAbd al-Raḥīm joined the movement of Sayyid Aḥmad Shahīd and died fighting at Balākot in 1830. Hādjī Imdād Allāh migrated from India in 1857 and settled at Mecca. He attracted a very large number of externalist scholars to his mystic fold. Many of the outstanding Indo-Muslim

(iv) REVIVAL OF THE NIẒĀMIYYA BRANCH:

- Shāh Kalīm Allāh Djahānābādī (d. 1142/1729) (Dihlī)
  - Shāh Niẓām al-Dīn (d.1142/1729) (Awrangābād)
    - Shāh Fakhr al-Dīn (d. 1199/1784) (Dihlī)
      - Nūr Muḥammad (d. 1205/1790) (Mahārān, in Bahawalpur)
        - Muḥammad ʿĀḳil (d. 1229/1813) (Čačrān, Pandjāb)
          - Gul Muḥammad Aḥmadpuri (d. 1243/1827) (author of *Takmilah-i Siyar al-Awliyā᾿*)
        - Ḥāfiẓ Djamāl (d. 1226/1811) (Multān)
          - Khudā Bakhsh (Multān)
            - Allāh Bakhsh (d. 1901) (Taunsa)
              - Ḥāfiẓ Mūsā (d. 1906) (Taunsa)
            - Shams al-Dīn (d. 1300/1882) (Siyāl, Pandjāb)
              - Mihr ʿAlī Shāh (Gulra, Pandjāb)
              - Ghulām Ḥaydar ʿAlī Shāh (d. 1908) (Djalālpur, Pandjāb)
            - Muḥammad ʿAlī (d. 1266/1849) (Khayrābād, U.P.)
            - Hādjī Nadjm al-Din (d. 1287/1870) (Fatḥpur, near Djhundjhunu, Rādjputāna)
              - Ḥakīm Muḥammad Ḥasan (d. 1904) (Amroha)
        - Shāh Muḥammad Sulaymān (d. 1267/1850) (Taunsa, near Dera Ghazī Khan)
      - Shāh Niyāz Aḥmad (d. 1250/1834) (Bareilly)
        - Sayyid Niẓām al-Dīn (Bareilly)
          - Shāh Muḥyī al-Dīn (Bareilly)

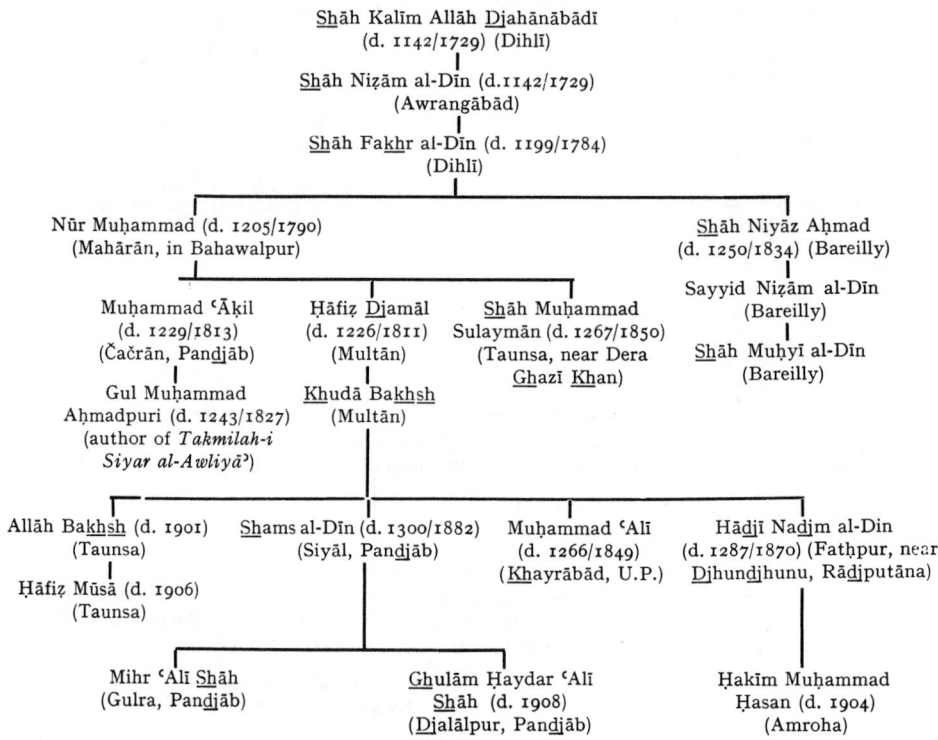

ʿulamāʾ of the post-1857 period, like Mawlānā Ras͟hīd Aḥmad Muḥaddit͟h of Gangu, Mawlānā Muḥammad Ḳāsim Nanawtawī, Mawlānā As͟hraf ʿAli Thānawī, Mawlānā Maḥmūd al-Ḥasan Deobandī, Sayyid Sulaymān Nadawī, Mawlānā Ḥusayn Aḥmad Madanī, Mawlānā K͟halīl Aḥmad, Mawlānā Muḥammad Ilyās Kandhlawī, Mawlānā Aḥmad Ḥasan Muḥaddit͟h Amrohwī, may be counted amongst his spiritual descendants. Almost all the great *ʿulamāʾ* of Deoband [*q.v.*] are spiritually associated with the Čis͟htiyya *silsila* through him.

The Niẓāmiyya branch of the Čis͟htiyya *silsila* was revitalised by S͟hāh Kalīm Allāh Dj̲ahānābādī. He belonged to that famous family of architects which had built the Tādj̲ Maḥall of Agra and the Dj̲āmiʿ Masdj̲id of Dihlī, but he dedicated himself to spiritual work and infused new life into the almost defunct Čis͟htī organization. After S͟hayk͟h Naṣīr al-Dīn Čirāg͟h, he was the greatest Čis͟htī saint who revived the old traditions and strove to build up a central organization of the *silsila*. His disciples spread in the distant south also. His chief *k͟halīfa*, S͟hayk͟h Niẓām al-Dīn, worked in Awrangābād. The latter's son, S͟hāh Fak͟hr al-Dīn, came to Dihlī and set up a mystic centre there. It was through his two *k͟halīfas*, S͟hāh Nūr Muḥammad of Mahārān and S͟hāh Niyāz Aḥmad of Bareilly, that the *silsila* spread in the Pandj̲āb, N.W. Frontier, and U.P. S͟hāh Nūr Muḥammad's disciples set up *k͟hānaḳāhs* at the following places in the Pandj̲āb: Taunsa, Čačrān, Kōt́ Mithan, Aḥmadpur, Multān, Siyāl, Gulra, and Dj̲alālpur. S͟hāh Niyāz Aḥmad worked mainly in Dihlī and U.P.

B: Ideology

The early Čis͟htī mystics of India had adopted the *ʿAwārif al-Maʿārif* of S͟hayk͟h S͟hihāb al-Dīn Suhrawardī as their chief guide book. On it was based the organisation of their *k͟hānaḳāhs*, and the elder saints taught it to their disciples. The *Kashf al-Maḥdj̲ūb* of Hudj̲wīrī was also a very popular work and S͟hayk͟h Niẓām al-Dīn Awliyāʾ used to say: "For one who has no spiritual guide, the *Kas͟hf al-Maḥdj̲ūb* is enough". Apart from these two works, the *malfūẓāt* (conversations) of S͟hayk͟h Niẓām al-Dīn Awliyāʾ, S͟hayk͟h Naṣīr al-Dīn Čirāg͟h, S͟hayk͟h Burhān al-Dīn G͟harīb and Sayyid Muḥammad Gīsū-Darāz give a fairly accurate idea of the Čis͟htī mystic ideology. (i) The cornerstone of Čis͟htī ideology was the concept of *waḥdat al-wudj̲ūd* (Unity of Being). It supplied the motive force to their mystic mission and determined their social outlook. The early Čis͟htī saints, however, did not write anything about *waḥdat al-wudj̲ūd*. Masʿūd Bakk's *Mirʾāt al-ʿĀrifīn* and his *dīwān*, *Nūr al-ʿAyn*, gave currency to these ideas and his works became a popular study in the Čis͟htī *k͟hānaḳāhs*. Later on, S͟hayk͟h ʿAbd al-Ḳuddūs wrote a commentary on Ibn al-ʿArabī's books and he was followed by S͟hayk͟h Niẓām al-Dīn Thānesarī, who wrote two commentaries on ʿIrāḳī's *Lamaʿāt*. One of his *k͟halīfas*, S͟hayk͟h ʿAbd al-Kārim Lāhurī, wrote a Persian commentary on the *Fuṣūṣ al-Ḥikam*. S͟hayk͟h Muḥibb Allāh of Allāhābād was a very powerful exponent of the ideology of *waḥdāt al-wudj̲ūd*. Awrangzīb, who was more influenced by the school of S͟hayk͟h Aḥmad Sirhindī, ordered his books to be burnt. (ii) The Čis͟htīs looked down upon possession of private property as a negation of faith in God. They rejected all worldly goods and material attractions (*tark-i dunyā*) and lived on *futūḥ*, which were not demanded as charity. (iii) They believed in pacifism and non-violence and considered retaliation and revenge as laws of the animal world. They lived and worked for a healthy social order—free from all dissensions and discriminations. (iv) In no form was contact with the state permitted. "There are two abuses among the mystics", says an early Čis͟htī mystic, "*dj̲irrat* and *muḳallid*. *Muḳallid* is one who has no master; *dj̲irrat* is one who visits kings and their courts and asks people for money". (v) The *summum bonum* of a mystic's life, according to Čis͟htīs, is to live for the Lord alone. He should neither hope for Heaven nor fear Hell. Man's Love towards God may be of three kinds: (a) *maḥabbat-i Islāmī*, *i.e.*, love which a new convert to Islam develops with God on account of his conversion to the new faith; (b) *maḥabbat-i muwahhibī*, *i.e.*, love which a man develops as a result of his 'effort' in the way of following the Prophet; and (c) *maḥabbat-i k͟hāṣṣ*, *i.e.*, love which is the result of cosmic emotion. A mystic should develop the last one. (vi) The Čis͟htī mystics did not demand formal conversion to Islam as a pre-requisite to initiation in mystic discipline. Formal conversion, they said, should not precede but follow a change in emotional life. The Čis͟htī attitude contrasted sharply with the Suhrawardī principles in this respect.

C: Practices

The following practices were adopted by the Čis͟htīs in order to harness all feelings and emotions in establishing communion with Allāh: (i) *D͟hikr-i Dj̲ahr*, reciting the names of Allāh loudly, sitting in the prescribed posture at prescribed times; (ii) *D͟hikr-i K͟hafī*, reciting the names of Allāh silently; (iii) *Pās-i Anfās*, regulating the breath; (iv) *Murāḳāba*, absorption in mystic contemplation; (v) *Čilla*, forty days of spiritual confinement in a lonely corner or cell for prayer and contemplation. The efficacy of audition parties (*samāʿ*) in attuning a mystic's heart to the Infinite and the Eternal was also emphasised. Some Čis͟htī mystics believed in *Čilla-i maʿkūs* ("inverted *Čilla*") also. One who practised it tied a rope to his feet and had his body lowered into a well, and offered prayers in this posture for forty nights.

D. Literature

The literature of the *silsila* may be considered under five heads: (a) *malfūẓāt* (conversations) of the saints, (b) *maktūbāt* (letters) of the saints (c) works on mystic ideology and practices, (d) biographical accounts of saints and (e) poetical works. Only major and representative works have been indicated here.

(a) Malfūẓāt: The *malfūẓ* literature of the Čis͟htī saints throws valuable light on their thought and activities. The art of *malfūẓ*-writing was introduced in India by Amīr Ḥasan Sidj̲zī, who compiled the conversations of S͟hayk͟h Niẓām al-Dīn Awliyāʾ in his *Fawāʾid al-Fuʾād*, Nawal Kishore 1302. Other important collections of *malfūẓāt* are the following: *K͟hayr al-Madj̲ālis*, conversations of S͟hayk͟h Naṣīr al-Dīn Čirāg͟h, compiled by Ḥamīd Ḳalandar (ed. K. A. Niẓāmī, Aligarh); *Surūr al-Ṣudūr*, conversations of S͟hayk͟h Ḥamīd al-Dīn Ṣūfī, compiled by his grandson (MSS Ḥabībgandj̲ and personal collection; see *Proceedings of the Indian History Congress*, Nagpur Session, 1950, 167-169); *Aḥsan al-Aḳwāl*, conversations of S͟hayk͟h Burhān al-Dīn G͟harīb, compiled by Mawlānā Ḥammād Kās͟hānī (MS personal collection, see *J.Pak.H.S.*, vol. iii Part I, 40-41). *Dj̲awāmiʿ al-Kalām*, conversations of Gīsū-Darāz, compiled by Sayyid Muḥammad Akbar Ḥusaynī (Uthmāngandj); *Anwār al-ʿUyun*, conversations of Shaykh Aḥmad ʿAbd al-Ḥaḳḳ (compiled by Shaykh ʿAbd al-Ḳuddūs), Aligarh 1905. *Laṭāʾif-i Ḳuddūsī*, conversations of Shaykh ʿAbd al-Ḳuddūs by Rukn al-Dīn, Delhi 1311; *Fakhr al-Ṭālibīn* (conversations of Shāh Fakhr al-Dīn, compiled by Rukn al-Dīn Fakhrī), Delhi 1315; *Nāfaʿ al-Sālikīn*, conversations of Shāh Sulaymān of Taunsa, by Imām al-Dīn, Lahore 1285. The following collections of the conversations of the Čishtī saints, *Anīs al-Arwāḥ*, *Dalīl al-ʿĀrifīn*, *Fawāʾid al-Salikīn*, *Asrār al-Awliyāʾ*, *Rāḥat al-Ḳulūb*, *Rāḥat al-Muḥibbīn*, *Miftāḥ al-ʿĀshiḳīn*, *Afḍal al-Fawāʾid*, are apocryphal, but are useful in so far as they represent the popular interpretation of Čishtī ideology.

(b) Maktūbāt: *Ṣaḥāʾif al-Sulūk*, letters of Aḥmad Faḳīr, Djhadjdjar; *Bahr al-Maʿānī*, letters of Sayyid Djaʿfar Makkī, Murādābād 1889; *Maktūbāt-i Ashrafī*, letters of Sayyid Ashraf Djahāngīr Simnānī (MS Aligarh); *Maktūbāt* of Sayyid Nūr Ḳuṭb-i ʿĀlam (MS Aligarh); *Maktūbāt-i Ḳuddūsī* of Shaykh ʿAbd al-Ḳuddūs (Delhi); *Maktūbāt-i Kalīmī* of Shāh Kalīm Allāh Djahānabādī, Delhi 1301. Copies of some letters said to have been addressed by Khwādja Muʿīn al-Dīn to Khwādja Ḳuṭb al-Dīn are also available, but their authenticity has not been established.

(c) Works on mystic ideology and practices: The two earliest Čishtī works on mystic ideology are in the form of aphorisms—the *Mulhamāt* of Shaykh Djamāl al-Dīn Hānswī, Alwar 1306, and *Mukh al-Maʿani* of Amīr Ḥasan Sidjzī (MS Muslim University Library, Aligarh). The *Uṣūl al-Samāʿ* of Fakhr al-Dīn Zarradī, Djhadjdjar 1311, contains an exposition of Čishtī attitude towards music parties. Amongst other Čishtī works, the following may be particularly noted: Rukn al-Dīn ʿImād, *Shamāʾil-i Anḳiyya* (MS As. Soc. of Bengal); ʿAbd al-Ḳuddūs, *Gharāʾib al-Fuʾād* (Muslim Press, Djhadjdjar); Niẓām al-Dīn Balkhī, *Riyāḍ al-Ḳuds*, Bidjnor 1887; Shāh Kalīm Allāh, *Muraḳḳa-i Kalīmī*, Delhi 1308; *Siwa al-Sabīl* (MS Rampur); Niẓām al-Dīn Awrangābādī, *Niẓām al-Ḳulūb* (Delhi 1309); Fakhr al-Dīn Dihlawī, *Niẓām al-Aḳāʾid* (Urdu trans., Delhi 1312); *Risāla ʿAyn al-Yaḳīn*, Delhi.

(d) Biographical works: The earliest biographical account of the Čishtī saints of the first cycle is found in Mīr Khurd's *Siyar al-Awliyāʾ* compiled in the 8th/14th century. Late in the 19th century, Khwādja Gul Muḥammad Aḥmadpurī wrote a *Takmila* to the *Siyar al-Awliyāʾ*, Delhi 1312. Other important biographical works include, Djamālī, *Siyar al-ʿĀrifīn*, Delhi 1311; Niẓām al-Dīn Yamanī, *Laṭāʾif-i Ashrafī*, Delhi 1395; Tādj al-Dīn, *Risāla Ḥāl Khānawāda-i Čisht* (MS personal collection); Bahā *alias* Rādjā, *Risala Aḥwāl Pīrān-i Čisht* (MS personal collection); ʿAlī Aṣghar Čishtī, *Djawāhir-i Farīdī*, Lahore 1301; ʿAbd al-Rahmān, *Mirʾāt al-Asrār* (MSS, Storey 1005); Allāh Ḍiyāʾ, *Siyar al-Aḳṭāb*, Lucknow 1881; Muʿīn al-Dīn, *Maʿāridj al-Wilāyat* (MS personal collection); ʿAlāʾ al-Dīn Barnawī, *Čishtiyya-i Bihishtiyya* (MSS., Storey 1008); Akram Baraswi, *Iḳtibās al-Anwār*, Lahore 1895; Muḥammad Bulāḳ, *Maṭlūb al-Ṭālibīn* (MSS, Storey 1014), *Rawḍa al-Aḳṭāb*, Delhi 1304; Mīr Shihāb al-Dīn Niẓām, *Manāḳib-i Fakhriyya*, Delhi 1315; Raḥīm Bakhsh, *Shadjarat al-Anwār* MS, personal collection); Muḥammad Ḥusayn, *Anwār al-ʿĀrifīn*, Lucknow 1876; Nadjm al-Dīn, *Manāḳib al-Maḥbūbayn*, Lucknow 1876; Ghulām Muḥammad Khān, *Manāḳib-i Sulaymānī*, Delhi 1871; Aḥmad Akhtar Mīrzā, *Manāḳib-i Farīdī*, Delhi 1314; Hādī ʿAlī Khān, *Manāḳib-i Ḥāfiẓiyya*, Kanpur 1305; Nithār ʿAlī, *Khawāriḳ-i Hādwiyya*, Delhi 1927.

(e) Poetical works: The *dīwān*s attributed to Khwādja Muʿīn al-Dīn and Khwādja Ḳuṭb al-Dīn Bakhtiyār are apocryphal. The *Surūr al-Ṣudūr* says that Shaykh Ḥamīd al-Dīn had left poetic compositions in Arabic, Persian and Hindwī. Only a few couplets are now available. The earliest poetical work of an Indian Čishtī mystic is the *Dīwān-i Djamāl al-Dīn Hānswī*, Delhi 1889. Amīr Khusraw, though associated with the Čishtī order, did not produce any work exclusively on mysticism, but some of his poems contain verses which throw light on mystic tendencies of the period. Masʿūd Bakk's *Dīwān*, Yūsuf Gadā's *Tuḥfat al-Naṣāʾiḥ*, Lahore 1283, and Shāh Niyāz Aḥmad's *Dīwān-i Bāy Niyāz*, Agra 1348, are steeped in Čishtī ideology.

Bibliography: Besides works cited in the article, see: ʿAbd al-Ḥaḳḳ Muḥaddith, *Akhbār al-Akhyār*, Delhi 1309; Ghulām Sarwar, *Khazīnat al-Aṣfiyāʾ*, Lucknow 1873; Mushtāḳ Aḥmad, *Anwār al-ʿĀshiḳīn*, Ḥaydarābād 1332. ʿĀshiḳ Ilāhī, *Tadhkirat al-Khalīl* (Meerut); Sayyid ʿAbd al-Ḥayy, *Nuzhat al-Khawāṭir*, Ḥaydarābād; Ashraf ʿAlī Thanawī, *Al-Sunnat al-Djilliya fi 'l-Čishtiyya al-ʿUliyya*, Delhi 1351; Muḥ. Ḥabīb: *Shaykh Naṣīr al-Dīn Čirāgh as a Great Historical Personality*, in *Islamic Culture*, April 1946; idem, *Čishtī Mystic Records of the Sultanate Period*, in *Medieval India Quarterly*, Vol. I, no. 2; K. A. Niẓāmī; *Taʾrīkh-i Mashāʾikh-i Čisht*, Delhi 1953; idem, *The Life and Times of Shaykh Farīd al-Dīn Gandj-i Shakar*, Aligarh 1955; idem, *Early Indo-Muslim Mystics and Their Attitude towards the State*, in *Islamic Culture*, October 1948-January 1950. (K. A. Nizami)

ČITR [see GHĀSHIYA]

ČIWI-ZĀDE, Ottoman family of scholars, two of whom held the office of *Shaykh al-Islām* in the 10th/16th century; they take their name from the *mudarris* Čiwi Ilyās of Menteshe (d. 900/1494-5).

1. Muḥyi al-Dīn Shaykh Muḥammad ('Kodja Čiwizāde'), the son of Čiwi Ilyās, b. 896/1490-1, was appointed *Ḳāḍī* of Cairo in 934/1527-8, *Ḳāḍī ʿasker* of Anadolu in 944, and *Shaykh al-Islām* (on the death of Saʿdī Ef.) in Shawwāl 945/Feb. 1539. He was dismissed (the first *Shaykh al-Islām* not to hold office for life) in Radjab 948 (?or 949), on the pretext that he had given an unsound *fatwā* (Luṭfī Pasha, *Taʾrīkh*, 390): the real reason was probably his hostility to *taṣawwuf* (*Shaḳāʾiḳ* [Medjdī], 446, and cf. Ḥ. Kh. [Flügel], iv, 429). In 952/1545 he replaced Abu 'l-Suʿūd, now *Shaykh al-Islām*, as *Ḳāḍīʿasker* of Rumeli, in which office he died (Shaʿbān 954/Sept. 1547).

His brother ʿAbdī Čelebi, who trained the young Ferīdūn [*q.v.*], was *Bash-Defterdār* from 954/1547 (cf. L. Forrer, *Rustem Pascha*, 145) until his death in 960, and his son-in-law Ḥāmid Ef. was *Shaykh al-Islām* from 982/1574 to 985.

2. Muḥammad, son of the above, b. 937/1531, was successively *Ḳāḍī* of Damascus (977/1569), Cairo, Bursa, Edirne and Istanbul, then *Ḳāḍī ʿasker* of Anadolu (983/1575) and of Rumeli (985), in which posts he won a great reputation for uprightness. Having incurred the enmity of Sokollu Meḥemmed Pasha, he was dismissed, but in 989/1581 he was re-appointed to Rumeli; he became *Shaykh al-Islām* in the same year, and died in office (28 Djum. I 995/6 May 1587).

His son Muḥammad Ef. (d. 1061/1651) and his grandson ʿAṭāʾullāh Ef. (d. 1138/1725) both rose to be *Ḳāḍīʿasker*.

Works: Besides the recorded works of Muḥyi al-Dīn (Ḥ. Kh. [Flügel] nos. 5990, 8721 [*fetwās*, = *GAL* II², 569, to which add MS. Esad Ef. 958] and 11585; *GAL* S II 642, S III 1304) and Muḥammad (Ḥ. Kh. nos. 774 [MS. Nur-iʿ Osm. 2061, which is now lost] and 8805 [MSS. Nur-iʿ Osm. 1959, Ist. Un. Lib. AY 610/3]; *GAL* II² 573 [where the Nur-iʿ Osm. reference should read 2060]), there are in the various collections in the Süleymaniye Library of Istanbul several *risālas*, attributed simply to 'Çivizade'.

Bibliography: The main sources are, for Muḥyi al-Dīn, *Shaḳaʾiḳ* [Medjdī], 446; for Muḥammad, ʿAṭāʾī's *dhayl* to the *Shaḳāʾiḳ*, 292; and for both, Taḳī al-Dīn al-Tamīmī, *al-Ṭabaḳāt al-saniyya fī tarādjim al-Ḥanafiyya* (in MS.). Further references in *IA*, s.v. Çivizāde [M. Cavid Baysun]; detailed biographies of these and other members of the family in the unpublished thesis *Çivizade ailesi* by Şerafettin Tunçay (Istanbul Univ. Lib., Tez 1872). (V. L. Ménage)

CLAN [see ĀL]

COFFEE [see ḲAHWA]

COIMBRA [see ḲULUMRIYA]

ČOKA [see ḲUMĀSH]

ČOKA ADASÎ, the Turkish name for Kythera (Cerigo), one of the Ionian islands. In early Ottoman times possession was disputed or shared between the Venetian state and the Venieri. Čoka Adasî was an important post for watching shipping, especially after the loss of the Morea, and was often attacked. In 943-4/1537 the Turks carried off 7000 captives; many survivors fled to the Morea. Čoka Adasî was again raided in 1571 and 1572, when an indecisive naval battle took place there. It was taken by the Turks in 1127/1715 but restored at the Peace of Passarovitz. It now became the easternmost Venetian colony and lost all importance, though it was again raided in the war of 1787-92.

Bibliography: V. Lamansky, *Secrets d'état de Venise*, St. Pétersbourg 1884, 641-2, 660-70; C. Sathas, Μνημεῖα, vi, 1885, 286-311; allusions in many travellers and chroniclers, especially Ḥādjdjī Khalīfa, *Tuḥfat al-Kibār*. (C. F. Beckingham)

ČÖLEMERIK (old form, DJŪLĀMERG or DJULAMERIK), a small town in eastern Anatolia, in the extreme south-east of the present-day region of Turkey, 37° 45′ N, 43° 48′ E, altitude 5,413 ft. (1650 m.), surrounded by mountains of over 9,840 ft. (3000 m.), about 3 km. from the Great Zab, a tributary of the Tigris. It is the capital of the *wilāyet* of Hakkâri; in the 19th century it was the capital of a *sandjaḳ* of the same name, in the *wilāyet* of Van, formerly belonging to the *ḥukūmet* of Ḥakkārī (Kātib Čelebi, *Djihānnümā*, 419). The place was destroyed in the First World War, but rebuilt again in 1935. At the census of 1950 it numbered 2,664 inhabitants (the *ḳaḍāʾ* had 14,473 inhabitants). There are hot sulphur springs nearby.

Andreas assumes (cf. Pauly-Wissowa, i, 1699; see also M. Hartmann, *Bohtān*, in *Mitteilungen der Vorderasiatischen Gesellschaft* 1896, 143) that Čölemerik is identical with the τὸ χλωμάρων of antiquity. This view is opposed by Marquart (*Ērānshahr*, 158 f.). The place Čölemerik has lent its name to a branch of the Kurds, the Djūlamerkiye; concerning these cf. Ibn Faḍlallāh al-ʿUmarī (*Notices et Extraits* xiii, 317 ff.).

Bibliography: in addition to works already mentioned in the article: Ritter, *Erdkunde*, xi, 625 ff.; E. Reclus, *Nouvelle géographie universelle*, ix, 429 ff.; G. Hoffmann, *Auszüge aus syrischen Akten persischer Martyrer*, 230; W. F. Ainsworth, *Travels and Researches in Asia Minor*, ii, 283; S. Martin, *Mémoires sur l'Arménie*, i, 177 ff.; H. Binder, *Aus Kurdistan*, 165; Lehmann-Haupt, *Armenien einst und jetzt*, passim; V. Cuinet, *La Turquie d'Asie*, ii, 716 ff.; *Geographical Journal*, xviii, 132; *IA*, iii, 441 f. (Besim Darkot).

(Fr. Taeschner)

COLOMB-BÉCHAR, chief town of the department of the Saoura (Organisation Commune des Régions Sahariennes), created by a decree of 7 August 1957.

This town is quite recent; before the French occupation, which dates from 13 November 1903, a few villages, with no historical importance, had been built unevenly along the banks of the Oued Bechar (Wādī Bashshār), which sustained a scanty group of palms. From 1857 the region had been explored by Captain de Colomb, whose name has been used for the new town; to this has been joined the name Bechar which, according to local tradition, derives from the fact that a Muslim sent to explore the region by a Turkish sultan (?) of the 15th century, brought back a flask of clear water; hence the epithet, taken from the root *b . sh . r* (to bring good news), which would be given to him and to the region from which he came.

The French occupation, following on Franco-Moroccan talks, was designed to protect southern Oran against incursions of Berber tribes from Tafilalt and neighbouring regions. At first a military post, Colomb-Béchar became in 1905 the terminal of a railway line from Oran Tell, and an important caravan centre, then in 1919 the main town of a mixed commune and in 1930 the main town of the territory of Ain Sefra (ʿAyn Ṣafrāʾ) (territories of southern Algeria). At the time of the Second World War, the coal mines which had been discovered in 1917 in the neighbourhood of the town were fully exploited, from 1941; at the same time the decision was made to build the railway from the Mediterranean to the Niger, which gave a new stimulus to the town. Since the war the output from the surrounding coal basin has remained at roughly 300,000 tons a year; in 1956 plans were made to build a thermo-electric power station, and important mineral deposits were discovered in the region. Finally the French government has installed at Colomb-Béchar and in the surrounding district an important practice centre for guided missiles. The result of this is that the population has risen from 750 inhabitants in 1906, to more than 16,500 in 1954, 3,350 of whom are Europeans (according to the census of 1954).

Bibliography: Dr L. Céard, *L'oasis de Colomb-Béchar*, in *Arch. de l'Inst. Pasteur d'Algérie*, 1933, and *Bull. Comité Afrique Française*, 1931, (nos. 4 to 7); A. G. P. Martin, *Les oasis sahariennes*, Algiers 1908; Lyautey, *Vers le Maroc. Lettres du Sud-Oranais* (1903-06), Paris 1937; I. Eberhardt, *Dans l'ombre chaude de l'Islam*, Paris 1926; J. P. Cambo, *Le "combinat" de Colomb-Béchar*, in *Encycl. mens. d'O.-M.*, suppl. to no. 47 (July 1954), doc. no. 30. (R. Le Tourneau)

COLUMN [see ʿAMŪD]

COMMERCE [see TIDJĀRA]

COMMUNICATIONS [see BARĪD, ṬARĪḲ, ULAḲ, etc.]

COMORS [see ḲUMR]

COMPANIONS [see ṢAḤĀBA]

CONAKRY [see KONAKRY].

CONGO, River and Country in Africa. The river forms the sole outlet of the great Central African basin, which is limited on the east by the western flanks of the Great Rift, on the north by the Monga mountains, on the west by the Cristal range, and on the south by the Lunda plateau. Since its tributaries drain areas both to the north and to the south of the Equator, the Congo maintains a relatively constant flow. Its waterways are broken here and there by cataracts, especially between Stanley Pool and the sea, but they nevertheless provide long navigable stretches which have permitted a certain amount of movement, both of people and of trade, through an otherwise impenetrable forest region. In the recesses of the great forests Africa's most primitive people, the pygmies, have maintained to this day a distinctive way of life based mainly on hunting and gathering. Along or near the rivers, and nowadays increasingly along the roads which are beginning to traverse the forest region, live negroid tribes, most of whom speak languages of the Bantu family, and all of whom use iron tools and are to some degree cultivators as well as hunters and fishermen. Doubtless on account of their relative inaccessibility, the forest tribes have in general remained the most backward of the Bantu peoples.

It is only the central part of the Congo basin, however, which is densely forested. The higher country all round its periphery is mostly covered with the light forest known as "orchard bush", in which grain crops can be grown by the simple, "slash and burn" system of shifting cultivation. In the east and in the west there are even considerable stretches of open savannah grasslands suitable for cattle-raising. Above all, these peripheral regions have been relatively open to the influences of migration and conquest, and it is consequently in these regions that the indigenous peoples have achieved their most significant political groupings. To the north of the forest on the Nile-Congo watershed the multiple states of the Zande are the result of seventeenth and eighteenth century colonization and conquest from the southern fringes of the Sudan. To the east of the forest, in the highlands of the Western Rift, the Kingdoms of Ruanda and Urundi and their related states are the creation of conquering immigrants from the Nilotic Sudan or South-West Ethiopia, who appear to have been in the area since the fourteenth or fifteenth centuries. To the west of the forest, in the highlands of light bush and open savannah separating the Congo basin from the Atlantic seaboard, the important kingdom of the Bakongo, with which the Portuguese entered into relations towards the end of the fifteenth century, and which then extended its influence in some sense from the Gaboon to Angola, had been built by another immigrant minority, stemming perhaps from the direction of Lake Chad. The Congo kingdom had many southward offshoots, among them certainly the kingdom of the Bakuba on the upper Kasai. The Luba-Lunda states of the Congo-Zambezi watershed, were equally founded by immigrants, but whether these came from the west or the east of the forest is not yet established.

The ideas diffused into western Bantu Africa by these movements were essentially remnants from the ancient world of the Nile Valley. They came from the still unislamized southern fringes of the Sudan. Meanwhile, for nearly four hundred years, from the late fifteenth century to the mid-nineteenth, European influences played remotely on a Congo basin whose inhabitants were still solidly pagan and animist. The dominant European interest in the region was the slave-trade, which soon undermined and killed off the early attempts at Christian evangelization. Portuguese mulatto traders, called *pombeiros*, operating from Loanda and other ports in Angola during the seventeenth and eighteenth centuries, penetrated deeply into the southern periphery of the Congo basin, and it is likely that in the copper-bearing region of the Katanga they occasionally encountered traders from the Swahili ports on the East African coast, who were probably no more seriously Muslims than the *pombeiros* were Christian. The indications are, indeed, that such early long-distance trade as there was in eastern Bantu Africa before the nineteenth century was conducted more by Africans from such interior tribes as the Nyamwezi and the Bisa than by coastmen whether Arab or Swahili.

It was not, therefore, until the nineteenth century, with the penetration of the southern Sudan by slave and ivory traders from Egypt, and still more with the penetration of East Africa by subjects of the Būsaʿīdī dynasty of Zanzibar, that Muslims began in any numbers to reach the borders of the Congo basin. The Arab settlement at Ujiji, from which dhows crossed to the Congolese shore of the Tanganyika Lake, was founded within a few years of 1840. It was from then until the partition and occupation of tropical Africa by the European powers in the late 'eighties and early' nineties of the century that the serious commercial exploitation of the eastern and central parts of the Congo Basin by Muslim Arabs and Swahili mainly took place. The foundation by King Leopold II of the Belgians of the Congo Independent State resulted in the suppression of the slave-trade and in the elimination of the Arab and Swahili war-lords whose activities had been so vividly described by Livingstone, Stanley and other explorers. But many of the Arabs and their East African followers settled permanently in the Congo under its new colonial administration, and, as in so many other parts of Africa, the transition from freebooting exploitation to a more settled form of petty commerce marked an intensification of religious proselytism.

The great majority of the Congo Muslims, who number to-day about 200,000, are S̲h̲āfiʿīs and belong to the Ḳādirī *ṭarīḳa*. There are a few hundred K̲h̲od̲j̲as [*q.v.*], mainly in Ruanda-Urundi and in the eastern part of the Kivu Province, also in Stanleyville and Kasongo; they are active in trade, and are well-organized and well instructed. The Aḥmadiyya [*q.v.*] number only a few dozens, but are active in propaganda by distributing books and literature.

In the Eastern Province, the Kivu Province and Ruanda-Urundi there are at least 175 recognized mosques. There are Ḳurʾānic schools at Rumungwe, Lake Nyanza, Stanleyville, Ponthierville, Kirundu and Kindu. The great centre of attraction, however, is Ujiji, where there is an important *madrasa*, attended by young people who desire a little instruction in Arabic.

Islamized villages have a mosque, a brotherhood banner (drapeau de confrérie), a *muʿallimu* and an *imām*. Unlike the Zanzibaris, the Muslims of the eastern Congo are not well instructed. There are some who read al-Damīrī or al-Suyutī. But in general their reading matter is limited to popular devotional books of the Ḳādiriyya. The initiation to the *Ṭarīḳa*, in the form known as *murīdī*, which is widespread in Sénégal too, is also highly esteemed by the negro, who finds membership both dignified and authoritative. The mosques which are specially designed are of the Zanzibar type, but the majority are nothing more than large huts. Only a few educated people know any Arabic. The *lingua franca* is Kiswahilī, the Bantu language showing some Arabic influence, which is spoken as a mother tongue by the people of the Zanzibar coast. The negro Muslims who have started to enter the western Congo from the North, from the Middle Congo Republic and Chad, sometimes have a much higher cultural standard. Many of them are merchants, who sell books of devotion and talismans inscribed in Arabic. The Muslim customary courts are becoming increasingly subject to a Shafiʿī version of the *sharīʿa*.

The limited cultural level to which black Muslims attain, leaves them with too little Arabic and even with too little Swahili to understand the Islamic propaganda broadcast by radio. Among the books currently in favour one finds, besides the Ḳurʾān, the *Miʿrādj* of al-Dardīr, a work by a Zanzibar Shaykh called Ḥasan b. Amīr al-Shīrāzī; *al-ʿIḳd al-iḳyān ʿalā Mawlid al-Djīlānī*; the *Kitāb Dalāʾil al-Khayrāt*, enriched with numerous accessory texts such as the *Ḥizb al-Barr*, the *Ḥizb al-Baḥr*, the *Ḥizb al-Naṣr* of al-Shādhilī, etc. To this should be added the full or partial Swahili translation of the Ḳurʾān, published by the Aḥmadiyya Society of Lahore, the sūrat Yāsīn in Swahili, a treatise on *Mirathi* (inheritance) by Shayikh al-Shīrāzī, and a very popular treatise on prayer called "Sula na Manrisho Yake".

Bibliography: J. B. Labat, *Relation historique de l'Ethiopie occidentale, contenant la description des royaumes du Congo, Angolla et Matamba*, Paris 1753; Abbé Proyart, *Histoire du Loango, Kakongo et autres royaumes d'Afrique*, Paris 1778; R. Avelot, *Les grands mouvements de peuples en Afrique, Jaga et Zimba*, Paris 1912; Delafosse et Poutrin, *Enquête coloniale . . .*, Paris 1930; P. Marty, *Études sur l'Islam au Sénégal, au Soudan, en Guinée sur la Côte d'Ivoire, au Dahoney*, Paris 1917-1926; A. Gouilly, *l'Islam en A.O.F.*, Paris 1926; *Notes et Études Documentaires*, no. 1152 (1947), no. 1642 (1952); Lieut. L. Nekkech, *Le Mouridisme depuis 1912*, St. Louis du Sénégal 1952; J. Maes and Boone, *Les peuplades du Congo Belge*, Brussels 1931; idem, *Bibliographie du Musée du Congo Belge sous le titre*: *Bibliographie éthnographique du Congo Belge*, Brussels 1932; Foureau, *D'Alger au Congo par le Tchad*, Paris 1902; Casati, *Dieci anni in Equatoria*, Milan 1891; R. P. Sacleux, *Dictionnaire Swahili-Français* (with Arabic etymologies), Paris 1939-41; R. P. Vanden Eynde, *Grammaire Swahili*, Brussels n.d.; Cornet, *Le Congo physique*, Brussels 1938; G. Hardy, *Vue générale de l'Histoire d'Afrique*[4], Paris 1942; Deschamps, *Les religions de l'Afrique*, Paris n.d.; H. Baumann and Westermann, *Les peuples et les civilisations de l'Afrique*, trans. Hamburger, Paris 1951; V. L. Grottanelli, *I. Bantu* (*Le Razze e i Popoli della Terra di R. Biasutti*), iii, 445-643, Turin n.d. 1955; *Revue de l'Université de Bruxelles*, 1954, 5-16, and 1957, 2-3, devoted to Congo questions; P. Ceulemans, *La Question Arabe et le Congo* 1883-1892, Brussels 1959; H. M. Stanley, *Through the dark continent*, 2 vols., London 1878; idem, *Twenty-five years' progress in Equatorial Africa*, London 1897; idem, *In darkest Africa*, London 1904; R. P. Henri Neyrand, *L'Evolution religieuse de l'A.E.F.*, in *Études Américaines*, *L'A.E.F.*, Paris n.d., 17; G. Eichtal, *De l'état actuel et de l'avenir de l'Islamisme dans l'Afrique centrale*, Paris 1841; D. Westermann, *Geschichte Afrikas*, Wiemar 1952; A. Abel, *Documents concernant le Bahr al Ghazal* (1893-1894), in *Bulletin de l'Académie Royale des Sciences coloniales*, 1954, 1385-1409; idem, *Les musulmans noirs du Maniéma et de la province Orientale*, Coll. de l'Institut de Sociologie Solvay, Brussels 1959; *Annuaire du Monde Musulman*.

(Ed., article based on information supplied by A. Abel and R. A. Oliver).

CONSTANTINE [see ḲUSṬANṬĪNA]

CONSTANTINOPLE [see ISTANBUL]

CONSTANTINUS AFRICANUS (Constantine the African), who first introduced Arab medicine into Europe, was born in Tunis in the early 5th/11th century (1010 or 1015 A.D.), and died at Monte Cassino in 1087.

His arrival in Salerno marked the beginning of what historians have labelled the 'golden age' of its famous medical school. But about the life of the man himself singularly little is known, and the details can only be sketched in conjecturally.

Various facts relating to him are to be found in the works of Petrus Diaconus who entered Monte Cassino in 509/1115, less than 30 years after Constantine's death. But they were adapted to suit the purposes of a story rather than set down objectively for their own sake. Like most other science historians, Petrus Diaconus traces Constantine's place of birth to Carthage (he probably means Tunis). By the age of 39 or 40, after many adventures, he had found his way to Italy. Petrus asserts that beforehand he had travelled to Egypt, Baghdād, India and Ethiopia, learning on the way Hebrew, Syriac, Chaldean, Greek, Ethiopian and even 'Indian'. His great talents roused such jealousy upon his return to Tunisia that, in order to avoid any harmful consequences, he left the country for Sicily. Karl Sudhoff is at variance with Petrus, and maintains that he journeyed to Italy as a merchant. It is there that he is said to have become acquainted with the reigning prince's brother, who was a doctor. His experiences made him realise the poverty of medical literature in Latin, and he returned to study medicine for three years in Tunisia; then, having collected together several treatises on Arab medicine, he departed, with his precious treasure, for southern Italy. The ship ran into a storm off the coast of Lucania, outside the gulf of Policastro, and the manuscripts were badly damaged. Constantine managed to salvage some of them, and when he arrived in Salerno he became a Christian convert.

It is not yet possible to establish the exact date of these events. But it is certain that he translated into Latin the best works on Arab medicine which had appeared up to the 5th/11th century, albeit omitting to acknowledge the names of their authors and thus earning the reputation of a plagiarist. He adapted the writings to the conditions of his new homeland, Italy. Many passages which he considered prolix were condensed, and other parts where the meaning remained obscure were simply translated literally. Nevertheless, Constantine's work infused new life into the medical school of Salerno, and indeed into the teaching of medicine in Europe for centuries to come. The most important translations are: (i) works of Greek origin which had been translated into Arabic, especially by Ḥunayn b. Isḥāḳ and his followers: maxims, prognoses and diet in the severe illnesses of Hippocrates, together with notes by Galen, the Great Therapeutics of Galen (*megatechne*) and the Small Therapeutics to Ġlaucon (*microtechne*), and pseudo-Galenian works; Ḥunayn b. Isḥāḳ's edition of Galen's introduction to therapeutics, with notes by ʿAlī b. Riḍwān (an Egyptian doctor of the 5th/11th century) (ii) works by Arab authors: the Oculistics (*al-ʿas̲h̲r maḳālāt fi 'l-ʿayn* of Ḥunayn b. Isḥāḳ (*Constantini liber de oculis*); the works of Isḥāḳ b. Sulaymān al-Isrāʾīlī (about 286/900) on the elements, urine, fever and diet; the *Zād al-Musāfir* of Ibn al-D̲j̲azzār, translated under the title *Viaticum*; the medical encyclopaedia *Kāmil al-Ṣināʿa al-Ṭibbiyya* of ʿAlī b. al-ʿAbbās al-Mad̲j̲ūsī (Persian, 4th/10th century) translated under the title *Pantechne*; Constantine's book *De Melancholia* was originally the *Kitāb al-Malīk̲h̲ūliyā* of Isḥāḳ b. ʿImrān (late 9th-early 10th century). Finally, Constantine translated and claimed the authorship of several less important works by al-Rāzī and others unknown by name.

The works were poorly translated into Latin and full of technical Arab expressions which had simply been transcribed. Constantine was nevertheless responsible for extending the knowledge of classical medicine as it existed in Europe at the beginning of the Middle Ages, and bringing into circulation many important Greek and Arab works.

Bibliography: Becavin, *L'école de Salerne et la medecine salernitaine* (Ph. D. thesis in medicine), Paris 1888; B. Ben Yahia, *Les origines arabes de "De melancholia" de Constantine*, in *Revue d'Histoire des sciences et de leurs applications*, vii/2 (1954), 156-162; idem, *Constantin l'Africain et l'école de Salerne*, in *CT*, iii/3, (1955), 49-59; Choulant, *Handbuch d. Bücherkunde f. d. ältere Medezin*, Leipzig 1841, 253-56; R. Creuz, *Der Arzt Constantinus Africanus von Monte Cassino*, in *Stud. und Mitt. z. Gesch. d. Benediktinerordens* New Series, XVI, 1929,1-44; Daremberg, *Histoire des sciences médicales*, i, 1870; idem, *Notices et extraits des manuscrits médicaux*, Paris 1853, 86; Petrus Diaconus, *Chronica Mon. Casinensis*, Lib. III; idem, *De viribus illustribus Casinensibus*, cap. 25, in Fabricius, *Bibl. Grec.* xiii, 123; Modestino del Gaizo, *La scuola medica di salerno Studiata nella storia e nelle legende*, Naples 1896; F. H. Garrison, *An Introduction to the history of medicine*, Philadelphia 1829; E. Gurlitt, *Geschichte der Chirurgie*, i, 1898, 670-72; F. Hartmann, *Die Literatur von Früh- und Hochsalerno*, thesis Leipzig 1919, 9-14; J. Hirschberg, *Über das älteste arabische Lehrbuch d. Augenheilkunde*, in *S. B. Ak. Wien*, xxix (1903); H. Lehmann, *Die Arbeitsweise des Const. Afri. und d. Joh. Africius*, in *Archiv f. Gesch. d. Mathematik.* xii (1930), 272-81; E. H. Meyer, *Geschichte der Botanik*, iii, (1856), 471, 484; A. Mieli, *La science arabe et son rôle dans l'évolution scientifique mondiale*, Leiden 1939; A. Mosolff, *Zahnheilkundliche Randbemerkungen zu einem Viaticum-Text*, thesis Leipzig 1924, in *Isis* vii, 1925, 536; M. Neuburger, *Geschichte der Medizin*, Stuttgart 1911, ii, 287 ff., K. Nord, *Zahnheilkundliches aus den Schriften Konstantins von Africa*, thesis etc., Leipzig 1922; S. di Renzi, *Storia documentata della scuola medica di Salerno*, ii, Naples 1857, 802; Ch. Singer, *A Legend of Salerno*, in *John Hopkins Hospital Bul.*, xxviii, 64-69; idem, *The original of the medical school of Salerno*, in *Essays presented to Sudhoff*, 38, Zurich 1923, in *Isis*, vii, 535; idem, *Introd. to the History of Science*, ..., M. Steinschneider, *Die europäischen Übersetzungen zu dem Arabischen*, in *S. B. Ak. Wien*, cxil-cli; idem, *Virchow's Archiv*, xxxvii, 351-410; K. Sudhoff, *Konstantin der Afrikaner und Medizinisches von Salerno*, in *Sudhoffs Arch. d. Gesch. d. Medizin*, xxiii, 293-98; L. Thorndike, *A History of magic and experimental science*, New York 1922, chap. xxxii.

(B. BEN YAHIA)

CONSTANZA [see KÖSTEND̲J̲E]

CONSUL (Arab. *Ḳunṣul*; Pers. *Ḳunṣūl*; Turk. *Konsolos*), consuls as representatives of the interests of foreign states in Islamic countries (and similarly in Byzantium). The institution of the consul was formed in the 12th and 13th centuries in the Italian merchant republics. The Genoese put their possessions in the Crimea (see KIRIM; since 1266), nominally subject to the K̲h̲ān of the Golden Horde, in the charge of a consul (B. Spuler: *Die Goldene Horde*, Leipzig 1943, 392-8, with further bibl.; E. S. Zevakin and N. A. Penčko: *Očerki po istorii genuèzskik̲h̲ koloniy* . . ., ('*Sketches on the History of the Genoese Colonies*') in *Istoričeskiye Zapiski* 3, 1938, 72-129). For the most part called Bailo [see BALYOS] until the 15th century, these representatives of foreign states in Islamic countries (for the first time in 1238, when Venice had a representative in Egypt) were occupied above all with the protection of the merchants of their nations, the adjustment of difficulties among them, and the regulation of all questions having to do with trade.

It was only when Ottoman hegemony extended over the entire east and south coasts of the Mediterranean as well as the Balkan peninsula, that it became necessary to grant to the ambassadors of the individual powers at Constantinople consuls in other places. For the first time in 1528, France obtained the right to provide its own consul in Alexandria, recently become Ottoman. He was able in all circumstances to negotiate directly on behalf of his countrymen with the local authorities, to adjust internal difficulties and to regulate financial conditions (including questions of inheritance). He might import his personal needs free of customs, and ships despatched by him were not subject to distraint or injury. The right to maintain a consul was extended to other cities in the treaty between the Porte and France in 1535, thus granting the latter a considerable extension of its influence, especially along the Syrian-Lebanese coast as well as in Asia Minor (a consulate in Aleppo since 1557; cf. the maps of the French Consulates in 1715 in P. Masson, *Histoire du Commerce Français* . . ., Paris 1896, p. xxxviii of the appendix). In 1580 England received corresponding rights. Between 1606-15 the German Emperor followed and later in the 17th century Venice, the Netherlands and Sweden. Only after the Peace of Küčük Ḳaynard̲j̲a [*q.v.*] in 1774, could Russia establish consulates (in particular in the Balkans and the Holy Land). Persia followed in 1839. All consuls, as well as ambassadors, were regarded as hostages to guarantee the behaviour of their home powers, and were repeatedly arrested and otherwise impeded.

Out of the consular rights the "Capitulations" developed, confirmed for the first time specifically in a treaty with France in 1740 (though in fact existing already in the 16th century). They conceded to the consuls extensive juridical and civil rights, and released foreign subjects more and more from local jurisdiction (for details cf. TÜRKIYE, History). Beside these, local Honorary Consuls appeared in increasing number in the 19th century, who held certain diplomatic rights, so that this position was much sought after. From 1862 Turkey fought with growing intensity against the distortion of this privilege, and a considerable limitation of the abuses was attained. After the gradual abrogation of the Capitulations combined with the renunciation of them by foreign states, the consuls in the Islamic world assumed the same position which they occupy internationally today.

In her own behalf Turkey first appointed consuls in foreign lands in 1802 (Turk. *Shehbender*; or, rarely at first, *Ḳonṣolos*), frequently from among Greeks and Levantines in the first decades.

Bibliography: General: A. M. Candioti, *Historia de la institución consular*, Buenos Aires 1925. Near East: F. Martens, *Das Konsularwesen und die Konsularjurisdiktion in Orient*, Berlin 1874; M. Tayyib Gökbilgin in *IA*, vi, 836-40 (with further bibl.); B. Spuler, *Die europ. Diplomatie in Konstantinopel*..., in *Jahrbücher für Kultur u. Geschichte der Slaven*, New Series, xi (1935), 208-10 (Consuls, with literature and catalogue of the Consulates); Frasherli Mehdī, *Imtiyāzāt-i edjnebiyyeniñ taṭbīḳāt-i Ḥāḍīrasî*, Samsun 1325/1907; *Sālnāme-i Neẓāret-i khāridjīye*, Constantinople 1885 and often.

Individual States: E. Watbled in *RA*, xvi/1872, 20 ff.; F. Rey: *La protection diplomatique et consulaire dans les Échelles du Levant et de Barbarie*, Paris 1899; N. G. Svoronos: *Inventaire des correspondances des Consuls de France au Levant, i: Salonique et Cavalle* (1686-1792), Paris 1951; Ahmed Refik, *Türkler ve kraliçe Elizabeth*, Constantinople 1932; M. Epstein, *The early history of the Levant company (to 1640)*, London 1908; A. N. Kurat, *Türk-ingiliz münasebetlerinin başlangıcı ve gelişmesi*, Ankara 1953.

Capitulations: F. A. Belin, *Des capitulations et des traités de la France en Orient*, Paris 1870; N. Sousa, *The capitulatory régime of Turkey. Its history, origin and nature*, Baltimore 1933; O. Nebioğlu, *Die Auswirkungen der Kapitulationen auf die türk. Wirtschaft*, Jena 1941; Habib Abi Chahla, *L'extinction des capitulations en Turquie et dans les régions arabes*, Paris 1924.

Juridical: G. Aristarchi Bey, *Législation Ottomane*, 7 vols, Constantinople 1873-88 (esp. ii, 403-9).

See further: Gibb and Bowen: *Islamic Society and the West*, i/1 and 2, London 1950-7; and the articles BALYOS, BERATLÎ, IMTIYĀZ, MUSTAʾMIN, and WENEDIK (Venezia); TÜRKIYE, History; MIṢR, History (including the collections of documents mentioned there). (B. SPULER)

ČOPAN-ATA (Turkish "Father-Shepherd"), the name of a row of hills 1/2 mile long on the southern bank of the Zarafshān [*q.v.*], close by the city walls of Samarḳand [*q.v.*]. There is no written evidence for this name before the 19th century; up to the 18th century, it was referred to in written sources (Persian) as Kūhak ('little mountain'), and the Zarafshān (only known as such in the written language since the 18th century) also sometimes carried this name. Under the name of Kūhak, the range is mentioned in Iṣṭakhri (*BGA* I, 318), and it contained quarries and clay pits for Samarkand.

There is an aetiological legend which gives the following explanation: "well over a thousand years before Muḥammad" there was an enemy besieging Samarḳand. The inhabitants of the town prayed fervently for deliverance, and in answer a mountain came and buried the attackers, having been transplanted from Syria, complete with a shepherd on it. Čopan-Ata is also regarded as a Muslim saint, and the shrine to him, which is on the summit of the hill, is attributed to Tīmūr (thus in al-Ḳandiyya, partly edited by W. Barthold, *Turkestan, MSS. I*, St. Petersburg 1900, 48/51).

Upon the Čopan-Ata the troops of the Khān of Bukhārā made a vain attempt to oppose the advancing Russians under general Konstatin Petrovič von Kauffmann on May 13th (new style) 1868. The latter succeeded in occupying Samarḳand the following day, and since then it has belonged to Russia.

Bibliography: W. Barthold, *Turkestan*, 86; Le Strange, 464.—On individual aspects: V. Vyatkin, in the *Spravočnîe knižki Samarkandskoy oblasti* vi-viii, Samarḳand 1893/1901; Abū Ṭāhir Khodja, *Samariyya*, Persian ed. by N. Veselovskiy, St. Petersburg 1904. —Illustrations: G. Pankrat'ye, *Âl'bbom istoričeskikh pamyatnikov goroda Samarkanda*, no. 31 and 38 (Shrine and remains of a mediaeval bridge). (W. BARTHOLD-[B. SPULER])

COPTS [see ḲIBṬ]

CORAN [see ḲURʾĀN]

ČORBADJÎ (literally: soup-provider). (1) The title applied among the Janissaries to commanders of the *orta*s and the *agha bölükleri*, though in official Ottoman terminology the commanders of the *djemāʿat ortalarî* were known as *Serpiyādegān* or (the Turkish equivalent of this Persian term) *Yayabashî*, while commanders of the *agha bölükleri* were called *Odabashî*.

As the 101 *djemāʿat ortalarî* were prior in foundation to the 61 *agha bölükleri*, the *Čorbadjî*s of the former had certain privileges over those of the latter: on frontier duty they kept the keys of the fortresses; they could ride on horseback in the presence of their superiors; they wore yellow gaiters and shoes. In the *agha bölükleri*, on the other hand, yellow gaiters and shoes were the prerogative of the *Odjaḳ Ketkhudāsî* and the *Muḥdir Agha*, the other *Čorbadjî*s wearing red.

The crested headdress generally worn on ceremonial occasions by the *Čorbadjî*s was called *ḳalafat* or *čorbadjî kečesi*. The crest of the *Yayabashî*s' *ḳalafāt* was of cranes' feathers, whereas that of *Čorbadjî*s of the *agha bölükleri* was of herons' feathers. The ordinary headdress of all *Čorbadjî*s was a red *ḳalafāt* narrow at the bottom and broad at the top. The *Čorbadjî* applied the bastinado to minor offenders among his men. His aide was known as the *Čorbadjî Yamaghî*.

Sometimes the *Čorbadjî*s were entrusted with police duties, thus performing the function of the *Subashî*. At the Čardaḳ, the customs station by the Yemish quay in Istanbul, there was a *Čardaḳ Čorbadjîsî*, who commanded the 56th Janissary *orta*, assisted the *ḳāḍī* of Istanbul who supervised the city's food-supply, and was responsible for maintaining public order in this locality.

*Yayabashî*s were appointed to collect the *devshirme* boys who were recruited into the *ʿAdjemī Odjaghî* from the provinces. The *Čorbadjî*s of the *ʿAdjemī Odjaghî* were under the orders of its commander, the *Istanbul Aghasî*.

(2) The title of *Čorbadjî* was also given to the village notables called *Mukhtar* and *Aḳ-ṣaḳal*, who entertained travellers. Later, until a half-century ago, it became an appellation of merchants and rich Christians. In colloquial Turkish it is still used for 'boss', 'skipper'.

Bibliography: *Ḳawānīn-i Yeničeriyān*; I. H. Uzunçarşılı, *Kapıkulu ocakları*, Ankara 1943; idem, *Tarihi Lugat*; Djewād Pasha, *Taʾrīkh-i*

ʿAskerī-i ʿOthmānī, Istanbul 1297; Maḥmud Shewket Pasha, *ʿOthmānlî teshkīlāt we ḳiyāfet-i ʿaskeriyyesi*, Istanbul 1325; Aḥmed Wefīḳ Pasha, *Lehdje-i ʿOthmānī*; Marsigli, *L'état militaire de l'empire Ottoman*, Paris 1732 = Nazmi Bey, *Osmanlı imparatorluğunun zuhur ve terakkisinden inhitâti zamanına kadar askerî vaziyeti*, Ankara 1934; M. d'Ohsson, *Tableau général*..., Paris 1788-1824; *The Military Costume of Turkey*, London 1818; M. Z. Pakalın, *Tarih deyimleri ve terimleri*, Istanbul 1946-56.

(I. H. Uzunçarşılı)

CORDOVA [see ḲURṬUBA]

COREA [see AL-SĪLĀ]

CORINTH [see KORDOS]

ČORLU, town in E. Thrace, the Byzantine Τζουρουλὸς (for the various forms of the ancient name see Pauly-Wissowa, s.v. Tzurulon (E. Overhummer]); it lies on the main road and railway between Istanbul and Edirne, 155 kms. by rail from Istanbul, facing N. over the Čorlu Su, a tributary of the Ergene. The town was taken by the Ottomans early in the reign of Murās I. In Djum. I 917/Aug. 1511 Bāyezīd II defeated Prince Selīm near Čorlu, at a place called Ṣirt-köyü by Luṭfī Pasha (*Taʾrīkh*, Ist. 1341, 202).

There were extensive *waḳfs* at Čorlu for Meḥemmed II's *külliyye* at Istanbul (cf. M. Tayyib Gökbilgin, *Edirne ve Paşa Livasî*, Ist. 1952, 300 ff.). When Ewliyā Čelebi visited it in 1061/1651 (*Seyaḥat-nāme*, III, 295 ff.) it had 3000 houses, in 15 Moslem and 15 Christian *maḥalles*, and was thriving centre of trade with 18 *khāns*. It was in a rich sheep-rearing region and was renowned for its cheese. At this time it was the centre of one of the five *ḳaḍāʾs* of the *sandjaḳ* of Vize (Ḥādjdji Khalfa, *Djihān-numā* = Hammer, *Rumeli und Bosna*, Vienna 1812, 19). It was the third stage on the main road from Istanbul: in 1717 Lady Mary Wortley Montague visited a *ḳonaḳ* built here as a rest-house for the Sultan (Letter xxxv).

Čorlu is now the centre of a *kaza* of the *vilayet* of Tekirdağ, population of the town (1955) 17,025.

(V. L. Ménage)

ČORLULU [see ʿALĪ PASHA]

COROMANDEL [see MAʾBAR]

ČORUH (Čorukh). I. River in the extreme north-east of Anatolia, flowing mainly through Turkey, but emptying into the Soviet Russian area of the Black Sea.

II. *Wilāyet* on the Black Sea, called after the river of the same name (cf. I) in the extreme north-east of Turkey. The modern *vilayet* of Čoruh covers roughly the same area as the former *sandjaḳ* of Lazistan which belonged to the *wilāyet* of Trabzon (Trebizond). Until the war between Russia and Turkey in 1878 (Treaty of San Stefano), Batum was the capital of the *sandjaḳ* of Lazistan. Subsequently, the capital of the *sandjaḳ*, or of the *wilāyet*, Lazistan became Rize. In 1935, Rize became a *vilayet* of its own, and Artvin became the capital of the remainder of the *vilayet* of Čoruh. According to the last census (1950) the *vilayet* of Čoruh had 174,511 inhabitants, and its capital Artvin had 4,547 inhabitants. Its *Ḳaḍā*'s are: Artvin, Ardanuč, Borčka, Fîndîklî, Hopa, Šavšat and Yusufeli.

Bibliography: G. Jäschke, *Die grösseren Verwaltungsbezirke der Türkei seit* 1918, in *MSOS*, 38th Annual number, (1935), ii, 81-104.

(Fr. Taeschner)

ČORUM, town in the north of Central Anatolia, 40° 34′ north, 34° 55′ east, some 7 km. east of the Čorum Čay, a tributary of the Mecitözü, which in turn flows into the Čekerek Irmak, a tributary of the Yešil Irmak. It lies in a large fertile valley and is the capital of the *wilāyet* of the same name. The *wilāyet* has the following *ḳaḍā*'s: Čorum, Alaca, Iskilip, Mecitözü, Osmancîk and Sungurlu. Before the Republic, the *ḳaḍāʾ* of Čorum formed part of the *sandjaḳ* of Yozgat belonging to the *wilāyet* of Ankara, formerly a *sandjaḳ* (*liwaʾ*) in the *Eyālet* of Sīwās (or Rūm). According to the last census (in 1950), the town had 22,835 inhabitants, the *ḳaḍāʾ* had 87,965, and the *wilāyet* 342,290.

Čorum has erroneously been taken to be the Tavium of antiquity. The latter has been proved to have been situated near Nefezköy, south of Sungurlu, in the *wilāyet* of Yozgat (concerning this, cf. the article on Tavium by W. Ruge in Pauly-Wissowa, iv, cols. 2524-26).

The modern Čorum shows few traces of historical interest. Its main Mosque, Ulu Djāmʿ, is a modern building (1909), but probably erected on the foundations of an older building of the 18th or 19th century. It contains a beautiful large Minbar of late Saldjūḳ times, which is said to have come from Karaḥiṣār.

The village of Elvančelebi, some 20 km. east of Čorum, belongs to the Kaza Mecitözü in the *wilāyet* of Čorum. There are the Tekye (mentioned by Kātib Čelebi, *Djihānnümā*, 625, l. 20, as Sheykh ʿUlwān Tekyesi, and also by Ewliyā Čelebi, *Seyāhat-nāme*, ii, 410, l. 8), *turbe* and mosque of Elvan Čelebi, the son of the famous poet ʿĀshîḳ Pasha (died in 733/1333, [*q.v.*]), and descendant of Baba Ilyās, the founder of the Dervish Order of the Bābāʾiyya [see BĀBĀʾĪ]. The shrine of Elvan Čelebi used to be a much frequented place of pilgrimage. Dernschwam visited it as a member of the retinue of the Imperial Envoy Busbecq in 1555 on his way to Amasya (cf. Hans Dernschwam's *Tagebuch einer Reise nach Konstantinopel und Kleinasien* (1553/55), ed. Franz Babinger, Munich and Leipzig 1923, 201-203, with a not particularly clear plan in Dernschwam's hand); concerning Elvan Čelebi in general, cf. Neşet Köseoğlu, *Elvan Çelebi*, in the periodical *Çorumlu*, of 1944, no. 46, 1373-79; no. 47, 1405-08; no. 48, 1437-41; in no. 11 of 1939 there are pictures of the shrine of Elvan Čelebi).

In some *ḳaḍā*'s of the *wilāyet* of Čorum there are famous Hittite excavations, particularly Boğazköy (Hattušaš) in the *ḳaḍāʾ* of Sungurlu, and also Alaca Hüyük in the *ḳaḍāʾ* of Alaca.

Bibliography: S. Sāmī, *Ḳāmūs al-Aʿlām*, iii, 1886 f.; Kātib Čelebi, *Djihānnümā*, 625; Ewliyā Čelebi, *Seyāhat-nāme*, ii, 407-410.

(Fr. Taeschner)

COS [see ISTANKÖY]

COSTUME [see LIBĀS]

CÔTE D'IVOIRE, the usual name of the Ivory Coast, a Republic, and member of the French Community. It is situated on the coast of the Gulf of Guinea, adjoins Ghana to the east, Liberia and the Republic of Guinea to the west, and the French Sudan and the Upper Volta to the North. It extends over 519,000 square kilometres and has a population of 2,500,000, including 12,000 non-Africans.

Although the first French settlements on the coast were founded at the end of the seventeenth century, colonization dates only from the end of the nineteenth century. The Ivory Coast became a self-governing colony in 1893, then, in 1900, it became part of the Government-General of French

West Africa. In 1957 it enjoyed a semi-autonomous domestic régime within the group of territories, with its Territorial Assembly and Government Council at Abidjan. Its administrative organization is that of the rest of French West Africa: circles, subdivisions and communes. After the referendum of 1958 the Ivory Coast, with its new status of autonomous Republic, refused to federate with the new state of Mali (formed by the union of Senegal with the French Soudan), and formed with the former territories of Upper-Volta, Dahomey and Niger the Benin-Sahil Alliance.

From south to north, it covers a narrow belt of lagoons, a densely forested belt about 300 kilometres wide, and, finally, a belt of Sudan type savanna. In the south, the population belongs to the Guinean and Apollonian groups, and, in the North, to the Sudanese and Voltaic groups.

The economy is based on agriculture (coffee, timber, bananas, cocoa, oil, cotton) with a little livestock-rearing and fishing. Industrialization has hardly been tackled, although some prospecting has been undertaken with a view to mining. The chief towns are: Abidjan, the capital and port (130,000), Bouaké (25,000), Grand-Bassam, Bondoukou.

The influence of Christianity is widespread in the south, with 160,000 Catholics, 65,000 Protestants, and syncretistic sects.

The number of Muslims is about 450,000, found mainly in the north, especially among the Malinké or Mandé tribes. But at the same time Islam seems to be making rapid inroads among the animist tribes of the Savannas and among the town immigrants.

The first Islamic settlement on the Ivory Coast must go back to the thirteenth century, at the height of the Māli ascendancy throughout the north of the country. The chief centres were Touba, Kong, Bondoukou, Odienné and Séguéla. Muslim influence seems to have receded after the collapse of the Malinké power (15th century). It had a reflux of strength during the first half of the nineteenth century, when the influence of El Hadj Omar Tall made itself felt throughout the whole of western Sudan. At the end of the century, Samory Touré lent his authority to proselytizing, and forcibly—albeit temporarily—converted a section of the Senoufo animists of the North. But, at the same time, he massacred the Malinké Muslims that resisted his conquest, and, above all, annihilated, in 1897, the kingdom of Kong which had remained the main seat of Islamic culture in the region. After the defeat of Samory, Islam fell into another temporary decline, from which it recovered fairly quickly, thanks to the sociological conjuncture that arose out of colonization.

It was spread by the influence of the *Dioula*, Malinké, or sometimes Hausa, traders, who had settled along the great trade routes and dealt chiefly in cola with the farmers from the forest region. Every year it made further progress towards the South, and eventually counted converts even among the coastal population. In addition to the traditional centres are found to-day important centres at Man, Bouaké, Gagnoa, Bouna, Daloa, Samatéguéla and Boundiala, as well as Abidjan.

The chief brotherhood is the Tidjāniyya, which forms the majority everywhere except at Man. Its adherents are divided more or less equally between the "twelve grains" who owe obedience to El Hadj Omar, and the "eleven grains" or Hamallists, followers of Shaykh Hama Allāh. Hamallism has, in addition, given rise to a new way, known as Yaʿkūbite after its founder, Yakouba Sylla, whose teaching is reminiscent of that of the Senegalese *Mourid*s of Ahmadou Bamba (work of the *talibé* on behalf of the Shaykh, importance of economic activity).

The Ḳādiriyya brotherhood exists in all regions, but is as important as the Tidjāniyya only in the Man district. It is considered favourable to the interests of the Wahhābīs, whose importance has developed considerably since 1946 under the influence of rich Mecca pilgrims and of *Karomoko* (scholars) educated in Egypt or Arabia. The chief Wahhābite centre is Bouaké.

Occasional Mahdists are to be found—these seem to be under Wahhābite influence. And, on the coast, is a small Aḥmadiyya community, formed around natives of Ghana and Nigeria. Certain dissident sects of the coastal region show Christian, Muslim and animist influences.

The level of Islamic teaching has never recovered from the massacres of Samory Touré, in spite of the recent endeavours of the young Wahhābīs and of certain Hamallists.

Bibliography: Marty, *Études sur l'Islam en Côte d'Ivoire*, Paris 1922; Gouilly, *L'Islam dans l'AOF*, Paris 1952; Le Grip, *Aspects actuels de l'Islam en AOF*, in *L'Afrique et l'Asie*, Paris 1953 and 1954; Cardaire, *L'Islam et le terroir africain*, Koulouba (Soudan) 1954; Trimingham, *Islam in West Africa*, Oxford 1958. (P. Alexandre)

ČOWDORS [see ČAWDORS]

CRAC [see KERAK]

CRAC DES CHEVALIERS [see ḤIṢN AL-AKRĀD]

CREATION [see ḤUDŪTH, IBDĀʿ, KHALḲ]

CREED [see ʿAḲĪDA]

CRETE [see IḲRĪTISH]

CRIMEA [see ḲIRĪM]

CROJA [see KROYO]

CRUSADES. Originally applied to military and religious expeditions organized in Western Europe and intended to take back from and defend against Islam the Holy Places of Palestine and nearby Syria, the term was later extended to all wars waged against "infidels" and even to any undertaking carried out in the name of a worthy or supposedly worthy cause; naturally these extensions of meaning are not part of our present concern.

The first Crusade (1096-99), following on from expeditions against the Muslims in the West, led to the establishment around Jerusalem, Tripoli, Antioch and Edessa of four States constituting (and later including Cyprus, then the Latin Empire of Constantinople) the Latin East, which from then on until the recapture of its last citadel Acre by the Muslims in 1291 was an essential factor in the history of the Middle East. The second Crusade started by the fall of Edessa bore no concrete results; the third, started by the fall of Jerusalem, ensured the maintenance of "Frankish" possessions on the Syro-Palestinian coast; the fourth was only concerned with Constantinople, the fifth failed at Damietta in Egypt, the sixth was more of a diplomatic journey by Frederick II and brought about the temporary restitution of Jerusalem to the Franks, the seventh led by St. Louis after the loss once more of the Holy City ended in another disaster at Damietta and the eighth, which brought the same king to Tunis, ended with his death. One might add to this traditional number of Crusades other less important ones and later Crusades against the Ottomans (Nicopolis, Varna, etc.). The Crusades in Syria-Palestine alone had a lasting effect on the history of Muslim countries, in view of the Frankish dominance in the East, uninterrupted for nearly two centuries, which was initiated by the first Crusade and maintained by those that followed.

In an encyclopaedia of Islam there can of course be no question of giving the history even of only these Crusades in its entirety; it would even be somewhat odd to speak of them at all, were it not that the Crusades when considered in terms of Islam give rise to certain problems which alone will be discussed here.

The specific character of the Crusades was not and could not be understood by Muslims. The very term, *ḥurūb al-ṣalībiyya*, used to designate them in modern Arab literature, was unknown to ancient authors, who referred to Crusaders by the plain ethnical term "Franks", and seems to have made its appearance during the Ottoman period in Christian circles of the East influenced by French culture. The theory of the Crusade, a war for the defence or liberation of oppressed co-religionists, differs from the theory of the *d̲j̲ihād*, a war for the expansion of Islam; but in practice almost the very reverse appears to have obtained at the time of the first Crusade, *d̲j̲ihād* in the majority of Muslim countries being no more than a memory and Christendom from the time of Charlemagne onwards having elaborated campaigns for the expansion of Christianity by force of arms. No doubt, in one sense the Crusades appear as a reaction, which had gradually been desired and made possible, against the humiliation of four centuries caused by the Muslim conquest of half the Mediterranean basin; but the example of Spain and Sicily proves that the Christian West did not need any deterioration in the generally reasonable treatment of Christians in Muslim countries as a spur to move onto the offensive or counter-offensive. In the East it is true that the Turkoman invasion of Asia Minor revived amongst a particular social group the tradition of Muslim Holy War in the form of *g̲h̲azwa*, bringing disaster to Byzantine Christendom; but in the old Muslim countries and particularly in Palestine the forming of the Sald̲j̲ūḳid Empire brought no fundamental change to the lot of autochthonous Christians or to the treatment of foreign pilgrims; the precise motivation of crusading, however sincere it was, could not therefore occur to the Muslim mind. Muslims obviously saw that they were dealing with Christian warriors who as such were attacking Islam, but apart from the distance from which they came they saw in them roughly the equivalent of the Byzantines whose Christian-inspired attacks and counter-attacks they had been sustaining for two centuries.

The Crusaders' conquests only affected territory which was incompletely Islamized, relatively small and quickly reduced by gradual Muslim reconquest, and even in Syria-Palestine did not reach any of the large Muslim centres. Nevertheless, the constant menace to vital sea and land routes between Muslim countries in the Middle East, the knowledge of Muslim abasement under Frankish rule, above all the repetition of Crusades, the non-assimilation of Franks into the native *milieu* and the permanence of a state of at least "cold" war finally conferred indisputable importance on the Crusades and the existence of the so-called "Latin" East in the history of Middle Eastern Islam. It would be interesting to examine more thoroughly than has hitherto been the case how Muslims, according to time and place, reacted to this phenomenom.

The Crusades found the Muslim Middle East in a state of division and dissension which alone made their initial success possible. Preceding generations had seen many examples of Islamo-Christian co-operation in Syria even against other Christians or Muslims. Although the Frankish invasion brought death or exile to many Muslims in Syria-Palestine, minor chieftains and certain isolated populations apparently at first assumed that it would be possible to adapt themselves to a state of small-scale war alternating with periods of peace, such as the former lord of S̲h̲ayzar, Usāma b. Munḳid̲h̲, by drawing on his early memories, was able to depict for us in his Memoirs. Soon, however, more directly threatened or more intensely Muslim communities, angered by the disgraceful indifference to the Frankish danger of Muslims beyond Syria-Palestine, attempted to rouse them from it by for example demonstrating in Bag̲h̲dād. Although individual volunteers, subsidies (particularly for prisoners' ransoms) and exhortations were sometimes forthcoming from the rest of the Muslim world, the backbone of resistance came really from the immediate neighbours of the Franks. A necessary condition for that, and this was bound to be one consequence of the Crusades, was some degree of *rapprochement* between various Muslim elements which only recently had been suspicious of each other: Arabs from the plains and the towns, Turks from the official armies that had come into being under the Sald̲j̲ūḳid regime, Turkomans lacking discipline but ready for *g̲h̲azwa*, warlike Kurds joining up with the Turkish armies that shortly before they had been fighting and so on. D̲j̲azīra constituted the hinterland, a source of manpower, such as Syria with its meagre resources could never be, and there followed a process of political unification between the two regions (remaining however somewhat incomplete in D̲j̲azīra). From a religious point of view, the Frankish menace certainly contributed without being its sole cause to the progress of Sunnism, which was already developed in the Sald̲j̲ūḳid domains of Irano-Mesopotamia, but until then scarcely of any importance in Syria. For one thing, intransigent elements denounced the heterodox as accomplices of the Franks and responsible for the misfortunes of Islam; more important, however, moderate S̲h̲īʿīs and even sometimes the Fāṭimids, no longer sustained by unanimous Ismāʿīlism, in the face of common enemies rallied to the Sunnī Turkish princes; the only group to remain outside this alliance were the Assassins, violent and irreconcilable enemies of Sunnī orthodoxy, who were massacred by the Muslim majority and who sometimes collaborated with the Franks from their frontier strongholds. Naturally, the anti-Crusade movement never affected the whole of the Muslim population even amongst the neighbours of the Franks; devout Muslims lamented the fact that some of their brethren, who were subjects or neighbours of the Franks, found it less dangerous to come to terms with them than to fight them and minor princes were hesitant about involving themselves in coalitions which could only serve to increase the authority of the more important. The ability of Zengī, Nūr al-Dīn and Saladin lay in realizing, each in his own manner, that the struggle against the Franks, by necessitating and favouring the unification of Muslims, played into the hands of anyone able to lead such a movement, although it is not possible for us of course, any more no doubt than it was for them, to say how far they were prompted by ardent conviction and how far by self-interest. This policy appeared to reach its final objective when after Jerusalem Saladin conquered almost the whole of the Latin East.

It would be interesting to know whether in the Muslim States concerned the war against the Franks or their neighbours brought about any deeper or broader changes than this partial "moral rearmament". The period of the Crusades certainly coincides with a remarkable rise of inland Syria, starting with Damascus, then of Egypt which replaced Ba<u>gh</u>dād, linked too closely with the Iranian States, as the liveliest area of Arab Islam; but it is difficult to indicate the exact role of the various factors in this development, as it is to say whether the militarization of the politico-social order common to the whole of the Muslim world was more extensive here than elsewhere. In the art of warfare it is probable that some progress in siege armament and artillery is due to contact with the Franks; the mutual borrowings which appear to have taken place between the two sides in the technique of fortification have still never been properly studied. Peaceful trading relations between Frankish and Muslim territories co-existed with war; but Alexandria, not Acre, was the great international trading centre of the Mediterranean and the fall of the Latin East was to have little effect on commerce.

It would be normal to expect the anti-Frankish reaction to have brought about some original movement of ideas. But Islam was no longer in a progressive phase and the conflict was after all limited. Subject to future research, therefore, the impression is that there was not really any ideological fermentation. The ancient themes of *<u>dj</u>ihad* were rediscovered, the old accounts (pseudo-Wāḳidī) of the Conquests and anti-Byzantine *<u>gh</u>azwa* were taken out and developed, emphasis was laid on devotion to the holy places of Jerusalem: but there was nothing really new and it must be admitted that the struggle against the Crusaders did not give rise to any doctrinal study of holy war or any popular works comparable with the epics about the Conquests or anti-Byzantine wars.

Furthermore, diplomatically, whereas Saladin in particular tried to play off Westerners and Byzantines against each other, no unity comparable with the unity, however slight, of Western Christendom against Islam was ever achieved between the East and West of the Muslim world, for each part was involved in its own struggles with neighbouring Christians. Even in the East, leaving aside the Iranians who were far away and shaken by successive crises, the Turks of Asia Minor, after involuntarily setting the Crusades in motion by their invasion, practically restricted their efforts to attacks against Byzantium and, showing little interest in Syria, only took some part in the struggle against the Crusaders in the first century of the Latin East, when the latter crossed their territory. The Caliphate itself does not appear to have taken a very deep interest in the anti-Frankish struggle.

Furthermore, at the end of Saladin's reign, the very seriousness of the Frankish defeat stirred the West, so that before his death in spite of all efforts he had to resign himself to certain losses and to the maintenance of a Frankish seaboard, emphasizing the extent of material sacrifices made practically in vain. Whence arose under the Ayyūbids the desire for a new policy which, recognizing both the presence of Franks in the trade ports of Syria-Palestine and the lessening of the Frankish menace, now that, left to their own devices, the Eastern Franks could hardly contemplate further aggrandisement, sought to set up a *modus vivendi* economically favourable to both sides. This policy, compromised by the Crusading activities of the West, nevertheless continued a fairly successful existence for half a century, finding its most spectacular and in the eyes of the devout its most scandalous expression when, with certain reservations, al-Kāmil restored Jerusalem to Frederick II. Could such a policy have been kept up for a long time? The unleashing of the Mongol conquest made it in any case impracticable. That invasion, much more dangerous for the time being than the Crusades could ever be, produced in the Mamlūk State, established in Egypt and Syria as the final redoubt of Muslim resistance, an uncompromising tension of all forces and the unquestionable predominance of an intransigent army. Some of the Franks had come to terms with the barbarians: their extermination or expulsion became a matter of supreme urgency and this time Europe did not prevent it.

With the exception of the Armenians in the North, native Christians had remained practically outside the Crusades; Muslims therefore did not at first change their attitude to local Christians and even occasionally supported members of the Greek Church who had serious grounds for complaint against Latin dominance, as well as the Jews. Tolerance of this kind contrasted with the treatment of Muslims under Frankish rule who, except in some special localities, had neither mosque nor *ḳāḍī* and were frequently considered as virtual enemies or spies. The over-quoted passage of Ibn <u>Dj</u>ubayr, shaming his co-religionists for Muslim satisfaction with good Frankish administration in the rich district of Tyre, cannot outweigh many cases where the opposite applied nor can it the legal status of Muslims; because of its warlike spirit, the Latin East was backward compared with the understanding which the Norman sovereigns of Sicily and the Spaniards were showing at the same time. In the long run the presence of Franks eventually jeopardized the native Christians of Muslim countries as well. For the lack of any future possibility of triumphing by the force of arms prompted the Franks to try to establish relations with Christians of Muslim states. It was inevitable that such a move should give rise to at least some suspicion amongst the Muslims. The most unfortunate individual case was that of the Maronites. This purely Lebanese minority living entirely within Frankish territory had rallied to the discipline of the Church of Rome and to a certain extent, in the coastal towns at least, had become intermingled with the Franks. Muslim reconquest did not wipe out the danger of Frankish attacks on the Syrian coast and, to prevent any Maronite complicity, the Mamlūks had many of the Maronite districts along the coasts evacuated. The fortunes of the Armenians, who had been the Mongols' quartermasters and were linked politically with the Christian West, were even less happy; in the fourteenth century their Cilician kingdom was destroyed and its population decimated. Generally speaking, the hardening of the Muslim attitude was bound to undermine the position of Christians and it is necessary to realise that the Crusades alone must bear, if not the sole responsibility, at least the greater part of it, for a development completely opposite to their avowed object.

Did they at least help to increase the interpenetration of peoples, the knowledge of Islam in the

West, or of the West in Muslim countries? It would of course be paradoxical to contend that among the members of the two geographically close populations there was no exchange of knowledge. But examination of institutions in the Latin East shows fewer borrowings from the Muslim past and less social intermingling than in the Christian States of Sicily and Spain. Similarly, from a cultural point of view, objective comparison leads to the categorical conclusion that where the West has acquired knowledge of Muslim civilization, it has done so mainly through Spain or Sicily and not through Western settlements in the East or Crusaders from the West; moreover, Islam as such nearly always remained misunderstood and the few accurate ideas about it that the West finally acquired are due to the efforts of missionaries, in other words to work undertaken in an entirely different spirit from the spirit of the Crusades. As for the Muslims, although some showed a certain curiosity about the Franks in the East or about a Western leader as exceptional as Frederick II, it must be acknowledged that their historians, geographers and anti-Christian polemists still had after the Crusades the same few notions about the European West, gleaned from their co-religionists in the West, that they had had before. Therefore, and contrary I regret to current opinion, it seems to me an anachronism to repeat with those who have worked on the cultural or political influence, indeed a very real one, of modern France in the East, or written within that context, that the Crusades laid their foundations; if in their own way they bore witness to the beginning of a process of interpenetration, the atmosphere they created proved subsequently more of a hindrance than a help.

Bibliography: The Arabic sources of the history of the Crusades are catalogued in C. Cahen, *La Syrie du Nord à l'époque des Croisades*, 1940, 33-94, without however certain elucidations which may be found particularly in (besides a forthcoming work by N. Elisséeff on Nūr al-Dīn) H. A. R. Gibb, *The Arabic sources for the life of Saladin*, in *Speculum*, xxv (1950); B. Lewis, *The sources for the history of the Syrian Assassins*, *ibid.*, xxvii (1952); H. Gottschalk, *al-Malik al-Kāmil*, 1958, Introduction. The five volumes of *Historiens Arabes* in the *Recueil des Historiens des Croisades* published by the Académie des Inscriptions suffer from lack of method in the choice of extracts and insufficient care in the establishment and translation of texts (not to mention their inconvenient format); they have still not yet however been replaced by editions or above all, for those who need them, by better translations. Since 1940 have appeared—and we quote only the essential—a French translation by R. Le Tourneau of Ibn al-Ḳalānisī's Damascus chronicle (*Damas de 1075 à 1154*, French Institute in Damascus, 1952), vol. i of a new and this time good edition of Abū Shāma's *K. al-Rawḍatayn* by M. A. Ḥilmī (Cairo 1957), as well as an edition of his *Dhayl* (Cairo 1947); the first two volumes, less important than those to follow, of a good edition of Ibn Wāṣil's *Mufarridj al-Kurūb* by al-Shayyāl (Cairo 1953 and 1957); an edition of the Ayyūbid part of al-Makīn b. al-ʿAmīd's chronicle by C. Cahen (in *BEO*, Damascus, xv, 1955-57); the edition of part of Ibn ʿAbd al-Ẓāhir's life of Baybars, under the title *Baybars the First*, by S. F. Sadeque, Oxford and Dacca 1956; the first two volumes out of the three of the excellent edition of (Kamāl al-Dīn) Ibn al-ʿAdīm's *Zubda* by Sāmī Dahān (Fr. Inst. Damascus, 1951 and 54) and, by the same editor, the part on Damascus of Ibn Shaddād's *Aʿlāḳ* (Fr. Inst. Damascus, 1956), with the part on Aleppo edited by D. Sourdel (*ibid.*, 1958); of the extant half of the *Life of Baybars* by the same author (in the absence of any edition) there is a Turkish translation by Şerefuddin Yaltkaya, Istanbul 1941; an edition by C. Zurayk and S. Izzedin, 1939-42, of the two volumes by Ibn al-Furāt on the years 672-696; an edition at Ḥaydārābād, 2 vol. 1954-55, of the part of Yūnīnī covering the years 664-670; and finally for the years 689-698 an analysis of Djazarī by J. Sauvaget, 1949. None of these authors of course deals specifically with the Crusades. A good number of selected and translated texts, together with useful introductions, has been given by Fr. Gabrieli, *Storici Arabi delle Crociate*, 1957.

For the general history of the Crusades in their Eastern setting reference should be made to the general works of Grousset, Runciman, my *Syrie du Nord* and the collective *History of the Crusades* by the University of Philadelphia under the supervision of K. M. Setton, vol. i (twelfth century) 1955, vol. ii (thirteenth century) in the press, and three further volumes on the later Crusades, institutions and civilization. A broadly conceived general bibliography of the Crusades will be found in H. E. Mayer, *Bibliographie zur Geschichte der Kreuzzüge*, Hanover 1960. It seems useful here only to indicate the few studies devoted particularly to aspects of the problems treated above: C. Cahen has given the outlines of a forthcoming *Autour des Croisades, Points de vue d'Orient et d'Occident*, in *En quoi la Conquête turque appelait-elle la Croisade* (*Bulletin de la Faculté des Lettres*, Strasbourg, Nov. 1950), *An Introduction to the First Crusade* (*Past and Present*, 1954) and *Les Institutions de l'Orient Latin*, in *Oriente e Occidente, XII Convegno Volta*, 1956. The only other studies which need be quoted here are: H. A. R. Gibb, *The achievement of Saladin* in *Bull. of the John Rylands Library*, 1952; A. S. ʿAṭiya, *The Crusades, Old ideas and new conceptions*, in *Cahiers d'Histoire Mondiale/Journal of World History*, ii/2, 1954; and, on a much broader theme, U. Monneret de Villard, *Lo studio dell' Islam nel XII e XIII secolo*, in *Studi e Testi*, cx (1948), and A. Malvezzi, *L'islamismo e la cultura europea*, n.d. [1957] (the history of the knowledge of Islam).

(C. Cahen)

CRYSTAL [see BILLAWR]

ČU, a river in Central Asia, 1090 km. long, but not navigable because of its strong current. It is now known as *Shu* (Barthold, *Vorl.* 80) by the Kirgiz who live there (and it probably had this name when the Turks lived there in the Middle Ages); Chinese: *Su-yeh* or *Sui-she*. modern Chinese: Čʿuci (for the problem of the indication of Ču = Chinese 'pearl' with the 'Pearl River' [Yinčü Ögüz] in the Orkhon Inscriptions, cf. the article SIR DARYĀ). The river Ču has its source in Terskei Alaltau, and then flows to the north-east until 6 km. from the western end of the Issik Kul [*q.v.*], known as Ḳočḳar in its upper regions (for the first time in Sharaf al-Dīn ʿAlī Yazdī, ed. Ilāhdād, i, Calcutta 1885, 274). It send a branch (called the Kutemaldi) to the lake, whose outlet it earlier was. Subsequently the Ču turns northwards through the Būghām (Russian: Buam) ravine (this is mentioned first in Sharaf al-

Dīn, *loc. cit.*; in Gardīzī, 102: Djīl, supposedly 'narrow'), which lies to the north-west of the western end of the Issik Kul, and then flows in a north-westerly direction. In this region it receives the waters of the Great and the Little Kebin from its right, and the Aḳsu and Kuragati from the left. The river then flows through dreary waste-land in its middle and lower course. 110 km. east of the Āmū Daryā [*q.v.*], it ends in the small desert lake Saumal-Kul.

The regions adjoining the upper Ču, which were good grazing land and could be easily irrigated, were already inhabited in the times of the Middle Siberian Andronovo culture (1700-1200 B.C.) (Bernstamm, 20). Later on, Sacae and Wusun (pseudo Tokharians?) lived on its banks. In the 6th and 7th centuries, these were joined by the Soghdians (see SUGHD) (Altï Čub Soghdaḳ, in the Orkhon inscriptions: Bernstamm, 269). Archaeological traces of these peoples have been found and described by the Soviet expert Aleksandr Natanovič Bernstamm (1910-1956). From his research, it has become evident that Syrian and some Byzantine influences had reached as far as this, and that the traffic from Further Asia to the Land of the Seven Rivers (Yeti Suw; Russ. Semireč'e; cf. also Ili) passed through this region along two ancient trade-routes (through the Kastek pass to the Ili valley, and through the Būghām pass to the south side of the Issik Kul). Thus two cultures met on the banks of the Ču (down to the Land of the Seven Rivers and the Farghāna Basin [Bernstamm, 147, 262]).

In 776, the Ḳarluḳ [*q.v.*] occupied the valley of the Ču and that of the Ṭarāz (Talas), and the area along both sides of the Alexander Mountains. The Tukhs(ī) also settled there (*Ḥudūd al-ʿĀlam*, 300; Barthold, *Vorl.*, 75). Sūyāb [*q.v.*] was the *capital* of the Ču valley (Kāshgharī, iii, 305; Hsüan-Čuang, ed. St. Julien, Paris 1857-8); the residence of the ruler of this area was usually in Ḳuz Ordu (Balāsāghūn; [*q.v.*]). Judging from the traces of settlements found, the valley was well populated at that time. The inhabitants developed a particular multi-coloured style in ceramics, and later also a distinct special form of ornamental Kūfic writing. There was a marked distinction between them and the other Transoxanians (Bernstamm, 157, 161/66).

Islamic armies reached the western part of the Ču valley only once, in 195/810 (battle against Kūlān, cf. Ibn al-Athīr, vi, 164), and the name of the river is not mentioned in Muslim sources of pre-Mongol times, although there is mention of some of the places in the region (Ibn Khurradādhbih (*BGA* VI, 29); Ḳudāma, *K. al-Kharādj* [*BGA*], 206). Islam reached the population only in the 4th/10th century, and even around the year 372/982, only a part of the inhabitants of Ṭarāz and Nawēkath had become Muslims (*Ḥudūd al-ʿĀlam*, 119, no. 93; 358, with mention of individual places); Nestorian Christianity was widespread for a considerably longer time. The rule of the Ḳara Khitāy [*q.v.*] followed that of the Ḳarluḳs in 535/1141. Thus there was a renewed influence of Chinese cultural elements (Nephrit, Sung porcelain) in the area, and these mixed again with those of Transoxania (Bernstamm, 168, 171 f.). Meanwhile, the numerous wars of the 6th/12th and 7th/13th centuries resulted in a decrease of the population of the Ču valley. Where the Chinese traveller Čʿang Čʿun still met several towns and villages in 616/1219, and crossed the Ču by a wooden bridge (E. Bretschneider, *Med. Researches*, i, London 1888, 71 f., 129 f.; A. Waley, *The Travels of an Alchemist*, London 1931), many ruins are reported already in 658/1259. At that time (651/1253), the region formed the border line between the areas of influence of the two Mongol Khāns Batu [*q.v.*] and Möngke (Mangū [*q.v.*]). Shiban (Shaybān), the founder of the "Blue" (White) Horde (see BĀTŪʾIDS) had his winter quarters here. But the main cause of virtual de-population of the area, was war amongst the Mongols in the 8th/14th century (see ČAGHATĀY), plague (acccording to epitaphs of 739/1338), and the campaigns of Tīmūr [*q.v.*]. Our sources for these last already fail to mention any place-names in the Ču valley. The Nestorian settlements near Pishpek and Toḳmaḳ [*q.v.*], of which we have epitaphs of the 7th/13th and 8th/14th centuries, also seem to have perished at this time. Muḥammad Ḥaydar Dūghlāt, *Taʾrīkh-i Rashīdī*, ed. N. Elias and E. D. Ross, London 1895-98, 364 f., *ca.* 1546, mentions only ruins with a minaret rising above them. The modern name Burana for a tower in the ancient Toḳmaḳ also derives from Manāra (according to Perovskiy in the *Zap. Vost. Otd.*, viii, 352).

Later the Ču valley occasionally came under the Kalmuks and the (Ḳara-) Kirghiz. Then it came under the rule of the Khāns of Khoḳand, who founded the fortresses of Pishpek (in the Khoḳand historians' writings: Pishkek) and Toḳmaḳ on the Ču. These came into Russian hands in 1860. Since then the Ču valley has belonged to Russia, and has become a target of eastern Slav settlement (cf. Herrmann, *Atlas*, 66-67). The upper course is in the Kirgiz S.S.R., the middle and lower reaches in the Kazak S.S.R. Since 1932, a great agricultural combine (hemp and other fibre plants) has developed in the area of the middle Ču. Two arms of the "Great Ču Canal" have been under construction since 1941; these should irrigate a further area. The Turksib railway crosses the river near the station of Ču, thus opening it up to traffic.

Historical Maps of the region of the Ču: A. Herrmann, *Atlas of China*, 1925, several maps, 37 and 60 in particular; *Ḥudūd al-ʿĀlam*, 279, 299; Bernstamm, maps ii and iii (at the end). Islamic Maps: C. Miller, *Mappae Arabicae*, iv 78/82, 86*-91*.

Bibliography: E. Chavannes, *Documents sur les Tou-kiue (Turcs) Occidentaux*, St. Petersburg 1903, 79, 85; *Ḥudūd al-ʿĀlam*, index; W. Barthold, *Zwölf Vorlesungen*, Berlin 1935, index; idem, *Four Studies*, Leiden 1956, index s.v. *Archaeology*; A. N. Bernstamm (Bernshtam), *Istoriko-arkheologičeskie očerki Tsentral'nogo Tyan'-Shanya i Pamiro-Alaya*, Moscow-Leningrad 1952 (*passim*; compare above and index under *Ču* and *Čuyskaya dolina*) (*Materiali i issledovaniya po arkheologii SSSR* 26). Christianity near Toḳmak: D. Chwolson, *Syrisch-nestorianische Grabinschriften aus Semirjetschie*, St. Petersburg 1890; *Neue Folge*, St. Petersburg 1897; P. K. Kokovtsov, *K siroturetskoy épigrafikě Semirěč'ya* (*Izv. Imp. Ak. Nauk* 1909, 773 f.); J. Dauvillier, *Les provinces Chaldéennes „de l'extérieur" au Moyen-Age*, in the *Mélanges Cavallera*, Toulouse 1948, 261-316; B. Spuler, *Die nestorianische Kirche*, in the *Handbuch der Orientalistik* viii, 1959 (the two last include further bibliography). Geography: W. Leimbach, *Die Sowjetunion*, Stuttgart 1950, 253; Brockhaus-Efron: *Entsiklopedičeskiy slovar'* 38 B (76), p. 932; 39 A (77), p. 27; *BSĖ* lxii, 695, 745; 2. ed., xlvii, 444, 464 (only geographical information). (B. SPULER)

ČŪBĀNIDS (ČOBANIDS), a family of Mongol *amīrs* claiming descent from a certain Sūrghān

Shīra of the Suldūz tribe who had once saved the life of Čingiz Khān. The most notable members of this family were:

(1) Amīr Čūbān. An able and experienced military commander, Amīr Čūbān, according to Ḥamd Allāh Mustawfī, fought his first battle in Rabīʿ II 688/April-May 1289 (*Tāʾrīkh-i Guzīda* (GMS), 588); thereafter he served with distinction under the Ilkhāns Arghūn, Gaykhātū, Ghāzān and Uldjāytū [*qq.v.*]. He was appointed *amīr al-umarāʾ* by Abū Saʿīd in 717/1317, and married the latter's sister Dūlandī. During the reign of Abū Saʿīd, who succeeded Uldjāytū at the age of twelve, Amīr Čūbān acquired great power in the affairs of state; in addition, all the important provinces of the Ilkhānid empire were governed by his sons. In Radjab 719/Aug.-Sept. 1319 a group of *amīr*s plotted to assassinate Amīr Čūbān, but the latter, supported by Abū Saʿīd, crushed the revolt with great severity. After the death of Dūlandī, Amīr Čūbān married Abū Saʿīd's other sister, Sātī Beg (719/1319). In 725/1325 Amīr Čūbān prevented Abū Saʿīd from marrying his daughter Baghdād Khātūn [*q.v.*], who was at that time the wife of Shaykh Ḥasan Buzurg the Djalāʾirid. Abū Saʿīd determined to break the power of the Čūbānids and, two years later, when Amīr Čūbān was absent in Khurāsān, he put to death Amīr Čūbān's son Dimashḳ Khwādja and issued orders for the execution of Amīr Čūbān at Harāt and of his family throughout the Ilkhānid dominions. Amīr Čūbān, forewarned, advanced as far as Rayy and attempted to negotiate with Abū Saʿīd, but without success. Deserted by most of his troops, he fled back to Harāt and took refuge with Malik Ghiyāth al-Dīn the Kurt. A few months later (Oct.-Nov. 1327, or perhaps in Muḥarram 728, which began on 17 Nov. 1327), the rewards offered by Abū Saʿīd induced Malik Ghiyāth al-Dīn to put to death Amīr Čūbān and his son Djilaw Khān. Their bodies were taken to Medina for burial.

(2) Dimashḳ Khwādja. The third son of Amīr Čūbān, Dimashḳ Khwādja remained at court in 726/1326 when his father left to defend Khurāsān against the Mongols of the house of Čaghatay, and became the virtual ruler of the Ilkhānid empire. His dissolute nature provided Abū Saʿīd with the excuse for destroying the Čūbānids which he had been seeking. Dimashḳ Khwādja was convicted of a liaison with a member of the royal harem, and was put to death on 5 Shawwāl 727/24 August 1327. One of his daughters, Dilshād Khātūn, was later married first to Abū Saʿīd (734/1333-4), and then to Shaykh Ḥasan Buzurg the Djalāʾirid.

(3) Tīmūrtāsh, the second son of Amīr Čūbān. He had acted as *wazīr* to Uldjāytū. In 716/1316 he was appointed by Abū Saʿīd governor of Rūm, and for the first time carried Mongol arms to the shores of the Mediterranean. In 721/1321-2 he rebelled; he minted coinage in his own name, had his name included in the *khuṭba*, and styled himself the Mahdī. His father Amīr Čūbān took him a prisoner to Abū Saʿīd, but the latter pardoned him for the sake of Amīr Čūbān. After the execution of his brother Dimashḳ Khʷādja, he fled to Egypt. At first the Mamlūk sultan al-Nāṣir Muḥammad treated him with great honour, but the intrigues of enemies of the Čūbānid family, and Abū Saʿīd's repeated demands for the extradition of Tīmūrtāsh, were a source of embarrassment to the Mamlūk sultan, who eventually decided to put him to death on 13 Shawwāl 728/21 August 1328.

(4) Ḥasan b. Tīmūrtāsh, known as Ḥasan Kūčūk to distinguish him from his rival Shaykh Ḥasan Buzurg the Djalāʾirid. After the death of Abū Saʿīd in 736/1335, he gained the support of his father's followers in Rūm by a ruse, and in Dhu 'l-Ḥidjdja 738/July 1338 he defeated Ḥasan Buzurg near Nakhčiwān. He then gave his allegiance to the princess Sātī Beg, the widow of Amīr Čūbān and Arpa Khān, at Tabrīz (739/1338-9), and came to terms with Ḥasan Buzurg. The following year he transferred his allegiance to a descendant of Hülegü, Sulaymān Khān, to whom he married Sātī Beg. For some years he continued to wage war on his rival Ḥasan Buzurg and the various puppet khāns nominated by the latter, but on 27 Radjab 744/15 December 1343, he was murdered at Tabrīz by his wife ʿIzzat Malik. See further the article ilkhānids.

Bibliography: Ibn Baṭṭūṭa, 116 ff.; H. H. Howorth, *History of the Mongols*, iii, London 1888, index s.v. Choban; ʿAbbās ʿAzzāwī, *Taʾrīkh al-ʿIrāḳ bayn Iḥtilālayn*, 3 vols., Baghdād 1353-7/1935-9, index; Ḥāfiẓ Abrū, *Dhayl-i Djāmiʿ al-Tawārīkh-i Rashīdī* (ed. K. Bayānī), Tehran 1317 solar/1938, *passim*; *Taʾrīkh-i Shaykh Uways* (ed. J. B. Van Loon), The Hague 1954, *passim*; B. Spuler, *Die Mongolen in Iran*², Berlin 1955, *passim*; Muʿīn al-Dīn Naṭanzī, *Muntakhab al-Tawārīkh-i Muʿīnī*, ed. J. Aubin, Tehran 1336 S./1957, index; *EI*¹, s.v. suldūz.

(R. M. Savory)

CUENCA [see kūnka]

ČUKA [see ḳumāsh]

ČUKUROVA [see cilicia]

ČULÎM. The term 'Tatars of Čulîm' (in Russian 'Čulîmtzî', a word invented by Radloff, *Aus Sibirien*, i, 211) includes several small Turkish-speaking groups of Central Siberia whose ancestors would have been Selkups of the Ob' and Ketes of the Yenisseĭ brought under Turkish influence by the Altaic tribes originating in the south and by the Tatars of Baraba [*q.v.*] and of Tobol' [*q.v.*] originating in the west.

The Tatars of Čulîm form three principal blocks: 1. On the river Kiya, tributary of the Čulîm, in the *oblast'* of Kemerovo who were formerly called "Ketzik" (to the south of the town of Mariinsk) and "Küerik" (to the north of that town). 2. On the central Čulîm, in the district of Ačinsk of the *Krraĭ* of Krasnoyarsk, whom ancient ethnographers called "Tatars of Meletzk". 3. On the lower Čulîm and the Ob', in the districts of Asino and Ziryansk of the *oblast'* of Tomsk, formerly known as "Tatars of Tomsk".

The present number of the Tatars of Čulîm is unknown. The Russian census of 1897 counted 11,123. The censuses of 1926 and 1939 included them with the "Tatars of the Volga". S. A. Tokarev, *Étnografiya narodov SSSR*, Moscow 1958, 428-429, estimates their number at 11,000. They speak a Turkish dialect akin to the Kîzîl speech of the Hakas, but strongly Russianized.

Previously Shamanists, the Tatars of Čulîm officially adopted orthodox Christianity in the 18th century. Sunnī Islam of the Ḥanafī school was brought to them in the second half of the 19th century by the Tatars of Ḳazan, but it has made no appreciable progress.

Nowadays the Tatars of Čulîm are dispersed among the Russian villages and are exposed to Russian cultural influence; they adopt Russian as their chief language, and merge fairly quickly into the Russian masses.

Bibliography: Ivanov, *Tatarî Čulîmskie*, in *Trudî Tomskogo oblastono Muzeya*, ii, Tomsk 1929;

A. M. Dul'zon, *Čulīmskie Tatarī i ikh yazīk*, in *Učenīe Zapiski Tomskogo Gosud. Pedagogič. In-ta*, ix, Tomsk 1925. (CH. QUELQUEJAY)

ČŪPĀN, 'herdsman, shepherd'. This word of Iranian origin was adopted by Turkish peoples in close contact with the Iranian language-area, namely speakers of the dialects of the S.W. group of Turkish languages (Anatolia and neighbouring areas) and the S.E. group (Čaghatay etc.). This derivation is supported by the fact that the word is not found in Turkish languages outside these two groups.

Shubān or *shabān*, the form in general use in modern Persian (= herdsman, < Phl. *špāna* < Late Av. **fšupāna*; cf. *fšūmā* 'owner of herds'), must have passed into Turkish via the *č*- dialects (cf. *Shāh-nāma, čōbān, čōpān*; Kāš *čepūn, čūpūn, čapō*; Kurd. *čuvān*, 'herdsman'; *čīpan* 'butcher' [*Grundr. d. iran. Philologie*, i, 13, 148 etc.; ii, 71, 79, 89, 188, 195]). In modern dictionaries of Persian there are attested besides *shubān* (popular pronunciation *shabān*) and *shūbān* (cf. also *shubāngāh* 'mansio pastoris' [Vullers]), the forms *čobān* 'a shepherd, a horsekeeper' (*čobānī* 'a pastoral office'), *čopān* (Steingass), *čūban*, vulg. *čoban* (Redhouse, '1. a shepherd, 2. a man who has charge of any kinds of beasts out at pasture, 3. a rustic, a boor'), *čūbān* (Zenker), *čūpān, čūbān* (Shaksp. *ğawpān*).

The fact that there is no general word for 'shepherd' in Turkish can be explained in the light of the historical development of Turkish society: in the economic life of the nomadic Turks stock-raising was the main activity of the whole tribe, and thus the idea of the herding of beasts as a distinct occupation had not developed. When later, with the increasing complexity of society, the occupation came into existence this task must have been delegated by the Turks, who formed the governing class, to non-Turks, as the Iranian origin of the word indicates.

Though the verbs *kü-, küdez-, küzet-* etc. were in general use in Old Turkish with the meaning of 'protect' 'guard', it is clear that they had not yet acquired the meaning of 'tend animals'; cf., *e.g.*, *ḳoyuġ ked küdezgil* 'guard the sheep well' (*Kutadgu Bilig*, 5164), *ḳoyuġ ked küdezip yorı* (*KB* 1413); *küzet* 'guard' (Index), *küdezči* (*yorıġlı binigli küdezčisi ol, KB* 1741). For a use with a meaning approaching that of 'shepherd' cf. *KB* 1412 (*budun ḳoy sanı ol begi ḳoyčısı: boġırsaḳ kerek ḳoyḳa ḳoy kütčisi* 'the people are like sheep and the *beg* is their shepherd: the shepherd must be kind to the sheep'), 5590 (*tarıġčı tarıġḳa irig bolsunı: yime yılḳıčı igdiš öklitsüni* 'let the farmers work hard at their farming, and those that tend the animals see that they increase').

Among the Ḳazan Turks the word *kütüčī* (< *küt-*, Ott. *güt-*; *kütü* = Ott. *sürü*, but Ott. *sürücü* has developed with a different meaning) is used; from which no doubt comes the Čuvash *kĕtüčĕ* or *kĕtü păxaka*. Among the Ḳazaḳ and the Kīrghīz, for whom stock-raising still constitutes the main activity, the words *malšı* (< *mal-čı*) and *baḳtašı* are generally used instead of *čoban*, or, if greater precision is required, the expressions *ḳoyšu, ğılḳıšı, sıyıršı, tüyeši* etc. are employed. The examples given by W. Barthold in *EI*[1] for the use of the word *čoban* for the inferior classes and for the ruling members of society are not of general application: the first belongs to a very late period, while the name of the Amīr Čoban, who was viceroy in Iran in the reign of Abū Saʿīd (1316-1327), is more probably connected with the word *čupan*, defined by Maḥmūd Kāshgharī as 'village headman's assistant'.

In Turkish languages in which the word *čoban* is used, it is found not only in the derivatives *čobanğa, čobanlık*, but in a number of compounds, chiefly for plant-names (many of them no doubt calques from Persian), *e.g.*, *čoban değneği* (*tayağı, tarağı*) 'knot-grass', *č. püskülü* 'ilex aquiflium, holly', *č. düdüğü* 'hazel', *č. dağarğığı* 'a creeper', *č. kaldıran* 'lychnis calcedonia', *č. kalkıdan* 'caltrop', *č. iğnesi* 'cranes-bill'; *č. kepeği*, 'sheepdog', *č. kušu* 'a bird like a sparrow', and especially *čoban aldatan* (*č. aldatğučı, č. aldatḳıčı*, cf. TTS IV).

The expression of particular interest for cultural history is *čoban yıldızı* 'the planet Venus', in which one sees the mutual influence of T. *čolpan* and P. *čuban*. *Čolpan* (Čagh. Ott. Tar. O.T.), *čolpon* (Kır.), *čulpan* (Ḳazan), *šolpan, šulpan* (Ḳaz.), *čolmon* (Tel.), *čulmon* (Alt.), *čolban* (Shor), *čölbön* (Tob. Leb.) and *tsolman* (*čolman, čolmun, čolbun*) (Mong.). *Čolpan* (*č. yulduz* [or *yulduzı*], *tañ čolmonu iñir čolmonu* ['morning- and evening-star']) has in this case presumably been identified with *čoban*.

With Čoban-Ata, the name of a line of hills on the S. bank of the Zarafshān near Samarḳand (which derives, according to W. Barthold in *EI*[1], from a legend of a shepherd seen on the hills, or from the name of a Muslim saint) cf. Kīrghīz *Čolpan-Ata* 'the guardian of the sheep' and hence 'sheep', *Kamber-Ata* 'guardian of the horses', *Čıčan-Ata* 'guardian of the goats', *Oysul-Ata* 'guardian of the camels' (and hence 'horses', 'goats', 'camels' respectively).

(R. RAHMETI ARAT)

ČŪPĀN-ATA [see ČOPAN-ATA]

ČUWASH (ČUVASH), (native name Čăvash), a Turkish-speaking people of the Middle Volga, numbering (in 1939), 1,369,000, who form the Soviet Socialist republic of the ČUVASH (18,300 square kilometres, 1,095,000 inhabitants in 1956), situated on the southern bank of the Volga, to the west of the Autonomous Soviet Socialist Republic of the Tatars. The Čuvash also inhabit the neighbouring regions: the Autonomous Republics of Tataristān and Bashkiria, the *oblast'*s of Ulianovsk, Kuybīshev, Saratov, and in Western Siberia.

The name Čuvash only appears in its present form in Russian chronicles of later than the 15th century, and is not found in such Arabic writers as Ibn Faḍlān, al-Muḳaddasī, Yāḳūt, etc., yet the Čuvash are according to general opinion, one of the oldest established peoples in the Volga region. Their origin is still the subject of controversy. According to a theory which has now been abandoned, the Čuvash were descendants of the Khazars (Hunfalvy, *Die Ungern Magyaren*, 1881; Fuks, *Zapiski o Čuvashakh i čeremisakh Kazanskoy Gubernii*, Ḳazan 1840). Other writers trace their descent to the Burṭās [*q.v.*] or the Huns (for example W. Barthold, *Sovremennoe sostoyanie i bližayshie zadači izučeniya istorii turetskikh narodov*, Moscow 1926, 5). More popular and more likely is the theory that they are of Bulghār origin, which is based, among other things, on the analogy between the present-day Čuvash language and the funeral inscriptions found in the ruins of the town of Bulghār and on the Danube. Several historians and linguists have defended this theory and it still has many supporters: Husein Feizkhanov, Il'minskiy, *O fonetičeskikh otnosheniyakh meždu čuvashskim i türkskimi yazīkami*, in *Izv. Arkh. Obshč. v*, (1965) 80-84. N. I. Ashmarin, *Bolgarī i Čuvashī*, St. Petersburg 1902, Howorth, etc.; A. P. Kovalevskiy, *Čuvashī i Bulgarī po dannīm Akhmeda ibn Fadlana*, Čeboksarî 1954, and P. N. Tretyakov, *Vopros o proizkhoždenii Čuvashskogo naroda v svete arkheologičeskikh dannîkh*, in *SE*, iii, 1950, 44-53, trace the descent of the Čuvash from the Bulghār tribe of the Savak (or Savaz) who, contrary to the Bulghārs properly so-called, refused to adopt Islam and remained animists.

Finally, according to a new theory, based on the existence of a pre-Turkish Finno-Ugrian substratum in the Čuvash language which has been recognized for some time by the majority of Soviet ethnologists, the ancestors of the Čuvash were Finno-Ugrian tribes who were influenced by Turkish culture through various Turkish tribes originating in the south or the south-east, before the arrival of the Bulghārs on the Middle Volga in the 7th century.

The infiltration of Turkish culture among the Finno-Ugrians continued during the Bulghār era until the 13th century or even later, under the Golden Horde and the Khanate of Ḳāzān. Whatever their racial origins may be, the Čuvash, a Turkish-speaking people, but animists (they were converted to Christianity in the 18th and 19th centuries) were exposed to the influence of Islam by contact with the Muslims, the Bulghārs, and then the Tatars; this influence is be found particularly in certain terms such as "*psemelle*", the word by which prayers begin, "*pikhampar*" (payghambar), 'wolf-god', "*kiremet*", 'spirit'. Other Čuvash, placed in immediate contact with the Tatars of Ḳazan, were converted to Islam. This phenomenon, which began at the time of the Khānate of Ḳazan, continued almost to the present day. It is impossible to appreciate its extent, for the Čuvash who were converted to Islam adopted the language of the Tatars, at the same time as their religion, and were "Tatarized". Tokarev, *Étnografiya narodov SSSR*, Moscow 1958, considers that at the beginning of the 19th century the Čuvash were three times as numerous as the Tatars in the "government" of Ḳazan, while in the census of 1897, their number was twice as small as that of the Tatars. According to him this decrease is due to the fact of "Tatarization" alone. Finally among the Čuvash who are animists or Christians, and the Muslim Čuvash there were still to be found at the beginning of the 20th century several semi-Muslim groups, such as, for example, the *Nekreshčenîe Kryasheni* of the district of Kaybitzk of the Autonomous Soviet Socialist Republic of Tataristān, who are semi-islamized animists, or again the Čuvash group of the region of Ulianovsk, who were considered before 1917 as Christians of the Orthodox church, while still observing the Muslim festivals and the fast of Ramaḍān.

Bibliography: V. G. Egorov, *Sovremmenîy Čuvashskiy Yazîk*, Čeboksarî 1954; P. N. Tret'yakov, *Vopros o proizkhoždenii čuvashkogo naroda v svete arkheologičeskikh dannîkh*, in *SE*, iii 1950; V. Sboev, *Čuvashi v bîtovom, istoričeskom i religioznom otnosheniyakh*, Moscow 1865; N. I. Ashmarin, *Bolgarî i Čuvashî*, in *Izv. Obshč. Arkh. Ist. i Étn. pri Imp. Kaz. Univ-te.*, xviii, Ḳazan 1908; V. K. Magnitskiy, *Materialî k ob'yasneniyu staroy čuvashskoy verî*, Ḳazan 1881; A. Ivanov, *Ukazatel' knig, broshyur, žurnal'nîkh i gazetnîkh statey na russkom yazîke o čuvashakh v svyazi s drugimi inorodtzami Srednego Povolž'ya*, 1756-1906, Ḳazan 1907; idem, *Izvestiya Obsh. Arkh. Ist. i Étn.*, xxiii, fasc. 2, 4; Koblov, *O tatarizatzii inorodtzev privolžskogo kraya*, Ḳazan 1910.

(Ch. Quelueqʃay)

CYPRUS [see ḲUBRUS]

CYRENAICA [see BARḲA]

D

AL-**DABARĀN** [see NUDJŪM].

ḌABB, the thorn-tail lizard (*Uromastix spinipes*). Cognate synonyms exist in other Semitic languages.

The animal, found in abundance in the homeland of the Arabs, is often mentioned and described in ancient poetry and proverbs. Much of the information on the animal derives from just these sources which are freely quoted in later zoological works. The *ḍabb* was eaten by the ancient Arabs who relished it as tasty food; still it is reported that the tribe of Tamīm, who were especially fond of eating it, were ridiculed on that account by other Arabs. In Islamic times, the lawfulness of its use as human food was expressly pointed out by some *ḥadīth*s. Bedouin eat it to the present day.

The *ḍabb* is described as clever but forgetful; it may even not find its way back to its hole, wherefore it chooses a conspicuous place for its habitation. It digs its hole in solid ground—whereby its claws become blunt—lest it collapse under the tread of hoofed animals. It does not brood over the eggs but lays them in a small cavity of the soil and then covers them with earth. The young hatch after forty days and are able to take care of themselves (autophagous). The *ḍabb* lays seventy eggs and more, which resemble the eggs of the pigeon. Its tail is jointed. It has such great strength in its tail that it can split a snake with it. If it is killed and left for one night and then is brought near a fire, it will move again. It devours its young when hungry and eats its vomit again; yet it is highly capable of enduring hunger, being second, in this respect, only to the snake. It likes eating dates. Its teeth are all of one piece. It is afraid of man but lives on friendly terms with the scorpion, which it takes into its hole as a protection from the human foe. It does not leave its hole in winter. When exposed to the sun, it assumes various colours like the chameleon. It lives seven hundred years and more. When old it foregoes food and is satisfied with air. The male has two penes and the female two vulvae. A certain kind has two tongues. The *ḍabb* drinks little or does not drink at all and voids one drop of urine in every forty days.

Some of the fabulous accounts have their origin in ancient popular tradition, mainly laid down in poetry and proverbs, as pointed out in the zoological works themselves.

Various medicinal properties were ascribed to the heart, spleen, skin, blood, fat and dung of the *ḍabb*. Its significance when seen in dreams has been treated by Damīrī and in special works on that subject.

Bibliography: ʿAbd al-Ghanī al-Nābulusī, *Taʿṭīr al-Anām*, Cairo 1354, ii, 58; Damīrī, s.v. (transl. Jayakar, ii, 195 ff.); Dāwūd al-Anṭākī, *Tadhkira*, Cairo 1324, i, 207; Goldziher, *Ẓâhiriten*, 81; J. Euting, *Tagebuch*, i, 107; Ibn Ḳutayba, *ʿUyūn al-Akhbār*, Cairo 1925-30, ii, 72, 73, 79, 96, 98 (transl. Kopf, 46, 47, 54, 72, 74); Ibshīhī, *Mustaṭraf*, bāb 62, s.v.; G. Jacob, *Beduinenleben*², 6, 24, 95; Ḳazwīnī (Wüstenfeld), i, 437 f. (transl. Wiedemann, *Beitr. z. Gesch. d. Naturw.*, liii, 259 f.; I. Löw, *ZA* xxvi, 145 ff.; G. W. Murray, *Sons of Ishmael*, 1935, 90 f.; al-Mustawfī al-Ḳazwīnī (Stephenson), 19; Nuwayrī, *Nihāyat al-Arab*, x, 155 ff. (L. Kopf)

DĀBBA, (plur. *dawābb*), any living creature which keeps its body horizontal as it moves, generally quadruped. In particular, beast of burden or pack-animal: horse, donkey, mule, camel (cf. Lane, s.v.).

Burāḳ, the legendary steed ridden by the Prophet at his ascension (*miʿrādj*), is given the name *dābba* by al-Ghīṭī and in the commentaries. The word acquires a particular significance from its use in the Ḳurʾān, XXVII, 82 in the sense of the archetypal "Beast", equivalent to the term θήριον in the Apocalypse of St. John. The text is laconic and gives no explanation: "And when the final word has been spoken against them (cf. XXVII, 85), we shall call forth before them *the Beast sprung from the earth*, that shall tell them that mankind had no faith in our signs". The formula is no doubt based purely on recollections of the Apocalypse: καὶ εἶδον ἄλλον θήριον ἀναβαῖνον ἐκ τῆς γᾶς ... (Rev., xiii, 11).

Exegesis carried out in the course of time has derived from the text, which has been reconsidered in respect of certain images relating to the Day of Judgment. Commentaries by al-Ṭabarī, al-Zamakhsharī, al-Rāzī, and al-Bayḍāwī repeat each other. The key point is, apparently, a *ḥadīth* which has been traced back to the Prophet (al-Ṭabarī): "I said: Oh Prophet of God, where will it (the Beast) appear? He answered: from the greatest of mosques, a thing sanctified by God. While Jesus shall perform the *Ṭawāf* in the House of God, and with him the Muslims, the Earth shall tremble beneath their feet at the movements of the vast Beast. And Ṣafā shall be torn apart at the place where it will appear". The Beast will emerge at Ṣafā. The forefront of its head will have a hairy mark, and its ears will be entirely covered with hair. Those who try to capture it will not succeed, nor will those who take to flight escape from it. It will speak Arabic. It will name people as either "believers" or "ungodly". The believers it will leave, their faces gleaming like stars, and between their eyes it will inscribe the word "believer"; as for the ungodly, it will set between their eyes the black mark of the ungodly.

Other traditions have extended this last part: it is with Moses' rod that the Beast will mark the believer with a white spot, which will expand until it makes the whole face gleam, whilst Solomon's seal, affixed to the nose of the ungodly man, will spread until all his features become black.

Around this nucleus later traditions have given rise to a mass of detail, some concerned with the Beast's essential actions: the Imām of the Mosque of Mecca, on its third appearance will recognize it as the sign of Universal Death (al-Ṭabarī). It will make men ashamed of their ungodliness or hypocrisy (*id.*). It will emphasize that it is now too late to begin to pray, and will castigate this belated way of returning to God. For al-Zamakhsharī, it is the "watchful" (*djassās*). The involuntary element of caricature in its appearance seems to derive from the desire to combine all the figurative features of the animal kingdom. One tradition insists upon its gigantic size: "only its head will appear, which will reach the clouds in the sky" (al-Zamakhsharī; Fakhr al-dīn al-Rāzī), a conception which seems to be influenced by the description of the appearance of Gehenna recorded in the Ps. Ghazzālī, *al-Durra al-fākhira* (Brockelmann, I, 538, no. 6; S I, 746, no. 6; cf. comm. on *Ḳurʾān*, XVIII, 100). Abū Hurayra [*apud* Rāzī] says that the horns on its bull-like head are a parasang apart. It will appear three times. Al-Zamakhsharī makes it travel in turn through the Maghrib, the East, Syria and the Yemen, proclaiming the vanity of all religions foreign to Islam. Al-Rāzī speaks of a long period of hiding in the mosque at Mecca between its second and third appearances.

All these descriptions which, one after another, betray the influence of vague notions deriving from the Scriptures, popular and apocalyptic accounts, are of late date. Al-Rāzī stresses that "out of all this there is nothing authentic in the Book, unless the words attributed to the Prophet are genuine".

In any case, it is not the Beast of the Apocalypse since it arrives *after* judgement has been pronounced (al-Rāzī states that the *warrāḳs* interpret the words "and when the final word has been spoken against them" in this sense). This is confirmed by traditions which depict it denouncing the futility of sinners seeking too late to be converted, after the time when, according to the Ḳurʾān, repentance will no longer avail. This explains the confusion with the idea of Gehenna in the Ps. Ghazzālī. (A. Abel)

ḌABBA b. Udd b. Ṭābīkha b. al-Yās (Khindif) b. Muḍar b. Nizār b. Maʿadd was the eponymous hero of the well known Arab tribe of that name. With their "nephews" ʿUkl b. ʿAwf, Taym, ʿAdī, and Thawr b. ʿAbd Manāt b. Udd, Ḍabba formed a confederacy called al-Ribāb. The Ribāb were in alliance with Saʿd b. Zayd Manāt, the greatest clan of Tamīm. This alliance has never been broken by the other confederates. These, indeed, were formations of rather moderate size, whereas the Ḍabba by means of their power sometimes were able to follow their own policy.

Of the three clans of Ḍabba, Ṣuraym had in the course of the 7th/13th century shrunk to a small number of families. But the second, Bakr, had vastly increased, thus leaving the once powerful Banū Thaʿlaba far behind.

From the second half of the 6th/12th century onwards, the domiciles of al-Ribāb were in the region al-Shurayf between the right bank of Wādī Tasrīr and the depression al-Sirr. In the spring they used to migrate to (Baṭn) Faldj and to the sands of the Dahnāʾ by way of Tiʿshār (= Ḳayʿiyya?) or Wādī al-ʿAtk farther south. But as their spring pastures lay as late as the eighties far in the N.W., in regions held in other seasons by Asad [*q.v.*] and Dhubyān, we may conclude that their domiciles before this time were farther in the west than they were later on.

We find al-Ribāb mentioned for the first time in the *Dīwān* of ʿAbīd b. al-Abraṣ (no. 17, 12) as fighting against Asad (not later than 540). In the eighties Ḍabba and Tamīm stood their ground in a long battle against the Kilāb (b. Rabīʿa b. ʿĀmir b. Ṣaʿṣaʿa [*q.v.*]) and ʿAbs (yawm al-Ḳurnatayn = al-Suʾbān, Aws b. Ḥadjar, no. 1, 9; 16; 17, 3-15; Labīd, no. 16, 41-42; ʿAntara in *Six Poets*, ed. Ahlwardt, no. 7, 19). Some years later al-Aswad, brother to al-Nuʿmān III of al-Ḥīra, began to restore by several campaigns in Arabia the lost prestige of the dynasty. The Ribāb hesitated to surrender until al-Aswad set on them Asad and Dhubyān. Next year al-Ribāb, together with mercenaries of al-Ḥīra, led by al-Aswad, defeated the Kilāb at Arīk. One year later Asad and Ḍabba again defeated the Kilāb and other ʿĀmir b. Ṣaʿṣaʿa (al-Aʿshā, ed. R. Geyer, no. 1, 62-74; The *Naḳāʾid* of Djarīr and al-Farazdaḳ, ed. Bevan, 240, 18-19; Yāḳūt, 1, 229; The *Mufaḍḍaliyyāt*, ed. Lyall, no. 96, 8-19; 99, 9). Their last feat in the *Djāhiliyya* was the murder of Bisṭām b. Ḳays, the hero of the Shaybān (of Bakr b. Waʾil [*q.v.*]), who were driving away their herds (E. Bräunlich, *Bisṭām Ibn Qais*, Leipzig 1923).

There is hardly any information on their conversion to Islam. In the first division of the population of al-Kūfa Ḍabba seem to be missing. Mentioned are only "the remaining Ribāb". That is to say, Ḍabba together with Bakr and Ṭayyiʾ formed the quarter missing in the enumeration Ṭabarī 1, 2495. The bulk of the tribe emigrated to Baṣra. In the Battle of the Camel they fought against ʿAlī. Later on they belonged to the quarter, *khums*, of Tamīm. The same applies to Khurāsān, where the Tamīm numbered (in 96/715) 10,000 warriors led by Ḍirār b. Ḥuṣayn, scion of the old leading family of Ḍabba.

The part of the tribe remaining in Arabia used to camp in the region S.W. of modern Kuwayt. In 287/900 308 Ḍabba joined the Basrian army against the East Arabian Carmathians, but suspecting coming defeat, deserted at a distance of a two days' march from Ḳaṭīf.

There is no outstanding poet amongst the Ḍabba, but a number of soldiers, judges and administrators in Umayyad and ʿAbbāsid times, *e.g.*, Abū Ḥātim ʿAnbasa b. Isḥāq, 238-242 AH governor of Egypt, a righteous man, the last Arabian ruling Egypt, and the last Amīr lead in prayer and hold Friday services.

Bibliography: Ibn al-Kalbī, *Djamhara*, MS. London, 111a-115b; Ṭabarī, index; Ibn Saʿd, index; Masʿūdī, *Tanbīh*, 394; Ibn Ḥazm, *Djamharat ansāb al-ʿArab*, ed. E. Lévi-Provençal, 194; Kindī, *Governors and Judges of Egypt*, ed. Guest, 200-202; U. Thilo, *Die Ortsnamen in der altarabischen Poesie, Schriften der M. Frh. v. Oppenheim-Stiftung*, 3, Wiesbaden 1958. (W. CASKEL)

AL-ḌABBĪ, ABŪ DJAʿFAR AḤMAD B. YAḤYĀ B. AḤMAD B. ʿAMĪRA, an Andalusian scholar of the 6th/12th century. According to the information that he gives us in his works concerning himself and his family, he was born at Vélez, to the west of Lorca, and he began his studies in Lorca. He travelled in North Africa (Ceuta, Marrākush, Bougie) and even reached Alexandria, but he appears to have spent the greater part of his life at Murcia. He died at the end of Rabīʿ II 599/beginning of 1203. Of his writings only a biographical dictionary of Andalusian scholars is preserved, preceded by a short survey of the history of Muslim Spain which continues and completes the introduction of ʿAbd al-Wāḥid al-Marrākushī (*Histoire des Almohades*, ed. Dozy). In addition al-Ḍabbī was closely connected with the *Djadhwat al-muḳtabis* of al-Ḥumaydī, which goes as far as 450/1058, and which he completed with the help of later biographical works. His collection of biographies, entitled *Bughyat al-multamis fi Taʾrīkh Ridjāl Ahl al-Andalus*, was edited in 1885 by Codera and Ribera (vol. iii of the *Bibl. Arabico-Hispana*).

Bibliography: Maḳḳarī, *Analectes*, ii, 714; Amari, *Bibl. ar. sic.*, i, 437; Wüstenfeld, *Geschichtschreiber*, no. 282; Pons Boygues, *Ensayo*, no. 212; Brockelmann, S I, 580. (C. F. SEYBOLD*)

AL-ḌABBĪ, ABŪ ʿIKRIMA [see AL-MUFAḌḌAL].

DĀBIḲ, a locality in the ʿAzāz region of northern Syria. It lies on the road from Manbidj to Anṭākiya (Ṭabarī, iii, 1103) upstream from Aleppo on the river Nahr Ḳuwayḳ. In Assyrian times its name was *Dabigu*, to become *Dabekôn* in Greek. It lies on the edge of the vast plain of Mardj Dābiḳ where, under the Umayyads and ʿAbbāsids, troops were stationed prior to being sent on operations against Byzantine territory. The Umayyad caliph Sulaymān b. ʿAbd al-Malik lived in Dābiḳ for some time, and after his death and burial there in Ṣafar 99/Sept. 717 his successor ʿUmar b. ʿAbd al-ʿAzīz was appointed caliph. According to al-Masʿūdī, his tomb was desecrated by the ʿAbbāsids, but the version told by al-Shābushtī conflicts with this (*K. al-Diyārāt*, Baghdād 1951, 149).

In the Ayyūbid era pilgrims visited a monument called *maḳām Dāwūd* on Mt. Barṣāyā near Dābiḳ. The spot today has the name Nabī Dāwūd.

Dābiḳ is known above all for the decisive battle which was fought there on 15 Radjab 922/24 August 1516 between the armies of the sultan Kanṣūh al-Ghūrī and the Ottoman sultan Selīm I. The Ottoman artillery proved superior, the bravest elements of the Mamlūk cavalry were decimated, and Kanṣūh himself was killed. The Ottoman victory paved the way for their occupation of Syria and Egypt.

Bibliography: Balādhurī, *Futūḥ*, 171, 189; Ṭabarī, index; Masʿūdī, *Murūdj*, v, 397 and 471; Harawī, *K. al-Ziyārāt*, ed. J. Sourdel-Thomine, Damascus 1953, 6 (trans. 11); Ibn al-ʿAdīm, *Zubda*, ed. S. Dahān, i, Damascus 1951, 41, 56, 57, 63, 67; Ibn Shāddad, *La Description d'Alep*, ed. D. Sourdel, Damascus 1953, 29, 138-39; Yāḳūt, ii, 513; G. Le Strange, *Palestine under the Moslems*, London 1890, 61, 426, 503; R. Dussaud, *Topographie historique de la Syrie*, Paris 1927, 468, 474; M. Canard, *Histoire des H'amdânides*, I, Algiers 1951, 225; Wellhausen, *Das arabische Reich*, Berlin 1902, 165 ff.; N. Jorga, *Geschichte des osmanischen Reiches*, ii, Gotha, 1909, 336; D. Ayalon, *Gunpowder and firearms in the Mamluk Kingdom*, London 1956, index.
(D. SOURDEL)

DABĪḲ (variant forms *Dabḳa* and *Dabḳū*) was a locality in the outer suburbs of Damietta, noted for the manufacture of high quality woven material, which it exported to the whole of the Muslim empire. The location of Dabīḳ cannot be fixed more exactly. It is found mentioned along with other cities that have disappeared, such as Shaṭā, Tinnīs, or Tūna, which were probably on the islands of Lake Menzāleh.

Fine cloths embossed with gold were made there, and, during the Fāṭimid period, turbans of multicoloured linen. These textiles were so sumptious that *dabīḳī* soon became known, and its fame grew to such an extent that the word came to designate a type of material. *Dabīḳī* came to be manufactured more or less everywhere, at Tinnīs and at Damietta, in the Delta, at Asyūṭ, in Upper Egypt, and even in Persia, at Kāzirūn. The quality of the cloth made at Dabīḳ must have dropped, because, according to al-Idrīsī, although these materials were very fine, they could not be compared with those of Tinnīs and Damietta, and this fact can already be deduced from the customs tariff of Djedda, given by al-Muḳaddasī.

At the present moment, three fragments of material are known—one ʿAbbāsid and two Fāṭimid—that include in their inscriptions the name of Dabīḳ.

The place name is not mentioned by Ibn Mammātī, who, however, mentions the *dabīḳī*.

Ibn Duḳmāḳ (v, 89) and Ibn Ḏjiʿān (76; ʿAbd al-Laṭīf, *Relation de l'Egypte*, 638) mention a place called Dabīḳ in the province of Gharbiyya, but this cannot be the town in the Damietta neighbourhood, which these two writers treat separately (Ibn Duḳmāḳ, v, 78; Ibn Ḏjiʿān, 62 and ʿAbd al-Laṭīf, 630).

For the same reason of distance, one could not possibly identify the old Dabīḳ with the modern Dabīdj, twelve kilometres south of Sinballāwayn, which could, on the other hand, well be the Dabīḳ of Ibn Duḳmāḳ and Ibn Ḏjiʿān.

Bibliography: Yaʿḳūbī-Wiet, 194-195; Ibn Khurradāḏhbih 83; Idrīsī, *Maghrib* 186-187; Nāṣir-i Khusraw, 141; Muḳaddasī, 54, 104, 193, 443; Ibn Mammātī, 81; Maḳrīzī, ed. Wiet, ii, 84; iii, 200, 215; iv, 82 (with a long bibliography), 247; Le Strange, 294; Salmon, *Introduction à l'histoire de Bagdadh*, 136, 138, 140; J. Maspero and Wiet, *Matériaux pour servir à la géographie de l'Egypte*, 178; R. B. Serjeant, *Islamic Textiles*, in *Ars islamica*, xiii, 89, 94, 97, 98, 100; xv, 76; Wiet, *Tissus et Tapisseries*, in *Syria*, xvi, 282-283; Kühnel, *Dated Tiraz Fabrics*, 107; *RCEA* iii, 902; vi, 2033, 2175. (G. WIET)

DABĪL [see DWĪN]

DABĪR, SALĀMAT ʿALĪ, MĪRZĀ, LAKHNAWĪ, an Urdū poet, who devoted himself to writing and reciting highly devotional elegies on the death of the martyrs of Karbalā. He was a son of Mīrzā Ghulām Ḥusayn, who is claimed to be a grandson of Mullā Hāshim Shīrāzī (a brother of the famous Ahlī of Shīrāz, d. 934/1536-7). Salāmat ʿAlī was born in Ballīmārān, Dihlī on 11 Ḏjumāda I 1218/29 August 1803; he accompanied his father as a child to Lucknow and there received a good education. He studied all the usual Persian and Arabic texts on religious and foreign sciences (*manḳūl wa maʿḳūl*) from well-known ʿulamāʾ of the city. He had finished his studies by the time he was 18. He began to write poetry at an early age (c. 1230 or 1232) and continued doing so along with his studies, under the guidance of Mīr Muẓaffar Ḥusayn Ḍamīr of Gurgāon. He soon acquired fame and won the appreciation of the rulers of Awadh, members of their family and the noblemen of the Court. For about 60 years of his life he wrote *marthiya*s (elegaic poems). Towards the end of his life he became almost blind. He, therefore, gladly accepted the suggestion of Wāḏjid ʿAlī Shāh, then living in Calcutta in exile, that he should go there for treatment; he reached there about Dhu 'l-Ḥidjdja 1290/c. Jan. 1874. A successful operation by a German eye-specialist, who was staying with Wāḏjid ʿAlī Shāh in Calcutta, restored his sight. He returned to Lucknow, where he had spent the major part of his life, and which he had only left for short periods in the disturbances of 1857 he had moved to Sītāpur for a while; about 1858 he went to Kānpur and in 1859 to ʿAẓīmābād; he visited ʿAẓīmābād again in 1292/1875 and died there on 30 Muḥarram 1292/8 March 1875, he was buried in his own house in a lane which is now known as *Kūča-i Dabīr*, after him. In his old age he suffered much tribulation on account of his loss of sight, and he was grieved by the death of a grown-up son and of a brother.

Dabīr is described as a pious, ascetic, generous, hospitable and serious-minded person. As a poet he was extremely prolific, and had the gift of composing good verses quickly. His compositions consisted mostly of *marthiya*s, *Salām*s (for them see *al-Mīzān*, 485) and *rubāʿī*s (*Ḥayāt-i Dabīr*, i, 272). His rival in this genre of poetry was his contemporary Mīr Anīs, who appeared in Lucknow long after Dabīr had established his fame as a poet. Their rivalry divided their admirers into two rival groups called Dabīrīs and Anīsīs and a considerable literature was produced on their comparative merits and failings (see, for example, Shiblī Nuʿmānī, *Muwāzana Anīs wa Dabīr*, Āgra 1907; Sayyid Nāẓir al-Ḥasan Fawḳ Raḍawi, *al-Mīzān*, ʿAlīgaṛh n.d.; ʿAbd al-Ghafūr Khān Nassākh, *Intikhāb-i Naḳs* 1879; Mīrzā Muḥammad Riḍā Muʿdjiz, *Taṭhīr al-Awsākh*; Mīr Afḍal ʿAlī Daw, *Radd al-Muwāzana*, etc. etc.).

While Anīs is usually praised for the simplicity of his style, easy flow of his verse, and his relatively eloquent (*faṣīḥ*) descriptions, Dabīr is eulogized for his brevity, freshness of his poetical ideas (*maḍāmīn*) and frequent and full use of rhetorical figures, and his touching laments and wailings (Urdū: *bayn*). As an Arabic and Persian scholar he drew freely on the literatures of these languages, incorporating in his poems materials taken from the Ḳurʾān, *ḥadīth* and the works on *Maḳātil*, etc. (cf. a comparative view quoted in *Ḥay. Dab.*, i, 290: The Mīr is eloquent and sweet (*faṣīḥ wa namakīn*)). The fact remains that it was due to the efforts of these two poets that *marthiya* attained such an important position in Urdū Poetry.

Works: Most of Dabīr's poems have been lithographed, though some are still unpublished. These editions are marred by interpolations, *e.g.*, (1) an edition of *marthiya*s in 2 vols. (*Ḥay. Dab.* i, 624); (2) *Daftar-i Mātam*, 20 vols. Lucknow 1897. For an analysis of the contents see *Ḥay. Dab.*, i, 276 ff. These *marthiya*s etc. were lost in the disturbances of 1957 and after, and were collected again later; (3) *Marāthī-i Dabīr*, 2 vols. (*ibid.* i, 490, 493); (4) *Marthiya-i Mīrzā Dabīr*, 2 vols., Lucknow 1875-76 (several editions in the following years), Kānpur 1890-99 (several editions in the following years); (5) *Marthiyahā-yi Mīrzā Dabīr*, Lucknow 1882 (several editions in the following years)); (6) *Abwāb al-Maṣāʾib*, a prose work, relating to the story of Joseph, compared to the story of the martyr of Karbalā, Dihlī (*Ḥay. Dab.*, i, 280); (7) *Rubāʿiyyāt Mīrzā Dabīr*, Lucknow n.d., containing 197 *rubāʿī*s. A smaller collection of these was also published along with those of Anīs in Āgra.

In his younger days the Mīrzā also composed three *dīwān*s of *ghazal*s, but later destroyed, lost or withdrew them.

Bibliography: In addition to the references given in the text: Mīr Muḥsin ʿAlī, *Sarāpā-Sukhun*, Lucknow 1292/1875, 108; Mīr Ṣafdar Ḥusayn, *Shams al-Duḥā*, Lucknow 1298/1880-81; Sayyid Afḍal Ḥusayn, *Thābit Raḍawī Lakhnawī*, *Ḥayāt-i Dabīr*, Lahore, vol. i, 1913, vol. ii, 1915; Muḥammad Ḥusayn Āzād, *Āb-i Ḥayāt*, Lahore 1883, 550-562; Rām Bābū Saksena, *A History of Urdu Literature*, Allāhābād 1940, 131 f. (Urdū version by Mirzā Muḥammad ʿAskarī, Lucknow 1952, 248 f.); Abu 'l-Layth, *Lakhnaʾū kā Dabistāni-Shāʿiri*, Lahore c. 1955, 690 f.; J. F. Blumhardt, *Cat. of Hind. Printed Books in the Br. Mus.*, London 1889, col. 7, 6, 308, *Suppl.*, London 1909, col. 421. (MOHAMMAD SHAFI)

DABISTĀN AL-MAD̲H̲ĀHIB, "The school of religions", a work in Persian describing the different religions of and in particular the religious situation in Hindustān in the 11th/17th century; it is the most complete account in the Persian language, later than the *Bayān al-adyān* (6th/12th century), which is accurate but concise, and than the *Tabṣirat al-ʿawāmm* (7th/13th century), written from the S̲h̲īʿite point of view. The sources of the *Dabistān* derive partly from the sacred books of the different religious persuasions, partly from verbal information given to the author, and partly from the latter's personal observations. In many chapters he also makes use of the earlier Arabic literature concerning these matters. First of all the religion of the Pārsīs is examined extensively; then that of the Hindūs; after some very short chapters concerned with the Tibetans, the Jews and the Christians, the author passes to the study of Islam and its sects; finally there are some chapters on the philosophers (the Peripatetics and the Neo-platonists) and on the Ṣūfīs. For a long time Muḥsin Fānī was thought (mistakenly) to be the author of this work; in some manuscripts he is mentioned solely in his capacity as the author of a *rubāʿī* which is quoted (see trans. by Shea-Troyer, i, 3); it was certainly an enlightened believer in the Pārsī religion who wrote the *Dabistān*, and we must probably accept those manuscripts which, in agreement with Sirād̲j̲ al-Dīn Muḥammad Arzū (in a passage from his *Tad̲h̲kira*), attribute its composition to Mūbad S̲h̲āh or Mullā Mūbad (cf. also Ouseley, *Notices*, 182). It is apparent from the book itself that the author was born in India shortly before 1028/1619, went to Āgra as a youth, spent several years in Kas̲h̲mīr and at Lahore, visited Persia (Mas̲h̲had) and acquired some knowledge of the west and south of India. The *Dabistān* was finished no doubt between 1064 and 1067/1654-57.

Bibliography: *Dabistān al-mad̲h̲āhib* (Calcutta 1224/1809; other editions from Tehran, Bombay, Lucknow; *The Dabistan or school of manners*, trans. David Shea and Anthony Troyer, Paris 1843, 3 vols. (not always accurate); *JA*, vi, (1845) 406-11; Rieu, *Cat. Persian Mss. of the British Museum*, i, 141 & iii, 1081. (Useful references to other catalogues of manuscripts and to old translations of isolated chapters): Éthé, *Cat. of the Persian Mss. of the India Office Library*, i, no. 1369 (useful references to other catalogues of manuscripts). (J. HOROVITZ-[H. MASSÉ])

ḌĀBIṬ, in Turkish *zabit*, an Ottoman term for certain functionaries and officers, later specialized to describe officers in the armed forces. In earlier Ottoman usage *Ḍābiṭ* seems to indicate a person in charge or in control of a matter or of (? the revenues of) a place (*e.g. Ewḳāf ḍābiṭi, Wilāyet ḍābiṭi* etc.; examples, some with place-names, in Halit Ongan, *Ankara'nın I Numaralı Şer'iye Sicili*, Ankara 1958, index, and L. Fekete, *Die Siyāqat-Schrift*, i, Budapest 1955, 493 ff.; cf. the Persian usage in the sense of collector — Minorsky, *Tad̲h̲kirat al-Mulūk*, index). The term seems to have remained in occasional use in this sense until quite a late date (see for example Gibb and Bowen, i, 259, and Dozy, *Suppl.* s.v.). By the 11th/17th century, however, it was already acquiring the technical meaning of army officer. In a *fāʾide* inserted under the year 1058/1648-9 Naʿīmā remarks that in the janissary corps the seniors of each *oda* are as *ḍābiṭs* (*ḍābiṭ gibidir*) to the other soldiers (*nefer*), and proceeds to name the ranks of the janissary officers (Naʿīmā⁴, iv, 351). By the 12th/18th century the term was already in common use in this sense (*e.g.* Resmī, *K̲h̲ulāṣat al-Iʿtibār*, 5, '*rid̲j̲āl we ḍābiṭān*') and documents cited by D̲j̲ewdet (i, 360; vi, 367 etc.). From the time of the westernizing reforms onwards it becomes the standard Ottoman equivalent of the European term 'officer'. In the Turkish republic it has been replaced by *subay*, but it remains current in the Arab successor states of the Ottoman Empire. (B. LEWIS)

ḌABṬ, assessment of taxable land by measurement, applied under the later Dihlī sultanate and the Mug̲h̲als; land so measured is called *ḍabṭī*. See ḌARĪBA, 6.

ḌABṬIYYA, in Turkish *zabtiyye*, a late Ottoman term for the police and gendarmerie. Police duties, formerly under the control of various janissary officers, were placed under the jurisdiction of the Serʿasker ([*q.v.*] see also BĀB-I SERʿASKERĪ) in 1241/1826, and in 1262/1846 became a separate administration, the *Ḍabṭiyye Mus̲h̲īriyyeti* (Luṭfī viii 27-8). At about the same time a council of police (*med̲j̲lis-i ḍabṭiyye*) was established, which was later abolished and replaced by two quasi-judicial bodies, the *dīwān-i ḍabṭiyye* and *med̲j̲lis-i taḥḳīḳ*. After several further changes the *mus̲h̲īriyyet* became a ministry (*neẓāret*) of police in 1286/1870. On 17 July 1909 the name ministry of *Ḍabṭiyye* was abolished and replaced by a department of public security (*Emniyyet-i ʿUmūmiyye*) under the Ministry of the Interior.

Bibliography: ʿOt̲h̲mān Nūrī, *Med̲j̲elle-i Umūr-i Belediyye*, i, Istanbul 1338/1922, 934 ff. Laws and regulations on police matters will be found in the *Destūr*, (French translations in G. Young, *Corps de Droit Ottoman*, Oxford 1905-6, and G. Aristarchi, *Législation ottomane*, Constantinople 1873-88. See further KARAKOL, S̲H̲URṬA. (B. LEWIS)

DĀBŪYA (DĀBŌĒ), the founder of the Dābūyid dynasty in Gīlān [*q.v.*]. The tribe claimed to be of Sāsānid extraction through Dābūya's father, Gīl Gāwbāra. Their residence was the town of Fūman [*q.v.*]. The dynasty clung to Zoroastrianism for a long time, and repeatedly defended the land against the Arabs, until the last ruler, K̲h̲ūrs̲h̲īd̲h̲ II (758/60, 141 or 142 A.H.) had to flee before the superior force of the ʿAbbāsids, and put an end to his own life in Daylam (Ṭabarī, iii, 139 f.). One of his daughters, whose name is unknown, became the wife of the Caliph al-Manṣūr.

The names of the members of the dynasty are as follows: Dābōē, 40 to 56/660-1 to 676.—His brother K̲h̲ūrs̲h̲īd̲h̲ I, 56 to 90/676 to 709.—His son Farruk̲h̲ān, 709 to 721-22, 90 to 103 A.H., who took the title Ispāhbad̲h̲ [*q.v.*] ("leader of the army"), and warded off an Arab assault in 717.—His son Dād̲h̲burzmihr (Dād̲h̲mihr), 103 to 116/721-22 to 734.—His brother Sārūya (Sārōē), for a few months in 116/721-22.—K̲h̲ūrs̲h̲īd̲h̲ II, the son of Dād̲h̲burzmihr, 116 to 141 or 142/721-22 to 758-60 (see above).

A dynasty descended from Dābūya's brother Pād̲h̲ūspān (title), ruled until 1567 and 1576 respectively (from 1453 in two branches) in Rūyān [*q.v.*] and some neighbouring districts.

Bibliography: Ibn Isfandiyār, *Taʾrīk̲h̲-i Ṭabaristān*, Tehran 1942 (to which I had access only in E. G. Browne, *An abridged translation of the history of Ṭabaristan .... by .... Ibn-i Isfandiyar ....*, Leiden and London 1905, index [GMS II]); *Sehir-eddin's* [= *Ẓahīr al-Dīn .... al-Marʿas̲h̲ī's*] *Geschichte von Tabaristan ....*, ed. Bernhard Dorn (*Mohammedanische Quellen ....*, vol. i), St. Petersburg 1850, 319 ff.; idem, in *Mém.*

Ac. Imp. St. Pétersbourg, xxiii, 1877, 103; G. Melgunof, *Das südliche Ufer des Kaspischen Meeres* ...., trans. by J. Th. Zenker, Leipzig 1868, 48 ff.—Family trees: F. Justi, *Iranisches Namenbuch* (1895), 433/35; E. de Zambaur *Manuel de généalogie* ....[2], Pyrmont 1955, 186-190.—Coins: A. D. Mordtmann in *ZDMG*, xix (1865), 485; xxxiii (1879d), 110. (B. SPULER)

DACCA [see ḎHĀKĀ].

ḌĀD, 15th letter of the Arabic alphabet, conventional transcription *ḍ*; numerical value, according to the oriental order, 800 [see ABḎJAD].

The definition of the phoneme presents difficulty. The most probable is: *voiced lateralized velarized interdental fricative* (see J. Cantineau, *Consonantisme*, in *Semitica*, iv, 84-5). According to the Arab grammatical tradition: *riḵhwa madjhūra muṭbaḳa*. For the *makhradj*, the *shadjiriyya* of al-Khalīl (al-Zamakhsharī, *Mufaṣṣal*, 2nd ed. J. P. Broch, 190, line 20) is difficult to define exactly (see De Sacy, *Gr. Ar.*[2], i, 26, n. 1; M. Bravmann, *Materialien*, 48 and 51). The most plausible meaning for *shadjr* is 'commissure of the lips' according to al-Khalīl's own explanation (*Le Monde Oriental*, 1920, 45, line 8): *mafradj al-fam* (repeated in *Mufaṣṣal*, ibid.; Raḍī al-Dīn al-Astarābādhī, *Sharḥ al-Shāfiya*, iii, 254, line 6); *ḍ* is thus in the lateral position.

Sībawayh represents *ḍ* as a lateral simply, and thus describes the *makhradj*: 'between the beginning of the edge of the tongue and the neighbouring molars' (Sībawayh, Paris edition, ii, 453, lines 8-9): a retracted lateral, for this beginning is to be taken as starting from the root of the tongue, and *lām* follows *ḍ* (ibid., lines 9-11; *Mufaṣṣal*, 188, line 19). This does not indicate, for the peculiarity of *istiṭāla* of *ḍ*, a great extent for the place of articulation but rather a dwelling on it, a special prolongation of it. In modern Arabic dialects the passage from *ḍ* to *ḷ* is known (Landberg, *Ḥaḍramoût*, 637), but the almost universal treatment of *ḍ* is its confusion with *ẓ* (voiced emphatic interdental fricative), whose evolution it shares [see ẒĀ']. One is thus led to include in the articulation of *ḍ* an activity of the tip of the tongue in the region of the teeth similar to the corresponding lateralized articulation of modern South Arabian (Mehri, Shkhawri, but not the lateralized occlusive of Soḳoṭri), whence the definition proposed above.

A lateral character is to be claimed for *ḍ*, as N. Youshmanov, G. S. Colin, J. Cantineau, and others have done (J. Cantineau, *Consonantisme*, 84). The *ḍ* phoneme of Classical Arabic continues an autonomous phoneme of common Semitic which is even more difficult to define precisely. M. Cohen sees in it a consonant 'of the dental region of which the articulation was doubtless lateral: *ḍ* [conventional transcription]. As an emphatic, this consonant may anciently have formed one of a lateral series (triad?)' (*Essai comparatif*, 149). In Classical Arabic *ḍ* is isolated.

In ancient Semitic, the South Arabian inscriptions assign a special character (of unknown pronunciation) to the phoneme corresponding with the *ḍ* of Classical Arabic. Geez does the same, but in the traditional nunciation it is a *ṣ*; *ṭ* in South Ethiopic. It is represented in Akkadian, Hebrew, and Ugaritic, by *ṣ*, but in Aramaic by *ḳ* in the oldest texts (preserved in Mandean), then by *ʿ*, a special evolution which represents a thorny problem. See the Table of correspondences in W. Leslau, *Manual of Phonetics*, 328.

For the phonological oppositions of the *ḍ* phoneme

in Classical Arabic see J. Cantineau, *Esquisse*, in *BSL* (No. 126), 96, 7th; for the incompatibles, *ibid.*, 134. In view of the latter, J. Cantineau would see in *ḍ* a *lateralized* rather than a *lateral* consonant (*ibid.*, no. 1).

Ḍ undergoes few assimilations in Classical Arabic (see J. Cantineau, *Cours*, 69).

The Arabs saw in *ḍ* one of the *khaṣā'iṣ* 'special features' of their language (Ibn Djinnī, *Sirr ṣināʿa*, i, 222; al-Suyūṭī, *Muzhir*[3], i, 329) and boasted of it (see the line of al-Mutanabbī quoted by Ibn Djinnī, *ibid.*). But Sībawayh (ii, 452, lines 14-5, 17 f.) already registers a corrupt pronunciation: *al-ḍād al-ḍaʿīfa* (M. Bravmann, *Materialien*, 53). In fact the articulation of *ḍād* has disappeared in the modern dialects and Ḳur'ānic recitation and either *ẓ* (voiced velarized interdental fricative) or *ḍ* (voiced velarized dental plosive) is used, according to the treatment of the phoneme in dialect.

In Persian and in Urdū, *ḍād* is a voiced alveolar fricative, and no differentiation is made in pronuncation between *dh*, *z*, *ḍ* and *ẓ*.

Bibliography: in the text and s.v. ḤURŪF AL-HIDJĀ'. (H. FLEISCH)

DADALOGHLU, ĀSHIḲ MŪSĀ-OGHLU WELI, 19th century Turkish folk poet (1790?-1870?), was a member of the Afshār tribe which lived in the Taurus Mountains in S. Anatolia. His father was also a poet and took his *makhlaṣ* from the same family name. It is said that for a time Dadaloghlu acted as imām in the villages and as secretary to the tribal chiefs. As a result of government action against his tribe, which rebelled because it was unwilling to undergo conscription or taxation, he was transported with the rest of the Afshārs to the village of Sindel near ʿAzīziyye in the province of Sīwās (1866-8). It is difficult to establish how well founded are reports that at the end of his life he returned to the Čukurova region and recited his poems in the bazaars of Adana. His poems were not collected during his lifetime. Among them are to be found the chief forms of folk poetry such as *türkü*, *koshma*, *semaï*, *varsaghi*, and *destān*. He embellished and enriched the story of Genč ʿOthmān in a number of poems with a local setting. His poetry is harsh and emotional in manner and shows the pure and sincere feelings of a bold, daring, upright, and sensitive tribesman. From passages in his poems one can understand the warlike psychology and nomadism of the society in which he lived. He was one of the last powerful representatives of epic, lyric, and pastoral Turkish folk poetry and story-telling which had continued ever since the composition of *Dede Korkud* and of which *Köroghlu* and *Karadja oghlan* are the leading examples.

Bibliography: Djewdet Pasha, *Tedhākir*, (Tadhkira 26-30), Istanbul Inkılâp Kütüphanesi, autograph; idem, *Maʿrūḍāt*, in *TOEM*, 87-93, 1925; Ahmed Şükrü, *Dadaloğlu, Halk Bilgisi Mecmuası*, i, 1928; Köprülüzade Mehmet Fuat *XVIInci asır sazşairlerinden Kayıkcı Kul Mustafa ve Genç Osman hikâyesi*, Istanbul 1930; Halid Bayrı, *Halk Bilgisi Haberleri*, 1933; Ali Rıza, *Cenupta Türkmen Oymakları*, Ankara 1933; Sadettin Nüzhet Ergun, *Türk Halk Edebiyatı Antolojisi*; Taha Toros, *Dadaloğlu*, Adana 1940; Cahit Öztelli, *Köroğlu ve Dadaloğlu*, Varlık Yayınları, Istanbul 1953. Halide Hoşgör, *Halk edebiyatında Kahramanlık Türküleri*, Istanbul University Library, thesis 1128 (unpublished); Semiha Karacabey, *Dadaloğlu*, Istanbul University Library, thesis 1752 (unpublished). (A. KARAHAN)

DADJĀDJA, the domestic fowl. The word is a noun of unity which, according to Arab lexicographers, may be applied to both the male and the female. Alternative pronunciations are *didjādja* and *dudjādja*. In more recent local usage (cf. Jayakar, Malouf), *didjādjat al-baḥr* and *didjādjat al-ḳubba* denote certain kinds of fish, just as the corresponding Hebrew דָּג.

The animal, which is not mentioned in the Hebrew Bible, was known to the Arabs from pre-Islamic times. Djāḥiẓ reports (ii, 277 f.) that it was given to poets as a reward for their literary achievements. Although it eats dung, it is permitted as human food by Islamic law because the Prophet was seen partaking of it.

The ample information on the fowl and its eggs, which is given in Arabic zoological writings, can partly be traced back to Aristotle's *Historia Animalium*. The fowl has no fear of beasts of prey except the jackal, an inherent enmity existing between the two. It is fearful at night and therefore seeks an elevated sleeping place. It shares the characteristics of both birds of prey and seed-feeding birds, since it eats flesh as well as grains. The hen lays, mostly one egg a day, throughout the year, except in the two winter months (in Egypt, according to Nuwayrī, all the year round without interruption); if she lays twice a day it is a portent of her approaching death. The chicken is produced from the white of the egg, while the yolk provides the nourishment for the embryo. From elongated eggs female chickens are born and males from round ones. Two chickens are produced from double-yolked eggs. If the hen while sitting hears thunder, the eggs are spoiled; if she is old and weak, the eggs have no yolk and produce no chickens. She also lays eggs without being covered by the cock (wind-eggs), but such eggs produce no chickens. When hens become fat they no longer lay, just as fat women do not become pregnant.

The sources mention and describe several kinds of *dadjādj*, some of them reaching the size of a goose. Numerous medicinal uses of eggs, fat, bile, gizzard, dung, etc. are mentioned by Arab zoologists and pharmacologists, partly from classical sources. The meat was considered a wholesome food, although its continual eating was said to cause gout and piles. Half-cooked eggs were credited with special efficacy as an aphrodisiac. The significance of fowl when seen in dreams has been treated in pertinent works.

The Arab astronomers give the name *al-Dadjādja* to the constellation of the Swan, which is also called *al-Ṭā'ir*.

Bibliography: ʿAbd al-Ghanī al-Nābulusī, *Taʿṭīr al-Anām*, Cairo 1354, i, 220 f.; Damīrī, s.v. (transl. Jayakar, i, 766 ff.); Dāwūd al-Anṭākī, *Tadhkira*, Cairo 1324, i, 139; Djāḥiẓ, *Ḥayawān*², index; Ibn al-ʿAwwām, *Filāḥa* (transl. Clément-Mullet), ii/b, 242 ff.; Ibn Ḳutayba, *ʿUyūn al-Akhbār*, Cairo 1925-30, ii, 71, 92 (transl. Kopf, 44, 68); Ibshīhī, *Mustaṭraf*, bāb 62, s.v.; Ḳazwīnī (Wüstenfeld), i, 32, 413 f.; al-Mustawfī al-Ḳazwīnī (Stephenson), 70 f.; Nuwayrī, *Nihāyat al-Arab*, x, 217 ff.; A. Malouf, *Arabic Zool. Dict.*, Cairo 1932, index. (L. Kopf)

AL-**DADJDJĀL,** the "deceiver", adjective of Syriac origin, *daggālā*, joined to the word *mᵉshīḥā* or *nᵉbīyā* (Peshitto, Matth., xxiv, 24). In Arabic, used as a substantive to denote the personage endowed with miraculous powers who will arrive before the end of time and, for a limited period of either 40 days or 40 years, will let impurity and tyranny rule the world which, thereafter, is destined to witness universal conversion to Islam. His appearance is one of the proofs of the end of time. The characteristics attributed to him in Muslim eschatological legends combine features from Christ's sermon to his disciples (Matth. xxiv, Mark xiii) with some elements taken from the Apocalypse of St. John of Patmos (xi 7, xii, xiii, xx 5-18, 8-10).

These elements reappear in the pseudo-apocalyptic literature of later periods. After the invasions of the Huns, St. Ephraem makes him appear from Chorasé (Chorasène, Khurāsān), in his sermon on the end of time (Scti. Ephremi Syri, *Sermo II de fine extremo*, trans. T. J. Lamy, iii, 187-214, §§ 9-13). His essential activity is to lead the crowds astray, to accomplish miracles (short of restoring the dead to life), to kill Elias and Enoch, the two witnesses put forward by God against him—they will immediately come to life again—and finally to be conquered and dismembered at the coming of the Son. The Ps. Methodius (*Monumenta SS. Patr. Orthodoxographa graeca*, Bale 1569, 99) speaks of a "son of the destruction" coming from Chorasé, and finally perishing at the hands of the king of the Romans, before the Second Coming. In a similar passage, the relationship being unconcealed, the Apocalypse of Baḥīrā speaks in the same terms of one Ibn al-Halāk who will perish at the hands of the angel of Thunder (MS. Arab. Paris, 215, f° 171).

Unknown in the Ḳur'ān, the same figure appears in Muslim traditions. Ibn Ḥanbal repeats the legends about the ass on which he rides, the sinners and hypocrites who attend him, his end before Jesus (iii, 867, iii, 238, ii, 397-98, 407-408). Similarly, in the *Kitāb al-Fitan* of the two *Ṣaḥīḥ*s, there is a chapter *Bāb dhikr al-Dadjdjāl*, which describes him as a corpulent, red-faced man with one eye and frizzy hair, who brings with him fire and water, the water being of fire and the fire of cold water. The Prophet will have announced his coming and will have prayed to God for help against his *fitna*. Conquering the world, he will be unable, at Medina (and Mecca), to cross the barrier formed by angels standing at the gates of the town (al-Bukhārī, ed. Munīriyya, ix, 107-110). These traditions derive their details from St. Ephraem: he will bring with him a mountain of bread and a river of water, and also the episode, though condensed and distorted, of his meeting with Elias and Enoch (an upright man among upright men who will denounce him, and whom he will kill and bring to life again, but will be powerless to put to death once more). On his brow he will bear the mark *Kāfir* (for detailed references see art. by Wensinck in *Shorter Encyclopaedia of Islam*, 67, and s.v., *Handbook of Early Muhammadan Tradition*).

Later apocalyptic writings: the revelations of Kaʿb al-Aḥbār (Ms. Arab. Paris, 2602, f° 128 sqq., cf. f° 134 v°), *Ṣayḥat al-Būm fī ḥawādith al-Rūm* (ibid. f° 119, 120 v°), *Shams al-Ghuyūb fī ḥanādis al-Ḳulūb* (Ms. Arab. Paris, 2669, f° 55n-56 v°), and also the Christian pamphlet on the capture of Constantinople in 1204, repeating the old Revelations of Sibylla, daughter of Herael (Ms. Arab. Paris, 70, 74, f° 126 v° ff., 178, f° 175 ff.), reproduce the description of Dadjdjāl's coming, his false miracles, his conquests and his end. But clearly in the Muslim apocalypses it is at the hands of the Mahdī that the false claimant who had usurped his title is to perish, whilst the Revelation of Sibylla makes him die at the hands of Jesus, at the very moment of the end of time. These accounts insist upon Dadjdjāl's beauty and powers of seduction, and repeat the episode of the righteous men denouncing him. The apocalypse of Sibylla believes that the decisive proof of his imposture is his inability to raise up the dead.

In considering these eschatological documents it appears that, from the 11th century at least until the 16th century, Judeo-Christian traditions regarding Dadjdjāl remained alive and formed an indispensable element in descriptions of the period preceding the Judgment. Conflating two traditions, ʿAbd al-Ḳāhir al-Baghdādī, *K. al-Farḳ bayn al-Firaḳ* (Cairo 1910, 266 and 332-333) regards him as the ultimate term of comparison to describe false doctrine and going astray—though his sedition is only to last 40 days—and recalls that Christians believed that he would perish at the hands of Jesus who, in that way, would be converted to Islam after killing pigs, scattering wine and taking his place for prayer at the Kaʿba.

The body of legend about Dadjdjāl is completed by statements about his origin. Apocalyptic texts make him come from the most remote regions. In St. Ephraem and the apocalypse *Shams al-Ghuyūb* (Ms. Paris, 2559), he comes from Khurāsān (cf. Ibn al-Wardī, al-Bīrūni). According to Ps. Kaʿb al-Aḥbār and the *Ṣayḥat al-Būm* (Ms. ar. Paris, 2502), he must come from the West. Geographers and travellers of the classical period state that he dwelt in the countries which the *ʿAdjāʾib al-Hind* habitually peopled with extraordinary beings, following the traditions of the Alexander Romance. Generally it was the East Indies which were the chosen place, from the time of Ibn Khurradādhbih and al-Masʿūdī to Ibn Iyās. A giant, false prophet, king of the Jews, representations of him vary according to the degree of literary information available or the predominating prejudices. It is interesting to note the allusion to the legend of Prometheus which makes him live chained to a mountain on an island in the sea (*Mukhtaṣar al-ʿAdjāʾib*, 130; al-Masʿūdī, *Murūdj*, iv, 28) where demons bring him his food. (A. Abel)

ḌAFĪR, an important, purely nomadic camel-breeding Sunnī (Mālikī) tribe of south-western ʿIrāḳ, whose *dīra* has been for the last 150 years in the steppe south of the Euphrates and Shaṭṭ al-ʿArab from the neighbourhood of Zubayr to that of Samāwa. Their immigration into ʿIrāḳ, dating from about 1220/1805, was caused by bad relations with the then powerful and fanatical rule of Ibn Saʿūd, who forcibly demanded their obedience. Their earlier history traces legendary origins in Nadjd and even in the Ḥidjāz; but in fact the modern tribe represents evidently a conglomeration of various *badw* elements from many parts of Arabia, more or less unified by the ruling family of Ibn Suwayṭ. Tribal traditions record many wars and raids of the usual Arab type, with the Muṭayr, Banī Khālid, Shammar and others. They were, while still in Nadjd, occasionally tributary to the Shammar, the Shaykh of Kuwayt, and the family of Ibn Saʿūd.

Administratively, the Ḍafīr are now grouped under the *liwā* headquarters of Baṣra, but move seasonally into Kuwayt territory or that of Saʿūdī Arabia. Their relations with the Turkish and ʿIrāḳ Goverments since the early 13th/19th century have been fairly good, with lapses especially when they habitually looted caravans on the Nadjf—Ḥāʾil road; and they have now lost much of their wild and inaccessible, though not their nomadic, character. Varying, but on the whole amicable, relations have been maintained with the Muntafiḳ, their eastern and riverain neighbours; bad, with the Muṭayr and Shammar and ʿAniza. The tribe was heavily involved in the serious raiding into ʿIrāḳ by Saʿūdī (chiefly Muṭayr) forces in the period 1340/1344 (1921/25).

Bibliography: ʿAbbās al-ʿAzzāwī, *ʿAshāʾir al-ʿIrāḳ*, Baghdād 1365/1937, vol. i; S. H. Longrigg, *ʿIraq 1900 to 1950*, Oxford 1953.

(S. H. Longrigg)

DAFN AL-DHUNŪB [see Dhunūb, dafn al-].

DAFTAR, a stitched or bound booklet, or register, more especially an account or letter-book used in administrative offices. The word derives ultimately from the Greek διφθέρα "hide", and hence prepared hide for writing. It was already used in ancient Greek in the sense of parchment or, more generally, writing materials. In the 5th century B.C. Herodotus (v, 58) remarks that the Ionians, like certain Barbarians of his own day, had formerly written on skins, and still applied the term *diphthera* to papyrus rolls; in the 4th Ctesias (*in* Diodorus Siculus ii, 32; cf. A. Christensen, *Heltedigtning og Fortællingslitteratur hos Iranerne i Oldtiden*, Copenhagen 1935, 69 ff.) claimed, somewhat unconvincingly, to have based his stories on the βασιλικαὶ διφθέραι—presumably the royal archives—of Persia. The word also occurs in pre-Islamic and even pre-Christian Jewish Aramaic texts (V. Gardthausen, *Griechische Paläographie*[2], i, Leipzig 1911, 91 f.; M. Jastrow, *A Dictionary of the Targumim etc.*[2], New York 1926, 304. Attempts to derive it from an Iranian root meaning to write (also found in *dabīr*, *dīwān*) are unconvincing; on the other hand, in view of the testimony of the Arab authors, it is probable that the word reached Arabic via Persian.

I. The Classical Period

In early Islamic times *daftar* seems to have been used to denote the codex form of book or booklet, as opposed to rolls and loose sheets. It was at first applied to quires and notebooks, especially those said to have been kept by some collectors of traditions as an aid to their memories; later, when sizable manuscript books come into existence, it was applied to them also (N. Abbott, *Studies in Arabic Literary Papyri*, i, Chicago 1957, 21-24; cf. Goldziher, *Muh.St.*, ii, 50-52 and 180-1. Stories of personal libraries and record collections in the first century A.H. must be treated with caution, cf. the comments of J. Schacht on the spurious tradition of the archives of Kurayb, *On Mūsā b. ʿUqba's Kitāb al-Maghāzī*, *AO*, 1953, xxi, 296-7. On the earliest Arabic papyrus quires see A. Grohmann, *The Value of Arabic Papyri*, *Proc. of the Royal Soc. of Hist. Studies*, i, Cairo 1951, 43 ff.).

The creation of the first Islamic record office is usually ascribed to the Caliph ʿUmar, who instituted the muster-rolls and pay-rolls of the fighting-men (see dīwān). The initial form of these is not known, but before long they were probably kept on papyrus, which after the conquest of Egypt became the usual writing material in the administrative offices of the Caliphate. The papyri show that records of land, population, and taxes were kept in Egypt; surviving documents include quires as well as rolls and loose sheets, though the latter seem to have been the usual form, and no quire in Arabic appears until a comparatively late date (see A. Grohmann, *New Discoveries in Arabic Papyri. An Arabic Tax-Account Book*, *BIE*, xxxii, 1951, 159-170. In general, the Umayyad Caliphs seem to have followed Byzantine bureaucratic practices, and kept their records on papyrus. This did not lend itself to the codex form. There was, however, also another bureaucratic tradition. The Sāsānids clearly could not have relied on supplies of imported Egyptian papyrus for their administration, and made use of a variety of prepared skins as writing materials (cf. Ibn al-Nadīm, *Fihrist*, 21). According to Ḥasan al-Ḳummī, quoting Hamadānī on the authority of al-Madā'inī (*Ta'rīkh-i Ḳumm* 180), the Sāsānid Emperor Kobād kept a land-tax office at Ḥulwān; this is indirectly confirmed by Ya'ḳūbī's story (*Ta'rīkh*, ii, 258) of the procuring, in Mu'āwiya's time, of lists of Sāsānid domain lands from Ḥulwān (A. K. S. Lambton, *Landlord and Peasant in Persia*, London 1953, 15 n. 1). It is possible that some of the army lists of the earlier period, at least in the ex-Persian provinces, were already in codex form. Balādhurī (*Futūḥ* 450; ed. Cairo 1901, 455) has 'Umar say to the Banū 'Adī "if the *daftar* is closed (*yuṭbaḳ*) on you', and explains it as meaning "if you are registered last". Abū Muslim is said to have prepared a pay-roll called *daftar* instead of the usual *dīwān* of his followers in Khurāsān in 129/766-7 (Ṭabarī, ii, 1957, 1969; see further N. Fries, *Das Heerwesen der Araber zur Zeit der Omaijaden*, 1921, 9; W. Hoenerbach, *Zur Heeresverwaltung der Abbasiden*, *Isl.*, xxix, 1949-50, 263). These may, of course, be no more than a projection backwards, by later historians, of a term common in their own time, though it is significant that the first example comes from the East.

According to the bureaucratic tradition, it was Khālid b. Barmak who, during the reign of al-Ṣaffāḥ, introduced the codex or register into the central administration. Until that time, says Djahshiyārī (fol. 45 b; ed. Cairo 89) the records of the *dīwāns* were kept on *ṣuḥuf*; Khālid was the first to keep them in *daftars*. Maḳrīzī (*Khiṭaṭ*, i, 91) goes further and says that the *ṣuḥuf mudradja* (? papyrus rolls, cf. Ḳalḳashandī, *Ṣubḥ*, i, 423—*adrādj min kāghid waraḳ*) which had hitherto been used were replaced by *dafātir min al-djulūd*—parchment codices. In the time of Hārūn al-Rashīd, Khālid's grandson, Dja'far b. Yaḥyā al-Barmakī, was responsible, it is said, for the introduction of paper. In this story there is some element of exaggeration. An incident told by Djahshiyārī (fol. 79 b; ed. Cairo 138) shows that under Manṣūr papyrus was still much used in government offices, and the supply from Egypt a matter of concern; it was still used under Hārūn al-Rashīd, and even as late as the time of Mu'taṣim, an abortive attempt was made to set up a papyrus factory, with Egyptian workmen, in Sāmarrā (W. Björkman, *Beiträge zur Geschichte der Staatskanzlei im islamischen Ägypten*, Hamburg 1928, 7; A. Grohmann, *From the World of Arabic Papyri*, Cairo 1952, 23 ff., 45 ff., 52; *Corpus Papyrorum Raineri Archiducis Austriae*, iii, *Series Arabica*, ed. A. Grohmann, i/I, *Allgemeine Einführung in die arabischen Papyri*, Vienna 1924, 32 ff., 54 ff., etc.). It is, however, broadly true that from the accession of the 'Abbāsids the register in codex form came to be the normal method of keeping records and accounts in government offices. Its use was confirmed and extended with the general adoption of paper from the 9th century onwards, and from this time the term *daftar* is in the main confined to administrative registers and record-books. The system of *daftars* seems to have been first elaborated in Iran and 'Irāḳ. In Egypt papyrus remained in use until the 4th/10th century, but the eastern form of *daftar* seems to have been introduced even before the general adoption of paper. Surviving specimens of papyrus account-books in quire form (described by A. Grohmann, *New Discoveries* . . , and idem, *New Discoveries* . . II, *BIE*, xxxv, 1952-3, 159-169) tally fairly closely with literary descriptions of the *daftar* in eastern sources (see below). From Egypt the *daftar* spread to the western Islamic world. In 373/985, al-Muḳaddasī (239) found it worthy of note that the people of Andalusia had their account-books as well as their Ḳur'āns on parchment. (On writing materials see further DJILD, KĀGHID, ḲIRṬĀS, RIḲḲ, WARAḲ).

Types of Daftar.

With the development of elaborate bureaucratic organizations, the keeping of *daftars* became a task calling for special skills and knowledge, and *daftars* of many different types emerge. The first systematic account that we possess of the records and registers of a Muslim administrative office is that given by Muḥammad b. Aḥmad al-Khwārizmī in the late 4th/10th century. He enumerates the following:

(1) *Ḳānūn al-Kharādj*—the basic survey in accordance with which the *Kharādj* is collected.

(2) *Al-Awāradj*—Arabicized form of *Awāra*, transferred; shows the debts owed by individual persons, according to the *Ḳānūn*, and the instalments paid until they are settled. (On *Awāradj* see V. Minorsky in his edition of *Tadhkirat al-Muluk*, London 1943, 144; to be modified in the light of W. Hinz, *Rechnungswesen*, 120 ff.).

(3) *Al-Rūznāmadj*—day-book; the daily record of payments and receipts.

(4) *Al-Khatma*—the statement of income and expenditure presented monthly by the *Djahbadh*.

(5) *Al-Khatma al-Djāmi'a*—the annual statement.

(6) *Al-Ta'rīdj*—an addition register, showing those categories (*abwāb*) which need to be seen globally, arranged for easy addition, with totals. Receipts for payments made are also registered here.

(7) *Al-'Arīḍa*—a subtraction register, for those categories where the difference between two figures needs to be shown. It is arranged in three columns, with the result in the third. Such is the *'Arīḍa* showing the difference between the original and the revised figures, the latter being usually smaller, (that is, presumably, the estimates and the amounts actually received. This seems to be the meaning of *aṣl* and *istikhrādj*, rather than income and expenditure, as assumed by Cevdet and Uzunçarşılı. On *istikhrādj* in the sense of revision cf. Uzunçarşılı, *Medhal*, 278 and Hinz, *Rechnungswesen* 18, On *Aṣl* cf. Māwardī, *al-Aḥkām al-Sulṭāniyya*, ed. Enger 373, ed. Cairo 209. The expression *dafātir-i aṣl wa istikhrādj* occurs in a text from Saldjūḳ Anatolia—O. Turan, *Türkiye Selcukları hakkında Resmi Vesikalar*, Ankara 1958, text xxvi). These are itemized in the first and second columns, with the differences between them in the third column. Grand totals are shown at the foot of each of the three columns.

(8) *Al-Barā'a*—a receipt given by the *Djahbadh* or *Khāzin* [*qq.v.*] to taxpayers. (It is not clear whether Khwārizmī means a register of copies and receipts, or is merely naming the *barā'a* as a kind of document).

(9) *Al-Muwāfaḳa wa 'l-djamā'a*—a comprehensive accounting (*ḥisāb djāmi'*) presented by an *'āmil* on relinquishing his appointment. If it is approved by the authority to whom he presents it, it is called *muwāfaḳa*, if they differ, it is called *muḥāsaba*.

Passing to the registers of the army office (*dīwān al-djaysh*), Khwārizmī lists:

(10) *Al-Djarīda al-Sawdā'*—prepared annually for each command, showing the names of the soldiers, with their pedigree (*nasab*), ethnic origin (*djins*), physical descriptions (*ḥilya*), rations, pay etc. This is the basic central register of this *dīwān*.

(11) *Radjʿa*—a requisition (*ḥisāb*) issued by the paymaster (*muʿṭī*) for certain troops stationed in outlying areas, for one issue of pay (*ṭamaʿ*) on reference to the *dīwān*.

(12) *Al-Radjʿa al-Djāmiʿa*—a global requisition issued by the head of the army office for each general issue (*ṭamaʿ*) of army pay, rations, etc.

(13) *Al-Ṣakk*—an inventory (*ʿamal*—cf. Dozy, *Suppl.* ii, 175) required for every *ṭamaʿ* showing the names of the payees, with numbers and amounts, and bearing the signed authority to pay of the sultan. The *Ṣakk* is also required for the hire of muleteers and camel-drivers.

(14) *Al-Muʾāmara*—an inventory of orders issued during the period of the *ṭamaʿ*, bearing at its end a signed authorization (*idjāza*) by the sultan. A similar *muʾāmara* is prepared by every *dīwān*.

(15) *Al-Istiḳrār*—an inventory of the supplies remaining in hand after issues and payments have been made.

(16) *Al-Muwāṣafa*—a list (*ʿamal*) showing the circumstances and causes of any changes occurring (*i.e.*. transfers, dismissals, deaths, promotions, etc.).

(17) *Al-Djarīda al-Musadjdjala*—the sealed register. The *Sidjill* (seal) is the letter given to an envoy or messenger, authorizing him, on arrival, to recover the expenses of his journey from any *ʿĀmil*. The *Sidjill* is also the judicial verdict (*maḥḍar*) prepared by a *ḳāḍī*.

(18) *Al-Fihrist*—a repertory of the inventories and registers in the *dīwān*.

(19) *Al-Dastūr*—a copy of the *djamāʿa* made from the draft.

Finally, Khwarizmī gives the names of three registers (*daftar*) used by the scribes of ʿIrāḳ. They are (as given in the edition) (1) الانجيذج

(2) الاوشنج

(3) الدروزن

The third is explained as a register of the land measurement survey (*misāḥa*). (Khwārizmī, *Mafātīḥ al-ʿUlūm*, ed. Van Vloten, 54-8, cf. Mez, *Renaissance*, 103, Eng. tr. 109, where however Mez's meaning is not very clearly rendered. An abridged Turkish paraphrase of Khwārizmī's text was made, in the light of Ottoman bureaucratic experience, by M. Cevdet, *Defter*, 88-91; there is also a rather more rapid Turkish summary by I. H. Uzunçarşılı, *Osmanlı Devleti Teşkilâtına Medhal*, Istanbul 1941, 479-480. This last has been translated into German by B. Spuler, *Iran in früh-islamischer Zeit*, Wiesbaden 1952, 338 n. 1).

It is probable that Khwārizmī's account refers to Samanid rather than ʿAbbāsid offices in this first instance. It is, however, almost certainly applicable in great part to ʿAbbāsid administration, and much of what he says is attested by passing references in the historians of ʿIrāḳ and Persia.

Khwārizmī's registers fall into two main groups, the fiscal and the military, which may now be considered separately.

Fiscal Registers.

The most important register of the tax-office is the *Ḳānūn*, the survey of land and taxable crops, (this would seem to be the meaning of the term *ḳānūn* in Māwardī, *Al-Aḥkām al-Sulṭāniyya*, ed. Enger 370, ed. Cairo 207).

This served as the basis for the assessment and collection of the land-tax and was thus the main instrument and authority for the department's activities. The term *Ḳānūn*, already recognized by Khwārizmī as arabicized Greek (*yūnāniyya muʿarraba*), was employed chiefly in ʿIrāḳ and the East, and was still in use in the 13th and 14th centuries, when it designated a kind of cadastral and fiscal survey (M. Minovi and V. Minorsky, *Nasīr al-Dīn Tūsī on Finance, BSOAS*, x, 1940, 761, 773, 781; Hinz, *Rechnungswesen*, 134 ff.). In later times the term *ḳānūn* in this sense seems to have fallen out of use, and was replaced by others. In Egypt the term *mukallafa* was used to designate the land survey registers, which were prepared by a *māsiḥ* and arranged by villages (Grohmann, *New Discoveries* . . , 163). According to Maḳrīzī, *Khiṭaṭ*, i, 82, a new survey was made in Egypt every thirty years. (For specimens of [land-tax registers from Egypt, on papyrus rolls, see A. Dietrich, *Arabische Papyri*, Leipzig 1937, 81 ff. (see further DAFTAR-I KHĀḲĀNĪ, MISĀḤA, RAWK, TAḤRĪR and TAPU).

The *Rūznāmadj* or *Rūznāmče* is mentioned in an anecdote attributed to the time of Yaḥyā b. Khālid al-Barmakī. A Persian taunts an Arab with the dependence of Arabic on Persian for terms and nomenclature, "even in your cookery, your drinks, and your *dīwāns*", and cites the word *Rūznāmadj*, as an example in the last-named group. (Muḥammad b. Yaḥyā al-Ṣūlī, *Adab al-Kātib*, Cairo 1341, 193). A passage in Miskawayh throws some light on how the *Rūznāmadj* was kept, in the treasury, in early 4th/10th century Baghdad. In 315/927, he tells us, the wazīr ʿAlī b. ʿĪsā 'relied on Ibrāhīm b. Ayyūb (a Christian treasury official, appointed head of the *Dīwān al-Djahbadha* in the following year—ʿArīb, *Tab. Cont.* 135; on him see also Ṣūlī, *Akhbār al-Rāḍī* 199; Hilāl al-Ṣābī, *Wuzarāʾ*, 136, 279, 296) to report to him on financial matters, to instruct the Treasurer (*Ṣāḥib bayt al-māl*) concerning his daily disbursements, and to require of him the weekly presentation of the *Rūznāmadjāt*, so that he might quickly know what had been paid out, what received, and what the deficit was (*mā ḥalla wa-mā ḳabaḍa wa-mā baḳiya*). The previous practice in making up the account (*khatma*) had been to present a monthly statement to the *dīwān* in the middle of the following month'. (*Tadjārib al-Umam*, ed. Amedroz, i, 151-2).

Two other passages in the same work indicate that the functionary in the treasury whose task it was to prepare the *khatma* was the *Djahbadh* [*q.v.*] (ibid., 155 and 164. The rendering of these passages in the English translation of Miskawayh by D. S. Margoliouth does not bring out their technical significance). Two documents of the time of al-Muḳtadir, quoted in the *Taʾrīkh-i Ḳumm*, shows how the *Rūznāmadj* functioned in Ḳumm and Fārs. Here the writer (*Kātib*) of the *Rūznamādj* is distinct from the *djahbadh*, and is a government official. His task is to register the sums received in taxes and issue receipts, called *Barāʾa* [*q.v.*], and to act as a kind of auditor on the operations of the *Djahbadh* (*Taʾrīkh-i Ḳumm*, 149 ff.; cf. Ann K. S. Lambton, *An Account of the Tarikhi Qumm, BSOAS*, xii, 1948, 595; C. Cahen, *Quelques problèmes économiques et fiscaux de l'Iraq Buyide* ... *AIEO*, x, 1952, 355. On the *Rūznāmadj* see further F. Løkkegaard, *Islamic Taxation in the Classic Period*, Copenhagen 1950, 149 and 159). In Ayyūbid Egypt Ibn Mammātī still includes the preparation of the *Rūznāmadj* and the *Khatma* among the duties of the *Djahbadh* (*Kitāb Ḳawānīn al-Dawāwīn*, ed. A. S. Atiya, Cairo 1943, 304), For examples of *Rūznāmadj* from Egypt see Grohmann, *New Discoveries* . .; for a discussion of the systems of accountancy they reveal, C. Leyerer,

Die Verrechnung und Verwaltung.. See further ḤISĀB and MUḤĀSABA.

Many scattered references to the *daftar*s kept in ʿAbbāsid offices will be found in the writings of Miskawayh, Hilāl, and others especially interested in administrative affairs. Some idea of the scale and presentation of the accounts of the state may be gathered from a few individual balance sheets of imperial revenue and expenditure that have been preserved by the historians. The earliest, dating from the time of Hārūn al-Rashīd, is preserved by Djahshiyārī (fol. 179a-182b; ed. 281-8) and, in a variant version, by Ibn Khaldūn (*Muḳ*. i, 321-4= Rosenthal, i, 361-5. See further R. Levy, *The Social Structure of Islam*, Cambridge 1957, 317-320. A budget for 306/908 is given by Hilāl, *Wuzarāʾ*, 11-22, and was analysed, together with other sources, by A. von Kremer, *Über das Einnahmebudget des Abbasiden-Reiches, Denkschrift d. Phil. hist. Kl. d. Wiener Ak.*, xxxvi, 1888, 283-362. A statement of the revenues of the privy purse (*Bayt māl al-Khāṣṣa*) in the 4th/10th century is given by Miskawayh (Mez 115-6. See further BAYT AL-MĀL).

Military Registers.

The muster-rolls of fighting-men date back to the beginnings of the Islamic state. These tribal rolls were, however, of quite a different character from the regular army lists described by Khʷārizmī. It may be that Abū Muslim was the first to introduce the *daftar* of soldiers; certainly the practice became general under the ʿAbbāsids. Besides Khʷārizmī's notes, we have a fuller description of the army lists kept in the *dīwān al-djaysh* in Ḳudāma's treatise on the land-tax, and in a late anonymous treatise on tactics (Tr. Wüstenfeld, in *Das Heerwesen der Muhammedaner*, Göttingen 1880, 1-7. Both are examined, with other evidence, by W. Hoenerbach, *Zur Heeresverwaltung* ... 269 ff. See further ʿATĀʾ). Similar lists were kept in the *dīwān al-djaysh* and *dīwān al-rawātib* (army office and pay office) of the Fāṭimids in Egypt (Ḳalḳashandī, *Ṣubḥ*, vi, 492-3 = Wüstenfeld, *Die Geographie und Verwaltung von Ägypten*, Göttingen 1879, 190-1). The common term for the army lists was *Djarīda*.

Diplomatic Registers.

Khʷārizmī's description is confined to financial and statistical registers—to accounts, inventories and the like in the tax and pay offices. Besides these there were also letter-books and other diplomatic registers, used in the chancery offices. A description of those kept in the Fāṭimid chancery (*dīwān al-rasāʾil*) is given by the Egyptian scribe Ibn al-Ṣayrafī (463-542/1070-1147). In the 12th chapter of his *Ḳānūn Dīwān al-Rasāʾil* (ed. ʿAlī Bahdjat, Cairo 1905, 137-141, Fr. trans. by H. Massé in *BIFAO*, xi, 1914, 104-8; cf. Ḳalḳashandī, *Ṣubḥ*., i, 133-5, where they are given in a slightly different order, and Björkman, *Beiträge*, 24-5), he considers the registers (*daftar*) and memoranda (*tadhkira*; Massé translates 'bulletin') which should be kept in this office, and the qualities of their keeper. This, he says is one of the most important tasks in the *dīwān*. The registrar must be reliable, long-suffering, painstaking, and work-loving, and should keep the following memoranda and registers.

(1) Memoranda (*tadhākīr*) of important matters (*muhimmāt al-umūr*) which have been dealt with in correspondence, and to which it may be necessary to refer. These memoranda ((*tadhākīr*) are much easier for reference than papers in bundles (*aḍābīr*; Massé translates 'dossier'). All letters received must therefore, after being answered, be passed to the registrar, who will consider them and record what is needed in his memoranda, together with any reply sent. He will assign a number of sheets (*awrāḳ*) in his memoranda to each transaction (*ṣafḳa*), with an appropriate heading. He will then register incoming letters, noting their provenance, date of arrival and contents, together with a note of the reply sent or, if such be the case, of the fact that no reply was sent. He will continue this to the end of the year, when he will start a new *tadhkira*.

(2) Memoranda of important orders (*awāmir*) in outgoing letters, in which are noted also the contents and dates of arrival of replies received to them. This is to ensure that orders are not disregarded and left unanswered.

(3) A register (*daftar*) showing the correct forms of *inscriptio* (*alḳāb*), *salutatio* (*duʿāʾ*), etc. to be used for various officials and dignitaries, as well as foreign rulers and other correspondents abroad, in different types of letters and diplomas. For each office or post (*khidma*) there should be a separate sheet (*waraḳa mufrada*) showing the name of its occupant, his *laḳab*, and his *duʿāʾ*. Changes and transfers must be carefully noted.

(4) A register of major events (*al-ḥawādith al-ʿaẓīma*).

(5) A specification (*tibyān*) of ceremonial (*tashrīfāt*) and robes of honour (*khilʿa*), to serve as a model when required. This should show grants made, with sartorial details, and prices.

(6) A repertory (*fihrist*), by year, month, and day, of incoming letters, showing provenance, date of arrival with a summary or, if needed, a transcript of the text.

(7) The same for outgoing letters.

(8) A repertory of diplomas, brevets, investitures, safe-conducts, etc. This is to be prepared monthly, accumulated yearly, and restarted each new year.

Finally, Ibn al-Ṣayrafī refers to the need to record Arabic translations of letters received in foreign scripts (*khaṭṭ*) such as Armenian, Greek or Frankish.

According to Ḳalḳashandī (*Ṣubḥ*, i, 139, cf. Björkman, *Beiträge*, 39), these Fāṭimid registers were in general maintained in the Cairo chancery until the end of the 8th/14th century. It is clear that this system of chancery registration and records originated in the eastern lands of the Caliphate, and continued there in one form or another, through the Middle Ages. Its later development can be seen in the Ottoman *Mühimme Defteri*, *Aḥkām Defteri*, *Tewdjīhāt Defteri*, *Teshrīfātdjī Ḳalemi Defteri*, etc.

II. The Turkish and Mongol Period.

In bureaucratic practice, as is in most other aspects of government and administration, the period of domination by the Steppe peoples, Turks and Mongols, brought noteworthy changes. Some of these may be due to Chinese influences, penetrating through the Uygurs, the Karakhitay, and above all through the Asian Empire of the Mongols. It seems likely that the system of registration owes something to East Asian examples (see for example Djuwaynī, i, 24-5 = Boyle, i, 33-4, and Rashīd al-Dīn, *Djāmiʿ al-Tawārīkh*, ed. Blochet, 39-40, 56-7; cf. ibid. 483 on the *daftar*s of Pekin), but this whole question is still in need of further investigation.

Despite some evidence of reorganization under the Great Saldjūḳs, the registrars and book-keepers of the Sultanate, as well as of Saldjūḳid Anatolia and Ayyūbid Egypt, seem to have continued many of the practices of the preceding period. What development there is seems to be in technical matters, especially in the collection and presentation of statistical data. Some idea of bureaucratic practice in the Sultanate of Rum can be obtained from Ibn Bībī, *Al-Awāmir al-ʿAlaʾiyya*, facsimile ed. Ankara 1956 (ed. N. Lugal and A. S. Erzi, part 1; Ankara 1937; abridgment, Houtsma, *Recueil*, ii; German trans. H. W. Duda, Copenhagen 1959; Turkish adaptation by Yazi̊dji̊oghlu ʿAlī, Houtsma, *Recueil*, iii). Registers were kept at the *Dīwān-i Aʿlā*, and dealt with land and tax matters. As new territories were acquired or recovered, new surveys were conducted (Ibn Bībī, 146, Antalya; 153-4, Sinop; 428, Akhlāṭ). An addition by Yazi̊dji̊oghlu (*Recueil*, iii 105—not in Ibn Bībī) tells that during the reign of ʿIzz al-Dīn Kaykāwūs the office of *Ṣāḥib-i Dīwān* and the care of the finance registers (*emwāl defātiri*) were entrusted to Khʷādja Badr al-Dīn Khurāsānī, 'who was unequalled in the lands of Rūm in his knowledge of *khaṭṭ, balāgha, inshāʾ, siyāḳat*, and *ḥisāb*' [*qq.v.*]. At the same time Khʷādja Fakhr al-Dīn ʿAlī Tabrīzī was put in charge of *inshāʾ* and *maktūbāt*, and each of the 12 *daftar*s in the *dīwān-i wizārat* entrusted to a competent master (*ustād*). On another occasion the office of *amīr-i ʿāriḍ* was entrusted to Shams al-Dīn, also a specialist in *inshāʾ* and *siyāḳat* (Ibn Bībī 127), Yazi̊dji̊oghlu adds the explanation that this office involved the control of the military registers (*čeri defteri*, *Recueil*, iii, 109. For similar appointments to the *dīwān al-ʿarḍ* by Sandjar see *K. ʿAtabat al-Kataba*, edd. Muḥ. Ḳazwīnī and ʿAbbās Iḳbāl, Tehran 1329, 39-40, 72-3). Another passage in the same work (*Recueil*, iii, 210) speaks of 24 registrars, 12 in the *dīwān-i wizārat* dealing with land and taxes, and 12 in the *dīwān-i ʿāriḍ* dealing with the lists of soldiers, pay and fiefs. A poem cited by Yazi̊dji̊oghlu (254-5), repeats these figures, but awakens doubt of their authenticity by linking them with the recurring figure 12 in the Oghuz legend. The same poem claims complete coverage in the registration of lands (Cevdet 91-3).

From the Il-Khānid period we have, for the first time, detailed treatises on public accounting. Two important works, the *Saʿādat-nāma* of Falak ʿAlā-i Tabrīzī (compiled 707/1307) and the *Risāla-i Falakiyya* of ʿAbd Allah b. Muḥammad b. Kiyā al-Māzandarānī (ca. 767/1363) were discovered and analysed by Zeki Velidi [Togan] (*Moğollar devrinde Anadolu'nun Iktisadî Vaziyeti, THITM*, i, 1931, 1-42). A Tīmūrid manual, written in Herāt ca. 845/1441, was discovered by Adnan Erzi (W. Hinz, *Ein orientalisches Handelsunternehmen im 15 Jahrhundert, Welt des Orients*, 1949, 313-40) and a complete budget (*Djāmiʿ al-Ḥisāb*) of 738/1337-8 found by Z. V. Togan. The first two were studied in great detail by W. Hinz (*Das Rechnungswesen*), to whom we also owe a critical edition of the second of them (*Die Resalä-ye Falakiyyä*, Wiesbaden 1952).

These works reveal a system of book-keeping based on seven main registers, as follows:

(1) *Rūznāma*—'Daybook', Arabicized form *Rūznāmadj*, also called *Daftar-i Taʿlīḳ*.

(2) *Daftar-i Awāradja*—cash-book, showing the balance of moneys in hand.

(3) *Daftar-i Tawdjīhāt*—register of disbursements.

(4) *Daftar-i Taḥwīlāt*—an off-shoot of the preceding, dealing with disbursements for stocks and running expenses in state establishments and enterprises.

(5) *Daftar-i Mufradāt*—budget register showing the income and expenditure by cities, districts, and provinces.

(6) *Djāmiʿ al-Ḥisāb*—the master-ledger, from which the annual financial reports were prepared.

(7) *Ḳānūn*—the survey and assessment book, or Domesday Book of the Empire.

(For a full discussion of these registers, and of the variations in usage and nomenclature, see Hinz, *Rechnungswesen*, 113-137).

III. The Post-Mongol States.

As in so many other respects, the Muslim states of the post-Mongol period seem to have followed, to a very large extent, the bureaucratic practices of the Il-Khāns, some of which can be recognized as far afield as Mamluk Cairo, Ottoman Istanbul and Mughal Delhi. Of these states only one, the Ottoman Empire, has left a collection of registers that has survived to the present day, though individual *daftar*s have come to light in other parts. The Ottoman *daftar*s have been discussed elsewhere (see BAŞVEKALET ARŞIVI, DAFTAR-I KHĀḲĀNĪ, DIPLOMATIC, MÜHIMME DEFTERI, SIDJILL, etc.), and need not, therefore, be described here. Numbers of Ottoman registers have also come to light in the ex-Ottoman territories in Europe, Asia and Africa. For a description of their material form see L. Fekete, *Die Siyaqat-Schrift*, i, 70 ff.

Bibliography: For a general discussion see the unfortunately incomplete article of M. Cevdet, published in Osman Ergin's *Muallim M. Cevdet'in Hayatı, Eserleri ve Kütüphanesi*, Istanbul 1937, appendix, 69-96; on finance registers C. Leyerer, *Studien zum Rechnungswesen der arabischen Steuerämter, ArO*, xii, 1941, 85-112; idem, *Die Verrechnung und Verwaltung von Steuern im islamischen Ägypten, ZDMG*, N.F. 28, 1953, 40-69; W. Hinz, *Das Rechnungwesen orientalischer Reichsfinanzämter im Mittelalter, Isl.*, xxix, 1950, 1-29, 113-141; on military registers W. Hoenerbach, *Zur Heeresverwaltung der Abbasiden, ibid.*, 257-290. On Ottoman finance registers, L. Fekete, *Die Siyaqat-Schrift in der türkischen Finanzverwaltung*, i, Budapest 1955, 67-110; on the *Ḳāḍī*'s registers Halit Ongan, *Ankara'nın I Numaralı Şer'iye Sicili*, Ankara 1958, and J. Kabrda, *Les anciens registres turcs des Cadis de Sofia et de Vidin, ArO*, xix, 1951, 329-392; on Safavid Persia V. Minorsky, *Tadhkirat al-Mulūk*, London, 1943; on Central Asia, M. Yuldashev, *The State Archives of XIX century feudal Khiva*, in *Papers by the Soviet Delegation at the xxiii. International Congress of Orientalists, Iranian, Armenian and Central Asian Studies*, Moscow 1954, 221-30. Some *daftars* have been published in full. The earliest Ottoman survey register was edited by H. Inalcık, *Hicri 835 Tarihli Sûret-i Defter-i Sancak-i Arvanid*, Ankara 1954; an Ottoman survey register of Georgia was edited by S. Jikia, *Gurjistanis vilaiethis didi davthari. Defteri mufassali vilâyeti Gürcüstan.* Great register of the vilayet of Gurdjistan. Vol. 1, Turkish text. Vol. 2, Georgian translation. Izdatel'stvo Akademii Nauk Gruzinskoy SSR: Tiflis, 1941-1947. (B. LEWIS)

DAFTAR-I KHĀḲĀNĪ, the collection of registers in which were entered, during the Ottoman period, the results of the surveys made every 30 or 40 years until the beginning of the 11th/17th century, in accordance with an old administrative and fiscal practice.

The imperial registers or *Daftar-i Khāḳānī* consisted primarily of a list of the adult males in the villages and towns of the Empire, giving, by the side of their names and the names of their fathers, their legal status, their obligations and privileges according to the economic and social class to which they belonged, and the extent of the lands which they possessed.

These registers also contain a great deal of information on the way in which the land was used (fields, orchards, vineyards, rice-fields, etc.), on the number of mills, on sheep and bee-hives, with an indication of their approximate fiscal value in aspers.

Nevertheless the fiscal information contained in the registers is not confined to this agricultural inventory. They also refer to fisheries and mines as well as to the proceeds from customs, fairs, markets and weighhouses, with their locations, their regulations and the volume of the transactions carried out.

We can also, by referring to the *daftar-i khāḳānī*, obtain an exact idea of the distribution of the revenues of the country as between the imperial domain, the military fiefs, *waḳf*s and private properties (*mulk*). These registers in fact constitute a survey showing the form of ownership of each estate with a summary of the successive changes which it underwent.

The compilation of the registers arose from the administrative organization of the Empire. The great majority of Ottoman officials, both civil and military, did not draw salaries from the budget of the central government but were allowed, in return for their services, to levy taxes on a given region on their own account. Thus at the beginning of the 10th/16th century the possessors of *timar*s alone, whose numbers had risen to about 35,000, appropriated more than half of the taxes levied on the territory of the Empire. This proportion moreover was to rise throughout the 17th century together with the number of timariots.

In order for this system to operate successfully it was essential to know every detail of the different sources of the Empire's revenues, and to follow their modifications step by step through a given period. In this way it was possible to examine whether the emoluments, whose amounts were entered in the registers, and the deeds of grant (*berāt* [*q.v.*]) issued to the beneficiaries, tallied with the taxes they actually levied. During the period of expansion, when the population and the resources of the Empire were constantly increasing, the frequent surveys always disclosed new surpluses in the State revenues.

But from the 11th/17th century onwards the central power, as a result of the anarchic mismanagement of State affairs, did not possess the authority necessary to carry out these surveys. The disorganization of the institution of *timar*s moreover rendered the value of these measures illusory.

In addition to these "detailed registers" (*daftar-i mufaṣṣal*) in which were listed the results of the surveys, auxiliary registers were also required, in which were noted, as they occurred, changes in the distribution of the *timar*s, thus avoiding the additions and corrections which would otherwise have had to be made in the "detailed registers". For the system in force at the beginning of the 10th/16th century two or even three kinds of auxiliary books were used:

1. *Daftar-i idjmāl* or "synoptic inventory". This register was a summary based on the detailed register, omitting the names of the inhabitants and giving the revenues only as lump sums for each unit. The *idjmāl* can cover all classes of ownership in a *sandjaḳ*, but is normally limited to one or two; there are thus *idjmāl*s of *timars*—*i.e.*, nominal rolls of timariots, with brief statements of their holdings and revenues; *idjmāl*s of domain, *waḳf*, and *mulk*.

2. *Daftar-i derdest* or "book of changes". This register was a list of the villages or towns constituting the nucleus of the military fiefs. It showed the successive changes which each fief had undergone and the authorities could, on consulting it, easily determine the fiefs escheated or without possessors.

3. *Daftar-i rūznāmče* or "daybook", into which were copied as they occurred the deeds of grant (*berāt*) issued to new fief-holders.

Each time a new survey was made, the old registers were replaced by new and consigned to the archives of the register-office (*daftarkhāne*). The greater part of the old registers were lost or destroyed during their removal from one repository to another. There remain nevertheless over a thousand in the Başvekalet Arşivi [*q.v.*] at Istanbul as well as a few in certain Turkish and foreign archives and libraries. Among these registers are some which date from the time of Murād II (824-55/1421-51) and of Meḥemmed II the Conqueror (855-86/1451-81), and which allude to still earlier surveys.

The archives section of the survey and land register office, at Ankara, includes a complete collection of the registers relating to the last surveys made during the reigns of the sultans Selīm II (974-82/1566-74) and Murād III (982-1003/1574-95). To these registers have been added the results of the surveys made in such provinces as Crete, conquered after this date, or the Morea, recaptured from the Venetians. Even today this collection is, on rare occasions, consulted in lawsuits.

In this collection the "detailed registers" number 254, the "synoptic inventories" (*idjmāl*) 116, the "books of changes" (*derdest*) 169, and the "daybooks" (*rūznāmče*) 1363 volumes. The "detailed registers" contain about 300 pages, 15 cms. across and 42 cms. down.

During the period of more than three centuries which has elapsed since the last survey, these records have been brought up to date each time it has been necessary to register the modifications which have occurred in the legal status of certain lands upon the creation of new *waḳf*s. The fact that certain judgments made in favour of privileged individuals and relating to law-suits concerning the boundaries of villages and pastures have been entered in these registers only increases their value. Nevertheless it would be wrong to believe that all the transactions carried out by the registry office have found a place in these documents.

Certain writers have suggested that the *daftar-i khāḳānī* constitute a land-register. But in the system of domain-lands (*arāḍī-i mīriyye*), the peasant has never been the owner of the land which happens to be in his possession, and he could not therefore dispose of the title-deed. He could indeed transfer the possession of the land which he occupied, but this act, which took place under the control and with the approval of the local lord (*sipāhī*), was not made the subject of an entry in the imperial registers. Only from the second half of the 19th century onwards was a land register, in the modern sense of the word, established in Turkey.

Bibliography: Ö. L. Barkan, *Les grands recensements de la population et du territoire de l'Empire Ottoman*, in *Revue de la Faculté des*

Sciences Economiques de l'Université d'Istanbul, ii, 1940, 21-34, 168-79; idem, *Essai sur les données statistiques des registres de recensements dans l'Empire Ottoman aux XVème et XVIème siècles*, *JESHO*, i, 1, 1957; B. Lewis, *The Ottoman Archives as a Source for the History of the Arab lands*, *JRAS*, 1951, 139-155; idem, *Studies in the Ottoman Archives* I, *BSOAS*, xvi, 3, 1954, 469-501; H. Inalcık, *Hicri 835 tarihli Suret-i defter-i Sancak-i Arvanid*, Ankara 1954; I. H. Uzunçarsılı, *Osmanlı devletinin merkez ve bahriye teşkilatı*, Ankara 1948, 95-110; L. Fekete, *Die Siyāqat-Schrift in der türkischen Finanzverwaltung*, Budapest 1955. See further BAŞVEKALET ARŞIVI, DAFTAR, TAḤRĪR, TAPU. (Ö. L. BARKAN)

DAFTARDĀR, in Turkish *defterdār*, keeper of the *daftar* [*q.v.*], an Ottoman term for the chief finance officer, corresponding to the *Mustawfī* [*q.v.*] in the eastern Islamic world. According to Ḳalḳa-shandī (*Ṣubḥ*, iii, 485, 494, 525, 526), the title *Ṣāḥib al-Daftar* already existed in the Fāṭimid administration, for the official in charge of the *Daftar al-Madjlis*, that is, of accounts and audits. The title *Daftarkhʷān—Daftar*-reader—appears in the time of Saladin (B. Lewis, *Three Biographies from Kamāl ad-Dīn*, in *Fuad Köprülü Armağanı*, Istanbul 1953, 343), and reappears in the Muslim West (Maḳḳarī, *Analectes*, i, 660). The title *Daftardār* seems to originate with the Il-khāns, who appointed a *daftardār-i dīwān-i mămalik* or *daftardār-i mamālik* to make and keep the registers (Uzunçarşılı, *Medhal*, 229-30; Köprülü, *Bizans* 204-5; Hammer, *Geschichte der Goldenen Horde*, Pest 1840, 497-501).

The Ottoman *ḳānūnnāmes*, from the 9th/15th century onwards, show the development of the office of *defterdār* in the Ottoman Empire. In the *Ḳānūnnāme* of Meḥemmed II, the chief *Defterdār* is already a high ranking official who, under the general supervision of the Grand Vezir, is the officer responsible (*wekīl*) for the Sultan's finances (*Ḳānūnnāme-i Āl-i ʿOthmān*, *TOEM suppl.* Istanbul 1330, 10). He is named immediately after the Grand Vezir, and is comparable with him in status. At the *Dīwān* he sits immediately after the Grand Vezir and the two *Ḳāḍīʿaskers*, and shares with them the right to issue fermans on matters within his jurisdiction. He has the right of personal access to the Sultan, who rises to greet him (*ibid.*, 10-11, 16-17, 23-5). His duties include the presentation of an annual report or balance sheet of income and expenditure, for which he is rewarded with a robe of honour. His emoluments may be an appanage (*Khāṣṣ* [*q.v.*]) worth 600,000 aspers, or a Treasury stipend (*sālyāne*) of from 150,000 to 240,000 aspers a year. In addition, the *Defterdars* are entitled to a registration fee (*ḥaḳḳ-i imḍā*) of 1,000 aspers per load (*yük* = 100,000 aspers) on all grants of *Khāṣṣ*, whether by farm or by commission (*iltizām* or *emānet* [*qq.v.*]; to a collection fee (*Kesr-i mīzān*) of 22 aspers per thousand on moneys paid into the Treasury, and to an issue in kind from the produce collected in tithes from the Imperial domains. On retirement they received a pension of 80,000 aspers. (*ibid.* 28-9). The chief *defterdār* (*bashdefterdār*) presided over a hierarchy of lesser finance officers; first the ordinary finance officers (*Māl defterdārī*), then, under them, their adjutants (*Defterdār ketkhudāsī*), and under them the registrars of *tīmārs* (*Tīmār Defterdārī*), all with a recognized and established ladder of promotion. From the time of Bāyazīd II the *Bashdefterdār* was concerned chiefly with Rumelia, and was also known as *Rumeli Defterdārī*. A second *Defterdār*, the *Anadolu Defterdārī*, was appointed to deal with the revenues of Anatolia. In the early 10th/16th century a further *defterdār*'s office was set up in Aleppo, to look after the remoter Asian provinces. Its head was called *Defterdār-i ʿArab wa ʿAdjam*. This office was later subdivided, with separate offices in Diyārbakr, Damascus, Erzurum, Aleppo, Tripoli, and elsewhere. In the mid-16th century a separate office for Istanbul was established, and at the end of the century yet another for the Danubian provinces. This last was of short duration. The three main offices came to be known as the first, second, and third divisions (*shiḳḳ-i ewwel, thānī, thālith*) corresponding to Rumelia, Anatolia, and the remoter provinces. A fourth division was set up by Selim III to deal with the budget of the new style army (see NIẒĀM-I DJEDĪD); it was abolished with the latter. In 1253/1838 the office of the *Defterdār* was renamed Ministry of Finance (*Māliyye* [*q.v.*]), but the term *Defterdār* remained in use for provincial directors of finances.

Bibliography: Meḥmed Zeki, *Teshkilāt-i ʿAtīḳada Defterdar*, *TTEM*, 15th year, 1926, 96-102, 234-244; Köprülüzade M. Fuat, *Bizans Muesseselerin Osmanlı Muesseselerine tesiri hakkında bâzı Mülâhazalar*, *THITM*, i, 1931, 201-5 (= M. Fuad Köprülü, *Alcune Osservazioni intorno all' influenza delle Istituzioni bizantine sulle Istituzioni ottomane*, Rome 1953, 44-8); Pakalın, s.v.; Gibb-Bowen, index; Hammer- Purgstall, index; *IA* s.v. (by İ. H. Uzunçarşılı). (B. LEWIS)

DĀGH, the *takhalluṣ* of Nawwāb Mīrzā Khān (originally called Ibrāhīm, *Āʾīna-i Dāgh*), one of the most distinguished Urdū poets of modern times. He was a son of Nawwāb Shams al-Dīn Khān, ruler of Fīrūzpur Djhirkā, and Wazīr Begam (usually called Čhoṭī Begam). Nawwāb Mīrzā was born in Čāndnī Čawk, Dihlī on 12 Dhu 'l-Ḥidjdja 1246/25 May 1831 (cf. his horoscope in *Djalwa-i Dāgh*, 9). When Shams al-Dīn Khān was hanged (Oct. 1835) for his part in the murder of Mr. W. Fraser, Resident of Dihlī, Nawwāb Mirzā Khān's mother remarried, and he went and lived in Rāmpūr in 1844, because of the influence of his aunt, ʿUmda Khānam, a member of the *harīm* of Nawwāb Yūsuf ʿAlī Khān. There he studied Persian with Mawlawī Ghiyāth al-Dīn. His mother, in the meanwhile (1844), entered the *harīm* of Mīrzā Muḥammad Sulṭān Fatḥ al-Mulk (= Mīrzā Fakhrū). a son and the heir-apparent of Abū Ẓafar Bahādur Shāh. Nawwāb Mirzā (then 13 or 14 years old) also came to the Dihlī Fort and received his regular education there. He studied the usual Persian texts, learned calligraphy from Sayyid Muḥammad Amīr Pandja Kash (d. 1857, Ghulām Muḥammad, *Tadhkira-i Khwushnawīsān*, Calcutta 1910, 71 f.) and Mīrzā ʿIbād Allāh Beg (*ibid.*, p. 73); he also learned horsemanship and the use of various arms. But above all his sojourn in the Fort brought him into contact with the famous poets of the day, who assembled in the Fort for the *mushāʿaras* (poetical contests). This environment developed his latent aptitude for writing poetry. He began to write *ghazals* in Urdū at an early age and when Shaykh Muḥammad Ibrāhīm Dhawḳ adopted him as his pupil, his genius blossomed fully. The tutorship of Dhawḳ lasted from 1844 to 1854 and in this period Dāgh took part in the *mushāʿaras* both of the Fort and the City. But Fatḥ al-Mulk's death (10 July 1856) forced him to leave the Fort. About ten months later followed the upheaval of 1857, after which Dāgh once again went to his aunt in Rāmpūr but occasionally visited Dihlī and sometimes stayed there. When Kalb ʿAlī Khān succeeded Nawwāb Yūsuf ʿAlī Khān (d. 21 April 1865) as Nawwāb of Rāmpūr, Dāgh had the honour of becoming his companion (14 April 1866). He was also appointed Superintendent (*dārūgha*) of the stables and carpet stores (*farrāsh-khāna*) at Rs. 70 p.m. Towards the end of the same year he had the privilege of accompanying the Nawwāb to Calcutta and a few years later (1289/1872-3) of performing the *ḥadjdj* in the retinue of the Nawwāb. Rāmpūr in this period was a rendezvous of distinguished poets, such as Amīr, Djalāl, etc. (see *Nigār*, 46) and Dāgh had ample opportunities of shining in their company. From here he visited Calcutta (and several other cities) in connexion with his love-affair described by him in the *Faryād-i Dāgh* (a *mathnawī*). The death of the Nawwāb (23 March 1887) scattered many of the poets; Dāgh resigned his post (July 1887), and a few months later left Rāmpūr (Dec. 1887), after serving the State for about 22 years. He visited Ḥaydarābād-Deccan, and after some years, was appointed (26 Djumāda II 1308/6 Feb. 1891) the *Ustād* or instructor (in poetry) of the Niẓām (Maḥbūb ʿAlī Khān), and in 1309/1891 was paid Rs. 450/- p.m. (local currency) retrospectively from the date of his arrival in Ḥaydarābād; this sum was raised to Rs. 1000 in 1312/1894 and he received many other favours.

In 1312/1894 he received from the Niẓām the titles of "Bulbul-i Hindūstān, Djahān Ustād, Nāẓim Yār Djang, Dabīr al-Dawla, Faṣīḥ al-Mulk, Nawwāb Mīrzā Khān Bahādur". He appears to have been signing his name only as Faṣīḥ al-Mulk Dāgh Dihlawī (see Nūrī opp. 12). His only son died at Rāmpūr; he adopted a daughter. He had an attack of paralysis and died on 9 Dhu 'l-Ḥidjdja 1322/14 Feb. 1905, and was buried on the ʿĪd day, in Ḥaydarābād. "Nawāb Mīrzā Dāgh" is the chronogram of his death. Dāgh was a tall person, with a somewhat pock-marked face and dark complexion, and he wore a beard. He had a pleasant personality, with a fine sense of humour, courtly manners, and an intense love of music.

His works: Dāgh composed four or five *dīwāns*. The earliest, comprising his poems of the Dihlī period up to 1857, is said to have been lost in that year, but was, later, partly rewritten by him from memory (Nūrī, 89); others say that he had it in Ms. form with marginal amendments by Dhawḳ. The other *dīwāns* were: *Gulzār-i Dāgh*, Rāmpūr 1296/1878-9; *Āftāb-i Dāgh*, Lucknow 1302/1884; *Mahtāb-i Dāgh*, Ḥaydarābād-Deccan 1310/1893; *Yādgār-i Dāgh* comprising his poems from 1310 till his death in 1322. The last one is said to have been lost, and was not published (*Wāḳiʿāt-i Dihlī*, ii, 451 f.). Dāgh's pupil Aḥsan Mārahrawī published in 1323/1905 what he could collect of the *Yādgār-i Dāgh* (Kāẓimī, 208) to which an appendix was published at Dihlī by Lāla Srī Rām. The above five *dīwāns* contain about 14,800 verses mainly in *ghazal* form, but there are also *ḳaṣīdas*, *rubāʿīs* etc. (Kāẓimī, 210). Dāgh also published in 1300/1882 the *mathnawī* called *Faryād-i Dāgh*. He composed a *dīwān-i muḥāwarāt* also (more than a thousand verses) which was surrendered by his relatives to Āṣaf Djāh VI.

Dāgh's prose: (i) *Inshā-i Dāgh*, his letters, collected and published by Aḥsan Mārahrawī, Dihlī 1941; (ii) *Zabān-i Dāgh*, his private letters collected and published by Rafīḳ b. Aḥsan Mārahrawī, Lucknow 1956. We may also mention *Bazm-i Dāgh*, (a diary compiled by Aḥsan & Iftikhār-i ʿĀlam, both of Mārahra, who had stayed with Dāgh for nearly 4 years from 15 August 1898 onwards) Lucknow 1956. The authenticity of these documents has been challenged (see Tamkīn Kāẓimī, *Dāgh*, 163 ff.).

Several selections from Dāgh have also appeared, viz. *Muntakhab-i Dāgh* (Allāhābād 1939), *Bahār-i Dāgh*, Lāhore 1940, *Kamal-i Dāgh* (Āgrā), and *Dīwān-i Dāgh* or *Intikhāb-i Dāgh* (Lucknow).

The art of Dāgh: Dāgh is famous for the purity and the charm of his diction, the easy and unaffected flow of his verse, and the simplicity and elegance of his style, all of which are especially suited to the *ghazal*. The artistic and realistic expression he gave to his amatory and other experiences made his appeal direct and vehement. His command of language is remarkable. He uses idiomatic phrases frequently and with masterly aptness (cf. Walī Aḥmad Khān, *Muḥāwarāt-i Dāgh*, Dihlī 1944; the author collects 4464 such phrases, arranges them alphabetically with brief explanations and citations from Dāgh; an earlier attempt by Aḥsan in his *Faṣīḥ al-Lughāt*, on similar lines, remained incomplete and only a few were published in some issues of the *Faṣīḥ al-Mulk* magazine). Dāgh made a powerful impression on Urdū poetry, especially on the *ghazal*, which he made once again primarily a vehicle of emotional expression couched in easy and simple language, free from unfamiliar, harsh-sounding Arabic and Persian words, as used, *e.g.*, by the school of Nāsikh and Ātish (cf. *Nigār*, 19). In fact, he defined Urdū as the language which is free from Persianisms (Nūrī, 65, 170; cf. *Djalwa-i Dāgh*, 142, for Dāgh's conception of what good Urdū poetry should be in form). Out of the three periods of his literary work, the earliest ends with his stay in Rāmpūr. In this he had already acquired the main characteristics of his poetry, *viz.*, a graceful and clear expression,—simple, fresh and forceful, and the boldness of his ideas. These were developed still further in the second or the Rāmpūr period, which is his best. His expressions become extremely sweet and elegant, almost unparalleled in Urdū literature, and the novel, dramatic and bold ways in which he clothes his ideas with words is to be rarely met with in other poets (*Kamāl-i Dāgh*, 50 f.). These outstanding features are embodied in the *Gulzār-i Dāgh* and the *Āftāb-i Dāgh*. The last of the three periods, that of Ḥaydarābād-Deccan, is the period of decay. The language is as correct, as perspicuous and smooth as ever, the composition is ingenious but there is nothing more. Towards the end, he became too fond of introducing in his verses idiomatic expressions. The characteristics of the period are to be seen in *Yādgār-i Dāgh*. Dāgh has been severely criticized for the low and degrading ideals which he consistently kept before himself when writing love poetry (cf. Čakbast, *Maḍāmīn-i Čakbast*, Allāhābād, 1936, 69 f.), but his poetry to a considerable extent reflected the general trends of the effete society of his time (see *Nigār*, 18, 49).

He had numerous pupils in all parts of India (*Djalwa-i Dāgh*, 125; *Nigār*, 28, 131), a fact which shows the great popularity which his style had gained in the country (but see *Mirʾāt al-Shuʿarāʾ*, ii, 36).

Bibliography: Mīrzā Ḳādir Bakhsh, Ṣābir, of Dihlī (wrote in 1270-71 A.H.), *Gulistān-i Sukhun*, Dihlī 1271, 220; ʿAbd al-Ghafūr Khān, Nassākh, of Calcutta, *Sukhun-i Shuʿarāʾ* (compiled 1269-81/1852-64, Nawalkishor Press 1291/1874, 157; Amīr Aḥmad Mīnāʾī, *Intikhāb-i Yādgār* (comp. 1289-90/1872-3), lithogr. 1297/1880, Part ii, 128; Nawwāb S. Nūr al-Ḥasan Khān Bahādur, *Ṭūr-i Kalīm* (comp. 1297/1880) Āgra 1298/1881, Part i, 31; Nawwāb S. ʿAlī Ḥasan Khān Bahādur, *Bazm-i Sukhun* (comp. 1297 A.H.), Āgra 1298 A.H., 46; ʿAlī Nadjaf of Rāmpūr, *Ghunča-i Iram* (comp. 1299/1881-2), Calcutta 1301/1883-4), 88; Ṣafīr Bilgrāmī, *Tadhkira Djalwa-i Khiḍr*, Āra 1302/1884, i, 266; ʿAlī Aḥsan Mārahrawī, *Djalwa-i Dāgh* (comp. 1319/1901), Ḥaydarābād 1320/1902; Nithār ʿAlī, Shuhrat, of Dihlī, *Āʾīna-i Dāgh*, Lahore 1905; ʿAbd al-Djabbār Khān Ṣūfī Malkāpūr, *Maḥbūb al-Zaman* (a *tadhkira* of the Deccan poets) comp. 1326/1908, Ḥaydarābād-Deccan 1329/1911, Vol. i, 417; Srī Rām of Dihlī, *Khumkhāna-i Djāwīd* (comp. 1915-6), Dihlī 1917, ii, 104-136; Ross Masʿūd, *Intikhāb-i Zarrīn* (comp. 1912, Badaʾūn 1922, 175; Ṭālib of Allāhābād, in *Urdū* (Quarterly), Awrangābād, April and July, 1931; Djamīl Aḥmad, *Urdū Shāʿirī*, Nawalkishor Press, 1931, 161-65; Ḥakīm ʿAbd al-Ḥayy, *Gul-i Raʿnā*[4] (comp. 1340/1921-2), Aʿẓamgaṙh 1370, 417; ʿAbd al-Salām Nadawī, *Shiʿr al-Hind*, ʿAẓamgaṙh, i, 301-23; R. B. Saksena, *A History of Urdu Literature*, Allāhābād 1940 (Urdū tr. Mīrzā Muḥammad ʿAskarī, *Taʾrīkh-i Adab-i Urdū*, Lucknow n. d., 426-40); Djalāl al-Dīn Aḥmad Djaʿfarī, *Taʾrīkh-i Mathnawiyyāt-i Urdū*, Allāhābād, 218-220; Ḥāmid Ḥasan Ḳādirī, *Kamāl-i Dāgh*, Āgra 1935; ʿAbd al-Shakūr Shaydā, of Ḥaydarābād, *Bayāḍ-i Sukhun* (comp. 1355/1936), Ḥaydarābād 1936, 162; Nūr Allāh Muḥammad Nūrī, *Dāgh*, Ḥaydarābād 1355 A.H.; Sīmāb Akbarābadī, *Ḥayāt-i Dāgh*; ʿAbd al-Kādir Sarwarī, *Urdū Mathnawī kā Irtiḳāʾ* (comp. 1358/1940), Ḥaydarābād, 123; Sh. ʿAbd al-Ḳādir, *Famous Urdu Poets and Writers*, Lahore 1947, 88-106; Bashīr al-Dīn Aḥmad of Dihlī, *Wāḳiʿāt-i Dār al-Ḥukūmat, Dihlī* 1337/1919, ii, 447-459; Muḥammad Yaḥyā Tanhā, *Mirʾāt al-Shuʿarāʾ*, Lahore 1950, ii, 33-45; the *Nigār* (magazine) ed. Niyāz Fatḥpūrī, *Dāgh Number*, etc., Lucknow 1953; Rafīḳ Mārahrawī, *Bazm-i Dāgh*, Lucknow 1956; Āftāb Aḥmad Ṣiddīḳī, *Gulhā-yi Dāgh*, Dacca 1958; Mawlānā ʿArshī Rāmpūrī, *Kuč̣h Dāgh ke mutaʿallaḳ* (1958; an article in Ms.); Waḥīd Ḳurayshī, *Dāgh* (1960; art. in Ms.); Tamkīn Kāẓimī, *Dāgh*, Lahore 1960.

(MUHAMMAD SHAFĪ)

DĀGHISTĀN "land of the mountains"; this name is an unusual linguistic phenomenon, since it consists of the Turkish word *dāgh*, mountain, and of the suffix which, in the Persian language, distinguishes the names of countries; this name seems to have appeared for the first time in the 10th/16th century). An autonomous Republic of the R.S.F.S.R. with an area of 19,500 sq. miles and a population of 958,000 inhabitants (1956), it is made up of two quite distinct parts: the Caucasian Range and the cis-Caspian Steppes, bordered in the north by the Terek and the Kuma, in the south by the Samur on one side and the Alazan, a tributary of the Kura, on the other.

Before the Russian conquest, the mountainous part of Dāghistān and the plain which lay beside the sea were never for very long united under the domination of one people or one dynasty. The coastal plain itself divided into two parts by the pass of Derbend, only 2 kms. wide. The southern section belonged principally to the civilized states of Asia Minor, while the northern section lay in the power of the nomadic kingdoms of southern Russia. Since history began, neither the people of the south nor those of the north have exerted any important influence on the ethnography of the mountain region. Before the establishment of Russian power, no foreign conqueror had succeeded in permanently subduing the inhabitants of this region. From time to time these people seized different parts of the coastal plain but each time these conquerors soon broke all political connexion with their brothers who remained in the mountains.

The southern part of the coastal plain as far as Derbend belonged in ancient times to Albania. North of this region, probably in the mountains, dwelt some small tribes whom Strabo (ch. 503) called Δῆγαι or Γῆλαι. Both the Romans and the Persians who succeeded them in the 4th century had to defend the pass of Derbend against the nomadic peoples. The condition in which the Arab conquerors found these regions suggests that the culture of the Sāsānid Empire and perhaps Mazdaïsm had some influence on the inhabitants of the neighbouring mountains. Some princes of these countries possessed Persian titles, *e.g.*, the Ṭabarsarān-Shāh, who governed a district west of Derbend. There also dwelt in Ṭabarsarān the Zirīhgarān (from the Persian *zirīh*, breast-plate), famous armourers whose funeral customs, described by Abū Ḥāmid al-Andalusī (*Tuḥfat al-Albāb*, ed. Ferrand, *JA* 207 (1925), 82-3; also text in Barthold, *Zapiski Vostoč. Otdel. Arkheol. Obshčestva*, xiii, 0104) and others, seem to owe their origin to Persian religious influence. It appears that Christianity began to spread in Albania in the 4th and 5th centuries and thence to the tribes in the steppes and mountains of Dāghistān.

In spite of the success of Arab arms in the north of Dāghistān, notably under the Caliph Hishām (105-125/724-743), when Maslama b. ʿAbd al-Malik first established with some degree of permanence the Arab power at Derbend, this town nonetheless retained its importance as a frontier fort under the Arabs as under the Sāsānids. There, as everywhere, close relations with the neighbouring peoples seem to have deepened in the wake of the Arab conquest. It was nevertheless the Christians and the Jews who first profited from this resurgence of activity, and only afterwards the Muslims. The Khazars are supposed to have adopted Christianity under the Armenian patriarch Sahak III (677 to 703 A.D.). In the time of Hārūn al-Rashīd (170-193/786-809), the Jews succeeded in winning to their faith the sovereign and the nobility of this people.

The geographers of the 4th/10th century furnish us with exact information on the ethnographic distribution of Dāghistān and the spread of the three religions through this country. At that time the Arabs held, in addition to Derbend, the neighbouring castles which were only one *farsakh* or three miles away from the town, according to al-Masʿūdī, ii, 40). A Muslim, son of the sister of ʿAbd al-Malik, amīr of Derbend, ruled over Ṭabarsarān. Ibn Rusta (De Goeje ed., 147 ff.) relates that the sovereign of the neighbouring kingdom of Khajdān (a true account according to Marquart, *Osteuropäische und Ostasiatische Streifzüge*, 492) professed the three religions simultaneously and observed Friday with the Muslims, Saturday with the Jews and Sunday with the Christians. In al-Masʿūdī (*Murūdj*, ii, 39) the same prince appears as a Muslim and was even said to have had drawn up a genealogical tree showing his connexion with the Arab race. He was, however, the only Muslim initiate in his country. Further north reigned another Muslim, Barzbān, prince of the Gurdj. North of his principality lived the Christian Ghumīḳ; still further north lay the impenetrable mountains of the Zirīhgarān, where the three religions each had their adherents, and finally the country of the Christian prince of Sarīr (which corresponds to present-day Avaristān), who bore the title of Fīlān<u>sh</u>āh or Ḳīlān<u>sh</u>āh. According to Ibn Rusta, only the inhabitants of the royal castle, built on a high mountain, were Christian; the prince's other subjects were pagan. According to al-Iṣṭa<u>kh</u>rī, Sarīr's frontier was only two *farsa<u>kh</u>* away from the seaboard town of Samandar. Governed by a Jewish prince related to the king of the <u>Kh</u>azars, Samandar lay four days' march from Derbend according to al-Iṣṭa<u>kh</u>rī, eight days' march according to al-Masʿūdī. It was probably situated in the northern part of the coastal region where the town of Ṭarkī or Ṭar<u>kh</u>ū was later built. It is described as a flourishing city where there were, some say, 4000, others, 40,000 vineyards; there the Muslims had their mosques, the Christians their churches, and the Jews their synagogues. On the west the country of Samandar bordered the land of the Alans.

The Arabs seem to have given the name of Lakz (Lezgians) to the people of southern Dā<u>gh</u>istān, whose geographical position they do not elsewhere indicate with any precision. According to al-Balā<u>dh</u>urī (De Goeje ed., 208), the land of the Lakz lay in the plain which stretched from Samur to the town of <u>Sh</u>āberān, south of present-day Dā<u>gh</u>istān. According to al-Masʿūdī (*Murū<u>dj</u>*, ii, 5), on the other hand, the Lakz people dwelt in the highest mountains of the region. Among these were the "infidels" who were not subject to the prince of <u>Sh</u>irwān. "Strange stories" went round about their family life and customs. The mention of <u>Sh</u>irwān shows that al-Masʿūdī imagined the country of the Lakz to lie in the mountainous region of upper Semur. At first the Russians only used the name of "Lezgians" for the tribes of southern Dā<u>gh</u>istān, as opposed to the "highlanders" of the northern territories or "*Tawli*", from the Turkish *taw*—mountain.

During the succeeding centuries, Islam seems to have made but slow progress in Dā<u>gh</u>istān. In 354/965, the power of the <u>Kh</u>azars was shattered by the Russians. Then the southern part of this state itself suffered the ravages of war. It was the Christian Alans who, it seems, profited from this upheaval, for their territory, at the time of the Mongol conquest, stretched much further to the east than in the 4th/10th century. At the time of their first incursion into these countries, according to Ibn al-A<u>th</u>īr (xii, 252), the Mongols encountered north of Derbend first the people of the Lakz who then included "Muslims and infidels", further north some other half-Muslim tribes—ancestors of the Avars—and lastly the Alans. According to William of Rubruk who visited these countries in November 1254, the mountains were inhabited by Christian Alans; "between the mountains and the sea" lived the Saracen Lezgians (Lesgi), that is to say Muslims; however Rubruk himself gave the name of "castellum Alanorum" to a fortress situated only one day's march north of Derbend. The Mongols at that time had still not succeeded in subjugating these tribes. It was necessary to assign to special detachments the defence of the passes leading from the mountains to the plain, in order to defend the herds grazing on the steppe against the raids of the highlanders (cf. Fr. M. Schmidt, *Rubruk's Reise*, Berlin 1885, 84 ff.).

In the 13th and 14th centuries, the region which stretched to the pass of Derbend, and partially the territories situated to the south of this town also, formed part of the empire of the Golden Horde. It is in the history of the campaigns of Tīmūr (797-798/1395-1396) that the names of the two chief peoples of Dā<u>gh</u>istān, the Ḳaytāḳ (or Ḳaytā<u>gh</u>) and the Ḳāzī-Ḳūmūḳ (now Laks) appear for the first time in their modern forms. The territory of the Ḳaytāḳ, next to the pass of Derbend, belonged to the empire of To<u>kh</u>tami<u>sh</u>. <u>Sh</u>araf al-Dīn Yazdī (*Ẓafar-nāma*, India ed. i, 742 sqq.) describes the Ḳaytāḳ as people "without religion" (*bī-dīn*) or of "bad faith" (*bad ki<u>sh</u>*) which shows that they were still not subject to Islam. According to Barbaro (Ramusio, *Viaggi*, ii, 109-a), there were among the Ḳaytāḳ even in the 15th century many Greek, Armenian or Roman Catholic Christians. On the other hand, the prince of the Ḳaytāḳ (<u>Kh</u>alīl Beg), mentioned by Afanasid Nikitin in his account of the voyage (1466), bore a Muslim name.

The Ḳāzī-Ḳūmūḳ were Muslim and were regarded as the champions of Islam against the pagan peoples around them. Their prince was called <u>Sh</u>awkal. North of the Ḳāzī-Ḳūmūḳ lived the A<u>sh</u>kū<u>dj</u>a (modern Dar<u>gh</u>ins), who had not yet become Muslim. The account of Tīmūr's campaigns also mentions the town of Tarḳi. Between the Ḳāzī-Ḳūmūḳ and the Ḳaytāks, and therefore in the land of the present-day Köbeči, dwelt the Zirīhgarān who had retained their ancient fame as smiths and who offered to the conqueror coats-of-mail of their own making.

The Tīmūrid conquest and the Ottoman occupation (from 865-1015/1461-1606) marked the further advance of Islam into Dā<u>gh</u>istān. From the beginning of the 10th/16th century, the Muslim faith won over the infidel populations in Dā<u>gh</u>istān, often by recourse to force. From this period dates the somewhat superficial conversion to Islam of the Dar<u>gh</u>ine (A<u>sh</u>kū<u>dj</u>a) people and the permanent conversion of the Ḳaytāḳ. The Avars as well were gradually brought over to Islam, but Christianity survived amongst them throughout the 15th century, whilst the Andis and the Didos peoples remained firmly pagan. The Zirīhgarān (Kubačis), converted to Islam in the 15th century, preserved traces of Christianity until the end of the 18th century. The Lezgians were also superficially converted after the Tīmūrid period.

The Islamic conversion is not the only aspect of the historical evolution of Dā<u>gh</u>istān at this time, in which we must include the formation of the feudal principalities which provided Dā<u>gh</u>istān with the political structure which remained until the 19th century.

The feudal principalities which appeared or developed at that time claimed ancestry from the Arab conquest, but these fanciful allegations are today strongly disputed.

The account of Tīmūr's campaigns shows decisively that the situation in which the Ottomans found Dā<u>gh</u>istān during their short domination dates from the 9th-15th to 10th/16th centuries only. Nevertheless this situation has been carried back to the first centuries of the *hi<u>dj</u>ra* by a historical tradition only invented during this era. Just as the Jews, perhaps before the Arab conquest, had located in Dā<u>gh</u>istān certain events in their legends and history (cf. Marquart, *Streifzüge*, 20), just as today those called Da<u>gh</u>-Čufut or "mountain Jews" still claim that their ancestors were formerly led into these regions by the conquering Assyrians or Babylonians, so also did the Muslim peoples all claim to have been converted to Islam by Abū Muslim and the princes all claim to be descended from the Arab governors whom he left in Dā<u>gh</u>istān. The title of Maʿṣūm, borne by the prince of Ṭabarsarān, was identified with the Arabic word *maʿṣūm*. Likewise Arabic etymologies were invented for the Ḳaytāḳ title of *ūsmī* ("renowned", from *ism* = "name") and for the Ḳāzī-Ḳūmūḳ's *s̲h̲āmḳh̲āl*. The word *s̲h̲āmkh̲āl* was alleged to derive from S̲h̲ām = Syria. Another root was also found for this word, namely *s̲h̲āh-baʿl*. It is not impossible that such etymologies also had some influence on the pronunciation of the titles in question. It is obviously not by chance that the title of the prince of the Ḳāzī-Ḳūmūḳ appeared in the oldest Russian documents in the same form (*s̲h̲ewḳal* or *s̲h̲awḳal*) as in S̲h̲araf al-Dīn Yazdī. Clearly the Persians and the Russians could not have corrupted *s̲h̲āmkh̲āl* into *s̲h̲awḳal* independently of each other; it is more likely if we assume that the present form of the title only took shape under the influence of the etymology described above. The subjects of the *s̲h̲āmkh̲āl*, the Ḳāzī-Ḳūmūḳ, claimed to have been distinguished under Abū Muslim as defenders of the faith and to have won at that time from the Arabs the title of "*G̲h̲āzī*" or victors.

Three great feudal principalities dominated Dāg̲h̲istān in the 9th-10th/15th-16th centuries: the the S̲h̲āmkh̲ālat Ḳāzī-Ḳūmūḳ, the Ūsmīyat of Ḳaytāḳ and the Maʿsūmat of Ṭabarsarān.

The first historical Ḳaytāḳ prince who bore the title of *ūsmī* seems to have been Aḥmad Kh̲ān, who died in 996/1587-88. He is credited with having founded the village of Madjālīs, where the representatives of the people assembled to discuss their affairs. He is supposed to have ordered the bringing together of the statutes of the popular law in a code to which the judges or *ḳāḍīs* had to conform, a measure which was considered a "great audacity" (*djasārat-i ʿaẓīma*) by Mīrzā Ḥasan Efendi, the author of *Āth̲ār-i Dāg̲h̲istān*, 65).

Towards the middle of the eleventh century (1050/1640), a number of the Ḳaytāḳ separated from their compatriots and proceeded to the regions south of Dāg̲h̲istān. Husayn Kh̲ān, leader of these emigrants, succeeded in setting up a new principality at Sāliyān and Kūba. The Ottoman traveller Ewliyā Čelebi (*Siyāḥat-nāma*, ii, 291 ff.) met these Ḳaytāḳ emigrants in 1057/1647 between S̲h̲aki (today Nukh̲a) and S̲h̲amākh̲ī. The glossary compiled by Ewliyā Čelebi proves that the Ḳaytāḳ did not then, as today, speak Lezgian but Mongol.

The *s̲h̲āmkh̲āls* of the Ḳāzī-Ḳūmūḳ (today the Laks) extended their domination little by little beyond their mountains north-east as far as the coast, into Turkish country (Ḳumīḳ). In the 10th/16th century, these princes used to spend the winter at Būynāḳ, a village on the coastal plain, and the summer at Kumukh̲ in the mountains. In 986/1578 at Būynāḳ died the *s̲h̲āmkh̲āl* Čūbān, whose possessions were then divided among his sons. These divisions naturally weakened the power of the dynasty. The Ḳāzī-Ḳūmūḳ who stayed in the mountains slowly proceeded to make themselves entirely independent of their ruling house. After the death of the *s̲h̲āmkh̲āl* Sūrkh̲āy-Mīrzā, in 1049/1639-40, the *s̲h̲āmkh̲āls* only ruled the coastal region, at Būināḳ or Tārkh̲ū (Tarḳi). None of the later *s̲h̲āmkh̲āls* ever returned to Kumukh̲, where the tombs of the first princes are still to be seen.

It was at this time that the Russians revived their efforts to seize, after Astrakh̲ān, the countries of the northern Caucasus, among them Dāg̲h̲istān. In 1594 a Russian detachment commanded by Prince Kh̲vorostīnin succeeded in taking Tārkh̲ū and in constructing a fortress on the Ḳoi-Su or Sulaḳ. It was not long, however, before the Russians suffered defeat by the sons of the *s̲h̲āmkh̲āl* and were compelled to withdraw over the Sulaḳ. A fresh attack in 1604, directed by Buturlin and Pleshčeev against Tārkh̲ū, was still less successful.

The period between the Ottoman occupation and the Russian conquest is distinguished in Dāg̲h̲istān by the flowering of the Arab culture which attained its zenith in the period of S̲h̲āmil. During the 17th century a galaxy of Dāg̲h̲istān scholars gathered round S̲h̲aykh̲ Ṣāliḥ al-Yamanī (born in 1637—died at Mecca in 1696): his most famous disciple was Muḥammad Mūsā of Kudatli, who disseminated his teachings in Dāg̲h̲istān and died in Aleppo in 1708. In the 18th century parties of Dāg̲h̲istān scholars went to Damascus and Aleppo to learn there the Arab language and the s̲h̲arīʿa. This period of cultural renascence was also a period of juridical organization—a codification illustrated by the Code of Umma Kh̲ān, the Avar, and the laws of Rustum Kh̲ān, *ūsmī* of Ḳaytāḳ.

With this flowering of Islamic culture in the Arabic language there coincided on the political level an anarchic dispersion when Dāg̲h̲istān, divided into manifold clans and rival kingdoms, wavered between Turkish and Persian influence, passing alternately from one to the other. This political dispersion confirmed the weakness of Dāg̲h̲istān and inevitably provoked a foreign conqueror.

From the 16th century onwards three powers, Persia, Turkey and Russia, claimed possession of Dāg̲h̲istān. The native princes allied themselves now with one, now with another, of these three powers. Not until the 19th century was the contest finally terminated, to Russia's advantage. After 986/1578 the prince of Ṭabarsarān, following the example of the *s̲h̲āmkh̲āl* and of the *ūsmī*, made his submission to the Sultan. When, in 1015/1606, S̲h̲āh ʿAbbās restored Persian power in these regions, the *ūsmī* joined with him, whilst the *s̲h̲āmkh̲āl* remained loyal to the Turks. One of the clauses of the peace treaty concluded in 1021/1612 stipulated that the *s̲h̲āmkh̲āl* and the other princes loyal to the Porte would not suffer any reprisals on the part of Persia. The *ūsmī* Rustam-Kh̲ān having crossed over to the Turks in 1048/1638, his rival the *s̲h̲amkh̲āl* won the favour of the S̲h̲āh, who confirmed him in his honours. He had moreover already received a similar investiture from the Tsar Michael (*Ath̲ār-i Dāg̲h̲istān*, 81).

When, under the feeble government of the S̲h̲ah Husayn, the Ṣafawid empire fell into decline, Dāg̲h̲istān itself became the stage for a movement directed against Persian domination. At the head of this movement there was Čulāḳ-Sūrkh̲ay-Kh̲ān who had just founded a new principality in the land of the Ḳāzī-Ḳūmūḳ. Allied with the *ūsmī* and the *mudarris* Ḥādjdjī Dāwūd, the leader of a pupolar movement, he succeeded in taking S̲h̲amākh̲ī in 1124/1712. Then the allies sent to Constantinople an embassy which obtained for them robes of honour from the Sultan, titles and diplomas and the favour of being received into the number of the subjects of the Porte. It was then that the intervention of Russia altered the course of events. Three hundred Russian merchants had been killed at S̲h̲amākh̲ī, and Peter the Great seized this as a pretext for intervention. He directed an expedition against Persia and occupied Derbend in 1722. Soon afterwards the other provinces on the west coast of the Caspian sea had themselves to submit to Russia. By the treaty of partition of 1724, Russia's rights over this coast were likewise recognized by the Porte.

The Russian occupation was not at that time of

very long duration. Nādir Shāh succeeded in restoring the unity of the Persian empire, and Russia gave back to him, by the treaty of 1732, all the countries south of the Kura and also, by the treaty of 1735, the territory contained between the Kura and the Sulaḳ. When the Russians had contrived to defeat an expedition of Tātars from the Crimea into Dāghistān, the Porte likewise gave up its claims. As for the native population, it opposed the new Shāh with unyielding resistance, especially in the mountains. It was only on the coast that Nādir Shāh succeeded in establishing his power in any lasting fashion. In 1718 the *shāmkhāl* ʿĀdil Girāy had taken an oath of loyalty to Peter the Great and had aided him in his campaign of 1722; as, however, he later revolted against the Russians, he had been deported to Lapland in 1725 and the dignity of *shāmkhāl* had been abolished. Nādir Shāh restored this dignity and conferred it on Khāṣ Pūlād-Khān, the son of ʿĀdil Girāy. The people of the mountains remained independent, owing to persistent attacks, particularly those of 1742 and 1744.

After the murder of Nādir Shāh in 1160/1747, Persia was for half a century without a government strong enough to maintain its power in this frontier region. The provinces of the empire themselves could not be defended against the incursions of the princes of Dāghistān. In this way the town of Ardabil was sacked by the *usmī* Amīr Ḥamza. In turn the Russians, in spite of the treaty of 1735, began to wield influence in Dāghistān once more. The traveller Gmelin was captured in the country of the *usmī* and put to death in 1774, and in 1775 a Russian detachment commanded by Madem came and devastated the region. In 1784 the *shāmkhāl* Murtaḍa ʿAlī once more joined Russia. In 1785 the establishment of the post of governor of the Caucasus consolidated Russian domination over these countries. A religious movement instigated by Turkey and directed by Shaykh Manṣūr affected Dāghistān only superficially; most of the princes refused to support the movement.

The Ḳādjārs, when they had succeeded in reuniting all the Persian provinces in one empire, strove once more to annex the lands of the Caucasus. But this time Russia was not disposed to give up her claims without a struggle, as she had with Nādir Shāh. The war began in the last year of the reign of Catherine II, in 1796. Derbend was occupied by the Russians but soon after evacuated by command of the Emperor Paul. In 1806 the town was recaptured, and this put an end to Persian domination in Dāghistān. It was, however, only by the peace treaty of Gulistān, in 1813, that Persia finally renounced her claims over the country.

The resistance offered to the Russians by the native princes and by their peoples in particular continued longer. In 1818 nearly all the princes of Dāghistān, with the exception of the *shāmkhāl*, formed an alliance against the Russians. This rebellion was not put down by the Governor Yermolov without difficulty. The title of *usmī* of the Ḳaytāḳ was abolished in 1819, that of *maʿṣūm* of Ṭabarsarān in 1828. After 1830 the princes who were allowed to remain accepted Russian officer advisers at their sides. The masses, excited by their preachers to a holy war against the infidels, resisted more tenaciously than their rulers. Since the end of the 18th century the adherents of the order of the Naḳshbandiyya had penetrated into Dāghistān and there disseminated their doctrines successfully. About 1830 the leaders of the order had stirred up among the Avars a popular movement directed both against the ruling house, against the intrusion of the infidels and in favour of the restoration of the *sharīʿa* in place of the *ʿādāt*. The chief leader of the rebels was Ghāzī Muḥammad [*q.v.*], called Kazi Mulla by the Russians and praised by his pupils as a great expert in Arab sciences (*ʿulūm ʿarabiyya*).

On 17th (29th) of October 1832, Ghāzī Muḥammad was surrounded and killed by a Russian detachment in the village of Gimri. His successor, Ḥamza Beg [*q.v.*] also died in 1834 near Khūnzāḳ. The third leader of the rebellion, Shāmil [*q.v.*] was more fortunate. The inferior of his predecessors in learning, he excelled them in his qualities of administrator and leader. For twenty-five years he maintained in the mountains the struggle against the Russians. He gained his greatest successes in the years 1843 and 1844 when the Russians occupied only the coast and the southern regions. In the mountains many Russian strongholds had been taken by the highlanders. After 1849, Shāmil was once more confined to the western part of the mountain region, but he continued the struggle for another ten years.

After the fall of Shāmil who, on 25th August (6th September) 1859, yielded to Prince Baryatinsky, the Russians restored for a while the authority of the Avar princes, deeming it opportune to consolidate the power of the princes and the nobility in order to destroy with their support the influence of the priesthood. But the Russian authorities soon abandoned this policy. The royal house of the Avars was dispossessed in 1862, and soon afterwards the other princes in their turn had to abdicate the semblance of sovereignty which still remained to them. The deposition of the *shāmkhāl* took place in 1865. Dāghistān was then given the organization which it retained until the Revolution of 1917. In 1877, during the Russo-Turkish war, the population took up arms again. On 8th (20th) September the rebels succeeded in taking the fortress of Kumukh. In Ḳaytāḳ and Ṭabarsarān the descendants of the old ruling houses re-assumed the titles of *usmī* and of *maʿṣūm*. But meanwhile the war changed to the advantage of the Russians who soon put down the insurrection.

After the extremely savage civil war in Dāghistān (1917-20), the Soviet regime was set up in the autumn of 1920. On the 13th of November there was proclaimed the Autonomous Socialist Soviet Republic of Dāghistān with Makhač-Ḳala for the capital.

The population of this republic consists now of a majority of Muslims and a minority of non-Muslim immigrants: Russians, Ukrainians, Jews both autochthonous (Dāgh-Čufut) and immigrant (Ashkenazim).

The Muslim population contains three great linguistic groups:

I. The Ibero-Caucasians which divide into three sub-groups speaking languages distinct from each other:

(a) The Avaro-Ando-Dido group (cf. AVAR, ANDI, DIDO and ARČI), in 1959 268,000 strong in the northern part of mountainous Dāghistān. It contains the Avar (or Khunzak) people, eight small Andi nationalities (Andis proper, Akhwakhs, Bagulals, Botlikhs, Godoberis, Čamalals, Ḳaratas and Tindis) inhabiting the high bowl of the Ḳoysu of Andi, five small Dido nationalities (Didos proper or Tzezes, Bežeta, Khwarshis, Ginukhs and Khunzals) and the Arčis.

The Avars possess a literary language, have absorbed the other nations in the group whose languages are not set down in writing, and form with them one sole Avar "nation".

(b) The Dar<u>gh</u>ino-Lak group (cf. DAR<u>GH</u>IN, LAK, ḲAYTĀḲ, KUBAČI) which numbered 222,000 in 1959 in the west-central part of mountainous Dā<u>gh</u>istān, and which contain the Dar<u>gh</u>ins (formerly A<u>sh</u>kū<u>dj</u>a), the Laks (formerly Ḳāzī-Ḳūmū<u>kh</u>) and two small peoples, Ḳaytāḳ and Kubači (formerly Zirīhgarān).

The Dar<u>gh</u>in and the Lak possess literary languages; the Ḳaytāḳ and the Kubači are without these and have merged into the Dar<u>gh</u>in nation.

(c) The Samurian group in southern Dā<u>gh</u>istān (cf. LEZG, TZA<u>KH</u>UR, RUTUL, ṬABARSARĀN and <u>SH</u>ĀH-DĀ<u>GH</u> peoples), 279,000 strong in 1959, contain two nations with a literary language, the Lezgians (223,000) and the Ṭabarsarān (35,000), and three small peoples destined to merge into the Lezg nation: Agul (8,000), Rutul (7,000) and Tza<u>kh</u>ur (6,000). To this group are connected the five peoples of <u>Sh</u>āh-Dā<u>gh</u> (numbering about 15,000) in northern Ā<u>dh</u>arbay<u>dj</u>ān (<u>Dj</u>ek, Krïz, <u>Kh</u>aputz, Budu<u>kh</u> and <u>Kh</u>inalug), who have been greatly influenced by Turkey and who are merging into the Ā<u>dh</u>arī nation.

II. The Turks are represented in Dā<u>gh</u>istān by the Ā<u>dh</u>arīs in the plain round Derbend and in the low valley of the Samur; by the Ḳumïḳs [*q.v.*] who numbered 135,000 in 1959 in the cis-Caspian plains north of Derbend to the Terek; and by the Nogays [*q.v.*] (41,000 in 1959) in the steppes between the Terek and the Kuma. The Ḳumïḳs and the Nogays, like the Ā<u>dh</u>arīs, possess literary languages.

III. The Iranophone peoples are represented by the Tāts [*q.v.*] who numbered several thousands around Derbend, and the mountain Jews or Dā<u>gh</u>-Čufut (about 12,000) in the villages of the plain, Jewish in religion but speaking Tātī.

Dā<u>gh</u>istān is a multi-national republic, the only one in the Soviet Union which was not founded on one nation or one dominant nationality (*narodnost'*). In the terms of the Constitution (art. 78), she possesses ten official literary languages: Avar, Dar<u>gh</u>īn, Lak, Lezg, Ṭabarsarān, Ḳumïḳ, Nogay, Ā<u>dh</u>ari, Tātī (in its Jewish form used by the Dā<u>gh</u>-Čufut) and Russian. These languages are used as teaching languages in the primary schools, but of the autochthonous languages only Avar, Dar<u>gh</u>in, Lak and Ḳumïḳ have newspapers. It thus appears that these four nations are destined to become poles of attraction and that in the end they will absorb the other groups.

Bibliography: As well as general works on the Caucasus, there is a rich literature on Dā<u>gh</u>istān in Russian. A bibliography (134 titles of works and articles) will be found in A. Bennigsen and H. Carrère d'Encausse, *Une République soviétique musulmane: le Dā<u>gh</u>istān, aperçu démographique*, in *REI* 1955, 7-56, and another more complete version appended to the work *Narodï Dagestana*, Moscow, Acad. Sc., 1955 (137 titles of which 79 are of pre-revolutionary works and titles and 58 later than 1918); Turkish sources in *IA* s.v. (by Mirza Bala). For further details see the bibliographies of the articles on the peoples mentioned in the text. (W. BARTHOLD-[A. BENNIGSEN])

AL-ḌAḤḤĀḲ [see ZUHĀK].

AL-ḌAḤḤĀK B. ḲAYS AL-FIHRĪ, ABŪ UNAYS (or ABŪ ʿABD AL-RAḤMĀN), son of a blood-letter (*ḥa<u>djdj</u>ām*, Ibn Rusta, *BGA* vii, 215), head of the house of Ḳays. He is reported to have been of a vacillating character (*<u>dj</u>aʿala yuḳaddimu ri<u>dj</u>l*^{an} *wa-yuʾa<u>khkh</u>iru u<u>kh</u>rā*, *A<u>gh</u>ānī* xvii, 111) and this is borne out by his changing attitude towards the ruling Umayyad house, in which he proved easy to influence. He was a keen follower of Muʿāwiya, first as head of the police (*ṣāḥib al-<u>sh</u>urṭa*), and then as governor of the *<u>dj</u>und* of Damascus. In the year 36/656, al-Ḍaḥḥāk defeated the ʿAlid al-A<u>sh</u>tar near al-Mar<u>dj</u> (between Ḥarrān and al-Raḳḳa), and the latter had to retreat to Mosul. At Ṣiffīn, he commanded the Syrian infantry. In 39/659-60, Muʿāwiya sent him against the ʿAlids with 3,000 men. He went to the Ḥi<u>dj</u>āz via al-<u>Th</u>aʿlabiyya, al-Ḳuṭḳuṭāna etc., and temporarily stopped the pilgrim traffic, until, at ʿAlī's order, Ḥu<u>dj</u>r b. ʿAdī al-Kindī, at the head of 4,000 men, forced him to retreat to Syria. In 55/674-5, or perhaps even in 54, Muʿāwiya nominated him as governor of Kūfa, in succession to ʿAbd Allāh b. <u>Kh</u>ālid b. Asīd, but deposed him again in 58. In 60/680, Muʿāwiya was dying, and made al-Ḍaḥḥāk and Muslim b. ʿUḳba joint regents; he dictated his last will to them, charging them to give it into the hands of his successor Yazīd, who was away from Damascus at the time. Al-Ḍaḥḥāk led the prayer for the dead, and worked for the succession of Yazīd, being recognized by him as governor. During his illness, Muʿāwiya II had chosen him to lead the prayers in Damascus until such time as a new Caliph should be elected.

During the time of general strife and intrigue after the death of Muʿāwiya II in 64/684, al-Ḍaḥḥāk—together with the governors of Ḥimṣ and Ḳinnasrīn—went over to the side of the rival caliph ʿAbd Allāh b. al-Zubayr. At first he did this secretly, but later openly. Ibn al-Zubayr then made him governor of Syria, putting under him the other governors with pro-Zubayr leanings. Marwān b. al-Ḥakam, who had attended Muʿāwiya II's funeral, and was at that time the oldest and most respected of the Umayyads, considered the position so hopeless that he left for Mecca, to pay homage to Ibn al-Zubayr, and to intercede for an amnesty for the Umayyads. On the way, however, he met ʿUbayd Allāh b. Ziyād in A<u>dh</u>riʿāt. The latter was on his way from ʿIrāḳ to Damascus, and reproached him severely, finally deciding him to turn back, which he did, going first of all to Palmyra. In Damascus, the crafty ʿUbayd Allāh suggested to al-Ḍaḥḥāk that he should break with Ibn al-Zubayr, and become the head of the Ḳuray<u>sh</u> himself and be recognized as their ruler. Al-Ḍaḥḥāk succumbed to this temptation, but within three days he had to yield to the revolt of his followers, who could find no blame in Ibn al-Zubayr, so he veered over to his side again. These vacillations lost him the confidence of his people, and at the same time he naturally became an object of suspicion to the Zubayrids. At this point, ʿUbayd Allāh gave him the fateful advice to leave the town, to collect an army, and to fight for Ibn al-Zubayr. So he left—apparently at ʿUbayd Allāh's instigation—and went to Mar<u>dj</u> Rāhiṭ, whilst ʿUbayd Allāh himself remained in Damascus. Also at ʿUbayd Allāh's instigation, Marwān accepted the homage of the people at Palmyra, married the mother of the two sons of Yazīd, and asked Ḥassān b. Mālik b. Baḥdal al-Kalbī, Yazīd's very powerful uncle, to come to Palmyra. When he refused, Marwān lost heart again, went to al-<u>Dj</u>ābiya where —after Ḥassān eventually gave up his position under pressure of the majority—he was elected caliph. After that, ʿUbayd Allāh had him recognized in Damascus as well.

In this way, it was possible for Marwān to lead

the warriors assembled in al-Djābiya, and all his followers from Damascus, against al-Ḍaḥḥāk. In 64/684, a momentous battle took place near Mardj Rāhiṭ, lasting for 20 days and ending with a victory of the Kalb over the Ḳays. Al-Ḍaḥḥāk himself was killed in battle and his followers fled. His son ʿAbd al-Raḥmān b. al-Ḍaḥḥāk, however, became governor of Medina under Yazīd b. ʿAbd al-Malik. Ibn ʿAsākir still knew the house and the beautiful bath of al-Ḍaḥḥāk near the city wall of Damascus (*Taʾrīkh Madīnat Dimashḳ*, ed. Ṣ. Munadjdjid, ii/1, Damascus 1954, 140), and even al-ʿAlmawī (died 981/1573) tells of a mosque, supposedly that of al-Ḍaḥḥāk b. Ḳays, on the southern side of the citadel (H. Sauvaire, in *JA*, 9e série, tome vi, 1895, 442, and vii, 1896, 386).

The course of events following the death of Muʿāwiya II is by no means as clear cut as might appear from the above: accounts vary considerably, but Ibn Saʿd's report is, for factual reasons, the most acceptable on the whole.

Bibliography: Ibn Saʿd, v, 27-30, vi, 13, 35; Ṭabarī, i, 3283, 3447, ii, 170, 172, 181, 188, 197, 202, 433, 468-74, 477-9, 482; Ibn al-Athīr, iii, 317, 416, 426, iv, 5, 120-5; idem, *Usd al-ghāba*, Būlāḳ 1286, 37 f.; Yaʿḳūbī, ii, 229 f., 283 f., 304 f.; Dīnawarī, *al-Akhbār al-Ṭiwāl* (ed. Guirgass), 164, 183 f., 192, 239 f.; Ibn Ḳutayba, *Maʿārif* (ed. Wüstenfeld) 33, 179, 210; idem, *al-Imāma wa 'l-Siyāsa*, Cairo 1356, i, 174, 177 f.; Masʿūdī, *Murūdj*, v, 198, 201; idem, *Tanbīh*, 307-9; Ibn Abī Ḥātim al-Rāzī, *al-Djarḥ wa 'l-Taʿdīl*, ii/1, (Ḥaydarābād 1952, 457, no. 2019; Ibn Ḥibbān, *Mashāhīr ʿulamāʾ al-amṣār* (Bibliotheca Islamica 22), no. 368; Ibn Ḥadjar, *Iṣāba* (Cairo 1358) ii, 199; Ibn ʿAbd al-Barr, *Istīʿāb* (printed together with the *Iṣāba*) ii, 197 f.; Djāḥiẓ, *al-Bayān wa 'l-tabyīn II* (ed. Hārūn), 131 f.; Ibn ʿAbd Rabbih, *ʿIḳd*, Cairo 1367-82, iii, 308, iv, 87 f., 362, 369, 372-4, 391-7; *Aghānī*, xv, 44, 46, xvi, 34, xvii, 111; Ibn Rusta, 209, 215; Wellhausen, *Das arabische Reich*, 107-112; Buhl, *ZA*, 27 (1912), 50-64; Caetani, *Chronographia*, 394 f., 442 f., 586, 598, 608, 636, 654, 735, 737; Lammens, *MFOB*. iv (1910), 237, v (1911), 107, 110; idem, *Études sur le siècle des Omayyades*, 203 f., 207; idem, *L'avènement des Marwānides et le califat de Marwān Ier* (*MFOB*. xii, 1927, fasc. 2 *passim*, see index).

(A. Dietrich)

AL-ḌAḤḤĀK B. ḲAYS AL-SHAYBĀNĪ, Khāridjite leader, opponent of Marwān b. Muḥammad (= Marwān II). During the disturbances which followed the murder of the Caliph al-Walīd II, the Khāridjites resumed their campaign in Djazīra and pushed forward into ʿIrāḳ, their leader at first being the Ḥarūrite Saʿīd b. Bahdal, and, after his death of the plague, al-Ḍaḥḥāk b. Ḳays al-Shaybānī, an adherent of the above-mentioned Ibn Bahdal. Several thousand fighters assembled under the standard of al-Ḍaḥḥāk; there were even among them Ṣufrites from Shahrazūr, who, at that time, according to al-Balādhurī, *Futūḥ*, 209, were contesting, with Marwān, the possession of Armenia and Ādharbaydjān, and there were also old women who, dressed in male armour, fought bravely in his ranks. For some months in ʿIrāḳ, two governors had been at war with each other; one of them, ʿAbd Allāh, son of ʿUmar II [*q.v.*], represented the Caliph Yazīd b. al-Walīd (= Yazīd II) and was supported by the Yemenites, and the other, al-Naḍr b. Saʿīd al-Ḥarashī, was the nominee of Marwān b. Muḥammad, and had the support of the Muḍarites. When the Khāridjites advanced, these two governors joined forces against the threat. In spite of their joint efforts, they were beaten in the month of Radjab 127/April-May 745, and al-Kūfa was evacuated. Ibn al-Ḥarashī returned to the domain of Marwān, and Ibn ʿUmar withdrew into the fortress of Wāsiṭ, but in the month of Shaʿbān of the same year, he was besieged there by al-Ḍaḥḥāk. After a few combats he ceased all resistance (Shawwāl 127/August 745), and, although a Ḳurayshite and a member of the ruling family, paid homage to the rebel. Ibn Kathīr, obviously struck by the enormity of this, diminishes its seriousness; he says that Ibn ʿUmar pressed the Khāridjite to oppose Marwān, promising to follow him if he killed the latter. Al-Ḍaḥḥāk, now master of al-Kūfa, did not delay there; invited by the inhabitants of al-Mawṣil, he entered that town and expelled the government officials (according to Ibn Kathīr, he marched against Marwān, and, on the way, he seized al-Mawṣil, at the invitation of the inhabitants). It is certain that he was popular. The sources imply that people flocked to his banner because he paid extremely well, but the real reason must have been that the ideas of the Khāridjites filled the masses with enthusiasm; the movement had acquired towards the end of the Umayyad dynasty a scope and an intensity that it had never known. Al-Ḍaḥḥāk's army is said to have numbered 120,000 men. Even the Umayyad Sulaymān, son of the Caliph Hishām, took his place alongside the Khāridjites, with his *mawālī* and his soldiers, although they had proclaimed him Caliph. Marwān, then busy besieging Ḥimṣ, asked his son ʿAbd Allāh, whom he had left at Ḥarrān, to march against al-Ḍaḥḥāk, but ʿAbd Allāh, beaten, retreated into Niṣībīn and was besieged there by the Khāridjite. Finally Marwān, who had meanwhile seized Ḥimṣ, himself marched against al-Ḍaḥḥāk. The battle took place at al-Ghazz on the territory of Kafartūthā (al-Masʿūdī, *Murūdj*, vi, 62: between Kafartūthā and Raʾs al-ʿAyn) towards the end of 128/Aug.-Sept. 746. Al-Ḍaḥḥāk fell in a fray, and his body was not discovered by Marwān's men until the following night. His successor, Khaybarī, was also killed when he attempted to renew the attack.

Bibliography: Ṭabarī, ii, 1898-1908/1913-1917, 1938-1940 and index, Ibn al-Athīr, v, 251, 253-256, 265 ff., Ibn Kathīr, *Bidāya*, Cairo 1348 ff.; x, 25 ff., 28; Theophanes, *Chronographia*, A. M., 6236 ff.; M. J. de Goeje and P. de Jong, *Fragmenta historicorum arabicorum*, l, 140, 158-160, 163 ff. (from the *Kitāb al-ʿUyūn wa-l-ḥadāʾiḳ fī akhbār al-ḥaḳāʾiḳ*); Sibṭ Ibn al-Djawzī, *Mirʾāt*, MS British Mus. Add. 23,277, f. 229v°; J. Wellhausen, *Die religiös-politischen Oppositionsparteien im alten Islam*, Berlin 1901, 49 ff.; *ibid.*, *Das ar. Reich*, 242-244.

(L. Veccia Vaglieri)

DAHISTĀN, erroneous spelling of Dihistān [*q.v.*].

DAHLAK Islands, a group of islands off the west coast of the Red Sea, opposite Muṣawwaʿ (Eritrea), with their centre about 40° 10′ E., 15° 45′ N. Of about 125 islands, including tiny islets, rocks and reefs, the two largest are Dahlak al-Kabīr and Nūra. Others are Nokra, Dohol, Harat Kubarī, Daraka and Dinifarikh. All are flat and low, with deeply indented coasts and scanty rain and vegetation; some are normally or seasonally inhabited, to a total in all of 1500 to 2500 persons, Tigré-speaking Muslims who closely resemble the Samhar coastal tribesmen. They represent an Ethiopian base with an admixture of Arabs, Danākil, Somālīs and Sūdānīs. The islands afford miserable grazing for goats and camels, with some humble sea-trading, fishing, recovery of mother-of-pearl (and, in former times, pearls), and quarrying. The Italians, who used Nokra Island as a penal station for undesired politicians as well as prisoners, drilled unsuccessfully for petroleum in 1357-59/1938-40.

The derivation of the name is unknown; the islands are referred to to as ʾΕλαία in Artemidorus and the Periplus, and as Aliaeu by Pliny. Occupied by the Muslims in the 1st/7th century, Dahlak al-Kabīr was used as a place of exile or prison by the Umayyad Caliphs (whose détenus included the poet al-Aḥwas and the lawyer Arrāk) and later by the ʿAbbāsids. About the 3rd/9th century the islands passed under the Yamanī coastal dynasty of Zabīd, and in probably the 6th/12th achieved independence as an amīrate both wealthy (thanks to trade and ruthless piracy) and highly civilized, as many recovered documents and elegant Kūfic inscriptions testify. Allied at times with (or menaced by) the Mamlūks of Egypt, and with claims to rule part of the neighbouring mainland including Muṣawwaʿ, the Dahlak amīrs (called "kings" by Maḳrīzī) still fell intermittently under Ethiopian or Yamanī suzerainty. The Amīr ruling when the Portuguese appeared in 919/1513 was Aḥmad b. Ismāʿīl, whose opposition to the newcomers was punished by a devastation of his islands; but he was later restored as a Portuguese vassal. Adhesion to the cause of the Muslim conqueror and liberator Aḥmad Grañ against the Portuguese led, after temporary success and the appointment of Aḥmad Ismāʿīl's successor as Governor of Harkiko, to a second devastation and a mass evacuation of the islanders. Reoccupied, the islands fell easily to the Turkish fleets later in the century, and their fortunes were thereafter those of rarely-asserted Turkish suzerainty, actual or nominal dependence on Muṣawwaʿ, and temporary Egyptian Government in the second half of the 13th/19th century. When the Italians colonized Eritrea in 1885, the Dahlak Islands had long since ceased to offer any claims to interest. They became a Vice-Residenza, with headquarters at Nokra, in the Commissariato of Bassopiano Orientale. This was abolished as a separate administrative unit under the British occupation of Eritrea (1360-72/1941-52) and that of Ethiopia from 1372/1952 onwards.

Bibliography: C. Conti Rossini, *Storia d'Etiopia*, Milan 1928, Vol. i; Issel, *Viaggio nel Mar Rosso*, Milan 1889; R. Basset, *Les Inscriptions de l'île de Daklak*, in *JA*, Paris 1893; A. Pollera, *Le Popolazioni indigene dell'Eritrea*, Bologna 1935; G. Wiet, *Roitelets de Dahlak*, in *BIÉ*, 1952, 89-95. (S. H. LONGRIGG)

DAḤLĀN, SAYYID AḤMAD B. ZAYNĪ, born in Mecca towards the beginning of the 19th century, was from 1288/1871 Muftī of the Shāfiʿīs and *Shaykh al-ʿUlamāʾ* (head of the corporation of scholars and therefore of the body of teachers in the *Ḥaram*) in his native city. When the Grand Sharīf ʿAwn al-Rafīḳ, because of a dispute with the Ottoman Governor ʿUthmān Pasha, removed himself to Madīna, Daḥlān followed him there but died soon afterwards from the fatigue of the journey in 1304/1886. Particularly in his later years, Daḥlān was very active as an author. He not only covered the traditional Islamic sciences which were studied in Mecca in his time, but produced a number of treatises on controversial topical questions, and became the solitary representative of historical writing in Mecca in the 19th century. The most successful of his writings on traditional subjects were a commentary on the *Ādjurrūmiyya* (see IBN ĀDJURRŪM) and an edifying biography of the Prophet, known as *al-Sīra al-Zayniyya*, both of which were often printed. His *al-Durar al-Saniyya fi 'l-Radd ʿala 'l-Wahhābiyya* provoked a chain of pro-Wahhābī and anti-Wahhābī replies and counter-replies. His polemics against Sulaymān Effendi, one of two rival Turkish *shaykhs* of the Naḳshibandī *ṭarīḳa* in Mecca, who competed for the leadership of the Naḳshibandīs in Indonesia, and against the learned *shaykh* Muḥammad Ḥasab Allāh of Mecca, whose scholarly reputation equalled his own were not free of personal interest. Of his works on history, *al-Futūḥāt al-Islāmiyya*, a history of the Islamic conquests until the time of the author, is remarkable for the light it throws on his attitude to the contemporary Mahdist rising in the Sudan, and his history of Mecca, *Khulāṣat al-Kalām fi Bayān Umarāʾ al-Balad al-Ḥarām*, until the year 1095/1684 a short extract from the chronicle of al-Sindjārī (Brockelmann, II, 502), is a most valuable source for the events in Mecca during the following two centuries, including the rise of the Wahhābīs, their first rule over the Ḥidjāz, the fight of the Sharīfs against them, the restitution of Ottoman rule by Muḥammad ʿAlī, and the disorders in Djidda of 1274/1858. Being a friend of the family of the ruling Sharīfs, Daḥlān had access to the best written and oral information. The giving of *fatwā*s formed, of course, an important part of his activities, and some of his decisions were incorporated in the current handbooks of Shāfiʿī doctrine; in his last years, however, he handed over this routine work to his assistant or *amīn al-fatwā*, Sayyid Muḥammad Saʿīd Bābaṣēl (Brockelmann, II, 650, S II, 811). Snouck Hurgronje has drawn a detailed picture, based on close acquaintance, of his person and background.

Bibliography: Snouck Hurgronje, *Verspr. Geschr.*, iii, 65-122 (with two extracts from the *Khulāṣat al-Kalām*); Brockelmann, II, 649 f., S II, 810 f.; ʿAbd al-Ḥayy al-Kattānī, *Fihris al-Fahāris*, i, 290-2; Sarkīs, *Muʿdjam al-Maṭbūʿāt*, 990-2. (J. SCHACHT)

AL-**DAHNĀʾ**—in Saʿūdī Arabia—a long, narrow arch of *nafūd* or dune desert, varying in width from 10 to 75 km., extending around an eastward curve for a total length of over 1,000 km., connecting the Great Nafūd of the northwest with the Empty Quarter (al-Rubʿ al-Khālī [*q.v.*]) of the south, lacking in natural water sources except along the fringes, but furnishing a favourite area of pasturing.

In the past separating the interior area of al-Yamāma from the coastal region of al-Baḥrayn, al-Dahnāʾ today serves as an informal boundary between the Province of Nadjd and the Eastern Province (until 1953 the Province of al-Ḥasā or al-Aḥsāʾ). Its western edge formed a major sector of the westerly boundary of the petroleum concession granted in 1933 to American interests, although an area of potential priority extended still farther west. Beginning with the first well in 1957, an oil field has been discovered in the sand belt itself and adjacent easterly thereto—the Khurayṣ field, some 120 km. west of the immense Ghawār field and *ca.* 150 km. west of al-Hufūf (in the oasis of al-Ḥasā).

Al-Dahnāʾ is the easterly and much more continuous of two parallel strips of sand desert extending from al-Nafūd generally south-eastward (see DJAZĪRAT AL-ʿARAB, esp. p. 536[1]). According to tribal toponymy it begins in the north-easterly Nafūd projection some 50 km. west of Darb Zubayda, which crosses it roughly along the line of longitude 43° 32′ E., and ends far southward with the brownish *ʿirḳ*s of al-Duhm, which lie in the latitude of the district of al-Aflādj (to the west) and the well Muḳaynima (to the east), or just above 22° N. The final link with the southern sands is formed by the continuing band of ʿUrūḳ al-Rumayla, which joins the Empty Quarter slightly below the line of 20° N.

The upper portion of al-Dahnāʾ runs between the desert of al-Ḥadjara on the north and the upland of al-Taysiyya on the south, to the ancient channel of Baṭn al-Rumma (modern Wādī al-Rumah—Wādī al-Bāṭin). Here, just south of the small Wādī al-Adjradī, the Dahnāʾ sands spread south-westward so as to be connected, through the *nafūd* of al-Sayyāriyyāt, with those of Nafūd al-Maẓhūr and Nafūd al-Thuwayrāt in the westerly sand chain. Thereafter, al-Dahnāʾ continues between and roughly parallels the two arcs formed by the low, stony plateau of al-Ṣummān (classical al-Ṣammān), a part of which is called al-Ṣulb, on the east, and the lofty escarpment of Djabal Ṭuwayḳ on the west, but is longer than either. Closer on the west is the escarpment of al-ʿArama (not al-ʿArma), which is much shorter, ending southward at the discontinuous channel of Wādī Ḥanīfa—Wādī al-Sahbāʾ, through which the sand belt is crossed by the Saʿūdī Government Railway, completed in 1951. Beyond this second great channel, al-Dahnāʾ continues between the southerly Ṣummān (Ṣummān Yabrīn, etc.) on the east, and the eastward-sloping, gravelly limestone region of al-Biyāḍ on the west. Running on under the name of ʿUrūḳ al-Rumayla to join the sands of the Empty Quarter, the southernmost portion of the sand strip has to the east the gravel plains of Abū Baḥr and Raydāʾ, and to the west the lower part of al-Biyāḍ and the terminal stretch of Wādī al-Dawāsir (here called Wādī al-Aṭwāʾ).

Narrower in its northern and southern terminal reaches, al-Dahnāʾ attains its greatest width in the portion lying between the two ancient but now sand-choked *wādī* channels, and exhibits here its most striking features. In the area of Ḥawmat al-Niḳyān, which lies athwart the crossing of Darb al-Mubayḥīṣ above the line of 26° 30′ N., over 100 tall pyramidal dunes tower above the huge, long sand ridges and reach heights up to 175 m. These massive formations, which are also called "star dunes", seemingly ride upon the *ʿirḳ*s, but they actually rest upon their own bedrock and are separated from the surrounding sand massifs by peripheral hollows.

In normal seasons a choice pasture land to shepherds, al-Dahnāʾ has been described by travellers as a difficult barrier, because of its long, high *ʿirḳ*s and its lack of water. The dread which it inspired in those who were strangers to it is reflected in the account of how in 12 A.H., during the Wars of the *Ridda* an expedition to al-Ḳaṭīf and Dārīn temporarily lost its camel transport during the night of crossing and was saved from death only by the miraculous appearance of a lake of sweet water. (Caetani, *Annali*, ii-2, 722, with refs. to al-Ṭabarī, Ibn al-Athīr, Yāḳūt, and the *Kitāb al-Aghānī*).

In addition to descriptions of Darb Zubayda with its chain of cisterns, we have, from Arabic sources, information regarding other and even earlier routes crossing al-Dahnāʾ. However, the details of toponymy from a long-past era are often difficult to reconcile with those of the present, in which there are many changes. A motorable crossing (with connexions to Medina, Mecca, and al-Riyāḍ) more or less follows Darb Zubayda between Birkat al-Djumayma, on the Saʿūdī-ʿIrāḳī border, and the *ḳalīb* of Zarūd, in Shāmat Zarūd south-west of al-Taysīya. Two motor crossings, which connect with this route and offer better travel to Zarūd *via* the *ḳalīb* of Turaba, branch from Līna (on the outer edge of al-Dahnāʾ, with old wells cut through stone; the junction of several motor and caravan tracks to al-ʿIrāḳ). One leads first westward by Darb Līna to Buraykat al-ʿAshshār (beside Darb Zubayda, in al-Dahnāʾ), and thence south-westward by Darb Ḳabʿa. The other runs south-westward over Darb Umm Udhn to Birkat al-ʿArāʾish in al-Taysīya, and continues in the same direction *via* Darb Umm Ṭulayḥa to join Darb Ḳabʿa and to cross ʿIrḳ al-Maẓhūr north-west of Turaba.

It is the presence of lasting wells which fringe al-Dahnāʾ, or lie sufficiently near, that has made it possible for the Badw to take advantage of the normally abundant pasturage of the sand belt. However, it is common for tribal groups, going forth with their camels, goats, and sheep from summering places (*maḳāyiẓ*) at more distant wells or villages, to spend in al-Dahnāʾ (as also in other sand deserts) all or most of the cooler portion of the year, keeping in their tents little or no water, and depending for sustenance on the milk from their animals. When rainfall has made the herbage plentiful and succulent, the animals, described as *djawāzī* or *madjziya* (classical verb: *djazaʾa, yadjzaʾu*), often remain at pasture without watering for as long as four or even six months.

The excellence and amplitude of the pastureland of al-Dahnāʾ are described by Yāḳūt, who says that it has been mentioned by many poets, especially Dhu ʾl-Rumma.

Groups now pasturing regularly in al-Dahnāʾ are of the following tribes: in the north, from al-Nafūd to the wells of al-Bushūk, Shammar, and from al-Bushūk to Wādī al-Adjradī and the *zabāʾir* of al-Sayyāriyyāt, Ḥarb; therefrom to Darb al-Mubayḥīṣ, Muṭayr; thence to the crossings of the main north-south motor track and Darb al-ʿArʿarī, Subayʿ (with also some of Suhūl); thence through all the remaining portion of al-Dahnāʾ and through ʿUrūḳ al-Rumayla, al-Dawāsir. Groups of al-ʿUdjmān and of Ḳaḥṭān also range in the southern part of the pasture area of Subayʿ and the northern part of that of al-Dawāsir—*i.e.*, east of the wells of Ḥafar al-ʿAtk, Rumāḥ and al-Rumḥiyya, and Ramlān, al-Djāfiyya, and Siʿd. In addition, some of al-Ṣulaba range in the northerly area of al-Dahnāʾ.

There is little use in attempting to identify the "mountains" or "swords" of sand in al-Dahnāʾ as mentioned by various sources, especially Yāḳūt. The names have changed too much. Likewise, there is no profit in belabouring the question of the origin and meaning of the name *al-Dahnāʾ* itself. The name has often been explained as meaning "red". For the root *DHN*, there persists the sense of paucity of moisture (as in *dahan al-maṭar al-arḍ*), from which may have been derived the senses connected with ointment and oil, including cooking-fat and, in modern times, oil-base paints. The people use *ʿabl* (or *arṭā*)—which grows widely in al-Dahnāʾ—for tanning, but the resulting colour is expressed by *ḤMR*, not by *DHN*, which is reserved to the application of fat to make the leather pliable and soft. One association of redness in the language of the people concerning this desert may be found in the occasionally heard expression *arḍ madhūna*, which is explained as distinguishing the sands of al-Dahnāʾ, as of a brownish or a duller red, from those of al-Nafūd, which are said to be of a lighter shade of red. At the same time, the people also equate *arḍ madhūna* with *arḍ mundahina*, land only lightly or superficially moistened by rain.

Yāḳūt, in both the *Muʿḏjam* and the *Mushtarik*, lists several other places and topographical features under the name *al-Dahnāʾ* or *al-Dahnā*.

Bibliography (in addition to the geographers and historians mentioned above): Admiralty, *A Handbook of Arabia*, London 1916-17; anon., *Ḥudūd al-ʿĀlam* (ed. Minorsky), London 1937; Ibn Bulayhid, *Ṣaḥīḥ al-Akhbār*, Cairo 1370 A.H.; R. E. Cheesman, *In Unknown Arabia*, London 1926; H. R. P. Dickson, *The Arab of the Desert*, London 1949; idem, *Kuwait and Her Neighbours*, London 1956; Ibn Ḏjubayr, *Riḥla* (ed. Wright), Leiden 1907; D. G. Hogarth, *The Penetration of Arabia*, London and New York 1904; G. E. Leachman, *A Journey in Northeastern Arabia*, in *GJ*, xxxvii, 1911; idem, *A Journey Through Central Arabia*, in *GJ*, xliii, 1914; Roy Lebkicher, George Rentz, and Max Steineke, *The Arabia of Ibn Saud*, New York 1952; J. G. Lorimer, *Gazetteer of the Persian Gulf, ʿOmān, and Central Arabia*, Calcutta 1908-15; Alois Musil, *Northern Neḡd*, New York 1928; W. G. Palgrave, *Central and Eastern Arabia*, London 1865; Lewis Pelly, *A Visit to the Wahabee Capital, Central Arabia*, in *JRGS*, xxxv, 1865; H. St. J. B. Philby, *Across Arabia: from the Persian Gulf to the Red Sea*, in *GJ*, lvi, 1920; idem, *The Heart of Arabia*, London 1922; idem, *The Empty Quarter*, New York 1933; Barclay Raunkiaer, *Gennem Wahhabiternes Land paa Kamelryg*, Copenhagen 1913 (English trans. without maps and ills., *Through Wahabiland on Camel-Back*, Arab Bureau, Cairo 1916; German trans. by W. Schmidt, *Auf dem Kamelrücken durch das Land der Wahibiten*, 1917); Ameen Rihani, *Ibn Saʿoud of Arabia*, London 1928; G. F. Sadleir [Sadler], "Account of a Journey from Katif ... to Yamboo ...", *Transactions ... Lit. Soc. of Bombay*, iii, London 1823; idem, *Diary of a Journey Across Arabia ...* (comp. by P. Ryan), Bombay 1866; ʿUmar Riḍā Kaḥḥāla, *Ḏjughrāfiyat Shibh Ḏjazīrat al-ʿArab*, Damascus 1364/1945; Ferdinand Wüstenfeld, *Die Strasse von Baçra nach Mekka ...*, in *Abh. K. G. W. Gött.*, xvi, 1871; idem, *Bahrein und Jemâma, nach Arabischen Quellen ...*, *ibid.*, xix, 1874. Maps: Series by the U. S. Geological Survey and Arabian American Oil Company under joint sponsorship of the Ministry of Finance and National Economy (Kingdom of Saʿūdī Arabia) and the Department of State (U.S.A.). Scale 1 : 2,000,000: The Arabian Peninsula, Map 1-270 B-1 (1950). Scale 1 : 500,000 (geographic): Southern Ṭuwayḳ, Map I- 212 B (1956); Northern Ṭuwayḳ, Map I-207 B (1957); Western Persian Gulf, Map I-208 B (1958); Darb Zubaydah, Map I-202 (in press 1960). *The Times Atlas of the World, Mid-Century Edition* (Bartholomew), map of Arabia in Vol. II, London 1960. (C. D. MATTHEWS)

AL-**DAHNADJ**, Persian *dahna, dahāna, marmar-i sabz* ('green marble'), Turkish *dehne-i frengī*, malachite, the well known green copper-ore. The description of the mineral in the *Rasāʾil Ikhwān al-Ṣafā* goes back to the pseudo-Aristotelian lapidary. According to that, the malachite is formed in copper mines from the sulphur fumes which combine with copper to form layers. Its colour is compared to that of the chrysolith (*zabardjad*), although it does appear in different shades: dark green, veined, the shade of peacock's feathers, and pale green, with all intermediate shades. Frequently all the shades appear in one piece, as it developed in the earth, layer by layer. The stone is a soft one, and therefore looses its gloss with the years. Tīfāshī, following Balīnās (Apollonius of Tyana), explains how the very best copper is gained from it. There is new malachite and old, from Egypt, Kirmān, and Khurāsān. The very best kind is the old Kirmānian. The stone has been found in ancient Egyptian graves, usually in the form of amulets (scarabs), statuettes, and cut stones. Our detailed description of malachite comes from al-Rāzī, who also treats of the following: 1) its calcination (*i.e.*, its decomposition and the burning up of sulphur and oils which it contains), which can take place in 4 different ways; 2) its ceration, due to salts and borax, each again in 4 different ways; 3) its sublimation.

Taken in powder form and with vinegar, it is regarded as a powerful antidote to poison; on the other hand. it will harm a person who has not been poisoned, and then causes serious inflammations. If rubbed on the sting of a scorpion or a bee, it will reduce pain; it has also been used against leprosy and to cure diseases of the eye. Evidence in poetry can be found in al-Shammākh (*LA*, s.v. *dahnaḏj*).

Bibliography: *Rasāʾil Ikhwān al-Ṣafā* (ed. Bombay), ii, 81; Tīfāshī, *Azhār al-Afkār* (new edition of the translation by C. Raineri Biscia, Bologna 1906, 94); Ḳazwīnī, *ʿAḏjāʾib* (*Cosmography* ed. Wüstenfeld), i, 224; Ibn al-Bayṭār (ed. Būlāḳ 1291) ii, 117 f. (= Leclerc, *Traité des Simples*, ii, 132); Clément-Mullet, in *JA*, 6e série, tome xi (1868), 185 f.; Steinschneider, *WZKM*, xii (1898), 83; Ruska, *Das Steinbuch aus der Kosmographie des Al-Qazwini (Beilage zum Jahresbericht 1895/96 der prov. Oberrealschule zn Heidelberg)*, 22; idem, *Das Steinbuch des Aristoteles* 103 f., 145-147; idem, *Al-Rāzī's Buch Geheimnis der Geheimnisse*, 44, 86, 149 f., 177 f., 197 f.; Barhebraeus, *Muntakhab Kitāb Ḏjāmiʿ al-mufradāt li-Aḥmad .... al-Ghāfiḳī* (ed. Meyerhof and Sobhy) i/3, Cairo 1938, 117 (Arab.), 530 (Engl.); Wiedemann, *Beiträge* xxx, 227 (*SBPMS Erlg.*, xliv, 1912) after Ibn al-Akfānī, *Nakhb al-Dhakhāʾir*. (A. DIETRICH)

DAHOMEY, a corridor 418 miles long by 125 miles wide, between Togoland and Nigeria, is one of the earliest known countries on the Gulf of Guinea.

The coast is low-lying, fringed with lagoons, while the central zone is formed of table-land and isolated mountains; the northern part is higher, slanted across by the mountains of Atacora, which rise to about 800 metres. In the south especially, the humidity is high and the temperature fairly constant although there are two rainy and two dry seasons.

The population of Dahomey, nearly two million inhabitants, is chiefly composed of Fon (central region), Goun and Yoruba (south-east region), Adja (south-west), Bariba, Somba, and Fulani (northern region).

The principal town is Cotonou (87,000 inhabitants), although Porto-Novo has always been the administrative capital.

In contact with Europeans since the seventeenth century, Dahomey was particularly affected by the slave trade, which helped also to increase the wealth of certain of its kingdoms, notably that of Abomey.

It was this last which put up the longest and fiercest resistance to French penetration (1892).

Dahomey, which entered the federation of French West Africa in 1899, played a great part in its development, through the agency of its élites who had emigrated to the various other territories. Together with Senegal, it was one of the first to form political movements, which demonstrated their strength well before the second world war.

Dahomey, like most of its neighbours on the Gulf of Guinea who have been influenced by the Benin cultures, has retained the strong animistic foundation upon which rests the life of its civilization.

The social and religious organization of the country, where animism was the state religion, forbade the introduction of any foreign doctrine and it was not until the fall of the kingdom of Abomey that Christianity could begin to spread.

Islam could nowhere take root very deeply nor bring about large conversions as the chiefs and the local princelings were before the end of the nineteenth century never willing to renounce their beliefs, neither among the archaic clan societies of north-west Dahomey called *Somba*, nor in the feudal Bariba societies of the north-east region which was still crossed by the caravan routes marked out by the Islamic caravanserais, nor in the kingdoms of the south, absolute monarchies where the king was the all-powerful repository of the ancestral traditions which he revived each year in honour of his predecessors.

The Muslim penetration probably began from the north-east; a little commercial colony of the Mali Empire was set up in the thirteenth century in the region which is today Sokoto: the travellers of the time called it Guangara. It was from there that the waves of caravans departed for present-day Ghana, land of the kola. Salt, slaves and other products from the north, sometimes even from Libya, came down to the south-west while kola nuts passed up to the Nigerian and the Hausa lands, crossing North Dahomey. Thus there were quickly established little Muslim colonies called *Wangara* or *Maro*(in Dahomey) which soon blossomed into important centres like Parakou, Djougou or Kandi.

These foreign settlements remained near the local chiefs, whose domains were crossed by the caravan routes; they founded families and so introduced Islam, which slowly developed, by the simple device of local marriages.

Later on, the conquest of the Songhai empire by the Moroccans, at the beginning of the 17th century, brought about the withdrawal towards the Niger of a group of Muslim Songhai called Dendi. These established themselves probably in the extreme north of modern Dahomey and formed the second wave of the Islamic influence. The third wave corresponded to the immigration of the Fulani shepherds, who spread out during the 18th century over the whole of the northern half of Dahomey. Although their religion was still tinged with traces of animism, it formed none the less an Islamic centre which converted a great many of the former slaves or Gando, with whom they maintained permanent contact.

At length, in the last years of the eighteenth century, Islam also entered by the south-east and Porto-Novo, the present capital of Dahomey, soon contained some Muslim Yoruba merchants, who had come from Ilorin and from the west of modern Nigeria. They quickly increased, converted certain Yoruba families of Dahomey and also some descendents of the slaves who had returned from Brazil bearing Portuguese names.

Although it is difficult to draw up statistics, we can reckon that, of a total Dahomey population of 1,800,000 inhabitants, between 230 and 240 thousand are Muslim, of whom only 100,000 are practising devotees.

The greater part of them are Tidjānī; some, particularly among the older people, belong to the Ḳādiriyya order. There are a few Hamallists in the north. In spite of this near-unity of sect, a difference of belief set some Muslims, Yoruba in origin, against the natives of the northern regions (Hausa-Zerma-Fulani-Dendi), who claimed to practise their religion with greater orthodoxy. These two aspects of Islamic Dahomey are to be met chiefly at Porto-Novo (Islamic Yoruba) and at Parakou (the Islamic north), which were soon called upon to become the two great Muslim capitals, Djougou having slowly to give place to its neighbour Parakou, where some conversion movements had already been born and where there were established some of the masters of the Ḳurʾān who possessed a new and more dynamic conception of their religion.

It is probable that, in the years to come, the religious leaders and the *imāms* will be chosen more and more from among the most educated notables and no longer, according to heredity, from the families connected with the animist chiefs. This explains the rise today of the schools of the Ḳurʾān in North Dahomey in particular, where religious learning is always an object of prestige.

Bibliography: Akindele and Aguessy, *Le Dahomey*, Paris 1955; Akindele and Aguessy, *Contribution à l'étude de l'histoire de l'ancien royaume de Porto-Novo*, in *Mémoires IFAN*, xxv; d'Albeca, *Les établissements français du golfe du Benin*, Paris 1889; S. Berbain, *Le comptoir français de Juda au XVIIIe siècle*, in *Mémoires IFAN*, iii; G. Brasseur and Brasseur Marion, *Porto Novo et sa palmeraie*, in *Mémoires IFAN*, xxxii; Brunet and Giethlen, *Dahomey et dépendances*, Paris 1900; A. Burton, *A mission to Gelele, King of Dahomey*, London 1864; Desanti, *Du Dahomey au Benin Niger*, Paris 1945; Ed. Dunglas, *Contribution à l'Histoire du Moyen-Dahomey*, 3 vols. (*Études Dahoméennes*, xix, xx, xxi), Porto-Novo; Ed. Foa, *Le Dahomey*, Paris 1895; R. Grivot, *Réactions dahoméennes*, Paris 1945; P. Hazoume, *Le pacte de sang au Dahomey*, Paris 1937; idem, *Doguicimi*, Paris 1938; M. J. Herskovits, *Dahomè — an ancient West African Kingdom*, New York 1938; M. Hubert, *Mission Scientifique au Dahomey*, Paris 1908; H. Le Herisse, *L'ancien royaume du Dahomey*, Paris 1911; J. Lombard, *Cotonou, ville africaine* (*Études Dahoméennes*, x); B. Maupoil, *La géomancie à l'ancienne Côte des Esclaves*, Paris 1943; P. Mercier, *Carte ethno-démographique de l'Afrique Occidentale*, v, *IFAN* Dakar; M. Quenum, *Au pays des Fons*, Paris 1938; Skertchly, *Dahomè as it is*, London 1874; Cl. Tardits, *Porto-Novo*, London 1958; P. Verger, *Dieux d'Afrique*, Paris; idem, *Notes sur le culte des Oricha et Vodoun*, in *Mémoires IFAN*, v; R. Cornevin, *Histoire des peuples de l'Afrique noire*, Paris 1960, index.

(J. Lombard)

DAHR, time, especially infinitely extended time (cf. Lane; al-Bayḍāwī on Ḳ. 76.1). The pre-Islamic Arabs, as is shown by many passages in their poetry, regarded time (also *zamān*, and *al-ayyām*, the days) as the source of what happened to a man, both good and bad; they thus give it something of the connotation of Fate, though without worshipping it (W. L. Schrameier, *Über den Fatalismus der vorislamischen Araber*, Bonn 1881; Th. Nöldeke, *Encyclopedia of Religion and Ethics*, i, 661 b; for possible parallels cf. A. Christensen, *Iran*, 149 f., 157—Zurvān as both time and fate; Kronos, Chronos, as father of Zeus; cf. also R. C. Zaehner, *Zurvan*, Oxford 1955, esp. 254-61. This view is ascribed to pagans in the Ḳur'ān, 45. 24/23, "They say ... we die and we live and only *dahr* destroys us". Pre-Islamic conceptions probably influenced the Islamic doctrine of predestination (W. Montgomery Watt, *Free Will and Predestination in Early Islam*, London 1949, 20 ff., 31). Tradition supplies evidence of an attempt to identify God with *dahr*; Muḥammad is reported to have said that God commanded men not to blame *dahr* "for I am *dahr*" (*e.g.*, al-Bukhārī, *Tafsīr* on 45. 24/23; *Adab*, 101; *Tawḥīd*, 35; al-Ṭabarī, *Tafsīr* on 45. 24/23; further references in Wensinck, *Concordance*, s.v. *ādhā*, *khayb*; a possible connexion with funeral rites is noted by Goldziher, *Muhammedanische Studien*, i, 254); the Ẓāhiriyya [*q.v.*] are said to have reckoned *dahr* as a name of God (but cf. I. Goldziher, *Die Ẓâhiriten*, Leipzig 1884, 153 ff.). Many traditionists tried to interpret the tradition so as to avoid the identification (cf. Goldziher, *op. cit.* 155; Ibn Ḳutayba, *Ta'wīl Mukhtalif al-Ḥadīth*, Cairo 1326, 281-4). The *mutakallimūn* show no interest in the point, and al-Ghazzālī is able to use *dahr* for the views of the Dahriyya [*q.v.*], which are independent of pre-Islamic Arab sources (*Tahāfut al-Falāsifa*, ed. M. Bouyges, Beirut, 1927, 208.1). By poets and prose writers the word continued to be used in the pre-Islamic way (cf. al-Mutanabbī, ed. F. Dieterici, Berlin, 1861, 473, 576); a biographer says that *al-zamān*, time, and *al-ayyām*, the days, took away al-Ghazzālī (al-Subkī, *Ṭabaḳāt al-Shāfi'iyya*, Cairo 1324, iv, 109).

(W. Montgomery Watt)

DAHRIYYA, holders of materialistic opinions of various kinds, often only vaguely defined. This collective noun denotes them as a whole, as a *firḳa*, sect, according to the *Dictionary of the Technical Terms*, and stands beside the plural *dahriyyūn* formed from the same singular *dahrī*, the relative noun of *dahr*, a Ḳur'ānic word meaning a long period of time. In certain editions of the Ḳur'ān it gives its name to *sūra* LXXVI, generally called the *sūra* of Man; but its use in XLV, 24 where it occurs in connexion with the infidels, or rather the ungodly, erring and blinded, appears to have had a decisive influence on its semantic evolution which has given it a philosophical meaning far removed from its original sense. These ungodly men said: "There is nothing save our life in this world; we die and we live, and only a period of time (or: the course of time, *dahr*) makes us perish". The word has as yet no philosophical specification; according to the commentaries of al-Bayḍāwī and the Djalālayn, it signifies "the passage of time" (*murūr al-zamān*), according to al-Zamakhshari "a period of time which passes" (*dahr yamurru*) in XLV, 24, and an interval of time of considerable length in LXXVI, 1. The idea of a long period of time became increasingly dominant, and finally reached the point of signifying a period without limit or end, to such an extent that certain authors used *al-dahr* as a divine name, a practice of which others strongly disapproved (Lane, s.v. *dahr*; see also *Dictionary of the Technical Terms*, i, 480). The vocalization given in the new edition of the *Rasā'il Ikhwān al-ṣafā'*, Beirut 1376/1957, iii, fasc. 9, 455, is *duhriyya*; this had already been attested by linguists who considered it to be in conformity with the transformation which vowels often undergo in the *nisbas* (Sībawayhi, ed. Derenbourg, ii, 64, 19-21). Al-Djurdjānī, *Ta'rīfāt*, s.v., emphasizes the perenniality and defines *al-dahr* as "the permanent moment which is the extension of the divine majesty and is the innermost part (*bāṭin*) of time, in which eternity in the past and eternity in the future are united".

According to the explanation given by al-Bayḍāwī, a semantic link with the material world must be understood, for *dahr*, he says, basically denotes the space of time in which this world is living, overcoming the course of time. The doctrine of the *dahriyya* was subsequently denoted by the same term, and in this way al-Ghazālī, among others, speaks of "professing the *dahr*", *al-ḳawl bi 'l-dahr* (*Tahāfut*, ed. Bouyges, 19). The translation "fatalists", sometimes used, cannot be justified. The relative *dahrī* will therefore have two philosophical connotations. It denotes, firstly, the man who believes in the eternity of the world whether in the past or in the future, denying, as a result of this opinion, resurrection and a future life in another world; secondly, the *mulḥid*, the man who deviates from the true faith (Lane, s.v. *dahrī*; cf. for the first meaning given, Pococke, *Notae miscellanae*, Leipzig 1705, 239-240, under the transcription *Dahriani*). To place the whole of human life in this world is to lead swiftly to a hedonistic morality, and it is in this sense that the first literary use of the word has been noted, in the *Kitāb al-Ḥayawān* by al-Djāḥiẓ (Cairo 1325-6/1906-7) in which, in an over-wide generalization no doubt made under the influence of *sūra* XLV, 24, *dahrī* denotes the man who "denies the Lord", creation, reward and punishment, all religion and all law, listens only to his own desires and sees evil only in what conflicts with them; he recognizes no difference between man, the domestic animal and the wild beast. For him it is a question only of pleasure or pain; good is merely what serves his interests, even though it may cost the lives of a thousand men (vii, 5-6). It follows from the principles accepted by the *dahriyyūn* that they reject popular superstitions, the existence of angels and demons, the significance of dreams and the powers of sorcerers (al-Djāḥiẓ, *ibid.*, ii, 50). Some of them, however, on the basis of rationalist analogies, apparently admitted the metamorphosis of men into animals (*maskh*, *ibid.*, iv, 24).

The *dahriyya* are defined in the *Mafātīḥ al-'ulūm* (ed. Van Vloten, Leyden 1895, 35) as "those who believe in the eternity of the course of time"; the *Ikhwān al-ṣafā'* call them the *azaliyya*, those who believe in the eternity of the cosmos, as opposed to those who attribute to it a creator and a cause (ed. Bombay 1306, iv, 39; ed. Beirut 1376/1957, iii, 455). In this respect the *Mutakallimūn* are opposed to them, affirming the beginning in time of bodies and of the world created by God, and to this adding an affirmation of the divine attributes, God being alone eternal and alone powerful (*ibid.* Bombay 39-40 and Beirut 456). Like the *Mutakallimūn* in general, the Judaeo-Arab theologian Sa'adyā (d. 942) refutes their doctrine, first in his commentary on *Sēfer Yeṣīrah* (ed. Lambert, Paris 1891), and later in the first book of his *Kitāb al-Amānāt wa 'l-I'tiḳādāt* (ed. Landauer, Leyden 1880), in three pages (63-5) on the doctrine known by the name *al-dahr*, which regards not only matter as eternal but the beings of the world which we see as invariable; this sect limits knowledge to the perceptible: "no knowledge save of what is accessible to the senses" (64, l. 13). His translation of Job also alludes to it, for he renders *ōraḥ ʿōlām* by *madhāhib al-dahriyyīn*; cf. also several passages in his commentary on Proverbs (B. Heller, in *REJ*, xxxvii (1898), 229).

Abū Manṣūr ʿAbd al-Ḳāhir b. Ṭāhir al-Baghdādī does not mention them among the sects, in the *Kitāb al-farḳ bayn al-firaḳ*, but he refers to them several times among the unbelievers, particularly the philosophers who looked on the heavens and stars as a fifth element escaping corruption and destruction, and who even believed in the eternity of the world (ed. Badr, Cairo 1328/1910, 102, 106 with typogr. error, 206, 346). He also compares them with the Christians, without any explanation, 157.

Al-Ghazālī for his part also looked on the *dahriyya* rather as an order of philosophers who throughout the centuries expressed a certain current of thought which was never without some representative. He does not always regard them in the same way. In the *Munḳidh min al-Ḍalāl* (ch. III, Cairo 1955, 96-97), he speaks of them as forming the first category (*ṣinf*) in chronological order. They were then a "sect (*ṭāʾifa*) of the ancients", denying a Creator who governs the world and the existence of a future world, professing that the world has always been what it is, of itself, and that it will be so eternally. He likens them to the *zanādiḳa*, who also included another, and more numerous, branch, the *ṭabīʿiyyūn*, naturalists. The *dahriyya* seem to make the perenniality of the world the centre of their doctrine, whilst the *ṭabīʿiyyūn* insist upon the properties of temperaments and deny, not creation but paradise, hell, resurrection and judgement. Against these two categories there stands a third, the deists, *ilāhiyyūn*, who came later and included Socrates, Plato and Aristotle. They refuted the errors of the first two groups, but they were not always followed by the Muslim philosophers, such as Ibn Sīnā and al-Fārābī. Both were particularly singled out in the *Tahāfut al-Falāsifa* by al-Ghazālī (ed. Bouyges, Beirut 1927, 9) who with reference to them demonstrates the "Incoherence of the philosophers" (according to the translation preferred by M. Bouyges to "Destruction" of the philosophers), at the same time proving the incapacity (*taʿdjīz*) of the adversaries. For the two Muslims strove against those who denied the Divinity, though not without avoiding theories which led them to be classed by al-Ghazālī among the *dahriyya*. To the latter, who are also given the name *dahriyyūn*, are attributed the following theses: they deny a Cause which might be "causative of causes" (65, l. 3-4); the world is eternal and has neither cause nor creator; new things alone have a cause (133, l. 6 and 206, l. 5). Here there are only two groups of philosophers and not three, that of the "followers of truth" (*ahl al-ḥaḳḳ*) and one other, that of the *dahriyya* (133, l. 6). Now there are philosophers who believe that the world is eternal and, nevertheless, demonstrate that it is the work of a Creator (*ṣāniʿ*), a reasoning which al-Ghazālī declares to be contradictory (133, l. 6 ff.). In fact, Ibn Sīnā returns to this subject on many occasions, and he was clearly persuaded of the force of his reasoning. Al-Ghazālī, apparently not convinced, compares the *falāsifa* with the *dahriyya* (95, l. 6) on account of the ambiguity in a reasoning which allows that the work may be God's, provided that he had not planned to carry it out but had acted from necessity. This was very much what Ibn Sīnā maintained, believing that if God made some plan, his action would be determined by some external factor, which is inadmissible. Al-Ghazālī also finds fault with the theses which hold that from One only One can emerge (95-132), that matter is eternal, with the four elements on one hand, on the other the fifth, incorruptible element which forms the celestial bodies; all of these are reasons for classing those who hold these theories with the *dahriyya* (206, l. 5 ff.). In the *Tahāfut al-Tahāfut* (ed. Bouyges 1930), Ibn Rushd does not make the same strictures as al-Ghazālī; he does not name the *dahriyya* (see Index, 654) who only appear under this denomination in the summary of al-Ghazālī's theses (414, l. 5), but he uses *dahr* not only in the original sense of "period of time" (95, l. 1 and 120, l. 3) but also in the sense of the well-known philosophic doctrine wrongly attributed to the *falāsifa* (415).

The *dahriyya* appear as a sect, properly speaking, in the definitions of Ibn Ḥazm and al-Shahrastānī. The former ascribes to the *dahriyya* the doctrine of the eternity of the world, and the corollary that nothing rules it, whilst all the other groups think that there was a beginning and that it was created, *muḥdath* (*Kitāb al-Fiṣal*, Cairo 1317, i, 9). He starts by giving the five arguments of the *dahriyya* who are called (11, l. 9) "those who profess the *dahr*", *al-ḳāʾilūn bi 'l-dahr*. These may be summed up as follows: 1. "We have seen nothing which was newly produced (*hadatha*) unless it arose from a thing or in a thing". — 2. What produces (*muḥdith*) bodies is, incontestably, substances and accidents, that is to say, everything that exists in the world. — 3. If there exists a *muḥdith* of bodies, it is either totally similar to them or totally different, or similar in certain respects and different in others. Now a total difference is inconceivable, since nothing can produce something contrary or opposite to itself, thus fire does not produce cold. — 4. If the world had a Creator (*fāʿil*), he would act with a view to obtaining some benefit, of redressing some wrong, which is to act like the beings of this world, or else by nature, which would render his act eternal. — 5. If bodies were created, it would be necessary that their *muḥdith*, before producing them, should act in order to negate them, negation which itself would be either a body or an accident, which implies that bodies and accidents are eternal (10-11). After refuting these arguments in turn, Ibn Ḥazm gives five counter-arguments of his own, continuing the discussion (11-23) into the following chapter which is devoted to "those who say that the world is eternal and that, nevertheless, it has an eternal Creator".

Al-Shahrastānī begins the second part of his *Kitāb al-Milal wa 'l-Niḥal*, in which the philosophical sects are enumerated, with those who "are not of the opinion" that there is "a world beyond the perceptible world", *al-ṭabīʿiyyūn al-dahriyyūn*, "the naturalists who believe in *dahr*, who do not expound an intelligible [world]", *lā yuthbitūn maʿḳūlan*, this last word being in the singular (ed. Cureton, 201, l. 7). A second passage, "sometimes, on the other hand, . . . they also admit the intelligible, (ed. Cureton, 202, l. 15)" seems to apply not to the naturalists who believe in *dahr* but to the *falāsifa dahriyya*, that is to say, very probably to Ibn Sīnā and al-Fārābī, contrasting them with the naturalists; this fits well with the position of the two philosophers who, for their part, strenuously affirm that an intelligible world exists. Thus the *dahriyya*, while having features in common, on the one hand with the naturalists, and on the other with the philosophers, could not be identified with either. The passage, however, remains obscure. In the *Kitāb Nihāyat al-iḳdām* (ed. Guillaume, Oxford 1931, with partial translation) al-S̲h̲ahrastānī records several discussions between the *dahriyya* (trans. materialists) and their adversaries (29, l. 1; 30, l. 15,' 123, l. 10, 126, l. 9), on the origin of the world, including the theory of atoms moving about in primal disorder. The mode of reasoning of the *dahriyya* appears sophistical, but the refuters who rely on the movements of Saturn adduce no proof. The origin of the world through the fortuitous encounter of atoms wandering in space is an opinion also attributed to the *dahriyya* by D̲j̲amāl al-Dīn al-Ḳazwīnī, *Mufīd al-ʿulūm wa-mubīd al-humūm*, Cairo 1310, 37.

The 19th century brought definition to a word that for so long had been somewhat loosely used. European natural sciences, penetrating the East, gave rise to a stream of very simplified but materialistic ideas which were the source of unexpected problems in Islam. (For an Ottoman ferman of 1798, refuting the Dahrī doctrines of the French Revolution, see Amīr Ḥaydar Aḥmad S̲h̲ihāb, *Taʾrīk̲h̲ Aḥmad Bās̲h̲ā al-D̲j̲azzār*, edd. A. Chibli and I. A. Khalifé, Beirut 1956, 125 ff.; cf. B. Lewis in *Journ. World Hist.*, i, 1953, 121-2). The question of materialism was raised in an extremely acute form in India. After the Mutiny of 1857-8, Sayyid Aḥmad K̲h̲ān realised that the Muslims could not challenge the British supremacy until they had assimilated western science and methods. In 1875 he founded the college of ʿAlīgaṙh [*q.v.*], later to be a University, combining English culture with the study of Muslim theology. Deeply impressed by the concepts of *conscience* and *nature*, he took the laws of nature as criteria of religious values. This new conception spread, giving, with the Arabic termination, the qualifying word *naturī*, which became *nayčarī*, plural *nayčariyyūn*, from transcription of the English pronunciation; in Persian *nayčeriyyé*. It was presented as a sort of new religion, appearing in the *Census of India*, where its followers were called *nečari*. These events exercised considerable influence on the whole of India, and made it necessary for orthodox Islam to take position.

D̲j̲amāl al-Dīn al-Afg̲h̲ānī [*q.v.*] wrote a violent reply in Persian, as early as 1298/1878, with his *Refutation of the Materialists*, the translation of which into Urdū was lithographed in Calcutta in 1883; it was translated into Arabic by Muḥammad ʿAbduh and first published (1st. ed. Beirut 1303/1885) under the title *Risāla fī ibṭāl mad̲h̲hab al-dahriyyīn wa-bayān mafāsidihim wa-it̲h̲bāt anna 'l-dīn asās al-madaniyya wa 'l-kufr fasād al-ʿumrān*, then (2nd. ed., Cairo 1312, 3rd ed., Cairo 1320/1902) under the title *al-Radd ʿalā 'l-dahriyyīn* (French translation A.-M. Goichon, Paris 1942), while the original title included *al-nays̲h̲uriyyīn*, clearly denoting the meaning given to *dahrī* which is therefore the translation of naturalistic-materialistic. In this short work D̲j̲amāl al-Dīn traces back this doctrine to the Greek philosophers in terms recalling those of al-G̲h̲azālī; he traces its history, such as he represents it, in the first chapter; it finishes with Darwin. His refutation is, throughout, superficial.

While materialism was spreading, particularly through Arabic translations of European works like Büchner's *Kraft und Stoff*, translated by S̲h̲iblī S̲h̲umayyil (Alexandria 1884), a contrary movement was taking shape. The history of this struggle between two irreconcilable conceptions is far from finished; it would require considerable research, but has no place here. In the various works mentioned above, the terms *māddiyya* and *māddiyyūn* have, in fact, always been used as synonyms of *dahriyya* and *dahriyyūn*; these latter finally disappeared, replaced by the more exact term. They no longer occur in the contemporary vocabulary in Egypt (information supplied by R. P. Jomier) and, without being in a position to make the same observation in respect of other countries, we can nevertheless remark that they are no longer found in certain publications in Muslim India.

Bibliography: in the text; see also W. L. Schrameier, *Über den Fatalismus der vorislamischen Araber*, Bonn 1881, 12-22; M. Horten, *Die philosophischen Systeme der spekulativen Theologen im Islam*, Bonn 1912, index s.v. Dahriten.

(I. Goldziher-[A. M. Goichon])

DAḤS̲H̲ŪR, a place in the province of D̲j̲īza, some 40 kms. south of Cairo, to the west of the Nile on the edge of the desert. A necropolis and pyramids dating from the first dynasties of the Old Kingdom are situated there. These relics of the age of the Pharaohs are mentioned by al-Harawī and al-Maḳrīzī without a precise description being given. Abū Ṣāliḥ speaks of a great church and an important monastery there.

The present-day hamlet is insignificant and the name continues to be well known solely on account of the pyramids.

Bibliography: Ibn Mammātī, 138; al-Harawī, *Ziyārāt*, 39; Abū Ṣāliḥ, fol. 53; Yāḳūt, ii, 633; Maḳrīzī, ed. Wiet, ii, 120, iii, 39, iv, 122; ʿAlī Pas̲h̲a, xi, 67; Maspero and Wiet, *Matériaux pour servir à la géographie de l'Égypte*, 94.

(G. Wiet)

DĀʿĪ (rarely, dāʿiya), "he who summons" to the true faith, was a title used among several dissenting Muslim groups for their chief propagandists. It was evidently used by the early Muʿtazilites [*q.v.* in *EI*[1]]; but became typical of the more rebellious among the S̲h̲īʿīs. It appears in the ʿAbbāsid mission in K̲h̲urāsān; and in some Zaydī usage. It was ascribed to followers of Abu 'l-K̲h̲aṭṭāb. It was especially important in the Ismāʿīlī and associated movements (which were called *daʿwa*, "summons"), where it designated generically the chief authorized representatives of the *imām*.

Among the Ismāʿīlīs, at the height of the movement, the *dāʿīs* were organized hierarchically. (They have been compared to Christian bishops). The terms applied to the several ranks varied according to context (and probably the manner of ranking was not rigidly fixed). The chief of the *dāʿīs*, mouthpiece of the *imām*, was called *bāb* [*q.v.*] or *dāʿī al-duʿāt*. The greater dāʿīs (nominally, at least, the top twelve of them) were called *ḥud̲j̲d̲j̲a*, "proof" of the truth, or, perhaps earlier, *naḳīb*; they seem each to have been in charge of a district (*d̲j̲azīra*, island) where the *daʿwa* was preached. In some works, the *ḥud̲j̲d̲j̲a* was called *lāḥiḳ* and the *dāʿī* was called *d̲j̲anāḥ* (cf. W. Ivanow, *Studies in Early Persian Ismailism*, Leiden 1948, 2nd ed. Bombay 1955, ch. ii). Each *dāʿī* was apparently assigned to a particular territory, within which he evidently had extensive authority over the faithful, initiating new converts and admitting them by steps into the esoteric doctrine, the *bāṭin* [*q.v.*]. He was assisted by subordinates, entitled *maʾd̲h̲ūn* (licensed to preach), *mukāsir* (persuader), etc.

Except where the *imām* himself was in power as Caliph, the *daʿwa* was usually a secret, conspiratorial movement. Accordingly, while a *dāʿī* in Ismāʿīlī-held lands had a high position in the state (the *dāʿī al-duʿāt*, at the head of all official religious matters, seems to have been on a level with the *wazīr*, if not united with him in one person), the *dāʿīs* in other lands often had adventurous lives and sometimes ended bloodily. Many served as military leaders, particularly before the Fāṭimid state was established (for instance, the Ḳarmaṭian leaders; and Abū ʿAbd Allāh al-S̲h̲īʿī, who led Berber tribesmen in the revolt which established al-Mahdī in the Mag̲h̲rib). Later, they still had to have a gift for political intrigue (some tried to convert the leading figures at the local court, or even the *amīr* himself; thus al-Muʾayyid fi 'l-Dīn al-S̲h̲īrāzī at the Būyid court), for they were not only preachers but agents of the Fāṭimid state. Nevertheless, the *dāʿīs* were often independent scholars; vigorous theological and philosophical controversies were carried on among them, and the chief Ismāʿīlī books seem to have been written by *dāʿīs*, many of the most important by those labouring in hostile Iran.

In the parallelism drawn between the Ismāʿīlī *ḥudūd*, religious ranks, and the principles of cosmic emanation from the One, the *dāʿī* was sometimes associated with "time" or with the *k̲h̲ayāl*, "fantasy". For such purposes, the *ḥud̲j̲d̲j̲a* formed a separate rank between the *dāʿī* and the *imām*, as did the *bāb* [*q.v.*].

The title *dāʿī* came to mean something different in each of the sects which issued from the classical Fāṭimid Ismāʿīlism. Among the first Druzes, the *dāʿīs* performed similar functions, but formed a rank directly dependent on the fifth of the great *ḥudūd*, the *tālī* (Bahāʾ al-Dīn); cosmically, they embodied the *d̲j̲idd* ("effort"). Subsequently they became superfluous. The Nizārīs ("Assassins") inherited the Ismāʿīlī organization in the Sald̲j̲ūḳ domains, which seems to have been headed by the *dāʿī* of Iṣfahān; *dāʿī* became the ordinary title for the chief of the sect, resident from the time of Ḥasan-i Ṣabbāḥ at Alamūt (in the name of an unknown *imām*), until in 559/1164 the then *dāʿī* proclaimed himself the actual *imām*. (Ḥasan-i Ṣabbāḥ was evidently also regarded as *ḥud̲j̲d̲j̲a* in a special sense). The Ṭayyibī *daʿwa* of the Yaman separated from the official Fāṭimid organization under a *dāʿī muṭlaḳ*, an "absolute" or sovereign *dāʿī*, who claimed to be the representative of the true line of *imāms*, themselves in *satr*, occultation. The *dāʿī* had full authority over the community, and the Ṭayyibīs split more than once over his person; in the mid-twentieth century there are two main rival *dāʿīs*, one seated traditionally in the Yaman (Sulaymānī) and one seated in Bombay (Dāʾūdī).

For bibliography, see ISMĀʿĪLĪS.

(M. G. S. HODGSON)

DĀʿĪ, AḤMAD B. IBRĀHĪM, Turkish poet of the end of the 8th/14th and the beginning of the 9th/15th century. The scanty information about his life is scattered in his works and in *tedhkires*. A *ḳāḍī* by profession, he began to gain prominence as a poet at the court of the Germiyān in Kütahya under princes Sulaymān and Yaʿḳūb II. He seems to have travelled a great deal in Anatolia and in the Balkans. During the chaotic years of struggle between the sons of Bāyezīd I after the battle of Ankara (804/1402), he entered the service of one of them, *amīr* Sulaymān in Edirne, whose court had become a gathering place for many famous men of letters of the period such as Aḥmedī, his brother Ḥamzawī and Sulaymān Čelebi. He continued to flourish at court under Meḥemmed I (816/1413-824/1421) and became tutor to his son, the future Murād II. The sources do not agree on the date of Dāʿī's death; Ḥād̲j̲d̲j̲i K̲h̲alīfa gives the year 820/1427, but there is evidence that he might still have been living during the first years of Murād II (824/1421-848/1444) (I. H. Uzunçarşılı, *Kütahya Şehri*. Istanbul 1932, 213). With the exception of Sehī (*Ted̲h̲kire*, 56) who has a short but appreciative note on him, until recently both Ottoman and modern scholars have considered Dāʿī a minor poet as but a few of his works were known. Since many of his works, specially an incomplete copy of his *dīwān* and his remarkable *mat̲h̲nawī Čeng-nāme*, have come to light (Ahmed Ateş, *Türk Dili ve Edebiyatı Dergisi*, 3-4, 172-4) Dāʿī has proved to be an outstanding poet of his period, without doubt superior in richness of inspiration, originality, mastery of technique and fluency of style to many of his contemporaries.

Apart from various religious treatises (I. H. Ertaylan, *Ahmed-i Dâʿî*, Istanbul 1952) Dāʿī is the author of: (i) *Dīwān*; the only known copy is in Burdur Waḳf Library no. 735; it is incomplete and not arranged alphabetically, containing his later poems: six *ḳaṣīdas* two of which are dedicated to Meḥemmed I and 199 *g̲h̲azals*. (ii) *Čeng-nāme*, called wrongly *D̲j̲enk-nāme* by some sources (Gibb, *Ottoman Poetry*, i, 256) and confused with S̲h̲ayk̲h̲og̲h̲lu's *Faraḥ-nāme* (*K̲h̲urs̲h̲īd-nāme*) by others (ʿĀlī, *Kunh al-Ak̲h̲bār* and Bursalî Meḥmed Ṭāhir, *ʿOt̲h̲manlî Müʾellifleri*, s.v.) is a *mat̲h̲nawī* of over 1400 couplets, dedicated to Amīr Sulaymān in 808/1405. In this allegory, the human soul is symbolized by the harp, whose heavenly music is a sign of its divine origin and which seeks the mystic paths of return to oneness with God. In a cheerful party on a flower-strewn lawn in spring, the poet asks the harp why it is so sad yet plays joyful melodies. Thereupon the four parts of the instrument tell him their stories: the silk of the strings came from worms which fed on the flesh of Job before eating the leaves of mulberry trees; the wood of the frame was a beautiful cyprus; the parchment covering the wood a gentle gazelle which was cruelly killed by hunters, and the hairs of the key were from the tail of a magnificent horse killed by the Tatars. This *mat̲h̲nawī* full of vivid description and rich imagery, told in a moving and colourful style of unusual fluency compares favourably with the best contemporary narratives and even with those of the classical period. (iii) *Tarassul*, a letter-writer which became a classic and long remained a popular hand-book (Sehī, *Ted̲h̲kire*, 56); (iv) *Muṭāyabāt*, a small book of 12 light poems; (v) *Waṣiyyat-i Nūs̲h̲irwān-i ʿĀdil*, a short didactic *mat̲h̲nawī*, probably translated from the Persian; (vi) *ʿUḳūd al-D̲j̲awāhir*, a short Persian rhyming vocabulary, written for the use of his princely pupil, the future Murād II; (vii) Persian *Dīwān*, autograph copy written in 816/1413 is in Bursa, Orhan Library no. 66; it is dedicated to K̲h̲ayr al-Dīn Hād̲j̲d̲j̲i K̲h̲alīl Bey; (viii) *Tafsīr*, translation of Abu 'l-Layt̲h̲ al-Samarkandīʿs Ḳurʾān commentary, with an introduction in verse, both in simple language and unadorned style, dedicated to Umur Bey b. Timurtas̲h̲ (Üniversite Library T. Y. 8248); (ix) also attributed to Dāʿī, a translation of the *Tad̲h̲kirat al-Awliyāʾ*, ʿAṭṭār's well known biographies and sayings of Muslim mystics.

Bibliography: The *Ted̲h̲kires* of Sehī, Laṭīfī, Ḳînali-zāde Ḥasan Čelebi, and the biographical section in ʿĀlī's *Kunh al-Ak̲h̲bār*, s.v.; Hammer-Purgstall, *Gesch. d. Osm. Dichtkunst*, i, 72; Gibb, *Ottoman Poetry*, i, 256 ff.; I. H. Ertaylan, *Ahmed-i Dâʾî*, Istanbul 1952, a voluminous collection where *facsimile* editions of the Turkish *Dīwān* and the *Čeng-nāme* and extracts from other works have been put together with all available data from sources; A. Bombaci, *Storia della letteratura turca*, Milan 1956, 297-9. (Fahir İz)

ḌAʿĪF [see al-djarḥ wa'l taʿdīl].

DAḲAHLIYYA, name of an Egyptian province in the eastern region of the Delta. It owes its name, which is an Arabicized form of the Coptic Tkehli, to the town called Daḳahla which was situated between Damīra and Damietta, a little closer to the latter than the former. At one time famous for its paper mills, it is now but an insignificant village.

The province was created at the end of the 5th/11th century and it has survived till today with some changes in its boundaries. At present it extends along the eastern bank of the Damietta branch of the Nile, which marks its western boundary, and ends on the south-east at the province of Sharḳiyya. Its chief town is now Manṣūra.

Bibliography: Ibn Khurradādhbih, 82; Ḳudāma, 48; ʿAlī Pasha, xi, 17; Maspero and Wiet, *Matériaux pour servir à la géographie de l'Égypte*, 90, 186-91. (G. Wiet)

DAKAR [see Supplement].

DAKHAN (Deccan). This word is derived from the Sanskrit word *dakshiṇa* 'right (hand)', hence 'south', since the compass points were determined with reference to the rising sun. The conventional line dividing north India from the south is formed by the south-western spurs of the Vindhyas along with their continuation called the Satpuṛās; peninsular India to the south of this line is usually further divided into (i) Deccan proper, extending up to the Tungabhadra, and (ii) south India extending right up to the southernmost tip of the peninsula. Physically also these two parts form two distinct units. For, while the Deccan plateau is formed by the great lavaic upland slowly rising from a point a few miles west of the deltas of the Godāvarī and the Krishṇa ending abruptly in the Western Ghāṭs, the country lying to the south of the Tungabhadra and touching the port of Goa has a distinct crystalline character. The Deccan proper, therefore, may be said to consist of five sections, *viz.*, (i) the western section enclosed by the sea and the Western Ghāṭs, called the *dēsh*, the original home of the Marāṭhas; this has extended beyond the Ghāṭs to include the whole territory with Aḥmadnagar and Poona as its principal towns; (ii) the area known as Berār during the Middle Ages and which is now known according to the ancient appellation of Vidarbha, with Nāgpur as its principal town; (iii) Marāṭhwāda, the Marāṭhi-speaking part of the old Ḥaydarābād State with its centre at Awrangābād; (iv) Tilangāna where Telugu is the mother-tongue of a large part of the population, with Ḥaydarābād as its historical and cultural capital; (v) the south-western portion populated mainly by the Kannadigās, with Bīdjāpur as its chief town.

Even if we disregard the legendary war between Rāma and Rāvaṇa, the Aryanization of the Deccan up to the far south must have been complete by the end of the Mawrya rule. There is little to relate between the fall of the Mawryas and rise of the Āndhras who ruled practically the whole of the Deccan plateau for five hundred years. We also read of the Ikshvakus of Nāgardjunakoṇḍa, the Vakaṭakas of Berar, the Western Čālukyas of Badāmī and Kālyanī, the Rāshṭrakūtas of Malkhēd, the Eastern Čālukyas of Vengī, the Yādavas of Deogiri and the Kākatīyas of Warangal, who ruled in different parts of the Deccan during the centuries preceding the Muslim conquest.

The first contact of the Deccan with the Muslims of the north was in 693/1294 when ʿAlāʾ al-Dīn, nephew of Sulṭān Djalāl al-Dīn Fīrūz Khaldjī of Dihlī, marched to Deogiri [see dawlatābād] and forced the Yādava Radja Rāmačandra to pay tribute. It was, however, not till 718/1318 that this kingdom, which extended to most of the Marāṭha country, was annexed to the Dihlī Empire. Sulṭān Muḥammad b. Tughluḳ not merely added the dominions of the Kākatīyas of Warangal to his Empire but annexed a large portion of south India as well, making Deogiri his second capital and renaming it Dawlatābād [*q.v.*]. But he could not control his far-flung empire effectively, and in 746/1345 his Deccan nobles, the *amīrān-i ṣadah*, revolted and chose Ismāʿīl Mukh as the first independent Muslim ruler of the Deccan. He was replaced by Ẓafar Khān as king, with the title of ʿAlāʾ al-Dīn Ḥasan Bahman Shāh in 748/1347, who thus became the founder of the Bahmanī kingdom [see bahmanids]. The Bahmanids spread their Empire over the whole of the Deccan from sea to sea and ruled it first from Aḥsanābād-Gulbarga [see gulbarga] and then from Muḥammadābād-Bīdar [see bīdar]. Towards the end of the 15th and the beginning of the 16th centuries the governors of the Bahmanid provinces became first autonomous and then independent, and the Deccan was finally divided into the five kingdoms of Aḥmadnagar, Bīdjāpūr, Berār, Bīdar and Golkoṇḍā under the Niẓāmshāhī, ʿĀdilshāhī, ʿImādshāhī, Barīdshāhī and Ḳuṭbshāhī dynasties respectively. Berār and Bīdar were soon absorbed into Aḥmadnagar which was itself annexed to the Mughal Empire during the reign of Shāh Djahān in 1042/1633. The turn of the extinction of Bidjapur and Golkoṇḍa did not come till 1097/1686 and 1098/1687 when the Emperor Awrangzīb ʿĀlamgīr annexed these two kingdoms to his vast Empire. But the Mughal authority in the Deccan was undermined by the continuous raids of the Marāṭhas who established a separate kingdom under Shivadjī in 1085/1674 and which forced the Emperor to direct his strategy from Awrangābād where he died in 1119/1707. The next important date in the history of the Deccan is 1136/1724 when Niẓām al-Mulk Āṣaf Djāh [*q.v.*] defeated Mubāriz Khān at Shakarkhēṛa and established his hegemony over the whole of the Deccan. The dynasty of the Āṣafdjāhīs ruled the Deccan first from Awrangābād and then from Ḥaydarābād [*q.v.*] effectively till 1948 when the Ḥaydarābād State was integrated into the Indian Union. The Niẓām, Sir Mīr ʿUthmān ʿAlī Khān, Āṣaf Djāh VII, was appointed *Rādjpramukh* or constitutional head of the state by the President of the Indian Union and acted as such till 1956 when the Ḥaydarābād State was partitioned between Andhra Pradesh, Bombay State and Mysore State more or less according to linguistic affinities.

Bibliography: R. G. Bhandarkar, *Early History of the Dekkan down to the Mahomedan Conquest*, 2nd. ed. Bombay 1895; S. K. Aiyangar, *South India and her Muhammadan Invaders*, London 1921; J. S. King, *History of the Bahmani Dynasty*, London 1900; Sherwani, *The Bahmanis of the Deccan, an Objective Study*, Ḥaydarābād, n. d,; J. D. B. Gribble, *History of the Deccan, Vol. I*, London 1936; Yūsuf Ḥusayn Khān, *Niẓāmu 'l-Mulk Aṣaf Jāh I.*, Mangalore 1936.

(H. K. Sherwani)

DAKHANĪ [see URDŪ],

AL-**DĀKHIL** [see ʿABD AL-RAḤMĀN].

DAKHĪL. The dictionaries (*LA*, *TA*, etc.) give a general meaning, "interior, inward, intimate", and two particular derived meanings, (1) guest, to whom protection should be assured, and (2) stranger, passing traveller, person of another race. The first of the particular meanings relates to an institution of nomadic common law which guarantees protection, in traditional ways, to whoever requests it. Although the concept has at all times existed, it has never been incorporated into Islamic law, which has no technical term corresponding to it. In its practical application, the institution combines elements of the complex system of ties of hospitality to which general opinion seems to assimilate the rights of the *dakhīl* and of a very old law of refuge in private households which is attested all over the Semitic world (cf. DJIWĀR). See in particular the detailed analysis by A. Jaussen, *Coutumes des Arabes au pays de Moab*, Paris 1948, 202-20, and Burckhardt's notes on the same subject in *Notes on the Bedouins*, London 1831, i, 329-38; see also Layard, *Narrative of a second expedition to Assyria*, London 1867, ch. VI, 139-62, and Caskel, *apud* Oppenheim, *Die Beduinen*, Leipzig 1939, i, 29.

From this last meaning, several meanings of the word as a technical term in philology, regarded as "late" by the lexicographers, have been derived, notably (1) "a foreign word borrowed by the Arabic language", like *dirham*, and (2) metrical term denoting the consonant preceding the rhyming consonant, the *dakhīl* itself being preceded by an *alif* (cf. ʿARŪḌ). (J. LECERF)

DĀKHLA WA KHĀRDJA [see AL-WĀḤĀT].

DAKHNĪ [see URDŪ].

DAḲĪḲĪ, ABŪ MANṢŪR MUḤAMMAD B. AḤMAD (or Muḥammad b. Muḥammad b. Aḥmad), the poet to whom we owe the oldest known text of the national epic in the Persian language. His place of birth is uncertain (Ṭūs, Bukhārā, Balkh or Samarḳand); he was born between 318 and 329/930 and 940, for he was at least twenty years old when he became panegyrist to the amīrs of Čaghāniyān, then of the Sāmānid amīr Manṣūr b. Nūḥ (350-366/961-976); further, Firdawsī, who continued after him the composition of *The Book of the Kings* (*Shāh-nāma*), assures us that Daḳīḳī was a young man when he began this work, at the behest of the amīr Nūḥ. b. Manṣūr, 366-387/976-997; Daḳīḳī therefore did not die before the time of this prince; and Firdawsī resumed the composition of the *Shāh-nāma* about 370/980, after the murder of his precursor by a slave (a murder provoked by his bad character (*khūy-i bad*) according to Firdawsī).

In the anthologies (*Lubāb al-Albāb*, *Madjmaʿ al-Fusaḥāʾ*, *Tardjumān al-Balāgha* etc.) there are lyrical pieces and fragments which bear witness to Daḳīḳī's precocious skill, his subtle and delicate mind, his easy style. But the work by which he is immortalized is the part of the *Shāh-nāma* (about a thousand lines) incorporated in the poem by his successor, Firdawsī: the reign of the king Goshtāsp, the appearance and the deeds of Zardosht (Zoroaster), and the war against their Chionite enemies.

The Zoroastrian faith of Daḳīḳī seems to assert itself in one of his *rubāʿis* and in other of his poems, in spite of his Muslim names. Did he remain Zoroastrian at heart? If he had been sincerely attached to Islam, would he, in undertaking the composition of the *Shāh-nāma* on the order of the Sāmānid amīr (a strictly orthodox Muslim), have straightway extolled the rise of Zoroastrianism and the war which it provoked? Howbeit, it is very probable, if not certain, that he chose this episode because he had at his disposal a copy of the *Memorial of Zarīr* (*Ayatkār-i Zarīrān*), a text from the Sāsānid period in Pahlawī verse (as E. Benveniste has shown) from which he drew direct inspiration. It may be that he had also put into verse other episodes from the *Shāh-nāma*, if we take into consideration some of his poems, epic in style and metre, scattered through the anthologies (*tadhkira*).

What remains of Daḳīḳī's lyrical poems shows his remarkable ability to vary his inspiration according to the descriptive, bacchic or amorous styles; quotations from his verse, numerous in the Persian anthologies and dictionaries, give proof of the lasting fame he enjoyed after his too-short career. Indeed his collaboration in the *Shāh-nāma* is as important for its own value as for the light it throws on the sources of the great national poem of Īrān.

Bibliography: Firdawsī, *Book of the Kings* (*Shāh-nāma*), ed. and trans. J. Mohl, 4to edition, iv, 358-730; 12mo edition, iv, 287 ff.; ed. Vullers-Landauer iii, 495-1747; Tehran ed. 1934-35 (pub. Beroukhim), vi; E. Benveniste, *Le Mémorial de Zarēr*, in *JA*, ccxx, (1932), no. 2, 245 ff. Lyrical poems: G. Lazard, *Les premiers poèmes persans*, critical edition, annotated, translation and bio-bibliography (in the press).

(CL. HUART-[H. MASSÉ])

AL-**DAḲḲĀḲ,** ABŪ ʿABD ALLĀH, Moroccan saint born at Sidjilmāsa. He and a certain Abū ʿAbd Allāh Muḥammad b. ʿUmar al-Aṣamm who was assassinated in 542/1147-8 belonged to one of the small circles of Ṣūfīs generally disapproved of by authority. This Abū ʿAbd Allāh had already been imprisoned at Fez at the same time as some of his companions, among whom one was al-Daḳḳaḳ, who on the orders of Tāshufīn b. ʿAlī the Almoravid was afterwards released.

No one knows the date of birth of this saint, nor that of his death. All the same, one can be sure that towards the middle of the 6th/12th century he had become known as a disciple of Ṣūfism at Fez, where his *aḥwāl* had aroused the kindly sympathy of Ibn al-ʿArīf and Ibn Barradjān, both of whom died in 536/1141.

If we may believe al-Tādilī, al-Daḳḳāḳ went to and fro between Sidjilmāsa and Fez. It was in Fez that he met Abū Madyan at a time when the latter, seeking instruction, was studying the *Riʿāya* of al-Muḥāsibī under the direction of Abu 'l-Ḥasan b. Ḥirzihim and the *Sunan* of al-Tirmidhī with Ibn Ghālib. Al-Daḳḳāḳ and a person of the name of Abu 'l-Salāwī initiated him into Ṣūfism (*Tashawwuf*, 319). It is because he was one of the masters of Abū Madyan that al-Daḳḳāḳ has not sunk into obscurity.

He led a life of renunciation, and was, it seems, before all else, a disciple of Ṣūfism rather than a scholar. His manner of claiming sanctity and the satisfaction which he felt when it was acknowledged has something displeasing about it. He died at Fez, most probably, according to A. Bel, at the latest in the last quarter of the 6th/12th century. He is buried in the cemetery of Bāb al-Gīsa.

Bibliography: A. Bel, *Sidi Bou Medyan et son maître Ed-Daqqâq à Fès*, in *Mélanges René Basset*, Paris 1923, i, 31 ff.; al-Tādilī, *Al-Tashawwuf ilā Ridjāl al-taṣawwuf*, ed. A. Faure, Rabat 1958, 135-7.

(A. FAURE)

DAḲŪḲĀʾ (or Daḳūḳ), a small town in the D̲j̲azīra province of the ʿAbbāsid empire, some 25 miles S.E. of Kirkūk on the Mosul-Bag̲h̲dād trunk-road, was known to the later Arab geographers and perhaps emerged into urban status, though never eminence, in the 5th/11th century. Some medieval brickwork and a minaret survive. The later and present name (from 9th/15th century, or earlier) was Ṭāwūḳ or Ṭāʾūḳ. The town, on flat ground immediately west of the foothills, stands healthy and well-watered beside the broad Ṭāʾūḳ Chay, a trickle in summer but a formidable flood after winter rains: this now flows into the ʿAẓaim river, and thence to the Tigris, but passed into the great Nahrawān canal when that existed. In modern ʿIrāḳ Ṭāʾūḳ, with some 2,000 Kurdish and Turkish-speaking inhabitants, is today a *nāḥiya* headquarters, partially modernized, and an agricultural and market centre for the surrounding Kurdish tribesmen (Dāʾūdīyya and Kākaʾī) and Turkoman villagers. The ʿIrāḳ Railways line, and the main road, cross the Ṭāʾūḳ Chay by modern bridges. A well-known shrine of Zayn al-ʿĀbidīn b. Ḥusayn is 1.5 miles distant.

Bibliography: Le Strange, 92, and the Arab authorities there noted. ʿAbd al-Razzāḳ al-Ḥasanī, *al-ʿIrāḳ Ḳadīm^an wa Ḥadīth^an*; Sidon 1367/1948, 197. Undersigned's own observations.

(S. H. Longrigg)

DĀL, 8th letter of the Arabic alphabet, transcribed *d*; numerical value 4, in accordance with the order of the letters in the Syriac (and Canaanite) alphabet, where *d* is the fourth letter [see abd̲j̲ad]. It continues a *d* of common Semitic.

Definition: *voiced dental occlusive*; according to the Arab grammatical tradition: *s̲h̲adīda, mad̲j̲hūra.* For the *mak̲h̲rad̲j̲*: *niṭʿiyya* according to al-K̲h̲alīl (al-Zamak̲h̲s̲h̲arī, *Mufaṣṣal*, 2nd ed. J. P. Broch, 191, line 1), who places the point of articulation at the *niṭʿ* (or *niṭaʿ*), the anterior part of the hard palate, 'its striped part' (Ibn Yaʿīs̲h̲, 1460, line 19) and so: *prepalatal.* This articulation has left traces in modern dialects (Lebanon, Syria: M. Bravmann, *Materialien*, 69; H. Fleisch, *Zahlé*, in *MUSJ*, xxvii, 78). Another tradition, based on the *Kitāb* of Sībawayh (Paris edition, ii, 453, line 13), which has been much more generally followed, indicates 'the bases of the central incisors', and so: *alveolar*. For the phonological oppositions of the *d* phoneme, see J. Cantineau, *Esquisse*, in *BSL* (No. 126), 99, 12th; for the incompatibles *ibid.*, 134.

Variants: in the mountain dialects of N. Morocco *d* may become *d̲h̲* after a vowel; *d* in Classical Arabic and in the modern dialects has numerous conditioned variants (assimilations), see J. Cantineau, *Cours*, 37-8, 41-2.

Bibliography: in the text, and s.v. Ḥurūf al-Hid̲j̲āʾ.

(H. Fleisch)

(ii) — Various modifications of *dāl* in languages other than Arabic in which an adaptation of the Arabic script is used may be mentioned here.

In the Indo-Aryan languages there are two series of "d-like" sounds, the dental and the retroflex (also called cerebral, cacuminal, or even, perversely, lingual), the latter produced by the under side of the tongue tip being curled back to strike the hard palate in the post-alveolar position, the concave upper surface of the tongue forming a secondary resonating chamber within the oral cavity. Both sounds may in addition be accompanied by aspiration. In Pas̲h̲to and Urdū the dental is represented by the unmodified *dāl*, the retroflex (transcribed in the Encyclopaedia by *ḍ*) by *dāl* modified in Pas̲h̲tō by a small subscript circle (ډ), in Urdū by a small superscript *ṭā* (ڈ; this was originally ڐ). The aspirated varieties of both are now always written with the "butterfly" (*dūčas̲h̲mī*) *hā*, the "hook" variety of *hā* being reserved for intervocalic *ẖ*, hence the contrast دہی *dahī* 'curds', but دھی *dhī* 'daughter'.

In Sindhī the retroflex *ḍāl* is represented by ڊ, aspirated *dāl* (*dha*) by ڌ, and aspirated *ḍāl* (*ḍha*) by ڍ. Sindhī, in common with other languages of Western India, has in addition a series of implosive consonants (implosive *b*, *d̲j̲*, *ḍ* and *g*); the implosive *ḍ* (*ḏa*) is represented by ڏ.

Bibliography: *Linguistic Survey of India*, Vols. x (Pas̲h̲tō), viii/1 (Sindhī), ix/1 (Urdū); D. N. MacKenzie, *A standard Pashto* in *BSOAS*, xxii/2 (1959), 231-5; R. L. Turner, *Cerebralization in Sindhī* in *JRAS*, 1924, 555-84; idem, *The Sindhī recursives ...*, *BSOS*, iii/2, (1924), 301-15; Mohiuddin Qadri, *Hindustani Phonetics*, Paris n.d. (1931?); also the articles pas̲h̲tō, sind̲h̲ī, urdū.

(J. Burton-Page)

DALĪL (Gr. σημεῖον) is an ambiguous term; it can mean sign or indication, every proof through the inference of a cause from its effect or the inference of the universal from the particular in opposition to the proof from a strictly deductive syllogism in which the particular is deduced from the universal; and finally it is used as synonymous with proof, ἀπόδειξις, *burhān* generally.

Aristotle treats the "proof from a sign" in the last chapter of his *Analytica Priora.* According to him "proof from a sign" is an enthymeme, *i.e.*, a syllogism in which one premiss is suppressed (ἐνθύμημα, *ḳiyās iḍmārī* or *ḳiyās īd̲j̲āzī*) in which from a fact another fact, anterior or posterior in time, is inferred (although Aristotle says "anterior or posterior", the example he gives infers an anterior fact and for the Arab philosophers the inference is always the inference of a cause from its effect). He gives as an example that from a woman having milk it is inferred that she has conceived. He states that this enthymeme can be fully expressed in the following way: all women who have milk have conceived, this woman has conceived, therefore she has milk. This would seem to imply that for this type of reasoning the enthymeme is not a necessary condition and that the conclusion provides absolute evidence, although a "sign", according to Aristotle, is always an accident and there is no necessary proof for the accidental. We find in Avicenna the same definition and the same example (*Nad̲j̲āt*, p. 92) and he adds that *dalīl* can mean both the middle term of the syllogism (in this case "having milk") and the enthymeme itself.

This type of reasoning is the only one for which Aristotle reserves the name of "proof from a sign". The Arab philosophers, however, give the term a wider meaning, based on the distinction made by Aristotle in his *Analytica Posteriora* between the proof that a thing is, τὸ ὅτι, *burhān anna* and the proof why a thing is, the proof of its cause or reason, τὸ διότι, *burhān lima*. The proof *why* a thing is is preceded by the proof *that* a thing is, for one can ask only why a thing is, when one knows that it is. The proof that a thing is starts from the particular, the fact, the effect perceived, and infers the cause from its effect, and it is for this reason that the Arab philosophers call it a *dalīl*; on the other hand the proof why a thing is starts from the universal, the cause, and deduces the particular effect from its cause. The distinction is confused through the ambiguity of the term "cause" which in Aristotelian philosophy can mean both the logical reason of a thing's being such and such, its formal cause, *e.g.*, the reason that Socrates is mortal is that he is a man, and the ontological cause of a thing's becoming, *e.g.*, this fire is the cause of the burning of this wood. I cannot discuss this here *in extenso*, but will give only Avicenna's examples from his *Nadjāt* (103, 105) which show clearly the confusion between the logical and the ontological, so usual in Aristotle. As an example of the *burhān lima* he gives: a great heat has changed this wood, everything a great heat has changed is burnt, therefore this wood is burnt; and as an example of the *burhān anna*: this wood is burnt, therefore a great heat has burned it. According to Avicenna the difference between the two syllogisms is that in the former the middle term (*i.e.*, a great heat) is both the cause (*i.e.*, the logical reason) of our conviction of the truth of the conclusion and the cause (*i.e.*, the ontological cause) of the major term (*i.e.*, the being burnt) in reality, whereas the latter gives us only the subjective conviction of the truth of the conclusion. That is to say in the *burhān anna* we can, purely logically, infer from the particular effect its formal cause, for being burnt implies the act of burning, and since being burnt is but the actualisation of the potentiality of heat, heat and the fact of being burnt are practically identical; in the *burhān lima* the ontological cause and the logical reason are identified.

The Arab philosophers hold also with Aristotle (*Anal. Prior.*, ii, 23) that through a syllogism based on a perfect induction of particular facts, that is the enumeration of all the particular cases, we can arrive at a universal proposition (cf. *e.g.*, Avicenna, *De demonstratione* [from his *Shifāʾ*], 31-2).

There is still another type of reasoning mentioned by Aristotle (*Anal. Prior.*, ii, 24) in which from a particular case a general principle may be inferred, reasoning by example, παράδειγμα, *mathal*. Avicenna gives in his *Nadjāt*, 90-91, as an example an argument of the theologians: the world is produced in time, because it is composed of parts, therefore it is like a building; now the building is produced in time, therefore the world is produced in time.

Aristotle had neglected in his logic the hypothetical and disjunctive syllogisms which were studied in his school by Theophrastus and Eudemus, but the Stoics for whom all argument is based on the inference of an event from another event, on the inference of the posterior from the anterior (or the reverse in prognostics), on the inference of a particular cause from a particular effect, that is on the inference from signs or symptoms, σημεῖα, a concept which becomes one of the most important elements of their logic, are chiefly concerned with the study of the hypothetical and disjunctive syllogisms and, indeed, inferences from actual events which imply a time-element, find an easier expression in a hypothetical than in a categorical syllogism. The example of σημεῖον given by Aristotle, becomes in Stoic logic a stock example in their syllogism: if this woman has milk, she has conceived, now she has milk, therefore she has conceived, and Avicenna in his *Ishārāt*, 84-5, gives an example of the difference between *burhān lima* and the *burhān anna* in a hypothetical form. Reasoning by example, regarded by Aristotle as a categorical syllogism, or as the Stoics call it reasoning by analogy (*ḳiyās*), takes in their logic a hypothetical form and becomes one of their principal arguments, since according to them all knowledge transcending the evidence of the senses proceeds by way of analogical inference. The analogical syllogism was the first one the Arabs became acquainted with (it may well be that because of this the term *ḳiyās* becomes later the general name for syllogism, just as the term *dalīl* becomes the general term for proof), the Muʿtazila, the rationalistic theologians in Islam, called by their adversaries *ahl al-ḳiyās*, used analogical reasoning for their interpretation of the Ḳurʾān and as a basis for criticizing traditions, and Shāfiʿī was aware that *ḳiyās* is based on signs, *dalāʾil* and examples, *mithāl* (cf. J. Schacht, *The Origins of Muhammadan Jurisprudence*, London 1950, 124 and 128). Ghazzālī in his logical works emphasizes the importance of the hypothetical syllogism in all juridical matters and the Ashʿarīs, nominalists like the Stoics and who with them deny the existence of Aristotle's forms and formal causes, base their arguments on analogical reasoning or as Averroës says (*Tahāfut al-Tahāfut*, Bouyges, p. 522) on what they call "sign".

Bibliography: in the text.

(S. van den Bergh)

DALLĀL (ar.) "broker", "agent". *Dallāl*, literally "guide"; is the popular Arabic word for *simsār, sensal*. In the *Tādj al-ʿArūs* we find, on the word *simsār*: "This is the man known as a *dallāl*; he shows the purchaser where to find the goods he requires, and the seller how to exact his price". Very little is known from the Arabic sources about the origins of these brokers, who have been of such great importance in economic affairs. The *dallāl* corresponded to the Byzantine μεδίτης. In the absence of any systematic earlier studies, only certain items of information collected at random can be given here. Law-books warn the *dallāls* of the need to be on their guard against the dishonest tricks customary in commerce (Ibn al-Ḥādjdj, *Kitāb al-Madkhal*, iii, 75). In fact the *dallāls* frequently recommended to purchasers goods which they knew to be inferior and always took sides with the seller against his customer. Their profession which, at times, was invested with an official character, was known as *dilāla*. The word al-dallāl occurs in early times as a surname (*Tādj al-ʿArūs*). Under the Fāṭimids, certain articles could only be sold through the intermediary of *dallāls* (al-Muḳaddasī, 213_6). In the time of the Mamlūks, the 2% commission which from the earliest days had been paid to these brokers was made subject to a charge, as a result of which the *dallāl* had to give up half his profits in taxes: the loss, naturally enough, he speedily passed on to his clients. This operation was known as *niṣf al-samsara* (Maḳrīzī, *Khiṭaṭ*, i, 89_5). A somewhat similar custom was to be found in northern Syria (cf. Sobernheim in the *Corpus Inscriptionum Arabicarum*, ii, no 55 and the account given by C. H. Becker in *Isl.* i, 100). The principal transactions were concluded in the maritime customs offices. There the *dallāls* acted at the same time as interpreters when any deailngs with the Franks were required. Commercial treaties fixed precisely what fees were due to these agents and interpreters (Amari, *Diplomi Arabi*, 106, 203). Heyd, *Levantehandel*, i, gives a wide range of details about this kind of transaction. For the Western Mediterranean one should consult de Mas Latrie, *Traités de paix et de commerce*, Paris 1866, 189. Later it was the West which monopolized questions of brokerage (cf. Schaube, *Handelsgeschichte der romanischen Völker des Mittelmeergebietes*, 761).

It was, however, not only for their transactions with foreigners, but also for business matters amongst themselves, that the Eastern peoples made use of the *dallāls* (see, for example, the notes on Ottoman brokerage dues in B. Lewis, *Studies in the Ottoman Archives, I, BSOAS*, xvi, 1954, 495 ff.). Furthermore, the latter also acted as independent traders, selling, for example, old clothes on their own account (*Description de l'Égypte, État moderne*, xviii/II, 321). The name *dallāl* was also applied to the hawker auctioning goods in the secondhand clothing market and, still more frequently, to the small intermediary and agent. The way of life of these agents has been well described by Lane, *Manners and Customs of the modern Egyptians*[5], ii, 13. Women are also found taking the part of agents. Known as *dallāla*, they act as intermediaries for harems of a superior sort (Lane, *op. cit.* I, 200, 239, 242). For other meanings of the word *dallāl* cf. Dozy, *Supplément*, s.v.

(C. H. Becker*)

II. — In the Muslim West, the *dallāl* is exclusively an intermediary who, in return for remuneration, sells by public auction objects entrusted to him by third parties. In the large towns the *dallāls* are grouped in specialized guilds, supervised by a syndic (*amīn*) who compels them to give a guarantee of good faith (*ḍāmin*). They chiefly concerned themselves with manufactured goods sold by artisans to the shopkeepers: slippers, locally woven fabrics, carpets, jewellery etc.; industrial raw materials such as hides (green or tanned), wool (untreated or yarn); commodities sold in bulk, such as oil, butter, honey, local soap, henna, eggs, fruit and vegetables; livestock, animals for both riding and baggage; furniture, books and old clothes. Before the French Protectorate was established in Morocco they were also engaged in the sale of slaves of both sexes.

The word has passed into Persian and Turkish (*tellāl*) and, from the latter, into various Balkan languages (modern Greek *tellâles*). Besides *dallāl* (*dellīl* in Granada), Spanish Arabic used *sawwāḳ*.

In the Muslim West today *dallāl* is quite distinct from *barrāḥ* "town crier" and from *simsār* [*q.v.*] "broker, business agent".

In the large towns the feminine *dallāla* denotes a "dealer in women's clothes" who frequents the houses of the rich, offering the women fabrics, clothes and jewellery.

Bibliography: Le Tourneau, *Fès avant le protectorat*, 1949, 306-14; Kampffmeyer, *Texte aus Fes*, 13; idem, *Weitere Texte aus Fes und Tanger*, 71. (G. S. Colin)

DALTĀWA, the headquarter town of the *Ḳaḍā* of Khāliṣ in the *liwā* of Diyālā, central ʿIrāḳ (44° 30′ E, 33° 50′ N). The population of the town —all settled ʿIrāḳī Arabs, with Shīʿī predominance over Sunnī—was some 10,000 in 1367/1947, and that of the *ḳaḍā* 70,000; the two dependent *nāḥiyas* are those of Khān Banī Saʿd and Manṣūriyya (formerly Dalī ʿAbbās). The name Daltāwa is said by ʿIrāḳī scholars to be a corruption of an original Dawlatābād.

Surrounded by date-gardens, the town is watered from the Khāliṣ canal, an important offtake from the Diyālā, right bank. Though still largely old fashioned, and never very healthy, the town now contains a number of new streets and buildings, especially Government offices and institutions; modern services and communications have been greatly developed during the last 30 years. Though nowhere mentioned in mediaeval writers, because then of little importance, the town is certainly of some antiquity, and was watered from the Nahrawān-Diyālā canal system.

Bibliography: ʿAbd al-Razzāḳ al-Ḥasanī, *al-ʿIrāḳ Ḳadīm*[an] *wa Ḥadīth*[an], Sidon 1367/1947.

(S. H. Longrigg)

al-**DALW** [see Nudjūm].

DĀM [see sikka].

DĀMĀD, a Persian word meaning son-in-law, used as a title by sons-in-law of the Ottoman Sultans. Under the early Sultans, princesses (*sulṭān*) of the reigning house were occasionally given in marriage to the vassal princes of Asia Minor, for example, to the Ḳaramānoghlu, and even to the vezirs and generals of the sovereign; the case of the saint Amīr Sulṭān of Bursa, who married a daughter of Bāyazīd I is, however, unique not only for that but also for later periods. We afterwards find Grand Vezirs, Kapudan Pashas, Aghas of Janissaries, Bostāndjībashīs and other high officials as sons-in-law of the Sulṭān; the best known are Ibrāhim Pasha, the favourite of Sulaymān I, Rustem Pasha (husband of Mihrimāh), Sokollu Meḥemmed Pasha (husband of Asmākhān), Ibrāhīm Pasha (son-in-law of Meḥemmed III), Ibrāhīm Pasha under Aḥmed III etc. (cf. Hammer, *GOR*, index, s.v. *Sulṭānin*). The title *dāmād* was applied to some of them both by their contemporaries and in historical writings and remained current to the end of the empire (*e.g.*, Dāmād Maḥmūd Pasha, Dāmād Ferīd Pasha [*q.v.*] etc.).

The marriage ceremonies were celebrated with great splendour and are minutely described in the Ottoman chronicles as well as by western travellers (cf. Hammer, *GOR*, index s.v. *Hochzeit und Vermählung*); the dowry had been fixed by Sulaymān I at 100,000 ducats and the appanage (*Khāṣṣ*) brought in 1000-1500 aspers daily. (Venetian *Relazione* of 1608, in Barozzi-Berchet, 72; Hammer, viii, 211); in addition a large palace was usually bestowed on the princesses. Till the time of Sulaymān I the Dāmāds were usually sent into the provinces as governors to prevent them having any personal influence on the affairs of the Sublime Porte, (Kočibey, ed. of 1303, 94, 97). Etiquette compelled the Dāmād to put away the wives he already had and to take no further wives (cf. the Venetian *Relazione* already quoted, 103 ff. and Hammer, iv, 103); he became the slave of his wife and this relationship finds expression in the form of address used between the spouses (cf. the above reports, 72, 104; de la Mottraye, *Voyages*, 338 ff.; Hammer, *Staatsverfassung*, i, 476-84 = *GOR*, viii, 211-13; C. White, *Three Years in Constantinople*, iii, 180 ff.). The statement that sons born of such marriages were done away with at birth (Eton, *Survey of the Turkish Empire*[3], 101; Hammer, *GOR*, iv, 463), may be disproved (cf. Djewdet, vi, 196 ff., *Relazioni* loc. cit., 181, 372); only in earlier times they were debarred from all public offices (*Relazioni* 181).

Bibl. in addition to that given in the article: Ismail Hakkı Uzunçarsılı, *Osmanlı Devletinin Saray Teşkilâtı*, Ankara 1945; A. D. Alderson, *The Structure of the Ottoman Dynasty*, Oxford 1956, 97-8. On the use of the title *Küregen* by the sons-in-law of Mongol rulers see Djuwayni-Boyle, 174 n. 11; Mostaert and Cleaves, *Trois Documents Mongols*, *HJAS*, 1852, 474; and article Gūrkhān.

(J. H. Mordtmann*)

al-**DĀMĀD,** "son-in-law", an honorific title given to Mīr Muḥammad Bāḳir b. Shams al-Dīn Muḥammad al-Ḥusaynī al-Astarābādī, called also *al-Muʿallim al-Thālith*, the "third teacher" in philosophy after al-Fārābī. This title properly belongs to his father who was the son-in-law of the famous Shīʿī theologian ʿAlī b. al-Ḥusayn b. ʿAbd al-ʿĀlī al-Karakī, called *al-Muḥaḳḳiḳ al-Thānī* (Brockelmann, S II, 574), but it was extended to the son, who is more correctly called Dāmādī or Ibn al-Dāmād. Born at Astarābād, Mīr-i Dāmād spent his childhood at Ṭūs from where he went to Iṣpahān, most probably for preliminary studies. Educated at Mashhad, among his teachers are counted his maternal uncle, al-Shaykh ʿAbd al-ʿĀlī b. ʿAlī (the *mudjtahid*), and al-Shaykh ʿIzz al-Dīn Ḥusayn b. ʿAbd al-Ṣamad al-ʿĀmilī.

A noted divine, he is, however, chiefly esteemed for his attainments as a scholastic theologian (*mutakallim*), and two of his numerous works, *al-Ufuḳ al-Mubīn* (also called by the author, at four places in the text, *al-Ṣirāt al-Mustaḳīm*) and *al-Sabʿ al-Shidād*, are still prescribed, in spite of their being the writings of a Shīʿī *mudjtahid*, in the religious institutions of India and Pakistan, run and managed exclusively by the Sunnīs, as courses of logical studies. For a long period of 36 years, from 984 to 1025 (1576-1616), he remained actively engaged in philosophical and scholastic discussions and religious polemics.

Mīr-i Dāmād was also a poet of no mean order and composed verses under the pen-name of *Ishrāḳ*. Specimens of his poetry are given in the *Madjmaʿ al-Fuṣahāʾ*, the *Riyāḍ al-ʿĀrifīn* and the *Ātash-Kada* (see Bibliography). Muḥammad Ḥasan "Zulālī" al-Khwānsārī (d. 1024/1615), the well-known author of the imaginative *mathnawī* "*Maḥmūd u-Ayāz*", was a great admirer of Mīr-i Dāmād.

The *Taʾrīkh-i ʿĀlam Ārā-yi ʿAbbāsī*, written in 1025/1616, fifteen years before the death of Mīr-i Dāmād in 1040/1630, describes him as skilled in most of the sciences, especially philosophy, philology, mathematics, medicine, jurisprudence, exegesis and tradition. It further mentions about a dozen of the works of Mīr-i Dāmād which shows that long before 1025/1616, his fame as a writer and author of distinction had been established.

Held in great esteem, rather awe, by Shāh ʿAbbās Ṣafawī I (996-1039/1587-1629), at whose Court he wielded great influence, and his successor Shāh Ṣafī I, Mīr Bāḳir rose morally also above most of his contemporaries who were engaged in the ignoble pursuits of "petty jealousy and mutual disparagement" (cf. John Malcolm, *History of Persia*, London 1815, i, 258-9). Among the notable pupils of Mīr-i Dāmād was Mullā Ṣadrā-i Shīrāzī [*q.v.*], the celebrated philosopher, accounted as the greatest in modern times in Iran.

Mīr Bāḳir died between al-Nadjaf and Karbalāʾ, during a visit to the holy places in ʿIrāḳ, in 1040/1630 and was buried in al-Nadjaf.

He was a prolific writer; a full list of his Arabic works is given by Brockelmann (S II, 579). Chief of these are: *al-Ufuḳ al-Mubīn* which has been the subject of numerous commentaries. Mawlawī Faḍl-i Ḥaḳḳ of Khayrābād, a famous theologian and *mutakallim* of India, was very fond of teaching this book. Baḥr al-ʿUlūm [*q.v.*] has written *taʿlīḳāt* (glosses) on it. *Al-Ṣirāt al-Mustaḳīm* and *al-Ḥabl al-Matīn*, are also on logic. Concerning the former a Persian poet says: "May the Muslim never hear nor the *kāfir* ever see the *Ṣirāt al-Mustaḳīm* of Mīr-i Dāmād".

His other notable works are: *al-Ḳabasāt* (composed in 1034/1624) on the *ḥudūth* (Creation) of the Universe and the Eternity of God, etc.; *Shāriʿ al-Nadjāt* (in Persian), on the principles of religion and jurisprudence, comprising an introduction, five books and a conclusion; *Sidrat al-Muntahā*, a commentary of the Ḳurʾān; *al-Djidhawāt*, (in Persian), a treatise on the mystic meanings of the detached letters (*ḥurūf muḳaṭṭaʿāt*) in the Ḳurʾān and also containing a discussion as to why the body of Moses, composed of organic matter, survived the divine *tadjallī* while Mount Sinai was (according to tradition) reduced to ashes. This work, specially composed for Shāh ʿAbbās Ṣafawī, is divided into 12 preliminary chapters and a large number of sections, each termed *djidhwa*; *Taḳwīm al-Īmān* or *al-Taḳwīm fī 'l-Kalām*, on the philosophy of *īmān*; and *al-Taḳdīsāt*, on the divine dispensation. He has also left two separate *dīwāns*, in Arabic and Persian.

Bibliography: Ibn Maʿṣūm, *Sulāfat al-ʿAṣr*, Cairo 1334/1915, 485-7; Iskandar Beg Munshī, *Taʾrīkh-i ʿĀlam Ārā-yi ʿAbbāsī*, Tehran 1313-14/1896-7, 109, 658; Muḥammad Bāḳir al-Khwānsārī, *Rawḍāt al-Djannāt fī Aḥwāl al-ʿUlamāʾ wa 'l-Sādāt*, Tehran 1347-1928, i, 114-6; Faḍl Allāh al-Muḥibbī, *Khulāṣat al-Athar*, Cairo 1281/1864, iv, 301-2; Muḥammad b. Ṣādiḳ, *Nudjūm al-Samāʾ*, Lucknow 1303/1885-6, 46; Iʿdjāz Ḥusayn al-Kantūrī, *Kashf al-Ḥudjub wa 'l-Astār ʿan Asmāʾ al-Kutub wa 'l-Asfār*, Calcutta 1330/1912, index (under Muḥ. Bāḳir b. Muḥ. al-Ḥusaynī al-Dāmād); Sarkīs, *Muʿdjam al-Maṭbūʿāt*, col. 860; C. Brockelmann, S II, 579-80; *Fihrist Kitāb Khāna-i Dānishgāh-i Īrān*, (compiled by Muḥammad Taḳī Dānish-Puzhūh), Tehran, 1332/1953, iii, 152 (where several other references are found); Muḥammad b. Hasan ..... al-Ḥurr al-ʿĀmilī, *Amal al-Āmil fī ʿUlamāʾ Djabal al-ʿĀmil*, 498; Muḥammad b. Sulaymān Tunakābunī, *Ḳiṣaṣ al-ʿUlamāʾ*, Tehran 1304/1886, 145, 238-40 (also Urdū translation by Mīr Nādir ʿAlī Raʿd, Ḥaydarābād 1340-1/1921-3); ʿAbd al-ʿAzīz "Djawāhir al-Kalām", *Risāla dar Faḍīlat al-ʿIlm wa 'l-Ulamāʾ* (MS.); Riḍāʾ Ḳulī Khān Hidāyat, *Madjmaʿ al-Fuṣaḥāʾ*, Tehran 1295/1878, vii, 2; Luṭf ʿAlī Khān Ādhar, *Ātash-Kada*, 1299/1882, 159; Riḍāʾ Ḳulī Khān Hidāyat, *Riyāḍ al-ʿĀrifīn*, Tehran 1305/1888, 166-7; Browne, iv, 256-7, 406-7, 426-9 and index; ʿAbbās al-Ḳummī, *al-Kunā wa 'l-Alḳāb*, al-Nadjaf 1376/1956, ii, 206-7; Bakhtāwar Khān, *Mirʾāt al-ʿĀlam* (MS.); Muḥammad Riḍāʾ "Bandah", *Zīnat al-Tawārīkh*, fol. 553; "Āghā" Aḥmad ʿAlī, *Haft Āsmān*, Calcutta 1873; Rieu, *Catalogue of Persian MSS. in the British Museum*, ii, 835; Muḥammad Muḥsin Aghā Buzurg al-Ṭihrānī, *Al-Dharīʿa*, ii, Nadjaf 1355, 261 (and elsewhere, under the entries referring to his works). (A. S. BAZMEE ANSARI)

DĀMĀD FERĪD PASHA, one of the last Grand Vezirs of the Ottoman Empire. Meḥmed Ferīd, son of Ḥasan ʿIzzet, a member of the Council of State (Shūrā-yi Dewlet), was born in Istanbul in 1853, served in minor diplomatic posts, and, upon his marriage (1886) to ʿAbd al-Ḥamīd II's sister Medīḥa, was made member of the Council of State and senator, and given the rank of Pasha. In 1911 he became co-founder and chairman of the Ḥürriyet we Iʾtilāf Fïrḳasï [*q.v.*]. After the Ottoman defeat he served his brother-in-law Meḥmed VI as Grand Vezir (4 March to 2 October 1919 and 5 April to 21 October 1920). His policy of accommodation to the victor powers in hopes of winning lenient peace terms proved as futile as his attempts to suppress the national resistance movement in Anatolia under Kemal [Atatürk]. Nationalist pressure forced his resignation in October 1919. Restored to office after the reinforced Allied occupation of Istanbul, his government was responsible for issuing the well-known anti-nationalist *fetwās* (signed by the *shaykh al-Islām* Dürrizāde ʿAbd Allāh [*q.v.*]) and dispatched troops against the nationalists in Anatolia. On 10 August 1920 his cabinet signed the peace treaty of Sèvres, but the growing strength of the nationalists soon caused his final dismissal. In September 1922 he left Istanbul for Nice, where he died on 6 October 1923.

Bibliography: Mahmud Kemal Inal, *Osmanlı devrinde son sadrıazamlar*, Istanbul 1940-53, 2029-2094; *Millī newsāl* 1340 (1924), 352; Tarık Z. Tunaya, *Türkiyede siyasī partiler*, 1952, 315, 451-55; Ali Fuat Türkgeldi, *Görüp işittiklerim*², 1951; *WI*, 1928-9, 1-154; Kemal [Atatürk], *Nutuk* (see 1934 edn., index); İbrahim Alâettin Gövsa, *Türk meşhurları ansiklopedisi*, 1946, 136.

(D. A. Rustow)

ḌAMĀN (A.), in Islamic law, the civil liability in the widest meaning of the term, whether it arises from the non-performance of a contract or from tort or negligence (*taʿaddī*, literally "transgression"). Prominent particular cases are the liability for the loss of an object sold before the buyer has taken possession (*ḍamān al-mabīʿ*), for eviction (*ḍamān al-darak*), for the loss of a pledge in the possession of the pledgee (*ḍamān al-rahn*), for the loss of an object that has been taken by usurpation (*ḍamān al-ghaṣb*), and for loss or damage caused by artisans (*ḍamān al-adjīr, ḍ. al-ṣunnāʿ*). The depositary and other persons in a position of trust (*amīn*, [*q.v.*]) are not liable for accidental loss but they lose this privileged position through unlawful acts, *e.g.*, using the deposit, whether the loss is caused by the unlawful act or not. Questions of *ḍamān* are treated sporadically in numerous sections of the works on *fiḳh*, and it forms the subject of a number of special treatises.

Ḍamān in the sense of suretyship, guarantee, is a liability specially created by contract; it is synonymous with *kafāla* [*q.v.*]. In a wider sense, *ḍamān* is used of the risk or responsibility that one bears with regard to property of which one enjoys the profit, as in the old legal maxim, which was put into the form of a *ḥadīth* attributed to the Prophet, *al-kharādj bi 'l-ḍamān* ("profit follows responsibility").

Bibliography: al-Djurdjānī, *Kitāb al-Taʿrīfāt*, s.v.; Tahānawī, *Dictionary of the Technical Terms*, s.v.; (the entry in Lane, *Arabic-English Lexicon*, contains several mistakes); E. Fagnan, *Additions aux Dictionnaires Arabes*, s.v.; Fuḍayl b. ʿAlī al-Djamālī, *K. al-Ḍamānāt fi 'l-Furūʿ* (Brockelmann, II, 573, S II, 645; J. Schacht, in *Abh. Pr. Ak. W., Phil.-hist. Kl.*, 1928, no. 8, § 43; 1929, no. 6, § 22; 1931, no. 1, § 33); Ghānim b. Muḥammad al-Baghdādī, *Madjmaʿ al-Ḍamānāt*, Cairo 1308 (Brockelmann, II, 492, S II, 502; J. Schacht, in *Abh. Pr. Ak. W., Phil.-hist. Kl.*, 1928, no. 8, § 45; 1929, no. 6, § 23; 1931, no. 1, § 34); Maḥmūd Efendi b. Ḥamza al-Ḥamzāwī, *al-Taḥrīr fī Ḍamān al-Maʾmūr wa 'l-Āmir wa 'l-Adjīr*, Damascus 1303 (Brockelmann, S II, 775); al-Ḥasan b. Raḥḥāl al-Maʿdānī (Brockelmann, S II, 696), *K. Taḍmīn al-ṣunnāʿ*, introduction, text, transl. and notes by J. Berque, Algiers 1949 (Bibliothèque Arabe-Française, XIII); J. Schacht, *G. Bergsträsser's Grundzüge des Islamischen Rechts*, 64 f.; D. Santillana, *Istituzioni di Diritto Musulmano Malichita*, II, index s.vv. *ḍamān, responsibilità, rischio*; J. Schacht, *The Origins of Muhammadan Jurisprudence*, 123, 181, 270; Wensinck, *Concordance et Indices de la Tradition Musulmane*, s.v.; E. Tyan, *La responsabilité délictuelle en droit musulman*, Paris 1926; F. M. Goadby, in *Journal of Comparative Legislation*, 1939, 62-74; E. Schram-Nielsen, *Studier over Erstatningslaeren i Islamisk Ret*, Copenhagen 1945 (with résumé in French); J. Lapanne-Joinville, in *Revue Algérienne*, 1955/I, 1-24, 51-75.

(Ed.)

ḌAMĀN, in the financial sense, 'farming' (of taxes). See BAYT AL-MĀL.

DAMANHŪR, a name derived from the ancient Egyptian Timinhur, the city of Horus. It is not surprising that a number of cities of this name are to be found, almost all in the Nile Delta.

I. Damanhūr al-Shahid, Damanhūr "of the Martyr", one of the northern suburbs of Cairo. This was the name still used by Yāḳūt, but the village was later known as Damanhūr Shubrā, a name which was however already known to al-Muḳaddasī. Ibn Mammātī calls it simply Damanhūr. The two names are sometimes inverted and certain authors speak of Shubrā Damanhūr or even Shubra 'l-Shahīd. This kind of phenomenon is frequent enough in Egypt, especially when it is necessary to distinguish one place from others of the same name. Shubrā is also called Shubra 'l-Khayma or Shubra 'l-Khiyām, Shubrā "of the tents".

There was once a Christian reliquary in this place containing the bones of a martyr. On 8th Bashans (3rd May) each year, the town celebrated a holiday while the people accompanied this casket in procession to the Nile, into which it was plunged in the hope of promoting the success of the river's annual flood. There was no doubt excessive drinking on this day and the feast was forbidden in 702/1302. It was re-established in 738/1338 but was definitely suppressed in 755/1354 and the relic burnt.

Bibliography: Abū Ṣāliḥ, fol. 45; Ibn Mammātī, 371; Muḳaddasī, 54, 194, 206; Yāḳūt, ii, 601; Ibn Duḳmāḳ, v, 46; Maḳrīzī, ed. Wiet, i, 292-6; the same, *Sulūk*, i, 941 (trans. Quatremère, ii, b, 213); Ibn Taghrībirdī, ed. Cairo, viii, 202-3; Ibn Djīʿān, 7; Quatremère, *Mémoires sur l'Égypte*, i, 360; Amelineau, *Géographie de l'Égypte*, 113-5 (to be consulted with caution); J. Maspero and G. Wiet, *Matériaux*, 108-110, 217.

II. Damanhūr, capital of the province of Buḥayra, the ancient Hermopolis Parva of the Byzantine era. Since the name is ancient it can hardly be called an Islamic creation, but nothing is heard of it in the chronicles until the time of the Arab conquest. The important locality is Ḳarṭasa, the only name known to the ancient authors, who mention it as the capital of a pagarchy (*kūra*).

The oldest reference is to be found in Ibn Mammātī, who calls it Damanhūr al-Waḥsh. Ibn Djubayr and Yāḳūt passed through it. To them it was an urban centre of medium size surrounded by a wall. Ibn Mammātī mentions a canal named after the city, the Bahr Damanhūr. The sultan Barḳūḳ restored its fortifications, in order better to resist the incursions of the Bedouin; furthermore the town had suffered greatly in the earthquake of 702/1302. Damanhūr increased in importance and according to Ibn Duḳmāḳ, it possessed a Friday mosque, schools, caravanserais and covered markets. It was, then, not only the capital of the province of Buḥayra, but also the residence of a senior Mamlūk officer commanding the whole of the Delta. The post road, skirting the desert from Cairo to Alexandria, had a stage post there and there was also a carrier pigeoncote.

According to Sonnini the town was "large but

badly built, almost all the houses being made either of mud or of bad quality brick. It is the centre of the trade in cotton, which is gathered in the vast and beautiful plains surrounding it".

On 30th April, 1799, a French company was massacred there by the troops of Mahdī Aḥmad; the reprisals were terrible.

Damanhūr is now a heavily populated town. The railway between Cairo and Alexandria has a station there, and it is the centre of a network of secondary railway routes.

Bibliography: Ibn ʿAbd al-Ḥakam, 83; *Synaxaire, Patrologia Orientalis*, xvii, 565, 1107; Idrīsī, *Maghrib*, 160; Ibn Mammātī, 169, 226-7; Ibn Djubayr, 44 (trans. Gaudefroy-Demombynes, 45); Yāḳūt, ii, 601; Ibn Furāt, ix, 86; Ibn Duḳmāḳ, v, 101; Ḳalḳashandī, iii, 406, xiv, 376 (trans. Wüstenfeld, 111); Maḳrīzī, *Sulūk*, i, 944 (trans. Quatremère, ii, *b*, 216); Ẓāhirī, 35, 117, 119 (trans. Venture de Paradis, 55, 197, 201); Ibn Taghrībirdī, ed. Cairo, xi, 291, xii, 113-4; Ibn Djīʿān, 116; Quatremère, *Mémoires sur l'Égypte*, i, 361-3; Dehérain, *Histoire de la Nation Égyptienne*, v, 436; J. Maspero and Wiet, *Matériaux*, 146-7, 175-8, 180-1, 183, 185, 194.

Other places of the same name are mentioned in geographical lists but not described.

Bibliography: Muḳaddasī, 55; Ibn Mammātī, 134, 135; Ibn Duḳmāḳ, v, 89; Ibn Djīʿān, 78; Amelineau, *Géographie de l'Égypte*, 116.

(G. Wiet)

DAMASCUS [see DIMASHḲ].

DAMĀWAND, the highest point in the mountains on the borders of Northern Persia (cf. ALBURZ), somewhat below 36° N. Lat. and about 50 miles north-east of Tehran. According to de Morgan it rises out of the plateau of Rēhne to a height of 13,000 feet above it. The various estimates of its height differ: Thomson estimates it at 21,000 feet (certainly too high), de Morgan at 20,260 feet, Houtum Schindler at 19,646, Sven Hedin at 18,187, and in the last edition of Stieler's *Handatlas* (1910) it is given as 18,830 feet. Its summit, perpetually snow-clad and almost always enveloped in clouds, is visible several days' journey away, as Yāḳūt tells us from his own experience. In fine weather and favourable light it may be seen, according to Melgunof, from the Caspian sea, a distance of over 260 versts (162 miles). Ḳazwīnī's statements on this point are exaggerated, but it is certain that the Damāwand massif commands the whole coastlands of Māzandarān (the mediaeval Ṭabaristān).

Geologically Damāwand is of recent origin, as is clear from its volcanic nature which is apparent in several features. There are as many as 70 craters on this mountain mass; from one of them, which is covered with thick deposits of sulphur, rises the conical peak. There are also many sulphur springs on it; Ḳazwīnī mentions "the springs of Damāwand from which smoke arises by day and fire by night". Damāwand is the centre of the earthquake zone which stretches throughout Māzandārān. It is clear from the earlier accounts of Arab travellers that the internal activity of the central volcano had not then quite ceased as it has now.

Damāwand is rich in minerals, particularly anthracite. Sulphur is found in immense quantities; the finest quality, the best in Persia according to Polak, *Persien*, Leipzig 1865, ii, 178, is found just below the summit of the mountain, where it is collected in the summer months by the people of Ask and Damāwand and sold by them. Around the foot of Damāwand rise numerous mineral springs, of which two in particular—one in the little town of Ask, the other somewhat further north on the Herāz (Herhaz)—enjoy a great reputation as baths. The majority deposit considerable sediment; for example Ask is built on such alluvium (Polak, *op. cit.*, ii, 229). The apricots grown in the valleys of Damāwand are highly esteemed in Persia. (Polak, *op. cit.*, ii, 146).

Like the other giants of Eastern Asia, such as Ararat, Damāwand was long regarded as inaccessible; this opinion, which was widely held, is found repeatedly in the Arab geographers, although one successful ascent is mentioned (see ʿAlī b. Razīn's statement in Ḳazwīnī, 159). Oliver (1798) was the first European traveller to visit the mountain, without however being able to reach the summit. The first complete climb was by W. Taylor Thomson in 1837; he was followed in 1843 by the botanist Th. Kotschy and in 1852 by the Austrian engineer Czarnotta. H. Brugsch and Baron Minutoli seem also to have reached the summit in 1860; (see Petermann's *Geographische Mitteilungen*, 1861, 437). In more recent years a number of further successful ascents have been undertaken by Napier and others, usually from Ask; cf. particularly Sven Hedin, *Der Demāwend* in *Verh. der Gesellsch. f. Erdkunde*, Berlin, xix, 304-22.

In the ancient history of Persia Damāwand is the scene of the legendary history of the Pēshdād and Kayān rulers. Even at the present day the people of Māzandarān point out the different places which were the scenes of the wonderful deeds of Djamshīd, Farīdūn, Sām, Zāl, Rustam and other heroes immortalized in the *Shāhnāma*. Damāwand is also the abode of the fabulous bird Sīmurgh. From ancient times the prison of the cruel king Ḍaḥḥāḳ (O. Iran. Dahāka, also Bēwarasp) has been located here. Farīdūn (O. Iran. Θraētaona) is traditionally said to have shut him up in a cavern on the summit of this mountain, and here, in the belief of the local populace, the imprisoned tyrant lives to this day; the dull sounds which are periodically heard inside the mountain are thought to be his groans, and the vapour and smoke which escape from fissures and springs on the mountain-face are his breath. Obviously the volcanic properties of Damāwand have been responsible for these legends. According to another story the demon Ṣakhr, imprisoned by Solomon, is also locked in Damāwand. As the highest mountain in Persia, Damāwand is thought by the Persians to be that on which Noah's Ark rested. On the wealth of Damāwand legends cf. Yāḳūt, ii, 606, 610; Ḳazwīnī; Melgunof, 22 ff.; Grünbaum in *ZDMG*, xxxi, 238-9.

Formerly on the slopes and in the valleys of Damāwand there were many fortified places. Nowadays the most important place is the small town called Damāwand after the mountain and situated on its south-western spurs (according to de Morgan, 6425 feet above sea level). It is said to be very ancient, and according to Mustawfī was formerly called Pishyān. The beautiful valley of Damāwand, watered by two rivers and including ten villages as well as the town of Damāwand, no longer belongs to Māzandarān but to ʿIrāḳ ʿAdjamī. Because of its elevated situation the climate is very pleasant; for this reason the Shāhs of Persia used to delight in spending the summer in its valleys. The ultra-Shīʿī sect of the ʿAlī Ilāhī [*q.v.*] has a large number of adherents among the inhabitants of this region.

The name of Damāwand appears in Persian and Arabic sources in a number of different forms: Persian Danbāwand (Vullers, Lex. Persico-Lat., i, 907b), Damāwand (ibid., 902b), Dēmāwand (ibid., 955b) and Dēmawand (ibid., 956b); Ar. Dunbāwand, Dubāwand, Dumāwand. The oldest form of the name appears to be Dunbāwand, while the usual modern one is Damāwand (Demāwend). On the different ways of writing the name, see Quatremère, *Hist. des Mongols,* 200 ff.; Fleischer's ed. of Abu 'l-Fidā', *Histor. Anteislamica,* Lips. 1831, 213 ff., 232; H. Hübschmann, *Armenische Grammatik,* Leipzig 1897, 17.

Bibliography: *BGA,* passim; Yāḳūt, ii, 544, 585, 606 ff.; Ḳazwīnī, *Kosmographie* (ed. Wüstenfeld), i, 82, 158 ff., 198; *Marāṣid al-Iṭṭilā'* (ed. Juynboll), i, 388, 408; v, 429, 432, 483; Quatremère, *Hist. des Mongols,* 200 ff.; Le Strange, 371; K. Ritter, *Erdkunde,* viii, 10, 502-5, 550-70; Fr. Spiegel, *Eranische Altertumskunde,* Leipzig 1871, i, 70; W. Ouseley, *Travels in var. countries of the East,* London 1819 ff., iii, 326-34; W. Taylor Thomson in *JRGeog.S,* viii (1838), 109 ff.; Hommaire de Hell, *Voy. en Turquie et en Perse,* Paris 1854 ff., with accompanying *Historical Atlas,* Pl. 74, 76a; Th. Kotschy in *Petermann's Geogr. Mitteil.,* 1859, 49 ff.; J. E. Polak, *Persien,* Leipzig 1865, i, 313, 315, 349; ii, 146, 178, 229; G. Melgunof, *Das südl. Ufer des Kasp. Meeres,* Leipzig 1868, 21-7, 52, 149, 183; F. v. Call-Rosenberg, *Das Lārthal bei Teherān u. der Demāwend* in *Mitteil. der Geog. Ges. in Wien,* N.F. ix (1876), 113-42; G. Napier's account in *Alpine Journal,* 1877, 262-5, and in *Petermann's Geogr. Mitteil.,* 1877, 434; Tietze, *Der Vulkan Demāwend in Persien,* in *Jahrb. der k. k. geolog. Reichsanst.,* Vienna 1877, vol. xxvii; de Morgan, *Mission scientif. en Perse. Étud. géograph.,* i, Paris 1894, 115, 120-33, with good views; Sven Hedin, *Der Demāwend* in *Verh. der Ges. f. Erdkunde* (Berlin), xix, 304-22; Sarre in *ZG Erdk. Birl.* 1902, 100 ff.; Mas'ūd Mayhān, *Djughrāfiyā-yi mufaṣṣal-i Īrān,* Tehran 1310/1932, index s.v.; Firdawsī, *Shāh-nāma,* ed. and tr. J. Mohl, 1878, vii, Index s.v. Demavend, Zohak; H. Massé, *Croyances et coutumes persans,* index ii, s.v. Démavend. (M. STRECK*)

DĀMGHĀN a town on the main highway between Tehran and Mashhad, some 344 km. east of Tehran; also, a station on the railway between Tehran and Mashhad. At an altitude of 1115 metres, it has a population of 9,900 (1950). One km. to the south of the town is the mound called Tappa Ḥiṣār where excavations conducted by the University of Pennsylvania in 1931 uncovered prehistoric burials and the plaster-decorated remains of a building of the Sāsānid period. The oldest Islamic structure—possibly the earliest surviving mosque in Īrān—is the Tārī Khāna, believed to date from the 3rd/9th century. Attached to this mosque is a minaret of the 5th/11th century. Several tomb towers of the Saldjūḳ period survive: the Pīr 'Alamdār dated 417/1026, the Čihil Dukhtarān dated 446/1054, and the Imām-zāda Dja'far. The minaret of the Masdjid-i Djāmi' is dated 500/1106.

Bibliography: Iḳbāl Yaghmānī, *Djughrāfiyā-yi Ta'rīkhī-yi Dāmghān,* Tehran 1326/1947, 36 ff.; *Rāhnāmā-yi Īrān,* Tehran 1330/1951, 92; *Farhang-i Djughrāfiyā-yi Īrān,* Tehran 1330/1951, vol. 3, 116. (D. N. WILBER)

DAMIETTA [see DIMYĀṬ].

ḌAMĪR [see NAḤW].

AL-**DAMĪRĪ,** MUḤAMMAD B. MŪSĀ B. 'ĪSĀ KAMĀL AL-DĪN, was born in Cairo about the beginning of the year 742/1341 (according to a note in his own handwriting quoted by al-Sakhāwī, 59) and died there in 808/1405. Later dates of his birth, as given in some sources (745/1344 or 750/1349), would hardly be consistent with certain details of his biography. His *nisba* is derived from the northernmost of the two townlets both called Damīra near Samannūd in the Delta.

After first gaining his livelihood as a tailor in his native town he decided to become a professional theologian, choosing as his main teacher the famous Shāfi'ī scholar Bahā' al-Dīn al-Subkī [*q.v.*], with whom he became closely associated for years. He also studied under Djamāl al-Dīn al-Asnawī (Brockelmann I, 110, S II, 107), Ibn al-'Aḳīl, the renowned commentator of Ibn Mālik's *Alfiyya* (Brockelmann II, 108, S II, 104), Burhān al-Dīn al-Ḳīrāṭī (Brockelmann II, 15, S II, 7) and others. His biographers point out his great competence in Muslim jurisprudence, *ḥadīth* science, Ḳur'ānic exegesis, Arabic philology and *belles lettres.* His younger contemporary, al-Maḳrīzī [*q.v.*], in his *'Uḳūd,* speaks of him with love and admiration.

Having been authorized to teach the usual branches of Muslim education and to give *fatwās,* al-Damīrī took up suitable posts in several places of learning and devotion (al-Azhar, the Djāmi' of al-Ẓāhir, the *madrasa* of Ibn al-Baḳarī, the Ḳubba of Baybars II, etc.), where he held lectures and delivered sermons and exhortations, apportioning his time in turn to the different institutions. A member of the Ṣūfī community established in the Khānḳāh Ṣalāḥiyya (previously known as Dār Sa'īd al-Su'adā'; cf. 'Alī Mubārak, iv, 102, Maḳrīzī, *Khiṭaṭ,* Būlāḳ 1270, ii, 415), he was celebrated for his ascetic life and credited with performing miracles. Although as a youth inclined to gluttony, he later made it a habit to fast almost continually, indulged in prayers and vigils and performed the pilgrimage six times between the years 762-799/1361-97. During his stay in Mecca and Medina he completed his education with several local scholars, held lectures and gave *fatwās* and married twice. After his last pilgrimage he stayed in Cairo until his death. He was buried in the Ṣūfī graveyard beside the Djāmi' of Sa'īd al-Su'adā' (cf. 'Alī Mubārak, iv, 102 ff.).

Al-Damīrī's fame as an author rests on his *Ḥayāt al-Ḥayawān,* a para-zoological encyclopaedia, through which he became known both in the east and the west. He wrote it, as stated in the preface, not because of a natural disposition for such an undertaking, but in order to correct false notions about animals which were entertained even by the learned of his time. The work, completed in draft in 773/1371-2, is not only a compendium of Arabic zoology but also a store house of Muslim folklore, described in part in the researches of J. de Somogyi. The author did not restrict himself to the purely zoological aspect of his subject matter but also treated, often at great length, all that pertains to the animals mentioned in any way whatsoever. In addition, he made frequent digressions into other fields, the most remarkable of which is a survey of the history of the Caliphs (s.v. *iwazz*), which occupies about the thirteenth part of the whole work.

The articles, arranged alphabetically according to the first letters—not the radicals—of the anima names, generally contain discussions of the following items: 1) philological aspects of the animal's name;

2) description of the animal and its habits; 3) mention of the animal in the *ḥadīth*-literature; 4) its lawfulness as human food according to the different *madhāhib*; 5) proverbs bearing upon it; 6) medicinal and other properties (*khawāṣṣ*) of its different parts; 7) its meaning when occurring in dreams. The work contains 1069 articles but treats of a much smaller number of animals, real and imaginary (among them the *Burāḳ* [*q.v.*]), since one and the same animal is frequently entered under different names. Being no professional naturalist, the author often entertained superstitious and fabulous notions without any attempt at criticism. He merely transmitted and rearranged traditional knowledge basing himself on hundreds of sources which have been analysed, though not quite satisfactorily, by J. de Somogyi. There are three recensions of the work—a long, a short and an intermediate one—of which the long one is available in at least 13 Oriental impressions (in addition to those mentioned by Brockelmann also Cairo 1315-16, 1321-22, 1353), while a critical edition is still awaited. There exist also several abridgements and adaptations, a Persian translation from the 17th century and a more recent Turkish translation. The English translation of Jayakar extends only to the article *Abū Firās* (about three quarters of the whole) and is not quite satisfactory from the philological point of view.

Of al-Damīrī's other writings only three are extant (see Brockelmann). His last work was a five volume commentary on the *Sunan* of Ibn Mādja [*q.v.*], entitled *al-Dībādja*, of which, however, he was not able to finish a clean copy before he died.

Bibliography: ʿAlī Mubārak, *al-Khiṭaṭ al-Djadīda*, xi, 59; Brockelmann, II, 172 f.; S II, 170 f.; S III, 1260; *Ad-Damîrî's Ḥayât al-Ḥayawân*, transl. from the Arabic by A. S. G. Jayakar, London & Bombay, 1906-08, Introduction; Ḥādjdjī Khalīfa, i, 696 f.; idem, ed. Flügel, index, 1127, no. 4759; Ibn al-ʿImād, *Shadharāt*, year 808; al-Sakhāwī, *al-Ḍawʾ al-Lāmiʿ*, x, 59 ff.; Sarton, *Introduction to the History of Science*, iii/b, 1168 f., 1214, 1326, 1639; al-Shawkānī, *al-Badr al-Ṭāliʿ*, ii, 272; J. de Somogyi, *Index des sources de la Ḥayât al-Ḥayawân de ad-Damîrî*, in *JA*, July-September 1928, 5 ff. (based merely on the Cairo edition 1284); idem, *Biblical Figures in ad-Damīrī's Ḥayāt al-Ḥayawān*, *Dissert. in honorem E. Mahler*, 1937, 263 ff.; idem, *ad-Damīrī's Ḥayāt al-Ḥayawān*, *Osiris*, ix (1950), 33 f.; idem, *ad-Damīrī Ḥayāt al-Ḥayawānja* (in Hungarian), *Sem. St. in Memory of I. Löw*, 1947, 123 ff.; idem, *Chess and Backgammon in ad-Damīrī's Ḥayāt al-Ḥayawān*, *Ét. or. à la mém. de P. Hirschler*, 1950, 101 ff.; idem, *Medicine in ad-Damiri's Hayat al-Hayawan*, in *JSS*, ii (1957), 62 ff.; idem, *The Interpretation of Dreams in ad-Damīrī's Ḥayāt al-Ḥayawān*, in *JRAS*, 1940, 1 ff.; *Die Chalifengeschichte in Damîrî's "Ḥayât al-Ḥayawân"*, in *Isl.*, xviii (1929), 154 ff.; idem, *A History of the Caliphate in the Ḥayāt al-ḥayawān of ad-Damīrī*, in *BSOS* viii (1935-37), 143 ff.; E. Wiedemann, *Beitr. z. Gesch. d. Naturw.*, liii, 233 f.; H. A. Winkler, *Eine Zusammenstellung christlicher Geschichten im Artikel über das Schwein in Damîrî's Tierbuch*, in *Isl.*, xviii (1929), 285 ff. (L. KOPF)

ḌAMMA [see ḤARAKA].

AL-**DAMMĀM**, a port on the Persian Gulf and capital of the Eastern Province of Saudi Arabia. The name formerly designated a tower fort, located at 26° 27′ 56″ N., 50° 06′ 06″ E., on a reef near the shore north of the present town. The origin of the fort is not known, although the structure razed in 1957 to make way for a small-craft pier appeared to date from the time of the redoubtable Djalāhima sea captain Raḥma b. Djābir [*q.v.*]. Ibn Djābir built a fort at al-Dammām after allying himself with Āl Saʿūd about 1809, but the Saʿūdīs destroyed it in 1231/1816 when he deserted their cause to attack al-Baḥrayn. Two years later he assisted the Turco-Egyptian forces of Ibrāhīm Pāshā to capture al-Ḳaṭīf and re-established himself in al-Dammām. He immediately rebuilt the fort, which with its dependent fortifications and village settlement on the adjoining shore became the base for his naval activities against Āl Khalīfa of al-Baḥrayn. In 1242/1826 Āl Khalīfa and Banī Khālid captured al-Dammām, following the death of Raḥma b. Djābir in a naval engagement with the blockading Baḥraynī fleet. For the next seventeen years al-Dammām remained a possession of al-Baḥrayn. During this period Āl Khalīfa permitted the ʿAmāʾir section of Banī Khālid and members of Banī Hādjir to settle there. In 1259/1843 ʿAbd Allāh Āl Khalīfa, having been dispossessed by his grand-nephew Muḥammad, which was soon invested by a Saʿūdī force on land and a Baḥraynī fleet. Fayṣal b. Turkī Āl Saʿūd occupied the fort in 1260/1844, to the disillusionment of Bishr b. Raḥma b. Djābir, who had participated in the campaign in the expectation of recovering his paternal estate. In 1260/1852 Āl Saʿūd, having fallen out with Muḥammad Āl Khalīfa, re-established the sons of ʿAbd Allāh at al-Dammām. An attempt by these exiles to recover al-Baḥrayn led Britain to demand that Āl Saʿūd evict them; when this was not done, they were driven out by a brief British naval bombardment in 1278/1861. In 1282/1866 the garrison of al-Dammām repulsed a British naval force which sought to destroy the fort in retaliation for an incident at Ṣūr in Oman. A Turkish expedition captured al-Dammām in 1288/1871 in the course of occupying a large part of eastern Arabia. Under Turkish administration the fort fell into disrepair, and al-Dammām declined to a minor settlement of fishermen, which figured occasionally in the piratical exploits of the Banī Hādjir. In 1326/1908 Lorimer described it as an abandoned ruin. The site reverted to Saʿūdī rule as a result of the conquest of al-Ḥasā by ʿAbd al-ʿAzīz Āl Saʿūd in 1331/1913. The present town was founded by members of the tribe of al-Dawāsir [*q.v.*], who moved from al-Baḥrayn to the mainland in 1341/1923 to escape British reprisals following clashes with Shīʿī elements on the island. For twenty years al-Dammām remained an insignificant fishing village. In 1357/1938 the California Arabian Standard Oil Company (now the Arabian American Oil Company) discovered oil at nearby al-Ẓahrān [*q.v.*] (Dhahran) on a geological structure which was named the "Dammam Dome". Al-Dammām experienced little growth until its selection in 1365/1946 as the site of a modern deep-water port and the starting point for a railroad leading to the national capital of al-Riyāḍ. The port, which consists of a pierhead connected to the mainland by a trestle and causeway 10.7 km. in length, was opened in 1369/1950 and has since been expanded. In 1372/1953 the capital of the Eastern Province was transferred from al-Hufūf in the oasis of al-Ḥasā to al-Dammām. Al-Dammām has grown rapidly since then and has developed various municipal services, and a limited amount of trade and industry. The town's population was estimated in 1960 at 35,000.

Bibliography: Muḥammad al-Nabhānī, *Al-Tuḥfa al-Nabhāniyya*, Cairo 1342; ʿUt͟hmān ibn Bis͟hr, *ʿUnwān al-Mad͟jd*, Cairo 1373; J. G. Lorimer, *Gazetteer of the Persian Gulf*, Calcutta 1908-15; H. St. J. B. Philby, *Saʿudi Arabia*, London 1954. (H. W. ALTER)

DAMNĀT (DEMNATE, DEMNAT), a small Berber town situated on the edge of the Great Atlas in Morocco, 120 km. east of Marrākush, at an altitude of 960 m., on a small hill overlooking the fertile valley (barley, beans) of the Oued Tassawt, the slopes of which are covered with olive-trees and vines. The town is surrounded by a rectangular wall and includes a *məllāḥ* (Jewish quarter); in fact almost half the population, which stands at about 4,000, consists of Jews, whose numbers however are diminishing regularly. Local trade on a large scale in oil, leather and livestock is carried on at the market which is held on Sundays; in addition, tribes from the Atlas and Sahara used to bring their products (hides, wool, dates), bartering them for such manufactured goods as they needed. Demnat thus appears to have owed part of its prosperity to its situation on the route leading from Marrakus͟h to Meknès and Fez in one direction, and to the Draa (Darʿa) and the Tafilalt in the other; but, without exception, the Arab geographers made no mention of it although its foundation certainly dates from ancient times. Leo Africanus appears to be the first to mention it, though he does not give the name of the town (according to a suggestion put forward by G. S. Colin, Adimmei which appears in Épaulard's trans. on p. 115 may be a mistake for Adimnat) and only mentions a place named El Madina (trans. Épaulard, 130-1), the description of which does in fact correspond closely with that of Demnat. Leo stressed the importance of the Jewish community and of the local leather-work; he also noted the lack of security on the roads, every merchant finding it necessary to maintain "an arquebusier or a cross-bowman". For the rest, the history of the town is little more than a series of disturbances caused either by jealousy of the Jewish population's wealth, or by dynastic rivalries in which the town was the stake. During the 19th century Demnat began to be of concern to the Western Powers who were obliged to intervene to protect the Jews from persecution by the authorities; as a result, on 17 S͟haʿbān 1304/11 May 1887, sultan Mawlāy Ḥasan resolved to give them a separate *məllāḥ*, which they still occupy and which formed the subject of a monograph by P. Flamand, *Un Mellah en pays berbère*: *Demnate* (*IHEM*, Notes et Documents, x), Paris 1952 (see further, idem, *Les communautés israélites au Sud-Morocain*, Casablanca 1959). Some years earlier, however, Ch. de Foucauld who stayed at Demnat on the 6th and 7th October 1883 was able to note (*Reconnaissance du Maroc*, Paris 1888, 77-8) that the Jews were treated with exceptional generosity by the Muslims with whom they lived "pell-mell". The two elements of the local population in fact lived together on good terms with each other; their long-standing association had given rise to affinities in practical matters, particularly in regard to the veneration of saints, even though one could not always tell if they were Muslim or Jewish or in fact if they had ever existed (see L. Voinot, *Pèlerinages judéo-musulmans au Maroc* (*IHEM*, Notes et Documents, iv), Paris 1948, 25 sqq., 60-1); 4 km. south-east of Demnat there still exists a grotto known by the name of Imi n-ifri (opening of the grotto) where Jews and Muslims celebrate a pagan ritual at a miraculous spring (L. Voinot, *op. cit.*, 27-8; E. Doutté, *Missions au Maroc*: *En tribu*, Paris 1914, 216-17).

Seven years before the capture of Demnat by Col. Mangin (1912), Said Boulifa stayed there and made a study of the Berber dialect of the Ahl Demnat (*Textes Berb. en dial. de l'Atlas marocain* (Pub. École des Lettres d'Alger, xxxvi), Paris 1908-9); as a result the local dialects, which are important by reason of their situation at the edge of the two large groups in the South (*tas͟həlḥit*) and Centre (*tamazik͟ht*), have been the subject of research carried out by E. Laoust (*Étude sur le dialecte berbère des Ntifa*, Paris 1918, and *Mots et Choses Berbères*—an ethnographical work—Paris 1920).

Leo Africanus noted that Demnat possessed a number of legal experts, but the true Damnātī rarely figure in Arabic literature; however, we may note ʿAlī b. Sulayman al-Damnātī, author of a commentary on the *Sunan* of Abū Dāwūd entitled *Darad͟jat mirḳāt al-ṣuʿūd ilā Sunan Abī Dāwūd*, published in Cairo in 1928.

Bibliography: given in the article.

(CH. PELLAT)

AL-**DAMURDĀS͟HĪ**, AḤMAD, Egyptian historian of the 12th/18th century. Nothing is known of his life beyond the fact that he held the post of *katk͟hudā* of the ʿAzabān regiment in Cairo, but he may have been a relative of the *rūznāmed͟ji* Ḥasan Efendi al-Damurdās͟hī, who flourished in the early 11th/17th century, and about whose doings he is well informed). His chronicle, *al-Durra al-muṣāna fī ak͟hbār al-kināna*, covers the period 1099-1169/1688-1755. It reveals unfamiliarity with Arabic, and the sense is sometimes garbled or obscure. Nevertheless it is valuable, both as a detailed record of events in Cairo, and as perhaps the sole extant chronicle of Ottoman Egypt composed by a member of the military élite. There are considerable differences in phraseology, and even in data, between the British Museum and Bodleian manuscripts: the former is unique among known copies in giving the name of the author. One recension of *al-Durra* seems to have been used as a source by al-D͟jabartī for his *ʿAd͟jāʾib al-āt͟hār*; for example, D͟jabartī's second legend of the origins of the D͟hu ʾl-Faḳāriyya and Ḳāsimiyya factions, and his list of the *ṣand͟jaḳ beys* at the beginning of the 11th century H. are closely paralleled in *al-Durra*: (D͟jabartī, i, 23-4; BM. Or. 1073, 5a-6b; Bodl. MS. Bruce 43, 2a-(3a). (P. M. HOLT)

DĀNAḲ [see SIKKA].

DANĀḲIL, DANĀḲLA [see DANḲALĪ].

DANCE [see RAḲṢ].

AL-**DĀNĪ**, ABŪ ʿAMR ʿUTHMĀN B. SAʿĪD B. ʿUMAR AL-UMAWĪ, Mālikī lawyer and above all, "reader" of the Ḳurʾān, born at Cordova in 371/981/2. After having made his pilgrimage to Mecca and spent some time in Cairo between 397/1006 and 399/1008, he returned to his birthplace but was soon forced to flee, first to Almeria and finally to Denia (Dāniya, whence his *nisba*), where he settled down and died in 444/1053.

Among more than 120 works which he wrote and enumerated himself in an *urd͟jūza*, only about ten are known (see Brockelmann, I, 407, S I, 719); two of them deal with questions of grammar, and the others with matters connected with the "readings", a science in which Abū ʿAmr al-Dānī had become famous. His most celebrated works are the *K. al-Muḳniʿ fī Maʿrifat Rasm Maṣāḥif al-Amṣār* (see S. de Sacy, *Notices et Extraits*, viii, 290) and *al-Taysīr fī ʾl-Ḳirāʾāt al-Sabʿ* (ed. O. Pretzl, Istanbul

1930), which was the one most studied according to the evidence of Ibn Khaldūn (*Prolégomènes*, ii, 456); *al-Muḥkam fī Naḳṭ al-Maṣāḥif* has recently been edited in Damascus (1379/1960) by ʿIzzat Ḥasan.

Bibliography: *EI*¹, s.v. AL-DĀNĪ, by Moh. Ben Cheneb; Ḍabbī, no. 1185; Ibn Bashkuwāl, no. 873; Ibn Khayr, *Fahrasa*, index; Maḳḳarī, *Analectes*, i, 550; Yāḳūt, ii, 540; Ibn Farḥūn, *Dībādj*, Fez 1316, 191; Dhahabī, *Ḥuffāẓ*, iii, 316; Suyūṭī, *Ṭabaḳāt al-Ḥuffāẓ*, xiv, 5; Freytag, *Einleitung*, 386; Wüstenfeld, *Geschichtsschreiber*, 197; Amari, *Bibl. Ar. Sic.* ii, 579; Pons Boygues, *Ensayo*, no. 91; Nöldeke, etc., *Gesch. des Qorâns*, iii, 214 ff. (ED.)

DĀNISHGĀH [see DJĀMIʿA].

DĀNISHMENDIDS, a Turcoman dynasty which reigned in northern Cappadocia from the last quarter of the 5th/11th century until 573/1178. The origins and first conquests of its founder, Amīr Dānishmend, are obscure. Appearing in Cappadocia during the years of anarchy which followed the death, in 781/1085, of the Saldjūḳid Sulaymān b. Kutlumish, he became involved in the events of the First Crusade. When historians became interested in him they resorted to legends or imagination to fill the gaps in their knowledge. But it was above all the epic romance of which he was made the hero that gave rise to an imbroglio of historical facts which is difficult to unravel. The oral epic tradition about Dānishmend was put into writing for the first time in 643/1245 by Mawlānā Ibn ʿAlāʾ; this first romance, now lost, was rewritten in 761/1360 by ʿĀrif ʿAlī. This romance which attributes to Dānishmend a legendary relationship with the famous epic heroes Abū Muslim and Sayyid Baṭṭāl and which is conceived as a sequel to the Romance of Sayyid Baṭṭāl, very soon gave rise to error through the fault of certain Ottoman historiographers who could not distinguish between historical truth and legend. The chief culprits were the historians of the 10th/16th century, ʿĀlī and Djenābī who, by treating the romance as a historical document, mingled legendary elements with history in their works. These errors which were to be repeated by historians in succeeding centuries, Ḳaramānī, Kātib Čelebī, Münedjdjim-bashī and Hezārfenn, have been reproduced in the works of orientalists who made use of these sources. Those scholars who attempted to determine which parts of the story were, in their view, in disagreement with historical data often succeeded only in further confusing the facts. When Dānishmend appears in the historians' account of the First Crusade he is already master of Sebastea, the Iris Valley with Eudoxias (Toḳat), Comana, Amasya, Neocaesarea where he resided, and Gangra; he controlled the route from Ankara to Caesarea, the towns of the Pontic coast paid him tribute, and his foraging parties laid waste the shores of the Black Sea, making incursions into Georgia and Armenia. Later he was to make a further conquest, Melitene, and it is in connexion with Ḳilidj Arslan b. Sulaymān's expedition against this town in 490/1096-1097 that Dānishmend is first mentioned in history. The sultan having laid siege to Melitene which was defended by the Armenian governor Gabriel, Dānishmend appeared on the scene and made peace between the opposing leaders. These events were interrupted by the capture of Nicaea by the Crusaders in 490/1097. In the summer of the same year Dānishmend, together with the other Turkish amīrs, took part in the harassing attacks to which the Crusaders were to be subjected throughout their march across Anatolia. But soon afterwards an important occurence was to bring him into prominence: in Ramaḍān 493/July 1100 one of the most eminent of the Crusaders' leaders, Bohemund of Antioch, when going to the help of Melitene which was besieged by Dānishmend, fell into the hands of the amīr who imprisoned him in the fortress of Neocaesarea. The following year the Franco-Lombard Crusade coming to the rescue of Bohemund took the Cappadocia route and was defeated by Dānishmend. In September of that year the amīr took part in the massacre of the Crusade's last army, made up of contingents from Aquitaine and Bavaria, which was wiped out near Heraclea in Cappadocia. A year later, Dānishmend entered Melitene after a siege lasting for three years and, by his generosity, won the praise of a population made up of different races and creeds. In Shaʿbān 496/May 1103 the amīr freed Bohemund with whom he had concluded an alliance against their common enemies, Byzantine and Saldjūḳid. But the death of Dānishmend which took place in the year 497/1104 prevented Bohemund from reaping the benefits of this alliance and allowed Ḳilidj Arslan to take part of his rival's territory, as well as the town of Melitene. Dānishmend's eldest son, Amīr Ghāzī, succeeded his father. Intervening in the dynastic struggles which divided the sons of Ḳilidj Arslan who had died in 500/1107, he helped his son-in-law Masʿūd in 510/1116 to take Ḳonya. Then, in alliance with Tughrul Arslan, prince of Melitene, and his *atabek* Balak, in 514/1120 he defeated the amīr of Erzindjān, Ibn Mengüdjek, and his ally the duke of Trebizond; but he set free his prisoner Ibn Mengüdjek who was also his son-in-law, an act which was a source of dissension between the allies. In 518/1124, on the death of Balak, Amīr Ghāzī recaptured Melitene. Intervening in the war then being waged between Masʿūd and his brother Malik ʿArab, prince of Ankara and Ḳasṭamonu, he defeated the latter and in 521/1127 captured Caesarea and Ankara from him. ʿArab appealed for help to Byzantium, but Amīr Ghāzī also took Gangra and Ḳasṭamonu and imposed his authority over Cappadocia. In 523/1129, on the death of the Armenian prince Thoros, Amīr Ghāzī intervened in Cilicia, in the following year defeated Bohemund II of Antioch, brought the Armenian prince Leon into subjection and ravaged the Count of Edessa's lands. He then had to turn against John Comnenus who in 527/1132 took Ḳasṭamonu from him. Amīr Ghāzī who had given refuge to Isaac Comnenus, then revolted against his brother, and recaptured the town in the following year. In reward for his victories over the Christians the caliph al-Mustarshid and the sultan Sandjār granted him the title of Malik, but when the envoys reached Melitene they found the amīr on his deathbed and it was his son Muḥammad who was invested in his place, in 528/1134. John Comnenus at once resumed hostilities and, in 529/1135, recaptured Ḳasṭamonu and Gangra, but these two towns fell once more into the hands of the Turks as soon as the Emperor had withdrawn. The reign of Malik Muḥammad is marked by a series of unsuccessful attempts by John Comnenus, in both Cilicia and the pontic region at different times, to recapture the strongholds which had been taken by the Dānishmendids, as well as by the amīr's inroads into the territories of the count of Marʿash. In 536/1142, Malik Muḥammad died at Caesarea which he had rebuilt and where he had resided. It was his brother Yaghibasan, governor of Sebastea, who proclaimed himself amīr at the expense of his nephew Dhu 'l-Nūn, and who married the dead man's widow. By thus usurping power, the new amīr caused the break up of the amīrate which was to lead to the fall of the dynasty; while Dhu 'l-Nūn seized Caesarea, Yaghībasan's brother ʿAyn al-Dawla made himself master of Elbistān and then of Melitene. Henceforth there were three rival branches whose interests were sometimes upheld, sometimes opposed by the Saldjūḳids. However the dynasty survived while Yaghībasan lived, in spite of his continual wars with his father-in-law Masʿūd and subsequently, with his brother-in-law Ḳīlīdj Arslan II. The emperor Manuel who had at first allied himself with the Saldjūḳids as a means of preventing the Dānishmendids' incursions into Byzantine territory, in 553/1158 took Yaghībasan's side against Ḳīlīdj Arslan II and imposed his authority over Dhu 'l-Nūn. The following year marks the opening of hostilities between Ḳīlīdj Arslan and Manuel, while at the same time war flared up between the rival dynasties as a result of Yaghībasan's abduction of Ḳīlīdj Arslan's fiancée, the daughter of the Ṣalṭuḳid amīr of Erzurūm, who was married to Dhu 'l-Nūn. But the death of Yaghībasan in 559/1164 gave rise to dynastic quarrels which provided Ḳīlīdj Arslan with his opportunity to destroy the amīrate. Yaghībasan's widow married Dhu 'l-Nūn's nephew—Ismāʿīl b. Ibrāhīm, aged sixteen, and proclaimed him amīr. In order to protect the interests of Dhu 'l-Nūn, against whom he was afterwards to turn, Ḳīlīdj Arslan invaded the Dānishmendids' territories. In 567/1172, as a result of a palace revolution during which Ismāʿīl and his wife perished, Dhu 'l-Nūn was called to Sebastea and proclaimed amīr. He was at once attacked by Ḳīlīdj Arslan, and appealed for help to his father-in-law Nūr al-Dīn, *atabek* of Damascus, whose intervention compelled Ḳīlīdj Arslan to hand back the territories he had taken from Dhu 'l-Nūn. Nūr al-Dīn withdrew, leaving a relief garrison in Sebastea. But Nūr al-Dīn died in 569/1174 and Ḳīlīdj Arslan at once seized Sebastea, the Iris valley with Toḳat and Comana, then Amasya, and proceeded to lay siege to Neocaesarea. Dhu l'-Nūn appealed for help to Manuel. In spite of the emperor's efforts the Byzantines were defeated, the Saldjūḳids took possession of Neocaesarea, and Dhu 'l-Nūn was put to death by poison on Ḳīlīdj Arslan's orders in 570/1175. In the surviving Melitene branch discord reigned among the three sons of Dhu 'l-Ḳarnayn b. ʿAyn al-Dawla, who had died in 557/1162. The eldest, Naṣr al-Dīn Muḥammad, was dethroned in 565/1170 in favour of his brother Fakhr al-Dīn Ḳāsim; but the latter, who was barely fifteen years old, was killed in a riding accident on his wedding day; and it was from the third brother, Afridūn, that Naṣr al-Dīn Muḥammad took back the town in 570/1175 and reigned for three years under Ḳīlīdj Arslan's suzerainty. But in 573/1178 the Saldjūḳid occupied Melitene, and so came the end of the Dānishmendids. According to Ibn Bībī, Yaghībasan's three sons Muẓaffar al-Dīn Mahmūd, Ẓahīr al-Dīn Ili and Badr al-Dīn Yūsuf entered the Saldjūḳids' service and helped Ghiyāth al-Dīn Kaykhūsraw I to regain his throne; in gratitude the monarch rewarded them by giving them important positions and restoring some of their possessions (cf. *al-Awāmir al-ʿAlāʾiyye*, Ankara 1956, 76 ff.).

Bibliography: Matthew of Edessa, *Chronicle*, trans. E. Dulaurier, Paris 1858; Michael the Syrian, *Chronicle*, trans. J. B. Chabot, iii; Anna Comnena, ed. B. Leib, iii, 18, 76, 200, 201, 210; Niketas Choniates, ed. Bonn, 27, 29, 46, 152, 159; Kinnamos, ed. Bonn, 14, 15, 16; William of Tyre, *Receuil Hist. Crois. Hist. Occ. I.*, ix, 396-397; Albert of Aix, *Rec. Hist. Crois., Hist. occ. IV*, 524, 525, 526, 567, 573, 576, 581, 611-4; Ibn al-Athīr (ed. Tornberg), x, 203, 204, 237; xi, 9, 52, 203-4, 207, 209, 237, 257-8, J. Laurent, *Sur les Emir Danichmendites jusqu'en* 1104, in *Mélanges Iorga*, Paris 1933, 449-506; Mükr. Halil Yınanc, art. Danişmendliler, in *IA*; also, *Türkiye Tarihi*: *Selcuklular Devri*, Istanbul 1944, 89-103; I. Mélikoff, *La Geste de Melik Dānişmend*, i, Paris 1960 (see bibliography). (I. Mélikoff)

DĀNIYA, Span. Denia, capital of the north-eastern district of the province of Alicante, the most southerly of the three present-day provinces which used to make up the ancient kingdom of Valencia (Castellon de la Plana, Valencia, Alicante). This town of 50,000 inhabitants is situated at the south-east tip of the Gulf of Valencia (Sinus Sucronensis), north of the mountain Mongó (in Arabic Djabal Ḳāʿūn) which is 2,190 feet high. Because of its good harbour, north-west of the ancient Promontorium Artemesium, Ferrarium or Tenebrium (to-day Cabo de S. Antonio, S. Martin or de la Nao), Denia was an ancient foundation of the Phocians (of Massilia/ Marseilles or of Emporium Ampurias) in the sixth century A.D., and was first called τὸ Ἡμεροσκοπεῖον (Strabo), Hemeroscopium, "the watch of the day"; then, because of the famous temple of Artemis of Ephesus erected on the castle hill, Artemisium; in Roman times this became Dianium (the city of Diana) which later gave the Arabic Dāniya (with the *imāla* Däniya) and finally became Denia in Spanish. Although allied to the Romans, it was nevertheless spared by the Carthaginians since it was a Greek colony. Cato achieved a victory over the Spanish in the neighbourhood of this town before 195. The liberator of Spain, Sertorius, found his last point of support there, as well as a powerful naval base; according to the most likely evidence it was there that he was assassinated in 73. Caesar punished the town because it sided with Pompey (Dianium Stipendiarium); under the Roman Empire it became nevertheless an extremely flourishing municipality, as can be seen from the excavations that have been made there. It soon became Christian, and in the 7th century a bishopric was created there, four of whose prelates took part in the councils of Toledo. It possesses a fragment of the Paleo-Christian tomb of Severina in mosaic and other much more primitive remains which testify to its new faith. But it was under Arab domination, after the country had been conquered by Ṭāriḳ in 94/713, that it reached its highest stage of development (50,000 inhabitants, as it has to-day). On the other hand, we know almost nothing about the period of the migration of the peoples and the Goths. Denia began to play a certain part in the rebellions against ʿAbd al-Raḥmān I, but this part became considerably greater after the fall of the Caliphate in 403/1013, when the ʿĀmirid Abu 'l-Djaysh Mudjāhid, [*q.v.*] a manumitted slave of ʿAbd al-Raḥmān b. al-Manṣūr (called in western sources Musett or Mugeto), at first with the assistance of the learned co-regent (*khalīfa*), al-Muʿayṭī (405-21/1015-30), took possession of Denia and the Balearic Islands [see mayurḳa] (405-36/1014-1045) and succeeded in surpassing the other *Reyes de Taifas* in learning and wealth. He surrounded himself with scholars and was a distinguished commentator on the Ḳur'ān. Denia was at that time one of the most important cities of the Levante and the country round it, where the fields were cultivated almost without interruption throughout the year, was very rich. The semi-insular kingdom of Denia played a very important part also as a naval base and in its dockyard was constructed the greater part of the fleet which Mudjāhid used for piracy and with which, after he had seized the Balearic Islands, he undertook his celebrated expedition to Sardinia (406/1015). His son ʿAlī, called Iḳbāl al-Dawla, was taken prisoner by the Germans at the same time that his father was put to flight and pursued by the Christian coalition which retook the island. Ransomed after several years of captivity, he succeeded his father in 436/1044, and reigned for 32 years until 468/1076. Born of a Christian mother and brought up in captivity, he became a Muslim, but possessed none of his father's qualities. Dissolute, miserly and a coward, he confined himself to wringing all he could out of his subjects, and his only undertaking consisted of sending a large ship full of food in 446 or 447 (1054-55) to Egypt, where famine was raging; it came back full of money and jewels. When his brother-in-law, al-Muḳtadir, wanted to enlarge his frontiers on the Denia side, ʿAlī was incapable of resisting him, and his subjects abandoned him, delivering the town up to al-Muḳtadir who sent ʿAlī to Saragossa where he died in 474/1081-2. Al-Mundhir succeeded his father, al-Muḳtadir, in the kingdom of Denia, and his son, Sulaymān, continued to rule under the suzerainty of the Banū Batīr until 484/1091. In the same year the Almoravids had just taken Almeria, which they seized along with Murcia, Játiva and Denia, all of which fell later into power of the Almohads. In the spring of 599/1203, these last concentrated in the harbour of Denia a powerful squadron and landing party, who, on their way to attack the Banū Ghāniya [*q.v.*] at Majorca, put in at Ibiza and seized Palma in September of the same year. Denia was at that time governed by Muḥammed b. Isḥāḳ, who had succeeded his father Isḥāk b. Ghāniya on the throne of Majorca but had been deposed by his brothers because of his adhesion to the Almohads; the Almohad sultān al-Manṣūr had recommended him strongly in his will. In 641/1244, Denia was finally taken from the Muslims by James I of Aragon (Don Jaime el Conquistador), and one of his captains, the German Carroz, undertook the redivision of its lands. In 725/1325, it was given to the Infante, Don Pedro, whose descendants, the royal dukes of Gandía, ruled the County from 1356 up to the time that the Catholic Kings made it a Marquisate. In 1610, it lost most of its population through the expulsion of the industrious Moors by Philip III, and from that time on was of no importance. However, in the War of the Spanish Succession, Denia, whose harbour was fortified, fought stubbornly on the side of the Archduke, was besieged three times by Philip V, and taken in 1708. In 1812-3 it was occupied by the French.

The most famous Arab scholar of Denia is the great commentator on the Ḳur'ān, al-Dānī [*q.v.*] Abu ʿAmr ʿUthmān b. Saʿīd.

Bibliography: Roque Chabas, *Historia de la Ciudad de Denia*, 2 vols., Denia 1874-76; Madoz, *Dicc. geogr.-estadistico-histór.*, vii, 37-78; Idrīsī, *Desc. de l'Afrique et de l'Espagne*, 192; Yāḳūt, ii, 540 (the harbour of Denia is called here al-Summān); B. al-Bustānī, *Dā'irat al-Maʿārif*, vii, 572; *Marāṣid al-Ittilāʿ*, v, 426; Ibn al-Khaṭīb, *Aʿmāl al-Aʿlām*, 250-4; *Les "Mémoires" du Roi Ziride ʿAbd Allāh*, in *al-And.*, iv/1, 42-4; ʿAfīf Turk, *El-Reino de Zaragoza en el siglo XI (V de la hégira)*, thesis, 149-59; *al-Ḥulal al-Mawshiyya*, 62. — Numismatics: F. Codera, *Tratado de Numismática arábigo-española*, Madrid 1879, 174-81; F. Caballero-Infante, *Estudio sobre las Monedas Árabes de Denia*, in *El Archivo*, iv, Denia 1889; A. Vives y Escudero, *Monedas de las dinastías arábigo-españolas*, Madrid 1893, 212-21. See also art. MUDJĀHID.

C. F. SEYBOLD-[A. HUICI MIRANDA])

DĀNIYĀL. Muslim tradition has retained only a weak and rather confused record of the two biblical characters bearing the name Daniel, the sage of ancient times mentioned by Ezekiel (xiv, 14, 20 and xxviii, 3) and the visionary who lived at the time of the captivity in Babylon, who himself sometimes appears as two different people. Furthermore, the faint trace of a figure from the antiquity of fable combining with the apocalyptic tone of the book handed down in the Bible under the name Daniel, makes Dāniyāl of Muslim legend a revealer of the future and eschatological mysteries, and even lends his authority to astrological almanacs (*Malḥamat Dāniyāl*) of extremely mediocre quality.

Apocalyptical revelations are attributed to Daniel the Elder, it being suggested that a book recording such predictions was found in the coffin supposed to contain the remains of Dāniyāl (whoever he might be) which was brought to light at the time of the Muslim conquest of Tustar, and buried again with the body at the command of Caliph ʿUmar; according to a legend told by al-Bīrūnī, Dāniyāl acquired his knowledge in the Treasure Cave; Muslim sources moreover hand down, besides a garbled version of chapter xi, some authentic quotations from the Book of Daniel. Perhaps it is this Daniel whom the *K. al-Tīdjān* (70) places on the same footing as Luḳmān [*q.v.*] and Dhu 'l-Ḳarnayn [*q.v.*]: three characters considered by some as prophets not apostles or simply as just but not inspired men.

Other traditions treat as two characters the Daniel of the destruction of the first Temple in Jerusalem and the captivity in Babylon: an elder Daniel and a son of the same name; the former, son of the Judaean king Jehoiakim, the latter becoming an uncle to Cyrus by marriage (a garbled reference to the marriage of Ahasuerus and the Jewess Esther; moreover, another tradition has Ahasuerus converted to Judaism by Mordecai and taught by Daniel and his three companions).

Muslim tradition has retained, somewhat distorted, episodes related in the Book of Daniel: the presence of Daniel and his companions in the court of Bukht-Naṣṣar [*q.v.*]—Nebuchadnezzar; Nebuchadnezzar's dreams; the friction between Daniel and his detractors (here presented as Magi) and his miraculous delivery from the lions' den; Belshazzar's feast and the deciphering of the mysterious writing. Nebuchadnezzar's being driven temporarily to dwell with the beasts of the field is also to be found here and al-Thaʿlabī is even able to narrate the king's death in a version forming one of the numerous variants of the folk theme used by Schiller in his ballad *Der Gang nach dem Eisenhammer* (see Stith-Thompson, *Motif-Index*, K. 1612, iv, 414). The character of Daniel is also introduced in the framework of stories which in the Bible centre round Ezra and Nehemiah: Ahasuerus did not allow Daniel and his three companions to return to the Holy Land, but he permitted Daniel, a great judge and a viceroy throughout his reign, to take from the royal treasure all that Nebuchadnezzar had taken from Jerusalem and restore it to the Jews.

Bibliography: Yaʿḳūbī, 70 (Dutch version, G. Smit, *Bijbel en Legende bij den arabischen Schrijver Jaʿqubi*, 82); Ṭabarī, i, 647, 652-4, 665-8, 717; Masʿūdī, *Murūdj*, i, 117, 120, ii, 115, 128; Ps.—Balkhī, *al-Badʾ wa ʾl-Taʾrīkh*, ii, 156 f./144; 165/150 sq.; iii, 114 f./118 f. and cf. index; Thaʿlabī, *ʿArāʾis al-Madjālis*, 198-202; Bīrūnī, *Āthār* (*Chronology*), 15-17/18-20, 302/300. On the tomb and coffin of Dāniyāl, see also Muḳaddasī, 417 (cf. C. Cahen, in *Arabica*, 1959, 28); Harawī, *K. al-Ziyārāt*, ed. J. Sourdel-Thomine, 69, transl., *Guide des lieux de Pèlerinage*, 154, n. 4 (cf. M. Schreiner, *ZDMG*, liii, 58 f.) and *EI*[1], article SŪSAN. *Malḥamat Dāniyāl*, cf. G. Levi Della Vida, *Elenco*, 98. See also R. Basset, *Mille et un Contes* ..., iii, 125-8 (observations by B. Heller in *REJ*, lxxxv, 134 f.) and B. Heller, *Encyclopaedia Judaica*, 5, 773 f. (G. VAJDA)

DĀNIYĀL, called Sulṭān Dāniyāl in the histories, the youngest and favourite son of the Mughal emperor Akbar, born Adjmēr 2 Djumāda I 979/22 September 1571. In 1008/1599 he was appointed military governor of the Deccan, and after his conquest of the city of Aḥmadnagar (1009/1601) he was honoured by Akbar and given the province of Khāndēsh, fancifully named Dāndēsh after him. He is described as well-built, good-looking, fond of horses, and skilful in the composition of Hindūstānī poems. He figures in Abu ʾl-Faḍl's lists of the grandees of the empire (*Āʾin-i Akbari*, i, 30) as a commander of 7000. He died of *delirium tremens* at Burhānpur on 9 Dhu ʾl-Ḥidjdja 1013/28 April 1605.

Bibliography: see AKBAR.

(J. BURTON-PAGE)

DANḲALĪ, (plural Danāḳil), a tribe occupying the western Red Sea coast from the neighbourhood of Zūla (39° 15′ E, 15° 10′ N) to French Somaliland, and spreading inland over territory of extreme heat and desolation to the foot of the main escarpment of Ethiopia and astride the Dessié—ʿAṣṣāb road. Mainly but no longer exclusively nomadic, with some cattle-owning sections, they have formed many semi-permanent hamlets and a few larger villages on the coast and inland, where a few practise agriculture. Fishing and salt-mining are other occupations. The larger permanent villages today contain markets and police posts, and are gradually losing the complete isolation of centuries. The prevailing standard of life is extremely low, thanks to conditions of abnormal severity and (in the past) to pitiless and ever-repeated raiding from the Ethiopian highlands. The Danḳalī character is reckoned as suspicious, unstable and savage; early attempts at European exploration based on ʿAṣṣāb was met by murderous resistance, and no European survivor returned from the expeditions of Müntzinger (1875), Giuletti (1881), or Bianchi (1884).

The Danāḳil appear to represent a Hamitic base with much absorption in the past of Arab, Somālī, and other stock. Their own origin-legends, all mythical but faintly reflecting actual invasions and upheavals, seek to explain the presence of a phenomenon familiar elsewhere in Eritrea and northern Ethiopia—that of a relatively small ruling caste superior in status, freedom and economic privilege to a larger serf-caste: a distinction which cuts across the division into the subtribes and communities of which the Danḳalī nation is composed. Divided between 1303/1885 and 1372/1952 between Eritrean (that is, Italian and British) and Ethiopian rule, the people had at no time—or have now no remaining trace of—political unity or any more cohesion than can be based on common language, religion, and living-conditions; the only potentate commanding more than sub-tribal or group prestige has been the Sultan of Aussa, resident at Sardo. The Danāḳil in 1954 numbered probably about 50,000 to 80,000 souls.

The Danḳalī language, also called ʿAfar, can be placed as a dialect of the lower-Kushite branch of the Southern Hamitic group. It is close to the Saho language (of the plateau-dwelling tribes west and south of Zūla), and has links with the Somālī dialects.

Bibliography: M. Nesbitt, *La Dankalia esplorata*, Florence 1930; O. Dante, *La Dankalia Settentrionale*, Asmara 1909; A. Pollera, *Le Popolazioni indigene dell' Eritrea*, Bologna 1935; British Military Administration of Eritrea (per S. F. Nadel), *Races and Tribes of Eritrea*, Asmara 1943; D. Buxton, *Travels in Ethiopia*, London 1949. (S. H. LONGRIGG)

DAR, a Persian word meaning "door" or "gate", found in many Iranian and Turkic languages. It is synonymous with Arabic *bāb* and is used similarly, *e.g.*, *dar-i ʿaliyya*, *dar-i dawlat*, and in India *dar-bār* (durbar). In a special sense it refers to the ruler's court, or in extension, to a government bureau, already in pre-Islamic Iran. In Pahlavi it was usually written with the heterogram *BB′*.

(R. N. FRYE)

DĀR, (dwelling place), house. The two words most commonly used to designate a dwelling place, *bayt* and *dār*, have, etymologically, quite different meanings. *Bayt* is, properly speaking, the covered shelter where one may spend the night; *dār* (from *dāra*, to surround) is a space surrounded by walls, buildings, or nomadic tents, placed more or less in a circle. *Dārat*[un] is the tribal encampment known in North Africa as the *duwwār*. From the earliest times there has been in Muslim dwellings a tendency to arrange around a central space: the park, where the shepherd's flock will be sheltered from the blows of enemies; the courtyard, where the non-nomadic family will live cut off from inquisitive strangers. The first house which Islam, in its infancy, offers for our consideration, is that built by Muḥammad, on his arrival in Medina, as a dwelling place for himself and his family, and as a meeting place for believers. The courtyard surrounded by walls is its essential feature. A shelter from the sun, intended to protect the faithful at prayer, runs alongside the wall on one side. Rooms built along another side were occupied by the Prophet's wives and were added to as a result of his subsequent unions.

Tradition brings us an interesting detail on the subject of these rooms. Their entrance on to the courtyard was fronted by a porch of palm branches which could be shut off, if required, by curtains of camel-hair. This front annexe of the room, which recalls the *riwāḳ*, the movable screen of the nomadic tent, which keeps the dwelling in touch with the outside world, and plays the part of a vestibule, was to be perpetuated in the Muslim house.

This arrangement, of a central open space, surrounded by habitable rooms, certainly does not belong exclusively to the Arab world. This disposition is also characteristic of the primitive Roman house, with its *atrium*, and the Hellenic house with its peristyle; it must have been adopted very early by the Mediterranean countries. But this type of domestic architecture seems to offer an ideal framework for Muslim life. It is well adapted to the patriarchal view of the family and creates for it an enclosed sphere; it conforms easily with the element of secrecy dear to the private life of the Muslim, and this idea is reflected in the architectural arrangement both in elevation and in plan. Houses in European towns look out widely upon the street, the elegance and luxury of the façade are for the architect an object of very considerable attention, and for the owner of the house, a sign of wealth; on the other hand the Muslim dwelling, however rich, presents a most sober external appearence—bare walls pierced by a massive and ever closed door, and by few and narrow windows. The main concern of this domestic architecture is with the central open space. The courtyard seems almost the principal room of the dwelling, and the façades which surround it offer the builder a rich and varied aesthetic theme, —but one whose charm is only accessible to the occupants.

If the customs moulded by Islam contribute to the relative unity of the dwellings, this unity derives even more clearly from the climatic conditions which affect the majority of Muslim countries. The latter, as is well known, almost all occupy a long east-west region in which rain is rare, the sun fierce, and the heat of summer intense. The scarcity of rain and the steppe-like arid character of these countries make water, be it pool or fountain, a much appreciated element of comfort and adornment—one which plays its part in the decoration of palaces as well as in more modest dwellings. The fierce sun and hot summer motivate the arrangement of underground recesses such as the *sarādīb* (sing. *sardāb*) of ʿIrāḳ and Persia, or the building of rooms which are well ventilated but lit only by a subdued light, such as the *īwān*. The *īwān* is a room enclosed by three walls, opening out in the whole width of the fourth side, like an enormous gaping flat-based ledge, and is generally roofed by a cradle-vault (semi-cylindrical). Open to the space of the courtyard, it recalls the *riwāḳ* of the Arab tent; it can act as a reception room and is not without similarity to the *prostas* of the Greek house; yet it does seem to be a genuinely Iranian creation. In the Parthian palace of Hatra (2nd. century A.D.) it is revealed in all its majesty. It was to become a characteristic theme of the architecture of the Sāsānids. The most famous example is the Ṭāḳ-i Kisrā, the palace of Ctesiphon, built by K͟husraw Anūs͟hirwān (551-579 A.D.). The Mesopotamian architects working for the ʿAbbāsids were to make the *īwān* one of the essential elements of their monumental compositions. The palace of Ctesiphon clearly inspired the builder who created, in 221/836, the great *īwān* of the palace of al-Muʿtaṣim at Sāmarrā [*q.v.*]. It is to be found on a smaller scale in 147/764 in the palace of Uk͟hayḍir; this princely dwelling exhibits courtyards surrounded by buildings. In two of the courts, two *īwān*s open out face to face, each preceded by a gallery, along the whole width of the courtyard. This symmetrical arrangement, with two wide galleries facing each other and the *īwān*s opening out in the far wall, used according to the season—summer and winter—has been perpetuated in the houses of modern ʿIrāḳ. The gallery, or wide room, giving on to the courtyard through three bays, is called a *tarma*; the *īwān* is flanked by two small rooms (called *ōda*) which re-establish the rectangular scheme. However, by the 3rd/9th century this architectural idea (wide ante-room, deep *īwān* with lateral rooms whose doors open on the ante-room) moved towards the West and began to reach the Mediterranean world. In some houses of al-Fusṭāṭ (old Cairo) generally attributed to the Ṭūlūnids, the *īwān* plays an important role. The courtyard, which one reaches by one of the corners, is framed by walls, and the four sides contain *īwān*s, some deep, others shallow and rather like wide, flat-based ledges. On one of the sides there is an ante-room with three bays, and at its far end we find a central *īwān* and the two flanking rooms. The arrangement of the wide ante-room and the deep *īwān* forms a characteristic T shape. These Ṭūlūnid dwellings, built in brick like the monuments of the period, comprise several storeys. They were provided with a system of conduits which brought fresh water and carried away dirty water. Their courtyards were decorated with pools and plants. In two houses, a fountain is built into one of the rooms and the water is channelled into the courtyard pool. In the rooms of rectangular shape, the short sides of the rectangle and the long wall facing the entrance are often cut into by level ledges, a sort of atrophied *īwān*s, where seats could be placed.

Before following up the westward migration of these elements of domestic architecture shown by the Ṭūlūnid houses, it seems worthwhile to indicate how they have changed on the spot, and what can be found of them, modified by Turkish influence, in the modern dwellings of Egypt. The courtyard is still an important element in these dwellings, but it is no longer in the centre of the building. It stands in front of them, accessible by a curved corridor. The visitor can be received here, in a low room (*tak͟htabos͟h*), opening out widely on the ground floor, or in a loggia (*maḳʿad*) which stands above it and dominates the courtyard. If the visitor is entering the interior of the house, he will be received in the *selāmlīk*. Its principal element is a large room (*mandara*) whose central part, a substitute for the courtyard, is paved, adorned with a fountain and surrounded by two or three *īwān*s—or rather, *līwān*s, as the word has come to be used in local parlance. These *līwān*s, raised above floor level, are furnished with carpets and divans. The *ḥarīm* is completely separate from the *selāmlīk* and is accessible by a door opening onto the courtyard and by a staircase. The *ḳāʿa*, its principal room, is not dissimilar to the *mandara*, for here, too, one finds a central space and lateral extensions. But it is different, and derives more evidently from the ancient courtyard, for the walls surrounding the central space rise to the level of the terraces, and carry a lantern which lights the interior.

The dwelling with the central courtyard, with the characteristics inherited from the Iranian tradition being adapted to the domestic theme of the Roman world, spread early across the Mediterranean countries of Islam. Evidences of this expansion have been found in archaeological researches in recent years. Excavations lately undertaken at Ṣabra-Manṣūriyya, the town founded in 335/947 by the Fāṭimid al-Manṣūr at the gates of al-Ḳayrawān, have revealed a palace with walls of clay once decorated with ceramic marquetry. Here we find the arrangement of the wide ante-room and the deep *īwān* with two rooms alongside. From the same period, or possibly a little earlier, the castle of the Ṣanhād͟jī Amīr Zīrī at As͟hīr, dated about 324/935, is interesting for the use of courtyards and for the rigorous symmetry of the rooms which surround them. Five rooms exhibit flat-based ledges cut into the wall facing the entrance; these inner recesses are fronted on the outside by rectangular fore-parts.

About a hundred years later, at Ṣanhādja in the Berber territory, the palaces of the Ḳalʿa of the Banū Ḥammād were being constructed. Three of these royal dwellings have been excavated. *Dār al-baḥr*, the largest, owes its traditional name to the sheet of water which entirely occupied a large courtyard. Above the huge pool were the state rooms. A second courtyard was surrounded by buildings presumably for domestic use: storerooms for provisions and a bath intended for guests. The flat-based ledges, probably derived from the *īwān* which certainly was already well known to Sāsānid architects, give variety to the interior construction of the rooms. In another Ḥammādid palace, the *Ḳasr al-Manār*, castle of the Fanal, the four sides of a central room, once no doubt roofed by a cupola, are hollowed out in this fashion: a similar cruciform plan is seen in Palermo in the pavilion of the Zīza, built by the Norman kings (Twelfth Century). One of these ledges contains a fountain whose water flows in a canal across the room as in Ṭulūnid houses in al-Fusṭāṭ, already mentioned.

The survival of the Asiatic elements taken over by domestic architecture in North Africa can be seen in Sedrata, a town in the Sahara founded by the Khāridjī Berbers south of Ouargla, which was inhabited from the tenth to the twelfth centuries. Houses recovered from the sand contain rooms giving on to multiple courtyards. In addition to buildings provided with storerooms for provisions, the house includes state-rooms richly decorated with plaster sculptures, sometimes roofed by a cradle-vault which joins two half-cupolas on shell-shaped corbels. Some of the rooms are preceded by galleries opening, as at al-Fusṭāṭ, by three bays onto the courtyard. The room follows the T-plan, consisting of a wide shallow room, and the *īwān* in the wall facing the entrance. The two ends of the wide room each show a raised couch framed by an overhanging arch.

We do not know when and how this type of house, with its combination of Persian and ʿIrāḳī elements, reached Muslim Spain and the Maghrib. Many fashions derived from Baghdād or from Sāmarrā were imported by the Western Caliphs, especially in the 3rd/9th century, and made a mark in Andalusia. Perhaps in this way we can explain certain of the architectural elements revealed by the Castillejo of Murcia, attributed to Ibn Mardanish (541-66/1147-1171). Here we find wide rooms, at the end of which there is a narrow room preceded by a fore-part. The inner rectangular courtyard is designed in the manner of a garden divided by two paths intersecting at the centre—a characteristic Persian theme. Two overhanging pavilions on the shorter sides of the rectangle mark the position of the paths. This type of dwelling, transplanted into Muslim Spain, takes on an incomparable beauty and amplitude in the Alhambra, the palace of the Naṣrid kings of Granada. It is known that the principal buildings of this royal habitation, the work of Yūsuf I (735-55/1335-1354) and of Muḥammad V (755-93/1354-1391) are arranged around two rectangular patios. One of them (Patio de los Leones) is divided by two paths in the shape of a cross, dominated by two overhanging pavilions on the shorter sides of the rectangle, as at the Castillejo of Murcia. Water plays an important part in the décor of these courtyards, filling the pool of Alberca and playing over the basins of the famous Fountain of the Lions. Galleries and wide ante-rooms opening on to the court-yards lead to state-rooms, such as the splendid Ambassadors' Room which is in the Comares tower, the outstanding feature of the enclosure. The wide rooms have, at each end, a recess, a lateral *īwān*, bounded by an overhanging arch, as in the houses of Sedrata.

This theme of garden-courts, with fountains, and crossing paths, which certainly seems to have come from Īrān, must have reached Maghrib even in the Middle Ages. It survives in the charming *riyāḍs*, the interior gardens found in Fez and Marrakesh. The Algerian house, especially in Algiers itself, is quite different. The vestibule (*sḳīfa*), very long, and bordered by seats, leads on through a curved corridor, or by a staircase, into the courtyard. The latter is enclosed by the columns and horseshoe arches of four galleries; a fountain plays in the centre. The rooms beneath the galleries, on the ground floor or on the upper storeys, are very wide and rather shallow, the limited height being necessitated by the weak bearing of the ceiling beams. Opposite the door is a recess containing a divan. In this we can see a degenerate form of the *īwān*, whose movements we have traced from ʿIrāḳ. In Algiers, this median recess has a fore-part supported by arms set at an angle into the façade. This, there can be little doubt, is an eastern fashion, imported by the Turkish masters of the town. In the villas of the suburbs, the less restricted space makes this overhang unnecessary; the fore-part rises from ground-level. On the upper storey, it develops into a sort of small salon, a belvedere with windows on the three sides, and frequently surmounts the entrance porch. The Tunisian house is a little different, the rectangular court-yard having galleries only on the two shorter sides. The principal rooms follow the T-plan, with the wide room (*bayt*), the deep *īwān* (*ḳbū*), and the two small rooms alongside, (*maḳṣūra*, plu. *mḳāṣer*).

Bibliography: Caetani, *Annali dell'Islam*, i, 376 ff., 433 ff.; Creswell, *Early Muslim architecture*, i, 3-6, ii, 53 ff.; Lowthian Bell, *Palace and mosque of Ukhaidir*, Oxford 1914; Herzfeld, *Die Ausgrabungen von Samarra*, Berlin 1923-1927; Viollet, *Un palais musulman du IXe siècle* (*Mémoires de l'Académie des Inscriptions*), 1911; Watelin, *Sasanian building*, in Pope, *Survey of Persian art*, i, 585; A. Bahgat and A. Gabriel, *Fouilles à Al-Foustat*, 1921; Pauty, *Les palais et les maisons de l'Egypte musulmane*, (Institut français du Caire) 1933; Mostafa Sliman Zbiss, *Comptes rendus de l'Académie des Inscriptions*, 1952, 512; P. Blanchet, *Comptes rendus de l'Académie des Inscriptions*, 1898, 520; L. Golvin, *Le Maghreb central à l'époque des Sirides*, 1957, 180 ff.; Gallotti, *Le jardin et la maison arabe au Maroc*, 2 vol., 1926; Gavault, *Notice sur la bibliothèque-musée d'Alger*, in *RA*, 1894; G. Marçais, *L'architecture musulmane d'Occident*, 1954; idem, *Salle, antisalle*, in *AIÉO Alger*, 1952.

(G. Marçais)

DAR-I ĀHANĪN. Persian "the iron gate", also called Derbend-i Āhanīn. The Arabic form is *Bāb al-Ḥadīd*, old Turkish *Tämir qapiy*. A name used for various passes in the eastern Islamic world. The most famous pass called *dar-i āhanīn*, is the pass in Mā warāʾ al-Nahr (Transoxiana), in the Baysuntau Mountain Range near the modern village of Derbent located on the old road between Samarḳand and Tirmidh.

Perhaps the earliest mention of this "Iron Gate" is in the account of the Chinese pilgrim Hsüan Tsang who went through the pass about 630 A.D. and described it briefly. The first mention of this pass under its Persian name is in al-Yaʿḳūbī, *Buldan*, 290, 5. In later times this pass was considered the boundary between Mā warā᾽ al-Nahr and the lands dependent on Balkh. The pass is frequently mentioned in Islamic literature, but the first European to visit the site was Clavijo who passed here in 1404 and mentioned a customs house from which Timur received revenue. The pass is mentioned by Sharaf al-Dīn Yazdī, *Ẓafarnāma*, ed. M. Ilahdād, Calcutta, 1887, I, 49, and the *Bāburnāma*, ed. Beveridge, 124, under the Mongolian name *qa᾽alya* (in Arabic script *ḳahalghah*). The name Buzghāla Khāna, later applied to the pass, is first mentioned by Muḥ. Wafā Karmīnagī, *Tuḥfat al-Khānī* (uncatalogued, in the former Asiatic Museum, Leningrad f. 184b) in the description of a campaign by Muḥ. Raḥīm Khān in 1171/1757. A road runs through the pass today but it is no longer of any importance.

Bibliography: T. Watters, *On Yuan Chwang's Travels in India*, London 1904, i, 100-2. Yaʿḳūbī-Wiet, 105; Niẓām al-Dīn Shāmī, *Ẓafarnāma*, ed. F. Tauer, Prague 1956, ii, 252 (s.v. *ḳahalghah*); Ruy Gonçalez de Clavijo, *Narrative of the Embassy to the Court of Timur*, tr. C. R. Markham, London 1859, 122. (R. N. FRYE)

DĀR AL-ʿAHD, "the Land of the Covenant", was considered as a temporary and often intermediate territory between the *Dār al-Islām* [*q.v.*] and the *Dār al-Ḥarb* [*q.v.*] by some Muslim jurists (see Al-Shāfiʿī, *Kitāb al-Umm*, Cairo 1321, iv, 103-104; Yaḥyā b. Ādam, *Kitāb al-Kharādj*, trans. A. ben Shemesh, Leiden 1958, 58). Al-Māwardī (*Kitāb al-Aḥkām al-Sulṭāniyya*, trans. E. Fagnan, Algiers 1915, 291) states that of the lands which pass into the hands of the Muslims by agreement, that called Dār al-ʿAhd is the one the proprietorship of which is left to their previous possessors on condition that they pay *kharādj*, and this *kharādj* is the equivalent of *djizya*. In case of the breach of the agreement their land becomes *Dār al-Ḥarb*. When the Imām accepts their request to submit and pay *kharādj*, war against them is prohibited (Yaḥyā, 58). But in theory these lands are in the end to be included in the *Dār al-Islām*.

Abū Ḥanīfa, however, holds the opinion that such a land can be considered only as part of the *Dār al-Islām*, and there can be no other territory than the *Dār al-Islām* and the *Dār al-Ḥarb*. If people in such a land break the agreement they are to be considered as rebels.

But, there existed, even in early Islam, a type of tributary lands which conformed to the theory defended by al-Shāfiʿī. Under Muʿāwiya the Armenian princes obtained, in return for the payment of *kharādj*, agreements from him guaranteeing their land and autonomous rule (see, J. Markwart, *Südarmenien und die Tigrisquellen*, Vienna 1930, 457, and ARMĪNIYA).

More precise information on the conditions affecting such lands is provided by the examples in Ottoman history. In the *ʿahdnāme*s granted by the Ottoman sultans to the tributary Christian princes (see Fr. Kraelitz, *Osmanischen Urkunden in türkischer Sprache*, Vienna 1922, 42-106; Fr. Babinger, *Beiträge zur Frühgesch. der Türkenherrschaft in Rumelien*, Munich 1944, 21; Ferīdūn, *Munsha᾽āt al-Salāṭīn*, ii, Istanbul 1265, 351-380) we find that submission and the payment of a yearly tribute (*kharādj*) by the Christian prince, with the request of peace and security on the one hand and the Sultan's grant of *ʿahd wa amān* [*q.v.*] on the other, are the essential points for the conclusion of an *ʿahd*. It is absolutely an act of grant on the part of the Sultan. In the *ʿahdnāme*s it is often stipulated that the tributary prince is to be 'the enemy of the enemies of the Sultan and the friend of his friends'. Besides these, further conditions were usually imposed, such as the sending of hostages to pay homage in person to the Sultan every year, and the provision of troops for his expeditions. In his *ʿahdnāme* the Sultan promises by oath peace, protection against the internal and external enemies of the prince, respect of the religion, laws and customs of the country (cf. Ferīdūn, ii, 355), no colonization of Muslim people there, and no interference by Ottoman officials in internal affairs. A *ḳapi-ketkhudā* of the prince represents him at the Porte. His people could freely enter and trade in Ottoman territory. Following Ḥanafī opinion, the Ottoman Sultan considered them as his own *kharādj*-paying subjects and the land as his own land (cf. Kraelitz, 57, doc. 7); Ferīdūn, ii, 358). If the circumstances changed, the Sultan could increase the amount of the tribute. If the prince failed to fulfill any of his obligations toward the Sultan, he would declare him a rebel and his land *Dār al-ḥarb*. If the Sultan saw fit, he could bring the land under his direct rule. But the first step in expanding the *Dār al-Islām* was usually to impose a yearly tribute. Most of the Ottoman conquests were achieved through it (cf. İnalcık, *Ottoman Methods of Conquest*, in *Stud. Isl.*, ii, 103). See also DĀR AL-ṢULḤ.

Bibliography: in addition to the references in the text: M. v. Berchem, *La propriété territoriale et l'impôt foncier*, Leipzig 1886; F. Løkkegaard, *Islamic Taxation in the Classic Period*, Copenhagen 1950; M. Khadduri, *War and Peace in the Law of Islam*, Baltimore 1955; M. Hamidullah, *Muslim Conduct of State*, Lahore 1954. (HALIL İNALCIK)

(AL-)**DĀR AL-BAYḌĀ᾽,** the Arab name for Casablanca, the principal city in Morocco. In Arab dialect Dār l-Bēḍa, formerly Anfā [*q.v.*].

After the Portuguese had destroyed Anfā in the 15th century, the town remained in ruins, sheltering but a few Bedouins and being occasionally used by ships as a watering-place. The Portuguese named the locality Casabranca, after a white house, overlooking the ruins, which served as a landmark for their ships. The Spanish transformed the name into Casablanca, the present European name of the city. The Arab name is its literal translation.

The ʿAlawid Sulṭān Sīdī Muḥammad b. ʿAbd Allāh had the city rebuilt in the 18th century, probably subsequent to the Portuguese evacuation of Mazagan in 1769. Fearing that the Christians would one day return to the attack, he wished to fill the gap in the defences which existed between Rabāṭ and Mazagan. The bastion, or *sḳāla*, provided with artillery emplacements, was similar to those at Rabāṭ and Larache. It is thought that he repopulated the city by setting up two *idālā*s, one of Shlūḥ of Ḥaḥa (a Berber tribe giving its allegiance to the Makhzen, in the Agadir region), the other of Bwākher (ahl al-Bukhārī) of Meknès. Right to this day one of the oldest mosques in the city is named *djāmiʿ al-shlūḥ*. Travellers to Casablanca in the early 19th century described it as a mass of ruins used more for camping than for permanent settlement. Like Feḍāla and Manṣūriyya, it was a stopping-place on the journey between Rabāṭ and Marrākesh.

In 1782 the trade in corn, Casablanca's main export, was granted to a Spanish company in Cadiz, and in 1789 to the Compaña de los Cinco Gremios Mayores of Madrid. But following the revolt organized by the Shāwiya governor, who had established his residence in Casablanca, Sulṭān Mawlāy Sulaymān closed the port to commerce in 1794, and summoned back to Rabāṭ the Christian traders who had set up business there. It was not reopened until 1830, by Mawlāy ʿAbd al-Raḥmān b. Hishām.

European traders began to return from 1840 onwards, and the influx was particularly great in 1852. The first ones were representatives of French manufacturers in Lodève. They were sent in quest of raw wool, in an attempt to free themselves of dependence on the English market. They were followed by English traders from Gibraltar, by Germans, Portuguese, and Spaniards. The first European vice-consul in Casablanca was appointed in 1857. Thereafter, despite periods of stagnation due to European economic crises or to local causes (*e.g.*, droughts and epidemics), the small foreign colony grew continually. Steamship companies (notably the French line Paquet) called regularly at Casablanca. Trade expanded, and in 1906 the port's traffic (imports plus exports valued at 14 million gold-francs) exceeded that of Tangier.

Following the loan of 1904 and the Conference of Algeciras in 1906, French officials took over control of the Casablanca customs post, and a French company undertook improvements to the port facilities. These events constituted a threat to the Shāwiya tribe which inhabited the surrounding countryside, and on 30 July 1907 they attacked and killed some European workers in a quarry outside the city walls. The intervention of a French warship provoked the sacking of the city, during which the Jewish quarter suffered particularly severely. The French replied by a bombardment on August 5th, and two days later 2000 troops under the command of General Drude were sent ashore from a French squadron. Spain also sent a squadron of assault troops. The French expeditionary force gradually occupied the whole of the Shāwiya territory by driving back the warlike tribes, and the train of events ended with the establishment of the French Protectorate in 1912.

As a result of the decision of its first Resident General, Lyautey, to make it the principal port of Morocco, the city underwent an enormous expansion. No doubt the decision would have been very different if Casablanca had not already known considerable economic prosperity. This arose in part from the presence of a sizeable European colony, in part from the need to supply material to the Expeditionary Force. The modern port is completely man-made. It has 4,870 m. of deep-water quays, and is protected from the open sea by a breakwater 3,180 m. long. In 1956 it registered 8$^1/_2$ million tons of traffic.

The census of 1952 showed a population of 680,000 (to be compared with 20,000 in 1907): 472,920 Muslims, 74,783 Jews (more than a third of the total Jewish population in Morocco), and 132,719 foreigners (of whom 99,000 were French).

The old city consisted of 3 districts: Medina (middle-class), Tnaker (working-class, not entirely built-up), Mellāḥ (Jewish). Today the whole area, its walls still in part intact, is called Old Medina, and to the W. and S.W. it has extended beyond the walls. The whole of the Jewish population lives there, mingled with the Muslims. The European districts have grown up around Old Medina, particularly to the E. and S., and further Muslim districts have been built outside these, the principal one being an immense area of 200,000 inhabitants, New Medina. The shanty-towns on the outskirts of the city, to which countryfolk flocked in search of work, have now been largely replaced by working-class dwellings, constituting quarters such as Muḥammadiyya to the E. (formerly the 'Central Quarries'), Sīdī ʿUthmān to the S. (formerly Ben Msīk), and Ḥasaniyya City, formerly Derb Jdīd (*al-darb al-djadīd*) to the S.W. The main centre of industry is in the N.E. along the road to Rabat. It contains the headquarters of most of the country's light industries, and is the most important industrial region in Morocco.

Bibliography: Aḥmad b. Khālid al-Nāṣirī al-Salāwī, *Kitāb al-Istiḳṣāʾ*, *4e partie, Chronique de la dynastie alaouite du Maroc* (1631-1894), trans. E. Fumey, in *Archives Marocaines*, Paris 1906-7, i, 332, 359, ii, 3-5; M. Rey, *Souvenirs d'un voyage au Maroc*, Paris 1844, 12-15; Georges Bourdon, *Ce que j'ai vu au Maroc, Les journées de Casablanca*, Paris 1908; *Villes et tribus du Maroc. Casablanca et les Chaouiya*, i, Mission scientifique au Maroc, Paris 1915; Dr. F. Weisgerber, *Casablanca et les Chaouiya en* 1900, Casablanca 1935; J. Célérier, *Les Conditions géographiques du développement de Casablanca*, in *Revue de Géogr. Maroc*, May 1939; F. Joly, *Casablanca-Éléments pour une étude de géographie urbaine*, in *Cahiers d'Outre-Mer*, April-June 1948; J. L. Miège and E. Hugues, *Les Européens à Casablanca au XIXème siècle*, (1856-1906), Paris 1954. (A. ADAM)

DĀR AL-ḌARB, the mint, was an indispensable institution in the life of mediaeval Middle Eastern society because of the highly developed monetary character of its economy, particularly during the early centuries of Muslim domination. The primary function of the mint was to supply coins for the needs of government and of the general public. At times of monetary reforms the mints served also as a place where obliterated coins could be exchanged for the new issues. The large quantities of precious metals which were stored in the mints helped to make them serve as ancillary treasuries.

Soon after their conquest of the Middle East, the Arabs made use of the mints inherited from the former Byzantine and Sāsānid regimes. It was only during the Umayyad period that the Muslim administration began to interfere with the minting organization. This was manifested in the setting up of new mints (*e.g.*, Kūfa, Wāsiṭ) by al-Ḥadjdjādj, in the famous coinage reform of ʿAbd al-Malik [see DĪNĀR], and in the centralizing measures of Hishām who drastically reduced the number of mints. The policy of Hishām, obviously influenced by Byzantine minting traditions, could not be maintained for long by the ʿAbbāsid caliphate. During the reign of Hārūn al-Rashīd the office of *nāẓir al-sikka* (inspector of coinage) was set up. Although by this measure the caliphate relinquished its direct authority over the mints in favour of a subordinate agency, it still defended the principle of a centralized minting system. But this office seems to have disappeared with the shrinking of the political and administrative authority of the ʿAbbāsids. The increased number of mints whose operations were necessitated by rapidly expanding trade and industrial activities, and the rise of many petty rulers asserting their control over these mints, led to a complete decentralization of minting, a situation closely resembling that which existed under the Sāsānids.

The assumption of control over the mints was one of the elements indicating the assertion of independent power by rulers. It was symbolized by the inclusion of their names in the inscriptions on the issues of their mints, hitherto an exclusive prerogative of the caliphs. By this measure, also, they declared themselves responsible for the quality of their coinage. To safeguard the integrity of the coinage, and consequently the interests of the general public, the mints were submitted to the legal authorities (*e.g.*, *ḳāḍī al-ḳuḍāt* in Fāṭimid Egypt and Syria, and a *ḳāḍī* in 11th century Baghdād) whose agents personally assisted at the minting processes. In spite of this system, the confidence of the general public was abused by the rulers who exploited their mint prerogatives by illegal monetary speculations. The usual method was to declare the coins in circulation invalid, and order their exchange against the new, secretly debased issues, obtainable in the official mints.

The staff of the mint consisted of clerical and manual employees. The former were in charge of book-keeping and of internal security. The manual workers, such as the *sabbākūn* (melters) and *ḍarrābūn* (minters), carried out the actual coining operations. A special position among the craftsmen was occupied by the *naḳḳāsh* (die-sinker) whose professional activities were restricted to engraving only.

Coins issued by Muslim mints were struck of gold, silver and copper [see DĪNĀR, DIRHAM, FALS]. Precious metals for coining consisted of bullion which was supplied by the official authorities as well as by private customers. The latter delivered also obliterated coins and 'foreign' coins which were prohibited on local markets. A prescribed percentage of such deliveries was retained by the mint as a coining levy. The money cashed from the customers was spent on the wages of the minters, on the costs connected with minting operations, as well as on a special government tax. During the period of flourishing trade activities which entailed intensive minting operations, the proceeds from the mint yielded a substantial income to the government. But the economic regression of the late Middle Ages drastically diminished the demand for coinage, with detrimental effects on the position of the mints and the profits derived from them. It then became practicable to farm out the mints, an expedient resorted to, for instance, by Mamlūk Egypt.

Bibliography: Abu 'l-Ḥasan ʿAlī b. Yūsuf al-Ḥakīm, *al-Dawḥa al-mushtabika fī ḍawābiṭ dār al-sikka*, ed. Ḥ. Muʾnis, Madrid 1379/1959; Ibn Khaldūn, *al-Muḳaddima*, tr. F. Rosenthal, New York 1958, i, 464 and *passim*; Nābulusī, *Lumaʾ al-ḳawānīn al-Muḍiyya fī Dawāwīn al-Diyār al-miṣriyya*, in C. A. Owen's *Scandal in the Egyptian Treasury*, *JNES*, 14, ii, 1955, 75-6; Ibn Baʿra, *Kashf al-Asrār al-ʿIlmiyya bi Dār al-Darb al-miṣriyya*, (cf., A. S. Ehrenkreutz, *Extracts from the Technical Manual on the Ayyūbid Mint in Cairo*, in *BSOAS*, xv, 1953, 432-47); A. S. Ehrenkreutz, *Contributions to the knowledge of the fiscal administration of Egypt in the Middle Ages*, in *BSOAS*, xvi, 1954, 502-14, containing further bibliographical references on the subject of Islamic mints; idem, *Studies in the monetary history of the Near East in the Middle Ages*, in *JESHO*, 2, ii (1959), 128-61.

(A. S. EHRENKREUTZ)

Ottoman period. — The Ottoman mint is generally known as *Ḍarbkhāne-i ʿĀmire* but also *ḍarrābkhāne*, *nuḳrakhāne* and *dār al-ḍarb*. The first coin from an Ottoman mint was an *aḳče* [*q.v.*] struck in Bursa probably in 727/1326-7 (cf. I. H. Uzunçarşılı, *Belleten* xxxiv, 207-221). On the *aḳče*s and *manghir*s, copper coins, of Murād I and Bāyazīd I no place-name is found (H. Edhem, *Meskūkāt-i ʿOthmāniyye*, Istanbul 1334, no. 1-58), but we know that under his sons there were mints in Bursa, Amasya, Edirne, Serez and Ayasoluḳ (Ephesus) (see H. Edhem, nos. 59-138).

The first Ottoman gold coin was struck in Istanbul in 882/1477-1478 (I. Artuk, *Fatih Sultan Mehmed namına kesilmiş bir sikke*, in *Ist. Arkeoloji Müzesi Yıllığı*, no. 7), but already in 828/1425 and even before the Ottoman mints must have produced Venetian gold ducats, *Frengī filori* or *aflūrī* (Fr. Babinger, *Zur Frage der osmanischen Goldprägungen im 15. Jahrhundert*, in *Südost-Forschungen*, vol. xv, 1956, 552). A regulation (R. Anhegger-H. Inalcık, *Ḳānūnnāme-i Sulṭānī ber mūceb-i ʿörf-i ʿOsmānī*, Ankara 1956, nos. 1 and 58) makes it clear that *Frengī filori* was struck in the mints of Istanbul, Edirne and Serez (Serres) under Meḥemmed II.

In their expanding empire the Ottomans established new mints in the commercially and administratively important cities and in the centres of gold and silver mines. Thus, under Bayazıd II, new mints were established in Ankara, Karatova (Kratovo), Kastamoni, Gelibolu (Gallipoli) in addition to those in Istanbul, Bursa, Edirne, Serez, Ayasoluk, Novar (Novaberda, Novobrdo), Üsküb (Skoplje), Amasya, Tire and Konya, which existed already under Meḥemmed II. Under Süleymān I, gold coins were struck in his name in Aleppo, Damascus, Miṣr (Cairo), Āmid, Baghdād and Algiers. In Shaʿbān 953/October 1546 a new mint was established in Djandja, a small town to the north of Erzindjān, when rich silver and gold mines were found there. The mints in Morava (Gilan), Novaberda, Sidrekapsa and Serebrenica (Srebrnica) owed their existence to the rich silver and gold mines (see R. Anhegger, *Beiträge zur Geschichte des Bergbaus im osmanischen Reich*, Istanbul 1943, 131-212). The Ottoman laws required that all bullion produced in the country or imported from abroad be brought directly to the *ḍarbkhāne*s to be coined. Also upon the issue of a new *aḳče* those possessing the old were to bring it to the mint. The special agents, *yasaḳ-ḳulus*, were authorized to inspect any person for bullion or old *akče* (see *Belleten*, xliv, 697, doc. 2, and Anhegger-Inalcık, *Ḳānūnnāme*, no. 2, 5, 58) and the gold or silver imported by foreigners was exempted from the customs duties. The state levied a duty of one fifth on all silver coined at the *ḍarbkhāne* which corresponded to the difference between the real and face values of the *aḳče* (*Belleten*, xliv, 679 and Anhegger-Inalcık, no. 58).

As a *muḳāṭaʿa* [*q.v.*], this revenue was usually farmed out at auction to the highest bidder. The contractor, *ʿāmil*, was to pay it in regular instalments to the public treasury (see Anhegger-Inalcık, no. 15). Spandugino (ed. Ch. Schefer, Paris 1896, 57) tells us that each new issue of *aḳče* under Meḥemmed II brought a revenue of 800 thousand gold ducats. The *muḳāṭaʿa* of the Bursa *aḳče* mint alone amounted to 6000 ducats in 892/1487 (see *Belleten*, xciii, 56). All the mints in the empire could be farmed out as one single *muḳāṭaʿa* (Anhegger-Inalcık, no. 15). But an *ʿāmil* in turn could farm out at his own responsibility the local *ḍarbkhāne*s to others. The *ʿāmil* employed *emīn*s and *wekīl*s to assist him. Though he was responsible for the revenue of the mint its actual operation and control were in the hands of the employees appointed by the state, namely an *emīn* or *nāẓir* who had its supervision (Anhegger-Inalcık, no. 13), a *ṣāḥib-i ʿayār* who was the director and in this capacity responsible for all the technical and legal requirements (Anhegger-Inalcık, no. 14, and, Ewliyā Čelebī, *Seyāḥatnāme*, x, 135) and an *ustād* or *usta* who supervised the actual minting processes. Under him the technicians and workers were divided into several groups, the *ḳāldjiyān* who prepared the standard ingots by melting the metal, the *kehledān*s or *kehledār*s who made them into plates to be minted and the *sikke-zen*s or *sikke-kün*s who, under strict supervision, prepared the steel moulds. There were also *dīdebān*s, watchers, *khazīne-dār*s treasurers, *kātib*s, scribes etc.

Minting was arranged on the basis of *newbet*, a system of turn; at each turn 13065 *dirhams* [*q.v.*] of silver were delivered from the capital out of which 3000 were placed in the *khazīne*, treasury, and 10,000 were delivered to the *ustād* to be minted, 65 *dirham*s were accepted as the legal loss.

The general supervision of the *ḍarbkhāne* and of its accounts was the responsability of the local *ḳāḍī* who kept there his own *emīn* (Anhegger-Inalcık, no. 13). It was the *ḳāḍī*'s duty periodically to see the accounts and send the balance sheets, *muḥāsabāt-i ḍarbkhāne*, to the central government (a *defter* of the *muḥāsebāt-i ḍarbkhāne-i Bursa* of the first half of the 10/16th century is now in Belediye Kütüphanesi, Istanbul, Cevdet yazm. no. 0.59).

In the *berāt*s given to the *ʿāmil*s and *emīn*s it was made clear how much they should pay for the bullion purchased and how many coins should be minted from each 100 *dirham*s of it; all this reflected the monetary policy of the state.

Until 865/1460 out of each 100 dirhams of silver 265 or 278 *aḳče* were struck, but it was 355 or 400 *aḳče* under Meḥemmed II, 500 under Süleyman I and 1000 in 996/1588. The original Ottoman monetary system based on *aḳče* was disrupted from this time on (for the causes, see *Belleten*, lx, 656-684). The spoiled and adulterated (*züyūf* and *čürük*) *aḳče*s invaded the market. The renewed attempts to put right the quality and value of it, the so called *taṣḥīḥ-i sikke*, failed (see M. Belin, *Essais sur l'his. économique de la Turquie*, Paris 1865, 118 ff.; I. Ghālib, *Taḳwīm-i Meskūkāt-i ʿOthmāniyye*, Istanbul 1307, 220-226). In 1010/1601 the use of bad and old *aḳče* was prohibited once more and the rate of *sagh* ("good") *aḳče* was fixed at 120 *aḳče* to one gold piece of 1 *dirham* and 1 1/2 *ḳīrāṭ* [*q.v.*]. In the following period the Ottoman mints showed little activity and many of them were closed down. In the 11th/17th century only were the mints of Istanbul, Cairo, Baghdād, Tripoli, Tunis and Algiers steadily active. The main reason for this situation was that Europeans, realizing the big profit to be made from the difference in price of silver, began increasingly to import their silver coins in the Levant (in 1614 the French alone imported 7 million *écu*). First *riyāl*s, Spanish *reales*, then in the 11th/17th century *arslānī*, *esedī* or *abū kalb gurush*, Dutch *Loewen riksdaler*, and the *ḳara-gurush*, German thalers, invaded the Levantine markets. The import of these coins was free of duty, but the mark *saḥḥ* had to be struck on them in the Ottoman *ḍarbkhāne*s as a condition of free circulation, because Europeans were increasingly importing counterfeit coins specially struck for the Levant. In 1010/1601 one gold coin was rated officially at 400, and one *gurush* (piastre) at 160, *aḳče* (Başvekâlet Arşivi, Fekete tasnifi, no. 3043). Eventually the *gurush* was made the Ottoman monetary unit, as the *aḳče* became too small in value as a result of the continual debasements and devaluations, and the abundance and cheapness of the commercial silver. The first Ottoman *gurush* of 6 *dirham*s of silver was struck in imitation of the German thaler in 1099/1688 (see I. Ghālib, 237, 254). It was rated 4 *para* (*pāre*), which was struck first under Murād IV. Pieces of half a *gurush*, *niṣfiyye*, and a quarter, *rubʿiyye*, were also struck.

The new system opened a new era in the history of the Ottoman coinage. The *aḳče* ceased to be the basic unit, though it was struck until 1234/1819; special care was then taken to improve the quality of the coins struck (see I. Ghālib, 230). New *ḍarbkhāne*s were opened in Edirne, Izmir (Smyrna) and Erzurum for gold and others at Tawshan-tashî in Istanbul and in Bosna-Saray for copper coins in 1100/1689. New machines and techniques were adopted (Rāshid, *Taʾrīkh*, Istanbul 1282, ii, 383, 394). On 13 Djumādā I, 1139/6 January 1727, the chief imperial *ḍarbkhāne* was transferred from its old location at the Sīmkeshkhāne to its new buildings in the first court of the Topḳapı-sarayî (Küčük Čelebī-zāde ʿĀṣim, *Taʾrīkh*, Istanbul 1282, ii, 443). During the same period, for better control, the provincial *ḍarbkhāne*s were again closed down. In 1132/1720 the silver coins struck were the *gurush* of 8 *dirham*s and 12 *ḳīrāṭ*, the *zolota* of 6 dirhams and 4 *ḳīrāṭ*, the *para* of 2-3 1/4 *ḳīrāṭ* and the *aḳče* of 3/4-1 3/4 *ḳīrāṭ* in weight. The *gurush* and *zolota* contained 60% pure silver (I. Ghālib, 280).

As the Ottoman government always considered minting as a source of revenue to meet its financial difficulties, the new silver coins, too, became subject to adulteration, and all attempts at reforms (*taṣḥīḥ-i sikke*), failed (I. Ghālib, 303, 327, 407; A. Djewdet, *Taʾrīkh*, iv, Istanbul 1275, 122; v, Ist. 1278, 289). The situation became most confusing under Maḥmūd II, and, eventually under ʿAbd al-Medjīd, by the *ferman* dated 26 Ṣafar 1256/29 April 1840, Western principles of monetary policy were accepted as a guide by the government (see the text in S. Sūdī, *Uṣūl-i Meskūkāt-i ʿOthmāniyye we ednebiyye*, Istanbul 1311, 76-104). Enlarged by the new buildings, the *ḍarbkhāne-i ʿāmire* was completely modernized by the machines and specialists brought from England (see H. Ferid, *Naḳd ve iʿtibār-i mālī, Meskūkāt*, Istanbul 1333, 215-222). In 1259/1843 new gold and silver coins known as Medjīdī were struck (see I. Ghālib, 422-445).

Bibliography: In addition to the references in the text: S. Lane-Poole, *The Coins of the Turks in the British Museum*, Class xxvi, Catalogue of Oriental Coins in the British Museum, vol. viii, London 1883; E. von Zambaur, *Contributions à la numismatique orientale*, *Numismatische Zeitschrift*, vol. 36, 43-122; vol. 37, 113-98; M. Kāẓim, *Ḍarbkhānenin aḥwāl-i dākhiliyyesi*, in *TOEM* I, 551-7; A. Refik, *Onaltıncı asırda Istanbul hayatı*, Istanbul 1935, 68-76; Ewliyā Čelebī, *Seyāḥatnāme*, i, Istanbul 1314, 564-7, x, Istanbul 1938, 135; P. Masson, *Hist. du commerce français dans le Levant au XVIIe siècle*, Paris 1896, xxxii-iii, 493-5; I. Artuk, *Fatih'in sikke ve madalyaları*, Istanbul 1946; O. Nūrī [Ergin], *Medjelle-i Umūr-i Belediyye*, i, İstanbul 1922.

(HALIL İNALCIK)

India. — The earliest coins of Muslim rulers to circulate in India—disregarding the insignificant issues from the early Arab kingdom of Sind in the 1st/8th century—were the bilingual *ṭanka*s struck at Lahore by Maḥmūd of Ghaznī in 418/1027 and 419/1028; after Lahore became the residence of the Ghaznawid princes small billon coins were occasionally struck there, but nothing is known of the mints they employed. Muʿizz al-Dīn Muḥammad b. Sām struck coin at Lahore, Dihlī and

'Parashawar' (Pēshāwar) as well as at Ghaznī and, after the conquest of Kanawdj [*q.v.*] in 590/1194, there also; these coinages were assimilated in weight series as well as in design to the existing coinages of north India, and included gold money—a convenient way of using the proceeds of plunder and war booty to maintain the local currency and simultaneously proclaim the victor's success. Muḥammad b. Sām's lieutenant Yīldīz struck coin in his own and his master's joint names: small *dihlīwālas* assimilated to the local billon currency, first at Karmān, including also some gold and silver, and later in billon only at Dihlī. The outline of the Čawhān horseman was retained in the designs, frequently also the Karmān bull of Shiva, which seems to indicate that Hindū craftsmen were still employed in the production of coin. Up to the death of Muḥammad b. Sām no gold or silver money had been struck in India, with the exception of the Kanawdj gold pieces. Silver appears to have been coined first by Shams al-Dīn Iletmish: silver *tankas* of an original weight of 175 grs. His reign clearly brought a time of experimentation for his mint, for the weights and designs of his early coins are very diverse; by 632/1234-5 a stable design for the silver coinage seems to have been reached, which was taken as a model for his later gold coinage. Billon, however, remained the most frequent currency, supplemented by smaller coin in copper. The silver struck up to this time was very impure. His mints were extended to Multān and Nāgawr, and the coins of his successors continue his series from the same mints: Ghaznī is still frequent, and Parwān, a town with nearby silver mines, also appears. By the time of Sulṭāna Raḍiyya, 634-7/1236-9, the mints had been extended east to Bengal, and Lakhnawtī appears as a mint-name on silver *tankas*. Assays of the Dihlī coinages of about this time show from 990 to 996 grains of silver per 1000, while the Bengal mintings fall below this, from 989 to as low as 962. By the time of Ghiyāth al-Dīn Balban, 664-86/1265-87, the Bengal coinage had become independent of Dihlī, where a period of settled rule had allowed the mint procedure to become stabilized; Balban's reign is notable for the appearance of a regular gold coinage on the silver models.

In the reign of ʿAlāʾ al-Dīn Muḥammad Shāh, 695-715/1295-1315, the expense of the army caused him to contemplate reducing the silver *tanka* from 175 to 140 grs.; but gold *tankas* remained at the nominal 175 grs., often crudely struck, and the gold *hūns* of his southern conquests seem to have been re-struck as camp currency, with no attempt to bring them up to the standard of the northern mints: their average fineness is described in the *Āʾīn-i Akbarī*, i, 5, as 8.5 parts in 12, whereas ʿAlāʾ al-Dīn's Dihlī coinage was 10.5 parts in 12. Devagiri now appears as a mint-town, including a gold issue in 714/1314-5. ʿAlāʾ al-Dīn's successor Ḳuṭb al-Dīn Mubārak Shāh, 716-20/1316-20 struck at 'Ḳuṭbābād' (= Dihlī?) new *square* gold and silver pieces of standard weight, also square copper pieces of 66 and 33 grs.

Ghiyāth al-Dīn Tughluḳ continued the Dihlī series almost unchanged, and also struck coin on his expedition to Bengal in 724/1324; but his son, Muḥammad b. Tughluḳ, has been called a "prince of moneyers": his numismatic types are characterized by novelty of form and variety of weight as well as by perfection of execution. Gold coin was struck at Devagiri, later renamed Dawlatābād [*q.v.*], and at Sulṭānpur (= Warangaḷ), up to the 200 grs. *dīnār*; the Dihlī coinage was much subdivided: the *tanka* was reckoned at 64 *kānīs*, and coins of 1, 2, 6, 8, 12, 16 and the full 64 *kānīs* are known. The *kānī* was further divided into 4 copper *fals*. Besides this system is a partially decimal system of 25, 50 and 100 *kānīs*: the 50-*kānī* piece, called *ʿadalī*, of 140 grs. silver, replaces the silver *tanka* as the largest silver piece of the coinage; the new *dīnār* exchanged at 8 old silver *tankas* or 10 *ʿadalīs*, a fictitious rate in terms of the relative values of gold and silver. The complete scheme of the sub-divisional currency was later conflated to mix silver and copper in arbitrary proportions to produce coins of similar size but different intrinsic values; this brought in the 'black *tanka*', containing only 16.4 grs. silver, valued at one-eighth of the old silver *tanka*. According to Abu 'l-Faḍl (*Āʾīn-i Akbarī*, i, 7, s.v. *Ḍarrāb*) the metal was cast into round ingots and cut by hand; since the black *tanka* was of the same size as the silver *tanka*, the same dies could be—and were—used for both, thus speeding and easing the work of the mint workmen. The uniform small size of the dies required less labour in the striking and resulted in increased efficiency of the mint.

In 731-2/1330-2 appeared Muḥammad b. Tughluḳ's 'forced currency', brass tokens nominally valued at one *ʿadalī*; the experiment failed owing to inadequate precautions against forgery. Tokens were turned out in thousands by local artisans, but after three years all were called in and redeemed. The whole operation thus became virtually a temporary loan from the sultan's subjects which was repaid at a swingeing rate of interest. The issues reverted to normal after this, except for some gold and silver coins of 741-3/1340-3, struck in the name of the Egyptian caliphs.

Fīrūz Shāh Tughluḳ, 752-90/1351-88, continued the 175 gr. gold *tanka*, but not its silver counterpart. Gold coin became more plentiful, thus relieving silver of its earlier responsibility, and mints concentrated on fractional issues, including small pieces in mixed silver and copper; assays of the 140 gr. pieces show 12, 18 or 24 gr. of pure silver. The later Tughluḳid sultans, and the Sharḳī sultans of Djawnpur, followed the Fīrūzian tradition with little change.

After the sack of Dihlī by Tīmūr the mints were in decline. Gold largely disappeared, thanks to Tīmūr's depredations, and the Sayyid Khiḍr Khān struck coin in the names of Fīrūz and other of his predecessors, (but not in Tīmūr's name, as Firishta asserts), using the original dies.

In the Deccan, mints were first established under the Bahmanīs [*q.v.*]; before these were set up at Aḥsanābād-Gulbarga and elsewhere, goldsmiths and dealers in bullion had been authorized to make money without reference to a royal stamp, and the currency was protected by the guild of craftsmen. Interesting among the later Deccan coinages are the silver *lārīns*, 'fish-hook' money, struck by ʿAlī II of Bīdjāpur, which became a standard Indian Ocean trading currency in the 10th/16th century (see G. P. Taylor, *On the Bījapur lārī or larin*, *JASB*, NS vi, 1910, 687-9).

The Mughals. Bābur's reign, 932-7/1526-30, was virtually a military occupation, and Humāyūn's was hardly a period of stability; this is reflected in their coinage, which seems to have been struck irregularly and to follow Central Asian patterns and a Central Asian system, probably depending on imported workmen. Both struck silver *shāhrukhīs* at Agra,

Lahore, Dihlī and Kābul, and Bābur uses Urdū, 'camp', as a mint-name; many of Humāyūn's gold coins are mintless, and his copper is anonymous.

The interrex S͟hīr S͟hāh, 945-52/1538-45, who had an intimate practical knowledge of local conditions, commenced the reform of the coinage later fully implemented by Akbar: a new 178 gr. standard for silver and 324 gr. for copper, the rupee (*rūpiya*) and *dām* respectively, with fractional divisions to correspond; the abolition of billon; and a great increase in the numbers of mints (over 25). Many silver and copper coins are without mint-name; sometimes this seems to be a result of the dies being too large for the discs.

Humāyūn in his brief second regnal period left the Sūrī system unchanged; Akbar, however, while retaining the system in principle, greatly elaborated the number of coin-types—Abu 'l-Faḍl (*Āʾīn-i Akbarī*, i, 10) enumerates over 30 without being exhaustive. (cf. Hodivala, *Studies*, iii). The *Āʾīn-i Akbarī* mentions the working of the mint in detail. in charge is the *darūg͟hā*, assisted by the *amīn*; the *ṣayrafī* is responsible for maintaining the fineness; the *mus͟hrif* keeps a day-book of the expenditure; merchants, weighmen, smelters and ingot-makers are other non-craftsman officials. After the ingots have been refined, melted and recast they are cut by the *ḍarrāb* and stamped by the *sikkačī* from dies cut by the engraver who holds the rank of *yūzbās͟hī* (*sic*; see YŪZBAS͟HĪ). The methods of extracting and separating the metals, refining silver and gold, and testing for fineness (*banwārī*) are fully described (*Āʾīn*, i, 4-9). From the statistics of *Āʾīn*, i, 12, it is clear that any individual could bring bullion to the mint where it would be converted into coin, after refining, on the owner defraying the cost of the minting operations and paying a seignorage to the state of 5½ per cent. Abu 'l-Faḍl also specifies the depreciation in face value to be allowed for wear of the coinage: *e.g.*, for gold, the *muhr* when struck was worth 400 *dāms*, although smaller *muhrs* were current of 360 *dāms*; as long as the loss in weight were no more than three rice-grains no allowance was made, but when it had lost from four to six its value was 355 *dāms*; after losing up to a further three rice-grains it was valued at 350 *dāms*; after losing further weight it ceased to be current and was considered as bullion. As a precaution against fraud by reducing full coins to the permitted legal deficiency the emperor ordered that official weights be made in the mint, and that revenue collectors should not demand payment in any particular species of coin. Abu 'l-Faḍl enumerates four mints for gold; ten more where silver and copper were struck; and 28 more for copper only. Over the entire reign gold is known from 21 mints, silver from 45, copper from 64. For the complete coin-system, see SIKKA.

D͟jahāngīr's and S͟hāhd͟jahān's system was similar, except for their gigantic pieces up to 1000 *tōlās* in weight (1 *tōlā* = 185.5 grs.) which were used as presents to distinguished persons or hoarded as bullion reserves, and the *nit͟hārs* of about 40 grs. in gold or silver. With Awrangzīb's imposition of the *d͟jizya* [*q.v.*] in 1090/1679 he caused the square silver *dirham s͟harʿī* to be struck in order to facilitate payment at the canonical rates; this was repeated in similar circumstances in 1129/1717 by Farruk͟hsiyar. The latter adopted the policy of farming out the mints, which led to many independent chiefs and states striking their own coin in the Mug͟hal emperor's name; this was in fact done by the British East India company, and S͟hāh ʿĀlam's coinage with wreaths of roses, shamrocks and thistles, commemorating Lord Lake's entry into Dihlī in 1803, shows a very extraneous influence in the Imperial mint.

The Mug͟hal coinage in general shows great diversity of mints—well over 200 are known—and a constant search for variation. The inscriptions could vary for each month of the year; for some years D͟jahāngīr struck round and square rupees in alternate months, and later varied the month names by zodiacal signs. Emblems appear on the coins from the time of Humāyūn; sometimes these appear to have marked a change of mint-masters, sometimes they were distinctive mint-marks. That the practice of the later Mug͟hal mints was substantially the same as that recorded by Abu 'l-Faḍl is shown by the *Hidāyat al-ḳawāʾid* of 1126/1714-5 which records the current mint rules (quoted by W. Irvine, *Mint rules in* 1126 *A.H.*, in *Proc. A.S.B.*, 1898, 149-52) and prescribes a differential revenue to be exacted from Muslim and Hindū merchants: the latter when specially appointed (*mahād͟janān ki muḳarrarī bās͟hand*) pay less than the Muslim rate of 2½ per cent, otherwise ½ per cent more.

Bibliography: Evidence for the history of the mint under the Dihlī sultanate is numismatic only; cf. E. Thomas, *The chronicles of the Pathán kings of Dehli*, London 1871; H. Nevill, *Mint towns of the Dehli Sultans*, *JASB*, NS xvii, 1921, 116-30; idem, *The currency of the Pathan Sultans*, ibid. 21-30 (corrects Thomas on many points of detail); R. Burn, *Muhammad Tughluq's forced coinage*, *JASB*, N.S. xxix, 1933, N. 5-6; H. N. Wright, *The Sultans of Delhi*: *their coinage and metrology*, Dihlī 1936; S. H. Hodivala, *Historical Studies in Mug͟hal Numismatics*, Calcutta 1923; C. R. Singhal, *Mint-towns of the Mug͟hal emperors of India* (Memoir iv, NSI), Bombay 1953; idem, *Bibliography of Indian Numismatics*, ii (*Muhammadan and later Series*), Bombay 1952.

(J. BURTON-PAGE)

DĀR AL-FUNŪN [see D͟JĀMIʿA].

DĀR FŪR, "the land of the Fūr", a province of the Republic of the Sudan, formerly a Muslim sultanate.

Geography and inhabitants.

Dār Fūr was one of the chain of Muslim states composing *bilād al-Sūdān*. Its eastern neighbour was Kordofān, from which it was separated by a tract of sand-hills. To the west lay Waddāī. The Libyan desert formed a natural boundary on the north, while the marshes of the Baḥr al-G͟hazāl [*q.v.*] marked the southern limits. Dār Fūr comprises three main zones: a northern zone, the steppe fringe of the Sahara, providing grazing for camel-owning tribes but little cultivation; a central zone (14° 30′ N to 12° N) with rainfall ranging from 12″ to 25″ (in the mountains), a country of settled cultivators; a southern zone of heavy rainfall (25″-35″), inhabited by cattle-owing nomads, the Baḳḳāra [*q.v.*]. In the central zone, the massif of D͟jabal Marra, rising to 3024 metres, runs from north to south. The northern and southern regions of Dār Fūr are locally known as *Dār al-Rīḥ* and *Dār al-Ṣaʿīd* respectively.

The central zone is a meeting place of routes. The *Darb al-arbaʿīn* [*q.v.*] (Forty Days' route) ran from Asyūṭ through K͟hārd͟ja and Salīma to Kūbayh (Cobbé, Browne), where a small mercantile town developed. Another route connected Dār Fūr with Tripoli and Cyrenaica. Kabkābiyya, lying west of D͟j. Marra was the mercantile centre on the route to Waddāī and the western *bilād al-Sūdān*. The route to Kordofān and the east was a pilgrimage road, although some pilgrims preferred the long route through Egypt. Besides such articles as ivory and ostrich feathers, Dār Fūr exported slaves, obtained from the pagan lands to the south. Many of these went by the *Darb al-arbaʿīn* to Egypt. The construction, completed in 1911, of a railway linking El Obeid (*al-Ubayyiḍ*) in Kordofān with Khartoum and Port Sudan, followed by the annexation of Dār Fūr in 1916, ended the importance of the old routes to the north. The capital was finally settled in 1206/1791 at its present site of El Fasher (al-Fā<u>sh</u>ir [*q.v.*]). The *fā<u>sh</u>ir*, or residence of the sultan, had previously varied from reign to reign, the earliest sultans ruling from <u>Dj</u>. Marra.

The inhabitants of Dār Fūr are of varied ethnic origins. The Fūr, (see A. C. Beaton, *The Fur*, in *Sudan notes and records*, xxix/1, 1948, 1-39), are a negroid people, originating in <u>Dj</u>. Marra, who succeeded in imposing their hegemony on the surrounding tribes. From the Kun<u>dj</u>āra, one of the three tribes of the Fūr, sprang the royal Kayra clan, and also, traditionally, the Musabbaʿāt, who established a sultanate in Kordofān. According to tradition, the dominant people in the region before the Fūr was the Tun<u>dj</u>ur, and, before them, the Dā<u>dj</u>ū: elements of both still survive in Dār Fūr. Arab immigration has played an important part in the ethnic pattern. Tribal groups connected with the great irruption of the <u>Dj</u>uhayna into the eastern *bilād al-Sūdān* in the 8th/14th century are now represented by the camel-Arabs of the northern zone and the Baḳḳāra of the south. The name of Fazāra, once commonly applied to a group of camel-Arabs, is now obsolete. Among the Baḳḳārī tribes, the Rizayḳāt and Taʿāi<u>sh</u>a may be noted. Individual immigrants, coming from the arabized Nubians of the Nilotic Sudan, Barābra [*q.v.*], Danāḳla [see DANḲALĪ] and <u>Dj</u>aʿaliyyīn [*q.v.*], have made an important contribution to the development in Dār Fūr of Islamic culture and trade. The present-day population of the province amounts to 1,328,559 (*Sudan Almanac, 1959*).

Chronology.

The chronology of the dynasty before the eighth sultan, ʿAbd al-Raḥmān al-Ra<u>sh</u>īd, is uncertain. Browne believed that Sulaymān Solong reigned c. 130-150 years before his time, *i.e.*, c. 1640-60; while al-Tūnusī, who makes the foundation of Dār Fūr contemporary with that of Waddāī and Kordofān, asserts that the event occurred not more than 200 years previously, *i.e.*, c. 1640 (Tūnusī, *Ouadây*, 75). <u>Sh</u>uḳayr's chronology, which refers Sulaymān Solong to the mid-9th/15th century, by incorporating a block of inert names, is a late tradition and clearly fictitious. Nachtigal gives the commencement of Sulaymān Solong's reign as 1596, which seems too early.

Sultans with dates of accession.

1. Sulaymān Solong c. 1050/1640
2. Mūsā b. Sulaymān
3. Aḥmad Bakr b. Mūsā
4. Muḥammad Dawra b. Aḥmad Bakr
5. ʿUmar b. Muḥammad Dawra c. 1156/1743-4
6. Abu 'l-Ḳāsim b. Aḥmad Bakr c. 1163/1749-50
7. Muḥammad Tayrāb b. Aḥmad Bakr c. 1170/1756-7
8. ʿAbd al-Raḥmān al-Ra<u>sh</u>īd b. Aḥmad Bakr 1202/1787
9. Muḥammad Faḍl b. ʿAbd al-Raḥmān 1215/1800-1
10. Muḥammad Ḥusayn b. Muḥammad Faḍl 1254/1838-9
11. Ibrāhīm b. Muḥammad Ḥusayn 1290/1873
(Annexation of Dār Fūr to the Egyptian Sudan; 1291/1874)
Shadow-sultans of the Khedivial and Mahdist periods:
12. Ḥasab Allāh b. Muḥammad Faḍl
13. Bū<u>sh</u> b. Muḥammad Faḍl
14. Hārūn b. Sayf al-Dīn b. Muḥammad Faḍl
15. ʿAbd Allāh Dūd Ban<u>dj</u>a b. Bakr b. Muḥammad Faḍl
16. Yūsuf b. Ibrāhīm
17. Abu 'l-<u>Kh</u>ayrāt b. Ibrāhīm
The revived sultanate:
18. ʿAlī Dīnār b. Zakariyyā b. Muḥammad Faḍl 1316/1898
(Annexation of Dār Fūr to the Anglo-Egyptian Sudan; 1916)

Traditions of the early sultanate.

In the absence of any native chronicle, we are dependent for information on foreign observers. Of these, the most important are the Tunisian Arab, Muḥammad b. ʿUmar al-Tūnusī, whose visit of eight years began in 1218/1803; the German, Gustav Nachtigal, who was in Dār Fūr in 1894; the Austrian, Rudolf v. Slatin, governor 1881-3; and the Lebanese, Naʿūm <u>Sh</u>uḳayr, an intelligence official of the Condominium, whose principal informant was <u>Sh</u>ay<u>kh</u> al-Ṭayyib, (d. 1902), formerly *imām* to sultan Ibrāhīm.

The discrepancies in the traditional genealogies of the Kayra were noticed by al-Tūnusī, Nachtigal and <u>Sh</u>uḳayr. These genealogies are more or less sophisticated attempts to schematize traditions associated with folk-heroes, the chief of whom are Aḥmad al-Maʿḳūr, Dālī, and Sulaymān Solong (*i.e.*, "the Arab"). The many variants of tradition cannot be detailed here. Aḥmad al-Maʿḳūr, an Arab of Tunis, of Hilālī or ʿAbbāsid descent, is represented as the ancestor of the Tun<u>dj</u>ur rulers who preceded the Kayra, or as the link (by marriage) between Tun<u>dj</u>ur and Kayra. His son (or more remote descendant), Dālī, was the organizer and legislator of the Fūrāwī state. A descendant of Dālī, Sulaymān Solong, usually described as the son of an Arab woman, is credited with the introduction of Islam, and is the first of the historical rulers. Aḥmad al-Maʿḳūr may represent a genuine memory of Arab intermixture with the Tun<u>dj</u>ur (or Fūr) or may be a late invention to antedate the coming of the Arab element. The epithet *al-Maʿḳūr*, "the Lame" is probably the arabicization of a non-Arab name: it is explained in Slatin and <u>Sh</u>uḳayr by an obvious legend. Dālī (or Dalīl Baḥr) may have been an historical individual, or may embody the traditions of the Kayra rulers before the coming of Islam. Sulaymān Solong, a warrior and administrator, is Dālī's Muslim counterpart and may have absorbed traditions originally connected with him. Sulaymān was probably not the founder of the Kayra dynasty, but simply the first Muslim ruler. The claims that the royal clan was descended from the Banī Hilāl or the ʿAbbāsids are sophistications, reflecting North African and Nilotic Sudanese influences respectively. The two claims are, of course, incompatible. There is more verisimilitude in a tradition that the Kayra, together with the Musabbaʿāt and the ruling house of Waddāī, were descended from the Fazāra. This is in harmony with the tradition that Sulaymān's conquests were achieved in alliance with the nomad Arabs.

While Sulaymān may have begun the introduction of Islam into Dār Fūr, the full islamization of the region was a slow process. The persistence of non-islamic customs into the 19th and 20th centuries is noted by all observers. The religious teachers (*faki* for *faķīh*; *fuķarā'* is invariably used as the plural), came mainly from the western *bilād al-Sūdān*, and from the Nilotic region, both areas where the Mālikī school predominates. Little is recorded of the sultans who immediately followed Sulaymān: his second successor, Aḥmad Bakr, is remembered as the father of many sons, five of whom were sultans after him. The traditions of both Dār Fūr and Waddāī preserve the recollection of a series of wars between the two sultanates, beginning in the time of Aḥmad Bakr and continuing until Muḥammad Tayrāb, early in his reign, made peace with sultan Djawda of Waddāī. Both ʿUmar and Abu 'l-Kāsim are said to have been killed in these wars, in which the advantage generally lay with Waddāī.

The later sultanate.

Fuller traditions begin with the reign of Muḥammad Tayrāb, who died only 16 years before the visit of al-Tūnusī. He is represented as luxury-loving and pacific, but his reign ended in war against sultan Hāshim, the Musabbaʿāwī ruler of Kordofān. The pretext for hostilities was found in Hāshim's aggression against the eastern frontier of Dār Fūr, but al-Tūnusī suggests that Tayrāb's real motive was to secure the succession for his son, Isḥāķ, at the expense of the surviving sons of Aḥmad Bakr. Isḥāķ, entitled *al-khalīfa*, "the successor", was left as regent in the capital, while the sultan's brothers and ministers accompanied Tayrāb on campaign. Hāshim was expelled from Kordofān and sought refuge with the Fundj sultan of Sinnār, while the Fūrāwī army occupied his dominions. The legend that Tayrāb advanced as far as Omdurman (*Umm Durmān*) and defeated an ʿAbdallābī army is not mentioned by al-Tūnusī or Nachtigal, and is a later elaboration, probably of the Mahdist period. Tayrāb died at Bāra in Kordofān, poisoned, it is said, by his grandees.

Tayrāb's death was followed by a succession struggle between the partisans of Isḥāķ and those of the sons of Aḥmad Bakr. The latter finally chose as their sultan the posthumous son of Aḥmad Bakr, ʿAbd al-Raḥmān al-Rashīd, a pious and scholarly youth. His election was brought about by Muḥammad Kurra, a eunuch of the late ruler, whom ʿAbd al-Raḥmān appointed as his chief minister. Kurra subsequently led another expedition into Kordofān, which he governed for some years. ʿAbd al-Raḥmān's reign witnessed the progress of both trade and religion, developments which may be ascribed to Nubian immigration into Dār Fūr at this time, in consequence of the decline of Fundj power in the Nilotic Sudan. Increased contact with the outside world, through trade with Egypt, is indicated by the exchange of presents between ʿAbd al-Raḥmān and the Ottoman sultan, by the visit of the English traveller, W. G. Browne, in 1793-6, and by the correspondence with Bonaparte in 1799 (French text in *Pièces diverses et correspondance relatives aux opérations de l'armée d'Orient en Égypte*, Paris, An IX; 187, 216-7). A Mamlūk refugee from Bonaparte was granted asylum in Dār Fūr, but was killed for plotting against the sultan.

ʿAbd al-Raḥmān's young son, Muḥammad Faḍl, was installed as sultan by Muḥammad Kurra in 1215/1800-1, but a rift grew between the ruler and his minister, and Kurra was killed in Radjab 1219/Oct.-Nov. 1804. Faḍl's long reign was a period of declining power. An expedition sent by Muḥammad ʿAlī Pasha of Egypt, under his son-in-law, the *daftardār* Muḥammad Bey Khusraw, defeated the Fūrāwī viceroy of Kordofān, the *maķdūm* Musallim, at Bāra in 1821, and annexed the province. Revolt in the Nile valley, however, deflected the *daftardār* from the conquest of Dār Fūr. Muḥammad ʿAbd al-Karīm Ṣābūn, the sultan of Waddāī, devastated the vassal state of Dār Tāma and laid it under tribute. Faḍl assisted a brother of Ṣābūn to obtain the throne of Waddāī after his death, but failed to establish a protectorate. The Baķķāra, especially the Rizayķāt, also gave much trouble.

Faḍl's successor, Muḥammad Ḥusayn, was threatened by a pretender, Muḥammad Abū Madyan, a son of sultan ʿAbd al-Raḥmān. Muḥammad ʿAlī Pasha, who claimed Dār Fūr by virtue of a *farmān* of sultan ʿAbd al-Madjīd (13 February 1841; see J. C. Hurewitz, *Diplomacy in the Near and Middle East*, New York, 1956; i, 120), supported Abū Madyan, and an expedition was prepared. The project was abandoned on the death of the ambitious *ḥükümdār* of the Egyptian Sudan, Aḥmad Pasha Abū Widān, in Ramaḍān 1259/Sept.-Oct. 1843. Relations between Ḥusayn and the viceroys Saʿīd and Ismāʿīl were friendly. In the later years of Ḥusayn's reign, his sight failed, and affairs were directed by his sister, the *iya basi* Zamzam.

His successor, sultan Ibrāhīm, soon became involved in hostilities over the Rizayķāt with al-Zubayr Raḥma Manṣūr, the Sudanese merchant-prince who controlled the western Baḥr al-Ghazāl. Al-Zubayr invaded Dār Fūr from the south, in collusion with the *ḥükümdār* Ismāʿīl Pasha Ayyūb, who brought a force from the east. Ibrāhīm was defeated by al-Zubayr, and killed at the battle of Manawāshī on 24 Oct. 1874. Dār Fūr was annexed to the Egyptian Sudan.

The Khedivial and Mahdist Periods.

Fūr resistance, based on Dj. Marra. continued under a series of shadow-sultans. The first, Ḥasab Allāh b. Muḥammad Faḍl, surrendered to al-Zubayr, and was sent, with a large number of Fūrāwī princes and notables, to Egypt. His brother and successor, Būsh, raised an alarming revolt, but was killed by al-Zubayr's son, Sulaymān. A further revolt, in 1877, against newly imposed taxation, found a leader in Hārūn, a grandson of Muḥammad Faḍl. He besieged El Fasher, the provincial capital, but was driven back to Dj. Marra, and was killed in 1880 by al-Nūr Bey Muḥammad ʿAnķara, subsequently a Mahdist officer. Another grandson of Muḥammad Faḍl, ʿAbd Allāh Dūd Bandja, next assumed the sultanate in Dj. Marra.

The outbreak of the Mahdist revolution in 1881 produced a critical situation in Dār Fūr, since many of the military and administrative officers were sympathizers with the Mahdi, like them a riverain Sudanese, while both the Fūr and the Rizayķāt wished to throw off khedivial rule. After the Mahdi's capture of El Obeid and defeat of the Hicks expedition (January and November 1883), Slatin, the Austrian governor, was isolated, and he surrendered in December to Muḥammad Bey Khālid, formerly sub-governor of Dāra, whom the Mahdi had appointed as his agent in Dār Fūr.

In 1884, a Mahdist force captured Dūd Bandja, who subsequently became a Mahdist officer. After the Mahdi's death in 1885, Muḥammad Khalid concerted a plot with the Ashrāf (the Mahdi's relatives), to oust the new sovereign, the Khalīfa ʿAbd Allāh b. Muḥammad [*q.v.*]. He marched on Omdurman with considerable forces, but was intercepted and arrested at Bāra (April 1886). He had left to govern Dār Fūr a son of sultan Ibrāhīm named Yūsuf, who in 1887 revived the sultanate. A force under ʿUthmān Ādam, the governor of Kordofān, defeated and killed Yūsuf early in 1888. ʿUthmān now assumed the governorship of Dār Fūr also.

A few months later, Mahdist authority in Dār Fūr crumbled, in consequence of a revolt, originating in Dār Tāma under a messianic *fakī*, Abū Djummayza. He was joined by the shadow-sultan of the Fūr, Abu 'l-Khayrāt (a brother of Yūsuf b. Ibrāhīm) with his supporters. The Mahdist forces were heavily defeated in two battles, but Abū Djummayza died of smallpox and his followers were routed outside El Fasher (February 1889). Abu 'l-Khayrāt fled to Dj. Marra, where he was killed by his slaves in 1891. ʿUthmān Ādam re-established his authority in the province, especially over the Baḳḳāra, who had supported the Mahdia against the khedivial administration, but were now resentful of Mahdist control. The Khalīfa's tribal policy, executed by ʿUthman Ādam, rested on three bases; the substitution of new nominees for the hereditary chiefs, the enforced migration (*hidjra*) of tribes to Omdurman, and the exploitation of tribal rivalries. The great migration of the Taʿāīsha, the Khalīfa's own tribe, was set on foot by ʿUthmān Ādam in 1888, and had important consequences for the Mahdist state.

ʿUthmān Ādam died in 1891, and was succeeded as governor by Maḥmūd Aḥmad, like himself a relative of the Khalīfa. In 1894, a Belgian expedition from the Congo reached the southern fringe of the province and concluded a treaty with the chief of the Farūḳī tribe, but withdrew shortly afterwards, (see A. Abel, *Traduction de documents arabes concernant le Bahr-el-Ghazal*, in *Bull. de l'Académie royale des Sciences coloniales*, xxv/5, Brussels 1954, 1385-1409). In 1896, Maḥmūd was recalled to Omdurman, to command the forces sent against the Anglo-Egyptian invasion.

The reign of ʿAlī Dīnār and subsequent history

When the Mahdist state fell in 1898, ʿAlī Dīnār, a grandson of Muḥammad Faḍl, who had had a chequered career in the Mahdia (see *A fragment from Ali Dinar*, in *Sudan notes and records*; xxxiv/1, 1953, 114-6), seized El Fasher and installed himself as sultan. Nominally a vassal of the Condominium government in Khartoum, he long imitated with success the Khalīfa's policy of excluding Europeans from his dominions. He was challenged by a survivor of the Mahdist régime, Sanīn Ḥusayn, who had held Kabkābiyya since ʿUthmān Ādam's time and now attempted unsuccessfully to obtain the protection of the Condominium government. Sanīn was not finally defeated until 1908. Like his predecessors, ʿAlī Dīnār had difficulty in asserting his authority, on the one hand over the Baḳḳāra, on the other, over the buffer states between Dār Fūr and Waddāī. This western frontier problem became more serious with the French occupation of Waddāī in 1909. The French, while accepting Dār Fūr proper as within the British sphere of influence, wished to occupy the buffer states. Although the British, through the Condominium government, vigorously supported Fūrāwī claims, the sultan, after prolonged hostilities, succeeded only in holding Dār al-Masālīt. Finding himself pressed by the extension of French power, and exasperated by a series of local grievances against the Condominium government, ʿAlī Dīnār was sympathetic to the Ottomans in the First World War. On the pretext of forestalling an attack from Dār Fūr, the Condominium government sent a force against him. The sultan's army was defeated near El Fasher on 22 May 1916. and he himself was killed on 6 November.

The removal of ʿAlī Dīnār, was followed by a settlement of the western frontier with the French. The final compromise in 1919 allowed Dār Fūr to retain Dār Ḳimr and two-thirds of Dār al-Masālīt, part of which had been ceded by its ruler to the French in 1912. The delimitation of the boundary was completed in 1924. The pacification of Dār Fūr did not prove difficult, although there was a belated rising under a messianic *fakī* at Nyala in 1921. As a consequence of its late annexation, Dār Fūr did not share in the early phase of development of the Anglo-Egyptian Sudan: it remained an isolated and backward province until the last years of the Condominium. The opening-up of air communications from 1947, the development of schools, and the construction of a railway line through southern Kordofān to Nyala (completed in April 1959) are indicative of the fuller integration of Dār Fūr in the modern Sudan.

Administrative history.

The administrative system under the Kayra sultans was described by al-Tūnusī and, more systematically, by Nachtigal. It had few Islamic features. Almost all the titles were Fūrāwī, not Arabic; the chief exception being the sultan's personal representatives (*maḳdūm*, pl. *maḳādīm*), who were usually appointed for a term of years and exercised overriding powers in their provinces. The royal women (sing., *mayram*) held a dignified position; the queen-mother was the second person in the realm, but more real power was possessed by the *iya basi*, usually the sultan's sister. Slaves and eunuchs played an important rôle: the chief minister, who was also *ex officio* governor of the eastern province, was a eunuch. The powers of this functionary were reduced after the death of the kingmaker, Muḥammad Kurra. A tradition that sultan Abu 'l-Ḳāsim was deserted in battle by his relatives because of his inclination to the blacks probably marks an increase in the military rôle of the ruler's slave-household at the expense of the free clansmen. A reorganization of the slave-army was carried out by sultan Muḥammad Ḥusayn, who equipped his troops with firearms. Besides the slave-solidiers, the forces included warriors summoned at need by the provincial authorities. Islamic influences are chiefly seen in the practices of the royal chancery and in the reception of the *Sharīʿa* according to the Mālikī school. The ancient customary law was not however disused: the "Book of Dālī", in which it was said to be codified, is probably mythical, or may be a generic term for attempts to commit custom to writing, (cf. A. J. Arkell, *The history of Darfur*: 1200-1700 *A.D.* III, in *Sudan notes and records*, xxxiii/1, 1952, 145-6).

After the conquest by al-Zubayr, the administration was assimilated, as far as circumstances allowed, to that of other parts of the Egyptian Sudan. A governor (*mudīr ʿumūm Dār Fūr*) had his headquarters at El Fasher, while sub-governors (*mudīrs*) were stationed at El Fasher, Shakkā (to control the Rizayḳāt territory), Dāra (on the route from the south to the capital), and Kabkābiyya (on the route to Waddāī). The governors have been listed by R. L. Hill, *Rulers of the Sudan*, 1820-1885, in *Sudan notes and records*, xxxii/1, 1951, 85-95.

The Mahdist régime inherited the problems and administrative structure of its predecessor. Dār Fūr, later combined with Kordofān in the Province of the West (*ʿImālat al-Gharb*), was ruled by a military governor (*ʿāmil*—originally *amīr*—*ʿumūm Dār Fūr*), who commanded a force composed of tribal levies (*awlād al-ʿArab*) and black troops (*djihādiyya*). Many of the latter, as well as of the military and civil officials had previously served the khedivial administration. The governor was in frequent correspondence with Omdurman, but had his provincial treasury (*bayt al-māl*).

The revived sultanate under ʿAlī Dīnār reproduced many features of the Khalīfa's central administration. Essentially it was a military autocracy under which the ancient Fūrāwī offices and the system of *maḳdūms* alike became obsolete, while special deputies (*mandūb*, plur. *manādīb*) gathered the revenue and represented the sultan in the provinces. Favourites and slaves had much influence at the centre. The influence of the Mahdia can be seen in the organization of a hierarchy of *ḳādīs*, and in the system of taxes, which closely resembled that of the Khalīfa.

After the annexation of Dār Fūr in 1916, the province was administered by a British governor and district commissioners, who at first were army officers. Experiments in "native administration" resulted in some useful devolution, primarily of judicial functions, to local notables, but also produced an anachronistic attempt to create or revive large native authorities. This curious reversal of the policy previously followed by successive sultans and governors was too artificial to succeed generally. In the last decade of the Condominium, Dār Fūr shared in the rapid constitutional changes. Local government councils were formed and representatives were sent to the various central deliberative bodies. The coming of independence on 1 January 1956 did not affect the administrative structure, in which Sudanese officials had already filled the higher cadres, previously occupied by British. The military *coup d'état* of November 1958 did not directly affect provincial administration, but the continued existence of the local government councils is necessarily precarious. For the administration under ʿAlī Dīnār and the Condominium, see G. D. Lampen, *History of Darfur*, in *Sudan notes and records*, xxxi/2, 1950, 203-8.

Bibliography: W. G. Browne, *Travels in Africa, Egypt, and Syria*, London 1799, 180-350; Muḥammad b. ʿUmar al-Tūnusī, *Tashḥīdh al-adhhān bi-sīrat bilād al-ʿArab wa 'l-Sūdān*, lith. Paris 1850; tr. Perron, *Voyage au Darfour par le cheykh Mohammed Ebn-Omar El-Tounsy*, Paris 1845; Al-Tūnusī, tr. Perron, *Voyage au Ouadây*, Paris 1851; G. Nachtigal, *Sahara und Sudan*, iii, Leipzig 1889, 355-446; R. C. [von] Slatin, *Fire and sword in the Sudan*, London 1896, 30-278; Naʿūm Shuḳayr, *Taʾrīkh al-Sūdān*, Cairo 1903, ii, 111-48, iii, 68-84, 93-6, 185-92, 451-5, 458-65, 533-4, 546-9, 672; H. A. MacMichael, *A history of the Arabs in the Sudan*, Cambridge 1922, i, 52-128; idem, *The Anglo-Egyptian Sudan*, London 1934, 125-37; R. [L.] Hill, *A biographical dictionary of the Anglo-Egyptian Sudan*, Oxford 1951, various notices; P. M. Holt, *The Mahdist state in the Sudan*, Oxford 1958; 66-8, 127-30, 132-46; Numerous articles in *Sudan notes and records*, Khartoum 1918-. Information supplied by A. B. Theobald, whose article, *Darfur and its neighbours under Sultan ʿAli Dinar*, is to appear in *Sudan notes and records*. The government archives in Khartoum contain a very considerable body of material relating to the Mahdia, the rule of ʿAlī Dīnār and the Condominium period.

(P. M. Holt)

DĀR AL-ḤADĪTH. I. Architecture [see SUPPLEMENT].

II. Historical development. The name *Dār al-ḥadīth* was first applied to institutions reserved for the teaching of *ḥadīths* in the sixth century of the Hidjra. The conclusion that until that time *ḥadīths* were learned through the journeys called *ṭalab al-ʿilm*, there being no special schools for the science of *ḥadīth* (cf. Goldziher, *Muh. Stud.* ii, 186), is not consonant with the results of the study of materials now available. Hence, among other matters connected with *ḥadīth*, the effects of the misunderstanding of the nature and object of the *ṭalab al-ʿilm* journeys need to be investigated (cf. F. Sezgin, *Buharî'nin kaynakları hakkında araştırmalar*, 23-36; idem, *Islam Tetkikleri Enst. dergisi* 1957, II/i, 24).

In his treatise *al-Amṣār dhawāt al-āthār* (MS Veliyeddin 463/3, 90b-93a), al-Dhahabī (d. 748/1347-8) gives us comprehensive information about the centres for hadīth-study and their distribution in different centuries throughout the Muslim world. Interest in the science of *ḥadīth* and the study of it had continued for centuries without intermission in Syria, where the first Dār al-Ḥadīth was founded, one of the centres (with an interruption of 90 years) being Jerusalem (*op. cit.*, 93b).

Until special institutions for the study of *ḥadīth* were set up, the teaching of this, as of other branches of religious learning, was carried out in the mosques. *Muḥaddiths*, unwilling that such instruction should be given to a few people only in private residences, encouraged the use of public places (cf. *e.g.*, al-Khaṭīb, *Taʾrīkh Baghdād*, ii, 33). Al-Bukhārī (d. 256/870), who as a young man came to Basra at the beginning of the 3rd/9th century, instituted *ḥadīth*-lectures in the mosque there, which were attended by thousands of students (*op. cit.*, ii, 16-17). In Cairo in the 3rd century a pupil of al-Shāfiʿī was giving *ḥadīth*-lessons in the Mosque of Ibn Ṭūlūn (*Ḥusn al-muḥāḍara*. Cairo 1299, i, 182). When later the institutions known as *dār al-ʿilm* or *madrasa* were founded, *ḥadīth*-studies were, to some extent, attracted to them from the mosques and the private houses of the teachers. Nevertheless schools reserved for the teaching of *ḥadīth* began to be opened from the 4th/10th century onwards; thus the *ḥadīth*-school set up for Abū ʿAlī al-Ḥusaynī (d. 393/1003) in Nīshāpūr had about a thousand students, and *ḥadīth*-schools were founded for Ibn al-Fūrak (d. 406/1015-6), Abu 'l-Ḳāsim al-Ḳushayrī (d. 465/1072-3) and Rukn al-Dīn al-Iṣfahānī (d. 418/1027) (cf. Wüstenfeld, *Imam Schafiʿi*, i, 156, ii, 229, iii, 284). In the Sunnī Dār al-ʿilm which al-Ḥākim bi-amrillāh founded at Cairo in 400/1009-10, two Mālikī professors gathered around them the experts in *fiḳh* and *ḥadīth* (al-Dhahabī, *Duwal al-Islām*, Ḥaydarābād, i, 186).

The first institution to be called specifically Dār al-Ḥadīth was founded by the Atabeg Nūr al-Dīn (d. 569/1173-4) (al-Nuʿaymī, *al-Dāris fī taʾrīkh al-madāris*, Damascus 1948, i, 99, cf. *Muh. Stud.* ii, 187). Though Nūr al-Dīn was himself Ḥanafī, he limited this school to Shāfiʿīs (Wüstenfeld, *Die Akademien der Araber und ihre Lehrer*, 69), and set over it the historian and *muḥaddith* ʿAbd Allāh b. ʿAsākir (d. 571/1175-6) (al-Nuʿaymī, *op. cit.*, i, 100). There were many *waḳf*s for this institution and the people attached to it (Abū Shāma, *Al-Rawḍatayn*, Cairo 1956, i, 23). Ibn ʿAsākir was succeeded by his son al-Ḳāsim (d. 600/1203-4) (al-Nuʿaymī, *op. cit.*, i, 100). Al-Nuʿaymī gives the names of the rectors of this *ḥadīth*-school down to Ibn Rāfiʿ (d. 718/1318). The opening of this first Dār al-Ḥadīth was followed by the establishment of numerous similar institutions to which leading historians and *muḥaddith*s were attached, mostly in Damascus and its neighbourhood (for which al-Nuʿaymī records the names of 16), but spreading immediately all over the Muslim world: thus ʿAbd al-Laṭīf al-Baghdādī (d. 629/1231-2), on going to Mosul in 585/1189, found such a dār al-ḥadīth on the ground floor of the Madrasa of Ibn Muhādjir (Ibn Abī Uṣaybiʿa, ii, 204); in 622/1225 al-Malik al-Kāmil Nāṣir al-Dīn founded in Cairo a dār al-ḥadīth inspired by the Dār al-Ḥadīth al-Nūriyya, setting over it Abu ʾl-Khaṭṭāb b. Diḥya. Maḳrīzī notes that in 806/1403-4 it had so far declined as to have as its head an ignorant young man, a mere child (*Khiṭaṭ*, Cairo 1270, ii, 375). In the time of Ibn Duḳmāḳ (d. 845/1441-2) two of the 73 *madrasa*s in Cairo were dār al-ḥadīths (*Intiṣār*, Cairo 1299, 99).

After the establishment of the first *dār al-ḥadīth*s, institutions known as Dār al-Ḳurʾān wa ʾl-Ḥadīth, for the teaching of both Ḳurʾān and *ḥadīth*, made their appearance: the first institutions of this type were set up by Sayf al-Dīn al-Malik al-Nāṣirī (d. 741/1340-1) (for this and two other institutions cf. al-Nuʿaymī, *op. cit.*, i, 123-8).

The Dār al-ḥadīth, as an independent institution or as one of many departments of a *madrasa*, survived until recent centuries in the Muslim world: thus according to Mudjīr al-Dīn (d. 927/1521), of the madrasas of Jerusalem, over 40 in number, one was called Dār al-Ḳurʾān and another Dār al-Ḥadīth (Sauvaire, *Hist. de Jérus. et Hebr.*, 139). In the Ottoman period the teachers of the dār al-ḥadīth opposite the Suleymāniyye Mosque were appointed from among the most senior and renowned of all the *mudarris* (*Taʾrīkh-i Djewdet*, Ist. 1309, i, 111). In the last two or three centuries *dār al-ḥadīth*s, like *madrasas* in general, have lost their importance as centres of learning. (FUAT SEZGIN)

DĀR AL-ḤARB ('the Land of War'). This conventional formula derived from the logical development of the idea of the *djihād* [*q.v.*] when it ceased to be the struggle for survival of a small community, becoming instead the basis of the "law of nations" in the Muslim State. The Ḳurʾān, in its latest texts on the holy war, IX, 38-58, 87, makes this "holy war" a major duty, a test of the sincerity of believers, to be waged against unbelievers wherever they are to be found (IX, 5). This war must be just, not oppressive, its aim being peace under the rule of Islam.

The Ḳurʾān does not as yet divide the world into territories where peace and the faith of Islam reign, (*dār al-Islām* [*q.v.*]), territories under perpetual threat of a missionary war (*dār al-ḥarb*), or, of course, territories covered by agreements and payment of tribute (*dār al-ʿahd, dār al-ṣulḥ* [*qq.v.*]).

The *ḥadīth*, it is true, traces back the idea of *dār al-ḥarb* to the Medina period. In any event, the classical practice of so regarding territories immediately adjoining the lands of Islam, and inviting their princes to adopt this religion under pain of invasion, is reputed to date back to the Prophet who invited Caesar and Chosroes (and the Jews) to be converted (al-Bukhārī, *Kitāb al-Djihād*, §§ 147, 148, 149, 151 and *K. al-Maghāzī*, § 416; see also al-Ḳalḳashandī, *Ṣubḥ*, Cairo 1915, 6, 15). Historically, the invitation to the people of the Yamāma is the prototype (cf. al-Balādhuri, *Futūḥ*). This traditional concept, which ended by committing the Muslim community (or State) and its princes to war, either latent or openly declared, with all its non-Muslim neighbours (the adjective denoting the latter is *ḥarbī* or, more especially, *ahl al-ḥarb*) is classical and is elaborated in the most widely read law books (*e.g.*, the definitions in the *Kitāb al-Djihād* of the *Durar al-ḥukkām fī sharḥ ghurar al-aḥkām* of Mullā Khusraw, where the *ahl al-ḥarb* are defined as those who have refused to be converted after being duly invited on the best terms, and against whom any kind of warfare is henceforth permissible in keeping with the rules of *sūra* IX). In classical times, the kings of the *dār al-ḥarb* are rebels: the emperor of Byzantium is *malik al-Ṭāghiya* (al-Ṭabarī, *Annals, passim*). Classically, the *dār al-ḥarb* includes those countries where the Muslim law is not in force, in the matter of worship and the protection of the faithful and *dhimmī*s. A territory of the *dār al-Islām*, reconquered by non-Muslims of any description, thereby becomes a territory of the *dār al-ḥarb* once again, provided that (1) the law of the unbelievers replaces that of Islam; (2) the country in question directly adjoins the *dār al-ḥarb*; (3) Muslims and their non-Muslim *dhimmī*s no longer enjoy any protection there. The first of these conditions is the most important. Some even believe that a country remains *dār al-Islām* so long as a single provision (*ḥukm*) of the Muslim law is kept in force there. The definition of the *dār al-ḥarb*, like the idea of *djihād*, has in the course of time been modified by the progressive loss of unity and strength in the Muslim State. The conception of hostility to neighbouring countries has equally been modified by the evolution of ideas in Islamic territories and is tending to be secularized. The proclamation of a holy war, at a time of international crisis and for psychological reasons, is an innovation (cf. Snouck Hurgronje, *The Holy war "made in Germany"*, New York 1915, = Verspreide Geschriften, iii, 257 ff.).

Bibliography: Majid Khadduri, *War and Peace in the law of Islam*, Baltimore 1955, 52, 53, 143, 144, 156-7, 171-4, 224-8 and bibliography; L. Gardet, *La Cité musulmane*, 95 ff. (A. ABEL)

DĀR AL-ḤIKMA, "house of wisdom", used by Arab authors to denote in a general sense the academies which, before Islamic times, spread knowledge of the Greek sciences, and in a particular sense the institute founded in Cairo in 395/1005 by the Fāṭimid caliph al-Ḥākim. Since the short-lived appearance of the *Bayt al-Ḥikma* [*q.v.*] of al-Maʾmūn, several libraries had been founded in ʿIrāḳ and Persia providing not only information on traditional learning, but also an introduction to classical sciences (*ʿulūm al-awāʾil*) (see DĀR AL-ʿILM).

Such establishments were very successful in Egypt under the Fāṭimids, where Shīʿī doctrines provided a favourable climate for the development of Greek sciences. The Cairo palace soon housed a large collection, and one of its librarians was the writer al-Shābushtī (d. 388/998). The vizier of al-ʿAzīz, Yaʿḳūb b. Ḳillis (d. 380/990), organized meetings of men of letters, jurists, and theologians in his own residence, and granted them financial allowances, but this initiative was soon overshadowed by the *Dār al-ḥikma* (sometimes *dār al-ʿilm*) which al-Ḥākim housed in the north-western part of the western Palace. It contained a library and reading-room, and served as a meeting-place for traditionists, jurists, grammarians, doctors, astronomers, logicians and mathematicians. The Cairo *Dār al-ḥikma* was administered by the *Dāʿī al-duʿāt*, who invited learned men to meet there twice weekly. It was closely associated with the propagation of Shīʿī doctrine, and charged to give instruction in Ismaʿīlī doctrine, which has also been called *ḥikma* since the time of al-Muʿizz (see al-Ḳāḍī al-Nuʿmān, *K. al-Madjālis*, after Dachraoui, *Arabica*, 1960). In 435/1045 a new catalogue was prepared, and it listed at least 6500 volumes on astronomy, architecture and *falsafa*. The institute was closed at the end of the 5th/11th century by the vizier al-Afḍal, but al-Maʾmūn reopened it in 517/1123 in another building, to the south of the eastern Palace. It had already been looted in 461/1068, in the reign of al-Muntaṣir during the civil wars, and when the Fāṭimid dynasty came to an end (567/1171) the library was once more closed. Ṣalāḥ al-Dīn sold the palace treasures, including the books, but fortunately some of them were re-purchased by enlightened men such as al-Ḳāḍī al-Fāḍil.

Bibliography: Maḳrīzī, *Khiṭaṭ*, Būlāḳ ed., i, 408-9, 445, 458-60; ii, 342, 363, 481; Cairo ed., ii, 253-5, 313, 334-7; iv, 158, 192, 377; Kindī, 600, 640; al-Ḳifṭi, 440; Ibn Khallikān, Cairo ed., 1949, vi, 28; O. Pinto, *Le biblioteche degli Arabi*, Florence 1928, 16, 25, 26; Mez, *Renaissance*, 169-70; M. Canard, *Le cérémonial fatimite* . . ., in *Byzantion*, xxi (1951), 364 (D. SOURDEL)

DĀR AL-ʿILM, "house of science", the name given to several libraries or scientific institutes established in eastern Islam in the 3rd/9th and 4th/10th centuries. After the disappearance of al-Maʾmūn's *Bayt al-Ḥikma* [*q.v.*], a man of letters called ʿAlī b. Yaḥyā al-Munadjdjim (d. 275/888), friend of al-Mutawakkil and, later, al-Muʿtamid, built a library at his own expense in his residence at Karkar, near Baghdād. It was called *Khizānat al-Kutub*, and was open to scholars of all countries (Yāḳūt, *Irshād*, v, 459, 467). Another writer and poet, the Shāfiʿī *faḳīh* Djaʿfar b. Muḥammad b. Ḥamdān al-Mawṣilī (d. 323/934), founded the institute named *Dār al-ʿilm* at Mosul; it was also equipped with a library open to everyone (Yāḳūt, *Irshād*, ii, 420). During the Buwayhid era further libraries were opened in other towns, and they did much to spread Shīʿī doctrines. The one in Shīrāz was founded by ʿAḍud al-Dawla, and was frequented by the geographer al-Muḳaddasī (449). Others in al-Baṣra and Rām Hormuz were founded by a certain Ibn Sawwār, and were associated with the Muʿtazilite school. The al-Rayy library (Muḳaddasī, 391, 413; Yāḳūt, *Irshād*, ii, 315; Ibn al-Djawzī, *Muntaẓam*, ix, 53) was later burnt down as a centre of heterodoxy upon the orders of Maḥmūd of Ghaznī.

But the most important establishment was the *Dār al-ʿilm* which the vizier Abū Naṣr Sābūr b. Ardashīr founded in Baghdād during the reign of Bahāʾ al-Dawla. It was housed in a building in the al-Karkh quarter, and dated from 381/991 or 383/993. It contained more than 10,000 books, some of them models of calligraphy, on all scientific subjects. It was governed by two *sharīf*s and a *ḳāḍī*, and after Sābūr's death the Shīʿī poet al-Sharīf al-Murtaḍā is thought to have taken over its administration. We also have the names of some of those who were appointed librarians, such as the grammarian Abū Aḥmād ʿAbd al-Salām, otherwise known as al-Wādjikā (d. 405/1014) (a friend of Abu 'l-ʿAlāʾ al-Maʿarrī) and the secretary Abū Manṣūr Muḥammad b. ʿAlī (d. 418/1027). Sābūr's library was used by numerous scholars, in particular by Abu 'l-ʿAlāʾ al-Maʿarrī during his short stay in Baghdād (399-400/1009-1010), and it also received the works of contemporary writers such as the Fāṭimid secretary Aḥmad b. ʿAlī b. Khayrān (d. 431/1039). It was finally burnt down when the Saldjūḳs reached Baghdād in 447/1055-56. The vizier ʿAmīd al-Mulk al-Kundurī was able to save only a few books from destruction.

It is thought that a Sunnī *Dār al-ʿilm* was founded at Fusṭāṭ in 400/1010 by the Fāṭimid caliph al-Ḥākim; it was governed by two Mālikī scholars, but after three years they were put to death and the library was suppressed (Ibn Taghrībirdī, ii, 64, 105-106).

Bibliography: *Taʾrīkh Baghdād*, iii, 93; Ibn al-Djawzī, *Muntaẓam*, vii, 172, 273; viii, 205; Ibn al-Athīr, ix, 71, 246-7, x, 5; Yāḳūt, i, 799; Yāḳūt, *Irshād*, i, 242; Ibn Khallikān, Cairo ed. 1949, ii, 100; Bundarī, ed. Houtsma, 18; Ibn al-ʿImād, *Shadharāt*, iii, 104 (*s.a.* 383); Abu 'l-ʿAlāʾ al-Maʿarrī, *Risālat al-Ghufrān*, ed. Yazīdjī, 73, 184; *Siḳt al-zand*, Cairo 1319, 1901, 103, 127; Mez, *Renaissance*, 167-9; O. Pinto, *Le biblioteche degli Arabi*, Florence 1928, 8-9, 14-5, 23; K. ʿAwwād, *Khazāʾin kutub al-Irāḳ al-ʿāmma*, in *Sumer*, 1946/2, 218-23 (in Ar.); H. Laoust, *La vie et la philosophie d'Abou-l-ʿAlāʾ*, in *BEO*, x, 1943-4, 127-9; idem, *La profession de foi d'Ibn Baṭṭa*, Damascus 1958, xxii-xxiii; G. Makdisi, *The Topography of eleventh century Baghdād*, in *Arabica*, vi (1959), 195-6. (D. SOURDEL)

DĀR AL-ISLĀM, 'the Land of Islām' or, more simply, in Muslim authors, *dārunā*, 'our Country' is the whole territory in which the law of Islam prevails. Its unity resides in the community of the faith, the unity of the law, and the guarantees assured to members of the *umma* [*q.v.*]. The *umma*, established in consequence of the final revelation, also guarantees the faith, the persons, possessions and religious organization, albeit on a lower level, of *dhimmīs*, the followers of the creeds of Christianity and Judaism which sprang from earlier revelations, and of the Zoroastrians (*Madjūs*) [cf. DHIMMA, DJIZYA]. Until the beginnings of contemporary history Islam's oecumenical aspirations were maintained. *Ḥadīth*s going back to the Prophet, *e.g.*, a *ḥadīth* on the capture of Rome (al-Bukharī, *Djihād*, § 135-139), are the source of these aspirations. In the classical doctrine, everything outside *dār al-Islām* is *dār al-ḥarb* [*q.v.*]. However, the historic example of Nadjrān (al-Balādhurī, *Futūḥ*, section *fī ṣulḥ Nadjrān*) and, at a later date, that of Nubia are proof of the permissibility of truces (*hudna, ṣulḥ*) concluded with the sovereigns of neighbouring territories, who preserve their internal autonomy in exchange for tribute which constitutes an external and formal recognition of the Muslim sovereign's authority (cf. DĀR AL-ʿAHD, DĀR AL-ṢULḤ).

Bibliography: Muḥammad ʿAbduh, *Risālat al-Tawḥīd*; L. Gardet, *La cité musulmane*, 26 and note 203 ff.; H. A. R. Gibb, *The Evolution of*

Government in Early Islam, in *Stud. Isl.*, 4; O. Turan, *The ideal of World Domination among the Mediaeval Turks*, *ibid*. (A. ABEL)

DĀR AL-MAḤFŪẒĀT AL-ʿUMŪMIYYA. The Egyptian State Archives, consisting of the administrative records of the governments of Egypt from the start of the sixteenth century until the present time, and stored at the Citadel and in the Abdine Palace in Cairo. The extant archives of the Ottoman treasury and administration in Egypt from the time of its conquest by Selīm I in 922/1517 until it became autonomous under Muḥammad ʿAlī at the start of the nineteenth century are located at the Citadel (*al-Ḳalʿa*) archives, which were built by Muḥammad ʿAlī in 1242/1827 to store the materials remaining after a disasterous fire in 1235/1820. A very few late-Mamlūk documents and registers, less important nineteenth-century administrative records, and all registers of births and deaths in Egypt are also kept at the Citadel, but the bulk of the nineteenth and twentieth century Egyptian government records are kept at the Abdine Palace in Cairo.

Materials remaining from the Ottoman administration fall into two broad classifications—registers (*dafātir*) and individual documents (*awrāḳ*). There are two basic types of Ottoman administrative registers, those containing copies of orders and decrees, written in the *Dīwānī* script, and those containing financial data, written in the *Siyāḳat* script. Most of the registers of Ottoman orders and decrees stored in Egypt were destroyed in the fire of 1820, and such materials are available only in the published collections of Ferīdun and Ḥayret Efendi (see bibliography) and in the *Mühimme-i Miṣr* registers kept in the *Başvekâlet Arşivi* [*q.v.*] in Istanbul. The materials remaining in the Citadel archives are principally financial registers and a few individual documents. In addition, the archives possess numerous private collections seized by the State upon the death of their owners. The nineteenth and twentieth-century archives kept in the Abdine Palace are far more comprehensive and complete and include copies made in recent times of materials concerning Egypt found in the principal European archives.

Registers of the deliberations of the *Dīwān* of Ottoman Egypt and of judicial archives since late Mamlūk times are found in the archives of the religious courts (*al-Maḥkama li 'l-Aḥwāl al-Shakhṣiyya*) in Cairo.

Bibliography: S. J. Shaw, *Cairo's Archives and the History of Ottoman Egypt*, in *Report on Current Research, Spring* 1956, Middle East Institute, Washington, D.C., 1956, 59-72; J. Deny, *Sommaire des Archives Turques du Caire*, Cairo 1930; Muḥammad Aḥmad Ḥusayn, *al-Wathāʾiḳ al-Taʾrīkhiyya*, Cairo 1945, 93-4; B. Lewis, *The Ottoman Archives as a source of History for the Arab Lands*, in *JRAS* (1951), 139-155; Michaud and Poujoulat, *Correspondance d'Orient*, 1830-1831, vi, Paris 1835, 292-3. For some published collections of documents from the archives of Ottoman Egypt, see: *Recueil de Firmans Impériaux Ottomans adressés aux valis et aux Khédives d'Egypte, 1006 A.H. 1322 A.H.*, Cairo 1934; Muṣṭafā Ḥayret Efendī el-Sīwāsī, *Inshāʾ-i Ḥayret Efendī*, Būlāḳ 1241/1825; Aḥmed Ferīdūn, *Munshaʾāt al-Salāṭīn*, 2 vol., Istanbul 1274/1857-8; G. Talamas Bey, *Recueil de la correspondance de Mohamed Ali, Khédive d'Egypte*, Cairo 1913. On the palaeography and diplomatic of these and other Ottoman administrative materials, see DIPLOMATIC.

(S. J. SHAW)

DĀR AL-MUṢANNIFĪN [see DĀR AL-ʿULŪM (d.)].

DĀR AL-NADWA, a kind of town hall in Mecca in the time of Muḥammad. The building was to the north of the Kaʿba, on the other side of the square in which the *ṭawāf* took place. It was the gathering place of the nobles (*malaʾ*). The Dār al-Nadwa is said to have been built by Ḳuṣayy [*q.v.*], who is taken to be the ancestor of the Ḳuraysh and founder of the Kaʿba. He bequeathed it to ʿAbd al-Dār and then to ʿAbd Manāf and his son Hāshim and Hāshim's descendants. "All matters of import to the Ḳuraysh" are said to have taken place there up to the coming of Islam: marriages, councils of war, advice on public matters, the clothing of marriageable girls, circumcision (*ʿadhr*) of boys, bestowing of standards of war. It—or rather, the square in front of it—is also regarded as the beginning and end of all Meccan trade caravans (Ibn Saʿd, I, i, 39). Henri Lammens, following a suggestion by Martin Hartmann, reasoned from these and other indications that the Dār al-Nadwa in the old days was not a profane but a sacred building which served for the enactment of social-religious rites (*Les sanctuaires préislamites*, 27-33; cf. G. Levi Della Vida, art. ḲUṢAIY, in *EI*[1]). His proof lacks, however, sufficient basis.

To begin with, the Dār al-Nadwa remained after the rise of Islam. Muʿāwiya bought it, and subsequently it served the Umayyads and the first ʿAbbāsids as a residence during their pilgrimages. Hārūn al-Rashīd had a different building extended as a residence (the so-called Dār al-ʿImāra). After that, the Dār al-Nadwa fell more and more into decay. At the end of the 3rd/9th century, under the Caliph al-Muʿtaḍid, it was given columns, arcades and galleries, and incorporated as an annexe to the Masdjid al-Ḥarām.

Bibliography: Ibn Hishām, 80, 83, 323 f., 789; Ibn Saʿd, i/1, 39 f.; Wüstenfeld, *Die Chroniken der Stadt Mekka*, i, (1858), 65-7 (Azraḳī); iv (1861), *passim*; Ṭabarī, i, 1098 f.; *al-Fāsī*, *Shifā al-gharām*, i (Mecca 1956), 226 f., 234-6; Caussin de Perceval, *Essai sur l'histoire des Arabes avant l'Islamisme*, i, (1847), 237, 250 f.; Caetani, *Annali*, i (1905), Introduction § 78; Snouck Hurgronje, *Mekka*, i (1888), 12; Gaudefroy-Demombynes, *Le Pèlerinage à la Mekke* (1923), 151 f.; H. Lammens, *La Mecque à la veille de l'Hégire* (*MFOB*, ix, 3, Beirut 1924), 72-4, 226, 301; idem, *Les sanctuaires préislamites dans l'Arabie occidentale* (*ibid*., xi, 2, 1926), 39-173; Article ḲUṢAIY, in *EI*[1] (G. Levi Della Vida).

(R. PARET)

DĀR AL-SAʿĀDA [see SARAY].

DĀR AL-SALĀM, "Abode of Peace", is in the first place a name of Paradise in the Ḳurʾān (vi, 127; x, 26), because, says Bayḍāwī, it is a place of security (*salāma*) from transitoriness and injury, or because God and the angels salute (*sallama*) those who enter it. Hence it was given to the city of Baghdād by al-Manṣūr, as well as Madīnat al-Salām (cf. BAGHDAD, and also the geographical lexicon of Yāḳūt, *ad init.*). For the capital of Tanganyika see DAR-ES-SALAAM.

(T. H. WEIR*)

DAR-ES-SALAAM, capital of the British administered United Nations Trusteeship Territory of Tanganyika, formerly German East Africa, lies in Lat. 6° 49′ S. and Long. 39° 16′ E. The settlement of

Mzizima (Swahili: the healthy town) was first made in the 17th century A.D. by Wabarawa, of mixed Arab-Swahili stock from Barawa, south of Mogadishu. The present name, a contraction of Bandar al-Salām ("haven of welfare") at least dates from 1862, when Sayyid Madjīd, Sultan of Zanzibar, built a palace and other buildings there, of which a few survive. So does his main street, "Barra-rasta" (Hind. *baṛā rāstā*, lit. 'big road'), now "Acacia Avenue". Its modern prosperity dates from 1888, when it became a station of the German East Africa Company, and, in 1891, the seat of the Imperial Government. In 1916, during the First World War, it was taken by the British forces, and has since been the capital of the British administration. In 1957 the population comprised 93,363 Africans, 2,545 Arabs, 4,479 Europeans, 2,460 Goans, 23,263 Indians, 1,718 Pakistanis, 11 Somali and 903 others. Probably about 85,000 Africans, 12,500 Indians and Pakistanis, the majority of Arabs and all the Somali, are Muslims.

At first a quiet, if imposing official capital, Dar-es-Salaam is now a busy commercial port. A railway bifurcating at Tabora connects it with Lakes Tanganyika and Victoria, while roads, some metalled, reach all parts of the Territory. A complete rebuilding of official buildings is in progress. The mass of the buildings are modern, and, if the African quarter retains its traditional style, as a whole the town has an occidental appearance.

As on the rest of the coast, and in many towns inland, Islam is the majority religion. Of a gross territorial population of 8¹/₂ m., there are probably 2 m. Muslims and almost as many Christians. Swahili, a Bantu language, has a vocabulary approximately 25% Arabic in origin: it is the coastal tongue from near Mogadishu to the Rovuma and the *lingua franca* far inland into the Belgian Congo. Except for a small number of Aḥmadiyya, who have published a Swahili translation of the Ḳur'ān, East African Muslims are Sunnīs of the Shāfi'ī rite. The *sharī'a* is administered for them in Dar-es-Salaam by a Liwali, with appeal to the civil courts. Since earlier than the 1st century A.D. there has been a constant drift of Arab migration along the coast, and possibly Islam reached it in the 7th century. There were already Shāfi'īs when Ibn Baṭṭūṭa visited the coast in 731/1331. Most of the present Arabs are from Shiḥr, but some derive from other parts of the Ḥaḍramawt and Maskaṭ, the latter being Ibāḍīs. There are a few from the Comoros. The wealthiest inhabitants of Dar-es-Salaam are Indians, of whom probably half are Muslims. Khodjas (Ismā'īlīs of the Nizārī branch) predominate, and their head, Āghā Khān IV, was ceremonially enthroned there in 1957. Other Shī'īs are the Ithnā 'Asharīs and the Bōhorās. There is a small group of Mayman, and of Sunnīs from Pakistan. There are numerous mosques. Some thirty Ḳur'ānic schools are conducted by Africans. The followers of the Āghā Khān conduct their own secular schools, one reaching secondary level, and certain charitable institutions. Apart from private lectures, there is no advanced Islamic religious instruction.

Bibliography: C. H. Becker in *EI*[1]; *Materialien zur Kenntnis des Islam in Deutsch Ost-Afrika*, in *Isl.*, ii, 1 ff.; C. Velten, *Prosa und Poesie der Suaheli*, Berlin 1907; B. Krumm, *Words of oriental origin in Swahili*, 1940; E. C. Baker, *Dar-es-Salaam, 1860 to 1940*, in *Tanganyika Notes and Records no. 20*, 1945; 1957 Census Report, Government Printer, Dar-es-Salaam. (G. S. P. FREEMAN-GRENVILLE)

DĀR AL-SHIFĀ' [see BĪMĀRISTĀN iii].

DĀR AL-ṢINĀ'A (also, but more rarely: *Dār al-ṣan'a*). Etymologically, this compound can be translated "industrial establishment, workshop". In fact it is always applied to a State workshop: for example, under the Umayyads in Spain to establishments for gold and silver work intended for the sovereign, and for the manufacture and stock-piling of arms. But the sense most widely used is that of "establishment for the construction and equipment of warships": *dār ṣinā'a li-inshā' al-sufun*; or simply *dār al-inshā'*, which also occurs. This does not include the arsenals which we are to consider later, while the construction of private merchant ships is not dealt with. See BAḤRIYYA, MILĀḤA, SAFĪNA, USṬŪL.

From the Arabic compounds *dār al-ṣinā'a, dār al-ṣan'a* the words for "arsenal" and "wet-dock" in the "mediterranean" languages are derived: Castilian *ataruzana, arsenal, darsena*; Catalan *darsanale, drasena*; Italian *arsenale, darsena*; Maltese *tarzna, tarznar*. It is probably from an Italian dialect that Ottoman Turkish borrowed its *tersāne* (sometimes "returkicized" as *tersḵẖāne*, on the analogy of *topḵẖāne* "arsenal for artillery"); the word passed into several languages from the early Ottoman Empire: modern Greek τερσανας, Syrian Arabic *tarsḵẖāne*, Egyptian Arabic *tarsāne* and *tarsaḵẖāne*.

Eastern Mediterranean. It was naturally in the eastern Mediterranean that the first arsenals in the service of the Muslims operated, partly inherited from the romano-byzantine Empire. Victorious on land, the Arabs remained exposed to reprisals by sea, which they tried to prevent by making use of the experience of the indigenous populations until, before long, they themselves took the offensive. Mu'āwiya, when still only governor of Syria, was the first to organize an arsenal at Acre, in 28/649, for the Cyprus expedition; the arsenal was later transferred to Tyre, where it was combined with a fortified dock, closed at night with a chain, in which vessels took refuge. Nevertheless, al-Mutawakkil thought it expedient to restore the arsenal to Acre, and Ibn Ṭūlūn, when he was put in charge of it, had it fortified (by the grandfather of the geographer al-Muḳaddasī) on the model of the one at Tyre. It is possible that smaller establishments also existed at times at Tripoli and Lādhiḳiyya (Latakia); however, apart from the sea they were eclipsed, in the extreme north, by the riverside works at Tarsus which combined the activities of the holy war on land and sea until, as the result of a revolt, the Caliph al-Muḳtadī had its fleet burnt in 287/900 and, fifty years later, the Byzantines regained possession of it. The Crusades gave the final blow to these establishments which were probably already weakened by disorders and political divisions, and it does not seem that the Mamlūks subsequently restored them even at Beirut, which had become the chief town on the littoral.

Egypt. It was also Mu'āwiya, when Caliph, who was responsible for the reopening of the Egyptian arsenals which the autonomous rulers of Egypt were, from the 3rd/9th century onwards, to bring to their fullest and most lasting development. The first to operate were those which the Byzantines had owned, at Ḳulzum (Clysma)—later to be replaced by Suez—which, thanks to the restoration of the canal linking it with the Nile, served both the Red Sea and the Mediterranean, and at Alexandria. Other naval centres were later established at Rosetta, Damietta and Tinnīs on the mouths of the Nile, and to protect them from Byzantine raids the ʿAbbāsids (al-Mutawakkil in particular) had them fortified and equipped with enclosed harbours like those in Syria. Numerous papyri provide evidence of requisitions of men and materials, made from the Umayyad period onward, to meet the needs of these arsenals. Nevertheless, the most secure, and consequently most highly developed, arsenal was the one established on the Nile near Fusṭāṭ (later Cairo), at first on the island of Rawḍa, in 54/674; probably damaged by Marwān II who had the ships burnt to prevent the ʿAbbāsids from pursuing him (132/750), it was reorganized during the naval struggles of the 3rd/9th century with the Byzantines by al-Mutawakkil (238/853); the island at that time was called Djazīrat al-ṣināʿa. The fortifications which it had possessed in the time of the Byzantines (under the name of Babylon), and which had fallen into disrepair since the conquest, were restored by Ibn Ṭūlūn, who also carried out the work of rebuilding the fleet. The decisive effort was however made by the Ikhshīdids in the following century, to meet the Fāṭimid threat. As it was at that time impossible to defend the arsenal from attack owing to its insular position, Ibn Ṭughdj had the island made into a garden, and gave orders for another arsenal to be set up on the river bank at Fusṭāṭ at the place then called Dār bint al-Fatḥ. It seems however that under the Fāṭimids the two arsenals operated alternately or simultaneously; the wazīr al-Maʾmūn al-Baṭāʾiḥī in 516/1122 tried to rationalize shipbuilding by making the arsenal at Misr (Fusṭāṭ), now enlarged, specialize in *shawānī* and "State vessels", and the Island arsenal in *shalandiyyāt* and *ḥarbiyyāt*. A third arsenal operated in the quarter known as al-Maḳs, north of the town, at the time of the early Fāṭimids, but we know nothing more about it; a fleet fitted out against Byzantium was burnt there in 386/996. The events of the Crusades and the troubles at the end of the dynasty proved fatal to the fleet and to the Cairo arsenals which disappeared in flames. Saladin attempted to re-establish shipbuilding at Alexandria, and in the Mamlūk period we once again hear of a fleet fitted out at the time of the Cyprus expedition; but these were sporadic efforts occurring at long intervals and, roughly speaking, although there had been sudden fluctuations in shipbuilding even earlier, it is safe to say that the Egyptian arsenals disappeared in face of the Italian domination over the Mediterranean.

The Muslims in Crete had an autonomous naval base at Khandaḳ in the 3rd-4th/9th-10th centuries.

The West. The oldest arsenals in the West were necessarily somewhat newer than those in the East, but some of them were perhaps to survive longer, and the East at times tried to make use of the West in this respect as a reserve of materials and equipment.

Ifrīḳiya. The oldest arsenal in the West was at Tunis [*q.v.*]. It was founded in about 75/694 by the governor Ḥassān b. al-Nuʿmān on the orders of the Umayyad Caliph in the East, ʿAbd al-Malik b. Marwān. A thousand Copts, together with their families, were brought from Egypt to undertake the work of building and arming a fleet intended to guard the coast of Ifrīḳiya and, in particular, to conquer Sicily.

Other maritime arsenals were recorded at Al-Mahdiyya, Sousse (= Sūsa) and Bougie (= Bidjāya).

Al-Andalus. It was only in the first quarter of the 4th/10th century that the Umayyads in Spain built arsenals. In fact they needed fleets, firstly to resist the Norman attacks, and subsequently to support their policy of intervention in North Africa against the Fāṭimids. The most important arsenal was at Almeria (= al-Mariyya). Others are recorded at Tortosa (= Ṭurṭūsha), Denia (= Dāniya), Almuñecar (= al-Munakkab), Málaga (= Mālaḳa), Gibraltar, Saltés (= Shalṭīsh), Santa Maria de Algarve (= Shantamariyya), Silves (= Shilb), Alcacer do Sal. There was, perhaps, one at Cadiz (= Ḳādis), a fief of the Banū Maymūn, whose family provided several *ḳāʾids* for the Almoravid fleets, and also in the Balearics.

Western Maghrib. The two oldest are those at Ceuta and Tangier, on the straits of Gibraltar, intended at first for merchant ships. With the advent of the three great Berber-Moroccan dynasties, the Almoravids, Almohads and Marinids, these arsenals became military establishments. They supplied warships and transport vessels, making it possible to keep command of the straits and to allow the passage of armies sent to defend Muslim Spain.

The other principal arsenals known in the Middle Ages were at Algiers (this was to be particularly developed later, after the Ottoman occupation), Oran, Hunayn, Bādis, al-Maʿmūra (now al-Mahdiyya at the mouth of the Subū), Salé and Anfā (now Casablanca).

Sicily. We cannot say if the Muslims established arsenals in the places they occupied on the island or the Italian mainland in the 3rd/9th and 4th/10th centuries. It is probable that there were some in Sicily, at Palermo and Messina.

Indian Ocean and neighbouring seas. In general, the Indian Ocean with its Muslim branches the Red Sea and the Persian Gulf were peaceful areas compared with the Mediterranean; many pirates were to be found there, but no hostile naval power. Police forces consequently proved sufficient, and it is probable that merchant ships, built as we know without nails, were often used by them; there seems to have been no true arsenal of the Mediterranean type. However, apart from Ḳulzum which has already been referred to, it is certain that the Fāṭimids maintained a fleet with ʿAydhāb as its base, to safeguard pilgrims and merchants in the Red Sea on their way to the Yemen. There is little doubt that shipbuilding was carried out in the large eastern commercial ports: Aden, at an earlier period Basra (or rather its outer harbour and precursor Ubulla), Sīrāf, later replaced by Kīsh, Ṣuhār then Mascat in ʿUmān, and perhaps also in Muslim towns on the coast of west India and east Africa; apart from Ubulla, it is difficult to be certain of their status and political character, and even there the dockyards were not able to remain in operation after the 5th/11th century when the maritime activity of Baṣra and Sīrāf began to decline considerably.

The Timber-Supply. The arsenals were naturally set up either within a short distance of districts producing timber for shipbuilding (pine and cedar, oak, acacia *labakh* or *sanṭ* in Egypt, sycamore and to some extent palm and fig) or else in a favourable situation for importing it from Italian, Indian (teak, coconut palm) and East African merchants, not to mention the raiders of the Anatolian coasts. Of the various causes of the decline in ship-building after the 5th/11th century, one may be the increasing shortage of timber.

Bibliography: A. H. Fahmy, *Muslim sea-power in the Eastern Mediterranean, 7th-10th century*, 1950; Ekk. Eickhoff, *Seekrieg und Seepolitik zwischen*

Islam und Abendland (650-1040), Univ. Saarland 1954; M. Lombard, *Arsenaux et bois de marine dans la Méditerranée musulmane (7e-11e siècles)*, in "*Le Navire*, etc." (Travaux du 2e Colloque d'histoire maritime, 1957), Bibl. Gén. Éc. Htes. Ét., VIe sect.; W. Hoenerbach, *Araber und Mittelmeer, Anfänge und Probleme arabischer Seegeschichte*, in *Zeki Velidi Togan Armağanı*, 1955; G. Wiet, in *CIA Égypte*, 2, 165-9 (Mémoires publ. Inst. Franc. archéol. or. 52); E. Lévi-Provençal, *L'Espagne musulmane au Xe s.*, 152; idem, *Hist. Esp. Mus.* i, 244, 367; idem, *La péninsule ibérique au Moyen Age*, 271; R. Brunschwig, *Deux récits de voyage inédits en Afrique du Nord*, 189; idem, *La Berbérie orientale sous les Ḥafṣides*, i, 347, 382; H. Terrasse, *Les portes de l'arsenal de Salé*, in *Hesp.*, 1922, 357; G. S. Colin, *Fès, Port de mer*, in *Bull. de l'Ens. Public du Maroc*, no. 183 (1945); G. F. Hourani, *Arab seafaring in the Indian Ocean*, 1951.—A diploma of nomination to command of a sea-town with arsenal is contained in Ḳudāma, *K. al-Kharādj*, ms. Istanbul 13v° ff., (ms. Paris 17v° ff.). For the Ottoman Empire, not treated here, I. H. Uzunçarşılı, *Osmanlı devletinin merkez ve bahriye teşkilâtı*, 1947, and TERSĀNE.

(G. S. COLIN and CL. CAHEN)

DAR AL-ṢULḤ 'the House of Truce', territories not conquered by Muslim troops but by buying peace by the giving of tribute, the payment of which guarantees a truce or armistice (*hudna, ṣulḥ*). The two historic examples of such a situation, which were evidently the starting-point for the whole theory, are Nadjrān and Nubia. Muḥammad himself concluded a treaty with the Christian population of Nadjrān, guaranteeing their security and imposing on them certain obligations which were later looked on as *kharādj* [*q.v.*] by some, and as *djizya* [*q.v.*] by others (for the whole question see Balādhurī, *Futūḥ*, 63 ff.; Sprenger, *Leben Mohammads*, 3, 502 ff.; M. Hamidullah, *Documents sur la diplomatie musulmane*, 78 ff., *Corpus*, no. 79 ff.). In the course of events this protectorate proved to be of no use to the inhabitants of Nadjrān on account of their geographical situation. For Nubia it was somewhat different. Thanks to their skill in archery the Nubians were able for centuries to defend themselves against Muslim attack and to preserve their independence. As a result, ʿAbd Allāh b. Saʿd in 31/652 concluded a treaty (*ʿahd*) with them imposing not a poll-tax (*djizya*) but merely a certain tribute in slaves (*baḳt* [*q.v.*]). On the other hand, some were not prepared to admit that, besides the *Dār al-Islām* and *Dār al-ḥarb*, [*qq.v.*], there existed a third category of territories excluded from Muslim conquest, and they held that in this instance it was in reality a question, not of a *ṣulḥ* or *ʿahd*, but merely of an armed truce (*hudna*) and the implementation of reciprocal undertakings (see Balādhurī, *Futūḥ*, 236 ff.; al-Maḳrīzī, *Khiṭaṭ*, ed. Wiet, iii, 290 f.; Ibn ʿAbd al-Ḥakam, *Futūḥ Miṣr*, ed. Torrey, 189). This somewhat vague theory also provided a basis upon which it seemed possible to establish contractual relations with Christian countries; presents sent by the latter were consequently looked on as a *kharādj*. The legal theory was expounded as follows by al-Māwardī. All the territories more or less directly under Muslim control can be divided into three categories; (1) those which have been conquered by force of arms; (2) those which have been occupied without battle after the flight of their rulers; (3) those which have been acquired by treaty, this third category including two instances which depend on whether the property (a) becomes common property (*waḳf*) of the Muslim community, or whether (b) it remains in the hands of the former proprietors; in the first instance the former proprietors can in fact remain on their land and become *dhimmīs*; they pay *kharādj* and *djizya* and their country becomes *Dār al-Islām*; in the second instance, the proprietors of the land keep their estates by contract and from their revenues pay a *kharādj* which is considered as a *djizya*, and collected until they are converted to Islam; their territory is considered neither as *Dār al-Islām* nor *Dār al-ḥarb* but as *Dār al-ṣulḥ* or *Dār al-ʿahd* [*q.v.*], and their estates can always be alienated or mortgaged without restriction; if the property is transferred to a Muslim, the land is no longer liable for *kharādj*; this state of affairs will continue so long as the proprietors observe the clauses of the treaty, and the *djizya* for which they are liable cannot be increased since they are not in the *Dār al-Islām*. However, according to Abu Ḥanīfa, if their territory became *Dār al-Islām* they would then be *dhimmīs* and subject to *djizya*. As regards the situation created by a rupture of the treaty, the various schools are not in agreement. According to al-Shāfiʿī, the country, if it is then conquered, belongs to the first category, that is to say, territories acquired by force; and if it is not conquered, it becomes *Dār al-ḥarb*. According to Abu Ḥanīfa, the the land becomes *Dār al-Islām* if there are Muslims there or if it is separated from the *Dār al-ḥarb* by Muslim territory, and its non-Muslim inhabitants are themselves considered as rebels (*bughāt*); if neither of these conditions applies, the land becomes *Dār al-ḥarb*. Others, on the contrary, claimed that in both cases it becomes *Dār al-ḥarb* (see *al-Aḥkām al-sulṭāniyya*, Cairo 1298, 131 ff.). It is evident that the position was irregular and ambiguous. Al-Māwardī himself (150 and 164) includes this *Dār al-ṣulḥ* in his enumeration of Muslim territories (*bilād al-Islām*) and al-Balādhurī does not observe this distinction when discussing *kharādj*.

In the period immediately following the Crusades numerous treaties, the details of which we possess, were concluded with Christian princes or princelings (treaties with the king of Armenia, the princess of Tyre, the Templars of Anṭarṭūs, etc.; cf. al-Maḳrīzī, *Histoire des Sultans Mameluks*, trans. Quatremère, ii, 201 ff., 206 ff., 218 ff.). For details and forms, and the traditional justifications of truce agreements concluded between Muslim sovereigns and non-Muslim princes, see al-Ḳalḳashandī, *Ṣubḥ*, xiii, 321 ff.; xiv, 7 ff.

Bibliography: Yaḥyā b. Ādam, *K. al-Kharādj*, ed. Juynboll, 35 ff.; al-Tabarī, *K. Ikhtilāf al-Fuḳahāʾ*, ed. Schacht. 14 ff; Juynboll, *Handbuch*, 240, 344 ff.; 348; M. Khadduri, *War and peace in the law of Islam*, Baltimore 1955; A. Abel, in *Revue internationale des droits de l'antiquité*, ii, 1949, 1-17; idem, in Société Jean Bodin, *Session de 1958 (Bruxelles) sur la Paix: La Paix dans l'Islam*; H. Kruse, *The Islamic doctrine of international treaties* (in preparation; cf. *Islamic Quarterly*, i, 1954, 152 ff.).

(D. B. MACDONALD-[A. ABEL])

DĀR AL-TAḲRĪB [see IKHTILĀF].

DĀR AL-ṬIBĀʿA [see MAṬBAʿA].

DĀR AL-ṬIRĀZ [see ṬIRĀZ].

DĀR AL-ʿULŪM or the "House of Sciences", (a) an establishment for higher instruction founded in 1872 by ʿAlī Pasha Mubārak [*q.v.*]. Its aim was to introduce a certain number of students of al-Azhar [*q.v.*] to modern branches of learning by means of a five year course, in order to fit them for teaching in the new schools. In fact, as other centres were created in Cairo for the teaching of science, its curriculum was remodelled a number of times and the exact sciences were relegated to the background. The length of the course was reduced to four years. Attached as a Faculty since 1946 to the University of Cairo (formerly Fuʾād), Dār al-ʿUlūm endeavours to be at the same time Arabic and Islamic, and is proud to be the great Muslim Teachers' Training College of Egypt, influential through the teachers and inspectors who have been trained there. The students are divided into sections: four for Arabic language and three for Islamic studies. The diploma given on completion of the course is equivalent to a Bachelor's degree, and can be followed by a Master's degree or a Doctorate. Since 1951-2, apart from the students of al-Azhar, men who have passed the government secondary schools' 'Baccalauréat' (*tawdjīh*) have been admitted, and since 1953-4, a certain number of women students. Formerly, as at al-Azhar, the teaching was free and a modest sum was given to the students monthly, but now teaching fees are charged, with special concessions for those who undertake to become teachers. In 1957-8, there were 1,715 students as well as some scholarship holders completing their education in European universities.

Bibliography: Muḥammad ʿAbd al-Djawwād, *Taḳwīm Dār al-ʿUlūm, al-ʿadad al-māsī* (1872-1947), Cairo 1952; the same, *Mulḥaḳ al-ʿadad al-māsī* (1946-1959), Cairo [1959]. (J. JOMIER)

(b) the religious institution at Deoband [*q.v.*].

(c) Farangī Maḥall. In a house known as the Farangī Maḥall in Lucknow, granted by Awrangzīb to his family as compensation for loss of property on the murder of his father in 1103/1691, Niẓām al-Dīn started two years later a *madrasa* which came to be known as Dār al-ʿUlūm Farangī Maḥall. Mullā Niẓām al-Dīn's fame rests mainly on the introduction of a syllabus of religious instruction called *dars-i Niẓāmiyya*, an improvement on the syllabus said to have been originally drawn up by Fatḥ Allāh al-Shīrāzī, a well-known scholar of Akbar's court. Much stress is laid in this syllabus on the rules of Arabic grammar, logic, and philosophy, while practically no attention is given to modern disciplines. There has more recently been a persistent demand for a change in the curriculum, so far unsuccessfully.

With the establishment of the Dār al-ʿUlūm at Deoband the Farangī Maḥall institution lost the pre-eminence it had enjoyed since the time of Awrangzīb, and has now receded into the background; in recent times it has been politically active: in the early 1920s the *ʿulamāʾ* of the Farangī Maḥall championed the cause of the Ottoman Khilāfa, and played a prominent rôle during Muslim League agitation in the late 1930s for the creation of Pākistān.

Bibliography: Walī Allāh Farangī Maḥallī, *al-Aghṣān al-Arbaʿa li 'l-Shadjarāt al-Ṭayyiba dar Aḥwāl-i ʿUlamāʾ-i Farangī Maḥall* ..., Lucknow 1298/1881; Alṭāf al-Raḥmān, *Aḥwāl-i ʿUlamāʾ-i Farangī Maḥall*, Lucknow (?) 1907; ʿAbd al-Bārī, *Āthār al-Uwal* (not available to me); S. M. Ikrām, *Rūd-i Kawthar*, Karachi n.d., 582-92; ʿInāyat Allāh, *Tadhkira-i ʿUlamāʾ-i Farangī Maḥall* (not available to me); Shiblī Nuʿmānī, *Maḳālat-i Shiblī*, iii, Aʿẓamgaṙh 1351/1932, 102-5; ʿAbd al-ʿĀlāʾ, *Risāla Ḳuṭbiyya* (ms.); Walī Allāh Farangī Maḥallī, *ʿUmdat al-Wasāʾil* (ms.); Raḍī al-Dīn Maḥmūd Anṣārī, *Aghṣān al-Ansāb* (ms.).

(d) The Nadwat al-ʿUlamāʾ, Lucknow, was founded in 1312/1894 by a band of progressive *ʿulamāʾ* who nominated Mawlawī Sayyid Muḥammad ʿAlī Kānpūrī as the first *nāẓim*, with the declared object of reforming the current system of religious education and effecting a rapprochement between the various factions of the *ʿulamāʾ* by the establishment of an Islamic *dār al-ʿulūm* which would not only provide education in both religious and temporal sciences but would also offer technical training. In 1316/1898 the primary classes were started, and a year later the great library was founded, round which later grew up the Dār al-Muṣannifīn, also known as the Shiblī Academy, an institute of Islamic research with the monthly *Maʿārif* as its organ. In 1322/1904 Shiblī Nuʿmānī [*q.v.*] joined the Nadwat al-ʿUlamāʾ as its secretary, and in 1326/1908 the present buildings were opened. Its periodical *al-Nadwa* appeared first in 1322/1904 under Shiblī's editorship. Under Shiblī's guidance the Nadwa became the first institution in India to adopt modern methods of critical research; it was, however, a synthesis of the Deoband and ʿAlīgaṙh ideologies, and failed to imbibe either the spirit of orthodoxy characteristic of Deoband or the purely rationalistic attitude of ʿAlīgaṙh. Its foremost scholar was Sayyid Sulaymān Nadwī, whose completion of the Urdū biography of the Prophet, started by Shiblī, is a blending of the seemingly divergent views of East and West in the field of historical research. The Nadwa, however, was not successful in the religious sphere; its leaders were not orthodox, and could not instil into their students the spirit of classical Islam. The result was that the Nadwa came to be known merely as an educational institution with Arabic as the medium of instruction, and its reputation as a seat of learning and Islamic research is now on the decline.

Bibliography: Sayyid Sulaymān Nadwī, *Ḥayāt-i Shiblī*, Aʿẓamgaṙh 1362/1943, 301-19, 352, 396 ff., 412-59, 539; S. M. Ikrām, *Mawdj-i Kawthar*, Karachi n.d., 206-18; *Maʿārif* (*Sulaymān Number*), Aʿẓamgaṙh Ramaḍān 1374/May 1955, 252-83; W. Cantwell Smith, *Modern Islam in India*, London 1946, 294, 296. (A. S. BAZMEE ANSARI)

DĀRĀ, DĀRĀB, Persian forms (adopted by Arab writers) of the name of the Achaemenian king familiarly known under the hellenized form *Dareios* (Darius). Dārāb, and its abbreviation Dārā, are directly derived from the ancient Persian Darayahvahav- (Bartholomae, *Altiranisches Wörterbuch*, 738; the different grammatical cases attested by Persian inscriptions, in Tolman, *Ancient Persian Lexicon and Texts*, 1908, s.v. *darayavau*; for the ancient historians of these kings, *Gr. I. Ph.*, ii, index, s.v. Dareios).

The sources of information about these princes collected by Arab and Persian writers are legendary rather than historical (cf. preface by J. Mohl, *Livre des Rois*, 12mo ed., v, 1877). The Persian poet Firdawsī (*op. cit.*, v), of later date than the Arab historians, was inspired by their accounts particularly in regard to the reign of Alexander (Iskandar), but he combined them with elements from Persian legends. His account, even when stripped of poetic elaborations, is fuller than those of the Arab historians, even the earliest in date, al-Ṭabarī. A short summary follows (Dārāb and Dārā are Darius II and Darius III respectively).

Goshtāsp (Vishtāspa, the Greek Hystaspe), king of Persia, named as his successor his grandson Bahman, son of Isfandyār (Vahman, derived from the Avestan Vohū Manah, "Good Thought"), in whom we recognize Artaxerxes (Artakhshatra) Longhand. In accordance with the *kheṭuk-das* (*kvaetvadaθa*) practice, Bahman married his own daughter Homāy ("who appears to represent in popular legend Parysatis", historically the wife of Darius II, to quote J. Mohl); Bahman got her with child; before his death, he declared her to be queen of Persia, and named as his successor the child whom she was to bear. From the time of its birth, the mother entrusted her child to a nurse who reared it secretly; when it was eight months old, the queen placed it in a box filled with treasure and committed it to the waters of the Euphrates; two spies set by the queen to keep watch brought her news that a washerman had rescued the baby. He and his wife, having lost their son, adopted the child and named it Dārāb (Persian: *dar āb*, "in the water", popular etymology); he grew up and questioned his parentage. A war broke out; he took part in it, came to the notice of the queen, then won great renown; the Persian commander-in-chief spoke to the queen of him and led her to recognize a jewel which she had fastened on her infant's arm. On Dārāb's return she had him proclaimed king. He founded Dārābgird, defeated first the Arabs and then king Faylaḳūs (Philip of Macedon); he compelled him to pay tribute and married his daughter. He was however repelled by her foul breath and sent her back, pregnant, to her father. She gave birth to a son whom she named Iskandar, after the plant *iskandar* (*iskandarus*, gr. σκόροδον) which had cured her complaint. Philip had Iskandar recognized as his own son. Dārāb for his part had had by another wife a son named Dārā. Then the two young princes becames kings. Iskandar, refusing to give Dārā the requisite tribute, conquered Egypt and invaded Persia which he hoped to take over from his half-brother; disguised as an ambassador he came to Dārā's camp and was received with great pomp; he was, however, recognized, took to flight and succeeded in escaping, subsequently inflicting four defeats on Dārā. Dārā was assassinated by his ministers who informed Iskandar; horrified by the news, the latter hurried to his half-brother whom he found on his death-bed. Dārā spoke with nobility of God's almighty power, and asked Iskandar to marry his daughter Rushanak (Roxane) and to treat the Persians well. Iskandar who became king of Persia made further conquests. (The *Deeds of Alexander*, *Iskandar-nāma*, written by the Persian poets Niẓāmī, Amīr Khusraw, Djāmī, only describe Dārā's defeat, with further moralizing upon the fickleness of fortune.

Accounts given by the Arab historians differ only in certain details from that of Firdawsī. In the Chronicle by al-Ṭabarī (Persian version, trans. Zotenberg, i, 508 ff.), the infant Dārāb was saved from the water by a miller; Homāy, when told of this, entrusted her son to him with the words (in Persian): *dar* ("look after him!"), whence the name Dārā (another popular etymology); "it is also said that he was called Dārāb because he had been found *in the water*" (*dar āb*); Homāy voluntarily told her son the secret of his birth when he reached his twentieth year; on Iskandar's refusal to give tribute, Dārā had a symbolical message sent to him (racket, ball, sack of sesame) very similar to that sent by the Scythians to Darius I (Herodotus, iv, 131-33; and cf. E. Doblhofer, *Le déchiffrement des écritures*, French trans. 1959, 24); as a result of Dārā's injustice and wickedness, his soldiers deserted and his two chamberlains murdered him with the complicity of Iskandar who was hypocrite enough to be present at Dārā's death-bed and then to punish his assassins. Ḥamza of Ispahan is very brief (*Annals*, ed.-trans. Gottwaldt, 28-9), as is al-Masʿūdī (*Murūdj*, ii, 127) who gives the same name (Dārā) to both Darius II and III. In al-Thaʿālibī's *History of the kings of the Persians* (ed. and trans. Zotenberg, 393 ff.), there is the same fanciful derivation of the name Dārāb, an account practically identical with al-Ṭabarī's, also insisting on Dārā's wickedness and Iskandar's duplicity. The same account appears in al-Maḳdisī's *Book of the Creation* (ed. and trans. Cl. Huart, iii, 154-9), with the exception that Iskandar, after refusing to pay tribute, thought better of it and sent it with an apology: Dārā gave him his daughter's hand.

Just as the Pseudo-Callisthenes had made Alexander heir to the kings of Egypt, so the legendary history of Persia made Iskandar a half-brother of Darius III with whom he disputed the throne (possibly a confused allusion to Cyrus the Younger's revolt against his brother Artaxerxes II in 401).

Dārā (or Daras-Anastasiopolis) is a fortress situated between Mardīn and Naṣībīn, captured from the Greeks by Chosroes I during the campaign in 540 (Nöldeke, *Gesch. der Perser ... zur Zeit der Sasaniden*, 239, and A. Christensen, *L'Iran sous les Sassanides*[2], 372 and 445).

Bibliography: In addition to the references given in the article: Firdawsī, *Shāhnāma*, ed.-trans. J. Mohl, in fol., v and trans. in 12, v; ed. Teheran 1934-35 (pub. Beroukhim), vi; Ṭabarī, index.

(B. Carra de Vaux-[H. Massé])

DARʿA [see ADHRIʿĀT].

DARʿA. This is the name both of a river of south Morocco which rises on the southern slope of the High Atlas and flows into the Atlantic south of the Djebel Bānī, and of a Moroccan province which stretches along the two cultivated banks of this water-course from Agdz as far as the elbow of the river Darʿa, for a distance of about 120 miles in a generally north-west to south-east direction.

This province is traditionally divided into eight districts corresponding with the wider parts of the valley which are separated by mountain barriers forming narrows. From north to south these are: Mazgīta, Ayt Saddrāt, Ayt Zarrī, Tinzūlīn, Tarnāta, Fazwāta, Ktāwa and Mḥammid.

It is populated by generally Berber-speaking tribes and by coloured people who can be divided into *ʿabīd*, slaves imported from the Sahara and negro countries, and *ḥarāṭīn*, who have a dark skin but whose features are not negroid, and who are thought to be the most ancient occupants of the region. Jews, apparently of Berber origin, complete the sedentary population of more than 100,000. At least up to the submission of Darʿa to the French Protectorate in 1932, the sedentary population lived in subjection to the sometimes Arab, but mainly Berber, nomad tribes of the surrounding mountains.

Darʿa has been inhabited from a very early date and must certainly have had an eventful history since it is a productive region in the midst of areas which are almost desert. Traditions lead us to believe that the Jews played an important part politically up to the 10th century and that Islam was brought there by a descendant of the founder of Fez in the first half of the 3rd/9th century. Later, at the end of the 4th/10th century, Darʿa came under the domination of the Maghrāwa (belonging to the Zenāta) who had settled in Sidjilmāsa.

With the Almoravids, Darʿa really enters on to the historical scene, for it served as an advance post for their penetration into Atlantic Morocco, as is witnessed by the ruins of a fortress which dominates Zagora. From the second half of the 5th/11th century on, Darʿa was part of the Moroccan empire created by the Almoravids, then by the Almohads and the Marīnids. The Maʿḳil Arabs infiltrated there towards the end of the 7th/13th century and exercised a dominating influence.

In the 10th/16th century, this province was the cradle of the first Sharīfian dynasty of the Saʿdīs [*q.v.*] and was the place from which the sultan Aḥmad al-Manṣūr started on his expedition to the Sudan (1591). This shows, in a very striking manner, the role of Darʿa as a point of contact between Morocco and the Sahara. Thanks to the trade with Gao and Timbuctoo at the beginning of the 11th/17th century, this region enjoyed a brief period of prosperity.

Held more or less by the ʿAlawī sultans, Darʿa was the centre of an important religious brotherhood, the Nāṣiriyyīn, which spread widely at the beginning of the 11th/17th century around the *zāwiya* of Tamgrūṭ. It was practically independant when Ch. de Foucauld crossed it in April 1884; its history then was essentially one of tribal and clan rivalries. The region was occupied by French troops between 1930 and 1932, almost without any fighting.

To-day, this overpopulated and poor region provides Casablanca and various other towns with a considerable number of workers, for its almost stagnant agriculture is very far from being able to support its growing population. This emigration is usually a temporary one, linked with the vicissitudes of its climate and agriculture (*Naissance du prolétariat marocain*, Paris, n.d., 67-9).

Bibliography: Bakrī, *Descr. de l'Afrique sept.*, tr. de Slane, 338, 343; Idrīsī,, 70-1; Leo Africanus, tr. Épaulard, i, 30-2, ii, 422-4; Marmol, *De l'Afrique*, tr. Perrot d'Ablancourt, Paris 1667, iii, ch. ix ff.; Rohelfs, *Mein erster Aufenhalt in Marokko*, Norden, 1885; Ch. de Foucauld, *Reconnaissance au Maroc*, Paris 1888, 208-11, 285-95; H. de Castries, *Notice sur la région de l'oued Draa*, in *Bull. Soc. Géogr.*, Paris, Dec. 1880; de Segonzac, *Au coeur de l'Atlas*, Paris 1910; Dj. Jacques-Meunié, *La nécropole de Foum le-Rjam, tumuli du Maroc présaharien*, in *Hesp.* xlv (1958), 95-142; J. Meunié and Ch. Allain, *La forteresse almoravide de Zagora*, in *Hesp.*, xliii (1956), 305-23; *Villes et tribus de Maroc*, ix, *Tribus berbères*, ii, *Districts et tribus de la haute vallée du Draʿ*, by G. Spillmann, Paris 1931, 1-201; G. Spillmann, *La zaouia de Tamgrout et les Nasiriyine*, in *Afr. Fr.*, Aug.-Sept. 1938, and *Les Ait Atta du Sahara et la pacification du Haut Dra*, Rabat 1936; F. de la Chapelle, *Une cité de l'oued Dra sous le protectorat des nomades*, in *Hesp.*, ix (1929), 29-42; Dj. Jacques-Meunié, *Les oasis des Laktaoua et des Mehamid*, in *Hesp.* xxxiv (1947), 397-429, and *Hiérarchie sociale au Maroc présaharien*, in *Hesp.*, xlv (1958), 239-69).

(R. Le Tourneau)

DĀRĀ SHUKŌH, eldest son of Shāh Djahān and Mumtāz Maḥall, was born near Adjmēr on 19 Ṣafar 1024/20 March 1615. He received his first *manṣab* [*q.v.*] of 12,000 *dhāt*/6000 *sawār* in 1042/1633, as also the *djāgīr* of Ḥisār-Fīrūza, regarded as the appendage of the heir-apparent. The same year he was given the nominal command of an army despatched to defend Ḳandahār which was threatened by the Persians, and again in 1052/1642 when the threat was renewed. The attack, however, did not materialize. In 1055/1645, he was given the governorship of the *ṣūba* of Ilāhābād to which were added the *ṣūba*s of Lahore in 1057/1647, and Gudjarāt in 1059/1649. Though he took some interest in Lahore and constructed a number of buildings and market-places, he left the other *ṣūba*s to be governed by deputies, himself remaining at the court. By 1058/1648, he had attained the *manṣab* of 30,000/20,000 (which incidentally was the highest rank attained by Shāh Djahān before his accession).

Following the failure of two attempts to recover Ḳandahār from the Persians (who had captured it in 1059/1649), Dārā was deputed to lead a third expedition for its recapture in 1062/1652. Although the siege was vigorously pressed, and forts in Zamīndāwar taken, Ḳandahār itself defied capture. The failure of the campaign, due partly to a division in Dārā's camp as also his lack of experience, adversely effected his prestige as a political and military leader.

On his return, Shāh Djahān associated him more closely than ever with the affairs of the state, bestowing upon him unprecedented honours, and the rank of 60,000/40,000 (1067/1657). It seems that Shāh Djahān, having clearly marked out Dārā as his successor, wanted to avoid a struggle for the throne on his death, a position which his younger sons were not prepared to accept. In 1067/1657, when Shāh Djahān fell ill, his younger sons, fearing that Dārā might use the opportunity to seize power, advanced towards Āgra on a plea of meeting the Emperor, thereby precipitating a war of succession (see Awrangzīb). Awrangzīb and Murād raised the slogan of Dārā being a heretic (*mulḥid*) and the orthodox faith being in danger from his constant association with Hindū *yōgī*s and *sanyāsī*s. However, the slogan of religion does not seem to have influenced significantly the actual alignment of the nobles. Dārā was defeated, first at the battle of Sāmūgaṛh near Āgra (7 Ramaḍān 1068/8 June 1658), and then at Deorāʾī near Adjmēr (28 Djumādā II 1069/23 March 1659). Shortly afterwards he was captured by an Afghān noble, Malik Djīwan, with whom he had taken shelter. He was brought to Dihlī and executed (22 Dhu 'l-Ḥidjdja 1069/10 Sept. 1659), a formal charge of heresy being laid against him. Dārā's elder son, Sulaymān Shukōh, soon followed him to the grave, a younger son, Sipihr Shukōh, being imprisoned at Gwāliyār.

Although Dārā had an undistinguished political and military career, he was one of the most remarkable figures of his age. A keen student of ṣūfism and of *tawḥīd*, he came into close contact with leading Muslim and Hindū mystics, notably Miyān Mīr (d. 1045/1635) and Mullā Shāh (d. 1071/1661) of the Ḳādirī order (becoming a disciple of the latter in 1050/1640), Shāh Muḥibb Allāh Ilāhābādī, Shāh Dilrubā, Sarmad the famous heterodox monist, and Bābā Lāl Dās Bayrāgī, a follower of Kabīr. A number of contemporary paintings showing Dārā in the company of ṣūfīs and *sanyāsī*s have been preserved.

Dārā was a prolific writer. His works include: *Safīnat al-awliyāʾ* (1050/1640) and *Sakīnat al-awliyāʾ* (1052/1642), dealing with the lives of *ṣūfī* saints, the latter with those of the Ḳādirī order; *Risāla-i Ḥaḳḳ numā* (1056/1646) and the rather rare *Ṭarīḳat-i ḥaḳīḳat*, both based on well known *ṣūfī* works; his *Dīwān*, also known as *Iksīr-i aʿẓam*, recently brought to light, containing verses and quatrains in a pantheistic strain; *Hasanāt al-ʿārifīn* (1062/1652) containing the aphorisms of *ṣūfī* saints belonging to various orders; *Mukālama-i Bābā Lāl wa Dārā Shukōh*, a record of his discussions with Bābā Lāl in 1063/1653; *Majmaʿ al-baḥrayn*, (1065/1655), perhaps his most remarkable work, being a comparative study of the technical terms used in *Vedānta* and Ṣūfism; and the *Sirr-i akbar* (1067/1657), his most ambitious work, being a translation of fifty-two principal Upanis͟hads which Dārā claims to have completed in six months with the aid of learned pandits and *sanyāsīs*. In additiòn to this, with Dārā's patronage and support, fresh translations into Persian were made of a number of Hindū religious works such as *Yōga-Vas͟his͟hta*, the *Gītā* and the mystic drama *Prabōdha-Čandrōdaya*. Dārā was also a good calligraphist, and patronized the arts: an album (*Muraḳḳaʿ*) of calligraphic specimens and Mug͟hal miniatures was presented by him to his wife Nādira Begam (d. of Parwīz) in 1051/1641-42 with a preface written by him.

In some of his later writings, Dārā shows considerable acquaintance with Hindū philosophy and mythology. He was attracted by a number of ideas which have obvious parallels in Hindū philosophy, such as the triune aspect of God, the descent of spirit into matter, cycles of creation and destruction, etc. However, he was opposed to the practice of physical austerities advocated by the exponents of *yōga* and favoured by many *ṣūfīs*, arguing that God desired not to inflict punishment but that He should be approached with love. Like a number of eminent Muslim thinkers (cf. Mīr ʿAbd al-Wāḥid, *Ḥaḳāʾiḳ-i Hindī*, 1566) Dārā came to the conclusion that there were no differences except purely verbal in the way in which Vedānta and Islam sought to comprehend the Truth. Dārā's translation of the Upanis͟hads which he regarded as "the fountain-head of the ocean of Unity", was a significant contribution in the attempt to arrive at a cultural synthesis between the followers of the two chief faiths in the country, being the first attempt to comprehend and to make available to the educated Muslims these fundamental scriptures of the Hindūs.

It may be doubted if Dārā's interest in gnosticism was motivated by political considerations. From an early age, Dārā felt that he belonged to the circle of the select who were marked out for the attainment of divine knowledge. Though some sections of orthodox opinion had accused him of heresy and apostasy as early as 1062/1652, it does not seem that Dārā ever gave up his belief in the essential tenets of Islam, affirming them at more than one place. Nor does the undoubted pantheistic strain in his writings go beyond what had been considered permissible for *ṣūfīs*. The opposition of these orthodox elements to Dārā stemmed from a deeper conviction, viz., that emphasis on the essential truth of all religions would in the long run weaken the position of Islam as the state religion, and effect their privileges. It was thus closely related to Dārā's position as an aspirant for the throne.

Dārā occupies a pre-eminent place among those who stood for the concept of universal toleration and who desired that the state should be based on the support of both Muslims and Hindūs, and remain essentially above religion. His defeat in the war of succession did not, by any means, imply the defeat of the trend he represented.

Bibliography: J. N. Sarkar, *History of Aurangzeb*[2], i, ii, Calcutta 1925; K. R. Qanungo, *Dara Shukoh*[2], Calcutta 1952; Bikrama Jit Hasrat, *Dārā S͟hikūh: Life and Works*, Vishwabharati 1953 (contains full list of mss. and editions of Dārā's works); *Risāla-i Ḥaḳḳ Numā*, *Mamaʿ al-Baḥrain and Mandak Upanishad* (ed. by S. M. Riḍā D͟jalālī Nāʾīnī with introduction by T. Chand), Tehran 1957; T. Chand, *Dara Shikoh and the Upanishads*, in *IC*, 1943; S. K. Rahman, *Sarmad and his Quatrains*, in *Calcutta Review*, 1943; C. B. Tripathi, *Mirza Raja Jai Singh* (unpublished thesis), Allahabad University, 1953; I. A. Ghauri, *Responsibility of the Ulema for the Execution of Dara Shikoh*, in *J. Pak. H. S.*, 1959; M. Athar Ali, *Religious Issue in the War of Succession: 1658-59*, in *Ind. Hist. Cong. Proc. 1960*; *Ḥaḳāʾiḳ-i Hindī*, Hindi tr. by S. A. A. Rizvi, Banāras 1957.

(Satish Chandra)

DĀRĀBD͟JIRD (modern Dārāb), a town in the province of Fārs in the district of Fasā, situated 280 kilometres east of S͟hīrāz at an altitude of 1188 metres and with a population of 6,400 people (1950). In Iranian legend the foundation of this town is ascribed to Dārāb, father of Dārā (Darius III Codomannus). The Sāsānīd ruler Ardas͟hīr rose to power by revolt from his post as military commander at Dārābd͟jird. The stone-strewn remains of the Sāsānid town lie 8 kilometres south-west of the modern village. The outline of the fortification walls exist as does the debris of a fire temple, located at the centre of the site. Six kilometres south-east of the modern village is a Sāsānid rock-cut relief known as the Naḳs͟h-i Rustam or as the Naḳs͟h-i S͟hāpūr. In the immediate vicinity is a spacious cruciform hall hewn into a rocky hillside, known as the Masd͟jid-i Sangī. Although it bears inscriptions dated 652/1254 and the title of the Sulṭān Abū Bakr, the hall is probably of the approximate period of the rock-cut relief.

Bibliography: Muḥammad Naṣīr Mīrzā Āḳā Furṣat Ḥusaynī S͟hīrāzī, *Āt͟hār-i ʿAd͟jam*, Bombay 1314/1896, 97-9, pls. 7-9; Le Strange, 288 ff.; A. Christensen, *L'Iran sous les Sassanides*, Copenhagen 1944, 86-7; *Farhang-i D͟jug͟hrāfiyā-yi Īrān*, Tehran 1330/1951, vol. 7, 95. (D. N. Wilber)

DARABUKKA, a vase-shaped drum, the wider aperture being covered by a membrane, with the lower aperture open. The body is usually of painted or incised earthenware, but carved and inlaid wood, as well as engraved metal are also used. In performance it is carried under the arm horizontally and played with the fingers. The name has regional variants: *darābukka* (or *ḍarābukka*), *dirbakki* and *darbūka*. Dozy and Brockelmann derive the word from the Syriac *ardabkā*, but the Persian *dunbak* is the more likely, although the lexicographers mistakenly dub the latter a bagpipe. The name *darabukka*, and its variants, is quite modern although a دربلة (a copyist's error for دربكة) is mentioned in the *Alf layla wa layla*. The type is to be found in ancient Egypt. The *dirrīd͟j* is mentioned by Al-Mufaḍḍal b. Salama (d. 319/930) although he wrongly thought that it was a kind of *ṭunbūr*, as do many Arabic lexicographers, but we know that it was a drum from Al-Maydānī (d. 518/1124). Ibn Mukarram (d. 710/1311) says that the correct vocalization is *durrayd͟j*, and that form—with variants—is to be found in the Mag͟hrib. The كريج and كربج found in Al-Maḳḳarī, are doubtless misreadings of دريج. Al-S͟haḳundī (d. 628/1231) uses the Berber name *agwāl* for this drum, and that is still the name used in the Mag͟hrib, although Höst calls it *akwāl*, whilst it is the *gallāl* of Algeria. In Tripolitania the name *tabdaba* is popularly used, and in Egypt *ṭabla*.

Bibliography: *EI*[1], Suppl., s.v. ṬABL, 215-6;

J. Robson, *Collection of Oriental writers on music*, iv, 14, Bearsden 1938; Farmer, *Studies in Oriental musical instruments*, 1st Series, 86-7, London 1931; G. A. Villoteau, *Description de l'Égypte. État moderne*, i, 996, Paris 1813; E. W. Lane, *Modern Egyptians*, 366-7, London 1860; A. Lavignac, *Encyclopédie de la Musique*, v, 2794, 2932, 3076, Paris 1922; Delphin et Guin, *Notes sur la poésie et la musique arabes*, 43-4, Paris 1886; Al-Maḳḳarī, *Analectes*, i, 143, Leiden 1955-61; Höst, *Nachrichten von Marokos und Fes*, 262, tab. xxxi, 9, Copenhagen 1787; H. Hickmann, *La Daraboukkah*, in *BIÉ*, xxxiii, 229-45, Cairo 1952. Specimens are exhibited at New York (Crosby Brown, Nos. 335, 345), Brussels (Conservatoire, nos. 112, 330-4, 680), and Paris (Conservatoire, nos. 954-7, 1457). (H. G. Farmer)

AL-**DĀRAḲUṬNĪ**, Abu 'l-Ḥasan ʿAlī b. ʿUmar b. Aḥmad b. Mahdī b. Masʿūd b. al-Nuʿmān b. Dīnār b. ʿAbdallāh, was born in Dār al-Ḳuṭn, a large quarter of Baghdad, whence he got his *nisba*, in 306/918. He was a man of wide learning who studied under many scholars. His studies included the various branches of *Ḥadīth* learning, the recitation of the Ḳur'ān, *fiḳh* and belles-lettres. He is said to have known by heart the *dīwān*s of a number of poets, and because of his knowing the *dīwān* of al-Sayyid al-Ḥimyarī he was accused of being a Shīʿī. His learning was so wide that many people felt there was no one like him. His biographers speak in fulsome terms of him. For example, al-Khaṭīb al-Baghdādī calls him "the *imām* of his time". Abu 'l-Ṭayyib al-Ṭabarī (d. 450/1058) called him *Amīr al-Mu'minīn* in *Ḥadīth*. This was the subject for which he was specially famous. He had studied it under many masters in Baghdād, al-Baṣra, al-Kūfa and Wāsiṭ, and when he was of mature age he travelled to Egypt and Syria. He became so famous as a traditionist that every *ḥāfiẓ* who came to Baghdād visited him and acknowledged his pre-eminence. Among the many who studied *Ḥadīth* under him were al-Ḥākim al-Naysābūrī (d. 405/1014) and Abū Ḥāmid al-Isfarā'inī (d. 406/1015). He died towards the end of 385/995 and was buried in the cemetery of Bāb al-Dayr near the grave of Maʿrūf al-Karkhī.

He contributed greatly to the advance of the critical study of Muslim traditions. His works, not all of which have survived, therefore deal primarily with the science of Tradition. His *Kitāb al-Sunan* (publ. Dihlī, 1306 and 1310) covers the normal ground of works of this nature. Al-Khaṭīb al-Baghdādī says it could have been produced only by one who was versed in *fiḳh* and acquainted with the conflicting views of the schools. It is said that he went to stay with Djaʿfar b. al-Faḍl, Kāfūr's *wazīr*, in Egypt because he heard that Djaʿfar wished to compile a *musnad*. Al-Dāraḳuṭnī is said to have helped him, or to have complied it for him. Whichever it was, he was richly paid for his trouble. His *Kitāb al-askhiyā' wa 'l-adjwād* has been edited by S. Wajahat Husain and published in *JASB*, n.s., xxx, 1934. It consists of stories of generosity. His *Kitāb ʿilal al-ḥadīth*, on weaknesses in traditions, was dictated from memory to al-Barḳānī. His *Kitāb al-afrād*, on traditions from one man or from one district only, is noted by Weisweiler as possibly the earliest book on the subject. Among other books on *ḥadīth* he wrote *Ilzāmāt ʿalā 'l Ṣaḥīḥayn*, in which he collected sound traditions not given by al-Bukhārī and Muslim which fulfilled their conditions. One other book which may be mentioned here is his *Kitāb al-Ḳirā'āt*, on Ḳur'ān readings, in which he began by stating the principles of the subject. He was the first writer to do so.

Bibliography: *Ta'rīkh Baghdād*, xii, 34-40; Samʿānī, 217a; Dhahabī, *Ḥuffāẓ*, iii, 186-90; al-Subkī, *Ṭabaḳāt al-Shāfiʿiyya al-kubrā*, ii, 310-12; Yāḳūt, ii, 523; Yāḳūt, *Udabā'*, ii, 406; vi, 8; Ibn Khallikān, Būlāḳ, i, 470; Yāfiʿī, *Mir'āt al-Djanān*, ii, 424-6; Ḥādjdjī Khalīfa, ed. Flügel, 23 times—see index; al-Djazarī, *Ghāyat al-nihāya fī ṭabaḳāt al-ḳurrā* (*Bibl. Isl.*, viiia), i, 558f., no. 2281; Ibn al-Ṣalāḥ, *ʿUlūm al-ḥadīth* (Aleppo, 1350/1931), 213, 241; Sarkis, *Dict. encyc. de bibl. arabe*, 856 f.; M. Weisweiler, *Istanbuler Handschriften zur arabischen Traditionsliteratur* (*Bibl. Isl.* x), nos. 54, 71n., 92; Brockelmann, I, 173 f., S I, 275. (J. Robson)

DARAN (deren) [see the article atlas].

AL-**DARAZĪ**, Muḥammad b. Ismāʿīl, was one of a circle of men who founded the Druze religion [see durūz]. He was not an Arab, and is called Nashtakīn in the Druze scriptures; according to Nuwayrī (who calls him Anūshtakīn), he was part Turkish and came from Bukhārā. He is said to have come to Egypt in 407 or 408/1017-18 and to have been an Ismāʿīlī *dāʿī* [see dāʿī and ismāʿīliyya], in high favour with the Caliph al-Ḥākim, allegedly to the point that high officials had to seek his good graces. He may have held a post in the mint (Ḥamza accuses him of malpractices with coinage).

He is said to have been the first who proclaimed publicly the divinity of al-Ḥākim; he is also accused, as heretics commonly were, of teaching *tanāsukh* (reincarnation) and *ibāḥa* (antinomianism) regarding the rules against wine and incest, though this latter is most unlikely. It is possible that his doctrine was a popularizing version of Ismāʿīlism such as the *dāʿī*s often warned against. His key treatise is said to have taught that the (divine) spirit embodied in Adam was transmitted to ʿAlī and (through the *imāms*) to al-Ḥākim. This would differ from orthodox Ismāʿīlism presumably in exalting ʿAlī over Muḥammad, imāmate over prophecy; and then in making public the secret *ta'wīl* (inner meaning of scripture) and probably denying the continued validity of the letter of revelation, *tanzīl*. For the commentator of Ḥamza's letters calls his followers Ta'wīlīs, who are accused by the Druzes of altogether rejecting the *tanzīl*. Ḥamza himself deems it necessary to remind al-Darazī that the inner truth and its outer form are always found together. He also accuses him of recognizing only the humanity of al-Ḥākim, not his divinity; which would follow, in Ḥamza's eyes, from his identifying al-Ḥākim with ʿAlī, the *asās*, who is a mere *imām*, leader of men, and far from the indefinable *One*, to Whom as such no functions can be assigned.

Al-Darazī seems to have gained a number of followers among al-Ḥākim's admirers, evidently with the approval of al-Hākim himself. Ḥamza, evidently claiming priority with al-Ḥākim, regarded al-Darazī as insubordinate and acting rashly on his own initiative; for instance, publicly attacking the Ṣaḥāba though warned against this. Ḥamza refused to let him see his doctrinal writings; he criticized the symbolism of the title al-Darazī first assumed, "sword of the faith", only to be worse offended when al-Darazī assumed instead a title, *sayyid al-Hādiyyīn*, "chief of the guided", which overreached Ḥamza's own title, *al-Hādī*, "the guide". He claims that some of al-Darazī's followers had at one time acknowledged Ḥamza's claims to leadership in the movement, and that al-Darazī himself had done so, having been converted by an agent of Ḥamza, ʿAlī b. Aḥmad al-Ḥabbāl—who subsequently supported al-Darazī. Sacy thinks Ḥamza regarded him as the *Ḍidd*, Ḥamza's Rival as *imām*, who would as such have a major cosmic rôle. But many of al-Darazī's followers, most notably a *dāʿī* al-Bardhaʿī, had from the first rejected Ḥamza as unauthorized by al-Ḥākim.

It seems that al-Darazī, probably in 408/1017-18, took the step of making public, with al-Ḥākim's private but not open blessing, a demand for acceptance of the divinity of al-Ḥākim—according to Sibṭ Ibn al-Djawzī, by reading his treatise in the main mosque of Cairo. This occasioned several riots, which engulfed Ḥamza also, and which evidently caused the whole movement to lose favour; it was probably this which forced Ḥamza to suspend his own preaching during 409. The Druze accounts are allusive, and other accounts seem to confuse several episodes, leaving the riots and the manner of al-Darazī's death unclear. Ḥamza's letters in 410/1019-20 seem to presuppose his death, which the Druze commentator places in 410, and imply that it was Ḥamza himself who—having denounced al-Darazī and others to al-Ḥākim—brought about his death on al-Ḥākim's orders. Ḥamza then tried to win over his followers, promising to intervene with al-Ḥākim for some who were in jail.

Sibṭ Ibn al-Djawzī makes al-Darazī withdraw secretly, on al-Ḥākim's orders, to Syria to preach, because people there readily accept novelties—which sounds like a later explanation of Druze geography. His name, in the form *Durzī*, was applied to the Druze community, probably not because it was he who first converted those of Syria—local tradition assigns this task to others—but because the whole movement was first associated with him in the public mind; thus al-Anṭākī applies the name "Daraziyya" to Ḥamza's own followers. The notion sometimes found, that either licentious teachings or loose moral practices among subsequent Druzes are to be traced to al-Darazī, is unsupported.

For bibliography see the article DURŪZ. Among Ḥamza's letters are especially relevant : *al-Ghāya wa 'l-naṣīḥa, al-Riḍā wa 'l-taslīm,* and *al-Subḥa al-kāʾina*. In Silvestre de Sacy's *Religion des Druzes*, the chief references are, in Vol. i, ccclxxxiii-cccxci, 99-113; in Vol. ii, 157-90 (and *errata*). See also Yaḥyā al-Anṭākī, continuation of Eutychius, in *Scriptores Arabici*, text, ser. iii, Vol. vii, second part, edd. L. Cheikho, B. Carra de Vaux, H. Zayyat, Beirut 1909, 220-4. (M. G. S. HODGSON)

DARB [see MADĪNA].

ḌARB [see DĀR AL-ḌARB and SIKKA].

DARB AL-ARBAʿĪN, one of the principal routes linking *bilād al-Sūdān* with the north, obtained its name from the forty days' travelling-time required to traverse it. W. G. Browne, the only European to have gone the whole way (in 1793) took 58 days from Asyūṭ to "Sweini" (al-Suwayna) near the southern terminus. Muḥammad ʿUmar al-Tūnusī in 1803 covered the same distance in 60 days. Starting from Asyūṭ, the route ran to the Khārdja oasis, an outpost of Ottoman Egypt. Thence it proceeded across the desert to al-Shabb, a watering-point where, as the name indicates, alum is found. At the next oasis, Salīma, a branch diverged to the Nubian Nile, which it attained a little above the Third Cataract at Mūshū, the frontier-post of the Fundj dominions. This route was followed in 1698 by Ch. J. Poncet (see his *Voyage to Aethiopia*, ed. Sir William Foster, in *The Red Sea and adjacent countries at the close of the seventeenth century*, (Hakluyt Society, Second Series, no. C), London 1949). From Salīma the Darb al-arbaʿīn proper continued across the deserts to al-Suwayna, the frontier post of Dār Fūr, where the caravans were held to await the sultan's pleasure. The route ended at Kubayh (*Cobbé*, Browne), about 35 miles NW of the sultan's residence at al-Fāshir. Kubayh, which is now deserted, was in the 18th and early 19th centuries an important town, principally inhabited by merchants, many of whom were immigrants from Nubia. The Darb al-arbaʿīn was the route followed to Egypt by the *ḳāfilat al-Sūdān*, which brought slaves, camels, ivory, ostrich feathers and gum, and returned with metal manufactured goods and textiles. During the 19th century, in consequence of the political changes of the eastern *bilād al-Sūdān*, and the decline of the slave-trade, the Darb al-arbaʿīn lost its importance, and only sectors of it are now occasionally used.

Bibliography: W. G. Browne, *Travels in Africa, Egypt, and Syria*, London 1799. Muḥammad ʿUmar al-Tūnusī, *Tashḥīdh al-adhhān bisīrat bilād al-ʿArab wa 'l-Sūdān*, lith. Paris 1850, 46-51; tr. Perron, *Voyage au Darfour par le ckeykh Mohammed Ebn-Omar El-Tounsi*, Paris 1845. W. B. K. Shaw, *Darb El Arbaʿin* in *Sudan Notes and Records*, xii/1, 1929, 63-71 (with photographs).
(P. M. HOLT)

ḌARB-KHĀNA [see DĀR AL-ḌARB].

DARBAND [see DERBEND].

DARBUKKA [see DARABUKKA].

DARD, one of the four pillars of Urdū literature and one of the greatest of Urdū poets, Khʷādja Mīr (with the *takhalluṣ* of Dard) b. Khʷādja Muḥammad Nāṣir "ʿAndalīb" al-Ḥusaynī al-Bukhārī al-Dihlawī, claimed descent from Khʷādja Bahāʾ al-Dīn Naḳshband and in the 25th step from the Imām Ḥasan al-ʿAskarī [*q.v.*]. Born in 1133/1720-21 in the decadent Imperial Dihlī, Dard received his education at home, mostly from his father, a very well-read man and the author of *Nāla-i ʿAndalīb*, a voluminous Persian allegory dealing with metaphysical and abstruse problems and of another Ṣūfī work, *Risāla-i Hūsh Afzā* (still in MS.). Casual references in Dard's work *ʿIlm al-Kitāb* (*vide infra*) show that on the completion of his studies he had attained proficiency in both the traditional and rational sciences. Starting life as a soldier he tried hard to secure a *djāgīr*, but soon withdrew from everything worldly and devoted himself, when barely 20 years of age, to a life of privation, austerity and asceticism. In 1172/1758-9, when he was 39 years old, he succeeded his father as the spiritual head of the local Čishtīs and Naḳshbandīs, and, despite the disturbed conditions prevailing in the capital in the wake of Nādir Shāh's invasion of 1152/1739 and Aḥmad Shāh Abdālī's incursions of 1175/1761, he did not leave Dihlī, being the only Urdū poet of note not to do so.

A great Ṣūfī, he passionately loved music and contrary to those who believed in the maxim "*al-ghināʾ ashadd min al-zināʾ*" (music is more heinous than adultery), he not only fraternized with the leading musicians of the town but also regularly held musical concerts (*madjālis-i samāʿ*) twice a month at his home, which were attended, among others, occasionally even by the ruling monarch Shāh ʿĀlam Bahādur Shāh I [*q.v.*]. In one of his works *Nāla-i Dard* (p. 37) he describes devotional music (*samāʿ*) "as ordained by God".

Essentially a Ṣūfī writer, Dard's first work *Asrār al-Ṣalāt*, was written during *iʿtikāf*, while he was still a lad of 15 years of age. It is a small tract dealing with the seven essentials of *al-Ṣalāt.* In 1166/1752 was begun *Risāla-i Wāridāt*, a collection of quatrains depicting the spiritual experiences of the author, and completed six years later in 1172/1758. His *magnum opus*, apart from his select Urdū *dīwān*, is, however, the *ʿIlm al-Kitāb*, a voluminous commentary on *Risāla-i Wāridāt*, comprising 648 very closely-written large-size pages. It is entirely on *sulūk* and is profusely interspersed with long Arabic quotations. Its style is sober and staid but powerful and the arguments adduced are cogent and sound. This book can be safely ranked with some of the outstanding works of S͟hāh Walī Allāh al-Dihlawī [*q.v.*], dealing with the same subject. It was followed by the supplementary works : *Nāla-i Dard, Āh-i Sard* and *Dard-i Dil.*

His other works are : *S͟hamʿ-i Maḥfil* (composed 1195-99/1780-84); a short Persian *dīwān* (Dihlī, 1309/1891-2); an Urdū *dīwān* (first published at Dihlī in 1272/1855 and later frequently printed); *Ḥurmat-i G͟hināʾ*, in defence of devotional music and *Wāḳiʿāt-i Dard*, also on mystic problems. All these works have been published.

For an estimate of his quality and importance as a poet see URDŪ LITERATURE.

Dard died at an advanced age on 24 Ṣafar 1199/ 6 January 1785 and was buried in the old cemetery (now abandoned and converted into a public park) of S͟hāhd͟jahānābād, outside the Turkomān Gate. His tomb, along with that of his father and the attached small mosque, is still preserved and visited by the local Muslims.

Bibliography: All the relevant *tad͟hkira*s of Urdū poets especially: Mīr Taḳī Mīr, *Nikāt al-s͟huʿarāʾ* 49 ff., Mīr Ḥasan, *Tad͟hkira-i s͟huʿarāʾ-i Urdū*[2], 66 ff., Ḳudrat Allāh Ḳāsim, *Mad͟jmūʿa-i nag͟hz*, Lahore 1933, i, 240 ff.; ʿAlī Ibrāhīm K͟hān K͟halīl, *Gulzār-i Ibrāhīm*, ʿAlīgaṙh 1935, 126-9; Garcin de Tassy, *Histoire de la littérature hindouie et hindoustanie*[2], Paris 1870, s.v.; Preface to his *dīwān*[2] (Badāʾūn 1933) by Ṣadr-Yār D͟jang Ḥabīb al-Raḥmān K͟hān S͟hirwānī; Rām Bābū Saksēna, *A history of Urdu literature*[2], Allāhābād 1940, 55-9 (the entire notice is almost a literal translation of the Urdū preface by S͟hirwānī); T. Grahame Bailey, *A history of Urdu literature*, Calcutta 1932, 50-1 and index; Sayyid ʿAbd Allāh, *Baḥt͟h o-Naẓar*, Lahore 1952, 9-26; Muḥammad ʿAẓmat Allāh K͟hān, *Maḍāmīn-i Aẓmat*, Ḥaydārābād (Deccan) 1942, ii, 1-64 (a critical study of Dard's *taṣawwuf*); Ḳiyām al-Dīn Ḳāʾim, *Mak͟hzan-i Nikāt*, 38 ff.; S͟hams al-ʿUlamāʾ Muḥammad Ḥusayn Āzād, *Āb-i Ḥayāt*, s.v.; *Oriental College Magazine* (articles by A. D. Nasīm), Lahore iv/31, i/32, i/33, ii-iii/34 (Aug., Nov., 1955, Nov., 1957, Feb.-May, 1958); S. Nāṣir Nad͟hīr Firāḳ, *Mayk͟hāna-i Dard*, Dihlī n.d.; G͟hulām Hamadānī Muṣḥafī, *ʿIḳd-i T͟hurayyā*, s.v.

(A. S. BAZMEE ANSARI)

DARDANELLES [see ČANAḲ ḲALʿE BOG͟HAZÎ].

DARDIC AND **KĀFIR LANGUAGES**, the description now generally applied to a number of what are in many respects very archaic languages and dialects, spoken in the mountainous N.W. corner of the Indo-Aryan (IA) linguistic area, in Afg͟hānistān, Pākistān and Kas͟hmīr. With the exception of Kas͟hmīrī, they are numerically insignificant, and have no written history. The others are known only from vocabularies and grammatical sketches, etc., the oldest dating from about 1830. There is still a great lack of adequate grammars, vocabularies, and collections of texts.

In the following account there is a departure from the normal transcription conventions of the Encyclopaedia: the symbol *ṣ* is used for a voiceless retroflex sibilant ('cerebral *s*'), *not* for *ṣād*; similarly the symbol *ṇ* is used for the retroflex nasal.

The Dardic and Kāfir languages may be roughly grouped as follows:

I. Kāfir Group. (*a*) Katī (Bas͟hgalī), spoken, in two main dialects, in the Ramgel, Kulum, Ktiwī and Bas͟hgal valleys in north Nūristān (Kāfiristān); (*b*) Prasun (Wasī-veri; Veron) in a small valley wedged in between the Katīs in Ktiwī and Bas͟hgal; (*c*) Aṣkūṇ (with Wāmāī), south of Katī, between the Alingar and Peč rivers; (*d*) Waigalī (Wai-alā), in the Waigal valley, south-east of Prasun. There is a not inconsiderable dialect variation, and especially Gambīrī, spoken in the Tregam valley east of Waigal towards the Kunar, differs in many respects from ordinary Waigalī. The Kāfir languages have certainly occupied their isolated valleys since very ancient times. (*c*) and (*d*) have been more exposed to outside influences than (*a*) and (*b*); the last language has undergone such violent sound-changes that it has become incomprehensible to its nearest neighbours.

Dardic group. II. (*e*) Kalaṣa, spoken in two dialects by the Kalaṣ tribe, who are still mainly pagan, in S. Chitral (Čitrāl), chiefly in the west side valleys. Closely related to Kalaṣa is (*f*) Khowār, the principal language of Chitral, spoken, with little dialect variation, by the Khō tribe (see CHITRAL, ii). Khowār has adopted a number of words from Wak͟hī, as well as from some Middle Iranian languages (cf. *BSOS*, viii, 294 ff.). These two languages represent the earliest wave of IA penetration into the Hindu Kush region.

III. (*g*) Damēlī, in one village in an east side valley of Chitral, between Mirkhani and Arandu. It has adopted a number of Kāfirī words, and has little connexion, except the geographical one, with (*h*) Gawar-Bātī (Narisātī), spoken in a few villages on the Kunar river, on both sides of the Chitral-Afg͟hān frontier. There is a tradition that this language was brought in from Swāt a few hundred years ago. (*i*) Remnants of dialects of a somewhat similar type are found further south, in Ningalām on the Peč (nearly extinct), and in S͟humās͟ht, in N. E. Pas͟haī territory.

IV. (*j*) Pas͟haī, spoken in numerous and widely differing dialects, from the lower Kunar in the east, through Lag͟hmān, and right up to Gulbahār on the Pand͟js͟hīr. The number of speakers may well run into the 100,000 guessed at in the *LSI*. Pas͟haī is descended from the ancient languages of Hindū and Buddhist civilization in Nagarāhāra, Lampāka and Kapis͟ha, and there is still a marked difference of vocabulary between the east and west dialects. A few numerals of Pas͟haī type have been recorded in Al-Bīrūnī's India.

V. (*k*) Bas͟hkarīk (Gāwrī/Gārwī), in the upper Pand͟jkora valley, above Dīr, and in three villages at the head-waters of the Swāt valley; (*l*) Torwālī, in the upper Swāt valley, below Bas͟hk; (*m*) Maiyā̃, with a number of related dialects (Kanyawālī, Dubērī, Čilis, Gowro, etc.), in the Indus valley region between the Ṣinā and the Pas͟htō speaking areas. Maiyā̃ is also called Kōhistānī, but this term is also used for (*k*) and (*l*); in some respects it approaches (*p*); (*n*) Woṭapūrī (nearly extinct) and Kaṭārḳalāī, on and near the Peč, just above Čig͟ha Sarāʾī on the lower Kunar. Connected with (*k*) and (*l*), but containing forms of a more ordinary Lahndā [*q.v.*] type, is (*o*) Tirāhī, in a few villages S.E. of Djalālābād, driven out of Tirāh by the Afrīdīs and probably the remnant of a dialect group once extending from there, through the Pēshāwar district, into Swāt and Dīr.

VI. (*p*) Ṣiṇā, spoken in many dialects in Gilgit, Čilās, etc., as far south as Gurez in Kashmīr, and towards the east isolated in Drās and Ḋah Hanū in Baltīstān, formerly even beyond Leh; (*q*) Phalūṛā, an archaic offshoot of (*p*), spoken in a few villages in S. E. Chitral. A related dialect, Sāwī, is spoken south of Gawar-Bātī; (*r*) Ḋumākī, the speech of the Ḋomas (musicians and blacksmiths) in Hunza, speaking Burushaskī [*q.v.* in Supplement]. It is influenced by (*p*), but has complex affinities with languages further south.

VII. (*s*) Kashmīrī, in the Kashmīr valley, with Kashtawārī as a true dialect, and other dialects strongly influenced by Ḋōgrī, etc.

The nomenclature and classification of these languages have been much discussed. E. Kuhn, in an important article in the *Album Kern* (1882) used the non-committal geographical term "Hindu Kush dialects". Pischel, *Grammatik der Prākrit-Sprachen*, 28, called them "Dardū and Kāfir dialects", employing the name Dard in the extended sense, accepted since. He thought that they were related to the so-called Piśāca dialect of Prākrit. This theory was further elaborated by Grierson in a series of publications, but no cogent linguistic arguments have been offered in support of it. According to Grierson the Dardic (or "Modern Piśāca") languages are not IA, but contain a number of Iranian features, and constitute a separate third branch of Indo-Iranian (IIr). Grierson divides the Dardic and Kāfir languages into (*A*) Kāfir group (= I, III, IV + (*e*) and (*o*); (*B*) Khowār (= (*f*)); (*C*) Dard group (= V, VI, VII). His classification has, in the main, been accepted in such recent works as *Les langues du monde* (2nd. ed. 1952), and Mhd. Shahidullah's article in *Indian Linguistics, Turner Jubilee Volume*, ii, 1959, 117. On the other hand, Sten Konow (*JRAS*, 1911, 1 ff.), drawing attention to some undoubtedly un-Indian features of Bashgalī (Katī), came to the conclusion that this language was of Iranian origin, and agreed with Grierson that the whole group must be separated from IA. Finally, Sköld (*ZDMG*, 81, LXXIV) went so far as to contend that the real Kāfir group (I) was not at all IIr, but a separate branch of the IE family.

In order to avoid confusion, it is important to distinguish between I (Kāfir group) and the rest (Dardic, II-VII). The latter languages, apart from some Kāfirī admixtures in (*g*), and in a few isolated cases in (*e*) and (*h*), contain absolutely no features which cannot be derived from Old IA. They have simply retained a number of striking archaisms, which had already disappeared in most Prākrit dialects. Thus for example the distinction between three sibilant phonemes (*s*, *ś* (*sh*), *ṣ*), or the retention, in the western dialects, of ancient *st*, *ṣṭ*. The loss of aspiration of voiced stops in some Dardic dialects is late, and in most of them at least some trace of the aspiration has been preserved. There is not a single common feature distinguishing Dardic, as a whole, from the rest of the IA languages, and the Dardic area itself is intersected by a network of isoglosses, often of historical interest as indicating ancient lines of communication as well as barriers. Dardic is simply a convenient term to denote a bundle of aberrant IA hill-languages, which in their relative isolation, accentuated in many cases by the invasion of Paṭhān tribes, have been in a varying degree sheltered against the expanding influences of IA Midland (*Madhyadesha*) innovations, being left free to develop on their own.

In the Kāfir group (I) the situation is an entirely different one. Although very heavily overlaid by IA (Dardic) words and forms, these dialects have retained several decidedly un-Indian features. The complete loss of aspiration of voiceless as well as voiced stops (*e.g.*, Katī *kur* 'ass'; *dyūm* 'smoke': S. Kalaṣa *khār*; *dhūm*) must go back to an extremely remote period, since we also find, *e.g.*, Katī (*d*)*zim* 'snow'; *djāṙ* 'to kill': cf. Sanskrit *hima-*; *han*. Cf. also Katī (*d*)*zāṙ* 'to know'; *dji* 'bowstring', both with unaspirated *dj* in Sanskrit. In this respect Kāfirī follows Ir. as against IA in abolishing the distinction between aspirated and unaspirated sounds, while retaining the one between ancient IE palatal and palatalized velar stops. In most other respects, however, such as in the preservation of *s*, it agrees with IA: Kāfirī *ċ* (= *ts*) corresponding to Skt. *ś*, Avestan *s* (*e.g.*, in Katī *duċ* 'ten') is an archaic feature, and still more so is the retention of dental *s* after *u*, as in *musä* 'mouse'. The vocabulary of Kāfirī contains a number of words not known from IA; some of these appear also in Iranian, *e.g.*, *kan-*, etc., 'to laugh', cf. Pers. *khand*; *washpīk*, etc., 'wasp', cf. Ir. Pamir dialect, Yidgha *wofshio*; Prasun *yase* 'belt', cf. Av. *yāh-*; etc. Other words are found only in Kāfirī, and, in a few cases, in some of the adjoining Dardic dialects.

We are, therefore, entitled to posit the existence of a third branch of IIr, agreeing generally with IA, but being situated on the Ir side of some of the isoglosses which, taken as a whole, constitute the borderline between IA and Ir. This branch had also retained archaisms of its own, and must have separated from the others at a very early date. The present-day Kāfir languages represent, so to speak, the decayed ruins of this original building, largely rebuilt and reconstructed with the help of foreign (IA) material, but with the outlines of the original structure still visible.

Bibliography: (see also article CHITRAL, ii): G. Buddruss, *Beitr. zur Kenntnis der Pašai-Dialekte*, Wiesbaden 1959; idem, *Kanyawali, Proben eines Maiyā-Dialektes*, Munich 1959; idem, *Die Sprache von Woṭapūr und Kaṭārqalā*, Bonn 1960; T. Grahame Bailey, *Grammar of the Shina language*, London 1924; G. A. Grierson, *Linguistic Survey of India* (cited above as *LSI*), viii/2, with bibliography up to 1919; idem, ibid. i/1 (Tirāhī); idem, *A Dictionary of the Kashmiri language*, Calcutta 1932; D. L. R. Lorimer, *Phonetics of the Gilgit dialect of Shina* in *JRAS* 1924; idem, *The forms and nature of the transitive verb in Shina* in *BSOS*, iii; idem, *The conjugation of the transitive verb in the principal dialects of Shina*, *JRAS* 1927; idem, *The Ḍumāki language*, Nijmegen 1939; G. Morgenstierne, in *Norsk Tidsskrift for Sprogvidenskap*: Aṣkūṇ (Vols. ii and vii); Damēlī, (ibid., xii); Shumāshti (xiii); Khowār (xiv); Prasun (xv); Wāmāī, Gambīrī, Woṭapūrī (xvi); Waigali (xvii); S. E. Dardic (= Kōhistānī) (with F. Barth), (xviii); idem, *AO* viii (Torwālī); Tirāhī (ibid., xii); Bashkarīk (xviii); idem, *Det Norske Videnskaps-Akademi i Oslo, Skrifter, Hist.-Filos. Klasse*, Phalūṛ (1940, v); Gawar-Bātī (1950, i); idem, *Indo-Iranian Frontier Languages*: *Pashai texts and vocabulary*, iii, 2 and 3. (G. MORGENSTIERNE)

DARDĪRIYYA, name of the Egyptian branch of the Khalwatiyya [*q.v.*] order. See also ṬARĪḲA.

DARDISTĀN, the name given to the area, lying between the Hindū Kush and Kāghān, between lat. 37° N. and long. 73° E., and lat. 35° N. and long. 74° 30′ E., the country of the Dardas of Hindū mythology. In the narrowest sense it embraces the Shinā-speaking territories, *i.e.*, Gilgit, Astor, Gurayz, Čilās, Hōdur, Darēl, Tangir etc., or what is now known as Yāghistān. In a wider sense the feudatory states of Hunza, Nāgar and Chitrāl [*q.v.*] (including the part known as Yāsīn), now forming the northern regions of Pakistan, comprise Dardistān; in the widest sense parts of what was till very recently known as Kāfiristān. Herodotus (iii, 102-5) is the first author who refers to the country of the Dards, "placing it on the frontier of Kashmīr and in the vicinity of modern Afghānistān". He, however, does not use the name "Dard" while referring to the country; on the other hand Strabo (xv) and Pliny (*Natural History*, xi) call the people inhabiting the area as *Derdae* or *Dardae*. The Dards are the "Darada" of the Sanskrit writers, a region to which Buddha sent his missionaries and *bhikshus*. These areas once formed the stronghold of Buddhism and even to this day numerous Buddhist remains and relics are found there. The Dards are "an independent people which plundered Dras in the last year, has its home in the mountains three or four days' journey distant and talks the *Pakhtu* or Daradi language. Those whom they take prisoners in these raids, they sell as slaves" (*Voyage par Mir 'Izzetulla in* 1812 in Klaproth's *Magasin Asiatique*, ii, 3-5).

Strangely enough the Dards have no name in common, each tribe inhabiting a different valley carrying a different name, derived mostly from the areas inhabited by them.

The history of Dardistān, a name first given to the entire country by Dr. G. W. Leitner after his visit in 1866, is the history of its component parts, namely Hunza, Nāgar, Chitrāl, parts of Baltistān, Ladakh, Gilgit etc. [*qq.v.*]. The main enemy of the Dards, otherwise a peace-loving people, was the Dōgrā State of Kashmīr under its first ruler, Gulāb Singh. He led a number of expeditions against the Dards. In 1850 a large Sikh army sent against Čilās met with an ignominious defeat. Next year, a force 10,000 strong under Bakhshī Hari Singh and Dīwān Hari Čand succeeded in destroying the fort of Čilās and scattering the hill tribes who had come to the assistance of the Čilāsīs.

A little-known fact about the outlying states of Hunza and Nāgar is that they never owed any allegiance to Kashmīr except that they occasionally sent a handful of gold dust to the Mahārādjā and received substantial presents in return. These two states have rather more than once punished Kashmīr when attempting agression, but they have never been hostile to the Dōgrā Kingdom.

The prevailing religion in the whole of Dardistān is Islam; a form of Shīʿīsm is met with in Hunza, Nāgar and parts of Chitrāl, although the latter is predominantly Sunnī. The Mawlāʾīs, as they call themselves, profess to be good Muslims with strong leanings towards the seventh Shīʿī *imām*. They, however, owe allegiance to the Āghā Khān. The *Kalām-i Pīr*, a book in Persian, an edition of which was published by Ivanow (Bombay 1935), is held in high esteem among the Mawlāʾīʿs. (See further ISMĀʿĪLIYYA).

Čamarkand in Yāghistān became the centre of the remnants of the *Mudjahidīn*, the followers of Sayyid Aḥmad Barēlwī [*q.v.*] after their defeat and dispersal in 1246/1831 at Bālākoṭ in the Kāghān valley, at the hands of the Sikh forces led by Prince Shīr Singh, a son of the Lahore Chieftain, Randjīt Singh. Because of the suspected revolutionary and subversive activities of these *Mudjāhidīn* and their descendants, entry into Yāghistān from British India and subsequently from Pakistan was regulated by permits. This system was, however, abolished by the Pakistan Government in 1959.

Bibliography: G. W. Leitner, *Dardistan in* 1866-1886 *and* 1893, Woking n.d.; idem, *The Hunza and Nagyr Handbook*, Calcutta 1889 and 1893; idem, *The languages and races of Dardistan* (Part II of this work deals exhaustively with the flora and fauna, rivers, mountains, the occupations etc. of the people of Dardistān); idem, article in *Asiatic Quarterly Review*, January 1892. See also the articles CHITRĀL, HUNZA and NĀGAR, and Muḥammad ʿAlī Ḳaṣūrī, *Mushāhadāt-i Kābul wa Yāghistān*, Karachi n.d.

(A. S. BAZMEE ANSARI)

AL-**DARDJĪNĪ**, ABU 'L-ʿABBĀS AḤMAD B. SAʿĪD B. SULAYMĀN B. ʿALĪ B. ĪKHLAF, an Ibāḍī jurist, poet and historian of the 7th/13th century, author of a historical and biographical work on the Ibāḍīs, the *Kitāb Ṭabaḳāt al-Mashāyikh*. He belonged to a pious and learned Berber-Ibāḍī family from Tamīdjār, a place in the Djabal Nafūsa in Tripolitania. His ancestor, al-Ḥādjdj Īkhlaf b. Īkhlaf al-Nafūsī al-Tamīdjārī, an eminent *faḳīh*, lived in the neighbourhood of Nefṭa in the Djarīd [*q.v.*]. Son of Īkhlaf, the pious ʿAlī, who lived in the second half of the 6th/12th century, earned his living by trading with the Sudan. In the course of one of his trading journeys, in the year 575/1179-80, he is said to have converted the pagan king of Mālī in the western Sudan to the Ibāḍī faith, but this is a legend (cf. J. Schacht, in *Travaux de l'Institut de Recherches Sahariennes*, xi, 1954, 21 f.). His son, the famous lawyer Sulaymān, who was the grandfather of Abu 'l-ʿAbbās, lived at Kanūma in the Djarīd; he was regarded as a saint. The father of Abu 'l-ʿAbbās, Saʿīd, who was a distinguished traditionist, settled at Dardjīn al-Sufla 'l-Djadīda near Nefṭa.

We do not know much about the life of al-Dardjīnī. He must still have been very young when he went to Ouargla in 616/1219-20, where he spent two years studying with the Ibāḍī *shaykh*s of this city. Afterwards he returned to the Djarīd, where we find him engaged in historical studies at Tozeur in 633/1235-6. Later he lived for some time on the island of Djarba, where he was highly regarded by the *ʿazzāba* (Ibāḍī scholars). It was at the request of these that he conceived the idea of writing the *Kitāb Ṭabaḳāt al-Mashāyikh*.

The *Kitāb al-Djawāhir al-Muntaḳāt*, of Abu 'l-Ḳāsim b. Ibrāhīm al-Barrādī [*q.v.*], gives some information on the origins of this work.

"Here", says al-Barrādī, "are the circumstances in which Abu 'l-ʿAbbās came to write his book. Al-Ḥādjdj ʿĪsā b. Zakariyyāʾ had just arrived from ʿOmān bringing various works with him ..... His brothers in the east had asked him to send them a work containing biographies of the earliest Ibāḍīs and recounting the virtues of the western forebears. Al-Ḥādjdj ʿĪsā consulted the learned *ʿazzāba* who were then to be found in Djerba and told them of this desire of their co-religionists in the east. They thought first of the book of Abū Zakariyyāʾ, but they recognized that it was not sufficiently complete, and that the style of the author, who was accustomed to the Berber language and hence not very accurate in the rules of Arabic grammar or the propriety of its terminology, was often defective. They thought then of having a new work compiled on the history of the Rustumids and the virtues of the ancient doctors. No-one was more suitable than Abu 'l-ʿAbbās to fulfil this task worthily and it was to him that it was confided".

The *Kitāb Ṭabaḳāt al-Mashāyikh* exists only in some manuscript copies (a few in the Mzab and one in the collection of the late Z. Smogorzewski). It consists of two distinct parts of which the first is merely a reproduction of the *Kitāb al-Sīra wa-Akhbār al-Aʾimma* of Abū Zakariyyāʾ Yaḥyā b. Abī Bakr al-Wardjlānī, or rather of the first part of this chronicle. It contains a history of Ibāḍī penetration into North Africa, of the installation of the Ibāḍī imāmate and of the imāms of the Banū Rustum family, and finally some biographies of Ibāḍī doctors of Maghribī origin. The second part, the original work of al-Dardjīnī, is a collection of biographies of doctors and other celebrated Ibāḍīs, divided in the customary way into twelve classes, each class covering a period of fifty years. The first four classes of the work cover the biographies of the eastern Ibāḍī doctors of the 1st/7th and 2nd/8th centuries. The author found it pointless here to give biographies of famous personages from the Maghrib, having reproduced the corresponding part of the work of Abū Zakariyyāʾ. The sources of the biographies of these eastern scholars are sometimes very old. The eight classes which follow, on the other hand, are confined to biographies of Ibāḍī shaykhs of Maghribī origin. The last 4 classes, indeed, deal only with persons from Ouargla, the Oued Rīgh, the Oued Souf, the Djarīd and the island of Djerba, and are therefore of no more than a local importance.

Al-Dardjīnī used a large number of sources in the second part of his book, among others the historical and biographical works of Maḥbūb b. al-Raḥīl al-ʿAbdi (2nd/8th century) and Abu 'l-Rabīʿ Sulaymān b. ʿAbd al-Salām al-Wisyānī (6th/12th century). He included in his work some curious passages which are of great value for students of Ibāḍī history, for example the rules concerning the constitution of the *ḥalḳa* laid down by the great Ibāḍī scholar, Abū ʿAbd Allāh Muḥammad b. Bakr al-Nafūsī (5th/11th century), and the *khuṭba* pronounced at Medina by the famous Ibāḍī chieftain, Abū Ḥamza al-Shārī (2nd/8th century). The exquisite language of of the *Kitāb Ṭabaḳāt al-Mashāyikh* surpasses by far in elegance all other Ibāḍī works of North African origin, and the author has corrected the style of his Maghribī sources, as can be seen from a comparison with the original text of the chronicle of Abū Zakariyyāʾ.

Al-Dardjīnī is also the author of a *dīwān* and of letters in verse. As a jurist, he decided a number of questions on the division of inheritances, which al-Djīṭālī [*q.v.*] put together afterwards.

The date of his death is unknown, but it was undoubtedly in the second half of the 7th/13th century.

Bibliography: Abu 'l-Faḍl Abu 'l-Ḳāsim b. Ibrāhīm al-Barrādī, *Kitāb al-Djawāhir al-Muntaḳāt*, lithogr. Cairo, 1302/1884-5, 11, 215 f., 219; Abu 'l-ʿAbbās Aḥmad b. Saʿīd al-Shammākhī, *Kitāb al-Siyar*, lithogr. Cairo 1301/1883-4, 164, 178, 453-61 and *passim*; A. de C. Motylinski, *Bibliographie du Mzab. Les livres de la secte abadhite*, in *Bulletin de Correspondance Africaine*, iii (1885), 29, 38-43; Brockelmann, I, 336, S I, 575; T. Lewicki, *Notice sur la chronique ibāḍite dʾad-Darǧīnī*, in *RO*, xiii (1936), 146-72; J. Schacht, *Bibliothèques et manuscrits abadites*, in *RA*, C (1956), 397. (T. Lewicki)

DARGĀH, Pers., lit. "place of a door" [see DAR], usually "royal court, palace" in Persia, but in India with the additional specialized sense "tomb or shrine of a *pīr*".

DARGHIN, name of a Muslim Ibero-Caucasian people in Dāghistān formerly inhabiting the pre-Caspian plains and then, in the 12th century, driven back towards the mountains by the Ḳumīḳs who had come from the North. The Soviet census of 1926 gives the number of 126,272 Darghins who, in 1954, had increased to 158,000. The Darghins are grouped in the sub-alpine and mid-alpine zones of central Dāghistān, and they form the greater part of the population in the districts of Sergo-Ḳalʿa, Akūsha and Dakhadaev. They are intermingled with Avars and Laks in the districts of Levashi and Tzudakhar, and with Ḳumīḳs and Ḳaytāḳs in the districts of Ḳaytāḳ (Madjālīs). They form isolated communities in the districts of Ḳarabudakhkent (*awl*s of Gubden and Gurbuki), Buinaksk (*awl*s of Ḳadar, Ḳaramakhi and Djankurbī), Agul (*awl*s of Amukh and Čirakh) and Gunib (*awl*s of Miamugi). Finally, in 1944 several Darghin *awl*s emigrated towards the steppes of north Dāghistān to the district of Shuragat.

The earliest information concerning the Darghins was given by Arab historians of the 4th/10th century in the *Darband-nāma*. After the Arab conquest the feudal principality of the Usmī of Ḳaytāḳ was established in the south-west part of the Darghin territory with its centre at Ḳalʿa Ḳuraysh, near the present *awl* of Kubači, whilst other Darghin clans were found in the dependency of the Lak Shamkhalat of Ḳazi-Ḳumuḳ. After the end of the 8th/14th century when the Shamkhālat became weakened by the pressure of the Darghin clans allied with the Avars, the Darghin territory was divided between the principality of the Ūsmī of Ḳaytāḳ, which reached its apogee in the 16th and 17th centuries, and the free clans (*djamāʿa*) which were joined together in unions or federations of clans. These were originally four in number: Akūsha, Usala-Tabun, Makhala-Tabun, Khürkili-Tabun; to these, six others were added by force of arms at the beginning of the 19th century: Keba-Dargwa, Kutkula, Sergala-Tabun, Usmī-Dargwa, Vakun-Dargwa and Čirakh. The administration of these federations reverted to the *ḳāḍī* of Akūsha. This patriarchal structure was maintained until the Russian conquest in the 19th century.

The Darghin language is divided into three dialects: Urakhi (or Khürkili), spoken by the cattle-breeders of the high plateaux; Tzudakhar, spoken by the artisans and traders in the plains, and Akūsha which is clearly differentiated from the other two and serves as a basis for the literary language used also by the Kubačis and Ḳaytāḳs. But Turkish (*ḳumīḳ*, *azeri*) and Russian linguistic influence is considerable and the majority of Darghins are bilingual: in primary schools teaching is carried out in Darghin, in secondary schools only Russian being used. Darghin literature is of recent creation. The earliest works do not go back beyond the 19th century, and Soviet literature is only represented by a few writers, the best-known being the poet Rashid Rashidov.

At the beginning of the 20th century the Darghin literary language was transcribed in Arabic characters. In 1920 a new modified Arabic alphabet was introduced (called the new *adjem*, with 43 letters). This gave way in 1928 to the Latin alphabet which in turn was replaced in 1938 by the Cyrillic alphabet.

In 1958 eight Darghin newspapers were published: one Republican journal at Makhač-Ḳalʿa, and seven district journals.

The Darghins are Sunnī Muslims of the Shāfiʿi sect, with the exception of two *awls*, Kurush and Miskindjī, whose inhabitants up to the time of the revolution were twelver Shīʿīs. Their Islamization which had begun in the 11th century became decisive in the 16th century, on the elimination of the last Jewish and Christian traces. In the 15th century some at least of the Darghins were still not Muslims, since the *Ẓafar-nāma* (i,777 ff.) cites among the "infidel" tribes of Dāghistān who resisted Tīmūr the "Ashkudja" (who can be indentified with the *awl* Akūsha).

Until the revolution of 1917 the social structure of the Darghins was based on the division into clans, *tukhum*, and the great patriarchal family, *djins*. If in the 19th century the *tukhum* had already lost its economic significance, the customs deriving from it decayed more slowly.

Polygamy was always rare among the Darghins and endogamy fell into decline from the 19th century: the ritual of marriage remained traditional, but though marriage with infidels was for a long time impossible, marriages with Russians became comparatively frequent after 1917. Abduction was often practised in former times, particularly by those who could not pay the obligatory *kalīm*, but the *kalīm* persists.

Conquered by the Russians for the first time in 1819 (capture of Akūsha), and then for the first in the second time in 1844, the Darghins were threatened before the revolution with assimilation by both the Avars and the Ḳumīḳs at the same time. The Soviet authorities, wishing to ensure their protection, as a unique "nationality" possessing a literary language, favoured their consolidation with two small neighbouring peoples, the Ḳaytāḳs and the Kubačis, both also threatened with extinction.

The Darghins practise agriculture in the plains and horticulture at the foot of the mountains; and they take up their flocks and herds of sheep, cattle and horses to the summer pastures in the mountains. Kubača is celebrated for the local handicrafts of jewellery and goldsmiths' work, and Sulevkent for pottery. Industry is scarcely developed; there are canning factories at Akūsha, Levashi and Tzudakhar.

Bibliography: C. N. Abdoullaev, *Russko-darginskiy slovarʾ*, Makhač-Ḳalʿa 1950; A. Bennigsen and H. Carrère d'Encausse, *Une république soviétique: le Daghestan*, in *REI*, 1955, 6-56; A. A. Bokarev, *Kratkie svedeniya o yazīkakh Dagestana*, Makhač-Ḳalʿa 1949; E. I. Kozubskiy, *Pamyatnaya knižka Dagestanskoy oblasti*, Temir Khān-Shurā, 1895; Meshčaninov and G. P. Serdučenko, *Yazīki Severnogo Kavkasa i Dagestana*, Moscow-Leningrad 1949; Z. A. Nikol'skaya, *Étnografičeskoe opisanie darginskogo kolkhoza "Krasnīy Partizan"*, in *Sov. Etn.*, ii (1950); L. Žirkov, *Grammatika darginskogo yazīka*, Moscow 1926, 103. See also AVARS, DĀGHISTĀN, DERBEND, ḲAYTĀḲS, KUBAČIS, LAKS, LEZGS.

(CH. QUELQUEJAY)

DARĪ, a Persian word meaning "court (language)" from *dar* [*q.v.*]. In Arabic authors such as al-Maḳdisī (335), Yāḳūt (iii, 925), and *Fihrist* (19), we find the *Darī* language (also *Fārsī Darī*) described as the spoken and written language of the (Sasanian) court. It was also the language of government and literature. After three centuries of Muslim rule in Persia it was written down in the Arabic script, and came to be called *Fārsī* or New Persian. The fact that New Persian literature arose and flourished in Khurāsān and Transoxiana because of political reasons (Iranian dynasties of the Ṭāhirids and Sāmānids) has caused some difficulty. The language was basically a West Iranian dialect, hence the name Fārsī after the province. In Islamic times, if not before, elegant Darī diverged more and more from the rather stilted language of the Pahlavi books, kept alive primarily by Zoroastrian priests. By the time of the Mongol conquest of Īrān the term Darī had gone out of use.

Bibliography: E. Bertels, *Persidskiy dari-tadžikskiy*, *SE*, iv, 1950, 55-66; R. N. Frye, *Die Wiedergeburt Persiens um die Jahrtausendwende*, in *Isl.* xxxv, 1960, 42, for further literature.

(R. N. FRYE)

ḌARĪBA, one of the words most generally used to denote a tax, applied in particular to the whole category of taxes which in practice were added to the basic taxes of canonical theory. These latter (*zakāt* or *ʿushr*, *djizya* and *kharādj*, etc.) and their yield in the "classical" period, have been covered in a general survey in an earlier article, BAYT AL-MĀL, and a detailed description of the methodes of assessment and collection will be given under their respective titles, in particular under KHARĀDJ; along with *kharādj* and *zakāt* will be included associated taxes and payments linked with them or levied on other categories of agricultural or pastoral wealth; finally, in the article DJIZYA will be found a discussion of the problem of the original distinction between *djizya* and *kharādj*. Apart from *djizya* which, as a poll-tax, is not concerned with the nature of the wealth, the above-mentioned taxes which form the basis of the official fiscal system of Islam are essentially concerned with agriculture and stock-breeding; only the theoretical definition of *zakāt* makes it possible to include the products of industry and commerce, but only with the Muslims and, as we shall see, is far from embracing all the effective forms of taxes to which they were subject; and no canonical tax covers the fiscal dues which the State arrogates to itself to recover certain costs of the conduct of its administration. It is of this whole group of taxes, usually called *ḍarāʾib* or *rusūm*, and often stigmatized by theorists, on account of their more or less extra-canonical character, under the name *mukūs*, that we shall attempt to speak here although, precisely because they are poorly represented in doctrinal treatises as well as in papyri, any research into them is made under more difficult documentary conditions than is the case with canonical taxation, and they have been scarcely noticed by historians.

In the practice of the last years of the Prophet's life, treaties concluded with certain communities of *dhimmīs* had allowed them to make payments in kind with goods useful to the Muslims, if they produced them; after the conquest, and on a larger scale, stipulations of the same sort had again been expressed for the benefit of the army of occupation; and for many centuries the same element occurs in the taxes paid by certain provinces with important specific products, either natural or manufactured. It is however clear that it was always a question of the method by which the total contribution from the province was compounded, and not of specific taxes on industry or the trade of individuals. As regards *zakāt*, this of course includes a levy on possessions in the form of precious metals (money included) or merchandise, as on other categories of wealth, as soon as they exceeded an estimated 200 dirhams, the figure regarded as marking the limit between "rich" and "poor"; but in fact it amounted to a preferential tariff granted to Muslims within the framework of a more general tax levied on traders of all faiths: it was to be confirmed in the rule that the Muslim should pay 1/40 = 2.5%, the *dhimmī* 1/20 = 5%, and the foreign merchant 1/10 = 10%. In the *zakāt* thus conceived two principles are combined: as regards foreigners, it is a matter simply (and explicitly in the account of the innovations attributed to caliph ʿUmar on this question) of conformity with international usage, and the rate of 10% was instituted in reciprocity with the usual rate levied by Byzantium on foreign merchants; for the native merchant, the relation between *dhimmī* and Muslim is the same for the levy on commercial goods as for the *kharādj* and the land tithe, and the conception of the tax appears to be inspired by what it is for livestock, (except that it is paid in money and not in kind) in the sense that it is an annual levy on the total trading capital, and not a tax on the profits from trading operations. Dionysius of Tell-Mahré describes at the beginning of the ʿAbbāsid period a procedure of this sort for levying the "*ʿushr* tithe" on merchants, which, however, he seems to regard as exceptional in its severity or in its very nature; the schedule that such a conception implies, with an official fixing of values and a distinction between consumer goods and those intended for trade, obviously presents great difficulties particularly to a merchant when travelling, for, on introducing himself to officials in a new province, he has to prove that he has already made the obligatory annual payment, since no administration could be satisfied by the Muslim's right, however valid in theory, to determine the amount of his *zakāt* himself and even to pay it direct to the "poor"; the conception of an annual payment became impracticable at the time of the political fragmentation of Islam, no State being prepared to be deprived of the proceeds of a tax on the ground that it had already been paid to another, and Ibn Djubayr, for example, complains that the Alexandria customs-post taxes pilgrims without enquiring whether they have already paid their *zakāt*, and moreover without distinguishing between goods for private consumption and goods for trade, and between pilgrims and merchants. All this helps us to understand that what was taking place was a reorganization and development of the kind of taxes which had been known to the pre-islamic empires and which more or less must have survived the conquest in the framework of local institutions, particularly for towns enjoying a "treaty" which left them free to compound their tributes from such of their resources as suited their rulers.

A first group of taxes belongs to what might be called customs, dues and tolls (*marāṣid, maʾāṣir*). There exist customs such as those on the frontiers which are well organized, on the great international trade routes, and from the very first naturally at the ports (Ubulla, the fore-port of Baṣra, kept the name of *al-ʿashshār*, the tithe-man. The "tithe" levied there can only have been taken in kind on certain merchandise, and for the most part it was therefore necessary to pay in cash according to an official estimate of value; in this way there were evolved certain kinds of customs tariffs such as the one preserved in the *Mulakhkhaṣ* (see *Bibl.*). In theory no customs-post should exist except on the frontiers of Islam, for the foreign merchant is in law indebted only to the Muslim community as a whole; in fact, from the start every large region seems to have had autonomy in customs, and this state of affairs became general everywhere, irremediably so after the establishment of many separate principalities. In addition there were often town-dues at the gates of towns, and tolls on the trade routes, particularly the water-ways, from which the *ḥadjdj* itself was not exempt. The theoretical justification for such dues, insofar as one was looked for, is in this case less clear than for customs; it may in certain cases, as also for other dues to be discussed later, be a question of taxes for the use of a route belonging to the State; in general, variations of this "protection", *ḥimāya* or *khafāra*, became widespread and, although the normal taxation implied such protection, payments had to be made to the *imām*, to local authorities of all kinds and, in bedouin countries, to the tribes, according to immemorial custom; payment generally is calculated on a "load" of an ass or camel. Finally, although the jurists ignore the point, we must add that in addition to dues for the import of goods others, for export (to obtain authorization), were sometimes imposed or substituted, as in other mediaeval societies. The result of all this was that, contrary to what one might expect, the Muslim world, even at the time of its on the whole great political unity, did not allow goods to circulate with any real freedom from those restrictions which so impeded them in, for example, the more divided European communities.

A second category of dues can be grouped under the heading of the renting of lands or buildings belonging to the State. The State, rediscovering ancient habits or regulations under the ʿAbbāsids, sometimes looked upon itself as the proprietor perhaps of the whole territory of a town, but invariably of the ramparts and public highways, calculated on the basis of a width of forty cubits; everything that had in fact been established or built on this land had to recognize the ownership of the State by paying rent; in practice all the shops in the souks and markets in public places were subject to this charge. Dionysius of Tell-Mahré again provides us with evidence from the reign of al-Mahdī, of whom we know in particular from al-Yaʿḳūbī that he introduced dues on the *sūḳ*s in Baghdād, and from others that he made the same innovation in Egypt. This did not however signify that the State did not recognize some sort of ownership by occupants of shops or houses standing on rented land, since in fact it left them free to dispose of them normally by inheritance, sale, *waḳf* etc. It regarded itself as having a more direct ownership of the *khān*s and *funduḳ*s, to enter which it was of course necessary to pay; in Egypt, this was true of many shops.

With regard to the *khān*s, there was also *ḥimāya*, protection of goods, to be provided. The same justification was given for the dues which the State required from individuals wishing to make use of the post (*barīd*), weights and measures, as well as certain instruments in which it retained a monopoly and, of course, the profit made from minting money. Ovens, presses, and mills also came into this category although private ones also existed, which were subject to taxes similar to those applying to trades in general.

Indeed, it seems clear that, whether or not under the pretext of *zakāt*, the State levied certain dues collectively on various organized trades or industrial establishments—without prejudice to secondary taxes on regulation, packing, etc., in the case of goods in which it had a monopoly or whose export it regulated (fabrics from Egypt and Fārs, among others). In addition, dues were charged on certain sales (especially of livestock) and on the exercise of brokerage which was particularly indispensable in commercial dealings with foreigners. We make no mention here of manufactures in which the State retained a monopoly, or of the fifth on mines, treasure trove, etc.

Dues for *ḥimāya* appeared frequently, though it is not always possible to distinguish between those which do or do not merge with certain of the dues noted above. Originally it was, generally speaking, a matter of demands from individuals or from local police, but subsequently the State replaced these beneficiaries, while keeping up their demands. We leave aside the question of State duties on legacies. The drawing up of any written legal deed also of course incurred a tax.

The *waḳf*s in principle were independent of the State, on condition that taxes were paid to it unless they had been renounced; but it tended to take over control, paying a fixed allocation to the parties concerned, while keeping the surplus : a kind of manipulation of property in mortmain.

It should not, however, be imagined that the various sorts of taxes and dues that we have just noted always coexisted everywhere and to the same degree. Of course it was Egypt which was the fiscal paradise, following the tradition of Antiquity. It is possible that at the start the conqueror, satisfied with the payment of poll-tax and other taxes and grants of land agreed upon by the terms of surrender, failed to pay attention to other sources of revenue which had been added by earlier régimes; subsequently, when equivalent measures were re-established, the Muslims accused the Copts of having appropriated them, though one cannot be certain if they meant that these revenues had fallen into private ownership, or that the local powers had embezzled the proceeds. Tradition, simplifying a more complex process that had been initiated earlier, attributes to Ibn al-Mudabbir, head of Egyptian finances on the eve of the Ṭūlūnid régime (mid 3rd/9th century), the particular responsibility for introducing the policy of new extra-canonical taxes. Succeeding régimes, according as to whether they were impelled by a desire for legality and popularity or by financial needs, alternately abolished and re-established all or part of these taxes which no doubt reached their fullest development during the difficult times of the last Fāṭimids; part of them (but not the customs) was later abolished by Saladin, with the loss of 100,000 dinars, and the report which has been preserved is one of the principal sources of our knowledge; but Saladin's successors re-established and perfected them (al-Maḳrīzī, *Khiṭaṭ*, i, 103 ff., Ibn Mammātī, ed. Atiya, chap. 5).

In ʿIrāḳ, tradition and the strength of custom did not allow such a fiscal system to be established, and the fact that the ʿAbbāsids had not the ability or the means to utilize for their own advantage the revenues from commerce like those from agriculture perhaps forms a part, which is difficult to evaluate, of their financial difficulties. Ibn Rāʾiḳ was said to be the first to set up a toll-house at the very gates of Baghdād. It was naturally the Būyids who in particular made repeated efforts to introduce in ʿIrāḳ a system similar to that of the Fāṭimids; ʿAḍud al-dawla, the best organizer of the dynasty, and his immediate successors tried to impose dues on the fine textile products which were the livelihood of great numbers of Baghdād artisans: popular riots compelled them finally to abandon the project, and the same was true of the attempt to place dues on mills, etc. In the time of the Būyids, Baṣra was notorious for the severity of its *ḍarāʾib*, as was Fārs; in Īrān, on the other hand, Iṣfahān in particular and the whole territory of the Sāmānids had moderate *ḍarāʾib*.

This very diversity raises a problem. It is indeed found in all sections of the fiscal organization, which was adapted to economic conditions and inherited different traditions, according to the region. But here there is another point. In principle, the Muslim has the right to pay his *zakāt* direct to the "poor", and if, as happened in fact, he paid it to specialized agents, it was understood that the money had to go direct to the true beneficiaries, and not pass into the coffers of the State, which was taken to imply that it was spent on the spot and not centralized in the capital; furthermore, we have indicated that various taxes had to be regarded as *ḥimāya*, which clearly meant that the beneficiaries were those who provided this *ḥimāya*, the local authorities. It can hardly be doubted that the police, either in their official form as *shurṭa*, or as *aḥdāth* militia etc. were the recipients in particular of the proceeds of certain taxes in particular. From all this it emerges that the *Bayt al-Māl* was not the recipient of all the taxes that we have noted. We must not, however, go too far in the opposite direction. In fact, all the *mukūs* abolished by Saladin had very clearly been profitable to his treasury, and it was no less clear that, to swell his own fortunes, ʿAḍud al-dawla in Baghdād made the fiscal efforts to which we have referred. Customs, which affected Muslims and non-Muslims alike, were in fact regarded as being unrelated to *zakāt* and profited the Treasury. The same was true of the proceeds from rents. However, it was a principle of the Muslim fiscal administration that local expenditure was met from the proceeds of local taxes, only the surplus being sent to the Treasury; the latter did not provide any means of evaluation or control for the *ḍarāʾib*, or for the *kharādj* and other basic taxes. In fact, without exception, the *ḍarāʾib* do not appear in the ʿAbbāsid "budgets" that still survive. However, the proceeds from certain *ḍarāʾib* perhaps formed part of the revenues of the caliph's or sovereign's private treasury, with which he thus contributed to the obligatory "good works".

Economic and international circumstances have sometimes brought about appreciable modifications in the system of *ḍarāʾib* and, more particularly, customs. Al-Ghazālī granted that the tariff could be lowered, even for infidels, if it was advantageous to the community to encourage the import of certain goods. From the 6th/12th century, this was in fact the object of the treaties concluded with the "Franks", setting up differential tariffs according to the goods, and sometimes even conferring on those nations' merchants advantages superior to those legally enjoyed by the Muslims. Naturally, this was not a practice peculiar to the Muslim States: Byzantium concluded similar treaties. It appears indeed that certain Muslim groups like the *Kārimī*s with the Indian Ocean trade were allowed to enjoy preferential tariffs at the end of the Middle Ages (according to the *Mulakhkhaṣ*, see *Bibl.*).

Bibliography: neither *fiḳh* works nor papyri

provide documentation on the aspect of financial history considered here (apart from the doctrinal definition of commercial *zakāt* and taxes on the non-Muslims which *fiḳh* approximates to it). Information is to be found either in geographers such as Muḳaddasī or, for certain countries, in various chroniclers and authors of technical treatises on administration, of which only a few examples can be quoted here; for Mesopotamia, Dionysius of Tell-Mahré, Syriac Chronicle, ed. trans. J. B. Chabot (see Cl. Cahen, *Fiscalité*, etc., in *Arabica*, 1954), Miskawayh, *Tad̲j̲ārib*, ed. trans. Margouliouth (*The eclipse of the Abbasid Caliphate*), with sequel by Abū S̲h̲udjāʿ Rud̲h̲awārī; for Egypt, in addition naturally to the materials in Maḳrīzī, *K̲h̲iṭaṭ*, particularly i, 103 ff., Ibn Mammātī, *Ḳawānīn al-dawāwīn*, ed. Atiya 1943, Nābulusī, *Ak̲h̲bār al-Fayyūm* ed. B. Moritz (see Cl. Cahen, *Impôts du Fayyum*, in *Arabica*, 1956; for Arabia, G. Wiet, *Un Décret du sultan Malik Ashraf à la Mecque*, in *Mélanges Massignon*, III, 1957, and in particular the Yemenī *Mulak̲h̲k̲h̲aṣ al-fitan*, on which see the article by Cl. Cahen and R. B. Serjeant in *Arabica*, 1957; on Syria, Kamāl al-Dīn b. al-ʿAdīm, *Zubda*, ed. S. Dahan, i, 163 ff. (on the treaty of 358/969 with Byzantium), and ʿIzz al-Dīn b. S̲h̲addād, *al-Aʿlāḳ*, ed. D. Sourdel, 150 (see Sauvaget, *Alep*, 253-4), and, for the D̲j̲azīra, the same, provisionally in *REI*, 1934, 111-2. The treaties with the Franks are given in Mas Latrie, *Traités ... concernant les relations des Chrétiens avec ... l'Afrique septentrionale*, 1866; G. Müller, *Documenti sulle relazioni delle citta toscane coll'Oriente*, 1879; Tafel and Thomas, *Urkunden zur älteren Handelsgeschichte Venedigs*, 3 vols. of *Fontes Rerum Austriacarum*, 2nd. s., xii-xiv, 1856-57. For the later Middle Ages, see the Italian technical treaties such as the *Pratica della Mercatura* by Pegolotti, ed. A. Evans, Cambridge Mass. 1936.

As regards the modern literature, besides the information given earlier in Aghnides, *Mohammedan theories of finance*, New York 1916; A. Mez, *Renaissance*, viii; R. Heffening, *Das Islamische Fremdenrecht*, 1925, various works by Arabic-speaking scholars should now be added: ʿAbd al-ʿAzīz Dūrī, *Taʾrīk̲h̲ al-ʿIrāḳ al-iḳtiṣādī fi 'l-ḳarn al-rābiʿ al-hid̲j̲rī*, Bag̲h̲dād 1948; ʿAbbās al-ʿAzzāwī, *Taʾrīk̲h̲ al-ḍarāʾib al-ʿirāḳiyya*, Bag̲h̲dād 1959; M. ʿAwwād, *al-Maʾāṣir fi 'l-Islām*, Bag̲h̲dād 1950; Rās̲h̲id al-Barawī, *Ḥālat Miṣr al-iḳtiṣādiyya fī ʿahd al-Fāṭimiyyīn*, Cairo 1943.

(Cl. Cahen)

(2) — West. The history of fiscal systems in the Mag̲h̲rib is still to be written, and perhaps may never be written. The texts are few and difficult to interpret, the terminology vague. The writers show little interest in the subject and apart from off-handed and scattered references restrict their remarks to conventional statements such as that "Such-and-such a king, on his accession, abolished illegal taxes and imposed only those allowed by the S̲h̲arīʿa". Scholars have fought shy of this unrewarding topic. The present writer has made an attempt to handle the subject for the period ending with the collapse of the Almohade régime (*see Bibliography*) and R. Brunschvig appears to have exhausted it for the Ḥafṣids. References apart from these are laconic. In any case it appears to be unlikely that more material would make the picture clearer, at least for the first few centuries of Muslim rule, simply because the subject actually is vague. The turbulent history of the country gave no opportunity for the establishment of a lasting fiscal tradition. Tax-collection, like the other functions of government, was generally organized *ad hoc*. The government took what revenue it could as opportunity offered without overmuch scruple. The S̲h̲arīʿa was generally acknowledged to be the only proper regulator of fiscal methods, but it was just as generally ignored in practice. It may be supposed that the townspeople as a rule came under a more or less regular taxation system; but the country people, and particularly the nomads, were less accessible to the central administration, who could often extract tribute from them only by sending out what were virtually military expeditions often manned by outsiders not bound by any feeling of *esprit de corps* with the taxpayers. Some taxes were, according to the S̲h̲arīʿa, to be collected in kind, but for N. Africa we have little more than hints to show that, at one time or another, the government accepted payment in this form. There is some evidence that certain taxes were occasionally farmed out, but this seems in the Mag̲h̲rib to be a late development first reported under the Almoravids and sporadically mentioned thereafter. There is no clear distinction between the privy purse and the public treasury.

Governors under the Caliphs.—There are no contemporary texts. They collected *ṣadaḳa* and *ʿus̲h̲ūr* and *d̲j̲izya* but there is no clear indication of what these terms implied; later writers tend to interpret them in the light of legal doctrines which became established later. It seems as though the multitude of newly-converted Muslims led to the same difficulties in Ifrīḳiya as it had in ʿIrāḳ 20 years before, and there was an ill-fated attempt by Yazīd b. Abī Muslim to deal with them as Ḥad̲j̲d̲j̲ād̲j̲ had done. In the earliest days the *k̲h̲ums* had some importance and there were even attempts to treat the vanquished populations themselves as booty.

Ag̲h̲labids.—New tax names (*maẓālim, ḳabālāt*) appear, without definitions, and a distinct reference to the conversion of the tithe from a proportion, in kind, of produce, to a fixed sum per area.

Idrīsids.—Little information. The Jews of Fez were obliged to pay the *d̲j̲izya*.

Rustamids.—This period affords the only (and probably idealized) account of the distribution of the agricultural produce accruing from taxation.

Fāṭimids.—The taxation system seems to take on a better-organized aspect, though this may be an illusion due to the nature of the sources. For the first time we hear of a cadastral survey and of *tawẓīf* or *tawzīʿ* ("apportionment" of tax?), and an attempt to establish the fiscal system on a rational and regular footing. Customs or *octroi* dues are first mentioned.

Zīrids, Hammādids, Berber Principalities (Mag̲h̲rāwa, B. Ifren, etc.), Almoravids.—Information is very sparse, but Ibn K̲h̲allikān describes the Almoravids' tax-collecting detachments composed of European mercenaries.

Almohades.—ʿAbd al-Muʾmin is traditionally remembered as the one who introduced *k̲h̲arād̲j̲* into the Mag̲h̲rib. However this may be understood it probably symbolizes some striking innovation on his part. These is in fact an obscure account by Ibn Abī Zarʿ of a land-survey which preceded the levying of *k̲h̲arād̲j̲*.

The *ṣāḥib al-as̲h̲g̲h̲āl* (first mentioned in connexion with Manṣūr) was an important official in charge of finance. There seems to have been only one at any given time and he is always mentioned among the high officers of state. The *mus̲h̲rif*, on the other hand, was a provincial official whose duties are not defined (but see the Ḥafṣid *mus̲h̲rif* below). We hear of *k̲h̲azāʾin* and *buyūt al-amwāl* "treasuries" but can only make guesses as to what these terms indicate.

Ḥafṣids.—A passage in Zarkas̲h̲ī (text 102, tr. 188) indicates a vast proliferation of taxes but in fact there is nothing to indicate that they were not in fact just as numerous in former times. The Ḥafṣids took over the title of *ṣāḥib al-as̲h̲g̲h̲āl*, and presumably his office, from the Almohades. Later this official is referred to as *munaffid̲h̲*. His subordinates are called *ʿummāl*. The *mus̲h̲rif* is in evidence here also but now as head of the maritime customs, with his subordinates called *mus̲h̲tag̲h̲il*. There were *octroi* duties (*maks*) collected by an official (he may have been a tax-farmer) called *makkās*. Tax-farming seems to have played a very minor rôle in the Ḥafṣids' fiscal policies. Many communities escaped close central control and were taxed only intermittently, when forced. One receives the impression that the taxes did not bear unduly hardly on the taxpayer; the system seems in general to have been mild and regular.

Marīnids.—Since the Marīnids inherited the Almohade machinery *en bloc* presumably their taxation system resembled that of the Almohades; but information is almost entirely lacking. Under Abū Saʿīd, however, tax-farming (if ʿUmarī is to be believed) was the rule; his successor Abu 'l-Ḥasan "abolished the illegal taxes". (*Masālik al-abṣār*, tr. Gaudefroy-Demombynes, 170-1).

Beylerbeys, Pas̲h̲as, and Deys of Algiers.—Little is known, but the pillaging expeditions (*maḥalla*) sent out by the Beys into the countryside may perhaps be looked upon as part of a fiscal system. The Turkish government exploited the country to its utmost with the aid of *mak̲h̲zan* tribes and military colonies (*zmāla*) who were exempted from taxation; but its power hardly extended beyond the chief towns and the main lines of communication.

Ḥasanī Sharīfs (Saʿdīs).—During the days of the last Marīnids and the B. Waṭṭāṣ much of Morocco had lost the habit of paying taxes. The first Saʿdīs seem to have levied only an occasional tax in kind called *nāʾiba*, but later this became more or less permanent and payable in cash. The *k̲h̲arād̲j̲* was re-introduced, not without revival of an old controversy concerning the legal status of the lands of the Mag̲h̲rib. Certain monopolies were farmed out. and the Sultan took a percentage of the proceeds of piracy. Taxation was not only crushingly heavy, but it had extortion added to it. The Ḥasanī *mak̲h̲zan* is a prime specimen of a government organized solely to exploit the resources of the country for its own profit.

Filālī S̲h̲arīfs (ʿAlawīs).—Mawlāy Muḥammad (1171/1757-1204/1789) is said to have established sundry market and commodity taxes, but it is difficult to believe that this was really an innovation. At Fez, perhaps elsewhere also, they were sometimes farmed out to the governor. Apart from these indirect taxes collectively called *mustafād* the treasury received the "legal" taxes *zakāt* and *ʿus̲h̲ūr* (the distinction between these two terms, originally synonymous, is not clear), and the *nāʾiba* mentioned above. Customs dues and the *hadāyā* (customary "gifts" to the Sultan at the feasts) were received directly by the Sultan. The authority of the tax-collectors was reinforced by contingents of the *gīs̲h̲* (*i.e.*, *d̲j̲ays̲h̲*) tribes, who were exempt from tax.

Beys of Tunis.—The subject is obscure and still awaits the investigation for which the sources would probably prove quite abundant, but the picture seems to be similar in general to that under the Beys of Algiers. Though from about 1112/1700 onwards the Beys were accepted as a national hereditary dynasty they and their administration continued to be a parasite on the Tunisian body politic, concerned more with exacting the maximum for their private profit than with maintaining a sound and equitable fiscal system. Their failure in this respect and their indebtedness to foreign creditors was one of the main causes of the imposition of the French protectorate in 1882.

Bibliography: Few writings are devoted exclusively to fiscal matters. The list below includes most of those which attempt to deal with the topic in any detail.

R. Brunschvig, *La Berbérie orientale sous les Ḥafṣides, des origines à la fin du XVme siècle*, 2 vols., Paris 1940-7, ii, 66 ff.; J. F. P. Hopkins, *Early Muslim government in Barbary*, London 1958; Michaux-Bellaire, *Les impôts marocains*, in *Archives Marocaines*, i; idem, *L'organisation des finances au Maroc*, in *Archives Marocaines*, xi; Lécureuil, *Historique des douanes au Maroc*, in *Arch. Mar.*, xv; Donon, *Le régime douanier du Maroc et le développement du commerce marocain jusqu'à nos jours*, Paris; J. Ganiage, *Les origines du protectorat français en Tunisie*, Paris 1959.

(J. F. P. Hopkins)

(3) — Ottoman Empire. In the Ottoman system the taxes were divided into two groups, *ḥuḳūḳ-i s̲h̲arʿiyye* and *rusūm-i ʿurfiyye*. The former included *ʿus̲h̲r* [*q.v.*] or *ondalıḳ*, *k̲h̲arād̲j̲*, *d̲j̲izya* [*q.v.*], *k̲h̲ums-i s̲h̲arʿī* levied on mi... rals mined and *g̲h̲anīma* [*q.v.*]. Other Islamic taxes objected to by some legists, such as *maks* [*q.v.*], were included rather among the *ʿurfī* taxes by the Ottomans (for the *s̲h̲arʿī* taxes dealt with by the Ottoman legists see Mollā K̲h̲usrew, *Durar al-ḥukkām fī s̲h̲arh g̲h̲urar al-aḥkām*, Istanbul 1258, 129-43). On the other hand they added to the *ʿus̲h̲r* an *ʿurfī* tax called *salāriyye* or *salārlîk* which raised it from one-tenth to one-eighth, and collected some additional dues, *rusūm* or *ʿādāt*, on hives, fisheries, hay, and vegetables. Also *d̲j̲izya* was somewhat modified in its application in the Ottoman empire.

The *ʿurfī* taxes [see ʿURF] were those assessed by the Sultan and, in origin, were mostly pre-Ottoman local taxes. They were recorded by the Ottoman *taḥrīr* [*q.v.*] *emīn*s and proclaimed in the *ḳānūn-nāme*s (see ḲĀNŪN) of the sand̲j̲aḳs. With the development of *ʿurf* this kind of taxation grew in importance, though from the 10th/16th century there appeared a strong tendency to accommodate these taxes, at least formally, to the *S̲h̲arīʿa*.

The *ʿurfī* taxes, generally called *rusūm* or *ʿādāt*, were divided into various categories: 1. Up to the late 10th/16th century the basic *ʿurfī* taxes were *čift resmi* and *ispend̲j̲e* [*qq.v.*]. The latter was paid by every adult non-Muslim at the rate of 25 *akče* [*q.v.*] per person. Widows paid it at the rate of 6 *akče* under the name of *bîwe resmi*. 2. Of the taxes levied on livestock the most important was *ʿādet-i ag̲h̲nām* or *ḳoyun resmi* which was usually 1 *akče* for two sheep, collected directly for the central treasury. The pasturage due, called *yaylaḳ resmi*, *otlaḳ resmi* or *resm-i čerāg̲h̲ah* was usually one sheep or its money equivalent for each flock of sheep of 300 which passed over to another *sandjaḳ*, *ḳaḍā* or *tīmār*. It was paid to the person holding the land as *tīmār* or *khāṣṣ* (see TĪMĀR). 3. The dues called *bād-i hawā* [*q.v.*] or *ṭayyārāt* were principally such dues levied on occasional cases as *djerā'im* or *ḳanluḳ*, fines, *ʿarūsāne* or *gerdek resmi* or *nikāh akčesi* bridegroom due, *yawa* and *ḳačḳun*, dues paid while recovering runaway cattle or slaves, *ṭapu resmi*, a due paid on entering into possession of a *čiftlik* [*q.v.*]. *Djerā'im* was also called *niyābet*, because for each case a decision of a *nā'ib* appointed by the local *ḳāḍī* was necessary. 4. The principal imposts on trade were *bādj* or *tamgha*, market dues, paid per load; *ḳapan* (*ḳabbān*) and *mīzān* or *terāzū rusūmu*, duties levied at the public scales. There were also *gümrük*, customs duties, *gečid resmi*, tolls levied at mountain passes and river fords, *köprü ḥaḳḳi*, bridge-toll. 5. The state established monopolies on the trade of such commodities as salt, rice, wax-candles, soap, sesame and lumber. The monopoly of minting was also a large source of revenue [see DĀR AL-ḌARB]. 6. The *ʿawāriḍ-i dīwāniyye we tekālīf-i ʿurfiyye* [see ʿAWĀRIḌ] were in origin certain services which the state required from its subjects to fulfil in emergency, but *bedel*, cash substitute for them, could be given instead and from the late 10th/16th century this became a regular tax collected directly for the central treasury. 7. The fees paid by persons for whom a document, *berāt*, *tedhkire*, *ṣūret-i defter* etc., was issued at a government office were another important source of revenue for the treasury. The rates were carefully fixed by law. The tax collectors or other officials sent by the Sultan were authorized to collect *ʿā'idāt*, fees and remunerations, for themselves, and these in the period of the decline of the Empire became the source of many abuses.

In addition to these *ʿurfī* taxes there were some dues in contradiction to the *Sharīʿa* or to Ottoman administrative principles, which, nevertheless, continued to be levied either by the state or *tīmār*-holders as *bidʿat*s. For example the treasury could not give up the large revenue obtained from the *bidʿat-i khinzīr* or *domuz bidʿati*, pig-tax. There were, however, some *bidʿat*s called *bidʿat-i merdūde* ('rejected innovation') which were absolutely prohibited as against *bidʿat-i maʿrūfe* ('acknowledged innovation').

After its conquest each *sandjaḳ* had its own *ḳānūn* embodying the *ʿurfī* taxes. Most of them were taken over from the pre-Ottoman regimes, but after a period of adjustment the Ottomans usually extended their own *ḳānūn-i ʿOthmānī* with typically Ottoman taxation. It seems to have formed still under strong local influences, Saldjūḳid and Byzantine in western Anatolia and Thrace in the late 8th/14th century. Its main characteristics can be seen in the *ḳānūnnāme*s of western Anatolia which were extended to eastern Anatolia toward 947/1540. These characteristics were simplicity and the policy of abolition of all kinds of feudal services and dues. An excessive burden of local and feudal dues was replaced by a few taxes such as *čift resmi*, *ispendje* and *ʿādet-i aghnām*. It was provided that no tax should be levied twice under different names. This system did much in consolidating the Ottoman rule in Anatolia and Rumeli. But when in the late 10th/16th century a profound economic and financial crisis shook the established order, and the rates of *ʿawāriḍ*, *djizya* and the other taxes paid in cash were raised in an attempt to adjust them to the depreciation of the currency (see *Belleten*, no. 60), and and the exactions of the *ʿaskerī* class [see ʿASKARĪ] in the provinces became more and more arbitrary, the whole Ottoman tax system underwent a fundamental change.

In the collection of taxes two basic systems were followed, the *ḥawāla* and *muḳāṭaʿa* or *iltizām* [*qq.v.*] systems. *Aʿshār* [see ʿUSHR] as well as *čift resmi*, *ispendje*, *bād-i hawā* and most of the other *ʿurfī* taxes were assigned as *tīmār*s to the members of the *ʿaskerī* class who collected them themselves in their respective *tīmār* lands. In view of the difficulties for the central government in collecting taxes in kind, such as *aʿshār*, and of the lack of adequate means of communication, this system was maintained as the best possible method at that time. In essence *tīmār* was a form of *ḥawāla*. The distribution and assignment of *tīmār*s were made by *taḥrīr* and all this made a vast department of financial administration called *daftar-i khāḳānī* [*q.v.*] under a *nishāndjī* [*q.v.*]. The total sum of the revenues in this section was about 200 million *akče* or about 3.5 million gold ducats in 933/1527-934/1528. Income unrecorded in the *defter*s [see BAŞVEKÂLET ARŞIVI] was to be collected by officers of the Sultan called *mewḳūfdju* or *mewḳūfātdjī*, under the *defterdār*, directly for the treasury.

Except for the *aʿshār*, *sharʿī* taxes, *resm-i berāt* and *tedhkire* and *bayt al-māl* (that is, escheated properties), *mewḳūfāt*, and the revenues from the imperial domains [see KHĀṢṢ] were collected for the central treasury, *khizāne-i ʿāmire*, either directly by *ḳul*s, men of slave origin at the Porte, or through the *iltizām* system.

The following is an official statement of the revenues from these sources for the provinces of Rumeli, Anadolu, Karaman, Dhulkadriye and Rūm in the fiscal year of 933/1527-934/1528 (*İstanbul Üniv. İktisat Fakültesi Mecmuası*, XV, 1-4, 269).

muḳāṭaʿāt	71,524,055 *akče*
djizya	46,056,305 *akče*
resm-i berāt and *tedhkire*	1,897,625 *akče*
bayt al-māl, *mewḳūfāt* and *mā-beyn*	1,928,257 *akče*

This was about one fifth of the total amount of the state revenues in the same year. The most important item in it, *muḳāṭaʿāt*, included the revenues of the Imperial domains (*Khāṣṣ-i Humāyūn*), state monopolies, *khums-i sharʿī*, customs duties and imposts on trade. The *muḳāṭaʿāt* were usually farmed out to the *mültezim*s or *muḳāṭaʿa ʿāmili* under the system of *muḳāṭaʿa* [*q.v.*], and their accounts were kept in the *muḳāṭaʿa defterleri* in the *defterkhāne-i ʿāmire* (one of the oldest and most important of these *defter*s covering the reign of Meḥemmed II is in the *Başvekâlet* Archives, Istanbul, nos. 176, 6222, 7387).

The *iltizām* system was essential for the Ottoman finances from the beginnings of the state and was also used by the big *tīmār*-holders. Upon an order, *ḥawāla*, of the Sultan payments were made for state expenses directly by the *mültezim*s. From the 10th/16th century onwards, the *iltizām* system became dominant throughout the empire and the *muḳāṭaʿa*s began to be farmed out for much longer periods; by the 12th/18th century the governors of some provinces became *mültezim*s at the same time, which made them virtually autonomous. As the central authority weakened the abuses of the system grew until in 1255/1839, by the rescript of Gülkhāne, *iltizām*, termed a 'destructive instrument', was abolished. The system of *emānet*, a system of collection of *muḳāṭaʿa* revenues directly by salaried employees called *emīn*, was made general and *muḥaṣṣils*, financial heads in the *sandjaḳs* [*q.v.*] with full responsibilities, were appointed. But the decrease in the state revenues under the new system compelled the government to restore *iltizām* which lasted to the end of the Empire.

Bibliography: *Ḳānūnnāme-i Āl-i ʿOthmān*, ed. M. Arif, supplements to *TOEM*, 1330-31; Fr.-Greifenhorst Kraelitz, *Ḳānūnnāme Sultan Mehmeds des Eroberers*, in *MOG*, i, 13-48; *ʿOthmānlī Ḳānūnnāmeleri*, in *MTM*, i-iii; Ö. L. Barkan, *XV. ve XVI. asırlarda Osmanlı imparatorluğunda ziraî ekonominin hukukî ve malî esasları, I:Kanunlar*, Istanbul 1943; O. N. Ergin, *Medjelle-i Umūr-i Belediyye*, i, Ist. 1922; A. Refik Altınay, *16. asırda Istanbul Hayatı*, Ist. 1935; L. Fekete, *Die Siyāqat-Schrift in der türkischen Finanzverwaltung*, 2 vols., Budapest 1955; Ö. L. Barkan, *Osmanlı imparatorluğu "Bütce" lerine dair notlar, Ist. Üniv. Iktisat Fakültesi Mecmuası*, xv, 1-4 (1953-4), 238-329; xix, 1-4 (1957-8), 219-332; idem, *Bazı büyük şehirlerde eşya ve yiyecek fiatlarının tesbit ve teftişi hususlarını tanzim eden kanunlar, TV*, vii/40, ix, 168-177; J. Kabrda, *Les anciens registres turcs des cadis de Sofia et de Vidin et leur importance pour l'histoire de la Bulgarie, ArO*, xix, (1951), 329-92; R. Anhegger and H. Inalcık, *Ḳānūnnāme-i Sulṭānī ber Mūceb-i ʿÖrf-i ʿOsmānī*, Ankara 1956; N. Beldiceanu. *Actes de Mehmed II et de Bayezid II* .., Paris-Hague 1960; M. de M. D'Ohsson, *Tableau général de l'empire othoman*, vii, Paris 1824, 233-73; Hammer-Purgstall, *Staatsverfassung*; A. Heidborn, *Les Finances ottomanes*, Vienna-Leipzig, 1912; Gibb-Bowen, i/2, 1-69; R. Mantran, *Règlements fiscaux ottomans. La police des marchés de Stamboul au début du XVI*ᵉ *siècle*, in *CT* IV, 1956, 213-41; idem, *Un document sur* l'Iḥtisāb *de Stamboul à la fin du XVII*ᵉ *siècle*, in *Mélanges Louis Massignon*, iii, 127-49; R. Mantran, and J. Sauvaget, *Règlements fiscaux ottomans*; *les provinces syriennes*, Beirut 1951; B. Lewis, *Studies in the Ottoman Archives-I*, in *BSOAS*, xvi, 1934, 469-501; B. A. Cvetkova, *Impôts extraordinaires et redevances à l'État dans les territoires bulgares sous la domination turque* (in Bulgarian), Sofia 1958; idem, *Contribution à l'étude des impôts extraordinaires en Bulgarie sous la domination turque, RO*, xxiii (1959), 57-65; idem, *The System of Tax-farming* (*iltizam*) *in the Ottoman Empire during the 16th-18th centuries with reference to the Bulgarian lands*, (in Bulgarian) in *Izvestiya na Instituta za pravni nauki*, Bulgarian Academy of Sciences, xi/2, 1960, 195-223; H. Inalcık, *Osmanlılarda Raiyyet Rüsûmu, Belleten* xcii (1959), 575-610.

(HALIL İNALCIK)

(4) — Post-Ottoman Egypt. In the years immediately preceding the Napoleonic invasion of Egypt in 1798, the Egyptian government's principal source of revenue was derived from numerous taxes levied on the land. These fell into three main categories: (1) *al-māl al-ḥurr*; (2) *māl* (or *khidmat*) *al-kushūfiyya*; and (3) supplementary taxes, the *muḍāf* and *barrānī*. The government farmed out all these land taxes to *multazims* who collected them through their agents, most of whom were members of the Copt corporation.

The first of these taxes, *al-māl al-ḥurr*, was composed of the *mīrī* and the *fāʾiẓ*. The *mīrī* was a fixed tax, part of which was destined for the Sultan's Private Treasury in Istanbul while the remainder was kept in Egypt to support the cost of local government. The *fāʾiẓ* went to the concessionaires of *iltizāms* (tax farms), the amount of this tax being fixed by the terms of the concession. To increase their profits, the *multazims* eventually demanded the payment of extraordinary taxes (*muḍāf* and *barrānī*), collecting them regularly despite their illegality. The *māl al-kushūfiyya* paid for the military and administrative expenses within the Egyptian provinces. All these taxes were paid either in specie or in kind.

The government's other sources of revenue included a succession tax (*ḥulwān*) paid by those heirs of *multazims* who desired to inherit tax farms; the *djizya* [*q.v.*]; fixed tax on customs duties, which the tax farmers of customs were required to remit to the government; a tax levied on certain government officials whose functions involved the collection of recognized dues; duties on boats navigating Egyptian waters; duty on the corporation of goldsmiths; various levies on trades, merchants, and *wikālas*, *i.e.*, buildings designed for the reception of merchants and their goods; the proceeds from grants of tax farms on the sale or manufacture of various products; and profits from the mint. About a quarter of the revenue obtained from these sources was sent to Istanbul along with the *mīrī* on land and some Egyptian produce for use in the *saray* and naval arsenal.

This fiscal system remained substantially the same during the three-year period of the French occupation of Egypt. Napoleon announced shortly after his arrival in Cairo in July 1798 that he wished to change none of the existing institutions or traditional taxes but planned only to eliminate arbitrary exactions and to introduce a regular system of tax collection. Indeed, the only change he made at the outset was to join the lands formerly held by Mamlūk *multazims* to the state domain for the profit of the French Republic (approximately two-thirds of the land of Egypt). Napoleon then confirmed the non-Mamlūk *multazims* in their *iltizāms*. Taxes continued to be collected by the Copts, under the supervision of French inspectors.

When Muḥammad ʿAlī became Pasha of Egypt in 1805, he altered the fiscal system radically by expropriating the *multazims* and the beneficiaries (*mutaṣarrif*) of *al-rizaḳ al-aḥbāsiyya*, state lands which had been illegally endowed with the characteristics of *waḳf* property. *Waḳfs* on houses and gardens, *i.e.*, endowments based on *milk* property, were not affected, however, since they were considered sound or legal *waḳfs*. As compensation for their loss, the *multazims* received a pension and the right to cultivate their *waṣiyya* lands (the portion of the *iltizāms* which had been assigned to *multazims* for their exclusive enjoyment). Neither was heritable; upon the death of the *multazims*, these pensions ceased and the *waṣiyya* lands reverted to the state. The beneficiaries of *rizḳa* lands also received a life pension while the state assumed the responsibility of maintaining mosques and charitable institutions, which had depended for their support upon revenues from these lands.

A cadastre of all cultivated (*maʿmūr*) lands was carried out in 1813-14; registers were prepared, listing the names of landholders, the quantity of land held, and the amount of the *mīrī*, now a single tax replacing the former complex schedule of taxes and rated according to the fertility of the land and ease of irrigation. The only lands excluded from the cadastral registers were the *waṣiyya* lands of the expropriated *multazims* and the uncultivated or uncultivable land (the so-called *abʿādiyya* land). The rate of the land tax did not remain fixed at the 1813-14 level, but was augmented periodically as the Pasha's need for revenue mounted; nor did all the land remain under direct government supervision. Instead, Muḥammad ʿAlī assigned estates to members of his family, to favourites, and to foreigners. Some of these estates were known as *čiftlik* [*q.v.*]; others as *abʿādiyya* (estates reclaimed from lands uncultivated at the time of the 1813-14 cadastre and granted on favourable terms); and *ʿuhda*s, estates consisting of bankrupt villages whose taxes were collected by their new landholders (*mutaʿahhid*s) rather than by members of the government hierarchy. The substance of the land (*raḳaba*) of all these estates was retained by the state, the landholders possessing only usufructuary rights (*taṣarruf*).

Along with his land reforms, Muḥammad ʿAlī also monopolized all money crops (cotton in particular), creating in consequence of this new policy an important source of revenue for the government.

Other innovations, as well as the retention of taxes antedating Muḥammad ʿAlī, are reflected in the extant budgets of this period. Receipts fell into three major categories: (1) direct taxes; (2) customs and *appaltos*, farms for the collection of duties on sundry items granted by the government for one or more years; and (3) profits from agriculture and industry. Direct taxes incorporated taxes on property, i.e., *mīrī* (land tax), tax on date trees, on successions to city properties and gardens, duties on *wikāla*s, bazaars, and houses; taxes on persons, called *furdat al-ruʾūs*, a personal tax amounting to 3 per cent on known or supposed revenue of all the inhabitants of Egypt, which was paid by all government employees, including even foreigners, by Egyptian employees of non-government establishments, by *fallāḥīn*, and by artisans and merchants, the *d̲j̲izya*, and a duty on dancers, prostitutes, jugglers, and conjurers; taxes on things, i.e., duties on boats navigating Egyptian waters, fish of the Nile, salt, fruit, butchers' shops, hides, tallow, smelting of silver, galloons for goldsmiths, animals, irrigation implements (*sāḳiya*s and *s̲h̲ādūf*s), exportation of cereals from Egypt, tax on textile looms, stamp duty, quarantine and lock dues, profits of the mint and the Transit, and miscellaneous duties; octrois, *i.e.*, octroi on eatables and duty on grain entering Cairo.

Revenues from customs and *appalto*s included customs collected at Damietta, Rosetta, Būlāḳ, Old Cairo, Deraoui, Asyūṭ, Suez, D̲j̲idda, al-Ḳuṣayr, and for merchandise coming overland from Syria; and *appalto*s on fish of Lake al-Manzala, Lake Ḳārūn, and Baḥr Yūsuf, on wines, spirits, and liqueurs, on senna, on oil from linseed and other seeds. Profits from agriculture and industry were obtained from the sale of cotton, sugar, indigo, opium, henna, honey and wax, safflower, flax, linseed, seed (sesame, lettuce, and *Carthamus*), raw silk, rosewater, rice, tobacco, wheat, beans, barley, maize, lentils, cotton goods, linen goods, silks, calicos and handkerchiefs, raw and tanned hides, horns, natron (carbonate of soda), nitre, sal-ammoniac, lime, plaster, tiles, and mats. In addition, the government obtained revenues from freight carried by government boats, gums (from Sinnār), coffee (from al-Yaman), and elephant tusks.

In general, Muḥammad ʿAlī's fiscal system endured until the British occupation of Egypt. Ibrāhīm Pas̲h̲a introduced nothing new during his short reign, while ʿAbbās altered the system very little, although he economized on those projects begun by his grandfather which seemed wasteful. He abolished those *ʿuhda*s whose proprietors had failed to comply with the terms of their concessions, and suppressed the octrois. He also relieved the tax burden of the peasants by removing a large part of the *furdat al-ruʾūs*.

His successor, Saʿīd Pas̲h̲a, changed the existing fiscal system, somewhat, by ending the monopoly system and opening the country to free trade, allowing foreign merchants to deal directly with the Egyptian peasants. To compensate for the loss of revenue from government monopolies, he introduced a new policy regarding land taxes. Former tax-free lands were now taxed, some with the *k̲h̲arād̲j̲*, and others with the *ʿus̲h̲r*, the rate of taxes being substantially increased as well. In 1853, during ʿAbbās's reign, the revenues from the land tax had amounted to 348,398 purses or £ 1,741,995; by 1858, Saʿīd had increased them to 501,898 purses or £ 2,509,492, almost a 50 per cent increase on land taxes alone (Green, May 1, 1858, in F.O. 78/1401). In addition, Saʿīd reinstated the entire *furdat al-ruʾūs*, adding it to the land tax.

Saʿīd's Land Law of 1858 introduced an important innovation of long-range significance. Under this law, the right to inherit, mortgage, and retain land permanently was granted to existing landholders, provided they paid their taxes. If these taxes were not paid within five years, the landholders were deprived of their lands permanently. This time limit, imposed by the new law, constituted a real change from traditional practices. Formerly, a peasant who had failed to pay taxes on his *athar* land (land held on usufructuary tenure but passed from father to son for generations) was dispossessed until such time as he was able to meet his obligations. In this way, he could always hope to recover his land, no time limit existing which could for ever alienate him from it. Indeed, the class most favoured by the Land Law of 1858 proved to be that of the rich landholders rather than of the poorer peasants. The ill effects of this law were particularly felt in the next reign. Those peasants who had over-extended their credit during the cotton boom of the 1860's were greatly in debt when the market collapsed at the end of the American Civil War. Consequently, many peasants, unable to pay their taxes, lost their land. To make matters worse, Ismāʿīl's excessive demands deprived still more peasants of their land because of their inability to pay the government. The Khedive took advantage of the peasants' plight to add more and more of their land to his private estates, until he eventually possessed one-fifth of the agricultural land of Egypt, which he exploited for his own profit.

Khedive Ismāʿīl resorted to numerous expedients to increase his revenues. Among these was his *Muḳābala* Law of 1871 which provided that all landholders agreeing to pay six years' taxes in advance would be permanently exempted from 50 per cent of their land tax, whether *k̲h̲arād̲j̲* or *ʿus̲h̲r*. This fiscal device failed to meet Ismāʿīl's expectations because many landholders refused to take advantage of it. Ismāʿīl was no sooner removed from office when the law was abrogated (1880) and taxes reimposed on all land. With the British occupation of the country in 1882, the fiscal functions of the Egyptian government passed into the hands of the British administrators.

Bibliography: Articles by Comte Estève, *Mémoire sur les finances de l'Égypte depuis sa conquête par le sultan Selym Ier, jusqu'à celle du général en chef Bonaparte*, Michel-Ange Lancret, *Mémoire sur le système d'imposition territoriale et sur l'administration des provinces de l'Égypte, dans les dernières années du gouvernement des Mamlouks*, and P. S. Girard, *Mémoire sur l'agriculture, l'industrie et le commerce de l'Égypte*, in *Description de l'Égypte, État Moderne*, 1st ed., Paris, 1809, 1813, 1822; Silvestre de Sacy, *Sur la nature et les révolutions du droit de propriété territoriale en Égypte, depuis la conquête de ce pays par les musulmans jusqu'à l'expédition de François*, published in three parts in *Mémoires de l'Institut Royal de France*, i, Paris 1815, 1-165, v, Paris 1821, 1-75, and vii, Paris 1824, 55-124; ʿAbd al-Raḥmān al-Djabartī, *ʿAdjāʾib al-āthār fi 'l-tarādjim wa 'l-akhbār*, 4 vols., Cairo 1322/1904-5; Gibb-Bowen, i, Chapters V and VI, ii, 40-2; Georges Rigault, *Le Général Abdallah Menou et la dernière phase de l'expédition d'Égypte* (1799-1801), Paris 1911; Helen Anne B. Rivlin, *The Agricultural Policy of Muḥammad ʿAlī in Egypt*, Cambridge, Massachusetts 1961; Boutros Ghali, *Rapport de S. E. Boutros Pacha Ghali, membre de la commission d'enquête de l'impôt foncier, présenté à cette commission le* 18 *février* 1880, in *Répertoire de la législation et de l'administration égyptiennes*, ed. Philippe Gelat, Supplément, Alexandria 1890; Viscount Milner, *England in Egypt*, London 1909; The Earl of Cromer, *Modern Egypt*, London 1908; G. Douin, *Histoire du Règne du Khedive Ismail*, 3 vols., Cairo 1933-41; Pierre Crabitès, *Ismail the Maligned Khedive*, London 1933; David S. Landes, *Bankers and Pashas*, Cambridge, Massachussetts 1958; diplomatic and consular records for Egypt deposited at the Public Record Office in London and in the Archives du ministère des affaires étrangères in Paris. (HELEN RIVLIN)

(5) — Persia. There is, on the whole, a remarkable continuity of practice in the matter of taxation in Persia from early Islamic times down to the 20th century; but whereas there was in early times an attempt to reconcile existing practice with Islamic theory and sporadic efforts to abolish non-sharʿī taxes, after the break with tradition in early Mongol (Ilkhānid) times, in spite of the Islamization of the administration under Ghāzān Khān and his successors, the general tendency was away from the Islamic theory of taxation towards a multiplication of taxes and dues and a greater variety of usage. Moreover, since there was no longer even an outward attempt to make the tax administration conform to the ideal of Islamic theory, the tendency towards arbitrary action increased; but the general principles of the tax system, the methods of assessment and collection, and the main problems to be faced did not vary greatly and such changes as took place prior to the 20th century were of degree rather than of a more fundamental kind. New dynasties and new rulers did not involve fundamental changes in the tax administration. The tax regime of Uzun Ḥasan, laid down between 874/1470 and 882/1477, is alleged still to have been operative in Ṣafawid times. Many oft he main features of the Ķādjār tax administration are already to be seen under the Ṣafawids, the period of Afshār and Zand rule having brought little that was new in the field of taxation. At no time, however, did a uniform system prevail throughout the country. In general the amount of money in circulation was limited; commerce was not highly developed and there was difficulty in transporting and remitting large sums of money, all of which affected the system of administration in general and of taxation in particular. Further, the tendency for the silver currency to depreciate makes it difficult to evaluate accurately the changes which took place in the amount of tax levied and its relative incidence. Money going into the Royal Treasury is alleged by various foreign observers to have been hoarded and seldom to have reappeared in circulation; but as against this the money thus accumulated would seem not infrequently to have been dissipated on military expeditions, accession gratuities to secure the throne against rival claimants, and other emergencies; while the frequency with which the pay of the army and the official classes was in arrears suggests that the treasury was not always as full as might be supposed were the surplus revenue hoarded. In any case by the latter part of the 19th century there was a constant struggle to provide revenue to meet the growing demands of the administration and an extravagant court. No very clear distinction was made between the revenue of the state and the ruler's private income; any surplus eventually found its way into the royal purse. In the Ṣafawid period there was a broad distinction between funds belonging to the state (*māl-i maṣāliḥ*), administered by the *mustawfī al-mamālik* under the Grand Wazir, and the funds belonging to the royal household (*māl-i khāṣṣa*), administered by the *mustawfī* of the *dīwān-i khāṣṣa*, corresponding roughly to the earlier division between the *dīwān* and the *dargāh*. How early this distinction is found is uncertain. Chardin affirms that it was first introduced by Shāh Ṣafī (A.D. 1629-42); in any case there was considerable overlapping between the two divisions. By Ķādjār times the distinction between them such as it was had disappeared. The general tax structure and the broad division into "fixed" taxes (*māl wa djihāt* and later *māliyāt*) and extraordinary levies and requisitions, and the purposes to which the revenue was devoted, namely the payment of the army, salaries of officials, pensions, and the upkeep of the royal court, were largely the same. Whereas, however, under the Ṣafawids large areas of the empire were alienated from the direct control of the central government and little supervision exercised over the tax administration of these areas, there was an attempt under the Ķādjārs to centralize the tax administration; but the farming of the taxes to governors and others made nonsense of this and by the 20th century chaos prevailed in the tax administration. Collection was profoundly unsatisfactory; such checks and controls as had been devised had broken down, and the system was oppressive in its operation.

The most important of the "fixed" taxes were those levied on the land or its produce. A great variety of practice existed as regards both the method and rate of assessment. Moreover the extent of the area subject to the payment of land tax varied considerably. Much of the land as stated above was alienated from the direct control of the government in the form of *tiyūl*s and *suyūrghāl*s, which carried full or partial immunity from taxation. The latter were granted mainly on crown lands, *waķf* land, and dead lands. According to Chardin the the Ṣafawid empire was divided into "provinces" (*mamālik*), *i.e.*, indirectly administered areas, and directly administered territory (*khāṣṣa*); the governors of the former, he affirms, remitted to the central government only a lump sum by way of a present (*pīshkash*) at the new year and a proportion of the produce and products of the province for the use of the royal court and workshops, retaining the remainder of the provincial revenue for the expenses of the provincial administration. To what extent such provincial governors under the Ṣafawids and those of the provincial governors who farmed the revenues of their provinces under the Ḳād̲j̲ārs exercised freedom of action in the assessment and collection of taxes is not entirely clear. In either period the *mustawfī*s of the central government prepared and sent, usually annually, to the provinces detailed assessments of the provincial districts, known as *dastūr al-ʿamal*, according to which, or on the basis of which, the *mustawfī*s in the provinces allocated the tax demand among the provincial population. It is also not clear to what extent *waḳf* land was exempt from taxation. It seems in any case unlikely that those *waḳf*s of which the ruling monarch was the *mutawallī* paid tax; Curzon states that *waḳf* land was exempt from taxation, but it may be that exemption was, in fact, not automatic but granted by a special decree or *farmān*. After the grant of the constitution in 1906, *waḳf*s of which the reigning S̲h̲āh was *mutawallī* were exempted from taxation on the grounds that the income of the S̲h̲āh was not taxable; other types of *waḳf*s were subject to taxation.

The land tax was assessed in three main ways: by measurement, as a proportion of the produce, or in a lump sum. The assessments were not made at regular intervals and were frequently hopelessly out of date; though where the tax due was assessed as a definite proportion of the crop, the government tax collectors of necessity estimated this annually. The most common form of assessment by Ḳād̲j̲ār times was the computation of the revenue due from a town or village in a lump sum; this had the advantage of avoiding annual visits by the tax collectors to assess the amount of the crop. The tax due, assessed partly in cash and partly in kind, was known as the *bunīča* of the area; it included from about the middle of the 19th century also the number of soldiers which the area was required to provide or a sum equivalent to the wages of a given number of soldiers. The final allocation of the tax demand among the population of the town or village was made locally. Special remissions on account of natural calamities or in return for some special service were granted from time to time and occasionally became permanent. More often, however, additional levies were made on account of arrears or to meet some emergency or special need, and the general tendency was for these to become part of the regular assessment. Further by the manipulation of the conversion rates (*tasʿīr*) by which taxes assessed at an artificial currency rate or in kind were converted into cash, the rate of taxation was increased. The assessments being usually out of date, it frequently happened that a village which had declined in prosperity and whose inhabitants had decreased on account of war, famine, emigration or some other cause, would be over-assessed and the amount of taxation due from the individual taxpayers automatically raised. Conversely villages which had increased in prosperity or had been newly developed were often under-assessed.

The rate of the land tax varied; it was affected by the nature of the crops grown and sometimes by the type of irrigation. Under Uzun Ḥasan's tax regime the rate at which tax was levied on the produce of the land varied from 14 to 20 per cent of the produce; in addition dues were levied on each plough-land. Under the Ṣafawids a somewhat similar situation presumably prevailed; Chardin, however, states that the tax on silk and cotton was one third of the produce. The rate in Ḳād̲j̲ār time seems to have been in the main some 20% of the crop; though a tradition affirms that prior to the reign of Fatḥ ʿAlī Shāh the rate was one tenth. This rate seems unlikely, however, to have been generally current. In any case a wide variety of practice existed. On grain crops the tax demand was paid in kind, the grain thus obtained being stored in government granaries and held against emergencies such as military expeditions and famine, or in some cases sold at fixed prices to the local population. Where the tax demand was made in kind as a fixed proportion of the crop it was presumably usually levied on the threshing floor before the division of the crop between the landlord and the peasant.

The extent of crown lands fluctuated. In cases where they were directly administered land tax as such was not levied, the whole of the produce after the deduction of the peasant's share going to the treasury. If leased, the rent paid by the tenant presumably included, or was in lieu of, land tax, and resembled an ordinary crop-sharing agreement. Under the Ṣafawids the land round Iṣfahān was largely crown land and administered by a special *dīwān* under the *mustawfī-i k̲h̲āṣṣa*.

In addition to the tax on the land or its produce water dues in the case of large rivers were levied. Pasture dues and a herd tax were also collected in some areas from both the settled and the semi-settled population; but their incidence and method of assessment varied. Among the other "fixed" taxes was a tax on real estate (other than agricultural land), such as baths, shops, water-mills, and caravanserais etc. (*mustag̲h̲allāt*), computed in early Ḳād̲j̲ār times at 20 per cent of the estimated annual proift. Malcolm alleges that there had been large increases in crown property of this nature owing to confiscations after the fall of the Ṣafawid and later dynasties. Where such property was rented by the crown to tenants, the rent presumably included, or took the place of, the tax levied on privately owned property of this kind. A poll-tax was paid by non-Muslims, Jews, Armenians, and Zoroastrians; and by foreigners unless granted special immunity. This derived from the canonical poll-tax or *d̲j̲izya*. Various other sections of the community, including certain tribal groups, also paid what amounted to a poll-tax (*sarāna, sar-s̲h̲umārī*). There are references in various documents to some kind of house or family tax (*k̲h̲āna-shumār*). Poll-taxes were finally abolished by the law of 20 Ād̲h̲ar 1305 A.H. (solar)/1926.

Taxes were levied on the craft guilds, except where special immunities were granted, by a group assessment, also known as *bunīča*. In Iṣfahān in Ṣafawid times the *kalāntar* and *naḳīb* of Iṣfahān would assemble the guilds in the first three months of the year and the *naḳīb* would fix their *bunīča* with the *kadk̲h̲udā* of the guild, this being subsequently allocated among the individual members of the guild. In practice, however, in the same way as the assessment of the land tax tended to become out of date so too was the *bunīča* of the guilds often out of date. Craft guilds continued to pay tax in this way until 1926, when this form of tax was abolished by the law of 20 Ād̲h̲ar 1305 A.H. (solar).

As regards taxes on merchants there appears to have been no uniform practice. Certain commodities were from time to time subject to special taxes. For example the *Tad̲h̲kirat al-Mulūk* mentions taxes on the tobacco trade. Market taxes were also in some cases levied. The main fixed taxes to which merchants were subject were road tolls (*rāhdārī*) and customs dues. The former were usually levied at so much per animal load at each town, the rate at which they were levied varying. Customs duties were paid on merchandise at the port of entry or exit. In the Ṣafawid period a duty of 10 per cent was levied by the customs houses in the Persian Gulf; on other frontiers the duty was levied per load. Certain exemptions and reductions were granted to various foreign merchants. By the Treaty of Turkomančay (1828) an *ad valorem* tariff of 5% was imposed on imports and exports by Russian merchants; in due course equivalent treatment was demanded by and granted to other nations. Persian merchants paid only 2 per cent but were subject in addition to road tolls. The revision of the customs tariff in 1903 was prejudicial to Persia and partial to Russia. The customs and road tolls were usually farmed in each district.

A levy on mines and pearl fisheries was made at the rate, in Ṣafawid times, of one third of the produce. Similarly a levy of 2 per cent on coins (*wād̲j̲ibī*) is mentioned. The mints were also a regular source of revenue in Ḳād̲j̲ār times. In the latter part of the 19th century the post and telegraphs became an additional source of revenue.

Numerous other dues made up the "fixed" revenue. Here again a great variety of practice existed and there is little detailed information on the rates at which these various dues were levied. Many of them were still levied in the 20th century. Millspaugh notes that some two hundred miscellaneous taxes existed in 1922. Included among these dues were those paid to afficials, local and otherwise, which did not necessarily go through the officials of the revenue department and were in many cases collected locally and constituted the whole or a large part of the salary of the officials in favour of whom they were levied. The holders of *tiyūl*s, annual grants, and *suyūrg̲h̲āl*s in Ṣafawid times paid a certain percentage of their assignments to various officials ranging from the *wakīl* of the supreme *dīwān* to the *daftardār* and other minor officials. More onerous than these, however, because more arbitrary in their incidence were the dues collected by local officials as their perquisites of office.

A further charge on the peasants and some of the craft guilds was labour service exacted by the state or a money payment taken in lieu of this. The incidence of labour service varied from place to place and it is difficult to assess it in money terms. The exaction of such service however could not fail to degrade the station of the peasant and artisan and to emphasize his subjection to authority.

The liability of the taxpayer was not limited to the payment of "fixed" taxation; perhaps the most onerous forms of taxation to which he was subjected were constituted by extraordinary levies, of which *ṣādirāt* and *suyūrsāt* were the most widespread and the most burdensome, and "presents" (*pīs̲h̲kas̲h̲*), casual and otherwise. *Ṣādirāt* comprised levies made to meet special expenditure such as that occasioned by a military expedition, the construction or repair of a royal building, or some special festivity, or simply to make good a deficit in the revenue. According to the nature of the occasion the whole country or a district or section of the community only was subjected to the levy. Its incidence was arbitrary in the extreme and its levy gave great scope for the show of partiality and the exercise of injustice. *Suyūrsāt* consisted of levies made for the keep and expenses of military forces, government officials, and foreign envoys passing through the country and like the *ṣādirāt* bore heavily upon the peasantry. Presents (*pīs̲h̲kas̲h̲*) were of two kinds, "casual" and "regular". The latter were remitted annually at the New Year and in some cases on certain religious festivals, such as the *ʿīd-i mawlūd*, by provincial governors, chiefs of tribes, and high officials. The amount of these presents was fixed broadly by custom. The occasions for the levy of casual presents were various. On the assumption of office by governors and high officials a payment, virtually equivalent to purchase money, was often expected and made; the grant of a *k̲h̲ilʿa* in many cases would cost its recipient a sum commensurate with his position in society; the progress of the shah through a district would involve the presentation of presents by all and sundry; similarly the visit of the Shah to the house of a favoured minister would impose upon the latter and his family and retainers heavy expenses in the form of presents; further, the heirs of the numerous body of persons who received pensions from the state had frequently to purchase the renewal of these grants, as did also the holders of *tiyūl*s and their heirs. This system of *pīs̲h̲kas̲h̲* extended throughout the administration; not only did the Shah expect and receive *pīs̲h̲kas̲h̲*, his governors and ministers also demanded and received similar treatment in the areas under their jurisdiction and from their subordinates.

Another irregular source of revenue, the extent of which, though difficult to compute, was no doubt considerable was confiscation (*muṣādara*) from officials dismissed from office, fines, and bribes. To these were added from the second half of the 19th century A.D. onwards considerable sums received from monopolies, concessions, and royalties.

In the latter part of the reign of Nāṣir al-Dīn various steps were taken to unify the tax administration of the country, abolish certain of the irregular taxes and requisitions, increase the revenue, and improve collection. A decree of 1303/1885-6 laid down certain changes in the collection of the revenue and attempted to define the financial responsibility of the governor. Instructions were issued for a new land survey and the levy of land tax at the rate of 10 per cent of the produce and various dues in 1307/1889-90. These and other measures were not, however, attended by any marked degree of success and were not operative throughout the country.

Full figures cannot be given for the total revenue owing to the impossibility of computing the extent of the revenue outside the "fixed" taxes. According to the *Tad̲h̲kirat al-Mulūk* the state revenue (*i.e.*, excluding revenue from the *k̲h̲āṣṣa*) in late Ṣafawid times amounted to c. 800,000 *tūmān*s. 61 per cent of this came from taxes registered in the *awārija*, which Prof. Minorsky thinks may have been land taxes; levies including rents from real estate excluding agricultural land, etc. accounted for 14.5 per cent, mines for 2 per cent, and produce and products remitted to the royal workshops for 1.5 per cent. According to the same source the total cost of the army and administration was 491,986 *tūmān*s 57,000 *dīnār*s, of which 396,792 *tūmān*s went to amīrs and governors. The first charge on the provincial revenues was the cost of the provincial administration. Under the Ḳād̲j̲ārs in addition to the regular tax assessment the provincial governors levied a sum known as *tafāwut-i ʿamal* for the expenses of the administration. Only after defraying local expenses and the payment of special drafts made on the local revenue by the central government was any surplus remaining remitted to the central treasury. According to Malcolm the "fixed" revenue in the early 19th century A.D. amounted to about three millions sterling. Local estimates put the receipts from Naw Rūz presents at two fifths of the "fixed" revenue, from fines one fifth of the "fixed" revenue, and the sum levied by public requisitions two fifths of the "fixed" revenue, the total revenue of the Shah being thus estimated at c. 6 millions sterling, only a proportion of which was paid in cash and large deductions being made for the expenses of collection before remission to the central government. Curzon estimates the "fixed" revenue at 55,369,516 *tūmāns* (or £ 1,652,820, converted at 33½ *ḳirāns* to the £ sterling, the rate prevailing in 1888), comprising taxes in cash 36,076,757 *tūmān*s, in kind (converted at government rates) 10,100,983 *tūmān*s, customs 8,000,000 *tūmān*s, and posts, mints, telegraphs, etc. 1,191,776 *tūmāns*. Expenditure, excluding local charges for the collection of revenue, reductions for bad harvests, etc., he estimated at 42,233,472 *tūmān*s (£ 1,260,700), comprising maintenance of government buildings 2,633,472 *tūmān*s, and the army, central administration, pensions, allowances, and the Shah's establishment, etc. at 21,600,000 *tūmān*s, showing a surplus of 13,136,044 *tūmāns* (£ 392,121). These figures, however, do not give a true picture of revenue and expenditure since not only is the revenue derived from sources other than "fixed" taxes and dues omitted, but also expenses for military expeditions and equipment, foreign journeys, and unforeseen emergencies. The total picture was far less favourable and such reserves as may have been accumulated were rapidly dissipated in the second half of the 19th century A.D. and the early years of the 20th century. Foreign loans were contracted to make good budgetary deficits, for the servicing of which the customs were mortgaged. By 1911 there was an annual deficit of c. 6,000,000 *tūmāns*, which in fact was usually increased to some 11,000,000 *tūmān*s because the "fixed" taxes were not collected in full. By 1922 there had been considerable changes in the proportions of the total revenue derived from different sources; nearly half the revenue was derived from the customs tariff, and oil royalties constituted a not inconsiderable part of the national revenue.

The grant of the Constitution in 1906 marks the beginning of a new phase in the tax system of Persia. Under the constitution the approval of the National Assembly was necessary for the regulation of all financial matters, the preparation and execution of the budget, the imposition of new taxes, the reduction and exemption of existing taxes, the sale and transfer of national resources and property, and the grant of concessions. One of the first actions of the newly convened National Assembly in 1907 was to appoint a committee to examine the question of financial reform. As a result of their labours the number and amount of the pensions and grants paid to individuals were reduced, the revenue assessments of the provinces were revised and the *tafāwut-i ʿamal* abolished; *tiyūl*s were also abolished, and conversion rates (*tasʿīr*) abrogated. In the same year a Frenchman, M. Bizot, was appointed financial adviser for two years; he had no powers and his mission proved abortive. In 1911 an American, Mr. W. M. Shuster, was appointed Treasurer-General of Persia with a view to reorganizing the chaotic and archaic state of the financial administration. He was forced, however, by Russian diplomatic pressure to leave the country after some months. The finances of the country continued in a state of disorder and during the first world war the administration broke down. In 1922 another American, Dr. A. C. Millspaugh, was appointed Administrator-General of the Finances, and it is from this date that the reform in the tax system of the country promised by the constitution really began and the foundations of a modern system of taxation were laid.

Bibliography: Josafa Barbaro and Ambrogio Contarini, *A Narrative of Italian Travels in Persia in the 15th and 16th Centuries* (Hakluyt Society, 1st ser., vol. 49); E. G. Browne, *The Persian Revolution of 1905-6*, Cambridge 1910; J. Chardin, *Voyages du Chevalier Chardin, en Perse, et autres lieux de l'Orient* ... (ed. L. Langlès), 10 vols., Paris 1811; G. N. Curzon, *Persia and the Persian Question*, 2 vols., London 1892; G. Demorgny, *Les Institutions financières de la Perse*, Paris 1915, Djamālzādeh, *Gandj-i Shāyagān*, Berlin 1919, R. Du Mans, *Estat de la Perse en 1660*, Paris 1890; J. B. Fraser, *Narrative of a Journey into Khorasān in the years 1821 and 1822*, London 1825; Mochar Ghadimy, *Les Finances de la Perse*, Paris 1920; Great Britain, Department of Overseas Trade, *Report on the Finances and Commerce of Persia*, 1925-7, by E. R. Lingeman, 1928; J. Greenfield, *Die Verfassung des Persischen Staats*, Berlin 1904; Sir Thomas Herbert, *Some Yeares Travels* (3rd ed., 1665); W. Hinz, *Das Steuerwesen Ostanatoliens im 15. und 16. Jahrhundert* in *ZDMG*, c.i. (New Series, xxv, 1950); E. Kaempfer, *Amoenitatum exoticarum* etc., Lemgo 1712; J. Macdonald Kinneir, *A Geographical Memoir of the Persian Empire*, London 1813; A. K. S. Lambton, *Landlord and Peasant in Persia*, *OUP*, 1953; I. de Laet, *Persica, gen regni Persici status variaque itinera et atque par Persiani*, Leiden 1633; E. Lorini, *La Persica economica contemporanea e la sua questione monetaria*, Rome 1900; Sir J. Malcolm, *The History of Persia from the Most Early Period to the Present Time*, 2 vols., London 1829; A. C. Millspaugh, *Americans in Persia*, Washington, 1946; idem, *The American Task in Persia*, New York and London 1928; idem, *The Financial and Economic Situation of Persia*, Washington 1926; F. Mochaver, *L'Evolution des finances iraniennes*, Paris 1938; ʿAbdullāh Mustawfī, *Sharḥ-i zindagī-i man*, 3 vols., Tehran 1945-6; H. Nafiçy, *L'Impôt et la vie économique et sociale en Perse*, Paris 1924; A. Olearius, *Voyages très curieux et très renommés faits en Moscovie, Tartarie, et Perse*, 2 vols. in one, Amsterdam 1719; The Royal Institute of International Affairs, *The Middle East*, London 1959; P. Sanson, *Voyage on relation de l'Etat présent du royaume de Perse*, Paris 1695; W. M. Shuster, *The Strangling of Persia*, London and New York 1912; E. Stack, *Six Months in Persia*, 2 vols., London 1882; *Tadhkirat al-Mulūk*, Persian text in facsimile tr. and explained by V. Minorsky (G.M.S., London, Leyden 1943); L. Tigranov, *Iz obshčestvenno-ékonomičeskikh otnosheniy v Persii*, St. Petersburg 1909; A. T. Wilson, *Persia*, London 1932.

(ANN K. S. LAMBTON)

(6) — India (a) The Sultanate of Dihlī. The fiscal administration of the Sultanate of Dihlī was modelled to a considerable extent upon the pattern evolved under the ʿAbbāsids. One of the earliest *wazīr*s was Fakhr al-Dīn ʿIṣāmī, who had served at Baghdād before he joined the court of Iletmish (607-33/1210-35) (Firishta, i, 117). The sultans, however, had to take into consideration Hindū traditions, especially in their agrarian policies.

Their fiscal administration, therefore, was based upon precedents developed by the Muslim administrators and jurists of the Eastern Caliphate with an admixture of Hindū traditions. The reconciliation of Islamic law and patterns with native tradition did not prove too difficult because of certain similarities between the two.

A group of taxes payable only by the Muslims came under the category of *zakāt*. The State does not seem to have levied the *zakāt* on personal property, but left it to the discretion of the individual to fulfil his duty in this respect. The State demand on the produce of the *ʿus͟hrī* lands, the prescribed *ʿus͟hr* being 5% or 10% of the gross produce, was levied by the State like other revenue. The *ʿus͟hrī* lands formed an insignificant proportion of the total area under cultivation. All imports paid a *zakāt* of 2½%. In the case of non-Muslim merchants the rate was doubled. This was the only tax paid by non-Muslims which was classified as *zakāt*.

Property left by Muslims dying without heirs belonged to the State and was earmarked for charitable purposes. The property of a *d͟himmī* dying in similar circumstances was handed over to his community.

Dj̲izya was levied in accordance with the rulings of the Ḥanafī jurists. Buddhists and Hindūs were recognized as *d͟himmī*s along with 'the peoples of the Book'. Muḥammad b. Ḳāsim, the conqueror of Sind, first extended the status of *d͟himmī*s to Buddhists and Hindūs and no subsequent ruler withdrew it. The sultans of Dihlī assessed *dj̲izya* in their own money; they charged ten, twenty, and forty *ṭanka*s per annum, in accordance with the income of the assessee (S͟hams-i Sirādj̲ ʿAfīf, *Taʾrīk͟h-i Fīrūzs͟hāhī*, Calcutta 1890, 383). Imbecile old men, cripples, the blind, and those who had not enough to pay the tax after defraying the cost of their living, were excused. Women and children also were exempt. Non-Muslim servants of the State also were not required to pay the *dj̲izya*. The Brāhmans remained exempt most of the time. Only Fīrūz S͟hah (752-90/1351-88) demanded *dj̲izya* from the Brāhmans, who protested and made a demonstration in front of the palace (*ibid*, 382-4). The sultan did not forego the tax in its entirety, but he relented to the extent of assessing all Brāhmans according to the lowest rate. Even this assessment was paid by charitably inclined rich Hindūs who wanted to relieve the Brāhmans of the burden. This is the only instance on record of a public protest against *dj̲izya*. The Hindūs perhaps did not find the idea of a poll-tax difficult to accept because it was also embedded in their own tradition. The Gaharwars of Kanawdj̲ had levied *Turus͟hkaḍanḍa*, either from the Muslims resident in their dominions or from all their subjects, as a contribution to defence against the encroachments of the Turks. Even during the British period a poll-tax was levied by some Rajput states.

The most important source of revenue and the mainstay of the financial stability of the Sultanate was *k͟harādj̲*. The bulk of the cultivated area in the Sultanate consisted of *k͟harādj̲ī* lands. Some grants to Muslims were classified as *ʿus͟hrī* lands; any other land in the possession of a Muslim or a *d͟himmī* was considered to be *k͟harādj̲ī*. There was no *arḍ al-mamlaka*. The territories of tributary chiefs, so long as they remained true to their agreements, were treated as *ṣulḥī*. From these areas the State received only a fixed sum of money stipulated at the time of the treaty. The State did not concern itself with the internal administration of such areas or with the relations between the peasants and tributary chiefs.

The principle of the *k͟harādj̲ al-muḳāsama* was applied to the *k͟harādj̲ī* lands. This was found convenient because the Hindūs were used to various forms of sharing the produce of their lands with the State, as they recognised that the State was entitled to a share of the agricultural produce. As the share of the State was traditionally considered to be a defined percentage of the actual produce, the basic principle of *k͟harādj̲ al-muḳāsama* was acceptable to the Hindūs. Thus the requirements of the *s͟harʿ* and Hindū tradition could be easily reconciled and there was no need to create confusion by any radical change in the principles of assessing the State demand on agricultural produce. The Hindūs had developed various methods of sharing the produce with the State before the establishment of Muslim rule. These included actual sharing through grain heaps of equal size, appraisement and the division of the field. Through long experience appraisement gained considerable accuracy and, because of its convenience, was widely adopted. Gradually the average yield in a unit of homogeneous area came to be so well established in popular knowledge that it was sufficient to measure the area under cultivation to calculate the yield. All these developments were intended to spread the time of assessment so that the harvest would not lie in the open field awaiting the arrival of the assessment team. The village accountant, the *paṭwārī*, kept a record of the area cultivated and the crops raised in every season. He also kept a record of the average yield. These traditional methods, called Sharing, Appraisement and Measurement, were left almost intact by the sultans of Dihlī. The sultans encouraged Measurement, because they found this device a more convenient method of accounting and collection. Its great weakness was that it worked satisfactorily only in normal seasons. If the rains failed or the area suffered from some other disaster, the normal yields could not be expected. It was then necessary to revert to Appraisement or Sharing. If the peasant felt that the Appraisement was not fair, he could always elect Sharing. This was an insurance against excessive assessment.

The proportion of the State demand to the gross produce varied in accordance with local tradition. In the areas conquered and brought under effective administration up to the reign of ʿAlāʾ al-Dīn K͟haldj̲ī (695-715/1296-1316) the prevailing proportion was a fifth of the yield; because of the increased expenditure upon the army on account of Mongol pressure, ʿAlāʾ al-Dīn raised it to the maximum allowed under the *s͟harʿ*: a half (I. H. Qureshi, *The Administration of the Sultanate of Dehli*, Karachi 1958, 103 ff.). G͟hiyāt͟h al-Dīn Tug͟hluḳ again reduced it to a fifth. When his son Muḥammad b. Tug͟hluḳ (725-52/1325-51) tried once more to increase the level in the Dōʾāb by ten to twenty per cent, there was rebellion. A fourth of the gross yield seems to have been stabilized as the recognized demand before S͟hīr S͟hāh (945-52/1538-45) came to the throne (*ibid.*, 111-9). However, in certain desert areas, the demand was as low as a seventh; there also seem to have been certain outlying provinces, such as Gudj̲arāt, where it was a half.

The spoils of war, technically called *g͟hanīma*, were shared between the State and the soldiers. Legally the State was entitled to a fifth, but because the soldiers were paid salaries out of the Public Exchequer, the sultans considered it fair to give a fifth to the soldiers and to deposit four fifths in the public treasury. Under Fīrūz Shāh the legal ratio was restored (ʿAyn al-Mulk Māhrū, *Inshāʾ-i Māhrū*, Letter xv. [MS. in Bankipore Public Library, Patna, India]). The State was also entitled to a fifth of all minerals, provided they were capable of being melted and bearing an imprint. The same applied to treasure trove, if it consisted of unstamped bullion or of money minted before the Muslim conquest.

In addition to the above taxes, local imposts were continually imposed in spite of repeated abolitions by the State. These went mostly into the pockets of the local authorities and did not contribute to the income of the State. They had come down from very early times and were so deep-rooted in the habits of the people that their effective abolition was difficult. They were not excessive and were generally petty levies on certain professions and the sale of a few commodities (Qureshi, *op. cit.*, Appendix H, 244 ff.).

The fiscal administration of the Sultanate was vested in the *dīwān-i wizārat*, which was presided over by the *wazīr*. He was assisted by a deputy. The *mushrif-i mamālik* was the accountant-general, and the *mustawfī-i mamālik* the auditor-general (ʿAfīf, *op. cit.*, 419-20). Every provincial capital had its own *dīwān-i wizārat* which was a replica of the central *dīwān-i wizārat* and functioned under its control (Qureshi, *op. cit.*, 200-1). Every *pargana*, the smallest unit of revenue administration, consisting of a number of villages, had its *ʿāmil* under whom there was an accountant, a treasurer and a field survey and assessment staff. The village accountant and registrar, called *patwārī*, kept all records concerning cultivation, assessment and yields (*ibid.*, 208, 209).

The *zakāt* on imports was assessed and collected at the local *sarā-i ʿadl*. *Ghanīma* was administered by the *dīwān-i ʿarḍ*; the property of Muslims dying heirless went to the office of the local *ḳāḍī*.

Bibliography: MSS. sources: Shams-i Sirādj ʿAfīf, *Tāʾrīkh-i Fīrūzshāhī*, Calcutta 1890; Ḍiyā al-Dīn Baranī, *Tāʾrīkh-i Fīrūzshāhī*, Calcutta 1862; Fīrūz Shāh, *Futūḥāt-i Fīrūzshāhī*, British Museum MS. Or. 2039; idem, *Sīrat-i Fīrūzshāhī*, MS. in Bankipore Public Library, Patna, India; ʿAbd al-Ḥamīd Muḥarrir Ghaznawī, *Dastūr al-Albāb fī ʿIlm-i ʾl-ḥisāb*, MS. in Rampur State Library, Rampur, India; Yaʿḳūb Muẓaffar Kirmānī, *Fiḳh-i Fīrūzshāhī*, India Office Library MS. IOL 2987; Muḥammad ʿAlī Kūfī, *Čačnāma*, Dihlī 1939; ʿAyn al-Mulk Māhrū, *Inshā-i Māhrū*, MS. in Bankipore Public Library, Patna, India.

Modern Works: Agha Mahdi Husain, *Le Gouvernement du Sultanat de Delhi*, Paris 1936; W. H. Moreland, *The Agrarian System of Moslem India*, Cambridge 1929; I. H. Qureshi, *The Administration of the Sultanate of Dehli*, Karachi 1958; R. P. Tripathi, *Some Aspects of Muslim Administration*, Allāhābād 1936.

(I. H. Qureshi)

(b) The early Mughals. No conspicuous modification of the system described above was attempted until the time of Shīr Shāh. Bābur and Humāyūn made no changes in the existing system, largely the result of Sikandar Lōdī's improvements, which they adopted in its entirety; the statistical returns of Bābur's times were based on the rent-rolls of Sikandar Lōdī, and all calculations were made in accordance with Sikandar's prescriptions on standards and computation. Both Bābur and Humāyūn granted new *djāgīrs*. The account of the reconstruction of the central administration in Humāyūn's reign (Khwand Amīr, *Humāyūn-nāma*, see Bibliography) suggests that there was no change in the work of the revenue ministry, now called *dīwānī*.

The interrex Shīr Shāh was the first ruler to rationalize taxation, especially in respect of the chief source, the land. He tried to counteract the recurring tendencies to impose extra-legal taxes on the cultivators, but there is no evidence that he conscientiously applied the Islamic principles of taxation: *djizya* and *zakāt* are not mentioned in contemporary records, although the later *Taʾrīkh-i Dāwūdī* gives an extensive list of the sources of state income under heads other than land-revenue: sales tax, conveyance duty, ground rent from market vendors, tax on sugar refinery, ferry tax, grazing tax, cattle tax, profession tax from various artisans, gambling tax, and *djizya* and pilgrim tax on Hindūs. Shīr Shāh is said to have forbidden the realization of transit dues and octroi, but how far this prohibition was effective is doubtful; it is probable that a distinction was made between *djāgīr* and *khāliṣa* territories. Property of intestates most probably escheated to the state. Presents to the Emperor do not seem to have been exploited by Shīr Shāh. The changes he introduced in respect of *kharādj* lands seem to have been the result of the practical experience he acquired in administering the *djāgīr* his father had been assigned under the Lōdīs. Sharing of the ripened crop (*ghallābakhshī*) and appraisement [(*kankūt, muḳtaʿī*) or visual estimation of the standing crop, the hitherto prevailing systems of assessment, were found difficult to operate effectively owing to the large numbers of personnel needed to apply them and because of the temptations for collusion between *riʿāya* and official; in their place measurement (*ḍabṭ*) was reintroduced wherever practicable; Bengal and Multān remained under appraisement until within Akbar's time, and in the latter province when taken for Shīr Shāh in 950/1543 the governor was ordered to observe the customs of the Langāhs and take no more than one-fourth of the produce as revenue (*Taʾrīkh-i Shīr Shāhī*, tr. Elliot, iv, 399); elsewhere one-third was taken, reckoned by an averaging system: for all the principal staples the good, medium, and bad yields per *bīghā* were added and then divided by three to give the 'average produce' (*maḥṣūl*) per *bīghā*; of this one-third was taken as the state's share (*Āʾīn-i Akbarī*, i, 297 ff.; tr. Jarrett, ii, 62 ff.); the obvious effect of this was to over-assess the bad lands and under-assess the good. This was presumably only applied in the *khāliṣa*-lands; no information is available on revenue collection in the *djāgīr* lands, which were still being granted by Shīr Shāh.

The ten years following Shīr Shāh's death in 952/1545 were a period of confusion; it is reasonable to assume that his methods persisted, since they were adopted in Akbar's reign. It is recorded (*Taʾrīkh-i Dāwūdī*, tr. Elliot, iv, 479-81) that Islām Shāh replaced *djāgīrs* by cash salaries, but this seems to have been a temporary measure.

Under Akbar most of the general sources of revenue (*sāʾir*) described above continued unchanged, except that the *djizya* and the tax on Hindū pilgrims were early abolished. Customs duty, only 2½ to 3 per cent *ad valorem*, was exacted at the ports (classified as major (*bandargāh*) and minor (*bāra*); 27 *bandargāhs* and 45 *bāras* are mentioned in the *Mirʾāt-i Aḥmadī*, *Khātima*, 239) by a *mutasaddī* with a large staff, and at the land frontiers. Certain internal transit duties were also levied, including ferry taxes. Other regular taxes included those on salt—in some districts accruing to the provincial revenue, in others to the central administration—; fisheries, particularly the Bengal fish-tanks; *rāhdārī*, a road tax for merchants in exchange for protection; and *pandārī*, a sales tax. Regular revenue from non-tax sources included that from copper, zinc, and silver mines (*Āʾīn*, index); mints (6,174,500 *dām* is mentioned as mint income in the *Mirʾāt-i Aḥmadī*, I. O. Ethé 3599, f. 728b), which were established in the principal towns of the empire (R. B. Whitehead in *JASB*, N.S. viii, 1912, 425-531; N.S. xi, 1915, 231-7; G. P. Taylor in *JASB*,N.S. x, 1914, 178-9; see also DĀR AL-ḌARB, c.); and tribute from vassal chiefs (*e.g.*, the revenue of the *ṣūba* of Adjmēr amounted to over 7,200,000 rupees, three-quarters of which comprised tribute from Rādjpūt chiefs; other tributary domains were in Gudjarāt, Uṙisā and Central India). Irregular revenue included presents on appointment (*salāmī*), escheat through intestacy or forfeiture, treasure trove, and *khums* (one-fifth of war booty reserved for the imperial exchequer).

The greatest single source of recurrent revenue was from the land, demanded under several different systems during Akbar's long reign, and documented in great detail in the *Āʾīn-i Akbarī* and other contemporary texts (see Bibliography). The old methods of *ghallābakhshī* (which prevailed in Sindh when the *Āʾīn* was compiled, for where there are no records of any survey or measurement) and *kankūt* remained in force for some areas, but the most favoured system, *ḍabṭ*, was subject to a number of experiments in the first twenty-four years of the reign. First Shīr Shah's schedule of assessment rates was adopted for general use by the regent, Bayrām Khān, on the basis of a demand of a prevailing rate of one-third of the average produce, stated in grain. "From the beginning of this eternal reign, every year unavaricious and high-minded experts used to ascertain prices and lay them before the royal court; and taking the schedule of crop yield and the prices theroof, used to fix the schedule of demand rates (*dastūr*); and this caused great vexation" (*Āʾīn*, i, 347, trans. I. H. Qureshi in *JPakHS*, i/3, 1953, 208); but by the tenth year the uniform schedules gave place to differential schedules based on local price rates, the measuring instruments had been standardized, and land had been classified in accordance with the time it had been cultivated (*bandjar*, uncultivated for five or more years; *puladj*, cultivated for more than five years; *puladj* land lying fallow for a short time was *paṙawtī*, but for three of four years was called *čačar*; when *bandjar* land was brought under cultivation the demand was one-fifth of the norm for the first year, increasing yearly until the full *puladj* rate was attained; there was a similar differential rate for *čačar*; *paṙawtī* was untaxed but paid the full *puladj* rate on being taken into cultivation again). The *ḍabṭ* system was abolished in the *khāliṣa* lands in the thirteenth year (976/1569) under the specially appointed Shihāb al-Dīn Aḥmad Khān, who discontinued the annual assessment and established a *nasaḳ* ((*Akbar-nāma*, ii, 333), not precisely defined but assumed to be a form of assessment analogous to *kankūt* administered through the *muḳaddams* (according to Moreland, Appx.D, "group-assessment", where the term is discussed).

A new system was introduced in the fifteenth year (978/1571) when Muẓaffar Khān and Rādjā Ṫoḋar Mal were appointed to the *wizāra*, having been set in motion in the eleventh year (on the dating question, see Moreland, Appx.E), described in *Āʾīn*, i, 347: *ḳānūngos* ("interpreters of customs", accountants and registrars of the *pargana* [*q.v.*]) prepared new schedules of produce separately for each *pargana*, and on the basis of returns for the whole empire (*taḳsīmāt al-mulk*) a new *maḥṣūl* was determined by estimate, and hence a new valuation (*djamʿ*) made by applying the new schedules to actual or estimated crop areas (actual areas being on hand for the *khāliṣa* lands).

In the nineteenth year (982/1575) Akbar, requiring to pay salaries by cash rather than by assignment, decided that the areas of the *parganas* of the Empire should be re-examined, and the extent of all land, including that *bandjar* or *čačar*, which on cultivation could be expected to yield one crore (*karōṙ*, 10 million) *ṫankās* should be separated and entrusted to an official called *karōṙī*, who was to be responsible for effecting the cultivation of the *bandjar* land and realizing the correct demand (*Ṭabaḳāt-i Akbarī*, B.M.Or. 2274, f. 203), so that in the course of three years all the waste land should be brought under cultivation, improving the condition of the *riʿāya* and benefitting the treasury (Badāʾūnī, ii, 189). But after a successful start the system broke down under the rapacity of the *karōṙīs* and the corruption of their collectors and clerks. The period of this breakdown coincides with Shāh Manṣūr's *de facto* tenure of the *dīwānī* in the absence of Ṫoḋar Mal on military duty. On Todar Mal's return in the twenty-sixth year (985/1577) he resorted to ferocious measures to bring the collectors to account, and the following year an Imperial commissioner (*amīn al-mulk*) was appointed in Fatḥ Allāh Shīrāzī, invited from the court of Bīdjāpur, to both of whom the final system is due.

Previously, in the twenty-fourth year (987/1579-80), the practice of assignment of *djāgīrs* having been re-established, a new valuation was made, calculated on the data of the previous ten years' operation of Ṫoḋar Mal's assessment rates, described in a notoriously difficult passage of the *Āʾīn* (i, 347), known as *Āʾīn-i dahsāla* (tr. Qureshi, *loc. cit.*; see Bibliography for earlier translations and interpretations): the ministry held the correct figures for the preceding five years, and those for five years before were taken from reliable sources. One-tenth of the total was declared to be the average produce (*harsāla*) and would be taken as the basis of valuation for the ensuing year; deductions were made for partial or complete failure of crops in any area. This decennial average was re-computed each year; demand rates were now fixed in cash, not grain, thus obviating the necessity for yearly revision of the commutation rates. In the provisions the *parganas* are grouped into assessment circles, each with its own schedule (*dastūr*). This system is attributed to Akbar himself.

The final system maintains this ideal of valuation but improves its administration (*Āʾīn*, i, 285-8). Ṫoḋar Mal's proposals of the twenty-seventh year are incorporated in a code of practice which was periodically amended. Village records are kept by the *paṫwārī*, but were available to the State officials. The collector was required to familiarize himself with local agriculture and to extend cultivation wherever possible; to this end the headman was to be allowed up to 2½ per cent share in the results, and was authorized to reduce the sanctioned rates on high-grade crops, and to depart from the system of *ḍabṭ* if the *riʿāya* elected *ghallābakhshī*, *kankūt*, or *nasaḳ*; the *riʿāya* was to know in advance the extent of his liability to the State. These regulations were applied, successfully, in the *khāliṣa* lands; there is insufficient information on their operation in *djāgīrs*.

Bibliography: Khwānd Amīr, *Humāyūn-nāma*, Eng. tr. in H. M. Elliot and J. Dowson, *The history of India as told by its own historians*, v, 116-26; ʿAbbās Sarwānī, *Taʾrīkh-i Shīr Shāhī*, Eng. tr. in Elliot and Dowson, *op. cit.*, iv, 305-433; ʿAbd Allāh, *Taʾrīkh-i Dāwūdī*, partial Eng. tr. in Elliot and Dowson, *op. cit.*, iv, 434-513; Abu 'l-Faḍl, *Āʾīn-i Akbarī*, 3 vols., Bibl. Ind. Calcutta; Eng. tr. by H. Blochmann vol. i) and H. S. Jarret (vols. ii and iii), Bibl. Ind. Calcutta. Blochmann's tr. contains many errors of interpretation of fiscal questions, especially i, 347; improved trs. of this in Moreland, *op. cit.* below, and Qureshi, *JPakHS*, i/3, 1953, 208; idem, *Akbar-nāma*, 3 vols, Bibl. Ind. Calcutta; Eng. tr. H. Beveridge, Bibl. Ind. Calcutta; ʿAbd al-Ḳādir Badāʾūnī, *Muntakhab al-Tawārīkh*, 3 vols. and Eng. tr., Bibl. Ind. Calcutta; Khwādja Niẓām al-Dīn Aḥmad, *Ṭabaḳāt-i Akbarī*, Lucknow lith. 1292/1875, also B.M.Or. 2274; ʿAlī Muḥammad Khān, *Mirʾāt-i Aḥmadī*, 3 vols., GOS Baroda; W. H. Moreland, *The agrarian system of Moslem India*, Cambridge 1929 (cited above as Moreland); idem, *The agricultural statistics of Akbar's empire* in *JUPHS*, ii/1, 1919, 1-39; idem, *A Dutch account of Mogul administrative methods* in *JIH*, iii/3-iv/1, 1923, 69-83; idem, *Akbar's land revenue arrangements in Bengal* in *JRAS* 1926, 43-56; Sri Ram Sharma, *Assessment and collection of the land revenue under Akbar* in *IHQ*, xiv, 1938, 705-34; idem, *The administrative system of Sher Shah*, in *IHQ*, xii, 1936, 381-605; P. Śaran, *Sher Shah's revenue system* in *JBORS*, xvii, 1931, 136-48; I. H. Qureshi, *The administration of the sultanate of Dehli*, Karachi 1958; idem, *The parganah officials under Akbar* in *IC*, xvi, 1942, 87-93; idem, *Akbar's revenue reforms* in *JPakHS*, i, 1953, 205-17 (includes improved translation of *Āʾīn*, i, 347); other references in Pearson, pp. 632-3, 638-47.

(c) The later Mughals. The schedules of cash-rates adapted to the varying productivity of different regions were discarded at some time during the reign of Djahāngīr in favour of the earlier principle of *nasaḳ*; the seasonal *ḍabṭ*, effective enough under such a strong administration as Akbar's, would have been less so under a weak or unsupported ministry. Djahāngīr's memoirs reveal his own lack of interest in fiscal questions, and it is assumed that he neglected the administration; there is indeed a dearth of contemporary information on the fiscal history of his reign, although the summary financial history collected in the later *Maʾāthir al-Umarāʾ* ([*q.v.*]; ii, 813 ff.) confirms this assumption in the statement that the annual expenditure rose to treble the annual income from the *khāliṣa*-lands. This instability is reflected in the frequency with which *djāgīrs* changed hands (cf. the accounts of W. Hawkins and E. Terry, in *Early Travels*, 83, 91-3, 114, 326, and of Pelsaert, *Remonstrantie*, Eng. trans. in W. H. Moreland and P. Geyl, *Jahāngīr's India*, Cambridge 1925, 64 ff.; for the contemporary situation in Gudjarāt cf. *De Remonstrantie van W. Geleynssen de Jongh*, The Hague 1929); some *djāgīr*-holders of high provincial office appear to have been appointed to their posts on farming-terms (Roe, 210; Terpstra, Appx. vi). An innovation of Djahāngīr's time is the introduction of the *āltamgha*, a grant of land given under the emperor's seal which required his direct personal authority to vary, and thus constituted the nearest approach to land-ownership, as now understood, in the Mughal period (*Tūzuk*, 10; cf. *Bādshāh-nāma*, ii, 409).

For Shāhdjahān's reign there is even less contemporary description of practices than for Djahāngīr's, although the account in the *Maʾāthir al-Umarāʾ* indicates that on his accession he designated as *khāliṣa* sufficient land to yield a revenue of 150 lakhs of rupees, and fixed the expenditure ceiling at 100 lakhs; the expenditure later greatly exceeded this figure, but the *khāliṣa* income was correspondingly increased. A later writer (Bindrāban, *Lubb al-Tawārīkh-i Hind.*, tr. in Elliot and Dowson, vii, 170 ff.) refers to agrarian orders having been issued by the emperor, but these have not been discovered, and the nature of his systems can best be inferred from Awrangzīb's early orders, referred to below. There is, however, a record of the practice in this reign in one area: the Deccan provinces had been brought almost to economic ruin as a result of the wars of conquest, and during Awrangzīb's second viceregal period their revenue systems were reorganized, from about 1062/1652, by Murshid Ḳulī Khān [*q.v.*] who retained plough rents where the state of agriculture was primitive, and elsewhere introduced *ghallābakhshī* and *ḍabṭ*, the former being introduced on differential scales for the first time in India, verying with the nature of the crop and with the nature of the source of water on which the crop depended; assessment rates were fixed at a low figure and were accompanied by positive measures to restore prosperity by repopulating and reorganizing the ruined villages and by capital advances. His achievements in the Deccan had apparently no reaction on the administration in the north.

The state of the revenue system when Awrangzīb came to the throne, and his measures towards a reform, can be gauged from two early *farmāns* of the 8th and 11th regnal years (1076/1665-6 and 1079/1668-9), with preambles containing descriptions of the systems of assessment then in force, with their defects, and the procedures to be adopted in future (texts with Eng. tr. in Jadunāth Sarkār, *The revenue regulations of Aurangzib ...*, in *JASB*, n.s. ii, 1906, 223-55); the former constitutes a manual of practice addressed to the provincial *dīwān* and his staffs, but intended to be applicable also for the staffs employed by *djāgīr*-holders, while the latter was issued with the object of ensuring an assessment and collection of revenue, throughout the whole empire, in accordance with the principles of Islamic Law. This latter *farmān* is based on the *Fatāwā-i ʿĀlamgīriyya* [*q.v.*] of contemporary jurists, whose authorities were the law-books and commentaries of the central Islamic lands rather than the practical conditions of agriculture in India, with consequent distortions of interpretation of the situation: *e.g.*, reference to peasants as though they held proprietary rights over the land; to a distinction between *ʿushr* and *kharādj* land, not applicable in India; and detailed rules for land under dates and almonds, irrelevant in India.

The first *farmān* is the more practical: revenue from the *khāliṣa* lands was expended by the emperor, not the viceroy, and was assessed and collected by the central *dīwānī* through the provincial *dīwāns*. There is to be increased control over the local staffs, and the central authority must be kept informed of actual agricultural conditions by more detailed annual returns from each village; there is set out a development policy through extension of cultivation, increase of the area under high-grade crops, and the erection and maintenance of irrigation works; the old standard demand of one-third became the new minimum demand, with the maximum raised to one-half—in practice presumably generally demanded, since the officials' primary duty was to increase the revenue. Assessment was usually by *nasaḳ*, usually of a whole village but on occasion of an entire *pargana*; the *nasaḳ* could be refused, in which case revenue could be obtained by *ḍabṭ* or *ghallābakhshī* at the discretion of local officials; cash-payments of revenue were usual, although Sarkār has shown (*Studies*, 217) that in parts of Uṙisā revenue was paid in kind. The demand was assessed as a lump sum at the beginning of the year, distributed over the peasants by the headmen; these were paid as the crops matured, and passed their collections to the officials after having set aside their own portions as "village expenses"—a further exaction on an already oppressed peasantry. Provision was made for the occurrence of such calamities as drought, frost, or low prices (the second *farmān* makes a distinction between calamities occurring before and those falling after the crops were cut). That these regulations were intended to set a standard of procedure in the *djāgīr*-lands is shown by a provision requiring the provincial *dīwān* to report on the loyalty and efficiency of the assessors and collectors employed in the *djāgīrs*.

A distinction is drawn in the second *farmān* between two forms of tenure, *muḳāsama* and *muwaẓẓaf*; under the former, revenue was paid only when the land was cultivated, while under the latter revenue was paid whether the land was cultivated or not. The latter was thus a form of contract-holding, where a fixed sum was paid for the occupation of land irrespective of its produce. There seems to be no prior record of this tenure in Muslim India, although the frequency of such holdings at the beginning of the British period, and the fact that they had been long known in Udaypur, never under Muslim administration, would indicate that they were no new institution. Here the administration recognizes the existence of certain rights to retain or dispose of a holding; a *muwaẓẓaf*-holder was ordinarily succeeded by his heir, and he could lease, mortgage or sell his rights.

Although the necessity for full and punctual collection of revenues is stressed, there is no explicit provision for action to be taken in case of default; but it is recorded in other sources that a cultivator's wives and family could be sold into slavery in such cases (cf. Bernier, 205; Manrique, i, 53).

Stress is laid in these *farmāns* on the need for keeping peasants on the land, for absconding had by this time become a serious problem; that the scarcity of cultivators was due to flight and not to death through warfare or epidemics is shown by several contemporary reports (*e.g.*, Bernier's letter to Colbert, *Travels*, 200 ff., esp. 205; also 226, 232): the severity of the administration drove large numbers to the towns or camps, or to territories under Hindū rule.

After Awrangzīb's reign the *djāgīr* seems to have become unremunerative and consequently unpopular (cf. Khʷāfī Khān, *Muntakhab al-Lubāb*, Bibl. Ind., i, 622 ff.), on account of the lack of cultivators and the general uncertainty of tenure; also an assignee could no longer rely on the authority of the emperor and had frequently to repel other claimants to the revenue by force of arms: *de facto* possession had more force than title. The place of the *djāgīr* is taken more and more by a stipend in cash, and territorially the most important unit of revenue is the *taʿalluḳ* [*q.v.*]; the *khāliṣa* areas were frequently farmed out in the later years of Awrangzīb and under his successors, and the large tax-farms in Bengal became the forerunners of the system of *zamīndārī* [*q.v.*]. The revenues thus passed out of the control of the imperial authority as such, and the later fiscal history more properly belongs to the period of British India.

Bibliography: *Tūzuk-i Djahāngīrī*, lith. ʿAlīgaṙh 1864, Eng. tr. Rogers and Beveridge, London 1909-14; Muḥammad Hāshim Khʷāfī Khān, *Muntakhab al-Lubāb*, Bibl. Ind., 1869; partial Eng. tr. in Elliot and Dowson, vii, 207 ff.; ʿAbd al-Ḥamīd Lāhawrī, *Bādshāhnāma*, Bibl. Ind., 1867; *Maʾāthir al-Umarāʾ*, Bibl. Ind., 1887-95; ed. W. Foster, *Early travels in India*, London 1921; ed. Foster, *The embassy of Sir Thomas Roe to India, 1615-19*, 2nd ed. London 1926; Fray Sebastian Manrique, *Itinerario de las Missiones orientales*, Eng. tr. as *The travels of Fray Sebastian Manrique, 1629-43*, London 1926-7; François Bernier, *Travels in the Mogul Empire*, ed. and tr. A. Constable, London 1891; J. van Twist, *Generale Beschrijvinge van Indien*, Amsterdam 1648; W. H. Moreland, *The agrarian system of Moslem India*, Cambridge 1929; H. Terpstra, *De Opkomst der Wester-Kwartieren van de Oost-Indische Compagnie*, The Hague 1918; Jadunāth Sarkār, *Studies in Mughal India*, 1919; idem, *Mughal Administration*², 1924; idem, *The revenue regulations of Aurangzib* in *JASB*, n.s. ii, 1906, 223-55; H. Beveridge, *Aurangzeb's revenues* in *JRAS*, 1906, 349-53; Y. K. Deshpande, *Revenue administration of Berar in the reign of Aurangzeb, 1679 A.D.*, in *Proc. Ind. Hist. Rec. Comm.*, xii, 1929, 81-7; Sh. Abdur Rashid, *A valuable document relating to revenue administration during Awrangzib's reign*, in *JPakHS*, ii, 1954, 26-34.

(d) Other Indian dynasties. Materials for the fiscal systems of the outlying regions are very scanty. For the fragmentary records of Gudjarāt and Mālwa see those articles; for post-Mughal Bengal see ZAMĪNDĀRĪ. For the Bahmanīs there is no information beyond Firishta's remarks that *djāgīr*-holdings were common and that there were reserved *khāliṣa*-areas (*Muntakhab al-Tawārīkh*, Kānpur lith., 320, 356).

For Aḥmadnagar there is no contemporary account of the reforms of Malik ʿAnbar [*q.v.*], although an account has been given by Grant Duff, *History of the Mahrattas*, Bombay 1826, from Maraṭhī sources, according to which Malik ʿAnbar abolished farming and substituted a collection of a percentage of the actual produce in kind; after some seasons this was commuted for a cash payment, fixed annually on the basis of cultivation, the State claiming one-third or two-fifths of the total value.

In Golkonḍa in the 11th/17th century the kingdom appears to have been entirely under the farming system, the amount payable having been settled annually by auction (cf. Methwold, *Relations of the Kingdom of Golckonda*, in *Purchas his Pilgrimes*, London 1625); farming is said to have persisted in this region until abolished by Sir Salar Jang in 1853 (*Imperial Gazetteer of India*, xiii, 280).

Bibliography: In the text.

(P. Śaran and J. Burton-Page)

7. Indonesia [See SUPPLEMENT].

DĀRIM [see TAMĪM].

AL-DĀRIMĪ, ʿABDALLĀH B. ʿABD AL-RAḤMAN B. AL-FAḌL B. BAHRĀM B. ʿABD AL-ṢAMAD ABŪ MUḤAMMAD AL-SAMARḲANDĪ belonged to the B. Dārim b. Mālik, a branch of Tamīm. He travelled in search of traditions and learned them from a number of authorities in al-ʿIrāḳ, Syria and Egypt. Among those who transmitted traditions on his authority were Muslim b. al-Ḥadjdjāj and Abū ʿĪsā al-Tirmidhī. Al-Dārimī lived a simple, pious life devoted to study, and acquired a reputation for knowledge of *Ḥadīth*, reliability, truthfulness and sound judgement. He was asked to accept office as *ḳāḍī* in Samarḳand but refused. The sulṭān insisted, so he accepted the office, but after acting once he asked to be excused and this was granted. He was born in 181/797 and died in 255/869. His writings were mainly concerned with *Ḥadīth*, but he is also credited with a Ḳurʾān commentary. Al-Khaṭīb al-Baghdādī says he compiled *al-Musnad* and *al-Djāmiʿ*, but one wonders whether these may not be alternative titles for the same work. His collection of traditions is commonly called *al-Musnad* (publ. Kānpur 1293, Ḥaydarābād 1309, Dihlī 1337, Damascus 1349), but this word is appropriate only if understood in the wider sense common in earlier times. It should be called *al-Sunan*, as the material is arranged according to the subject-matter. This work has not been treated on an equality with the six canonical books, but Ibn Ḥadjar al-ʿAsḳalānī considered it superior to Ibn Mādja's *Sunan*. It is much shorter than any of the six books. Ḥādjdjī Khalīfa mentions three other works, two of them excerpts from his *Musnad*, but they have not survived.

Bibliography: Ibn Abī Ḥātim, *Kitāb al-djarḥ wa 'l-taʿdīl*, Ḥaydarābād 1372/1953, ii, 2, 99; *Taʾrīkh Baghdād*, x, 29-32; al-Samʿānī, 218ab; Dhahabī, *Ḥuffāẓ*, ii, 105 f.; Ibn Ḥadjar al-ʿAsḳalānī, *Tahdhīb al-tahdhīb*, v, 294-6; Ibn al-Ṣalāḥ, *ʿUlūm al-ḥadīth*, Aleppo 1350/1931, 42; Ibn al-ʿImād, *Shadharāt*, ii, 130; Ḥādjdjī Khalīfa, ed. Flügel, ii, 492; iii, 628; v, 109 f., 530, 539 f.; Sarkis, *Dict. Encyc. de bibl. arabe*, Cairo 1928-30, 857 f.; Goldziher, *Muh. St.*, ii, 258-60; M. Weisweiler, *Istanbuler Handschriften zur arabischen Traditionsliteratur* (*Bibl. Islam.*, x, 1937), no. 50; Brockelmann, I, 171 f., S I, 270.

(J. ROBSON)

ḌARĪR, MUṢṬAFĀ, Turkish author of the 7th/14th century. Very little is known of his life. He was born blind (*ḍarīr*) in Erzurum where he studied; later he travelled in Egypt, Syria and Karaman. His works which have come down to us are : 1. *Tardjumat al-Ḍarīr*, an enlarged free translation, interspersed with many original verse passages, of Abu 'l-Ḥasan al-Bakrī al-Baṣrī's (6th/13th century) version of the *sīra* of Ibn Isḥāḳ, filled with stories and legends borrowed from various sources. It consists of five volumes and was written by the order of the Mamlūk sultan of Egypt Al-Manṣūr ʿAlāʾ al-Dīn ʿAlī; it was completed in 790/1388 and presented to the sultan al-Ṣāliḥ Ṣalāḥ al-Dīn Ḥādjdjī. The chapter on the birth of the Prophet seems to have inspired the corresponding chapter in Sulayman Čelebi's *Mewlid* (Ahmed Ateş, *Vesîletü'n-Necât, Mevlid*, Ankara 1954, 55-7); 2. a free translation of Wāḳidī's *Futūḥ al-Shām*, which relate the conquest of Syria under the caliphs Abū Bakr and ʿUmar, completed in Aleppo in 795/1392; 3. a translation of the Hundred *Ḥadīths*; 4. *Yūsuf we Zulaykhā*, a recently discovered *mathnawī* (Istanbul Univ. Library no. 311, 862). None of these works has yet been edited. Ḍarīr shows remarkable mastery of *ʿarūḍ*; his verse is fluent and he often reaches the heights of lyric poetry. His pleasant and simple prose is one of the best specimens of early Turkish narrative style.

Bibliography: *Istanbul Kütüphaneleri Tarih-Coğrafya Yazmaları Katalogları*, Seri I, fasc. 1-9, Istanbul, 1943-9, 305-7, 404-10; Alessio Bombaci, *Storia della letteratura turca*, Milan, 1956, 227-8.

(FAHİR İZ)

ḌARIYYA, a village and a watering place in Nadjd located at 42° 56′ N., 24° 46′ E., on the Darb al-Sulṭānī pilgrim route from al-Baṣra to Mecca (*Handbook*, ii, 189). The village was a much frequented halting place for pilgrims, for the junction with the route from al-Baḥrayn was here. The district of Ḍariyya, according to Ibn Bulayhid, was a wide territory in Nadjd celebrated by the poets in pre-Islamic times for its sweet water and pasturage. The famous Ḥimā Ḍariyya is said to have been named after the village and was part of the district (Yāḳūt, iii, 457). There is some doubt as to when the *ḥimā* was first reserved. Yāḳūt states that Ḍariyya was set aside by Kulayb [*q.v.*], the legendary hero of the War of Basūs, whose burial ground, according to traditions handed down by the Ṭayyiʾ, lies within the confines of the *ḥimā* in the mountains of al-Nīr. The site of this grave was well known among the Arabs as late as the 15th century, for al-Samhūdī, who completed his work in 886/1481, reports that Adjwad b. Zāmil al-Djabrī, the lord of al-Ḥasā and al-Ḳaṭīf (called by the author, Raʾīs Ahl Naghd), had heard of the shrine from the local Arabs and visited it (al-Samhūdī, ii, 227). Al-Bakrī, however, claims that Ḥima Ḍariyya was first reserved for the state by ʿUmar b. al-Khaṭṭāb for the camels given as *ṣadaḳa* or taken in battle. The statement by al-Hamdānī (172, 24) that Ḥimā Ḍariyya and Ḥimā Kulayb are not the same but are separated by the mountains of al-Nīr, which Yāḳūt himself recognizes as an independent *ḥimā*, supports al-Bakrī. It is likely that Ḍariyya was one of the many *ḥimās* of the *djāhiliyya* epoch which later changed their names (Ibn Bulayhid, iii, 244). The Ḥemmey on Doughty's map is probably an approximation of the older Ḥimā Kulayb. According to al-Ṭabarī (i, 1107) and Yāḳūt (ii, 290), Ḍariyya derives its name from Ḍariyya, the mother of Ḥulwān, the son of ʿUmrān and grandson of Ḳuḍaʿa. Al-Hamdānī says that Ḍariyya was the daughter of Rabīʿa b. Nizār.

The *ḥimā* reserved by ʿUmar originally extended 6 miles in each direction from the village of Ḍariyya. Owing to the continuous increase in livestock, which reached a total of about 40,000 in the time of ʿUthmān the *ḥimā* was enlarged about 10 miles in at least one direction (al-Bakrī, iii, 860). The land, which was under the control of the Amīrs of Medina, was released by the ʿAbbāsid Caliph al-Mahdī and is said to have yielded, as private property, an annual tribute of 8,000 dirhams in the early ʿAbbāsid period. At that time the territory was chiefly inhabited by the Kilāb, against whom Muḥammad had sent troops in A.H. 6 and 7. Ḍariyya was not without strife, for al-Ahwāzī mentions that al-Rabtha, a neighbouring pilgrim station and *ḥimā*, was destroyed in the year 319/931 through continuous warfare between its people and those of Ḍariyya.

Today, by-passed by modern roads, Ḍariyya is a poor settlement with about 20 wells and only a few scattered palms, lying in desolate steppe terrain at the edge of one of the dikes in the granite shield underlying the western plateau. Western writers have frequently confused it with al-Dirʿiyya [*q.v.*], the former Wahhābī capital (cf. Wüstenfeld). Among European travellers in the area, Philby is the first to have visited and described Ḍariyya and its companion village Miska, about 6 kilometers to the north (*The Land of Midian*, 9, 52). He mentions Kūfic inscriptions found on rocks in Ḍariyya, attesting to its former prominence as a pilgram station. Ḍariyya is in territory now occupied by ʿUtayba and Ḥarb, tribes which figured as makeweights in the struggles of the late 18th and early 19th centuries among the S̲h̲arīfs of Mecca and the ruling families of Ras̲h̲īd and Saʿūd for domination of Nad̲j̲d.

Bibliography: Cf. *EI²*, ii, 924. In addition: al-Samhūdī, *Wafā' al-Wafā'*, ii, 228; Ibn Bulayhid, *Ṣaḥīḥ al-Ak̲h̲bār*, iii, 11, 244; J. J. Hess, *Isl.* (1917) 106; Moritz, *Arabien*, 50: Doughty, *Travels in Arabia Deserta*, ii, 492; Philby, *The land of Midian*, 9, 52; Admiralty, *Western Arabia and the Red Sea*, 1946, 189. (PHEBE MARR)

AL-**DARʿĪYYA** [see AL-DIRʿIYYA]

DARḲĀWA, plural of the *nisba* Darḳāwī, a religious brotherhood founded in north Morocco at the end of the 18th century by an Idrīsī *s̲h̲arīf*, Mawlāy al-ʿArbī al-Darḳāwī. His name is supposed to come from the appelation of one of his ancestors who used to be called Abū Darḳa, the man with the leather shield. He was the pupil at Fās of another Idrīsī *s̲h̲arīf*, ʿAlī b. ʿAbd al-Raḥmān al-Djamal, an adept of the mystical doctrine of al-S̲h̲ād̲h̲ilī [*q.v.*], and after the latter's death, he organized a brotherhood inspired by this doctrine. The seat of this group was at first the *zāwiya* of Bū Brīḥ in the tribe of the Banū Zarwāl (on the right bank of the Oued Warg̲h̲a), then, after 1863, the *zāwiya* of Amad̲j̲d̲j̲ūṭ (Amjot) not far from there, where it is still located and where each year at the end of September the annual festival (*mawsim*) of the brotherhood is celebrated. Many pilgrims go there on this occasion.

The Darḳāwa brotherhood has spread above all in the north and east of Morocco and in the west of Algeria. In Morocco especially it has brought together adepts from every kind of social class, including the Sharifian court: the sultans, Mawlāy ʿAbd al-Raḥmān (1822-1859) and Mawlāy Yūsuf (1912-1927) belonged to it. At the end of the 19th century, the number of Darḳāwa in Algeria was estimated at about 14,500, and in 1939, at almost 34,000 in Morocco.

The doctrine of the Darḳāwa appears perfectly orthodox; it insists essentially on the necessity of man's consecrating himself as far as possible to the contemplation of divinity and to the mystic union with God. To attain this the Darḳāwī must pray as often as he can, and particularly during the sessions of prayer (*d̲h̲ikr*) which are held regularly in the customary meeting-places of the brotherhood. These sessions aim at provoking ecstasy by means of the recitation of pious formulas, mystical poems, song and dance. An excellent description of them is to be found in the *Essai sur la mystique musulmane* of E. Dermenghem, the preface to his translation of the *K̲h̲amriyya* of Ibn al-Fāriḍ (Paris 1931, 64, n. 1). In order better to detach themselves from the world, certain adepts go so far as to live as wanderers, a staff in their hands, clothed miserably, and with a rosary of a hundred beads round their necks. The majority content themselves with paying as little attention as possible to wordly matters, and with taking no part in any form of public life.

Nevertheless, on several occasions the Darḳāwa have played a part in politics: one of them, Ibn al-S̲h̲arīf, provoked serious agitation in the Turkish province of Oran which lasted for several years (1803-9); but for the moderation of the sultan Mawlāy Sulaymān (1792-1822), this agitation might have ended in the annexation of western Algeria by Morocco. Soon afterwards, various groups of Darḳāwa took an active part on the Berber revolt of the last years of Mawlāy Sulaymān's reign, and the head of the brotherhood was even imprisoned for a time. After the death of Mawlāy Sulaymān, the Darḳāwa took hardly any further part in the political life of Morocco, even in the troubled years at the beginning of the 20th century. On the other hand, they played a certain part during the first years of the French conquest of Algeria by opposing the Amir ʿAbd al-Ḳādir, who was accused of making common cause with the French after the Desmichels (1834) and Tafna (1837) treaties.

Bibliography: Mawlāy al-ʿArbī al-Darḳāwī, *Rasā'il*, lith. Fās, 1318/1900-01; Muḥammad b. D̲j̲aʿfar al-Kattānī, *Salwat al-Anfās*, lith. Fas 1316/1898-9, *passim*, and especially i, 176, 267, 358; Nāṣirī, *K. al-Istiḳṣā'*, Cairo 1312/1894-5, iv, 140; Zayyānī, *Turd̲j̲umān al-muʿrib*, ed. Houdas, Paris 1886, 100-2; L. Rinn, *Marabouts et K̲h̲ouan*, Algiers 1884, 231-64; O. Depont and X. Coppolani, *Les Confréries Musulmanes*, Algiers 1897, 503; A. Joly, *Étude sur les Chadeilias*, Algiers 1907; G. Drague, *Esquisse d'Histoire Religieuse du Maroc*, Paris n.d.,251-73. (R. LE TOURNEAU)

DARNA, in modern pronunciation Derna, a town on the northern coast of Cyrenaica which is to-day the second most important in the region after Beng̲h̲āzī. It is situated in a little plain along the banks of a *wādī* of the same name, bounded by the plateau of the al-D̲j̲abal al-Ak̲h̲ḍar, which forms a steep slope to the south and touches the sea to the east and west, but thanks to its never-failing springs it is rich in palms (8,000) and in orange and other fruit trees. Darna owes its origin to the Greeks who founded one of their colonies in the neighbourhood. Darnis, as their trading post was called, did not become a *polis* and was not one of the five cities combined into a federation in the time of Alexander the Great, which gave the country its name, Pentapolis. It is probable that it developed only in the time of the Ptolemies. Darna shared the fate of the Pentapolis and with it became a Roman possession in 96 B.C., in accordance with the will of Ptolemy Apion, who renewed a decision already made in 155 B.C. by Ptolemy Physcon (= Ptolemy VII, Euergetes II Neoteros); concerning these facts, an important inscription discovered at Cyrene, and the bibliography, see Romanelli, *Cirenaica*, 1-24. Under the Byzantines, Darna was the seat of a bishopric which already existed at the time of the Council of Nicea in 325. On the conquest of Pentapolis by the Muslims, see BARḲA. According to Yāḳūt, it was at Darna that the governor of the country, Abū S̲h̲addād Zuhayr b. Ḳays al-Balawī, was killed in 76/695 (or in 74/693?), as he was hastening to meet the Greeks who had disembarked there in an attempt to recapture the region. Yāḳūt says that his tomb, and those of others killed in the battle, were well-known. Under the Arabs Darna fell into decay; if this were not proved by the complete silence of the Arab geographers with regard to it, it would be possible to deduce it from the fact that its prosperity was always linked to the exploitation of its soil and that the conquering Arabs were never farmers. Its harbour was not as good as others in Cyrenaica, and its site was at some distance from the route followed generally by the Arab armies and the caravans of merchants and pilgrims, which passed about 90 kms. to the south (by ʿAyn al-Ghazāla, al-Tamīmī and al-Makhīlī). It was from the end of the 15th century on, or even later, that Darna revived thanks to the immigration of Andalusians, coming less from Andalusia than from other places in North Africa where they had already found refuge. Accurate information on the arrival of these farmers of Spanish origin goes back to the 17th century: a Turkish Pasha called Ḳāsim, returning from Tripoli to Constantinople, had noticed the fertility of the Darna region and, after having obtained a concession from the Sublime Porte, established himself there with the Andalusians; later on his lieutenant requested the help of the Bey of Tunis in transferring there other Andalusians who had been living in Tunis. Eight hundred colonists were then brought to Darna in four ships (1637). These facts are confirmed by the authors of two well-known *riḥla*s, al-ʿAyyāshī (d. 1091/1679) and Ibn Nāṣir al-Darʿī (d. 1129/1717), who tell us that Darna was colonized by Andalusians in about 1040/ 1631-2. Before this date, according to these travellers, the town had been in ruins for a long time. It had therefore begun to prosper again when the Dey of Tripoli, Muḥammad (1041-59/1632-49), who wanted to keep all the threads of trans-Saharian trade in his own hands, and did not like foreign expansion in the cities of Cyrenaica, made an expedition against Benghāzī (1638) and Awdjila (1640), for part of the caravans from Fezzān and from Bornu used to reach the Mediterranean coast by way of this oasis. Darna must also have fallen into the power of this Pasha, because we learn that its population was unwilling to bear the yoke of Tripoli and that Muḥammad's successor, the Dey ʿUthmān, marched against the town in 1656. As a consequence of this attack, Darna was left almost deserted, so great was the number of the dead and the exiled. However, it soon revived again; even to-day it venerates the memory of Muḥammed Bey (presumably, Muḥammad b. Maḥmūd, governor for the Pasha of Tripoli: see Ibn Ghalbūn, *Cronaca*, or a rich private person of Anatolia), because he, towards the end of the 17th century, gave attention to the irrigation system and achieved various other public works, notably the construction of the Great Mosque, which has 42 cupolas and the only minaret in the town. The daring and hardihood of the people of Darna continued to cause trouble even to the government of the Ḳaramanlī; Aḥmad I tried in 1715 to subdue Benghāzī and Darna once and for all. In the time of Warthīlānī, who, too, described in a *riḥla* his journey of 1179/1765-1181/1767, there was continual struggle between the inhabitants of the town and the people of Miṣrāta; in the time of Ibn Nāṣir, these last formed the garrison, and perhaps later (see Ibn Ghalbūn), after they had become established there, became part of the population. In short, just as the Bedouins of Cyrenaica, who were at all times the true masters of the region, were turbulent, so were the foreign immigrants in the principal towns. Only famines and epidemics, frequent enough in this country, weakened the tendency to rebellion. Warthīlānī tells us about a famine which caused a temporary cessation of hostilities, and Della Cella of an epidemic of plague which in 1816 reduced the population from 7,000 to 500. In 1805, Darna was the scene of a surprise attack; it was bombarded and occupied by irregular troops (400 men) with the support of three ships of the United States, because that country's naval representative for Barbary, William Eaton, intended to march from Egypt against Tripoli via Cyrenaica, in order to punish the Pasha of this town, Yūsuf Ḳaramanlī, for his corsairs' attacks against United States ships, since the direct attempts of the American fleet against Tripoli had met with failure; he had persuaded the elder brother of the Pasha, Aḥmad, (Ahmet, Hamet, in the western sources), who was considered the legitimate ruler, to join the expedition. Nevertheless, these troops did not advance much farther than Darna, for a treaty between Yūsuf and the United States put an end to this strange adventure. In 1835, after the long interval of Ḳaramanlī [*q.v.*] rule, Cyrenaica came back under the direct government of Constantinople, and Darna, one of the three *ḳaḍā*s of the *sandjaḳ* of Benghāzī, was useful to it in exercising a precarious control, which grew gradually stronger, over the interior and Marmarica. The government did its utmost to develop the land between Marsā Sūsa and Darna. When Italy decided to take possession of Libya and declared war on Turkey (29th September 1911), one of the first actions was the bombardment of Darna (30th September) and its occupation (16th October). The population of the town was then about 9,500. Under the Italians, Darna became a very beautiful and well cared for city which even tried to attract tourists. During the first world war it remained in Italian hands, and one of the places from which later the reconquest of Cyrenaica began. During the second world war, it passed several times from the hands of the Italians and Germans into that of the allies before its final occupation by the English in January 1943. It suffered much damage in the course of these operations.

Darna now forms part of the United Kingdom of Libya, following on Italy's renunciation of her colonies in the Peace Treaty (10th February 1947) and the proclamation of the kingdom (24th December, 1951). Notwithstanding the importance that the Sanūsiyya has in Cyrenaica, this *ṭarīḳa* has only one *zāwiya* in Darna, whereas 14 other *ṭarīḳa*s are represented there, some of them for as long as 150 years. One of the 70 warriors killed at the side of the above mentioned Zuhayr al-Balawī, Sīdī Bū Manṣūr al-Fārisī, whose tomb stands in the cemetery, has given his name to that part of the town which stretches along the right bank of the *wādī*.

Bibliography: For Darna in ancient times: J. P. Thrige, *Res Cyrenensium*, Copenhagen 1828, reprinted Verbania 1940 (Ital. trans., Verbania 1940) P. Romanelli, *La Cirenaica romana*, Verbania 1943 (these volumes have appeared in the collection *Storia della Libia*); among the Arab geographers, Yāḳūt, *Muʿdjam*, s.v. *Darna*, mentions the place but is confused in his information. For the events of the Berber period: C. Bergna, *Tripoli dal 1510 al 1850*, Tripoli 1925, 123 f., 149; Ch. L. Féraud, *Annales Tripolitaines*, Tunis 1927, 100-4, 109-11, 149, 319 f.; E. Rossi, *La cronaca araba tripolina di Ibn Ġalbūn (sec. XVIII) tradotta e annotata*, Bologna 1926, 101, 116 f., 150; ʿAyyāshī, *al-Riḥla al-ʿAyyāshiyya*, Fez 1316, i, 108 f. (passage copied by Warthīlānī, 232); Ibn Nāṣir al-Darʿī, *al-Riḥla al-Nāṣiriyya*, Fez 1320 (passage copied by Warthīlānī, 609 f.); Warthīlānī, *Nuzhat al-anẓār fī faḍl ʿilm al-taʾrīkh wa 'l-akhbār = al-Riḥla al-Warthīlāniyya*, Algiers 1326/1908, 608 f. For the occupation of Darna by the Americans in 1805: E. Dupuy, *Americains et Barbaresques (1776-1824)*, Paris 1910, 231-272; *Encyclopaedia Britannica*, s.v. *Eaton*,

William; V. H. Serrano, *Libya, the new Arab kingdom*, Ithaca 1956, 127-31. On 18th century European travellers: *Enciclopedia Italiana*, s.vv. *Cirenaica*, *Esplorazioni*; A. Cervelli, extract from his travel diary, in *Recueil de Voyages et Mémoires de la Societé de Géographie de Paris*, ii, 1825, P. Della Cella, *Viaggio da Tripoli di Barberia alle frontiere occidentali dell'Egitto fatto nel 1817*, Milan 1826 (1st ed. Genoa 1817), 165-70. On the last period of Turkish domination: Fr. Coro, *Settantasei anni di dominazione turca in Libia*, 1937, 102. For the period of the Italian occupation, see the bibliography in the *Enciclopedia Italiana*, s.v. *Cirenaica*, For the modern period: E. E. Evans-Pritchard, *The Sanusi of Cyrenaica*, Oxford 1954, index; N. A. Ziadeh, *Sanūsīyah, a study of a revivalist movement in Islam*, Leiden 1958, index; idem, *Barḳa, al-dawla al-ʿarabiyya al-th̲āmina*, Beirut 1950, 8 f., 18 f.; I.S.O., Playfair, *History of the Second World War, The Mediterranean and the Middle East*, I . . ., London 1954 . . ., index; E. Rossi, *Il Regno Unito della Libia*, in *OM*, xxxi (1951), 157-177 (ibid. bibliography, 162 (1)); road-map of the region of Darna (1 : 400,000) in *Bollettino geografico del Governo della Cirenaica, Servizio Studi*, no. 9; *Guida d'Italia del Touring Club italiano, Possedimenti e colonie*, Milan 1929, 484-7.

(L. Veccia Vaglieri)

DARS̲H̲AN, also less correctly darsan, a Sanskrit word (*darśana*, from the root *dṛś* "see") meaning "showing, being visible"; hence, the ceremonial appearance of a king to his subjects. This Hindū practice was adopted by the Mug̲h̲al emperor Akbar (*Āʾīn-i Akbarī*, i, 73) and his immediate successors. The English traveller Coryat records that D̲j̲ahāngīr in Āgra used to present himself three times a day from a canopied window. The failure of S̲h̲āhd̲j̲ahān to appear during his illness at the end of 1067/September 1657 led to rumours of his death. The practice of *dars̲h̲an* was at first followed by Awrangzīb, but abandoned by him in 1078/1668 as savouring of idolatry.

(J. Burton-Page)

DĀRŪG̲H̲A. The word is derived from the Mongol *daru-*, 'to press, to seal' and was used to denote a chief in the Mongol feudal hierarchy (K. H. Menges, *Glossar zu den Volkskundlichen Texten aus Ost. Turkistan*, ii, Wiesbaden 1955, 714 s.v. *dorγa*; B. Vladimirtsov, *Le régime social des Mongols*, Paris 1948, 181, 209, 214; P. Pelliot, *Notes sur l'histoire de la Horde d'or*, Paris 1950, 73). In 617-8/1221 there was a Mongol *dārūk̲h̲ači*, or representative of the head of the empire, in Almālīg̲h̲ beside the native ruler. The duties laid upon him included the making of a census of the inhabitants, the recruitment of local troops, the establishment of postal communications, the collection of taxes, and the delivery of tribute to the court (W. Barthold, *Turkestan* [2], 401). The term is first met with in Persia in the Ilk̲h̲ānid period and by Tīmūrid times it had virtually superseded the term *s̲h̲iḥna*, the *dārūg̲h̲a* exercising broadly similar functions to the *s̲h̲iḥna*. In his main capacities he belonged to the military hierarchy. The functions of the *dārūg̲h̲a* in the Ṣafawid period were sometimes those of the governor of a town (Olearius, *The Voyages and Travels* . . . ., London 1669, 304; Chardin, *Voyages*, ed. Langlès, Paris 1811, v, 260); but more commonly he was a kind of police officer, usually under the *dīwānbegī*. His duty was to prevent misdeeds, tyranny, brawls, and actions contrary to the *s̲h̲arīʿa*, such as prostitution, drinking, and gambling (*Tadhkirat al-Mulūk*, Persian text in facsimile tr. and explained by V. Minorsky, London and Leiden 1943, 77b ff.; Tavernier, *Collections of Travels* . . . ., 222, 232). He had power to fine and punish offenders and was himself responsible for the return of stolen goods (*Tadhkirat al-Mulūk*, *ibid.*). Fees, known as *dārūg̲h̲āna*, were levied in his favour (*Tadhkirat al-Mulūk*, 90b; Du Mans, *Estat de la Perse en 1660*, Paris 1890, 39). In the 12th/18th and 13th/19th centuries the main functions of the *dārūg̲h̲a* in Persia continued to be those of a police official acting under the city governor. He regulated prices, weights and measures, preserved order in the towns and bazaars, and supervised the morals of the people; his jurisdiction, which tended to become restricted to the bazaar, encroached upon and in some cases superseded that of the *muḥtasib*. In the capital he appears to have kept special registers of certain crafts which performed labour service for the crown (cf. P. A. Jaubert, *Voyage en Arménie et en Perse*, Paris 1821, 334). The office of *dārūg̲h̲a* was still found at the beginning of the Constitutional period (see E. Aubin, *La Perse d'aujourd'hui*, Paris 1908, 37, 109; *De Téhéran à Ispahan* in *RMM.*, June-July 1907, 459; and *Le Chiisme et la nationalité persane* in *RMM.*, 1908, 482); but with the new forms of government his office became an anomaly, the various functions formerly exercised by him being taken over by the municipalities and the police force.

The term *dārūg̲h̲a* was not, however, applied exclusively to an official whose functions were those of a town governor or police officer. There are several instances of the appointment of a *dārūg̲h̲a* over a tribal group, whose functions were clearly rather different from those of the *dārūg̲h̲a* of a town or the *dārūg̲h̲a* of the bazaar. For example ʿAbd al-Razzāḳ states that Tīmūr used sometimes to send a *dārūg̲h̲a* and a *muḥaṣṣil* to collect the taxes due from the Hazāra near Harāt (*Maṭlaʿ al-Saʿdayn*, ed. Muḥammad S̲h̲afīʿ, ii, 1297). There was also a *dārūg̲h̲a* of the Turkomans in Astarābād in Ṣafawid times (cf. Ḥasan Rūmlū, *Aḥsan al-Tawārīk̲h̲*, ed. and tr. C. N. Seddon, Baroda, 1931-4, 346-7); and under the Ḳād̲j̲ārs the taxes of various Turkoman tribes appear to have been collected by a *dārūg̲h̲a* (cf. *Rūznāma-yi Dawlat-i ʿAliyya-i Īrān*, 2 Rabīʿ I 1280, 26 Muḥarram, 1287). There are other cases also of a *dārūg̲h̲a* being appointed over special sections of the population. Thus, the *dārūg̲h̲a* of the Mad̲j̲ūsiyān of Yazd is mentioned c. 1054/1644 (Muḥammad Mufīd, *D̲j̲āmiʿi Mufīdī*, B.M. Or. 210, f. 363b). It is not stated what his functions were; they may well have been to collect the taxes due from the Zoroastrian community and to enforce any special regulations relating to that community.

Under the Ṣafawids the term *dārūg̲h̲a* was also used to denote a kind of head clerk controlling the staff of the larger government departments; such were the *dārūg̲h̲a* of the *farrās̲h̲k̲h̲āna* and the *dārūg̲h̲a* of the *daftark̲h̲āna* (*Tadhkirat al-Mulūk*, ff. 91a-b, 141; Tavernier, 222). This usage of the term *dārūg̲h̲a* continued in the Ḳād̲j̲ār period.

In Muslim India the term *dārūg̲h̲a* was used to denote an official in the royal stables (Abu 'l-Faḍl, *Āʾīn-i Akbarī*, tr. Blochmann, i, 53). In British India it was used to designate the native head of various departments; and from 1793 to 1862-3 the local chief of police was also known as the *dārōg̲h̲a* (H. Yale and H. C. Burnell, *Hobson-Jobson*, London 1903, 297-8). In Georgia in Ṣafawid times the *dārūg̲h̲a* was a police officer working in conjunction with the *mouravi* (constable) and *melik* (Armenian burgomaster) and the *kadk̲h̲udā* (see the charters analysed by M. F. Brosset in *Histoire de la Georgie*).

Bibliography: See text above and G. Le Strange, *Clavijo's Embassy to Tamerlane 1403-1406*, London 1928, 304; idem, *Don Juan of Persia*, London 1926, 46; J. Fryer, *Travels*, London 1698, 339; W. Francklin, *Observations on a Tour from Bengal to Persia*, 130-1, 146-7; Krushinsky, *The History of the Revolution in Persia*, Dublin 1729, 80; E. S. Waring, *A Tour to Sheeraz by the Route of Kazroon and Feerozabad*, London 1807, 67; Sir J. Malcolm, *History of Persia*, London 1829, ii, 324; M. Tancoigne, *A Narrative of a Journey into Persia*, London 1820, 238-9, J. B. Fraser, *Travels and Adventures in the Persian Provinces on the Southern Banks of the Caspian Sea*, London 1826, 149; R. B. M. Binning, *A Journal of Two Years Travel in Persia, Ceylon, etc.*, London 1857, i, 337-9; A. K. S. Lambton, *The Evolution of the office of Dārūgha*, in *Mardum Shināsī*, Tehran [nos. 1-3], 1338 s./1959-60. (A. K. S. Lambton)

al-**DĀRŪM**, the name of a coastal plain in Palestine, and later in particular the name of a famous fortress of the time of the Crusades, is to be found in the works of Arab authors with both these meanings. The Hebrew *dārōm* from which it is derived and to which it corresponds in the Arabic version of Deuteronomy, XXXIV, 3°, appeared in a few passages of the Old Testament for south as a cardinal point, or any country situated in the south (F. M. Abel), and it was later applied especially to the south-west of Judea, a low-lying region distinct both from Sephela which bordered it on the north and the southern, desert territory of the Negeb. The Byzantine name Daromas, which corresponded to this ancient Darom, was equally applied to the south-west section of the vast district of Eleutheropolis (see bayt djibrīn), while not including the town itself. However, this distinction was forgotten in Arab times and al-Dārūm, according to the evidence of al-Muḳaddasī, was identified with the territory surrounding Bayt Djibrīn, and it shared its history from the time of its conquest under the Caliphate of Abū Bakr.

As to the Palestinian citadel of al-Dārūm, the Daron of the Crusaders, it stood on the road from Gaza to Egypt on the site marked to-day by the ruins of Dayr al-Balaḥ, to assure the defence of the Latin kingdom of Jerusalem from this side. Attacked especially by Salāḥ al-Dīn, then conquered by him in 583/1187 at the time of his re-occupation of the greater part of Palestine, it was later besieged, taken, and then dismantled by Richard Cœur de Lion and the Franks of the Third Crusade in 588/1192, but was still counted in the Mamlūk period as one of the fortresses depending directly on the *nāʾib* of the district of Gaza, on the coastal border of the province of Damascus.

Bibliography: F. M. Abel, *Géographie de la Palestine*, Paris 1933-8, especially i, 420-3; G. Le Strange, *Palestine under the Moslems*, London 1890, 437; A. S. Marmardji, *Textes Géographiques*, Paris 1951, 71-2; Caetani, *Annali*, index (ii, 1299); Ṭabarī, index; *BGA*, indices; Yāḳūt, ii, 525; Ibn al-Athīr, especially xi, 326, 361, and xii, 52-3; *Hist. Or. Cr.*, i to v, indices; Ibn Shaddād, *Aʿlāḳ*, Southern Syria, ms. Leiden 800, fol. 139 b; R. Grousset, *Hist. des Croisades*, Paris 1934-6, index, especially ii, 559-62 and iii, 85-7; M. Gaudefroy-Demombynes, *La Syrie à l'époque des Mamelouks*, Paris 1923, especially 14 and 50. (J. Sourdel-Thomine)

ḌARŪRA, necessity (also *iḍṭirār*), in works of *fiḳh* has a narrow meaning when it is used to denote what may be called the technical state of necessity, and a wider sense when authors use it to describe the necessities or demands of social and economic life, which the jurists had to take into account in their elaboration of the law which was otherwise independent of these factors.

I. The state of necessity, whose effects recall those of violence, does not result from threats expressed by a person, but from certain factual circumstances which may oblige an individual, finding himself in a dangerous situation which they have brought about (shipwrecked, dying of hunger or thirst in the desert, for example), to do some action forbidden by the law, or to conclude a legal transaction on very unfavourable terms in order to escape from the danger which threatens him. The Ḳurʾān contains numerous verses which, directly or indirectly, legitimize on grounds of necessity certain acts which in principle are forbidden (II, 168; V, 5; VI, 119; XVI, 116). Ibn Nudjaym derived from this a maxim which became famous: *al-ḍarūrāt tubīḥ al-maḥẓūrāt*, which the Ottoman *Madjalla* (art. 21) reproduced literally and which may be translated: "Necessity makes lawful that which is forbidden".

The effects of the state of necessity of which the writers here fixed the conditions and limits, are more or less drastic according to the domain of *fiḳh* in which they occur.

a) In what concerns prohibitions of a religious character (the prohibition against eating pork or dead animals, or against drinking blood or other liquids regarded as impure, for example), it is admitted without difference between the Schools, that necessity legitimizes the non-observance of these rules. It follows—and this is the opinion which has prevailed in doctrine—that one is even obliged to disregard them in a case of danger.

b) Most of the offences committed under the rule of necessity (for example, the theft of food, a shipwrecked person's throwing into the sea the goods of another shipwrecked person in the same boat if it is too heavily laden) are excused and do not give rise to any form of punishment, although they do not cancel any civil responsibility. Three offences are never legitimized, let alone simply excused, whatever may be the circumstances in which they are committed (apart from legitimate defence). They are: murder, the amputation of a limb, or serious wounding likely to cause death; in these cases the evil inflicted is equal, if not superior, to that which the perpetrator of the offence has endeavoured to avoid, and there is no reason to favour him rather than the victim.

c) Jurists have not paid much attention to the effect of legal transactions (sale, lease) committed under necessity. They regard it only as a case of violence (*ikrāh*) to be decided according to the rules which govern violence in general. Nevertheless, in treatises on *fiḳh* rules are found relating to a sale concluded in a state of necessity, when one of the parties (buyer or seller) exploits the circumstances which force the other to buy or sell. The Ḥanafīs call such a sale *fāsid*; the writers of the other schools decree that the price should not be that so agreed, but the habitual price of something equivalent (*thaman al-mithl*).

II. *Ḍarūra* is used in a much wider sense by the commentators when they try to justify by practical necessity, solutions which the lawyers of the first centuries of the Hidjra adopted by *istiḥasān* or *istiṣlāḥ* rather then by the rules of reasoning by analogy (*ḳiyās*). In these very numerous cases, the word is no longer synonymous with constraint, but signifies practical necessity, the exigencies of social and economic life. This is why other expressions such as *ḥādja* or *taʿāmul al-nās* or *maṣlaḥa* are frequently used. It is almost exclusively in S̲h̲āfiʿī law, which does not recognize *istiḥsān*, that these divergencies from *ḳiyās* had to be justified by reason of necessity, then taken in its narrower sense (al-G̲h̲azzālī, *al-Mustaṣfā*, Cairo 1322, i, 284 ff.).

Ḍarūra in its wider meaning takes into consideration the existence in Muḥammadan law of rules and who'e institutions which reasoning by strict analogy (*ḳiyās*) would have condemned, but which the "necessities" imposed, for instance contracts of hire and lease (*idjāra*) and of mercantile partnership (*s̲h̲arika*), loan of money (*ḳarḍ*), the agricultural contract of *muzāraʿa*, several kinds of sale including the *salam* sale, and a number of rules concerning details which have no other justification.

> Bibliography: I. Ibn Nud̲j̲aym, *al-As̲h̲bāh wa-'l-naẓāʾir*, ed. Cairo, 43; *al-Baḥr al-rāʾiḳ*, Cairo 1334, viii, 71 ff.; Kāsānī, *Badāʾiʿ al-ṣanāʾiʿ*, Cairo 1328/1910, vii, 175 ff.; Ibn ʿĀbidīn, *Radd al-muk̲h̲tār*, ed. Cairo, iv, 146, v, 124; Ḥaṭṭāb, *Commentary on K̲h̲alīl*, Cairo 1329, iii, 233 ff.; Ibn Ḳudāma, *al-Mug̲h̲nī*, 2nd ed. of *al-Manār*, Cairo, xi, 75, 79-80; ʿAbd al-Ḳādir, ʿAwda, *al-Tas̲h̲rīʿ al-d̲j̲anāʾī al-islāmī²*, Cairo 1379/1959, i, 576-81.
>
> II. ʿAbd al-Wahhāb K̲h̲allāf, *Maṣādir al-tas̲h̲rīʿ al-islāmī fīmā lā naṣṣ fīhi*, Cairo 1955, especially 62; D. Santillana, *Instituzioni di Diritto Musulmano Malichita*, Rome 1925, i, nos. 22 to 25.

On the "necessity" in theologica, see IḌṬIRĀR.

(Y. Linant de Bellefonds)

DARWĪSH (Darwēs̲h̲) is commonly explained as derived from Persian and meaning "seeking doors", *i.e.*, a mendicant (Vullers, *Lexicon*, i, 839a, 845b; *Gr. I. Ph.*, i/1, 260; ii, 43, 45); but the variant form *daryōs̲h̲* is against this, and the real etymology appears to be unknown. Broadly through Islam it is used in the sense of a member of a religious fraternity, but in Persian and Turkish more narrowly for a mendicant religious called in Arabic a *faḳīr*. In Morocco and Algeria for dervishes in the broadest sense, the word most used is *Ik̲h̲wān*, "brethren", pronounced *k̲h̲uān*. These fraternities (*ṭuruḳ*, plural of *ṭarīḳa* [q.v.], "path", *i.e.*, method of instruction, initiation and religious exercise) form the organized expression of religious life in Islam. For centuries that religious life (see TAṢAWWUF) was on an individual basis. Beyond the single soul seeking its own salvation by ascetic practices or soaring meditations, there was found at most a teacher gathering round himself a circle of disciples. Such a circle might even persist for a generation or two after his death, led by some prominent pupil, but for long there was nothing of the nature of a perpetual corporation, preserving an identity of organization and worship under a fixed name. Only in the 6th/12th century—the troubled times of the Sald̲j̲ūḳ break-up—did continuous corporations began to appear. The Ḳādirites, founded by ʿAbd al-Ḳādir al-D̲j̲īlānī [q.v.] (d. 561/1166), seem to have been the first still-existing fraternity of definitely historical origin. Thereafter, we find these organizations appearing in bewildering profusion, founded either

by independent saints or by split and secession from older bodies. Such historical origins must, however, be sharply distinguished from the legends told by each as to the source of their peculiar ritual and devotional phrases. As the origin of Ṣūfism is pushed back to the Prophet himself, and its orthodoxy is thus protected, so these are traced down from the Prophet (or rather from Allāh through Gabriel and the Prophet) through a series of well-known saints to the historic founder. This is called the *silsila* or "chain" of the order, and another similar *silsila* or apostolic succession of Heads extends from the founder to the present day. Every darwīs̲h̲ must know the *silsila* which binds him up to Allāh himself, and must believe that the faith taught by his order is the esoteric essence of Islam, and that the ritual of his order is of as high a validity as the *ṣalāt*. His relationship to the *silsila* is through his individual teacher (*s̲h̲ayk̲h̲*, *murs̲h̲id*, *ustād̲h̲*, *pīr*) who introduces him into the fraternity. That takes place through an *ʿahd*, "covenant", consisting of religious professions and vows which vary in the different bodies. Previously the neophyte (*murīd*, "willer", "intender") has been put through a longer or shorter process of initiation, in some forms of which it is plain that he is brought under hypnotic control by his instructor and put into rapport with him. The theology is always some form of Ṣūfism, but varies in the different *ṭarīḳa*s from ascetic quietism to pantheistic antinomianism. This goes so far that in Persia dervishes are divided into those *bā-s̲h̲arʿ* "with law", that is, following the law of Islam, and those *bī-s̲h̲arʿ* "without law", that is, rejecting not only the ritual but the moral law. In general the Persians and the Turks have diverged farther from Islam than the Syrians, Arabs or Africans, and the same *ṭarīḳa* in different countries may assume different forms. The ritual always lays stress on the emotional religious life, and tends to produce hypnotic phenomena (auto and otherwise) and fits of ecstasy. One order, the K̲h̲alwatiyya [q.v.], is distinguished by its requiring from all its members an annual period of retreat in solitude, with fasting to the utmost possible limit and endless repetitions of religious formulae. The effect on the nervous system and imagination is very marked. The religious service common to all fraternities is called a *d̲h̲ikr* [q.v.], a "remembering", that is, of Allāh (Ḳur. XXXIII, 41 is the basic text), and its object is to bring home to the worshipper the thought of the unseen world and of his dependence upon it. Further, it is plain that a *d̲h̲ikr* brings with it a certain heightened religious exaltation and a pleasant dreaminess. But there go also with the hypnosis, either as excitants or consequents, certain physical states and phenomena which have earned for dervishes the various descriptions in the west of barking, howling, dancing, etc. The Mawlawīs, founded by D̲j̲alāl al-Dīn al-Rūmī (d. at Konya in 672/1274), stimulate their ecstasies by a whirling dance. The Saʿdīs used to have the Dawsa [q.v.] and still in their monasteries use the beating of little drums, called *bāz*. The use of these is now forbidden in the Egyptian mosques as an innovation (*bidʿa*; Muḥammad ʿAbduh, *Taʾrīk̲h̲*, ii, 144 ff.). The Saʿdīs, Rifāʿīs and Aḥmadīs have particular feats, peculiar to each *ṭarīḳa*, of eating glowing embers and live serpents or scorpions and glass, of passing needles through their bodies and spikes into their eyes. But besides such exhibitions, which may in part be tricks and in part rendered possible by a hypnotic state, there appear amongst dervishes automatic phenomena of clairaudience and clairvoyance and even of levitation, which deserve more attention than they have yet received. These, however, appear only in the case of accepted saints (*walīs*: [*q.v.*]), and are explained as *karāmāt* [*q.v.*] (χαρίσματα) wrought by Allāh for them. But besides the small number of full members of the orders, who reside in the monasteries (*khānḳāh, ribāṭ, zāwiya, takiyya* or *takya*) or wander as mendicant friars (the Ḳalanderīs, an order derived from the Bakṭāshīs, must wander continually), there is a vast number of lay members, like Franciscan and Dominican tertiaries, who live in the world and have only a duty of certain daily prayers and of attending *dhikrs* from time to time in the monasteries. At one time the number of regular dervishes must have been much larger than now. Especially in Egypt under the Mamlūks, their convents were very numerous and were richly endowed. Their standing then was much higher than it is now, when dervishes are looked down upon by the canon lawyers and professed theologians (*ʿulamā*) in the essential contest of intuitionists on the one hand and traditionists and rationalists on the other. For this division see further under TAṢAWWUF. Now their numbers are drawn mostly from the lower orders of society, and for them the fraternity house is in part like a church and in part like a club. Their relation to it is much more personal than to a mosque, and the fraternities, in consequence, have come to have the position and importance of the separate church organizations in Protestant Christendom. As a consequence, in more recent times, the governments have assumed a certain indirect control of them. This, in Egypt, was exercised by the Shaykh al-Bakrī, who was head of all the dervish fraternities there (*Kitāb bayt al-Ṣiddīḳ*, 379 ff.). Elsewhere there is a similar head for each city. The Sanūsīs [*q.v.*] alone, by retiring into the deserts of Arabia and North Africa and especially by keeping their organization inaccessible in the depths of the Sahara, have maintained their freedom from this control. Their membership is also of a distinctly higher social order than that of the other fraternities. As women in Islam have generally the same religious, though not legal, status as men, so there are women dervishes. These are received into the order by the shaykh; but are often instructed and trained by women, and almost always hold their *dhikrs* by themselves. In mediaeval Islam such female dervishes often led a cloistered life, and there were separate foundations and convents for them with superiors of their own sex. Now, they seem to be all tertiaries. To give a complete list of fraternities is quite impossible here. Besides the separate articles referred to above, see, also, the articles on the various Ṣūfī leaders and orders.

Bibliography: The bibliography on this subject is very large, and the following is only a selection: Depont and Coppolani, *Les confréries religieuses musulmanes*, Algiers 1897; A. Le Chatelier, *Les confréries musulmanes du Hedjaz*, Paris 1887; Goldziher, *Vorlesungen*, 168 ff., 195 ff.; Lane, *Modern Egyptians*, chaps. x, xx, xxiv, xxv; J. P. Browne, *The Derwishes, or Oriental Spiritualism*, London 1868, ed. with introd. and notes by H. A. Rose, Oxford and London, 1927; Hughes, *Dictionary of Islam*, s.v. *Faqīr*; D'Ohsson, *Tableau général de l'Empire Othoman*, ii, Paris 1790; Sir Charles N. E. Eliot, *Turkey in Europe*, London 1900; E. G. Browne, *A Year among the Persians*, London 1893; T. H. Weir, *Shaikhs of Morocco*, Edinburgh 1904; B. Meakin, *The Moors*, London 1902, chap. xix,; H. Vambéry, *Travels in Central Asia*, London 1864, and all Vambéry's books of travel and history; W. H. T. Gairdner, *The 'Way' of a Mohammadan Mystic* (in *MW*, April 1912 ff.); D. B. Macdonald, *Dervish* in *Encyclopaedia Britannica*, ed. xi, but to be corrected by above, also his *Religious Attitude and Life in Islām*, Chicago 1909, and *Aspects of Islām*, New York 1911, both by index; Aḥmad Amīn, *Ḳāmūs al-ʿādāt ... al-miṣriyya*, Cairo 1953, 199; For the present state of the brotherhoods, L. Massignon, *Annuaire du monde musulman*, iv, 1954, 426; index no. 4, esp. on the Shaykh al-Bakrī, ibid. 274, after the list of congregations; more generally, L. Massignon, *Annuaire du monde musulman*, iii, 1929, 457-61: *ṭarīḳa*; idem, art. ṬARĪḲA in *EI*[1]; P. J. André, *Contribution à l'étude des confréries religieuses musulmanes*, 1956. For the various meanings of the word and the two proposed etymologies see Vullers, *Lexicon persico-latinum*, s.v.; Dozy, *Suppl.*, s.v. *drwz*. Miniatures: Ph. W. Schulz, *Die Persisch-islamische Miniatur-malerei*, pl. 156, 165; pl. 188 (caricature).

(D. B. MACDONALD *)

DARYĀ-BEGI, DERYĀ-BEYI, sea-lord, a title given in the Ottoman Empire to certain officers of the fleet. In the 9th/15th century the term *deryā-beyi* or *deñiz-beyi* is sometimes used of the commandant of Gallipoli [see GELIBOLU], who had the rank of Sandjaḳ-beyi, and was the naval commander-in-chief until the emergence of the Kapudan Pasha [*q.v.*]. In the 10th/16th century the Kapudan Pasha became, as well as an admiral, the governor of an *eyālet*, which consisted of a group of ports and islands [see DJAZĀ'IR-I BAḤR-I SAFĪD]. This province, like others, was divided into Sandjaḳs, the governors of which were called *deryā-beyi* instead of *sandjaḳ-beyi*. The *deryā-beyis* and the officers under them held appanages and fiefs like the feudal cavalry; they were required to serve with the fleet, and to supply, equip, and man one, two, or three galleys, according to the importance of their sandjaḳs. Their fiefs were administered by the department called *Deryā Ḳalemi*, sea office, which also handled the *mensūkhāt* [*q.v.*]. The *deryā-beyis* usually held their appointments for life, and transmitted them to their sons. Their ships were auxiliary to the main fleet.

Bibliography: Marsigli, *Etat militaire de l'Empire ottoman*, i, The Hague 1732, 144-5; M. D'Ohsson, *Tableau général de l'Empire othoman*, vii, Paris 1824, 424; Hammer-Purgstall, *Staatsverfassung*, ii, 252-3; I. H. Uzunçarşılı, *Osmanlı devletinin merkez ve bahriye teşkilâtı*, Ankara 1948, 421, 427, 423; Gibb-Bowen, 1/i, 102.

(B. LEWIS)

DARYĀ-YI SHĀHĪ [see URMIYA]

DASKARA, name of four places in ʿIrāḳ, viz: 1. a town on the Diyālā N. E. of Baghdād, 2. a village in the district of Nahr al-Malik W. of Baghdād, 3. a village near Djabbul, S. of Baghdād, 4. a village in Khūzistān (cf. Yāḳūt, ii, 575; *Marāṣid*, i, 402; cf. Muḳaddasī, 26).

Daskara is arabicized from the Pahlavi *dastakarta* (Dastkarta, Dastakrta), modern Persian Dastadjird [*q.v.*]; it means a post, a village, a town or simply level ground (see Herzfeld, *Geschichte der Stadt Samarra*, Hamburg 1948, 44; J. Markwart, *A catalogue of the provincial capitals of Eranshahr*, Rome 1931, 59; Djawālīḳī, *Muʿarrab*, 67; A. Geiger, in *WZKM*, xlii, 1935, 124; Eddi Shīr, *al-Alfāẓ al-Fārisiyya al-Muʿarraba*, 64; Vullers, *Lexicon Persico-Lat.*, i, 871-2, 878 (s.vv. *Daskara, Dastikār, Dastakarta*); Fleischer in Levy, *Chaldaeisches Wörterb.*, ii, 577 (contra ii, 430ᵃ); Perles, *Etymol. Studien*, 83; H. Hübschmann, *Armenische Grammatik* (1897), 135, Yāḳūt, ii, 575).

The best known is Daskara I, 16 parasangs (c. 88 km.) by the post road east of Baghdād (Ibn Khurradādhbih, 18-19) just above the 34° N. Lat. It is the modest successor of Sasanian Dastadjird [*q.v.*], probably a caravan post which developed into an important town. Its association with Hurmizd I (272-3) who very probably rebuilt it (cf. Yāḳūt, v, 575 and Ḥamza al-Iṣfahānī), and with Khusraw Parvēz (590-608) who made it his permanent residence, account for its name Daskarat al-Malik (The King's Daskara) (Herzfeld, *Samarra*, 44; Ibn al-Athīr, i, 348, 363).

In 628, Heraclius reduced it to a heap of ruins, and a few years later the Arab conquests followed.

In the Islamic period, Daskara (or Daskarat al-Malik) was the centre of an agricultural district (*ṭassūdj*) in Astān Shādh Ḳubādh, and a caravan station of some importance on the Khurāsān road. (Ibn Khurradādhbih, 13, 41; Yaʿḳūbī, *Buldān*, 270). In early Islamic history Daskara became a Khāridjite stronghold (Ibn al-Athīr, iii, 290, 313; Ṭabarī, i, 3310, 3388; ii, 890, 896. Even in the 3rd/9th century the Khawāridj were associated with it, ibid. iii, 1689-90, 2108).

Daskara, as a village or small town, grew gradually and attained some prosperity in the 3rd/9th century (See Ḳudāma, 238 for the revenue of the *ṭassūdj* of Daskara). Ibn Rusta considered Daskara a big town (164). Iṣṭakhrī (318-321/930-933) and Ibn Ḥawḳal (c. 367/977) describe it as a flourishing town, surrounded by date groves and abundant cultivations. They refer to a clay fortress probably constructed by the Arabs. (Iṣṭakhrī, 87; Ibn Ḥawḳal, i, 246). However, Muḳaddasī (375/985) found it a small town with one long market (121; cf. 53). Daskara declined further and in the 7th/13th cent. Yāḳūt followed by the *Marāṣid* spoke of it as a mere village (Yāḳūt, ii, 575; cf. iii, 227; *Marāṣid*, i, 402). It is not known when Daskara was deserted.

Arab geographers were impressed with the ruins of old Dastadjird. Yaʿḳūbī (*Buldān*, 270) refers to the wonderful buildings of old Persian kings, while Ibn Rusta (164) mentions a Sasanian palace surrounded by a high wall.

The ruins of Dastadjird-Daskara are seen now about 9 miles south of Shahrubān, left of the Diyālā (Herzfeld described them in 1905). The ruins of Muslim Daskara are called Eski Baghdād. They occupy a quadrangular area of about half a square mile surrounded by a wall with round towers (Sarre-Herzfeld, *Iranische Felsreliefs*, Berlin 1910).

Bibliography: in addition to sources quoted in the article: Yāḳūt, *Mushtarik* (ed. Wüstenfeld), 179; Abū Dulaf, *al-Risāla al-thāniya* (ed. and tr. V. Minorsky), Cairo 1955; Le Strange, 62, also 48, 80; Ritter, *Erdkunde*, ix, 445, 500-10.

(A. A. Duri)

DASTADJIRD, Arabicized form of the Persian Dastagard, the name of a number of towns in the Sasanian empire. See DASKARA.

DASTŪR [see DUSTŪR].

DASTĀN [see ḤAMĀSA].

AL-**DASŪḲĪ,** BURHĀN AL-DĪN **IBRĀHĪM** B. ABI 'L-MADJD **ʿABD** AL-**ʿAZĪZ,** nicknamed ABU 'L-ʿAYNAYN, founder of the Dasūḳiyya order, also known as the Burhāniyya or Burhāmiyya, the followers being generally called Barāhima. Born most probably at the village of Marḳus in the Gharbiyya district of Lower Egypt in the year 633/1235 according to Shaʿrānī in *Lawāḳiḥ* (but 644/1246 according to Maḳrīzī in *Kitāb al-Sulūk* and 653/1255 according to Ḥasan b. ʿAlī Shāmma the commentator on his *ḥizb*) he spent most of his life in the neighbouring village of Dasūḳ or Dusūḳ where he died at the age of 43 and was buried. His father (buried at Marḳus) was a famous local *walī* and his maternal grandfather Abu 'l-Fatḥ al-Wāsiṭī (Shaʿrānī, *Lawāḳiḥ*, i, 176) was the leading Rifāʿī *khalīfa* in the Gharbiyya district. It would seem that Wāsiṭī, in conjunction with a disciple of his, Muḥammad b. Hārūn (*ibid.*, ii, 3), possibly in rivalry to Ibrāhīm's father, were the first to start a legend concerning the saintliness of Ibrāhīm when they credited him with having certified to the beginning of Ramaḍān by refusing to take his mother's breast on the day of his birth at the end of Shaʿbān. After a brief study of Shāfiʿī law, Ibrāhīm became a mystic. He left no children but was succeeded after his death by his brother Shaykh Mūsā.

His works include *al-Djawāhir* (quoted at length in Shaʿrānī's *Lawāḳiḥ*) a collection mostly of instructions to novices and homiletic injunctions, *al-Djawhara*, which enumerates his *karāmāt*, and *al-Ḥaḳā'iḳ*, a record of intimate conversations (*munādjāt*) with God. Ibrāhīm was also the author of several *ḳaṣīdas*, two of which are quoted in *Lawāḳiḥ* (see also Dār al-Kutub, Cairo, *Fihrist* Taṣawwuf no. 319 Madjāmīʿ) a *ṣalāt* (*ibid.*, no. 2593) and a *ḥizb*. *Al-Djawāhir*, his major work, consistently argues the compatibility of *ḥaḳīḳa* and *sharīʿa*. Only in ecstasy is *taklīf* dropped. Inner purity is the central theme. Adherence to the *sharīʿa* is not by word of mouth, nor is Ṣūfism a matter of outward garb or residence in *zāwiya*s. It is the inward action "*ʿamal djuwwānī*" that counts, inasmuch as one's real *zāwiya* is one's heart. The *walī* is in intimate communion with God "*muttaṣil*", and the strictest obedience to him is enjoined. Love, *taslīm* (complete trust, *i.e.*, in the *walī*) and self-mortification "*dhabh al-nafs*" are the true path of the Ṣūfī. Although the *karāmāt* listed in the *Djawhara* are extravagant, yet they were not unusual for the times. In his *Ḥaḳā'iḳ* occurs the moving prayer that Ibrāhīm made to God that his body be so enlarged that it should fill up all Hell to ransom mankind. It is evident that Ibrāhīm owed no allegiance to any other Ṣūfī. In the *Djawhara* he stated that at the age of seven he had exceeded in rank all the other saints with the exception of ʿAbd al-Ḳādir (thus affirming his independence of Rifāʿī and Badawī) but later he stated that at a ceremony in heaven God ordered him to invest all saints with the *khirḳa* saying: "O Ibrāhīm, you are the *naḳīb* over them all". The Prophet at the time was by his side but ʿAbd al-Ḳādir was behind him and Rifāʿī behind ʿAbd al-Ḳādir.

Ibrāhīm receives the briefest note from Maḳrīzī (*Kitāb al-Sulūk*, i, 739), and commenting on a certain Khayr al-Dīn Abu 'l-Karam, the Dasūḳī *khalīfa* who died in 890/1485, Ibn Iyās (ii, 228) merely says "*la baʿsa bihi*". But Ḳā'it Bay seems to have had great respect for Ibrāhīm, for he visited the sanctuary in 884/1479 (*ibid.*, ii, 189) and enlarged the building (Mubārak, *Khiṭaṭ*, xi, 7). Shaʿrānī devotes more space in the *Lawāḳiḥ* (i, 143-58) to Ibrāhīm (mostly quotations from *al-Djawāhir*) than to any other saint and it is possible that this was the starting point of a Dasūḳī revival. In 1168/1754

Ḥasan b. ʿAlī S͟hāmma wrote the first commentary on Ibrāhīm's *ḥizb* entitled *Masarrat al-ʿaynayn bi-s͟harḥ ḥizb Abi 'l-ʿAynayn* (Cairo *Fihrist*, Taṣawwuf 184 Mad̲j̲āmīʿ, and Sarkis 762) abridged by ʿAlī b. Aḥmad al-Ṣayrafī in *Kas͟hf al-g͟hāmma muk͟htaṣar al-S͟hayk͟h Ḥasan S͟hāmma* (*ibid.*, 2097). Another commentary on the *ḥizb* is by Muḥammad al-Bahī (*ibid.*, 2594) whilst a commentary on his *ṣalat* was written by a certain ʿAbd al-Ḥayy in 1271/1862 (*ibid.*, 2593). It would seem that Ibrāhīm's reputation rested to a large extent on his *ḥizb* and its efficacy in fulfilling wishes, driving away *d̲j̲inn* and its general curative and protective powers. According to Bahī, the famous 18th century Egyptian saint Muḥammad al-Hifnī used Ibrāhīm's *ḥizb*, which was usually read after the morning and sunset prayers.

According to D̲j̲abartī (iv, 176) the Burhāmiyya together with the Rifāʿiyya, Ḳādiriyya and Aḥmadiyya are the *aṣḥāb al-ʿas͟hā'ir*, *i.e.*, processions. Their founders were frequently referred to as the four *aḳyān*. A full description of the Dasūḳī *mawlid*s is in Mubārak (*K͟hiṭaṭ*, xi, 7). There were three *mawlid*s held in the three Coptic months of Barmūda, Tūbah, and Misrā respectively. The second and third lasted eight days each, but the third is *al-mawlid al-kabīr*. The Khedive Ismāʿīl enlarged the Dasūḳī sanctuary, and in 1293/1876 Ibrāhīm Pas͟ha, Ismāʿīl's son, presented it with a new *kiswa*. In his *Salsabīl al-muʿīn*, Sanūsī sums up the characteristics of the Burhāniyya, as he calls the order, as being *al-d̲h̲ikr al-d̲j̲ahrī*, self-mortification *mud̲j̲āhadāt*, and the formula "*Yā Dā'im*".

Bibliography: Muḥammad Bulḳīnī, *Ṭabaḳāt al-S͟hayk͟h Aḥmad al-S͟harnūbī*, Cairo 1280; Ṣāliḥ b. Mahdī *al-ʿAlam al-s͟hāmik͟h*, Cairo 1328, 476, T. Tawil, *Al-Taṣawwuf fī Miṣr*, Cairo 1946, *passim*; A. Le Chatelier, *Les confréries musulmanes*, Paris 1887, 190, and Lane, *Modern Egyptians*, i, 303-7. (WALID KHALIDI)

AL-DASŪḲĪ, AL-SAYYID **IBRĀHĪM** B. **IBRĀHĪM** (ʿABD AL-G͟HAFFĀR), a descendant of Mūsā, brother of the Ṣūfī Ibrāhīm Dasūḳī (see the preceding article) born in 1226/1811 in a poor family following the Mālikī ritual. After completing his elementary education in his native place of Dasūḳ, he attended the lectures of distinguished S͟hayk͟hs at the Azhar Mosque, among whom was the celebrated Mālikī Muḥammad ʿIllīs͟h (d. 1299/1882). After himself lecturing in the Azhar for a short time, he entered the employment of the state in 1248/1832 where on account of the accuracy of his knowledge of Arabic philology he received the office of corrector of the text-books destined to be used in the higher educational institutes and was ultimately appointed *bas͟h-muṣaḥḥiḥ* (chief reader) at the government printing office in Būlāḳ in the time of the K͟hedive Ismāʿīl Pas͟ha. He was for a period also assistant editor of the official gazette *al-Waḳā'iʿ al-Miṣriyya*. He died in 1300/1883. His claim to a place in this work is based on the fact that, on the recommendation of Fresnel, he was employed during E. W. Lane's second residence in Cairo with him for several years as a trusted collaborator in the preparation of and collection of material for Lane's *Arabic-English Lexicon*, for which Lane in his preface gave him a glowing testimonial. Even after Lane's return to England, Dasūḳī continued to assist him with extracts from Arabic works (preface, i, xxii, xxiii). We possess a memoir prepared for the former Egyptian minister ʿAlī Mubārak's encyclopaedic work in *sad̲j̲ʿ* from the pen of Dasūḳī in which he describes his meeting and intercourse with Lane, his impression of his personality, his domestic arrangements and mode of life in Cairo, his intercourse with Muslims there (including S͟hayk͟h Aḥmad, immortalized in the preface to the *Manners and Customs of the Modern Egyptians*), his singular mastery of the Arabic idiom ("as if he were an ʿAdnānī or a Ḳaḥṭānī"), their joint method of studying the authorities on Arabic philology and their work on the utilization of these materials for the *Lexicon*, Lane's generosity to his Arab collaborators, etc., in the fullest detail. This article is an important document for the biography of the great English Arabist.

Bibliography: ʿAlī Mubārak, *al-K͟hiṭaṭ al-D̲j̲adīda li-Miṣr al-Ḳāhira wa-mudunihā wa-bilādihā al-ḳadīma wa 'l-s͟hahīra*, Būlāḳ 1305, xi, 9-13; S. Lane-Poole, *Life of E. W. Lane*, 117 ff. (I. GOLDZIHER)

AL-DASŪḲĪ, IBRĀHĪM B. **MUḤAMMAD** B. ʿABD AL-RAḤMĀN, a Ṣūfī of repute, b. 833/1429, d. in Damascus S͟haʿbān 919/October 1513, author of collections of prayers (*wird*, *ḥizb*).

Bibliography: Ibn al-ʿImād, *S͟had̲h̲arāt*, year 919; Brockelmann, II, 153; S II, 153. (C. BROCKELMANN *)

DĀTĀ GAND̲J̲ [see HUD̲J̲WĪRĪ].

DAT̲H̲ĪNA (דתנת in Ḳatabanic inscriptions), a district in South Arabia, situated between the lands of the ʿAwd̲h̲illa (see art. ʿAWD̲H̲ALĪ), in the north-west and the ʿAwāliḳ (see art. ʿAWLAḲĪ), in the east. It belongs to the Western Aden Protectorate and has ca. 8000 inhabitants. The country is called by Hamdānī *g͟hā'iṭ*, a steppe, a description still applicable to the greater portion of it. The climate is dry and the soil is fertile only in the north-east, where it produces tobacco, wheat and maize. Dat̲h̲īna is inhabited by two large tribes, the Ahl em-Saʿīdī (al-S.) and the ʿÖlah (al-ʿUlah: ʿUlah al-Kawr and ʿUlah al-Baḥr). The chief market is al-Ḥāfa (also called Sūḳ Ahl em-Saʿīdī(. In a wider sense Dat̲h̲īna also includes the districts of the Mayāsir and Ḥasana tribes in the east; here is also the town Mōdiya (em-Awdiya "the *wādī*s"), since 1944-5 the headquarters of the Government.

Dat̲h̲īna is a very ancient country, mentioned in the inscriptions. Hamdānī gives many details on it in his *D̲j̲azīra*. By that time it probably also comprised the territory now belonging to the ʿAwd̲h̲illa. It was inhabited by the Banū Awd, who spoke very good Arabic. The main Wādīs are: W. Dat̲h̲īna, al-Ḥār, Tārān, al-G͟hamr, al-Ḥumayrā', al-Maʿwarān, Ṣaḥb, ʿUruffān, Marrān, ʿAzzān, and Ḍurā. Among the numerous settlements are mentioned: Āt̲h̲ira, al-K͟hanīna, al-Muwas͟hs͟haḥ (once the largest town in Dat̲h̲īna) etc. The big mountain al-Kawr (K. ʿAwd̲h̲illa) at one time belonged to Dat̲h̲īna; minor hills are D̲j̲abal Aswad and Rā'is͟h.

There are other places called (al-)Dat̲h̲īna or Dafīna; the geographers mention a town between Baṣra and Mecca, the name of which is usually recorded as al-Dafīna.

Bibliography: Ryckmans, *Les noms propres*, i, 330; Hamdānī, *D̲j̲azīra* (ed. Müller), 78, 80, 91 ff., 96, 125, 134; (trad. Forrer) 102, 126, 141 ff., 153 ff.; Yāḳūt, *Muʿd̲j̲am*, ii, 550; Sprenger, *Die alte Geographie Arabiens*, Berne 1875, 81, 187, 275 ff.; H. v. Maltzan, *Reise nach Südarabien*, Brunswick 1873, 269-74; C. Landberg, in *Arabica*, iv, 1897, 9-35; idem, *Études sur les dialectes de l'Arabie méridionale*, ii: Datînah, 1-3 1905-13), *passim*; idem, *Glossaire Datînois*, i-iii (1920-42), *passim*; Doreen Ingrams, *A Survey of social and economic conditions in the Aden Protectorate*, Eritrea, 1949, 27, 34; v. Wissmann and Höfner, *Beiträge zur hist. Geographie des vorislam. Südarabien*, Wiesbaden 1953, 60 ff., *et passim*. Map: Southern Arabia: Aden Protectorate, Sheet 1, by v. Wissmann, 1957; Scale 1 : 500.000 (with special plan of Dat͟hīna 1 : 250.000).

(O. Löfgren)

DĀʾŪD, DĀʾŪD b. K͟HALAF, etc. [see dāwūd, dāwūd b. k͟halaf, etc.].

DAWĀʾ [see adwiya].

DAʿWA, pl. *daʿawāt*, from the root *daʿā*, to call, invite, has the primary meaning call or invitation. In the *Ḳurʾān*, XXX, 24, it is applied to the call to the dead to rise from the tomb on the day of Judgement. It also has the sense of invitation to a meal and, as a result, of a meal with guests, *walīma*: al-Buk͟hārī, *Nikāḥ*, 71, 74; *LA*, xviii, 285. It also means an appeal to God, prayer, vow: al-Buk͟hārī, *Daʿawāt*, beginning and 26, *Wuḍūʾ*, 69, *Anbiyāʾ*, 9 (Abraham's prayer, cf. *Ḳurʾān*, II, 123), 40 (Solomon's prayer, cf. *Ḳurʾān*, XXXVIII, 34; see also *Ḳurʾān*, II, 182; X, 89; XIII 1; XV; XL, 46 (to which al-Ṭabarī, *Tafsīr*, 24, 45, gives a gloss *duʿāʾ*). The *daʿwat al-maẓlūm*, prayer of the oppressed, always reaches God: al-Buk͟hārī, *Maẓālim*, 9 (cf. *D̲j̲ihād*, 180). The *daʿwa* of the Muslim on behalf of his brother is always granted: Muslim, *D̲h̲ikr*, 88. The word is applied to a vow of any kind (*e.g.*, al-Masʿūdī, *Murūd̲j̲*, vii, 361; Ibn al-Muʿtazz, *Rasāʾil*, Cairo, 1365, 53: *daʿwa bi ʾl-s̲h̲ifāʾ*). It can also have the sense of imprecation or curse. Finally, it can be synonymous with *daʿwā*, signifying action, case, lawsuit.

In the religious sense, the *daʿwa* is the invitation, addressed to men by God and the prophets, to believe in the true religion, Islam: Ḳurʾān, XIV, 46. The religion of all the prophets is Islam, and each prophet has his *daʿwa*, an idea which has been developed, with the addition of heterodox elements, by the Ismāʿīlīs (see S. Guyard, *Fragments relatifs à la doctrine des Ismaéliens*, in *Not. et Extr.*, xxii (1874), 193; al-Maḳrīzī, *K̲h̲iṭaṭ*, i, 393, 31; cf. Hodgson, *The Order of Assassins*, 1955, 200 ff.). Muḥammad's mission was to repeat the call and invitation: it is the *daʿwat al-Islām* or *daʿwat al-Rasūl*. As we know, the Infidels' familiarity with, or ignorance of, this appeal determined the way in which the Muslims should fight against them. Those to whom the *daʿwa* had not yet penetrated had to be invited to embrace Islam before fighting could take place: see Abū Yūsuf, *Kitāb al-k̲h̲arād̲j̲*, Fr. trans. Fagnan, 295; al-Māwardī, *Aḥkām*, ch. 4, *ḳism* 2; al-Buk͟hārī, *Siyar*, 101. Elsewhere De Goeje, *BGA*, iv, 235 noted *daʿwa* in al-Muḳaddasī, 311, 5 in the sense of *invitatio ad vitam beatam* and Goldziher, *Muh. St.*, i, 61 in the meaning of *s̲h̲iʿār*.

The word *daʿwa* is also applied to the propaganda, whether open or not, of false prophets: see, *e.g.*, al-D̲j̲āḥiẓ, *Kitāb al-tarbīʿ*, ed. Pellat 75.

By a natural extension *daʿwa* also denotes the content of this appeal, the religious law, and the words *daʿwa, sunna, s̲h̲arīʿa, dīn*, are often used interchangeably. Lastly the word can be applied to those who have heard this appeal by the Prophet Muḥammad, the Islamic community, considered as a united body as a result of this appeal, and to some extent the word becomes a synonym of *umma*. Thus in al-Muḳaddasī, *BGA*, iii, 244, n.c.; cf. Abū Ḥanīfa al-Nuʿmān, *S̲h̲arḥ al-ak̲h̲bār*, in Ivanow, *The Rise of the Fatimids*, text, 4. Note also *id̲j̲timāʿ al-daʿwa* in the sense of *id̲j̲timāʿ al-kalima* (*BGA*, iv, 236).

In the politico-religious sense, *daʿwa* is the invitation to adopt the cause of some individual or family claiming the right to the imāmate over the Muslims, that is to say civil and spiritual authority, vindicating a politico-religious principle which, in the final analysis, aims at founding or restoring an ideal theocratic state based on monotheism. The whole organization responsible for attracting the greatest possible number of people to this idea and for giving power to their representatives, as well as propaganda for this purpose, is thus called *daʿwa* which can often be translated as mission or propaganda. The *daʿwa* is one of the means of founding a new empire, as Ibn K̲h̲aldūn noted, *Proleg.*, ii, 111 and 118, Rosenthal, ii, 121 and 129. Such was the ʿAbbāsid *daʿwa* which was, strictly speaking, propaganda for a member of the Prophet's family denoted impersonally by the name *al-Riḍā min Āl Muḥammad*, the accepted member of the family of Muḥammad, of which the ʿAbbāsids took advantage after the claims of the heir of the ʿAlid Muḥammad b. al-Ḥanafiyya were handed down to the ʿAbbāsid Muḥammad b. ʿAlī. This is the *daʿwat Banī Hās̲h̲im* or *daʿwat Banī ʾl-ʿAbbās*: al-Ṭabarī, ii, 1467; Ibn Abī Ṭāhir Ṭayfūr, 288. The *ṣāḥib al-daʿwa* is the person in whose name the propaganda is carried out, but the term also denotes the actual head of the organization; thus Abū Muslim is called *ṣāḥib daʿwat Banī Hās̲h̲im* (al Ṭabarī, iii, 129). Propaganda was carried out by missionaries devoted to the cause: *dāʿī*, pl. *duʿāt*, sometimes *naḳīb*, pl. *nuḳabāʿ*.

In the same way one speaks of the *daʿwa* of the ʿAlids who were persecuted by the ʿAbbāsids and took refuge in Ṭabaristān and Daylam, where they made their claims to the imāmate and founded a short-lived state (Ibn K̲h̲aldūn, *Proleg.*, ii, 122, Rosenthal, ii, 133), or of the Almohad *daʿwa* (*ibid.*, ii, 123, Rosenthal, ii, 134). Every adventurer claiming prophetic powers and seeking to win authority used the same tactics and had his *daʿwa* (see above).

The word *daʿwa* is well-known as applied to the wide-spread Ḳarmaṭī-Ismāʿīlī propaganda movement appealing to Muslims to give their allegiance to an imām descended from Ismāʿīl b. D̲j̲aʿfar al-Ṣādiḳ, a movement which resulted firstly in the Ḳarmaṭī revolt in Syria-Mesopotamia in 289-294/902-907 (see al-Ṭabarī, iii, 2218 ff.), and later in the establishment in North Africa of the Fāṭimid dynasty. In this context the word takes on a particular shade of meaning from the fact that, in conformity with the S̲h̲īʿite idea of the permanence of the revelation through the person of the imām, this *daʿwa* had come to complete the Prophet's *daʿwa*. The latter had preached faith in one single God, without the other articles of the faith, a thing permitted only to Muḥammad, but that was no longer sufficient: see a saying of D̲j̲aʿfar al-Ṣādiḳ in the *Kitāb S̲h̲arḥ al-ak̲h̲bār* by Abū Ḥanīfa al-Nuʿmān (Ivanow, *The Rise of the Fatimids*, text, i, trans., 104-105), where we see that the *daʿwa* (here called *duʿāʾ*) must be renewed by the Mahdī; cf. also article 65 of *Tād̲j̲ al-ʿAḳaʾid* by Sayyidunā ʿAlī b. Muḥammad, in Ivanow, *A creed of the Fatimids*; also al-S̲h̲ahrastānī, Cairo 1347, ii, 26: *kānat lahum daʿwa fī kull zamān*.

Ismāʿīlī propaganda was at first secret, so long as the imām was not sufficiently strong and had to remain in hiding. It was in this way that it was exercised in the East, the Yemen and North Africa (cf. B. Lewis, *The origins of Ismāʿīlism*, 19, 52, 73 etc.), and that in the Mag̲h̲rib the *dāʿī* of the Mahdī ʿUbayd Allāh took over power from his master. Abū Ḥanīfa al-Nuʿmān's book describing the beginnings of Fāṭimid propaganda in the Yemen and North

Africa and the establishment of the dynasty in the Maghrib is entitled *Kitāb iftitāḥ al-daʿwa waʾbtidāʾ al-dawla*. When the imām was strong enough and at the head of a state, he made his *daʿwa* public (*aẓhara daʿwatahu*: Ibn Khaldūn, *Proleg.*, i, 363, Rosenthal, i, 413). Unlike the ʿAbbāsid *daʿwa* which ceased once the dynasty was established, the Fāṭimid *daʿwa* did not cease but, on the contrary, became organized and even more extensive from the time the dynasty was established in Cairo. Though overt in the Fāṭimid possessions or in territories won over to the doctrine, it continued in secret in other parts, except that it was proclaimed openly in favourable districts (thus the *dāʿī* al-Muʾayyad fi 'l-Dīn preaching to the Buwayhid Abū Kālīdjar: see the *Sīra Muʿayyadiyya*, ed. M. Kāmil Ḥusayn, Cairo 1949, 43 ff.). Missionaries were each entrusted with some specified province, denoted by the term island (*djazīra*: for this name and these divisions see Ivanow, *Rise*, 20 and M. Kāmil Ḥusayn, *Fī adab Miṣr al-Fāṭimiyya*, Cairo 1950, 19). In Persia it was known by a name recalling its Egyptian origin, *daʿwat-i Miṣriyān* (Ivanow, *Rise*, 140). From the purely political aspect this propaganda could be effected by those who were merely sympathizers, but for doctrinal matters it was carried out by means of preaching by the *dāʿīs* whose head, *dāʿī al-duʿāt* or chief missionary—whose duties were also called *daʿwa* (al-Ḳalḳashandī, *Ṣubḥ*, x, 434)—had his headquarters in Cairo. In general, the political aim was to convince the Muslims that the *imām* alone, divinely inspired, aided by God and guardian of the secrets transmitted to ʿAlī by the Prophet, could give mankind good guidance, and that dynasties other than the Fāṭimids descended from Ismāʿīl b. Djaʿfar were usurpers and illegitimate, rotten with vices and neglectful of the most sacred duties of religion. The expression *ḳiyām* (*iḳāmat*) *al-daʿwa al-hādiya* clearly shows the task of directing humanity undertaken by the *imāms* and upon which their missionaries had to insist. It occurs, for example, in letters from caliph al-Mustanṣir to the Ṣulayḥid queen of the Yemen, of Fāṭimid persuasion (*Rasāʾil al-Mustanṣir*, ed. ʿAbd al-Munʿim Mādjid (Magued), Cairo 1954, no. 46, p. 157) or in missionaries' investiture diplomas (al-Ḳalḳashandī, *Ṣubḥ*, ix, 19, 8, x, 435, 7 a f.) or in an Ismāʿīlī oath (Shihāb al-Dīn al-ʿUmarī, *Taʿrīf*, 158; cf. B. Lewis, *The origins* .... 59-60, Arabic trans., 141, and in *BSOAS*, xii, 1948, 597-8). In addition, M. Canard, *L'impérialisme des Fāṭimides et leur propagande*, in *AIEO*, Algiers, iv, (1942-1947), gives a survey of the methods used by Fāṭimid propagandists to demonstrate the justice of the dynasty's claims and its exclusive merits, and to denigrate and weaken its enemies, whether Byzantine, Umayyad or ʿAbbāsid.

The propaganda was also concerned with education and initiation in doctrine. The doctrine of the sect is indeed a combination of political, religious, juridical and philosophical instruction forming a secret, esoteric side (*bāṭin*, whence the name Bāṭiniyya also given to the sect and misinterpreted by Ibn Khaldūn, i, 363, Rosenthal, i, 413, who makes it refer to the *satr* of the *imām*), founded upon the allegorical interpretation of the Ḳurʾān and the laws of Islam, and another overt, exoteric side (*ẓāhir*), the first reserved for the intellectual élite of the faithful (*awliyāʾ*), the second for those from whom only fidelity to the imāms was required, together with the various obligations it entailed (see the *Kitāb al-Himma* by Abū Ḥanīfa al-Nuʿmān), and the accomplishment of the religious duties of Islam. Doctrinal propaganda and instruction went together, and more exclusively juridical or philosophico-scientific instruction also had propaganda objectives. This we can see, as early as 385/995, in a lecture given on Fāṭimid *fiḳh* at the al-Azhar mosque, with a list of names of those present, and then by the wazīr Ibn Killis in his own house; Yaḥyā b. Saʿīd, *Patr. Or.*, xxiii/3, 434 (226). In 385/995, a vast crowd thronged to the lectures on "Science of the *ahl al-bayt*" given by Ḳāḍī Muḥammad b. al-Nuʿmān in the palace; eleven men perished, crushed to death. In 395/1005 the caliph al-Ḥākim compelled people to "enter the *daʿwa*", that is to say to attend lectures by the chief *ḳāḍī* ʿAbd al-ʿAzīz b. Muḥammad b. al-Nuʿmān who arranged sessions at the palace on different days, attended either by men or women, or else by dignitaries; there too there was a crowd so dense that men and women perished in the press. From other information we learn that the chief *dāʿī* directed the *daʿwa* sessions, known as *madjālis al-ḥikma*, in a section of the palace called al-Muḥawwal, where the *dāʿī* had a special *madjlis* and his own chair (*kursī al-daʿwa*). He had the oath administered to those who were being converted to the Fāṭimid doctrine, and received offerings of silver from those present (*al-nadjwā*). The lectures which he had carefully prepared with the help of his *naḳībs* and official *faḳīhs* who worked and taught at the *dār al-ʿilm* or *dār al-ḥikma* [*qq.v.*], founded by al-Ḥākim in 395/1005, a kind of university with a library, were submitted to the caliph before being read. As has been noted above, there were separate sessions for men and women. According to Ibn al-Ṭuwayr (525-617/1131-1220), those for men were held in the great hall of the palace (*al-īwān al-kabīr*), those for women in the *madjlis al-dāʿī*. On the other hand al-Musabbiḥī (366-420/977-1029) records five different sessions, one for the *awliyāʾ*, one for the élite of the senior administrative and palace officials, one for the people and visitors from the interior of the country, another for women (at the al-Azhar mosque), and another for women from the palace (for all these points see al-Maḳrīzī i, 341-42 and ii, 390-391). According to al-Ḳalḳashandī (iii, 487), it was at the *dār al-ʿilm* that the juridical meetings of the chief *dāʿī* were held, and the taking of oaths by converts to the Fāṭimid doctrine. But it is not absolutely certain that the religious and doctrinal lectures based on allegorical interpretation were held in this place (M. Kāmil Ḥusayn, *Fī adab Miṣr al-Fāṭimiyya*, Cairo 1950, 32). Incidentally we know that at Aleppo at the time of the amīr Riḍwān, who died in 507/1113, there was a *dār al-daʿwa*: Ibn Shiḥna, 27; Kamāl al-Dīn b. al-ʿAdīm, in *Rec. Hist. Cr. Or.*, iii, 589-90; Abu 'l-Maḥāsin, *Nudjūm*, Cairo, v, 205, s.a. 507.

We have a detailed account of the procedure apparently used by Ismāʿīlī missionaries to gain neophytes for their philosophico-religious theses imbued with the neo-platonic theory of emanation, their cyclic conception of the world and imāmate, the way in which they made use of allegorical interpretation (*taʾwīl*) of the Ḳurʾān and the laws of Islam to attain their ends, and the different methods used, according to the religion of those whom they were trying to win over. According to this account which is found in al-Maḳrīzī, i, 391 ff. and with greater detail in al-Nuwayrī (translation in S. de Sacy, *Exposé de la religion des Druzes*, i, Introduction), the initiation of neophytes (*al-madʿū*) was only completed after nine periods of instruction, each one of which was called *daʿwa*. This system was attributed to the alleged founder of Ismāʿīlism, ʿAbd

Allāh b. Maymūn al-Ḳaddāḥ. In it we see how they proceeded gradually to reveal the secrets of the doctrine, the *taʾwīl* and the *taʾwīl al-taʾwīl* (for this last expression see al-Masʿūdī, *Tanbīh*, 395, trans. 501, and cf. Goldziher, *Vorlesungen*², 246; Fr. trans., 206). Ivanow has on several occasions (*An Ismailitic Work by Naṣīru d-dīn Ṭusī*, in *JRAS*, 1931, 534; *The organization of the Fatimid propaganda*, in *JBBRAS*, xv (1939), 11 and *Rise*, 133 in the chapter *The Myth of ʿAbdu ʾl-lāh b. Maymūn al-Qaddāḥ*) challenged the existence of these nine degrees of initiation for converts to Ismāʿīlism with a gradual revelation of the mysteries. According to him, this is a misinterpretation of the hierarchy of the *ḥudūd al-dīn*, a kind of Fāṭimid "clergy" (for this expression see Ivanow, *Organization*, 8, and a note in M. Canard's translation of the *Sīrat Jaudhar*, 52); these nine degrees have no connexion with either the ancient or modern grades of initiates, there is no trace of it either in the literature of the sect or in controversial literature; he similarly rejects any comparison with initiation in Masonic lodges and their secret ceremonies. It is however difficult to believe that it is merely an invention. The nine degrees were known before al-Maḳrīzī and al-Nuwayrī, from Sunnī sources, not as stages in initiation but as stages (*marātib, daradjāt*) in the Machiavellian tricks (*ḥiyal*) to recruit new adherents and detach them from their religion (Sunnī interpretation, as opposed to the true religious fervour of the Fāṭimids). Each stage bears a name corresponding to the dialectical and psychological method used; the names given to these stages by al-Baghdādī, *Farḳ*, ed. Cairo 1367/1948, 179 ff. are: *tafarrus, taʾnīs, tashkīk, taʿlīk, rabṭ, tadlīs, taʾsīs*, after which come the oaths (*aymān*), and then complete detachment (*khalʿ*). (See also al-Ghazālī, *Kitāb faḍāʾiḥ al-Bāṭiniyya* (Goldziher, *Streitschrift des G. gegen die Bāṭinijja Sekte*, 40 and p. ٤ ff.), and M. Kāmil Ḥusayn, *Fī adab* . . ., 19 ff.).

The question remains obscure. Various methods of propaganda and discussion were used, but the period of their full development can hardly be taken back to the time of the beginnings of Ismāʿīlism. The outline given by al-Nuwayrī and al-Maḳrīzī seems to be of later date.

The word *daʿwa* does not only have the sense of appeal and propaganda. We have seen above its use to denote the Islamic community. Similarly, in connection with the Fāṭimids and Ismāʿīlīs, it has the sense of doctrine, religion, community, sect, party of the imām. Ivanow, *Organization*, 18-19, noted this polyvalence. *Daʿwa* can even be equated with zone of obedience, empire, dynasty. Ibn Ḥawḳal says (57-8) that the lands of the Maghrib are in the *daʿwa* of the Commander of the Faithful al-Muʿizz li-Dīn Allāh, and that (221) Kirmān is in the *daʿwa* of the people of the Maghrib. In the *Kitāb al-Himma* by Abū Ḥanīfa al-Nuʿmān, chap. 7, *man shamalathu daʿwat al-imām* denotes the caliph's subjects, as a whole. *Shuyūkh al-daʿwa* in the *Sīrat Jaudhar* (trans. 54, cf. Ivanow, *Rise*, V 9) is synonymous with *shuyūkh al-dawla*. For this use in the sense of dynasty see also al-Iṣṭakhrī, 36, 4 and 296, 4: *sawād daʿwat Banī ʾl-Abbās*, the black colour of the ʿAbbāsid dynasty (*BGA*, iv, 236); al-Maḳrīzī, *Sulūk*, i, 18. Finally we may note that *daʿwa* is the equivalent of *madhhab* among the Wahbī Ibāḍites who call themselves *ahl al-madhhab* or *ahl al-daʿwa* (T. Lewicki, *La répartition géographique des groupements ibāḍites dans l'Afrique du nord au Moyen Age*, in *RO*, xxi, 1957).

In the Ismāʿīlī community there was a schism after the death of al-Mustanṣir in 487/1094, when his son Mustaʿlī was proclaimed in opposition to his other son Nizār. A group of Ismāʿīlīs refused to recognize Mustaʿlī, and there were two branches or parties in the community, the Mustaʿlians and the Nizārīs. The former were called *al-daʿwa al-ḳadīma*, the old, and the latter *al-daʿwa al-djadīda*, the new *daʿwa*. This schism became permanent. When Āmir, Mustaʿlī's successor, was assassinated in 524/1130 by the Nizārīs, before dying he handed over his authority to ʿAbd al-Madjīd, the future Ḥāfiẓ, his cousin, as his son Ṭayyib was a minor. The latter disappeared or entered the *satr*. The *daʿwa ḳadīma* was also called *daʿwa ṭayyibiyya*, and was perpetuated in the Yemen where the Ṣulayḥid queen spread the *daʿwa* for the imām al-Ṭayyib. It is is this *daʿwa ḳadīma*, or Mustaʿlian or Ṭayyibī *daʿwa*, which is today represented by the Bohoras in India, whilst the *daʿwa djadīda* or Nizārī *daʿwa*, made famous by Ḥasan b. Ṣabbāh and the Hashīshiyya (Assassins), is today represented by the Khodjas. For these two branches of the Ismāʿīlian *daʿwa* see Ibn Khaldūn, i, 363, Rosenthal, i, 413; al-Shahrastānī, ed. Cureton, 147, 150-152, ed. Cairo 1347, ii, 26, 28-31; Hodgson, *The Order of Assassins*, index. The Nizārīs or Assassins of Syria, also called Fidāʾiyyūn, who with their fortresses played an important part at the time of the Crusades, were conquered by the Mamlūk Baybars in 671/1278. They continued to occupy a certain number of places. They were then known by the name *al-ṭāʾifa al-ismāʿīliyya bi-ḳilāʿ al-daʿwa*; they called themselves *aṣḥāb al-daʿwa al-hādiya*, or *mudjāhidūn*, and had at their head an *atābek* appointed by Cairo (see al-Ḳalḳashandī, i, 122; iv, 146, 235, 309; ix, 254). For modern Islamic propaganda and the propagandist school founded by Rashīd Riḍā in the island of Rōḍa near Cairo, called *Dār al-daʿwa wa'l-irshād* ("House of propaganda and direction"), see Goldziher *Richtungen*, 343-4.

Bibliography: In addition to the works referred to in the text, see: De Goeje, *Mémoire sur les Carmathes du Bahrain et les Fatimides* 16 ff., 23 ff., 27 ff.; Casanova, *La doctrine secrète des Fatimides d'Égypte*, in *BIFAO*, xviii (1921); Ḥusain F. al-Hamdānī, *The history of the Ismāʿīlī Daʿwat and its literature during the last phase of the Fāṭimid Empire*, in *JRAS*, 1932, 126-136; M. Kamil Husayn, edition of *al-Madjālis al-Mustanṣiriyya*, Cairo 1946, Introduction; M. Kāmil Ḥusayn and M. Muṣṭafā Hilmī, edition of *Rāḥat al-ʿaḳl* by Aḥmad Ḥamīd al-Dīn al-Kirmani, Cairo 1952, Introduction; M. Kāmil Ḥusayn, *Fī adab Miṣr al-Fāṭimiyya*, Cairo 1950, 19 ff.; Ivanow, *Brief survey of the evolution of Ismailism*, 1952; A. M. Magued, *Institutions et cérémonial des Fatimides*, Cairo 1953-5, i, 177 ff.; Muṣṭafā Ghālib, *Taʾrīkh al-daʿwa al-ismāʿīliyya*, Damascus 1954 (not consulted); Bayard Dodge, *Ismāʿīliyyah and the origins of the Fatimids*, in *The Muslim World*, Oct. 1959, 299-300. The work by B. Lewis, *The origins of Ismāʿīlism*, Cambridge 1940, has been translated into Arabic by Kh. A. Jallu and J. M. Rajab, Cairo 1947 (see 164 ff. and *passim*).

(M. Canard)

DAʿWĀ, action at law. According to a well-known formula the *daʿwā* is defined as: "the action by which a person claims his right, against another person, in the presence of a judge" (*Madjalla*, art. 1613). A case submitted to an arbitrator is, equally, a *daʿwā*. The plaintiff is termed *muddaʿī*, the defendant *muddaʿā alayh* and the object of the claim *muddaʿā* or, more popularly—though less accurately, as certain writers note,—*muddaʿā bihi*. We also meet, particularly in the Mālikī *madhhab*, the terms *ṭālib* (plaintiff) and *maṭlūb* (defendant). The parties to the suit are called, in the dual, *khaṣmān*. and in the plural, *khuṣūm* or *khuṣamāʾ* (opponents)—(singular *khaṣm*); more concretely each party is the *khaṣm* of the other. The contentious argument itself is the *khuṣūma* (additional synonyms, though of a slightly less technical character, are *nizāʿ*, *munāzaʿa* and *tanāzuʿ*).

The fact that the *daʿwā* envisages two contesting parties excludes from this notion the process in which the magistrate effects *ex officio* the exercise of certain rights such as measures to safeguard the public welfare.

But in every case which involves the three essential elements of contentious process there is a *daʿwā*, whatever the judicial authority before whom the action is brought and whatever the nature of the interest in issue.

A *daʿwā* exists, therefore, in the following cases: in the suit brought by an individual, the victim of an offence against the person, who claims the application of the law of talion (*ḳiṣāṣ* [*q.v.*]) or the payment of compensation (*diya* [*q.v.*]); in the case of prosecutions for various "legal" offences sanctioned by public penalties (*ḥudūd*) (see ḤADD) when brought in the exclusive or partial interest of the victim, such as the offences of theft or fornication; in the case of criminal prosecutions *ex officio* where the victim intervenes as plaintiff as well as in every case of the exercise of the so-called *ḥisba* action, a kind of *actio popularis*, based on the principle that every Muslim, apart from any personal grievance, is authorized to stand in the rôle of prosecutor for any infringement of the law (see ḤISBA); and finally in the action brought in accordance with the extra-ordinary procedure of the *maẓālim* [*q.v.*].

Certain conditions are required for the "validity" (*ṣiḥḥa*), that is to say the acceptability, of the *daʿwā*: there must be an adequate determination of the object of the claim, of the identity of the parties, and of their capacity. The person who does not possess ordinary legal capacity, but who simply has the ability to discriminate, may go to law, provided, however, he is authorized to do so by his guardian or the judge. In a real action the defendant must necessarily be the person in possession of the object in dispute (*ṣāḥib al-yad*).

A *daʿwā* which does not satisfy all these conditions may, however, be subsequently rectified by the fulfilment of the condition(s) in question, such rectification being termed *taṣḥīḥ al-khuṣūma*. This may be accomplished solely upon the initiative of the plaintiff or upon the order of the judge.

The parties may appear in person or through a representative, who may be either appointed by the party (*wakīl*) or, as in the case of the guardian (*waṣī*) or the *walī* of those lacking capacity, required by the law. In the case of things which are open to the use of the general public such as sea-water or the public highway, every person is entitled to go to law to defend his right of user. In the event of litigation between defined groups, such as villages in relation to communal property, such as forests, pastures, etc., a single member of each of the groups may go to law in the name of the group whether as plaintiff or defendant, provided, however, it is a question of groups whose number is "unlimited" (*ḳawm ghayr maḥṣūr*), such a group being, according to the general opinion, one whose number exceeds one hundred persons.

Certain estates of property, such as *waḳf*s, which are regarded as a legal entity, appear in process of law through the medium of their qualified representatives. The same applies to an inheritance prior to its distribution: in principle each heir may appear as plaintiff or defendant in the name of the succession.

The court which is competent to entertain a *daʿwā* is the court of the domicile or of the place of simple residence of the defendant. This rule is equally applicable in the case of immovable property. In the Mālikī *madhhab*, however, it is admitted that in this latter case competence also belongs to the court of the *situs* of immovable. Where there exists in the same locality a number of judges—as will be the case when judges are appointed for the different *madhhab*s, or when there is an ordinary judge and a judge appointed to hear suits concerning military personnel (*ḳāḍī ʿaskar* [*q.v.*]), the choice of the competent court rests with the defendant. However, all these rules of competence are not of a peremptory nature; they may be avoided by the common agreement of the parties.

The appearance of the parties, is, in principle, a necessary condition precedent to the fighting of the issue; there does not exist, in Islamic Law, a procedure of judgment in default of appearance. Further, various procedures of indirect coercion are laid down with the object of securing the appearance of a recalcitrant defendant. As a last resort, the judge will appoint for such a defendant an official representative (*wakīl musakhkhar*).

In another system, followed notably in the Shāfiʿī *madhhab* and in the Shīʿī doctrine, the view is maintained that the appearance of the duly named defendant is not a necessary condition of the *daʿwā*: the procedure runs its course in the ordinary way in his absence, but without being for that reason considered as a procedure of default; further the judgment delivered will have precisely the same validity as a judgment delivered in the presence of the defendant.

Essentially the process is an oral one; and while the parties may be allowed to present their pleas in written form, the writing nevertheless will have no validity until it is orally confirmed by the litigant before the judge.

The term *dafʿ* is used for the reply which tends to traverse the *daʿwā*—and, by extension, for every reply made by a party in contradiction of a plea raised by his opponent.

It is upon the plaintiff that the burden of proof falls. The methods of legal proof are acknowledgement or confession (*iḳrār*), the oath (*yamīn*), testimony (*shahāda*), which is the normal proof *par excellence*, writing (*khaṭṭ*) and legal presumptions (*ḳarāʾin*).

One particular form of testimony is the *tawātur*. This consists of the affirmation of a fact by a number of persons (a minimum of twenty-five according to a fairly widespread opinion) so large as logically to exclude any possibility of fraud or lying. It is not necessary in this case that the strict conditions of testimony properly so-called—such as the condition that the witness should have personal knowledge of the attested fact, or the condition of moral integrity (*ʿadāla*, [*q.v.*])—should be observed. But in spite of this the *tawātur* is superior to all other modes of proof with the exception of confession.

Writing in itself has no evidential value; it is a

valid mode of proof only in so far as it is orally confirmed by duly qualified witnesses.

In the event of the defendant failing to put in a voluntary appearance with the plaintiff it is a matter of some controversy whether the suit is to be regarded as started by the simple action itself of the plaintiff, or whether there can be no question of continuing the process further and naming the defendant until there has first been a preliminary enquiry by the judge to establish that there is at least a *prima facie* ground for the action.

The system of proof is a 'legal' system, in the sense that once proof has been provided according to the dictates of the law and is in conformity with the facts alleged, it binds the judge, whatever his own inner conviction may be. Hence one arrives at solutions like the following: in the case where two contending parties, each of whom claims exclusive ownership of a certain chattel, both adduce a regular form of proof supporting their allegations, it will be incumbent upon the judge to decide that they are co-owners in equal shares; or even, according to one opinion, it will be necessary to draw lots (*ḳurʿa*) to determine the title to the property.

The trial terminates with the judgment (*ḥukm*). Since the system of Muslim judicial organization is a system of a single jurisdiction, the judgment of the *ḳāḍī* is not subject to an appeal before a superior jurisdiction, which does not exist. This principle, however, is subject to two important reservations. In the first place, in periods or in areas where there exists an organized procedure of *maẓālim*, any person who feels himself a victim of injustice as a result of the workings of the public services, may demand redress by presenting a petition to the sovereign authority. In the second place, the suit may be reopened either before the same judge or before another judge—the successor in office of the judge who delivered the decision, or in fact any judge who may be on other grounds competent—in order to determine the case afresh. Furthermore the principle of *res judicata* is, to a large extent, unknown to Islamic law. Although it would be difficult to indicate here the precise scope of this rule, which is, indeed, beyond a certain point a matter of controversy, it may simply be pointed out that the authorities are unanimous in holding that a judgment may be contested and, in suitable circumstances, withdrawn or annulled where there is an infringement of an undisputed rule of law.

The right of action at law is extinguished by prescription, the period of which varies, according to different opinions, from three to thirty-six years. In the Ottoman Empire the period was fixed at fifteen years, except in certain cases, such as those relating to a *waḳf* fund, where the period was extended to thirty-six years. The law further recognizes certain causes of suspension or interruption of the period. Prescription functions as a procedural bar, which paralyses the exercise of the right of action; it does not affect the substantive right itself.

In the final stage of Islamic law in the Ottoman Empire, as represented by the code known as *Medjelle-i aḥkām-i ʿadliyye* [*q.v.*], which was promulgated between the years 1870 and 1877, the old system of the *daʿwā* was reformed in a number of particulars, notably by the recognition of the intrinsic probative value of writing (art. 1736), by the acceptance of the principle of *res judicata* (art. 1837), and by the introduction of procedure in default of appearance (art. 1833 ff.). These modifications ran parallel with the modernization of the judicial organization, established in accordance with European models and based upon the principles of benches of judges and the institution of a hierarchy of courts with systems of appeal.

Bibliography: The chapter *Daʿwā* in the works of *fiḳh*; Ibn ʿAbd al-Raḥmān, *Raḥmat al-umma fi-'khtilāf al-aʾimma*, edited by ʿAbd al-Ḥamīd, Cairo n.d., 310 ff.; *Medjelle*, art. 1613 ff.; Querry, *Recueil de lois concernant les musulmans schyites*, Paris 1877, ii, 385 ff.; T. W. Juynboll, *Handbuch des islamischen Gesetzes*, Leiden 1910, 313 ff.; L. Milliot, *Introduction à l'étude du droit musulman*, Paris 1953, 683 ff.; M. Morand, *Études de droit musulman algérien*, Algiers 1910, 313 ff.; E. Tyan, *Histoire de l'organisation judiciaire en pays d'Islam*, ii, Lyons 1943, 21 ff., 141 ff., 390 ff., 477 ff.; idem, *La procédure du défaut en droit musulman*, in *Stud. Isl.*, 1957, 115 ff. (E. Tyan)

DAWĀDĀR, also Dawātdār, Duwaydār and Amīr Dawāt, the bearer and keeper of the royal inkwell. Under the ʿAbbāsids the emblem of office of the *wazīr* was an inkwell. The post of *dawādār* was created by the Saldjūḳs, and was held by civilians. Sultan Baybars transferred it to a Mamlūk Amīr of Ten. Under the Baḥrī Mamlūks the *dawādār* did not rank among the important amīrs, but under the Circassians he became one of the highest amīrs of the sultanate, with the title Grand Dawādār (*dawādār kabīr*), and with a number of *dawādārs* under him. The office of *dawādār* ranked among the seven most important offices of the realm. There was competition between the *raʾs nawba* and the *dawādār kabīr* for the fifth and sixth places, possession of which alternated irregularly between them. Some *dawādārs* even became sultans. One of the *dawādār*'s duties during the later Mamlūk period was to decide which of the members of the *ḥalḳa* [*q.v.*] were fit to join in military expeditions; in addition, he regularly visited Upper Egypt, and sometimes the regions of Djabal Nābulus, al-Sharḳiyya, and al-Gharbiyya, in order to collect taxes and gather in the crops. These trips would take place amid great pomp, and the sources discuss them at great length. They were accompanied by cruel oppressions of the local population. At the close of the Mamlūk era, enormous power was concentrated in the hands of the *dawādār*; thus for example Amīr Yashbak was, in addition to his duties as *dawādār*, also *amīr silāḥ*, *wazīr*, *ustādār*, *kāshif al-kushshāf* (inspector-general), *mudabbir al-mamlaka*, and *raʾs al-maysara*; no previous Mamlūk amīr had accumulated such a great number of offices, though exactly the same offices were accumulated by the *dawādār* Ṭūmānbāy, who later became sultan. In the Ottoman and Safavid empires the *dawādārs* (called *divittār* and *dawātdār*) were functionaries with scribal duties in the chanceries.

Bibliography: I. H. Uzunçarşılı, *Osmanlı devleti teşkilâtına medhal*, Istanbul 1941, 91, 96 and index; D. Ayalon, *Studies on the structure of the Mamluk army*, in *BSOAS*, xvi, 1954, 62-3, 68-9. (D. Ayalon)

DAWĀʾIR, plural of *dāʾira*, group of families attached to the service and the person of a native chief in Algeria. Before the French conquest, the name of *dawāʾir* (local pronunciation *dwāyr*) was borne especially by four tribal groups encamped to the south-west of Oran and attached to the service of the Bey of that city, although there were other *dawāʾir*, for example in the Titteri. They were organized as a militia, living on the products of the land put at their disposition by the Turkish government and the profit from expeditions against tribes who were unruly or refused to pay their taxes. The Zmāla, their neighbours, played the same part.

Local tradition, as discovered after the French conquest, held the members of these groups to be the issue of troops whom the Moroccan sultan, Mawlāy Ismāʿīl, had brought into the region to fight against the Turks in 1701. The campaign having failed, a number of Moroccan soldiers passed into the service of the Turks and formed a *makhzen* tribe, placed under the command of two local families.

Dawāʾir and Zmāla had the privilege of levying the taxes only in the district called Yaʿḳūbiyya in the southern region of Oran, which extended from the neighbourhood of Mascara and the mountains of Tlemcen to the Djabal ʿAmūr. Apart from this task, the Dawāʾir were charged with policing the tribes of the western region of Oran, and accompanied the Bey on all his expeditions. They were completely devoted to the Turks.

When the Turkish régime collapsed suddenly after the French expedition of 1830, the Dawāʾir found themselves deprived of their chief reason for existence and sought someone else under whom they could serve. They first embraced the cause of the envoy of the Moroccan sultan, Mawlāy ʿAbd al-Raḥmān, who had come to occupy Tlemcen in 1830 at the request of part of the population, But the Moroccan régime did not last long and they found themselves once again out of employment.

The Amīr ʿAbd al-Ḳādir tried in his early days to enrol them into his service, but their chief, Muṣṭafa b. Ismāʿīl, had already entered into negotiations with the French general in command at Oran, and did not respond to the Amīr's advances. Nevertheless, a part of the tribe joined ʿAbd al-Ḳādir. He tried to win over the rest in 1833 and seemed at one time to have succeeded, but Muṣṭafā b. Ismāʿīl, already an old man, found the authority of the young Amīr difficult to bear and separated himself finally from him. He shut himself up in the citadel (*mashwar*) of Tlemcen with fifty families of the Dawāʾir and the Kulughlī [*q.v.*] of the town. At that time, other groups of Dawāʾir were submitting to the French and were settled around Misserghin. The whole tribe treated with General Trezel at the camp of le Figuier near Oran on 16th June 1835, and became again in the service of France, the *Makhzen* group that they had been in the days of the Turks. Muṣṭafā b. Ismāʿīl, who remained at Tlemcen, was aided by the French early in 1836 and took back his place as head of the Dawāʾir. In this position, he co-operated with them in the struggle of the French against ʿAbd al-Ḳādir, and was appointed a brigadier by Louis-Philippe. He was assassinated at the age of almost 80 after the capture of the *smala* of ʿAbd al-Ḳādir (1843). His death brought to an end the greatest period in the history of the Dawāʾir.

Bibliography: Anon., *Douair et Zmala*, Oran 1883; Pellissier de Raynaud, *Annales algériennes*, 3 vols., Paris and Algiers 1854, *passim*; W. Ezterhazy, *Notice sur le Maghzen d'Oran*, Algiers 1838, and *De la Domination Turque dans l'ancienne Régence d'Alger*, Paris 1840, 266 ff.; Desmichels, *Oran sous la Commandement du général Desmichels*, Paris 1835, *passim*; Nāṣirī, *K. al-Istiḳṣā*, Cairo 1312, iv, 184-192; M. Emerit, *L'Algérie à l'Époque d'Abd al-Kader*, Paris 1951, *passim*; R. Tinthoin, *Colonisation et Évolution des Genres de Vie dans la Région Ouest d'Oran de 1830 à 1885*, Oran 1947, *passim*. (A. Cour-[R. Le Tourneau])

DAWʿAN (sometimes Dūʿan), one of the principal southern tributaries of Wādī Ḥadramawt. Dawʿan, a deep narrow cleft in al-Djawl, runs c. 100 km. almost due north to join the main wādī opposite the town of Haynan. The precipitous walls of Dawʿan are c. 300 m. high; its towns nestle against the lower slopes with their palm groves lying in the valley bed below. The valley is formed by the confluence of two branches, al-Ayman (pronounced *layman*) and al-Aysar (pronounced *laysar*), with al-Ayman often reckoned an integral part of Dawʿan proper. Among the cluster of settlements in al-Ayman are al-Ribāṭ al-Khurayba, al-Rashīd, and al-Maṣnaʿa. Just below the juncture of al-Ayman and al-Aysar is the town of Ṣīf, after which come Ḳaydūn and al-Hadjarayn [*q.v.*], the last of which sometimes gives its name to the lower reaches of the valley. North of al-Hadjarayn is the comparatively recent shrine of al-Mashhad with the tomb of al-Sayyid ʿAlī b. Ḥasan al-ʿAṭṭās. Wādī al-ʿAyn empties into the valley from the east and Wādī ʿAmd from the west. The name Wādī al-Kasr (Kasr Ḳamāḳish in al-Hamdānī) is given to the lowest stretch where the stream beds of ʿAmd, Dawʿan, and al-ʿAyn run together. The towns of Ḥawra and al-ʿAdjlāniyya are on the right bank.

A motor road leads from al-Mukallā to the interior past Kawr Saybān, the highest peak in the region, and then past the sacred summit of Mawlā Maṭar to upper Dawʿan.

Relics of Sabaean times have been found in the valley, and the ruins of Ghaybūn lie south of al-Mashhad. The name Dawʿan has been detected in Ptolemy's Thauane (Thabane) and in the Toani, a tribe mentioned by Pliny. The valley lays within the territory of Kinda, and the royal house of Ākil al-Murār came from Dammūn at al-Hadjarayn. In al-Hamdānī's time the Imām of the Ibāḍīs in Ḥadramawt had his seat in Dawʿan, perhaps on the site now known as al-Khurayba. Later the upper valley became the stronghold of Āl al-ʿAmūdī, whose ancestor, al-Shaykh Saʿīd b. ʿĪsā (d. 671/1272-3 and buried in Ḳaydūn) is said to have been the first to introduce Ṣūfism into Ḥadramawt. The Bedouin tribes of Saybān and al-Dayyin in the highlands showed great reverence for the *shaykh*s of this family, but the religious basis of its influence did not keep the *shaykhs* from squabbling among themselves, and they could not resist the expanding power of the Ḳuʿayṭī Sultanate of al-Mukallā at the close of the 19th century. Dawʿan now forms a *liwāʾ* of the Sultanate with al-Hadjarayn as the northern limit. The house of Bā Ṣurra of Saybān provides the provincial governors, but Āl al-ʿAmūdī has recovered something of its old standing, its main centre now being at Biḍa in al-Ayman.

Many of the people of Dawʿan have emigrated to Aden, East Africa, and Java. For sentimental reasons a number of the rich emigrants maintain homes and gardens in the valley, the only export from which is honey.

Bibliography: Hamdānī; Muḥammad b. Hāshim, *Taʾrīkh al-Dawla al-kathīriyya*, i, Cairo 1367; Ṣalāḥ al-Bakrī, *Taʾrīkh Ḥadramawt al-siyāsī*, Cairo 1354-5; idem, *Fī djanūb al-djazīra al-ʿarabiyya*, Cairo 1368; M. de Goeje in *Rev. Colon. Internat.*, 1886; H. von Wissmann & M. Höfner, *Beiträge zur hist. Geog.*, Wiesbaden 1953; L. Hirsch, *Reisen*, Leiden 1897; D. van der Meulen & H. von Wissmann, *Ḥadramaut*, Leiden 1932; W. Ingrams, *A Report on ... Hadhramaut*, London 1937; idem, *Arabia and the Isles*², London 1952. (G. Rentz)

AL-DAWĀNĪ, MUḤAMMAD B. ASʿAD DJALĀL AL-DĪN, was born in 830/1427 at Dawān in the district of Kāzarūn, where his father was Ḳāḍī; he claimed descent from the Caliph Abū Bakr whence his *nisba* al-Ṣiddīḳī. He studied with his father and then went to Shīrāz where he was a pupil of Mawlānā Muḥyī 'l-Dīn Gūsha Kinārī and Mawlānā Humām al-Dīn Gulbārī and Ṣafī al-Dīn Īdjī. He held the office of *Ṣadr* under Yūsuf b. Djahānshāh, the Ḳarā Ḳoyūnlū, and after resigning this office became Mudarris of the Begum Madrasa, also known as the *Dār al-Aytām*. Under the Āḳ Ḳoyūnlū he became Ḳāḍī of Fars. During the disorders which occurred in Fārs at the time of the break-up of the Āḳ Ḳoyūnlū kingdom and the wars between them and Shāh Ismāʿīl Ṣafawī, Djalāl al-Dīn took refuge in Lār and Djurūn; and when Abu 'l-Fatḥ Beg Bayāndur took possession of Shīrāz, he set out for Kāzarūn but died some days after reaching the encampment of Abu 'l-Fatḥ in 908/1502-3. He was buried at Dawān. He wrote numerous commentaries on well-known works of philosophy and mystical literature and a number of dogmatic, mystic, and philosophical treatises in Arabic. His commentary on the *Tahdhīb al-Manṭiḳ wa 'l-Kalām* of al-Taftazānī (d. 791/1389), Lucknow 1264, 1293 (with glosses by Mīr Zāhid), and his *Risālat al-Zawrāʾ*, completed in 870/1465 (Cairo 1326 with *Taʿlīḳāt*) have been printed. His best known work is the *Lawāmiʿ al-Ishrāḳ fī Makārim al-Akhlāḳ*, better known as the *Akhlāḳ-i Djalālī*, which he wrote in Persian (lith. Calcutta, 1283/1866-7, translated into English by W. T. Thompson, *Practical Philosophy of the Muhammedan People*, London 1839).

It is a 'modernized' and 'popular' version of the *Akhlāḳ-i Nāṣirī* of Naṣīr al-Dīn Ṭūsī, made at the command of Uzun Ḥasan, the Aḳ Ḳoyunlū ruler, to whom it is dedicated (Persian text, 16). Djalāl al-Dīn admits his debt to Naṣīr al-Dīn (321). The *Akhlāḳ-i Nāṣirī* is divided into three parts, ethics, economics, and politics; the first part is a translation and reworking of an Arabic treatise by Abū ʿAlī Aḥmad b. Muḥammad b. Yaʿḳūb b. Miskawayh, entitled *Kitāb Ṭahārat al-Aʿrāḳ fī Tahdhīb al-Akhlāḳ*; the second derives from Bryson through an essay entitled *Tadābīr al-Manāzil* by Abū ʿAlī b. Sīnā; and the third is based on al-Fārābī's *Madīna Fāḍila* and *Kitāb al-Siyāsa al-Madaniyya*. The *Akhlāḳ-i Djalālī* follows a similar arrangement. Djalāl al-Dīn, like Naṣīr al-Dīn Ṭūsī, argues the necessity of a supreme law, a governor, and a monetary currency. The law he interprets to be the Sharīʿa and the governor that person distinguished by the support of God and possessing such qualities as would enable him to lead individual men to perfection. Government was either righteous, in which case it was the imāmate, or unrighteous in which case it was the rule of force. He does not lay down any conditions of election or deposition for the ruler. Any righteous ruler was the shadow of God upon earth, His representative (*khalīfat allāh*), and the deputy (*naʾib*) of the prophet Muḥammad (236). It is, doubtless, in this sense that Djalāl al-Dīn addresses his patron, Uzun Ḥasan, as caliph. The righteous ruler maintained the equipoise of the world, for the preservation of which co-operation between men was needed. Djalāl al-Dīn recognizes two types of civilization, righteous and unrighteous, which, following al-Fārābī and Naṣīr al-Dīn Ṭūsī, he calls the "good city" (*madīna-i fāḍila*) and the "unrighteous city" (*madīna-i ghayr-i fāḍila*); and subdivides the latter into the "ignorant city" (*madīna-i djāhila*), the "profligate city" (*madīna-i fāsiḳa*), and the "wicked city" (*madīna-i ḍālla*) (260-1). Within the good city there were several intellectual grades among the citizens and a differentiation of function. Equity demanded that each class should be kept in its proper place and each individual engaged in that occupation to which he was fitted and wherein he could attain to perfection (266). Righteous government, the imāmate, consisted in the ordering of the affairs of the people in such a way that each might arrive at that degree of perfection which lay in him (269). Unrighteous government was force, and consisted in the subjugation of the servants of God and the devastation of His territories (270). In order to preserve the equipoise of civilization, society was to be resolved into four classes; (i) men of learning, such as the *ʿulamāʾ*, *fuḳahāʾ*, *ḳāḍīs*, scribes, mathematicians, geometricians, astronomers, physicians, and poets; (ii) men of the sword; (iii) merchants, craftsmen, and artisans; and (iv) agriculturalists, without whom, Djalāl al-Dīn states, the continued existence of the human race would be impossible (277-8). He then, still following Naṣīr al-Dīn Ṭūsī, divides men into five classes according to their moral nature: (i) those who were by nature righteous and who influenced others, whom Naṣīr al-Dīn describes as the choicest of creation, whom the ruler should treat with the utmost respect and consider to be over the other classes; and whom Djalāl al-Dīn declares to be such people as the *ʿulamāʾ* of the Sharīʿa, the *shaykhs* of darwīsh orders, and mystics; (ii) those who were by nature good but had no influence over others; (iii) those who were neither righteous nor unrighteous; (iv) those who were evil but had no influence over others; and those who were evil and had an influence over others (279-81). He then discusses the means to be adopted to coerce the evil and the need for the ruler to enquire personally into the affairs of his subjects (282 ff.). The final section of the work, also based on the *Akhlāḳ-i Nāṣirī* contains a number of political maxims attributed to Plato and Aristotle.

Djalāl al-Dīn's *ʿArḍ Nāma*, written for Sulṭān Khalīl when he was governor of Fārs on behalf of his father Uzun Ḥasan, has been translated into English by V. Minorsky, *A Civil and Military Review in Fars in* 881/1476, in *BSOS*, x/1, 141-78.

Bibliography: Khwāndamīr, *Ḥabīb al-Siyār* (Bombay 1857) iii, 4, 111; Ḥasan Rūmlū, *Aḥsan al-Tawārīkh* (ed. C. N. Seddon, Baroda, 1931), i, 71-2; Ḥādjdjī Mīrzā Ḥasan Fasāʾī, *Fārs Nāma-i Nāṣirī*, Tehran, lith., 1894-6, ii, 250; Rieu, *Catalogue of the Persian Manuscripts in the British Museum*, ii, 442*b*; Brockelmann, II, 217; Storey, i, 2, 1277; Browne, iii, 442; E. I. J. Rosenthal, *Political Thought in Medieval Islam*, Cambridge 1958, 210-23. On Dawānī's influence in the Ottoman empire, see S. Mardin, *The Mind of the Turkish Reformer 1700-1900*, in *The Western Humanities Review*, xiv, 1960, 418 ff.

(ANN K. S. LAMBTON)

DĀWAR [see ZAMĪN-I DĀWAR].

DAWĀR, an encampment of Arab Bedouins in which the tents (sing. *khayma*) are arranged in a circle or an ellipse, forming a sort of enceinte around the open space in the middle (*murāḥ*) where the cattle pass the night; this very ancient way of laying out an encampment is still to be found among the Bedouins of the east (northern Syria, Mesopotamia) and among all the nomads or semi-nomads of North Africa. The name of *dawār* which is given to it appears already in the writings of certain travellers and geographers of the middle ages. In the East, the exact form of the word is *dawār* or *dwār*; in the Maghrib, it is *dūwār* or *dawwār* (pl. *dwāwīr*). The number of tents of which a *dawār* is composed can vary greatly; it can be as many as several hundreds, or no more than ten. Many different reasons, such as abundance or scarcity of pasturage, security or the lack of it, etc., bring about the splintering of the same Bedouin group into *dawārs* of little importance, or its reunion into *dawārs* of considerable size. Beside this term, which has in a way become the generic one, one finds for less important groups the dialectal representatives *rasm*, *ḥilla*, *nazla*, *farīḳ*, etc. In the administrative language of Algeria, the word *douar* no longer bears its original primitive meaning, but is employed to designate an administrative area, either nomad or sedentary, placed under the authority of the same chief, *ḳā'id*, or *shaykh*. The word *dawār* was known in Arab Spain. The *Vocabulista* (ed. Schiaparelli) gives it as the equivalent of the Latin *mansio*, without further definition. In modern Spanish *aduar* means a gipsy camp.

Bibliography: Dozy, *Supplément aux Dictionnaires Arabes*, i, 473; on the *dawār* of the Bedouin of the east: Burckhardt, *Voyages en Arabie* (French. trans.), iii, 24; von Oppenheim, *Vom Mittelmeer zum Persischen Golf*, ii, 44; A. Musil, *Arabia Petraea*, iii, 130-1 and fig. 180; on the *dūwār*, *dawwār* of the Maghribī Arabs, cf. Delphin, *Recueil de Textes pour l'Étude de l'Arabe Parlé*, 284; A. Bernard and N. Lacroix, *L'évolution du nomadisme en Algérie*, 276 ff.; Urquhart, *Pillars of Hercules*, i, 452; *Archives Marocaines*, iv, 105, 106; Loubignac, *Textes Arabes des Zaër*, 129, 215, 304; Marmal, *Descripción general de Africa*, i, ch. xxiv, fol. 36 v. (W. MARÇAIS-[G. S. COLIN])

DAWĀRO, one of the Muslim trading states of southern Ethiopia. It was a long narrow strip of territory lying immediately east of Bāli, and included the great Islamic centre of Harar. It seems to have reached the Webi Shabelle in the south, and the edge of the Danāḳil lowlands in the north, where, with Bāli, it met the state of Ifāt. It is clear, however, that for a time at least, and as early as the reign of ʿĀmda Ṣyon I of Ethiopia, there was an isolated continuation of Dawāro on the north side of the lower course of the Hawaš river, which included part of the present sultanate of Awssa. Dawāro first appears in Ethiopic records in the reign of ʿĀmda Ṣyon I (1312-42). Like the other Muslim states of Ethiopia it was under a king of its own (called *makuannen* in the History of ʿĀmda Ṣyon, BM. MS. Orient. 821, fol. 43), who was tributary to the king of Ethiopia. Under ʿĀmda Ṣyon the king, Hāydārā, revolted and joined the rebellious peoples of Adal; but it was conquered, and remained a dependency of Ethiopia till after 1548 when Fanu'el was governor under Gālāwdēwos. According to al-ʿUmarī, though only five days' journey in length and two days' in breadth, it maintained a large and powerful army; the inhabitants were Ḥanafites. Al-Maḳrīzī repeats the account of al-ʿUmarī. The name Dawāro was applied also locally to the small Sidamā state of Kullo west of the Omo because this area was colonized by refugees from Dawāro during the war of Ethiopia with Aḥmad Grañ (1527-42); but there was no other connexion between Kullo and Dawāro.

Bibliography: Perruchon, *Histoire des guerres d'ʿAmda Ṣyon*, *JA*, 1889, 271-363, 381-493; I. Guidi, *Le canzoni geez-amariña*, 1889, nos. viii and x; Perruchon, *Les Chroniques de Zar'a Yaʿeqôb et de Ba'eda Mâryâm*, Paris 1893; ʿUmarī, *Masālik al-Abṣār*, tr. Gaudefroy-Demombynes, Paris 1927; Maḳrīzī, ed. F. T. Rinck, Leiden 1790; Beckingham and Huntingford, *Some Records of Ethiopia, 1593-1646*, London 1954. (G. W. B. HUNTINGFORD)

AL-**DAWĀSIR** (singular: Dawsarī), a large tribe based in central Arabia. The Dawāsir are remarkable for the way in which many of them have spread abroad and won success in areas and endeavours remote from their original environment, while at the same time even the settled elements among them have retained an unusually strong sentiment of tribal solidarity and attachment to the *mores* of their Bedouin forebears.

Whatever the origins of the tribe, the Dawāsir became primarily identified with Wādī al-Dawāsir in southern Nadjd (the closest of the populated districts there to al-Rubʿ al-Khālī) and with al-Aflādj [*q.v.*]. Although the mainstream of Dawsarī emigration has flowed off towards the north and east, Dawāsir (emigrants or relics clinging to an earlier home?) are found to the south and west in Raghwān near Mārib and in al-Khurma in the Ḥidjāz mountains. North of al-Aflādj, Dawāsir are numerous in the districts of al-Khardj (where they predominate in the principal town, al-Dalam), al-ʿĀriḍ, al-Maḥmal, and Sudayr. Among the towns for which they have provided rulers or judges or other prominent citizens in recent centuries are al-Bīr and Thādiḳ in al-Maḥmal; and al-Madjmaʿa, Djalādjil, al-ʿAwda, and al-Ghāṭ in Sudayr (Ibn Bishr, ii, 142-4, gives the biography of a famous Dawsarī judge of Ḥuraymilā). Dawāsir live in al-Zilfī on the borders of al-Ḳaṣīm, but not many have moved farther north.

The pride of the Dawāsir is the house of the Sudayrīs (al-Sadārā). Their name comes from Sudayr, where for about four centuries they have lived in al-Ghāṭ. In the 13th/19th century Aḥmad b. Muḥammad al-Sudayrī was an illustrious lieutenant of Āl Saʿūd, and his descendants have been intimately associated with this dynasty ever since. A daughter of his was the mother of King ʿAbd al-ʿAzīz (d. 1373/1953), and a great-granddaughter of his bore the King seven sons, two of whom (Fahd and Sulṭān) were Ministers in the Saudi Arabian Government in 1379/1960. In 1369/1950 thirteen of the Sadārā held provincial or district governorships in Saudi Arabia; through this one family Dawāsir have reached into every corner of the Kingdom.

On the Persian Gulf Dawāsir coming from Nadjd via Bahrayn have founded the new towns of al-Dammām [*q.v.*] and al-Khubar, in which they are prospering. Others live in Bahrayn and Ḳaṭar. From Bahrayn some have migrated to the Iranian shore, and from Ḳaṭar a few to the island of Dalmā. In ʿIrāḳ there are Dawāsir in al-Zubayr, and a stretch of Shaṭṭ al-ʿArab is called the district of the Dawāsir, whose name is also given to river islands there.

The tribe consists of two principal divisions, ʿIyāl Zāyid and the Taghāliba, originally independent of each other. Neither claims an ancestor called Dawsar ("strong camel"), though Dawsar occurs as a tribal name in classical sources. The plural Dawāsir is popularly derived from the phrase *al-da yāsir* (sometimes given as *al-dalyāsir* with an intrusive *lām*), the meaning and application of which are obscure. ʿIyāl Zāyid's eponym is Zāyid al-Malṭūm ("the Slapped"—not al-Maltub as in Philby, etc.), whose name appears in the tribal war-cry. Zāyid's identity is uncertain; frequently mentioned as a progenitor of his is ʿUmar al-Khaṭṭāb (without *ibn*), but the ordinary tribesman knows him only vaguely as one of the Ṣaḥāba. In legend both Zāyid and the Taghāliba are associated with Sadd Mārib (pronounced Māridz), and Zāyid is said to have led the tribe from there into Wādī al-Dawāsir. Rather early sources speak of the Dawāsir as an offshoot of ʿĀʾidh, which may be plausible if ʿĀʾidh was in fact a branch of ʿUḳayl [*q.v.*], as ʿAdnānite ʿUḳayl once occupied the valley now known as Wādī al-Dawāsir. Against this identification are various indications, admittedly inconclusive, that ʿIyāl Zāyid are Ḳaḥṭānite rather than ʿAdnānite. ʿIyāl Zāyid are sometimes called Banī Zinwān, legend holding that Zāyid's mother had been falsely accused of adultery.

The other principal division, the Taghāliba, has a firm tradition of descent from Taghlib (pronounced Tughlub) b. (not *bint*) Wāyil, which is not impossible, as this ʿAdnānite tribe was in the forefront of eastern Arabian affairs well beyond the heyday of the Ḳarmaṭians. For unclear reasons the Taghāliba, particularly the section of the Khiyālāt, are referred to as ʿAbāt al-Dawāsir. The union between the two principal divisions is traced back to al-ʿIrʿir, the ancestor of Āl Ḥuḳbān of the Taghāliba, whose daughter is said to have been Zāyid al-Malṭūm's mother.

The most important sections of ʿIyāl Zāyid are the Masāʿira, Āl Ḥasan, the Ridjbān, the Makhārīm, the Wadāʿīn, the Badārīn (including the Sadārā), the Ghiyāthāt, the Sharāfā, and the Ḥarādjīn. The foremost chief is Ibn Ḳuwayd of the Masāʿira, who leads a semi-nomadic life in the hamlet of al-Ḳuwayz in Wādī al-Dawāsir. The Taghāliba consist of five sections: the ʿUmūr, the Maṣārīr, the Mashāwiya, Āl Ḥuḳbān, and the Khiyālāt.

The Dawāsir first appear by name about the 7th/13th century, when they were in contact with Āl Faḍl of Ṭayyiʾ, the Amīrs of the Syrian Desert, and with the Mamlūk Sultans in Cairo, who got horses from Arabia. The Dawāsir are called a tribe of the Yemen, and Ibn Badrān (of the Badārīn) is named as their chief.

Beginning in 851/1447-8, details on the history of the Dawāsir become more abundant and precise. In that year Zāmil b. Djabr, the Djabrid [*q.v.*] lord of al-Ḥasā and al-Ḳaṭīf, defeated the Dawāsir and ʿĀʾidh in al-Khardj. In the following year Zāmil led a large force of Bedouins and townsmen against the Dawāsir in their own valley (the first mention of the valley as Wādī al-Dawāsir) to punish them for their many raids on the nomads of al-Ḥasā. Later Zāmil's son Adjwad launched four separate expeditions against the Dawāsir without reaching their valley on any of them. With the decline of Djabrid power, the Dawāsir multiplied their attacks on caravans carrying merchandise from al-Ḥasā to Nadjd.

Of the 43 battles involving the Dawāsir which are recorded for the period between 851 and 1164/1751, fifteen were fought against Ḳaḥṭān. Other principal opponents were Subayʿ, Āl Maghīra, Āl Kathīr, and the Fuḍūl. Usually the Dawāsir had fewer friends than foes; no other tribe stood by them steadfastly, but on occasion even some of their opponents mentioned above, such as Ḳaḥṭān, joined their side, such being the evanescent loyalties of desert warfare.

The favourite battleground for the Dawāsir was the watering place of al-Ḥarmaliyya near al-Ḳuwayʿiyya, where no less than six encounters took place. In the broader district of al-Khardj the Dawāsir fought seven or eight battles, and four in al-ʿArama. The Dawāsir engaged in most of their strife on territory not their own; other tribes seem to have lacked the temerity to assault them in their homeland.

About 1100/1689 pressure by the Dawāsir forced Āl Ṣabāḥ [*q.v.*] and Āl Khalīfa [*q.v.*], both of ʿAnaza, to migrate from al-Haddār in al-Aflādj to the Persian Gulf, where they in time became the rulers of Kuwayt and Bahrayn. As the power of Āl Saʿūd [*q.v.*] grew during the 12th/18th century, the Dawāsir were among the last of the great tribes of Nadjd to adhere to the reform movement of Shaykh Muḥammad b. ʿAbd al-Wahhāb. In 1199/1784-5 Rubayyiʿ b. Zayd of the Makhārīm swore allegiance to Āl Saʿūd, whose mainstay in Wādī al-Dawāsir he remained for the rest of his days. The Ridjbān and the Wadāʿīn resisted the progress of the reform movement in the valley, supported first by the Ismāʿīlī lord of Nadjrān and then by Ghālib, the Sharīf of Mecca. As the domains of Āl Saʿūd expanded, the Dawāsir fought for them in the west side by side with their old enemies Ḳaḥṭān. In 1212/1809 Dawāsir were among the Bedouins who raided Ḥaḍramawt. The large army annihilated by Muḥammad ʿAlī of Egypt at Bisl in 1230/1815 contained a contingent of Dawāsir.

When Āl Saʿūd returned to power after the capture of al-Dirʿiyya by Muḥammad ʿAlī's forces in 1233/1818, both Turkī b. ʿAbd Allāh and his son Fayṣal maintained Amīrs in Wādī al-Dawāsir. The tribesmen were not always obedient subjects; in 1243/1827-8, for instance, Turkī disciplined Bedouin elements of the Dawāsir for their lawlessness.

About 1845 a number of Dawāsir arrived in Bahrayn, having come from Nadjd by way of the island of al-Zakhnūniyya, where they sojourned for a few years. In Bahrayn they settled in the towns of al-Budayyiʿ (cf. the Dawsarī town of al-Badīʿ in al-Aflādj) and al-Zallāḳ.

During the civil war between Fayṣal's sons ʿAbd Allāh and Saʿūd, the chief of al-Sulayyil in Wādī al-Dawāsir and the Ismāʿīlī lord of Nadjrān championed Saʿūd's cause. In 1283/1866-7 ʿAbd Allāh's forces under his brother Muḥammad crushed Saʿūd and his partisans at al-Muʿtalā in Wādī al-Dawāsir and during the next year ʿAbd Allāh himself spent two months in the valley inflicting condign punishment on its inhabitants. After the death of Saʿūd in 1291/1875, the Dawāsir supported his sons in the struggle which led to a temporary eclipse of Āl Saʿūd, whose rule in Nadjd was supplanted by that of Āl Rashīd of Ḥāʾil. Āl Rashīd is said to have kept a small force in Wādī al-Dawāsir in the closing years of the 19th century.

Following the recapture of al-Riyāḍ by ʿAbd al-ʿAzīz Āl Saʿūd in 1319/1902, Wādī al-Dawāsir was quickly brought back into the fold, though ʿAbd al-ʿAzīz had no easy time in keeping the peace among the turbulent elements of the Dawāsir, who if not fighting with each other were often at war with Āl Murra to the east or Āl Murra's cousins of Yām to the south-west.

In 1336/1918 Philby became the first Westerner to visit Wādī al-Dawāsir and provide an accurate description of it. The valley in recent years has remained a backwater of the new Kingdom of Saudi Arabia, scarcely touched by the material progress being achieved in many other parts. Wādī al-Dawāsir, once an important way station for the coffee trade between the Yemen and Nadjd, has been replaced by Bīsha in the 20th century. The present centre of influence of the Dawāsir is in their government positions and their new towns on the Persian Gulf.

In the old days Dawāsir would go from their valley to the Gulf to work as pearl-divers every summer. Now many who reside on the Gulf shore are landowners, merchants, contractors, and laborers in the oil industry.

In Nadjd the Dawāsir have been Ḥanbalīs since the time of Ibn ʿAbd al-Wahhāb. Along the Persian Gulf some are Mālikīs, while on the Iranian side a number have embraced Shīʿism.

Wādī al-Dawāsir is one of the great eastward trending channels which cut through the long wall of Ṭuwayḳ. The Wādī's ancient tributaries, the valleys of Bīsha, Ranya, and Tathlīth, descend from the Ḥidjāz mountains and meet in the basin of Hadjlat al-Mukhatmiyya (for al-Mukhātimiyya?), where a sand barrier now prevents their waters from reaching the Wādī save in exceptional years (the Tathlīth *sayl* flooded the Wādī the year before Philby's first visit). The name Wādī al-Dawāsir is sometimes restricted to the western part of the valley, in which are found the capital of the whole district, al-Khamāsīn; its sister town, al-Lidām (incorrectly shown as Dam on many maps); and the westernmost settlements known as al-Farʿa. Like al-Khamāsīn, a number of other towns bear the names of units of the tribe, such as al-Sharāfā and al-Walāmīn (a subsection of the Wadāʿīn). South of the gap in Ṭuwayḳ lies Tamra, which earlier lent its name to the valley, if the identification of ʿAḳīḳ Tamra with Wādī al-Dawāsir is accepted. East of the gap is the oasis of al-Sulayyil, whence the principal route to the north leads to al-Aflādj. The lower course of the Wādī, called al-Aṭwā, disappears to the east in the sands of al-Rumayla, the southerly extension of al-Dahnāʾ [*q.v.*].

Bibliography: Ḥamad Ibn Laʿbūn, *Taʾrīkh*, Mecca 1357; Aḥmad Ibn Faḍl Allāh, *al-Taʿrīf*, Cairo 1312; ʿUthmān Ibn Bishr, *ʿUnwān al-madjd*, Cairo 1373; Ibrāhīm Ibn ʿIsā, *ʿIḳd al-durar*, Cairo 1954-5; J. G. Lorimer, *Gazetteer of the Persian Gulf*, Calcutta 1908-15; H. St J. B. Philby, *The Heart of Arabia*, London 1922; idem, *Arabian Jubilee*, London 1952; idem, *Arabian Highlands*, Ithaca, N. Y. 1952; Max Freiherr von Oppenheim & Werner Caskel, *Die Beduinen*, iii, Wiesbaden 1952. Also information received from members of the tribe and Arab scholars in Saudi Arabia. (G. Rentz)

AL-DAWḤA (Doha), the capital and only major city of Ḳaṭar, a Persian Gulf state. Al-Dawḥa is located at 25° 17′ N, 51° 32′ E in the SW corner of a natural shallow-draught harbour formed by two reefs in a bay (*dawḥa* in Persian Gulf Arabic) on the east coast of Qatar (Ḳaṭar) Peninsula. A former fishing village, al-Bidʿ, on the site is now a quarter of the city.

Little is known of al-Dawḥa before 1238/1823, when the British Political Resident in the Persian Gulf visited the town and reported that it was a dependency of Bahrain (al-Baḥrayn). The nature of this relationship, however, varied with changing circumstances. During the early 13th/19th century al-Dawḥa apparently belonged to Bahrain, which in turn paid Āl Saʿūd of Nadjd *zakāh* collected from al-Dawḥa by the British Resident, with whom both Bahrain, in 1235/1820, and Muḥammad b. Thānī, for al-Dawḥa in 1285/1868, had agreed to keep the maritime truce. After a Turkish force occupied al-Dawḥa in 1288/1872 and proclaimed it part of the so-called Sandjaḳ of Nadjd, the town still maintained close relations with Bahrain, Āl Saʿūd of Nadjd, and the British. Other parts of Qatar were treated occasionally as belonging to Bahrain, Abu Dhabi (Abū Ẓabī) or Nadjd until after the departure of the Turks. In 1335/1916, ʿAbd Allāh Āl Thānī as "Shaikh of Qatar" signed an agreement placing Qatar in a "special treaty relationship with H. M. Government". Its status has more recently been defined as that of "a British-protected state". As such, it remains the concern of the British Foreign Office, while British Protectorates proper, such as those in southern Arabia, come under the Colonial Office.

The ascendancy of al-Dawḥa derives from the destruction of the rival city of al-Zubāra in 1312/1895 and from the production of oil from a field at Dukhān, the oil being shipped from a marine terminal at Musayʿīd (incorrectly shown on most maps and in much other printed matter as Umm Said). In 1318/1900 al-Dawḥa was a pearling port of some 12,000 inhabitants in nine *farīḳs* or quarters, sprawling for almost two miles (three km.) along the waterfront on the rocky edge of the desert and dominated by the Ḳalʿat al-ʿAskar or Ḳaṣr Kunāra, as the Turkish garrison called it. This fort still stands in the quarter of the Kalʿat al-ʿAskar, in which are the finest shops and residential areas. Until recently the town proper had no water or gardens; today water is piped in or extracted from sea water by a distillation plant. The hereditary mansion of Āl Thānī still stands in the quarter of al-Dawḥa, from which the town derives its name, but the family now has palaces in the western suburb of al-Rayyān. The present population of al-Dawḥa, which may be roughly estimated at 20-30,000, forms the major part of the total population of Qatar. The city possesses a modern hospital and a small airport which affords connexions with international flights out of Dhahran (al-Ẓahrān) in Saudi Arabia and al-Muharraḳ in Bahrain. The British Political Agent is the only representative of a foreign government resident in al-Dawḥa.

Bibliography: Ibn Bishr, *ʿUnwān al-madjd*, Cairo 1373; Muḥammad al-Nabhānī, *al-Tuḥfa al-nabhāniyya*, Cairo 1342; C. U. Aitchison, *A Collection of Treaties* ..., xi, Dihlī 1933; J. G. Lorimer, *Gazetteer of the Persian Gulf* ..., Calcutta 1908-1915. (R. L. Headley)

DAWLA, 1) an Arabic word signifying the period of an individual's rule or power but also often employed in the meaning of "dynasty". The root *d-w-l* may occur in Akkadian *dālu* "to wander around aimlessly" (*The Assyrian Dictionary*, iii, 59) and Syriac *dāl* "to move, to stir" (Brockelmann, *Lex. Syr.*², 144 b). However, the basic meaning of Arabic *d-w-l* is clearly "to turn, to alternate" (relating it to *d-w-r*?). The Ḳurʾān has *nudāwiluhā* "We cause (days) to alternate" (III, 140/134) and *dūlatan* "something whose ownership is passed around" (LIX, 7/7). In addition, the *ḥadīth* uses *adāla* "to cause someone to obtain his 'turn' (success, victory)", and the famous report of the *Sīra* (Ibn Hishām, 1011) on Muḥammad's death mentions that it took place when it was ʿĀʾisha's regular "turn" (*daw/ūlatī*) for Muḥammad to visit her. The meaning "turn, time (of success, holding office, etc.)" is often attested in early times, as, for instance, in the verses of Farwa b. Musayk in which, however, one of the two occurrences of *dawla* is occasionally replaced by another word (*LA*, s.v. *ṭ-b-b*; al-Ṭabarī, i, 735). It appears to have been the starting point for the development of the meaning "dynasty".

How *dawla* acquired this meaning remains to be investigated. There is nothing to indicate a pre-Islamic origin. Tribal terms, such as *banū* or *āl*, continued to be used in Islam. Genuine verses antedating early ʿAbbāsid times and containing *dawla* in the meaning of "dynasty" have not yet been signalized. Prose references are open to the suspicion of anachronism. Thus, it seems unlikely that an Umayyad general should have blamed a son of the caliph ʿUthmān in these words: "we are fighting for your dynasty (*dawlatikum*) while you betray it" (al-Balādhurī, *Ansāb*, IVB, 39). An increase in the use of the word is noticeable in the earliest ʿAbbāsid documents, some of which may have been transmitted with literal accuracy. In his speech to the Kūfans upon his accession, al-Saffāḥ said: "... you have reached our time, and God has brought to you our *dawla* (time of success)" (al-Ṭabarī, iii, 30). Al-Manṣūr, advising al-Saffāḥ to kill Abū Muslim, praises the strength of "our *dawla*" (*ibid.*, iii, 85; P. K. Hitti, *History of the Arabs*[6], 286). Al-Saffâḥ speaks of Abū Muslim's *dawla* (time in office) (al-Ṭabarī, iii, 86), and, in a document of doubtful historicity, he refers to those who "disrupt the rope of the *dawla* (dynasty)" (*ibid.*, iii, 104). A few years later, al-Manṣūr speaks of those who supported the ʿAbbāsid *dawla* (*ibid.*, iii, 339, but cf. the earlier, similar passage, iii, 32, where *dawla* means "victory"). In a paraphrase of al-Manṣūr's last will, reference is made to the *dawla* (reign) of al-Mahdī (*ibid.*, iii, 454). The evidence is inconclusive. It seems that at the beginning of the ʿAbbāsid period, the term *dawla* was by no means well established in the meaning of "dynasty". However, the word was frequently used by the ʿAbbāsids with reference to their own "turn" of success. Thus it came to be associated with the ruling house and was more and more used as a polite term of reference to it. Soon, one could speak of the supporters and members (*aṣḥāb, ridjāl*) belonging to the *dawla*, the supporters and members of the dynasty; again, the precise date of the earliest occurrence of such usage as yet eludes us.

It has been assumed that Persian political speculation along the lines of the Polybian ἀνακύκλωσις τῶν πολιτειῶν contributed to the formation of the concept *dawla* "dynasty". Such an assumption may find some slender support in the suggestion advanced here that it was the ʿAbbāsids who gave prominence to the term by stressing the significance of their "turn". However, no conscious application of any political theory seems to be involved, notwithstanding the fact that *dawla* occurred later in connexion with speculations about cycles of political power. Al-Kindī, in his *Risāla fī mulk al-ʿArab* (ed. O. Loth, in *Morgenländische Forschungen, Festschrift Fleischer*, Leipzig 1875) usually paired *dawla* with *mulk*. Cf. also al-Rāzī, *Fī amārāt al-iḳbāl wa 'l-dawla* (ed. P. Kraus, *Razis Opera Philosophica*, Paris 1939), where *dawla* means "political success".

2) *Al-dawla* as the second element in titles. At the end of the 3rd/10th century, the *wazīr* al-Ḳāsim b. ʿUbayd Allāh Ibn Wahb was granted the title Walī al-Dawla "Friend of the Dynasty", which then also appeared on al-Muktafī's coinage; specimens dated 291/904 are common, but the existence of any dated 290 is doubted by G. C. Miles. Muslim authors stress that this is the first occurrence of a title composed with *dawla*. Al-Ḳāsim's son, al-Ḥusayn, continued the tradition inaugurated by his father when al-Muḳtadir solemnly bestowed upon him the title of ʿAmīd al-Dawla "Support", which was also inscribed upon coins. This happened in al-Muḥarram 320/February 932 (ʿArīb, 167; Miskawayh, in *Eclipse*, i, 223, trans. iv, 250).

Occasional use of descriptive composites with *dawla* can be traced for the immediately following years. At about this time, we also find a musician and littérateur nicknamed Djirāb al-Dawla "Bag" (*Fihrist*, 135); however, he is said to have chosen this nickname himself in order to ridicule the Būyids (Yāḳūt, *Irshād*, ii, 62 f.). In any case, titles composed with *dawla* came into their own when in Shaʿbān 330/April 942, the Ḥamdānids Ḥasan and ʿAlī were granted the titles Nāṣir al-Dawla "Helper" and Sayf al-Dawla "Sword", respectively. Soon after (beg. 946), the three Būyid brothers claimed *dawla* titles as a sign that they had assumed control in Baghdād and the East. They received the titles Muʿizz al-Dawla "Fortifier", ʿImād al-Dawla "Support", and Rukn al-Dawla "Pillar". Bestowal of these titles was not a meaningless gesture but a highly significant step indicating cession by the caliph of most of the powers of his office.

The Ḥamdānids and the Būyids continued the use of *dawla* titles, and their example was followed in their time, for instance, by the Ghaznawids and Ilek-Khāns in the East and even some of the *reyes de taifas* in Spain. The Fāṭimids also bestowed occasional *dawla* titles upon their highest officials. But the tenth century was hardly over when *dawla* titles lost greatly in significance. They were at first supplemented and eventually replaced by other similar titles; this marked the beginning of the excessive use of titles in Muslim countries, which we find occasionally criticized by Muslim authors. A comprehensive study of post-Būyid occurrences of *dawla* has not yet been made. In the twelfth century, for instance, a court physician was called Amīn al-Dawla "Trusted Supporter" (Hibat Allāh b. al-Tilmīdh) (for *dawla* titles of non-Muslims, cf. al-Ḳalḳashandī, *Ṣubḥ*, v, 490 f.; Ḥ. Zayyāt, in *al-Mashriḳ*, xlii, 1948, 8 ff.). However, while composites with *dawla* were reduced to merely honorific appellations, it can fairly be said that they always denoted high standing in the community. In India, for instance, they continued to be used by some rulers, and, until the abolition of honorary titles in 1935, Persian cabinet ministers often received titles composed with *dawla*.

Bibliography: Al-Bīrūnī, *Chronology*, 132-3; Hilāl al-Ṣābīʾ, *Rusūm dār al-khilāfa*, in al-Suyūṭī, *Awā'il*, Baghdād 1369/1950, 83; al-Ḳalḳashandī, *Ṣubḥ*, i, 431, v, 442, 490 f.; M. van Berchem, in *ZDPV*, xvi, 1893, 93 n. 1; F. Babinger, in *Isl.*, xi, 1921, 20 n. 3; A. Mez, *Renaissance*, 133 n. 1; J. H. Kramers, in *AO*, v, 1927, 53-67; E. de Zambaur, *passim*; H. Bowen, *The Life and Times of ʿAlī Ibn ʿĪsá*, Cambridge 1928, 59; Ḥ. Zayyāt, in *al-Mashriḳ*, xlii, 1948, 7-12; G. C. Miles, *Rare Islamic Coins*, New York 1950, 42 f.; B. Spuler, *Iran*, 223; M. Canard, *Histoire de la dynastie des H'amdanides*, i, Algiers, 1951, 426; E. Tyan, *Institutions du droit public musulman*, ii, Paris, 1956, 26 f.; Ḥasan al-Bāshā, *al-Alḳāb al-Islāmiyya*, Cairo 1957, 410, 512, and *passim*.

3) From its original meaning, *dawla* developed quite a few specialized connotations (cf. Dozy, *Suppl.*, i, 476 f., and the dictionaries of Muslim languages other than Arabic; further, for instance, A. J. Maclean, *A Dictionary of the Dialects of Vernacular Syriac*, Oxford 1901, 62 b). In modern times, an adjectival formation *dawlī* or *duwalī*—from *dawla*, or its pl. *duwal*, in the meaning of "nation" (< state < government < dynasty)—has become accepted in Arabic as the current term for "international".

(F. Rosenthal)

DAWLAT GIRAY (918/1512-985/1577), styled the Taḥt-alghan or Daghtī-alghan (Conqueror of the

Capital), Khān of the Crimea from 958/1551 to 985/1577. He was the son of Mubārek Giray, and was appointed *ḳalghay*, first heir to the throne, by Saʿādet Giray Khān in 938/1532. When he was made Khān in 958/1551 with the firm support of the Ottomans, the latter increased their influence in the Crimea. He vigorously continued the anti-Russian policy of his predecessor, and made an alliance with the Jagellons against Russian in 959/1552. He made several expeditions against Moscow but could not prevent the capture by the Russians of the two sister Khānates of Ḳazan [*q.v.*] and Astrakhān [*q.v.*]. When the Ottomans failed to get control of the lower Volga in their expedition of 977/1569, they encouraged the Khān to continue the war against Russia. In 979/1571, breaking Russian resistance on the Oka river, he reached Moscow and burned it down, whence his cognomen. The following year, when the Czar rejected the Khān's claims on Ḳazan and Astrakhān, he made a new expedition but was severely defeated at Molodi near Moscow.

His co-operation with the Ottomans in the Polish elections against Russia was more successful (see *Belleten*, no. 46, 390). He died in Ṣafar 985/April-May 1577. His reign was marked by the vital struggle of the Crimean Khānate against Russia for the heritage of the Golden Horde in the Volga basin, and by the further integration of the Crimea in the Ottoman empire. Mention should be made of the Great Mosque that he built at Gözleve in 979/1571. Six of his eighteen sons became Khān after him (see *Giray* in *IA*).

Bibliography: Meḥmed Riḍā, *Al-Sabʿ al-sayyār fī akhbār al-mulūk al-Tātār*, ed. Kāẓim Bik, Kazan 1832, 93-101; Ḥalīm Giray, *Gulbun-i Khānān*, Istanbul 1278, 18-21; ʿAbd al-Ghaffār, *ʿUmdat al-Tawārīkh*, in *TOEM*, 112; H. Feyizkhanoghlu-V. Zernov, *Ḳirīm yurtuna wa ol taraflargha dāʾir bolghan yarlīḳlar wa ḥatlar*, St. Petersburg 1864, 558 ff.; Ferīdūn, *Munshaʾāt al-salāṭīn*, Istanbul 1265, ii, 541; 558-59; A. Refīḳ, *Baḥr-i Khazar-Ḳaradeniz ḳanalī ve Ejderkhan seferi*, in *TOEM*, vol. 8, no. 43, 1-14; H. Inalcık, *Osmanlı-Rus rekabetinin menşei ve Don-Volga kanalı teşebbüsü*, *Belleten*, xii, No. 46, 368-90.

(HALIL INALCIK)

DAWLAT-SHĀH (AMĪR) B. ʿALAʾ AL-DAWLA BAKHTĪSHĀH, a Persian writer from a family owning estates at Isfarāʾ in in the Khurāsān. His father was one of the most intimate courtiers of Shāh-Rukh, son of Tīmūr; he himself took part in the battle fought by the Timurids Abu'l-Ghāzī Sulṭan Ḥusayn and Sulṭan Maḥmūd near Andakhūd. He was about fifty years of age when he began to write his *Tadhkirat al-shuʿarāʾ* ("Memorial to the Poets"), which he finished in about 892/1487 towards the end of his life, the date of his death being unknown. In his *Madjālis al-nafāʾis* (chap. VI), Mīr ʿAlī Shīr Nawāʾī, the famous minister, writer and patron of letters and the arts (cf. Browne, iii, 437), praises Dawlat-Shāh for renouncing the society of the great in order to devote himself to study and to writing his book. This "Memorial to the Poets", the earliest of the *tadhkira* [*q.v.*] made known through von Hammer's translation, is divided into seven parts, each containing information on twenty or so poets and the princes who were their patrons; there is an introduction on the art of poetry; the concluding section is devoted to seven poets who were contemporaries of the author, and to the glorification of the Timurid prince Abu 'l-Ghāzī Sulṭān Ḥusayn b. Manṣūr b. Bayḳarā, who was himself a man of letters (Browne, iii, 390 and 439). This concise anthology of poems which for the most part are well chosen is very useful in literary history, especially for the study of 8th/14th and 9th/15th century poets; but many mistakes have been detected in the notes on the princes and poets, while the judgments expressed on their talents are very often lacking in critical sense.

The eldest son of Fatḥ ʿAlī Shāh was also called Dawlat-Shāh; born at Nawā on 7 Rabīʿ II 1203/6 January 1789, he was for many years governor of Kirmān-shāhān, and died on 26 Safar 1236/3 December 1820 on his return from his campaign against Maḥmūd Pasha; he has left a number of poems.

Bibliography: editions: Bombay, 1887; *The Tadhkiratu'sh-shuʿarā*, ed. E. G. Browne, London 1901. Translation: *Geschichte der schönen Redekünste Persiens* .... by J. von Hammer, Vienna 1818. Riḍā Ḳulī Khān, *Madjmaʿ al-fusaḥā*, i, 26; Belin, in *JA*, i, (1861), 245; Browne, iii, index, *sub nom.*; idem, *The Sources of Dawlat-shah*, in *JRAS* 1899, 37-60; list of other *tadhkira* in *Gr.I.Ph.*, ii, 213-6.

(CL. HUART-[H. MASSÉ])

DAWLATĀBĀD, a hill fort lat. 19° 57′ N., long. 75° 15′ E., ten miles N.-W. of Awrangābād, now in Mahārāshtra State, was called Deogiri (properly Devagiri), "the Hill of God", in pre-Muslim times as the capital of the Yādavas, originally feudatories of the Western Čālukyas but independent since 1183 A.D., after which they continued to rule the territory from Deogiri independently. ʿAlāʾ al-Dīn, nephew of Sulṭān Djalāl al-Dīn Fīrūz Khaldjī of Dihlī, actuated by reports of the immense wealth of Deogiri, reached there by forced marches in 693/1294 and invested the fortress. Rāmčandra, the then Rādjā, taken by surprise, was ultimately forced to surrender to the invaders huge quantities of gold, silver and precious stones, which became ʿAlāʾ al-Dīn's bait to lure Fīrūz to his death, as well as agree to the cession of Eličpur to the Dihlī Empire. Rāmčandra failed to remit the revenues of Eličpur and in 706/1307 a force commanded by Kāfūr Hazārdīnārī, then Malik Nāʾib, was sent against him; but on making his submission to Kāfūr he was courteously sent to the capital where he offered sumptuous gifts in lieu of tribute. His ready pardon and official appointment as governor of Deogiri, with the title of *Rāy-i Rāyān*, has been attributed to ʿAlā al-Dīn's superstitious regard for Deogiri as the talisman of his wealth and power. But his son and successor, Shankara, having defied the Dihlī hegemony, Kāfūr was again sent south in 713/1313, where he assumed the government of the state having put Shankara to death. Shankara's son-in-law Harapāla proclaimed his independence some three years later, and the new Dihlī sultan, Ḳuṭb al-Dīn Mubārak Khaldjī, personally led an expedition south, slew Harapāla, re-annexed the Deogiri lands, and built in 718/1318 the g eat Djāmiʿ masdjid there (see Monuments, below).

The next important date in the history of Deogiri was when Muḥammad b. Tughluḳ decided in 727/1327 that, since Dihlī was not sufficiently central in his dominions, Deogiri should be renamed Dawlatābād and become his capital. Officials were at first encouraged to settle there, but in 729/1329 the entire population was compelled to move to Dawlatābād as a punitive measure (Baranī, 481 ff.; Ibn Baṭṭūṭa, iii, 314 ff.), and from there as a base of operations order was restored in the Deccan. But shortly thereafter Mughal raids in north India necessitated Muḥammad's return to Dihlī and Dawlatābād reverted to its status as a southern garrison. It was at Dawlatābād that Ismāʿīl Mukh was elected their leader by the Amīrān-i Ṣadah in . . ./1346 and it was again there that a year later Ẓafar Khān, who had defeated the Dihlī army, superseded Ismāʿīl and became the first Bahmanid sulṭān. The Bahmanīs retained Dawlatābād as a garrison on their northern frontier and improved its defences; the conspicuous Čānd mīnār dates from their occupation. It passed to the Nīẓām Shāhīs of Aḥmadnagar in 905/1500, becoming their capital in 1009/1600. The Mughal emperor Shāhdjahān clearly considered possession of Dawlatābād to be the key to dominion over the Deccan, and in 1043/1633 it was taken for the Mughals by Mahābat Khān after a fierce siege (ʿAbd al-Ḥamīd Lāhawrī, *Bādshāh-nāma*, Bibl. Ind., 496-536). Salābat Djang secured Dawlatābād for the Niẓām al-Mulk in 1170/1757, but lost it three years later to the Marāthās.

Dawlatābād once boasted of the Fatḥābād mint (for the name Fatḥābād given to Dawlatābād in the time of Muḥammad I Bahmanī, see *Burhān al-Maʾāthir*, 1936 ed., 17) where coin was struck from 761-6 A.H.; it was also the centre of a paper-making industry.

Bibliography: in addition to references above, see Bilgrami and Willmott, *Historical and Descriptive Sketches of H.H. the Nizam's Dominions*; T. W. Haig, *Historical Landmarks of the Deccan*; *Imperial Gazetteer of India, Hyderabad State.*

(H. K. Sherwani)

(*ii*) Monuments. The earliest building work at Dawlatābād (apart from the rock-cut caves of the 1st century B.C.) is the scarping of Devagiri, a single conical hill of rock some 200 m. high commanding a natural pass. This scarping, dating at least from the early Yādava times, results in the entire circuit of the rock presenting a vertical face 50 to 65 m. high, above a water-filled moat of rectangular section dug a further 15 m. into the rock (a causeway across the moat leading to a rock-cut shrine shows its Hindū provenance). The utilization of stone of Hindū workmanship in later Islamic building indicates the former existence of a town on the sloping ground to the east.

It is on the east that the triple apron of fortification lies, dating in origin from the time of Muḥammad b. Tughluḳ. The outermost wall is the curtain of the outer town, which is traversed from south to north by the Awrangābād—Khuldābād [*qq.v.*] road; the town (called ʿAnbarkōṭ in ʿAbd al-Ḥamīd Lāhawrī, *Bādshāhnāma, passim*) is an area about 2 km. north-south by a maximum of 1 km. east-west; the second wall encloses an area of 1.2 km. by 0.4 km. to the west of the first, called Kaṭak (= Sanskrit *kaṭaka*) by Ibn Baṭṭūṭa and Mahākōṭ ("great fort") by Lāhawrī, and is entered through a hornwork formed by a succession of rounded bastions [see BURDJ, iii]; a less elaborate entrance in the third apron leads to the citadel, Devagiri (Bālākōṭ of Lāhawrī) through a steep flight of steps, the rock-cut moat crossed by a narrow stone bridge, a tunnel through rock-cut chambers and re-used Djayn caves emerging some 15 m. higher, a broad rock staircase leading to a Mughal *bāradarī*, and finally another flight of 100 steps to the acropolis, a platform 50 m. by 36 m., on which guns are mounted. All three walls are defended by external ditch and counterscarp; they all show signs (by heightening in work of smaller stone) of modification during the Bahmanī period. Of interest in the defence works are: (1) the bridge over the final moat, with its central portion about 3 m. below the level of each side, approached by steep flights of steps from counterscarp and gallery. The height of water in the moat must have been under control, so that the central portion of the bridge could be submerged; (2) the long tunnel, at the head of which was an iron barrier which could be rendered red-hot by lighting a fire on it (for a different interpretation see Sidney Toy, *The strongholds of India*, London 1957, 38 ff., criticized by J. Burton-Page in *BSOAS*, xxiii/3, 1960, 516 ff.); midway is a rock-cut look-out post.

The mosque of Ḳuṭb al-Dīn Mubārak Khaldjī of Dihlī (inscr. 718-1318) is perhaps the earliest Muslim monument. Largely an improvisation out of temple material, it has tapering fluted corner buttresses and a corbelled dome, and is some 78 m. square in overall plan (illustration in *Ann. Report, Arch. Dept. Hyd.*, 1925-6, Pl. III); the *miḥrāb* has since been filled with an idol.

The mosque has no minaret; fulfilling this function, however, is the Čānd mīnār, 30 m. high, of about 840/1435, similar in shape to the towers of Maḥmūd Gāwān's *madrasa* at Bīdar [*q.v.*] but with three galleries supported by elaborate brackets. In addition to its function as a *mīnar* of the mosque, it was also an observation post, since it commanded the dead ground on the north-east.

The palaces are mostly in ruins; noteworthy are the *bāradarī* mentioned above, built for Shāhdjahān's visit in 1046/1636, and the Čīnī maḥall in Mahākōt, of the Niẓām Shāhī period, with fine encaustic tile-work; the latter was used as a state prison for the last Ḳuṭb Shāhī ruler, Abu 'l-Ḥasan (Khʷāfī Khān, *Muntakhab al-Lubāb*, ii, 371 ff.).

Bibliography: There is no monograph on Dawlatābād as a site; in addition to references in the text, see S. Piggott, *Some ancient cities of India*, Bombay 1945, 78 ff. (including sketch-map).

(J. Burton-Page)

AL-**DAWLATĀBĀDĪ**, Shihāb al-Dīn Aḥmad b. Shams al-Dīn b. ʿUmar al-Zāwulī al-Hindī, an eminent Indian scholar of the 9th/15th century, was born at Dawlatābād in the Deccan. He completed his studies in Dihlī at the feet of Ḳāḍī ʿAbd al-Muḳtadir and Mawlānā Khʷādjgī, two eminent disciples of Shaykh Naṣīr al-Dīn Čirāgh-i Dihlī. When Tīmūr invaded India, Shihāb al-Dīn left Dihlī and settled at Djawnpur where Sulṭān Ibrāhīm Sharḳī (804-844/1400-1440) received him with honour and appointed him as the *ḳāḍī al-ḳuḍāt* of his kingdom. Later on he conferred upon him the title of *Malik al-ʿUlamāʾ*. Firishta says that he was held in such high esteem by the Sulṭān that a special silver chair was provided for him in the court. He died at Djawnpur in 848/1445.

Shihāb al-Dīn was a prolific writer. According to Shaykh ʿAbd al-Ḥaḳḳ Muḥaddith Dihlawī and Muḥammad Ghawthī Shaṭṭārī he enjoyed some reputation as a Persian poet also. Of his compositions, the following are particularly noteworthy: *Sharḥ al-Hindī*, a commentary on the *Kāfiya* (for Mss, *Contribution of India to Arabic Literature*, Zubaid Ahmad 401); *Sharḥ uṣūl al-Bazdawī*, (Ms. in possession of M. Abul Kalām Azād); *Al-ʿAḳaʾid al-Islāmiyya*, on scholastic theology (Ms, Rampur, 314); *al-Irshād*, on Arabic syntax, (printed at Ḥaydarābād); *Muṣaddiḳ al-faḍl*, commentary on the famous *Ḳaṣīda Bānat Suʿād*, (printed at Ḥaydarābād); *Baḥr al-mawwādj*, a Persian commentary on the Ḳurʾān, dedicated to Sulṭān Ibrāhīm Sharḳī (for Mss,

Storey 10, 1193); *Ta'rīkh al-Madīna* (Storey, 427); *Fatāwā-i Ibrāhīm Shāhī*; *Badā'iᶜ al-bayān*; *Manāḳib al-sādāt*, on the merits and prerogatives of the descendants of the Prophet, (Storey 211, 1261).

Bibliography: ᶜAbd al-Ḥaḳḳ Muḥaddith Dihlawī, *Akhbār al-akhyār*, (Dihlī 1309) 175-6; Muḥd. Ghawthī Shaṭṭārī, *Gulzār-i abrār*, (Ms. As. Soc. of Bengal 47 V); Muḥd. Ṣādiḳ, *Ṭabaḳāt-i Shāhdjahānī*, (Ms. British Museum f. 60); Ghulām ᶜAlī Azād, *Ma'āthir al-kirām*, (Agra, 1910) 188-189; Faḳīr Muḥammad, *Ḥadā'iḳ al-Ḥanafiyya*, (Nawal Kishore, Lucknow, 1906) 316; Raḥmān ᶜAlī, *Tadhkira-i ᶜulamā'-i Hind*, (Nawal Kishore, Lucknow, 1914), 88-9; Nūr al-Dīn, *Tadjallī-i Nūr*, (Djawnpur, 1900) ii 33; Zubaid Ahmad, *The Contribution of India to Arabic Literature*, 167 ff.; Storey 9-10; Brockelmann II, 220.

(K. A. Nizami)

DAWR [see supplement].

DAWRAḲ, formerly a town in south-western Khūzistān, was also called Dawraḳ al-Furs, 'Dawraḳ of the Persians' and sometimes al-Madīna, 'the Town'. The original Persian name was Darāk. In the middle ages Dawraḳ was the capital of a district which was sometimes called after it and was sometimes known as Surraḳ. Dawraḳ lay on the banks of the river of the same name, which was a tributary of the Djarrāḥī; it was connected by canal with the Kārūn [*q.v.*]. It was famous for its veils and for its sulphur springs. Pilgrims from Kirmān and Fārs used to pass through Dawraḳ on their way to and from Mecca. As late as the 4th/10th century a fire-temple and some other remarkable buildings dating from the Sāsānid era were still to be seen in the town. Dawraḳ was described in the *Ḥudūd al-ᶜĀlam* (130) as a pleasant, prosperous and wealthy town. Towards the close of the 10th/16th century the Banī Tamīm occupied Dawraḳ and the surrounding area, but they were ousted by Sayyid Mubārak, of the Mushᶜashaᶜ dynasty of Ḥawīza, the well-known *Wālī* of ᶜArabistān (Khūzistān) about the year 1000/1591-2. In 1029/1619-20 the *Beglerbegī* of Fārs conquered Dawraḳ and its district (see the *Ta'rīkh-i ᶜĀlam-ārā-yi ᶜAbbāsī*, 675). Subsequently the district was occupied by a branch of the Afshār tribe [*q.v.*], but they were displaced by Shaykh Salmān of the Kaᶜb [*q.v.*] during the reign of Nādir Shāh [*q.v.*]. Shaykh Salmān built a new town, which he called Fallāḥiya, five miles to the south of Dawraḳ, which thereafter fell into ruin. In order to protect Fallāḥiya against the Huwala and other hostile tribes, Shaykh Salmān erected a strong fort there and built a mud wall two miles in circumference round the town. When Layard visited Fallāḥiya a century later, he found this wall in bad repair; he stated, however, that the many canals and water-courses surrounding it would provide a formidable barrier to invasion if strongly defended (*Description of the province of Khuzistan*, in *JRGS*, 1846, xvi, 39; see also his *Early adventures in Persia, Susiana and Babylonia*, London 1887, ii, 57).

In 1933 the name of Fallāḥiya was changed to Shādagān; it is the capital of the sub-district (*bakhsh*) of the same name which forms part of the *shahristān* of Khurramshahr (formerly known as Muḥammara). The date-groves and rice fields surrounding the town are watered by irrigation canals; wheat is also grown. In the town there are some 400 houses, 120 shops, two mosques and two schools; the population, including that of the surrounding district, is about 20,000. The swampy area between Shādagān and the coast of the Persian Gulf is still known as Dawraḳistān. The name is also preserved in the Khawr Dawraḳ, a northern arm of the Khawr Mūsā, the large inlet of the Gulf which bounds Dawraḳistān on the east and north-east.

Bibliography: in addition to references in the text: *BGA*, *passim*; Balādhurī, *Futūḥ*, 382, 415; Yāḳūt, ii, 618, 620; *Marāṣid al-Iṭṭilāᶜ*, (ed. Juynboll), i, 414, v, 502-3; Ḳazwīnī, *Kosmographie* (ed. Wüstenfeld), 191; J. Macdonald Kinneir, *A geographical memoir of the Persian Empire*, 88-9; J. H. Stocqueler, *Fifteen months' pilgrimage through untrodden tracts of Khuzistan and Persia*, i, 72; Ritter, *Erdkunde*, ix, 158-60; Le Strange, 242; G. N. Curzon, *Persia and the Persian Question*, ii, 322-3; Razmārā and Nawtāsh, *Farhang-i djughrāfiyā-yi Īrān*, vi, 228.

(L. Lockhart)

DAWS [see azd].

DAWSA (Dōsa), literally "trampling", a ceremony formerly performed in Cairo by the Shaykh of the Saᶜdī *ṭarīḳa* on the *mawlids* [*q.v.*] of the Prophet, of al-Shāfiᶜī, of Sulṭān Ḥanafī (a celebrated Saint of Cairo who died in 847/1443; *Khiṭaṭ djadīda*, iii, 93, iv, 100), of Shaykh Dashṭūṭī (or Ṭashṭūshī), another saint; Lane, *Modern Egyptians*, chap. xxiv; *Khiṭaṭ djadīda*, iii, 72, 133, iv, 111), and of Shaykh Yūnus (see below). These took place by day; a similar ceremony was performed by the Shaykh al-Bakrī, the head of the *ṭarīḳas* in Egypt, on the *mawlid* of Dashṭūṭī by night. The ceremony has been described at length by Lane (*loc. cit.*, with drawing; another description, with a drawing by the artist C. Rudolf Huber, who was an eye-witness, in G. Ebers, *Aegypten*, Stuttgart and Leipzig 1879-80, ii, 129 ff.); it consisted, in short, of as many as three hundred members of the *ṭarīḳa* lying down with their faces to the ground and the Shaykh riding over them on horseback. It was believed that by a special *karāma* [*q.v.*], inherent in the *ṭarīḳa*, no one was ever injured, and by such physical contact the *baraka* [*q.v.*] of the Shaykh was communicated to his followers. The same ceremony was performed elsewhere (Lady I. Burton, *The inner life of Syria*, etc., chap. x, for Barze near Damascus; Muḥammad b. ᶜUmar al-Tūnisī, d. 1274/1857, in *Voyage au Ouaday*, tr. A. Perron, 700). In other *ṭarīḳas*, *baraka* has been ascribed to rubbing with the feet of the Shaykh and even to the dust on which he has trodden. The use of the horse by Saᶜdī *ṭarīḳa* has been associated with the rank of its founder as a descendant of the Prophet. The origin of the Cairo *dawsa* is obscure; the legend has it that when Shaykh Yūnus, the son of Sa'd al-Dīn al-Djībāwī, the founder, came to Cairo his followers asked him to establish for their usage a *bidᶜa ḥasana* (good innovation) which by its *karāma* would prove his rank as a saint; he thereupon made them cover his path with round and smooth vessels of glass, and he rode over them without breaking one. This his successors could not do, and prostrated men were substituted for the glass (Goldziher, in *ZDMG*, 1882, 647 f.; Muḥammad Rashīd Riḍā, *Ta'rīkh ... Muḥammad ᶜAbduh*, ii, 147 ff., 2nd. ed., ii, 139 ff.). This Shaykh Yūnus is said by some to be buried outside the Bāb al-Naṣr (Goldziher, *loc. cit.*; *Khiṭaṭ Djadīda*, ii, 72). Saᶜd al-Dīn is commonly assigned to the second half of the 7th/13th century. The date is quite uncertain, and there may have been confusion with the ecstatic (*madjdhūb*) Shaykh Yūnus al-Shaybānī, the founder of the Yūnusī *ṭarīḳa* (al-Maḳrīzī, *Khiṭaṭ*, Būlāḳ 1270, ii, 435). The *dawsa* was abolished by the Khedīw Muḥammad Tawfīḳ in 1881, after the Chief Muftī of Egypt had given a *fatwā* in which he declared it a *bidʿa ḳabīḥa* (evil innovation), involving undignified treatment of Muslims. For some time afterwards, on the mornings of those *mawlid*s some members of the Saʿdī *ṭarīḳa* lay down in front of the door of their Shaykh and let him walk over them (A. Le Chatelier, *Les Confréries Musulmanes du Hedjaz*, 225), but this, too, has now been discontinued.

Bibliography: in addition to the references given: ʿAlī Pasha Mubārak, *al-Khiṭaṭ al-djadīda*, iv, 112; O. Depont and X. Coppolani, *Les confréries religieuses musulmanes*, 329 ff.).

(D. B. Macdonald*)

DĀWŪD, the biblical David. David is mentioned in several places in the Ḳurʾān, sometimes together with his more famous son and successor Solomon (Sulaymān). He kills Goliath (Djālūt, *Sūra* II, 251). God grants him the rule of the kingdom (*ibid.*) and enforces it (XXXVIII, 20). He makes him a "*khalīfa* on earth" (*i.e.*, the successor of an earlier generation of rulers, XXXVIII, 26). He gives him knowledge (*ʿilm*) and wisdom (*ḥikma*), and the ability to do justice (*ḥukm*, esp. XXI, 78 f.; XXXVII, 21-24, 26; *faṣl al-khiṭāb*, XXXVII, 20). He gives him a *zabūr* (book, psalter, IV, 163; XVII, 55), and makes the birds and mountains his servants, so that they unite in his praise (XXI, 79; XXXIV, 10; XXXVIII, 18 f.). God also instructs him in the art of fashioning chain mail out of iron (XXXIV, 10 f.; XXI, 80). Together with Solomon, he gives judgment in a case of damage to the fields (XXI, 78). The fable of the rich man and the poor man, which Nathan tells the king (2 Sam, xii, 1-4), is retold in a somewhat modified form (XXXVIII, 21-23). There is no mention of the wrong David did to Uriah, but the subsequent verses show that the king feels himself to be guilty. His prayer for forgiveness is heard (24 f.).

The *ḥadīth* stresses David's zeal in prayer, and especially in fasting. Ḳurʾān commentators, historians, and compilers of the "Tales of the Prophets", specifically mention David as a prophet and add further material from Jewish (and Christian) tradition, including the story of Saul's jealousy of David, and that of the wife of Uriah (this as proof of David's 'temptation', *Sūra* XXXVIII, 24), and the story of Absalom and his early death. The details —especially in the later (and also in the mystical) works—are fantastically elaborated. The title *khalīfa fi 'l-arḍ* (*Sūra* XXXVIII, 26) is interpreted as 'God's delegate on earth'. David's readiness to do penance is mentioned in particular. Another favourite theme is David's gift in singing psalms. His voice has a magic power: it weaves its spell not only over man, but over wild beasts and inanimate nature.

There is proof of the name of Dāwūd (or Dāwud) in pre-Islamic times. There are poems which mention a Dāwūd, or his son, as a maker of coats of chain mail. Perhaps this refers to a Jewish armourer. In any case, presumably even in pre-Muḥammadan times, he was identified with King David (Horovitz, *Koranische Untersuchungen*, 109 f.). In the Ḳurʾān, the name is spelled Dāwūd (< Hebrew Dāwīḏ), or *Dʾwd* (Dāwud) throughout. Later on, the form Dāʾūd (with hamza) became common.

Bibliography: Bukhārī, *Ṣaum* 59, *Anbiyāʾ* 37-9; Muslim, *Ṣiyām* 182-97; Ṭabarī, i, 554-6, 559-72; idem., *Tafsīr*, Cairo 1321, ii, 375-81; xvii, 34-7; xxii, 40 f.; xxiii, 77-87; Ibn al-Athīr, *Chronicon* (ed. Tornberg), i, Leiden 1867, 153-9; Masʿūdī, *Murudj*, i, Paris 1861, 106-10; Thaʿlabī, *Ḳiṣaṣ al-Anbiyāʾ*, Cairo 1292, 235-54; Kisāʾī, *Ḳiṣaṣ al-Anbiyāʾ*, Leiden 1922, 252-78; Ghazzālī (supposed author), *Al-Durra al-fākhira* (ed. L. Gautier, Geneva-Basle-Lyons 1878), 74-6, transl. 63 f. (trans. by M. Brugsch, Hanover 1924, 83-5); Hudjwīrī, *Kashf al-maḥdjūb* (trans. by R. A. Nicholson, GMS XVII, 1911), 402 f.; G. Weil, *Biblische Legenden der Muselmänner*, Frankfurt 1845, 202-24; R. Basset, *Mille et un contes, récits et légendes arabes*, iii, Paris 1927, 89-99; M. Grünbaum, *Neue Beiträge zur semitischen Sagenkunde*, Leiden 1893, 189-98; J. Walker, *Bible characters in the Koran*, Paisley 1931, 41-4; H. Speyer, *Die biblischen Erzählungen im Qoran*, Gräfenhainichen o.J., 369, 372, 375-82, 403 f.; J. Horovitz, *Koranische Untersuchungen*, Berlin and Leipzig 1926, 109-11.

(R. Paret)

DĀWŪD b. ʿAlī b. **KHALAF** al-Iṣfahānī Abū Sulaymān, the *imām* of the school of the Ẓāhiriyya ([*q.v.*]; also called Dāwūdiyya) in religious law. An extreme representative of the tendency hostile to human reasoning and relying exlusively on Ḳurʾān and *ḥadīth*, Dāwūd not only rejected personal opinion (*raʾy*) as al-Shāfiʿī [*q.v.*] had done, but, as far as he could, systematic reasoning by analogy (*ḳiyās*) which al-Shāfiʿī had admitted and tried to regularize, and he made it his principle to follow the outward or literal meaning (*ẓāhir*) of Ḳurʾān and *ḥadīth* exclusively; he also restricted the concept of consensus (*idjmāʿ*) to the consensus of the Companions of the Prophet, and rejected the practice of allegiance (*taḳlīd*) to a single master which in his time had come to prevail in the other schools of religious law. In all these respects, his doctrine represents a one-sided elaboration and development of that of al-Shāfiʿī and his school.

Dāwūd's family came from a village near Iṣfahān; he was born in Kūfa in 200-2/815-8. He studied *ḥadīth* under well-known authorities in Baṣra, Baghdād and Nīsābūr, and then settled in Baghdād where he became highly esteemed as a teacher and muftī. His biographers praise him for his piety, humility and asceticism. Nothing is known of his teachers in *fiḳh* proper; his father was a Ḥanafī, and he himself is called a fanatical adherent (*mutaʿaṣṣib*) of al-Shāfiʿī, a description which fits both the starting-point and the later development of his own doctrine, and he occupies an honoured place in the biographical works of the Shāfiʿī school. In theology, he is reported to have held the opinion that the Ḳurʾān as it exists on the "well-preserved tablet", was uncreated, but as it exists in the actual copies, produced in time, and Aḥmad b. Ḥanbal is said to have refused to meet him on account of this.

Dāwūd was the author of numerous treatises (see a more or less contemporary list in the *Fihrist*), some of them extremely long (up to 3000 folios), covering legal theory (*uṣūl*) and all branches of positive law (*furūʿ*); nothing of all this has survived, and we depend for statements of his doctrine on questions of detail on later authors (*e.g.*, al-Subkī, and particularly Ibn Ḥazm [*q.v.*], and some of the works on *ikhtilāf*), who however do not always distinguish between Dāwūd's own opinions and those of his followers. The Ḥanbalī author Muḥammad al-Shaṭṭī (1307/1889-90), at the suggestion of the muftī of Damascus, Maḥmūd b. Ḥamza Effendi al-Ḥamzāwī (d. 1305/1887-8), collected many of these opinions and compared them with the corresponding Ḥanbalī doctrines (*R. fī Masāʾil al-Imām Dāwūd al-Ẓāhirī*, Damascus 1330). The school of the Ẓāhiriyya disappeared in due course, and for this reason their opinions and those of their *imām*, Dāwūd, are not taken into account in establishing the consensus of the scholars, although a number of Shāfiʿī scholars take, theoretically at least, a more accomodating view (see al-Nawawī and, in more detail, al-Subkī). Dāwūd died in Baghdād in 270/884 and was buried there. His son, Muḥammad b. Dāwūd [*q.v.*], was a famous man of letters.

Bibliography: *Fihrist*, i, 216 f.; *Tāʾrīkh Baghdād*, viii, no. 4473; Samʿānī, s.v. al-Ẓāhirī; Ibn al-Djawzī, *al-Muntaẓam*, v/2, no. 164; al-Nawawī, *Biographical Dictionary*, ed. Wüstenfeld, 236 ff.; Ibn Khallikān, s.v.; al-Yāfiʿī, *Mirāt al-djanān*, ii, 184 f.; al-Subkī, *Ṭabaḳāt al-Shāfiʿiyya*, ii, 42 ff.; Wüstenfeld, *Der Imām el-Schāfiʾi*, no. 46; Ibn Kathīr, *al-Bidāya wa ʾl-Nihāya*, xi, 47 ff. (Year 270); Ibn al-ʿImād, *Shadharāt al-Dhahab*, ii, 158 f.; Ibn Taghribirdi, Cairo, iii, 47 ff. (Year 270). Goldziher, *Die Ẓāhiriten*, 27 ff. and *passim* (fundamental work); Brockelmann, I, 194 f.; idem, S I, 312; Schacht, *Esquisse*, 56 f. (J. Schacht)

DĀWŪD al-ANṬĀḲĪ [see al-anṭaḳī].

DĀWŪD b. ʿAbd Allāh b. Idrīs al-**FAṬĀNĪ** or Faṭṭānī, *i.e.*, from Patani on the N.E. coast of the Malay Peninsula, a Malay author living in Mecca in the first half of the 13/19th century. He belonged to the Shaṭṭāriyya order. He wrote popular tracts as well as extensive handbooks on Shāfiʿite *fiḳh*, theology and orthodox mysticism. All these works are translations from the Arabic into Malay, more literal than those of ʿAbd al-Ṣamad al-Palimbānī [*q.v.*]. They aim at a public not learned enough to read Arabic fluently, but familiar, to a certain degree, with the structure of the language. His earliest dated work was finished in 1224/1810, the latest in 1259/1843. Most of his works are compiled from various Arabic sources, but it seems that sometimes he followed one model only, *e.g.*, in his translation of al-Ghazzālī's *Minhādj al-ʿābidīn ilā Djannat Rabb al-ʿĀlamīn*, and in *al-Bahdja al-wardiyya fī ʿaḳāʾid ahl al-djamāʿa al-sunniyya*, a Malay version of ʿAbd al-Raḥmān b. ʿAbd al-Salām al-Ṣaffūrī's commentary on the *Manẓūma fi ʾl-tawḥīd* by Aḥmad b. ʿAbd al-Raḥmān al-Djazāʾirī (printed Mecca 1331; on the title-page the *manẓūma* is erroneously ascribed to Ibn al-Wardī; the complete text of the Arabic *manẓūma* is incorporated in this edition). Another remarkable work is *Kanz al-minan ʿalā ḥikam Abī Madyan*, translated from a commentary on the maxims of Abū Madyan Shuʿayb b. al-Ḥusayn al-Andalusī (printed Mecca 1328; the maxims are quoted in Arabic). A popular treatise on marriage law by Daud Patani was lithographed in Singapore, 1287, and some other treatises a few years later in Bombay. His main works were printed in Mecca c. 1302, and from 1328 onward his descendants, still living in the holy city, reprinted some of his works and published some others for the first time. There are MSS. of Malay works by Daud Patani in Cambridge (Scott coll.), Djakarta, Leiden and London (R.A.S.) but none of them unpublished.

Bibliography: C. Snouck Hurgronje, *Mekka*, ii, 386; H. H. Juynboll, *Catalogus v. d. Mal. en Sund. hss. der Leidsche Univ. Bibl.*, 276; Ph. S. van Ronkel, *Catalogus der Mal. hss. in het Museum v. h. Bat. Gen. v. K. en W.*, 374, 378, 382, 385, 401; C. O. Blagden, *List of Malay books*, in *JRAS* 1899, 125 no. 50; R. O. Winstedt, *A history of Malay literature*, in *JSBRAS* xvii/3, 1940, 104.

(P. Voorhoeve)

DĀWŪD KHĀN KARARĀNĪ, younger son of the governor of Bengal under Shīr Shāh, Sulaymān Kararānī, who later asserted his independence, was raised to the Bengal throne in 980/1572 by the Afghān nobles who had deposed his elder brother Bāyazīd. Intoxicated by a sense of power he defied the Mughal emperor Akbar and attacked his outpost at Ghāzīpur in 982/1574. Munʿim Khān [*q.v.*], sent to oppose him, occupied his capital at Ṫānḋā and compelled him to retreat into Uṙīsā; he counter-attacked at the important battle of Tukarōʾī [*q.v.*] (= Mughalmārī), but when Mughal reinforcements arrived he sued for peace and paid tribute to Akbar, being permitted to retain the province of Uṙīsā. In 983/1575 Munʿim Khān died and in the following confusion Dāwūd attacked and regained Bengal. Khān Djahān and Ṫoḋar Mall renewed the Mughal attack in 984/1576, when Dāwūd was captured and executed, and Bengal finally passed into Mughal hands.

Bibliography: Abu ʾl-Faḍl ʿAllāmī, *Akbar-nāma*, iii, 22, 70-3, 93 ff., 118 ff., 177-8; tr. Beveridge, iii, 30 ff., 97 ff., 130 ff., 169 ff., 248 ff.; idem, *Āʾīn-i Akbarī*, tr. Blochmann, 2nd. ed. 334, 350, 404, 407, 411. (J. Burton-Page)

DĀWŪD PASHA, Ḳara (? — 1032/1623), Ottoman Grand Vizier. The year of his birth is uncertain, but, in a "relazione" submitted to the Signoria in 1612, Simone Contarini, who had been Venetian Bailo at Istanbul, mentions a Dāwūd Pasha, whom he describes as a Croat in origin and at that time about 46 years old. According to the Ottoman sources, however, Ḳara Dāwūd Pasha was of Bosnian descent. He was trained in the Palace Schools, being appointed in due course to the office of *čuḳadār* (*čuhadar*). During the reign of Sulṭān Meḥemmed III (1003-1012/1595-1603) he became Ḳapidji Bashi and later, in the reign of Sulṭān Aḥmed I (1012-1026/1603-1617), was made Beglerbeg of Rūmeli in 1013/1604. Dāwūd Pasha served thereafter against the Djalālī [*q.v.*] rebels in Asia Minor and also in the Eriwān campaign against the Ṣafawīds of Persia in 1021/1612. He held the office of Ḳapudan Pasha [*q.v.*] for a short time during the first reign of Sulṭān Muṣṭafā I (1026-1027/1617-1618) and also accompanied Sulṭān ʿOthmān II (1027-1031/1618-1622) on the campaign of Choczim (Ḥotin) against the Poles in 1030/1621. Dāwūd Pasha was married to a sister german of Sulṭān Muṣṭafā. Māh-Peyker, the Wālide Sulṭān (*i.e.*, the mother of Muṣṭafā I) used her influence to secure the elevation of Dāwūd Pasha to the Grand Vizierate (9 Radjab 1031/20 May 1622), when her son Muṣṭafā became Sulṭān for the second time (1031-1032/1622-1623). Dāwūd Pasha at once carried out the execution of Sulṭān ʿOthmān II, who had just been deposed from the throne. On 3 Shaʿbān 1031/13 June 1622 Dāwūd Pasha was dismissed from the office of Grand Vizier. The conflict of factions at the Porte brought about in the end his own execution in Rabīʿ I 1032/January 1623. He was buried in the mosque of of Murād Pasha at Istanbul.

Bibliography: Pečewī, *Taʾrīkh*, ii, Istanbul A.H. 1283, 386 ff., *passim*; Ḥādjdjī Khalīfa, *Fedhleke*, ii, Istanbul A H. 1287, 19 ff., *passim*, 33-4, 46; Naʿīmā, *Taʾrīkh*, ii, Istanbul A.H. 1283, 224 ff., *passim*, 235 ff., *passim*, 248-52; *Ambassade en Turquie de Jean de Gontaut Biron, Baron de Salignac 1605-1610. Correspondance Diplomatique et Documents Inédits*, ed. Comte Théodore de Gontaut Biron, in *Archives Historiques de la Gascogne*, fasc. xix, Paris 1889, 9, 11, 186; R. Knolles, *The Generall Historie of the Turkes . . . . Together with the Lives and Conquests of the Othoman Kings and Emperours*, London 1639: *A Continuation of the Turkish History from .... 1620 untill .... 1628. Collected out of the Papers and Dispatches of Sir Thomas Rowe*, 1408, 1412, 1417-8; S. Purchas, *Purchas His Pilgrimes*, viii, Glasgow 1905, 343-59, *passim* ("The Death of Sultan Osman"); *The Negotiations of Sir Thomas Roe in his Embassy to the Ottoman Porte from the Year 1621 to 1628 inclusive*, ed. S. Richardson, London 1740, 42, 47, 51, 125-6; A. Galland, *La Mort du Sultan Osman, ou le Retablissement de Mustapha sur le Throsne, traduit d'un Manuscrit Turc ....*, Paris 1678, 143-5, 166, 169, 171-2, 194-5, 196, 199, 201-2; M. Steinschneider, *Die Geschichtsliteratur der Juden*, i, Frankfurt 1905, § 146; M. A. Danon, *Contributions à l'histoire des Sultans Osman II et Mouçtafà I*, in *JA*, onz. sér., xiv, Paris 1919, 69 ff. and 243 ff., *passim*; *Le Relazioni degli Stati Europei lette al Senato dagli Ambasciatori Veneziani nel secolo decimosettimo*, edd. N. Barozzi and G. Berchet, ser. V: *Turchia*, i, Venice 1866, 142 (*Relazione di Simon Contarini, 1612*) and 294 (*Relazione .... del Bailo Cristoforo Valier*, 1616); E. de Hurmuzaki, *Documente privitóre la Istoria Romănilor*, Supplement i/1, Bucharest 1886, 197 ff. and 200 ff.; Hammer-Purgstall, iv, 549, 551 ff., 558-9, 571 ff.; Zinkeisen, iii, 749, 750, 754, 760; N. Jorga, *Geschichte des osmanischen Reiches*, iii, Gotha 1910, 445 ff.; I. H. Uzunçarşılı, *Osmanlı Tarihi*, iii/2, Ankara 1954, 375-6; ʿO͟thmān-zāde Aḥmed Tāʾib, *Ḥadīḳat al-Wuzarāʾ*, Istanbul A.H. 1271, 67 ff.; Ḥusayn b. Ismāʿīl, *Ḥadīḳat al-D͟jawāmiʿ*, Istanbul A.H. 1281, i, 204; Sāmī, *Ḳāmūs al-Aʿlām*, iii, Istanbul A.H. 1308, 2110-1; *Sid͟jill-i ʿO͟thmānī*, ii, 325; *IA*, s.v. Davud Paşa. (V. J. Parry)

DĀWŪD PAS͟HA, Ḳod͟ja, Darwīs͟h, d. 904/1498, Ottoman Grand Vizier. Of Albanian origin, he came through the *dews͟hirme* to the Palace School. In 876/1472, as beylerbeyi of Anadolu, he fought under Prince Muṣṭafā, *wālī* of Konya, against the Aḳ-ḳoyunlu Yūsufča Mīrzā. In the battle against Uzun Ḥasan at Otluk-beli in 878/1473, he was in command of the vanguard. He served in the Bog͟hdan campaign of 881/1476 and, as beylerbeyi of Rumeli, in the operations in Albania and the siege of Is͟hkodra (883/1478). After the accession of Bāyezīd II he was made vizier and shortly afterwards, in 888/1483, succeeded Isḥāḳ Pas͟ha as Grand Vizier, remaining in this post for 15 years. During this period he went on only two campaigns, the operations against the Mamluks in 892/1487, when he re-occupied Adana and Tarsus and reduced the Wārsāḳs to obedience, and the Albanian campaign of 891/1492, when he took Tepedelen and defeated the Albanian forces (though according to one source he remained at Üsküb to guard against a possible Hungarian attack from the north). He was dismissed from the Grand Vizierate on 4 Rad͟jab 902/8 March 1497 and ordered to live at Dīmetoḳa (with a yearly pension of 300,000 *akčes*). The reason for his dismissal was that the flight of the Aḳ-ḳoyunlu Göde Aḥmed Bey, a grandson of Meḥemmed II, to Tabrīz was attributed to Dāwūd Pas͟ha's negligence. Two years later, in 4 Rabī ʿI 904/20 october 1498, he died and was buried in the *türbe* before the *miḥrāb* of his mosque in Istanbul.

He is described as a capable and upright statesman and a patron of learning. In foreign policy he supported Venice. He was one of the richest statesmen of his time: the *resm-i ḳismet* due to the *ḳāḍiʿasker* on his estate amounted to no less than 2,000,000 *aḳčes*. The mosque which he built in the quarter which bears his name exists today, together with an *ʿimāret*, a *čes͟hme*, a school and a *medrese*. There are also an *iskele* and a *ḳaṣr* named after him. The Dāwūd Pas͟ha Ṣaḥrāsī, on which the Dāwūd Pas͟ha Barracks now stands, was for centuries a famous camping-ground for the Ottoman army. His sons Muṣṭafā Pas͟ha and Meḥemmed Bey are mentioned in the sources.

Bibliography: *IA*, s.v. (by I. H. Uzunçarşılı); Hammer-Purgstall, *GOR*, ii, 309 ff. and index; Leunclavius, *Hist.*, 644 ff.; Kantemir, *Gesch. d. Osm. Reiches*, 428; *al-S͟haḳāʾiḳ al-Nuʿmānīya*, *Ḥadīḳat al-wuzarāʾ*, *Ḥadīḳat al-d͟jawāmiʿ* (s.vv.); for his *waḳfs*, T. Gökbilgin, *Edirne ve Paşa Livası*, Istanbul 1952, index. (M. Tayyib Gökbilgin)

DĀWŪD PAS͟HA (1181-1267/1767-1851), the last Mamlūk ruler of Turkish ʿIrāḳ, was acquired in Bag͟hdād as a Georgian slave-boy by Sulaymān Pas͟ha (the Great), marriage with whose daughter, together with his own good looks, charm, learning and ostentatious piety, assisted him in his upward career in the civil service under his patron, as confidential secretary, treasurer, *daftardār*, and finally *ḳahya*. By opportunism, violence and a skilful balancing of forces—Kurds, Mamlūks, the court, the mob, the tribes—Dāwūd, aged 50 years, obtained the Pas͟halīk for himself in 1233/1817, and assured it by the assassination of his predecessor (Saʿīd Pas͟ha), and by timely generosity. He ruled for fifteen years. He adopted a vigorous (at times a treacherous) tribal policy, preserved fair order, chastised the notoriously turbulent Yazīdīs and the mid-desert ʿAnaza, kept a watch on endless Kurdish princely schisms and threats, and contrived to stop a serious Persian invasion (1239/1823). Under orders from Istanbūl, he disbanded the Janissary forces in Bag͟hdād, raised and armed new-type regiments, and—fitfully, jealously and inconsistently—permitted a marked increase of European methods, traffic and trade. He constructed numerous public works, and maintained a luxurious court and entourage. His decline and fall (1247/1831) was inevitable in the changing atmosphere of the Turkish government; immediately, it was brought about by his persistent insubordination to the Istanbul authorities, whose emissary (and his own successor as *wālī*) was able to evict and replace him thanks to a devastating flood in Bag͟hdād and a terrible visitation of plague. Arrested and captive, Dāwūd was surprisingly well treated, re-promoted to important offices in both Europe and Asia, and, high in royal favour, became in 1261/1845 Guardian of the Holy Shrine at Madīna. He died in 1267/1851, after a career of extraordinary vicissitudes.

Bibliography: S. H. Longrigg, *Four Centuries of Modern ʿIraq*, Oxford 1925, 234-274; the Appendix on sources (328 ff.) particularizes the Arabic and Turkish sources (partly in MS.), and European travellers. C. Huart, *Histoire de Bagdad dans les Temps Modernes*, Paris 1901.

(S. H. Longrigg)

DĀWŪD PAS͟HA, first Ottoman *mutaṣarrif* (governor) of Mount Lebanon (1861-1868). He was an Armenian Catholic, born in Constantinople in March 1816. He spent his early years with a French family at Galata; later he married an English wife whom he abandoned before being appointed *mutaṣarrif*. He began his public career as an attaché to the Ottoman Embassy in Berlin, serving next as Ottoman consul general in Vienna. Transferred back to Constantinople, he held several posts in the

Ministry of Interior. In 1857 he was put in charge of the government publications; and in the following year he became superintendent of the Telegraph Office, where he introduced a number of improvements. In that same year, he assisted the Foreign Minister Fu'ād Pasha in applying for a foreign loan. Finally, in 1861, he was appointed to the governorship of Mount Lebanon by the Porte in conjunction with the European Powers. Sent to Beirut with the rank of Vizier, he established the seat of his government in Dayr al-Ḳamar and organized the new administration in a manner satisfactory to all parties concerned. Among other things, he organized the gendarmerie of Mount Lebanon, built roads and bridges, and established a number of schools, and his wise government soon restored peace, order, and good will in Lebanon. Appointed at first to govern the country for three years, the term of his administration was extended for five more years. During his second term, however, he met with a strong resistance from some of the traditional leaders in the Mountain, and was therefore advised to resign from the governorship in 1868, before the end of his term. He next served as Minister of Public Works, and was sent to Europe to negotiate a loan. But, having somehow incurred disfavour with the Porte, he preferred to remain in Europe. He died in Biarritz on 9 Nov. 1873—1292/1875 according to *Sidjill-i ʿOthmānī*.

Dāwūd Pasha was described by a contemporary as an able statesman and administrator, a good linguist, and a lover of learning. Among other things, he was a member of the Berlin Academy of Sciences.

Bibliography: Buṭrus al-Bustānī, *Kitāb dā'irat al-maʿārif*, vii Beirut 1883, 576-7; Sh. Sāmī Frashëri, *Ḳāmūs al-aʿlām*, iii, Istanbul 1308 A.H., 2111; *Sidjill-i ʿOthmānī*, iv, 874; Jouplain, *La Question du Liban*, Paris 1908, 484; G. Vapereau, *Dictionnaire universel des contemporains*, Paris 1880, 507. (K. S. Salibi)

DĀWŪDPŌTRĀS, a rival branch of the tribe to which also belonged the Kalhōrās, one time rulers of former Sind. They and the Kalhōrās both claimed descent from Abu 'l-Faḍl al-ʿAbbās b. ʿAbd al-Muṭṭalib. The rulers of the former princely state of Bahāwalpūr, now merged with West Pakistan, belong to the Dāwūdpōtrās, who unlike their collaterals, the Kalhōrās, take pride in calling themselves the ʿAbbāsīs. Their claim to nobility and high birth appears, however, based more on tradition, hallowed through a long period of rulership and authority, than on unimpeachable information derived from reliable sources.

The genealogical tables, contained in some of the local Persian histories, such as the *Mir'at-i dawlat-i ʿAbbāsī* and the *Djawāhir-i ʿAbbāsiyya*, are defective and on close examination appear to have been hastily composed at the behest of royalty. However, some references in the older and more authentic works like the *Ma'āthir al-Umarā'*, (i, 825) show that both the Dāwūdpōtrās and the Kalhōrās were commonly believed to be the descendants of al-ʿAbbās [*q.v.*].

The common ancestor of both the Kalhōrās and the Dāwūdpōtrās, of whom something is known to history, is believed to be one Muḥammad Čannēy Khān (variants: Čaynay Khān, Čīnā Khān, Čannī Khān, Djīhna *alias* Čīnah Khān), whose father Ḳā'im is said to have migrated to Sind from Iran *via* Kēč-Mukrān in c. 259/873, long before the advent of the Ghaznawids in the Indo-Pakistan sub-continent. But this date is both doubtful and improbable. Most of the works make no mention of Ḳā'im. They instead mention one Miyān Odhānā, who is said to have lived the life of a *shaykh* with numerous followers. In the fifth generation from him was one Thull Khān (Fatḥ Allāh Khān?) whose son, Bhallā Khān (Bahā' Allāh Khan?) was the father of Čannēy Khān. Čannēy Khān was succeeded to the tribal chieftainship by his sons Muḥammad Mahdī and Dāwūd Khān, the latter inheriting a copy of the Ḳur'ān, the *tasbīḥ* (rosary) and the prayer-carpet (*muṣallā*) belonging to his father; while the family-sword and his turban fell to the share of Muḥammad Mahdī whose descendants came to be known as the Kalhōrās after his son, Ibrāhīm *alias* Kalhōrē Khān.

As a result of family feuds, Dāwūd Khān I had to leave the place and shift for himself. He is stated to have founded a new settlement near the town of Wāndjī, now untraceable. He was followed by his son, Maḥmūd Khān and grandson Muḥammad Khān as the leaders of the tribe. During the chieftainship of Dāwūd Khān II, a son of Muḥammad Khān, the tribe had greatly multiplied and felt the need to enlarge its territory. The descendants and retainers of this Dāwūd Khān II came to be known as the Dāwūdpōtrās irrespective of the fact whether they were the issue of his body or had only spiritual or temporal attachment with him. This explains the fact why certain families of purely Sindhī origin, mainly engaged in the weaving profession and living in the Shikārpūr and Dādū districts of West Pakistan, still proudly call themselves Dāwūdpōtrās. Some foreign writers (for instance, R. F. Burton, *A History of Scinde*, London 1850, 410), not fully acquainted with the origins of the Dāwūdpōtrās, were led to believe that the Dāwūdpōtrās as a tribe were of indigenous origin and weavers by profession. In according recognition as equal members to all those who did not belong to the family or the clan of Dāwūd Khan II, the Dāwūdpōtrās simply revived the old Arab custom of admitting manumitted slaves (*mawālī*) into the family fold or the clan. The prevalence of this Arab custom among them also lends support to their claim to being of Arab stock and descent.

Dāwūd Khān II was followed by eight chiefs, of whom only Bahādur Khān II deserves mention. He is credited with having laid the foundations of the town of Shikārpūr in 1026/1617. The dates of birth and death of all the Dāwūdpōtrā chiefs who preceded Ṣādiḳ Muḥammad Khān I (1136/1723-1159/1746), the founder of the House of Bahāwalpūr [*q.v.*], are practically unknown, none of them being important enough for history to record his annals.

One of the Dāwūdpōtrā chiefs, Mubārak Khān I, assisted the Mughal prince Muʿizz al-Dīn, a grandson of Awrangzīb ʿĀlamgīr, and the then *sūbadār* of Multān [*q.v.*] and Lahore [*q.v.*], in crushing the uprising of the Mīrānīs, a powerful Balūč tribe of Dēra Ghāzī Khān, in 1114/1702. As a reward for this military assistance, the towns of Shikārpūr, Bakhtiyārpūr and Khānpūr were granted to him as a *djāgīr*. The town of Shikārpūr became thereafter the seat of his clan. Most of his time was spent in fighting fraternal battles against the rival Kalhōrā chief, Yār Muḥammad Khān *alias* Khudā-Yār Khān. A grim battle lasting over a week was fought in which both the sides lost heavily. Contemporary accounts show that the Dāwūdpōtrās suffered grievously and had to seek for a truce. It was purely a faction fight, a dynastic feud, which determined the future course of events. Coupled with subsequent encounters between the rival factions this battle culminated in the separation and demarcation of their respective spheres of influence and control.

The Dāwūdpōtrās, in the final phase, emerged successful, as they were able to conserve and consolidate their hard-won possessions, while their rivals, the Kalhōrās, were ousted by the Tālpūrs who, in their turn, gave way to the British when the latter occupied Sind in 1842, seven years before the annexation of the Pandjāb and the termination of the short-lived Sikh rule. Mubārāk Khān I abdicated in 1136/1723 in favour of his son Ṣādiḳ Muḥammad Khān ʿAbbāsī I and died three years later in 1139/1726. An ambitious ruler, he first annexed Uččh [*q.v.*] followed by a part of the Mughal *sūba* of Multān and the fort of Ḍērāwar, wrested from Rāwal Akhī Singh of Djaysalmēr, whose forefathers had held it for long. In 1152/1739 when Nādir Shāh Afshār invaded India, Ṣādiḳ Muḥammad Khān I waited on him at Dērā Ghāzī Khān, and was granted the title of *Nawwāb*. In addition to what he had added to his possessions by the sword he was granted the *parganahs* of Sīwastān and Lārkāna. In 1159/1746 Shikārpūr, his ancestral home, was attacked by the rival Kalhōrā chief, Khudāyār Khān. Ṣādiḳ Muḥammad Khān lost his life in the contest, and was succeeded by Muḥammad Bahāwal Khān I who, the very next year, founded some towns including that of Bahāwalpūr, which ultimately gave its name to the state. It was during the rule of Bahāwal Khān I that the state came to command respect and gained in political stature. The irrigation canals dug under his orders opened up a new era of prosperity for the otherwise arid regions of the state of Bahāwalpūr. Meanwhile the power of the Dāwūdpōtrās continued to increase. On the death of Bahāwal Khān I in 1163/1749 Muḥammad Mubārak Khān II was unanimously elected by the Dāwūdpōtrās to succeed him. In 1165/1751 Djahān Khān Pōpalzaʾi, the commander-in-chief of the Durrānī forces, first attacked Uččh and then marched on Bahāwalpūr at the instance of ʿAlī Muḥammad Khān Khākwānī, the leaseholder of Dēra Ghāzī Khān. A pitched battle was fought near Khānpūr which resulted in the rout of the enemy, and Bhāwalpūr gained in stature. In 1173/1759 Rāwal Rāy Singh of Djaysalmēr surrendered the border fort of Ḍerāwar which had been recaptured from the Amīr of Bahāwalpūr. Two years later Ghulām Shāh Kalhōrā, the ruler of Sind, who several times in the past had received help from the ruler of Bahāwalpūr, attacked the state timing his invasion with the onslaught of Aḥmad Shāh Abdālī [*q.v.*], banking on the confusion that was to prevail in the wake of the Afghān king's invasion. He had to be appeased by surrendering Ghulām Shāh's brother, ʿIṭr Khān, who had taken refuge in Bahāwalpūr, after an unsuccessful attempt against the former.

On his death in 1186/1772 he was succeeded by Muḥammad Djaʿfar Khān, his nephew, who on accession at the age of 12 years assumed the title of Bahāwal Khān II. In 1191/1777 Multān was lost to the Sikhs and was never recovered thereafter. In 1194/1780 Shāh ʿĀlam II, Emperor of Delhi, honoured him with a *khilʿat* and bestowed on him the titles of Rukn al-Dawla, Nuṣrat Djang, Ḥāfiẓ al-Mulk. In 1201/1785 Tīmūr Shāh Durrānī attacked the Nawwāb's principality, and captured and plundered the town of Bahāwalpūr which was subsequently set on fire and destroyed. The fortress of Ḍērāwar was also captured and garrisoned with Durrānī troops. Tīmūr Shāh even carried away his son, prince Mubārak Khan ʿAbbāsī, as a hostage and set him up as the ruler of the state virtually deposing Bahāwal Khān II. Tīmūr Shāh was so severe in his punishment that he also carried away to Kābul the cannon captured from Bahāwalpūr. Till 1203/1788 Bahāwal Khān II was engaged in mopping-up operations against the Durrānīs having earlier placed prince Mubārak Khān, on his return to Bahāwalpūr, under detention.

The threat of Durrānī invasion to his possessions over, he turned to aggression and began to annex the neighbouring areas. His territorial ambitions aroused the suspicions of Makhdūm Ḥāmid Gandj Bakhsh of Uččh, a descendant of Makhdūm-i Djahāniyān Djalāl al-Dīn Bukhārī [*q.v.*] who, in close collaboration with the neighbouring chiefs, revolted in 1214/1799 against the Nawwāb and defied attempts at his capture. He also incited the ruler of Bīkānēr to invade the state, set prince Mubārak Khān free, and proclaimed him the Nawwāb. After some sharp encounters with the rebels and their confederates, the state forces under prince ʿAbd Allāh Khān (afterwards known as Nawwāb Ṣādiḳ Muḥammad Khān II), succeeded in restoring peace. The disgruntled Makhdūm, who wielded considerable influence in the state, again rebelled in 1221/1806 at the instance of Shāh Shudjāʿ al-Mulk of Kābul. This attempt also failed and two years later the Nawwāb entered into a treaty of friendship with the British Government. Thereafter complete peace prevailed in the state and people from Lahore, Dihlī, Dēra Ghāzī Khān and Multān, etc., who felt insecure under the Sikh rule and the disturbed conditions in India, migrated to Bahāwalpūr.

On the death of Bahāwal Khān in 1805 he was succeeded by his son ʿAbd Allāh Khān, in supersession to his elder brother, prince Wāḥid Bakhsh, who was put to death. As already mentioned, ʿAbd Allāh Khān assumed the title of Ṣādiḳ Muḥammad Khān II, on his accession. The greater part of his reign of 15 years (he died in 1825) was spent in either repelling the attacks of the Amīrs of Sind, suppressing the rebellions of his own *umarāʾ* or defending his conquered territories. Among other notable events of his reign was the capture of Dēra Ghāzī Khān in 1234/1818 by Shāh Shudjāʿ with the military assistance provided by the Amīr himself. The very next year he was, however, dispossessed by Randjīt Singh, the ruler of Lahore, who made over Ḍēra Ghāzī Khān (see ḌĒRADJĀT) to the Amīr of Bahāwalpūr in consideration of an annual sum of 250,000 rupees. During the rule of his successor, Raḥīm Yār Khān entitled Muḥammad Bahāwal Khān III (1825-52), Dēra Ghāzī Khān along with Muẓaffargarh and Multān were irretrievably lost to Bahāwalpūr, having been conquered in 1235/1819 by the French military adventurer, General Ventura, for his Sikh master, Randjīt Singh. The Nawwāb wreaked his vengeance by providing a contingent 23,000 strong to the British for the capture of Multān, which fell in 1848 to Herbert Edwardes, the founder of Bannū [*q.v.*], and was annexed to the dominions of the East India Company.

On his death in 1852 he was succeeded by Saʿādat Yār Khān, entitled Ṣādiḳ Muḥammad Khān III. The latter's coronation ceremony was performed by the Makhdūm of Uččh, a happy result of the reconciliation reached between the ruling family and the head of the most powerful spiritual group in the state. His harsh treatment of his brothers caused the eldest, prince Ḥādjdjī Khān, to rise against him. Subsequently Ṣādiḳ Muḥammad

Khān was deposed and imprisoned in a grain silo in the fort of Dērāwar. A small allowance was later settled on him and he was deported to Lahore, where he lies buried. Ḥādjdjī Khān assumed the title of Fatḥ Khān, but soon alienated the support of the Dāwūdpōtrās, who continued to intrigue unsuccessfully against him. He died, after a rule of five years, in 1858. He was followed by Raḥīm Yār Khān entitled Muḥammad Bahāwal Khān IV (1858-66), whose otherwise uneventful reign was marred by internal disturbances and commotions culminating in his death through poisoning. He was succeeded by his minor son, Ṣādiḳ Muḥammad Khān IV. On attaining his majority in 1879 he was formally invested with the ruling powers by the Government of British India, the state having accepted British paramountcy in 1849 on the annexation of the Pandjāb. Close on his accession the Dāwūdpōtrās broke out into a rebellion which was, however, ruthlessly suppressed and its leader put to death.

During the minority of the ruler the state was administered by the Chief Political Officer and Agent to the Lieutenant-Governor of the Pandjāb for Bahawalpur Affairs. A very popular ruler, he was known as "Ṣubḥ-i Ṣādiḳ". The 'Shāhdjahān' of the House of Bahāwalpūr, he constructed a number of beautiful palaces, in the construction of which foreign and local artisans were employed. Of these, two, the Ṣādiḳ-Gaṛh Palace and the Nūr Maḥall Palace, deserve mention.

He was succeeded in 1899 by Mubārak Khān, entitled Muḥammad Bahāwal Khān V, a lad of 16 years and the first Bahāwalpūr prince to have received education at the Aitchison College, Lahore. He died in the prime of youth in 1907 at Aden while on his way back home from a pilgrimage to Mecca.

He was succeeded by his infant son, Ṣādiḳ Muḥammad Khān V (1907-56), then only three years old. During his minority, the affairs of the state were managed by a Council of Regency presided over by the late Mawlawī Sir Raḥīm Bakhsh, a native of Ṫhaskā Mīrāndjī (Gurāhm) near Ambālā. His efficient administration, anxiety for public weal combined with piety and philanthropy won him much admiration. In 1947 Bahāwalpūr acceded to Pākistān and rendered much useful service to the new state, especially in the rehabilitation of the uprooted refugees from India, who were then pouring in in large numbers. In 1956 the state of Bahāwalpūr ceased to exist as an independent unit when it was merged with West Pākistān, on the creation of the One Unit.

Bibliography: Dawlat Ray, *Mirʾāt-i Dawlat-i ʿAbbāsī*, Dihlī 1850 (materially different from the Brit. Mus. MS, Rieu iii 951 a); Muḥammad Aʿẓam Ḥāshimī, *Djawāhir-i ʿAbbāsiyya* (MS); Djān Muḥammad Khān Maʿrūfānī, *Taʾrīkh-i Bahāwal Khān* (Punjab University Library MS); Aʿẓam Ḥāshimī, *Iḳbāl-nāmah-i Saʿādat Āyāt* (MS); Anon., *Khulāṣa-i Tawārīkh-i ʿAbbāsiyya* (an abridgement of a work by Sayyid Nūr Allāh, not available to me); Shahamet Ali, *The History of Bahawalpur* (an abridged English translation of a Persian work by Pīr Ibrāhīm Khān Khʷēshgī Ḳaṣūrī, British Agent at Bahawālpūr 1840-56); *Gazetteer of the Bahawalpur State*, Lahore 1908; H. B. Edwardes, *A year on the Punjab frontier in 1848-9*, London 1851, ii, 314, 319, 344, 377; Ghulām Rasūl Mihr, *Taʾrīkh-i Sindh* (*ʿAhd-i Kalhōrā*), Karachi 1958, i, 42, 48-60, 100-19 and *passim*; Sayyid Murād Shāh, *Taʾrīkh-i Murād* (MS); Nazeer Ali Shah, *Sadiqnamah*, Lahore 1959; ʿAṭāʾ Muḥammad Shikārpūrī, *Tāzah Nawāʾ-i Maʿārik*, Karachi 1960, index; Hittō Rām, *Taʾrīkh Dēra Ghāzī Khān*, Lahore 1875; idem, *Taʾrīkh-i Balūčistān*; Ḥafīẓ al-Raḥmān, *Taʾrīkh-i Bahāwalpūr* (in Urdū); ʿAzīz al-Raḥmān, *Subḥ-i Ṣādiḳ*², Bahāwalpūr 1943; F. G. Goldsmid, *A Memoir on Shikarpur*, Bombay Government Records; see also the article BAHĀWALPŪR, and C. U. Aitchison, *A Collection of Treaties, Engagements and Sanads relating to India*, ix, Calcutta 1892.

(A. S. BAZMEE ANSARI)

ḌAYʿA, plu. *ḍiyāʿ*, estate. The word can mean generally a rural property of a certain size, but is understood in a more precise sense in fiscal contexts. It is known that at the time of the Conquests the local people were left in possession of their lands, subject to their paying the *kharādj*; it was later understood that the conversion of the landowner would not change the fiscal status of the land. In contradistinction to the *kharādj* lands there were the original properties of the Arabs, especially in Arabia, and the grants made in favour of notables or their dependents by the Caliphs from public property, the *ḳaṭāʾiʿ* (the plural of *ḳaṭīʿa*) [see *iḳṭāʿ*]: in practice, the primitive *ḳaṭāʾiʿ* were assimilated into the Arab properties. These were not subject to the native taxes, but the Muslim had to pay out of the revenues that he drew therefrom the *zakāt*, comparable in land matters to the tithe *ʿushr* [*q.v.*]. It was the group of tithe-lands which came to be called *ḍiyāʿ*, whatever the origin of the land, and which appertained in fiscal matters to a *Dīwān al-ḍiyāʿ* as distinct from the *Dīwān al-kharādj*. It inevitably came about that some great landowners might possess numerous *ḍiyāʿ*, but the term *ḍayʿa* means not the group but each estate, the extent of which is sometimes less and rarely more than the area of a village. It was not unknown for the owner of a *ḍayʿa* to be a notable living on the estate, but usually they were rural properties owned by townspeople. During the first centuries of Islam, *ḳaṭīʿa* and *ḍayʿa* described different aspects of the same thing; when, later on, it became customary to distribute to the soldiers, as *iḳṭāʿ*, the *kharādj* of certain districts, in time amounting to the quasi-possession of those districts, the term *ḍayʿa* became distinct from this new *iḳṭāʿ* and continued to describe only estates of the old sort, now mostly in the hands of "civilians".

It follows from this that the holder of the *ḍayʿa* was not usually its cultivator. He maintained on the land, appointing a bailiff (*wakīl*) for their management, some peasants, usually share-croppers [see MUZĀRAʿA]. Here it must be understood that the rents payable by the *muzāriʿ* being of the same order as the taxes payable by the possessor of *kharādj* land, the real difference of status between the two categories of land rests less in an inequality in peasant conditions at the bottom—otherwise it would be difficult to explain why there was no migration from one to the other—than in the social hierarchy which required the fiscal revenues of the *kharādj* to go directly and entirely to the State, whilst on the tithe-lands the peasant rents went for the greater part to the holder of the *ḍayʿa*, who passed on to the State only a small part (a fifth in the case of the half crop of a *muzāraʿa*). The social rôle of the formation of the *ḍiyāʿ* was to ensure the existence of an aristocracy. The real difference between the *kharādj* lands and the tithe-lands faded in this respect as the practice developed of granting to local chiefs the levying of taxes on their subjects, on condition that they made an outright payment to the State (*muḳāṭaʿa*), or to soldiers the right to the taxes of certain districts, on condition that they paid the tithe (usually a fifth of the *kharādj*) to the State (later, without any further payment). Certainly in law the holder of these revenues was not the landowner but in fact the difference gradually diminished, and many *ḍiyāʿ* were in fact enlarged by the surrounding lands through the workings of the practice of recommendation, *ildjāʾ* [*q.v.*]. The theory moreover, recognizing of necessity past encroachments, permitted the Caliph in the public interest to convert *kharādj* lands into tithe-lands.

The biggest owner of *ḍiyāʿ* during the ʿAbbāsid epoch was the Caliph himself, whose *ḍiyāʿ* were called *khāṣṣa*; then came the princes of the Caliph's family, the amīrs of the army, the heads of the administration and afterwards the merchants and other well-to-do citizens who had put a part of their savings in landed property; in general, very few of the notables lived in the country itself. On the other hand the estates directly maintained by the State (*sulṭāniyya, dīwāniyya*) were likewise divided into *ḍiyāʿ*; according to the state of the budget they could be disposed of, recovered, rounded off, or new estates created from land formerly uncultivated; no doubt this is the explanation of the formula *ḍiyāʿ mustaḥdatha* which is found in the ʿAbbāsid budgets; occasionally there is added the group of estates sequestrated from a very great official, such as the *furātiyya* of the *wazīr* Ibn al-Furāt, which were usually left to the management of an *ad hoc dīwān*, and even restored to its former owner in case of a turn of fortune. The allocation of the *ḍiyāʿ* obviously did not correspond to the original distribution, since in most cases they could be freely transmitted by inheritance, or sold (which seems to have been common), or transformed into *waḳf*, etc.; the only ones not to enjoy this were those which were a result of an *iḳṭāʿ-ṭuʿma*, given with a life-title, or those attached to the discharge of a temporary office.

Bibliography: See BAYT AL-MĀL, KHAṢṢ, IḲṬĀʿ, ʿUSHR. It is impossible to give here all the sources in which *ḍiyāʿ* occur, judicial, chronological, geographical etc. Many references will be found in Fr. Løkkegaard, *Islamic Taxation*, by consulting the word *ḍayʿa* in the index. See also A. von Kremer, *Das Einnahmebudget des Abbasiden Reiches v. Jahre* 306 *H.*, in *Denkschr. K. Akad. d. Wiss. Wien*, xxxvi, 1888, especially 292 ff., and ʿAbd al-ʿAziz Dūrī, *Taʾrīkh al-ʿIrāḳ al-iḳtiṣādī*, Baghdād 1948, chap. ii. (CL. CAHEN)

DAYBUL (Dēbal or Dēwal), the ancient port-town of Sind, which contained a *dēwal* (temple) of *al-budd* (Balādhurī, *Futūḥ*, Cairo ed., 442), situated on the mouth of a creek (*al-khawr*) and to the west of the Mihrān, *i.e.*, the Indus, was the first place to fall to Muḥammad b. al-Ḳāsim al-Thaḳafī [*q.v.*], who led a punitive expedition against Rādjā Dāhir, the ruler of Sind, in 92/711-12, who was alleged to have connived at an act of piracy committed at Daybul on some boats carrying Muslim men and women on their way to Mecca and ʿIrāḳ from Ceylon. A flourishing town, a centre of sea-borne commerce and trade, it was inhabited largely by traders and artisans belonging mostly to the Mēd tribe. Two earlier attempts by the Arabs under ʿUbayd Allāh b. Nabhān and Budayl b. Ṭahfa al-Badjalī to conquer Daybul by sea having ended in failure, Muḥammad b. al-Ḳāsim decided to march against it by the land-route. His plans met with success, the *mandjanīḳ*, used by the Arabs for the first time in India, proving an effective weapon of war. The tower of Daybul, surmounted by a dome 40 yds. high from which flew a huge red flag, overshadowing the entire town, housed a Buddhist *stūpa* (*manārat al-budd*) or the *dēwal*, after which, it appears, the town itself came to be known as Dēwal (Dēbal, pronounced by the Arabs as Daybul). A huge stone hurled by the *mandjanīḳ* wrought havoc with the tower and brought it down with a thundering crash. The post and the gigantic flag, considered by the local population as a symbol of impregnability, fell to the ground. After the fall of the town Muḥammad b. al-Ḳāsim offered liberal terms to the vanquished non-Muslims and assured them of full protection as *dhimmīs*. He also built a mosque, the first to be constructed on the soil of Sind, and settled 4,000 Arab families in a new quarter, built by him. The ruined *stūpa* remained in a state of neglect and disrepair for a long time until it was partially restored and converted into a prison-house by ʿAnbasa b. Isḥāḳ al-Ḍabbī, governor of Daybul under al-Wāthiḳ Bi'llāh [*q.v.*], about 232/846.

According to the Arabic chronicles (Ṭabarī, *sub anno*, Ibn al-Djawzī, *Muntaẓam* v/2, 143) a terrible earthquake destroyed a large part of the town in 280/893, at the same time killing many thousands of the inhabitants. The town, however, survived the catastrophe and seems to have been rebuilt as it was long in existence thereafter having been visited, among others, in as late as c. 637/1239 by Raḍī al-Dīn Ḥasan b. Muḥammad al-Ṣaghānī [*q.v.*], who strangely enough refers to the old practice of the wealthy classes of Daybul of indulging in acts of piracy and buccaneering. In 618/1221 Djalāl al-Dīn Khʷārizm-shāh after his defeat at the hands of the Tātars came to Sind, attacked and captured Daybul and built a Djāmiʿ Masdjid there on the site of an idol-temple. This means that even in the 7th/13th century idolatry was prevalent in Daybul and that there was a considerable number of non-Muslims residing there.

Various attempts have been made to identify and locate the ruined city of Daybul but they have met with little success. The description of the town, as given by Arab writers and travellers, beyond supplying useful information on the past glory of the town, has been of little use otherwise. The Pakistan Archaeological Department undertook large-scale excavations for the first time in 1958 at the site of Bhambōr, another ruined city, presumed by some scholars to be the original town of Daybul. But the uncovered topography of the Bhambōr mound and the archaeological finds so far (1960) discovered there have failed to provide any conclusive evidence that the ruins of Bhambōr are those of Daybul. Iṣṭakhrī makes separate mention of the town of Daybul and the idol temple of Bahamburā (Bhambōr).

During the early part of Muslim occupation it was a great centre of culture and learning and al-Samʿānī (*Kitāb al-Ansāb*, fol. 236 b) and Yāḳūt mention a large number of traditionists who flourished here.

The destruction of Daybul, its probable causes and the subsequent total disappearance of the town, despite its large size, a big population and its having been in existence till a very late date, are problems which have so far defied all attempts at a satisfactory solution.

Bibliography: Sulaymān al-Mahrī, *Ḳalādat al-shamūs wa istikhrādj ḳawāʾid al-usūs*, (not available to me); Ibn Khurradādhbih, *al-Masālik wa 'l-Mamālik*, Leiden 1306, 62 ff.; al-Masʿūdī, *Murūdj* (Cairo ed.), i, 378;al-Iṣṭakhrī, 175 ff.; Ibn Ḥawḳal, 317, 328; Yāḳūt, ii, 638; al-Nuwayri, *Nihāyat al-ʿArab*, (not available to me);

al-Ḳalḳas͟handī, *Ṣubḥ al-Aʿs͟hā*ʾ, v : 64; *Ḥudūd al-ʿĀlam*, 372; al-Idrīsī, *Nuzhat al-Mushtaḳ* (extracts), ʿAlīgaṛh 1954, 28; Abdul Hamid Khan, *Towns of Pakistan*, Karachi n.d., 59-69; *Journal of the Sind Historical Society*, May 1934, 3 ff.; J. McMurdo in *JASB*, 1834; Sulayman Nadwī in *JPakHS*, i, 1953, 8-14; N. B. Baloch, *The most probable location of Daibul, the first Arab settlement in Sind*, in *Dawn*, Karachi, February (4, 18), 1951; D̲j̲uwaynī, ii, 94, 142-8; D̲j̲uwaynī-Boyle, ii, 411 ff.; Sidi Ali Reis, *Travels and Adventures*, London 1899, 38; *Čačnāma* (ed. U. M. Daudpota), Dihlī 1358/1936, 89-91, 100-10; al-Bīrūnī, *Ḳānūn-Masʿūdi*, Ḥaydarābād 1955, ii, 552; *Marāṣid al-ʿIṭṭilāʿ*, Tehrān 1310/184; al-Balād̲h̲urī, *Futūḥ* 432, 435-8, 443; Le Strange 331; H. Cousens, *The Antiquities of Sind*, Calcutta 1925, 124 ff.; Elliot and Dowson, *The history of India as told by its own historians*, London 1867, index; H. G. Raverty, *The Mihran of Sind*, Calcutta 1892 (special issue of *JASB*); M. R. Haig, *The Indus Delta Country*, London 1894, 42 ff.; J. Abbot, *Sind*, Oxford 1924, 43-55; al-Bīrūnī, *Kitāb mā li 'l-Hind* (transl. E. Sachau, London 1914, 205, 208, 260, 316; Yaʿḳūbī, ii, 330-1, 345-6, 448; Ṭabarī, i. 868; Ibn al-At̲h̲īr, *Taʾrīk̲h̲* (Cairo ed.), iv, 257-8; Minhād̲j̲-i Sirād̲j̲, *Ṭabaḳāt-i Nāṣirī* (transl. Raverty, i, 294, 295 *n*, 452 *n2*; D̲j̲awālīḳī, *Muʿarrab*, 67; Muḥammad Ṭāhir Nasyānī, *Taʾrīk̲h̲-i Ṭāhirī* (MS), Muḳaddasī, 481-4; *TA*, under the root *D'B'L*; N. B. Baloch, *The most probable site of Debal*...., in *IC*, xxvi/3, 1952, 35-49.

(A. S. Bazmee Ansari)

DAYDABĀN, from Persian *dīdebān*, a term applied at different times to certain categories of sentinels, watchmen, inspectors, etc. It already appears as the name of a profession in the *Rasāʾil Ik̲h̲wān al-Ṣafā* (8th *risāla* of 1st series, ed. Cairo, i, 210; cf. *IC*, 1943, 147), together with the *Nāṭūr*. In classical Ottoman usage the term, pronounced *Dīdebān*, was applied to the Customs-house guards, whose chief was the *Dīdebān bas̲h̲ī*. It was also given to the watchmen on the fire-towers in Istanbul, as well as to naval and military look-outs.

Bibliography: Dozy, *Supplément*, i, 481; I. H. Uzunçarşılı, *Osmanlı Devleti teşkilâtından Kapıkulu Ocakları*, i, Ankara 1943, 394; M. Z. Pakalın, i, 450. (Ed.)

ḌAYF. From the basic meaning "to incline towards, to set (of the sun), swerve, glance off (of an arrow)", the verbal root comes to mean "to turn aside (from one's road)" and "to halt, on a visit to someone", whence for the noun the sense of "guest"; the meaning "host"—recalling the ambivalence of the French *hôte*—also occurs, but very much later, as indicated by Dozy, *Suppl.* ('maître de maison'). The social implications of the right to protection were earlier associated with the word *d̲j̲ār* [*q.v.*], the corresponding Hebrew word *gēr* (but not exactly parallel; see d̲j̲iwār) attesting the same Semitic institution. It is curious that the root of this word shows the some semantic derivation from "deviate" to "descend, stay with someone". For a short bibliography, see dak̲h̲īl. (J. Lecerf)

DAYĪ, Turkish word meaning "maternal uncle", which seems to have been used to designate official functions only in the Regencies of Algiers and Tunis. It probably began as a sort of honorific title (comparable to the word *alp*, used by the ancient Turks), and must have been difficult to acquire, as its bearer had to have demonstrated his prowess on land and sea in the Mediterranean (Pakalın, i, 407-8). This usage would conflict with the legend in which the father of the Barbarossas is supposed to have told his sons to obey K̲h̲ayr al-Din [*q.v.*] for "he will be your day" (Venture de Paradis, *Alger au XVIIIe siècle*, in *RA*, 1896, 257).

Another use of the honorific title was to designate a lower rank in the Janissary militia; towards the end of the 10th/16th century in Tunis, the name was born by the heads of the 40 sections of the militia. In 1591 these *dayīs* elected one of their number to the command of the army; this supreme *dayī* held the whole of the power in the Regency of Tunis, at least from 1594, allowing the *beylerbeyi-pas̲h̲a* to remain in office but with only nominal power (Pierre Dan, *Histoire de la Barbarie et de ses Corsaires*, Paris 1637, 144-5). Ḥamūda b. Murād, when he came into power in 1640 allowed the title of *dayī* to continue, but the person who bore it was no longer the head of the Regency, even if he remained one of its highest dignitaries.

After 1705, the word *dayī* is no longer to be found among the titles conferred by the Ḥusaynid sovereigns, but still appears in the Tunisian hierarchy, in the ninth rank, according to Muhammad Bayrām al-K̲h̲āmis al-Tūnusī (*Safwat al-Iʿtibār*, Cairo 1302/1885, ii, 2-3); it is found in several diplomatic documents of the eighteenth century, particularly in the treaties drawn up between the Regency of Tunis and France on 16th December, 1710, 9th November, 1742, and 4 Ventôse, Year X. The word at that time referred to a high judicial officer. It seems to have continued up to the middle of the 19th century.

In Algiers, after 1671, when the Corsair Captains took over the power of the Ag̲h̲as (see art. algeria (ii) (2), the title of *dayī* was borne by the head of the Regency. This was not yet the case at the beginning of the seventeenth century, when Pierre Dan was in Algiers.

Elected at first by the company (*ṭāʾifa*) of corsair masters, the *dayī* was elected by the officers of the army after 1689. Thirty *dayīs* succeeded each other in power between 1671 and 1830. In theory their power was limited by the control of the *dīwān* of the militia; in fact if the *dayī* had a strong personality, he enjoyed an absolute power.

The *dayī* resided in Algiers, first in the palace of the D̲j̲anīna, on the site where the archbishop's palace now stands, then after 1816, in the fortress called the Ḳaṣba, which dominates the Muslim town. The private life of the ruling *dayī* was strictly regulated: he lived apart from his family, except on Thursday afternoons and the night of Thursday/Friday, which he could spend in his private house. No woman could enter his palace, except for a public audience. He was entitled only to the high pay of a Janissary and to allocations of provisions, but he received numerous presents as well, so that several *dayīs* amassed considerable fortunes. Fourteen of them died a violent death.

Bibliography: No books or articles are specially concerned with the function of *dayī*; some scattered information can be found in sources or studies relating to the Turkish regencies of Algiers and Tunis. (R. Le Tourneau)

DAYLAM, geographically speaking, the highlands of Gīlān [*q.v.*]. In the south, the lowlands of Gīlān proper are bounded by the Alburz range; the latter forms here a crescent, the eastern horn of which comes close to the Caspian coast (between Lāhīd̲j̲ān and Čālūs). In the centre of the crescent there is a gap through which the Safīd-rūd, formed on the central Iranian plateau, breaks through towards the Caspian Sea. Before entering the gorge at Mandjīl the river, flowing here from west to east, receives a considerable tributary, the Shāh-rūd, which, rising in the district of Ṭālaḳān and flowing east to west, skirts the southern face of the Alburz wall. On its southern side the basin of the Shāh-rūd is separated by a line of hills from the plain of Ḳazwīn [*q.v.*], while on its right side it is fed by a number of streams flowing down the southern slopes of the Alburz. The principal of these tributaries is that watering the valley of Alamūt [*q.v.*]. The valleys of the Shāh-rūd and its tributaries seems to be the cradle of the Daylamite tribe. Though belonging to the basin of the great river of Gīlān (the Safīd-rūd), 'Daylam proper' (*al-Daylam al-maḥḍ*) is in fact separated from it by the Alburz wall. The Daylamites also occupied the northern slopes of the mountain and its ramifications stretching towards the sea (see *Ḥudūd al-ʿĀlam*), and Daylam formed here a wedge between Gīlān and Ṭabaristān [*qq.v.*].

While Gīlān is marshy and unhealthy but highly fertile, the highlands of Daylam, much less favoured by nature, were inhabited by a robust and enterprising race of men ready to emigrate or serve abroad. The geographical term 'Daylam' followed the destinies of the Daylamite expansion in the 4th/10th century, and came to comprise many other neighbouring lands (see below).

The ancient period. The remote origins of the Daylamites are uncertain. They probably belonged to a pre-Iranian stock. The name of the peak of Dulfak (or Dalfak), which rises on the right bank of the Safīd-rūd gorge to the north-east of Mandjīl, has been compared to the name of the ancient tribe of Δρίβυκες. The name of the Daylamites is known to many classical writers. In the 2nd century B. C. Polybius, v, 44, mentions the northern neighbours of Media: *Δελυμαῖοι, *Ἀναρίακαι, ('non-Aryans'), Καδούσιοι, Ματιάνοι. In the 2nd century A.D., Ptolemy, vi, 2, places *Δελυμαΐς to the north of Choromithrene (Khʷār-u Waramīn, to the south-east of Rayy), and to the west of the Tapuri (Ṭabaristān). On the Iranian side the information begins to emerge only in Sāsānian times. Before the decisive victory of Ardashīr the Sāsānian over Ardavān the Arsacid the latter is said to have mobilized "the troops of Rayy, Damāwand, Daylamān, and Patishkhʷārgar" (*Kārnāmak-i Artakhshīr*, tr. Nöldeke, 47). This would suggest Arsacid influence established among the population of the southern face of the Alburz range. At first the Sāsānians treated the Daylamites with caution (see Marquart, *Ērānšahr*, 126) but gradually the latter became conspicuous both in the army and at the court. Kāwādh sent an expedition against Iberia (Georgia) under the command of a "Persian" whose name Boēs (**Bōya*) and title Οὐαρίζης (**wahriz*) point, however, to his Daylamite connexions (see Procopius, *De bello persico*, i, 14). Under Khusraw Anūshīrwān a detachment of Daylamites is mentioned (ca. 552 A.D.) at the siege of Archeopolis (now Tsikhe-Godji) in Lazica where they were used as expert cragsmen, while the Turkic Sabirs were leading the frontal attack (see Procopius, *De bello gothico*, iv, 14 ed. Dindorff, 529-30). A few years later the Daylamites carried out an unsuccessful night attack on another corps of Sabirs employed by the Byzantines (see Agathias, iii, 17) According to Procopius, the "Dolomites" lived in inaccessible mountains; they were never subjects of the kings of Persia, and served them only as mercenaries. They fought on foot, each man being armed with a sword and a shield, and carrying three javelins (*acontia*) in his hands, which corresponds to the later Islamic descriptions.

Khusraw I's famous expedition to the Yemen (ca. 570 A.D.) consisted of 800 prisoners from Daylam and neighbouring places, and was led by an old man, also released from prison, bearing the title of *wahriz* [*q.v*]. When under Kāwādh and Khusraw the passes of the Caucasus were fortified and military colonies settled near them, the names of the latter reflected their origin from Daylam and its neighbourhood (see below, Toponymy). The conspiracy against Khusraw's successor Hurmizd IV, which resulted in his overthrow in 590 A.D., was led by Zoanab, the chief of the "Dilimitic" people (Theophylactus Simocatta, iv, 3, 1).

Daylam and the Arabs. During the Arab invasion the Daylamites took up an indecisive position when the people of Ḳazwīn invoked their help, but, supported by the people of Rayy, they opposed Nuʿmān b. Muḳarrin sent by the caliph ʿUmar. The Daylamites, led by their king (chief?) Mūtā (or Mūrthā), were defeated on the river Wādj in Dastabay (*Dasht-pay, *i.e.*, the "edge of the plain" stretching between Rayy and Hamadān) (Ṭabarī, i, 265 (*sub* 22/642)). Balādhurī, 317-25, and other historians mention seventeen Muslim expeditions into Daylam, from the time of ʿUmar I to that of al-Maʾmūn, which were reflected in Arabic poems (see Kasrawī, 4-20). The poet Aʿshā Hamdān (d. 83/702) was kept a prisoner by the Daylamites, though the place-names he quotes (Ḳ.līsm, Ḳayūl, Ḥāmin, Lahzamīn) seem to refer to the region of Damāwand (Wīma?). Nevertheless Daylam preserved its independence. The Muslim strongholds against them were in the south: Ḳazwīn; and in the north-east, on the frontier of Ṭabaristān: the fortifications on the rivers Kalār and Čālūs.

Language and religion. The name of the king Mūtā (?) sounds unusual, but when in the 9th and 10th centuries A.D. Daylamite chiefs appear on the stage in large numbers, their names are clearly pagan Iranian, not of the south-western "Persian" type, but of the north-western variety: thus Gōrāngēdj (not Kūrānkīdj, as formerly deciphered) corresponds to Persian *gōr-angēz* "chaser of wild asses", Shēr-zil to *shēr-dil* "lion's heart", etc. Iṣṭakhrī, 205, distinguishes between Persian and Daylamī and adds that in the highlands of Daylam there was a tribe that spoke a language different from that of Daylam and Gīlān.

There may have been some Zoroastrians and Christians in Daylam, but practically nothing is known about the pagan creed of the Daylamites. According to Bīrūnī, (*al-Āthār*, 224) they followed the law established by the mythical Afrīdūn who ordered men to be masters in their family and called them *kadhkhudhā*. Rather enigmatically Bīrūnī adds that this institution was abrogated by the ʿAlid *al-Nāṣir al-Uṭrūsh (see below) and thus they reverted to the condition in which people were living in the time of the tyrant Ḍaḥḥāk Bīwarāsp, when "devils and demons" (*al-shayāṭīn wa 'l-marada*) dwelt in their houses and they were powerless against them.

Apart from the *kadhkhudhā*s exercising the rights of *pater familias*, the Daylamites had their local rulers of whose existence we can judge by such titles as *Wardān-shāh*, *wahriz* (cf. Hübschmann, *Armen. Gramm.*, 78: *vahrič-i vahričay* "vahriz of Vahriz"), and even kings (see above, Mūtā). The rôle of the latter becomes clearer only in the 9th and 10th centuries A.D. in connexion with their collaboration with the ʿAlids.

The ʿAlids. At an early date the mountain fastnesses of Daylam served as places of refuge for the ʿAlids who had been obliged to flee from the ʿAbbāsids. The earliest known refugee was Yaḥyā b. ʿAbd Allāh, whose two brothers had been executed and who himself joined a rebel brother of Hārūn al-Ras͟hīd. He came to Daylam in 175/791, but soon surrendered to the Barmakid Faḍl b. Yaḥyā. It appears that in the meantime the caliph used pressure on the king of Daylam both by threats and by offers of money (cf. Ṭabarī, *anno* 176; Yaʿḳūbī, ii, 462).

The D̲j̲ustānids. When in 189/805 Hārūn arrived in Rayy he summoned the rulers of the Caspian region and let the lord of Daylam, Marzubān b. D̲j̲ustān, go with a gift of money and a robe of honour; no payment of tribute is mentioned in this case, while such an obligation was imposed on the other kings. Although this is the first time that we hear of the family of D̲j̲ustān, it is likely that the leniency of Hārūn had a connexion with the events of 175/791 when the same king (or his father?) must have been the ruler. Provisionally we can take Marzubān as the first in the list of the ruling *Banū D̲j̲ustān*.

The next king known to us is Wahsūdān b. D̲j̲ustān; the interval between Marzubān (who is mentioned in 189/805) and Wahsūdān (who was still living in 259/872, cf. Ṭabarī, iii, 188) is too great to consider them as brothers. The consensus (Justi, Vasmer, Kasrawī, Ḳazwīnī) is now to insert between them D̲j̲ustān I (No. 2), putative son of No. 1, Marzubān, and father of No. 3, Wahsūdān. In fact under 201/816 Ṭabarī reports that ʿAbd Allāh b. K̲h̲urdad̲h̲bih in the course of his victorious campaign in Daylam captured a king called Abū Laylī. Laylī (or Līlī) is known in Daylam as a man's name (cf. the adventurer Laylī b. Nuʿmān), and the question is whether he is identical with D̲j̲ustān (no. 2) or whether he was a usurper or a local ruler (of Lāhīd̲j̲ān?).

The situation in Daylam becomes clearer with the advent on the frontier of Daylam of the line of Ḥasanid sayyids, clever politicians and able warriors who succeeded in involving the Daylamites in their struggles and schemes, although no obligation of professing Islam had yet been imposed on them.

Sayyid Ḥasan b. Zayd *al-dāʿī al-kabīr* (no. I) stood at the head of a rising in Čālūs and Kalār in 250/864 and protected the inhabitants against the Ṭāhirid governor who wished to appropriate the common lands which served for collecting fuel and as grazing grounds (Ṭabarī, iii, 1524). According to Iṣṭak̲h̲rī, 205, before the time of Ḥasan b. Zayd, Daylam had been considered as the 'territory of unbelief' (*Dār al-kufr*) from which slaves had been taken, but the ʿAlids had intervened on behalf of the Daylamites. Wahsūdān b. D̲j̲ustān (no. 3) swore allegiance to Ḥasan b. Zayd, but soon after broke with him and died.

The *Taʾrīk̲h̲-i D̲j̲īl wa Daylam* (quoted by D̲j̲uwaynī, iii, 271) reports that in 246/860 a D̲j̲ustānid began the construction of a building (*ʿimāra*) on Mt. Alamūt, in which the kings of Daylam took pride. It is more likely that this enterprise marked not the end of the long reign of Wahsūdān but the beginning of that of his energetic son D̲j̲ustān II (no. 4). The latter invited the *dāʿī* to send his representatives to Daylam, and under the auspices of the ʿAlids took Rayy from the Ṭāhirids and occupied Ḳazwīn and Zand̲j̲ān. In 253/867 the caliph al-Muʿtazz sent an army under Mūsā b. Bug̲h̲ā, who wiped out the successes of D̲j̲ustān. In 259/872 the latter made a second, though unsuccessful, attempt to occupy Rayy, and continued to assist the *dāʿī* in his struggle against the Ṣaffārids. In 270/883 Ḥasan b. Zayd died and was succeeded by his brother Muḥammad b. Zayd, called *al-dāʿī al-ṣag̲h̲īr*, to whom also D̲j̲ustān swore allegiance (no. II).

The worst experience befell Daylam ca. 276/889 when the K̲h̲urāsānian soldier of fortune Rāfiʿ b. Hart̲h̲ama, acting on behalf of the Sāmānids, ousted Muḥammad b. Zayd from D̲j̲urd̲j̲ān. The *dāʿī* sought refuge in Daylam. The troops of Rāfiʿ occupied Čālūs, but the sayyid, assisted by D̲j̲ustān, surrounded them. Then Rāfiʿ himself moved forward. Muḥammad b. Zayd retreated to Gīlān, while on the heels of D̲j̲ustān Rāfiʿ marched from Čālūs to Talaḳān, and for three months (summer of 278/891) this region was plundered by the invaders. D̲j̲ustān gave a promise not to assist the sayyid, and Rāfiʿ went on to occupy Ḳazwīn and Rayy (see Ibn al-At̲h̲īr, vii, 303, and Ibn Isfandiyār, ed. Eghbal, 252-4). In 279/892 Rāfiʿ, seeing himself threatened from many sides, suddenly swore allegiance to the *dāʿī* and returned D̲j̲urd̲j̲ān to him, on the understanding that he would send him 4000 Daylamite stalwarts. By threats and promises the Ṣaffārid ʿAmr b. Layt̲h̲ prevented the *dāʿī* from helping Rāfiʿ and the latter had to flee to K̲h̲ʷārizm where he was killed in 283/November 896. Four years later (287/October 900) Muḥammad b. Zayd fell in a battle against a Sāmānid commander.

After a short interval the ʿAlid cause was taken up by the Ḥusaynid Ḥasan b. ʿAlī (Nāṣir al-Dīn, al-T̲h̲āʾir, al-Uṭrūs̲h̲ "the deaf" (no. III), who despite the shortness of his reign (301-4/904-7) is regarded as the greatest of the ʿAlid rulers. According to Ṭabarī (iii, 2296) the world had never known such justice as that of al-Uṭrūs̲h̲. He had lived for thirteen years among the Daylamites, and succeeded in converting to the Zaydī creed a considerable number of people "between the farther (eastern) side of the Safīd-rūd and Āmul". To confirm this achievement al-Uṭrūs̲h̲ had the fortifications of Čālūs razed to the ground. He was recognized by D̲j̲ustān, and although their first campaign against the Sāmānids was a failure, the next year, after a pitched battle of forty days, the Sāmānids were driven out of the Caspian provinces.

The enigmatic phrase of Bīrūnī, referred to above, concerning Nāṣir's action in disrupting the ancient authority of the *kad̲h̲k̲h̲ud̲h̲ā* may hint at the influence of Islamic institutions which had established control over isolated households. Such a trend of events must have been resented by the D̲j̲ustānids, and some historians (Awliyāʾ Āmulī, *Taʾrīk̲h̲-i Rūyān* (750/1349), ed. Tehran, 77; Ibn Wāṣil, *al-Taʾrīk̲h̲ al-Ṣāliḥī* in Dorn, *Muhamm. Quellen z. Gesch. d. Kasp. Meeres*, iv, 474) mention a period of struggles between D̲j̲ustān and Nāṣir, though apparently before the latter's advent in 301/913. He died on 5 S̲h̲aʿbān 304/31 January 917, after having appointed as his successor his son-in-law, the Ḥasanid Ḥasan b. al-Ḳāsim (no. IV).

At about the same time, after a reign of forty years, D̲j̲ustān was assassinated. The perpetrator of this crime was his brother ʿAlī b. Wahsūdān (no. 5), whom in 300/912 the ʿAbbāsids had already appointed their financial agent (*istaʿmala*) in Iṣfahān. He was dismissed in 304, but in 307/919 the ʿAbbāsid commander Muʾnis, who had just taken prisoner Yūsuf b. Abi 'l-Sād̲j̲, reappointed ʿAlī as the governor of Rayy, Ḳazwīn, and Zand̲j̲ān. In the same year he was killed in Ḳazwīn by Muḥammad b. Musāfir (Kangarī, or Sallārī, of the second Daylamite dynasty of Tārom), who being married to the clever Kharāsūya, daughter of Djustān b. Wahsūdān (no. 4) wished to avenge his father-in-law (not his "nephew", as in Ibn al-Athīr, viii, 76). With his political attitude, ʿAlī b. Wahsūdān could hardly have been recognized in the whole of Daylam. However, we learn that when the Ḥasanid Ḥasan b. al-Ḳāsim (the *dāʿī* no. IV) was captured in Ṭabaristān and delivered to ʿAlī to be sent to Baghdād, ʿAlī had him imprisoned in his "ancestral fortress" of Alamūt (see Ibn Isfandiyār, ed. Eghbal, 281). Immediately after ʿAlī's death, his other brother Khusraw Fīrūzān, who apparently had acted as ʿAlī's *locum tenens*, released the sayyid. Khusraw Fīrūzān (no. 6) marched against Ibn Musāfir but was killed by him. Khusraw's son Mahdī (no. 7) also took up arms against the Kangarid, but was defeated and took refuge with the new rising star of Daylam, Asfār b. Shīrōya or Shīrawayh [*q.v.*].

The epigons. With this event (ca. 315/927) ends our direct information about the Djustānids, but remnants of the dynasty may still have carried on, at least in a part of their dominions. When Ibn Musāfir had dealt with his Djustānid opponents (nos. 5, 6, 7), the former amīrs of the ʿAlids and Djustānids had already spread over the Iranian plateau, and Daylam proper lay at the mercy of Ibn Musāfir. In a report in which an official (some time before 379/989) summed up the history of Shamīrān (Tārom) for the Būyid minister Ibn ʿAbbād (see Yāḳūt, iii, 149-50, as explained by Kasrawī, i, 130-4), he states that the Musāfirid ruled over the whole of the mountainous *Ustāniya and (thus?) appropriated a part of Daylam, whereas the descendants of Wahsūdān (no. 3) b. Djustān had to content themselves with the region of *Lāʾidjiya. The same terms appear in the anti-Daylamite and pro-Turkish tract which the secretary Ibn Ḥassūl presented (ca. 450/1058) to al-Kundurī, the *wazīr* of Tughril-beg (see *Faḍāʾil al-Atrāk*, ed. ʿA. al-ʿAzzāwī, *Belleten*, iv/14-5, (1940) 31). Ibn Ḥassūl explains that *Ostān is the highlands, and *Lāʾidj (wrongly printed *Lāndj*) the lowlands of Daylam, the former being in the possession of the Wahsūdānid (here Kangarid) governors, and the latter in the possession of the Djustānid kings. These independent reports indicate that soon after the death of Djustān b. Wahsūdān (no. 4) his possessions were split up and the Wahsūdānids (here children of the *Kangarid* Wahsūdān b. Muḥammad of Tārom) had taken possession of the highlands of Daylam (presumably the "*ostān*", *i.e.*, "home, centre" of the Djustānids). The latter must have migrated to the neighbourhood of Lāhīdjān (*i.e.*, the coastal area of Daylam, of which ten districts are enumerated in the *Ḥudūd*).

On the contrary, when Sulṭān Tughril was operating near Ḳazwīn (Ibn al-Athīr, *anno* 434/1042) the king of Daylam appeared before him with a tribute; then separately Ibn al-Athīr mentions the submission of the *Salār* of Ṭarm (Tārom). We have to conclude either that the Djustānids had succeeded in reoccupying a part of their dominions, or that the tribute was paid by the Lāhīdjān branch. The latter surmise is more likely, for Nāṣir-i Khusraw in his *Safar-nāma* states that in 438/1046 a levy (*bādj*) was collected at the crossing of the Shāh-rūd (near its confluence with the Safīd-rūd) on behalf of the *amīr-i amīrān* who was "(one) of the kings of Daylamān". Nāṣir describes then his visit to Shamīrān whose ruler bore the title of "Marzubān al-Daylam Djīl-i Djīlān (*sic*) Abū Ṣāliḥ"; his name was Djustān Ibrāhīm and he possessed "many castles in Daylam". This must have been the great-grandson of Wahsūdān of Tārom (see MUSĀFIRIDS), and it appears as though the *bādj* on the Shāh-rūd was levied also in his name.

The story of the *dāʿīs* ends with the rule of the above-mentioned Ḥasanid Ḥasan b. Ḳāsim (no. IV), son-in-law (*khatn*) of al-Uṭrūsh. Although he was nominated by Nāṣir himself, struggles for the succession began between him and the sons of Nāṣir, and after the death of the latter the Daylamite amīrs, involved in complicated struggles, fought for their own supremacy. Ḥasan b. Ḳāsim was killed ca. 316/928 by Mardāwidj b. Ziyār, then the ally of Asfār b. Shīrōya.

Daylamite expansion. The result of the ʿAlids' activities was that the Daylamites, partly converted to the Zaydī creed, developed strong oppositionary tendencies with regard to the caliphate, and that in their numerous fights for the ʿAlids they greatly improved their military skill and became conscious of their strength. The revolts of the Sādjid Yūsuf b. Dīwdād (in 295/907 and in 304-7/916-9) and his final recall before his death in 315/928 opened the field for a chaotic succession in Rayy of Sāmānid governors, Turkish slaves, and ʿAlids of Daylam. An important branch of the Musāfirids of Tārom had expanded towards Ādharbaydjān and Transcaucasia (see Minorsky in *BSOAS*, xv/3, 1953, 514-29), while quite new elements appeared on the central plateau of Īrān: first Asfār b. Shīrōya who ca. 315/927 had proclaimed himself king, then the Ziyārids (316-434/928-1042), for a short time in Rayy in Iṣfahān, and later in the south-eastern corner of the Caspian Sea whither they had had to withdraw under the impact of the more important Būyids [*q.v.*]. This period is known to us through such sources as Masʿūdī, *Murūdj*, ix, 4-15; Miskawayh, in *Eclipse*; Ibn Isfandiyār, ed. Eghbal, 224-301, tr. Browne, 162-223; and such subsidiary mentions as are found in the historians of the Sāmānids, cf. Gardīzī, *Zayn al-akhbār*; Ibn Faḍlān, in his *Riḥla*, etc.

Having occupied the major part of the Iranian plateau (except Khurāsān held by the Sāmānids) the Būyids, who rose in 320/932, occupied Baghdād in 334/946, and for 109 years held the caliph under their ʿAlid tutelage. Under their shadow a great number of local dynasties of Iranian origin (Daylamite and Kurdish) sprang up in the peripheral areas: the Musāfirids; the Kurdish Shaddādids of Gandja (340-409/951-1018) and their branch of Ani (451-559/1059-1163); the Kākūyids [*q.v.*] of Hamadān and Iṣfahān (398-443/1007-51); the Kurdish Ḥasanūyids [see ḤASANAWAYHIDS] in the region of Kirmānshāh (348-406/959-1015); the Kurdish ʿAnnāzīds [*q.v.*] in Ḥulwān and on the western slopes of the Zagros (381-511/991-1117); the Kurdish Marwānids [*q.v.*] of Mayyāfāriḳīn and Diyārbakr (380-478/990-1085), etc. The weakness of the Daylamite régime consisted in the dispersion of the not too numerous elements of Daylam over too vast an area; the splitting up of the dynasty into several rival branches; and finally the Turko-Daylamite antagonism in the army (see below). The first great blow to the Būyid power was the occupation of Rayy by the Ghaznawid Maḥmūd in 420/1029; the definite end came under the impact of Tughril-beg who in 447/1055 arrested the last Būyid of Baghdād, al-Malik al-Raḥīm. In Fārs, the last scions of the Būyid house carried on for a few more years as vassals of the Saldjūḳs, (see Bowen in *JRAS*, 1929, 229-45). Outside their country, the Daylamites continued to serve as mercenaries. Niẓām al-Mulk, *Siyāsat-nāma*, ch. xix, still recommends the employment of 100 Daylamites together with 100 Khurāsānians as palace guards of the Saldjūḳs. Isolated colonies of Daylamites survived in many places before they were absorbed by the local populations.

Toponymy. The area over which generations of Daylamites scattered throughout the ages is very wide, but, in view of the chronological difficulties involved, it is better to combine the references under a single heading. Thus the Babylonian name of the island of Dilmun (Baḥrayn) still merits consideration, while the name of Bandar-i Daylam on the southern coast of Fārs seems to date back to the Būyid period. In the sub-Caucasian region the existence of military settlements of the Sāsānian times is reflected in such names as Layzān or Lāʾizān (now Lahīdj) connected with Lāhīdjān. The name of Shīrwān is probably linked with that of Shīr (in Arabic Shirriz) lying at the confluence of the rivers of Ṭalaḳān and Alamūt, cf. *Ḥudūd*, ch. xxxii, § 24, and Djuwaynī, iii, 425 (note of M. Ḳazwīnī). Even the title of the king of Sarīr (Avaria) figuring in Balādhurī, 196, as Wahrarzān-shāh, may prove to be linked with the title *wahriz*, cf. Minorsky, *History of Sharvān*, 1958, 23-5. The so-called "Zāzā", living north of Diyārbakr up to Pālū and Darsim and still speaking an Iranian language, call themselves *Dimlä*, which name F. C. Andreas identified with Daylam. The (now turkicized) tribe Dumbulī, active in the region of Khoy by the beginning of the 19th century, seems also to be connected with the Dimlä. It is noteworthy that Agathias, iii, 17, speaking of the *Dilimnitai* troops fighting in Lasica, says that their homes (perhaps of that particular group?) lay in the neighbourhood of Persian lands "on the middle course of the Tigris", *i.e.*, (if the "Tigris" is not a mistake for the Safīd-rūd) in the region where the Zāzā live nowadays. The traveller Abū Dulaf, ed. Minorsky, Cairo 1955, § 25, mentions a place called Daylamastān at seven *farsakh*s east of Shahrazūr whence "in the days of the ancient kings of Persia" the Daylamites used to send their raiding parties into the Mesopotamian lowlands. The borough of Daylamān lying west of Lāhīdjān may be the witness of the transfer of the Daylamite centre from *Ostān (see above) to the region of Lāhīdjān. North-west of Lake Urmiya the centre of Salmās was until recently called Dilmaḳān; south-west of Lake Urmiya near an important Zagros pass one finds a district called Lāhīdjān (see SĀWDJ-BULAK in *EI*[1]). Several other villages bearing the name Lāhīdjān are known in the basin of Lake Urmiya, north of Mt. Savalan (Lāhī), etc.

Territory and peoples. The earlier Muslim geographers, such as Ibn Khurradādhbih, Yaʿḳūbī, Ibn Rusta, Ibn Faḳīh, have little to say on Daylam, but ample information on the country and its inhabitants is supplied by the geographers and historians after the rise of the Daylamite dynasties in the 4th/10th century. Already Iṣṭakhrī had described under Daylam all the southern coast of the Caspian and the lands forming a belt to the south of the Alburz range (including Rayy and Ḳazwīn). Muḳaddasī (who lived in the heyday of the Daylamite dominion) adds to it all the coasts of the Caspian comprising the Khazar kingdom at the estuary of the Volga.

Iṣṭakhrī (possibly following Balkhī) places the capital of the Djustān family at Rūdhbār. The editor of Djuwaynī, iii, 434, M. Ḳazwīnī, has presented weighty arguments for identifying it with the Rūdhbār of Alamūt, which would mark the latter valley as the home (*ostān*) of the dynasty of Daylam. In Ibn Ḥawḳal's text, which is mainly based on Iṣṭakhrī, the capital of the Djustānids is placed at al-Ṭarm, which is a slip probably on the part of a scribe or reader, for al-Ṭarm (Tārom) was the capital not of the Djustānids but of the later Musāfirids [*q.v.*]. More complicated is the identification of B.rwān, which according to Muḳaddasī, 360, was the capital (*ḳaṣaba*) of Daylam. The place was devoid of amenity, as opposed to the fertile Tālaḳān (in the Shāh-rūd valley) which in the author's opinion would have been more suitable for the capital. The residence of the government (*mustaḳarr al-sulṭān*), in B.rwān, was called Shahristān, where the treasure was kept in a deep well (Ẓahīr al-Dīn spells Shahr-astān, perhaps Shahr-*Ostān "the town of Ostān", see above). Muḳaddasī names separately Samirūm (*sic*) the capital of the Salāarwand rulers (Musāfirids) of the Tārom region, and Khashm the town of the ʿAlid *dāʿīs*, in eastern Gīlān, situated by a bridge.

Iṣṭakhrī, 205, describes the Daylamites as lean, having "light" (probably "fluffy") hair, rash, and inconsiderate. They practised agriculture and had herds but no horses. According to Muḳaddasī, 368-9, the Daylamites were good-looking and wore beards. Some valuable data on "Daylam proper" and Gīlān are given in the *Ḥudūd al-ʿĀlam*, ch. xxxii, §§ 24-5: Daylam consisted of ten districts in the Caspian lowlands, and three, *Wustān, Shīr (apparently Shirriz of the Arabic sources), and Pazhm, in the mountains.

Customs. Many habits and customs of the Daylamites struck the contemporary authors. Their men were extremely hardy and capable of enduring great privations (Miskawayh, *Eclipse*, i, 140). Particularly mentioned among their armament are javelins (*zhopīn*) and tall shields painted in gay colours and carried by assistant lads. Set side by side these shields formed a wall against the attackers. Special men throwing javelins with burning naphtha (*mazārīḳ al-nafṭ wa 'l-nīrān*) were also used in their army (see *Eclipse*, i, 282). A poetical description of Daylamite warfare is given in Gurgānī's *Wīs wa Rāmīn*, ed. Minovi, ch. xcix. The great disadvantage of the Daylamites was their lack of cavalry; they were obliged to operate jointly with Turkish mercenaries (whose armament was more complete, *Eclipse*, ii, 336) and basic rivalry between them disrupted the army.

Reference is often made to the extravagance of the Daylamite lamenting over their dead, and even over themselves in misfortune (Muḳaddasī, 369; *Eclipse*, ii, 162; iii, 260). In 352/963 Muʿizz al-Dawla introduced public mourning (*niyāḥa*) in Baghdād for the *imām* Ḥusayn (Ibn al-Athīr, viii, 406; Tanūkhī, *Nishwār*, tr. Margoliouth, 219; but see Hilāl b. Muḥassin on the temporary character of the performance, *Eclipse*, iii, 458, *sub* 393), and this institution may be responsible for the later Persian *taʿziya*s in the month of Muḥarram (cf. A. E. Krïmskiy, *Perskiy teatr*, Kiev 1921).

Ca. 200 A.D. the Syrian sage Bardesanes reports that the women of Gīlān work in the fields (*Leges regionum*, Patrologia Syriaca, ii/1, 1907, ed. F. Nau, 586). Eight centuries later the author of the *Ḥudūd* writes that the Daylam womenfolk are engaged in agriculture like men. According to Rudhrāwarī, *Eclipse*, iii, 313, they were "equals of men in strength of mind, force of character, and participation in the management of affairs". The Daylamites practised endogamy within their tribes, and marriages were concluded by direct agreement between the parties (Muḳaddasī, 368-9).

The Ismāʿīlīs. The Fāṭimid Ismāʿīlī propaganda had been rampant in the environs of Rayy even since the beginning of the 3rd/9th century (see S. M. Stern, in *BSOAS*, xxiii, 1960, 56-90). Asfār of Daylam and Mardāwidj of Gīlān had accepted the new teaching (Baghdādī, *Farḳ*, tr. A. Halkin, Tel-Aviv 1935, 113; Rashīd al-Dīn, *Ismāʿīliyān*, ed. Dānishpazhūh, Tehrān 1338/1959, 12). Under the last Būyids the Daylamites in Fārs adhered to the doctrine of the Seven Imāms, and the penultimate Būyid Marzubān Abū Kālīdjār (d. 440/1048) lent his ear to the preacher al-Muʾayyad who was finally expelled from Fārs (*Sīrat al-Muʾayyad fi ʾl-Dīn*, Cairo 1949, 43, 64; cf. *Fārs-nāma*, 115). The strong position of Daylam and the oppositionary tendencies of the population naturally attracted Ḥasan-i Ṣabbāḥ, who first sent his propagandists into Daylam, and then in 483/1090 seized the town of Alamūt, which was then held by an ʿAlid called Mahdī as a fief from Malik-shāh (Djuwaynī, iii, 174). Thus for the next 166 years the great stronghold of Daylam was transformed into a danger-spot on the very doorstep of Saldjūḳ territory and a threat to the whole Sunnī world. The efforts of the Saldjūḳs to liquidate Alamūt were unsuccessful, but they caused much harm to the population; cf. the expedition of Arslan-tash in 485/1092, that of the son of Niẓām al-Mulk in 503/1109, that of Shīrgīr before 511/1117. The last reminiscence of the Būyids in Daylam is Djuwaynī's report, iii, 239, on the deed of one of their scions, Ḥasan b. Nāmāwar, who in 561/1166 stabbed to death the master of the Ismāʿīlīs because, despite his being his brother-in-law, he disliked his propaganda.

The Mongols and after. The total destruction of the fortresses of the Assassins (Alamūt, Lamassar, Maymūn-diz) by the troops of Hulāgū in 654/1256, and the extermination of the followers of the last master of the Assassins, dealt a terrible blow to the original highlanders of Daylam. The Shāh-rūd valley became easily accessible from Ḳazwīn (cf. the account of the operations of Öldjeytū Khān, who in 706/1307 invaded Gīlān and reached Lāhīdjān; *Taʾrīkh-i Uldjāytū*, Bibl. Nat., Supp. 4197, fol. 42v).

At a later period the highlands of Daylam were more or less controlled by the dynasty of the *kār-kiyā* of eastern Gīlān (Biyapīsh) whose centre was at Lāhīdjān. They gradually eliminated their Hazāraspī princes of Ashkawar, the last scions of the Ismāʿīlīs of Alamūt, and the clan of Kūshīdj of Daylamān and Rūdhbār. In 819/1416 the sayyid Raḍī of Lāhīdjān invited the Daylamites to the bank of the Safīd-rūd and had two or three thousand of them murdered with their chiefs (Ẓahīr al-Dīn, *Taʾrīkh-i Gīlān*, ed. Rabino, Rasht 1330, 57, 118, 122-6).

The most recent movement in the history of Daylam is the uprising of the Ahl-i Ḥaḳḳ [*q.v.*] leader Sayyid Muḥammad in Kalār-dasht in October 1891 (see Minorsky, *Notes sur la secte des Ahlé-Ḥaqq*, Paris 1920-1, 51).

No complete enquiries have been carried out on the population of Daylam proper, but H. Rabino, *Le Guilan*, 280, states that the original Daylamites are found only in Kalārdeh and Čawsāl (in winter) and in Kalač-khānī (in summer). The inhabitants of Daylamān (south-west of Lāhīdjān) have sold their lands and now live at Barfdjān (mentioned in the *Ḥudūd* as a canton in the lowlands of Daylam).

Bibliography: Given in the course of the article. The *Taʾrīkh-i Djīl wa Daylam*, dedicated to the Būyid Fakhr al-Dawla (who according to G. C. Miles ruled in Rayy 373-87/984-97), and used by Djuwaynī, iii, 270, is now lost. No Djustānid coins have yet been discovered. Marquart., *Ērānšahr*, 126-7; H. L. Rabino, *Les provinces Caspiennes*, in *RMM*, xxxii, 1915-6, 227-384 (Daylamān, Lāhīdjān, Rān-i kūh); R. Vasmer, *Zur Chronologie d. Ǧastaniden*, in *Isl.*, iii/2, 1927, 165-86, and 483-5; A. Kasrawī, *Pādshāhān-i gumnām*, 1928, i, 23-37 (Djustāniyān) — a valuable work; V. Minorsky, *La domination des Dailamites*, Soc. des Études Iraniennes, no. iii, 1932, 1-26; M. Ḳazwīnī, annotations to Djuwaynī, iii, 306-9 (ʿAlids), 432-45 (Djustānids); *İA*, s.v. Deilem (A. Ateş).

(V. MINORSKY)

DAYN [see SUPPLEMENT].

DAYR, a word of Syriac origin denoting the Christian monasteries which continued to function after the Arab conquest of the Middle East. If we are to believe the lists drawn up by Arab writers, they were very numerous, particularly in ʿIrāḳ (along the Tigris and Euphrates valleys), Upper Mesopotamia, Syria (Stylite sanctuaries in the vicinity of the "dead cities"), Palestine and Egypt (along the whole length of the Nile valley). They were often named after a patron saint (Dayr Mār Yuḥannā near Takrīt, Dayr Samʿān in northern Syria) or founder (Dayr ʿAbdūn in ʿIrāḳ), but also occasionally after the nearest town or village (Dayr al-Ruṣāfa in Syria) or a feature of the locality (Dayr al-aʿlā near Mosul, Dayr al-Zaʿfarān in Upper Mesopotamia). Monks, called *dayyār* or *dayrānī*, lived in the *dayr*s (also known in ʿIrāḳ as *ʿumr*, a word of uncertain origin). The monasteries were often no more than simple hermitages, particularly if they were located in remoter parts. Usually however they consisted of several buildings—a church (*kanīsa* or *bīʿa*), cells (*ḳilliya*, pl. *ḳalālī*, or *kirḥ*, pl. *akrāḥ* and *ukayraḥ*, words of Syriac origin, the second being strictly speaking ʿIrāḳī), and outbuildings such as shops and inns. The *dayr* in fact constituted a centre of agricultural development, and drew revenue from the lands which were cultivated to meet its needs (vineyards, olive groves and palm plantations). Hermitages and convents were made defensible either by the construction of fortifications or by the careful choice of site (*e.g.*, on mountain-sides, or even set into the rock face and thus cut off from normal means of entry).

The Christian monasteries were centres of religious and intellectual life during the early years of Islam. For instance, the liturgical rules adopted in the 3rd-4th/9th-10th centuries by the Nestorian church were formulated in the Dayr al-aʿlāʾ of Mosul (see J. M. Fiey, *Mossoul chrétienne*, Beirut 1959, 126-32). They also played an important role in diffusing the works of classical Greece, generally translated into Syriac and then into Arabic, and in some instances they built up large libraries, such as the notable collection in St. Catherine's monastery on Mount Sinai (see A. S. Atiya, *The Arabic manuscripts of Mount Sinai*, Baltimore 1955). Furthermore, some ʿIrāḳī monasteries and the Christian communitites attached to them proved an important source of official clerks in ʿAbbāsid times. They took part in the administration of the empire, and if they adopted the Islamic faith they even had the right to be appointed vizier (see DAYR ḲUNNĀ).

The monasteries were also an important factor in the political and social life of the Islamic world.

They were open without distinction to virtually all travellers, including notabilities, and indeed often provided a safer stopping-place than elsewhere. At the Dayr Murrān [*q.v.*] near Damascus, for example, there was a princely residence nearby (confused with the monastery by some authors), and sovereigns or governors were sometimes accommodated in the *dayr* itself. This was the case in the Dayr al-aʿlaʾ of Mosul, the Dayr Zakkī of al-Raḳḳa, or the monastery of al-Anbār where Hārūn al-Ras͟hīd and his retinue stopped in 187/803—it was here that D͟jaʿfar the Barmakid was executed (Ṭabarī, III, 675, 678). Upon his arrival in Egypt the Fāṭimid al-Muʿizz lived for some months in the monastery of al-Gīza. There are ample records showing that during their hunting excursions rulers and princes visited the local monasteries, where they were offered food and drink by the monks. Muslim visitors were also attracted to the monasteries on account of the taverns usually attached to them, and there they were free to drink as much wine as they wished. Each monastery solemnly celebrated an annual festival, and the buildings were generally surrounded by places of entertainment and even debauchery, particularly if they were situated near a large town. This explains why so many of the monasteries figure in bacchic and erotic poetry, and why there are so many stories relating to the questionable behaviour of some of their inhabitants. Indeed, Arab authors of the 3rd/9th and 4th/10th centuries even wrote whole books about them by collecting poems and stories in which they were mentioned. Only one is still in existence, the *Kitāb al-Diyārāt* of al-S͟hābus͟htī (d. 388/998). But the names of several other books are known, written by His͟hām al-Kalbī, Abu 'l-Farad͟j al-Iṣfahānī, the poet al-Sarī al-Raffāʾ, the two brothers al-K͟hālidiyyān and al-Sumaysāṭī.

After the Arab conquest the monasteries and churches were subject to special conditions laid down by jurists. Although the existing monasteries remained intact, the monks were forbidden to put up new buildings, or even to repair damage incurred through wear and tear or accidental causes. In reality, however, the fortunes of the monasteries varied with the times, and periods of toleration were followed by periods of persecution. The tax regulations governing the occupants of the monasteries were a subject of continual discussion. The monks were initially exempt from poll-tax (*d͟jizya*), and the tradition was often later confirmed by jurists. But some maintained that exemption applied only to those living in poverty, and the S͟hāfiʿīs even went so far as to assert that the exemption was unjust. From the chroniclers it would seem that in the Umayyad age some governors subjected monks in Egyptian monasteries to personal taxation, and others in the ʿAbbāsid age granted exemption only in certain circumstances. The question was raised again during the caliphate of al-Muḳtadir, when in 313/925 ʿAlī b. ʿĪsā, chief inspector of taxes in Egypt, demanded that exemption given to the monks of Wadi 'l-Naṭrūn be withdrawn; the caliph did not accede to his wishes, and in 366/976 al-Ṭaʾiʿ announced once more that the *d͟jizya* should not apply to poor monks (see DHIMMA).

The 5th/11th century was the beginning of a period of increasing hardship for the Christian monasteries. They had to contend with successive Sald͟jūḳid and Mongol invasions, a growing insecurity (*e.g.*, Turcoman raids into Upper Mesopotamia), the worsening of relations with the Muslims at the time of the Crusades, and the progressive disappearance of former small Christian communitites.

In ʿIrāḳ the monasteries near Bag͟hdād and Samarrā perished, whilst many of those in Egypt were abandoned and became overrun by the sand (some of them have been discovered in recent excavations). After the Mongol invasion Christian monastic life was confined to a few groups of monasteries, primarily in Upper Mesopotamia, the Mosul and Mardin region (the monasteries of Ṭūr ʿAbdīn), the Sinai desert, and Egypt (at Wādī 'l-Naṭrūn and near the Red Sea). In Palestine and Syria, great monastic centres before the Arab conquest, there remained no more than a few scattered monasteries, mostly near Jerusalem and in Anti-Lebanon. In the Lebanon itself on the other hand monasticism found a new lease of life, particularly in the 15th century when the Maronite patriarchate was established in the mountains at the monastery of Ḳannūbīn.

During the age when they flourished, Christian monasteries took part in the artistic life of the region, and it is instructive to compare the decorative techniques used in some of them with Muslim works of the same period. Particularly interesting in this respect are the Dayr al-Suryānī at Wādi'l-Naṭrūn in Egypt, containing stucco ornamentation influenced by the style of Samarrā, and the Mār Behnām monastery near Mosul, some parts of which date back to the 6th/12th century. Furthermore, the illuminating of some manuscripts copied in the monasteries bears a resemblance to that of the oldest Islamic miniatures, which seem to have inherited some features of their style and workmanship.

Bibliography: Ḥ. Zayyāt, *al-Diyārāt al-Naṣrāniyya fi 'l-Islām*, in *Mas͟hriḳ*, 1938, 219-417; A. Fattal, *Le statut légal des non-Musulmans*, Beirut 1958, 174-203, 270-2; al-S͟hābus͟htī, *K. al-Diyārāt*, ed. K. ʿAwwad, Bag͟hdād 1951; Bakrī, *Muʿd͟jam*, ed. Wüstenfeld, i, 359-81; Yāḳūt, ii, 639-710 and iii, 724-6; ʿUmarī, *Masālik*, Cairo ed., i, 254-386; A. S. Marmardji, *Textes géographiques arabes sur la Palestine*, Paris 1951, 72-9; Maḳrīzī, *Khiṭaṭ*, Būlāḳ ed., ii, 501-9; Cairo ed., iv, 409-37; *The churches and monasteries of Egypt*, attributed to Abū Ṣāliḥ the Armenian, trans. Evetts-Butler, Oxford 1895; E. A. Wallis Budge, *The chronography of Gregory Abū 'l-Faradj* (*Bar Hebraeus*), London 1932, introduction; R. Honigmann, *Le Couvent de Barsauma et le patriarcat jacobite d'Antioche et de Syrie*, Louvain 1954; N. Abbott, *The monasteries of the Fayyum*, in *AJSL*, liii (1937), 13-33, 73-96, 159-79; H. C. Evelyn White, *The monasteries of the Wadi n'Natrūn*, 2 vols., New York, 1926-33; S. Flury, *Die Gipsornamente des Dēr es-Sūrjānī*, in *Isl.*, vi (1916), 71-87; F. Sarre and E. Herzfeld, *Archäologische Reise im Euphrat und Tigris Gebiete*, ii, Berlin 1911, 247; J. Leroy, *Moines et monastères du Proche-Orient*, Paris 1958; idem, *Les manuscrits syriaques à peintures conservés dans les bibliothèques d'Europe et du Proche-Orient* (to appear shortly).

(D. SOURDEL)

DAYR ʿABD AL-RAḤMĀN, a place in the vicinity of Kūfa, next to Ḳanāṭir Rās al-D͟jālūt (Ṭabarī, ii, 701), near Ḥammām Aʿyun (Ṭabarī, ii, 703). It was the assembly point of the Kūfan army which was sent by al-Ḥad͟jd͟jād͟j under the command of al-D͟jazl against the K͟hārid͟jites (Ṭabarī, ii, 902) and of Ibn al-Ashʿath (Ṭabarī, ii, 930). Al-Ḥārith b. Abī Rabīʿa encamped there in his revolt against al-Mukhtār (Ṭabarī, ii, 759). (SALEH A. EL-ALI)

DAYR AL-ʿĀḲŪL, a town in ʿIrāḳ 15 parasangs (c. 83 km.) south east of Baghdād on the Tigris (Yāḳūt, ii, 676-7. Muḳaddasi, p. 134 gives the distance as two stages, while Ibn Faḍl Allāh al-ʿUmarī, *Masālik al-Abṣār*, Cairo 1924, i, 263, makes it 12 parasangs or c. 67 km.). The town probably grew around a Christian monastery, and was the centre of an agricultural district (*ṭassūdj*) in central Nahrawān.

Ibn Rusta (300/912) mentions its Friday mosque and its market, thus indicating some prosperity. Besides, it was a post where tolls on merchandise carried in boats (*maʾāṣir*) were levied. (Ibn Rusta, 186). Iṣṭakhrī (318-21/930-3) speaks of it as being similar to other towns north of Wāsiṭ, moderate in size with cultivations around (Iṣṭakhrī, 87). Half a century later, the author of *Ḥudūd al-ʿĀlam* (372/982) describes it as a prosperous town, while Muḳaddasī (ca. 375/985) considers it the most important town on the Tigris between Baghdād and Wāsiṭ. It was flourishing, well populated, and had markets with many branches at a distance from the mosque (Muḳaddasī, 123).

Dayr al-ʿĀḳūl is famous in history for the decisive battle fought there in 262/876 between Yaʿḳūb b. al-Layth al-Ṣaffār and the army of the Caliph al-Muʿtamid, led by his able brother al-Muwaffaḳ, in which the rebellious governor suffered his first serious defeat and a great danger for the Caliphate was averted (cf. Ṭabari, iii, 1893; Masʿūdī, *Murūdj*, viii, 41 ff.; Weil, *Geschichte der Chalif.*, ii, 441; Müller, *Isl.*, I, 583; Nöldeke, *Sketches* (1892), 195 ff.).

Then the town began to decline, and when Yāḳūt wrote of it, (beginning of 7th/13th century), followed verbatim by the *Marāṣid al-Iṭṭilāʿ*, the period of its prosperity was already past. The decline of the Caliphate, the ruin of the Nahrawān canal, and the alteration in the course of the Tigris largely account for that. Yāḳūt found it one Arab mile (1848 metres) east of the river; it stood alone in a desolate area. (Yāḳūt, ii, 676; *Marāṣid*, i, 435).

Maps of Arab geographers show the gradual change in its position in relation to the Tigris. Balkhī (308/920) and Iṣṭakhrī put it directly on the east bank of the Tigris. (Sousa, *al-ʿIrāḳ fi 'l-Khawāriṭ al-Ḳadīma*, Baghdād 1960, nos. 12 and 18, cf. the map of Muḳaddasī no. 23 and Djayhānī no. 27). Ibn Ḥawḳal shows the river slightly removed westward (ibid no. 22). Abū Saʿīd al-Maghribī (685/1236) puts it at a distance east of the Tigris, thus confirming Yāḳūt (ibid., map no. 32).

It seems that the town revived again, for Ḥamd Allāh Mustawfī (d. 740/1339) describes it as a big town with humid air, as it was surrounded by gardens and palm trees (*Nuzhat al-Ḳulūb*, 46). However, ʿUmarī (d. 748/1347) talks of the fine buildings of the monastery, but refers to Dayr al-ʿĀḳūl as a big village (*Masālik al-Abṣār*, i, 256-7).

Dayr al-ʿĀḳūl ultimately became utterly deserted. Its site may be identified now among the ruins called locally al-Dayr, consisting of three mounds east of the Tigris, north of modern ʿAzīziyya (see T. Hāshimī, *Mufaṣṣal Djughrāfiyat al-ʿIrāḳ*, Baghdad 1930, 529).

The name Dayr al-ʿĀḳūl, though seemingly Arabic (lit. monastery of the camel-thorn [*Alhagi Maurorum* or *Hedysarum Alhagi*]) is almost certain to be, like so many pre-Islamic names in ʿIrāḳ, of Aramaic origin. The Arabic *ʿāḳūl* reproduces the Aramaic *ākola*, 'bend'; therefore the name means 'the monastery of the bend of the river'. *Ākōla* exists elsewhere as a place name in ʿIrāḳ as the name of the suburb of Kufa, a name given on account of a well marked bend in the Euphrates as is expressly stated in Syriac sources (cf. Nöldeke, in *SBAk. Wien*, cxxiv, Abh. IX, 43).

Bibliography: References are in the article. The following are to be noted: Sumer, x, 1954, 120; Le Strange, 35; idem, in *JRAS*, 1895, 41; K. Ritter, *Erdkunde*, x, 191, 232. (A. A. DURI)

DAYR AL-AʿWAR, a place in ʿIrāḳ named after a member of the clan of Umayya b. Ḥudhāfa of the Iyād tribe (Balādhurī, *Futūḥ*, 283; Hamdānī, *Buldān*, 182; Yāḳūt, ii, 644). It is therefore an Iyādī Dayr (Hamdānī, 135, quoting al-Haytham b. ʿAdī; Bakrī, 69, quoting Ibn Shabba). Hamdānī's identification of it with Dayr al-Djamādjim, *loc. cit.*, is probably an error, since no other source confirms it.

Dayr al-Aʿwar was mentioned in the description of the march of the Sāsānian general Rustam from Ctesiphon to Ḳādisiyya following the route Kūthā Burs (ancient Bursippa)—Dayr al-Aʿwar—Milṭaṭ —Nadjaf, where he pitched his camps (Ṭabarī, i, 2254). This Dayr was also mentioned when Sulaymān b. Ṣurad, after leaving Kūfa with the Tawwābīn, chose it as the assembly point for his followers before he moved to Aḳsās Mālik and Karbala (Ṭabarī, ii, 548; Balādhurī, *Ansāb*, v, 209). It was mentioned also when Ḥamīd b. Ḳuḥṭuba moved south along the route Karbala—Dayr al-Aʿwar—ʿAbbāsiyya (Ṭabarī, iii, 15); when al-Ḥasan b. Ḳaḥṭaba followed a similar route (Ṭabarī, iii, 18); and finally when Saʿīd and Abu 'l-Buṭṭ passed through Dayr al-Aʿwar in their advance from Nīl to check Harthama's armies which were stationed in Shāhī, a village on the Surā canal.

These texts show that Dayr al-Aʿwar is located west of Burs and east of Nadjaf; it is also south of Karbala, Surā and Shāhī, and north of ʿAbbāsiyya and Nīl; they also show that it was known up to the 3rd/9th century.

The Kūfan rebel ʿUbayd Allāh b. al-Ḥurr is said to have withdrawn to Dayr al-Aʿwar after having been defeated by ʿUmar b. Ubayd Allāh at the time of Muṣʿab (Ṭabarī, ii, 775; Ibn al-Athīr, iv, 241).

Bibliography: in the text.

(SALEH A. EL-ALI)

DAYR AL-DJAMĀDJIM, a place in ʿIrāḳ, near Kūfa. It was originally owned by the Iyād tribe before its migration from ʿIrāḳ (Bakrī, 69, quoting Ibn Shabba; Hamdānī, *Buldan*, 135, quoting al-Haytham b. ʿAdī).

Various etymological explanations of its origin have been given: Abū ʿUbayda states that its name was derived from the wooden cups that were made in it (*Naḳāʾiḍ*, 412; Ibn Ḳutayba, *Maʿārif*, 156; Bakrī, *Muʿdjam*, 574; Yāḳūt, ii, 112, 652). Other authorities assert that it was named after the buried skulls of the casualties of the battle between Iyād Bahrā (al-Sharḳī, *Futūḥ*, 283; Hamdānī, *Buldān*, 182) or between Iyād and the Sāsānians (Ibn al-Kalbī, *Futūḥ*, 283; Ibn Shabba in Bakrī, 70; Masʿūdī, *Tanbīh*, 175). Yāḳūt (ii, 652) states that its name was derived from a well in a saline land.

Dayr al-Djamādjim is west of the Euphrates (Bakrī, 70, 573, quoting Ibn Shabba) on the high-lands of Kūfa (Iṣfahānī in Bakrī ,573; Yāḳūt, ii, 652) near ʿAyn al-Tamr and Fallūdja [*q.v.*] (Ṭabarī, ii, 1073) and is about 7 parasangs from Kufah.

The description of the battle of Djamādjim (83/

702) shows that this Dayr is near Dayr Ḳurra, nearer to Kūfa and the Euphrates (Iṣfahānī in Bakrī, 592; Yāḳūt, ii, 685), i.e. south-east of Dayr Ḳurra [*q.v.*].

In Islamic history Dayr al-Djamādjim is known as the battlefield of the war between al-Ḥadjdjādj and ʿAbd al-Raḥmān b. al-Ashʿath (see IBN AL-ASHʿATH) in 83/702, the latter supported by most of the Arab Kūfans as well as by some non-Arab Mawālī. The long negotiations had failed; al-Ḥadjdjādj, supported by Syrian Arab reinforcements, defeated Ibn al-Ashʿath, who retreated to Maskin, leaving al-Ḥadjdjādj the unrivalled master of Kūfa and enabling him to assert his control over that city by taking severe measures against his opponents. On the battle see Ṭabarī ,ii, 1070 ff.; Yaʿḳūbī, 332; Masʿūdī, *Tanbīh*, 315, and *Murūdj*, iv, 304; Ibn Ḳutayba, *Maʿārif*, 156; Abū Yūsuf, *Kharādj*, 57; Ibn al-Athīr, iv, 376 ff.

Bibliography: in the article.

(SALEH A. EL-ALI)

DAYR AL-DJĀTHALĪḲ, a name given to two monasteries in ʿIrāḳ. The first stands in the district (*ṭassūdj*) of Maskin, which is watered by the Dudjayl canal. This canal flows off from the west bank of the Tigris south of Sāmarrā and takes a southward course on almost the same line as modern Dudjayl till it reaches the neighbourhood of Baghdād. Maskin is to be located about 9-10 parasangs (50-55 km.) north of Baghdād. Its ruins seem to keep their old name and are called Kharāʾib (ruins of) Maskin; they are by the west bank of the modern Dudjay some 3 km. south of Smeika village (see Sousa, *Rayy Sāmarrā*, i, 191. Abū Ṣakhar could not be the ruins of Maskin as Streck thought; it is by the old course of the Tigris; see ibid., map 6, facing 192).

The place of Dayr al-Djāthalīḳ was near Maskin (cf. Balādhurī, *Ansāb*, v, 337). It seems probable that its remains are what is called "Tel al-Dayr", now some 6 km. S. E. of Smeika village. These ruins show a square building of bricks with a square courtyard higher than the neighbouring ground. (Sousa, *op. cit.*, i, 196-7).

Dayr al-Djāthalīḳ owes its fame in Arab history to the decisive battle fought in its neighbourhood in 72/691 between the Caliph ʿAbd al-Malik and Muṣʿab b. al-Zubayr, governor of ʿIrāḳ for his brother, the anti-Caliph, ʿAbdallāh b. al-Zubayr. The Zubayrī poet ʿAbd Allāh b. Ḳays al-Ruḳayyāt calls it "The Day of the *Dayr*". Muṣʿab was defeated and killed (see Balādhurī, *Ansāb*, v, 343, 350, 355; Masʿūdī, v, 246 ff.; *Aghānī*, viii, 132, x, 147, xvii, 162; Ṭabarī, ii, 806, 818, 812; Yaʿḳūbī, ii, 317; Wellhausen, *Das Arab. Reich* (1902) 120-123).

A mausoleum was built on the spot where Muṣʿab was buried which soon became an object of pilgrimage. It is likely that the dome of Imām Manṣūr is the tomb of Muṣʿab (see Balādhurī, *Ansāb*, v, 337; Sousa, *op. cit.*, i, 198. Balādhurī also states (p. 350) that the place of the battle is called Khirbat Muṣʿab, a desert where—as people claim—nothing grows).

The name 'Monastery of the Catholicos' points to the fact that the head of the Nestorians stayed here at times.

The second Dayr al-Djāthalīḳ was a great monastery in Western Baghdād (see M. Streck, *Die Alte Landschaft Babylonien*, i, 167; Le Strange, *Baghdād*, 210; Shābushtī, *al-Diyārāt*, ed. G. ʿAwwād, 221-224; R. Bābū Isḥāḳ, *Naṣārā Baghdād*, 1960, 104-108).

Bibliography: References are mentioned in the article. The following are to be noted: Yāḳūt, ii, 251, 260; *Marāṣid al-Iṭṭilāʾ*, ed. Juynboll, 1850 ff., i, 426; v, 539; Sousa, *Ray Sāmarrāʾ*, i, (Baghdād 1448), 198 ff.; M. Streck, *Die Alte Landschaft Babylonien*, ii, 190, 236; Shābushtī, *Diyārāt* (ed. G. ʿAwwād), Bagdad 1951, 221-4. (A. A. DURI)

DAYR KAʿB, an Iyādī Dayr (Balādhurī, *Futūḥ*, 283) in ʿIrāḳ on the main Ctesiphon-Kūfa route which passes through Kūtha—Dayr Kaʿb—Muzāḥimiyya (near Ḳissayn)—Kūfa (Ṭabarī, ii, 60; Iṣfahānī, *Maḳātil al-Ṭālibiyyin*, 63). The Muslim armies, in their advance on Ctesiphon after their victory in Ḳādisiyya, defeated a Sāsānian detachment under command of Nukhayridjan (*Futūḥ*, 262).

(SALEH A. EL-ALI)

DAYR ḲUNNĀ, a locality in ʿIrāḳ some 90 km. south of Baghdād and a mile from the left bank of the Tigris. The name comes from a large monastery still flourishing in ʿAbbāsid times; it consisted of a church, a hundred cells, and extensive olive and palm plantations, all enclosed by thick walls. On the occasion of the feast of the Holy Cross many people flocked to the monastery. It seems that it was abandoned at the time of the Saldjūḳid occupation, and geographers of the 7th/13th century record that only the ruins then remained.

Dayr Ḳunnā is famous primarily on account of the families of high officials, both Christians and converts to Islam, which came from there. The best known is the Banu 'l-Djarrāḥ family, of which the viziers al-Ḥasan b. Makhlad, Muḥammad b. Dāwūd and ʿAlī b. Īsā were members. The secretaries of Dayr Ḳunnā played a considerable political role in the late 3rd/9th and early 4th/10th centuries. In al-Muʿtamid's reign they sought to obtain general recognition of the Nadjrān convention which granted certain privileges to Christians, and supported the conspiracy of Ibn al-Muʿtazz (296/908). Once converted to Islam, they were devout Sunnīs, tried to restore the waning authority of the Caliphate, and were influenced by the preachings of al-Hallādj (of whose disciples at least one was from Dayr Kunnā). But the open hostility of the pro-Shīʿī groups frustrated all efforts to restore the Sunnī caliph's authority and bring about a reconciliation between Christians and Muslims.

Bibliography: Yāḳūt, ii, 687-8; Shābushtī, *K. al-Diyārāt*, Baghdād 1951, 171-6, 248-50; Bakrī, *Muʿdjam*, ed. Wüstenfeld, i, 381; ʿUmarī, *Masālik al-Abṣār*, ed. A. Zakī Pasha, 256-8; Ṭabarī, iii, 1961; Le Strange, 36-7; M. ʿAwwād. *Dayr Ḳunnā*, in *Machriq*, xxxvii, 1939, 180-98; L. Massignon, in *Vivre et penser* (*Revue biblique*), IInd series, 1942, 7-14; idem, in *Dieu vivant*, iv, 1946, 18, 22; A. Fattal, *Le statut légal des non-Musulmans*, Beirut 1958, 32; D. Sourdel, *Le vizirat ʿabbāside*, Damascus 1959-60, index. (D. SOURDEL)

DAYR ḲURRA, a place named after a certain Ḳurra of the Umayya b. Ḥudhāfa clan (Hamdānī, *Buldān*, 182; Yāḳūt, *Muʿdjam*, ii, 685, quoting Ibn al-Kalbī) of the Iyād tribe (Balādhurī, *Futūḥ*, 283; Bakrī, 592, quoting Ibn Shabba), and is therefore to be considered as an Iyādī Dayr in origin (Hamdāni, 135, quoting al-Haytham b. ʿAdī; Bakrī, 698, quoting Ibn Shabba). Al-Iṣfahānī claims that Ḳurra was a Lakhmī (Bakrī, 592; Yāḳūt, ii, 685) and that the Dayr was established during al-Mundhir's reign (Bakrī, *loc. cit.*).

Dayr Ḳurra was mentioned in early Islamic history as the place through which a detachment of the Sāsānian army passed in its retreat after the battle of Ḳādisiyya (Ṭabarī, i, 2357) and where al-Ḥadjdjādj had encamped during the battle of

Djamādjim [see DAYR AL-DJAMĀDJIM]. This Dayr is about 7 parasangs from Kūfa; it is far from, and not on the borders of, Karbala, as A. Musil erroneously locates it in his study (*Middle Euphrates*, 411).

(SALEH A. EL-ALI)

DAYR MURRĀN, name of two former Christian monasteries in Syria. The name is of obscure origin; the Arab etymology *dayr al-murrān*, "ash-tree convent", is suspect, and Syriac does not offer a satisfactory explanation. The better known of the two monasteries was near Damascus, though its exact location cannot be determined. It was on the lower slopes of the Djabal Ḳaysūn, overlooking the orchards of the Ghūta, near the gateway of Bāb al-Farādīs and a pass (*ʿaḳaba*) where we may see in all probability the Baradā [*q.v.*] gorge. It was a large monastery, embellished with mosaics in the Umayyad era, and around it was built a village and, one presumes, a residence in which the caliphs could both entertain themselves and keep watch over their capital. Dayr Murrān often figured in poems of the time. Its estates no doubt benefited from the improvements to the river Nahr Yazīd carried out by the caliph Yazīd I. He was staying there when, before his accession, his father asked him to lead the expedition against Constantinople. Al-Walīd I died there in 96/715, and it is thought that al-Walīd II established his residence there. The ʿAbbāsid caliphs and their representatives visited or lived there on various occasions, as did Hārūn al-Rashīd, al-Maʾmūn, who built a watch-tower on the mountainside and had a new canal dug, and al-Muʿtaṣim. Radja b. Ayyūb set up his headquarters there when al-Wāthiḳ sent him to Damascus to put down the revolt of the Ḳays.

Dayr Murrān was made well-known in the 4th/10th century by the poets Abu 'l-Faradj al-Babbaghāʾ (al-Thaʿālibī, *Yatīma*, i, 180), and Kushādjim and al-Ṣanawbarī of Aleppo. In the Ayyūbid era it was also mentioned by a geographer and by a panegyrist of Ṣalāḥ al-Dīn.

It has been incorrectly asserted by some that the tomb of the Umayyad caliph ʿUmar b. ʿAbd al-ʿAzīz was in this Dayr Murrān. It was in fact in the other monastery of the same name on a hill overlooking Kafarṭāb, near Maʿarrat al-Nuʿmān, in northern Syria. The latter was also called Dayr al-Naḳīra and Dayr Samʿān. Although it probably no longer existed in Ayyūbid times, the locality was still inhabited, and it was the home of a holy figure, the *shaykh* Abū Zakariyyā al-Maghribī. He was known to chroniclers of the 7th/13th century, and was visited by the sultan Ṣalāḥ al-Dīn in person. He was buried near the tomb of ʿUmar (J. and D. Sourdel, *Annales archéologiques de Syrie*, iii, 1953, 83-8).

Bibliography: Ṭabarī, ii, 1270, 1792; Yaʿḳūbī, ii, 272; Ibn al-Athīr, vi, 372; *Aghānī*, vi, 195; vii, 55; xvi, 33; Bakrī, *Muʿdjam*, ed. Wüstenfeld, i, 362; Ibn ʿAsākir, *Taʾrīkh madīnat Dimashḳ*, ed. Ṣ. Munadjdjid, ii, Damascus 1954, 41, 104, 166; Ibn Shaddād, *La description de Damas*, ed. S. Dahān, Damascus 1956, 282-7; Yāḳūt, i, 865; ii, 696-7; iv, 480, 604; Ibn Shākir al-Kutubī, *ʿUyūn al-tawārīkh*, after H. Sauvaire, *Description de Damas*, in *JA*, 1896, 381, 407; ʿUmarīʿ, *Masālik al-Abṣār*, ed. A. Zakī Pāshā, i, 353-6; H. Lammens, *Études sur le règne du calife omaiyade Moʿâwiya Ier*, Paris 1908, 377-8, 444-5; R. Dussaud, *Topographie historique de la Syrie*, Paris 1927, 184, 298; M. Kurd ʿAlī, *Ghūṭat Dimashḳ*, Damascus 1368/1949, 241-3; Ḥ. Zayyāt, in *Mashriḳ*, xliii (1949), 425-48.

(D. SOURDEL)

DAYR MŪSA, a place near Kūfa on the way to Surā (Ṭabarī, ii, 644). Al-Ashʿath chose it as an assembly point for his troops after ʿAlī had sent him to fight the Khāridjites (Ṭabarī, i, 3422-4). Al-Mukhtār reached this Dayr in his bidding farewell to Yazīd b. Anas whom he sent to occupy Mosul (Ṭabarī, ii, 644). (SALEH A. EL-ALI)

DAYR SAMʿĀN, the name of various places in Syria, often confused by writers past and present, which corresponded to the sites of Christian monasteries still flourishing during the first centuries of Islam. Among the monasteries to which the name Simeon, common in Syria, was given, were Dayr Murrān [*q.v.*] near Maʿarrat al-Nuʿmān, whose name Dayr Samʿān was also incorrectly applied to the Dayr Murrān at Damascus, and the Byzantine constructions built on hill-tops (called in every case Djabal Samʿān) in the region of Antioch. The most important of the monasteries was 40 km. north-west of Aleppo, and owed its fame to a Stylite who lived there, Simeon the Elder. In the 4th/10th century it suffered severely during the wars between Byzantines and Arabs and, later, between Fāṭimids and Ḥamdānids. By Ayyūbid times it had probably been abandoned. Nevertheless one of the most interesting archaeological sites in northern Syria today is the remains of the 'basilica of St. Simeon' together with the ruins of the extensive quarters which accommodated pilgrims (to which the modern word *dayr* refers in particular). In the Middle Ages the Muslims transformed the basilica into a fortress called Ḳalʿat Samʿān. A second monastery, situated on the road from Antioch to Suwaydiyya, commemorated the Stylite Simeon the Younger, and it is no doubt to this Dayr Samʿān that the description by Ibn Buṭlān, reproduced by Yāḳūt (ii, 672), applies.

Bibliography: Ibn al-ʿAdīm, *Zubda*, S. Dahān ed., i, Damascus 1951, 224; J. Lassus, *Sanctuaires chrétiens de Syrie*, Paris 1947, index, s.v. Deir Semʾân, Qalʾat Semʾân, Mont Admirable; G. Tchalenko, *Villages antiques de la Syrie du Nord*, iii, Beirut 1958, 92, 100, 119, 124; Howard C. Butler, *Ancient architecture in Syria* (*Publications of the Princeton University archaeological expeditions to Syria in 1904-1909*), Division ii, Leiden 1919.

(D. SOURDEL)

DAYR AL-ZŌR, a small Syrian town, 195 m. above sea-level, on the right bank of the Euphrates. A suspension bridge 450 m. long, completed in 1931, crosses the river a short distance down-stream from the town. In 1867 it became the chief town of a *sandjaḳ* and later of a *muḥāfaẓa*, and today it has a modern aspect about it. The majority of its 22,000 inhabitants are Sunnī Muslims, and the small Christian minority comprises mainly Armenian refugees from former Turkish possessions. There are three mosques and several Orthodox and Roman Catholic churches. It is an important military centre, and also a stopping-place on the road from Aleppo and Damascus to Hasatché, Mosul and Baghdād. It thus takes the part played in the Middle Ages by Raḥbat Mālik and Ḳarḳīsiya.

It was probably the site of the ancient town of *Auzara*, from which, via the transposition Azuara, the name Dayr al-Zōr is derived. Its meaning is now explained as "convent set in a grove", referring to the clusters of tamarisks alongside the river. We may suppose that in the immediate neighbourhood of Dayr al-Zōr lay the Dayr al-Rummān mentioned by Yāḳūt (ii, 662) between al-Raḳḳa and Khābūr.

Bibliography: V. Cuinet, *La Turquie d'Asie*, ii, Paris 1890, 275 ff.; A. Musil, *The Middle Euphrates*, New York 1927, 1-3, 254; R. Dussaud, *Topographie historique de la Syrie*, Paris 1927, 456, 483-4; M. Canard, *Histoire des H'amdânides*, i, Algiers 1951, 95 (D. SOURDEL)

DAYṢĀNIYYA, Daysanites or Disanites, disciples of Bar Dīṣān, Bardesanes, Ibn Dayṣān, the celebrated syncretist heresiarch of Edessa, 154 (or 134)-201 A.D., co-disciple and contemporary of Abgar the Great. Arab authors writing of the dualists have placed him among the false prophets, between Zoroaster (Zaradu_sh_t) and Marcion (Marḳiyūn), after Manes (Mānī). The account of him which they give is very schematic and far from reliable. One may wonder if their knowledge of the Dayṣāniyya was confined to a chapter taken from one of the historians of the dualists, hitherto the sole source (*e.g.*, Abū ʿĪsā al-Warrāḳ). They give neither a biography of the author nor details of his descent. The doctrine attributed to him is a somewhat general dualism, regarded solely from the point of view of what may be called the physical state of being, in conformity with the constant preoccupation of Arab writers dealing with religions and sects, and which from the start envisages a theodicy. The Dayṣāniyya, taking light and darkness as the primal elements, looked upon them as the sources of good and evil respectively, with the distinction that light was active, living, perceptive and endowed with the fundamental attributes of life, knowledge and power, as against darkness which was purely passive, devoid of these attributes and endowed merely with existence. The cosmogonal drama stems from the determination of light to penetrate the darkness, by deliberate action, and so to bring about salvation. From this voluntary action it is then unable to free itself through some physical misfortune, the cause of which is not explained. Arab authors writing of the doctrine of Bar Dīṣān and his disciples differentiate between two doctrinal tendencies: some believe that in darkness there is a tendency, among the superior forms, to unite with the lower ranks of the creatures of light, who are subsequently unable to free themselves from this union; others consider the intermingling of light and darkness to be an action consciously undertaken by light, and followed by unexpected results inherent in the physical nature of darkness.

Alongside these ideas we may set those which emerge from the information invariably given by the Christian heresiologists, headed by Eusebius, Epiphanius, St. John of Damascus and the Syriac authors Theodore Bar Kouni, Elias of Nisibis, Moses Bar Kepha and St. Ephraem, and thereby may make some useful comparisons. We know that Bar Dīṣān, after receiving a pagan education, studied and reflected upon this cosmological system, influenced by the emanationist and Hermetic doctrines that were called astrology. For him, as for the rest of his contemporaries, the world was the result of the action upon beings of the influence of the spheres, exerted in succession by either the Monad or the Dyad. Persian influences, which underlie the beliefs of the region of Edessa where Bardesanes lived, are no doubt the basis of the dualist conception which, according to Arab writers, can be discovered in his natural philosophy. On the basis of the cosmological ideas provided by his education Bardesanes developed an interpretation of Christianity as it appeared to an inhabitant of Edessa who had grown up in Hierapolis in the house of a priest of the Syrian goddess, at the very time Lucian of Samosata described the ceremonies performed there (Lucian was born about 120 A.D.).

It is, no doubt, in his interpretation of Salvation that the origin must be found of the myths about the mingling of light and darkness, as given by Ibn al-Nadīm and al-_Sh_ahrastānī. The *Dialogue on the Laws on the Lands*, the principal surviving work of Bar Dīṣān—with the very remarkable text on Destiny preserved by Eusebius—allows us to understand his basic philosophy as distinguishing between the physical state of being, horologically dependent upon the stars (it is possible to find an echo of his argumentation against the belief in astrological determinism in the chapter Ibn Ḥazm devotes to refuting the astrologers, Cairo ed., iv, 24), and the moral destiny which, like the escape from darkness, results from the contradiction between the irremediably determined nature of matter and the free nature granted to man by his Creator, who made him in his own image. Moreover this God is, above all, the co-ordinator and creator of a hierarchy of beings whose original characters and affinities he has defined, and in conformity with which this world is constantly built up and destroyed. It is furthermore a world of failure—and here the Manichaean spirit is revealed—where God in his patience allows confusion and promiscuity until, after the passing of 6,000 years, he will recreate a world all whiteness, light and good.

Bardesanes' reputation as an astrologer, despite his own very clearly defined attitude, was finally fixed by St. Ephraem who fought against him in his own town of Edessa, wrote sermons against him and composed hymns which were destined to supplant those by Bardesanes. Posterity, while recognizing his attitude against Marcion, nevertheless included him in the line of Manichaeans, alongside Marcion. The Arab authors followed suit. For the Christian heresiologists his philosophy, elaborated under the influence of Valentinism, is tainted with Manichaeism.

Bibliography: Ibn al-Nadīm, Cairo edn., 474; _Sh_ahrastānī, on the margin of Ibn Ḥazm, Cairo, ii, 70-2; ʿAbd al-Ḳāhir al-Bag_h_dādī, Cairo 1910, 333; Bāḳillānī, ed. MacCarthy, Beirut, 67 ff.; Eusebius, apud *Patr. Graec.*, xx, 397-400, 573; v. Philosophumena, *Patr. Graec.*, xvi, col. 170/599; Merx, *Bardesanes von Edessa*, Halle 1863; F. Nau, *Bardisane l'Astrologue. Le livre des lois des pays*, Paris 1899; idem, *Dictionnaire de Théologie catholique*, s.v. (with bibliography). (A. ABEL)

ḌAYZAN [see AL-ḤAḌR].

DAZA [see TŪBŪ].

DEAD SEA [see BAḤR LŪṬ].

DEBDOU [see DUBDŪ].

DECCAN [see DAKHAN].

DEDE, literally "grandfather, ancestor", a term of reverence given to the heads of Darwī_sh_ communities, as alternative for *ata* and *baba*. The meaning "father" is attested in _Gh_uzz as early as the *Dīwān lug_h_āt al-Turk* (compare C. Brockelmann, *Mitteltürkischer Wortschatz*, Budapest and Leipzig 1928, under *dädä*). In western Turkish heroic tales, the term is also used (again as an alternative for *ata*) for the rhapsodes, thus Ḳorḳūt Ata, or Dede Ḳorḳūt [*q.v.*]. Concerning its use preceding a proper name in ancient Anatolian, cf. Ismail Hakkı Uzunçarşılı, *Osmanlı teşkilâtına methal*, Istanbul 1941, 173 (Dede Bâli in a Germiyān deed of foundation).

Dede, following the name, is used predominantly

in Mewlewī Derwīsh circles. It is also used as a term of respect for various wonder-working holy men in Istanbul and Anatolia, as reported by Ewliyā Čelebi (cf. Ewliyā Efendi, *Travels*, translated by Hammer, i, 2, 21, 25; ii, 97, 213).

With this meaning, Dede has also entered the Persian language (*dada*, plur. *dadagān*) (compare F. Steingass, *Persian-English Dictionary*, London 1830, s.v.). In the terminology of the Ṣafawid *ṭarīḳa*, *dada* denoted one of the small group of officers in constant attendance on the *murshid* (cf. *Tadhkirat al-Mulūk*, 125, n. 4).

Bibliography: other than the works already mentioned in the article: J. T. Zenker, *Türkisch-Arabisch-Persisches Handwörterbuch*, Leipzig 1866, s.v. 1; Hüseyin Kadrî, *Türk lûgati*, Istanbul 1928; Şeyh Süleyman Buhârî, *Lûgat-i çagatay ve türkîi osmanî*, Istanbul 1928; Abū Ḥayyān, *Kitāb al-idrāk li-lisān al-Atrāk*, ed. A. Caferoğlu; *İA*, iii, 506 (Mecdud Mansuroğlu). (Fr. Taeschner)

DEDE AGHAČ, now Alexandropolis, town on the Aegean coast of Thrace, founded in 1871, after the construction of the branch railway from the main Rumeli line. Being an outlet for the products of the hinterland it prospered rapidly, so that in 1300/1883 it supplanted Dimetoḳa as the centre of a *sandjaḳ* (*mutaṣarrīflīḳ*) of the *wilāyet* of Edirne. In 1894 the *sandjaḳ* of Dede Aghač comprised the *ḳaḍās* of Dede Aghač, Enez (Inos) and Sofrulu; the *ḳaḍā* of Dede Aghač comprised three *nāḥiyes*, Feredjik, Meghri and Semadrek, and 41 villages. This was the position until the region was lost as a result of the Balkan War of 1912-3. Two mosques were built in the town, one in the Muṣliḥ al-Dīn quarter in 1877, the other, in the Arab style, in the Ḥamīdiyye quarter in 1890, in the court-yard of which the *mutaṣarrif* Trabzonlu Hüseyn Rüshdī Pasha is buried. In 1894 there were some 1500 houses in Dede Aghač. In the village of Fere-īlīdjalarī there were foundations of Ghāzī Ewrenos Beg [*q.v.*] and of (Ḳodja) Dāwūd Pasha [*q.v.*].

Bibliography: *Edirne Sālnāmesi* for 1310 and 1317; ʿAlī Djewād, *Memālik-i ʿOthmāniyyenin taʾrīkh we djoghrāfyā lughātī*, i, Istanbul 1313; Bādi Aḥmed, *Riyāḍ-i Belde-i Edirne*, iii (Bayezid Library, Istanbul). (M. Tayyib Gökbilgin)

DEDE ḲORḲUT, a Turkish collection of twelve tales in prose, interspersed with verse passages, the oldest surviving specimen of the Oghuz epic and one of the most remarkable monuments of the Turkish language. They are named after the sage, a legendary character, who appears in each tale; he is the poet-singer who re-composes and recites each narrative, and bestows his blessings upon all. He is strongly reminiscent of the poet-magicians of the shamanistic era. The only existing complete manuscript is in Dresden (H. O. Fleischer, *Catalogus codicum man. orientalium* ... no. 86) of which J. H. von Diez made a copy for the Berlin Library (A. Pertsch, *Die Hand. Verzeichnisse* ... vi, no. 203). The works of von Diez (*Denkwürdigkeiten von Asien*, i, Berlin-Halle 1815, 399-457) and W. Barthold (*Zapiski Vostočnago Otdeleniya, Imp. Russ. Arkh. Obshčestva*, viii, 1894, 203-218; also ix, 1895; xi, 1898; xii, 1899; xv, 1904; xix, 1910) and the first edition of the book by Kilisli Muʿallim Rifʿat (*Kitāb-ī Dede Ḳorḳut ʿalā lisān-ī ṭāʾife-i Oghūzān*, Istanbul, 1332/1916) are based on the Berlin copy. The first edition in transcription with a long historical-bibliographical introduction by Orhan Şaik Gökyay (see bibliography) also uses the Berlin copy with some emendations from the Dresden copy. In 1950 Ettore Rossi discovered a second incomplete manuscript in the Vatican Library (*Un nuovo manoscritto del "Kitāb-i Dede Qorqut"* in *RSO*, xxv (1950), 34-43), which he published in facsimile with an Italian translation of the whole work and a 95-page introductory study. In 1958 Muharrem Ergin published a new transcription of the whole text with the facsimiles of both the original manuscripts and an introduction. A promised second volume will contain an index, grammar and notes. The work also aroused interest in Ādharbaydjān (for a criticism, on ideological grounds, see *Ost-Probleme*, iii, no. 35, 1951). An edition of the text appeared in Baku in 1939, and a Russian translation, based an a manuscript left by Barthold, in 1950.

The publication of the complete text in 1916 gave great impetus to Dede Ḳorḳut studies, and since then a growing number of scholars have been occupied with elucidating many historical, literary, linguistic, ethnological and folkloristic problems of the work. Despite the remarkable contributions of the above-mentioned authors and other scholars (among them M. F. Köprülü, A. Inan, P. N. Boratav, Hamid Araslı, Walter Ruben, Faruk Sümer, M. F. Kırzıoğlu, etc.) these problems continue to be controversial and there is still disagreement as to the date, authorship, the origin of the existing text, the identity of the heroes and of the place-names, etc. As research stands at present, we can cautiously assume that these stories were collected from oral tradition and put together and polished by an unknown author, probably during the second half of the 9th/15th century. They seem to be mainly based on the reminiscences of the Oghuz Turks concerning their life in their original home in Central Asia. In the present text they relate the life of the Oghuz Turkish tribes in north-eastern Anatolia, the deeds of their prince Bayundur Khan and their chief Salur Kazan Beg, of his wife Burla Khātun, and his son Uruz and their companions, their battles against other Turkish tribes and against the Black Sea Greeks and Georgians. The effect of Islamic culture is superficial. The pre-Islamic elements have strong common characteristics, in expression, style and content, with Anatolian and Central Asian popular literature. Some of the tales (*e.g.*, Beyrek) still live in Turkish folklore in slightly altered versions, and two tales (Depegöz and Deli Dumrul) show striking resemblances to Greek legends (Cyclops and Admetus) (cf. C. S. Mundy, *Polyphemus and Tepegöz*, *BSOAS*, xviii, 1956, 279-302).

Bibliography: Detailed bibliographical data are given in the following works : Orhan Şaik Gökyay, *Dede Korkut*, Istanbul 1938; Ettore Rossi, *Il Kitab-ı Dede Qorqut*, Vatican 1952; P. N. Boratav, *Korkut Ata*, in *İA*; idem, *Dede Korkut hikâyelerindeki tarihî olaylar ve kitabın telif tarihi*, *TM*, xiii, 1958, 30-62; Muharrem Ergin, *Dede Korkut Kitabı*, i, *Giriş-Metin-Facsimile*, Ankara 1958. For a recent study of the language of the work see E. M. Demircizade, *Kitabı Dede Korkud dastanlarının dili*, Baku 1959. A German translation of the text was published by J. Hein, *Das Buch des Dede Korkut*, Zurich 1958.

(Fahir İz)

DEDE SULṬĀN, epithet of a great religious fanatic by name of Bürklüdje Muṣṭafā, who was prominent in Anatolia in the time of Meḥemmed I (further information under BADR AL-DĪN B. ḲĀḌĪ SAMĀWNĀ). (Fr. Taeschner)

DEFTER [see DAFTAR].

DEFTER-I KHĀḲĀNĪ [see DAFTAR-I KHĀḲĀNĪ].

DEFTERDĀR [see DAFTARDĀR].

DEFTER EMINI, the title given in the Ottoman Empire to the director of the Daftar-i Khāḳānī [*q.v.*].

DEHĀS, a river in northern Afghānistān, explained by Ibn Ḥawḳal, 326, as *dah-ās* "(that which drives) ten mills". It rises in the Band-i Amīr massif in the mountains of Kūh-i Bābā (Bāmiyān district), and flows in a general northerly direction through several natural lakes, past Mad(a)r and Ribāt-i Karwān, finally reaching the region of Balkh [*q.v.*]. This area, especially the southern part, is dependent on the river for its irrigation and its consequent fertility—especially Siyāhgird, on the route to Tirmidh, as well as the suburb Nawbahār. Because of its importance for Balkh, the Dehās was also called Nahr Balkh (*e.g.*, *Ḥudūd al-ʿālam*, 73, 211, no. 24); in the Middle Ages, however, this was also one name for the Āmū Daryā [*q.v.*], Today the river is called Balkh-āb. The neglect of the irrigation system in the late middle ages and in modern times has caused the once fruitful country-side to revert to marsh land, and brought about the complete decline of the Balkh region.

In ancient times the Dehās was known as Βάκτρος or Ζαριάσπης and reached as far as the Oxus (Strabo, xi, 4, 2 (516); Pauly-Wissowa, *Real-Encyclop.*, ii, 2814). Since Islamic times its waters have become dispersed in canals or in swamps.

Bibliography: Iṣṭakhrī, 278; Le Strange, 420; J. Markwart, *Erānšahr*, 1901, 230; idem, *Wehrot*, Leiden 1938, 3 ff., 45, 169; W. K. Fraser-Tytler, *Afghanistan*, London 1950, index s.v. Balkh; A. Foucher, *De Kaboul à Bactres*, in *La Géographie*, xlii, 1924, 147-61. See also Bibliography to BALKH. Maps: *Ḥudūd al-ʿĀlam*, 339; Fraser-Tytler, 11.

(B. SPULER)

DEHHĀNĪ, KHODJA, Anatolian poet of the 7th/13th century, one of the earliest representatives of the *dīwān* poetry. Almost nothing is known about his life except that he came from Khurāsān and was at one time at the court of the Saldjūḳ sultan ʿAlāʾ al-Dīn Ḳayḳūbād III, for whom he wrote a Saldjūḳid *Shāhnāma* of 20,000 couplets which has not come down to us (M. F. Köprülü, *Anadolu Selçuklu Tarihinin Yerli Kaynakları*, in *Belleten*, vii, 27, 396-7). Only ten of his poems survive; they have been assembled from various *naẓīra* collections and published from 1926 onwards (see bibliography). Dehhānī, unlike his contemporaries, does not dwell on mystical or religious-didactic themes, but sings, with remarkable mastery of *ʿarūḍ* and a flowing style, worldly love, wine and other set themes of *dīwān* poets.

Bibliography: Köprülüzāde Meḥmed Fuʾād, *Khodja Dehhānī*, in *Ḥayāt*, i, 1, Ankara 1926; idem, *Selçuklu devri edebiyatı hakkında bazı notlar*, in *Ḥayāt*, iv, 103, Ankara 1928; Mecdut Mansuroğlu, *Anadolu Türkçesi*, xiii *asır*, *Dehhānī ve Manzumeleri*, Istanbul 1947.

(FAHİR İZ)

DEIR EZ-ZOR [see DAYR AL-ZŌR].

DELHEMME [see DHUʾ L-HIMMA].

DELHI, DELHI SULTANATE [see DIHLĪ, DIHLĪ SULTANATE].

DELI, Turkish adjective, meaning "mad, heedless, brave, fiery" etc. In the Ottoman empire the *deli*s were a class of cavalry formed originally in the Balkans (Rumeli, [*q.v.*]) at the end of the 9th/15th or the beginning of the 10th/16th century. Although later official usage, abandoning their true name, styled them *delīl* (guides), they continued to be popularly known by their original name until recent times.

The *deli*s were recruited partly among Turks and partly from Balkan nations such as the Bosniaks, Croats, and Serbs. At first they were private retainers in the suites of the Beylerbeyi (*Beglerbegi*, [*q.v.*]) of Rumeli and of the border beys. They were called *deli*, "mad", on account of their extraordinary courage and recklessness. The caliph ʿUmar was considered the patron of their *odjaḳ*s. Their motto was *yazïlan gelir basha*, "what is written (*i.e.*, destined) will come to pass".

The *deli*s were armed with curved scimitars, concave shields, spears, and maces (*bozdoghan*) attached to their saddles. They wore hats made of the skin of wild animals, such as hyenas or leopards, trimmed with eagles' feathers, and their shields were also decorated with such feathers. Their clothes and horsecloths were made of the skins of lions, tigers and foxes, and their breeches of wolves' or bears' skins, with the hairy side showing. Their calf-length spurred boots, pointed at the toes and high at the back, were known as *serḥaddlïḳ* or border boots. Their horses were renowned for their strength and endurance. They received a fixed salary from the Beylerbeyi or the Beys whom they served. In his *Ṭabaḳāt al-Mamālik fī Daradjāt al-Masālik*, Djelālzāde Muṣṭafā Čelebi mentions the *deli*s of the Bey of Semendere, Yaḥyā Pasha-zāde Bālī Bey, in connexion with the Mohacz expedition, and describes their clothes. In the first half of the 10th/16th century the forces of *deli*s of Yaḥyā Pasha-zāde Bālī Bey and Meḥemmed Bey and of Ghāzī Khusrew, Bey of the *sandjaḳ* of Bosnia, were famous in the Balkans; Khusrew Bey had 10,000 *deli*s in addition to his other forces.

The cavalry organization of the *deli*s spread later to Anatolia, where *deli*s were numbered among the retainers of *vezīr*s and Beylerbeyis. The clothes of *deli*s were changed in the 12th/18th century, when they were seen to wear pipe-like hats some twenty-six inches long, made of black lambskin with a turban wound round them.

Fifty to sixty *deli*s made up a company (under a standard, *bayraḳ*), groups of several companies being commanded by a *delibashï*. A new recruit was attached to the retinue of the *agha* [*q.v.*]; after learning the customs of the *odjaḳ* and proving his worth he took an oath to serve the Faith and the State and to be steadfast in battle. At the end of the ceremony, which included prayers, the recruit would then be entered as an *agha-čiraghï* (apprentice to an *agha*), a *deli*'s hat being ceremonially placed on his head. *Deli*s breaking their oath, failing to observe the rules of the *odjaḳ*, or deserting from the battlefield, were expelled and deprived of their hat. In the middle of the 11th/17th century a *deli*'s daily pay amounted to 12 or 15 aspers (*aḳče*s), according to Rycaut; Marsigli, writing at a later date, says that *deli*s were paid only while on active service.

The *deli*s served the state well in the 10th/16th and 11th/17th centuries, but later they became disorganized like the other military units. *Deli*s deprived of a patron, either through the dismissal of the *wālī* whom they served, or as a result of being paid off, wandered about in search of a new patron, raiding villages in the meantime. In the second half of the 12th/18th century their depredations were centred in the regions of Kütahya and Ḳonya. A *delibashï* by the name of Ḳodja-Bashï, who stood at the head of a numerous band, was notorious at Kütahya towards the end of the century. while the *delibashī* Ismāʿīl terrorized the region of Ḳonya in 1801. In the rebellion which took place in Ḳonya in 1803 against the "new army" (*niẓām-i djedīd*), Ismāʿīl assisted the rebels and, entering Ḳonyā, shut off the *ḳāḍi* ʿAbd al-Raḥmān Pasha who had been appointed *wālī* of Ḳonya.

The riotousness of the *deli*s reached its peak at the end of the 12th/18th and the beginning of the 13th/19th centuries, when they were a grave evil to the people of Anatolia. This prompted the Grand Vizier Yūsuf Ḍiyā Pasha to decide in Aleppo, on his return from the Egyptian expedition, to reorganize the *delis*. He had some of them sent to Baghdād, while those in his retinue were not demobilized but taken to Istanbul and billeted in the barracks at Üsküdar. The numerous *deli*s of the factious Gurdjī (Georgian) ʿOthmān Pasha in Rumeli were also brought to Istanbul and billeted in the Dāwūd Pasha barracks. Later all the *deli*s in Istanbul, amounting to 200 companies (*bayraḳs*) were sent off to Baghdād.

In 1829 after the Russian-Ottoman war, 2000 *deli*s commanded by 18 *delibashī*s and one *hāyṭabashī* (leader of armed band) moved into Anatolia and, gathering in the region of Ḳonya, tried to take up brigandage again. Sultan Maḥmūd II, determined to carry through his reforms, succeeded however in eliminating them, a remnant fleeing to Egypt and Syria. Of those who stayed behind, those who disobeyed the order to settle on the land were defeated by the *wālī* of Ḳaraman Esʿad Pasha.

(İ. H. Uzunçarşili)

DELI-ORMAN is the historical name of a district, the greater part of which lies in north-eastern Bulgaria and the remainder in southern Roumania. But as the term is a popular one, exact boundaries cannot be given. It is usually applied to the triangle, the apex of which is at the town of Rusčuk, and the two arms formed by the Danube and the Rusčuk-Varna railway, while the base is somewhat undefined and runs at a certain distance from the coast of the Black Sea. On the north-east, Deli-Orman is bounded by the Dobruja, in the south by the Bulgarian provinces of Tozluk and Gerlovo. The most important places in Deli-Orman are the towns of Balbunar, Kemanlar and Razgrad on Bulgarian territory and Akkadînlar and Kurtbunar on Roumanian.

The name Deli-Orman is of Turkish origin and means something like "wild forest, primeval forest". The country was actually at one time covered with primeval forest of which considerable stretches still survive at the present day. The wooded character of the district contrasts strongly with the flat and treeless Dobruja.

The name is also extended to the land on the left bank of the Danube, where in the Wallachian plain between the mouths of the Aluta and Vede lies a district called Teleorman (C. Jireček, *Einige Bemerkungen über die Überreste der Petschenegen und Kumanen, sowie die Völkerschaften der sogenannten Gagauzi und Surguči im heutigen Bulgarien*, in *Sitzungsber. d. K. böhmischen Gesellschaft der Wiss., Philos.-gesch. Klasse*, Year 1889, 11). According to Jireček, the name was formerly applied to the whole of the hilly forest country lying in front of the Carpathians in southern Moldavia and eastern Wallachia. Tomaschek thinks he recognizes the name Teleorman in a corrupt place-name in the Byzantine writer John Kinnamos of the 12th century. If he is right, the name Deli-Orman would be pre-Ottoman and come from an earlier North Turkish immigration.

Deli-Orman only a generation ago was still inhabited predominantly by Turks, but since the middle of the 19th century Bulgarian colonization has been steadily increasing. Nevertheless the Turks still form a considerable percentage of the population. One hears Turkish spoken everywhere, as is also the case in the provinces of Tozluk and Gerlovo adjoining on the south.

The Turks of this district form a particular type; they are remarkable for their tall stature and athletic build. Their language reveals dialectical peculiarities which are not found elsewhere in the Ottoman Turkish system but can be paralleled among the Christian Gagauz of Bessarabia. These peculiarities form the reason why they are regarded by some students as descendants of the Turkish Bulgars (K. and Ch. V. Škorpil, *Pametnici na gr. Oddessos-Varna*, Varna 1898, 4-6) and sometimes as descendants of the Kumans (V. Moškov, *Turetskiya plemena na Balkanskom poluostrově*, in *Izv. Imp. Russk. Geogr. Obshčestva*, xl, 1904, 409-17). But a strict philological analysis proves no more than that their language shows certain North Turkish features which perhaps go back to an old North Turkish stratum in the population. This stratum was however assimilated in two waves of southern Turkish elements which came later (cf. T. Kowalski, *Les Turcs et la langue turque de la Bulgarie du Nord-Est*, in *Mémoires de la Commission Orientaliste de l'Académie Polonaise des Sc. et des Lettres*, no. 16, 1933). Nevertheless it is significant that in the Balkan Peninsula the most compact mass of Turks is found not in the south-east but in the north-east, which makes very probable the hypothesis of a very early Turkish settlement in the lands south of the lower Danube. Turkish immigration in the Saldjūḳ period (6th/12th century) to the neighbouring Dobruja appears to be a historical fact (cf. F. Babinger, in *Isl.*, xi, 1921, 24).

In the Ottoman period Deli-Orman was a place of refuge for all kinds of political and religious refugees. It therefore still offers a great variety of sects. It was from here that in 819/1416 Shaykh Badr al-Dīn began his missionary career (F. Babinger, *Schejch Bedr ed-Dīn, der Sohn des Richters von Simāw*, in *Isl.*, xi, 1921, 60). At various periods different teachings, usually strongly tinged with Shīʿism, have found an asylum here. To this day there are in Deli-Orman considerable remnants of the followers of ʿAlī, who are here called ʿAlawī or Kîzîlbash (Redheads). Their headquarters seem to be the little town of Kemanlar (plural of Kemal with peculiar dissimilation of the two *l* sounds) in the vicinity of which is the famous, now disused, monastery of the Bektāshī saint Demir Baba (F. Babinger, *Das Bektaschi-Kloster Demir Baba*, in *MSOSAs.*, xxxiv, 1931; Babinger calls my attention to Ewliyā Čelebi, *Seyāḥatnāme*, v. 579, where there is a reference to Demir Baba as a disciple of Ḥādjdjī Bektāsh). There is a short poem (*nefes*) composed in honour of this sanctuary by the Bektāshī poet Derdli Kātib of Shumen (11th/17th century) in N. E. Bulgaria (Sadettin Nüzhet, *Bektaşî Şairleri*, Istanbul 1930, 55 ff.).

A remarkable feature is the wrestling bouts, apparently connected with the worship of Bektashī saints, which are the favourite amusement of the Turkish population of Deli-Orman. Indeed this little explored region is an interesting field for research not only for Turkologists but also for students of Islam.

Bibliography: In addition to references in the text: F. Kanitz, *Donau-Bulgarien und der Balkan*, iii,

Leipzig 1879 (with full indexes); C. Jireček, *Das Fürstenthum Bulgarien*, Prague-Vienna-Leipzig1891 (indexes); W. Stubenrauch, *Kulturgeographie des Deli-Orman*, in *Berliner Geographische Arbeiten*, fasc. iii, 1933 (with full references).—On the problem of population: L. Miletič, *Staroto bîlgarsko naselenije v sěveroiztočna Bîlgaraija*, Sofia 1902; S. S. Bobčev, *Za deliormanskitě Turci i za Kîzîl-basite*, in *Sbornik na Bîlgarskata Akademija na Naukitě*, xxiv, 1929.—On the language question: D. G. Gadžanov, two short notices in *Anzeiger der philos.-hist. Kl. d.k. Akad. d. Wiss, in Wien*, year 1911, no. v. and year 1912, no. iii; T. Kowalski, *Compte rendu de l'excursion dialectologique en Dobroudja, faite du 10 septembre au 1er octobre 1937* in *Bull. Intern. Acad. Polon. Philolog.*, 1938, i/3, 7-12; idem, *Les éléments ethniques turcs de la Dobroudja*, in *RO*, xiv, 1939, 66-80; J. Eckmann, *Razgard Türk ağzı, Türk Dili ve Edebiyatı hakkında araştırmalar*, Istanbul 1953, 1-25; P. Wittek, *Les Gagaouzes = Les gens de Kaykaus* in *RO*, xvii, 1953, 12-24; J. Németh, *Zur Einteilung der türkischen Mundarten Bulgariens*, Sofia 1956; A. Caferoğlu, *Die anatolische und rumelische Dialekte*, in *Philologiae Turcicae Fundamenta*, i, 1959, 239-60; G. Doerfer, *Das Gagausische*, *ibid.* 260-71; I. Conea and I. Donat, *Contribution à l'étude de la toponymie pétchénègue-comane de la Plaine Roumaine du Bas-Danube* in *Contributions Onomastiques*, Bucarest 1958, 139-67.

(T. Kowalski-
[J. Reychmann and A. Zajączkowski])

DELVINA, former residence of an Ottoman *sandjaḳ-bey* in Albania. In Ottoman times Delvina (so in Turkish and Albanian; Gk. Δέλβινον, Délvinon) formed a *sandjaḳ* of the Rumelian governorship. It stands 770 ft. above sea level, about 10½ miles from the shores of the Ionian sea, and consists of one single bazar street set in the midst of olive, lemon and pomegranate trees, surmounted by the ruins of an old, perhaps Byzantine, stronghold. The inhabitants numbered about 3000 before 1940, of whom two-thirds were Muslims and the remainder Orthodox Christians, as well as a few (about 40) Jews, all of whom subsisted by cattle-breeding, fisheries, olive plantations, and retail trade. Delvina, as principal town of the *sandjaḳ* of the same name, contains several mosques and Greek-Orthodox churches, and was formerly well fortified against the attacks of a population frequently restive under Ottoman dominion.

The history of Delvina in the Middle Ages is nebulous. In Byzantine times, probably also even earlier, it played a part of some importance, as is shown by the church of St. Nicholas (Kisha Shën Kollit bë Mesopotam) erected by the ruler Constantine IX Monomachos (1042-54)—of which some significant remains were until recently in existence; cf. Ph. Versanis, Βυζαντιακός νάος ἐν Δελβίνῳ, in Ἀρχαιολογικόν Δελτίον, i (1915), 28-41, and S. Stoupi, Μοναστήρια τοῦ Δελβίνου, in Ἠπειρωτικὴ Ἑστία, iv (1959), 331 ff.—and likewise the imposing outworks of the castle which must have had a part to play in feudal times in Albania. An illustration of the church of St. Nicholas in its present state of conservation is to be found in *Historia e Shqipërisë*, Tirana 1959, 191, fig. 30. Since the establishment of Ottoman domination (end of the 9th/15th century) until well into the 19th century Delvina was a bulwark against the independent minded Albanians of the Himara region, who were constantly in conflict with their overlords. In the 10th/16th century Delvina was also a centre of the Khalwetī order of dervishes, which was spread in the direction of Albania about 937/1530 by one Yaʿḳūb Efendi of Yanina, to be later supplanted by the Bektāshīs. The Khalwetīs attracted a considerable following there, and some of the 12 mosques, two madrasas, and baths owed their beginnings to the adherents of this order. Yūsuf Sinān, son of the same Yaʿḳūb Efendi, has expatiated upon this point in detail in his *Menāḳib-i Sherīf* [sic] *we ṭarīḳanāme-yi pīrān we meshāyikh-i tarīḳat-i ʿaliyye-yi Khalwetiyye*, Istanbul 1290/1873; cf. H. J. Kissling in *ZDMG*, ciii, 1953, 264.

Delvina is depicted as a sizeable colony by Ewliyā Čelebi in the *Seyāḥatnāme*, viii, 668 ff.; it had first come into contact with the Ottomans in 835/1431-2 through the incursions of Sinān Pasha (cf. Ḥādjdjī Khalīfa, *Taḳwīm al-tawārīkh*, Istanbul 1146, 104), but was not definitely brought under subjection until 944/1537, by the Albanian Ayās Pasha [*q.v.*] in the reign of Sulaymān the Magnificent (cf. Fr. Babinger, *Rumelische Streifen*, Berlin 1938, 9 ff.). The pentagonal castle, open towards the east, in the interior of which was the residence of the fort governor, a mosque, powder-magazine, and granaries, made a deep impression on the Ottoman globe-trotter. The largest mosque of that time was the Khunkār Djāmiʿi, founded by Bāyezīd II, which has long since disappeared. Nothing has remained of all the Islamic places of worship of older times, with the exception of the mosque of Ḥadjdjī Aḥmed Agha built in 1269/1872.

In 1913 Delvina came within the newly established principality of Albania, having formerly belonged to Greece (cf. L. von Thallóczy, *Illyrisch-albanische Forschungen*, i, Munich and Leipzig 1916, 360 (Delvina in 1847), and ii, 240 (transfer to Albania); also Edith P. Stickney, *Southern Albania 1912-1923*, Stanford 1926, *passim*.

Bibliography: In addition to references above: *Rumeli und Bosna geographisch beschrieben von Mustafa Ben Abdalla Hadschi Chalfa*, tr. J. von Hammer, Vienna 1812, 130 (whence the misspelling "Delonia"); M. F. Thielen, *Die europäische Türkey*, Vienne 1828, 58 ff. (also "Delonia"); Fr. Babinger in Karl Baedeker, *Dalmatien und die Adria*, Leipzig 1929, 250; Delvina was seldom visited and described by travellers, but cf. W. Leake, *Travels in Northern Greece*, i, London 1835; cf. here the important statements made by Frashëri, *Ḳāmūs al-aʿlām*, iii, Istanbul 1308/1889, 2153, with detailed information on Delvina up to 1890. For the 17th century the most important source is Ewliyā Čelebi, *Seyāḥatnāme*, viii, 668 ff.; on the opposition of the Albanian population to the Ottomans at the end of the 15th century cf. Fr. Babinger, *Das Ende der Arianiten*, *SBBayr. Ak.*, phil.-hist. Kl., 1960, Fasc. 4, 19 ff., and the sources, mostly ms., there enumerated. On the Delvina basin cf. H. Louis, *Albanien. Eine Landeskunde*, Stuttgart 1927, 9 ff., esp. 102. See further ARNAWUTLUḲ.

(Fr. Babinger)

DEMİRBASH, literally iron-head, a Turkish term for the movable stock and equipment, belonging to an office, shop, farm, etc. In Ottoman usage it was commonly applied to articles belonging to the state and, more especially, to the furniture, equipment, and fittings in government offices, forming part of their permanent establishment. The word Demirbash also means stubborn or persistent, and it is usually assumed that this was the sense in which it was applied by the Turks to King Charles XII of Sweden. It is, however, also possible that the nickname is an ironic comment on his long frequentation of Turkish government offices.

Bibliography: *BSLP*, 1960/1, XXXIII.

(ED.)

DEMIR KAPİ [see DAR-I ĀHANĪN].

DEMNAT [see DAMNĀT].

DEMOKRAT PARTİ, Turkish political party, registered on 7 January 1946. In the general elections held in July of the same year, the party put up 273 candidates for 465 seats; sixty one of them were elected, forming the main opposition group. The first party congress, held on 7 January 1947, formally adopted the party programme and charter. As a result of various internal disagreements, notably the secession of a group of deputies who formed the National Party (*Millet Partisi*) in July 1948, the strength of the Democrat Party in the Assembly had fallen by 1950 to 31. Their influence in the country, however, continued to grow, and in the general election of May 1950 they won a clear majority. The *Demokrat Parti* now took over the government of the country, and remained in power for the next ten years. A series of cabinets was formed, Celâl Bayar and Adnan Menderes retaining the offices of President and Prime Minister respectively. In the general elections of 1954 the D. P. won an increased majority, but in the election of 1957 they were able to win only a popular plurality, which, however, gave them a clear parliamentary majority over a divided opposition. After a period of mounting discontents the *Demokrat Parti* was ousted from power by the revolution of 27 May 1960 (see TÜRKIYE, history). It was formally dissolved on 29 September 1960.

Bibliography: K. H. Karpat, *Turkey's politics, the transition to a multi-party system*, Princeton 1959, 408-31 and *passim*; Tarık Z. Tunaya, *Türkiyede Siyasî Partiler*, Istanbul 1952, 646-92; B. Lewis, *Democracy in Turkey*, in *MEA*, x, 1959, 55-72; G. Lewis, *Turkey: the end of the first Republic*, in *World Today*, September 1960, 377-86; surveys of events in *COC*, *MEA*, *MEJ*, *OM*.

(ED.)

DEMOTIKA [see DIMETOKA].

DENEB [see NUDJŪM].

DENIA [see DĀNIYA].

DEÑİZLİ, chief town of the *wilāyet* of the same name, in south-western Anatolia. Situated in a fertile plain which has been inhabited since the earliest times, Deñizli in the 14th century replaced Lādīķ, the ancient *Laodiceia ad Lycum*, whose ruins stand at Eski Ḥiṣār, on the Çürük Şu, a tributary of the Büyük Menderes, near the railway station of Gondjali, 9 km. from Deñizli. Built in the 3rd century B.C. by the Seleucid Antiochus II on the site of the ancient Diospolis (Pliny, v, 105), Laodicaea controlled an important meeting point of trade routes, and in Roman times was ranked as one of the principal towns of Phrygia (Strabo, xii, 578). Until the end of the 11th century Laodicaea was Byzantine, but it was then disputed between the Comneni and the Saldjūķid Turks who took possession of it on several occasions. Alexis I captured it from them in 491/1098 and held it temporarily (Anna Comnena, ed. Leib, iii, 27). In 513/1119, it was recaptured and fortified by John Comnenus (Cinn., 5; Nicetas, 17); although sacked in 553/1158 and 585/1189 by Turkish tribes who had settled at about that time in the district, it nevertheless remained in the hands of the Byzantines (Cinn., 198; Nicetas, 163, 523) until 602/1206, on which date Theodore Lascaris was forced to cede Laodicaea and Chonae (now Honaz) to Manuel Mavrozomes, father-in-law of Ghiyāth al-Dīn Kaykhusraw I (Nicetas, 842; Houtsma, *Rec. de textes rel. à l'hist. des Seldj.*, iii, 66-7; iv, 26). However in 655/1257 ʿIzz al-Dīn Kaykāwus II gave the town to Michael Palaeologus in order to secure his help against his brother Rukn al-Dīn and the latter's allies, the Mongols; but the little Greek garrison could no longer hold out (Acropolitus, 153-4) and two years later the town was once again in the hands of the Turcomans. It is at about this time, in eastern documents, that together with Lādīķ one first finds a mention of Ṭoñuzlu; this name was later to be changed to Deñizli, and it was to take the place of Lādīķ in the 14th century. In 659/1261 the chief Turcoman of the district, Meḥmed Beg—who must not be confused with the Ķaramānid of the same name who died in 675/1277, nor with Meḥmed Beg Aydînoghlu who died in 734/1334—rose in revolt against ʿIzz al-Dīn Kaykāwus and conquered the district; then, refusing allegiance to the Saldjūķid princes, he asked Hūlāgū for a charter of formal investiture for the towns of Ṭoñuzlu, Khōnās (Honaz) and Ṭālamānī (Dalaman). Thus the first Turcoman principality of Deñizli was founded, but it was short-lived: in 660/1262, at the request of Rukn al-Dīn, Hūlāgū marched against Meḥmed Beg who was defeated and put to death. His son-in-law ʿAlī Beg became chief of the Turcomans of the region, while the towns of Lādīķ and Khōnās were included in the possessions which were granted, in 669/1271, to the sons of the vizier Fakhr al-Dīn ʿAlī. It was, no doubt, in order to regain his independence that ʿAlī Beg took part, in 675/1277, in the revolt of Djimrī and Meḥmed the Ķaramānid; but he was defeated by the sultan's army and put to death. However, as a result of the weakness of the central authority, the Ṭoñuzlu-Lādīķ region fell into the hands of the Turcoman amīrs of Germiyān who in the last quarter of the 13th century seized the town of Kütāhya and lost no time in proclaiming their independence. According to the accounts of al-ʿUmarī and Ibn Baṭṭūṭa who visited the town in 730/1330 and 732/1332, Ṭoñuzlu and the surrounding district were at that time in the hands of an amīr of the Germiyān family, Yînandj Beg. However the town, though still prosperous, lost its value owing to the conquests of the Turcoman amīrs of Menteshe who, at the end of the 13th century, took possession of the sea-coast of Caria; Ṭoñuzlu which was disputed between the amīrs of Menteshe and the Germiyān thereby lost its position as a frontier post and could no longer remain the centre of a principality of any great importance. In 792/1390, the district of Ṭoñuzlu-Lādīķ was restored to the Ottoman empire at the same time as the amīrate of Germiyān. Temporarily given back to the Germiyān by Timūr who stayed in the town in the autumn of 1402, Ṭoñuzlu served as a residence, in the reign of Bāyezīd II, for one of his sons; it was at that time the chief town of a *liwāʾ* attached to the *eyālet* of Anatolia. In the 17th century it was reduced to the rank of *ķaḍāʾ* attached to the *sandjaķ* of Kütāhya. It was at that time that the name Ṭoñuzlu was replaced by Deñizli, under which name the town was mentioned in the accounts of Ewliyā Čelebi and Kātib Čelebi. According to these travellers, Deñizli was then divided into 24 districts and included 7 mosques; a small fort protected the bazaar, whilst the population was housed outside the town proper, in gardens and fields; this situation still remains to the present day and, despite the allegations of European travellers in the 19th century, it is not the consequence of the terrible earthquake which struck the town in 1702, when 12,000 people perished. Although Deñizli has never managed to regain the position of importance it enjoyed in the Middle Ages, since the Republic was established it has once again become increasingly prosperous. In 1891 a railway line was built connecting Deñizli, via Gondjalî, with the Izmir-Eğridir line; Deñizli, which since the end of the 19th century had been the chief town of a *sandjaḳ* attached to the *wilāyet* of Aydîn, after the Republic became the chief town of the *wilāyet* of Deñizli. The population consisted of 19,461 inhabitants in 1940 (compared with 15,787 in 1927). Deñizli now possesses a Lycée and is a centre for agricultural products (fruit, cereals, tobacco, cotton, sesame, poppy-seed) and handicraft industries (tanning, weaving, carpet-making). The remains of the ancient towns scattered about the region (ruins of Laodicaea, Hierapolis, Hydrela, Kolossai, Chonae) also make it an important tourist centre.

Bibliography: Houtsma, *Recueil*, iii, 66-7, iv, 26, 288-9, 308, 333; ʿUmarī in *Not. et Ext. des MSS de la Bibl. Nat.*, xiii, 358-9; Ibn Baṭṭūṭa, ed. Defrémery and Sanguinetti, ii, 270-7; Ewliyā Čelebī, *Seyāḥatnāme*, ix, Istanbul 1935, 192-5; Kātib Čelebī, *Djihānnümā*, ed. Ibrāhīm Müteferrika, Istanbul 1145/1732, 634; Pauly-Wissowa, xii, s.v. *Laodikeia*; W. M. Ramsay, *The cities and bishoprics of Phrygia*, i, Oxford 1895, 32-83; V. Cuinet, *La Turquie d'Asie*, iii, Paris 1894, 614-28; A. Philippson, *Reisen und Forschungen im westlichen Kleinasien*, iv, Gotha 1914, 67-70, 85-107; I. H. Uzunçarşılı, *Kitabeler*, ii, Istanbul 1929, 181-209; Cl. Cahen, *Notes pour l'histoire des Turcomans d'Asie Mineure*, in *JA*, ccxxxix (1951), 335-40; Besim Darkot, *İA*, iii, s.v. Deñizli. (I. Mélikoff)

DEOBAND, in the Sahāranpur district of Uttar Pradesh, is a place of great antiquity but its early history is shrouded in myth and romance. In one of the many groves which almost surrounds the site there is an ancient temple of Devī. On this account the name is supposed to be a corruption of *Devī-ban*, 'forest of the goddess'. The earliest recorded reference to it is found in the *Āʾīn-i Akbarī* where Abu 'l-Faḍl refers to a fort of 'baked bricks in Deoband'. Monuments of earlier periods are, however, found in Deoband. The Čhattā Masdjid is considered to be one of the oldest monuments of Deoband, dating back to the early Paṭhān period. According to tradition, Shaykh ʿAlāʾ al-Dīn known as *Shāh-i Djangal Bāsh*, who lies buried here, was a pupil of Ibn al-Djawzī and a disciple of Shaykh Shihāb al-Dīn Suhrawardī. Some mosques and other buildings constructed during the reigns of Sikandar Lodi (894-923/1489-1517), Akbar (963-1014/1556-1605), and Awrangzīb (1068-1118/1658-1707) are still extant.

Deoband is known to-day for its great seat of Muslim religious learning, the *Dār al-ʿUlūm*, founded by Ḥādjdjī Muḥammad ʿĀbid Ḥusayn with the support of three eminent scholars in the Education Department, and to which Mawlawī Muḥammad Ḳāsim was appointed as patron-principal in 1282/1867. During the last 90 years this institution has attained an unrivalled place amongst Muslim religious institutions. It combines the characteristics of three different types of religious institutions which existed in Dihlī, Lucknow and Khayrābād during the 13th/19th century. The institutions of Dihlī emphasized the teaching of *tafsīr* and *ḥadīth*; the institutions of Lucknow [see DĀR AL-ʿULŪM, (*c*), (*d*)] took to *fiḳh*, while Khayrabād [*q.v.*] specialized in *ʿilm al-kalām* and philosophy. Deoband represents a synthesis of these three experiments, but its main emphasis has been on the traditions established by Shāh Walī Allah and his Dihlī school of *muḥaddithīn*. It attracts students from many different parts of the Muslim world. Residential accommodation is provided for nearly 1500 students. The buildings of the *Dar al-ʿUlūm* comprise a mosque, a library, and a number of separate lecture halls for *ḥadīth*, *tafsīr*, *fiḳh* etc. Its library, though without a catalogue, is one of the biggest manuscript libraries in India. It comprises 67,000 Arabic, Persian and Urdū books, both printed and manuscript. The system of instruction is traditional and the emphasis is more on building up a religious personality than on imparting knowledge with a view to fulfilling the requirements of the modern age. The institution has, therefore, produced mainly religious leaders though its contribution in the political sphere cannot be ignored. Many of those associated with it have been in the forefront of the national struggle for freedom. The principal officers of the *Dār al-ʿUlūm* are: *Sarparast* (patron), *muhtamim* (secretary), *Ṣadr mudarris* (principal) and *Muftī*. Very eminent persons like Mawlānā Rashīd Aḥmad Ganguhī, Mawlānā Muḥammad Yaʿḳub, Mawlānā Ashraf ʿAlī, Shaykh al-Hind Maḥmūd Ḥasan, Mawlānā Anwar Shāh Kashmīrī and Sayyid Ḥusayn Aḥmad Madanī have filled these posts. The present secretary, Mawlānā Muḥammad Ṭayyib is a grandson of the founder of the institution. The *Djamiʿat ʿUlamāʾ-i Hind*, a very influential organization of the Indian *ʿUlamāʾ*, derives its main ideological strength from the *Dār al-ʿUlūm*.

Bibliography: *District Gazetteers of the United Provinces*, ii (Lucknow 1921), 224-35; Sayyid Maḥbūb Riḍwī, *Taʾrīkh-i Deoband*, (Deoband 1372 A.H.); Mawlānā Muḥd. Ṭayyab, *Ḥālāt-i Dār al-ʿUlūm Deoband*, (Deoband 1378 A.H.); G. M. D. Ṣufī, *Al-Minhādj*, (Lahore 1941); Muḥammad Miyān, *ʿUlamāʾ-i Ḥaḳḳ*, Part I (Morādābād 1939) 49 ff; S. M. Ikram, *Mawdj-i Kawthar*, Lahore n.d.; Imdād Ṣābirī, *Farangiyŏ ka djāl*, Dihlī 1949, 177-89; W. Cantwell Smith, *Modern Islam in India*, London 1946, 294-7; Muḥammad Yaʿḳūb Nānawtawī, *Sawāniḥ ʿUmarī* (*Muhammad Ḳāsim*), Deoband n.d., 14-5; Ḥusayn Aḥmad Madanī, *Safarnāma Asīr-i Māltā*..., Deoband n.d. (on the character and political activities of Shaykh al-Hind Maḥmūd Ḥasan, the first student and son of a co-founder); Maḥbūb Riḍawī, *Dār al-ʿUlūm Deoband kī taʿlīmī khuṣūṣiyyāt*, Deoband n.d.; idem, *Dār al-ʿUlūm Deoband ek naẓar mē*, Deoband n.d.; M. O'Dwyer, *India as I knew it, 1855-1905*, London 1925, 178-81, 189; Manāzir Aḥsan Gaylānī, *Sawāniḥ Ḳāsimī*, Deoband n.d. (K. A. Nizami)

DĒRADJĀT, name of a tract lying between the River Indus to the east and the Sulaymān Mountains to the west, including the modern districts of Dēra Ismāʿīl Khān and Dēra Ghāzī Khān. The name Dēradjāt is a supposed Persian plural of the Indian word *déra*, "tent, encampment", and means the "country of the *deras*", that is, of the three towns Dēra Ismāʿīl Khān, Dēra Ghāzī Khān, and Dēra Fatḥ Khān, founded by Balōč leaders in the early 10th/16th century. (See BALŌČISTĀN). These three towns were all close to the R. Indus, and have been liable to damage by erosion; hence the modern towns show much rebuilding, especially Dēra Ismāʿīl Khān which was largely destroyed under Sikh rule. The mints of Dēradjāt and Dēra under the Durrānī kings were at Dēra Ismāʿīl Khān and Dēra Ghāzī Khān respectively; copper coins were also struck at Dēra Fatḥ Khān. Afghāns form the most important element in the population, especially in the Dāmān or western part, and the Balōč are numerous in the south. (M. LONGWORTH DAMES*)

DERBEND, a town of Dāghistān [*q.v.*], called Bāb al-Abwāb [*q.v.*] by the Arabs in the Middle Ages. Only the modern period is described under this heading.

Having belonged to Russia from 1722 to 1735, Derbend was restored to the Persians, and Nādir Shāh attempted to restore to it its former importance; but after the death of this sovereign it passed into the hands of the Khān of Kūba, Fatḥ ʿAlī (1765). Recaptured by the Russians in 1796, it was soon evacuated, to be ultimately occupied on 21 June/3 July 1806.

Under Russian domination the town has lost its former military importance. It has, however, retained traces of its past as a fortified town, carefully preserved. Of the two walls which formerly enclosed the town and the citadel, the one most badly damaged is the south wall, now reduced to four gates and three towers, whereas the north wall, with its 8 gates and 30 towers, is still intact over almost all its length.

To the north of the town lies the Arab cemetery of Ḳïrḳlar, which dates from the 8th/14th century. The old congregational mosque constructed in 783/1381-2 out of a Christian church, several mosques of the 17th and 18th centuries, and a few very old caravanserais, remain practically intact. Remains of the old irrigation system bear witness to a very advanced technical civilization.

The economic development of the old fortified city is very remarkable. It is favoured by a well-cultivated soil (supporting vines and fruit-trees), a sub-soil rich in petroleum and natural gas, the proximity of the sea which makes it an important fishing-port, and finally the Bakū—Makhač—Ḳala railway which allows for the transport of merchandise and the multiplication of food industries which make use of the local produce.

At the beginning of this century Muslims made up about 57 per cent of the population, against 18 per cent of Russians, 16 per cent Jews, and 7 per cent Armenians. At that time there was a penetration of socialistic ideas under the influence on the one hand of the Bolshevik organizations of Tiflis and Bakū, on the other of political exiles like I. V. Maligine and some others. The first agitators at Derbend were the Russian railway workers, whose rôle became apparent in the 1905 revolution. In December 1917 Soviet power was established in the town and entrusted to the workers' and soldiers' Soviet set up in the February revolution. From July 1918 to March 1920 the town was stricken with civil war; the power was in the hands of local nationalists ranged against the Bolsheviks, who had to appeal to the Red Army to establish their authority. Since the creation of the Republic of Dāghistān, Derbend has become the capital of the district of that name, and in importance the second town of the Republic. In 1956 its population was 41,800.

Bibliography: W. Barthold, in *Zapiski vost. otd. Imp. Russkago Arkh. Obshč.*, xix, XI ff., 073 ff.; xxi, IV ff.; idem, DERBEND, in *EI*[1]; E. I. Kazubskiy, *Istoriya goroda Derbenta* 1806-1906, Temīr Khān Shurā 1906; Abbas Kuli Agha, *Gulistān-i Iram*, Baku 1926; M. I. Artamonov, *Nastoyashčiy Derbent*, in *Archéologie soviétique*, 1946; N. B. Baklanov, *Pamyātniki Dagestana*, viii, 1, Leningrad 1955. See also the Bibliography to BĀB AL-ABWĀB. (H. CARRÈRE D'ENCAUSSE)

DERDLİ, İBRAHİM, Turkish folk poet (1186-1261/1772-1845) born in Shahnalar, a forest village in the province of Bolu. At the death of his father, he tried his fortune in Istanbul but was soon forced to go back to his native province. He then spent ten years in Egypt and travelled extensively in Anatolia where he became one of the leading poet-singers of the period. Again in Istanbul under Maḥmūd II, he became a popular figure of the coffee-houses frequented by folk poets and wrote his famous *ḳaṣīda* on the fez, praising this newly introduced headgear, and enjoyed for a short time the favour of the court. Falling into disgrace, he left Istanbul and wandered again in Anatolia and, after an unsuccessful attempt at suicide, died in Ankara.

In his poems in *ʿarūḍ*, written in an awkward language, he is an unskilled imitator of *dīwān* poets, particularly of Fuḍūlī [*q.v.*]. His poems written in the traditional syllabic metre, though not perfect in language and style, echo in sincere tones his vagrant and nonchalant character, and reflect his endless sufferings in his chequered life.

Bibliography: *Dīwān*, lithograph edition, 1329/1913; Ahmet Talât, *Aşık Derdli, Hayatı-Divanı*, Bolu 1928; M. F. Köprülü, *Türk Sazşairleri Antolojisi*, xii, Istanbul 1940; Cahit Öztelli, *Derdli ve Seyrani*, Istanbul 1953. (FAHİR İZ)

DEREBEY, 'valley lord', the Turkish name popularly given to certain rulers in Asia Minor who, from the early 12th/18th century, made themselves virtually independent of the Ottoman central government in Istanbul. The Ottoman historians usually call them *mutaghallibe*, usurpers, or, when a politer designation was needed, *Khānedān*, great families. The derebeys became in effect vassal princes, ruling over autonomous and hereditary principalities. In time of war they served, with their own contingents, in the Ottoman armies, which came to consist to a large extent of such quasi-feudal levies. Though given, as a matter of form, such titles as *muḥaṣṣil* and *mütesellim*, ostensibly as representatives of the titular governors, they were effectively independent within their own territories. Unlike the usurping pashas who had won similar autonomies in other Ottoman provinces, the Anatolian derebeys had deep local roots, and could count on powerful local loyalties. Being under no pressure, as were the pashas, to extract a quick return during a brief tenure of power, they were able to adopt more constructive policies, taking care for public security, the development of trade, and the well-being of their subjects, Muslim and non-Muslim alike. The travellers attest their good government, and the regard in which they were held by their people. The Porte found itself obliged to tolerate them and afford them some form of recognition, proceeding against them only if they openly rebelled against it. The war with Russia in 1182/1768-1188/1774 brought new opportunities, and helped to extend the derebey regimes over most of Anatolia. By the beginning of the 19th century only the *eyālet*s of Karamān and Anadolu were still under direct administration by governors sent from Istanbul. During the reign of Selīm III the derebeys reached the summit of their powers, and even began to play an important rôle in the affairs of the court and capital. Some of them, notably the Ḳara ʿOthmān-oghlu and the Čapan-oghlu, supported the reforms of Selīm III, while their rivals the Djānīkli bitterly opposed them. While on the one hand the struggle between reformers and reactionaries in the capital was confused with the rivalries of the feudal chiefs, on the other the clash between the Čapan-oghlu and the Djānīkli in central and eastern Anatolia assumed the appearance of a quarrel over the Sultan's New Order (see NIẒĀM-I DJADĪD). Where the derebeys did apply the New Order in their territories, they seem to have done so for their own purposes and to their own profit, using goverment money to strengthen their own armed forces. (For examples of abuse and corruption in the application of the New Order by the derebeys see ʿĀṣim, i, 111-3; cf. Akçura 140, Miller 100-101).

The leading derebeys played a role of some importance in the political struggles of 1807-8, and the victory of the Bayraḳdār Muṣṭafā Pasha seemed to consecrate their power. One of his first tasks, after becoming Grand Vezir, was to convene a great imperial assembly in Istanbul, to which he invited dignitaries of various types from all over the Empire. The great derebeys from Anatolia came to Istanbul in person, with large forces of armed retainers, and seem to have played a considerable part in the proceedings. A deed of agreement (*Sened-i Ittifāḳ*) confirmed their rights, privileges, and autonomies, which were now, for the first time, officially defined and ratified (Shānīzāde, i, 66-73; Djewdet, *Taʾrīkh*², ix, 3-7 and 278-83; Uzunçarşılı, *Alemdar*, 138-44; Miller, 283-91. On the *Sened-i Ittifāḳ* see further A. Selçuk Özçelik in *İstanbul Üniv. Hukuk Fak. Mec.* xxiv, 1959, 1-12).

Sultan Maḥmūd II, who had thus been compelled, at the dawn of the 19th century, to recognize the privileges of a feudal baronage, was determined to end them; the 19th century provided him with the means. After the conclusion of the war with Russia in 1812, he turned his attention to the task of establishing the authority of the central government in the provinces. By a series of political, military, and police actions he overcame rebellious pashas and autonomous derebeys alike, and replaced them by appointed officials sent from Istanbul. (For the impressions of a contemporary Western observer see A. Slade, *Record of travels in Turkey, Greece etc.*, i, London 1832, 215 ff.). The work of centralization was continued under his successors; the last major military expedition was that of 1866, sent to subjugate the surviving derebey dynasties in the Čukurova district, such as the Menemendji-oghlu, the Kökülü-oghlu, and the Kozan-oghlu of Kozan (Djewdet, *Maʿrūḍāt*, in *TTEM*, 14/91, 1926, 117 ff.). Though the autonomous principalities of the derebeys had disappeared, the term derebey remained part of the Turkish political vocabulary, used to designate large-scale hereditary landlords, especially in southern and eastern Turkey, who exercised quasi-feudal rights over their peasantry (see for example the remarks of K. H. Karpat in *Social themes in contemporary Turkish literature*, *MEJ*, 1960, 34-5).

The best known Derebey families were:

1) The Ḳara ʿOthmān-oghlu of Aydîn, Manisa, and Bergama; they ruled the sandjaḳs of Saruhan and Aydîn and their influence extended from the Great Menderes river to the coast of the sea of Marmara. [See ḲARA ʿOTHMĀN-OGHLU].

2) The Čapan (Čapar, Djabbār)-oghlu of Bozok, of Turkoman origin, practically contemporary with the Ḳara ʿOthmān-oghlu. They ruled the sandjaḳs of Bozok (Yozgad), Kayseri, Amasya, Ankara, Niğde, and, at the height of their power, also controlled Tarsus. The first member of the family whose name is known was Aḥmed Pasha, the mutaṣarrif of Bozok, who was deposed by order of the Porte in 1178/1764-5. (Wāṣif, i, 233 ff., 268). He was succeeded by his son Muṣṭafā Bey, who was murdered by his body-guard in 1196/1781 (Djewdet, *Taʾrīkh*², ii, 171-2); he in turn was followed by his brother Sulaymān Bey, the most powerful of the Čapan-oghlu, who played a rôle of some importance during the reigns of Selīm III, Muṣṭafā IV, and Maḥmūd II. After his death in 1229/1814, his lands reverted to the direct authority of the Porte. Descendants of the family held high offices under the Sultans as governors and generals. One of them, Čapanzāde Agāh Efendi (1832-1885), played a pioneer rôle in the development of Turkish journalism (see DJARĪDA). Another led an anti-nationalist band during the War of Independence. Their name survives in a Turkish proverbial phrase, with the meaning of a hidden snag.

3) The family of ʿAlī Pasha of Djānīk, in Trebizond and its neighbourhood. The founder of the family, Djānīkli ʿAlī Pasha [*q.v.*] was succeeded by his two sons Miḳdād Aḥmed Pasha (executed in 1206/1791-2) and Ḥusayn Baṭṭāl Pasha (d. 1215/1801). After holding the offices of Kapîdjî-bashî, governor of Aleppo, and governor of Damascus, Baṭṭāl Pasha became governor of Trebizond in 1202/1787-8. In 1201/1787 he led his forces against Russia, but in 1205/1790 was defeated and taken prisoner. The town of Battalpashinsk commemorates his name. After a period of disgrace, he was reappointed, thanks to Russian intercession, in 1213/1798-9. His elder son, Khayr al-Dīn Rāghib Pasha, governor of Afyūn Ḳara Ḥiṣār, was dismissed and executed in 1206/1791-2, when the independent political power of the Djānīklis ended. This family opposed the military reforms of Selīm III, which were supported by their rivals the Čapan-oghlu and the Ḳara ʿOthmān-oghlu. Ṭayyār Maḥmūd Pasha, a younger son of Ḥusayn Baṭṭāl, was active against the reforms, and in 1805-7 was in exile in Russia. He returned to Turkey in 1807, and was appointed Ḳāʾimmaḳām to the Grand Vezir during the brief interval of reactionary rule under Muṣṭafā IV. A few months later he was dismissed and executed by Maḥmūd II.

These three were the most important derebey dynasties, and ruled in western, central, and eastern Anatolia respectively. Among lesser dynasties mention may be made of the Ilyās-oghlu of Kush Adasî (Scala Nuova, near Ephesus), who ruled the sandjaḳ of Menteshe as far south as Bodrum from about the middle of the 18th century; the Küčük ʿAlī-oghlu, who ruled in Payas and for a while Adana, and the Yîlanlî-oghlu of Isparta and Eghridir, and the region of Antalya.

Bibliography: The Ottoman chronicles pay some attention to the Derebeys, but tend to gloss over their independent status and represent them as servants of the Porte. More realistic information will be found in Western sources, notably in diplomatic and consular reports and in the writings of travellers and archaeologists. These may be supplemented, especially for names and dates, from the numerous local inscriptions. Some attention has been given to the derebeys in recent Turkish work on local history (as in the important studies of M. Çagatay Uluçay on Manisa), but the subject still awaits detailed examination.

On the Ḳara-ʿOthmān-oghlu, see Kgl. Museum, *Altertümer von Pergamon*, i, Berlin 1885, 84-91; F. W. Hasluck, *Christianity and Islam under the Sultans*, ii, Oxford 1929, 597-603; Ç. Uluçay,

Karaosmanoğullarına ait bazı Vesikalar, in *Tarih Vesikaları*, ii, 1942-3, 193-207; 300-8; 434-40; idem, *Manisa Ünlüleri*, Manisa 1946, 54-62; on the Čapan-oghlu, J. Macdonald Kinneir, *Journey through Asia Minor* ..., London 1818, 84 ff.; Georges Perrot, *Souvenirs d'un voyage en Asie Mineure*, Paris 1864, 386 ff.; on the Djānīkli, Djewdet, *Ta'rīkh*², iii, 144 ff.; iv, 29 f.; v, 133 ff., 254 ff.; on the Ilyās-oghlu, P. Wittek, *Das Fürstentum Mentesche*, Istanbul 1934, 109-110. In general, see Yusuf Akçura, *Osmanlı Devletinin Dağılma Devri*, Istanbul 1940; I. H. Uzunçarsılı, *Alemdar Mustafa Pasha*, Istanbul 1942; idem, *Osmanlı Tarihi*, iv/I, Ankara 1956, 318-9, 436-7, 612-5; A. F. Miller, *Mustafa Pasha Bayraktar*, Moscow 1947; Gibb-Bowen, i/I, 193 ff.; B. Lewis, *The Emergence of Modern Turkey*, London 1961, 38, 74, 441-2. (J. H. Mordtmann-[B. Lewis])

DERGĀH [see dargāh].

DERNA [see darna].

DERSIM, area in eastern Anatolia: bordered on the north by the ranges of the Monzur Dagh (3188 m.) and the Mercan Dagh; on the west by the northern source of the Euphrates (the Kara Su); on the south by its southern source (the Murat Su); and on the east by its tributary, the Piri Su. The area is of a predominantly hilly character, and (in the country districts) inhabited by Kurds. At one time, Dersim, under the name of Čemishkezek (the capital at that time) was a *liwā* of the *eyālet* of Diyārbekir. Dersim became a *wilāyet* temporarily in the 19th century, but in 1888 it came under the *wilāyet* of Maʿmūret al-ʿazīz (Harput) as a *sandjak*, with the capital Hozat and the *ḳaḍā's* Ovadjıḳ, Čemishkezek, Čarsancak, Mazgird, Pertek, Kozičan, Kīzīlkilise, and Pah. During the reorganization in the administration of the Turkish Republic, Dersim once more became a *wilāyet* under the name of Tunceli [*q.v.*].

Towards the end of the 19th century, the *sandjak* of Dersim had 63,430 inhabitants, of whom 15,460 were Sunnī Turks, 12,000 were Kurds, 27,800 Ḳīzīl-Bāsh (Shīʿīs), 7,560 were Gregorian and 610 Protestant Armenians.

Bibliography: Kātib Čelebi, *Djihānnümā*, 439; V. Cuinet, *La Turquie d'Asie*, vol. ii, Paris 1892, 384 ff.; Ch. Samy-Bey Fraschery, *Ḳāmūs al-Aʿlām* (*Dictionnaire Universelle d'Histoire et de Géographie*), iii, Istanbul 1308/1891, 2131 f.; Naşit Hakkı Uluğ, *Derebeyi ve Dersim*, Ankara 1932. (Fr. Taeschner)

DERVISH [see darwīsh].

DERWĪSH PASHĀ (?-1012/1603)—the historian Pečewī refers to him (ii, 132) as Derwīsh Ḥasan Pasha—was born at Mostar in the Herzegovina and, in the reign of the Ottoman Sultan Selīm II (974-982/1566-1574), entered the Palace service, where, in the course of his education, he revealed an interest and ability in literature and poetry. During the reign of Sulṭān Murād III (982-1003/1574-1595) he became one of the Imperial Falconers (*doghandji*) and won the favour of the Sultan through the *ḳaṣīdes* and *ghazels* which he presented to him. At the order of Murād III he rendered from Persian into Turkish verse the *Shāhnāme* of the poet Bannāʾī, giving to his work the title of *Murādnāme*. Derwīsh Agha rose to the rank of *doghandjī bashī* and, according to Pečewī (ii, 132) acted as *ḳapu ketkhudā* of the Sultan. Pečewī (*loc. cit.*) describes him as a poet of force (*shāʿir-i metīn*) and a man who, in good qualities and knowledge, could vie with the greatest of the *ʿulemā'*. It is possible that he did not go out from the Palace service until the reign of Meḥemmed III (1003-1012/1595-1603). During the long war of 1001-1015/1593-1606 between the Austrian Habsburgs and the Ottomans Derwīsh Pasha was charged with the defence of the Hungarian fortress Istoni Belgrād (Stuhlweissenburg) in 1007/1599. He was at this time Beglerbeg of Bosnia. Derwīsh Pasha, again as Beglerbeg of Bosnia, shared also in the Ottoman reconquest (1011/1602) of Istoni Belgrād, which the Imperial forces had taken in the previous year (1010/1601). He was removed from the Beglerbeglik of Bosnia in 1011/1602, the office being then given to Deli Ḥasan Pasha, hitherto one of the leaders of the Djelālī rebels in Asia Minor. Derwīsh Pasha remained on the Hungarian front and fought in the campaign of 1012/1603, but was slain in battle near Pest on 4 Ṣafar 1012/14 July 1603.

Bibliography: Pečewī, *Ta'rīkh*, Istanbul A.H. 1281-3, ii, 132, 228, 229, 271 ff.; Ḥādjdjī Khalīfa, *Fedhleke*, Istanbul A.H. 1286-7, i, 126, 179, 198; Naʿīmā, *Ta'rīkh*, Istanbul A.H. 1281-3, i, 226, 227, 298, 330, 331; Ewliyā Čelebi, *Seyāḥatnāme*, vi, Istanbul A.H. 1318, 211 ff.; Hammer-Purgstall, *Histoire*, vii, 557 and viii, 35; *Wissenschaftliche Mittheilungen aus Bosnien und der Hercegovina*, i, Vienna 1893, 511; *Sidjill-i ʿOthmānī*, ii, 329; Sâdeddin Nüzhet Ergun, *Türk Şâirleri*, iii, 1172 ff.; *İA.*, s.v. Derviş Paşa (M. Cavid Baysun). (V. J. Parry)

DERWĪSH PASHA (?-1015/1606), Ottoman Grand Vizier, was of Bosnian origin. He served in the corps of *Bostāndjīs*, becoming *ketkhudā* of the corps and then being raised, through the favour of the Wālide Sulṭān, to the office of *Bostāndjī bashī* in 1013/1604. Derwīsh Pasha was set in charge of affairs at Istanbul, when Aḥmed I visited Bursa in 1014/1605. He was made Ḳapudān Pasha, with the rank of Vizier, in Ramaḍān 1014/January 1606 and became Grand Vizier in Ṣafar 1015/June 1606. His tenure of the office was, however, brief, for the enemies whom he had made during his rapid rise to the Grand Vizierate so undermined the confidence which the Sultan reposed in him, that Aḥmed I had him executed in Shaʿbān 1015/December 1606. The Ottoman chroniclers describe Derwīsh Pasha as a harsh, unjust and incompetent man, but the English ambassador at Istanbul, Lello, took a much more favourable view of him and indeed refers to him (Lello-Burian, 27) as "the stouteste and pollitic-quest" of the Grand Viziers that he had known.

Bibliography: Pečewī, *Ta'rīkh*, Istanbul A.H. 1281-1283, ii, 293, 294, 316, 319, 322, 324-9, 354; Ḥādjdjī Khalīfa, *Fedhleke*, Istanbul A.H. 1286-7, i, 251, 271, 275-82, 288; Naʿīmā, *Ta'rīkh*, Istanbul A.H. 1281-3, i, 407, 434, 441-53 *passim* and ii, 157; *The Report of Lello, Third English Ambassador to the Sublime Porte*, ed. O. Burian (Ankara Üniversitesi Dil ve Tarih-Coğrafya Fakültesi Yayınları no. 83), Ankara 1952, 23-7, 29-32; *Ambassade de Jean de Gontaut Biron. Correspondance Diplomatique et Documents Inédits, 1605-1610*, ed. Comte Théodore de Gontaut Biron, in *Archives historiques de la Gascogne*, fasc. 19, Paris 1889, 6, 7, 21, 25-8, 33, 50, 51, 55, 57, 61, 63, 66, 71, 78-84 *passim*, 88, 90, 93-110 *passim*, 127; Hammer-Purgstall, *Histoire*, viii, 68, 92, 95-103 *passim*, 182; I. H. Uzunçarşılı, *Osmanlı Tarihi* (Türk Tarih Kurumu Yayınlarından, XIII Seri, no. 16²), iii, Pt. 2, 362-3; ʿOthmān-zāde Tā'ib, *Ḥadīḳat al-wuzarā'*, Istanbul A.H. 1271, 54 ff.; *Sidjill-i ʿOthmānī*, ii, 329; Sāmī, *Ḳāmūs al-Aʿlām*, iii, Istanbul A.H. 1308, 2136; *İA*, s.v. Derviş Paşa (M. Cavid Baysun). (V. J. Parry)

DERWĪSH MEḤMED PASHA. (c. 993?-1065/1585?-1655), Ottoman Grand Vizier, was of Čerkes (Circassian) origin. As *ketkhudā* of Ṭabānî Yassî Meḥmed Pasha, Grand Vizier (1041-6/1632-7) in the reign of Sulṭān Murād IV (1032-49/1623-40), he shared in the Eriwān campaign of 1044-5/1635 against the Ṣafawīds of Persia and became thereafter Beglerbeg of Shām, an appointment that he held, according to Ibn Djumʿa, in 1046/1636-7. At the time of Murād IV's campaign against Baghdād in 1048/1638 he was Beglerbeg of Diyārbekir, but in 1049/1639 became Beglerbeg of Baghdād, receiving soon afterwards the rank of Vizier. Derwīsh Meḥmed Pasha remained at Baghdād for three years. During the course of his subsequent career he served as Beglerbeg of Aleppo, of Anadolu, of Silistria and of Bosnia. Appointed to Silistria for the second time in 1059/1649, Derwīsh Meḥmed Pasha was given also a special assignment, *i.e.*, command over the land defences of Čanaḳ-Ḳalʿe Boghazî (the Dardanelles) with the object of driving off the naval forces of Venice, which, in the course of the Cretan War begun in 1055/1645, were then blockading the Straits—a task that he accomplished with success in Djumādā I/May 1649. There followed a second tenure of office as Beglerbeg of Anadolu in 1061/1651, at which time he was entrusted with the defence of Bursa against the threatening advance of the Djelālī rebels in Asia Minor. Derwīsh Meḥmed became *Ḳapudān Pasha* in 1062/1652 and then in Rabīʿ I 1063/March 1653 was raised to the Grand Vizierate, which he held thereafter until Dhu 'l-Ḥidjdja 1064/October 1654, when, disabled with paralysis, he was removed from office. Derwīsh Meḥmed Pasha, noted as one of the wealthiest of the great Ottoman dignitaries of his time, died on 5 Rabīʿ I 1065/13 January 1655 and was buried in the cemetery of the mosque of ʿAtīḳ ʿAlī Pasha at Čemberlitash in Istanbul.

Bibliography: Pečewī, *Taʾrīkh*, Istanbul A.H. 1281-3, 447; ʿAbd al-ʿAzīz Ḳaračelebizāde, *Rawḍat al-Abrār*, Istanbul A.H. 1248, 591, 592, 599, 603, 634; Ḥādjdjī Khalīfa, *Fedhleke*, Istanbul A.H. 1286-7, ii, 167, 185, 186, 197-201 *passim*, 205, 215-8 *passim*, 325, 343, 377, 381, 385-97; Naʿīmā, *Taʾrīkh*, Istanbul A.H. 1281-3, iii, 244, 292, 295, 350, 351, 360, 367, 380, 420, 429, 431, 432, 442-3; iv, 11, 73, 108, 227, 228, 380, 385, 386, 390; v, 151, 162, 163, 208, 255, 275, 276, 283 ff. *passim*, 304, 314, 324, 396 ff., 441-4; and vi, 22-9; Hammer-Purgstall, *Histoire* ix, 324, 325, 356, 359, 362 and x, 24, 131, 217, 218, 303, 305, 322-32 *passim*, 344, 347-52 *passim*, 357, 390, 391; S. H. Longrigg, *Four centuries of modern Iraq*, Oxford 1925, 82, 109; H. Laoust, *Les Gouverneurs de Damas sous les Mamlouks et les premiers Ottomans (658-1156/1260-1744). Traduction des Annales d'Ibn Ṭūlūn et d'Ibn Ǧumʿa* (Institut Français de Damas), Damascus 1952, 206; I. H. Uzunçarşılı, *Osmanlı Tarihi* (Türk Tarih Kurumu Yayınlarından, XIII Seri, no. 16[3]), iii/2, Ankara 1954, 406-8; ʿOthmānzāde Tāʾib, *Ḥadīḳat al-wuzarāʾ*, Istanbul A.H. 1271, 98 f..; *Sidjill-i ʿOthmānī*, ii, 331; Sāmī, *Ḳāmūs al-Aʿlām*, iii, Istanbul A.H. 1308, 2138; *İA*, s.v. Derviş Mehmed Paşa (M. Cavid Baysun).

(V. J. Parry)

DERWĪSH MEḤMED PASHA (1142-91/1730-77), Ottoman Grand Vizier, son of Yaghlîḳčî ("oil-cloth merchant") Ḳadrī Agha, was born in Istanbul in 1142/1730. (References to his having been born in 1146/1733-4 are probably wrong.) Derwīsh Meḥmed Efendi entered the service of the State as assistant seal-keeper to the *defterdār* (treasurer) Behdjet Efendi. He then became *dewātdār* (secretary or steward) of Nāʾilī ʿAbdullāh Pasha, Silāḥdār ʿAlī Pasha and Saʿīd Meḥmed Pasha, in that order. Promoted *defterdār kesedārî* (treasury cashier), he became finance clerk (*māliyye tedhkiredjisi*) during the expedition of 1181/1768. On 22 Dhu 'l-Ḳaʿda 1185/26 February 1772, while the army was camped at Shumnu (Shumen), he became *defterdār* of the first division (*shiḳḳ*). Although he left that post when the army returned to Istanbul, he was re-appointed to it on 6 Ramaḍān 1188/25 November 1774. On 3 Ṣafar 1189/5 April 1775 he became steward (*kedkhudā*) to the Grand Vizier, being finally appointed Gand Vizier himself on 7 Djumāda I 1189/6 July 1775.

Having in this way come to power in the period which followed the conclusion of the treaty of Küčük Kaynardja, Derwīsh Meḥmed Pasha made use of the authority which Sultan ʿAbd al-Ḥamīd I was in the habit of granting to his Grand Viziers, to procure a pleasurable life for himself instead of trying to make good the damage suffered by the Empire during the war. The laxity of his conduct of State affairs combined with gossip about him led to his dismissal on 8 Dhu 'l-Ḳaʿda 1190/19 December 1776 and to his exile in Gallipoli. Nevertheless, he was appointed on 2 Muḥarram 1191/10 February 1777 to be *wālī* (governor) of Khanya (Canea in Crete). He fell ill, however, during his voyage out and died in Sakîz (Chios), being buried in the mosque of Ibrāhīm Pasha. Derwīsh Meḥmed Pasha was a man of quiet disposition whose services to the State were negligible. Nevertheless, he built or, at least, repaired some pious establishments in Istanbul (in the districts of Eyyūb and of Üsküdar-Scutari), in Bursa and in Egypt. The fact that some of these were *tekkes* (*tekyes*) suggests that he had *ṣūfī* sympathies.

Bibliography: Wāṣif, *Taʾrīkh* (Istanbul 1219 A.H.) ii, 197 ff.; Djewdet Pasha, *Taʾrīkh* (Istanbul 1309 A.H.), ii, 11, 24, 49 ff. 70; iv, 246; Aḥmed Djāwid, sequels to *Hadīḳat al-Wuzarāʾ* (published with latter) (Istanbul 1271) 27 ff. (*İA*)

DERWĪSH MEḤMED PASHA (1178-1253/1765-1837), Ottoman Grand Vizier, son of Rüstem Agha from Anapoli (Nauplion) in Mora (Peloponnesus). He received his training as seal-keeper (*mühürdār*) of the Grand Vizier Aḥmed Pasha, also of Peloponnesian origin, thanks to whose protection he was appointed *mīr-i mīrān* (Pasha of the second class) and *sandjaḳ-beyi*. He became later tax-collector (*muḥaṣṣil*) of the *liwā* of Ḥamīd, while in 1232/1817 he served as *mutaṣarrif* (with the rank of *wezīr* or Pasha) of Khudāwendigār, Eskishehir and Ḳodja-ili. The most influential functionary in the Empire, Ḥālet Efendi, wanted at that time to see a weak Grand Vizier and he, therefore, advised Sultan Maḥmūd II to appoint Derwīsh Meḥmed Pasha, who became Grand Vizier on 27 Ṣafar 1233/6 January 1818. During his two-year tenure of office Derwīsh Meḥmed Pasha did not succeed in imposing his authority: he was even unable to ensure the security of Istanbul, where he refrained from punishing the gang leaders, preferring instead to propitiate every one. Although this conduct was agreeable to the leading functionaries and particularly to Ḥālet Efendi, the Sultan realized the Grand Vizier's impotence, but chose to keep him for some time in order to safeguard the honour of the office. Finally on 19 Rabīʿ I 1235/5 January 1820 the Sultan dismissed him and banished him to Gallipoli. On 11 Rabīʿ II 1236/16 January 1821 he was appointed nevertheless, governor of Damascus with additional jurisdiction over the *liwā* of Nablūs and with the additional function of *amīr al-ḥadjdj* (official responsible for the pilgrims). In this capacity he quarrelled with ʿAbdullāh Pasha, the *wālī* of Ṣaydā (Sidon), whom he besieged in Acre in accordance with the orders of the Sublime Porte. When, however, the latter was pardoned, Derwīsh Meḥmed Pasha was transferred to the *eyālet* (province) of Anatolia, where the tyrannical behaviour of his son-in-law Ḥamdī Bey led to complaints by the people of Kütahya (Cotyleaum), as a result of which Derwīsh Meḥmed Pasha was dismissed, stripped of the rank of *wezīr*, deprived of his property and exiled to Afyūn-Ḳara-Ḥiṣār, whence he was later transferred, at his own request, to Bursa. In Rabīʿ I 1253/June 1837 he was appointed *Shaykh al-Ḥaram* (governor of Medina), but died (in Ramaḍān/December of the same year) at Yanbūʿ on his way there.

A man of weak and kindly temperament, Derwīsh Meḥmed Pasha is one of the least forceful of the Ottoman Grand Viziers. Some pious works in Bursa and in Istanbul are ascribed to him.

Bibliographie: Shānīzāde ʿAṭāʾullāh Efendi, *Taʾrīkh* (Istanbul 1290-1 A.H.) ii, 304, 331, 356 ff.; iii, 88 ff., 149; Djewdet Pasha, *Taʾrīkh* (Istanbul 1301 A.H.), xi, 38, 72, 80; xii, 23, 84 ff., 125; Luṭfī Efendi, *Taʾrīkh* (Istanbul 1302 A.H.), v, 88 ff.; Rifʿat Efendi, *Ward al-Ḥadāʾiḳ* (lith. Istanbul), 15. (M. Cavid Baysun)

DESTOUR [see dustūr].

DEVE BOYNU, literally "camel's neck", a Turkish geographical term used to designate certain mountain passes and promontories. The most celebrated mountain pass known as Deve Boynu is that between Erzurum [*q.v.*] and Ḥasan-Ḳalʿe, which played an important part in the defence of Erzurum. The transit road leads from Trebizond (ṭarabzun, [*q.v.*]) to Īrān, and the Erzurum-Kars railway passes through it (see F. B. Lynch, *Armenia Travels and Studies, 1898*, London 1901, ii, 194 ff.; E. Nolde, *Reise nach Innerarabien, Kurdistan und Armenien*, 1895, 260 ff.). Another pass known as Deve Boynu is situated near Göldjük and is crossed by the Elâziz-Ergani (Diyār-Bakr, [*q.v.*]) road (see Hommaire de Hell, *Voyage en Turquie*, iv, 83; E. Chaput, *Voyages d'études géologiques et géomorphogéniques en Turquie*, 193 ff.). There are other passes (between Gaziantep (ʿAyntāb, [*q.v.*]) and Besni in the Ḳaradagh mountains) and villages (*e.g.* between Elbistan and Göksu) known by that name. Other similar place-names are Deve Geçidi ("Camel Pass"), a village and valley north-west of Diyār-Bakr; Deve Çayırı ("Camel pasture"), a village west of Gürün; Deve Tepesi ("Camel hill"), a peak in the Bulgar Daghī mountains, see T. Kotschy, *Reise in den Kilik. Taurus*, 1858, 201); Develi ("connected with camels"), name of inhabited localities and a mountain. Similar place-names occur in Syria and ʿIrāḳ. In ancient Assyria Gaugamela (Aramaic Gab Gamela,) where the famous battle was fought, meant "camel's back" (Pauly-Wissowa, vii, 865, s.v. Gaugamela). Pīrī Reʾīs mentions three promontories known as Deve Boynu on the Aegean coast of Anatolia (*Kitāb-i Baḥriyye*, 140, 151, 240). Modern maps show another promontory known as Deve Boynu at the western tip of the Dadya peninsula, and there is also a Deve Boynu promontory on the southern coast of Lake Van [*q.v.*]. (Besim Darkot)

DEVEDJI, a Turkish word meaning cameleer, the name given to certain regiments of the corps of janissaries [see yeni čeri], forming part of the *Djemāʿat*, and performing escort duties with the supply columns. They were also called by the Persian term *shuturbān*. The Devedjis originally formed the first five *orta*s of the *Djemāʿat* (four according to D'Ohsson), and were later augmented to include many others. They wore heron's feathers in their crests (see sorguč); when attending the *dīwān* they wore velvet trimmed with sable and lynx fur. Devedji officers enjoyed high precedence among the *orta*s. According to Marsigli, the captains of the first five *orta*s were always preferred to the command of garrison centres. Their chief, the Bashdevedji, ranked high in the ladder of promotion, after the Khāṣṣeki Agha and above the Yaya-bashī [*qq.v.*].

Bibliography: Marsigli, *L'État militaire de l'Empire ottoman*, The Hague 1732, i, 72; D'Ohsson, *Tableau général de l'empire othoman*, vii, Paris 1824, 343; Hammer-Purgstall, *Histoire*, iv, 217, 436; idem, *Staatsverfassung*, ii, 209; Aḥmed Djewād, *Taʾrīkh-i ʿAskerī-i ʿOthmānī*, Istanbul 1299 A.H., 12 etc.; I. H. Uzunçarşılı, *Osmanlı Devleti teşkilâtından Kapıkulu Ocakları*, i, Ankara 1943, index; Gibb-Bowen i/I, 321-2. (B. Lewis)

DEVELI ḲARA ḤIṢĀR [see Ḳara Ḥiṣār].

DEVSHIRME, verbal noun of T. *devshir-* 'to collect' (with various spellings, cf. *TTS* s.v. *derşürmek*), Ottoman term for the periodical levy of Christian children for training to fill the ranks of the Janissaries (see yeni čeri) and to occupy posts in the Palace service and in the administration (Gr. παιδομάζωμα). The same verb is used in the earliest Ottoman sources (Giese's *Anon.* 22, l. 12 = Urudj 22, l. 4) for the 'collection' of the fifth part of prisoners from the *dār al-ḥarb* due to the Sultan as *pendjik* [*q.v.*], from whom, according to tradition, the Janissary corps was first raised in the early years of the reign of Murād I; but the date of the institution of the *devshirme* in its narrower sense of a levy of *dhimmī* children is still uncertain (Idrīs Bidlīsī's attribution of it to Orkhān is certainly anachronistic, although, having been followed by Saʿd al-Dīn and Hammer, it long enjoyed general acceptance). The earliest contemporary reference to the *devshirme* so far known appears in a sermon preached in 1395 (*i.e.*, in the reign of Bāyezīd I) by Isidore Glabas, the metropolitan of Thessalonica, lamenting the 'seizure of the children by the decree of the amīr' (Ὁμιλία περὶ τῆς ἁρπαγῆς τῶν παιδίων κατὰ το τοῦ ἀμηρᾶ ἐπίταγμα, first noticed by O. Tafrali, in *Thessalonique au XIVème siècle*, 1913, 286 f., and discussed by S. Vryonis Jr. in *Isidore Glabas and the Turkish Devshirme* in *Speculum* xxxi, 1956, 433-43); the second oldest appears in Sinān Pasha's letter, of 1430, to the inhabitants of Ioannina, promising them if they submitted exemption from πιασμὸν παιδίων (cf. K. Amantos, in Ἑλληνικά ix, 1936, 119). Bartholomaeus de Jano, in his letter written in 1438, says (Migne *Patr. Graec.* vol. 158, col. 1066): '[Murād II] *decimam puerorum partem de Christianis, quod prius numquam fecerat* (sic, not *fuerat* as in *EI*[1]), *nuper accepit* ...', which has been interpreted as indicating that it was Murād II who introduced the *devshirme*; however in the light of Isidore Glabas's reference it seems rather that Murād re-introduced it, perhaps after it had been suspended in the years of confusion following the battle of Ankara (as is stated by ʿAṭā I 33) and as part of his re-organization of the Janissaries (Sphrantzes 92).

Although Idrīs Bidlīsī maintained, on the ground that most of the *dhimmī*s had been conquered by force (*be-ʿanwa*), that the *devshirme* was in accordance with the *sharʿ*, this argument seems not to have commended itself to Saʿd al-Dīn (cf. V. L. Ménage in *BSOAS*, xviii, 1956, 181-3), and the *devshirme* does appear in fact to have been an infringement of the rights of the *dhimmī*s (see DHIMMA). It has been suggested however that a justification of the *devshirme* might have been drawn from the Shāfiʿī doctrine that Christians converted since the Descent of the Ḳurʾān (and hence most of the rural population of the Balkans, but not the Greeks) were not entitled to the status of *dhimmī* (cf. P. Wittek, *Devshirme and Sharīʿa, BSOAS*, xvii, 1955, 271-8).

With certain exceptions (see below) all the Christian population of the European domains of the Empire, and later the Asiatic domains as well, was liable to the *devshirme.* In the 16th century, the *devshirme* was entrusted to a Janissary officer, usually a *yaya-bashī* (for the ranks eligible for this duty cf. I. H. Uzunçarşılı, *Kapukulu Ocakları*, i [hereafter *KkO*], 15), who went to the district where the levy was to be made, accompanied by a *kātib*, and taking with him a letter from the Agha of the Janissaries, a *berāt* of authorization, and (according to Navagero [see *Bibl.*]) a supply of uniforms. In each *ḳaḍā* criers summoned the children to gather, accompanied by their fathers and by the priests, who brought the baptismal registers. Under the supervision of the *ḳāḍī* and the *sipāhī*s, or their representatives, the officer selected the best of the children of the ages eligible. The age-limits reported in European accounts vary greatly, from as low as eight years old to as high as 20 (cf. Lybyer 48); relatively late Ottoman documents (of 1601, 1621, 1622 and 1666) prescribe the limits 15-20 (*KkO*, 95, 98; A. E. Vakalopoulos [see *Bibl.*] 286 f.). For each group of 100-150 children two registers were made, listing their names, parentage, ages and descriptions; one remained with the recruiting-officer, the other went with the *sürüdjü* ('drover') who conducted the impressed children to Istanbul (see especially documents in *KkO*, 92-7). The local *reʿāyā* were obliged to pay a special tax to meet the cost of the uniforms (*KkO*, 17 f., 22 n.).

On arriving in Istanbul the children were inspected both for their physique and for their moral qualities as revealed by the science of Physiognomy (*ḳiyāfa*, [*q.v.*]; cf. ʿĀlī, *Künh*, v, 14 f.; id., *Mevāʿidüʾn-Nefāʾis*, Istanbul 1956, 21; Postel, iii, 3). The best were taken directly into the Palace service or distributed to high dignitaries; the rest were hired (for 25 *aḳčes* a head, according to Navagero [1553]: one ducat according to Busbecq; two ducats according to Ḳoči Beg) to Turks in Asia Minor, and later—already by the middle of the 16th century [Navagero, Busbecq, Chesneau]—in Rūmeli as well, to work on the land for some years, learn Turkish and assimilate Muslim ways (the term for this training period was *Türk üzerinde olmak*, cf. *KkO*, 115 ff.). The lads were called in as required to fill vacancies in the *ʿadjamī odjaḳ* (see ʿADJAMĪ OGHLAN).

In principle the *devshirme* was not applied to children of townsfolk and craftsmen, as being sophisticated and less hardy than peasant lads (*KkO*, 18, 39), though these rules were often abused: *devshirme*s were levied regularly in Athens in the middle of the 16th century (cf. the chronicle in *Ecthesis Chronica*, ed. S. Lampros, 1902, 86). As married lads were not taken, the Christian peasantry often married their children very young (Gerlach, 306). Regions which had submitted voluntarily to the Ottomans seem to have been exempt from the *devshirme* (cf. Des Hayes): certainly exemption is specified among the terms granted, for example, to Galata (cf. E. Dalleggio d'Alessio in Ἑλληνικά xi, 1939, 115-24), Rhodes (cf. Charrière, *Négociations*, i, 92; Fontanus in Lonicerus [1584 ed.] i, 423) and Chios (cf. P. Argenti, *Chius Vincta*, 1941, cxliii, 208 ff.). The inhabitants of Istanbul, perhaps as being townsfolk, were in practice not liable (Gerlach 48; and cf. the story in the *Historia Patriarchica* [Bonn ed. 167, discussed by J. H. Mordtmann in *BZ*, xxi, 1912, 129-144] that Meḥemmed II had granted them *amān*). Moldavia and Wallachia were never subject to the *devshirme* (Cantemir, 1734 ed., 38, and cf. *KkO*, 14 n., Jorga, iii, 188); the Armenians seem to have been exempt at first (Thevet, 799 b, but cf. *KkO*, 17), but were so no longer in later years (Ḳoči Beg). Freedom from the *devshirme*, temporary or permanent, was also included occasionally among the exemptions from taxes and *ʿawāriḍ* granted to various groups of *reʿāyā* in return for services rendered directly to the State, *e.g.*, miners, guardians of passes and dwellers on main roads, or to some dwellers on *waḳf*-lands (*KkO*, 109-14; Ö. L. Barkan, *Kanunlar*, 72, 85; *relazione* of Garzoni [1573] in Albèri, 3rd ser., i, 396); these exemptions were strictly checked and liable to be withdrawn (*KkO*, 97-101).

The Muslims of Bosnia were in a special position. According to a late Ottoman source (Shamʿdānī-zāde, *Marʾī al-tawārīkh*, Istanbul 1338, 454) the Christian population embraced Islam *en masse* upon the Ottoman conquest in 867/1463, but requested that their children should nevertheless be eligible for the *devshirme.* Though the Islamization of the peasantry was not in fact instantaneous (cf. B. Djurdjev, BOSNA, 1265 b above), there is a record of a recruitment of 1000 lads for the Janissaries from the Muslim population of Bosnia and Herzegovina as early as 921/1515 (Ferīdūn², i, 472). Here the converted Bosnians are called *Poturnāk* (cf. A. V. Soloviev, in *Byzantion*, xxiii (1953), 73-86); they are called *Potur ṭāʾifesi* in a document of 981/1573 (*KkO*, 103), and the recruited lads *Potur oghullarī* in a document of 998/1589 (*KkO*, 108), which defines them as 'circumcised but ignorant of Turkish', and which warns the beylerbey against recruiting boys who are '*Türkleshmish*', *i.e.*, Turkish-speaking. An undated list preserved in the Topkapu archives (published by R. M. Meriç in *Ist. Enst. Dergisi*, iii, 1957, 35-40) gives the names and descriptions of 60 boys (whose ages range from 13 to 19) recruited from the *ḳaḍā* of Yenipazar; the names show that 44 of them are Muslim-born and 16 Christian-born, the latter being identified both by their (new) Muslim names and by their (former) Christian names. It is said that these Muslims of Bosnia were not distributed for training, but mostly drafted straight into the Palace or into the *odjaḳ* of the *bostāndjī*s, [*q.v.*] (*KkO*, 19, referring to the *Ḳawānīn-i Yeničeriyān*, a work composed under Aḥmed I—see *Bibl.*).

Many of the European reports suggest that the *devshirme* was made at regular intervals, estimates ranging from every five years to annually (references in Zinkeisen, iii, 216 and Lybyer, 51). More probably it took place on an *ad hoc* basis according to need—infrequently in the reign of Meḥemmed II, when the Janissaries were relatively few and *pendjik* prisoners abundant (cf. Cippico [1472] in Sathas, *Docs. in-*

édits . . ., vii, 281: '*se non possono avere prigioni*' = Basle ed. 1544, ii, 51; Iacopo de Promontorio-de Campis [ca. 1480] ed. Fr. Babinger, 1957, 36: '*manchandoli* [*i.e.*, prisoners] *preda rape de figlioli de christiani subditi soi*'), then at more and more frequent intervals throughout the 16th century, until at the end of the century the ranks of the Janissaries were in effect opened to all comers; thereafter, when recruitment was no longer dependent upon the *devshirme*, levies were spasmodic.

Again, many reports maintain, erroneously, that the *devshirme* officials recruited a fixed proportion of children, often stated to be a 'tithe', though estimates range as high as one in five (Spandugino, Thevet) and even one in three (anon. report of 1582 in Albèri, 3rd ser., ii, 245; Palerne [also 1582]). A *fermān*, said to be of the early 16th century (*KkO*, 92 ff.) shows that—at that time, at least—the number of boys to be levied was calculated beforehand on the basis of one boy (aged 14 to 18) from every 40 households.

Reports of the numbers taken also vary greatly, Postel's being as high as 10-12,000 a year. According to Gerlach (34) a *devshirme* of 1573 (documents in *KkO*, 103 ff. show that it covered both Rūmeli and Asia Minor) produced 8000 boys. Saʿd al-Dīn calculated that in the 200 years and more that it had been in force the *devshirme* had produced over 200,000 converts to Islam (i, 41), *i.e.*, an average of 1000 a year, which is the figure given by Shamʿdānīzāde (*loc. cit.*). However, there was much abuse by the recruiting officers, who levied more children than their warrants permitted, selling the surplus for their private profit (Spandugino); they also grew rich on bribes, both from Christians who bought their children off, and from non-Christians who smuggled their children in (Gerlach, 48, 306; Roe, *Negotiations*, 534; Selānikī 263 f., referring to the *devshirme* of 998/1589-90, for which cf. the documents in *KkO*, 102 f.).

When the *devshirme* was extended to Asia Minor is not clear. In 1456 the Greeks of the west coast appealed to the Grand Master of Rhodes for help against the Turks 'who take (πέρνουν) our children and make Muslims of them' (Miklosisch and Müller, *Acta*, iii, 291), but this complaint may refer only to piracy. Trabzon was liable to the *devshirme* at various times throughout the 10th/16th century (*KkO*, 15 n., 19); it may be that the *devshirme* was extended from this (formerly Christian) district over the rest of Asia Minor. Kartal had been subject to the *devshirme* before 945/1538 (*KkO*, 111 f.); the *sandjaḳ*s of Sis and Kayseri were visited shortly before 972/1564 (*KkO*, 126), and the districts of Bursa, Lefke and Iznik before 984/1576—the year in which Gerlach visited Ulubad and found it liable to the *devshirme* (257). In 981/1573-4 there was an extensive *devshirme* not only in Rūmeli but also in the area Begshehri-Marʿash and around Biledjik (*KkO*, 103-6, 127), no doubt that which, according to Gerlach (34), brought in 8000 boys in January 1574. The *devshirme* reached as far as Batum in 992/1584 (*KkO*, 107), and in 1032/1623 almost the whole of Asia Minor was covered (*KkO*, 94 ff. and cf. 22 n.); in the latter year, that following the murder of Sultan ʿOthmān, Greece too was visited 'to fill the seraglio' (Roe, *Negotiations*, 534).

By the beginning of the 11th/17th century, the ranks of the Janissaries had become so swollen with Muslim-born 'intruders' that frequent recruitments by *devshirme* were no longer necessary. Although according to Lithgow (*Rare Adventures*, 1906, 106 and 149) the *devshirme* was 'absolutely abrogated' by Aḥmed I, levies were made throughout the century, but sporadically: according to the *relazione* of Foscarini (1637) there had then been no levy for twelve years (Barozzi-Berchet, v/ii, 86). There was a *devshirme* however in the next year, 1048/1638 (*Fedhleke*, ii, 211), and it was not, as Hammer believed (*GOR*, v, 244, and hence Zinkeisen, iv, 166), the last; for according to Rycaut (*Present State*, i, ch. 4) the Janissary leader Bektāsh Agha demanded (in 1061/1651) that henceforth the 'yearly' collection of children should be abolished, and only the children of Janissaries be admitted 'for the service of the Grand Signior'; and Ewliyā Čelebi (i, 598) speaks of a *devshirme* in Rūmeli every 7 years, when 7-8,000 boys were collected at Üsküb, brought to Istanbul, and placed directly into the various *odjaḳ*s (the preliminary training in Anatolia evidently being by now abandoned, cf. *KkO*, 24 f.). Rycaut found that in his time (he was in Istanbul from 1660) the *devshirme* was 'in a great part grown out of use' (*op. cit.*, i, ch. 18) and 'wholly forgotten' (iii, ch. 8); so too Quirini (1676) reported that there had been no *devshirme* since 1663 (Barozzi-Berchet, V/ii, 160, and cf. Hammer *GOR*, vii, 555), and Morosini (1680) spoke of it as taking place only every twenty years or so (*op. cit.*, 219); article 3 of the Ottoman-Polish treaty of Buczacz (1083/1672) provided that the inhabitants of Podolia would be exempt 'if a *devshirme* is ordered' (Rāshid², i, 285), a phrase implying that the practice was by then irregular and infrequent. All the same there were *devshirme*s in 1666 (Vakalopoulos, 286) and 1674 (Hammer-Purgstall, *GOR*, vi, 299), the latter at least intended only to recruit staff for the Palace. Very shortly after his accession in 1115/1703 Aḥmed III ordered that the turbulent *bostāndjī*s should be enrolled in the Janissaries and 1000 *devshirme* boys be collected to replace them (Rāshid², iii, 88 f., Hammer-Purgstall, *GOR*, vii, 91); there may be a connexion between this and an attempt to carry out a *devshirme* in Greece in April 1705 (Vakalopoulos, 292). This is the latest record of a *devshirme* so far known, though Uzunçarşılı has found a *berāt* of 1150/1738 exempting a Christian subject from taxes and his son from the *devshirme* (*KkO*, 68 f.).

Bibliography (further to references given in the text): Zinkeisen, iii, 215-230, which is based mainly on the Venetian reports in Albèri (the most circumstantial being that of Navagero [1553!, Albèri, 3rd ser., i, 48 ff.) and Gerlach's *Tagebuch*, 34, 48, 306; J. H. Mordtmann, DEWSHIRME in *EI*¹ (1912) and references there (most of which have been incorporated above); Ḳoči Beg, Ist. 1303, 27 f. = tr. Bernhauer, *ZDMG*, xv, 284 = Ist. 1939, 28; A. H. Lybyer, *The Government of the Ottoman Empire* . . ., 1913, 49 ff.; F. W. Hasluck, *Christianity and Islam under the Sultans*, 1929, ii, 484 ff.; W. L. Wright, *Ottoman Statecraft*, 1935, index; Barnette Miller, *The Palace School of Muhammad the Conqueror*, 1941, 74 ff., 174 f.; D. Pephanes, Τὸ Παιδομάζωμα, Athens 1948 (not seen); Gibb-Bowen, index; J. A. B. Palmer, *The Origin of the Janissaries*, in *Bull. of the John Rylands Library*, xxxv, 1953, 448-481; A. E. Vakalopoulos, Προβλήματα τῆς ἱστορίας τοῦ παιδομαζώματος, in Ἑλληνικά xiii, 1954, 274-293.

References in European travel-books etc. must be treated with caution, for authors frequently borrow without acknowledgement from their predecessors: thus the reference in Rycaut (*Present State*, i, ch. 10) to an annual *devshirme* of

2000 boys mostly from the Morea and Albania derives, presumably via Withers, from Bon (Barozzi-Berchet, v/i, 77), who was writing 60 years earlier, as does that in Baudier, and the account in B. de Vigenère's *Illustrations* (1650 ed., col. 49) largely from Postel. The following references seem to be independent: Spandugino, *Petit Traicté*, ed. Schefer 1896, 102 ff., 144 f., = Sathas, *Documents inédits*, ix, 212 f., 225; J. Chesneau, *Le Voyage de M. d'Aramon*, ed. Schefer 1887, 44 f.; A. Geuffroy, *Briefve Description* (appendix to preceding) 242 f.; G. Postel, *De la république* ..., 1560, iii, 22 ff.; A. Thevet, *Cosmographie Universelle*, 1575, 799 b, 808 b, 817 b (engraving); N. de Nicolay, *Navigations*, 1568, 79 ff.; S. Schweigger, *Neue Reysbeschreibung*, 1608, 168 ff.; Busbecq, *De Acie* ..., 1581, 152 f. = Eng. tr. by N. Tate, 1694, 400 f.; J. Palerne, *Peregrinations*, 1606, 412 f., 502 f.; H. de Beauvau, *Relation Journalière*, 1619, 68; L. Des Hayes, *Voiage de Levant*, 1624, 137 ff.

These accounts can be controlled from the archive-material given by I. H. Uzunçarşılı in *Osmanlı Devleti teşkilâtından Kapukulu Ocakları*, i, 1943, 1-141 (this includes nearly all the documents published by Aḥmed Refīḳ in *Edebiyyāt Fakültesi Medjmūʿasi*, v, 1926, 1-14, and on it is based I. H. Uzunçarşılı's article Devşirme in *IA*); Uzunçarşılı refers frequently to a work *Ḳawānīn-i Yeničeriyān* in his private library: this seems to be identical with the work, composed under Aḥmed I, which is described in *İst. Kit. Tarih-Cografya Yazmaları Katalogları*, i/10, 813 (MS Esad Ef. 2068) and of which MS Revan 1320 contains another copy (cf. L. Forrer in *Isl.*, xxvi, no. 62).

(V. L. Ménage)

DEWLET [see dawla].

DEY [see dayī].

DHABĪḤA: a victim destined for immolation according to Muslim law, in fulfilment of a vow, *nadhr*, for example, or for the sacrifice of *ʿaḳiḳa*, or on the occasion of the feast of the 10th day of Dhu 'l-ḥidjdja (then called *ḍaḥiyya*), or in order to make atonement for certain transgressions committed during the *ḥadjdj* (the victim in this case being known as *hadī*).

This *dhabīḥa* must be slaughtered according to a strict ritual known as *dhakāʾa*. Its form does not differ from the ritual slaughter of animals permitted as food: hence it is with this type of slaughter that we shall now concern ourselves. The differences between the various schools of law in this regard are comparatively unimportant. However, on this question, as with the rest of *fiḳh*, in order to adopt not only a theoretical but also a sociological point of view, it would be necessary to show what the actual practice on this matter has been throughout the world of Islam as whole. On this subject we shall limit ourselves to a single observation.

The matter is briefly referred to in the Ḳurʾān (v, 4, vi, 147) and dealt with at greater length in the collections of traditions and the texts of *fiḳh*.

1. What animals are proper subjects for ritual slaughter? The list does not coincide exactly with that of the animals that are permissible as food. For in the first place there are those animals which may be eaten without any necessity of ritual slaughter—grasshoppers or fish, for example (these latter, indeed, may be eaten even if found dead); in the second place there are special rules, which are not our present concern, applicable to hunting, and finally the foetus which is almost at term is permissible as food if its mother has been ritually slaughtered. On the other hand it is recommended that animals which are not lawful food should be slaughtered according to ritual in order to avoid any prolonged suffering. Nevertheless it is, in general, with a view to being able to eat the animal concerned that a ritual slaughter takes place, and this is the more so since the *dhabīḥa*, the sacrificial victim, is normally eaten. It may be remarked that a ritual slaughter makes the flesh of the animal lawful even if the animal is already sick or mortally wounded and the slaughter does no more than accelerate its end.

2. Who may perform ritual slaughter? It is lawful, although blameworthy, for the people of the Book to perform it on behalf of Muslims. On the other hand it is in no way prohibited, nor, even, is it reprehensible (contrary to a curious superstition which prevails in North Africa, for example) for a woman to kill an animal such as a chicken. (One observer has reported that at Tangier, if women are of necessity obliged to do this, they place a phallic symbol between their thighs). All those authorized to act as slaughterers must be in possession of their mental faculties.

3. How is the slaughter (*dhakāʾa*) effected? Four methods of killing may be distinguished of which only the first two need concern us: the *dhabḥ*; the *naḥr* (see below); the wounding or *ʿaḳr* (which is important with regard to the theory of hunting); any other method of killing. For the *dhabīḥa* to be validly put to death and the animal concerned to be permissible as food then either the *dhabḥ* or the *naḥr* should be employed according to the circumstances. Otherwise the dead animal will be regarded as carrion (*mayta*) and therefore legally unfit for consumption except in the case of absolute necessity. At the moment of slaughter it is obligatory to have the necessary intention and to invoke the name of God. The *dhabḥ* is the normal method of slaughter, for the *naḥr* is applicable only to camels (there are some differences of opinion among the schools as to the obligatory or simply praiseworthy character of these provisions). The *dhabḥ* consists of slitting the throat, including the trachea and the oesophagus; (as for the two jugular veins there are divergencies between the schools); the head is not to be severed. Preferably the victim should be laid upon its left side facing in the direction of the *ḳibla*. As for the *naḥr*, it consists of driving the knife in by the throat without it being necessary to cut in the manner prescribed above, the camel remaining upright but at the same time facing the *ḳibla*. There are some casuistic discussions regarding the nature of the instrument to be used. More important is the fact that many provisions of *fiḳh* bear witness to an anxiety that the victims should be spared any unnecessary suffering. In particular the knife ought to be well sharpened; the practice of collective slaughtering is condemned, as too is that of cutting off part of an animal or removing its skin (except in the case of fish) before it is dead.

Bibliography: The collections of traditions contain chapters on the subject—of a greater or lesser scope—such as Buk̲h̲ārī, tr. Houdas and Marçais, iv, 72; so too do all the books of *fiḳh*, usually in the context of hunting (*e.g.*, K̲h̲alīl, *Muk̲h̲taṣar*, tr. Guidi, i, 315 ff., and tr. Bousquet, i, 85 ff.; S̲h̲īrāzī, *Tanbīh* (tr. Bousquet, i, 108 ff.)). We might also note the classical treatises of *ik̲h̲tilāf*, which have not yet been translated—for example, Ibn Rus̲h̲d, *Bidāya*; S̲h̲aʿrānī, *Mīzān*, etc.; E. Gräf, *Jagdbeute und Schlachttier im islamischen Recht*, Bonn 1959. See also ṢAYD.

(G.-H. BOUSQUET)

DHAFĀR [see ẒAFĀR].

DHAHAB, gold, played an important part in various areas of the life of Muslim society. The main reason for the significance of the metal was its economic assets. These were referred to in the Ḳurʾān. Apart from implicitly alluding to the value aspect of gold (*Sūra* III, 85), the Ḳurʾān alludes to the attraction of 'hoarded ḳinṭārs of gold' for people (*Sūra* III, 12) and warns against hoarding since 'those who treasure up gold and silver and do not expend them in the way of Allāh' would meet with a painful punishment (*Sūra* IX, 34). The problem of gold was also discussed by Muslim jurists who determined its taxability and regulated property laws in respect of lands possessing gold deposits (cf. al-Māwardī, *Les Statuts gouvernementaux*, trad. E. Fagnan, Algiers 1915, 252-3, 426-7, 447-8).

Since gold, along with silver, constituted the basis for the official Muslim monetary system (see DĪNĀR), a sufficient supply of this metal was essential for general economic stability. This was secured by the exploitation of gold mines situated in the Muslim Empire, as well as by the influx of bullion from the adjacent countries. Although mediaeval sources refer to many mining areas (cf. D. M. Dunlop, *Sources of gold and silver in Islam according to al-Hamdani (10th Century A.D.)*, in *Stud. Isl.* viii, 1957, 29-49), the region of Wādī ʿAllaḳī was particularly famous for intensive mining activities (cf., al-Yaʿḳūbī, *Les pays*, trans. G. Wiet, Cairo 1937, 190), while that of Ghāna for the excellent quality of its ore (cf., *Description de l'Afrique septentrionale par el-Bekri*, trans. de Slane, 177). It seems that the exploitation of gold mines was not subject to the monopolistic pressure of Muslim political authorities (cf. C. H. Becker, *Islamstudien*, Leipzig 1924, i, 189; also, al-ʿUmarī, *Masālik al-Abṣār fī Mamālik al-Amṣār*, trans. Gaudefroy-Demombynes, Paris 1927, i, 58). The total volume of gold circulating in the Near East during various periods of Muslim domination can hardly be ascertained. It is nevertheless possible to infer on the basis of textual and abundant numismatic evidence that the Muslim Empire was well provided with gold. But a tremendous war expenditure connected with the operations of the Crusaders, a gradual re-establishment of European hegemony in the Mediterranean balance of trade, and a later absorption of West Sudanese gold by the Portuguese, led to a drastic draining of Near Eastern gold reserves (cf. M. Lombard, *Les bases monétaires d'une suprématie économique. L'or musulman du VIIe au XIe siècle*, in *Annales* [*Économies, Sociétés, Civilisations*], 2, 1947, 142-60; F. Braudel, *Monnaies et civilisations. De l'or du Soudan à l'argent d'Amérique*, *ibid.*, i, 1946, 9-22).

As in the pre-Islamic period, the use of gold in jewellery, ornamental crafts, in manuscript illuminations and in calligraphy, was widely practised during the Middle Ages (Aḥmad b. Mīr-Munshī, *Calligraphers and painters*, transl. V. Minorsky [*Freer Gallery of Art Occasional Papers*, vol. 3, ii], Washington, D.C., 1959). A prominent place in the goldsmithing production was held by Baghdād (cf. Cl. Cahen, *Documents relatifs à quelques techniques iraquiennes au début du onzième siècle*, in *Ars Islamica*, xv-xvi, 1951, 23-8). Gold woven robes and gold vessels, whose use was condemned by Muslim tradition, were also in demand. The fashion of collecting such luxury objects prevailed particularly during the Buwayhid regime (cf. E. Kühnel, *Die Kunst Persiens unter den Buyiden*, in *ZDMG*, 106, i, [N.F. 31], 1956, 78-92).

The natural properties of gold were studied by Muslim alchemists. Although they still accepted the theory of transmutation of metals (cf. G. Sarton, *Introduction to the history of science*, 2/ii, 1045), they were well acquainted with various chemical processes, such as cupellation, the separation of gold and silver by means of nitric acid, and the quantitative chemical analysis of gold-silver alloys (cf. E. J. Holmyard, *The makers of chemistry*, Oxford 1931, 77).

Finally, gold was used by Muslim medicine. It was considered particularly effective in diseases of the eye, melancholia, palpitation of the heart, alopecia, etc. Instruments of gold were preferably used for the piercing of holes in the ear, as well as for cauterization (cf. Ibn al-Bayṭār, ed. Leclerc, *Notices et extraits*, ii, 150-151).

See also KHAZAF.

(A. S. EHRENKREUTZ)

AL-**DHAHABĪ** [see AḤMAD AL-MANṢŪR].

AL-**DHAHABĪ**, SHAMS AL-DĪN ABŪ ʿABD ALLĀH MUḤAMMAD B. ʿUTHMĀN B. ḲĀYMĀẒ B. ʿABD ALLĀH AL-TURKUMĀNĪ AL-FĀRIḲĪ AL-DIMASHḲĪ AL-SHĀFIʿĪ, an Arab historian and theologian, was born at Damascus or at Mayyāfāriḳīn on 1 or 3 Rabīʿ II (according to al-Kutubī, in Rabīʿ I) 673/5 or 7 October 1274, and died at Damascus, according to al-Subkī and al-Suyūṭī, in the night of Sunday-Monday on 3 Dhu 'l-Ḳaʿda 748/4 February 1348, or, according to Aḥmad b. ʿIyās, in 753/1352-3. He was buried at the Bāb al-Ṣaghīr.

His Life. His main lines of study were Tradition and canon law.

He began to study Tradition at Damascus in 690/1291 or 691/1291-2 under Yūsuf al-Mizzī, ʿUmar b. Ḳawwās, Aḥmad b. Hibat Allāh b. ʿAsākir, and Yūsuf b. Aḥmad al-Ḳamūlī. He continued his studies in Tradition in several Islamic centres, especially at Cairo where he stayed longest, under the best authorities of his time. The number of his teachers is said to have surpassed 1,300, whose biographies he collected in his *Muʿdjam*. The most important of them were: at Baʿlabakk ʿAbd al-Khāliḳ b. ʿUlwān, and Zaynab bint ʿUmar b. al-Kindī; in several towns of Egypt al-Abarḳūhī, ʿĪsā b. Aḥmad al-Muʾmin b. Shihāb, Abū Muḥammad al-Dimyāṭī and Abu 'l-ʿAbbās al-Ẓāhirī; at Mecca al-Tūzarī; at Ḥalab Shawḳar al-Zaynī; at Nābulus al-ʿImād b. Badrān; then at Alexandria Abu 'l-Ḥasan ʿAlī b. Aḥmad al-ʿIrāḳī and Abu 'l-Ḥasan Yaḥyā b. Aḥmad al-Ṣawwāf; and lastly at Cairo Ibn Manṣūr al-Ifrīḳī and chiefly Ibn Daḳīḳ al-ʿĪd who was well-known for his discrimination in selecting his pupils.

He studied canon law with Kamāl al-Dīn b. al-Zamlikānī, Burhān al-Dīn al-Fazārī, and Kamāl al-Dīn b. Ḳāḍī Shuhba. He was an adherent of the Shāfiʿī school.

Having obtained licence for teaching from Abū Zakariyyā b. al-Ṣayrafī, Ibn Abi 'l-Khayr, al-Ḳāsim al-Irbilī, and others, he became Professor of Tradition at the *madrasa* Umm al-Ṣāliḥ in Damascus; however, he was unable to succeed his teacher Yūsuf al-Mizzī at the *madrasa* al-Ashrafiyya of the same city because he could not subscribe to the conditions made by the founder of the institute concerning the canon law school of the Professor of Tradition.

The fields of research he mostly excelled in were Tradition, canon law, and history. He had an indefatigable energy, having been at his studies day and night, even when he was struck by blindness which befell him, according to Abu 'l-Fidā' and ʿUmar b. al-Wardī, in 743/1342-3, or, according to others, as early as 741/1340-1. He had a great many excellent pupils, among whom we particularly mention ʿAbd al-Wahhāb al-Subkī, the author of the *Ṭabaḳāt al-Shāfiʿiyya al-Kubrā*, whose father Taḳī al-Dīn al-Subkī, the famous Shāfiʿī doctor of law, was his most intimate friend.

His many-sided qualities were acknowledged both by his contemporaries and his later biographers. By the latter he was commonly referred to as *muḥaddith al-ʿaṣr* ("traditionist of the age") and *khātam al-ḥuffāẓ* ("the seal [*i.e.*, the last] of the *ḥāfiẓ*s"). Al-Kutubī praised him with select poetical phrases. According to Ṣalāḥ al-Dīn al-Ṣafadī, "he had nothing of the rigidness of the traditionists or the stupidity of the historians; on the contrary, he was a lawyer of spirit, and was at home in the opinions of people". Ibn Ḥadjar al-ʿAsḳalānī composed a beautiful *ḳaṣīda* in praise of his excellent qualities.

On the other hand, we also find opinions adverse to his reputation. His own most eminent pupil al-Subkī reproached him with reviling even his own Shāfiʿī school, in addition to the Ḥanafīs and the Ashʿarīs, and extolling the theological tendency known as al-Mudjassima. Similarly, Abu 'l-Fidā' and ʿUmar b. al-Wardī, while admitting that he was an historian and traditionist of a high rank, state that towards the end of his life, when he became blind, he compiled biographies of some of his living contemporaries which, based on the biased information of his young admirers, quite unwittingly tarnished the good reputation of certain persons.

His Work. As an author he was not as prolific as Ibn al-Djawzī before him or al-Suyūṭī after him; however, some of his works have attained a high standard in East and West alike. Like practically all the post-classical Arab authors he too was a compiler, but his works are distinguished by careful composition and constant references to his authorities. It is for these peculiarities that his works on Tradition, especially on the *ʿilm al-ridjāl*, have become very popular.

A) History. His greatest work is the *Ta'rīkh al-Islām* ("History of Islam"), printed together with his *Ṭabaḳāt al-mashāhīr wa 'l-aʿlām* at Cairo from 1367/1947-6 onwards, an extensive history of Islam, beginning with the genealogy of the Prophet Muḥammad and ending with the year 700/1300-1. It follows the system of the *Kitāb al-muntaẓam* of Ibn al-Djawzī [*q.v.*], containing both the general narrative (*al-ḥawādith al-kā'ina*) and the obituary notices of the persons who died in the several years (*al-mutawaffūn*). The whole work is divided into "classes" (*ṭabaḳāt*) of decades, so that it contains seventy "classes" altogether. In each decade first comes the general narrative, subdivided into the several years; then follow the "classes" of the obituary notices, equally subdivided into the several years, and ended by the obituary notices of persons whose exact dates of death could not be stated. The relation of the extent of the general narrative to that of the obituary notices is, on an average, 1 to 6 or 7.

The system of the general narrative of the first three centuries is entirely different from that of the last four centuries. For the first three centuries it is very short, giving only the gist of the matter and being but a concise compendium of al-Ṭabarī's [*q.v.*] chronicle; it enumerates the notable persons who died in the year concerned, then the leaders of the annual pilgrimage, and last the political events. For the last four centuries the order is quite inverted. First come the detailed annual records of political history, with constant references to the authorities consulted; then there follow those of local and administrative history, especially of Baghdād and Damascus; then the so-called "strange things" (*al-ʿadjā'ib*), *i.e.*, the curiosities and striking phenomena of the year are recorded; then comes the enumeration of the leaders of the annual pilgrimage from Baghdād and Damascus, and last the list of the names of the notabilities who died in the year concerned. The literary value of the general narrative is in its recording of events neglected by Ibn al-Athīr [*q.v.*] in his *al-Kāmil fi 'l-ta'rīkh*, such as 1) the history of the Saldjūḳs, Ayyūbids, and the Mongol invasion; 2) the internal development of Islam, especially the Bāṭinīs and the Shīʿīs; 3) Western Islam. Al-Dhahabī's tendency is, therefore, to record the development of the *whole* of Islam although his narrative is more detailed for Syria and Egypt than for other countries.

The obituary notices record the biographies of all the caliphs and minor rulers of both the Eastern and the Western Islam; then the viziers, generals, and functionaries of rank; then the jurisconsults and theologians of all the schools of canon law as well as other scholars; and last the poets, whose biographies contain numerous quotations from their works. The obituary notices in general follow the scheme of the *ṭabaḳāt*-works; they have far greater historical value than the general narrative has.

The *Ta'rīkh al-Islām* was continued by at least six hands; three of these continuations are extant: 1) from 701/1301-2 to 740/1339-40 by al-Dhahabī himself; 2) from 701/1301-2 to 786/1384-5 by ʿAbd al-Raḥīm al-ʿIrāḳī and his son Aḥmad (died in 826/1422-3), only the latter's work being extant; 3) from 701/1301-2 to 790/1388 by Ibn Ḳāḍī Shuhba (died in 851/1447-8) in his *Al-iʿlām bi-ta'rīkh al-Islām*.

Owing to the voluminous character of the *Ta'rīkh al-Islām* it was abridged many times. Six abridgments were made by al-Dhahabī himself:

1) *Kitāb duwal al-Islām* or *al-Ta'rīkh al-ṣaghīr* ("Small History"), published at Ḥaydarābād in 1337/1918-9.

2) *al-ʿIbar fī akhbār al-bashar mimman ʿabar* (*Muntakhab al-ta'rīkh al-kabīr*), an abridgment of the biographical "classes".

Whereas these two works combined give a fairly good synopsis of the whole of the *Ta'rīkh al-Islām*, the following are extractions from the biographical "classes" (*ṭabaḳas*) only.

3) *Tadhkirat al-ḥuffāẓ*, published at Ḥaydarābād in 1332-3/1914-5 in five volumes. The best known abridgment and continuation of the work was done by al-Suyūṭī [*q.v.*] under the title *Ṭabaḳāt al-ḥuffāẓ*, published by F. Wüstenfeld at Göttingen in 1833-4. Al-Suyūṭī's continuation was also published at Damascus in 1347/1928-9.

The *Tadhkirat al-ḥuffāẓ* is also the basis of the *Ṭabaḳāt al-Shāfiʿiyya* of Ibn Ḳāḍī Shuhba.

4) *al-Iṣāba fī tadjrīd asmā al-Ṣaḥāba*, an alphabetical list of Muḥammad's Companions, based chiefly on the *Usd al-ghāba* of Ibn al-Athīr, printed at Ḥaydarābād in 1315/1897-8.

5) *Ṭabaḳāt al-ḳurrā' al-mashhūrīn*, published in 7 parts in *al-Hidāya* (an Arabic periodical in Turkey), iv, 1331/1912-3 and ff.

6) *Siyar aʿlām al-nubalāʾ*, printed in 2 vols. at Cairo n.d.

7) *al-ʿIbar fī khabar man ʿabar*, a transcript, enlarged in some passages, of al-Ḏhahabī's work under the same title (see above no. 2) by Ibn Ḳāḍī Shuhba (d. 851/1447-8).

8) A similar recension of the same work by Ibn al-Shammāʿ (d. 936/1529-30), extending to 734/1333-4.

9) *al-Mukhtaṣar min Taʾrīkh al-Islām wa Ṭabaḳāt al-mashāhīr wa ʾl-aʿlām*, by Ibn Ildekiz al-Muʿaẓẓamī al-ʿĀdilī al-Ayyūbī.

Two other historical works of al-Ḏhahabī are extant:

Mukhtaṣar li-Taʾrīkh Baghdād li ʾbn al-Dubaythī, a synopsis of the history of Baghdād according to Ibn al-Dubaythī (died in 637/1239-40).

Mukhtaṣar akhbār al-naḥwiyyīn li ʾbn al-Ḳiftī, a synopsis of Ibn al-Ḳiftī's (d. 646/1248-9) History of the Grammarians.

B) Tradition. His works of this category are nearly all of lexicographical character.

Tadhhīb Tahdhīb al-kamāl fī asmā ʾl-ridjāl, an improved edition of the *Tahdjīb al-kamāl fī asmā ʾl-ridjāl* of Ibn al-Nadjdjār (died in 643/1245-6).

al-Mushtabih fī asmā ʾl-ridjāl, ed. by P. de Jong at Leiden in 1881.

Mīzān al-iʿtidāl fī naḳd (or *tarādjim*) *al-ridjāl*, published at Lucknow in 1301/1883-4, at Cairo in 1325/1907-8, at Ḥaydarābād in 1329/1911-1331/1913, and the letter *hamza* only at Istanbul in 1304/1886-7. It was extracted by Ibn Ḥadjar al-ʿAskalānī (died in 852/1448-9) in his *Lisān al-mīzān*.

Bibliography: Brockelmann, II, 46-8; S II, 45-7 (with enumeration of the Oriental references and the manuscripts); G. Sarton, *Introduction to the history of science*, iii, *the fourteenth century*, Baltimore 1947-8, 963-7; Fr. Rosenthal, *A history of Muslim historiography*, Leiden 1952, 30 (n. 8), 129-30; J. de Somogyi, *The Taʾrīkh al-islām of adh-Ḏhahabī*, in *JRAS* 1932, 815-55; idem, *Ein arabisches Kompendium der Weltgeschichte. Das Kitāb duwal al-islām des aḏ-Ḏahabī*, in *Islamica* 1932, 334-53; idem, *A Qaṣīda on the destruction of Baghdād by the Mongols*, in *BSOS* 1933, 41-8; idem, *Aḏ-Ḏhahabī's Taʾrīkh al-islām as an authority on the Mongol invasion of the Caliphate*, in *JRAS* 1936, 595-604; idem, *Ein arabischer Bericht über die Tataren im Taʾrīḥ al-islām des aḏ-Ḏahabī*, in *Islamica* 1937, 105-30; idem, *Aḏh-Ḏhahabī's record of the destruction of Damascus by the Mongols in 699-700/1299-1301*, in *Ignace Goldziher Memorial Volume I*, Budapest 1948, 353-86. (Moh. Ben Cheneb-[J. de Somogyi])

DHAHABIYYA, Persian name of the Kubrāwiyya [*q.v.*] order. See also ṬARĪḲA.

DHAHRAN [see ẒAHRĀN].

ḌHĀKĀ (DACCA) — (literally 'concealed', but origin obscure) is the capital of East Pakistan. The city is situated at the head of the waterways about a hundred miles from the sea, in a region which has had throughout history a premier position in this province of rivers and flooded plains. The Hindū capital was at Vikramapura, then favourably situated on the Dhaleshwarī river, where the line of old fortification can still be seen, but more important are the tomb and mosque (built 888/1483) of Bābā Ādam Shahīd, a pioneer Muslim saint. Sonārgāon on the Meghnā river was the early Muslim capital, which was famous for the seminary of Shaykh Sharf al-Dīn Abū Tawwāma, a Ḥanafī jurist and traditionist of great renown in the 7th/13th century, for the lively court maintained by the romantic Sulṭān Ghiyāth al-Dīn Aʿẓam Shāh in the late 8th/14th century, and for the fine muslin industry through the period. The place is full of ruined tombs, mosques and inscriptions, the most famous being the tomb of Aʿẓam Shāh and the remains of the Khānḳāh of Shaykh Muḥammad Yūsuf, who emigrated from Persia in the 8th/15th century. Later the local rebel chief ʿĪsā Khān made Sonārgāon and its neighbourhood his headquarters, but the town was destroyed in 1017/1608 by the Mughal soldiery under Shaykh Islām Khān Čishtī. The temporary Mughal camp, which was located in the old Thānā of Ḏhākābāzū, came to be developed as the new Mughal capital of the *ṣūba* of Bengal under the name of Djahāngīrnagar, after the reigning Mughal emperor Djahāngīr.

The capital city stood on the northern bank of the Burigangā, the river Dulāy of the Muslim historians, about eight miles above its confluence with the Dhaleshwarī and far away from the recurring floods. It was well protected against the raids of the Arakanese Maghs and the Portuguese pirates in the 11th/17th century by a system of river fortresses, which still survive at Munshīgandj, Narāyangandj and Sonakanda. The Mughal city spread out beyond the Hindū localities, well-laid with gardens, palaces, markets, mosques and minarets, which are all associated with the names of the Mughal officers. Of the princely governors Shāh Shudjāʿ, the ill-fated brother of the Mughal emperor Awrangzīb, and Muḥammad Aʿẓam, the latter's son, had a great reputation in Eastern India. From their time have been inherited the Baṛā Katrā (the great market quadrangle), the ʿĪdgāh and the fort of Awrangābād, commonly called Lāl Bāgh, the last still showing its terraced walls, bastions, gateways, a mosque and a beautiful mausoleum (partly in marble) of Bībī Parī, one of the wives of Muḥammad Aʿẓam. Of the other governors Mīr Djumlā is better known for his conquest of Assam, and Shāyista Khān for his twenty-five years' service in Bengal, his final conquest of Čatgāon in 1076/1666, his lavishly kept harem, and above all the numerous mosques and mausolea built by him in the provincial Mughal style, wrongly called by the people the Shāyistā Khānī style of architecture. Though the Mughal seat of government was transferred to Murshīdābād in 1118/1706, Dacca never lost its importance. It remained the centre of the flourishing muslin industry and many other luxury arts of the East, which attracted the foreign merchants, and as early as the middle of the 17th century we find here factories being established by the Dutch, French and British.

With the introduction of British rule and the growing importance of the city of Calcutta, Dacca lost its premier place in Bengal. In 1905 it was again made the capital of the newly created province of Eastern Bengal and Assam—an administrative measure to favour the Muslims which was annulled because of the growing opposition from Hindū nationalists. In 1906 Dacca witnessed the foundation of the All India Muslim League with the object of protecting the rights of the Muslims of the subcontinent. Many of the red-faced buildings of the newly-developed Ramna in Dacca were built at this time. In 1921 the University of Dacca was founded mainly to meet the demands of the local Muslims. It became a centre of both education and political training for the rising talents of Muslim Bengal. Today Dacca (population 432,853 in 1951) is the second capital of Pakistan and is fast growing into a modern city with its industrial suburban town of Narāyangandj. The old Mug̲h̲al city still survives with its numerous mosques and mausolea, but its lanes and by-lanes are being broadened, in line with the new developments in the city. Dacca shares fully in the rebirth of the Muslims of Pakistan.

Bibliography: Mīrzā Nathan, *Bahāristān-i-G̲h̲aybī*, Engl. tr. by M. I. Borah, Gawhati 1936; C. D'Oyly, *Antiquities of Dacca*, London 1824-30; *Taʾrīk̲h̲-i-Nuṣratd̲j̲angī*, in *Memoirs of the Asiatic Society of Bengal*, Vol. ii, no. 6, Calcutta 1908; J. Taylor, *Topography and statistics of Dacca*, Calcutta 1840; Sayīd Awlād Ḥasan, *Antiquities of Dacca*, Dacca 1904; F. B. Bradley Birt, *The romance of an Eastern capital*, London 1906; Raḥmān ʿAlī Tays̲h̲, *Tawārīk̲h̲-i Ḍhākā* (Urdū), 1910; A. H. Dani, *Dacca, a record of its changing fortunes*, Dacca 1956; idem, *Muslim architecture in Bengal*, Dacca 1961.   (A. H. DANI)

DH̲ĀKIR, KĀs̲ĪM BEY, the foremost Ād̲h̲arbāyd̲j̲ānī poet and satirist in the first half of the 19th century. He was born probably in 1786, at Penāhābād in the K̲h̲ānate of Ḳarabāg̲h̲ (now S̲h̲ūs̲h̲a, Nagorno-Karabak̲h̲skaya Avtonom. Oblast). He belonged to the clan of Djawāns̲h̲īr, a renowned family of *bey*s.

In his satirical poetry he relentlessly castigated the religious fanaticism of the Mollās as well as corruption and all kinds of abuses by the *beyzāde*—the local aristocracy—and the Czarist administration officials. His criticism of the latter resulted in his being persecuted by the governor of Ḳarabāg̲h̲, Prince Konstantin Tarkhanov, who took advantage of illegal actions in which a nephew of the poet was involved, to have him deported to Baku for some time. Upon the intervention of his friends he was allowed to return to his family estate, where he spent most of his lifetime.

There have been preserved and partly published (see M. A. Resulzade in the bibliography to this article) a number of complaints and appeals for help (*s̲h̲ikāyat-nāma*) which Dh̲ākir addressed, in brilliant verse, to influential fellow-countrymen such as Mīrzā Fatḥ ʿAlī Ak̲h̲und-zāda [*q.v.*] and the first Ād̲h̲arbāyd̲j̲ānī novelist Ismāʿīl Bey Ḳutkas̲h̲īnlī (who had risen to the rank of general in the Russian army). His much esteemed style was obviously influenced by the great 18th century poet Mollā Panāh Wāḳif (1717-97). Like his predecessor, he preferred the simple, popular lyric forms applied by the ʿās̲h̲iḳ folk literature, such as "Ḳos̲h̲ma" and "Kerayli̊", but he also wrote a number of poems in Persian and in traditional metric forms, as well as some pieces in rhymed prose (*e.g., Darwīs̲h̲ we ḳīz*). His fables in verse (*Tülkü we s̲h̲īr, ḳurd, čaḳḳal we s̲h̲īr, Tülkü we ḳurd* etc.) follow the widespread oriental tradition set by the "*Kalila and Dimna*", but may be also influenced by Krĭlov's (1768-1844) genial adaptations. In his works a number of Russian words—mostly taken from the terminology of administration and selected to suit his satirical purpose—made their first appearance in Ād̲h̲arī Turkish.

The first publications of poetry by Dh̲ākir seem to have appeared in 1854 (in the official Tiflis newspaper *Kavkaz*) and 1856 (within an anthology published in Temir-K̲h̲ān S̲h̲ūra —now Buinaksk, Dāg̲h̲istān—by Mīrzā Yūsuf Nersesov Ḳarabāg̲h̲ī).

Although there is reason to believe that Āk̲h̲und-zāda had planned a complete edition of Dh̲ākir's works after the latter's death in 1857, no such edition was printed in the pre-Soviet era.

The manuscripts of Dh̲ākir's *dīwān* are kept in the fund of the Academy of Sciences of the Ād̲h̲arbāyd̲j̲ān SSR (Niẓāmī-Institute of Literature, inventory no. 15).

Bibliography: Gasĭm Bäy Zakir, *Äsärlär*, Baku 1953 (in Ād̲h̲arī); A. Bergé, *Dichtungen transkaukasischer Sänger des XVIII. und XIX. Jahrhunderts in aserbaidschanischer Mundart*, Leipzig 1868; F. Gasĭmzade, *XIX äsr äsrbaydžan ädäbiyyatĭ tarĭk̲h̲i*, Baku 1956, 212-31; K. Mamedov, *Gasĭm Bäy Zakir*, Baku 1957 (in Ād̲h̲arī); M. A. Resulzade, *Azerî türklerinin hayat ve edebiyatĭnda neşʾe: Zâkir*, in *Azerbaycan Yurt Bilgisi*, iii, 1934, 113 ff.   (H. W. BRANDS)

DHĀL, 9th letter of the Arabic alphabet, here transcribed *d̲h̲*; numerical value 700, in the Eastern system [see ABD̲J̲AD].

Definition: voiced interdental fricative; according to the Arabic grammatical tradition: *rik̲h̲wa mad̲j̲hūra*. For the *mak̲h̲rad̲j̲*: *lit̲h̲awiyya* in al-K̲h̲alīl (al-Zamak̲h̲s̲h̲ari, *Muf.*, 191, line 2, 2nd ed. J. P. Broch) indicates a position of the tongue on the *lit̲h̲a* "gum", therefore *gingival*. Ibn Yaʿīs̲h̲ (1460, line 21, ed. G. Jahn) records a position quite close to this, "the base of the central incisors", and therefore *alveolar*. Sībawayh (ii, 453, line 14, ed. Paris), much more widely accepted (*e.g.* Ibn Djinnī, *Sirr ṣināʿa*, i, 53, line 3), indicates an interdental properly speaking "from between the tip of the tongue and the tips of the central incisors".

D̲h̲ is the continuation in classical Arabic of a similar (or analogous) articulation in common Semitic (see S. Moscati, *Sistema*, 28-29); retained in epigraphic South Arabic, in Mehri, S̲h̲k̲h̲awri, and partly in Ugaritic; represented by *z* in Akkadian, Hebrew-Phoenician, Ethiopian (ancient and modern), by *d* in Aramaic and in Soḳoṭri. In modern Arabic dialects the following principle can be stated: interdental fricatives are preserved unchanged in the speech of nomads or former nomads; they have changed into the corresponding occlusives in the speech of settled populations. Following this principle we shall find *d̲h̲* or *d*; for the details and the nuances see J. Cantineau, *Cours*, 50-54. In classical Arabic *d̲h̲* is subject to numerous conditioned corruptions (assimilations), see *ibid.*, 47-49.

For the phonological oppositions of the phoneme *d̲h̲* see J. Cantineau, *Esquisse, BSL* (no. 126) 96 5°; for the incompatibilities, see *ibid.*, 134.

Bibliography: in the text and under ḤURŪF AL-HID̲J̲Āʾ.   (H. FLEISCH)

2. In Persian, and in Urdū which largely depends on Persian practice, *d̲h̲āl* is not distinguished in pronunciation from *ze, ḍād* and *ẓāʾ*. Its use in the writing systems of these languages is not, however, confined to borrowings of Arabic words with *d̲h̲āl*, for it occurs in words of certain Iranian origin.

Most cases of the occurrence of *d̲h̲āl* in Persian words arise since modern Persian represents a κοινή: in some Middle Iranian dialects post-vocalic *d* developed a spirant pronunciation, and is in fact shown fairly consistently as *d̲h̲āl* in the oldest Modern Persian mss, while in others the occlusive pronunciation persisted. The confusion between the dialects, and their mutual influence, has led to the general reintroduction of *dāl*, in spelling and pronunciation, for post-vocalic *d*, although cases of the spirant pronunciation, later > *z*, have resulted in the occasional retention of *d̲h̲āl* in some words.

The few cases of variation between *dāl* and *d̲h̲āl* in Indian languages are the legacy of borrowings from Persian at different periods; thus Urdū *kāghadh* (pron. *kāghaz*), 'paper', appears in early 16th century Hindī texts as *kāgad*, also in Marāṯhī, Dakhnī Urdū, and in the Dravidian languages Kannaḍa and Telugu (*kāgadʷ*); similar variations in *gunbadh*: gunbad, 'dome' (Kann. *gumbadʷ*).

(J. BURTON-PAGE)

DHAMĀR (or Ḏhimār, see Yāḳūt s.v.), a district (*mikhlāf*) and town in South Arabia, south of Ṣanʿā, on the Ṣanʿā-ʿAdan road, near the fortress of Hirrān. The district of Ḏhamār was very fertile and had rich cornfields, splendid gardens, and many ancient citadels and palaces. On account of its fertility it was called the Miṣr of Yaman. The horses of Ḏhamār were famed throughout Yaman for their noble pedigree.

Amongst places which are mentioned as belonging to the district of Ḏhamār are the following: Aḍraʿa, Balad ʿAns, Baraddūn, al-Darb, Dalān and Ḏhamū-rān (the women of these two places had the reputation of being the most beautiful in all South Arabia), Ḏhū Ḏjuzub, al-Talbūʿ, al-Tunan, Thamar, Raḵhama (Hamdānī mentions a Ruḏjma), al-Samʿāniyya, Sanabān, Ṣhawkān, al-ʿAḏjala, al-ʿAshsha, al-Ḳaṭāyṭ, Ḳaʿra, Ḳunubba, Muḵhdara, al-Malla al-ʿUlyā and al-Malla al-Suflā, Nahrān, and al-Yafāʿ; among Wādīs: Banā, Ḵhubān, Surba or Suraba (a large Wādī, with many water-mills), Shurād and Māwā; among mountains: Isbīl (near which on the black hill of ʿŪsī was a hot spring called Ḥammām Sulaymān, "bath of Solomon", where people sought relief from leprosy) and Ṣayd (a high mountain with the citadel Sumāra); among citadels: Barʿ, Ḥayāwa, Dathar, al-Rabaʿa, ʿAwadān, ʿUyāna, al-Kawna, Hirrān, Baynūn [*q.v.*], and Hakir.

Not far from Ḏhamār there were popularly believed to be remains of the throne of Bilḳīs (*ʿArsh Bilḳīs*), consisting of several pillars near a large stream which could only be crossed at the risk of one's life; but the explorer Niebuhr, who visited Ḏhamār, could find no trace of it.

The town of Ḏhamār used to be the headquarters of the Zaydiyya sect, and had a famous *madrasa* attended by 500 students, from whose numbers arose many famous scholars. Its inhabitants included many Jews and Banians. After the fail of the kingdom of the Zaydī Imāms of Ṣanʿā, Ḏhamār lost its importance and now enjoys but a miserable existence.

Bibliography: Hamdānī, *Ḏjazīra*, ed. Müller, 55, 80, 104 ff., 107, 135, 189; trad. Forrer, 103, 144, 169-72, 179, 248; Yāḳūt, *Muʿḏjam*, ii, 721 ff., and *passim*; Niebuhr, *Beschreibung von Arabien*, Copenhagen 1772, 235; Sprenger, *Die alte Geographie Arabiens*, ... 1875, 73; H. v. Maltzan, *Reise nach Südarabien*, Brunswick 1873, 399; Ibn al-Muḏjāwir, ed. Löfgren, 190; Naṣhwān, ed. ʿAẓīmuddīn Aḥmad, 39; von Wissmann and Höfner, *Beiträge zur hist. Geogr. des vorislam. Südarabien*, Wiesbaden 1953, 21, 61.

(J. SCHLEIFER-[O. LÖFGREN])

AL-ḎHAMMIYYA, "the people of the blame", is a name given by heresiographers to those who held certain disapproved doctrines. Ṣhahrastānī (134) and Maḳrīzī (*Ḵhiṭaṭ*, Būlāḳ 1270 A.H., ii, 353) apply it to Ṣhīʿīs who claimed that Muḥammad was originally an agent of ʿAlī (the real prophet) but blameably summoned men to himself instead—a position noted (without a name) by Aṣhʿarī (*Maḳālāt al-Islāmiyyīn*, ed. Md. Muḥyī al-Dīn ʿAbd al-Ḥamīd, Cairo 1950, 82), and ascribed also to al-Ṣhalmaghānī [*q.v.*]. Maḳrīzī explains that ʿAlī was silenced by being given Fāṭima. Ṣhahrastānī says they believed

ʿAlī was a god. Both associate them with ʿAlbāʾ (or ʿUlyān, etc.) b. Ḏhirāʿ al-Dawsī (or Asadī or Sadusī), who in Masʿūdī (*Murūḏj*, iii, 265; cf. v, 475) and Ibn Ḥazm (cf. I. Friedlaender, *Heterodoxies of the Shiites*, in *JAOS*, xxix, 102-3) seems to be the originator of the ʿAlawiyya or ʿAyniyya, who exalted ʿAlī's rôle in revelation above Muḥammad's without disapproving Muḥammad.

The name is also applied by Baghdādī (*Farḳ*, 169) to Abū Hāshim b. al-Ḏjubbāʾī and his followers among the Muʿtazilites, whose niceties of psychological analysis led them into seeming to assert that a man could be condemned for a sin he had not yet committed. Muṭahhar al-Maḳdisī (*K. al-badʾ wa 'l-taʾrīkh*, ed. Cl. Huart, Paris 1916, v, 143) gives a different explanation of the same name. He also ascribes the name to one group of Karrāmiyya (145).

(M. G. S. HODGSON)

DHANAB [see NUḎJŪM].

DHĀR, an ancient town on the scarp of the Vindhyas overlooking the Narbadā valley, and since 1956 the headquarters of Dhār district, Madhya Pradesh, India. It stood on the main routes from Dihlī to the Dakhan and to Gudjarāt. From the 3rd/9th to the end of the 7th/13th centuries it was a capital of the Paramāras who ruled Mālwā first as Rāṣhtrakūṭa feudatories and then as independent monarchs. The most powerful of these, Vākpati II (or Muñḏja) and Bhoḏjadeva I, receive mention in many Muslim histories of India. Bhoḏja's troops may have joined Ānandapāla in 399/1008 against Maḥmūd of Ghaznī, while Ḏjagaddeva, 480/1087-497/1104, defeated Ghaznavid forces in the Pandjāb. Undermined by Čawlukya and Yādava onslaughts and attacked by Ḳuṭb al-Dīn Aybak in 596/1199, Iletmiṣh in 632/1234 and Ḏjalāl al-Dīn Ḵhaldjī in 690/1291 and 692/1293, the Ḏhār Paramāras broke up in confusion at the end of the 7th/13th century.

In 705/1305 ʿAlāʾ al-Dīn's general ʿAyn al-Mulk Multānī defeated the Paramāra Rādjā Mahlakdeva and his minister Gogadeva, slaying both. Dhār was taken and ʿAyn al-Mulk appointed governor of Mālwā. Until 804/1401 Dhār remained the seat of the governors of Mālwā appointed from Dihlī. In 731/1330-31 Muḥammad b. Tughluḳ struck token *tanka*s at Dhār. He himself was at Dhār during the famine of 736/1335. His appointment of ʿAzīz Ḵhammār as *shiḳḳdār* of Dhār, with instructions to curb the *amīrān-i ṣada*, led to the massacre of over eighty of them at Dhār and precipitated the fatal revolts of 745/1345 onwards. The last governor, Dilāwar Ḵhān [*q.v.*], was appointed prior to 793/1390.

From 801/1399 to 804/1401 Dhār entertained Sultan Maḥmūd Tughluḳ, a refugee from Tīmūr, at Dhār, but on Maḥmūd's return to Dihlī Dilāwar Ḵhān declared himself independent at Dhār. His son, Alp Ḵhān, succeeded him in 808/1405 with the title Hūshang Ṣhāh. Accused of parricide, he was attacked at Dhār and carried off prisoner by Muẓaffar Ṣhāh of Gudjarāt, whose brother Naṣrat Ṣhāh was appointed governor at Dhār. His extortion provoked rebellion and he was expelled from Dhār, where Hūshang Ṣhāh was reinstalled in 811/1408.

Thereafter Hūshang Ṣhāh made Māndū his capital, as did his successors. The importance of Dhār consequently declined, though during the struggle between the sons of sultan Ghiyāth al-Dīn, in 905-06/1499-50 Nāṣir al-Dīn made Dhār his headquarters, as did his son, Ṣhihāb al-Dīn, when he rebelled in 916/1512.

In the Mughal period, though visited by Akbar and Ḏjahāngīr, Dhār was merely one of the sixteen *maḥal*s of Māndū *sarkār*, chiefly notable, as befitted Pīrān-i Dhār, for extensive *suyūrghal* grants. Its importance, as a strong fort on the Dihlī-Dakhan communications, revived with the Mughal-Marāṭhā struggle. South Mālwā was first invaded in 1111/1699, and in 1115/1703 the fawdjdār of Māndū took refuge from the Marāṭhās in Dhār. From 1129/1717 Shāhū granted *mokāsā*s to his generals in southern Mālwā, and from 1135/1722 Dhār was allotted to Udādji Pawār. The Mughal governor Girdhār Bahādur and his cousin Dayā Bahādur refused Udādjī's demands and repelled Marāṭhā attacks until both were killed at the Amdjherā pass below Dhār on 25 Djumādā I 1141/29 November 1728.

From 1141-42/1729 the Marāṭhās collected dues from Dhār *maḥall*, though the fort, strengthened by Girdhār's son and successor Bhawāni Rām, held out and Muḥammad Khān Bangash defeated the attacks made on Dhār from 6-18 Ramaḍān 1143/15-27 March 1731 by Malhār Holkār. But on 15 Ramaḍān 1150/6 January 1738 Niẓām al-Mulk conferred Mālwā on the Peshwā, who allotted the Dhār territories to Yashwant Rāo Pawār. (Dhār fort was only taken on 6 Shawwāl 1153/25 December 1740). Dhār state, which came under British protection in 1234/1819, remained under Pawār rulers until 28 May 1948 when it was merged in Madhya Bhārat, and in 1956 in Madhya Pradesh.

Bibliography: *Central India gazetteer*, v, 389-515; *EIM*, 1909-10, 1-29; D. C. Ganguly, *History of the Paramara dynasty*, Dacca 1933; H. N. Wright, *The sultans of Delhi*; *their coinage and metrology*, Delhi 1936, 167; R. Sinh, *Malwa in transition*, Bombay 1936; *History and culture of the Indian people*, vi, *the Delhi sultanate*, Bombay 1960. See also DILĀWAR KHAN; MĀLWĀ; MĀNḌŪ.

(J. B. HARRISON)

2. — Monuments. From the architectural point of view the monuments of Dhār are important only as illustration of the earliest phase of the Mālwā style, one of the characteristic provincial styles of Indian Islamic architecture (see HIND, Architecture). The earliest mosque building is that in the tomb enclosure of Kamāl al-Dīn Mālawī (locally called Kamāl Mawla), a disciple of Niẓām al-Dīn Čishtī of Dihlī; the oldest grave inscription in this enclosure is of 795/1392-3, which records that the ruling sovereign was Maḥmūd Tughluḳ, whose local representative was Dilāwar Khān [*q.v.*]. This, and the slightly later Djāmiʿ masdjid, are both adaptations from pillaged Hindū temple material, of trabeate construction; the outer portico of the Djāmiʿ masdjid shows an attempt to integrate the trabeate façade by the interposing of pointed arches, of no structural significance, between the columns, the forerunner of the arrangement in the mosque of Malik Mughīth at Māndū [*q.v.*]. The Djāmiʿ masdjid bears inscriptions of 807/1404-5 on the east entrance, and of 15 Radjab 807/17 January 1405 on the north entrance (presumably misread by Djahāngīr, *Tūzuk-i Djahāngīrī*, Persian text 201-2); for these see *EIM*, 1909-10, 11-2 and plates III and IV. A third mosque of similar style and date is the so-called School of Rādjā Bhodj, which owes its misnomer to numerous paving slabs and pillar stones carved with mnemonic rules of Sanskrit grammar.

Later buildings almost all owe their origin to the first Khaldjī ruler of Mālwā, Maḥmūd Shāh (839/1436-873/1469), including the restoration of perhaps the oldest Muslim tomb in Dhār, that of ʿAbd Allāh Shāh Čangāl, who is said to have converted "Rādjā Bhōdj" to Islam; it has been disputed whether this refers to Bhōdja I (1010-1053), a broad-minded and tolerant but nevertheless strict Shayva Hindū—in which case this *pīr* could perhaps have come to Mālwā with the army of Maḥmūd of Ghaznī—, or to Bhōdja II (1280-1310), at a time when conversion to Islam might have been politically expedient for the ruler of a small state; nothing is known of this *pīr*, and the story of Bhōdja's conversion is now regarded as most doubtful, but the inscription erected by Maḥmūd Shāh in 859/1455 (*EIM*, 1909-10, 1-5 and Plate I; 42 couplets of Persian verse, one of the longest Persian inscriptions in India) shows the then implicit belief in this tradition. To Maḥmūd Shāh is due also the restoration of the tomb of Kamāl al-Dīn (inscription over doorway of 861/1456-7); a tomb opposite the *pīr*'s is said by local tradition to be Maḥmūd's own.

The Djāmiʿ masdjid is known in later times as the Lāṭ masdjid, from the iron pillar (*lāṭ*) — probably a victory pillar of a local Paramāra king in the early 13th century, cf. *ASI*, *Annual Report*, 1902-3, 203—lying outside; this pillar bears an inscription recording Akbar's brief stay in Dhār in 1008/1599, its position showing that the pillar had already fallen.

The fort, now empty of internal buildings, is said to have been built by Muḥammad b. Tughluḳ on his way to the conquest of the Deccan; no adequate description of it exists.

Bibliography: E. Barnes, *Dhar and Mandu*, in *JBBRAS*, xxi, 1904, 340-54; idem, *Conservation of ancient buildings at Māṇḍū and Dhâr*, in *ASI*, *Annual Report*, 1903-4, 30-45; C. E. Luard, *Dhār state gazetteer*, Bombay 1908, 106-12; G. Yazdani, *The inscription on the tomb of ʿAbdullāh Shāh Changāl at Dhār*, in *EIM*, 1909-10, 1-5 and Plate I; idem, *Remarks on the inscriptions of Dhār and Māṇḍū*, in *EIM*, 1911-2, 8-11; Zafar Hasan, *The inscriptions of Dhār and Māṇḍū*, in *EIM*, 1909-10, 6-29.

(J. BURTON-PAGE)

DHARRA, a term denoting, in the Ḳurʾān or *ḥadīth*s, the smallest possible appreciable quantity. The Ḳurʾān uses it five times, in the expression *mithḳāl al-dharra*, "the weight of a *dharra*",—to extol the Omniscience of God (X, 61; XXXIV, 3), or His absolute Omnipotence (XXXIV, 20), or His supreme Justice in retribution: IV, 40 and the celebrated text XCIX, 7-8 "He who shall have done the weight of one *dharra* of good shall see it; he who shall have done the weight of one *dharra* of evil shall see it".

Commentators on the Ḳurʾān and interpreters of *ḥadīth*s have explained *dharra* by two images, both of which go back to Ibn ʿAbbās. 1). From the most usual meaning of the root: powder, dust. The *dharra* is the dust which remains clinging to the hand after the rest has been blown off (the sense recollected in *tafsīr*, for example, by Khāzin in xcix, 7-8); or the weightless dust, seen when sunlight shines through a window (*id.*, iv, 40). 2). The image of the "red (black) ant", by a kind of equivalence *dharra-namla* (al-Zamakhsharī): "the weight of the head of a red ant", (Khāzin iv, 40); "little ant" (xcix, 7-8); "little red ant" (x, 61), etc.—The *dharra* is also said to be equivalent to "the hundredth part of a grain of barley".

In translation *dharra* is generally rendered as "atom" (cf. R. Blachère: "weight of an atom", except for iv, 40: "weight of an ant"). L. Massignon, *Passion d'al-Ḥallādj*, Paris 1922, 550, gives *dharra* in the sense of atom with *nuḳta* ("point") in order to explain the *djawhar fard* ("elemental substance") of the *kalām* and the *falsafa*. It is noticeable, however, that *dharra* was not generally used as the technical term to denote the philosophical atomism of Democritus, Epicurus and the Muslim "atomists". Two technical expressions were used in preference: *djuzʾ* [*q.v.*], "part" (indivisible), and *djawhar fard*. On the other hand, modern Arabic readily renders the atom of modern physics by *dharra* (*djuzʾ* becoming "molecule").

Thus Arabic vocabulary is careful to distinguish between three terminologies: 1) physical sciences: *dharra*, atom; 2) mathematical sciences: *nukta*, geometrical point (thus Ibn Sīnā, *Risāla fi 'l-Ḥudūd*); 3) philosophy: *djuzʾ* and *djawhar fard*, "atom",—and in this way to emphasize that the last usage does not include the atom of modern physics. (L. Gardet)

DHĀRWĀR, a district in the Belgaum division of the Indian State of Mysore. It has an area of 5,305 square miles and a population of 1,575,386 of whom 15% are Muslims (1951 Census). Until the 7th/13th century it remained free from the Muslim invader. In the following century it formed part of Muḥammad b. Tughluḳ's extensive empire. After the decline of Tughluḳ power its geographical position, especially its proximity to the Rāyčūr Dōʾāb, made it a bone of contention between the Bahmanī kingdom of the Deccan and the Hindū empire of Vidjayanagar. From about 972/1565 it seems to have been conquered by the ʿĀdil Shāhī sultans of Bīdjāpur who retained it until their power was crushed by Awrangzīb in 1097/1686. With the disintegration of the Mughal empire in the 12th/18th century it was frequently overrun by plundering Marāṫhā forces. For a time it was annexed to Ḥaydar ʿAlī's kingdom of Mysore but, in 1791, during the reign of Tipu Sulṭān, the fort of Dhārwār was taken by an Anglo-Maratha force under Captain Little and Paraśurāma Bhāu (see Grant Duff's *History of the Mahrattas*, vol. ii, 197-201, Oxford 1921 and Wilk's *Mysoor*, vol. ii, 483-8, Mysore 1932). After this it remained in Marāṫhā hands until their defeat by the British in 1817. In 1857-8 Bhāskar Rāo (Bābā Sāhib), the chief of Nargūnd in Dhārwār, who had been refused permission to adopt an heir by Lord Dalhousie, rose in revolt and murdered Charles Manson, the British Commissioner and Political Agent for the Southern Maratha Country. This resulted in the execution of Bhāskar Rāo and the forfeiture of the Nargūnd estate (see *Indian Mutiny*, Kaye and Malleson, vol. v, 164-72, London 1889). Dhārwār was administered as part of Bombay until the reorganization of 1956 when it was transferred to the new State of Mysore.

(C. Collin Davies)

DHĀT. In Muslim philosophy this term is used in several senses. As a general term it can mean "thing", like the words *shayʾ* and *maʿnā*; next, it signifies the "being" or "self" or even "ego": thus *bi-dhātihī* means "by itself" or "by his self"; but most commonly *dhāt* is employed in the two different meanings of "substance" and "essence", and is a translation of the Greek οὐσία. In its former usage as "substance" it is the equivalent of the subject or substratum (ὑποκείμενον) and is contrasted with qualities or predicates attributed to it and inhering in it. In the second sense of "essence", however, *dhāt* signifies the essential or constitutive qualities of a thing as a member of a species, and is contrasted with its accidental attributes (*aʿrāḍ* [see ʿarad]). In this sense it is the equivalent of *māhiyya* [*q.v.*] and corresponds to the Greek τό τι ἦν εἶναι. Some Muslim philosophers distinguish, within the essence, its prior parts from the rest and apply the description "essential" (*dhātī*) to the former: *dhātī* is the conceptually and ontologically prior part of the essence of a thing. Derivative from this second sense of the term is the distinction between the essential and the temporal order. Thus ordinarily a cause is said to be both essentially and temporally prior to its effects. Some causes are, however, not temporally prior to their effects but only essentially; this is the case with the relationship between God and the world according to Muslim philosophers who reject the idea of temporal creation.

Both these meanings of *dhāt* as essence and substance, however, are combined and often confused, like the term corresponding to *djawhar* [*q.v.*] by Aristotle and his followers. This is because essence is regarded as being constitutive of the substance which is a substance only in so far as it is constituted by this essence. The term *dhāt*, from the point of view of this ambiguity in meaning, is especially relevant to the philosophico-theological doctrine of God and His Attributes. The Muʿtazila and the philosophers deny Divine Attributes and declare God to be a simple substance or pure Essence; in this case simple substance and simple essence coalesce and are identical with one another. The Attributes are then construed either as negations or as pure relations. Although both the Muʿtazila and the philosophers agree in the denial of Divine Attributes, their reasons for doing so are very different. The Muʿtazila were moved to deny Attributes through the theological anxiety that affirmation of these would be contrary to strict monotheism. The philosophers' reasoning, on the other hand, is the result of the rational search for a simple being from which all multiplicity and composition—existential and conceptual—should be excluded, but which at the same time should "explain" the multiplicity of existing things. In this they were followers of Plotinus. The Islamic orthodoxy devised a formula according to which Attributes are "neither identical with God nor other than Him".

The Ṣūfī theosophy, which became widely influential during the later middle ages of Islam, found another way of reconciliation between philosophy and orthodoxy. According to this theory God, as absolute, is pure and simple Being without any Attributes; but through a series of "descents" or "determinations" He becomes progressively determinate. In this pantheistic world-view the mystic, in his upward march towards communion with God, passes through a series of theophanies (*tadjalliyāt*) from the levels of Names and Attributes to the final theophany of the Absolute.

Bibliography: al-Thānāwī, *Dictionary of Technical Terms*, s.v. (F. Rahman)

DHĀT al-HIMMA [see dhu 'l-himma].

DHĀT al-SAWĀRI [see supplement].

DHĀTĪ, Turkish poet, b. 875/1471 in Balıkesir. The son of a modest bootmaker, as a boy he practised his father's craft but soon gave it up, moving to the capital during the reign of Bāyezīd I where, following his natural inclinations, he devoted his life to poetry. An easy and prolific versifier, he made a living from the gifts of the notables of the day, to whom he dedicated *ḳaṣīdas* (among others, to the sultans Selīm I, Suleymān I, to Djaʿfer Čelebi and Ibn Kemāl). In his old age he practised geomancy in a shop which soon became a sort of literary club for men of letters, where Dhātī helped and encouraged many young talents (such as Tashlīdjalī Yaḥyā

Khayālī, Bāķī). A "bohemian", unmarried and a heavy drinker, he died in 953/1546 at Istanbul, in poverty.

Apart from a voluminous *dīwān*, his major work is *Sham' we Pervāne*, a *mathnawī* of nearly 4000 couplets interspersed with *ghazals*, which develops one of the favourite themes of *mathnawī* literature (for a fairly good copy, see Süleymāniye (Lala Ismā'īl) no. 443).

With no regular education and training, Dhātī taught himself all the knowledge which was required by a *dīwān*-poet. Much appreciated by his contemporaries and early *tedhkire*-writers, unduly neglected later, Dhātī was a poet of remarkable talent and skill, and contributed to the refinement of language and style of *dīwān*-poetry, and thus became a link between Nedjātī and Bāķī.

Bibliography: The *tedhkires* of Laṭīfī, Kînalîzāde Ḥasan Čelebi, and the biographical section of 'Ālī's *Kunh al-Akhbār*, s.v.; Gibb, *Ottoman Poetry*, ii; M. Fuad Köprülü, *Divan Edebiyatı Antolojisi*, Istanbul 1934, 133; A. Bombaci, *Storia della letteratura turca*, Milan 1956, 336.

(Fahir Iz)

DHAWḲ, "taste", is a technical term used in philosophy, in aesthetics (especially literature), and in Ṣūfism.

1. In philosophy [see FALSAFA] *dhawḳ* is the name for the gustatory sense-perception. Following Aristotle, it is defined as a kind of sub-species of the tactual sense, localized in the gustatory organ, the tongue. It differs from tactual sense, however, in that mere contact with skin is not sufficient for gustation to occur: besides contact, it needs a medium of transmission, viz. the salival moisture. The salival moisture, in order to transmit tastes faithfully, must be in itself tasteless, otherwise it will impose its own taste upon the object of gustation, as is the case with patients of bile. The problem is discussed whether the tasted object "mixes" with the saliva and thus its parts are directly tasted, or whether the object causes a qualitative change in the saliva, which is then transmitted to the tongue. The answer is that both are conjointly possible and it is therefore held that if it were possible for the object to be transmitted without this moisture gustation could occur all the same, unlike, for example, vision, for which a medium is absolutely necessary. Nine kinds of taste—which are joint products of the tactual and gustatory sensations—are enumerated by Avicenna.

2. In aesthetics, *dhawḳ* is the name for the power of aesthetic appreciation; it is something that "moves the heart". But although it is psychologically subjective, it nevertheless requires objective standards (*idjmā'*) for objectivity and verification, "just as the taste of sugar is private, nevertheless its sweetness is something universally agreed upon by consensus".

3. The aesthetic definition of *dhawḳ* already stands at the threshold of the mystic use of the term. In its mystical usage this term denotes the direct quality of the mystic experience. The Christian mystics had also used the term (*e.g.*, the αἴσθησις καρδίας and γεύσις of Bishop Diadochus), although it would occur naturally to a mystic endeavouring to distinguish direct experience from discursive knowledge. The metaphor of "sight" is also often used, but *dhawḳ* has more qualitative overtones of enjoyment and "intoxication" (*sukr*) besides the noetic element which it shares with the term "sight". Thus, Djalāl al-Dīn Rūmī says "you cannot appreciate the intoxication of this wine unless you taste it". Kamāl al-Dīn in his *Iṣṭilāḥāt al-ṣūfiyya* states that *dhawḳ* is the first stage of *wadjd* (ecstasy), the two further stages being *shurb* (drinking) and *riy* (satisfaction). According to some, however, *wadjd* is a higher stage than *dhawḳ*. These distinctions, however, are later, and concern the doctrine of Ṣūfism rather than its practice.

Dhawḳ is also commonly used to denote insight or intuitive appreciation, generally of any phenomenon whatsoever, and implies the previous acquisition and exercise of a skill. A doctor, for example, may *on the basis of* his previous experience be able to identify a novel disease by *dhawḳ*; or a historian, in face of conflicting evidence on a point, may be able to decide by a kind of "historical intuition".

Bibliography: in addition to the references above, and general works on philosophy and literary aesthetics, see al-Thānawī, *Dictionary of technical terms*, s.v.; al-Djurdjānī, *K. al-Ta'rīfāt*.

(F. Rahman)

DHAWḲ, Muḥammad Ibrāhīm Shaykh, Urdū poet b. Dihlī 11 Dhu 'l-Ḥidjdja 1204/18 December 1790 (so Āzād; in 1203 according to a contemporary Calcutta newspaper, cf. *Nawā-i Adab*, 45), the only son of Sh. Muḥammad Ramaḍān, a trusted servant of Nawwāb Luṭf 'Alī Khān of Dihlī. His early schooling in Persian and Arabic was in the mosque-school of Ḥāfiẓ Ghulām Rasūl Shawḳ, a poet and a pupil of Shāh Naṣīr (Sheftā, 150), who inspired the young learner with a love for reading and writing poetry. Dhawḳ later became a pupil of Shāh Naṣīr and followed his style, but after some time, when a rupture had taken place between the pupil and the teacher, he began to write successfully in the style of the well-known masters of Urdū poetry, particularly Sawdā. He was now attending *mushā'aras* and acquiring fame as a young poet (cf. Sprenger, 222; Ḳāsim, *Madjmū'a-i Naghz*, ii, 385: Dhawḳ was about 17 when this was written). He intensified his study of the sciences (medicine, music, astrology, etc.) when an opportunity came for him to complete his education, and the technical terms of these stood him in good stead later when he came to write *ḳaṣīdas*. His reputation grew rapidly, and Mīr Kāẓim Ḥusayn, an old class-fellow, introduced him to Abū Ẓafar, the heir apparent of Akbar Shāh II, whose poetical compositions he was in due course appointed to correct, roughly from 1816 (cf. Karīm al-Dīn, *Tadhkira-i Nāzninān*, 118; but cf. also his *Ṭabaḳāt*, 459). On presenting a *ḳaṣīda* to Akbar Shāh he received the title of *Khāḳānī-i Hind*, by which Shefta (between 1831-3) calls him. After the prince ascended the throne, as Bahādur Shāh II, in 1837, Dhawḳ became his laureate, and his pay, formerly between Rs. 4 and 7, was raised to 30, later to 100, rupees. In his old age he was made a Khān Bahādur, and received many other favours after reciting his court odes in the 'Īd *darbārs* and other ceremonial occasions. He died on 23 Safar 1271/15 November 1854 (Sābir, 224 ff., quoting also Ẓafar, and an elegy of Sōz, particularly 237, line 10).

Dhawḳ was of rather small stature, with a dark pock-marked face (the result of a childhood attack), bright eyes, and a loud but pleasant voice. He had a good memory, and knew a large number of Persian verses by heart. He was a religious-minded man, of the Shī'a persuasion according to Karīm al-Dīn's information, contented and kind-hearted (he wrote no satires). His only son Muḥammad Ismā'īl (called in the *Nawā-i Adab*, 49, Wakār al-Dawla Muḥammad Ismā'īl Khān) survived him for only a few years.

He was a prolific writer, as his contemporaries (Ṣābir, Sayyid Aḥmad Khān, Ānwar, Āzād and others) testify, but much of his work was lost in the disturbances of 1857-8. According to Shēfta, who used to meet him occasionally, 106, and Ṣābir, 223, he did not arrange his poems in the form of a *dīwān*; according to Āzād Dhawḳ compiled a *dīwān* when 15 or 16 years old, though its fate is unknown. Ẓafar also refers to a *dīwān* of Dhawḳ (*Hindustānī*, April 1945, 40). The earliest edition of the *dīwān*, 186 pp., was lithographed in Dihlī in 1859; no reference to it occurs in the subsequent editions. An attempt to collect his work was made by Ḥāfiẓ Ghulām Rasūl Wīrān (the blind pupil of Dhawḳ, who had associated with him for some 20 years and who knew a large number of his poems by heart) and his co-editors Ẓahīr and Anwar (for whom see Saksena, 156 ff.; Bailey, 74 ff.); as well as taking dictation from Wīrān, Ẓahīr and Anwar made use of various *tadhkira*s and of the note-books of the poet's pupils. This *dīwān* (2393 *bayts*) was lithographed in Dihlī in 1279/1862-3, with an Urdū colophon and Anwar's Persian preface (20 pp.) appended to the book; it was later lithographed several times, without the Persian preface, in Kānpur, Dihlī, Mīraʾth, etc. The largest edition was produced by Āzād, in his old age (1885-9 ?) just before his mind became finally deranged; he states that soon after Dhawḳ's death he and the poet's son, Muḥammad Ismāʿīl, collected Dhawḳ's poems after the labour of many months. This collection was published from Lahore in 1890 (Blumhardt, *Suppl. Cat.*, 319), and is composed mostly of *ghazal*s, 24 or 25 *ḳaṣīda*s, and some fragments (5040 *bayt*s in all), with interesting prefatory and marginal notes. Several pages of rare verses of the poet have been quoted from a *Nigāristān-i Sukhan* in the *Muʾāṣir*. More of his unpublished verses can be collected from old *tadhkira*s. This and what follows would justify a new critical edition of the *dīwān*.

In a critical examination of Āzād's edition (Ph. D. thesis, 1939) Muḥammad Ṣādiḳ claims that Āzād revised and improved Dhawḳ's juvenile work, in some cases slightly, in others drastically; later, in 1944-7, Professor Maḥmūd Shērānī proved the interpolations throughout the *dīwān* even more fully and conclusively, and the same is shown by Āzād's copy of the *dīwān* (edition of 1279 A.H.; now in Dr. Ṣādiḳ's possession) which bears emendations in his own handwriting.

As a poet Dhawḳ enjoyed great popularity among his contemporaries who praised him for handling *ghazal*s, *ḳaṣīda*s and other verse forms with equal facility. He owed his great prestige partly to his being a teacher of Bahādur Shāh II, partly to his writing in a style which was, unlike Ghālib's, easily intelligible to all. His work shows great technical skill; the language he uses is perfect in its eloquence, purity, sweetness and naturalness of expression; he uses idioms in a masterly manner, and his similes and metaphors have novelty and beauty. His ideas are well-arranged and often fresh, and his allusions have grace and elegance. Generally speaking, however, he has not the subjectivity of Dard or Mīr; his *ghazal*s, therefore, lack what *ghazal*s must have —effect and warmth of feeling. In the *ḳaṣīda*, however, he was much more successful, and is regarded as the best *ḳaṣīda*-writer, next to Sawdā, in Urdū. On the whole he shared the tastes of Nāsikh and Ātish of Lucknow, rather than those of the Dihlī school. Gradually public opinion has swung more in the direction of the rival school represented by Ghālib and Muʾmin.

Bibliography: Ḳāsim, Ḳudratallāh, *Madjmūʿa-i Naghz*, completed 1221/1806-7, Lahore 1933; Ibn Amīnallāh, Ṭūfān, *Tadhkira-i Shuʿarāʾ-i Urdū kā*, Dihlī 1844 (not available to me); Muṣṭafā Khān Shēfta, *Gulshan-i Be-khār*, compiled between 1832 and 1835, 2nd ed., lith., Dihlī 1837; Karīm al-Dīn, *Guldasta-i Nāzanīnān*, Dihlī 1261/1845, 118 (cites 549 *bayt*s of Dhawḳ); idem, *Ṭabaḳāt-i shuʿarā-i Hind*, Dihlī 1848, 458; Mirzā Ḳādir Bakhsh Ṣābir, *Gulistān-i sukhan*, Dihlī 1271/1854-5; *Nigāristān-i sukhan* (not available to me, but see *Muʾaṣir* (Urdū quarterly), x-xi, Patnā 1957; Wīrān—Zahīr—Anwar, *Dīwān-i Dhawḳ*, Dihlī 1279/1862-3; Sayyid Aḥmad Khān, *Āthār al-ṣanādīd*, Lucknow 1900; A. Sprenger, *Catalogue of the Arabic, Persian and Hindustany mss. of the libraries of the King of Oudh*, Calcutta 1854, 222 (notice based on Shēfta, see above, and Aʿẓam al-Dawla Mīr Muḥammad Khān Sarwar, *ʿUmda-i Muntakhaba*, completed between 1216 and 1246 A.H.); Nassākh, *Sukhan-i shuʿarāʾ*, composed 1281, Lucknow 1291/1874, 166 ff.; M. Garcin de Tassy, *Histoire de la littérature hindouie et hindoustanie*[2], Paris 1871, iii, 339, 364; Sayyid ʿAlī Ḥasan Khān, *Bazm-i sukhan*, Āgra 1298/1881, 51; Sayyid Nūr al-Ḥasan Khān, *Tadhkira Ṭūr-i Kalīm*, Āgra 1298/1881; J. F. Blumhardt, *Catalogue of Hindustānī printed books in the library of the British Museum*, London 1889, col. 231; idem, *A supplementary catalogue* ..., London 1909, col. 323; Muḥammad Ḥusayn Āzād, *Dīwān-i Dhawḳ* (the life of Dhawḳ as given in this and the following work is to be used cautiously); idem, *Āb-i Hayāt*, Lahore 1907, 420; Srī Rām, *Khumkhāna-i Djāwid*, Dihlī 1917, iii, 269; Shāh Muḥammad Sulaymān, *Intikhāb-i ghazaliyāt-i Dhawḳ* (with *Muwāzana-i Dhawḳ wa Ghālib*), Budāyūn 1925 (?); T. Grahame Bailey, *History of Urdu literature*, Calcutta 1932, 70 and index; Muḥammad Rafīk Khāwar, *Khāḳānī-i Hind* (*ēk muṭālaʿa*) Lahore 1933; Muḥammad Ṣādiḳ, *Maulvī* [*sic*] *Muhammad Husain Āzād: his life, works and influence* (Ph. D. thesis, 1939, Appx. viii, VII, now in the Panjab University library); Rām Bābū Saksenā, *History of Urdu literature*, Allāhābād 1940, 152-6, 16, 29; Ḳāḍī Ghulām Amīr, *Bihtarīn ghazal-gō*. Lucknow 1941; Firāḳ Gorakhpurī, *Andāze*, Allāhābād, xcii (1937), cii (1944); Kalīm al-Dīn Aḥmad, *Urdū shāʿirī par ēk naẓar*[2], Paṭnā 1952, i, 113; *Hindustānī* (Urdū quarterly), Allāhābād, 1944, i, iv; 1945, all issues; 1946, i; 1947, i; Sayyid Masʿūd Ḥasan Riḍawī, *Āb-i Hayāt kā tanḳīdī muṭālaʿa*, Lucknow 1953, 59, 69; *Nawā-i Adab* (Urdū quarterly), Bombay, ix/3 (July-September 1958), 41; Sayyid Imdād Imām Athar, *Kāshif al-ḥaḳāʾiḳ*, Lahore 1959, i, 29 ff., 258 ff., 280 ff.

(MUHAMMAD SHAFI)

DHAWWĀḲ [see ČASHNAGĪR].

AL-**DHIʾĀB**, "the wolves", a South Arabian tribe whose lands lie between the territory of the Lower ʿAwāliḳ [*q.v.*] and the Lower Wāḥidī [*q.v.*]. There are also considerable settlements of the Dhiʾāb in the country of the Lower Wāḥidī itself, the villages of which are largely occupied by them. The soil is unfertile and mostly prairie-like pasture land. In the east of the distict is a mountain of some size, the Djabal Ḥamrā, over 4000 ft. high. The chief place is the fishing village of Ḥawra (al-Ulyā) with an important harbour.

The Dhiʾāb are a very wild, warlike tribe of

robbers, and are therefore feared throughout South Arabia. They are *Ḳabāʾil* (free, independent tribes) and are considered as genuine Ḥimyarīs; their slogan (*ṣarkha*, *ʿazwa*) is: *anā dhēb* (*dhib*) *Ḥamyar* (*Ḥimyar*), "I am the wolf of Ḥimyar". They have no common sultan, and the various branches of the tribe are ruled by Shaykhs, called *Abū*, "father", whom they heed only in case of war. The most influential Shaykh of the Dhiʾāb lives in ʿIrḳa (ʿIrgha).

Bibliography: H. v. Maltzan, *Reise nach Südarabien*, Brunswick 1873, 224, 235 ff.; C. Landberg, in *Arabica*, iv, 1897, 19 ff.; v, 1898, 230 ff.; von Wissmann and Höfner, *Beiträge zur hist. Geogr. des vorislam. Südarabien*, Wiesbaden 1953, 76, 92, 98 ff. (J. Schleifer-[O. Löfgren])

DHIʾB, the wolf. Most of the cognate forms in other Semitic languages have the same significance. Numerous synonyms and sobriquets are found in Arabic, such as *sirḥān, uways, sīd, abū djaʿda*, etc. In local usage, *dhiʾb* may also denote the jackal (Jayakar, Malouf), yet Hommel's assumption (303, n. 1) that this was the only meaning of the word in ancient Arabic (so also Jacob) is inconsistent with its use in the Sūra of Joseph (Ḳurʾān, XII, 13, 14, 17), where it stands for the biblical 'evil beast' (Gen. xxxvii 20, 33).

Ample mention of the *dhiʾb* is made in ancient Arabic poems, proverbs, popular traditions and *ḥadīths*, some of which are quoted in later zoological writings. Other information given by Arab zoologists goes back to foreign sources, such as Aristotle's *Historia Animalium* and the ancient *Physiologus* literature.

Since *dhiʾb*, in the Arabic script, is similar to *dubb* (= bear), the two words were easily confused and, consequently, the behaviour and properties of one animal have sometimes been attributed to the other.

The *dhiʾb* is described as extremely malignant, quarrelsome and cunning. It is quick of hearing and possesses a powerful sense of smell. It feeds on flesh only but eats herbs when ill. It can go without food for a long time, whence the proverb: "More hungry than a wolf". *Dāʾ al-dhiʾb* (lit.: the wolf's disease) is a metaphorical expression for hunger. Its stomach (according to some: its tongue) is able to dissolve a solid bone but not a date stone. Its penis consists of bone. The female is robuster and more courageous than the male. If a hyena is killed or caught, the *dhiʾb* takes care of her young. Some authors state that the wolf goes single and does not associate, while others describe its behaviour in aggregation; no one separates from the pack, as they do not trust one another. When one becomes weak or is wounded, it is eaten by the others. When asleep, they keep the right and left eye open alternately to keep watch on one another. The wolf is always prone to attack men in contrast to other wild animals which do so only when old and unable to hunt. It assails a person from behind, not from the front. A man who shows no fear of it remains unmolested, but is attacked when afraid. Only ravenous wolves are aggressive. When a wolf has designs on a flock of sheep, it howls so that the dog hears and runs in the direction of the sound; the wolf then goes to the other side where there is no dog and snatches the sheep away. It makes its raids preferably just before sunrise when shepherd and dog are both tired from the night watch.

Some of the information on the wolf belongs to the field of superstition, *e.g.*: If a man carries with him the fang, skin or eye of a wolf, he will overcome his opponents and be loved by all people. The wolf also played a part in Arabic oneiromancy. Its blood, brain, liver, bile, testicles, dung and urine were used for various medicinal purposes.

Bibliography: ʿAbd al-Ghanī al-Nābulusī, *Taʿṭīr al-anām*, Cairo 1354, i, 229 f.; Damīrī, s.v. (transl. Jayakar, i, 834 ff.); Abū Ḥayyān al-Tawḥīdī, *Imtāʿ*, i, 144, 165, 171 f., 177, 183, 186; ii, 31, 105 (transl. Kopf, in *Osiris* xii [1956], index, s.vv. *dhiʾb*, *dhiʾba* and *wolf*); Dāwūd al-Anṭākī, *Tadhkira*, Cairo 1324, i, 150 f.; Djāḥiẓ, *Ḥayawān*[2], index; Hommel, *Säugethiere*, 303 ff., 441; Ibn Ḳutayba, *ʿUyūn al-Akhbār*, Cairo 1925-30, ii, 79, 82, 88 (transl. Kopf, 54, 57 f., 64); Ibn al-Bayṭār, *Djāmiʿ*, Būlāḳ 1291, ii, 127 f.; Ibshīhī, *Mustaṭraf*, bāb 62, s.v.; G. Jacob, *Beduinenleben*[2], 18 f.; A. Malouf, *Arabic Zool. Dict.*, Cairo 1932, 47 f.; Ḳazwīnī (Wüstenfeld), i, 395 f.; al-Mustawfī al-Ḳazwīnī (Stephenson), 29 f.; Nuwayrī, *Nihāyat al-arab*, ix, 270 ff.; E. Wiedemann, *Beitr. z. Gesch. d. Naturw.*, liii, 284. (L. Kopf)

DHIHNĪ, Bayburtlu, Turkish folk-poet, b. towards the end of the 12th/18th century in Bayburt. Educated in Erzurum and Trabzon, he spent ten years in Istanbul and later travelled in the provinces on minor governmental duties; he was for a short time in the service of Muṣṭafā Reshīd Pasha. He spent the last four years of his life in Trabzon and died in a village nearby while on his way to his home town (1275/1859).

His background, somewhat different from that of the usual folk poet, led him to imitate classical poets, and he even composed a complete *dīwān* of traditional poetry in *ʿarūḍ*. But he remained a poor and awkward imitator of *dīwān* poets and his fame rests entirely on a few poems, written in the folk tradition, which he himself tried to ignore and did not include in his *dīwān*. Dhihnī, as a folk poet, is strongly under the influence of classical poets and his poems are full of the figures, images, and similes of *dīwān* poetry. In spite of this he succeeds in capturing the spirit of the genuine folk poet of the early 19th century. His famous *koshma* about his home town was written when he saw Bayburt in utter ruin, after its evacuation by the Russians in 1828.

Bibliography: Ziyaeddin Fahri, *Bayburdlu Zihni*, Istanbul 1928; İbnülemin Mahmud Kemal, *Bayburdlu Zihni*, in *Türk Tarih Encümeni Mec.*, i, 1929; M. Fuad Köprülü, *Türk Sazşairleri Antolojisi*, Istanbul 1940, iii, 450. (Fahir İz)

DHIKR, reminding oneself. "Remind thyself of (*udhkur*) thy Lord when thou forgettest" (*Ḳurʾān*, XVIII, 24). Thus: the act of reminding, then oral mention of the memory, especially the tireless repetition of an ejaculatory litany, finally the very technique of this mention. In *taṣawwuf* the *dhikr* is possibly the most frequent form of prayer, its *muḳābal* ("opposite correlative") being *fikr* [*q.v.*], (discursive) reflection, meditation. In his *Ṭawāsīn*, in connexion with Muḥammad's "nocturnal ascension", al-Ḥalladj declares that the road which passes through "the garden of *dhikr*" and that which takes "the way of *fikr*" are equally valid. For the Ṣūfīs the Ḳurʾānic basis of the *dhikr* is the above-quoted text (cited, among others, by al-Kalābādhī) and XXXIII, 41: "O ye who believe! Remember (*udhkurū*) Allah with much remembrance (*dhikr*^{an} *kathīr*^{an})". *Ḥadīths* are often quoted in support and in praise of the practice.

As an ejaculatory litany tirelessly repeated the *dhikr* may be compared with the "prayer of Jesus" of the oriental Christians, Sinaitic then Anthonic, and also with the *djapa-yōga* of India and the Japanese *nembutsu*, and this quite apart from historical threads which may have played a rôle in one direction or another. One may recognize in these modes of prayer, without denying possible influences, a universal tendency, however climates and religious beliefs may differ.

Traditions of the Brotherhoods:—The *dhikr* may be uttered aloud (*djalī*) or in a low voice (*khafī*). At the beginning the formula must always be articulated. In the Muslim brotherhoods (*ṭarīḳa*) [*q.v.*] there is a double tradition: that of solitary *dhikr* (aloud or whispered). and that of collective *dhikr* (aloud). It is the first which the major texts of the great spiritual writers envisage: "The Ṣūfī retires by himself to a cell (*zāwiya*) ... After sitting in solitude he utters continously "God (Allāh)" being present with his heart as well" (al-Ghazzālī, *Iḥyā'*, iii, 16-7). Several brotherhoods (the Shadhiliyya and their offshoots Khalwatiyya, Darḳāwa, etc.) stress the advantages of solitary *dhikr* and seem to make it a condition of the *dhikr al-khawāṣṣ* (of the "privileged", those well advanced along the spiritual path). Others (Raḥmāniyya, etc.), without excluding the entry into solitude, stress the dangers of it and recommend, at least for a long time, "sessions" (*ḥaḍra*) or "circles" (*ḥalḳa*) of collective *dhikr*. The latter is without doubt as old as the solitary *dhikr*; but in its liturgico-technical form, with prescribed attitudes regulating the respiratory rhythm as well as the physical posture, it seems to have been born at a relatively late date, about the 8th/13th century, betraying Indo-Iranian influence among the Mawlawiyya ("Whirling Dervishes") of Ḳonya, and Indian through Turko-Mongol influence (cf. the descriptions by the Mongol ex-functionary Simnānī, 13th-14th centuries). This technicality, which must have been introduced progressively, extends its influence to the experience of the solitary *dhikr* itself (cf. in the Christian Orient the connexions between the "prayer of Jesus" and the hesychastic technique).

The "sessions" generally take the form of a kind of liturgy which begins with the recitation of Ḳur'ānic verses and prayers composed by the founder of the brotherhood. This is the *ḥizb* or the *wird* [*qq.v.*], often accompanied by the "spiritual oratorio" (*samā'*). *Wird, samā'*, and physical posture during the recitation of the *dhikr* vary with the brotherhoods (see, for the Maghrib, Rinn, *Marabouts et Khouan*). For the *dhikr* itself the best summary is the *Salsabīl al-mu'īn fi'l-ṭarā'iḳ al-arba'īn* of Muḥammad al-Sanūsī (d. 1276/1859) printed on the margin of the same author's *Masā'il al-'ashr*, where there is a condensed account of the essential characteristics of the *dhikr* practised by the forty preceding brotherhoods, of which the Sanūsiyya claim to have adopted the essential. The collective *dhikr* sessions described by Western writers are generally classifiable as "*dhikr* of the commonalty (*al-'awāmm*)". One of the best-observed accounts is that of the Raḥmāniyya by W. S. Haas. It requires correction and completion (*e.g.*, in connexion with the interpretation of the formula used); in any case it can hardly exhaust the subject.

Description of the experience:—Whether collective or solitary, the recitation of the *dhikr* presupposes a preparation. This is the aim of the *ḥizb* and *wird* in the "sessions". But a general preparation is necessary ("renouncing the world to lead an ascetic life" says al-Ghazzālī) and always the intention of the heart (*niyya*). The part played by the *shaykh* ("spiritual director") is a capital one. It is he who directs and regulates the recitation in the collective sessions; it is he who must guide the solitary disciple step by step. The beginner is recommended to close his eyes and to place the image of his *shaykh* before his mind. The disposition of the "circle" in the collective *dhikr* is carefully regulated. He who recites the *dhikr* in solitude is enjoined to sit in an attitude of *tarabbu'* (with legs crossed) or on his heels. The position of the hands is specified. It is recommended that the disciple should perfume himself with benzoin and wear ritually pure clothing.

The formula chosen may vary according to tradition and according to the spiritual advancement attained by the Ṣūfī. A customary formula for the commencement is the "first *shahāda*", *lā ilāh illā 'llāh*. The Shādhilī method is: "One begins the recital from the left side (of the chest) which is, as it were, the niche containing the lamp of the heart, the focus of spiritual light. One continues by passing from the lower part of the chest on the right upwards to the upper part, and so on to the initial position, having thus, so to speak, described a circle" (Ibn 'Iyāḍ). There is another (slightly different) description of the Shādhilī *dhikr* by al-Sanūsī, and a description of the Raḥmānī *dhikr* (same formula) in the late work of Bāsh Tārzī, *Kitāb al-minaḥ*, 79-80, etc.

A formula for advanced adepts (sometimes for solitary beginners, sometimes from the beginning of "collective" sessions) is the "Name of Majesty" *Allāh*. The utterance is accompanied by two movements, says Bāsh Tārzī (ibid., 80): (1) "strike the chest (with the head) where the corporeal heart (which is cone-shaped) is, saying *Allāh* with the head inclined over the navel; (2) raise the head as you pronounce the *hamza* (*'A*) and raise the head from the navel up to a level with the brain, then pronounce the remainder of the formula (*llāh*) on the secret navel". The *dhikr* known as that of the Ḥallādjiyya, according to al-Sanūsī, is: *Allāh*, with the suppression of *Al* and with the vocalization *lāha, lāhi, lāhu* (cf. L. Massignon, *Passion d'al-Ḥallādj*, 342). Al-Sanūsī warns that this procedure may only be used in solitude and by "a man aware of what the result will be". (It appears that the modern 'Alīwiyya brotherhood of Mostaghanem has re-adopted this procedure).

Other formulae are proposed by Ibn 'Aṭā' Allāh of Alexandria, Simnānī, Bāsh Tārzī, etc. in accordance with gnostic hierarchies where spiritual progress is matched with the vision of "coloured lights" which is the sign of it: *Huwa, al-Ḥaḳḳ, al-Ḥayy, al-Ḳayyūm, al-Ḳahhār.*

The duration of the experience is regulated either by the *shaykh*, or, in solitude, by numbers, with or without the help of a rosary (*subḥa*): 300, 3,000, 6,000, 12,000, 70,000 repetitions (cf. the 6,000 or 12,000 "prayers of Jesus" daily of the "Russian Pilgrim" and the Japanese liturgy "of the million" (*nembutsu*). The invocation may finally become unceasing, without care about the exact number. Control of the respiration seems mostly to be concomitant, but it appears more deliberate in the Hamaylī *dhikr* (6th/12th century) and Simnānī's descriptions and also in the counsels of Zayn al-Milla wa 'l-Dīn (no doubt Khawāfī) the commentator on Anṣārī's *Manāzil*.

The *dhikr* as an internal experience:—One of the best sources is the *Miftāḥ al-falāḥ* of Ibn

ʿAṭāʾ Allāh of Alexandria, the second Grand Master of the S̲h̲ād̲h̲ilī order. Reference may also be made, on the one hand, to al-Kalābād̲h̲ī's chapter on the d̲h̲ikr and the matter-of-fact description of G̲h̲azzālī, and, on the other hand, to the numerous gnoses of later times (Zayn al-Dīn, Bās̲h̲ Tārzī, Amīn al-Kurdī Naḳs̲h̲bandī, etc.). Three main stages may be distinguished, each being subdivided; it is to be noted that these progressive stages are found again in the writings of Malay Ṣūfism.

(1) *Dhikr* of the tongue with "intention of the heart" (the mere "*d̲h̲ikr* of the tongue" without *niyya* is rejected, for it would be "just routine, profitless", says Bās̲h̲ Tārzī). (a) At the first step, there is a voluntary recitation, with effort, in order to "place the One Mentioned in the heart" according to the exact modes of utterance and physical postures taught by the s̲h̲ayk̲h̲; it is firstly to this level that the foregoing descriptions apply. (b) At the second step the recitation continues effortless. The disciple, says G̲h̲azzālī (*Iḥyāʾ*, iii, 17), "leaves off the movement of the tongue and sees the word (or formula) as it were flowing over it". Cf. the similar testimony of those who have experienced the "prayer of Jesus" and the Japanese *nembutsu*. However, three elements are still present: the subject conscious of his experience, the state of consciousness, and the One Mentioned: d̲h̲ākir, d̲h̲ikr, mad̲h̲kūr (cf. the triad of Yoga-Sūtra, i, 41: receptive subject, act of reception, object received). The "effortless" step may be compared with the *dhāraṇā* stage of Yoga experience, "fixation" (of mental activity).

(2) *Dhikr* of the heart
"The Ṣūfī reaches a point where he has effaced the trace of the word on his tongue, and finds his heart continuously applied to the d̲h̲ikr (al-G̲h̲azzālī, ibid. Same testimony in *Account by a Russian Pilgrim*). Here also there are two steps: (a) with effort (cf. Ibn ʿAṭāʾ Allāh, *Miftāḥ*, 4), *i.e.*, with the obscure desire to "maintain the formula" which results in something like a pain felt in the physical heart; (b) effortless: this presence is expressed in a sort of hammering of the formula by the beating of the physical heart (same in *Russian Pilgrim*) and by the pulsation of the blood in the veins and the arteries, with no utterance, even mental, of the words, but where the words nevertheless remain. This is a mode of "necessary presence", where the "state of consciousness" dissolves into an *acquired* passivity. Cf. the step of "absorption" (*dhyāna*) of Yoga. Al-G̲h̲azzālī's analysis in the *Iḥyāʾ* halts at this stage. "It is in his (the disciple's) power to reach this limit, and to make the state lasting by repulsing temptations; but, on the other hand, it is not in his power to attract to himself the Mercy of the All-High". This important distinction is reminiscent of al-Ḥallād̲j̲'s exclamation to God: "You are my ravisher, it is not the d̲h̲ikr which has ravished me!" (*Dīwān*, 53). Later traditions no longer draw this distinction. Ibn ʿAṭāʾ Allāh's monograph speaks of a third stage, for which the second is an effective preparation.

(3) *Dhikr* of the "inmost being" (*sirr*)
The heart (ḳalb) was the seat of the "knowledge of divine things"; the "inmost being" (*sirr*), "a substance more subtle than the spirit (rūḥ)" will be the place of the "vision" (mus̲h̲āhada) of them. It is also the place where the tawḥīd takes place, the declaration of divine unity and the unification of the self with the self, and the self with God. The writers often associate this third stage of the d̲h̲ikr with the state of iḥsān, spiritual perfection and beauty. The "arrival" of the "d̲h̲ikr of the inmost

being" is known by this, that "if you leave off the d̲h̲ikr it does not leave you, and the whole being of the Ṣūfī becomes 'a tongue uttering the d̲h̲ikr'" (*Miftāḥ*, 6). The slave of God "has disappeared (g̲h̲āʾib) both from the d̲h̲ikr and the very object of the d̲h̲ikr" (ibid.). Thus no duality must remain. But a twofold step is distinguished even here: (a) fanāʾ ʿan al-d̲h̲ikr wa ʾl-mad̲h̲kūr ... ilā ʾllāh, annihilation away from the d̲h̲ikr and its object ... towards God; (b) fanāʾ ʿan al-fanāʾ ... bi'llāh, annihilation away from the annihilation... in God.

It seems that this state may be compared with the entry into *samādhi* of Indian Yoga (or at least the "samādhi with seed"; any equivalence with the "samādhi without seed" should be more closely examined): "becoming one alone" (cf. the Indian *kaivalya*) conceived as abolition in God, generally in the line of "monism of the Being" (waḥdat al-wud̲j̲ūd). The personality of the Ṣūfī has, it as were, "disappeared" in the act of abolishing all acts. Ibn ʿAṭāʾ Allāh's description of the d̲h̲ikr al-sirr goes as far as possible in expressing this.

Accompanying phenomena and explicatory gnoses:—Ibn ʿAṭāʾ Allāh describes the d̲h̲ikr of the tongue as sounds of voices and rhythms "within the periphery of the head". Explanation: "the son of Adam is a mixture of all substances, noble and base", and the sounds heard come from each of the "constituent elements of these substances" (*Miftāḥ*, 5); the d̲h̲ikr liberates the harmony established between the microcosm and the macrocosm (cf. the period of "cosmization" of Yoga). The d̲h̲ikr of the heart resembles "the buzzing of bees, without a loud or disturbing noise" (ibid.) and is accompanied by luminous and coloured phenomena, at this stage intermittent. Al-G̲h̲azzālī drew attention to this apparition of "lights" which "sometimes pass like a flash of lightning and sometimes stay, sometimes last and sometimes do not last, sometimes follow each other different from one another, sometimes blend into one single mood" (loc. cit.). He explains them as "gleams of truth" released by God's good will, but other authors later describe them as intrinsically and obligatorily bound up with the d̲h̲ikr experience.

Later writers describe these luminous phenomena as being even more brilliant at the step of the d̲h̲ikr of the inmost being, of which they become the particular mark. This time "the fire of the d̲h̲ikr does not go out, and its lights do not flee ... You see always lights going up and others coming down; the fire around you is bright, very hot, and it flames" (*Miftāḥ*, 6). Yoga describes similar phenomena. Moreover it would be rewarding to make a comparison and a distinction between the Ṣūfī analyses and either the Buddhist "objective" illumination or the "uncreated light of the Thabor" of the oriental forms of Christianity. Various late authors establish other successive stages from the d̲h̲ikr of the inmost being which are also marked by variously coloured luminous phenomena. The descriptions vary with the texts and do not seem to affect the structure itself of the experience. This is the hierarchy proposed by Simnānī: grey smoke (corporeal envelope); blue (physical soul); red (heart); white light ("inmost being"); yellow (spirit [rūḥ]); black (subtle and mysterious principle, k̲h̲afiyya); green (reality [ḥaḳīḳa], the state of the perfect soul "which sums up all the other states" as Bās̲h̲ Tārzī states).

These rising and falling lights are held to be "divine illumination"; no longer a gift from Mercy, as al-Ghazzālī believed, but an effect linked to the experience according to the extent to which the *dhikr* of the inmost being has liberated the divine element in the human spirit directly "emanating" from God (cf. the "trace of the One" of Plotinus). The *dhikr* also effects a direct communication with the "worlds" [see ʿĀLAM, § 2]. The *dhikr* of the tongue and its "cosmization" effects entry into the world of *djabarūt*, All-Power. The higher stages introduce into the domain of *malakūt* "angelic substances"; they may even lead to *lāhūt*, the world of the Divine Essence. "If you recite the *dhikr* with your inmost being, recite with yourself the Throne with all its worlds until the *dhikr* unites with the Divine Essence (*dhāt*) (*Miftāḥ*, 7). One is reminded here of the entry into the "Pure Land" of the *Jōdo* promised to the disciples of the Japanese *nembutsu*.

These gnostic visions, which in Ibn ʿAṭāʾ Allāh are relatively sober, later become involved in the extreme, as in the above-quoted text of Ibn Amīn al-Kurdī.

Interpretations:—Al-Ḥallādj, al-Kalabādhī, etc., speak of the *dhikr* as a *method* of reminding one's self of God, of helping the soul to live in God's presence; but without for this reason underestimating the discursive method of *fikr*. Al-Ghazzālī portrays the *dhikr* as *the* way of the Sufis, but still preserves, so it seems, the *method* aspect of its nature: a method of unifying the disciple's spirit and preparing him to receive, if the Lord wills, the supreme Mercies. Ibn ʿAṭāʾ Allāh informs us at the beginning of the *Miftāḥ* that to the best of his belief no monograph has yet been devoted to the *dhikr*. If this is true, then the developments *ex professo* in the theory and practice of the *dhikr*, and the absolutely capital importance assigned to it, may be dated from the 6th/12th century. Ibn ʿAṭāʾ Allāh no longer speaks of it as a preparatory or concomitant method, but as an effective technique, up to its consummation: entry into the domain of *lāhūt*. Later works insist even more on technique—voice, breathing, posture, etc., give themselves up to long disquisitions on the gnostic theme, and never cease to see in the *dhikr* pursued to its last steps a "guarantee" of attainment. This emphasis on technique (where non-Muslim influences are at work) dates from the period when Ṣūfism was dominated by the One-ness of Being (*waḥdat al-wudjūd*); man, in respect of his most "spiritual" aspects, is considered to belong by nature to the divine.

Now the direct effect of experiencing the *dhikr* seems to be a monoideism working on the One Mentioned, "realizing" that perpetual (conscious) "re-remembering" which the first Ṣūfīs demanded of it (cf. the "prayer of Jesus" of the Sinaitic Fathers). But as techniques progressed the ever more numerous analyses are marked by the "cosmization" of the *dhikr* of the tongue, the influence of the *dhikr* of the heart on the circulatory system, and the probable influence of the *dhikr* of the inmost being on the para- and ortho-sympathetic systems, and it seems as though we are in the presence of a control by this monoideism on the individual's subconscious, not to say unconscious, zones. In this case we are dealing with an equivalent of the *djapa-yoga*, almost certainly bringing about a twisting-back of self on self towards an ineffable grip of the first act of existence. The conceptualizations of the *waḥdat al-wudjūd* remain faithful to their monist view of the world by calling this movement of "enstasis" *fanāʾ ... billāh*.

This "attainment" is the fruit of a difficult technique of natural spirituality based on long asceticism. It is understandable that certain brotherhoods should have sought the equivalent (or what they thought to be the equivalent) by purely physical procedures: the sacred dances of the Mawlawiyya, the cries of the "Howlers", not to mention stimulating and stupefying drugs. Thus one arrives finally at veritable counterfeits which have not been without effect on the opposition by the *nahḍa* of contemporary Islam to the brotherhoods and its distrust of Ṣūfism.

To sum up: we find, in the course of the history of Ṣūfism, two distinct lines of utilization of the *dhikr*. The first and oldest makes it simply a method of prayer, without excluding other methods, where technique appears only in rudimentary form. The second, which became dominant, sees in it a guarantee of efficacity in attaining the highest "states" (*aḥwāl*) by virtue of a seeking after *ittiḥād* conceived as a (substantial) identification with the divine. This latter tendency often yields to the attraction of "procedures" and gnoses which become ever more extravagant. The testimony of Ghazzālī in the *Iḥyāʾ* stands at the hinge of the two lines—nearer to the first, and yet bearing witness already to the appearance of technique.

Bibliography: I. *Muslim works*. An exhaustive list would be very long. We shall restrict ourselves to recalling and specifying the chief sources used in the article: Kalābādhī, *Kitāb al-taʿarruf li-madhhab ahl al-taṣawwuf*, ed. Arberry, Cairo 1352/1933, ch. 47; Ḥallādj, *K. al-ṭawāsīn*, ed. Massignon, Paris (Geuthner), 1913, 33; id., *Dīwān*, 2nd ed., ed. Massignon, Paris (Geuthner), 1955; Abū Ḥāmid al-Ghazzālī, *Iḥyāʾ ʿulūm al-dīn*, Cairo 1352/1933, iii, 16-7; Ibn ʿAṭāʾ Allāh of Alexandria, *K. miftāḥ al-falāḥ wa-miṣbāḥ al-arwāḥ*, Cairo n. d. (often printed on the margin of Shaʿrānī, *e.g.*, Cairo 1321/1903); Zayn al-Dīn al-Khawāfī, *Al-waṣiyya al-ḳudsiyya*, MS. B.N. Paris, fonds arabe 762 (pointed out and studied by S. de Beaurecueil); Ibn ʿIyāḍ, *K. al-mafākhir al-ʿaliyya fi 'l-maʾāthir al-shādhiliyya*, Cairo 1355/1937, 108-13 and *passim*; Bāsh Tārzī, *K. al-minaḥ al-rabbāniyya*, Tunis 1351/1932; Muḥammad al-Sanūsī, *op. cit.*, to which may be added most of the Ṣūfī manuals, including Abū Ṭālib al-Makkī, *Ḳūt al-ḳulūb*, Cairo 1351/1932, etc.; in translation: Hudjwīrī, *Kashf al-maḥdjūb*, tr. Nicholson, *GMS*, xvii, *passim* (see Index); extract from Muḥammad Amīn al-Kurdī al-Naḳshbandī, *Tanwīr al-ḳulūb*, 3rd ed., Cairo, 548-58, unsigned French tr. as appendix to Jean Gouillard, *Petite Philocalie de la Prière du Cœur*, *Cahiers du Sud*, 1953.

II. *Western works*: A. le Chatelier, *Les confréries musulmanes du Hedjaz*, Paris 1887; Depont and Coppolani, *Les confréries religieuses musulmanes*, Algiers 1897; Goldziher, *Vorlesungen*, index s.v. *Dhikr*; J. P. Browne, *The Derwishes, or oriental spiritualism*, London 1868; Hughes, *Dictionary of Islam*, s.v. *Zikr*; D. B. Macdonald, *Religious attitude and life in Islām*, Chicago 1909, index s.vv. *Darwīsh* and *Dhikr*. For the primary meaning of *dhikr* = recollection, remembering, see for example, M. Gaudefroy-Demombynes, *Mahomet*, Paris 1957, 517-9; for the technical meaning: Louis Rinn, *Marabouts et Khouan*, Algiers 1884; W. S. Haas, *The zikhr of the Rahmanija-Order in Algeria*, in *MW*, January 1943; Louis Massignon, *Passion d'al-Ḥallādj*, Paris 1922, Index; idem, *Recueil de textes inédits*, Paris 1929, 143, ref. to Fleischer,

ZDMG, xvi, 235; idem, *Le souffle dans l'Islam*, in *JA* 1943-5; idem, *L'idée et l'esprit dans l'Islam*, in *Eranos-Jahrbuch* 1945; Louis Gardet, *La mention du Nom divin en mystique musulmane*, in *Revue Thomiste* 1952, iii and 1953, i; S. de Beaurecueil, *Les Recommandations du Shaykh Zayn al-Dīn*, *Cahiers* (Cairo), Sept. 1952; Mircea Eliade, *Le Yoga*, Paris 1954, 220-3, 392; A. H. Johns, *Malay Ṣūfism*, in *J. Malayan Branch RAS*, August 1957, 98-9.

(L. Gardet)

DHIMMA, the term used to designate the sort of indefinitely renewed contract through which the Muslim community accords hospitality and protection to members of other revealed religions, on condition of their acknowledging the domination of Islam. The beneficiaries of the *dhimma* are called *dhimmīs*, and are collectively referred to as *ahl al-dhimma* or simply *dhimma*. An account of the doctrinal position of Islam vis-à-vis the religions in question, and of the polemics between the two sides, is given in the article ahl al-kitāb; for a detailed account of the various religious communities see madjūs, naṣārā, ṣābiʾūn and yahūd. Mention is made here only of the general characteristics of the Muslim attitude to non-Muslims, as expressed in their institutions and social practices.

The bases of the treatment of non-Muslims in Islam depend partly on the attitude of the Prophet, partly on conditions obtaining at their conquest. Muḥammad is known to have first tried to integrate the principal Jewish groups at Medina into a rather loose organization, then opposed them violently, and finally, after the expansion of his authority across Arabia, concluded agreements of submission and protection with the Jews of other localities such as Khaybar, and with the Christians of, *e.g.*, Nadjrān; this last action alone could and did serve as precedent in the subsequent course of the Conquest. The essential Ḳurʾānic text is IX, 24: "Fight those who do not believe ... until they pay the *djizya* ..." which would imply that after they had come to pay there was no longer reason for fighting them. The conditions at the time of the conquest consisted essentially of the enormous numerical superiority of non-Muslims over Muslims in the conquered countries, and of their generally favourable bias towards the Arabs (because of the vexations to which they had been subjected by the official Churches); the natural, and indeed the only possible, policy was to extend to the inhabitants of the new territories the conception that had been tested experimentally in Arabia,—a flexible attitude in the absence of which no régime of the conquerors could have endured.

However, the precise nature of the earliest régimes, which varied according to the conditions obtaining at each conquest, is difficult to determine exactly, since the relevant texts have often been altered, and sometimes fabricated from the whole cloth, as a consequence of the differing concerns of Muslims and non-Muslims at later periods. Certain regulations have the temporary character of the demands made on a subject population by an army of occupation: dwellings, food-supply, intelligence, and security against espionage (it is as an example of this that we must understand the prohibition, on which later rigorists were to insist, of the wearing by *dhimmīs* of Arab dress, since in fact the natives and the Arabs dressed differently). But the essential—and lasting—stipulation concerns the payment of the distinguishing tax or *djizya* [*q.v.*], which was later to develop into a precise poll-tax, and which, expressing subjection, was to inaugurate the definitive fiscal status of the *dhimmīs*; this was in conformity with the usual custom of all mediaeval societies where non-dominant religious communities were concerned. Precautions must have been taken to avoid clashes between different communities, which at first enjoyed such friendly relations that buildings could be divided between Christians and Muslims; but it was only in the *amṣār* that restrictions on the right to construct new religious buildings could already from that time be maintained. The preservation by each community of its own laws and peculiar customs, as well as its own leaders—this also in conformity with the attitude of all mediaeval societies—must have resulted in the first place from the situation as it was rather than from any formal decision. The autochthonous non-Muslims, who were often unaccustomed to bear arms, were only exceptionally called upon for military services.

The *dhimmī* is defined as against the Muslim and the idolater (with reference to Arabia, but this is scarcely more than a memory); also as against the *ḥarbī* who is of the same faith but lives in territories not yet under Islam; and finally as against the *mustaʾmin*, the foreigner who is granted the right of living in an Islamic territory for a short time (one year at most). Originally only Jews and Christians were involved; soon, however, it became necessary to consider the Zoroastrians, and later, especially in Central Asia, other minor faiths not mentioned in the Ḳurʾān. The Zoroastrians, by committing to writing the previously orally transmitted Avesta, attained the status of *Ahl al-kitāb*; but more generally the Muslims, without waiting for such a step, and whether or not there existed recognized communal chiefs to guarantee the unbroken performance of the agreements, in fact accorded to the subject believers of most religions an effective status comparable to that of the *dhimmīs* properly so-called, except for a few points of inferiority of which one or two examples will be given.

Soon, however, Islam was reinforced numerically, organized itself institutionally, and deepened culturally. Polemics began to make their appearance between the faiths, and the Muslims sought to delimit more clearly the rights of those who were not Muslims. The measures for Islamization of the state introduced by ʿAbd al-Malik already included, as it turned out, an indirect threat to the *dhimmīs*; it is, however, to ʿUmar b. ʿAbd al-ʿAzīz that tradition, doubtless partially based on truth, attributes the first discriminatory provisions concerning them. The only other Umayyad of note in this connexion is Yazīd II, on a special matter which will be referred to later; thereafter one must come down to Hārūn al-Rashīd, and more especially to al-Mutawakkil, to encounter a policy really hostile to the *dhimmīs*. But always, through the centuries, the evolution of ideas has shown two aspects at once different and interdependent. On the one hand are the doctrinaires, found mainly among the *fuḳahāʾ* and the *ḳāḍīs*, who have interpreted the regulations concerning *dhimma* in a restrictive way, developing a programme which, if not one of persecution, is at least vexatious and repressive. From time to time a sovereign, either through Islamic zeal or through the need for popularity amongst them, ordains measures to the doctrinaires' satisfaction; sometimes, also, there are outbursts of popular anger against the *dhimmīs*, which in some cases arose from the places occupied by *dhimmīs* in the higher ranks of administration, especially that of finance.

But indeed, on the other hand, we must recognize that current practice fell very much short of the programme of the purists, which was hardly ever implemented except in the great Muslim centres and in the capitals, and was even then incomplete and sporadic; the different juridical schools are moreover not all in agreement, and some of them reiterate rules without any practical effect. On the whole the condition of the *dhimmīs*, although unstable in its minor practical aspects, was until about the 6th/12th century in the west, and the 7th/13th in the east, essentially satisfactory, in comparison with, say, that of the admittedly smaller Jewish community in the neighbouring Byzantine empire.

The principal directions in which the strengthening of Islamic control operated were as follows. On the one hand people like the *zindīḳs*, Manichaeans and those under their influence, who were suspected of wishing to propagate false doctrines within Islam, were excluded from the benefits of the *dhimma*; so too, of course, were those who, like the Mazdakites of Bābak, called in question the very political domination of Islam. As far as the *dhimmīs* in the traditional sense are concerned, their rights held good, and it could even be said that their financial situation had become closer to that of the Muslims than it was at first, since the converted possessors of *kharādj* lands had to continue to pay this *kharādj*, which the Arabs from the time of the conquest had not paid, and, though they did not pay the *djizya*, had to pay the *zakāt* on their other income. The *dhimmīs* moreover retained the autonomy of their own internal law, the stipulations of which formed the subject of treatises compiled at that time, and although they were able, if they wished, to apply to a Muslim judge (who would then often adjudicate according to Muslim law), they continued normally to resort to their own chiefs where these existed. Nevertheless, in relations between *dhimmīs* and Muslims, the two parties were not treated equally; thus, the Muslim could marry a *dhimmī* woman, but a *dhimmī* could not marry a Muslim woman; a *dhimmī* could not own a Muslim slave, although the converse was permitted; at the frontier the *dhimmī* merchant, although paying only half the rate paid by the *ḥarbī*, would pay double the rate for Muslims (20%, 10%, 5%); in criminal law it was frequently considered, in spite of the contrary opinion of the Ḥanafīs, that the blood-wit (*diya* [*q.v.*]) for a *dhimmī* was less (1/2 or 2/3) than that for a Muslim—less still in the case of a Zoroastrian—a principle the equivalents of which are encountered in all societies at this time. Finally the *dhimmī* had, according to the doctrine going back in part to the time of ʿUmar b. ʿAbd al-ʿAzīz, to wear distinguishing articles of dress, in particular the *zunnār* belt, the original intention of which was perhaps merely to prevent administrative errors but which gradually came to be regarded as a sign of humiliation, and was accompanied by complementary restrictions such as the prohibition of fine cloth, noble steeds, uncut forelocks, etc.; in fact, it would appear that these regulations, often variable in their detail, had never been respected for any length of time (whence their repetition by pietistic sovereigns), and it is even doubtful whether there was any real desire to apply them outside Baghdād and the great Islamic centres. On the other hand, although there may have been a natural tendency for town-dwellers to reside in different districts according to their faiths, there were no precise quarters, nor *a fortiori* any obligatory quarters, for *dhimmīs* of any kind. On the contrary, it was the close association of Muslims and non-Muslims in everyday life that provided the *raison d'être* of the restrictions mentioned above. Similarly, although there may have been some professional specialization, such as the trade of dyeing in the hands of the Jews, in general the mixture of faiths among all trades is the striking characteristic of society in "classical" times.

Although there was obviously no "liberty of conscience", as it would now be understood, in any Muslim society, Islam tolerated the religions of the *dhimmīs* subject to the following restrictions: it was forbidden to insult Islam, to seek to convert a Muslim, and apostasy was forbidden (all this, in principle, subject to the death penalty). The child of a mixed marriage was Muslim. As regards places of worship, the jurists are almost unanimous in interpreting restrictively the undertaking made on behalf of Muslims to uphold them, in the sense that this promise could apply only to those buildings which were in existence at the time of the advent of Islamic power; hence new building was forbidden, and rigorists opposed even the reconstruction of buildings fallen into decay. The practice of earlier centuries shows that these probibitions were rarely made absolute, and that as long as money was available the construction of new buildings was usually possible, even in Muslim centres like Fusṭāṭ and Cairo, and *a fortiori* in the regions where there was a non-Muslim majority during the greater part of the middle ages, such as certain districts in Upper Mesopotamia. Yazīd II had forbidden figure-representations in these buildings, but this order—linked with the iconoclastic movement, regarded favourably by many monophysite Christians, which was shortly afterwards to show itself so strongly at Byzantium—was certainly not enforced in any lasting way. There were also various limitations on the outward expressions of worship, such as processions and the use of bells, though these were never general in the earlier centuries of Islam. Only in Arabia, most strictly in the Holy Cities, was permanent residence by *dhimmīs* forbidden, following measures some of which go back to ʿUmar—although temporary exceptions made under the Umayyads and ʿAbbāsids were numerous, and indeed Jews lived in the Yemen until a few years ago.

Of course, those Muslims who interpreted the early pledges on the *dhimma* restrictively endeavoured to find textual authority for their attitude, as did the Christians who opposed them. Thus appeared the allegedly ancient Pact of ʿUmar on the one hand—which in its complete form is not attested before the end of the 5th/11th century—and on the other the Edict of the Prophet to the Christians, a pious fraud of Nestorian monks of the 3rd/9th century. In addition there came gradually into prominence a person, the *muḥtasib* [*q.v.*], who, entrusted with the maintenance of order in the streets and markets, was to include within his province the control of the *dhimmīs*.

The domain from which one might have expected, from a doctrinal point of view, to see *dhimmīs* excluded is that of government; but in fact this is not the case. Originally the Arabs would, without their assistance, have been unable to carry out the duties of an administration which was primarily the administration of the non-Muslim population. Later Christian bureaucrats, Nestorians in ʿIrāḳ and, more permanently, Copts in Egypt, were able to uphold family positions acquired in the face of the competition of Muslims, who turned more readily towards other professions, and to whom authority would in any case have found it difficult to entrust duties whose Islamic legality was questionable; the *dhimmīs*, whose situation depended more on the favour of prince or vizier, were more faithful to them. Nowhere had Jews and Christians played a more important part in these matters than in Egypt under the Fāṭimids; much the same position arose, however, at certain periods in Spain, and even in the east, al-Māwardī, the theoretician of Caliphal revival, admits—legitimizing past instances—that even a *dhimmī* vizier was possible, provided that his vizierate was 'executive' (*tanfīdh*) and not with power to command, *i.e.*, that in practice he should neither exercise explicit political responsibility for major political decisions nor, in particular, sit in judgment over Muslims or take the initiative in matters where Islam was concerned. Obviously, it happened on many occasions that the condition upon which a *dhimmī* could secure or retain a high post was that he should become a convert to Islam; but the bonds of clientship and patronage still held, and the official new Muslim could protect the *dhimmī* staff to whom he was used.

Moreover, since the *dhimmīs* remained to some extent under the jurisdiction of their own leaders, it followed that the latter were officially invested by the Muslim ruler—to whom the community did not hesitate to appeal when they disagreed on a candidate. The Jews thus came officially under the government of their Exilarch, and the Christians of different denominations similarly under that of their respective Catholicoi and Patriarchs; in this respect the position of the Zoroastrians is less clear. In ʿIrāḳ, the Catholicos of the Nestorians had some precedence within the entire Christian community.

One single persecution of the *dhimmīs* has been recorded in the classical centuries of Islam, that of the Fāṭimid al-Ḥākim [*q.v.*], which made a considerable impact in both East and West, because of its severity and of the destruction of the Holy Sepulchre; this was, however, the work of a visionary caliph, whose decision, difficult to explain, may not derive from ordinary processes of reasoning; he himself, at the end of his reign, retracted his measures, and his successors until the end of the dynasty restored the previous tradition of an extremely broad toleration. Even the Ayyūbid conquest, which adversely affected the Armenian community, hardly impaired the administrative position of the Copts. The restriction of *dhimmīs* in special quarters in Jerusalem was an exceptional move on the part of the Fāṭimids, and was intended to ensure their safety.

One cannot, therefore, say that it was persecution which led in some cases to the diminution and in others the complete disappearance of non-Muslim communities. The factors, essentially social, involved in this process cannot be discussed here; it must, however, be emphasized that the general position of the *dhimmīs* was gradually transformed by the fact that they passed almost everywhere from the position of a majority to that of a minority community. Moreover, instead of consisting, as previously, of a variety of communities, the gradual disappearance of Christians (foreigners excepted) in the Maghrib, of Christians also in Central Asia a little later, and of Zoroastrians in Īrān, bring it about that in some regions the category of *dhimmī* had practically ceased to exist, while in others it had come to comprise only the Jewish community, more tenacious but by now almost exclusively urban. These proportions were of course to be reversed after the establishment of the Ottoman empire in Europe, but this represented a new phenomenon which was to lead to no modification in the rest of the Muslim world.

It cannot be denied that from the last three or four centuries of the Middle Ages there was a general hardening against *dhimmīs* in Muslim countries, helped materially and morally by the change in numerical proportions. Before proceeding further, however, it must be noticed that this hardening of opinion was contemporary with that which appeared in Christendom against the Jews and against Muslims where there were any, without our being able to say to what extent there was convergence, influence, or reaction. On the other hand it must be emphasized that the populace were more easily excited as a result of the deterioration in the economic climate, and that generally changes in the Muslim attitude had been occasioned more by political than by religious considerations. Hitherto there had been scarcely any difference in the treatment accorded to Christians and Jews (at most they were distinguished by prescribed differences in dress); but it later came about that some categories of *dhimmīs* were looked on as friends of foreign powers and were worse treated, and naturally some Christians were in this respect more of a target than the Jews. There is nothing in mediaeval Islam which could specifically be called anti-semitism.

Although it has sometimes been considered that the formation of the Saldjūḳ empire aggravated the condition of the Christian community, this is only very marginally true. The Saldjūḳids, partly because the numerical proportions of the various communities made it less of a natural conclusion, employed Christian functionaries less than their predecessors, whence doubtless there were a few less safeguards in the life of the community; nothing, however, was directly changed in the régime of which they were the beneficiaries. In Asia Minor the Turkish conquest evidently caused much suffering and loss to Byzantine Christendom, but inter-denominational relations became singularly good once a stable political situation had been established. Contrary to what might have been expected, the Crusades had at first no noticeable effect on the condition of the *dhimmīs*, because the eastern Christians were not of the Latin rite and maintained on the whole an attitude of correct loyalty to their masters—except for the Armenians, who were only to be met with locally. The first suspicions seem to have mounted against the Copts at the time of the Frankish expeditions into Egypt; there may also have been some in Syria and the neighbouring lands after the penetration of Latin missionaries, whose ministries were in vain precisely because it was impossible for the local Christian communities to come into contact with them without becoming politically suspect. The climax came with the Mongol invasions which, wherever they occurred, were of temporary advantage to the Christians, as there were Christians in the Mongol ranks, and because the Mongols held the balance between the various faiths; several acts of excess by Christians against Islam followed locally; but finally Muslim reaction made the Christians pay for their behaviour, and the expansion of intolerant nomads to the detriment of cultivators was a grave blow to rural Christian communities in Armenia and Upper Mesopotamia even when these were under Mongol control. Tīmūr's massacres, and the rivalries between Turkomans in the 7th/15th centuries, heightened the drama.

In the Mamlūk state the native Christians, the Maronites even more than the Copts, suffered the repercussions of the struggle against the Mongols, the perpetuation of the state of war maintained against the Franks on the mediterranean coastline, and the growing supremacy of western merchants over their eastern rivals. The Mamlūk government tried in general to uphold the earlier legal system, but it was able neither to prevent popular violence stirred up by extremists, especially in 721/1321, nor to resist the pressure of jurists, such as Ibn Taymiyya, who insisted on an increasingly vexatious interpretation of the law regarding *dhimmīs*. Not only were the regulations on dress periodically renewed, though still with doubtful efficacy, but the regulations on mounts were narrowed so as to allow the *dhimmīs* nothing better than indifferent donkeys, and a new restriction was introduced—which has an Italian parallel—which forbade them to possess houses higher than those occupied by Muslims (thus indicating incidentally that they did not live in special quarters). Care was in general taken that nothing in their everyday social comportment might tend to conceal the evidence of their inferiority vis-à-vis Muslims; an attempt was made to embarrass the *dhimmī*'s trade by regulations, always temporary, against the sale of wine; there was a growing repugnance on the part of certain Muslims to associate with non-Muslims, and their religious buildings were destroyed on various pretexts; there was a partial exclusion of *dhimmīs* even from the administrative offices themselves. From this period date also treatises specially written against the *dhimmīs* (no longer merely religious polemics), to say nothing of chapters inserted in works of *fiḳh*.

In the West the Almoravids, and even more the Almohads, had adopted, earlier than the East, an intolerant policy, which is partly explained by the suspicions entertained of their Christian subjects of complicity with the Spaniards of the northern kingdoms who were already intent on the Reconquista, although the Jews suffered no less, whence for example the emigration of Maimonides to the East; *dhimmīs* ceased to be employed in the administration, the distinctive badges reappeared, etc. In the Maghrib there started to appear for the Jews, henceforth the only *dhimmīs*, special quarters (*mallāḥ*, *ḥāra*) which remind one of the European ghetto, and they were authorized to live in certain towns only. They regained, however, some influence after the arrival of their co-religionists who had been expelled from Christian Spain. It must be remembered that this country, for long tolerant, moved at the end of the Middle Ages towards the expulsion of all non-Christians, Jews and Muslims alike; this was achieved at the beginning of the 17th century after two centuries of ill-treatment.

Objectivity requires us to attempt a comparison between Christian and Muslim intolerance, which have partial resemblances and partial differences. Islam has, in spite of many upsets, shown more toleration than Europe towards the Jews who remained in Muslim lands. In places where Christian communities did not die out it may have harassed them, but it tolerated them when they did not seem too closely bound up with western Christianity (as in Egypt and Syria); it has bullied them more roughly in Spain, after a long period of toleration, in the face of the Reconquista (it is impossible to say how the Maghrib would have tolerated Christian communities there while Spain was expelling its Muslims, since except for foreigners there were none). What one may emphasize is that, although religious factors obviously contributed to the intolerance shown in particular by the Almohads, it is political factors which in general outweighed strictly religious intolerance in Islam. Finally, it was at the time of the expulsions from Spain and the religious wars in the West that the constitution of the Ottoman empire restored—albeit without modifying the situation in other Islamic countries—the spectacle of an Islamo-*dhimmī* symbiosis which was none the less remarkable for having been indispensable for the maintenance of the régime, as it had been for the Arab conquerors in the 1st/7th century. The Jews found asylum there, the Armenians and Greeks, in the 18th century, backed by Christian Europe, attained to positions of the highest importance. The later deteriorations are connected with the history of nationalist movements and the change in the notion of the State, which, gradually reaching all Muslim peoples, has emptied the concept of *dhimmī* of its traditional content. No more can be done here than merely to mention this last phase [see ḲAWMIYYA, MILLA and WAṬAN].

Bibliography: It is obviously impossible to enumerate here all the sources, which might include almost all Islamic legal and historical literature, with additions from the geographers, the *adab* authors, etc. An extensive, but incomplete, list will be found in Fattal, cited below. One might notice the importance, for the earlier period, of Balādhurī and Abū Yūsuf; later of Māwardī; then of the works on *ḥisba*, omitted by Fattal (see Gaudefroy-Demombynes, in *JA*, ccxxx, 1938, and ʿArīnī's edition of Shayzarī, Cairo 1946); and in general the Christian chronicles, either Arabic, like the *History of the Alexandria Patriarchs* and the historical chronicle of Mari (ed. Gismondi, 1909), or non-Arabic, like the Syriac chronicle of Michael the Syrian (ed. Chabot); mention may also be made of the Jewish documents, mainly in Arabic, of the *Geniza*. Some smaller works specially directed against the *dhimmīs* date from Ayyūbid and Mamlūk times, such as al-Nābulusī, *Tadjrīd* (fragments edited by Cl. Cahen in *BIFAO*, lix, 1960; complete edition in prepation by M. Perlmann); Ghāzī b. al-Wāsiṭī, *Radd ʿalā ahl al-dhimmā*, ed. and trans. R. Gottheil, in *JAOS*, xli, 1921; the *Fetwa sur la condition des dhimmīs*, etc., trans. Belin, in *JA*, 4e série, xviii-xix, 1851-2; the *Tract against Christian officials* of al-Asnawī, ed. M. Perlmann, in *Goldziher Mem.*, ii, 1958. On this literature in general see Perlmann, in *BSOAS*, 1942.

In the modern literature there are two general studies worthy of notice: A. S. Tritton, *The Caliphs and their non-Muslim subjects*, London 1930 (Arabic trans. Ḥasan Ḥabashī, Cairo n.d.), and Ant. Fattal, *Le statut légal des non-musulmans en pays d'islam*, Beirut 1958. Neither however can be considered as complete, nor to have sought to portray and explain the evolution and the differentiation in the condition of the *dhimmīs*. Deeper studies, but limited to the category of the Jews, are: S. D. Goitein, *Jews and Arabs*, New York 1955; the numerous but scattered passages relevant to the world of Islam in S. Baron, *History of the Jews*, iii-vii (up to the 12th century), New York 1957-9; E. Strauss[-Ashtor], *History of the Jews in Egypt and Syria under the Mamlūks* (in Hebrew), 2 vols., Jerusalem 1944-51; E. Ashtor, *History of the Jews in Muslim Spain*, (in Hebrew), i, *711-1002*, Jerusalem 1960. The fuller and more diverse history of the Christians has not been the subject of any special study; for religious polemics, see AHL AL-KITĀB. An important work on the Christians in Spain is I. de las Cagigas, *Los Mozarabes*, 2 vols., Madrid 1947-8; E. Cerulli, *Etiopi in Palestina*, 2 vols., Rome 1943, deals in fact with the entire religious history of that country. For the Zoroastrians the only collected references are to be found in works on Iranian history, such as B. Spuler, *Iran in früh-islamischer Zeit*, Wiesbaden 1952 (expanded English translation in the press). Some general information on *dhimmīs* as a whole in Mez, *Die Renaissance des Islams*, ch. iv; Cl. Cahen, *L'Islam et les Minorités confessionelles*, in *La Table Ronde*, 1958; E. Strauss[-Ashtor], *The social isolation of Ahl adh-dhimma*, in *P. Hirschler Memorial Book*, Budapest 1950; N. Edelby, *Essai sur l'autonomie juridictionnelle des Chrétientés d'Orient*, in *Arch. d'Hist. du Droit Oriental*, 1952; O. Turan, *Les souverains Seldjoukides et leurs sujets non-musulmans*, in *Stud. Isl.*, i, 1953. More detailed bibliography appears in the articles on the various religions. On the Ottoman period, see F. W. Hasluck, *Christianity and Islam under the Sultans*, 2 vols., Oxford 1929; Gibb-Bowen, 1/2, ch. xiv. (CL. CAHEN)

DHIMMA. The term *dhimma*, in its legal sense, bears two meanings, the first of which, that of the works on *Uṣūl* (legal theory), is equivalent to the notion of capacity, and such is the definition of it given by the classical doctrine. The *dhimma* is the legal quality which makes the individual a proper subject of law, that is, a proper addressee of the rule which provides him with rights or charges him with obligations. In this sense the *dhimma* may be identified with the legal personality. It is for this reason that every person is endowed with a *dhimma* from the moment of birth. Equally it follows that the *dhimma* disappears with the person at death.

But the *dhimma*, an attribute of the personality, is never used exclusively, by the Muslim legal theoreticians, in relation to a person's estate. It embraces all kinds of proprietary and extra-proprietary rights. Thus the duty of the ritual prayer binds the person insofar as it is endowed with a *dhimma*. So completely is the *dhimma* identified with the legal personality that certain authors have been able to assert that it is a useless notion and even devoid of any real meaning (Taftāzānī, *al-Talwīḥ*, ii, 726).

In its second sense, that of the legal practitioners, the term goes to the root of the notion of obligation. It is the *fides* which binds the debtor to the creditor. The bond of the obligation requires the debtor to perform a given act (*fiʿl*), and this act will be obtained at the demand of the creditor, *muṭālaba*. In the case of a real right (*ḥaḳḳ fi'l ʿayn*) on the contrary no bond exists: there will be no case of exacting any performance from a specified person. For this reason, then, there will be no question of *dhimma*. Some authors have so completely identified the idea of *dhimma* with that of obligation that in their view *dhimma* is properly undertaking, *ʿahd*, or guarantee, *ḍamān*. Others restrict the term to contractual obligations (al-Nasafī, *Iṣṭilāḥāt al-ḥanafiyya*, 65).

But in actual fact *dhimma* is never identical with obligation: it is properly the basis of an obligation. Once *fides* has been brought into existence the object of the right will exist in the seat of rights which is the person. It is at this stage that the second sense given to the term by the legal practitioners merges with that of the theoreticians of Islamic law. The *dhimma* is not only the bond which ties the creditor to the debtor but is, in particular, the seat of it. But here it embraces only rights of debt properly so-called. Thus it is that the obligation to give alms to those in need is not held to exist in the *dhimma*. It must be particularly noted that, as distinct from Western law, a right of debt with which the *dhimma* is charged is restricted to the right which exists in relation to a sum of money or other fungible goods. It is therefore only the obligation termed *dayn* that has its basis in the *dhimma*. The case will be the same if the obligation is one of future performance (*istiṣnāʿ*). But if the obligation exists in regard to a specific object it will be termed *ʿayn* and this obligation will lie outside the *dhimma*. In this case indeed the obligation cannot be *in futuro* and on the other hand is not discharged, in case of non-performance, by payment of damages.

It results that the idea of obligation in Islamic law is of a quite different structure according as to whether it is or is not directed towards a specific object.

In the first case it does not create a legal bond since it cannot be *in futuro*. In the second case the creditor's purpose is to bind his debtor, and this bond is established on the basis of the *dhimma*. Obligation, then, will properly be, as it has been defined by Muslim lawyers, an incorporeal right existing in the *dhimma* of the debtor. Thus the *dhimma* becomes, in the final analysis, the equivalent of what is termed in modern law, the debtor's estate.

Bibliography: Chafik Chéhata, *Essai d'une théorie générale de l'obligation en droit musulman*, Cairo 1936, i, 171, § 263; Juynboll, *Handbuch*, 263; idem, *Handleiding*⁴, 268; Santillana, *Istituzioni*, index; Taftāzānī, *al-Talwīḥ*, Cairo 1304 H., and other works on *uṣūl*; Ibn ʿĀbidīn, *Radd al-muḥtār*, iv; Ibn Nudjaym, *al-Baḥr al-rāʾiḳ*, vi, 204; Kāsānī, *Badāʾiʿ al-ṣanāʾi*, v and vi; Mīkhāʾīl ʿĪd al-Bustānī, *Mardjiʿ al-ṭullāb*, Beirut 1914, index.

(CHAFIK CHEHATA)

DHIMMĪ [see AHL AL-DHIMMA].

DHIRĀʿ, originally the part of the arm from the elbow to the tip of the middle finger, then the measure of the cubit, and at the same time the name given to the instrument for measuring it. The legal cubit is four handsbreadths (*ḳabḍa* = index finger, middle finger, ring finger, and little finger put together), each of six fingerbreadths (*aṣbaʿ* = middle joint of the middle finger) each the width of six barley corns (*shaʿīra*) laid side by side. A considerable number of different cubits were in common use in Islam. Roughly speaking they can be grouped around the following four measures: the legal cubit, the "black" cubit, the king's cubit, and the cloth cubit. The point of departure for all these calculations is the cubit of the Nilometer on the island of al-Rawḍa of the year 247/861, which, on an average, measures 54.04 cm.

1) The legal cubit (*al-dhirāʿ al-sharʿiyya*), is the same as the Egyptian hand cubit (*dhirāʿ al-yad*, also called *al-dhirāʿ al-ḳāʾima*), the Joseph cubit (*al-dhirāʿ al-Yūsufiyya*, called after Ḳāḍī Abū Yūsuf, who died in 182/798), the post cubit (*dhirāʿ al-barīd*), the "freed" cubit (*al-dhirāʿ al-mursala*), and the thread cubit (*dhirāʿ al-ghazl*), measuring 49.8 cm. (In ʿAbbāsid times, a cubit measured only

some 48.25 cm. in Baghdād; this can possibly be traced back to the caliph al-Maʾmūn (170-218/786-833) who reorganized surveying).

2) The "black" cubit (*al-dhirāʿ al-sawdāʾ*), fixed as above at 54.04, is identical with the "common" cubit (*al-dhirāʿ al-ʿāmma*), the sack-cloth cubit (*dhirāʿ al-kirbās*), and the cubit in common use in the Maghrib and in Spain, *al-dhirāʿ al-Rashshāshiyya*. The "black" cubit came into use in ʿAbbāsid times, but was not introduced, as is often stated, by al-Maʾmūn, who had measurements carried out in the legal cubit.

3) The originally Persian "king's" cubit (*dhirāʿ al-malik*), since the caliph al-Manṣūr (136/754-158/775) known as the (great) Hāshimī cubit (*al-dhirāʿ al-Hāshimiyya*). It measured eight *ḳabḍa* instead of six, and measured on an average 66.5 cm. It is identical with the Ziyādī cubit (*al-dhirāʿ al-Ziyādiyya*), which Ziyād b. Abīhi (died 53/673) used in the survey of ʿIrāḳ, and which is therefore also known as the survey cubit (*dhirāʿ al-misāḥa*); it is also identical with the "work" cubit (*dhirāʿ al-ʿamal*), and probably also with the cubit *al-dhirāʿ al-hindāsa*, which measures 65.6 cm.

4) The cloth cubit, which is also known in Levantine commerce as pic, varied from town to town. The Egyptian cloth cubit (*dhirāʿ al-bazz*, also called *al-dhirāʿ al-baladiyya*, identical with the late-mediaeval *dhirāʿ al-ḥadīd*, or "iron" cubit, which seems to have been originally the same as the "black" cubit) measured 58.15 cm., the cloth cubit of Damascus 63 cm., the widely accepted cloth-cubit of Aleppo 67.7 cm., that of Baghdād 82.9 cm., and that of Istanbul 68.6 cm.

Other cubit measures: beside the "great", there was also a "small" Hāshimī cubit of 60.05 cm., also known as *al-dhirāʿ al-Bilāliyya*, after Bilāl b. Abī Burda (died 121/739), a ḳāḍī in Baṣra. The Egyptian carpenter's cubit (*al-dhirāʿ bi 'l-nadjdjārī*) was identical with the architects' cubit (*al-dhirāʿ al-miʿmāriyya*), and measured ca. 77.5 cm. (standardised at 75 cm. in the 19th century). The ʿAbbāsid "house" cubit (*dhirāʿ al-dūr*) which was introduced by ḳāḍī Ibn Abī Laylā (died 148/765) measured only 50.3 cm. The "scale" cubit (*al-dhirāʿ al-mīzāniyya*), introduced by the caliph al-Maʾmūn, was chiefly used for measuring canals, and measured 145.6 cm.; it was double the length of the cubit of the caliph ʿUmar (*al-dhirāʿ al-ʿUmariyya*) which was 72.8 cm. The Persian cubit (*dharʿ*, generally called *gaz*) was in the Middle Ages either the legal cubit of 49.8 cm. or the Iṣfahān cubit of 8/5 *dharʿ-i sharʿi* = 79.8 cm. In the 17th century, there was a "royal" cubit (*gaz-i shāhī*) of 95 cm. in Iran; the "shortened" cubit (*gaz-i mukassar*) of 68 cm. was used for measuring cloth; this was probably the cloth cubit of Aleppo. Today, 1 *gaz* = 104 cm. in Īrān. There was also a "royal" cubit (*dhirāʿ-i pādishāhī*) in Mughal India which consisted of 40 fingerbreadths (*angusht*) = 81.3 cm.

Subdivisions of the cubit: basically, there were six handsbreadths (*ḳabḍa*) to the cubit; the *ḳabḍa* of the legal cubit was thus 8.31 cm., that of the common or "black" cubit was 9 cm. In the 19th century, the *ḳabḍa* in Egypt was even 16.1 cm. The *ḳabḍa*, in turn, consisted basically of four fingerbreadths (*aṣbaʿ*); the *aṣbaʿ* of the legal cubit was thus 2.078 cm., and that of the "black" cubit 2.25 cm. In Egypt, the *aṣbaʿ* is officially established at 3.125 cm. The fingerbreadth (*angusht*) of the Mughals was standardized at 2.032 cm. by the emperor Akbar at the end of the 10th/16th century.

Multiples of the cubit: the *bāʿ* or 'fathom', also known as *ḳāma*, is basically 4 legal cubits = 199.5 cm., or approximately 2 metres, and thus the thousandth part of a mile (*mīl*). Today in Egypt, the *bāʿ* = 4 "carpenter's" cubits = 3 metres. The *ḳaṣaba*, or measuring rod (Persian *nāb*; *bāb* is a reading error) is predominantly used in surveying. The Fāṭimid al-Ḥākim bi-amri'llāh (375-411/985-1021) introduced the *ḳaṣaba Ḥākimiyya*, which measured $7^1/_7$ "black" cubits, on the norm of 3.85 metres, established by a French expedition to Egypt. In 1830, the *ḳaṣaba* was established at 3.55 metres. The *ashl* or "rope" (Persian *ṭanāb*) equals 20 *bāʿ* = 60 Hāshimī cubits = 80 legal cubits = 39.9 metres; 150 *ṭanāb* or 3 *mīl* equal one parasang (*farsakh*) = 5985 metres = approx. 6 km.

Bibliography: W. Hinz, *Islamische Masse und Gewichte*, Leiden 1955, 54-64; A. Grohmann, *Einführung und Chrestomathie zur arabischen Papyruskunde*, Prague 1954, 171-178; W. Popper, *The Cairo Nilometer*, Berkeley 1951, 102-105.

(W. Hinz)

DHOLKĀ [see GUDJARĀT].

DHŪ, DHĪ, DHĀ, demonstrative forms based on the demonstrative element *dh*. The variety of their uses precludes these forms from being regarded as a single declined word; thus:

Dhū was the relative pronoun, invariable, of the Ṭayyiʾ; corresponding to the Hebrew *zū*, the poetic form of the relative pronoun.

Dhī forms part of the masc. relative pronoun *alladhī*; but *allatī* in the feminine. The opposition *dh/t* marks the gender. Corresponding to *dhī* are the Aramaic biblical relative, invariable, *dī* (*d^e* in syr.), the Geez masc. demonstrative *ze*, acc. *za*.

Dhā masc. sing. demonstrative (near object), diminutive *dhayyā*; *dhī* for the feminine, the opposition *ā/ī* then marking the gender here. J. Barth understood it as *ē/ī*, maintaining the existence of an ancient sound *ē*, from which followed his sharp controversy with A. Fischer (*ZDMG*, 1905, 159-61, 443-8, 633-40, 644-71; J. Barth, *Sprachwissenschftl. Untersuch.*, i, Leipzig 1907, 30-46). *Dhā* occurs most often either reinforced with *hā-*: *hādhā*, or combined with other demonstratives: *dhāka, dhālika*. Corresponding with *dhā* are the Geez feminine sing. demonstrative *zā*, Hebr. *zōt*^{h} (= **dhā* + *t*), the Geez masc. relative *za*.

Once in the nominal form with the sense: "he of", then "who has", "possessor of", *dhū* follows the Ist declension, taking the dual and the external plural. But it is always followed by a noun in the dependent grammatical phrase (common noun, according to the requirements of the Arab grammarians: al-Zamakhsharī, *Muf.*, § 130, 2nd ed. Broch; al-Ḥarīrī, *Durra*, ed. H. Thorbecke, 138). Thus *dhū māl*^{in} "possessor of money", pl. *dhawū māl*^{in} or (elegantly)*ulū māl*^{in}; for the feminine with the same construction: *dhātu māl*^{in}, pl. *dhawātu māl*^{in} (or *ulātu māl*^{in}). See W. Wright, *Ar. Gr*^{3}, i, 265 D, in *Lisān* the art.: *dhū wa-dhawāt*, xx, 344/xv, 456; *Muf.*, § 122, for expressions like *dhāta yawm*^{in} "a day", *dhāta 'l-yamīni* "on the right".

Dhū, having this meaning of "possessor of" or "who has", was suited to provide surnames or nicknames (*laḳab*), *e.g. Dhu 'l-Ḳarnayn* (for Alexander), which have sometimes become the most commonly known name for some individual, e.g. the poet *Dhu 'l-Rumma*. For the kings or princes of the Yemen (such as *Dhū Yazan*) it has become an autonomous word with internal plural; these are the *adhwāʾ al-yaman* (see Wright, *ibid.*, 266 A and *Lisān*, *ibid.*), [see ADHWĀ']. In addition, two Muslim names of months: *Dhu 'l-ḥidjdja*, *Dhu 'l-ḳa'da* [see TA'RĪKH, i].

Bibliography: in the text. In addition: J. Barth, *Die Pronominalbildung in den semitischen Sprachen*, Leipzig 1913, 103-16, 152-8; for modern dialects: W. Fischer, *Die demonstrativen Bildungen der neuarabischen Dialekte*, The Hague 1959, 57-98. (H. FLEISCH)

DHU 'L-FAḲĀR, the name of the famous sword which Muḥammad obtained as booty in the battle of Badr; it previously belonged to a heathen named al-'Āṣ b. Munabbih, killed in the battle. It is mentioned in the *Sīra* (ed. Saḳḳā, etc., 1375/1955), ii, 100, and in several *ḥadīths* (see for example Ibn Sa'd, ii, 2, section: *fī suyūf al-Nabī*. The expression Dhu 'l-Faḳār is explained by the presence on this sword of notches (*fuḳra*) or grooves (cf. the expression *sayf mufaḳḳar*). According to a tradition, the sword bore an inscription referring to blood-money which ended with the words *lā yuḳtal Muslim bi-kāfir* "no Muslim shall be slain for an unbeliever". The proverbial expression *lā sayf illā Dhu 'l-Faḳār* has often been inscribed on finely engraved swords, from the middle ages down to our own times, throughout the Muslim world. The words *wa-lā fatā illā 'Alī* are sometimes added, because, although Muḥammad's sword, after belonging to 'Alī, passed into the possession of the 'Abbāsid caliphs, it became an attribute of 'Alī and an 'Alid symbol. Muslim iconography represented it with two points, probably in order to mark its magical character (the two points were used to put out the eyes of an enemy; for a representation of a sword with two points, among other magic objects, see V. Monteil, in *REI*, 1940/i-ii, 22). Dhu 'l-Faḳār became a proper name which is found more particularly among Shī'īs.

Bibliography: F. W. Schwarzlose, *Die Waffen der alten Araber*, Leipzig 1886, 152; G. Zawadowski, *Note sur l'origine magique de Dhoû-l-Faqâr*, in *En Terre d'Islam*, 1943/I, 36-40. (E. MITTWOCH*)

DHU 'L-FAḲĀRIYYA, (alternatively *Faḳāriyya*, *Zulfaḳāriyya*); a Mamlūk household and political faction in Egypt during the 17th and 18th centuries.

(1) Origin and first ascendancy. The eponymous founder of the household, Dhu 'l-Faḳār Bey, is a shadowy figure, who seems to have flourished in the first third of the 17th century, but is not mentioned by contemporary chroniclers. The account (in Djabartī, *'Adjā'ib al-Āthār*, i, 21-3) which makes Dhu 'l-Faḳār and the rival eponym, Ḳāsim, contemporaries of sultan Selīm I is legendary. The political importance of the Faḳāriyya began with the *amīr al-ḥadjdj* Riḍwān Bey, a *mamlūk* of the eponym (Muḥammad al-Muḥibbī, *Khulāṣat al-Āthār*, Būlāḳ, 1290; ii, 164-6). He held the command of the Pilgrimage for over twenty years until his death in Djumādā II 1066/April 1656. The grandees of his household dominated the Egyptian political scene until Ṣafar 1071/October 1660, when their rivals, the Ḳāsimiyya faction, joined with the Ottoman viceroy to overthrow them. Their forces and leaders were dispersed, several of the Faḳārī beys being put to death at al-Ṭarrāna by the Ḳāsimī, Aḥmad Bey the Bosniak.

(2) The Ḳāsimī ascendancy. For over forty years after the Ṭarrāna episode, the Faḳāriyya remained in a state of diminished power and prestige. The Ḳāsimiyya, although the dominant faction, did not display the arrogance and turbulence *vis-à-vis* the viceroys which had characterized the Faḳāriyya during their ascendancy. The disturbances of this period originated mainly in the garrison of Cairo. By 1123/1711-12, however, a dangerous political polarization had developed. The Faḳāriyya and Ḳāsimiyya were allied respectively with the much older factions of Sa'd and Ḥarām among the Egyptian artisans and nomads. In a quarrel between the Janissaries and 'Azabs in that year, the Faḳāriyya supported the former and the Ḳāsimiyya the latter. The Ḳāsimiyya-'Azab combination was ultimately victorious, but the death during the fighting of Īwāẓ ('Iwaḍ) Bey, the leading Ḳāsimī grandee, opened a vendetta between the two factions which dragged on for two decades. Finally in 1142/1729-30, the Faḳāriyya succeeded in extirpating their rivals, and restoring their own ascendancy.

(3) The second ascendancy of the Faḳāriyya. The architect of the Faḳārī triumph, another Dhu 'l-Faḳār Bey, (who was assassinated on the eve of victory), came, not from the original Mamlūk household deriving from Riḍwān Bey, but from a household established by a regimental officer of Anatolian (*Rūmī*) origin, Ḥasan Balfiyya, *agha* of the Gönüllüs, who flourished in the late 11th/17th century. Another branch of this household stemmed from Muṣṭafā al-Ḳāzdughlī, also an Anatolian, who entered the service of Ḥasan Agha. The predominance of the Ḳāzdughliyya branch was established by Ibrāhīm Kâhya, who in 1156/1743-44 allied with Riḍwān Kâhya al-Djulfī to oust 'Uthmān Bey, a *mamlūk* of the late Dhu 'l-Faḳār Bey and holder of the supremacy (*ri'āsa*) in Egypt. The Ḳāzdughliyya, hitherto a regimental household, now entered the beylicate, several of Ibrāhīm Kâhya's *mamlūks* being appointed beys, both before and after his death in Ṣafar 1168/November-December 1754. Amongst them was Bulut Kapan 'Alī Bey, usually called 'Alī Bey the Great (see 'ALĪ BEY). In spite of the inveterate rivalry among the Ḳāzdughliyya grandees, they maintained their ascendancy, ultimately embodied in the duumvirate of Ibrāhīm Bey and Murād Bey, until the French invasion under Bonaparte in 1798.

Bibliography: Abū 'Abd Allāh Muḥammad b. Muḥammad b. Abi 'l-Surūr, *al-Rawḍa al-zahiyya* and *al-Kawākib al-sā'ira*, (Brockelmann, II, 297-8; 8, 409); the author was a friend of Riḍwān Bey; Anonymous, *Zubdat ikhtiṣār ta'rīkh mulūk Miṣr al-maḥrūsa*, (B.M., Add. 9972); anonymous fragment, Bibliothèque nationale, MS. arabe 1855; 'Abd al-Raḥmān b. Ḥasan al-Djabartī, *'Adjā'ib al-Āthār fi 'l-tarādjim wa 'l-akhbār*, Būlāḳ 1290. See also P. M. Holt, *The exalted lineage of Riḍwān Bey: some observations on a seventeenth-century Mamluk genealogy*, in *BSOAS*, xxii/2, 1959, 221-30. (P. M. HOLT)

DHU 'L-ḤIDJDJA [see TA'RĪKH, i].

DHU 'L-HIMMA or DHĀT AL-HIMMA, name of the principal heroine of a romance of Arab chivalry entitled, in the 1327/1909 edition, *Sīrat al-amīra Dhāt al-Himma wa-waladihā 'Abd al-Wahhāb wa 'l-amīr Abū (sic) Muḥammad al-Baṭṭāl wa-'Uḳba shaykh al-ḍalāl wa-Shūmadris al-muḥtāl*, which, in the subtitle, describes itself as "the greatest history of the Arabs, and the Umayyad and 'Abbāsid caliphs, comprising the history of the Arabs and their wars ..... and including their amazing conquests". Also known is the title *Sīrat al-mudjāhidīn wa-abṭāl al-muwaḥḥidīn al-amīra Dhū (sic) 'l-Himma wa-'Abd al-Wahhāb* etc. (catalogue of Vienna MSS by Flügel, ii, 13). Cf. also Brockelmann, S II, 65 and Sarkis, *Dict. encycl.*, xi, 1930, 2008.

The main subject of this romance is the Arab

war against the Byzantines from the Umayyad period until the end of al-Wāthiḳ's caliphate, that is to say it covers in principle the first, second and third centuries of the Hidjra, but also reflects later events. Though this is the general character of the romance, it also has an equally important but individual character as the history of the rivalry between two Arab tribes, the B. Kilāb and the B. Sulaym, the key to a whole series of vicissitudes in the *Sīra* and to the course of action taken by the leading figures, and it may indeed be regarded as the epic of the B. Kilāb tribe. In the edition noted above it covers a total of 5084 pages in 8vo with 27 lines to the page, in 7 volumes of 10 sections (*djuzʾ*) each, with 64 pages in each section except for sections 69 and 70 which have 92 and 158 pages respectively.

The name of the heroine appears in different forms. She is often called simply Dalhama or al-Dalhama, and this might be her original name, the feminine of Dalham, a well-known proper name and appellation signifying wolf. It has been regarded as a vulgarism for a name beginning with *dhū* (cf. *Abu 'l-* becoming *Bal*), which could be reconstructed as Dhu 'l-Himma, and then, as it refers to a woman, as Dhāt al-Himma, the woman of noble purpose. In the edition and the different manuscripts all these forms occur concurrently, even Dhu 'l-Himma al-Dalhama or Dhu 'l-dalhama. It is by the name Delhemma that the romance is most generally known. But whilst several of the characters have a historical prototype, the heroine herself seems never to have existed historically.

Contents of the romance. The starting point is the history in the Umayyad period of the rivalry between two Ḳaysī tribes in the Ḥidjāz, the B. Kilāb and the B. Sulaym, the former belonging to the ʿĀmir b. Ṣaʿṣaʿa group, a section of the Hawāzin who, with the Sulaym, are one of the two principal branches of Ḳays ʿAylān. The head of the Kilāb was Djandaba b. al-Ḥārith b. ʿĀmir b. Khālid b. Ṣaʿṣaʿa b. Kilāb, while the head of the Sulaym was Marwān b. al-Haytham. It was the latter, a favourite of the Umayyad caliph, who, despite the superiority which Djandaba had won by his exploits, held the *imāra* (command) over the Arab troops. But after Djandaba's death his son al-Ṣaḥṣāḥ, having saved the daughter of caliph ʿAbd al-Malik b. Marwān, and sister of Maslama b. ʿAbd al-Malik, when she was attacked by Bedouin brigands on her return from the pilgrimage, won Maslama's friendship and, thanks to him, was given the *imāra*. It was as head of the Arab tribes that he took part with Maslama in a great expedition against Constantinople, in the course of which he had romantic adventures in a fortress (a monastery in the corresponding episode in the ʿUmar al-Nuʿmān's tale in the 1001 Nights) inhabited by a Greek princess who fell in love with him after a show of resistance and whom he carried off. He was the hero in the fighting outside Constantinople against the emperor Leo and his generals and allies, one of whom was the queen of Georgia, Bakhṭūs. After foiling the devilish plots of Shammās, a monk, he entered the town as victor with Maslama, had a mosque built there and had Shammās crucified.

The romance then relates al-Ṣaḥṣāḥ's adventures in the desert with other women, one of whom was a *djinniyya*, his death while hunting, the disputes over the succession between his two sons Ẓālim and Maẓlūm, the birth of Ẓālim's son, al-Ḥārith, and Maẓlūm's daughter, Fāṭima who, having been carried off in a raid with her nurse and foster-brother Marzūk by the B. Ṭayy, grew up among that tribe, became a fearsome amazon and was given the name of Dalhama (Dhāt al-Himma). Returning to her own tribe as a result of romantic events too lengthy to describe here, she continued to astound the Kilāb by her exploits. It was in these circumstances that the revolution which brought the ʿAbbāsids to power took place. The amīr of the B. Sulaym at that time, ʿAbd Allāh (ʿUbayd Allāh) b. Marwān, supported the ʿAbbāsid cause and obtained from al-Manṣūr command over the tribes which from then onwards was lost by al-Ṣaḥṣāḥ's successor. Delhemma persuaded the Kilāb, despite their initial reluctance, to support the new dynasty. The Byzantines having taken advantage of the change of dynasty to regain the initiative, war broke out again and the two tribes, Kilāb and Sulaym, took part in it at the caliph's request, acquiescing in ʿUbayd Allāh's leadership. They freed Āmid, captured Malaṭya and took up positions to defend the frontiers, the Sulaym at Malaṭya, the Kilāb in the nearby fortress of Ḥiṣn al-Kawkab.

It was after this development that Delhemma's cousin al-Ḥārith, son of the Kilābī amīr Ẓālim, succeeded in overcoming the rebellious heroine's repugnance to love and marriage, aided by a drug (*bandj*) supplied by the *faḳīh*, later *ḳāḍī* ʿUḳba, of the Sulaym tribe, and made her the mother of a child, ʿAbd al-Wahhāb who, as a result of the strange circumstances in which the conception took place, was black. ʿAbd al-Wahhāb was educated by his mother and, on reaching manhood, became the head of the Kilāb and the Blacks who formed a group under his leadership; he was the chief hero of the romance together with Delhemma, and won fame in the incessant wars against Byzantium. At his side was al-Baṭṭāl, a Sulaymī and pupil of the *ḳāḍī* ʿUḳba, playing an important part but relying on cunning rather than on force of arms. In the perpetual rivalry that existed between the two tribes al-Baṭṭāl took the side of the Kilāb, left Malaṭya for the Kilāb's fortress and became the implacable enemy of the *ḳāḍī* ʿUḳba who was secretly converted to Christianity and had become a traitor to Islam and the Byzantines' most valuable auxiliary. The amīr of Malaṭya and head of the Arab tribes was now ʿAmr b. ʿAbd Allāh (ʿUbayd Allāh). Although he had concluded a pact of fraternity with ʿAbd al-Wahhāb and had been rescued by Delhemma from the hands of the Byzantines and their allies the "Christianized Arabs", a band whom Delhemma's ephemeral husband al-Ḥārith had led into Greek territory and placed at the emperor's service, he remained in a state of veiled hostility to the Kilāb and their leaders. If the Byzantines had valuable assistants like ʿUḳba and the "Christianized Arabs", the Muslims also had accomplices in Byzantine territory, in a small group of crypto-Muslims organized by Māris, the emperor's personal chamberlain, and his brother and sister, and also, near Malaṭya, an ally in the person of Yānis, of the imperial family and lord of a Greek fortress which he put at the disposal of the Muslims.

In the reign of al-Mahdī a great battle with the emperor Theophilus took place at Mardj al-ʿUyūn. Then the narrator, after a romantic account of al-Mahdī's death, takes us to the reign of Hārūn al-Rashīd, whom he speaks of as the immediate successor of al-Mahdī, and in Byzantium to the reign of Manuel, son of Theophilus. It was at this point that the great duel between al-Baṭṭāl and ʿUḳba began, each trying to seize his adversary and have him put to death, and, as the Sulaym, their amīr and the caliph supported and defended ʿUḳba whose treason they refused to acknowledge despite the proof provided by Delhemma, ʿAbd al-Wahhāb and al-Baṭṭāl, in consequence the Kilāb only took part in the war to save the situation when it had been rendered critical by the Byzantines' successes in capturing and even advancing beyond Malaṭya, or else to fight against the emperor and the caliph who were linked together in an unnatural alliance against the Kilāb, or else to go off into far distant lands beyond Byzantium to rescue ʿAbd al-Wahhāb's wife and daughter. Adventures which cannot be related here led al-Baṭṭāl into the West, whence he brought back a Frankish king whom he converted, and a little later to the Maghrib, returning with a contingent of Berbers. Subsequently the two tribes were reconciled and secured victories over the Byzantines near the Cilician Gates, recapturing Malaṭya from them and imposing a truce.

The narrator then tells, after the death of Hārūn al-Rashīd, of the war between al-Amīn and al-Maʾmūn in which the Kilāb fought against al-Amīn whilst the Sulaym supported him. The amīrs of the Kilāb who had been summoned to Baghdād, with the exception of al-Baṭṭāl who had escaped, were arrested by ʿAmr at the instigation of Zubayda, she in turn being inspired by ʿUḳba. A fratricidal struggle then broke out between the Sulaym, reinforced by troops from ʿIrāḳ, and the Kilāb and ʿĀmir. The Kilāb overcame the Sulaym and the ʿAbbāsid troops, reached Baghdād, attacked the palace, set free the Kilābite amīrs and took al-Amīn prisoner, but were persuaded by ʿAbd al-Wahhāb and Delhemma to release him. However, some of the Kilāb still continued to support al-Maʿmūn.

The emperor Michael, Manuel's successor, taking advantage of the civil war between al-Amīn and al-Maʾmūn, on ʿUḳba's advice renewed hostilities. Al-Maʾmūn, who had been supported by al-Baṭṭāl, came to the throne but had Delhemma, ʿAbd al-Wahhāb and the Kilābī amīrs who had helped al-Amīn arrested. The caliph, following the not disinterested advice of ʿUḳba, the emperor's ally, set off in the direction of al-Raḳḳa and was captured, together with the Kilābīs whom he had taken with him, and they were all carried off to Constantinople. Delhemma was at once freed by al-Baṭṭāl. The others regained their liberty under cover of a war against the emperor that had been launched by a king named Kushānūsh, grandson through his father of the king of the Bulgars (al-Burdjān) and through his mother descended from Nestor, king of the Maghlabites (sic). Kushānūsh captured Constantinople, and then in his turn renewed the struggle with Islam and penetrated as far as Baṣra. He was finally captured by the Kilāb and beheaded by Delhemma herself. Thanks to the Kilāb, the emperor was freed and restored to the throne, and he decided for the future to give them the tribute which, in the past, he had paid to the caliph, a step which led to some jealousy of the Kilāb. However, the emperor resumed war against the caliph whom he compelled to take refuge in Persia with the Sulaym. Once again it was the Kilāb who saved the situation. Then they hastily started new operations, this time by sea, with the help of the amīr of Tarsus, ʿAlī al-Armanī, against the king of a remote island named Ḳarāḳūna who was holding some Kilābī women captive. But on hearing that al-Maʾmūn had come to lay siege to Constantinople and been captured with the help of the Franks, they hurried to the rescue, fought a naval engagement and laid siege to the city; they captured the emperor and then, reinforced by an army commanded by the future caliph al-Muʿtaṣim, they set al-Maʾmūn free; he had however been wounded by ʿUḳba and died. Al-Muʿtaṣim took over power, at al-Baṭṭāl's request set free the emperor Michael, who was to pay tribute, and gave orders to return to Malaṭya where for the time being he effected a reconciliation between the Kilāb and the Sulaym, later returning to Baghdād.

But soon afterwards he was won over by the amīr ʿAmr to the side of the Sulaym and ʿUḳba. He came to Malaṭya with the intention of invading Byzantine territory, arrested Delhemma, ʿAbd al-Wahhāb and the Kilābī amīrs, and also al-Baṭṭāl shortly afterwards, while ʿAmr released ʿUḳba whom al-Baṭṭāl after prolonged search had finally captured. An attempt by the Kilāb to rescue the prisoners on their way to Baghdād failed on account of the superiority of al-Muʿtaṣim's and ʿAmr's forces. Thereafter the Kilāb seem to have been powerless against the Sulaym and ʿAmr. Those of the Kilāb and ʿAbd al-Wahhāb's Blacks who were unwilling to submit to ʿAmr emigrated to Egypt. While the amīrs were held prisoner in Baghdād the emperor, urged on by ʿUḳba, launched an expedition. But he was soon besieged in his capital by Baḥrūn, the king of the island of Ḳamarān, and dethroned. Baḥrūn then invaded the Muslim territories, took Malaṭya, captured ʿAmr and later the caliph, and marched on ʿIrāḳ. It was then that the Kilābī amīrs were released during a riot. They at once out to fight Baḥrūn, defeated him and released his prisoners, and helped the caliph to recapture Constantinople and restore the emperor to his throne. They took the town of ʿAmūdā the Great, towards which Baḥrūn had fled, and once again freed the caliph who had been captured for the second time.

However, the emperor Michael had died and been succeeded by the usurper Armānūs (Romanus), who expelled the Muslims from Constantinople and was joined by Baḥrūn. Fighting continued, and an interminable series of adventures brought the Kilāb to the kingdom of Kordjāna, bordering on the country of the Abkhāz, in their search for Delhemma who was still a prisoner, while the Sulaym accompanied by the caliph had returned to Malaṭya. Then followed a great offensive by Armānūs who took Malaṭya and went as far as Mosul. The Kilāb, who through ʿUḳba's intrigues had been expelled from the frontier by the caliph, nevertheless saved the situation. Then the caliph became suspicious of ʿAmr, but the latter returned to favour, set out an on expedition, and was defeated. Finally Armānūs was overcome and surrendered. He was soon compelled to seek help from the Muslims against his enemy king Karfanās who, with the Saḳāriḳa and the Malāfiṭa (Amalfitans) captured Constantinople. The caliph sent the Sulaym against him. Karfanās captured ʿAmr, defeated the caliph al-Muʿtaṣim and reached Āmid. At that point ʿAbd al-Wahhāb intervened. Karfanās was killed and Armānūs regained the throne.

The narrator, who is not unaware that al-Muʿtaṣim led an expedition against Amorium in 223/838, does not fail to describe it in a fanciful way, with certain characteristics which recur in an already legendary account by Ibn al-ʿArabī in his *Muḥāḍarāt al-abrār wa-musāmarāt al-akhyār*, ii, 64. Then he had Armānūs dethroned by his own son Bīmund. The latter maltreated al-Baṭṭāl, who had fallen into the hands of Armānūs, and thereby provoked ʿAbd al-Wahhāb and ʿAmr to intervene. The latter was made prisoner. Delhemma then came to the rescue, killed Bīmund and restored Armānūs to the throne.

ʿUḳba once more contrived to turn the caliph against the Kilāb, and the Sulaym and Kilāb were again at war, when the caliph called in Armānūs against the Kilāb. There followed a long series of exploits in the course of which, outside Constantinople, Delhemma killed a Frankish king, Mīlāṣ, who had come for the Crusade and conquest of Jerusalem, ʿAbd al-Wahhāb was carried off by the Pečenegs, ʿUḳba and al-Baṭṭāl continued their perpetual game of hide and seek, and Armānūs took and sacked Malaṭya. Armānūs was later dethroned and strangled by Fālūg̲h̲us (Paleologos?) whom Delhemma forced to keep peace. He resumed the war but was beaten and compelled to pay tribute and to rebuild in Constantinople Maslama's mosque which had fallen into ruin. ʿUḳba, whom al-Baṭṭāl had captured, was nearly crucified in Constantinople, but he managed to escape and returned to the caliph; he hatched a new plot against the Kilāb and procured the arrest of ʿAbd al-Wahhāb and al-Baṭṭāl, and it was only by the vizier's help that they escaped from the sentence of death by drowning in the Tigris. Nevertheless, ʿAmr and the Sulaym continued to fight against the Kilāb.

A new emperor named Michael twice sent expeditions against the Muslims, the second time with a Frankish king Takafūr. He took Malaṭya but it was recaptured by the caliph and ʿAbd al-Wahhāb; it was then that al-Muʿtaṣim, after seeing ʿUḳba performing his devotions in the underground church in his house in Malaṭya, became convinced of his treason and no longer defended him, even suspecting ʿAmr also of being a Christian.

We come now to the final section of the romance, section 70, which like the preceding one is almost three times longer than the others. It is given up to a description of two important events: the pursuit of ʿUḳba through various countries from Spain to the Yemen, his capture and crucifixion on the Golden Gate at Constantinople in spite of the intervention of a vast army of Christian peoples led by 17 kings; the murderous ambush into which the Muslims fell on their way back, in the Defile of the Anatolians, from which the only survivors were the caliph with 400 men, al-Baṭṭāl and some of his companions, as well as Delhemma, ʿAbd al-Wahhāb and a number of men who had been shut up in a cave and given up for lost, but were miraculously saved by a genie. Soon afterwards al-Muʿtaṣim died.

His successor al-Wāt̲h̲iḳ decided on a reprisal expedition against Constantinople. The emperor was captured and executed. Until then, Muslim conquerors had limited themselves to making the emperors pay tribute. From that time, a Muslim governor was appointed in Constantinople in the person of a son of ʿAbd al-Wahhāb who had the mosque rebuilt with great splendour. The amīr ʿAmr had been killed in the disaster of the Defile of the Anatolians, and was succeeded at Malaṭya by his son al-D̲j̲arrāḥ.

At this point the narrator describes the deaths, first of Delhemma, then her son ʿAbd al-Wahhāb, after their return from Mecca, in a state of piety, while al-Baṭṭāl ended his life at Ankūriya (a corruption of Ancyra-Angora through contamination with ʿAmmūriya-Amorium), saddened by the news that, from the time of al-Wāt̲h̲iḳ's successor, al-Mutawakkil (or in some manuscripts al-Muḳtadir), the Byzantines had regained the initiative, reconquered the whole territory between Ankara and Malaṭya, and sent out endless expeditions against the Muslim countries. He died and was buried in the mosque at Ankara, but his tomb, being concealed, escaped the notice of his foes. Islam was to remain in this critical situation until the coming of the Turks (Sald̲j̲ūḳid?—in some versions there is reference to Čerkesses, hence to the Mamlūks), with their king Āḳ Sunḳur, who recaptured Ankara and discovered al-Baṭṭāl's tomb.

Elements in the romance. Different elements enter into the creation of Delhemma. Firstly, a bedouin element which might be described as "antarian", since it is what occurs in the *Sīrat ʿAntar*, which may have served as a model, as comparisons sometimes appear between some personage and ʿAntar, whose horse Abd̲j̲ar is mentioned. In the preamble of a Berlin manuscript the narrator, after giving al-Ṣaḥṣāḥ's genealogy, says that the events which he is about to describe took place after the death of ʿAntar b. S̲h̲addād. To this element belong, in the first part of the romance, the intertribal raids and battles, the exploits of al-Ḥārit̲h̲, his son D̲j̲andaba, and later of al-Ṣaḥṣāh and Delhemma herself, tales of pursuits and horse-stealing, al-Ṣaḥṣāḥ's romantic encounters with first Laylā, then Amāma, then a d̲j̲inniyya. In the last analysis these bedouin tales go back to pre-islamic antiquity. It is noteworthy that Islam only plays a subsidiary part (doxology, Muslim talismanic formulae) although the importance of the *d̲j̲ihād* is stressed from the start.

The most important element is the pseudo-historical, for the romance claims to be an accurate history of the Arabs. This element appears as the often very vague recollection of a certain number of facts and historical personages, garbed in romantic trappings and presented in an imaginary way, with constant disregard for chronology and probability. In the internal history of the Umayyad period we find traces of the history of Maslama b. ʿAbd al-Malik and of the eulogy of him spoken by ʿAbd al-Malik on his death-bed; Maslama's renunciation of the throne in favour of al-Walīd rests on a historical basis, Maslama as the son of a non-Arab mother having been barred from the caliphate for that reason. The ʿAbbāsid propaganda and the story of Abū Muslim find an echo in the romance, like the founding of Bag̲h̲dād by al-Manṣūr. The incident of the Zindīḳ in al-Mahdī's time is transformed into a meeting of 12,000 zindīḳs with renegade Arabs acting in the service of Byzantium. It would be fruitless to reveal the improbabilities and inventions in the story of al-Mahdī's succession, or the account of the Barmakids interwoven with ʿUḳba's intrigues. Similarly a K̲h̲ārid̲j̲ī, in revolt against Hārūn al-Ras̲h̲īd, is endowed with the same characteristics as the Ḳarmaṭī in al-Muḳtadir's time, for he carries off the Black Stone. In the account of al-Baṭṭāl's adventures in the West there is an incredible farrago in which the Spanish Umayyad called His̲h̲ām al-Muʾayyad and described as the imām *mahdī*, the Mulat̲h̲t̲h̲ama (Almoravids) whose king ʿAbd al-Wadūd (a recollection of the ʿAbd al-Wādids of Tlemcen) pays tribute to the Frankish king of Andalusia, and the Maṣāmida (Almohads) all appear. Turks are mentioned in the Muslim army from the time of Hārūn al-Ras̲h̲īd. We have seen how the war between al-Amīn and al-Maʾmūn is described in terms of the rivalry between the Kilāb and Sulaym. There is only a very brief allusion to the founding of Sāmarrā by al-Muʿtaṣim.

As regards the Arabo-Byzantine war, it is the historical element which plays the chief part. Thus, in the first part Maslama's expedition against Constantinople in 97-9/715-7 is the central event, around which all the romantic episodes are grouped. Al-Baṭṭāl who in actual fact took part in it is not mentioned here because he has been relegated to the second part of the romance. This part, which is based primarily on the Arabo-Byzantine war, reflects several important events of the ʿAbbāsid period, above all the establishment of a group of fortresses west of the Euphrates, with Malaṭya at the centre, dating from the period of al-Manṣūr, a fact well-known from al-Balādhurī. Then came al-Muʿtaṣim's great expedition against Amorium, which inspired several episodes in the romance, either under Hārūn al-Rashīd's caliphate or under al-Muʿtaṣim himself. Finally, and in particular, there is the fact that the amīr of Malaṭya, ʿAmr b. ʿUbayd Allāh, is no other than the historical personage of that name of the 11th century, for whom see M. Canard, *Un personnage de roman arabo-byzantin*, in *RAfr.*, 1932 and H. Grégoire, *L'épopée byzantine et ses rapports avec l'épopée turque et l'épopée romane*, in *Bull. de la Cl. des Let. et des Sc. Mor. et Pol. de l'Ac. roy. de Belgique*, 5th series, volume xvii, and articles in *Byzantion*, v and vi. And as we know from Byzantine historians that ʿAmr was closely connected with the Paulician dissidents, we can deduce that the situation of the Greek Yānis al-Mutaʿarrab, poised between the two camps in his fortress near Malaṭya, reflects the position of the Paulician Carbeas.

If the romance does not trace the Arabo-Byzantine war after the reign of al-Wāthiḳ (227-32/842-7), later events certainly inspired the narrators. It is probable that the disastrous defeat which the Arabs suffered at the end of al-Muʿtaṣim's reign is the counterpart of the defeat in which ʿAmr perished in 249/863. There are many allusions to situations in the 10th century, in the period of the Ḥamdānids. Apart from Malaṭya, the frequent references made to Shimshāt, Ḥiṣn Ziyād (also in the form Kharpūt, which takes us to a still later period), Mayyāfāriḳīn, Dārā, Āmid and the celebrated Byzantine stronghold Kharshana (Charsianon kastron) call to mind Sayf al-Dawla's campaigns. The emigration on two occasions of renegade Arab groups to Byzantium recalls the emigration of the B. Ḥabīb described by Ibn Ḥawḳal. Various Greek names also seem to suggest the events of the 10th century. No doubt it is Corcuas, the conqueror of Melitene, who can be recognized in Ḳarḳiyās, the Domestikos in al-Dimishḳī, Nicephores (Phocas) in Takafūr. In section 47, p. 34 there is a direct reference to John Tzimisces and his siege of Āmid. Armanus suggests Romanus Lecapenus. For the rest, many names and episodes take us to an even later epoch. From the start, the rivalry for the *imāra* between the two tribes reveals a situation which belongs, not to the Umayyad, but rather to the Ayyūbid period, when command of the Syrian tribes was held by one dominant tribe, but at that time the rivalry was between the Kilāb and the Yemeni Faḍl. The ceremonial forms of salutation, hospitality and procession, and the general use of titles are reminiscent of the Fāṭimid, Ayyūbid or Mamlūk ceremonial forms and titles. The Crusades and the Saldjūḳid period are the source of many names of persons and peoples. Among the Christian, or presumably Christian, peoples in addition to the Bulgars, Armenians and Franks, we find ʿAmāliḳa (Amalekites!), Georgians (Kurdj), Abkhāz, Alans, Pečenegs (al-Badjnāk), Amalfitans (Malāfiṭa), Venetians (Banādika), Saḳāliba, Maghlabites (the Byzantine Μαγγλαβίτης = Latin manuclavium, lictor), Zaghāwira, Dūḳas (sic). As names of individuals we find Kundafarūn (Godefroy, cf. Kundafarī in Yāḳūt, i, 207, ii, 381 and Gontofrè in book x of the *Alexiad*), Fransīs, Ghaytafūr who is certainly king Tafūr in the *Chanson d'Antioche*, Bīmund (Bohemund) etc. Certain names of Christians, Greek or French, are simply taken from antiquity and to some extent garbled: Iflāṭūn, Christopher, Pythagoras, Ptolemy. These names reveal a very superficial knowledge of history and geography on the part of the narrators who, on the other hand, seem to be better documented on Christian practices, religious festivals and formulae (*e.g.*, *Kyrie eleison*, sect. 4, 39; 20, 4; 59, 26), the sign of the cross, the emperor's crown topped with a cross, and on certain Byzantine customs (games in the hippodrome, humiliation of prisoners by having a foot placed on the back of the neck, etc.).

The description of land-battles is full of clichés, but the description of naval battles which have inspired prose or verse accounts seem to be more realistic. There is, for example, (sect. 18, 35) a detailed description of the use of Greek fire, *ḳawārīr al-naft*, boarding with the help of grappling-irons and several names of ships.

Folklore element. As in all romances and *Futūḥ* works, Delhemma contains a mass of features derived from folklore, of which we shall only specify a few: tricks to make the enemy kill each other, the description of wonderful objects (automatic birds, talismanic statues), amazons, the use of the *bandj*, etc. In the story of the queen of Georgia, Bakhtūs, which occurs in the first part, one can detect features which go back, through the legend of queen Thamar, to that of Zenobia. The theme of the camel-skin cut into strips in order to obtain a larger area for the building of the mosque in Constantinople is the same as the legend of Dido. Certain names (Kayḳābūs, Ḳilīdj b. Ḳābūs) suggest an Irano-Saldjūḳid influence, rather than the Iranian legend.

Composition of the romance. I have tried to show, in an article entitled *Delhemma, Sayyid Baṭṭāl et Omar al-Noʿmān*, in *Byzantion*, xii (1937), 183 ff., following an article by H. Grégoire in *Byzantion*, xi (1936), 571 ff., on the subject of the relegation of the personage of al-Baṭṭāl, the hero of the Umayyad period, to the legend of ʿAmr b. ʿUbayd Allāh, amīr of Malaṭya in the ʿAbbāsid period, that the romance of Delhemma is made up of two parts which are each a version or fragment of two cycles of different periods and origins. The first and shorter part goes back to a bedouin and Syrio-Umayyad cycle (other fragments of which are incidentally extant) describing the adventures of the Umayyad amīr Maslama b. ʿAbd al-Malik and of personages of the B. Kilāb tribe related to Maslama through his wife. Though this part does not include the historical heroes of the Umayyad period, al-Baṭṭāl and his companion ʿAbd al-Wahhāb who have been relegated to the second part, al-Baṭṭāl's exploits have been put under the name of the Kilābī amīr al-Ṣaḥṣāḥ. The second, the principal and longer part of the romance, very closely related to the Turkish Sayyid Baṭṭāl, represents not only the Turkish romance but also a cycle which H. Grégoire and I have called a Melitenian cycle on account of the part played by Malaṭya-Melitene and its amīr ʿAmr b. ʿUbayd Allāh, of the B. Sulaym tribe in the ʿAbbāsid period. This must originally have been the epic of the B. Sulaym and their famous amīr.

As a result of al-Baṭṭāl's popularity the Sulaym must have appropriated the personage who is described in the romance as being of Sulaymī origin. In H. Grégoire's opinion, this change in respect of al-Baṭṭāl was determined by the fact that in the expedition during which he met his death, he was accompanied by an amīr of Malaṭya named Ghamr, a name easily confused with ʿAmr, and his relegation has also involved a similar change in respect of ʿAbd al-Wahhāb. A later stage in the development of the romance was the fusion of the two cycles and the appropriation of the Melitenian cycle by the B. Kilāb, to their advantage, for the reasons I have given in the article under reference (the submission of the amīrs of Malaṭya to Byzantium in the 10th century, which was frowned upon by Islam; and, on the other hand. the important rôle played by the B. Kilāb in the Byzantine war in the 10th centuries, and their eminence in north Syria). It is in this way that the end of the first part, in which we see the birth and childhood of Delhemma, al-Ṣaḥṣāḥ's granddaughter, and then of her son ʿAbd al-Wahhāb, forms a transition with the second part where the Kilābīs take their place in the Melitenian cycle, that ʿAbd al-Wahhāb, historically an Umayyad *mawlā* of unknown origin, becomes a Kilābī and the principal character, with his mother, that al-Baṭṭāl is represented as voluntarily leaving the B. Sulaym in order to join the B. Kilāb, and that ʿAmr b. ʿUbayd Allāh, the central hero of the Melitenian cycle as he is in the Turkish romance under the name ʿUmar b. al-Nuʿmān (cf. also the story in the 1001 Nights of the same name) becomes a personage not only less important than ʿAbd al-Wahhāb but also less attractive, since the narrators give all their sympathies to the B. Kilāb. Moreover, it is known from Ḳalḳashandī, *Ṣubḥ*, i, 340 and iv, 231, that in his time the romance was regarded as having been written to glorify the B. Kilāb of north Syria who claimed to be adherents of ʿAbd al-Wahhāb.

Date of composition of the romance. It goes without saying that it is impossible to give an exact date for the composition of this romance as we have it in the published edition and in the manuscripts which differ little from it. It is probable that, if the first outlines of the Syrio-Umayyad cycle were traced as early as the Umayyad period, and those of the Melitenian cycle shortly after the death of amīr ʿAmr in 249/863, it was at a much later date, and under the inspiration of the spirit of hostility to the Crusaders, that an epic of the Arabo-Byzantine wars followed by the Islamo-Frankish wars finally took shape. Positive references to an epic of this sort do not go back beyond the 12th century. The Egyptian historian al-Ḳurṭī, writing at the time of vizier Shāwar and the Fāṭimid caliph al-ʿĀḍid (555-67/1160-72), speaks of the *Aḥādīth al-Baṭṭāl* and the 1001 Nights as being known in his time (al-Maḳrīzī, *Khiṭaṭ*, i, 485, ii, 181; cf. Macdonald, in *JRAS*, 1924, 381), a detail which should be added to the article AL-BAṬṬĀL. Samaʿwal b. Yaḥyā al-Maghribī, a Jew converted to Islam in 558/1163, says that before his conversion he took pleasure in reading stories and romances and collections of legendary histories like the *Dīwān akhbār ʿAntara*, the *Dīwān Delhemma wa 'l-Baṭṭāl* (see *Bibl.* to AL-BAṬṬĀL). If we can accept a tradition from al-Mughultāʾī reported in the *Tazyīn al-aswāḳ* by Dāwūd al-Antākī (ed. Būlāḳ, 1279, 55), a Maghribī shaykh was said to have heard the *Sīrat al-Baṭṭāl* recited in Cairo, at the time of al-Ḥākim. Thus a romance dealing with al-Baṭṭāl, or with both Delhemma and al-Baṭṭāl, was known in the Fāṭimid period, and it is difficult to tell if it is a question of one and the same romance, or of two separate romances. A *Sīrat al-Baṭṭāl* is also mentioned by al-Ḳalḳashandī, xiv, 149, l. 9. Can we go back even further? According to H. Grégoire (*ZDMG*, lxxxviii, 213-32), the basis of Delhemma's history and the tale of ʿUmar al-Nuʿmān (see also my article *Un personnage* ...) must have been known in about 390/1000 in north Syria since it served as a source for the Byzantine epic Digenis Akritas.

After this period we find other mentions of Delhemma. In the 8th/14th century Ibn Kathīr (see *Bibl.* to AL-BAṬṬĀL), repeating what Ibn ʿAsākir had said of al-Baṭṭāl, adds that the *Sīra* put out under the name of Delhemma, al-Baṭṭāl, amīr ʿAbd al-Wahhāb and *ḳāḍī* ʿUḳba is no more than a tissue of lies, like the *Sīra* of ʿAntara or the one (on the Prophet) by al-Bakrī [*q.v.*]. In the 16th century, the jurist al-Wansharīshī, in his *al-Miʿyar al-mughrib* (see the analysis by Amar, in *Arch. Marocaines*, xi (1908), 456-7 and the lith. ed. vi, 52), says that it is not permitted to sell historical romances like the one on ʿAntar or the "Dalhama". Today, the disfavour shown by the most critical circles has become even more marked: see the modern contempt for this literature, in Brockelmann, S II, 62.

The author or authors of the romance. In the edition, no author is named, but there is a list of *rāwīs*. A manuscript analysed by Ahlwardt begins: *ḳāla Nadjd b. Hishām al-Hāshimī al-Ḥidjāzī*, as though in reference to the author. But in another, six *rāwīs* are listed, Nadjd being the third. The edition gives ten *rāwīs*, of whom Nadjd, with the ethnic al-ʿĀmirī, that is to say, of the tribe of ʿĀmir who plays a large part in the romance with the related Kilāb, is the last. These persons are unknown and one can scarcely draw any conclusions from the fact that the one has the *nisba* at al-Shimshāṭī, and the other at al-Marʿashī, that is to say, lands situated on the Arabo-Byzantine frontier. The fact that a *rāwī* is stated to have been present at the event described (sect. 18, 64), dated 190 A.H. is merely a device by the narrator.

Conclusion. Such then is this long romance of which our analysis gives only an incomplete idea, so complicated are the adventures of the characters, prolonged at will by the author by means of repetition, the constant return of similar situations, the artificial duplication of characters with identical rôles etc. Such as it is, this epic of the Arabo-Byzantine wars and of the B. Kilāb succeeded in pleasing a popular Muslim public by exalting the *mudjāhidūn* and their successes in battles and against adversaries that were often imaginary. A simple-minded audience accepted all this with enthusiasm as though it were fact. In addition to the epic character, with its accounts of combats and great feats of arms, the dramatic or melodramatic element is not lacking; the narrator is adept in holding his listeners spell-bound waiting for some climax, through agonizing situations, sudden changes of fortune whether happy or unhappy, and by various means rousing sympathy or antipathy. The comical element, at times of a somewhat crude sort, appears fairly frequently, particularly in scenes portraying disguise, abduction or theft, and in the more or less childish devices employed by al-Baṭṭāl and ʿUḳba, the use of various mountebank tricks of which al-Baṭṭāl is past master, when for example he appears as a Christian king with his *ghulām*, in the guise of Christ and the twelve apostles (cf. a similar story in *Murūdj al-dhahab*, viii, 175).

The personages are simple in character. They resemble each other and always act in the same way, according to the type they represent. The language is incorrect or careless, but at the same time it pretends to seem learned by making a show of rhymed prose and redundant and assonant epithets in descriptions (horses, arms, clothing, combats, receptions, processions). Verse which plays the same part as in the 1001 Nights is relatively infrequent, but section 70 contains a passage of 472 lines of verse in which al-Baṭṭāl himself reviews his exploits.

Bibliography: In addition to works referred to in the article, see M. Canard, *Les expéditions des Arabes contre Constantinople dans l'histoire et la légende*, in *JA*, ccviii (1926), 116 ff.; idem, *Delhemma, épopée arabe des guerres arabo-byzantines*, in *Byzantion*, x, 1935; idem, *Les principaux personnages du roman de chevalerie arabe* Ḍāt al-Himma wa-l-Baṭṭāl, in *Arabica*, viii, 1961, 158-73. Mentions or fragmentary analyses in Perron, *Femmes arabes*, 352-3; Lane, *Modern Egyptians*, ed. 1836, ii, 146-162; M. Hartmann, in *OLZ*, 1899, 103; Chauvin, *Bibl. des ouvr. arabes*, iv; Kosegarten, *Chrestomathie*, 68-83 (extract: Djandaba and Ḳattālat al-Shudjʿān); analysis of the beginning and end of the romance by W. Ahlwardt (*Die Handschr.- Verzeichnisse der kgl. Bibl. zu Berlin*, xx. Band; *Verzeichnis der arab. Handschr.*, viii. Band, Berlin 1896; *Grosse Romane*, no. 10, 107 ff.).—Besides the edition noted above, there is another dated 1298 H. (M. CANARD)

DHU 'L-ḲAʿDA [see TAʾRĪKH, i].

DHU 'L-ḲADR, Turkmen dynasty, which ruled for nearly two centuries (738/1337-928/1522) from Elbistan over the region Marʿash-Malatya, as clients first of the Mamlūk and later of the Ottoman Sultans. Name: The use in Arabic sources of the spellings Dulghādir and Ṭulghādir and in one of the dynasty's inscriptions of Dulḳādir (see R. Hartmann, *Zur Wiedergabe türkischer Namen* ..., Berlin 1952, 7; this spelling occurs also in *Bazm u Razm*, Istanbul 1918, 456) indicates that the Arabicized forms Dhu 'l-Ḳadr and Dhu 'l-Ḳādir, usual in the later Ottoman sources, are a folk-etymology ('powerful') of a (presumably Turkish) name or title : A. von Gabain has suggested *tulga* + *dar*, 'helmet-bearer' (*Isl.* xxxi, 115).

The founder of the dynasty, Zayn al-Dīn Ḳaradja b. Dulḳādir, first mentioned as penetrating Little Armenia with 5000 horsemen in 735/1335, was the leader of Bozoḳ clans whose summer-pastures were in the east range of the Anti-Taurus and who wintered in the valley east of the Amanus range. In the confusion following the death of the Ilkhān Abū Saʿīd, Ḳaradja Beg seized Elbistan and procured from the Mamlūk Sultan a diploma recognizing him as *nāʾib* (738/1337). The rest of his life was spent in struggles with his neighbours and in revolts against Egyptian suzerainty. Defeated at last by a strong force led by the governor of Aleppo, he escaped capture, but was eventually surrendered to the Egyptians by his rival Muḥammad b. Eretna and executed (754/1353).

Ḳaradja's son and successor Khalīl, seeking revenge for his father's betrayal, seized Kharput from the Eretna-oghlu and began to menace Malatya. The Sultan sought to depose him; after several inconclusive expeditions, in 783/1381 the Egyptian forces, driving Khalīl out of Elbistan and advancing as far as Malaṭya, procured his temporary submission. Sultan Barḳūḳ finally resolved to dispose of the turbulent Khalīl by craft and had him murdered (788/1386).

The Turkmens recognized as his successor his younger brother Sūlī, who defeated an Egyptian army near Göksün and allied himself with the rebellious Mamlūk Mintash. Sūlī sent troops to take part in the revolt of the Syrian governors against Barḳūḳ (791/1389); he remained loyal to Mintash for a time after Barḳūḳ's recovery of power, but was obliged to submit in 793/1391. Four years later Barḳūḳ, learning that Sūlī had offered to guide Tīmūr's army into Syria, sent an expedition against him and Sūlī narrowly escaped capture. Barḳūḳ eventually had him murdered (800/1398); but at this juncture the Ottoman Sultan Bāyezīd I arrived on the scene, drove Sūlī's son Ṣadaḳa from Elbistan, and installed Khalīl's son Nāṣir al-Dīn Muḥammad (801/1399). In 803/1400, Tīmūr, whose army had been harassed by the Dhu 'l-Ḳadr Turkmens during the siege of Sivas, ravaged Muḥammad's territories, and on his return from Syria sent a force to attack the Dhu 'l-Ḳadr nomads near Tadmur (Sharaf al-Dīn Yazdī, *Ẓafar-nāma*, Calcutta ed. ii, 270 ff., 346).

Throughout his long reign Muḥammad remained on friendly terms with Egypt, and also with the rising Ottoman state. In 815/1412 he sent troops to assist Meḥemmed I, who had married one of his daughters, against Mūsā (Neshrī, ed. Taeschner, i, 122, 136 f.). He took part in the Egyptian punitive expedition against the Ḳaraman-oghlu in 822/1419, and after its withdrawal defeated him and sent him prisoner to Cairo; for these service the Sultan al-Muʾayyad made over Kayseri to him (where, in 835/1432, he built the Khātūniyye medrese). The Ḳaraman-oghlu Ibrāhīm re-took Kayseri (O. Turan, *Tarihi Takvimler*, 40), but in 840/1436 Muḥammad appealed for help to the Ottoman Sultan Murād II, who captured the city and restored it to him (*İA*, art. Karamanlılar [Şihabeddin Tekindağ], 324 f.). In 843/1440, to restore the temporarily interrupted harmony with Egypt, Muḥammad visited Cairo and married one of his daughters to Čaḳmaḳ; he died, over 80 years of age, in 846. Bertrandon de la Broquière, travelling through Syria in 1432, encountered nomads attached to the Dhu 'l-Ḳadr-oghlu north of Ḥamā, and noted, on passing through his territories, that this prince "a en sa compaignie trente mil hommes d'armes Turquemans" (*Le voyage d'outremer*, ed. C. Schefer, 82, 118).

The twelve-year reign of Muḥammad's son Sulaymān passed uneventfully. In 853/1449 Murād II, seeking an ally against the Ḳaraman-oghlu and the Ḳara-ḳoyunlu sultan (Ducas, 224), married the future Meḥemmed II to Sulaymān's daughter Sitt Khatun (see F. Babinger, *Mehmed's II Heirat mit Sitt-Chatum* (1449), in *Isl.* xxix, 1950, 217-35).

During the reign of Sulaymān's son Malik Arslan (858/1454-870/1465) the principality was menaced by Uzun Ḥasan, who seized Kharput, and Ottoman-Egyptian intrigues for control of the region became intensified. Malik Arslan was murdered, at the instigation of his brother Shāh-budaḳ and with the connivance of the Mamlūk Sultan Khosh-ḳadem, who installed Shāh-budaḳ. But Meḥemmed II sent against him his own candidate Shāh-suvār, another brother (his diploma [see *Bibl.*], dated 14 Rabīʿ II 870/4 December 1465, appointed him *wālī* over his ancestors' domains "and all the dispersed Bozoḳlu and Dhu 'l-Ḳādirlü", *i.e.*, the nomads). Shāh-suvār drove out Shāh-budaḳ, and gained such successes over the Egyptians that he threw off Meḥemmed's protection (see *Ibn Kemāl, VII. defter* [facsimile], ed. Ş. Turan, 429-33). The Egyptians retaliated, took him prisoner to Cairo and executed him (877/1472), and re-installed Shāh-budaḳ. (Shāh-suvār alone of the Dhu 'l-Ḳadr rulers is said to have struck coins, cf. ʿĀrifī [see *Bibl.*], 430, 763).

Another brother, ʿAlāʾ al-Dawla (whose daughter was married to Prince Bāyezīd and had borne him the future sultan Selīm I), sought Meḥemmed's protection (Ibn Kemāl, 433-7) and in 884/1479 drove out Shāh-budaḳ. During the Ottoman-Mamlūk war of 890-6/1485-90, ʿAlāʾ al-Dawla began to incline towards Egypt, so that the Ottomans made an unsuccessful attempt to depose him in favour of Shāh-budaḳ, who had changed sides and was now sandjaḳ-bey of Vize (ʿĀshiḳpashazāde, ed. ʿĀlī, 234-8; Saʿd al-Dīn, ii, 63-5). During the next twenty years ʿAlāʾ al-Dawla remained at peace with the Ottomans, but came into conflict with Shāh Ismaʿīl, who in 913/1507 sacked Elbistan (destroying the monuments of the dynasty) and Marʿash. When Selīm I marched against Shāh Ismāʿīl the aged ʿAlāʾ al-Dawla refused to assist the Ottoman army, so that on his return Selīm sent against him Khādim Sinān Pasha and ʿAlī, the son of Shāh-suvār, an Ottoman sandjaḳ-bey. ʿAlāʾ al-Dawla was defeated and killed (Rabīʿ II 921/June 1515) and his head sent to Cairo (Saʿd al-Dīn, ii, 293-7; Ferīdūn, *Munshaʾāt*², I, 407-413).

ʿAlī Beg, appointed in his stead, distinguished himself in Selīm's Egyptian campaign; but by playing the major part in suppressing the Djalālī revolt and the rebellion of Djān-birdi he aroused the jealousy of Ferhād Pasha, who procured Suleymān I's consent to his killing ʿAlī Beg and all his family (Shaʿbān 928/July 1522). Thereafter the region was administered as an Ottoman beglerbegilik, 'Dhu 'l-Ḳadriyya', with its headquarters at Marʿash (from which it was later named); in the 17th century it comprised five sandjaḳs, Marʿash, Malaṭya, ʿAyntāb, Kars (modern Kadirli) and Sumeysat (ʿAyn-i ʿAlī in P. von Tischendorf, *Lehnswesen* . . ., 60, 72).

Under Ottoman suzerainty the Dhu 'l-Ḳadr-oghullari enjoyed the privileges of a mediatized ruling house (*e.g.*, in the *alḳāb*, cf. Ewliyā, *Seyāḥatnāme*, i, 170) and were in the 17th century still reckoned among the 'famiglie del Regio sangue' (Sagredo, *Memorie istoriche* . . ., Venice 1677, 1068). Members of the family appear, sometimes in official positions, throughout the Ottoman period (see ʿĀrifī, 694-6).

Dhu 'l-Ḳadirlü was the name of a large *ulus* of tribesmen, widely spread not only in E. Anatolia but also in Ṣafawid domains, where they formed an influential element in the state (*Tadhkirat al-Mulūk*, tr. and comm. V. Minorsky, GMS New Series xvi, London 1943, 14-19).

Bibliography: Mordtmann's article in *EI*¹ was mainly based on Münedjdjimbashî, iii, 167-71, ʿĀlī, *Künh* iv/3, 38-45, and Hammer-Purgstall. See further ʿĀrifī, *Elbistān ve Marʿashda Dhu 'l-Ḳadr (Dūlghādir) oghullari ḥukūmeti*, in *TOEM*, v, 358-77, 419-31, 509-12, 535-52, 623-9, 692-7, 767-8, and (inscriptions) vii, 89-96; *İA*, art. Dulkadırlılar (Mordtmann's article in *EI*¹ much expanded by M. Halil Yinanç with many new facts, especially for the 14th century, from Arabic sources; *İA*, art Elbistan, by M. Halil Yinanç. Letters of Meḥemmed II to and concerning Shāh-suvār are found in *Fatih devrine ait münşeat mecmuasi* (= Vienna, Nationalbibl. MS H.O. 161), ed. N. Lugal and A. Erzi, Istanbul 1956 (the diploma of appointment at 41); see also *Belleten*, xxi, 1957, 279. A *ḳānūn* of ʿAlāʾ al-Dawla, confirmed by the Ottomans, is included in Ö. L. Barkan, *Kanunlar*, Istanbul 1943, 119-24 (on the introduction of Ottoman administration see also *İA*, art. Elbistan, 229), and *Arşiv Kılavuzu* I (index s.v. Alâüddevle) notes some letters of his in the Topkapu Sarayı archives. For the Dhu 'l-Ḳadirlü tribesmen see firstly F. Sümer, *XVI. asırda Anadolu, Suriye ve Irakta yaşayan Türk aşiretlerine umumî bir bakış*, in *Iktisat Fak. Mecm.*, xi (1949-50), 509-23 (esp. 512-3); sporadic references to them appear in the various articles of F. Sümer and F. Demirtaş concerning the tribesfolk.

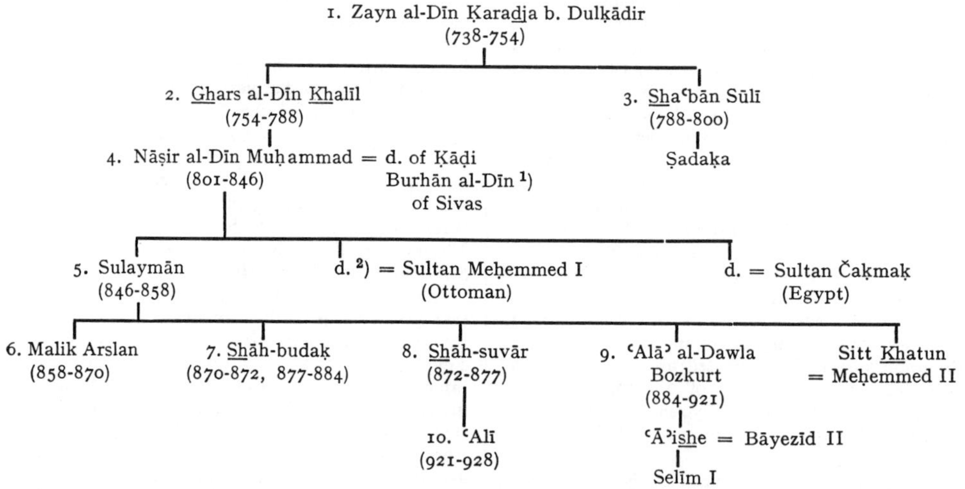

¹) ʿĀshiḳpashazāde, ed. Giese, 66; her name was perhaps Miṣr Khatun (Kh. Edhem, *TOEM*, v, 456).
²) Perhaps named Emīne, see Kh. Edhem, *Düvel*, 309n.

(This table shows only the ruling members of the line and their dynastic alliances; for a full genealogy see the table in *İA*, art. Dulkadırlılar, 660, which corrects and expands those of Khalil Edhem (*Düwel-i Islāmiyye*, 312) and E. de Zambaur (*Manuel de Généalogie* . . ., 158 f.).

(J. H. Mordtmann-[V. L. Ménage])

DHŪ ḲĀR, name of a watering-place near Kūfa, in the direction of Wāsiṭ (Yāḳūt, iv, 10), where one of the most famous Arab *ayyām* [*q.v.*] took place. In contrast with most other clashes between Arabian tribes, this one had a historical importance because the Bakr b. Wā'il tribe (a coalition of all its clans except the Banū Ḥanīfa) put other Arabs to flight (Taghlib, Iyād, etc.) among whom, significantly, were regular Persian troops. Even if the battle was no more than a skirmish (though sources speak of several thousand combatants) it showed the Arabs that the Persians were not as invincible as had been supposed. Caetani points out that it was not mere coincidence that several years later, the same Bakr b. Wā'il tribe, led by al-Muthannā b. Ḥāritha, took the initiative in making the first incursions into ʿIrāḳ; it was henceforth well aware of the Persian weakness when faced with an Arab coalition. The date of the battle is uncertain (variously put at the year of Muḥammad's birth(!), or when he began preaching, *i.e.*, ten years before the *hidjra*, or immediately after the flight to Medina, or some months after Badr, *i.e.*, 2-3/623-625) but the account left of it allows us to place it within a very restricted period. Details vary, and are partly legendary; some of them however can be accepted as authentic, and indicate that the battle occurred soon after certain well-known historical facts. These details attribute the cause of the conflict to the imprisonment of the last Lakhmid leader, al-Nuʿmān b. al-Mundhir, by Khusraw Parwīz (Abarwīz in Arab sources) From them it is possible to reconstruct the train of events: the Sāsānid made an error of judgment in replacing the Lakhmid monarchy by a system of direct government. The Bakr b. Wā'il were either incited by al-Nuʿmān's imprisonment followed shortly by his death, or else, suddenly freed from their fear of this guardian of the frontiers, they devoted themselves to plundering, and the Sāsānid resolved to punish them. His troops, however, were defeated and pursued as far as the Sawād, and through a combination of circumstances the expected reprisal did not ensue. The end of al-Nuʿmān's reign has been put at 602 A.D. (605 by Caetani), and the government of the Taghlibid Iyās b. Ḳabīṣa, who followed the Lakhmid sovereign with a *marzubān* at his side lasted until 611. The date of the battle can therefore be restricted to the years between 604 and 611 A.D. (Caussin de Perceval, *Essai*, ii, 185, puts it at 611; Noeldeke, *Geschichte*, 347, n. 1., between 604-610; Goldziher, *Muh. Stud.*, i, 103, at 611; Caetani, *Annali*, Intr. § 230, at 610).

A famous *ḥadīth* bears witness to the great importance which the Arabs attached to this military success; the Prophet is recorded as having said "It is the first time that the Arabs have got the upper hand of the Persians, and it is through me that God has helped them (*nuṣirū*)". Poets and story-tellers of the *ayyām* have perpetuated the fame of this battle; many poems are recorded by al-Ṭabarī and in both the *Aghānī* and the *ʿIḳd*; the traditions of the event have been collected together principally by Abū ʿUbayda [*q.v.*], and in time provided the material of popular romances, such as (according to Goldziher, xvi, 6-43) the romance of ʿAntar, and (according to Mittwoch, *EI*¹, s.v. DHŪ ḲĀR) the romance entitled *K. Ḥarb Banī Shaybān maʿa Kisrā Anūshirwān*.

The *yawm* of Dhū Ḳār is also known by the names of other places situated near the watering-place, such as al-Ḥinw (*i.e.*, the *ḥinw*, "the curve", of Dhū Ḳār or of Ḳurāḳir), al-Djubābāt, al-ʿUdjrum or Dhu 'l-ʿUdjrum, al-Ghazawān, al-Baṭḥā' (*i.e.*, the *baṭḥā'*, the "wide valley", of Dhū Ḳār).

At Dhū Ḳār another battle took place, between the Bakr and Tamīm tribes, but it is of no historical interest (*ʿIḳd*, Cairo 1305, iii, 73).

Bibliography: Yaʿḳūbī, i, 246, ii, 47; Ṭabarī, i, 1015-37; Th. Noeldeke, *Geschichte der Perser und Araber*, 310-45; Ibn al-Athīr, i, 352-8; Ibn al-Wardī, Cairo 1285, i, 117; *Aghānī*, x, 132-40 (summarized in Nuwayrī, *Nihāya*, Cairo, xv (1949), 431-5 = end of *fann* v, *ḳism* iv, *bāb* v) and index s.v. Ḳār; Masʿūdī, *Murūdj*, ii, 227 ff.; iii, 205-9; idem, *Tanbīh*, ed. al-Ṣawī, Cairo 1928, 207-9 (trans. Carra de Vaux, 318-21); Maydānī, *Amthāl*, in the *bāb* 19 (ed. Freytag, iii, 557); *ʿIḳd*, Cairo, 1305, iii, 90-3 (at the end of *K. al-durra al-thāniya*); Bakrī, *Muʿdjam* (ed. Wüstenfeld), 723; Yāḳūt, iv, 10-12 (s.v. Ḳār); A. P. Caussin de Perceval, *Essai sur l'histoire des Arabes avant l'Islamisme*, Paris 1847-8, ii, 171-85; G. Rothstein, *Die Dynastie der Laḫmiden in al-Ḥīra*, Berlin 1899, 120-3; L. Caetani, *Annali*, Intr. § 230 & Note 1; year 12, §§ 135 and 136; I. Goldziher, *Muh. Studien*, i, 103 ff; Djād, Badjawī and Abū Faḍl Ibrāhīm, *Ayyām al-ʿArab*, Cairo 1361/1942, 6-39. (L. VECCIA VAGLIERI)

DHU 'L-ḲARNAYN [see ISKANDAR].

DHU 'L-KHALAṢA (or KHULAṢA). Dhu 'l-Khalaṣa refers to the sacred stone (and the holy place where it was to be found) which was worshipped by the tribes of Daws, Khathʿam, Badjīla, the Azd of the Sarāt mountains and the Arabs of Tabāla. "It was a white quartziferous rock, bearing the sculpture of something like a crown. It was in Tabāla at the place called al-ʿAblā', *i.e.*, White Rock (*TʿA*, viii, 3) between Mecca and the Yemen and seven nights' march from the former (*i.e.*, approximately 192 kilometres or 119 miles). The guardians of the sanctuary were the Banū Umāma of the Bāhila b. Aʿṣur" (Ibn al-Kalbī, *Aṣnām*, 22 f.). As the rallying point for a good many tribes, the sanctuary acquired the name *al-Kaʿba al-Yamāniya* in contrast with the Meccan sanctuary which was called *al-Kaʿba al-Shāmiyya* (Ibn Saʿd, i/1, 55), whence there arose occasional confusion with the legendary church built by Abraha in order to drawn Arabs away from Mecca (Yāḳūt, ii, 461, iv, 170). Can the divinity referred to by this characteristic be identified with the idol bearing the name al-Khalaṣa "built in the lower part of Mecca" by ʿAmr b. Luḥayy [*q.v.*]? We are told that, "It was adorned with necklaces; offerings of wheat and barley were made to it; milk was poured over it [as libations]; sacrifices were offered and ostrich eggs placed on it" (al-Azraḳī, 78).

The form of worship thus outlined suggests an agrarian goddess. She was also a cleromantic goddess, as is shown by the belomantic practices carried out in her sanctuary (cf. *Semitica*, viii, 1958, 59, 67). The arrows at Dhu 'l-Khalaṣa were called *al-āmir* (ordering), *al-nāhī* (forbidding), and *al-mutarabbiṣ* (expecting) (*Aghānī*, viii, 70, etc.). Legend has it that before leaving to avenge his father Imru 'l-Ḳays consulted the oracle at Dhu'l-Khalaṣa. Seeing 'forbidding' emerge he became angry, broke the arrow and continued on his way. "From then on until the advent of Islam and its destruction by Djarīr b. ʿAbd Allāh al-Badjalī, nobody ever consulted the arrows again (*ibid.*; Ibn Saʿd, i/2, 78). From the time of Ibn al-Ḳalbī (*op. cit.*, 23) the stone of Dhu 'l-Khalaṣa was used as the threshold in the entry to the mosque of Tabāla.

A *ḥadīth* of eschatological character is recorded

about the idol according to which the prophet said: "The hour will not come until the women of Daws crowd about Dhu 'l-Khalaṣa, worshipping it as in the past" (Ibn al-Kalbī, *l.c.*, 23; Wensinck, *Concordance*, i, 85).

Bibliography: All traditional data has been assembled in Yāḳūt, ii, 461-3, which uses Ibn al-Kalbī, *K. al-Aṣnam*, ed. Ah. Zakī Pasha, after R. Klincke-Rosenberg, Thesis, Leipzig 1941, 22 f. and 29 (English translation by N. A. Faris, Princeton 1952, 29-32). Cf. J. Wellhausen, *Reste*², Berlin 1897, 45-8. (T. Fahd)

DHU 'L-KIFL, a personage twice mentioned in the Ḳur'ān (XXI, 85 and XXXVIII, 48, probably second Meccan period), about whom neither Ḳur'ānic contexts nor Muslim exegesis provides any certain information. John Walker (*Who is Dhu 'l-Kifl?*, in *MW*, xvi (1926), 399-401) would like the name to be understood in the sense of "the man with the double recompense" or rather "the man who received recompense twice over", that is to say Job (Ayyūb [*q.v.*]; cf. Job xlii, 10). Without being certain, this explanation does not lack probability; in any case, no better suggestion has been put forward. Muslim exegesis either adopts a similar opinion in making Dhu 'l-Kifl the second name of Ḥizḳil [*q.v.*] = Ezekiel, or else identifies him with an imaginary Bishr (Bashīr), son of Ayyūb (as early as Ṭabarī, *Annales*, i, 364). "Etymological" speculations about the meaning of *kifl* or the derivatives of the root *KFL* (double, caution, subsistence) have helped to swell the legends that have been woven round the rather insignificant figure in the Ḳur'ān; thus, for example, Dhu 'l-Kifl assumes the role of Obadiah, Ahab's pious *major domo* who, according to the Bible (I Kings, xviii, 4) kept and fed a great number of prophets.

The figure of Dhu 'l-Kifl reappears elsewhere in certain edifying accounts in which another person of the same name is presented as typical of the sinner who, having overcome some particularly strong temptation, gains his eternal reward.

As with many other historical or legendary personages, various local traditions attribute to Dhu 'l-Kifl burial places far removed from each other.

Bibliography: Commentaries on the two passages in the Ḳur'ān; Thaʿlabī; *ʿArā'is al-Madjālis*, Cairo edition 1371, 155; other references in the very elaborate article by I. Goldziher in *EI*¹; in addition to the note by J. Walker quoted *supra*, there is also J. Horovitz, *Koranische Untersuchungen*, 113 (which adds nothing to Goldziher). For the theme of the repentant sinner, see the Judeo-Arab legend edited in the original language by J. Obermann (*Studies in Islam and Judaism, The Arabic Original of Ibn Shâhîn's Book of Comfort*, New Haven 1933, 129 ff.), and the introduction by H. Z. Hirschberg to his Modern Hebrew version of this text, *Rabbēnu Nissīm ... mi-Ḳayruwān, Ḥibbūr yāfeh mēha-yeshūʿāh*, Jerusalem 1954, 63-9.—The burial of Dhu 'l-Kifl: Harawī, *K. al-ishārāt ilā maʿrifat al-Ziyārāt*, ed. J. Sourdel-Thomine, 76, trans. by the same *Guide des lieux de Pèlerinage*, Damascus 1957, 174 (in which the figure is identified with Ḥizḳīl). (G. Vajda)

DHU 'L-NŪN, ABU 'L-FAYḌ Thawbān b. Ibrāhīm al-Miṣrī. This early Ṣūfī was born at Ikhmīm, in Upper Egypt, about 180/796. His father was a Nubian and Dhu 'l-Nūn was said to have been a freedman. He made some study of medicine and also of alchemy and magic and he must have been influenced by Hellenistic teaching. Saʿdūn of Cairo is mentioned as his teacher and spiritual director. He travelled to Mecca and Damascus and visited the ascetics at Lubbān, S. of Antioch; it was on his travels that he learnt to become a master of asceticism and self-discipline. He met with hostility from the Muʿtazila [*q.v.*] because he upheld the orthodox view that the Ḳur'ān was uncreated: he was condemned by the Egyptian Mālikī ʿAbd Allāh b. ʿAbd al-Ḥakam for teaching mysticism publicly. Towards the end of his life he was arrested and sent to prison in Baghdād, but was released by order of the caliph Mutawakkil [*q.v.*] and returned to Egypt; he died at Djīza in 246/861.

He was called "the head of the Ṣūfīs", a great teacher who had many disciples during his lifetime and afterwards. A few books on magic and alchemy, attributed to him, have survived, but his mystical teaching is found only in what has been transmitted by other writers, including his great contemporary, al-Muḥāsibī. There are many of his prayers recorded and also some poems of fine quality. He was the first to explain the Ṣūfī doctrines and to give systematic teaching about the mystic states (*aḥwāl*) and the stations of the mystic way (*maḳāmāt*). He taught the duty of repentance, self-discipline, renunciation and otherworldliness. Self, he considered, was the chief obstacle to spiritual progress and he welcomed affliction as a means of self-discipline. Sincerity in the search for righteousness he calls "the sword of God on earth, which cuts everything it touches". Solitude helps towards this end, "for he who is alone sees nothing but God, and if he sees nothing but God, nothing moves him but the Will of God".

Dhu 'l-Nūn was the first to teach the true nature of gnosis (*maʿrifa*), which he describes as "knowledge of the attributes of the Unity, and this belongs to the saints, those who contemplate the Face of God within their hearts, so that God reveals Himself to them in a way in which He is not revealed to any others in the world". "The gnostics are not themselves, but in so far as they exist at all they exist in God". The gnostic needs no state, he needs only his Lord in all states. Gnosis he associates with ecstasy (*wadjd*), the bewilderment of discovery. Dhu 'l-Nūn used the word *ḥubb* for love to God, which means, he says, to love what God loves and to hate what God hates. But the love of God must not exclude love to man, for love to mankind is the foundation of righteousness. He is one of the first to use the imagery of the wine of love and the cup poured out for the lover to drink.

Dhu 'l-Nūn was a practical mystic, who describes in detail the journey of the soul on its upward way to the goal, and gives the Ṣūfī conception of the unitive life in God.

Bibliography: al-Sulamī, *Ṭabaḳāt al-Ṣūfiyya* (ed. J. Pedersen), i, 23-32; Abū Nuʿaym, *Ḥilya*, ix, 331-95; ʿAṭṭār, *Tadhkirat al-Awliyā'* (ed. R. A. Nicholson), i, 114-34; Djāmī, *Nafaḥāt al-Uns* (ed. Nassau Lees), 35-18; Ibn ʿAsākir, *Ta'rīkh*, v, 271-88; L. Massignon, *Lexique technique*, 206-13, 238; Brockelmann, S I, 214. (M. Smith)

DHU 'L-NŪNIDS, in Arabic Bānū Dhi 'l-Nūn, a prominent family of al-Andalus, originally Berbers of the tribe of Hawwāra. Their name appears to be the Arabicization of an earlier Zannūn (cf. Ibn ʿIdhārī, *Bayān*, iii, 276) which would explain the alternative spelling Dhunnūn (adj. Dhunnūnī). In the 5th/11th century, during the first period of the 'Party Kings' (*Mulūk al-Ṭawā'if*), the Dhu 'l-Nūnids ruled, with Ṭulayṭula (Toledo) as their capital, from Wādi 'l-Ḥidjāra (Guadalajara) and Ṭalabīra (Talavera) in the N. to Murcia in the S.

The original territory of the Banū Dhi 'l-Nūn lay E. of Toledo in the *kūra* (administrative district) of Shantabariyya (represented by modern Santaver near the confluence of the Guadiela and the Tagus) where as early as the amīrate of Muḥammad I (238-73/852-86) we find established Sulaymān b. Dhi 'l-Nūn, a descendant in the fourth generation of a certain al-Samḥ, who is said to have been present at the conquest of al-Andalus. In this region of the Middle Frontier (*al-thaghr al-awsaṭ*) or, as is also given, of the Northern Frontier (*al-thaghr al-djawfī*), the family played an active part, frequently in opposition to the reigning dynasty, until the end of the Caliphate of Cordova.

In the troubles of the *Fitna* (literally 'sedition') after 399/1009 the Dhu 'l-Nūnids rallied at first to Sulaymān al-Mustaʿīn (died 407/1016), but soon ʿAbd al-Raḥmān al-Miḍrās b. Dhi 'l-Nūn and his son Ismāʿīl, who is said to have received from Sulaymān the double vizirate and the title Nāṣir al-Dawla (Ibn Ḥayyān, quoted Ibn Bassām, iv/1, 110), struck out a line of their own. According to Ibn Ḥayyān, Ismāʿīl was the first of the 'Party Kings' to break with the central authority and was imitated in this by the others, but when and how he actually did so are not known. It is usually said that he began to rule in Toledo after the *ḳāḍī* Ibn Yaʿīsh in 427/1035. But this is evidently too late. The date of the death of Ibn Yaʿīsh is given by Ibn Bashkuwāl (ed. Codera, 628) as 419/1028-9. We also have an inscription of Ismāʿīl in Toledo dated 423/1032 with the titles Dhu 'l-Riʾāsatayn (cf. above) and al-Ẓāfir, 'the Triumphant', which must be placed after his accession (E. Lévi-Provençal, *Inscriptions arabes d'Espagne*, 66). As king in Toledo Ismāʿīl was beset by difficulties on all sides, including war with the Christians (Ibn Saʿīd, *Mughrib*, ii, 15-16), but he made good his position and survived till 435/1043, when he was succeeded by his son Yaḥyā, called al-Maʾmūn.

Early in his reign al-Maʾmūn was attacked by Sulaymān b. Hūd of Saraḳusṭa (Saragossa), and subsequently both he and Ibn Hūd at different times leagued themselves with the Christians, who were able to operate practically unopposed in Muslim territory. The death of his rival in 438/1046 put an end to these anxieties, at least temporarily, and al-Maʾmūn was free in the next decades to occupy himself elsewhere. He intervened profitably in the E. of al-Andalus, wresting Valencia from the hands of a descendant of al-Manṣūr b. Abī ʿĀmir in 457/1065 (see art. BALANSIYA). In 464/1072 he received Alfonso VI, who had been defeated by his brother Sancho of Castile at the battle of Volpejares (Golpejera), and retained him as guest in Toledo for 9 months. The main object of al-Maʾmūn's ambition was Cordova, the former seat of the Caliphate, held by the Djahwarids till 461/1069. To secure help against Ibn Hūd, he had been obliged to support the claims to the Caliphate of the pseudo-Hishām, maintained by the ʿAbbādids of Seville, which his father al-Ẓāfir had always denied. But even though thus compromised, he was able to gain possession of Cordova, which had passed to the ʿAbbādids, in 467/1074-75, shortly before his own death in the same year.

Al-Maʾmūn was succeeded at Toledo by his grandson Yaḥyā al-Ḳādir, whose ineptitude was speedily shown by the assassination of the *wazīr* Ibn al-Ḥadīdī, hitherto a principal support of the Dhu 'l-Nūnid regime. Al-Ḳādir lost Cordova and Valencia and, faced by dissension at home and by the hostility of the other 'Party Kings', he took the disastrous decision of applying for help to Alfonso VI. He was brought back to Toledo, which he had been obliged to leave, by Christian arms and later installed by Alfonso in Valencia, in return for the cession of Toledo, but was assassinated in 485/1092. With al-Ḳādir ended the rule of the Dhu 'l-Nūnids. Toledo itself had passed into the hands of the Christians in 478/1085.

Less well-endowed than the ʿAbbādids, the family produced perhaps only one man of literary distinction, Arḳam b. Dhi 'l-Nūn, brother of Ismāʿīl al-Ẓāfir (Ibn Saʿīd, *ibid.*, 14), and at first their court appears to have been deficient in poetical talent (Ibn Bassām, *ibid.*, 111, 114). This state of affairs must have radically altered under al-Maʾmūn, since we know the names of many literary men and scholars who flourished under Dhu 'l-Nūnid protection, among them the *ḳāḍī* Ṣāʿid, author of the well-known *Ṭabaḳāt al-Umam*, valuable for the history of science, and the famous astronomer al-Zarḳāla (Azarchiel), who may have been employed as engineer by al-Maʾmūn in some of his constructions at Toledo. The luxury of al-Maʾmūn's court became proverbial in the expression 'the circumcision-feast of Ibn Dhi 'l-Nūn' (*al-iʿdhār al-Dhunnūnī*), given in honour of his grandson (an eye-witness description in Ibn Bassām, iv/1, 99 ff., paraphrased by E. Lévi-Provençal, *Islam d'Occident*, 119-120).

Bibliography: Ibn Bassām, *al-Dhakhīra fī maḥāsin ahl al-djazīra*, ed. Cairo, 1364/1945, iv/1, 99-132, also i/2, 124-9; Ibn Saʿīd, *al-Mughrib fī ḥulā 'l-maghrib*, ed. Shawḳī Ḍayf (*Dhakhāʾir al-ʿArab*, x), ii, 11-4; Ibn ʿIdhārī, *al-Bayān al-mughrib*, iii, ed. E. Lévi-Provençal, Paris 1930, 276-83, also 266-7; Ibn al-Khaṭīb, *Aʿmāl al-aʿlām*, ed. E. Lévi-Provençal, Rabat 1353/1934, 204-10; Maḳḳarī, *Nafḥ al-ṭīb*, ed. Leiden, i, 126 ff., 288; ii, 672 ff., 748; E. Lévi-Provençal, *Alphonse VI et la prise de Tolède*, in *Islam d'Occident* (*Islam d'Hier et d'Aujourd'hui*, t. vii), 109-35 (reprinted from *Hespéris*, t. xii, 1931, 33-49); D. M. Dunlop, *The Dhunnunids of Toledo*, in *JRAS*, 1942, 77-96; idem, *Notes on the Dhunnunids of Toledo*, in *JRAS*, 1943, 17-9; A. Prieto y Vives, *Los Reyes de Taifas*, Madrid 1926, 52-5, 133-5, 213-9 (chiefly numismatics); G. C. Miles, *Coins of the Spanish Mulūk al-Ṭawāʾif*, *Hispanic Numismatic Series*, no. 3, American Numismatic Society, New York 1954, 122-34; Daniel of Morley, *Liber de naturis inferiorum et superiorum*, ed. K. Sudhoff, *Archiv für die Geschichte der Naturwissenschaften und der Technik*, viii, 1918, 33 (12th century Latin reference to architectural works of the Dhu 'l-Nūnid period). (D. M. DUNLOP)

DHŪ NUWĀS, YŪSUF ASHʿAR, pre-Islamic king of the Yemen. According to a tradition probably deriving from Wahb b. Munabbih (*Tīdjān*, 2 ff.) and repeated by the Arab chroniclers (Ibn Ḳutayba, *Maʿārif*, 277; al-Dīnawarī, *Akhbār*, 63; al-Ṭabarī, i, 540 ff.; Ibn Khaldūn, *ʿIbar*, i, 90; al-Masʿūdī, *Murūdj*, i, 129 etc.), Lahayʿa b. Yanūf (Lakhīʿa, Lakhīʿa Yanūf Dhū Shanātir; al-Ṭabarī, i, 540; see also Ibn al-Athīr, ii, 250) abandoning himself to unnatural practices with the sons of the aristocracy, the young Dhū Nuwās, who in Arab traditions is generally known as Zurʿa b. Tibbān Asʿad, and who took the name Yūsuf after his conversion to Judaism (Ibn al-Athīr, ii, 252, calls him Yūsuf Shuraḥbīl), was placed on the throne by the Ḥimyarites after he had assassinated Laḥayʿa b. Yanūf to escape from his attentions. On the subject of his reign, which is said to have lasted 38 years, tradition tells in particular of the persecutions to which he subjected the Christians of Nadjran [see AṢḤĀB AL-UKHDŪD] and the invasion of the Yemen by the Negus at the request of the emperor of Constantinople. Dhū Nūwās was conquered by Aryāt, (who had Abraha under his command, and threw himself into the sea.

In the *Martyrium St. Arethae* he is called Δουναας (nom.) and Δουναav (accus.) (Nöldeke, *Geschichte*, 174, 3) (Theophanus calls him Dimianus, which Nöldeke believes incorrect, the name belonging to an Ethiopian king). Thus the epithet Dhū Nuwās does not seem to be an invention of Arab traditions which explain it by his curly hair (al-Hamdānī, *Iklīl*, viii, 137); but a certain Dhū Ghaymān and Nuwās, lord of a fief, is mentioned in *CIH*, 68, li (cf. M. Hartmann, *Islamische Orient*, ii, 292 ff.). However, *The Book of the Himyarites* (A. Moberg, lxxiv, 34a; D. Smith, 456, 3) and the *Chronique de Seert* (v, 2, 330-1) call our Dhū Nuwās Masrūḳ; brought up in the Jewish faith by his mother (from Nisibis), he reigned after his father. The inscription Ry 446 = Ry 510, (*Muséon* lxv, lxvi), whose author was the South Arabian king Maʿdīkarib Yaʿfur, at that time (631 sab. = 522 A.D.) on a campaign in central Arabia against al-Mundhir III of al-Ḥīra, and various pieces of evidence show that Dhū Nuwās Masrūḳ had succeeded Maʿdīkarib on the throne. If the *Chronique* is authentic, Yūsuf Dhū Nuwās must be his predecessor's son. The two inscriptions Ry 507 = Ḥima 444 (Philby 158, *Muséon*, lxiv, 93 ff.) and Ry 508 (*Muséon*, lxvi), discovered in 1952 by G. and J. Ryckmans confirm the historical existence of Yūsuf Dhū Nuwās; they describe the operations conducted against the Christians and Abyssinians in Ẓufār, Mukhā and Nadjrān in 633 sab. = 524 A.D. by a South Arabian king who can be conclusively identified with Yūsuf Dhū Nuwās. Between the dates of Ry 510 (522 A.D.) and Ry 508, Ry 507 (524, March, April, July-September 524 A.D.) we note the date of the letter from Simeon Bēth Arsham (cf. J. Ryckmans, *Persécution*, 18) written on the 20 January 524 and addressed to the Christians, telling of the coming of the new king and his persecution of the Christians. E. Glaser has however remarked that the Sabaean year began between January and February. It emerges that Dhū Nuwās, Yūsuf Ashʿar had come to power at the end of 523 A.D. Simeon Bēth Arsham's letter seems to establish this fact. Simeon was sent by Justinian I to negotiate a peace with al-Mundhir III at that time, in 524, to Ramla in the Syrian desert. It was there that the letter came from the king of Ḥimyar telling al-Mundhir: "this king whom the Abyssinians sent to us is dead, therefore I have become king of the whole Ḥimyarite region" (cf. J. Ryckmans, *Muséon*, lxvi, 329; Guidi, *Lettera*, 480 ff.).

John Posaltes' hymn and Simeon's letter, as I. Guidi has shown, must refer to the second persecution, that is to say to the period of Negus Ella Aṣbaha's second expedition. The letter from James of Sarug to the Ḥimyarites dated 521 A.D. (Guidi, *Lettera*, 479), must relate to an earlier and less general persecution. This letter and other facts from Abyssinian and Greek sources suggest that the persecution had in fact already started before Dhū Nuwās, during the reign of his predecessor Maʿdīkarib Yaʿfur. According to a tradition from Ibn al-Kalbī (al-Ṭabarī, above; Ibn al-Athīr, *Kāmil*, i, 254), the Negus must have made two expeditions. In the first, Dhū Nuwās by means of a ruse succeeded in wiping out the occupation forces. After installing a viceroy, the Negus withdrew to Ethiopia, leaving an Ethiopian garrison on Ḥimyarite territory. According to Cosmas Indicopleustes, the Negus (Sidney Smith, *Events*, 454) tried to establish Abyssinian claims to the Ḥimyarite territory from 518 A.D. Abyssinian sources suggest that the Christians paid their tribute to the Negus himself.

On the other hand, Maʿdīkarib Yaʿfur, the author of Ry 510, can be identified with his homonym of CIH 621 = RES 2633 (640 sab. = circa 530 A.D.; cf. Philby, *Muséon*, lxiii, 271-5). One explanation is therefore possible: Maʿdīkarib Yaʿfur may have abdicated as he could not restore the economic autochthonous situation. His régime must have been in financial difficulties, with the result that he was compelled to seek a large credit from a Nadjrānī Christian, Raḥma (A. Moberg, 26a, 43b). Then Yūsuf Ashʿar, Dhū Nuwās and other leading Ḥimyarites, specially those of Ry 508, Ry 507 and a certain number of those of RES 4069 and Ist. 7608 bis must have joined together to seize power and unleash the persecutions (cf. Philby, *Muséon*, lxiii, 271 ff.). The Dhū Yazan tribe must have taken a leading part in these activities. Sharāḥīl Yaḳbul Dhū Yazan acted for Yūsuf Ashʿar in the persecutions at Ẓufar and Nadjrān. Sumayfaʿ Ashwā (Ist. 7608 bis ll. 1-2) whom the Abyssinians chose as king of Sabaʾ after the defeat of Dhū Nuwās (G. Ryckmans, lix; J. Ryckmans, *Muséon*, lxvi, 337-8; *The Book of the Ḥimarites*, 54a and c/xvii-ix; see also Smith, *Events*, 459) was grandfather of Sharāḥīl Yaḳbūl Dhū Yazan; this tribe must be the same as king Yūsuf's (J. Ryckmans, *Muséon*, lxvi, 337). At the beginning of his reign, Yūsuf Ashʿar invited the king of Ḥīra, al-Mundhir, just when the latter was leading a campaign against Byzantium in the Syrian desert, to follow his example and exterminate all Christians who would not deny Christ.

Then Yūsuf Ashʿar began a savage onslaught on the Christians and Abyssinians, first of all at Ẓufar where he destroyed and burnt the church (Ry 508 ll. 2-3; Ry 507 l. 4; cf. *The Book of the Ḥimyarites*, 7b). Then turning to the neighbouring Christian tribe of al-Ashʿar, he ordered his commander Sharāḥīl Dhū Yazan to march against Mukhā (Ry 508, 3-4). In the operations in the two inscriptions, casualties in the battles amount to 14,000 killed, with 11,000 prisoners. At Nadjrān, where the siege was said to have lasted some months, the king asked the Nadjrānīs for guarantees to prevent any invasion by the South. Meanwhile a certain Daws Dhū Thuʿlubān fled and informed the emperor Justinian I. Simeon Bēth Arsham arranged that the news should reach the monophysites in Tarsus and Antioch. An Ethiopian army then intervened, at Justinian's request, in May 525 A.D. (J. Ryckmans, *Persécution*, 18-22) and the Negus occupied the Yemen (see Bury, *Later Roman Empire*, ii, 324; Smith, *Events*, 451) at the head of 120,000 men (70,000 according to al-Ṭabarī, i, 548) who came down on Bāb al-Mandab (J. Ryckmans, lxvi, 334-5; Budge i, 262; Smith, 458).

According to Syrian evidence, Dhū Nuwās Ashʿar was killed (A. Moberg, Ch. XLII; Philby, *Background*, 120). We can see from what ensued that a split occurred among king Yūsuf's allies (cf. Smith, 549; Ibn Khaldūn, *ʿIbar*, i, 92). Sumayfaʿ Ashwā, viceroy to the Negus in 525, was among Yūsuf's supporters in 524. Inscriptions and *The Book of the Himyarites* are in agreement about the Jewish king's successor, whom Ella Aṣbaḥa gave to the Ḥimyarites (see Smith, 459, B.H. 54b); it is a question of king Sumayafaʿ Ashʿwa (in Procopius, *Wars*, i, xx, 3-8, he is called Esimiphaeus) of Inst. 7608 bis, l. 1, a Christian convert of the royal family. J. Ryckmans and A. F. L. Beeston think that RES 2633 = CIH 621, the date of which, 640 sab., must indicate his death, not that of Dhū Nuwās Yūsuf (*Persécution*, 8-9). This inscription must relate to Abraha's revolt against king Sumayfaʿ Ashʿwa in about 530 A.D. (see also Procopius, *Wars*, supra). According to this thesis, the Sabaean era started in about 109 B.C., and not in 115. It is by this system of dating, which conforms better with the evidence of inscriptions and traditions, that the inscriptions quoted in this article have been dated.

Bibliography: J. B. Bury, *Later Roman Empire*, ii; A. Moberg, *The Book of the Himyarites*, Lund 1924; Sidney Smith, *Events in Arabia in the 6th Century*, in *BSOAS*, xvi, 3, 1954, 425-68; Ibn Munabbih, *Tidjān*, Ḥaydarābād; Ibn Khaldūn, *ʿIbar*, Cairo 1936; Ṭabarī, Cairo 1939; Hamdānī, *Iklīl*, viii; Budge, A. E. Wallas, *History of Ethiopia*, London 1928; E. Glaser, *Zwei Inschriften über den Dammbruch von Marib*, 1879; Th. Nöldeke, *Geschichte der Perser und Araber zur zeit der Sasaniden*; G. Ryckmans, *Répertoire d'epigraphie sémitique*, iv-vii; J. Ryckmans, *Institutions monarchiques en Arabie méridionale*, 1951; idem, *La Persécution des chrétiens himyarites au sixième siècle*, 1956; I. Guidi, *Della lettera di vescovo di Simeone Beth Aršam*, in *Rend. C. Lincei*, 1881; *Corpus Inscriptionum Semiticarum*, iv (abbreviated CIH); H. Philby, *Background of Islam*, Alexandria 1947.

(M. R. Al-Assouad)

DHU 'L-RUMMA, lit. 'he who wears a piece of cord', nickname given to the famous Arab poet Ghaylān b. ʿUḳba, who died in 117/735-36.

He earned the name on account of a small charm which he hung around his neck by a piece of string. He was from the Ṣaʿb b. Milkān clan, an offshoot of the ʿAdī tribe which originated from the ʿAbd Manāt peoples of Central Arabia. On his mother's side he was related to the Asad tribe. If we accept that he died at the age of forty, his date of birth would be 77/696. This information is however open to doubt, as it is based on a very obscure passage in one of his poems (see Ibn Ḳutayba, 334, l. 7). He came from a family rich in poetical talent (see *Aghānī*[1], xvi, 111); and was known as the 'transmitter' (*rāwī*) of the poet al-Rāʿī [*q.v.*]. Later in his life, in Baṣra, he was regarded as an authority on poetry (*Aghānī*[3], vi, 88), but is said not to have divulged the fact that he knew how to read and write (see Ibn Sallām in *Aghānī*[1], xvi, 121, and Ibn Ḳutayba, 334). There is every reason to think that during his life he remained in close contact with his tribal group in Central Arabia; numerous anecdotes have come to us of his relations with the very aged governor of Yamama, Muhādjir (see *Aghānī*[1], xvi, 112, 115, and *Aghānī*[3], viii, 54—panegyric in his honour by the poet). Other anecdotes throw light on Dhu 'l-Rumma's activities in Kūfa (*ibid.*, xvi, 122) and, above all, in Baṣra, where he frequently came into contact with the ḳāḍī-governor Bilāl b. Abī Burda (d. after 120/738). Certain works addressed to this generous patron are evidence of the protection which he granted the poet (see Ibn Ḳutayba, 341. Ibn Sallām in *Aghānī*[1], xvi, 121 bottom, 128 ff.). It was in Baṣra, moreover, that Dhu 'l-Rumma met the reader (*ḳārī'*) ʿAnbasa and the grammarians Abū ʿAmr al-ʿAlā' [*q.v.*], Yūnus [*q.v.*] and ʿIsā b. ʿUmar (see *Aghānī*[8], xvi, 122 bottom; Ibn Sallām, 128; Ibn Ḳutayba, 334). The city was also the scene of his disputes with other poets from eastern Arabia; on one occasion, Ru'ba accused him in front of Bilāl b. Abī Burda of the shameless plagiarism of his own poems (see *Aghānī*[1], xvi, 121 and 123-5; also Ḳutayba, 339). The controversies with Djarīr [*q.v.*] were a result of the open preference which Dhu 'l-Rumma showed for the poetry of al-Farazdaḳ; his diatribes with the Tamīmī Hishām seem to have given rise to some of the choicest anecdotes in Baṣra (see *Aghānī*[3], viii, 55, and *ibid.*[8], xvi, 117). We have only a few facts of doubtful authenticity on his love affairs with Mayya and a certain Kharḳā'; they were later developed into a sort of novel. His thoughts on religion also remain obscure, there being but a few references to the Ḳur'ān in his poems, *e.g.*, *Dīwān* no. 7 verse 30, no. 22 verses 35 & 79 (cf. anecdotes in *Aghānī*[1], xvi, 128). His death, at a relatively young age, has been put at about 117/735 (for other estimations see Schaade in *EI*[1], s.v., and references). According to a story originating from two sources in Baṣra, an unknown person reported his burial at Huzwā, on the borders of Dahmā.

As was normal for the times, Dhu 'l-Rumma's works were diffused orally by *rāwīs*, one of whom is known by name (see *Aghānī*[1], xvi, 112, l. 27). Many stories attributed to him circulated among the nomads of eastern Arabia (*ibid.*, xvi, 112), and, although often of doubtful authenticity, they have helped preserve his poetry for later generations. In time, oral accounts were written down in the form of a *Dīwān*, and by the end of the 3rd/9th century two collections existed, one by Thaʿlab and the other, a more complete edition, by al-Sukkari (cf. *Fihrist*, 158, l. 20). In Macartney's work, the collection attributed to Dhu 'l-Rumma is extensive, comprising 87 complete poems to which the author has added 149 fragmentary works. Most of the poems are exceptionally long. Sometimes they are improvised for a particular occasion, *e.g.*, nos. 31, 33 (in praise of Muhādjir), 57 (traditional *ḳaṣīda* in honour of Bilāl), 81 (an allusion to events of which nothing is known historically). More often than not they are lyrical odes written in a style common to Bedouin poets of the time, beginning with a description of deserted camps, followed by some reflections on the poet's lover, and ending with a description of his camel and its wanderings across the desert. His beloved Mayya is mentioned in nearly all of them (nos. 4, 7, 10, 11, 17, 22, 28 etc.). The study of his works poses several well-known problems. Some pieces are fragmentary (*e.g.*, the end of no. 60, *ḳaṣīda*, is missing), others are of dubious origin because of the inconsistent sequence of themes treated in them. Some seem to have no more than a lexicographical inspiration, and were no doubt composed to meet the demands of certain learned men of Baṣra and Kūfa. If we are to believe Ḥammād 'the Transmitter', many poems full of *pathos* were written in Kūfa by persons using Dhu 'l-Rumma's name (see *Aghānī*[1], xvi, 122, l. 156 ff.). Moreover, it may well be asked whether certain elegaic poems were not included in the collection simply because they contained references to Mayya. From the 3rd/9th century onwards, the historical character of Dhu 'l-Rumma began to change and he took his place among those famous Arab lovers who were victims of unrequited passion; in this case, the hero pines away for Mayya, who is married to a rich *sayyid*, and his songs addressed to Kharḳā' are designed only to arouse his Lady's jealousy (ref. *Aghānī*[1], xvi, 113, 114, 119 ff., 125, quoting Ibn al-Naṭṭāḥ; cf. Ibn Ḳutayba 334-6, where the story, from an unknown source, is in a very conventional romantic manner).

Although this epic of love has been much elaborated (cf. mention of title in *Fihrist*, 306, l. 22), it has nevertheless retained traces of its Bedouin origin, as is shown by comparison with a story in al-Hamadhānī's [*q.v.*] *Maḳāmāt* [*q.v.*] (Beirut 1924, 43), which the author adapted from an old story of central Arabian origin.

Dhu 'l-Rumma's prestige stood particularly high with the Baṣra grammarians (see *Aghānī*[1], xvi, 113 ff.), although this assertion must be qualified with some reservations (see Ibn Sallām, 125, & Ibn Ḳutayba, 333). It was the profuse richness of the poet's descriptions of the camel, onager and oryx and the desert which aroused admiration; the great beauty of his elegies was also acknowleged, hence the large number of his verses which were set to music (*Aghānī*[1], xvi, 129 ff.), of which we may mention a *Kitāb akhbār Dhu 'l-Rumma* composed by Isḥāḳ al-Mawṣilī (title in *Fihrist*, 142, l. 19). But it was nevertheless the lexicographers whom Dhu 'l-Rumma interested most, and, to give but one example, numerous verses of his are quoted in the dictionary *Lisān al-ʿArab*. This is due to the great number of rare expressions used by the poet. On the other hand, he is quoted only 6 and 20 times respectively in the *Bayān* of al-Djāḥiẓ and the *ʿIḳd* of Ibn ʿAbd Rabbih. Set in the perspective of his age and society, Dhu 'l-Rumma is one of the great figures in the tradition of eastern Arabian poetry. His excessive use of rare terms was a common tendency in poets (*e.g.*, Ruʾba, [*q.v.*]) who were in close contact with the philologists and grammarians of ʿIrāḳ; the frequent appearance of the *radjaz* metre in his *Dīwān* underlines his close relationship with certain of his contemporaries. He terminates a line of poets who, even in their own age, were considered 'behind the times'.

Bibliography: Ibn Sallām, *Ṭabaḳāt*, ed. Hell, 17, 125-8; Ibn Ḳutayba, *Liber Poesis*, ed. De Goeje, 29, 41, 333-42; *Aghānī*[3], vi, 88, vii, 238, viii, 52-6, 58, 199 and *Aghānī*[1], xvi, 110-30; Ibn Khallikān, *Wafayāt*, Cairo 1310, i, 404-6; Ibn al-Nadīm, 158, 306; Ḳurashī, *Djamhart ashʿār al-ʿArab*, ed. Sandūbī, 360-74; quotations by Djāḥiẓ, *Bayān*, ed. Hārūn, index; by Ibn ʿAbd Rabbih, *Iḳd*, ed. ʿUryān, index; by Yāḳūt, *Muʿdjam*, index; R. Geyer, *Altarabische Diiamben*, Leiden 1908, 69-86; Smend, *De Dsur-Rumma poeta*, Bonn 1874; C. H. H. Macartney, *The Dîwân of Chailan ibn ʿUqbah known as Dhû r-Rummah*, Cambridge 1919, xxxviii, 676. (R. Blachère)

DHU 'L-SHARĀ is the soubriquet of a god borrowed from the Nabataeans, known in Aramaic as *dshr*, *Dusares* (E. Littmann, *Thamūd und Ṣafā*, 30). These soubriquets for gods formed from the pronoun *dhū* (feminine *dhāt*) were of frequent use in Southern Arabia (G. Ryckmans, *Les religions arabes préislamiques* 2, 44-5; W. Caskel, *Die alten semitischen Gottheiten*, 108-9). According to Ibn al-Kalbī, Dhu 'l-Sharā was a divinity of the Banu 'l-Hārith of the tribe of the Azd (*Kitāb al-Aṣnām*, ed. Aḥmad Zakī[2], 37). Ibn Hishām records that Dhu 'l-Sharā "was an image belonging to Daus and the *ḥimā* was the temenos which they had made sacred to him; in it there was a trickle of water from a rivulet from the mountain" (Ibn Isḥāḳ's *Sīra*, ed. Wüstenfeld, 254; trans. A. Guillaume, *The Life of Muhammad*, 176). This tradition is resumed in the *Ḳamūs*: *dhu 'l-sharā ṣanam daws*. The tradition arose from confusion among the Arabs between Duserani, "the worshippers of Dusares", a naming for the Nabataeans, and the tribe of Daws (R. Dussaud and F. Macler, *Mission dans les régions désertiques de la Syrie moyenne*, 67, n. 3).

Dhu 'l-Sharā is attested in Thamudic and Ṣafaitic. Its only trace in Thamudic is on an inscription from the region of Tabūk, in the Aramaic form *dshr* (Jaussen-Savignac 658[1], according to the reading of A. van den Brauden, *Les inscriptions thamoudéennes*, Louvain 1950, 451). Ṣafaïtic has the name of this god in the form *dhshr* (*CIS*, v 57, etc.) and in the Aramaic forms *dshr* (*CIS*, v 88 etc.) and *dshry* (*CIS*, v, 2955). The name *Dhu 'l-Sharā* means "The One from Sharā", the local god of the Sharā range, the southernmost tip of the chain of mountains to the south-east of the Dead Sea (A. Musil, *The Northern Heğâz*, New York 1926, 252-5; R. Dussaud, *La pénétration des Arabes en Syrie*, 30; W. Caskel, *Die alten sem. Gottheiten*, 109). The name of this god was Aʿara, as is shown by several Nabataean inscriptions dedicated to Dū Sharā Aʿara (*CIS*, ii 190; *RES* 83, 696; J. Cantineau, *Le nabatéen*, ii, nos X-XII, 21-4). This name might belong to a root *ghry*; in Arabic, *gharā* means "to coat with a sticky substance". At Ḥīrā, in the kingdom of the Lakhmids, there were known to be two obelisks (*ghariyān*) daubed with the blood of sacrifices (H. Lammens, *L'Arabie occidentale avant l'Hégire*, 146 and 167). Aʿara would then be the god whose bethel was daubed with blood. It was the same with Dusares (Suidas, *Lexicon*, s.v. Θευσαρης) whose bethel was a black, rectangular, uncarved stone and who was the object of bloody sacrifices (D. Sourdel, *Les cultes du Hauran à l'époque romaine*, 59; R. Dussaud, *Pénétration*, 40 and n. 4; J. Starcky, *Palmyréniens, Nabatéens et Arabes du Nord*, 222). The confusion of Dusares with the god Ares is due to Suidas who "takes Θευσαρης, a defective form of Dusares, for the god Ares" (M.-J. Lagrange, *Études sur les religions sémitiques* 2, 210, n. 1).

From the fifth century B.C. the god Aʿara was identified with Dionysos, according to Herodotus: "Dionysos, with Urania, is the only god whose existence they [the Arabs] recognize . . . They call Dionysos Orotalt, Urania Alitat" (*Hist.* iii, 8). Aʿara can be recognized in the part *Oro*, whatever may be the case with its second part *talt* or *tal* (C. Clermont-Ganneau, *Recueil d'archéologie orientale*, V, Paris 1903, 109-15; R. Dussaud, *Pénétration*, 45). Alitat, clearly, is the goddess Allāt. Hesychius (s.v.) identifies Dusares with Dionysos: Δουσάρης τὸν Διόνυσον· Ναβαταῖοι. Aʿara Dhu 'l-Sharā being none other than Dionysos the god of vegetation, "it may be concluded that during the occupation of Djebel esh-Sharâ by the Edomite Arabs the vine prospered there and that before the arrival of the Greeks the god of vegetation Orotal (Aʿara) had soon been identified with Dionysos" (R. Dussaud, *op. cit.*, 56). J. Perrot's excavations in the Negev and the recent experiments of the botanist M. Evenari, who has restored a Nabataean agricultural settlement dating from early in the Christian era, on the site of the former city of Subeita, prove that the fertility of the land in that desert area was ensured by the construction of terraces, dams and channels, irrigated by periodic rainfall and flooding. This explains how Dionysos-Dusares came to be represented on reliefs decorated with vine-branches, particularly on the lintels of Ḳanawāt and Suwayda (R. Dussaud, *Pénétration*, 57-61; see M. Dunand, *Le musée de*

Soueida, Paris 1934, nos 1, 2 and 3; D. Sourdel, *Les cultes du Hauran*, 64, expresses certain doubts on these identifications). Similarly, the statue of a bearded god at Ghariya-Shubayḥ, holding a horn of plenty filled with bunches of grapes, seems indeed to represent Dusares (R. Dussaud, *op. cit.* 61; see D. Sourdel, *op. cit.* 64, who does not share this opinion).

An eagle with outspread wings was probably the symbol of Dusares. It figures above the entrance to numerous Nabataean tombs at Hegra (see particularly Jaussen and Savignac, *Mission*, i, pl. xxxvi and fig. 160; ii, *Atlas*, pl. xli, xliii, xliv and xlv). Jaussen and Savignac see in it the symbol of Dusares, who might have been assimilated in Zeus the sun god (*Mission*, i, 400-401). An eagle figures also on one of the lintels of Suwayda (M. Dunand, *op. cit.*, n. 2); attributing it to Dusares in this relief "is not subject to doubt" (R. Dussaud, *op. cit.*, 60). R. Dussaud sees Dusares on an altar relief from a Nabataean temple to that god in Siʿ (formerly Seia in the Ḥawrān; see R. Dussaud, *Topographie historique de la Syrie antique et médiévale*, Paris 1927, 368-9), dating from early in the Christian era (D. Schlumberger, *La Palmyrène du Nord-Ouest*, Paris 1951, 97 n. 3). But the altar is dedicated to Zeus Kyrios (R. Dussaud, *Pénétration*, 57). This assimilation, as does also the assimilation of Dusares to Helios in the Roman era, nevertheless raises problems which are far from resolved (D. Sourdel, *op. cit.*, 63-5), and it should be noted that, while Strabo may associate Dionysos with Zeus Ouranos, he never identifies them with each other in any way (Strabo, xvi, 1, 11).

In the Hellenistic period Dionysos gave his name to the town of Suwayda, Dionysias, formerly called Soada, in Djabal Drūz. The Greek inscription [Waddington 2309 = CIG 4617] describes Dionysos as the founder of Dionysias: πρωνοία κυρίου κτίσλου Διονύσου. The identification of Suwayda with Dionysias has been established by the remains of an inscription, engraved on a milestone between the towns of ʿAtil (formerly Athela) and Suwayda: ... ὅροι Διον[υσιά]δος ... [ὅ]ροι Ἀθελεν[ῶ]ν (R. Dussaud and F. Macler, *Mission*, 247-248, Greek no. 23). This confirms that during the Nabataean occupation the worship of Dusares had spread into the Ḥawrān and adjacent areas. Several Nabataean inscriptions were dedicated to Dhu 'l-Sharā *dy bbṣrʾ*, "who is at Boṣrah" (*CIS*, ii 218; *RES* 83; see J. Cantineau, *Le nabatéen*, ii, 21, no. X 36,; no. VII).

According to Epiphanius (*Contra Haeres.*, LI, 22, 9-12), the Nabataeans celebrated on the sixth of January (formerly in the East the Christian feast of the Nativity) the feast of Dusares, the son of the virgin Χααβου (correction for Χααμου; R. Eisler, in *ARW*, xv (1912), 630). Epiphanius records this tradition with apologetical purpose, "with a view to showing that also the pagans had the notion of the virgin birth of a god" (D. Sourdel, *Les cultes du Hauran*, 67). But Epiphanius's account rests on a linguistic confusion: Χααβου "virgin" (in Arabic *kuʿba, kaʿiba*) is in fact the Arabic *kaʿba* "cube" (a word belonging to the same root), whence *kaʿba*, "stele" or "bethel", the term which designates the Kaʿba of Mecca. This tradition is perhaps only a reminiscence of the worship of the bethel personifying Dhu 'l-Sharā. In Aramaic bethel is *mōtab* "seat". According to J. Starcky, coins from Boṣra presenting the legend of "Dusares the god", as might also three egg-shaped bethels resting on a support, may give some idea of Dusares' "seat", represented by the support (*Palmyréniens, Nabatéens et Arabes*, 221).

According to Ibn Hishām (see above) the *kaʿba* or bethel of Dhu 'l-Sharā was in a *ḥimā*, a sacred enclosure also called *ḥaram*. According to a scholion in the *Dīwān* of the Hudhaylīs (J. Wellhausen, *Reste*, 51), the *ḥaram* was itself enclosed in the *sharā*, which covered a greater area: *al-sharā mā kāna ḥawl al-ḥaram wa-huwa ashyaʾu 'l-ḥaram*. Thus Dhu 'l-Sharā, the god of Djabal Sharā, becomes also "the master of the sacred enclosure" (M.-J. Lagrange, *Études sur les religions sémitiques*², 184-5). Nevertheless, that is only a secondary meaning of the name Dhu 'l-Sharā.

Also known are the Nabataean theophorous proper names ʿAbddūsharā, Taymdūsharā (references in J. Cantineau, *Le nabatéen*, ii, 126 and 256), and the Arabic proper name ʿAbd dhī Sharā (J. Wellhausen, *Reste*², 3).

Bibliography: *CIS*, ii and v; *RES*, i-iv; Ibn Hishām, ed. Wüstenfeld, Göttingen, 1858-60 (translated by A. Guillaume, see below); C. Clermont-Ganneau, *Recueil d'archéologie orientale*, v, Paris 1903, 109-15; R. Dussaud and F. Macler, *Mission dans les régions désertiques de la Syrie moyenne*, Paris 1903; M.-J. Lagrange, *Études sur les religions sémitiques*², Paris 1905; A. Jaussen and R. Savignac, *Mission archéologique en Arabie*, i-ii, Paris 1909-20; Ibn al-Kalbī, *Kitāb al-aṣnām*, ed. Aḥmad Zakī², Cairo 1924 (French summary by M. S. Marmardji, *Les dieux du paganisme arabe d'après Ibn al-Kalbî*, in *Revue biblique*, xxxv (1926), 397-420; translations by R. Klinke-Rosenberger, *Das Götzenbuch Kitâb al-Aṣnâm des Ibn al-Kalbî*, Leipzig 1941, and N. A. Faris, *The Book of idols*, Princeton 1952); J. Wellhausen, *Reste arabischen Heidentums*², Berlin 1897; H. Lammens, *L'Arabie occidentale avant l'Hégire*, Beirut 1928; J. Cantineau, *Le nabatéen*, i-ii, Paris 1930, 1932; E. Littmann, *Thamūd und Ṣafā*, Leipzig 1940; G. Ryckmans, *Les religions arabes préislamiques*², Louvain 1951; D. Sourdel, *Les cultes du Hauran à l'époque romaine*, Paris 1952; A. Guillaume, *The Life of Muhammad, a translation of Ishāq's* Sīrat Rasūl Allāh, London 1955; R. Dussaud, *La pénétration des Arabes en Syrie avant l'Islam*, Paris 1955; J. Starcky, *Palmyréniens, Nabatéens et Arabes du Nord avant l'Islam* (in M. Brillant and R. Aigrain, *Histoire des religions*, iv), Paris 1956, 201-37; W. Caskel, *Die alten semitischen Gottheiten in Arabien* (in S. Moscati, *Le antiche divinità semitiche*), Rome 1958, 95-117.

(G. RYCKMANS)

DHŪ YAZAN [see SAYF].

DHUBĀB, the fly. Some authors state that word is used also for other insects, such as bees, hornets, butterflies or moths (*farāsh*), etc. According to Arab lexicographers, it is either a singular or else a collective noun, in which case *dhubāba* is used for the singular. Cognate synonyms are found in other Semitic languages, *e.g.*, Hebrew זְבוּב, Aramaic דִּבָּבָא.

The fly is often mentioned and described in ancient Arabic poems and proverbs. A *ḥadīth* has it that there are flies in hell to torture the condemned. Numerous kinds are mentioned by Arab zoologists, some of them bearing specific names and some being distinguished by their colour (black, blue, red, tawny [*aṣfar*]). Another distinction is made according to the supposed origin of the different varieties: Some are said to be produced by spontaneous generation, in putrescent substances or in the body of certain animals (lion, dog, camel, horse, cattle, etc.), to

which they adhere exclusively; others are born by sexual procreation. The flies that molest man are produced in dung. Certain places are pointed out as man.
particularly infested with flies, such as the town of Wāsiṭ. In some region flies are said to be eaten by man

The fly lives no longer than forty days (based on a *ḥadīth*). It belongs to the 'sunny' animals, appearing in summer and vanishing in winter. It is killed by intense heat or cold. It is active during day time and rests at night. It likes sweet and loathes certain substances, as oil, camphor and arsenic. It hunts bugs (*baḳḳ*) and gnats (*baʿūḍ*) and is eaten itself by bats, spiders, reptiles and other animals. If it were not for the flies' hunting bugs, it would be intolerable for man to live in houses. The tips of the fly's feet are rough so that it may not slip on smooth surfaces. The sources mention several devices for keeping flies away from human habitations.

In various ways flies were used for medicinal and cosmetic purposes: rubbed over the sting of a hornet they relieve the pain; burnt and mixed with antimony they increase the beauty of the eyes of women, etc. Their significance when seen in dreams was treated in pertinent writings.

A work entitled *Kitāb al-dhubāb* (probably a lexicographical treatise) is attributed by Ḥādjdjī Khalīfa (ed. Flügel, v, 85, no. 10120) to Abū ʿAbd Allāh Muḥammad b. Ziyād al-Aʿrābī, who, but for the year of his death, 333 A.H. as given by Ḥ.Kh., could be identical with the well known philologist Ibn al-Aʿrābī (Brockelmann, S I, 179).

Bibliography: ʿAbd al-Ghanī al-Nābulusī, *Taʿṭīr al-Anām*, Cairo 1354, i, 229; Damīrī, s.v. (transl. Jayakar, i, 816 ff.); Dāwūd al-Anṭākī, *Tadhkira*, Cairo 1324, i, 148; Djāḥiẓ, *Ḥayawān*², index; Euting, *Tagebuch*, i, index s.v. *Fliegen*; Ibn al-Bayṭār, *Djāmiʿ*, Būlāḳ 1291, ii, 123; Ibn Ḳutayba, *ʿUyūn al-Akhbār*, Cairo 1925-30, ii, 72, 75, 98, 104 (transl. Kopf, 46, 50, 74, 79); Ibn Sīda, *Mukhaṣṣaṣ*, viii, 182 ff.; Ibshīhī, *Mustaṭraf*, bāb 62, s.v.; Ḳazwīnī (Wüstenfeld), i, 434 f. (transl. Wiedemann, *Beitr. z. Gesch. d. Naturw.*, liii, 257 f.); al-Mustawfī al-Ḳazwīnī (Stephenson), 72 f.; Nuwayrī, *Nihāyat al-arab*, x, 298 ff. (L. Kopf)

DHUBYĀN [see GHAṬAFĀN].

DHUNNŪNIDS [see DHU'L-NŪNIDS].

AL-**DHUNŪB, DAFN**, burial of offences, a nomadic practice which consists of a make-believe burial of the offences or crimes of which an Arab is accused. According to Shihāb al-Dīn al-ʿUmarī (*al-Taʿrīf bi 'l-muṣṭalaḥ al-sharīf*, Cairo 1312, 165 ff.), almost the only source, this curious ceremony was practised as follows. A delegation consisting of men who had the full confidence of the culprit appeared before an assembly of notables belonging to the tribe of the victim, to whom they said: "We wish you to perform the *dafn* for So-and-so, who admits the truth of your accusations". The delegates then enumerated all the offences of their client. The plaintiff agreed, dug a hole in the ground, and said: "I throw into this hole all the offences with which I charge So-and-so, and I bury them as I bury this hole". He then filled in the hole and levelled the ground.

According to the same author, the practice of *dafn* was sometimes also applied to the *amān* [*q.v.*]. However, contrary to the customs of the nomadic Arabs, who recognized only oral confessions, the offences which were forgiven were also recorded in a written document.

This practice, about which we have little information, seems to have been current in the time of al-ʿUmarī. By the present day it would seem to have completely disappeared.

Bibliography: see also Ibn Nāẓir al-Djaysh, *Tathḳīf al-taʿrīf*, ms. Escorial, Arabic mss., no. 550, fol. 97-8; al-Ḳalḳashandī, *Ṣubḥ*, xiii, 352-5; Chelhod, *L'enterrement des délits chez les Arabes*, in *RHR*, April-June 1959, 215-20. (J. Chelhod)

ḌIBĀB [see ʿĀMIR B. ṢAʿṢAʿA].

DĪBĀDJ [see ḲUMĀSH].

AL-**DIBDIBA**, an extensive gravel plain in north-eastern Arabia, bounded roughly on the east by the depression of al-Shaḳḳ (which forms the western boundary of the Saudi Arabia-Kuwait Neutral Zone), on the west by the *wādī* of al-Bāṭin, and on the south by the gravel ridge of al-Warīʿa. The plain extends northward from Saudi Arabia into the Shaikhdom of Kuwait for a distance of about 20 kms. It has an area of c. 30,000 sq. kms. and is remarkable for its firm, almost featureless surface, sprinkled with pebbles of limestone, quartz, and igneous rock carried from central and western Arabia during the Pleistocene by the Wādī al-Ruma al-Bāṭin drainage system. Al-Dibdiba is drained internally, with rain water collecting in shallow, silt-floored basins (*khabārī*; sing., *khabrā'*). It is part of the traditional *dīra* of Muṭayr and is now a favourite winter grazing area of several north-eastern tribes. The plain was once famous for its gazelle hunting. The term *dibdiba* (pl. *dabādib*) is applied by some of the Bedouins to any flat, firm-surfaced area and is related to the classical *dabdaba*, referring to the drumming sound of hooves on hard earth.

Maps: Series by the U. S. Geological Survey and Arabian American Oil Company under joint sponsorship of the Ministry of Finance and National Economy (Kingdom of Saudi Arabia) and the Department of State (U. S. A.). Scale 1:500,000 (geographic); Wādī al-Bāṭin, Map I-203 B (1959); Northern Ṭuwayḳ, Map I-207 B (1957).

(J. Mandaville)

DIʿBIL, poetic nickname of ABŪ ʿALĪ MUḤAMMAD B. ʿALĪ B. RAZĪN AL-KHUZĀʿĪ, ʿAbbāsid poet, born 148/765 and died 246/860. His birthplace is uncertain; the cities of Kūfa and Ḳarḳīsiya are given as his places of birth. According to the accounts in the *Kitāb al-Aghānī*, he spent his youth in Kūfa from which he was forced to flee because of some mischievous activity. Diʿbil's apprenticeship as a poet was under the tutelage of Muslim b. al-Walīd [*q.v.*]. However, he soon made a reputation for himself as is indicated from his relationship with Khalaf al-Aḥmar (d. 180/796) and Marwān b. Abī Ḥafṣa (d. 181/797). The most probable date for Diʿbil's entry into the circle of Hārūn al-Rashīd (d. 193/809) lies between 795-809.

Being pro-Shīʿite and famous for his poem praising ʿAlī al-Riḍā [*q.v.*] he generally attacks the ʿAbbāsid caliphs from Hārūn to al-Mutawakkil (d. 247/861). However, Diʿbil's loyalty appears to be motivated also by monetary considerations so that we find him praising them on occasion. If Diʿbil is famous for his satires—at times of the vilest content—he is also capable of expressing a fine sentiment and an appreciation of nature. The simplicity and directness of his expression share and give additional evidence of this tendency which has become characteristic of the early ʿAbbāsid age.

Ibn Rashīḳ places him in the *Ṭabaḳa* of Abū Nuwās [*q.v.*] and al-Buḥturī rates him above Muslim b. al-Walīd. Diʿbil's rivalry with Abū Tammām [*q.v.*], whom he excluded from his *Kitāb al-shuʿarā'*, is based not only on literary grounds but also on political-religious foundations, since Abū Tammām was lukewarm to the S͟hīʿa and was pro-North-Arab.

Diʿbil's *Book of the Poets,* whose date of final composition is post 231/846, and whose fragments are cited in works from the 9th to the 17th century, is important in Arabic literary history since it forms a link between the *Ṭabaḳāt* of al-Djumaḥī (d. 230/845) and the *Kitāb al-S͟hiʿr* of Ibn Ḳutayba (d. 276/889), Diʿbil's pupil. Moreover, since Diʿbil was chiefly interested in the minor poets of the Islamic period—including those of the category of Hārūn al-Ras͟hīd, ʿAbd Allāh b. al-Zayyāt (d. 233/847), and Aḥmad b. Abī Duʾād (d. 240/854)—his work can be regarded as a defence of the "modern poets" which preceded and anticipated that of the *Kitāb al-S͟hiʿr* by Ibn Ḳutayba.

Bibliography: Brockelmann, I, 78, S I, 121-2; *Fihrist,* 161; *Ag͟hānī,* xviii, 29-60; Ibn Ḳutayba, *al-S͟hiʿr* (De Goeje), 593-541; *Taʾrīk͟h Bag͟hdād,* viii, 382-5, ii, 342; iv, 143; Ibn al-Djarrāḥ, *al-Waraḳa,* Cairo 1373/1953, 17, 123; Ibn al-Muʿtazz, *Ṭabaḳāt al-s͟huʿarāʾ al-muḥdat͟hīn,* ed. A. Eghbal, London 1939 (GMS, NS., xiii), 124-7; Masʿūdī, Murūdj, index; al-Marzubānī, *Muʿdjam,* Cairo 1354/1935, 244; al-Āmidī, *al-Muʾtalif,* Cairo 1354/1935, 168; Ibn Ras͟hīḳ, *al-ʿUmda,* Cairo 1325/1907, i, 64; Ibn Hadjar, *al-Iṣāba,* Cairo 1358/1939, ii, 102; idem, *Lisān al-mīzān,* ii, 430-2. (L. Zolondek)

ḌIDD, ναντίον, "contrary" is one of the four classes of opposites, ἀντικείμενα, *mutaḳābilāt,* as discussed by Aristotle in his Categories x (and also in his Metaphysics v, 10). There are four classes of opposites: 1) relative terms; 2) contraries; 3) privation and possession; 4) affirmation and negation. The fact that there are contraries implies that there must be a substratum in which they inhere, for it is impossible, even for God, to change, *e.g.,* the White into the Black, although a white thing may become black. There are things which have necessarily one of two contraries, *e.g.,* illness and health, for every animal is either sick or healthy (Galen, however, distinguishes three conditions of the body, *corpus salubre, corpus insalubre* and *corpus neuter*) and there are contraries which allow an intermediate term, for not all bodies are necessarily black or white. The question whether there is an intermediate term between virtue and vice was much debated by the Stoics who originally denied this, for whether a man is a hundred stadia from his aim or only one stadium, he is equally not there. In Islam the question whether there is a medium term between faith and unbelief was much discussed and those theologians who asserted that belief is based only on *taṣdīḳ* assent, (for faith as a θεοσεβείας συγκατάθεσις see for example, Clemens Alexandrinus, *Strom,* ii, 2.8) held that faith can be neither increased nor diminished.

Ḍidd is used also as a translation of the Greek prefix ἀντί. So ἀντίδοτον is translated by *ḍidd al-samm* or simply by *al-ḍidd.*

Bibliography: See, *e.g.,* Ibn Rus͟hd, *Talk͟hīṣ Kitāb al-Maʿḳūlāt* (ed. Bouyges), Beirut 1932, 92; Ibn Sīnā, *al-Maʿḳūlāt,* ed. Cairo 1958, 241. See also AḌDĀD. (S. van den Bergh)

DIDJLA, the Arabic name (used always without the article *al-*) of the easterly of the "Two Rivers" of ʿIrāḳ, the Tigris. The name is a modernized and Arabicized form of the Diglat of the Cuneiform, and occurs as Ḥiddeḳel in the Book of Genesis.

The river (Dicle Nehri in modern Turkish) rises in the southern slopes of the main Taurus, south and south-east of Lake Golcük. Its upper course, with its many constituent tributaries, drains a wide area of foothills and plain, which formed the northern half of the ʿAbbāsid province of Djazīra) in which stood the important towns of Āmid (modern Diyarbakır), Mayyāfāriḳīn, and many others. Among the early tributaries the Arab geographers (Ibn Sarābiyūn, Muḳaddasī, Yāḳūt) name the Nahr al-Kilāb (alternatively Nahr al-D͟hiʾb), the Wādī Ṣalb, Wādī Sātīdamā and Wādī al-Sarbaṭ. Identifications of these are not certain with the modern tributaries which are notably (in their Turkish forms) the Zulkarneyn Suyu, the Ambar-Çay, the Pamuk Çayı, the Batman Suyu and the Garzan Suyu. At the point where the river bends from eastward to southward, at the modern Til or Till (medieval Tall Fāfān) the Bohtan Çayı enters from the east, and at least doubles the discharge of the Didjla: this, the Wādī al-Zarm of the Arab geographers, drains the high mountains south of Lake Vān including the areas of Bidlīs (modern Bitlis), and Sīʾird (modern Siirt). Above this junction, 50 miles to the west, lay the important town of Ḥiṣn Kayfā, modern Ḥasankayf.

Between the entry of the Bohtan Çayı and that of the Greater Zāb, Arab geographers mention as tributaries the Nahr Baznā, the Nahr Bāʾynāt͟hā (or Bāsānfā, or Saffān) the Būyār and the Wādī Dūs͟ha. The identification of these with each of the present-day hill streams is uncertain. The K͟hābūr al-Ḥasaniyya (modern K͟hābūr) with its tributary the Iṭayzil Su, forms today the Turkish-ʿIrāḳī boundary. The town of Ḥasaniyya (probably the modern Zak͟ho) contained a famous bridge. No main tributary except the Abu Maryā (modern Wādī al-Murr, joining the Didjla at Eski Mosul, the former Balad), and many small left-bank flood-channels, comes in south of the K͟hānbūr till the Greater Zāb is reached, 30 miles below the great city of Mosul (al-Mawṣil), itself a Sāsānid city which grew to greatness under the Umayyads.

The Greater Zāb (al-Zāb al-Aʿẓam) which rises partly in the Ḥakārī mountains and partly in those which form the Perso-ʿIrāḳī frontier, contribute a highly important volume to the Didjla. The same is true of the Lesser Zāb, which joins the river some 60 miles to the south, having drained a wide sector of the Perso-ʿIrāḳī frontier region. The point of junction of the Greater Zāb was in the middle ages marked by the town of Ḥadīt͟ha, that of the Lesser Zāb by Sinn; neither of these survives. There are no intermediate tributaries, but it is possible that a stream or streams, rising in Djabal Sindjār, may in some periods have found an outlet for their flood water into the Didjla near Ḳalʿa S͟harḳaṭ.

Below the point where the river cuts through Djabal Ḥamrīn (at al-Fatḥa) it appears that, at or above Takrīt, the Wādī T͟hart͟hār (which may in some flood seasons have drawn water from the (western) K͟hābūr drainage-area, which belongs more naturally to the Euphrates) poured its waters into the Tigris passing by al-Ḥaḍr: Yāḳūt speaks even of a formerly navigable Euphrates-Tigris channel in this area. Lands in the Didjla drainage area above Takrīt have at all periods been rain-irrigated, and have therefore risked drought but not floods; skin-bucket water-lift devices (the modern *karad*) assured crops along the river-banks. The great mediaeval (and in part much more ancient) canal-system of ʿIrāḳ began below Takrīt. The Nahr al-Isḥāḳī, doubtless a partially-controlled spring-flood channel, took off from the right bank and after the expenditure of its waters in irrigation poured the remainder into the river below Sāmarrā. South of the latter the Dudjayl took off also from the right bank, and (it is said) was sometimes augmented from the tails of Euphrates canals; it returned to the river at varying points south of ʿUkbarā. The course of the main river between a point south of Sāmarrā and one not far north of Baghdād (that is, for some 70 miles) lay in ʿAbbāsid times some five to twelve miles west of its modern channel, with the towns of Ḳādisiyya, al-ʿAlth, ʿUkbarā and Rashīdiyya on its banks. Many flood-season irrigation canals led off from this stretch of the river which later, when partially or wholly abandoned (perhaps by the 7th/13th century), was known as the Shuṭayṭ or Little River.

On the left bank the great Ḳāṭūl-Tāmarrā-Nahrawān waterway, probably initiated in Sāsānid times and improved under the early ʿAbbāsids, took off from the main river near Dūr (15 miles above Sāmarrā), and ran, at a maximum distance of 30 miles from it and nearly parallel, to re-join the Didjla near (modern) Kūt al-Amāra (medieval Mādharāyā) having received into its left bank, and somehow disposed of, the very important waters of the ʿUẓaym and the Diyālā which—especially the latter—are today major tributaries of the Didjla. (See NAHRAWĀN and DIYĀLĀ). Important canals taking off from the right bank of the Nahrawān system included the Khāliṣ (which still exists under that name, but with different alignment) and the Bīn; the waters of these made possible a closely-cultivated area north of Baghdād, and in part supplied the city itself.

Bringing Euphrates water, thanks to its proximity in this area (minimum, 20 miles) and to the slight eastward dip of central ʿIrāḳ, a number of large canals took off from that river and poured the unutilized portion of their waters into the Didjla at various points between Baghdād city and Mādharāyā. These were the Nahr al-ʿĪsā (approximately but not identically the modern Ṣaḳlāwiyya), the Ṣarṣār and the Malik (corresponding to the modern Abū Ghurayb and Raḍwāniyya), the Kūthā and the Nīl, the last of which took off just above Ḥilla (and the ruins of Babylon) and joined the Didjla not far above (modern) Kūt. Alike on these canals, on the main river channel, and on the parallel Nahrawān system, a relatively dense population lived in mediaeval times, cultivating by flow-water and lift.

Mādharāyā marked the spot from which, downstream, the greatest difference between the mediaeval and modern courses of the river was manifest. In ʿAbbāsid times the present course, by way of modern ʿAlī al-Gharbī, Ḳalʿa Ṣāliḥ and ʿAmāra was unimportant or (unless in high flood) non-existent; the main river ran down or near the channel of the (present) river Ḥayy or Gharrāf, past the great mediaeval but now vanished city of Wāsiṭ, and the sites of the modern towns of Ḥayy, Ḳalʿa Sikr, and Shaṭra. The change to the modern course of the Didjla (which had also probably prevailed in pre-Islamic antiquity), permitting to the Gharrāf a far smaller but considerable discharge, took place gradually from late ʿAbbāsid times onwards and was (on the evidence of European travellers) nearly complete by the 10th/16th century. Under the ʿAbbāsids the Didjla, like the Euphrates, poured its waters, except in so far as used for irrigation higher up, into the swamps (al-Baṭāʾiḥ) about 60 miles below Wāsiṭ, a vast area of water which, corresponding to but much larger than the Ḥammār Lake of today, took the full flood-discharge of both the great ʿIrāḳī rivers, and was in its turn drained into the Persian Gulf by the single water-way called in the Middle Ages Didjla al-ʿAwraʾ (one-eyed Didjla), and in modern times the Shaṭṭ al-ʿArab. Ḳurna stood on the Shaṭṭ al-ʿAwraʾ a little below its point of emergence from al-Baṭāʾiḥ, and below it villages and towns were continuous. Dry land, created by the deposited silt of the Two Rivers and of the Kārūn, had in early ʿAbbāsid times pushed out as far as (modern) Ābādān, and later ruined this seaport by advancing further. Many irrigation canals (including those serving Baṣra, the Maʿḳil and Ubulla canals) took off from the Didjla al-ʿAwraʾ in the area today covered by extensive date gardens and numerous villages. Seagoing ships of the Caliphs could ascend the Didjla through the swamp to well above Wāsiṭ.

Although, as mentioned above, the Didjla has changed its course in more than one area since the Middle Ages, and although an idea of the canal system derived from it can be gained from the contemporary geographers and from remaining traces, it is evident that this system was under constant modification between the 2nd/8th and the 7th/13th centuries, until it was substantially destroyed by the Mongols in the middle of the latter. The alignment and degree of water control, and the discharge of the canals, varied from century to century; most were seasonal flood-channels without head-works, and the solution if any found for disposal of the devastating annual floods does not satisfactorily appear. Nevertheless, irrigation from the Didjla—and rain cultivation in the north—undoubtedly supported a population perhaps three times more numerous than that of today, in a host of cities and villages now forgotten. During the centuries following the ruin caused by Hūlāgū (656/1258) conditions fell to a low point of disorganization, misery and stagnation, during which the régime of the river deterioriated and all control was lost. No serious study of its problems was made thereafter until the 14th/20th century.

The efforts of the modern ʿIrāḳ Governments have been concentrated on such irrigation works as will stabilize the course of the river, prevent the extremely serious annual flooding of the country side—and almost of Baghdād itself—and regulate and conserve the water for summer irrigation upon which, in central and southern ʿIrāḳ, all cultivation other than precarious spring crops must depend. Many control works have been built, notably in 1357/1938 the Kūt Barrage which regulates the supply into the Ḥayy (Gharrāf) river; many more, and major flood-disposal arrangements—for instance, on the Greater Zāb, and by utilizing the Wādī Tharthār—are in hand or planned. But the immense difference between the high water and the low water discharge of the river, varying between some 6000 to 300 cubic metres a second at Baghdād, due to seasonal melting of snow in the north and to winter and spring rains, and the inadequacy of the river bed to take the flood water, combine to render the Didjla peculiarly difficult to control or utilize. The important extension of irrigation by mechanical pump from the Didjla has been a striking feature of the period since 1346/1927.

The river contains large quantities of indifferent or low-quality fish.

In modern as in ancient and mediaeval times, all the traditional types of river-craft—skin-borne rafts floating downstream from Mosul or the Zābs, bitumen-covered coracles, sailing-craft and paddled skiffs of every size have been and are in use. They have been supplemented regularly between Baṣra and Baghdād (and rarely and precariously between Baghdād and Mosul) by river steamers since 1256/1840, and by motor-launches and tugs. In addition to public passenger and goods services, the work of river-steamship fleets has made an important contribution in both World Wars; the navigational difficulties are, nevertheless, formidable. The railway, of which a first German-made section (Baghdād-Sāmarrā) was opened in 1332/1914, now runs from Baghdād to Mosul along the right bank of the river, and north of Mosul branching westward joins the Turkish system. Main roads, successors to immemorial tracks, follow the course of the river in many areas. The river passes through the administrative provinces, in Turkey, of Diyārbakır, Siirt and Mardin, and in ʿIrāḳ those of Mosul, Irbīl, Baghdād, Kūt al-Amāra, ʿAmāra and Baṣra.

Bibliography: Iṣṭakhrī, i, 72-7, 90; Ibn Ḥawḳal, 138, 162; Muḳaddasī, 20, 124, 136, 144; Ibn Khurradādhbih, 174; *BGA* = vii, 94-6; Masʿudī, *al-Tanbīh*, 52 ff.; Ibn Sarābiyūn, in *JRAS* 1895, 1-76, 255-315; Masʿūdī, *Murūdj*, i, 223-30; Yāḳūt, ii, 551 ff., and *passim*; Abu 'l-Fidāʾ, *Taḳwīm*, 53-5; Dimashḳī (ed. Mehren), 95-8; Ḳazwīnī (ed. Wüstenfeld), i, 178.

Le Strange; M. Streck, *Die alte Landschaft Babylonien*, Leyden 1901; E. Herzfeld, *Memnon*, i, 89-143 and 217-38; W. Willcocks, *The irrigation of Mesopotamia*, Cairo 1905; A. Sousa and J. D. Atkinson, *ʿIraq irrigation handbook*, Baghdād 1944/6; M. Ionides, *The régime of the rivers Euphrates and Tigris*, London 1937; S. H. Longrigg, *ʿIraq 1900 to 1950*, London 1953.

(R. Hartmann-[S. H. Longrigg])

DIDO, a people comprising five small Ibero-Caucasian Muslim nationalities, whose total number reaches, according to a 1955 estimate, some 18,000. Ethnically close to the Andi [*q.v.*] and the Avar [*q.v.*], they inhabit the most elevated and inaccessible regions of Central Dāghistān, near to the Georgian frontier.

It is necessary to distinguish:

1. The Dido proper (Tsez Tsunta), numbering about 7,200, distributed in 36 *awl*s along the upper reaches of the Ori-Tskalis.

2. The Bežeta (Kapuči, Kapčui, Beshite, Khwanal), the most developed of the Dido peoples (2,500 in the 1926 census, 2,580 in 1933), who inhabit the three *awl*s of Bežeta, Khodjar-Khota, and Tladal, in the district of Tlarata.

3. Khwarshi (Kwan), 1561 in 1920, 1614 in 1933, living in five *awl*s on the upper reaches of the Ori-Tskalis shortly before it flows into the Koysu of Andi.

4. The Khunzal (Gunzal, Nakhad, Enzeli, Enseba, Gunzeb), 799 in 1920, 616 in 1933, in the four *awl*s of Tlarata district on the upper reaches of the Avar Koysu.

5. The Ginukh, numbering a few hundreds.

The Dido peoples were converted to Islam by the Avars, and like them are Sunnīs of the Shāfiʿī rite. Each Dido race has its own language, not committed to writing, belonging to the Avar-Ando-Dido group of the Dāghistān branch of the Ibero-Caucasian languages, but the Dido are in general bilingual, and Avar serves as their cultural language.

The geographical position of the Dido peoples has protected them from external influences, and because of this they have retained patriarchal customs and Muslim traditions more than have the Andi. The Avar influence is less noticeable among them, except for the Bežeta, than among the Andi; and their integration within the Avar nation is less advanced. Russian linguistic influence is barely noticeable.

The economy of the Dido remains traditional; they subsist by fodder-production (maize, potatoes), by sheep-raising over changing pasture-lands, and by terraced horticulture. They are well-known for their craftsmanship: goldsmiths' work among the Dido and the Bežeta, and leatherwork among the Khunzal.

Bibliography: A. Bennigsen and H. Carrère d'Encausse, *Une République soviétique musulmane*, in *REI*, 1956; A. A. Bokarev, *Kratkie Svedeniya o yazïkak Dagestana*, Makhač-Ḳalʿa 1949; A. Dirr, *Materialï dlya izučeniya yazïkov i narečiy ando-didoyskoy gruppï*, in *Sbornik materialov dlya opisaniya mestnostey i plemen Kavkaza*, xl, Tiflis 1909; I. V. Megelidze, *Zvukovoy sostav tseskogo (didoyskogo) yazïka*, in *Yazïk i mïshlenie*, vi, vii, Moscow 1926. See also Bibliography of DĀGHISTĀN, AVAR, ANDI.

(Ch. Quelquejay)

DIENNÉ, a town in the Sudan Republic, 360 km. SW of Timbuctoo and 200 km. ENE of Segou. Geographical position: lat. 13° 55′ N.—long. 4° 33′ W. (Gr.). Altitude: 278 m.

The etymology of this name (often wrongly spelt Djenné) is unknown but the most likely is Dianna = the little Dia (Dia is an ancient Sudanese town, 70 km. to the NW.). Dienné was mentioned for the first time in 1447 by the Genoese Malfante, under the name Geni.

The town is situated in the flood-area of the Niger and the Bani, 5 km. from the left bank of the latter river, to which it is connected by a navigable channel. It is built on a hill of sandy clay not subject to flooding, though surrounded by water particularly during the flood season, which normally lasts from August to February; and it is then that movement in the district is easiest, owing to the network of navigable channels between the Bani and the Niger, the most important and most freely used being the Kouakourou channel. In the dry season the town is linked up with surrounding districts by tracks which can be used by motor vehicles.

In area, Dienné extends for 900 m. from east to west, and 600 m. from north to south. Until the end of the 19th century it was surrounded by a brick wall; this was destroyed by the French who also cleared and laid out a large square in the town.

The population which has remained the same since 1900 is about 6,300; of these, 3,000 are Diennenké, 1,600 Fulani and 1,600 Bozo. Several languages are spoken, Songhai, Bozo and Fula among others.

The date on which the town was founded is not known. The *Taʾrīkh al-Sūdān*, trans. Houdas, 23, mentions a first settlement at Zoboro, the foundation of the town in about 150/767 and the conversion to Islam in about 500/1106. It seems more likely that the actual date of founding was later: M. Delafosse puts it at about 648/1250 and attributes it to Soninke merchants, the Nono; according to him, the inhabitants' conversion to Islam followed in about 700/1300. Legend has it that a Bozo virgin, Tapama, was immured alive in the walls at the instigation of magicians, in order to ensure the future prosperity of the town.

When chief Konboro was converted he pulled down his palace and, on the foundations, built the great mosque which remained standing until about 1830 when it was destroyed by Shaykhu Aḥmadu.

Konboro's descendants remained in power until the Songhai conquest.

In spite of the well-known passage in *Taʾrīkh al-Sūdān* (26) stating that from the time the town was founded the inhabitants of Dienné were never conquered by any king until the day when Sonni Ali imposed his authority over them, there is a strong possibility that, after 735/1335, the city belonged to Mali. It must have regained its liberty fairly soon, before being captured by Sonni Ali (872/1467).

The Songhai domination was very favourable to Dienné and it seems that it was from this time onwards in particular that it became a commercial centre of the highest importance in the Sudan. In direct communication with Timbuctoo by river, it was also situated at the head of the overland routes leading to the gold mines of Bitou (Bonduku region, Ivory Coast), Lobi and Bouré. It was the great entrepot for salt from Teghaza on its way via Timbuctoo to the countries in the south.

The first account to speak of the town is the *Descripçam* ..... by Valentim Fernandes (1506): "Gyni is a large town built of rock and limestone, surrounded by a wall. To it come the merchants visiting the gold mines. These dealers belong to one particular race, the *Ungaros* (*Wangara*), who are red or brownish ..... When these Ungaros come to Gyni, each merchant brings with him 100 or 200 or more negro slaves to carry salt on their heads from Gyni to the gold mines, and to bring back gold. Merchants who trade with the gold mines deal in considerable sums. Some of them undertake a deal which may amount to 60,000 *mithḳāl*; even those who are content merely to take salt to Gyni make 10,000 *mithḳāl* ..... The Ungaros only come to Gyni once a year".

Leo Africanus (1525) repeats the theme of the town's prosperity, describing it under the name Ghinea (ii, 465-485).

This prosperity was maintained throughout the 16th century, and even to the beginning of the Moroccan domination. In fact Dienné followed the fate of her sister town, Timbuctoo, which from 1000/1591 was occupied by the Moroccans of Djūdhar. The *ḳāʾid*s of Timbuctoo had no difficulty in compelling Dienné to recognize their overlordship. In Dienné the Moroccan authority was represented by a pasha, a *ḥākim* assisted by an *amīn* or treasurer and a *ḳāʾid* in command of the troops.

In the middle of the 17th century the *Taʾrīkh al-Sūdān* once again described (22 ff.) a town at the height of prosperity: "This town is large, flourishing and prosperous; it is rich, and enjoys Heaven's blessing and favour .... Dienné is one of the great markets of the Muslim world. It is the meeting-place for merchants with salt from the mines of Teghaza and others bringing gold from the Bitu mines. Almighty God has drawn to this blessed town a certain number of scholars and men of piety, strangers in this country who have come here to live".

The town's two-fold reputation for commerce and religion continued even after the decline of Timbuctoo in the 17th and 18th centuries; protected by its marshes, Dienné was able to hold its own in spite of the attacks of the Bambara [*q.v.*] who for a time even succeeded in making themselves masters of the Dienneri but were unable to take the capital.

After 1818, Shaykhu Aḥmadu founded the Fulani empire of Massina and took Dienné after a well-conducted siege. He drove out part of the population and built a new mosque (on the site now occupied by the school) in place of the old one which he allowed to fall into ruin. He left the administration of the city to the people of Dienné, but he was represented by an *Amīru mangal*, military commander. It was at this time (1828) that René Caillié visited the town. The Fulani rule lasted until 1861-1862 when al-Ḥādjdj ʿUmar conquered Dienné. In 1893, Colonel Archinard took possession in the name of France. By bringing peace to the Sudan, French rule paradoxically enough led to the decline of Dienné, for what had previously been the source of its strength, its isolated position surrounded by flood-waters, in the 20th century became a source of weakness. The town's commercial functions were taken over by Mopti which is situated at the confluence of the Bani and the Niger, and is connected by a dyke with dry land. Dienné is no more than a second-rate local market and centre of the administrative sub-division.

The town has kept its beautiful old houses, built in the style which was peculiar to itself, now widespread and known as the "Sudanese style"; the old mosque, built before the 19th century, has been rebuilt in the old style on the same foundations.

Bibliography: P. de Cenival and Th. Monod: *Description de la Côte d'Afrique de Ceuta au Sénégal par Valentim Fernandes (1506-1507)*, Paris 1938; *Taʾrīkh al-Fattāsh*, trans. O. Houdas and M. Delafosse, Paris 1913; *Taʾrīkh al-Sūdān*, trans. O. Houdas, Paris 1900; Leo Africanus, *Description de l'Afrique*, trans. Épaulard, Paris 1956, ii, 464-5; R. Caillié, *Journal d'un voyage à Tombouctou et à Dienné dans l'Afrique Centrale*, Paris 1830, ii, ch. 18; *Reisen und Entdeckungen in Nord und Zentral Afrika in 1849-1855*, Gotha 1857-8, iv; F. Dubois, *Tombouctou la mystérieuse*, Paris 1896, ch. v-vi; Ch. Monteil, *Monographie de Djénné*, Tulle 1903; A. H. Ba and J. Daget: *L'Empire du Macina*, i (1818-1853), IFAN, Bamako 1955. (R. Mauny)

DIFRĪGĪ [see diwrīgī].

DIGLAL, the title of the hereditary ruler of the Banī ʿĀmir tribal group in the Agordat district of western Eritrea and in the eastern Sudan; he is also senior member of the aristocratic Nabtab class or caste, who, for historical reasons no longer possible to elucidate, form the superior stratum in every Banī ʿĀmir section. The title is believed of Fundj origin, and may recall days when the tribe was, in the 10th/16th and 11th/17th centuries, intermittently tribute-paying to the Nilotic but Muslim Fundj dynasty of Sennar. The insignia of the Diglal's position include notably a red velvet three-cornered hat of unique design.

The Diglal, whose relations with Ethiopian, Italian and British rulers of Eritrea have varied in the manner usual with feudal or tribal potentates, has at his best exercised good control over the lawless, scattered and wholly nomadic Banī ʿĀmir, themselves numerous (some 60,000 in Eritrea in 1936-44, and 30,000 in the Sudan), varied in origin (containing an original Hamitic base with large admixtures of Sudani, Ethiopian and Nilotic stocks), and speaking the Beja or Tigré languages according to subtribe or section. Indeed, the Diglal's traditional position, unchallenged for four centuries, has been a main unifying force in a group otherwise highly heterogeneous.

He lives normally in a main settlement of the Dagga (Dega, Dāga), a term which, by origin the "camp" of himself and his immediate circle, now signifies that section of the Banī ʿĀmir (numerically the largest) which contains the Diglal's family, retainers and slaves, and the descendents and numerous accretions of these.

Bibliography: A. Pollera, *Le Popolozioni indigene dell' Eritrea*, Bologna 1935; British Military Administration of Eritrea (per S. F. Nadel), *Races and tribes of Eritrea*, Asmara 1943; S. H. Longrigg, *Short history of Eritrea*, Oxford 1945. (S. H. LONGRIGG)

DIGURATA [see OSSETES].

DIHISTĀN, name of two towns, and their respective districts in north-eastern Īrān:

1) A town north-east of Harāt, the capital of the southern part of the Bādghīs [*q.v.*] region, and the second largest town in that region ("half the size of Būshandj"), and according to Yāḳūt (i, 461), the capital of the whole of Bādghīs around the year 596/1200. The town was situated upon a hill in a fertile area, and near a silver mine; it was built of brick. In 98/716-7, Dihistān is mentioned as the seat of a Persian *dihḳān* (Ṭabarī, ii, 1320); ca. 426/1035, it came into the possession of a Turkish *dihḳān* (these titles persisted amongst the Turks) by the agency of the Saldjūḳs (to whom the Ghaznawids had left it). In 552/1158, it was the residence of the Oghuz prince Ikhtiyār al-Dīn Aytaḳ, who, as the only ruler of this district, became subject to Khwārizmshāh Il Arslan (Bayhaḳī, *Ta'rīkh-i Bayhaḳ*). The Khwārizmshāh Sulṭān Shāh was robbed of his succession by his brother Tekesh, and fled with his mother Terken (Islamicized: Turkān) to Dihistān in 569/1174. Following this, Tekesh occupied the town of Dihistān, and had Terken executed; Sulṭān Shāh succeeded in escaping further to the Ghūrids (Ibn al-Athīr, xi, 247/53). The town does not appear to have played an important part later on. It is probably to be equated with the modern shrine Khwādja Dihistān.

Bibliography: Iṣṭakhrī, 268 f.; Ibn Ḥawḳal 319 f.; Muḳaddasī, 50, 298, 308; Ḥamd Allāh Mustawfī, *Nuzha*, 153, trans. (1919), 151; Le Strange, 414 f.; J. Marquart, *Ērānšahr* ..... (1901), 150; J. Markwart (= idem), *Wehrot und Arang* (1938), 40; W. Barthold, *Turkestan*, 308, 335, 338; Spuler, *Iran*, 311.

2) A region rich in agriculture, to the north of the lower Atrek [*q.v.*], which waters its southern section. Its capital is Akhur (4 days' journey to the north of Djurdjān), which, according to Muḳaddasī (358 f.), also bore the name of Dihistān, and was on the route from Djurdjān to Khwārizm. There was also a frontier fortification (Ribāṭ) by the name of Dihistān, with beautiful mosques and an active market (Muḳaddasī, 358, compare also *ibid.*, 312, 367, 372; and see below). W. Barthold regards this fortress as the capital of the whole region in the 12th century, and bases this view on Yāḳūt (i, 39). Islamic data concerning the area are not consistent and lack clarity: according to Ibn Ḥawḳal (i, 277, 286; ii, 388, 398), the region was sparsely populated, and only by fishermen from the Caspian Sea. Muḳaddasī, on the other hand, reckons the 24 villages of this area amongst the most densely populated of the region of Djurdjān.

According to the Middle Persian list of towns, Dihistān was founded by the Arsacid Narsahē (J. Marquart, *Ērānšahr* [1901], 54, 73, 310); in Islamic times, the Sāsānid Ḳubādh b. Fīrūz (Pērōz) is mentioned (Ḥamd Allāh Mustawfī, *Nuzha*, [1915], 160; trans. [1919], 157; comp. also index). In the 4th/10th century, the area was a border region [against the 'heathen' Turks], and even Ḥamd Allāh, 212 (trans. 205) mentions it as such in the 14th century. At this time it can only have referred to a few nomad tribes between Khwārizm and the Üst Yurt, as by then, Islamization—even of the Mongols of Transoxania—was complete.

The *Ḥudūd al-ʿālam*, ed. V. Minorsky (1937), 60, mentions the peninsula *Dihistānān Sūr* (?), inhabited by fishermen and birdhunters, which W. Barthold takes to be the modern Cape Ḥasan Ḳulī (to the north of the mouth of the Atrek). This is hardly possible, if Iṣṭakhrī's data (219) are correct: he states that there are 50 parasangs between the mouth of the river Djurdjān and this peninsula, and this would get on to the region of the Bay of Ḳzîl Suw (Russian: Krasnovodsk).

V. Minorsky, *Ḥudūd*, 386, connects the name of Dihistān with the name of the ancient *Daher* (Δάαι) (concerning these, compare W. Tomaschek in Pauly-Wissowa, *Realencyklopädie*, iv, 12 [1901], col. 1945/6). Today, the ruins of Ribāṭ Dihistān (as can be gathered from an inscription in a mosque of the beginning of the 13th century) are known as Mashhad-i Miṣriyyān [*q.v.*].

Bibliography: In addition to references in the text: *Ta'rīkh-i Bayhaḳī*, Tehran 1946, index [but note that the vocalization Dahistān demanded on 135[5]—in view of the derivation from Δάαι—contradicts Yāḳūt and the other Islamic sources]; Samʿānī, *K. al-ansāb*, 1922 (GMS xx), fol. 234 v (gives the correct vocalization); Nikbī (in Narshakhī, ed. Ch. Schefer), 144; Gg. Hoffmann, *Syr. Akten pers. Märtyrer* (1880), 277-81; W. Barthold, *K istorii orosheniya Turkestana* (History of irrigation in Turkestan) (1914), 31-7; Le Strange, 337-82; Spuler, *Iran*, 430, 455, 464[4]; *Ḥudūd al-ʿĀlam*, index. (B. SPULER)

DIHḲAN, arabicized form of *dehkān*, the head of a village and a member of the lesser feudal nobility of Sāsānian Persia. The power of the *dihḳāns* derived from their hereditary title to the local administration. They were an immensely important class, although the actual area of land they cultivated as the hereditary possession of their family was often small. They were the representatives of the government vis-à-vis the peasants and their principal function was to collect taxes; and, in the opinion of Christensen, it was due to their knowledge of the country and people that sufficient revenue was provided for the upkeep of a luxurious court and the cost of expensive wars (*L'Iran sous les Sasanides*[2], Copenhagen 1944, 112-3). Masʿūdī divides the *dihḳāns* into five classes, distinguished from one another by their dress (*Murūdj*, ii, 241). Persian legend imputes their origin to Vēghard, brother of the legendary king Hūshang (Christensen, *Le premier homme et le premier roi dans l'histoire légendaire des iraniens*, i, 144, 150, 151, 153, 155, 159). After the Arab conquest the *dihḳāns* continued to be responsible for local administration and the collection of tribute from the protected communities; many of them were converted to Islam and largely retained their lands (von Kremer, *Culturgeschichte*, ii, 160). In Transoxania, where immediately before the Arab invasion the *dihḳāns* had enjoyed perhaps greater influence than in Persia in that their power was not limited by that of the monarchy and the Zoroastrian clergy, the local rulers as well as the landowners were designated by the term *dihḳān* (Barthold, *Turkestan*, 180-1; and see Narshakhī, *Ta'rīkh-i Bukhārā*, ed. Mudarris Riḍavī, 7, 72). The power of the Ṭāhirids and Sāmānids was largely founded on their community of interest with the *dihḳāns*; but by the end of the Sāmānid period the *dihḳāns* had become discontented and were in part responsible for the eventual overthrow of the Sāmānid dynasty by Bughrā Khān Hārūn b. Mūsā, the Ilak Khān (Barthold, 257, 307). With the spread of the *iḳṭāʿ* system in the 5th/11th century and the depression of the landowning classes the position and influence of the *dihḳāns* diminished. With this the term *dihḳān* became debased and by the 5th/11th century it was also used to denote a peasant, in which sense it is used by Nāṣir-i Khusraw (*Dīwān*, Tehrān 1304-7 A.H. solar, 557) and Kāʾūs b. Iskandar (*Ḳābūs nāma*, G.M.S., 138). On the other hand under the Saldjūḳs the *dihḳāns* appear to have continued to exist in the eastern part of the empire as village heads or landowners. The term would appear to have this sense in a document issued by the *dīwān* of Sandjar (*ʿAtabat al-kataba*, ed. ʿAbbās Iḳbāl, Tehrān 1950, 53, 55) and in a diploma for the *miʿmār* of Khʷārazm belonging to the latter half of the 6th century A.H. (Bahāʾ al-Dīn Muḥammad Muʿayyad Baghdādī, *al-Tarassul ilā 'l-tarassul*, ed. Bahmanyār, Tehrān 1315 A.H. solar, 113, 114). Similarly Nadjm al-Dīn Rāzī uses the term *dihḳān* to mean landowner (*Mirṣād al-ʿibād*, Tehrān 1312 A.H. solar, 294 ff.). Naṣīr al-Dīn Ṭūsī (*Akhlāḳ-i Nāṣirī*, Lahore, lith., 180-1) and Djalāl al-Dīn Dawānī (*Akhlāḳ-i Djalālī*, lith., 278), however, seem to use *dihḳān* simply in the sense of peasant, which is its meaning in modern Persia also. In Turkistan farmers are called *dihḳān* (*RMM*, xiii, 1911, 568).

Bibliography: Firdawsī, *Shāhnāma* (ed. Mohl, viii, ff.); M. C. Inostrančev, *Sasanidskie Etiudi*; Quatremère, *JA*, 2 ser., xvi, 532; P. Horn, *Gr.I.Ph.*, i, 2, 178; Nöldeke, *Gesch. der Perser*, 440; Max Van Berchem, *Propriété territoriale*, 25; A. V. Kremer, *Culturgeschichtl. Streifzüge*, 14; Wellhausen, *Das arabische Reich und sein Sturz*, Berlin 1902; Bartold, *Die Rolle der Gebiete des kaspischen Meeres in der Geschichte des muslimanischen Welt*, Baku 1924, 21; K. H. Menges, *Drei Ozbekische Texte*, in *Isl.*, xxi, 179; F. Løkkegaard, *Islamic taxation in the classic period*, Copenhagen 1950; D. C. Dennett, *Conversion and the poll tax in early Islam*, Harvard 1950, 22-3, 29-30, 32-3; F. W. Cleaves, *Daruγa and Gerege* in *Harvard Journal of Asiatic Studies*, 1953, 237; A. K. S. Lambton, *Landlord and Peasant in Persia*, Oxford 1953.

(ANN K. S. LAMBTON)

AL-DIHLAWĪ, NŪR AL-ḤAḲḲ [see NŪR AL-ḤAḲḲ AL-DIHLAWĪ].

AL-DIHLAWĪ, SHĀH WALĪ ALLĀH, the popular name of ḲUṬB AL-DĪN AḤMAD ABU'L-FAYYĀḌ, a revolutionary Indian thinker, theologian, pioneer Persian translator of the Ḳurʾān, and traditionist, the first child of the 60-year-old Shāh ʿAbd al-Raḥīm al-ʿUmarī of Dihlī, by his second wife, was born in 1114/1703 at Dihlī, four years before the death of Awrangzīb. A precocious child, he memorized the Ḳurʾān at the early age of seven and completed his studies with his father, both in the traditional and rational sciences, at the age of fifteen. On the death of his father in 1131/1719 he succeeded him as the principal of the religious college, *Madrasa Raḥīmiyya*, which Shāh ʿAbd al-Raḥīm had founded, at Dihlī. This institution, in later years, produced a galaxy of brilliant scholars and was the fore-runner of the famous *Dār al-ʿUlūm* at Deōband [*q.v.*]. In 1143/1730 Walī Allāh went on a pilgrimage to Mecca and Medina and stayed in al-Ḥidjāz for 14 months before returning to India in 1145/1732. He took advantage of his stay in Medina to learn *ḥadīth* from eminent scholars like Abū Ṭāhir al-Madanī, ʿAbd Allāh b. Sālim al-Baṣarī, and Tādj al-Dīn al-Ḳalʿī, all of whom he held in high esteem (*Anfās al-ʿārifīn*, 191-3, 197-200). After his return from al-Ḥidjāz he devoted himself to writing along with his old profession of teaching. He died in 1176/1762, the author of more than forty works (*Nuzhat al-khawāṭir*, vi, 407 f.). He lies buried in the family graveyard beside his father and his equally illustrious son, Shāh ʿAbd al-ʿAzīz al-Dihlawī, in the Mēnhdīyān cemetery of Old Dihlī, behind the modern Central Jail.

Basically an altruist, Shāh Walī Allāh may be called the founder of Islamic modernism. He was much ahead of his times, a revolutionary thinker who attempted, although with little success, the reintegration of the socio-economic and the religio-ethical structure of Islam. His chief merit, however, lies in the propagation of the doctrine of *taṭbīḳ* (conciliation) which he skilfully applied even to such controversial problems as the *khilāfa* and the conflict between dogmatic theology and mysticism.

The reform movement outlined by Shāh Walī Allāh, which found full expression in the religio-military campaigns of Sayyid Aḥmad Barēlawī [*q.v.*] and Shāh Ismāʿīl, the grandson of Walī Allāh, revolved round his concept of *maṣlaḥa*, *i.e.*, the establishment of a kind of welfare state based on the "relationship of man's development with the creative forces of the Universe". The time and the environment were both unsuited for the success of such a revolutionary movement. The inevitable result was that the movement, although launched with a great deal of fervour, soon lost impetus when faced with realities. On the other hand, the Wahhābī movement launched by his contemporary, Muḥammad b. ʿAbd al-Wahhāb, [*q.v.*] succeeded, as it sternly refused to accept the idea of compromise, which constitutes the kernel of Shāh Walī Allāh's thought; he even attempted to reconcile such antithetic theories as the *waḥdat al wudjūd* [see IBN AL-ʿARABĪ] and *waḥdat al-shuhūd* [see AḤMAD SIRHINDĪ].

His mission failed because both he and his successors failed correctly to assess the impact of contemporary forces and the increasing conflict of the East and West consequent on the growth of European influence in India, especially those parts of the country where Muslims dominated.

His chief works are: (a) Arabic, (i) *Ḥudjdjat Allāh al-bāligha*, his *magnum opus*, a unique work on the secrets of religion (*asrār al-dīn*), also dealing with various other subjects such as metaphysics, politics, finance and political economy. It was in this book (ed. Bareilly 1285/1868; Cairo 1322-3/1904-5), now prescribed as a course of study at al-Azhar and in the Sudan, that he propounded his revolutionary theory of "*fakk kull niẓām*" (down with all systems!). The book has also been translated into Urdū (Lahore 1953, Karachi n.d.); (ii) *al-Musawwā*, a commentary on the *Muwaṭṭaʾ* of Mālik b. Anas; (iii) *al-Fatḥ al-khabīr* ...... the fifth and the last chapter of his Persian work *al-Fawz al-kabīr fī uṣūl al-tafsīr*, but with the above independent title (Lucknow 1289/1872); it is a pithy but highly useful dissertation on the principles of the science of Ḳurʾānic exegesis; (iv) and (v) *al-Budūr al-bāzigha* and *al-Khayr al-kathīr*, both on the *ʿilm al-asrār*, a branch of *taṣawwuf* dealing with its truths and realities (Dābhēl n.d.); (vi) *al-Inṣāf fī bayān sabab al-ikhtilāf*, a masterly survey of the causes of the juristic differences between the various sects of Islam and the evolution of Islamic jurisprudence; (b) Persian, (vii) *Tafhīmāt-i Ilāhiyya*, partly in Arabic, contains *inter alia* addresses to the various groups in Muslim society, pinpointing their vices, failings and weaknesses; (viii) *ʿIḳd al-d̲j̲īd fī bayān aḥkām al-id̲j̲tihād wa 'l-taḳlīd*, a scholarly survey of the two problems mentioned (Dihlī 1344/1925; partial Eng. transl. by M. Dā'ūd Rahbar in *MW*, xiv/4, 346-587) (ix) *Fatḥ al-Raḥmān bi tard̲j̲amat al-Ḳur'ān*, an annotated Persian translation of the Ḳur'ān, by far his greatest achievement, published several times in India and still in great demand; (x) *al-Muṣaffā*, a sister volume to the *al-Musawwā*, being a commentary on the *Muwāṭṭā'*; (xi) *Izālat al-k̲h̲afā' ʿan k̲h̲ilāfat al-k̲h̲ulafā'*; basically a vindication of the *k̲h̲ilāfa* of the first two caliphs, Abū Bakr and ʿUmar al-Fārūḳ, but also comprising an exhaustive discussion of the doctrine of the *k̲h̲ilāfa*, political theory in Islam, the basic principles of economics (*tadbīr al-manzil*), the *id̲j̲tihād* as practised by ʿUmar b. al-K̲h̲aṭṭāb and the significance of his judgments etc.; practically the same discussion figures in (xii) *Ḳurrat al-ʿaynayn fī tafḍīl al-s̲h̲ayk̲h̲ayn*; (xiii) *Alṭāf al-ḳuds*, (xiv) *Fuyūḍ al-ḥaramayn* (Ar.); (xv) *Hamʿāt* (Ar.) (Urdū translation: *Taṣawwuf kī ḥaḳīḳat awr uskā falsafa-i ta'rīk̲h̲*, Lahore 1946); (xvi) *Satʿāt* (Ar.) and (xvii) *Lamʿāt* (Ar.), all deal with the different aspects of *taṣawwuf* as viewed by S̲h̲āh Walī Allāh; (xviii) *Anfās al-ʿārifīn*, contains an account of his ancestors, the *mas̲h̲ā'ik̲h̲* with whom they contracted their *bayʿa*, and the teachers of the author. This work is very useful for a critical appreciation of S̲h̲āh Walī Allāh and the evolution of his religio-political thought.

Bibliography: S̲h̲āh Walī Allāh, *Anfās al-ʿārifīn* (comprising his autobiography called *al-D̲j̲uzʿ al-laṭīf fī tard̲j̲amat al-ʿabd al-ḍaʿīf*, (Eng. tr. by Hidāyat Ḥusayn in *JASB* 1912, 161-75), Dihlī 1335/1917; ʿAbd al-Ḥayy Nadawī, *Nuzhat al-k̲h̲awāṭir*, Ḥaydarābād (Deccan) 1376/1957, vi, 398-415; Ṣiddīḳ Ḥasan, *Itḥāf al-nubalā'*, Cawnpore 1288/1871, 1448; idem, *Abd̲j̲ad al-ʿulūm*, Bhopāl 1295/1878, 912 ff.; idem, *al-Ḥiṭṭa bi d̲h̲ikr ṣiḥāḥ al-sitta*, Cawnpore 1283/1866; Brockelmann, II, 418 and index; Storey i, 20-2, 179; ii, 1020-1, 1137, 1201, 1253, 1263; Muḥsin b. Yāḥyā al-Tirhutī, *al-Yāniʿ al-d̲j̲anī fī asnād al-S̲h̲ayk̲h̲ ʿAbd al-G̲h̲anī*, Dihlī 1287/1870, 113-38; G̲h̲ulām Sarwar Lāhōrī, *K̲h̲azīnat al-Aṣfiyā'*, Cawnpore 1333/1914, ii. 373; Zubayd Aḥmad, *Contribution of India to Arabic literature*, Allāhābād 1946, 28-31; *A history of the Freedom Movement*, Karachi 1957, 491-541; Yūsuf Husayn, *Glimpses of medieval Indian culture*, Bombay 1957, 60-3; F. Rahman, *The thinker of crisis: Shah Waliy-Allah*, in *Pakistan Quarterly*, Karachi (Summer) 1956, 44-8; Raḥmān ʿAlī, *Tad̲h̲kira-i ʿulamā'-i Hind*, Lucknow 1899, 250; Muḥammad Isḥāḳ, *India's contribution to the study of Hadith literature*, Dacca 1955, 172-8; ʿUbayd Allāh Sindhī, *Ḥizb Imām Walī Allāh*, Lahore 1942, 13n[1], 43n[1]; idem, *S̲h̲āh Walī Allāh kī siyāsī taḥrīk*, Lahore n.d.; *J Pak. H.S.*, (S̲h̲āh Walī Allāh's conception of *id̲j̲tihād*), vii/iii, July 1959, 165-94; M. Sag̲h̲īr Hasanal Maʿṣūmī: *An appreciation of S̲h̲āh Walīyullāh al-Muḥaddit̲h̲ ad-Dihlawī*, in *IC*, October 1947, 340 ff.; K̲h̲alīḳ Aḥmad Niẓāmī, *S̲h̲āh Walī Allāh Dihlawī kē siyāsī maktūbāt*, (ed. K. A. Niẓāmī), ʿAlīgaṙh 1950; S̲h̲iblī Nuʿmānī, (*Ta'rīk̲h̲-i*) *ʿilm al-kalām*, Āẓamgaṙh 109-19; Raḥīm Bak̲h̲sh, *Ḥayāt-i Walī*, Dihlī 1319/1901; *Kalimāt-i ṭayyibāt*, (a collection of Persian letters of S̲h̲āh Walī Allāh, Mīrzā Maẓhar D̲j̲ān-i D̲j̲ān and others), Murādābād, 1305/1887, 15; Manāẓir Aḥsan Gaylānī, *Tad̲h̲kira-i Ḥaḍrat S̲h̲āh Walī Allāh*, Ḥaydarābād (Deccan), 1946; Ismāʿīl Gōdharawī, *Walī Allāh*, Dihlī n.d.; Muk̲h̲tār Aḥmad, *K̲h̲āndān-i ʿAzīzī*, Kānpur n.d., 1-26; *Maktūbāt S̲h̲āh Walī Allāh*, Dihlī n.d.; Abū Muḥammad Imām K̲h̲ān Naws̲h̲ahrawī, *Tarād̲j̲im ʿulamā'-i ḥadīt̲h̲ Hind*, Dihlī 1938, 4-48; S̲h̲araf al-Dīn Muḥammad al-Ḥusaynī, *al-Wasīlat ilā 'llāh*; S̲h̲āh G̲h̲ulām ʿAlī al-Dihlawī, *al-Maḳāmāt*; *al-Furḳān* (ed. Muḥammad Manẓūr Nuʿmānī), Bareilly (special issue)[2] 1941; Bānkīpur (Arabic) Cat., V/i, 5-6; Bas̲h̲īr al-Dīn Aḥmad, *Wāḳiʿāt-i Dār al-Ḥukūmat-i Dihlī*, Dihlī 1337/1919, ii, 286; Bas̲h̲ir Aḥmad, *S̲h̲āh Walī Allāh ke ʿimrānī naẓariyyē*, Lahore 1945; Muḥammad Ikrām, *Rūd-i Kawt̲h̲ar*, Karachi n.d., 487-564; Faḳīr Muḥammad Lāhōrī, *Ḥadā'iḳ al-Ḥanafiyya*, Lucknow 1906, 447; A. J. Halepota, *Philosophy of Shah Wali Allah of Delhi* (in Press); *Maʿārif* (Āẓamgaṙh), xxii/5, 341 ff.; Amīr al-Riwāyāt, *Arwāḥ-i t̲h̲alāt̲h̲a* (ed. Muḥammad Ṭayyib), Deōband n.d., 44; *Malfūẓāt-i ʿAzīziyya* (Persian text), 40, 93 (Urdū transl., Meerut 1315/1897); F. M. Asiri, *S̲h̲āh Walī Allāh*, in *Viśva-Bharalī Annals*, iv (1951); K. A. Nizami, *S̲h̲āh Walī Allāh and Indian politics in the eighteenth century*, in *IC*, Jubilee Number, 1951; Muhammad Dā'ūd Rahbar, *Shāh Walī-ullāh and Ijtihād*, in *MW*, xlv/4, october 1955; ʿUbayd Allāh al-Sindī, *Kitāb al-tamhīd* (MS. in Arabic); for an appreciation by an Egyptian scholar see D̲j̲. al-S̲h̲ayyāl, *Muḥāḍarāt ʿan al-ḥarakāt al-iṣlāḥiyya.*, Cairo 1957, 34-51.

(A. S. Bazmee Ansari)

DIHLĪ. 1. — History. The city of Dihlī, situated on the west bank of the river D̲j̲amnā [*q.v.*] and now spread out between 28° 30′ and 28° 44′ N. and 77° 5′ and 77° 15′ E., was the capital of the earliest Muslim rulers of India from 608/1211 (see DIHLĪ SULTANATE), and remained the capital of the northern dynasties (with occasional exceptions: Dawlatābād, Āgrā, and Lahore (Lāhawr), [*qq.v.*], were the centres favoured by some rulers) until the deposition of Bahādur S̲h̲āh in 1858; from 1911 it became the capital of British India, and after 1947 of Independent India.

The usual Romanized form of the name is Delhi, based on the commonest form in the earlier Muslim usage Dihlī; the common spellings in Urdū, Hindī (certainly from the time of the *Prithī Rād̲j̲ Rāsō* of the 7th/13th century), and Pand̲j̲ābī represent *Dillī*. The etymology is obscure; for some popular etymologies see A. Cunningham, *ASI*, i, 137 ff.

It has become popular to speak of "the seven cities of Delhi"; but the number of centres of government in the Dihlī area has in fact been nearer double that number. These are here described in approximate chronological order; all appear on the accompanying map, on which those which are no longer in existence are marked with an asterisk.

The earliest settlement was Indrapat, Sanskrit *Indraprastha*, a tell on which the present Purānā Ḳilʿa stands, supposed to have been built in legendary times by the Pāṇḍavas; the site is certainly old, and potsherds of Painted Grey ware and Northern Black Polished ware, types dating back to the 5th century B.C., as well as Kushan fragments of the 1st and 2nd centuries A.D., have been discovered there (see *Ancient India*, x-xi, 1955, 140, 144). The region of Dihlī seems to have been almost abandoned thereafter, for the next settlement dates from the 9th or 10th century, the Tomār city now known as Sūrad̲j̲ Kuṇḍ, where a large masonry tank and an earthwork are still in existence. More extensive are the remains of the Čawhān Rādjpūt town, dating probably from the 10th century A.D., which existed immediately prior to the Muslim conquest. On a small hill in the south-west of this region a citadel, Lālkōt, was built *circa* 1052 A.D. by Ānang Pāl, and around the town an outer wall was thrown, as a defence against the Muslim invaders, by Prithwī Rādj in about 576/1180 (Cunningham, *ASI*, i, 183). Subsequent to the conquest a mosque, known as Masdjid Ḳuwwat al-Islām, was built in 588/1192 by Ḳuṭb al-Dīn Aybak, who later commenced the building of the adjoining *mīnār* not only as a *maʾdhana* but also as a commemoration of his victory; for these, their extensions by Shams al-Dīn Iletmish and ʿAlāʾ al-Dīn Khaldjī, and other buildings in this so-called "Qutb site" see Monuments, below. The systematic refortification and extension of these old Hindū walls was effected by the earliest governors and monarchs to form the first Muslim city of Dihlī, known by the name of its former occupant as Ḳilʿa Rāy Pithorā. An indication of the extent of these walls and of their periods is given in the sketch-map, Fig. 1; for a discussion of the archaeological evidence see J. D. Beglar, *ASI*, iv, 1874, 6 ff.

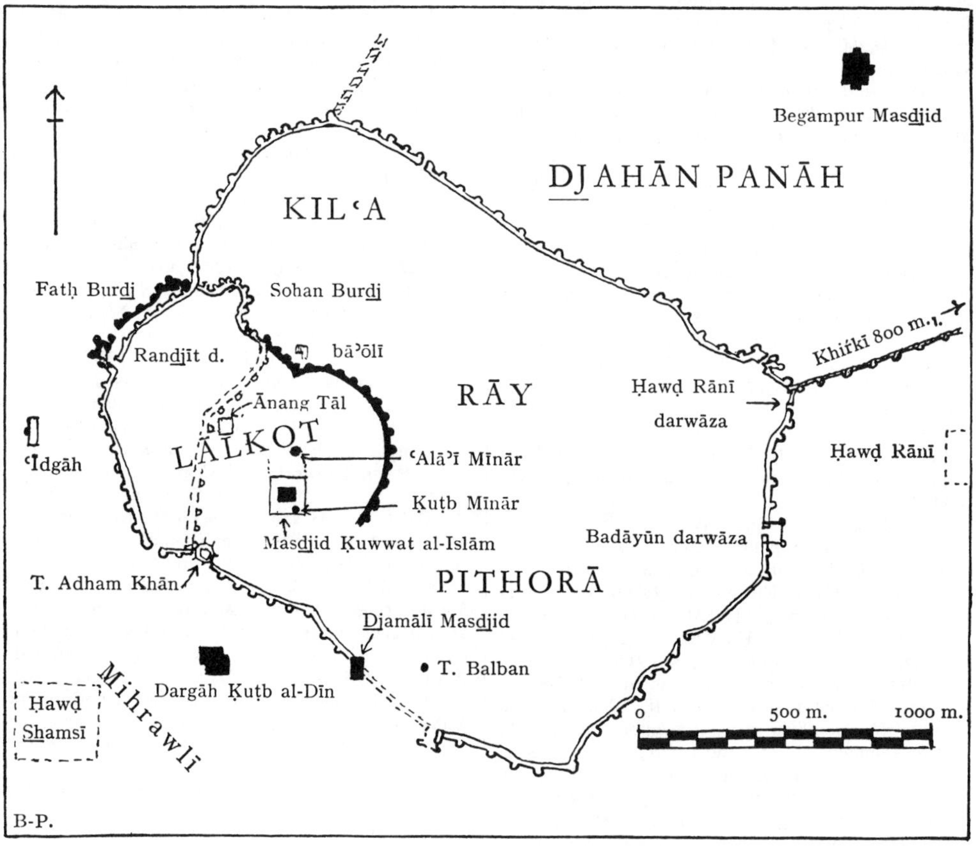

Fig. 1

Old Hindū walls — Walls removed by ʿAlāʾ al-Dīn — Extension of ʿAlāʾ al-Dīn, c. 700/1300 — T = Tomb

Ḳilʿa Rāy Pithorā remained the only regular residence of the Dihlī sultans until Muʿizz al-Dīn Kayḳubād built his palace at Kilōkhŕī, then on the banks of the Djamnā (Briggs, *Ferishta*, i, 274), in about 688/1289; this was occupied, completed, and its suburbs extended, by Djalāl al-Dīn Fīrūz Khaldjī in and after 689/1290. It has now fallen completely into desuetude. Even in Djalāl al-Dīn's case the older city seems to have had a higher prestige value, and he moved his court there as soon as it was politically practicable so to do. The sultan ʿAlāʾ al-Dīn Khaldjī effected many improvements and repairs, including the west gate (Randjīt darwāza) of Lālkōt (Amīr Khusraw, trans. in Elliott and Dowson, iii, 561); he commenced also the extension of the citadel of Lālkōt, see Beglar, *loc. cit.*, and Fig. 1. As a protection against the invading Mongols he first established a camp on the plain of Sīrī to the north, later encompassed it by entrenchments, and finally walled it, in about 703/1303. The location of Sīrī has been questioned (*e.g.*, by C. J. Campbell, *Notes on the history and topography of the ancient cities of Delhi*, in *JASB*, xxxv, 1866, 206-14); but the descriptions of Ibn Baṭṭūṭa, iii, 146, 155, and Tīmūr, *Malfūẓāt-i Tīmūrī*, trans. in Elliott and Dowson, iii, 447, and the ruins and lines of defences on the ground, enabled Campbell's views to be convincingly refuted by Cunningham in *ASI*, i, 207 ff. All that now remains within the walls is the comparatively modern village of Shāhpur.

Hardly a "city of Delhi", but an important site in its history, is the group of buildings, the earliest of which date from Khaldjī times, surrounding the shrine of the Čishtī saint Niẓām al-Dīn Awliyā', which make up what Piggott has described as the "squalid but entertaining complex" now known officially as "Nizamuddin" (for plan, and description of these buildings, see Monuments, below).

Some of the most ambitious building projects in the time of the Dihlī sultanate were conceived during the rule of the following Tughluḳ dynasty. Firstly, Ghiyāth al-Dīn Tughluḳ selected a site some 8 km. to the east of Ḳilʿa Rāy Pithorā, immediately after his defeat of the converted Hindū Nāṣir al-Dīn in 720/1320, for the building of his capital Tughluḳābād. The trace of the outer enceinte is approximately a half-hexagon, within which are a more strongly defended palace area, and an even stronger citadel; there are the ruins of a mosque in the city area, and the layout of the streets and houses of the streets and houses of the city, which shows it to have been well populated, can be seen from the aerial photograph in *Ancient India*, i, Plate IX. On the south of the city was formerly an artificial lake, in which stands the tomb of Ghiyāth al-Dīn, connected to the citadel by a fortified passage supported on arches, itself fortified. Connected with Tughluḳābād by a causeway on the south-east, which formed a *band* to retain the waters of the lake, is the subsi-

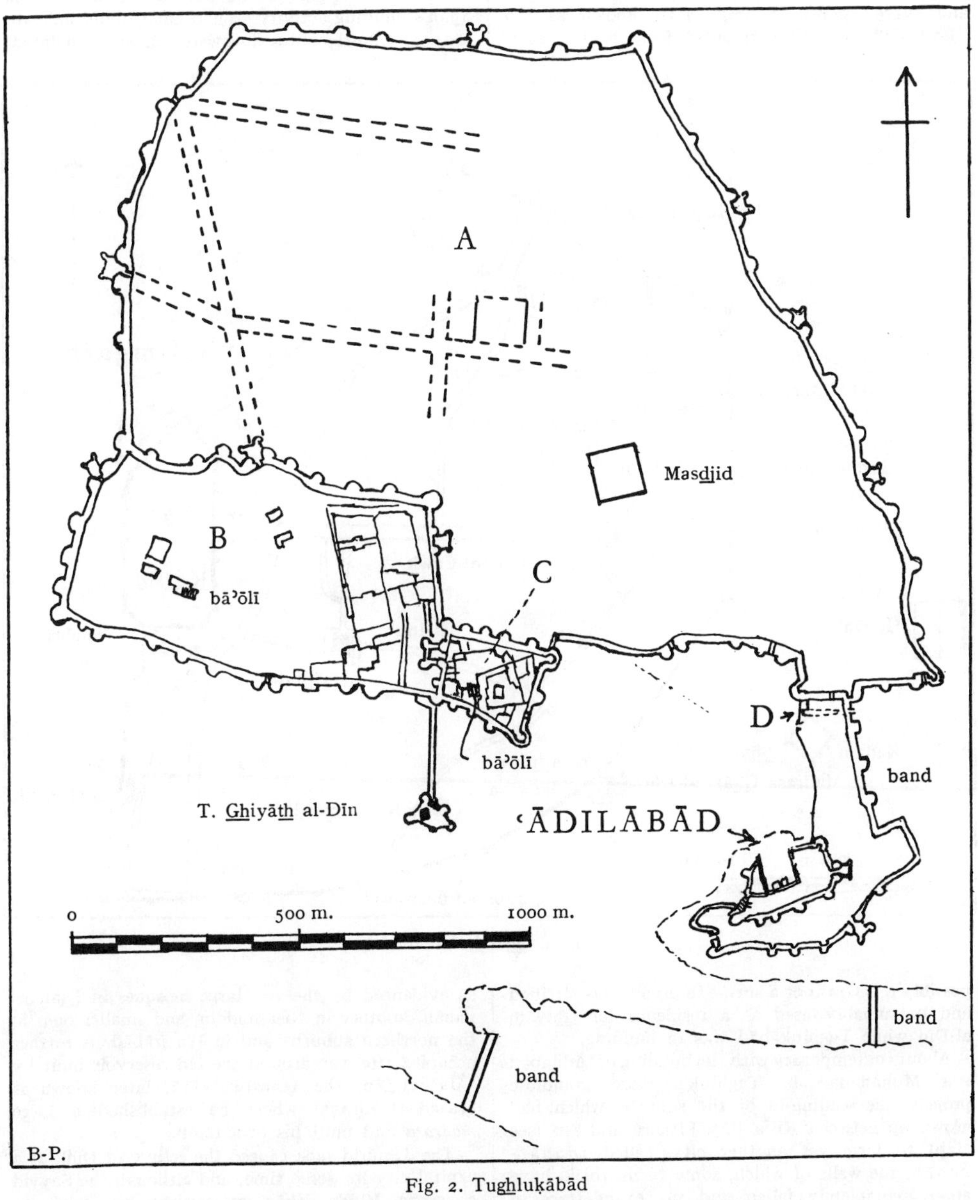

Fig. 2. Tughluḳābād

A: City B: Palace C: Citadel D: Sluices

diary fort of ʿĀdilābād built by his son Muḥammad b. Tug͟hluḳ c. 725/1325, but abandoned by him, together with Tug͟hluḳābād, in 729/1329 on his transfer of the capital to Dawlatābād [*q.v.*]. For these sites see Fig. 2, and the excellent article of Hilary Waddington, *ʿĀdilābād: a part of the "fourth" Delhi*, in *Ancient India*, i, 60-76, with photographs and survey plans. A small fort, known as the "Barber's" or "Washerman's" fort, to the east, machicolations, containing a palace complex, the remains of a fine mosque, and an extraordinary pyramidal structure built as a plinth for a column of As͟hoka brought from near Ambālā; the isolated Ḳadam S͟harīf and the nearby ʿĪdgāh show the western extent of the city to have been no further than the later S͟hāhd͟jahānābād. The extent of Fīrūz S͟hāh's building activity around Dihlī would indicate that the suburbs in his time were still well populated,

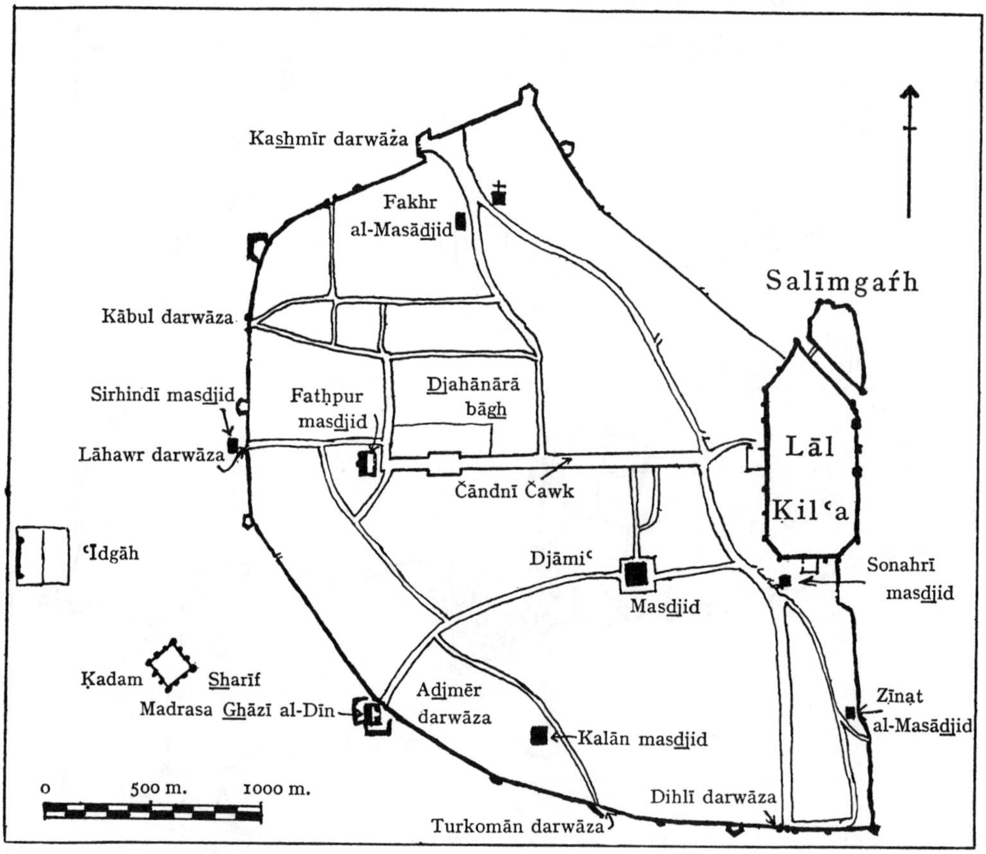

Fig. 3. S͟hāhd͟jahānābād

possibly a *madrasa* or a shrine in origin, was fortified and presumably used as a residence for G͟hiyāt͟h al-Dīn while Tug͟hluḳābād was in building.

About contemporary with the building of ʿĀdilābād was Muḥammad b. Tug͟hluḳ's more grandiose project, the walling-in of the suburbs which had grown up between Ḳilʿa Rāy Pithorā and Sirī (see Map) to form yet another city, called D͟jahānpanāh, the walls of which, some 12 m. thick, have almost completely fallen and the exact trace of which cannot easily be located; for the sluice built into this wall near the village of Khiŕkī, the Sāt Pulāh, see *Monuments*, below.

Muḥammad's successor Fīrūz Tug͟hluḳ was responsible for the building of another city, Fīrūzābād, extending from Indrapat to Kus͟hk-i S͟hikār some 3 km. north-west of the later city of S͟hāhd͟jahānābād, and now largely covered by that latter city. Its buildings were dilapidated by later builders, especially S͟hīr S͟hāh Sūrī and S͟hāhd͟jahān, and all that remains is the citadel, known as Fīrūz S͟hāh Kōŧlā, its walls reduced to below the level of their as evidenced by the two large mosques in D͟jahānpanāh, another in Nizamuddin, and smaller ones in the northern suburbs and in Wazīrābād. A further occupied site was around the old reservoir built by ʿAlāʾ al-Dīn, the Ḥawḍ-i ʿAlāʾī, later known as Ḥawḍ-i K͟hāṣṣ, where he established a large *madrasa* and built his own tomb.

The Tīmūrid sack caused the eclipse of Dihlī as a capital city for some time, and although the Sayyid governor K͟hiḍr K͟hān established his court at K͟hiḍrābād, and Mubārak S͟hāh his at Mubārakābād, both on the D͟jamnā, and the latter sultan built also his own tomb in the fortified village Mubārakpur (also Mubārikpur, Mubārik [*sic*] S͟hāh Kōŧlā), the Sayyids and their successors the Lōdīs built no further cities at Dihlī. The Lōdīs, indeed, moved their seat of government to Āgrā, and Dihlī became little more than a vast necropolis, the plains between Sirī and Fīrūzābād being covered with tombs and mausolea of this period; especially K͟hayrpur, 2 km. west of Nizamuddin, a region 1 km. west of Mubārikpur ("Tīn Burd͟j", *i.e.*, "three towers"), and a region on the road to Ḥawḍ-i Khāṣṣ (Kharērā); there was also some building in the region of the reservoir of Iletmish, Ḥawḍ-i Shamsī, south of the village of Mihrawlī.

After the Mughal invasions in the early 10th/16th century [see MUGHALS] Humāyūn settled at Dihlī and started the building of a citadel, Dīnpanāh, on the mound of the old Indrapat in 940/1533, but was dispossessed by the usurper Shīr Shāh Sūrī. Shīr Shāh took over and completed the building of Dīnpanāh, as the citadel of a new city, to which no particular name is given, little of which remains except the northern gate, near Fīrūz Shāh Kotlā, and the southern gate, opposite the citadel, as most of the stone was removed for the building of Shāhdjahānābād. His son and successor Islām Shāh, popularly called Salīm Shāh, built on the Djamnā the fortress Salīmgaṛh as a bulwark against the return of Humāyūn in about 957/1550. Humāyūn's return five years later added nothing to the Dihlī buildings, and the next two Mughal rulers preferred to reside at Āgrā and Lahore; some buildings at Dihlī date, however, from their time, especially the complex of monuments around Humāyūn's tomb (see S. A. A. Naqvi, *Humāyūn's tomb and adjacent buildings*, Dihlī 1947). Shāhdjahān also reigned at Āgra for 11 years, but the inconveniences there caused him to remove to Dihlī (*ʿAmal-i Ṣāliḥ*, fol. 575-6; Manucci, *Storia do Mogor*, i, 183) and found there on 12 Dhu 'l-Ḥidjdja 1048/16 April 1639 (so the contemporary historians and inscription in the Khʷābgāh; 9 Muḥarram 1049/12 May 1639 according to the *Maʾā-thir al-Umarāʾ*, iii, 464, and Sayyid Aḥmad Khān) a new fort, the citadel of his new city (Fig. 3) Shāhdjahānābād, known as the "Red Fort", Lāl ḳilʿa, which was completed after 9 years. The walling of the city proceeded at the same time, and it was enriched with many more buildings in the reign of Shāhdjahān and his successors (notably the Djāmiʿ masdjid, commenced two years after the completion of the fort), who made no further expansions of any of the successive cities. Shāhdjahānābād continued to be the capital of the Mughal rulers—except for Awrangzīb, who spent much time in the Deccan and died at Awrangābād [*q.v.*]—although other sites around continued to be used; *e.g.*, the Humāyūn's tomb complex, Nizamuddin, and the *dargāh*s of Rōshan Čirāgh-i Dihlī in Djahānpanāh and of Ḳuṭb al-Dīn Kākī at Mihrawlī were all used as burial places for the later Mughal rulers, and at Mihrawlī is a small summer palace used by the latest Mughals.

With the fall of the Mughal dynasty in 1858, the destruction of many buildings by the British during and after the mutiny, and the transfer of the capital to Calcutta, Dihlī became a town of less importance, the head of a local administration and a garrison town. The British expansion was to the north of Shāhdjahānābād, where the Civil Lines were established; here the capital was transferred in 1911, and the building of the new city commenced, originally known as Raisena, later New Delhi, *Naʾī Dillī*. Later expansion has been westwards of Shāhdjahānābād in the Sabzī Mandī, Karōl Bāgh, and Ṣadr Bāzār quarters; south of Khayrpur and on the road to Mihrawlī; and around the Cantonment, north of the Gurgāʾōn road, and the new airport of Pālam.

Some confusions of nomenclature, omitted in the above description, must be mentioned. Lālkōt and Ḳilʿa Rāy Pithorā were known as "Old Dihlī" as long ago as Tīmūr's time, and this phrase was in regular use in the early British period; since the building of New Delhi the expression "Old Delhi" has often been falsely applied to Shāhdjahānābād. After the building of Shāhdjahān's new fort, Lāl ḳilʿa, the older fort of Humāyūn and Shīr Shāh was regularly known as the "Old Fort", Purānā Ḳilʿa or Ḳilʿa-i kuhnā.

2. — Monuments. As the buildings of Dihlī present the earliest monuments of a settled Islamic power in the sub-continent, and as it was there that the first characteristic Indian Islamic styles developed, the influence of which was to spread far and wide from Dihlī itself, the account of the monuments given here is confined to a simple description of the major works, arranged chronologically, and an account of the architectural features of the monumental complexes of buildings of different periods.

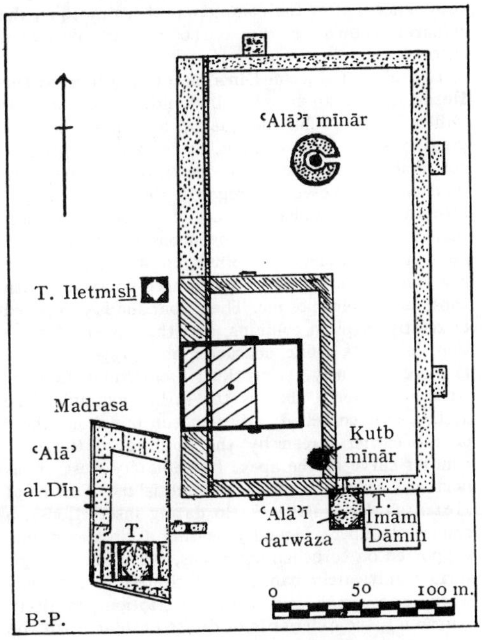

Fig. 4. Masdjid Ḳuwwat al-Islām

Plinth of Hindū temple — Iletmish
Ḳuṭb al-Dīn Aybak — ʿAlāʾ al-Dīn

For a treatment of the styles, with plates and detailed drawings, see HIND, Architecture.

The earliest phase of Muslim building in Dihlī is represented, as in the earliest stages in other sites (see ADJMĒR, BHARŌČ, BĪDJĀPUR, DAWLATĀBĀD, DHĀR, DJAWNPUR, GAWṚ, GUDJARĀT, MĀNḌŪ, TRIBĒNI) by the re-utilization of pillaged Hindū temple material. This applied to the first mosque constructed in India, Ḳuṭb al-Dīn Aybak's Masdjid Ḳuwwat al-Islām, earliest inscription 587/1191-2, in Ḳilʿa Rāy Pithorā: on a temple plinth 37.8 m. by 45.4 m. is constructed the central court, 65.2 m. by 45.4 m., with colonnades of three bays on the east and two on north and south; the western *līwān* is four bays in depth, originally with five domes covering voids in front of the *miḥrāb* recesses, its roof raised at the north end to accomodate a *zanāna* gallery. The *līwān* is separated from the mosque courtyard by a great arched screen, added 595/1199, whose arches do not conform with the spacing of the columns and *miḥrāb*s behind. The columns of the arcades were taken from some twenty-seven Hindū and Dj̲ayn temples, arranged haphazard, often set one over another to give the necessary height, ranged to support a roof made from ceiling slabs of similar temples, the sculptured figures mutilated and roughly covered with plaster, sometimes turned face inwards. The screen arches are corbelled, ogee at the top, some 2.5 metres thick, the central arch 13.7 m. high with a span of 6.7 m. The whole surface of this *maḳṣūra* is covered with carving, Hindū floral motifs and arabesques, and vertical lines of *nask̲h̲*. In the court-yard stands a pillar of rustless malleable iron from a temple of Vis̲h̲nu of the Gupta period (4th century A.D.), doubtless placed there by the builders not only as a curious relic but also as a symbol of their triumph over the idolaters. At the south-east corner of the mosque Ḳuṭb al-Dīn commenced, after the completion of his mosque, the minaret known as the Ḳuṭb mīnār, described below.

The reign of Ḳuṭb al-Dīn's successor, S̲h̲ams al-Dīn Iletmis̲h̲, saw an increase in building, not only at Dihlī. To the Dihlī mosque he attempted to give greater scale and dignity by extensions of the colonnades and the great *maḳṣūra* screen—symmetrically disposed as regards the new *miḥrāb*s, columnar bays, and the arches of the *maḳṣūra*, thus indicating a design of homogeneous conception; the new *ṣaḥn* included the *mīnār*, to which he added also, and its entrances were arranged co-axially with those of the old mosque. The colonnade is composed of relatively plain columns, and the screen decoration, including Kūfic character and *ṭug̲h̲ra* devices, is more obviously the work of a craftsman familiar with his material than is the earlier example. The arches, still corbelled, differ in contour from those of the earlier screen by the absence of the ogee counter-curve at the apex. Immediately west of his northern extension of the mosque is the Tomb of Iletmis̲h̲ (c. 632/1235 ? No dating inscriptions), a square chamber, originally bearing a circular dome, supported on corbelled squinches, the whole interior surface intricately banded with arabesques, diaper-work, and *nask̲h̲* and Kūfic inscriptions (entirely Ḳur'ānic); the exterior is of dressed ashlar, with the arched openings on north, east and south in red sandstone; red sandstone is also used for the interior, with marble on the *miḥrāb* wall and the cenotaph; the true grave is in a subterranean *tahk̲h̲āna*.

The Ḳuṭb mīnār was extended by Iletmis̲h̲ by the addition of three further storeys, to a total height of 69.7 m. (Cunningham, *ASI*, i, 195), completed c. 626/1229. The angle of slope is about $4^1/_2$ degrees from the vertical, and the four storeys are separated by balconies supported by stalactite corbelling. Each storey is fluted—developing probably the polygonal outline of the prototype *mīnār* at G̲h̲aznī —the lowest having alternately rounded and angular flutes, the second all rounded, the third all angular; the upper storeys, the work of Fīrūz Tug̲h̲luḳ (see below), are plain. Each of the three lowest storeys is decorated with wide encircling bands of Arabic inscriptions in *nask̲h̲* (dating inscriptions, panegyrics of Muʿizz al-Dīn Muḥammad b. Sām and S̲h̲ams al-Dīn Iletmis̲h̲, Ḳur'ānic verses); features of typically Hindū origin are almost entirely absent.

To the reign of Iletmis̲h̲ belongs the first instance in India of a monumental tomb, the mausoleum of his son Nāṣir al-Dīn Maḥmūd, at Malikpur, of 629/1231. This stands within a plinth some 3 m. high in an octagonal cell, the top of which projects into a court-yard with a plain enclosure wall pierced by corbelled arches, with arcades of Hindū columns on the east and west walls; that on the west forms a small mosque, with central portico and *miḥrāb*. The external gateway bears the dating inscription in Kūfic characters (non-Ḳur'ānic inscriptions in Kūfic are known only here, at the Masdj̲id Ḳuwwat al-Islām, and at Adj̲mēr); the corner towers appear to be part of Fīrūz Tug̲h̲luḳ's restorations (*Futūḥāt-i Fīrūz S̲h̲āhī*, ʿAlīgaṙh ed. 1943, 16). The tomb is locally known as "Sulṭān G̲h̲ārī", presumably on account of the crypt (*g̲h̲ār*) in which Nāṣir al-Dīn is buried, but this name is not known before Sayyid Aḥmad K̲h̲ān, *Āt̲h̲ār al-Ṣanādīd*, lith. Dihlī 1848, 206-8. For a detailed study see S. A. A. Naqvi, *Sulṭān G̲h̲ārī, Delhi*, in *Ancient India*, iii, 1947, 4-10 and Plates I-XII.

During the reigns of the suceeding sovereigns no buildings of note were erected until the reign of the K̲h̲aldj̲ī ruler ʿAlā' al-Dīn, except for the tomb of the sultan Balban, d. 686/1287, in the south-east of Ḳilʿa Rāy Pithorā, larger than the tomb of Īletmis̲h̲, with side chambers leading off the main hall, in which appears for the first time the use of the true voussoired arch. This marks not only a technical advance in construction but also a strengthening of Islamic building tradition, as opposed to that of the impressed Hindū craftsmen.

ʿAlā' al-Dīn K̲h̲aldj̲ī's extensions to the citadel of Lālkoṭ, and the building of Sirī, have been mentioned above. He started a grandiose plan of extension to the Ḳuwwat al-Islām mosque to the north and east; a few columns remain, and the foundations of the north gateway, to show the extent of this, and of the great arched *maḳṣūra* screen which was intended to be twice as long as the two previous screens combined, and of twice the scale; in the northern court-yard stands the incomplete first storey of a gigantic *mīnār*, its diameter at base twice that of the Ḳuṭb mīnār. The most notable feature of these extensions is the southern gateway, the ʿAlā'ī darwāza, of exceptional architectural merit: a square building of 10.5 m. internal dimension, with walls 3.4 m. thick, is surmounted by a flat dome, with lofty (10.7 m. from ground level to apex) arches on east, south and west, and a smaller trefoil arch on the north leading to the new eastern extension of the court-yard. The three large arches, and the squinches which support the dome, are of pointed horse-shoe shape, voussoired, with on the intrados a fringe of conventionalized spear-heads. A similar style is seen in the Dj̲amāʿat K̲h̲āna mosque at the *dargāh* of Niẓām al-Dīn, the first example in India of a mosque built with specially quarried materials, not improvised from Hindū material. (For a discussion of this mosque see M. Zafar Hasan, *A guide to Niẓāmu-d-Dīn* (= *Memoir ASI*, x), 1922). Apart from the early building (*madrasa*?) at Ḥawḍ ʿAlā'ī (= Ḥawḍ-i K̲h̲āṣṣ), the only other structure of ʿAlā' al-Dīn at Dihlī is his tomb and madrasa to the south-west of the Masdj̲id Ḳuwwat al-Islām, now much ruined; the series of small cells on the west wall show for the first time in India domes supported by a corbelled pendentive. The location of this building and all others in the "Qutb site" is shown on Fig. 4; for an extensive description of all the monuments and archaeological work see J. A. Page, *Historical Memoir on the Qutb, Delhi* (= *Memoir ASI*, xxii), 1925; idem, *Guide to*

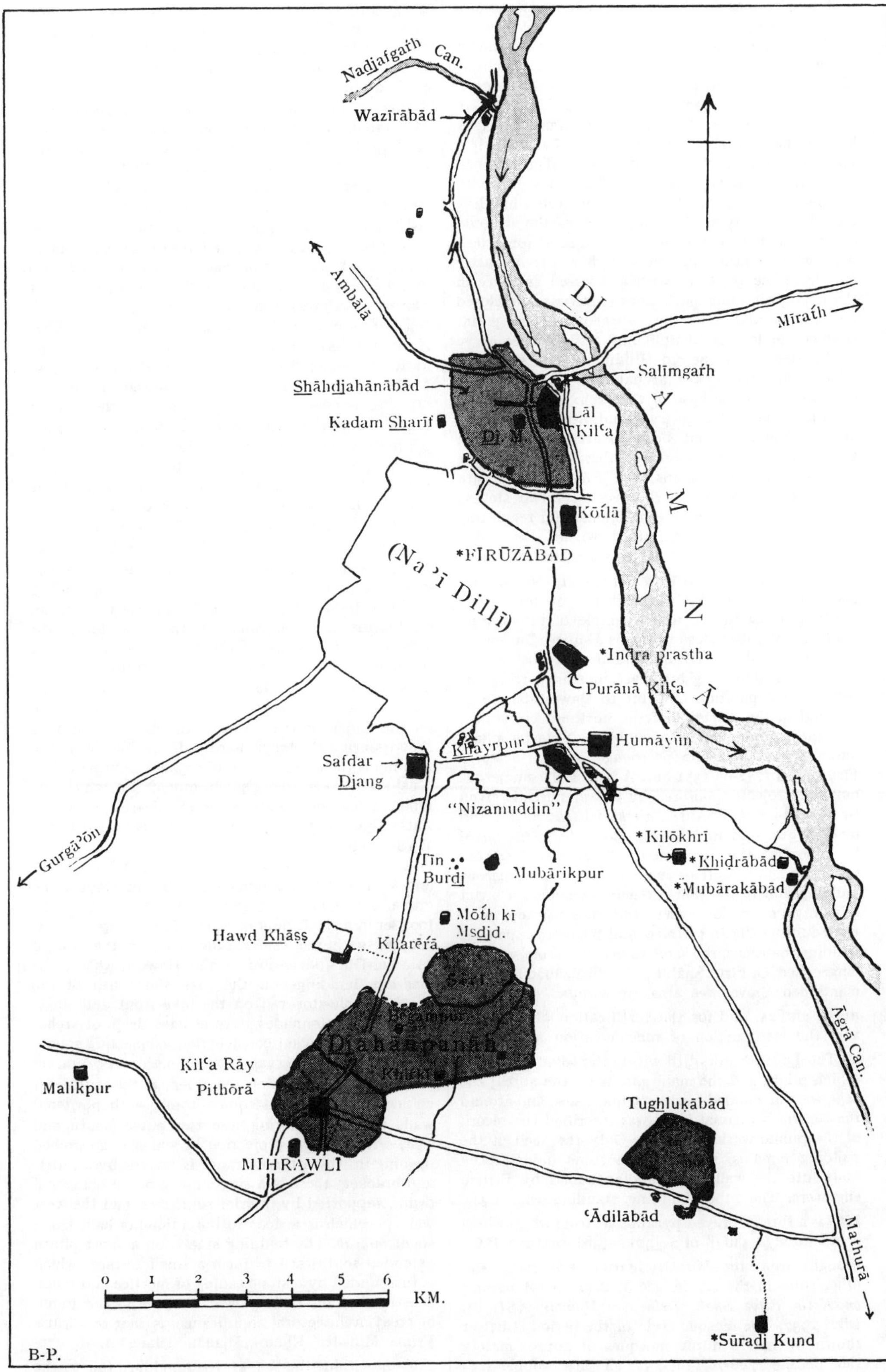
Nadjafgaṙh Can.
Wazīrābād
Ambālā
DJAMNĀ
Mīraṫh
Salīmgaṙh
Shāhdjahānābād
Lāl Ḳilʿa
Ḳadam Sharīf
Dj. M.
Kōṫlā
*FĪRŪZĀBĀD
(Na'ī Dillī)
*Indra prastha
Purānā Ḳilʿa
Humāyūn
Khayrpur
Safdar Djang
"Nizamuddin"
Gurgā'ōn
*Kilōkhrī
*Khiḍrābād
*Mubārakābād
Tīn Burdj
Mubārikpur
Mōṫh kī Msdjd.
Ḥawḍ Khāṣṣ
Khiṙkī
Sīrī
Bēgampur
Djahānpunāh
Ḳilʿa Rāy Pithōrā
Malikpur
Khiṙkī
Tughluḳābād
MĪHRAWLĪ
ʿĀdilābād
Āgrā Can.
Mathurā
0 1 2 3 4 5 6
KM.
*Sūradj Kund
B-P.

the Qutb, Delhi, (abridged from above), Dihlī 1938; best illustrations in H. H. Cole, *The architecture of Ancient Delhi,* London 1872.

The achievements of Ghiyāth al-Dīn, the founder of the Tughluḳ dynasty, are confined to the building of the city of Tughluḳābād (see above, History), and his own two tomb buildings; for the first of these see MULTĀN; the second, commenced after leaving the Pandjāb and coming to Dihlī as sovereign, forms an outwork on the south side of Tughluḳābād (see Fig. 2 above), an irregular pentagon with bastions at each angle, with the tomb-building placed diagonally at the widest part of the enclosed court-yard. This mausoleum is of red sandstone faced with white marble, its walls with a strong batter (25° from the vertical), with a recessed archway in the north, east and south sides (the west side closed for the *miḥrāb*) with the "spear-head" fringe introduced under the Khaldjīs and a slight ogee curve at the apex. Here the old Hindū trabeate system is joined with the newer arcuate by a lintel being imposed across the base of the arch.

Muḥammad b. Tughluḳ's foundation of ʿĀdilābād and Djahānpanāh has been mentioned above; in the walling of the second of these is a sluice or regulator of seven spans, the Sāt pulāh, with subsidiary arches and end towers, its two storeys of seven arches holding the mechanism for regulating the level of a lake contained within the walls. Another building of his time, near the village of Begampur, is the Bidjay Manḍal, which has been supposed to be the remains of his Ḳaṣr-i hazār sitūn, with the first example of intersecting vaulting in India; close to this is a superb but nameless tomb, and the Bārah Khambā (see below).

Muḥammad b. Tughluḳ's act in transporting the entire *élite* population of Dihlī to Dawlatābād [*q.v.*] resulted in the dispersal of the northern craftsmen, and the introduction of a rubble-and-plaster phase under the enthusiastic patronage of his successor Fīrūz Shāh (752-90/1351-88). A list of the numerous building projects sponsored by this monarch is given by Shams-i Sirādj ʿAfīf, *Taʾrīkh-i Fīrūz Shāhī,* and by Firishta, and in his own *Futūḥāt-i Fīrūz Shāhī* he describes the monuments of his predecessors which he had rebuilt or renovated. These numerous building and restoration projects demanded a strict economy: plans for every undertaking were submitted to the *Dīwān-i wizāra*, and the more expensive building materials, red sandstone and marble, were no longer used. Of Fīrūz Shāh's cities, Fīrūzābād has been mentioned above; see also DJAWNPUR, FATḤĀBĀD, ḤIṢĀR FĪRŪZA, and for the fortification of the *kōṭlā* and the introduction of machicolation see BURDJ, iii. The Djāmiʿ masdjid within the *kōṭlā* stands on a high plinth and the main gate is on the north; the *ṣaḥn* was surrounded by deep triple aisles, and around the central octagonal *ḥawḍ* was inscribed the record of the public works of Fīrūz. Only the shell of the building remains, much of the stone having been built into the walls of Shāhdjahānābād by British engineers. The other building standing within the *kōṭlā* is a three-storeyed pyramidal structure on which is mounted a pillar of Ashoka (3rd century B.C.) brought from the Mīraṭh district. For these and other ruins in the citadel see J. A. Page, *A memoir on Kotla Firoz Shah, Delhi* (= *Memoir ASI*, lii) Dihlī 1937. The mosque style of the period is better shown by half a dozen mosques of approximately the decade 766-76/1364-75: all are rubble-and-plaster, presumably originally whitewashed, with pillars and Hindū-style brackets and eaves in local grey granite, with prominent gateways, many-domed roofs, and tapering ornamental pillars flanking the gateways. The simplest is the mosque in the *dargāh* of Shāh ʿĀlam at Wazīrābād (= Tīmūrpur), a simple west *līwān* of five bays, with three domes, within which is the earliest example in Dihlī of a *zanāna* gallery in the rear corner of the *līwān*; the large (court-yard 68.0 by 75.3 metres) Begampur mosque in the north of Djahānpanāh has the *ṣaḥn* surrounded on all sides by a domed arcade, and the west *līwān* has a tall arched pylon in the centre of its façade which completely masks the large central dome; the Sandjar mosque (also called Kālī [black] masdjid) at Nizamuddin has the central court-yard divided into four smaller courts each 13.1 by 10.1 metres by a cruciform arcade one bay in depth, as well as the domed arcading on all sides (*ASI, Annual Report*, xxvii, Plate I); the Khiṛkī mosque, at Khiṛkī village in the south of Djahānpanāh close to the Sāt Pulāh, has a similar arrangement, but the crossing arcades are of three ranks of arches, as are the side *līwāns*: hence only the four courts, each 9.8 metres square, are open in the total area of about 52 m. square; the Kalān (this also sometimes miscalled 'Kālī) masdjid, within the walls of the later Shāhdjahānābād, is smaller with a single open court and surrounding domed arcades. This, the Khiṛkī mosque, and the Djāmiʿ masdjid in the *kōṭlā*, are all built on a high plinth over a *tahkhāna* storey, and the mosques themselves are approached by high flights of steps. The Kalān masdjid was no doubt the main mosque of the new Fīrūzābād suburbs, but the size of the Begampur and Khiṛkī mosques implies that the older cities still maintained a considerable population. The northern suburbs were further provided for by the Čawburdjī mosque on the Ridge, now so altered through various uses that its original plan is hardly discernible; near the mosque is the remains of Fīrūz Shāh's hunting lodge, Kushk-i Shikār or Djahān-numā, to which he repaired for consolation after the death of his son, Fatḥ Khān, in 776/1374. This prince is buried in the Ḳadam Sharīf, a fortified enclosure (see BURDJ, iii, and *ASI Annual Report*, xxii, 4 and Plates III*c* and *d*) in which is a domed arcade surrounding the grave, over which is a stone print of the Prophet's foot set in a small tank of water. Fīrūz's own tomb is coupled with the *madrasa* he built on the site of ʿAlāʾ al-Dīn's structure at the Ḥawḍ-i Khāṣṣ; the *madrasa* buildings on the east and south of the *ḥawḍ*, double-storeyed on the lake front and single behind, are colonnades, several bays deep, of arches or lintel-and-bracket construction, connecting square domed halls at intervals, extending about 76 m. on one shore and 120 m. on the other; at the south-east corner is the 13.7 m. square tomb, with plastered walls slightly battering, the two outer (south and east) with a slight projection in which is an arched opening in which the entrance is framed by a lintel-and-bracket; there is a single dome on an octagonal drum, supported by interior squinches, and the west wall, in which is a door to the adjoining hall, has a small *miḥrāb*. The building stands on a short plinth extended southward to form a small terrace, which is surrounded by a stone railing of mortice and tenon construction resembling woodwork. Another tomb, of great architectural significance, is that of Fīrūz's Prime Minister Khān-i Djahān Tilangānī, d. 770/1368-9, within the *kōṭ* at Nizamuddin; this is the first octagonal tomb at Dihlī (although the tomb-chamber at Sulṭān Ghārī is octagonal also), and is surrounded by a verandah, each side of which has three arched openings surmounted by a wide *čhadjdjā* or eaves-stone; there is a central dome, and eight smaller dome-like cupolas, one over each face. The prototype of this tomb has been sought in the Dome of the Rock in Jerusalem; it formed the model for many royal tombs of the subsequent "Sayyid", Lōdī and Sūrī dynasties. One of the latest buildings of the Tughluḳs is the tomb of the *shaykh* Kabīr al-Dīn Awliyāʾ (probably of the time of Nāṣir al-Dīn Maḥmūd, after 796/1394); although an indifferent and half-scale copy of the tomb of Ghiyāth al-Dīn Tughluḳ, it is of interest in indicating a revival of sympathy for the earlier polychromatic style, a reaction against the Fīrūzian austerity.

On Fīrūz Shāh's tunnels at Dihlī, see H. Hosten, in *JASB*, n.s. vii (1911), 99-108; viii (1912), 279-81; ix (1913), lxxxiii-xci.

Since the major structures at the shrine of Niẓām al-Dīn are of this time the complex is described here (Fig. 5). The entrance gate bears the date 780/1378-9, within which is a large *bāʾōlī* [*q.v.*] flanked by two tombs and a two-storeyed mosque, all of Fīrūzian appearance; the *bāʾōlī* is named Čashma-i dil kushā (= 703/1303-4 by *abdjad*). A further gate leads to the shrine enclosure; the shaykh's tomb dates from the time of Akbar, replacing an earlier one built by Fīrūz Tughluḳ, but has been much restored since, the dome being an addition of Akbar Shāh II in 1823; the Djamāʿa khāna mosque, to the west of the tomb, has already been referred to. To the south of the enclosure are numerous graves (Djahānārā, daughter of Shāhdjahān; Muḥammad Shāh, d. 1161/1748; Djahāngīr, son of Akbar II; Amīr Khusraw, a contemporary of the *shaykh*, although the tomb is early 11th/17th century; and others); outside the east wall of the court is the square polychromatic tomb of Atga Khān, foster-father of Akbar, d. 969/1562, of a style similar to that of Humāyūn (see below). Some 60 m. south-east of this tomb is the Ćawnsaṫh Khambe, a grey marble pavilion of excellent proportions forming the family burial place of Atga Khān's son, Mīrzā ʿAzīz Kōkaltash, d. 1033/1624. The adjoining *kōṫ* and Tilangānī tomb have already been described. For a full account of all these buildings see M. Zafar Hasan, *A guide to Niẓāmu-d-Dīn* (= *Memoir ASI*, X), Calcutta 1922.

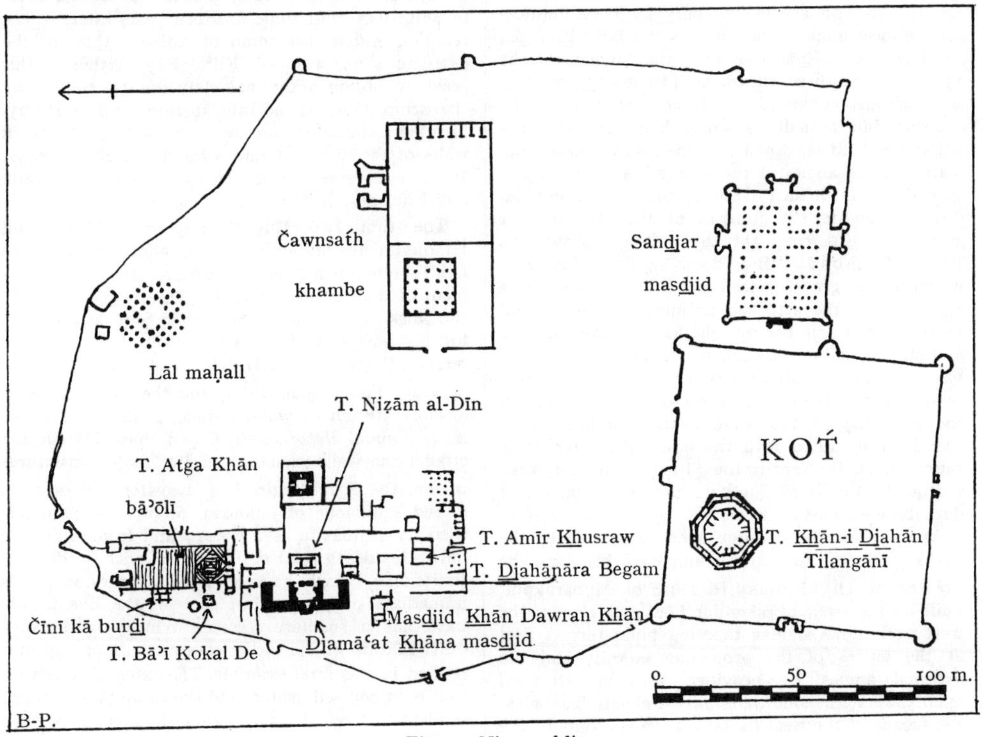

Fig. 5. Nizamuddin

Another *dargāh* largely dating from Fīrūzian times is that of Naṣīr al-Dīn Čirāgh-i Dihlī, d. 757/1356 (see ČISHTIYYA); the east gate is of 775/1373, but the tomb has been much modernized; the walls enclosing the shrine and village were built by Muḥammad Shāh in 1142/1729; beside stands one of the alleged tombs of Bahlōl Lōdī.

The "Sayyid" and Lōdī dynasties produced no great building projects; their monuments consist entirely of tombs, except for one significant mosque, and the principal ones are concentrated in three sites: Khayrpur, Mubārakpur, and south of Mu-djāhidpur on the road to Ḥawḍ-i Khāṣṣ. The tombs are of two distinct types, square and octagonal, in both cases with a large central dome, frequently also with open *čhatrīs* above the parapets. The earliest octagonal example is that of Mubārak Shāh, d. 838/1434, in Kōṫlā Mubārakpur, an improvement on the style of the Tilangānī tomb although the dome is not high enough and the octagonal *čhatrīs* over each face are too crowded. The tomb of Muḥammad Shāh, ten years later, removes these defects by raising the drum of the dome and the *čhatrīs*, and adding a *guldasta* at each angle of the verandah parapet. The tomb of Sikandar Lōdī, c. 924/1518, at the north end of Khayrpur, is of similar proportions but without the *čhatrīs*, and the dome has an inner and outer shell; the mausoleum stands in a fortified enclosure, on the west wall of which is an arrangement of arches resembling an *ʿīdgāh*, presumably an outdoor *miḥrāb*. The tomb of Mubārak has a detached mosque, but that of Muḥammad has none. All tombs have sloping buttresses at the angles.

The square tombs probably all date from the last quarter of the 9th/15th century, but they lack inscriptions and are known only by very uninformative local names. The finest is the Baŕē Khān kā gumbad, "Big Khān's dome", the largest (height 25 m.) of the three known as Tīn burdj, west of Mubārakpur, apparently of three storeys from the exterior, but actually a single hall; this and the adjoining "Little Khān's dome" have octagonal *čhatrīs* in the angles of the square below the drum, as had the Dādī kā ("Grandmother's) and Potī kā ("Granddaughter's") gumbad of the Mudjāhidpur group. At Khayrpur are the best preserved, the Baŕā Gumbad ("Big dome"), date 899/1494, which has no graves within and is locally said to be a gateway to the attached mosque, court-yard and *madjlis-khāna* (?). The mosque has massive tapering and sloping pillars at each rear angle, each with a band of fluting, alternately rounded and angled, reminiscent of the lowest storey of the Ḳuṭb mīnār; the east façade has wide central arches whose spandrels are filled with the best cut-plaster decoration in Dihlī. Near is the Shīsh gumbad, very similar to the Baŕā gumbad, but with courses of dark blue encaustic tile work.

Apart from the mosque mentioned above, the Lōdīs produced one major example of this class, the isolated Moŕh kī masdjid south of Mubārakpur, built by the *wazīr* of Sikandar Lōdī c. 911/1505; the west wall shows similar tapering pillar-turrets, but at the angles of the projecting *miḥrāb*, and the external angles are provided with two-storeyed open towers; the side walls have trabeate balconies; the façade of the west *līwān* has the contours of the arches emphasized by the recession of planes of the intrados, and the central arch is emphasized further by a pylon-like structure of the same height as the remainder; the *līwān* side domes are supported on stalactite pendentives; white marble, red sandstone, and coloured encaustic tiles are used in the decorative scheme, as well as fine cut-plaster; it is aesthetically one of the liveliest buildings in the whole of Islamic art in India. Other buildings of the Lōdīs are few: a structure (*madrasa*?), incorporating a small mosque, known as the Djahāz maḥall, on the east side of the Ḥawḍ-i ʿAlāʾī at Mihrawlī, a few small *bārādārīs* and *maḥalls* near Nizamuddin, and the residence (Bārah Khambā), with enclosed court-yard and three-storeyed tower, at Begampur.

In the unsettled days of the early Mughal conquest the Lōdī mode seems to have continued: the Djamālī mosque, of 943/1536, in the south of Ḳilʿa Rāy Pithōrā, has fine ashlar masonry, five *līwān* arches with recession of planes in the intrados, and the central archway sunk in a larger arch, with a spearhead fringe, in a central propylon rising above the general level of the façade, with a single central dome; to the north is the insignificant-looking oblong building over the tomb of Faḍl Allāh [*q.v.*], *takhalluṣ* Djamālī, with the best colour decoration in Dihlī on its ceiling. A continuation of the octagonal tomb style is in that of ʿĪsā Khān Niyāzī, of 954/1547-8 and hence in the reign of Islām Shāh Sūrī; the construction is similar to the preceding examples, including the closed west wall and *miḥrāb*, but more encaustic tile remains; a separate mosque stands on the west of the octagonal court-yard, of grey quartzite and red sandstone, the central bay of the three set in a projecting portico, with a central dome and *čhatrīs* over the side bays. The tomb-building has sloping buttresses at each angle, and is the last building in Dihlī so treated. (For these buildings see S. A. A. Naqvi, *Humāyūn's tomb and adjacent buildings*, Dihlī 1947, 21-4). The last octagonal tomb in Dihlī was built some fourteen years later, in the reign of Akbar, the tomb of Adham Khān in the extreme south-west of Ḳilʿa Rāy Pithōrā; this seeks to obtain additional elevation by converting the drum of the dome into an intermediate storey, arcaded externally, and without *čhatrīs*; the thick walls of the drum contain a labyrinth of stairways. Its general effect is rather spiritless. (Photograph and brief description in Cole, *op. cit.*).

The first two Mughal emperors, Bābur and Ḥumāyūn in his first period, added nothing to Dihlī's monuments, except perhaps the commencement of the Purānā Ḳilʿa; this, however, was mostly the work of the usurper Shīr Shāh Sūrī, as a citadel for his new city. Of the city only two gateways remain, the northern (Lāl, Kābulī or Khūnī darwāza), opposite Fīrūz Shāh Kōŕlā, and the southern, with a short stretch of walling, near Purānā Ḳilʿa (see *ASI*, *Annual Report*, xxii, 6 and Plate II). Of the citadel the walls remain, and two major structures within, the Shīr Manḍal, a two-storeyed octagon of red sandstone of unknown original purpose but used by Humāyūn as a library and from which he fell to his death; and the mosque, with no distinctive name, which has the Djamālī mosque as its immediate prototype: but each of the five façade bays has a smaller recessed archway, and every other feature of the earlier mosque is improved and refined in this later example. The external construction is in coursed ashlar, and the *līwān* façade in red sandstone, some of it finely carved, embellished with white marble and polychromatic encaustic tile work; inside the central dome is supported by two ranks of squinches, and in the side bays stalactite pendentives support the roof; the rear wall has tapering turrets on each side of the *miḥrāb* projection, and an open octagonal turret at each angle.

The first major building of the Mughals in Dihlī is the tomb of the emperor Humāyūn, of a style already prefigured in the small tomb of Atga Khān at Nizamuddin; the foundations of it were laid in 976/1568-9 (so Sangīn Beg, *Siyar al-Manāzil*, MS in Dihlī Fort Museum; 973/1565 according to Sayyid Aḥmad Khān, followed by most later writers) by his widow, employing the Persian architect Mīrzā Ghiyāth, although the enclosure wall had been started some five years before. In a large square garden enclosure (340 m. side; this is the first *čārbāgh* garden in India still preserving its original plan) stands the mausoleum building, 47.5 m. square on a plinth 95 m. square, 6.7 m. high; each face is alike, having a central rectangular fronton containing an immense arch, flanked by smaller wings each containing a smaller arch; these wings are octagonal in plan and project in front of the main arches. The central chamber is surmounted by a bulbous double dome on a high collar, around which are *čhatrīs* over the corner wings and portals. The entire building is in red sandstone, with a liberal use of white and coloured marble. Neighbouring structures are the small Nāʾī kā gumbad, "Barber's dome"; the Nīlā Gumbad, "Blue dome", earlier than Humāyūn's tomb and therefore not the tomb of Fahīm Khān, d. 1035/1626, as often stated; the "Afsarwālā" tomb and mosque; the ʿArab Sarāʾī; and the tomb of ʿĪsā Khān already described (see Fig. 6 for plan of this complex; full description of these buildings in S. A. A. Naqvi, *Humāyūn's Tomb and adjacent buildings*, Dihlī 1947). Not far to the south is the tomb of ʿAbd al-Raḥīm [*q.v.*], Khān-i Khānān, d. 1036/1626-7, a similar structure but smaller and without the octagonal corner compartments—hence a more obvious forerunner of the wards to the river. The dīwān-i ʿāmm is of red sandstone, with slender double columns on the open sides; this and the palace buildings on the east have engrailed arches, stand on low plinths, and most have open *čhatrīs* at each corner of the roof. Through the palaces runs an ornamental canal, the Nahr-i Bihisht, which flows south from the Shāh Burdj, water being brought from a point thirty *kōs* up the Djamnā (through the Western Djamnā canal; for the history of this, which dates from the time of Fīrūz Shāh Tughluḳ, see J. J. Hatten, *History and description of government canals in the Punjab*, Lahore n.d., 1-3); this has a plain marble channel, which in the Rang maḥall flows into a large tank in which is set a marble lotus, having previously passed, in the royal

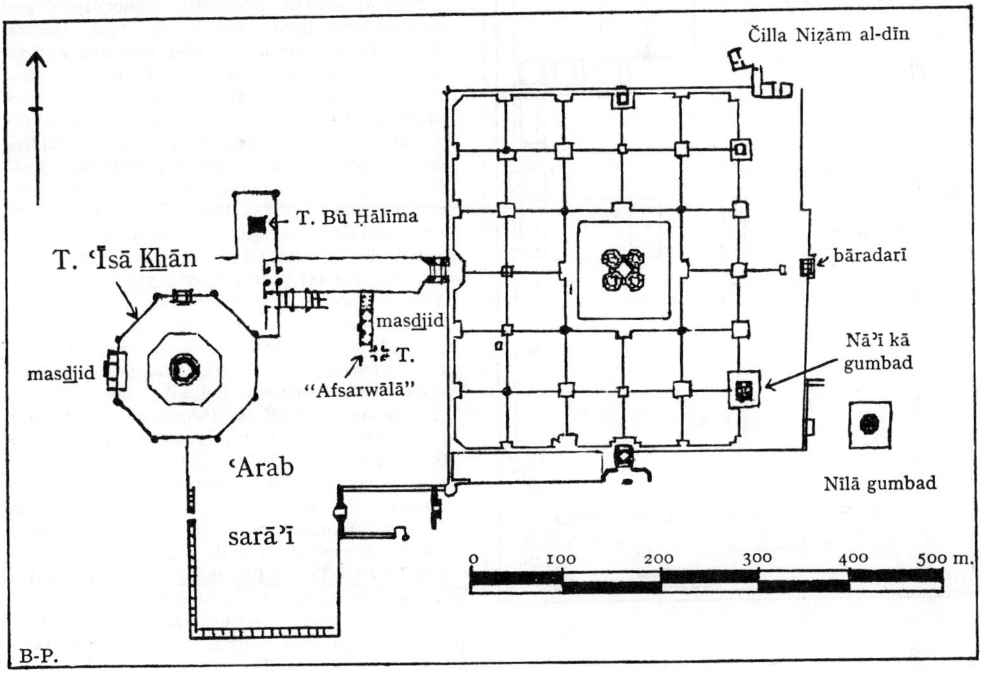

Fig. 6. Humāyūn's tomb

Tādj Maḥall than Humāyūn's tomb; the white marble of this building was later stripped off by Āṣaf al-Dawla, *wazīr* of Awadh. Other early Mughal buildings are the Lāl čawk or Khayr al-manāzil (the latter name a chronogram, 969 = 1561-2), a mosque built by Māham Anaga, foster-mother of Akbar, with double-storeyed chambers on east, south and north forming a *madrasa* (*ASI, Annual Report*, xxii, 6 and Plate I a and b; inscr., *Memoir ASI*, xlvii, 10); and the mosque of Shaykh ʿAbd al-Nabī, *ṣadr al-ṣudūr* of Akbar, between Fīrūz Shāh Kōtlā and the Purānā Ḳilʿa, built 983/1575-6 (see M. Zafar Hasan, *Mosque of Shaikh ʿAbdu-n Nabī* (= *Memoir ASI*, ix), Calcutta 1921).

The main phase of Mughal building in Dihlī was the construction of Shāhdjahānābād and the Red Fort, Lāl ḳilʿa, founded 1048/1638. The main features of Mughal palaces and other buildings will be described in MUGHALS; a brief account only is given here. Within the palace enclosure, about 950 by 505 m., are a central court, containing the Dīwān-i ʿāmm; flanking this, two open spaces containing gardens; and, on the eastern wall, the range of palaces facing inwards to the gardens and out-private apartments, under a screen bearing a representation of the "Scales of Justice", Mīzān-i ʿadl. Off these apartments is the external octagonal balcony, the Muthamman Burdj, from which the emperor gave the darshan [*q.v.*]. The Rang maḥall and the Dīwān-i khāṣṣ are the most lavishly ornate of these palaces, built and paved in white marble, the piers of the arches inlaid with floral designs in *pietra dura*; the latter building contained the fabulous Peacock Throne (*Takht-i ṭāʾūs*), taken to Persia by Nādir Shāh in 1152/1739 and there broken up (G. N. Curzon, *Persia and the Persian question*, i, 321-2). The disposition of these and the other buildings is shown in the plan, Fig. 7.

The fort originally contained no mosque; the Mōtī masdjid was added by Awrangzīb in 1073/1662-3, entirely of white marble, with a curved "Bengali" cornice over the central bay. For the fort and its buildings, see G. Sanderson, *A guide to the buildings and gardens, Delhi Fort*[4], Dihlī 1937.

The Djāmiʿ masdjid of Shāhdjahānābād (named *Masdjid-i Djahān-numā*), built 1057-9/1648-50, stands on an open plain to the west of the Lāl Ḳilʿa, its high basement storey, with blind arches on all sides, built on an outcrop of the local Aravallī ridge. The gates on north, east and south have an external opening in the form of a half-dome with a smaller door in the base of each. The east gate, used as the royal entrance, is the largest. The *līwān* surrounding the court is open to the outside, and has a square *burdj*, surmounted by an open *čhatrī*, at each angle. The western sanctuary is a detached compartment 79 m. by 27.5 m. with the

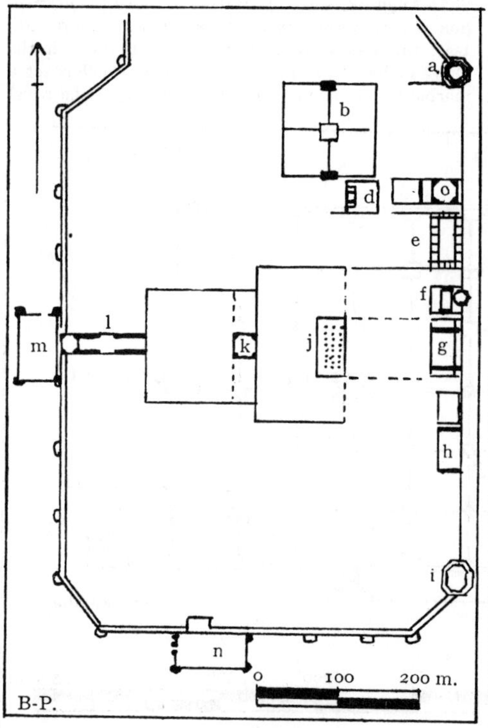

Fig. 7. Lāl ḳilʿa

a — Shāh burdj b — Ḥayāt Bakhsh bāgh c — Ḥammām d — Mōtī masdjid e — Dīwān-i khāṣṣ f — Kh^{w}ābgāh & Muthamman burdj g — Rang maḥall h — Mumtāz maḥall i — Asad burdj j — Dīwān-i ʿamm. k — Nawbat khāna l — Čhattā čawk m — Lāhawr darwāza n — Dihlī darwāza

court-yard (99 m. square), with a wide central arch flanked by five smaller bays of engrailed arches on each side, and a three-storeyed minaret at each front angle; above are three bulbous domes of white marble with slender vertical stripes of black marble. The mosque as a whole is in red sandstone, with white marble facings on the sanctuary, and white marble vertical stripes on the minarets. Nearly contemporary is the Fatḥpurī masdjid at the west end of Čandnī Čawk, the main street of Shāhdjahānābād, of similar style but less refinement, with a single dome; there is a mosque school within the enclosure. A smaller mosque of similar style, but with the three domes more bulbous and with equal black and white marble stripes, is the Zīnat al-Masādjid, c. 1112/1700, in the east (river) quarter of Shāhdjahānābād.

Of the latest Mughal phase must be mentioned the Mōtī masdjid in the *dargāh* of Ḳuṭb al-Dīn Awliyāʾ at Mihrawlī (early 12th/18th century); the tomb, madrasa, and mosque of Ghāzī al-Dīn Khān, father of Āṣāf Djāh, in a hornwork outside the Adjmēr gate of Shāhdjahānābād (1122/1710), and where the Arabic school is still maintained; the gateway of the Ḳudsiya Bāgh, north of the Kashmīr Gate, c. 1163/1750, and the elegant diminutive mosque (Sonahrī masdjid) of Djāwid Khān, of fawn-coloured sandstone, of the same time; and the finely-proportioned fawn sandstone tomb of Safdar Djang, d. 1166/1753, standing in the last great Mughal garden. One British building is worth mention, St. James's church, built by Col. James Skinner in Palladian style in 1824. The vast building projects of New Delhi (*Naʾī Dillī*) show occasional reminiscences of the glory of Mughal building, but have no further Islamic significance.

Bibliography: Specialist monographs and articles have been cited in the text. General works: H. C. Fanshawe, *Delhi Past and Present*, London 1902; H. Sharp, *Delhi: its story and buildings*, London 1921; G. Hearn, *The seven cities of Delhi*, Calcutta 1928 (not generally reliable); P. Brown, *Indian Architecture: Islamic period*, Bombay n.d., *passim*; Sayyid Aḥmad Khān, *Āthār al-Ṣanādīd*, Dihlī 1263/1847, lith., 2nd ed. Dihlī 1270/1854, later liths. Lucknow 1876, 1900, and Cawnpore (Kānpur) 1904; Fr. trans. by Garcin de Tassy in *JA*, V^{e} série, xv, 508-36; xvi, 190-254, 392-451, 521-43; xvii, 551-60; based on Aḥmad Khān: Carr Stephen, *The archaeology and monumental remains of Delhi*, Simla etc. 1876; *Journal of the Archaeological Society of Delhi*, 1850, *passim*; J. Ph. Vogel, *Catalogue of the Delhi museum of archaeology*, Calcutta 1908, Appx. II (*The sultans of Delhi and their existing monuments* ....), 60-71; cf. also W. Franklin, *An account of the present state of Delhi*, in *Asiatick Researches*, iv, 419-32 (1795). For inscriptions at Dihlī, see specially J. Horovitz, *A list of the published Mohamedan inscriptions of India*, in *EIM*, 1909-10, 30-144; *Memoir ASI*, xlvii. (J. Burton-Page)

DIHLĪ SULTANATE, the principal Muslim kingdom in northern India from its establishment by Iletmish (608-633/1211-1236) until its submergence in the Mughal empire under Akbar (963-1014/1556-1605). The establishment of the Dihlī sultanate was made possible by the Indian campaigns of the Ghūrid Muʿizz al-Dīn Muḥammad b. Sām and his lieutenant Ḳuṭb al-Dīn Aybak. Having recovered Ghaznī from the Ghuzz in 568/1173, in 571/1175 Muḥammad b. Sām captured Multān and Učč, hoping to by-pass the Ghaznawid possessions in the Pandjāb. A severe defeat near Mount Ābū in 574/1178 by Mūlarādjā II, the Čālukya ruler of Gudjarāt, induced the Ghūrids not to persist with the southern route into Hindūstān via the Gumal pass. The capture of Peshāwar in 575/1179, of Siālkoṭ in 581/1185, and of Lahore finally in 582/1186, ended Ghaznawid rule in India and placed the Ghūrids in a favourable strategic position *vis-a-vis* the Rādjput clans. Defeated however at Tarāʾīn (Tarāorī) in 587/1191 by the Čawhāns (or Čāhamānas) under Pṛithvīrādja, Muʿizz al-Dīn returned the following year with an army, said by Firishta to be of 120,000 horse, decisively to defeat the Čawhāns at the same place. Although Hānsī, Kuhrām and Dihlī (588/1192) were occupied, the political fragmentation of northern India prevented Ghūrid victories from having more than a temporary and local result. The Gāhaḍavāla chief, Djayačandra was defeated and slain near Čandāwar on the Djamnā in 590/1194 and Banāras occupied, but even so Ḳuṭb al-Dīn Aybak had to fight hard to retain Koyl and

Adjmēr and Muʿizz al-Dīn had to enter India himself in 592/1195-6 to take Bayāna, the stronghold of the Djadon Bhaṭṭī Rādjpūts. Thereafter, however, until the year of his death, Muʿizz al-Dīn left Ḳuṭb al-Dīn a free hand in Hindūstān. In 592/1196, the latter defeated an attempt by the Mhers, in alliance with the Čālukyas, to retake Adjmēr and in the following year defeated the Čālukyas near Mt. Ābū without however attempting permanently to occupy their territory. Turning his attention to the upper Ganges, Aybak occupied Badāʾūn in 594/1197-8 and Kanawdj in 595/1198-9. In 597/1200-1, Gwāliyār was taken and the Bundelkhanḍ area was penetrated in 599/1202-3 with the capture of Kālāndjara (Kālindjar).

When, in 602/1206, Muʿizz al-Dīn was assassinated at Damyak on the Indus (on the identity of the assassins see Habibullah, *The foundation of Muslim rule in India*, 79), the Ghūrid position in India was that of a precarious military occupation. Holding only the chief towns of the Pandjāb, Sind and the Ganges-Djamna Dōʾāb, the Ghūrid forces were menaced by the Khokars along their line of communication with Ghaznī and were faced by a resurgence of the Rādjpūts in Bundelkhanḍ (Kālindjar had been retaken by the Čandelas) and around Gwāliyār which had been retaken by the Parihāras. Moreover the Gāhaḍavālas were still active in the districts around Farrukhābād and Badāʾūn. The Rādjpūt clans had but melted into the countryside hoping to re-emerge and take control when the Turkish invaders had passed on. Indeed, by accepting Pṛithvīrādja's son and the Rāy of Gwāliyār Sallakshaṇapāla as tributaries, the Ghūrids may have testified to their limited political rôle in Hindūstān and their principal pre-occupation with their extra-Indian rivalry with the Khʷārazm-Shāh and the Ḳara-Khitay.

That the consolidation of the Ghūrid position in Hindūstān was still a secondary consideration even after Muʿizz al-Dīn's death is evident from the subsequent career of Ḳuṭb al-Dīn Aybak. Said by his panegyrist Fakhr-i Mudabbir to have been appointed *walī ʿahd-i Hindūstān* by Muʿizz al-Dīn shortly before 602/1206, on his master's death Ḳuṭb al-Dīn moved from the neighbourhood of Dihlī to Lahore and assumed power there. (Statements that he assumed the title of sulṭān are not corroborated by numismatic or inscriptional data and are not consonant with others that he sought and obtained a patent of manumission and a diploma as *malik* of Hindūstān from Ghiyāth al-Dīn Maḥmūd, nephew of Muʿizz al-Dīn and ruler of Fīrūz Kūh). Maintaining his headquarters at Lahore, he fended off Tādj al-Dīn Yildiz who claimed the Ghūrid conquests in Hindustan; when, in 605/1208 Yildiz moved out of Ghaznī into the Pandjāb, Ḳuṭb al-Dīn promptly drove him back and occupied Ghaznī himself, only in turn to be expelled by the people of Ghaznī after the proverbial 'forty days'.

It is significant that no efforts by Ḳuṭb al-Dīn to extend the conquests in Hindūstān are recorded in the four years before his death at Lahore in an accident at *čawgān* in 607/1210.

Ḳuṭb al-Dīn was succeeded at Lahore by his son Ārām Shāh, but at Dihlī a group of military officers set up Iletmish, *muḳtaʿ* of Badāʾūn and son-in-law of Aybak. Ārām Shāh was slain while marching on Dihlī. However, before Iletmish was secure, he had first to put down a revolt by the Turkish *djāndārs* of Dihlī.

Shams al-Dīn Iletmish (Iltutmish), an Ilbārī Turk, may be regarded as the founder of an independent sultanate of Dihlī. (The correct form of the name is Iletmish, as shown by Hikmet Bayur in *Belleten*, xiv, 1950, 567-88). His reign saw three main political developments—the severance of political ties between the Turks and Afghāns in Hindūstān and Central Asia, the achievement of primacy in Muslim India by the ruler of Dihlī, and the firm grasping of the main strategic centres of the north Indian plain by the forces of Dihlī. But in 608/1211, another former Muʿizzī slave, Nāṣir al-Dīn Ḳabāča, the ruler of Multān, had taken advantage of the struggle between Ārām Shāh and Iletmish to occupy Lahore, Tādj al-Dīn Yildiz had not abandoned his claim to the Ghūrid conquests in India and numerous Hindū chiefs were threatening the Turkish hold over Badāʾūn, Kanawdj and Banāras. Rādjāsthān also had slipped out of Dihlī's feeble grasp.

Placating Yildiz by acceptance of the *čhatr* and *dūrbāsh* of sovereignty and by not stirring when the latter's troops drove Ḳabāča from Lahore, Iletmish tightened his hold over Sarsūtī and Kuhrām east of the Satladj and when, in 612/1215, Yildiz was forced out of Ghaznī into the Pandjāb by the forces of the Khʷārazm-Shāh, Iletmish was able to defeat and capture him at Tarāʾīn (Tarāorī). He still did not hasten, however, to occupy Lahore.

Čingiz Khān's attack upon the Khʷārazm-Shāh hastened the political isolation of the Turks in India. Iletmish refused to be drawn into the struggle between the Mongols and Djalāl al-Dīn Khʷārazm-Shāh [*q.v.*], watching the latter erode Ḳabāča's position in the Pandjāb and Sind. Taking advantage of Ḳabāča's difficulties, Iletmish occupied Lahore and in 625/ 1228 drove Ḳabāča from Multān and Učč to a death by drowning in the Indus. Although Iletmish occupied Siālkoṭ (and Lahore when he could), by drawing back his effective frontier east of the Beās, he managed to avoid a head-on clash with the Mongols before his death.

In the east, where Muḥammad Bakhtiyār Khaldjī had overcome the Sena kingdom in Bengal in 600-2/1203-6, Iletmish repelled Ghiyāth al-Dīn ʿIwāz Khaldjī's encroachments in Bihār in 623/1225; in the following year the latter was slain by Iletmish's eldest son Nāṣir al-Dīn Maḥmūd. Towards the end of 627/1230, Iletmish invaded Lakhnawtī and slew the Khaldjī chief Balka.

Against the Rādjpūts, Iletmish was successful in capturing, at least temporarily, Ranthambhor in 624/1226, Mandor in 625/1227, Gwāliyār in 629/1231, and in plundering Bhīlsā and Udjdjayn (Ujjain) in 632/1234-5. Nevertheless his lieutenants were worsted in encounters with the Čawhāns of Bundī and the Čandelas of Narwar and even in the Dōʾāb Hindū chiefs needed constant overawing.

The appearance of an independent Muslim power in north India was however signalized by Iletmish receiving, in 626/1229, a robe of honour and the title of *Nāṣir Amīr al-Muʾminīn* from the ʿAbbāsid caliph, al-Mustanṣir.

That the Dihlī sultanate had 'settled in' in northern India by the end of Iletmish's reign is suggested by its capacity to survive faction, Mongol pressure and sapping by Hindū chiefs during the years immediately following. Within ten years of Iletmish's death, the *muḳtaʿ*s and officials had accepted and deposed four of his children or grandchildren, Rukn al-Dīn Fīrūz (633/1236), Raḍiyya (634-7/1236-40), Muʿizz al-Dīn Bahrām, (637-9/1240-2) and ʿAlāʾ al-Dīn Masʿūd (639-44/1242-6).

Stability was not achieved until the reign of Nāṣir al-Dīn Maḥmūd (644-64/1246-66) during whose time effective authority was exercised by Ghiyāth al-Dīn Balban as *nā'ib*. Most sources picture Nāṣir al-Dīn as a pious recluse, but from the evidence of ʿIṣāmī's *Futūḥ al-Salāṭīn*, it is possible that this is an exaggeration. (See also K. A. Nizami, *Balban, the regicide*, in bibl.).).

The ceaseless struggle required of the Turks and Afghāns in Hindūstān to maintain Dihlī as the principal, let alone the paramount, power at this time, is emphasized by the career of Balban both as *nā'ib* and sultan. Ceaseless military activity was demanded. In 645/1247, Balban plundered the areas between Kālindjar and Karra; in 646/1248, he led an unsuccessful raid against Ranthambhor and in 649/1251 he marched against Čahaŕadeva, the Djadjapella ruler of Gwāliyār and Narwar. In 652/1254 he campaigned against the Katehriyas whose activities always threatened the hold of Dihlī over Badā'ūn and Sambhal, north of the Ganges. Depredations by the Yaduvanshī Rādjpūts of the northern Alwār area, the 'Mewātīs', were endemic in the last decade of Nāṣir al-Dīn Maḥmūd's reign, with raids against Hānsī in 655/1256 and even as far as the environs of Dihlī itself.

Early in Balban's own reign (664-86/1266-87), he cleared the forests near Dihlī of marauders and pacified the Bhodjpur, Patīyālī and Kampil districts, stationing garrisons of Afghāns there. One historian of the next century, Ḍiyā' al-Dīn Baranī, depicts Balban as consciously pursuing, in his own reign, a purely defensive policy and as concerned mainly to hold the western marches against the Mongols. That this is probably an *ex post facto* rationalization, provoked by the contrast with the succeeding period, is suggested by the fierceness of Balban's reaction to trouble in Lakhnawtī in the 1280's when he put forth a great military effort to suppress Tughril who had assumed independence under the title of Sulṭān Mughīth al-Dīn. Dihlī was not always so mindful of events in Bengal. Although Balban strengthened the frontier strongholds of Dīpālpur, Sāmāna and Bhātinda and posted his favourite son Muḥammad to Multān and Lahore, the Mongols were too preoccupied with the quarrels between the Čaghatāys and the Il-Khānids and their rivalry in Afghānistān to be a serious threat to the Dihlī sultanate in Balban's time.

As Muḥammad was killed in a skirmish with the Mongols in 684/1286, and Balban's second son Bughrā Khān preferred his *iḳṭāʿ* of Lakhnawtī, Balban was succeeded by his grandson, Muʿizz al-Dīn Kayḳubād who, young and frivolous, proved incapable of withstanding the intrigues of ambitious ministers and the faction struggles between groups of Turks and Khaldjīs. Eventually, succumbing to paralysis, he was displaced by his infant son, Kayūmarth, a puppet in the hands first of the Turks and then of the Khaldjīs. The Khaldjī leader, Djalāl al-Dīn, accepted the status of *nā'ib* to Kayūmarth; after about three months, finding that, in order to protect himself against the jealousies of other nobles, he needed the title to as well as the reality of power, Djalāl al-Dīn assumed the sultanate himself (689/1290).

By Muslim historians of a later generation, the end of Balban's dynasty was regarded as signalizing the end of the Turkish sultanate of Dihlī. In the sense of the race of the sultan this is so, but not in the sense that the ruling élite had hitherto been exclusively Turkish. Djalāl al-Dīn Khaldjī had been Balban's *muḳtaʿ* of Sāmāna before becoming *ʿāriḍ-i mamālik* under Muʿizz al-Dīn; and Balban's *ʿāriḍ-i mamālik*, ʿImād al-Mulk Rāwat, was a converted Hindū. The outcome of the diversification of the Muslim ruling groups through immigration, intermarriage and concubinage with the subject population was to become more evident under the Khaldjīs, but Baranī's rhetoric, for example, cannot conceal the fact that the process had already gone a considerable way under Balban.

Djalāl al-Dīn Khaldjī's assassination by his nephew, ʿAlā' al-Dīn, has enabled Baranī, agalnst the evidence of events and the testimony of Amīr Khusraw's *Miftāḥ al-Futūḥ*, to fasten upon him the character of an ageing, indulgent and gullible valetudinarian. Actually, he suppressed a revolt by Balban's former officers in Shaʿbān 689/August-September 1290, besieged Ranthambhor (though unsuccessfully) in 690/1291 and defeated a Mongol foray in 691/1291-2. He also pillaged Mandor and Udjdjayn (Ujjain) at the end of 691/1292.

But it was under ʿAlā' al-Dīn Khaldjī (695-715/1296-1315) that, for a brief period, the Dihlī sultanate attained an imperial status in the sub-continent. ʿAlā' al-Dīn was probably born about 666/1267-8. A participant in the Khaldjī coup against Balban's family and the other military officers, he was appointed *muḳtaʿ* of Karra in 690/1291 from whence he raided Bhīlsā and then, in 695/1296, unbeknown to Djalāl al-Dīn Khaldjī, the Yādava kingdom of Devagiri (Deogir). Loaded with booty, he was met on the Ganges near Mānikpur by Djalāl al-Dīn who appears to have been so avid to share the spoils that he was careless of his own safety. Fear of the influence of powerful enemies at court feeding his ambition, ʿAlā' al-Dīn had his uncle slain.

Supported by his brother Almās Beg, ʿAlā' al-Dīn bought over many *malik*s and *amīr*s by money and promotion. Within a few months of his accession, he had captured the surviving sons of Djalāl al-Dīn Khaldjī and their supporters and blinded, imprisoned or executed them.

The reign was noteworthy in that serious attacks upon Hindūstān by the Čaghatay Mongols of Transoxiana were repulsed, the influence of Dihlī over Rādjāsthān was greatly extended and profitable raids, which made possible the introduction of a Muslim ruling class there later, were made against the Hindū kingdoms of the Deccan and the far south. The historian Baranī details important changes in the system of administration and measures to control the prices of necessities at headquarters and thus lessen the cost of a large army. (See Baranī, *Ta'rīkh-i-Fīrūz Shāhī*, Bib. Ind. ed., 282-8, 302-19). There are hints of unwonted activity in these spheres in other contemporary or near-contemporary evidence. It is not clear from the evidence why ʿAlā' al-Dīn should have succeeded in winning the co-operation of the military and official classes for reforms which adversely affected them.

The rivalry between Dawā Khān, great-great grandson of Čaghatay and ruler of Transoxiana, and the Great Khāns in the east in alliance with the Il-Khāns in the west, led to an effort by Dawā to expand in the direction of Afghānistān and Hindūstān. The first Mongol invasion of ʿAlā' al-Dīn's reign, into the Pandjāb in 697/1297-8, was worsted at Djalandhar and the second, into Sīwistān in 698/1299 was equally abortive. A third, later the same year, under Ḳutlugh Khwādja, son of Dawā, reached Kīlī near Dihlī before it too was defeated. The invasion of Ṭarghī in 702-3/1303 invested Dihlī and appears to have been thwarted of success only by ʿAlāʾ al-Dīn Khaldjī's entrenchments at Sīrī. (On the location of Sīrī, see *ASI*, i, Simla 1871, 207-12). Other incursions were defeated at Amroha in 705/1305, and near the Rāwī in 706/1306 by Malik Kāfūr and Malik Tughluḳ. But although Dihlī was almost uniformly successful against the Čaghatay Mongols, the cessation of major attacks during the latter half of ʿAlāʾ al-Dīn's reign was probably caused more by an intensification of antagonism between the Il-Khāns and Dawā's successors than by discomfiture in Hindūstān; Malik Tughluḳ appears to have been kept busy combatting minor forays as *muḳtaʿ* of Dīpālpur.

ʿAlāʾ al-Dīn had not waited upon security from the Mongols before expanding the sultanate in India itself. In 698/1299, Gudjarāt was invaded and Khambāyat plundered. (See K. S. Lal, *History of the Khaljīs*, 83, on the date of this expedition). In 700/1301, Ranthambhor, in 702/1303 Čittor, in 705/1305 Māndū were captured, to be followed in 708/1308 by the capture of Siwāna and in 711/1311-2 of Djālor. These victories in Rādjāsthān were essential to the success of ʿAlāʾ al-Dīn's expeditions south of the Narbadā. The Yādava kingdom of Devagiri was laid under tribute in 706-7/1307, the Kākatīya kingdom of Telingāṇa in 709/1309-10. In 710/1311, with the help of the Hoysāla Ballāladeva of Dwārasamudra, Malik Kāfūr invaded the Pāndya kingdom in the far south, returning laden with spoils to Dihlī in 711/1311.

The successes of ʿAlāʾ al-Dīn Khaldjī's reign may be attributable partly to the personal drive of a sultan requiring, as his uncle's murderer, to go on living dangerously, partly to the financial appeal of his earliest Deccan raid and the conquest of Gudjarāt to the soldiery, and partly to the services of Indian-born Muslims and converted Hindū slaves. Moreover, he treated defeated Hindū rulers in a conciliatory way, receiving them at court and marrying into their families. (He himself married a daughter of Rāmadeva of Devagiri and his son Khiḍr Khān married "Duwal Rānī" (correctly Devaldevī), daughter of Rāy Karan of Gudjarāt). It is significant that he was content to reduce the Hindū kingdoms of south India to a tributary status. His administrative measures will be mentioned under a general reference to the political institutions of the Dihlī sultanate.

ʿAlāʾ al-Dīn Khaldjī did not however succeed in perpetuating the sultanate in his family. On his death, his *nāʾib* Malik Kāfūr raised ʿAlāʾ al-Dīn's six-year-old son ʿUmar Khān to the throne as Shihāb al-Dīn ʿUmar Khaldjī, blinding Khiḍr Khān and Shādī Khān before himself being murdered by the palace *payk*s. ʿAlāʾ al-Dīn's third son Ḳuṭb al-Dīn Mubārak Shāh Khaldjī then ascended the throne. During his reign (716-20/1316-20), a revolt in Gudjarāt was suppressed, Devagiri was garrisoned and Telingāṇa and the far south raided again. However, Ḳuṭb al-Dīn was murdered by a Hindū convert, his favourite Khusraw Khān Barwārī (on his name and origin see: Hoḍīvālā, *Studies in Indo-Muslim history*, i, 369-71), who assumed the title of Sulṭān Nāṣir al-Dīn Khusraw Shāh.

Tradition formed under the Tughluḳs depicts his rule of four months as that of an avowed Hindū infidel; it is evident however that Ḳuṭb al-Dīn was unpopular among important elements of the military classes [there had been plots against his life in 718/1318 when coins were struck in favour of one Shams al-Dīn Maḥmūd Shāh (see R. B. Whitehead, *Some rare coins of the Pathan sultans of Delhi*, in *JASB*, 1910, Numismatic Supplement xiv, 566-7; *Shamsu-d-din Maḥmūd of Dehli*, in *JASB*, 1912, Numismatic Supplement xvii, 123-124; H. Nelson Wright, *The sultans of Delhi; their coinage and metrology*, Dihlī 1936, 109-10; K. S. Lal, *op. cit.* 330-2, 337-8)]. Historians favouring the Tughluḳs state that many Muslims either accepted office under him or refused to join Malik Tughluḳ's revolt, or fought energetically on the Barwārī's behalf. It is stated that Hindū Khokhar chiefs also supported the Tughluḳs. However, Ghāzī Malik, later Ghiyāth al-Dīn Tughluḳ, encouraged by his son Malik Fakhr al-Dīn Djawnā, marched on Dihlī, defeating the forces of Nāṣir al-Dīn Khusraw Shāh twice, capturing and executing him.

According to Ibn Baṭṭūṭa, (*Riḥla*, ed. Defremery and Sanguinetti, iii, 201), Ghiyāth al-Dīn Tughluḳ was a Ḳarawna Turk. (On this see Wolseley Haig, *Five questions in the history of the Tughluq dynasty of Dihli*, in *JRAS*, July 1922, 319-21). He appears to have risen to the appointment of *wakīl-dār* under Muʿizz al-Dīn Kayḳubād and first to have obtained the post of *muḳtaʿ* under Djalāl al-Dīn Khaldjī. His reign (720-5/1320-5) saw a further campaign against Telingāṇa, the repulse of a Mongol raid, a raid into Djādjnagar and an expedition to Lakhnawtī to re-assert Dihlī's suzerainty. Ghiyāth al-Dīn Tughluḳ met his death under a collapsing hunting pavilion at Afghānpur. The complicity of Muḥammad b. Tughluḳ in his father's death has been exhaustively argued (see Syed Moinul Haq, *Was Mohammad bin Tughlak a parricide?*, in *Muslim University Journal*, Aligarh, v/2, October 1938, 17-48). In the light of Ḍiyāʾ al-Dīn Baranī's apparently genuine mystification at the event, the absence of condemnation of Muḥammad b. Tughluḳ (whom he condemns fiercely on other counts) and the unnecessarily elaborate and haphazard method of killing alleged, Muḥammad b. Tughluḳ is, in this article also, adjudged innocent of his father's death.

The reign of Muḥammad b. Tughluḳ (725-52/1325-51) appears to have been a watershed in the history of the Dihlī sultanate. At the outset, Dihlī's authority was, according to Ḍiyāʾ al-Dīn Baranī, recognized in twenty-three provinces, and the picture drawn by Ibn Baṭṭūṭa in the 730/1330's is one of Dihlī's power and magnificence. Yet by 752/1351 the power of Dihlī south of the Narbadā was clearly forfeit and revolt endemic elsewhere. Baranī's interpretation of Muḥammad b. Tughluḳ's troubles is too redolent of his general philosophy of history (see P. Hardy, *Historians of medieval India*, 36-9, 124-5) to be acceptable as it stands (it hardly explains the military support the sultan enjoyed until his natural death, for instance).

Perhaps the decision which did most, in the long term, to undermine the sultan of Dihlī's authority was Muḥammad b. Tughluḳ's attempt to make Deogir (Dawlatābād [*q.v.*]) a second capital and to settle numbers of Muslims belonging to the ruling *élite* in the Deccan. During the two previous reigns, the temptation among Muslims of the Deccan armies to plot against the Dihlī sultan had been shown to exist. By changing the Khaldjī policy of suzerainty over south India for one of settlement in south India, Muḥammad b. Tughluḳ unintentionally ensured that such temptations would be successful. The relationship of other projects of the sultan—an expedition said to have been aimed at the conquest of Khurāsān, but probably at the seizure of Peshāwar or Ghaznī (Baranī's geographical statements are vague and uncorroborated, while ʿIṣāmī speaks of a Pes͟hāwar expedition about the same date), a disastrous campaign against Ḳarāčil in the Kumāon-Gaṙhwāl region of the Himālayan foothills, the issue of token currency [see DĀR AL-ḌARB]—to the many rebellions has not been satisfactorily established. It was perhaps important that the Dihlī-Dōʾāb area was afflicted by a disastrous famine in 736/1335-6. In all, Muḥammad b. Tug͟hluḳ was called upon to put down twenty-two rebellions, the most important of which, as resulting in a permanent loss of hegemony, were in Maʿbar (735/1334-5), Gulbargā (740/1339), Warangal (746/ 1345-6) and Deogir, which led to the proclamation, in 748/1347, of an independent sultanate under ʿAlāʾ al-Dīn Bahman S͟hāh [see BAHMANIDS]. Muḥammad b. Tug͟hluḳ died near Ṫhaṫṫhā while in pursuit of one Tag͟hī, a Turkish rebel, who had taken refuge with the Sammas of Sind. It is noteworthy that tradition in *ṣūfī* or *ṣūfī*-influenced writing is generally hostile to Muḥammad b. Tug͟hluḳ. (He is known to have welcomed a pupil of Ibn Taymiyya to his court (see K. A. Nizami, *Some aspects of k͟hānqah life in medieval India*, in *Stud. Isl.*, viii, 1957, 69).)

Muḥammad's successor, his cousin Fīrūz b. Rad͟jab, selected by the army in Sind, was apparently *persona grata* to the *ṣūfīs* of the time; the extant accounts of the reign are mainly panegyrical and in the *manāḳib* idiom; they depict him as pious and benevolent, shunning war and devoting himself to building. Nevertheless, before old age came upon him, he seems to have been no more pacific than Dihlī sultans usually were. He led expeditions to Lakhnawtī in 754/1353-4 and in 760/1359, followed by a foray into D͟jād͟jnagar in 761/1360 and Nagarkoṫ 762/1361. Other campaigns followed to Ṫhaṫṫha in 767-8/1366-7, Etāwā in 779/1377 and Katehar in 782/1380. Fīrūz S͟hāh Tug͟hluḳ did however refrain, despite an invitation, about 767/1366, from disaffected leaders in the Bahmanī sultanate, from attempting to recover Dihlī's former possessions south of the Narbadā. The impression of prosperity and contentment among all sections of the population given in ʿAfīf's *Taʾrīk͟h-i Fīrūz S͟hāhī* was probably heightened by the contrast with the period after Tīmūr's incursion into Hindūstān, when the work was written.

Perhaps Fīrūz's longevity (he died in 790/1388) had removed all restraint from the frustrated ambitions of his descendants, for after his death his sons and grandsons fell to struggling for the throne without regard for the consequences for the sultanate. By 796/1393-4, there were two would-be sultans, Maḥmūd, son of Muḥammad the third son of Fīrūz S͟hāh Tug͟hluḳ, with headquarters in old Dihlī, and Nuṣrat K͟hān, son of Fatḥ K͟hān the eldest son of Fīrūz, with headquarters in Fīrūzābād, the new capital built by Fīrūz S͟hāh Tug͟hluḳ to the north-east of old Dihlī. It was not surprising that the *muḳtaʿ*s of the provinces seized their opportunity to become independent or to raise their terms for supporting one or other of the contestants.

Upon a scene of political disintegration burst Tīmūr's invading army. Crossing the Indus in Muḥarram 801/September 1398, capturing Bhatnagar but by-passing Dīpālpur and Sāmāna, Tīmūr defeated the forces of Sulṭān Maḥmūd before Dihlī and occupied and sacked Dihlī itself. The consequent political anarchy is reflected in the purely local scale of the events recorded in the histories of the period. The possessor of Dihlī itself became merely one of many military chiefs, both Muslim and Hindū, struggling to widen the area in north India from which they drew revenue, or to increase their military following. Some of Dihlī's former officers succeeded in assuming complete independence of Dihlī. In 808/1406 Hūs͟hang S͟hāh put the seal on his father Dilāwar K͟hān's independent rule in Mālwā with a proclamation of an independent sultanate; in 810/1407 Ẓafar K͟hān did the same in Gud͟jarāt. In the east, the area of Awadh and Tirhut became the centre of the independent power of D͟jawnpur under the eunuch Malik Sarwar (D͟jawnpur appears to have become formally independent of Dihlī in 803/1400). K͟hāndes͟h in the valley of the Tāptī, Kālpī and Mahoba in eastern Rād͟jāsthān also became independent in the period immediately after Tīmūr's invasion.

Dihlī itself, a capital city without an empire, came in 817/1414 into the possession of the 'Sayyid' K͟hiḍr K͟hān, governor of Multān, Maḥmūd, the last of the Tug͟hluḳs, having died the previous year. He lay claim to a title no higher than Rāyāt-i Aʿlā and, according to the *Taʾrīk͟h-i Muḥammadī*, (B.M. Or. 137, folios 311b-312a) acknowledged the suzerainty of S͟hāh Ruk͟h, Tīmūr's son. K͟hiḍr K͟hān and his 'Sayyid' successors, Mubārak S͟hāh (824-37/1421-34) and Muḥammad b. Farīd (837-49/1434-45) were obliged to play the part of provincial rulers, struggling with the Rāys of Katehar, Etāwā, Čandwar, Bayānā, Gwāliyār for the acknowledgment of suzerainty by the payment of tribute. The possession of Dihlī and its historic claims was worth so little at this time that in 855/1451 the last of the Sayyids, ʿAlāʾ al-Dīn ʿĀlam S͟hāh, peacefully relinquished Dihlī to the Lōdī Afg͟hān, Bahlūl, contenting himself until his death in 883/1478 with possession of the district of Badāʾūn, a possession which, illustrative of the particularist outlook of the time, Bahlūl was equally prepared peacefully to allow.

There are now extant no records strictly contemporary with the Lōdī period of the sultanate; moreover some authors in Mug͟hal times tend to romanticize the Lōdīs under the influence of pro-Afg͟hān sentiment. It is incontrovertible that considerable Afg͟hān immigration into India occurred (it is said with the deliberate encouragement of Bahlūl) and that during Bahlūl's reign (855-94/1451-89), the Loḥānis, the Sūrs, the Sarwānīs, the Niyāzīs and the Karranīs come into prominence as settlers in India.

Bahlūl Lōdī was the grandson of Malik Bahrām who had migrated to Multān during the reign of Fīrūz S͟hāh Tug͟hluḳ. Bahlūl succeeded his uncle Malik Sulṭān S͟hāh as governor of Sirhind and acquired Lahore becoming *K͟hān-i K͟hānān* under Muḥammad b. Farīd. He was invited to take over at Dihlī by Ḥamīd K͟hān, the *wāzīr* of ʿAlāʾ al-Dīn ʿĀlam S͟hāh. Bahlūl succeeded in widening the area of Dihlī's influence. He pacified the Dōʾāb, reduced Etāwā, Čandwar and Rewārī and, in 856/1452, defeated an attempt by sultan Maḥmūd S͟harḳī of D͟jawnpur to seize Dihlī itself. Another attempt by sultan Ḥusayn S͟hāh in 880/1475 was also defeated. Desultory warfare between Dihlī and D͟jawnpur continued until, in 884/1479 Bahlūl succeeded in occupying D͟jawnpur itself and seating his son Bārbak S͟hāh on the throne. Much of Bahlūl's success is attributed to his dexterous handling of his Afg͟hān *amīrs*; he is reputed to have avoided any extreme assertion of the authority of the sultanate and to have limited his demands upon his *d͟jāgīrdārs* to military service.

Bahlūl's third son, Niẓām Khān (Sikandar Lōdī), was preferred as successor by the Afghān chiefs. Sikandar completed the incorporation of Djawnpur into the Dihlī kingdom, deposing Bārbak Shāh, and campaigned in Bihār where the fugitive Ḥusayn Shāh had taken refuge. In order to control the Etāwā, Koyl, Gwāliyār and Dholpur areas more effectively, he founded Āgra in 910/1504, but the latter years of his reign (894-923/1489-1517) saw incessant military activity in this region.

His successor, Ibrāhīm (923-32/1517-26), was soon faced by a Loḥānī and Farmūlī revolt under the nominal leadership of Djāl Khān, a younger brother, in Djawnpur and Bihār where the tradition of independence of Dihlī at that time was still strong. Although Ibrāhīm enjoyed some successes, Dawlat Khān, governor of the Pandjāb appealed to the Mughal Bābur at Kābul to intervene in Hindūstān, as also did ʿĀlam Khān, Ibrāhīm's uncle who claimed Dihlī for himself. Bābur, proving more adept at using them than they at using him, marched on Dihlī to defeat and kill Ibrāhīm Lodī at Pānīpat in Radjab 932/April 1526. But this victory merely established Bābur as one of the serious contenders for empire in Hindūstān. The Afghāns melted into the countryside or withdrew into Bihār out of Bābur's immediate reach, waiting on events and by no means reconciled to Mughal supremacy.

The Afghān sultanate of Dihlī was temporarily restored by Shīr Shāh Sūr and his son Islām Shāh. Farīd Khān's (Shīr Shāh's) grandfather had migrated to Hindūstān during the reign of Bahlūl Lōdī; his father Miyān Ḥasan Khān receiving under Sikandar Lōdī the *parganas* of Sahsarām, Ḥādjīpur and Kharpur Tānda near Banāras in *djāgīr* for the maintenance of 500 horsemen. Shīr Shāh, who was born about 1472 (see P. Saran, *The date and place of Sher Shāh's birth*, in *Journal of the Bihar and Orissa Research Society*, xx, 1934, 108-22, and Ishwari Prasad, *Life and times of Humayun*, Calcutta 1955, 96 *fn.*) was given the management of his father's *parganas* about 917/1511. Losing them to his half-brother Sulaymān, in 933/1527 he took service with Bābur only to leave him the following year to place himself under Bahar Khān Loḥānī who had set himself up as Sultan Muḥammad Shāh in southern Bihār. In 936/1529, after Muḥammad Shāh's death, Shīr Khān ruled in co-operation with Dudū, the mother of the boy successor Djalāl Khān. Shīr Khān temporarily lost his position in Bihār to the Lōdī claimant Maḥmūd b. Sikandar Lōdī. His rivals were however discomfited by the Mughal Humāyūn at the battle of Dawra 937/1531, with the help of Shīr Khān's neutrality. His spirited defence of Čunār rallied the Afghāns of Bihār around him and he consolidated his position in Bihār by defeating an invasion by the forces of the Bengal ruler Maḥmūd Shāh at Suradjgarh in 940/1534. Counter-attacking, by Dhu 'l-Ḳaʿda 944/April 1538, the sultanate of Bengal was at his feet with the occupation of the capital Gawr.

Alarmed at the rise of Shīr Khān, Humāyūn moved eastward from Āgra in Ṣafar 944/July 1537 only to waste six months besieging Čunār. Losing an opportunity to secure Shīr Khān's submission as a tributary, Humāyūn marched on to Bengal only to meet defeat at Čawnsa in Ṣafar 946/June 1539. He was again defeated near Kanawdj in Muḥarram 947/May 1540 and forced to flee to Lahore and then via Multān to Sind from whence he eventually made his way to Ḳazwīn.

Shīr Shāh secured his position in the west by occupying the Pandjāb, founding a stronghold, Rohtās, near Balināth; Multān was also occupied in 950/1543. Shīr Shāh took up Dihlī's perennial struggle with the Rādjpūts with the capture of Rāysen in 950/1543 and campaigns against Mārwār in 950-1/1544. He was killed while besieging Kālindjar in Rabīʿ I 952/May 1545.

His successor, Islām Shāh Sūr (952-60/1545-53), the younger son of Shīr Shāh, though far from adroit in handling the Afghān chiefs, managed to hold Shīr Shāh's dominions together until his death. He is criticized by later Afghān writers for attempting to curb the powers of the *djāgīrdārs*.

On his death the throne was seized by Mubāriz Khān, a nephew of Shīr Shāh who took the title of Muḥammad ʿĀdil Shāh. This was the signal for the collapse of any unifying authority in the area of the Dihlī sultanate. Tādj Khān Karranī in Gwāliyār, Ibrahīm Khān Sūr, Aḥmad Khān Sūr in Lahore and Muḥammad Khān Sūr in Bengal threw off their allegiance. Upon this scene of political confusion Humāyūn re-entered in 962/1555, occupying Lahore in Rabīʿ II 962/February 1555, defeating the Afghāns at Sirhind in Shaʿbān 962/June 1555 and entering Dihlī the following month. It was not however until after Humāyūn's death (Rabīʿ I 963/January 1556) that the Mughal victory at Pānīpat over Hemū, the Hindū general of Muḥammad ʿĀdil Shāh, guaranteed that the Mughals would not be expelled from India again.

Under Akbar, the Dihlī sultanate merged imperceptibly into the Mughal empire, distinguished from that empire less by the character of its institutions (for Akbar built more upon Khaldjī and Tughluḳ foundations than his panegyrists acknowledge) than by the narrower extent of its authority, its failure to guard the north-west marches and its failure to hold Rādjāsthān for any appreciable period.

Despite the rhetoric of Muslim historians of the period and the undoubted achievements of the Khaldjīs and the early Tughluḳs, the Dihlī sultanate made no violent break with the later Rādjpūt political tradition that rulers in Hindūstān sought paramountcy rather than sovereignty, that is, acknowledgment of their superior rights in the spheres of military service and revenue enjoyment rather than a general control over the people at large. This is hardly surprising when it is remembered that at no time did the Turks and the Afghāns succeed in reducing the Hindū chiefs to disarmed impotence. The panegyrics of Muslim historians require correction by the inscriptional evidence cited, for example, in H. C. Ray, *The dynastic history of Northern India*, i, Calcutta 1931, 544-7, 565; ii, Calcutta 1936, 729-35, 908, 1096-1103, 1132-4, 1190-5 (see also *Cambridge History of India*, iii, *Turks and Afghans*, Chapter xx), which shows clearly that the Rādjpūt clans remained politically active away from the principal centres of Turkish military occupation; the emergence of the Hindū chiefs into prominence in the 9th/15th century is explicable only on the basis that they had been there all the time, concealed from view by the earlier Muslim historians. It is important to recall that except for a short period under the Khaldjīs and Tughluḳs, Rādjāsthān was generally independent of Dihlī. Moreover the Ghūrid conquest of Hindūstān was undertaken by a military *élite* of Turks, Khaldjīs and Afghāns, accustomed at home to a predatory relationship with the economically productive sections of the population but leaving them a large measure of autonomy in law and custom. Although there was a large and continuing (though imperfectly documented) migration of Muslims to India during the sultanate period, it was largely a movement of professional classes and did not involve economic and social displacement of the mass of the Hindū population. The bulk of the Muslim 'working' population consisted of converts made in the group or the products of intermarriage and concubinage. Neither their own political traditions nor their political necessities would suggest more than the minimum interference, political and administrative, by the Muslim conquerors with the principal unit of Indian social life, the village community. (It is probable that the Muslim *d̲j̲āgīrdārī* contingents living in the villages near the larger towns had some social and cultural impact upon the local population).

The relations of the Dihlī sultanate with the Hindū population were dominated usually by considerations of policy rather than of religion. Hindū chiefs were acceptable as tributaries and Hindū cultivators as tax-payers. Hindū clerical assistance in leyying the land revenue and Hindū bankers' services in providing sultans with ready cash were indispensable. The description of the place of the Rād̲j̲pūts at Muḥammad b. Tug̲h̲luḳ's court by Ibn Baṭṭūṭa, following upon K̲h̲ald̲j̲ī marriages with Rād̲j̲pūt families, suggests that Akbar's policy of conciliating the Rād̲j̲pūts was not without precedent in the sultanate period. It cannot be regarded as established, without question, that the sultans of Dihlī normally levied *d̲j̲izya* as a discriminatory tax on non-Muslims as such. It is suggested that many statements in Indo-Muslim historians to that effect may be discounted as attempts to depict, for the comfort and edification of the pious, an ideal Muslim ruler. Moreover, where the terms *k̲h̲arād̲j̲* and *d̲j̲izya* are found together, it is suggested that they are being used as conventional legal terms, with emotive intent, for what was in fact the tribute or land revenue customarily paid to a paramount power. In support of this latter hypothesis, it may be noted that in his *Fatāwa-yi D̲j̲ahāndārī*, Ḍiyāʾ al-Dīn Baranī speaks of Hindū Rāys taking *k̲h̲arād̲j̲* and *d̲j̲izya* from Hindū *mus̲h̲rik*s and *kāfir*s (India Office Library MS. 1149, f. 119a). However, for a contrary (and indeed the more usual) view of this very controversial question, see, *e.g.*, Ishwari Prasad, *History of mediaeval India*, 475-6; A. L. Srivastava, *The sultanate of Delhi*, Agra 1950, 443-5; and *The advanced history of India*, index, *s.v. jizya*, 1051.

The Muslim ruling *élite* was ethnically heterogeneous. Turks from the steppe, Afg̲h̲āns and K̲h̲ald̲j̲īs were dominant until Balban's time, but Hindū converts soon made their appearance in important offices (see P. Saran, *Politics and personalities in the reign of Nasir-uddin Mahmud, the Slave*, in *Studies in medieval Indian history*, Delhi 1952) and later, under the K̲h̲ald̲j̲īs and Tug̲h̲luḳs, sometimes played a dominant rôle (*e.g.*, Malik Kāfūr, K̲h̲usraw K̲h̲ān Barwārī and K̲h̲ān-i D̲j̲āhān Maḳbūl, *wazīr* of Fīrūz S̲h̲āh Tug̲h̲luḳ). Muḥammad b. Tug̲h̲luḳ was reported to have encouraged Muslims to come to India to take service under him. As in Mug̲h̲al times, the Indian-born Muslim of Hindū stock did not enjoy the same prestige as did descendants of the original conquerors or Muslim immigrants. Although Ḳuṭb al-Dīn Aybak, Iletmis̲h̲ and Balban, their principal commanders and *muḳtaʿ*s, and the K̲h̲ald̲j̲ī favourites Malik Kāfūr and K̲h̲usraw K̲h̲ān, began as slaves in the royal household, the position of slaves in administration and war under Dihlī followed the G̲h̲aznawid and Sāmānid precedents. Slavery was not the only or indeed the principal road to power; slaves formed merely one source of recruitment to the ruling *élite*.

The headquarters administration of the Dihlī sultanate followed familiar Sāmānid and G̲h̲aznawid lines. The *wakīl-i dār* and the *amīr-i ḥād̲j̲ib* were to be found managing the sultan's household and regulating access to him; the *wazīr*, the *ʿāriḍ-i mamālik*, the *barīd-i mamālik* and the *ḳāḍī al-mamālik* appear to have exercised broadly the same functions as under the Sāmānids and G̲h̲aznawids.

The administrative, the military and the salary *iḳṭāʿāt* (cf. A. K. S. Lambton, *Landlord and Peasant in Persia*, London 1953, 61-64), are clearly discernible under the Dihlī sultanate. The provincial governor, in the period from Balban to Fīrūz S̲h̲āh Tug̲h̲luḳ, *wālī* or *muḳtaʿ* was an official, transferable at will, commanding the local military forces and paid personally by the grant of a revenue assignment or by a percentage of the provincial revenues. He was supposed to remit the revenue, surplus to local expenditure, to headquarters, where a record was kept of the numbers of the provincial contingents and the anticipated revenue. This system broke down after the Tug̲h̲luḳs when the distinction between the administrative and the military *iḳṭāʿ* became blurred, governors became semi-independent tributaries with their own private armies, and the process of revenue audit also became spasmodic. The military assignment, or grant of the revenue from villages for the recruitment and upkeep of a body of cavalry, is reported to have existed under Balban; ʿAlāʾ al-Dīn K̲h̲ald̲j̲ī is said to have resumed many such assignments and to have paid his soldiers in cash. An Arabic source (*Masālik al-abṣār fī mamālik al-amṣār* of S̲h̲ihāb al-Dīn al-ʿUmarī, trans. Otto Spies *etc.*, *Muslim University Journal*, Aligarh, March, 1943, 28-9) written in Egypt during the reign of Muḥammad b. Tug̲h̲luḳ states that the troops of the Dihlī sultan were paid in cash from the *dīwān*. The encomiast ʿAfīf clearly indicates that during the time of Fīrūz S̲h̲āh Tug̲h̲luḳ the military assignment was common, though there are passages which suggest that the assignee was not always allowed the personal management of his assignment. In the 'Sayyid' and Lōdī periods payment of troops by the grant of *d̲j̲āgīr*s or assignments, which the *d̲j̲agīrdār* managed himself and over which the sultan's *dīwān* exercised minimal supervision, was usual. It is clear that there was throughout the sultanate period a tension between the sultan, like ʿAlāʾ al-Dīn K̲h̲ald̲j̲ī, with a preference for an extension of the *k̲h̲āliṣa* land, or area under direct revenue administration from which the troops could be paid in cash, and the Muslim military class with a preference for assignments which they managed themselves. Neither the sultan nor the military class ever wholly succeeded in obtaining their wishes throughout the whole area of the sultanate. Probably ʿAlāʾ al-Dīn K̲h̲ald̲j̲ī succeeded more in managing the assigned areas than in abolishing all such grants of revenue. The accounts of S̲h̲īr S̲h̲āh give a vivid picture of the opportunities open to a *d̲j̲āgīrdār* or military assignee in the Afg̲h̲ān period to become the *de facto* ruler of the area of the *d̲j̲āgīr* and aspire to a provincial sultanate or even to the throne of Dihlī itself. S̲h̲īr S̲h̲āh did not himself, as sultan, abolish *d̲j̲āgīrdār*s but set a limit to their influence by maintaining a large army recruited by himself and financed by a more extensive *k̲h̲āliṣa* area.

Evidence on the sub-organization of a province

(*iḳṭāʿ* or *wilāyat*)—which in any event denoted that area around the principal town which the *wālī* or *muḳṭaʿ* could control rather than a clearly defined administrative area—is scanty. There are references to *shiḳḳdār*s in the time of Muḥammad b. Tughluḳ and *fawdjdār*s rather later; these probably represented military commands subordinate to the *wālī* or *muḳṭaʿ* rather than regular heads of a definite administrative subdistrict. Shīr Shāh is said however to have appointed *shiḳḳdār-i shiḳḳdārān* to the unit known as the *sarkār* under the Mughals. The existence of the *pargana* or *ḳaṣaba* as a revenue district of a number of villages is well attested. Shīr Shāh is said to have appointed a *shiḳḳdār* and an *amīn* to each *pargana* to control the police and the revenue aspects of its work respectively. Below the *pargana* was the village community with which the Muslim official dealt through its *muḳaddam* or headman and *paṭwārī* or village accountant. In the 9th/15th century *shiḳḳ* is sometimes used to denote a province — a sign perhaps of the smaller political scale of that period.

In the collection of the land revenue, the Dihlī sultanate, its revenue officers and assignees, did not depart seriously from the principles and practices of the pre-Muslim period—of demanding a proportion of the gross produce of the soil assessed either by sharing the harvest (*ḥukm-i ḥāṣil*), by estimating its probable yield (*ḥukm-i mushāhada*) or by measurement of the area under cultivation and assessment according to a standard rate of demand per unit area according to the crop sown (*ḥukm-i misāḥat*). For the best account of the known changes and permutations in the sultanate period, see W. H. Moreland, *The agrarian system of Moslem India*, Cambridge 1929; see also ḌARĪBA, 6(a).

Bibliography: In addition to references in the text: — Materials in Persian and Arabic: Storey, 68, 71-8, 90, 92-104, 107-8, 283-7, 433-50, 493-516, 529-40, 1310-3. To the editions there listed add: — Amīr Khusraw, *Miftāḥ al-futūḥ*, ed. Shaykh Abdur Rashid, Aligarh 1954; Abdullah, *Taʾrīkh-i Dāwūdī*, ed. Shaykh Abdur Rashid, Aligarh 1954; *Taʾrīkh-i Fīrūz Shāhī-yi Ḍiyāʾ al-Dīn Baranī*, i, ed. Shaykh Abdur Rashid, Aligarh 1957; ʿIṣāmī, *Futūḥ al-Salāṭīn*, ed. A. S. Usha, Madras 1948; ʿAbd Allāh Muḥammad b. ʿUmar al-Makkī, *Zafar al-Wālih bi Muẓaffar wa Ālih*, ed. as *An Arabic history of Gujarat* by E. Denison Ross, three vols., London 1910, 1921 & 1928—see index under the various sultans of Dihlī; al-Ḳalḳashandī, *Ṣubḥ al-aʿshā*, trans. Otto Spies, *An Arabic account of India in the 14th Century*; Stuttgart 1936; Ibn Baṭṭūṭa, *Riḥla*, English translation by Mahdī Husayn of the part relating to India, Baroda 1953); Sir Henry M. Elliot and J. Dowson, *The history of India as told by its own historians*, vols. ii-v, London 1869-73. See also reprint of vol. ii with introduction, commentary and additional bibl. by Muhammad Habib, Shaykh Abdur Rashid and Khaliq Ahmad Nizami, Aligarh 1952. S. H. Hodīvālā, *Studies in Indo-Muslim history*, two vols. Bombay 1939 and 1957, is an indispensable commentary upon Elliot and Dowson; P. Hardy, *Historians of medieval India*, London 1960. Articles on the sources not given in Pearson, below, include: K. Z. Ashrafyan, *"Tarikh-i Firuz Shakhi" Afifa kak istoričeskii istočnik*, (ʿAfīf's 'Taʾrīkh-i Fīrūz Shāhī' as an historical source) *Učenie Zapiski Instituta Vostokovedeniya*, xviii, 1957, 407-41; K. A. Nizami, *The so-called autobiography of Sultan Mohammad bin Tughluq*, in *Studies in medieval Indian history*, Aligarh 1956, 76-85; Mahdi Husayn, *Critical study of the sources for the history of India 1320-1526*, in *IC*, xxxi, 4, October, 1957, 314-21; P. Hardy, *The Oratio Recta of Baranī s Taʾrīkh-i Fīrūz Shāhī—fact or fiction?* in *BSOAS*, xx, 1957, 315-21; idem, '*The Tarikh-i Muhammadi by Muhammad Bihamad Khani*, in *Essays presented to Sir Jadunath Sarkar*, ed. Hari Ram Gupta, Hoshiarpur 1958, 181-90; S. M. Imamuddin, *Some Persian literary sources of the Afghan history of India*, in *IC*, 1, Jan. 1959, 39-49.

General Aids: Pearson, pp. 620-7 *passim*, 629-33, 305-10 *passim* (epigraphy), 319-21 *passim* (numismatics); C. R. Singhal, *Index to the numismatic Supplements xxxiii to xlvii* (*Articles* 200-350) *in the JRASB 1919-1938*, in *JRASB*, third series iii, 1937, Numismatic Supplement xlvii, i-xiv; E. Thomas, *The chronicles of the Pathān kings of Dehli*, London, 1871; J. Tod, *Annals and antiquities of Rajasthan*, ed. W. Crooke, three vols., Oxford 1920. An Ottoman account of the Sultans of Dihlī will be found in the universal history of Munedjdjimbashī (d. 1113/1702). (Turkish version, *Ṣaḥāʾif al-akhbār*, Istanbul 1285/1868, ii, 602-6, iii, 121-30. The Arabic original is still unpublished).

Monographs and Articles not listed in Pearson: A. B. M. Habibullah, *The foundation of Muslim rule in India*, Lahore 1945; M. A. Ahmad, *Political history and institutions of the early Turkish empire of Delhi*, (*1206-1290 A.D.*), Lahore 1949; (ed.) R. C. Majumdar, *The struggle for empire* (*History and culture of the Indian people*, v), Bombay 1957; K. A. Nizami, *The religious life and leanings of Iltutmish*, in *Studies in medieval Indian history*, Aligarh 1956, 15-47; S. L. Rathor, *A plea against the charge of usurpation by Iltutmish*, in *IC*, xxxii, 4, Oct. 1958, 262-7; P. Saran, *Politics and personalities in the reign of Nasir uddin Mahmud, the Slave*, in *Studies in medieval Indian history*, Delhi 1952; K. A. Nizami, *Balban, the regicide*, in *Studies in medieval Indian history*, Aligarh 1956, 48-62; K. S. Lal, *History of the Khaljis, 1290-1320*, Allāhābād 1950; P. L. Gupta, *The coinage of the Khilji sultans of Delhi*, in *Journal of the Numismatic Society of India*, xix, 1, 1957, 35-47; N. Venkataramanya, *The early Muslim expansion in South India*, Madras 1942; A. L. Srivastava, *Historicity of Deval Rani Khizr Khan*, in *IC*, xxx, 1, Jan. 1956; E. E. Oliver, *The Chagatāi Mughals*, in *JRAS*, new series xx, 1888, 72-128; R. Grousset, *L'Empire Mongol 1re phase* (*Histoire du monde publié sous le direction de M. F. Cavaignac*, iii) Paris 1941, *appendice, Khanat de Djaghatai et Inde*, 364-74; Dasaratha Sharma, *New light on Alāʾuddin Khaljī's achievements*, in *IHQ*, xxxii, 1956, 96-8; Ishwari Prasad, *A history of the Qaraunah Turks in India*, Allāhābād 1936; Agha Mahdi Husayn, *Rise and fall of Muḥammad bin Tughluq*, London 1938; Mawlāna ʿAbd al-Raḥmān, *Muḥammad Shāh ibn Tughluk*, (Urdū), in *Oriental College Magazine* Lahore iii, 1, 1926 and iii, 2, 3 & 4, 1927; A. Rahim, *The nature of the Afghan monarchy and the position of the Afghan chiefs*, in *JPak.HS*, iv, 2, April, 1956, 116-32, and *Islam Shah Sur*, in *JPakHS*, iv, 4, Oct., 1956; S. M. Imamuddin, *The nature of Afghan monarchy in India*, in *IC*, xxxii, 4, Oct., 1958, 268-75; M. M. Nagar, *On some Moham-*

madan coins in the State Museum Lucknow, in *Journal of the Numismatic Society of India*, xx, pt. ii, 1958, 202; N. B. Roy, *Anecdotes of Sher Shah, from the manuscript of Tarikh-i Daudi*, in *IC*, xxxii, 4, Oct., 1958, 250-61; *some interesting anecdotes of Sher Shah from the rare Persian MS. of Tazkirat-ul muluk*, in *JASB*, (Letters), xx, 2, 1954, 219-26. Kalikaranjan Qanungo, *Sher Shah*, Calcutta 1921.

Political Institutions. See Pearson, for periodical articles arranged under dynasties. R. P. Tripathi, *Some aspects of Muslim administration*, Allāhābād 1936; I. H. Qureshi, *The administration of the sultanate of Dehli*, Lahore 1942, third ed. Lahore 1958; W. H. Moreland, *The agrarian system of Moslem India*, Cambridge 1929; M. B. Ahmad, *The administration of justice in medieval India*, Aligarh 1941; Agha Mahdi Husayn, *Le gouvernement du sultanat de Delhi*, Paris 1936; Ibn Hasan, *The central structure of the Mughal empire*, London 1936, 41-51; P. Saran, *The provincial government of the Mughals (1526-1658)*, Allahabad 1941, 26-63; Satesh Chandra Misra, *Administrative systems of the Surs (Shīr Shāh and his successors)*, in *IC*, xxxi, 4, Oct., 1957, 322-34; K. Z. Ashrafyan, *K istorii razvitiya lennoi sistemi v Deliiskom Sultanate v. XIV v.* (The history of the development of feudal land ownership in the Dihlī Sultanate in the fourteenth century), in *SO*, iv, 1957, 51-62; A. K. Bhattacharyya, *Some agricultural and irrigational activities of the Muslim rulers in medieval India*, in *Indo-Iranica*, ix, 3, 1956, 69-71.

General Works. J. Mill, *The history of British India*, i, London 1817; Mountstuart Elphinstone, *The history of India*, two vols., London 1841; J. Talboys Wheeler, *The history of India*, iv, pt. *i*, *Mussulman Rule*, London 1876; S. Lane-Poole, *Mediaeval India under Mohammedan rule*, London 1903; V. A. Smith, *Oxford history of India*, third ed., P. Spear, Oxford 1958; Ishwari Prasad, *History of mediaeval India*, first ed., Allahabad 1925; ed. Sir Wolseley Haig, *Cambridge history of India, iii, Turks and Afghans*, 1928; J. C. Powell Price, *A history of India*, London 1955; S. R. Sharma, *Studies in medieval Indian history*, Sholapur 1956; Ḳārī Muḥammad Bas̲h̲īr al-Dīn Pandit, *Taʾrīk̲h̲-i Hindī-i Ḳurūn-i wusṭā* (Urdū), Aligarh 1949; Yusuf Hikmet Bayur, *Hindistan tarihi* (in Turkish), i, Ankara 1946; R. C. Majumdar, H. C. Raychaudhuri & Kalikinkar Datta, *An advanced history of India*, London 1948; R. C. Majumdar (ed.), *The Delhi Sultanate*, Bhāratīya Vidya Bhavan, Bombay 1960; Awadh Bihari Pandey, *The first Afghan empire in India (1451-1526)*, Calcutta 1956; Muhammad Abdur Rahim, *History of the Afghans in India A.D. 1545-1631* with especial reference to their relations with the Mughals; K. A. Nizami, *Some aspects of religion and politics in India during the 13th century*, Aligarh 1961; Olaf Caroe, *The Pathans 550 B.C.-A.D. 1957*, London 1958, 124-50. (P. Hardy)

DIHLĪ SULTANATE, ART. With the exception of the coinage [see sikka] and a very few ceramic fragments (a few described in J. Ph. Vogel, *Catalogue of the Dehli museum of archaeology*, Calcutta 1908; for the pottery fragments of the ʿĀdilābād excavations see H. Waddington, in *Ancient India*, i, 60-76), the only body of material for the study of the art of the Dihlī sultanate is monumental. Most of the monuments are in Dihlī itself and are described s.v. dihlī. The remainder are mostly described under the appropriate topographical headings, and are listed here in more or less chronological order.

The first major undertaking outside Dihlī was at Ad̲j̲mēr [*q.v.*], where Ḳuṭb al-Dīn Aybak built the mosque, known as Aṛhāʾī din kā d̲j̲hōmpṛā ("Hut of two-and-a-half days"), at about the same time as the Masd̲j̲id Ḳuwwat al-Islām at Dihlī, to which Iletmis̲h̲ added a *maḳṣūra* screen as he had done to the Dihlī example. Other buildings attributed to Iletmis̲h̲ include a large masonry tank, the Ḥawḍ-i S̲h̲amsī, and an *ʿidgāh* and mosque at Badāʾūn [*q.v.*]; for the last, one of the largest mosques in India, see J. F. Blakiston, *The Jami Masjid at Badaun and other buildings in the United Provinces* (= *Memoir ASI*, xix), Calcutta 1926, and Cunningham, *ASI*, xi, 1880. In Nagawr [*q.v.*] is a fine gateway, the Atarkin kā darwāza, c. 627/1230, and at Bayānā, about 80 km. south-west of Āgra, is a mosque made out of temple spoil with corbelled arches similar to those of the Dihlī mosque; known as the Ukhā mandir, it was later reconverted to temple use. Of the time of Balban is a *mīnār* at Koyl (see ʿalīgaṛh), demolished in 1862, described in *ʿAligarh Gazetteer*, v, 218.

Noteworthy buildings of the K̲h̲ald̲j̲ī dynasty include the bridge over the Gambērī river at Čitawr built by ʿAlāʾ al-Dīn in c. 703/1303, and the Ukhā masd̲j̲id of Ḳuṭb al-Dīn Mubārak (716-20/1316-20) at Bayānā, with colonnades of temple pillars but typical K̲h̲ald̲j̲ī arches with their "spear-head" fringe.

G̲h̲iyāt̲h̲ al-Dīn Tug̲h̲luḳ's buildings after his accession were confined to Dihlī; for his previous buildings see multān. His son, Muḥammad b. Tug̲h̲luḳ, carried the Dihlī craftsmen south to Dawlatābād [*q.v.*], whence the Dihlī style spread to the Deccan (see bahmanis, monuments). Fīrūz S̲h̲āh Tug̲h̲luḳ was responsible for the early buildings of the towns of D̲j̲awnpur, Fatḥābād, Ḥiṣār and Lalitpur [*qq.v.*], and the last Tug̲h̲luḳ, Maḥmūd S̲h̲āh, for the D̲j̲āmiʿ masd̲j̲id at Irič [*q.v.*], the arches of which anticipate the recession of planes characteristic of the Lōdīs (there is not general agreement about the date of this building; the interpretation of Blakiston, *op. cit.*, seems the most plausible).

The Lōdī dynasty's buildings outside Dihlī are mainly at Āgra, Kālpī, Lalitpur, and Hansī, [*qq.v.*], to which must be added the fine tomb of Muḥammad G̲h̲awt̲h̲ at Gwāliyar [*q.v.*], of c. 972/1564, which is Lōdī in spirit if not in date. The Čawrāsī Gumbad at Kālpī is said to be the mausoleum of one of the Lōdī sultans, who is not further identified (cf. Blakiston, *op. cit.*).

For the buildings of the Sūrī dynasty see especially rōhtās, rōhtāsgaṛh, sahsarām, and the bibliography to bihār.

See also hind, Architecture.

(J. Burton-Page)

DIḤYA (or Daḥya) b. K̲h̲alīfa al-Kalbī, Companion of the Prophet and a somewhat mysterious character. He is traditionally represented as a rich merchant of such outstanding beauty that the Angel Gabriel took his features; and, when he arrived at Medina, all the women (*muʿṣir*, see *LA*, root. *ʿṣr*) came out to see him (Ḳurʾān, LXII, 11, may be an allusion to this occurrence). There is no reason to accept the suggestion put forward by Lammens (*EI*[1], *s.v.*) of some commercial connexion with Muḥammad; we only know that a sudden death put a stop to a projected marriage between a niece of Diḥya and the Prophet, that the latter died just as he was about to marry a sister of the Kalbī and that Diḥya, to whom Ṣafiyya [*q.v.*] had been allotted after the capture of Khaybar, had to renounce her, to receive instead a cousin of the young captive.

After being present, if not at Uḥud, at least at the Khandaḳ, Diḥya commanded a small detachment at the battle of the Yarmūk, but it was his "diplomatic" activities in particular which have been pointed out. As a Kalbī he was bound to have an intimate knowledge of the districts along the Syrian *limes*, and his business allowed him to move freely everywhere without arousing suspicion; for this reason, he was probably used as a secret agent. Tradition however simply reports that, in 6 or 7, he was given the task of conveying to Heraclius a message from the Prophet inviting him to be converted to Islam, and that on his return the caravan was plundered by the Djudhām, against whom Muḥammad was compelled to send Zayd b. Ḥāritha. Several orientalists have noted legendary characteristics in the account of these events and have called into question the authenticity of the letter addressed to Heraclius; M. Hamidullah has recently applied himself to the task of refuting their arguments and even of finding evidence concerning the fate of the original document which may still be in existence (see *Arabica*, 1955/i, 97-110).

After the conquest of Syria, it is surprising that Diḥya should disappear from the scene; one source makes him withdraw to Egypt, but most biographers state that he settled in Damascus (al-Mizza = Mezzé), where he died in the caliphate of Muʿāwiya, in about 50/670.

Bibliography: Djāḥiẓ, *Ḥayawān*, i, 299, vi, 221; Muḥ. b. Ḥabīb, *Muḥabbar*, 65, 75, 90, 93, 121; Ibn Ḳutayba, *Maʿārif*, 114; Ibn Saʿd, *Ṭabaḳāt*, iii/1, 173, iii/2, 52, iv/2, 184-5, viii, 46, 114, 115; Ṭabarī, i, 175 ff., 1741, 2093, 2154, ii, 1836, iii, 2349; Ibn Ḥanbal, *Musnad*, i, 262, ii, 107; Ibn Hishām, *Sīra*, index; Ibn ʿAbd al-Barr, *Istīʿāb*, s.v.; Bakrī, *Muʿdjam*, 530; *Aghānī*, vi, 95; Nawawī, *Tahdhīb*, 239-40; Ibn Ḥadjar, *Iṣāba*, no. 2390; Caetani, *Annali*, s.a. 6; I. Goldziher, *Ẓâhiriten*, 178-9; Buhl, *Das Leben Muhammeds*, 245; *Gesch. des Qor.*, i, 22-4, 186; H. Lammens, *Moavia*, Ier 292-3; Gaudefroy-Demombynes, *Mahomet*, Paris 1957, 74, 180; M. Hamidullah, *Le Prophète de l'Islam*, Paris 1959, 2 vol., index (with complementary bibl.).

(H. LAMMENS-[CH. PELLAT])

DĪK, the cock. The word is perhaps of non-Semitic origin. No cognate synonyms seem to exist in the other Semitic languages, except in modern South Arabian (Leslau, *Lexique soqoṭri*, 1938, 126).

The cock is mentioned quite often in ancient Arabic poems and proverbs and in the *ḥadīth*. In zoological writings it is described as the most sensual and conceited of birds. It is of feeble intelligence, as it cannot find its way to the hen-house when it falls from a wall. Yet it possesses a number of laudable properties: it is courageous and enduring, bold and clever in fighting other cocks and in defending its hens. The numerous hens with which it mates at the same time are treated by it impartially; it apportions to them grains even when hungry itself, its generosity having become proverbial. The best cocks (for eating) are those which do not crow yet. For fecundation a cock of two years should be chosen. Its vigour is recognizable by a round comb, a short mandible, a black pupil of the eye, etc. A good fighting cock is distinguished by its red comb, its thick neck, etc.

The cock lays one small egg in its whole life-time, the cock's egg (*bayḍatu 'l-ʿuḳr*). Its testicles are big; they are tasty and easy to digest. Castrated cocks yield meat fatter and tastier than that of any other animal; yet the Prophet, according to a *ḥadīth*, forbade their castration. When castrated their comb and 'beard' wither. Several kinds of *dīk* with various epithets (*hindī*, *nabaṭī*, *zandjī* etc.) are mentioned in the sources. According to Nuwayrī, the *dīk* in a town of Sind reaches the size of an ostrich.

It is one of the most remarkable characteristics of the cock that it apportions its crowing correctly to the different hours of the night, whether the night is 9 or 15 hours long. People are delighted by its crowing; the sick, when hearing it, feel alleviation of their pains, and even God, according to a *ḥadīth*, likes its voice. The Prophet was fond of white cocks and used to keep one in his house.

There is an angel in the form of a gigantic cock in Paradise, immediately below the throne of Allāh; by his crowing, which is repeated by all the cocks in the world, he announces the hours of prayer (M. Asín Palacios, *La escatologia musulmana en la Divina Comedia*, 2nd ed., Madrid and Granada 1943, 50 ff.; E. Cerulli, *Il "Libro della Scala"*, Vatican City 1949, 98 ff. (§ 69) and plate 4 (opp. 49); R. Ettinghausen, in *Convegno di Scienze Morali Storiche e Filologiche* (XII Convegno "Volta", Rome 1957, 362 f.; J. Berque, *Les Arabes*, Paris 1959, 17.). The Barghawāṭa [*q.v.*] determined the times of their prayers by the call of the cock, and did not eat him (al-Bakrī, ed. de Slane, 139 f.).

Although the *dīk* is the male of the *dadjādja* [*q.v.*] it is treated in most of the sources under a separate heading. Its medicinal properties, however, are mentioned by Ibn al-Bayṭār and Dāwūd al-Anṭākī in the chapters of *dadjādj*. Mainly its flesh and a gravy soup prepared therefrom, its bile, brain, comb and blood were put to medicinal use.

Djāḥiẓ, who mentions quite often a dispute between *ṣāḥib al-dīk* and *ṣāḥib al-kalb*, seems to quote from an anonymous work belonging to that kind of literature which has been treated by Steinschneider in his *Rangstreit-Literatur* (*SBAk. Wien, phil.-hist. Kl.*, 155, Abh. 4, 1908).

Bibliography: Suyūṭī, *K. al-wadīk fī faḍl al-dīk*, Cairo 1322 (Brockelmann, II, 198, and S II, 193, no. 245); Aḥmad b. Aḥmad al-Fayyūmī al-Gharḳāwī, *Al-Ishārāt wa 'l-dalā'il ilā bayān mā fī 'l-dīk min al-ṣifāt wa 'l-faḍā'il* (Brockelmann, S II, 438); ʿAbd al-Ghanī al-Nābulusī, *Taʿṭīr al-anām*, Cairo 1354, i, 219 f.; Abū Ḥayyān al-Tawḥīdī, *Imtāʿ*, i, 144, 187 (transl. Kopf, *Osiris*, xii [1956], index); Damīrī, s.v. (transl. Jayakar, i, 800 ff.); Djāḥiẓ, *Ḥayawān*², index; Ibn al-ʿAwwām, *Filāḥa* (transl. Clément-Mullet), ii/b, 243; Ibn Ḳutayba, *ʿUyūn al-Akhbār*, Cairo 1925-30, ii, 78, 89 (transl. Kopf, 53, 65); Ibshīhī, *Mustaṭraf*, bāb 62, s.v.; Ḳazwīnī (Wüstenfeld), i, 412 f.; al-Mustawfī al-Ḳazwīnī (Stephenson), 71 f.; Nuwayrī, *Nihāyat al-arab*, x, 219 ff.; J. Schacht and M. Meyerhof, *The medico-philosophical controversy between Ibn Butlan of Baghdad and Ibn Ridwan of Cairo*, Cairo 1937, 73 ff., 79 f. (English), 37 f., 44 ff. (Arabic); J. Henninger, *Über Huhnopfer und Verwandtes in Arabien und seinen Randgebieten*, in *Anthropos*, xli-xliv, 1946-9, 337-46.

(L. KOPF)

DĪK AL-DJINN AL-ḤIMṢĪ, surname of the Syrian Arabic poet ʿAbd al-Salām b. Raghbān b.

ʿAbd al-Salām b. Ḥabīb b. ʿAbd Allāh b. Ra<u>gh</u>bān b. Yazīd b. Tamīm. This latter had embraced Islam at Muʾta [*q.v.*] under the auspices of Ḥabīb b. Maslama al-Fihrī [*q.v.*], whose *mawlā* he became. The great-grandfather of the poet, Ḥabīb, who was head of the *dīwān* of salaries under al-Manṣūr, gave his name to a mosque at Ba<u>gh</u>dād, mas<u>dj</u>id Ibn Ra<u>gh</u>bān (al-<u>Dj</u>āḥiẓ, *Bu<u>kh</u>alāʾ*, ed. Ḥā<u>dj</u>irī 327, trans. Pellat, index; al-<u>Dj</u>ah<u>sh</u>iyārī, 102; Le Strange, *Baghdad*, 95). Dīk al-<u>Dj</u>inn, born at Ḥimṣ in 161/777-8, died under the caliphate of al-Mutawakkil, in 235 or 236/849-51, without ever having left Syria. He is said to have had a frivolous and happy-go-lucky disposition. A moderate <u>Sh</u>īʿī, as the elegies on al-Ḥusayn b. ʿAlī b. Abī Ṭālib prove, he was associated particularly with Aḥmad b. ʿAlī al-Hā<u>sh</u>imī and his brother <u>Dj</u>aʿfar, to both of whom he addressed panegyrics. He also composed epigrams and erotic poems in the taste of the times. Arab critics do not recognize any superior talent in him, although his work has largely spread beyond the bounds of his native land. The Ḳayrawānīs of the 5th/11th century however have not failed to extract therefrom a particularly obscure and complicated verse (Ibn Ra<u>sh</u>īḳ, *ʿUmda*, i, 147; Ibn <u>Sh</u>araf, ed. and tr. Pellat, 85; A. Benhamouda, in *Bull. des Ét. Ar.*, March-April 1949, 65). The few fragments which have come down to us are of interest only since the poet upholds the equality of the rights of his compatriots, the Arabized Syrians, with those of the true Arabs, and since he seizes the opportunity to write on the conflicts between the Northern and Southern Arabs.

Bibliography: in addition to the references in the text: *A<u>gh</u>ānī*[1], xii, 142-9 (= Beirut ed., xiv, 49-65); Ibn <u>Kh</u>allikān, no. 394, tr. de Slane, ii, 133); <u>Th</u>aʿālibī, *Yatīma*, i, 66, 172; Goldziher, *Muh. St.*, i, 156; Brockelmann, S I, 137.

(A. SCHAADE-[CH. PELLAT])

DIKKA, or *dikkat al-muballi<u>gh</u>*. During the prayer on Fridays (or feast-days) in the mosque, a participant with a loud voice is charged with the function of *muballi<u>gh</u>*. While saying his prayer he has to repeat aloud certain invocations to the imām, for all to hear. In mosques of any importance he stands on a *dikka*. This is the name given a platform usually standing on columns two to three metres high, situated in the covered part of the mosque between the *miḥrāb* and the court. In Cairo numerous undated platforms are to be found. The oldest dated inscription, with the word *d-k-t*, dates back to Sulṭān Ḳāytbāy (end of the 9th/15th century). Mosques of the Ottoman period have their *dikka* in the form of a rostrum against the wall opposite the *miḥrāb*. Nowadays, a microphone is used to amplify the *muballi<u>gh</u>*'s voice.

The *dikka* should not be confused with the *kursī al-sūra*, the place where the ritual reader of the Ḳurʾān sits cross-legged. The term *dikka* is also used to describe a kind of wooden bench of secular usage.

Bibliography: Van Berchem, *CIA*, *Egypte*, index.

(J. JOMIER)

DILĀWAR <u>KH</u>ĀN, founder of the kingdom of Mālwa [*q.v.*], whose real name was Ḥasan (Firi<u>sh</u>ta, Nawalkishore ed., ii, 234); or Ḥusayn (Firi<u>sh</u>ta, Briggs's tr., iv, 170; so also Yazdani, *op. cit.* below); or ʿAmīd <u>Sh</u>āh Dāwūd (*Tūzuk-i <u>Dj</u>ahāngīrī*, tr. Rogers and Beveridge, ii, 407, based on the inscriptions of the <u>Dj</u>āmiʿ mas<u>dj</u>id (= Lāt mas<u>dj</u>id) in Dhār, cf. Zafar Hasan, *Inscriptions of Dhār and Māndū*, in *EIM*, 1909-10, 11-2 and Plates III and IV). He was believed to be a lineal descendant of Muʿizz al-Dīn Muḥammad b. Sām, <u>Sh</u>ihāb al-Dīn <u>Gh</u>ūrī, and this belief is reflected in the dynastic name <u>Gh</u>ūrī usually given to himself and his descendants. During the reign of Fīrūz Tu<u>gh</u>luḳ a title had been granted to him and a *manṣab* conferred on him. From an inscription on a gravestone discovered in the enclosure of the shrine of *<u>shaykh</u>* Kamāl al-Dīn Mālwī at Dhār it is established that in 795/1392-3 Dilāwar <u>Kh</u>ān was the governor of Mālwa. The date of his assumption of the pseudonym of Dilāwar <u>Kh</u>ān is not known precisely, but most probably this was the title conferred on him by Fīrūz <u>Sh</u>āh Tu<u>gh</u>luḳ, whose son Muḥammad <u>Sh</u>āh had appointed him as the *ṣūbadār* of Mālwa (the inscription referred to curiously mentions the name of the regnant sovereign as Maḥmūd <u>Sh</u>āh).

Dilāwar <u>Kh</u>ān unhesitatingly offered protection and refuge to the runaway Tu<u>gh</u>luḳ monarch Nāṣir al-Dīn Maḥmūd <u>Sh</u>āh when Tīmūr attacked India in 801/1398. His devotion and loyalty to this ill-starred monarch, however, incurred the resentment of his ambitious son Alp <u>Kh</u>ān (later Hū<u>sh</u>ang <u>Gh</u>ūrī [*q.v.*]) who disapproved of his father's homage to his fugitive overlord and removed himself to Māndū [*q.v.*] where he put in order and consolidated the fortress-buildings. On the departure of Maḥmūd Tu<u>gh</u>luḳ for Dihlī in 804/1401 Dilāwar <u>Kh</u>ān, who had since 795/1392 ceased to send to Dihlī the balance of the revenue collections, proclaimed his independence, much instigated by his son Alp <u>Kh</u>ān (cf. Briggs, *Ferishta*, iv, 169). Dilāwar <u>Kh</u>ān did not, however, live long to enjoy the fruits of freedom, and died suddenly in 808/1405; his sudden death gave rise to a suspicion, shared by some of the high-ranking army commanders, that he had been poisoned by his ambitious son, and Muẓaffar <u>Sh</u>āh I, ruler of the neighbouring kingdom of Gu<u>dj</u>arāt, long had the same impression and ultimately made the desire to avenge his old friend and sworn brother-in-arms the reason for his attack on Mālwa.

<u>Dj</u>ahāngīr's record (*Tūzuk-i <u>Dj</u>ahāngīrī*, Lahore ed., 431) of the year of construction of the <u>Dj</u>āmiʿ mas<u>dj</u>id at Dhār as *ha<u>sh</u>t ṣad wa haftād* (870) is apparently a misreading of the line in the inscription on the east gate referred to above, since Dilāwar <u>Kh</u>ān had died in 808/1405; the inscription on the north entrance (*EIM*, 1909-10, 12 and Pl. IV) gives the date of its construction as Ra<u>dj</u>ab of *sabʿ wa <u>th</u>amāni miʾa* (807). Other buildings of Dilāwar <u>Kh</u>ān are the mosque which bears his name at Māndū (insc. of 808/1405, *EIM*, 1909-10, 20-1 and Pl. XII/1) and the Tārāpur gate of that fort (Ins. of 809/1406, ibid., 19 and Pl. VII/2); the latter inscription, though attributing its erection to Dilāwar <u>Kh</u>ān, is presumably a reference to the date of its completion after his death.

Bibliography: Muḥammad Hādī Kāmwar <u>Kh</u>ān, *Haft Gul<u>sh</u>an* (ms), *faṣl* 3; Firi<u>sh</u>ta, *Gul<u>sh</u>an-i Ibrāhīmī*, Nawalkishore ed., ii, 234; *Tūzuk-i <u>Dj</u>ahāngīrī*, Eng. tr. Rogers and Beveridge, London 1909, ii, 407 ff.; E. Barnes, *Dhar and Mandu*, in *JBBRAS*, xxi, 1900-3, 339-91, *passim*; J. Fergusson, *History of Indian and Eastern Architecture*, London 1910, 541; G. Yazdani, *Mandū: the City of Joy*, Oxford 1929; Amīr Aḥmad ʿAlawī, *<u>Sh</u>āhān-i Mālwa*, Lucknow n.d., 14-7. See also DHĀR; MĀLWA; MĀNDŪ.

(A. S. BAZMEE ANSARI)

DILĀWAR PA<u>SH</u>A (?-1031/1622), Ottoman Grand Vizier, was of Croat origin. He rose in the Palace service to the rank of Ča<u>sh</u>nigīr Ba<u>sh</u>ī, becoming thereafter Beglerbeg of Cyprus and then, in Dhu 'l-Ḥidjdja 1022/January 1614, Beglerbeg of Baghdād. As Beglerbeg of Diyārbekir—an appointment bestowed on him in 1024/1615—he shared in the Erivān campaign of 1025/1616 against the Ṣafawids of Persia. His subsequent career until 1030/1621 is somewhat obscure. The Ottoman chronicles (cf. Pečewī, ii, 366; Ḥādjdjī Khalīfa, i, 392; Naʿīmā, ii, 166) state that a certain Muṣṭafā Pasha, killed in action during the last hostilities of the Ottoman-Ṣafawid war (1024-7/1615-8), was Beglerbeg of Diyārbekir at the moment of his death in 1027/1618. A Venetian "relazione" of July 1620 mentions the removal of Dilāwar Pasha from the Beglerbeglik of Diyārbekir, the office being now given to the "Silidar del Re" (cf. Hammer-Purgstall, viii, 267). Dilāwar Pasha fought—once more as Beglerbeg of Diyārbekir (cf. Ḥādjdjī Khalīfa, i, 406; Naʿīmā, ii, 194)—in the Choczim (Ḥotin) campaign of 1030/1621 against the Poles. It was on 1 Dhu 'l-Ḳaʿda 1030/17 September 1621, in the course of this war, that Sultan ʿOthmān II (1027-31/1618-22) raised Dilāwar Pasha to the Grand Vizierate. His tenure of the office was destined to be brief. He lost his life on 8 Radjab 1031/19 May 1622 during the revolt of the Janissaries which led to the deposition and death of ʿOthmān II. Dilāwar Pasha built a large khān at Čār-Malik, between al-Ruhā' (Urfa) and Bīredjik, and another khān—not completed until the time of Sulṭān Murād IV (1032-49/1623-40)—at Sīdī Ghāzī (Seyyid Gâzî).

Bibliography: Pečewī, *Ta'rīkh*, ii, 368, 378, 382, 383; Ḳaraçelebizāde, *Rawḍat al-abrār*, 544, 546, 547, 549; Ḥādjdjī Khalīfa, *Fedhleke*, i, 375, 393, 406, 407, 410, 411 and ii, 1, 8, 10-16 *passim*, 31; Ṣolaḳzāde, *Ta'rīkh*, 702-14 *passim*; Naʿīmā, *Ta'rīkh*, ii, 142, 168, 194, 201-19 *passim*; Naẓmīzāde, *Gulshan-i khulafā'*, Istanbul A.H. 1143, 66v; M. Sertoğlu, *Tuği tarihi*, in *Belleten*, xi, 1947, 489-514 *passim*; Ferīdūn, *Munsha'āt al-salāṭīn*, ii, 429 ff.; M. A. Danon, *Contributions à l'histoire des Sultans Osman II et Mouçtafa I*, in *JA*, onz. sér., xiv, Paris 1919, 69 ff. and 243 ff., *passim*; A. Galland, *La mort du Sultan Osman ou le retablissement de Mustapha sur le throsne, traduit d'un manuscrit Turc ....*, Paris 1678, 29, 35, 41, 60, 79, 82, 85, 98, 104, 105, 117; M. Steinschneider, *Die Geschichtsliteratur der Juden*, i, Frankfurt 1905, § 146; S. Purchas, *Purchas his Pilgrimes*, viii, Glasgow 1905, 343-59 *passim* ("The Death of Sultan Osman"); R. Knolles, *The Generall Historie of the Turkes ... together with the Lives and Conquests of the Othoman Kings and Emperours: A Continuation of the Turkish History from .... 1620 untill .... 1628. Collected out of the Papers and Dispatches of Sir Thomas Rowe ....*, London 1638, 1406-18 *passim*; *The Negotiations of Sir Thomas Roe in his Embassy to the Ottoman Porte from the Year 1621 to 1628 inclusive*, ed. S. Richardson, London 1740, 42-51 *passim*; Hammer-Purgstall, *Histoire*, viii, 214, 242, 243, 267, 278, 281-91 *passim*, 298, 302; Zinkeisen, iii, 744-9 *passim*; N. Jorga, *Geschichte des osmanischen Reiches*, iii, Gotha 1910, 444; I. H. Uzunçarşılı, *Osmanlı tarihi*, iii/2, Ankara 1954, 375; ʿOthmānzāde Aḥmed Ta'ib, *Ḥadīḳat al-wuzarā'*, 31; Sāmī, *Ḳāmūs al-aʿlām*, iii, Istanbul A.H. 1308, 2151; *Sidjill-i ʿOthmānī*, ii, ii, 339; *İA*, s.v. Dilâver Paşa (M. Tayyib Gökbilgin).

(V. J. Parry)

DİLSİZ, in Turkish tongueless, the name given to the deaf mutes employed in the inside service (*enderūn*) of the Ottoman palace, and for a while also at the Sublime Porte. They were also called by the Persian term *bīzabān*, with the same meaning. They were established in the palace from the time of Meḥemmed II to the end of the Sultanate. Information about their numbers varies. According to ʿAṭā', three to five of them were attached to each chamber (*Koghush*); Rycaut speaks of 'about forty'. A document of the time of Muṣṭafā II (d. 1115/1703), cited by Uzunçarşılı, dealing with the distribution of cloth to the palace staff, mentions one mute in the *ḥarem*, two mutes and a dwarf (*djüdje*) in the Privy Chamber (*Khāṣṣ oda*), a chief mute, chief dwarf, six mutes and two dwarfs in the Treasury Chamber (*Khazīne Koghushu*), a chief mute, chief dwarf, and ten mutes in the Campaign Chamber (*Seferli Koghushu*).

The mutes received pay and pensions, and had special uniforms and ceremonial dress. Their chiefs were called *bashdilsiz*—chief mute. Though deaf mutes from birth, they are said to have been men of intelligence, and to have had an elaborate sign language in which they communicated among themselves and received orders from their superiors. According to Bon, many of them could write 'and that very sensibly and well'. Their duties were to act as guards and attendants, and as messengers and emissaries, in highly confidential matters, including executions.

Bibliography: *Ta'rīkh-i ʿAṭā'*, i, 171-2, 283; Robert Withers, *A description of the Grand Seignor's seraglio* (adapted from Ottaviano Bon, *Il serraglio del gransignore* [1608]), *Purchas his Pilgrims*, ii/II. London 1625 (repr. Glasgow 1905, vol. ix), chap. VII (also repr. J. Greaves, London 1650, 1653, 1737); P. Rycaut, *History of the Present State of the Ottoman Empire*[4], London 1675, ch. viii, 61-2; D'Ohsson, *Tableau général de l'Empire othoman*, vii, Paris 1824, 45; Hammer-Purgstall, *Staatsverfassung*, ii, 57; Gibb-Bowen, i/I, 80; I. H. Uzunçarşılı, *Osmanlı Devletinin Saray Teşkilâtı*, Ankara 1945, 330; Pakalın, i, 237. There are descriptions and pictures of the deaf-mutes in a number of western accounts of the Ottoman court.

(B. Lewis)

DIMASHḲ, Dimashḳ al-Shām or simply al-Shām, (Lat. Damascus, Fr. Damas) is the largest city of Syria. It is situated at longitude 36° 18′ east and latitude 33° 30′ north, very much at the same latitude as Baghdād and Fās, at an altitude of nearly 700 metres, on the edge of the desert at the foot of Djabal Ḳāsiyūn, one of the massifs of the eastern slopes of the Anti-Lebanon. To the east and the north-east the steppe extends as far as the Euphrates, while to the south it merges with Arabia.

A hundred or more kilometres from the Mediterranean behind the Lebanon and Anti-Lebanon, a double barrier of mountains which rise to 3,000 metres, the city, which is deprived by these of sea-winds and cloud, gives the impression already of belonging to the desert. The seasons are capricious, the winter short but severe with very occasional snowfalls. The rains which come in December, January and February, this last being a particularly wet month, are by no means abundant (in fact the city only has from 250 to 300 mm. as against 850 to 930 at Bayrūt [*q.v.*]. The spring, sudden and short, lasts for only a few weeks at the end of March and the beginning of April, followed by a relentless summer. From May to November there is absolute dryness, the daily temperature exceeds 35° centigrade in the shade and the glaring light accentuates the shadow. At the end of November the first heavy showers wash the dust from the leaves; it is autumn. In this semi-desert type of climate vegetation sufficiently abundant and above all sufficiently lasting to support animals or man would scarcely be expected. But nature had fixed the site of Dimashḳ in advance. It was at the point where the Baradā [q.v.], the only perennial water-course of the region, emerges on to the plain after crossing the mountain-side and before losing itself in the desert. By means of an ingenious system of irrigation, man learned how to use this water, succeeded in wrenching from the desert a corner of ground which responded to his needs, and even made of it one of the richest agricultural regions of all "Hither Asia", the Ghūṭa [q.v.], which Muslim tradition likes to regard as one of the three earthly paradises (the others are Samarḳand and al-Ubulla; Ibn ʿAsākir, Taʾrīkh, 169). Thus with its situation between the desert and the mountains, its fertile soil and abundant water, it was able to support human habitation on a scale which from the dawn of time has caused it to be regarded as a metropolis.

Difficulties of communication between the town and the sea forced Dimashḳ to turn towards the interior. Protected on the west by the mountains, endowed with an excellent water supply, situated along the road which crosses Syria from north to south, and in the middle of a rich oasis, the city served as a market for the nomads and as a halt for the caravans which joined the Euphrates to the Nile; the incessant movement of men and goods was not unlike the activity of a great maritime port. Turned towards the desert, many times attacked but never destroyed, Dimashḳ offers us, against this unchanging background, evidence of a history of several thousands of years.

We have no precise knowledge of the epoch in which the city was founded. Nevertheless the excavations made in 1950 to the south-east of Dimashḳ at Tell al-Ṣāliḥiyya have disclosed an urban centre dating from the fourth millennium. When we compare the rudimentary equipment even of Bronze Age man with the complexity of the irrigation system, we can understand that the prosperity of this city in the middle of the second millennium must have been the result of a long and slow development.

Dimashḳ enters into history with the mention made of her in the Tell al-Amarna tablets. She is named as one of the towns conquered in the 15th century B.C. by the Pharaoh Thutmoses III who occupied Syria for a time.

In the 11th century B. C. Dimashḳ was the flourishing capital of the land of Aram referred to in the history of Abraham (Genesis, X, 22, XIV, 15); even to-day Muslims venerate the Masdjid Ibrāhīm at Berzé, to the north of Damascus, which according to tradition was the birthplace of Abraham. It seems that it was at this time that the Aramaeans introduced its grid-like plan with straight streets and rectangular intersections, similar to that which existed in the second millennium in Babylon and Assyria. The city owed the development of its canal system to the Aramaeans; we know from the Old Testament history of Naʿamān the Leper (II Kings, V) that the Abāna was already flowing alongside the Baradā before the 10th century B.C., while the Nahr Tawrā with its Aramaean name, which had been dug along the slopes of the Ḳāsiyūn, irrigated the region to the north and north-east of the city and played an important part in the agricultural economy of the oasis.

The town was conquered by David (II Kings, viii, 5-6) but in the century of Solomon, the king of Dimashḳ fought successfully the Assyrian kings to the north and the kings of Israel to the south. In 732 B.C. the Assyrian troops of Tiglatpilezer III put an end to the kingdom of Dimashḳ; they took the town and despoiled the temple and palace, part of whose furniture was rediscovered in 1930 in Upper Mesopotamia. For this period of the city's history, as for the successive occupations by the Assyrians in the 8th century, the Babylonians in the 7th century, the Achaemenids in the 6th century, the Greeks in the 4th century and the Romans in the 1st century B.C., see K. Wulzinger and C. Watzinger, Damascus, i, Die Antike Stadt, and the articles of J. Benzinger in Pauly-Wissowa, iv, 2042-8, Jalabert in the Dictionnaire d'archéologie chrétienne et de liturgie of Cabrol and Leclercq, art. Damas, iv, 1920, col. 119-46, R. Janin in the Dictionnaire d'histoire et de géographie ecclésiastiques of R. Aubert and E. van Cauwenbergh, xiv, 1957, col. 42-7.

The conquest of Alexander the Great in 333 B.C. is an important date, for Dimashḳ, lost to the Achaemenids, was now to come for several centuries, up to the time of the Arab conquest in 14/635, under western influence. Three stages can be distinguished in the Hellenistic period; first a Ptolemaic foundation in the 3rd century B.C., then the raising of the town to the rank of a capital by the Seleucid Antiochus IX of Cyzicus (111 B.C.), and finally the installation of a new Greek colony about the year 90 B.C. under Demetrius III. As a Seleucid capital Dimashḳ became important once again and began to be developed according to Hellenistic urban planning. At the side of the Aramaean town, where stood the temple which since the 9th century B.C. had dominated the development of the city, there arose a twin city, that of the Greeks, following a normal procedure when two cultures of quite different character are obliged to exist upon the same site. Elements of Hellenistic urban architecture appeared such as the street with side arcades, traces of which are to be found to the east of the Umayyad Mosque, or the agora of which we are reminded by the still-existent Zuḳāḳ al-Sāḥa, or the small blocks of houses with the standard size of 100 by 45 metres with the longer side orientated north-south.

In 85 B.C. the town fell for the first time into the hands of the Nabataeans who had come from Petra under the rule of Aretas III, the Philhellene. These fresh arrivals constructed a new quarter to the east of the Hellenistic city, which mediaeval Arab historians called al-Naybaṭūn. In addition, they made on the the slopes of the Djabal Ḳāsiyūn above the Nahr Tawrā a canal which was reconstructed under the Umayyads and then took the name of Nahr Yazīd.

In 64 B.C. Pompey proclaimed Syria a Roman province, but Dimashḳ was not its capital and the imperial legates installed themselves in Antioch. From 37 to 54 A.D., under Aretas IV Philopator, the Nabataeans became for a second time masters of Dimashḳ with the approval of Rome. It was at this period that Saul, the future St. Paul, came to visit the important Jewish colony of the city in order to seek out Christians and was himself converted to Christianity by Ananias whose chapel, excavated in 1921, is still preserved to-day. Under Hadrian (beginning of the 2nd century) Dimashḳ was given the rank of metropolis. Septimus Severus and Caracalla carried out many public works there and Alexander Severus set it up as a Roman colony after the year 222.

Rome brought internal peace and administrative order, which in their turn brought amazing prosperity to the town. The upward trend of its economy led to a considerable influx of population and goods and the city very soon became too small. The Romans therefore imposed a new urban plan and set about combining the original Aramaean town with the Hellenistic one to form a new city. The state occupied itself mainly with projects of general interest such as the city walls and additional canals to provide extra water.

Rectangular walls measuring 1500 by 750 metres were built on the right bank of the Baradā to protect the inhabitants against pillaging nomads. Strengthened by a *castrum* in the north-east corner, the entry took on the appearance of a vast quadrangle which could be entered by seven gates: to the east, the Eastern Gate (Bāb Sharḳī), to the south the Kaysān Gate and the Little Gate (Bāb al-Ṣaghīr), to the west the al-Djābiya Gate, and to the north the Gate of the Gardens (Bāb al-Farādīs), the Djīnīḳ Gate and the Thomas Gate (Bāb Tūmā). Important remains of these walls and gates are still visible to-day. The growth in the population necessitated the construction of an aqueduct, *al-Ḳanawāt*, to provide drinking water which functions up to the present time. New blocks of houses in the southern part of the rectangle settled the problem of finding homes for the newcomers. Two great colonnaded streets were new features of the urban picture. One of these important thoroughfares, 25 metres wide and with arcades on either side, joined Bāb Sharḳī to Bāb al-Djābiya, crossing the city from east to west and corresponding with the *decumanus* of Roman cities. This road, the present Sūḳ Midḥat Pasha, is still referred to by foreigners as the 'Street called Straight' from the allusion to it in Acts, IX, 11. In the middle we can still see to-day one of the three Roman arches which used to stand there, and in a little semi-circular *tell* on its south side, crossed obliquely by a small alleyway, is the site of the ancient theatre. The second colonnaded street was the ancient road joining the temple and the *agora*, which was now turned into a *forum*. The temple, which was dedicated to Jupiter of the Damascenes, the successor to Hadad, god of storms, was partially rebuilt and altered on several occasions, especially in the second and third centuries A.D. Part of the *peribolus* (enclosure), two of whose corner towers serve as bases for minarets, is to be found in the outer wall of the Great Mosque. The eastern propylaea are to be seen in the present day Djayrūn to the east of the Great Mosque, while the western propylaea, which are ornamented with a wide pediment, are visible at Bāb al-Barīd to the west of the sanctuary. Finally it is also known that the Circus, which perhaps replaced the Stadium, was situated on the site of the present Boulevard de Baghdād, north of a cemetery outside the Gate of the Gardens, where Roman sarcophagi have been found.

Medieval Arab nomenclature has preserved in other ways the memory of certain Roman districts such as al-Dīmās, corresponding with the ancient *demosion*, al-Fūrnaḳ which recalls the furnaces or pottery kilns, and again al-Fusḳār, which seems to show that at this end of the Street called Straight there once stood the *foscarion* where the *fusca* was made and sold.

Many of the ancient remains must have disappeared beneath the earth whose level has risen by more than four metres in some places since the Roman period, but the plan of the city as it was laid out at the beginning of the 3rd century A.D. was hardly altered up to the arrival of the Muslims. The Roman city, in fact, formed the skeleton of the mediaeval one.

The Romans were succeeded by the Byzantines. Syria became a part of the Eastern Empire after the death of Theodosius in 395. When Dimashḳ became the outpost of Byzantium, a new urban element, the church, appeared there. First of all the Temple of Jupiter was rebuilt and transformed into the cathedral which was dedicated to St. John the Baptist. The head of Yaḥyā b. Zakariyyāʾ is preserved in a crypt now situated in the Great Mosque and is venerated alike by Christians and Muslims. The present Orthodox Patriarchate stands on what was once the site of the Church of St. Mary.

The weakening of the Ghassānids and the Persian wars of the 6th century ruined the Syrian economy. In 612 the soldiers of Khusraw II occupied Dimashḳ, the majority of whose population was Jacobite Monophysite and hostile to the Melkite Byzantines. Well received, the Sāsānids did not ravage the town as they were to do later (614) in Jerusalem. In 627 on the death of the Persian monarch, the city was evacuated and the following year Heraclius returned to Syria.

The Muslim Conquest.—After first the dissolution of the Ghassānid Phylarchate and then the devastations of the Persians, the Arabs of the Ḥidjāz must have had no difficulty in conquering Syria. Each year Arab expeditions crossed the Byzantine frontier; in Djumāda I 13/July 634 Khālid b. al-Walīd's men crossed Palestine and then went up towards the north along the route of the Djawlān. The Byzantines offered some resistance to the north of al-Ṣanamayn in the Mardj al-Ṣuffar before turning back to Dimashḳ in Muḥarram 14/March 635. A few days later, the Muslims were at the gates of the city. Khālid b. al-Walīd established his general headquarters to the north-east of the town; an ancient tradition puts his camp near the existing tomb of Shaykh Raslān outside Bāb Tūmā. A blockade aimed at hindering a reunion of the Byzantine troops flung back into Dimashḳ with any army which might come to their aid from the north. The dislike of the population of Dimashḳ for Byzantine rule brought a group of notables, among them the bishop and the controller-general, Manṣūr b. Sardjūn, father of St. John of Damascus, to engage in negotiations to avoid useless suffering for the people of the city. In Radjab 14/September 635 the Eastern Gate was opened to the Muslims and the Byzantine troops retired to the north. There are several traditions concerning the capture of the city. The most widely spread is that of Ibn ʿAsākir (*Taʾrīkh*, i, 23-4) according to which Khālid b. al-Walīd forced his way through the Bāb Sharḳī, sword in hand, while Abū ʿUbayda b. al-Djarrāḥ entered by the Bāb al-Djābiya after having given them the *amān*, and the two generals met in the middle of the *Kanīsa*. Another version, that of al-Balādhurī (*Futūḥ*, 120-30), says that Khālid received the surrender of the city at Bāb Sharḳī and that Abū ʿUbayda entered by force of arms at Bāb al-Djābiya; the meeting of the two commanders is said to have been at al-Barīṣ, towards the middle of the Street called Straight near the church of al-Maḳsallāt (Ibn ʿAsākir, *Taʾrīkh*, i, 130). By demonstrating that Abū ʿUbayda was not in Syria in the year 14, Caetani has destroyed the validity of these traditions. Lammens (*MFOB*, iii, 255) has tried to save them by proposing to substitute the name of Yazīd b. Sufyān for that of Abū ʿUbayda. In any case, Lammens has shown the unlikelihood of a division of the town, a legend which seems to have come into being only at the time of the Crusades.

The Muslims guaranteed the Christians possession of their land, houses and churches, but forced them to pay a heavy tribute and poll tax.

In the spring of 15/636, an army commanded by Theodorus, brother of Heraclius, made its way towards Dimashk. Khālid b. al-Walīd evacuated the place and reformed his troops at al-Djābiya before entrenching himself near the Yarmūk to the east of Tiberias. It was there that on 12 Radjab 15/20 August 636 the Byzantine army was put to flight by Khālid who, after this success, returned to Medina. This time the conquest of Syria and Dimashk was to be the work of Abū ʿUbayda b. al-Djarrāḥ. The town capitulated for the second time in Dhu 'l-Kaʿda 15/December 636, and was finally integrated into the dominion of Islam.

The fall of Dimashk was an event of incalculable importance. The conquest put an end to almost a thousand years of western supremacy; from that time on the city came again into the Semitic orbit and turned anew towards the desert and the east. Semitic by language and culture, Monophysite and hostile to the Greek-speaking Orthodox Church, the people of Dimashk received the conquerors with unreserved pleasure, for they felt nearer to them by race, language and religion than to the Byzantines, and, regarding Islam as no more than another dissident Christian sect, they hoped to find themselves more free under them. At Dimashk more than elsewhere circumstances seemed as if they ought to have favoured Arab assimilation to Greek culture but in fact Hellenization had not touched more than a minute fraction of the population who for the most part spoke Aramaic. While the administration continued to maintain Byzantine standards, religious controversies arose and contributed towards the formation of Muslim theology. Assimilation took place in the opposite direction so that the positive result of the conquest was the introduction of Islam, which within half a century succeeded in imposing Arabic, the language of the new religion, as the official tongue.

The Caliph ʿUmar nominated Yazīd b. Abī Sufyān [*q.v.*] as governor of the city. The more important of the conquerors installed themselves in houses abandoned by the Byzantines (Ibn ʿAsākir, *Taʾrikh*, xiii, 133-44). The town had made a deep impression on the nomads who referred to it as the 'beauty spot of the world', but the lack of space and above all of pasturage led the Bedouins to camp at al-Djābiya. Dimashk very soon took on the character of a holy city, for traditions recognized here places made famous by the prophets, and pilgrimages began to increase. People went chiefly to the Djabal Kāsiyūn to visit Adam's cave, the Cave of the Blood where the murder of Abel was thought to have taken place, or the Cavern of Gabriel. At Berzé, Abraham's birthplace was honoured; the tomb of Moses (Mūsā b. ʿImrān) was regarded as being situated in what is now the district of Kadam. Jesus (ʿĪsā b. Maryam) was cited among the prophets who had honoured the town; he had stayed at Rabwa on the 'Quiet Hill' (Kurʾān, XXIII, 50) and would descend at the end of time on to the white minaret sometimes identified as that of Bāb Sharkī, sometimes as the eastern minaret (*maʾdhanat ʿĪsā*) of the Great Mosque, in order to fight the Antichrist.

The Umayyads.—In 18/639 Yazīd b. Abī Sufyān died of the plague; his brother, Muʿāwiya, succeeded him in command of the *djund* of Dimashk. In 36/656, after the death of ʿAlī, Muʿāwiya was elected Caliph and, leaving al-Djābiya, he fixed his residence in Dimashk. The Umayyads were to carry the fortunes of the new capital to their highest point; for a century it was the urban centre of the metropolitan province of the Caliphate and the heart of one of the greatest empires that the world has ever known.

The domination of the conquerors did not at first bring any changes in the life of the city since the Muslim element was no more than an infinitesimal minority; arabization was slow and Christians predominated at the court up to the reign of ʿAbd al-Malik. At this time the growth in the number of Muslim subjects provoked a reaction which caused Arabic to replace Greek as the official language of the administration. At the beginning of the dynasty, discipline, prosperity and tolerance were the order of the day, but later on civil strife culminated in anarchy and in the end of Umayyad rule. Troubles broke out in the city, fires increased in number, even the walls had been demolished by the time that Marwān II installed himself in his new capital, Ḥarrān, in 127/744.

The change of régime was reflected in the urban plan only by the erection of two buildings closely connected with each other, the palace of the Caliph and the mosque, which did not alter the general aspect of the city. Muʿāwiya was content to remodel the residence of the Byzantine governors to the south-east of the ancient *peribolus* on the site of the present-day gold- and silversmith's bazaar; it was called *al-Khaḍrāʾ*, 'the Green (Palace)'. This name must in fact have been given to a group of administrative buildings as was also the case in Constantinople and later at Baghdād. At the side of the palace, which under the ʿAbbāsids appears to have been transformed into a prison, was situated the *Dār al-Khayl* or Hostel of the Ambassadors. The Caliph Yazīd I improved the water supply by reconstructing a Nabataean canal on the slopes of the Djabal Kāsiyūn above Nahr Tawrā which was given the name of Nahr Yazīd which it still bears to-day. Al-Ḥadjdjādj, the son of the Caliph ʿAbd al-Malik b. Marwān, built a palace outside the walls to the west of Bāb al-Djābiya whose memory is preserved in the name of the district of Kaṣr al-Ḥadjdjādj.

It is to Caliph al-Walīd I that we owe the first and one of the most impressive masterpieces of Muslim architecture, the Great Mosque of the Umayyads. The Church of St. John continued to exist under the Sufyānids and Muʿāwiya did not insist on including it in the *masdjid*. The Gallic bishop, Arculf, passing through Dimashk about 50/670, noted two separate sanctuaries for each of the communities (P. Geyer, *Itinera Hierosolymita, Saeculi iv-viii*). Conversions grew in number and the primitive mosque, which was no more than a *muṣallā* situated against the eastern part of the south wall of the *peribolus*, became too small. ʿAbd al-Malik laid claim to the church and proposed its purchase but the negotiations failed. "By the time that Caliph al-Walīd decided to proceed with the enlargement of the mosque, the problem had become difficult to solve. There was no free place left in the city, the *temenos* had been invaded by houses and there remained only the agora where the Sunday markets were held. In spite of previous agreements, he confiscated the Church of St. John the Baptist from

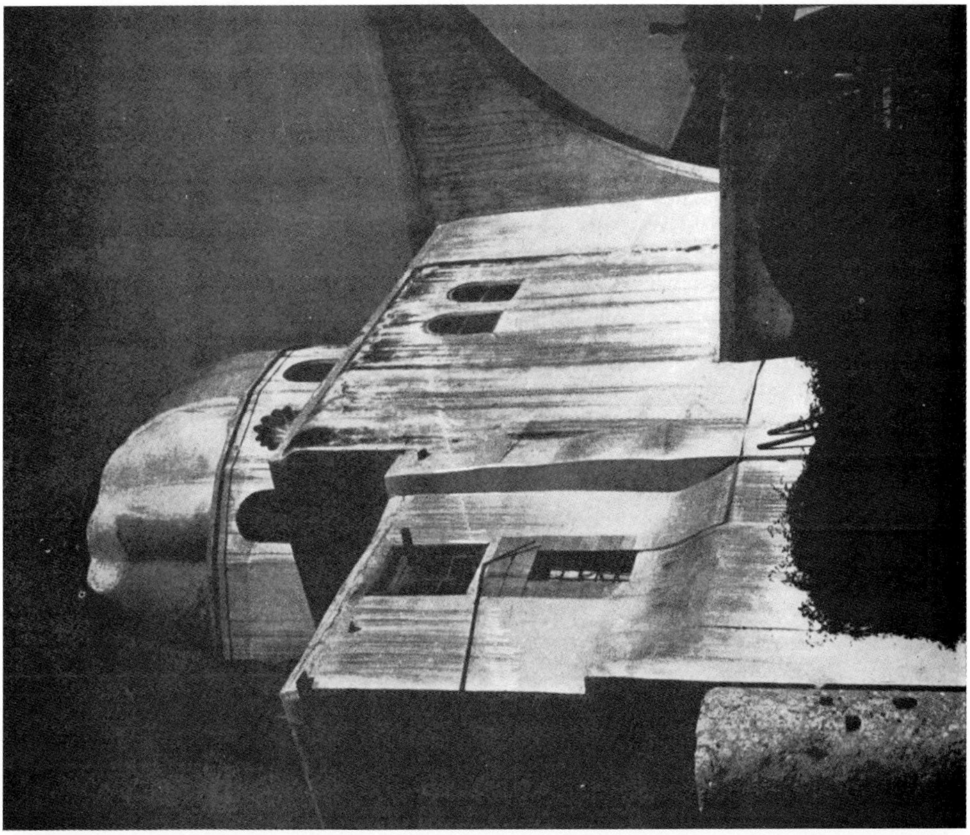

1. Mausoleum of Ṣalāḥ al-Dīn, eastern façade
By courtesy of the General Directorate of Antiquities, Damascus

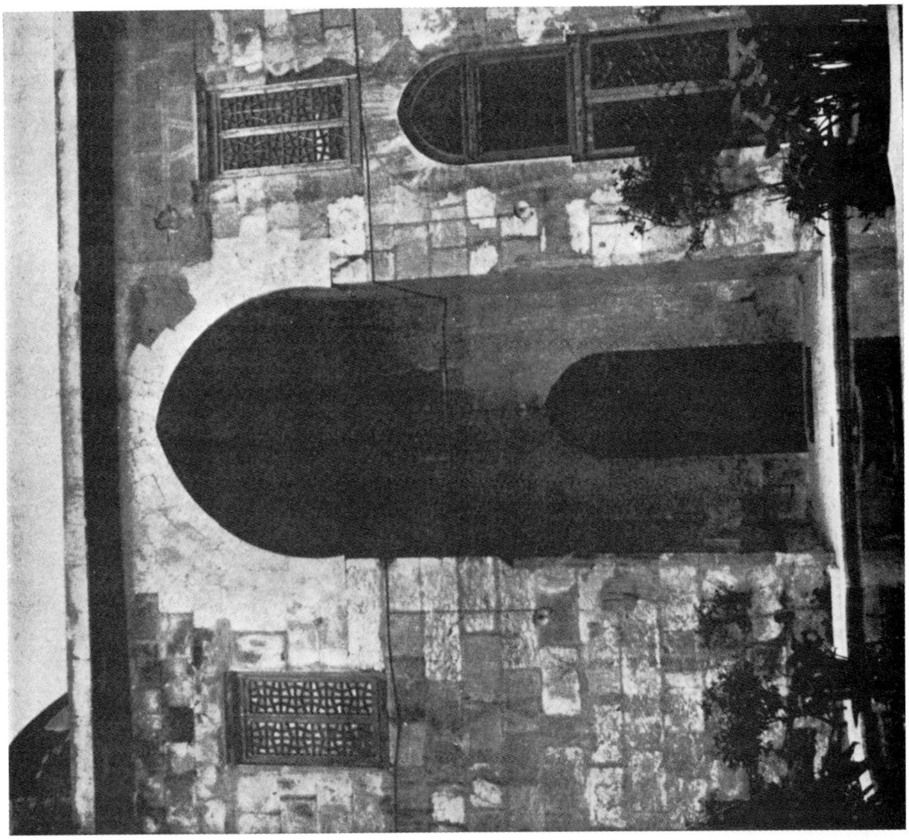

2. Courtyard of the Madrasa al-ʿĀdiliyya, eastern façade
By courtesy of the General Directorate of Antiquities, Damascus

3. Wooden cenotaph from a tomb within the mausoleum of Ṣalāḥ al-Dīn
By courtesy of the General Directorate of Antiquities, Damascus

4. Entrance to the Madrasa al-ʿĀdiliyya
By courtesy of the General Directorate of Antiquities, Damascus

5. Courtyard of the Madrasa al-Nūriyya, interior of the eastern façade
By courtesy of the General Directorate of Antiquities, Damascus

6. Stalactite ornamentation on the dome of the Madrasa al-Nūriyya
By courtesy of the General Directorate of Antiquities, Damascus

7. Madrasa al-Nūriyya, exterior façade
By courtesy of the General Directorate of Antiquities, Damascus

8. Dome of the Māristān of Nūr al-Dīn, exterior view
By courtesy of the General Directorate of Antiquities, Damascus

9. Māristān of Nūr al-Dīn, façade and doorway
By courtesy of the General Directorate of Antiquities, Damascus

10. Courtyard of the Māristān of Nūr al-Dīn, west façade
By courtesy of the General Directorate of Antiquities, Damascus

the Christians, giving them in exchange, however, several other places of worship which had fallen into disuse". A legend which tells of the division of the Church of St. John between Christians and Muslims springs from an error in translation. Neither al-Ṭabarī (*Annales*, ii/2), nor al-Balādẖurī (*Futūḥ*, 125), nor al-Masuʿdī (*Murūd̲j̲*, v, 363) mentions the division of the church. The text of Ibn al-Muʿallā which Ibn ʿAsākir and Ibn D̲j̲ubayr have helped to spread, speaks of a division of the *kanīsa* where the Christian sanctuary adjoined the *muṣallā* of the Muslims. We must take the word *kanīsa* in a broad sense as meaning place of prayer, that is to say the open-air *ḥaram* of the ancient sanctuary (J. Sauvaget, in *Syria*, xxvi, 353) which can also be called *masd̲j̲id*. Fascinated by the plan of the mosque in which they hoped to discover an ancient Byzantine basilica, certain authors, of whom Dussaud is one, have stated that the Christian hall of prayer was divided between the two communities. Lammens admits, however, that the construction of the cupola must be attributed to al-Walīd. All those who have studied it on the spot, such as Thiersch, Strygowski, Sauvaget and Creswell, agree with only some slight differences of opinion in regarding the Great Mosque as a Muslim achievement. In 86/705, al-Walīd had everything within the *peribolus* of the ancient temple demolished (al-Farazdaḳ, *Dīwān*, 107-109), both the Church of St. John and the little chapel which stood over the three cubits square cript, in which there was a casket containing the head of St. John the Baptist (Yaḥyā b. Zakariyyāʾ). Only the surrounding walls made of large stones and the square corner towers were allowed to remain. In this framework, approximately 120 by 80 metres in size, the architects placed to the north a court-yard surrounded by a vast covered portico with double arcades. "Along the whole length of the south wall of the *peribolus*, extended in the same direction as that in which the faithful formed their ranks for prayer, an immense hall made a place of assembly for the Muslim community". In the middle was an aisle surmounted by a vast cupola. In the east the "*miḥrāb* of the Companions" served as a reminder of the primitive *masd̲j̲id*. In the west a new door, Bāb al-Ziyāda, was opened in the wall to replace the central portico which had been blocked up. "Finally, in the centre of the north wall a high square minaret showed from afar the latest transformation which had come to the old sanctuary of Damascus". The walls of the building were hidden in some places under marble inlays, in others under mosaics of glass-paste. The Great Mosque was built in six years and "by the vastness of its proportions, the majesty of its arrangement, the splendour of its decorations and the richness of its materials" it has succeeded in impressing the human imagination down the centuries. A Muslim work in its conception and purpose, it was to be "the symbol of the political supremacy and moral prestige of Islam".

Two new Muslim cemeteries were made in addition to that of Bāb al-Farādīs: the first was situated at Bāb Tūmā but the one in which most of the Companions of the Prophet were to lie was to the south of the city outside Bāb al-Ṣag̲h̲īr.

The ʿAbbāsid period.—ʿAbd Allāh b. ʿAlī, uncle of the new Caliph Abu 'l-ʿAbbās al-Saffāḥ, having put an end to the Umayyad dynasty, took Dimas̲h̲ḳ in Ramaḍān 132/April, 750 and became its first ʿAbbāsid governor. Umayyad buildings were sacked, the defences dismantled, tombs profaned. A sombre era began for the city which dwindled to the level of a provincial town, while the Caliphate installed its capital in ʿIrāḳ. A latent state of insurrection reigned in the Syrian capital. Under al-Mahdī (156-68/775-85) a conflict between Ḳaysīs and Yamanīs flared up into a vain revolt led by an Umayyad pretender called al-Sufyānī, with the support of the Ḳaysīs. Under the Caliphate of Hārūn al-Ras̲h̲īd, the movement against Bag̲h̲dād became more broadly based; in 180/796, the ʿAbbāsid ruler sent a punitive expedition under the command of D̲j̲aʿfar al-Barmakī. Order was only temporarily re-established and the authority of the ʿAbbāsid governors was continually being put to scorn. In an endeavour to restore calm, the Caliph al-Maʾmūn made a first visit there in 215/830, but the troubles continued. He made a second visit in 218/833, the year of his death. In 240/854 a violent revolt ended in the execution of the ʿAbbāsid governor of Dimas̲h̲ḳ, but troops of the Caliph succeeded in restoring order. Four years later the Caliph al-Mutawakkil tried to transfer his capital to the Syrian metropolis but only stayed there 38 days before returning to Sāmarrā.

In 254/868 a Turk of Buk̲h̲ārā, Aḥmad b. Ṭūlūn [*q.v.*], was appointed governor of Egypt by the Caliph of whom he was no more than a nominal vassal. He seized the opportunity of the Caliphate's being so much weakened by the successive revolts of the Zand̲j̲ to occupy Dimas̲h̲ḳ in 264/878. His son, K̲h̲umārawayh [*q.v.*], succeeded him in 270/884 and continued to pay an annual tribute to the Caliph-Sultan in order to remain master of Egypt and Syria. He was assassinated at Dimas̲h̲ḳ in D̲h̲u 'l-Ḥid̲j̲d̲j̲a 282/February 896. In the course of the last years of Ṭūlūnid power, the Ḳarmaṭians [*q.v.*] appeared in Syria and helped to increase the centres of political and social agitation. The decline of the Ṭūlūnids and the growing activity of the Ḳarmaṭians who got as far as besieging Dimas̲h̲ḳ forced the Caliph to dispatch troops who reduced the Ḳarmaṭians to order in 289/902 and lifted the siege of Dimas̲h̲ḳ whose governor, Ṭug̲h̲d̲j̲ b. D̲j̲uff, a Turk from Transoxania, re-allied himself with the ʿAbbāsid general, Muḥammad b. Sulaymān, without difficulty, and as a reward was appointed governor of Egypt by the Caliph. In this country his son, Muḥammad, founded the dynasty of the Ik̲h̲s̲h̲īdids [*q.v.*] in 326/938. Recognizing the nominal suzerainty of the ʿAbbāsids, the new dynasty went to the defence of Dimas̲h̲ḳ against the Ḥamdānids. In 333/945 an agreement was reached, the Ik̲h̲s̲h̲īdids holding the town in return for paying a tribute to the masters of Ḥalab. When Muḥammad died at Dimas̲h̲ḳ in 334/946 chaos was born again both there and in Cairo.

The Fāṭimids [*q.v.*] replaced the Ik̲h̲s̲h̲īdids in Cairo in 357/968. With their coming, first in Egypt and then in Syria, a S̲h̲īʿite Caliphate was installed which was the enemy of Bag̲h̲dād. At the beginning of the 11th century, Dimas̲h̲ḳ was in a difficult situation; the Ḥamdānids were putting on pressure from the north, the Fāṭimids from the south, not to mention Byzantine movements, Ḳarmaṭian activities and Turkoman invasions. At one time the city was occupied by the Ḳarmaṭians but in 359/970 the Fāṭimids expelled them, not without causing a certain amount of fire and destruction in the town. The Fāṭimid domination only aggravated the situation for the city, where the Mag̲h̲rabī soldiers in the pay of Cairo exasperated the population. It was a century of political anarchy and decadence. The riots sometimes turned into catastrophe, for the majority of the houses were built of unfired brick with framework and trusses of poplar trees, and any fire could have grave consequences; such was the case in 461/1069 when one which broke out owing to a brawl between Damascenes and Berber soldiers caused serious damage to the Great Mosque and the city.

The Turkish domination.—A Turkoman chief, Atsīz b. Uvak [q.v.], who had been in the pay of the Fāṭimids, abandoned their cause and occupied Dimashḳ on his own account in 468/1076, thus putting an end to Egyptian rule. Threatened by his former masters, Atsīz hastened to strengthen the citadel and endeavoured to form an alliance with Malik Shāh [q.v.] whom he asked to help him. In reply, the Saldjūḳid sultan gave the town in appanage to his brother, Tutush [q.v.]. He arrived in Dimashḳ in 471/1079, re-established order and got rid of Atsīz by having him assassinated. The era of violence continued. In 476/1083, Muslim b. Ḳuraysh besieged the city; the Fāṭimid aid which he expected failed to arrive and Tutush succeeded in setting the city free. He died fighting his nephew, Barkyārūḳ [q.v.], in 488/1095. His sons divided his domain. Riḍwān installed himself at Ḥalab and Duḳāḳ at Dimashḳ. The latter put the direction of his affairs into the hands of his atabeg, the Turk Ẓahīr al-Dīn Tughtakīn, who from that time on seems to have been the real ruler of Dimashḳ. His political position was a delicate one for he had against him the Fāṭimids, the Saldjūḳids of Baghdād and, after 490/1097, the Franks as well.

On the death of Duḳāḳ (Ramaḍān 497/June 1104), Tughtakīn exercised his power in the name of the young Tutush II who died soon afterwards. From then on, the atabeg was the only master of Dimashḳ and his dynasty, the Būrids [q.v.], remained there until the arrival of Nūr al-Dīn in 549/1154. During the quarter of a century of Tughtakīn's reign, there was a remarkable improvement in the state of the city, both morally and economically. On his death in Ṣafar 522/February 1128, he was succeeded by his son, Tādj al-Mulūk Būrī. The Bāṭiniyya [q.v.], who had already made themselves felt in Dimashḳ by killing the Amir Mawdūd in 507/1113, redoubled their activities supported by the Damascene vizier, Abū ʿAlī Ṭāhir al-Mazdaḳānī. In 523/1129 Būrī had this vizier killed. This was the signal for a terrible massacre, the population, out of control, exterminating some hundreds of Bāṭiniyya. The survivors did not long delay their revenge; Tādj al-Mulūk Būrī was the victim of an attempt on his life in 525/1131 and died as a result of his wounds a year later in Radjab 526/May-June 1132. The two succeeding princes were also assassinated, the one, Ismāʿīl, by his mother in 529/1135, the other, Shihāb al-Dīn Maḥmūd, by his enemies in 533/1139.

In 534/1140 the military leaders brought to power the young Abū Saʿīd Abaḳ Mudjīr al-Dīn, who left the direction of his affairs to his atabeg, Muʿīn al-Dīn Unur. On the atabeg's death ten years later Abaḳ took over the power himself but was obliged to accept the guardianship of Nūr al-Dīn who finally chased him out of Dimashḳ.

The situation of the Būrids was not easy. Invested with their power by the Caliph, they defended an advance position on the road to Fāṭimid Egypt, while the replenishment of their grain supplies was dependent on two regions, the Ḥawrān and the Biḳʿa, which were threatened by the Latin kingdom of Jerusalem. It was necessary at certain times to negotiate with the Franks, while at the same time they had to account for this conduct to Baghdād.

A new threat hung over Dimashḳ from the beginning of 524/1130, that of the Zangids, who at that time became masters of Ḥalab. In order to cope with them, the Būrids on more than one occasion obtained the help of the Franks, but as these last themselves attacked Dimashḳ in 543/1148, new agreements with them became no longer possible. The city was obliged to seek other alliances in order to safeguard its recently re-established economy.

Before Tughtakīn succeeded in restoring order, Dimashḳ had known three centuries of anarchy. Delivered up to the arbitrary power of ephemeral governors and their agents, the population lived under a reign of terror and misery. Hence the quest for security which haunted them determined the lay-out of its streets. They had to live among people whom they knew and who knew each other and be near to those who lived a similar kind of life. It was from this starting-point that they were able to make a new beginning in their corporate life.

The plan of the city, which had changed very little since Roman times, from the beginning of the 4th/9th century on became broken up into numerous water-tight compartments. Each district (ḥāra) barricaded itself behind its walls and gates and was obliged to form itself into a miniature city provided with all the essential urban constituents such as a mosque, baths, water supply (tāliʿ), public bakery, and little market (suwayḳa) with its cook-shop keepers; each had its own chief (shaykh) and group of militia (aḥdāth [q.v.]).

This breaking up of the ancient town was accompanied by a complete religious segregation since each community had its own sector of the city, the Muslims in the west near the citadel and the Great Mosque, the Christians in the north-east and the Jews in the south-east. The whole appearance of the city changed, houses no longer opening directly on to the streets. From this time on, there sprang up along the ancient roads of the city streets (darb) each of which served as the main thoroughfare of its own district and was closed at both ends by heavy gates. It branched out into little lanes (zuḳāḳ) and blind alleys.

Nevertheless there still existed in the city some elements of unity. These were the fortified outer walls which protected the town, the Great Mosque of the Umayyads, its religious and political centre where official decrees were proclaimed and displayed, and finally the sūḳs which, under the supervision of the muḥtasib, furnished provisions and manufactured goods. Commercial activities went on in the same places as in the Roman epoch. One sector was on the great thoroughfare with the side arcades and another on the street with the columns which, to the east of the Great Mosque, led from the temple to the agora. These highways had been completely changed. The arcades had been occupied by shops, the roadway itself invaded by booths, and in each of the commercial sectors there had developed a maze of sūḳs. One of the centres of the ancient Decumanus was the Dār al-Biṭṭīkh which, as in Baghdād, was the actual fruit-market, while not far from the ancient agora the Ḳayṣariyyas were much frequented. In these covered and enclosed markets, like civil basilicas based on Byzantine models, trade in valuable articles such as jewels, embroideries carpets and furs, was carried on.

When tranquillity returned under Tughtakīn, new districts were built, al-ʿUḳayba to the north, Shaghūr to the south, and Ḳaṣr al-Ḥadjdjādj to the south-west. At the gates of the city, tanneries produced raw materials for the leather workers, two paper-mills functioned from the beginning of the 9th century, and many water-mills ground various fatty substances.

Of the period preceding the Būrids, the only monument which still exists is the cupola of the Treasure-house (*Bayt al-Māl*) built in the Great Mosque in 161/778 by a governor of the Caliph al-Mahdī.

During the reign of Duḳāḳ, the city's oldest hospital was built to the west of the Great Mosque, and there also in 491/1098 the first *madrasa*, the Ṣādiriyya, was constructed for the Ḥanafīs.

The first *khānaḳāh* of Dimashḳ, the Ṭāwūsiyya, once contained the tombs of Duḳāḳ and his mother, Ṣafwat al-Mulk, but the last traces of it disappeared in 1938. Intellectual activity and Sunnī propaganda developed in the city under the Būrids. The Shāfiʿīs had their first *madrasa*, the Amīniyya, by 514/1120, whereas the first Ḥanbalī one, the Sharafiyya, was not built until 536/1142. On the eve of Nūr al-Dīn's capture of Dimashḳ seven *madrasas* were to be found there but there was still none for the *madhhab* of the Imām Mālik.

Dimashḳ under Nūr al-Dīn.—A new era began for the city with the arrival of Nūr al-Dīn in 549/1154. In establishing his residence at Dimashḳ, this prince, already master of Ḥalab, set a seal on the unity of Syria from the foot-hills of Cilicia to the mountains of Galilee. For the first time since the Umayyads, Dimashḳ was to become once again the capital of a vast Muslim state, unified and independent. Nūr al-Dīn's politics imprinted his character on the city which assumed the rôle of rampart of Muslim orthodoxy as opposed to the Fāṭimid heretics and the infidel Franks. A recrudescence of fanaticism showed itself at this time; its one and only aim was the triumph of Sunnī Islam and all efforts were concentrated on the *djihād* [*q.v.*]. Great centre of the Sunnīs, its fame was heightened by a large number of new religious buildings, mosques and *madrasas*. Dimashḳ retrieved at this time both its military importance and its religious prestige.

Works of military defence were carefully planned and carried out. The surrounding city walls were strengthened, and new towers built, of which one can still be seen to the west of Bāb al-Ṣaghīr. Some gates such as Bāb Sharḳī and Bāb al-Djābiya were merely reinforced, others provided with barbicans (Bāb al-Ṣaghīr and Bāb al-Salām). A sector of the north part of the city wall was carried forward as far as the right bank of the Baradā, and a new gate, Bāb al-Faradj, was opened to the east of the citadel, while Bāb Kaysān to the south was blocked up.

Nūr al-Dīn carried out works at the citadel itself, strengthening Bāb al-Ḥadīd and building a large mosque. Finally, in keeping with the military life of the city, two great plots of ground were reserved for the training of cavalry and for parades, the Maydān al-Akhḍar to the west of the the town and the Maydān al-Khaṣā to the south.

Religious and intellectual life was very highly developed and here two families played leading rôles, the Shāfiʿī Banū ʿAsākir and the Ḥanbalī Banū Ḳudāma who came originally from the now district of al-Ṣāliḥiyya, outside the walls on the slopes of the Ḳāsiyūn, in 556/1161. Places of prayer multiplied; Nūr al-Dīn himself had a certain number of mosques restored or constructed. An especially energetic effort was made to spread Sunnī doctrine and traditions and Nūr al-Dīn founded the first school for the teaching of traditions, the Dār al-Ḥadīth. There remain only ruins of this little *madrasa* whose first teacher was the Shāfiʿī historian, Ibn ʿAsākir. Other new *madrasas* were built, for the most part Shāfiʿī or Ḥanafī. It was at this time that the first Mālikī *madrasa*, al-Ṣalāḥiyya, was begun, to be finished by Ṣalāḥ al-Dīn. It was to the initiative of Nūr al-Dīn that we owe the construction of the great *madrasa*, al-ʿĀdiliyya, now the home of the Arab Academy. Begun about 567/1171, it was only finished in 619/1222.

Another new institution owed to Nūr al-Dīn was the Dār al-ʿAdl, which later on became the Dār al-Saʿāda. A high court of justice occupied the building to the south of the citadel; there, in the interests of equity, the prince grouped representatives of the four *madhhabs* around the Shāfiʿī *ḳāḍī 'l-ḳuḍāt*.

New forms showing an ʿIrāḳī influence appeared in Damascene architecture, notably the dome with honey-comb construction outside, to be found on the funerary *madrasa* of Nūr al-Dīn which was built in 567/1171, and in the cupola over the entrance to the *Māristān* whose portal is ornamented with stalactites. This hospital, one of the most important monuments in the history of Muslim architecture, was founded by Nūr al-Dīn to serve also as a school of medicine. An accurate inventory of the 12th century monuments of Dimashḳ is to be found in the topographical introduction drawn up by Ibn ʿAsākir for his *Taʾrīkh madīnat Dimashḳ*. By the end of Nūr al-Dīn's reign the number of places of worship had risen to 242 *intra muros* and 178 *extra muros*.

The Ayyūbid period.—In 569/1174 on the death of Nūr al-Dīn his son, al-Malik al-Ṣāliḥ Ismāʿīl, whose *atabeg* was the Amīr Shams al-Dawla Ibn al-Muḳaddam, inherited his father's throne. In Dimashḳ, where a powerful pro-Ayyūbid party had been in existence since the time when Ayyūb, father of Ṣalāḥ al-Dīn [*q.v.*], had been governor, plots were hatched among the amīrs. The young prince was taken to Ḥalab while Ibn al-Muḳaddam remained master of the city. To ensure its stability, the amīr negotiated a truce with the Franks, an agreement which upset one section of public opinion. The agents of Ṣalāḥ al-Dīn presented him as the champion of Islam and won over the population of Dimashḳ to their side. The former Kurdish vassal of Nūr al-Dīn took over the waging of the Holy War and entered Dimashḳ in 571/1176. During the years which followed fighting hardly ever ceased; it was the time of the Third Crusade and the Muslims were dominated by a desire to throw the Franks back to the sea. At last, in 583/1187, the victory of Ḥaṭṭīn [*q.v.*] allowed Islam to return to Jerusalem. Some months after having made peace with the crusaders, Ṣalāḥ al-Dīn, founder of the Ayyūbid dynasty [*q.v.*], died on 27 Ṣafar 589/4 March 1193 at Dimashḳ. Buried first at the citadel, his body was to receive its final sepulchre in the al-ʿAzīziyya *madrasa* to the north of the Great Mosque. After the sovereign's death fierce fighting broke out between his two sons and his brother. Al-Afḍal [*q.v.*], who in 582/1186 had received Dimashḳ in fief from his father, tried to retain his property, but in 592/1196 he was chased out by his uncle, al-ʿĀdil, who recognized the suzerainty of his nephew, al-ʿAzīz, successor of Ṣalāḥ al-Dīn in Cairo. Al-ʿAzīz died three years later and after lengthy disputes, al-ʿAdil was recognized as head of the Ayyūbid family in 597/1200. Under the rule of this spiritual heir of Ṣalāḥ al-Dīn there began a period of good organization and political relaxation. Cairo from that time on became the capital of the empire but Dimashḳ remained an important political, military and economic centre. Al-ʿĀdil died near Dimashḳ in 615/1218 and was buried in the al-ʿĀdiliyya *madrasa*. Al-Malik al-Muʿaẓẓam ʿĪsā, who had been his father's lieutenant in Syria since 597/1200, and who had received the province in fief in 604/1207, endeavoured to remain independent in Dimashḳ, but the twists and turns of political life brought him at the beginning of 623/1226 to mention in the *khuṭba* the Khʷārazm-shāh, Djalāl al-Dīn [*q.v.*], who thus became nominal suzerain of the city. When al-Muʿaẓẓam died in 624/1227 his son, al-Malik al-Nāṣir Dāwūd, succeeded him under the tutelage of his *atabeg*, ʿIzz al-Dīn Aybak. Very soon afterwards, the Amīr al-Ashraf arrived from Diyār Muḍar, eliminated his nephew, Dāwūd, and installed himself in Dimashḳ in 625/1228.

On the death of al-Kāmil, who had succeeded al-ʿĀdil in Cairo in 635/1138, there had begun a period of decline. Fratricidal disputes started again. In order to hold on to Dimashḳ, al-Malik al-Ṣāliḥ Ismāʿīl allied himself with the Franks against his nephew, al-Ṣāliḥ Ayyūb, master of Egypt. With the help of the Khʷārizmians, Ayyūb was victorious over him in 643/1245 and once again Dimashḳ came under the authority of Cairo. Ayyūb died in 646/1248, his son, Turanshāh, disappeared presumably assassinated a few months later, and in 648/1250, the prince of Ḥalab, al-Malik al-Nāṣir Yūsuf, seized Dimashḳ of which he was the last Ayyūbid ruler. The Mongol threat was, indeed, now becoming more imminent; Baghdād fell in 656/1258 and less than two years later the Syrian capital was taken in its turn.

The arrival of Nūr al-Dīn had undoubtedly brought about a renaissance in Dimashḳ, but the circumstances of the reign of Ṣalāḥ al-Dīn had put a stop to the evolution of the city.

Progress began again under the Ayyūbids when Dimashḳ became the seat of a princely court. The growth in population and new resources which such a promotion implied had repercussions on its economic life, all the more appreciable since the calm reigns of al-ʿĀdil and his successor brought a peaceful atmosphere. This improvement in economic activity went side by side with the development of commercial relations. From that time on, Italian merchants began to come regularly to Dimashḳ. Industry took an upward trend; its silk brocades remained as famous as ever, while copper utensils inlaid or not, gilded glassware and tanned lambskins were also much in demand. The markets (*sūḳs*) stayed very active and at the side of the Ḳayṣariyyas, warehouses (*funduḳ*) multiplied in the town, while the Dār al-Wakāla, a depôt of merchant companies, gained in importance.

To strengthen their resistance against both family cupidity and the threats of the Franks, as well as to bring the system of defence up to date with the progress of the military arts, the Ayyūbids made changes and improvements in the outer walls and the citadel of Dimashḳ. The work on the walls was confined to the gates; Bāb Sharḳī and Bāb al-Ṣaghīr were strengthened in 604/1207 by al-Muʿaẓẓam ʿĪsā; al-Nāṣir Dāwūd rebuilt Bāb Tūmā in 624/1227; Bāb al-Faradj was reconstructed in 636/1239; lastly, al-Ṣāliḥ Ayyūb remodelled Bāb al-Salām in 641/1243, adding a square tower which may still be seen at the north-east corner of the walls. Complete reconstruction of the citadel, a piece of work which took ten years, was begun in 604/1207. A new palace with

a throne-room was built in the interior to serve as a residence for the Sultan, while the military offices and financial services were installed in new locations there. The present-day arrangements, indeed, go back to this period and although the citadel was burnt down and dismantled by the Mongols, two of these 7th/13th century towers still remain almost intact.

The general prosperity allowed the Ayyūbids to practise an exceptionally generous patronage of writers and scholars. Dimashḳ at this time was not only a great centre of Muslim cultural life but also an important religious stronghold. The Sunnī politics of the dynasty showed themselves in the encouragement which its leaders gave, following the custom of the Saldjūḳids and the Zangids, to the propagation of the Islamic faith and of orthodoxy. Civil architecture flourished at this time also. Princes and princesses, high dignitaries and senior officers rivalled each other in making religious foundations and Dimashḳ was soon to become the city of *madrasas*; the number of these—twenty are mentioned by Ibn Djubayr in 1184/1770—was to quadruple in a single century. (On the Ayyūbid *madrasas*, see Herzfeld in *Ars Islamica*, xi-xii, 1-71). From then on, the *madrasa* with its lecture-rooms and its lodgings for masters and students, began, like the mosques, to be combined more and more often with the tomb of its founder (see, for example, the ʿĀdiliyya and the Muʿaẓẓamiyya). Linked with the funerary *madrasa*, there appeared also at this time the *turba* of a type peculiar to Dimashḳ. The mausoleum consisted of a square chamber whose walls were decorated with painted stucco, above which four semi-circular niches and four flat niches symmetrically placed formed an octagonal zone surmounted by a drum composed of sixteen niches of equal size upon which rested a sixteen-sided cupola. This was the typical way of erecting a cupola over a square building. The first example whose date we know is the mausoleum of Zayn al-Dīn, built in 567/1172. Among the monuments of this kind which can still be seen to-day are the following of the 6th/12th century: the Turbat al-Badrī, the al-Nadjmiyya *madrasa*, the al-ʿAzīziyya *madrasa* where the tomb of Ṣalāḥ al-Dīn is situated, and the mausoleum of Ibn Salāma, built in 613/1216. Most characteristic of Ayyūbid architecture is its sense of proportion; the buildings have façades of ashlar of harmonious size, and the alternation of basalt with limestone forms a decorative motif whose finest example, perhaps, is the Ḳilīdjiyya *madrasa*, completed in 651/1253. The dimensions of the cupolas are such that they seem to sink naturally into their urban background.

The 7th/13th century was one of Dimashḳ's most brilliant epochs. It had once more become "a political, commercial, industrial, strategic, intellectual and religious centre" and most of the monuments which still adorn the city date from this period.

The Mamlūk period (658-922/1260-1516).—A new phase began in the history of Dimashḳ when in Rabīʿ I 658/March 1260 the troops of Hūlāgū entered the city. The governor fled, the garrison was forced to retreat towards the south, the Prince al-Malik al-Nāṣir and his children were made prisoners. The Ayyūbid dynasty had come to an end. The invasion stopped at ʿAyn Djālūt [*q.v.*] where the Mamlūks, under the command of the Amīrs Ḳuṭuz and Baybars, put the Mongols to flight. These then evacuated Dimashḳ which was given by the powerful Kurdish family of the Ḳaymarī into the hands of the Sultan of Egypt's troops. The Christians of the city suffered reprisals for their attitude with regard to the Mongols, and the Church of St. Mary was destroyed at this time. From then on Cairo, where since 656/ 1258 a shadow Caliphate had been maintained, supplanted Dimashḳ which became a political dependency of Egypt.

It was still to be the most important city of the Syrian province, the mamlaka or niyāba of Dimashḳ. (For its administrative organization, see Gaudefroy-Demombynes, La Syrie à l'époque des Mamelouks, Paris 1923, 135-201). The first great Mamlūk sultan, al-Malik al-Ẓāhir Baybars [q.v.], interested himself especially in Dimashḳ which he visited frequently during his reign (658-76/1260-77). He reconditioned the citadel which served as a residence for the sultan when he visited the city; in it also were to be found the mint, the arsenal, a storehouse of military equipment, food reserves, a mill and some shops. This veritable "city" served also as a political prison (see J. Sauvaget, La Citadelle de Damas, in Syria, xi (1930), 50-90 and 216-41).

On the Maydān al-Akhḍar to the west of the town Baybars built a palace with black and ochre courses of masonry, the famous Ḳasr al-Ablaḳ, of which the Sultan Muḥammad b. Ḳalāwūn was later to build a replica in Cairo. In the 10th/16th century the Ottoman Sultan Sulaymān erected the takkiyya on the site of this building. Baybars died in this ḳaṣr in 676/1277 and on the orders of his son, al-Malik al-Saʿīd, was buried in the al-Ẓāhiriyya madrasa where the National Library is now situated. During his long reign of seventeen years Dimashḳ had only four governors but after the death of Baybars it was to undergo a long period of political anarchy punctuated by frequent rebellions.

Dimashḳ was the second city of the empire and the post of governor was given to eminent Mamlūks, usually coming from the niyāba of Ḥalab. The possibility of rivalry between the governor of Dimashḳ and the Sultan was diminished by the presence of the governor of the citadel. There were, in fact, two governors, the nāʾib of the city who received his diploma of investiture from the Sultan and who resided to the south of the citadel at the Dār al-Saʿāda where he gave his audiences, and the nāʾib of the citadel who had a special status and represented the person of the Sultan. The constant rivalry between these two dignitaries and the amīrs of their circles was sufficient pledge of the maintenance of the Sultan's authority. A change of Sultan in Cairo usually provoked a rebellion on the part of the governor of Dimashḳ. Thus when al-Saʿīd, Baybars' son, was dismissed from the throne and succeeded by the Sultan al-Malik al-Manṣūr Ḳalāwūn [q.v.], the governor, Sunḳur al-Ashḳar, refused to recognize his authority. Supported by the amīrs and strengthened by a fatwā given him by the ḳāḍi 'l-ḳuḍāt, the celebrated historian, Ibn Khallikān, Sunḳur seized the citadel whose governor, Ladjīn, he imprisoned, and proclaimed himself Sultan in Djumādā II 677/October-November 1278. He had the khuṭba said in his name until Ṣafar 679/ June 1280, when the troops of Ḳalāwūn were victorious over him, following the defection of certain Damascene contingents. Sunḳur fled to al-Raḥba on the Euphrates. Ladjīn, now freed, was proclaimed governor of the city. A new Sultan often decided to change the governor; thus ʿIzz al-Dīn Aybak was relieved of his office in 695/1296 on the succession of al-Malik al-ʿĀdil Kitbughā, who nominated Shudjāʿ al-Din Adjirlu. After the deposing

of Kitbughā, who was imprisoned in the citadel of Dimashḳ, Ladjīn, who became Sultan, nominated Sayf al-Dīn Ḳipčaḳ governor in 696/1297. The latter put himself at the disposition of prince Ghāzān [q.v.] and accompanied him at the time of his incursion into Syria. In 699/1300 the Mongol army entered Dimashḳ; it seized the Great Mosque but did not succeed in taking the citadel where the Mamlūks had entrenched themselves. The whole sector of the town between these two strongpoints underwent serious damage and the Dār al-Ḥadīth of Nūr al-Dīn suffered. When the Mongols evacuated the city, Ḳipčaḳ betook himself to Egypt and rejoined the new Sultan al-Malik al-Nāṣir Muḥammad b. Ḳalāwūn. In 702/1303 a new Mongol threat hung over the city, but the advance was repulsed. From the beginning of 712/1312, in the course of the third reign of Muḥammad b. Ḳalāwūn, Dimashḳ had, in the person of Tankiz, a governor of true quality whose authority was recognized by the Syrian amīrs. Viceroy of Syria in fact as well as name, he inspired respect in the Sultan whose nominal representative he was for almost a quarter of a century. The prosperity which this period brought allowed intellectual life to flourish. This was the epoch of the Muslim reformer Ibn Taymiyya, and of the historian al-Ṣafadī. In 717/1317 Tankiz built the mosque where his tomb was to be placed extra muros. Some years later he had work done on the Great Mosque; finally in 739/1339, he founded a Dār al-Ḥadīth. On the succession of the new Sultan, al-Malik Abū Bakr, he fell suddenly into disgrace, was arrested in Dhu 'l-Ḥidjdja 740/June 1340 and imprisoned at Alexandria where he died of poison.

From 730/1340 until 784/1382, the time when Ibn Baṭṭūṭa was visiting the Muslim East, twelve Baḥrī sultans succeeded each other in Cairo, while a dozen governors occupied the position of nāʾib of the city. Some of them had charge of its destiny on more than one occasion. It was a continual struggle stirred up by the ambitions of one or another and aggravated by the audacity of the zuʿar, whose militias, intended for self-defence, neglected their proper duties and, often with impunity, terrorized the population.

The succession of Barḳūḳ [q.v.] in 734/1382 brought a new line of Circassian Sultans to power who are also called Burdjīs.

In 791/1389 Dimashḳ fell for some weeks into the power of Yilbughā al-Nāṣirī, a governor of Ḥalab who had revolted against the Sultan. Master of Syria, he penetrated the walls of Dimashḳ, overthrew an army sent by Barḳūḳ and made his way towards Egypt. He was defeated in his turn but in Shaʿbān 792/July-August 1390 we find him once again governor of Dimashḳ.

Although warned of the progress of Tīmūr, Barḳūḳ did not have time to reinforce the defences of his territory for he died in 801/1399. In Dimashḳ, Sayf al-Dīn Tanibak who had governed the city since 795/1393, revolted against Faradj, the new Sultan, and marched on Egypt. He was beaten near Ghazza, made prisoner and executed at Dimashḳ. Syria, torn apart by the rivalries of the amīrs, fell an easy prey to Tīmūr. The Mongol leader advanced as far as Dimashḳ and it was in his camp near the town that he received the memorable visit of Ibn Khaldūn. The Sultan Faradj, coming to the aid of the Amīr Sudun, Barḳūḳ's nephew, was forced to turn back, following a series of defections. After its surrender the city was given over to pillage but the citadel held out for a month. Many were the victims of fires which caused serious damage. The Great Mosque itself was not spared nor the Dār al-Saʿāda. In 803/1401, Tīmūr left Dimashk, taking with him to Samarkand what remained of qualified artisans and workmen. This mass deportation was one of the greatest catastrophes in the history of the town. After the Mongols' departure, the Amīr Taghrībirdī al-Ẓāhirī became the governor of a devastated city, despoiled and depopulated. The exhausted country had to face a thousand difficulties. Two long reigns gave Dimashk the opportunity of rising from its ruins: that of Sultan Barsbāy (825-41/1422-38) and, more important, that of Ḳāʾitbāy [*q.v.*] whose rule from 872/1468 until 901/1495 brought a long period of tranquillity. Moreover between 16 Shaʿbān and 10 Ramaḍān 882/23 November and 16 December 1477 this Sultan paid a visit to Dimashk where the post of governor was held by the Amīr Ḳidjmas, whose rapacity remains legendary. The civil strife had swallowed up large sums of money and the amīrs did not hesitate about increasing the number of taxes and charges. The Sultans themselves would often use violent means of procuring a sum of money with which the taxes could not provide them, nor did they scruple about reducing their governors to destitution by confiscating their fortunes. Under the last Mamlūks corruption even won over the *ḳāḍī*s who, in return for a reward, were willing to justify certain measures against the law. After Ḳāʾitbāy, there began once again a régime of violence and extortions which ended only with the reign of Ḳānṣūh al-Ghawrī (905-22/1500-16). This last Mamlūk Sultan had to defend himself against the Ottomans who had invaded Syria. He died in battle in Ramaḍān 922/mid-October 1516, and the troops of Selīm I made their entry into Dimashk.

Paradoxically enough, a large number of buildings were constructed in the city during this tragic period. The Mamlūks, who lived uncertain of what the next day would bring, tried at least to secure themselves a sepulchre, so that mausoleums and funerary mosques multiplied although they built few *madrasas*.

There were no innovations in the art of this period, for any lack of precedent frightened these parvenus. At the beginning of Mamlūk times they built according to Ayyūbid formulas. The al-Ẓāhiriyya *madrasa*, now the National Library, where Baybars' tomb is situated, was originally the house of al-Aḳīḳī, where Ayyūb, father of Ṣalāḥ al-Dīn, had lived, and the modifications made in 676/1277 were limited to the addition of a cupola and an alveoled gate.

The only new type of building was the double mausoleum, of which that of the old Sultan Kitbughā, built in 695/1296, was the first example in Dimashk.

In 747/1346 Yilbugha, then governor of the city, erected a building on the site of a former mosque whose plan was inspired by that of the Great Mosque. It was in this sanctuary, situated near the modern Mardja Square, that the new governor put on his robe of honour before making a solemn entry into the city.

The artistic decadence which became more pronounced in the course of the 8th/14th century came into the open at the beginning of the 9th/15th century after the ravages of Tīmūr. At this time everything was sacrificed to outward appearances and the monument was no more than a support for showy ornamentation. This taste for the picturesque manifested itself in the minarets with polygonal shafts, loaded with balconies and corbelling whose silhouettes were to change the whole skyline of the city. The first example was the minaret of the Djāmiʿ Hishām, built in 830/1427. Polychromatic façades grew in popularity and even inlays were added. The al-Ṣabūniyya mosque, finished in 868/1464, and the funerary *madrasa* of Sibay called the Djāmiʿ al-Kharrāṭīn, built in the very early years of the 9th/16th century, are two striking examples of the decadence of architecture under the last Mamlūks.

It is interesting to notice that most of these Mamlūk monuments were built *extra muros*. There was no longer room within the city walls and the city "burst out" because, paradoxically, "there was an immense development of economic activity during this sad period". "All the trades whose development down the course of the centuries had been assisted by the presence of a princely court, had now to satisfy the demand for comfort and the ostentatious tastes" of military upstarts who thought only of getting what enjoyment they could out of life and of impressing the popular imagination with their display. Dimashk, while remaining the great market for the grain of the Ḥawrān, became also a great industrial town, specializing in luxury articles and army equipment. This activity was reflected by a new extension of the *sūḳ*s which was accompanied by "a sharp differentiation between the various trading areas according to their type of customer". A new district, Taḥt Ḳalʿa, developed to the north-west of the town below the citadel. In the Sūḳ al-Khayl, whose open space remained the centre of military life, groups of craftsmen installed themselves whose clients were essentially the army and who left the shops inside the city walls to other groups of artisans. Wholesale trade in fruit and vegetables also went outside the town; a new Dār al-Biṭṭīkh was set up at al-ʿUḳayba where the amīrs and the members of their *djund* lived.

Towards the middle of the 9th/15th century there appeared the first symptoms of an economic crisis. The state, whose coffers were empty, lived on its wits, but commerce still remained active as is demonstrated by the accounts of such travellers as Ludovico de Varthema (*Itinerario*, v-vii) who visited Dimashk in 907/1502. The city profited from the very strong trading activity between western Europe and the Muslim East, but the hostility of the people of Dimashk and the despotic nature of its governors prevented European merchants from founding any lasting establishments likely to acquire importance. Merchants arrived bringing a above all cloth from Flanders, stocked themselves up with silk brocades, inlaid copper-work and enamelled glassware, and then departed. The effects of the discovery of the Cape of Good Hope did not immediately make themselves felt; it was excessive taxation rather which was beginning to slow down trade on the eve of the coming of the Ottomans.

The Ottoman Period (922-1246/1516-1831). — On 25 Radjab 922/24 August 1516 the Ottoman troops, thanks to their well-trained infantry and the superior firing power of their artillery, put the Mamlūk cavalry to flight at Mardj Dābiḳ near Ḥalab. This success gave the Sultan Selīm I a conquest of Syria all the more swift since the majority of the *nāʾib*s rallied to the Ottoman cause. There was practically no resistance at Dimashk where the Mamlūk garrison retreated and the Sultan made his entrance into the town on 1 Ramaḍān 922/28 September 1516. The Mamlūk detachments protecting Egypt were beaten three months later near Ghazza. The commander of the Syrian contingents,

Djanbirdī al-Ghazālī, joined forces with Selīm and was allowed to return to the post of governor of Dimashḳ to which he had been nominated by Ḳānṣūh al-Ghawrī, the last Mamlūk Sultan.

The arrival of the Ottomans seemed no more to the Damascene population than a local incident and not as a remarkable event which was to open a new era. To them it was merely a change of masters; the Mamlūks of Cairo were succeeded by another group of privileged foreigners, the Janissaries who had come from Turkey. Fairly quickly, however, there was a reaction on the part of the amīrs and Djanbirdī surrounded himself with all the anti-Ottoman elements. On the death of Selīm I in 927/1521 the governor of Dimashḳ refused to recognize the authority of Sulaymān, proclaimed himself independent and seized the citadel. The rebel quickly became master of Tripoli, Ḥimṣ and Ḥamā, and marched against Ḥalab which he besieged without success, then returning to Dimashḳ. Sulaymān sent troops which crossed Syria and in a battle at Ḳābūn, to the north of Dimashḳ, on 17 Ṣafar 927/27 January 1521, the rebellious governor was killed. The violence and pillaging of the Turkish soldiery then sowed panic in Dimashḳ and its surroundings. A third of the city was destroyed by the Janissaries.

Under the rule of Sulaymān, the political régime changed and the administration showed some signs of organization. In 932/1525-6 the Ottomans made their first survey of the lands, populations, and revenues of Dimashḳ (see DAFTAR-I KHĀḲĀNĪ and B. Lewis, *The Ottoman Archives as a source for the history of the Arab lands*, in *JRAS*, 1951, 153-4, where the registers for Dimashḳ are listed). Dimashḳ was no more than a modest *pashalīk* in the immense empire over which the shadow of the Ottoman Sultanate extended. Most certainly the city no longer had the outstanding position in the game of political intrigue which it had enjoyed in the century of the Circassians. Pashas, accompanied by a Ḥanafī *ḳāḍī* and a director of finance but with no authority over the garrison, succeeded each other at a headlong rate; between 923/1517 and 1103/1679 Dimashḳ was to have 133 governors. A list of them and an account of these years is to be found in H. Laoust, *Les gouverneurs de Damas sous les Mamelouks et les premiers Ottomans*, Damascus 1952.

Early in the 12th/late in the 17th century there was a change of feeling in the empire; the Sultans lost their authority and remained in the Seraglio, and the Ottoman frontiers receded, but they still remained wide enough to shelter Dimashḳ from enemy attempts. Furthermore the population had internal troubles at that time. The offices of State were farmed out during this period; the holders and especially the governors, wanting to recover the cost of their position as quickly as possible, put pressure on the people; corruption became the rule and lack of discipline habitual. Nevertheless Dimashḳ was not without a certain prosperity thanks to the two factors of trade and the pilgrimage to Mecca.

As early as 942/1535, France concluded with the Porte a Treaty of Capitulations which opened Turkish ports to its traders and enabled them to do business throughout the eastern Mediterranean. European merchants, three-fifths of whom at the end of the 18th century were French, imported manufactured goods and exported raw materials and spices. Despite the very high custom duties, the bad behaviour of officials and even, to some extent, the insecurity, external trade remained very lucrative and political events never succeeded in stopping the broad movements of commerce. At Dimashḳ, as in other parts of Syria, the native Christians served as intermediaries between the Europeans and both the Turkish administration and the population which spoke an Arabic that in the course of four centuries had taken in many Turkish loan-words. The intensity of the commercial traffic justified the construction of numerous *khāns* which served as hotels, as well as exchanges and warehouses, for the foreign traders. In the oldest *khāns*, such as the Khān al-Ḥarīr, built in 980/1572 by Darwīsh Pasha and still in existence to-day, we find the usual Syrian arrangements: a court-yard, generally square, surrounded by an arcaded gallery on to which open the shops and stables, while the floor above is reserved for lodgings. Certainly the Venetian *funduḳ* which came into being in Damascus after 1533 would have had the same arrangements. Early in the 18th century this plan was modified; the central space became smaller and was covered with cupolas, the merchandise thus being protected in bad weather. This was a new type of building and specifically Damascene. Still to be seen to-day is the Khān Sulaymān Pasha, built in 1144/1732, whose central court is covered by two great cupolas, and most important of all, the Khān Asʿad Pasha, constructed in 1165/1752, which is still alive and active. This masterpiece of architecture is a vast whole, square in plan, covered by eight small cupolas dominated by a larger one in the middle which is supported by four marble columns.

Trade with Europe was carried on via the ports of the *wilāyet* of Dimashḳ, the most important of which was Ṣaydā.

The Ottoman Sultan, having become protector of the Holy Cities, showed a special interest in the pilgrimage to Mecca. This became one of Dimashḳ's main sources of income. Being the last stop of the *darb al-ḥadjdj* in settled country, the city was the annual meeting-place of tens of thousands of pilgrims from the north of the empire. This periodical influx brought about intense commercial activity. The pilgrims seized the opportunity of their stay in order to prepare for crossing the desert. They saw to acquiring mounts and camping materials and bought provisions to last three months. At the given moment, the Pasha of Dimashḳ, who bore the coveted title of *amīr al-ḥadjdj*, took the head of the official caravan accompanying the *maḥmal* and made his way to the Holy Cities under the protection of the army. On the way back, Dimashḳ was the first important urban centre and the pilgrims sold there what they had bought in Arabia, whether coffee or black slaves from Africa.

Once past the Bāb Allāh which marked the extreme southern limits of the town, the caravans passed for three kilometres through the district of the Maydān, where cereal warehouses and Mamlūk mausoleums alternated without a break between them. This traffic to the south helped to develop a new district near the ramparts outside Bāb Djābiya; this was to be the quarter of the caravaneers. These found equipment and supplies in the *sūḳ*s where, side by side with the saddlers and blacksmiths, the curio dealers installed themselves as well. This district owed its name of al-Sināniyya to the large mosque which the Grand Vizier, Sinān Pasha, *wālī* of Dimashḳ, had built between 994/1586 and 999/1591; its minaret covered with green glazed tiles could be seen from a very long way off. Some years earlier, in 981/1574, the governor, Derwīsh

Pas͟ha, had had a large mosque, whose remarkable faïence tiles are worth admiring, built in the north of this quarter. This mode of decoration arrived with the Ottomans when the art of Constantinople was suddenly implanted in Dimas͟hḳ. A new architectural type also appeared in the urban landscape, that of the Turkish mosque, schematically made up of a square hall crowned by a hemispherical cupola on pendentives, with a covered portico in front and one or more minarets with circular shafts crowned by candle-snuffer tops at the corners. The first example of this type in Dimas͟hḳ was the large mosque built on the site of the Ḳaṣr al-Ablaḳ by Sulaymān Ḳānūnī in 962/1555 according to the plans of the architect, Sinān. This mosque, indeed, formed part of a great ensemble which is still called to-day the Takkiyya Sulaymāniyya. The covered portico of the hall of prayer opens from the south side of a vast court-yard; on the east and west side there are rows of cells with a columned portico in front of them; on the north stands a group of buildings which used to shelter the kitchens and canteen but which since 1957 has housed the collections of the Army Museum. Active centres of religious life were to spring up both around the ʿUmariyya *madrasa* at al-Ṣāliḥiyya, and around the mausoleum of Muḥyi 'l-Dīn al-ʿArabī, where in 959/1552 the Sultan Selīm I had an *ʿimāret* constructed to make free distributions of food to the poor visiting the tomb of the illustrious *ṣūfī*, or again at the Takkiyya Mawlawiyya built in 993/1585 for the Dancing Dervishes to the west of the mosque of Tankiz. The fact that all these great religious monuments of the Ottoman period were built *extra muros* shows that the Great Mosque of the Umayyads was no longer a unique centre of assembly for the Muslim community and definitely confirms the spread of the city beyond the old town.

With the progress of artillery the ancient fortifications of Dimas͟hḳ became outdated, but on the other hand the peace which reigned over the empire diminished the value of the surrounding walls which at this time began to be invaded by dwelling-houses, while the moats which had become a general night-soil dump were filled with refuse.

Within the ramparts the streets were paved, cleaned and lit at the expense of those living along them, as under the last Mamlūks. If the piety of the population showed itself in the construction of public fountains (*sabīl*), the *madrasa*s and *zāwiya*s, in contrast, were deserted by many in favour of the coffee-houses which multiplied and added to the number of meeting-places for the people. The only monument worth notice *intra muros* apart from the *k͟hān*s is the palace which the governor Asʿad Pas͟ha al-ʿAẓm had built to the south-east of the Great Mosque in 1162/1749. The whole body of buildings is grouped according to the traditional arrangements of a Syrian dwelling of the 18th century with a *salāmlīk* and a *ḥarāmlīk* decorated with woodwork in the Turkish style. This palace is at present occupied by the National Museum of Ethnography and Popular Art.

The Modern Period (1831-1920).—Between 1832 and 1840, Egyptian domination was to bring to Dimas͟hḳ, which had for centuries remained outside the main current of political events, a relative prosperity. In 1832 Ibrāhīm Pas͟ha, the son of Muḥammad ʿAlī, after crossing Palestine came to seize Dimas͟hḳ, where revolts against the Ottomans had preceded his arrival. The population aided the Egyptian troops who put the Ottomans to flight near Ḥimṣ, then at the end of July inflicted a new defeat on them near Ḥalab and forced them back across the Taurus.

The Egyptian regime lasted a decade and allowed the return of Europeans who up to that time had not been able to enter the town in western clothes and had been forced to submit to all kinds of irritating formalities. In spring 1833 the Sultan ceded the viceroyalty of Syria to Muḥammad ʿAlī and Ibrāhīm Pas͟ha governed it in his father's name. From that time on, foreign representatives came and settled in Dimas͟hḳ. Very liberal and tolerant on the religious side, Ibrāhīm Pas͟ha founded a college in Damascus where some six hundred uniformed pupils received both general and military instruction. Many administrative buildings were put up even to the sacrifice of some ancient monuments such as the Tankiziyya, which was turned into a military school and remained so until after 1932. A new residence, the Sérail, was built for the governor. This, which was erected outside the walls to the west of the city facing Bāb al-Ḥadīd, was soon to bring about the creation of a new district, al-Ḳanawāt, along the Roman aqueduct. The buildings of Dar al-Saʿāda and the Iṣṭabl, where in 932/1526 there had existed a small zoological garden dating from the Mamlūks, were transformed into a military headquarters which only ceased to exist in 1917, while in this same sector of the city the best patronized shops were grouped together in the Sūḳ al-Arwām. In J. L. Porter's *Five Years in Damascus*, 2 vols., London 1855, an interesting picture of the city in the middle of the 19th century is to be found. In 1840, after having re-established order and peace, Ibrāhīm Pas͟ha made a first attempt at reform (see BALADIYYA and MAD͟JLIS) and proposed an independent and centralized government. Europe, and above all Palmerston, was opposed to the ambitions of Muḥammad ʿAlī; they profited therefore by the discontent provoked by the introduction of conscription to rouse the population against Ibrāhīm Pas͟ha who was forced to evacuate Dimas͟hḳ. His attempt at reform was not followed up and the Damascenes fell back under Ottoman domination. A violent outburst of fanaticism was to break the apparent calm of life there. Bloodthirsty quarrels having arisen between the Druzes and the Maronites of the south of Lebanon, public opinion was stirred up in Damascus and on 12 July 1860 the Muslims invaded the Christian quarters and committed terrible massacres, in the course of which the Amīr ʿAbd al-Ḳādir, exiled from Algeria, was able by his intervention to save some hundreds of human lives. This explosion was severely punished by the Sultan and, at the end of August 1860, provoked the landing of troops sent by Napoleon III.

From the beginning of this period European influence made itself felt in the cultural and economic spheres. Foreign schools of various religious denominations were able to develop, thanks to subventions from their governments. The Lazarist Fathers had had a very active college since 1775, and a Protestant Mission had been functioning since 1853. New establishments were opened after 1860 such as the British Syrian Mission and the College of Jesuits (1872). Education of girls was carried on by the Sisters of Charity. Midhat Pas͟ha made an attempt to develop state education but it was no more than an attempt and was not followed up. Cairo was the true intellectual centre at this time, and it was Cairo's newspapers, *al-Muḳtataf* and *al-Muḳattam*, which were read in Dimas͟hḳ. *Al-S͟hām*, the first Arabic language newspaper edited and printed in

Damascus, was not to appear until 1897. Little by little, however, the Syrian capital was to become one of the centres of Arab nationalism. As in the other towns of Syria, secret revolutionary cells showed themselves very active in the last quarter of the 19th century and periodically exhorted the population to rebel. It was even said that Midḥat Pas̲h̲a, author of the liberal constitution of 1876, protected the movement after he had become governor of Dimas̲h̲ḳ in 1878. The great reformer had a population of about 150,000 to administer and accomplished lasting good in the city, chiefly in matters concerned with public hygiene and improvement of the traffic system, which since carriages had come on the scene had grown very inadequate in the old town. The governor replaced a number of alleyways in the *sūḳ*s with broader streets. The western part of the Street called Straight was widened and given a vaulted roof of corrugated iron; this is the present day Sūḳ Midḥat Pas̲h̲a. To the south of the citadel the moat was filled in and its place occupied by new *sūḳ*s, while the whole road joining Bāb al-Ḥadīd with the Great Mosque was made wide enough for two-way carriage traffic and was given the name Sūḳ Ḥamīdiyya. New buildings were put up at this time on vacant lots to the west of the town around the Mard̲j̲a, the "Meadow". These were a new "sérai", seat of the civil administration, a headquarters for the military staff, the town-hall, the law-courts, a post-office and a barracks. The Ḥamīdiyya barracks, which was newly fitted out and arranged after 1945, was to be the kernel of the present-day university. The Christian quarter of Bāb Tūma saw the rise of fine houses where European consuls, missionaries, merchants and so on, settled themselves, while the old town began to empty; there were no longer any gaps between the suburbs of Suwayḳāt and al-Ḳanawāt to the west, or those of Sarūd̲j̲a and al-ʿUḳayba to the north-west. A new colony of Kurds and of Muslims who had emigrated from Crete settled at al-Ṣāliḥiyya, which gave the quarter the name of al-Muhād̲j̲irīn. The situation of this suburb on the slopes of the D̲j̲abal Ḳāsiyūn attracted the Turkish aristocracy who built beautiful houses surrounded by gardens there. At this time also relations with the outer world became easier and to the two *locanda*s existing before 1860 were added new hotels for the foreigners who, after 1863, were able to travel from Bayrūt to Dimas̲h̲ḳ by stage-coach over a road newly constructed by French contractors. Further progress was made in 1894 when a French company opened a railway between Bayrūt, Dimas̲h̲ḳ and the Ḥawrān. Later on a branch from Rayyāḳ to the north went to Ḥimṣ and Ḥalab. Then ʿIzzat Pas̲h̲a al-ʿAbīd, a Syrian second secretary to the Sultan, conceived the idea of a Damascus-Medina line to make the pilgrimage easier. From this time on, the Sultan was to be on friendly terms with Kaiser Wilhelm II, who had visited Dimas̲h̲ḳ in the winter of 1898, and so the construction of this line was placed in German hands. The narrow gauge Ḥid̲j̲āz railway was inaugurated in 1908; it allowed pilgrims to reach the Holy City in five days instead of the forty which it had taken by caravan. In this same year, an army officers' movement forced the Sultan to restore the Ottoman constitution which had been suspended for 31 years and it was not long after this that ʿAbd al-Ḥamīd II was overthrown. This news was greeted in Dimas̲h̲ḳ with large-scale popular manifestations and many firework displays, but their happiness was to be of short duration. The spirit of liberalism which had led Kurd ʿAlī to bring to the city his review, *al-Muḳtabas*, which he had founded in Cairo three years earlier as a daily paper, was deceptive. Indeed after 1909 the Ottoman authorities banned it and the only resource for the Arab nationalists was to band themselves together again in secret societies.

The declaration of war in 1914 was to have grave consequences for Dimas̲h̲ḳ. At the end of that year, D̲j̲emāl Pas̲h̲a was appointed Governor-General of Syria, Lebanon and Palestine, and Commander-in-Chief of the 4th Ottoman army with headquarters in Dimas̲h̲ḳ. This town rapidly became the great General Headquarters of the combined German and Turkish forces and their operational base against the Suez zone. D̲j̲emāl Pas̲h̲a soon showed himself a mediocre general but a very energetic administrator. He had hoped to win the people of Dimas̲h̲ḳ over to the Turkish cause but was soon forced to give up this idea. It was in Dimas̲h̲ḳ, in the circle of the family al-Bakrī, that the Amīr Fayṣāl, son of Ḥusayn, the S̲h̲arīf of Mecca, was won over to the idea of Arab revolt in April 1915; he met with members of the secret societies *al-Fatāt* and *al-ʿAhd*, at that time. At the end of May, Fayṣal returned from Constantinople and shared in the elaboration of a plan of action against the Turks with the co-operation of the British. They arrived ultimately at the famous "Protocol of Damascus" asking Britain to recognize Arab independence and the abolition of capitulations. In January 1916, Fayṣal was in Damascus again and was still there on 6 May when D̲j̲emāl Pas̲h̲a had twenty-one partisans of the Arab cause hanged. This event, the "Day of the Martyrs", is still commemorated every year. On 10 June, the revolt broke out in the Ḥid̲j̲āz, where the S̲h̲arīf Ḥusayn proclaimed himself "King of the Arabs". It was not until 30 September 1918 that Turkish troops evacuated Dimas̲h̲ḳ. On 1 October Allied forces, including units of the Amīr Fayṣal, entered the city. In May 1919 elections took place to appoint a National Syrian Congress and in June this congress decided to reject the conclusions at which the Peace Conference of Paris had arrived concerning the mandates. On 10 December a national Syrian government was formed in Dimas̲h̲ḳ. On 7 March 1920 the National Congress proclaimed Syria independent and elected Fayṣal as king. The Treaty of San-Remo in April 1920 gave the mandate over Syria to France, in the name of the League of Nations. But this decision roused serious discontent in Dimas̲h̲ḳ and other large Syrian towns. On 10 July the National Congress proclaimed a state of siege and introduced conscription, but on 14 July General Gouraud, High Commissioner of the French Republic, gave an ultimatum to Fayṣal who accepted its terms. Popular agitation grew in Dimas̲h̲ḳ and on 20 July the Arab army had to disperse a large meeting of the people. French troops were sent to Syria to put the agreement which had been concluded into force. On 24 July fighting broke out at Mayṣalūn and on 25 July the French entered Dimas̲h̲ḳ. King Fayṣal was forced to leave the country and power passed into the hands of the High Commissioner. The mandate had begun.

The Contemporary Period.—The period of the mandate was marked by expressions of hostility to the mandatory power, which sometimes took the form of strikes, sometimes of more violent outbreaks.

The most serious revolt which broke out in 1925 in the D̲j̲abal Durūz, under the leadership of the

Amīr Sulṭān al-Aṭrash, succeeded in taking Dimashk. At the end of August the rebels, newly arrived in the suburbs of the city, were repulsed. The population did not openly support them until they came back a second time, when on 15 October 1925 serious rioting occurred in the city which caused General Sarrail to bombard it on 18 October. In April 1926 a new bombardment put an end to a rising in the Ghūṭa and the city, but tranquillity was not restored until the following autumn.

From 1926 onwards the town began to develop in the western sense of the word very quickly. Undeveloped quarters between al-Ṣāliḥiyya and the old city were rapidly built up and from then on, the suburbs of al-Djisr, al-ʿArnūs and al-Shuhadāʾ provided homes for a growing number of Europeans and Syrians without any segregation of ethnic groups. The Christians of Bāb Tūma left the city walls in greater and greater numbers to set up the new district of Ḳaṣṣāʿ. To avoid chaotic development, the French town-planner, Danger, in 1929 created a harmonious and balanced plan for the future town, and its working out was put into the hands of the architect, Michel Écochard, in collaboration with the Syrian services. New roads, often tree-lined, were made and the ancient Nayrāb became the residential quarter of Abū Rummāna which continued to extend towards the west. New suburbs were developed to the north of the old city between the Boulevard de Baghdād and the Djabal Ḳāsiyūn, and to the north-east towards the road to Ḥalab. In view of the growth of the population and in the interests of public health the drinking water was brought from the beginning of 1932 by special pipelines from the powerful spring of ʿAyn Fīdja in the valley of the Baradā.

Dimashk suffered very much less in the Second World War than in the first. In June 1941 British and Free French troops entered Syria. On 16 September 1941 General Catroux proclaimed its independence, but there was no constitutional life in Dimashk until August 1943. It was then that Shukrī al-Ḳuwwatlī was elected President of the Republic. On 12 April 1945 the admission of Syria to the United Nations Organization put an end to the mandate, but a new tension was to be felt in Franco-Syrian relations. They reached a culminating point on 29 May 1945, when the town was bombarded by the French army. The British intervened in force to restore order and some months later foreign troops finally evacuated Syria.

From 1949 until 1954 Dimashk was shaken by a series of military *coups d'état*. In 1955 Mr. Shukrī al-Ḳuwwatlī became President of the Republic again and from 1956 on discussions were broached with a view to a Syro-Egyptian union. On the proclamation of the United Arab Republic in 1958 Dimashk became the capital of the northern region; but after the *coup d'état* of the 28th September 1961 it again became the capital of the Syrian Arab Republic.

Ruled by a municipal council, the city in 1955 had a population of 408,800 of whom 90% were Sunnī Arabs. Important groups of Kurds, Druzes and Armenians were also to be found there.

Numerous cultural institutions make Dimashk an intellectual centre of the first rank. The Arab Academy (*al-Madjmāʿ al-ʿIlmī al-ʿArabī*), founded in June 1919, on the initiative of Muḥammad Kurd ʿAlī, is situated in the al-ʿĀdiliyya *madrasa*, while opposite this, the al-Ẓāhiriyya *madrasa* houses the National Library which possesses more than 8,000 manuscripts. The Syrian University, which originated from a school of medicine (1903) and a school of law (1912), was founded on 15 June 1923. In 1960 it had about 10,000 students divided into six faculties. The National Museum of Syria, founded in 1921, has been installed since 1938 in premises specially devised for the preservation of its rich collections (Palmyra, Doura Europos, Ras Shamra, and Mari rooms). The *Direction générale des antiquités de Syrie*, created in 1921, is housed in the same buildings. Many bookshops, a dozen or so cinemas, radio and television transmitting stations, help make Dimashk give a very modern impression. It is an important centre of communications with its railway connections with ʿAmmān and beyond that, ʿAḳaba, terminus of the Dimashk-Ḥimṣ line and its prolongation (D.H.P.), its motor-roads, Bayrūt-Baghdād and al-Mawṣil as well as Jerusalem-ʿAmmān-Bayrūt, and its Class B international aerodrome situated at Mizza. It is also the greatest grain market of the Ḥawrān and a centre of supplies for the nomads and peasants of the Ghūṭa. These not only find many foreign products in its *sūḳ*s but also goods specially manufactured to fit the needs of the country-dweller. There exists also a class of artisans which specializes in luxury goods such as wood inlays, mother of pearl mosaics, silk brocades and engraved or inlaid copper work. Wood turners and glass blowers are also very active.

The protectionist measures of 1926 brought a remarkable upward trend to industry and thus it was that a first cloth factory (1929), a cement works at Dummar (1930) and a cannery (1932) were founded one after the other. Modern spinning mills were installed in 1937, and by 1939 there were already 80 factories representing 1500 trades. A large glass-works was put up to the south of the city at Ḳadam in 1945, while to the east many tanneries and dye-works ply their centuries-old activities. Since 1954 an important international exhibition and fair has been held at the end of each summer on the banks of the Baradā. This has helped to establish Dimashk as a great commercial and industrial centre of the Arab Near East.

Bibliography: in addition to the references in the text: on geography: R. Thoumin, *Géographie humaine de la Syrie Centrale*, Tours 1936, 237-59; Ch. Combier, *La climatologie de la Syrie et du Liban*, in *Revue Géogr. Phys. et Géol. Dynam.*, vi (1933), 319 ff.; R. Tresse, *L'irrigation dans la Ghouta de Damas*, in *REI*, 1929, 459-576; R. Thoumin, *Notes sur l'aménagement et la distribution des eaux à Damas et dans sa Ghouta*, in *BEO*, iv (1934), 1-26.—Arabic texts: Rabaʿī, *K. Faḍāʾil al-Shām wa-Dimashḳ*, ed. S. Munadjdjid, *RAAD*, 1951; Ibn ʿAsākir, *Taʾrīkh madīnat Dimashḳ*, i, ed. S. Munadjdjid, *RAAD*, 1951; ʿAbd al-Ḳādir Badarān, *Tahdhīb Taʾrīkh Dimashḳ li'bn ʿAsākir*, 7 vols., Damascus 1911-29; Ibn Shaddād, *Al-Aʿlāḳ al-khaṭīra (Description de Damas)*, ed. S. Dahan, *PIFD*, 1956; Yūsuf b. ʿAbd al-Hādī, *Thimār al-maḳāṣid fī dhikr al-masādjid*, ed. Asʿad Ṭalas, *PIFD*, 1943; Nuʿaymī, *Al-Dāris fī taʾrīkh al-madāris*, ed. Djaʿfar al-Ḥasanī, 2 vols., *RAAD*, 1948-51; Muḥammad Kurd ʿAlī, *Khiṭaṭ al-Shām*, 6 vols., Damascus 1925-29; Yāḳūt, *Muʿdjam al-Buldān*, s.v. *Dimashḳ*; Ibn al-Ḳalānisī, *Dhayl taʾrīkh Dimashḳ*, ed. Amedroz, Leyden 1906; Harawī, *K. al-Ziyārāt*, ed. J. Sourdel-Thomine, *PIFD*, Damascus 1953, 10-6, (trans. idem, *PIFD*, Damascus 1957, 24-40). — Translations and general works: G. Le Strange, *Palestine under the Moslems*, London 1890, 224-71; Ibn Djubayr, *Journeys*, trans. M. Gaudefroy-Demombynes, 3 vols., Paris 1949-56; Ibn Baṭṭūṭa, *The Travels of .....*, trans. H. A. R. Gibb, i, Cambridge 1958, 118-157; H. A. R. Gibb, *The Damascus chronicle of the Crusades*, London 1932; R. Le Tourneau, *Damas de 1075 à 1154*, *PIFD*, 1950; M. Gaudefroy-Demombynes, *La Syrie à l'époque des Mamelouks*, *BAH*, Paris 1923, 135-201, 312-48; H. Lammens, *La Syrie, précis historique*, Beirut 1921; *Sovremennaya Siriya*, publ. A.N.S.S.R., Moscow 1958; P. Hitti, *Syria, a short history*, London 1959; R. Dussaud, *Topographie historique de la Syrie*, *BAH*, iv, Paris 1927, 291-322; R. Mantran and J. Sauvaget, *Règlements fiscaux ottomans relatifs aux provinces syriennes*, *PIFD*, 1951, 3-34; Cl. Cahen, *Mouvements populaires et autonomisme urbain dans l'Asie Musulmane du Moyen Age*, in *Arabica*, v (1958), 225, 250; vi, (1959), 25-26, 233-65.—Works on the city and its monuments: H. Sauvaire, *La description de Damas*, in *JA*, 3rd series, iii-vii, 1894-96, *Index général* by E. Ouéchek, *PIFD*, 1954; K. Wulzinger and C. Watzinger, *Damaskus*, i, *Die antike Stadt*; ii, *Die islamische Stadt*, 2 vols., Berlin 1921-24; J. Sauvaget, *Le plan antique de Damas*, in *Syria*, xxvi (1949), 314-58; idem, *Monuments historiques de Damas*, Beirut 1932; idem, *Esquisse d'une histoire de la ville de Damas*, in *REI*, 1934, 422-80; K. A. C. Creswell, *A short account of early Muslim architecture*, London 1959, 60 ff.; *Monuments ayyoubides de Damas*, *PIFD*, Damascus 1938-50, 4 fasc. by J. Sauvaget, M. Écochard and J. Sourdel-Thomine; M. Écochard and Ch. le Coeur, *Les Bains de Damas*, 2 vols., *PIFD*, 1942-3; E. Herzfeld, *Damascus: studies in architecture*, in *Ars Islamica*, ix, 1-53, x, 13-70, xi-xii, 1-71, xii-xiv, 118-38 (see J. Sauvaget, *Notes .....*, in *Syria*, xxiv, 211-28); J. Sourdel-Thomine, *Les anciens lieux de pèlerinage damascains d'après les sources arabes*, in *BEO*, xiv, 65-85; H. S. Fink, *The Rôle of Damascus in the history of the Crusades*, in *MW*, xlix (1959), 41-53; N. Elisséeff, *Les monuments de Nūr ad-Dīn*, in *BEO*, xiii, 5-43; idem, *Corporations de Damas sous Nūr al-Dīn*, in *Arabica*, iii (1956), 61-79. (N. Elisséeff)

al-DIMASHḲĪ, Shams al-Dīn Abū ʿAbd Allāh Muḥammad b. Abī Ṭālib al-Anṣārī al-Ṣūfī, known as Ibn Shaykh Ḥittīn, author of a cosmography and other works. He was *shaykh* and *imām* at al-Rabwa, described by Ibn Baṭṭūṭa as a pleasant locality near Damascus, now the suburb of al-Ṣāliḥiyya, and d. at Ṣafad in 727/1327. Al-Dimashḳī's best known work, *Nukhbat al-dahr fī ʿadjāʾib al-barr wa 'l-baḥr* is a compilation dealing with geography in the widest sense, and somewhat closely resembling the *ʿAdjāʾib al-makhlūḳāt* of al-Ḳazwīnī. Though the author's standpoint is conspicuously uncritical, his book contains a good deal of information not to be found elsewhere. Less well known but also of considerable interest is another work of al-Dimashḳī, *al-Maḳāmāt al-falsafiyya wa 'l-tardjamāt al-ṣūfiyya* (see E. G. Browne, *Handlist of the Muḥammadan MSS preserved in the library of the University of Cambridge*, 217-218, no. 1102), fifty *maḳāmas* forming an encyclopaedia of physical, mathematical and theological information, placed in the mouth of one Abu 'l-Ḳāsim al-Tawwāb (*i.e.*, the Penitent), on the authority of Abū ʿAbd Allāh al-Awwāb (*i.e.*, the Repentant). Al-Dimishḳī has also left a defence of Islam, *Djawāb risālat ahl djazīrat Ḳubrus*, in which traces of Ṣūfī mysticism appear (see E. Fritsch, *Islam u. Christentum im Mittelalter*, Breslau, 1930, 33-36). Another work of his has been printed: *al-Risāla* (variant: *al-Siyāsa*) *fī ʿilm al-firāsa* (Cairo 1300 A.H.); but *Maḥāsin al-tidjāra* (Cairo 1318 A.H.) attributed to Shams al-Dīn by Brockelmann (correctly *K. al-ishāra ilā maḥāsin al-tidjāra*, tr. H. Ritter, in *Isl.*, vii, 1917, 1-91) was written by Abu'l-Faḍl Djaʿfar b. ʿAlī al-Dimashḳī.

Bibliography: A. F. Mehren, *Cosmographie de Chems-ed-Din Abou Abdallah Mohammed ed-Dimichqui*, Arabic text, St. Petersburg 1866, transl. *Manuel de la Cosmographie du Moyen Age*, Copenhagen 1874; Brockelmann, II, 130, S II, 161, *GAL*², ii, 161. (D. M. Dunlop)

DIMETOḲA, also called Dimotiḳa, a town in the former Ottoman Rumeli. Dimetoḳa lies in western Thrace, in a side valley of the Maritsa, and at times played a significant role in Ottoman history. The territory has belonged to Greece since the treaty of Neuilly (27 November 1919), again bears its pre-Ottoman name of Didymóteikhon, and lies within the administrative district (Nomos) of Ebros. It has a population of about 10,000, and is the seat of a bishop of the Greek church as well as of an eparch (provincial governor). It is situated near the junction of the Saloniki—Alexandroupolis—Dimetoḳa line with the Orient line.

Dimetoḳa, which was called Didymóteikhon (Διδυμότειχον) by the Byzantines, fell first into Ottoman hands in Muḥarram 763/November 1361, according to the Florentine chronicler Matteo Villani (cf. F. Babinger, *Beiträge zur Frühgeschichte der Türkenherrschaft in Rumelien (14.-15. Jhdt.)* = *Südosteuropäische Arbeiten*, xxxiv, Munich 1944, 46). Dimetoḳa had been defended by a castle encircled by a double wall, built for protection on a conical hill, and provided with strong fortifications under the ruler Matthew Cantacuzenus; it was probably the commander Ḥādjdjī Ilbegi who brought it into Ottoman possession. Murād I, before the conquest of Adrianople early in 762/1361 (cf. F. Babinger, in *MOG*, ii (1926), 311 ff.), set up his court there. The Burgundian traveller and diplomat Bertrandon de la Broquiere (see his *Voyage d'outre-mer*, ed. Ch. Schefer, Paris 1892, 172 ff., 180) has vividly depicted its appearance in 1443; from this it may be seen that Dimetoḳa, as the first residence of the new Ottoman lords—their final removal to Adrianople/Edirne cannot have followed until about 766/1365—was built and beautified with especial care, although the layout of the fortifications of that time goes back for the most part to Byzantine times. The rich and broad hunting grounds of the surrounding country made Dimetoḳa a favourite resort of early Ottoman rulers, such as the prince and claimant to the Sultanate Mūsā Čelebi, and Bāyazīd II, who was born there in Dhu 'l-Ḳaʿda 852/January 1449 to the 15 year-old future Sultan Meḥemmed II. The planning of the royal palace and its additions owed its origin to this circumstance. The first design was brought to completion under Murād I (Cf. Ḥādjdjī Khalīfa, *Rumeli und Bosna*, trans. J. von Hammer, Vienna 1812, 65). Bāyazīd II, weary of wordly cares, proposed to spend the rest of his life there, to avoid persecution by his son Selīm I, but died en route—probably poisoned—on 10 Rabīʿ I 918/26 May 1512, not far from Hafsa (on the place of death cf. Hammer-Purgstall, *GOR*, ii, 365 ff., 625). The Swedish king Charles XII (1697-1718) fared rather better when, before reaching Stralsund, he stayed in Dimetoḳa from February 1713 to October 1714, and managed to evade pursuit by an adventurous ride.

A graphic description of Dimetoḳa in the year

1080/1670 is given by the Ottoman globe-trotter Ewliyā Čelebi [*q.v.*] in the eighth volume of his *Siyāḥatnāme* (73 ff.; cf. the abridgement in H. J. Kissling, *Beiträge zur Kenntnis Thrakiens im 17. Jahrhundert* = *Abh.K.M.*, xxxii/3 (1956), 81 ff.). At that time the sole Muslim in the fortress of the city was its commandant (*dizdār*), for the inner castle (*derūn ḥiṣār*) consisted of a hundred tumbledown houses occupied by "unbelievers". Dimetoḳa was the seat of a judge and the administrative centre of a district (*nāḥiye*). The upper fortress measured, according to Ewliyā Čelebi, 2500 paces in circumference, and the outer double walls of stone were defended by "a hundred" towers. There was no moat, no space for one being available. The citadel (*ič ḳalʿe*) of the upper fort is arranged on two vertical levels; one part is commonly called the "Maiden's tower" (*Ḳiz ḳalʿesi*). From Ewliyā Čelebi's detailed description of the defensive arrangements of Dimetoḳa it is specially noticeable that the royal palace, which was at that time no longer much used, lay in the upper fortress, and could be reached through doors accessible only to the sultan. The lower city (*varoš*) was divided in Ewliyā Čelebi's time into twelve wards (*maḥalle*) and consisted of 600 multi-storeyed tiled houses. In Dimetoḳa at that time there were twelve places of worship, the most important of these being that with which sultan Bāyazīd I graced his usual abode. The remainder are smaller mosques (*mesdjid*), many of which our traveller mentions by name; they owe their origin for the most part to the well-to-do Ottoman dignitaries established there. Sultān Bāyazīd I had a Ḳurʾān school erected in Dimetoḳa, which next to that of Urudj Pasha is the most important of the four in existence. Of the baths, the so-called "Whisper Bath" (*fîsîltî ḥammāmî*), with its "Ear of Dionysus", is also mentioned by Ḥādjdjī Khalīfa (*op. cit.*, 66). According to the *Sālnāme* of Edirne, 1309/1891-2, 208, it was still standing and widely famous. There was no *bazzistān*, although the market (bāzār) was dominated by some 200 potters' stalls, whose wares, especially the red Dimetoḳa glasses, beakers, dishes and jugs enjoyed a great reputation. The chief produce of Dimetoḳa and its environs is grapes and quinces.

There were numerous graves of holy men, who found their last resting place in or near Dimetoḳa; Ewliyā Čelebi gives a list of them by name, from which it appears that they belonged entirely to the Bektashī order; from the evidence of Ottoman toponymy the hinterland of Dimetoḳa towards the west must have been to a very great extent a centre of the dervishes, particularly those of the Bektashīs (cf. H. J. Kissling, *op. cit.*, 83, n. 310). In more modern times Dimetoḳa, out of the way from the bustle of the world, had practically no part to play under the Ottomans, and gradually declined.

Bibliography: in addition to references in the text, cf. *Sālnāme-i Edirne*, 18th ed. 1309, 203-9; 28th ed. 1319, 996 ff.; Sāmī Bey Frashëri, *Ḳāmūs al-aʿlām*, iii, Constantinople 1308/1891, 2216 ff.; Ami Boué, *Recueil d'itinéraires dans la Turquie d'Europe*, i, Vienna 1854, 102 ff. European travellers have hardly touched Dimetoḳa and its surroundings and have left no descriptions.

(F. Babinger)

DIMYĀṬ (Damietta), a town of Lower Egypt situated on the eastern arm of the Nile, near its mouth. Dimyāṭ, which was an important town before the Muslim conquest, was captured by a force under al-Miḳdād b. al-Aswad, sent by ʿAmr b. al-ʿĀṣ. As a Muslim town, it suffered repeated naval raids, at first from the Byzantines and subsequently from the Crusaders. After an attack in Dhu 'l-Ḥidjdja 238/June 853, al-Mutawakkil ordered the construction of a fortress at Dimyāṭ as part of a general plan to fortify the Mediterranean coast. Dimyāṭ, as the key to Egypt, played a particularly important part in the conflicts between Franks and Muslims at the end of the Fāṭimid dynasty and in Ayyūbid times. When Ṣalāḥ al-Dīn al-Ayyūbī was vizier of Egypt, the Franks under Amalric I of Jerusalem besieged Dimyāṭ, but were compelled to withdraw in Rabīʿ I 565/December 1169. Dimyāṭ was twice more the centre of important military operations. The great Crusading expedition of 615-8/1218-21 (see Hans L. Gottschalk, *Al-Malik al-Kāmil von Egypten und seine Zeit*, Wiesbaden 1958, 58-70, 76-88, 104-15) succeeded in capturing the town but was ultimately forced to capitulate by al-Kāmil. In Ṣafar 647/June 1249 Dimyāṭ was taken by Louis IX, shortly before the death of al-Ṣāliḥ, but was restored to Muslim rule on Louis's subsequent capitulation. The Baḥriyya Mamlūks, who then formed the ruling élite of Egypt, decided to end its military importance. The walls and town, except for the mosque, were demolished in 648/1250-1; while in 659/1260-1 the river-mouth itself was blocked to sea-going ships by order of Baybars I. The devastation of Dimyāṭ was no doubt the cause of the extinction of its famous textile industry, although a new urban centre, which took the old name, soon arose on a site south of the former town. In the Mamlūk and Ottoman periods, Dimyāṭ was used as a place of banishment. In Rabīʿ I 1218/July 1803 the Ottoman viceroy of Egypt, Meḥmed Khüsrev Pasha, who had been expelled from Cairo by a revolt of Albanian troops, was compelled to surrender at Dimyāṭ, where he had fortified himself, to a force commanded by Meḥmed ʿAlī and the Mamlūk grandee, ʿUthmān Bey al-Bardīsī.

Bibliography: The principal data are given in Maḳrīzī, *al-Mawāʿiẓ*, ed. Wiet, iv/2, 37-80; and ʿAlī Mubārak, *al-Khiṭaṭ al-djadīda*, xi, 36-57 (largely a reproduction of Maḳrīzī). For a full bibliography, see Maspero-Wiet, *Matériaux*, 92-3.

(P. M. Holt)

AL-DIMYĀṬĪ, ʿAbd al-Muʾmin b. Khalaf Sharaf al-Dīn al-Tūnī al-Dimyāṭī al-**Shāfiʿī**, traditionist born in 613/1217 on the island of Tūnā between Tinnīs and Damietta; at the end of his career he was professor at the Manṣūriyya and at the Ẓāhiriyya in Cairo, where he died in 705/1306. Apart from the works listed by Brockelmann, to be supplemented by the recent study of A. Dietrich, *ʿAbdalmuʾmin b. Xalaf ad-Dimyāṭi'nin bir muhâcirûn listesi*, in *Şarkiyat Mecmuasi*, iii (1959), 125-55) he has left a dictionary of authorities, often cited and used by subsequent historians and biographers, called *Muʿdjam Shuyūkh*; it only survives at the present time in a single incomplete manuscript (Tunis, *Aḥmadiyya*, 911-2,—about 1185 entries out of the 1250 contained in the complete work) which was written at the author's dictation. In this document are contained the *Ḥadīth*, and also other texts collected by al-Dimyāṭī in the course of his numerous voyages in Egypt, the two holy cities, in Syria, Djazīra and in ʿIrāḳ between 636/1238 and 656/1258; these, together with the numerous reading-certificates which accompany them, will be the subject of a monograph by G. Vajda. Apart from his own works, al-Dimyāṭī is one of the most important figures of the last third of the 7th/13th century in the field of the handing down of traditions.

Bibliography: Brockelmann, II², 88; S. II, 79 (to the sources quoted may be added *al-Durar al-Kāmina*, ii, 417, no. 2525 and Ibn Rafiʿ, *Muntakhab al-Mukhtār*, in the edition of ʿAzzāwī, 120-2, no. 104; for Dimyāṭī as a transmitter of traditions, see also Ahlwardt, *Verzeichniss . . . Berlin*, no. 9648 (ix, 193 f.); G. Vajda, *Les certificats de lecture . . .* 12; Ahmed Ateş, in *RIMA*, iv, 1, 1958, 14.

(G. Vajda)

AL-DIMYĀṬĪ, al-Bannāʾ. Aḥmad b. Muḥammad b. Aḥmad b. Muḥammad b. ʿAbd al-Ghanī al-Dimyāṭī, known as al-Bannāʾ, though he had some local reputation in Lower Egypt as a pillar of the Nakshbandiyya order of dervishes, owes his fame to his work *Itḥāf fuḍalāʾ al-bashar* on the Ḳurʾānic variants of the Fourteen Readers. He was born at Dimyāṭ where he had the usual education of a Muslim youth under local teachers, till he was able to journey to Cairo, where he studied *ḳirāʾāt*, *ḥadīth* and Shāfiʿī *fiḳh* under al-Muzāḥī and al-Shabrāmulsī, and was able to hear such contemporary masters as al-Adjhūrī, al-Shawbarī, al-Ḳalyūbī and al-Maymūnī. At the conclusion of his studies he went on pilgrimage to Mecca where he studied *ḥadīth* under al-Kūrānī. On his return to Dimyāṭ he published his *Itḥaf*, on which he had apparently been at work while in the Ḥidjāz, and in which he collected the variant readings of Ibn Muḥayṣin of Mecca, al-Yazīdī of Baṣra, al-Ḥasan of Baṣra, and al-Aʿmash of Kūfa, as well as the more commonly studied Ten Readers, prefacing the whole with an excellent study on the science of *ḳirāʾāt*. He also made a one volume digest of the famous *al-Sīra al-Ḥalabiyya*, and compiled a treatise, *al-Dhakhāʾir al-muhimmāt*, on the signs which precede the coming of the Last Day. After a second pilgrimage to the Holy Cities he journeyed to the Yemen, where he was initiated by Shaykh Aḥmad b. ʿAdjīl into the Nakshbandiyya fraternity. On his return to Egypt he established himself as a marabout in the sea-side village of ʿEzbet al-Burdj. During a third pilgrimage he died at Medina in Muḥarram 1117/April-May 1705, and was buried in the Baḳīʿ. Besides the *Itḥāf*, which has been printed at Constantinople in 1285/1868-9, and at Cairo in 1317/1899-1900, he wrote smaller works on Ḳurʾānic readings, of which MSS survive, and the gloss he made to al-Maḥallī's commentary on the *Waraḳāt* of Imām al-Ḥaramayn has been printed at Cairo in 1303/1885-6 and again in 1332/1913-14.

Bibliography: al-Djabarti, *ʿAdjāʾib al-Āthār*, i, 89, 90, copied into ʿAlī Pasha Mubārak's *Khiṭaṭ Djadīda*, xi, 56; Sarkis, *Bibliographie*, col. 885; Brockelmann, II, 327; S. II, 454).

(A. Jeffery)

AL-DIMYĀṬĪ, Nūr al-Dīn or Aṣīl al-Dīn; his dates are uncertain but almost certainly not before the end of the 7th/13th century; author of a *ḳaṣīda* in *lām* on the names of God (see al-asmāʾ al-ḥusnā and dhikr); each verse of this *ḳaṣīda* is reputed to possess mysterious virtues, given in detail by the commentaries of which the text has several times been the object (the best-known is that by the Moroccan mystic, Aḥmad al-Burnusī Zarrūḳ, d. 899/1493). The *ḳaṣīda Dimyāṭiyya* holds a considerable place in the worship of the semi-literate, in particular in North Africa. A translation of it was made into Ottoman Turkish in 1257/1841 by Ibrāhīm b. Meḥmed Ṣāliḥ al-Ḳādirī al-Kasṭamūnī al-Istānbūlī, and printed in the following year at Istanbul, together with several *taḳrīẓ* and the Arabic text, under the title of *Farāʾid al-Laʾālī fī bayān asmāʾ 'l-mutaʿālī*. A fragment of another work of the same kind attributed to al-Dimyāṭī is preserved, with a commentary, in the ms. Paris, B.N. Arabe 1050, fol. 138-139, while an imitation, not without vulgarisms in its language, was written by a certain Maḥmūd Hizza al-Dimyāṭī (printed as an appendix to *Badīʿ al-maḳāl* by an anonymous Andalusian, with the title of *al-Istighfār al-asmā fī naẓm asmāʾ Allāh al-ḥusnā*, Būlāḳ 1319/1901).

Bibliography: J. Goldziher, in *Orientalische Studien . . . . Nöldeke*, i, 317-20; E. Doutté, *Magie et Religion en Afrique du Nord*, 199-211; G. Levi Della Vida, *Elenco* 55-66; Brockelmann, S II, 361, note.

(G. Vajda)

DĪN, I. Definition and general notion. It is usual to emphasize three distinct senses of *dīn*: (1) judgment, retribution; (2) custom, usage; (3) religion. The first refers to the Hebraeo-Aramaic root, the second to the Arabic root *dāna*, *dayn* (debt, money owing), the third to the Pehlevi *dēn* (revelation, religion). This third etymology has been exploited by Nöldeke and Vollers. We would agree with Gaudefroy-Demombynes (*Mahomet*, 504) in not finding it convincing. In any case, the notion of "religion" in question is by no means identical in Mazdaism and Islam. On the contrary, the two first etymologies, Hebrew and Arabic, seem to interact, and the meanings are nothing like so diverse as has sometimes been stated. Thus the semantic dialectic of Arabic causes *dayn* "debt which falls due on a given date" to pass to *dīn* "custom" (cf. *EI*¹, s.v., art. by Macdonald). "Custom, usage", in its turn, leads to the idea of "direction" (given by God), *hudā*; and to judge (the sense of the Hebrew root) is to guide each one in a suitable direction, hence to give retribution. In Gaudefroy-Demombynes' view the "Day of Judgment" (*yawm al-dīn*)" is the day when God gives a direction to each human being". Elsewhere the Arabic philologists freely derive *dīn* from *dāna li-. . .* "submit to". *Dīn* henceforth is the corpus of obligatory prescriptions given by God, to which one must submit.

Thus *dīn* signifies obligation, direction, submission, retribution. Whether referring to the Hebrew-Aramaic sense or the ancient Arabic root, there will remain the ideas of debt to be discharged (hence obligation) and of direction imposed or to be followed with a submissive heart. From the standpoint of him who imposes obligation or direction, *dīn* rejoins the "judgment" of the Hebrew root; but from the standpoint of him who has to discharge the obligation and receive the direction, *dīn* must be translated "religion"—the most general and frequent sense.

There is no doubt about this translation. But the concept indicated by *dīn* does not exactly coincide with the ordinary concept of "religion", precisely because of the semantic connexions of the words. *Religio* evokes primarily that which binds man to God; and *dīn* the obligations which God imposes on His "reasoning creatures" (*aṣḥāb al-ʿuḳūl*, as Djurdjānī says). Now the first of these obligations is to submit to God and surrender one's self to Him. Since the etymological sense of *islām* is "surrender of self (to God)", the famous Ḳurʾānic verse then shows its full meaning: "This day I have perfected your religion (*dīn*) for you and completed my favour unto you, and have chosen for you as religion *al-Islām*" (V 3; cf. II 126, III 19).

These few remarks cast some light on and perhaps

oversimplify the difficulties encountered in translating the *dīn* of Ḳurʾānic verses into Western languages. (1) The sense of judgment (and retribution) is quite frequent in the *sūras* of the Meccan period: four times taken absolutely and 12 times in the expression *yawm al-dīn*. (2) The sense of religion is suitable in the other cases. It is true that R. Blachère several times, and appropriately, translates it by "act of worship" (*culte*) (e.g. II, 189; XLII, 11 and 20, etc.). Notice XLII, 11: "Discharge the debt of worship" (*acquittez-vous du Culte*), which evokes the primitive Arabic sense of debt, owing. But if we recall that *dīn* is defined by the obligations and prescriptions laid down by God, it must be admitted that the *culte* is the essential part of *dīn*. (Moreover Muslim authors often associate *ʿibāda*, the act of worship proper, and *dīn*). Finally sundry Ḳurʾānic expression must be indicated which are found again in subsequent elaborations: *al-dīn al-ḳayyim* "the immutable religion": "The Judgment (*ḥukm*) rests with Allāh only Who hath commanded you that ye worship none save Him. This is the immutable religion" (XII, 40); *dīn al-ḥaḳḳ*, "the religion of Truth": "He it is Who hath sent this Messenger with the guidance (*hudā*) and the religion of Truth" (XLVIII, 28); *al-dīn ḥunafāʾ*, "religion practised as a *ḥanīf* [*q.v.*]" (XCVIII, 5); *al-dīn al-k͟hāliṣ*, "the pure religion" (XXXIX, 3). The three texts cited above (V, 3; IX, 36; and XLVIII, 28) emphasize the relationships of meaning between *dīn* on the one hand and, on the other, *islām* (surrender of self to God), *ḥukm* (judgment), and *hudā* (right direction). Other references could be given.

II. Content of the notion of *dīn*

There are numerous Ḳurʾānic verses which associate the worship of God, or the prayer due to God, and the religion (or *culte*), *e.g.*, XXXIX 14, etc. A well-known *ḥadīt͟h* (Buk͟hārī, ii, 37) unites under "the teaching of religion" (a) the contents of the faith (*īmān*), (b) the practice of *islām*, (c) *iḥsān* or interiorization of the faith ("to adore God as though one saw him"). It later became common to define *dīn* by these three elements.

We now come to a few elaborations of doctrine. The Ḥanafī-Māturīdī text *Fiḳh Akbar II* defines religion as an appellation including faith, *islām*, and all the commandments of the Law. The *Kitāb al-tamhīd* of the As͟hʿarī Bāḳillānī devotes a short chapter to the meaning of *dīn*. He distinguishes several possible meanings: (1) judgment in the sense of retribution (in the expression *yawm al-dīn*); (2) judgment in the sense of decision (*ḥukm*); (3) doctrine (*mad͟hhab*) and religious community (*milla*), implying faith, obedience, and the practice of a given belief; in this last sense there may be more than one religion (cf. below); (4) *dīn al-ḥaḳḳ*, which is *islām* (and Islam): allowing one's self to be led by God and abandoning one's self to Him. In his *Taʿrīfāt*, D̲j̲urd̲j̲ānī defines *dīn* as a divine institution (*waḍʿ*) which creatures endowed with reason receive from the Apostle. Similar definitions are repeated in the treatises of the As͟hʿarī school. Thus in Bād̲j̲ūrī's elementary manual *dīn* is "the corpus of prescriptions (*aḥkām*) which God has promulgated through the voice of His Apostle".

Thus the Māturīdīs willingly make faith an element in religion; the As͟hʿarīs stress the prescriptions to be observed. As for the Ḥanbalī school, their accent falls on the "authentic tradition" taken in the widest sense. The Ḳurʾān and the Sunna—therein lies religion (*ʿAḳīda I* of Ibn Ḥanbal); Ibn Taymiyya repeats that it is "the whole of religion". Hence the assertion that *dīn* is *taḳlīd* (*Ṭabaḳāt al-ḥanābila*, i, 31), endowing *taḳlīd* with a positive value of faithfulness to the Prophet (contrarily to other schools who see it primarily as pure acceptance, passive and non-reasoning). L. Massignon writes that, for Ibn Ḥanbal (*Passion d'al-Ḥallād̲j̲*, 669), *dīn* may be understood as "devoting our religious observances to God", as distinct from *islām* (external practices) and *s͟harīʿa* (observance of legal precepts): the whole constitutes faith (*īmān*). Thus understood *dīn* is nourished by the Tradition and supererogatory acts of piety. Besides the Ḥanbalīs associate *dīn* with the act of worship (*ʿibāda*) which is "action", and with right guidance (*hudā*). Now the first act of worship is prayer (*ṣalāt*). Ibn Taymiyya quotes several Traditions where prayer is stated to be "the basis of religion"; "those (then) who cause it to be observed and themselves observe it preserve their religion" (cf. *Siyāsa*, tr. Laoust, 19). He is pleased to reproduce the dictum of the "Ancients", which makes *īmān* the complement of *dīn*: "Religion and faith consist of word, action, and the fact of following the Sunna" (*Maʿārid̲j̲*, tr. Laoust, 76). Commenting on the author's thought, M. Laoust stresses that "religion" is "above all a law" (ibid., 79 n.). Finally, the contemporary writer Ras͟hīd Riḍā, whose links with Ibn Taymiyya are well known, presents religion as "the act of worship, the care to avoid bad and blameworthy deeds, to respect right and justice in social relationships, and to purify the soul and prepare it for the future life; in a word [it consists of] all the laws whose aim is to bring man near to God" (*K͟hilāfa*, 192; tr. Laoust, 156). This concept, though losing nothing of its specifically Muslim character, reminds one of the more usual meaning of *religio*.

III. *Dīn wa-milla; dīn al-ḥaḳḳ*

In order to set forth clearly the elements of the problem *dīn* is often distinguished from terms with related meanings or made more specific by a determinative which limits its connotation.

Ibn Ḥanbal employed *milla* in the sense of *dīn* (cf. Massignon, *loc. cit.*, n. 4), and, as we have seen, Bāḳillānī noted that *dīn* could be synonymous with *milla* or, in a more restricted sense, with *mad͟hhab*. D̲j̲urd̲j̲ānī (*Taʿrīfāt*, 111) distinguishes a shade of meaning: *dīn* and *milla* agree in respect of their essence, but are distinct in respect of their signification. Both go back to the idea of Law, divine positive legal prescriptions (*s͟harīʿa*). Here we come across the usual As͟hʿarī position again. *Dīn*, says D̲j̲urd̲j̲ānī, is the Law as something obeyed; *milla* (a word of Aramaic origin: word, revelation) is the Law gathering men in a community; *mad͟hhab* is the Law to which one strives to return. *Dīn* relates to God, *milla* to the Apostle (*rasūl*), *mad͟hhab* to the founder of a school, the *mud̲j̲tahid* who strives to know and interpret the Law. It is to be noted that in the Ḳurʾān *milla* is used now to designate the "religion of Abraham", which is already essentially Islam, now to designate the communities of "possessors of the Scripture".

But Islam alone is *dīn al-ḥaḳḳ*, the "religion of Truth". Each time that this expression appears in the Ḳurʾān it is to affirm that the "religion of Truth" has the primacy over the "whole of religion", that is over all the domain of religion, and so over any other religion (*e.g.*, XLVIII, 27; IX, 33; and parallel text LXI, 9). Opposite to *dīn al-ḥaḳḳ* is *al-dīn al-mubaddal* "corrupted religion", "like that of the polytheists or the Zoroastrians" says Ibn Taymiyya (*Maʿārid̲j̲*, tr. Laoust, 87). Tradition, especially that of the Ḥanbalīs (*e.g.*, Barbahārī, cf. Laoust, *La profession de foi d'Ibn Baṭṭa*, 4, n. 1), distinguishes *ḥaḳḳ*, what comes from God, *i.e.*, the Ḳur'ān; *sunna*, what was established by the Prophet; *djamā'a*, the common practices and beliefs of the Companions. Thus we have on the one hand *dīn al-ḥaḳḳ*, revealed religion, and on the other *al-dīn al-'atīḳ* "the ancient religion" understood as Islam as practised by the Companions (from whom Barbahārī exludes 'Alī). This latter expression is connected with the Ḥanbalite conception of *taḳlīd*.

Dīn al-ḥaḳḳ is to be compared with and distinguished from the other Ḳur'ānic expression *al-dīn al-ḳayyim* "the immutable religion": it is Islam referred to the faith of Abraham (VI, 162, here synonymous with *dīn ḥunafā'*) or considered as bound to laws testifying to the order of the universe (IX, 36) and recapitulated in the worship of God alone (XII, 40). Note finally that one of the characteristics of the *dīn al-ḥaḳḳ* is to be a "religion of the golden mean", "far from extremes". Several Muslim apologists, arguing from *Ḳur'ān* II, 137 where the determinative is applied to the Community (*umma*) and on the other hand from the phrase "no constraint in religion" (II, 256, cf. XXII, 78), like to present Islam as a religion of the "golden mean". This is a theme which readily re-occurs when a writer wishes to urge a balanced solution on the opponents of his school (*madhhab*); thus Ibn 'Asākir, in his defence of Ash'arism, or Ibn Taymiyya, in his solution of this or that legal problem (*e.g.*, *Siyāsa*, tr. Laoust, 31). In the opposite direction a severe warning is addressed to the "People of the Book" (Jews or Christians) who "are extravagant" or "exaggerate" in their religion (*Ḳur'ān* II, 171; V, 77; cf. VII, 31); those who do not practise *dīn al-ḥaḳḳ* must be combated.

IV. *Dīn wa-dunyā, dīn wa-dawla*

Dīn, distinct from *milla* and *madhhab*, is opposed to *dunyā*. The nearest translation would be the *relations* of the spiritual and the temporal. *Dīn*: the domain of divine prescriptions concerning acts of worship and everything involved in spiritual life; *dunyā*: "domain of material life", as M. Laoust translates (*dunyā* appears besides as the opposite correlative to *ākhira*: "this world" and "hereafter".

Dīn and *dunyā* are undoubted opposites. The Ṣūfīs stress the ascetic's disdain in the face of *adhā 'l-dunyā*. But the most traditional tendency is to subordinate *dunyā* to *dīn*, to make "this base world" in some way included in the "domain of religion". The Ḥanbalī school is insistent on this. It is "an act of religion (*diyāna*)" says Ibn Baṭṭa, "to give good advice to the imāms and all the other members of the Community, whether in the domain of religion (*dīn*) or that of material life (*dunyā*)" (tr. Laoust, 129-30). Ibn Taymiyya quotes Ḥasan al-Baṣrī with approval: "Religion is good advice, religion is good advice, religion is good advice". Religion and state are closely bound to each other: "exercise of a public office is one of the most important duties of religion; we would add that public office is essential to the very existence of religion". Again: "Thus it is a duty to consider the exercise of power as one of the forms of religion, as one of the acts by which man draws near to God" (*Siyāsa*, tr. Laoust, 172-4). "Social order and peace" are indispensable to the exercise of religion. Commenting on Ibn Taymiyya's political doctrine, M. Laoust writes: "Religion (*dīn*) is intimately bound up with the temporal (*dunyā*)", (*Doctrines sociales et politiques d'Ibn Taymiyya*, 280).

The contemporary Salafiyya school puts the elements of the problem somewhat differently. By a modernized apologetic, Muḥammad 'Abduh intends above all to show the conformity of reason (*'aḳl*) and *dīn*. Rashīd Riḍā, having set forth what in social life is an integral part of the religious domain (cf. quotation above), enumerates everything which depends on it in a wide sense: respect for life, honour, other people's property, an attitude based on sound counsel, shunning of sin, iniquity, violence, deceit, abuse of confidence, unjust wastage of other people's property; in other words the domain of morality. Thus it is a question, both here and there, of an equivalence between "the rights of God and of men", according to the classic distinction of Muslim jurists. But Rashīd Riḍā adds that there is a third order of facts, which no longer depends on the domain of *dīn*: everything to do with "administrative, juridical, political, and financial organization" (*Khilāfa* 92/154). Two concepts may be brought up here: (1) the principle of distinction established by Ibn Taymiyya between the prescriptions of the Ḳur'ān, as distinct from the beliefs (*'aḳīdāt*) and laws concerning the acts of worship (*'ibādāt*), which are untouchable, ethics (*akhlāḳ*) (in certain cases) and social relationships (*mu'āmalāt*) (more generally) are capable of adaptation to time and place; (2) the prescriptions of the Ḳur'ān taken as a whole (domain of *dīn*) do not by any means legislate in detail for the actual organization of social life; this organization must be, and it is sufficient that it be, subservient to those prescriptions. Thus we see the sketch, according to a traditional line of reflection, of a possible principle of distinction between the "spiritual" and the "temporal" derived not so much from the *object* of the prescriptions as from their *source* ("revealed" or not).

The Muslim Brethren vie with one another in repeating that Islam is at one and the same time *dīn* and *dawla* (government, domain of politics). The principle of distinction is by no means abolished. *Dīn* and *dawla* are not identical. But Islam, which is the link between the two, includes both. According to this view there is a distinction between *dīn*, domain of religion, and Islam, which is religion, true enough, but temporal Community also. The Muslim "laicists" or "progressives", on the contrary, tend to identify *dīn* with Islam, and to see in the latter a "religion" in the Western sense of the word.

V. *Uṣūl al-dīn*

Apart from this latter case, where modern Western influence is obvious, *dīn* and Islam are distinct. Sometimes Islam, as the practice of the Ḳur'ānic faith, is one of the elements of *dīn* (*ḥadīth* quoted above, Bukhārī, ii, 37); and sometimes *dīn* is one of the elements of Islam understood as an organized politico-religious Community (e.g. Islam is *dīn* and *dawla*). In current language *dīn* is employed absolutely in the sense of *dīn al-ḥaḳḳ* and then becomes the religious expression and spiritual radiation of Islam itself. Such is the connotation of the frequent proper names where *dīn* is a determinative (*e.g.*, Muḥyī —, Fakhr —, Nūr —, Ṣalāḥ —, Taḳī al-Dīn, etc.).

But if we translate *dīn* by "religion" or "spiritual domain" we must not forget that the Muslim concept denotes above all the Laws which God has promulgated to guide man to his final end, the submission to these laws (thus to God), and the practice of them (acts of worship). The expression *uṣūl al-dīn* "sources (or bases) of religion" is to be taken in this sense.

The advanced course in the great mosques is

often shared by three faculties (cf. an old official syllabus of al-Azhar, *REI* 1931, 241-75: *kulliyyat al-lug͟ha al-ʿarabiyya* ["faculty of Arabic language"], *k. al-s͟harīʿa* [centred on *fiḳh*], and *k. uṣūl al-dīn* ["theology" and apologetics]). As a matter of fact the writers on *ʿilm al-kalām* often used the term *uṣūl al-dīn* (or *al-diyāna*) to denote an introduction to or a résumé of dogmatics, and so we have the titles of well-known works: *Al-ibāna ʿan uṣūl al-diyāna* (As͟hʿarī); *Maʿālim uṣūl al-dīn* (Fak͟hr al-Dīn Rāzī), etc. The *Uṣūl al-dīn* of ʿAbd al-Ḳāhir al-Bag͟hdādī deals with the methods (*asbāb*) towards knowledge and their degree of certitude. The expression *ʿulūm al-dīn* made famous by G͟hazzālī's great work there signifies the body of knowledge on the spiritual plane. The "religious sciences" as properly understood, in the technical sense of organized disciplines, are rather to be called *al-ʿulūm al-s͟harʿiyya* (as often) or (more rarely, and also by G͟hazzālī) *dīniyya.*

Bibliography: The quotations in the body of the article are completed and specified by: I. Muslim Works. *Fiḳh Akbar II*, tr. Wensinck, *The Muslim creed*, Cambridge 1932, 194; Ibn Baṭṭa, *Kitāb al-s͟harḥ wa 'l-ibāna ʿalā uṣūl al-sunna wa 'l-diyāna*, text and tr. in Henri Laoust, *La profession de foi d'Ibn Baṭṭa*, Damascus 1958 (see Index); Abū Bakr al-Bāḳillānī, *Kitāb al-tamhīd*, ed. R. J. McCarthy, Beirut 1957, 345; Ibn Taymiyya, *Maʿāridj al-wuṣūl ilā maʿrifat anna uṣūl al-dīn*, tr. H. Laoust, *Contribution à une étude de la méthodologie canonique de Taḳī al-Dīn Aḥmad b. Taymiyya*, Cairo 1939 (Index s.v. Religion); idem, *Kitāb al-siyāsa al-s͟harʿiyya*, tr. Laoust, *Le traité de droit public d'Ibn Taimiya*, Beirut 1948, Index; Djurdjānī, *Kitāb al-taʿrīfāt*, ed. Flügel, Leipzig 1845, 111; Bādjūrī, *Ḥās͟hiya ... ʿalā Djawharat al-tawḥīd*, Cairo 1352/1934, 9-10; Muḥammad ʿAbduh, *Risālat al-tawḥīd*, Cairo 1353/1935, 124-9; Ras͟hīd Riḍā, *Al-k͟hilāfa aw al-imāma al- ʿuẓmā*, Cairo (Manār) 1341/1922, 92 (tr. Laoust, *Le califat dans la doctrine de Ras͟hīd Riḍā*, Beirut 1938, 154-5). (See also the principal *tafsīrs* on the Ḳur'ānic texts concerning *dīn*, *e.g.*, Ṭabarī, i, 51).

II. Western Works. References given by D. B. Macdonald (*EI*[1]), especially for the etymology and meaning of the word: Lane, *Lexicon*, 944; Nöldeke, *ZDMG*, xxxvii, 534, n. 2; *Gr.I.Ph.*. i/1, 107, 270; i/2, 26, 170; ii, 644; Vollers, in *ZA*, xiv, 351; Juynboll, *Handbuch*, 40, 58. These are supplemented by: Louis Massignon, *Passion d'al-Ḥallādj*, Paris 1922, 669; Henri Laoust, *Essai sur les doctrines sociales et politiques de Taḳī-d-Dīn Aḥmad b. Taimīya*, Cairo (IFAO) 1939, 280, 312, 453; L. Gardet and M. Anawati, *Introduction à la théologie musulmane*, Paris 1948, 375; M. Gaudefroy-Demombynes, *Mahomet*, Paris 1957, 504-5.

(L. Gardet)

DĪN-I ILĀHĪ (Divine Faith), the heresy promulgated by the Indian Mug͟hal emperor Akbar [*q.v.*] in 989/1581. The heresy is related to earlier *Alfī* heretical movements in Indian Islam of the 10th/16th century, implying the need for the reorientation of faith at the end of the first millennium of the advent of the Prophet. Among its formative inspirations was Akbar's reaction to the decadence and corruption of contemporary *ʿulamā'*, his eclecticism and religious tolerance, and the intellectual scepticism of his chief associate Abu 'l-Faḍl ʿAllāmī. Ethically, the *Dīn-i Ilāhī* prohibited sensuality, lust, misappropriation, deceit, slander, oppression, intimidation and pride. To these was added the Djayn dislike of animal slaughter and the Catholic value of celibacy. Nine of the ten virtues enjoined were presumably derived directly from the Ḳur'ān: liberality, "forbearance from bad actions and repulsion of anger with mildness", abstinence, avoidance of "violent material pursuits", piety, devotion, prudence, gentleness, kindness; while the tenth was the ṣūfistic "purification of soul by yearning for God". Ritually, it was a kind of solar monotheism with an exaggerated preoccupation with light, sun and fire, showing primarily Zoroastrian, and secondarily Hindū and *ṣūfī* influences.

The brunt of the orthodox Muslim criticism of Akbar's age was focussed on its indirect suggestion of extolling the emperor to a status of prophethood, even of divinity in such manifestations as the mutual greetings of his disciples *Allāhu Akbar* and *Djalla djalāluhu* hinting flatteringly at Akbar's name; though these were also familiar formulae of *ṣūfī d͟hikr*. Actually Akbar discouraged enrolment to his sect on the plea: "Why should I claim to guide men before I myself am guided?" The number of its adherents did not exceed nineteen. Akbar seems to have regarded it as a spiritual club confined to those of the élite of his court whose devotion to himself, by his own encouragement, had assumed the form of an esoteric and heterodox personality cult. The *Dīn-i Ilāhī* did not claim to possess a revealed text, and did not develop a priest-craft. The apologetics of Akbar in diplomatic correspondence with ʿAbd-Allāh K͟hān Ūzbek [*q.v.*], stressed that the basis of his religious faith was essentially rationalistic, affirmed Akbar's attestation of faith as a Muslim, and denied any claim on his part to prophethood or divinity. On the other hand Abu 'l-Faḍl quotes Akbar as confessing, at least figuratively, to cessation from Islam.

Though electically influenced by other religions, the *Dīn-i Ilāhī* derives its essential tenets from various streams of orthodox and heterodox ṣūfism. Its preoccupation with light was an exaggeration of the Suhrawardiyya emphasis on *nūr*; Akbar's personality cult was inspired by Ibn al-ʿArabī [*q.v.*] and al-Djīlī's doctrines of the 'Perfect man'; the use of the Emperor's name in salutation was giving a heterodox significance to familiar *ṣūfī* formulae of *d͟hikr*; the ritual of the initiation of a disciple was based on the Čis͟htiyya example.

Some features of the ritual of sun and fire, specially at one stage Akbar's recitation of one thousand Sanskrit names for the sun, suggest Hindū influence; but it is remarkable that very little was borrowed from either orthodox Hinduism or the Bhakti movement. The sect had only one Hindū member, Rājā Bīrbal, while Akbar's trusted administrators like Bhagwān Dās and Mān Singh were opposed to it.

The trend of recent scholarship is to treat the *Dīn-i Ilāhī* as a heresy within Islam, rather than a form of apostasy. In Akbar's own age Muslim orthodoxy treated it with some apprehension, and although it died out with him, it set in motion a strong orthodox reaction represented in Naḳs͟hbandiyya ṣūfism by S͟hayk͟h Aḥmad Sirhindī and in theological studies based on *ḥadīt͟h* by S͟hayk͟h ʿAbd al-Ḥaḳḳ Dihlawī.

Bibliography: Abu 'l-Faḍl ʿAllāmī, *Ā'īn-i Akbarī*, i (Eng. tr. by H. Blochmann), Calcutta 1927, 50-8, 64, 110-5, 157-76; *ibid*, ii (tr. by Jarrett) Calcutta 1891, 30; *ibid*, iii (tr. by Jarrett), Calcutta 1948, 426-49; idem, *Maktūbāt*, Lucknow 1863, ii, 26; ʿAbd al-Ḳadīr Badāyūnī, *Muntak͟hab al-tawārīkh*, Calcutta 1868-9, ii, 200-8, 255-87, 301-26, 336-9, 356, 391-2, 399; Muḥsin-i Fānī, *Dabistān-i madhāhib* (Eng. tr. by D. Shea and A. Troyer, Paris 1843, iii, 48-105); ʿInāyat Allāh Khān "Rāsikh", *ʿInāyat nāma*, India Office Pers Ms. 549, ff. 20b-21a; Vincent A. Smith, *Akbar, the Great Mogul*, Oxford 1927, 209-22, 237; F. W. Buckler, *A new interpretation of Akbar's "Infallibility" decree of 1579*, in *JRAS*, 1924, 591-608; Sri Ram Sharma, *The religious policy of the Mughal emperors*, Oxford 1940, 18-68; Makhanlal Roychoudhury, *The Dīn-i Ilāhī*, Calcutta 1941; Shaykh Muḥammad Ikram, *Rūd-i Kawthar*, Karachi n.d., 47-82; E. Wellesz, *Akbar's religious thought reflected in Mogul painting*, London 1952; Y. Hikmet Bayur, *L'Essai de réforme religieuse et sociale d'Ekber Gürkan ....*, in *Belleten*, ii, 1938, 127-85; Aziz Ahmad, *Akbar, hérétique ou apostat?*, in *JA*, 1961, 21-38; Correia Afonso, *Father Xavier and the Muslims of the Mughal empire*, 1957.

(AZIZ AHMAD)

DĪNĀDJPUR: a district in East Pakistan; population (1951) 1,354,432.

In 1947 the district was partitioned, and its southern part was given to India. The name has been wrongly derived from Dinwadj or Danudj, identified with king Danudja Mardana Deva, whose coins are dated in Sáka 1339-40 = A.D. 1417-18. This king has nothing to do with Rādjā Ganesá, whose original estate was at Bhatoriya in this district and who played an important role in the early 9th/15th century Muslim history of Bengal. *Dīnādj* is a non-Aryan term, which with the Sanskrit ending *pur* makes the full name of the town and district. Such non-Aryan terms are common in the place names of Bengal. The district is famous for the fortified remains of the old city of Devkoṭ, the ancient Koṭivarsha, about 18 miles south-south-west of Dīnādjpur, now marking the boundary between India and Pakistan, just on the Indian side of the railway station Hilly. It was at this place that Muḥammad Bakhtiyār Khaldjī, the first Muslim conqueror of Bengal, returned from his ill-fated Tibetan expedition and died in 602/1206. There is also to be found the famous *dargāh* of Shaykh al-Mashāyikh Mawlānā ʿAṭāʾ Waḥīd al-Dīn, who died in the middle of the 8th/14th century. Another important saint, Shāh Ismāʿīl Ghāzī, who died a martyr's death in the third quarter of the 9th/15th century in fighting against the non-Muslim rulers of this area, has a memorial *dargāh* at Ghoṛāghāṭ, 18 miles east of Hilly. The third important place is Mahisantosh, spelt in Persian works as Mahisūn, which was a centre of Muslim education during the early Muslim rule.

Bibliography: *Eastern Bengal District Gazetteers*: *Dinadjpur*, Allāhābād, 1912; A. Cunningham, *ASI*, xv, Calcutta 1882; G. H. Damant, *Notes on Shāh Ismāʿīl Ghāzī, with a sketch of the contents of a Persian Ms. Risālat ush-Shuhdā*, in *JASB*, 1874; A. H. Dani, *The House of Rādjā Gaṇeśa of Bengal* in *JASB*, 1952; idem, *Bibliography of the Muslim inscriptions of Bengal*, Dacca 1957.

(A. H. DANI)

DĪNĀR (pl. *danānir*), the name of the gold unit of currency in early Islam. The word derives from Greek δηνάριον (Latin, *denarius*), originally signifying a silver coin but in post-Constantinian times commonly synonymous with *solidus, denarius aureus* or νόμισμα χρυσοῦν. The Arabs were familiar with the word and with the Roman and Byzantine gold coin before Islam (*Ḳurʾān*, ed. Flügel, iii, 68; and cf. J. Stepková in *Numismatický Sborník*, iii, 1956, 65).

The earliest type of Arab dīnār, undated but attributable to approximately the year 72/691-2, and struck almost certainly at Damascus, imitates the *solidus* of Heraclius and his two sons but with specifically Christian symbolism deleted and an Arabic religious legend added. A new type, more distinctly Arab, that of the "standing sword-girt Caliph", appears at the Umayyad capital with an issue dated 74/693-4 and is repeated in 76 and 77; but in the latter year ʿAbd al-Malik's coinage reform drastically affects the style of the dīnār which henceforth, with very rare exceptions, is purely epigraphic. In North Africa and Spain the early dīnār (*ḳūḳī*) has an independent history: before approximately the year 85/704 the unit and its fractions imitates the Carthaginian *solidus* of Heraclius but bears Muslim legends in abbreviated Latin translation; thereafter until the year 95/713-4 the portraits are deleted and dates are sometimes given in indiction years; Hidjra dates appear in 95, bilingual legends in 97/715-6, and just after the turn of the century both Ifrīḳiya (Ḳayrawān) and al-Andalus (Cordoba) issue dīnārs of purely Arab type, differing only in minor detail from the reformed dīnār of the East. The minting of gold in al-Andalus ceases in 106/724-5 (except for an anomalous unpublished issue of 127/744-5) and is not resumed until 317/929 under ʿAbd al-Raḥmān III.

The weight standard of the early transitional dīnār appears to have been the same as that of the Byzantine *solidus*, *i.e.*, approximately 4.55 grams. With ʿAbd al-Malik's reform, however, the weight was reduced to 4.25 grams. The accuracy of this latter figure is attested not only by the weights of well-preserved dīnārs but by the evidence of Egyptian glass dīnār and dīnār fraction weights dating from the end of the first to the end of the second century A.H. The reduced standard of the post-reform dīnār resulted from a decision to redefine the mithḳāl (*i.e.*, dīnār) in convenient terms of 20 Syro-Arabian ḳīrāṭs of 0.2125 grams in place of such cumbersome terms as $21^3/_7$ ḳīrāṭs, or "22 ḳīrāṭs less a fraction", etc., which had been employed by the Arabs in pre-Islamic times to express the weight of the mithḳāl. The latter was doubtless based on the Attic drachm theoretically weighing 4.37 grams but actually, as circulated in Arabia, falling somewhat below that weight. While in general the weight standard of the dīnār was maintained in most parts of the Islamic world down to the 4th century of the Hidjra, thereafter extreme irregularity occurs both in weight and purity. In any case the dīnār usually passed by weight rather than tale, except where payments were made in sealed purses (*ṣurra*) of coins of guaranteed weight and fineness.

The half dīnār (*niṣf, semissis*) and the third dīnār (*thulth, tremissis*) were struck in North Africa and Spain in the transitional period and in the early years of the 2nd/8th century, while glass weights for these fractions (2.12 and 1.41 grams) continued to be issued until the third quarter of that century. The quarter dīnār (*rubʿ*) was introduced by the Aghlabids in North Africa early in the 3rd century and subsequently was issued in large quantities by the Fāṭimids both in North Africa, and in Sicily where in due course it became the well-known *tari d'oro*; as well as in Spain under ʿAbd al-Raḥmān III and his successors and some of the *Mulūk al-Ṭawāʾif*.

With respect to fineness the standard of the early dīnār was exceptionally high. The post-reform Umayyad dīnār ranges between 96% and 98% fine and this same standard prevails by and large during the ʿAbbāsid period. Exceptions are the years of civil war between al-Amīn and al-Maʾmūn, the period between the end of Ṭūlūnid and the beginning of Ikhshīdid rule in Egypt and the Buwayhid period in Baghdād. Less debased but still below the early standard is the gold of the Caliph al-Nāṣir and his successors who resumed the striking of dīnārs and multiples in their own names in Baghdād during the last years of the Caliphate. In Egypt under the Fāṭimids the standard exceeds 98% and even approximates 100% under al-Āmir; under Saladin it falls below 90% but rises again to 98-100% under his successors, particularly under al-Kāmil. "There existed neither in the West nor in the East dīnārs of a standard excelling the standard *al-Āmiri al-Kāmili*" (Ibn Baʿra, writing between 615 and 635 A.H.). Reliable statistics for the fineness of the dīnār in the period of its decline in the East are lacking (Ghaznawids, Saldjūḳs, Khwarizmshāhs, etc.), but it is evident from the appearance of preserved specimens and from limited technical data available that in eastern Khurāsān in the 5th and 6th centuries A.H. the alloy is low-grade electrum containing a large percentage of silver. Electrum fractions also appear among the *Mulūk al-Ṭawāʾif* in Spain. Silver and copper "dīnārs" of eastern Irān and Transoxiana are known in Mongol and post-Mongol times (see v. Schrötter, *op. cit.* in bibliography).

For the division of the dīnār into various theoretical fractions, see *Dānaḳ*, *Ḳīrāṭ*, *Ḥabba*, s.v. SIKKA.

In outward appearance the dīnār of the Caliphates and of most independent dynasties differs very little. The prototype carries the *shahāda* and part of Ḳurʾān CXII in the field or area, and the "prophetic mission" (Ḳurʾān IX, 33) and a formula stating the date of striking in words in the circular margins. The ʿAbbāsids alter the legends and arrangement slightly. Down to the year 170/786-7 the dīnār is anonymous; thereafter the name of the official charged with the administration of the coinage begins to appear; some of the issues of al-Amīn and al-Maʾmūn bear their names, and from the time of al-Muʿtaṣim the Caliph's name appears regularly. Until the year 198/813-4 there is no indication of the mint, but beginning with that year at Miṣr (Fusṭāṭ) and subsequently at Madīnat al-Salām (Baghdād), Ṣanʿā, Dimishḳ, al-Muḥammadiyya (Rayy), Marw, Surra-man-raʾa (Samarra) and many other cities, the name of the mint regularly appears in the date formula. Gradually other legends are added, such as the name of the heir-apparent, supplementary religious legends and eventually the names of independent dynasts and princes. The Fāṭimids, while not entirely abandoning the style of the prototype, introduce Shīʿite legends and a type in which the inscriptions are arranged in concentric circles.

The word dīnār disappears from the coinage in the 6th century A.H. in the West, in the 7th/13th century in the East and in India, and in the 8th/14th century in Egypt. As a money of account the word was widely used both during and after its circulation as an actual coin.

The influence of the dīnār on the economy of western Europe, its rôle in mediaeval international commerce along with the Byzantine *solidus* or *nomisma* have been discussed at length, notably by Pirenne, Monneret de Villard, Block, Lombard, Lopez, Bolin, Grierson (synthesis and bibliography conveniently assembled by F.-J. Himly in *Rev. Suisse d'Histoire*, v, 1955, 31); and it was inevitable that it should on occasion be imitated as other popular media of exchange have at various times been imitated (*e.g.*, the florin, the ducat, etc.). Most important was the Crusader bezant (*besantius saracenatus*, *sarrazinas*, etc., etc., the Arabic *dīnār ṣūrī*), chiefly imitating Fāṭimid coins of al-Mustanṣir and al-Āmir. In the western Mediterranean the dīnār gave rise to the *mancus*, a European term used not only to describe the Arab dīnār and as an accounting term, but also, with qualifying proper names, to designate various Christian imitations of the 5th/11th century in Spain (cf. P. Grierson in *Rev. belge de phil. et d'histoire*, xxxii, 1954, 1059, and J. Duplessy in *Rev. Numismatique*, 1956, 101). The original *marabotino* (*maravedi*, etc.) of Alphonso VIII of Castile was an imitation of the Murābiṭ dīnār with Christian legends in Arabic character.

Sauvaire (see bibliography) lists numerous adjectives and nouns which occur in written sources qualifying or describing various types of dīnārs. To these may be added: *Atābakī* (Zangid), *tūrī* (for *tari* ?, *JAOS* 1954, 163), *djayshī* (Dozy, *Suppl.*), *Ḥākimī* (Fāṭimid), *Ḥasanī* (Fāṭimid), *al-kharīṭa* (for special occasions, Herzfeld, *Geschichte ... Samarra*, 195), *ʿadad* ("counted", ἀρίθμια νομίσματα, papyri), *sawā* ("correct weight", papyri), *ṭarā* ("fresh", "uncirculated", papyri), *ḳawāmī* (Buwayhid, *Ars Islamica* 1951, 23), *mithḳālī* ("full weight", papyri), *mudawwara* (Fāṭimid, with concentric legends ?), *musaṭṭara* (Fāṭimid, with legends in parallel lines ?), *mashkhaṣ* or *mushkhaṣ* ("with effigies", *i. e.*, European, *BSOAS*, 1953, 72, *JESHO* 1958, 48), *mashriḳī* ("eastern", papyri), *muẓaffarī* (Shah-i Arman, *JAOS* 1954, 163), *maʿsūl* ("correctly counted out", papyri), *malikī* (Zurayʿid, *Num. Zeitschrift* 47, 1914, 172), *munaḥḥat* ("clipped", papyri), *nizārī* (Fāṭimid), *yūsufī* (Muwaḥḥid, Ibn Khallikān).

The word dīnār as a denomination applied to coins of various metals including nickel, copper, etc., bearing no relationship to the classical Arab unit, has survived in modern times: *e.g.*, Ḳādjārs (Nāṣir al-Dīn Shāh and successors, and the Pahlavī dynasty), ʿIrāḳ (1 dīnār, paper money = 1000 fils), Yugoslavia (1 dinar = 100 para).

(See also DIRHAM, MITHḲĀL, ḲĪRĀṬ, SANADJĀT and SIKKA).

Bibliography: al-Maḳrīzī, *K. Shudhūr al-ʿuḳūd*, various eds. including Tychsen (1797), Istanbul (1298 A.H.), L. A. Mayer (1933), A.-M. de St.-Elie (1939); E. v. Bergmann, *Die Nominale der Münzreform der Chalifen Abdulmelik*, in *SBAk.* Wien, 1870, 239; H. Sauvaire, *Matériaux pour servir à l'histoire de la numismatique et de la métrologie musulmanes* (*JA*, 1879-82); convenient summary of this comprehensive, indispensable work by S. Lane-Poole in *NC* 1884, 66-96; R. Vasmer in F. v. Schrötter, *Wörterbuch der Münzkunde* (Berlin-Leipzig, 1930), s.v. Dinar; J. Walker, *A catalogue of the Arab-Byzantine and post-reform Umaiyad coins* (*Cat. of the Muhammadan coins in the British Museum*, ii, London 1956); A. Grohmann, *Einführung und Chrestomathie zur arabischen Papyruskunde* (*Monografie Archivu Orientálniho*, xiii/1, Prague 1955); A. S. Ehrenkreutz, several articles on the dīnār and its standard of fineness in *JAOS* 1954, 162, 1956, 178, and *JESHO* 1959; G. C. Miles, *Some early Arab dinars* in American Numismatic Society *Museum Notes*, iii, 1948, 93; idem, *The numismatic history of Rayy* (N.Y., 1938); idem, *Fāṭimid coins* (N.Y., 1951); idem, *The coinage of the Umayyads of Spain* (N.Y., 1950); the various catalogues of Arab glass weights (see SANADJĀT); P. Grierson, *The monetary reforms of ʿAbd al-Malik* in *JESHO*, 1960, 241; the numerous catalogues of papyri (full bibliographies in A. Grohmann's *Arabic papyri in the Egyptian Library*) and of coin collections, notably those of London (Lane-Poole), Paris (Lavoix), Berlin (Nützel), Istanbul (Ismāʿīl Ghālib, Aḥmed Tevḥīd, Khalīl Edhem), and W. Tiesenhausen's compendium of Umayyad and ʿAbbāsid coins, *Moneti vostočnago Khalifata*. The bibliographical details are available in L. A. Mayer's *Bibliography of Moslem Numismatics*², London 1954. (G. C. MILES)

DĪNĀR (MALIK), name of one of the Oghuz chieftains who set themselves up at Khurāsān after the dislocation of the kingdom of the Saldjūḳid Sandjar; unable to maintain his position there before the pressure of the Khʷārizmian state, he found a way to profit from the dissensions among the Saldjūḳids of Kirmān to lay hands on that principality (582/1186) and to hold it, in spite of hostilities on the borders of Sistān, Fārs, and the Persian Gulf, until his death in 591/1195. After his death, however, Kirmān in its turn became absorbed within the Khʷārizmian empire, on account of insufficient Oghuz immigration.

Bibliography: Almost the only source for the history of Kirmān in this period lies in the *Badāʾiʿ al-azmān fī waḳāʾiʿ Kirmān* of the contemporary Afḍal al-Dīn Kirmānī, the text of which, reconstituted from later compilers (especially Ḥasan Yazdī), was published by M. Bayānī in 1331/1952, but was already almost equally well accessible in Muḥammad b. Ibrāhīm's *History of the Saldjūḳids of Kirmān* ed. by Th. Houtsma as vol. i of his *Recueil de textes relatifs à l'histoire des Seldjoucides*, and analysed by him in an article in *ZDMG*, 1885; also to be consulted is the special apologetic work of Afḍal al-Dīn on Malik Dīnār, *ʿIḳd al-ʿUlā*, ed. Tehran 1311/1932, and the *Risāla* recently discovered and published by A. Iḳbāl, 1331/1952, which continues the history of Kirmān until 612/1215 (excellent editorial preface on Afḍal al-Dīn). Isolated references in Ibn al-Athīr, xi, 116, 248-9, and xii, 198; and Djuwaynī, *Taʾrīkh-i Djahāngushā*, ed. Muḥ. Ḳazwīnī, ii, 20-2 (Khurāsānian period). (CL. CAHEN)

DĪNAWAR (sometimes incorrectly written Daynawar) in the middle ages was one of the most important towns in Djibāl (Media); it is now in ruins. The exact location is 34° 35′ Lat. N. and 47° 26′ E. Long. (Greenwich). The ruins are situated on the north-eastern edge of a fertile plain 1600 metres above sea level which is watered by the Čam-i Dīnawar. This stream, after traversing the precipitous Tang-i Dīnawar, joins the Gamas-Āb near the rock of Bisitūn; the Gamas-Āb is a tributary of the Ḳara Sū which, in its lower reaches, is known as the Karkha. When Ibn Khurradādhbih (ed. de Goeje, 176) stated that the Nahr al-Sus (Karkha) rose in the neighbourhood of Dīnawar, he was obviously regarding the Čam-i Dīnawar as its real source.

The foundation of Dīnawar dates from the Seleucid era, if not earlier. As at Kangāwar (42 km. east by south), there was a Greek settlement there; recent excavations have brought to light a stone basin decorated with busts of Silenus and satyrs, thus making it probable that the cult of Dionysus had been introduced there by the Greeks (see R. Ghirshman, *Iran*, 236).

Dīnawar surrendered to the Muslim Arabs immediately after the battle of Nihāwand in the year 21/642. In Muʿāwiya's reign it was renamed Māh al-Kūfa. In the administrative division of the Caliph's empire, Māh al-Kūfa appears not only as the name of the town of Dīnawar, but also as that of two districts of Djibāl, Dīnawar comprising the upper lands and Ḳarmīsīn (Kirmānshāh) the lower. In the west Māh al-Kūfa was bounded by the district of Ḥulwān, in the south by Māsabadhān, in the east by Hamadhān and in the north by Ādharbāydjān (see Ḳudāma in *BGA* (ed. de Goeje), vi, 243 ff.). There has been some controversy as to the meaning of the word Māh in such names as Māh al-Kūfa and Māh al-Baṣra (Nihāwand). Some Arab authors have maintained that Māh was a Persian noun equivalent in meaning to the Arabic *ḳaṣaba* 'town' or 'capital', while Balʿamī, in his Persian translation of Ṭabarī, stated that it was a Pahlawī word meaning 'province' or 'kingdom' (see Zotenberg's French version, iii, 480); it is to be noted that this explanation is not given in the Arabic text. A more probable explanation is that Māh is equivalent in meaning to the ancient Māda or Media. It is noteworthy that all geographical names which are compounded with Māh and can be fairly definitely located (cf. for example Māh al-Baṣra) belong to Media. In the case of Māh al-Kūfa, it has been said that the place was so called because the taxes raised from it and its district were applied for the benefit of the citizens of Kūfa. On the word Māh, see in particular Nöldeke in *ZDMG*, xxxi, 559 ff. and his *Gesch. der Perser und Araber zur Zeit der Sasaniden* (1879), 103, and J. Marquart, *Ērānšahr*, Berlin 1901, 18-19.

In the Umayyad and ʿAbbāsid periods Dīnawar was very prosperous. In the 4th/10th century it was, according to Ibn Ḥawḳal, only one-third less in size than Hamadhān. Muḳaddasī praised its well-built bazaars and its rich orchards. The confusion that broke out in the last years of al-Muḳtadir's reign (d. 320/932) temporarily ruined the town. When the rebellious general Mardāwīdj of Gīlān seized the whole province of Djibāl after defeating the troops sent against him by the Caliph, Dīnawar also fell into his hands (319/931), and several thousands (the figures vary from 7,000 to 25,000) of the inhabitants perished soon afterwards. Ḥasanwayh (Ḥasanūya), a Kurdish prince living in this region, founded a small independent kingdom of which the capital was Dīnawar; he was able to retain possession of it for nearly 50 years (until his death in 369/979). Ḥamd Allah Mustawfī (*Nuzha*, 106) described Dīnawar as a small town, with a temperate climate and abundant water, producing crops of corn and also fruit. Half a century after Mustawfī's time, Dīnawar was completely destroyed by Tīmūr and has never been rebuilt.

Theodore Strauss, who visited the ruins of Dīnawar in 1905, stated that: "The site of Dīnawar is indicated only by mounds of earth which have been ransacked several times in the search for coins; numerous finds are still being made especially by peasants tilling the fields" (See his *Eine Reise im Westlichen Persien*, in Petermann's *Geog. Mitteil.*, 1911, 65). Strauss also stated that traces can still be seen in the adjacent Tang-i Dīnawar of an ancient road hewn out of the rock which probably connected Dīnawar with Baghdād.

Bibliography: in addition to the references in the text: *BGA* (ed. de Goeje), *passim*, particularly, iii, 395-6, v, 259, vi, 119 ff., 226 ff., 243 ff., vii, 271; Balādhurī, *Futūḥ*, 194, 306-8, 310; Masʿūdī, *Murūdj*, iii, 263, ix, 24, 25, 31; Yāḳūt, ii, 704, iv,

407; Ḳazwīnī (ed. Wüstenfeld), ii, 250; *Aghānī*, Tables, 752; Le Strange, 189, 227; A. v. Kremer, *Culturgeschichte des Orients unter den Chalifen* (1875), i, 337-8, 365; Nöldeke, in *ZDMG*, xxviii, 102; Weil, *Chalifen*, i, 93; ii, 620 (wrongly vocalized Deinewr); J. de Morgan, *Mission Scientif. en Perse, Études Géograph.*, ii, 95 ff.; *Guides Bleus*: *Moyen Orient*, Paris 1956, 705.

(L. Lockhart)

al-DĪNAWARĪ, Abū Ḥanīfa Aḥmad b. Dāwūd, Arab scholar of the 3rd/9th century. The name of his grandfather, Wanand, indicates that he was of Iranian origin. In spite of the great value attached to his work by later authors very little has been handed down about his life except a short notice by Ibn al-Nadīm (*Fihrist*, 78), copied by Yāḳūt with additional notices about the year of his death, which according to various sources fell in 281 or 282/894-5 or before 290/902-3; an appreciation of his work quoted from the *K. Taḳrīẓ al-Djāḥiẓ* by Abū Ḥayyān al-Tawḥīdī and an anecdote about his meeting in Dīnawar with the philologist al-Mubarrad (*Irshād al-arīb*, 1, 123-7; an extract in ʿAbd al-Ḳādir al-Baghdādī, *Khizānat al-adab*, 1, 25-26). That he lived in Dīnawar is corroborated by what is said by the astronomer ʿAbd al-Raḥmān al-Ṣūfī, who in the year 335/946-7 saw the house in Dīnawar that served him as an observatory (*Ṣuwar al-kawākib*, Ḥaydarābād 1373/1954, 8). His philological studies he prosecuted in ʿIrāḳ, where he is said to have learned both from Baṣran and Kūfan teachers, especially from the two grammarians al-Sikkīt and his son Ibn al-Sikkīt (see also Suyūṭī, *Bughyat al-wuʿāt*, Cairo 1326, 132).

Dīnawarī belonged to the epoch of Arabic literature which was dominated by the spirit of al-Djāḥiẓ [*q.v.*] to whom he may be compared (as did Abū Ḥayyān al-Tawḥīdī) in consideration of his interests in the "philosophical" studies of the Hellenistic learning (*ḥikmat al-falsafa*) and the Arabic humanities alike. Unlike Djāḥiẓ, however, he had a clear disposition for a systematical approach, which was from the very beginning applied by the masters of the philological schools of ʿIrāḳ to materials treated by them. It may be that this disposition was connected also with his mathematical genius attested by works of his in the field of the exact sciences, which were cultivated by scholars of Iranian origin like himself. From the beginning, Arabic philology, the study of pre-Islamic literature and culture, had been associated with Ḳurʾānic studies; a commentary on the Ḳurʾān is mentioned by the bibliographers among his works. These studies may have corresponded also to his temperament, because he is characterized as pious and ascetic (*wariʿ zāhid*).

Of his mathematical works, one on Indian arithmetic (*K. al-baḥth fī ḥisāb al-Hind*) and another on algebra (*K. al-djabr wa 'l-muḳābala*), nothing has been preserved. A work on astronomical geography (*K. al-Ḳibla wa 'l-zawāl*) was plagiarized by Ibn Ḳutayba, according to Masʿūdī (*Murūdj*. vii, 335). For his *K. al-anwāʾ*, which was estimated by al-Ṣūfī as most complete in its kind (*op. cit.*, 7), he tried to check, by observations of his own, the statements made by the Bedouins and collected by the philologists concerning the *anwāʾ* [*q.v.*].

To later authors Dīnawarī is especially known as the author of the *K. al-nabāt*, the main purpose of which is lexicographical, to collect all available tradition, oral and literary, about names and terminations in the field of plants and plant life as documented by verses of poetry or by authorities on Bedouin dialects. In this field he had predecessors among the philologists (see al-nabāt). The work of Dīnawarī incorporated their material and added to it collections and observations of his own. To later generations it was the standard work in the field and was to a great extent quoted by lexicologists from Ibn Sīda [*q.v.*] on. Of the two sections into which it was divided the first contained a series of monographs some of which go far beyond the field of "botany" proper, treating with themes that have a more or less indirect connexion with the world of plants; see B. Silberberg, *Das Pflanzenbuch des Dînawarî* in *ZA* xxiv, 1910: 225-65, xxv, 1911: 39-88. Two volumes of the original work have come down to us, the 5th containing the last part of the monograph section and the letters *alif* to *zāy* of the alphabetical section (ed. by B. Lewin, *Uppsala Universitets Årsskrift* 1953: 10), and the 3d (M. S. Salisbury 77, Yale Univ. Libr.; an edition of this together with the monograph part of the 5th vol. is under preparation to appear in *Bibliotheca islamica*).

The only work of Dīnawarī's that has come down to us in its full extent is his historical work *al-Akhbār al-ṭiwāl* (ed. by V. Guirgass, Leiden 1888; Preface, variantes et index par I. J. Kračkovskij, Leiden 1912). That this work, in spite of its literary and scholarly qualities, never met with great approval and popularity in the Arab speaking world may be due to accidental circumstances rather than to a deliberate disregard. Its title was known to bibliographers from Ibn al-Nadīm on, but the author is never called a historian. History is seen from an Iranian point of view; thus the Prophet is mentioned so to speak in a marginal note of the history of Anūsharwān; Islam and the Arabs appear on the scene when invading Persia; the Umayyads are treated with only as far as the religious and political movements involving the eastern part of Islam are concerned, etc. This tendency towards promoting Iranian views may be due, not to anti-Arab feelings, but to the sources on which he drew. His chief aim was certainly to write a book of literary and entertaining qualities. For this reason he omitted the *isnāds* of the *akhbār*, took the liberty of choosing, among different traditions about one and the same event, the one that suited him and insisted on points of dramatic value; *e.g.*, the days of Ḳādisiyya, Ṣiffīn and Nahrawān, the death of Ḥusayn, the *fitna* of Ibn al-Ashʿath etc., narratives which belong to the finest products of Arab historiography.

Bibliography: in the article. (B. Lewin)

al-DĪNAWARĪ, Abū Saʿīd (Saʿd) Naṣr b. Yaʿḳūb, is a writer chiefly remembered as author of *al-Ḳādirī fi 'l-Taʿbīr* (composed in 397/1006 and dedicated to al-Ḳādir Bi'llāh 381-422/991-1020), which is the oldest authentic Arabic treatise on oneirocriticism and an excellent synthesis of everything that was known on the subject at the time. Its sources were Arabic: Ibn Sīrīn [*q.v.*] to whom innumerable interpretations are attributed; Greek: Artemidorus of Ephesus, whose *Oneirocritica* translated into Arabic by Ḥunayn b. Isḥāḳ (died 260/873; cf. *Fihrist*, 255, MS A 4726 in the Istanbul University Library; edition being prepared) is reproduced almost in its entirety in this learned compilation. As for Christian and Byzantine sources, al-Dīnawarī would have used the Arabic original of the Greek treatise known as Ἀχμετ υἱὸς Σηρείμ, written by a Christian and translated into Latin by Leo Tuscus in 1160 [see ibn sīrīn[. The same work would have served him for Hindū and Persian sources. The author makes frequent reference to interpretations imputed to the Jews and has numerous quotations from the Bible.

Bibliography: *al-Ḳādirī fi 'l-taʿbīr* is still unpublished; 29 MSS. are known. It was translated into Persian (AS 1718) and following Ḥādjdjī Khalīfa (ii, 312, no. 3068), translated into Turkish verse by Shihāb al-Dīn Aḥmad b. ʿArabshāh (died 854/1450). On this work and Arabic oneirocritical literature, cf. T. Fahd, *Les Rêves en Islam*, in *Sources Orientales*, ii, Paris 1960, 125-58.

(T. Fahd)

DINDĀN, the *laḳab* of Abū Djaʿfar Aḥmad b. Ḥusayn, a Shīʿī traditionist of the 3rd/9th century. His father was a reliable authority who related traditions of the Imāms ʿAlī al-Riḍā, Muḥammad al-Djawād, and ʿAlī al-Hādī; originally from Kūfa, he lived for a while in Ahwāz, where Dindān was born. Dindān also related traditions on the authority of his father's masters, but was regarded as a *ghālī*, extremist, and his reliability as a relator was impugned. He wrote several books, among them *Kitāb al-iḥtidjādj*, *K. al-anbiyāʾ*, *K. al-mathālib*, and *K. al-mukhtaṣar fi 'l-daʿwāt*; none of them appears to have survived. He died and was buried in Ḳumm.

These data are found in twelver Shīʿī biographical and bibliographical sources (*e.g.*, *Tusys List of Shyʾah Books*, edd. Sprenger and ʿAbd al-Ḥaqq, Calcutta 1853, 26; Ibn Shahrāshūb, *Maʿālim al-ʿulamāʾ*, ed. Eghbāl, Tehrān 1934, 10; Astarābādī, *Minhādj al-maḳāl*, Tehran 1307, 34). The reference to Dindān's extremist views is amplified in a group of Sunnī sources, dealing with the genesis of Ismāʿīlism. (*Fihrist* 188; Baghdādī, *Farḳ*, 266, tr. A. S. Halkin, *Moslem schisms and sects*, Tel-Aviv 1935, 108; Maḳrīzī, tr. Quatremère, in *JA*, 1836, 132, etc.). In these Dindān appears as one of the founders of the sect, in association with ʿAbd Allāh b. Maymūn [*q.v.*]. He is said to have played an active part in both the formulation and propagation of Ismāʿīlī doctrines, and in addition to have provided large sums to finance the *daʿwa*. According to the *Fihrist*, he was secretary to Aḥmad b. ʿAbd al-ʿAzīz b. Abī Dulaf (d. 280/893). His name and pedigree are variously distorted in these sources, but remain recognizable. His grandfather's name is given, with various corruptions, as Čahār Lakhtān, 'four parts'—obviously a nickname. Abu 'l-Maʿālī (*Bayān al-adyān*, ed. Eghbāl, 36, tr. Massé in *RHR*, 1926, 57) makes Čahār Lakhtān an associate of Dindān and ʿAbd Allah b. Maymūn in founding the Bāṭinī sect, and attributes to him the role of financier.

The much better informed Shīʿī sources make it clear that Dindān lived in the 3rd century. While therefore he may have been a secretary of Ibn Abī Dulaf, he cannot have been associated with ʿAbd Allah b. Maymūn, who lived and died during the 2nd/8th century. He may well, however, have played some part in the early history of Ismāʿīlism, though it is noteworthy that neither his name nor any of his works appear to have been preserved by the Ismāʿīlīs.

Bibliography: M. J. De Goeje, *Mémoire sur les Carmathes . . .*[2], Leiden 1886, 15; L. Massignon, *Esquisse d'une bibliographie Carmathe*, in *A volume of Oriental Studies presented to E. G. Browne*, Cambridge 1922, 331; B. Lewis, *The origins of Ismāʿīlism*, Cambridge 1940, index; S. M. Stern, *Abu'l-Qasim al-Busti and his refutation of Isma'ilism*, in *JRAS*,, 1961, 28-9. (B. Lewis)

DIOSCORIDES [see DIYUSḲURIDĪS].

DIPLOMACY [see ELČI, MUʿĀHADA, SAFĪR].

DIPLOMATIC

i. Classical Arabic

1) Diplomatic has reached the status of a special science in the West, and the results of such research are accessible in good manuals (like Harry Bresslau's *Handbuch der Urkundenlehre für Deutschland und Italien*, 2nd. ed. 1931). Much less work has been done on Arabic documents: the material is very scattered, and not yet sufficiently collated to permit detailed research. Yet Arabic documents have aroused interest for some considerable time: a number have been published, and the editing of Arabic papyri of the first centuries of Islam in particular has added materially to our knowledge. It is thus not mere chance that so much of the groundwork for the establishment of a science of Arabic diplomatic should have been done by a papyrologist (Grohmann), and it is to be hoped that the publishing of further papyri will advance work in that direction. It is indeed of very special advantage to possess original documents of so early a date, particularly as there are not so many Arabic documents of the later centuries. Some collections have become known only recently, and it is to be hoped that here, too, more material will be discovered. Numbers of important Arabic documents have already come to light in the *Geniza* collections and among the manuscripts in the St. Catherine's Monastery on Mount Sinai. Documents of the Mamlūk period are preserved in archives in Italy and Spain.

Arabic manuals for secretaries also form part of the material on which a science of Arabic diplomatic can be based, and these are preserved in great number. In part, they consist of theoretical explanations and advice to scribes, in part of practical examples in the text; these, however, are usually no more than model forms without either names or dates. It is obviously difficult to decide to what extent these texts are authentic, that is to say to what extent they are based on original documents. Such manuals gradually grew and became more complete, until in the time of the Mamlūks they reach encyclopaedic extent in Ḳalḳashandī's *Ṣubḥ al-aʿshā fī ṣināʿat al-inshāʾ*. This great work is an essential source book for the study of documents, and therefore its author may be regarded as the most important precursor of scientific Arabic diplomatic. Here too, of course, it is hard to tell to what extent Ḳalḳashandī had himself seen the originals of the numerous texts he gives. It is known that he did have access to the archives, and that many more texts survived then than do today. We are not so certain about the older texts: Ḳalḳashandī probably based his work largely on literary sources (some of which he names), but we can hardly expect a critical treatment of these.

The following is an attempt at a survey, based on Bresslau's classification, in order to get nearer to a complete picture.

2) Composition of Documents. The same division which is observed in occidental documents is also to be found in Arabic ones; namely the introductory protocol, the text, and the closing protocol.

A. The introductory protocol is known as *ṭirāz* and *iftitāḥ*. *Ṭirāz* is the name of the protocol in the Arabic papyri: to begin with the formulae were bilingual, Greek-Arabic, and later Arabic-Greek; later on, purely Arabic. There is considerable variety in the wording, and extensive material has been published by Grohmann. The purpose seems to have been to endow the document with a certain authenticity, but as far as the validity of Arabic documents goes, it is without import. From the 4th/10th century it was omitted altogether, and the term *ṭirāz* is now used only in the sense of the inscription of names on clothes. Ḳalḳas̲h̲andī knows it only in this sense, and uses the term *iftitāḥ* for the introduction of documents, for example *iftitāḥ al-kutub* and *iftitāḥ al-mukātaba*. He calls the individual parts of this *iftitāḥ fawātiḥ*; they are *basmala*, *ḥamdala*, *tas̲h̲ahhud*, *ṣalwala* (*taṣliya*), *salām*, and *baʿdiyya* (*ammā baʿdu*). Each of these terms has its own history; thus the *ṣalwala*, for example, is said to have been added only in the year 797.

The *ʿunwān*, a direction or address, is also part of the introduction. It was formerly known as *min fulān ilā fulān* or *li-fulān min fulān*, and developed from there. Ḳalḳas̲h̲andī collected 15 different forms. The designation of the sender in the *ʿunwān* was *tard̲j̲ama*, which developed from the simple *ak̲h̲ūhu* or *waladuhu* to *al-mamlūk al-Nāṣirī* etc. There is also evidence of the use of *tafdiya* for sender, developing from the ancient *d̲j̲aʿalanī 'llāhu fidāʾaka* through numerous intermediate forms, as early as ʿAbbāsid times. The formulae of benediction for the addressee, which were called *duʿā* and were taken very seriously, were even more varied. Developing from inconspicuous beginnings in Umayyad times, there was a whole system of gradation under the ʿAbbāsids. Scribes appear to have compiled lists of these *adʿiya* fairly early on, which became more detailed when distinctions in rank became more and more minute in the times of the Fāṭimids and Mamlūks, when every *laḳab* had its own precise *duʿāʾ*.

The different personal names (*asmāʾ*, *kunā*, *alḳāb*, *nuʿūt*) also underwent considerable development, and details concerning them are naturally of great importance in the interpretation of documents. Ḳalḳas̲h̲andī devoted his third *maḳāla* to them, and the material which he collected is very extensive. Here too, the development is towards ever increasing complexity. Under the Umayyads, *ism* and *kunya* were sufficient, but *laḳab* and *naʿt* became current under the ʿAbbāsids. There was a veritable inflation of terms in Mamlūk times, which is borne out by Ḳalḳas̲h̲andī's lists of 152 *alḳāb* and 372 *nuʿūt*. These can be checked with Caetani's *Onomasticon*.

B. The term used for the actual text is *matn*, in letters also *mā bayn al-salāmayn*, because they usually began and ended with *salām*. The text can be cast in either a subjective or an objective form: objective, as for instance *hād̲h̲ā mā* . . . There are definite terms for different parts of the text: *e.g.*, in letters of appointment the *isnād* mean the decisive words *an yuʿhada ilayhi*, etc. The *waṣiyya* is the part in which the duties of the nominee are specified in detail. Such details are important for the consideration of the ethics of civil servants and throw light on lesser known offices.

C. The concluding protocol consists of the *k̲h̲awātim* : *istit̲h̲nāʾ* = *in s̲h̲āʾ allāhu taʿālā*, often run together in writing, though some authorities state that this should have a line to itself. *Taʾrīk̲h̲* = dating, sometimes omitted and a separate subject of enquiry, see 14 below. *ʿAlāma* = signature of the person drawing up the document; this was known popularly, with great lack of respect as 'crow's foot' (*rid̲j̲l g̲h̲urāb*), often in particularly large writing (*al-ṭūmār al-kāmil*); in the *ik̲h̲wāniyyāt* this was in the margin. Ḳalḳas̲h̲andī, for example, has *ḥasab al-marsūm al-s̲h̲arīf* and *bi 'l-is̲h̲āra al-ʿāliya al-wazīriyya* as *mustanadāt* of the closing phrases. The *ḥamdala*, *ṣalwala*, *ḥasbala* and others are religious closing phrases, and amongst these one might perhaps list the *ḥr*, which Ḳalḳas̲h̲andī did not understand, and explains as a second *ḥasbala* or mere padding (more correctly, perhaps, a mere differentiatory sign under the letter *ḥ*).

3. Types of Documents. Grohmann has made an attempt to submit Arabic documents to the same kind of classification as European ones: with and without legal content, public and private documents, cancellarial and non-cancellarial documents, mandates, diplomas, evidential and business documents etc. The Arabs, Ḳalḳas̲h̲andī in particular, likewise classified their documents clearly.

A. The following are general terms: *kitāb*, *wat̲h̲īḳa*, *ṣakk*, *sanad*, *ḥud̲j̲d̲j̲a*, *sid̲j̲ill*, *ẓahīr*. *Kitāb* is frequently explained by such additions as *k. al-ins̲h̲āʾ*, *k. al-nikāḥ*, *k. al-ṭalāḳ*, *k. al-iʿtimād* and others. A more limited meaning was attached to the other ones, but the Fāṭimids had a preference for *sid̲j̲ill*, and in the Mag̲h̲rib, for *ẓahīr*.

B. At the beginning, documents of state were apparently also just known as *kutub*, although quite early on a distinction was made between *kutub ʿāmma* or *muṭlaḳāt*, and *kutub k̲h̲āṣṣa*, and these were further sub-divided into *k. al-aymān*, *k. al-awḳāf*, *k. al-mulūk*, *k. al-sid̲j̲ill*, and others, according to their contents. Their inclusion under the heading of 'state documents' gives this a very wide meaning. Consequently, the exchange of letters concerning matters of state was called *mukātabāt* by the ʿAbbāsids, and the chancellery the *dīwān al-mukātabāt*. This was also usual in Egypt, under the Fāṭimids, Ayyūbids, and Mamlūks. There were also *rasāʾil* and *dīwān al-rasāʾil*. *Murāsalāt* and *tarassul* were also known, though these appear to have been less common. *Ins̲h̲āʾ* and *muns̲h̲aʾāt* were used, and *dīwān al-ins̲h̲āʾ* was already known in ʿAbbāsid times, then, especially under the Fāṭimids and Mamlūks, it became the general term for chancellery (cf. 6 below).

C. Letters of Appointment. *Wilāyāt* = offices are dealt with in detail under that heading by Ḳalḳas̲h̲andī in his 5th *maḳāla*. Generally, however, compound terms appear to have been more common, such as *wilāyat al-ʿahd*, *w. al-dīwān*, *w. al-ḥisba*, *w. al-Ḳāhira* and others. Thus there is, for instance, a term like *nusk̲h̲at sid̲j̲ill bi-wilāyat al-Ḳāhira*. *Tawliya* was the right to appoint, but this, in Mamlūk times, rested with the governors of Syria only, not with those of Egypt. The following terms for the different grades of appointment were, at least in Mamlūk times, more common than these general terms: *bayʿa*, *ʿahd*, *taḳlīd*, *tafwīḍ*, *marsūm*, *tawḳīʿ*, *mans̲h̲ūr*. Each of these has its own history.

(*a*) *bayʿa* [*q.v.*] = the homage paid to a Caliph. Under the Fāṭimids, this reached particular importance, and reports of it were written in the capital and sent to the provinces, where the governor accepted the oath of allegiance from the subjects.

(*b*) *ʿahd* = contract in general, but here the contract between a caliph and his successor, or a sultan, in particular; and later also the contract between a sultan and his successor, or the sultan and rulers of smaller lands. Ḳalḳas̲h̲andī classifies all these as appointments. He believes that the first two are traceable back to the Prophet, but he describes the latter as developments which took place only under the Ayyūbids after the death of Nūr al-Dīn.

(*c*) In the actual letters of appointment of officials, there was also one supreme grade, called *ʿahd*, which concerned only the highest officials. It has not been usual since the time of the Fāṭimids.

(*d*) *taḳlīd* was a much used term for high officials such as *wazīr*s and *ḳāḍī*s, although under the Mamlūks it was restricted to very special high officials such as the confidential secretary = *kātib al-sirr*.

(*e*) *tafwīḍ*, applied to supreme *ḳāḍī*s, appears to have been used in Mamlūk times only. It may have been introduced by Shihāb al-Dīn b. Faḍl Allāh (?).

(*f*) *marsūm*, used for military personnel, also seems to appear in Mamlūk times only. By this, Shihāb al-Dīn b. Faḍl Allāh means minor documents which are not connected with appointments (of these, the more important with *basmala*, and the less important, such as passes, without), but Ḳalḳashandī distinguishes between major and minor *marāsīm* : *mukabbara* for the appointment of the commander of a fortress, and military persons of medium rank, *muṣaghghara* for the lower ranks. The latter are said to be rare (presumably because they were normally given a *manshūr*).

(*g*) *tawḳīʿ*: to begin with this seems to have been the ruler's signature, which was appended in the chancellery (whilst *ʿalāma* was a kind of motto written in the ruler's own hand, like a signature, at the bottom of documents). The *tawḳīʿ ʿalā 'l-ḳiṣaṣ* may well have developed from this. Later on, *tawḳīʿ* was also used for letters of appointment: to begin with, quite generally (thus Ibn Faḍl Allāh, perhaps even Ayyūbid); but later only for the lesser officials, and in Ḳalḳashandī for the fourth and lowest group of the *mutaʿammimīn* = turban wearers.

(*h*) *manshūr*. In the first centuries, this was a pass for peasants in Egypt, apparently designed to curb increasing movement away from the land. In ʿAbbāsid times, it was the name given to grants of fiefs; under the Fāṭimids it denoted certain letters of appointment; rather general appointments under the Ayyūbids; but under the Mamlūks, it became restricted to feudal grants, in different grades according to size and writing. The wording was short and precise, there were no instructions (*waṣāyā*), neither was there the sultan's signature, but a kind of tughra can occasionally be found at the head.

D. Contracts. The general terms *ʿahd*, *ʿaḳd*, and *mīthāḳ* appear as early as the Ḳurʾān, and seem to have been usual at all times. *ʿAhd* [*q.v.*] seems to have been used particularly for political agreements; *ʿaḳd* [*q.v.*] for civil contracts, often more clearly defined by an additional genitive, such as *ʿaḳd al-nikāḥ*, *ʿaḳd al-dhimma*, *ʿaḳd al-ṣulḥ*. *Mīthāḳ* seems to have been less common. Ḳalḳashandī does not mention it, but Ibn Faḍl Allāh's *Taʿrīf* mentions *mawāthīḳ* and *muwāthaḳa*. Ḳalḳashandī uses the terms *hudna* and *muhādana* for an armistice, giving examples from ʿAbbāsid and Mamlūk times. He pays particular attention to the form which the oath takes, and states that such contracts have not been current in more recent times. He knew the terms *muwādaʿa*, *musālama*, *muḳādāt*, and *muwāṣafa* as having the same meaning, but these were probably all less usual. Neither did the terms *faskh* and *mufāsakha*, for revocation by one or both parties, appear frequently. See further SHURŪṬ.

E. Documents of a predominantly business nature. These include not only grants of fiefs (see C (*h*) above) and annual tax settlements, but also the *musāmaḥāt* and the *tarkhāniyyāt*. The former concerned tax-relief, probably only in Mamlūk times, and were divided into large (*ʿiẓām*), issued in the name of the sultan, and small (*ṣighār*) in the name of the governor. Dues thus cancelled were called *mukūs*, *djihāt mustaḳbaḥa*, *munkarāt*, and *bawāḳī* (ref. balance of tax due). Some were valid for merchants and all their goods, others only for certain sums. The *ṭarkhāniyyāt* were concessions granting aged officials exemption from taxes, and possibly also a fixed salary (*maʿlūm*). In the case of the military, they were called *marsūm*, and in others *tawḳīʿ*.

F. Documents of a predominantly legal nature. Such were *amān* [*q.v.*], safe-conducts either for whole tribes or for individuals, in particular for foreigners in Islamic territory, though later also for Muslims "whose attack is feared, and especially those who have renounced their allegiance", so that, if possible, they might yet be recalled to obedience. The drawing up of such documents gradually came to form the bulk of the work of a *dīwān*. Ḳalḳashandī endeavours to trace both varieties back to the time of the Prophet and gives examples from Umayyad, ʿAbbāsid, Fāṭimid, and Mamlūk times. Some documents refer to an application of the *mustaʾmin* (*e.g.*, *innaka dhakarta raghbataka*), others do not.

Yarlīgh = Ferman, extensively used by the Turks, and introduced as far as Mamlūk Egypt by consular traffic, but only in its limited meaning of a pass for foreign ambassadors.

Iṭlāḳāt was the name given to documents reaffirming decisions of former rulers; sometimes, however, they were simply called *tawḳīʿ*. The Fāṭimid proclamation of the year 415/1024 (ed. Grohmann, *RSO*, 32, 641) can be added to the three texts cited by Ḳalḳashandī.

Dafn, the burying of sins, is said to have been known in pre-Islamic Arabia, but appears to have fallen into disuse (perhaps replaced by the *amān* ?) [see DHUNŪB, DAFN AL-].

Taḳālīd ḥukmiyya were occasionally written for the *ḳāḍī*s; they were appointments either in the form of diplomas or mere *mukātabāt*.

Isdjālāt al-ʿadāla were certificates of good character of witnesses. They are known both in the papyri, and later right into Mamlūk times. The *ʿalāma*, date, and *ḥasbala* at the end were written by the *ḳāḍī* himself, and witnessed by the scribes.

al-tawḳīʿ ʿalā 'l-ḳiṣaṣ, *i.e.*, the decision of petitions in open court, is said to have been the custom even in Sāsānid times. In Islam under the Umayyads, and under Hārūn al-Rashīd, the right of *tawḳīʿ* is said to have been transferred to Yaḥyā al-Barmakī. Egyptian governors exercised this right, too, but it seems to have been forgotten after the Ṭūlūnids, and not revived until the Fāṭimids fostered and developed it. The decision was made immediately, and was noted briefly on the back by the 'owner of the fine pen', then, after instruction (*taʿyīn*) by the head of the *dīwān*, it was fully executed by the 'owner of the broad pen'. The right of decision remained with the head of the *dīwān al-inshāʾ*, even under the Mamlūks. The Sultan himself also presided in court, and Ḳalḳashandī reports six different ways of submitting a petition. This *tawḳīʿ* was so popular that the people applied the term *tawḳīʿ* to the profession of the scribe, and called the scribes themselves *muwaḳḳiʿūn*.

ʿAḳd al-nikāḥ. Marriage contracts; legal documents in which the economic details were of special importance (*ḥawāʾidj al-ʿurs*, *nuskhat ṣadāḳ*), though the attestation of equality, the undertaking to pay the remainder of the marriage portion, and the rejection of all claims in case of divorce, etc., were likewise important.

Fatwā. Whereas certain qualities were demanded of the muftī, there does not appear to have been any set form for the *fatwā*. A customary form did, however, emerge, as can be seen from the many collections, and a certain brevity appears to have been typical.

Waḳfiyya, deed of *waḳf*, also traced back to the Prophet. Lawyers have laid down regulations for the content and form of endowments, and the deciding words *waḳaftu*, *ḥabastu*, *sabbaltu*, as well as the exhortation that it must be neither sold, nor given away, nor bequeathed, appears in every such deed. Such texts are extant in the original, in literature, and carved in stone. The numerous endowments affected the economic situation adversely, and the state found a solution for this in large scale confiscations, as also—in more modern times—in supervision by Ministries of *Awḳāf*.

Waṣiyya, last will and testament, legacy. The content is laid down by law in detail, the form appears to be free, but two witnesses are prescribed.

Waṣāyā dīniyya were large and ornate documents for reading from pulpits, in order to inculcate the rules of Islam. They were of particular importance at the time of the Sunnī restoration after the fall of the Fāṭimids, but appear also in the Maghrib.

Yamīn. Oaths played an important part in the ceremonies of homage (*bayʿāt*), and the *aymān al-bayʿa*, introduced by al-Ḥadjdjādj, were famed for being particularly strong. The Fāṭimids systematically extended these oaths, particularly in view of the fact that their subjects were of a different faith. Later, too, the oaths had their significance when they sealed contracts, or were made on attaining office or entering certain professions.

ʿUmra. These were documents for pilgrims to Mecca, who there made the *ʿumra*; these appear to have been rather rare.

Idjāzāt were frequently issued on behalf of scholars and writers, *e.g.*, for *futyā*, *tadrīs*, *riwāya*, often in the form of large sized *farkhat al-shāmī*.

Mulaṭṭifāt were sent by the Fāṭimids to the governor of a province when he took up his office, and also when honours were bestowed (*khilaʿ*, *tashārīf*). *Mulāṭafa* was also the term applied to letters accompanying appointments or presents.

Tadhkira were the orders laid down for the higher officials, ambassadors, and commanders of fortresses. These were chiefly concerned with income and expenditure.

Taḳrīẓ recommending books or poems occur occasionally.

4. Transmission and multiplication of documents. Naturally, the Arabs recognized a difference between draft, original, and copy (*musawwada*, *aṣl*, *nuskha*). A capable copyist (*nāsikh*) might advance to being a *munshiʾ* (Ṣūlī 118). Ibn al-Ṣayrafī 142 mentions copying as an important occupation, and also mentions a fair-copyist (*mubayyiḍ*). Copies are marked with *nusikha* or *nusikhat*, and, like originals, could be attested by *ṣaḥḥ*. The copies were kept, and it may well be that some collected works of the *inshāʾ* literature were compiled from collections of drafts or books of copies.

There are innumerable examples of the transmission of documents, in historical works. M. Hamidullah has collected no fewer than 269 texts attributed to the period before 652 (*Documents sur la diplomatie musulmane à l'époque du Prophète et des khalifes orthodoxes.* Suivi de: *Corpus des traités et lettres diplomatiques de l'Islam*, Paris 1935. Also in Arabic: *al-Wathāʾiḳ al-siyāsiyya fi 'l-ʿahd al-nabawī wa 'l-khilāfa al-rāshida*). This has of course no bearing on the unsettled question of their authenticity.

5. Archives. The preservation of originals and copies in archives was already customary in the Ancient Orient and in Greek Egypt. It may therefore be assumed that the Arabs likewise knew of the practice at an early date, and indeed we find a short précis on the back of some papyri, intended to facilitate storing and reference. But there is no evidence of the existence of a central archive, as there was in Greek times. Barthold in 1920 treated the question of the preservation of documents in the states of the Islamic orient (*Arkhivnïe Kursï*, i, Petrograd 1920; cf. *Islamica*, iv, 145). Perhaps one might be permitted to regard the documents drawn up between Hārūn al-Rashīd and his sons Amīn and Maʾmūn in 186/802, and sent to Mecca to be hung up in the *Kaʿba*, as being kept in a kind of archive in that holy place.

There was a proper archive in Fāṭimid times, and Ibn al-Ṣayrafī (*Ḳānūn*, 142) calls the archivist *khāzin* [*q.v.*], and stresses his importance. He praises the Baghdād archive *al-khizāna al-ʿuẓmā* as a model. It was the archivist's task to file the originals of incoming documents, and the copies of the outgoing ones according to months, in folders with headings (*iḍbāra yaktub ʿalayhā biṭāḳa*). A certain decline in this practice seems to have set in in Mamlūk times, and there were periods when the *dawādār* of the confidential secretary sufficed as an archivist.

6. Chancelleries. A. Whether the Prophet himself had a chancellery in which his famous writings to the rulers of the world were written is not certain, although we do have a whole list of scribes of the Prophet, among them the first caliphs. According to one report, ʿUmar is said to have set up the first chancellery and called it *dīwān* [*q.v.*], a word which might go back to the Persian *dīwān*, or even the Assyrian *dep*, and in fact, a certain parallel with Persian administration can be discerned. Yet it would appear to have been a *dīwān* for matters of finance and the army, rather than an actual chancellery of state.

B. In Umayyad times, the official language—which had hitherto been Persian in the east and Greek in the west—became Arabic. This *taḥwīl al-dīwān ilā 'l-ʿarabī* was carried through by al-Ḥadjdjādj in the east, and by ʿAbd al-Malik in the west. It was indeed a disaster when all the *dīwān*s were burnt in the battle near Dayr al-Djamādjim [*q.v.*] in 82/701. Otherwise we know little about Umayyad chancelleries. A special office for the sealing of documents (*dīwān al-khātam*) is said to have been introduced because of an attempted forgery under Muʿāwiya. Some innovations are said to have been made by Walīd b. ʿAbd al-Malik, when papyrus appears to have become better and the writing more beautiful; though here, as on other occasions, ʿUmar b. ʿAbd al-ʿAzīz is said to have reverted to the customs of his forebears. The custom of the caliph's hearing and deciding complaints in open session (*al-tawḳīʿ ʿalā 'l-ḳiṣaṣ*) is said to have come into being under the Umayyads. The scribes then had to record the caliph's decisions in writing. The most famous of the Umayyad scribes was ʿAbd al-Ḥamīd b. Yaḥyā [*q.v.*], who was active from the time of Sulaymān to the end of the dynasty. He appears to have enriched the scribal art in respect of both form and content, and he was probably influenced by the Persians. Not all the writings attributed to him have, however, been authenticated.

C. ʿAbbāsid Chancellery. The ʿAbbāsids do

not appear to have taken over much of the Umayyad administration. They developed a completely new scheme, in which Persian influence—still only latent in Umayyad times—came to the fore. The *kātib* became *wazīr*, and the state chancellery became known as *dīwān al-rasāʾil* or *dīwān al-inshāʾ*. We have only scanty reports (and those particularly from Ibn ʿAbdūs al-D̲j̲ahs̲h̲iyārī and Maḳrīzī) of its organization and the way it functioned. Some innovations are attributed to the Barmakids. Thus, for example, K̲h̲ālid b. Barmak is said to have introduced parchment books (*dafātir min al-d̲j̲ulūd*) instead of scrolls (*ṣuḥuf mudrad̲j̲a*), Yaḥyā b. K̲h̲ālid is said to have enlarged the *basmala* by the *taṣliya*, and Hārūn al-Ras̲h̲īd is said to have bestowed the right of the *tawḳīʿ ʿala ʾl-ḳiṣaṣ* on him. The *tawḳīʿāt* of D̲j̲aʿfar b. Yaḥyā were copied, collected, and studied as models of erudition. Al-Mahdī is said to have decreed that scribes should be free every Thursday, and it became a working day again only under al-Muʿtaṣim. The following were famous scribes and *wazīr*s of the ʿAbbāsids: Ibn Muḳla (died 328/940), Ibn al-ʿAmīd (died 360/970), and Abū Isḥāḳ al-Ṣābiʾ (died 384/994), and many innovations are traced back to them. One used to quote: *Futiḥat al-rasāʾil bi-ʿAbd al-Ḥamīd wa-k̲h̲utimat bi-Ibn al-ʿAmīd*. We hear little of the working of the state chancellery in later ʿAbbāsid times, but it will still have served as an example to the chancelleries in Egypt and other countries.

D. Chancelleries in Egypt. Papyri are the main source for the earliest days, and Grohmann has attempted to describe the administration of the provinces from these in *From the world of Arabic papyri*, 114 ff. Of course, Egypt had no state chancellery at that time, although it did have one for the provinces which dealt with the exchange of letters with the capital. A seal of the conqueror of Egypt, ʿAmr b. al-ʿĀṣ (died ca. 43/663), has survived by chance, and there are a number of letters by Ḳurra b. S̲h̲arīk (died 96/714), which exhibit the uniform style of a chancellery.

It was not until around 258/872, when Aḥmad b. Ṭūlūn became independent, that a chancellery on the Bag̲h̲dād pattern was introduced in the general development of his administration. Its first head was Ibn ʿAbd Kān, and some of his documents became famous. Other scribes were Ibn al-Dāya (died 340/951), and four brothers of the Banu ʾl-Muhād̲j̲ir family, descendants of ʿAbd al-Ḥamīd b. Yaḥyā.

The first report of an exchange of letters between Egypt and a non-Islamic country dates from the time of the Ik̲h̲s̲h̲īdids: at the time when Muḥammad b. Ṭug̲h̲d̲j̲ (323-35/935-46) wished to write to the Byzantine co-emperor Romanus I (920-944), he asked several scribes to submit their drafts, and chose that of Nad̲j̲īramī.

Thanks to Ibn al-Ṣayrafī we know a great deal more about the Fāṭimid chancellery. His *Ḳanūn dīwān al-rasāʾil* is practically a treatise on the chancellery. It is dedicated to the wazir al-Afḍal (487-515/1094-1121). After a foreword, the work consists of what amounts to a chancellery programme; even if it was in fact put into practice, this still leaves the following questions unanswered: what was the *dīwān* like before? On what pattern did he model his suggestions? Did he evolve them himself, or in imitation of Bag̲h̲dād or even Byzantium? According to Dölger, there are certain similarities with Byzantium; but how did Ibn al-Ṣayrafī come to hear of them? Could it be through Monte Cassino

(cf. Roemer, *Staatsschreiben der Timuridenzeit*, 7)? From Ibn al-Ṣayrafī we learn many details of the duties of civil servants in the state chancellery, which he calls *dīwān al-rasāʾil*, also *dīwān al-mukātabāt*, and (in his later work *al-Is̲h̲āra ilā man nāla rutbat al-wizāra*) *dīwān al-inshāʾ*. He distinguishes 12 different kinds of officials: 1) the head (*raʾīs*, *mutawallī*, *ṣāḥib*), 2) a secretary for correspondence with rulers (*mukātabat al-mulūk*), 3) one for the decision of complaints (*al-tawḳīʿāt fī riḳāʿ al-maẓālim*) with two under him (*ṣāḥib al-ḳalam al-daḳīḳ*, and *ṣāḥib al-ḳalam al-d̲j̲alīl*), 4) one for nominations and official proclamations (*inshāʾāt*), 5) one for correspondence with the important men in the country, especially the governors of the provinces, 6) one for letters of investiture (*manās̲h̲īr*), 7) one fair-copyist (*mubayyiḍ*), 8) one copyist (*nāsik̲h̲*), 9) one keeper of bound model texts (*tad̲h̲ākir*), 10) an archivist (*k̲h̲āzin*), 11) a keeper (*ḥād̲j̲ib*), 12) a translator (*mutard̲j̲im*), who was only consulted when the need arose. Thus the departments of the *dīwān* were: documents of state, appointments, decisions of complaints and occasional documents such as proclamations of important events (*al-kutub fī ʾl-ḥawādit̲h̲ al-kibār waʾl-muhimmāt*), passes (*amānāt*), texts of oaths (*kutub al-aymān waʾl-ḳasāmāt*), and others.

There is no special text giving us information concerning the chancellery of state in the time of the Ayyūbids, but there are a few details in the *Rasāʾil* of al-Ḳāḍī al-Fāḍil, and in Ibn Mammātī, al-Nābulusī, and Ibn S̲h̲īt̲h̲. Al-Ḳāḍī al-Fāḍil describes his admission to the *dīwān al-inshāʾ* by a stringent examination. Cliques and intrigues in the *dīwān* are also mentioned. Ibn S̲h̲īt̲h̲ describes conditions in the province of Syria, and pays special attention to the form of the documents. There is a detailed description of the *Tard̲j̲ama* of the sender; *duʿāʾ*, *nuʿūt*, and *ʿunwān* are treated in detail, and so is collaboration with other *dīwān*s.

Our most extensive sources date from Mamlūk times, namely from S̲h̲ihāb al-Dīn b. Faḍl Allāh (d. 749/1349), in his *al-Taʿrīf bi ʾl-muṣṭalaḥ al-s̲h̲arīf* (with three commentaries: *Tat̲h̲ḳīf*, *ʿUrf*, and *Laṭāʾif*); and, above all, there is Ḳalḳas̲h̲andī's (died 821/1418) great encyclopaedia *Ṣubḥ al-aʿs̲h̲ā* (with *muk̲h̲taṣar Ḍawʾ al-ṣubḥ*). Of late Mamlūk times, we have the Paris MSS *Dīwān al-inshāʾ*, and K̲h̲alīl al-Ẓāhirī (died 872/1468), *Zubdat kas̲h̲f al-mamālik*. Ḳalḳas̲h̲andī may be regarded as the main source, particularly as he did a great amount of historical research, and gives a survey of earlier developments. His work can thus be regarded as a precursor of an Arabic diplomatic. Amongst the heads of the *Dīwān al-inshāʾ*, the families of Banū ʿAbd al-Ẓāhir and Banū Faḍl Allāh became famous and continued to improve their position. The title *kātib al-sirr* emerged under Ḳalāʾun, and under Nāṣir Muḥammad b. Ḳalāʾun, the head acquired the right of the *tawḳīʿ ʿalā ʾl-ḳiṣaṣ*, and precedence over the *wazīr*. The number of employees rose with the increasing importance of the office. The higher employees bore the title of *kātib al-dast*, the others *kātib al-dard̲j̲*. Although their numbers increased, their status in the public eye diminished. The head also succeeded in bringing official mail and the whole of the news service gradually under his control.

The spheres of work were the same as under the Fāṭimids, but they were enlarged and differentiated. Foreign correspondence in particular had grown very much, through contact with almost the whole of the world which was then known. Foreign languages and interpreters were of importance. The exchange of letters with governors became increasingly complicated as the number of grades, titles and addresses increased. Offices (*wilāyāt*) also became more numerous, demanding further written work, and one now distinguishes 5 different grades of officials (cf. C 3 above). The *tawḳīʿāt ʿalā 'l-ḳiṣaṣ* continued, as did a whole group of occasional documents such as contracts, passes, oaths, amnesties etc.

E. Compared with Egypt our knowledge of chancelleries in the other Arab countries, such as the Maghrib and al-Andalus, is scanty. In these, the term *ẓahīr* was commonly applied to all documents. Ibn al-Khaṭīb (died 776/1374) became famous with his *Rayḥānat al-kuttāb*, which is frequently quoted by Ḳalḳashandī. Cf. below, ii.

7. Probative force of documents. Islamic law accepts only proof brought by witnesses, and rejects written testimony in principle. Nevertheless, in the actual practice of law, documents have achieved great importance. Incidentally, contracts seem to have appeared in writing in Arabia even in pre-Islamic times. The seal (*khātam*), which is of very long standing in the Orient, was an important means of authentication in Arabic documents. This seal was not replaced, as it was in the West, by the use of a signature, for the document was not valid unless a seal appeared on it, even if it was signed. The Prophet is said to have had a silver seal with the inscription: *Muḥammad Rasūl Allāh.* The earliest known seal is that of ʿAmr b. al-ʿĀṣ, which has the picture of a bull.

8. Development of Documents. Petitions and preliminaries also occur amongst Arabic documents. Petitions (*ḳiṣaṣ*) naturally preceded decisions (*tawḳīʿ*), and were the instigation of their formulation. The actual text of the *tawḳīʿ* was generally short and to the point, so that mention of the petition was hardly possible. The *fatwā*, too, was preceded by an investigation, and the state of affairs was described more or less explicitly in a set formula which omitted names. Contracts were often preceded by lengthy negotiations, but there is no mention of these preliminaries in the actual text of the contract.

9. Procedure and authentication, stages of authentication. Of the nine stages of authentication which are known in western documents, only a few can so far be traced in Arabic ones. Ibn al-Ṣayrafī (108 f.) mentions revision and correction as *muḳābala* and *iṣlāḥ*. During the consultation with the ruler, the head of the *dīwān* merely indicated the main points of the reply, whilst the reply itself was drawn up by the relevant secretary. Then he compared the reply with the excerpt, corrected omissions and errors if need be (there is also mention of a special corrector = *mutaṣaffiḥ*), and only then did he submit the completed reply to the ruler to be signed. The latter then added his signature (*ʿalāma*), but the address (*ʿunwān*) had to be written by the head of the *dīwān* himself, in order to give visible proof that he was aware of the contents and accepted responsibility for it. In order to be put into effect, the document required the *taʿyīn* for the charge of carrying out the decision, which was summarized on the reverse of the *ḳiṣṣa*; this charge had to be assigned in writing by the head of the *dīwān*. According to the rank of the secretary who was ordered to carry this out, it had different phrasing and placing, *e.g.*, *yuktab bi-dhālika* or *li-yuktab bi-dhālika* (cf. Ḳalḳashandī, vi, 210). Great attention was obviously paid to the elegance of the fair copy, and the Fāṭimids had a special fair-copyist (*mubayyiḍ*) who was responsible for all types of documents (cf. Ibn al-Ṣayrafī, 133 f.). Nothing is said concerning the reading of this fair copy to the ruler, or about its handing over.

10. Intercessors and witnesses. The religious intercession (*shafāʿa*) of the Prophet is well known in Islam. There are also intercessions of a secular nature, such as on the occasion of the handing in of a petition to the ruler, or on standing surety for a debtor. Ḳalḳashandī, ix, 124 gives early and late textual examples, and, in xiii, 328, an *amān* in which the intercessor is referred to as follows: *inna M.b. al-Musayyib saʾala fi amrikum wa-dhakara raghbatakum fi 'l-khidma.*

11. Model documents for use by scribes. In the West, set forms were always used, from the days of ancient Rome to the end of the Middle Ages. As early as the first century, there are some Arabic papyri which prove that letters and documents were written in a certain set form, and one may therefore assume the presence of models, although none is extant. Later Arabic formularies, the so-called *inshāʾ* works, are an independent genre of literature. Of these, three types can be distinguished: 1) collections of models similar to the formularies of the West, 2) treatises on stylistics and rules concerning the drawing up of the documents, similar to the Western *artes* or *summae dictaminis*, 3) a mixture of both, that is to say, formularies with theoretical commentary, or theoretical treatises with examples from practice, similar to the ones found in the West from the 12th century onwards. The most important of the many (over 50) Arabic *inshāʾ* works are probably the following: al-Ṣūlī (d. 335/946), *Adab al-kuttāb* (type 2); Abū Isḥāḳ al-Ṣābiʾ (d. 384/994), *Rasāʾil* (type 1); Ibn al-Ṣayrafī (d. 542/1147), *Ḳānūn dīwān al-rasāʾil* (type 2); al-Ḳāḍī al-Fāḍil (d. 596/1200), *Rasāʾil* (type 1); Shihāb al-Dīn b. Faḍl Allāh (d. 749/1349), *al-Taʿrīf bi'l-muṣṭalaḥ al-sharīf* (type 3); al-Ḳalḳashandī (d. 821/1418), *Ṣubḥ al-aʿshā fi ṣināʿat al-inshāʾ* (type 3). As examples of preliminaries, one might perhaps mention those known as *iṭlāḳāt*, which confirmed decisions of earlier rulers. These naturally refer to the older decisions, but there is no evidence of a complete list as an *insertum*.

12. Copies. There are many examples of official facsimiles or copies in the West, but I know of no Arabic ones. But there were grounds for them, too, such as the loss of an original, or the accession of a new ruler. There are Arabic examples of illegal imitations or forgeries. As early as Ṣūlī (143), there is mention of forgery from *miʾat alf* to *miʾatay alf*, which is given as the reason for introducing the *dīwān al-khātam* of the Umayyads. Ḳalḳashandī (xiii, 104) writes on Tamīm al-Dārī's first investiture with land, and Shihāb al-Dīn b. Faḍl Allāh (*Masālik*, i, 173) claims to have seen the original. This can hardly have been anything other than a forgery. Hamidullah seems to accept the documents attributed to the Prophet as genuine, but some internal evidence would argue against the authenticity of some of them. Concerning forged papyri cf. Grohmann, *Chrestomathie* 35.

13. The language of the documents. Whilst much thorough work has been done on the development of Latin in the Middle Ages, only the main outline of the development of modern literary Arabic from Classical and Middle Arabic is known (cf. ʿARABIYYA). This development is of great importance for the interpretation or documents. A special branch is the emergence of rhymed prose

(*sadj*ᶜ), on which there are the treatises by Zakī Mubārak (*La prose arabe au 4ᵉ siècle de l'hégire*, thesis, Paris 1931; also in Arabic, *al-Nathr al-fannī fi 'l-ḳarn al-rābiᶜ*, 2 vols., 1352/1934). The zenith of *sadj*ᶜ was, in documents as elsewhere, the time of the Mamlūks. The infiltration of the vulgar tongue into the language of the documents poses a further question. It can already be traced in the papyri and later it repeatedly led to errors on the part of the scribes. This is dealt with in detail by Ṣūlī (129) and Ḳalḳashandī (i, 148 ff.).

14. Dating. Just as in the West, dating (*ta'rīkh*) brought a wealth of problems. Even the normal *hidjra* dating offered many possibilities, such as dating according to nights and days, feast-days, parts of the month etc.; but Ḳalḳashandī (vi, 234 ff.) treats no less than 19 older eras and one younger era, that of Yezdegird. Most of them were of little importance. Only the Christian and the Coptic occurred frequently. A special problem was the adjustment between the lunar and the solar year (*sana hilāliyya* and *kharādjiyya*) for the purposes of taxes. As far back as ᶜAbbāsid times, special documents, *fi taḥwīl al-sana*, were written when the need arose. [see TA'RĪKH].

15. Writing materials. Extensive work has been done on writing materials by papyrologists, the most recent being by Grohmann, (*Chrestomathie* 63 ff.). Apart from the usual materials (papyrus up to the 11th century, parchment, paper), there were the rarer materials, such as cloth (especially for marriage contracts), wood, stone, wax, bones and potsherds. Size (*ḳaṭ*ᶜ, in Ṣūlī *miḳdār*) also differed greatly, and so did the kinds and the prices. Ḳalḳashandī gives several recipes for the ink (*ḥibr*, *midād*). [See DJILD, KĀGHAD, ḲIRṬĀS, RIḲḲ, WARAḲ].

16. Script in documents. Although much groundwork has been done by Moritz, Tisserand, Cheikho, and others there is as yet no full scholarly history of Arabic script (cf. KHAṬṬ). Grohmann investigated the script of the papyri (*Chrestomathie* 88-103). As far as later documents are concerned, observation of the peculiarities of different types of script, the use of diacritic marks and differential signs, must suffice in order to decide the age of undated pieces approximately. Certain formulae, numbers, notes on records etc. often appear in a shortened cursive hand which one might almost call shorthand. Grohmann (*Chrestomathie* 83) discusses the writing materials, and Ḳalḳashandī (ii, 430) lists no less than 17 terms, the precise meaning of which can hardly be determined in the absence of drawings. Codes and hidden allusions may always have played a part, as in Ṣūlī (186) (*tardjama*), and Ḳalḳashandī (ix, 229, *taᶜmiya*, later *ḥall al-rumūz*). They even occur in a papyrus (Grohmann, *Chrestomathie* 103[2]).

17. Sealing. Ṣūlī (139) and Ḳalḳashandī (iii, 273) were already interested in seals (*khātam*), and in Europe too the shape and use of Arabic seals has roused a certain amount of interest since Hammer. According to Grohmann (*Chrestomathie* 129 f.), one should distinguish between the use of a seal to replace the signature as a means of authentication, the attaching of a seal by way of recognition and ratification, and sealing on the part of witnesses. [See KHĀTAM].

Bibliography: Information concerning the extensive literature on Arabic papyri now probably best found in A. Grohmann, *Einführung und Chrestomathie zur arabischen Papyruskunde*, 1955, iv-viii. Cf. also *Die Papyri und die Urkundenlehre*, 107-30. Works in Arabic: al-Ṣūlī, *Adab al-kuttāb*, ed. M. Bahdjat al-Atharī, Cairo 1341 A.H.; Ibn al-Ṣayrafī, *Ḳānūn dīwān al-rasā'il*, ed. ᶜAlī Bahdjat, Cairo 1905; Shihāb al-Dīn b. Faḍl Allah, *al-Taᶜrīf bi 'l-muṣṭalaḥ al-sharīf*, Cairo 1312 A.H.; al-Ḳalḳashandī, *Ṣubḥ al-aᶜshā fī ṣināᶜat al-inshā'*, i-xiv, Cairo 1331-8/ 1913-9. Index in W. Björkman, *Beiträge zur Geschichte der Staatskanzlei im islamischen Ägypten*, Hamburg 1928, 87-177. Older publications of documents by S. de Sacy, Amari, Cusa, de Sousa, Remiro, Ribera, and others, are collected by G. Gabrieli, *Manuale* 255-288. Concerning more recent publications, cf. H. R. Roemer, *Über Urkunden zur Geschichte Ägyptens und Persiens in islamischer Zeit*, in *ZDMG* 107, 1957, 519-38 (this also mentions an Egyptian project of editing Fāṭimīd and Mamlūk documents); A. Grohmann and Pahor Labib, *Ein Fatimidenerlass vom Jahre 415/1024*, in *RSO* 32, 1957, 641-54 (which mentions a projected series of *Monumenta diplomatica arabica*); J. Wansbrough, *A Mamluk letter of 877/1473*, in *BSOAS*, xxiv/2 (1961), 200-13; S. D. Goitein, *The Cairo Geniza as a source for the history of Muslim civilization* in *Stud. Isl.*, iii, 1955, 75-92; G. E. El-Shayyal, *Madjmūᶜat al-wathā'iḳ al-Fāṭimiyya*, i, Cairo 1958; Ḥasan al-Bāshā, *Al-Alḳāb al-Islāmiyya*, Cairo 1937. See further DAFTAR, SIDJILL, etc.

(W. BJÖRKMAN)

ii. — MAGHRIB

In the Maghrib the external characteristics of documents (format, colour of paper, kinds of script, etc.) as well as the choice of protocols and formulae appear always to have been simpler than in the East.

To be mentioned, however, is the introduction by the Moroccan Almohad dynasty (*al-Muwaḥḥidūn*) of a sign manual of authentication called *ᶜalāma*. This consisted of the precatory formula *wa 'l-ḥamdu li-llāhi waḥdah*! elegantly inscribed in large, thick letters, with a ligature of the *hā'* and the *dāl* in the final word, and followed by a "terminal sigla" (see below). This mark of authentication was written afterwards at the top of the document, in a broad space left free for this purpose by the scribe, below the *basmala* and the *taṣliya*, of which it was a complement.

Of a "unitarian" nature, this formula was possibly used by the mahdī Ibn Tūmart himself in some of his epistles. His successor ᶜAbd al-Mu'min certainly used it in his famous *Risālat al-Fuṣūl* (see E. Lévi-Provençal, *Documents inédits d'histoire almohade*, Arabic text, 13). But it is Yaᶜḳūb al-Manṣūr (580-95/ 1184-99) whom the *Ḳirṭās* (ed. Fās 1305, 154) considers to have been the first to use this formula as an *ᶜalāma* and to write it with his own hand. Indeed, it was not until under this ruler that the formula appeared, as a dynastic device, on the Almohad *dīnar*s (see Lavoix, *Cat. mon. mus.*, Espagne et Afrique, 303-308) replacing the earlier formula *al-ḥamdu li-llāhi rabbi 'l-ᶜālamīn*.

The Almohad Ḥafṣid rulers of Ifrīḳiya expanded the formula by adding *wa 'l-shukru li'llāh*. Later, the Naṣrids of Granada chose *wa-lā ghāliba illa 'llāh* "and there is no conqueror but God", very likely in memory of the name of their eponymous ancestor Naṣr ("divine aid which grants victory"). Moreover their first ruler chose the *laḳab*: al-Ghālib bi'llāh.

These two dynastic devices, Ḥafṣid and Naṣrid, appeared as well on their coins and some monuments.

Left at first to the ruler himself, the responsibility for inscribing the *ᶜalāma* was later entrusted to a very high confidential official, a kind of head chancellor or keeper of the seal called *ṣāḥib al-ʿalāma*. It was most often a scholar of great distinction; thus it was that Ibn al-Abbār [*q.v.*] and Ibn Khaldūn [*q.v.*] filled this office at Tunis. According to the importance of the document to be authenticated, it could have an *ʿalāma kubrā* or an *ʿalāma ṣughrā*, whose inscription was entrusted to two chancellors of different rank.

In Morocco the use of the Almohad *ḥamdala* as *ʿalāma* continued to the end of the Saʿdian dynasty. But it became much more stylized and ended by becoming a kind of tracery of arabesques, difficult to decipher, and possibly in imitation of the Turkish *ṭughrā* [*q.v.*]. This very artistic *ʿalāma* of the Saʿdians, for them a sort of coat of arms, is found on their guns, some of their coins, and in the ornament of their palaces. In the last years of the Saʿdian dynasty as well as the manual *ʿalāma*, use was made of a stamp in ink engraved on an oval seal.

The succeeding Moroccan dynasty, that of the ʿAlawids, abandoned entirely the Almohad *ʿalāma*, both manual and stamped. The sole mark of authentication became the ink stamp of a round seal (*ṭābiʿ*), large or small according to the importance of the document, placed below the blank space between the *ḥamdala* and the *taṣliya*.

Yet another particularity of Maghrib diplomatic must be noted. To mark the end of the text in a document, a terminal sigla was splaced immediately after the date, consisting of an initial *hāʾ* with a tail curving towards the right, which it is tempting to read, not without reason, as an abbreviation of the verb *intahā* ("it is concluded"). In any case it cannot be an abbreviation of the postscript (*tawḳīʿ*) *ṣaḥḥ hādhā* or *ṣaḥīḥ dhālik* ("this is authentic") which appears at the end of diplomas conferring privileges and favours, often written by the ruler in his own hand.

We might add that some Moroccan documents, of the Waṭṭāsids and Saʿdians, are dated in "Greek numerals" which also appear on some of their coins, and that the Saʿdian sultan Aḥmad al-Manṣūr made use of a cryptographic writing.

The principal types of Maghribī documents are the following:

ẓahīr (for *kitāb ẓahīr*), pl. *ẓahāʾir*, in the Moroccan dialect *ḍahīr*, pl. *ḍwāher*. This is a diploma of investiture or of immunity from taxes, tolls, and forced labour, especially in favour of *sharīf*s or *murābiṭ*s.

tanfīdha, a diploma conferring a life pension or personal usufruct of a property belonging to the royal domain. These first two kinds of letters-patent are also called *ṣakk*.

risāla or *barāʾa* (in dialect *brā*), a letter addressed to a community, in order to announce an important event (the appointment of a new governor, victory over the enemy or rebels, etc.), or in order to exhort or to admonish. These official communications were generally read from the *minbar* in the mosque on Friday. Several Moroccan ʿAlawid sultans, among them Sayyidī Muḥammad b. ʿAbd Allāh and Mawlāy Sulaymān b. Muḥammad, acquired a solid reputation as letter-writers in this *genre*.

bayʿa, the "contract of allegiance" concluded between notables and the new ruler.

Bibliography: Ibn Khaldūn, *Muḳaddima*, ed. Bulak 1274, 120, 129: trans. de Slane, *Prolégomènes*, i, xxxi, ii, 26, 63; Rabino, *Contribution à l'histoire des Saadiens*, in *Archives berbères*, iv (1920), 1; H. de Castries, *Les signes de validation des chérifs saadiens*, in *Hespéris*, i, (1921), 231; E. Tisserant and G. Wiet, *Une lettre de l'almohade Murtaḍā au pape Innocent IV*, in *Hespéris*, vi (1926), 27; E. Lévi-Provençal, *Un recueil de lettres officielles almohades*, in *Hespéris*, xxviii (1941), 1. The text and the notes of the last three articles provide a basic bibliography, which can be supplemented by S. de Sacy, *Mémoires d'histoire et de littérature orientales*, Paris 1832, 119 and 149; G. S. Colin, *Contribution à l'étude des relations diplomatiques entre les Musulmans d'Occident et l'Égypte*, in *Mélanges Maspero*, iii, 197, Cairo 1935; idem, *Note sur le système cryptographique du sultan Aḥmad al-Manṣūr*, in *Hespéris*, vii (1927), 221; L. Di Giacomo, *Une poétesse grenadine du temps des Almohades*, in *Hespéris*, xxxiv (1947), 64-65; R. Brunschvig, *La Berbérie orientale sous les Ḥafṣides*, ii, 61; Cusa, *I Diplomi greci ed arabi di Sicilia*, Palermo 1868; ʿAbd Allāh Gannūn, *Rasāʾil Saʿdiyya—Cartas de historia de los Saadies*, Tetuan 1373/1954; M. Nehlil, *Lettres chérifiennes*, (collection of 128 official documents of the Moroccan ʿAlawid dynasty, in facsimile), Paris 1915. The collection of *Sources Inédites de l'histoire du Maroc* contains in transcription, as well as plates, numerous Moroccan diplomatic documents.

(G. S. Colin)

iii. — Persia

The origins of Persian diplomatic are to be found in the period of the foundation of Turkish states in Persian territory. While in the chancelleries of the Ṭāhirids and Sāmānids, who in so many respects were influenced by Iranian culture, Arabic was employed and efforts to introduce Persian (in the form of a "court language", [see dari]) failed, Maḥmūd of Ghazna (389-421/999-1030) declared Persian the official language and thus provided for its introduction into the chancellery. A similar development took place under the Saldjūḳs (see B. Spuler, *Iran*, 245-6). It is impossible to say to what extent Arabic documents served as models for Persian, though the strong Arabic influence can very likely be traced back to this early period. The relations between the ruler of Ghazna and the Caliphal court necessitated the translation of Persian documents into Arabic as well as of Arabic into Persian. There were in addition a number of Turkish elements, considerably increased during the Ilkhānid period by elements of Mongol-Turkish origin, which for centuries were to influence in particular the external form of documents and other written communications.

Categories of documents. These correspond broadly with the types described above for Arabic documents. An important distinction is between documents which attest and documents which command. The first consist of legal deeds or certificates which were recorded and confirmed by witnesses with seal and signature (*muhr wa niwishta*), for example, *ḳabāla* (deed of purchase, confirmed by a judge), *tamassuk* (bill or receipt), *ʿaḳd-nāma* or *nikāḥ-nāma* (marriage contract), *wakālat-nāmča* power of attorney), *bayʿ sharṭ-nāmča* (deed of sale), *waṣiyyat-nāma* (testament), *waḳf-nāma* (act for the establishment of a pious foundation). These documents (*sidjillāt-i sharʿiyya*) belong primarily to the sphere of competence of the authorities for religious law. In contrast to these, documents containing orders were the exclusive prerogative of the organs of state, executed by the ruler or his deputies and recorded in the chancellery. In principle an "official document" (*farmān*) can be found for every expression of the ruler's will. In practice they may be divided according to contents into the following groups: deeds of appointment, of investiture (*iḳṭāʿ*, in the Mongol and post-Mongol period: *soyūrg̲h̲āl*; *musallamī*, tax-exemption; *tiyūl*, office-holder's fief; *waẓīfa*, grants to religious from foundations or state funds; the awarding of a robe of honour, *k̲h̲ilʿa*, etc.), treaties, passports, judicial decisions of the ruler, and orders of a general nature to governors and officials. In the Seld̲j̲ūḳ period the terminology appears to have been still largely undeveloped. In addition to *farmān*, the most general term, *mans̲h̲ūr* (*manās̲h̲īr*) refers to documents of the greatest diversity, while others are *taḳlīd*, *tafwīḍ*, *taslīm*, *mit̲h̲āl* (*amt̲h̲ila*), and *mans̲h̲ūr-i taḳlīd* or *tafwīḍ* (see Rieu, *Cat. Pers. Mss in the Brit. Mus.*, London 1879, i, 389; Ethé, *Cat. Pers. Mss in the Ind. Off. Library*, i, 1131; Muntad̲j̲ab al-Dīn Badīʿ Atābeg al-D̲j̲uwaynī, *ʿAtabat al-kataba*, *passim*). The expression *nis̲h̲ān* appears in the Tīmūrid period (see Roemer, *Staatsschreiben der Timuridenzeit*, Wiesbaden 1952, *passim*) and is used until the 17th century (see Chardin, *Voyages du Chevalier Chardin en Perse*, ed. Langlès, Paris 1811, ii, 97). Synonymous with *nis̲h̲ān* is *maktūb*, occasionally used in the Tīmūrid period (Niẓām al-Dīn S̲h̲āmī, *Ẓafar-nāma*, ed. F. Tauer, ii, 264, index). Decrees were further called *ḥukm* (Ḥāfiẓ-i Abrū/Tauer, *Cinque opuscules*, 83, index), *tawḳīʿ* (originally only the signature of the ruler and later his seal as well, see below) or *mit̲h̲āl* (S̲h̲āmī/Tauer, ii, 299). The Mongol designation *yarlīg̲h̲*, alone or in the combination *ḥukm-i yarlīg̲h̲*, remained in use until the end of the 15th century (S̲h̲āmī/Tauer, ii, 274). A distinction according to diverse introductory formulae (see below), though not according to contents, appears in the 9th-10th/15th-16th centuries: *parwānča* and *ḥukm* with solemn formulae are contrasted with simpler documents designated by *raḳam* (see H. Busse, *Untersuchungen zum islamischen Kanzleiwesen an Hand turkmenischer und safawidischer Urkunden* (Abhandlungen des Deutschen Archäologischen Instituts Kairo, Islamische Reihe), i, Cairo 1959, 67); the acts of subordinate authorities are now evidently called *mit̲h̲āl* (*mit̲h̲āl-i dīwān al-ṣadāra*: Papazyan no. 17, 970/1562). In the Ḳād̲j̲ār period the designations depend upon the issuing authority: only the decrees of the Shah are called *farmān*; acts of governors of royal origin are called *raḳam* (*arḳām*); those of other governors *ḥukm* (see Greenfield, *Die Verfassung des persischen Staates*, Berlin 1904, 115). In less official language, however, almost all of the expressions listed above occur (see S. Beck, *Persische Konversationsgrammatik*, Heidelberg 1914, ii, 211 ff.).

Distinct from deeds and orders in the strict sense are the letters concerned with domestic and foreign affairs (*maktūb*, *kitābat* or *risāla*). Like the former they are provided with an official attestation and have a fixed external and internal form, but lack a legal content, as for example in the letters confirming friendly relations (*ik̲h̲wāniyyāt*). There is a form for every occasion, such as congratulation (*adʿiyyāt*), condolence (*taʿziyat-nāma*), etc. Into the 9th/15th century foreign correspondence, based on a Mongol pattern, preserved in part the form of a decree, from which, however, it tended to depart under the Ṣafawids in the 11th/17th century. Owing to their legal contents "border-books" (*sinūr-nāma*, examples in Evoğlu Ḥaydar, *Ins̲h̲āʾ*, see Rieu, i, 390) approach the form of decrees. The same may be said of letters-patent for envoys. Letters from the royal hand (*dast-k̲h̲aṭṭ-i humāyūn* or *mubārak*), the highest in rank, assume a middle position between documents and other writings, their contents ranging from the personal execution of an act by the ruler to confidential communications.

The internal structure of documents and writings has in the course of nine hundred years of Persian chancellery history scarcely changed—that is, until modern times. The documents begin with an invocation to God (*invocatio*) frequently combined with a devotional ejaculation (*al-ḥukm li'llāh*, *al-mulk li'llāh*). These formulae, together with the formula of promulgation, the *arenga* and the *narratio*, constitute the protocol, which is followed by the most important part of the document, the *dispositio*. In the *arenga* the execution of the document in general terms, mostly of a religious character, is established, partly by the abundant use of Ḳurʾānic citations, verse, and rhetorical analogy. Here, in contrast to other parts of the document which are bound by more rigid formulae, the writer is free to display his literary talent. Evidence of this art is to be found, however, in pronounced form more frequently in *ins̲h̲āʾ* works than in original documents. The *narratio* on the other hand contains the essential transaction, for the most part a report of the proposition (*ʿarḍa-dās̲h̲t*) of the petitioner, while in documents of confirmation the proposed act, or, depending upon the affair in question, several acts are included completely or in their most important parts (*insertio*). In the *narratio* appear for the first time the name and title of the addressee, who is always referred to in the third person, and afterwards only by *mad̲h̲kūr*, *mazbūr*, *mus̲h̲ār ilayhi* and *mūmā ilayhi*. The full titles can, in artistic combinations with *panāh*, *dastgāh*, *niẓām*, etc., be extended for several lines. The formulae of promulgation (such as *farzandān wa wuzarā ... bi-dānand ki*) are placed before the *arenga* or *narratio*, but can be omitted. The *arenga* closes frequently with the phrase *ammā baʿd*.

The nucleus of the document is the *dispositio*, or decision of the ruler: in appointments and investitures the office and date of the nomination or object of the investiture are given in more detail (*circumscriptio*), while in other acts the decision or command is set forth. The *dispositio* is expressed in either active (that is, the ruler refers to himself in the first person plural: *muḳarrar farmūdīm wa arzānī dās̲h̲tīm*), or passive form, (*muḳarrar farmūda s̲h̲ud ki*). Vestiges of an original first person singular were preserved in isolated phrases into the 17th-18th centuries: *s̲h̲āh bābam*, *d̲j̲add-i buzurgwāram* (accompanied by blessings). The transition from the *narratio* to the *dispositio* is accomplished by means of set formulae: frequently *bināʾan ʿalayhi*, *binā bar īn*, *li-had̲h̲ā*, or *mī-bāyad ki*. To the *dispositio* in cases of appointments and investitures, prescriptions (*adhortatio*) for the addressee or officials and persons concerned might be added, usually introduced by *sabīl wa ṭarīḳ*. In contrast to the formulae of promulgation, where the highest dignitaries are named first, they appear here at the end. The accountants (*mustawfiyān*) are often directed to register the document (*dar dafātir ʿamal namāyand*). Finally a prohibition might follow, forbidding the annual request for a renewal, with the directive "may this apply in all similar cases". Except for the *invocatio* all of these parts which precede and succeed the *dispositio* may be omitted, in which case the document consists only of the *dispositio*. Most frequently, however, the order is *narratio—dispositio*—conclusion (date etc.). In this case the entire text is included between *čūn* (beginning of the *narratio*) and *binā bar īn* (*dispositio*). In the *narratio* or in the *dispositio* by means of *siyāḳat* script directions for registration of the document might be given; should these instead be written on the reverse side (*ẓahr, ḍimn*), this is indicated by a remark in the text.

The documents close with a phrase in which reference is made to the seal (*corroboratio*), and with the Islamic date: *kutiba fī* (as early as Rashīd al-Dīn, ed. Jahn, *GMS*, n.s. xiv, 222) or *taḥrīr*[an] *fī*. The day of the month, in Arabic numerals as well as in Persian ordinals, disappears almost completely in the 10th/16th century. The Persian day of the week is occasionally given (Papazyan, no. 18, 977/1570). The first day of the month is called *ghurra*, the last *salkh*. The names of the months appear with their customary attributes: *Muḥarram al-ḥarām, Ramaḍān al-mubārak*, etc. The year was at first written in Arabic, replaced by Arabic numerals from the 10th/16th century on. Until the 10th/16th century the *Hidjra* year was usually accompanied by the corresponding year of the animal cycle, which was used even later (with the *Hidjra* year) with reference to dates in the *dispositio*. Up to the end of the 9th/15th century the place of issue was named after the date: *ba-maḳām, ba-madīna* or *ba-dār al-salṭana*. With some exceptions this later disappears. In Turcoman documents, beneath the date and place name, is an *apprecatio*: *rabbī ikhtim bi'l-khayr wa'l-iḳbāl* (see Busse, *Untersuchungen*, no. 2). In the 10th/16th century this phrase was moved to the right-hand margin and shortened to *khutima bi'l-khayr* or *khutima*, later disappearing altogether. Similarly, until the end of the 9th/15th and beginning of the 10th/16th centuries, to the right below the text and perpendicular to it, was a reference to the secretary and other officials who might have participated in the preparation of the text: *parwānča-yi ashraf-i aʿlā, ba-risāla* (name), *ba-wuḳūf* (name). From the beginning of the 11th/17th century this remark can be found in altered form on the reverse side of the document (see below).

The external form of the documents has been more subject to change than the internal form. The periods of modification are roughly the following: Pre-Mongol—Mongol—Tīmūrid and Turcoman—Ṣafawid to the beginning of the 14th/20th century. The *tughra*—[*q.v.*] was employed by the Saldjūḳs and the rulers of Khwārizm (in *ʿAtabat al-kataba* a *wazīr-i tughra* is mentioned, no. 16; for Khwārizm see al-Nasawī, *Sīrat al-sulṭān Djalāl al-Dīn Mängübärdī*, ed. Ḥāfiẓ Aḥmad Ḥamdī, Cairo 1953, 324). While here they consisted evidently only of the name and titles of the ruler, in the Mongol period was added, in addition to *bahādur* (after 1319, see Spuler, *Mongolen*², 197 and 271), after the name the phrase *üge manu* ("an order from us"). In Tīmūr's documents the phrase reads in Turkish translation: *Tīmūr gūrkān sözümüz* (see Fekete, *Arbeiten der grusinischen Orientalistik auf dem Gebiet der türkischen und persischen Paläographie und die Frage der Formel sözümüz*, in *AO Hung.* vii (1957), i, 14). In this form the *tughra* was preserved on particular documents throughout the Turcoman period into the 11th/17th century, and was employed by the khāns of Bukhārā as well as by the Golden Horde in southern Russia (see Fekete, *op. cit.*, 14). In Aḳ Ḳoyunlu documents the *tughra* is combined with the *tamgha* which appears on their coinage (see Hinz, *Irans Aufstieg zum Nationalstaat im fünfzehnten Jahrhundert*, Berlin and Leipzig 1936, 106 and the illustration opposite 104). An innovation for the world of Islam was the Uyghur practice introduced by the Mongols of indenting the first lines of the text, as well as emphasizing (owing indirectly to Far Eastern influence) the name of the ruler and the word *yarlīgh* by beginning a new line (see Busse, *Die Entwicklung der Staatsurkunde in Zentralasien und Persien von den Mongolen bis zu den Safawiden*, in *Akten des XXIV. Internationalen Orientalisten-kongresses München*, Wiesbaden (1959), 372-4). With insignificant changes this usage can be observed as late as the 11th/17th century in documents with a *tughra*, from which it was also extended to other documents. During the rule of the Ṣafawid Ismāʿīl I (1501-24) the *tughra* disappeared from certain documents, though the first two lines of the text continued to be indented. The seal, earlier at the bottom of the document, came generally to be placed at the top (where it is still, in the form of a crest). There was a new development under the second Ṣafawid Ṭahmāsp I (1524-76), in that the *tughra*, written by the head of the chancellery (*munshī al-mamālik*), appeared now in red or gold ink in two forms as an introductory phrase (while the indenting of the first two lines was dropped): *farmān-i humāyūn shud* and *farmān-i humāyūn sharaf-i nafādh yāft*. At the beginning of the 11th/17th century was added the phrase (written in black ink by the *wāḳiʿa-niwīs*, equivalent to the *madjlis-niwīs* or *wazīr-i čap*): *ḥukm-i djahān-muṭāʿ shud*. In documents of the *dīwān begi* the same formula appears in red ink (see *Tadhkirat al-Mulūk*, ed. and tr. V. Minorsky, London 1943, fol. 21b, 24b, 40a). A further differentiation had already begun to develop (the first example in Papazyan no. 3, 866/1462), in that the *tughra* in documents emanating from members of the royal family had instead of *sözümüz* the term *sözüm* ("my order"), to be found up to the end of the 10th/16th century (see Puturidze no. 17, 1591). There appeared further in the 10th/16th century in the documents of governors the formula *amr-i ʿālī shud* (also in combination with the *tughra* containing *sözüm*: Puturidze no. 76, 1051/1642), and in the 11th/17th century *muḳarrar ast ki*. Under Ismāʿīl II (1576-77) the phrase *amr-i dīwān-i ashraf-i aʿlā* was used in certain decrees (Papazyan no. 19, 984/1577). Documents of the authorities in the central government bore in the 11th/17th and beginning of the 12th/18th centuries the imperial seal but contained no introductory phrase (see Busse, *Untersuchungen*, 65). The same is true even today for letters of the Shāh, which begin directly with the name and title of the addressee. Diverse introductory phrases characteristic of different kinds of documents remained in use in the Post-Ṣafawid period. The formula *farmān-i humāyūn shud* continued to appear in the acts of the Afshars, though combined with *biʿawn Allāh taʿālā* (later *aʿūdhu bi'llāh taʿālā*), while the strokes of the letters were curved into an artistic shape similar to a row of treble clefs. In Ḳādjār documents is the phrase *ḥukm-i djahān-muṭāʿ shud* (with *al-mulk li'llāh taʿālā*), while in the acts of Muẓaffar al-Dīn Shāh (1896-1907) *farmān-i humāyūn shud* reappears (see Beck, *op. cit.*, ii, 342-3 and facsimile). The *tughra* in gold ink was preserved. The phrase *ḥukm-i djahān-muṭāʿ shud* (without additions) appears even in the late Afshar and in some Zand documents, retaining the same simple form of the Ṣafawid period. The acts of Nādir Shāh prior to his coronation (8 March 1736; the nominal ruler was the Ṣafawid ʿAbbās III, 1732-6) contained the phrase *farmān-i*

ʿālī shud (with *bi-ʿawn* ...) already in the peculiar form described above. After 1736 *farmān-i ʿālī shud* was replaced by *farmān-i humāyūn shud. Farmān-i ʿālī shud* (without additions and in simpler form) is also to be found in the documents of Karīm Khan Zand (1750-96), who was content to hold the actual power under the nominal rule of the Ṣafawid Ismāʿīl III. His predecessor the Bakhtiyārī leader ʿAlī Mardān Khān, also unofficially Shah, employed the introductory phrase *ḥukm-i wālā shud* (without additions). Here tendencies towards a practice which was definitively established in the Ḳādjār period become apparent: documents emanating from governors belonging to the royal family bear the formula *ḥukm-i wālā shud*, while other governors must content themselves with *ḥukm-i ʿālī shud* (customary as early as the Ṣafawid period; see *Sayyid al-inshāʾ*, Tehran 1327/1919; Beck, *op. cit.*, i, 451 and 455). Modern edicts (with an obvious European influence) contain the following protocol: crest (a lion and sun). *farmān-i muṭāʿ-i mubārak—aʿlā-haḍrat-i humāyūn-i shāhinshāhī—ba-taʾīdāt-i khudāwand-i mutaʿāl—mā* ("we")—*Pahlawī shāhinshāhī Īrān.* Seal. Here parts of the old formulae are combined into one.

Scripts and writing materials. Owing to the lack of original documents nothing is known of the kinds of script used in the Saldjūḳid chancellery. The *tughra* was written with a "broad pen" (*ḳalam-i ghalīẓ*; see Spuler, *Iran*, 362). It may be presumed that the variety of scripts developed in the late ʿAbbāsid period (see *Fihrist*, ed. Flügel, 4 ff.) continued to be cultivated in the chancellery in the 5th/11th century. The earliest Persian fragment, a deed of sale (see Margoliouth, in *JRAS* 1903, 761 ff.), indicates tendencies towards *taʿlīḳ*, which later came into general use. The Mongol documents of the Ilkhans were of course written in Uyghur script, still used in the Turkish documents of the Tīmūrids in the 9th/15th century though with an interlinear transcription in Arabic script (see Kurat, *Topkapı Sarayı ... yarlık ve bitikler*, Istanbul 1940, 195 ff.: an act of Abū Saʿīd 873/1468). In the post-Mongol chancelleries *taʿlīḳ* had become firmly established, though some parts (*invocatio, tughra*) were occasionally written in *thulth*. In the 10th/16th century *nastaʿlīḳ* came into use, though *shikasta* script was also employed. The development towards *shikasta*, which did not attain its pure form until the 11th/17th century, had been evident in the *taʿlīḳ* of the 8th/14th century.

From the beginning the writing material used was probably paper, a domestic product in the Near East from the end of the 3rd/9th century. As early as the end of the 9th/15th century, as in other Islamic states, a part of the paper was obtained from Europe; Chardin (*Voyages*, iv, 271 f.) bears witness to this at any rate for the second half of the 11th/17th century in Persia. Better grades of paper came from Balkh, Bukhārā and Samarḳand. The format varied in breadth from 15 to 30 cm; some documents were several metres long (for example, Busse, no. 3: 263 cm), consisting of separate sheets pasted together.

Mongol decrees were already richly decorated in coloured (red and gold) inks, especially in those parts which were emphasized by means of *elevatio*. The same is true into the 11th/17th century for documents with a *tughra*, in which, especially, gold ink was used for the *invocatio*, prayers, the *tamgha* (in Aḳ Ḳoyunlu decrees), Ḳurʾānic citations, and words on the right-hand margin. Gold and red inks were used abundantly in documents with introductory formulae, with the exception of those with *ḥukm-i djahān-muṭāʿ shud*, which with this phrase were executed completely in black. The use of coloured inks was dropped also in the documents emanating from provincial authorities. In writing, a large margin was left at the top and on the right, in which only words to be stressed were written. The lines rise, especially in the early period, slightly to the left; occasionally, in order to prevent later insertions, the last word of the line was extended to reach the left-hand edge of the paper. Until the end of the 9th/15th century the beginning of the *dispositio* was indicated by particularly large letters (see Busse, no. 3). In letters to foreign rulers the name of the addressee is placed above the text; the place in the text in which it was to be inserted (after the execution of the title) was indicated by a small space.

Seals. Originally, decrees and writings (except for those with a seal?) were attested by the ruler's flourish (*tawḳīʿ* or *imḍā*), in the place of which the seal (alone?) must have early appeared. In any event into the 10th/16th century the expression *tawḳīʿ* in the *corroboratio* refers to the seal; not until the 11th/17th century was *tawḳīʿ* replaced by the (long overdue) designation *muhr*. Shāh Ismaʿīl included in his edicts the phrase *huwa Allāh al-ʿādil* (Papazyan no. 19, 984/1577), though it was an exception; in principle the seal was enough. Not until the Ḳādjār period did the seal require a countersign (*tughra*) by the Shah (see Greenfield, *op. cit.*, 197; Beck, *op. cit.*, facsimile: *saḥḥa* below the first line). The ruler's seal was originally at the bottom of the document. The Mongol square seal was also used on paste-joints, in order to preclude the possibility of later insertions, though in the 9th/15th century the seal appeared only at the bottom (see Kurat, *op. cit.*, 19). At the beginning of the Ṣafawid period, in acts of the ruler and those of the central government, the seal was put in the place of the *tughra* at the top of the document. In the decrees of governors with the *tughra*: *ḥukm-i ʿālī shud*, the seal remained at the end, while those governors who were princes placed their seals to the right of the *tughra* (similar to the *pençe* of the Ottoman viziers). Correspondence (*maktūbāt*) was sealed on the reverse side (see *A chronicle of the Carmelites in Persia and the Papal mission of the XVIIth and XVIIIth centuries*, 2 vols., London 1939, plate opposite 95 in vol. i). In the Mongol chancellery seals for the various affairs of state were stamped in different colours, such as blue, red (or gold), green, and black (see Spuler, *Mongolen*, 293). For the square seal still to some extent used by the Tīmūrids, gold ink was employed; later all seals were stamped in black. In addition to square seals (Ghāzān Khān had introduced different kinds of seals for the different branches of government; see Rashīd al-Dīn, ed. Jahn, 292) the Tīmūrids also had round seals, often stamped at the top of the document (see J. Deny, *Un soyurgal du Timouride Shah Rukh en écriture ouigure*, in *JA* 245 (1957), 253-66). The use of different seals for different kinds of documents, of which there were tendencies under Ismāʿīl I, reached full development in the later Ṣafawid period: "great" seals (*muhr-i sharaf-i nafādh* and *muhr-i humāyūn*) were used in documents with the introductory formulae *farmān-i humāyūn sharaf-i nafādh yāft* and *farmān-i humāyūn shud*, while "small" seals (*muhr-i angushtar-i āftāb-āthār*), or signet rings, were used for documents with *ḥukm-i djahān muṭāʿ shud*. The inscription in the large seals partly contained the names of the twelve *imāms*, that in the small seals contained only the ruler's name, frequently combined with the title *banda-yi shāh-i wilāyat* (servant of the king of holiness, that is, ʿAlī). Chardin gives evidence also of a square seal (Plate XXXI, and v, 461). The large seals were round (occasionally with an upper extension in the shape of a roof), and the small seals rectangular or in the form of a shield (plates in Rabino di Borgomale, *Coins, medals and seals of the Shahs of Iran, 1500-1941*, place of publication not given, 1945, plate 3). The seals of the ruler were later for the most part rectangular with an upper extension in the form of a roof. The lion and sun (*shīr wa khūrshīd*) appears in the seal as early as 1159/1746 (Chubua, no. 47). Large (rectangular with extension) and small (oval) seals are still to be found in the Ḳādjār period (plates in Rabino, *op. cit.*, 4). The governors' seals were in the Ṣafawid period mostly rectangular or oval (some isolated examples are round) with inscriptions containing the name of the office-holder and a religious device. These were not much changed. Imperial authorities employed during the Ṣafawid period a special round "dīwān-seal" (*muhr-i musawwada-yi dīwān-i aʿlā*). Originally in the custody of the keeper of the seal (*muhr-i dār*), the seals passed in the early Ṣafawid period into the safe-keeping of harem officials (see Roemer, *Der Niedergang Irans nach dem Tode Ismaʿils des Grausamen* (1577-81), Würzburg 1939, 44), in whose protection they remained in the later Ṣafawid period. The actual sealing was executed by officials with the title *dawāt-dār* (see DAWĀDĀR), while the keepers of the seal placed only a small stamp on the reverse side (see *Tadhkirat al-Mulūk*, ed. Minorsky, fol. 41a ff.).

Before delivery to the addressees the documents were sent through different departments of the financial administration (*daftar khāna-yi humāyūn aʿlā*), where high officials supplied flourishes and seals, and other officials confirmed the entry of the documents in various registers (*daftar, dafātir*) by means of seals and annotations (*muhr wa khaṭṭ*) (other than for example in the Ottoman administration, where these remarks were placed on the draft, that is, as mere bookkeeping comments; see Fekete, *Die Siyaqat-Schrift in der türkischen Finanzverwaltung*, i, Budapest 1955, 67, 68 note 2). While flourishes and comments were placed, in Fāṭimid decrees for example, between the last lines (see Grohmann in *RSO*, xxxii (1957), 641-54), in Persia they appear early on the reverse side from and written in a direction perpendicular to that of the text. This procedure was already to be found in Ilkhān documents (see Cleaves in *HJAS*, xiv (1951), 493-526). In this respect Ghāzān Khān also introduced obligatory prescriptions (see Rashīd al-Dīn, ed. Jahn, 291-6). A series of seals and comments are also to be found on Tīmūrid (see Deny, *op. cit.*), Turcoman and early Ṣafawid documents (see Busse, *Untersuchungen*, 77 ff.). A definitive system was introduced at the beginning of the 11th/17th century and remained substantially in effect until the end of the Ḳādjār period. The flourishes consist of a religious device (for example, *tawakkaltu ʿalaʾllāh*), while the registration comments contain a reference to the nature of the business, for example, *thabt-i daftar-i tawdjīh-i dīwān-i aʿlā shud* ("it has been entered in the outgoing register of the high dīwān"), or simply *saḥḥa* ("correct"). In the later Ṣafawid period flourishes and seals were applied to all documents by the grand vizier (*iʿtimād al-dawla*), by the *ṣadr* and officials who belonged to the *arkān-i dawlat*, such as the *ḳurči bashī* and *ḳullar aḳasī*, on documents which fell within their jurisdiction, while registration comments and seals were applied by the *mustawfī al-mamālik* (or—*khāṣṣa*), *lashgar-niwīs*, *ṣāḥib-tawdjīh, nāẓir-i daftar-khāna-yi aʿlā, darūgha-yi daftar-khāna-yi aʿlā*, and others. The documents were brought first to the *mustawfī*, then circulated in the various departments, returning finally to the *mustawfī*. The registration comments of the imperial officials (*sarkār-i mamālik*) differed from those of the officials for the royal domain (*sarkār-i khāṣṣa-yi sharīfa*) in composition: for example *ba-naẓar rasīd* (imperial), *thabt-i daftar-i naẓārat shud* (royal domain). In contrast to those documents which were registered in the *daftar-khāna* (*arḳām-i daftarī*), are those which were not registered (*arḳām-i bayāḍī*) because they did not concern the financial administration or because they were to be kept secret (see *Tadhkirat al-Mulūk*, fol. 42b; and Busse, *Untersuchungen*, 79).

The documentary commission was given orally by the ruler or a high official directly, or in writing by way of the "relator", to the chancellery. The actual process was then, even in the Mongol period, entered on the document (see Hinz, *Die Resālā-yi Falakiyyä des ʿAbdollāh ibn Mohammad ibn Kiyā al-Māzandarānī*, Wiesbaden 1952, fol. 44a ff.). In Turcoman documents into the 10th/16th century the annotation was placed on the lower right-hand front (see above), but from the beginning of the 11th/17th century it is to be found on the reverse side: in an oral commission from the ruler *bi'l-mushāfa al-ʿalīya al-ʿāliya*, otherwise *huwa ḥasab al-amr al-aʿlā*. In the latter case beneath this formula the relator was named: *az ḳarār-i niwishta* ... when the relator was the grand vizier; otherwise *ba-risāla*. The phrase *ḥasab al-amr al-aʿlā* was omitted when the grand vizier or another official had given the commission (see Busse, *Untersuchungen*, 69 ff.). In post-Ṣafawid documents such annotations appear to have been omitted. After all of the formalities had been seen to the documents were rolled together with the writing inside and pressed flat. Letters to foreign rulers were often sent in richly ornamented covers of brocade, protected against unauthorized view by a special seal.

In the early period documents and correspondence were prepared in the imperial chancellery (*dār al-inshāʾ, dīwān al-rasāʾil*) under the authority of the *munshī al-mamālik*. From the 11th/17th century on, documents with the introductory formula (*tughra*) *ḥukm-i djahān-muṭāʿ shud* (in black ink) were executed in the chancellery of the *wāḳiʿa-niwīs*, who was also responsible for letters addressed to foreign princes. There was also a subdivision in the jurisdiction for the empire and for the royal domain: documents relating to imperial affairs (with the introductory formulae *farmān-i humāyūn sharaf-i nafādh yāft* and *farmān-i humāyūn shud*) were prepared by the *munshī al-mamālik*, those for the royal domain by the *wāḳiʿa-niwīs*. In addition to these two authorities separate departments of the *daftar-khāna* were also authorized to execute documents, in the Ṣafawid period for example, the *lashgar-niwīs* and the secretariats of the *ḳullar aḳasī, tubčī bāshī, tufangčī bashī*, and others. These documents contained no introductory formulae (*tughra*). The provincial authorities had their own chancelleries. Solemn documents were independent pieces of writing; on less important occasions, though the other formalities were preserved (seal, *tughra*), the resolution was placed in the upper margin of the petition (*ʿarḍa-dāsht*). Supplementary remarks and additions by subordinate officials were until the 9th/15th century written between the lines, later in the right hand margin (with the phrase *muḳarrar ast ki* and seal). In solemn edicts the ruler could make additions in his own hand (*ḥāshiya ba-khaṭṭ-i mubārak*).

In addition to the Persian section there were, as was mentioned before, in the chancellery departments for foreign languages as early as the Ghaznawids. Especially comprehensive in this respect, corresponding to the many nationalities involved, was the Ilkhānid chancellery (see Hinz, *Die persische Geheimkanzlei im Mittelalter*, in West-östliche Abhandlungen, Wiesbaden 1954, 345). The Tīmūrids corresponded with the Ottomans partly in Arabic and partly in Eastern Turkish (Rieu, i, 389; Kurat, *op. cit.*, 195 ff.), the Ṣafawids in Ottoman Turkish (see Fekete, *Iran Şahlarının iki türkçe mektubu*, in *TM*, v (1935), 269-74). During the Ḳādjār period French became the principal foreign language of the chancellery, a position which it has preserved.

Original deeds and deeds of confirmation may be distinguished according to the occasion of their issue. Confirmations were necessary upon the death of the incumbents of hereditary offices and fiefs, and general upon a change of government. The prohibition at the conclusion of many documents "a renewal (*tadjdīd*) shall not be requested annually" was very likely of a precautionary nature. In practice an annual renewal does not seem to have been customary. For practical reasons possessors of documents might have issued verified copies of these which carried the same degree of authority as the originals. Edicts which concerned larger groups of people or the population of an entire community were frequently posted in the form of inscriptions in public buildings and places (see Barthold/Hinz, *Die persische Inschrift an der Mauer der Manūcehr-Moschee zu Ani*, in *ZDMG*, ci (1951), 241-69; and Hinz, *Steuerinschriften aus dem mittelalterlichen Vorderen Orient*, in *Belleten*, xii (1949), 745-69).

The oldest original documents preserved belong to the Ilkhān period (largely Mongol letters to European princes). Some Persian documents of the 8th/14th and 9th/15th centuries are to be found in Persia (and bordering territories), and in European archives and museums. Only Ṣafawid and later documents have been found in greater quantity. Especially rich in this respect are Georgian (M. Chubua, *Persidskie firmanî i ukazî Muzeya Gruzii*, i, Tbilisi 1949; and V. S. Puturidze, *Gruzino-persidskie istoričeskie dokumentî*, Tbilisi 1955) and Armenian sources (A. D. Papazyan, *Persidskie dokumentî matenadarana*, 2 vols., Erivan 1956-60). A small collection of Ṣafawid documents (of which two are Turcoman) is located in the British Museum (Rieu, *Suppl.* 252-60, the greater part having been published by Busse, *Untersuchungen*). Isolated documents and letters are to be found in the Vatican (*A Chronicle of the Carmelites in Persia*, Appendix B) and in Italian archives (see F. Gabrieli, *Relazioni tra lo scià 'Abbas e i Granduchi di Toscana Ferdinando I e Cosimo II*, in *Rend. Lin.* 1949), in Poland (H. S. Szapszal, *Wyobrazenia swietych muzulmanskich*, Wilna 1934, 26-48), in Sweden (see K. V. Zettersteen, *Türkische, tatarische und persische Urkunden im Schwedischen Reichsarchiv*, Uppsala 1945), in Austria (Vienna), and in Germany (Dresden, see Fekete, *Iran Şahlarının . . .*). In Persia there are large and small collections in private archives in Teheran (Ḥusayn Shāhshāhānī, Maḥmūd Farhād Muʿtamid, Khān Malik) and Tabrīz (Muḥammad and Ḥusayn Āḳā Nakhdjuwānī), other collections in the Archaeological Museum in Teheran, in the Čihil-Sutūn pavilion in Iṣfāhān, in the Armenian church in New Djulfā, and in the Sanctuary Library (*kitāb-khāna-yi āstāna*) in Mashhad. In Germany there is a small collection of documents, assembled in 1938-9 by Wilhelm Eilers (Würzburg) in Persia (original documents and copies of inscriptions), in the possession of Hans R. Roemer (Mainz). In two articles the latter has brought together the material known up to 1957: *Vorschläge für die Sammlung von Urkunden zur islamischen Geschichte Persiens*, in *ZDMG*, civ (1954), 362-70; and *Über Urkunden zur Geschichte Agyptens und Persiens in islamischer Zeit*, in *ZDMG*, cvii (1957), 519-38.

Bibliography: V. Minorsky, *Some early documents in Persian*, in *JRAS* 1942, 181-94; 1943, 86-99; A. Mostaert and F. W. Cleaves: *Trois documents mongols des Archives secrètes vaticanes*, in *HJAS*, xv, 1952, 419-506; F. W. Cleaves, *The Mongolian documents in the Musée de Téhéran*, in *HJAS*, xvi, 1953, 1-107; P. Wittek, *Ankarada bir ilhani kitabesi*, in *THITM*, i, 1931, 161-4; V. Minorsky, *A soyūrghāl of Qāsim b. Jahāngīr Aq-qoyunlu 903/1498*, in *BSOS*, ix, 1937, 926-60; idem, *A Mongol decree of 720/1320 to the family of Shaikh Zāhid*, in *BSOAS*, xvi, 1954, 515-27; Ann K. S. Lambton, *The administration of Sanjar's empire as illustrated in the ʿAtabat al-kataba*, in *BSOAS*, xx, 1957, 367-80; Maḥmūd Mīrāftāb, *Dastūr al-kātib fī taʿyīn al-marātib*, Ph.D. thesis, Göttingen 1956; *Arşiv Kılavuzu*, edited by the administration of the Topkapı Sarayı Museum, 2 fasc., Istanbul 1938-40; J. Aubin, *Note sur quelques documents Aq qoyunlu*, in *Mélanges L. Massignon*, 1956, 123-47; idem, *Note préliminaire sur les archives du Takya du Tschima-Rud*, Tehran 1955; Khan Malek, *Un ferman d'Abu Nasr Hasan Bahadur*, in *Āthār-i Irān*, iii, 1937-39, 203-6; W. Hinz, *Zwei Steuerbefreiungsurkunden*, in *Documenta islamica inedita*, Berlin 1952, 211-20; H. Horst, *Ein Immunitätsdiplom Schah Muḥammad Khudābandäs vom Jahre 989/1581*, in *ZDMG*, cv, 1955, 289-97; idem, *Zwei Erlasse Šāh Ṭahmāsps I*, in *ZDMG*, cx 1961, 301-9; Ann K. S. Lambton, *Two Ṣafavid soyūrghāls*, in *BSOAS*, xiv, 1952, 44-54; Khanikoff, *Lettre de M. Khanikoff à M. Dorn* (16 *Sept.* 1856), in *Mélanges Asiatiques*, St. Petersburg, iii, 1857, 70-4 (late Ṣafawid document); C. Speelman, *Journal der Reis van de Gezant der O. J. Compagnie Joan Cunaeus near Perzie in 1651-1652*, ed. A. Hotz, Amsterdam 1908 (numerous documents in verbatim translation); Maḥmūd Farhād Muʿtamid, *Taʾrīkh-i rawābiṭ-i siyāsī-yi Īrān wa ʿuthmānī*, Tehran n.d. (numerous Ḳādjār *dast-khaṭṭ-hāy-i humāyūn* in facsimile); H. L. Rabino di Borgomale, *Une lettre familière de Fath Ali Chah*, in *RMM*, xl-xli, 1920, 131-5; Muḥammad Ḥasan Khān, *Mirʾāt al-buldān-i Nāṣirī*, 3 vols., Tehran 1294 (text of some 70 documents); idem, *Kitāb-i taʾrīkh-i munṭaẓam-i Nāṣirī*, 2 vols., Tehran 1298-9 (about 30 documents, of which 21 are Ṣafawid); for a more detailed account see H. Busse, *Persische Diplomatik im Überblick. Ergebnisse und Probleme*, in *Isl.*, xxxvii, 1961.

(H. Busse)

iv. — Ottoman Empire

Diplomatic in Ottoman Turkey can be traced back to the beginnings of the Empire in the 8th/14th century. The diplomatic system was fashioned after the pattern brought by Asiatic Turks who in turn followed diplomatic models that were developed by the states of Central Asia, thus presenting a blend of Uyg͟hur and Chinese traditions. On the other hand its organization was largely based on European practice, especially that established by the Byzantine Empire. The Tatar documents (those of the Golden Horde and of the Crimean Tatars) mainly followed Central Asian models and showed influence of Uyg͟hur and indirectly of Chinese diplomatic usage. This fact is evidenced by Persian documents dating from the 16th to 17th century which use the title-forms of *sözümüz* (see L. Fekete, *Arbeite der grusinischen Orientalistik auf dem Gebiete der türkischen und persischen Palaeographie und die Frage der Formel "sözümüz"*, in *AOHung.*, vii, 1, 1957). The documents of Ottoman Turkey from the 15th century represent a set of more or less consistent patterns (see F. Kraelitz-Greifenhorst, in *SbAK Wien* 1921 and *TOEM*, xxviii, P. Wittek, in *WZKM*, 1957). The documents, their general names being *ewrāḳ* or *wet͟hiḳa*, were issued by the chancellor's office of the Sublime Porte; solemn public documents proclaimed by sultans or announced by viziers were issued by the office of the so-called *beylik* or *beylik ḳalemi*, a special department of the central office of the Porte, formally known as *dīwān-i humāyūn ḳalemi*. The secretary, the scribe and the official in charge of the whole department (*beylikd͟ji*) attached their signatures to the documents, before they were sent to the *reʾīs efendi* for his stamp (the *resīd*). More important deeds were checked by the *nis͟hānd͟jī* and had to bear his *tug͟hra*. In the office of *takwīl* documents such as letters of appointments, proclamations and letters-patent were renewed or ratified. The documents called *ted͟hkere* were issued by the office of the *büyük ted͟hkered͟ji* and those of the fisc were made out by the clerks of the *defterdār*. Officials of lower rank in the capital as well as in the provinces had their own secretariats and were endowed with the authority to issue their own documents (see J. Hammer, *Staatsverfassung und Staatsverwaltung des osman. Reichs*, Wien, 1815; I. H. Uzunçarşılı, *Osmanlı devleti teşkilâtı*, 1945, and also BEYLIK above).

The documents were of two main trends. On the one hand there were proclamations, messages, and pronouncements, as for instance public edicts of the sultan, called *nāme, mektūb, kitāb, yazî, biti, tewḳīʿ*. The most solemn was the royal proclamation called *k͟haṭṭ-i-humāyūn*. These terms have never been very precise in meaning. Quite frequently the same document bore one or another name. The same is the case with various documents falling into the second category, of orders, edicts and ordinances such as *fermān, emr, ḥükm, buyuruldu* ([*q.v.*] see also I. H. Uzunçarşılı, *Buyuruldu*, in *Belleten*, 5/19, 1941), and deeds of appointment (*berāt*). The most solemn public documents bore names consisting of several words, *e.g.*, *ʿahd nāme, mülk nāme* (or *temlīk nāme*), *ṣulḥ nāme*. Of another category were the deeds called *nis͟hān* (denoting also patent letters, diplomas, or charters), *mens͟hūr* (a deed of nomination to an office or rank), *mit͟hāl*, *ʿarḍ ḥāl* (Tk. *arzuhal*) etc. Documents would at times bear elaborate names, *e.g.*, *nis͟hān-i s͟herīf ʿālīs͟hān, fermān-i bes͟hāret-i ʿunwān* etc. These names concerned exclusively documents promulgated by the ruler or by his highest officials and clerks of the public offices. There were, too, numerous acts issued by officials of lower ranks, such as *ted͟hkere, telḫīṣ, taḥrīr, defter, sid͟jill* etc., while the documents (diplomatic notes) presented to the Turkish government by members of the foreign diplomatic corps were called *taḳrīr*. Another group of documents issued by religious authorities (especially by the *s͟heyk͟h al-islām*), the so-called *fetwā*, concerned rulings in disputes and controversies.

The body of a Turkish document shows a great similarity to a European document. It is quite probable that its form and shape were imitated from the Byzantine model. The Turkish document can be divided into two parts; the first (the opening and concluding formulae) bears the character of protocol while the middle part contains the essential text. There are particular formulae which are also found in any Turkish document: *erkān*: (1) *daʿwet*, being an invocation composed of the formula containing the name of governor (the Bey's name). This would range from the simplest *huwa* to the longest titles (numerous examples are quoted by Fr. Kraelitz, *Osmanische Urkunden in türkischer Sprache*, in *SbAK Wien* 1921). A little space that follows the initial formula somewhat to the right hand side (in the documents issued by the Sultan only) is succeeded by (2) *tug͟hra*, the device or the sign of the sultan, named also *nis͟hān-i humāyūn, tewḳiʿ*, or *ʿalāmet*, and of different design for each sultan. This device contains the name of the sultan and all his titles and other distinctions with the formula *muẓaffer dāʿimā*. All this is encased in an ornamental design, always with the same motifs and shape. The *tug͟hra* was drawn and painted with particular care by a clerk specially assigned to this work, the *tug͟hra-kes͟h*. It was made in colours. The origin of *tug͟hra* is not certain (see I. H. Uzunçarşılı, in *Belleten* v, 1941; P. Wittek, in *Byzantion* xviii, 1948 and xx, 1956; F. Kraelitz-Greifenhorst, in *MOG* i; F. Babinger, *Sarre-Festschrift* 1925; P. Miyatev, *Tugrite na osmanskite sultani ot XV-XX wek*, in *Godischnik na plovdivska narodna biblioteka i muzei 1937-1939*, Sofia 1940; E. Kühnel, *Die osmanische Tughra*, Wiesbaden 1955; and TUG͟HRA). The documents issued by higher officials bore instead of the *tug͟hra* another sign, the *pence*. It was usually placed not at the beginning but on the left hand or right hand margin or at the foot of the scroll. Sometimes it was called *imḍā* or erroneously *tug͟hra* (see F. Kraelitz-Greifenhorst, *Studien zur osmanischen Urkundenlehre*, i; *Die Handfeste (Penče) der osmanischen Wesire*, in *MOG*, ii). (3) The *ʿunwān*, that is, the title of the person in whose name the document was made, was, especially in sultanic documents, of considerable length and worded in solemn form beginning with the traditional *benki* . . . (see Orgun Zarif, *Tuğralarda el muzaffer daʿima duası ve Şah unvanı, Türk Tarih, arkeol. ve etnogr. dergisi*, Istanbul 1949). (4) The *inscriptio* or the title of the person to whom the document was addressed (*elḳāb*), especially in documents of great importance, was also very long, and was introduced with the formula *sen ki* or *ḥālā*. Beside the name and titles of the addressee it contained (as regards Christian rulers) certain long-established formulae, *e.g.*, "the paragon of the highest princes of Jesus", "the pattern of the most illustrious dignitaries of the people of Messiah", etc. The addressee's name was followed by (5) *duʿāʾ*, *e.g.*, by a brief clause expressing the good wishes of the sender, an equivalent to a certain extent of a salutation in European documents. If the person addressed was a Muslim the clause contained also a blessing, an invocation to Allāh for protection over his person, etc. If the letter was addressed to a Christian, this formula would contain an allusively worded hope for his future conversion to Islam, *e.g.*, *khutimat ʿawāḳibuhu bi'l-khayr*, see J. Østrup, *Orientalske Høflighedsformler*, Copenhagen 1927, 85-8 (German tr., *Orientalische Höfflichkeit*, Leipzig 1929). The *duʿāʾ* concludes the introductory part of the protocol. The transition to the contents proper of the document is achieved through a special expression, *e.g.*, "when this writing comes to your hand, let be known that", then follows (6) *naḳl-i iblāgh* or *taṣrīḥ*, that is the main body of the letter or document which tells of the reasons for writing it, of favours bestowed or letters which have preceded it, sometimes introduced by means of the *areng*, *i.e.*, excuses and apologies that would occasionally contain a quotation from the Ḳurʾān, or a proverb, etc. In documents dispatched to foreign rulers no distinction is made between the narrative part and the succeeding one, which is (7) a *dispositio* with the opening words *ḥükm* or *emr*. This bears the main decision or resolution, either being strengthened by the use of the word *teʾkīd* and the formula, such as for instance *shöyle bilesiz* together with *laʿnet*, a threat of punishment in case of disobedience to orders (in relation to superior authorities). Then follows (8) an attesting formula, corresponding to the European *corroboratio* as *biti taḥḳīḳ bilüb, iʿtimad ḳīlasīz*. The dating or (9) *taʾrīkh* is marked by means of an Arabic formula, *e.g.*, *taḥrirᵃⁿ fī*. Then comes the decade of the month, the name of the month, and the year. The numerals are written in letters without any diacritic signs. To the names of the months there are usually added such descriptive definitions as *ramaḍān-i sherīf*. Instead of the name of the day there we find the monthly decades indicated. The first one is called *awāʾil*, the second, *awāsiṭ*, the third *awākhir*. The first day of the month is called *ghurre*, the last one, *salkh*, the middle of the month, *muntaṣaf*. To indicate particular months abbreviations are used. This rule is followed in documents written in the *siyāḳat* script. From the abbreviated forms the names of the quarters of the year are made (the first is *müshir*, the second *redjedj*, the third *reshen* and the fourth *ledhedh*) see J. H. Mordtmann, in *Isl.* ix; F. Kraelitz-Greifenhorst, in *Isl.*, viii; J. Mayr, *Islamische Zeitrechnungen*, in *MSOS*, xxx, 1927; H. Šabanović, *Izrazi evaᵉ il, ewasit i evahir u datamima turskih spomenika*, in *Prilozi za Orijentalnu filologiju*, i, 1950. (10) The place of promulgation or announcement comes after the date and here the usual formula is *be-meḳām-i* .... Then the name of the town is given (sometimes accompanied with an appropriate epithet), which frequently is descriptively defined. If the writing was made out on a journey or in camp, the phrase *be yurt* is used. Last comes (11) the seal *mühür*, *khātem*, serving to attest the document. It is impressed in China ink on the moistened paper. The seal is of various sizes and shapes, round, oval, square, polygonal etc. It contains the name of the writer, religious formulae and ornamental elements (see İ. H. Uzunçarşılı, in *Belleten*, iv, 1940; also MUHR). On the front page of the writing or on its back there are attached various attesting formulae for ensuring its validity, *e.g.*, *ṣḥ* (= *ṣaḥiḥ*) inserted by the officials of the chancellery to attest to the authenticity and correctness of the document. There frequently occur abbreviated forms of certain terms, *e.g.*, *m* in the meaning of *merḳūm* (= mentioned), *la* instead of *Allāh*, etc.

As a matter of course documents of the Turkish chancery were written in the vernacular (in Turkish), but there are also other documents in Greek, Old Slavonic (Cyrillic characters), Hungarian, with the genuine *tughra* or *penče* attached to them. Sometimes a translation in Italian, Polish etc. accompanied the Turkish text, or its transcription in Latin, Greek or Armenian characters. The documents of the Ḳazan Khāns and those of the Golden Horde that were dispatched to the sultans in the 15th century were written in the Uyghur language and bore the specific characteristics of Central Asian diplomatic documents.

Turkish diplomatic practice led to the development of a specific technique for writing more formal and solemn documents. The left hand side of each line was rounded upward and resembled a sabre with a curved point. For the sake of more intricate ornamentation the last letter in each line was inscribed in oval shape (usually *nūn*, *rāʾ* or *tāʾ*). The script used was the *dīwānī*, also known as *tewḳiʿ* in its various forms (see under KHAṬṬ). Not infrequently the invocation would be written in *thuluth* while the rest of the text would be written in the *dīwānī* characters. Documents signed by inferior officials were written in *neskhī* and *dīwānī* (see Mahmut Yazır, *Eski yazıları okuma anahtarı*, Istanbul, 1942). Fiscal documents were written in the *siyāḳat* characters which are very difficult to read (see L. Fekete, *Die Siyāqat-Schrift in der türkischen Finanzverwaltung*, i-ii, Budapest 1955; N. Popov, *Paleografski osobenosti na čislitelnite imena v pismoto siyakat*, Sofia, 1955).

Official papers are usually written with a rather broad margin (*kenār*) on the right hand side. It is covered with notes and remarks (*der kenār*), suggesting the main points to be worked into the body of the answer.

The usual ink used for writing was black China ink; in some words the black letters were covered with gold dust (*altīn rīg* or *rīh*).

Waxpaper, frequently imported from Italy, with watermarks was used (see F. Babinger, in *OM*, xi, 1931). The sheets were of elongated rectangular shape about 50 cm. long and 20 cm. wide; the letters of sultans, solemn acts of alliance were at times several metres long.

Generally the document was folded in pleats breadthwise so that when it was unfolded the introductory part with the forms of courtesy etc. would be the first to be read. Longer documents were rolled up like scrolls. Each document was kept in a satin bag, *kise*, tied up and having a slip of paper sticking out that contained the address or *ḳulaḳ*.

Copies (*ṣūret*) were made and sewn together into files (*munshaʾāt*). They would contain the bare text only, with no remarks, notes, *tughra*, or stamp. The legal formula which was usually placed on the right side close to the first lines of the text stated (usually in Arabic) the conformity of the copy with the original and was called *imḍā* or *tewḳiʿ -i ḳāḍī* (see F. Kraelitz-Greifenhorst, *Legalisierungsformeln in Abschriften osmanischer kaiserlicher Erlässe und Handschreiben*, in *MOG*, ii, 1926). In order to indicate that this was a copy only and not an original, such phrases were used as *yazīlidjak*, *gönderiledjek*, *irsāl olunan*. Also registers of documents were kept with entries which contained transcripts or summaries, the so-called *defter* or *sidjill*.

The development of the style and phraseology of the Turkish diplomatic document continued till about the 17th century, when the forms crystallized and acquired their uniform character. In the 19th century the lettering looked exactly like print. The style and wording of Turkish documents had their effect upon the somewhat different tradition and usage of the Crimean Tatars, as they also left their mark upon Persian diplomatic practice. A certain number of letters sent out by the Chancellor's office of the Persian *pādishāh* in the 17th and 18th centuries were written in Turkish (see L. Fekete, in *Türkiyat Mecmuası*, v, 1936).

The copies of the documents and incoming correspondence were kept in special offices from which Turkish archives later developed (see BAŞVEKALET ARŞIVI and F. Bajraktarević, *Glavni Carigradski arhivi i ispisi iz niega* in *Prilozi za orijentalnu filologiju i istoriju jugosl. naroda*, vi-vii, Sarajevo 1958).

Numerous Turkish documents are extant in the countries once forming part of the Turkish Empire—in Egypt (see J. Deny, *Sommaire des Archives turques du Caire*, Cairo 1930), Tunisia (see R. Mantran, in *Les Cahiers de Tunisie*, 1957, 341 ff.); Bulgaria (see V. Todorov-Hindalov in *Godischnik na Narodna Biblioteka*, Sofia 1923; P. Mutafčiev in *Mitteilungen des deutsch. wissenschaft. Instituts in Sofia*, Sofia 1943; P. Miyatev in *Levéltári Közlemények*, 1936; B. Nedkov in *Istoričeski Pregled*, x/2, 1954), Yugoslavia (see F. Giese in *Festschrift Jacob*; G. Elezović, *Turski izvori za istoriju Jugoslavena*, Belgrade 1932; H. Šabanović, *Turski diplomatički izvori*, in *Prilozi za orijentolnu filologiju*, i, Sarajevo 1950; R. Muderizović, *Turski dokumenti v dubrovackom arhivu*, in *Glasnik Zem. Muz.*, Sarajevo, 1938, v. L.); Rumania (see M. Guboglu, *Documentele turçești din arhivele Statului*, Bucharest 1957). Less numerous are Turkish documents in Greece (see E. Rossi, in *OM*, xxi, 1941). A great many of them, either through diplomatic channels or as booty or through trade relations, became part of foreign collections. Especially rich are the collections in those countries that maintained close diplomatic and other relations with Turkey: in Austria (see F. Zsinka, in *KCA*, i); Germany (on the Berlin and Dresden collections—see L. Fekete in *Levéltári Közlemények*, 1928-1929); Hungary; Poland (see E. Zawaliński, in *RO* xiv, 1938 and Z. Abrahamowicz, *Przegląd Orient.*, 1954, 2); Italy (see A. Bombaci, in *RSO*, xviii, 1939 and xxiv, 1949; L. Fekete in *Levéltári Közlémenyek*, 1926); the Soviet Union. Numerous documents are found in Sweden (see K. V. Zetterstéen, *Türkische, tatarische und persische Urkunden im schwedischen Reichsarchiv*, Uppsala 1945), Denmark (see H. Duda, *Mitteil. d. Instit. f. Oesterreich. Geschichtsforschung*, lviii, 1950), Great Britain (see P. Wittek, *The Turkish documents in Hakluyt's 'Voyages'*, in *Bull. of Inst. of Hist. Research*, xix, 1942; and A. N. Kurat, *Ingiliz devlet arşivinde ... Türkiye tarihine ait bazı malzemeye ait*, in *AÜDTCFD*, 1949), Czechoslovakia and in other countries (see the bibliography by J. Reychman and A. Zajączkowski, *Zarys dyplomatyki osmańsko-tureckiej*, Warsaw 1955, English edition in the press). Many collections are still to be classified, some are being catalogued at present.

The fullest and most comprehensive bibliography of published Turkish documents is given by A. Zajączkowski and J. Reychman (English edition).

The first textbook of Turkish diplomatic was published by L. Fekete, *Bevezetés a hodoltság török diplomatikájába*, Budapest 1926, with an introduction followed by a series of photographed documents. The introduction contained valuable information on the progress of research in this particular field of the history of diplomatic.

In 1955 in Warsaw there was published a textbook by A. Zajączkowski and Jan Reychman: *An outline history of Ottoman Turkish Diplomatic* (*Zarys dyplomatyki osmańsko-tureckiej*). An English version of this book, under the title: *A manual of Ottoman Turkish Diplomatics*, revised and considerably enlarged, is in the press. In 1958 a Rumanian scholar M. Guboglu published a new book: *Paleografia, și diplomatica turco-osmană*, Bucharest 1959, which beside the facsimiles contains 203 Turkish documents from Rumanian archives. In this book the author gives new and useful information on the subject of Turkish diplomatic and documents.

Bibliography: in addition to the works mentioned above: F. Babinger, *Das Archiv des Bosniaken Osman Pascha*, Berlin 1931; L. Fekete, *L'Édition des chartes turques et ses problèmes*; in *Körösi Csoma, Arch.*, i, 1939; G. Jacob, *Türkisches Hilfsbuch*, i, Berlin 1917; H. Scheel, *Die Schreiben der türkischen Sultane an die preuss. Könige*, Berlin 1930; *Tarih Vesikaları*, Ankara 1941-58; P. Wittek, *Zu einigen frühosmanischen Urkunden*, i-iv; in *WZKM*, liii-lvi (1957-60); L. Fekete, *A török oklevelek nyelvezete és forrásértéke* in *Levéltári Közlemények*, iii, 1925; see also under BAŞVEKALET ARŞIVI, BERĀT, BEYLIK, BUYURULDU, DAFTAR, DĀR AL-MAḤFŪẒĀT AL-ʿUMŪMIYYA, KHAṬṬ, MUHR, SIDJILL, TUGHRA, WATHĪḲA.

(J. Reychman and A. Zajączkowski)

DĪR, a princely state, which acceded to Pakistan in 1947, with an area of 2,040 sq. miles and a population of 148, 648 in 1951, lies to the south of Čitrāl in 35° 50′ and 34° 22′ N. and 71° 2′ and 72° 30′ E., taking its name from the village of Dīr, seat of the ruler, lying on the bank of a stream of the same name and a tributary of the Pandjkōřā. Politically the Dīr territory roughly comprises the country watered by the Pandjkōřā and its affluents. The state gained prominence in the second half of the 19th century for its hostility to the cause of the *mudjāhidīn*, remnants of the defeated forces of Sayyid Aḥmad Barēlawī [*q.v.*], with their headquarters first at Asmast (Samasta) and later at Čamarkand in Yāghistān.

The present Nawwāb of Dīr, Prince Muḥammad Shāh Khusraw, is a member of the Akhund Khēl, a branch of the Pāyandah Khēl subtribe of the Yūsufzaʾīs. The founder of the ruling family, like those of the sister states of Swāt, Amb and Čitrāl, was one Mullā Ilyās *alias* Akhund Bābā, who flourished in the 11th/17th century. His grandson, Ghulām Bābā, however, is said to be the first to have discarded the rôle of a religious leader and assumed worldly power. It was his great-grandson, Ghazzan Khān b. Ḳāsim Khān b. Ẓafar Khān who, with a force 10,000 strong, joined the tribal *lashkar*s during the Ambēylā Campaign of 1863 directed by the British-Indian troops against the *mudjāhidīn* of Sayyid Aḥmad Barēlawī and their allies. He, however, withdrew his contingent when he found that the scales had turned in favour of the invaders. He was succeeded by his son, Raḥmat Allāh Khān, who, aware of his weak title, gained the throne with the monetary assistance of the Mahārādjā of Kashmīr. In 1875 Raḥmat Allāh Khān, offended at the misbehaviour of the Kashmīr agent, broke off relations with the Mahārādjā and threw off his suzerainty. On his death in 1884 his son Muḥammad Sharīf Khān came to the throne and soon started a series of campaigns and skirmishes against the neighbouring state of Čitrāl [*q.v.*]. The forces of Muḥammad Sharīf Khān were, however, completely defeated and the Mihtar Amān al-Mulk of Čitrāl acquired great influence in Dīr. Muḥammad S̲h̲arīf K̲h̲ān had to take refuge in Swāt [q.v.] with whom his principality had been almost constantly at war. He made several unsuccessful attempts to regain from Amān al-Mulk his territory, which in 1890 was conquered by the adventurer, ʿUmrā K̲h̲ān, chief of Djandōl. Five years later in 1313/1895, Muḥammad S̲h̲arīf K̲h̲ān succeeded with the moral and material backing of the British forces, in recovering Dīr and even capturing S̲h̲īr Afḍal, pretender to the throne of Čitrāl.

In 1897 the title of Nawwāb was conferred on Muḥammad S̲h̲arīf K̲h̲ān who had, the same year, annexed a part of the upper Swāt territory, the old enemy of his House. This title was, in all probability, conferred on him in recognition of his services to the British in dissuading the Dīr tribes from participating in the djihād which Mullā Saʿd Allāh K̲h̲ān of Bunēr, nicknamed Sartōr (crazy) Faḳīr, had launched against the alien government. A close ally of the British Government, in receipt of an annual allowance amounting to 26,000 rupees, Muḥammad S̲h̲arīf K̲h̲ān died in 1904 and was succeeded by his son Awrangzīb K̲h̲ān (Bāds̲h̲āh K̲h̲ān). He soon fell out with his younger brother, Miyān Gul Djān, who in alliance with the disaffected sections of the population of Dīr, marched against his elder brother and captured, in Djumādā I 1323/June 1905, two of the Dīr fortresses. Peace was, however, restored through the efforts of the British Chief Commissioner of the North-West Frontier Province. It proved short-lived and fighting broke out between the two brothers again in 1911-12. This period of internecine war came to a close with the death of Miyān Gul in Djandōl in 1914.

In 1917, while World War I was still in progress, Bāds̲h̲āh K̲h̲ān helped ʿAbd al-Matīn K̲h̲ān, a son of ʿUmrā K̲h̲ān, to regain the principality of Djandōl but soon afterwards occupied it himself. This act was characterized as usurpation and betrayal of the worst kind. The Sultan of Turkey, in an appeal issued in Muḥarram 1336/October 1917 to the war-like tribes of Yāg̲h̲istān, exhorted the Nawwāb of Dīr to give up creating discord among the tribesmen and restore Djandōl to its rightful ruler. In 1919 the oppressed people of Swāt, under Miyān Gul Gul S̲h̲āhzāda, threw off Bāds̲h̲āh K̲h̲ān's rule but the British forced S̲h̲āhzāda in 1922 to withdraw from the area conquered by him. On his death in 1925 Bāds̲h̲āh K̲h̲ān was succeeded by his eldest son, Muḥammad S̲h̲āh Djahān K̲h̲ān, the deposed ruler. In 1930 when the entire north-west frontier of India was ablaze he placed his resources at the disposal of the British Government for quelling the Red Shirt disturbances in Pēs̲h̲āwar and the surrounding area. The same year existing boundaries between Dīr and Swāt were confirmed, putting an end to centuries-old hostilities.

A great part of the Dīr territory is divided into small K̲h̲ānates, held by the Nawwāb's relations. There have recently (1959) been some disturbances in the state but these were described as mostly agrarian rather than political in nature.

In 1960 Muḥammad S̲h̲āh Djahān K̲h̲ān was deposed, arrested and interned by the Government of Pakistan on serious charges of misgovernment and maladministration. He was succeeded by his eldest son, Prince Muḥammad S̲h̲āh K̲h̲usraw, who was formally installed as the Nawwāb of Dīr on 9 November 1960 at Čakdara, in the Malākand Agency.

Bibliography: C. U. Aitchison, Treaties, Engagements and Sanads ..., Delhi 1933, xi. 417-46; G̲h̲ulām Rasūl Mihr, Sarguzas̲h̲t-i Mudjāhidīn, Lahore 1956, 348, 359, 365, 368, 489, 530; Imperial Gazetteer of India, Oxford 1908, 360-1; W. W. Hunter, The Indian Musulmans, Calcutta 1945, 29; Memoranda on the Indian States, Delhi 1940, 210-15; also see the article SWĀT. (A. S. BAZMEE ANSARI)

DIR [see SOMALI].

ḌIRĀR B. AL-K̲H̲AṬṬĀB B. MIRDĀS AL-FIHRĪ, a poet of Mecca. Chief of the clan of Muḥārib b. Fihr in the Fidjār [q.v.], he fought against the Muslims at Uḥud and at the battle of the Trench, and wrote invectives against the Prophet. He was however converted after the capture of Mecca, but it is not known if he perished in the battle of Yamāma (12/633) or whether he survived and went to settle in Syria.

Bibliography: Sīra, ed. Saḳḳā, etc., Cairo 1375/1955, i, 414-5, 450, ii, 145-6, 254-5; Ṭabarī, index; Muḥ. b. Ḥabīb, Muḥabbar, 170, 176, 434; Buḥturī, Ḥamāsa, index; Ibn Sallām, Ṭabaḳāt, ed. S̲h̲ākir, 209-12; Ag̲h̲ānī, iv, 5=ed. Beirut, iv, 144-5; Ibn Ḥadjar, Iṣāba, no. 4173; Ibn ʿAsākir, vii; Nallino, Litt., 74. (ED.)

DIRE DAWA, important road, rail, and air communication centre and chief commercial town in Eastern Ethiopia, situated 35 miles North-West of Harar [q.v.] and thus within the cultural orbit of this major Muslim city in the Ethiopian Empire. The name is most probably derived from the Somali Dir-ḍabo 'limit of the Dir' (the Dir being the confederation of Somali tribes which inhabit the vast arid region between Dire Dawa and Djibuti), but it is possible that the Amharicized form is meant to reflect a popular etymology from the Amharic dire dawa 'hill of uncultivated land'. Dire Dawa owes its comparatively recent origin and importance to the Addis Ababa-Djibuti railway which climbs from the desolate Dankali plain to this first great centre of sedentary population at the edge of the escarpment at an altitude of just below 4000 feet. The total population (estimated between 30,000 and 50,000) includes Ethiopians proper as well as Gallas, Somalis, Italians, French, Greeks, Indians, and Arabs. The ill-starred Emperor, Lidj Iyasu, built a mosque at Dire Dawa during the First World War, while during the Second the town became the headquarters of the British Reserved Areas Administration after the reconquest of Ethiopia in 1941. The Islamic culture of the Muslim population of Dire Dawa and its hinterland varies considerably and includes remnants of pagan practices. The S̲h̲āfiʿī is the most generally accepted mad̲h̲hab in this area.

Bibliography: Guida dell'Africa Orientale Italiana, Milan 1938, 432 ff. (street plan 435; area map 448); Reale Società Geografica Italiana, L'Africa Orientale, Bologna 1936 (index under Dire Dawa); Chamber of Commerce, Guide Book of Ethiopia, Addis Ababa 1954 (index under Dire Dawa); Lord Rennell of Rodd, British military administration of occupied territories in Africa, 1941-1947, H.M. Stationery Office 1948 (index under Dire Dawa); J. S. Trimingham, Islam in Ethiopia, Oxford 1952 (for general characteristics of Islam in this area). (E. ULLENDORFF)

ḌIRG̲H̲ĀM ("Lion"), Fāṭimid amīr and wazīr; his full name Abu 'l-As̲h̲bāl al-Ḍirg̲h̲ām b. ʿĀmir b. Sawwār, he received the agnomens of Fāris al-Muslimīn, S̲h̲ams al-k̲h̲ilāfa, and, when he was vizier of the last Fāṭimid al-ʿĀḍid, the title of al-Malik al-Manṣūr, the victorious king, according to a protocol issued by Riḍwān [*q.v.*]. He was Arab in origin and was perhaps descended from the former kings of Ḥīra, to judge from the dynastic names of al-Lakhmī and al-Mundhirī that he bore.

The first mention of him is made in 548/1153. He was among the detachment charged with relieving the garrison of ʿAsḳalān led by the future vizier al-ʿAbbās together with Usāma b. Munḳidh [*q.v.*]. It was during the advance of this company that the murder of the vizier Ibn al-Sallār [*q.v.*] was planned, and was carried out by Naṣr, the son of al-ʿAbbās; the latter, advised of this, returned to Cairo with his company and seized the vizierate (Muḥarram 548/April 1153). Al-ʿAbbās was overthrown by Ṭalāʾiʿ b. Ruzzīk in 549/1154. The latter, whose trust Ḍirghām seems to have received (Abu 'l-Maḥāsin calls him "one of the emirs of Banū Ruzzīk"), made him commander of the corps of Barḳiyya which he had just formed. He rose in the hierarchy and became *nāʾib al-bāb*, that is to say lieutenant of the *ṣāḥib al-bāb* or grand chamberlain. He distinguished himself as commander of the army sent by Ṭalāʾiʿ against the Franks, which gained a victory at Tell al-ʿAdjūl in Palestine on the 15 Ṣafar 553/19 March 1158. The following year, together with Ruzzīk, son of the vizier, he triumphed over the rebel Bahrām in Upper Egypt near Aṭfīḥ (Derenbourg, *Oumara du Yémen*, i, 1-3, ii, 127). During the vizierate of Ruzzīk, Ṭalāʾiʿ's successor, Ḍirghām, was sent with an army to stop the expedition of the king Amalric I who, in September 1162, invaded Egypt in order to claim the tribute already promised by Ṭalāʾiʿ. Ḍirghām (Dargan of Guillaume de Tyr, in *RHC. Occ.* i/2, 890-1), was defeated and fell back on Bilbays. But, taking advantage of the rising of the Nile, he breached its dikes in order to flood the adjoining plain and Amalric had to withdraw into Palestine (Derenbourg, *op. cit.*, ii, 203-4, 208-9). Immediately afterwards, he took part in the putting down of a rebellion in the province of al-Gharbiyya.

But there soon broke out the revolt of Shāwar, the powerful prefect of Ḳūṣ, which was to end with his victory and the death of Ruzzīk. When Shāwar's success was certain, Ḍirghām, in spite of his good relations with Ruzzīk whom he had instructed in horsemanship and knightly pursuits (al-Maḳrīzī, *Khiṭaṭ*, ii, 78), did not hesitate to leave him and go over to the side of Shāwar, who became vizier (Ṣafar 558/January 1163). Shāwar, in whose circle he remained, made him grand chamberlain or *ṣāḥib al-bāb* (Abu 'l-Maḥāsin, v, 338, 10), the most important office after the vizierate. But Ḍirghām, supported by his brothers and a considerable part of the army, was not long in forming a faction against the vizier and, after nine months of the vizierate of Shāwar, revolted against him, although Shāwar, according to the Continuator of the *History of the Patriarchs of Alexandria*, had made him swear forty oaths that he would not betray him (Derenbourg, ii, 246). In Ramaḍān 558/August 1163 Shāwar was driven from Cairo and took refuge in Syria where he sought the support of Nūr al-Dīn in regaining the vizierate. Ḍirghām had Ṭayy, the eldest son of Shāwar, put to death, and on 29 Ramaḍān/31 August he was invested with the vizierate with the title of al-Malik al-Manṣūr.

He had three brothers, Nāṣir al-Dīn Humām, Nāṣir al-Muslimīn Mulham and Fakhr al-Dīn Ḥusām. The first, after his brother's accession to the vizierate, took the title of Fāris al-Muslimīn which Ḍirghām had formerly borne. According to al-Maḳrīzī, during his vizierate Ḍirghām was dominated by his brothers Humām and Ḥusām.

Fortune did not smile on Ḍirghām for very long, and difficulties soon arose. Aware of Shāwar's preparations for revenge, he attempted to start negotiations with Nūr al-Dīn by promising him his allegiance and an advantageous alliance against the Franks. Nūr al-Dīn gave an evasive reply. And perhaps it was at the instigation of Nūr al-Dīn that Ḍirghām's messenger was seized by the Franks of Karak on his return from Damascus. Thwarted in this and disturbed by the attitude of the *amīr*s of the corps of the Barḳiyya, who had given him powerful support in winning the vizierate but some of whom envied him and were negotiating with Shāwar, Ḍirghām trapped them in an ambush and massacred seventy of them, not counting their followers. Historians do not fail to point out that these executions removed men of ability and weakened Egypt dangerously.

Amalric however had not given up his scheme to conquer Egypt, and at the end of 1163 or at the beginning of 1164 his advance-guard invaded Egyptian territory. Ḍirghām, after failing to bring over Nur al-Dīn to his cause, decided to negotiate with Amalric and offered him, on condition that he withdrew his troops, a peace treaty, the delivery of hostages, and the payment of an annual tribute to be levied until a date fixed by the king. But Shāwar had finally gained the support of Nūr al-Dīn, who in Djumādā I 559/April 1164 sent into Egypt with Shāwar an army commanded by Shīrkūh which included Saladin his nephew. It crossed unhindered the territory controlled by the Franks who were prevented from taking action by a manoeuvre of Nūr al-Dīn. Mulham the brother of Ḍirghām (Ḥusām according to al-Maḳrīzī), who was sent against the invaders with a large but, according to Shāwar, inglorious army, was surprised near Bilbays and put to flight at the end of April 1164. This caused panic at Cairo, where Shīrkūh and Shāwar soon appeared. Several battles took place between the troops of Shāwar and those of Ḍirghām. In order to raise some resources Ḍirghām made the mistake of seizing the possessions of the orphans, and so alienated the population. He was deserted by some of his troops; the corps of Rayḥānīs who had sustained some losses promised their aid to Shāwar. Ḍirghām, after trying in vain to muster some supporters and accompanied by no more than 500 cavaliers, presented himself at the palace of the Caliph, who refused to admit him and advised him to have a care to his own life. The desertions continued until he retained only thirty cavaliers. He took to flight followed by the curses of the people while Shāwar's troops entered Cairo. Overtaken between Cairo and Fusṭāṭ, Ḍirghām was dragged from his horse and killed near the mausoleum of al-Sayyida Nafīsa in Ramaḍān 559/July-August 1164, or, according to certain traditions, at the end of Djūmādā II/24 May 1164 or in Radjab/May-June 1164. His three brothers were likewise killed soon afterwards. His corpse remained without burial for two or three days and his head was carried on a pikestaff. He was buried near Birkat al-Fīl and a cupola was raised over his tomb. His vizierate had lasted only nine months.

ʿUmāra al-Yamanī and al-Maḳrīzī praised Ḍirghām whom they consider among the greatest *amīr*s and bravest cavaliers. He combined with his physical qualities (skill at polo, archery, wielding the spear, and feats of prowess at tilting in the ring) a gift for penmanship, for poetry (he composed some fine *muwashshaḥāt*) and for poetic criticism. ʿUmāra has spoken highly of his generosity, but has also noted that he was quick to turn against his friends, and it must not be forgotten that he betrayed successively Ruzzīk and Shāwar.

Bibliography: Ibn al-Athīr, Cairo edition 1303, xi, 108 f., 111 f., Tornberg edn., xi, 191, 196-7; Ibn Khallikan, Būlāḳ ed., i, 276 f., ii, 499 (trans. de Slane, i, 609 f., iv, 485 f.); Derenbourg, *Oumara du Yémen, sa vie et son œuvre*, i, (*Kitab al-Nukat* and *Extraits du Diwan*), 67 f., 73 f.; ii (*Vie de Oumara du Yémen*, 101, 166, 257 f., 281-303 and in the index; Kamāl al-Dīn Ibn al-ʿAdīm, *Taʾrīkh Ḥalab*, ed. S. Dahhān, ii, 316-7; Ibn Muyassar, *Akhbār Miṣr*, ed. Massé, 92, 97; Ibn Shaddād, *Sīrat Ṣalāḥ al-Dīn*, Cairo ed., 1346, 28-9; Abū Shāma, *Kitāb al-rawḍatayn*, in *RHC Or.*, iv, 107-8; Ibn Wāṣil, *Mufarridj al-Kurūb*, ed. Shayyal, i (1953), 137-9; Djamāl al-Dīn Ibn Ẓāfir, *Kitāb al-Duwal* . . . ., in Wüstenfeld, *Gesch. der Fatimiden-Khalifen*, 329 f.; Maḳrīzī, *Khiṭaṭ*, i, 338, 358, ii, 12 f., 78; Abu ʾl-Maḥāsin, *Nudjūm*, Cairo ed., v, 317, 338, 346-7; S. Lane-Poole, *Hist. of Egypt*, 175-8, *Saladin*, 80-2; Röhricht, *Gesch. des Königreichs Jerusalem*, 314 f., and G. Schlumberger, *Campagnes du roi Amaury Ier*, 36 f. (with dates to be rectified); G. Wiet, *Hist. de la Nation Égyptienne*: *L'Égypte arabe*, 284, 287 f., 291-4; idem, *Précis de l'hist. de l'Égypte*, 196; Grousset, *Hist. des Croisades*, ii, 447-8, 453-4 and in the index. For the poetic gifts of Ḍirghām, cf. M. Kāmil Ḥusayn, *Fī adab Miṣr al-Fāṭimiyya*, 138, 178, 199-200. See also the articles AL-ʿĀḌID, CRUSADES, RUZZĪK, SHĀWAR, SHĪRKŪH, ṬALĀʾIʿ B. RUZZĪK. (M. CANARD)

DIRHAM. 1. The name of a weight, derived from Greek δραχμή. Traditionally the *dirham kayl* or *sharʿī* weighed from 50 to 60 average-sized, unshelled *shaʿīra* or *ḥabba*, and was theoretically divided into 6 *dānaḳ*, the latter being calculated variously between 8 and 10 *shaʿīra*. So numerous and contradictory are the reports on the weight of the dirham and its relationship to other Arab metrological units in different parts of the Islamic world and at different times that they cannot be summarized here, and the reader is referred to such works as Sauvaire's *Matériaux* and Grohmann's *Einführung* (see bibliography under DĪNĀR). Efforts to define the weight of the traditional dirham in terms of modern metric grams have resulted in various figures, most of them probably erroneous. Cf. W. Hinz, *Islamische Masse u. Gewichte* (*Handbuch der Orientalistik, Ergänzungsband* 1, *Heft* 1, Leiden 1955, 2 ff.), where also 19th and 20th century legal definitions in different countries are to be found. Although most Muslim states have now officially adopted the metric system, the dirham and other traditional weights continue irregularly in use in various trades. In present-day Egypt, the dirham is defined as weighing 3.12 grams; two actual goldsmith's brass dirham weights of the year 1953 are found to weigh 3.1322 and 3.1335 grams respectively.

2. The silver unit of the Arab monetary system from the rise of Islām down to the Mongol period. The earliest Arab dirhams (*baghlī*) were imitations of the late Sasanian *drahms* of Yezdigird III, Hormuzd IV and (chiefly) Khusraw II. The Sāsānian iconography was retained, but a Kūfic religious inscription was added to the margin; on a few issues the name of the Caliph (Muʿāwiya and ʿAbd al-Malik) and on most issues the name of the provincial governor and the abbreviated mint name and date according to the Hidjra, Yezdigird or post-Yezdigird era (all in Pahlevi characters), were engraved. About the year 72/691-2 (American Numismatic Society *Museum Notes* vii, 1957, 191) and for a few years thereafter variations of the conventional type, including the use of more Kūfic legends and innovations in iconography more suitable to Islam, were experimented with, but in the year 79/698-9 ʿAbd al-Malik's monetary reform drastically altered the style of the dirham, which thenceforth, with few exceptions, was, like the dīnār, purely epigraphic. The post-reform dirham was at first anonymous, but in the course of the 2nd and 3rd centuries A.H. the names of governors, heirs-apparent, Caliphs, etc. were added. The name of the mint and the date, in words, was always present. In Umayyad times the chief dirham mints were located in former Sāsānian administrative centres, but silver was struck also in Damascus, North Africa and Spain. Wāsiṭ, founded in 84/703-4, appears to have been the most prolific of Umayyad dirham mints, and it is possible that the administration of the silver coinage was centred in this city and that the dirham dies were engraved there.

Little change in the style and general appearance of the dirham occurred under the various independent dynasties down to the end of the 4th/10th century, except that the legends on the Fāṭimid dirham were usually arranged in concentric circles. There followed a period of silver famine in the East when the output of silver coinage was relatively insignificant (cf. R. P. Blake in *Harvard Journal of Asiatic Studies*, 1937, 291, where the study of this phenomenon is broached but not investigated to the depth which it deserves); but with the rise of the Mongols in the mid-7th/13th century, dirhams and multiples thereof, differing in design from the "classical" type, were again issued in immense quantities. For the late Fāṭimid *dirham waraḳ*, the Ayyūbid *dirham Nāṣirī* and *Kāmilī*, and Mamlūk dirhams, see P. Balog in *BIE*, xxxiii, 1950-1, and v. Schrötter, s.v. *dirhem*. In the West the dirham declines in quality with the fall of the Umayyad dynasty of Spain, is restored in somewhat altered form under the Murābiṭs, and undergoes a complete change in style and weight with the Muwaḥḥids, when the square dirham (*murabbaʿ*), also imitated by the Christians in France (the *millares*), is introduced (corpus and bibliography in H. W. Hazard, *The numismatic history of late medieval North Africa*, N.Y. 1952).

With regard to the weight of the classical Arab dirham, statistics (unpublished) show that the highest frequency group of the Sāsānian drachm of Khusraw II falls between 4.11 and 4.15 grams. The Arab-Sasanian dirham was definitely lighter, approximately 3.98 grams. After the reform of 79 A.H., an entirely new standard is adopted with the result that thenceforth until the middle of the 3rd/9th century, when weights begin to be very erratic, the peak weight of the dirham consistently lies between 2.91 and 2.95 grams (A.N.S. *Museum Notes*, ix, 1960, see bibliography). The corrected figure, allowing for loss of weight, is 2.97 grams, which conforms exactly with the traditional theoretical figure based on the classical Arab formula which pronounced the weight of the dirham to be 7/10 that of the *mithḳāl* (dīnār), *i.e.*, $^{7}/_{10} \times 4.25 = 2.97$ (see s.v. DĪNĀR). Dirham glass weights fall slightly below this figure; and a special category of glass weights establishes the fact that there were in Egypt dirhams of 13 *kharrūbas*, weighing still less.

The rate of exchange between dīnār and dirham fluctuated widely at different times and in different parts of the empire. The jurists speak of 10 (or 12) dirhams to the dīnār in the time of Muḥammad, but subsequently there is plentiful evidence to show that the dirham at times sank as low as 15, 20, 30 and even 50 (see the numerous textual citations by Sauvaire, Lane-Poole in *NC* 1884, Grohmann in *Einführung*, etc.). P. Grierson (*op. cit.* under DĪNĀR) has attempted to explain the economic bases of the mint and market gold-silver ratios, with particular reference to Byzantine-Arab relationships.

Both typologically and economically the dirham exerted a strong influence on Byzantium and the West. The Byzantine *miliaresion*, introduced in the second quarter of the 8th century after a generation during which virtually no silver coinage was issued in Constantinople, was clearly inspired by the dirham, and many *miliaresia* of the 8th and 9th centuries were actually struck on Arab dirham planchets. There is some reason to believe also that the style of the Carolingian *denier* or *denar* may have been influenced by the dirham. The great importance of Arab silver in commerce between the lands of the Eastern Caliphate on the one hand and Russia, eastern Europe, Scandinavia and the Baltic regions on the other, is abundantly documented by the immense numbers of dirhams and fragments of dirhams found in these areas in hoards dating from four clearly defined periods between 780 and 1100 A.D. (comprehensive summary and full bibliography in U. S. L. Welin in *Kulturhistorisk Leksikon for nordisk middelalder*, i, Copenhagen 1956, s.v. *Arabisk mynt*). Dirhams also have been found in lesser numbers in England and France (cf. J. Duplessy in *Rev. Numismatique* 1956, 101).

Beginning in the 5th/11th century, dirhams of base silver (billon) and copper were struck by various dynasties (late Buwayhid, Ḳarakhānid, Khʷārizm-shāh, etc.). The large, thick copper dirhams of the Artuḳids (in the coin catalogues "Urtuḳids"), Zangids and Ayyūbids, with figured types resembling those of Hellenistic, Roman provincial, Byzantine and other coinages, and occasionally exhibiting original Islamic iconography, constitute a unique phenomenon so far unsatisfactorily explained and deserving of further study (best illustrations in the British Museum and Istanbul catalogues and in S. Lane Poole, *Coins of the Urtuḳi Turkumáns*, London 1875; cf. also J. Karabacek, in *Num. Zeitschr.*, 1869, 265).

Bibliography: In addition to the bibliography under DĪNĀR and the works cited in the body of the present article, see R. Vasmer in F. v. Schrötter, *Wörterbuch der Münzkunde* (Berlin-Leipzig, 1930) s.v. *Dirhem* (with valuable bibliography); J. Walker, *A Catalogue of the Arab-Sassanian Coins* (*A Cat. of the Muhammadan Coins in the British Museum*, i, London 1941); U. S. L. Welin, in *Kulturhistorisk Leksikon for nordisk middelalder*, iii (Copenhagen, 1959), s.v. *Dirhem*; G. C. Miles, *Byzantine miliaresion and Arab dirhem*: *some notes on their relationship* in *American Numismatic Society Museum Notes* ix (1960), 189-218; idem, *The Iconography of Umayyad Coinage* in *Ars Orientalis* iii (1959), recent bibliography; idem, "*Trésor de dirhems du IXᵉ siècle*", in *Mémoires de la Mission Archéologique en Iran*, xxxvii, 1960, 67-145 (detailed study of a large hoard of dirhams found at Susa).

(G. C. MILES)

AL-DIRʿIYYA (or al-Darʿiyya), an oasis in Wādī Ḥanīfa [*q.v.*] in Nadjd, the capital of Āl Saʿūd [*q.v.*] until its overthrow in 1233/1818. The oasis lies c. 20 km. north-west of al-Riyāḍ, the present capital. The wadi flows south-east through the upper part of the oasis and then bends to the east before passing the main settlements. Beyond these settlements the high cliff of al-Ḳurayn forces the wadi to make a sharp turn to the south-west. The road from al-Riyāḍ descends the cliff by Nazlat al-Nāṣiriyya to enter the wadi opposite Shaʿīb Ṣafār, the largest tributary on the right bank. On the left bank just below the pass lies the cultivated plot of al-Mulaybīd.

The wadi is a narrow ribbon threading the oasis from one end to the other, hemmed in by abrupt cliffs on both sides. The flash floods coursing down the wadi may be as few as two or as many as fifteen a year; as soon as they are gone the wadi is dry. In many places the date gardens occupy a raised step above the valley floor which is protected from the floods by a levee (*djurf*) of large stone blocks sometimes three metres high. On occasion the floodwater surges over the levee and reaches the base of the cliff (*djabal*) at the outer edge of the palms. The houses are built either among the palms or on the heights above.

The settlements farthest up the wadi are al-ʿIlb and al-ʿAwda, both among the palms on the right bank. Below these is Ghaṣība, now a complete ruin, on the high ground on the left bank opposite the tributary al-Bulayda. The tributary Ḳulayḳil runs along the eastern side of Ghaṣība. After the wadi bears eastwards the left bank is lined with a series of settlements, among them being the low-lying al-Budjayrī, the home of the reformer Shaykh Muḥammad b. ʿAbd al-Wahhāb and the many *ʿulamāʾ* among his progeny, Āl al-Shaykh. A mosque stands on the site where the Shaykh was accustomed to worship, and his grave is not far off, though, in keeping with his doctrine, it is not an object of visitation. On the right or southern bank facing these settlements is the promontory of al-Ṭurayf thrusting into the pocket between Wādī Ḥanīfa and Shaʿīb Ṣafār; here rise the majestic ruins of the palaces where the princes of Āl Saʿūd once lived and held court—in Philby's words, "the noblest monument in all Wahhabiland". The buildings, made of clay save for the pillars of stone, have a grace and delicacy of ornamentation unusual in Nadjd. Near the north-western corner of the fortified enclosure is the highest point in al-Ṭurayf, the citadel known as al-Darīsha (it is noteworthy that in Nadjd, the wellspring of Arabic, the common words for window, *darīsha*, and gate, *darwāza*, are both Persian in origin). Leading up to the citadel from the shelf of palms below is a ramp called Darb Fayṣal after Fayṣal b. Saʿūd, one of the captains guarding the town when Ibrāhīm Pasha besieged it in 1233/1818. The most impressive palace still standing is Maḳṣūrat ʿUmar on the brink of the northern cliff. Near it is the congregational mosque of al-Ṭurayf in which the Imām ʿAbd al-ʿAzīz was assassinated in 1218/1803. The ruins of al-Ṭurayf are gradually disintegrating because of the ravages of time and the development of a new settlement which is spreading from the foot of the promontory up to its shoulder.

According to the chroniclers of Nadjd, al-Dirʿiyya was first settled in 850/1446-7 when Māniʿ b. Rabīʿa al-Muraydi was given Ghaṣība and al-Mulaybīd by his relative Ibn Dirʿ of Ḥadjar al-Yamāma. Māniʿ was an emigrant from the east; his former home, said to have been called al-Dirʿiyya, is reported to have been in the region of al-Ḳaṭīf, but its exact location is not known. Some genealogists state that the Marada, the kinsfolk of Mānīᶜ, belong to Banū Ḥanīfa, while others advocate a descent from ᶜAnaza, which appears to be the prevailing view among members of Āl Saᶜūd.

After Mānīᶜ various branches of his descendants took turns in ruling al-Dirᶜiyya. Gh̲aṣība seems to have been the original centre and strong point; no record has been found of when it was supplanted by al-Ṭurayf, which topographically enjoys an even greater degree of impregnability. In 1133/1721 Saᶜdūn b. Muḥammad Āl Gh̲urayr of Banū Kh̲ālid, the lord of al-Ḥasā, plundered houses in al-Ẓuhayra, Malwī, and al-Surayḥa, all settlements still existing along the left bank.

In 1139/1726-7 Muḥammad b. Saᶜūd Āl Muḳrin, a direct descendant of Mānīᶜ, became the independent ruler of al-Dirᶜiyya, including Gh̲aṣība. At that time the primacy among the towns of central Nad̲j̲d was held by al-ᶜUyayna, farther up the valley, under the domination of Āl Muᶜammar of Tamīm. ᶜAbd Allāh b. Muḥammad, the most powerful representative of this house, died the same year Muḥammad b. Saᶜūd came to power in al-Dirᶜiyya. Muḥammad b. Saᶜūd won a good reputation as a secular lord. In 1157/1744 Sh̲ayk̲h̲ Muḥammad b. ᶜAbd al-Wahhāb chose al-Dirᶜiyya as his new home when requested to leave al-ᶜUyayna, his native town, by ᶜUth̲mān b. Aḥmad Āl Muᶜammar. The Sh̲ayk̲h̲ and Muḥammad b. Saᶜūd made a compact to work together in establishing the true version of Islam throughout the land of the Arabs.

The spiritual force of Ibn ᶜAbd al-Wahhāb and the military skill of Muḥammad b. Saᶜūd and his son ᶜAbd al-ᶜAzīz and grandson Saᶜūd brought virtually the whole of the Arabian Peninsula under the authority of al-Dirᶜiyya by the early 13th/19th century. Ibn Bis̲h̲r records his own eye-witness description of the capital in the time of Saᶜūd. Much of the land now given over to palms was then occupied by buildings. Particularly vivid are Ibn Bis̲h̲r's vignettes of the market in the valley bottom, the sunrise religious assembly in the same spot attended by Saᶜūd and his resplendent corps of *mamlūk*s, Saᶜūd's hearing of petitions and dispensing of largesse to his subjects and guests, and the diligent Islamic instruction given by the sons of the Sh̲ayk̲h̲. Saᶜūd was said to own 1,400 Arab horses, of which 600 were taken on campaigns by Bedouins or his *mamlūk*s. He had 60 cannon, half of which were of large size. For Nad̲j̲d, al-Dirᶜiyya had become a very cosmopolitan and expensive centre: visitors from Oman, the Yemen, Syria, and Egypt thronged its bazaar; shops rented for as high as 45 riyals a month, and houses sold for 7,000 riyals. So much building went on that there was a great scarcity of wood.

The first and only European to see al-Dirᶜiyya while it flourished was J. L. Reinaud, an Arabic-speaking Dutchman (or Englishman?) sent there in 1799 by Samuel Manesty, the East India Company's Resident in al-Baṣra, to negotiate with the Imām ᶜAbd al-ᶜAzīz. Reinaud, who spent a week in the oasis, remarks on the simplicity of the ruler's establishment and the sullen hospitality of the inhabitants.

When Ibrāhīm Pas̲h̲a of Egypt advanced into Nad̲j̲d with the intention of breaking the power of Āl Saᶜūd, ᶜAbd Allāh b. Saᶜūd, who had succeeded to the rule in 1229/1814, fortified himself in al-Dirᶜiyya instead of using the superior mobility of his forces to harass the enemy's over-extended lines of communication. Ibrāhīm, establishing himself athwart the wadi at al-ᶜIlb, began a siege which lasted about six months. The attack consisted of a ponderous advance step by step down the wadi, accompanied by a piecemeal reduction of the numerous towers and barricades of the defenders scattered about the heights on either flank. Ibrāhīm moved his headquarters from al-ᶜIlb down the wadi to Ḳarī Ḳuṣayr (now known in memory of his army as Ḳurayy al-Rūm), a tributary descending from the north. Sweeping around the oasis, the invader's horse fell on the town of ᶜIrḳa farther down the wadi. Progress was impeded by the explosion of Ibrāhīm's ammunition depot, but ᶜAbd Allāh b. Saᶜūd failed to exploit this opportunity. Once a new supply of ammunition had been built up, Ibrāhīm resumed pressure on the main front and fought his way into the palm grove of Mus̲h̲ayrifa south of the tributary al-Bulayda, thus gaining access to the promontory of al-Ṭurayf from the heights to the west. A resolute offensive launched at all points brought about the surrender of the capital in D̲h̲u 'l-Ḳaᶜda 1233/September 1818. After staying in al-Dirᶜiyya a short time, Ibrāhīm returned to Egypt. On his orders the place was systemically torn down in 1234/1819. According to Captain Sadleir, a British officer who saw it almost immediately afterwards, "the walls of the fortification have been completely razed by the Pacha, and the date plantations and gardens destroyed. I did not see one man during my search through these ruins. The gardens of Deriah produced apricots, figs, grapes, pomegranates; and the dates were of a very fine description; citrons were also mentioned, and many other fruit trees, but I could only discern the mutilated remains of those I have mentioned. Some few tamarisk trees are still to be seen."

An attempt was soon made to restore al-Dirᶜiyya as the capital. As many members of Āl Saᶜūd had been killed during the siege or carried off to Cairo, Muḥammad b. Mus̲h̲ārī of the old princely house of Muᶜammar of al-ᶜUyayna, a nephew on the distaff side of the great Saᶜūd, established himself in al-Dirᶜiyya before the end of 1234/Oct. 1819 with the aim of rebuilding the oasis and making himself the head of the reform movement in Nad̲j̲d. A few months later, in 1235/1820, Mus̲h̲ārī b. Saᶜūd appeared in al-Dirᶜiyya, and Ibn Muᶜammar swore allegiance to him as scion of Āl Saᶜūd. Having once tasted power, Ibn Muᶜammar dreamed of regaining it and rebelled against Mus̲h̲ārī b. Saᶜūd. Another member of Āl Saᶜūd, Turkī b. ᶜAbd Allāh, a cousin of the great Saᶜūd, now returned to the scene after having escaped Ibrāhīm Pas̲h̲a's dragnet. Turkī sided with his relative Mus̲h̲ārī b. Saᶜūd, but the Egyptian forces got hold of Mus̲h̲ārī and he died in captivity in 1236/1821. In revenge Turkī put Ibn Muᶜammar to death. After taking al-Dirᶜiyya, Turkī also occupied al-Riyāḍ, but the Egyptian troops quickly drove him out. In 1236/1821 Ḥusayn Bey, the new Egyptian commander, ordered all the people who had settled in al-Dirᶜiyya with Ibn Muᶜammar to go to T̲h̲armadāʾ, the new Egyptian headquarters. After their departure al-Dirᶜiyya was destroyed for the second time, trees being cut down and the torch set to whatever was inflammable. In T̲h̲armadāʾ about 230 men from al-Dirᶜiyya were paraded on orders from Ḥusayn Bey and slaughtered in cold blood. The obliteration of al-Dirᶜiyya was complete. When Turkī in 1240/1824 gained strength enough to challenge the Egyptian forces, he attacked them in al-Riyāḍ, which he chose as the new capital for his realm in preference to the twice desolated home of his forefathers.

In 1281/1865 Colonel Pelly, the British Resident in the Persian Gulf, passed through al-Dirʿiyya on the way to al-Riyāḍ; the place seemed to him "utterly deserted". The modern oasis, now encroaching on the territory of its forerunner even in the hallowed precincts of al-Ṭurayf, was described by Philby after his visit in 1336/1917.

Bibliography: Ḥusayn b. Ghannām, *Rawḍat al-afkār*, Bombay n.d.; ʿUthmān b. Bishr, *ʿUnwān al-madjd*, Cairo 1373; *von Zachs Monatliche Correspondenz*, 1805 [Reinaud's journey]; J. B. L. J. Rousseau, *Description du pachalik de Bagdad*, Paris 1809; L. A. Corancez, *Histoire des Wahabis*, Paris 1810; F. Mengin, *Histoire de l'Égypte*, Paris 1823; G. Sadlier [Sadleir], *Diary of a journey across Arabia*, Bombay 1866; L. Pelly, *Report on a journey to the Wahabee capital of Riyadh*, Bombay 1866; H. St. J. B. Philby, *The heart of Arabia*, London 1922. (G. RENTZ)

DİRLİK, a Turkish word meaning living or livelihood. In the Ottoman Empire it was used to denote an income provided by the state, directly or indirectly, for the support of persons in its service. The term is used principally of the military fiefs (see TIMAR), but also applies to pay (see ʿULŪFA), salaries, and grants of various kinds in lieu of pay to officers of the central and provincial governments. It does not normally apply to tax-farms, the basis of which is purchase and not service.

Bibliography: Djaʿfer Čelebi, *Maḥrūse-i Istanbul fetḥnāmesi*, *TOEM* suppl. 1331, 17; *Koçi Bey Risalesi*, ed. Ali Kemali Aksüt, Istanbul 1939, 84; ʿAbd al-Raḥmān Wefīḳ, *Tekālīf ḳawāʿidi*, i, Istanbul 1328, 243-4; Pakalın, i, 455; Gibb-Bowen, i/1, 47, 238. (B. LEWIS)

DIŪ, an island off the southern point of Saurashtra (Sawrāshṭrā, Sōraṭh), India, with a good harbour clear of the dangerous tides of the Gulf of Cambay. Taken from the Čuḍasāmas in 698/1298-99 by the generals of ʿAlāʾ al-Dīn Khaldjī, probably lost a few years later, it was recovered by Muḥammad b. Tughluḳ in 750/1349.

In 804/1402 Muẓaffar Khān, governor for the last Tughluḳs and first sultan of Gudjarāt, built mosques, appointed ḳāḍīs and installed a garrison in Diū. By 834/1431 Diū was a flourishing port furnishing ships for the Gudjarātī fleet. From 916/1510 it became the seat of the governors of Soraṭh, of whom the most famous was Malik Ayāz. He made Diū a great emporium, built the fort and harbour defences and threw a bridge to the mainland suburb of Goglā. Though in 914/1509 his fleet and that of the Mamlūk admiral Amīr Ḥusayn were crushed in Diū harbour by the Portuguese viceroy Francisco d'Almeida, he was able to persuade Sultan Muẓaffar II to withdraw his offer of Diū made to Albuquerque in 919/1513 and to repulse Portuguese fleets in 926/1520 and 927/1521.

Malik Ayāz died in 928/1522 and was succeeded at Diū by his son Isḥāḳ. Isḥāḳ rebelled in 933/1526-27 and offered Diū to the Portuguese; their fleet was forestalled and defeated by the new governor Ḳawām al-Mulk, but next spring so crushed the Diū fleet under his son that Ḳawām al-Mulk was replaced by Malik Tūghān, second son of Malik Ayāz.

In 937/1531 Tūghān, aided by the timely arrival of two Ottoman generals, Amīr Muṣṭafā and Khwādja Ṣafar, defeated a full-scale attack by the viceroy Nuno da Cunha.

In 942/1535 Sulṭān Bahādur Shāh, a refugee from Humāyūn, and the Mughal emperor both offered Diū to the Portuguese. Nuno da Cunha chose the less formidable Bahādur Shāh with whom he signed a treaty of military aid in return for Diū on 27 Rabīʿ II 942/25 October 1535.

In 943/1536 Bahādur Shāh, having expelled the Mughals, returned to Diū. He invited Nuno da Cunha to come north, and having failed to tempt him ashore, visited his galleon. On his way back to the shore he was killed in a scuffle with the Portuguese, 3 Ramaḍān 943/13 February 1537.

The Portuguese thereupon seized the palace, treasury and arsenals in Diū, and in 943/1537 proclaimed Muḥammad Zamān Mīrzā sultan, in return for his confirmation of their position in Diū. He was defeated outside Diū, however, and in 945/1538 Khwādja Ṣafar laid siege to the island. The siege was intensified after the arrival of Khādim Sulaymān Pasha [*q.v.*], governor of Egypt, with a powerful fleet, but after three months, distrust between Ottomans and Gudjarātīs and reports of Nuno da Cunha's approach led to the break-up of the siege and the conclusion of peace, 6 Shawwāl 945/25 February 1539.

On 20 Rabīʿ II 953/20 April 1546 Khwādja Ṣafar opened a second siege of Diū which lasted seven months and cost the lives of the Khwādja and his son before the viceroy João de Castro routed the Muslim forces and lifted the siege on 19 Dhu 'l-Ḳaʿda 953/11 November 1546.

For many years the Portuguese from Diū fort controlled all seaborne traffic from Gudjarāt through a system of *cartazes* or passes. Though in 1079/1668 and 1086/1676 Diū was overrun and sacked by Arabs the Portuguese were able to use Mughal decline to extend their control over the whole island and its mainland suburb. They retained them until December 1961.

Bibliography: M. S. Commissariat, *A history of Gujarat*, i, London 1938; A. B. de Braganca Pereira, *Os Portugueses em Diu*, Bastora n.d. (J. B. HARRISON)

DIVAN [see DĪWĀN].

DIVINATION [see KIHĀNA, also DJAFR, FAʾL, IKHTILĀDJ, RAML, TAʿBĪR].

DIVORCE [see ṬALĀḲ].

DĪW (originally *dew*, Avestan *daeva*, Sanskrit *dēva*), in Persian the name of the spirits of evil and of darkness, creatures of Ahriman, the personification of sins; their number is legion; among them are to be distinguished a group of seven principal demons, including Ahriman, opposed to the seven Amshaspand (Av. *aməša spənta*, the "Immortal Holy Ones"). "The collective name of the *daiva* designates ... exclusively the inimical gods in the first place, then generally other supernatural beings who, being by nature evil, are opposed to the good and true faith .... These *daiva*, these *dēv* have become increasingly assimilated to the ogres and other demoniac beings whose origins are to be found in ancestral beliefs" (A. Christensen). In the Iranian epic Kayūmarth, the first of the civilizing kings of Īrān, and then his son and his grandson, fought the Black Dīw and his hordes; Tahmurath, his great-grandson, deprived them of power, and they taught him writing (Firdawsī, *Shāh-nāma*, Fr. tr. J. Mohl, i, 19-32); Djamshīd, son of Tahmurath (ibid., 35), controlled the *dīw*s (as Solomon did the *djinn*s in the Muslim legend [see SULAYMĀN B. DĀWŪD]); these, on his orders, constructed palaces and other buildings, then took him to heaven on a day later called *nawrūz*; under the following dynasty, that of the

Kayanids in the course of the war against the king of Māzandarān—a country frequented by the *dīws* (ibid., 421 ff.)—the hero Rustam, champion of the king Kay-Kawūs, killed the *dīw* Arzang whose hordes he dispersed, and then the White Dīw whose blood, which he carried to the king of Īrān, cured him of incipient blindness (cf. the fish-gall which restored sight to Tobit). In the *Garshāsp-nāma* (see ASADĪ) that hero, the great-grandfather of Rustam, several times opposed *dīws* of monstrous form (*Livre de Gerchasp*, tr. Massé, ii, 46, 48, 129-31, 190).

It is impossible to mention here all the *dīws* who appear in Persian literary or popular sources : most frequently the term *dīw* is juxtaposed to the Arabic epithets *ʿifrīt*, *shayṭān*, *tāghūt*; for example, the Dīws with Cows' Feet (*dīw-i gāw-pāy*: Saʿd al-Dīn Warāwīnī, *Marzubān-nāma*, ed. Muḥammad Ḳazwīnī, 79 ff.; M. Nizāmuʾd-dīn, *Introduction to the Jawāmiʿ ul-ḥikāyāt of Muḥammad Awfī*, 163). In modern popular tales *djinn* is generally substitued for *dīw*; but *dīw* remains, *e.g.*, in H. Massé, *Contes en persan populaire*, nos. 27 and 29; or it may be associated with both *djinn* and *parī* (*e.g.*, Ria Hackin and A. A. Kohzad, *Légendes et coutumes afghanes*, 17 and note). According to the Shīʿas, men, *dīws*, and *djinns* will receive reward or punishment at the day of resurrection (*Tabṣirat al-ʿawāmm*, ed. Iqbal, 210). Ḥamd Allāh Mustawfī Ḳazwīnī mentions a Dīw River (*Dīw rūd*, district of Djiruft, Kirmān), so called because of its rapid current (*Nuzhat al-ḳulūb*, tr. Le Strange, 217, 139).

Bibliography: For the various senses of *dīw* and its use in metaphor and composition: Vullers, *Lexicon persico-latinum*, and Desmaisons, *Dictionnaire persan-français*; *dīw* occurs frequently in Firdawsī (see F. Wolff, *Glossar zu Firdosis Schahname*, s.v. *dīw*, *dēv*; and *Shāh-nāma*, ed. and Fr. tr. J. Mohl, 1878, vii, index, s.v.); Spiegel, *Eranische Altherthumskunde*, 11, 126-36; A. V. W. Jackson, in *Gr.I.Ph.*, ii, 139, 165, 175, 196, 646 ff., 662; A. Christensen, *Essai sur la démonologie iranienne*, 60 (*dīws*, *parīs* and dragons in the neo-Persian epic), 67 (*dīws* in Arabic and Persian texts), 71 (*dīw* and *djinn*), 92 (conclusions). On the *dīws* in Persian secondary epics: Firdawsī, *op. cit.*, i, introd., 68 note 1, 70 note 1, 72, 77, 87). Popular beliefs: H. Massé, *Croyances et coutumes persanes*, ii, chap. XIII and index III: *dīv*. On the Armenian *dews*: Christensen, *op. cit.*, 87; F. Macler, *Les dew arméniens* (text and facsimile mss.). There are few miniatures representing the *dīws*, apart from those illustrating the epics; some confuse *dīws* and *parīs*; see E. Blochet, *Enluminures ... de la Bibliothèque Nationale*, plates 20, 64b, 75, 78a, 106b, 117a; Sakisian, *La miniature persane*, plate 78; Ph. W. Schulz, *Die persische-islamische Malerei*, plates 14 and 63, 31, 172 (*dīws* and *parī*); *Iran*: *Miniatures de la Bibliothèque Impériale de Téhéran* (New York Graphic Soc.—Unesco), plate 6 (*dīw* in the aspect of a man).

(CL. HUART-[H. MASSÉ])

DĪWĀN, a collection of poetry or prose [see ʿARABIYYA; PERSIAN LITERATURE; TURKISH LITERATURE; URDŪ LITERATURE and SHIʿR], a register, or an office. Sources differ about linguistic roots. Some ascribe to it a Persian origin from *dev*, 'mad' or 'devil', to describe secretaries. Others consider it Arabic from *dawwana*, to collect or to register, thus meaning a collection of records or sheets. (See Ḳalḳashandī, *Ṣubḥ*, i, 90; *LA*, xvii, 23-4; Ṣūlī, *Adab al-kuttāb*, 187; Māwardī, *al-Aḥkām al-sulṭāniyya*, 175; Djahshiyārī, *Wuzarāʾ*, 16-17; cf. Balādhurī, *Futūḥ*, 449). However, in administration, the term first meant register for troops (cf. Ṣūlī, *op. cit.*, 190; Kindī, *Wulāt*, 86; Balādhurī, *Futūḥ*, 454) and then any register. Only later was it used for office. It seems that the idea is foreign, but the term itself was in use earlier.

i. — THE CALIPHATE

ʿUmar I instituted the first *dīwān* (usually called *al-Dīwān*) in Islam (Djahshiyārī, *op. cit.*, 16). The sources ascribe this action to the need to organize the pay, register the fighting forces, and set the treasury in order. (Cf. Djahshiyārī, 16-17; Balādhurī, *Futūḥ*, 449-51; Maḳrīzī, *Khiṭaṭ*, i. 148; Yaʿḳūbī, *Taʾrīkh*, ii, 130; Abū Yūsuf, *Kharādj*, 25; Ṣūlī, *Adab*, 190-1; Abū Sālim, *al-ʿIḳd*, 154-5). Though some reports put this in 15 A.H., more reliable authorities prefer 20 A.H. (See Ṭabarī, iv, 162; Yaʿḳūbī, ii, 170; Maḳrīzī, *Khiṭaṭ*, i, 148-9; Balādhurī, *Futūḥ*, 450; Abū Yūsuf, 24).

This first *dīwān* was the *dīwān al-djund*. The register covered the people of Medina, the forces that participated in the conquests and those who emigrated to join garrisons in the provinces, together with their families. Some *mawālī* were included in the register, but this practice was not continued. With the names, pay and rations were indicated (Abū ʿUbayd, *al-Amwāl*, nos. 562, 567, 568; Ṭabarī, iv, 163). A committee of three genealogists carried out the registration, by tribes, and pay depended on past services to Islam and relationship to the prophet. Registration by tribes continued till the end of the Umayyad period. (Abū Yusuf, 24, 26-7; Ṭabarī, iv, 162-3; Yaʿḳūbī, *Taʾrīkh*, ii, 132; Abū ʿUbayd, *Amwāl* nos. 569, 520, 577; Balādhurī, *Futūḥ* 450 ff.; 457-9, Maḳrīzī, *Khiṭaṭ*, i, 149-50). Similar *dīwāns* (of *djund*) were set up in provincial capitals like Baṣra, Kūfa and Fusṭāṭ (cf. Djahshiyārī, 21, 23; Thaʿālibī, *Laṭāʾif*, 59). Besides, Byzantine and Sāsānian *dīwāns* of Kharādj continued to function in the provinces as before (Djahshiyārī, 38; cf. 3).

The Umayyad Period. — The *dīwān al-kharādj* of Damascus became the central *dīwān* and was now called '*al-dīwān*' to indicate its importance. It looked after the assessment and levying of land taxes. Under Muʿāwiya (d. 60/680) the *dīwān al-rasāʾil* (correspondence) took shape. The Caliph would read all correspondence and make his comments, and then the secretary (*kātib*) would draw up the letters or documents required (Djahshiyārī, 24, 34; Ḳalḳashandī, i, 92). Muʿāwiya established the *dīwān al-khātam* or 'office of the seal', where a copy of each letter or document was made and kept while the original was checked, sealed and dispatched. It was set up as a check to prevent forgery (Djahshiyārī, 25; Thaʿālibī, *Laṭāʾif*, 16; Nabia Abbott, *Ḳurrah papyri*, 14; See also Grohmann, *CPR*, iii, Bd. I/1, 17 ff). Balādhurī states that Ziyād b. Abīh, governor of ʿIrāḳ, first organized it under Persian influence (*Futūḥ*, 464). Muʿāwiya also initiated the *dīwān al-barīd* (post office), which was later reorganized by ʿAbd al-Malik (d. 86/705) (see further BARĪD).

The *dīwān al-djund* carried out, at intervals, censuses of the Arabs by tribes to keep its registers up to date. The *dīwān* of Egypt made three censuses during the 1st/7th century, the third by Ḳurra b. Sharīk in 95 A.H. (Kindī, *Wulāt* 86; Maḳrīzī, *Khiṭaṭ*, i, 151.

The *dīwān al-nafaḳāt* (expenditure), which is very probably a continuation of a Byzantine office, kept account of all expenditure (cf. Djahshiyārī, 3).

It seems to be closely linked to the treasury (*Bayt al-Māl* [*q.v.*], Djahshiyārī, 49). The *dīwān al-ṣadaḳa* was founded to assess the *zakāt* and *ʿushr* [*qq.v.*]. A *dīwān al-mustaghallāt* was established, apparently to administer government lands in cities, and buildings, especially *sūḳ*s rented to the people. The *dīwān al-ṭirāz* was responsible for making banners, flags, official costumes and some furniture. The name of its secretary was inscribed on the cloth (cf. Djahshiyārī, 60; Ṣābī, *Rasāʾil*, i, 141).

Each province had a *dīwān* of *kharādj* to which all revenue came (*li-wudjūhi 'l-amwāl*), a *dīwān* of *djund* and a *dīwān* of *rasāʾil* (Djahshiyārī, 21, 23, 24, 27, 36, 44-5, 60, 61, 63-4). The chief secretary of a *dīwān* received three hundred dirhams a month under Ḥadjdjādj (Djahshiyārī, 61).

ʿAbd al-Malik initiated the policy of Arabization in the *dīwān*s, *ṭirāz* and currency. Hitherto, the *dīwān*s of *kharādj* used local languages: Persian in ʿIrāḳ and Persia, Greek in Syria, and Coptic and Greek in Egypt, and followed previous practices of book-keeping and recording. Even local seals and dates were frequently used. Arabic forms and formulas were introduced and previous calendars adjusted to the Muslim lunar year. (See *PERF* Nos 566, 559, 566, 586, 587, 572, 589, 601; *CPR* III Bd. I, Teil I 87, Teil II c-ci). Arabic was occasionally used (the first available papyrus dates from 22 A.H. *PERF* no. 558) before it became the official language. However, local languages were occasionally used far into the 2nd/8th century (cf. Grohmann, *Étude de papyrologie*, i, 77-9; P. Lond IV, 417; Nabia Abbott, *op. cit.*, 13-14). The arabization of the *dīwān*s was effected in the Empire by stages. In 78/697 Ḥadjdjādj arabized the *dīwān*s of ʿIrāḳ (Djahshiyārī, 39; Balādhurī, *Futūḥ*, 300-1; Ṣūlī, *Adab*, 192); then in 81/700 ʿAbd al-Malik arabized the *dīwān*s of Syria (Balādhurī, *Futūḥ*, 193; Djahshiyārī, 40; Sūlī, *Adab*, 192-3). The *dīwān*s of Egypt followed in 87/705 (Kindī, *Wulāt*, 80; Ibn ʿAbd al-Ḥakam, *Futūḥ*, 122; Maḳrīzī, *Khiṭaṭ*, i, 150). Finally, the *dīwān*s of Khurāsān were arabized under Hishām in 124/742 (Djahshiyārī, 63-4). *Dhimmī*s, who were the bulk of secretaries in these *dīwān*s were to be removed, but some continued to be employed. The *mawālī* were always employed (cf. Djahshiyārī, 61, 67, 38-40, 51; Tritton, *The Caliphs and their non-Muslim subjects*, Ch. ii; Kindī, *Wulāt*, 80; Balādhurī, *Futūḥ*, 193; von Kremer, *The Orient*, 196-7).

The ʿAbbāsid period. — The ʿAbbāsids extended and elaborated the Umayyad system of *dīwān*s, and provided a central bureaucratic direction through the office of *wazīr* [*q.v.*].

Under Saffāḥ a *dīwān* for confiscated Marwānid lands was established (Djahshiyārī, 90). It probably developed into the *dīwān al-ḍiyāʿ*, which looked after caliphal domains (ibid, 277).

Under Manṣūr a temporary *dīwān* for confiscations (*muṣādara*) was created to look after confiscated properties of political enemies (Yaʿkūbī, iii, 127; *al-Fakhrī*, 115). A *dīwān al-aḥshām* is mentioned; it probably looked after people in the service of the palace (Wiet-Yaʿkūbī, *Les Pays*, 15). There was a *dīwān al-riḳāʿ* (petitions) responsible for collecting petitions to be presented to the Caliph (Ibn Ṭayfur; *Taʾrīkh Baghdād*, vi).

During the reign of Mahdī, in 162/778, we hear of *dīwān*s of *zimām* (control), one for each of the existing *dīwān*s. In 168/784 a central *dīwān*, *zimām al-azimma*, was established to control all *zimām*s. These *dīwān*s checked the accounts of the *dīwān*s, supervised their work and acted as intermediaries between single *dīwān*s and the *wazīr* or other *dīwān*s (Djahshiyārī, 146, 166, 168; Ṭabarī, x, 11; Balādhurī, *Futūḥ*, 464). The *dīwān al-maẓālim* was created to look into complaints of the people against government agents. Judges sat in this *dīwān* (*Fakhrī*, 131).

The *dīwān al-kharādj*, it seems, looked after all land taxes, while the *dīwān al-ṣadaḳa* confined its work to the *zakāt* of cattle (cf. Yaʿkūbī, *Buldān*, 11; Abū Yūsuf, *Kharādj*, 80-1). It had different sections, including one of *djahbadha* to check accounts and to examine the quality of items of revenue (Djahshiyārī, 220 1; Tanūkhī, al-Faradj, i, 39-40 [see further DJAHBADH]). Another section was the *madjlis al-ʿaskudār*, where a record was made of incoming and outgoing letters and documents with the names of people concerned. The same section is found in the *dīwān al-barīd* and in the *dīwān al-rasāʾil* (Djahshiyārī, 199; Khʷārizmī, *Mafātīḥ al-ʿulūm*, 42, 50). Letters of the *dīwān al-kharādj* were checked in the *dīwān al-khātam*, and delays here led Rashīd to permit his wazīr to send the letters directly (Djahshiyārī, 178).

Under Mutawakkil we hear of a *dīwān al-mawālī wa 'l-ghilmān*, which may be another version of the *dīwān al-aḥshām*. It was concerned with slaves and clients of the Palace whose number was very large (Yaʿkūbī, *Buldān*, 23).

The *dīwān al-khātam*, also called *dīwān al-sirr* (confidential affairs) (Djahshiyārī, 177), was of special importance because of the close relation its head kept with the Caliph (cf. Ṭabarī, x, 51-2).

In the provinces there were local *dīwān*s of *kharādj*, *djund* and *rasāʾil* which were smaller copies of the central *dīwān*s (cf. Djahshiyārī, 141, 142, 177, 220-1).

A distinguished *kātib* was sometimes appointed over more than one *dīwān* (ibid., 266; cf. 179). Until the time of Maʿmūn the salaries of *kuttāb* ranged between 300 dirhams and ten dirhams a month (Djahshiyārī, 23, 126, 131-2. Djāḥiẓ states that the highest in pay after Maʿmūn was that of *kātib al-kharādj* (cf. *Three essays*, ed. Finkel, 49). (See further KĀTIB).

*Dīwān*s reached full development during the 3rd-4th/9th-10th centuries.

The *dīwān al-kharādj* usually kept copies of records of local *dīwān*s. But by the middle of the 3rd/9th century each province had a special *dīwān* (of *kharādj*) in the capital. Muʿtaḍid combined these *dīwān*s and organized them into one *dīwān* called *dīwān al-dār* (or *dīwān al-dār al-kabīr*). Under his successor Muktafī, it was reorganized in three *dīwān*s: *dīwān al-mashriḳ* for Eastern provinces, *dīwān al-maghrib* for Western provinces, and *dīwān al-sawād* for ʿIrāḳ. ʿAlī b. ʿĪsā considered the *dīwān al-sawād* "the most important *dīwān*" (Miskawayh, *Tadjārib al-umam*, i, 152). However, under Muḳtadir a central office (*dīwān al-dār*) still remained. The three *dīwān*s remained under the *wazīr*, or one secretary next to him, and were still considered sections of the *dīwān al-dār* (Ṣābī, *Wuzarāʾ*, 123-4, 131-2, 262; Yāḳūt, *Irshād*, i, 226; ʿArīb, 42; Miskawayh, i, 151-2; Bowen, *ʿAlī b. ʿĪsā*, 31-2). It seems that '*dār*' or palace refers to the *dār al-wizāra* or ministerial residence (cf. Ṣābī, *Wuzarāʾ*, 131). The secretary of the *dīwān al-dar* was authorized to communicate directly with the *ʿummāl* (Ṣābī, *Wuzarāʾ*, 177). After the Buwayhid occupation (334/945) we hear only of *dīwān al-sawād* because of the dismemberment of the caliphate (cf. Ṣābī, *Tāʾrīkh*, 467-8).

The *dīwāns* of *kharādj* kept a record of the areas of lands, the rates of taxation in money or in kind, and the measures used. (Māwardī, *op. cit.*, 182-3; Khwārizmi, *Mafātīḥ*, 37). They received the revenue of *kharādj*, *djizya* and *zakāt* (al-Ḥasan b. ʿAbd Allāh, *Āthār al-uwal* (Bulāḳ 1295/72. Māwardī's reference to *dīwān* [*al-ʿushr* could only mean a section of this *dīwān*. Māwardī, 182).

When the *dīwān al-dār* was formed, the relevant *dīwāns* of *zimām* were combined in one (Ṣābī, *Wuzarāʾ*, 73, 84; idem, *Taʾrīkh*, 468). The *zimām* was "guardian of the rights of *Bayt al-Māl* and the people" (Māwardī, 189). It kept another copy of the documents concerning lands in the *dīwān al-kharādj* and checked assessments, orders for payments and receipts (Māwardī, 190-1). An *iḳṭāʿ* granted by Muʿtaḍid, and passed by the Wazīr and the secretary of *dīwān al-dār*, was not passed by the secretary of *dīwān al-zimām* until he checked the *iḳṭāʿ* in his records (Ṣābī, *Wuzarāʾ*, 683).

The *dīwān al-nafaḳāt* dealt with all *dīwāns*. It examined accounts of their expenses and drew its reports (al-Ḥasan b. ʿAbd Allāh, *op. cit.*, 71). By the end of the 3rd/9th century it dealt mainly with the needs of *Dār al-Khilāfa* (Mez (Arabic), i, 125; cf. Ṣābī, *Wuzarāʾ*, 11 ff.). It kept records of recurring and of current expenditures (Ṣābī, *Wuzarāʾ*, 16), and had sub-sections dealing with various heads of expenditure (cf. Mez (Arabic) i, 125-6). There was a *zimām* of *nafaḳāt*, and in 315/927 its secretary held the *zimām* of treasury stores (*khazāʾin*) as well (Ṣūlī, *Akhbār al-Rāḍī wa 'l-Muttaḳī*, 61; Miskawayh, i, 152).

The *dīwān* of *Bayt al-Māl*, also called *al-dīwān al-sāmī*, kept classified records of the sources of money and goods, coming to the Treasury, and maintained stores (*khizāna*) for the different categories of revenue, and a small *dīwān* for each, such as *dīwān al-khizāna* (for cloth and money), *dīwān al-ahrāʾ* (for cereals), and *dīwān khizānat al-silāḥ* (for arms) (al-Ḥasan b. ʿAbd Allāh, *op. cit.*, 72; cf. Ṣābī, *Wuzarāʾ*, 16). This *dīwān* checked all items of income, and all expenditure had to be passed by it. The secretary's mark on all cheques and orders of payment was required by the *wazīr* (Mez (Arabic), i, 126-7). Usually, the *dīwān* drew up monthly and yearly balance sheets. (In 315/927 ʿAlī b. ʿĪsā requested weekly sheets. Miskawayh, i, 651-2; Ṣābī, *Wuzarāʾ*, 303, 306).

The *dīwān al-djahbadha* branched off from the *Bayt al-Māl*. ([*q.v.*] See further DAFTAR, DJAHBADH). The *dīwān al-ḍiyāʿ* administered domains of the treasury (Hamadānī, *Takmila*, 18; Miskawayh, i, 21; cf. Ṣābī, *Rasāʾil*, i, 139). Yet we hear at times of more than one *dīwān* for *ḍiyāʿ*. In 325 A.H. there was a *dīwān al-ḍiyāʿ al-khāṣṣa wa 'l-mustaḥdatha* (*i.e.*, Caliphal and newly acquired domains) and *dīwān al-ḍiyāʿ al-Furātiyya* (*i.e.*, Domains on the Euphrates) (Ṣābī, *Wuzarāʾ*, 123-4; Miskawayh, i, 152).

In 304/916 Ibn al-Furāt established a *dīwān al-marāfiḳ* (lit. aids; bribes, *i.e.*, which were paid by governors, obviously from riches accumulated by dubious means). The *marāfiḳ* amounted then to 100,000 dinars per year from Syria and 200,000 dinars from Egypt. ʿAlī b. ʿĪsā forbade the *marāfiḳ* because they corrupted administration (Miskawayh, i, 44, 108, 241-2; Ṣābī, *Wuzarāʾ*, 31-2, 81).

While every *dīwān* dealing with finance had a *zimām*, all *dīwāns* of *zimām* were occasionally put in one hand. In 295/907 the *wazīr* of the one-day Caliph Ibn al-Muʿtazz put all the *uṣūl* (*dīwāns* proper) under ʿAlī b. ʿĪsā and the *dīwāns* of *zimām* under Ibn ʿAbdūn (Miskawayh, i, 60). In 319/931 the *zimāms* were put under one secretary and the *uṣūl* under the *wazīr* (Miskawayh, i, 226). This was repeated in 325/936-7 and in 327/938-9 (Ṣūlī, *Akhbār al-Rāḍī wa 'l-Muttaḳī*, 87, 147).

The *dīwān al-djund* kept a register of the forces classified according to their ranks, and their pay or *iḳṭāʿ*. It consisted of two sections, one dealing with pay (*ʿaṭāʾ* [*q.v.*]) and expenses, and the other with recruiting and classification (*taṣnīf*) (Djāḥiẓ, *Three essays*, 49; Ḳudāma calls them *madjlis al-Taḳrīr* and *madjlis al-Muḳābala*, Mez (Arabic), i, 165. See also Māwardī, 179-80). This *dīwān* had a *zimām*, called *dīwān zimām al-djaysh*, to supervise its accounts and expenditure (Miskawayh, i, 152).

The *dīwān al-rasāʾil* was directly under the *wazīr* or under a secretary. Letters and documents were drafted by the first secretary on the instructions of the *wazīr* (or Caliph) and when approved by him the final copy was made. Sometimes, a special calligrapher (*muḥarrir*) made the last copy. At intervals of three years, letters and documents were sent to the great store (*al-khizāna al-ʿuẓmā*) to be finally classified and indexed (Ḳalḳashandī, i, 96; Ibn al-Ṣayrafī, *Ḳānūn dīwān al-rasāʾil*, 94, 100-3, 108 ff., 116, 118, 144-5; Djāḥiẓ, *Three essays*, 49; Khwārizmī, *Mafātīḥ*, 50; cf. Ṣābī, *Wuzarāʾ*, 109 where *dīwān al-kharāʾiṭ* is used). The *dīwān al-faḍḍ*, probably a section of the *dīwān al-rasāʾil* in origin, received letters and documents, opened and classified them, put indications of their contents on the back, presented them to the *wazīr* and kept a record of them. (Mez (Arabic), i, 130-1; Ibn al-Ṣayrafī, *op. cit.*, 108; Tawḥīdī, *al-Imtāʿ wa 'l-muʿānasa*, i, 98). In 315, *Faḍḍ* and *Khātam* were combined in one *dīwān* (Miskawayh, i, 152).

In 301 A.H. ʿAlī b. ʿĪsā established a *dīwān al-birr*, to administer pious endowments and charitable gifts (*wuḳūf* and *ṣadaḳāt*). The revenue was spent on the holy places, in Mecca and Medina, and on volunteers in the Byzantine front (Miskawayh, i, 257; cf. 151). The *dīwān al-ṣadaḳāt* continued to levy the *zakāt* of cattle. In 315/927 one secretary looked after the two *dīwāns* of *birr* and *ṣadaḳāt* (Miskawayh, i, 152; Ṣābī, *Rasāʾil*, 111).

Mention is made of a *dīwān al-ḥaram* which looked after the affairs of the female section of the palace (Miskawayh, i, 152).

There was a *dīwān* to administer confiscated property, called *dīwān al-muṣādarīn* (Ṣābī, *Wuzarāʾ*, 306, 311). Two copies of confiscations were made, one for the *dīwān*, and the other for the *wazīr* (Miskawayh, i, 155). A *dīwān* was created to administer confiscated estates, *dīwān al-ḍiyāʿ al-maḳbūḍa* (Ṣābī, *Wuzarāʾ*, 21, 30; cf. Miskawayh, i, 84; cf. Hamadānī, *Takmila*, 83 where a *dīwān al-mukhālifīn* is mentioned, as administering the property of *Muʾnis*.

It is clear that sections of a *dīwān* were sometimes called *dīwāns*, while some *dīwāns* were short-lived and were set up for temporary needs. Besides, more than one *dīwān* were sometimes put under one secretary (cf. Ṣābī, *Wuzarāʾ*, 27, 123-4).

In the reign of Muʿtaḍid, the two days rest was resumed, Tuesday for relaxation and Friday for prayers (Ṣābī, *Wuzarāʾ*, 223).

Salaries of the heads of *dīwāns* varied. At the beginning of the 4th/10th century, the secretary of the *dīwān al-sawād* received 500 dinars per month and the secretary of *the dīwān al-ʿaṭāʾ* 10 dinars. In 314, ʿAlī b. ʿĪsā reduced salaries by one third, so the secretary of the *dīwān al-sawād* got $333^1/_2$ dinars, and the secretaries of the *dīwān al-fadd* and *dīwān al-khātam* 200 dinars each. The secretaries of the *dīwān al-mashrik* and *dīwān al-ḍiyāʿ al-khāṣṣa wa ʾl-mustaḥdatha* 100 dinars each, the secretary of the *dīwān al-dār* 500 dinars, and the secretary of the *dīwāns* of *zimām*, together with his *kuttāb*, 2700 dinars (Ṣābī, *Wuzarāʾ*, 31, 84, 177, 178, 314; cf. ibid. 20-1; Miskawayh, i, 68). Measures of economy led ʿAlī b. ʿĪsā to reduce the year to 8-10 months of pay, and this became a common practice (Ṣābī, *Wuzarāʾ*, 314; Miskawayh, i, 152.

In the Buwayhid period (334-447/945-1055), we still hear of a *dīwān al-sawād* with a secretary and an assistant-secretary (*khalīfa*), and of a *dīwān al-ḍiyāʿ* (or *al-ḍiyāʿ al-khāṣṣa*) (Ṣābī, *Taʾrīkh*, year 390 A.H., 401-2, year 392 A.H., 467-8; Miskawayh, ii, 120-1; Abū Shudjāʿ, *Dhayl Tadjārib al-umam*, 147). The central *dīwān* for finance was now called *al-Dīwān*; it was under the *wazīr* or a secretary next to him in importance (cf. Miskawayh, ii, year 338 A.H., 242, 263, 266; Abū Shudjāʿ, 143). In 389/999, a special *dīwān* was set up to levy the *ʿushr* on silk cloth made in Baghdād (Ṣābī, *Taʾrīkh*, 364). The *dīwān al-nafakāt* continued (Miskawayh, ii, 120-1) with a special *zimām* to check expenditure in accounts and in amount (cf. Ṣābī, *Tāʾrīkh*, 353, 357). However, there was the *dīwān al-zimām* to supervise financial *dīwāns* (ibid., 467-8). The *dīwān* of the Treasury was called *dīwān al-khazāʾin* or *dīwān al-khazn* (Abū Shudjāʿ, 76, Ṣābī, *Taʾrīkh*, 368; Khwārizmī, *Mafātīḥ*, 41). The head of its *dīwān* was the *khāzin* or *nāẓir*, and at times, the mint (*dār al-ḍarb*) was put in his charge (Abū Shudjāʿ, 250-1). Al-Tawḥīdī, however, mentions a special *dīwān* for the mint called *dīwān al-nakd wa ʾl-ʿiyār wa dār al-ḍarb* (*Imtāʿ*, i, 98).

The *dīwān al-djund* was divided into two *dīwāns*, one for the Daylamites and the other for the Turks (the two main elements of the army) and called *dīwān al-djayshayn* (Ṣābī, *Taʾrīkh*, 467-8). There was however one head or paymaster, called *al-ʿāriḍ* (Abū Shudjāʿ, 258).

The Fāṭimids. — Fāṭimid *dīwāns* are basically related to the ʿAbbāsid. The *dīwān al-rasāʾil* is here *dīwān al-inshāʾ*; its head is *ṣāḥib dīwān al-inshāʾ* or *kātib al-dast al-sharīf*. The detailed account of this *dīwān* given by Ibn al-Ṣayrafī shows that it was similar to the ʿAbbāsid *dīwān*. (See Ibn al-Ṣayrafī, *Ḳānūn dīwān al-rasāʾil*, ed. A. Bahjat, Cairo 1905; Maḳrīzī, *Khiṭaṭ*, ii, 244, 306; iii, 140; Ḳalḳashandī, iii, 490; i, 103; x, 310; Ibn al-Ḳalānisī, *Dhayl taʾrīkh Dimashk*, 80; Shayyāl, *al-Wathāʾiḳ al-Fāṭimiyya*, 365).

The *dīwān al-djund* was called *dīwān al-djaysh*, or *dīwān al-djaysh wa ʾl-rawātib* (office of troops and salaries). It consisted of two sections: the *dīwān al-djaysh*, under a *mustawfī*, dealing with the recruitment, equipment and inspection of the troops, and the *dīwān al-rawātib* dealing with pay. However, other references show that the two *dīwāns* were often separate, the first under *ṣāḥib dīwān al-djaysh* and the latter concerned with salaries of the military and civilians (See Maḳrīzī, *Khiṭaṭ*, ii, 242; Ḳalḳashandī, iii, 492-3, 495, cf. Ibn al-Ṣayrafī, *Ishāra*, 25, 47; Maḳrīzī, *Ittiʿāẓ*, year 542; Shayyāl, *Wathāʾiḳ*, 304). The Fāṭimids, who attached great importance to the fleet, had a *dīwān al-ʿamāʾir* to look after the construction of ships and their forces (Ḳalḳashandī, iii, 496).

Accounts of the *dīwāns* of finance are involved. The *dīwān al-madjlis* seems to have been the central bureau. It had different sections, one of which dealt with fiefs (*iḳṭāʿāt*). It was probably similar to the ʿAbbāsid *'al-Dīwān'*. It made the estimate of the budget (*istīmār*) when required, after getting estimates from all *dīwāns* (Maḳrīzī, *Khiṭaṭ*, ii, 236 ff.; i, 160-2; cf. ii, 245; Shayyāl, *Wathāʾiḳ*, 325). The *dīwān al-naẓar* had general control over the *dīwāns* of finance (*amwāl*) and over their officials. It seems to correspond to the central *dīwān* of *kharādj* of the ʿAbbāsids (cf. Shayyāl, *Wathāʿiḳ*, 304, i, Ibn al-Ṣayrafī, *Ishāra* 35; Maḳrīzī, *Khiṭaṭ*, ii, 241; Ḳalḳashandī, iii, 493). The *dīwān al-taḥḳīḳ* was linked to *dīwān al-naẓar*, but its function was to check the accounts of other *dīwāns* of finance. It is parallel to the ʿAbbāsid central *zimām* (Maḳrīzī, ii, 242; Ḳalḳashandī, iii, 493, i, 401; Ibn Muyassir, *Akhbār*, 43).

The *dīwān al-khāṣṣ* looked after the financial affairs of the palace (Maḳrīzī, *Ittiʿāẓ*, 200). The office of *waḳf* was the *dīwān al-aḥbās* (Ḳalḳashandī, iii, 494-5). The *dīwān al-mawārīth al-ḥashriyya* was instituted to administer escheated and heirless property (Ibn Muyassir, 56; Ḳalḳashandī, iii, 496).

The *Maẓālim* [*q.v.*] were presented to the Caliph or *wazīr*. There was a *dīwān al-tawḳīʿ*, with two secretaries, to deal with them (Maḳrīzī, *Ittiʿāẓ*, 307; Ḳalḳashandī, 491).

Salaries of secretaries varied. The secretary for *inshāʾ* got 150 dinars monthly, that of *naẓar* 70, of *bayt al-māl* 100, of *taḥḳīḳ* 50, and the secretaries of *djaysh*, *tawḳīʿ madjlis* and *iḳṭaʿ* 40 dinars each. Lesser secretaries got 5-10 dinars (Ḳalḳashandī, iii, 526; Maḳrīzī, *Khiṭaṭ*, ii, 243). Non-Muslims were widely employed in the *dīwāns* and this led to occasional reactions against them (cf. Ibn al-Ḳalānisī, 59; Ibn al-ʿIbrī, *Taʾrīkh*, 370; Ibn al-Ṣayrafī, *al-Ishāra*, 34, 35, 48, 53. cf. Tritton, *op. cit.*, ch. ii).

The 11th-13th centuries. — Since the Buwayhid period, the *dīwān al-rasāʾil* had been called *dīwān al-inshāʾ*, and its secretary *kātib al-inshāʾ* (Abū Shudjāʿ 153-4; Ibn al-Djawzī, *Muntaẓam*, ix, 55; x, 125; Ibn al-Fuwaṭī, *Ḥawādith*, 16; Ibn al-Sāʿī, *Djāmiʿ*, ix, 222). The central bureau was *al-Dīwān* (cf. Ibn al-Djawzī, ix, 91, 27, 28, 29, 83). It was headed by the *wazīr*, and at times by a secretary called *ṣāḥib al-dīwān* (Ibn al-Djawzī, x, 56, 165, 125). Later it was called *al-dīwān al-ʿazīz* (cf. al-Fuwaṭī, 47, 63, 88; Ibn al-Sāʿī, *Djāmiʿ*, ix, 285).

Finances were primarily the concern of *dīwān al-zimām*, which in effect carried the work of *dīwān al-kharādj*; fief farmers and governors sent revenue to it (Ibn al-Sāʿī, ix, 16). It had two sections: the main *dīwān* headed by a *kātib* (*kātib al-zimām*) (cf. Ibn al-Djawzī, ix, 150, 223, x, 27, 124) later called *ṣadr*, and the other section headed by a *mushrif* who supervised the work of the *dīwān* and the revenue (Ibn al-Sāʿī, ix, 98-9, 118; Ibn al-Fuwaṭī, 16, 62, 63). Each province (or district) had such a *dīwān* headed by a *nāẓir* and a *mushrif* (Ibn al-Fuwaṭī, 63, 101).

Al-makhzan al-maʿmūr replaced, in time, *al-makhzan* (treasury) used for *Bayt al-Māl*, and its head *ṣāḥib al-makhzan* was replaced by *nāẓir* or *ṣadr*. This *dīwān* supervised the mint also (cf. Ibn al-Djawzī, x, 24-5, 52, 125; ix, 125, 155, 216). His standing was very high (cf. Ibn al-Djawzī, ix, 203). In 594/1198 the *ṣadr* of this *dīwān* was given authority over all *dīwāns* (Ibn al-Sāʿī, ix, 250). It had many sections each headed by a *nāẓir* (for example *khizānat al-ghallāt*. Ibn al-Fuwaṭī, 7, 37. cf. Ibn al-Djawzī, ix, 83; x, 52; Ibn al-Sāʿī, ix, 103, 127. He describes the ceremony of appointment, 141). Here, again, there was a *mushrif* to supervise the work of the *makhzan*. Obviously, *ishrāf* replaces the old *zimām* (Ibn al-Fuwaṭī, 103; Ibn al-Sāʿī, ix, 20, 229).

The *dīwān al-djawālī* (*i.e.*, poll-tax) looked after assessing and levying the poll-tax. (See DJAWĀLĪ, DJIZYA). A new bureau, *dīwān al-tarikāt al-ḥashriyya*, appeared to administer heirless property (Ibn al-Sāʿī, 107; Ibn al-Djawzī, x, 68). The *dīwān al-ʿaḳār*, headed by a *nāẓir*, looked after buildings, such as shops, owned by the state (Ibn al-Fuwaṭī, 63; cf. Ibn al-Djawzī, x, 243). Building and repairs, however, were the concern of another bureau called *dīwān al-abniya* (building bureau). It had engineers and architects among its staff (Ibn al-Sāʿī, ix, 93, 184). In 635/1237-8 it participated in repairing the walls of Baghdād (Ibn al-Fuwaṭī, 111). The *dīwān al-ḥisba* was usually under the *Ḳāḍī al-Ḳuḍāt*, or under a deputy (Ibn al-Sāʿī, ix, 16; Ibn al-Fuwaṭī, 64).

Non-Muslims worked with Muslims in financial offices to the end of the Caliphate. Occasionally restrictions against them were enforced, but only temporarily. In 533/1139, Jews and Christians were expelled from *al-Dīwān* and *al-Makhzan* only to be returned after one month (Ibn al-Djawzī, x, 78). The repetition of such orders (like that of al-Nāṣir li-Dīn Allāh in 601 A.H.) shows that they were not enforced and non-Muslims continued to be employed (Ibn al-Sāʿī, ix, 162).

Bibliography: Given in the article. See further Nabia Abbott, *The Ḳurrah papyri*, Chicago 1938; *British Museum Greek Papyri IV, the Aphrodito Papyri*, ed. H. I. Bell, London 1910; *National Bibliothek Papyrus Erzherzog Rainer* Vienna 1894; *Corpus Papyrorum Raineri Archiducis Austriae III*, ed. Adolf Grohmann, 1923-4; H. F. Amedroz, *Abbasid administration in its decay . . .*, in *JRAS*, 1913, 823-42; H. Bowen, *The life and times of ʿAlī b. ʿĪsā*, Cambridge 1928; A. A. Duri, *al-Nuẓum al-Islāmiyya*, i, Baghdād 1950; R. Levy, *The social structure of Islam*, Cambridge 1957, 325 ff.; S. A. Q. Husaini, *Arab administration*, Madras 1949, 76 ff., 149 ff.; Mez, *Renaissance*, chapter VI; (Arabic tr. by A. H. Abū Rīda, 2 v., Cairo 1920-1); D. Sourdel, *Le vizirat ʿabbāside de 132/750 à 324/934*, Damascus 1961.

(A. A. DURI)

ii. Egypt.

Three periods may be distinguished in the development of the Egyptian *dīwān*, though, since continuity in administrative institutions tends to be stronger than changes of governments, there are in reality no clear cleavages: (1) the time when Egypt was a province of the great Muslim Empire (18/649-358/969); (2) the Fāṭimid caliphate (358/969-567/1171); (3) the Ayyūbid and Mamlūk period (567/1171-923/1517).

The sources for the first section are scattered remarks in the earlier and later historians and manuals for *kuttāb* as well as the growing number of Arabic papyri. For the second and third periods the manuals and encyclopaedic works for *kuttāb* provide ample materials which increase by the end of the mediaeval period; and the historians supplement the actual facts rather than the more theoretical explanations of the former. Among the latter al-Maḳrīzī's (d. 845/1442) *al-Khiṭaṭ* is of outstanding importance, as he gives a nearly continuous history of the Egyptian administration from the Muslim conquest until his own time (ed. Būlāḳ, i, 81 ff., 397 ff.; ii, 215 ff.), besides many important additions in the scattered "vitae" and the descriptions of buildings etc.

(1) The Muslims carried on the administrative practice in Egypt that the Byzantines had established with the help of the resident Christian population, even allowing them the use of the Coptic language.

Since the term *dīwān* was not in use in Egypt under the Byzantines, we may deduce that it was brought by the new masters. Severus b. al-Muḳaffaʿ (living about 1000 A.D.; see IBN AL-MUḲAFFAʿ, ABU'L-BASHAR) reports that the second governor ʿAbd Allāh b. Saʿd b. Sahl (24/644-35/656, [*q.v.*] "established the *dīwān* at Miṣr (al-Fusṭāṭ) to which all the taxes of Egypt were paid" (*History of the Patriarchs of Alexandria*, ed. C. F. Seybold 103; ed. B. T. Evetts (*Patr. Orient.* v) i, 50, quoted by N. Abbott, *The Kurra papyri*, 13, and D. C. Dennett, *Conversion and poll tax*, 74). Unfortunately the Muslim sources do not offer any confirmation either for the establishment of a central revenue office, or the use of the word *dīwān* for it at such an early time. Al-Maḳrīzī relates (*Khiṭaṭ*, i, 94, 2-10) that the governor Maslama b. Mukhlid al-Anṣārī (47/667-62/682; al-Kindī, ed. Rh. Guest 38-40; Maḳrīzī, *Khiṭaṭ* i, 301, 18-27) appointed an official to go round among the immigrant Arabs each morning to inquire about changes in their family status, or the arrival of guests, and to report it to the *dīwān*. The governor would then advise the *ahl al-dīwān* (the officials of the *dīwān*) to pay the increased pensions. This narration indicates the existence of an organized office called *dīwān*, as well as its concern with registration and the payment of pensions to the immigrant Arabs. The same use of the term *dīwān* also appears in a note by al-Kindī (ed. Guest 71; Maḳrīzī, *Khiṭaṭ* i, 94, 10-3): the first *dīwān* was established in Egypt by ʿAmr b al-ʿĀṣ, the second by ʿAbd al-ʿAzīz b. Marwān, the third by Ḳurra b. Sharīk [*q.v.*], the fourth by Bishr b. Ṣafwān. After the establishment of the fourth *dīwān* nothing worth mentioning happened except the admission of the Ḳays into the *dīwān* during the caliphate of Hishām b. ʿAbd al-Malik b. Marwān (105/724-125/743). Al-Kindī (ed. Guest 76) refers to that event in the year 109/727: 3000 families of the Ḳays were transferred to Egypt together with their *dīwān*s. These notes show that the term *dīwān* was used from an early time to denote (*a*) the pension lists of the Muslim-Arab tribes, (*b*) that these lists accompanied the tribe wherever it moved, (*c*) that consequently the *dīwān* (pension list) of the Ḳays was transferred to Egypt and there added to the other already existing *dīwān*s.

During the second half of the 1st/7th century, the use of the term *dīwān* to denote central government offices must have become more general. We read (al-Kindī, 58-9; al-Maḳrīzī, *al-Khiṭaṭ*, i, 98, 11-15) that the change-over from Coptic to Arabic in the Egyptian *dīwān*s took place in 87/705 (cf. ed. Wiet, ii, 58). This can only mean that in the above-mentioned year the term *dīwān* was already the name of the central government office at al-Fusṭāṭ. The first independent director of finances (*ʿāmil al-kharādj*) was Usāma b. Zayd al-Tanūkhī who was appointed in 96/715 by the caliph Sulaymān b. ʿAbd al-Malik on the death of the governor Ḳurra b. Sharīk. That Usāma worked with the help of a *dīwān* is shown by the report of al-Maḳrīzī (*Khiṭaṭ*, i, 77, 37-8, 3) that ʿUmar b. ʿAbd al-ʿAzīz (99/717-101/720) abolished the poll-tax for Muslims and notified the *dīwān* (*al-kharādj*?) about it. In

105/725 the governor al-Ḥurr b. Yūsuf sent officials of the *dīwān* against Coptic peasants in order to enforce the payment of higher taxes. Two years later the well-known *ʿāmil al-kharādj* Ibn Ḥabḥāb (C. H. Becker, *Beiträge*, ii, 107-10) set up lists of taxpayers which were carefully put together and provided with detailed information for the *dīwān al-kharādj* (al-Maḳrīzī, *Khiṭaṭ*, i, 74, 24 & 99, 10). *Aṣḥāb al-ahrāʾ* (officers of the government granary) are already mentioned in a papyrus dated Shawwāl 90/August-September 709; it seems likely that they were officials of the *dīwān al-ahrāʾ* listed later by al-Nābulusī (C. H. Becker, *Pap. Schott-Reinhardt* 70, 37 & 49; see below). — The *dīwān al-barīd* (*dīwān* of the post) is alleged by al-Maḳrīzī (*Khiṭaṭ*, ii, 226, 27-9; W. Björkmann, *Staatskanzlei*, 18 note 3) to have preceded the *dīwān al-inshāʾ* in early times; and A. Grohmann (*Studien z. hist. Geogr. und Verw.* 35) takes it for granted that revenue-offices with a director (*ʿāmil*) and his deputy existed in the main places of the provinces (*kūra*) besides many other offices. The existence of the *dīwān asfal al-arḍ* (*dīwān* of Lower Egypt) is proved by a papyrus dated 143/761 (C. H. Becker, *Pap. Schott-Reinhardt*, 36, note 9; A. Grohmann, *APEL* IV 143; see below).

An increase of the number of *dīwān*s can be noticed in the years shortly before the rise of the Ṭūlūnids (al-Maḳrīzī, *Khiṭaṭ* i, 107, 28-9; C. H. Becker, *Beiträge* ii, 144; A. Grohmann, *Zum Steuerwesen im arabischen Ägypten*, in *Actes d. V. Cong. Int. d. Pap.*, Brussels 1938, 132): The famous director of finances Ibn Mudabbir introduced new taxes on pasture and fishing (*marāʿī, maṣāyid*) and established a special *dīwān* for their administration. On the other hand an order of the caliph al-Muʿtaṣim terminated the pension-rights of Arab settlers and therefore presumably of the relevant *dīwān*s. The seat of the *dīwān al-kharādj* at al-Fusṭāṭ was at first a building near the mosque of ʿAmr; the *mutawallī 'l-kharadj* (inspector of finances) used to sit in public in the mosque itself in order to assess the fiefs. Aḥmad b. Ṭūlūn transferred the seat of the *dīwān* to the mosque of Aḥmad b. Ṭūlūn where it remained until the Fāṭimid period (al-Maḳrīzī, *Khiṭaṭ*, i, 82, 3-15).—A papyrus dated 301/913 describes the local tax-office as *dīwān al-kharādj* (A. Grohmann, *APEL* IV², 227). The *de facto* independence of Egypt under Aḥmad b. Ṭūlūn from the Baghdād caliphate was shown by the foundation of the *dīwān al-inshāʾ* (chancellery of state) as first head of which was appointed Abū Djaʿfar Muḥammad b. ʿAbd Kān (d. 278/868, al-Ḳalḳashandī, i, 95; W. Björkman, 18-9; Zaki Mohammad Hassan, *Les Tulunides*, 191-216 & 280-2).

(2). The Fāṭimid period. Our main sources are (*a*) for general information (1) al-Ḳalḳashandī (iii, 490-6; Wüstenfeld, 188-94); (2) al-Maḳrīzī (*Khiṭaṭ*, i, 397-402); (3) for the last decades of the Fāṭimid dynasty and the first years of the Ayyūbids Ibn Mammātī (*Ḳawānīn al-dawāwīn*, viii and ix); (*b*) for the *dīwān al-inshāʾ* especially Ibn al-Ṣayrafī's *Ḳānūn dīwān al-inshāʾ*. The reports of al-Ḳalḳashandī and al-Maḳrīzī are largely based on the lost *Nuzhat al-muḳlatayn fī akhbār al-dawlatayn al-Fāṭimiyya wa 'l-Ṣāliḥiyya* by al-Murtaḍā Abū Muḥammad ʿAbd al-Salām b. Muḥammad b. al-Ṭuwayr al-Kaysarānī, life-time unknown (Ḥādjdjī Khalīfa, (ed. G. Flügel) vi, 334, no. 13720; R. Guest, *Writers, books, etc., in the Khiṭaṭ*, in *JRAS*, 1902, 117; C. H. Becker, *Beiträge*, i, 29-30; W. Björkman, 26 note 1, 83). According to Ibn al-Ṭuwayr (al-Ḳalḳashandī, iii, 93; al-Maḳrīzī, *Khiṭaṭ*, i, 397, 32 ff.; see also al-Nābulusī, *Lamʿa* chapter iii, in Cl. Cahen, *Quelques aspects* ...., 103) the first central administrative office and the mother of all the other *dīwān*s had been the *dīwān al-madjlis* (*dīwān* of the council) in which the whole of the administration was concentrated. A number of clerks sat there in their own rooms with one or two assistants (*muʿīn*). The chief of this *dīwān* was responsible for the grant of fiefs (*iḳṭāʿāt*; C. H. Becker, *Islamstudien*, i, 226; W. Björkman, Index; Cl. Cahen, *Evolution de l'iḳṭāʿ*, in *Annales ESC* 1953), and his decisions were called *daftar al-madjlis* (record of the council). The different departments of the *dīwān al-madjlis* dealt with such topics as alms, gifts, clothing and administration of the private purse of the sultan. Our sources do not state whether that *dīwān* existed already before the Fāṭimids or when its splitting up into different independent *dīwān*s took place. But it seems probable that the *dīwān al-madjlis* was the predecessor of the *dīwān al-amwāl*, and that the *dīwān al-inshāʾ* existed side by side with it.

The following list of *dīwān*s culled from the above-mentioned sources can not claim to be a complete one. It should be kept in mind that the different offices styled *dīwān* do not rank on the same level, as *dīwān* denotes sometimes even provincial branches of central offices.

(i) *Dīwān al-inshāʾ*, or *al-rasāʾil*, or *al-mukātabāt* (chancellery of state) is subdivided into three departments: 1) *Ṣaḥābat dīwān al-inshāʾ wa 'l-mukātabāt*, or *dīwān al-naẓar* (head office or control-office). Its head was called *raʾīs* (head), or *mutawallī* (superintendent), or *ṣāḥib* (master), or *mushidd* (director), and addressed as *al-shaykh al-adjall* (excellency). His exalted position resulted from his influence with the caliph to whom he brought the papers of state and whom he advised on their answering. He was assisted, according to Ibn al-Ṣayrafī, by two high-rank officials, The other two departments of the *dīwān al-inshāʾ* were (2) the office of appeal (*tawḳīʿāt bi 'l-ḳalam al-daḳīḳ*) which dealt with the caliph's decisions about complaints which any person could bring before him during a public audience, and (3) the registrar's office (*tawḳīʿāt bi 'l-ḳalam al-djalīl*), which executed the decisions of the office of appeal, with copious legal notes to the petitioner. Other minor offices of the *dīwān al-inshāʾ* included (*a*) the bureau for correspondence with foreign princes (*mukātaba ila 'l-mulūk*), (*b*) the appointments board (*inshāʾāt, taḳlīd*), (*c*) the bureau for correspondence with high officials in the provinces and nobles (*mukātaba ila umarāʾ al-dawla wa-kubarāʾihā*), (*d*) the bureau for the letters-patent (*manāshīr*), secret decrees (*kutub liṭāf*) and copies (*nusakh*). Besides these departments four clerks of lesser rank are mentioned, who, however, do not conduct independent bureaus: the copyist (*nāsikh*), a clerk for the safe-keeping of records in systematic order so that they could be used as models for later usage, the keeper of original documents (*khāzin*) and the chamberlain (*ḥādjib*) who takes care that no unauthorized person trespasses into the presence of the chief of the *dīwān* (Ibn al-Ṣayrafī-Massé, Index; al-Ḳalḳashandī, i, 130 & iii, 490 ff.; W. Björkman 20 ff.; al-Maḳrīzī, *Khiṭaṭ* i, 402).

(ii) *Dīwān al-djaysh wa 'l-rawātib* (*dīwān* of the army and the salaries) is divided into three departments: (*a*) *dīwān al-djaysh* a kind of war office as well as military administration; its principal must be a Muslim; (*b*) *dīwān al-rawātib*, the central pay office for all receivers of salaries from the *wazīr* down to the cavalry trooper (cf. A. Mez, *Renaissance* 74-6); (*c*) *dīwān al-iḳṭā*ᶜ (*dīwān* of fiefs and pensions) for civilians, as the military personnel belonged to the *dīwān al-rawātib* (al-Ḳalḳa<u>sh</u>andī, iii, 492-3; al-Maḳrīzī, *<u>Kh</u>iṭaṭ* i, 401-2).

(iii) *Dīwān al-amwāl* (*dīwān* of finance, the treasury) was divided into fourteen departments, also called *dīwān*, which are enumerated by al-Ḳalḳa<u>sh</u>andī (iii, 493-6) and much more briefly by al-Maḳrīzī (*<u>Kh</u>iṭaṭ*, i, 400-1). Ibn Mammātī offers a list of seventeen employees of the class of civil servants (*asmā*ʾ *al-mustak<u>h</u>damīn min ḥamal al-iḳlīm*) which apparently belonged to the staff of the *dīwān al-amwāl*; but it is not always clear to which of the 14 departments these 17 groups correspond (ed. A. S. Atiya 297-306). (*a*) *Naẓar al-dawāwīn*, or *dīwān al-naẓar* (control-office of the *dīwān*). The head of it is *ex officio* the chief of the *dīwān al-amwāl*, *i.e.*, the chancellor of the exchequer. Ibn Mammātī distinguishes between the *nāẓir* of the *dīwān* (the controller, auditor) who checked and countersigned the accounts and the *mutawallī* (superintendent) who was responsible for all business (C. H. Becker, *Islamstudien* i, 170, 173; (*b*) *dīwān al-taḥḳīḳ* (*dīwān* of official enquiry (cf. Dozy s.v.) was founded by al-Afḍal b. Badr al-<u>D</u>jamālī [*q.v.*] in 501/1107-8, when a Jew and a Christian were employed as its heads; later on it was not filled for most of the time (Ibn al-Ṣayrafī/Massé 82 note 1); (*c*) *dīwān al-ma<u>dj</u>lis* (see above xxx) only administered royal gifts, alms etc.; (*d*) *dīwān <u>kh</u>azāʾin al-kiswa*, *dīwān* of the storehouses of clothing; about the numerous storehouses see the long lists in al-Ḳalḳa<u>sh</u>andī, iii, 475 ff. and al-Maḳrīzī, *<u>Kh</u>iṭaṭ*, i, 408 ff.; (*e*) *Dīwān al-ṭirāz* (*dīwān* of the embroidered garment-factories and storehouses). The *dīwān* maintained several branches at places where the factories were situated, *e.g.*, Alexandria, Damietta, Tannīs (Ibn Mammātī 330-1; A. Grohmann. *Stud. z. hist. Geogr. u. Verw.*, 44); (*f*) *dīwān al-aḥbās* (*dīwān* of endowments). Since its foundation by the caliph al-Muᶜizz in 363/974 the *dīwān* dealt with the administration of pious foundations (*waḳf* [*q.v.*]); its officials were Muslims only (al-Maḳrīzī, *<u>Kh</u>iṭaṭ*, ii, 295 ff.; Cl. Cahen, *Le régime des impôts*, in *Arabica*, iii, 24-5; (*g*) *dīwān al-rawātib* (*dīwān* of wages). It is not clear what the relation had been between this *dīwān* and the office of the same name in the *dīwān al-<u>dj</u>ay<u>sh</u>*. It seems possible that this *dīwān al-rawātib* had been a kind of predecessor to the *dīwān al-<u>kh</u>aṣṣ* (the *dīwān* of the private fund of the caliph; al-Ḳalḳa<u>sh</u>andī, iii, 495 and 457); (*h*) *dīwān al-Ṣaᶜīd* (*dīwān* of Upper Egypt); (*i*) *dīwān Asfal al-arḍ* (*dīwān* of Lower Egypt); (*j*) *dīwān al-<u>th</u>u<u>gh</u>ūr* (*dīwān* of the frontier districts). The marches of Alexandria, Damietta, Tannīs and ᶜAy<u>dh</u>āb formed an administrative unity for the purpose of levying import-taxes from the merchants at the ports (*al-<u>kh</u>ums* and *mat<u>dj</u>ar* [see MAKS]; Ibn Mammātī 325-7); (*k*) *dīwān al-<u>dj</u>awāli wa 'l-mawārī<u>th</u> al-ḥa<u>sh</u>riyya* (*dīwān* of the poll tax and estate duty of *<u>dh</u>immīs*; F. Løkkegaard, *Islamic Taxation* 51 & 140-1; C. H. Becker, *Islamstudien*, i, 172; Ibn Mammātī 306, 317-8 and 454; Cl. Cahen, *Le régime des impôts*, in *Arabica*, iii, 24; (*l*) *dīwān al-<u>kh</u>arā<u>dj</u>ī wa 'l-hilālī* (*dīwān* of the lawful and illegal taxes). F. Løkkegaard, 185-6; C. H. Becker, *Islamstudien*, i, 177-9). Ibn Mammatī enumerates several officials connected with this *dīwān*: *al-<u>dj</u>ahba<u>dh</u>* (the tax collector), *al-<u>sh</u>āhid* (the notary) who countersigned the invoices, *al-māsiḥ* (the surveyor), etc.; (*m*) *dīwān al-kurā* or *al-iṣṭiblāt* (*dīwān* of the horses or the stables); (*n*) *dīwān al-<u>dj</u>ihād* or *al-ᶜamāʾir* (*dīwān* of the holy war, or the navy). Its seat was in the dockyards at Cairo, and it served as administrative centre for the navy (Ibn Mammātī, 340-1).

(3). The Ayyūbid period. The political and religious break which the end of the Fāṭimid caliphate meant for Egypt was counterbalanced by the administrative continuity clearly demonstrated by the leading personality: the last *ṣāḥib dīwān al-in<u>sh</u>āʾ*, al-Ḳāḍī al-Fāḍil Muḥyī al-Dīn, [*q.v.*], was kept on by Saladin in the same office and later on created *wazīr*. Hence al-Ḳāḍī al-Fāḍil and his numerous pupils form a link between the two periods. As already mentioned Ibn Mammātī's *Ḳawānīn al-dawāwīn* can serve as a contemporary source for the first half of the Ayyūbid period; for the second half two other contemporary authors have come down: Ibn <u>Sh</u>ī<u>th</u> al-Ḳura<u>sh</u>ī and ᶜU<u>th</u>mān al-Nābulusī. Like Ibn Mammātī, Ibn <u>Sh</u>ī<u>th</u> al-Ḳura<u>sh</u>ī was a pupil of al-Ḳāḍī al-Fāḍil whose high esteem he gained by his skill in poetry and prose. He went to Damascus where he became the head of the *dīwān al-in<u>sh</u>āʾ* and the friend of al-Muᶜaẓẓam b. al-ᶜĀdil (d. 624/1227). *Maᶜālim al-kitāba*, being a guide to the correct form of letter-writing for clerks of the *dīwān al-in<u>sh</u>āʾ*, offers but one chapter dealing with our theme (pp. 23-32). The *dīwān al-in<u>sh</u>āʾ* is in the eyes of Ibn <u>Sh</u>ī<u>th</u> the most important government office, hence its head (*ṣāḥib al-dīwān*) should be of a moral standard that corresponds to his exalted rank and the high esteem he enjoys among his colleagues. His next subordinate to whom he forwards the answering of letters and deeds was called *mutawallī kitābat al-in<u>sh</u>āʾ*, (superintendent of the secretariat of the chancellery). Other offices enumerated by Ibn <u>Sh</u>ī<u>th</u>: *dīwān al-<u>dj</u>uyū<u>sh</u>* whose chief (*kātib al-<u>dj</u>ay<u>sh</u>*) holds a lower rank than the *ṣāḥib dīwān al-in<u>sh</u>āʾ*, and needs an account-book (*<u>dj</u>arīda*) with the names and fiefs of all the military personnel to be in a position to pay out their salaries, even if no head of the *dīwān al-iḳṭā*ᶜ should have been appointed. The *dīwān al-iḳṭā*ᶜ apparently was an independent office, whose head was of lower rank than that of the *dīwān al-<u>dj</u>ay<u>sh</u>* and both worked together with and under the control of the *ṣāḥib dīwān al-naẓar* who is the same person as the *ṣāḥib dīwān al-māl*, *i.e.*, the chancellor of the exchequer. This important appointment is carried out directly by the sultan. The assistant to the *ṣāḥib dīwān al-māl* is called *mustawfī* (bookkeeper); other ranks of the treasury include the *<u>sh</u>āhid bayt al-māl* (notary of the treasury), the *mu<u>sh</u>rif* (the supervisor), the *<u>dj</u>ahba<u>dh</u>* (the tax-collector) and the *<u>kh</u>āzin* (the recorder). Al-Nābulusī enumerates only the following *dīwān*s: (*a*) *dīwān al-<u>dj</u>uyū<u>sh</u>*, (*b*) *dīwān al-in<u>sh</u>āʾ*, (*c*) *dīwān al-aḥbās* that had grown into an independent ministry out of a branch office of the *dīwān al-amwāl* in the Fāṭimid period (above xx), (*d*) *dīwān al-māl* which is divided into two departments (i) *dīwān bi 'l-aᶜmāl* (*dīwān* for the provinces) and (ii) *dīwān bi 'l-bāb* (*dīwān* for the court). These two names and the offices are new ones; the first one seems to have taken the place of the *dīwān al-Ṣaᶜīd*, *dīwān asfal al-arḍ* and *dīwān al-<u>th</u>u<u>gh</u>ūr*; it administered the *<u>kh</u>arā<u>dj</u>ī* and *hilālī* taxes in these provinces. The *dīwān bi 'l-bāb* managed the *zakāt*, and *<u>dj</u>awālī*, and *wawārī<u>th</u>* duties as well as the control (*naẓar*) of all other treasure departments including the former *dīwān al-taḥḳīḳ*, *dīwān al-ma<u>dj</u>ālis*, etc.

A wider and vaguer use of the term *dīwān* is found in such expression of the *Lumᶜa al-ḳawānīn* as *dīwān khazā'in al-silāḥ* (*dīwān* of the arsenal), *dīwān sāḥil al-sanaṭ* (*dīwān* of the acacia-coast, Ibn Mammātī, ed. A. S. Atiya 347-8; al-Maḳrīzī, *Khiṭaṭ* ed. Wiet ii, (*MIFAO* xiii, 1913) 108 note 4), and *dīwān al-aḥrā'* (see above xxx). Al-Nābulusī also mentions the *dīwān al-zakāt*, *dīwān al-mawārīth* and *al-dīwān al-nabawī* (*dīwān* for the descendants of the Prophet) an office otherwise known as *niḳābat al-ashrāf*, whose head was called *naḳīb al-ashrāf* (syndic of the Prophet's descendants (W. Popper, *Egypt and Syria* 101, 15; W. Björkman, Index).

(4). The Mamlūk period. The administration under the Mamlūks shows an increasing influence of the military class (*arbāb* or *aṣḥāb al-suyūf*) over the civilians, the *kuttāb* (*arbāb al-aḳlām*), in many governmental departments, such as exercised by the *ustādār*, the *dawādār* [*qq.v*], etc. Ibn Khaldūn considers it as typical sign of "senility" of an epoch and a dynasty, as in such a situation "the sword" has the advantage over "the pen" (ii, 41, tr. Rosenthal ii, 47; I. Goldziher, *Ueber Dualtitel*, in *WZKM* xiii (1899), 321-9). Two reforms of administration have been tried which both affected the *dīwāns*: Sultan al-Nāṣir Muḥammad b. Ḳalā'ūn (709/1309-741/1341) abolished for the first time in 710/1310 the *wizāra* and divided its functions between four officials: *nāẓir al-māl* (controller of the exchequer), *shādd al-dawāwīn* (superintendent of the *dīwāns*), *nāẓir al-khāṣṣ* (controller of the private funds of the sultan; W. Popper, *Egypt and Syria*, 97: "controller of privy funds) and *kātib al-sirr* (secretary of state; al-Ḳalḳashandī, iv, 28; al-Maḳrīzī, *Khiṭaṭ*, ii, 227, al-Sulūk, ii, 2, 93 & 103). And again the first Circassian Mamlūk sultan, al-Ẓāhir Sayf al-Dīn Barḳūḳ (784/1382-801/1208, [*q.v.*]) strengthened the *dīwān al-khāṣṣ* by surrendering to it the administration of the *thaghr* of Alexandria (see above) and established the *dīwān al-mufrad* (*dīwān* of the special bureau) for the control of stipends, clothing of the royal Mamlūks etc., and all that at the expense of the *wizāra*. The *wazīr*, however, becomes chancellor of the exchequer and was put "in charge of collecting all the different kinds of taxes" being "the highest rank among the men who are in charge of financial matters", and thus Ibn Khaldūn explains why many Copts were chosen for that and similar appointments who are "familiar with these matters since ancient times" (Ibn Khaldūn, ii, 15 & 20; tr. Rosenthal, ii, 19 & 25. Maḳrīzī, *Khiṭaṭ*, ii, 223, 28; Gaudefroy-Demombynes, *Syria* xliii; W. Popper, *Egypt and Syria*, 96-8). (i) The *dīwān al-inshā'*, called also *kitābat al-sirr* (Maḳrīzī, *Khiṭaṭ*, ii, 225, 36 ff.; al-Ḳalḳashandī, iv, 30; al-Ẓāhirī, *zubda* 99-100) still executed many of its former functions (see above xxx). Its chief, the *kātib al-sirr*, enjoyed the highest esteem among the hierarchy of civil servants (W. Popper, *Egypt and Syria*, 97; Maḳrīzī, *Khiṭaṭ*, ii, 226, 37); but he was responsible to the *dawādār* [*q.v.*], a *ṣāḥib al-sayf*, a sign of the influence of the military caste. He had been the head of the sultan's civil cabinet who received the postbag and forwarded it to the sultan, or presented foreign ambassadors to the sovereign (al-Ḳalḳashandī, iv, 19). On the other hand the *kātib al-sirr* gradually took over the function of *ṣāḥib al-barīd*; the first holder of both offices had been Awḥad al-Dīn ʿAbd al-Wāḥid b. Ismāʿīl al-Ḥanafī (d. 786/1385; Maḳrīzī, *Khiṭaṭ*, i, 78; Abu 'l-Maḥāsin b. Taghrībirdī, *Manhal* no 1483; W. Björkman, *Staatskanzlei*, 41 & note 3). The *dīwān al-inshā'* was concerned with (*a*) correspondence (*mukātabāt*) with foreign powers as well as with the provincial authorities. Al-Ḳalḳashandī, therefore, asks for the knowledge of foreign languages among the officials of that *dīwān* such as Turkish, Persian, Greek and 'Frankish' *al-farandjiyya* (Latin?); *Ṣubḥ al-aʿshā'*, i, 165-7; Björkman, *Staatskanzlei*, 44 and note 1); (*b*) appointments (*wilāyāt*), including the oath of allegiance (*bayʿa*) and the document of investiture for the sultan's successor (*ʿahd*) as well as the governors of the provinces (*taḳlīd*) and other officials (*tafwīḍ*, *tawḳīʿ*; al-Ḳalḳashandī, i, 252; Björkman, *Staatskanzlei* 48, 52); (*c*) the royal decisions upon complaints of the common folk (*tawḳīʿāt ʿala 'l-ḳiṣaṣ*, see above, al-Ḳalḳashandī, vi, 202 ff.; Björkman, *Staatskanzlei* 52-3). (ii) *Dīwān al-djaysh*, or *dīwān al-djuyūsh al-manṣūra* administered the grant of fiefs of army personnel (al-Ḳalḳashandī, i, 102), hence sometimes called *dīwān al-iḳṭāʿ*; al-Ḳalḳashandī, iii, 457; Björkman, *Staatskanzlei* 51, note 2). Its chief, *nāẓir al-djaysh* (controller of the army-*dīwān*), often a *Ḳāḍī*, was assisted by the inspector of the *dīwān al-djaysh* (*ṣāḥib dīwān al-djaysh*) and numerous other officials called *shuhūd*, *kuttāb*, etc. (Popper, *Egypt and Syria*, 97). According to al-Ẓāhirī (*zubda* 103) the *dīwān al-djaysh* was divided into two regional sections, *dīwān al-djaysh al-Miṣrī* and *dīwān al-djaysh al-Shāmī*. (iii) *Dīwān al-khāṣṣ* gained its importance under the sultan al-Nāṣir Muḥammad b. Kalā'ūn (see above xxx; Maḳrīzī, *Khiṭaṭ* ii, 227, 10 reports its existence already under the Fāṭimids) and it grew in influence during the following decades until it reached its peak at the beginning of the reign of al-Ẓāhir Barḳūḳ in 790/1388 when it absorbed the *dīwān al-khizāna* (*dīwān* of the storehouses; Maḳrīzī, *Khiṭaṭ*, ii, 227, 15 ff.; Popper, *Egypt and Syria* 97, 4). (iv) *Dīwān al-mufrad* (*dīwān* of the special bureau) was founded by al-Ẓāhir Barḳūḳ when he replaced the *wizāra* with it (Maḳrīzī, *Khiṭaṭ*, ii, 223, 28 ff.; al-Ḳalḳashandī, iii, 457, mentions an office of that name already under the Fāṭimids). Its real head was the *ustādār* [*q.v.*], a *ṣāḥib al-sayf* who even was appointed sometimes (titular) *wazīr* (Popper, *Egypt and Syria*, 93, 9; al-Ẓāhirī, *zubda* 107, tr. 178). Under the *ustādār* the *nāẓir* (controller) of the *dīwān al-mufrad* directed with the help of a large staff the obligations of that *dīwān* such as "stipends, clothing, fodder, etc., for the Sultan's mamlūks" (Popper, 97). (v) The *dīwān al-amwāl* exercised the control of all the financial manipulations, and was responsible for the payment of salaries, and keeping of accounts (al-Ḳalḳashandī, iv, 29 ff.; Maḳrīzī, *Khiṭaṭ*, ii, 224, 7 ff.). His chief was the *wazīr*, but he, too, became more and more subordinate to the *ustādār* like the *nāẓir dīwān al-mufrad*; hence the high esteem of that office declined (Popper, *Egypt and Syria*, 96; Ibn Khaldūn, ii, 20-1; tr. ii, 25). And disastrous appointments showed the real state of affairs such as when in 868/1464 a certain "wholesale butcher", Shams al-Dīn Muḥammad al-Babāwī, was made *wazīr* and *nāẓir al-dawla*, or again in 870/1466 the "money-changer", Ḳāsim Yughayta/Shughayta, both men without education (Abu 'l-Maḥāsin b. Taghrībirdī, ed. Popper, vii, 724-5 & 738-9; tr. Popper, iv 58, 67; Ibn Iyās, unpublished pages 136, 2 & 160, 4-5). The *nāẓir al-dawla* (sometimes the vizier, sometimes working with the vizier) functioned as the head of the exchequer and under him were numerous accountants (*mustawfī*), notaries (*shāhid*), etc. As mentioned already the supervision of the *dīwān al-amwāl* extended over a number of offices called *dīwān* or *naẓar* dealing with different branches of administration, *e.g.*, *naẓar bayt al-māl* which according to Maḳrīzī no longer existed at his time (*Khiṭaṭ*,

224, 36-7), *naẓar al-mawārīth al-ḥashriyya* (control-office of heirless property; Popper, *Syria and Egypt*, 99, 17), *naẓar al-murtadjaʿāt* also called *naẓar al-sulṭān* (control-office of reclaims; W. Popper, *loc. cit.* 99, 18; al-Ḳalḳashandī, iv, 33) its head being called *mustawfī al-murtadjaʿāt*, *naẓar al-wadjh al-ḳiblī* and *naẓar al-wadjh al-baḥrī* (control-office of Upper and Lower Egypt respectively), *dīwān al-istīfāʾ* (*dīwān* for the payment of salaries), *dīwān al-aḥbās* (*dīwān* of pious foundations), *dīwān al-zakāt* (*dīwān* of alms), etc. The historians provide ample examples for the working of that complicated machinery, the disastrous effect of its inefficiency aggravated by the incessant changes of the leading personnel as well as of the rulers and the cruel arbitrary system of punishments (*muṣādara*) that accompanied every change.

Bibliography: In addition to references in the article: A recent list of publications of Arabic papyri in A. Dietrich, *Arabische Briefe aus der Papyrussamlung der Hamburger Staats- und Universitätsbibliothek*, Hamburg 1955; a list of the indispensable works of A. Grohmann in *Isl.*, xiii (1957), 2-4; A. Grohmann, *Studien zur historischen Geographie und Verwaltung des frühmittelalterlichen Ägypten*, Vienna 1959 (Ost. Akad. d. Wiss. Phil.-hist. Kl. Denkschr. 77Bd., 2. Abh.); C. H. Becker, *Beiträge zu Geschichte Ägyptens unter dem Islam*, i/2, Strassburg 1902-3; idem, *Papyri Schott-Rheinhardt*, i, Heidelberg 1906; idem, *Islamstudien*, i/2, Leipzig 1924-32; D. C. Dennett, *Conversion and poll tax in early Islam*, Cambridge, Mass., 1950 (Harvard Historical Monograph xxii); F. Løkkegaard, *Islamic taxation in the classic period*, Copenhagen 1950; Zaki Mohamed Hassan, *Les Tulunides*, Paris 1933; Cl. Cahen, *Evolution de l'iqṭāʾ du IXᵉ au XIIIᵉ siècle*, in *Annales ESC*, viii, (1953), 25-52; idem, *Le régime des impôts dans le Fayyum ayyubide*, in *Arabica*, iii (1956), 8-30; idem, *Histoires Coptes d'un cadi médiéval*, *BIFAO*, lix, (1960), 133-50; M. Gaudefroy-Demombynes, *La Syrie à l'époque des mamelouks*, Paris 1923; W. Popper, *Egypt and Syria under the Circassian Sultans 1382-1468 A.D.*, Berkeley and Los Angeles 1955 f. (University of California Publications in Semitic Philology, vol. 15 & 17); D. Ayalon, *The system of payment in Mamluk military society*, in *JESHO*, i, 37 ff. & 257 ff.; idem, *The plague and its effect upon the Mamluk army*, in *JRAS*, 1946, 67-73; idem, *Studies on the structure of the Mamluk army I*, in *BSOAS*, xv (1953), 203-28; *II*, ibid. 448-76; *III*, ibid., xvi (1954), 57-90; idem, *Gunpowder and firearms in the Mamluk kingdom*, London 1956; A. N. Poliak, *Les révoltes populaires en Égypte à l'époque des Mamlouks et leurs causes économiques*, in *REI*, viii (1934), 251-73; idem, *Feudalism in Egypt, Syria, Palestine and the Lebanon, 1250-1900*, London 1939; Ibn Iyās, Muḥammad b. Aḥmad, *Unpublished pages of the chronicle of Ibn Iyas, A.H. 857-873/A.D. 1453-1468*, Cairo 1951; Ibn Khaldūn, *Muḳaddima*, tr. F. Rosenthal. Vol. i-iii, New York 1957; Abū Bakr b. ʿAbd Allāh al-Dawādārī, *Die Chronik des Ibn Dawādārī*, ix, ed. H. R. Roemer, Cairo 1960.

(H. L. GOTTSCHALK)

iii. Muslim West.

A. So far as Muslim Spain is concerned, we do not know how much of the civil and military administration of the Visigoths, which unquestionably was influenced by the Byzantine system, was found and adopted by the first conquerors at the beginning of the 2nd/8th century.

In the 4th/10th century, in the Umayyad period, three basic *dīwāns* are known to have been in operation, corresponding with the three essential needs of a State, each directed by a special minister (*wazīr* or *ṣāḥib*). These were:

1.—The Chancellery and State Secretariat, *dīwān al-rasāʾil* (= *al-tarsīl*) *wa'l-kitāba*, which dealt with official correspondence, both incoming and outgoing, and also with the drafting of various diplomas and commissions (*sidjillāt*, *ṣukūk*).

2.—The Ministry of Finance, *dīwān al-kharādj wa 'l-djibāyāt*, *dīwān al-ashghāl* or *al-aʿmāl* (+ *al-kharādjiyya* or *al-māliyya*), *dīwān al-ḥisbān*, *dīwān al-zimām*, which was responsible for the collection of various taxes, supervision of tax-collectors, and keeping of accounts of revenue and expenditure. Connected with it by more or less direct links was the *Dīwān al-khizāna* which looked after the State's secular treasury, and separate from the *Bayt al-Māl* which was religious in character.

3.—The Ministry of the Army, *dīwān al-djaysh*, *dīwān al-djund*, *dīwān al-ʿasākir*, *dīwān ahl al-thughūr*, which had three different functions; keeping up to date the financial records of the regular army; keeping accounts and giving the army their pay (*arzāḳ*) and active service gratuities (*ʿaṭiyyāt*); distributing gifts of estates to senior officers (*iḳṭāʿāt*). But it had no share in the command of troops or direction of campaigns.

After the Umayyads, a similar tripartite organisation, though naturally on a much reduced scale, was found at the "satraps' "court (*mulūk al-ṭawāʾif*), and later at the Naṣrids'.

With regard to North Africa before the Almohad period (6th/12th century), we know practically nothing about the *dīwāns*.

In 554/1159 the Almohad ʿAbd al-Muʾmin, after imposing his authority over North Africa from Wādī Nūl to Barḳa, had a survey made of his empire, with the aim of compiling a register for the assessment of land taxes (*kharādj*), payable in kind and money; from this we can deduce that a special fiscal *dīwān* was either set up or developed.

Another Almohad, Yaʿḳūb al-Manṣūr (580-95/1184-94) introduced the practice of *ʿalāma*, the formula of authorization written in large lettering at the head of despatches and commissions, the text of which was: *wa'l-ḥamdu li-llāhi waḥdah.* At first this was inscribed by the sovereign himself; later the insertion of *ʿalāma* was entrusted to the High Chancellor. The practice was maintained by the Ḥafṣids and Marīnids, and was observed until the end of the Saʿdids. The Naṣrids alone did not adopt it.

In other respects the Almohad *dīwāns* correspond with those of the Umayyads in Spain. But the High Chancellery tended to become the *dīwān al-inshāʾ*. This organization was maintained in Ifrīḳiya by the Ḥafṣids, and in Morocco by the Marīnids. However, several *diwāns* were often put together and held simultaneously by a single statesman belonging to one or other of the great ministerial families.

From the 10th/16th century there is very little information about the operation, or indeed the existence, of *dīwāns* in North Africa. In Morocco we only know of the *dīwān al-djaysh* which included all regular troops, at first Arab and later negro (*ʿAbīd* or *Ḥarāṭīn*). As these troops (more particularly the *ʿAbīd*) had often made and deposed ʿAlawid sultans, their *dīwān* sometimes appeared to be a kind of royal Council.

After the disastrous Tetuan war (1860), sultan Muḥammad III b. ʿAbd al-Raḥmān tried to establish a modernized *dīwān al-djaysh*, but his attempt proved abortive.

Bibliography: Ibn Khaldūn, *Muḳaddima*, ed. Būlāḳ 1274, 114-20: trans. de Slane, 2nd part, 1-29; E. Lévi-Provençal, *L'Espagne musulmane au Xᵉ siècle*, 69, 128; Ibn Faḍl Allāh al-ʿUmarī, *Masālik al-abṣār*, trans. Gaudefroy-Demombynes, in the index, s.v. *Dīwān*. For Morocco under the Saʿdids and ʿAlaouits, cf. Aḥmad al-Nāṣirī, *Kitāb al-Istiḳṣāʾ*, trans. Fumey (= *Archives Marocaines*, vol. ix and x), i, 46, 66, 94, 128, 178, 239, 283; ii, 240.

B. From the Almohad period (6th/13th century), in those ports open to trade with Christian Europe (from al-Mahdiyya in Ifrīḳiya to Ceuta, and also in Almeria), the existence has been established of special offices which were subordinate to the *dīwān al-ashghāl*, and whose function was to collect tithes (*aʿshār*) and other incidental taxes (*malāzim*) which were imposed upon European importers. This sort of office was in general called simply *al-dīwān*; but more detailed titles are also encountered: *dīwān al-baḥr* and in particular *dār al-ishrāf ʿalā ʿimālat al-dīwān* "supervisory headquarters for the levying of customs-duties". The local official in charge was called *mushrif*.

To facilitate the operation of customs, and in addition to ensure the safety of Christian merchants and their merchandise, one or more entrepots (one for each nation) were situated very close to the *dīwān*; these were *funduḳ* or *ḳaysāriyya*, the eastern equivalents of which were *khān* and (*dār al-*)*wikāla*.

As an exception, offices of this sort also operated in capital cities situated inland, as for example at Tlemcen and Fez. In the latter town, the "office for the tax" levied on cloth imported from Europe which Leo Africanus (beginning of 10th/16th century) recorded as being in the *ḳaysāriyya* there must correspond with the small commercial quarter, still known today as *Ed-Dīwān*, immediately north of the present *ḳaysāriyya*.

The word *dīwān*, taken in this narrow sense (which must have been the one best known to European merchants), is evidently the origin of the Italian *dogana* and the Spanish *aduana*, and so of the French *douane*. But the loss of the *-ī-* and the addition of the final *-a* in the two first borrowings cause difficulty. In Granada (end of 9th/15th century), P. de Alcala still gave, as the Arabic translation of the Spanish *aduana*, the word *dīwên*.

However that may be, the present-day term in Morocco is *dīwāna*, perhaps influenced by the Spanish form. In the other Maghribī languages as in eastern languages, that is to say in the Arabic-speaking countries which were annexed to the former Ottoman empire, the words for "Customs" are borrowed from the Turkish *gümrük* which goes back to the Latin *commercium* through demotic Greek.

Bibliography: Ibn Djubayr, *Riḥla*, ed. De Goeje, for Alexandria (39-40) and ʿAkkā (302); De Mas Latrie, *Relations et commerce de l'Afrique septentrionale*, 1886, 166, 335; *Hespéris*, xii (1931), 162 (for Ceuta).

C. From the middle of the 10th/16th century *dīwāns* made their appearance in the Turkish principalities of Algiers, Tunis and Tripoli. At that time the word denoted a clique of senior officers who were appointed to assist and, more particularly, to supervise the leading Turkish official of the locality.

It was no doubt on the precedent of these cliques that, at the beginning of the 11th/17th century, the Moors living in the *ḳaṣaba* of Rabat set up their *Dīwān* or Council (contemporary European texts refer to them as *duan, duano, duana*), the members of which exercised supervision over the Governor.

In its present use in dialect, the word *dīwān* is sometimes applied to the "councils" which the Saints, and also *djinns*, are reputed to hold from time to time. It is partly for this reason that the word is sometimes used in the sense of "plot, cabal".

Bibliography: See the articles ALGERIA, LIBYA, TUNISIA; de Castries, *Les trois républiques du Bou-Regreg*, in *Sources inédites de l'histoire du Maroc* (Holland, 1st series, V, i-xxviii), in which the author is mistaken with regard to "douane".

In the East, special systems of writing were used in government offices, notably the *dīwānī* for chancery and diplomatic usage, and the *siyāḳ* or *siyāḳa*, including a system of numerical abbreviations, for fiscal and financial records. In the Muslim West the accountants in the financial offices made use of a series of 27 figures called *rusūm* (or *ḥurūf*) *al-zimām* "abbreviations or characters of the great book", the Byzantine origin of which is established. See also KHAṬṬ.

Bibliography: G. S. Colin, *De l'origine grecque des "chiffres de Fès"*, in *JA*, 1933, 193.

(G. S. COLIN)

iv. Īrān

The term *dīwān* was variously used to mean the central government in general, in which sense it was also more specifically known as the *dīwān-ī aʿlā*, the office or place in which government business was transacted and the "civil" administration as opposed to the "military" administration, though the dividing line between them is sometimes difficult to establish. By the mid-19th century the term *dīwān* in the sense of the central government had been largely replaced by *dawla* or *dāʾira-i dawla*. Secondly the term *dīwān* was used to mean a government department in general, in which sense it was eventually replaced by *wizāra*, *dāʾira*, and *idāra*. These *dīwāns* varied according to the exigencies of the time. The adjective *dīwānī* is similarly used. Thus, *muhimmāt-i dīwānī* meant the affairs of the central administration; *takālīf-i dīwānī* were taxes or dues (of a non-canonical nature) imposed by the *dīwān*. Applied to land *dīwānī* meant state land in contradistinction to crown land or private estates.

Barthold's statement that "throughout the whole system of the eastern Muslim political organization there runs like a red thread the division of all organs of administration into two main categories, the *dargāh* (palace) and *dīwān* (chancery)" (*Turkestan*, 227) is, perhaps, an over-simplification; there was, almost inevitably, because of the intensely personal nature of power, a tendency for the dividing line between the competence of the various officials to be a shifting one. The general tendency in the early phases of Ilkhān, Ṣafawid, and Ḳādjār rule, for obvious reasons, was for the central administration to be relatively simple and for the differentiation between the various organs of government to increase with the passage of time. This is noticeable especially in the Ṣafawid and Ḳādjār periods.

The *dīwān-i aʿlā* covered the whole field of administration; but it was concerned primarily with three aspects; the issue of diplomas and decrees; financial administration; and the administration of justice (apart from cases of personal status which came under the *sharʿi* courts). The first two fell within the purview of the *wazīr*; the last, so far as it was delegated, was delegated, not to the *wazīr*, who lacked the power to execute decisions, but rather to "military" officials. In Salḏjūḳ times the sultan or his officials as well as conducting state business in the *dīwān-i aʿlā* also held from time to time a *dīwān-i maẓālim*. Under the Tīmūrids and Ṣafawids the chief judicial official was the *dīwānbegī*, who was usually a member of the military classes. The tradition of personal administration, including the administration of justice, by the ruler continued into Ḳādjār times (Malcolm, *History*, London 1829, ii, 308), and the royal residence in which state business of all kinds was transacted by the ruler (and by the governors in the provinces) in general, and the audience hall in particular, was known as the *dīwānkhāna*.

The central administration had little influence in the field of policy or over the appointment of governors, which was in the hands of the sultan or the *shāh*. Large areas of the empire were also alienated from its control in the form of *iḳṭāʿs* or *tiyūl*s. There was, nevertheless, a remarkable continuity of administrative tradition in Persia, especially in the field of finance, which was that aspect of the central government which was most highly organized. This tradition stretches back from the mid-19th century (after which administrative changes influenced by the example of western European countries began to take place) to Ṣafawid and Tīmūrid times, and it can, in spite of certain innovations made by the Ilḵhāns, be traced back still further to the period of the Great Salḏjūḳs. That this continuity should have been preserved was, perhaps, largely due to the fact that the members of the bureaucracy were drawn almost exclusively from the settled population and served the successive dynasties. Thus, the administrative personnel of the early Ṣafawid empire was largely composed of officials who had served the preceding Turkoman dynasties; similarly the bureaucratic officials of the Ilḵhāns had served the dynasties ruling in Persia before the Mongol conquest. Equally striking is the extent to which high office under the early Ḳādjārs was held by the ministers and officials of the Zands, who had ruled before them.

The most important official of the central administration was the *wazīr* [q.v.]. His power was delegated to him by the ruler, and might, and sometimes did, range over the whole field of government, "civil", "military", and religious. The personal factor was of immense importance in deciding the extent of his authority and influence. For a brief period under the early Ṣafawids the chief official of the state came to be known as the *wakīl* [q.v.], the term *wazīr* being used mainly for the head of a department or ministry and for the head official of the provincial administration under the governor. In the later Ṣafawid period the chief official of the central government was called the *wazīr-i aʿẓam* and had the title *Iʿtimād al-dawla*; under the Ḳādjārs the chief minister, who was called the *ṣadr-i aʿẓam*, also sometimes bore this title.

In Great Salḏjūḳ times the wazīrate was the keystone of the central administration; the *wazīr*, when he was at the height of his power, supervised all aspects of the administration over which the central government had control, including especially finance. Sources of revenue were in some measure regulated by him; and his main business was to increase the revenue. The principal *dīwān*s under him were the *dīwān al-inshāʾ wa ʾl-ṭughrāʾ* (sometimes known as the *dīwān-i rasāʾil*), which dealt with incoming and outgoing correspondence, and the *dīwān al-zimām wa ʾl-istīfāʾ* (also known as the *dīwān-i ishrāf*), which dealt with financial affairs. It is not without interest that two of the main departments of the central government in the 19th century were under the *munshī al-mamālik* and the *mustawfī al-mamālik* respectively. The *dīwān al-zimām wa ʾl-istīfāʾ* was divided into two main sections, one under the *mustawfī al-mamālik* and the other under the *mushrif al-mamālik*. Their relative importance varied. In post-Salḏjūḳ times the two offices tended to be independent, the former being concerned with revenue matters and the latter with inspection and control. The main object on which the revenue was expended was the army; it therefore followed that even when the revenue was alienated in the form of assignments (*iḳṭāʿs*) from the control of the central government the records of these transactions should have been kept in a department of the central government, the *dīwān-i ʿarḍ* (cf. *ʿAtabat al-kataba*, ed. ʿAbbās Iḳbāl, Tehrān 1950, 39-40, 76, and see DAFTAR).

After the reign of the first three sultans the importance of the *wazīr* declined relative to that of the *mustawfī* [q.v.]. Faḵhr al-Mulk b. Niẓām al-Mulk, the *wazīr* of Barkyāruḳ, was, for example, overshadowed by the *mustawfī* Madjd al-Mulk al-Balāsānī (Bundārī, *Dawlat al-Salḏjūḳiyya*, Cairo 1318, 79). Further, whereas in the early period there was no intermediary between the sultan and the *wazīr*, in the later period the *wakīldār* and *amīr ḥādjib* were interposed between them (Bundārī, 86, 107, 175; Ibn al-Athīr, xi, 59); and as the wazīrate decreased in influence there was a tendency for the ruler to deal with the heads of the various *dīwān*s directly and not through the *wazīr* (cf. Rashīd al-Dīn, *Djāmiʿ al-tawārīkh*, B.M. Add. 7628, f. 251a). This is not to say that in the early period all *dīwān* business invariably went through the *wazīr* or that in the later period the reverse was the case.

In addition to the two major *dīwān*s of the central government there were various *dīwān*s which dealt with special aspects of financial affairs and land, such as the *dīwān-i khāṣṣ* (concerned with crown lands) and the *dīwān-i awḳāf* (*ʿAtabat al-kataba*, 33, 52 ff.). The pattern of the central government was to some extent repeated in the provinces. The governor had his *dīwān*, known sometimes as the *dīwān-i ayālat* (cf. *ʿAtabat al-kataba*, 79). There was a *dīwān-i istīfāʾ* in the principal districts, for example in Marw and Bisṭām (*ʿAtabat al-kataba*, 56, 46); and a number of *dīwān*s dealing with various aspects of the financial administration. Thus in Rayy Ḳiwām al-Dīn Ināndj Ḳutlugh Bilgā, who was governor on behalf of Sandjar, was ordered in his deed of appointment to hold the *dīwān-i ʿamal* and the *dīwān-i shihnagī* in his own residence (*sarāy*) (*ʿAtabat al-kataba*, 73). Similarly the document appointing Tādj al-Dīn Abu ʾl-Makārim *raʾīs* of Māzandarān on behalf of Sandjar laid down that he should hold the *dīwān-i muʿāmilāt wa ḳismāt* in his own residence (*ʿAtabat al-kataba*, 26). Cases concerning the levy of dues, public contraction, and taxation were apparently in some cases referred to the *dīwān-i riyāsat* (A. K. S. Lambton, *The administration of Sanjar's empire*, in *BSOAS*, 1957, xx, 386). The extent to which the heads of these various *dīwān*s had freedom to appoint and dismiss their subordinates probably varied. Muʿīn al-Dīn, who was appointed *shiḥna* of Djuwayn by Sandjar, was given freedom to dismiss his subordinates but was instructed to confirm the appointment of the *kadkhudā* of the *dīwān* ('*Atabat al-kataba*, 61). There are also cases recorded of Saldjūk women having *dīwān*s (cf. '*Atabat al-kataba*, 61; Khʷāndamīr, *Dastūr al-wuzarā³*, Tehrān, 190).

With the Mongol invasion of Persia there was to some extent a break with tradition; much of the earlier administrative structure nevertheless remained, or was revived after the adoption of Islam by the Ilkhāns; and the officials of the bureaucracy and the religious institution with their various *dīwān*s were again found alongside the officials of the "military" government. The foremost minister of state continued to be known as the *wazīr*, or, sometimes, in his position as the representative of the ruler as the *nā³ib* (Spuler, *Mongolen²*, 282). There was, however, a tendency to remove financial affairs from the direct supervision of the *wazīr* and to entrust these to an official known as the *ṣāḥib dīwān*, who tended at times to overshadow the *wazīr*. It seems not unlikely that the Ilkhāns intended in this way to lessen the likelihood of the *wazīr* gaining an undue ascendancy. Djuwaynī as *wazīr* shared power with Madjd al-Mulk Yazdī, the *mushrif al-mamālik*, for several years from 677/1279; and from 699-718/1300-18 there were joint *wazīr*s at the head of the administration. In this, however, the Ilkhāns may have been merely following the example of earlier rulers in Central Asia (cf. Pritsak, *Die Karachaniden*, in *Isl.*, xxxi/1, 24). This practice of appointing two officials to hold office jointly was subsequently adopted on various occasions by the Ṣafawids. When Rashīd al-Dīn was appointed *ṣāḥib dīwān* in 699/1299-1300 he was charged with the general supervision of the kingdom, especially the tax administration, and among other things crown lands, the appointment of the officials of the bureaucracy, the post (*yām*), and the development of the country. (Waṣṣāf, Bombay 347). Under the *ṣāḥib dīwān* was the *mustawfī al-mamālik* and various departments dealing with different aspects of the finances, including a *dīwān-i khāliṣāt* (Waṣṣāf, 349).

Under the Tīmūrids, although there was an attempt in theory to reaffirm the principles of *sharʿī* government and to return to the traditional forms, in practice the distinction between the "civil" and "military" branches of the administration, which broadly coincided with the dichotomy between Turk and Tādjīk (*i.e.*, Persian) was clearly marked. Under Ḥusayn Bāykara the *dīwān-i aʿlā*, the supreme organ of government was divided into the *dīwān-i buzurg-i amārat* (under the *dīwānbegī*), which dealt with military affairs, and the *dīwān-i māl* (under a *wazīr*), which was concerned with "civil" affairs (Roemer, *Staatsschreiben der Timuridenzeit*, 169 ff.).

It seems likely that the administrative pattern of the Ilkhānid empire was inherited by the Ḳara Ḳoyunlu (Minorsky, *The Aq-Qoyunlu and land reforms*, in *BSOAS*, 1955, xvii/3), but little is known of the details of the organization of their various *dīwān*s apart from their tax administration. There is mention of the *dīwān-i tawādjī* and the *dīwān-i parwānačī* (Minorsky, *Persia in A.D. 1478-90: An abridged translation of Faḍlullāh b. Rūzbihān Khunjī's Tārīkh-i ʿalam-ārā-yi amīnī*, London 1957, 28, 101). For a survey of the administrative organization of the Ilkhāns in Persia see I. H. Uzunçarşılı, *Osmanlı devleti teşkilâtına medhal*, Istanbul 1941, specially 187 ff.

Information on the central administration is considerably fuller for Ṣafawid times than for the preceding periods. It is, however, extremely difficult to establish a dividing line between the various aspects of the *dīwān-i aʿlā*, which was both the royal court and the central government; similarly there was not always a clear demarcation of the functions of the members of the bureaucracy, the military officials, and the officials of the religious institution. The internal organization of the *dīwān-i aʿlā* was under the *ishīk-aḳāsī-bāshī* (*Tadhkirat al-Mulūk*, ff. 7b, 13a ff.). The master of ceremonies of the Ḳādjār court was similarly designated. There appears to have been something in the nature of a state council, to which certain members of the *dīwān-i aʿlā* belonged; this council seems to have been outside the traditional pattern of the central administration. Alessandri states that Ṭahmāsp held a daily council attended by twelve sultans (*i.e.*, provincial governors and therefore members of the military classes) and those of his sons who were at court (*A narrative of Italian travels in Persia*, Hakluyt, 220-1). The functions of this council appear to have been purely advisory. The *Tadhkirat al-Mulūk* states that the *ḳūrčī-bāshī*, *ḳullar-āḳāsī*, *ishīk-āḳāsī-bāshī*, *tufangčī-āḳāsī*, *wazīr-i aʿzam*, *dīwānbegī*, and *wāḳiʿa-niwīs* "had from early times belonged to the council of amīrs of the *umarā-yi djānkī* and at the end of the reign of Shāh Sulṭān Ḥusayn the *nāẓir*, *mustawfī al-mamālik*, and the *amīr-shikār-bāshī* were also, on some occasions, included in the council. If the council met on the subject of sending an army commander (*sipahsālār*) to some outlying part of the empire, the presence of the *sipahsālār* at the *djānkī* was a necessary condition" (ff. 7b-8a). Minorsky considers the institution to be of Mongol or Tīmūrid origin. Chardin maintains that there was no council of state similar to the European institution; Sanson, on the other hand, states that all decisions were taken in the King's Council (*Tadhkirat al-Mulūk*, 113-4). Under the Ḳādjārs the *djānkī* does not appear to have been a regular part of the central government administration, but to have been a tribal council dealing with affairs concerning the Ḳādjār tribe, which presumably normally sat under the *ilkhānī*. Malcolm mentions a case of treason by a "high noble" of the Ḳādjār tribe being tried about 1808 by a *djānkī* (*History*, ii, 327n.).

The highest official of the *dīwān-i aʿlā* under Ismāʿīl and Ṭahmāsp was the *wakīl*, who was the *alter ego* of the shāh as the *wazīr*, in his heyday, had been of the sultan; his competence extended virtually over the whole field of the administration. The use of the term *wakīl* for the chief official of the *dīwān-i aʿlā* appears to have died out in the middle of the 10th/16th century and to have been replaced by the term *wazīr-i aʿzam*, who held the title of Iʿtimād al-dawla. After 920/1514 his office tends to be referred to as the *niẓārat-i dīwān-i aʿlā*, *niẓārat-i dīwān*, or *dīwān-i wizāra* (R. M. Savory, *The principal offices of the Safawid state*, in *BSOAS*, xxiii/1, 1960, 91-105 and xxiv/1, 1961, 65-84). In due course an elaborate system of administrative procedure was evolved. As head of the *dīwān-i aʿlā* the *wazīr* confirmed official appointments; documents concerning these matters and the pay of officials went through an office called the *daftarkhāna-i humāyūn-i aʿlā* under a special *wazīr*. Documents concerning the pay of the "standing army" (*ḳūrčī*s, *ghulām*s, *tufangčī*s, and members of the *topkhāna*) went through the relative department (*sarkār*), which was under a *wazīr* and *mustawfī* and staffed by secretaries belonging to the *dīwān* (*Tadhkirat al-Mulūk*, f. 58 ff.). Letters of appointment and salary grants for "civil" and military officials as well as being sealed by the *wazīr-i a'zam* were also sealed by the *lashkar-niwīs* of the *dīwān-i a'lā*, who was also *wazīr* of the department (*sarkār*) of the eunuchs, falconers (*ḳūsh̲čiyān*), ushers (*yasāwulān*), and doorkeepers (*ḳāpūčiyān*) (*Tad̲h̲kirat al-Mulūk*, f. 65a ff.).

Among his other duties as head of the *dīwān-i a'lā* the *wazīr* checked the legality of the proceedings of officials and presided over the financial affairs of the state (*Tad̲h̲kirat al-mulūk*, 115); this last was, in effect, his most important function. Like his predecessors in the wazīrate in earlier times, it was his duty to exert himself in increasing the revenue (*Tad̲h̲kirat al-mulūk*, f. 8b). The financial administration was divided into two main departments, the *dīwān-i mamālik* under the *mustawfī al-mamālik* and the *dīwān-i k̲h̲āṣṣa* under the *nāẓir-i buyūtāt* (also called the *nāẓir-i buyūtāt-i sarkār-i k̲h̲āṣṣa*). The exact relationship of the *wazīr-i a'zam* to the *nāẓir-i buyūtāt* and the nature of his control over the *dīwān-i k̲h̲āṣṣa* are not entirely clear. The budget of the *buyūtāt* was apparently submitted to the *wazīr-i a'zam* (*Tad̲h̲kirat al-Mulūk*, f. 16a). Under the *mustawfī al-mamālik* there were various officials in charge of different tax offices (*daftar*), parallel offices in many cases being in existence to deal with the relevant matters according to whether they were situated in *mamālik* or *k̲h̲āṣṣa* areas. These included a *daftar-i mawḳūfāt* (*Tad̲h̲kirat al-Mulūk*, f. 71a) and a *daftar-i baḳāyā* (Iskandar Mun̲s̲h̲ī, 'Ālam-ārā, 765). A special department, the *sarkār-i fayḍ āt̲h̲ār*, at Mas̲h̲had administered the *waḳf*s of the shrine of the Imām Riḍā ('Ālam-ārā, 258 *bis*, 654). General supervision of *waḳf*s was carried out by the *dīwān al-ṣadāra* under the *ṣadr-i a'zam* (H. Busse, *Untersuchungen zum islamischen Kanzleiwesen*, Cairo 1959, 204). Some of the provincial *ṣadr*s also had *dīwān*s or *sarkār*s (cf. a diploma dated A.H. 1077 for the *mustawfī* of the *mawḳūfāt* of Yazd, *Dj̲āmi'-i mufīdī*, B.M. Or. 210, ff. 168b-170b; and Busse, 132).

The *dīwān-i mamālik* was concerned with the administration of provinces and districts which were administered by governors and were alienated from the direct control of the central government. The *dīwān-i k̲h̲āṣṣa* was concerned with areas directly administered by the central government under *wazīr*s. The extent of the indirectly administered areas relative to the directly administered varied (*Tad̲h̲kirat al-mulūk* 24 ff., A. K. S. Lambton, *Landlord and Peasant in Persia*, Oxford 1953, 108). With the increase in the extent of the *k̲h̲āṣṣa* which took place under S̲h̲āh Ṣafī the importance of the *dīwān-i k̲h̲āṣṣa* was presumably enhanced; the *nāẓir-i buyūtāt-i sarkār-i k̲h̲āṣṣa* is mentioned as the greatest of the offices of the *dīwān* in the time of S̲h̲āh Ṣafī, (*Dj̲āmi'-i Mufīdī*, f. 338b-339a). The *mustawfī* of the *dīwān-i k̲h̲āṣṣa* appears to some extent to have been subordinate to the *mustawfī al-mamālik* and hence to the *wazīr-i a'zam* (*Tad̲h̲kirat al-mulūk*, ff. 27b-28a). Iṣfahān, as the capital, enjoyed, perhaps, a special position. The *sarkār-i fayḍ āt̲h̲ār* and the *sarkār-i intiḳālī* dealt with special categories of land (presumably *waḳf*s and land resumed by the state); the administration of crown lands appears to have been under the *wazīr* of Iṣfahān. All three departments were under the general supervision of the *wazīr-i a'zam* of the *dīwān-i a'lā* (*Tad̲h̲kirat al-Mulūk*, ff. 71a ff.).

The *buyūtāt*, i.e., the Royal Household, was administered by the *wazīr-i buyūtāt* under the general supervision of the *nāẓir-i buyūtāt*. It was divided into a number of offices (*daftark̲h̲āna*) and workshops (*kārk̲h̲āna*), each under a *ṣāḥib dj̲am'* and a *mus̲h̲rif*,

the former responsible for its general activities and the latter for administrative routine (*Tad̲h̲kirat al-Mulūk*, 140).

The department corresponding to the former *dīwān-i ins̲h̲ā'* was known under the Ṣafawids as the *dār al-ins̲h̲ā'* and was under the *mun̲s̲h̲ī al-mamālik* (*Tad̲h̲kirat al-Mulūk*, ff. 39b-40a; Busse, 59 ff.).

The *dīwān-i a'lā* under the Ḳādj̲ārs was broadly speaking modelled on the practice of the Ṣafawids. As the royal court its procedure from the time of Fatḥ 'Alī onwards was elaborate. The administration of the royal household, which comprised a number of offices which were collectively known as the *buyūtāt*, was, however, more clearly separated from the *dīwān-i a'lā* than had previously been the case. So far as the *dīwān-i a'lā* in the central government was concerned, its organization was less elaborate than in Ṣafawid times; and there was no longer a distinction between the *mamālik* and *k̲h̲āṣṣa* departments. Āḳā Muḥammad K̲h̲ān apparently attended to the details of the administration largely in person; the rule of Fatḥ 'Alī was also personal, but during his reign the administration was expanded. The chief official of the *dīwān-i a'lā* was the *ṣadr-i a'zam*; his power varied with the relative energy, indolence, and competence of the s̲h̲āh. Under Āḳā Muḥammad K̲h̲ān the *ṣadr-i a'zam*, Ḥādj̲dj̲ī Ibrāhīm, is said to have presided over all the departments of state (Malcolm, ii, 308-9). The two most important departments were under the *mustawfī al-mamālik* and the *lashkar-niwīs* respectively; the latter was concerned with the pay and levy of the military forces, which was closely bound up with the tax administration. Under Fatḥ 'Alī the office of *mun̲s̲h̲ī al-mamālik* again became important. The internal administration of these various departments appears to have been of a relatively rudimentary nature under the early Ḳādj̲ārs. Morier, writing in 1809, states that the offices of the ministers and secretaries of state were situated in the s̲h̲āh's palace where they assembled every day to be ready whenever the s̲h̲āh might summon them (*A journey through Persia*, London 1812, 216); but in fact the ministers often had to set up their departments wherever they happened to be. Āḳā Muḥammad K̲h̲ān and Fatḥ 'Alī both spent much of their time on military expeditions and in camp (as also did their successors); and they were normally accompanied on these occasions by their ministers. In such circumstances government departments had to function without any elaborate administrative apparatus. Malcolm states that "the accounts of the receipts and disbursements throughout the ecclesiastical, civil, revenue and military branches of the government, are kept with much regularity and precision" (*History*, ii, 310). In fact, these records were largely treated as the personal property of the officials who made them; and so far as they concerned the revenue assessment, by the middle of the century they often bore little relation to conditions as they were. The *dīwān* of the *mustawfī al-mamālik* was organized on a geographical basis, the tax assessment and records of a given area being placed in charge of a *mustawfī*, who was known as the *mustawfī* of that district. Separate departments dealt with crown lands (*k̲h̲āliṣa*) and *waḳf*s and other special aspects such as arrears (*baḳāyā*).

The provincial administration was delegated to the governor, who often attended to the details of this in person. In the case of a powerful provincial governor, especially if he were a Ḳādj̲ār prince, the provincial court tended to be a replica (on a smaller scale) of the *dīwān-i aʿlā*. The most important provincial official was the *wazīr*, who was normally appointed by the *dīwān-i aʿlā*. His main responsibility was to ensure that the governor remitted the provincial tax quota to the central government.

Bibliography: see authorities quoted in the text. (ANN K. S. LAMBTON)

v. India

The term *dīwān*, meaning a government department, appears to have been first introduced into India during the rule of the Ghaznawids with the seat of their administration at Lahore. Ariyaruk, the Commander of India appointed by Sultan Maḥmūd, had all the wealth which be had accumulated during his viceroyalty in India confiscated on his dismissal and recall to Ghazna. A great part of this fortune must have come from *kharādj* (land-revenue) for whose collection and disbursement there must have existed a separate department. Narshakhī (cf. *Taʾrīkh-i Bukhārā*, ed. Schefer, 24) mentions the existence of no less than 10 *dīwāns* under the Ghaznawids, including the *dīwān-i wizāra* or revenue department (cf. also Abu 'l-Faḍl Bayhaḳī, *Taʾrīkh-i Bayhaḳī*, ed. Said Naficy, Teheran 1319 s/1940, 53, 180, 792). Bayhaḳī was himself on the staff of the *dīwān-i risāla* (*dīwān-i inshāʾ*) during the rule of Masʿūd b. Maḥmūd. Moreland's contention [see Bibl.] that the word *dīwān* was first used by Indian historians to denote a department or a ministry in the 7th/13th and 8th/14th centuries is, therefore, erroneous. The term was in use much earlier.

During the Sultanate period its use was mainly confined to the minister for revenue, who was ordinarily the *wazīr* himself, and his department, the revenue ministry. A new department, on its creation, was also known as the *dīwān*, such as the *dīwān-i risāla* or the *dīwān-i maẓālim*. During the same period the word was also used for the military department, which too was under the control of the *wazīr*, although under the Ghaznawids, this department was known separately as the *dīwān-i ʿarḍ*.

This system of government seems to have been fully developed during the Sultanate period as we find quite a number of departments in existence. These included: (i) *dīwān-i wizāra*, which dealt mainly with finance (cf. Shams Sirādj ʿAfīf, *Taʾrīkh-i Fīrūz Shāhī* (Pers. text, 419-20); (ii) *dīwān-i ʿarḍ*, the military department, under the *ʿĀriḍ-i Mamālik* who was sometimes the Sultan himself; (iii) *dīwān-i Risāla*, which dealt with religious matters, endowments, and grants of *madad maʿāsh*, and which was controlled by the *ṣadr al-ṣudūr*, who also combined the office of the *ḳāḍī-i mamālik* or Chief Judge of the realm; (iv) *dīwān-i inshāʾ*, the same as the *dīwān-i khātam*, first established by Muʿāwiya b. Abī Sufyān, or *dīwān-i risālat*, under the Ghaznawids. It dealt with all official correspondence, a prototype of the modern, but more complex and highly developed, secretariat; (v) *dīwān-i maẓālim*, which dealt with courts of *Maẓālim* [*q.v.*] jurisdiction, the *sharīʿa* courts being administered by the *dīwān-i ḳaḍāʾ*, under the *ṣadr al-ṣudūr* or the *ḳāḍī al-ḳuḍāt*; (vi) *dīwān-i ishrāf*, under the *mushrif* or the accountant-general, which dealt with the accounts received from the provinces or other departments. These were audited by the sister department controlled by the *mustawfī al-mamālik*. During the reign of Fīrūz Tughluḳ (cf. ʿAfīf, Pers. text, 409-10) the *mushrif* dealt with the income and the *mustawfī* with the expenditure only. Fīrūz Shāh Tughluḳ had also set up a separate *dīwān*, under a *mutaṣarrif*, for the royal *kārkhānas* (factories), whose accounts were, however, audited by the *dīwān-i wizāra*. There occurred a slight change in the designation of the *wazīr* during the Mughal period, who came to be known as the *dīwān-i kull* and his colleagues in the same department as mere *dīwāns*, with such other appellations as denoted their functions and duties such as the *dīwān-i tan* or the *dīwān-i khāliṣa*.

Another significant change under the Mughals was that the head of the department of revenue and finance came exclusively to be known as the *dīwān*. During the reign of Akbar the word *wazīr* in this sense was seldom used, having been replaced by the term *dīwān*, which had come to denote a person rather than an institution or a government department. However, in the reign of his son, Djahāngīr, the old practice was revived and the term *wazīr* again came into vogue. It was during the reign of Shāhdjahān that the *wazīr* came to be known as the *dīwān-i kull* and his other colleagues in the department as *dīwāns*, with the addition of such epithets as showed their designations. For some time the two words *wazīr* and *dīwān* remained almost synonymous, and even in private business, a person who managed a high officer's or a wealthy person's financial affairs came to be known as a *dīwān*. Dayānat Khān was the *dīwān* of Mumtāz Maḥall in the first year of Shāhdjahān's reign (*Maʾāthir al-umarāʾ*, Eng. tr. by A. H. Beveridge, i, 484). Even to this day male members of some families, both Hindū and Muslim, proudly carry the hereditary honorific of *Dīwān*, once borne by some illustrious ancestor.

The revenue ministry, under the *dīwān*, was consequently known as *dīwānī*, a term which was destined to survive in the *dīwānī* (civil) and *fawdjdārī* (criminal) courts of the British days, which still form a part of the legal structure of Pakistan.

During the Mughal period the *dīwān* performed multifarious duties. He was not only responsible for the disposal of revenue papers, but also drafted urgent royal letters and *farmāns*. He also granted interviews to the agents of the princes, provincial governors and high nobles. The mounting of the guard, under the command of a nobleman, round the imperial palace at night was also a part of his duty. He had to submit revenue collection and expenditure returns to the emperor who was in this way kept informed of the finances of the State. As an administrative functionary, he allocated duties to all high dignitaries on first appointment, received regular reports from them, and also had powers to grant leave. He was also in charge of all official records which were deposited in his office (for a detailed list of these records, see Jadūnāth Sarkār, *Mughal administration*[4], Calcutta 1952, 29-32).

His colleagues, the *dīwān-i khāliṣa* and the *dīwān-i tan*, had separate duties to perform. The former, *inter alia*, examined the accounts prepared by the revenue department, checked up the *ṭūmār-i djamʿ* (record of total standard assessment) of the *khāliṣa* (Crown lands), prepared the estimates of expenditure (*barāwurd*) on the troops and the emperor's personal staff and retinue. The *dīwān-i tan* was responsible, *inter alia*, for the submission of all matters to the emperor, which dealt with the *djāgīrs* or cash disbursements including the drafting of *farmāns*, memoranda, *parwānas* etc. for the grant of *madad maʿāsh* to scholars, the *ʿulamāʾ*, *ḳāḍīs* etc.

The office of the provincial *dīwān* was next in

importance to that of the *sipāhsālār* only. The provincial *dīwān* having been appointed directly by the emperor on the recommendation of the central *dīwān*, was, in no way subordinate to the governor. He obtained his orders from the central *dīwān* and was only responsible to him; the idea was to keep the *fiscus* independent of gubernatorial control and thus minimize dangers of misappropriation, defalcation and embezzlement of public money as well as of the insurrection of the *ṣūbadārs*. The *Mir'at-i Aḥmadī* (Baroda 1928, i, 163-70) quotes a *farmān* of Akbar giving in a comprehensive form the duties of a provincial *dīwān*, who according to this *farmān*, should be a "trustworthy and experienced person who has already served some high noble in the same capacity". His duties entailed heavy responsibilities as he was supposed to scrutinize the accounts of the revenue collectors (*ʿāmils*) and report corrupt ones for dismissal. He sometimes also acted as the provincial auditor.

As time passed, the powers of the *dīwān* increased greatly. Not only could he make grants up to 99,000 *dāms* but could also sign the deeds for the grant of *dj̲āgīrs* and *a'imma* lands, which technically were defective and void without the Imperial seal or the signature of the central *dīwān*. In spite of this the *dīwān* did not enjoy a rank equal to that of the *ṣūbadār* who, as head of the executive, enjoyed a higher status, prestige and honour in the public eye than the 'chancellor of the exchequer'.

The provincial *dīwān* was assisted in his duties by a *pīs̲h̲kār* or personal assistant, who was appointed by an imperial *sanad* under the seal of the central *dīwān*, a *dārūg̲h̲a* or office superintendent, a *mus̲h̲rif* and a *taḥwīldār-i daftark̲h̲āna* (record-keeper), all holding a *manṣab*. Among the lower staff the *mirdhā* (process-server) occupied an influential position in the public eye and was generally held in great respect.

In 11th-12th/17th-18th centuries the term *dīwānī* came to be used only for the revenue administration in contrast to the *niẓāmat* or *fawdj̲dārī*, terms which denoted the general administration, concerned primarily with the maintenance of law and order. Even to this day civil courts in the Indo-Pakistan sub-continent are known as *dīwānī* courts, as distinguished from the criminal or *fawdj̲dārī* courts. In this sense the word owes its origin to the appointment of the East India Company as the *dīwān* of the Province of Bengal. The management of the Company found it desirable to establish their own court of justice which they named the *Dīwānī ʿAdālat*, *i.e.*, court of the *dīwān*.

In some of the former princely States in India, now merged with the Indian Union, the chief minister was known as the *Dīwān*. The word also formed part of two of the titles *Dīwān Ṣāḥib* and *Dīwān Bahādur*, conferred by the British Indian Government; their use was, however, restricted to South Indian celebrities.

The use of the word in expressions like the *Dīwān-i ʿāmm* (Hall of Public Audience) and the *Dīwān-i k̲h̲āṣṣ* (Hall of Special Audience) in the Mug̲h̲al forts at Lahore, Agra, Dihlī, and elsewhere, is a faint echo of its original meaning. In the houses and mansions of the great or well-to-do people, in days gone by, there was a separate apartment known as the *Dīwān-K̲h̲āna*, equivalent to the modern drawing-room, but reserved exclusively for the use of the male members of the family or their guests and visitors.

Bibliography: In addition to the authorities quoted in the text: S. M. Jaffar, *Mediaeval India* . . . (The Ghaznawids), Peshawar 1940, 242-54; idem, *Some cultural aspects of the Muslim rule in India*, Peshawar 1950, 25-9, 51, 110; Jadunath Sarkar, *Mughal administration*[4], Calcutta 1952, 25-40, 53-4; Ishtiaq Husain Qureshi, *The administration of the sultanate of Delhi*[2], Lahore 1944, index; Ibn Hasan, *The central structure of the Mughul empire*, London 1936 (Urdū transl. entitled *Dawlat-i Mug̲h̲liyya kī Hay'at-i Markazī*, Lahore 1958), index; P. Saran, *The provincial government of the Mughals*, Allāhābād 1941, 189-97; R. P. Tripathi, *Some aspects of Muslim administration*, Allāhābād 1936; W. H. Moreland, *The agrarian system of Moslem India*[2], Allāhābād n.d., xiv-xv, 78, 109, 133 ff., 148, 197, 271; Rieu, iii, 926a, (gives a list of *wakīls*, *dīwāns*, etc., from the reign of Akbar to that of Muḥammad S̲h̲āh).

(A. S. Bazmee Ansari)

vi. — Ottoman. [see dīwān-i humāyūn].

DĪWĀN al-S̲H̲ŪRĀ [see madjlis al-s̲h̲ūrā].

DĪWĀNĪ [see k̲h̲aṭṭ].

DĪWĀN-I HUMĀYŪN, the name given to the Ottoman imperial council, until the mid 11th/17th century the central organ of the government of the Empire. Evidence on the *dīwān* under the early Sultans is scanty. According to ʿĀs̲h̲ıḳpas̲h̲azāde (ch. 31; ed. N. Atsız, *Osmanlı tarihleri*, Istanbul 1949, 118; German trans. R. Kreutel, *Vom Hirtenzeit zur hohen Pforte*, Graz 1959, 66), the practice of wearing a twisted turban (*burma dülbend*) when attending the *dīwān* was introduced during the reign of Ork̲h̲ān. Probably a kind of public audience is meant. The Egyptian physician S̲h̲ams al-Dīn b. Ṣag̲h̲īr, sent by Barḳūḳ to treat Bāyazīd II, describes how the Ottoman ruler used to hold public audience in the morning and dispense justice to the people (quoted by Ibn Ḥadjar in the *Inbā' al-g̲h̲umr, anno* 805; Şevkiye Inalcık, *Ibn Hacer'de Osmanlı'lara dair haberler*, in *AÜDTCFD*, vi/3, (1948), 192, 195; cf. Tas̲h̲köprüzāde Kemāl al-Dīn Meḥmed, *Ta'rīk̲h̲-i Ṣāf*, Istanbul 1287, 34). ʿĀs̲h̲ıḳpas̲h̲azāde (ch. 81; text 155-6, tr. 134) speaks of the pas̲h̲as holding a *dīwān* when Meḥemmed I was dying, and of a daily *dīwān* at the Porte (*ḳapu*), and again (ch. 122; text 190-1, tr. 195) of a similar *dīwān* of the pas̲h̲as on the death of Murād II. From these, and parallel narratives in Nes̲h̲rī and other early chroniclers, it may be inferred that by the early 9th/15th century it had become a regular practice for the Sultan to preside over a council of the pas̲h̲as, and that during the interregnum between the death of a Sultan and the arrival of his successor the *dīwān* could, exceptionally, be held by the pas̲h̲as on their own. Meḥemmed II seems to have been the first Sultan to give up the practice of presiding over the meetings of the *dīwān*, relinquishing this function to the Grand Vizier. According to an anecdote recorded by later historians the reason for this was that a peasant with a grievance came to the *dīwān* one day and said to the assembled dignitaries: "Which of you is the Sultan? I have a complaint". The Sultan was offended, and the Grand Vizier Gedik Aḥmed Pas̲h̲a suggested to him that he might avoid such embarrassments by not appearing at the *dīwān*. Instead, he could observe the proceedings from behind a grille or screen (Solaḳzāde, *Ta'rīk̲h̲*, 268; Muṣṭafā Nūrī Pas̲h̲a, *Netā'idj al-wuḳūʿāt*[2], i, Istanbul 1327, 59; ʿAbd al-Raḥmān S̲h̲eref, *Topḳapu Sarāy-i humāyūnu*, in *TOEM*, i/6, 1911, 351). Whatever the truth of the anecdote, the withdrawal of the Sultan is confirmed by the *Ḳānūn* of Meḥemmed II, which states clearly that the Sultan sits behind a screen (*dj̲anāb-i s̲h̲erīfim pes-i perdede oturup* (*ḳānūnnāme* 23)). This practice continued until the time of Suleymān Ḳānūnī, who ceased to attend the meetings of the *dīwān* even in this form (Koču Bey, *Risāle*, ch. 2, ed. A. K. Aksüt, Istanbul 1939, 20-3; German trans. by W. F. A. Behrnauer in *ZDMG*, xv, (1861), 275 ff. cf. Hammer-Purgstall, *GOR*, iii, 489; *Histoire*, vi, 282).

Constitution and procedure. The *Ḳānūn* of Meḥemmed II, which purports to set forth the practice of the Sultan's father and grandfather, lays down the constitution of the *dīwān-i humāyūn* in some detail. The *dīwān* met every day; those attending were, in order of precedence, the Grand Vizier, the other viziers, the ḳāḍīʿaskers, the defterdārs, and the nis̲h̲ānd̲j̲ī. If the nis̲h̲ānd̲j̲ī had the rank of vizier or beylerbey, he sat above the defterdārs; if that of sand̲j̲aḳ-beyi, below the defterdārs. When they came, they were received with obeissance by the Chief Pursuivant (*Čaʾus̲h̲-bas̲h̲ī*) and by the Intendant of the Doorkeepers (*Ḳapīd̲j̲īlar Kâhyasī*). Four times a week a meeting was held in the audience chamber (*arḍ odasī*), attended by the viziers, ḳāḍīʿaskers, and defterdārs, at which the Sultan was present behind a grille (*ḳānūnnāme* 13, 23). In former times, it had been the practice of the Sultans to dine with the viziers, but Meḥemmed had abolished this (ibid. 27).

In the course of the 10th/16th century the membership of the *dīwān* was somewhat extended. A document of 942/1536, quoted by Ferīdūn (*Muns̲h̲eʾāt al-Selāṭīn*², i, 595) authorizes the Beylerbey of Rumeli to attend the *dīwān* but excludes the Beylerbey of Anatolia. Later, in recognition of the growing importance of naval affairs, the Ḳapudān Pasha was added. The Ag̲h̲a of the Janissaries, however, was only a member if he held the rank of vizier. Besides the full members of the *dīwān*, a number of other dignitaries were in attendance, though they had no seats in the council-chamber and did not participate in the deliberations. Among these were the Chief Secretary (*reʾīs al-kuttāb* [*q.v.*]), head of the chancellery; the Chief Pursuivant; the Intendant of the Doorkeepers, who maintained liaison between the Grand Vizier and the Sultan; the financial secretaries (see MUḤĀSABA); the *dīwān* interpreters (see TERD̲J̲UMĀN); the police chiefs [see S̲H̲URṬA], and a number of other palace and administrative officers who might be called upon to carry out the decisions of the *dīwān*, with their assistants, clerks, and messengers.

During the 10th/16th century, the *dīwān* met regularly four times a week, on Saturday, Sunday, Monday and Tuesday. Its proceedings began at daybreak, and dealt with the whole range of government business. The morning was normally devoted to public sessions, and especially the hearing of petitions and complaints, which were adjudicated by the relevant member of the *dīwān*, or by the Grand Vizier himself. About noon, the mass of petitioners and other outside visitors withdrew, and lunch was served to the members of the *dīwān*, who then proceeded to discuss what business remained. Withers (after Bon) makes it clear that the council was purely consultative, the final responsibility resting with the Grand Vizier: "Dinner being ended, the chief Vizier spendeth some small time about general affairs, and taking counsel together (if he pleaseth and thinks it fit) with the other Bashaws; at last he determineth and resolveth of all within himself, and prepareth to go in unto the King (it being the ordinary custom so to do, in two of the four Divan days, *viz.* upon Sunday, and upon Tuesday) to render an account briefly unto his Majesty of all such businesses as he hath dispatched" (ed. Greaves 1747, 616). Besides the regular *dīwān* meetings, certain special *dīwān*s were held. These were 1) the *ʿulūfe dīwānī* or *g̲h̲alebe dīwānī*, held quarterly for the distribution of pay and supplies to the Janissaries and other 'slaves of the gate' (see ḲAPU-ḲULU), and also for the reception of foreign ambassadors, 2) the *ayak dīwānī*—foot *dīwān* —an extraordinary or emergency meeting presided over by the Sultan or army-commander. It was so-called because all present remained standing. (On these two, see I. H. Uzunçarşılı, *Osmanlı devleti teşkilâtından kapukulu ocakları*, i, Ankara 1943, index, and idem, *Osmanlı devletinin saray teşkilâtı*, Ankara 1945, 225-9).

Place of meeting. The *dīwān* building, usually known as *dīwānk̲h̲āne*, stands in the second court of the Topḳapu palace, between the Middle gate (*Ortaḳapu*) and the Gate of Felicity (*Bāb al-seʿāde*). The present structure was erected during the reign of Suleymān Ḳānūnī, by order of the Grand Vizier Ibrāhīm Pas̲h̲a, and repaired in 1792 and 1819. In earlier times the *dīwān* met in another building, later referred to as the 'old *dīwānk̲h̲āne*'. The council chamber was known as *ḳubbe-altī*, 'under the dome', and those viziers who had the right to attend the *dīwān* were called 'the dome viziers' (see further WAZĪR). Overlooking the council-chamber was a screened enclosure, known as the *ḳaṣr-i ʿādil* or *ḳafes*, from which the Sultan could observe the proceedings. This was directly connected with the *ḥarem* quarters. Adjoining the *dīwānk̲h̲āne* were the offices and quarters of the various viziers, and the office of the Grand Vizier, known as *Divit* (= *dawāt*) *odasī* (cf. DAWĀDĀR). (On these buildings, see ʿAbd al-Rahmān S̲h̲eref, *Topḳapu-Sarāy-i humāyūnu*, in *TOEM*, i/6, 1911, 329-64, especially 350 ff.).

Administration. The main branches of the central administration, functioning under the *dīwān-i humāyūn*, were as follows :

(1) *Dīwān ḳalemi*, also called *Beylik* or *Beylikd̲j̲i ḳalemi*, the central chancery office, headed by the *Beylikd̲j̲i*, the senior chancery officer under the *reʾīs al-kuttāb*. This office was responsible for drafting, issuing, and filing copies of all edicts, regulations (*Ḳānūn*), decrees and orders other than those concerned with finance. Treaties, capitulations, privileges and exequaturs issued to foreign powers were also, for a time, the concern of this department.

Besides the chancery, there were two departments dealing with questions of personnel, *viz*:

(2) the *Taḥwīl ḳalemi*, also called *nis̲h̲ān* or *kese ḳalemi*, which issued orders and kept records on appointments to the rank of vizier, beylerbey, sand̲j̲aḳ-beyi, and *mawlā—i.e.*, *ḳāḍī* of a *wilāyet*, as well as appointments and transfers to *timar*s and *ziʿāmet*s [*qq.v.*] (see further TAḤWĪL).

(3) the *Ruʾūs ḳalemi*, which was concerned with appointments to all ranks and posts other than those covered by the *Taḥwīl ḳalemi*, the emoluments of which came from treasury or *waḳf* funds. These included religious as well as civil and military posts.

Apart from these three main offices, there were two other branches, headed by the *Tes̲h̲rīfātd̲j̲ī* and the *Waḳʿanuwīs* [*qq.v.*], dealing respectively with ceremonial and with historical records. A later addition was the office of the *Āmedī* or *Āmeddji* [*q.v.*], who headed the personal staff of the *Re'īs al-kuttāb*. This was concerned with the conduct of relations with foreign states, and with the maintenance of liaison between government departments and the palace.

Some of the staff employed in these offices received salaries; others, of lower status, were paid with *tīmārs* and *zi'āmets*. The latter could be promoted to salaried appointments. The more important established officials had the rank of *khwādjegān* [*q.v.*]. Their subordinates were called *khalīfe*.

Decline of the *Dīwān-i humāyūn*. The growing importance of the Grand Vizierate as against the palace led to the practice of the *Ikindi dīwānī*, a meeting held in the Grand Vizier's residence after the afternoon prayer (*ikindi*), to deal with unfinished business left over from the *dīwān-i humāyūn*. This body came to meet five times a week, and gradually took over a large part of the real work of the *dīwān-i humāyūn*. The transfer of the effective control and conduct of affairs from the palace to the Grand Vizierate was formalized in 1054/1654, when Sultan Meḥemmed IV presented the Grand Vizier Derwīsh Meḥmed Pasha with a building that served both as residence and as office (see BĀB-I 'ĀLĪ and PASHA ḲAPUSU). To this new institution most of the administrative departments formerly under the *dīwān-i humāyūn* were, in time, transferred. By the 18th century the *dīwān-i humāyūn* had dwindled into insignificance. A new form of *dīwān* appeared under the reforming sultans Selīm III and Maḥmūd II, who established special councils to plan and apply the reforming edicts (see TANẒĪMĀT). These in time evolved into a system of cabinet government.

Bibliography: an early statement, from an Ottoman official source, on the constitution and functioning of the *dīwān-i humāyūn* will be found in the Ḳānūn of Meḥemmed II, dealing with the officers and organization of the government (*Ḳānūnnāme-i āl-i 'Othmān*, ed. Meḥmed 'Ārif, *TOEM* Supplement 1330 A.H. 13 ff.; 23 ff. The existing copy contains revisions dating from the reign of Bāyazīd II). This description may be supplemented from information in the Ottoman chronicles (notably the *Hasht Bihisht* of Idrīs Bidlīsī [*q.v.*], reign of Meḥemmed II), and the foreign sources (*e.g.*, G. M. Angiolello [Donado da Lezze] *Historia turchesca*, ed. I. Ursu, Bucarest 1909, 130 ff.). The subsequent development of the institution may be traced in later *ḳānūns* (*e.g.*, that of 1087/1676, published in *MTM*, i/3, (1331 A.H.), 506 ff.) and later foreign descriptions (*e.g.*, the very full account written by the Venetian Bailo Ottaviano Bon in 1608, *Il Serraglio del gran Signore*, in N. Barozzi and G. Berchet, edd., *Relazioni degli stati europei lette al Senato...*, 5 ser., i, Venice 1866 (English adaptation by Robert Withers, *A Description of the Grand Seignor's Seraglio, Purchas' Pilgrims* ii/II, London 1625, repr. Glasgow 1905, ix, 322ff.; also in John Greaves, *Miscellaneous Tracts...*, ii, London 1650 and later reprints), P. Rycaut, *History of the present state of the Ottoman Empire*[4], London 1675, Bk i, ch. xi, 77 ff. From about the middle of the 10th/16th century, the development and functioning of the *dīwān-i humāyūn* and the various administrative departments and services which it controlled can be followed in great detail in the records preserved in the Ottoman archives. A classification and description will be found in Midhat Sertoğlu, *Muhteva bakımından başvekâlet arşivi*, Ankara 1955, 13-14 (see also BAŞVEKÂLET ARŞIVI). The fullest general description of the *dīwān-i humāyūn* and its administration is that of I. H. Uzunçarşılı, *Osmanlı devletinin merkez ve bahriye teşkilâtı*, Ankara 1948, 1-110. Briefer accounts will be found in Djewdet[2], i, 43 6 (summarizing Wāṣif); D'Ohsson, *Tableau général de l'empire othoman*, vii, Paris 1824, 211-32; Hammer-Purgstall, *Staatsverfassung*, 412-36; idem, *GOR*, index; A. H. Lybyer, *The government of the Ottoman Empire in the time of Suleiman the Magnificent*, Cambridge Mass. 1913, 187-93; Zinkeisen, *Geschichte des osmanischen Reiches*, iii, Gotha 1855, 117-25; Gibb-Bowen, i/1, 115 ff. and index; Pakalın, i, 462-6, including a passage from the unpublished *Ḳawānīn-i teshrīfāt* of Nā'ilī 'Abd Allāh Pasha (d. 1171/1757); Sertoğlu, *Resimli Osmanlı tarihi ansiklopedisi*, Istanbul 1958, 78-81. On the early Ottoman and Saldjūḳid background, see I. H. Uzunçarşılı, *Osmanlı devleti teşkilâtına medhal*, Istanbul 1941, 42-4, 95-8; V. A. Gordlevsky, *Izbrannie sočineniya*, i, Moscow 1960, 166-77; Mustafa Akdağ, *Türkiye'nin iktisadî ve içtimaî tarihi*, i, 1243-1453, Ankara 1959, 217-23, 323-33.

(B. LEWIS)

DĪWĀNIYYA, a town of central 'Irāḳ, on the Ḥilla branch of the Euphrates, (at 44° 55′ E, 32° N.), midway between Ḥilla and Samāwa. With a population of some 12,000, almost all Shī'ī Arabs, it is the headquarters of a *liwā'* (total population, 508,000 according to the 'preliminary figures' of the 1957 census with the dependent *ḳaḍās* of Samāwa, 'Afak, Shāmiyya, Abū Ṣukhayr, and Dīwāniyya itself; the tribes included in the *liwā'* are among the largest and least amenable of the middle Euphrates, and whether in Turkish times or the British occupation (notably in 1336/39, 1919/20) or under the 'Irāḳ government (notably in 1354/57, 1935/38), have frequently embarrassed the government by faction and disobedience calling for punitive expeditions; the influence of the Nadjaf *'ulamā'* is strong. The town, built mainly on the left bank and with only small date-gardens, is now extending to the right and has been greatly modernized in recent years with improved streets, bazaars and public buildings. A new steel bridge has replaced the ancient pontoons, and passable roads and the 'Irāḳ Railways and a landing-ground serve the town and district. It is an important military station.

Dīwāniyya under its present name dates only from about 1271/1854, when it was formed as a settlement of the Khazā'il *shaykhs* for the accomodation of the office and reception room (*dīwān*) of their tax-gatherers. The Turkish government adopted it soon afterwards as headquarters of a *ḳaḍā*, and merchants, officials, and a military and police garrison augmented the existing matting dwellings and mud-huts, and inaugurated the modern town.

In site, however, and as an important middle-Euphrates tribal, administrative and intermittently military station, it seems to have continuity with the Ḥiska of earlier (post-medieval) centuries. It and its district were disorganized and largely deserted by the tribesmen and cultivators when the Euphrates increasingly abandoned its eastern (Ḥilla) channel from 1298/1880 onwards in favour of the Hindiyya channel; but conditions were restored by the erection of the Hindiyya barrage in 1330/1912.

Bibliography: S. H. Longrigg, *Four centuries of modern 'Iraq*, Oxford 1925, and *'Iraq 1900 to*

1950, Oxford 1953; ʿAbd al-Razzāḳ al-Ḥasanī, *al-ʿIrāḳ Ḳadīmᵃⁿ wa Ḥadīthᵃⁿ*, Sidon 1947.
(S. H. Longrigg)

DIWRĪGĪ or DIFRĪGĪ, now DIVRIGI, a small town in modern Turkey, situated on the confines of Armenia and Cappadocia on one of the routes leading from Syria and Upper Mesopotamia to the Anatolian plateau. Through it runs a torrent which flows into the Çaltı Irmak, a tributary of the Kara Su (northern Euphrates). This chief town of a *ḳaḍāʾ* in the province of Sivas, situated among market gardens and orchards which make it a pleasant resort—archaeological remains alone testify to its former prosperity in the Middle Ages—is now no more than a very scattered village, part of which is deserted (in about 1930 it had less than 4000 inhabitants). It stands at the bottom of a fertile valley, the old quarters of the town clustered together on the right bank, along with the ruins of the citadel.

The ancient Byzantine Tephrikè, which must not be confused, as is sometimes done, with the Nikopolis of Pompey, and which Arab authors of the early centuries knew by the name of al-Abrīk or al-Abrūk, "capital of the Paulicians" (G. Le Strange, *Al-Abrīk, Tephrikè*, in *JRAS*, 1896, 733-41, and Pauly-Wissowa, s. v. *Tephrikè*), known to have been long occupied by Manichaean sectarians who were persecuted by the emperors of Constantinople and aided by the caliphs of Baghdād. But the most important period in its history followed the annexation of the country to Islam, shortly after the battle of Manāzgird in 464/1071 and the partial conquest of Armenia and Asia Minor by the Saldjūḳid sultan Alp Arslan. The upper Kara Su region, with Erzindjan as its capital, was in fact entrusted to a Turcoman officer serving under this prince, Amīr Mangudjak, whose possessions were thus adjacent to those of Malik Dānishmend who had settled in Kayseri and Sivas, and a second small Mangudjakid independent state was subsequently organized around Divrigi until, in 625/1228, it was compelled to recognize the suzerainty of the more powerful Saldjūḳids of Rūm. It was at this period that the chief monuments in the town were erected, with inscriptions revealing the genealogy of this branch of the Mangudjakids (see table in *CIA*, *Asie mineure*, i, 90). Then the history of Divrigi, which though sacked on several occasions, by the Mongols among others, still continued to depend upon minor local dynasties, is consequently somewhat obscure. For a time reunited with the Ottoman possessions by Bāyezīd I in 801/1397, it was recaptured by the Mamlūks who have left many epigraphic traces of their occupation and, along with the other Taurus frontier-zones which for a time protected their empire, from the Divrigi territory they created the third of the great Armenian districts forming the mountain marches of the province of Aleppo, connected with Malaṭya and Cairo by a post road. Finally, in the reign of Selīm I in 922/1516, Divrigi was to become Ottoman for several centuries.

The dismantled castle which dominates the town was probably founded in ancient times, but the present fabric apparently dates entirely from the Middle Ages (inscriptions of 634/1236-7, 640/1242-3 and 650/1252). The mosque of *amīr* Shāhanshāh or Ḳalʿe Djāmiʿi, built in 576/1180-1, is still well-known, but the most remarkable building in the town, and indeed one of the most curious Turkish monuments in the whole of Anatolia is, beyond question, the architectural group comprising the great mosque and the adjoining hospital, built in 626/1228 for Aḥmad Shāh, grandson of the previous sovereign, and his wife Tūrān Malik by the skill of a native craftsman of Akhlāṭ. The rich decoration of the three doorways is no less effective than that of the vaults which have been used to cover these buildings. One must search far in the East to find parallels to these features. Various mausolea of the same period, aedicules built on an octagonal base, crowned with a pyramid of stone and containing a domed burial chamber, are also noteworthy, in particular the tomb of Shāhanshāh, known by the name of Sitte Malik Türbesi, and the tomb of the *amīr* Ḳamar al-Dīn, both of which were built in 592/1192-6. On the other hand, it is profitless to seek to identify in present-day Divrigi the site of the strange place of pilgrimage, venerated both by Muslims and by Christians and housing in a grotto the mummified bodies of "martyrs of the time of ʿUmar b. al-Khaṭṭāb", which the shaykh ʿAlī al-Harawī, whose account has been reproduced by Yāḳūt, had the opportunity to visit at al-Ubrūḳ, doubtless the present locality of Ubruk which appears on maps between Konya and Ak Saray.

Bibliography: Ibn Rusta, 93; Masʿūdī, *Murūdj*, viii, 74; *al-Tanbīh*, 151, 183; Maḳdisī, *Livre de la création*, ed. trans. Cl. Huart, iv, 54; Harawī, *K.al-ziyārāt*, ed. trans. J. Sourdel-Thomine, Damascus 1953 and 1957, 59-60 (trans., 133-5); Yāḳūt, i, 87-8; Ibn Bībī, ed. Houtsma, iv, 210, 318; Ḥamd Allāh Mustawfī, *Nuzha*, 96; Ḥādjdjī Khalīfa, *Djihānnüma*, 624; Ewliyā Čelebi, *Siyāḥatnāme*, iii, 210-4; Le Strange, 119; M. Gaudefroy-Demombynes, *La Syrie à l'époque des Mamelouks*, Paris 1923, 98; J. Sauvaget, *La poste aux chevaux dans l'empire des Mamelouks*, Paris 1941, 56; Cuinet, *Turquie d'Asie*, i, 685. For inscriptions and monuments see: M. van Berchem and H. Edhem, *CIA*, *Asie mineure*, i, 55-110; A. Gabriel, *Monuments turcs d'Anatolie*, ii, Paris 1934, 169-89 and pl. lxii-lxxix; J. Sauvaget, *Décrets mamlouks de Syrie*, in *BEO*, xii, 1947-8, 52-5 (decree of 891/1486-7); *İA* s. v. (art. by Besim Darkot). (J. Sourdel-Thomine)

DIYA, a specified amount of money or goods due in cases of homicide or other injuries to physical health unjustly committed upon the person of another. It is a substitute for the law of private vengeance. Accordingly it corresponds exactly to the compensation or *wergeld* of the ancient Roman and Germanic laws. Etymologically the term signifies that which is given in payment. The *diya* is also called, though very much more rarely, *ʿaḳl*.

In a restricted sense—the sense which is most usual in law—*diya* means the compensation which is payable in cases of homicide, the compensation payable in the case of other offences against the body being termed more particularly *arsh*.

The historical origin of the institution lies in pre-Islamic customary practice, where it was closely bound up with the social organization of Arabia. This rested upon a tribal basis, with the absence of any political authority, even within the individual tribe, and a system of private justice tempered to some extent by the practice of voluntary submission to arbitration. In matters of homicide particularly the principle of the exercise of personal vengeance (*thaʾr* [*q.v.*]) reigned supreme, apart from the possibility of voluntary renunciation of the right against the payment of *diya*. The amount of this was, in principle, fixed—at least in the area in which Islam was born—at one hundred head of camels, although there are certain traditions which speak of ten camels only. A strong solidarity, as much active as passive, united the members of the tribe in the application of the system: the tribe as a whole was obliged to share in the payment of the *diya*, just as vengeance itself could be exercised upon members of the tribe other than the culprit himself. In the opposite case, and where the nearest blood-relative of the victim was himself unable to exact vengeance, any other qualified fellow-tribesman could take his place.

Islam did not interfere with the basic system; various Ḳur'ānic texts even expressly confirmed it. They indicated, however, certain modifications, among which the most important was the rule which made compensation obligatory in the case of accidental homicide.

On the other hand the integration of the ancient custom in the Ḳur'ānic revelation perforce had the effect of fixing this custom in a definite form in the law and thus constituting, in principle, a barrier to any further development.

It was, however, soon to find itself out of tune with the new Islamic society such as was to develop rapidly into a community unified in principle and, in particular, organized as a State.

Working under the influence of such opposing demands the jurists constructed a theory of the *diya* (and of the law of private justice (see ḲIṢĀṢ)) in which divergent trends are readily apparent. This theory is, in general, the same in both the Sunnī and the Shīʿī doctrine, apart from certain differences on secondary points, some of which will be noted below.

The operation of the institution is confined to the field of homicide and a certain number of injuries to the body which will be defined below and which are restricted by enumeration to such effect that outside their bounds the developed common law of civil liability and the precise calculation of damage asserts its sway. *Diya*s are sometimes optional and sometimes obligatory.

They are optional in the case of offences committed deliberately (*ʿamd*). In the case of homicide the condition of intention is interpreted restrictively: notably it is necessary that the murder should have been committed with a weapon intrinsically likely to kill. In the absence of this last condition there is quasi-deliberate (*shibh ʿamd*) homicide where the *diya* is no longer optional. The Mālikī *madhhab* does not recognize this separate category: whatever the means employed might be, as soon as the intention to kill is established the *diya* remains optional.

There are, however, a certain number of cases where an *ʿamd* offence does not entail a right of vengeance and for which the *diya* is no longer optional, such as infanticide, murder which is not the direct and immediate result of the assault, etc. (see ḲIṢĀṢ).

The *diya*s are obligatory in all cases other than those of deliberate offences which entail a right of vengeance.

Controversy exists among the different schools on the question as to whether the choice of the optional *diya* in place of *ḳiṣāṣ* depends solely upon the wishes of the victim or his heirs, or whether the agreement of the offender is necessary for the choice to be effective.

In the absence of a contrary agreement between the parties there is a fixed tariff for the amount of the *diya*. In principle it consists of camels of different ages and sex. The *diya* in cases of homicide is one hundred camels, split into five categories equal in number: twenty four-year-old, twenty three-year-old, twenty two-year-old and twenty one-year old female camels and twenty one-year-old male camels. Subject, however, in the matter of this division, to divergent juristic opinions, if the homicide is deliberate or quasi-deliberate, the value of the *diya* is increased (*diya mughallaẓa*) comprising now only female camels of the first four categories described.

The *diya* for accidental homicide is also due in full in all cases of total loss of an organ or of a physiological or intellectual function. In cases of partial loss the amount of the *diya* is in proportion to the part lost: a half of the total *diya* for the loss of an arm, a leg, an eye or an eyelid; a quarter for the loss of eyelashes; a tenth for the loss of a finger or toe; a twentieth for a tooth, etc.

The remaining physical injuries for which a *diya* or *arsh* is prescribed and for which, again, the amount is determined by reference to the *diya* of homicide are the following: the *djā'ifa*, a wound penetrating the interior of the body, and the *āmma* (or *ma'mūma*), a wound penetrating the brain: 1/3rd of the *diya*; the *munaḳḳila*, a fracture with displacement of a bone: 3/20ths; the *hāshima*, a fracture of a bone: 1/10th; the *mūḍiḥa*, a wound laying bare the bone: 1/10th.

All other injuries lie outside the system of the *diya* and are dealt with on the basis of what is called *ḥukūmat ʿadl*, *i.e.*, an assessment of the actual harm suffered. This remains, however, under the influence of the *diya* system inasmuch as compensation is determined by a comparison with an injury for which a fixed *diya* is established and it cannot, in any case, exceed the amount of the *diya*.

The proviously cited amounts of *diya* or *arsh* are due in full only where the victim is a Muslim, of the male sex and of freeborn status. The *diya* of a woman is half that of a man. According to the Mālikīs, however, who are here followed by al-Shāfiʿī, this reduction to half is only applicable where the *diya* exceeds a third of the full *diya*; but if, for example, the offence is one for which it would have been due at the rate of a quarter of the full *diya*, this same amount will be due to the woman.

The *diya* of the *dhimmī* or the *musta'min* (a non-Muslim foreigner, temporarily admitted to Muslim territory—in the case of the foreigner who is not *musta'min* nothing is due) is at the rate of one third or one half in the opinion of the majority, though the Ḥanafīs admit an equal rate. In every case the *diya* is due only where the offence is committed in Muslim territory. As for the slave, he is outside the system when he is the victim (see below for his position when he is the offender). Since he is assimilated to property, if he is killed or is the victim of some injury to his physical well-being, his master will be entitled to an amount of compensation equivalent to the loss he himself suffers from this fact. Such compensation may even exceed the amount of the relevant *diya*, except, according to a minority opinion, in the case of murder, where the compensation may not exceed this amount.

Although, according to the original principle, the *diya* consists of camels, it was very soon recognized that it could eqally well be paid in gold coinage (1000 dinars) or silver coinage (10,000 or 12,000 dirhams according to different versions which, without doubt, depend upon the variations in gold and silver currency rates). According to certain opinions the *diya* may consist of cattle (200), sheep (1000) or clothing (200 garments). Opinions differ, however, on the point as to whether the choice of the mode of payment depends upon the agreement of the parties or belongs to the guilty party or to the judge; or whether one or the other of the modes is obligatory in circumstances where it would constitute the mode of payment most widely or exclusively used in the locality where the debt is to be exacted, or whether the *diya* in camels is the fundamental obligation and it is only in circumstances where the provision of payment in this form is impossible that recourse may be had to the other forms.

As to the matter of deferred payment of the full *diya*, the majority opinion (S̲h̲āfiʿī, Mālikī and Ḥanbalī) draws a distinction according as to whether the offence is deliberate or not. In the former case the *diya* may be demanded within the year in which the offence was committed; while in other cases it may be paid over a period of three years in instalments of one third. According to the Ḥanafīs the *diya* may, in all cases, be paid within the three year period.

Where the *diya* is equal to one third of the full *diya*, payment may be exacted, in all cases and according to all opinions, in the course of the first year. Where the *diya* exceeds one third of the full *diya* the same controversy exists as in the matter of the full *diya*; the second third may also be exacted within the first year in the case of a deliberate offence according to the majority opinion, while according to the Ḥanafīs it may be paid in the course of the second year.

The legal nature of the *diya* is complex and is marked by diverse and contradictory characteristics which are the result of its origin and subsequent development. It appears at one and the same time as a manifestation of the law of private vengeance, as a measure to safeguard the public order and as a means of compensation for loss suffered.

The creditor of the *diya* is the victim; in the case of homicide it will be the victim's heirs according to the order of succession; it is not precisely the circumstances of the victim of the loss which will be the determining factor.

The debtor of the *diya* was, at the outset, the tribal group—referred to, in these circumstances, as the *ʿāḳila* [*q.v.*]—to which the culprit belonged; and this is the explanation for the comparatively high amount of the *diya*. The principle of this collective responsibility was firmly maintained in theory; but in fact it was progressively impaired, eventually disappearing altogether; it is avoided in the case of deliberate offences, as we have seen. The responsibility of the *ʿāḳila*, having previously been the primary one, became subordinate to that of the culprit himself; it was now regarded as no more than the act of a beneficiary towards a debtor without means; and then, in recognition of the fact that the tribal organization had disappeared in developed Islamic society, the place of the *ʿāḳila* was taken by the State itself, whose responsibility, in turn, eventually disappeared. In cases where there is a number of culprits the *diya* is divided among them *per capita*.

If the perpetrator of the offence is a slave, again a distinction is drawn according as to whether the offence is deliberate or accidental. In the former case there is ground for *ḳiṣāṣ* just as in the case of a freeman, unless, according to one opinion, the victim or his heirs should choose to surrender the slave. In the view of the majority, however, the choice of the successful prosecutor lies solely between *ḳiṣāṣ* and outright pardon.

A secondary practice connected with that of *diya* and *ḳiṣāṣ* is that of *ḳasāma* [*q.v.*]. When the corpse of a murdered person is found in a locality—tribe, village or district—and the identity of the culprit is not discovered, fifty persons from the local population are asked to take an oath that they have no knowledge of the identity of the perpetrator of the offence. In default of such oaths, the obligation to pay the *diya* will fall upon the local population. This practice also, as was observed by an author of the 6th/12th century, eventually disappeared.

The survival of the *diya*.

The system of the *diya* survives in the present contemporary period in two principal forms according to circumstances.

Among the Bedouin tribes, with their innate hostility towards a State organization, the system of private vengeance tempered by the practice of the *diya* still survives upon a basis of customs which are analogous to ancient Arabian customs in several particulars—though they differ from tribe to tribe—and which often contradict the precepts of the Ḳurʾān and the rules of Islamic law. The efforts of the governments concerned have not been able to achieve more than the imposition upon these groups of certain regulations of a procedural character and of limited scope.

Thus, among the Arab tribes of Egypt, Jordan and Syria there is a fairly general custom which renders the *diya* obligatory in all cases save those of deliberate homicide. The composition of the *diya* varies from tribe to tribe—40 male camels only, 40 male camels and a virgin girl, a sum of money (in Egypt, for example, £E 400, or 300 or 150 etc.). The *diya* of a woman is usually greater than that of a man; among certain tribes it even reaches four times or eight times the amount of a man's *diya*. As regards proof of the offence, the system of ordeal, by fire and water particularly, is often practised. Among certain tribes a procedure of *ḳasāma* is in evidence.

The survival of the system in communities more fully developed and politically organized is essentially attributable to the religious character which it had acquired. A typical example in this regard is provided by the Ottoman Empire, where, despite the modernization of the law towards the middle of the 19th century, and notwithstanding the fact that the principle of the rule of compensation (properly so-called) for loss suffered had been enunciated and the system of public law had been duly organized, the right of the interested parties to demand the application of *ḳiṣāṣ* and, finally, the *diya*, was retained, notably under the terms of the penal code of 1863. The amount of the *diya* was officially fixed at £T 224.

All this has now, in actual fact, disappeared from positive legislative enactments; but traces, hard to erase, of the former state of things still persist. In certain countries such as Syria the courts, in spite of the spirit and the letter of legislation, such as a civil code and a penal code wholly modern in inspiration and in force since 1949, still continue to pronounce liability for *diya*s, the amount of which, in cases of homicide, is always fixed as a lump sum of money, and is greater or less according as to whether it is a case of deliberate or accidental homicide.

Bibliography: S̲h̲ayk̲h̲zāde, *Mad̲j̲maʿ al-anhur*, ed. Aḥmad b. ʿUt̲h̲mān, 1328/1910, ii, 614 ff.; Dardīr on Dasūḳī, Commentary on the *Muk̲h̲taṣar* of K̲h̲alīl, 14, 258 ff.; Ibn ʿAbd al-Raḥmān al-Dimas̲h̲-

ḳī, *Raḥmat al-umma fī ikhtilāf al-aʾimma*, ed. ʿAbd al-Ḥamīd, Cairo, 255 ff.; Ibn al-Humān, *Fatḥ al-ḳadīr*, Cairo, viii, 244 ff.; Ibn Ḳudāma, *Mughnī*, 3rd. ed. Rashīd Riḍā, Cairo 1367/1947, vii, 636 ff., viii, 1 ff.; Khirshī, Commentary on the *Mukhtaṣar* of Khalīl, viii, 2 ff.; Querry, *Recueil de lois concernant les musulmans chiites*, Paris 1871, ii, 541 ff.; Shāfiʿī, *Kitāb al-Umm*, Cairo 1903, vi, 2 ff.; Abou-Heif, *La diya* (Arabic translation from the French), Cairo 1932; Hakim, *Le dommage de source délictuelle et son évaluation en droit musulman*, thesis (typewritten), Beirut 1955, 1 ff.; Juynboll, *Handbuch*, 295 ff., 353; Tyan, *Système de responsabilité délictuelle en droit musulman*, thesis, Lyon 1926, 13 ff. (E. Tyan)

ḌIYĀ GÖKALP [see gökalp, ziya].

ḌIYĀ PASHA [see ziya].

ḌIYĀFA [see ḍayf, mihmān, musāfir].

DIYĀLĀ, an important river of east-central ʿIrāḳ. Its name, of unknown origin and meaning, is ancient, appearing in antiquity as Σίλλα or Δέλας or Dialas; its upper waters are known as the Sirwān or (originally and more correctly) Shirwān, as known to Yāḳūt, and this name is in common use for most of its length. It forms a left-bank tributary of the Didjla (Tigris), navigable only by small craft, and with a discharge formidable in the flood season (March-May), slight in the later summer and autumn.

The river rises in western Persia, where the many hill-streams (often dry in the summer and autumn) which unite to form its principal tributaries drain (1) the area north of Kirmānshāh, (2) the area both north and south of Sanandadj (Senna, Siḥna) in the Ardalān province, (3) the Perso-ʿIrāḳī frontier area around Mariwān, (4) the westerly area of Kirmānshāh province, west of Karind, opposite (ʿIrāḳī) Khāniḳīn and (Persian) Ḳaṣr-i Shirīn. The first three of these sources have made their contributions before the main stream of the Sirwān crosses the frontier; the tributaries are known locally by various names, all flowing in valleys of great natural beauty and inhabited, from time immemorial, by Persian-Kurdish tribesmen. The contribution from area (4) of those suggested above forms the Alwānd river (the Ḥulwān river of ʿAbbāsid times, called from the famous town of that name) and enters immediately west of Khāniḳīn, in ʿIrāḳ. The Tandjera stream, draining the Shahrizūr valley (Sulaymāniyya *liwāʾ*), also forms an ʿIrāḳī contribution; there are others of lesser importance. The middle course of the river, until realignment by the Frontier Commission of 1333/1914, marked the Turko-Persian boundary in so far as that had by then been stabilized; but areas west of this sector, now forming part of Khāniḳīn *ḳaḍā*, were then assigned to Turkey as "Transferred Territories".

The river greatly changes its character in its middle and lower course, where it flows first through undulating, then through flat country, diminishing its speed of flow, and lending itself to important use for irrigation. Near the point where it breaks through the Djabal Ḥamrīn a series of major canals takes off, and maintains extensive date gardens and winter and summer crops. These are notably, from the right bank, the Khāliṣ canal, which waters Daltāwa [*q.v.*], and from the left bank the Rūz (on which stands Balad Rūz), the Maḥrūt, and the Khurāsān. The intensive cultivation and famous ruits of the Diyālā *liwāʾ*—itself named from the r iver, of which it contains nearly the whole length in ʿIrāḳ (*liwāʾ* headquarters at Baʿḳūba, dependent ḳaḍās of Khāniḳīn, Mandalī, Khāliṣ, and Baʿḳūba) —are due entirely to the presence of these canals, and to water-lift irrigation by *Karad* and mechanical pump from the main stream. This irrigation system is similar to, but less than and not identical to, that prevailing in the 3rd/9th to 7th/13th centuries, before its ruin by the Mongols; but in that age, or most of it, the Diyālā waters below the Djabal Ḥamrīn discharged into the great Tāmarrā-Nahrawān canal (see didjla, and nahrawān), and were extensively canalized from it; a major part was probably delivered to the Tigris at or near the present mouth, 10 miles below Baghdād. Technically, the relation between the Diyālā (with its capacity for sudden and formidable flooding) and the Nahrawān canal-system, remains obscure; nomenclature varies in the Arab geographers, who do not distinguish between canals and mere flood-channels, and at times even identify the Diyālā with the Nahrawān or Tāmarrā. The mediaeval cities dependent on the Diyālā and its connected canals included Nahrawān, Bādjisrā, Baʿḳūba, Daskara and Djalūlā. The area astride its lower course was closely administered and sustained hundreds of villages and a dense population; traces of Sāsānian and older sites indicate that this had always been a favoured region. The main road from Baghdād to, and through, the province of al-Djibāl—the Khurāsān highway—ran through it, and largely followed the course of the river; this is still the case; the motor-road running from Baghdād to and across the Persian frontier follows substantially the old alignment by way of Baʿḳūba, Shahrabān, Ḳizil Rubāṭ, Khāniḳīn, and Ḳaṣr-i Shirīn. The metre-gauge railway to Khāniḳīn, constructed in and after 1337/1918, follows a similar line; railway bridges exist at Baʿḳūba and at Ḳaraghān, where the Kirkūk-Irbīl line branches off.

Bibliography: For the Arab geographers, see bibliography under didjla; equally for the relevant works of Streck, Le Strange, Willcocks, and Longrigg. (S. H. Longrigg)

DIYĀR BAKR, properly "abode of (the tribe of) Bakr", the designation of the northern province of the Djazīra. It covers the region on the left and right banks of the Tigris from its source to the region where it changes from its west-east course to flow in a south-easterly direction. It is, therefore, the upper basin of the Tigris, from the region of Siʿirt and Tell Fāfān to that of Arḳanīn to the north-west of Āmid and Ḥiṣn al-Ḥamma (Čermük) to the west of Āmid. Yāḳūt points out that Diyār Bakr does not extend beyond the plain.

Diyār Bakr is so called because it became, during the 1st/7th century, the habitat of an important portion of the Rabīʿa tribe of Bakr b. Wāʾil [*q.v.*]. The latter had already moved forward, following the tribal wars of the pre-Islamic period, into Mesopotamia. Having stayed for some time in the region of al-Kūfa, the Bakrī groups spread out towards the north. It was at the time of the conquests under the caliphate of ʿUthmān, while Muʿāwiya was governor of Syria and the Djazīra, that some Muḍarī and Rabīʿī tribes were settled in the unoccupied lands of this region on the orders of the government. Muʿāwiya installed these Muḍarīs in what came to be called the Diyār Muḍar and the Rabīʿīs in what came to be called the Diyār Rabīʿa. Al-Balādhurī, who gives us this information, does not mention the Bakrīs expressly, who were included in the Rabīʿī group, but it is probable that it was in the same manner and at the same time that they established themselves in the Diyār Bakr. This appellation does not however mean that this territory was inhabited by Bakrīs alone; on the other hand, there were Bakrīs elsewhere.

The Diyār Bakr and the Diyār Rabīʿa, since the two groups were connected, are sometimes spoken of jointly under the single name of Diyār Rabīʿa (Yāḳūt, ii, 637).

The principal towns of the Diyār Bakr are Āmid, the capital, Mayyāfāriḳīn, Ḥiṣn Kayfā, and Arzan, which strictly speaking is part of Armenia. The territory of the Diyār Bakr has, from the administrative point of view, generally followed the destiny of the Djazīra. It has, however, sometimes formed, with neighbouring Armenia, a distinct and quasi-independent government. ʿĪsā b. al-Shaykh al-Shaybānī, from 256/870 to 269/883, and his descendants ruled over the Diyār Bakr until the reconquest of Āmid by the caliph Muʿtaḍid in 286/899. The same situation recurred in Ḥamdānid times when Diyār Bakr and Armenia were in the hands of the Amīr of Aleppo, Sayf al-Dawla, at the same time as northern Syria. After the death of the latter in 356/967 Diyār Bakr returned to the Ḥamdānid Abū Taghlib of al-Mawṣil. With the rest of the Djazīra, it fell under the domination of the Buwayhid ʿAḍud al-Dawla in 367/978, but after the death of the latter in 372/983 it passed into the hands of a Kurdish chief, Bādh (the Kurds were also inhabitants of this part of the Djazīra), then to those of his nephew Abū ʿAlī b. Marwān, who disputed the Diyār Bakr lands with scions of the Ḥamdānid family, but remained in control, and was the founder of the Marwānid dynasty.

From Diyār Bakr comes the name of the Bakrī frontier posts (*al-thughūr al-bakriyya*) enumerated in M. Canard, *Histoire de la dynastie des Ḥamdānides*, i, 254-61, and cf. 846 ff., which are situated in the north and north-west of the province.

ii. The formation of the Saldjūḳ empire faced the Marwānids with a new problem. From the beginning they rejoiced in their increasing power, causing the *khuṭba* to be read in the name of the Sultans as well as of the Caliphs. The Saldjūḳs were in no hurry to suppress a principality which was functioning as a buffer state between themselves and Byzantium. The Marwānids, however, were unable to prevent some Turcoman infiltrations, some of which were accompanied by plunder. The collapse of the Byzantine power and the policy of the third Saldjūḳ, Malikshāh, which tended to reabsorb autonomous states, were in the long run a danger to the Marwānids; the Banū Djahīr [*q.v.*], originally from Diyār Bakr, whose resources they knew, were able to convince Malikshāh and Niẓām al-Mulk [*q.v.*] of the interest of a conquest, which these latter entrusted to them; it was a bitter struggle, since the population was attached to a dynasty which guaranteed their autonomy, and took two years of campaigning (476-7/1084-5). Scarcely, however, had Diyār Bakr been thus directly annexed to the Saldjūḳ empire when the troubles which followed after the death of Malikshāh (485/1092) restored to them an autonomy of a different kind. A series of small Turcoman dynasties had set themselves up at Āmid (Īnālids), Arzan, Isʿird, etc., the most important of which was soon to become that of the Artuḳids [*q.v.*] at Mārdīn, Ḥiṣn Kayfā, Mayyāfāriḳīn and Kharpūt, and, after 578/1183, Āmid as well. It is true that this family was divided into two branches often at rivalry, and that it ran counter to the ambitions of the Saldjūḳids of Rūm, of the princes of Akhlāṭ, and especially the Zangid governors, then princes, of al-Mawṣil; nevertheless Diyār Bakr seems to have enjoyed in the 6th/12th century a relative material and cultural prosperity. More serious for the Artuḳids was to be the ambition of the Ayyūbids [*q.v.*], who aimed, for reasons of military recruitment, at setting foot in this country which was in part peopled by their Kurdish congeners. After 580/1185 Ṣalāḥ al-Dīn occupied Mayyāfāriḳīn, which afterwards fell to the lot of two successive sons of his brother al-ʿĀdil, then in 630/1233 to the son of the latter, al-Kāmil; the Saldjūḳs of Rūm, however, had occupied Kharpūt, and penetrated right into the heart of the Diyār Bakr country by the conquest of Āmid (638/1241). Diyār Bakr was thus politically divided when the Mongol invasion took place. In the face of this invasion, Artuḳids and Ayyūbids had no differences, and both Mayyāfāriḳīn and Mārdīn succumbed after severe sieges (657/1259 and 659/1261), but the Mongols allowed two small dynasties, an Artuḳid one at Mārdīn and an Ayyūbid one at Ḥiṣn Kayfā, to remain, under their suzerainty; these recovered some degree of autonomy as the dislocation of the empire of the Ilkhāns proceeded. The region, however, became the prey of nomadic pastoral tribes, especially Kurds in the north and Turcomans in the south, whose attacks against the rural Christian communities of Ṭūr ʿAbdīn contributed to the Islamization of this region which had hitherto not proceeded very far. On the eve and the morrow of Tīmūr's devastations (especially at Mārdīn), Diyār Bakr was the stake in the struggles with which the two great confederations of the Aḳ-Ḳoyunlu and the Ḳara-Ḳoyunlu occupied themselves; the former, masters of Āmid, made themselves masters of the whole of Diyār Bakr having taken Mārdīn from the Ḳara-Ḳoyunlu, and then Ḥiṣn Kayfā from the Ayyūbids. Diyār Bakr was, however, occupied for a time by the troops of Shāh Ismāʿīl, founder of the Ṣafawī dynasty in Persia (913/1507), and fell, for three centuries, into Ottoman hands in 922/1516.

It must be borne in mind that, in the terminology of the Saldjūḳids of Rūm, Diyār Bakr referred to the western confines of the province, which were all that they possessed, whereas in that of the Mongols it often refers to all the Djazīra, including the Diyār Muḍar and the Diyār Rabīʿa.

iii. Diyār Bakr, in its Turkish form Diyarbakır, is the name by which the Turks called the capital of the province, Āmid, which they also called Ḳara ("black") Āmid, on account of the black colour of its ramparts and its houses, built of basalt (or millstone); this is noted by the Arab geographers, and is perhaps alluded to in a verse of al-Mutanabbī (ed. Barḳūḳī, i, 182; cf. Vasiliev, *Byzance et les Arabes*, ii/2, 316). A proverb relates that all there is black, dogs, walls, and hearts.

Only the Āmid of Arab times is described here. This was built on the left bank of the Tigris on a plateau which runs down abruptly to the river, which runs beside the enceinte on three sides, the fourth being protected by a moat and an outer wall.

Āmid was taken without a fight in 19/640 at the time of the conquest of the Djazīra by ʿIyāḍ b. Ghanm. It was besieged by al-Muʿtaḍid who put paid to the attempt at independence of the small Shaybānī dynasty (see above), and the walls of the town were dismantled; at the time of al-Muḳtadir, however, in 297/910, they were restored. An inscription commemorating this restoration is still legible on the Mārdīn gate. Āmid fell into the hands of the Buwayhids in about 368/978. It was also the target of several attacks by the Byzantines, such as in 347 and 348/958 and 959 by the Domesticos John Tzimisces, and again when the same Tzimisces was emperor, in 972, 973 and 974 A.D. In the course of that of 973 the Domesticos Melias was taken prisoner. But the accounts of the historians of these sieges are often vague, contradictory and in part legendary. At all events, at the time when al-Muḳaddasī was writing, in 375/985, Āmid, capital of Diyār Bakr, had become a frontier post threatened in consequence of the success of the Byzantines, and Ibn Ḥawḳal seems to have foreseen that it would fall into Greek hands.

Āmid was renowned for its woollen and fine linen products, said to be "Greek" and "in the Sicilian style" (al-Muḳaddasī, 145).

Bibliography: i. (to the 10th century): Le Strange, 109 ff., where reference to the geographers will be found; M. van Berchem, *Arabische Inschriften aus Armenien und Diyarbekr*, in Lehmann-Haupt, *Materialen zur ältesten Geschichte Armeniens und Mesopotamiens*, Abh. G. W. Gött., ix/3, 22; idem, *Inschriften Max Oppenheim*, i, *Arab. Inschr.*, 71, 91-2; M. van Berchem and J. Strzygowski, *Amida*; J. Strzygowski, *Kara-Amid*, in *Orientalisches Archiv*, i/5; Sarre and Herzfeld, *Archäologische Reise im Euphrat- und Tigrisgebiet*, ii, 363; G. Bell, *Amurath to Amurath*, 322 ff.; J. Laurent, *L'Arménie entre Byzance et l'Islam*, index; Amedroz, *The Marwanids*, in *JRAS*, 1903; M. Canard, *Hist. de la dynastie des H'amdânides*, i, 77 ff., 572 ff., 795, 799, 838 ff. *et passim*; Margoliouth, *The eclipse of the Abbasid caliphate*, index. On Amida in Roman times, see Chapot, *La frontière de l'Euphrat*, 323 ff.

ii. The sources are those of the history and general geography of the periods covered, for which see AḲ-ḲOYUNLU, ARTUḲIDS, AYYŪBIDS; the only references specifically to Diyār Bakr are Ibn al-Azraḳ al-Fāriḳī (Marwānid part ed. B. A. L. Awad and M. S. Ghorbal, Cairo 1959; Artuḳid part analysed by Cl. Cahen in *JA*, 1935), and the anonymous Vienna ms. analysed by Cl. Cahen in *JA*, 1955; in Persian, the *Kitāb-ı Diyārbakriyya* of Abū Bakr Tihrānī (ed. Faruk Sümer); in Syriac, the chronicle published by Ottomar Behnsch, *Rerum saeculo XV in Mesopotamia gestarum*, Bratislava 1838.—Modern works: Cl. Cahen, in *JA* 1935 and 1955; M. H. Yınanç and Faruk Sümer, in the articles Diyarbekir, Akkoyunlu and Karakoyunlu in *İA*. (M. CANARD and CL. CAHEN)

iv. Ottoman period. In 923/1527 the district of Diyār Bakr was conquered by the Ottomans, who organized the newly conquered territories into an extensive province (*wilāyet*) centred on the city of Āmid, and including the districts of Diyār Bakr, Mawṣil, Diyār Rabīʿa and Diyār Muḍar, as well as the territory of Bitlis (Bidlīs). Later, at the time of Sultan Sulaymān the Magnificent, when ʿIrāḳ was conquered, another *wilāyet* was formed at Ūrfa, while the territory of Bitlis was included in the *wilāyet* of Vān which had been formed in the territory of Akhlāṭ. The province of Diyār Bakr remained, nevertheless, one of the largest and most important Ottoman provinces, and during four centuries of Ottoman government, protected from invasion and wars, it began to recover some of its prosperity. Its position near the Persian frontier gave it special importance. Its first *beylerbeyi* was Bïyïklï ("the mustachioed") Meḥmed Pasha, who had taken the city of Āmid from the Persians and was, therefore, known as the Conqueror (Fātiḥ Pasha). Other famous governors, who numbered Grand Viziers among them, included Khusrew, Rustem, Iskender, Behrām, Özdemir (Oz-ṭemür)-oghlu ʿOthmān, Čighāla-zāde Sīnān, Ḥāfiẓ Aḥmed, Bosnalï Khusrew, Ṭayyār Meḥmed, Melek Aḥmed, Ḳaplan Muṣṭafā, Dalṭaban Muṣṭafā, Köprülü-zāde ʿAbd Allāh, Ḥekīm-oghlu ʿAlī, Ḥasan, Reshīd Meḥmed, Esʿad Mukhliṣ and Kurt Ismāʿīl Pashas. Both Bïyïklï Meḥmed Pasha and Özdemir-oghlu are buried within the enclosure of the Fātiḥ Pasha mosque, founded by the former. Other *wālī*s are also buried in the same mosque. Two inscriptions made in the name of Suleymān the Magnificent are in existence, an Arabic one in the court-yard of the Ulu(gh) Djāmiʿ and a Persian one on the gate of the Ič-Ḳalʿe (Inner Castle or Keep). A long decree (*fermān*) drawn up in Turkish in the name of Sultan Meḥemmed IV is engraved in the Djāmiʿ-i Kebīr (Great Mosque) (Basrı Konyar, *Diyarbekir tarihi*, ii, 130-3).

As the centre of an important province and the base and winter quarters of the armies against Persia, Āmid was also the headquarters of a *beylerbeyi* having a large number of troops under his command. Sultan Suleymān the Magnificent visited Āmid on 22 Rabīʿ II 942/20 October 1535, on his return from the Persian expedition, when he went up to the Castle, prayed in the Ulugh Djāmiʿ and spent some twenty days in the city, and also in 961/1554 when he stayed for eight days on his way out to the second Persian expedition. Sultan Murād IV visited Āmid in 1047-8/1638 on his way out to the Baghdād expedition and also on his return in 1049/1639 when he ordered the execution of the famous and very popular Shaykh Maḥmūd Urmewī, known as the *shaykh* of Rūmiyya.

Of the Ottoman *wālī*s Khusrew, Iskender, Behrām, Naṣūḥ, Murteḍā, Melek Aḥmed, Dalṭaban ʿAlī and Ismāʿīl Pashas built one mosque each in the city, while Ḥasan Pasha had an inn (*khān*) built. Another *khān* is ascribed to Melek Aḥmed Pasha. Baths were built by Meḥmed, Iskender and Behrām Pashas and a *dār al-ḳurrā'* by Köprülü-zāde ʿAbdullāh Pasha. Sarï (yellow or fair) ʿAbd al-Raḥmān Pasha founded a library. In 1815 Suleymān Pasha repaired the walls.

Āmid, now known as Diyārbakr, also became an important cultural centre in Ottoman times. In the 10th/16th century it bred the poet Ibrāhīm Gulshenī, who also founded a *tarīḳa* (religious order), and the historian Ḳāḍī Ḥuseyn. It was during that century that the famous historian Muṣliḥ al-Dīn Lārī was *mufti* of Āmid. Many poets are known as Āmidī in the 12th/18th century, including Labīb, Ḥāmī, Wālī and Aḥmed Murshidī, as also the physician Aḥmed Riḍā, the mathematician Ismāʿīl and the theologian Küčük Aḥmed-zāde Abū Bakr. Later local notables included the poets Refīʿ, Rāghib and Ṭālib in the 19th century, as also the historian, belletrist and poet Saʿīd Pasha, while in modern times there are the latter's sons Suleymān Naẓīf and Fā'iḳ ʿAlī Beys, ʿAlī Emīrī Efendi, the founder of the *Millet* library, and the political thinker Ziya (Ḍiyā) Gökalp. The ʿAbd al-Djalālī-zāde family which gave many distinguished Pashas to the service of the Ottoman Empire is also of Diyārbakr origin. Descendants of tribal chiefs in the Ḳara-Ḳoyunlu and Aḳ-Ḳoyunlu States, of 10th/16th century governors and of regional notables can still be found in the city.

In the second half of the 19th century the Diyārbakr region, like other Ottoman provinces, was the scene of opposition and sometimes of revolts of local *amīrs*, tribal chiefs and other notables who did not wish to accept the reforms carried out in the Ottoman Empire. This led to long drawn out punitive operations, as a result of which local chiefs, such as Bedr Khān Pasha, were forced to submit, or were punished, sometimes by exile. Leaders of nomadic or settled tribes, however, succeeded in maintaining their influence, even although their official titles had been abolished, only instead of gathering round *amīrs* or tribal chiefs, these notables gave allegiance to the *shaykhs* of *derwīsh* orders (*ṭarīḳa*). Led by shaykh Saʿīd, the latter rebelled in 1925 against the reforms which the new Republican government of Turkey sought to carry out. The revolt started in Khani and spread before long to most of the Diyārbakr region. The rebels were, however, beaten back before the walls of Diyārbakr, after which the Government, which had proclaimed a partial mobilization, rapidly quelled the rebellion. In 1928 an Inspectorate-General was formed in the regions of Diyārbakr and of Akhlāṭ with the object of promoting reforms. While it was in existence a small rebellion was quelled at Ṣāṣūn.

The city of Diyārbakr is always named Āmid in all writings up to the end of the 10th/16th century. It then began to acquire its present name, which was the name of the province of which it had become the centre, the name of Āmid being gradually forgotten. Under the Republic the form Diyarbakır was officially adopted, in place of the earlier Diyarbekir.

Bibliography: Among Ottoman geographers and travellers, Kātib Čelebi (*Djihannumā*) gives some information, Ewliyā Čelebi very much more (*Siyāḥatnāme*, iv, 24 ff.). There are useful data on the social and cultural conditions in the region of Diyārbakr in the *Menāḳib* of Ibrāhīm Gülshenī. Interesting information on local customs is given in the chapter on Diyārbakr written by Bakr Fayḍī (in the author's private library). At the end of the 19th century Diyārbekirli Saʿīd Pasha gives the mediaeval Islamic history of the city in his *Mirʾāt al-ʿibar*: he does not, however, add very much to the data of Ibn al-Athīr and Munedjdjim-Bashī. Detailed information on local scholars and writers is given in ʿAlī Emīrī Efendi, *Tadhkira-i shuʿarā-i Āmid* (Istanbul, 1227). The second volume of this work has not, however, been printed. There is further information in the same writer's *Diyārbekir Vilāyeti*, Istanbul 1918, in his *Mirʾāt al-fawāʾid* and in the magazine *Āmid* which he published. For more recent Turkish work on the history of the city and province see Basri Konyar, *Diyarbekir tarihi, kitābeleri, yıllığı*, Ankara 1936; Ibrahim Tokay, *Diyarbakır*, Istanbul 1937; Osman Eti, *Diyarbakır*, Diyarbakır 1937; Kadri Günkut, *Diyarbakır tarihi*, Diyarbakır n.d.; Kâzim Baykal and Süleyman Savci, *Diyarbakır şehri*, Diyarbakır 1942. Much useful information will also be found in the *Sālnāmes* of Diyārbakr.

Data on the city and region can also be found in European travellers from the 16th century onwards. Scholars have also described the region and the archaeology, geography and history of the city. For local monuments and inscriptions see van Berchem and Strzygowski, *Amida* (Heidelberg 1910) (reviewed by Khalīl Edhem in *TOEM* 1st year, no. 6, 1329, 365-77). Further information on inscriptions is given by J. Sauvaget and Basrı Konyar. See also the extensive bibliography in A. Gabriel, *Voyages archéologiques dans la Turquie orientale* (Paris 1940). (Mükrimin H. Yinanç)

Monuments. One of the most remarkable characteristics of the present-day town of Diyārbakr is without doubt the archaeological wealth of this city of black stone, with its old quarters still surrounded by walls which give the site its character and which, throughout the middle ages, gave a strategic value to this locality which is otherwise lacking in natural protection. The well preserved enceinte naturally attracted the attention of 19th century European travellers, as well as admiration from all visitors to the stronghold since the Arab conquest (for example, the account of Nāṣir-i Khusraw). But not until the serious archaeological investigation made on the spot by A. Gabriel, re-opening the joint study to which M. van Berchem and J. Strzygowski had formerly bent themselves on the basis solely of photographic material, was it possible to recognize in it one of the most eloquent witnesses of military art in the mediaeval Near East. The site shows a rampart of regular trace, somewhat modified by certain configurations in the terrain (the original town was in fact situated on the edge of a plateau bounded by escarpments on the side of the Tigris), displaying on a perimeter of more than 5 km. a curtain flanked by towers and contreforts, before which were a fausse-braie and a ditch, now filled in, interrupted by several monumental gates and by breaches of recent date. The layout of the curtain (8 to 12 m. high, 3 to 5 m. broad, built of masonry rubble between two matching facings), with its chemin de ronde protected by a crenellated parapet and its arched gallery running at certain places under the chemin de ronde,—the disposition of the square, polygonal or circular flanking towers, of varying dimensions, with powerful basalt piers equipped with lower casemates and with upper rooms or platforms arranged for defence,—the roman elements still in place between the circular salients of the gates now called the Kharpūt, Urfa and Mārdīn gates, all combine with epigraphic evidence to show the antiquity of an enceinte which indeed underwent successive alterations after the Arab conquest but "which remains the most important and the most complete example of Byzantine fortification of the 4th century" (A. Gabriel). No less significant, however, is the nature of the works which were carried out later,—on the one hand, during the ʿAbbāsid period, indicated particularly by the restoration of the principal gates (dismantled by al-Muʿtaḍid, then rebuilt by al-Muḳtadir, as inscriptions of 297/709 testify)—on the other, under the Marwānids, Saldjūḳids and Artuḳids who undertook at different times partial repairs to the curtain and towers on the western front (indicated both by inscriptions and by underpinning of coursework), or more important works of reconstruction attested by those enormous circular bastions of the Artuḳid period, Ulu Badan and Yedi Kardash, which are over 25 m. in diameter and encompass previous works within their complex systems of casemates and galleries—and, finally, under the Ottomans, who were content to keep the enceinte of the town in repair but directed their main efforts to the citadel, on the north-east corner of the rampart, extended it, and substituted their own works for the ruins of the former palace of the Artuḳids.

In the interior of the enceinte the great mosque, Ulu Djāmiʿ, is noteworthy, whose abundant inscriptions, scattered in the greatest disorder on a heterogeneous composition in which re-utilized older material dominates, have provoked a clash of opinions concerning its origin and history. In fact the most probable conclusions, with regard to both the actual state of the building and the vicissitudes (fire in particular) which, according to textual information, it must have undergone, tend to show it as a specifically Islamic construction, modified however continually under the different masters of the country "from Malik Shāh down to the Ottoman sultans of the 16th and 17th centuries". Mention must also be made of some Artuḳid *madrasas*, with a central court surrounded by porticos and with a great interior *īwān*, like the Masʿūdiyya and Zindjiriyya *madrasas*, as well as the numerous Ottoman mosques, with a prayer-hall entered by a simple portico and covered by a cupola on a polygonal drum, which were built in the years after the capture of the town in 920/1514. Other interesting remains of this last period, marked for Diyārbakr by a real commercial prosperity, belong to the field of civil architecture, shown by the great caravanserais and spacious houses of an original type, built alike in fine ashlar.

The structural qualities of these various works should not let it be forgotten that there developed at Diyārbakr in the middle ages a school of very capable sculptors, who not only left some reliefs on their walls, not without artistic merit (Artuḳid reliefs often representing animal forms), but also brought a remarkable impetus to the particular style of decorative writing which then was most favoured for the exterior enrichment of monuments. The inscribed bandeaux of the 5th/11th century at Diyārbakr, which have already been the subject of intensive research by S. Flury (a real pioneer in this field), constitute the best examples of this ornamental epigraphy of Upper Mesopotamia the influence of which was to be felt in neighbouring lands and whose luxuriance, with its "incessant variations of detail brought to an initial type by an incomparable richness of invention" (J. Sauvaget, in *Ars Islamica*, 1938, 214), has been emphasized.

Bibliography: M. van Berchem, *Arabische Inschriften, apud* M. von Oppenheim, *Inschriften aus Syrien, Mesopotamien und Kleinasien*, Leipzig 1909, 71-100 (nos. 114-25); M. van Berchem and J. Strzygowski, *Amida*, Heidelberg-Paris 1910; S. Flury, *Islamische Schriftbänder Amida-Diarbekr*, Basle-Paris 1920 (= *Bandeaux ornementés à inscriptions arabes*, in *Syria*, 1920-1, 235-49, 318-28, 54-62); A. Gabriel, *Voyages archéologiques dans la Turquie orientale*, with a *Recueil d'inscriptions arabes* by J. Sauvaget, Paris 1940, 85-205, 310-38 (nos. 38-108). (J. Sourdel-Thomine)

DIYĀR MUḌAR, a name formed in the same way as Diyār Bakr [*q.v.*], is the province of the Djazīra whose territory is watered by the Euphrates and its tributary the Balīkh as well as by the lower reaches of the Khābūr. It extends on both banks of the Euphrates from Sumaysāṭ (Samosata) in the north to ʿAnā (ʿĀnāt) in the south. The principal town of the Diyār Muḍar was al-Raḳḳa on the left bank of the Euphrates; other major towns were Ḥarrān on the Balīkh, Edessa (al-Ruhā, Urfa), capital of Osrhoene, and Sarūdj to the south-west of Edessa. Those places situated on the Euphrates after its confluence with the Balīkh, such as al-Ḳarḳīsiyā' and al-Raḥba, were sometimes united in a special district known as the "Euphrates Road".

For most of the time the Diyār Muḍar formed part of the government of the Djazīra, but was sometimes separated from it. Such was the case in Ḥamdānid times when it formed part of the amīrate of Aleppo with Sayf al-Dawla. After him it reverted to the amīrate of al-Mawṣil, and later fell into the power of the Buwayhids like the rest of the Djazīra; then it became the capital of the small Numayrī dynasty (Banū Numayr), which was brought to an end by the Saldjūḳs. On the other hand, the Diyār Muḍar was often overrun by the Byzantine armies in the 4th/10th century, and in the 5th/11th century the Byzantine empire succeeded in annexing Edessa and its district, in 423/1032.

Bibliography: Le Strange, 86 ff., 101 ff.; Cl. Cahen, *La Syrie du Nord*, 110 ff.; Margoliouth, *The eclipse of the Abbasid caliphate*, index; M. Canard, *Hist. de la dynastie des H'amdânides*, i, 86 ff., 795 ff., 838 ff., et *passim*; D. S. Rice, *Medieval Harran*, in *Anatolian Studies*, ii, (1952), 36-83. (M. Canard)

ii.—After the Byzantine conquest of Edessa, the Diyār Muḍar, which continued to be a communication territory without real autonomy, was divided into two parts, one in the north under Christian domination, partially colonized by Armenians, the other in the south, with Ḥarrān as its principal centre, where the dominant influence was that of the Numayrī Arabs. From 457/1065, however, the country sustained the repercussions of Turkish expansion; it was troubled by marauding bands, and then at the beginning of 463/1071 it was crossed by the Saldjūḳ sultan Alp Arslan who, on his way to Syria, at one point besieged Edessa, and in 471/1078 by Tutush, brother of the new sultan Malikshāh. In the same year Ḥarrān and Sarūdj were incorporated, at the same time as Aleppo, in the principality of the ʿUḳaylid of al-Mawṣil, Muslim b. Ḳuraysh [*q.v.*], a nominal vassal of Malikshāh, and Edessa into the state of the Graeco-Armenian Philaretes, master of the western Taurus and later of Antioch. Finally the two divisions of the Diyār Muḍar fell into the hands of Malikshāh himself, with al-Mawṣil and northern Syria, in 479/1086.

Nevertheless, Saldjūḳ domination in this frontier region was fairly lax, and the disorders following the death of Malikshāh (485/1082) maintained at Edessa an Armenian rulership which was practically autonomous. The Crusade at the end of 1097 renewed for a half-century the partition commenced by the Byzantine conquest. Although the Franco-Armenian county of Edessa, as well as the lands to the south of the western Taurus along the middle Euphrates, formed its northern part, Ḥarrān, seat of an ephemeral Turkish principality at the beginning of the 6th/12th century, was cast with the lot of Aleppo between the hands of the Artuḳids and the Zangids. In 553/1158 Zangī granted it in fief to ʿAlī Küčük, the holder of Irbil to the east of al-Mawṣil, in order to ensure the recruitment of the Turco-Kurdish contingents who were responsible for its defence, which was strategically important; his successors, the Begteginids [*q.v.*], held it for half a century. The ʿUḳaylid Arab seignory which held sway at Ḳalʿat Djaʿbar was suppressed by Nūr al-Dīn [*q.v.*] in 558/1163. Thanks to the disturbances which marked the succession of this prince, the Diyār Muḍar was occupied by Ṣalāḥ al-Dīn [*q.v.*], who granted it first to his nephew Taḳī al-Dīn ʿUmar, then to his brother al-ʿĀdil. The latter, who had become master of the Ayyūbid heritage, assigned it to his son al-Ashraf (597/1201), who in 624/1227 exchanged it for Damascus with his brother al-Kāmil of Egypt. Al-Kāmil incorporated it in the government set up in the east for the benefit of his son al-Ṣāliḥ Ayyūb who, threatened by the anti-Ayyūbid coalition following the death of al-Kāmil, granted it to the Khwārizmians, recent fugitives from Asia Minor (635/1238). The later defeat of these latter and the fall of the Ayyūbid dynasty in Egypt caused the region to pass into the hands of the Aleppo Ayyūbid al-Nāṣir Yūsuf, from whose time dates the administrative description of ʿIzz al-Dīn b. Shaddād; but in 658/1260 it was conquered by the Mongols, who were already in control of Asia Minor and Mesopotamia.

Henceforward the function of the Diyār Muḍar changed. Reconquered by the Mamlūks, who replaced the Ayyūbids in Egypt and Syria, they established a frontier with the Mongols of Persia, and later with the Turcoman dynasties who succeeded them at the end of the 8th/14th century. Successive invasions ruined the land, especially in the south, and Ḥarrān declined irretrievably, although Edessa was the capital of the province. As in the neighbouring regions of the north, east and west, the Turcoman element, here especially of the tribe of the Döger, increased its influence. At the end of the 8th/14th century, the region was again laid waste by Tīmūr. In the following century the fact that it served as a base for the inconclusive expansionist attempts of the Mamlūks towards the east gave it no security. It fell without difficulty into the hands of the Aḳ-Ḳoyunlu of Diyār Bakr, under the nominal suzerainty of the Mamlūks, and then to the Ottomans at the same time as Syria and Mesopotamia. It is remarkable that the bounds of the Arab population remain today much as they were at the time of the Crusades, so that the modern frontier between Turkey and Syria cuts the Diyār Muḍar in two, as it was cut in the 5th/11th and 6th/12th centuries.

Bibliography: The sources of the history and geography of this period are to the found especially, for almost all the Djazīra, in ʿIzz al-Dīn b. Shaddād, *Aʿlāḳ*, iii, analysed by Cl. Cahen in *REI*, 1934. (Cl. Cahen)

DIYĀR RABĪʿA, a name formed in the same way as Diyār Bakr [*q.v.*], is the most eastern and the largest province of the Djazīra. It includes three regions: that of the Khābūr and its tributary the Hirmās (Djaghdjagh) and their sources, *i.e.*, the slopes of the Ṭūr ʿAbdīn; that which is contained between the Hirmās and the Tigris, the former Bēth ʿArabāyē with the Djabal Sindjār; and that on both banks of the Tigris between Tell Fāfān and Takrīt, which marks the boundary with ʿIrāḳ. The lower reaches of the two Zābs are also included in this last region. The principal towns are the capital Mosul (al-Mawṣil) on the left bank of the Tigris, Balad, Djazīrat Ibn ʿUmar, al-Sinn, and in the west Barḳaʿīd, Sindjār, Nāṣibīn, Mārdīn and Raʾs al-ʿAyn.

The history of the Diyār Rabīʿa is often confused with that of al-Mawṣil. It was marked by numerous Khāridjī revolts, which also affected other regions of the Djazīra, as much in the Umayyad period as in the ʿAbbāsid. In the first period they were further complicated by the rivalries between the Caliphal governors of the Djazīra and Syria. An account of the troubles which afflicted the Diyār Rabīʿa in the ʿAbbāsid period is given in Suleiman Saigh, *Histoire de Mossoul*, Beirut 1923-8, i, 73 ff.; L. Veccia Vaglieri, *Le vicende del Ḫārigismo in epoca abbaside*, in *RSO*, xxiv, (1949), 31 ff.; M. Canard, *Hist. de la dynastie des Ḥamdānides*, i, 291 ff.

The Diyār Rabīʿa is the region from which sprang the Taghlibī family of the Ḥamdānids, who took part in these Khāridjī revolts and founded thereafter the quasi-independent amīrate of al-Mawṣil, which during the reign of Nāṣir al-Dawla consisted principally of the Diyār Rabīʿa. After the conquest of the Ḥamdānid amīrate of al-Mawṣil by the Buwayhids, the attempt on the part of the last Ḥamdānids, Ibrāhīm and Ḥusayn, to reconstitute this amīrate to their advantage at the time of the Buwayhid Bahāʾ al-Dawla (379-403/989-1012) was opposed on the one hand by the Marwānid of Diyār Bakr [*q.v.*], and on the other by the ʿUḳaylid amīr Muḥammad b. al-Musayyab, who had originally helped the two princes and had received three places in the Diyār Rabīʿa in return. The latter became ruler of al-Mawṣil, and was only nominally subject to the Buwayhid of Baghdād. He was the founder of the ʿUḳaylid dynasty of al-Mawṣil, to which the Saldjūḳs put an end.

Bibliography: in addition to the references given in the text, see: Le Strange, 87 ff.; M. Canard, *Hist. de la dynastie des H'amdânides*, i, 97 ff., 291 ff., 573 ff. *et passim*, where will be found information on the sources for the topography of the different regions of the Diyār Rabīʿa; Margoliouth, *The eclipse of the Abbasid caliphate*, index.

(M. Canard)

ii.—In the middle of the 5th/11th century the Diyār Rabīʿa sustained the repercussions of the Turkish advance. From 433-5/1041-3 it was ravaged by the first band of Turcomans, who were finally massacred. When in 447/1055 the Saldjūḳ sultan Tughrīl Beg was enthroned at Baghdād by the ʿAbbāsid caliph, the ʿUḳaylids, fearing for their Shīʿa faith and for their pastures, resisted his summons, and it was in their territories that the coalition of Arab adversaries of the sultan was organized, grouped under the former Buwayhid general al-Basāsīrī [*q.v.*], who was now adhering to the Fāṭimid caliph of Cairo (449-51/1057-9). The ʿUḳaylid Ḳuraysh however decided in due time to rally to Tughrīl Beg, who for his part in this frontier region preferred to content himself with his vassal status. The ʿUḳaylid principality thus remained until 479/1086, the son of Ḳuraysh, Muslim, recently suspected of intrigues with Egypt, having met his death in a battle in Syria, and Malikshāh, the third Saldjūḳ sultan, having thereupon annexed his dominions without a struggle. After the death of this sovereign the Saldjūḳ empire broke up, and the Diyār Rabīʿa followed the fortunes of al-Mawṣil, which was governed by a series of increasingly independent generals, one of whom, Zangī, appointed in 521/1127, finally made himself independent and founded the Atabek dynasty of al-Mawṣil. This lasted for about a century, although quarrels between its members, certain of which received Ayyūbid support, had on occasion detached Sindjār or Djazīrat Ibn ʿUmar from al-Mawṣil. Their former slave and minister Badr al-Dīn Luʾluʾ succeeded the Zangids in the 7th/13th century; he was led to pay homage to the Mongols for a time in 642/1244, but his sons, who had opened relations with the Mamlūks, were dispossessed in 659/1261. Subsequently al-Mawṣil and the Diyār Rabīʿa, in front of the Kurds and Turcomans of Diyār Bakr and the Mamlūk governors of the Diyār Muḍar, were the foundation of the power in the Djazīra of the Persian Ilkhāns, then of their Djalāʾirid [*q.v.*] successors, the Ḳara-Ḳoyunlu and Aḳ-Ḳoyunlu Turcomans, and finally the Ṣafawids, until their incorporation in the Ottoman empire which was completed only in 1047/1637. In spite of Persian attacks, the province remained Ottoman until 1918, but having absorbed no true Turkish population, unlike Diyār Bakr, was not integrated into the new Turkey. The odd disposition of frontiers divides it between ʿIrāḳ and Syria.

See further the articles DJAZĪRA, DJAZĪRAT IBN ʿUMAR, AL-MAWṢIL, NAṢĪBĪN, SINDJĀR, and ZANGIDS.

Bibliography: The sources are those of the general history of the period; the only special work is *Histoire des Atabeks de Mossoul* of Ibn al-Athīr (ed. and Fr. trans. in *Recueil des Hist. des Croisades, Hist. Arabes*, ii/2), which, however, is particularly devoted to the exploits of Nūr al-Dīn, who reigned at Aleppo and not al-Mawṣil. The *Aʿlāḳ* of ʿIzz al-Dīn b. Shaddād describes the Diyār Rabīʿa (see Cl. Cahen, in *REI*, 1934), but does not give the developments promised about al-Mawṣil). (Cl. Cahen)

AL-**DIYĀRBAKRĪ**, Ḥusayn b. Muḥammad b. al-Ḥasan, 10th/16th century author of a once popular history of Muḥammad, entitled *Taʾrīkh al-khamīs fī aḥwāl nafs nafīs* and preserved in numerous MSS and printed twice (Cairo 1283, 1302). The work is furnished in addition with a brief sketch of subsequent Muslim history. The brief enumeration of Ottoman rulers at the end stops in some MSS with Süleymān Ḳānūnī but usually ends with Murād III (982/1574). The author is also credited with a detailed description of the sanctuary in Mecca. There is much confusion concerning his identity. According to Ḥādjdjī Khalīfa (ed. Flügel), iii, 177, the *Taʾrīkh* was finished in 940/1534, and its author lived in Mecca and died in the 960s/1550s. His date of death is now given as 990/1582 on the basis of an identification with Judge Karam al-Dīn Ḥusayn al-Mālikī of Mecca, who was appointed judge of Medina in 982/1574-5 (al-ʿAydarūsī, *al-Nūr al-sāfir*, 380-3; Ibn al-ʿImād, *Shadharāt*, viii, 419 f.), but proof for this identification is not available. The unpublished works of al-Nahrawālī may decide the question. However, the identification is unlikely if only in view of Istanbul mss. of the *Taʾrīkh*, such as Topkapusaray, Aḥmed III 3044, which was written at the latest around 960/1553 and which states that the work was completed in 935/1528-9 (and which represents an earlier recension breaking off, originally, with the caliphate of Yūsuf al-Mustanṣir in Egypt); or Damad Ibrahim 898, dated Wednesday, 28 Ṣafar 941/(Tuesday) 8 September 1534, and stating that the work was completed on Sunday, 8 Shaʿbān 940/23 February 1534 (see Ḥādjdjī Khalīfa, *loc. cit.*).

Bibliography: Brockelmann, II, 500, S II, 514, III, 1293; *ʿOthmānlî müellifleri*, iii, 118 f. A further ms. of the *Risāla fī dharʿ al-Kaʿba* in Istanbul, Bagdatlî Vehbi 1142, 10b-16a. (F. Rosenthal)

DIYUSḲURIDĪS, is the most correct transcription of the Greek Διοσκορίδης; other forms, such as Diyāsḳūridūs, allow a certain Syriac influence to be admitted. In Islam the name always refers to Pedanius Dioscorides (Ist. century B.C.), born at Anazarbe in Cilicia, whose name when fully arabicized is Diyusḳuridīs al-ʿAyn Zarbī. What the Muslims in the Middle Ages knew of him and his work can be found summarized in the *Ṭabaḳāt al-aṭibbāʾ wa ʾl-ḥukamāʾ* by Ibn Djuldjul, ed. Fuʾad Sayyid, Cairo 1955, 21). After Galen (Djālīnūs [*q.v.*]) (377/987), he is the doctor most frequently quoted by Muslims. His περί ὕλη ἰατρικῆς, which was already considered by Galen to be a definitive manual of *materia medica* and which has been the foundation of Muslim pharmacology [see ADWIYA] is known in Arabic by different names: *Hayūlā ʿilādj al-ṭibb*, *Kitāb al-adwiya al-mufrada* and *Kitāb al-ḥashāʾish*. It was an original translation from Greek into Syriac which provided the basis for the Arabic version; this was made by Iṣṭifān b. Basīl, with the original text before him, and corrected by Ḥunayn b. Isḥāḳ [*q.v.*] in Baghdād in the 3rd/9th century; it was the only complete translation made in the Muslim world. This translation, like the earlier Greek text, was issued in two versions: 1) the original edition of Dioscorides, which arranged simple drugs systematically in groups, divided the work into five books; to these were added up to three later apocryphal books on poisons.—2) for ease of reference, alphabetical order was introduced, an arrangement which lent itself to expansion of the text.

The Arabic text of Dioscorides was disseminated *in extenso* or in fragments throughout the whole Muslim world and has helped later pharmacological studies in the Arabic language. Two great difficulties have been evident from the start: the first a question of natural history, from the fact that botanical species were not the same everywhere; the second, a linguistic and lexical difficulty, for it was not easy to name the different species without ambiguity. The original Arabic translation acknowledges these difficulties by introducing into the text the original Greek, Syriac and Iranian names.

For this reason, the marginal glosses are of the highest importance for the manuscripts of the *materia medica* of Dioscorides. One of the most precious, the codex copied at the imperial court of Byzantium for princess Anicia Juliana, is of great interest on account of the variety of its glosses which bear witness to the hazardous progress from East to West of Greek as well as Arabic manuscripts, giving proof of the continuous scholarly work which they have inspired. During the 4th/10th century the centre of this ceaseless labour was the caliphal court at Cordova where the monk Nicholas who had come from Constantinople, in collaboration with Ḥasdāy b. Shaprūṭ [*q.v.*] and others, adapted the old eastern Arabic version to the needs of western Hispano-Arabic nomenclature, a task which was continued by Ibn Djuldjul, Ibn Buklārish and others. A similar readaptation was carried out in the East by al-Ḥusayn b. Ibrāhīm al-Natīlī who dedicated his Arabic Dioscorides in 380/990-91 to prince Abū ʿAlī al-Samdjūrī of Ṭabaristān. Now, if Arabic pharmacology reached its apogee in al-Andalus with al-Ghāfiḳī and Ibn al-Bayṭār [*q.v.*], not only was use made of fragments of the text of Dioscorides, but also Ibn al-Bayṭār (7th/13th century) himself edited a *Tafsīr Kitāb Diyusḳuridīs*, a manuscript of which, with its glosses, is preserved at Mecca. Later the polygraph Abu 'l-Faradj—Bar Hebraeus (7th/13th century) wrote a résumé in Syriac entitled *Kethabha dhe Dhiosḳoridhus*. On the whole, the work of Dioscorides was known above all in the fragmentary form preserved by Ibn al-Wāfid, Māsawayh and others. Latin versions which for the most part were made in Toledo allowed mediaeval Europe to become acquainted, through the medium of two translations, with only part of his work; and the complete text of Dioscorides only became known in the West at the Renaissance. But fragments of the Arabic Dioscorides were also translated in the East, as is proved by the Armenian pharmacology of Amīr Dawlat (2nd half of the 15th century).

Any study of the *materia medica* of Dioscorides is incomplete if his iconography is omitted. Dioscorides himself used botanical drawings by Cratevas (Ist century B.C.), whose sketches are preserved in Greek and Arabic manuscripts. In their illustrations these manuscripts contain an additional element which may help to determine their origins. As for the iconography, in addition to the ancient source already mentioned, it sometimes reveals Byzantine traces, and at other times Iranian influence; by the nature of things the different Muslims schools of painting are reflected, as for example the Baghdād school or the later Persian schools. Particularly interesting as a Muslim botanist and one of the most original is Ibn al-Sūrī (d. 639/1241), who when botanizing in Syria took with him an artist who made drawings of plants for him at different stages of growth; it is astonishing that Ibn al-Bayṭār does not quote this author who was his contemporary. In the iconography of the Arabic Dioscorides we have a proof that Diyusḳuridīs became the point of fusion of all the earlier traditions, enriched by the Muslims' observations of nature.

Bibliography: Pauly-Wissowa, s.v. Dioskurides; G. Sarton, *Introduction to the history of Science*, i, 258-60, 611, 613, 678, 680, 682, 728, ii, 52, 54, 79, 84, 649, 663, 976, 1073; L. Leclerc, *De la traduction arabe de Dioscoride*, in *JA*, ix (1867), 5 ff.; M. Meyerhof, *Die Materia Medica des Dioskorides bei den Arabern*, in *Quellen u. Studien zur Gesch. d. Naturwissenschaften u. Medizin*, iii, (1933), 72 ff.; H. P. J. Renaud, *Le Mustaᶜīnī d'Ibn Beklāreš*, in *Hesp.*, x (1930), 135; C. E. Dubler, *Le "Materia Medica" de Dioscorides, transmision medieval y renacentista*, i and ii, Barcelona 1953-1957; Aḥmad ᶜĪsā Bey, *Taʾrīkh al-nabāt ᶜind al-ᶜArab*, Cairo 1363/1944, 38 ff.; Muṣṭafā al-Shabābī, *Tafsīr Kitāb Diyusḳūrīdis l-Ibn al-Bayṭār*, in *RIMA*, iii/I (May 1937), 105 ff.; F. E. Day, *Mesopotamian manuscripts of Dioscorides*, in *The Metropolitan Museum of Art Bulletin*, May 1950; K. Weitzmann, *The Greek sources of Islamic scientific illustrations*, in *Archaeologica Orientalia in Memoriam Ernst Herzfeld*, 250 ff.

(C. E. Dubler)

DIZFŪL, the capital of the district (*shahristān*) of the same name in the VIth *ustān* (Khūzistān) of Persia, is situated in 32° 23' N. Lat. and 48° 24' E. Long. (Greenwich), on the left bank of the Āb-i Diz or Dizfūl-rūd. This river, which rises in the neighbourhood of Burūdjird, flows into the Kārūn [*q.v.*] at Band-i Ḳīr (ᶜAskar Mukram, [*q.v.*]). The town, which stands 200 metres above sea level, is built on a conglomerate formation; many of the inhabitants have made cellars (*sardābs*) under their houses in this formation, into which they retire during the heat of the day in summer. Dizfūl (Persian Dizpūl = 'Castle bridge') takes its name from the fortress which was built to protect the well-known bridge over the river there. The piers of this bridge, like those of the even more famous bridge at Shūshtar [*q.v.*], are undoubtedly Sāsānid; their construction may have been supervised by Roman engineers in the time of Shāpūr I (see D. L. Graadt van Roggen, *Notice sur les Anciens Travaux Hydrauliques en Susiane*, in J. de Morgan's *Mémoires de la Délégation en Perse*, Paris 1905, vol. vii, 187). The arches and superstructure are of later origin and have frequently been repaired. According to Mustawfī (740/1339-40), this bridge had 42 arches, while ᶜAlī of Yazd (828/1424-5) stated that it had 28 large and 27 small arches, making 55 in all (these authors doubtless regarded as arches the supplementary vents over the piers which were made in order to ease the pressure on the structure when the river was greatly in flood).

The name Dizfūl did not come into use until the 6th/12th century; previously it had been known as Andālmishk or Andāmishk (this name is now borne by the small town on the Trans-Iranian railway 11 km. to the north of Dizfūl). The older Arab geographers gave the town various names, such as Ḳasr al-Rūnāsh, Ḳanṭarat al-Rūm ('the Roman Bridge'), Ḳanṭarat al-Rūd ('the River Bridge') and Ḳanṭarat al-Zāb (Zāb repeatedly occurs as a river name; it is from the Semitic root זוב 'to flow').

Procopius, in his *Caesareensis* (Book I, v, 7-9, 28 and 29) has given an interesting account of a 'castle of oblivion' (τὸ τῆς Λήθης φρούριον) somewhere in Persia where persons of high degree were incarcerated; no one, under pain of death, was allowed to speak of it. Neither Procopius nor the Arab and Persian writers who also mentioned this castle gave its precise location, but, according to Armenian sources, it was at Andāmishn, which H. Hübschmann, in his *Armenische Grammatik* (Leipzig 1897, 19), has identified with Andāmishk, that is, Dizfūl.

Dizfūl, like Shūshtar, was for long overshadowed by the neighbouring city of Gundī-Shāpūr. Later, when Gundī-Shāpūr fell into ruin, Dizfūl became more prosperous, but it and the surrounding district suffered when the wonderful hydraulic system of the Sāsānids fell into disrepair. Although Dizfūl escaped destruction by the Mongols, it afterwards submitted to the rule of the Il-Khāns. In 1393 it offered no resistance to Tīmūr. It is said that, shortly after its surrender to Tīmūr, Khʷādja ᶜAlī, the grandson of Shaykh Ṣafī [*q.v.*] of Ardabīl, visited Dizfūl and converted its inhabitants to Shīᶜism by temporarily stopping the flow of the Āb-i Diz by a display of his supernatural powers. Nādir Shāh [*q.v.*] visited Dizfūl on several occasions; in order to protect it against the Lurs, he built a fortress called Diz-i Shāh some miles to the north-east.

Muḥammad ᶜAlī Mīrzā, one of the sons of Fatḥ ᶜAlī Shāh [*q.v.*], had the famous bridge repaired in the early years of the 19th century, but exceptionally heavy floods in 1832 swept away the parts that had been so carefully restored. It was at this time that the cultivation of indigo was introduced on a large scale in the neighbourhood. Much indigo was produced until the importation of foreign dyes made the industry uneconomic. Dizfūl was also noted for its reed pens, which were for long considered the best in the east and were exported far and wide. The raw material for this industry was supplied by the inexhaustible reed-beds in the so-called Baṭīḥa, the marshes of the lower reaches of the Tigris and Euphrates.

Owing to very severe outbreaks of plague and cholera at Shūshtar in 1831 and the following year, Dizfūl for a short while supplanted it as the capital of Khūzistān. About the middle of the 19th century, Loftus estimated the population of Dizfūl at between 15,000 and 18,000, all of whom were Muslim except some 30 Mandaean families. Wells, in 1883, gave the total as 20,000, while Herzfeld, in 1907, estimated it at only 15,000, including Persians, Kurds, Lurs and Arabs. At the present time (1962), the population is approximately 50,000. Many of the inhabitants, like those at Shūshtar, are *Sayyids* or descendants of the Prophet. In the town are some 35 mosques and a large number of tombs of saints; in the suburb of Rūband is the shrine of Sulṭān Ḥusayn which closely resembles that of the Prophet Daniel at Susa (Shūsh).

Quite recently the bridge over the Āb-i Diz has been extensively repaired; in the process, a number of the old arches have been replaced by three modern spans.

Dizfūl and the surrounding area will undoubtedly benefit greatly when the big dam across the Āb-i Diz which is now (1959) under construction in a gorge 12 miles to the north-east of the town has been completed, as it will not only provide sufficient water to irrigate a large area, but it will also supply electricity on a large scale to northern and central Khūzistān.

Bibliography: *BGA*, *passim*; Yāḳūt, i, 372 (s.v. Andāmish); iv, 111 (s.v. Ḳaṣr Rūnāsh); Sir W. Ouseley, *Travels in various countries of the East*, London 1819, i, 358 ff.; Sir A. H. Layard, *Description of the province of Khuzistan*, in *JRGS*, London 1846, 56-64; W. K. Loftus, *Travels and researches in Chaldaea and Susiana*, London 1857, 310-4; London 1846, 56-64; idem, *Early adventures in Persia, Susiana and Babylonia*, London 1887, ii, 293; Sir A. H. Houtum-Schindler, in *ZGErdk. Berl.*, 1879, 38 ff.; H. L. Wells, *Surveying tours in Southern Persia*, in *Proceedings of the Roy. Geograph. Society*, 1883; J. Dieulafoy, *La Perse, la Chaldée et la Susiane*, Paris 1887, 647-52; E. Herzfeld, in Petermann's *Geograph. Mitteil.*, 1907, 73-5; Razmārā and Nawtāsh, *Farhang-i djughrāfiyā-yi Īrān*, vi, 161; L. Lockhart, *Persian cities*, London 1959, chapter xx.

(L. Lockhart)

DJAʿALIYYŪN: (1) A group of tribes in the Republic of the Sudan. The principal tribes of this group, mainly sedentary in their way of life, inhabit the banks of the main Nile from the Dongola [*q.v.*] region southwards to the Fifth (Sabalūḳa) Cataract. Other tribes and clans in Kurdufān (Kordofan) and elsewhere attach themselves to this group. The link among the tribes of the Djaʿaliyyūn is traditionally expressed in genealogical form: their eponymous founder (rather than ancestor) is said to have been a certain Ibrāhīm known as *Djaʿal* (*i.e.*, "he made", because he made himself a following from those whom he relieved in a famine). More realistically, the common element of the Djaʿaliyyūn group may be seen in a Nubian strain in their ancestry. The Danāḳila, or northern tribes of the group still speak a Nubian tongue. They are separated from the southern Djaʿaliyyūn by the Shayḳiyya. Although no memory of Nubian speech survives in the southern sector of the group, the name of Berber [*q.v.*] may well indicate an ancient linguistic enclave or frontier (cf. the Barābra [*q.v.*] further north). Migration from the Nile valley, a recurrent historical phenomenon, probably accounts for the numerous claims to Djaʿalī descent made in other parts of the Sudan, *e.g.*, by the Hamadj of the Sinnār region, and by a group of tribes lying west of the Nile whose names are derivatives of the root DJ-M-ʿ, "to gather"—a clear indication of synthesis. Elsewhere a ruling clan claims descent from the marriage of a Djaʿalī immigrant with a local woman, *e.g.*, the Nabtāb among the Bedja [*q.v.*] Banī ʿĀmir, and the dynasty of the hill-state of Taḳalī in the Nūba Mountains. The rise of the Shayḳiyya confederacy in the 17th and 18th centuries produced a notable migration of Danāḳila-Djaʿaliyyūn which affected the culture and commerce of Dār Fūr [*q.v.*]. Tradition also represents Ibrāhīm Djaʿal as a descendant of al-ʿAbbās: this may be regarded as a later sophisticated pedigree of a type not uncommonly adopted by parvenu groups. ʿAbbāsī has thus become virtually synonymous with Djaʿalī in Sudanese usage. The claims of the dynasties of Dār Fūr and Waddāy to ʿAbbāsid descent should be understood in this sense.

(2) The name of Djaʿaliyyūn in a more restricted sense is commonly and currently applied to a specific tribe, the most southerly member of the riverain group, which has its territory (*dār*) between the Atbara-Nile confluence and the Sabalūḳa Cataract. It is probably the "kingdom of Al Ğaʿl" mentioned by the Jewish traveller, David Reubeni, who passed through its territory in 1523. During the Fundj period, the Djaʿaliyyūn were dependent upon their southern neighbours, the ʿAbdallāb, whose hereditary chief, the Wad ʿAdjīb, was paramount over the Arab tribes under the sultan of Sinnār. From the late 10th/16th century until the Turco-Egyptian conquest, the tribe was ruled by chiefs (*mukūk*, sing. *makk*) of the Saʿdāb clan. Their capital was at Shandī (Shendi) on the right bank of the Nile. At the time of Bruce's visit (1772) the effective ruler was an ʿAbdallābiyya princess, the widow of the late *makk*. Under the last *makk*, Nimr Muḥammad, the Djaʿalī tribal kingdom was far more important than that of the ʿAbdallāb, whose power was much decayed. At the time of Burckhardt's visit (1814) Shandī was the principal trading-centre of the eastern geographical Sudan, as it was the meeting-place of routes from the interior of Egypt and the Red Sea. During the Turco-Egyptian invasion, *Makk* Nimr submitted to the *serʿasker* Ismāʿīl Kāmil Pasha (23 Djumādā II 1236/28 March 1821). When Ismāʿīl returned from Sinnār in the following year, he was entertained at Shandī by Nimr. A quarrel over the slave-tribute, a matter then causing great tension in the newly annexed territories, led to Ismāʿīl's assassination, which in turn touched off a revolt of the Djaʿaliyyūn and the tribes to their south. The rising was bloodily suppressed by the *defterdār* Meḥmed Khüsrev Bey, the *serʿasker* in Kurdufān. Shandī was devastated, and the sister-town of al-Matamma, on the left bank of the Nile, became the principal urban centre of the tribe. In general, however, the Djaʿaliyyūn, sharpwitted folk with great trading ability, profited under Turco-Egyptian rule. Djaʿaliyyūn of the dispersion were numerous in Kurdufān and Dār Fūr, especially in the Arab-negroid southern fringe, where conditions were particularly favourable to petty traders (*djallāba*). The involvement of the *djallāba* in slave-trading led to severe measures being taken against them by the governor-general C. G. Gordon Pasha in 1879. It is therefore not surprising that many of the Mahdī's supporters were Djaʿaliyyūn of the dispersion. The Djaʿaliyyūn and other riverain tribes were prominent in the early years of the Mahdist state, but the Khalīfa ʿAbd Allāh [*q.v.*] transferred political power increasingly to the Baḳḳāra [*q.v.*]. When Kitchener began his great advance towards Omdurman, the Djaʿalī chief of al-Matamma, ʿAbd Allāh Saʿd, refused to obey the Khalīfa's order to evacuate the town (which was to form the base for the Mahdist forces), and sent for help to the *serdār*. This could not be given; al-Matamma was retaken by Mahdist troops, and ʿAbd Allāh Saʿd was killed (30 Muḥarram 1315/1 July 1897). Under the settled rule of the Condominium, the Djaʿaliyyūn gained from the increasing opportunities for trade and education, and are ubiquitous throughout the territories of the present Republic of the Sudan.

Bibliography: H. A. MacMichael, *A history of the Arabs in the Sudan*, Cambridge 1922; i, 197-

236 and Index. S. Hillelson, *David Reubeni, an early visitor to Sennar*, in *Sudan Notes and Records*, xvi/1, 1933, 55-66. James Bruce, *Travels to discover the source of the Nile*, 2nd edn., Edinburgh 1805; vi, 436 ff.; J. L. Burckhardt, *Travels in Nubia*, London 1819, 277 ff.; R. Hill, *Egypt in the Sudan*, London 1959, Index; P. M. Holt, *The Mahdist state in the Sudan*, Oxford 1958, Index.

(P. M. Holt)

DJABĀ [see BENNĀK].

DJĀBA (variants: Ibn Rusta : *N. djāba*; Yaʿḳūbī: *N.h.nāya*, *Kanbāya*; al-Idrīsī: *Djāfa*; *ibid*, MS. Cairo: *Ḥāba*; again, *ʿĀba*, *Ghāba*, *ʿĀna*, etc. occurring in the same list of kings separately in Ibn Khurradādhbih and al-Idrīsī are perhaps a dittography of *Djāba*) represents the name of the former hill-state of Chamba (old name *Čampā*). The ancient capital of the state was Brahmapura (or Vayrāṭapaṭṭana). Hiuen Tsang describes the kingdom as 667 miles in circuit, and it must have included the whole of the hilly country between the Alaknanda and Karnālī rivers (Law, *Historical geography*). Later, the city of Chamba became the capital. On 15 April 1948 it was merged into Himāčal Pradesh to be centrally administered by the Union Government of India.

Djāba is generally used by the Arab writers as the title of the rulers of Chamba, who were probably Sūryavamśī Rādjpūts. According to Ibn Rusta, the king enjoyed an honourable position (among the kings of India) and belonged to the *Salūḳī* (race). The term *Salūḳiyyīn*, which undoubtedly applies to the ruling dynasty of Chamba, seems to have been wrongly used for the country in *Ḥudūd al-ʿālam* (for the *salūḳī* hound, see KALB). There is difference of opinion among scholars with regard to the date of the foundation of the Chamba dynasty. The earliest Arabic source to mention Djāba is Ibn Khurradādhbih, and the first draft of his work was prepared in 231/846, although the original report upon which his information and that of other Arab writers was based was drawn up much earlier. It is therefore very likely that the city of Chamba existed during the early decades of the 9th century A.D.

Ibn Rusta and Marwazī state that the rulers of Chamba, on account of their pride (*sharaf*) took wives only from among themselves but the *Balharā* kings (the Rāshṭrakūṭas), married their ladies. Then, they were always at war with *al-Djurz* (the Gūrdjara-Pratīhāras) who also fought the Rāshṭrakūṭas and *al-Ṭāḳā* (Ṭakka-deśa east of Sialkoṭ). It may be deduced from the above information that the Rāshṭrakūṭas and the rulers of Chamba may have been allies, not only because they had a common enemy in the Gūrdjara-Pratīhāras, but also because they were related to each other, in the internecine wars for political supremacy in India at this period.

The Red Sandalwood, which according to Ibn Rusta was exported from Chamba, is the product of *Pterocarpus santalinus*, native of South India, Ceylon and the Philippine Islands; climatic conditions could not have favoured its growth in Chamba. Al-Bīrūnī says that the red sandalwood is رخت جندن, (= Skt. *rakta-čandana*) and was exported from Djawa.

The kingdom of Djābat al-Hindī, the Island of Djāba (Ibn Khurradādhbih), the Indian Djāba (*Ḥudūd al-ʿālam*) and Djāba Island (Ḳazwīnī, *ʿAdjāʾib*) are all the same place as *Zābadj* of other Arab writers and represent Java [*q.v.*].

Bibliography: Ibn Khurradādhbih, 16, 66, 67; Ibn Rusta, 135; *Sharaf al-Zamān Ṭāhir Marvazī on China, the Turks and India*, text, tr. and commentary by Minorsky, London 1942, 34, 143; al-Idrīsī, *India and the neighbouring territories*, ed. S. Maqbul Ahmad, ʿAlīgaṛh 1954, 22; idem, *Nuzhat al-mushtāḳ fi'khtirāḳ al-āfāḳ* (MS Cairo, 275); *Ḥudūd al-ʿālam*, 57, 91, 249-50; Yaʿḳūbī, *Taʾrīkh*, ed. Houtsma, Leiden 1883, 106; Ḳazwīnī, *ʿAdjāʾib al-makhlūḳāt wa gharāʾib al-mawdjūdāt*, ed. F. Wüstenfeld, Göttingen 1849, 112; C. V. Vaidya, *History of mediaeval Hindu India*, Poona 1921, i, 378; *District Census Handbooks*, vol. xxiv: Chamba District, Simla 1954, v, viii; David Ross, *The Land of the Five Rivers and Sindh*, London 1883, 204-5; S. M. H. Nainar, *Java as noticed by Arab geographers*, University of Madras 1953, 17-22; *Cyclopaedia of India, and Eastern and Southern Asia*, ed. Edward Balfour, Madras 1873; L. H. Bailey, *Standard cyclopedia of horticulture*, New York 1958; al-Bīrūnī, *Bīrūnī's Picture of the World*, ed. Zekī Valīdī Togan (*Memoir ASI*, liii), 71, 126; B. C. Law, *Historical geography of Ancient India*, Calcutta 1954, 72, 73; S. Q. Fatimi, *In quest of Kalah*, in *Journal, South East Asian History*, Singapore, i/2, 62-101.

(S. Maqbul Ahmad)

DJABAL, Mountain, see under the name of the Mountain.

AL-**DJABAL** [see AL-DJIBAL].

DJABAL-I BARAKĀT [see YARPŪT].

DJABAL AL-**ḤĀRITH** [see AGHRIDĀGH and DJUDĪ]

DJABAL ṬĀRIḲ, GIBRALTAR, the promontory of calcareous rock, a British possession, south-west of the Spanish province of Cádiz, almost at the southern extremity of Spain (length 4.6 km., breadth reaching 1.2 km.; area, 4.9 sq. km.; highest point 425 m.); the town extends the length of the western slope, which is fairly gradual, and numbers 28,000 inhabitants (British, Spanish, Jews and Moroccans) (including the garrison); it is as it were the key to the Mediterranean, and is fortified and studded with batteries on a gigantic scale. In the bay to the west, called the Bay of Gibraltar or of Algeciras, there was in antiquity the European column of Hercules, also called Calpe or Abyla Mons, facing the African column called Columna Abyla or Abenna, the modern Ceuta. Gibraltar commands, from the north-east, the whole strait between Europe and Africa, the Atlantic Ocean and the Mediterranean Sea; in antiquity this strait was called Γαδειρίτιδες Πύλαι, Fretum Gaditanum (from Gades, Cadiz) or Herculeum; the Arabs call it (*Khalīdj*) *al-Zuḳāḳ*, "(canal of) the alley" [see BAḤR AL-MAGHRIB]. Gibraltar received also the name of *Djabal al-Fatḥ* or *Djabal Ṭāriḳ* from the name of Ṭāriḳ b. Ziyād [*q.v.*], who landed there in 92/711. During the entire Arab period the port, the town and the citadel ("The Moorish Castle") on the north-west of the rock played a continual part as a sure base for vessels, while Algeciras, facing it across the bay, developed still further and became the prosperous principal town of the entire southern extremity of Andalusia. The Almohad caliph ʿAbd al-Muʾmin, on his return from the Ifrīḳiya campaign (554-5/1159-60) sent from Constantine orders to his son and successor Yūsuf, then governor of Seville, to construct a new town at Gibraltar which, with regard to the attacks aimed at Cordova, Granada and Seville, would serve as a base and as an assembly point for the large scale campaign he intended to undertake against the Christian kingdoms of the Peninsula. Yūsuf, from Seville, and his brother

ʿU͟thmān, from Granada, hastened to collect the necessary material and workmen for the foundation of a new and beautiful city with a cathedral mosque, palace for the Caliph and his children, and vast dwellings for the high officials of the empire, and for the troops, all, including gardens and orchards, supplied by water derived from mountain springs. The architect in charge of the works was al-Ḥadīdī; in the "Moorish Castle" remains of the fortifications erected at that time by the Almohads have been preserved up to the present day. ʿAbd al-Muʾmin arrived in Gibraltar in D͟hu 'l-Ḳaʿda 555/November 1160; he received the homage of the whole of al-Andalus with great pomp and, having organized a reception in which the poets took part, inspected and accelerated the work on the new city which he named *Madīnat al-fatḥ* "city of victory", he returned to Morocco in Muḥarram 556/January 1161, after a stay of two months. In 709/1309 Gibraltar was taken by Alonso Pérez de Guzmán, el Bueno, on behalf of Ferdinand IV of Castile, but in 733/1333 it fell into the hands of the Marīnids of Morocco, from whom the Naṣrid Yūsuf III Abu 'l-Ḥad͟jd͟jād͟j of Granada took it, but only in 813/1410, until the time when, on 24 D͟hu 'l-Ḳaʿda 866/20 August 1462, the town was finally conquered by the duke Guzmán de Medina Sidonia on behalf of Henry IV of Castile. From 1462 to 1502 it became, together with all the mountainous region of the Campo de Gibraltar, on the north-west (in substance the entire Sierra de los Gazules), a hereditary fief of the Guzmáns of Medina Sidonia, after which it reverted to the crown. In 947/1540 Gibraltar was pillaged by the Algerian corsair K͟hayr al-Dīn, but in 959/1552 it was powerfully fortified by Charles Quint; in 1019/1610 the admiral Don Juan de Mendoza embarked at Gibraltar the Moors who had been driven out of Spain in order to return them to Africa. In the war of the Spanish succession Gibraltar fell in 1704 into British hands, and subsequently had to sustain several difficult sieges, particularly in 1779-83 under General Elliott, against Spain and France.

Bibliography: Idrīsī, *Description de l'Afrique et de l'Espagne*, text 177, trans. 213; *Géographie d'Aboul féda*, text 68, trans. 85; *Marāṣid al-iṭṭilāʿ*, v, 23-4; Ibn K͟haldūn, *Histoire des Berbères*, trans. de Slane, iv, index; *Encyclopédie arabe* (*Dāʾirat al-maʿārif*), vi, 383-6; Seybold, *Zur spanisch-arabischen Geographie*: *die Provinz Cadiz*, Halle 1906, s.v. Cadiz; Baedeker, *Spanien und Portugal*[4] (with plan); Ibn ʿAbd al-Munʿim, *al-Rawḍ al-miʿṭār*, ed. Lévi-Provençal, text 121, trans. 148; A. Huici Miranda, *Historia politica del imperio almohade*, i, 197-8.

(C. F. Seybold-[A. Huici Miranda])

D͟JABALA, Djeblé, Lat. Gabala, Fr. Gibel, Zibel (not to be confused with Giblet-D͟joubayl) is a small port on the Syrian coast, situated 30 km. to the south of al-Lād͟hiḳiya, facing the island of Ruwad; it is one of the termini of the main road from K͟hurāsān, through the valley of the ʿAya al-S͟harḳī in contact with D͟jabal Bahirā and G͟hāb, where there are roads towards Apamée and Aleppo.

This town was an important commercial centre from the time of the Phoenicians, a Dorian colony in the 5th century B.C. and then a prosperous Roman town, surrounded by a coastal plain rich in agricultural products; it was conquered and its fortifications destroyed by ʿUbayda b. al-D͟jarrāḥ in 17/638; Muʿāwiya reorganized its defences and built a citadel separate from the Byzantine fortifications.

In the 4th/10th century, with the renewal of the power of the Byzantines, the town was occupied by them on two occasions (Nicephorus Phocas in 357/985, and John Tzimisces in 364/975). In 375/985 it once again became part of the *d͟jund* of Ḥimṣ. In 473/1080, *ḳāḍī* Abū Muḥammad ʿAbd Allāh b. Manṣūr, known by the name of Ibn Ṣulayḥa, drove the Byzantines out, and the town fell into the hands of the Muslims who kept an important Jacobite bishopric there. After the third attempt of the Franks, the *ḳāḍī* surrendered the town to the *atabeg* of Damascus Tug͟htakīn (S͟hawwāl 494/August 1101); a short time later the Damascan garrison was driven out and replaced by the Banū ʿAmmār of Tripoli.

In 502/1108-9 D͟jabala was captured by the Crusaders, its commerce was given to the Genoese and it became the seat of a Roman bishopric.

In 584/July 1188 Ṣalāḥ al-Dīn was called in by the inhabitants and captured the town, which became part of the empire of al-Ẓāhir. Between 1192 and 1285 D͟jabala was the object of rivalry between the Templars and the Hospitallers. In 1285 Sulṭān Ḳalāwūn took possession of it and joined it to the *niyāba* of Ḥamāh; throughout the Mamlūk occupation the town's prosperity benefited from the important pilgrimage to the tomb of the Ṣūfī Ibrāhīm b. Adham [*q.v.*] (d. 161/778).

In 1516 it remained for four centuries under Ottoman rule. Nowadays D͟jabala, surrounded by gardens, is no more than a small town where it is still possible to admire numerous traces of the past.

Bibliography: Yāḳūt, *Muʿd͟jam*[2], ii, 105-6; Le Strange, *Palestine under the Moslems*, 460; Dussaud, *Topographie Historique de la Syrie*, 136, 432; Grousset, *Croisades*, i, 128, 210, 444; ii, 824-6; Cl. Cahen, *Syrie du Nord*, 233, 428-9, 634.

(N. Elisséeff)

D͟JABALA, an isolated mountain (known locally as a *ḥadba*) located in Nad͟jd at about 24° 48′ N, 43° 54′ E, some 60 km. north-west of al-Dawādimī, 25 km. south and east of Nafī, and 15 km. west of Wādī al-Ris͟hāʾ. The mountain, which consists of reddish stone, rises abruptly from the surrounding gravel plains. About seven km. in length and three km. wide, D͟jabala runs from south-west to north-east with three main wādīs descending from its slopes on the south-east, the north-east, and the north-west, all of which eventually flow eastwards into Wādī al-Ris͟hāʾ. The local pronunciation of the name is D͟ja-bá-la (cf. Doughty's "Gabilly").

According to the classical Arab geographers, D͟jabala lay five days' journey from Had͟jr in al-Yamāma and was inhabited by the ʿUyayna brauch of Bad͟jīla. It had al-S͟hurayf on the east, whose water belonged to Banū Numayr, and on the west al-S͟haraf, whose water belonged to Banū Kilāb. None of these names is familiar to the present inhabitants of the area.

Before Islam the battle of Yawm D͟jabala (or *Yawm al-Nūḳ*) took place in one of the wādīs descending from this mountain; the Arabs number it with those of al-Kulāb and D͟hū Ḳār among the greatest battles. An unusually large number of Arab tribes took part. On one side were ʿĀmir b. Ṣaʿṣaʿa [*q.v.*], with whom ʿAbs amongst others had allied themselves; on the other side were practically all of Tamīm under the leadership of Laḳīṭ b. Zurāra, supported by D͟hubyān and Asad, detachments from al-Ḥīra led by the step-brother of the reigning king, and men of Kinda under the "two D͟jawna", members of the family then ruling in al-Baḥrayn. In spite of great numerical superiority, Tamīm and their allies, relying, as suggested by a remark of the poet Labīd, too much on one another, were utterly defeated. The prince Laḳīṭ fell, while Ḥādjib, one of his brothers, was taken prisoner and afterwards ransomed for a huge sum. This defeat shattered the last remnants of Kinda's power in Central Arabia; one of the tribe's leaders also fell in battle. The statements regarding the date of this battle are, as usual, contradictory and uncertain. According to some it took place 17 or 19 years before the birth of the Prophet, while others say it was fought in the year of his birth. Caussin de Perceval places it a few years later, and this must be the correct date, if the king of al-Ḥīra who sent reinforcements was, as is said, al-Nuʿmān b. al-Mundhir; his reign did not begin until about 580 A.D.

In 1347/1929 another memorable battle took place at Djabala between branches of ʿUtayba. Following the crushing defeat of the rebellious *Ikhwān* at al-Sabala by King ʿAbd al-ʿAzīz Āl Saʿūd, the Barḳā branch of ʿUtayba fled, under Sulṭān b. Bidjād Āl Ḥumayd, the paramount Shaykh of ʿUtayba and one of three leaders of the rebels. He and his men were eventually caught and beaten again at Djabala by ʿUmar Ibn Rubayʿān, in command of loyal elements of al-Rawḳa of ʿUtayba. Sulṭān himself managed to escape once more, but he was later taken prisoner. Like Tamīm on Yawm Djabala, the fugitive members of ʿUtayba may have been attempting to reach one of the waters of Djabala, either the *mishāsh* of ʿAṭiyya in the south-eastern wādī or the *ʿidd* of Muwādjih in the north-eastern wādī, the reputed site of the pre-Islamic battle.

Bibliography: Bakrī, *Geogr. Wörterbuch*, ed. Wüstenfeld, 229; Yāḳūt, ii, 24 ff.; Ahlwardt, *Anonyme arab. Chronik*, 127; Ṭabarī, i, 966; *Aghānī*, x, 34-47; Ibn ʿAbd Rabbihi, *al-ʿIḳd al-farīd*, iii, 46 ff.; Ibn al-Athīr, i, 435-8; Masʿūdī, *Tanbīh*, 204 ff.; *Kāmil*, ed. Wright, 129 ff., 273, 349, 659; Caussin de Perceval, *Essai de l'Histoire des Arabes*, ii, 475-84; Sprenger, *Alte Geogr. Arabiens*, 216; idem, in *ZDMG*, xlii, 337; Wellhausen, *Skizzen und Vorarbeiten*, vi, 20; Rothstein, *Die Laḥmiden*, 108 ff.; Huber-Brockelmann, *Die Gedichte des Lebīd*, 2; Philby, *Saʾudi Arabia*, London 1955; Dickson, *Kuwait and her neighbours*, London 1956.

(F. Buhl-[R. L. Headley])

DJABALA b. **al-AYHAM**, the last of the Ghassānid dynasts whose personality dominates the scene in the story of Arab-Byzantine relations during the Muslim Conquests and may evidence the resuscitation of the Ghassānid Phylarchate after its destruction during the Persian invasion in A.D. 614.

As the ally of Byzantium, Djabala fought against Muslim arms but lost twice, first at Dūmat al-Djandal and later at Yarmūk, after which battle he made his exit from military annals. But tradition has remembered him in beautiful anecdotes whether as a Muslim who could not endure the rigour of Islam's egalitarian ideal or an apostate to Christianity living amid glittering court surroundings in Constantinople and reminiscing on his former days in the Djawlān.

Bibliography: Balādhurī, *Futūḥ*, 135, 136; Ṭabarī, i, 2065, 2066, 2347; *Aghānī*[1], xiv, 2-8; Caetani, *Annali*, iii, 551 ff., 562, 936; iv, 506; v, 194 ff. (Irfan Kawar)

DJAʿBAR or **ḲALʿAT DJAʿBAR**, a ruined fortress situated on the left bank of the middle Euphrates, almost opposite Ṣiffīn. Also called Ḳalʿat Dawsar from the name by which this locality was known in the pre-Islamic period and in the early days of Islam (Pauly-Wissowa, iv, 2234: *to Dawsarōn*, which explains the Arab traditions connecting this name Dawsar with the king of al-Ḥīra, al-Nuʿmān b. al-Mundhir), it was described by ancient Arabic authors as a stopping-place on the route leading from al-Raḳḳa to Bālis (Ibn Khurradādhbih, 74; al-Tabarī, iii, 220). In the Mamlūk period it became a stage on the Ḥimṣ-Raʾs al-ʿAyn postal route.

The fortress owes its modern name to the Ḳushayrī Djaʿbar b. Sābiḳ who captured it in the time of the Saldjūḳids, but was forced to give it up to sultan Malikshāh. The latter handed it over to the last ʿUḳaylid of Ḥalab, Sālim b. Mālik, who had been expelled from his former possessions (479/1086-7), and Ḳalʿat Djaʿbar remained in the hands of Sālim's descendants for almost a century, apart from a brief occupation by the Franks (497/1102). Zankī, the powerful *atabeg* of al-Mawṣil, was assassinated there in 541/1146 while besieging it, and in 564/1168-9 the ʿUḳaylid Shihāb al-Dīn Mālik was forced to surrender it, in exchange for other districts, to Nūr al-Dīn who put up various buildings there; of these a minaret still survives. The importance of the Jewish colony at the time was noted by Benjamin of Tudela. Subsequently Djaʿbar passed into the hands of the Ayyūbids, and then the Mamlūks. Under the latter dynasty it was at first abandoned but the fortress, which had fallen into ruin in the time of Abu 'l-Fidāʾ, was restored at the end of al-Nāṣir Muḥammad's reign by governor Tankīz in 736/1335-6. Traces of the fortress still attract attention, standing above a steep chalky cliff and dominating the wide Euphrates valley, but no serious archaeological investigations have ever been conducted there. According to ʿĀshiḳpashazāde (chapter 2) and other early Ottoman historians, Sulaymān Shāh, the ancestor of the Ottoman Sultans, was drowned nearby; he was buried by the castle of Djaʿbar and commemorated by a tomb known as Mezār-i Türk or Türk Mezārī. The tomb was reconstructed by order of ʿAbd al-Ḥamīd II and retained as Turkish property by article ix of the Treaty of Ankara of 1921. This story is perhaps due to a confusion between Sulaymān Shāh, the putative grandfather of ʿOthmān I, and the Saldjūḳid prince Sulaymān b. Ḳutlumush [*q.v.*]. The tomb itself is in all probability not connected with either of them.

Bibliography: Ibn Khurradādhbih, 74, 98; Yāḳūt, ii, 84, 621; iv, 164; Harawī, *K. al-Ziyārāt*, ed. trans. J. Sourdel-Thomine, Damascus 1953-7, 63, 140; Abu 'l-Fidāʾ, *Géographie*, ed. Reinaud, 269, 276-7; Ibn al-ʿAdīm, *Zubda*, ed. S. Dahan, ii, Damascus 1954, index; Ibn al-Ḳalānisī, ed. Amedroz, Eng. trans. Gibb, French trans. R. Le Tourneau, index; Ibn al-Athīr, index; Ibn Iyās, ed. Būlāḳ, i, 168; M. Gaudefroy-Demombynes, *La Syrie à l'époque des Mamelouks*, Paris 1923, 103; Le Strange, 102; R. Dussaud, *Topographie historique de la Syrie*, Paris 1927, particularly 465; A. Musil, *Middle Euphrates*, New York 1927, 95; M. Canard, *Histoire de la dynastie des H'amdanides*, i, Algiers 1951, 88; Cl. Cahen, *La Syrie du nord à l'époque des Croisades*, Paris 1940, index, particularly 372 and 408; F. Sarre and E. Herzfeld, *Archäologische Reise im Euphrat- und Tigris-Gebiete*, Berlin 1911, i, 135; *RCEA*, ix, no. 3314; N. Elisséeff, *La titulature de Nūr al-Dīn*, in *BEO*, xiv (1952-54), 165-6; J. Sauvaget, *La poste aux chevaux*, Paris 1941, 56-7. (D. Sourdel)

DJABART, the name of the Muslims of Ethiopia. Originally the name of a region (Djabara or Djabart) in the territories of Zaylaʿ and Ifāt (cf. al-Maḳrīzī, *al-Ilmām*, Cairo 1895, 6 ff.), later applied to all the Muslim principalities of southern Ethiopia and, ultimately, to all Muslims living in Ethiopia. The term Djabart is sometimes also used by the Christian population of Ethiopia with reference to the Muslims of the Arabian peninsula and thus becomes identical with the term Muslim in general. In modern usage Djabart is almost invariably employed, in a narrow sense, to describe the Muslim nuclei in the Christian plateau provinces of Eritrea, Tigre, Amhara, Shoa, etc. The common form Djabarti is scarcely a *nisba* but rather shows the *-i* ending by which Tigriña and Harari dissolve final consonant clusters. According to Abyssinian tradition the word is derived from Ethiopic *agbərt* (pl. of *gabr*) "servants (of God)"—cf. the similar development in the case of *ʿibād*. In Amharic a Muslim is called *əslam* or *näggadʷe* ("trader").

The Djabarti live in families and small groups scattered throughout the Christian Abyssinian highlands. Ethnically and linguistically they are indistinguishable from their Christian neighbours. Their knowledge of Arabic is generally limited to the minimum necessary for an understanding of the Ḳurʾān. Some of them claim descent from the first Muslim refugees who were sent to Abyssinia by the Prophet. The majority, however, owe their conversion to the sultanates in south-east Ethiopia and to the invasion of Aḥmad Grañ. In general, the relations between Djabarti and Christians are friendly, though discrimination against them was not unknown in the past, particularly in the deprivation of *rəsti* (the hereditary land-right), which led many of them into commerce and handicrafts.

Estimates of their numbers vary greatly, but it seems safe to say that there are about 20,000 Djabarti in the three plateau provinces of Eritrea and not less than 50,000 in Ethiopia (these figures exclude, of course, the fairly large number of Muslims other than Djabarti in the narrow application of the term). They maintain a number of mosques and Ḳurʾān schools. In *madhhab* they belong to the Mālikiyya and Shāfiʿiyya. The Djabarti have a *riwāḳ* at al-Azhar in Cairo.

Bibliography: Djabartī, *ʿAdjāʾib*, Būlāḳ 1297, i, 385 ff ; E. Mittwoch, *Excerpte aus dem Koran in Amharischer Sprache*, in *MSOS As.*, 1906, iii; E. Cerulli, in *OM*, 1925, 614-5; A. Pollera, *Le popolazioni indigene dell'Eritrea*, Bologna 1935, 149-52; J. S. Trimingham, *Islam in Ethiopia*, Oxford 1952, 150-3. (E. ULLENDORFF)

AL-**DJABARTĪ**, ʿABD AL-RAḤMĀN B. ḤASAN, the historian, b. 1167/1753, d. 1825 or early 1826, was a descendant of a Ḥanafī family from al-Djabart [*q.v.*]. According to al-Djabartī the people of that region were very strict in their religion and were inclined to asceticism. Many of them went on foot to the Ḥidjāz, either as pilgrims or as *mudjāwirūn*. They had three *riwāḳ*s of their own: one in the mosque of Medina, one in the mosque at Mecca, and one in the mosque of al-Azhar at Cairo. The forefather of the Egyptian branch of the family of al-Djabartī, ʿAbd al-Raḥmān by name, who was al-Djabartī's "seventh grandfather", went first to Mecca and Medina, where he studied for a long time; he then reached Egypt and joined the *riwāḳ* of the people of al-Djabart in al-Azhar at the beginning of the 10th/end of 15th or beginning of 16th century. There he became the head (*shaykh*) of the *riwāḳ* and the leader of the Djabartī community. The office of the *shaykh* of the *riwāḳ* was inherited from father to son in al-Djabartī's family; all the holders of this office are described as very religious, ascetic and upright people.

From such a family rose a very great historian, who is undoubtedly a unique phenomenon in Muslim historiography. For in glaring contrast to the period of the Mamlūk sultanate (648-918/1250-1512), which abounds in rich, most detailed and accurate source material, hardly surpassed in either quality or quantity by the source material pertaining to any other region of Islam, the period of Ottoman rule in Egypt (918-1226/1512-1811 approximately) is conspicuous for the dearth of its historical sources written by contemporary inhabitants of the country. A very limited revival of historiography in Egypt, which took place towards the close of the 11th/17th century, did not change substantially this state of affairs. According to al-Djabartī's own testimony, the study of history was completely ignored and despised by his contemporaries. He himself would not have dealt with it had he not been ousted from public life. His knowledge of Muslim and Egyptian history up to 1100/1688 (the year with which his chronicle opens) seems to have been very limited; yet in spite of these handicaps, and in spite of the fact that he had written only a local history of a province belonging to a much wider empire, he succeeded in writing one of the most important chronicles of the Arab countries during the Muslim period.

Al-Djabartī's main historical work is his chronicle, entitled *ʿAdjāʾib al-āthār fi 'l-tarādjim wa 'l-akhbār*, which covers the years 1100/1688 to 1236/1821. He gives us two versions about its compilation: from the first version, which is somewhat unclear, it would appear that he started to take notes for his book regularly from 1190/1226-7. According to the second version, the Damascene historian al-Murādī, author of the biographical dictionary of famous people of the 12th/18th century (*Silk al-durar fī aʿyān al-ḳarn al-thānī ʿashar*) was the "main cause" of the compilation of the chronicle in its existing form. Al-Murādī asked and obtained the co-operation of Muḥammad al-Murtaḍā al-Zabīdī, the author of *Tādj al-ʿarūs*, who lived in Egypt, in the compilation of that work. Al-Murtaḍā was helped in this task by his pupil al-Djabartī. When al-Murtaḍā died in Shaʿbān 1205/April 1791 al-Murādī asked al-Djabartī to take his dead master's place. Al-Murādī died, however, in Ṣafar 1206/October of the same year, a fact which discouraged al-Djabartī from pursuing his collection of material. Somewhat later, however, an "internal urge" (*bāʿith min nafsī*) prompted the author to resume his work and add the chronicle of events "in the present order".

From the above it is made clear that as long as al-Djabartī worked for al-Murtaḍā and al-Murādī he collected material solely for biographies, and that only quite a long time after 1206/1791, when he decided to continue his work independently, did he start collecting purely chronological data as well. This explains the extremely large proportion of biographies in his book; it explains also why al-Djabartī concentrated on the 12th/18th century, for al-Murādī's biographical dictionary is devoted to persons of the same century. In any case, it is no mere accident that al-Djabartī's chronicle is called *al-Tarādjim wa 'l-akhbār*, biographies taking first place and the narrative only second. This fact acquires a considerably added significance if we recall that out of all the chronicles of Ottoman Egypt al-Djabartī's was the only one to include biographies in historical work. In the Mamlūk sultanate there developed an extremely rich biographic literature, unparalleled perhaps in any other Muslim country or region. This kind of historical writing died out completely in Egypt under the Ottomans until it was revived by al-Djabartī alone, as a result of *Syrian* influence. Whether he was also influenced by the Mamlūk biographical works is a matter which, in the state of our knowledge at present, cannot be ascertained.

Al-Djabartī wrote the first three volumes of his chronicle in their final form during the year 1220 and the beginning of 1221/1805-6; the fourth and last volume was compiled, seemingly, during the period which it covers, *i.e.*, the years 1221-36/1806-21. There is no doubt that he intended to continue the chronicle after the fourth volume, as may be inferred from his remark at the end of that volume. Whether he did continue it or not cannot be established with certainty.

Because of al-Djabartī's vehement attacks on Muḥammad ʿAlī and his regime, the publication of the *ʿAdjāʾib* was long forbidden in Egypt. A. von Kremer gives revealing evidence of the Egyptian government's attempt to suppress the book (*Aegypten*, ii, 326). Only towards the end of the 1870s was the ban on the book lifted. The first time any part of it was published without government interference was in 1878, when the press of the Alexandria newspaper *Miṣr* printed the section dealing with the French occupation; it was edited by Adīb Isḥāḳ, who called it *Taʾrīkh al-Faransawiyya fī Miṣr*. In 1297/1879-80, soon after the Khedive Tawfīḳ's accession to the throne, the whole chronicle was published for the first time at the Būlāḳ printing press—this is the standard edition. In 1302/1884-5, the chronicle was published again in *al-Maṭbaʿa al-Azhariyya* in the margins of Ibn al-Athīr's *K. al-Kāmil*. In 1322/1904-5, it was published as an independent book in *al-Maṭbaʿa al-Ashrafiyya*, Cairo. A French translation of the *ʿAdjāʾib*, called *Merveilles biographiques et historiques, ou Chronique du Cheikh Abd-El-Rahman El-Djabarti*, was published in Cairo at the Imprimerie Nationale, during the years 1888-96; it is an extremely inaccurate and bad translation and is very dangerous to use.

The chronicle is of immense importance for the whole period which it covers. As for the early part of that period, it is difficult to establish, in the present state of our knowledge, to what extent al-Djabartī relied on earlier sources which he has not cited; also, he might have erred about certain facts, some of which are important. Yet the general picture which he depicts of that early part reflects the history of the Egypt of that time in the clearest and truest way. For the later part of that period, and especially for the French occupation and the early reign of Muḥammad ʿAlī, he is undoubtedly the best extant source (for an enumeration and evaluation of the subjects with which the chronicle deals see D. Ayalon, *The historian al-Jabartī and his background*, in *BSOAS*, xxiii/2, 1960, 235-6).

A second chronicle written by al-Djabartī, called *Muẓhir al-taḳdīs bi-dhahāb dawlat al-Faransīs*, covers the few years of the French occupation of Egypt. Its compilation was finished at the end of Shaʿbān 1216/end of December 1801 or beginning of January 1802. In it al-Djabartī attempted to curry favour with the Ottomans by extolling them on the one hand and by denigrating the French on the other. It was published recently (in 1958?) by Muḥammad ʿAṭā under the title *Yawmiyyāt al-Djabartī* (two small volumes, nos 59 and 60 in the series *ikhtarnā laka*, Dar al-Maʿārif, Cairo). It was twice translated into Turkish, by the historian ʿĀṣım, and by the physician Bahdjat Muṣṭafā [*qq.v.*]. The latter's version, under the name *Taʾrīkh-i Miṣr*, was published in Istanbul in 1282 A.H.

Al-Djabartī also made an abridgment of Dāwūd al-Anṭāḳī's medical treatise *Tadhkirat al-Albāb*. According to Lane he also refined the language of the *Thousand Nights and One Night*, and "added many facetiae of his own and of other literati". This copy seems to have been lost.

Although al-Djabartī's knowledge of Muslim history was very limited, and although he did not have any personal contact with any important Muslim historian, he was very well situated to acquire first-hand information on events which took place in Egypt and especially in Cairo. His family, and particularly his father, Ḥasan, had strong and numerous connexions both among the ruling class (Mamlūks and Ottomans) and the class of the *ʿulamāʾ*. His father had the greatest share in moulding his character and shaping his outlook. He seems to have inherited from him the combination of Muslim piety and learning with the practical knowledge and understanding of a man of the world. Other persons who greatly influenced al-Djabartī were the above-mentioned Murtaḍā al-Zabīdī, Ḥasan al-ʿAṭṭār [*q.v.*] and Ismāʿīl al-Khashshāb.

Bibliography: (1) Autographs. For an example of the *ʿAdjāʾib* in the ʿIrāḳ Museum library see *RIMA*, i, 1955, 45; for an autograph of the *Muẓhir* in the Cambridge University library see E. G. Browne, *Handlist*, 1900, 207, no. 1058. Qq. 214. (2) Works and references in Arabic: ʿAlī Mubārak, *al-Khiṭaṭ al-Tawfīḳiyya al-djadīda*, *passim*; Djurdjī Zaydān, *Taʾrīkh ādāb al-lugha al-ʿArabiyya*, Cairo 1914, iv, 283-4; P. L. Cheikho, *al-Ādāb al-ʿArabiyya fi 'l-ḳarn al-tāsiʿ ʿashar*², Beirut 1924, 21; Sarkīs, i, col. 676; Khalīl Shaybūb, *ʿAbd al-Raḥmān al-Djabartī*, Cairo 1948 (no. 70 in the series *iḳraʾ*); Maḥmūd al-Sharḳawī, *Dirāsāt fī Taʾrīkh al-Djabartī, Miṣr fi 'l-ḳarn al-thāmin ʿashar*, 3 vols., Cairo 1955-6; Muḥammad Anīs, *al-Djabartī bayna Muẓhir al-taḳdīs wa-ʿAdjāʾib al-āthār, madjallat kulliyyat al-ādāb*, Cairo 1956, xviii, 59-70; Djamāl al-Dīn al-Shayyāl, *al-Taʾrīkh wa'l-muʾarrikhūn fī Miṣr fi'l-ḳarn al-tāsiʿ ʿashar*, Cairo 1955, 10 ff. (3) Works and references in European languages: D. B. Macdonald, art. DJABARTĪ in *EI*¹; Brockelmann, II, 364, 480; S II, 730; *Supplement to the catalogue of the Arabic mss of the British Museum*, London 1894, no. 571; G. Wiet, *Index de Djabarti* (Arabic title: *Fihris ʿAdjāʾib al-āthār*), Cairo 1954; Fr. Babinger, *Geschichtschreiber*, 340; Seetzen, *Reisen*, Berlin 1854, iii, 128-9; E. W. Lane, *Description of Egypt*, Brit. Mus. MS, Add. 34080, vol. i, fol. 215; idem, *Manners and customs of the modern Egyptians*, (first publ. 1836), Everyman's Library ed. 222; idem, *The Thousand and One Nights*, London 1889, i, 61, n. 28; 66, n. to ch. I; 201, n. 85; Giambatista Brocchi, *Giornale delle osservazioni fatte ne' viagi in Egitto, nella Siria e nella Nubia*, Bassano 1641-3, i, 151; A. Cardin, *Journal d'Abdurrahman Gabarti pendant l'occupation Française en Égypte*, Paris 1938; *Histoire scientifique et militaire de l'Expédition Française en Égypte*, Paris 1830-4, i, 10 *et passim*; A. von Kremer, *Aegypten*, Leipzig 1863, ii, 325-6; idem, *Beiträge zur Arabischen Lexikographie*, Vienna 1883-4; *Merveilles biographiques et historiques*, Cairo 1888, i, Introd.; Cl. Huart, *Littérature arabe*, Paris 1902, 415-6; J. Heyworth-Dunne, *Introduction to the history of education in modern Egypt*, 1938; idem, *Arabic literature in Egypt in the nineteenth century*, in *BSOS*, ix, 1938, 675-89; Gibb-Bowen, i, Parts I and II; Nicolas Turc, *Chronique d'Égypte 1798-1804*, ed. and tr. G. Wiet, Cairo 1950 (specially the glossary, 289-314, and the annotations to the Fr. trans., where al-Djabartī's chronicle is frequently used); Gamāl al-Dīn al-Šayyāl, *Al-Ŷabarti y su escuela*, in *Revista del instituto de estudios islámicos en Madrid*, vi, (1958), 91-101; D. Ayalon, *The historian al-Jabartī and his background*, in *BSOAS*, xxiii/2, 1960, 217-49. (D. AYALON)

DJABARŪT [see ʿĀLAM].

AL-**DJABBĀR** [see NUDJŪM].

DJABBUL, a town in Central Babylonia, on the east bank of the Tigris, a few hours' journey above Kūt al-ʿAmāra, and five parasangs (about twenty miles) south-east of Nuʿmāniya (the modern Tell Naʿmān). It is described as a flourishing place by the older Arab geographers; but, by Yāḳūt's time (beginning of the 7th/13th century) it had considerably declined. In course of time—we have no details of its decay—it fell utterly into ruins. This town must date from a very remote period; for the name of the Gambūlu, one of the most important Aramaic nomadic tribes, frequently mentioned in the first thousand years B.C., must have survived in Djabbul; they have left traces of their influence in modern topography in several other places. The ruins of Djabbul, which were known by the name Djumbul, Djanbal, or Djenbil as late as the first half of the 19th century according to the travellers Rich, Chesney and Jones, have now utterly disappeared owing to earthquakes. On the site where Chesney in 1833 had seen the ruins of a large town, no trace of them was to be seen in 1848 when Jones passed it; the Tigris had in the interval entirely engulfed the remains of the town.

Bibliography: *BGA*, *passim*; Yāḳūt, ii, 23; Le Strange, in *JRAS*, 1895, 43; Le Strange, 38; M. Streck, *Babylonien nach den arab. Geograph.*, ii, 1901, 307-9; idem, in *Mitteil. d. Vorderas. Gesellsch.*, xi, 1906, 222; Ritter, Erdkunde, x, 232; xi, 934; H. Kiepert, in *GErdk. Birl.*, 1883, 16. (M. STRECK)

AL-**DJABBŪL**, the ancient Gabbula, a place east-south-east of Ḥalab, watered by the Nahr al-Dhahab. The salt-mines there lent Djabbūl a certain economic importance in the middle ages as they still do, to which it probably also owed its position as an administrative centre in the political division of the Mamlūk kingdom.

Bibliography: M. Streck, *Keilinschriftl. Beiträge zur Geogr. Vorderasiens*, 20; Schiffer, *Die Aramäer*, 131 ff.; Yāḳūt, ii, 29; Ḳalḳashandī, *Ḍawʾ al-ṣubḥ*, Cairo 1324, 295; von Kremer, *Beiträge z. Geogr. des nördl. Syrien*, 18; Le Strange, *Palestine*, 460; Ritter, *Erdkunde*, xvii, 1694 ff. (R. HARTMANN)

DJĀBIR B. **AFLAḤ**, ABŪ MUḤAMMAD, the astronomer Geber of the middle ages; he was often confused with the alchemist Geber, whose full name was Abū ʿAbd Allāh Djābir b. Ḥayyān al-Ṣūfī. He belonged to Seville; the period in which he flourished cannot certainly be determined, but from the fact that his son was personally acquainted with Maimonides (d. 1204), it may be concluded that he died towards the middle of the 12th century. He wrote an astronomical work which still survives under two different titles; in the Escurial Ms. it is called *Kitāb al-Hayʾa* (the Book of Astronomy), in the Berlin copy it is entitled *Iṣlāḥ al-Madjisṭī* (correction of the Almagest). In it he sharply criticizes certain views held by Ptolemy; particularly rightly when he asserts that the lower planets, Mercury and Venus, have no visible parallaxes, although he himself gives the sun a parallax of about 3′, and that these planets are nearer the earth than the sun. The book is otherwise noteworthy for prefacing the astronomical part with a special chapter on trigonometry [see ABU 'L-WAFAʾ]. In his spherical trigonometry, he takes the "rule of the four magnitudes" as the foundation for the derivation of his formulae, and gives for the first time the fifth main formula for the right-angled triangle (cos A = cos a. sin B). In plane trigonometry he solves his problems with the aid of the whole chord instead of using the trigonometrical functions sine and cosine. The work was translated into Latin by Gerhard of Cremona and this translation was published by Petrus Apianus in Nuremburg in 1534.

Bibliography: Ibn al-Ḳifṭī (ed. Lippert), 319, 393; Ḥādjdjī Khalīfa, vi, 506; M. Steinschneider, *Zur pseudepigraphischen Litteratur*, Berlin 1862, 14 ff., 70 ff.; von Braunmühl, *Vorlesungen über Gesch. der Trigonom.*, Leipzig 1900, i, 81 ff.; H. Suter, *Abhandlungen zur Gesch. der mathem. Wissensch.*, x, 119, xiv, 176; Duhem, *Système du monde*, ii, 172-9; Sarton, *Introduction*, ii, 206, 1005, iii, 1521. (H. SUTER*)

DJĀBIR B. **ḤAYYĀN** B. ʿABD ALLĀH AL-KŪFĪ AL-ṢŪFĪ, one of the principal representatives of earlier Arabic alchemy. The genealogy quoted above is taken from the Fihrist, where on p. 354 the oldest biography of Djābir is preserved. His *kunya* given there is not Abū Mūsā, as usual, but Abū ʿAbd Allāh, although Ibn al-Nadīm himself states that al-Rāzī (d. 313/925 or 323/935) used to quote: "Our master Abū Mūsā Djābir b. Ḥayyān says ...". The biography shows not only complete uncertainty regarding facts, but also legendary elements; on the other hand, Ibn al-Nadīm contests the opinion that Djābir had never existed. The references to the Imām Djaʿfar al-Ṣādiḳ (d. 148/765) as Djābir's master to be found in the writings attributed to Djābir, and further references to the Barmakids (see below) have supported the tradition given by al-Djildakī (d. 743/1342) according to which Djābir was a contemporary of the first ʿAbbāsids. As for Djābir's historic personality, Holmyard has suggested that his father was "a certain Azdī called Ḥayyān, a druggist of Kūfa ... mentioned ... in connexion with the political machinations that, in the eighth century, finally resulted in the overthrow of the Umayyad dynasty". This would explain why Djābir has in some later sources the *nisba* Azdī.

It can no longer be denied that the list of Djābir's writings given in the *Fihrist* with reference to Djābir's own lists of his writings is on the whole correct. Many quotations from the books only known by name have recently been found in the writings preserved. They enabled P. Kraus to prepare a critical biography of the books belonging to the corpus, to arrive at a relative chronology of them, and to amend the list in the *Fihrist* (to his bibliography add *Ḥall al-rumūz wa mafātiḥ al-kunūz*, quoted in the *Shawḳ al-mustahām*, ed. J. v. Hammer, *Ancient alphabets*, 1810, 80).

But the time of the writings is not that suggested by the names of the persons occurring therein. The earliest evidence of their existence is found partly in the works of the alchemist Ibn Umayl (c. 350/961) and of the forger Ibn Waḥshiyya (c. 350/961), and partly in the *Fihrist* of Ibn al-Nadīm [*q.v.*].

The corpus was divided into several collections of which the most important are: the CXII books, incoherent essays on the practice of alchemy with many references to ancient alchemy (Zosimus, Democritus, Hermes, Agathodemon, etc.); the LXX books, a systematic exposition of the alchemical teaching of Djābir; the CXLIV books or *Kutub al-mawāzīn* ("Books of the balances"), an exposition of the theoretical and more philosophical foundations of alchemy and of all occult sciences; the D books, consisting of isolated treatises investigating more fully certain problems of the *Kutub al-mawāzīn*. These four collections also mark successive stages in the development of the Djābirian doctrine and in the composition of the corpus. To this have to be added other smaller collections dealing with alchemy in its relation to the commentaries on the works of Aristotle and Plato, then treatises on philosophy, astronomy and astrology, mathematics and music, medicine and magic, and finally religious works.

This vast body of literature, which comprises all the sciences of the ancients which passed to Islam, cannot be the work of a single author nor can it date back to the second half of the 2nd/8th century. All the facts combine to show that the corpus was compiled at the end of the 3rd/9th and beginning of the 4th/10th century.

The writings of Djābir in the first place present us with a problem in religious history. Just as the ancient alchemists who have been preserved are oriented towards Christian gnosis, so Djābir introduces into his system of sciences Muslim gnosis. This gnosis is not the primitive gnosis which developed in Shīʿī circles of the 1st/7th and 2nd/8th centuries as described to us by Muslim writers on heresy; it is rather the gnostic syncretism which was in vogue among the Shīʿī extremists (*ghulāt*) at the end of the 3rd/9th century, which, combining with revolutionary political tendencies, threatened the very existence of Islam. Djābir proclaimed the imminent advent of a new *imām* who would abolish the law of Islam and replace the revelation of the Ḳurʾān by the lights of Greek science and philosophy. The teachings of the corpus are the expositions of this new, purely spiritual, revelation, the representatives of which are the ʿAlid imāms.

From the point of view of his religious terminology, Djābir is closely connected with Ḳarmaṭianism (the Ḳarmaṭians who came to the front after 260/873 are even quoted in Djābir). The imām is called *nāṭiḳ* in contrast to *ṣāmit*; the degrees of initiation are called by the same terms as among the Ḳarmaṭians and the Fāṭimid Ismāʿīlīs (*bāb, hudjdja, dāʿī muṭlaḳ, sābiḳ tālī, lāḥiḳ*, etc.); the doctrine of the adversaries (*aḍdād*) of the imām is also developed. The history of the world is divided according to the successive revelations into seven stages, of which the revelation of the Djābirian imām is the last. Similarly the Muslim imāms who have succeeded one another from ʿAlī to the new Ḳāʾim number seven: Ḥasan, Ḥusayn, Muḥammad b. al-Ḥanafiyya [*sic*], ʿAlī b. Ḥusayn, Muḥammad b. al-Bāḳir, Djaʿfar al-Ṣādiḳ, Ismāʿīl (= Muḥammad b. Ismāʿīl = the new Ḳāʾim). Contrary to the Ḳarmaṭians and the Ismāʿīliyya, ʿAlī is not regarded as one of the seven imāms. He is a *ṣāmit*, a concealed divinity, superior to the *nāṭiḳ*, and the seven imāms are his terrestrial incarnations. In this Djābir's teaching resembles that of the sect of the Nuṣayrīs [*q.v.*]. With the Nuṣayrīs it also shares the conceptions of the three divine hypostases: *ʿAyn* (= ʿAlī), *Mīm* (= Muḥammad), *Sīn* (= Salmān); the *Sīn* being superior to the *Mīm* in Djābir's view. In this system the imām proclaimed by Djābir and called *Mādjid* or *Yatīm* is a direct emanation from the ʿAyn, after having passed the stages of the *Mīm* and the *Sīn*. As with all the Shīʿī *ghulāt* and particularly with the Nuṣayrīs, the doctrine of metempsychosis is accepted (terms: *tanāsukh, adwār, akwār, naskh, faskh, raskh, maskh*).

In the second place the writings of Djābir present problems connected with the history of the sciences in Islam. The corpus is devoted to the study of the following branches: alchemy (which always takes first place), medicine, astrology, magic (telesmology), the doctrine of the specific qualities of things (*khawāṣṣ*), and the artificial generation of living beings (*takwīn*). Granted that we are frequently ill-informed regarding the corresponding branches in ancient science, the writings of Djābir still enable us to restore to Greek science some interesting aspects which were thought to have been lost. The alchemy of Djābir is fundamentally distinct from all that has survived of ancient alchemy. It deliberately avoids hermetic allegorism (of Egyptian origin) represented in antiquity by the writings of Zosimus and others and revived in Islam by most of the alchemists like Ibn Umayl, the *Turba philosophorum*, Ṭughrāʾī, Djildakī, etc. The alchemy of Djābir is an experimental science based on a philosophical theory.

This philosophical theory comes for the most part from the physics of Aristotle. Djābir knows and quotes (often from the translations of Ḥunayn b. Isḥāḳ (d. 260/873-4) and his school) all the parts of Aristotle's work, as well as the commentaries of Alexander of Aphrodisias, Themistius, Simplicius, Porphyry and others. We also find quoted the writings of Plato, Theophrastus, Galen, Euclid, Ptolemy, Archimedes, the *Placita philosophorum* of Ps. Plutarchus, etc. Among these there are several of which the Greek originals are lost. No alchemical work of Islam reveals such vast knowledge of ancient literature or has such an encyclopaedic character as the writings of Djābir. In this they resemble the *Rasāʾil Ikhwān al-Ṣafā*, which, by the way, come from the same source.

The scientific terminology used by Djābir is without exception that introduced by Ḥunayn b. Isḥāḳ, which shows once more that the corpus could not have been composed before the end of the 3rd/9th century.

The fundamental principle in the science of Djābir is that of *mīzān* (balance). This term combines the most diverse speculations and shows very well Djābir's scientific syncretism. *Mīzān* means: (*a*) specific gravity (references to Archimedes); (*b*) the σταθμός of the ancient alchemists, meaning the measure in a mixture of substances; (*c*) a speculation on the letters of the Arabic alphabet, which are connected with the four elementary qualities (hot, cold, wet, dry). This *mīzān al-ḥurūf* is not only applied to all things comprised in the sub-lunary world, but also to metaphysical beings, like intelligence, the soul of the world, matter, space, and time. It was from neo-Pythagoreanism on the one hand and the Shīʿī speculations of the *djafr* [*q.v.*] on the other that Djābir borrowed this system; (*d*) *mīzān* is also the metaphysical principle *par excellence*, a symbol of the scientific monism of Djābir. In this sense it is opposed to the dualist principle of the Manichaeans. Neo-Platonic speculations on the One do not seem to have been without influence here; (*e*) lastly, *mīzān* derives from an allegorical explanation (*ta'wīl*) of the Ḳur'ānic references to the weighing at the day of judgment. This speculation is also found in Muslim gnosis and it is through it that Djābir connects his scientific system with this religious teaching.

The writings of Djābir seem to be closely connected with the pagan scholarship of the Ḥarrānian milieu. Djābir expressly refers to the Ṣābi'a when reproducing their discussions of certain metaphysical problems. The direct sources of his scientific system are the writings of Ps.-Apollonius of Tyana (Balīnūs [*q.v.*]), *Kitāb sirr al-khalīḳa* and others, apocryphal works which, according to a note by Muḥammad b. Zakariyyā al-Rāzī, were composed in the time of al-Ma'mūn and are found to be the best source for a knowledge of "Ḥarrānian" literature.

Djābir says that his knowledge was handed down to him by his master Dja'far al-Ṣādiḳ. It is to this "mine of wisdom" that all his knowledge goes back, he himself being only a compiler. In the religious hierarchy he ranks immediately after the imām. He further quotes as his master a certain Ḥarbī the Ḥimyarī, a monk (*rāhib*) and a man named Udhn al-Ḥimār. Among the contemporaries of Dja'far are mentioned the Barmakids Khalīd, Yaḥyā and Dja'far, to whom Djābir dedicated several of his treatises, and the members of the Shī'ī family of Yaḳṭīn.

All these statements belong to the realm of legend and are in contradiction to the internal evidence of the writings. Besides, a pupil of Dja'far named Djābir b. Ḥayyān is nowhere mentioned in Shī'ī literature and seems to be a pure invention. It is easily understood why the author of these works attributed them to a pupil of Dja'far, who was often regarded in Shī'ī literature as the representative of Greek learning and particularly of occult sciences. Moreover, Dja'far was the father of the seventh imām Ismā'īl, whose advent is announced in these writings.

The *Fihrist* of Ibn al-Nadīm says that there were in his time Shī'īs who doubted the authenticity of these writings. The philosopher and scientist Abū Sulaymān al-Manṭiḳī (d. ca. 370/980-1) has left in his *Ta'līḳāt* a note according to which he was personally acquainted with the author of the writings attributed to Djābir. He calls him al-Ḥasan b. al-Nakad al-Mawṣilī. We have no reason to doubt the authenticity of this statement even if it is certain that the writings of Djābir are not the work of a single author and even if the corpus underwent a fairly long evolution before attaining its present form. The *terminus ante quem* would be about 330/942.

The writings of Djābir considerably influenced the development of later Arab alchemy. All later writers quote them, and many wrote commentaries. Several books of the corpus were translated into Latin. The famous writings attributed to *Geber rex Arabum*, however, represent only a late recension by a Latin author of the 13th century A.D.

Bibliography: P. Kraus, *Jābir ibn Ḥayyān, Essai sur l'histoire des idées scientifiques dans l'Islam, I. Textes choisis*, 1935; idem, *Jābir ibn Ḥayyān, Contribution à l'histoire des idées scientifiques dans l'Islam*, I, *Le corpus des écrits jābiriens*, 1933; II, *Jābir et la science grecque*, 1942 (*MIE*, xliv and xlv; a third volume on Djābir's religious position was never finished). The *K. al-Mādjid* (*Textes choisis*, 115-25) has been translated and commented upon by H. Corbin, in *Eranos-Jahrbuch*, xviii, 1950. The *K. al-Sumūm wa daf' maḍārrhā* has been published and translated by A. Siegel, *Das Buch der Gifte des Ğābir ibn Ḥayyān*, 1958 (cf. M. Plessner, in *Isis*, li, 1960, 356 ff.). A complete German trans. of the LXX Books by M. Plessner is still unpublished.—Books later than Kraus's *magnum opus* are: E. J. Holmyard, *Alchemy*, 1957 (Pelican books); Ps.-Mağrīṭī, *Das Ziel des Weisen* (*Picatrix*), Ger. trans. H. Ritter and M. Plessner, 1962 (*Studies of the Warburg Institute*, xxvii). For the quotations from Ps.-Plutarchus, *Placita philosophorum*, in the corpus see 'A. Badawī's introduction to his ed. of the full text, *Aristotelis De anima, etc.*, in *Islamica*, xvi, 1954. For recent articles see Pearson, nos. 5121-47.

(P. KRAUS-[M. PLESSNER])

DJĀBIR B. ZAYD, ABU 'L-SHA'THĀ' AL-AZDĪ AL-'UMĀNĪ AL-YAḤMIDĪ AL-DJAWFĪ (al-Djawf in Baṣra) AL-BAṢRĪ, a famous traditionist, *ḥāfiẓ* and jurist, of the Ibāḍī sect. He was born in 21/642 in Nazwā (in 'Umān), and, according to tradition, became head of the Ibāḍī community of Baṣra upon the death of 'Abd Allāh b. Ibāḍ [*q.v.*]. He carried on the latter's policy of maintaining friendly relations with the Umayyads, and kept on good terms with the ruthless persecutor of the Azāriḳa, al-Ḥadjdjādj, through whom he even succeeded in obtaining regular payments from the state coffers. But towards the end of the first century of Islam he was exiled to the southern part of the Arabian peninsula, together with other Ibāḍī leaders, on account of a political disagreement with the governor of Baṣra. The date of his death has not been firmly established (93/711, 96/714, 103/721, 104/722).

At Baṣra he enjoyed an enormous prestige as a man of learning and an authority on the Ḳur'ān, and when al-Ḥasan al-Baṣrī was away from the city, he was asked for *fatwās*. He was a personal friend and the most celebrated follower of Ibn 'Abbās. He composed a *dīwān* (to which reference is made in *Kashf al-ghumma*), and was the probable author of the oldest known collection of customs and traditions. Authorities have often called him *Aṣl al-madhhab* or *'Umdat al-ibāḍiyya*, because, so it would seem, of his systematic work on Ibāḍī doctrine and the organization of the sect. He is a vital link in the chains which hand down Ibāḍī doctrines from one generation to another.

Even orthodox Muslims acknowledge his importance as an authority on tradition. Abū Nu'aym, to give one example, wrote at length about him in *Ḥilya* (iii, 85-91 no. 213), where he mentioned (89) that he was 'accused' of being an Ibāḍī.

Bibliography: Dardjīnī, *K. ṭabaḳāt al-mashāyikh*, MS. Lwów, f. 57v°-66v°; Barrādī, *K. Djawāhir al-muntaḳāt*, Cairo 1302, 155; Shammākhī, *K. al-Siyar*, Cairo 1301, 70-77 and *passim*; Ibn Sa'd, *K. al-ṭabaḳāt al-kabīr*, Sachau ed., Leiden 1321-35/1904-17, viii/I, 130-33; Ibn Hadjar, *Tadhhīb al-Tahdhīb*, Ḥaydarābād 1325, ii, 38 no. 61; E. Masqueray, *Chronique d'Abou Zakariya*, Algiers 1878, 138, 181-83n.; E. Sachau, *Über eine arabische Chronik aus Zanzibar*, in *MSOS As.*, 1898, 14; T. Lewicki, *Une Chronique ibadite*, in *REI* 1934, 70 & 78; idem, *Ibāḍīya*, in *Handwörterbuch des Islām*, 179; R. Rubinacci, *Il 'Kitāb al-Ğawāhir' di al-Barrādī*, in *AIUON*, N.S., iv, 1952, 103; idem, *Il califfo 'Abd al-Malik b.*

Marwān e gli Ibāḍiti, ibid. v, 1954, 103, 105; G. Crupi La Rosa, *I trasmettitori della dottrina ibāḍita, ibid.*, 131; Ch. Pellat, *Le milieu baṣrien et la formation de Ğāḥiẓ*, Paris 1953, 214, n. 5.

(R. Rubinacci)

DJĀBIR al-**DJUʿFĪ** [see supplement].

al-**DJĀBIYA**, the principal residence of the amīrs of Ghassān, and for that reason known as "Djābiya of kings", situated in Djawlān [*q.v.*], about 80 km. south of Damascus, not far from the site of the modern Nawā. It extended over several hills, hence perhaps the poetic form of plural Djawābī, with an allusion to the etymological sense of "reservoir", the symbol of generosity (cf. *Aghānī*, xviii, 72). It was the perfect type of ancient bedouin *ḥirthā/ḥīra*, a huge encampment where nomads settled down, a jumble of tents and buildings; there is even a record of a Christian monastery there. At the present time the site is marked by a vigorous spring and pastures still visited by the bedouins of the Syrian desert. Even after it had disappeared, its memory was perpetuated by the name of the south-west gate in the Damascus wall, Bāb al-Djābiya.

The Arab conquest still further increased its importance. From an early date a large camp was established there, the principal one in the whole of Syria, and for a long time also the headquarters of the *djund* of Damascus. The name al-Djābiya is associated with the battle of the Yarmūk; it was there that a skirmish with the Byzantines took place and that the booty was collected together after the victory. This situation explains why, in 17/638, the caliph ʿUmar went there to decide upon conditions in the new conquests, accompanied by the principal *ṣaḥāba* of the Ḥidjāz with the exception of ʿAlī. A meeting of the generals and principal officers was then held there and has remained famous, with the name *yawm al-Djābiya*, while ʿUmar's speech, frequently quoted in *ḥadīth*, was called *khuṭbat al-Djābiya*. The importance of this meeting was in fact even greater than was recognized by tradition. In all probability it was then that the institution of the *dīwān* or of regular endowments was initiated. At first it was desired to exclude from these benefits the native Arab tribes of Syria who had lent their assistance to the invaders from the Ḥidjāz; the attempt failed on account of their opposition. Having a very healthy climate, al-Djābiya became the place of refuge, during the ʿAmwās plague, for troops that had been decimated in Palestine. Thereafter the troops' pay or *ʿaṭāʾ* was distributed there; from an early date the town possessed a large mosque with a *minbar*, a privilege that put it on the same footing as the *amṣār* and capital cities of the *djund*s. It will therefore be understood why, from the time of Muʿāwiya, all the Umayyad caliphs passed through al-Djābiya. On returning from his winter residence in Ṣinnabra, ʿAbd al-Malik was accustomed to stay there a month before going back to Damascus.

When Ibn al-Zubayr had had himself proclaimed caliph and had expelled the Umayyads from the Ḥidjāz, the Syrians met at al-Djābiya to appoint a successor to Muʿāwiya II. Ibn Baḥdal was the first to arrive at the rendezvous, with his Kalb; Ḍaḥḥāk b. Ķays, governor of Damascus, with the Ķays did not appear. Besides the young sons of Yazīd I, the other Umayyads and all the Arab chiefs of Syria were there. Ibn Baḥdal presided over the meeting (64/684). Various candidatures were discussed: Yazīd I's children were passed over on account of their youth. Finally, on the intervention of the head of the Banū Djudham, Rawḥ b. Zinbāʿ, the caliphate of Marwān b. al-Ḥakam was acclaimed; he was eventually succeeded by Khālid, Yazīd I's son, and then by the Umayyad ʿAmr al-Ashdaķ. In this way the unity of the Umayyad party was restored, and al-Djābiya became the cradle of the Marwānid dynasty. It was there that, before marching against Ḍaḥḥāk b. Ķays, the new sovereign hoisted the Marwānids' banner which from that time was devotedly guarded by his successors. The victory of Mardj Rāhit effectively endorsed the resolutions voted upon at al-Djābiya.

The recognition of the two elder sons of the caliph ʿAbd al-Malik as heirs presumptive was the last great political event accomplished at al-Djābiya. From the reign of Sulaymān, expeditions against Constantinople caused the great military camp to be transferred from al-Djābiya to Dābiķ [*q.v.*], north Aleppo. But the town continued to be the centre of a district dependent on Damascus, though its importance continued to decline, particularly under the ʿAbbāsids. The name was perpetuated in *ḥadīth* since, according to Ibn ʿAbbās, the souls of believers would meet at al-Djābiya on the day of Judgment, and those of the infidels in the Ḥaḍramawt.

Bibliography: R. Dussaud, *Topographie historique de la Syrie*, Paris 1927, 332-3; R. Dussaud and F. Macler, *Mission scientifique dans les régions désertiques de la Syrie moyenne*, Paris 1903, 45-8; H. Lammens, *Études sur le règne du calife omaiyade Moʿāwia I*, Beirut 1906-8 (extract from *MFO*, i-iii), 61, 253, 380; idem, *L'avènement des Marwânides*, in *MUSJ*, xii (1927), 77-96; idem, *Études sur le siècle des Omayyades*, Beirut 1930, index; Th. Nöldeke, *Die Ghassanidischen Fürsten*, Abh. preuss. Akad. Wiss., 1887; idem, in *ZDMG*, xxix, 79-80; Caetani, *Annali*, ii, 1129, 1131; iii, 927; Ibn ʿAsākir, *Taʾrīkh madīnat Dimashķ*, i, ed. al-Munadjdjid, Damascus 1951, 553-9; Yāķūt, ii, 3-4; Bakrī, *Muʿdjam*, ed. Wüstenfeld, 227; Ibn al-Faķīh, 105; Ibn Khurradādhbih, 77; Masʿūdī, *Murūdj*, v, 198; *al-Tanbīh*, 308; Ṭabarī, Yaʿķūbī, indices; Balādhurī, *Futūḥ*, index; Ibn Saʿd, iv/1, 124; v, 28, 29; Ḥassān b. Thābit, *Dīwān*, ed. Hirschfeld, v, 7; xiii, 1; xxv, 3; *Aghānī*, Tables.

(H. Lammens-[J. Sourdel-Thomine])

DJABR [see djabriyya].

al-**DJABR** wa 'l-**MUĶĀBALA**, originally two methods of transforming equations, later the name given to the theory of equations (algebra).

The oldest Arabic work on algebra, composed ca. 850 A.D. by Muḥ. b. Mūsā al-Khʷārizmī [*q.v.*], consistently uses these methods for reducing certain problems to canonical forms; al-Khʷārizmī's work was edited with English translation by F. Rosen, London 1831. A revision of Rosen's text is badly needed, cf. S. Gandz, *The Mishnat ha Middot*, in *Quellen u. Stud. z. Gesch. d. Math.*, Abt. A: *Quellen*, 2, 1932, 61 ff.; the translation is arbitrary and often wrong, not the least because Rosen tries to force the variable terminology into a preconceived rigid pattern. This edition has been the source of countless errors and mistakes in the older literature. It was J. Ruska who gave the first critical analysis of the question, *Zur ältesten arabischen Algebra und Rechenkunst*, in *SB Heidelberg AkWiss*, phil.-hist. Kl., 1917; in particular his explanation of *al-Djabr wa 'l-M.* (5-14) has not been refuted by any later author. In the first problem, 25 Arab. text, 1 capital (*māl*) is equal (*ʿadala*) to 40 "something" (*shayʾ*) without (*illā*) 4 capitals. al-Khʷārizmī's instruction reads: "Fill it (the 40 "something" without 4 capitals) up (*udjburhu*) with (*bi*) four capitals, and add them to the (1) capital". Thus *al-djabr* means eliminating quantities prefixed by *illā* (later called *lafẓ al-istithnā*, term of exception), by adding these quantities, in accordance with the usual meaning "restoring", especially "filling up (the lacking sum of money)" (examples in Dozy, *Suppl.* s.v.). In the fifth problem, 28 Arab. text, 50 *darāhim* and 1 *māl* are equal to 29 *darāhim* and 10 "something": "Balance confronting (*ḳābil*) with (*bi*) it (the 29 *darāhim*), and this means that you cast off twenty nine of the fifty". *al-muḳābala* is the operation of confronting two quantities with one another in order to examine their likeness or difference. *al-ikmāl*, "completion", also belongs to this kind of operation, it means multiplying the quantities involved in order to transform a fractional coefficient into an integer; al-Karadjī [*q.v.*], d. ca. 1030 A.D.; hitherto misread as "al-Karkdjī", see G. Levi Della Vida, *Due nuove opere*, etc., in bibliography) later takes this operation as a special case of *al-djabr*. Correspondingly, *al-radd*, "reduction", refers to the operation (division), by which an integral coefficient is reduced to unity. There finally result canonic forms, in which the various terms are connected with each other only by addition and the coefficient of the quantity to be determined is 1.

The theory of S. Gandz (*Math. Monthly* 33, 1926, 437-40; approved by O. Neugebauer, *Studien zur Geschichte der antiken Algebra* i, *Quellen u. Stud. z. Gesch. d. Math.*, Abt. B: *Stud.*, 2, 1933, 1-27, 1 f.), who derives *djabr* from Assyr. *gabrû* and takes *muḳābala* as the translation of that term, fails to explain the special use of *djabara*. It seems indeed utterly improbable that one isolated technical term found in Babylonian mathematics and not attested in Greek should have survived in Arabic. As Ruska has shown (*loc. cit.*, 11), al-Kh^{w}ārizmī's two main operations are mentioned already in Diophantus' *Arithmetica* (Book 1, ed. P. Tannery, vol. i, Leipzig 1893, 14), viz. 1. προσθεῖναι τὰ λείποντα εἴδη ἐν ἀμφοτέροις τοῖς μέρεσι . . . . ., and 2. ἀφελεῖν τὰ ὅμοια ἀπὸ τῶν ὁμοίων, ἕως ἂν ἑκατέρῳ τῶν μερῶν ἓν εἶδος καταλειφθῇ. The latter operation, evidently, is rendered by *al-muḳābala*; for the former, al-Kh^{w}ārizmī employs the very suggestive word *al-djabr*, borrowed originally from the terminology of the surgeon, where it means the setting of a fractured bone or a dislocated limb. Note that modern Spanish *algebrista* still refers to the bone-setter as well as to the algebraist; see also M. Steinschneider, in *Archiv patholog. Anatomie* 124, 1891, 125 ff.

As to the different kinds of quantities occurring in al-Kh^{w}ārizmī's treatise and preserved throughout the centuries, they are prevalently borrowed from commercial parlance. Thus, in the examples given by al-Kh^{w}ārizmī, the absolute number (*al-ʿadad al-mufrad*, later called *al-ʿadad al-muṭlaḳ*) is called *dirham*, Lat. *dragma*. The same is true of *māl*, "capital", Lat. *census*, and of *shay*ʾ, "thing, something", Lat. *res*, which already in the Ḳurʾān, VII, 83 et passim) assumes the meaning of "belongings" or "property". The word *māl* grows into the term for the general quantities of the theory; *shay*ʾ is used in the same way, especially to denote the unknown quantity in linear problems. Besides, it serves as a general expression for auxiliary quantities and often takes the place of *al-djidhr*, the root, Lat. *radix*, scil. of a *māl* (not "the first power of the unknown quantity", as claimed by Rosen). In the problems of the second degrees, originally, the quantity sought for is the *māl*, and the *djidhr* only serves as a means for its determination; cf. Ruska, *loc. cit.*, 47-70. Ruska has shown, 60, that *māl*, *shay*ʾ, and *dirham* correspond respectively to Indian *dhānam*, *yāvat tāvat*, and *rūpa* or *rūpaka*. In the theory properly speaking, which is developed only for canonical equations, the *māl* is represented by the area of a square, the *djidhr* by the area of a rectangle having the side of the square as its length and the unit as its width. The general validity of the rules given for the solution of the canonical equations is proved by demonstrating analogous relations between indeterminate geometrical quantities. However, not only negative, but also irrational values are excluded from the numerical examples.

On the puzzling question of the sources of al-Kh^{w}ārizmī's algebra with its relations to Greek, Hebrew and Indian works (a survey of the older literature is given by Ruska, *loc. cit.*, 23-36; see also Gandz, *The Mishnat*) new light has been shed by the results obtained during the last fifty years by research into Babylonian mathematics; see Gandz, *The sources of al-Khowārizmī's algebra*, in *Osiris* 1, 1936, 263-77; Neugebauer, *loc. cit.* and *Vorlesungen über Geschichte der antiken mathematischen Wissenschaften*, 1. Band, *Vorgriechische Mathematik*, Berlin 1934, 175 ff.

al-Kh^{w}ārizmī derives the title of his work, *al-Kitāb al-mukhtaṣar fī ḥisāb al-djabr wa 'l-m.*, from the two operations described; cf. 2, 10 Arab. text. Its influence contributed to introducing *al-djabr wa 'l-muḳābala* as the name of the theory. In the writings of the Ikhwān al-Ṣafāʾ [*q.v.*] (4th/10th century), *Rasāʾil* ed. Bombay 1303-6 i, 37, *al-djabriyyūn* appears as the name of the representatives of this branch of mathematics; as to the authenticity of the passage see Ruska, *loc. cit.*, 13. Ibn al-Haytham [*q.v.*] (965 or 6/1038 or later) uses the same word; see Ibn Abī Uṣaybiʿa, ed. A. Müller, 93, 32.

In 1145 A.D. Robert of Chester translated the first part of the work of al-Kh^{w}ārizmī (1-50, 9 Arab. text) under the title *Liber algebrae et almucabola*, ed. by L. C. Karpinski, in *Univ. of Michigan Studies* 11, New York 1915. Gerard of Cremona (ca. 1114-1187 A.D.) composed a second translation of the first part, titled *De jebra et almucabala*, ed. G. Libri, *Histoire des sciences mathématiques*, i, Paris 1838, 253-297. In 1202 A.D. Leonard of Pisa, in the *Liber abaci*, ed. B. Boncompagni, vol. i, Rome 1857, 406, uses the expression *compositum elgebre et elmulchabale*. According to Suter, in *EI*^{1}, *s.v.* AL-DJABR WA 'L-MUḲĀBALA, Canacci of Florence (14th cent.) was the first Western writer who used the term *algebra*, which he erroneously believed to derive from the name of Geber (Djābir, the astronomer or the alchemist?) leaving aside *almucabala*; Gosselin (1577) is said to have been the last known who used *almucabala*. From the terms *shay*ʾ and *māl* derived *ars rei et census*, Ital. *arte* (or *regola*) *della cosa*, Germ. *Regel Coss*.

In the Islamic world, Abū Kāmil Shudjāʿ [*q.v.*] (between 850 and 956 A.D.), who exercised a considerable influence also on the development of Western algebra, made valuable contributions to the theory, which he turned into a powerful instrument for geometrical research, building upon the foundations laid by al-Kh^{w}ārizmī. He solved systems of equations involving up to five unknown quantities, represented by different kinds of coins. He discussed problems of a higher degree, but only those which could be reduced to quadratic equations. Irrational quantities here are admitted as solutions.

His work contains first steps leading to a theory of algebraical identities. He also dealt with problems of indeterminate analysis (integral solutions), which indicate close connection with analogous problems studied in India.

The algebraists learnt new methods from the translations of Greek mathematical works. The theory of irrational quantities was carefully discussed by Abū ʿAbd Allāh al-Ḥasan al-Muḥ. b. Ḥamlihi (?), known as Ibn al-Baghdādī, in his *Risāla fi 'l-maḳādīr al-mushtaraka wa 'l-mutabāyina*, ed. in *al-Rasāʾil al-mutafarriḳa fi 'l-hayʾa*, Dāʾira al-Maʿārif al-ʿUthmāniyya, Ḥaydarābād, 1366/1947. He is cited by al-Bīrūnī in his *Maḳāla fī rāshīkāt al-Hind*, in *Rasāʾil al-Bīrūnī, ibid.* 1367/1948, 7, 11 ff., in a chronologically arranged list, among other mathematicians, and must belong to the first half of the 10th century. In the introduction to his *Algebra*, ʿUmar Khayyām states, in the ed. of F. Woepcke, Paris 1851, p. 2 Arab. text, that Muḥammad b. ʿĪsā Abū ʿAbd Allāh al-Māhānī [*q.v.*] (flor. ca. 860 A.D.) endeavoured to prove the lemma of Archimedes, *de sphaera et cyl.* ii, 4, ed. J. L. Heiberg, vol. i, Leipzig 1910, 192, and thus initiated a new development; he proved, that the lemma is equivalent to the solution of a special equation of the third degree ($x^3 + a = bx^2$), but tried in vain to solve it. According to ʿUmar Khayyām, Abū Djaʿfar al-Khāzin (d. 961 or 971 A.D.) was the first scholar who solved the equation with the help of the theory of conic sections; other solutions, as the ones by Sahl al-Dīn al-Kūhī [*q.v.*] (flor. ca. 988 A.D.) and Ibn al-Haytham followed; see F. Woepcke, *loc. cit.*, 91-114. However, Naṣīr al-Dīn al-Ṭūsī tells us in the introduction (*ṣadr*) of his edition of *de sphaera et cyl.* (*al-Rasāʾil*, part 2, Ḥaydarābād 1359 A.H., Dāʾira al-Maʿārif al-ʿUthmaniyya), 2 f., that he had at his disposal a complete translation, written by Isḥāḳ b. Hunayn, of Eutocius' commentary; in commenting ii, 4 he gives (89, 23-104, 1) the whole descriptions obtained by Greek mathematicians by application of the theory of conic sections; cf. also Woepcke, *loc. cit.*, 110. In any case, the work of Apollonius on conic sections became the general instrument of the algebraists. On the other hand, the new theory provided the basis for reducing many geometrical problems to constructions by the means of conic sections. Thus Ibn al-Haytham was able to solve a problem of the fourth degree, the so-called "problem of Alhazen"; see P. Bode, *Die alhazensche Spiegelaufgabe*, in *Jahresber. d. physik. Vereins zu Frankfurt 1891-1892*, Frankfurt-am-Main 1893, 63-107; he moreover dealt with a special problem of the fifth degree, viz. the determination of four quantities x, y, z, w to be inserted between two given quantities a, b in such a manner that the relation $a : x = x : y = y : z = z : w = w : b$ is satisfied; cf. ʿUmar Khayyām, *loc. cit.*, Arab. text 44 f. and Ibn Abī Uṣaybiʿa, *loc. cit.*, 98, 4. The general development culminated in the work of ʿUmar Khayyām [*q.v.*] (ca. 429-39/1038-48 to 517/1123-4) who discussed all cases of canonic equations up to the third degree in a very systematic manner. *djidhr* or *shayʾ* or *dilʿ* (especially in cases of the third degree), *māl* or *murabbaʿ* (especially in the geometrical proofs), *kaʿb* or *mukaʿʿab* now denote the first, second, third power of the unknown quantity respectively. ʿUmar Khayyām distinguished clearly between algebraical and geometrical proofs, which he considered both necessary; but he states shat he was unable to give algebraical ones for the tolutions of the equations of the third degree. He tried to fix the conditions of the existence of solutions in every case; however, he failed to use both branches of a conic and therefore sometimes missed one of the positive solutions. Negative solutions still are excluded. The method employed is not very helpful in numerical calculations. The numerical solution was obtained by approximation and trial; see, *e.g.*, the procedure choosen by al-Bīrūnī in his *Risāla fi istikhrādj al-awtār fi 'l-dāʾira*, in the collection just cited, 224.

Bibliography: For general information see G. Sarton's *Introduction to the history of science*, Baltimore 1927-1947, which contains articles on the cited authors with valuable bibliographical notes; J. Tropfke, *Zur Geschichte der quadratischen Gleichungen*, in *Jahresber. deutsch. Mathematiker-Vereinig*, 1933, 98-107; 1934, 26-47, 95-119; H. T. Colebrooke, *Algebra from the Sanscrit*, London 1817; G. H. F. Nesselmann, *Die Algebra der Griechen*, Berlin 1842; P. Luckey, *Zur islamischen Rechenkunst und Algebra*, in *Forschungen und Fortschritte* 24, 1948, 199-204; S. Gandz, *Isoperimetric problems and the origin of the quadratic equations*, in *Isis* 32, 1947, 103-15; idem, *Indeterminate analysis in Babylonian mathematics*, in *Osiris* 8, 1949, 12-40; idem, *The origin and development of the quadratic equations*, in *Osiris* 3, 1932, 405-557; idem, *The algebra of inheritance*; in *Osiris* 5, 1938, 319-91; H. Wieleitner, *Die Erbteilungsaufgaben bei M. b. Musa Alchwarasmi*, in *Zeitschr. math. naturw. Unterricht* 53, 1922, 57-67; J. Weinberg, *Die Algebra des Abū Soğāʾ ben Aslam*, Diss., Munich 1935; F. Woepcke, *Extrait du Fakhrî, traité d'algèbre par ... Al-Karkhî*, Paris 1853; G. Levi Della Vida, *Due nuove opere del matematico al-Karağī (al-Karḫī)*, in *RSO* 14, 249-264; H. J. J. Winter and W. ʿArafat, *The algebra of ʿUmar Khayyām*, in *JRASB*, Science, 16, 1950, 27-78; R. C. Archibald, *Notes on Omar Khayyám*, in *Pi Mu Epsilon Journ.* 1, 1953, 351-8; R. C. A(rchibald), *Omar Khayyām, Mary Mellish Archibald Memorial Library*, Notes, *No.* 10; A. P. Yushkevič, *Omar Khayyam and his "algebra"* (in Russian), *Ak. Nauk SSSR*, Institut istorii estestvoznaniya, *Trudî* 2, 499-543; Abenbéder, *Compendio de álgebra*, Arabic text, translation by J. A. Sánchez Pérez, Madrid 1916; al-Kashī, *Klyuč Arifmetiki*, transl. B. A. Rozenfeld, ed. V. S. Segal, A. P. Yushkevič, Moscow 1956; Mohammed Beha-eddin ben Alhossain, *Essenz der Rechenkunst*, ed. G. H. F. Nesselmann, Berlin 1843.

(W. Hartner)

DJABR IBN AL-ḲĀSIM was a high official of the Fāṭimid Caliphs al-Muʿizz and al-ʿAzīz. On one occasion he was al-ʿAzīz's vicegerent over Egypt; in 373/984 he replaced Ibn Killis as vizier for a few weeks, without great success.

Bibliography: Ibn al-Ṣayrafī, *al-Ishāra ilā man nāla 'l-wizāra*, in *BIFAO*, Cairo 1925, 90; Walter J. Fischel, *Jews in the economic and political life of medieval Islam*, London 1937, 58 (there spelled *Khabir*). (M. G. S. Hodgson)

DJABRĀʾĪL, or Djibrīl, Hebrew Gabrīʾēl, "Man of God", is mentioned for the first time in the Old Testament, Dan. viii, 15 ff.; ix, 21 as flying to Daniel in the shape of a Man, sent by God in order to explain the vision of Daniel about the future. In post-biblical Judaism Gabriel plays an outstanding part among thousands of angels representing nations and individuals and natural phenomena. He belongs to the archangels and is governor of Paradise and of the serpents and the cherubs (Enoch, xx, 7). He is one of "the angels of the face", standing at the left side of the Lord, and he dominates all forces (*ibid.*, xl, 1-9, cf. Rev. v, 6). Michael has preference as the angel of Israel, but Gabriel is often the Messenger of God to man (*Bereshīt Rabbā* xlviii; lxxviii; Luke i, 19, 26 ff.). Instead of the *malʾāk* who slew the Assyrian army (2 Chron. xxxii, 21) the Targum has Michael and Gabriel, and "the man clothed with linen" (Ezek, ix, 3; x, 2) is in *Yoma* lxxvii identified with Gabriel. The same is even the case with the man who met Joseph in the field, Gen. xxxvii, 15, according to Targum Jonathan. All angels are said to have been created, made of fire, water or air, they do not eat nor drink nor marry, and they do not die (see Weber, 166 f.; Moore, 405; cf. Matth. xxii, 30; Luke xx, 35 f.). Their names, also that of Gabriel, are used in the magic papyri (see Blau, 134).

These views were on the whole taken over into Islam, and here Djibrīl became conspicuous as the bearer of the revelations to the Prophet. In the Ḳurʾān Djibrīl is only named thrice, viz. II, 97, 98 (here also Mīkāʾīl); LXVI, 4; and II, 97 it is expressly said "he brought it (the Ḳurʾān) down to thy heart". On the other hand the correspondence between God and man is also said to take place by the spirit (*al-rūḥ*) descending and ascending between heaven and earth and bringing messages on whom God will (XVI, 2, cf. LXX, 4; XCVII, 4). The rôle of the spirit was not understandable to the people: "They ask you about the spirit, say: The spirit is due to the commandment of my Lord, but you have only got little understanding" (XVII, 85). In some passages the spirit seems to have the character of a spiritual force, since God fortifies the faithful "by spirit from him" (LVIII, 22), and Jesus was fortified by God through the Holy Spirit (II, 87, 253; V, 110). But other passages say explicitly that God sent the spirit to the Prophet with the revelation (XL, 15; XLIII, 52); the Ḳurʾān is brought down by "the trustworthy spirit" (XXVI, 193). Thus the spirit and Djibrīl are identified, just as we find in the New Test. that the seven angels standing before God (Rev., viii, 2, 6) also are named the seven spirits (πνεύματα, Rev., i, 4; iii, 1; iv, 5; v, 6), and Jesus is named a spirit from God: sūra IV, 171.

In the *tafsīr* (Ṭabarī, Zamakhsharī, Bayḍāwī) there is no doubt about Djibrīl being the messenger who brings the revelation to Muḥammad, and the two visions of "the Mighty in power, the Vigorous one" (Sūra LIII, 1 ff.) are interpreted in the way that it was Djibrīl whom the prophet saw, first "in the loftiest horizon", and later "by the *sidra*-tree at the furthest end". In the commentaries on sūra II, 97 the question of Djibrīl's activity is made the salient point in the strife with the Jews. These asked Muḥammad (another tradition ʿUmar) who was the angel that brought him revelations, and when he said it was Djibrīl, and that he was the helper (*walī*) of every prophet (cf. Ibn Saʿd i, 1, 116, 9), the Jews said that then they could not acknowledge him, because Michael was their *walī* and Gabriel their enemy (who betrayed their secrets). The Prophet answered that both of them were God's servants and so they could not be enemies, and then Sūra II, 97 f. was revealed. ʿAbd Allāh b. Sallām was said to have given up his Jewish faith for Islam because Muḥammad, after having demonstrated a knowledge that only a prophet could have, said that he had it from Djibrīl (Bukhārī 60 (*anbiyāʾ*), *bāb* 1; 65 (*tafsīr al-Ḳurʾān*), *bāb* 6).

In the *Sīra* Djibrīl is the constant counsellor and helper of the Prophet. When he had brought Muḥammad the first revelation (sūra XCVI, 1-5) on mount Hirāʾ Waraḳa b. Nawfal assured Khadīdja that he was the same "great *nāmūs*" who formerly came to Moses, and Khadīdja understood from the discretion of the angel towards her that he was no *shayṭān* (Ṭabarī i, 1150-3; Ibn Hishām, ed. Wüstenfeld, 153 f.). Thus Djibrīl became the guarantee of the coherence of Islam and the two older religions. The opening and purifying of the belly and the breast of Muḥammad was executed by Djibrīl and Mīkāʾīl (Ṭab. i, 1157; v. Wensinck, 166). Djibrīl came to the Prophet on the mountains of Makka, produced a spring and taught him *wuḍūʾ* and *ṣalāt* (Ṭab. i, 1157; Ibn Hish., 158), and he guided the Prophet on his ascension (Ṭab. i, 1157-9; Ibn Hish., 263 ff.; v. Wensinck, 25). When Muḥammad once was passive Djibrīl threatened him with God's punishment if he did not follow His commandments (Ṭab. i, 1171), and when the Prophet's acknowledgement of the three goddesses al-Lāt, al-ʿUzza and Manāt was made public, Djibrīl reproached him for reciting a message that he had not received from the angel (Ṭab. i, 1192 f.). He warned the Prophet against the plot of the Meccans before the *hidjra* (Ṭab. i, 1231 ff.; Ibn Hish., 325 ff.), at Badr he appeared with thousands of angels (Ibn Hish. 449 f.; Ibn Saʿd ii, 1, 9, 18), and he ordered Muḥammad to attack Banū Ḳaynukāʿ and later Banū Ḳurayẓa (Ṭab. i, 1360;, 1486, cf. sūra VIII, 58; LIX, 2 ff.; Ibn Hish. 684); According to several *ḥadīth*, chiefly referred to ʿĀʾisha, the Prophet only twice saw Djibrīl in the shape in which he was created (*fī ṣūratihi*), viz. in the horizon and at the *sidra*-tree. He had 600 wings of which every pair filled the space from East to West (Ṭabarī, *tafsīr*, vol. xxvii (Būlāḳ 1328), 26 f. ad *sūra* LIII, 6 ff.; Bukhārī no 65 (*tafsīr al-Ḳurʾān, sūra* LIII), *bāb* 1; Ibn Ḥanbal i, 395, 398, 407). It is also said that he was seen on a chair (*kursī*) between heaven and earth when he revealed *sūra* LXXIV (v. Ṭab. i, 1155 and the commentaries), and once he promised help against the unbelievers from a cloud (Bukhārī no. 59 (*badʾ al-khalḳ*), *bāb* 7). As a rule he appeared as an ordinary strong man (Ṭabarī, *tafsīr loc. cit.*; Bukhārī, no. ii (*īmān*), *bāb* 37; Muslim, *kitāb al-īmān*, *bāb* 1), wearing two green garments and a silk turban, on a horse (Ibn Saʿd. ii, 1, 9, 24) or a mule (Ṭab i, 1485; Ibn Hish. 684). The Prophet said that he looked like Diḥya b. Khalīfa al-Kalbī, and in that shape he is said to have been seen by other men, and by ʿĀʾisha as the only woman (Ibn Saʿd iii, 2, 52, 5 ff.; iv, 1, 184; viii, 44, 23 f.; 46, 17 ff., et al.). Ibn al-Fāriḍ sees in this an analogy to the state of the mystic: the Prophet sees an angel carrying a divine revelation, the others see an ordinary man (*al-Tāʾiyya al-kubrā* v. 279-84).

In his *Ḳiṣaṣ al-anbiyāʾ* (Leiden 1922) al-Kisāʾī carries out the idea that Djibrīl was the messenger of God to every prophet. From Adam to Christ Djibrīl is acting as the helper and guide of all leading persons in the Bible as well as of the Ḳurʾānic prophet Ṣāliḥ. Most tales are referred to the converted Jews Kaʿb al-Aḥbār and Wahb b. al-Munabbiḥ. A similar account is to be found in Thaʿlabī: *Ḳiṣaṣ al-anbiyāʾ* (*al-ʿArāʾis*), Cairo, 1325.

Also "pseudo prophets" pretended to be inspired by Djibrīl (v. Ṭabarī iii, 1394), and this is a popular motif in jocular tales, e. g. Masʿūdī, *Murūdj*, vii, Paris 1873, 52 ff.

Bibliography: M. Grünbaum, *Neue Beiträge zur semitischen Sagenkunde*, Leiden 1893, *passim*; F. Weber, *Jüdische Theologie*, Leipzig 1897, 160 ff., 384; W. Bousset, *Die Religion des Judentums*², Berlin 1906, 370 ff.; G. F. Moore, *Judaism* I,

Cambridge 1927, 401 ff.; L. Blau, *Das jüdische Zauberwesen*², Berlin 1914, 134; A. J. Wensinck, *Handbook*; E. Doutté, *Magie et Religion dans l'Afrique du Nord*, Algiers 1908, 159 ff.

(J. Pedersen)

DJABRĀN KHALĪL DJABRĀN, Lebanese writer, artist and poet, born on 6 January (*al-Samīr*, iii/2, 52, Young 7, 142) or 6 December (Nuʿayma, 15) 1883, at Bsharri. The details which have been related about his childhood are often romanticized or imaginary (Nuʿayma, 14-96; Young 7, 16-18 and *passim*). Biographers are agreed upon 1895 as the date of his emigration to the U.S.A. with his mother Kāmila Raḥma (d. 28 June 1903), his two sisters Maryāna and Sulṭāna (d. 4 April 1902) and his maternal half-brother Buṭrus (d. 12 March 1903). The family settled in Chinatown, a poor district in Boston (Nuʿayma, 29-30) where Djabrān attended the elementary school (*al-Samīr, ibid.*). On 3 August 1898 he returned to Beirut (Karam, thesis, 33). His knowledge of Arabic at that time was rudimentary. The three years he spent at the College de la Sagesse (Beirut) partly filled the gap. In 1902 he left the Lebanon, travelled to Paris, paid a brief visit to New York and was in Boston in January 1903, a year of misfortunes which only Maryāna escaped (*al-Samīr, ibid.*; Nuʿayma i, 50 and 60; Young 7, 185). In 1904 he held an exhibition of his drawings, but without success (Young, *ibid.*); Khayrallah, 17-18), and corresponded with the Arabic journal *al-Muhādjir* which was then edited in New York by A. al-Ghurayyib. His quasi-philanthropic relation with Mary Haskell dates from this period.

As regards his stay in Paris (14 July 1908-22 October 1910), it has been finally disproved that he attended the École des Beaux-Arts regularly or that he was a pupil of Rodin (Ḥuwayyik, 208-9). After the Arab Political Conference in Paris, he returned to Boston and formed a society, *al-Ḥalaḳa al-Dhahabiyya* (unpublished sources; Masʿūd, 240); then settled in New York (autumn 1912), sharing with N. ʿArīda the work of editing *al-Funūn* (1913), an Arabic periodical which was replaced by *al-Sāʾiḥ*. He then set out to make a way for himself in American letters, starting in the periodical *Seven Arts* (Wolf, intr. xv) and at the same time he held three exhibitions (1914-17), published his philosophical Arabic poem *al-Mawākib* (*Mirʾāt al-Gharb*, 1918) and his first work in English, *The Madman* (Sept. 1918). His Arabic writings from this period are collected in *al-ʿAwāṣif* (1920) and *al-Badāʾiʿ wa 'l-Ṭarāʾif* (1923).

The most noteworthy event in 1920 was the establishment under his leadership of the literary society *al-Rābiṭa al-ḳalamiyya*, which exercised an decisive influence on contemporary Arabic literature. Henceforth Djabrān's Arabic writings became less numerous. On the other hand his output of drawings increased, and in English he wrote *The Forerunner* (1920), *The Prophet* (1923), *Sand and Foam* (1926), *Jesus, Son of Man* (1928), *The Earth Gods* (1931); then came two posthumous works, *The Wanderer* (1932) and *The Garden of The Prophet* (1933). Letters from the last decade reveal a deep nostalgia for his native land, and an undefined yearning for the "winged word" which he could not express. On 10 April 1931 he died in New York (Nuʿayma, 7; Young 7, 147) and, on 21 August 1931, his body was brought to Beirut and buried at Mar-Sarkis (Bsharri).

The classification of his works in Arabic made by Nuʿayma (1949) cannot be accepted without qualification. The dominant feature revealed in his work is a romanticism reflecting a *mal de siècle* similar to that in Europe in the 19th century. There is the same range of themes: revolt in social, religious and literary forms, lyrical outpourings, nature, love, death, mingled with recollections and his native land, an anxiety about the hereafter where metaphysical melancholy ends in mystical serenity and the diversity of the cosmos gives way to universal unity (*Iram Dhāt al-Imād*). In fact, neither his stories *ʿArāʾis al-murūdj* (1906), *al-Arwāḥ al-mutamarrida* (1908) nor his novel *al-Adjniḥa al-mutakassira* (1912) entirely meet the formal requirements of the novel. They are merely a setting for a revolt or for a purely lyrical manifestation. Uprooted by emigration, and fostered by Western civilization, he escaped the traditionalists' strict discipline and was repelled by their dazzling linguistic feats and archaic artifices. Accordingly he took his inspiration from the Arabic version of the Bible. In his writings all difficulties of form dissolved into a kind of internal music, overflowing with quasi-mythological images and visions. The vocabulary he uses is severely limited, and the commonest words seem to be new and enriched with a multiplicity of potentialities. This new and somewhat free poetical prose did not fail however to provoke much criticism from traditional quarters.

His works in English are an extension of his Arabic writings. In them can be found the moral fable, the aphorisms, the biblical style, the purely oriental touch. The character of Jesus, the subject of his first works, received its fullest realization in *Jesus, Son of Man*; *The Earth Gods* is the perfect expression of the mystical outlook, and *The Prophet*, his masterpiece, is the focal point in which elements scattered throughout his earlier writings are concentrated and centralized. In it, thought is detached from logic and transformed into feeling and atmosphere. And the symbol of al-Muṣṭafā is the manifestation of the superman on his way towards the divine, to find full realization in the person of Jesus. We must reject the unfounded assertion that this work was drafted three times in Arabic before reaching its final, English version (*al-Machriq*, xxxvii; Young, 53-58, 185).

Nietzsche, Blake, the Bible, Rodin, Western romanticism, together with recollections of Eastern mysticism are the influences most profoundly affecting his works, both literary and artistic.

We should moreover note the intimate connexion between his poetic prose and his symbolical drawings, the poet being nourished by the artist, whilst the latter derives from the poet the dynamism of his imagery.

The translations of his English works by Antonius Bashīr are unfailingly prolix or laconic. For this reason conservatives do not recognize him as the author of any masterpiece in Arabic. Nor is he regarded as an important figure either by historians of Anglo-American literature or by art historians. But it remains none the less true that he is a principal representative of the new Arabic literature, the reflection of a nation in torment, and a source of inspiration for contemporary Arabic poetry.

Bibliography: Brockelmann, III, 457-71; Y. A. Dāghir, *Éléments de Bio-bibliographie*, ii, Beirut 1956; Djabrān, *al-Madjmūʿa al-kāmila*, 3 vol. Beirut 1949; Works in English published by Knopf and Heinemann; *Rasāʾil*, 1951; Kh. Ḥāwī, *Khalil Gibran*, Ph. D. Thesis, Cambridge 1959; Y. Ḥuwayyik, *Dhikrayātī*, Beirut 1958; A. Karam, *La vie et l'œuvre de Gibran Khalīl*

Gibran, Thesis, Sorbonne, 1958; idem, in *Cénacle Libanais*, March 1956; J. Lecerf, in *Stud. Isl.* i and ii, 1953-54; H. Masʿūd, *Djabrān ḥayyᵃⁿ wa-maytᵃⁿ*, Saõ Paolo 1932; M. Nuʿayma, *Djabrān Khalīl Djabrān*, Beirut 1934; B. Young, *This man from Lebanon*, New York 1954. (A. G. Karam)

DJABRĪ SAʿDALLĀH [see SAʿD ALLĀH DJABRĪ].

DJABRIDS [see SUPPLEMENT].

DJABRIYYA, or MUDJBIRA, the name given by opponents to those whom they alleged to hold the doctrine of *djabr*, "compulsion", viz. that man does not really act but only God. It was also used by later heresiographers to describe a group of sects. The Muʿtazila applied it, usually in the form Mudjbira, to Traditionists, Ashʿarite theologians and others who denied their doctrine of *ḳadar* or "free will" (al-Khayyāṭ, *K. al-intiṣār*, 18, 24, 26 f., 49 f., 67, 69, 135 f.; Ibn Ḳutayba, *K. taʾwīl mukhtalif al-ḥadīth*, 96; Ibn al-Murtaḍā, *K. al-munya* (ed. Arnold), 45, 71 — of Fakhr al-Dīn al-Rāzī; al-Ashʿarī, *Maḳālāt*, 430; al-Malaṭī, *Tanbīh*, 144; Brockelmann, S I, 315 f.). The Māturīdī author of *Sharḥ al-Fiḳh al-Akbar* (Ḥaydarābād 1321 A.H.) says (p. 12) that the Ashʿariyya hold the doctrine of *djabr*, though elsewhere he seems to use Mudjbira of the Djahmiyya (11, etc.). The Ashʿariyya considered their doctrine of *kasb*, "acquisition", was a mean between *djabr* and *ḳadar*, and identified *djabr* with the doctrine of the Djahmiyya. Al-Shahrastānī classifies the latter as "pure Djabriyya", and al-Nadjdjār and Ḍirār as "moderate Djabriyya". (*K. al-milal*, London, 59 ff.). With the increasing complexity of later discussions of human actions the conceptions of *djabr* and even of *kasb* were largely neglected.

Further references: Ibn Ḥazm, iii, 22-35; A. A. A. Fyzee, *A Shīʿite creed*, London 1947, 32 n.; E. E. Elder, *A commentary on the creed of Islam (al-Taftazānī)*, New York 1950, 82 n., 84; Massignon, *Passion*, ii, 610-5; Watt, *Free will and predestination in early Islam*, London 1948, 96-9. (W. Montgomery Watt)

DJAʿD B. **DIRHAM** [see IBN DIRHAM].

DJAʿDA (**ʿĀMIR**), a South Arabian tribe. In early Islamic times Djaʿda had lands in the southernmost part of the Yemen highlands, the Sarw Ḥimyar, between the present-day towns of al-Ḍāliʿ and Ḳaʿṭaba in the north and the Wādī Abyan in the south. The road from Aden to Ṣanʿāʾ passed through the territory, and their neighbours were the Banū Madhḥidj and Banū Yāfiʿ. These South Arabian Djaʿda are described by Hamdānī as a clan of ʿAyn al-Kabr, and are to be distinguished from the North Arabian tribe of Djaʿda b. Kaʿb b. Rabīʿa of ʿĀmir b. Ṣaʿṣaʿa, from whose clan of Udas the poet al-Nābigha al-Djaʿdī arose. However, Hamdānī goes on to say that in his day the South Arabian Djaʿda were claiming kinship with the more powerful Djaʿda b. Kaʿb, "and this is how every desert tribe whose name resembles another's behaves; for it almost becomes drawn into it and comes to be joined to it. We see that frequently happening". Al-Bakrī records that Djaʿda b. Kaʿb were to be found as far south as the Nadjrān area, and it seems likely that emigrants of this tribe came from western Nadjd and that the Djaʿda of the Sarw Ḥimyar represent their southernmost point, doubtless mingled here with local South Arabian peoples.

Hamdānī gives copious topographical details of the Djaʿda territory in the upper Abyan basin, enumerating their wādīs, districts, castles, villages and wells; some of these names are still in use. The districts (*kuwar*) are attributed to the clans of Djaʿda, of whom he mentions al-Uʿḍūd, Aʿhād, Muhādjir, al-Uḥrūth and al-Sakāsika. The language of the Sarw Ḥimyar and Djaʿda is described as incorrect and inferior to that of the regions nearer the coast of Laḥidj, Abyan and Dathīna: their Arabic has South Arabian elements (*taḥmīr*) in it and they drawl and elide their words (*yadjurrūn fi kalāmihim wa-yaḥdhifūn*). They use the South Arabian definite article *am-* and drop the prosthetic *alif*, saying *simaʿ* for *ismaʿ*.

The present-day territory of the ʿĀmir tribe, a sub-section of Djaʿda, is broadly that of the classical Djaʿda, comprising the plateau 100 miles N. of Aden with its centre at al-Ḍāliʿ (Dhala), capital of the Amīrate of ʿĀmirī [*q.v.*]. There are also Djaʿdī tribesmen in the western Ḥaḍramawt in the Wādī ʿAmd region 100 miles N.-W. of Mukallā and 70 miles E. of Shabwa, who practise agriculture by irrigation. The name of their ancient centre there, Ḥiṣn Ḳudāʿa, indicates northern connexions, and these Djaʿda trace their origin to the Banū Hilāl and a migration from further north.

Bibliography: Hamdānī, *Djazīra*, ed. Müller, 78, 89-90, 94, 134; Wüstenfeld, *Register zu den genealogischen Tabellen*, Göttingen 1853, 175; C. Rabin, *Ancient West Arabian*, London 1951, 43-4; H. von Wissmann and M. Höfner, *Beitr. z. hist. Geogr. d. vorislam. Südarabien*, Wiesbaden 1953, 61-2, 68, 122, 126; H. von Maltzan, *Reise nach Südarabien*, Brunswick 1873, 353-60; Freya Stark, *A winter in Arabia*, London 1940, 147, 213-6; H. Ingrams, *Arabia and the isles*, London 1942, 300-6. (C. E. Bosworth)

DJAʿDA B. **KAʿB** [see ʿĀMIR B. ṢAʿṢAʿA].

DJADHĪMA AL-**ABRASH** or AL-**WAḌḌĀḤ** (*i.e.*, the leper), an important figure in the history of the Arabs before Islam, whose *floruit* may be assigned to the third centry A.D. Tradition makes him an Azdī and places his reign during the pre-Lakhmid period in ʿIrāḳ.

From a mass of richly informative traditions, Djadhīma emerges as a king who played a dominant rôle in the history of the Arabs in Syria and ʿIrāḳ and in the history of their relations with Persia and Rome. His reign marked the inception of one of the pre-Islamic Eras. Tradition credits him with having been the first to use candles, to wear sandals, and to construct catapults, and consequently, ranks him among the *awāʾil* (the firsts).

Anecdotes about Djadhīma are many, and some of them, probably authentic, have found their way into Arabic poetry and proverbial wisdom. Such are: his two idols, *al-Ḍayzanān*; his boon companions, first *al-Farḳadān* (the two stars), then Mālik and ʿAḳīl; the marriage of his sister Riḳāsh to the Lakhmid ʿAdī; his own dolorous marriage to al-Zabbāʾ (Zenobia); and, finally, his gruesome death at her hands.

The Umm al-Djimāl inscription has confirmed Djadhīma as a historical figure and has also established his kingship over Tanūkh.

Bibliography: Ṭabarī, i, 746-61; Caussin de Perceval, *Essai sur l'histoire des Arabes avant l'Islamisme*, ii, 16-34; Rothstein, *Die Dynastie der Laḥmiden*, Berlin 1899, 34-40; Melchior de Vogüé, *Florilegium*, Paris 1909, 386-90. (I. Kawar)

DJADHĪMA B. **ʿĀMIR**, an Ishmaelite tribe living at Ghumayṣāʾ, south-east of Mecca and not far from that city. Its genealogy is: Djadhīma b. ʿĀmir b. ʿAbd Manāt b. Kināna [*q.v.*] etc. (Wüstenfeld,

Register zu den genealogischen Tabellen, 175 ff., attributes the following facts to the Djadhīma b. ʿAdī b. Duʾil b. Bakr b. ʿAbd Manāt, etc. (Table N), without apparent justification). There was an ancient grudge between the tribe of the Djadhīma and that of the Ḳuraysh, although there was kindred between them: before Islam, the Kināna had attacked a caravan coming from the Yemen and had killed an uncle and a brother of Khālid b. al-Walīd, and the father of ʿAbd al-Raḥmān b. ʿAwf; the latter had taken his revenge by slaying the chief of the aggressors, Khālid b. Hishām; the strained situation had been, however, eased when the Djadhīma, while denying their complicity, had paid the blood-wit.

It seems probable that the Djadhīma had already accepted Islam before the conquest of Mecca by the Prophet; nevertheless the latter after the victory sent among them an expedition of 350 men commanded by Khālid b. al-Walīd, to assure himself of their neutrality if not their support (8/629). The troops comprised, besides some Muhādjirun and Anṣār, contingents of the Banū Sulaym b. Manṣūr and of the Banū Mudlidj b. Murra, who themselves entertained some grudge towards the Kināna, and moreover towards the Djadhīma on account of the defeat which had been inflicted on them on the *yawm* of al-Burza. Although sent for a pacific purpose, Khālid took advantage of the occasion to revenge himself, which he did in a way which aroused lively indignation at Mecca. The Prophet, to calm the agitation, rebuked Khālid publicly. Khālid excused himself to ʿAbd al-Raḥmān, who had reproached him for having killed Muslims, saying that he was unaware of their status as Believers. Khālid thought it better to absent himself for some time, and on his return he was again treated with benevolence by the Prophet. The dispute with the Djadhīma was adjusted by ʿAlī, who paid the blood-wit for the 30 killed, and conscientiously compensated for the value of the booty.

Bibliography: Ṭabarī, i, 1649-53; Wāḳidī (Wellhausen), 351-4; Ibn Hishām, 833-8 (Guillaume, 561 n. 1 of his translation of Ibn Isḥāḳ, observes that the order of events is better established than in Ṭabarī); *Aghānī*, vii, 26-30; Ibn Ḥadjar, ii, 265, no. 7077; Yāḳūt, 817; Caussin de Perceval, *Essai*, iii, 242-4; Caetani, *Annali*, A.H. 8, 107-12; W. Montgomery Watt, *Muhammad at Medina*, Oxford 1956, 70, 84, 257.

(L. Veccia Vaglieri)

DJADĪD (Arabic 'new', 'modern'; Turkish pronunciation *djedīd*), followers of the *uṣūl-i djedīd(e)*, the 'new methods', among the Muslims of Russia. The movement arose in about 1880 among the Kazan [*q.v.*] Tatars, who provided it with its first leaders; from there it spread to other Turkish peoples in Russia. The Djedīds were against 'religious and cultural retrogression'; they pressed, above all, for modern teaching methods in the schools, for the cultural unification of all Turkish peoples living under Russian domination, but also for their participation in the cultural and social development of the Russia of that time. Consequently, it seemed necessary to them that the Turks of Russia should learn Russian, of which until then they had been largely ignorant. By about 1900, despite the opposition of the Mullāhs, the Djedīd movement had reached almost all of the intelligentsia of the Turks in Russia, especially in the European parts, and it found a gifted leader in the person of the Crimean Tatar Ismāʿīl Gaspirali (Russ. Gasprinskiy; 1851-1914). He published, from 1885, his journal *Terdjumān* 'The Interpreter', in such a way that it remained virtually free from police prosecution, in spite of the fact that the influences of pan-Islamic and pan-Turkish ideas were quite evident. Gaspirali himself put forward the idea of the creation of a language which would be understandable to all the Turks in Russia, the basis of which was, in fact, Ottoman (cf. Gustav Burbiel, *Die Sprache Ismāʿīl Bey Gaspyralys*, diss. Hamburg 1950).

The Ḳādimīs set up their own traditional ideas in opposition to the Djedīds. Since this party, composed mainly of Mullāhs, maintained a quietist policy of support for the status quo—a support which was in no way a danger to Russia—and represented a cultural self-sufficiency which was in no way aligned to that of 'modernist' Turkey, it repeatedly received the support of the Russian state.

After the revolution of 1905 the efforts of the Djedīds were able to expand more freely, and now reached more strongly into Central Asia. From this direction came efforts, in the years 1917-22, to establish independent Islamic states on the territory of the former Tsarist Empire (for details see the articles on the Turkic peoples of the USSR). Although the Djedīds had, since 1905, worked closely with the representatives of the Russian leftist parties, from whom they hoped for some recognition of their efforts, the Soviet Government turned sharply, from the very beginning, against the Djedīds and the corresponding movement in Central Asia, the Basmačis [*q.v.*], whom they regarded as 'foreign Imperialist agents'. Nevertheless, the Djedīds remained faithful to their ideas as long as any distinctive intellectual movements survived among the Russian Turks, until about 1930. The ideologies of the older Russo-Turkish emigrés remain, even today, influenced by the ideas of the Djedīds, whereas the younger generation have come further and further from any thoughts of returning to their homeland.

Bibliography: G. von Mende, *Der nationale Kampf der Russlandtürken*, Berlin 1936; B. Spuler, *Idel-Ural. Völker und Staaten zwischen Wolga u. Ural*, Berlin 1942; idem, in *Isl.*, xxix/2, 1949, 142-216; Zarevand, *Turtsiya i pantyurkizm*, Paris 1930; B. Hayit, *Turkestan im XX. Jahrhundert*, Darmstadt 1957; C. W. Hostler, *Turkism and the Soviets*, London 1957; A. Bennigsen and Ch. Quelquejay, *Der "Sultangalievismus" und die nationalistischen Abweichungen in der Tatarischen Autonomen Sovetrepublik*, in *Forschungen zur Osteuropäischen Geschichte*, vii, Berlin 1959, 323-96; idem, *Les mouvements nationaux chez les Musulmans de Russie*, Paris/The Hague 1960; all the above contain further bibliographical references. The Soviet point of view is given in, *e.g.*, A. Arsharuni and Kh. Gabidullin, *Očerki panislamizma i pantyurkizma v Rossii*, Moscow 1931.

(B. Spuler)

AL-**DJADĪDA**, Arabic and the present-day official name of the ancient Mazagan (former Arabic name: al-Buraydja "the little fortress"), a maritime town of Morocco, situated on the Atlantic Ocean 11 km. south-west of the mouth of the wādī Umm Rabiʿ. Its population was 40,318 in 1954, of whom 1704 were French, 120 foreigners, and 3,328 Jews.

Some authors have considered that Mazagan arose on the site of Ptolemy's Ῥουσιβὶς λιμήν, Pliny's *Portus Rutubis*. The texts do not, indeed, say that there had ever been a town there, but merely an anchorage frequented by ships, and this seems to have been the case throughout the middle ages. The name of Mazagan seems to have appeared for the first time in al-Bakrī (5th/11th century). This geographer, enumerating the Atlantic Coast ports of Morocco, mentions one Mārīfen (de Slane's reading) which must certainly be restored as Māzīg͟han, the form attested by al-Idrīsī (6th/12th century). The same place-name recurs in a ms. collection of edifying anecdotes concerning the great saint of Azammūr, Mawlāy Abū S͟huʿayb, who also lived in the 6th/12th century; here Māzīg͟han appears as a fishermen's hamlet situated between the town of Azammūr and the *ribāṭ* of Tīṭ [*q.v.*]; the propinquity of these two relatively important centres impeded its development. The anchorage is marked on a whole series of planispheres and *portolani* of the 14th and 15th centuries (publ. Ch. de La Roncière, *Le découverte de l'Afrique au Moyen-Âge*, 1925), which give the forms Mesegan (1339 and 1373), Maseghan (1367), and Mazagem, forms intermediate between Māzīg͟han and the Mazagão of the Portuguese. These latter had, since the end of the 9th/15th century, come to load corn from the Dukkāla in the port of Mazagan for the provisioning of their capital. In 1502 a squadron commanded by a Portuguese gentleman, Jorge de Mello, caught by a storm in the straits of Gibraltar, is said to have been driven as far as Mazagan and to have landed there. The Portuguese accommodated themselves in an abandoned tower for protection against possible attack by the inhabitants. Shortly thereafter Jorge de Mello returned to Portugal and obtained royal permission to found a fortress at Mazagan. Although the account of these facts is only recorded by 18th century authors, it must be based on the actual events, for letters-patent of the king Dom Manuel, dated 21 May 1505, grant to Jorge de Mello the captaincy of the castle which he was authorized to build at his own expense at Mazagan. However, he did not avail himself of this privilege, because when, on 27 August 1513, the Portuguese army who were on their way to the conquest of Azammūr under the command of the Duke of Braganza disembarked at Mazagan there was no town and no fortress except for the old ruined tower (al-Buraydja). The difficulties of access to the port of Azammūr induced the Portuguese to establish a more accessible base at Mazagan.

During the summer of 1514 there was built, under the direction of the architects Diego and Francisco de Arruda, a square castle flanked with four angle towers. One of these bastions was formed out of the old tower al-Buraydja, whose name, for the present inhabitants, continues to refer to the Portuguese town. Most of the original castle still stands; most worthy of notice is a magnificent room the vaulting of which is supported by twenty-five columns and pillars, probably a huge granary built to receive the quit-rent, paid in grain, of the tribes subject to Portuguese protection rather than an armoury; this was later (1541) used as a reservoir. Since more than ten years previously the predicament of Portuguese strongholds on the coast, in the face of the religious and xenophobe movement roused by the accession and the conquests of the Saʿdī s͟harīfs, was so bad that the king of Portugal thought of abandoning many of his fortresses. The capture of that of Santa Cruz in Cape Ghir [see AGADIR-IGHIR] by the S͟harīf (12 March 1541) was a warning. John III resigned himself to evacuating Safi and Azammūr and concentrating in Mazagan, a more favourable and more easily defendable position, for all that he wished to leave some Portuguese forces in the south of Morocco. It was at this time that the walls of Mazagan received their present layout.

In preserving Mazagan the Portuguese wished to retain a base on the coast to guarantee the protection of the Indies route. They hoped also that the fortress might serve them as a springboard for the conquest of Morocco when conditions became favourable, but this was never to be realized. In fact, for over two hundred years while it remained in Portuguese possession Mazagan only furnished them with a pretext for obtaining papal bulls of Crusade, which furnished appreciable revenue to the treasury. But the tribes kept the town so tightly blockaded that the inhabitants were unable to venture outside the walls without military protection. The Muslims of the neighbourhood had founded, a mile or so from the town, two large villages, Faḥṣ al-Zammūriyyīn and Faḥṣ Awlād D͟huwayyib, the ruins of which still remain, where they ensconced themselves in order to maintain the blockade.

Badly provisioned by sea, often victims to famine and epidemics, the garrison and the population managed to live in fair security within the protection of their powerful walls, against which the tribesmen could do nothing, although on several occasions the stronghold sustained vigorous attack. In April 1562 Muḥammad, son of the Saʿdī sultan ʿAbd Allāh al-G͟hālib bi 'llāh, laid siege to Mazagan, but the besiegers became discouraged after two attacks had been repulsed. During the disorders which accompanied the decline of the Saʿdī dynasty the governors of Mazagan seem to have succeeded in opening the blockade and in re-establishing relations with the tribes. The *mudjāhid* Sīdī Muḥammad al-ʿAyyās͟hī, to remedy this offence, made an attack on the Portuguese in 1639 and inflicted some losses on them. Mawlāy Ismāʿīl, occupied with the siege of Ceuta, never seriously attempted to make himself master of Mazagan. The honour of reconquering it fell to his grandson Sīdī Muḥammad b. ʿAbd Allāh. The sultan came in person to besiege it at the end of January 1769. The fortress resisted victoriously for five weeks, but the order to evacuate came from Lisbon, and the governor capitulated on honourable terms, and troops and civilians returned to Portugal with their arms and baggage. In abandoning Mazagan, on 10 March 1769, the Portuguese left mines there, the explosion of which caused great damage; the sultan took possession of a devastated town, which he partly repopulated, but which remained in such a sorry state that it was called al-Mahdūma, "the ruin", until the time when, under the reign of Sīdī Muḥammad b. His͟hām, in 1240/1824-5, it was restored by Sīdī Muḥammad b. al-Ṭayyib, ḳāʾid of the Dukkāla and of the Tāmasna, who gave it the name of al-Djadīda.

Bibliography: St. Gsell, *Hist. ancienne de l'Afrique du Nord*, ii, 1928; Luis Maria do Couto de Albuquerque da Cunha, *Memorias para a historia da praça de Mazagão*, publ. Levy Maria Jordão, Lisbon 1864; Alfonso de Dornellas, *A praça de Mazagão*, Lisbon 1913; J. Goulven, *La place de Mazagan sous la domination portugaise*, Paris 1917; Vergilio Correia, *Lugares dalêm*, Lisbon 1923; Agostinho de Gavy de Mendonça, *História do cerco de Mazagão* 1562, Lisbon 1891; *Discurso da Iornada de D. Gonçalo Coutinho à villa de Mazagam*, Lisbon 1629; Jorge de Mascarenhas, *Descrição da fortaleza de Mazagão (1615-19)*, publ. Belisario Pimenta, Lisbon 1916; G. Höst, *Den Marokanske Kajser Mohammed ben Abdallah's Historie*, Copenhagen 1791; R. Ricard, *Mazagan* et le Maroc sous le règne du sultan Moulay Zidan (1608-27), Paris 1956, with the bibliography therein; Nāṣirī, *Kitāb al-istiḳṣā*, trans. Fumey in *AM*, ix and x; *Guides bleus, Maroc*, 1954, 172-7.

(G. S. COLIN and P. de CENIVAL)

DJADĪS [see ṬASM].

DJĀDŪ (DJADO) in Arabic, or *Brao* in Teda, designates at once the principal palm-grove and the bulk of a massif bounded by the 12° and 20° N. parallels and the 12° and 13° E. meridians. This massif is a short branch of the plateau of primary sandstones which, from Tassili of the Ajjers to the massif of Afafi, joins the Ahaggar to the Tibesti. Changes of level are not marked: one passes from 5-800 m. on the plateau to 450 m. at the foot of its western declivity; the impression of relief is given less by the height than by the appearance of the sandstones, looking almost like ruins, cut up, in bands running from north to south, by the beds of the "enneris". These intermittent streams flow towards a zone at the southern point of the massif where they expand; fed in part by the vast "impluvium" formed by the sandstone plateaux, their subterranean course is marked by the line of wells. The fall of the plateau to the west is marked in its northern part by the "gueltas" (Er Roui), and in the south-west by a string of oases.

The richness in underground reservoirs allows life to flourish in this region where the desert characteristics of the climate, violent temperature constrasts and extreme dryness, are very noticeable; there is a cold season from December to February (night temperature -3° or -4° C. [5 to 7 degrees of frost F.], day temperature 25° to 30° C. [77°-86° F.]), when violent sandstorms from the north-east obscure the horizon; from March the temperature rises rapidly to day maxima of 45° to 48° C. (113°-118° F.) with night temperatures of 16° to 20° C. (61°-68° F.). The rains fall at this time, very irregularly, the total annual rainfall varying between 2 and 50 mm., sometimes in a single shower. The intense evaporation explains the rhythm of the variations in the water-level in the wells and numerous springs at the southern end of the massif: from March to November the springs weaken and the ponds and some of the wells dry up; then, at the beginning of December, the level again rises, the ponds expand to an area of about 10 acres in the oases. Palms need no irrigation, and tomatoes, spices, millet, and tobacco grow in the gardens. There are numerous salt-mines. In the north and north-east of the massif the region of the "gueltas" and that of the wells are the *ḥādd* pasture-lands.

Djado is also favoured by its proximity to a crossing of caravan routes: the old commerce route from Murzuk to Chad, joined at this point by the route which runs to Ghat and Ghadames via In Ezzan, bifurcates, like the line of wells towards the south, on the one hand towards Fashi, running to Air or the Nigerian steppes, on the other towards Kawar and Chad; these were the traditional routes of the Sudan-Mediterranean traffic studied by Nachtigal, doubled across the Tenere by the local traffic carried by the *azalay* [*q.v.*].

The wealth in water and the ease of communication have been a twofold source of profit; but they have also been the cause of troubles, as the state of the oases testifies: the mud villages ranged one above another on the flanks of the mounds of derelict palm plantations are ruined; there are trunks to be seen, blackened by fire; a wholesale medley of undergrowth marks the reverted form of palm-groves planted and then abandoned; on the borders are traces of gardens, three of which remained in 1950; matting hovels are scattered on the surrounding sands. The sedentary Kanūrīs who built the villages were doubtless impoverished after the end of the 19th century by the decline in trade across the Sahara, particularly hard hit by the prohibition of slave traffic by the pasha of Murzuk in 1884, and were victims of marauding nomads into the bargain. Ajjer Tuaregs and Tedas would converge on Djado, either to fight or to form up in bands to batten on the caravans or to plunder Air. In any case the massif was a supply base, and so was sacked. The Kanūrīs fled, leaving their salt-workings and palm orchards in which the Tedas established themselves; the 1950 census shows that in a population of 450 inhabitants over 63 families, 53 families were originally from Tibesti, and only 7 were "Braouia", that is to say of mixed Teda and Kanūrī blood. The Tedas, attracted towards the south, would leave wives and children, the old men, perhaps a brother, in the oases, to take care of the propagation and cultivation of the palm plantations, and would return in August at harvest time, when the population of the oases would rise to some thousand persons.

The French administration attempted to revive these deserted oases, and from 1943 an *azalay* again worked the Djado road, while the palm orchards were in part restored. The Djado oasis produced for it alone some 60 tons of dates from 7000 trees; this production, with that of the other oases in the massif, Drigana and Djaba, and that of Kawar, represented 1/5 of the production of the former French West Africa, Mauretania producing the remaining 4/5.

Bibliography: J. Despois, *Le Fezzan*; Ch. and M. Le Cœur, *Enquêtes dans les confins nigériens* (*Cercles de Gouré et de Bilma*); Lt. le Rouvreur, *Notice sur le Djado* (roneo, C.H.E.A.M.); Administrative reports of the Bilma Circle.

(M. CH. LE CŒUR)

DJĀDŪ (DJADO), the old capital of the eastern region of the Djabal Nafūsa in Tripolitania, nowadays a large village in the Fassāṭō district situated on three hills of unequal height. The population of about 2,000—towards the end of the 19th century there were 500 houses—mostly consists of Berbers of the Ibāḍī tribe of Nafūsa. The ruins of the old town are nothing but a pile of broken stones and caves with a mosque in the centre. Near the mosque was formerly the business quarter and the market (*sūḳ*), near which one can still see today the site of the Jewish quarter, synagogue, and cemetery. According to J. Despois, to whom we owe this description, the former large settlement of "Old Djādū" has been replaced by five modern villages, Djado (Djādō), El Gsir (al-Gṣīr), Ouchebarî (Ushebarī), Ioudjelîn (Yudjlīn), and Temouguet (Temūdjeṭ). This information is not quite accurate. It appears, in fact, that at least two of these villages, Yudjlīn and Temūdjeṭ, have nothing to do with the old town of Djādū, and that they already existed alongside this town long ago. According to J. Despois, the present Djado would be about four centuries old. As for the old town, we do not know exactly when it was abandoned. The last mention of Djādū found in the Ibāḍī chronicles is connected with a celebrated Ibāḍī *shaykh* who lived in the 6th/12th century (al-Shammākhī, *Kitāb al-Siyar*, 541).

Little is known of the first days of Djādū. Nevertheless it appears that this town was founded long before the Muslim conquest of North Africa and that it owed its creation and prosperity to the fact that it was situated on the ancient highway joining the city of Tripoli (and probably Sabratha and Leptis Magna) with the Fezzān and the central Sudan (on this highway, see A. Berthelot, *L'Afrique saharienne et soudanaise. Ce qu'en ont connu les anciens*, Paris 1927, 274-6). It seems to us, in fact, that it is with the name Dj̲ādū that the tribal name Gadaiae mentioned by Corippus (549 A.D.) must be connected.

It must, however, be said that the first certain mentions of this town date from much later, the end of the 2nd/8th and the beginning of the 3rd/9th centuries. At this time we hear already of a caravan of traders composed of men from Dj̲ādū in an anecdote concerning the *s̲h̲ayk̲h̲* Abū ʿUt̲h̲mān al-Mazātī and related by the Ibāḍī biographer al-Dardj̲īnī [*q.v.*]. For some time, in the second half of the 3rd/9th and about the beginning of the 4th/10th century, Dj̲ādū, according to the Ibāḍī historians, was the political and administrative centre of the entire Dj̲abal Nafūsa. It was the residence of Abū Manṣūr Ilyās, the governor of the country appointed by the Rustamid *imām* of Tāhart, and later of Abū Yaḥyā Zakariyyāʾ al-Irdj̲ānī who ruled the Dj̲abal Nafūsa as an independent *imām*.

Dj̲ādū was at this time also a considerable commercial city. Ibn Ḥawḳal (367/977) says that it possessed a mosque and a *minbar*. According to Abū ʿUbayd al-Bakrī (461/1068), who got his information about the Dj̲abal Nafūsa from the geographical work of Muḥammad b. Yūsuf al-Warrāḳ (d. 363/973), Dj̲ādū was a large city with bazaars and a considerable Jewish population. According to this geographer the caravans going from Tripolitania to the town of Zawīla in the Fezzan (today Zuīla N.E. of Murzūḳ), a sizeable centre for the export of slaves to Ifrīḳiya and the neighbouring lands in the Middle Ages, used to pass through Dj̲ādū. A march of 40 days separated Zawīla from the Sudanese country of Kānem, with which the Dj̲abal Nafūsa, and in particular the town of Dj̲ādū, had close, but as yet very little studied, relations. In this connexion it is relevant that al-Dj̲anāwanī [*q.v.*], governor of the Dj̲abal Nafūsa on behalf of the *imām* of Tāhart in the first half of the 3rd/9th century, knew, besides Berber and Arabic, the language of Kānem (*lug̲h̲a kānamiyya*). Another fact attests the existence of close relations between Dj̲ādū and the Sudan: the name of the birthplace of al-Dj̲anāwanī, Īdj̲nāwun (situated below Dj̲ādū), which is known from the middle of the 2nd/8th century onwards, is the Arabicized form of the Berber *Ignawn*, an appellation still used today, which is the masculine plural of the Berber word *agnaw* "dumb > negro, black man" (cf. G. S. Colin, in *GLECS*, vii, 94-5). It is therefore probable that the village of Idj̲nāwun (Ignawn) "the Negroes" owes its name to an ethnic group of Sudanese origin, probably natives of Kanem, who had established themselves there some time previously to the 2nd/8th century (T. Lewicki, *Études ibāḍites nord-africaines*, i, Warsaw 1955, 94-6). So one may speak of Dj̲ādū as having been from that period at least a stage on the ancient track Tripoli-Zawīla-Kānem.

The inhabitants of other places in the Dj̲abal Nafūsa used to come to the market at Dj̲ādū, which was above all an economic centre for the whole of the eastern region of the country. It even had, about the 4th/10th century, a special magistrate in charge of the market of the town.

In spite of its mixed population Dj̲ādū was also an Ibāḍī religious centre of great importance. According to al-S̲h̲ammāk̲h̲ī it was a meeting-place for the Ibāḍī scholars of the country.

From a very distant period, the second half of the 2nd/8th century at least, Dj̲ādū was also a political centre, the chief town of the eastern region of the Dj̲abal Nafūsa, which is called in the old Ibāḍī chronicles "the region of Djādū", "Dj̲ādū and its villages", or "Dj̲ādū and its neighbourhood". This region comprised the present districts of Fassāṭo, al-Rūdj̲abān, and al-Zintān. We know the names of some fifteen villages and strongholds (*ḳuṣūr*) which existed in this neighbourhood in the early Middle Ages, as well as the names of several Ibāḍī Berber tribes who lived there side by side with the Nafūsa proper. Of these tribes the Banū Zammūr and the Banū Tārdayt deserve special mention. We do not know whether the region of Dj̲ādū enjoyed autonomy under the Rustamids and their governors in the Dj̲abal Nafūsa. But after the downfall of the imāmate of Tāhart, from the second half of the 4th/10th century onwards, at the time of the greatest economic prosperity of Dj̲ādū, there were *ḥākims* (local Ibāḍī chiefs) of this town (or perhaps of the whole region of Dj̲ādū) side by side with the *ḥākims* of the Dj̲abal Nafūsa. The first *ḥākim* "of the people of Dj̲ādū" whose name we know was Abū Muḥammad al-Darfī, a contemporary of the *ḥākim* of Nafūsa Abū Zakariyyāʾ al-Tindemirtī. He lived in the famous Dār Banī ʿAbd Allāh which was situated on the *sūḳ* of Dj̲ādū. This house, which afterwards became the meeting-place of the *s̲h̲ayk̲h̲s* of the town, was considered later to be one of the holy places of the Dj̲abal Nafūsa. After the death of Abū Muḥammad the office of *ḥākim* of Dj̲ādū passed to his son Abū Yaḥyā Yūsuf, who lived about 390/1000. Along with the *ḥākims* of Dj̲ādū there were also in the region of this town from the 4th/10th to the 5th/11th centuries *ḥākims* special to the Banū Zammūr.

Bibliography: Ibn Ḥawḳal, 95 and map between 66 and 67; Bakrī, text 9-10, tr. 25-6; Abu 'l-ʿAbbās Aḥmad b. Saʿīd al-S̲h̲ammāk̲h̲ī, *Kitāb al-siyar*, Cairo 1301/1883, 172, 203, 239, 242, 243, 244, 253, 255, 273, 284, 285, 286, 287, 288, 298, 299, 304, 306, 314, 320, 321, 324, 334, 339, 340, 341, 343, 541, 544; R. Basset, *Les sanctuaires du Djebel Nefousa*, in *JA* 1899, May-June 453, July-August 99, no. 89; A. de C. Motylinski, *Le Djebel Nefousa: Transcription, traduction française et notes avec une étude grammaticale*, Paris 1899, 89; Abu 'l-ʿAbbās Aḥmad b. Saʿīd al-Dardj̲īnī, *Kitāb ṭabaḳāt al-mas̲h̲āyik̲h̲*, Cracow MS. f° 89 v.; *Guida del Touring Club Italiano. Possedimenti e colonie. Isole Egee, Tripolitania, Cirenaica, Eritréa, Somália*, by L. V. Bertarelli, Milan 1929, 333; J. Despois, *Le Djebel Nefousa (Tripolitaine). Étude géographique*, Paris 1935, 245, 246, 269, 288, 289; T. Lewicki, *On some Libyon ethnics in Johannis of Corippus*, in *Rocznik Orientalistyczny*, xv, 1948, 125-6; idem, *Études ibāḍites nord-africaines*, Part i, Warsaw 1955, 37, 84-5, 88-92, 95-6, and *passim*; idem, *La répartition géographique des groupements ibāḍites dans l'Afrique du Nord au moyen âge*, in *Rocznik Orientalistyczny*, xxi, 1957, 332, 334-6; cf. also the bibliographies to the two articles by F. Beguinot: 'AL-NAFŪSA' in *EI*[1] and 'Nafūsa' in *Enciclopedia Italiana*, xxiv, 500-1. (T. LEWICKI)

DJADWAL, pl. *djadāwil*, primarily "brook, water-course", means further "table, plan". Graefe suggested that in this meaning it might derive from *schedula*; but perhaps one should rather think of *dj-d-l* "to twist", cf. S. Fraenkel, *Die aramäischen Fremdwörter im Arabischen*, 224, and the similar development of the meaning of *zīdj*, as stated by E. Honigmann, *Die sieben Klimata*, 1929, 117 ff. In this second sense the word becomes a special term in sorcery, synonymous with *khātim*; here it means quadrangular or other geometrical figures, into which names and signs possessing magic powers are inserted. These are usually certain mysterious characters, Arabic letters and numerals, magic words, the Names of God, the angels and demons, as well as of the planets, the days of the week, and the elements, and lastly pieces from the Ḳur'ān, such as the *Fātiḥa* [*q.v.*], the *Sūrat Yāsīn*, the "throne-verse", the *fawātiḥ*, etc. The application of these figures is manifold: frequently the paper on which they have been drawn is burnt in order to cense someone with its smoke; or the writing may be washed off in water and drunk (cf. Num., v, 23 ff.); along with the *daʿwa* (conjuration) and often also the *ḳasam* (oath) the *djadwal* forms the contents of an amulet (*ḥirz*, [*q.v.*]). The very popular *daʿwat al-shams*, for example, is prepared as follows: it is quadrangular, divided into 49 sections by six lines drawn lengthwise and six drawn across its breadth, and contains Solomon's seal and other peculiar figures: seven consonants, Names of God, names of spirits, the names of the seven kings of the *djinns*, the names of the days of the week, and the names of the planets. The underlying notion is that secret relationships exist between these various components, and the *djadwal* is therefore made to obtain certain certain results from the correlations of the elements composing it. The highly developed system of mystic letters, which is based on the numerical values of the Arabic letters, is very frequently used for the *djadwal*. A special class is formed by the squares called *wafḳ* [*q.v.*] in the fields of which certain figures are so arranged that the addition of horizontal, vertical and diagonal lines gives in every case the same total (*e.g.*, 15 or 34). The celebrated name *budūḥ* is nothing but an artificial talismanic word formed from the elements of the simple threefold magic square, *i.e.*, from the letters in the four corners in the alphabetical order of the *abdjad*,

4	9	2
3	5	7
8	1	6

expressed in *abdjad* by

د	ط	ب
ج	ه	ز
ح	ا	و

The name *budūḥ* evidently passed at an early date into South Arabic, became used there as a feminine proper name and as a feminine epithet, "fat", and was confused with the root بذخ (*LA*, iii, s.v. بذخ). It has no other meaning in Arabic. In magical books there are even a few cases of the word being personified (*e.g.*, *Yā budūḥ*, in Ḥādjdj Saʿdūn, *Al-fatḥ al-raḥmānī*, 21), although in popular belief Budūḥ has become a Djinnī whose services can be secured by writing his name either in letters or in numbers (*JA*, sér. 4, xii, 521 ff.; Spiro, *Vocabulary of colloquial Egyptian*, 36; Doutté, *Magie et religion*, 296, along with *Ḳayyūm* as though a name of Allāh; Klunzinger, Upper Egypt, 387). The uses of this word are most varied, to invoke both good and bad fortune: thus, in Doutté, *op. cit.*, against menorrhagia (234), against stomach pains (229), to render oneself invisible (275), against temporary impotence (295); Lane's Cairo magician also used it with his ink mirror, and so in several treatises on magic. It is also engraved upon jewels and metal plates or rings which are permanently carried as talismans, and it is inscribed at the beginning of books (like *kabīkadj*) as a safeguard, *e.g.*, in *Fatḥ al-djalīl*, Tunis 1290. By far its most common use is to ensure the arrival of letters and packages.

Besides the references above, see also Reinaud, *Monuments musulmans*, ii, 243 ff., 251 ff., 256. For the other meanings of *djadwal* cf. the notes s.v. in Dozy's *Supplément* and Redhouse's *Turkish and English lexicon*. The *K. al-budūḥ* by Djābir b. Ḥayyān mentioned in the *Fihrist* is in fact a *kitāb al-tadarrudj*, cf. P. Kraus, *Jābir ibn Ḥayyān*, i, 1943, p. 26, no. 47, and J. W. Fück, in *Ambix*, iv (1951), 128, no. 36.

Bibliography: *Ikhwān, al-Ṣafā'*, ch. i; Ibn Khaldūn, *Muḳaddima*, vi, ch. xxvii-xxviii, and Ibn Khaldūn-Rosenthal, iii, 156 ff.; al-Dayrabī, *Mudjarrabāt*, 1298, *passim*; al-Būnī, *Shams al-maʿārif*, i, ch. xvi; *Tadhyīl tadhkirat uli 'l-albāb li 'l-Anṭākī*, *passim*; Muḥammad b. Muḥmūd al-Āmulī, *Nafā'is al-funūn* (Pers. Encycl., lith., 1309, in folio), ii, 199 ff., sub *ʿilm-i wafḳ-i aʿdād*; Ṭāshköprüzāde, *Miftāḥ al-saʿāda*, i, 331, no. 182: *ʿilm aʿdād al-wafḳ*; al-Ḳazwīnī, *Āthār al-bilād* (*Kosmographie*, ii), 385 (credits Archimedes with the invention of the magic square); C. H. Becker, *Islamstudien*, i, 315; ii, 100; Lane, *Manners and customs* ..., ch. xi-xii; W. Ahrens, in *Isl.*, vii (1917), 186 ff., esp. 239; H. Winkler, *Siegel und Charaktere*, 1930, 55 ff.; P. Kraus, *Jābir ibn Ḥayyān*, ii, 73; E. Mauchamp, *La sorcellerie au Maroc*, n.d., 208 (magic letters); H. Hermelink, in *Sudhoffs Archiv*, xlii (1958), 199-217; xliii (1959), 351-4.

(E. Graefe-D. B. Macdonald-[M. Plessner])

AL-**DJADY** [see nudjūm].

DJĀF. A large and famous Kurdish tribe of southern (ʿIrāḳī) Kurdistān, and of the Sanandadj (Senna) district of Ardalān province of Western Persia.

The tribe, cattle-owning and seasonally nomadic, was centred in the Djawānrūd [*q.v.*] area of the latter province in the early 11th/17th century, and is first mentioned in connexion with the operations and Turko-Persian treaty of Sultan Murād IV. About 1112/1700, following bad relations with the Ardalān authorities, the main body of the tribe (estimated at 10,000 tents or families) moved into Turkish territory, leaving substantial sections in their own original homes. The Djāf who settled in the Turkish and border districts occupied, in summer, the highlands around Pandjwīn: in spring and autumn, the plain of Shahrizūr, with headquarters at Ḥalabdja: and in winter, lands dependent upon Kifrī, on the right bank of the Sīrwān (Diyālā). Other Djāf elements at various periods became incorporated with the Gūrān, others with the Sindjābī, others the Sharafbayānī, others the Bādjalān (all more or less astride the reputed frontier, which was not fixed until 1263/1847), and separated from their original tribe.

The main body of the Djāf, although grouped in many distinct sections, sometimes of formidable size and self-consciousness, showed fair general cohesion under capable leaders. For a century and a half (1112-1267/1700-1850) they intermittently (but never much more than nominally) formed part of the dependencies of the Bābān [*q.v.*] empire. Their nomadic habit and indiscipline involved them in endless quarrels with neighbours and settled folk, and their seasonal entry into, and close contacts in, Persian districts gave them a footing in both countries which made them for a century an element in Turko-Persian frontier politics: an element the more unmanageable by reason of their formidable numbers, and the rivalries between claimants for power among their own Beg-zāda, who frequently courted, or were championed by, both Governments in turn. Even after their nominal incorporation in the Turkish administrative system, about 1267/1850, and in spite of increasing contacts of their leaders with Turkish officialdom and forces, they remained effectively ungoverned until the first World War, dominated the area in which they camped and grazed (as well as the town of Ḥalabdja, which was a Djāf creation), and paid infrequent dues to the Treasury in the form of lump sums collected by their own chiefs. Since 1337/1918, however, a defined frontier, more effective government, and increasing tribal settlement have deprived the tribe of much of its former importance.

Bibliography: E. B. Soane, *Report on the Sulaimania district of Kurdistan*, Calcutta 1918; ʿAbbās al-ʿAzzāwī, *ʿAshāʾir al-ʿIrāḳ*, ii, Baghdād 1366/1947. Cf. also SENNA. (S. H. LONGRIGG)

MĪR **DJAʿFAR** or Mīr Muḥammad Djaʿfar Khān (*Siyar al-mutaʾakhkhirīn*, vol. ii in both the text and rubrics, and not Djaʿfar ʿAlī Khān), son of Sayyid Aḥmad al-Nadjafī, of obscure origin, rose to be the Nawwāb of Bengal during the days of the East India Company. A penniless adventurer, like his patron Mīrzā Muḥammad ʿAlī entitled ʿAlīwirdī Khān Mahābat Djang (see the article ʿALĪ WERDI KHĀN), he married a step-sister, Shāh Khānim, of ʿAlīwirdī and served his master and brother-in-law as a commandant, before the latter ascended the *masnad* of Bengal in 1153/1740 after defeating and killing Sarfrāz Khān, son and successor of Shudjāʿ al-Dīn, the Mughal *sūbadār* of Bengal. He fought, successfully on a number of occasions, against the Marāthās, who were then making inroads into Bengal. In one of the encounters on the banks of the Bhagīrthī in 1155/1741 he scattered and dispersed the *lashkar* of the Marāthā chieftain, Bhāskar Pandit. After the withdrawal of the Marāthās he was appointed *nāʾib-nāẓim* of Cuttack and *fawdjdār* [*q.v.*] of Medinīpur and Hidjlī. He, however, continued to held the office of paymaster (*bakhshī*) of the army, to which post he had been appointed in 1153/1740 by ʿAlīwirdī Khān. In 1160/1747 he was ordered to oppose the Marāthās, but he fled and fell precipitately on Burdwan. The same year he was deprived of this and other offices held by him for malversation and his insolence towards ʿAlīwirdī Khān, who had gone to his house to condole with him in a family bereavement. The next year, however, he was reinstated. In 1164/1751 he was again successful against Mīr Ḥabīb and his Marāthā confederates. On the accession of Sirādj al-Dawla, a grandson of ʿAlīwirdī Khān, to the *masnad* of Bengal, Mīr Djaʿfar was removed from the all-important office of *bakhshī* as by reason of his maturity, war experience, and high position, he was the only man whom Sirādj al-Dawla had reason to fear in a trial of strength. It must have been within the knowledge of Sirādj al-Dawla that Mīr Djaʿfar was an ambitious man and had on an earlier occasion during the life-time of ʿAlīwirdī Khān conspired to kill his master and patron and himself occupy the *masnad* of Bengal (*Siyar*, ii, 157). Soon after the death of ʿAlīwirdī Khān (1169/1756), Mīr Djaʿfar sent a secret letter to Shawkat Djang, the Nawwāb of Purnia, to attack Sirādj al-Dawla, assuring him of full support. Shawkat Djang needed no such invitation as he had refused to recognize the succession of Sirādj al-Dawla. Djaʿfar, however, did not slacken his efforts and in 1170/1757 entered into a secret treaty with Lord Clive, through William Watts, the chief of the English Factory in Ḳāsimbāzār, for the overthrow of Sirādj al-Dawla, who had by his various indiscretions alienated not only his own officers but even the influential Hindū bankers, the Djagat Sēths, whom he had threatened with circumcision. Not very sure of the support promised by Mīr Djaʿfar, Clive took the field at Plassey in 1170/1757. On the fall of Mīr Madan, the Chief of Artillery (*Mīr Ātash*) of Sirādj al-Dawla's army, the Nawwāb in utter despair called Djaʿfar to his tent and begged and implored him to "defend his honour". Djaʿfar, in spite of his having sworn on the Ḳurʾān, informed Clive of the helplessness of the Nawwāb and urged the English to advance at once and seize his camp. Next day Mīr Djaʿfar, instead of supporting the Nawwāb, retreated from the battlefield, thus facilitating the victory of the English. After the battle he returned to Murshīdābād, the capital, and was proclaimed Nawwāb by Clive. (S. C. Hill, *Bengal in 1756-57*, London 1905, ii, 437). A few days later he had Sirādj al-Dawla, who had been captured while fleeing and brought back to Murshīdābād, executed by his son Mīran, although the fallen Nawwāb abased himself by begging for mercy. Mīr Djaʿfar soon found that he was not in a position to fulfil his monetary commitments (£ 3,388,000) rashly entered into with the East India Company. In 1174/1769 he was deposed and supplanted by his son-in-law, Mīr Ḳāsim, partly because of his doubtful attitude during the attempted Dutch invasion of Bengal in 1173/1759 and partly because of his having been in arrears with his payments to the Company. The declaration of war against the Company by Mīr Ḳāsim in 1177/1763 and his ultimate defeat and flight into Awadh again brought Mīr Djaʿfar to the *masnad*, which he occupied till his death in 1178/1765. Taking account of the standards of the time, the prevailing atmosphere of political chicanery and doubtful entitlement to high offices of State, of the way his contemporary ʿAlīwirdī Khān had obtained the *niẓāmat* of Bengal, of Sirādj al-Dawla's incompetence and unpopularity, it is rather difficult to justify the charge of national treachery commonly levelled against Mīr Djaʿfar, much less to dub him "Lord Clive's jackass". His last years were not very happy or comfortable as he had contracted leprosy and was strongly addicted to sensual pleasures, opium, and *ḥashīsh*.

Bibliography: Ghulām Ḥusayn Ṭabāṭabāʾī, *Siyar al-mutaʾakhkhirīn*, Lucknow 1314/1897, vol. ii; Yūsuf ʿAlī Khān, *Taʾrīkh (Aḥwāl)-i Mahābat Djang* (in Persian, still in MS.); Karam ʿAlī, *Muẓaffarnāma*, I.O. (MS) no. 4075; *The history of Bengal*, ii (Muslim Period), ed. J. N. Sarkar, Dacca 1948, 469-70 and index; Robert Orme, *History of the military transactions of the British Nation in Indostan*; C. R. Wilson, *Early annals of the English in Bengal*, (2 vols.), London 1895-1917; Lucy S. Sutherland, *The East India Company in eighteenth-century politics*, Oxford 1952, index; George Dunbar, *India and the passing of empire*, London 1951, 86-9, 102

n. 6; J. Mill, *The history of British India*, (2 vols.), London 1817-18; H. Dodwell, *India*, (2 vols.), London 1936; G. R. Gleig, *History of the British empire in India*, (3 vols.), London 1830; *Cambridge History of India*, v; *A history of the Freedom Movement*, Karachi 1956, index; Jadunath Sarkar, *Fall of the Mughal empire*; Kālī Kinkar Datta, *ʿAlī Vardi and his times*, Calcutta 1939, index; F. N. Nikhilnath Ray, *Murshidabad kahani*, 247; Thompson and Garrat, *Rise and fulfilment of British rule in India*, 100-4; Alfred Lyall, *Growth and expansion of British rule in India*, 148, 143; J. N. Sarkar, *Bengal Nawabs*, Calcutta 1952; A. C. Roy, *Career of Mir Jafar Khan*, Calcutta 1953.

(A. S. BAZMEE ANSARI)

DJAʿFAR B. ABĪ ṬĀLIB, cousin of the Prophet and brother of ʿAlī, whose elder he was by ten years. When his father was reduced to poverty, his uncle al-ʿAbbās took Djaʿfar into his house to solace him, while Muḥammad took care of ʿAlī. Soon being converted to Islam (Djaʿfar occupies the 24th, or 31st, or 32nd place in the list of the first Muslims), he was among those who emigrated to Abyssinia (his name heads the second list given by Ibn Hishām, 209); his wife Asmāʾ b. ʿUmays followed him. When the Ḳuraysh sent Abū Rabīʿa Ibn al-Mughīra al-Makhzūmī and ʿAmr b. al-ʿĀṣ to the Negus to demand the detention of the émigrés, Djaʿfar, by reciting Ḳurʾānic verses on the Virgin (from Sūra XIX) before the sovereign, and at a subsequent audience verses on Jesus (from Sūra IV), obtained his protection for himself and his companions; it is even said that he converted him to Islam. During this period of exile the Prophet expressly commended Djaʿfar to the Negus; at the time of the famous Pact of Fraternity between *Muhādjirūn* and *Anṣār*, he allotted Muʿādh b. Djabal to him as adoptive brother, and, unless the tradition is in error, he considered him as present at the battle of Badr, since his name figures among the Badrites.

On his return from Abyssinia, Djaʿfar met the Prophet on the day of the capture of Khaybar (7/628). Muḥammad, embracing him with the greatest fervour, cried "I know not what gives me the greater pleasure, my conquest or the return of Djaʿfar".

The name of Djaʿfar is found in the sources in connexion with an episode concerning ʿAmmāra, daughter of Ḥamza the uncle of the Prophet. The girl had stayed at Mecca; to withdraw her from the pagans while respecting the pact of Ḥudaybiya, ʿAlī proposed to take her as wife to Medina. Zayd b. Ḥāritha protested that he was her *walī* in his capacity as Ḥamza's brother and heir, and that Djaʿfar was also on account of his kinship with her (he was Ḥamza's nephew and brother-in-law of ʿAmmāra's mother). Muḥammad agreed that Djaʿfar should be the girl's guardian, but restrained him from marrying her because of his double bond of relationship. Djaʿfar welcomed the decision of the Prophet, skipping (*ḥadjala*) around Muḥammad in the way in which the Abyssinians did around the Negus. It was on this occasion that the Prophet is reputed to have said "Thou art like me in thy features and thy manners (*ashbahta khalḳī wa khuluḳī*)".

In the year 8/629, when the Prophet decided to send an expedition beyond the Byzantine frontier, he appointed Zayd b. Ḥāritha as commander-in-chief, and, in case the latter should be killed, Djaʿfar, and then, as Djaʿfar's eventual replacement, ʿAbd Allāh b. Rawāḥa. All three fell in the battle of Muʾta (Djumādā I 8/629) and were buried in the same tomb which had no distinctive markings. A tomb is in existence at Muʾta on which Djaʿfar's epitaph in Kūfic characters is partly preserved, which shows the antiquity of the tradition concerning him. Djaʿfar fought and died bravely (at this time he was about forty years old); he is said to have hamstrung his horse before the battle so that he should have no means of flight, and that he was the first in Islam so to do; having had his hands cut off one after the other, he carried the standard against his chest with his stumps; more than sixty wounds were counted on his body. The Prophet, through his supernatural powers of perception, witnessed the battle from his *minbar*. The following day he went to Djaʿfar's house and revealed to his widow, by his tears, the sorrow which had fallen upon her.

Djaʿfar was the one of Muḥammad's kinsmen who most closely resembled him. He was surnamed Abu 'l-Masākīn (or Abu 'l-Masākin) for his charity towards the poor. After his death he was called Djaʿfar dhu 'l-djanāḥayn or Djaʿfar al-Ṭayyār fi 'l-djanna, as the Prophet declared that he had had a dream of him flying on two bloody wings among a group of angels in Paradise. The *Usd* and the *ʿUmdat al-ṭālib* say that he was also called Dhu 'l-hidjratayn because of his two emigrations, to Abyssinia and to Medina, which seems strange since, on account of his exile, he could not have had the opportunity of following Muḥammad on his *hidjra*.

Of the sons Djaʿfar had by his wife al-Asmāʾ, ʿAwn and Muḥammad fell at Karbalāʾ beside al-Ḥusayn; only ʿAbd Allāh gave him any descendants.

Ibn Abi 'l-Ḥadīd tells us of the arguments of those who considered the merits of Djaʿfar to be superior to those of ʿAlī: he had embraced Islam after puberty; he had died a martyr's death, whereas there was dispute as to whether ʿAlī's had been a *shahāda*, etc. Abū Ḥayyān al-Tawḥīdī has also treated of this subject in the 5th part of his *K. al-Baṣāʾir*.

Bibliography: Ibn Hishām, 159, 164, 209[10], 219, 221, 344, 781, 794-6; Ṭabarī, i, 1163 ff., 1184, 1610, 1614, 1616-8; ii, 329; iii, 2297 ff.; Wāḳidī (Wellhausen), 73, 83, 282, 287, 296, 302 ff., 309 ff., 433; Masʿūdī, *Murūdj*, iv, 159, 181, 182, 290, 449; v, 148; Ibn Khaldūn, ii App., 7, 16 ff., 39 ff.; Ibn al-Athīr, *Usd*, i, 286-9; Ibn Ḥadjar, *Iṣāba*, ii, 584, no. 8746; Ibn ʿInaba, *ʿUmdat al-ṭālib*, Nadjaf 1358, 19 ff.; Ibn Abi 'l-Ḥadīd, *Sharḥ Nahdj al-balāgha*, Cairo 1329, ii, 108 ff.; iii, 39-41; Caetani, *Annali*, index at end of 2nd volume; W. Montgomery Watt, *Muhammad at Mecca*, Oxford 1953, 88, 110, 111; idem, *Muhammad at Medina*, Oxford 1956, 54 ff., 380 ff. (for the explanation of the prohibition of Djaʿfar's marriage with ʿAmmāra). For the *ḥadīth* on the resemblance see Wensinck, *Concordance*, s.v. *shabaha*. For the tomb, and relevant bibliography, see Harawī, *Guide des lieux de Pèlerinage* [= *K. al-Ziyārāt*], trans. J. Sourdel-Thomine, Damascus 1957, 47.

(L. VECCIA VAGLIERI)

DJAʿFAR B. ʿALĪ B. ḤAMDŪN AL-ANDALUSĪ, a descendant of a Yemeni family which settled in Spain at an unknown date, subsequently moving to the district of Msīla, in the Maghrib, at the end of the 3rd/9th century at the latest. Like his father ʿAlī, he was at first a loyal supporter of the Fāṭimid cause, as Governor of Msila; then, probably inspired by jealousy of the Zīrids [*q.v.*] who were increasingly favoured by the Fāṭimid caliphs, he changed sides in 360/971 and swore obedience to the Umayyad caliph of Spain. After a few years in favour, he incurred the displeasure of the all-powerful *ḥādjib* al-Manṣūr b. Abī ʿĀmir [*q.v.*] who had him assassinated in 372/982-3.

Bibliography: M. Canard, *Une famille de partisans, puis d'adversaires des Fatimides en Afrique du Nord*, in *Mélanges d'histoire et d'archéologie de l'Occident musulman*, Algiers 1957, ii, 33-49, with references to sources in Arabic.

(R. Le Tourneau)

DJAʿFAR b. **AL-FAḌL** [see ibn al-furāt].

DJAʿFAR b. **ḤARB.** Abu 'l-Faḍl Djaʿfar b. Ḥarb al-Hamadhānī (d. 236/850), a Muʿtazilī of the Baghdād branch, was first a disciple of Abu 'l-Hudhayl al-ʿAllāf at Baṣra, and then of al-Murdār at Baghdād, whose asceticism he tried to imitate; this is what inspired him to give to the poor the large fortune which he had inherited from his father.

In agreement with the Muʿtazila, he defended the doctrine that God knows through Himself from all eternity, that His knowledge is His very being, and that the object of His knowledge can exist from all eternity. He said that we have, in the divine wisdom, the guarantee that God does not commit injustice and does not lie; indeed that we cannot reasonably conceive the idea of a God who in fact commits an injustice. The infidel who is converted by his own effort, he said, has greater merit than one who is converted by divine grace. Again in agreement with the Muʿtazila, he admitted that the Word of God—the Ḳur'ān—is created; it is therefore an accident and its place is the Prophet. He considered the soul to be essentially different from the body and united to it accidentally. He said that we act according to the last decision we have taken, provided it is not halted by another decision or by an obstacle.

Djaʿfar was a Zaydī: he said that the imāmate falls on the most worthy and not on the person who deserves it by right; and ʿAlī b. Abī Ṭālib is the most deserving in the community after the Prophet.

Bibliography: al-Ashʿarī, *Maḳālāt*, Istanbul 1929, 191, 202, 337, 373, 415, 557, 598; Ibn al-Nadīm, *Fihrist*, in *Muḥ. Shafiʿ Presentation Volume*, Lahore 1955, 65-6; Al-Baghdādī, *Farḳ*, 151; al-Malaṭī, *al-Tanbīh*, 27, 33; al-Khayyāṭ, *K. al-Intiṣār* (French trans. by Albert Nader, Beirut 1957), 7, 12, 66, 74, 89, 100, 113; Ibn al-Murtaḍā, *K. al-Munya* ed. T. W. Arnold, *The Muʿtazilah*, 41 ff.; ed. S. Diwald-Wilzer, *Die Klassen der Muʿtaziliten*, Wiesbaden 1961, 73 ff.; A. N. Nader, *Le système philosophique des Muʿtazila*, Beirut 1956 (index).

(Albert N. Nader)

DJAʿFAR b. **MANṢŪR AL-YAMĀN** [see supplement].

DJAʿFAR B. MUBASHSHIR al-Ḳaṣabī (also al-Thaḳafī), a prominent Muʿtazilī theologian and ascetic of the school of Baghdād, d. 234/848-9. He was a disciple of Abū Mūsā al-Murdār, and to some slight degree also influenced by al-Naẓẓām [*q.v.*] of Baṣra. Little is known of his life except some anecdotes about his abnegation of the world, and the information that he introduced the Muʿtazilī doctrine to ʿĀna [*q.v.*], and held disputations with Bishr b. Ghiyāth al-Marīsī [*q.v.*]. He is the author of numerous works on *fiḳh* and *kalām* (al-Khayyāṭ 81; *Fihrist* 37) and he had numerous disciples who, together with the disciples of his like-minded contemporary Djaʿfar b. Ḥarb [*q.v.*], were called Djaʿfariyya, a branch of the Muʿtazila of Baghdād, by later heresiographers. Nothing of his literary output seems to have survived, except one long quotation on various opinions concerning the Ḳur'ān, from which it appears that he had anticipated al-Ashʿarī's style of literary exposition (*Maḳālāt al-Islāmiyyīn*, 589-98). His principle in *fiḳh* was, according to al-Khayyāṭ (89), to follow the *ẓāhir* meaning of Ḳur'ān, *sunna* and *idjmāʿ*, and to avoid *ra'y* and *ḳiyās*, and among his writings are mentioned works directed against the *aṣḥāb al-ra'y wa- 'l-ḳiyās*, and against the *aṣḥāb al-ḥadīth*. His opinions in theology remain within the framework of the various doctrines held by the Muʿtazila; some of them seem directly to reflect his unworldly attitude, such as his definition of the world of Islām not as the "world of faith" but as the "world of unrighteousness" (*dār fisḳ*, in the technical meaning of the word; *Maḳālāt al-Islāmiyyīn* 464); this seems to have been the basis for Ibn al-Rēwendī's [*q.v.*] charge, repeated by later heresiographers but rejected as false by al-Khayyāṭ (81), that Djaʿfar regarded some Muslim sinners (*fussāḳ*) as worse than the Jews, Christians, Zindīḳs and Dahriyya. As regards the caliphate, Djaʿfar held, in common with Djaʿfar b. Ḥarb and al-Iskāfī [*q.v.*], that ʿAlī was the most meritorious of men after the Prophet, but that the appointment of his less meritorious predecessors before him was valid; he and the other Muʿtazila of Baghdād are therefore regarded as a branch of the Zaydiyya (al-Malaṭī 27).

Djaʿfar's brother, Ḥubaysh b. Mubashshir (d. 258/872), was a *faḳīh* and traditionist who is claimed both by Sunnī and by Shīʿa biographers (al-Khaṭīb al-Baghdādī, no. 4369; Ibn Ḥadjar al-ʿAsḳalānī, *Tahdhīb al-Tahdhīb*, ii, no. 363; al-Māmaḳānī, *Tanḳīḥ al-Maḳāl*, Nadjaf 1349 ff., no. 2237); it is reported that Djaʿfar refused to talk to him because he was a Ḥashwī (al-Masʿūdī, *Murūdj*, v, 443).

Bibliography: al-Khayyāṭ, *K. al-intiṣār*, ed. Nyberg, index; al-Ashʿarī, *Maḳālāt al-Islāmiyyīn*, ed. Ritter, index; al-Malaṭī, *K. al-Tanbīh*, ed. Dedering, index; Ibn al-Nadīm, *Fihrist*, in *Muḥ. Shafiʿ Presentation Volume*, Lahore 1955, 64; ʿAbd al-Ḳāhir b. Ṭāhir al-Baghdādī, *K. al-farḳ bayn al-firaḳ*, ed. Badr, 153 f.; al-Khaṭīb al-Baghdādī, *Ta'rīkh Baghdād*, no. 3608 (tradition from ʿAlī, of an ascetic tendency); al-Isfarā'īnī, *al-Tabṣīr fi 'l-Dīn*, Cairo 1359, 47; al-Shahrastānī, *K. al-milal wa 'l-niḥal*, ed. Cureton (cf. T. Haarbrücker, *Religionspartheien* etc., transl., index); Fakhr al-Dīn al-Rāzī, *K. firaḳ al-Muslimīn wa'l-Mushrikīn*, Cairo 1356, 43; al-Īdjī, *al-Mawāḳif*, ed. Soerensen, 338; Ibn al-Murtaḍā, *K. al-Munya*, ed. T. W. Arnold, *al-Muʿtazilah*, 43 f.; ed. S. Diwald-Wilzer, *Die Klassen der Muʿtaziliten*, Wiesbaden 1961, 76 ff.; A. S. Tritton, *Muslim theology*, index; W. M. Watt, *Free will and predestination in early Islam*, index; A. N. Nader, *Le système philosophique des Muʿtazila*, index.

(A. N. Nader and J. Schacht)

DJAʿFAR b. **MUḤAMMAD** [see abū maʿshar].

DJAʿFAR b. **YAḤYĀ** [see al-barāmika].

DJAʿFAR BEG (?-926/1520)—the "Zafir agà, eunuco" listed in the index to Marino Sanuto, *Diarii*, xxv, col. 832—was Sandjaḳ Beg of Gallipoli, *i.e.*, Ḳapudān or High Admiral of the Ottoman naval forces. He was appointed to this office, not (as *Ḳāmūs al-aʿlām* and *Sidjill-i ʿOthmānī* assert) in 917/1511, but in 922/1516. His tenure of the office coincided with the Ottoman conquest of Syria and Egypt (922-3/1516-7) and with the extensive naval preparations that Sultan Selīm I (918-26/1512-20) urged forward during the last of his reign. Djaʿfar Beg was noted for his harsh character (cf. Hammer-

Purgstall, *GOR*, iii, 7). His misdeeds brought about his execution at the beginning of the reign of Sultan Sulaymān Ḳānūnī (926-74/1520-66).

Bibliography: Saʿd al-Dīn, *Tādj al-tawārīkh*, Istanbul A.H. 1280, ii, 373, 389; Ḥādjdjī Khalīfa, *Tuḥfat al-kibār fī asfār al-biḥār*, Istanbul A.H. 1329, 23; Paolo Giovio, *Historiarum sui temporis tomus primus*, Paris 1558, lib. xvii, fol. 197r (= *La prima parte dell'istorie del suo tempo di Mons. Paolo Giovio .... tradotta per M. Lodovico Domenichi*, Venice 1560, 469); M. Sanuto, *I Diarii*, edd. Barozzi, Berchet, Fulin, Stefani, Venice 1879-1903, xxiv, col. 848, xxv, cols. 832-833, xxvi, col. 628, xxviii, col. 821 and xxix, col. 549; Hammer-Purgstall, *GOR*, ii, 533; iii, 7; Sāmī, *Ḳāmūs al-aʿlām*, iii, Istanbul A. H. 1308, 1818; *Sidjill-i ʿOthmānī*, ii, 69; *Arşiv kılavuzu*, fasc. I, Istanbul 1938, 88. (V. J. PARRY)

DJAʿFAR ČELEBI (864/1459-921/1515), Ottoman statesman and man of letters, was born at Amasya (for the date see E. Blochet, *Cat. des mss. turcs*, ii, 1-2), where his father Tādjī Beg was adviser to Prince (later Sultan) Bāyezīd. After rising in the theological career to *müderris*, he was appointed nishāndjī by Bāyezīd II (in 903/1497-8, see *Tâci-zâde Sa'dî Çelebi Münşeâtı*, ed. N. Lugal & A. Erzi, Istanbul 1956, 85). Suspected of favouring Prince Aḥmad in the struggle for the succession, Djaʿfar, with other of Aḥmad's partisans, was dismissed at the insistence of the Janissaries (Djumādā II 917/September 1511), but Bāyezīd's successor Selīm, appreciating his talents, restored him to office. After the battle of Čāldirān he was given Shāh Ismāʿīl's wife Tādjlī Khanum in marriage (see I. H. Uzunçarşılı in *Belleten*, xxiii, 1959, 611 ff.) and appointed ḳāḍiʿasker of Anadolu (Ferīdūn², i, 406, 464); back in Istanbul, however, he was accused of having encouraged the discontent of the Janissaries on the campaign and put to death (8 Redjeb 921/18 August 1515).

His poetical works consist of (1) a *Dīwān* (selections published by Gibb and S. Nüzhet, see Bibl.) and (2) *Hevesnāme*, composed in 899/1493-4, a Turkish *mathnawī* completely original in theme, containing a description of Istanbul and the account of an amatory adventure. He was reckoned especially skilful as a *munshī*. His ornate description of Meḥemmed II's capture of Constantinople, *Maḥrūse-i Istanbul Fetḥnāmesi*, was published from a MS owned by Khāliṣ Ef. as the supplement to *TOEM*, parts 20-1, 1331/1913 (simplified text in Latin transcription by Şeref Kayaboğazı, Istanbul 1953; further MSS: Ist. Un. TY 2634, Vienna 993/1 [see A. S. Levend, *Gazavātnāmeler*, 16]). He translated into Turkish a Persian *Anīs al-ʿārifīn* (Ḥādjdjī Khalīfa, ed. Flügel, no. 1448; MSS: Istanbul, Esad Ef. 1825, Un. TY 834). A collection of his official compositions (*Munshaʾāt*) was owned by Khāliṣ Ef., but seems now to be lost (for one specimen see Ferīdūn², i, 379 ff.). Djaʿfar was also a famous calligrapher and a patron of poets.

Bibliography: Sehī, 28; Laṭīfī, 117; Tashköprüzāde, *Shaḳāʾiḳ*, tr. Rescher 212 = tr. Medjdī 335 ff.; Gibb, *Ottoman poetry*, ii, 263-85; B. Meḥmed Ṭāhir, *ʿOsmānlı müʾellifleri*, i, 263; Babinger, 49 f.; S. Nüzhet Ergün, *Türk şairleri*, ii, 882-90; *IA*, s.v. Câfer Çelebi (M. Tayyib Gökbilgin). (V. L. MÉNAGE)

DJAʿFAR AL-ṢĀDIĶ ("the trustworthy"), Abū ʿAbd Allāh, son of Muḥammad al-Bāḳir, was a transmitter of *ḥadīth*s and the last *imām* recognized by both Twelver and Ismāʿīlī Shīʿīs. He was born in 80/699-700 or 83/702-3 in Medina, his mother, Umm Farwa, being a great-granddaughter of Abū Bakr. He inherited al-Bāḳir's following in 119/737 (or 114/733); hence during the crucial years of the transition from Umayyad to ʿAbbāsid power he was at the head of those Shīʿīs who accepted a non-militant Fāṭimī imāmate. He lived quietly in Madīna as an authority in *ḥadīth* and probably in *fiḳh*; he is cited with respect in Sunnī *isnād*s.

He made no sharp break with the non-Shīʿī majority—even a Shīʿī follower of his could appear in Sunnī *isnād*s (and his heir, ʿAbd Allāh, was accused by later Shīʿīs of Sunnī tendencies); but he seems to have been a serious Shīʿī leader nonetheless. He appears to have permitted his own *shīʿa*, his personal following, to regard him, like his father, as sole authoritative exponent of the *sharīʿa*, divinely favoured in his *ʿilm*, religious knowledge (and in principle as the only man legitimately entitled to rule). But he taught also a wider circle who consulted him along with other masters; Abū Ḥanīfa, Mālik b. Anas, and Wāṣil b. ʿAṭāʾ, among other prominent figures, are alleged to have heard *ḥadīth* from him. It is in his time, at the earliest, that distinctive Shīʿī positions in *fiḳh* begin to appear; but it is uncertain how far the subsequent Twelver or Ismāʿīlī (or Zaydī) systems may be ascribed to his teaching, though he is given a leading role in the two former.

At the time of Zayd's revolt (122/740), Djaʿfar served as symbol for those Shīʿīs who refused to rise; and during the revolutions after the death of al-Walīd (126/744), when most Shīʿīs were expecting that at last the ʿAlid family would come to power, he remained neutral. His support and possibly his candidacy may have been solicited by the Kūfa Shīʿa at the time of ʿAbbāsid victory, but he seems to have declined to recognize any other Shīʿī candidacy than his own, while, if he did think of himself, he held to the principle of *ḳuʿūd*, that the true *imām* need not attempt to seize power unless the time be ripe, and can be content to teach. At the time of the Shīʿī revolt of Muḥammad al-Nafs al-Zakiyya in the Ḥijāz (145/762), he was again neutral, leading the Ḥusaynids in their passivity in that largely Ḥasanid affair, and was left in peace by al-Manṣūr.

Djaʿfar attracted a circle of active thinkers, most of whom, like the majority of his *shīʿa*, lived normally in Kūfa (or some in Baṣra). The most fecund leader among the early Ghulāt, Abu 'l-Khaṭṭāb [*q.v.*], seems to have had close relations with him, and some radical ideas were attributed to Djaʿfar himself (but were later rejected by Twelvers as interpolations by Abu 'l-Khaṭṭāb). Before the latter was killed in 138/755, however, Djaʿfar repudiated him as going too far; this repudiation greatly disturbed some of his associates. It seems likely that though certain radical Shīʿī ideas helped to make his imāmate attractive in ʿIrāḳ, Djaʿfar made a point of keeping them within bounds. More technical philosophers also were associated with him and with his son, Mūsā, notably Hishām b. al-Ḥakam and Muḥammad b. al-Nuʿmān, nicknamed Shayṭān al-Ṭāḳ, who were inclined to an anthropomorphist system in contrast to that of the early Muʿtazilites with whom they disputed. Djaʿfar himself is assigned (with uncertain authenticity) a position on the problem of *ḳadar* which claims to be between determinism and free-will.

Djaʿfar died in 148/765 (poisoned, according to the unlikely Twelver tradition, on the orders of al-Manṣūr) and was buried in the Baḳīʿ cemetery in

Medina, where his tomb was visited, especially by Shīʿīs, till it was destroyed by the Wahhābīs. He left a cohesive following with an active intellectual life, well on the way to becoming a sect. But some of the differing tendencies which he had usually managed to reconcile now seem to have caused historic splits in it, occasioned by a disputed succession to his imāmate. He had designated Ismāʿīl, his eldest son (by an ʿAlid wife, Fāṭima, granddaughter of al-Ḥasan), but Ismāʿīl had died before his father—a fact which had troubled the faith of some of Djaʿfar's followers. A considerable body held by Ismāʿīl, some maintaining that he was himself not dead but only concealed; others passing on to his son Muḥammad b. Ismāʿīl. These formed the nucleus of the later Ismāʿīliyya, for whom Djaʿfar was the fifth imām. Most of Djaʿfar's following, however, accepted ʿAbd Allāh, Ismāʿīl's uterine brother and the eldest surviving son, on the ground that Djaʿfar had generalized that an *imām*'s successor must be his eldest son; but ʿAbd Allāh died without sons a few weeks later. The majority thereupon accepted Mūsā, whose mother was Ḥamīda, a slave (and whom some, including prominent philosophers, had hailed as *imām* from the start); these developed into the Twelver Shīʿa, for whom Djaʿfar was the sixth *imām*. A few asserted that Djaʿfar was not really dead, but absent, and would return as *mahdī* (these were called the Nāwūsiyya). Some of Djaʿfar's following looked to Mūsā's young brother Muḥammad, who later became the Imām of the Shumayṭiyya [*q.v.*].

Among most Shīʿīs, Djaʿfar has been regarded as one of the greatest of the *imāms* and as the teacher of *fiḳh* par excellence. The Twelvers, when referring to themselves as a *madhhab*, have called it the Djaʿfariyya. To Djaʿfar have been ascribed numerous utterances defining Shīʿī doctrine, as well as prayers and homilies; he has been ascribed, by both Sunnīs and Shīʿīs, numerous books, probably none of them authentic, dealing especially with divination, with magic, and with alchemy, of which the most famous is the mysterious *Djafr* [*q.v.*], foretelling the future. He is regarded as the chief teacher of the alchemist Djābir b. Ḥayyān (who did in fact revere him as a religious teacher). He is also regarded as a master Ṣūfī. Especially among the Shīʿa, so many sayings on all sides of all controverted questions have been ascribed to him that such reports are almost useless for determining his actual opinions in a given case.

Bibliography: Ṭabarī, ed. de Goeje, iii, 2509 f.; Ibn Khallikān, *Wafayāt al-aʿyān*, ed. M. Muḥyi 'l-dīn ʿAbd al-Ḥamīd, Cairo 1367/1948, i, 291 f. (no. 128); al-Ḥasan b. Mūsā al-Nawbakhtī, *Firaḳ al-Shīʿa*, ed. M. Ṣādiḳ Āl Baḥr al-ʿulūm, Nadjaf 1355/1936, 62-79. Other references in Julius F. Ruska, *Arabische Alchemisten*, ii, *Ǧaʿfar al-Ṣādiq, der Sechste Imām*, Heidelberg 1924 (see also Ruska, *Ǧābir ibn Ḥayyān und seine Beziehungen zum Imām Ǧaʿfar aṣ-Ṣādiq*, in *Isl.*, xvi, 264-66), and in the less critical Dwight M. Donaldson, *The Shi'ite religion*, London 1933, Chapter XII. See also, for his alleged works, Brockelmann, S I, 104; and Marshall G. S. Hodgson, *How did the early Shīʿa become sectarian?* in *JAOS*, lxxv, 1955, 1-13; ʿAbd al-ʿAzīz Sayyid al-Ahl, *Djaʿfar b. Muḥammad*, Beirut 1954.

(M. G. S. HODGSON)

DJAʿFAR SHARĪF B. ʿALĪ SHARĪF AL-ḲURAYSHĪ AL-NĀGŌRĪ, whose dates of birth and death are unknown, wrote his *Ḳānūn-i Islām* at the instigation of Dr. Herklots some time before 1832. He is said to have been "a man of low origin and of no account in his own country", born at Uppuēlūru (Ellore) in Kistna District, Madras, and was employed as a *munshī* in the service of the Madras government. He was an orthodox Sunnī, yet tolerant towards the Shīʿas, who had considerable influence in south India in his time, learned yet objective in his approach to his faith, knowledgeable in magic and sorcery yet writing of it in a deprecatory and apologetic tone, and a skilful physician of the Yūnānī school. In the course of his duties he met with Gerhard Andreas Herklots (b. 1790 in the Dutch colony of Chinsura in Bengal of Dutch parents, d. Wālādjābād 1834), who had studied medicine in England and had been appointed Surgeon on the Madras establishment in 1818. Herklots, struck by the lack of any information on the Indian Muslims comparable with the *Manners and customs of the Hindoos* of the Abbé Dubois, had started a collection of material when he met Djaʿfar accidentally, whom he encouraged to produce the work himself acting "merely as a reviser", occasionally suggesting "subjects which had escaped his memory".

The original was written in Dakkhinī Urdū, which Herklots had intended to publish also, but his death prevented this and the original has now been lost. To the translation Herklots added notes and addenda incorporating additional material from Mrs. Meer Hassan Ali's *Observations on the Mussulmauns of India*, 1832, and Garcin de Tassy's *Mémoires sur les particularités de la religion mussulmane dans l'Inde*, Paris 1831, that the work might embrace "an account of all the peculiarities of the Mussulmans . . . in *every part* of India". His *Qanoon-e-Islam* was published (London, late 1832) with a subvention from the East India Company.

Djaʿfar's account traces the religious and social life of the south Indian Muslims from the seventh month of pregnancy to the rites after death, with full descriptions of all domestic rites and ceremonies and festivals of the year, including necromancy, exorcism, and other matters of magic and sorcery; Herklots's appendix adds information on relationships, weights and measures, dress, jewellery, games, etc., and a glossary. The work was rearranged and partially rewritten by W. Crooke for the new Oxford edition of 1921, enhancing its value as an authoritative account of Indian popular Islam with particular reference to the Deccan. (J. BURTON-PAGE)

DJAʿFARIYYA [see FIḲH, ITHNĀ ʿASHARIYYA].

DJAFR. The particular veneration which, among the Shīʿas, the members of the Prophet's family enjoy, is at the base of the belief that the descendants of Fāṭima have inherited certain privileges inherent in Prophethood; prediction of the future and of the destinies of nations and dynasties is one of these privileges. The Shīʿī conception of prophecy, closely connected with that of the ancient gnosis (cf. Tor Andrae, *Die Person Muhammeds in Lehre und Glauben seiner Gemeinde*, Stockholm 1918, ch. vi) made the prophetic afflatus pass from Adam to Muḥammad and from Muḥammad to the ʿAlids (cf. H. H. Schaeder, in *ZDMG*, lxxix, 1925, 214 ff.). The Banū Hāshim, to whom ʿAlī b. Abī Ṭālib belonged, had long since claimed superiority over the Banū Umayya, as having prophecy as their appanage. Immediately after his conversion, seeing the armies of Muḥammad filing off ready for the conquest of Mecca, the Umayyad Abū Sufyān said to al-ʿAbbās, the Prophet's uncle, who was standing beside him, "Your nephew's authority has become very great!"; and al-ʿAbbās replied, "Yes, wretched one, that is Prophethood!" (Ṭabarī, iii, 1633).

A Bāṭinī tradition tells that the Prophet, when on the point of death, said to ʿAlī b. Abī Ṭālib, "O ʿAlī, when I am dead, wash me, embalm me, clothe me and sit me up; then, I shall tell thee what shall happen until the day of resurrection". When he was dead, ʿAlī washed him, embalmed him, clothed him and sat him up; and then Muḥammad told him what would happen until the day of resurrection (Ps. al-Dj̲aʿfī [read al-Dj̲uʿfī; cf. F. Wüstenfeld, *Register*, 7, l. 13], *K. al-Haft wa 'l-aẓilla*, ed. ʿA. Tāmir and I.-A. K̲h̲alīfé, Beirut 1960, 135; on the *K. al-dj̲afr*, attributed to ʿAlī, see Brockelmann, S I, 75). Here, clearly defined, is the *terminus a quo* of the *dj̲afr*, which in origin was identified with the *ḥidt̲h̲ān* and the *malāḥim*.

In the desperate struggle for the Caliphate carried on by the descendants of ʿAlī, early divided and weakened amongst themselves and suffering from the severe persecution of which they had been victims—notably in 237/851 under al-Mutawakkil—an esoteric literature of apocalyptic character arose, created in order to bolster the hopes of the adepts, who were near to despair, and to sustain in the minds of the ruling Caliphs that quasi-religious respect which they felt they should owe to the descendants of the daughter of the Prophet. This literature appears in different forms, all grouped under the generic name of *dj̲afr*, to which is often added the noun *dj̲āmiʿa* or the adjective *dj̲āmiʿ*. It is of a fatidical and sibylline character, and in its later form is summarized in a table in which the *dj̲afr* represents fate (*ḳaḍāʾ*) and the *dj̲āmiʿa* destiny (*ḳadar*). "It is", says Ḥādjdjī K̲h̲alīfa (ii, 603 ff.), "the summary knowledge (of that which is written) on the tablet of fate and destiny, which contains all that has been and all that which will be, totally and partially". The *dj̲afr* contains the Universal Intellect and the *dj̲āmiʿa* the Universal Soul. Thus, the *dj̲afr* tends to be a vision of the world on a supernatural and cosmic scale. Deviating from its original form of esoteric knowledge of an apocalyptic nature, reserved to the imāms who were the heirs and successors of ʿAlī, it became assimilated to a divinatory technique accessible to the wise whatever their origin, particularly to the mystics [see ʿILM AL-ḤURŪF]. Among the numerous authors who contributed to the development of this technique four great names must be cited: Muḥyī al-Dīn Abu 'l-ʿAbbās al-Būnī (d. 622/1225), in *S̲h̲ams al-maʿārif*, a work which exists in three recensions, the small, the mean, and the great; the last-named was edited in Cairo in 1322-4 (1903-6) in 4 vols. It should be noted that the small work called *Dj̲afr al-imām ʿAlī b. Abī Ṭālib* or *al-Durr al-munaẓẓam* . . ., attributed to Ibn ʿArabī (cf. ms Leipzig 833, 1; cf. Paris 2646; Aleppo-Sbath 57 and 390), is nothing but paragraphs 33 and 34 of the *S̲h̲ams al-maʿārif* (cf. Hartmann, *Eine arab. Apokalypse* . . ., 109 ff.). Muḥyī al-Dīn b. ʿArabī (d. 638/1240), *Miftāḥ al-dj̲afr al-dj̲āmiʿ* (mss. Istanbul-Hamidiye, Ism. Ef. 280; Paris 2669, 14, etc.). Ibn Ṭalḥa al-ʿAdawī al-Rādj̲ī (d. 652/1254), with the same title or under the title *al-Durr al-munaẓẓam fi 'l-sirr al-aʿẓam* (mss. Paris 1663/4; Istanbul, Amuca Hüseyin Paşa 348; Saray Ah. III, 3507, etc.). ʿAbd al-Raḥmān al-Bisṭāmī (d. 858/1454), with the same titles (mss. AS 2812/3; Vat. V. 1254; cf. Nicholson, in *JRAS*, 1899, 907).

In all these writings, and in many others, there is great confusion as to the procedures to be followed. Other heterogeneous elements, belonging to other forms of obscure thought, have been added; one finds the occult properties of the letters of the alphabet (*ḥurūf*) and of divine names (*al-asmāʾ al-ḥusnā*), gematria and isopsephy (*ḥisāb al-dj̲ummal*), the indication of the numerical value of a name which one wishes to keep secret, the transposition of letters in a single word, for the purpose of forming another word, the combination of letters composing a divine name with those of the name of the object desired (*al-kasr wa 'l-basṭ*), the substitution of one letter in a word by another according to the *atabas̲h̲* system (a table of concordance in which the first letter of the Hebrew alphabet corresponds to the last, the second to the penultimate, etc.), the formation of a word by putting together the first letters of the words of a phrase, in other words all the procedures made use of by the cabbala (cf. J. G. Février, *Histoire de l'écriture*, Paris 1948, Appx. III, 588-91).

These speculations on the numerical value of the letters have played a considerable part in Muslim mysticism, where not only the letters composing the divine names, but also the seven letters not found in the *fātiḥa*, have been the object of a special veneration. In the Islamic *ḥurūfiyya* neo-Platonic and cabbalistic traditions join with the speculations of certain exalted Ṣūfīs, to form a body of esoteric knowledge of such an obscurity that "only the Mahdī, expected at the end of time, would be capable of understanding its true significance" (Ḥadj̲dj̲ī K̲h̲alīfa, ii, 603). This diversity of procedure is further complicated by divergences in the methods of classification. Certain authors, in fact, follow the long alphabet (*alif, bāʾ, tāʾ, t̲h̲āʾ*, etc.) while others follow *al-abdj̲adiyya* (*alif, bāʾ, dj̲īm*, etc.). The first method is called *al-dj̲afr al-kabīr* and includes one thousand roots, the second *al-dj̲afr al-ṣag̲h̲īr* and includes only seven hundred. There is also a *dj̲afr mutawassiṭ* based separately on the lunar and solar letters; this last method is preferred by authors, and is used generally in talismanic compositions (Ḥādj̲dj̲ī K̲h̲alīfa, *loc. cit.*).

Beside this numerical and mystical aspect of the letters, which by its technical and mechanical character puts the *dj̲afr* on the level of the *zāʾirdj̲a* [*q.v.*], mention must be made of their astrological aspect. According to Ibn K̲h̲aldūn (*Muḳaddima*, ii, 191; Rosenthal, ii, 218; cf. 184, Rosenthal, 209) the S̲h̲īʿas gave the name of *dj̲afr* to a work of astrological predictions by Yaʿḳūb b. Isḥāḳ al-Kindī (d. after 256/870), which is probably that mentioned by Ibn al-Nadīm under the title *al-Istidlāl bi 'l-kusūfāt ʿalā 'l-ḥawādit̲h̲* (*Fihrist* 259; cf. the *Risāla fi 'l-ḳaḍāʾ ʿalā 'l-kusūf*, mss. Escurial, Casiri 913, 4; AS 4832, 27; for details, cf. De Goeje, *Mémoire sur les Carmathes*[2], Leiden 1886, 117 ff.). This work, in which al-Kindī establishes according to the eclipses the fortunes of the dynasty of the ʿAbbāsids until its downfall, was not to be found at the time of Ibn K̲h̲aldūn, who considered that it must have disappeared with the ʿAbbāsids' library, thrown into the Tigris by Hūlāgū after he had conquered Bag̲h̲dād and killed al-Muʿtaṣim, the last caliph. However, it appears that a part of this work reached the Mag̲h̲rib under the name of *al-Dj̲afr al-ṣag̲h̲īr*, and must have been there adapted to the dynasty of the B. ʿAbd al-Muʾmin.

According to the Ps. Dj̲āḥiẓ (*Bāb al-ʿirāfa wa 'l-zadj̲r wa 'l-firāsa ʿalā madh̲hab al-Furs*, ed. Inostranzev, St. Petersburg 1907, 4) this astrological aspect of the *dj̲afr* is of Indian origin; "*Al-dj̲afr*" he says, "is the knowledge of the [auspicious and inauspicious] days of the year, the knowledge of the direction of winds, of the appearance and withdrawal of lunar mansions . . . . The book called *al-dj̲afr* contains the predictions for the year, arranged according to the seasons and the lunar mansions; each group of seven lunar mansions, constituting a quarter of the year, is called *djafr*; they [the Persians] take omens from it for rains, winds, journeys, wars, etc. It is from India that the Chosroes and their people have learnt all these sciences ....".

The last and most important of the aspects of the *djafr* is the apocalyptic. This is properly the original aspect, already well developed under the Umayyads and much expanded in ʿAbbāsid times, in the form of books of oracles, called *kutub al-ḥidthān* (cf. references in De Goeje, *Carmathes*, 115 ff.). The starting-point of these speculations was the book of Daniel. Books of predictions attributed to Daniel were being read in Egypt in the year 61/680 (Ṭabarī, ii, 399; on the Arabic apocalypse of Daniel cf. the references in A. Abel, in *Stud. Isl.*, ii, (1954), 28 n. 2). Muḥammad b. ʿAbd al-Malik al-Hamadhānī (d. 521/1127), who continued al-Ṭabarī's chronicle up to 487/1095 (ms. Paris 1469, f° 45r, quoted by De Goeje, *Carmathes*, 225 ff.; cf. ed. A. J. Kanaan, in *Al-Machriq*, 1955 ff.; and cf. Ibn Khaldūn, *Muḳaddima*, ii, 198, Rosenthal 227-8) relates that under the vizierate of (Abū Djaʿfar) al-Karkhī (324/936) there was in Baghdād a bookseller, called al-Dāniyālī, who exhibited ancient books attributed to the prophet Daniel, in which there figured certain prominent persons together with their descriptions. He enjoyed great success with the statesmen (cf. an anecdote in Ṭabarī, iii, 496 ff., in the story of Mahdī, cited by Ibn Khaldūn, *Muḳaddima*, ii, 192, Rosenthal 219, illustrating the tricks employed by forgers in this genre of writing). This literature is also known under the name of *Malāḥim* (cf. the astrological mss. Berlin 5903, 5904, 5912 and 5915, the last two of which are attributed to Daniel, as is Istanbul-Bağdatlı Vehbi Ef. 2234). It has been widely diffused in the Maghrib. Written in verse or prose, sometimes even in dialect, it deals sometimes with events which were to happen within the Islamic community in general, sometimes with those concerning one dynasty in particular. The greater part of these writings is attributed to famous authors, although it is not possible to verify their authenticity. A list of *malāḥim* is given by Ibn Khaldūn (*Muḳaddima*, ii, 193 ff., Rosenthal 220 ff.), mostly of Maghribī origin and dealing in general with the Ḥafṣid dynasty. Two names in this list deserve particular attention: Ibn ʿArabī, in whose name there was current, in the time of Ibn Khaldūn, a *malḥama* entitled *Ṣayḥat al-būm* (on this work cf. A. Abel, in *Arabica*, v (1958), 6 n. 3), and al-Bādjarbaḳī (d. 724/1323) to whom a poem on the Turks is attributed. The latter belonged to the Ḳarandaliyya (or Ḳalandariyya; cf. references in Dozy, *Suppl.*, ii, 340), and founded a sect called al-Bādjarbaḳiyya (Ibn Khaldūn, *Muḳaddima*, ii, 199 ff., Rosenthal 229; cf. *TA*, vi, 283. Other sources on al-Bādjarbaḳī are cited by Rosenthal, 230 n.). There are also many citations from these *malāḥim* to be found in the writings of Ibn Abī Usaybiʿa (d. 668/1270) and al-Maḳrīzī (d. 845/1442; cf. De Goeje, *Carmathes*, 125 ff.).

Finally, one fact must be mentioned which enhances the prestige of the *djafr* in the eyes of the Shīʿa; this is its use in a spiritual and mystical interpretation of the Ḳurʾān as opposed to the traditional and lexicographical exegesis of the Sunnīs. Ibn Saʿd (ii, 101) attributes such an interpretation to ʿAlī b. Abī Ṭālib. From the latter it is said to have passed to Djaʿfar al-Ṣādiḳ (d. 148/763) through his uncle Zayd b. ʿAlī (d. 122/740); and Hārūn b. Saʿīd (Saʿd) al-ʿIdjlī (cf. Brockelmann, S I, 314) is said to have received this esoteric interpretation from Djaʿfar al-Ṣādiḳ [*q.v.*]. With regard to this, Ibn Khaldūn says: "It should be known that the *Kitāb al-Djafr* had its origin in the fact that Hārūn b. Saʿīd al-ʿIdjlī, the head of the Zaydiyya, had a book that he transmitted on the authority of Djaʿfar al-Ṣādiḳ. That book contained information as to what would happen to the family of Muḥammad in general and to certain members of it in particular. The [information] had come to Djaʿfar and to other ʿAlid personages as an act of divine grace and through the removal [of the veil, *kashf*] which is given to saints like them. [The book was] in Djaʿfar's possession. It was written upon the skin of a small ox. Hārūn al-ʿIdjlī transmitted it on [Djaʿfar's] authority. He wrote it down and called it *al-Djafr*, after the skin upon which it had been written, because *djafr* means a small [camel or lamb]. [*Djafr*] became the characteristic title they used for the book.

The *Kitāb al-Djafr* contained remarkable statements concerning the interpretation of the Ḳurʾān and concerning its inner meaning. [The statements in it] were transmitted on the authority of Djaʿfar al-Ṣādiḳ. The book has not come down through continuous transmission and is not known as a book as such. Only stray remarks unaccompanied by any proofs [of their authenticity] are known from it. If the ascription to Djaʿfar al-Ṣādiḳ were correct, the work would have the excellent authority of Djaʿfar himself or of people of his family who enjoyed acts of divine grace. It is a fact that Djaʿfar warned certain of his relatives about accidents that would occur to them, and things turned out as he had predicted." (*Muḳaddima*, ii, 184-5., Rosenthal 209-10). Many books of mystic exegesis and of divination bear the name of Djaʿfar al-Ṣādiḳ (cf. Brockelmann, S I, 104), notably a *Kitāb al-djafr* (B.M. 426, 10; cf. Steinschneider, *Zur pseudepigraph. Literatur*, 71). The foundation of this "pneumatic" exegesis seems to rest on this saying of Jesus: *Naḥnᵘ maʿāshir al-anbiyāʾ naʾtīkum bi 'l-tanzīl wa ammā 'l-taʾwīl fa-sayaʾtī bihⁱ al-Bāraḳlīṭ al-ladhī sayaʾtīkum baʿdī*, "We the Prophets bring ye the revelation; its interpretation the Paraclete [the Holy Spirit], who shall come after me, will bring ye" (Ḥādjdjī Khalīfa, 603; cf. John, xiv, 26).

Bibliography: In order sufficiently to cover the range of this literature, the lists of writings on the *djafr* to be found in the manuscript catalogues should be consulted, especially Ahlwardt, iii, nos. 4213-29, and *Fihrist al-kutub al-ʿarabiyya al-maḥfūẓa bi 'l-kutubkhāna al-khidīwiyya al-Miṣriyya*, v, 333 ff.; numerous *djafr* treatises are to be found in the various collections at Istanbul. The principal works of reference are: R. Hartmann, *Eine arabische Apokalypse aus der Kreuzzugszeit. Ein Beitrag zur Ǧafr-Literatur*, in *Schriften d. Königsberger Gelehrten Gesellschaft, Geisteswiss. Kl.*, Berlin 1924, 89-116 (Study of an extract of Ibn ʿArabī, *Muḥāḍarat al-abrār*, ed. Cairo 1324/1906, i, 197 ff., completed by the Berlin ms. no. 4219); cf. especially 108 ff.; A. Abel, *Changements politiques et littérature apocalyptique dans le monde musulman*, in *Stud. Isl.*, ii (1954), 23-43; idem, *Un ḥadīṯ sur la prise de Rome dans la tradition eschatologique de l'Islam*, in *Arabica*, v (1958), 1-14; I. Goldziher, *Vorlesungen*, 224 ff., 263 ff.; Fr. trans. Arin, Paris 1920; idem, in *ZDMG*, xli (1887), 123-5.

(T. FAHD)

AL-DJAGHBŪB, a small oasis to the south-east of Cyrenaica, the site of the tomb of Muḥammad b. ʿAlī al-Sanūsī, founder of the brotherhood of the Sanūsiyya. It is the furthest east, the smallest and the least prosperous of the oases along the important traditional route which leads from the valley of the Nile and Sīwa to Fezzan and the region of Tripoli, passing through a chain of depressions where are to be found the palm-groves of Djālo, Awdjīla, Marada, and Djufra, which are close to the 29th parallel.

The depression of Djaghbūb consists of a sinuous basin called Wādī Djaghbūb covering 700 sq. km., and going down to 29 m. below sea-level: in the north it is dominated by the plateau in sand and limestone of the Marmaric (Miocene period); this gives way in the south to soft hills covered by dunes of Libyan erg. The depression is carpeted in red earth and yellow sand and the beds occupied by *sebkhas* or, to the east, by salt lakes (*baḥr*).

The only traces of the distant past are the tombs dug out of the northern cliff, similar to those at Sīwa. Djaghbūb owes its existence to Muḥammad b. ʿAlī al-Sanūsī, who came from Cairo in 1856 with his family, followers and servants, and founded the mother *zāwiya* of the brotherhood on a slight hill to the N-E of the depression. Later a large mosque was built while gradually a town grew up, which, according to Duveyrier in 1881 had nearly 3,000 inhabitants, of which 750 were *tolba* and 2,000 slaves. But the departure in 1895 of Muḥammad al-Mahdī—the son of the founder of the town, who died in 1859—for Kufra, marked the start of the decadence of Djaghbūb, which is briefly mentioned by some travellers: Rohlfs (1869), Rosita Forbes and Hassanein Bey (1921 and 1923) and Bruneau de Laborie (1923). The town was occupied by the Italians in 1926: they put up two forts and encouraged agriculture. The British took it in 1941 and ceded it to Cyrenaica, a province of the Libyan federal union which was founded in 1951.

Djaghbūb is a very small settlement of 200 inhabitants. Its enclosure of huge dry stones surrounds the great mosque and the *zāwiya*, both of which have a large porticoed courtyard, their annexes and a small number of houses which are often two-storied. The tomb of Muḥammad b. ʿAlī al-Sanūsī, situated under the dome of the great mosque, is a place of pilgrimage for all the followers of the brotherhood, and the *zāwiya* a place of learning. Masters, *tolba* and officials of the *zāwiya* and the mosque form the greater part of the population, together with the negro servants who work in the few gardens in the date-grove; the latter consists of scarcely more than 2,000 cultivated date-palms; the gardens, watered by the brackish water of a shallow well, have been improved thanks to the drilling done by the Italians, who bored an artesian well of fresh water. There is practically no commercial activity.

Bibliography: A. Desio, *Risultati scientifici della missione alla oasi di Giarabub, 1926-1927*, Soc. Geogr. italiana, Rome 1928-31; E. Scarin, *Le oasi cirenaiche del 29° parallelo*, Florence 1937; G. Rohlfs, *Von Tripolis nach Alexandrien*, Bremen 1871; R. Forbes, *The secret of the Sahara. Koufra*, London 1921; Hassenein-Bey, *The lost Oases*, London 1921; Bruneau de Laborie, *Du Cameroun au Caire par le désert de Libye*, Paris 1924.

(J. DESPOIS)

AL-DJAGHMĪNĪ (or ČAGHMĪNĪ), MAḤMŪD B. MUḤAMMAD B. ʿUMAR, a well-known Arab astronomer, a native of Djaghmīn, a small town in Khwārizm. The dates of his birth and death are not precisely established, but it is very probable that he died in 745/1344-5 (cf. Suter, in *ZDMG*, liii (1899), 539). The following works of his have been preserved: (1) *al-Mulakhkhaṣ fi 'l-hayʾa* (Epitome of astronomy), which was very widely known and was frequently commented upon, notably by Ḳāḍīzāda al-Rūmī, by al-Djurdjānī, and by many others; a German translation of this work, by Rudloff and Hochheim, was published in *ZDMG*, xlvii (1893), 213-75; manuscripts of this work are to be found in many collections, *e.g.*, Berlin, Gotha, Leiden, Paris, Oxford, etc.—(2) *Ḳiwā 'l-kawākib wa ḍaʿfuhā* (The strong and weak influences of the constellations), preserved at Paris.—(3) *Ḳānūnča* (The little canon), a medical work, an extract from the canon of Ibn Sīnā, preserved at Munich, Gotha, etc., which has appeared in several lithograph editions.

Bibliography: Ḥādjdjī Khalīfa, vi, 113; Brockelmann, I, 473; II, 213; S I, 826, 865 (this author makes Djaghmīnī two authors of the same name: the first, d. 618/1221, is said to be the author of no. 1 above and of two arithmetical treatises; the second, a physician, d. 745/1344, of no. 3 above); Nallino, *Al-Battānī, Opus astronomicum, passim* (in index); Suter in *Abh. z. Gesch. d. mathem. Wissensch.*, x, 164; xiv, 177; Sarton, *Introduction*, iii, 699-700.

(H. SUTER-[J. VERNET])

DJĀGĪR, land given or assigned by governments in India to individuals, as a pension or as a reward for immediate services. The holder (*djāgīrdār*) was not liable for land tax on his holding (see ḌARĪBA), nor necessarily for military service by virtue of his tenure. See further IḲṬĀʿ.

DJAHĀN SHĀH (i) [see SUPPLEMENT].

DJAHĀN SHĀH (ii) [See MUGHALS].

DJAHĀNĀRĀ BĒGAM, the eldest daughter of Shāhdjahān and Mumtāz Maḥall (the lady of the Tādj at Āgrā) and their first child, was born on 21 Ṣafar 1023/23 March 1614. She bore the complimentary title of Fāṭima al-Zamān, which misled von Kremer followed by Macdonald (*The Religious Attitude and Life in Islam*, London, 205) into believing that her name was Fāṭima. To contemporary historians she is known by the Court title of Bēgam Ṣāḥib or Ṣāḥiba (ʿAbd al-Ḥamīd Lāhawrī, *Bādshāh-nāma* (text), i, 1178 and Muḥammad Ṣāliḥ Kanbōh, *ʿAmal-i Ṣāliḥ*, i 80) or Pādshāh Bēgam. After the death of her mother in 1041/1631, she enjoyed the status of the first lady of the realm, partly reflected in her aforesaid Court title. Throughout her life she remained staunchly devoted to her father and even kept company with him during his incarceration after his deposition by Awrangzīb, whose displeasure she earned through her excessive fondness for her brother, Dārā Shukōh [*q.v.*], his rival.

An accomplished lady, she is the author of two Ṣūfī works: (i) *Muʾnis al-arwāḥ* and (ii) *Ṣāḥibiyya*, an incomplete biography of her *pīr*, Mullā Shāh Ḳādirī. According to her own statement (see *Oriental College Magazine*, Lahore xiii/4, 16), she was the first woman in the line of Tīmūr to have taken to mysticism. Originally a disciple of Mullā Shāh Ḳādirī, she contracted her *bayʿa* in the Čishtī order [*q.v.*], and one of her works, *Muʾnis al-arwāḥ*, is on the life of Khwādja Muʿīn al-Dīn Čishtī [*q.v.*]. She wielded great influence during the reign of her father, and enjoyed an allowance of 600,000 rupees, half in cash and half in lands, settled on her by the Emperor; Awrangzīb doubled this amount during his reign. During Shāhdjahān's captivity she served as a link between the deposed emperor and the reigning monarch, Awrangzīb, all the important political correspondence passing through her. She died unmarried in 1092/1681 and was buried in Delhi, according to her wishes, in the compound of the shrine of Niẓām al-Dīn Awliyā' [see DIHLĪ, Monuments] in a simple marble tomb, built by herself and covered with grass at the top. The allegations against her by some European travellers that she had illicit relations with her own father, the deposed emperor, are baseless and may be disregarded.

The Djāmiʿ Masdjid at Āgrā, which had an attached madrasa, was built by Djahānārā. This is the first mosque of major dimensions built under the Mughals, except for Akbar's at Fatḥpur Sīkrī [*q.v.*].

Bibliography: Autobiographical statements at the end of the *Ṣāḥibiyya* (MS. Āpā-Rāo Bhōlā Nāth Library, Ahmadabad); ʿAbd al-Ḥamīd Lāhawrī, *Bādshāhnāma* (Bib. Ind.), i, I, 94; Muḥammad Ṣāliḥ Kanbōh, *ʿAmal-i Ṣāliḥ* (Bib. Ind.), i, 80; Muḥammad Sāḳī Mustaʿidd Khān, *Maʾāthir-i ʿĀlamgīrī* (Bib. Ind.) 213; Shāhnawāz Khān, *Maʾāthir al-Umarāʾ* (Bib. Ind.) s.v.; G. Yazdani, *Jahānāra* in *JPHS*, ii/2 (Calcutta 1914), 152-69; Maḥbūb al-Raḥmān, *Djahānāra* (in Urdū), ʿAlīgaṙh 1918; H. A. Rose, *Persian letters from Jahān Ārā, daughter of Shāh Jahān .... to Rāja Budh Parkāsh of Sirmūr*, in *JASB*, 1911, 449-58; K. R. Qanungo, *Dara Shukoh*, Calcutta 1935, i, 10; N. Manucci, *Storia do Mogor*, tr. W. Irvine, London 1907, i, 217 and index; Carr Stephen, *The archaeology and monumental remains of Delhi*, Calcutta 1876, 108-9; R. C. Temple, *Shahjahan and Jahanara*, in *Indian Antiquary*, xliv, 1915, 111-2; Nazākat Djahān Tīmūrī, Doctoral thesis Punjab University, 1959; Ṣabāḥ al-Dīn ʿAbd al-Raḥmān, *Bazm-i Tīmūriyya*, Aʿzamgaṙh 1367/1948, 447-455 (where other references especially on her poetic talents are given); Banarsi Prasad Saksena, *A History of Shahjahan of Dihli*, Allahabad 1932, index; Sayyid Aḥmad Khān, *Āthār al-Ṣanādīd*, Kānpur 1846, s.v.

(A. S. BAZMEE ANSARI)

DJAHĀNDĀR SHĀH, MUʿIZZ AL-DĪN, Mughal emperor *regnabat* 21 Ṣafar 1124/29 March 1712 to 16 Muḥarram 1125/11 February 1713. Born 10 Ramaḍān 1071/10 May 1661, eldest son of Bahādur Shāh [*q.v.*], at the time of his father's death he was governor of Multān. Pleasure-loving and indolent, he was able to participate actively in the struggle among Bahādur Shāh's sons for the throne only through the support of the ambitious Dhu 'l-fiḳār Khān, *mīr bakhshī* and *ṣūbadār* of the Deccan who was anxious to exclude ʿAẓīm al-Shaʾn from the succession and to win the *wizāra* for himself.

After three days fighting near Lahore, ʿAẓīm al-Shaʾn was defeated and killed. With the help of Dhu 'l-fiḳār Khān, Djahāndār Shāh disposed of his other brothers Djahān Shāh and Rafīʿ al-Shaʾn. At the time of his accession Djahāndār Shāh was 52 (lunar) years of age. His sybaritic tastes and devotion to the dancing girl Lāl Kunwar, quickly seized upon by contemporary historians as the explanation of his fate, certainly did nothing to restore the finances of the central government, nor did the intrigues of Lāl Kunwar's entourage against the *wazīr* Dhu 'l-fiḳār Khān make for vigour and loyalty in the administration.

In Shaʿbān 1124/September 1712, supported by the Sayyids of Bārha [*q.v.*] ʿAbd Allāh Khān and Ḥusayn ʿAlī Khān, whom Djahāndār Shāh had failed to conciliate, Farrukhsiyar, second son of ʿAẓīm al-Shaʾn, marched on Āgra from Paṭnā, defeating ʿIzz al-Dīn, son of Djahāndār Shāh. at Khwādja on the way. Hastily gathering an army, Djahāndār Shāh and Dhu 'l-fiḳār Khān marched to Āgra but were defeated on 13 Dhu 'l-ḥidjdja 1124/10 January 1713. Djahāndār Shāh fled to Dihlī to take refuge with the *wakīl-i muṭlaḳ* Asad Khān, father of Dhu 'l-fiḳār Khān. Father and son imprisoned him in the fort of Dihlī in the hope of mollifying Farrukhsiyar. The day before Farrukhsiyar's triumphal entry into Dihlī, Djahāndār Shāh was slain by his orders.

Bibliography: Nūr al-dīn Fārūḳī, *Djahāndār-nāma*, India Office Library Persian MS 3988, fol. 6b to end; Kāmrādj, son of Nam Singh, *ʿIbrat-nāma*, I.O. Library, Persian MS 1534, fols. 45a-47b; Mīrzā Mubārak Allāh, 'Waḍiḥ', *Taʾrīkh-i Irādat Khān*, I.O Persian MS 50, fols. 43, 58 to end; Muḥammad Ḳāsim "ʿIbrat' Lāhawrī, *ʿIbrat-nāma*, B.M. Or. 1934, fols. 57a-72b, 75a; Mīr Shafīʿ Wārid, *Mirʾāt-i wāridāt*, B.M. Add. 6579, fols. 126a-142b; Mīr Muḥammad Aḥsan Idjād, *Farrukhsiyar-nāma*, B.M. Or. 25, fols. 57b-93b; Muḥammad Ḳāsim, *Aḥwāl al-Khawāḳīn*, B.M. Add. 26, 244, fols. 36b-59b; Anon., *Taʾrīkh-i Sulṭanat-i Farrukhsiyar*, B.M. Add. 26, 245, fols. 36b-57b; Lāl Rām, *Tuḥfat al-Hind*, vol. ii, B.M. Add. 6584, fols. 80b-87a; Khāfī Khān, *Muntakhab al-lubāb*, Bibliotheca Indica, Part ii, Calcutta, 1874, *index*, 1086; Ghulām Ḥusayn Khān Ṭabāṭabāʾī, *Siyar al-mutaʾakhkhirīn*, *lith.* Lucknow, 1866, vol. ii, 381-93; F. Valentyn, *Oud- en Nieuw Oost-Indien*, vol. iv, Dordrecht & Amsterdam, 1726, 280-302; trans. as *Embassy of Mr. Johan Josua Ketelaar* by D. Kuenen-Wicksteed, in *Journal of the Punjab Historical Society*, x, 1, 1929, 1-94; For other references not available to me see: Storey, i, 600-10 *passim* and Satish Chandra, *Parties and politics at the Mughal court, 1707-1740*, ʿAlīgaṙh 1959; William Irvine, *Later Mughals*, Calcutta & London, 1921. *Cambridge History of India*, vol. iv, *The Mughul Period*, 1937, Chapter xi.

(P. HARDY)

DJAHĀNGĪR, the fourth Mughal emperor of India in the line of Bābur [*q.v.*], the first surviving child of Akbar, others born earlier having all died in infancy, was born on 17 Rabīʿ I 977/31 August 1569 of a Rādjpūt queen, called Miryam al-Zamānī, at (Fatḥpur) Sīkrī, near Āgrā, in the hermitage of a recluse Shaykh Salīm Čishtī, to whose intercession the birth of a son was attributed. The young prince was named Salīm after the Shaykh but Akbar always called him Shaykhū Bābā, scrupulously avoiding the Shaykh's name. History is silent on the conversion of Djahāngīr's mother to Islām either before or after her marriage to Akbar. Badāʾūnī's silence on the subject may, however, be taken to mean that she had embraced Islām before entering the *ḥarīm* of the emperor.

In spite of the best education that Akbar provided his son and successor, the youthful prince could not escape the prevailing atmosphere of political intrigue and chicanery which ultimately vitiated relations between father and son. In 1001/1591 Akbar fell seriously ill and in his agony accused Salīm of conspiring to poison him. This was the beginning of estranged relations which reached a climax in 1008/1599 when Djahāngīr revolted and proclaimed his independence at Allāhābād [*q.v.*].

His alleged romance with a palace-maid called Anārkalī, which resulted in a tragedy, finds no corroboration in history. The mausoleum known as Anārkalī's tomb, in Lahore (see S. M. Latif, *Lahore, its history, architectural remains . . .*, Lahore 1892, 186-7) is said to have been raised over the mortal remains of his lady-love by the baulked lover, prince Salīm. The marble sarcophagus, still preserved in a corner of the plain whitewashed octagonal building, bears the intriguing inscription "*madjnūn Salīm-i Akbar*". The entire affair is so shrouded in mystery that nothing convincing can be said about it. The unusual inscription while on the one hand may be interpreted to reveal the depth of prince Salīm's intense grief on the cruel death of his beloved, said to have been built up alive in a wall by the order of Akbar, on the other hints at a compromise having been reached between the emperor, as head of the royal family, and the demented prince, the heir to the 'Great Mogul'. Why none of the contemporary historians or Djahāngīr himself makes any mention of this tragedy is difficult to comprehend. Latif (*op. cit.*, 187) gives the date 1008/1599 as the date of Anārkalī's death. This date, according to him, is inscribed on the sarcophagus along with another date 1024/1615 and the words "in Lahore" which is considered to be the date of the construction of the mausoleum, but in 1008/1599 Djahāngīr was 31 (lunar) years of age and already married to a number of wives. Moreover, Djahāngīr was at Allāhābād in 1008/1599 when he rose in open revolt against his father. Was the cruel fashion in which Anārkalī was done to death the real cause of this rebellion? Akbar's leniency towards the rebel prince seems to be precalculated as he apparently wanted to soothe the lacerated heart of the erratic prince carried away by passion and distress by adopting a mild policy.

Akbar's attempts at a reconciliation were thwarted by the ambitious prince who in 1010/1601 marched at the head of a large army to Āgrā. On Akbar's showing signs of resistance the rebel prince retreated to Allāhābād where he assumed the royal title and set up a regular court. Temporary reconciliation was again brought about by the widow of Bayram Khān [*q.v.*], Salīma Sulṭān Bēgam, but the youthful prince soon after took to his old ways. He went back to Allāhābād where he again set up his Court. In the meantime Salīm was convinced that Abu 'l-Faḍl [*q.v.*], the talented minister of Akbar, was responsible for his troubles and that he was constantly poisoning the ears of the emperor against him. He, therefore, designed an attack on Abu 'l-Faḍl and while the latter was on his way back from the Deccan in 1011/1602 he was set upon by the retainers of the Bundēlā chieftain, Bīr Singh Dēw, who had been commissioned by Djahāngīr to perform the deed; his head was cut off and sent to Djahāngīr at Allāhābād. This cold-blooded murder was unjustifiable, but Djahāngīr was so much convinced of the villainy of Abu 'l-Faḍl that he felt no compunction, but rather was relieved at the removal of a stumbling-block from his way. (*Tūzuk-i Djahāngīrī*, tr. Rogers and Beveridge, i, 25).

On the death of Akbar in 1013/1605 Djahāngīr ascended the throne under the title of Abu 'l-Muẓaffar Nūr al-Dīn Muḥammad Djahāngīr Pādshāh-i Ghāzī, which also appears on some of his coins. Soon after his accession he had to face the rebellion of his eldest son Khusraw in 1015/1606. Although a reconcilation was effected, the emperor never forgave the audacity of his son, whose death in suspicious circumstances in 1031/1622 at Burhānpūr relieved Djahāngīr of considerable worry. The Sikh *guru* (spiritual leader) Ardjun, who had helped and sheltered Khusraw during his rebellion, was punished with death by the emperor. This punishment, however, was interpreted as an atrocious act on the part of the Mughal emperor, and it laid the foundations of that deep-rooted hostility which continued to embitter the relations between the Indian Muslims and the Sikhs over the centuries, at its worst during the supremacy of the Sikh general, Banda Bayrāgī, in the 12th/18th century, and during the large-scale disturbances in India on the eve of Independence in 1947.

In 1016/1607 Djahāngīr was able to crush a conspiracy to murder him while camping at Kābul. Four of the ringleaders were executed while prince Khusraw, the moving spirit, was partially blinded by the orders of the emperor. With his marriage to Nūrdjahān, daughter of Ghiyāth Bēg, known to history as Iʿtimād al-Dawla, in 1020/1611 Djahāngīr commenced a new phase in his life as a ruler. Contemporary sources make no mention of the popular story of Djahāngīr's passionate love for Nūrdjahān and the premeditated murder of her husband, ʿAlī Ḳulī Khān Istadjlū (Shīr Afkan), at the instance of Djahāngīr, in 1016/1607. None of the European travellers who visited India during the reign of Djahāngīr makes even an oblique mention of Djahāngīr's complicity in the murder of Shīr Afkan and his anxiety to marry Nūrdjahān, then known as Mihr al-Nisāʾ. After her marriage to the emperor, Nūrdjahān gradually assumed all power and wielded great influence in affairs of state. Her name, along with that of the emperor, was inscribed on gold coins and she came to be recognized as the *de facto* ruler.

The Shīʿī scholar Nūr Allāh al-Shūstarī, who had been appointed *ḳāḍī* of Lahore by Akbar and who had so far practised *taḳiyya*, successfully concealing his faith from the people, emboldened by the meteoric rise to power of Nūrdjahān, herself an orthodox Shīʿī, began to pronounce judgments which created doubts in the minds of the Sunnī majority. This led to a Court conspiracy against the *ḳāḍī*, then in the queen's favour. He was accused of professing the Shīʿī faith while boldly acting as a Sunnī *ḳāḍī*. This revelation resulted in his execution by order of the emperor, who punished him for practising a fraud (*Nudjūm al-samāʾ*, 15-6). This act of bigotry on the part of a latitudinarian and eclectic like Djahāngīr, whose own consort Nūrdjahān was a Shīʿī, is rather surprising but it shows, at the same time, the measure of influence that the disgraced theologians and *ʿulamāʾ* had again come to exercise in state affairs, after their calculated downfall during the reign of Akbar. No less surprising is Djahāngīr's estimate, based on intelligence reports, of *shaykh* Aḥmad Sirhindī [*q.v.*] whom he described as an impostor (*shayyād*), and his famous *Maktūbāt* as a tissue of absurdities (*Tūzuk*, Eng. tr., ii, 91-2). He was so much convinced of the *shaykh's* fraudulence that on the pretext of his having transcended the limits of Ṣūfic propriety in his *Maktūbāt* (i, no. 11), he ordered his imprisonment in the fort of Gwāliyār [*q.v.*], where political criminals were generally confined, but after a year or so revised his opinion and liberated him.

In 1032/1623 Djahāngīr had to face a filial revolt when prince Khurram (Shāhdjahān) rebelled, driven to this predicament by the machinations of

Nūrdjahān who wanted her son-in-law Shahryār, a step-brother of Shāhdjahān, to succeed to the throne once the latter was removed from the way. Khurram's rebellion, pursued all over India with the support of his own forces, amounted to a civil war which weakened Imperial prestige and greatly depleted the treasury; but the superior generalship of Mahābat Khān [*q.v.*] forced his surrender in Djumādā II 1035/ March 1626 after a revolt of three years.

An attempt by Mahābat Khān to seize Djahāngīr in 1035/1626 in order to remove him from the influence of Nūrdjahān and her brother Āṣaf Khān was at first successful, to the queen's discomfiture; but Āṣaf Khān, having first fled, later joined Mahābat Khān at Kābul at Nūrdjahān's instigation, and provoked dissension among the Imperial followers. On Mahābat Khān's flight and his subsequent alliance with Prince Khurram, Nūrdjahān appointed Khān-i Djahān Lōdī as Imperial commander, with orders to subdue the rebels; but her plans were thwarted by the death of Djahāngīr, whose health had been shattered by excessive drinking, his greatest weakness, pursued since his early youth. Some hagiological works attribute Mahābat Khān's conduct to the maltreatment and disgrace that Aḥmad Sirhindi suffered at the hands of Djahāngīr. It has further been claimed that prince Khurram, (Azad Bilgrami, *Subḥat al-mardjān*, Bombay 1303/ 1886, 49), Mahābat Khān and some other high-ranking nobles had secretly contracted their *bayʿa* with the *shaykh* and held him in high esteem; and that the treatment meted out to him was bitterly resented by them all. Before any decisive action could be taken against Mahābat Khān, Djahāngīr died while on his way to Bhimbar from Rādjawrī, on 27 Ṣafar 1037/28 October 1627 in the 58th solar year of his age and the twenty-second of his reign. His body was brought down to Lahore where it was laid to rest, without its receiving an appropriate funeral on account of the disturbed conditions, at a spot designated by Nūrdjahān over which she erected a magnificient mausoleum at her own expense. (For a description of the tomb, see LĀHAWR).

A well-read man, a patron of literature and art, a keen observer of men and matters, Djahāngīr was the most polished and cultured scion of the House of Tīmūr. He was a sensible ruler, kind-hearted and generous, who hated oppression and had a passion for justice. Immediately after his accession to the throne he ordered a chain of gold, adorned with bells, to be hung from the imperial palace in Āgrā which an aggrieved person could shake at any moment of the day or night and get justice. (See *Tūzuk*, Rogers and Beveridge, i, 7). He was lover of nature; Djahāngīr's *Tūzuk* is full of descriptions of the scenic beauty of Kashmīr and other lovely places and of the fauna and flora of the regions he visited. An accomplished prose-writer, his memoirs are in no way inferior to those of Bābur, although he sometimes portrays himself as a violent and unprincipled man whose personal account arouses our disgust and contempt. But unlike Bābur he must be credited with greater honesty and frankness in whatever he writes except in one or two instances when he deliberately tried to conceal the truth.

He makes no secret of his addiction to wine and opium, which ultimately ruined his robust health and hastened his end. He was exceedingly cruel sometimes, having once got a sodomite flayed alive and another castrated. Similarly he ordered the bones of Naṣīr al-Dīn Khaldjī, ruler of Mālwa, who was guilty of poisoning his father, to be exhumed and thrown into the Narbadā, when he visited Māndū [*q.v.*] in 1027/1617. As a rule, his reign brought peace and prosperity to the people; industry and commerce flourished; architecture, painting and literature progressed and on the political side there was stability and strength only marred by a few wars in Mewār and the Deccan, and some minor disturbances in Bengal as the ineffectual revolt of ʿUthmān Khān Afghān.

Bibliography: *Tūzuk-i Djahāngīrī* (with numerous variants), ed. Sayyid Ahmad Khan, Ghazipur 1864 (Eng. transl. Rogers and Beveridge, London, i 1909, ii 1914, Urdū transl. Lahore 1960); there is another version of the memoirs called *Taʾrīkh-i Salīm Shāhī* translated into English by Major David Price (Calcutta², 1906), quite unreliable being a forgery and a fabrication; Ṣamṣām al-Dawla Shāh Nawāz Khān, *Maʾāthir al-umarāʾ*, (Eng. transl. Beveridge), i, 573-4; Muʿtamad Khān, *Iḳbāl-nāmah-i Djahāngīrī*, (Bibl. Ind.), Calcutta 1865; Beni Prasad, *History of Jahangir*, Allahabad 1940 (contains an exhaustive bibliography and gives a fairly balanced account of Djahāngīr's reign; certain statements by the author are, however, not unbiased); *Cambridge History of India*, iv, s.v.; *Jahangir and the Jesuits* (transl. C. H. Payne), London 1939; *Calcutta Review*, 1869, xcviii, 139-40 (article by H. Blochmann); Ṣabāḥ al-Dīn ʿAbd al-Raḥmān, *Bazm-i Tīmūriyya* (in Urdū), Aʿẓamgaṙh 1367/ 1948, 128-68; Storey, i, 556-64; Mīrzā Muḥammad ʿAlī, *Nudjūm al-samāʾ* (for an authentic account of the death of Nūr Allāh al-Shūstarī) Lucknow 1302 A.H., 9-16; *Embassy of Sir Thomas Roe*, ed. William Foster (Hakluyt Society); Francis Gladwin, *The History of Hindustan during the reigns of Jahangir, Shah Jahan and Aurungzeb*, Calcutta 1788, (based mainly on Kamgār Ḥusaynī's *Maʾāthir-i Djahāngīrī*, still in MS.); V. A. Smith, *Oxford History of India*,⁴ *s.v.*; Dhakāʾ Allāh Dihlawī, *Taʾrīkh-i Hind* (in Urdū), vi, ʿAligaṙh 1917, the only detailed account in Urdū; ʿAbd al-Ḥayy Nadwī, *Nuzhat al-khawāṭir*, Ḥaydarābād 1375/1955, v, 120-22, (the only brief account in Arabic known to me).

For the buildings of Djahāngīr, see HIND, Architecture; MUGHALS; also ĀGRA, LĀHAWR, PALAMAŪ.

For the Mughal garden, which Djahāngīr specially developed, see BŪSTĀN, KASHMĪR, SRĪNAGAR.

For miniature painting, which reached its highest point in India under Djahāngīr's patronage, see HIND, Art.

Mughal coinage reached its highest point of elaboration in the variety of pieces and the refinement of designs during Djahāngīr's reign. For Djahāngīr's coins see SIKKA.

(A. S. BAZMEE ANSARI)

DJAHANNAM, Gehenna (Hebrew *gēhinnōm*, valley of the Gehenna); the Arabic word evokes etymologically the idea of "depth" (cf. *infernus*). Used very often in the *Ḳurʾān* as a synonym of *nār* ("fire"), *djahannam* must accordingly be rendered by the general idea of Hell. The same is true in traditions.

Exegetists and many treatises on *kalām* (or *taṣawwuf*) were, subsequently, to give it a particularized connotation. The description of the Muslim Hell, the problems relating to it and consequently the references to verses in the *Ḳurʾān* mentioning *djahannam*, are considered in the article NĀR; here only its restricted sense is considered. Here are two examples from among the most familiar:

1. Some traditionists like al-Baghawī, with an extremely literal and uncritical outlook, considering the precise wording of the dialogue (*taṣwīr*) in the *Ḳur'ān*, L, 30, between God and Gehenna, regard the latter as a fantastic animal of hell which they describe with endless hyperbole. It will be drawn along by 70,000 angels, its guardians, at the time of the resurrection, the width between the shoulders of each guardian angel being equal to 70 years' march, etc. The description, supported by *ḥadīth*, is repeated in al-Sha'rānī's *Mukhtaṣar* (for this sort of commentary in Muslim thought, see *Djanna*).

2. Descriptions which show hell as a place made up of concentric layers of increasing depth generally put Gehenna in the higher zone, that reserved for members of the Muslim community who have committed "grave sins" about which they have not repented and whom God, in accordance with his threats, decides to punish for a time with infernal torments. It is thereby admitted, even by those who uphold the eternity of hell, that Gehenna will cease to exist. It will be wiped out when the last repentant sinner among the believers leaves it to enter paradise. We may note that the etymological reference to the idea of "depth" is suppressed here.—This interpretation, which occurs in the *tafsīr* of Khāzin and elsewhere is freely expounded in the manuals of the Ash'arī school (e.g. al-Bādjūrī, *Ḥāshiya .... 'alā Djawharat al-tawḥīd*, ed. Cairo 1352/1934, 107). For the place of Gehenna in the circles of Hell according to Ibn 'Arabī, see the diagrams reproduced by Asin Palacios, *La Escatologia musulmana en la Divina Comedia*, Madrid-Granada 1943, 147.

Bibliography: in the article; detailed references will be given in the article NĀR.

(L. GARDET)

DJAHĀN-SŪZ, 'ALĀ' AL-DĪN ḤUSAYN B. AL-ḤUSAYN, Ghūrid ruler—poet, notorious for his burning of Ghazna in 546/1151. The cause of the violence between the Ghūrids and Bahrām Shāh of Ghazna [*q.v.*] would appear to have been an attempt by Ḳuṭb al-Dīn Muḥammad, (eldest brother of 'Alā' al-Dīn) to seize Ghazna through an intrigue with some of its inhabitants. Bahrām Shāh had him poisoned; an attempt by another brother, Sayf al-Dīn Sūrī, to avenge his brother ended, after the temporary occupation of Ghazna by the Ghūrid forces, in his ignominious death at the hands of Bahrām Shāh. Death (from natural causes) prevented another brother, Bahā' al-Dīn Sām, from action, whereupon 'Alā' al-Dīn marched against Bahrām, defeating him in three battles and occupying Ghazna. The city was probably sacked so ruthlessly through rage at the fickleness of its inhabitants but also with the intention of securing 'Alā' al-Dīn's rear for his wider ambitions against the Saldjūḳ possessions to the west and north of Ghūr. In the year following (547/1152), with Bahrām Shāh a fugitive in the Pandjāb, 'Alā' al-Dīn moved against Sandjar, in alliance with the *muḳṭa'* of Harāt, only to be defeated and captured at Awba near Harāt. He was released before Sandjar's quarrel with the Ghuzz in 548/1153 and appears to have ruled quietly at Fīrūz-Kūh until his death in 556/1161. Several of his poems in self-praise survive both in the histories and in the biographies of the poets.

Bibliography: Ibn al-Athīr, ed. Tornberg, xi, 89-90, 107-8; Minhādj b. Sirādj Djūzdjānī, *Ṭabaḳāt-i Nāṣirī*, trans. H. G. Raverty, Calcutta 1873-81, index, vol. ii, 7; Niẓāmī al-'Arūḍī al-Samarḳandī, *Čahār maḳāla*, ed. Mīrzā Muḥammad, Leyden and London 1910, index, 282; Muḥammad b. 'Alī b. Sulayman al-Rāwandī, *Rāḥat al-ṣudūr*, ed. Muḥammad Iqbāl, London 1921, 175-6; trad. M. C. Defrémery, *Histoire des Sultans Ghourides* (extract from Mīr Khwānd's *Rawḍat al-ṣafā*), Paris 1844, 7-15; Firishta, i, 87-90; Dawlatshāh, 75-6; 'Awfī, *Lubāb*, i, 38-9. Fakhr-i Mudabbir, *Ādāb al-ḥarb wa 'l-shudjā'a*, British Museum MS. Add. 16,853 fols. 170a-172b; Browne, ii, 107, 306, 338, 381. Other references (unavailable to me) are given in Ghulām Muṣṭafā Khān, *A history of Bahram Shah of Ghaznin*, in *IC*, xxiii, 3, July 1949.

(P. HARDY)

DJAHBADH (pl. DJAHĀBIDHA), a term of Persian origin, perhaps derived from a **gahbadh* in the Sāsānid administration, (the term is suggested by Herzfeld; Paikuli, gloss. N° 274) used in the sense of a financial clerk, expert in matters of coins, skilled money examiner, treasury receiver, government cashier, money changer or collector (*Tādj al-'Arūs*, ii, 558; Dozy, *Supplément*, i, 226; Vullers, *Lexicon Persicum*, i, 544; Ibn Mammātī, 304, etc.).

From the end of the 2nd/8th century on, bearers of this title in the time of the 'Abbāsid Caliphs Manṣūr, Harūn, and Mahdī are mentioned (Djahshiyārī; Mas'ūdī, vi, 227) also frequently in Arabic papyri (Karabaček, Becker, Grohmann, Dietrich, etc.).

In an economy based on bimetallism, *dīnār* and *dirham*, with their fluctuating weights and values and their diversity in circulation, the function of the Djahbadh assumed an ever-increasing importance, as manifested by repeated references in Arabic sources of the 3rd/9th and 4th/10th centuries to:

(a) *Māl al-Djahābidha*, also known as *Ḥaḳḳ al-Djahābidha*, which represents the fee of the Djahbadh for his services to the government, levied as a charge on the taxpayer and which, though somewhat dubious in its legality, became an integral part of the public budget (Kremer, *Einnahmebudget*; al-Ṣābī; *Ta'rīkh-i Ḳumm*; Løkkegaard).

(b) *Dīwān al-Djahbadha*, whose chief was required to prepare a monthly or yearly statement accounting for all the items of income and expenditure of the treasury (Ḳudāma b. Dja'far; Løkkegaard; Cl. Cahen; see further DAFTAR); and above all to:

(c) Individual bearers of the title *Djahbadh* by name with precise information about their activities.

The text of an official appointment of a *Djahbadh* (*Ta'rīkh-i Ḳumm*, 149-53) specifies his function, his salary, and his obligation "to be just and fair in the collection of taxes ... and to give an official receipt for all incoming amounts in the presence of witnesses".

The 4th/10th century Arabic sources (Miskawayh, Tanūkhī, Ṣābi, Ṣūlī, etc.) indicate that it was customary for viziers to have their own *Djahbadh* with whom they deposited large, legally or illegally acquired, amounts of money as the safest method of securing their fortune.

In the time of the 'Abbāsid Caliph al-Muḳtadir, (295-320/908-32), however, the Djahbadh emerged as a banker in the modern sense, who, in addition to his functions as an administrator of deposits and as a remitter of funds from place to place through the medium of the *ṣakk* and especially of the *suftadja* [*qq.v.*],—then a widely used instrument of the credit economy,—was called upon to advance huge sums to the Caliph, the viziers, and other court officials on credit terms with interest rates and securities.

The *D̲j̲ahābid̲h̲a* were mostly Christians and Jews whose appointment to this office despite their status as *D̲h̲immī* was legalized by a special decree issued in 295/908 by the Caliph (Muḳaddasī, ed. de Goeje, 183).

Among the *D̲j̲ahābid̲h̲a* listed in the sources were Ibrāhīm b. Yuḥannā, Zakariyā b. Yuḥannā, Sahl b. Naẓīr, Ibrāhīm b. Ayyūb, Ibrāhīm b. Aḥmad, Isrā'īl b. Ṣāliḥ, Sulaymān b. Wahb, etc., and, above all two Jewish merchants and bankers, Yūsuf b. Pink̲h̲ās and Hārūn b. ʿImrān of Bag̲h̲dād. They were appointed to the office of *D̲j̲ahbad̲h̲* of the Persian province of Ahwāz, and then became the court bankers (*D̲j̲ahābid̲h̲at al-Ḥaḍra*) of al-Muḳtadir and his viziers, and the pillars of the financial administration of their time. By virtue of their vast resources and commercial connexions, these Jewish merchants and *D̲j̲ahābid̲h̲a* and their associates were instrumental in establishing the first State bank in Islamic history (ca. 302/913), through which the urgent financial needs of the State could be satisfied and the financial ruin of the State staved off. The sources indicate the amounts they lent, the contracts they concluded with the vizier ʿAlī b. ʿIsā, and other details of the methods of their credit transactions. They were given interest on their loans and securities in the form of the tax revenues of the province of Ahwāz (Fischel).

Under the successors of al-Muḳtadir, the *D̲j̲ahabid̲h̲a* continued to play a rôle not only in Bag̲h̲dād, but also in Baṣra and other cities of the ʿAbbāsid Empire. Under the Buwayhid Amīrs mention is made of one ʿAlī b. Hārūn b. ʿAllān (d. 329/941), and of Abū ʿAlī b. Faḍlān (d. 383/993). At the beginning of the 7th/13th century, Abū Ṭāhir b. S̲h̲ibr, the "chief of the Jews in Bag̲h̲dād" occupied the position of a *D̲j̲ahbad̲h̲* (Ibn al-Fuwaṭī). In later centuries the *D̲j̲ahbad̲h̲* lost his central significance as a Court banker; his functions were equated with that of a ṣayrafī [*q.v.*] (Ḳalḳas̲h̲andī, Ṣubḥ, v, 466).

Bibliography: al-D̲j̲ahs̲h̲iyārī, *Kitāb al-wuzarā'*, Cairo 1938; Hilāl al-Ṣābī, *Kitāb al-wuzarā'*, ed. Amedroz, Leyden 1904; Ibn al-Fuwaṭī, *al-Ḥawādit̲h̲ al-d̲j̲āmiʿa wa 'l-tad̲j̲ārib al-nāfiʿa*, Baghdād 1351/1932, ed. Muṣṭāwfa D̲j̲awād; al-Miskawayh, *The eclipse of the ʿAbbasid caliphate*, ed. and tr. by H. F. Amedroz and D. S. Margoliouth, Oxford 1921; al-Tanūk̲h̲ī, *Nis̲h̲wār al-muḥāḍara*, ed. D. S. Margoliouth; i, London, 1922; ii, Damascus, 1930. Tr. i, London 1923; ii, Ḥaydarābād 1931; al-Ṣūlī, *Ak̲h̲bār al-Rāḍi wa'l-Muttaḳī* from the *Kitāb al-awrāq*, ed. J. Heyworth Dunne, London 1935; Fr. tr. Marius Canard, Algiers 1946, 1950; Ibn Mammātī, *Kitāb ḳawānīn al-dawāwīn*[2], ed. A. S. Atiya, Cairo 1943, 304; *Ta'rīk̲h̲-i Ḳumm*, Teheran 1934, 149-55; 159-61; Ḳalḳas̲h̲andī, *Ṣubḥ al-aʿs̲h̲ā*, v, 466; C. H. Becker, *Neue Papyri*, in *Isl.*, ii, 1911, 254 ff., no. 327; Cl. Cahen, *Quelques problèmes économiques et fiscaux de l'Iraq Buyide d'après un traité de mathématiques*, in *AIEO*, x, 1952, 326-36; A. Dietrich, *Arabische Briefe in der Papyrus Sammlung der Hamburger Staats- und Universitäts-Bibliotek*, Hamburg 1955; A. A. Dūrī, *Ta'rīk̲h̲ al-ʿIrāḳ al-iḳtiṣādī fi 'l-ḳarn al-rābiʿ al-hid̲j̲rī*, Baghdad 1948; A. Grohmann, *Probleme der Arabischen Papyrusforschung*, in *ArO*, v, 273-83; vi, 125-49; vii, 278; idem, *Griech. und Latein. Verwaltungstermini Chronique d'Egypt*, i, 13-14; J. v. Karabaček, *Mitteilungen aus der Sammlung der Papyrus Erzherzog Rainer*, Vienna 1886-7; A. v. Kremer, *Über das Einnahmebudget des Abbasidenreiches*, Vienna 1887, 8; A. K. S. Lambton, *An account of the Tārīkhi Qumm*, in *BSOAS*, xii, 1948, 594; idem, *Landlord and Peasant in Persia*, Oxford 1953, 42-5; F. Løkkegaard, *Islamic taxation in the classic period*, Copenhagen 1950, 158 ff.; L. Massignon, *L'influence de l'Islam au moyen âge sur la fondation et l'essor des banques juives*, in *B.Ét.Or.*, 1932; A. Mez, *Die Renaissance des Islam*, Heidelberg 1922; H. Zayyāt, *al-Mashriq*, 1937, 491-6; W. J. Fischel, *The origin of banking in medieval Islam*, in *JRAS*, 1933, 339 ff., 569 ff.; idem, *Jews in the economic and political life of medieval Islam*, London 1937; D. Sourdel, *Vizirat ʿabbāside*, Damascus 1959-60, index. (W. J. Fischel)

D̲J̲ĀHIDIYYA [see k̲h̲alwatiyya].

D̲J̲ĀHIL wa ʿĀḲIL [see durūz].

D̲J̲ĀHILIYYA, a term used, in almost all its occurrences, as the opposite of the word *islām*, and which refers to the state of affairs in Arabia before the mission of the Prophet, to paganism (sometimes even that of non-Arab lands), the pre-Islamic period and the men of that time. From the morphological point of view, *d̲j̲āhiliyya* seems to be formed by the addition of the suffix *-iyya*, denoting an abstract, to the active participle *d̲j̲āhil*, the exact sense of which is difficult to determine. I. Goldziher (*Muh. St.*, i, 219 ff.; analysis in *Arabica*, vii/3 (1960), 246-9), remarking that *d̲j̲āhil* is opposed to *ḥalīm* "administered" [see ḥilm], gives it the sense of "barbarous", and renders *d̲j̲āhiliyya* as "the time of barbarism", but he has not been followed to the letter by translators of the Ḳur'ān who render *d̲j̲āhil* as "not knowing God, the Prophet and the Law", or "lawless", and *d̲j̲āhiliyya* as "time of ignorance", "heathendom" (cf. however T. Izutsu, *The structure of the ethical terms in the Koran*, Tokyo 1959, index). The fact is that the nine attestations of *d̲j̲āhil* and the four of *d̲j̲āhiliyya* in the Ḳur'ān scarcely permit of their sense being precisely determined; however, in the feeling of Muslims and of the commentators, *d̲j̲āhil* is opposed to *ʿālim* "one who knows God, etc.", and *d̲j̲āhiliyya* to *islām* taken not in the sense of "submission to God" but rather that of "knowledge of God, etc." (compare the Druze terminology [see durūz], where *d̲j̲āhil* is opposed to *ʿāḳil*, and designates all those who have not been initiated into the mysteries of the sect.) The word *d̲j̲āhiliyya* as an abstract is thus applicable to the period during which the Arabs did not yet know Islam and the Divine Law, as well as to the beliefs current at that time. One the basis of Ḳur'ān, XXXIII, 33, where the expression *al-d̲j̲āhiliyya al-'ūlā* "the first *d̲j̲āhiliyya*" appears, one is inclined to distinguish two periods, the first *d̲j̲āhiliyya* extending from Adam to Noah (or to other prophets), and the second corresponding to the "Interval" between Jesus and Muḥammad [see faṭra]. The relative adjective *d̲j̲āhilī* formed from *d̲j̲āhiliyya* is applied to all which is anterior to Islam, in particular to the poets who died before Muḥammad's preaching; those who knew both periods are called *muk̲h̲ḍram*, and those born after Islam *islāmī*. The double opposition *d̲j̲āhilī*/*islāmī* and *d̲j̲āhiliyya*/*islām* thus marks an evolution and a departure from the primitive sense of *d̲j̲āhil*.

The history of the Arabs during the *d̲j̲āhiliyya* has been dealt with under al-ʿarab, the geography and ethnography under d̲j̲azīrat al-ʿarab, the language under ʿarabiyya, and nomadism under badw; on all these points the articles on the different regions, on the major tribes, and on the towns, should be consulted; for the economic situation see especially under TIDJĀRA.

A point calling for some remark is, rather than the true state of pre-Islamic Arabia, the distinctive characters attributed by Muslims to their pagan ancestors, that is to say the traits which allow their conception of *djāhiliyya* to be defined.

The ideas of the Muslims on pre-Islamic paganism are based on the Ḳurʾān and on traditions which, in spite of their contempt for everything before Islam, they have collected in the framework of their historical and linguistic researches; in the article ḲURʾĀN will be found a résumé of the pronouncements of the Sacred Book on earlier beliefs; in the articles ḤADJDJ and KAʿBA an account of the ancient cult and the history of the Sacred House; under ṢANAM a study of idolatry. Also to be consulted are the various articles on the principal divinities, and also the articles on the adepts of the revealed religions, NAṢĀRĀ and YAHŪD.

While attributing to the *djāhiliyya* the faults condemned in the Ḳurʾān, Muslims do not fail to recognize a certain number of virtues among the ancient Arabs, such as honour [see ʿIRḌ], generosity [see KARAM], courage and dignity [see MURUWWA], and hospitality [see ḌAYF].

For relevant information on social organization see ʿĀʾILA, ʿĀḲILA, ḲABĪLA, etc., and, for the position of women, NIKĀḤ and ṬALĀḲ. (ED.)

DJAḤĪM [see NĀR].

DJAHĪR (BANU), one of the families of government contractors characteristic of their period who almost completely monopolized the caliph's vizierate during the protectorate of the Great Saldjūḳids, and deriving their particular importance from that fact.

The founder of the political fortunes of the dynasty, Fakhr al-Dawla Abū Naṣr Muḥammad b. Muḥammad b. Djahīr, born in al-Mawṣil in 398/1007-8 of a family of rich merchants, entered the service of the Shīʿī ʿUḳaylid princes of that town; then, after one of them, Ḳirwāsh, fell in 442/1149, as a result of somewhat obscure feuds he went to Aleppo where at one time he was vizier to the Mirdāsid Shīʿī Muʿizz al-Dawla Thimāl, and finally (in about 446/1054?) he settled down with, and soon became vizier to, the Marwānid of the Diyār Bakr, Naṣr al-Dawla (401-53), a Sunnī and vassal of the Saldjūḳids from before the time of Tughrul Beg's entry into Baghdād (447/1055). After his protector's death, the rivalries between the sons apparently caused him some anxiety, and he was able to take advantage of the difficulties which caliph al-Ḳāʾim was experiencing in choosing a vizier who would be *persona grata* to the sultan and at the same time ready to safeguard the prerogatives of the caliphs, to have the post offered to himself (454/1062), for which no doubt he was further recommended by the administrative talents he had revealed at Mayyāfāriḳīn. The family was to hold the ʿAbbāsid vizierate almost without a break for half a century, and Fakhr al-Dawla himself was to remain as vizier, apart only from four months in 460-1/1068, until 471/1078 when once again he fell into disgrace, to be replaced, however, after some months by his son (born in 435) and close colleague ʿAmīd al-Dawla. Ibn Djahīr calculated that, if he was obliged on the one hand to defend the rights of the caliphate and to avoid wishing to appear to act without the caliph's orders, on the other hand he could only enjoy a really secure position if he maintained close personal relations with the sultanate and his eminent and powerful vizier (from the time of Alp Arslan's reign 455/1063), Niẓām al-Mulk; these ties were strengthened, after the incident in 460-1/1068, by the marriage of ʿAmīd al-Dawla to one of Niẓām's daughters, and then after her death (on the eve of the affair in 471/1078 which possibly her death precipitated) by his subsequent marriage to her niece: thanks to this it was possible at last to put a stop to the hostile intrigues of Göherāīn, the sultan's representative in Baghdād, in that year. However in the second half of Malikshāh's sultanate (463-85/1072-92), in face of the Saldjūḳid hold over Baghdād which was becoming increasingly severe, the caliph al-Muḳtadī (467-87/1075-94) in 476/1083 replaced the Djahīrids by Miskawayh's successor, Abū Shudjāʿ Rudhrawarī who, without being in any way anti-Saldjūḳid, was perhaps a truer representative of the vizier in his heart, and more attentive to the religious, orthodox aspect of the caliphate's own policy. It was then that the Djahīrids embarked on another venture, the explanation of which, if not from their point of view at least from that of the sultan's government, seems far from clear. Taking advantage of the Marwānids' difficulties, Fakhr al-Dawla in fact arranged that Malikshāh, who provided him with the necessary troops, should entrust him with the task of conquering the principality in which, it was true, he had maintained his interests and relations, but of which neither Malikshāh nor his predecessors had ever had cause to complain. Furthermore, the military operations were difficult, being complicated by the intervention of the ʿUḳaylid of al-Mawṣil, Muslim, who saw clearly that if an autonomous neighbouring state were to disappear, his own, which he had put to far more questionable uses, would not long survive, and even by the somewhat equivocal attitude of the Saldjūḳid Turkoman leader Artuḳ. Actual sieges were necessary to take Mayyāfāriḳīn, Āmid and other fortresses in the Diyār Bakr, and the war in which ʿAmīd al-Dawla's brother al-Kāfī Zaʿīm al-Ruʾasāʾ Abu 'l-Ḳāsim ʿAlī also took part was only concluded at the beginning of 478/1085. Fakhr al-Dīn hunted out and apparently squandered the Marwānids' treasure, appropriating a portion of it for himself, and from the end of that year Malikshāh thought it advisable in view of his unpopularity to replace him by a less self-seeking representative as head of government in the province. However, in 482 ʿAmīd al-Dawla obtained the right to farm taxes from the province, paying ten million dinars in three years, while his father received the administration of al-Mawṣil which meanwhile had also come into Malikshāh's possession; he won a good reputation with everyone by the remission of taxes, and the family was able to retrieve its fortunes before the death of Fakhr al-Dawla which occurred in al-Mawṣil in 483. In the following year Niẓām al-Mulk persuaded the caliph to reappoint ʿAmīd al-Dawla to the office of vizier which he was to retain after the death of the great Saldjūḳid administrator, Malikshāh and al-Muḳtadī until 493/1100; to govern the Diyār Bakr he had left his brother al-Kāfī as representative, later succeeded by his son.

But harsher times were to befall the family. In 487/1094, after Malikshāh's death, his brother Tutush took possession of the Diyār Bakr; after retaining al-Kāfī as vizier, perhaps for a short time, he recalled him and, under the Turkoman leaders who were to partition the province between themselves, we hear no more of the Djahīrids. In Baghdād the new sultan Barkyārūk, running short of funds during the wars he was obliged to wage against his brothers, and possibly not being certain of ʿAmīd al-Dawla's loyalty to his cause, had him arrested and fined an enormous sum on the charge of misappropriating or squandering the treasure from the Diyār Bakr and al-Mawṣil, and left him to die shortly afterwards in prison (493/1100). However, his brother al-Kāfī later became vizier to al-Mustaẓhir, the new caliph, from 496/1102-3 to 500/1106-7 and then, on the recommendation of the new sultan Muḥammad, from 502/1108-9 to 507/1113-4. Henceforward new families were to share the ʿAbbāsid vizierate among themselves. Nevertheless we do once again find a Niẓām al-Dīn Abū Naṣr al-Muẓaffar b. Muḥammad b. Djahīr as *ustādhdār*, and then vizier to the caliph from 535/1140-1 to 541/1146-7, so proving that the Djahīrids had not completely disappeared. But that is the final mention. The residence of Fakhr al-Dawla b. Djahīr at Bāb al-ʿĀmma had been destroyed by al-Mustaẓhir, and the new one, belonging to Niẓām al-Dīn at Bāb al-Azadj, soon fell into the possession of the caliphate.

Bibliography: Sources: Ibn al-Djawzī, *K. al-Muntaẓam*, viii, ix and x, ed. Ḥaydarābād, index; Ibn al-Azraḳ, *Taʾrīkh Mayyāfāriḳīn*, analysed in Amèdroz, *The Marwanid dynasty of Diyār Bakr*, in *JRAS* 1903, 136 ff.; Ibn al-Athīr, *al-Kāmil*, x and xi in Tornberg ed., index; Sibṭ b. al-Djawzī, *Mirʾāt al-zamān* (from Ghars al-Niʿma b. Hilāl al-Ṣābī), *passim* years 454 to 479 (not edited; the continuation not original); Ibn Khallikān, *Wafayāt* no. 711, and tr. De Slane, iii, 280; histories of the caliphs, such as Ibn al-Tiḳṭaḳa, *Fakhrī*, ed. Derenbourg, 394 ff.; and G. Makdisī, *An autograph diary* (of Ibn al-Bannāʾ), in *BSOAS*, xviii (1956), 254 with note 1. (CL. CAHEN)

AL-**DJĀḤIẒ**, ABŪ ʿUTHMĀN ʿAMR B. BAḤR AL-FUḲAYMĪ AL-BAṢRĪ, was a famous Arab prose writer, the author of works of *adab*, Muʿtazilī theology and politico-religious polemics. Born at Baṣra about 160/776 in an obscure family of *mawālī* from the Banū Kināna and probably of Abyssinian origin, he owes his sobriquet to a malformation of the eyes (*djāḥiẓ* = with a projecting cornea). Little is known of his childhood in Baṣra, except that from an early age an invincible desire for learning and a remarkably inquisitive mind urged him towards a life of independence and, much to his family's despair, idleness. Mixing with groups which gathered at the mosque (*masdjidiyyūn*) to discuss a wide range of questions, attending as a spectator the philological enquiries conducted on the Mirbad [*q.v.*] and following lectures by the most learned men of the day on philology, lexicography and poetry, namely al-Aṣmaʿī, Abū ʿUbayda, Abū Zayd, he soon acquired real mastery of the Arabic language along with the usual and traditional culture. His precocious intelligence won him admittance to Muʿtazilī circles and bourgeois salons, where conversation, often light, was also animated by problems confronting the Muslim conscience at that time: in the realm of theology, harmonizing faith and reason and, in politics, the thorny question of the Caliphate which was constantly brought up by the enemies of the ʿAbbāsids, the conflicts between Islamic sects and the claims of the non-Arabs. His penetrating observation of the various elements in a mixed population increased his knowledge of human nature, whilst reading books of all kinds which were beginning to circulate in Baṣra gave him some outlook on to the outside world. It is quite certain that the intellectual resources offered by his home town would have been fully adequate to give al-Djāḥiẓ a broad culture but the ʿIrāḳī metropolis, then at its apogee, had a decisive influence in helping to form his mind. It left its rationalist and realist imprint so clearly on him, that al-Djāḥiẓ might be considered not only one of the most eminent products of his home town, but its most complete representative, for the knowledge he subsequently acquired in Baghdād did not modify to any noticeable degree his turn of mind as it had been formed at Baṣra; Baṣra is the continuous thread running through all his works.

Although he probably began writing earlier, the first proof of his literary activity dates from roughly 200/815-6; it relates to an event which had a decisive effect on his subsequent career. Some works (the plural is no longer in doubt) on the imāmate, a very characteristic subject, won him the compliments of al-Maʾmūn and thereby that consecration by the capital coveted by so many provincials eager to have their talent recognized and so reach the court and establish themselves. From then on, without completely abandoning Baṣra, al-Djāḥiẓ frequently stayed for long periods in Baghdād (and later Sāmarrā) devoting himself to literary work of which an appreciable part, fortunately, has been spared the ravages of time.

In spite of some slender indications, it is not really known on what he relied for his income in Baṣra. In Baghdād, we know, he discharged for three days the functions of scribe and was very briefly assistant to Ibrāhīm b. al-ʿAbbās al-Ṣūlī at the Chancellery; it is also probable that he was a teacher, and he records himself an interview he claims to have had with al-Mutawakkil who, anxious to entrust him with the education of his children, finally dismissed him because of his ugliness. Although information about his private and public life is not readily forthcoming from either his biographers or himself, it appears from what knowledge we have that al-Djāḥiẓ held no official post and took on no regular employment. He admits, however, that he received considerable sums for the dedications of his books and we know that for a time at least he was made an allowance by the *dīwān*. These fragmentary indications are indeed confusing and tend to suggest that al-Djāḥiẓ who otherwise, unlike some of his fellow countrymen, does not appear to have led the life of a courtier, acted the part of an *éminence grise*, so to speak, or of unofficial adviser at least. We have seen already that the writings which won him the recognition of the capital dealt with the Caliphate and were certainly intended to justify the accession to power of the ʿAbbāsids; they were the prelude of a whole series of opuscules addressed to the authorities, if not inspired by them, and relating to topical events; notwithstanding some degree of artifice in *risāla*s beginning: "Thou hast asked me about such and such a question .... I answer thee that ...", it may be presumed that in many cases the question had in fact been asked and he had been requested to reply in writing. For, if he was never admitted to the intimacy of the Caliphs, he was in continuous contact with leading political figures and it is rather curious that he should have attached himself successively to Muḥammad b. ʿAbd al-Malik al-Zayyāt [*q.v.*], then after the latter's fall from favour (233/847) which almost proved fatal to both men, to the *Ḳāḍī al-ḳuḍāt* (d. 240/854) Aḥmad b. Abī Duʾād [*q.v.*] and to his son Muḥammad (d. 239/853) and finally to al-Fatḥ b. Khāḳān [*q.v.*] (d. 247/861).

He nevertheless retained ample independence and was able to take advantage of his new position to further his intellectual training and to travel (particularly to Syria; but al-Masʿūdī, *Murūdj*, i, 206, was to criticize him for having attempted to write a geography book—now almost entirely lost—without having travelled enough). In Baghdād also he found a rich store of learning in the many translations from Greek undertaken during the Caliphate of al-Maʾmūn and studying the philosophers of antiquity —especially Aristotle (cf. al-Ḥādjirī, *Takhrīdj nuṣūṣ arisṭaṭāliyya min K. al-Ḥayawān*, in *Madjallat kulliyyat al-ādāb*, Alexandria, 1953 ff.)—enabled him to broaden his outlook and perfect his own theological doctrine, which he had begun to elaborate under the supervision of the great Muʿtazilīs of the day, of whom al-Naẓẓām and Thumāma b. Ashras [*qq.v.*], who seems to have had a strong influence on him, should be placed in the first rank.

Towards the end of his life, suffering from hemiplegia, he retired to his home town, where he died in Muḥarram 255/December 868-January 869.

Like many Arabic writers, al-Djāḥiẓ had a very great output. A catalogue of his works (see *Arabica*, 1956/2) lists nearly 200 titles of which only about thirty, authentic or apocryphal, have been preserved, in their entirety; about fifty others have been partially preserved, whilst the rest seem irremediably lost. Brockelmann (S I, 241 ff.) has attempted to classify his works according to real or supposed subjects and gives us some idea of the breadth and variety of his interests. Considering only the extant works, which now for the most part are available in editions of varying quality, two broad categories may be distinguished: on the one hand, works coming under the head of Djāḥiẓian *adab*, that is to say intended in a rather entertaining manner to instruct the reader, with the author intervening only insofar as he selects, presents and comments on documents; on the other hand, original works, dissertations where his ability as a writer and to some extent his efforts as a thinker are more clearly shown.

His chief work in the first category is *K. al-Ḥayawān* (ed. Hārūn, Cairo n.d, 7 vols..) which is not so much a bestiary as a genuine anthology based on animals, leading off sometimes rather unexpectedly into theology, metaphysics, sociology etc.; one can even find embryonic theories, without it being possible to say how far they are original, of the evolution of species, the influence of climate and animal psychology, which were not to be developed till the nineteenth century. Following *K. al-Ḥayawān*, which was never completed, came *K. al-Bighāl* (ed. Pellat, Cairo 1955). *K. al-Bayān wa 'l-tabyīn* (ed. Hārūn, Cairo 1367/1948-50, 4 vols, and other editions) seems fundamentally to be an inventory of what have been called the "Arabic humanities", designed to stress the oratorical and poetic ability of Arabs; he attempts to justify his choice by positing the bases of an art of poetry, but he does so in an extremely disorderly fashion, as was pointed out by Abū Hilāl al-ʿAskarī, *K. al-Ṣināʿatayn*, 5, who decided to write a more systematic treatise.

Another quality of the Arabs, generosity, is emphasized in *K. al-Bukhalā* (ed. al-Ḥādjirī, Cairo 1948 and other editions; Ger. tr. O. Rescher, *Excerpti*..; Fr. tr. Ch. Pellat, Paris 1951), which is at the same time a portrait gallery, an attack on non-Arabs and an analysis of avarice, the equivalent of which is not to be found anywhere in Arabic literature. His acute powers of observation, his light-hearted scepticism, his comic sense and satirical turn of mind fit him admirably to portray human types and society; he uses all his skill at the expense of several social groups (schoolmasters, singers, scribes etc.) generally keeping within the bounds of decency; only *K. Mufākharat al-djawārī wa 'l-ghilmān* (ed. Pellat, Beirut 1957), dealing with a delicate subject, is marred by obscenity, whilst *K. al-Ḳiyān* (ed. Finkel), which is about slave-girl singers, contains pages of remarkable shrewdness. But this work really belongs to the second category, which includes the dissertations assembled by Kraus and Ḥādjirī: *al-Maʿād wa 'l-maʿāsh*, *al-Sirr wa ḥifẓ al-lisān*, *al-Djidd wa 'l-hazl*, *Faṣl mā bayn al-ʿadāwa wa 'l-ḥasad*, and several other texts published either by al-Sandūbī or in the *11 Risāla*. One might also add the politico-religious works, now for the most part lost, perhaps even deliberately destroyed when Sunnism finally triumphed over Muʿtazilism. Of those still extant, the most voluminous is *K. al-ʿUthmāniyya* (ed. Hārūn, Cairo 1374/1955; see *Arabica*, 1956/3) in which al-Djāḥiẓ asserts the legitimacy of the first three Caliphs, attacks the claims of the Shīʿa and thereby justifies the accession of the ʿAbbāsids to power. No less important is *K. Taṣwīb ʿAlī fī taḥkīm al-ḥakamayn* (ed. Pellat, in *Machriq*, July 1958), unfortunately incomplete and defective but clearly directed against the outdated partisans of the Umayyads, who again were enemies of the ʿAbbāsids. In this respect *Risāla fī 'l-Nābita* (or *fī Banī Umayya*) is interesting also (see Pellat's translation, in *AIEO Alger*, 1952), for it is nothing short of a report by al-Djāḥiẓ to the son of Aḥmad b. Abī Duʾād on the political situation, the causes of division in the community and the danger presented by the *nābita*, that is the neo-*ḥashwiyya*, who were reviving Muʿāwiya for their own ends and using the *kalām* to support their theses; *Risāla fī nafyi 'l-tashbīh* (ed. Pellat, in *Machriq*, 1953) is in the same manner. Revealing of the correspondences between government policy and al-Djāḥiẓ's activity are *K. al-Radd ʿalā 'l-Naṣārā* (see Allouche's translation, in *Hesp.*, 1939) and *Risāla fī manāḳib al-Turk*, dealing respectively with measures taken against the Dhimmīs and the forming of the Turkish guard. Generally speaking, in politics al-Djāḥiẓ shows himself a resolute Muʿtazilī, that is an apologist of the ʿAbbāsids against the pro-Umayyad movement of the Nābita, the Shuʿūbīs and the Shīʿa; but his highly personal manner of presenting facts tends to mislead his readers and in all probability the pro-ʿAlid al-Masʿūdī in *Murūdj*, vi, 55 ff. misunderstood the true significance of his writings. If the chronology of al-Djāḥiẓ's work could be established, one would probably see that after warning the authorities against the regression that might be the result of abandoning Muʿtazilism, he gave up the struggle once Sunnī reaction had won the day and from then on restricted himself to purely literary activity; the fact that he wrote *K. al-Bukhalāʾ* in the latter part of his life supports this hypothesis.

As in politics so in theology al-Djāḥiẓ was a Muʿtazilī, though his doctrine appears to offer hardly any original features; as the writings where he expounded are for the most part lost, one has to make do with occasional annotations in al-Khayyāṭ, *K. al-Intiṣār*, translated and edited by A. N. Nader, Beirut 1957, and with data supplied by the heresiographers (al-Baghdādī, *Farḳ*, 160 ff.; Ibn Ḥazm, *Fiṣal*, iv, 181, 195; al-Shahrastānī, on the margin of Ibn Ḥazm, i, 95-6; etc.; see also, Horten, *Die phil. Systeme der spekulativen Theologen im Islam*, 320 ff.; L. Gardet and M. M. Anawati, *Introd. à la Théologie musulmane*, index; A. N. Nader, *Le Système philosophique des Muʿtazila*, Beirut 1956, index) which summarize or indicate points where al-Djāḥiẓ differs from other Muʿtazilīs. Too little is known of the doctrine itself for one to be able to do more at this stage than simply refer to the article MUʿTAZILA, pending the completion of a thesis specifically concerned with the question.

Meanwhile, even though al-Djāḥiẓ's place in the development of Muslim thought is far from negligible, he is chiefly interesting as a writer and an *adīb*, for with him form is never overshadowed by content; even in purely technical works. If he is not the first of the great Arab prose writers, if in rhetoric ʿAbd Allāh b. al-Muḳaffaʿ [*q.v.*] and Sahl b. Hārūn [*q.v.*], to name but two, are his masters, nevertheless he gave literary prose its most perfect form, as was indeed recognized first by politicians who made use of his talent for the ʿAbbāsid cause and then by Arab critics who were unanimous in asserting his superiority and making his name the very symbol of literary ability.

Al-Djāḥiẓ's writing is characterized by deliberately contrived disorderliness and numerous digressions; the individuality of his alert and lively style lies in a concern for the exact term—a foreign word if necessary—picturesque phrases and sentences which are nearly always unrhymed, but balanced by the repetition of the same idea in two different forms; what would be pointless repetition to our way of thinking, in the mind of a 3rd/9th century writer simply arose from the desire to make himself clearly understood and to give ordinary prose the symmetry of verse; though difficult to render and appreciate in a foreign language, the flow of his sentences is perfectly harmonious and instantly recognizable. Nevertheless, for the majority of literate Arabs al-Djāḥiẓ remains, if not a complete buffoon, at least something of a jester; his place as such in legend can undoubtedly be attributed in part to his fame and his ugliness, which made him the hero of numerous anecdotes; but it must also be attributed to a characteristic of his writing which could not but earn him the reputation of being a joker in a Muslim world inclined towards soberness and gravity; for he never fails, even in his weightiest passages, to slip in anecdotes, witty observations and amusing comments. Alarmed at the dullness and boredom enshrouding the speculations of a good many of his contemporaries, he deliberately aimed at a lighter touch and his sense of humour enabled him to deal entertainingly with serious subjects and help popularize them. But he realized he was doing something rather shocking and one cannot help being struck by the frequency with which he feels it necessary to plead the cause of humour and fun; the best example is in *K. al-Tarbīʿ wa 'l-tadwīr* (ed. Pellat, Damascus 1955) a masterpiece of ironic writing, as well as a compendium of all the questions to which his contemporaries whether through force of habit, imitative instinct or lack of imagination offered traditional solutions or gave no thought at all. Without stepping outside the boundaries of the faith—this itself was something of a strain—he takes for granted the right to submit to scrutiny accepted attitudes to natural phenomena, ancient history and legends handed down as truths, to restate problems and skilfully suggest rational solutions. Nor is that all; for at a time when mediaeval Arabic culture was taking shape, he brought together what seemed of most value to him, drawing either on the Arab heritage, of which he was a passionate defender, or on Greek thought, always careful however to curb the intrusion of the Persian tradition, which he considered too dangerous for the future of Islam, into the culture he longed to bestow on his co-religionists. This vast undertaking, based on the spirit of criticism and systematic doubt in everything not directly concerned with the dogma of Islam, was unfortunately to be to a considerable extent narrowed and side-tracked in the centuries to follow. It is true that al-Djāḥiẓ was to have admirers as noteworthy as Abū Ḥayyān al-Tawḥīdī, imitators and even counterfeiters, who made use of his name to ensure greater success for their works; but posterity has only kept a deformed and shrunken image of him, seeing him at the most as a master of rhetoric (see Pellat, in *al-And.*, 1956/2, 277-84), the founder of a Muʿtazilī school—whose disciples no one bothers to enumerate—and the author of compilations to be drawn upon for the elaboration of works of *adab*, a sizeable share of recorded information on *djāhiliyya* and the early centuries of Islam.

Bibliography: The main biographies are those of Khaṭīb Baghdādī, xii, 212-22; Ibn ʿAsākir, in *MMIA*, ix, 203-17; Yāḳūt, *Irshād*, vi, 56-80. A general outline is to be found in manuals of Arabic literature, as also in: Sh. Djabrī, *al-Djāḥiẓ muʿallim al-ʿaḳl wa 'l-adab*, Cairo 1351/1932; Kh. Mardam, *al-Djāḥiẓ*, Damascus 1349/1930; Ṭ. Kayyālī, *al-Djāḥiẓ*, [Damascus] n.d.; Ḥ. Fākhūrī, *al-Djāḥiẓ*, Cairo [1953]; M. Kurd ʿAlī, *Umarāʾ al-bayān*, Cairo 1355/1937; Ḥ. Sandūbī, *Adab al-Djāḥiẓ*, Cairo 1350/1931; Ch. Pellat, *Le Milieu basrien et la formation de Ǧāḥiẓ*, Paris 1953; idem, *Ǧāḥiẓ à Bagdād et à Sāmarrā*, in *RSO*, 1952, 47-67; idem, *Ǧāḥiziana* in *Arabica*, 1954/2, 1955/3 and mainly 1956/2: *Essai d'inventaire de l'œuvre ǧāḥizienne*, with an account of mss, editions and translations (one should add to the bibliography: A. J. Arberry, *New material on the Kitāb al-Fihrist of Ibn al-Nadīm*, in *Isl. Research Assoc. Miscellany*, i, 1948, which gives the notice from *Fihrist* on Djāḥiẓ, missing in the editions; and also: F. Gabrieli, in *Scritti in onore di G. Furlani*, Rome 1957, on the *R. fī manāḳib al-Turk*; the Tunisian review *al-Fikr*, Oct. 1957 and March 1958, on the *R. al-Ḳiyān*); J. Jabre, *al-Djāḥiẓ et la société de son temps* (in Arabic, Beirut 1957 (?), not consulted here). It should be pointed out that in addition to the editions quoted in the course of the article, the following collections have been published: G. van Vloten, *Tria opuscula*, Leyden 1903; J. Finkel, *Three essays*, Cairo 1926; P. Kraus and M. T. Ḥādjirī, *Madjmūʿ rasāʾil al-Djāḥiẓ*, Cairo 1943 (a French translation of these texts is being prepared); Ḥ. Sandūbī, *Rasāʾil al-Djāḥiẓ*, Cairo 1352/1933; *Iḥdā ʿashrata risāla*, Cairo 1324/1906; O. Rescher, *Excerpte und Übersetzungen aus den Schriften des ... Ǧāḥiẓ*, Stuttgart 1931 (analytical translation of a good many texts). The texts in the three manuscript collections: Dāmād Ibrāhīm Pasha 949; Br. Mus. 1129 and Berlin 5032 (see *Oriens*, 1954, 85-6) have in a good many cases been published; those not yet published, along with some other texts of less importance, will be included in our *Nuṣūṣ Ǧāḥiẓiyya ghayr manshūra*. *K. al-ʿUrdjān*, etc. has been recently discovered in Morocco, but is of no great interest. (CH. PELLAT)

DJAHLĀWĀN (from Balōčī *djahla* "below" or "southern"), district of Pakistani Balōčistān, lying below Sarawān. Formerly part of the Khānate of Kalāt and one of the two great divisions of the

Brahōīs (or Brahūī). Area, 21,128 sq. miles, population unknown, estimated 100,000. The capital is Khuzdār and the population is mainly Brahōī with a few Balōč and Lōrīs. It is mainly a grazing country.

Bibliography: *Baluchistan Gazeteer*, vi, B, Bombay 1907; M. G. Pikulin, *Beludzhi*, Moscow 1959. (R. N. FRYE)

DJAHM B. **ṢAFWĀN**, ABU MUḤRIZ, early theologian, sometimes called al-Tirmidhī or al-Samarḳandī. He was a client of Rāsib (a *baṭn* of Azd) and appears as secretary to al-Ḥārith b. Suraydj, "the man with the black banner" who revolted against the Umayyads and from 116/734 to 128/746 controlled tracts of eastern Khurāsān, sometimes in alliance with Turks. Djahm was captured and executed in 128/746, shortly before al-Ḥārith himself. The basis of this movement of revolt, of which Djahm was intellectual protagonist, was the demand that government should be in accordance with "the Book of God and the Sunna of His Prophet" (al-Ṭabarī, ii, 1570 f., 1577, 1583, etc.); and the movement is therefore reckoned to the Murdji'a (al-Nawbakhtī, *Firaḳ al-Shī'a*, 6). Nothing further can be said with certainty about Djahm's own views, except that he argued for the existence of God against the Indian sect of Sumaniyya (Aḥmad b. Ḥanbal, *Radd 'alā 'l-Djahmiyya*, in *Dār ül-Fünūn Ilāhiyyāt Fakültesi Medjmū'asī*, v-vi (1927), 313-27). Other views ascribed to him are those of the sect of Djahmiyya [*q.v.*], which is not heard of until seventy years after his death, and whose connexion with him is obscure. (W. MONTGOMERY WATT)

DJAHMIYYA, an early sect, frequently mentioned but somewhat mysterious.

Identity. No names are known of any members of the sect, apart from the alleged founder Djahm [*q.v.*]. The basic fact is that "after the translation of the Greek books in the second century a doctrine (*maḳāla*) known as that of the Djahmiyya was spread by Bishr b. Ghiyāth al-Marīsī [*q.v.*] and his generation (Ibn Taymiyya, *'Aḳīda Ḥamawiyya*, *ap.* M. Schreiner in *ZDMG*, liii, 72 f.; lii, 544). A pupil of Abū Yūsuf (d. 182/798), Bishr (d. 218/833 or a little later) was questioned about his strange views under Ibrāhīm b. al-Mahdī (c. 202/817) (Ibn Abi 'l-Wafā', *al-Djawāhir al-muḍī'a*, i, nos. 1146, 371). Apart from this the early references to the Djahmiyya are by opponents, notably Aḥmad b. Ḥanbal (*al-Radd 'alā 'l-Zanādiḳa wa 'l-Djahmiyya*) and men of similar outlook, *e.g.*, Ibn Ḳutayba (*al-Ikhtilāf fi 'l-lafẓ wa 'l-radd 'alā 'l-Djahmiyya wa 'l-Mushabbiha*), al-Ash'arī (esp. *Ibāna*), Khushaysh (in al-Malaṭī, *Tanbīh*), Ibn Khuzayma (*K. al-Tawḥīd*); cf. *ZDMG*, liii, 73; Brockelmann, S I, 281 (p), 310 (3a); Ibn Radjab al-Baghdādī, *Histoire des Ḥanbalites*, Damascus 1951, i, 38, 40; W. M. Patton, *Aḥmed b. Ḥanbal and the Miḥna*, Leiden 1897, 37 f., 48. Aḥmad considered a Djahmī one who said the speaking (*lafẓ*) of the Ḳur'ān was created or who denied God's knowledge (H. Laoust, *Essai sur .... Aḥmad b. Taimīya*, 172, 261; Nu'aym b. Ḥammād, who died in prison about 231/846 when he denied the Ḳur'ān was created, said he had earlier been a Djahmī, Ibn 'Asākir, *Tabyīn kadhib al-muftarī*, 383 f.) and he attributed the growth of the sect to followers of Abū Ḥanīfa and 'Amr b. 'Ubayd in Baṣra (*Radd*, 315). Thus the Ḥanbalites in attacking the Djahmiyya may have been thinking of men usually reckoned as Mu'tazila (cf. H. Laoust, *Profession de Foi d'Ibn Baṭṭa*, 167-9). There is in fact a close similarity between the views of the Djahmiyya and those of a Mu'tazilī like Abu 'l-Hudhayl (cf. S. Pines, *Beiträge zur islamischen Atomenlehre*, 124-33). In course of time the Mu'tazila disacknowledged those who, while agreeing with them in many points, differed in the doctrine of *ḳadar* or 'free will' (al-Khayyāṭ, *Intiṣār*, 133 f.) and tried to minimize the resemblances between themselves and the Djahmiyya (*ibid.* 12). There is also criticism of the Djahmiyya by followers of Abū Ḥanīfa, probably prior to the advent of Bishr al-Marīsī (*al-Fiḳh al-akbar* I, § 10, *ap.* Wensinck, *Muslim creed*, 104; Ibn Abi 'l-Wafā, *op. cit.*, i, nos. 23, 61); but the Māturīdite author of *Sharḥ al-Fiḳh al-akbar* seems embarrassed by the reference in § 10, and brackets the Djahmiyya with the Ḳadariyya and Mu'tazila (19; cf. 30). Al-Baghdādī (*Farḳ*, 200; translation by A. S. Halkin, 14) says there were Djahmiyya in Tirmidh in his own time, some of whom became Ash'arites.

Doctrines. They held an extreme form of the doctrine of *djabr*, according to which men acted only metaphorically, as the sun "acts" in setting. They held the Ḳur'ān was created. They denied that God had a distinct eternal attribute of knowledge, considering that his knowledge of temporal events followed the occurrence of the event. More generally they denied the distinct existence of all God's attributies, and were therefore accused of *ta'ṭīl* (making God a bare unity) and called Mu'aṭṭila. For attributes of God, such as hand and face, occurring in the Ḳur'ān, they had a rational interpretation (*ta'wīl*). On the question of faith their views were a form of those of the Murdji'a.

Bibliography: al-Ash'arī, *Maḳālāt*, i, 279 f., with further references; Massignon, *Passion*, see Index; Montgomery Watt, *Free will and predestination*, London 1948, 99-104; 'Abdus Subhan, in *IC*, xi (1937), 221-7; A. S. Tritton, *Muslim theology*, London 1947, 62 f., with further references; Aḥmad b. Ḥanbal, *al-Radd 'alā 'l-Zanādiḳa wa 'l-Djahmiyya*, Cairo n.d., and *Dār ül-Fünūn Ilāhiyyāt Fakültesi Medjmū'asī*, v-vi (1927), 313-27; al-Dārimī (d. 282/895), *Kitāb al-Radd 'alā 'l-Djahmiyya*, ed. G. Vitestam (with introduction and commentary) Lund and Leiden 1960.

(W. MONTGOMERY WATT)

AL-**DJAHSHIYĀRĪ**, ABŪ 'ABD ALLĀH MUḤAMMAD B. 'ABDŪS, a scholar born in al-Kūfa, who played a political rôle at the beginning of the 4th/10th century on account of his relations with the viziers of the time. He succeeded his father in the office of *ḥādjib* to the vizier 'Alī b. 'Īsā, of whose personal guard he was in command in 306/912. Later, he is found among the supporters of Ibn Muḳla whom he helped to be proclaimed vizier and whom he concealed after his fall; several times he was imprisoned and fined, either by the viziers or by the amīrs Ibn Rā'iḳ and Badjkam. He died in 331/942.

Al-Djahshiyārī is principally known as the author of a *Kitāb al-wuzarā' wa 'l-kuttāb* which traced the history of the Secretaries of State and viziers until 296/908; only the first part, stopping at the beginning of al-Ma'mūn's caliphate, has been preserved for us intact. This work, which reveals the true spirit of inquiry of a chronicler as well as an undeniable taste for *adab*, lays quite as much emphasis upon men's characters and intellectual qualities as upon their administrative or political activities. Al-Djahshiyārī also wrote a voluminous chronicle of al-Muḳtadir's caliphate, from which certain passages are thought to have been recovered, and a collection of stories (*asmār*) which seems to be lost despite the opinion of those who would like to attribute to al-Djahshiyārī the *K. al-Ḥikāyāt al-ʿadjiba*, an anonymous work published recently (see *Arabica*, iv, 1957, 214).

Bibliography: on his life, see M. Canard, *Akhbâr ar-Râḍî billâh*, Algiers 1946, i, 143 n. 3; J. Latz, *Das Buch der Wezire und Staatssekretäre von Ibn ʿAbdūs al-Ğahšiyārī, Anfänge und Umaiyadenzeit*, Walldorf-Hessen 1958, 3-6; D. Sourdel, *Le vizirat ʿabbāside*, Damascus 1959-60, index; Ibn Khallikān, ed. Cairo 1948, vi, 23. On his writings, see *GAL*, S I, 219-20; in addition to the facsimile edition of the *Kitāb al-wuzarāʾ* by H. von Mžik (Leipzig 1926), the edition by Muṣṭafā al-Saḳḳāʾ, etc., which appeared in Cairo in 1357/1938, should be added; the pages devoted to the beginnings and the Umayyad period have been translated into German by J. Latz (*supra*); the character of the work has been studied by D. Sourdel, *La valeur littéraire et documentaire du "Livre des Vizirs" d'al- Ğahšiyārī*, in *Arabica*, ii, 1955, 193-210; the surviving fragments of the second part have been published or recorded by Mikhāʾīl ʿAwwād, in *MMIA*, xviii, 1943, 318-32 and 435-42, and D. Sourdel, *Mélanges L. Massignon*, iii, Damascus 1957, 271-99. On the *Akhbār al-Muḳtadir*, see D. Sourdel, *Mélanges L. Massignon*, iii, 271 n. 2. (D. Sourdel)

DJAHWARIDS. The terrible conflict brought about by the fall of the Umayyad Caliphate led the Cordovans, under the direction and advice of the influential and respected vizier Abū Ḥazm Djahwar b. Muxammad b. Djahwar, to declare incapable and expel from the city all the members of the imperial family. They proclaimed a form of republic (422/1031) at the head of which they placed the vizier, who had already demonstrated his great political talents at the court of Hishām II. Once elected, however, he refused to assume all the reigns of power, and formed a democratic government which administered all public affairs. He himself claimed to be no more than the executor of the Council's decisions on behalf of the people. Order and calm were restored at Cordova, the vizier earned the respect of the petty Berber kings in the neighbouring areas, and even the Banū ʿAbbād of Seville learned to leave him in peace. Trade took on a new lease of life, prices came down, and the ruins were repaired. His paternal government lasted for 12 years until his death in 435/1043. His son Abu 'l-Walīd Muḥammad, called al-Rashīd, succeeded him. Without assuming the title of Sultan, he followed the line of conduct established by his father. In order to avoid a rupture with al-Muʿtaḍid of Seville, he recognized the deceitful farce of Hishām II, and intervened as a mediator in the war between al-Muʿtaḍid and Ibn al-Afṭas of Badajoz. But he was not of the same mettle as his father, and, lacking the energy to command, he delegated the administration of his small state to his vizier Ibn al-Raḳā, who became the virtual sovereign of Cordova. He earned the hatred of Muḥammad's younger son, ʿAbd al-Malik, who, drawn into the intrigues of al-Muʿtaḍid, treacherously assassinated the vizier in Muḥarram 450/March 1058. Far from punishing him for the deed, his father appointed him crown prince, giving him a free hand in governing and the right to use Caliphate titles. The Cordovans rapidly developed a strong dislike for him on account of his illegal dealings. Whereas al-Muʿtaḍid dethroned the *reyes de taifas* of the south, ʿAbd al-Malik continued his arbitrary rule. In 461/1069, when al-Muʿtadid and the vizier Ibn Raḳā were dead, Ibn al-Afṭas saw his chance to seize Cordova, and ʿAbd al-Malik summoned the assistance of al-Muʿtamid. The latter sent a cavalry detachment of 1300 men, and they raised the siege set by Ibn al-Afṭas. But the Cordovans allowed al-Muʿtamid's generals to capture ʿAbd al-Malik and his aged father who had ruled for 25$^1/_2$ years, and they were both exiled to the island of Saltis, off Huelva, where the Odiel flows into the sea.

Bibliography: The main source is Ibn Ḥayyān, which is used by Ibn Bassām, *Dhakhīra*, i/2, 114, i/4, 182; Dozy, *Scriptorum arabum loci de Abbadidis*, Leiden 1846; Ibn ʿIdhārī, *Bayān*, iii, ed. Lévi-Provençal, 175-7; Ibn al-Khaṭīb, *Aʿmāl al-aʿlām*, ed. Lévi-Provençal, 168. (A. Huici-Miranda)

DJAḤẒA, Abu 'l-Ḥasan Aḥmad b. Djaʿfar b. Mūsā b. Yaḥyā al-Barmakī al-Nadīm (and also al-Ṭunbūrī, because he played the *tunbūr*, lute (Fr.: "pandore")). A philologist and transmitter of traditions, singer and musician, poet and wit and a descendant of the Barmakids. He was reputedly born in 224/839, and died at the age of a hundred, at Wāsiṭ in Shaʿbān 324/June-July 936. A man of very varied culture, but little religion, of doubtful morals and repulsive appearance (he was dirty and ugly, and owed his last name to a malformation of his bulging eyes), he is the hero of numerous stories—in which nonetheless he is shown as keeping the company of persons in high society: Ibn al-Muʿtazz (who apparently gave him his last name), al-Ḥasan b. Makhlad, Ibn Muḳla, Ibn Rāʾiḳ. Apart from the *Amālī* and a *dīwān*—what remains of the latter is mainly incidental writings—he has left a series of works enumerated by the *Fihrist* (208), about the kitchen, lute-players, astrology, and the life of al-Muʿtamid (*K. mā shāhada-hu min amr al-Muʿtamid*).

Bibliography: M. Canard, *Akhbâr ar-Râḍî billâh*, etc., i, 1440, note (biographical note and references); Bouvat, *Barmécides*, 104-5; Masʿūdī, *Murūdj*, viii, 261-2; *Aghānī*, index; Khaṭīb Baghdādī, iv, 65; Ibn Khallikān, i, 41; Thaʿālibī, *Thimār al-ḳulūb*, 183; Ibn Hadjar, *Lisān al-mīzān*, i, 146; Yāḳūt, *Muʿdjam al-udabāʾ*, ii, 241-82. (Ch. Pellat)

DJĀʾIZ, a term used in a general way to denote permissible acts, that is to say acts which are not contrary to a rule of the law. However, in the classical division of acts into five categories (*al-aḥkām al-khamsa*; cf. *Dict. Tech. Terms*, i, 379 ff.; I. Goldziher, *Die Ẓāhiriten*, 66 ff.; Juynboll, *Handbuch*, 59 ff.) adopted by the writers on *uṣūl* [*q.v.*] the permissible act is generally described as *mubāḥ*. It is thus quite as clearly differentiated from the act which is obligatory (*wādjib*) or merely recommended (*mandūb*), as from that which is forbidden (*ḥarām*) or simply considered reprehensible (*makrūh*).

In writings on *furūʿ*, that is to say of the Muslim jurisconsults, the term *djāʾiz* assumes a different significance. The juridical act which is not completely null and void (*bāṭil*) or merely defective (*fāsid*)—according to the Ḥanafīs—is regarded as *ṣaḥīḥ*, that is to say valid. It is the act carried out in conformity with the prescriptions of the law, and it must in principle produce all its effects. A valid act of this kind is certainly *djāʾiz*, or permissible; but the correct term to denote it is *ṣaḥīḥ*.

Ḥanafī authors, however, preferred to use the term *djāʾiz*, not to denote a valid act but, in particular, to specify that the act was legitimate or licit, in point of law. In their works, the study of each contract under consideration generally begins with a preamble in which the writer is at pains to state that the contract is *dj̲āʾiz* by reason of some text, or custom, or *omnium consensus*, or simply its practical usefulness (Chafik Chehata, *Théorie générale de l'obligation en droit musulman*, i, 105, no. 117). This is true of the contract of hire (Kāsānī, *Badāʾiʿ*, iv, 174); of guarantee (ibid., vi, 3); and of deposit (Sarak̲h̲sī, *Mabsūṭ*, xi, 108). In all these texts the writer raises the question whether the contract is or is not *dj̲āʾiz*, quite apart from the fact that it can be valid or not, according to whether the conditions of its conclusion or validity have or have not been fulfilled. Thus, with regard to the contract of *locatio operis* (*istiṣnāʿ*), the conditions of legality are made clear, independently of conditions of conclusion (*inʿiḳād*), validity (*ṣiḥḥa*), irrevocability (*luzūm*) or efficacity (*nafād̲h̲*) (Kāsānī, v, 209). Sometimes the term *mas̲h̲rūʿ* is used in place of *dj̲āʾiz*, as for example in the contract of crop-sharing (*muzāraʿa*) (Kāsānī, vi, 175); and in the contract of association (ibid., v, 220). In fact the *dj̲āʾiz* act is, correctly, the lawful act, *mas̲h̲rūʿ* in point of law. But lawful must here be understood in a special sense. It is not a question of the legality of the object or cause of the contract, but rather of the act considered in itself, as to how far it is sanctioned by law. And thus, in the final analysis, the term *dj̲āʾiz* as used by jurisconsults in writings on *furūʿ* by indirect means comes to approximate the term *mubāḥ* which is found in works on *uṣūl*, in the writings of *fiḳh* logicians.

Furthermore the term *dj̲āʾiz*, taken in the sense of *mas̲h̲rūʿ*, goes beyond the limits of juridical acts. It underlies the theory of criminal responsibility, since it is established that a lawful act cannot give rise to damages (*al-dj̲awāz al-s̲h̲arʿī yunāfī 'l-ḍamān*). Here again, by lawful act we must understand an act permitted by law, however prejudicial.

Certain authors, however, including Ḥanafīs, use the term to denote a valid contract. Thus for Ḳudūrī a contract vitiated by risk is looked upon as illegal (Ḳudūrī, *Muk̲h̲taṣar*, 60), in the same way as a contract whose object is illegal (ibid., 54). In both these texts the writer specifies that the contract is not *dj̲āʾiz*.

Finally it must be stated that, in non-Hanafī writers, the term *dj̲āʾiz* has assumed an entirely unexpected significance. In effect, in Mālikī as well as S̲h̲āfiʿī and Ḥanbalī writings, the contract is said to be *dj̲āʾiz* when it is revocable. (For the Mālikīs, see Ḳarāfī, *Furūḳ*, iv, 13; for the S̲h̲āfiʿīs, Suyūṭī, *As̲h̲bāh*, 141; for the Ḥanbalīs, Ibn Ḳudāma, iv, 119). Thus it is that the contract can be *dj̲āʾiz* for one of the parties, that is to say revocable by him, and not *dj̲āʾiz*, or irrevocable, for the other—just as it can be *dj̲āʾiz* for both, that is to say revocable by both parties (al-Aʿlawī, *Bug̲h̲yat al-mustars̲h̲idīn*, 112).

In logic, *dj̲āʾiz* means what is not unthinkable, whether it be necessary, probable, improbable, or possible (*Dict. Tech. Terms*, i, 207 ff.)

Bibliography: the works on *uṣūl*, e.g. al-Taftāzānī, *al-Talwīḥ*, 1304 H.; Chafik Chehata, *Théorie générale de l'obligation en droit musulman hanifite*, i, Cairo 1936; J. Schacht, *G. Bergstrasser's Grundzüge des islamischen Rechts*, 31-3; al-Kāsānī, *Badāʾiʿ al-Ṣanāʾiʿ*, Cairo 1327; al-Sarak̲h̲sī, *al-Mabsūṭ*, Cairo 1324. (CHAFIK CHEHATA)

DJ̲ĀʾIZA [see ṢILA].

DJ̲AKARTA, town on the north coast of Java, a few miles to the east of 107° E. Long. The name is believed to be the abbreviated form of Djajakarta, 'Victorious and Prosperous'; in its turn it was corrupted into Jakatra (Jacatra) by the first Dutch visitors (1610). Judging by the name, we may suppose old Djakarta to have been the residence of a more or less independent king who was Javanese by descent or by culture. The Dutch settlement was given the name Batavia, from Batavi, one of the Latin names for the Netherlanders; Jan P. Coen, local representative of the Dutch Chartered Company, decided to establish his headquarters here in 1619. In 1628 and 1629 Batavia was heavily attacked by Anjakrakusuma alias Sultan Agung, king of Mataram. The narrow escape was followed by a long period of peace and prosperity which made the Indonesians use the expression *untung Betawi*, 'Batavian luck'. Several stories were invented to explain that luck, the most interesting being the one which Cohen Stuart published in 1850 (*Geschiedenis van Baron Sakéndhèr*, Batavia); it says that Jan P. Coen was the son of a Javanese princess with a flaming womb who had been given in marriage to Sukmul, twin-brother of Sekèndèr (Iskandar D̲h̲u 'l-Ḳarnayn, Alexander the Great).

The town was the seat of a Dutch Governor-General from 1619 to 1942, with a British interregnum from 1811 to 1816. As such it developed into an international centre of trade, and within the Indonesian Archipelago into a centre of administration. Under the Chartered Company (1619-1799) it attracted a multitude of merchants, from various parts of Indonesia as well as from various foreign countries (China, India, Arabia). Especially in the second half of the existence of the Netherlands Indies (1800-1942) Batavia was the gateway for various kinds of missionary activities, in the field of religion as well as in the field of school education. Both factors—commerce and propaganda—have contributed to the cosmopolitan character of the town; it may be true that the majority of the Indonesian population is Muslim, it is as true that the town does not owe its importance, character and function to the Muslims as such.

From the view-point of Islamology it deserves attention that Batavia was an observation-post for the study of Muslim life ever since it came into existence as an Indonesian town under Dutch rule. When Snouck Hurgronje was appointed adviser to the Colonial Government for Muslim and native affairs (1889) his office in Batavia became a centre for theoretical and applied Islamology. The Batavian Faculty of Law, founded in 1924, had a chair for Muslim law and Islamology from the very beginning. This is why Indonesian Islam, in many respects different from the type of Islam which one finds in Egypt and similar countries, is fairly well known. See DJ̲ĀWĪ, INDONESIA, JAVA, SUMATRA.

Batavia became Djakarta once more in 1942, when the Japanese conquered Indonesia and put an end to the colonial empire of the Dutch. The Indonesian Republic, proclaimed in 1945 and recognized by the Dutch in 1949, maintained Djakarta as its capital. The town which counted a population of approximately 400,000 people in 1940, is rapidly growing. It still has a cosmopolitan character, though its present function might detract from this character in a near future. (C. C. BERG)

DJ̲AKAT [see ZAKĀT].

DJ̲AʿL [see TAZYĪF].

DJ̲ALĀʾIR, DJ̲ALĀʾIRID [see DJ̲ALĀYIR, DJ̲ALĀYIRID].

DJ̲ALĀL AL-DAWLA, honorific title of various princes, notably the Būyid (see below), the G̲h̲aznawid Muḥammad [*q.v.*], and the Mirdāsid Naṣr [*q.v.*].

DJALĀL AL-DAWLA, ABŪ ṬĀHIR B. BAHĀʾ AL-DAWLA, a Būyid, born in 383/993-4. When Sulṭān al-Dawla, after the death of his father Bahāʾ al-Dawla in 403/1012, was named *amīr al-umarāʾ*, he entrusted his brother Djalāl al-Dawla with the office of governor of Baṣra. The latter stayed there for several years without becoming involved in the private quarrels of the Būyids. In 415/1024-5 Sulṭān al-Dawla died and his brother Musharrif al-Dawla died in the following year. Djalāl al-Dawla was then proclaimed *amīr al-umarāʾ*, but, as he did not appear at Baghdād to take possession of his new dignity, an invitation was given instead to Abū Kālīdjār, son of Sulṭān al-Dawla, who was also unable to accept the office. When Djalāl al-Dawla heard that he was no longer named in public prayers he marched on Baghdād with an army, but was defeated and had to retreat to Baṣra. However, in Ramaḍān 418/October 1027 he entered the capital at the request of the Turks who were unable to keep on good terms with the population of Baghdād and were afraid of the influence of the Arabs. But friendly relations with the Turks were short-lived. In the following year an insurrection broke out in Baghdād, and Djalāl al-Dawla restored order only with difficulty. At the same time Abū Kālīdjār took possession of Baṣra without striking a blow and in 420/1029 succeeded in capturing Wāsiṭ. As Djalāl al-Dawla was preparing an expedition against Ahwāz, Abū Kālīdjār wanted to start peace negotiations; but Djalāl al-Dawla preferred to sack Ahwāz, and took prisoner the women of Abū Kālīdjār's family. At the end of Rābīʿ I 421/April 1030 the latter marched against Djalāl al-Dawla but was defeated after a three days' battle and had to flee, while the victor first took Wāsiṭ and then entered Baghdād. Baṣra was also conquered, but Abū Kālīdjār's troops soon reoccupied it, though in Shawwāl/October of the same year they suffered a further defeat near al-Madhār. In the capital, the insubordination of the Turkish mercenaries increased constantly, and the *amīr al-umarāʾ* soon lost the last vestiges of his authority. In 423/1032 Djalāl al-Dawla's palace was sacked, and he was obliged to leave the town and flee to ʿUkbarā, while Abū Kālīdjār was proclaimed *amīr al-umarāʾ* by the Turks in Baghdād. Abū Kālīdjār then came to Ahwāz and, as the amīrate held no particular attraction for him, Djalāl al-Dawla was able, after about six weeks, to return to his capital where, however, the situation was steadily worsening. In the following year his palace was once again attacked and pillaged, and for the second time the Būyid, who from now on was completely powerless, was forced to take to flight. This time he went to al-Karkh where he was protected by the Shīʿīs, remaining there until the rebels called him back to Baghdād. In the same year the governor of Baṣra, Abu 'l-Ḳāsim, revolted against Abū Kālīdjār who was intending to depose him, and called in Djalāl al-Dawla's son al-ʿAzīz to Baṣra. But in 425/1033-4 al-ʿAzīz was driven out, and the population again took an oath of loyalty to Abū Kālīdjār. During this period complete anarchy dominated the capital and in 427/1035-6 a new revolt broke out in the army which however was brought back to loyalty by the caliph's intervention. In 428/1036-7 Barsṭoghan, who was one of the most powerful Turkish leaders in Baghdād and whose position was threatened, called on Abū Kālīdjār for assistance. Once more Djalāl al-Dawla was driven out of Baghdād but, after being helped by Ḳirwāsh b. al-Muḳallid of Mawṣil and Dubays b. ʿAlī of Ḥilla, while the Daylamites broke away from the Turks in Baghdād, he was soon able to expel Barsṭoghan and occupy the capital. Barsṭoghan was taken prisoner and put to death, and Abū Kālīdjār at last made peace with Djalāl al-Dawla. The final reconciliation was sealed by the marriage of one of Djalāl's daughters with Abū Manṣūr, Abū Kālīdjār's son. On this occasion Djalāl al-Dawla took the ancient Persian title "king of kings", which in fact was far from justified by his own lack of authority and the general anarchy. In 431/1039-40 or, according to others, in 432/1040-1, he had to face a further Turkish revolt in the capital. Djalāl al-Dawla died on 6 Shaʿbān 435/9 March 1044, leaving the Būyid kingdom in a state of the deepest degradation.

Bibliography: see BUWAYHIDS.

(K. V. ZETTERSTÉEN)

SHARĪF **DJALĀL AL-DĪN AḤSAN,** d. 740/1339, first Sultan of Madura [*q.v.*]. A native of Kaythal in the Pandjāb, he is known from a well-inscription (cf. B. D. Verma, in *Epigraphia Indica, Arabic and Persian Supplement, 1955-6*, 109 ff.) to have been *nāʾib-i iḳṭāʿ* in the province of Maʿbar [*q.v.*] in 725/1324; later he was appointed governor by Muḥammad b. Tughluḳ (or, according to ʿIṣāmī, *Futūḥ al-Salāṭīn*, 449, was *kotwāl* [*q.v.*] at Madura and usurped the government), but shortly after this, in 735/1335, he proclaimed his independence under the title of Djalāl al-(Dunyā wa 'l)-Dīn Aḥsan Shāh at Madura, the old Pāndya capital, where he struck coin. Muḥammad's march south to crush the rebel was prevented by an outbreak of cholera at Warangal, which decimated his army, and the Dihlī sultan had no further opportunity of regaining his lost province. Djalāl al-Dīn was killed in 740/1339 by one of his officers who seized the throne as ʿAlāʾ al-Dīn Udawdjī Shāh; thus although he was the first independent sultan of Madura he founded no dynasty. One of his daughters, however, married the fourth sultan, and another daughter, Ḥūrnasab, married the traveller Ibn Baṭṭūṭa, who spent some time at the Madura court, and to whom much of the scanty knowledge of this small sultanate is due.

Djalāl al-Dīn is erroneously called Sayyid Ḥasan by Ḍiyāʾ al-Dīn Baranī (Eng. tr. Elliot and Dowson, *History of India* . . ., iii, 243) and Firishta (Eng. tr. Briggs, i, 423).

Bibliography: Ibn Baṭṭūṭa, iii, 328, 337-8; iv, 187 ff., 189, 190, 200; H. von Mžik, *Die Reise des Arabers Ibn Baṭūṭa durch Indien und China (14 Jhdt.)*, Hamburg 1911, 170 ff. and note; C. J. Rodgers, *Coins of the Musulmān kings of Maʿbar*, in *JASB*, lxiv/1, 49; E. Hultzsch, *The coinage of the sultans of Madura*, in *JRAS*, 1909, 667-83.

(J. BURTON-PAGE)

DJALĀL AL-DĪN ʿĀRIF (Celâleddin Ârif), Turkish lawyer and statesman, was born in Erzurum on 19 October 1875, the son of Meḥmed ʿĀrif, a writer of some repute. He received his education at the military *rüshdiyye* in Çeşme and the *Mekteb-i Sulṭānī* at Galatasaray (Istanbul), where he graduated in 1895. He studied law in Paris and began to practise it in Egypt in 1901. He returned to Turkey after the 1908 revolution and joined the Ottoman Liberal (*Aḥrār*) Party, the first group of this period to oppose the centralizing tendencies of the Union and Progress movement in the name of multinational equality within the Empire. He became a lecturer at the Istanbul Law School and president of the Istanbul Bar Association (1914-20). In 1919 he acted as defence counsel in the trial of the wartime Union and Progress cabinet. In the last

Ottoman Chamber of Deputies (*medjlis-i mebʿūthān*) he served as deputy for Erzurum, temporary presiding officer, and co-founder of the Nationalist *Felāḥ-i Waṭan* group; upon the death of Reshād Ḥikmet, he was elected (4 March 1920) President of the Chamber. Two weeks later, after the reinforced occupation of the capital and the adjournment *sine die* of the Chamber, he led the flight of deputies to Ankara, where he urged his colleagues to join the Grand National Assembly convened by Muṣṭafā Kemāl [Atatürk]. He became the Assembly's Second President (*reʾīs-i thānī*), Minister of Justice in the Ankara government (April 1920 to January 1921 and July to August 1922), and its diplomatic representative in Rome (1921-3). His differences with Kemāl became apparent as early as the autumn of 1920 during an extended stay in his native Erzurum. A proposal that ʿĀrif be appointed governor-general over the Eastern wilāyets went unheeded, and he in turn delayed for two months before accepting Kemāl's invitation to return to Ankara. During his brief second tenure as Minister of Justice he was considered one of the parliamentary leaders of the conservative opposition (*ikindji grub*) in the Assembly. After 1923 he retired from political and diplomatic life. He died in Paris on 18 January 1930.

Bibliography: *Istanbul Barosu Mecmuası*, February 1930; *WI*, x, 26-73; xii, 29-35; Hasan Basri Erk, *Meşhur Türk Hukukçuları*, Istanbul 1958, 419; Kemal (Atatürk), *Nutuk*, 1934 edn., i, 302-5, ii, 29-40; Tarık Z. Tunaya, *Türkiye'de Siyasi Partiler*, Istanbul 1952, 239, 539; *Talât Paşanın Hatıraları*, Istanbul 1958, 116-24.

(DANKWART A. RUSTOW)

DJALĀL AL-DĪN ḤUSAYN AL-BUKHĀRĪ, surnamed *Makhdūm-i Djahāniyān Djahāngasht*, one of the early *pīrs* of India, was the son of Sayyid Aḥmad Kabīr whose father Sayyid Djalāl al-Dīn-i Surkh had migrated from Bukhāra to Multān and Bhakkar [*q.v.*]. A descendant of Imām ʿAlī al-Naḳī, his father was a disciple of Rukn al-Dīn Abu 'l-Fatḥ, son and successor of Bahāʾ al-Dīn Zakariyyā [*q.v.*]. Born 707/1308 at Učch, where he also lies buried, he was educated in his home-town and in Multān but seems to have left for the Ḥidjāz at a very young age in search of more knowledge. He is reported to have visited, in the course of his extensive travels which earned him the sobriquet of *Djahāngasht*, Kāzarūn, Egypt, Syria (including Palestine), Mesopotamia, Balkh, Bukhāra and Khurāsān, in addition to Mecca and Medina. The *Safarnāma-i Makhdūm-i Djahāniyān* (Urdū transl. Lahore 1909), purporting to be an account of his travels, is full of supernatural stories and may, therefore, be regarded as apocryphal. A contemporary of ʿAbd Allāh al-Yāfiʿī al-Yamanī, with whom he read *al-Ṣiḥāḥ al-Sitta* in Mecca, and of Ashraf Djahāngīr al-Simnānī [*q.v.*], he received his *khirḳa* from Naṣīr al-Dīn Čirāgh-i Dihlī [*q.v.*]. He was appointed Shaykh al-Islām by Muḥammad b. Tughluḳ and forty *khānaḳāhs* in Sīwastān (modern Sēhwān) and its suburbs were assigned to him; but he left for the Ḥadjdj before taking up the appointment. Fīrūz Shāh Tughluḳ became deeply attached to him after his return, and held him in high esteem. The *shaykh* used to visit the sultan at Delhi every second or third year. He had also accompanied him on his expedition to Thaṭṭā in 764/1362. Fīrūz's religious policy, as outlined in the *Futūḥāt-i Fīrūz Shāhī*, was greatly influenced by the saint. He died on 10 Dhu 'l-Ḥidjdja 785/3 February 1384. Three collections of his *obiter dicta* are known to exist: i) *Khulāṣat al-alfāẓ djāmiʿ al-ʿulūm*, compiled by ʿAlāʾ al-Dīn ʿAlāʾ b. Saʿd al-Ḥasanī in 782/1380 (MS. Riḍāʾ Library, Rampur Urdū transl. "*al-Durr al-manẓūm fī tardjamat talfūẓāt al-Makhdūm*", Anṣārī Press. Dihlī n. d.); ii) *Sirādj al-hidāya*, compiled by ʿAbd Allāh in 787/1385 (MSS. Rampur, Aligarh, I.O.D.P. 1038); and iii) *Khizāna-i Djalālī* (also called *Manaḳib-i Makhdūm-i Djahāniyān*) compiled by Abu 'l-Faḍl b. Ridjāʾ ʿAbbāsī (only an incomplete MS. in A.S.B.). All these collections, especially the *Djāmiʿ al-ʿulūm*, are voluminous, and are written in a miraculous and supernatural strain. Another work based on his teachings is the *Khizānat al-fawāʾid al-Djalāliyya* composed in 752/1351 by Aḥmad Bahāʾ b. Yaʿḳūb (Storey, ii, 945).

Bibliography: Shams-i Sirādj ʿAfīf, *Taʾrīkh-i Fīrūz Shāhī*, Bibl. Ind., 514-6; Djamālī, *Siyar al-ʿārifīn*, Dihlī 1311/1896, 155-8; ʿAbd al-Ḥaḳḳ Muḥaddith Dihlawī, *Akhbār al-akhyār*, Dihlī 1332/1914, 141-3; Firishta, *Gulshan-i Ibrāhīmī*, Bombay 1831-2, ii, 779-84; Muḥ. Ghawthī Māndūwī, *Gulzār-i abrār* (MS.) no. 128; Yūsufī, *Maḥbūbiyya* (MS.) I.O.D.P. 658 (containing anecdotes of S. Djalāl al-Dīn and his descendants); Dārā Shukōh, *Safīnat al-awliyāʾ*, Kānpur 1884, 166; ʿAbd ʾal-Raḥmān Čishtī, *Mirʾat al-asrār* (MS.), ṭabaḳa xxi; Muḥ. Akram Barāsawī, *Sawatiʿ al-anwār*, (*Iḳtibās al-anwār*), Lahore 1895; ʿAbd al-Rashīd Kayrānwī, *Taʾrīkh-i Ḳādiriyya*, (MS.) fol. 47b; Ghulām Sarwar Lāhōrī, *Khazīnat al-aṣfiya*, Kānpur 1914, ii, 57-63; *Laṭāʾif-i ashrafī*, Dihli 1298/1880-1, i, 390-2, ii, 94; ʿAbd al-Ḥayy Nadwī, *Nuzhat al-khawāṭir*, Ḥaydarābād, i, 1350, 28-25; Ṣabāḥ al-Dīn ʿAbd al-Raḥmān, *Bazm-i ṣūfiyya* (in Urdū), Aʿẓamgaṙh 1369/1949, 394-440; ʿAlī Aṣghar Gudjarātī, *Tadhkira Sādat al-Bukhāriyya* (MS.); Riazul Islam, *Collections of the Malfuzat of Makhdum-i Jahanian (1307-1388) of Uchh*, in *Proceedings of the All Pakistan History Conference*, 1951 session, 211-6.

(A. S. BAZMEE ANSARI)

DJALĀL AL-DĪN KHALDJĪ [see DIHLĪ SULTANATE, KHALDJIDS].

DJALĀL AL-DĪN KHʷĀRAZM-SHĀH, the eldest son of Sultan Muḥammad Khʷārazm-Shāh [*q.v.*] and the last ruler of the dynasty. The spelling and pronunciation of his personal name (MNKBRNY) are still uncertain. Such forms as Mangoubirti, Mankobirti, etc., are based upon a derivation first proposed by d'Ohsson, from the Turkish *mengü* in the sense of "Eternal [God]" and *birti* (for *birdi*) "[he] gave"; but this etymology is now discredited. Muḥammad had originally designated his youngest son, Ḳuṭb al-Dīn Uzlagh-Shāh, as his successor, but shortly before his death on an island in the Caspian Sea had altered his will in favour of Djalāl al-Dīn. The princes, who had remained in attendance on their father throughout his flight, now left the island and landing on the Manḳīshlaḳ Peninsula made their way to Gürgāndj [*q.v.*], which they reached some little time before its investment by the Mongols. The discovery of a plot against his life caused Djalāl al-Dīn to leave the capital almost immediately and to make for the territories formerly allotted to him by his father and corresponding more or less to the modern Afghānistān. The Mongols had posted observation parties along the nothern frontiers of Khurasān but Djalāl al-Dīn succeeded in breaking through this cordon and reaching Ghazna, where he found himself at the head of a heterogeneous force of some 60,000 Turks, Khʷārazmīs and Ghūrīs. At Parwān to the north-east of Čarīkār he inflicted upon a Mongol army the only serious defeat that the invaders suffered during the whole campaign. However, deserted on the very battlefield by almost half of his followers he was obliged to retreat southwards pursued by Čingiz-Khān in person at the head of the main Mongol army. He was overtaken on the banks of the Indus and after offering desperate resistance (8 Shawwāl 618/24 November 1221) escaped to safety by riding his horse into the river and swimming to the farther side. After a successful expedition against a petty rādjā in the Salt Range Djalāl took the field against Nāṣir al-Dīn Ḳubača [*q.v.*], the ruler of Sind, and sought in vain to form an alliance with Sultan Shams al-Dīn Iletmish [*q.v.*] of Dihlī. He remained nearly three years in India and then decided to make his way to ʿIrāḳ-i ʿAdjam, where his brother Ghiyāth al-Dīn had now established himself. In 621/1224 he appeared in Kirmān, where Burāḳ Ḥādjib [*q.v.*] had seized power. Djalāl al-Dīn found it expedient to confirm him in his usurped authority before continuing his journey to Fārs, where he stayed only long enough to marry a daughter of the Atabeg Saʿd [*q.v.*], and to ʿIrāḳ-i ʿAdjam, where he was at once successful in dispossessing his brother. The winter of 621-2/1224-5 he passed in Khūzistān, his troops colliding with the forces of the Caliph al-Nāṣir. He then proceeded to attack and overthrow the Atabeg Öz-Beg [*q.v.*] of Ādharbāydjān, whose capital Tabrīz he entered on 17 Radjab 622/25 July 1225. From Ādharbāydjān he invaded the territory of the Georgians capturing Tiflis on Rabīʿ I 623/9 March 1226. Here he received a report that Burāḳ Ḥādjib had risen in revolt, and he travelled, according to Djuwaynī, from the Caucasus to the borders of Kirmān in the space of 17 days. Returning to the west he laid siege, on 15 Dhu 'l-Ḳaʿda 623/7 November 1226, to the town of Akhlāṭ [*q.v.*] in the territory of al-Ashraf [*q.v.*] but was obliged to raise the siege almost immediately owing to the severe cold. In the following year the Mongols reappeared in Central Persia and Djalāl al-Dīn engaged them in a great battle before the gates of Iṣfahān. The result was a Pyrrhic victory for the invaders who at once retreated northwards and had soon withdrawn beyond the Oxus. After another campaign against the Georgians Djalāl al-Dīn again, in Shawwāl 626/August 1229, laid siege to Akhlāṭ. With the fall of the town in Djumādā I 627/April 1230 he found himself involved in war with the combined forces of al-Ashraf and Kay-Ḳubād I [*q.v.*], the Sultan of Rūm. Defeated in the battle of Arzindjān (28 Ramaḍān 627/10 August 1230) he withdrew into Ādharbāydjān and had no sooner concluded peace with his opponents than he was threatened with the approach of new Mongol armies under the command of Čormaghun. A Mongol force overtook him in the Mūghān Steppe and he fled first to Akhlāṭ and then to the vicinity of Āmid. Here the Mongols made a night attack in his encampment (middle of Shawwal 628/17 August 1231): roused from a drunken sleep he made off in the direction of Mayyāfārīḳīn and met his death in a nearby Kurdish village, where he was murdered for reasons either of gain or of revenge. The ruler of Āmid recovered his body and gave it burial, but many refused to believe that he was dead, and time and again, in the years that followed, pretenders would arise claiming to be Sultan Djalāl al-Dīn.

Bibliography: Nasawī, *Histoire du Sultan Djelal ed-Din Mankobirti*, ed. and transl. O. Houdas, 2 vols., Paris 1891-5; Djūzdjānī, *The Ṭabaqāt-i-Nāṣirī*, transl. H. G. Raverty, London 1881; Djuwaynī, *The history of the world-conqueror*, transl. J. A. Boyle, 2 vols., Manchester 1958; Barthold, *Turkestan*; V. Minorsky, *Studies in Caucasian history*, London 1953; H. L. Gottschalk, *Al-Malik al-Kāmil von Egypten und seine Zeit*, Wiesbaden 1958; I. Kafesoğlu, *Harezmşahlar devleti tarihi*, Ankara 1956.
(J. A. Boyle)

DJALĀL AL-DĪN RŪMĪ b. Bahā' al-Dīn Sulṭān al-ʿUlamā' Walad b. Ḥusayn b. Aḥmad Khaṭībī, known by the sobriquet Mawlānā (Mevlânâ), Persian poet and founder of the Mawlawiyya order of dervishes, which was named after him, was born on Rabīʿ I 604/30 September 1207 in Balkh, and died on 5 Djumāda II 672/1273 in Ḳonya. The reasons put forward against the above-mentioned date of birth (Abdülbaki Gölpınarlı, *Mevlânâ Celâleddîn*³, 44; idem, *Mevlânâ Şams-i Tabrîzî ile altmış iki yaşında buluştu*, in *Şarkiyat Mecmuası*, iii, 153-61; and *Bir yazı üzerine*, in *Tarih Coğrafya Dünyası*, ii/12, 1959, 468) are not valid. His father, whose sermons have been preserved and printed (*Maʿārif. Madjmūʿa-i mawāʿiẓ wa sukhanān-i Sulṭān al-ʿulamā' Bahā' al-Dīn Muḥammad b. Ḥusayn-i Khaṭībī-i Balkhī mashhūr ba-Bahā'-i Walad*, ed. Badīʿ al-Zamān Furūzānfarr, Tehran 1333), was a preacher in Balkh. The assertions that his family tree goes back to Abū Bakr, and that his mother was a daughter of the Khwārizmshāh ʿAlā' al-Dīn Muḥammad (Aflākī, i, 8-9) do not hold on closer examination (B. Furūzānfarr, *Mawlānā Djalāl al-Dīn*, Tehrān 1315, 7; ʿAlīnaḳī Sharīʿatmadārī, *Naḳd-i matn-i mathnawī*, in *Yaghmā*, xii (1338), 164; Aḥmad Aflākī, *Ariflerin menkibeleri*, trans. Tahsin Yazıcı, Ankara 1953, i, Önsöz, 44). According to the biographical sources, he left Balkh because of a dispute with the Khwārizmshāh ʿAlā' al-Dīn Muḥammad and his protégé Fakhr al-Dīn al-Rāzī (d. 606/1209-10) and, when his son Djalāl al-Dīn was five years old (Aflākī, ed. Yazıcı, i, 161), *i.e.*, in 609/1212-3, emigrated to the west. In fact the sermons of Bahā' al-Dīn contain attacks on the Khwārizmshāh and the above-named religious philosopher. But according to the same book of sermons, he was in Wakhsh between 600/1203 and 607/1211, and in Samarḳand in 609/1212-3 (Maʿārif. ed. Furūzānfarr, *Muḳaddima*, 37 and *Fīhi mā Fīh*, ed. Furūzānfarr, 173 respectively). He must, however, have returned from Samarḳand to Balkh, as according to the sources the emigration took place from there. The date of 609/1212-3 for the emigration is in any case too early (*Isl.* xxvi, 117 ff.). As according to Aflākī he arrived in Malaṭya only in 614/1217, one may perhaps assume that he emigrated in 614/1217 or the year before. Whether his quarrel with the Khwārizmshāh was connected with the latter's hostile attitude towards the Caliph in Baghdād cannot be settled, but would be possible. In 616/1219 Bahā' al-Dīn was in Sivas, stayed for some four years in Akshehir near Erzindjan, went to Larende, probably in 619/1222, and stayed there for seven years. In Larende there is the tomb of Mawlānā's mother, Mu'mina Khātun (Azmı Avcioğlu, *Karaman'da mader-i Mevlânâ câmi ve türbesi*, in *Konya dergisi*, v, no. 35, 2088). Bahā' al-Dīn married his son in Larende to Djawhar Khātun, the daughter of Sharaf al-Dīn Lālā.

In the year 626/1228, at the request of the Saldjūḳ Prince ʿAlā' al-Dīn Kayḳubad, the family moved to Ḳonya, where Bahā' al-Dīn Walad died on 18 Rabīʿ II 628/1231 (Aflākī, i, 32, 56). A year after his death Sayyid Burhān al-Dīn Muḥaḳḳiḳ, an old pupil of his, came to Ḳonya to visit his former master, but found that he was no longer alive. Djalāl al-Din became a *murīd* of Sayyid Burhān al-Dīn until the latter's death nine years later. Burhān al-Dīn, however, withdrew to Kayseri after some time and died there, probably in 637/1239-40. His tomb is in Kayseri. According to Aflākī, Djalāl al-Dīn went to Aleppo and Damascus after the arrival of the Sayyid to complete his studies. Burhān al-Dīn is supposed to have made him aware that his father possessed, besides exoteric learning, other learning that could be won not through study but through inner experience. After the death of Burhān al-Dīn Djalāl al-Dīn was alone for five years. On 26 Djumādā II 642/1244 the wandering dervish Shams al-Dīn Muḥammad Tabrīzī came to Ḳonya and put up in the *khān* of the sugar-merchants. Djalāl al-Dīn met and talked to him; Shams asked him about the meaning of a saying of Bāyazīd Bisṭāmī, Djalāl al-Dīn gave the answer. According to Aflākī, Djalāl al-Dīn had already seen Shams once in Damascus (Furūzānfar, *Mawlānā*, 65-6). However that may be, the appearance of Shams-i Tabrīzī made a decisive change in the life of Mawlānā. In the Ṣūfī manner he fell in love with the dervish and took him into his home. It will be possible to say something about Shams's remarkable personality only when his collected sayings, the *Maḳālāt*, have been edited. He constantly wore a black cap (*kulāh*) and because of his restless wandering life was called *paranda* "the flier". Although, as his *Maḳālāt* show, he had the usual theological conceptions of his time, he tried to keep Mawlānā away from the study of books. It seems from his sayings that he had a certain bluntness of character. Shams-i Tabrīzī is called in the sources *sulṭān al-maʿshūḳīn*, "prince of the loved ones", and Mawlānā's son Sulṭān Walad, who knew Shams well, and was aware of the relationship Shams had with his father, develops in the *Ibtidānāma* a theory that there is another class of "lovers who have reached the goal" (*ʿāshiḳān-i wāṣil*) besides the "perfect saints" (*awliyāʾ-i kāmil*). Beyond these there is a further stage (*maḳām*), that of the "beloved" (*maʿshūḳ*). Until Shams appeared nobody had heard anything about this stage, and Shams had reached it. Shams showed Mawlānā this way of Ṣūfī love, and Mawlānā had to re-learn everything from him. Mawlānā's love for Shams-i Tabrīzī turned him into a poet, but at the same time caused him to neglect his *murīds* and disregard everyone but Shams. The *murīds* were angered by this and maintained that they were more important than the foreign, unknown dervish and are even said to have threatened Shams's life. Thereupon Shams fled on 21 Shawwāl 643/11 March 1246 to Damascus. But the *murīds* did not achieve their end. Mawlānā was quite disconcerted, and sent his son Sulṭān Walad to Damascus. Shams could not resist the spoken entreaties of Sulṭān Walad and the written poetical entreaties of Mawlānā, and returned on foot with Sulṭān Walad to Konya. But at once the *murīds* began to murmur again and took pains to keep Shams away from Mawlānā. Shams is said to have declared that he would now disappear for ever and no-one would be able to find him again. On 5 Shaʿbān 645/5 December 1247 Shams was murdered with the participation of Sulṭān Walad's brother ʿAlāʾ al-Dīn, or at his instigation, and the corpse was thrown into a well and later found and buried by Sulṭān Walad. It seems that his coffin has been discovered in the latest repairs done on the burial-place in Ḳonya, (A. Gölpınarlı, *Mevlânâ Celâleddîn*³, 83). It is understandable that Sulṭān Walad says nothing of this murder in the *Ibtidānāma*, not wanting to make the family scandal public. Shams's death was obviously kept from the Mawlānā, as he went to Damascus twice to look for him. His spiritual condition is depicted in touching verses by Sulṭān Walad (*Waladnāma* 56-7) : he became all the more a poet, devoted himself to listening to music and to dancing (*samāʿ*) to an extent that even his son obviously felt was immoderate, and found the lost Shams in himself. In most of his *ghazals* the *takhalluṣ* is not his own name, but that of his mystic lover.

Shams had, however, flesh and blood successors. In the year 647/1249 Mawlānā announced that Shams had appeared to him again in the form of one of his *murīds*, Ṣalāḥ al-Dīn Zarkūb of Ḳonya. He appointed the goldsmith, who was illiterate but distinguished by his handsomeness and pleasant character, as *khalaf*, and thus as the superior of the other *murīds*. He himself wanted to retire from the offices of shaykh and preacher. The *murīds* found that Shams al-Dīn, the Tabrīzī, had been more bearable than the uncultured goldsmith's apprentice from Ḳonya, whom they had known from childhood. Plans were even made to murder him, and then revealed. The *murīds* noticed that Mawlānā threatened to desert them completely, and they asked remorsefully for forgiveness. We may assume that the loyal attitude of Sulṭān Walad himself and the modest, pleasant personality of Ṣalāḥ al-Dīn helped to surmount this second crisis. For ten years Ṣalāḥ al-Din filled the office of a deputy (*nāʾib* and *khalīfa*), then he became ill and died, according to the inscription on his sarcophagus, on 1 Muḥarram 657/29 December 1258 (A. Gölpınarlı, *Mevlânâ'dan sonra Mevlevîlik*, 355). His successor, Čelebi Ḥusām al-Dīn Ḥasan, whose family came from Urmiya, was to be the inspirer of the Mathnawī. Ḥusām al-Dīn's father was the chief of the *akhis* in Ḳonya and the surrounding districts and so was known as Akhi Turk. Ḥusām al-Dīn lived with Mawlānā for ten years until the latter's death on 6 Djumāda II 672/18 December 1273; his appointment as Shaykh must therefore fall approximately in the year 662/1263-4, and there must therefore be five years between the death of his predecessor and his own taking office (according to this the statement in *Isl.* xxvi, 124-5, should be corrected). After Mawlānā's death Ḥusām al-Dīn offered the office of Khalīfa to Sulṭān Walad, the son of the master, who, however, declined. Ḥusām al-Dīn died in 683/1283.

On the people's insistence Sulṭān Walad now accepted the title of Shaykh and held it until his death on 10 Radjab 712/1312. He was followed by his son Ulu ʿĀrif Čelebi (d. 719/1319), followed by his brother ʿĀbid Čelebi, followed by his brother Wādjid Čelebi (d. 742/1341-2). A list of the Čelebis to the present day can be found in A. Gölpınarlı, *Mevlânâ'dan sonra Mevlevîlik*, 152-3, and in Tahsin Yazıcı's translation of the *Manāḳib al-ʿārifīn*, ii, 62-6 of the Önsöz.

The real history of the order begins with Sulṭān Walad. He founded the first branches of the order and helped it to gain greater respect. Already in the lifetime of Mawlānā the members of the order had the title Mawlawī (Aflākī, i, 1, 334). At first they were recruited from among artisans, which gave offence (Aflākī i, 151). The central part of the religious practices was held by listening to music, and dancing, which were indeed usual among other orders, but never had the greatest importance, as with the Mawlawīs. The dance ceremony in the regular, solemn form which is usual later, was, as Gölpınarlı has proved, first introduced by Pīr ʿĀdil Čelebi (d. 864/1460) (*Mevlânâ'dan sonra Mevlevîlik*, 99-100). On this ceremony cf. H. Ritter, *Der Reigen der tanzenden Derwische*, in *Zeitschrift für vergleichende Musikwissenschaft*, i; A. Gölpınarlı, *Mevlânâ'dan sonra*, 370-89, and *Mevlevî âyînleri* (Istanbul konservatuarı neşriyatı, Türk Klâsiklerinden VI-XV cild) 1933-9 publ. by Istanbul Music Conservatoire.

Mawlānā's piety and thought have not yet been the object of a thorough examination. Anyone undertaking such an examination would have to take care not to rely too much on the Mat̲h̲nawī commentaries, which read into the work the views of their own time or their personal views. Also the *Dīwān* of Mawlānā has only now become available in a critical edition, so that the examination can really begin. According to A. Gölpınarlı, himself a former Mawlawī dervish, the Mawlawīs do not regard their order as a Ṣūfī order in the strict sense. Gölpınarlı is inclined to connect the order with the Malāmatiyya movement from K̲h̲urāsān. Even in reading the sermons of Mawlānā's father one notices a gladness praised there which reminds one of the "merriness of hearts" (*ṭibat al-ḳulūb*) of the Ḳalandariyya, who are related to the Malāmatiyya (cf. Ritter in *Oriens*, viii, 360 and xii, 15). Some of the Čelebis lived like Ḳalandar dervishes, as Ulu ʿĀrif Čelebi, and still more his brother ʿĀbid Čelebi, and the Diwāne, Mehmed Čelebi, who was used in the expansion of the order (Gölpınarlı, *Mevlânâ'dan sonra*, 101-22). But of course this does not prove anything for Mawlānā himself. He appears to have been of a philanthropic, anything but fanatical, strongly emotional type, to judge from the countless love-poems in the *Dīwān*, easily inflamed, inclined to work off his excitement in the dance. Whether his religious ideas possess anything original besides the general mystical piety of his time, will have to be shown by the analysis of his works, which are :

1) The *Dīwān*, containing *g̲h̲azal*s and quatrains. There are also Greek and Turkish verses in this, the presence of which shows a certain connexion with sections of the common folk and also with the non-Muslim elements of the Ḳonya population. His *tak̲h̲alluṣ* is "K̲h̲āmūs̲h̲". This, however, is usually replaced with the name of S̲h̲ams-i Tabrīz. In some *g̲h̲azal*s Ṣalāḥ al-Dīn also appears as the *tak̲h̲alluṣ*. Former impressions and editions of the *Dīwān* have now been superseded by the good edition of Badīʿ al-Zamān Furūzānfar, *Kullīyāt-i S̲h̲ams yā Dīwān-i kabīr, mus̲h̲tamil bar ḳaṣāʾid wa g̲h̲azaliyyāt wa muḳaṭṭaʿāt-i fārsī wa ʿarabī wa tard̲j̲īʿāt wa mulammaʿāt az guftār-i Mawlānā D̲j̲alāl al-Dīn Muḥammad mas̲h̲hūr ba-Mawlawī*, Tehran 1336 ff., of which so far three volumes have appeared. Complete Turkish translation by ʿAbdülbaki Gölpınarlı, *Mevlânâ Celâleddîn, Dîvân-i kebîr*, Istanbul 1957 ff. So far three volumes have appeared. Of earlier selections and translations the following are still important: R. A. Nicholson, *Selected poems from the Dīvāni Shamsi Tabrīz, edited and translated with an introduction, notes and appendices*, Cambridge 1898; S. Bogdanov, *The Quatrains of Jalālu-d-dīn Rūmī and two hitherto unknown manuscripts*, in *JASB*, 1935, i, 65-80.

2) *Mat̲h̲nawī-i maʿnawī*. Didactic poetical work in double verses, in six *daftar*s. (The seventh *daftar* supposedly discovered by Rüsūk̲h̲ī Ismāʿīl Dede is spurious). The long poem was inspired by Ḥusām al-Dīn Čelebi, who suggested to Mawlānā that he should produce something like the religious *mat̲h̲nawī*s of Sanāʾī and ʿAṭṭār. Mawlānā is supposed to have at once pulled the famous eighteen verses of the introduction out of his turban already written. The rest he dictated to Ḥusām al-Dīn. The date when the work was begun is not known. We know only that between the first and second *daftar* was a pause of two years, caused by the death of Ḥusām al-Dīn's wife. The second *daftar* was started in 662/1263-4, as the poet says himself (ii, 7). Mawlānā dictated his verse whenever it occurred to him, dancing, in the bath, standing, sitting, walking, sometimes in the night until morning. Then Ḥusām al-Dīn read out what was written and the necessary corrections were made. The whole is composed very informally and without any thought of a well-planned structure. Thoughts hang together in free association, the interspersed stories are often interrupted and continued much later on. (On the style, cf. Nicholson's edition, 8-13 and the preface to Gölpınarlı's translation). The classic edition is that of R. A. Nicholson, *The Mathnawi of Jelálu'ddín Rúmi, edited from the oldest manuscripts available; with critical notes, translations and commentary*, London 1924-40 (*GMS*, vi, 1-8). Latest Turkish translation: Mevlâna, *Mesnevi, Veled Izbudak tarafından tercüme edilmiş, Abdülbaki Gölpınarlı tarafından muhtelif şerhlerle karşılaştırılmış ve esere bir açılma ilâve edilmiştir*, Istanbul 1942 ff. The fourth edition is now in the press. On European translations before Nicholson cf. his edition ii-xv; on Urdū translations cf. *Catalogue of the library of the India Office*, ii, vi, *Persian Books*, by A. J. Arberry, London 1937, 301-4. The best known earlier printed Turkish commentaries and translations are: Ankaralî Ismāʿīl Rüsūkhi, *Fātiḥ al-Abyāt*, Istanbul 1289, six volumes; Bursalî Ismāʿīl Ḥaḳḳi, *Rūḥ al-Mat̲h̲nawī* (Commentary on one part of the first *daftar*) Istanbul 1287; Sarî ʿAbdallāh Efendi (to the first *daftar*) Istanbul 1288, five volumes; translation in verse by Naḥīfī, Cairo 1268; ʿĀbidīn Pas̲h̲a, Istanbul 1887-8, six volumes. On the commentaries and translations written and printed in Īrān and India, and the earliest oriental editions cf. Nicholson, Introduction to i, 16-18; vii, Introduction 11-12 and the above-mentioned catalogue by Arberry, 301-4. On the Tehran edition of ʿAlā al-Dīn cf. ʿAlīnaḳī S̲h̲arīʿatmadārī, in *Naḳd-i matn-i Mat̲h̲nawī*, in *Yag̲h̲ma*, xii, 1338. On the sources of the stories in the Mat̲h̲nawī; Badīʿ al-Zamān Furūzānfarr, *Maʾāk̲h̲id̲h̲-i ḳaṣaṣ wa-tamt̲h̲ilāt-i Mat̲h̲nawī*, Tehran 1333 (see *Oriens*, viii, 356-8); on the *ḥadīt̲h̲*s quoted in the Mat̲h̲nawī: idem, *Aḥādīt̲h̲-i Mat̲h̲nawī mus̲h̲tamil bar mawāridī ki Mawlānā dar Mat̲h̲nawī az aḥādīt̲h̲ istifāde karde ast bā d̲h̲ikr-i wud̲j̲ūh-i riwāyat wa maʾāk̲h̲id̲h̲-i ānhā*, Tehran 1334.

3) *Fīhi mā fīh*. Collection of Mawlānā's sayings. (The title comes from a verse of Ibn al-ʿArabī). Cf. R. A. Nicholson, *The Table Talk of Jalalu'ddin Rumi*, in *Centenary Supplement to the JRAS*, 1924, 1-8. Edition by Badīʿ al-Zamān Furūzānfarr, Tehran 1330. Turkish translation: Mevlânâ Celâleddîn, *Fîhi mâ fîh. Çeviren, tahlilini yapan, açıklamasını hazırlayan Abdülbaki Gölpınarlı*, Istanbul 1959.

4) *Mawāʿiẓ macālis-i sabʿa. Mavlânâ'nin 7 öğüdüdür. Düzelten Ahmed Remzi Akyürek, mütercimi Rizeli Hasan Efendi-Oğlu*, Istanbul 1937.

5) *Maktūbāt. Mevlânâ'nın mektupları*. Düzelten *Ahmed Remzi Akyürek*, Istanbul 1937. Also Şerefeddin Yaltkaya in *Türkiyat Mecmuası*, 1939, vi, 323-45; Fuad Köprülü, in *Belleten* 1943, vii, 416.

Bibliography: H. Ritter, *Philologika XI. Maulānā Ǧalāl-addīn Rūmī und sein Kreis*, in *Isl.*, xxvi, 1942. (Life. Sources for biography, manuscripts of the works along with the works of his father, his son, and of S̲h̲ams-i Tabrīzī). The most important biographical sources are: Sulṭān Walad, *Ibtidānāma*, publ. by D̲j̲alāl Humāʾī, *Waladnāme, Mat̲h̲nawī-i Waladī bā taṣḥīḥ wa muḳaddima*, Tehran 1315; Farīdūn b. Aḥmad Sipahsālār,

Risāla-i Sipahsālār. Latest edition: Shams al-Dīn Aḥmad al-Aflākī al-ʿĀrifī, *Manāḳib al-ʿārifīn*, ed. Tahsin Yazıcı, i, Ankara 1959. (Türk Tarih Kurumu Yayınlarından.)

Translations: Cl. Huart, *Les saints des dervisches tourneurs. Récits traduits du persan et annotés*, 2 vols., Paris 1918 and 1922 (unreliable); Tahsin Yazıcı, *Ahmet Eflâkî, Âriflerin menkibeleri* (*Manāḳib al-ʿārifīn*), 2 vols., Ankara 1953 and 1954 (Dünya Edebiyatından Tercümeler. Şark-Islâm Klâsikleri: 26). On the value of the work as an historical source cf. Cl. Huart, *De la valeur historique des mémoires des dervisches tourneurs*, in *JA* 1922, 19, 308-17; Fuad Köprülü, in *Belleten*, 1943, 422 ff.

Portrayals: Badīʿ al-Zamān Furūzānfarr, *Mawlānā Djalāl al-Dīn Muḥammad mashhūr ba-Mawlawī*, Teheran 1315-17; H. Ritter, article Celâleddîn Rûmî in *İA*. (On other portrayals see Mawlawī ʿAbd al-Muḳtadir, *Catalogue of the Arabic and Persian manuscripts in the Oriental Public Library at Bankipore*, Calcutta 1908, i, 630); *Konya halkevi kültür dergisi, Mevlâna özel sayısı*, Istanbul 1943; Abdülbaki Gölpınarlı, *Mevlânâ Celâleddîn. Hayatı, Felsefesi, Eserleri, Eserlerinden secmeler*[3], Istanbul 1959; idem, *Mevlânâ'dan sonra Mevlevîlik*, Istanbul 1953; idem, *Konya'da Mevlâna Dergahının Arşivi*, in *Istanbul Üniversitesi Iktisat Fakültesi Mecmuası*, xvii, 1-4, 130-53.

On the meaning of the eighteen introductory verses of the Mathnawī: Ahmed Ateş, *Mesnevi'nin onsekiz beytinin mânası*, in *Fuad Köprülü Armağanı*, Istanbul 1953, 37-50. On Mawlānā's Turkish verses: Mecdut Mansuroğlu, *Calāladdīn Rūmī Türkische Verse*, in *Ural-Altaische Jahrbücher*, xxiv, 1952, 106-15; idem, *Mevlâna Celaleddin Rûmî'de Türkçe beiyit ve ibareler*, in *Türk Dili Arastırmaları Yıllığı, Belleten* 1954, 207-20. On the Greek verses of Mawlānā and Sulṭān Walad; P. Burguière and R. Mantran, *Quelques vers grecs du XIIIe siècle en caractères arabes*, in *Byzantion*, xxii, 1952, 63-80. (H. Ritter)

ii) It is not easy to summarize systematically the main lines of Djalāl al-Dīn's thought. He was not a philosopher (in his works there are often attacks against the vacuity of purely intellectual philosophy) and claimed not to be a classical poet (both in the *Dīwān* and the *Mathnawī* he proclaims his dislike for rhymes and poetical artifices) but above all he was a passionate lover of God who expressed his feelings in a poetically unorthodox, volcanic way, thus creating a style which is unique in the entire Persian literature. Historically, influences on him by the religious and philosophical thought of Ghazzālī, Ibn ʿArabī, Sanāʾī, and ʿAṭṭār have been traced. The importance of the influence of Ibn ʿArabī on him has been perhaps exaggerated. The following account outlines as shortly as possible some of the main trends in Djalāl al-Dīn's thought. Quotations from the *Mathnawī* are from Nicholson's edition mentioned in *Bibliography*.

God: The absolute transcendence of God seems conceived not only spatially and intellectually but even morally. God is Himself the Absolute Value, Good and Evil being relative to Him and both at His orders (ii, 2617 ff.). Reality is ordered in four "spaces": the Realm of Nothingness, of Phantasy, of Existence, of Senses and Colours (ii, 3092-7). God is beyond Nothingness and Being, He works in the Nothingness, which is His Workshop (ii, 688-90; ii, 760-2; iv, 2341-83). In this sense is difficult to speak of a real "pantheism" in Djalāl al-Dīn: in any case immanentism is totally foreign to his turn of mind.

Creation: Djalāl al-Dīn seems to accept the Ashʿarī idea of the discontinuity of time and creation. God creates and destroys all in discontinuous atoms of time (i, 1140-8). He creates things murmuring enchanting words in their ears while they are still asleep in the Nothingness (i, 1447-55).

The World: The non-human World is something created by God in preparation for the creation of Man. Nature is a hint of God: every tree that germinates from the dark earth extending its branches towards the sun is a symbol of the liberation of Spirit from Matter (i, 1335-6; 1342-8). Creation has been however progressive. In a famous passage (v, 3637 ff.) Djalāl al-Dīn sketches a theory of mystical evolution (not to be mistaken for a scientific and Darwinistic evolution). The emergence of Man (who always remained Man, even in his former stages of development) from the animal kingdom is a first step indicating further journeys to the realms of the Angels and of the Godhead.

Man: Man is not simply a compound of body and soul. The human compound is formed by a body, his manifest part, a deeper soul (*rūḥ*, ψυχή), a still more concealed mind (*ʿaḳl*) and, even deeper, a *rūḥ-i waḥy* (spirit partaking of Revelation) present only in Saints and Prophets (ii, 3253 ff.). Djalāl al-Dīn's spiritual anthropology does not accept an indiscriminate possibility for every one to reach the highest stages of sanctity. Prophets and Saints are "different" from ordinary men. In a very interesting passage Djalāl al-Dīn shows the pragmatic utility of bowing in veneration to the Holy Men: it is the only way of breaking the ever-reappearing humanistic pride and superbity of Man (ii, 811 ff.).

God speaks through the mouth of the "man of God". The Prophet, the Holy Man is the manifest sign of the Unity of God, he is above the normal human standards (i, 225-7).

Ethics: Djalāl al-Dīn is far from speaking the language of modern "liberal" religious thinkers. The exterior practices of worship are binding for all. The reason given for this is also of a typically Muslim pragmatic character: the exterior rites are useful, like the presents of a lover to his Beloved. If Love were purely a spiritual thing why should God have created the material World? (i, 2624 ff.). On the problem of freedom and destiny he acutely remarks that there is a great difference between the momentaneous act of God (*ṣunʿ*) and the result of that act (*maṣnūʿ*), between *ḳaḍāʾ* (the act of deciding or predestining) and *maḳḍī* (the predestined thing). One has to love the *ṣunʿ* of God, not his *maṣnūʿ* like an idolater (iii, 1360-73). When his spiritual eyes are open, man recognizes that he is, at the same time, totally "operated" and moved by God (i, 598 ff.) and totally free, of a freedom unmeasurably above the petty freedoms of ordinary men (i, 936-9). To reach this deeper freedom in God, efforts and action (*kūshish*) are necessary (i, 1074-7). Perfect examples of this supreme freedom are the Saints and the Prophets (i, 635-7).

Life after death: The nearness to God in the worlds beyond is never felt by Djalāl al-Dīn as a real absorption in God without any residue. The metaphors he uses to express *fanāʾ* in an interesting passage of the *Mathnawī* (iii, 3669 ff.) are for instance the following: the flame of the candle in the presence of the sun (but yet the candle exists and "if you put cotton upon it, the cotton will be consumed by the sparks") or a deer in presence of a lion, or, elsewhere, as red-hot iron in the fire, when iron takes the properties of fire without losing its own individual essence. In that state it can claim to be fire as well as iron. The soul near God becomes then one "according to whose desire the torrents and rivers flow, and the stars move in such wise as He wills" (iii, 1885 ff.). In another passage Djalāl al-Dīn tells of a lover who, as he reached the presence of his Beloved, died and "the bird, his spirit, flew out of his body" for "God is such that, when He comes, there is not a single hair of thee remaining" (iii, 4616, 4621). What an encouraging idea for a pantheist! But Djalāl al-Dīn is always ready to surprise us with some coup-de-scène. So the real end of the story is told some lines further, under the heading: "How the Beloved caressed the senseless lover that he might return to his senses" (iii, 4677 ff.). Djalāl al-Dīn goes even so far as to admit an element of activity in the otherworldly plane, so that the highest degree in the life of spirit "is not attainment but infinite aspiration after having attained": "... there is a very occult mystery here in the fact that Moses set out to run towards a Khiḍr ... This Divine Court is the Infinite Plane. Leave the seat of honour behind: the Way is thy seat of honour!" (iii, 1957 ff.).

Djalāl al-Dīn Rūmī's style: The style of the *ghazals* of Djalāl al-Dīn's *Dīwān* is conditioned by the fact that many of them were "sung" by the poet himself or were destined to be sung. A well known tradition shows us Djalāl al-Dīn improvising odes while gently dancing around a pillar in his school, and another story tells how he found one of his beloved pupils and companions, the already mentioned goldsmith Ṣalāḥ al-Dīn Zarkūb, while listening enraptured, in a street, to the rhythmic beat of his goldsmith's hammer. His powerful sense of rhythm is not always accompanied by equal attention to the strict rules of classical quantitative Persian poetry. He often complains against metres ("*mufta*ʿ*ilun mufta*ʿ*ilun mufta*ʿ*ilun* killed me!") and more than one verse both in his *Dīwān* and in his *Mathnawī* shows strong irregularities. In his *dīwān* two styles can be distinguished, a "singing" and a "didactic" style. Often some *ghazals* begin in the former (strong rhythm, double rhymes etc.) to pass slowly into the second or *vice versa*. In the *Mathnawī*, which is a single uninterrupted discourse, where the Speaker is often drawn by a word or a casual connexion of words to pass into ever newer subjects, anecdotes and sub-anecdotes, three styles can be distinguished. The purely "narrative" style; at the end, or during the telling of a story, however, comments are introduced in a "didactic" style. Here and there, either in the context of a story or of its comment, the author seems to be suddenly taken away as by rapture and then he uses his "ecstatic" style, in which some of the best verses of the *Mathnawī* are composed. Both the narrative and the didactic styles are of a remarkable simplicity and colloquialness, almost unique in the Persian literature of that time. Elements of colloquial language penetrate sometimes even into the more refined language of the *ghazals* and of the "ecstatic" style of the *Mathnawī*. We have even some verses of Djalāl al-Dīn containing a few words and sentences in colloquial Greek. Because of its strongly personal features Djalāl al-Dīn's style found practically no imitators, but it is highly—and rightly—valued by modern Persians (even by those who do not fully agree with his mystical views) and perhaps exerted a certain influence in the movement of simplification and modernization of Persian literature begun in the past century.

Bibliography: To the bibliography above add: Life: Aflākī, *Manāḳib al-*ʿ*ārifīn*, is partly translated in the Introduction to J. W. Redhouse, *The Mesnevī ... of Mevlānā ... Jelālu 'd-Dīn, Muḥammed, er-Rūmī. Book the first ... translated and the poetry versified*, London 1881, 1-135; Badīʿ al-Zamān Furūzān-farr, *Risāla dar taḥḳīḳ-i aḥwāl wa zindagānī-i Mawlānā Djalāl al-Dīn Muḥammad*, Tehrān 1315 s., 2nd ed. 1333 s. Books on Djalal al-Din: G. Richter, *Persiens Mystiker Dschelâl-eddin Rûmî*, Breslau 1933; Khalifa Abdul Hakim, *The metaphysics of Rumi*, Lahore n.d.; R. A. Nicholson, *Rúmí: poet and mystic*, ed. A. J. Arberry, London 1950; Afzal Iqbal, *The life and thought of Rumi*, Lahore 1956.

(A. Bausani)

DJALĀL AL-DĪN TABRĪZĪ [see TABRĪZĪ, DJALĀL AL-DĪN].

DJALĀL AL-DĪN THANESARĪ [see THANESARĪ, DJALĀL AL-DĪN].

DJALĀL ḤUSAYN ČELEBI (Celāl Hüseyin Çelebi), Turkish poet. He was born in Monastir, the son of a *sipāhī* (?-978/1571?). As a young man he went to Istanbul to study, later wandered in Syria where he found protectors through whose help he entered the court of prince Selīm, who liked his easy manner and gaiety and who kept him at his court when he ascended the throne as Selīm II. Djalāl remained a boon-companion of the Sultan until he became involved in political intrigues and religious controversies; he then had to leave court life and returned to his home-town where he died.

His *dīwān* has not come down to us. Many of his poems are collected in most *medjmu*ʿ*as*. His only surviving book is a small collection of *ghazels*: *Ḥusn-i Yūsuf*, not yet edited.

Bibliography: The *tedhkīres* of ʿAhdī, ʿĀshiḳ Čelebi, Kinali-zāde Ḥasan Čelebi, and the biographical section in ʿĀlī's *Kunh al-akhbār*, s.v.

(Fahir İz)

DJALĀL NŪRĪ [see ILERI, CELÂL NURI].

DJALĀL REDJĀʾĪZĀDE [see REDJĀʾĪZĀDE].

DJALĀLĀBĀD, principal town and administrative centre of the region of the same name in the Kirghiz SSR, situated in the plain of Kongar to the extreme south of the essentially mountainous region which is a prolongation of the Tian Shan and whose mean altitude is from 2000 to 3000 m., the lowest regions of the plains being no less than 500 m. This former small town, of no economic importance, is now a large industrial city supported by the cotton production of the hinterland. The urban population reflects that of the region, peopled since the remotest past by Kirghiz, to whom have been added Uzbeks in the southern part, also Tatars, Tadjiks, and Russians. (H. Carrère d'Encausse)

DJALĀLĪ (*Taʾrīkh-i Djalālī*), the name of an era and also that of a calendar used often in Persia and in Persian books and literature from the last part of the 5th/11th century onward. The era was founded by the 3rd Saldjūḳid ruler Sulṭān Malikshāh b. Alp Arslan (465-85/1072-92) after consultation with his astronomers. It was called Djalālī after the title of that monarch, Djalāl al-Dawla (not Djalāl al-Dīn as some later authors supposed). The era was also called sometimes *Malikī*. The epoch of the era (*i.e.*, its beginning) was Friday, 9 Ramaḍān 471/15 March 1079, when the vernal equinox occurred in about $2^{h.}$ $6^{m.}$ Greenwich time (in Iṣfahān $5^{h.}$ $33^{m.}$).

The names of the astronomers who helped in the matter of the reform of the calendar and advocated the institution of the era are given in some sources, and include the name of the famous mathematician and poet ʿUmar b. Ibrāhīm al-Khayyāmī [*q.v.*]. As he died at least 50 years after the reform, Khayyāmī, if he ever took part in that consultation, must have been very young.

By the term *Ta'rīkh-i Djalālī* is meant a new calendar instituted in 467/1075 by the above mentioned sultan Malikshāh. This was, as a matter of fact, rather a reform of the common Persian calendar that had remained in general usage in Īrān, side by side with the Arabian calendar with lunar year and months used by Muslims, after the downfall of the Persian empire and the domination of the Arabs in Īrān in the 7th century A.D. Through this reform the Persian vague year of 365 days was stabilized and brought into exact agreement with the astronomical tropic year of $365^1/_4$ days (or strictly speaking 365 days 5 hours and about 49 minutes). This regulation was effected by adding one day in every four and sometimes five years to the vague year, thus making it 366 instead of 365 days. This was in a way more or less similar to the Julian calendar.

The Persian year was, from the time of its institution probably in the 5th century B.C., a vague year of 12 months of 30 days each and five odd days (*andargāh*, Arab. *al-mustaraka*) added at the end of the year as intercalary days. This is believed to have been the original order which was re-established towards the end of the 4th/10th century in the great part of Persia by one of the Būyid kings of Fārs, who transferred the epagomenae from the end of Ābān where they then were, to the end of the 12th month where they remained in those parts of the country and also with the Zoroastrians of Īrān and the Pārsīs of India. As a matter of fact the place of the five supplementary or intercalary days, *i.e.*, the above mentioned *andargāh* (the so-called epagomenae) has not been always at the end of the year after the 12th month, but they had been periodically advancing in the civil year by being moved forward a month every 120 years. That is to say, after being at first at the end of the last month for 120 years, they were moved to the end of the first month, where they remained for another 120 years, and then they were again moved forward and put at the end of the second month and so on, until they were brought to the end of Ābān or the 8th month probably in the 5th century A.D. (of course after some 960 years from the institution of this process). This periodical and regular movement or change of the place of the epagomenae in the civil year was a consequence of the periodical shifting of the places of the six Zoroastrian religious festivals of 5 days each, called *gāhanbārs*, a whole month forward in the civil year once every 120 years, with a view of keeping those most important religious feasts fixed in their original astronomical places in the tropic year.

The epagomenae, which were, as a matter of fact, the Avestan 5 Gāθā days, also constituted one of those *gāhanbārs*, the sixth one, *i.e.*, the Avestan *Hamaspaθmaēδaya*, and hence it moved in the civil year in the same way as the other *gāhanbārs*. This operation of shifting forward the *gāhanbārs* periodically, and consequently the epagomenae as well, was considered, according to the reports in the Muslim books of chronology, as an intercalation of one month in the year (in reality in the ecclesiastic fix year) carried out by a special process which cannot be fully explained in this article.

The above mentioned periodical operation, executed more or less regularly in the pre-Islamic ages, ceased to be carried out during the last century or the last two centuries of the Sāsānid period, and was no longer carried out after the downfall of that dynasty and the Muslim conquest of Īrān. Therefore the epagomenae remained, as has already been said, at the end of Ābān till about 1000 A.D. in the southern provinces of Persia, and still later in the northern provinces of the country *e.g.*, in Māzandarān (and, as I have been recently informed, also in the district of Sangsar near Simnān) even at the present time.

The effect of the calendar reform of Malikshāh was (1) to fix the beginning of the Persian solar year in the day of vernal equinox. The New Year or the first day of the month Farwardīn, through the retrogression of the vague year (due to the neglect of the quarter of a day which the tropic year has in excess to the vague year of 365 days), had reached 26 February (Julian) in the year in which the reform was decided upon (467 A. H.). It was now brought forward to 15 March (Julian), which corresponded in that year to the day of vernal equinox; and (2) to provide a rule for keeping New Year's Day always fixed in the same astronomical point of time by counting every fourth (or sometimes fifth) year 366 days instead of 365. This was, in fact, an intercalation of one day every four or five years at the end of epagomenae, somewhat similar to that effected in the Julian year, where once in every four years (leap years) an intercalary day is placed at the end of February.

However, just as the above mentioned intercalation in the Julian calendar did not bring the Julian year into exact agreement with the tropic year, because the latter is about 11 minutes (at the present rate 11 minutes and 14.9 seconds) shorter than the Julian year, which is 365 and a quarter days, the difference amounted to about 45 minutes in 4 years or one day in about 128 years, and therefore a further adjustment was found necessary; the Djalālī year would have been as imperfect as the Julian if the intercalation of one day in the year were limited to every fourth year.

In both calendars a means for eliminating the imperfection was elaborated. While in 1582 A.D. the Pope Gregory XIII introduced a new arrangement in the order of the above mentioned four-yearly intercalation in the Julian year, by establishing a rule according to which this intercalation would be omitted in the last year of every century except in those divisible by 400, such as 1600, 2000, 2400 A.D. etc., the initiators of the Djalālī calendar or rather reform made the intercalation of one day in the year dependent on the vernal equinox occurring in the afternoon of the 366th day, provided that it had been in the preceding year before midday. The equinox or the exact point of time when the sun (in reality the earth) reaches the equinoctial point of the ecliptic, which in astronomy is conventionally called "the first point of Aries", was the real commencement of the year. In other words the Djalālī year, being a solar tropic year, always began on the vernal equinox and the exact time of this astronomical beginning could be found out every year by calculation. Thus the first day of the calendar year (civil year), or New Year's Day, was always the day on which the sun at midday was already in Aries, having entered that sign sometime between that point of time and midday of the preceding day.

Now as a rule every time the equinox occurred in the afternoon after having occurred the last time (*i.e.*, at the beginning of the preceding year) before noon, the year just coming to a close would be a leap year, *i.e.*, an intercalation of one day would be effected. This happened normally once in every four years, when the fourth year was of 366 days instead of 365. However, if in a given fourth year when, as has been said, an intercalation would normally have been due, the equinox did not fall in the afternoon but occurred before midday, even though it also occurred before noon in the preceding year, such a year in spite of the fact that it followed three successive common years (of 365 days each) would not be a leap or bissextile year and the intercalation would be effected only in the next year (*i.e.*, in the fifth year). The precise time of this quinquennial or five-yearly intercalation was never fixed by a regular rule by the reformers. It was left absolutely dependent on the result of the astronomical calculation each year, that is to say it was to be estimated by deductive method. A similar process is followed in the modern calendar of Persia instituted in 1925 A.D. It was, however, noticed that this case (the postponement of intercalation to the fifth year) occurred only after some 6 or 7 or 8 quadrennial intercalations. In other words some oriental astronomers like Ulūgh Beg (d. 1449) believed that the quinquennial intercalation would follow at times the sixth, and at other times the seventh, quadrennial ones, however without giving any regular sequence for the alternative cycles. Again, other astronomers like Ḳuṭb al-Dīn of Shīrāz (d. 1311) put the alternative periods as 7 and 8. This means that according to the former the quinquennial intercalation would fall in the 29th (instead of 28th) or 33rd (instead of 32nd) year, and according to the latter in 33rd or 37th year. If by alternative numbers the regular sequence were meant, the first system (that of Ulūgh Beg) would mean 15 intercalations in 62 years and the second (that of Ḳuṭb al-Dīn) 17 intercalations in 70 years. Possibly every author worked out these cycles according to his own opinion of the length of the tropic year.

By calculation on the basis of the length of the fraction of the day (over 365 days) in the tropic year, according to the modern measure, there will be still an error of one day in 3844 years in the case of 15 intercalations in 62 years and in 1470 years in the case of 17 intercalations in 70 years.

Some European scholars, misunderstanding the statements of the Oriental authors about the different cycles and the alternative periods, have discussed at length the question as to whether this or that cycle was more correct and corresponded to what they supposed to be the original plan of Malikshāh's astronomers. Golius, Weidler, Bailly, Montucla, Sédillot, Idler, Matzka, Ginzel and Suter have tried to find a more or less plausible solution and some of them have proposed formulae based, in fact, on their own calculation according to the modern opinion as to the length of the tropic year. Some of them have even credited the founders of the Djalālī calendar with such an ingenious system as to make the divergence between the Djalālī and tropic year possible only one day in every 10,000, 28,000, or even 400,000 years. The truth, however, is that as it has already been said, not only was no rule ever established by the men responsible for the institution of the Djalālī calendar for the cycles of the quinquennial intercalations, but even their own opinion of the length of the tropic year is not known with any certainty. Further, in order to find out whether the next leap year will be a quadrennial or quinquennial, several big cycles are proposed by different Oriental astronomers. These theories are given with details in an article by the present writer in *BSOS*, x/1, 115-6. They are conjectures worked out each according to the length of the tropic year in the opinion of its proposer. They have nothing to do with the supposed original scheme of the founders of the Djalālī era and calendar, which most probably never existed. Perhaps it is not necessary to add that not only were the calculations of the old astronomers of the Middle Ages at variance with each other, but also all of them differ from the modern measures of time (year and day). Therefore no rule proposed or thought of for the sequence of quadrennial and quinquennial intercalations would agree with the result of scientific observations of the present day. It is not impossible to work out a formula in accordance with the modern measures of the tropic year as Riyāhī did (see bibliography) in his treatise on the subject (in Persian). He puts the quinquennial intercalations in 440 Djalālī years in the 101st, 262nd, and 423rd or 68th, 130th, 192nd, 287th, 349th and 411th. But owing to the progressive changes in the measures of time, the shortening of the day, and so many other factors, no plan whatever can be permanently entirely correct. It must also be said that what astronomers until recent times conventionally considered to be the beginning of New Year's Day (namely midday), must be now discarded, and midnight (of Greenwich time) should be ādopted for the beginning of the day.

The question of whether the reform of Malikshāh took place in Iṣfahān, Rayy or Nīshāpūr is not very important from the astronomical point of view.

The Djalālī calendar found general usage in the greater part of Persia. The famous Persian poet Saʿdī used it in his verse about two centuries after its institution. In spite of losing ground to a certain extent, as a result of the extension of the Arabian calendar used generally by Muslims, it is still to-day commonly the means of time-reckoning in the cental part of Persia, especially by peasants and the inhabitants of many towns such as Kāshān, Yazd, Nāʾīn etc.

The year has 12 months of 30 days each, and five days (or 6 days in leap years) following the 12th months. A curious phenomena, however, is observed in a district, or rather a group of villages, near the small town of Natanz in the province of Kāshān, where the epagomenae follow the eleventh month (Bahman) instead of the twelfth. The principal place of the district is the village Abiyāna.

The names and length (*i.e.*, 30 days each) of the months of the Djalālī calendar are the same as those of the Persian calendar before the reform.

This seems to me to be unquestionable. Nevertheless, according to the famous author Ḳuṭb al-Dīn of Shīrāz, some astronomers adopted for the length of each month the period of time during which the sun remained in the corresponding sign of the zodiac, so that the first and second month, corresponding to Aries and Taurus, were each of 31 days long, and the 3rd month, corresponding to Gemini, 32 days and so on. Further, while most of the sources agree that the names of the months were the some as those of the common Persian year, some authors speak of the introduction of new names for the Djalālī months and even for the days of the month, of both of which a list is given by them. This list is to be found in a Persian treatise called *Sī faṣl* by the famous Naṣīr al-Dīn Ṭūsi, and elsewhere.

Bibliography: *Prolégomènes des tables astron. d'Oloug Beg* (ed. L. A. Sédillot), Paris 1853, 27-31 and 235, Persian text 309-13; Alfraganus, *Ele-*

menta astronomica (ed. J. Golius), Notae, 32-5; L. Ideler, *Handbuch der mathemat. u. techn. Chronologie*, Berlin 1826, ii, 512-58; Matzka, *Die Chronologie in ihrem ganzen Umfang*, Vienna 1844, 480; F. K. Ginzel, *Handbuch der mathemat. u. techn. Chronologie*, Leipzig 1906, i, 300-5; S. H. Taqizadeh, *Various eras and calendars used in the countries of Islam*, in *BSOS*, x/1, 108-17; Taḳī Riyāḥī, *Sharḥ-i taḳwīmhā-yi mukhtalif wa Mas'ala-yi Kabīsahā-yi Djalālī*, Teheran 1335 A.H. solar 1956 (in Persian). (S. H. Taqizadeh)

DJALĀLĪ [see SUPPLEMENT].

DJALĀLZĀDE MUṢṬAFĀ ČELEBI (ca. 896/1490-975/1567), known as 'Ḳodja Nishāndjī', Ottoman civil servant and historian, was the eldest son of the *ḳāḍī* Djalāl al-Dīn from Tosya (for whom see *Shaḳā'iḳ*, tr. Rescher, 297 = tr. Medjdī, 466). His talents having attracted the attention of Pīrī Pasha, in 922/1516 he turned from the scholarly career to become a clerk to the *dīwān-i humāyūn*. He was private secretary to Pīrī Pasha during his Grand Vizierate (924/1518-929/1523) and to his successor Ibrāhīm Pasha; his services in helping to regulate the affairs of Egypt after the revolt of Aḥmed Pasha were rewarded with the post of *ra'īs al-kuttāb* (931/1525). Just after the conquest of Baghdād in 941/1534 he was promoted to *nishāndjī* (Ferīdūn, *Munsha'āt*², i, 592), holding office with great distinction for 23 years: his state papers and the styles of address (*alḳāb*) which he instituted remained models to the Chancery for years afterwards (Pečevī, i, 43; Ḥuseyn, *Badā'iʿ al-Waḳā'iʿ*, Moscow 1961, 584 f.). In 964/1557 he was induced by Rustem Pasha to resign, with the post of *müteferriḳa-bashi*, but allowed to retain his *khāṣṣ* (amounting to 300,000 *akčes*, according to ʿAṭā'ī). While on the Szigetvar campaign he was re-appointed to his old office by Sokollu, immediately after Suleymān's death (cf. Selānikī, 46, 51). He died a little over a year later (Rebīʿ II 975/October 1567), and was buried by the mosque which he had built at Ayyūb, in the quarter known thereafter as Nishāndjī (*Ḥadīḳat al-Djawāmiʿ*, i, 295; Ewliyā, i, 393 f.).

Of his projected description of the whole Empire and its government in thirty books, *Ṭabaḳāt al-mamālik wa daradjāt al-masālik*, only the last, a very full and elaborate history of the reign of Suleymān to 962/1555, is known to exist, although a note in a MS copied by the author's son (cf. Uzunçarşılı [see Bibl.], 405) refers to the other books as having been written (perhaps only in draft). The work was highly esteemed and used by ʿĀlī, Pečevī, and Hammer-Purgstall, who also published with translation a short excerpt from the description of the campaign of 939/1532 (*Fundgruben des Orients*, ii, 143-54). Portions of the work exist independently in MS under such titles as *Mohāč-nāme, Feth-nāme-i Rodōs*, etc. Muṣṭafā Čelebi later wrote a detailed history of Selīm I, *Ma'āthir-i Selīm Khānī*, which depends in part on the relation of Pīrī Pasha (also used by Hammer-Purgstall; except translated by H. v. Diez, *Denkwürdigkeiten von Asien*, ii, 355-71).

The following works, all in Turkish, also survive: (1) *Mawāhib al-Khallāḳ fī marātib al-akhlāḳ*, a work on ethics; (2) *Dalā'il-i nubuwwat-i Muḥammadī*, a translation of Molla Miskīn's Persian *Maʿāridj al-nubuwwa*; (3) a short treatise entitled *Hadiyat al-mu'minīn*; (4) *Djawāhir al-akhbār fī khaṣā'il al-akhyār*, a translation of Sirādj al-Dīn ʿUmar's *Zahr al-kimām* (Brockelmann, S II, 377 f.). He wrote poems under the *makhlaṣ* Nishānī. One MS of a Ḳānūn-nāme is ascribed to Muṣṭafā Čelebi (cf. *Ist. Kit. Tarih-Coğ. Yazmaları Kat.* i/10, 805), but its editor Meḥmed ʿĀrif thinks the attribution false (*TOEM ʿilāve*, 1329, intr. v). The Istanbul catalogue ascribes to him also (791) the *ḳānūn-nāme* for Egypt published by Ö. L. Barkan (*Kanunlar*, Istanbul 1943, 355-87).

Bibliography: Sehī, 33 f.; Laṭīfī, 335-7; ʿAṭā'ī, 113 f.; Rieu, *CTM*, 49-51; B. Meḥmed Ṭāhir, *ʿOthmānlî Mü'ellifleri*, iii, 37-9; *EI*², s.v. (J. H. Mordtmann); Babinger, 102 f.; *İA*, s.v. Celâl-zâde (M. Tayyib Gökbilgin); I. H. Uzunçarşılı, *Tosyalı Celâlzâde Mustafa ve Salih Çelebiler*, in *Belleten*, xxii, 1958, 391-441. For Istanbul MSS of his works see further A. S. Levend, *Gazavât-nâmeler*, Ankara 1956, index, and F. E. Karatay, *Topkapı Sarayı .... Türkče Yazmalar Kataloğu*, Istanbul 1961, index. (V. L. Ménage)

DJALĀLZĀDE ṢĀLIḤ ČELEBI, Ottoman scholar, historian and poet, and younger brother of the famous *nishāndjī*, Djalālzāde Muṣṭafā Čelebi. Born in the last decade of the 9th century A.H. in Vučitrn (NW of Prishtina) where his father, Djalāl al-Dīn, was *ḳāḍī*, upon completing his studies under Kamāl Pasha-zāde and Khayr al-Dīn Efendi, the tutor of Sulṭān Sulaymān, he entered the normal teaching career, reaching the Ṣaḥn in 943/1536-7 and the Bāyazīdiyya in Edirne in 949/1542-3. His judicial appointments include Aleppo (951/1544), Damascus (953/1546) and Cairo (954/1547), from which latter post he retired in 957/1550 to settle in Ayyūb where he was later (966/1559) given the professorship of the local *madrasa*. Forced to retire by failing eyesight in 969/1561, he devoted himself to writing until his death at about the age of eighty in Rabīʿ I 973/September-October 1565. He is buried in the courtyard of his brother's mosque in Ayyūb. Of the seventeen works ascribed to him, the most famous is certainly his *Ta'rīkh-i Miṣr-i djadīd* (953/1547), a compilation from familiar Arabic sources and, unlike his other historical works, of no original value. More interesting are his translations from the Persian of the *Ḳiṣṣa-i Fīrūz Shāh* and ʿAwfī's *Djawāmiʿ al-ḥikāyāt*, representative works of a period when elegant Ottoman prose style was establishing its own aesthetic identity. Apart from his *Laylā wa Madjnūn*, his poetry has commanded little praise or admiration.

Bibliography: The most recent study on Ṣāliḥ is that of I. H. Uzunçarşılı, *Belleten*, lxxxvii (1958), 422-41, which enters into more detail than M. T. Gökbilgin's contribution to *İA*, iii, 63, and fully discusses his surviving works. Babinger, 100; Hammer-Purgstall, *Gesch. osman. Dichtkunst*, ii, 327; *Sidjill-i ʿOthmānī*, iii, 300 and *ʿOthmānlî Mü'ellifleri*, ii, 278, all contain inaccuracies. The most important source is ʿAṭā'ī, *Ḥadā'iḳ al-ḥaḳā'iḳ*, 47; aside from ʿAhdī's *Gulshan-i shuʿarā'* (Brit. Mus., Add. 7876, f. 23b) and Laṭīfī's *Tadhkirat al-shuʿarā'*, 218 (neither this text nor the Brit. Mus. ms., Or. 6656, f. 68b, containing the *ḳaṣīda* mentioned by Hammer-Purgstall), the other *tadhkiras*—viz., Ḳïnalïzāde Ḥasan Čelebi (Brit. Mus., Add. 24, 957), f. 157b; Bayānī (Millet, 757), f. 100; Riyāḍī (Nuruosmaniye, 3724), f. 93b; Ḳāfzāde Fā'iḍī, *Zubdat al-Ashʿār* (Şehid ʿAli Paşa, 1877), f. 57b—all derive from that of ʿĀshiḳ Čelebi (Süleymaniye, 268), f. 273b. ʿĀlī, *Kunh al-akhbār* (Esʿad Efendi, 2162), f. 411b, adds nothing of value to the above, nor do Ḥāfiẓ Ḥusayn Aywānsarāyī, *Ḥadīḳat al-djawāmiʿ*, i, 296, or Mustaḳīm-zāde Suleymān Efendi, *Tuḥfat al-khaṭṭāṭīn*, 229. For his *Laylā wa Madjnūn*, cf.

Agâh Sirri Levend, *Leyla ve Mecnūn hikâyesi* (Ankara 1959), 287 ff., and for certain of his historical works, ibid., *Ġazavāt-nāmeler* (Ankara 1956), index. The Bibl. Nat. possesses fragments, additional to those in the Istanbul libraries, of his translation of the *Ḳiṣṣa-i Fīrūz Shāh* (A.F. 103, Supp. 140), and the unique copy of his *dīwān* is in the Nuruosmaniye, no. 3846. (J. R. Walsh)

DJALĀYIR, DJALĀYIRID (djalāʾir, djalāʾirid). Originally the name of a Mongol tribe (see Rashīd al-Dīn, *Taʾrīkh-i Ghāzānī*, esp. *bāb* a), the term Djalāyir (and Djalāyirid) in Islamic history principally denotes one of the successor-dynasties that divided up the territories of the defunct Ilkhānid empire. The spelling 'Djalāyir' is given by al-Ahrī, the contemporary, and very likely official, chronicler of the dynasty. Djalāyirid genealogies usually begin with Īlkā Nūyān (hence the dynasty's other name Īlkānī), a follower of Hūlāgū, and proceed through Āḳbūḳā and Ḥusayn to Ḥasan "Buzurg", the founder of the dynasty, who was Ūlūs Beg and governor of Rūm under Abū Saʿīd.

When Abū Saʿīd died without heirs in 735-6/1335 A.D., the great chiefs of the Ilkhānid empire struggled to control the succession, and elevated in turn three obscure Hūlāgūids: Arpā (736/1335-6), Mūsā (736-7/1336), and Muḥammad (737-9/1336-8). These rapid changes at the top did not seriously disturb the structure of the empire: Muḥammad, the protegé of Ḥasan Buzurg, ruled over as large a realm as had Abū Saʿīd.

The breakdown of the empire began with the defeat of Ḥasan Buzurg and execution of Muḥammad by the Čubānid, Ḥasan "Küčük" (so-called to distinguish him from the Djalāyirid Ḥasan), in 738-9/1338. Ḥasan Küčük, who ruled in the name of Sātībek (739/1338-9) and Sulaymān (740-4/1340-3), could not control the whole Ilkhānid realm. Ḥasan Buzurg and his followers established themselves at Bagdad, and continued to dispute Čubānid authority, as did Eretna, the governor (and, after 741/1340-1), independent ruler) of Rūm, and the ruler of Khurāsān, Ṭughā Tīmūr. Ḥasan Küčük's attempts to subdue the Djalāyirids (741/1340-1) and Artanā (743-4/1343) failed. On his death in 743-4/1343, his brother, Malik Ashraf, seized power and forced Sulaymān and Sātībek to flee to Ḥasan Buzurg. Ashraf (who ruled in the name of a certain Anūshirwān) also failed to dislodge the Djalāyirids from Baghdād (748/1347-8), and, moreover, lost control of the provinces of Iṣfahān, Kirmān, Yazd and Shīrāz that had owed allegiance to Ḥasan Küčük.

Although Ḥasan Buzurg was instrumental in the breakdown of the Ilkhānid empire, he seems to have hoped rather for its restoration—on his own terms—than its collapse. He used only the title Ūlūs Beg that he had held under Abū Saʿīd, and either acknowledged legitimate Djingizids as sovereigns—Ṭughā Tīmūr (739/1338-9), 740-6/1340-5), Djihān Tīmūr (739-40/1339-40), and Sulaymān (746-7/1346)—or left sovereignty unattributed (746-57/1346-56).

Ḥasan Buzurg died in 757/1356, leaving Djalāyirid leadership to his son, Uways. When, in the same year, Sulṭān Djānībek of the Golden Horde overthrew Ashraf, the Djalāyirids in Baghdād recognized Djānībek as their sovereign. But the Mongol empire in Īrān was not to be renewed. Djānībek died in 758-9/1357, and his son, Bīrdībek, abandoned Ādharbaydjān to Ashraf's former supporters, led by a certain Akhīdjūk.

Uways now assumed personal sovereignty (759/1358), and undertook to annex Ādharbaydjān. His first campaign failed, but after his retreat, Muḥammad b. al-Muẓaffar, who had seized Fārs and Iṣfahān in the years following Ḥasan Küčük's death, raided Ādharbāydjān (760/1359), and so weakened Akhīdjūk that Uways' second invasion succeeded (761/1360).

There were further Djalāyirid successes during the years 762-5/1361-4, especially in Fārs, where the Muẓaffarid princes, Shāh Maḥmūd and Shāh Shudjāʿ, having deposed their father, Muḥammad, were quarrelling over the succession. Shāh Maḥmūd acknowledged Djalāyirid suzerainty, and was enabled by Uways to hold Iṣfahān and seize Shīrāz. But after 765/1364 a series of reverses precluded further Djalāyirid expansion. Until about 770/1368 Uways was busy suppressing revolts by the Shīrwānshāh, by Khʷādja Mirdjān in Baghdād, and by the Ḳaraḳoyunlu Turkomans in the Diyārbakr region. While meeting these challenges, Uways faltered in his support of Shāh Maḥmūd, who was driven from Shīrāz. Another enemy appeared in 772/1370-1, when Amīr Walī of Astarābād began to attack Rayy.

Uways died in 775-6/1374, and was succeeded by his son, Ḥusayn, after the great amīrs had murdered an unpopular elder son, Ḥasan. Other harbingers of decline appeared during Ḥusayn's reign (776-86/1374-82): Ḥusayn came to depend entirely upon Amīr ʿĀdil for leadership; and Ḥusayn's brothers, Shaykh ʿAlī, Aḥmad, and Bāyazīd, were left at large and even given positions of power despite the example Ḥusayn had set of profiting from a brother's murder. Abroad, the death of Shāh Maḥmūd in 776-7/1375 enabled Shāh Shudjāʿ to occupy Iṣfahān and attack Ādharbāydjān (777/1375-6, 783/1381); Amīr Walī continued to threaten the border at Rayy; and the Ḳaraḳoyunlu had again to be subdued (778-9/1377).

The dangers implicit in these conditions were soon realized. Shaykh ʿAlī rebelled in 780/1378-9, held Shūshtar against Ḥusayn and ʿĀdil, and, in 782/1381, seized Baghdād. Then, in 783/1382, ʿĀdil led the army against Rayy, leaving Ḥusayn at Tabrīz. Aḥmad, seeing Ḥusayn unprotected, gathered a force from his own domains in Ardabīl and slew his brother. When attacked in turn by Shaykh ʿAlī, coming from Baghdād, and by ʿĀdil, returning from Rayy with Bāyazīd, Aḥmad called in the Ḳaraḳoyunlu. Shaykh ʿAlī was killed, and ʿĀdil and Bāyazīd retreated to Sulṭāniyya.

Before Aḥmad could consolidate his position in Ādharbaydjān, the intervention of the Golden Horde and then Tīmūr drove him away. Aḥmad retired to Baghdād (787/1385), and later fled before Tīmūr to the Ottomans, and then to Egypt. After Tīmūr's death in 807-8/1405, Aḥmad regained Baghdād, and briefly reoccupied Tabrīz, only to be driven out by the Tīmūrid Abū Bakr, who was, in turn, ousted by the Ḳaraḳoyunlu. When Aḥmad tried again to take Tabrīz (812-3/1410), he was captured by the Ḳaraḳoyunlu, and executed on the pretext of having violated an agreement to cede Ādharbaydjān to Ḳarā Yūsuf Ḳaraḳoyunlu, made while they were fellow-exiles in Egypt.

Although Baghdād fell to the Ḳaraḳoyunlu in 814-5/1412, Djalāyirid princes survived in lower Mesopotamia for some years. The last of these, Ḥusayn II, fell during the siege of Ḥilla by the Ḳaraḳoyunlu in 835-6/1432.

Djalāyirid patronage has left us the khān and mosque of Mirdjān in Baghdād, Salmān Sāwadjī's poems, and the miniatures of Shams al-Dīn. Aḥmad, himself a poet, unsuccessfully offered his support to Ḥāfiẓ, who would not leave Shīrāz.

Bibliography: Abū Bakr al-Ahrī, *Taʾrīkh-i Shaykh Uways*, ed. and trans. J. B. van Loon,

The Hague 1954; Ḥāfiẓ-i Abrū, *Dhayl-i Djamiʿ al-tawārīkh-i Rashīdī*, ed. and trans. Kh. Bayānī; i-text: Tehran 1317s/1938; ii-trans.: Paris 1936; A. Markov, *Katalog Dželairidskikh monet*, St. Petersburg 1897; idem, *Inventarniy katalog musulmanskikh monet ... Ermitaža* (1 vol. and suppls.), St. Petersburg 1896, 1898; Lane-Poole, *Cat.*, vi and x; Cl. Huart, *Mémoire sur la fin de la dynastie des Ilékaniens*, in *JA*, 7ème sér., viii (1876); C. Defrémery, *Mémoire historique sur la destruction de la dynastie des Mozafferiens*, in *JA*, 4ème sér., iv (1844) and v (1845); Spuler, *Mongolen*²; H. Howorth, *History of the Mongols*, iii, London 1888; ʿAbbas al-ʿAzzāwī, *Taʾrīkh al-ʿIrāḳ bayn iḥtilālayn*, ii, Baghdād 1354/1936; M. H. Yınanç, art. Celāyir, in *İA*. See also ČUBĀNIDS.

(J. M. SMITH, JR.)

DJĀLĪ [see DJAWĀLĪ].

DJALĪLĪ, a family and quasi-dynasty in Mosul, where seventeen members held the position of *wālī* of that *wilāya* for various periods between 1139/1726 and 1250/1834. If legendary origins in eastern Anatolia can be ignored, the founder of the family, ʿAbd al-Djalīl, seems to have begun life as a Christian slave of the local and equally famous ʿUmarī family in the later 11th/17th Century. His son Ismāʿīl, a Muslim and well educated, attained the Pashalīḳ of Mosul by exceptional merits after a long career of public office, and governed it with distinction for some years from 1139/1726; and the easy succession of his son, Ḥādjdj Ḥusayn Pasha, in 1143/1730 to a position which, with interruptions, he was to hold eight times between then and his death in 1173/1759, showed that the family was already a firm claimant to hereditary rule of the province. Ḥādjdj Ḥusayn, an outstanding personality, attained lasting fame for his part in the defence of Mosul against Nādir Shāh, notably in 1156/1743; he held also at intervals other *wilāya*s and high positions in ʿIrāḳ and elsewhere in the Ottoman Empire, as did for the next fifty years his sons and relations, to an extent doubtless unique among ʿIrāḳī families before or since. The chronic tribal and country-side disorders of northern ʿIrāḳ, and of Mosul itself, at this period rendered all government precarious, and tenures shortlived; but a Djalīlī pasha, from the numerous descendents of Ḥādjdj Ḥusayn, was to be found in office at Mosul, struggling with the forces of anarchy and with the jealous factions—and on one occasion, the murderous attacks—of his own family discontinuously till 1250/1834, when the last *wālī* of the family, Yaḥyā Pasha, was displaced by a modernized central government. Eminent among these were Amīn Pasha (son of Ḥadjdj Ḥusayn) who was six times *wālī*, in part during his father's lifetime: his son, Muḥammad Pasha, who ruled the *wilāya* more or less at peace for 18 years (1204-22/1789-1807): and Aḥmad Pasha, who rebuilt the walls of Mosul at intervals from 1228/1813.

The local annals of the ninety years covered by Djalīlī pre-eminence in northern ʿIrāḳ are unedifying in their tale of violent, selfish and corrupt misgovernment, and are of interest mainly for the light they throw on the contemporary administration of the remoter Turkish provinces; but the virile persistence, and at times the superior qualities, of the effectively irreplaceable Djalīlī dynasty for so long a period entitles them to a place in history. Their descendants in Mosul are still numerous, but no longer influential.

Bibliography: S. H. Longrigg, *Four centuries of modern ʿIraq*, Oxford 1925, esp. 158, 176 f., 210, 242, 284, authorities specified on 328-30, and genealogical tree, 347. (S. H. LONGRIGG)

DJĀLĪNŪS, Arabic for Galen, born in Pergamon, in Asia Minor A.D. 129, died in Rome about 199; the last great medical writer in Greek antiquity, outstanding as an anatomist and physiologist as well as as a practising physician, surgeon and pharmacologist. He also became known as an influential though minor philosopher. More than 120 books ascribed to him are included in the last complete edition of his Greek works by C. E. Kühn (Leipzig 1821-33); they represent by no means his whole output: some works have survived in Arabic, Hebrew or Latin translation only, others are unretrievably lost.

Although Djālīnūs stands nowhere in the first rank, his popularity especially as a physician grew steadily in subsequent centuries, and he eventually became the most influential teacher of medicine together with Hippocrates (Buḳrāṭ [*q.v.*]) whom he had helped to establish as a model physician and a pattern of perfection, and whose treatises he had explained in many elaborate commentaries. When the teaching of Greek philosophy and medicine was definitely made part of the Christian syllabus of learning in ± 500, the preservation of the greater part of his numerous works was assured and his supreme position established for the next millennium. Whereas the far superior works of his predecessors in Alexandria and elsewhere have perished, his codification of the great achievements of the Hellenistic physicians, whose independence of mind he still understood and taught himself, was handed on to posterity and was instrumental in establishing a fundamentally unbroken tradition of scientific medicine which never lost sight of him.

As in the case of philosophy and other sciences, Syrian and Arabic medicine follow the late Greek syllabus almost without a gap. We are not too badly informed about the Syriac translations of Djālīnūs, by Sergius of Rāshʿayna (d. 536) and Job of Edessa (about 825) for instance. We have Ḥunayn b. Isḥāḳ's [*q.v.*] detailed survey of 129 major and minor works by Djālīnūs translated into Syriac and/or Arabic by himself and others, he actually lists 179 Syriac and 123 Arabic versions (cf. O. Neugebauer, *The exact sciences in antiquity*, Providence 1957, 180). This unduly neglected autobibliographical account by Ḥunayn was edited and translated into German by G. Bergsträsser in *Abh. K.M.* XVII/2, 1925 and XIX/2, 1932, cf. M. Meyerhof, in *Isis* VIII 1926, 658 ff.; *Byzantion* III, 1927, 1 ff.; *The legacy of Islam*, Oxford 1931, 316 ff., 346 ff. Ḥunayn's list is not even complete. The Arabs eventually came to possess translations of every work of Djālīnūs still read in Greek centres of learning during the 7th, 8th and 9th centuries A.D., and thus knew a number of medical and philosophical works of Djālīnūs which disappeared in the late Byzantine period.

There can be no doubt—although details have still to be ascertained and interpreted in monographs —that Galen's medical works in their entirety, his methods and his results, were fully digested and appreciated by all the later Arabic physicians and became an integral part of their medical learning, in their original form as well as in summaries, commentaries and new works based on them. This by no means applies only to such outstanding physicians as Muḥammad b. Zakariya al-Rāzi [*q.v.*] or Ibn Sīnā [*q.v.*] but to many others as well (cf., *e.g.*, J. Schacht-M. Meyerhof. *The medico-philosophical controversy between Ibn Butlan of Baghdad and Ibn Ridwan of Cairo*, Cairo 1937, passim). A comparison between D̲j̲ālīnūs and Ibn Sīnā's *Ḳānūn fi 'l-ṭibb* would yield very interesting results indeed. D̲j̲ālīnūs deserves a major chapter in any future history of Arabic medicine down to the first half of the 20th century. The Galen studies in medieval and Renaissance Europe owe very much to the Arab precedent and to Galen-translations from the Arabic.

A number of otherwise lost medical and philosophical works of D̲j̲ālīnūs has been recovered from Arabic translations, and it seems appropriate to mention them here.

Medical works: 1) M. Simon, *Sieben Bücher Anatomie des Galen*, 1906 (cf. G. Bergsträsser, *Hunayn ibn Isḥak und seine Schule*, Leiden 1913) with Ger. tr.; Eng. tr. by the late W. H. L. Duckworth, edd. M. C. Lyons and G. Towers, *Galen on anatomical procedures*; *the later books*, Cambridge 1962. 2) Ps.-Galenus *In Hippocratis de Septimanis Commentarius*, ed. G. Bergsträsser, *Corpus medicorum Graecorum*, xi/2.i. 3) M. Meyerhof-J. Schacht, *Galen über die medinischen Namen* in *Abh. Berl. Akad. Wiss.*, phil.-hist. Kl. 1931, no 3 (with Ger. tr.). 4) *In Hippocratis Epidemias* i, ii, vi/1-8, ed. E. Wenkebach-F. Pfaff, *Corpus medicorum Graecorum* v/10, 1.1; v/10, 2.2 (German translation only, cf. *Gnomon*, xxii, 1950, 226 ff.). 5) *Schrift über die Siebenmonatskinder*, ed. R. Walzer, in *RSO*, xv, 1935, 323 ff.; xxiv, 1949, 92 (with Ger. tr. 6) *On medical experience*, ed. R. Walzer, Oxford 1944 (with Eng. tr.).

Philosophical works: 1) *Summary of Plato's Timaeus*, see AFLĀṬŪN (with Latin translation). 2) Additional fragments of the medical commentary on the Timaeus, ed. P. Kahle, see AFLĀṬŪN (with Ger. tr.). 3) Epitome of Περὶ ἠθῶν, ed. P. Kraus 1939 (Arabic text and notes), cf. R. Walzer in *Classical Quarterly* 1949, 82 ff.; idem, in *Harvard Theological Review* 1954, 254 ff. S. M. Stern, *Classical Quarterly*, 1956, 91 ff. 4) *De demonstratione*: P. Kraus, *Jabir ibn Ḥayyān*, ii, Cairo 1942, passim; S. Pines, *Rāzī, Critique de Galien* in *Actes du Septième Congrès Internationale d'Histoire des Sciences*, 1953, 480 ff. 5) Statements on Jews and Christians: R. Walzer, *Galen on Jews and Christians*, Oxford 1949. 6) S. Pines, *A refutation of Galen by Alexander of Aphrodisias* in *Isis*, lii, 1961, 21 ff. 7) J. Schacht-N. Meyerhof, *Maimonides against Galen*, in *Bulletin of the Faculty of Arts in the University of Cairo*, vi, 1939, 54-84.

The Arabic versions of books by Galen which are preserved in the original Greek may often prove useful for the establishment of the Greek text, especially in cases where only late Greek manuscripts are available. Moreover, they are very important for the general history of medical terminology, and work in this direction has scarcely stated. The Arabic text of Galen's commentary on Hippocrates Κατ' ἰητρεῖον, ed. M. Lyons (with Eng. tr.) will be published in 1962 as part of the *Corpus Medicorum Graecorum*. A Ger. tr. of the Arabic text of Περὶ ἠθῶν by F. Pfaff is to be found in the *Corpus Medicorum Graecorum Supplementum*, iii, 1941.

A survey of Arabic MSS of Galen, as far as it could be established at the time of the compilation, is to be found in H. Diels, *Die Handschriften der antiken Ärzte*, Berlin 1906. Additions: H. Ritter-R. Walzer, *Arabische Übersetzungen griechischer Ärzte in Stambuler Bibliotheken* in *Berichte der Berliner Akademie*, phil-hist. Klasse, 1934 and in many miscellaneous publications.

An intensive and detailed study of Arabic medical writers will no doubt eventually yield more texts of Galen and will make it possible to write the history of his very important impact on the development of Arabic medicine.

Bibliography: In addition to references in the article: G. Sarton, *Introduction to the history of science, passim*; idem, *Galen of Pergamon*, Kensas Press 1954; D. Campbell, *Arabian medicine and its influence in the middle ages*, ii, Leiden 1926, 13-220; H. Schipperges, *Ideologie und Historiographie des Arabismus*, Wiesbaden 1961. (R. WALZER)

D̲J̲ĀLIYA (from Arabic *d̲j̲alā* [*ʿan*], to emigrate), used here for the Arabic-speaking communities with special reference to North and South America. About eighty per cent of these emigrants are estimated to have come from what is today the Lebanese Republic; fifteen per cent from Syria and Palestine and the rest from al-ʿIrāḳ and al-Yaman. Egypt's quota is negligible.

Overpopulation in mountainous Lebanon, whose soil was less fertile than its women, combined with political unrest, economic pressure and a seafaring tradition, found relief in migration to other lands. Egypt, the only country to which the Ottoman authorities before 1890 permitted emigration, offered a special attraction particularly after the British occupation in 1882. The response came from the Western-educated group, graduates of the American University of Beirut (then known as the Syrian Protestant College) and the Jesuit St. Joseph University. Clerks, government employees, physicians, pharmacists, teachers found rewarding employment in Egypt and the Sūdān. Two of the earliest and most influential learned magazines (*al-Muḳtaṭaf* and *al-Hilāl*) and of the newspapers (*al-Muḳaṭṭam* and *al-Ahrām*) were founded by such graduates. In addition a Syro-Lebanese commercial colony flourished mainly in Cairo and Alexandria and gained possession of about a tenth of the entire wealth of the land. Western Africa, where today Syro-Lebanese communities—with about 30,000 settlers—are sprinkled over the major cities, was not discovered until the late 1890's. South Africa claims about an equal number.

But the golden fleece lay in more distant horizons. The first recorded Arabic speaker to land in North America was a Christian Lebanese youth Anṭūniyūs al-Bis̲h̲ʿalānī, whose tombstone in a Brooklyn (N. Y.) cemetery gives 1856 as his date of death, two years after his arrival. But there was no mass movement until after the mid-1890's following the World's Fair at Chicago. The peak was reached in the pre-first World War period. For the thirteen years ending in 1913 the Commissioner General of Immigration reported 79,420 "Syrians" (which term then embraced Lebanese and Palestinians), of whom 4064 entered the United States in 1901 and 9211 in 1913, By that time there was hardly a village in Lebanon which could not claim an American citizen as its son. Decline began with the war followed by restricted quota imposed in 1924 by the United States government. Its official statistics indicate that in 1940 there were about 350,000 of Arabic-speaking origin; estimates in 1950 raise the figure to 450,000; but Lebanese government statistics released in 1958 make those of Lebanese descent alone in the United States 450,000.

The majority of these emigrants were Christians, who felt less strange in the Western world, and were recruited largely from the uneducated classes. Wherever these people went they carried along their cuisine, churches and Arabic printing press. By 1924 they had established two hundred and nineteen churches and missions scattered all over the larger commercial and industrial cities of the United

States. Since then nine mosques have been built, of which the most imposing is that of Washington, D.C., founded in 1952 and patronized by the embassies. Of the estimated 33,000 Muslims, mostly Palestinians and Yamanites, 5,000 live in Detroit, attracted by employment in the automobile factories. In 1924 New York housed six newspapers (in 1960 five) and three monthlies. The oldest newspaper extant, *al-Hudā*, celebrated on 22 February 1960 its sixty-second anniversary. A census taken in 1929 lists 102 Arabic periodicals and papers, extant and extinct, which saw the light in North America and 166 in South America [see DJARĪDA].

The first to reach Brazil was again a Lebanese in 1874. The movement acquired mass proportions in the 1880's following Emperor Pedro II's visit to Lebanon and Palestine. In 1892 an Ottoman-Brazilian treaty gave further impetus. Argentina was equally interested in new emigrants to develop its vast resources. The Syro-Lebanese community in Brazil is larger than that of the United States; that of Argentina numbers about 150,000, of Mexico 60,000. A number of streets in Latin American countries bear the names of Syria, Lebanon or of a citizen born there. In South America such emigrants felt more at home than in North America; they also prospered more and maintained a stronger Arab tradition. In wealth and influence the São Paulo colony, headed by the Jafet (Yāfit͟h) family—founded by a Christian from al-S͟huwayr, Lebanon—compares favourably with that of Cairo. In 1959 the São Paulo community maintained two sport clubs (one Syrian, one Lebanese), two chambers of commerce, one hospital, one orphanage, two secondary schools and a score of philanthropic organizations. Its Greek Orthodox Cathedral, begun in 1939, is the most imposing place of worship erected by Syro-Lebanese emigrants anywhere.

Though originating mostly in villages the bulk of the emigrants to the two Americas took to business. The general pattern was to start from peddling, carrying a *kas͟hs͟ha* (from Portuguese *caixa*) and knocking at doors, move on to shopkeeping and graduate to large store owning and perhaps to a leading position as a merchant or industrialist. Arabic papers abound in "success stories" of penniless emigrants developing into millionaires. Arabic-speaking merchants are credited among other things with contributing to the introduction and popularization of kimonos, lingeries, negligées, linens, laces, Oriental rugs and Near Eastern food articles. The "folks back home" were generally never forgotten. Remittances to relatives and friends in the course of the first World War have been credited with saving numberless lives. Even as late as 1952 Lebanese official statistics credit Lebanese emigrants with remittances to relatives, friends and religious and educational institutions amounting to $ 22,000,000. Descendants of emigrants have entered all kinds of professions. In 1959 California sent to the House of Repesentatives in Washington the first son of a Lebanese emigrant; in the same year a second-generation girl singer was admitted to the Metropolitan Opera in New York. In 1960 an American citizen whose father was born in Zaḥlah (Lebanon) was elected mayor of a large city (Toledo, Ohio).

More striking perhaps has been the literary contribution. New York boasted a literary circle, founded by Kahlil Gibran (D͟jabrān K͟halīl D͟jabrān, [*q.v.*]), whose influence has been felt throughout the Arab world. Its counterpart in São Paulo published for twenty years a magazine (*al-Andalus*) which had a wide vogue. These writers treated new themes, struck fresh notes, introduced modern styles and reflected the Western influences to which they were exposed in their adopted lands. By their writings, correspondence and return visits Arabic-speaking emigrants contributed substantially to the liberalizing, modernizing trend of their native lands. Some of the tenderest and most often quoted modern verses have been composed by Arabic poets in New York and São Paulo.

Legislative restrictions on immigration into the New World encouraged the movement into Australia where the Syro-Lebanese community is estimated at 20,000 largely clustered in Sydney.

The wave of migration which rolled from the eastern Mediterranean in the decade preceding the first World War sent sprinkles to the remotest corners of the habitable world. The Canadian community now counts about 30,000.

Bibliography: M. Berger, *Americans from the Arab world*, in *The World of Islam*, ed. James Kritzeck and R. Bayly Winder, London & New York 1960, 351-72); Tawfīḳ Ḍaʿūn, *Muk͟htārāt al-d͟jadīd*, São Paulo 1922; Wadīʿ Dīb, *al-S͟hiʿr al-ʿArabī fī al-mahd͟jar al-Amirkī*, Beirut 1955; ʿAbdo A. Elk͟holy, *Comparative analyses of two Muslim communities in the United States*, (Ms., Princeton University Library, 1960); E. Epstein, *Demographic problems of the Lebanon*, in *Royal Central Asian Journal*, xxxiii (April 1946), 150-4; Elie Safa, *L'émigration libanaise,*, Beirut 1960; Philip K. Hitti, *Anṭūniyūs al-Bis͟hʿalānī awwal muhād͟jir Sūrī ilā al-ʿālam al-d͟jadīd*, New York 1919; idem, *The Syrians in America*, New York 1924; Salīm al-Ḥuṣṣ, *al-Hid͟jra min Lubnān*, in *al-Abḥāt͟h*, xii, pt. 1 (March 1959), 59-72; Institute of Arab American Affairs, *Arabic-speaking Americans*, New York 1946; Nadīm al-Maqdissi, *The Muslims of America*, in *The Islamic Review*, xliii, no. 6 (June, 1955), 28-31; D͟jūrd͟j Ṣaydaḥ, *Adabunā wa-udabāʾunā fī al-mahād͟jir al-Amīrikiyya*[2], Beirut 1957; ʿAbdul D͟jalīl ʿAlī al-Ṭāhir, *The Arab community in the Chicago area* (Ms., University of Chicago Library, 1952); Fīlīb dī Ṭarrāzī, *Taʾrīk͟h al-ṣaḥāfa al-ʿArabiyya*, 4 vols., Beirut 1933; U. S. Department of Justice, *Annual Report of the Immigration and Naturalization Service in the fiscal year ended June* 30, 1954, Washington 1954, table 4 and *passim*; U. S. Bureau of the Census, *16th census of the United States*, 1940. *Population, nativity and parentage of the white population. Mother tongue*, Washington 1943, tables 1, 2, 4; U. S. Bureau of the Census, *U. S. Census of Population*, 1950, vol. iv, *Special reports. Nativity and parentage*, Washington 1954, table 12; M. Zelditch, *The Syrians in Pittsburgh* (Ms., University of Pittsburgh Library, 1936). (P. K. HITTI)

DJALLĀB, or, according to the dialect, DJALLĀBA or DJALLĀBIYYA, an outer garment used in certain parts of the Mag͟hrib, which is very wide and loose with a hood and two armlets. The *d͟jallāb* is made of a quadrangular piece of cloth, which is much longer than it is broad. By sewing together the two short ends a wide cylinder is formed. Its upper opening is also sewn up except for a piece in the centre where a hole is required for the head and neck. Holes are cut on each side for the arms. When the garment is put on, the seam joining the two short ends runs down the middle of the breast. The two seams which close the two ends of the upper part run along the shoulders and the upper part of the arms. The head and neck are put through the space left open in the middle of the upper end. The forearms come through the holes at each side; they would be left uncovered if armlets were not sewn on to the edges of the armholes. These armlets are very short. At their lower extremity is a slit (*nīfuk*) for the elbow and at the top a second slit (*fatḥa*) across, through which, when necessary (*e.g.*, for the ritual ablution) the bare fore-arm can be thrust. The *djallāb* is made either of native cloth or (in prosperous towns) of European. The former is woollen, rarely and only quite recently of cotton or cotton and wool. These cloths are dyed in different colours in different districts; red, brown, black, white, of uniform colour, striped or spotted. The European materials are thick, usually navy blue, black or dark grey.—The *djallāb* of native manufacture consists of a single piece of cloth, which is made of the required size. The hood is not added but consists of a quadrangular piece of cloth woven on, the sides of which are folded together behind and sewn. In the *djallāb* of European cloth, the hood is cut separately and put on. The seams of the *djallāb* are covered with braid and often ornamented with tassels, knots and rosettes.—The cut, the form of the *djallāb* and the hood, the ornamentation, the style of weaving, of sewing and of lining vary much in different districts.— This garment is called *djallāb* (*djallāba*, *djallābiyya*), throughout the greater part of Morocco and in the west of Algeria; it is also used in other parts of the Maghrib, *e.g.*, in the south of Algeria and in the Mzāb but it is given another name there. Among the Andalusian Muslims, however, the word *djallābiyya* was the name of a garment, the shape and use of which we do not know; in Egypt, we find a phonetic equivalent of the word, *gallābiyya* (with *g* for *dj*), but the garment it denotes is quite different from the *djallāb* of the Maghrib. The origin of the word is uncertain. Dozy considers the form *djallābiyya* to be the original one and *djallāb*, *djallāba* to be corruptions. He therefore gives the original meaning as "garment of a *djallāb*, *i.e.*, a slave dealer". This view seems philologically untenable. It is much more probable that *djallāb* is connected with the Old Arabic *djilbāb* "outer garment". The dissimilative dropping of the *b* in this word of foreign origin (cf. Nöldeke, *Neue Beiträge zur semitischen Sprachwissenschaft*, 53) is not surprising; moreover it has also taken place outside the Maghrib in the modern forms of the word *djilbāb*: thus for example in the dialect of ʿUmān we find *gillāb* with the meaning of "women's veil".

Bibliography: Dozy, *Dictionnaire détaillé des noms des vêtements ches les Arabes*, 122 ff.; idem, *Suppl.*, i, 204, 205, with numerous references; Budgett Meakin, *The Moors*, 58 ff., 59, 59, with an illustration; Mouliéras, *Le Maroc inconnu*, ii, 16; *Archives marocaines*, xvii, 122; Bel, *La population musulmane de Tlemcen*, Pl. xix, Fig. 17; Bel and Ricard, *Les industries et le travail de la laine à Tlemcen.* (W. Marçais)

DJĀLOR, a town in the Indian state of Rajasthan, some 75 miles south of Djodhpur on the left bank of the Sukrī river.

Although the troops of ʿAlāʾ al-Dīn Khaldjī had passed through Djālor on their return from the conquest of Gudjarāt in 696/1297, it was not then occupied by them. In Djumādā I 705/December 1305, however, that king sent ʿAyn al-Mulk, governor of Multān, on an expedition to Djālor, Udjdjayn and Čandērī; he was opposed by an army of 150,000 Hindūs on his entry into Mālwā, and his victory over them, which brought Udjdjayn, Dhār, Māndū, and Čandērī [*qq.v.*] into Muslim possession, so impressed the Čawhān rādjā of Djālor that he accompanied ʿAyn al-Mulk to Dihlī to swear his allegiance to ʿAlāʾ al-Dīn. Two years later this rādjā's arrogance caused ʿAlāʾ al-Dīn to attack Djālor, which was taken for Dihlī by Kamāl al-Dīn Gurg. On the weakening of the sultanate at ʿAlāʾ al-Dīn's death it seems to have relapsed into Čawhān possession.

At some time in the 8th/14th century a body of Lohānī Afghāns left their adoptive province of Bihār and came to Mārwāṛ, where they entered the service of the Čawhān rādjā of Djālor. On the latter's death by a trick at the hands of a neighbouring rādjā in 794/1392 their leader, Malik Khurram, assisted the rādjā's widow in carrying on the government, but after disagreements between the Afghāns and the Rādjpūts he established himself as ruler over the city and its fort, Songir (Sanskrit: *suvarṇa-giri* "golden hill"), and sought through Ẓafar Khān, *ṣūbadār* of Gudjarāt under the Tughluḳs, a *farmān* from Dihlī confirming his title; this was given, 796/1394. After Tīmūr's depredations in north India in 801/1399 the Djālorīs became independent rulers for a time, before later becoming feudatory to the new and powerful sultanate of Gudjarāt.

At some time in the early 10th/16th century the Djālorī family had added Pālanpur [*q.v.*] to its dominions, and by mid-century its ruler had acquired the title of Nawwāb. By about 1110/1699 the Nawwāb moved his seat from Djālor to Pālanpur, which remained an independent Muslim state until 1956; for the history of the dynasty, see PĀLANPUR.

Monuments. The fort of Djālor was built by the Paramāra Rādjpūts, and remained substantially unchanged under Muslim rule except for the modification of its perimeter wall for artillery. The oldest monument is the mosque in the city, built from temple spoil probably at the time of ʿAlāʾ al-Dīn, 56.4 m. square, with cloisters of three arcades on north, south, and east, broken by doorways, and a deeper three-domed *līwān* on the west. The latter is faced with a screen wall of later date, probably of the time of Muẓaffar II of Gudjarāt (917-32/1511-26); an inscription including the name of Muḥammad b. Tughluḳ stands over the north door, implying an extension or restoration in his time. The arcades have been enriched by the addition of graceful and delicate stone lattice screens of the middle Gudjarātī period. Known as the Tōpkhāna masdjid, it was for long used as an arsenal. A smaller mosque stands in the fort; although said by Erskine (*Rajputana Gazetteer*, iii A, 1909, 189 ff.) to have been built by ʿAlāʾ al-Dīn's armies, it seems to be in its present form entirely a construction of the period of Maḥmūd I (863-917/1458-1511) or Muẓaffar II of Gudjarāt, and bears an inscription of the latter.

Bibliography: Malik Sulaymān b. ʿAbd Allāh b. Sharf al-Dīn, *Khātim-i Sulaymānī*, on which the *History of Palanpur state* (in Gudjarātī) by H. H. Sir Taley Muhammad Khan, Nawab of Palanpur, is based; *Bombay Gazetteer*, v, 318 ff.; *Rajputana Gazetteer*, ii, 1879, 260, and second ed., 1909, iii A, 189 ff.; J. Tod, *Annals and antiquities of Rajasthan*, 2nd. ed. W. Crooke, Oxford 1920, iii, 1266-8; *Progress Report*, *ASI*, *Western Circle*, *year ending March 1909*, Bombay 1909, 54 ff.

(J. Burton-Page)

DJALŪLĀʾ, a town in ʿIrāḳ (Babylonia) and, in the mediaeval division of this province, the capital of a district (*ṭassūdj*) of the Shādh-Ḳubādh circle to the east of the Tigris, was a station on the important Khurāsān road, the main route between Babylonia and Īrān, and was at about an equal distance (7 parasangs = 28 miles) from Dastadjird [*q.v.*] in the south-west and from Khāniḳīn in the north-east. It was watered by a canal from the Diyālā (called Nahr Djalūlāʾ), which rejoined the main stream a little further down near Bādjisrā [*q.v.*]. Near this town, which seems from the statements of the Arab geographers to have been quite unimportant, the Arabs inflicted a severe defeat on the army of the Sāsānian king at the end of the year 16/637.

According to Mustawfī, writing about 740/1340, the Saldjūḳ sultan Malikshāh (465-85/1073-92) built at Djalūlāʾ a watch-house (*ribāṭ*, popularly *rubāṭ*) which probably served also as a caravanserai; after his time the place was usually called Ribāṭ Djalūlāʾ. This statement helps us to locate the site of Djalūlāʾ with certainty; for indeed there can be almost no doubt that Ribāṭ Djalūlāʾ must be identified with the modern Ḳīzīlrobāṭ, especially since the distances given by the Arab geographers for Djalūlāʾ apply perfectly to Ḳīzīlrobāṭ. Its geographical position is 34° 10′ N., 45° E.; it lies within the mountains, at the east end of the pass through the Djabal Ḥamrīn. The Diyālā flows by at some distance to the east of the town. The name Ḳīzīlrobāṭ ("red caravanserai") is popularly corrupted to Ḳazilābādh and Ḳazrābādh (cf. Petermann, *Reisen im Orient*, ii, 274) or abbreviated to Ḳizrabāṭ (cf. Herzfeld, in *Petermanns Geogr. Mitt.*, 1907, 51). Like its mediaeval predecessor, the modern Ḳīzīlrobāṭ is of only moderate importance; it still has no other rôle than that of a transit and relay station on an important caravan route.

Bibliography: in addition to references in the article BAʿḲŪBĀ, see in particular M. Streck, *Babylonien nach den arab. Geograph.*, i, 8, 15; Le Strange, 62; and, on Ḳīzīlrobāṭ, cf. Ritter, *Erdkunde*, ix, 418, 489; Ker Porter, *Reisen in Georgien, Persien u. Armenien*, etc., Weimar 1833, ii, 234.

(M. STRECK)

DJĀLŪT. The Goliath of the Bible appears as Djālūt in the Ḳurʾān (II, 248/247-252/251) (the line of al-Samawʾal where the name occurs is inauthentic), in assonance with Ṭālūt [*q.v.*] and perhaps also under the influence of the Hebrew word *gālūt*, "exile, Diaspora", which must have been frequently on the lips of the Jews in Arabia as elsewhere. The passage of the Ḳurʾān where he is referred to by name (his introduction in the exegesis of V, 25 seems to be sporadic and secondary) combines the biblical account of the wars waged by Saul and David (I Samuel xvii) with some traces of Gideon's expedition against the Midianites (Judges vii, particularly the episode of the water drinking test to select warriors.

Furthermore, Muslim tradition, tending to see in the Ḳurʾān account a prefiguration of the Battle of Badr, embroiders on the Haggadic development of the Bible story (for instance, the sling-stones given to David and their joining together into one, the latter detail borrowed from the Midrashic legend about the stones of Bethel, which Jacob put for his pillow); the same tradition attempts to link the giant Djālūt variously with the Amalekites (see ʿAmālīḳ), the ʿĀdites or the Thamudites, or even with the Berbers, no doubt in connexion with the Talmudic legend about the emigration of certain Canaanite tribes into "Africa" at the time of the Israelite conquest of Palestine (*Tosefta Shabbat*, vii, 25; Talmud of Jerusalem *Shebīʿit* vi, 2 [36c]; cf. H. Lewy, *MGWJ*, lxxvii, 1933, especially 178). With the help of these linkings, even though the Bible story in its authentic form must have been known to a writer as particular about first hand information as al-Yaʿḳūbī, Djālūt became a kind of collective name for the oppressors of the Israelite nation before David. The battle against Djālūt is localized in the Ghor or lower valley of the Jordan (see ʿAYN DJĀLŪT).

Bibliography: *K. al-Tīdjān*, Ḥaydarābād 1347/1928, 178 f.; Yaʿḳūbī, *Taʾrīkh*, 51 f. (Smit, *Bijbel en Legende*, 61 f.); Ṭabarī, i, 370-6, cf. 278-80; Masʿūdī, *Murūdj*, i, 105-8; iii, 241; Kisaʾī, *Vita Prophetarum*, 250-4; *Mukhtaṣar al-ʿadjāʾib* (*Abrégé des Merveilles*), translated by Carra de Vaux, 101; M. Grünbaum, *Neue Beiträge zur semitischen Sagenkunde*, 191 f.; J. Horovitz, *Koranische Untersuchungen*, 106; R. Blachère, *Le Coran*, 803-5.

(G. VAJDA)

DJAM [see FĪRŪZKŪH].

DJĀM, a village in Afghānistān (orchards, particularly of apricots) in the region of Ghūr [*q.v.*] on the Tagao Gunbaz, tributary on the left bank of the Harī Rūd, above Čisht; an hour's march away, by the confluence of the tributary and the main stream, stands a cylindrical minaret of harmonious proportions, with an octagonal base which carries three superposed stages of truncated conical form, with an interior staircase (over 180 steps); the height of this minaret (about 60 m.) puts it between the Ḳuṭb mīnār of Dihlī [*q.v.*] and the minaret of Bukhārā [*q.v.*]. One of the inscriptions on this minaret, which is entirely covered with a striking decoration, gives the name of the prince who ordered its construction: Ghiyāth al-Dunya wa 'l-Dīn Abu 'l-Fatḥ Muḥammad b. Sām, 5th Ghūrid sultan (558-99/1163-1202; cf. GHŪRIDS, and Wiet, *op. cit. infra*, 21-55). A. Maricq, who in 1957 discovered this minaret which previously had been known only by hearsay, considers it to have been a "tower of glory" as well as a minaret (as was the Ḳuṭb mīnār, so described in its inscription), the central point of the territories of the Ghūrid sultanate; furthermore, he has collected (*op. cit. infra*, 55 and 65) the texts and other evidence which allow this monument of Djām to be considered as the only apparent vestige of the town of Fīrūzkūh, the Ghūrid capital (contrary to identifications previously proposed, *e.g.*, FĪRŪZKŌH in *EI*[1]); this hypothesis calls for a meticulous examination of the site.

Bibliography: A. Maricq and G. Wiet, *Le minaret de Djām: la découverte de la capitale des sultans Ghōrides* (*XII*ᵉ-*XIII*ᵉ *siècles*), in *Mém. Delegation archéol. française en Afghanistan*, xvi, Paris 1959, 91 pp., 17 plates and two maps.

(H. MASSÉ)

DJAMʿ, DJAMĀʿA.—The aim of the present article is to clarify general ideas, and to show what system underlies the expression of grammatical number, as regards the Arabic plural and collective.

The Arabic language distinguishes between: 1) the singular, 2) dual, 3) plural, 4) collective. Arab grammarians have paid close attention to the first three: 1) the singular: *al-wāḥid*; *mufrad* is applied to the "simple" noun (as opposed to *murakkab*, applied to the "compound" noun) by the *Muf.* § 4; but it has also been used for "singular", likewise *fard* [*q.v.*].—2) the dual: *al-muthannā*, for units of two.—3) the plural: *al-djamʿ*, for units numbering three or more, with the subdivision: *djamʿ sālim* "sound plural", the external plural and *djamʿ mukassar* "broken plural", the internal plural. As regards 4), the collective, they have no general word to denote it. In relation to the noun of unity they have distinguished between: the *ism al-d̲j̲ins* "specific name", which possesses a noun of unity, made by means of the suffix *-aᵗ*, added *to it, e.g.*: *tamr* "dates", noun of unity *tamraᵗ* "a date"; the *ism al-d̲j̲amᶜ* which denotes a *d̲j̲amāᶜa* "collection, assembly of beings", but does not possess a noun of unity or else forms it in a manner different from that given above: without a noun of unity, like *ḳawm* "tribe, group to which one belongs", with noun of unity provided by another word, like *ibil* "camels", *baᶜīr* "a camel", or by another Form of the same root, like *rakb* "travellers" *rākib* "a traveller".

Note: A. Fischer has studied *Die Terminologie der arabischen Kollektivnomina* (*ZDMG*, xciv (1940), 12-24): *S̲h̲ibh al-d̲j̲amᶜ*, in the sense of *ism al-d̲j̲amᶜ* and the plural *as̲h̲bāh al-d̲j̲amᶜ*, recent terms (taken from the author of the *Baḥt̲h̲ al-maṭālib*), current in European grammars, are to be ignored; *asmā' al-d̲j̲amᶜ* can already be traced back to Ibn Yaᶜīs̲h̲ (*e.g.* 732, l. 6) (*asmā' al-d̲j̲umūᶜ* in the *Muf.* § 285). *Ism al-d̲j̲ins* (coll.) gave rise to amphibology with *ism al-d̲j̲ins* (common noun). Al-Us̲h̲mūnī (d. 900/1494) had already in his time defined the collective by *ism al-d̲j̲ins al-d̲j̲amᶜī*, a term at present in general use in Egypt, according to Fischer (20).

The article by A. Fischer will provide useful references for Arabic terminology, see in particular the text of al-Us̲h̲mūnī (*op. cit.* 21-22) on the difference between: *al-d̲j̲amᶜ*, *ism al-d̲j̲amᶜ*, *ism al-d̲j̲ins al-d̲j̲amᶜī*. In the latter, al-Us̲h̲mūnī (l. 12) puts the collectives with noun of unity in *-iyy-* (like *rūm*, *rūmiyy-*). The text can be compared with that of the *S̲h̲*. *S̲h̲*., ii, 193 ff.

I. — The external plural

A.—The external plural for rational beings (*al-ᶜuḳalā'*).

a) By reason of their constitution, agent-nouns and passive nouns of Forms derived from verbs are not capable of forming an internal plural; they form the external plural necessarily, where there is a question of rational beings: *mufaᶜᶜi/alūna*, *mufaᶜᶜi/alāt*, etc.; as for the IVth F., *mufᶜi/al* can form the internal plural, but one finds only a few examples of this (*Muf.* § 252); the external plural is normal for them. The Forms *faᶜᶜāl* (intensive agent-noun and noun of occupation), *fiᶜᶜīl*, *fuᶜᶜāl* (with one exception, *Muf.*, *ibid.*) take only the external plural for rational beings, similarly the relative adjective: *miṣriyyūna* "Egyptian (men)", *miṣriyyāt* "Egyptian (women)". These constructions are constant.

b) For the *ᶜuḳalā'*, the external plural is the proper plural of *fāᶜil* and *mafᶜūl* (agent-noun and passive noun which is exactly the *ṣifa* of the Arab grammarians), through and by reason of the verbal "value" which they contain, in the view of these grammarians: this is true of them considered as "participles". In proportion as they become substantives (*ism*), they become further removed from the position of "participles" and can take the internal plural. This is the principle which emerges from Ibn Yaᶜīsh's explanations, 625, in particular l. 14-9, on the subject of the masculine external plural (with exceptions: *Muf.* § 247 and 252). See also *S̲h̲*. *S̲h̲*., ii, 116, l. 9 ff.

c) This extends to adjectives (*ṣifa mus̲h̲abbaha*) of the Form *faᶜl*, *fiᶜl*, *fuᶜl*, *faᶜal*, *faᶜil*, *faᶜul*, *fuᶜul* (*Muf.* § 239; Ibn Yaᶜīs̲h̲, 625, l. 20-4); see (Ibn Yaᶜīs̲h̲, 626-8) examples and cases of internal plural. As for the numerous adjectives with a *long* vowel after the second root consonant (like *faᶜūl*), the internal plural is normal for them (unlike the preceding instances). The external plural can occur, especially in the case of *faᶜīl* in the active sense (*karīmūna*, *karīmāt*), as opposed to *faᶜīl* in the passive sense which cannot take it for the *ᶜuḳalā'*; (for *afᶜalu* see *Muf.* § 249).

This outline sufficently shows the Arab point of view; it remains, with the help of monographs, to define the usage of the authors themselves, particularly in their use of the external feminine plural for non-rational beings, like *wa-ḳudūrin rāsiyātin* (Ḳur'ān, XXXIV, 12/13) "and firm cooking-pots", *fī ayyāmin maᶜdūdātin* (Ḳur'ān, II, 199/203) "on days well numbered". Such instances are infrequent, less frequent than those of the internal plural (like *ayyām ḳalā'ilᵘ* "days few in number").

Used as a feminine singular substantive for non-rational beings, *fāᶜilaᵗ* and *mafᶜūlaᵗ* take the internal plural *e.g.*: *fā'idaᵗ* "utility", pl. *fawā'idᵘ*, *maḳṣūraᵗ* "small private room", pl. *maḳāṣīrᵘ*. This does not create any difficulties. It remains to examine the external plural for substantives *which are only substantives* (proper names included). The difficulty noted above, for the *ᶜuḳalā'*, arose precisely from the participial adjectives (the *ṣifa*) which can become substantives.

B. — The external plural for substantives and proper names.

a) Proper names: the question of the *ᶜuḳalā'* naturally affects the use of the plural of proper names and also of diminutives.

For the former, Sībawayhi (ii, ch. 350) leaves a choice between the external plural and the internal plural when the name is capable of forming it, *e.g.*: for Zayd (masc. proper name): *zaydūna* or *azyād*, *zuyūd*, for Hind (fem. proper name): *hina/idāt* (or *hindāt* of the Tamīm) or *ahnād*, *hunūd*; but *-āt* for the plural of men's proper names terminated by *-atᵘ*: *ṭalḥatᵘ* "Ṭalḥa", pl. *ṭalaḥāt* (according to the Baṣrians, 4th disputed question, Ibn al-Anbārī, *K. al-Inṣāf*, ed. Weil, 18 ff.).

As to the diminutive (like *s̲h̲uwayᶜir*, diminutive of *s̲h̲āᶜir* "poet"): for the masculine *ᶜuḳalā'*: *s̲h̲uwayᶜirūna*; *s̲h̲uwayᶜirāt* for the feminine; *-āt* for the plural of the diminutive for non-rational beings: *kitāb* "book", diminutive *kutayyib*, pl. *kutayyibāt*.

b) Substantives which are purely substantives: a small proportion reverts to the suffix *-ūna*: biliteral nouns like *sanaᵗ* "year": *sinūna* and some isolated ones, like *ᶜālam* "world": *ᶜālamūna*. The suffix *-āt* is used much more widely. It is given to:

1. feminine nouns with the suffix *-ā'u* or *-ā*: *ṣaḥrā'u* "desert" *ṣaḥrāwāt*, *d̲h̲ikrā* "memory" *d̲h̲ikrayāt*.
2. names of the letters of the alphabet: *alif*, *alifāt*.
3. names of the Muslim months: *ramaḍānᵘ*, *ramaḍānāt*.
4. infinitives of the derived Forms of verbs used as substantives: *taᶜrīf* "definition", *taᶜrīfāt*.
5. foreign nouns: *iṣṭabl* "stable", *iṣṭablāt*; the same, denoting men: *bās̲h̲ā* "Pasha", *bās̲h̲awāt*. The modern language still carries on this procedure: *tilifūn* "telephone", *tilifūnāt*.
6. biliteral nouns: *sanaᵗ* "year", *sanawāt* and a few isolated instances, some feminine like: *arḍ* "earth", *araḍāt*, others masculine like *d̲j̲amād* "mineral", *d̲j̲amādāt*.
7. a particular and important usage can be included here: agent-nouns or passive nouns of

all Forms of the verb and of adjectives with the suffix *-āt* are regarded as neuter, *e.g.*: *al-ṣāliḥāt* "Good" (Ḳurʾān, II 23/25, 76/82, etc.), *al-sayyiʾāt* "Evil" (Ḳurʾān, IV 22/18, VII 152/153, etc.), *al-makhlūḳāt* "creatures", etc. This usage still exists in modern Arabic: *al-mashrūbāt* "refreshments", etc.

To sum up, for the *ʿuḳalāʾ* the external plural is the proper plural of relative adjectives, the agent-nouns and passive nouns *fāʿil* and *mafʿūl*, *mufʿil/al* (and still more, Forms which take only the external plural), of the Forms *faʿʿāl*, *fiʿʿīl*, *fuʿʿāl*; for adjectives with one or two short vowels, the external plural is also given as the standard form (the *ḳiyās*) but not for the other adjectives subject to greater variation. With substantives, the *ʿuḳalāʾ* apply only in respect of proper names and diminutives. In this special treatment of rational beings is to be found the indication of a true *Class*, operative in classical Arabic. It was important to place it.

C.—External plural, plural for small numbers.

Another assertion by the Arab grammarians is that the external plural is a plural for small numbers (*Muf.* § 235, Ibn Yaʿīsh, 611-2) (which characteristic can cross its influence with the preceding). There is thus a way of explaining, in certain instances, the coexistence of the external plural and the internal plural for the same word, *e.g.*: *ḳarayāt* (small number), *ḳuraⁿ* (large number) for a singular *ḳaryaᵗ* "village". This seems to be particularly noticeable for the external plural in *-āt* and to have had an influence on dialects: the plural for a small number, described by E. F. Sutcliffe in *A grammar of the Maltese language*, London 1936, 36, is of this kind. The question of small numbers will occur again in connexion with internal plurals.

II—The internal plural

The internal plural is found sporadically (as it were, still on trial) in Western Semitic languages in the north (Hebrew-Aramaic) (Brockelmann, *Précis*, § 165). It is the Western Semitic languages in the south which made use of the procedure, particularly Arabic (only ten Forms of the internal plural in Geez). But from what do these internal plurals derive? Are they the plural of a singular following a genetic connection, or on the other hand are they independent words linked simply by the singular-plural relationship? This genetic connexion cannot be established: even in the case of sing. *fuʿlaᵗ*, pl. *fuʿal*, sing. *fiʿlaᵗ*, pl. *fiʿal*, the question is not clear (cf. below); some *fiʿlān* plurals are seen to come from a suffix *-ān*: **akhwān* > *ikhwān* "brothers", **djārān* > *djīrān* "neighbours", but the words thus pluralized are lost in the mass of internal plurals of the Form *fiʿlān*, independent of a singular. Thus the second position is adopted by many Orientalists (see Barth, *Nominalbildung*, 417-8). Internal plurals are therefore considered to be derived from collectives which are connected with abstract words (M. Bravmann has recently maintained the contrary view, in *Orientalia*, xxii, 1953, 7-8, but he is not convincing).

Internal plurals are collectives clarified by the plural: collectives offered a mass; through this use of the plural, individualities have become *distinct* in this mass (see below, III) and can be numbered (that is to say, counted precisely according to the different numbers), or else remain simply with a vague, not fixed, number—the *indeterminate* plural.

The human mind can easily make the transition from the collective to the indeterminate plural because, while being a true plural, it retains some subtle element of the former through the vagueness and imprecision of the number of units comprised. This explains how, in Arabic, the same word without any internal change or variation in its external form may be looked upon in one connexion as a collective and in another as an indeterminate plural. A good example is provided by Raḍī al-Dīn al-Astarābādhī (*Sh. Sh.*, ii, 196, l. 1-3) when he states explicitly that the *ism al-djins* (coll.) for the noun of unity with *-aᵗ*, takes the plural in *-āt* for a small number and uses the same form without *-aᵗ* for a large number, as for example for "ant": *namlaᵗ* (n. of un.) pl. *namalāt* (small number), *naml* (large number). This is his example (*loc. cit.*) even though there exists the internal plural for a large number *nimāl*. This concept of an *indeterminate plural*, for a vague number of units, brings an element of clarity, here and in other instances, *e.g.* for *ḳawm* (see below). A true plural, it forms a link and transition between collective and plural.

The link between collectives and abstract nouns, it seems to us, cannot be denied; a collective on the way to becoming an abstract word (this cannot be developed here (see my *Traité* § 71); conversely, an abstract word which becomes collective, *e.g.* *shabāb* "youth" (abstract word), *shabāb* "young people" (coll.). The collective thus proves to be the link between the abstract word and the internal plural. But not all collectives derive from an abstract word. Can one therefore refuse the language the power of *directly* creating, for natural masses, collectives to which it has opposed nouns of unity to designate separate members of these masses? In this question of the internal plural it is well to consider the complexity of the collective from which it derives, a complexity increased by the diversity of the collective *wazn*s, which have passed into the internal plural.

How has the relationship between singular and plural for internal plurals been established? Semantic analogies have been followed, *e.g.* *fiʿalaᵗ* for animals, and also formal analogies, *e.g.* the so-called plural of quadriliterals, also extensions purely analogical by simple propagation of a *wazn*. All this has varied from one region of the language to another, either in diachrony or in synchrony throughout the vast expanse of Arabia.

Behind the internal plurals lies a long and complicated history which we have no longer the means to unravel. In classical Arabic they appear as a product that had been moulded in the general process of internal flexion. A good way of approaching the question is to consider this product within the framework of internal flexion, according to the series affected: initial basis and development, as a sort of outline. No doubt an outline simplifies and neglects cross-currents, but it is not altogether without its value in introducing a systematic arrangement based on the general progress of the language.

In this way one can distinguish four main series, with progression in them according to the lengthening of the vowels, the gemination of the second root consonant or the use of the affix:

a) Series: *fiʿal*, *fiʿāl*, *fiʿālaᵗ* (*fiʿāl* + *aᵗ*), *afʿāl* (= **a* + *fiʿāl*, or *fiʿāl* > **fʿāl* > *afʿāl*, see below), *fiʿalaᵗ* (= *fiʿal* + *aᵗ* or secondary parallel formation of *fiʿāl*).

b) Series: *fuʿl*, *fuʿul*, *fuʿūl*, *fuʿūlaᵗ* (*fuʿūl* + *aᵗ*), *afʿul* (= **a* + *fuʿul*), *fuʿlān* (*fuʿl* + *ān*).

c) Series: *fiᶜl*, *fiᶜil* (these only collective), *fiᶜlaᵗ* (= *fiᶜl* + *aᵗ*), *afᶜilaᵗ* (= **a* + *fiᶜil* + *aᵗ*), *afᶜilāʾu* (= **a* + *fiᶜil* + *āʾu*), *fiᶜlān* (= *fiᶜl* + *ān*).

d) Series: *fuᶜal*, *fuᶜalaᵗ* (= *fuᶜal* + *aᵗ*), *fuᶜalāʾu* (= *fuᶜal* + *āʾu*), *fuᶜᶜal*, *fuᶜᶜāl*.

Out of series: *faᶜlā* (= *faᶜl* + *ā*) and *faᶜalaᵗ* (probably *faᶜal* + *aᵗ*). The internal plurals of quadriliterals will be discussed later. But *faᶜal* like *khadam* "servants" is a collective (*ism al-djamᶜ*), similarly *faᶜil* (like *ḥamir* "asses") and *faᶜal* for a singular *faᶜlaᵗ* (like *ḥalḳa* "ring", *ḥalaḳ*) is also a collective (*ism al-djins*).

As for *fuᶜal* (sing. *fuᶜlaᵗ*), *fiᶜal* (sing. *fiᶜlaᵗ*), they are indisputably acknowledged by Arab grammarians to be broken plurals. A problem arises with the development: *fuᶜa/ulāt*, *fiᶜa/ilāt*. Is this the plural of a plural (Brockelmann's solution, *Grundriss*, i, 430, Anm. 2)? Or merely the external plural of the singular *fuᶜlaᵗ*, *fiᶜlaᵗ* (with *supplementary* vowel for the second root consonant) (see Nöldeke, in *ZA*, xviii, 72)? Arab grammarians had proposed the solution adopted by Brockelmann; Ibn Yaᶜīsh refutes them (630, l. 6-8): *fuᶜa/ulāt*, *fiᶜa/ilāt*, applied in the usage for a small number [1]), cannot be the plural of a plural, a kind of plural which is valid for a large number. The question could be discussed further. The situation is not clear. But the solution is, more probably, to be found in the direction: simple external plural.

Internal plurals for a small number.

The distinction is made between plurals for a large number and plurals for a small number (3 to 10 inclusive) in the general teaching of Arab grammarians (see *e.g. Muf.* § 235). They did not invent it. But to what extent they fixed what had been a flexible usage, or imposed a distinction which departed from the spoken language and which was preserved only in the traditions of fine language (poetry), one cannot tell exactly. A study of the practice of the different authors will certainly produce interesting results. We know already that poets have not always conformed with rules. The language itself did not always provide the means to observe them, *e.g.* *ḳalam* "reed cut for writing" has only one plural *aḳlām* (plural for a small number), similarly *rasan* "horse's nose-band" *arsān*; on the contrary, *radjul* "man" *ridjāl*, *sabuᶜ* "wild beast" *sibāᶜ*, without a plural for a small number (according to Ibn Yaᶜīsh 612 l. 14; like Sībawayhi, he does not recognize any plural except *sibāᶜ*, see *LA*, x, 10 l. 16). The so-called internal plurals of quadriliterals are incapable of expressing the distinction, *e.g.*: *burthun* "talon, claws", pl. *barāthinu* (for a small or large number). From all this one can discern that in practice there was considerable variation. It remains to say that Arab grammarians have put forward, for a small number, the Forms *afᶜāl*, *afᶜul*, *afᶜilaᵗ* (in frequent association respectively with *fiᶜāl*, *fuᶜūl*, *fiᶜlān* for a large number), and *fiᶜlaᵗ* (seldom used), and besides the external plural noticed above. This subdivision of the internal plural was noteworthy.

Apart from this last (*fiᶜlaᵗ*), the other Forms (of

the plural for a small number) have the peculiarity of having an initial *hamza*. It seems to me that this *hamza* is not unconnected with the indication of the small number and acts in the linguistic sense as a formative prefix (however *afᶜilāʾu* is not considered as a plural for small numbers). Barth (*Nominalbildung*, 422, l. 16-17) already considered it to be "ein specifisches Mittel der Pluralbildung", but did not see how to explain its precise origin. It seems that some research work is to be done to investigate the possibility that a *hamza*, originally prothetic (in *fiᶜāl* > **fᶜāl* > *afᶜāl*), was later reinterpreted as a formative *hamza* and capable of generalization and of extension to other Forms.

The so-called internal plurals of quadriliterals.

The so-called formation of "quadriliterals" is considered separately. In fact it possesses a special characteristic. It includes not only quadriliterals properly speaking like *ᶜaḳrab* "scorpion", but words which, with three root consonants, add another as prefix, like *maktab* "place where one writes, office", or many words with a long vowel after the 1st or 2nd root consonant, like *fāris* "horseman", *ᶜadjūz* "old woman". The term quadriliteral becomes incorrect but it is useful and in fact does not cause any misunderstanding as to its significance. This Form of internal plural has one single type, that is to say (denoting the four possible consonants by dots) the pattern: *. a . ā . i .* and follows the second declension (special question). When applied to the examples given above, the formula gives *ᶜaḳāribu*, *makātibu*, *fawārisu*, *ᶜadjāʾizu*. It has the very considerable advantage that in the great majority of instances it is possible to predict the result whereas, for the other Forms (described in order above) since in most of the cases two or more Forms of internal plural are possible for a given singular, one is reduced in practice to learning every word with its plural.

An individual characteristic, and no doubt also an individual origin, but what is it? Brockelmann in *Grundriss* (i, 434 Anm.) was unable at that time to see any certain explanation. M. Bravmann (*Orientalia, loc. cit.* 20 f.) proposed a phonetic solution, taking as his starting-point **faᶜālt*, deriving from *faᶜālaᵗ*. This does not appear to be satisfactory; *faᶜāl* can be used, but in another manner, in a solution which I am describing very briefly here but which I shall develop later. It consists of these processes: adaptation of the Form *faᶜāl* (collective) to quadriliterals, on the analogy of *fuᶜayl* (diminutive) which became *fuᶜaylil* for quadriliterals, and of *fuᶜāl* which became *fuᶜālil* (even with quadriliteral roots of the pattern 1212); *faᶜāl* (collective) thus became *faᶜālil* (collective). This gives a collective to quadriliterals and makes it possible to represent, in this category, animals whose designation by a quadriliteral noun is not lacking in Arabic. Subsequently it was possible in the linguistic sense to interpret *faᶜālil* as having been augmented by an *ā*, internal, characteristic moved elsewhere, *e.g.*: *faᶜlā*, collective (then internal plural of *faᶜlānu*) could become *faᶜālā* (*kaslānu* "lazy", pl. *kaslā* and *kasālā*); *faᶜālā* thus opened up a way of propagating. From the collective the internal plural was easily derived.

Variations: *faᶜālīlu* when the singular quadriliteral noun contains a long vowel in the second syllable: *ᶜuṣfūr* "sparrow", *ᶜaṣāfīr*; *faᶜālilaᵗ*, secondary and parallel formation of *faᶜālīlu*, used especially for nouns of foreign origin: *tilmīdh* "disciple", *talāmīdhu* and *talāmidhaᵗ*.

---

1) Ibn Yaᶜīsh argues from the possibility of saying: *thalāthu rukabātin* "three knees". This is not the usual construction: according to the *Sharḥ al-Kāfiya* of Raḍī al-Dīn al-Astarābādhī, ii, 139 (ed. Constantinople 1275 A.H.), the general practice is to use the internal plural and not the external plural for numbers from 3 to 10.

III—The collective

It is important to have a clear conception of the collective. Collectives are not plurals. Plurals denote a plurality of *distinct* beings or objects, collectives on the contrary denote a sum or assembly of several objects, abstracting *from the component units* (see the *Lexique de la terminologie linguistique* by J. Marouzeau, Paris 1933, 41 and 145). The collective is the mass in which the individuality of those "massed together" is blurred: it is this mass which is envisaged and which constitutes as it were a unit, a kind of singular. A collective, considered purely as such, cannot be numbered, unless one wishes to indicate the plurality of the unit represented by the mass of its components. When the collective can be numbered to denote the plurality of the latter, it is a sign that it has ceased to belong to the collective category through becoming plural: the individuality of the "objects massed together" has become *distinct* (see above for the indeterminate plural).

At the beginning of this article the Arabs' terminology was explained: it now remains to examine the question of gender and the distribution of collectives in the light of the *ʿuḳalāʾ*.

The *ism al-d̲j̲ins* (n. of un. with *-aᵗ*) is formed for *natural* masses of *non-rational* beings, *e.g.* *naḥl* "bees", *naḥlaᵗ* "a bee", very rarely for objects made by man. As for gender, it can be considered as either masculine or feminine, according to *e.g.*: Ḳurʾān, LIV, 20 and LXIX, 7. This is the teaching of *Muf.* § 271, Ibn Yaʿīs̲h̲ 701, l. 20-2. But according to the *S̲h̲. S̲h̲.* (ii, 195, l. 2-3) the masculine is dominant.

The *ism al-d̲j̲ins* (n. of un. with *-iyy-*) is formed for the *ʿuḳalāʾ* (with very rare exceptions), *e.g.* *yahūd* "Jews", *yahūdiyy-* "a Jew". The question of gender is not discussed in grammars; according to the usage of the Ḳurʾān, *yahūd* is used as masculine plural or feminine singular (for the verb which precedes, *e.g.*: *ḳālat-i-l-yahūdu*).

The *ism al-d̲j̲amʿ* without an individual noun or with the individual noun provided by another word: masculine or feminine for the *ʿuḳalāʾ*, feminine for the others.

The *ism al-d̲j̲amʿ* with the noun of unity provided by another Form of the same root. It exists both for the *ʿuḳalāʾ* and for the others. Howell (i, 1145) does not express himself clearly, Wright (i, 181 A) is not sufficiently thorough. For Sībawayhi in his ch. 429 (ii, 210-1), the masculine is dominant; the same view is held by al-Astarābād̲h̲ī (*S̲h̲. S̲h̲.*, ii, 204, l. 7-8); Ibn Yaʿīs̲h̲ (673, l. 23-4) is even more positive.

As regards the *ʿuḳalāʾ*, there exists an important collective which Arab grammarians have not fitted exactly into their categories (*Muf.* § 267, Ibn Yaʿīs̲h̲ 695). It is formed by means of the suffix *-aᵗ* added to the agent-noun: *al-sābilaᵗ* "the travellers", *al-muḳātilaᵗ* "the combatants", *al-muslimaᵗ* "the Muslims", etc., and in particular to the relative adjectives: *al-marwāniyyaᵗ* "the Marwanids", *al-zubayriyyaᵗ* "the Zubayrites", etc. This procedure allows one to designate sects, groups, parties, and it is freely used in the modern language. Used in this manner, *-aᵗ* has formed the collective in the reverse way from that used for the *ism al-d̲j̲ins* (n. of un. with *-aᵗ*).

Note: *faʿl* (coll.) can provide a complete system, *e.g.*: *ṣaḥb* (coll.) "companions", *ṣāḥib* (n. of un.), *aṣḥāb* (plural for small number), *ṣiḥāb* (plural for large number), or else *ṭayr* (coll.) "birds", *ṭāʾir* (n. of un.), *aṭyār* (plural for small number), *ṭuyūr* (plural for large number). But this system cannot be generalized: it is not *ḳiyās* (al-Astarābād̲h̲ī, *S̲h̲. S̲h̲.*, ii, 203). One habitually says: *ṣāḥib* pl. *aṣḥāb*, *d̲j̲ālis* pl. *d̲j̲ulūs*, etc., but *genetically* these internal plurals derive from *faʿl* (coll.) and not from the noun of the Form *fāʿil*.

There are at least two aspects to the collective: the collective-unit, the mass considered as a sort of unit, whereby use in the singular is possible: *ḳawm karīm* "a noble tribe", *al-ḥamām al-muṭawwaḳ* "the ring-dove"; the collective-object which inclines towards the neuter, and hence the tendency to denote the anonymous mass by a feminine singular, even for rational beings: *ibil rāʿiyaᵗ* "grazing camels", *ḳawm sāfiraᵗ* "a nomadic tribe". The internal plurals of nouns have inherited from their former status as collectives the possibility of being treated in this way: *rid̲j̲āl kat̲h̲īraᵗ*. But if the component parts resume their distinct individuality in the mass, the collective passes into the indeterminate plural: *ḳawm kuramāʾᵘ*, *ḳawm mukrimūna* "noble people".

These different considerations have been able to exert their influence to a greater or lesser degree, and in the same way with greater or lesser regard for the *ʿuḳalāʾ*, among the various tribes throughout the vast territories of Arabia. Arab grammarians intended to portray the *ʿarabiyya* as an entity and have been at pains to show its unity and harmony. It was necessary to simplify the diversity, but by selecting which aspect? Hence the divergencies of opinion. Only precise monographs furnished with statistics and based on texts will give a clear view of the situation.

Bibliography: in the text; in addition, works discussing the genesis of internal plurals: H. Derenbourg, *Essai sur les formes des pluriels arabes*, Paris 1867, 105 (extract from *JA*, June 1867); St. Guyard, *Nouvel essai sur la formation du pluriel brisé en arabe*, Paris 1870, 32 (Biblioth. Ec. H.-E., Sc. Ph. Hist., 4); L.-Marcel Devic, *Les pluriels brisés en arabe*, Paris 1882, 24; J. Barth, *Die Nominalbildung in den semitischen Sprachen* 2, Leipzig 1894, 417-83; C. Brockelmann, *Grundriss der vergleichenden Grammatik der semitischen Sprachen*, i, Berlin 1908, 426-39; on the external plural, *ibid.*, 441-55. Lists of internal plurals in all instructional grammars, in particular W. Wright, *Arabic Gr.*³, i, Cambridge 1933, 199-234 or *Le pluriel brisé* by Mohammed-Ben-Braham, Paris 1897, viii, 121, using Arabic sources and following the Arab manner. Also J. H. Greenberg, *Internal a-plurals in Afroasiatic (Hamito-Semitic)*, in *Afrikanistische Studien* (Festschrift Westermann), Berlin 1955, 198-204.

For Arabic sources: *Kitāb* by Sībawayhi (Paris), ii: internal plurals: ch. 416, 418, 422, 424, 426, 427, 429-31; external plural: ch. 423, 425; plural of plurals: ch. 426; plural of biliterals: ch. 421; collectives: ch. 417, 419, 420, 429. *Mufaṣṣal* (quoted as *Muf.*) by Zamak̲h̲s̲h̲arī, 2nd, ed. J. P. Broch, § 234-61; *S̲h̲arḥ* by Ibn Yaʿīs̲h̲, ed. G. Jahn, 604-80, *S̲h̲arḥ al-S̲h̲āfiya* (quoted as *S̲h̲. S̲h̲.*) by Raḍī al-Dīn al-Astarabad̲h̲ī, 4 vols., Cairo 1358/1939, ii, 89-210.

On the external plural and its origin: W. Vycichl, in *RSO*, xxviii, 71-8; S. Moscati, *ibid.*, xxix (1954), 28-52 and particularly 178-80; W. Vycichl, *ibid.*, xxxiii, particularly 175-9 and on the plural in *-āt*, in *Aegyptus*, xxxii (1952), 491-4. On collectives, H. L. Fleischer, *Kleinere Schriften*, i, 256-8.

For all the questions discussed in this article: H. Fleisch, *Traité de philologie arabe*, i, Beirut 1961, §§ 59-63, 65, 101 and 102. (H. Fleisch)

DJAMĀʿA, meeting, assembly. In the religious language of Islam it denotes "the whole company of believers", *djamāʿat al-muʾminīn*, and hence its most usual meaning of "Muslim community", *djamāʿa islāmiyya*. In this sense *djamāʿa* is almost synonymous with *umma* [*q.v.*]. The two terms must, however, be distinguished.

The term *umma* is Ḳurʾānic. It means "people", "nation", and is used in the plural (*umam*). It acquires its religious significance particularly in the Medina period when it becomes, in the singular, "the nation of the Prophet", "the Community, *e.g.*, Ḳurʾān III, 110, etc.). The term *ḥizb Allāh*, "the party of God" is used in a similar sense on two occasions (V, 56; LVIII, 22). On the other hand, although √dj.m.ʿ is of very frequent usage, the word *djamāʿa* itself does not belong to the vocabulary of the Book. It was, however, very soon to appear, for example in the (diplomatic) "Documents" reproduced by Ibn Saʿd and ascribed by him to the Prophet. Letter from Muḥammad to the Ṣāḥib of Baḥrayn: "and that you enter into the Community (*djamāʿa*)". The use of this term was to become general in the *sunna*. We may restrict ourselves to two frequently cited *ḥadīth ṣaḥīḥ* of Ibn ʿAbbās: "Whosoever removes himself from the Community by the space of a single span, withdraws his neck from the halter of Islam", and: "Whosoever dies after being separated from the Community, dies as men died in the days before Islam (*djāhiliyya*)" (translation by H. Laoust).

In Western languages *umma* and *djamāʿa* are very often translated by this same word "community"; and Muslim writers, in fact, find no difficulty in using them interchangeably. (The famous *ḥadīth*: "my community does (or: will) never agree upon error" uses *umma*. Cf. Wensinck, *Handbook* 48 A.). If, etymology apart, one wishes to distinguish them: *umma* is the community as constituting a nation on a religious-legal basis; while *djamāʿa* is the whole body of believers united by their common faith. Both terms equally reflect "the desire to live together" (L. Massignon)—so characteristic of Islam—in accordance with the code of behaviour laid down by the Ḳurʾān for this world and for the hereafter. But it is to the head of *umma* that the study of the ideal structure of this Community as ordained by *siyāsa al-sharʿiyya* is best referred; while the term *djamāʿa* focuses our attention upon the bond which fashions from a group of individuals a community of believers. We may add that in current Islamic terminology, and even in actual popular sentiment, it is *umma* which first and foremost expresses the values of unity and solidarity.

It is by a doctrinal implication that *djamāʿa* comes to bear its technical religious sense. This "assembly of the believers" is united by its faith. It will, accordingly, stand opposed to those who "deviate" and those who "innovate" (even though these latter have not officially left the duly constituted Community, *umma*). And it will be identified with *al-djumla*, "the majority" of Muslims, as opposed to the sects which "are withdrawn apart". Al-Fuḍayl: "The hand of God rests upon the Community (*djamāʿa*). God looks not upon the innovators".

The most widely used expression which embodies this doctrinal significance is *ahl al-sunna wa 'l-djamāʿa* "the people of the Tradition and the Community"; here, Tradition (of the Prophet) and "assembly" of the believers are mutually supporting (cf. L. Veccia Vaglieri, in *Studi Orientalistici in onore di Giorgio Levi Della Vida*, ii, 573 ff.). From a slightly different standpoint, the *ahl al-ʿaḳd wa 'l-ḥall* ("the people who bind and loosen") are an equivalent body. They are the representatives of Community (*umma*) insofar as they give it expression by their consensus (*idjmāʿ* [*q.v.*]). *Djamāʿa* and *idjmāʿ* are two words from the same root; it may be said that the second is the agreement of the first. The two *ḥadīth* of Ibn ʿAbbās mentioned above, as well as that concerning the *umma*, are among the "divinely-revealed texts" which establish the *idjmāʿ*.

In fact, the extent of the *djamāʿa* was to become closely linked with the recognized concept of *idjmāʿ*. It is in the development of Ḥanbalī thought that we find a very particular attachment to the *djamāʿa* which was that of the first Muslims and of them alone; and it is a well-known feature of Ḥanbalī doctrine that the only *idjmāʿ* of value is the consensus of the Companions. Barbahārī, a Ḥanbalī of the 3rd-4th/9th-10th century, would define the *djamāʿa* as "the ancient religion" (*al-dīn al-ʿatīḳ*), by which we understand the practices, beliefs and customs of the Companions during the period of the first three "rightly guided" Caliphs (cf. Abu 'l-Ḥusayn b. al-Farrāʾ, *Ṭabaḳāt al-ḥanābila*, ii, 32-3, cited by H. Laoust, *Ibn Baṭṭa*, 9, n. 1). But if the *djamāʿa* in its strict sense is the community of the Companions, there remains the fact that every Muslim is bound, down through the centuries, to follow it and conform to it. "To follow the Community", *luzūm al-djamāʿa*, is a duty of the believer upon which the Ḥanbalīs have consistently insisted (e.g. Ibn Baṭṭa, *Ibāna*, 5/10). By the same token, "the *djamāʿa* of the Ancients" is kept alive down through the ages. At every epoch those Muslims who are wholly faithful to the Tradition are integrated in the *djamāʿa*. The first *credo* (*ʿAḳīda*, i) of Ibn Ḥanbal describes them as *ahl al-sunna wa 'l-djamāʿa wa 'l-athar*, thus joining to the first two terms the "precedent" of the Prophet and the Companions (cf. H. Laoust, *Ibn Baṭṭa*, 11, n. 1). The expression *ahl al-ḥadīth* ("traditionists") was to become an approximate equivalent, until the appearance of *ahl al-ḥaḳḳ*, which was to have a tendency to prevail later.

The stream of Ḥanbalī doctrine was to remain faithful to this notion of a Community centred upon the faith of the Ancients as the only absolutely authentic faith. Ibn Taymiyya for example was to speak of both *umma* and *djamāʿa*. He was to stress the obligation of the *ahl al-sunna wa 'l-djamāʿa* to follow the "precedents" (*āthār*) of the Prophet "just as much in the depths of their inmost beings (*bāṭin*) as in their external behaviour (*ẓāhir*)", and to follow in the same way the paths of the Companions (*Wāsiṭiyya*, 34, cf. H. Laoust, *ibid.*, 10,n.). This reverential attachment of Ḥanbalism to the *djamāʿa* finally arrives, in a manner of introverted devotion, at the point where the faithful of the Medina period grouped around Muḥammad are recalled, and where this ancient "religion" is revived by each generation of believers until the last hour of the end of time.

The same was not to hold good for the other schools. For example, to the extent that the *idjmāʿ* is understood (e.g. the Shāfiʿī school) to be the consensus of the scholars living in a given generation, and becomes the fourth "source" (distinct from the *sunna*) of Islamic law, *al-djamāʿa* loses its strict historical reference to the first years of Islam. Already al-Ṭabarī (cited by Rashīd Riḍā, *Khilāfa*, 14) had argued against a *djamāʿa* restricted to the group of the Companions. According to him the *luzūm al-djamāʿa* ought to be defined, without reference to any particular period, as the obedience of the Muslim community to the sovereign that it has chosen for itself; and "whosoever breaks his contract with the sovereign leaves the *djamāʿa*". The verb here employed which signifies "to obey the sovereign" evokes the notion of "the one who commands authority", and must be taken to refer to the Imām, the guide and leader of the Community. The *djamāʿa* will, therefore, be defined by reference no longer to the first Muslims alone, but to every Imām recognized as legitimate. It will become, according to this point of view, a factual reality rather than a value primarily doctrinal, and will thenceforth tend to be supplanted by *umma*.

This is most noticeable in the *ʿilm al-kalām*. Notwithstanding his affirmed respect for Ibn Ḥanbal, Abu 'l-Ḥasan al-Ashʿarī was to present his two celebrated *credo* of the *Ibāna* and the *Maḳālāt* simply as the agreement of the *ahl al-sunna*. Once only is the notion of "community" there in operation: the intercession of the Prophet for "the great sinners of the Community", and *umma* is the term employed (*Maḳālāt*, i, 322). In the *Lumaʿ* likewise, whether it is a question of the attitude (condemned as dissidence) of the Muʿtazilites, or of the consensus of the Community as the foundation of the *idjmāʿ*, it is always *umma* which alone appears. It was no part of the task of *kalām* to devote a chapter to *al-djamāʿa*. As for the works which deal with "Public law" they look at the *Imāma* or the *Khilāfa* from the aspect of the conditions of power, and have no concern to analyse the formal constituent elements of the Community. More and more it is the term *umma* which comes to epitomize the communal fervour of the believers.

And yet *djamāʿa*, with its connotation of doctrinal unity, never entirely disappeared from the technical vocabulary. It could be found, *passim*, in many works; such, too, is the case in the contemporary period. It is found also, incidentally, in the *Ẓuhr al-Islām*, 199, of Aḥmad Amīn citing Masʿūdī. The adjective *djamāʿī* was to retain the same sense. When Ibn ʿAsākir, in the 6th/12th century, wrote his apologetic biography of al-Ashʿarī, his purpose was to describe him as *sunnī*, *djamāʿī*, *ḥadīthī*: and one can recognize in these epithets the formula maintained by the Ḥanbalīs. *Djamāʿī* also must be understood to mean the supporter of the true doctrine of the Ancients. It remains to note that in general the Ashʿarīs call themselves "the people of the Tradition and the Truth", *ahl al-sunna wa 'l-ḥaḳḳ*,—this last word recalling quite accurately the technical sense of *djamāʿa*, but, as is easy to appreciate, with other connotations. In short, *al-djamāʿa*, when understood as a duly constituted *union* of Muslims, tends here to give way to the term *umma*; when it is taken to signify the *unity* of the true beliefs, it is consistently replaced by *al-ḥaḳḳ*.

As regards the contemporary period, mention must be made of the "reformist" movement of the *salafī*, which is broadly receptive to the influences of Ḥanbalī thought. It might, therefore, be expected that their scheme would refer to *djamāʿa*. In fact, and very logically, Rashīd Riḍā, in his analysis of the notion of *idjmāʿ*, examines, in his *Khilāfa*, the meaning of *al-djamāʿa*. But he does not hesitate to expand the strict sense given to it by the Ḥanbalīs, readily admits the definition of Ṭabarī referred to above, and identifies *djamāʿa* with the "men who bind and loosen" in each period. In the same paragraph he uses *umma* in a fairly approximate, but nonetheless not identical, sense. For him the *djamāʿa* is the whole group of those who hold the reins of authority and who must be followed when they are in agreement (*idjmāʿ*). It is the *umma* which is liable to be split by disturbances; the best line of conduct to observe, therefore, (the *ḥadīth* of Ḥudayfa b. al-Yaman) is to remain faithful to the *djamāʿa* and its Imām. Furthermore, the title of Rashīd Riḍā's chapter, "Concerning the power of the *umma* and the meaning of the term *djamāʿa*" is characteristic.

In the *salafī* sense, then, it may be said that the people who constitute the *djamāʿa* are those Muslims whose faith and truth are guaranteed and who are thereby in perfect line of continuity with the faith of the Ancients (*salaf*). To them belongs the right to designate the supreme Imām to whom they promise allegiance (*bayʿa*) in the name of all, and who, by the same token, will be the duly appointed leader of the entire *umma*. The *djamāʿa* only attains its full import when united with its Imām.

The same applies to the more restricted, more localized meaning of the word. Every assembly of Muslims gathered together in order to "perform the prayer" (*ṣalāt* [*q.v.*]) is a *djamāʿa*. This definition is eminently suitable for the obligatory ritual of the *ẓuhr* on Friday, *djumʿa*, which is, accordingly, the day of meeting par excellence; and the mosque, *djāmiʿ*, where the ritual is performed in the place which gathers together the believers. The same holds good for the obligatory prayers performed in congregation on the prescribed festivals. It is in relation to the congregational prayers that the two *credo* of al-Āshʿarī speak of *djamāʿa* in the singular in the *Maḳālāt*, i, 323, and in the plural in the *Ibāna*, 12. This *djamāʿa* of Muslims united in the performance of the prayer, as testimony to their faith, will be of a form and nature which is not so much determined by principle as fixed by the description of its own particular imām "little *imāma*".

Bibliography: as indicated in the text with the following particularizations or additions: Muḥammad Ḥamidullah, *al-Wathāʾiḳ al-siyāsiyya*, 2nd. ed., Cairo 1956, n. 67; W. Montgomery Watt, *Muḥammad at Medina*, Oxford 1956, 247, 360; H. Laoust, *Essai sur les doctrines sociales et politiques de Taḳī-d-Dīn Aḥmad B. Taimīya*, Cairo 1939 (v. Index, *djamāʿa*); idem, *La profession de foi d'Ibn Baṭṭa*, Damascus 1958 (v. Index); Abu 'l-Ḥasan al-Ashʿarī, *al-Ibāna ʿan uṣūl al-dīn*, Cairo edition 1348 A.H., 11-2; idem, *Maḳālāt al-Islāmiyyin*, Cairo 1369/1950, i, 322-3; Ibn ʿAsākir, *Tabyīn Kadhib al-muftarī fī mā nusiba ilā 'l-imām Abī 'l-Ḥasan al-Ashʿarī*, Damascus 1347 A.H. (cf. A. F. Mehren, *Exposé de la reforme de l'Islamisme ... in Travaux de la 3e session du Congrès International des Orientalistes*, ii; and the English translation of R. J. McCarthy, *The theology of al-Ashʿarī*, Beirut 1953, 147 ff.); Rashīd Riḍā, *al-Khilāfa aw al-Imāma al-ʿuẓmā*, Cairo 1341 A.H. (edition of *al-Manar*), 13-5 (French translation by H. Laoust, *Le Califat dans la doctrine de Rashīd Riḍā*, Beirut 1938, 21-5). (L. Gardet)

(ii) The word has been most regularly used in Morocco. In Algeria, records at least a hundred years old confirm the existence under the name "djemaa", of local administrative assemblies. Their competence to own property was confirmed as regards the patrimony of the "douar", but was suppressed politically and juridically (decree of 25 May 1863; ruling of 20 May 1868; decree of 11 September 1873, with particular reference to Kabylia). However, even before the 1914 war, public opinion was demanding a liberalization of the system. This was in part the aim of the 1919 reform which established elected "djemaas" within the "mixed commune". The administration was later to attempt, not without circumspection, to develop from these first assemblies the communal evolution of which they contained the nucleus.

As for Algeria, it was no doubt in the Berber regions, and especially in Kabylia, that the first observers had noted the most revealing features of these collective undertakings. The *thajmāʿth* (and variants), which included all the adults but paid regard to individual and family influences, and much nearer to a "senate" than to an *ekklesia,* met regularly, deliberated on all matters of concern to the village and showed a vitality which has endured side by side with official life, even to the point of continuing to exert influence, in certain cases, through the codification of the *ḳānūn*s, an accepted function of public law.

But it is in Morocco, in the High and Middle Atlas, that investigation has demonstrated the system functioning in its purest form. A constant theme of the research conducted up to the present time has been to bring out the triple incidence of these communal customs upon political life which becomes organized, within the canton, in a sort of spontaneous democracy, upon judicial life which is governed by regulations of extraordinary detail, and upon the tenure of property. In 1922, L. Milliot defined the *djamāʿa*s as "representative assemblies of the different groupings of tribe, subdivision, douar, family which make up Muslim society in Morocco. These groupings exercise over vast stretches of territory rights characterized by occupation in the form of cultivation leaving widely scattered areas of fallow-land, and grazing . . . .".

This economic aspect, stimulating the competition of the two systems of cultivation, the European and the native, the intensive and the extensive, has throughout the colonial period constituted a constant preoccupation for the legislator, administrator and judge through its actual effects on practical life. Juridical definitions have reflected the successive phases of the proceedings and have taken a particular turn in Algeria (*ʿarsh* or *sābga* (*sābiḳa*) land) in Morocco (*blād əj-jmāʿa* (*bilād al-djamāʿa*)), and lastly in Tunisia where this regulation seems to have reached its latest development. Tunisia, however, provides the example which reveals most clearly, through the interference that has taken place between private ownership of estates, collective property and religious foundations or *ḥubus*, both the richness and the danger of this form of tenure which is so exposed to spoliation from all sides.

The juridical designation of the *djamāʿa*, elevated to the small tribal or cantonal senate, gave rise in Morocco to an evolution that was taking shape at the time of the beginning of the Protectorate and which led to its acquiring a competence not merely with regard to property, but also in civil and penal matters. The culminating point was reached at the time of the celebrated "Berber dahir (*ẓahīr*)" of 16 May 1930 which the nationalist opposition, with the support of Islamic opinion throughout the world, at once denounced as an attack upon the religious Law. One of the first measures taken by Morocco after gaining independence was therefore the revocation of this dahir, and the establishment of lay judges incidentally contributed a further step towards modernity.

In short, whatever may be the hazards of this long history, they have served to emphasize the intimate connexion which, in the rural Maghreb, associates the use of this term with certain forms of effort by local groups and of its connexions with the soil. These forms, hitherto characterized by their anarchic particularity, seem at the present day to be adapting themselves to the demands of a more intensive agriculture and of administrative decentralization. That is why, particularly in Morocco, the *djamāʿa* is always found as the central point of programmes of reform. It is possible that, by remarkable sociological conjuncture, certain contemporary evolutions are being based upon the rich communal potentialities comprised, in the Maghreb, by the *djamāʿa*, an ancient word and a reality of long standing.

Bibliography: Property law: P. Lescure, *Du double régime foncier de la Tunisie*, 1900; L. Milliot, *Les terres collectives* (*blād Djemāʿa*)*—étude de législation marocaine*, 1922; F. Dulout, *Des droits et actions sur la terre arch ou sabga en Algérie*, 1929; A. Guillaume, *La propriété collective au Maroc*, 1960. Judicial procedure: A. Ribaut, *Les djemaas judiciaires berbères*, 1930; various articles and works by Henri Bruno, G. Surdon etc., listed in the excellent summary of J. Caillé, *La justice coutumière au Maroc*, 1945.—Administration and politics: in addition to the basic work of Hanoteau and Letourneux, *La Kabylie et les coutumes kabyles*[2], Paris 1893 and the thesis of Masqueray, *La formation des cités, etc.*, Paris 1886, cf. Maxime Champ, *La commune mixte algérienne*, 1933, 127 ff.; H. Brenot, *Le douar, cellule administrative de l'Algérie du Nord*, 1938.—The connexion between these different aspects emerges from sociological studies that have emphasized the various regional peculiarities in the Maghreb: cf. especially R. Montagne, *Les Berbères et le Makhzen*, 1930; L. Milliot, *Les institutions kabyles*, in *REI*, 1932; G. Marcy, *Le droit coutumier Zemmour*, 1949; G.-H. Bousquet, *Justice française et coutumes kabiles*, 1950; J. Berque, *Structures sociales du Haut-Atlas*, 1955; idem, *Droit foncier et intégration sociale au Maghreb*, in *Cahiers internationaux de sociologie*, 1958. (J. Berque)

DJĀMAKIYYA. A term current in the Muslim World in the later Middle-Ages equivalent to salary. Its origin is the Persian *djāma* = "garment", whence *djāmakī*, with the meaning of a man who receives a special uniform as a sign of investiture with an official post. From this came the form *djāmakiyya* with the meaning of that part of the regular salary given in dress (*malbūs, libās*) or cloth (*ḳumāsh*). Ultimately it took the meaning of "salary", exactly as the word *djirāya,* which meant originally a number of loaves of bread sent daily by the Sultan to someone, took the sense of salary in the terminology of the Azharīs during the Ottoman period. *Djāmakiyya* first seems to have acquired the sense of salary under the Saldjūḳs, since the official terminology of the Fāṭimids did not use the term. In his detailed study of the organization of the Fāṭimid Empire, al-Ḳalḳashandī uses only the Arabic term of *rātib* (pl. *rawātib*) (*Ṣubḥ*, iii), but the term appears already in texts concerning the later Saldjūḳs (*e.g.*, Ibn al-Athīr, *Taʾrīkh al-Atābika*), Zangids, and Ayyūbids (*e.g.*, Abū Shāma, *Kitāb al-rawḍatayn*, Ibn Wāṣil, *Mufarridj al-kurūb*, and al-Maḳrīzī, *al-Sulūk*). This last author, speaking of the *adjnād* (soldiers) mentions *mabāligh iḳṭāʿātihim* (revenues of their fiefs), *djāmakiyyātihim wa rawātib nafaḳātihim* (the regular payments necessary to cover their expenditure) (*Sulūk*, i, 52). The *djāmakiyyāt* most probably stands here for the part of the regular payment given in the form of dress or cloth. Later on the term was used under the Mamlūks to denote the part of the salary given in money: al-Ḳalḳashandī (*Ṣubḥ* iii, 457) says that the payments of the mamluks of the Sultan were composed of *djāmakiyyāt waʿalīf* (fodder) *wa kiswa* (dress). In the time of Baybars, al-Maḳrīzī uses the term *djāmakiyya* as equivalent to "salary" in general (*e.g.*, *djāmakiyyat al-ḳaḍāʾ*, iii, 475). But al-Nuwayrī (*Nihāyat al-arab*, Cairo 1931, viii, 205) specifies that the *djamakiyyāt* were the regular payments for a category of Mamlūks who worked as clerks (*al-mamālīk al-kitābiyya arbāb al-djāmakiyyāt*). This sense is most probably what he meant when he said later on: *wa asmāʾ arbāb al-istiḥḳāḳāt wa 'l-djāmakiyyāt wa 'l-rawātib wa 'l-ṣilāt* (viii, 218-9). In the Circassian period the *djāmakiyya* was the regular monthly pay of the army, paid at a special parade (*ʿarḍ*) in the sultan's court-yard (*al-ḥawsh al-sulṭānī*) usually beginning in the middle of the Muslim month. It was paid by *ṭabaḳa* [*q.v.*], each individual mamlūk being called by name. For details of the procedure and the rates of pay, see D. Ayalon, *The system of payment in Mamluk military society*, in *JESHO*, i, 1958, 50-6. For the further use of the term in the sense of "salary" see Dozy, *Suppl.* i, 1666.

Bibliography: Other than that included in the article: Alexandre Handjéri, *Dictionnaire français, arabe, persan et turc* (Moscow 1844), under "habit", and Steingass, *Persian-English Dictionary*, under *djāma*. (Hussain Monés)

DJAMAL [see ibil].

al-**DJAMAL**, "the camel" is the name of the famous battle which took place in the month of Djumādā II 36/November-December 656 near al-Baṣra between the Caliph ʿAlī b. Abī Ṭālib on the one hand, and the Prophet's widow ʿĀʾisha [*q.v.*] with the Companions of the Prophet Ṭalḥa b. ʿUbayd Allāh al-Taymī and al-Zubayr b. al-ʿAwwām [*qq.v.*] on the other. At that time it was these two companions who, after ʿAlī, had most authority among the Muslims.

ʿĀʾisha was completing the *ʿumra* in Mecca when she learned of the assassination of the Caliph ʿUthmān b. ʿAffān, and, on the way back to Medina, of the election of ʿAlī to the Caliphate at the same time as the riots in Medina where public order had broken down. Without revealing her intentions she turned back, and when she reached Mecca, gave a fiery speech near the Kaʿba accusing the rabble of the murder of ʿUthmān, and demanding the punishment of the culprits, for ʿUthmān, she said, had been killed 'unjustly' (*maẓlūm^{an}*) (al-Ṭabarī, i, 3098 etc.); with these words she was alluding to a verse of the Ḳurʾān (XVII, 32/35), which Muʿāwiya was to invoke later (see ʿalī b. abī ṭālib), and which prescribed revenge as a duty in such a case, thus establishing a *ḥadd* [*q.v.*]. She had been one of ʿUthmān's opponents (this was used against her to impugn her right to protest) but she would not condone his murder and made some characteristic remarks on this point (cf. al-Ṭabarī, i, 3097, Ibn Saʿd, iii, 1, 57-8); in particular she could not bear that ʿAlī, towards whom she had for long felt great animosity, should have taken advantage of the murder. Some time later (four months, it is said, after the death of ʿUthmān; al-Ṭabarī, i, 3102) Ṭalḥa and al-Zubayr arrived in Mecca; after rather violent discussions with ʿAlī, who refused them posts in the government, they had asked and obtained permission from him to go to Mecca to perform the *ʿumra*. A conspiracy was formed against ʿAlī, in which took part, besides the persons mentioned above, some Umayyads and other Muslims alarmed by the turn of events. ʿUthmān's assassination had caused a scandal, but the real causes of the rebellion were above all ʿAlī's indulgent attitude towards the culprits, which indicated that they would go unpunished, his weakness towards the dissidents who had become so arrogant and dangerous that several persons had fled, and his popularity-seeking anti-Ḳurayshī policy. In the provinces nearest to the Ḥidjāz, opposition to ʿAlī was strong; in Syria, Muʿāwiya had refused homage; Kūfa had rejected the governor sent by the Caliph, preferring the one already in office, Abū Mūsā al-Ashʿarī [*q.v.*]; elsewhere parties opposed to the newly elected Caliph had been formed. The rebels tried to choose the place offering the best prospects for the success of the insurrection, and in the course of a meeting the conspirators decided to go to Baṣra, in the hope of finding there the money and troops needed for the enterprise. ʿĀʾisha agreed to join the expedition; she was to rouse the people, as Ṭalḥa and al-Zubayr seemed hardly qualified for that rôle; not only had they so stirred up opinion against ʿUthmān that they could be accused of being murderers of the Caliph, but they had also paid homage to ʿAlī immediately after the election; in rebelling against him they were thus violating their pact, so that they had to claim, in order to justify themselves, that they had been forced to pay homage by violence. Ḥafṣa bint ʿUmar [*q.v.*], whose first intention was to follow the rebels, was dissuaded by her brother ʿAbd Allāh [*q.v.*]. After collecting several hundred men with their mounts (600 or 700?) they set off. ʿAlī, hearing of this, realized that he must react in order not to be isolated in Medina. After bringing together, slowly and with difficulty, a contingent of 700 warriors he too set out (according to al-Ṭabarī, i, 3139, the last day of Rabīʿ II). His aim was to intercept the insurgents, but he did not succeed in reaching them; at al-Rabadha, he learned that they had already passed that halt, and as he too needed money and troops, he set off again, in the direction of al-ʿIrāḳ. At the same time the rebels were hurrying to Baṣra. When, in a place called al-Ḥawʾab, dogs barked at the troops, ʿĀʾisha was on the point of giving up the adventure, as she remembered a sort of foreboding of the Prophet's, but they swore to her that this was not al-Ḥawʾab, and, with her mind at rest, she carried on (cf. Yāḳūt, *Muʿdjam*, ii, 352, etc.); this episode is worth mentioning only because of the importance attached to it in the sources. When they reached the outskirts of Baṣra, the rebel leaders opened negotiations and began to make propaganda. ʿĀʾisha, through an emissary and letters to certain notables in the town, tried to persuade the Baṣrans to join the insurrection, the aim of which, she proclaimed, was *iṣlāḥ*; a word that implied, for the rebels, the restoration of the law and its *ḥudūd* and hence revenge for ʿUthmān, the re-establishment of the disrupted social order, the placing of power in the hands of a Caliph legally elected by a committee or *shūrā*, but, for ʿAlī, the restoration of his authority, a return to the observance of the Sunna of the Prophet, and the suppression of privileges. The Baṣrans split into two parties: some followed the governor nominated by

ʿAlī, ʿUthmān b. Ḥunayf, who, without deliberately opposing the rebels, temporized while awaiting the arrival of ʿAlī; others made common cause with ʿĀʾisha and her two associates, whose forces had grown on the way. In a meeting at al-Mirbad, an esplanade three miles from Baṣra, the rebel leaders addressed the people and their propaganda was successful. Disorders followed, then a mêlée at the "place of the tanners" and on the following days fights near the Dār al-Rizḳ, or supply store (the sources do not agree on details). It is there that the chief of police, Ḥukaym b. Djabala, was killed. He was too pro-ʿAlī to stand aside and wait without acting. At last, an armistice was concluded: to settle who would hold power in the town of Baṣra, they were to await the return of a messenger sent to Medina to find out whether it was true that Ṭalḥa and al-Zubayr had been forced to pay homage to ʿAlī (evidently the governor was trying to gain time). In the meantime, the situation was not to be altered: the governmental palace, the great mosque, and the *bayt al-māl* were to stay in the hands of the governor Ibn Ḥunayf; but because of the significance attached to the leadership in prayer, it was agreed that this office would be performed by two *imāms*, the governor himself, and another nominated by the insurgents. Ṭalḥa and al-Zubayr quarrelled, as each wanted to have this function, but ʿĀʾisha decided that they would exercise it on alternate days, or, according to another version of the facts, that their respective sons Muḥammad and ʿAbd Allāh would exercise it in turn. The inquiry of the messenger sent to Medina was favourable to Ṭalḥa and al-Zubayr, but a letter which had reached the governor declared exactly the opposite of what they asserted. Consequently ʿUthmān b. Ḥunayf would not give up his office and a brawl broke out in the mosque. But the most serious fact was the assault made by the rebels on the *bayt al-māl*; they killed or made prisoner (and later decapitated) its guards who were Zuṭṭ [*q.v.*] and Sayābidja [*q.v.*]. The attackers moreover forced ʿUthmān b. Ḥunayf to leave the palace and pulled out his hair and his beard: he succeeded in getting himself released and joining ʿAlī by threatening them with reprisals against their families in Medina, where his brother Sahl was governor. In these brawls and fights, who were the aggressors? Some traditions praise the moderation of the rebels (ʿĀʾisha is said to have forbidden her men to use their hands except in self-defence) but it is evident that it was they who were the attackers, as they needed provisions and money, and were afraid of being caught later between the advancing forces of ʿAlī and those of the governor. With Baṣra occupied, the rebels published an order calling on the population to surrender all who had taken part in the siege of the House (the house of the Caliph ʿUthmān), called *nuffār* in the sources, so that they might be killed like dogs. The people obeyed and those killed, it was said, numbered six hundred (only Ḥurḳūṣ b. Zuhayr [*q.v.*] was able to escape because he was protected by his tribe). This slaughter and the distribution of gifts and supplies which Ṭalḥa and al-Zubayr made to their partisans angered part of the population of Baṣra, and 3,000 men went to join ʿAlī at Dhū Ḳār, among them the Banū ʿAbd al-Ḳays. The tribe of the Tamīm, the most important in Baṣra, on the other hand, remained neutral with its chief al-Aḥnaf b. Ḳays [*q.v.*].

While these events were taking place (the parleys with the governor had lasted, it is said, for twenty-six days), ʿAlī had advanced as far as Dhū Ḳār, for, instead of marching on Baṣra, he had preferred to approach Kūfa so as to win over its inhabitants to his cause. Unfortunately for him, the governor Abū Mūsā al-Ashʿarī, although he had recognized ʿAlī's election as valid, exhorted the Kūfans to stay neutral in the approaching civil war and the envoys sent by ʿAlī to Kūfa (al-Ashtar, Ibn ʿAbbās, al-Ḥasan, ʿĀmmār b. Yāsir) had to make a great effort to persuade part of the population (6, 7 or 12 thousand men?) to leave the town and join him. Abū Mūsā was deprived of his office. At last ʿAlī arrived on the outskirts of Baṣra and negotiations were opened between him and the insurgents. Although everyone was convinced that agreement was near, fighting began between the two armies. The same question arises here—who started it? According to some traditions, ʿAlī had ordered his men not to attack, and it was only after the murder of some of his partisans that he felt himself entitled to fight against opponents belonging to the *ahl al-ḳibla* (*Aghānī*, xvi, 132; al-Masʿūdī, *Murūdj*, iv, 314 ff. etc.). But al-Ṭabarī (i, 3181-3) reports another tradition which explains why and how the battle began: ʿAlī is said to have shown his intention of not according protection to the persons implicated in the murder of the Caliph ʿUthmān, and these, anxious about their fate, are said to have provoked the conflict by a sudden attack unknown to ʿAlī. The battle lasted from morning to sunset (according to the (pseudo-) Ibn Ḳutayba, Cairo 1377, 77, seven days). The sources differ on the date when it took place: the most frequent date is 10 Djumādā II 36/4 December 656, but according to Caetani (A.H. 36, § 200) the date 15 Djumādā II/ 9 December is to be preferred.

It is a striking fact that the warriors often belonged to the same tribes, to the same clans, and sometimes even to the same families, and they fought one another regardless of kinship. ʿĀʾisha was present during the fighting on a camel, in a palanquin the cover of which had been reinforced by plates of iron and other materials (al-Masʿūdī, *Murūdj*, iv, 315) and the camel was protected by a kind of armature (al-Dīnawarī, 159); at the end of the battle, the palanquin had so many arrows stuck in it that it looked like a hedgehog. ʿĀʾisha was not hit; all she received was scratch on an arm. The fighting round the camel was particularly fierce; the defenders followed one after the other while declaiming verses; those who fell handed the bridle of ʿĀʾisha's camel to other fighters and there were many dead (but the figures vary from 40 to 2,700). The victory went to ʿAlī, when his soldiers succeeded in hamstringing the camel, thus forcing the beast to lie down on its side with its precious burden. But even before this last episode the battle was virtually lost, as Ṭalḥa, struck by an arrow which many sources say was shot by Marwān b. al-Ḥakam [*q.v.*], had retired into a house where he soon died, and al-Zubayr, who was no longer very sure of the merits or prospects of his cause, had withdrawn from the battlefield after a talk with ʿAlī, who had reminded him of an episode of the past, and of certain sayings of the Prophet. Al-Zubayr was pursued by some Tamīmīs and treacherously killed in a lonely place (Wādī al-Sibāʿ); al-Aḥnaf b. Ḳays was suspected of instigating his murder (for the death of al-Zubayr, see also Ibn Badrūn, *Sharḥ Ḳaṣīdat Ibn ʿAbdūn*, ed. Dozy, Leiden 1848, 150-4).

The sources tell of a host of episodes concerning duels, the courage of the combatants, the verses declaimed by them, but they do not explain the development of the battle from the tactical point of view; the general picture that emerges from the mass of details is that, following the Arab custom, the battle consisted of a series of duels and encounters along the opposing ranks, and not of a general engagement. The most serious fighting was undoubtedly that which took place round the camel. It is impossible to calculate the numbers of combatants or of casualties because of the great variation in the figures (which vary, for the dead, between 6,000 and 30,000; the latter figure is considerably exaggerated, since for the forces of ʿAlī alone, the combined figure of the men who followed him from Medina and those who joined him later can hardly have exceeded 15,000 men). ʿĀʾisha was taken prisoner, but far from being ill-treated was shown great respect. ʿAlī decided, however, that she must return to Medina and on that point he was inflexible. He granted *amān* to all the insurgents, and certain compromised individuals (Marwān b. al-Ḥakam, for example) were able to join Muʿāwiya in Syria. An act which caused a stir among ʿAlī's partisans, and which provoked recriminations among the most fervent of them, was his refusal to allow them to take captive the women and children of the conquered or to seize their goods, with the exception of things found on the battlefield (al-Ṭabarī, i, 3227; al-Masʿūdī, *Murūdj*, iv, 316 ff., etc.); they asked why enemies whose blood it had been judged lawful to shed should be treated in this way; the Khāridjites made this afterwards one of their points of indictment against ʿAlī.

After the battle ʿAlī received the homage of the inhabitants of Baṣra, of which he nominated Ibn ʿAbbās governor (with Ziyād b. Abīhi at his side) thus causing the indignation of al-Ashtar, as two other sons of al-ʿAbbās had the same office, one in the Yemen, and the other in Mecca.

In the whole insurrection of al-Djamal, the preeminent personality is ʿĀʾisha; she appears as energetic, resolved (except for a moment at al-Ḥawʾab) to gain her end and respected in her decisions; while Ṭalḥa and al-Zubayr, under her orders, quarrelling with each other, making weak excuses to defend themselves against the accusation of having broken faith with ʿAlī, withdrawing during the battle instead of fighting to the death, look like men impelled only by ambition and at the same time lacking the energy and firmness necessary to succeed. Caetani assumed that there was an organizer of the enterprise behind the widow of the Prophet, namely Marwān, who followed the insurgents; the theory is attractive, but there is nothing to confirm it; if Marwān was in fact the insurgents' counsellor, he operated so discreetly that the sources hardly speak of his actions.

Bibliography: Ṭabarī, i, 3091-233 (in detail, excluding episodes: ʿAlī prepares to fight his opponents: 3091-6; ʿĀʾisha excites the people in Mecca and calls for vengeance for the murder of ʿUthmān, agreement and march of the rebels, who occupy Baṣra: 3096-106, 3111-38; march of ʿAlī halting in Dhū Ḳār: 3106-11, 3141-3, 3154 ff.; situation in Kūfa and ʿAlī's efforts to win the inhabitants to his cause, removal of Abū Mūsa: 3140 ff., 3145-54, 3172 ff., 3187 ff.; ʿAlī's march towards Baṣra: 3138-40; negotiations between ʿAlī and the rebels: 3155-8, 3175 ff.; events preceding the battle, neutrality of al-Aḥnaf; 3143-5, 3162-9; battle: 3174-98; ʿAlī and ʿĀʾisha after the battle: 3224-6, 3231; homage of the Baṣrans and nomination of Ibn ʿAbbās as governor of the town: 3229 ff.; Ṭabarī transl. Zotenberg iii, 658-64 (with some additions); Balādhurī, *Ansāb*, ms. Paris, ff. 467 recto-493 verso (contains traditions neglected by Ṭabarī: cf. G. Levi Della Vida, *Il Califfato di ʿAlī secondo il Kitāb Ansāb al-Ašrāf di al-Balāḏurī*, in *RSO*, vi (1913), 440-9); Yaʿḳūbī, ii, 209-13; Abū Ḥanīfa al-Dīnawarī, *al-Akhbār al-ṭiwāl*, 150-63; (pseudo) Ibn Ḳutayba, *K. al-Imāma wa 'l-siyāsa*, ed. Muḥ. Maḥmūd al-Rāfiʿī, Cairo 1322/1904, i, 88-133; idem, ed., Muṣṭafā al-Bābī al-Ḥalabī, second ed. 1377/1957, i, 52-79 (speeches, letters and details missing elsewhere); Masʿūdī, *Murūdj*, iv, 292 ff., 304-23, 324-37; idem, *Tanbīh*, 295; Ibn Miskawayh, *Tadjarib al-umam*, facsimile of the Istanbul ms., i, 518-62; Ibn al-Athīr, *Kāmil*, iii, 164-218 (résumé of Ṭabarī); Ibn Abi 'l-Ḥadīd; *Sharḥ ʿalā K. Nahdj al-balāgha*, Cairo 1329, ii, 77-82, 497-501 (passage interesting for details of the occupation of Baṣra); Ibn Kathīr, *Bidāya*, vi, 229-44 (with details missing elsewhere); Ibn Khaldūn, ii, App., 153-61 (good résumé of Ṭabarī). The résumés of Ibn Taghrībirdī, Dhahabī, and Abu 'l-Fidāʾ are not important. Much information about al-Djamal and especially about its episodes and the verses declaimed on that occasion are to be found scattered among the books of *adab* (such as Mubarrad; *Aghānī*; *ʿIḳd*; Bayhaḳī, *Maḥāsin*; Ibn Ḳutayba, *ʿUyūn*; Djāḥiẓ, *Bayān*; etc., and in biographical collections, *e.g.* in Ibn Saʿd; Ibn al-Athīr, *Usd*; Ibn Ḥadjar, *Tahdhīb*; Ibn Khallikān etc. The following are passages with a certain historic interest; Ibn Saʿd, iii, 1, 20; v, 26; *Aghānī*, xvi, 131; *ʿIḳd*, ed. Bulāḳ 1293, ii, 275-84; Ibn ʿAbd al-Barr, *Istīʿāb*, Ḥaydarābād 1318-9, 209 (part played by al-Zubayr), 213 ff. (part played by Ṭalḥa). Besides the well-known histories of Weil, A. Müller, and Muir, see also: Fr. Buhl, *ʿAlī som praetendent og Kalif*, Copenhagen 1921, 40-55; N. Abbott, *Aishah the beloved of Mohammed*, Chicago 1942 and especially Caetani, *Annali*, 36 A.H., §§ 21-302.

(L. VECCIA VAGLIERI)

DJAMĀL [see ʿILM AL-DJAMĀL].

DJAMĀL AL-DĪN AL-AFGHĀNĪ, AL-SAYYID MUḤAMMAD B. ṢAFDAR, was one of the most outstanding figures of nineteenth century Islam. Cultured and versed in mediaeval Muslim philosophy, he devoted his life and talents to the service of the Muslim revival. He was, in the words of E. G. Browne, at the same time a philosopher, writer, orator and journalist. Towards colonial powers he was the first to take the political attitude since adopted by many movements of national liberation. He is known above all as the founder of modern Muslim anticolonialism, admired unreservedly by many and considered by his opponents as a dangerous agitator. There is, on the other hand, a tendency to overlook the intellectual side of his personality, to forget his importance as a thinker. Notwithstanding the factors that crowded in on him (the decadence and lethargy of the Muslim countries, the increasing control of their economic and political life by European powers, the diffusion in the East of an atheism claiming its origin in Darwin) he had a clear view of the situation. It is with him that begins the reform movement which gave rise to the Salafiyya and, later, the Muslim Brothers. He expresses almost all the attitudes adopted between 1900 and 1950 by Muslim apologetics. By the spoken and written word he preached the necessity of a Muslim revival, both in thought (the need to throw off blind fatalism and give intelligence and freedom their proper place in life) and in action. Courageous and uncompromising, he aroused and strengthened the enthusiasm of his audiences wherever he went in his long years of exile. In Egypt he influenced the youth of Cairo and Alexandria, so that his personality left its mark both on future moderate leaders and partisans of immediate violence. He supported movements working for constitutional liberties and fought for liberation from foreign control (Egypt, Persia). He attacked Muslim rulers who opposed reform or did not show enough resistance to European encroachments. He even envisaged the possibility of political assassination. His ultimate object was to unite Muslim states (including Shīʿī Persia) into a single Caliphate, able to repulse European interference and recreate the glory of Islam. The pan-Islamic idea was the great passion of his life. He remained unmarried, made do with the absolute minimum in the way of food and clothing and took no stimulants other than tea and tobacco.

His family descended from Ḥusayn b. ʿAlī through the famous traditionist ʿAlī al-Tirmidhī, whence his right to use the title Sayyid. According to his own account he was born at Asʿadābād near Konar, to the east and in the district of Kābul (Afghānistān) in 1254/1838-9 to a family of the Ḥanafī school. However, Shīʿī writings give his place of birth as Asadābād near Hamadān in Persia; this version claims that he pretended to be of Afghān nationality, in order to escape the despotic power of Persia. He did in fact spend his years of childhood and adolescence in Afghānistān. At Kābul he followed the usual Muslim pattern of university studies and in addition began to pay attention to philosophy and the exact sciences, through the still mediaeval methods used at that time. Then he spent more than a year in India, where he received a more modern education, and made the pilgrimage to Mecca (1273/1857); on his return, he went back to Afghānistān and entered the service of the *amīr* Dūst Muḥammad Khān [*q.v.*], whom he accompanied on his campaign against Herāt. The *amīr*'s death led to civil war between his sons over the succession [see AFGHĀNISTĀN]. Djamāl al-Dīn taking sides with one of them, Muḥammad Aʿẓam, shared the short-lived successes of that prince as his minister. But when the rival faction under Shīr ʿAlī finally triumphed, he judged it prudent to leave the country. On the pretext of making the pilgrimage a second time (1285/1869), he went to India where he remained for less than two months; he was kept under observation by the British, and requested to leave as soon as possible. He then went to Cairo where he stayed for forty days, became acquainted with Azharīs and gave lectures in his home. Then he went to Constantinople (1287/1870). As he already enjoyed a brilliant reputation, the high society of the Turkish capital gave him an enthusiastic welcome. He was soon called to the council of public education and invited to give lectures at the Aya Sofya and the mosque of Sulṭān Aḥmed. But many were jealous of his success. A lecture given at the *Dār al-Funūn* on the usefulness of the arts gave rise to such criticisms (especially from the *shaykh al-Islām*, Ḥasan Fehmī) that he decided to leave Turkey. Certain of his words on the rôle of prophets in the organization of societies had been twisted to look like rationalism.

He went to Cairo (March 1871) with no thought of settling there; but the welcome he received made him decide to stay. The government made him an annuity of 12,000 Egyptian piastres without asking anything of him in exchange. Young men, among them Muḥammad ʿAbduh, the future chief muftī of Egypt, and Saʿd Zaghlūl, the future hero in the struggle for Egyptian independence, gathered round him. At his home he gave them lectures on various subjects, read to them from Muslim philosophy and generally broadened their outlook. A wider circle, composed of these same pupils and older people, would listen to him at the "Café de la Poste" speaking on literature, science, politics etc. He urged the young people to fight with the written word by going into journalism, considered as the modern method of influencing people's minds. He gave his encouragement to Adīb Isḥāḳ who founded the review *Miṣr*, then the daily *al-Tidjāra*; he helped found *Mirʾāt al-Sharḳ*. He contributed himself to these journals, but above all got his pupils to do so. He aroused patriotic resistance to European interference in the question of the Egyptian debt. In 1878 he joined the Scottish Freemasons; but, disillusioned, he founded an Egyptian lodge affiliated to the French *Grand Orient*, whose three hundred members formed the fieriest element of the nationalist youth. Politics were discussed in the lodge and plans for reforms drawn up. At that time, Djamāl al-Dīn was involved in all requests for a parliamentary régime. He is even said to have suggested to Muḥammad ʿAbduh the idea of assassinating the Khedive Ismāʿīl. The replacement of Ismāʿīl by the Khedive Tawfīḳ (1879) put an end to any such project. In bad odour with the conservative Azharīs and the Council of Ministers, closely watched by the British, Djamāl al-Dīn was finally expelled on the instigation of the latter (September 1879). Next he went to India, living under close scrutiny first at Ḥaydarābād, then at Calcutta, where the British requested him to remain as long as the ʿUrābī Pasha affair lasted. It was while staying in Ḥaydarābād that he composed in Persian his refutation of materialists [see DAHRIYYA]. He begins with an attack on Darwin's ideas and goes on to assert that only religion can ensure the stability of society and the strength of nations, whilst atheistic materialism is the cause of decay and debasement. He stresses this assertion by detailing all that belief in God and religion gives a society, first in terms of the collectivity: pride in the knowledge of one's superiority to animals and of belonging to the finest community, *i.e.*, Islam, and also in terms of the individual: fear of stricture, loyalty and truthfulness. He attributes the loss of political supremacy of certain states to materialism (Epicureanism in Greece, the doctrines of Voltaire and Rousseau in France etc.). He ends with an apologia for Islam, rendered antonomasically as religion.

During this time the situation in Egypt was becoming explosive. In 1881 ʿUrābī Pasha rose up against the Khedive, the Circassian officers in the army, and foreigners. It is certain that Djamāl al-Dīn's activities in Egypt had helped to stir up unrest. The revolt failed because of the British intervention of 1882 ending in the occupation of the country. Djamāl al-Dīn left India. We next find him in London in the spring of 1883, when Wilfrid Scawen Blunt met him. According to Blunt he had just returned from the United States where, after leaving India, he stayed for a few months with a view to naturalization. (This information given by Blunt without any explanation, cf. Browne, 401, is contested by all Arab studies on the subject; a letter from Djamāl al-Dīn to Muḥammad ʿAbduh written in Port Said on the 23 September—no mention of the year—bears simply the instruction to write to him in London where he is going. It can only refer to 23 September 1882 although a number of studies in Arabic prefer 1883. But let us look at his subsequent activities). On 18 May 1883 in the *Journal des Débats* of Paris he published a reply to the lecture which Ernest Renan had given at the Sorbonne on 29 March 1883 on *L'Islam et la science* and which had caused a great deal of feeling in Muslim circles in Paris. In his reply he asserted that Islam is compatible with science, that in the past there had been Muslim scientists, some of them Arabs; only the present state of Islam could support the opposite view. On 3 September 1883 Blunt met him in Paris. He was conducting a campaign against British policy in Muslim countries. Leading newspapers published articles by him which made an impact on influential circles (on the Eastern policy of Russia and Great Britain, the situation Turkey and Egypt, the importance and justification of the movement brought about in the Sudan by the Mahdī). But the outstanding feature of his stay in Paris was the joint publication with Muḥammad ʿAbduh, who had joined him and acted as his editor, of an Arabic weekly *Urwa al-Wuthḳā* (The Indissoluble Link). This journal was the organ of a secret Muslim society of the same name which financed it. The first number appeared on 15 Djumādā I 1301/13 March 1884 and the eighteenth and last on 26 Dhu 'l-Ḥidjdja 1301/16 October 1884. Sent free of charge to members of the association and anyone else requesting it, its entry into Egypt and India was barred by the British (confiscations and heavy fines for being in possession of it). In spite of various stratagems (such as sending it in closed envelopes, as Djamāl al-Dīn later revealed) it did not reach enough readers and had to lapse. Its influence was nevertheless considerable. It attacked British action in Muslim countries. It emphasized the doctrinal grounds on which Islam should lean, in order to recover its strength. In 1885 Muḥammad ʿAbduh left his mentor and went to Beirut; from then on the two men followed politically divergent paths. Muḥammad ʿAbduh temporized, concentrating mainly on reforms that were immediately possibl», above all in teaching. Djamāl al-Dīn continued as a lone pilgrim along the road to pan-Islamism.

In 1885, on the suggestion of W. S. Blunt, British statesmen approached Djamāl al-Dīn, in spite of the aggressive character of his anti-British activities, over steps to be taken with regard to the movement of the Mahdī in the Sudan. The discussions led to no practical result. Shortly afterwards (1886) Djamāl al-Dīn was invited by telegram to the court of Shāh Nāṣir al-Dīn in Tehran. He was given a lavish reception and was earmarked for high office. But very soon his increasing popularity and influence became offensive to the Shāh and he was forced to leave Persia "for health reasons". Next he went to Russia where he established important political contacts and on behalf of Russian Muslims obtained the Tsar's permission to have the Ḳur'ān and religious books published. He stayed there till 1889. On his way to the Paris World Fair he met the Shāh in Munich, and was persuaded by him to return to Persia. During his second stay there Djamāl al-Dīn had cause to realise how changeable the sovereign was. Djamāl al-Dīn had drawn up a plan of legal reforms; by criticizing it the jealous and scheming grand vizier Mīrzā ʿAlī Aṣghar Khān, *amīn al-sulṭān*, reversed the Shāh's favourable attitude. Djamāl al-Dīn retired to the sanctuary of Shāh ʿAbd al-ʿAẓīm near Teheran. In an asylum considered inviolable [see BAST], he remained for seven months, sourrounded by a group of admirers who listened avidly to his theories for politcal reform in the oppressed country. Urged by the grand vizier and spurning the right of asylum, the Shāh had him forcibly removed by 500 cavalry, put into chains and despite his delicate state of health taken as far as Khāniḳīn on the Turko-Persian border (beginning of 1891). From then on Djamāl al-Dīn showed nothing but hatred and a desire for vengeance towards the Shāh, an attitude which Aḥmad Amīn contrasts with the nobler feelings of other exiled reformers. From Baṣra, where he stayed just long enough to recover his health, he sent a scorching letter to Mīrzā Ḥasan-i Shīrāzī, the first *mudjtahid* of Sāmarrā, opposing the Shāh's decision of March 1890 to grant the tobacco rights of Persia to a British firm. He mentioned other concessions made to Europeans and accused the Shāh of wasting public moneys to the advantage of "the enemies of Islam". He also denounced other abuses and cruelty by members of the government, particularly ʿAli Aṣghar Khān (see this letter in Arabic in *Manār*, x, 820 ff., and in English in Browne, 15-21). His letter had swift results; the *mudjtahid* published a *fatwā* prohibiting the use of tobacco to all believers until the government cancelled the contract of concession. .The government had to give in and compensate the concessionaires. Djamāl al-Dīn then went to London for a year conducting a violent campaign through articles and lectures against the régime prevailing in Persia. He contributed particularly to the bilingual monthly review (in Arabic and English) *Ḍiyā' al-Khāfiḳayn*, "Radiance from the two hemispheres", which he helped to found (1892). He demanded the deposition of the Shāh. He looked especially to the professional men of religion, assuring them they were the ramparts of Islam against European designs. His repeated appeals, the feeling caused by his expulsion and the successful tobacco boycott were the beginning of a powerful movement for reform backed by the Persian religious authorities.

The closing years of Djamāl al-Dīn's life were clouded by sadness. He spent them so to speak in a gilded cage at Constantinople, where sultan ʿAbd al-Ḥamīd had twice summoned him through his ambassador in London (1892). After first declining, Djamāl al-Dīn consented to go. Was the sultan sincere in inviting the illustrious champion of a pan-Islamism, in which Turkey would have played a major part, and did he really intend to work with him towards its realization? Or, as Aḥmad Amīn suggests, did he want Djamāl al-Dīn near him to be able to neutralize his influence more effectively? It is difficult to say. The newcomer was given a fine house on the hill of Nishāntāsh, not far from the imperial palace of Yildiz. He received 75 Ottoman pounds a month and was allowed to keep contact with people wishing intercourse with him. The sultan behaved kindly towards his guest, listened to him to begin with at least and persuaded him to drop his resentful attitude to the Shāh. He even offered him the post of *shaykh al-Islām*, but he declined it. That was the turning-point. Intrigues and rivalries, especially on the part of Abu 'l-Hudā, the leading religious dignitary at the court, did the rest. Relations between the sultan and his guest became extremely frigid. Djamāl al-Dīn made several requests for permission to leave, which always met finally with a negative reply. We have some idea of his position at that time from the visitors he received. He was pained and dejected by the sight of so much cowardice around him. He criticized Muslims for their boastfulness and inactivity. His ideas were twisted so that he was accused, for example, of wanting to recognize the young Khedive ʿAbbās as Caliph because the latter had gone out of his way to meet him during a walk one day. But he continued to profess the same ideas on the need for constitutional liberties and on Islam, the one solid foundation of reformed Muslim states of the future. When on 11 March 1896 the Shāh fell victim to an assassin who was a loyal follower of Djamāl al-Dīn, he was accused of guiding the murderer's hand. He defended himself against the charge, notably in his statements shortly afterwards to the correspondent of the Paris newspaper *Le Temps*. But his position was even more precarious.

He died on 9 March 1897 from cancer of the chin; rumour had it that Abu 'l-Hudā ordered the doctor only to pretend to treat him, or even poisoned him. He was buried in the cemetery of Nishāntāsh. At the end of December 1944, his remains were taken to Afghānistān and laid to rest on 2 January 1945 in the suburbs of Kābul near ʿAlī-Ābād, where a mausoleum had been raised to him.

Despite his knowledge of Muslim theology and philosophy, Djamāl al-Dīn wrote little on these subjects. His treatise on the refutation of materialists was soon translated [see DAHRIYYA]. He has left an extremely succinct outline of the history of Afghānistān called *Tatimmat al-bayān* (lith. Cairo, undated, 45 p.) and the article *Bābī* in the *Dāʾirat al-Maʿārif* of Buṭrus al-Bustānī. But his pamphlets and political articles above all establish him as a commentator on current affairs. Apart from those in European languages, others in Arabic are to be found in the Egyptian press of about 1872-9 under his own name or such pseudonyms as Muẓhir b. Waḍḍāḥ; he later contributed to *al-ʿUrwa al-Wuthḳā* (anonymously) and to *Diyāʾ al-Khāfiḳayn* (signing al-Sayyid or else al-Sayyid al-Ḥusaynī). It should finally be noted that the intensification of the struggle against the Western colonial powers after the war of 1939-45 gave Djamāl al-Dīn a topical interest. Consequently, his life and ideas became the subject of several works published in Cairo and intended for the general public.

Bibliography: The Arabic translation of Djamāl al-Dīn al-Afghānī's work, *al-Radd ʿalā 'l-Dahriyyīn*, Cairo 1925, is preceded by a biography (7-19) taken from the review *al-Hilāl*, Cairo, 1 April 1897; Edward G. Browne, *The Persian Revolution of 1905-1909*, Cambridge 1919, contains a detailed biography based on original documents, appreciations and bibliography; Wilfrid Scawen Blunt, *Secret history of the English occupation of Egypt*, New York 1922; Rashīd Riḍā, *Taʾrīkh al-Ustādh al-Imām al-Shaykh Muḥammad ʿAbduh*, Cairo 1931, brings together documents, extracts of biographies, articles by Djamāl al-Dīn and articles from *al-ʿUrwa al-Wuthḳā*; the articles from that review have been reprinted several times in a single volume, first edition Beirut 1328/1910; L. Massignon, in *RMM*, xii (1910), 561 ff., and in *REI*, 1927, 297-301; Vollers, in *ZDMG*, xliii, 108; Ernest Renan, *L'Islam et la science*, lecture delivered at the Sorbonne on 29 March 1883, Arabic translation and refutation by Ḥasan Efendi ʿAṣīm (Cairo, lith., undated); German translation of the Renan lecture, Djamāl al-Dīn's reply and Renan's reply to that reply in Ernest Renan, *Der Islam und die Wissenschaft* etc., Basle 1883; two lectures by Djamāl al-Dīn (on education and trade) in *Miṣr* (Alexandria 1296, 5 Djumādā I); two articles on despotic governments (*fi 'l-ḥukūmāt al-istibdādiyya*) in *al-Manār*, iii. Considerable information is to be found in articles from periodicals on visits to Djamāl al-Dīn and interviews with him. Cf. in German *Berliner Tageblatt* (23 June 1896, evening edition) and *Beilage zur Allgemeine Zeitung* (Munich, 24 June 1896). Muḥammad al-Makhzūmī, *Khāṭirāt Djamāl al-Dīn*, Beirut 1931 (a fundamental work, reporting many conversations between the author and Djamāl al-Dīn, in the course of which most of the topics of modern Muslim apologetic are raised in turn); ʿAbd al-Ḳādir al-Maghribī, *Djamāl al-Dīn*, Cairo, collection *Iḳraʾ*, n. 68; Charles C. Adams, *Islam and Modernism in Egypt*, London 1933, 4-17; Aḥmad Amīn, *Zuʿamāʾ al-Iṣlāḥ fi 'l-ʿaṣr al-ḥadīth*, Cairo 1948, 59-120; Maḥmūd Ḳāsim, *Djamāl al-Dīn al-Afghānī, ḥayātuhu wa-falsafatuhu*, Cairo [undated, about 1955], with a hitherto unpublished letter; Maḥmūd Abūriyya, *Djamāl al-Dīn al-Afghānī*, Cairo 1958, a popularization but with an interesting bibliography; *Kabul almanack*, year 1323, 344-7 (in Pashtō).

(I. GOLDZIHER-[J. JOMIER])

DJAMĀL AL-DĪN AKSARAYĪ, a Turkish philosopher and theologian, who was born and died (791/1389?) at Aḳsaray. According to tradition Djamāl al-Dīn Meḥmed, who during his lifetime was known by the name of Djamālī, is said to have been the great-grandson of Fakhr al-Dīn Rāzī. He was appointed instructor at the *madrasa* of Zindjirli, at Aḳsaray, after learning by heart the *Ṣaḥāḥ*, al-Djawharī's Arabic lexicographical work, an indispensable requirement of anyone seeking to obtain this appointment. Like the ancient Greek philosophers he split up his very numerous pupils into three classes: those in the first class, known as *meshāʾiyyūn* (peripatetic), met outside the door of his house and accompanied their master to the *madrasa*, his lesson being given as they walked along; those in the second class, known as *riwāḳiyyūn* (stoics), awaited him under the pillars of the *madrasa* where their master, still standing, gave his second lesson; finally he went into the hall of the *madrasa* to join the pupils of the third class. The learned Molla Fenārī was one of his pupils; another scholar, Sayyid Sharīf Djurdjānī, attracted by the master's reputation, is said to have started out from Ḳaramān to come to attend his lectures, but the news of Djamāl al-Dīn's death interrupted his journey. According to a written tradition recorded by Ḥuseyn Ḥusām al-Dīn in his *Amasya taʾrīkhi* (a work which appeared in 5 vol. in Istanbul 1330-2 and 1927-35), Djamāl al-Dīn is said to have held office as *ḳāḍī ʿasker* to the governor of Amasya, Ḥādjdjī Shādgeldi, and to have retired to Aḳsaray in 783/1381 after the latter's defeat by the Amīr of Sivas, Ḳāḍī Burhān al-Dīn; however, this tradition derives from an unreliable source and must be treated with reserve. Writers differ as to the year of Djamāl al-Dīn's death: 1377 according to Brockelmann, 1389 according to Tahir Bursalı, 1388 according to Adnan Adıvar. His works in manuscript are divided among various libraries; with the exception of a moral treatise entitled *Akhlāḳ-i Djamālī*, they consist for the most part of commentaries; a commentary on *al-Ghāya al-ḳuṣwā* of al-Bayḍāwī; commentaries on theological works, *Sharḥ al-īḍāḥ*, *Sharḥ-i mushkilāt al-Ḳurʾān al-karīm*; on medical works, *Ḥāl al-mūdjiz*; on jurisprudence, *Ḥāshiyat-i multaḳā*; on syntax, *Sharḥ al-lubāb al-musammā bi-kashf al-iʿrāb*, etc.

Bibliography: Brockelmann, S II, 328; T. Bursalı, *ʿOthmānlī Müellifleri*, i, 265; A. Adnan Adıvar, *La Science chez les Turcs Ottomans*, Paris 1939, 17; *Türk Ansiklopedisi*, s.v. *Cemaleddin Aksarayı*. (I. MÉLIKOFF)

DJAMĀL AL-DĪN (T. Cemaleddin) **EFENDI**, 1848-1919, Ottoman Shaykh al-Islām, was born in Istanbul (9 Djumādā I 1264/13 April 1848), the son of the *ḳāḍīʿasker* Meḥmed Khālid Ef. Educated by his father and by private tutors, he attained the rank of *mudarris* and entered the secretariat of the Shaykh al-Islām's department. In 1295/1880 he was appointed Secretary (*mektūbdju*), with the rank of *mūṣile-i Süleymāniyye*, then became *ḳāḍīʿasker* of Rūmeli, and in Muḥarram 1309/August 1891 Shaykh al-Islām. He held office until 1327/1909, retaining his post in the cabinets formed immediately after the revival of the Constituent Assembly in 1908. He became Shaykh al-Islām again in 1912, in the cabinets of Ghāzī Aḥmed Mukhtār Pasha and Kāmil Pasha, but lost office with the fall of Kāmil Pasha's cabinet in the *coup* of 1331/1913. Like many prominent personalities who were known to be opposed to the Society for Union and Progress he was banished from Istanbul, and spent his last years in Egypt, where he died in Radjab 1337/April 1919. He is buried in Istanbul. A shrewd and affable man, he won the confidence of ʿAbd al-Ḥamīd II and managed to conform to the exigencies of his time. He was a writer of some power and an amateur of *dīwān* literature.

Bibliography: Başvekâlet Arşivi, sicill-i ahval defteri, no. 47, 143; *ʿIlmiyye Sālnāmesi*, Istanbul 1334, 615 ff.; Djamāl al-Dīn Efendi, *Khāṭirāt-i siyāsiyye*, Istanbul 1336; Aḥmad Mukhtār, *Inṭāḳ-i ḥaḳḳ*, Istanbul 1926; Ali Fuad Türkgeldi, *Görüp işittiklerim*, Ankara 1949, 24 ff. (CAVID BAYSUN)

DJAMĀL AL-DĪN HANSWĪ [see HANSWĪ, DJAMĀL AL-DĪN].

DJAMĀL AL-ḤUSAYNĪ, a complimentary title of the Persian divine and historian AMĪR DJAMĀL [AL-DĪN] ʿAṬĀʾ ALLĀH B. FAḌL ALLĀH AL-ḤUSAYNĪ AL-DASHTAKĪ AL-SHĪRĀZĪ, who flourished at Harāt during the reign of Sulṭān Ḥusayn the Tīmūrid (875-911/1470-1505); the probable date of his death is 926/1520. His known works are: (1) *Rawḍat al-aḥbāb fī siyar al-Nabī wa 'l-āl wa 'l-aṣḥāb*, a history of Muḥammad, his family and companions, written at the request of Mīr ʿAlī Shīr and completed in 900/1494-5 (Lucknow ed. 1297/1880-2, Turkish tr. Constantinople 1268/1852); (2) *Tuḥfat al-aḥibbāʾ fī manāḳib Āl al-ʿAbāʾ*, on the merits of Muḥammad, Fāṭima, etc.; (3) *Riyāḍ al-siyar*.

Bibliography: For details of MSS., and additional biographical information, see Storey, ii/1, 189-92, and i/2, 1254-5. (R. M. SAVORY)

DJAMĀL PASHA [see DJEMĀL PASHA].

DJAMĀLĪ, MAWLĀNĀ ʿALĀʾ AL-DĪN ʿALĪ B. AḤMAD B. MUḤAMMAD AL-DJAMĀLĪ, Ottoman Shaykh al-Islām from 908/1502 to 932/1526, also called simply ʿAlī Čelebi or Zenbilli ʿAlī Efendi, was of a family of *shaykhs* and scholars of Ḳaramān who had settled in Amasya. Djamālī was born in this city (Ḥ. Ḥusām al-Dīn, *Amasya taʾrīkhi*, i, Istanbul 1327, 105, 321). After his studies under such famous scholars as Mollā Khusraw in Istanbul and Ḥusām-zāde Muṣliḥ al-Dīn in Bursa Djamālī was appointed a *mudarris* at the ʿAlī Beg Madrasa in Edirne. His cousin, Shaykh Muḥammad Djamālī in Amasya, was using his influence in favour of Bāyazīd against Djem, rivals for the succession to Meḥemmed II (cf. Madjdī, *Ḥadāʾiḳ al-shaḳāʾiḳ*, Istanbul 1269, 285).

ʿAlī Djamālī had to resign when Ḳaramānī Meḥemmed, who favoured Djem, became grand vizier in 881/1476. But with Bāyazīd II's accession to the throne in 886/1481 Djamālī was again made a *mudarris* and then in 888/1483 a muftī in Amasya where he was appointed in addition a *mudarris* in the newly opened *madrasa* of Bāyazīd II (Ḥ. Ḥüsāmeddīn, iii, 235-6) in 891/1486. After a long service in various important *madrasas* in the empire he was eventually appointed a *mudarris* at the Themāniye Madrasa in Istanbul in 900/1495, thus reaching the highest degree in the career of *tadrīs*. His biography (Madjdī, 302-8) suggests that he retained a spiritual influence on Bāyazid II as did his cousin Shaykh Muḥammad.

ʿAlī Djamālī left Istanbul for the *ḥadjdj* but had to stay one year in Egypt where he learned of his appointment to the post of Shaykh al-Islām [*q.v.*] in Djumādā II 909/November-December 1503. Under Bāyezīd II, Selīm I, and Süleymān I he kept this post for twenty four years until his death in 932/1526.

By his personal influence and bold interferences in certain important governmental affairs (cf. Madjdī, 305-7) he was responsible for making the office of Shaykh al-Islām one of the most influential in the state. When Selīm I argued that his interference meant an infringement of the Sultan's executive power in the affairs of the sultanate which should be absolutely independent, Djamālī replied that as Shaykh al-Islām he was responsible for the Sultan's salvation in the other world. The Sultan eventually agreed to modify some of his decisions to meet Djamālī's objections. As a sign of his admiration Selīm wanted to confer on him the office of *Ḳāḍīʿasker* [*q.v.*] of both Rumeli and Anadolu. He declined the offer, saying that he would never accept a position in *ḳaḍā* [*q.v.*]. However, he was to overshadow the *ḳāḍīʿaskers* who were most influential in the government as the heads of the administration of *tadrīs* and *ḳaḍā*.

In the tradition of the *shaykhs* attached to the Ottoman Sultans, Djamālī was interested in *taṣawwuf* [*q.v.*] and was also called Ṣūfī ʿAlī Djamālī. He is said to be the author of a treatise on *taṣawwuf* entitled *Risāla fī ḥaḳḳ al-dawarān*. He was venerated as a *walī* after his death and various *manḳibas* were told about him. He was buried in the garden of the small mosque he had built in Zeyrek street in Istanbul. A selection of his *fatwās* were collected in *Mukhtārāt al-fatāwī*. He is also the author of a *Mukhtaṣar al-hidāya*.

Bibliography: Aḥmad Tashköprī-zāde, *al-Shaḳāʾiḳ al-nuʿmāniyya fī ʿulamāʾ al-dawla al-ʿOthmāniyya*, Ger. tr. O. Rescher, Istanbul 1927, Turkish tr. with additions by Muḥammad Madjdī, *Ḥadāʾiḳ al-shaḳāʾiḳ*, Istanbul 1269/1853, 302-8; ʿĀlī, *Kunh al-akhbār*, MS. in the list of Selīm I's ʿulamāʾ; Saʿd al-Dīn, *Tādj al-tawārīkh*, ii, 549-54; Ḥ. Ḥusām al-Dīn, *Amasya taʾrīkhi*, i, Istanbul 1327, 321; iii, 235-40, T. Spandouyn Cantacassin, *Petit traicté de l'origine des Turcqz*, ed. Ch. Schefer, Paris 1896, 112-3; *IA*, art. Cemâlî (M. Cavid Baysun). (HALIL INALCIK)

"DJAMĀLĪ", ḤĀMID B. FAḌL ALLĀH of Dihlī (d. 942/1536), poet and Ṣūfī hagiographer. He travelled extensively throughout the Dār al-Islām from Central Asia to the Maghrib, and from Anatolia to Yemen, meeting a number of prominent Ṣūfīs including Djāmī [*q.v.*], with whom he had interesting discussions in Harāt. His travels constitute a link between the Indian Ṣūfī disciplines and those of the rest of the Muslim world; while it is possible that the style of the Persian poetry of the court of Harāt travelled to India in his wake, creating the *sabk-i Hindī* of the 10th/16th century. Though a Ṣūfī, with a reputation for asceticism, Djamālī, like other Suhrawardī mystics before him, associated intimately with the Sultans of Dihlī. His relations with Sikandar Lodī were especially cordial, on whose death he wrote a *marthiya*. After the overthrow of the Lodīs by the Mughals [*q.v.*], he developed friendly relations with Bābur [*q.v.*] and Humāyūn [*q.v.*], often accompanying the later on his military expeditions. His son Shaykh ʿAbd al-Raḥmān Gadāʾī became *ṣadr* early in the reign of Akbar [*q.v.*].

He compiled a lengthy *dīwān* and a mystical *mathnawī*, *Mirʾāt al-maʿānī*; but his fame chiefly rests on *Siyar al-ʿārifīn*, a *tadhkira* of the Indian saints of the Čishtiyya and Suhrawardiyya orders, a classic of hagiography.

Bibliography: Works, *Dīwān* (unpublished), two known *mss* in the Rāmpūr Library (Nadhīr Aḥmad, no. 179), and in the private library of Ḥabīb al-Raḥmān Khān Shīrwānī, which also has a copy of his *Mirʾāt al-maʿānī*. *Siyar al-ʿārifīn*, *mss*: Lindesiana, no. 115; Rieu, i, 354a, 355a; Ethé 637-9; Berlin 590-1; Ivanow, Curzon 71; Bankipore, Suppt, i, 1782; ed. Dihlī 1311/1893. ʿAbd al-Ḥaḳḳ Dihlawī, *Akhbār al-akhyār*, Dihlī 1332/1914, 227-9; Niẓām al-Dīn Aḥmad, *Ṭabaḳāt-i Akbarī*, Bibl. Ind., i, 340; ʿAbd al-Ḳādir Badāʾūnī, *Muntakhab al-tawārīkh*, Calcutta 1864-9, i, 325-6; iii, 76-7; Abū Bakr Ḥusaynī, *Haft Iḳlīm*, no. 393; Ṣādiḳ Kāshmīrī, *Kalimāt al-sādiḳīn*, no. 91; Brindābandās Khʷushgū, *Safīna-i Khʷūshgū*, no. 43; Mubtalā, *Muntakhab al-ashʿār*, no. 137; Āzād Bilgrāmī, *Khizāna-i ʿĀmira*, Kānpur 1900, 177-9; Luṭf ʿAlī Beg Ādhar, *Ātashkada*, no. 751; Aḥmad ʿAlī Khān Sandīlawī, *Makhzan al-gharāʾib*, no. 493; Sayyid Aḥmad Khān, *Āthār al-ṣanādīd*, Dihlī 1270/1853, 47; Ghulām Sarwar, *Khazīnat al-aṣfiyāʾ*, Kānpur 1914, ii, 84; Raḥmān ʿAlī, *Tadhkira-i ʿulamāʾ-i Hind*, Lucknow 1894, 43; Yāsīn Khān Niyāzī, *Sikāndar Lodī aur uskē baʿd fārsī muṣannifīn*, in *Oriental College Magazine* (*OCM*), ix/3 (May 1933), 37-48; Ḥabīb al-Raḥmān Khān Shirwānī, *Taṣānīf-i Shaykh Djamālī Dihlawī*, in *OCM*, x/i (Nov. 1933), 145-59; Imtiyaz ʿAlī ʿĀrshī, *Istidrākāt*, in *OCM*, xi/i (Nov. 1934), 74-8; Shaykh Muḥammad Ikrām, *Āb-i Kawthar*, Lahore 1952; idem, *Armaghān-i Pāk*, Karachi 1953, 47.

(Aziz Ahmad)

DJAMBI [see PALEMBANG].

DJAMBUL [see AWLIYĀ ATA].

DJAMBUL DJABAEV, a popular Ḳazakh poet, illiterate and thus representing oral poetic tradition. Born in 1846 in Semireče of a nomadic family, he took the name Djambul (Džambul) from a mountain; later, in 1938, this name was to be given in his honour to the town of Awliyā Ata [*q.v.*] and to an *oblast'* of Ḳazakhistān. From an early age he was devoted to music and singing, and by them earned his living while still a youth; taking his inspiration from popular grievances, he often improvised poems which he sang, accompanying himself on the *dombra*; the best known are entitled "The Plaint", "The poor man's lot", etc. His first teacher was the popular poet Syuyumbay, but he soon surpassed him and was given the title of "father of the popular poets" (*akîn*).

After the October Revolution he employed his talents in the cause of the new régime and made himself its panegyrist, composing poems in praise of Lenin, Stalin and other important figures; he even celebrated China and the Spanish Republic (1937), and later, during the Second World War, the Red Army's feats of arms, particularly at Leningrad, while in an elegy he mourned the loss of his son who fell on the battlefield. His poetry is characterized by its great simplicity, though daring comparisons occur not infrequently.

The Soviet authorities who had previously awarded him the Order of Lenin and a Stalin Prize in 1941 were preparing to celebrate his centenary when he died in 1945.

His original works, transmitted orally or in writing, were collected and published in Alma Ata in 1946, at the same time and in the same town as the collected edition of his poems translated into Russian.

Bibliography: M. Abdîkadîrov, *Narodniy Pevets Stalinskoy épokhi*, 1946; M. Balakaev, *O yazîke Džambula*, in *Vestnik Akad. Nauk Kazakhskoy SSR*, 1947/6; *BSE*, xiv, 206-8 (with portrait).

(Ed.)

DJAMDĀR. The word *djamdār* is a contraction of Pers. *djāma-dār*, "clothes-keeper", cf. Dozy, *Suppl.* This word is not, as stated by Sobernheim in *EI*¹, a "title of one of the higher ranks in the army in Hindustān ...", although *djamʿdār*, popularly *djamādār*, Anglo-Indian Jemadar, "leader of a number (*djamʿ*) of men", is applied in the Indian Army to the lowest commissioned rank, platoon commander, but may be applied also to junior officials in the police, customs, etc., or to the foreman of a group of guides, sweepers, etc. (Ed.)

In Mamlūk Egypt the *djamdāriyya* (sing. *djamdār*), "keepers of the sultan's wardrobe", were all Royal Mamlūks (*mamālīk sulṭāniyya*). Many, but not all, of them belonged to the sultan's corps of bodyguards and select retinue (*khāṣṣakiyya*). A head or commander of the *djamdāriyya* was called *raʾs nawbat al-djamdāriyya*. Of these there were seven, according to Khalīl b. Shāhīn al-Ẓāhirī, *Zubdat kashf al-mamālik*, 115-6.

Bibliography: D. Ayalon, *Studies on the structure of the Mamluk army*, in *BSOAS*, xv/2, 1953, 214 and note 5 (bibliographical note).

(D. Ayalon)

DJĀMĪ, Mawlanā Nūr al-Dīn ʿAbd al-Raḥmān, the great Persian poet. He was born in Khardjird, in the district of Djām which is a dependency of Harāt, on 23 Shaʿbān 817/7 November 1414 and died at Harāt on 18 Muḥarram 898/9 November 1492. His family came from Dasht, a small town in the neighbourhood of Iṣfahān; his father, Niẓām al-Dīn Aḥmad b. Shams al-Dīn Muḥammad, had left that district and settled near Harāt; consequently the poet had for some time signed his works with the *takhalluṣ* Dashtī before adopting the *takhalluṣ* Djāmī. In the regular course of his studies, he became aware of his deep passion for mysticism, and took as his spiritual director Saʿd al-Dīn Muḥammad al-Kāshgharī, the disciple of and successor to the great saint Bahāʾ al-Dīn Naḳshband, founder of the order of the Naḳshbandīs [*q.v.*]. Two biographers, ʿAbd al-Ghafūr Lārī (his disciple, buried in 912/1506 beside Djāmī's tomb) and, in particular, Mīr ʿAlī Shir Nawāʾī, a famous minister and scholar, have described the events of his life: apart from two pilgrimages, one to Mashhad, the other to the holy cities of the Ḥidjāz (in 877/1472, with a further stay of four months near Baghdād, and about two months in Damascus and Tabrīz), he lived quietly in Harāt, dividing his time between his studies, poetry and spiritual exercises, honoured by the sovereigns of the time whom he in no way flattered with excessive panegyrics by dedicating his works to them. Bābur [*q.v.*] in his Memoirs says that he was without an equal in his time in the field of the concrete and speculative sciences; Meḥemmed II tried to attract him to Istanbul; Bāyezīd II sent two letters to him (reproduced in Ferīdūn Bey, *Munsha'āt*, i, 361-4); his influence on Turkish literature is well-known (Gibb, *Ottoman Poetry*, ii, 7 ff.). According to Dawlat-Shāh (who should be treated with caution), Djāmī is said at the end to have lost his reason; but ʿAlī Shīr Nawā'ī, who lived on intimate terms with him and was present during his last days, does not confirm this statement (which recalls St. Jerome's about the madness of the poet Lucretius). Djāmī's funeral, conducted by the prince of Harāt, was attended by great numbers; his tomb, near that of Saʿd al-Dīn his director, is well cared for. Of his four sons (he was son-in-law of Saʿd al-Dīn), three died in infancy, the fourth in early youth (when reading to him and commenting on Saʿdī's *Gulistān*, he conceived the idea of writing his *Bahāristān*).

His writings, which are both diverse and numerous, testify to the flexibility of his genius, the depth and variety of his knowledge, and his perfect mastery of language and style. Although he wrote a great deal in prose, he is mainly known for his poetic works; these consist, firstly, of seven *mathnawīs* [*q.v.*] collected together under the title *Haft awrang* ("the seven thrones", one of the names of the Great Bear) and, secondly, of three collections of lyric poems (*dīwān*) written from the time of his youth and arranged, towards the end of his life, under the following titles: *Fātiḥat al-shabāb* ("The beginning of youth", 884/1479), *Wāsiṭat al-ʿiḳd* ("The central pearl in the necklace", 894/1489), *Khātimat al-ḥayāt* ("The conclusion of Life", 895/1490)—on his lyric poetry: H. Massé, introd. to the translation of *Bahāristān*, 18 ff. The seven poems mentioned above are: *Silsilat al-dhahab* ("The chain of gold") dedicated to Sulṭān Ḥusayn Bayḳarā, written between that prince's accession in 873/1468, and Djāmī's journey to the Ḥidjāz in 877/1472: a series of anecdotes provides a framework for an exposé of philosophical, ethical or religious questions; *Salamān wa-Absāl*, 885/1480, dedicated to Yaʿḳūb Aḳ-ḳoyunlu, an allegorical romance in which the characters, in the words of Naṣīr al-Dīn Ṭūsī, "are symbols denoting the various degrees of the intellect" (ed. Forbes Falconer, 1850-6; Eng. tr. by E. Fitzgerald 1879, new edition with literal translation by A. J. Arberry 1956; Fr. tr. A. Bricteux, 1911, with an important introd.); *Tuḥfat al-aḥrār* ("The gift to the noble", 886/1481), a didactic poem of moral and philosophic character, written (as the two panegyrics inserted in the introduction show) in honour of Bahā' al-Dīn, founder of the order of Naḳshbandīs, and of the superior of the order, Nāṣir al-Dīn ʿUbayd Allāh, known by the name Khʷādja-yi Aḥrār (ed. Forbes Falconer, 1848); *Subḥat al-abrār* ("The rosary of the devout", of about 887/1482, written in honour of Sulṭān Ḥusayn Bayḳarā), similar to the last, but with mystical trends (ed. 1811, 1818, 1848); *Yūsuf wa-Zalīkha* (Zulaykha), 888/1483, the best known, written in honour of the same prince: a legendary life of Joseph, son of Jacob, treated in a mystical manner (ed. and Ger. tr. Rosenzweig, 1824; Eng. tr. R. T. H. Griffith, 1882; Fr. tr. A. Bricteux, 1927); *Layla wa-Madjnūn*, 1484, a romance with a theme of Arabic origin (Fr. tr. Chézy, 1805); *Khirad-nāma-yi Sikandarī* ("The wisdom of Alexander"), a didactic poem written in about 890/1485 in honour of Ḥusayn Bayḳarā: discussions between Alexander and certain philosophers on philosophical and moral questions.

Although earlier writers had already made use of identical or similar subjects, Djāmī did not allow their works to exert an influence upon these great poems: for example, the *Ḥadīḳat al-ḥaḳīḳa* of Sanā'ī and the *Djām-i djam* of Awḥadī upon the first; a lost work of Avicenna (known from the commentaries of Fakhr al-Dīn Rāzī and Naṣīr al-Dīn Ṭūsī) upon the second (cf. introd. by Bricteux, 47 ff.); the *Makhzan al-asrār* of Niẓāmī and the *Maṭlaʿ al-anwār* of Amīr-i Khusraw upon the third and fourth; the *Yūsuf wa-Zalīkha* attributed to Firdawsī upon the fifth; the Arabic *dīwān* attributed to Ḳays upon the sixth; Niẓāmī (*Iskandar-nāma*, 2nd part) and Amīr-i Khusraw upon the seventh. But if Djāmī is not the first to deal with these subjects, he has the ability to bring new life to the material by means of a style that is fresh, graceful, supple and highly distinguished, at times foreshadowing his successors' over-elaborate affectations, but nevertheless avoiding the complexities and obscure allusions in which Niẓāmī delighted; in addition to the revelation of the noblest moral qualities, in certain parts of these poems (especially in *Yūsuf* and *Salamān*), and in a number of lyric poems we find the language and the themes of pantheistic mysticism, challenging comparison with the works of the very greatest poets of Ṣūfism; if Djāmī is not, as he is often said to be, (perhaps through Dawlat-Shāh's influence) the last of the classical poets, he is probably the last of the great mystical poets.

Of his very numerous works in prose (commentaries on the Ḳur'ān, on the *ḥadīths*, and on mystical questions and poems—in particular on the *Khamriyya* of Ibn al-Fāriḍ), mention must be made of the highly prized collection *Nafaḥāt al-uns* ("The breath of divine intimacy", ed. Calcutta 1859), biographies of mystics, preceded by a comprehensive study of Ṣūfism (trans. Silvestre de Sacy, in *Not. et extr. des mss. B.N.*, xii (1831), 287-436; for this work, Djāmī made use of the *Tadhkirat al-awliyā'* of Farīd al-dīn ʿAṭṭār while completing it); the treatise *Shawāhid al-nubuwwa* ("Distinctive signs of prophecy"), which is clear and precise; the short treatise on mysticism *Lawā'iḥ* ("Shafts of light"), interspersed with invocations and poems (ed. and tr. Whinfield and Muḥammad Ḳazwīnī, Or. Translat. Fund, 1906); lastly, the *Bahāristān* (1478), a collection of memorable sayings, witticisms, striking anecdotes, short notes on poets and stories about animals (several ed.; Ger. tr. Schlechta-Wssehrd, 1846; Fr. tr. H. Massé, 1925).

Bibliography: the manuscript of the complete works (*Kulliyāt*) of Djāmī, in his own hand, is preserved in the Institute of Oriental Languages at Leningrad (cf. Victor Rosen, *Collections de l'Institut ... Les manuscrits persans*, 215-61). In addition to the references given in the article, see: *Gr. I. Ph.*, ii, 231-3 and 305-7; E. G. Browne, iii, index s.v. Jāmī; and in particular ʿAlī Aṣghar Ḥikmat, *Djāmī* (in Persian; Tehran 1320/1942: life and works, 1-228; selected pieces, 228-373).

(CL. HUART-[H. MASSÉ])

DJĀMIʿ [see MASDJID].

DJĀMIʿA. From the root *djamaʿa* (to bring together, to unite), this Arabic term is used to denote an ideal, a bond or an institution which unites individuals or groups, *e.g.*, *al-Djāmiʿa al-Islāmiyya* (Pan-Islamism); *Djāmiʿat al-Duwal al-ʿArabiyya* (League of Arab States); *Djāmiʿa* (University). This article is limited to the last-mentioned meaning and deals with university institutions in the Islamic countries.

Although *Djāmiʿa*, in this sense, includes, in popular and semi-official usage, traditional institutions of higher religious education (such as *al-Djāmiʿa al-Azhariyya*; see, for example, Muḥ. ʿAbd al-Raḥīm Ghanīma, *Taʾrīkh al-Djāmiʿāt al-Islāmiyya al-Kubra*, Taṭwān 1953), officially it is restricted to the modern university, established on western models. Thus, Law no. 184 of 1958, organizing the *djāmiʿāt* of the United Arab Republic does not name al-Azhar among these universities. This article will, consequently, deal with "modern" universities. It should be stressed, however, that in Islamic countries higher education had a remarkable tradition in the older institutions of the mosque, the *madrasa* and other centres of education and learning. For these traditional institutions, see the articles AL-AZHAR, DAR AL-ʿULŪM, DEOBAND, MASDJID, etc.

The term *djāmiʿa* seems to have come into use towards the middle of the 19th century, and to have been translated from "université" or "university". Buṭrus al-Bustānī does not have an article on it in his *Dāʾirat al-Maʿārif* (vi, Beirut 1882). Originally, it seems to have been used as an adjective qualifying *madrasa*. (The earliest such use I have been able to trace is by Aḥmad Fāris al-Shidyāḳ, in *al-Sāḳ ʿala al-sāḳ*, Paris 1855, 513, where he speaks of *madārisihim al-djāmiʿa*. But there may have been earlier ones. This adjectival form continued down to the early years of the twentieth century. See Djurdji Zaydān, *al-Hilāl*, viii/8, 15 January 1900, 24, and xii, 18 and 19, 1 July 1904, 590; *madrasat Oxford al-djāmiʿa*).

Furthermore, there was no clear distinction in those years between *djāmiʿa* and *kulliyya* which was used as equivalent to "college". Badger's *English-Arabic Lexicon* (London 1881) includes *madrasa djāmiʿa* as one of the Arabic equivalents of "college", whereas for "university" he gives: "*dār kulliyyāt al-ʿulūm*", and "*dār al-ʿulūm wa 'l-funūn*". Neither Bellot's *Vocabulaire arabe-français* (Beirut 1893), nor Hava's *Arabic-English Dictionary* (Beirut 1899), includes *djāmiʿa*, but both include *kulliyya*, the former translating it by "l'université" and the latter by "university, college".

Similarly, other dictionaries published in the nineteenth or early twentieth century either do not include *djāmiʿa* (such as al-Bustānī's *Muḥīṭ al-muḥīṭ*, 1867-70, Steingass, *Arabic-English Dictionary*, 1881, or Shartūnī's *Aḳrab al-mawārid*, 1889-93), or use it as an adjective qualifying *madrasa*, without distinguishing it properly from *kulliyya* (Abcarius, *English-Arabic Dictionary* 1903; Hammām, *Muʿdjam al-ṭālib*, 1907; Saadeh, *English-Arabic Dictionary*, 1911).

The first definite use of *djāmiʿa* in the technical meaning of university appears to have been in the movement of some intellectual leaders and reformers in Egypt in 1906 for the establishment of a *djāmiʿa miṣriyya*. On 12 October 1906 a group of such leaders, the most active among whom seems to have been Ḳāsim Amīn, met in the house of Saʿd Zaghlūl and formed a preparatory committee to appeal to the Egyptian people for funds for the establishment of a university (*djāmiʿa*) which, they decided, would be called "*al-Djāmiʿa al-Miṣriyya*" (Aḥmad ʿAbd al-Fattāḥ Badīr, *al-Amīr Fuʾād wa nashʾat al-djāmiʿa al-miṣriyya*, Cairo 1950, 6 ff.). From then on, the use of *djāmiʿa* began to be established in the Arab countries as equivalent to "university", whereas *kulliyya* is now reserved for a faculty or an independent college.

In other Islamic countries, other terms came into use, either derived from the national language, such as *Dānishgāh* (the abode of knowledge) in Īrān, or borrowed from the West such as "Üniversite" in Turkey, "University" (U. *Yūniwarsiṭī*) in Pakistan, and "Universitas" in Indonesia.

Survey of university activity in Islamic countries

In recent years, university education has undergone rapid and extensive development in Islamic countries. Established universities are yearly increasing their facilities, courses and student enrolments, and new universities are being planned or opened to meet the increasing demand for higher education. Any statement about them is likely to become out-of-date the time it is published. Consequently, only a general summary of their history and present situation will be attempted here. For current details the reader will have to consult the catalogues or handbooks of individual universities, national or regional handbooks or reports, or a general work of reference such as the *International Handbook of Universities*. No attempt will be made to refer to independent colleges, or any other institutions of higher learning that do not bear the name *Djāmiʿa* or its equivalent.

Since the establishment of universities is closely bound up with the cultural and national development of their respective countries, or regions, the following summary will follow the lines of the various cultural areas in the Islamic world.

United Arab Republic: Egypt. Technical and professional education began in Egypt in the reign of Muḥammad ʿAlī. The contacts which Egypt had with the West since Bonaparte's campaign and the autonomy it enjoyed within the Ottoman Empire laid the ground for the educational efforts and reforms under Muḥammad ʿAlī. Use was made of foreign, particularly French, advisors and professional men; educational missions were sent to Europe, and a number of specialized technical and professional schools were established, mainly to meet the needs of forming an army and a civil service on modern lines. The years 1824-37 witnessed a movement of active educational expansion. In 1827 a School of Medicine was established and was followed by various military Schools, and by Schools of Pharmacy, Maternity, Engineering, Agriculture, Civil Administration and Accountancy, Languages and Translation, etc. This movement received a set-back under ʿAbbās I and Saʿīd (1848-63). Most of these Schools were closed, but they were reopened under Ismāʿīl. In 1871, *Dār al-ʿUlūm* for the training of teachers of Arabic was opened; in 1880 a Teachers' Training College; and in 1882 a School of Administration (changed in 1886 to School of Law).

In 1906, there arose a movement for the establishment of a national university. A committee of prominent citizens and intellectual leaders was formed and funds were sought from the Government and the public. This university—commonly known as *al-Djāmiʿa al-Ahliyya* to distinguish it from the later state university—was opened on 21 December 1908. Its teaching was limited to courses in literature, history, philosophy, and social sciences, and a number of leading European orientalists and other professors were invited to teach in it. Following World War I, the Egyptian Government took steps to establish a state university. This university, consisting of the former national university as the nucleus of the Faculty of Letters, of the Schools of Law and Medicine already established and of a new Faculty of Science, was instituted by law in March 1925. It continued to develop by the incorporation of existing Schools into Faculties, or by the creation of new ones.

In 1938 a branch of this University was established in Alexandria comprising branches of the Faculties of Letters and of Law. In 1941 a third branch, of the Faculty of Engineering, was opened. In 1942 a full-fledged university was founded in Alexandria. This was followed by another university in Cairo in 1950. These three universities which in course of time came to bear the names of, respectively, Fuʾād I, Fārūḳ, and Ibrāhīm, have since the Revolution been called the Universities of Cairo, Alexandria and ʿAyn S̲h̲ams. Following a policy of spreading facilities of higher education throughout the country, the Egyptian Government began in 1954-55 to plan for another university in Asiūṭ. This university opened its doors in October 1957 with a Faculty of Science and a Faculty of Engineering. Other Faculties are being instituted gradually, the scientific ones taking precedence over others. Of the four universities in Egypt, the oldest and most developed is the University of Cairo. In addition to its twelve faculties and its various institutes in Cairo, it administers a branch in Khartoum comprising faculties of Law, Letters, and Commerce.

In 1919 the American University at Cairo was established. An independent private institution, it now includes a faculty of Arts and Sciences, a faculty of Education, a School of Oriental Studies, a Social Research Centre and a Division of Extension, and is smaller than the state universities in facilities, number of staff and students, and educational influence.

Syria. In 1902, under Ottoman rule, a School of Medicine was established in Damascus with Turkish as the medium of instruction. During World War I, it was transferred to Beirut, where a School of Law had been opened in 1912. Both institutions were closed at the end of the War. They were reopened in Damascus in 1919, with Arabic as the medium of instruction. In 1924, they were joined together in the Syrian University, which continued to be limited to them, until, with the gaining of independence, higher national education received a vigorous impulse. In 1946 four new Faculties were opened in the University: Letters, Science, Engineering (at Aleppo), and a Higher Teachers' College (later changed to Faculty of Pedagogy). In 1954-55, a Faculty of Holy Law (*S̲h̲arīʿa*) was added.

Following the formation of the U.A.R., the name of the Syrian University was changed into that of the University of Damascus. Law no. 184 of 1958, published on October 21, 1958 governed the organization of universities in the U.A.R. In addition to the five universities mentioned above, it instituted a University at Aleppo (which was due to open in 1960-61) and created the Higher Council of Universities, with seat in Cairo, to co-ordinate the activities of these institutions. Since 28 Sept. 1961, the former organization was reestablished in Syria.

Lebanon: The universities in Lebanon, in order of foundation, are: The American University of Beirut, the Université St. Joseph and the (state) Lebanese University, all of which are located in the capital, Beirut. The oldest, the American University of Beirut was established by the American missionaries in the sixties of the last century, but was from the start made separate from the Mission, and governed by an independent Board of Trustees. Its original name was the Syrian Protestant College and under this name it was granted a charter by the State of New York in April 1864. University work in the School of Arts and Sciences began in 1866. The School of Medicine opened in 1867, the School of Pharmacy in 1871, the School of Commerce in 1900, the School of Nursing and the Hospital in 1905. On November 18, 1920, the Board of Regents of the University of the State of New York changed the name of the institution into the American University of Beirut. In 1951, the School of Engineering was established, in 1952 the School of Agriculture and in 1954 the School of Public Health. The medium of instruction is English.

The Université St. Joseph was founded by the Jesuits in Beirut in 1875. It received the title of University from Pope Leo XIII in 1881, but in Arabic it continued for many years to be called *Kulliyyat Mār Yūsuf* (See Cheikho's article on its fiftieth anniversary, *Al-Machriq*, xxxiii 5, May 1925, 321 ff.). Originally, its higher instruction was limited to theology and philosophy. In 1883, under agreement between the Jesuits of Syria and the French Government, the School of Medicine was established, and, in 1888, the School of Pharmacy, both becoming in 1889 the *Faculté française de Médecine et de Pharmacie*. In 1902 was founded the Faculty of Oriental Studies which was closed with the rest of the University during World War I. In 1913, the School of Law was opened; in 1919, the School of Engineering; and in 1937 the Institute of Oriental Studies. The medium of instruction is French.

The Lebanese University started in 1951 with a Higher Teachers' Institute for the training of teachers for secondary schools. It was formally organized by Legislative Decree no. 25 of 6 February 1953 (revised by Leg. Decree no. 26 of 18 January 1955), but its activity remained restricted to the Higher Teachers' Institute with its two divisions, literary and scientific, of three years each leading to the Licence, and a fourth year of pedagogical training. In 1959 a Faculty of Law and Economic and Political Sciences was established, and in the same year a regulatory decree (no. 2883 of 16 June 1959) gave the University its inner constitution. This decree provided for faculties of Letters, Sciences, Law and Economic and Political Sciences, for a Higher Teachers' Institute and an Institute of Social Studies, and, like similar state university constitutions or charters, for other faculties, colleges or institutes which might later be created. Also, like other state universities in Arab countries, the language of instruction is Arabic, unless otherwise decided in particular fields.

ʿIrāḳ. Before World War I, there was only one institution of higher education in ʿIrāḳ: a School of Law. In 1923, the ʿIrāḳ Government decided to establish a university called *D̲j̲āmiʿat Āl al-Bayt*, but this plan was later abandoned. Instead, between 1920 and 1949, a number of Faculties or Colleges (Medicine, Education, Engineering, Business and Economics, etc.) were established and made dependent to various ministries. In 1951, a "Council of Higher Education" was set up to co-ordinate the work of these Faculties, "in preparation for the establishment of the ʿIrāḳī University". Following many commissions and reports, the University of Bag̲h̲dād was established by Law no. 60 of June 6, 1956. This Law provided for the establishment of a "Constituent Council" which was charged with the study of each of the existing Faculties and Colleges to decide on its inclusion in the University. On 15 September 1958 a new Law was issued to replace the previous one. According to it, the University is composed of the Faculties of Letters, Sciences, Law, Commerce, Education, Education (Women), Engineering, Agriculture, Medicine, Dentistry, Pharmacy, Veterinary Medicine and such other Faculties and Institutes as may be established in the future.

Saʿūdī Arabia: The King Saʿūd University was established in Riyāḍ by Royal Decree no. 17 of 21 Rabīʿ II 1377/14 November 1957. It started with a Faculty of Letters. In 1958 a Faculty of Science was added, and in 1959 a Faculty of Pharmacy and a Faculty of Commerce. Each of these Faculties is being developed at the rate of a class a year. A project has been drawn up for an extensive campus and ample building facilities, and plans are under study for curricular and other developments.

Kuwayt: The Government of Kuwayt asked a committee of experts to study the question of establishing a university in that Principality. The committee met in Kuwayt during the month of February 1960, and presented its recommendations to the Government.

Sudan: The University of Khartoum was officially constituted by Act of Parliament on 24 July 1956, seven months after the establishment of the new Republic of the Sudan. It developed from the University College of Khartoum, which was instituted in 1951 by the fusion of Gordon Memorial College and the Kitchener School of Medicine. The former had in 1945 grouped together the Schools which had been set up from 1936 onwards to give post-secondary training in Arts, Law, Public Administration, Engineering, Agriculture and Veterinary Science. The academic standard of the College was recognized in 1945 by the University of London which admitted it to Special Relationship. The Kitchener School of Medicine was founded in 1924, and from 1940 onwards its final examination was supervised by a visitor appointed by the Royal Colleges of Physicians and Surgeons of England.

The University of Khartoum includes at present the following Faculties: Agriculture, Arts, Economic and Social Studies, Engineering, Law, Medicine, Science, and Veterinary Science. The only other institution of higher education in the Sudan is the previously mentioned branch in Khartoum of the University of Cairo including faculties of Law, Letters, and Commerce.

Libya. The University of Libya was founded in 1955-56. The Law establishing it was issued on 15 December 1955. It started with a Faculty of Letters and of Pedagogy in Benghazi. Since then a Faculty of Commerce in Benghazi and a Faculty of Science in Tripoli have been added. Plans for the development of these Faculties and for the creation of new ones are under way.

Tunisia: al-Dj̲āmiʿ al-Aʿẓam, the traditional centre of higher religious instruction in Tunisia has in recent years been popularly called al-Dj̲āmiʿa al-Zaytūniyya, but the only post-secondary education it has given is in the fields of Islamic studies and of Arabic language and literature related to them. Modern university studies were recently started in schools or institutes on the French model and using generally the French language. Thus, the *Institut des Hautes Études*, founded in 1945 and attached to the Sorbonne, covered the fields of Law, Arabic Studies, Sciences, and Social Sciences. In 1960, the Tunisian University was founded incorporating existing institutions and establishing new ones. Law no. 2 of 1960 (31 March 1960) established the Tunisian University as a public institution, Decree (*Amr*) no. 98 of the same date set up its organization, and a ten-years plan for its development has been formulated.

Algeria: The University of Algiers was until 1962 a French university organized and administered as other French state universities. Growing out of a School of Medicine and Pharmacy (1859) and Schools of Law, Science and Letters (1879), it was formally established as a university in 1909. It included these Faculties and certain specialized institutes and used French as the medium of instruction.

Morocco: As in the case of other countries, modern higher instruction in Morocco started with separate institutions: the *Institut des Hautes Études Marocaines, Centres d'Études Juridiques* and *Centre d'Études Superieures Scientifiques.* With the acquisition of independence, there was a movement for the establishment of a national university. This university, the University of Rabāṭ, was inaugurated in December 1957, and was formally organized by royal decree (*Ẓahīr S̲h̲arīf* (no. 1.58.390 of 29 July 1959). It consists of Faculties of Holy Law (*S̲h̲arīʿa*), Legal, Economic and Social Sciences, Letters, Physical and Natural Sciences, and a Faculty of Medicine and Pharmacy to be established. Here again the relation of this University (and particularly its Faculty of Holy Law) with the traditional Islamic higher education centred around the celebrated Dj̲āmiʿ al-Ḳarawiyyīn in Fās depends upon future developments.

Turkey: Modern technical and professional education started in Turkey towards the end of the 18th and the beginning of the 19th century, to meet the needs of the army, navy and civil service. In 1773 a *Muhendisk̲h̲āne* [*q.v.*], or School of Engineering for the navy was set up and another for the army in 1796. These were followed by a School of Medicine (1827), and a school of Military Sciences (*Ḥarbiyye* [*q.v.*]) in 1834. In 1846 a committee on education recommended the creation of a state university, without however any practical result. A new start was made in 1859, with the foundation of a school for Civil Servants (*Mülkiyye* [*q.v.*]) which was reorganized and expanded in 1877. Many other higher schools followed, including finance (1878), law (1878), fine arts (1879), commerce (1892), civil engineering (1884), etc. In August 1900, after long preparation, the University of Istanbul, at first known as the Dār al-Funūn, was opened, and in 1908 the Schools of Medicine and of Law were incorporated in it. This University now includes Faculties of Medicine, Law, Economics, Letters, Science, and Forestry, and Schools of Dental Medicine and of Pharmacy.

Growing out of the *Muhendisk̲h̲āne*, the Technical University of Istanbul (Istanbul Teknik Üniversitesi) was established in 1944. It includes to-day five Faculties and several Institutes, for teaching and research in various fields of engineering. In 1946 the University of Ankara (Ankara Üniversitesi) was founded in the capital, incorporating the already existing Faculties of Law, Letters, Science, Medicine and Agriculture. Now it includes in addition Faculties of Veterinary Medicine, of Political Science and of Theology (*Ilâhiyat*).

In 1955 the Aegean University (Ege Üniversitesi) was established in Izmir. In 1956 Atatürk Üniversitesi was founded in Erzurum to serve the needs of eastern Turkey. This was done with the assistance of the University of Nebraska, under contract between this University and the Technical Cooperation Administration of the U.S.A. All these universities are state institutions. By the University Law of 1946, they were granted administrative and financial autonomy.

In 1957, the Middle East Technical University was established in Ankara, by special act of parliament, with certain unique features. The United Nations and Unesco have been closely associated with the Government of Turkey in the planning and development of this university. Whereas the other universities use Turkish as their medium of instruction, this uses English and hopes to attract students from other countries of the region.

Īrān: The oldest and the most important of the universities of Īrān is the University of Tehran, *Dānishgāh-i Tehrān*. Growing out of the polytechnic school, *Dār al-Funūn* (1851), and of other more recently established schools, it was constituted as a state university in 1934. It now includes eleven Faculties: Arts, Fine Arts, Islamic Sciences (*ʿUlūm-i Maʿḳūl wa Manḳūl*), Law, Science, Engineering, Agriculture (at Karadj), Medicine, Dentistry, Pharmacy and Veterinary Medicine. Other universities to serve the needs of the provinces have been established since World War II. In 1947, the University of Tabrīz (Ādharbāydjān) was founded, and was followed by the Universities of Mashhad (Khurāsān), of Shirāz (Fars), of Iṣfahān, and of Ahwāz (Khuzistān).

These provincial universities have as yet a limited number of Faculties (mostly professional), but their development in this short period indicates the concern of the Government of Īrān to extend the facilities of university education and to spread it throughout the country. The language of instruction in all the universities of Īrān is Persian.

Afghānistān: Higher university education in Afghānistān began with a Faculty of Medicine in 1932. Other Faculties were later established and all were incorporated in the University of Kābul, which was founded by Royal Decree in 1946. This University now includes Faculties of Medicine (including Women's Division and School of Nursing), Law and Political Science, Science, Letters, Islamic Law, Agricultural Engineering, a Women's Faculty (Social and Physical Sciences) and Institutes of Economics and of Education. Instruction is through the medium of Persian and Pashtō.

India and Pakistan: It was not until the early decades of the nineteenth century that schools and colleges on western models began to be established in the sub-continent of India. These institutions used English as the medium of instruction. Following the recommendations of Sir Charles Wood, the Universities of Calcutta, Bombay, and Madras were established in 1857, and remained for twenty-five years the only universities in India. In 1882 the University of the Panjab was created at Lahore, and in 1887 the University of Allāhābād. No other university was established before World War I. Subsequently there were two periods of rapid development of university institutions: 1915-1929, and after partition. The latest edition of the *Commonwealth Universities Handbook* (1960) lists thirty-seven universities in India, of which eighteen were established or achieved full university status after 1947. Of the six universities of Pakistan, only two, the University of the Panjab (1882) and the University of Dacca (1921), existed before independence, although many colleges were affiliated to universities in India before partition.

In India, two universities have been active in the field of higher education for the Muslim community. The older, the ʿAlīgaṙh Muslim University, has played its particular rôle in the intellectual life of this community. Founded in 1875 by the author and reformer Sir Sayyid Aḥmad Khān, as the Mohammedan Anglo-Oriental College, with the object of imparting to the Muslim youth a modern scientific education, it received its charter as a university in 1920, and has since its establishment served as an influential centre of Indian Muslim intellectual life. The other University, Osmania, at Ḥaydarābād, Deccan, was established in 1918 and has also paid special attention to Islamic studies. In addition to these two universities, there are Muslim colleges which either form part of, or are affiliated to, other Indian universities. Among other institutions of higher education, mention should be made of the Jamia Millia Islamia [*q.v.*] at Jamaniagar, Dihlī, whose courses in the arts and social sciences lead to an examination recognized by the government as equivalent to the B.A. degree of an Indian university.

In Pakistan, there are six universities: University of the Panjab at Lahore (1882), University of Dacca (1921), University of Sind (1947), University of Karachi (1950), University of Peshawar (1950), and University of Rajshahi (Rādjshāhī) (1953). Although these institutions are entirely secular and pursue liberal, scientific and professional education on modern lines, they are permeated by Islamic traditions and spirit.

The first universities established in the sub-continent of India in the middle of the last century took as their model the then newly established University of London. This University was at that time a purely examining body. Thus the early universities were slow to develop teaching of their own. At present, the universities of India and Pakistan are of various types, but most of them are both teaching and affiliating. Post-graduate teaching is generally carried on by the universities themselves, whereas first-degree teaching is still largely done by affiliated colleges under university supervision and examination arrangements.

Malaya and Singapore: The University of Malaya was founded in 1949 by the combined actions of the governments of the Federation of Malaya and the Colony of Singapore. It grew out of two existing colleges in Singapore, King Edward VII College of Medicine and Raffles College. Full university teaching began in Kuala Lumpur in 1957, and on the Singapore site in 1949-50. It includes teaching in arts, science, engineering, law and medicine. According to the new constitution which came into effect in 1959, the University now comprises two divisions of equal status, the University of Malaya in Singapore and the University of Malaya in Kuala Lumpur, each with its own principal, divisional council and divisional senate. These two divisions are equally represented on the central council of the University.

Indonesia: Although Faculties (largely professional) had been instituted in Indonesia in the period between the two World Wars, the movement for the establishment of universities began in 1949 and has progressed rapidly since the country acquired its sovereignty. These universities have incorporated previously-existing Faculties and created new ones. In 1949 Universitas Gadjah Mada was instituted at Djogdjakarta by merger of five Faculties, whose number has grown to eleven. Universitet Indonesia was founded in 1950 at Djakarta and now includes Faculties of Medicine, Law and Social Sciences, Philosophy and Letters, Economics, Mathematics and Natural Sciences (at Bandung), Technology (at Bandung), Veterinary Medicine (at Bogor) and Agriculture (at Bogor). Other Faculties of the University established at Surabaya, Bukitinggi and Makassar, have since formed the nuclei of separate universities: Universitas Airlangga (1954), Surabeja (also incorporating the former Faculty of Law of Universitas Gadjah Mada in Surabeja); Universitas Andalas (1956), Bukitinggi; and Universitas Hasanuddin (1956), Makassar. A new university is being established in Bandung independently of the Faculties of the Universitet Indonesia set up there.

In addition to the above, which are all state universities there are a number of private institutions. Of particular importance for us are the Universitet Islam Indonesia, Diogdjakarta (theology, social economics, law) and the Perguruan Tinggi Islam Indonesia, Medan (law and social sciences, theology).

Reference should finally be made to universities in some of the predominantly Muslim Republics of the U.S.S.R. which also serve the needs of the Muslim population, such as the Ādharbāydjān State University at Baku (1919), the Tadjik State University at Stalinabad (1948), and the Uzbek State University (1933). These Universities follow the pattern of universities in the Soviet Union, and use, along with Russian, local languages in their instruction.

Bibliography: As the majority of the universities in the Islamic countries are state institutions, the basic sources on their constitutions and organization are the government promulgated charters embodied in laws, decrees, or other government acts, as well as the catalogues, reports, or handbooks issued by the individual universities, national associations of universities, or the government ministries. For universities in Arab countries, Sāṭiʿ al-Ḥuṣri's *Ḥawliyyat al-thaḳāfa al-ʿarabiyya*, published by the Cultural Section of the League of Arab States (5 vols., Cairo, 1949-57), summarizes the governing legislation and other acts, and gives pertinent information on the programs and activities of the universities up to 1956. For Pakistan and India see the *Handbook of the Universities of Pakistan*, 1955-6 (Inter-University Board of Pakistan, 1956) and the *Handbook of the [Indian] Universities, 1953-4* (Inter-University Board of India, 1958). For universities in these two and other countries of the British Commonwealth, see *Commonwealth Universities Yearbook*, 1960, (37th edition, ed. J. F. Foster, London 1960). General information about universities (outside the Commonwealth and the U.S.A.) is given in the *International Handbook of Universities* (1st edition, ed. H. M. R. Keyes, International Association of Universities, Paris 1959). Discussions of various problems will be found in *Universität und moderne Gesellschaft*, edd. C. D. Harris and M. Herkheimer, Frankfurt 1959; *Science and Freedom*, 12, Oct. 1958; J. Jomier, *Écoles et universités dans l'Égypte actuelle*, in *MIDEO* 1955, ii, 135-60, 1956, iii, 387-90; H. de la Bastide, *Les universités islamiques d'Indonésie*, in *Orient*, no. 21, 1962, 81-4. For accounts of current university activity and development see the *Bulletin of the International Association of Universities* (quarterly, published since February 1953). The International Association of Universities (6, Rue Franklin, Paris, 16e) also maintains a documentation and information centre on universities, including those treated in this article.

(C. K. Zurayk)

DJĀMID [see naḥw and ṭabīʿa].

DJAMĪL b. ʿAbd Allāh b. Maʿmar al-ʿUdhrī, an Arab poet of the 1st/7th century, in literary tradition the most famous representative, and almost symbol of, the "ʿUdhrī(te)" school of poetry, with its chaste and idealized form of love. He is a quite authentic historical figure, although very few details of his life have come to light. He was born about 40/660, and spent his life in the Ḥidjāz and in Nadjd. It is also thought that, on the instigation of the parents of his beloved, he fled for a period to the Yemen in order to escape persecution by an Umayyad governor. Towards the end of his life he went to Egypt, where he made the governor ʿAbd al-ʿAzīz b. Marwān famous in his *ḳaṣīdas*, and it was there that he died in 82/701, still relatively young. Although most of the poems which have come to us are on the theme of love, we can also discern other aspects of his character and poetic ability. He was adept at composing *fakhr* and *hidjāʾ* poetry, was quarrelsome and quick at repartee, and devoted to the glories of his forefathers and his clan. (Although genealogists assert that the Banū ʿUdhra tribe originated from the south, he speaks of his ancestors' triumphs as those of the Maʿaddīs). But the outstanding historical image of Djamīl is that of the love-poet. Right from his early youth he was inflamed with love for his fellow tribeswoman Bathna, or Buthayna, of the Banu 'l-Aḥabb ʿUdhrī tribe, and the story of his deep and unhappy love is commemorated both in the work of the poet himself and in the stories of other men of letters of the 2nd/8th century (often based in part on Djamīl's own poems). Buthayna's parents refused him their daughter's hand, and she was married off to a certain Nabīh b. al-Aswad. After periods of reconciliation followed by periods of reproach, he eventually left Wādi 'l-Ḳurā, the camp of the ʿUdhra where his love had first become inflamed, and never returned. He remembered it in moving lines composed on his death-bed.

The *dīwān* of Djamīl (during whose lifetime the poet Kuthayyir ʿAzza was *rāwī*) circulated widely in the 3rd/9th century, and was studied and made known by philologists such as Ibn al-Anbārī and Ibn Durayd. But it was not preserved for posterity, and we have access to no more than a few fragments and extracts of Djamīl's poetry gleaned from anthologies and other literary sources (primarily from the *Aghānī*). They amount to some 800 verses, and bear the stamp of an unmistakably individual personality, although his originality has been somewhat clouded by the mass of imitators, and by the literary conventions of Djamīl's time which even he could not ignore. The story of his passionate love as it emerges from his poetry is much more than the normal run of such stories. He was the first to speak of love as an ever-present cosmic force which attracts a person from the moment he is born, and lives on after his death. True to the ʿUdhrī tradition, he constantly laid emphasis on the purity and nobility of love, the virtue of self-denial, the ability to worship the beloved one, and endure suffering oneself. There is with him no trace of the wanton and joking love described in the trifles of ʿUmar b. Abī Rabīʿa and others. He developed the Bedouin tradition of love, infusing into it his own deep personal experience, the poignant sincerity of which cannot be doubted. His poetry, together with that of ʿUmar, soon became classical (al-Walīd b. Yazīd was proud of his ability to write verse "in the manner of Djamil and ʿUmar"). Time has with good reason shown him to be the most perfect representative of the ʿUdhra poets, who "when loving, die".

Bibliography: The principal sources are *Aghānī*[3], viii, 90-154; Ibn Ḳutayba, *Shiʿr*, 260-8; Ibn Khallikān, no. 141 Wüstenfeld; Ibn Asākir, iii, 395-405 Badrān; F. Gabrieli, *Ǧamīl al-Udhrī. Studio critico e raccolta dei frammenti*, in *RSO*, xvii (1937), 40-71, 132-72; idem, *Contributi alla interpretazione di Ǧamīl*, in *RSO*, xviii (1938), 173-98; Oriental editions of fragments, by Bashīr Yamūt, Beirut 1934, and (much superior) by Ḥusayn Naṣṣār, Cairo 1958; R. Blachère, *Les principaux thèmes de la poésie érotique au siècle des Umayyades de Damas*, in *AIEO*, Algiers, v (1939-41), 82-128.

(F. Gabrieli)

DJAMĪL (b.) Nakhla al-Mudawwar, Arab journalist and writer, born in Beirut in 1862, died in Cairo on 26 January 1907. Djamīl came from a wealthy, intellectually active, Christian family, and grew up in conditions which were very favourable to his development as a writer. His father (1822-89), who had attended lectures on Arabic grammar, French, and Italian in Beirut, was an interpreter at the French Consulate, and a member of the Beirut town council; he also took part in editing the Beirut newspaper *Ḥadīḳat al-Akhbār*, as well as being a member of the *Société Asiatique*, Paris, and of *al-Djamʿiyya al-ʿilmiyya al-sūriyya*, Beirut.

Djamīl pursued Arabic studies, and also studied French language and literature at Beirut University. He soon began to show a preference for the history of the peoples of the ancient Orient. Later on, he became editor of several journals. He collaborated in the semi-monthly *al-Djinān*, and also in *al-Muḳtaṭaf*. The second of these moved its offices from Beirut to Cairo in 1888. Finally, he brought out the pan-Islamic paper *al-Muʾayyad* in Cairo.

Djamīl al-Mudawwar reached fame with his *Ḥaḍārat al-Islām fī Dār al-Salām*, Cairo 1888, [2]1905, [3]1932. This work is of great literary importance, because it is a completely new departure in Arabic literature. It was probably modelled on J. Barthélémy's (1716-95) *Voyage du jeune Anacharsis en Grèce*, and takes the form of letters. It quotes many sources and treats of early ʿAbbāsid times from al-Manṣūr to Hārūn al-Rashīd in a popular manner. Occasional references to the past of Islamic history and culture add further to the attraction of the book. The special quality of al-Mudawwar's presentation of history lies in the fact that he views the rule of the caliphs from the point of view of a Shīʿī Persian and friend of the Barmakids. Yet his view is also influenced by such great modernistic ideas as Panislamism and Nationalism, which appeared in the Islamic Orient at that time. As a document of modern Arabic thought, the *Ḥaḍārat al-Islām* is one of the most important works of the so-called renaissance of Arabic literature.

Al-Mudawwar also wrote *Taʾrīkh Bābil wa Āshūr*, a compilation based on European sources, which was improved and edited by Ibrāhīm al-Yāzidjī. From the French, he translated *ʿAṭlalā*, Beirut 1882 (F. R. de Chateaubriand's Red Indian tale of *Atala*), and *al-Taʾrīkh al-ḳadīm*, Beirut 1895, ed. Yūḥannā ʿAkkā, director of the catholic patriarchal school.

Bibliography: L. Cheikho, *Kitāb al-makhṭūṭāt al-ʿarabiyya li 'l-kataba al-naṣrāniyya*, Beirut 1924, 120, 187; *Taʾrīkh al-ādāb al-ʿarabiyya fi 'l-rubʿ al-awwal min al-ḳarn al-ʿishrīn*, ii, Beirut 1926, 22 f.; E. J. Sakīs, *Dictionnaire de bibliographie arabe*, Cairo 1929, 1721; Djirdjī Zaydān in *al-Hilāl*, xv, 1907, 338 ff. (this article is in Zaydān's *Tarādjim mashāhīr al-sharḳ*, ii, Cairo 1922, 223 ff.); *Taʾrīkh ādāb al-lugha al-ʿarabiyya*, iv, Cairo 1914, 293; Ph. de Ṭarrāzī, *Taʾrīkh al-ṣiḥāfa al-ʿarabiyya*, i, Beirut 1913, 111 f., 114 f.; ii, Beirut 1913, 45, 56; iii, Beirut 1914, 40; I. Kračkovskij, in *WI*, xii, 1930, 67 ff.; idem, in *MSOS*, xxxi, 1928, 189; Brockelmann, S III, 184 ff.; G. Graf, *Gesch. d. christlichen arabischen Literatur*, iv, Città del Vaticano 1951, 293 (Studi e Testi, 147); E. Köcher, *Untersuchungen zu Ǧamīl al-Mudauwars Ḥaḍārat al-islām fī Dār as-Salām*, Berlin 1958. (Dtsch. Akad. d. Wiss. zu Berlin, Inst. f. Orientf. Veröff. 43).

(E. Köcher)

DJAMĪL, ṬANBURĪ [see ṭanburī djamīl].

DJAMĪLA, a famous singer of Medina at the time of the first Umayyads. Tradition has it that she taught herself the elements of music and singing by listening to her neighbour Sāʾib Khāthir [*q.v.*] (d. 63/682-3). It became unanimously recognized that her great natural talent put her in a class of her own, and she founded a school where, among numerous lesser-known singers and *ḳiyān*, Maʿbad [*q.v.*], Ibn ʿĀʾisha [*q.v.*], Ḥabāba and Sallāma received their training. Artists as great as Ibn Suraydj [*q.v.*] would come to hear her, and would accept her critical judgments, while her salon was regularly frequented by such poets as ʿUmar b. Abī Rabīʿa, al-Aḥwaṣ, and al-ʿArdjī. When at one time she was on a pilgrimage, all the singers and musicians of the Ḥidjāz gathered to accompany her, or to welcome the 'star' of Medina to Mecca. They then accompanied her back to Medina, where an enormous festival of music and song lasted for 3 days. Although the story is of doubtful authenticity, being regarded as false by Abu 'l-Faradj al-Iṣfahānī himself, it is nevertheless an indication of the fame which has always surrounded the figure of Djamīla. The date of her death is unknown.

Bibliography: The basic reference-work is the *Kitāb al-Aghānī*, vii, 124-48 (Beirut ed., viii, 188-234); it has been extensively used by Caussin de Perceval, *Notices anecdotiques sur les principaux musiciens arabes des trois premiers siècles de l'Islamisme*, Paris 1874 (*JA*, 1873), and by ʿAmrūsī, *Al-Djawārī al-mughanniyāt*, Cairo n.d., 48-73.

(A. Schaade-[Ch. Pellat])

DJAMʿIYYA. This term, commonly used in modern Arabic to mean a "society" or "association", is derived from the root DJ - M - ʿ, meaning "to collect, join together, etc.". In its modern sense it appears to have come into use quite recently, and was perhaps first used to refer to the organized monastic communities or congregations which appeared in the eastern Uniate Churches in Syria and Lebanon at the end of the seventeenth and beginning of the eighteenth centuries (*e.g.*, *Djamʿiyyat al-Mukhalliṣ*, the Salvatorians, a Greek Catholic order founded c. 1708). In the middle of the nineteenth century the term came into more general use first in the Lebanon and then in other Arabic-speaking countries, to refer to voluntary associations for scientific, literary, benevolent or political purposes. Perhaps the first of them was *al-Djamʿiyya al-sūriyya*, founded in Beirut in 1847 through the efforts of American Protestant missionaries with learned tastes, for the purpose of raising the level of culture. Its members were all Christians, and included the famous writers Nāṣif al-Yāzidji and Butrus al-Bustānī [*qq.v.*], as well as a number of missionaries and the English writer on the Lebanon, Colonel Charles Churchill, then living near Beirut. The society met regularly until 1852; in 1857 it was succeeded by *al-Djamʿiyya al-ʿilmiyya al-sūriyya*, a larger society on the same model but including Muslims and Druzes; it had corresponding members in Cairo and Istanbul, including the reforming Prime Minister Fuʾād Pasha, and in 1868 received official recognition from the Ottoman government. In 1850 the French Jesuit missionaries in Beirut created a similar organization, *al-Djamʿiyya al-sharkiyya*; its membership was partly foreign, partly local and wholly Christian.

At a slightly later date there arose societies with more practical aims: for example, the first feminist society, *Djamʿiyyat bākūra Ṣūriyya*, founded in Beirut in 1881 or earlier, and a number of benevolent associations. Perhaps the first of these was *al-Djamʿiyya al-khayriyya al-islāmiyya*, founded in Alexandria in 1878, as an expression of the new public consciousness which was appearing in Egypt at that time. Its aim was to found national schools for boys and girls; one school was established in Alexandria and placed under the direction of the famous nationalist orator, ʿAbd Allāh al-Nadīm, but the ʿUrābī movement and British occupation put an end to it, as to a similar society, *Djamʿiyyat al-makāsid al-khayriyya*, founded in Cairo about the same time for the same purpose. A later organization, *al-Djamʿiyya al-khayriyya al-islāmiyya*, started in 1892, had more success: the great reformer of Egyptian Islam, *shaykh* Muḥammad ʿAbduh, was active in it, and it established a number of schools. The *Djamʿiyyat al-makāsid al-khayriyya* of Beirut, founded in 1880, had a similar success, and its schools for the Sunnī Muslim community of the Lebanon are still flourishing.

In an age when representative institutions did not exist, and newspapers were still new, such societies provided an opportunity for educated men to form political ideas and exert a certain pressure of opinion on the government. Some of them were political by implication, and in the 1870's the development of national consciousness and the comparative freedom of expression in Egypt led to the growth of specifically political associations. Among the earliest was *Miṣr al-fatāt* or the "Young Egypt" society, formed in Alexandria in 1879. It included ʿAbd Allāh al-Nadīm and other Muslim nationalists and a number of Lebanese Christian journalists working in Egypt; one of them, Adīb Isḥāk, published the journal of the society until it was suppressed. It had a programme of reforms—ministerial responsibility, equality before the law, liberty of the press, etc.—but could do nothing effective to carry it out, and only remained in existence for a year or so. More famous although scarcely more effective was the *Djamʿiyyat al-ʿurwa al-wuthkā*, a secret society of Muslims pledged to work for the unity and reform of the Muslim world, through the restoration of a true Islamic government, and more specifically for the liberation of Egypt from British control. The moving spirits in this society were the famous publicist Djamāl al-Dīn al-Afghānī and his disciple Muḥammad ʿAbduh. It was established in the period after the British occupation of Egypt, and appears to have had branches in several Muslim countries and an oath of initiation. Little is known of its activities, and perhaps in fact it did nothing except to sponsor the publication of the famous periodical *al-ʿUrwa al-wuthkā*, issued in Paris by al-Afghānī and ʿAbduh in 1884. Although this lasted for a few months only it had a far-reaching influence on educated Muslims, and the leading articles are still reprinted from time to time and widely read.

The use of the term *djamʿiyya* for political associations continued for some time. For example, the most famous of the Arab nationalist societies of late Ottoman days was called *al-Djamʿiyya al-ʿarabiyya al-fatāt*. Founded in Paris in 1911 by seven Arab students, its centre later moved to Damascus and its membership grew to two hundred. It played an important part in the secret negotiations between the Sharīf Ḥusayn and the British authorities in Cairo, which led to the revolt in Arabia against Turkish rule; the military leader of the revolt, Ḥusayn's son Fayṣal, was himself a member of the society. A generation later, in Egypt, there was founded another *djamʿiyya* which played an important role in politics: *al-Ikhwān al-Muslimūn* [*q.v.*], started in 1928 by Ḥasan al-Bannāʾ [*q.v*],, had the explicit purpose of bringing about a moral reform in Islam, but in course of time it became more openly political in its aims and methods, and in the confused decade after 1945 seemed near to taking over power in Egypt, until suppressed by the military régime in 1954. In general however the word *ḥizb* [*q.v.*] had by this time replaced *djamʿiyya* to refer to political movements, although the latter term still remained in use for charitable, cultural and other such voluntary organizations.

Bibliography: G. Graf, *Geschichte der Christlichen arabischen Literatur*, iii, 36; Dj. Zaydān, *Taʾrīkh adāb al-lugha al-ʿarabiyya*, iv, 67 ff.; G. Antonius, *The Arab awakening*, London 1938, 51 ff., 111 ff.; *al-Mashrik*, xii (1909), 32 ff.; Rashīd Riḍā, *Taʾrīkh .... al-shaykh Muḥammad ʿAbduh*, i, 283 ff., 726 ff.; J. M. Landau, *Parliaments and parties in Egypt*, Tel Aviv 1953, 101 ff.; I. M. Husaini, *The Moslem Brethren*, Beirut 1956; R. Hartmann, *Arabische politische Gesellschaften bis 1914*, in R. Hartmann and H. Scheel, *Beiträge zur Arabistik, Semitistik, und Islamwissenschaft*, Leipzig 1944, 439-67. On the *Djamʿiyyat al-Shubbān al-Muslimīn*, see Kampffmayer, in H. A. R. Gibb, ed., *Whither Islam*, London 1936.

(A. H. Hourani)

Ottoman Empire and Turkey

The most common term for "society" or "association" in Ottoman and modern Turkish is *djemʿiyyet* (*cemʿiyet* or *cemiyet*), to which partisans of *öztürkçe* prefer *dernek*, or more rarely, *birlik*. Since the late 19th century *djemʿiyyet* has been the word used for voluntary associations, secret or open, for political, benevolent, professional and other purposes. In the early twentieth century, political parties began to call themselves *firka* or, occasionally, *ḥizb*, both of these yielding, in common usage since the 1920's, to *parti*. Among the near-synonyms of *djemʿiyyet*, *endjümen* (*encümen*, from P. *andjuman* [*q.v.*]) designates (i) a parliamentary committee and (ii) a quasi-public organization such as the Turkish History and Turkish Language Societies, its *öztürkçe* equivalents in these two senses being, respectively, (i) *komisyon* and (ii) *kurum*; *heyʾet* or *heyet* ("committee") designates a temporary or *ad hoc* grouping; *gurup* or *parti gurubu* a parliamentary party; and *kulüb* (club) a more informal cultural, social, or convivial organization.

Legislation granting and regulating the right of association has been a product mainly of the 20th century. The Ottoman reform decrees of 1839 and 1856 promised civic equality and security of person and property, but the 1876 constitution for the first time included a specific if limited guarantee of freedom of association (art. 13: "Ottoman subjects have the right within the limits of existing laws and regulations to found all manner of associations for commercial, industrial, and agricultural purposes"), buttressed by promises of freedom of the press (art. 12: "... free within the limits of the law...") and of the right of individual and collective petition for redress of grievances (art. 14). The constitutional revision of 21 August 1909 left art. 13 unchanged but added a new art. 120 guaranteeing freedom of assembly and association generally, except for (i) associations offending against public morals, (ii) associations aiming at violation of the territorial integrity of the state or at a change of the constitution or the government or at setting various ethnic groups against each other, and (iii) secret societies. A Law of Association adopted at the same legislative session (*Djemᶜiyyetler Ḳānūnu* of 16 August 1909) elaborated these constitutional prohibitions and provided for registration of associations with the local civil authorities. The immediate political target of the 1909 legislation were "reactionary" political movements such as that leading to the abortive counter-revolution of 13 April 1909 (known, according to the Julian calendar then in effect, as *Otuz-Bir Mart Hadisesi*) and nationalist and secessionist tendencies among ethnic minority groups.

The 1909 Law of Associations remained in force until the end of the Ottoman period and (with two amendments: laws 353 and 387 adopted by the Ankara Grand National Assembly in 1923) under the First Republic until 1938. Article 70 of the 1924 constitution guarantees in summary fashion "the rights and freedoms of conscience, of thought, of speech and press, of travel, of contract, of work, of owning and disposing of property; of assembly and association and of incorporation...". A new Law of Associations (no. 3512) of 28 June 1938 specifically prohibited, among others, associations with aims contrary to the five of the Six Arrows (*altı ok*) of the Republican People's Party incorporated by 1935 amendment into art. 2 of the constitution (*i.e.*, republicanism, nationalism, étatism, secularism, and revolutionism (*inkılâpçılık*]); associations directed against the territorial integrity of the state or "disrupting political and national unity"; and associations based on "religion, confession, or sect", on "region", and on "family, congregation [*cemaat*], race, kind [*cins*], or class" (art. 9). Branches of international organizations or of those with headquarters outside Turkey also were outlawed, except where special permission should be granted by cabinet decree in the interests of international cooperation (art. 10). By a major amendment of 5 June 1946 (law no. 4919), the prohibitions against associations contrary to the Six Arrows and against those based on class were lifted, and that against regional associations limited to political parties. Other laws of the First Republic provided additional restrictions. Laws no. 334 (15 April 1923) and 556 (25 February 1925) prohibited propaganda for restoration of the sultanate or caliphate and the abuse of religion for political purposes. A decree of 1922 outlawed Communism, and one of 2 September 1925 closed the dervish orders. These prohibitions were incorporated into the Penal Code (*Türk Ceza Kanunu*) of 1926 (arts. 141 and 142 being directed chiefly against Communism and art. 163 against religious-political associations). Law no. 5018 of 20 February 1947 for the first time specifically regulated trade unions and employers' associations (both being termed *sendika*, from Fr. *syndicat*). The Constitution of the Second Republic of 9 July 1961 provides broad and specific guarantees of the freedom of association (art. 29: "Every individual is entitled to form associations without prior permission. This right can be restricted only by law for the purposes of maintaining public order or morality") and of the right to form trade unions and employers' associations (art. 46) and political parties (art. 56).

The actual development of associational life was at times broader and at times narrower than the legislative history would indicate. Until the 1908 revolution, political associations within the Empire took the form of secret conspiracies, often with headquarters in exile. Among the first were those organized by nationalists among the Christian minorities, notably the Greek *Ethnike Hetairia* (National Association) founded in Odessa in 1814, followed by the Armenian Hinčak party (Geneva 1887) and the Dashnaktsutiun (Armenian Revolutionary Federation, 1890). The earliest political movements among Ottoman Muslims lacked elaborate organization; rather they were short-lived and abortive conspiracies aimed at the quick overthrow of the reigning *sulṭān*. Such was the nature of the *Kuleli* Incident of 1859, the *Čiraghān* Incident of 1878 and the so-called Scalieri-ᶜAzīz Committee of the same year. A more elaborate society was formed in 1865 by a number of prominent literary and political figures with liberal and constitutionalist aims, including the poet Nāmīk Kemāl. When its members were banished or exiled in 1867, the centre of their activities shifted to Europe, where they adopted the name *Yeni ᶜOthmānlīlar* (New Ottomans) or *Jeunes Turcs*. From this time onward, "Young Turks" became the name commonly used by Europeans to designate the advocates of Ottoman constitutionalism; in Turkish, the name occurs only as a French loan word, *Jön Türk*. Returning from exile after the deposition of ᶜAbd al-ᶜAzīz, the original "Young Turks" played a leading rôle in the events leading to the adoption of the constitution of 1876. With the establishment of ᶜAbd al-Ḥamīd II's autocracy, the movement was at first eclipsed and then relegated once again to secrecy, banishment, and exile. In 1889, a number of students at the Army Medical College (*Mekteb-i Ṭibbiyye-i ᶜAskeriyye*) in Istanbul, including Ibrāhīm Temo and ᶜAbdullāh Djewdet, formed a secret political society known at first as *Teraḳḳī we Ittiḥād* and later as *ᶜOthmānlī Ittiḥād we Teraḳḳī Djemᶜiyyeti* (Ottoman Society of Union and Progress, later commonly known to Westerners as the Committee of Union and Progress). In Paris, the most prominent spokesman of the anti-Ḥamīdian exiles was Aḥmed Rīza (Riḍā), editor of the journal *Mechveret* (*i. e.*, *Meshweret*, "Consultation"). Defections and factionalism weakened the movement from time to time, whereas ᶜAbd al-Ḥamīd's repressive measures supplied a steady stream of new recruits both for the secret internal and for the exiled opposition movement. Thus, whereas Aḥmed Rīza considered himself an adherent of Comtean positivism and hence an advocate of strong central government, his rival "Prince" Sabāḥ al-Dīn formed a "Society for Individual Enterprise and Decentralization" (*Teshebbüth-ü Shakhṣī we ᶜAdem-i Merkeziyyet Djemᶜiyyeti*, Paris 1902). By 1906, the centre of gravity of the opposition movement had once again shifted from Europe to the Empire itself, where discontented military officers and civil servants spread the conspiracy to the provincial centres to which they were posted. That year a small Fatherland and Freedom Society (*Waṭān we Ḥürriyyet Djemᶜiyyeti*) was formed in Damascus with the participation of Muṣṭafā Kemāl (the later Atatürk) and a larger *ʿO*<u>*th*</u>*mānlī Ḥürriyyet* <u>*Dj*</u>*emʿiyyeti* in Salonica with participation of Ṭalʿat, <u>Dj</u>emāl (both later Pa<u>sh</u>as) and other prominent future figures. By the end of 1907, the Salonica group had absorbed the remnants of the Damascus society and merged with representatives of the Paris exile movement under the name of "Committee (or Society) of Union and Progress—a name adopted out of respect to its predecessors rather than a name acquired by direct inheritance" (Ramsaur, 122 f.). The successful revolution of 1908 was the result mainly of pressure of Macedonian army units enlisted into the conspiracy by this consolidated Salonica group.

From 1908 to the present, periods of proliferation of political and other voluntary associations have alternated with periods of suppression or coordination under the aegis of a single, powerful party. The number of parties and political associations listed for each of these periods in the index of Tunaya's work (772-7) may serve as a rough measure of this ebb and flow: 1814-1908: 18; 1908-13: 22; 1913-8: 2; 1918-23: 55; 1923-45: 5; 1945-52: 30. Among the many associations formed after the 1908 revolution were the New Generation Club (*Nesl-i* <u>*Dj*</u>*edīd Kulübü*, 1908, representing Sabāḥ al-Dīn's decentralist tendency), an Ottoman Press Association (*Maṭbūʿāt-i ʿO*<u>*th*</u>*māniyye* <u>*Dj*</u>*emʿiyyeti*, 1908), an Arab-Ottoman Brotherhood Society (1908), a pro-Unionist association of *ʿulemāʾ* (<u>*Dj*</u>*emʿiyyet-i Ittiḥādiyye-i ʿIlmiyye*, 1908), the Turkish Society (1908) and the Turkish Home Society (1911) both later (1913) merged and expanded into the Turkish Hearth (*Türk Od*<u>*j*</u>*a*<u>*gh*</u>*ī*, for the next two decades the most important association of Turkish nationalist intellectual and cultural leaders with branches throughout the country). The list of constituent organizations which on 17 April 1909 formed the Ottoman Unity Committee (*Heyʾet-i Müttefiḳa-i ʿO*<u>*th*</u>*māniyye*) to oppose the threat of counter-revolution provides an indication of the variety of political and semi-political associations which had sprung up in the capital in the first few months after the 1908 revolution (see Tunaya, 275 f.): Ottoman Society of Union and Progress, Ottoman Liberal Party, Da<u>sh</u>naktsutiun, Greek Political Society, Ottoman Democratic Party, Albanian Central Club, Kurdish Mutual Aid Club, Circassian Mutual Aid Club, Bulgarian Club, Club of *Mülkiyye* Graduates, Ottoman Medical Society, etc. Philanthropic and professional societies, such as the Red Crescent (*Hilāl-i Aḥmer* <u>*Dj*</u>*emʿiyyeti*, later called *Kızılay*), the Children's Aid Society (*Ḥimāye-i Eṭfal* <u>*Dj*</u>*emʿiyyeti*, today *Çocuk Esirgeme Kurumu*), and the Istanbul Bar Association also date back to this period. On the political scene, the Society of Union and Progress was the most powerful organization in the country, and for the next decade it became known as *the* Society—<u>*Dj*</u>*emʿiyyet tout court*—even though in 1913 it officially proclaimed its transformation into a political party. Meanwhile, adherents of Sabāḥeddīn and a continuous stream of dissidents from Unionist ranks formed a number of opposition parties, most of which eventually merged in the Freedom and Accord Party (*Ḥürriyyet we Iʾtilaf Fīrḳasī*, or, with its official French name, *Entente Libérale*) in 1911. But the coup d'état of January 1913 (*Bab-ī ʿAlī Waḳʿasī*) firmly entrenched the Unionists in power and the assassination of Maḥmūd <u>Sh</u>ewket in June of that year prompted a wave of stern suppression, including banishment of most Freedom and Accord leaders. For the next five years, the Union and Progress Party, led by Ṭalʿat and Enwer, ruled unchallenged, and control of government patronage and tightening wartime economic regulations gave it the opportunity to dominate such voluntary associations as continued to be active in public life.

The period following upon the Ottoman defeat in the first World War and the armistice of Moudros (30 October 1918) led to an intensive resumption of party and other associational activity in the capital. Many of the new groups were political parties trying to rally the anti-Unionist politicians for whom the discrediting and flight of the Unionist leaders had left an open field. The largest among these resumed the name Freedom and Accord Party, and for a time provided the major political support for the government of Dāmād Ferīd Pa<u>sh</u>a [*q.v.*] in 1919. Other, semi-political societies of the armistice period included the Kurdistan Resurrection (*Teʿālī*) Society, the National Unity Committee, the Society of the Friends of England and the Society for Wilsonian Principles (the last two respectively a collaborationist and a nationalist group), a Society for Mutual Aid Among Victims of Political Persecution (*Ma*<u>*gh*</u>*dūrīn-i Siyāsiyye Teʿāwün* <u>*Dj*</u>*emʿiyyeti*). Once again the list of societies adhering to a non-partisan effort at national unity, the National Congress (*Millī Kongre*) of 29 November 1918, gives an indication of the wide variety of associations then in existence. It reads, in part, as follows: Turkish Hearth, Children's Aid Society, Teachers' Colleges Alumni Association, Navy Society, Galatasaray Students' Home, Mutual Aid Society of Kabata<u>sh</u> (a quarter of Istanbul), Women's Employment Society (*Kadīnlarī Čalī*<u>*sh*</u>*tīrma* <u>*Dj*</u>*emʿiyyeti*), National Defence Society, Press Association, Teachers' Society, National Instruction and Physical Education Association, Bar Association, Painters' Society, Farmers' Association, National Association of Private Schools, Craftsmen's Society, Women's Welfare Association (<u>*Dj*</u>*emʿiyyet-i* <u>*Kh*</u>*ayriyye-i Niswāniyye*), Muslim Women's Employment Society, Society of Music-Loving Ladies, Society for the Modern Woman (*ʿAṣrī Ḳadīn* <u>*Dj*</u>*emʿiyyeti*), Society for the Promotion of Fine Arts, etc, etc. (Tunaya, 420). During this same period we also encounter the first parties with a specific appeal to the lower classes, notably the Workers' and Peasants' Socialist Party of Turkey, the Ottoman Labour Party, and the Socialist Party of Turkey (*ibid.*, 438, 458, 463).

While the capital and the central government were coming increasingly under the control of Allied occupation authorities, local societies were forming in most of the *wilāyet* and *ḳaḍā* seats of Anatolia and Eastern Thrace for the purpose of opposing Allied occupation, partition, and annexation plans. In the case of one of the earliest and most prominent of these, the Ottoman Committee for the Defence of Thrace and Pa<u>sh</u>aeli (Edirne, 2 December 1918), we know that it was prepared and founded at the behest of Ṭalʿat Pa<u>sh</u>a, who hoped that such local groups would be able to carry on the Unionist political cause after the defeat of the Empire and the demise of the central party organization (see Bıyıklioğlu, i, 123; cf. Rustow in *World Politics*, xi, 541). Since several similar organizations were founded in other important cities within a few days or weeks of each other, in some cases also with direct participation of local Unionist leaders (Ottoman Society for Defence of Rights of Izmir, 1 December 1918; Society for the Defence of Rights of the Eastern Wilāyets, founded in Istanbul, 4 December 1918, Erzurum branch opened 10 March 1919; Cilician Society, Adana 21 December 1918), one may infer that there may have been a more comprehensive central plan. Whereas the earlier nationalist organizations rallied to the slogan of "Defence of Rights" (*müdāfaʿa-i ḥuḳūḳ*), those formed in western Anatolia at the time of the Greek occupation of Izmir (May 1919) commonly called themselves "Rejection of Annexation" (*redd-i ilḥāḳ*) societies. Regional congresses of these groups were held throughout the summer of 1919 at Erzurum, Balîkesir, Alas͟hehir, and elsewhere. Whatever the antecendents of the Defence of Rights movement, its nation-wide consolidation was the result of the activities of Muṣṭafā Kemāl Pas͟ha [Atatürk] [*q.v.*], who was elected chairman of the Erzurum Congress and himself called for a nationwide congress at Sivas (4-11 September 1919) which repudiated the Union and Progress Movement, defined the foreign policy aims of the nationalist resistance movement in the so-called National Pact (*mīt͟hāḳ-i millī*), and created the consolidated Society for the Defence of Rights of Anatolia and Rumelia (*Anadolu ve Rumeli Müdāfaʿa-i Ḥuḳūḳ D͟jemʿiyyeti*). Following the reinforced occupation of Istanbul in March 1920, the convening of a Grand National Assembly at Ankara on 23 April created a *de facto* nationalist government which was to become the foundation of the First Turkish Republic (proclaimed on 29 October 1923).

In the Ankara Assembly Kemāl time and again faced a religious-conservative opposition, known as the Second Group, but the elections of 1923 resulted in the complete elimination of these opponents. Later that year the Defence of Rights Society was reconstituted as the People's Party, later as the Republican People's Party (*K͟halḳ Fîrḳasî*, *D͟jumhūriyyet K͟halḳ Fîrḳasî* [*q.v.*], and eventually *Cumhuriyet Halk Partisi*). The precipitate manner in which the Republic had been proclaimed and fears of personal rule by Kemāl led to the formation of a new opposition group, the Progressive Republican Party (*Teraḳḳîperver D͟jumhūriyyet Fîrḳasî*, 17 November 1924), led by Kemal's closest and earliest associates of the 1919-20 period. Following the Kurdish uprising of February-April 1925, this party was charged with complicity in the insurrection and dissolved by cabinet decree (3 June 1925) under authority of the Law for the Restoration of Order (*Taḳrīr-i Sükūn Ḳānūnu*, 4 March 1925). The following year, most of the members of its Assembly group were tried, and seven of them sentenced to death and executed, on unproven charges of complicity in the attempt on Kemāl's life discovered in Izmir.

Although the formation of opposition parties was never formally prohibited, the events of 1924-26 clearly discouraged any would-be founders for the next two decades. The only important exception was the short lived Free Republican Party founded (and reclosed within four months) at Kemāl's suggestion by his close friend Ali Fethi [Okyar] [*q.v.*] in 1930. The dissolution of the Turkish Hearth (see above) in 1931 (involving the conversion of its branches into People's Houses to be administered by the People's Party), the merger of the posts of *wālī* and *wilāyet* chairman of the Republican People's Party (1936), the formation of a new Press Association under the chairmanship of Atatürk's long-time journalistic spokesman Falih Rıfkı Atay (11 June 1935), and the Law of Association of 1938 (see above) were so many steps toward the complete coordination of all associational and political activities within a single official party. Earlier, the formation under Atatürk's personal auspices of the Turkish Historical Society and the Turkish Language Society (*Türk Tarih Kurumu* and *Türk Dil Kurumu*, 1932), provided a vehicle for Atatürk's concern with the promotion of a national-historical consciousness and of language reform.

A radical shift toward a policy of democratization and liberalization came at the end of the Second World War, first heralded in President İnönü's speech of 19 May 1945, and confirmed after some wavering by his pledge of impartiality between government and opposition parties of 12 July 1947. (The 1946 revision of the Law of Associations and the new Labour Code of 1947 were parts of the new political course). As a result, the formation of political and other associations multiplied in unprecedented fashion in the years after 1945. Tunaya lists as many as 14 parties founded during the single year of 1946. During the same year voluntary associations of national prominence were numerically distributed among various categories as follows: Craftsmen's Associations 343; sports clubs 246; social clubs 241; benevolent societies 100; town clubs 89; student societies 80; sports societies 79; civic improvement associations 79; scholarly associations 22; trade unions and employers' associations 20; health societies 17; journalists' associations 13 (*Türkiye Yıllığı* 1947, 266). The more liberal atmosphere also encouraged a secret revival of dervish orders which continued to be outlawed. (For specific cases of arrest see G. Jäschke, *Die Türkei in den Jahren 1942-51*, Wiesbaden 1955, index s.v. Derwischorden). Among these, the Tid͟janiyye attracted the greatest notoriety because of its campaigns for reintroduction of the Arabic version of the *ad͟hān* and of smashing statues of Atatürk. The latter subsided after the passage in 1953 of a new law for the protection of the memory of Atatürk which imposed heavy penalties on such activity.

A number of parties were disbanded after 1945 because of Communist leanings, notably the Socialist Toilers' and Peasants' Party of Turkey (closed 16 December 1946 by the Istanbul Martial Law Command) and the Socialist Party of Turkey (closed by the same decision, reopened after acquittal of its founders in 1950, and reclosed by court order on 17 June 1952). A number of other parties or associations of the extreme right were similarly dissolved, including the Islam Democratic Party (involved in an assassination attempt on the liberal journalist Ahmed Emin Yalman and closed by court order on 20 October 1952), the Great East (*Büyük Doğu*) Society (dissolved itself 26 May 1951 while on trial for "reactionary" activities and after its leader, Necip Fazıl Kısakürek had been apprehended on a gambling charge), and the pan-Turkist and racist Turkish Nationalists' Association (*Türk Milliyetçiler Derneği*, dissolved by court order 4 April 1953). (Information in this paragraph furnished to author by Turkish Ministry of the Interior, January 1954).

The advent to power of the Democratic Party under Celâl Bayar and Adnan Menderes as a result of the 1950 elections soon brought more systematic legal and extra-legal restrictions upon the freedom of association. Whereas the parties just listed consisted mainly of small groups of obscure men whose aims were repudiated by the vast majority of thoughtful citizens, the major targets of Menderes's repressive policies, it soon became clear, were the major opposition parties themselves. In December 1953, the assets of the Republican People's Party (in opposition since 1950) were taken over by the government treasury, and just before the 1954 elections the second largest opposition group, the Nation Party (*Millet Partisi*) was dissolved by court order on tenuous allegations of being in fact a religious association. The latter party soon reappeared as the Republican Nation Party, enlarged in 1957 into the Republican Nation Peasants' Party. Toward the end of the decade opposition parties were subject to stringent police controls at their meetings, suppression of their newspapers, and systematic harrassing of their leaders in their movements throughout the country. At the same time many voluntary associations were pressed into joining the Patriotic Front (*Vatan Cephesi*) under Democratic Party auspices. The overthrow of the Menderes regime in the revolution of 27 May 1960 brought a temporary moratorium on all political activities under the provisional government of General Gürsel's Committee of National Unity. With the proclamation of the Constitution of the Second Republic, political and associational freedoms were once again restored, although the leaders of the deposed Democratic regime of Bayar and Menderes remained barred from political activity for the time being.

Bibliography: Tevfik Bıyıklıoğlu, *Trakya'da Millî Mücadele*, 2 vols, Ankara 1955-6; F. von Kraelitz-Greifenhorst, ed., *Die Verfassungsgesetze des Osmanischen Reiches* (Osten und Orient iv/1: 1), Vienna 1919; B. Lewis, *The emergence of modern Turkey*, London 1961; E. E. Ramsaur, Jr., *The Young Turks*, Princeton 1957; D. A. Rustow, *The army and the founding of the Turkish Republic*, in *World Politics*, xi (July 1959), 513-52; T. Z. Tunaya, *Türkiye'de siyasi partiler*, Istanbul 1952; *Türkiye Yıllığı*, 1947, 266, and 1948, 240-96; *Türk Ansiklopedisi*, x, 151-4; *Türkiyede siyasi dernekler* (vol. ii only), Ankara: Emniyet Genel Müdürlügü, 1951; F. R. Unat, ed., *İkinci meşrutiyet ilâni ve otuzbir Mart hadisesi . . . Ali Cevat Beyin Fezleke'si*, Ankara 1960, 158-88.

(D. A. Rustow)

(iii)—Persia. The word which came to be commonly used in Persian for a voluntary society or association for literary, scientific, benevolent, or political purposes was *andjuman* [*q.v.*]. The terms *madjmaʿ*, *idjtimāʿ*, and *ittiḥādiyya* were less frequently used. The formation of *andjumans* in Persia was a relatively late growth. In a country where government was despotic and power arbitrary any group of persons regularly associating together was likely to be suspected of plotting against the state (cf. the story related in the *Siyāsat-nāma* of Niẓām al-Mulk, Persian text, ed. Schefer, 145 ff.); or of religious heresy, which was also closely bound up with opposition to the state, since an attack on orthodoxy implied a threat to the established order. This was perhaps a dilemma inherent in the very nature of the Islamic theory of state, which led the government to adopt an uncompromising attitude towards the unorthodox, thereby driving them to the very action which the government feared, namely the formation of secret societies, whose ultimate aim was the violent overthrow of the state. Further, co-operation between the citizens was mainly through associations such as the dervish orders and the craft guilds; and the *futuwwa* organizations, which in medieval Persia were connected at one extreme with the dervish orders and at the other with the craft guilds, and of which the *zūrkhāna* of modern Persia was in some measure an offshoot; and lastly perhaps even the factions, which had a vigorous life in some towns. Many of these various types of association were in some measure charitable associations also. These various factors to some extent account for the late growth of voluntary associations in Persia and their relative weakness in the nineteenth century when they were first found in any number.

The earliest *andjumans* mentioned in modern times are the literary societies which are recorded in early Ḳādjār times. That the first associations to be formed should have been literary societies is probably due to two factors: first there was a long tradition in Persia of literary discussion, and secondly a literary circle was less likely to draw the suspicion of the authorities upon itself than was any other type of association. Mention is made of a literary circle formed by the poet, Mushtāḳ (d. 1171/1757-8); and the formation of another some time prior to 1218/1803-4 in Iṣfahān by the poet Nishāt (d. 1244/1828-9) in imitation of the *andjuman-i mushtāḳ*. Nishāt's *andjuman*, which met weekly, was a centre for poets, men of letters, and Ṣūfīs (Ibrāhīm Safāʾī, *Nahḍat-i Adabī-i Īrān*, Tehrān n.d., 17). Sir Harford Jones Brydges describes literary gatherings which were attended by a mixed company of jurists, officers, merchants, and others, c. 1747 at the house of the poet Mīrzā Ḥusayn Wafā in Djīrāz (*The dynasty of the Kajars*, London 1833, cxlviii). The Ṣāḥib Dīwān, Mīrzā Muḥammad Taḳī ʿAlī Ābādī (d. 1256/1840-1) is also said to have formed a literary society in Zandjān and later in Shīrāz during the reign of Muḥammad Shāh (*Nahḍat-i Adabī-i Īrān*, 28-9). Wiṣāl (d. 1262/1845-6) formed a similar society in Shīrāz during the reign of Fatḥ ʿAlī Shāh (ibid., 35). It is difficult to know whether these literary societies really had any regular membership or were merely circles of literary-minded men. Iʿtiḍād al-Salṭana, at one time minister of education to Nāṣir al-Dīn (reg. 1848-96) mentions in an essay that as a young man at the beginning of Nāṣir al-Dīn's reign he liked having meetings with literary and mystically inclined persons and had formed a group which met nightly. It included poets, such as Ḳaʾānī, and learned men, such as Mīrzā ʿAbd al-Raḥmān Harawī, who later became one of the Bābī leaders (*Rasāʾil-i Mutaʿaddida*, Madjlis, ms. 1293).

Under Riḍā Shāh Pahlawī when freedom of political association was limited, a number of literary societies (known individually as *andjuman-i adabī*) were founded in Tehrān and the provinces under official and private inspiration.

During the reign of Nāṣir al-Dīn there was a gradual intellectual, or rather political, awakening; and with this there began a movement of revolt against internal corruption and misgovernment on the one hand and foreign intervention on the other. There was, however, at the time little political freedom and it was difficult for men to meet openly for political discussion, nor was there a free press in which they could express their views. This accounts both for the slowness with which the movement of revolt developed and also for the tendency to form secret or semi-secret societies. About the middle of the century there appear to have been attempts to organize societies known as *farāmūsh-khāna*, which are alleged to have been connected with freemasonry (though neither English nor French freemasonry apparently recognized these associations). On 12 Rabīʿ II 1278/19 October 1861 a notice appeared in the official gazette forbidding the organization of such groups.

One of the earliest societies to be formed during the reign of Nāṣir al-Dīn was the Madjmaʿ-i Ukhuwwat founded by ʿAlī Khān Ẓahīr al-Dawla b. Muḥammad Nāṣir Khān, the *Ishīkāḳāsībāshī* and son-in-law of Nāṣir al-Dīn. Ẓahīr al-Dawla succeeded Ṣafī ʿAlī Shāh as the leader of a group of Niʿmatallāhī dervishes who had gathered round Safī ʿAlī Shāh as their *pīr*. Although Madjmaʿ-i Ukhuwwat was something in the nature of a Ṣūfī fraternity rather than a literary or political society, it appears to have been regarded by some as the first of the "political" *andjumans* and on these grounds its premises were destroyed on the orders of Muḥammad ʿAlī Shāh after the bombardment of the National Assembly (Muʿayyir al-Mamālik, *Ridjāl-i ʿAṣr-i Nāṣirī*, in *Yaghmā*, ix/7, 1956, 326 ff.). Nevertheless the society appears to have continued in existence or to have been reformed (see Ḥusayn Samīʿī, *Manthūrāt ya munshaʾāt wa tarasullāt*, Tehrān n.d., 314 ff.).

Towards the end of Nāṣir al-Dīn's reign various secret or semi-secret associations started to meet in Tehrān and the provinces. When these *andjumans* (which came to be known individually by the term *andjuman-i millī*, *i.e.*, a national or popular society), first started to meet their deliberations appear to have been mainly confined to discussions on the desirability of the liberation of the people from the yoke of tyranny, and of the benefits which accrued from freedom, justice, and education. Their members were held together by discontent at existing conditions and a belief in the need for modernization. After the assassination of Nāṣir al-Dīn in 1896 the activities of the *andjumans* increased and their members advocated reform more openly. Their membership appears to have been drawn predominantly from the middle ranks of the *ʿulamā*. At this period the *andjumans* (or those of which we have records) seem to have considered their function to have been purely an educative one: to awaken the people to the evils of despotism and the benefits of freedom. Their members were apparently convinced that "progress" would inevitably result from the acquisition of the "new learning". With this in view they encouraged their members to found schools, which some of them did. In the second period of their existence after the grant of the constitution many of the *andjumans* themselves ran classes to combat illiteracy and even founded schools (Yaḥyā Dawlatābādī, *Ḥayāt-i Yaḥyā*, Tehrān n.d., ii, 207-8; E. G. Browne, *The Persian revolution of 1905-1909*, Cambridge 1910, 245). One of the late 19th century *andjumans*, the Andjuman-i Maʿārif founded in 1315/1897-8, was apparently specifically concerned with educational matters (*Tarbiyyat*, no. 90, 6 Dhu 'l-Ḥidjdjā 1315, Tehrān; ʿĪsa Ṣadīḳ, *Taʾrīkh-i farhangī-i Īrān*, Tehrān, 1957-8, 340). Some of the *andjumans* after the grant of the constitution published newspapers; but most of these were ephemeral (see Browne, *The press and poetry of modern Persia*, Cambridge 1914, and Muḥammad Ṣadr Hāshimī, *Taʾrīkh-i djarāʾid wa madjallāt-i Īrān*, 4 vols., Iṣfahān).

By 1903 discontent against the government had become more open and the need for reform seemed to the members of the *andjumans* more urgent. In 1904 a secret meeting of various groups which had hitherto been acting independently took place. They agreed to work for the establishment of a code of laws and the rule of justice and the overthrow of tyranny. The drew up a programme of action, or charter of association, consisting of eighteen articles; and set up a revolutionary committee of nine. The main purposes of the association were the dissemination of information, the establishment of contact with various classes of people inside and outside Persia, and the fanning of dissension among those opposed to their aims. (Malikzāda, *Taʾrīkh-i inḳilāb-i mashrūṭiyyat-i Īrān*, Tehrān n.d., ii, 8; and see also Malikzāda, *Zindagī-i Malik al-mutakallimīn*, Tehrān 1946). Somewhat later, in 1905, a group called the Andjuman-i Makhfī (the Secret Society) was formed. Its membership was mainly drawn from the religious classes. It, too, was concerned to restrain corruption on the one hand, and curtail foreign intervention in the affairs of Persia on the other. It was both nationalist and Islamic. It is clear from its proceedings as recorded in the *Taʾrīkh-i Bīdārī-i Īrāniyān* by Nāẓim al-Islām-i Kirmānī (Tehrān, 2nd edition, n.d.) that its members were convinced that the despotism and the tyranny of the government on the one hand and the possibility of intervention by Great Britain and Russia on the other constituted a threat to Islam, and secondly that they believed that all the ills of the country could be cured by education. The activities of this and other *andjumans* played an important part in preparing the people for modernization, canalizing the growing discontent, and bringing the disaffected elements together. Their members became active supporters of the constitutional revolution. About the end of 1905, or the beginning of 1906, after the conflict between the Shah and the "reformers" had become open, a group broke away from the Andjuman-i Makhfī and the Andjuman-i Makhfī-i Thānawī (the Second Secret Society) was formed. The original *andjuman* continued its activities for some months, but by June 1906, various of its members having been arrested, it ceased to exist.

With the grant of the constitution in August 1906 the Andjuman-i Makhfī-i Thānawī was reconstituted and numerous other *andjumans*, with local and professional affiliations, sprang up in the capital and the provinces. In Tehrān within a short space of time some two hundred *andjumans* were formed; some of the larger ones are said to have had several thousand members. Their purpose was to support the constitution, advocate reforms, watch over the actions of the government and its officials, and demand redress for the citizens in cases of real or alleged injustice. Two main types of *andjuman* came into existence: "official" *andjumans* and "popular" *andjumans*. The former were the provincial councils (*andjuman-i ayālatī wa wilāyatī*) which were originally set up in the provincial towns for the purpose of electing deputies to the National Assembly and were later recognized by Article 90 of the Supplementary Fundamental Laws promulgated on 7 October 1907. Article 91 lays down that they should be elected by the people and Article 92 states that they were to be free to exercise supervision over all reforms connected with the public interest. The second type of *andjuman*, the "popular" *andjuman*, was also recognized by the supplementary Fundamental Laws, Article 21 of which states "Societies (*andjumans*) and associations (*idjtimāʿāt*) which are not productive of mischief to religion or to the state and are not injurious to good order are free throughout the whole empire, but members of such associations must not carry arms, and must obey the regulations laid down by the law on this matter . . ."

The provincial councils varied a good deal from place to place. The Andjuman-i Ayālatī of Tabrīz, which had been set up for the purpose of the election of deputies to the new National Assembly, was dissolved by Muḥammad ʿAlī, the *walī ʿahd* and governor of Ādharbāydjān, as soon as the deputies had been elected. It reformed almost immediately as the Andjuman-i Millī though it subsequently appears to have been known by its original name (Karīm Ṭāhirzāda Bihzād, *Ḳiyām-i Ādharbāydjān dar inḳilāb-i mashrūṭiyyat-i Īrān*, Tehrān n.d. 148-9, 174 ff; cf. also Aubin, *La Perse d'aujourdhui*, Paris 1908, 40). After the *coup d'état* of 1907 it became, in the absence of the National Assembly, the focal point of the constitutional or nationalist movement in Persia. In Iṣfahān the Andjuman-i Muḳaddasī-i Millī-i Iṣfahān, opened on 6 Dhu'l Ḳaʿda 1324/22 December 1906, appears to have had executive as well as consultative functions and to have been run by the leading *ʿulamāʾ*, merchants, and citizens of the town (see the weekly paper published by the Andjuman-i muḳaddas-i millī-i Iṣfahān, 1907-8; and also Muḥammad Ṣadr Hāshimī, *op. cit.*, i, 290). The membership of the "popular" *andjuman*s also varied from place to place. They were more strongly developed in Tehrān, Tabrīz, Iṣfahān, and north Persia than in the south. Whereas prior to the grant of the constitution the Tehrān *andjuman*s were largely drawn from the religious classes and the intellectuals, in the second phase they had a strong connexion with the craft guilds; many of them also had local affiliations. In Tabrīz each street tended to have its own *andjuman*; and in Tehrān not only were there local *andjuman*s but the inhabitants of different districts and provinces who lived in Tehrān also formed their own *andjuman*s. In Ādharbāydjān from the first the *andjuman*s were opposed to the large landowners and had a strong "middle class" bias. In Iṣfahān, on the other hand, the *andjuman*s were largely dominated by the local religious leaders. In Rasht some of the members of the Andjuman-i Millī formed there are said to have been connected with the Social Democratic Party of Baku (Malikzāda, *Taʾrīkh-i inḳilāb-i mashrūṭiyyat-i Īrān*, ii, 264). In general, however, the members of the *andjuman*s had had no political experience, and there was a tendency on the part of some of them to an irresponsible interference in the administration of the country (Cf. Cd. 4581 Persia No. 1 (1909), no. 176, p. 143). In spite of this they played an important part in creating a public opinion in favour of constitutional reform and were the one support which the National Assembly had against the reactionary party. Further, through the contact which the *andjuman*s established with each other they fostered a certain sense of solidarity among those who were seeking to assert themselves against the arbitrary, and often tyrannical, rule of the provincial governors. Prior to this time any attempt by the people to assert themselves against the local authorities was likely to be isolated. The *andjuman*s created a sense of a community of interest and this gave the people in widely separated districts courage to act. The success of the *andjuman*s in providing a focal point for public opinion in support of the constitution was such that their opponents sought to counter this by infiltrating into existing *andjuman*s and by forming *andjuman*s themselves, hoping to confuse the issue by working in secret against the constitution under cover of nationalist associations.

Muḥammad ʿAlī, who succeeded his father, Muẓaffar al-Dīn, in January 1907, disliked the constitution from the start. After the appointment of Mīrzā ʿAlī Aṣghar Khān Amīn al-Sulṭān, the Atābak-i Aʿẓam, as prime minister in the late spring of 1907 there was a great increase in the numbers of the *andjuman*s, secret and otherwise, formed for the defence of the constitution (ʿAbdallāh Mustawfī, *Sharḥ-i zindagī-i man*, Tehrān 1945, ii, 244-6; memorandum by Churchill, enclosed by Sir Cecil Spring Rice to Sir Edward Grey in a letter dated 23 May 1907, Cd. 4581, no. 26, p. 27). Little was done to implement the constitution. Disorders were fomented in the provinces. Russia was suspected of aiding and encouraging the Shah against the National Assembly, and the belief grew that there was secret collusion between the Shah and the Amīn al-Sulṭān for the overthrow of the constitution and the sale of the country to Russia. On 31 August the Amīn al-Sulṭān was assassinated by a certain ʿAbbās Āḳā (who immediately afterwards shot himself). On the assassin's body was found a paper stating that he was devotee (*fidāʾī-i millī*) no. 41 of the Andjuman. Whether in fact such an *andjuman* whose members were thus known as *fidāʾī*s really existed remains an open question. There is, however, no doubt that the murder heightened the morale of the nationalists, and gave rise to the belief that the membership of secret societies whose members would not stop at political assassination to gain their ends was spreading. Popular sentiment approved the murder and regarded ʿAbbās Āḳā as the saviour of the country (Kasrawī, *op. cit.* (in Bibl.), 447 ff., Browne, *op. cit.*, 150 ff.).

An abortive attack by the court party on the National Assembly in the winter of 1907-8 was frustrated by the help of the Tehrān and provincial *andjuman*s. Some of them meanwhile began to raise volunteers for a kind of national militia. In June 1908 a more serious attack was made against the National Assembly. The *andjuman*s again rallied to its defence, this time in vain. The Cossack regiment bombarded the Assembly and the *andjuman*s were dispersed after a brief resistance. The Assembly was closed and a number of prominent nationalists were arrested and some executed. The organization of the nationalist resistance, which culminated in the deposition of Muḥammad ʿAlī and the restoration of the constitution in July 1909, largely devolved on the *andjuman*s. They were helped in this by *andjuman*s formed by Persian communities abroad, especially the Andjuman-i Saʿādat in Constantinople.

As soon as Muḥammad ʿAlī had closed the National Assembly he sent instructions to the provinces for all the *andjuman*s to be closed also (Kasrawī, *op. cit.*, 672). Immediate and effective resistance came from Tabrīz only. Government troops were expelled from the town, which was then blockaded, the siege being raised by Russian troops who opened the Julfa road in April 1909. The resistance of Tabrīz organized by the Andjuman-i (Millī-i) Ayālatī, although the nationalists were eventually forced to capitulate, gave the nationalists in other cities of Persia, especially Iṣfahān and Rasht, time to recover after the *coup d'état* of 1908. In Iṣfahān contact was eventually established between the *andjuman*s and the Bakhtiyārīs and in January 1909 Iṣfahān was taken. At the end of April a force of Bakhtiyārīs and nationalist fighters (*mudjāhidīn*) set out from Iṣfahān for the capital, while the Sipahdār-i Aʿẓam Muḥammad Walī Khān, who had been in command of the government troops outside Tabrīz and had gone over to the the nationalists and assembled a force of *mudjāhidīn* in Gīlān and Tunākabūn, marched on Tehrān from the neighbourhood of Ḳazwīn. The two forces entered Tehrān on 13 July and Muḥammad ʿAlī abdicated on 17 July.

With the restoration of the constitution the activities of the "popular" *andjuman*s declined. For a brief period in 1911 when renewed attempts to strangle the constitution were made they were again sporadically active; and various acts of violence were attributed to them. However, when the constitution was again suspended in 1911 on account of the opposition of the National Assembly to the Russian ultimatum demanding the dismissal of Mr. Morgan Shushter, the treasurer-general, the cumulative effect of internal disorders, the infiltration of hostile elements into the nationalist movement, and, above all, Russian pressure, discouraged, if it did not make virtually impossible, the emergence of a popular movement of protest. The "popular" *andjumans*, thus, had no longer a function to perform and so they disappeared from the political scene.

Bibliography: In addition to references on the text: A. K. S. Lambton, *Secret societies and the Persian Revolution of 1905-6*, in *St. Antony's Papers, no.* 4, *Middle Eastern Affairs*, no. 1, London 1958; idem, forthcoming article *The Political rôle of the Anjumans 1906-11* in *St. Antony's Papers*, Oxford, xvi; Kasrawī, *Taʾrīkh-i hidjdasāla-i Ādharbāydjān*, Tehrān 1933-41; *Central Asian Review*, iv/4; Nūrullāh Dānishwar ʿAlawī, *Taʾrīkh-i mashrūṭa-i Īrān*, Tehrān 1956-7; Morgan Shushter, *The strangling of Persia*, London 1912.

(A. K. S. Lambton)

(iv)—Tunisia. In Tunisia, the term *djamʿiyya* does not appear to have been in use before the 19th century. Khayr al-Dīn al-Tūnusī used it in 1284/1867 in the sense of academy, scientific association; charitable society; municipal or cantonal organization (*djamʿiyyat al-kāntūn*), agricultural or industrial association; parish, parish council; various groups of teachers, notables, officials, local magistrates, municipal councillors. In the field of economics he used *sharika* (but *djamʿiyya* for a joint-stock company). He even used the expression *al-sharikāt al-djamʿiyya* (*Akwam al-masālik*, 77).

In the twentieth century *djamʿiyya* signifies association, society, corporation, league, parliamentary assembly (*al-djamʿiyya al-waṭaniyya*) and includes so-called voluntary associations of every sort (*al-djamʿiyyāt al-ḥurra*).

Religious associations.—The oldest is the *Djamʿiyyat al-Awḳāf*, in charge of the public habous and with the right to inspect the endowments of private habous and Zaouias (*zawāyā*). It is social and religious in character. With it can be connected the *djamʿiyyāt khayriyya* (charitable), the first of which was founded in 1323/1905. In 1380/1902 the Yearbook (*Rūznāma*) added the *takāyā* (sing: *takiyya*), institutions dating from 1188/1774 under ʿAlī Pasha Bey). Neither the traditional Islamic organizations nor the confraternities (*ṭarīḳa*) bear this name. The non-confessional associations founded after 1900 added to their titles the adjective *islāmiyya* or *ʿarabiyya*, to be replaced by *tūnusiyya* or *waṭaniyya* between 1919 and 1938 (a period of intense Destour activity). In 1935 *shaykh* ʿAbd al-ʿAzīz al-Bawandī founded the *djamʿiyyat al-imlāʾāt al-ḳurʾāniyya* (Ḳurʾānic readings).

Political associations.—To the "evolutionist" group are attributed numerous foundations connected with music (al-Hilāl, 1322/1904 and al-Ḥusayniyya founded in 1907 in al-Naṣriyya), sport (al-Islāmiyya, 1905), the theatre (1905), etc. Special mention must be made, on account of its influence, of the "Association of North African Muslim students in France" (*Djamʿiyyat ṭalabat shamāl Ifrīḳiya al-muslimīn bi-Firansa*), which was presided over by several well-known Tunisians. From the time of its foundation (1934) the Neo-Destour created or controlled numerous associations (for example, *al-shubbān al-muslimūn*). In 1945 there occurred a characteristic regrouping of existing associations (agricultural labourers, workers, officials, students, and teachers, women, young people etc.). The word *ḥizb*, party, denotes a purely political association from the time of the foundation of the Young Tunisian Party (1907).

Economic associations.—The first of these appears to have been the association of food merchants: *Djamʿiyyat tudjdjār al-maʿāsh* (15 September 1888). After 1906 they became more numerous (at least nine societies were founded between 1910 and 1921); in this sphere, after 1906 *sharika* tends to replace *djāmʿiyya*. From 1888 to 1938, out of 38 societies only 6 bear this second name. At first societies had a symbolic name (*nahḍa, taʿāwūn, taʿāḍud*) with *sharika* as a secondary name, but soon *sharika* became their name. After 1900, as the development of such societies was curbed by the latent objection to loans subject to interest (*ribāʾ*), their Islamic character was stressed: *Islamic* Commercial Society (*al-Iḳbāt*, 1908). After 1910 the national aspect was emphasized: the *Tunisian* Islamic Society (*al-Taraḳḳī*, 1910), the National Commercial Society (*al-Amān*, 1914); and the still more significant title *al-Istiḳlāl al-iḳtiṣādī*.

Cultural associations.—The term *djamʿiyya* applies particularly to unaffiliated associations of this sort. The earliest in date (18 Radjab 1314/22 December 1896) was *al-Djamʿiyya al-khaldūniyya* whose aim was the teaching of modern science to Tunisian students, particularly those of the great mosque. The second (23 December 1905) was the Association of Former Pupils of Ṣādiḳī (*Djamʿiyyat Ḳudamāʾ talāmidhat al-ṣādiḳiyya*) which rapidly acquired great political importance. Groups with aims concerned with sport, music, the theatre etc. also adopted or at least implied the title *Djamʿiyya*.

New associations.—With the coming of independence (20 March 1957), the associations underwent a transformation (juridical reforms, a new political, cultural, social and economic orientation). Unions (*ittiḥād*) took the place of *Djamʿiyyāt*. However, the term remained in use for cultural associations, as is shown by the recently established "Cultural Associations Centre" (*Dār al-djamʿiyyāt al-thaḳāfiyya*).

Bibliography: Khayr al-Dīn al-Tūnusī, *Aḳwam al-masālik fī maʿrifat aḥwāl al-mamālik*, Tunis 1284/1867, *passim*; *al-Djamʿiyya al-khaldūniyya* (List of members), Tunis 1318/1900; Moh. Lasram, *Une association en Tunisie, la Khaldounia*, Tunis 1906; *Taḳrīr djamʿiyyat ḳudamāʾ talāmidhat al-madrasa al-ṣādiḳiyya*, Tunis 1924-25; Emile Lesueur, *Les associations agricoles en Tunisie*, Paris-Tunis 1906; ʿAbd al-Wahhāb, *Ḳawāʿid ʿilm al-iḳtiṣād*, Tunis 1338/1919; M. S. Mzali, *L'évolution économique de la Tunisie*, Tunis 1921, 69 ff.; Tāhir al-Ḥaddād, *al-ʿUmmāl al-tūnusiyyūn wa-ẓuhūr al-ḥāraka al-niḳābiyya*, Tunis 1346/1927; Chedly Khairallah, *Le mouvement Jeune tunisien*, Tunis n.d.; al-Fāḍil b. ʿAshūr, *al-Haraka al-adabiyya wa 'l-fikriyya fī Tūnis*, Arab League, 1955-56; Van Leeuwen, *Index des publications périodiques parues en Tunisie (1874-1954)*; J. Rousset de Pina-H. Pilipenko, *Récapitulation des périodiques officiels parus en Tunisie (1881-1955)*, Tunis 1956; Records (reports, publications) of associations and societies (in Arabic and French): a more detailed study is to appear in *IBLA*. (A. Demeerseman)

India and Pakistan.—In Muslim India the word *djamᶜiyya* is replaced by *djamīᶜat* or *djamāᶜat* as a term for religious or religio-political as distinct from purely political organizations. The term, in this sense, is of recent though not of modernist origin.

The *Djamāᶜat-i mudjāhidīn*, the religio-political organization formed by Sayyid Aḥmad Barēlwī, owed its name to its movement of *djihād* against the Sikhs in the early 19th century and later against the British. Essentially it based its programme on the teachings of Shāh Walī Allāh and his successors to purify Indian Islam from syncretic elements borrowed from Hinduism and to organize and strengthen the Muslim community socially and politically. It was a popular organization deriving its support from all cross-sections of Muslim society and operating its own *bayt al-māl* and law courts.

The *Djamīᶜat al-ᶜulamāʾ-i Hind* was founded in 1919 at the peak of the Indian Muslim agitation in favour of the Ottoman Khilāfat. Mawlana Maḥmūd Ḥasan, already a well-established religio-political leader was among its founders, and though the ᶜulamāʾ of the Farangī Maḥall [see dār al-ᶜulum] and members of the *Nadwat al-ᶜulamāʾ* also participated in it, the element of Deoband [*q.v.*] remained by far the most powerful. It supported the nationalist programme of the Indian National Congress and was opposed to separatist trends in Muslim politics and to the demand for Pakistan by the general Muslim consensus.

This led in 1945 to the formation, by a dissident group of Deobandī and other ᶜulamāʾ, of the *Djamīᶜat al-ᶜulamāʾ-i Islām*, under the leadership of Shabbīr Aḥmad ᶜUthmānī, which supported the Muslim League's demand for Pakistan. It moved to Pakistan in 1947, and during the various phases of that country's constitution-making championed the traditionalist view of the *sharīᶜa*. Another traditionalist organization which participated to some extent in the processes of constitution-making and legislation was the *Djamīᶜat al-ᶜulamāʾ-i Pākistān*.

The *Djamāᶜat-i Islāmī* differs from these traditionalist religio-political bodies in basing its programme strictly on fundamentalism. It was founded in 1941 by Abu 'l-ᶜAlāʾ Mawdūdī, with its centre at Paṫhānkoṫ, and moved to Pakistan in 1947, where it developed itself into a well-knit, well-organized religio-political group, extending its influence into urban and rural areas of West Pakistan and playing a controversial rôle on the question of the ideals and constitution of Pakistan as an Islamic state. Its fundamentalism is the complete antithesis of liberal modernism and vests all rights of legislation immutably in God alone, denying them to all human agencies, individual or collective, thus preaching a theocracy which is to be run by the consensus of the believers according to the letter of the revealed law.

Bibliography: Raḥmān ᶜAlī, *Tadhkira-i ᶜulamāʾ-i Hind*, Lucknow 1914; Sayyid Muḥammad Miyān, *ᶜUlamāʾ-i Hind kā shāndār māḍī*, Delhi 1942-61; ᶜUbayd Allāh Sindhī, *Shāh Walī-Allāh aur un kī siyāsī taḥrīk*, Lahore 1952; Sayyid Muḥammad ᶜAlī, *Makhzan-i Aḥmadī*, Agra 1882; Djaᶜfar Thānesarī, *Tawārīkh-i ᶜadjība*, Lahore; W. W. Hunter, *The Indian Musulmans*, Calcutta 1945; Abu 'l-Ḥasan ᶜAlī Nadwī, *Sīrat-i Sayyid Aḥmad Shahīd*, i, Lucknow 1938; Ghulām Rasūl Mihr, *Sayyid Aḥmad Shahīd*, Lahore 1952; idem, *Djamāᶜat-i Mudjāhidīn*, Lahore 1955; idem, *Sarguzasht-i Mudjāhidīn*, Lahore 1956; Ḥusayn Aḥmad Madanī, *Naksh-i ḥayāt*, Aᶜzamgaṙh; Shabbīr Aḥmad ᶜUthmānī, *Khutbāt*, Lahore n.d.; ᶜAlī Aḥmad Khān, *Djamāᶜ-i Islāmī*, Lahore n.d.; Abu 'l-ᶜĀlāʾ Mawdūdī, *Towards understanding Islam*, n.d., n.p.; idem, *The political theory of Islam*, Pathankot n.d.; idem, *The process of Islamic revolution*, Pathānkoṫ 1947; W. Cantwell Smith, *Modern Islam in India*, London 1946; L. Binder, *Religion and politics in Pakistan*, Los Angeles 1961. (Aziz Ahmad)

al-**DJAMMĀZ**, Abū ᶜAbd Allāh Muḥammād b. ᶜAmr b. Ḥammād b. ᶜAṭāʾ b. Yāsir, a satirical poet and humorist who lived in Baṣra in the 2nd-3rd/8th-9th centuries. Nephew of Salm al-Khāsir [*q.v.*], pupil of Abū ᶜUbayda, and friend of Abū Nuwās, of whom he has left an exceptionally accurate portrait (see al-Ḥuṣrī, *Zahr al-ādāb*, 163; idem, *Djamᶜ al-djawāhir*, 115). Unlike many of his contemporaries, he does not seem to have gained entrance to the court of Baghdād, despite his attempt during the reign of the caliph al-Rashīd. He therefore remained, poverty-stricken, in his native town, satisfying himself with amusing the local notabilities. But it is said that late in life he was called to the capital by al-Mutawakkil and presented with the sum of 10,000 dirhams; legend has it that he died of shock on the spot. This event must have taken place before 247/861, but his death has also been put at 255/868-9.

As a satirical poet he composed little other than *muḳaṭṭaᶜāt* of 2 or 3 verses, which were nevertheless remarkable for their malicious liveliness aimed, among others, at Abu 'l-ᶜAtāhiya and al-Djāḥiẓ. He was quick and scathing at repartee, but his humour, following the taste of the time, was in general very coarse.

Bibliography: Among old writers, it is to be noticed that Ḥuṣrī (*Zahr* and *Djamᶜ*, see index) frequently quotes anecdotes and lines of al-Djammāz; Khaṭīb Baghdādī, iii, 125-6, and Kutubī, *ᶜUyūn al-tawārīkh*, MS. Paris 1588, 149 a-b, carry a notice of him; Marzubānī, *Muwashshaḥ*, 278, and *Muᶜdjam*, 431, concentrate more on the work than the man. See also: Djāḥiẓ, *Ḥayawān*, i, 174-5, *Bayān* and *Bukhalāʾ*, index; Ibn Ḳutayba, *Mukhtalif*, 71; Ṭabarī, iii, 1412: Ibn al-Athīr, vii, 39; *Aghānī*, index; Thaᶜālibī, *Thimār al-ḳulūb*, 322; Ibn al-Shadjarī, *Ḥamāsa*, 275; ᶜAskarī, *Ṣināᶜatayn*, 50; Ḳālī, *Amālī*, iii, 46; Yāḳūt, *Irshād*, ii, 60. Biographical data and a number of lines are contained in Sandūbī, *Adab al-Djāḥiẓ*, 46-8; Hādjiri, in his edition of the *Bukhalāʾ* of Djāḥiẓ, 315, gives a summary of his biography. (Ch. Pellat)

DJAMNĀ, the usual modern Muslim spelling of the Indian river which rises in Tehrī in the Himālaya and falls into the Ganges at Allāhābād. Generally called Jamnā (older Jumna) on western maps, its Sanskrit name Yamunā has been largely re-adopted in modern India; it was known to Ptolemy as Διαμούνα, to Arrian as Ἰωβαρής, and to Pliny as *Iomanes*; the spellings *Gemini* (Roe) and *Gemna* (Bernier) occur among early European travellers. Early Muslim historians of India refer to it as جون.

Its depth and width have made it a natural frontier in the division of territory in north India, between the Pandjāb and the Doʾāb lands and between Awadh (Oudh) and the districts (Gwāliyār, etc.) to the south. Navigable for the greater part of its length in the plains, it was an important traffic route until the coming of the railways; this and the purity of its water have largely been responsible for its urban settlements in Dihlī, Mathurā (Muttra), Āgrā, Etāwā, Kalpī and Allāhābād [*qq.v.*].

Of its canals, the East Jumna canal was a British enterprise. The western canal, however, was begun by Fīroz Shāh Tughluḳ in 757/1356, as a monsoon supply channel to Ḥiṣār and Hansī [*qq.v.*]. In 976/1568 it was re-excavated, by Akbar's orders, and became a perennial water-course, as shown by the contemporary bridges at Karnāl, Safīdon, etc., and implied by the *sanad* of construction. It was further extended and improved in 1025/1626 by ʿAlī Mardan Khān. On the canals see J. J. Hatten, *History and description of government canals in the Punjab*, Lahore n.d. [see also NAHR].

The "Jumna musjid" of Forbes (1785) and other 18th-century writers is a misapprehension of Djāmiʿ (commonly Djamā, Djammā) masdjid.

(J. Burton-Page)

al-**DJAMRA**, lit. "pebble", (pl. *djimār*). The name is given to three halts in the Vale of Minā, where pilgrims returning from ʿArafāt during their annual pilgrimage (*ḥadjdj*) stop to partake in the ritual throwing of stones. The *Lisān al-ʿArab* explains that the place acquired its name either through the act of throwing, or through the stones themselves, which accumulate as more pilgrims perform the rite. Travelling from ʿArafāt, one comes first to *al-djamra al-ūlā* (or *al-dunyā*), then, 150 metres further on, to *al-djamra al-wusṭā*. They are in the middle of the main street of Minā, which runs in the direction of the valley itself. There is at each halt a square column of stonework surrounded by a trough into which the stones fall. 115 metres further on to the right, where the road leaves Minā and climbs towards the mountains in the direction of Mecca, the pilgrim comes to *djamrat al-ʿaḳaba* (also known as *al-kubrā* in *ḥadīth*), which consists of a wall and a basin sunk into the earth. The columns and wall are called 'the devils' (*Iblīs* or *Shayṭān*) by the people. The halts also sometimes go by the name *al-Muḥaṣṣab*, which is a plain lying between Mecca and Minā. The ritual stone-throwing is considered compulsory (*wādjib*) by the 4 schools, and exact procedural instructions are laid down. Any infraction invokes a penalty, ranging from the giving of food to a beggar to the offering of a victim for sacrifice.

On 10 Dhu 'l-Ḥidjdja, before the sacrifice of the Feast, the pilgrim throws 77 stones into the *djamrat al-ʿaḳaba*. On the 11th, generally between midday and sunset, he visits each *djamra* in turn, beginning with the *djamra al-ūlā*, and throws 7 stones into each one. He does the same on the 12th (and on the 13th should he still be in Minā). The stones normally come from Muzdalifa, although this is a custom and not an obligation, and they are about the size of a date-kernel or large bean. Burckhardt speaks of stones collected into actual heaps by some pilgrims. They are thrown from a short distance with a flick of the right thumb, rather like marbles. As he makes a throw, the pilgrim utters a *takbīr*, which some jurists consider is the essence of the rite. The crowd presses thick and excitedly round the *djimār*. Poets of the past recounted that the mob allowed them a glimpse of their beloved (see *e.g.* *Kitāb al-Aghānī*, vi, 30; Yāḳūt, iv, 427; Mubarrad, *Kāmil*, ed. Wright, 166, 13; cf. 370, 8 ff.). The Saʿūdī Arabian authorities have recently improved the means of access to the *djamrat al-ʿaḳaba*. In Arab countries, where stones are within easy reach, lapidation is an expression of hostility (cf. stones thrown at tombs which carry a curse). At *al-djamra* it is Satan who is stoned; there is an old story that Adam was the first person to drive Satan away there by stoning him. Another version attributes the event to Abraham, Hagar and Ishmael. The three *djimār* are said to mark the spots where each in turn was accosted by Satan, who wished to prevent the sacrifice of Ishmael. They all resisted the temptation, and repelled him with stones. There is no explicit mention of the Minā rites in the Ḳurʾān, but reference to them can be found in the biographies of Muḥammad and the *ḥadīth* (see for example Ibn Hishām, 970; Wāḳidī, Wellhausen, 417, 428 ff.; Ibn Saʿd, ii, 1, 125, viii, 224 ff.). They can be traced to an ancient pagan rite adapted by Islam. According to Ibn Hishām, 534, 17 (see also Wellhausen, *Maghrī*), in pagan times there existed blood-spattered stones, used in sacrifices, near the present heaps; cf. references to stone idols of al-Muḥaṣṣab in a poem of al-Farazdaḳ (Boucher ed., 30). Both van Vloten and Houtsma have given interpretations of the pre-Islamic significance of lapidation (cf. *EI*[1], and bibliography below). In a more detailed study, Gaudefroy-Demombynes suggested that it was an idolatrous cult of planetary origin, but warned that the present state of knowledge does not permit of a definitive answer being given (see ḤADJDJ).

Bibliography: Gaudefroy-Demombynes, *Le Pèlerinage à la Mekke*, Paris 1923; Ibrāhīm Rifʿat Bāshā, *Mirʿāt al-Ḥaramayn*, Cairo 1925, with photographs; Lane, i, 453e; Muḳaddasī, in *BGA*, iii, 76; Bakrī, *Geogr. Wörterbuch* (ed. Wüstenfeld), iv, 426-7, 508; Bukhārī, *Kitāb al-Ḥadjdj*, chap. *Ramy al-djimār*; Wensinck, *Concordances et Indices de la tradition musulmane*, Leiden; Azraḳī, (ed. Wüstenfeld), *Chroniken der Stadt Mekka*, i, 402-5; Burckhardt, *Reisen in Arabien*, 474-5; Snouck Hurgronje, *Het Mekkaansche Feest*, 159-61, 171-2; Van Vloten, in *Feestbundel aan de Goeje* (1891), 33 ff.; idem in *WZKM*, vii, 176; Th. Houtsma, in *Vers. Med. Ak. Amst.*, 1904, Literature section, series 4, vi, 154 ff.; Wellhausen, *Reste arab. Heidentums*[2], 111; Juynboll, *Handbuch*, 155-7.

(F. Buhl-[J. Jomier])

DJAMSHĪD (Avestan Yima Khshaēta "Yima the brilliant"), in abbreviated form Djam, an Iranian hero who has "remained alive in popular and literary tradition, from Indo-Iranian times until our own day (see the texts collected, translated and commented upon by A. Christensen, *Le premier homme et le premier roi dans l'histoire légendaire des Iraniens*, ii). To the Indian hero Yama, son of Vivasvant, sometimes immortal man become god, sometimes the first human to have suffered death and to have become its god (*Rig-Veda*, *Mahābhārata*, *Atharva-Veda*; cf. the texts in Christensen, *op. cit.*) there corresponds, in the texts from ancient Īrān, the hero Yima, son of Vīvahvant, a hero of the millennium when men, rescued from the influence of the *dīws* [*q.v.*] by the establishment of morality and religion, did not know hunger or thirst, heat or cold, old age or death; he founded towns and villages in thousands, kindled the three sacred fires, organized the social castes, preserved humanity from perishing by providing a safe, vast refuge, underground but nevertheless light, the *Var* (cf. Noah's ark), on the approach of a terrible winter followed by floods, provoked by a sorcerer or demon; but, according to the texts, he taught men, who were then simply vegetarians, to eat animal meat (hence his condemnation by the Avesta which forbids sacrifices of blood; cf. text and commentary in Christensen, *op. cit.*, ii); moreover, having fallen under the demon's influence, he believed he was God, lost his purity, gave himself up to profane pleasures and was forsaken by his glory (*kh^w^arəna*) which was of divine origin; it was in this way that he brought misery upon mankind and was reduced to living in hiding for a century; finally, on being discovered by the demons, on the order of their leader Azhi-dahāka (Azhdahag, Ẓaḥḥāk) he was sawed in the hollow tree in which he had taken refuge (a borrowing from Talmudic tradition: Christensen, *op. cit.*, 74); later, he was avenged upon Azhi-dahāka through Θraētaona (Farīdūn), a hero descended from the royal family who inherited the divine glory and re-established the monarchy which for some years had been usurped. Christensen has shown that three of the legend's principal characteristics recur in legends of various Iranian herous: the loss of divine favour as a result of a deadly sin (cf. Hartman, *Gayōmart*, 87), the building of a wonderful palace, immortality lost. According to the oldest texts, which find a reflection in al-Ṭabarī (Persian tr. by Balʿamī), Yima was the type of the first man to reign throughout the first millennium; but very soon legend credited him with predecessors: Gayōmart (Kayūmarth) and his children, Hūshang, Takhmōruv (Tahmūrath) whose reigns preceded his own, in the course of the first millennium (Christensen, *Premier homme*, i, 124 ff.).

Arabic and Persian texts deriving from the (lost) Pahlavi work *Kh^w^adāināmagh* differ as to the genealogy and chronology of these heroes. As an example we may note that only the *Shāh-nāma* of Firdawsī makes Djamshīd the son of Ṭahmūrath, unlike tradition which makes them brothers; again, several authors insert two or three generations between Hūshang and Djamshīd. In these works we find, developed to a lesser or greater extent (most of all in al-Ṭabarī, Balʿamī, Firdawsī, from the *Kh^w^adāināmagh*), details from the ancient texts summarized above (see the summaries and tr. in Christensen, *op. cit.*, ii). Popular tradition and Persian poetry have clung to two elements in the Djamshīd legend: the magic cup (*djām-i Djam*) in which he saw the universe (a very ancient legendary theme: Christensen, *op. cit.*, ii, 128 ff.), the celebration of the *nawrūz* (ibid., 138). Several Arab authors protest against the identification of Djamshīd with Solomon—which proves that this belief was widespread (Christensen, *op. cit.*, ii, 119), and hence the buildings which they are supposed in popular tradition to have erected: Takht-i Djamshīd ("Djamshīd's throne": Persepolis), Takht-i Sulaymān (Murghab), Masdjid-i mādar-i Sulaymān ("mosque of the mother of Solomon": tomb of Cyrus at Pasargadu). In short, Islamic authors do not add any notable element to the legend of Djamshīd; in their works we find borrowings from Avestan sources through the intermediary of Pahlavi texts and the *Khodāi-nāma* (*Kh^w^adāināmagh*); in general, they are agreed on the details of his civilizing work, but differ as to his genealogy.

Several historical personages bore the name of Djamshīd (or Djam); among others, the son of the Sāsānid king Kavadh I (Christensen, *L'Iran sous les Sassanides*, index: Zham; idem, *Les Kayanides*, 40), a son of the Ottoman sultan Meḥemmed II [see DJEM], Ghiyāth al-Dīn Djamshīd, who collaborated with Ulugh-Beg [*q.v.*] for his astronomical tables, *zidj* (Browne, iii, 386). According to Yāḳūt (*Muʿdjam*, ed. Wüstenfeld, ii, 118), "Djāmm (sic) is a town in Fars to which was given the name of Djamshīd son of Ṭahmūrath".

The poet Asadī [*q.v.*] of Ṭūs told of the romance between Djamshīd and the daughter of the king of Kābul with whom he had taken refuge from Ẓaḥḥāk, who pursued him as far as China (*Livre de Gerchasp*, i, 37-91, text and trans. Cl. Huart); Djamshīd's magic cup has given the name to a poem *djām-i Djam* [see art. AWḤADĪ; the vowel of the second Djam should be changed to a short *a*]; a romance in verse by Salmān of Savè [*q.v.*] tells of the love of Djamshīd, son of the emperor of China, and Khūrshīd, daughter of the emperor of Byzantium. As it is not possible to mention here all the poems in which Djamshīd features, we will limit ourselves to the *ḳaṣīda* by Manūčahrī (ed.-trans. Biberstein-Kazimirski, no. 57) on the wine-jar which the poet calls "Djamshīd's daughter", following the popular belief which credits Djamshīd with the invention of wine (cf. Muḥammad Muʿin, *Mazdayasna*, Tehran 1326/1948, 267 ff.); Djamshīd appears many times in the *ghazals* of Ḥāfiẓ (play of words on *djām* and *Djam*: ed. Kazwīnī-Ghanī, no. 78, 179, 431, 468).

Bibliography: in addition to the works mentioned in the text, see: Desmaisons, *Dict. persan-français*, art. Djam, the name denoting three sovereigns; *Gr. I Ph.* (s.v. Yima); A. Christensen, *Les Kayanides* (index: Yim); Sven S. Hartman, *Gayōmart* (index: Yim, Yima); E. Benveniste, *Les classes sociales dans la tradition avestique*, in *JA*, ccxxi (1932), 117 ff.; G. Dumézil, *Jupiter, Mars, Quirinus*, 45 ff.; Browne (index: Djamshid as named in lyric poetry); Dr. Safa, *Ḥamāsa-sarāʾī dar Īrān*, 396 ff.; idem, *Taʾrīkh-i adabiyāt-i Irān*, (index); H. Massé, *Croyances et coutumes persanes* (index I: Djamchīd).

(CL. HUART-[H. MASSÉ])

DJĀN-I DJANĀN [see MAẒHAR].

DJANĀB SHIHĀB AL-**DĪN** (CENAP ŞEHABETTIN) (1870-1934). Turkish poet and writer, one of the three representatives of the *Therwet-i Fünūn* school of literature (the others being Tewfīḳ Fikret and Khālid Ḍiyā (Ziya)).

He was born in Monastir. Upon the death of his father, an army officer, killed at the battle of Plewna (1876), he settled in Istanbul with his mother and attended, as a boarder, various military high schools, graduating from the military School of Medicine in 1889 as an army doctor. He spent four years in Paris completing his medical studies. On his return to Turkey he served in various Department of Health offices in the provinces and in Istanbul. After the Constitution of 1908 and during the First World War he tried political life without success. On retiring from government service he joined the staff of the Faculty of Arts of Istanbul University (1914) but had to resign in 1922, following a student protest about his hostile attitude towards the Nationalist movement in Anatolia. After the establishment of the Republic (1923), and after a vain attempt to win the favour of the new Government in Ankara, he lived until his death a relatively secluded life, contributing essays and occasional poems to the revived literary review *Therwet-i Fünūn*.

In his early youth Djanāb came under the influence of the last important group of supporters of the old school of literature and his first poems are in the classical tradition. But he soon freed himself of this influence and began to write poems strongly inspired by the work of the great modernist ʿAbd al-Ḥakk Ḥāmid and of Redja'īzāde Ekrem. On his return from Paris, where he had ample opportunity to study contemporary French literature, he definitely chose the modern school, which, led mainly by Redja'īzāde Ekrem and Tewfīḳ Fikret, was now developing round the literary review *Therwet-i Fünūn*. Djanāb was invited to join this review, which gave its name to the literary movement of the turn of the century. He became, after Fikret, the most successful and admired poet of the movement.

After 1908, the prose-writer eclipsed the poet, and with his numerous articles, political and literary polemics, essays, criticisms and travel notes, he came to be considered, by a whole generation, as the brilliant master of Turkish prose.

Ignoring completely all the new tendencies which were to revolutionize Turkish poetry and the Turkish language, Djanāb remained an adherent of 'Art for art's sake'. He was influenced in choice of words, concern with rhythm and unusual images by the French Parnassiens and to a lesser degree by the early Symbolists. Djanāb's comparatively few poems (collected after his death by Saadettin Nüzhet Ergun, see *Bibliography*) are all limited variations upon two themes: nature and love. Despite his obsession with metre and choice of words, which were often unearthed from the depths of Arabic and more particularly Persian dictionaries, he is no master of form. But his uncertainty, often awkwardness in form, does not prevent him from achieving at times an original and strangely attractive poetry, with unusual imagery and internal rhythm. "A silvery dew had fallen on the black leaf of night—The moon quivered like a dewdrop on the night".

Djanāb's prose is more ornate and very precious and equally full of rare Arabic and Persian words; it quickly became antiquated because of his failure to see the rapid and inevitable development of the Turkish literary language and style after 1910. In long and futile polemics, supported by his admirers, he fought a losing battle against the generation of young writers, supporters of "New Language" ("*Yeñi Lisān*"), led by the short story writer ʿUmar Seyf al-Dīn (Omer Seyfettin), who were determined to rid Turkish of the domination of Arabic and Persian grammar and vocabulary and introduce spoken Turkish, "the living Turkish" as they called it, into literature. When he realized his mistake in the 1920's and began experimenting with the "new language", it was too late: his day as writer was over. He collected some of his many essays and articles in *Ewrāḳ-i Eyyām*, Istanbul 1915, and *Nethr-i Ḥarb, Nethr-i Ṣulḥ*, Istanbul 1918; and his travel notes in *Ḥadjdj Yolunda*, Istanbul 1909, 1925, and in *Avrupa Mektūblari*, Istanbul 1919. He also wrote two plays: *Yalan*,1911, *Kôrebe*, 1917. His last book was a study on *William Shakespeare*, 1931.

Djanāb owes his important place in the history of Turkish literature to his remarkable contribution in the 1890's to the modern school of Turkish poetry, which completed the break with almost all the traditions of *dīwān* poetry and established for good the "westernized" type of Turkish poetry. In this, his role was second only to that of Tewfīḳ Fikret.

Bibliography: Rushen Eshref, *Diyorlar ki*, Istanbul 1918, 81-93 and *passim*; Sadettin Nüzhet Ergun, *Cenap Sehabettin, Hayati ve seçme siirleri*, Istanbul 1934; Ali Canip Yöntem, in *Aylik Ansiklopedi*, Istanbul 1945, i, 298-9; Kenan Akyüz, *Batı tesirinde Türk şiiri antolojisi*², Ankara 1958, 265-96. (FAHİR İZ)

AL-**DJANABA** (sing. Djunaybī), one of the leading tribes of Oman. Apparently at one time the strongest of all the Bedouin tribes there, the Djanaba still number enough nomadic members to rank as peers of the Durūʿ [*q.v.*] and Āl Wahība [*q.v.*] in the desert. The main divisions of the Djanaba are the Madjāʿila (sing. Madjʿalī, pronounced Mēʿalī), the Fawāris, Āl Dubayyān, and Āl Abū Ghālib, of which the first is recognized as paramount. The present chief (*rashīd*) of the tribe is Djāsir b. Ḥamūd, whose predecessors were the descendants of al-Murr b. Manṣūr.

Covering a wide territory, the Djanaba generally speaking fall into two groups, an eastern and a western. In the east many have settled along the coasts, in Ṣūr on the Gulf of Oman, which is shared with Banī Bū ʿAlī, and in the little ports of the coast of the Arabian Sea as far south as al-Djāzir. These settled folk have largely turned their hand to nautical affairs, and some have done well as merchants, trading to Bombay, Zanzibar, and the Red Sea. The nomads in the eastern group have large herds of camels and goats, which they keep on the coasts in winter and in the interior in summer, sheltering themselves in caves from the south-west monsoon. Some are skilful fishermen, especially in catching sharks.

The western group consists primarily of Bedouins, though some own property, *e.g.*, the chief of the tribe, Djāsir, who has land in ʿIzz, which is regarded as the tribal capital. Djāsir also has a claim to the island of Maṣīra, on which he stays for a time each year. The favourite range of the western Djanaba, the wadis in the vicinity of the town of Adam, lies east of the range of the Durūʿ.

The Djanaba belong to the Ghāfirī faction, in which they are allied with the Durūʿ in opposition to Āl Wahība, who are Hināwīs. The enmity between these tribes is no longer as bitter as it once was. In Djaʿlān the Djanaba are allies of Banī Bū ʿAlī. The Djanaba call themselves Sunnīs; Ibāḍī doctrines have not made much headway among them, though they respect the Ibāḍī Imām.

Bibliography: B. Thomas, *Alarms and excursions in Arabia*, Indianapolis, 1931; W. Thesiger, *Arabian sands*, London, 1959; ʿAbd Allāh b. Ḥumayd al-Sālimī, *Tuḥfat al-Aʿyān*, Cairo, 1332-47. Also information from inhabitants of Oman. (G. RENTZ)

DJANĀBA, the state of so-called major ritual impurity. It is caused by marital intercourse, to which the religious law assimilates any *effusio seminis*. One who is in this state is called *djunub*, and can only become ritually clean again by the so-called major ritual ablution (*ghusl* [*q.v.*]) or by the *tayammum* [*q.v.*]. On the other hand, the law prescribes for a Muslim in the state of so-called minor impurity the minor ritual ablution (*wuḍūʾ* [*q.v.*]). The distinction is based on the wording of Ḳurʾān, V, 6. The *djunub* cannot perform a valid *ṣalāt*; he may not make a *ṭawāf* round the Kaʿba, enter a mosque (except in cases of necessity), touch copies of the Ḳurʾān or recite verses from it; these last provisions are based on the traditional interpretation of Ḳurʾān, LVI, 77-9. *Djanāba* is also called "the major *ḥadath*" [*q.v.*], in opposition to the minor ritual impurity.

Bibliography: The chapters on *ṭahāra* in the

collections of traditions and the works on *fiḳh*; I. Goldziher, *Die Ẓâhiriten*, Leipzig 1884, 48-52.

(Th. W. Juynboll*)

al-**DJANADĪ**, Abū ʿAbd Allāh Bahāʾ al-Dīn Muḥammad b. Yaʿḳūb b. Yūsuf, Shāfiʿite jurist and historian of Yemen. His family was of the town of Ẓafār in Yemen although he resided most of his life in Zabīd where he apparently died in 732/1332. His only known extant work, *Kitāb al-sulūk fī ṭabaḳāt al-ʿulamāʾ wa 'l-mulūk*, is an important biographical dictionary of the learned men, primarily jurisconsults, of Yemen arranged by the towns in which they were born or lived. The dictionary proper is preceded by a long introduction comprising a political history of the country from the time of the Prophet to 724/1323-4, early recognized by the later historians of Yemen to be of the greatest value so that his work is quoted as a source by al-Khazradjī, al-Ahdal, Abū Makhrama, and others. The biographical portion was later continued by al-Khazradjī in his *Ṭirāz aʿlām al-zaman fī ṭabaḳāt aʿyān al-Yaman* and in the *Tuḥfat al-zaman fī aʿyān al-Yaman* by al-Ahdal. The *Sulūk* of al-Djanadī has not as yet been edited in its entirety although a portion of the historical introduction, that concerning the Fāṭimid *dāʿīs* in Yemen, has been edited and translated from the manuscript in the Bibliothèque Nationale (2127, Add. 767, foll. 30a-32b) by H. C. Kay in his *Yaman, its early mediaeval history* (London, 1892). To those manuscripts of the *Sulūk* listed by Brockelmann should be added the excellent copy in the Chester Beatty Library (no. 3110, i. & ii) and another in the Egyptian National Library in Cairo (25 Taʾrīkh); the latter is a recent photocopy of that in the library of the great mosque of Ṣanʿāʾ.

Bibliography: Brockelmann, II, 184, S II, 236; Ḥādjdjī Khalīfa, ed. Flügel, ii, 613; al-Sakhāwī, *Iʿlān* in Franz Rosenthal, *A history of Muslim historiography*, 406-7; Kay, pp. xii-xiv.

(C. L. Geddes)

al-**DJANĀḤIYYA** (or al-Ṭayyāriyya), the special partisans of ʿAbd Allāh b. Muʿāwiya [*q.v.*], great-grandson of Djaʿfar al-Ṭayyār Dhū 'l-Djanāḥayn. Though Djaʿfar and his son and grandson were highly respected by Shīʿīs, no political or religious party seems to have been attached to the family until ʿAbd Allāh took the leadership of the general Shīʿī revolt against the Umayyads in 127/744. The wider party of ʿAbd Allāh included for a time most politically active Shīʿīs (including some ʿAbbāsids), not to mention certain displaced Khāridjites; but the term *Djanāḥiyya* may be applied more particularly to those for whom ʿAbd Allāh had exclusive rights to the imāmate. These claimed that Abū Hāshim b. Muḥammad b. al-Ḥanafiyya had left the imāmate not to the ʿAbbāsids but to ʿAbd Allāh b. Muʿāwiya, then still a lad, in care of a certain Ṣāliḥ b. Mudrik. They are said to have believed that the *imām* knew the unseen, and that whoever knew the *imām* was exempt from other (presumably ritual) obligations. (It is doubtful if ʿAbd Allāh b. Muʿāwiya shared these opinions). Among them, Isḥāḳ (or ʿAbd Allāh) b. Zayd b. al-Ḥārith and his partisans are said to have believed in reincarnation and in the presence of the light of God in the *imām*. On the death of ʿAbd Allāh b. Muʿāwiya, some claimed he was withdrawn into the mountains of Iṣfahān, whence he would return to put an ʿAlid in power; others evidently accepted Isḥāḳ b. al-Ḥārith as *imām*.

Bibliography: see ʿAbd Allāh b. Muʿāwiya (to which add in particular Ṭabarī, ii, 1976 ff.); see also Masʿūdī, *Murūdj*, vi, 41, 42, 67-8; Nawbakhtī, *Firaḳ*, 29, 30, 31, 32, 35; Ashʿarī, *Maḳālāt*, 6, 22 (the group was strengthened by the Kaysānī Ḥarbiyya), 85; Baghdādī, *Farḳ*, ed. M. Zāhid Kawtharī, 142-3, 150, 152, 163, 193, 216 (ed. M. Badr, 235 ff.); Ibn Ḥazm, Cairo ed. iv, 137, 143; Shahrastānī, *Milal*, ed. Cureton, i, 113 (ed. on margin of Ibn Ḥazm), i, 156 (branch of the Hāshimiyya), trans. Haarbrücher, ii, 408); Ibn Nubāta al-Miṣrī, *Sarḥ al-ʿuyūn* (commentary of the *Risāla* of Ibn Zaydūn), Cairo ed., 241-4; Djāḥiẓ, *Ḥayawān*, iii, 488 and note (the Ḥamāsa of Buḥturī contains many of his verses), vii, 160; *Aghānī*, xi, 72 ff.; Thaʿālibī, *Thimār al-ḳulūb*, 261; I. Friedlaender, *The heterodoxies of the Shiʿites*, in *JAOS*, xxviii, 45, 71, and xxix, 44-5; Moscati, *Il testamento di Abū Hāshim*, in *RSO*, xxvii, 32-3, 46.

(M. G. S. Hodgson and M. Canard)

al-**DJANĀWANĪ** (also al-Djenāwunī), Abū ʿUbayda ʿAbd al-Ḥamīd, governor of the Djabal Nafūsa for the Ibāḍite *imāms* of Tāhart. He was a native of the village of Īdjnāwun (also Djenāwen, in Berber Ignaun) situated below the town of Djādū in the present district of Fassāṭo. He already enjoyed great prestige there about 196/811 during the stay of the *imām* ʿAbd al-Wahhāb b. ʿAbd al-Raḥmān b. Rustam in the Djabal Nafūsa. On the death of Abu 'l-Ḥasan Ayyūb he was elected governor of the Djabal Nafūsa by the people of the country and afterwards received the investiture from ʿAbd al-Wahhāb, probably a little before the death of the latter which occurred in 208/823. His governorship, the duration of which corresponded very nearly with the reign of the *imām* Aflaḥ b. ʿAbd al-Wahhāb (208/823-258/871), was troubled by the continuous war which he had to wage against the heretic Khalaf b. al-Samḥ, grandson of a previous Ibāḍite *imām* of North Africa, Abu 'l-Khaṭṭāb ʿAbd al-Aʿlā al-Maʿāfirī. Several episodes are known of this war which came to an end only after the victory which al-Djanāwanī achieved over Khalaf's army in 221/835. As a result of this victory the Djabal Nafūsa, whose population were fanatical partisans of the Rustamids, continued to be a province of the state of Tāhart until the latter's downfall.

Al-Djanāwanī was pious and learned. Besides Berber he also knew Arabic and the language of Kanem (*lugha kānamiyya*), a very strange fact. He is counted among the twelve *mustadjāb al-duʿāʾ* ('those whose prayers are answered') who inhabited the Djabal Nafūsa towards the end of the 2nd/8th century and the beginning of the 3rd/9th. He resided at Īdjnāwun which at this period became for a time the religious and political centre of the whole Djabal Nafūsa. The Ibāḍite tradition recorded by al-Shammākhī speaks of seventy Ibāḍī scholars who flocked there at that time from all the province governed by al-Djanāwanī.

Bibliography: *Chronique d'Abou Zakaria*, trans. with comm. by E. Masqueray, Paris-Algiers 1878, 144-74; Abu 'l-ʿAbbās Aḥmad b. Saʿīd al-Shammākhī, *Kitāb al-Siyar*, Cairo 1301/1883, 179-89; A. de C. Motylinski, *Le Djebel Nefousa*, Paris 1899, 88, n. 2; R. Basset, *Les sanctuaires du Djebel Nefousa*, in *JA* 1899, July-August, 95-6; T. Lewicki, *Études ibāḍites nord-africaines*, i, Warsaw 1955, 92-3, 131, and *passim*.

(T. Lewicki)

DJANĀZA (or Djināza, Ar.) a corpse, bier, or corpse and bier, and then, funeral. It was *sunna* [*q.v.*] to whisper the *shahāda* [*q.v.*] in the ear of a dying man whose face was turned towards Mecca. The dead body was washed by those of the same sex though there were exceptions; Abū Bakr [*q.v.*] gave orders that he should be washed by his widow. It was a mark of piety for one at the point of death to wash himself in readiness. The body was not stripped entirely and was washed several times, always an uneven number, and for the last *sidr* leaves or camphor was steeped in the water. If disease made it unwholesome to touch the body, it was enough to pour quantities of water over it. Washing began with the right side and the parts washed in the ritual ablution. Martyrs who fell in battle were not washed and were buried in their blood-stained clothes without prayers. Grave-clothes might be the every day garments, usually three, though sheets were used; white was the normal use though colours were allowed but not red. The eyes were closed, the jaw tied up and the graveclothes tied tightly but were loosened in the tomb. If the clothes were short they had to cover the head while the feet might be covered with reeds. The body was carried to the grave on an open bier with a cloth thrown over it, and there was an extra covering for a woman. Burial might be in the house but was more usual in a cemetery. The funeral moved quickly for, "If I am good, hurry me to God; and if I am bad, get rid of me quickly". It was better to walk in the procession than to ride and it was a work of merit to help carry the bier, if only for a few steps. A halt might be made at a mosque for prayers which differed from the *ṣalāt* [*q.v.*] because the mourners stood throughout. Prayers were said by the grave. A near relative officiated though the governor or a famous scholar might be asked to lead or might insist on doing so. The *imām* [*q.v.*] stood by the head of a man or by the trunk of a woman. Prayers were said over an infant if it had cried once but not over a suicide. Those sitting in the street should stand as a funeral passes. Women were not allowed to be present; this was to avoid the lamentation customary in the *Djāhiliyya* [*q.v.*] because lamentations added to the pains of the dead. The earth must not press on the body which must sit up to answer Munkar and Nakīr (see ʿADHĀB AL-ḲABR) so the grave was a pit with a narrower trench at the bottom or a niche hollowed out at the side; the trench was roofed with flagstones and the niche shut off by a wall of sun-dried bricks. Grave-diggers specialized in one or other of these forms and Muḥammad's grave depended on whether a "trencher" or a "nicher" came first. If this tale is true, these forms of burial existed before Islam but the details are so precise that the whole is suspect. The nearest relatives descended into the grave to put the body in position with the face towards Mecca and to loosen the grave-clothes. One man one grave is the rule; after the battle of Uḥud two bodies were put in one grave but one was taken away later; if a man and a woman had to be laid in one grave, there had to be a partition between them. Burial might be on the day of death or the following day but a hurried burial at night was not approved. Some held that the earth over a grave should be level though others allowed a small mound. Covering it with plaster and inscriptions was forbidden but headstones with name, date and sentences from the Ḳurʾān soon became common. Water was often sprinkled on the grave; rain watered that of a saint and in later times, if there was a horizontal stone, it had a hole in it to let water through. Coffins were not used at first but by the 6th century they were common. There might be a meal with gifts of food to the poor. Customs changed; women followed funerals, professional mourners were employed and masonry tombs became common.

Bibliography: Chapter *djanāʾiz* in the collections of traditions; Ibn Saʿd, *Ṭabaḳāt*, 2/ii, 60 ff. (burial of Muḥammad); Ibn Abi ʾl-Ḥādjdj, *Madkhal* (1929), 2, 220 ff., 281 ff., 3, 234-80 (middle ages); M. Galal, in *REI*, ii (1937), 131-300 (modern Egypt); Lane, *Modern Egyptians*, ch. 28; Hughes, *Dictionary of Islam*, s.v. *Burial*; I. Gruetter, in *Isl.*, xxxi (1953), 147-73, xxxii (1955), 79-04, 168-94; A. S. Tritton, in *BSOS* ix, 653-61.

(A. S. TRITTON)

DJĀNBĀZ. The Persian *djānbāz* 'playing with one's life; dare-devil' developed three meanings which, mainly through Ottoman Turkish, spread into a number of languages: 1. 'acrobat', especially 'rope-dancer', which is known in the east as far as Eastern Turki (*čāmbashči*), in the west in the Caucasus, Turkey, and Egypt (*ganbādhiya* 'rope-dancers', *gunbāz* 'gymnastics'), 2. 'soldier' [see article DJĀNBĀZĀN), 3. 'horse-dealer'; this latter word spread through Turkey (recorded in the 16th century: Gliša Elezović, *Iz Carigradskih Turskih Arhiva Mühimme Defteri*, Belgrade 1951, 115, no. 659) north as far as Rumania and south to Syria and Lebanon, often with pejorative development of the meaning: 'one who drives a hard bargain' (Bulgaria), 'merchant who demands exorbitant prices' (Syria), 'trickster' (Rum. *geambaş*).—Acrobats, known since antiquity, were always popular in the Near East, and, in particular, in the festivities given by the Ottoman sultans to the people of the capital they were never missing. 'A troupe of excellent Tumblers and Mountebanks (where of Turkey abounds aboue all the Regions of the Earth) ...' begins the description of such a festivity (Michel Baudier, transl. by Edward Grimestone, *The History of the Serrail and of the Court of the Grand Seigneur*, London 1635, 88 f.). The earliest reference to *djānbāz* in Ottoman times seems to be found in the description of a circumcision feast for the royal princes in Edirne in 1457 (here Laonikos Chalkokondyles translates the Turkish term, spelled τάμπεζιν instead of τζάμπεζιν, as 'rope-dancer', cf. Moravcsik, *Byzantinoturcica*, vol. 2, 252). From the 16th century we have many descriptions, often accompanied by illustrations, both in Turkish sources and narratives of European travellers, of the performances of various kinds of acrobats at public festivities; particularly famous was the circumcision feast which Murād III gave for his son Meḥemmed (III) in 990/1582. Ewliyā Čelebi's travel book offers interesting details about the *djānbāz* in the 17th century. In his account of the parade of the Istanbul guilds he mentions the guild of the acrobats (i, 625 f.), listing several names. He also mentions that the most outstanding rope-dancer, Meḥmed Čelebi of Üsküdar, was holding an imperial letter patent (*khaṭṭ-i sherīf*) by which he was appointed warden (*ser-česhme*) of all acrobats (here the term is *pehliwān*) of the empire, of whom a total of 200 masters were listed in his register (*defter*). Meḥmed Čelebi is again mentioned among the participants of a memorable show at Istanoz (now Zir, *vilâyet* of Ankara) where—we are told by Ewliya Čelebi (ii, 439-42, ed. Ozön, iii, 10-13)—all rope-dancers (here the narrower term *resenbāz* is used) assembled once every 40 years for a contest which resulted in the promotion of the apprentices to master's status. The sources for the 16th and 17th centuries can be found in Metin And, *Kırk gün, kırk gece, Eski donanma ve shenliklerde seyirlik oyunları*, Istanbul

1959. For the *djānbāz* in Istanbul's more recent past see Refik Ahmed, *İstanbul nasıl eğleniyordu?* Istanbul 1927, 83-86, and Musahipzade Celâl, *Eski İstanbul yaşayışı*, Istanbul 1946, 68 f.

(A. Tietze)

DJĀNBĀZĀN (Persian plural of *djānbāz*, see previous article)—the name of a military corps in the Ottoman Empire. It is not known when exactly the corps was founded, although it may have been in the reign of Orkhān Ghāzī [*q.v.*]. The *djānbāzān* served only in time of war, like the *ʿazab* [*q.v.*], *gharībān* and *čerekhōr* ("territorial" miners and sappers). Grzegorzewski (*Z sidzyllatów Rumelijskich epoki wyprawy wiedeńskiej*, Lwów 1912, 53 ff.) believes, however, that they were organized in 844/1440 by Murād II [*q.v.*] to meet the first Balkan expedition of John Hunyady and that they took part in the battle of Varna. The *djānbāzān* served in the vanguard and were charged with dangerous tasks. This fact led Hammer (*Staatsverfassung*, index) to class them with the irregulars known as *serden-gečti* (lit. "mad or wild adventurers"), *gönüllü* ("volunteers") and *deli* ("madmen", [*q.v.*]). Grzegorzewski followed by Babar (*Zur wirtschaftlichen Grundlage des Feldzuges der Türken gegen Wien im Jahre 1683*, Vienna/Leipzig 1916, 29 ff.) held, however, that they formed the personal body-guard of *Beglerbegis* [*q.v.*] and *sandjak begis*, like the *djāndārān*, while D'Ohsson (*Tableau général*, vii, 309) thought that, like the *gharībān*, the *djānbāzān* served as coastal militia in Anatolia.

The *djānbāzān* later joined the *yürüks* ("nomads", [*q.v.*]) and Tatars as well as the *yaya* ("infantry") and *müsellems* ("sappers") in forming support forces for the Janissaries (cf. Djelāl-zāde Nishāndjī, *Ṭabaḳāt al-mamālik fī daradjāt al-masālik*, Fātiḥ Library MS 4467, f. 8; I. Ḥaḳḳī Uzunçarşılı, *Osmanlı devleti teşkilâtında kapı kulu ocakları*, Ankara 1943, 2).

A *ḳānūnnāme* dating back to the middle of the 10th/16th century is in existence concerning the *djānbāzān* of Rumeli. It states that 10 *djānbāzān* formed an *odjaḳ*, that only one served at a time, the remaining nine paying 50 *aḳčes* each as *ʿawāriḍ-i dīwāniyye* [see ʿAWĀRIḌ]. The *ḳānūn-nāme* describes the *djānbāzān* as nomads, paying taxes (*bād-i hawā rusūmu*) to their own officers (*Su-bashî*). The relatives and dependants of the *djānbāzān* were assimilated to the corps, which could also be joined by outsiders, related by marriage, and by converts. The *djānbāzān* of Rumeli were considered part of the *yürük zeʿāmet* of Vize; they were subject to the same penal, taxation and other rules, and seem, therefore, to have come largely from the same stock. They were subject, however, to a more complicated system of *ʿawāriḍ* services (*Ḳānūnnāme-i Djānbāzān*, Başvekâlet Arşivi, Tapu Defterleri, no. 226). The *Ḳānūnnāme-yi Āl-i ʿOthmān* (v. *TOEM*) states that *djānbāzān* on active service should be considered as soldiers and that the "estate duty" (*resm-i ḳismet*) for any killed in war should be paid to the *ḳāḍī ʿasker*, if it exceeds 100 *aḳčes*, and in other cases to the *ḳāḍīs* of *wilāyets*. Later, however, all *djānbāzān* were considered soldiers and all duties became payable to the *ḳāḍī ʿasker* of Rumeli.

In 950/1543 the corps (*ṭāʾife*) of *djānbāzān* amounted to 39 and in 964/1557 to 41 *odjaḳs*. ʿAyn-i ʿAlī (*Ḳawānīn-i Āl-i ʿOthmān*, 45) gives their strength together with that of *ʿazabs* as 1280, of whom one tenth served at any one time. The corps was abolished towards the end of the 16th century (according to D'Ohsson under Selīm II) together with those of the *yaya* and *müsellems*.

The *djānbāzān* were cavalry troops and they also bred horses for the army. After their dissolution their name lived on in the form "*at djānbāzī*" meaning "horse broker". (M. Tayyib Gökbilgin)

DJĀNBULĀṬ, a family of *amīrs*, Durūz in religion and Kurdish in origin ("soul of steel" in this language), established in the Lebanon, where they formed the Djānbulāṭī party, active until the present day (common modern spellings: Djoumblatt, Jomblatt, etc.). The Djānbulāt, related to the Ayyūbids according to Lebanese tradition, appeared in the region of Killis during the latter half of the 10th/16th century (the Mamlūk Djānbulāt al-Nāṣirī, governor first of Aleppo and then of Damascus in 902-4/1497-9, sultan of Egypt for six months under the name of al-Malik al-Ashraf Abu 'l-Naṣr, d. 906-7/1501, seems to have no connexion with this family).

Djānbulāṭ b. Ḳāsim al-Kurdī (d. 980/1572), surnamed Ibn ʿArabī, perhaps by *taḳiyya*, suppressed brigandry in the sandjaḳ of Killis, where he hade been placed in charge by the Ottomans, and participated in the conquest of Cyprus. His son Ḥusayn (d. 1013/1604) evicted the wālī Naṣūḥ Pasha from Aleppo, whom he had assisted against the rebels of Damascus, and was executed at Van for having refused to join in an expedition against Īrān. ʿAlī, his son (Djānbulāṭoghlu to the Ottoman historians), rebelled in Aleppo and extended his rule in Syria; he aligned himself with the amīr of Mount Lebanon, Fakhr al-Dīn Maʿn, against Yūsuf al-Ṣayfa, also a Kurd, the governor of Tripoli, defeated the latter at Ḥamā, but then was reconciled to him; he established an independent amīrate from Ḥamā to Adana, failed to remit taxes to the Sultan, had the *khuṭba* recited in his own name, and raised an army of more than 30,000 men. He was conquered at Orudj in 1016/1607, as was his ally Fakhr al-Dīn; thanks to his uncle Ḥaydar, he received the pardon of the Sultan at Istanbul. Placed in command of Temesvar, he joined battle with the Janissaries, fled to Belgrade, and was decapitated in 1020/1611. The Djānbulāṭ, however, kept their command over Killis and thereafter remained faithful to the Sultan; a nephew of ʿAlī, Muṣṭafā, became bey of Rumeli. They seem to have left some remnants in the Lebanon, where one of these was imprisoned at Shakīf in 1019/1610, and where they struggled against Yūnis Maʿn during Fakhr al-Dīn's absence in Italy; the latter, however, after his return and before his new revolt, made a fresh appeal to the Djānbulāṭ of Killis.

Djānbulāṭ b. Saʿīd (d. 1050/1640), probably grandson of ʿAlī, finally emigrated to the Lebanon in 1040/1630 with his sons Saʿīd and Rabāḥ, settled in the Shūf, and, from 1041/1631, joined the campaigns of the amīr. His son Rabāḥ succeeded him, and ʿAlī, his grandson (d. 1124/1712), outlived his brothers Fāris and Sharaf al-Dīn, who were assassinated; he entered the service of the powerful Druze chieftain Ḳablān al-Ḳāḍī al-Tanūkhī, married his daughter, and inherited his fortune and his influence, which he increased by his generosity towards the common people. He helped the amīr Ḥaydar Shihāb to carry the battle of ʿAyn Dāra, 1123/1711, against the Yamanī "party". Before his death he wished to divide his fortune between his son-in-law ʿAlī and the amīr, but the Druzes bought back the latter's portion for ʿAlī's benefit. This son-in-law ʿAlī built the castle of Mukhtāra, finally established the local authority of his family, developed with the Djānbulāṭī "party" an opposition movement to the amīral power, and intervened in the dissensions of the Shihāb whom he looked upon as upstarts. In 1173-4/1760 he assured the succession of the amīr Manṣūr against his co-regent Aḥmad, then, deceived by him, brought the amīr Yūsuf to power, joined with him in an unhappy struggle against Ḍāhir al-ʿUmar, and later turned against him, won over by the intrigues of Djazzār. He died as an octogenarian in 1192/1778.

Bashīr Djānbulāṭ, grandson of ʿAlī (?), built the mosque of Mukhtāra on the model of that of Acre, and undertook important irrigation works; he helped the accession to power in 1202/1788 of the amīr Bashīr II Shihāb, and long supported him, but he set up his lieutenant ʿAbbās against him during the amīr's absence in Egypt; the latter on his return defeated him at Mukhtāra and had him strangled in 1240/1825. After the downfall of the Shihāb dynasty in 1841 the Ottomans preferred the Arslān to the too rich and powerful Djānbulāṭ for the Ḳāʾimaḳāmate of the Shūf. Saʿīd Djānbulāṭ, set aside in this way, took an active part in the bloody events of 1860; condemned to death, he died in prison in 1861. His son Nasīb continued after him the struggle for authority against the Arslān, whom he eliminated, at the end of the 19th century, from the Ḳāʾima-ḳāmate of the Shūf.

The Djānbulāṭī "party" (with a scarlet flag edged with green, bearing a hand and a dark green scimitar) was formed, not in the 17th century as is often supposed, but during the first half of the 18th, when the amīr Ḥaydar supported against ʿAlī Djānbulāṭ ʿAbd al-Salām Yazbak ʿAmād, who formed the Yazbakī "party". These parties do not continue, as is sometimes claimed, the classical Yamanī (totally eliminated from the mountains after ʿAyn Dāra) and Ḳaysī (with whom the Djānbulāṭ were always friendly) clans, but substitute for this traditional division an analogous one, some effects of which persist in the contemporary political life of the Lebanon.

Bibliography: G. Mariti, *Geschichte Fakkardins, Gross-Emirs der Druzen, und der übrigen Gross-Emiren bis 1773*, Gotha 1790; C. F. Volney, *Voyage en Egypte et en Syrie pendant les années 1783, 1784 et 1785*, 6th ed. Paris 1823, ii; H. Huys, *Relations d'un séjour de plusieurs années dans le Liban*, Paris 1850, i, 279; ii, 48, 78-80, 112, 126 etc.; Ṭannūs al-Shidyāḳ, *Akhbār al-aʿyān fī Djabal Lubnān*, Beirut 1859; M. von Oppenheim, *Vom Mittelmeer zum persischen Golf*, Berlin 1899, i, 30, 115, 150, 163, etc.; Ḥaydar Aḥmad al-Shihābī, *Taʾrīkh*, Cairo 1900-1; Jouplain, *La question du Liban*, Paris 1908; Michael of Damascus, *Taʾrīkh ḥawādith al-Shām wa Lubnān*, ed. Maʿlūf, Beirut 1912; H. Lammens, *La Syrie, précis historique*, Beirut 1921; P. K. Hitti, *The origins of the Druze people and religion*, New York 1928, 22; N. Bouron, *Les Druzes, histoire du Liban et de la montagne haouranaise*, Paris 1930; A. N. Poliak, *Feudalism in Egypt, Syria, Palestine and the Lebanon, 1250-1900*, London 1939, 44, 57, etc.; *İA*, s.v. Canbulat (M. C. Şihâbeddin Tekindağ); Adel Ismaïl, *Histoire du Liban du XVIIᵉ siècle à nos jours*; *I, Le Liban au temps de Fakhreddine II (1596-1633)*, Paris 1955; M. Chebli, *Une histoire du Liban à l'époque des émirs (1635-1841)*, Beirut 1955.

(P. Rondot)

DJĀNDĀR or Djandār, the name given to certain guards regiments serving the great Saldjūḳs and subsequent dynasties. Attached to the royal household, they provided the sovereign's bodyguard, and carried out his orders of execution. Their commander, the *amīr djāndār*, was a high-ranking officer; some of them are reported as becoming *atābaks* [*q.v.*]. Under the Saldjūḳs of Rūm, they formed an élite cavalry guard, and wore their swords on a gold-embroidered baldric. At the accession of ʿAlāʾ al-Dīn Kayḳobād I in 616/1219 he is said to have had a bodyguard of 120 djāndārs (Ibn Bībī, *El-Evāmirü 'l-ʿalāʾiyye*, facsimile ed. A. S. Erzi, Ankara 1956, 216). Under the Khʷārizm-Shāhs the djāndārs, as guards and executioners, held positions of great influence (Barthold, *Turkestan*, 378). Under the Ayyūbids the *amīr djāndār* was one of the highest ranking officers in the state; he remained so under the early Mamlūks [*q.v.*], the post being held by an amīr of a thousand. Later the office declined in importance, and from the middle of the 9th/15th century to the end of the Mamlūk Sultanate the djāndārs were common soldiers. From Mamlūk Egypt the term passed to North Africa, where it was used of the bodyguards of the Marīnids.

Bibliography: İ. H. Uzunçarşılı, *Osmanlı devleti teşkilâtına medhal*, Istanbul 1941, 37, 88-9, 382; D. Ayalon, *Studies on the structure of the Mamluk army-III*, in *BSOAS*, xvi/1, 1954, 63-4; *CIA*, *Egypte*, 77, 78, 291, 370, *Syrie* lix; W. Popper, *Egypt and Syria under the Circassian Sultans*, Berkeley-Los Angeles 1955, 94; H. Quatremère, *Histoire des Sultans mamlouks*, ia 14; *İA* ('Cândâr' by M. Mansuroğlu).

(Ed.)

DJANDARLİ, name of an Ottoman family of *ʿulemāʾ*-statesmen, prominent from ca. 750-905/1350-1500, five of whom held the office of Grand Vizier. The name, variously spelt in the early sources, in later works usually Čandarlî, appears in the oldest inscriptions as Djandarī, which has been explained as a *nisba* from Pers. *djāndār*, 'bodyguard' (so Fr. Taeschner and P. Wittek, in *Isl.* xviii, 83) or from a locality Djender or Čender near Sivrihisar (so I. H. Uzunçarşılı, in *Belleten*, xxiii, 457 f.).

(1) Khayr al-Dīn Khalīl b. ʿAlī (popularly 'Kara Khalīl') is said to have been *ḳāḍī* successively of Biledjik, Iznik and Bursa. Murād I, shortly after his accession, appointed him to the newly-created office of *ḳāḍīʿasker* [*q.v.*], and later (certainly by 783/1381, perhaps earlier, see *Belleten*, xxiii, 465-8) made him vizier; as the first Ottoman vizier to combine with the supervision of the administration the command of the army he is reckoned the first 'Grand Vizier'. He played a prominent part in the conquest of Western Thrace, Macedonia and Thessaly, and penetrated Albania (787/1385). Left in Rumeli as Murād's representative during the Karaman campaign, he died at Serres in 789/1387.

Khayr al-Dīn Pasha is credited by the chroniclers with the establishment of the corps of the *yaya* [*q.v.*] and later of the *yeni-čeri* [*q.v.*]. He was married to a daughter of Tādj al-Dīn Kurdī, *müderris* of the *medrese* of Iznik. Three sons of his are known: ʿAlī (2), Ibrāhīm (3) and Ilyās; the last is said to have been beglerbegi and to have died under Bāyezīd I; he had a son, Dāwud Čelebi, who died in 898/1492.

(2) ʿAlī Pasha [*q.v.*] served Murād I, Bāyezīd I and Emīr Suleymān as Grand Vizier, and died in 809/1406.

(3) Ibrāhīm Pasha's early career is obscure (he too seems to have been a partisan of Emīr Suleymān). In 808/1406 he was *ḳāḍī* of Bursa (*Belleten*, v, 560 f.). According to one account (Neshrī, ed. Taeschner, i, 133) he was sent by Mūsā Čelebi, after Emīr Suleymān's death, to Constantinople to demand tribute, and seized the opportunity to desert to Meḥemmed I,

who appointed him vizier (but ʿĀs̲h̲iḳpas̲h̲azāde [ed. Giese, 196] says he had been ḳāḍīʿasker to Meḥemmed, who made him vizier on occupying Bursa). A document of 818/1415 shows that he was in that year ḳāḍīʿasker (TTEM xvi, 379 and n. 11), and another of 823/1420 (Belleten, v, 561) that he was by then second vizier (Bāyezīd Pas̲h̲a being Grand Vizier). When, shortly after Murād II's accession, Bāyezīd Pas̲h̲a was killed by the pretender 'Düzme' Muṣṭafā, Ibrāhīm succeeded him as Grand Vizier and remained in office until his death, of the plague (O. Turan, Tarihî takvimler, 24), on 24 D̲h̲u 'l-Ḳaʿda 832/25 August 1429. Ibrāhīm Pas̲h̲a restored the influence of his family, weakened by their adherence to Meḥemmed I's rivals, and followed a cautious and prudent foreign policy.

(4) K̲h̲alīl Pas̲h̲a [q.v.], the eldest son of Ibrāhīm, was by 847/1443 Grand Vizier. He enjoyed Murād II's full confidence to the end of his reign, but the part he had played in recalling Murād to the throne in 850/1446 and the suspicion of having dealings with the Byzantine Emperor incurred the displeasure of Meḥemmed II, and he was executed (the first Grand Vizier so to suffer) shortly after the capture of Constantinople (857/1453).

His brother Maḥmūd C̲elebi was married to a sister of Murād II; taking part as sand̲j̲aḳ-bey of Bolu in the campaign of the Izladi Pass (847/1443-4) he was captured, but later ransomed (Nes̲h̲rī, ed. Taeschner, i, 172). Maḥmūd had a son, Suleymān C̲elebi, who died in 860/1455.

K̲h̲alīl's son Suleymān C̲elebi was by 851/1447 ḳāḍīʿasker; he predeceased his father (Med̲j̲dī, 126).

(5) Ibrāhīm Pas̲h̲a, son of K̲h̲alīl, was born in 833/1429-30. Documents (to those cited by Uzunçarşılı, İA s.v. Çandarlı, 356a, add M. T. Gökbilgin, Edirne ve Paşa Livâsı, 333, 203, 344, 327 etc.) show that he was ḳāḍī of Edirne at the time of his father's disgrace and remained in that office until 869/1465, when he was appointed ḳāḍīʿasker (thus Tas̲h̲köprüzāde's story of the poverty he suffered is to be rejected); by 878/1473 he was lala (with the rank of vizier) to Prince Bāyezīd (cf. also Ibn Kemal, VII. defter, ed. Ş. Turan, 1954, 399 ff.). After his accession, Bāyezīd II appointed him ḳāḍīʿasker of Rumeli in 890 and, in Ṣafar 891/February 1486, vizier (Saʿd al-Dīn, ii, 217, and cf. Gökbilgin, Edirne, 74-5, 418, 121). Second vizier by 893 (Ḳiwāmī, ed. F. Babinger, Istanbul 1955, 321), he succeeded Hersekzāde Aḥmed Pas̲h̲a as Grand Vizier in 903/1498, but died two years later while on the campaign against Lepanto.

Thereafter the family fell into relative obscurity. One son of Ibrāhīm, Ḥuseyn Pas̲h̲a, died after 940/1533-4 as beglerbegi of Diyārbekir, and another, ʿĪsā Pas̲h̲a, for a short time nis̲h̲ānd̲j̲î, died in 950/1543-4 as beglerbegi of Damascus; the latter's son K̲h̲alīl was lala to Prince Ork̲h̲ān, the son of Suleymān I's son Bāyezīd, and died in 976/1568-9 as defterdār of Budin.

Bibliography: Fr. Taeschner and P. Wittek, Die Vezirfamilie der G̲andarlyzāde (14./15. Jhdt.) und ihre Denkmäler, in Isl. xviii, 1929, 60-115 and ('Nachträge') xxii, 1935, 73-5 (full references to and discussion of the sources); İ. H. Uzunçarşılı, İA art. Çandarlı (mainly following the preceding but with some further details from archival sources etc.); idem, Çandarlızâde Ali Paşa vakfiyesi, in Belleten, v, 1941, 549-76; idem, Çandarlı (Cenderli) Kara Halil Hayreddin Paşa, in Belleten, xxiii, 1959, 457-77; İA art. Murad II (H. Inalcık). Further members of the family are named in documents in M. T. Gökbilgin, XV.-XVI. asırlarda Edirne ve Paşa Livâsı, Istanbul 1952 (see index, s.v. İbrâhim Paşa b. Halil Pş.). (V. L. MÉNAGE)

DJANDJĪRA [see ḤABS̲H̲Ī].

DJANFIDĀ K̲H̲ATŪN [see SUPPLEMENT].

DJANGALÍ, the name of a nationalist and reformist movement in Persia which came into being in 1915 in the forests (d̲j̲angal) of Gīlān under the leadership of Mīrzā Kūc̲ik K̲h̲ān, Iḥsān Allāh K̲h̲ān and a number of other liberals (āzādīk̲h̲ʷāhān) and constitutionalists (mud̲j̲āhidīn). The Dj̲angalīs (in Persian: d̲j̲angaliyān or aḥrār-i d̲j̲angal), whose slogans were freedom from foreign influence and the independence of Īrān under the banner of Islam, set up a revolutionary committee called Ittiḥād-i Islām, published a newspaper entitled Dj̲angal, and engaged as military instructors a number of German, Austrian and Turkish officers. The movement, which was financed by money extorted from the landowners of Gīlān, was given an added impetus by the Russian Revolution of 1917, and by 1918 had spread to other Caspian regions, notably the province of Māzandarān. In March 1918 the Dj̲angalīs were narrowly prevented from occupying Ḳazwīn. The territory held by the Dj̲angalīs lay across the path of the British force which had been dispatched from Hamadān to prevent German and Turkish penetration of the Caucasus and seizure of the Baku oilfields. After some fighting between the Dj̲angalīs and the British on the Mand̲j̲īl-Ras̲h̲t road, the British signed an agreement with Mīrzā Kūc̲ik K̲h̲ān on 12 August 1918 whereby they recognized the latter's authority in Gīlān; in return, Mīrzā Kūc̲ik K̲h̲ān agreed to suspend hostilities against the British, expel his German and Turkish instructors, and release his remaining British hostages. This agreement caused a split between Mīrzā Kūc̲ik K̲h̲ān, who represented the more moderate element among the Dj̲angalīs, and the radicals led by Iḥsān Allāh K̲h̲ān, and this dissension enabled the Persian Government's Cossack troops temporarily to disperse the Dj̲angalī forces.

The second phase of the Dj̲angalī movement was marked by open Bolshevik support, which changed its whole character. On 18 May 1920 the Red fleet bombarded Enzeli, and Soviet troops occupied Ras̲h̲t, the capital of Gīlān; a new committee was formed, and on 5 June 1920 Mīrzā Kūc̲ik K̲h̲ān, styling himself the "representative of the Persian Socialist Soviet Republic proclaimed in the city of Ras̲h̲t", announced the establishment of the Soviet Republic of Gīlān. The Gīlān Soviet, which remained in power until the autumn of 1921, confiscated the estates of the big landowners and distributed them among the peasants, but met with no success in its attempts to organize the Persian peasants into independent local Communist groups.

By the terms of the Soviet-Iranian treaty of 26 February 1921, the Soviet Government renounced the imperialist policies of the former Czarist Government towards Persia, and on 8 September 1921 Soviet forces were withdrawn from Persia. Deprived of Soviet support, the Dj̲angalī movement collapsed when faced by strong Persian forces under the leadership of Riḍā K̲h̲ān (later Riḍā S̲h̲āh [q.v.]), and by October 1921 the rebellion was over. Mīrzā Kūc̲ik K̲h̲ān was captured and executed.

Bibliography: Gen. L. C. Dunsterville, The adventures of Dunsterforce, London 1920, index s.vv. Jangali and Kuchik Khan; M. Martchenko, Kutchuk Khan, in RMM, xl-xli (1920), 98-116; G. Ducrocq, La politique du gouvernement des

Soviets en Perse, in *RMM*, lii (1922), 84 ff.; G. Lenczowski, *Russia and the West in Iran, 1918-1948*, New York 1949, 16 ff., 54 ff.; N. S. Fatemi, *Diplomatic history of Persia 1917-1923*, New York 1952, 217 ff.; Ḥusayn Makkī, *Taʾrīkh-i bīst-sāla-yi Īrān*, i, Tehran 1323 A.H. solar/1944, 239, 308 ff., 319 ff. (biographical information on Mīrzā Kūčik Khān); E. H. Carr, *The Bolshevik revolution 1917-1923*, iii, London 1953, index *s.v.* Kuchik Khan; D. Geyer, *Die Sowjetunion und Iran*, Tübingen 1955. (R. M. SAVORY)

DJĀNIDS, name of the dynasty which ruled Bukhārā [*q.v.*] from 1007/1599 to 1199/1785. It was descended from Djān(ī) b. Yār Muḥammad, a prince of the house of the Khāns of Astrakhań (Tatar *Azhdarhān* and *Ashtarkhān*) who had fled from his homeland before the advancing Russians to Bukhārā around 963/1556. It was from this homeland of his that the dynasty was also called Ashtarkhānids (for genealogy cf. ČINGIZIDS).

Djān married Zahrā Khanīm, a sister of the Shaybānid ruler ʿAbd Allāh II b. Iskandar [*q.v.*]. On the latter's death in 1006/1598 the empire that he had founded rapidly crumbled, and it was then that the son of this marriage, Bāḳī Muḥammad, was able to establish himself in the territory at the core of the state around Bukhārā in 1007/1599 (for more detailed information see BUKHĀRĀ); he died in 1014/1605-6. The state was strengthened by Imām Ḳulī Khān (1027-53/1611-43?), who secured internal order by the cruellest of methods and, thanks to his religious leanings, enjoyed the favour of the dervishes. He finally retired to undertake the *ḥadjdj* (1060/1650).

The most significant ruler of the dynasty was ʿAbd al-ʿAzīz (1055-91/1645-80), who was also outstanding as a Muftī. After his death the authority of the dynasty sank rapidly. The local princes (Biy) became almost independent, and the Farghānā valley was separated off as a Khōḳand [*q.v.*] Khānate on its own. Abu 'l-Fayḍ (1123-60/1711-47) became a plaything in the hands of the amīral family of Mangit [*q.v.*], whose members often held the position of an *Atalīk*. From 1167/1753-4 it was the Mangits who exercised the actual power within the state. The last Djānid Abu 'l-Ghāzī (1171-99/1757-85) was only nominally Khān, rather like the Čingizids in the case of Tīmūr. Yet the first completely independent Mangit ruler (since 1199/1785) continued to be related in marriage to the Djānids.

Under the Djānids Bukhārā was one of the centres of Sunnī orthodoxy; its leading rôle in defensive struggles against Shīʿī Persia was politically significant also. Furthermore, the state constantly had to do battle with penetrations of the Ḳazakhs and of the Khāns of Khiwa (*e.g.*, in 1099/1688), and also withstood attempts on the part of the Mughal ruler Shāhdjahān [*q.v.*] in the first half of the 11th/17th century to regain the homeland of his ancestors. Through the rivalries of the Biys and the growing pressure of taxation, however, the agriculture of the state deteriorated more and more, and commerce took other paths. Literary expression was in Persian rather than in Özbeg, and it consisted essentially of works of a traditional stamp; yet these works, as also the historical writings of this period (in spite of much Russian pioneer work) have not yet been fully investigated. The architecture is greatly inferior to that of the Tīmūrids.

Bibliography: Storey, i/2, 2, 375-86, 1301 (since then also published: Amīn Bukhārī [Storey no. 508, 378 ff.], *ʿUbaydallāh-nāma*, trans. and annotated A. A. Semenov, Tāshkent 1957; and Muḥammad Yūsuf al-Munshī, *Tadhkira-yi Muḳīm Khān* [cf. Storey no. 509, 379 ff.]). Cf. further Abu 'l-Ghāzī Khān, i, 120 ff. For general treatises, see H. H. Howorth, *History of the Mongols*, ii/2, London 1880; R. Grousset, *L'empire des Steppes*, Paris 1939; P. P. Ivanov, *Očerki po istorii Sredney Azii* (Outlines of the History of Central Asia, 16th to the middle of the 19th century), Moscow 1958, 67-114; E. Sarkisyanz, *Geschichte der oriental. Völker Russlands bis 1917*, Munich 1960, 186-90; B. Spuler, in *Handbuch der Orientalistik*, v/5, Leiden 1961; see also BUKHĀRĀ. For dynastic genealogies see Zambaur, 273 (data in some instances open to question). (B. SPULER)

DJĀNĪK (CANİK), an area along the Black Sea between Bafra and Fatsa, including the mouths of the rivers Kîzîl and Yeshil Irmak, as well as the mountainous regions to the east. It is called after the Tsan (Georg. *čan*, compare Macdonald Kinneir, *Journey*, 282)—a tribe of the Laz—and it has a mild climate and fertile soil; consequently, it is relatively densely populated (between 50 and 100 people per sq. km.). Until recent times, the name was applied to the *sandjaḳ* of Samsun [*q.v.*], and is applied even today to the beautiful mountain forests of Djanik Dağlarî along the Black Sea coast from Samsun to Ordu.

Djānīk once belonged to the Turkish principality of the Djāndār-oghlu of Ḳasṭamūnī, and together with this, it was incorporated into the Ottoman Empire by Sulṭān Bāyazīd I. After Bāyazīd's defeat at Ankara in 1402, Djānīk was re-established by Tīmūr, but it was later conquered by Meḥemmed I, becoming a *liwā* of the *eyālet* of Siwas with Samsun (which—next to Trabzon—is the most important port on the Black Sea) for capital. In more recent times, it was a *sandjaḳ* of the *wilāyet* of Trabzon, with the *ḳaḍā*s Ṣamṣūn, Fatsa, Üniye, Terme, Čarshamba, and Bafra. Under the Turkish Republic, the greater part of Canik forms the *vilâyet* of Samsun.

Bibliography: D. M. Girard, *Un coin dè de l'Asie Mineure, le Djanik . . .*, in *Muséon*, N.S. viii, (1907), 100-71). Kātib Čelebi, *Djihān-nümā*, Istanbul 1145, 623 f.; V. Cuinet, *La Turquie d'Asie*, i, Paris 1890, 86 ff.; Ch. Samy-Bey Frascheri, *Ḳāmūs al-aʿlām (Dictionnaire universelle d'Histoire et de Géographie)*, iii, 1308/1891, 1762 f.; *Trabzon wilāyeti sālnāmesi*; E. Banse, *Die Türkei*, 87-9; v. Hammer, *GOR*, i, index in X, s.v.; Münedjdjimbashî, *Ṣaḥāʾif*, iii, 36; *İA*, iii, 25 (Besim Darkot). (FR. TAESCHNER)

DJĀNĪKLI ḤĀDJDJI ʿALĪ PASHA, Ottoman soldier and founder of a Derebey [*q.v.*] family. He was born in Istanbul in 1133/1720-21, the son of Aḥmed Agha, a ḳapîdjî-bashî at the Imperial palace. As a youth he accompanied his elder brother Suleymān Pasha to Djānīk, where he eventually succeeded him as ruler with the title, customary among the autonomous derebeys, of *muḥaṣṣil* [*q.v.*]. During the Russo-Turkish war of 1182/1768-1188/1774, he held a number of military commands. Serving first in Georgia, he was appointed in Djumādā II 1183/September-October 1769 to the staff of the Serʿasker of Moldavia, where he distinguished himself in the fighting against the Russians and took part in the battle of Khotin, narrowly escaping capture. As a reward he was given the rank of vizier. In 1188/1774 he led an expedition to the Crimea and in 1190/1776 was appointed Serʿasker of Kars. In the meantime he had been able to consolidate his authority in

Djānīk, overcoming or winning over such opposition as existed, and to extend his dominions eastwards. In 1185/1771 he was recognized as *Wālī* of Trebizond, where his brother Süleymān Pasha had preceded him. The province was assigned to him as a *mālikāne* [*q.v.*]. Within the next few years his holdings were extended to include Sivas and Erzurum.

On 3 Dhu 'l-Ḥidjdja 1191/2 January 1778 he was again appointed Serʿasker of the Crimea and given the command of an expeditionary force which, with naval support, was to threaten the peninsula. This plan came to nothing. ʿAlī Pasha now had to deal with his Anatolian rival the Čapanoghlu (see DEREBEY), who, at the instigation of his enemies in Istanbul, launched an attack against him. Deprived of his offices and of his vizierial rank, he fled in 1193/1779 to the Crimea, where he sought refuge with the Khan, Shāhīn Giray. In Shaʿbān 1195/August-September 1781, thanks to the mediation of the Khan, he was pardoned and reinstated, recovering the rank of vizier and the control of his dominions. In 1190/1776 he presented a memorandum to the government on the reasons for the Turkish defeat in the Russian war and, more generally, on the reforms that were needed in the Empire. The work of a man of action, it deals with practical problems in simple, direct, and sometimes forceful language, and is a remarkable document of its time. An edition is in preparation. ʿAlī Pasha died in Shaʿbān 1199/June-July 1785.

Bibliography: Djewdet, *Taʾrīkh*², iii, 144-6; *Sidjill-i ʿOthmānī*, iii, 548-9; İsmail Hakkı Uzunçarşılı, *Osmanlı tarihi*, iv/I, Ankara 1956, 447-51, 509-11, iv/II, 1959, 32-3. ʿAlī Pasha's memorandum is mentioned by Djewdet (*loc. cit.*) and is preserved in Upsala (a rather free paraphrase of parts of it will be found in M. Norberg, *Turkiska Rikets Annaler*, v, Hernösand 1822, 1425-43).

(B. LEWIS)

DJANNA, "Garden", is the term which, used antonomastically, usually describes, in the Ḳurʾān and in Muslim literature, the regions of the Beyond prepared for the elect, the "Companions of the right". *E.g.*: "These will be the Dwellers in the Garden where they will remain immortal as a reward for their deeds on earth" (Ḳurʾān, XLVI, 14). Other Ḳurʾānic terms will be considered later either as synonyms or as particular aspects of the "Garden": *ʿAdn* and *Djannāt ʿAdn*. (Eden, *e.g.*, LXI, 12), *Firdaws* ("Paradise", sg. *farādis*, cf. παράδεισος XXIII, 11), the Dwelling of Salvation or of Peace (*dār al-Salām*, VI, 127; X, 25), of Sojourn (*al-Muḳāma*), XXXV, 35), of the true Life (*al-Ḥayawān*, XXIX, 64), Garden of Retreat or of Refuge (*djannat al-Maʾwā*, LIII, 15), of Eternity or Immortality (*al-Khuld*, XXV, 15), Gardens of Delight (*djannat al-Naʿīm*, X, 9), etc. Following current usage, we will translate *Djanna* as "Paradise", and cite *Firdaws* in its transliterated form.

(A) EVIDENCE FROM THE ḲURʾĀN

The description of Paradise, the presentation of the relationship between its delights and the "good deeds" (*ṣāliḥāt*) performed on earth by the believer, together with the description of Hell (*nār*, *djahannam*) and the torments awaiting the damned, form one of the major themes of Ḳurʾānic preaching. These passages constitute a form of *ṭarīḳa khiṭābiyya* ("way of eloquence") with frequent and urgent evocations of the blessed life. The schools were to differ on the interpretation of these verses.

It would take too long to classify and enumerate here the descriptive details of the Ḳurʾān. The essentials may be found in Ṣubḥī al-Ṣāliḥ, *Les Délices et les Tourments de l'Au-Delà dans le Coran*, doctoral thesis (Sorbonne 1954), typescript, 18 ff. The following summary is derived from it:—Location: "the garden of Retreat" is in heaven, near the "Lotstree of the Boundary (*al-Muntahā*)" (LI, 22, LIII, 14-5). Two texts which suggest a prosopopœia (*taṣwīr*) foretell that Paradise "shall be brought near" to the righteous (LXXXI, 13), "close unto them" (L, 31). There is mention of the gates of Paradise, of their guards and of the greetings with which they met the elect (XXXIX, 73). The size of Paradise is equal to that of earth and heaven together (*e.g.*, III, 133, LVII, 21). There will be pleasant dwellings for the chosen (XIX, 72) and pavilions where Houris are kept (LV, 72). Lofty gardens (LXXXVIII, 10), leaping fountains (*passim*), streams of living water (id.), of milk, wine and honey (XLVII, 15), fountains scented with camphor (LXXXVI, 5) or ginger (id., 17), shady valleys, all sorts of delicious fruits (*passim*), of all seasons and without a thorn ....

The life of Paradise is described in concrete details, especially in the Sūras of the first Meccan period (the Sūras of the other periods also refer to it): regal pomp (LXXXIII, 24), costly robes, scents, bracelets; the texts lay emphasis on the visions of exquisite banquets, served in priceless vessels (e.g. LII, 24) by immortal youths "like separate pearls", with meats and fruits to the heart's desire (LII, 22, LV, 54, etc.), where scented wines, never-failing goblets of a limpid liquid (LXXXVII, 47), "delight for those who drink" (XLVII, 15), bring neither drunkenness (XXXVII, 46-7) nor rouse folly or quarrelling (LXXXVIII, 35). "Eat and drink in peace, as a reward for your deeds, reposing on rows of couches!" (LII, 19-20),—couches inlaid with gold or with precious stones (LXVI, 15), etc.

The elect will rejoice in the company of their parents, their wives and children who were faithful (XIII, 23, XXXVI, 56, XL, 8, XLIII, 70). They will praise their Lord (XXXV, 34), bending towards each other in love, conversing in joy and recalling the past (e.g. XV, 47, LII, 25, etc.). "Pure consorts" are promised (II, 25, III, 15, IV, 57). Tradition has identified these with the Houris (*ḥawrāʾ*, pl. *ḥūr*), beings from the Other World "with modest looks and large fine eyes" (XXXVII, 48), "like the hidden pearl" (LXVI, 23), "whom We have created in perfection and whom We have kept virgin" (id., 34-5) "so that they have been touched by neither man nor demon before" (LV, 72-4).

A happy life, without hurt or weariness, neither sorrow, fear nor shame (Ṣubḥī al-Ṣāliḥ 24) where every desire and every wish is fulfilled (XVI, 31, 39). "The Pious will there enjoy what they desire and We will grant yet more (*mazīd*)" (L, 35). This "more", like the "addition" (*ziyāda*) of, X 26, is usually associated with the "approval" (*riḍwān*) of God foretold to the elect (thus, III, 15 *in fine*). Now, "to believers, God has promised Gardens where rivers flow, where they will rest immortal. He has promised them goodly dwellings in the gardens of Eden. (But) the approval of God is greater. That will be the great Victory' (IX, 72). The fruits of it will be nearness to God. God will bring the elect near to his Throne (*passim*), and "on that Day some faces will shine in contemplating their Lord" (LXXV, 22-23). This last text, understood in the sense given in our translation, was to serve as the accepted scriptural foundation for the dominating thesis of the "vision of God" (*ruy'at Allāh*) in Paradise (see below).

Ṣubḥī al-Ṣāliḥ, 12 ff., emphasizes a certain progression in the Ḳur'ānic annunciation of Paradise: the Sūras of the first Meccan period describe it with numerous brief, concrete details "in an ardent, brief and elliptical style, with the symmetry of antithesis". During the second and third Meccan periods "the descriptive elements become (...) more summary". Later we find "a more abstract means of evocation". Well-known is verse XIII, 35, *Mat͟hal al-d͟janna*, "the picture of the Garden promised to the Pious"; the later allegorical interpretations were to base themselves on it, making the concrete descriptions of Paradise the representation of an inexpressible reality. And it was during the Medina period that stress was laid on the divine "approval", joy above all others.

Does the Ḳur'ān refer to different sorts of Gardens organized hierarchically, or should we understand the terms used as synonyms? Either hypothesis can be accepted, according to the commentators. Let us simply consider two verses: "For those who fear the (Judgment) seat of their Lord, there will be two Gardens" (LV, 46), and "this side of the two, two Gardens" (id., 62); certain *tafsīr*s render *dūn* not by "this side of" like M. Blachère (en deçà), but by "above". Should we assume four distinct Gardens? A single description applies to each pair; and the descriptions of both groups are identical except for infinitesimal differences.

Relationships may be established between the Muslim Paradise and some earlier eschatological traditions, particularly Persian and Judeo-Christian, cf. as an example the comparison proposed by Grimme and Tor Andrae between the Ḳur'ānic descriptions and certain Syriac hymns by the Deacon Ephrem (cf. Tor Andrae, *Der Ursprung des Islams und das Christentum*, Fr. tr., *Les origines de l'Islam et le Christianisme*, Paris 1955, 151 ff.).

(B) Principal elaborations

How has Muslim thought interpreted the data of the Ḳur'ān? Laying aside the copious S͟hīʿī exegeses, we shall consider:—(1) *ḥadīt͟h* and so-called traditional commentaries; (2) developments of the "science of *kalām*"; (3) *falsafa* and *taṣawwuf*; (4) efforts at synthesis; (5) reformers and contemporary modernists.

1. Traditions and traditional exegesis

The *ḥadīt͟h*s devoted to Paradise and the life therein are very numerous. Their dominating tendency is a literalness which emphasizes the reality and the detail of sensual pleasure. The value attributed to them is variable. While many are considered *ṣaḥīḥ* (authentic), others are called *ḍaʿīf* (doubtful). Certain of them derive not from the Prophet, but from a Companion or a Follower (*ḥadīt͟h mawḳūf* or *maḳṭūʿ*). Among the many *ṣaḥīḥ*, if some are *mutawātir* (ensured by many lines of transmission), many are *ʿazīz* (rare), little known and vouched for by only two authorities; or even *aḥād* (unique), by one only. The *Musnad* of Ibn Ḥanbal abounds with descriptions of the joys of the Beyond. The two *Ṣaḥīḥ* (al-Buk͟hārī and Muslim) and the four *Sunan* reproduce numerous traditions on the same subject; see in particular al-Buk͟hari, *K. Bad' al-K͟halḳ*, c. 8, *K. al-Riḳāḳ*, c. 51, and especially *K. al-Tafsīr*. Muslim's commentators are in the habit of grouping eleven principal *ḥadīt͟h* reproduced by him, on the subject of Paradise. For a restatement and discussion of these sources, see Ṣubḥī al-Ṣāliḥ, *op. cit.*, 43 ff. A typical example of traditional exegesis is given in the *tafsīr* of al-Ṭabarī. It may be considered together with the abundant contribution from the "preachers", themselves inspired by the old "story-tellers" (*ḳaṣṣāṣ*) and "weepers" (*bakkā'ūn*), who in their concern to catch the popular imagination multiplied all kinds of extravagant concrete details. On the basis of these diverse sources, there were extensive and varied developments. It is impossible to give an exhaustive survey. Here are some points of reference, borrowed from authoritative compilations of *ḥadīt͟h*, or from al-Ṭabarī, or al-S͟haʿrānī (*Muk͟htaṣar*), who himself gives a summary of al-Ḳurtubī, etc.

Location:—most commonly Paradise is placed under the Throne of God, above the highest heaven. It is usually distinguished from the Eden of Adam. Traditional accounts of the "ascension" (*miʿrād͟j*, [*q.v.*]) of the Prophet describe in detail his progress across the levels and degrees of Paradise.

The Entrance:—the different levels of Paradise are reached through eight principal gates, the respective dimensions and distances of which are described (the figures are intended to give an impression of limitless space). Each level is in turn generally divided into a hundred degrees. The highest level, which is either in the seventh heaven or, better (see below), beyond, is sometimes called Eden, sometimes *Firdaws*, etc. According to an often-quoted *ḥadīt͟h* (*e.g.*, al-Buk͟hārī, *D͟janā'iz*, 7), the key to open these doors has three webs: the proclamation of the divine Unity (*tawḥīd*); obedience to God; and abstention from all unlawful deeds. Others add "the swords of battle on the path of God". The Prophet Muḥammad will enter first. The poor believers will precede the rich. Angels will welcome the elect to the strains of an exquisite Arab melody—Arabic being the only language in Paradise. A banquet of welcome awaits them and each dish is described at length. They will be led to dwellings made ready for them, "accompanied by their wives, their children, by houris and by youths" (Ṣubḥī al-Ṣāliḥ, 121). Note: though Paradise already exists, the descriptions of a happy Beyond are always related to the resurrection of the body. It is not until after the resurrection, the "gathering" (*ḥas͟hr*) and the Judgment, that the "Halls Eternal" will receive their guests.

The representation of Paradise. An eternal Spring will spread an everlasting light. One day in Paradise is equal to a thousand days on earth. The stuff of which it is made is of musk, gold and silver. The palaces are of gold, silver, pearls, rubies, topazes, etc.: descriptions which may be taken metaphorically, but which the commentaries usually see as concrete realities. The stream al-Kawt͟har (cf. Ḳur'ān, CVIII, 1), with a scent more subtle than musk, flows over pearls and rubies between banks of gold. Four rivers, whose names are given, spring from mountains of musk, flow between banks of pearls and rubies, and carry to the elect milk "of an unvarying flavour", wine "a delight to those who drink", "clearest" honey (cf. al-Ṭabarī, Ibn Ḥanbal, etc.). There are references to four mountains (Uḥud, Sinai, Lebanon, Ḥaṣīb), to a large valley, innumerable plains, wonderful fruit-trees. It would take a horse a hundred years at the gallop to emerge from the shade of the banana-tree (al-Buk͟hārī, *Riḳāḳ*, 114; *Musnad*, *passim*). A single leaf from the "Lote-Tree of the Boundary" could shade the whole Community of the Faithful. In Paradise there are horses and camels "of dazzling whiteness", perhaps goats and sheep, and winged *Rafraf* made of red rubies will serve as the mounts of the elect (al-Tirmidhī, *Djanna*, 88, etc.).

The pleasures of Paradise. Here too there is the same concern for extravagant and concrete descriptions. Each of the elect will have the same stature as Adam (60 cubits by 7), and the same age, 33 years, as Jesus. Their robes and adornments will be marvellous. The delights of eating and drinking are the occasion for a surfeit of endless detail, as are also the hours of rest which follow them. The Ḳur'ānic evocation of the Houris calls forth endless commentaries (cf. Ṣubḥī al-Ṣāliḥ, 133-40) which celebrate the carnal joys, "a hundred times greater than earthly pleasure", that the elect will derive from their perpetual virginity. But the female Believers who have been admitted to Paradise through the merit of their good deeds will rank 70,000 times greater than the Houris in the eyes of God.—The whole of Paradise will be drenched in glorious music: the angels, the elect, the creatures of Paradise, the hills, trees and birds all joining in the universal melody.

The Vision of God. The most wonderful melody of all is the voice of God greeting the elect. Several traditions (*e.g.*, al-Shaʿrānī, *Mukhtaṣar*, 118; Ibn al-Ḳayyim al-Djawziyya, *Hādī 'l-arwāḥ*, 225) speak of the visit that the elect will pay "each Friday" to the Most High, at his invitation, and after they have chosen "a fine face" at the "*suḳ* of Recognition". The men following the Prophet, the women in the train of his daughter Fāṭima, will cross the heavens, pass by the celestial *Kaʿba* surrounded by praying angels, draw near to the "Guarded Table" (*al-lawḥ al-maḥfūẓ*) where the Pen writes the divine decrees, and finally emerge on to the "terrace of the Throne", which is of musk. "The veil of light lifts" and God appears to his guests "like the moon at the full" (Ṣubḥī al-Ṣāliḥ, 148). He greets each and everyone with "Peace be with you", and the angels serve them. There is supreme bliss which surpasses all other joy.

These traditional concepts and their concrete details permeate the mind of the Islamic peoples. In considering their implications two comments are necessary. They are put forward as a continuous extrapolation of sensual earthly pleasures. If the "Vision of God" is the highest reward, even so that too is described as a sensual ocular sight. However, the famous *ḥadīth*, both *ṣaḥīḥ* and *mutawātir*, "I have prepared for my faithful servants that which no eye has seen, no ear heard, no human heart ever felt", is constantly quoted. A literalist exposition explains it by multiplying every earthly joy tens of thousands of times. But the idea of "without common measure", indeed the idea of "another order" of reality or existence, also has its place. This is certainly one of the leitmotifs of Ibn al-Ḳayyim al-Djawziyya (14th century), the well-known disciple of Ibn Taymiyya, in his *Hādī al-arwāḥ*.

2. "The Science of kalām".

Among the *mutakallimūn*, three fundamental attitudes may be distinguished: a) Muʿtazilī schools (which influence the *tafsīr* of al-Zamakhsharī). Their principle of "reason as the criterion of the Law" does not favour an allegorical or spiritual interpretation, but in the sense of a more restrained literal exposition, which treats as figurative any statement or description deemed rationally unacceptable. Applications: the anthropomorphisms applied to God or to the acts of God are interpreted metaphorically; the sensual delights of Paradise, on the contrary, are taken literally, but with the exclusion of all the hyperbole and all the traditional wonders. The Houris are like beautiful women, the fruits of Paradise like earthly fruits, etc. The future heresiographers (al-Ashʿarī, al-Baghdādī, al-Shahrastānī, al-Khayyāṭ) were to note that Abu 'l-Hudhayl does indeed allow the "corporeal pleasures" (*djismiyyāt*) of Paradise but that, with the rest of the school, he associates with them "spiritual" delights (*rūḥāniyyāt*). All the Muʿtazila, on the other hand, deny the vision of God and, by an appropriate grammatical exegesis, give a different interpretation to the Ḳur'ānic verses which mention it. In the same way they reject the present existence of Paradise which, according to them, will only be created at the Resurrection.

b) The first Ashʿarī school asserts the reality (*ḥaḳīḳa*) of the attributes of God as expressed by the anthropomorphisms of the text, the reality of the descriptions of Paradise, those deriving from the principal traditions as well as those of the Ḳur'ān, and the reality of the ocular but not spatialized vision of God, "like the moon at the full". In his *Ibāna*, Cairo ed. 15, al-Ashʿarī calls this last the "highest bliss": a "spectacular", not a transforming, vision (Massignon). Paradise, which will be eternal, already exists. But the emphasis is laid on the incomparable and ineffable nature of the conditions of the future life. In conformity with one of the great Ashʿarī principles, all that is said of it must be taken literally but *bilā kayf*, "without asking how". Not only have the pleasures of Paradise no common measure with earthly joys, but they bear no analogy to them; they are of a different nature.

c) The later Ashʿarīs (called "modern" by Ibn Khaldūn), in whom there is often a mixture of Ashʿarism properly so called and Māturīdism, adopt a *ta'wīl* (interpretation) which is perhaps more influenced by the *Falāsifa* than by the Muʿtazila. The most notable example is Fakhr al-Dīn al-Rāzī (12th-13th centuries). The principles of his exegesis are stated in his *Kitāb asās al-taḳdīs* (Cairo ed. 1327), and applied at length in the famous *Mafātīḥ al-ghayb* (Cairo ed. 1321), still known as the "great *tafsīr*". A broad metaphorical interpretation is given of the descriptions of Paradise as well as of the divine attributes. While allowing, with the school, the reality of the Beings of the Beyond, al-Rāzī concludes, in conformity with a *ḥadīth* of Ibn ʿAbbās, that there is equivocality between the names which describe them and the same names which describe things on earth (*Mafātīḥ*, viii, 280; cf. Ṣubḥī al-Ṣāliḥ, 245 ff.). He does not deny the sensual rewards of Paradise, the luxury, the feasts, the carnal relations with the Houris, but he underlines the "without asking how", and insists upon "the glorious divine presence which impregnates the soul with sanctity and spirituality" (viii, 281; tr. Ṣubḥī al-Ṣāliḥ).

A disputed question in the Kalām: is Paradise, especially under its name of Eden, or the Garden of Eden, the Eden where God placed Adam and Eve? The Muʿtazilī al-Djubbā'ī, who was at one time the teacher of al-Ashʿarī, placed Eden in the seventh heaven. A later opinion, which is supported by al-Iṣfahānī and which claims to follow Hanafī-Māturīdīs, considers the Eden of Adam an earthly garden, distinct from the heavenly Paradise. The commentaries which distinguish the two Edens in this way usually place Paradise above the seventh heaven.

One last detail. Some hierarchical plans ("stages") of Paradise are often allowed; but there was no consensus on the order of enumeration. A *ḥadīth* of Ibn ʿAbbās proposes: (1) (the highest circle) the dwelling of Majesty, (2) of Peace, (3) the garden of Eden, (4) of Refuge (or "Retreat"), (5) of Immortality, (6) of the *Firdaws*, (7) of Delights.—But in other texts the *Firdaws* is put at the summit; and in others again Eden. Certain opinions, less popular, define only four "dwellings" or gardens, and place Eden on the level of the fourth heaven. But it is generally accepted that, beyond the seventh heaven (or simply the highest heaven), and thus not cosmically located, Paradise, whether or not divided into plans or hierarchical divisions, has above it only the Stool (*kursī*) and the Throne (*ʿarsh*) of the Most High God. (See below the summary by al-Bādjūrī).

3. Falsafa and taṣawwuf.

Between al-Ashʿarī, who follows Ibn Ḥanbal, and the *tafsīr* of Fakhr al-Dīn al-Rāzī, the Hellenistic *falsafa*, during the course of these controversies, exerted some influence on the school. For the "philosophers", the future life begins, not with the Resurrection, but with the individual death; and the human soul separated from its body will know, in accordance with its nature, only intelligible joys. Ibn Sīnā in his exoteric works is careful not to deny the Resurrection; the same is true of Ibn Rushd, who, at the conclusion of the *Tahāfut al-tahāfut*, confines himself to declaring his respect for the prophetic teaching. But everything is determined by the conception of prophecy in question. In his "esoteric" *Risāla adḥawiyya fī amr al-maʿād* (ed. S. Dunyā, Cairo 1949), Ibn Sīnā clearly suggests that the Resurrection must be taken as a lesson meant for the people; the wise man must understand it as a symbol or allegory, for "opposed to the true happiness of man is the existence of his soul in the body, and (. . .) corporeal pleasures are different from true pleasures, and to return to the body would be a punishment for the soul" (53). Henceforth, in its deepest reality, the life of Paradise will be that of intelligible substances united with the Active Intellect and the Universal Intellect in which, as in a clear mirror, will shine the supreme Divine Lights. —Is then the apparent meaning of the Ḳurʾānic descriptions totally ignored? No. They are of value, in their literalness, for the "weak-minded" (*buhl*) who, although they have observed God's commandments on earth, will be incapable of rising to the life of pure intelligence. They will be experienced, in the strict sense, not as sensual delights, but as pleasures of the imagination, thanks to the heavenly Bodies (cf. *Nadjāt*, 2nd Cairo ed. 1357/1938, 298; see also *Ishārāt*, ed. Forget, Leiden 1892, 196 § 2; Ibn Sīnā, in order to put forward this opinion, takes shelter behind the authority of "certain teachers").

Avicenna's influence marks a break in the history of *taṣawwuf*. The first Ṣūfīs took Ḳurʾānic teaching literally, but focussed their hopes on the supreme bliss and reward, the vision of God. Well-known is the allegorical act of Rābiʿa, who wanted "to burn Paradise" (and "drown Hell") so that God might be loved for Himself alone and not for His rewards (and feared for Himself alone and not for His punishments). In some famous texts, al-Bisṭāmī objects to the "market of images" (the *sūḳ* of the traditional exegesis where the elect choose "a fine face" for "the visit on Friday"), and proclaims: "If in Paradise I were prevented from meeting Him, were it only for an instant, I would make life intolerable for the elect of Paradise" (cf. L. Massignon, *Lexique technique*, Paris 1954, 253). For al-Ḥallādj everything is turned towards the *ruyʾat Allāh*, dazzling but intermittent, in which the elect find happiness only "after the event".—Characteristic is the attitude of al-Muḥāsibī, of whom certain texts transpose the promised bliss into spiritual values, whilst his *Kitāb al-tawahhum*, in order to encourage popular piety, emphasizes the sensual and carnal descriptions.

The later Ṣūfīs took care not to remove the sensual character of the joys of Paradise, but they developed, often extensively, the "superior" spiritual sense, revealed by the *kashf* ("unveiling"). The most remarkable presentation is that of Ibn ʿArabī in his *al-Futūḥāt al-Makkiyya*. Paradise is an "abode of Life", *dār al-Ḥayawān*, overflowing with both sensual and spiritual joys. In *Futūḥāt*, i, 353 ff., he enumerates three Gardens or Paradises: "the Garden of the Exception" for children who died before attaining the age of reason, the *amentes*, the righteous who have not received the revealed Law, "and those for whom God destines it"; "the Garden of Inheritance" into which the souls in the "Exception" and the believers who have been punished for a time in Gehenna may enter; and lastly "the Garden of Works" where believers will be rewarded for their good deeds. This last is in turn subdivided into eight Gardens, each comprising a hundred degrees. The highest Garden is Eden (preceded by the *Firdaws*); and the highest degree of Eden, *al-Maʾwā*, is reserved for the Prophet (ii, 96). The second volume of the *Futūḥāt* takes up the traditional descriptions and gives a commentary based on distinctions between desire, pleasure and will. The eschatology of Ibn ʿArabī has been briefly summarized by Ṣubḥī al-Ṣāliḥ, 288 ff., and analysed in detail by Asín Palacios, *La escatalogia musulmana en la Divina Comedia*, Madrid-Granada 1943, 230 ff. and references given there. See particularly the diagrams reproduced on pp. 233, 262, 264, where the gardens of Paradise are drawn in concentric and ascending levels. Another representation (ibid., 235) in a pyramid of eight levels has been suggested on the basis of the *Maʿrifat-nāma* of Ibrāhīm Ḥakkī, studied by Carra de Vaux (*Fragments d'eschatologie musulmane*, Brussels 1895).

If we refer to *Futūḥāt* i, 353, it appears that the concrete eschatological descriptions of Ibn ʿArabī may all bear an allegorical meaning; and that they refer, not to two distinct Paradises, "earthly" and "heavenly", as Asín Palacios suggests, but to one single place of delights in which these two aspects join to make one: an application of the gnostic thesis of the author, which was developed in the *Fuṣūṣ al-Ḥikam* (Cairo ed. 1365/1946) where the world of the created being is the manifestation *ad extra* of the transcendent God. A text attributed to Ibn ʿArabī, but which is more probably from al-Ḳāshānī (cf. Ṣubḥī al-Ṣāliḥ, 312) gives to the Ḳurʾānic texts themselves an interpretation which is very spiritual and uses a very Avicennian terminology: where the "lofty beds" are the degrees of perfection, the brocade lining is the inward aspect of the soul, the Houris the heavenly Spirits.

4. Two essays in synthesis.

The *falāsifa* on one side and the many Ṣūfīs on the other were regarded with mistrust and often opposed by the official teaching. Nevertheless their influence was effective. The expansion of *Ṭarīḳas* ("brotherhoods") spread throughout the masses many Ṣūfī interpretations, sometimes but not always mixed with "philosophical" glosses. This resulted in some attempts at synthesis, clearly concerned to maintain the values of the faith. We will consider two of them.

Al-Ghazzālī.—The most important synthesis is that by Abū Ḥāmid al-Ghazzālī (earlier therefore than Ibn ʿArabī), in which are united the traditional currents, *kalām, falsafa* and *taṣawwuf*. In the *Iḳtiṣād* and the *Iḥyā'*, al-Ghazzālī defends the Ashʿarī thesis of the vision of God. The *Kitāb al-mawt wa-mā baʿdahu* of the last quarter of the *Iḥyā'* (Cairo ed. 1352/1933, iv, 381-468) reproduces extensively *ḥadīth* and traditional texts which describe the sensual pleasures and joys of Paradise. But the *Maḳsad al-asnā* (Cairo ed., n.d.), without rejecting them, insists on the superiority of spiritual bliss. Paradise is a "medium of bliss" of which only images are revealed to us. There is the same doctrine in *Mīzān al-ʿamal* (cf. tr. Ḥikmat Hashīm 5-6): it is because the pleasures of Paradise "are incomprehensible to the understanding of the commonalty of men" that they "assimilate them to the sensual pleasures which they know". Here we are very close to the theses of Ibn Sīnā. Al-Ghazzālī, however, differs radically from the "philosopher" in his teaching of the reality of the resurrection of the body. His own personal ideas seem to take shape as follows: the believers who can only conceive of sensual and material happiness will enjoy the pleasures of Paradise in the flesh; others will delight in imaginative pleasures; and others again, "the holy and the initiated (*ʿārifūn*)" will enjoy superior delights, intellectual and spiritual, which alone can satisfy them and of which the sensual delights described in the Law are only the image. Elsewhere the possibility is not ruled out that some of the elect may share in the three kinds of joy at the same time (cf. *Arbaʿīn*, 40, and Ṣubḥī al-Ṣāliḥ, 286).

An elementary manual of kalām.—The popular treatise on *kalām* by al-Bādjūrī (18th-19th centuries, *Ḥāshiya ... ʿalā Djawharat al-tawḥīd*, Cairo ed. 1352/1934), so often taught in the great mosques and the centres of the brotherhoods, contains only some sober observations on the subject of Paradise. Throughout his work al-Bādjūrī faithfully follows the traditional Ashʿarī line; reality in the literal sense of the texts, but *bilā kayf*, "without asking how"; he is sometimes not averse from admitting a double meaning, literal but also allegorical, and is receptive to Ṣūfī influences. He does not treat in detail the question of paradisiacal rewards, and confines himself to noting that "the whole of Paradise is abundantly supplied with all sorts of delights" (107). He centres his comments on the existence and the structure of the Garden. Existence: (1) Paradise has already been created (contrary to Muʿtazilī opinion), and the Eden of Adam and Eve is identified with the Dwelling Beyond; (2) it is an eternal abode which will never end (contrary to the Djahmīs).—Structure: three hypotheses are admitted, and al-Bādjūrī draws no conclusion (id.): (1) Paradise will consist of seven parts (and not of eight as proposed by Ibn ʿArabī), concentric and ascending circles. The Highest, which is in the centre, is the *Firdaws*, where the rivers part; and Eden comes in the second place; (2) four Gardens, according to the Ḳur'ān, LV, 46 and 62, which are named in ascending order: Delights, Refuge, Eden, *Firdaws*; (3) a single Abode to which the seven designations may be applied, each underlining one of its qualities.

5. Reformers and contemporary modernists (cf. Ṣubḥī al-Ṣāliḥ, Vth part.).

Muḥammad ʿAbduh (*Risālat al-tawḥīd*, Cairo 1353H., 203-4 on the "vision of God", *Tafsīr Djuz' ʿamma* ...., a commentary on the thirtieth part of the Ḳur'ān or the "thin suras", 1st ed., Cairo 1322/1904; an article from the *Manār*). The vision of God is possible, but is not of the same nature as an ocular vision on earth; it is by transforming their visual faculty that God will reveal himself to His elect. The literal, descriptive sense (localization and pleasures of Paradise) is upheld but soberly explained. The principle of *bilā kayf* is reaffirmed, especially on the subject of the joys dispensed by the Houris. Let us note finally that a critique of traditional sources is adumbrated. For Muḥammad ʿAbduh, the *ḥadīths*, even if *ṣaḥīḥ*, may only be retained if they are *mutawātir*, warranted by many lines of transmission. This principle leads him to reject the hyperboles of many literalist descriptions.

Rashīd Riḍā and his great *Tafsīr al-Manār*.—This important differentiation between the *ḥadīths* is taken up again and elaborated, even to the point of an internal criticism of certain *matn* (texts) of the traditions. Thus Rashīd Riḍā rejects as inauthentic those which promise to the elect Houris in abundance, and he refers to a *ḥadīth* reproduced by al-Bukhārī and Muslim, which awards to everyone in Paradise his earthly wife and a single Houri. The descriptions abounding in hyperbolical literalism are, he says, mistaken in not considering the spirit of the Arabic language, which requires that all anthropomorphisms be interpreted metaphorically. We should strive to understand the inner spirit of the Ḳur'ān which teaches both sensual and spiritual delights, but which places the second far above the former. For Rashīd Riḍā, the authentic *ḥadīth par excellence* is that which defines the blessed life as "that which no eye has seen, no ear heard" .... He criticizes in turn the descriptive hyperboles of many "literalists", the excessively rationalist principle of the Muʿtazila, the allegorism of the Ṣūfīs, and he attacks by name Ibn ʿArabī. Only the attempt to understand the actual text of the Ḳur'ān counts. If the spiritual life prevails over the life of the flesh, if the delights of Paradise are both sensual and intelligible, it is because that is the teaching of the Book. The vision of God is possible (contrary to the Muʿtazila) but "it is not a fundamental basis of the Islamic faith" (see Ṣubḥī al-Ṣāliḥ, 325-35, and ref. *Tafsīr al-Manār*).

In conclusion it may be useful to mention with M. Ṣubḥī al-Ṣāliḥ "the philological exegesis" presented by ʿAbd al-Ḳādir al-Maghribī who, in 1920, wrote a commentary on the twenty-ninth section of the Ḳur'ān, *djuz' Tabārak* (reissued in the work *ʿAlā hāmish al-Tafsīr*, Cairo n.d.). The author dismisses the literalist exegesis which presents the life of the Beyond in purely sensual terms: that would be to fail to take account of the incomparable power of expression of the text; he also dismisses the purely spiritual allegorical exegesis, for it derives only from subjective views. He requires an exegesis founded on the laws of the Arabic language, its eloquence and its use of metaphor. The terms describing the delights of Paradise aim at evoking the grandest possible conception of joy. We should then understand these terms literally, but as designating, in the Other World, concrete realities intrinsically different from those here below. It is thus we should understand the fleshly joys promised to the elect: consequently, the feasts of Paradise are by no means intended for the satisfaction of sensuality, and the delights offered by the Houris represent a reality inaccessible to human understanding, a noble pleasure in which the female believers will share.—The author adds that his exegesis is only one of the interpretations possible, and that a Muslim is free to prefer another.

The Egyptians Sayyid al-Ḳuṭb, Amīn al-Khūlī, and especially Muḥammad Aḥmad Khalaf Allāh, a disciple of the former, go even further than the *shaykh* al-Maghribī in the study of the "literary genres" of the Ḳurʾān. Azharī circles displayed violent opposition towards Dr. Khalaf Allāh.

In conclusion: the official teaching has never confirmed the exclusively allegorical and spiritual interpretations of Ḳurʾānic verse and *ḥadīth* concerning Paradise. Throughout the centuries two trends have co-existed: (1) the so-called traditional exegesis, which accepts many traditions and which endlessly multiplies concrete details about the life of Paradise and its sensual pleasures; (2) the attempts of *kalām*, of al-Ghazzālī, the Salafiyya reformers, etc., who retain indeed the obvious literal meaning of the Ḳurʾānic text, but take care not to amplify it; who insist on the intrinsic difference between the realities of the Beyond and earthly realities, emphasizing the primacy of the spiritual over the carnal order. Even without mentioning the "philological" exegesis of al-Maghribī, we may say that the attempts of Muḥammad ʿAbduh and of Rashīd Riḍā to perform an internal critique of the traditions may well open new perspectives to our knowledge of the *tafsīr*.

Bibliography: in the article. (L. Gardet)

DJANNĀBA, (Djannābā, Djunnāba), arabicized forms of Ganāfa, a town and port in the VIIth *ustān* (Fārs) of Persia. The name is a corruption of *Gand-āb*, 'stinking water', so called because of the bad quality of its water (see Ibn al-Balkhī, *Fārs-nāma*, 149 and Ḥamd Allāh Mustawfī, *Nuzha*, 130). Ganāfa is situated on the coast of the Persian Gulf in Lat. 29° 35′ N. and Long. 50° 31′ E. In former times it was an important manufacturing centre where cloths of good quality were produced. Pearl-fishing was also carried on from there. It was the birthplace of Abū Sulaymān al-Djannābī [*q.v.*], the well-known Ḳarmaṭian *dāʿī*. According to the *Ḥudūd al-ʿĀlam* (127), it was a large and flourishing town in the 4th/10th century. An oil pipe-line from the Gač Sarān oilfield (which lies 70 km. to the north-east) to the island of Khārag [*q.v.*], where tankers of the largest size will be loaded, is shortly to be constructed; it will enter the sea just to the north-west of Ganāfa. The town is connected with Būshahr [*q.v.*] by a dry weather road 156 km. in length. Agriculture, fishing and shipping repairs are carried out at Ganāfa, the population of which in 1951 was 2,235. The modern form of the name is Ganāveh.

Bibliography: in addition to the references in the text: *BGA*, *passim*: Yāḳūt, ii, 122; Fuch, *De Nino Urbe*, Lipsiae 1845, 10; Le Strange, 273-4, 296; P. Schwarz, *Iran im Mittelalter n. den Arab. Geogr.*, ii, 61, 63, 86; iii, 125-7: Monteith, in *JRGS*, 1857, 108: Tomaschek, *Die Küstenfahrt Nearchs* = *SBAk.Wien*, cxxl/8, 67; Razmārā and Nawtāsh, *Farhang-i djughrāfiyā-yi Īrān*, vii, 204. (L. Lockhart)

AL-DJANNĀBĪ, Abū Muḥammad Muṣṭafā b. Ḥasan b. Sinan al-Ḥusaynī al-Hāshimī, 10th/16th-century author of an Arabic historical work dealing with eighty-two Muslim dynasties in as many chapters, entitled *al-ʿAylam al-zākhir fī aḥwāl al-awāʾil wa'l-awākhir*, usually called *Taʾrīkh al-Djannābī*. A Turkish translation and abridgment were prepared by the author himself. Whether the accepted form of the *makhlaṣ* is correct or should be rather Djanābī cannot be decided in the absence of information as to whence it was derived. Al-Djannābī came from a distinguished Amasya family, studied and taught in various cities, and was for a short time judge of Aleppo. His younger brother was the poet Suʿūdī. Both died in the same year 999/1590.

Bibliography: Brockelmann, II, 387, S II, 411 f., III, 1281; *ʿOthmānli müellifleri*, iii, 40; F. Babinger, 108 f. (F. Rosenthal)

AL-DJANNĀBĪ, Abū Saʿīd Ḥasan b. Bahrām, was the founder of Ḳarmaṭian power in East Arabia. Born at Djannāba on the Fārs coast, he is said to have become a flour merchant at Baṣra. He was crippled on the left side. His first mission as a Ḳarmaṭian is said to have been as a *dāʿī* in southern Īrān, where he had to go into hiding from the authorities. He was then sent to (mainland) Baḥrayn, where he married into a prominent family and won followers rapidly, perhaps among a group formerly attached to the line of Ibn-al-Ḥanafiyya.

We find that in 286/899 he had subjected a large part of Baḥrayn and taken Ḳaṭīf. In 287 his partisans were in strength around Hadjar, the capital of Baḥrayn, and were approaching Baṣra. The Caliph Muʿtaḍid sent an army of 2,000 men against them, to which were added many volunteers. This army was cut to pieces; its general was taken prisoner, then set at liberty; the other prisoners were killed. About 290/903 Abū Saʿīd took Hadjar after a long siege, by cutting off the water supply; he then subjected Yamāma and invaded ʿUmān. In 300 his troops again invaded the district of Baṣra, but in 301/913 he was murdered by a slave, together with several of his high officers.

He left seven sons, of whom Saʿīd succeeded, to be replaced later by the youngest, the famous Abū Ṭāhir [see art. below]. Abū Saʿīd was venerated after his death. His partisans believed that he would return; a horse was always kept saddled at the door of his tomb. The Ḳarmaṭians of Baḥrayn called themselves Abū Saʿīdīs after him, and attributed to him the later constitution of their republic.

Bibliography: The sources are presented and in part translated in Silvestre de Sacy, *Exposé de la religion des Druzes*, Paris 1838, i, ccxi ff., and M. J. de Goeje, *Mémoire sur les Carmathes du Bahraïn et les Fatimides*[2], Leiden 1886, 31-47, 69-75. Add Masʿūdī, *Tanbīh*, transl. Carra de Vaux, 498-501. Important corrections are in Bernard Lewis, *Origins of Ismāʿīlism*, Cambridge 1940 (see index).

(B. Carra de Vaux-[M. G. S. Hodgson)

AL-DJANNĀBĪ, Abū Ṭāhir. Abū Ṭāhir Sulaymān b. Abī Saʿīd al-Ḥasan was one of the most famous chiefs of the small Ḳarmaṭian state of Baḥrayn and, for several years, the terror of the pilgrims and of the inhabitants of lower ʿIrāḳ. On the death of Abū Saʿīd [see art. above] in 301/913-4, or 300/912-3 according to al-Masʿūdī, his son Saʿīd succeeded him and governed with a council of notables (al-ʿIḳdāniyya). For some time the Ḳarmaṭians refrained from troubling the caliphate and were even on good terms with the government of the vizier ʿAlī b. ʿĪsā, who granted them privileges such as the use of the port of Sīrāf, in 304/916-7. In 307/919-20, however, there was an attack on Baṣra to support a Fāṭimid attempt against Egypt, according to Ibn Khaldūn (*ʿIbar*, iv, 89). At this time Abū Ṭāhir was not personally at the head of affairs, since he was still too young, having been born in Ramaḍān 294/June-July 907, and he seems not to have wielded any power before 311/923-4 when he appears, although aged then no more than 16, in Rabīʿ II/July-August 923, as commander of the Ḳarmaṭians who entered Baṣra by surprise at night. Escalading the walls, they established themselves in the town before any resistance could be organized, and spent seventeen days in pillage and massacre. As early as 305/917-8, however, Saʿīd, whom the sources depict as lacking energy and authority, had been deposed, perhaps at the instigation of the Fāṭimid ʿUbayd Allāh. The latter, according to Ibn Khaldūn, sent a letter of investiture to Abū Ṭāhir, whose reign is by some sources dated from this year.

The attack against Baṣra in 311/923-4 coincided with the removal of the vizier ʿAlī b. ʿĪsā whom his enemies represented as the ally of the Ḳarmaṭians. At the end of the same year Abū Ṭāhir attacked the pilgrim caravan returning from Mecca to al-Habīr, and took prisoner the amīr Abu 'l-Haydjāʾ ʿAbd Allāh b. Ḥamdān, who had been charged with the protection of the caravan. Abu 'l-Haydjāʾ and the prisoners were released some time afterwards at the same time as an envoy from Abū Ṭāhir arrived at Baghdād demanding the cession of Baṣra, Ahwāz and even other territories. This claim was rejected and, in 312/924-5, the pilgrims were again attacked and Kūfa was sacked by Abū Ṭāhir. In 315/927-8, having again plundered Kūfa, Abū Ṭāhir gained a great victory over the army sent against him by the caliph and commanded by Yūsuf b. Abi 'l-Sādj [*q.v.*], whom he captured and who was put to death in Dhu 'l-Ḳaʿda 315/January 928 in the course of the operations that followed. Advancing up the Euphrates, Abū Ṭāhir arrived at Anbār, crossed the river with the intention of marching on Baghdād, but was stopped by the army of Muʾnis [*q.v.*] thanks to the destruction, at the instigation of Abu 'l-Haydjāʾ, of the bridge on the Nahr Zubāra. He thereupon turned north and reached Raḥba, Ḳarḳīsiyyā and Raḳḳa, holding the inhabitants to ransom. Some detachments penetrated as far as Sindjār, Raʾs ʿAyn and Naṣībīn. Abū Ṭāhir did not return to Baḥrayn until the beginning of 317/February-March 929, when he had built a *dār al-hidjra* called al-Muʾminiyya (it is known that the Ḳarmaṭians called themselves *muʾminūn*), near al-Aḥsā, his capital.

The most sensational act of Abū Ṭāhir was his expedition against Mecca where the pilgrims were gathered and where he arrived on 7 Dhu 'l-Ḥidjdja 317/11 January 930. He killed the pilgrims in the mosque, removed everything of value in the holy house, and took away the Black Stone, having spent eight days in pillage and massacre. In 318/930 he possessed himself of ʿUmān. In 319/931 he was thought to be reattempting the conquest of ʿIrāḳ, but the Ḳarmaṭians went no futher than Kūfa where they remained for 25 days of pillage. According to De Goeje, the expedition was put off on account of the troubles which broke out in the Ḳarmaṭian state following the enthronement as *Mahdī* of an impostor set up by the vizier Ibn Sanbar and for some time recognized by Abū Ṭāhir himself (see below).

Since the pilgrimage had become impossible and the operations of Abū Ṭāhir were continuing (against Sīnīz in 321, and against Tawwadj in 322, that is to say against the coast of Fārs), the chamberlain of the caliph al-Rāḍī, Muḥammad b. Yāḳūt, in 322/934 entered into negotiations with Abū Ṭāhir for his recognition of the authority of the caliphate, the cessation of his interference with the pilgrims, and the return of the Black Stone; in return he would receive official investiture for the regions which he possessed or had conquered. Abū Ṭāhir refused to restore the Black Stone, but agreed to cease obstructing the pilgrims and offered to have the *khuṭba* read in the name of the caliph if he were allowed free use of the port of Baṣra. However, in 323/935 he again attacked the pilgrimage, defeated the caliphal troops between Kūfa and Ḳādisiyya, and occupied Kūfa for everal days before returning to Baḥrayn. Fresh negotiations were commenced in 325/937, by the *amīr al-umarāʾ* Ibn Rāʾiḳ, with Abū Ṭāhir who had again entered Kūfa. In reply to the demand of the Ḳarmaṭian, who wanted the caliph to give him 120,000 dinars per year in silver and supplies, Ibn Rāʾiḳ proposed that Abū Ṭāhir and his troops should consider themselves as enrolled in the service of the caliph and that this sum be considered as a salary. No agreement was signed. Finally, in 327/939, thanks to an ʿAlid of Kūfa, the pilgrimage was able to resume in consideration of a tribute of 25,000 (or 120,000) dinars and a protection due (*khifāra*) which was regularly levied by the Ḳarmaṭians on the pilgrims; this did not, however in any way prevent incursions into the south of ʿIrāḳ.

Abū Ṭāhir died of smallpox at the age of 38 in 332/943-4, and was succeeded by his brother Aḥmad.

The activity of Abū Ṭāhir raises questions as to what were his relations with Ismāʿīlism, whether he really considered the Fāṭimid caliph ʿUbayd Allāh to be the awaited *imām* and obeyed him, and whether it was at his secret request that he carried off the Black Stone and launched attacks against ʿAbbāsid territory. The question of the differences and the common ground between Ḳarmaṭians and Ismāʿīlīs, dealt with by Ivanow, *Ismaili tradition concerning the rise of the Fatimids*, 69 ff., and *Ismailis and Qarmatians* in *JBBRAS*, 1940, 78 ff., and B. Lewis, *The origins of Ismāʿīlism*, Cambridge 1940, ch. iii on the Ḳarmaṭians of Baḥrayn and particularly the Ḳarmaṭians and the Fāṭimids, will not be examined here; this account is restricted to a review of the facts concerning the history of Abū Ṭāhir. There are documents as much in favour of an adherence to the Fāṭimid caliphs as against (see the texts in B. Lewis, *op. cit.*). In their work on ʿUbayd Allāh al-Mahdī Ḥ. Ibrāhīm Ḥasan and T. Aḥmad Sharaf incline to the idea of secret and close relations between Abū Ṭāhir and the first Fāṭimid caliph, and a real subordination of the former to the latter (cf. also De Goeje, *passim*). Many sources indicate that Abū Ṭāhir recognized ʿUbayd Allāh as the *mahdī*, that he sent him the *khums*, and that he was his agent in Baḥrayn (see the declarations of the Ḳarmaṭian interrogated by ʿAlī b. ʿĪsā and of the secretary of Yūsuf b. Abi 'l-Sādj in Miskawayh, i, 167, 181, and cf. B. Lewis, *op. cit.*). Al-Dhahabī cites the words of Abū Ṭāhir : *Anā al-dāʿī ilā 'l-mahdī* (Ḥ. Ibrāhīm Ḥasan, 277). Abu 'l-Maḥāsin declares that he recognized ʿUbayd Allāh as *mahdī* on his return from Raḥba in 317/929; but the letter of ʿUbayd Allāh to Abū Ṭāhir which is cited in support of this theory, extracts from which are given by al-Baghdādī, is most probably apocryphal. Moreover, Abū Ṭāhir cannot have been very convinced of the legitimacy of ʿUbayd Allāh, since he considered as the awaited *imām* an impostor of Persian origin, the very name of whom varies in the sources, and enthroned him as such (it is said that he even proclaimed him as God). The attitude of Abū Ṭāhir is comprehensible if, as Ivanow says, the Fāṭimids were not regarded as *imām*s by the Ḳarmaṭians. Moreover, how did Abū Ṭāhir himself appear in the eyes of the Ḳarmaṭians? If we are to believe al-Dhahabī, some considered him as Prophet, some as the Messiah, some as the *Mahdī* himself, some as "he who prepares the way for the Mahdī" (*al-mumahhid ila 'l-mahdī*). At all events there is a curious mixture of phantasmagoria and realism about him, for he did not hesitate to put to death the impostor in whom he had believed when certain of the latter's acts had opened his eyes, and his politics towards the ʿAbbāsids is further evidence of realism.

It does not appear that the attacks of Abū Ṭāhir against the caliphal territories, whether Baṣra, Kūfa, etc., or the south-west region of Persia, could have had as their precise purpose to help the Fāṭimid caliphate in its attempts against Egypt; but everything which could weaken the ʿAbbāsid caliphate, to which Abū Ṭāhir as a Ḳarmaṭian was violently hostile, would help the Fāṭimids. Nevertheless he agreed to negotiate with the ʿAbbāsid caliphate, as has been shown, to obtain certain advantages, while keeping up relations with their enemies, such as the Fāṭimids, the Grand Mobed Isfandiyār, or the Daylamid Mardāwīdj who supported him, or the Barīdī, who offered him sumptuous presents on the occasion of the birth of his son and who took refuge with him for a time. In all, it could be said that if Abū Ṭāhir did assist the Fāṭimids, this was perhaps not on account of absolute devotion to their cause; he was carrying out a very personal policy. In his attitude to the practices and dogmas of Islam one must recognize, even making allowances for the exaggerations and slanders of the Sunnī authors, an extraordinary violence, which Ivanow explains (in *JBBRAS*, 1940, 82) by saying that the Ḳarmaṭians "regarded themselves as the followers of a new religion, revealed to supersede the now obsolete religion of Islam", and he compares this attitude with that of the original Islamic community in the face of Christianity and Judaism both of which refused to recognize their legitimate continuation by Islam. But his violent acts, even if the removal of the Black Stone was executed at the instance of ʿUbayd Allāh, as Defrémery and later De Goeje thought, could not have been openly approved by the caliph who was aspiring to supplant the ʿAbbāsids (cf. Ḥ. Ibrāhīm Ḥasan, 225-6).

Bibliography: The basic work remains that of De Goeje, *Mémoire sur les Carmathes du Bahraïn et les Fatimides*², Leiden 1886, where reference will be found to the works of historians and geographers and other authors, published or in manuscript. Of editions and translations later than this work: Miskawayh, i, 33-4, 121, 139, 167, 181 ff., 201, 330, 367; ii, 55 (with a long passage from al-Dhahabī on the history of the impostor in a footnote); Masʿūdī, *Tanbīh*, tr. Carra de Vaux, 149, 483, 484-92, 495-7; idem, *Murūdj*, viii, 285-6; Abu 'l-Maḥāsin, *Nudjūm*, Cairo ed., iii, 207, 211, 213, 217, 220, 224-5, 232, 245, 260, 264, 279, 281, 287; Hilāl al-Ṣābiʾ, *Wuzarāʾ*, 49, 56, 210, 314-6; Ṣūlī, *Akhbār al-Rāḍī wa 'l-Muttaḳī*, tr. i, 71, 77, 122, 152, 207; ii, 27, 66, 78; Baghdādī, *Farḳ*, ed. 1367/1948, 172-3, 175, 177-9; Ibn Khallikān, tr. de Slane, i, 246; Kutubī, *Fawāt*, i, 173-5. For modern works, other than those of Ivanow and B. Lewis mentioned in the article (there is an Arabic tr. of B. Lewis entitled *Uṣūl al-Ismāʿīliyya*, Baghdād 1947), see H. Bowen, *The life and times of ʿAlí Ibn ʿÍsà*, Cambridge 1928, index; Ḥasan Ibrāhīm Ḥasan and Ṭaha Aḥmad Sharaf, *ʿUbayd Allāh al-Mahdī*, Cairo 1947, 94, 176, 180 ff., 217 ff., 225 ff., 220 ff., 231, 277, 279, 302. For the episodes of Abu 'l-Haydjāʾ and Ibn Abi 'l-Sādj, see M. Canard, *Histoire de la dynastie des H'amdānides*, i, 352 ff., 355 ff. (M. Canard)

DJANZA [see GANDJA].

DJĀR [see DJIWĀR].

AL-**DJĀR**, once an Arabic port (*furḍa*) on the Red Sea, 20 days' journey south of Ayla, 3 from al-Djuḥfa. Until almost the end of the Middle Ages (when Yanbuʿ, which is situated further north, took over this function), al-Djār was the supply port of Medina, one day's journey away (this according to Yāḳūt, ii, 5; according to BGA, vi, 191 it was two days' journey; according to BGA, i, 19, and ii², 31 it was three). Al-Djār was half on the mainland, and half on an island just offshore. Drinking water had to be brought from the Wādī Yalyal, two parasangs distant. It was an important entrepôt for trade with Egypt, Abyssinia, India and China. The harbour of Ḳarāf (probably the Κοπαρ κώμη of Ptolemy), used for trade with Abyssinia, was situated on an island, a square mile in area,facing the town. There were many castles (*ḳuṣūr*) in al-Djār. Their beginnings must date back to the time of ʿUmar, who had two castles built here for the purpose of housing 20 ship-loads of grain (Yaʿḳūbī, ii, 177). By 1800, the name of the town no longer appears in descriptions of travel, and it was apparently replaced by Burayka (Burēka), which is the name of the bay of al-Djār. Extensive ruins found there may well be the remains of the old castles. The whole stretch of the Red Sea from Djudda to al-Ḳulzum was referred to as al-Djār in antiquity.

In the time of the Prophet, those who had taken part in the second great emigration to Abyssinia returned in two ships to al-Djār, and then went on to Medina (Ibn Saʿd, i/1, 139; Ṭabarī, i, 1571). ʿUmar gave ʿAmr b. al-ʿĀṣ the order to bring Egyptian grain to Medina by sea via al-Djār (Balādhurī, *Futūḥ* 216; Ibn Saʿd, iii/1, 224; Yaʿḳūbī, ii, 177), and this supply-route—though occasionally interrupted by pro-ʿAlid risings (in 145/762: Ṭabarī, iii, 257)—remained the usual one until the time of the Caliphate of al-Manṣūr. The trade in assignments (*ṣukūk*) for grain from the stores in al-Djār, the earliest recorded instance of promissory notes, ie recorded in the *ḥadīth* and in the discussions of ths scholars of Medina (Mālik, *al-Muwaṭṭaʾ*, sections *al-ʿīna* and *djāmiʿ bayʿ al-ṭaʿām*, with al-Zurḳānī's commentary; Ibn ʿAbd al-Ḥakam, *Futūḥ Miṣr*, ed. Torrey, 166 ff.; G. Jacob, *Die ältesten Spuren des Wechsels*, in *MSOS*, xxviii/2, 1925, 280-1). The name of al-Djār is also frequently linked with reports of unrest on other occasions: for instance in 230/814-5 (Ṭabarī, iii, 1336), 266/879-80 (Ṭabarī, iii, 1941), under al-Muḳtadir (Abu 'l-Faradj al-Iṣfahānī, *Maḳātil al-ṭālibiyyīn* 706, Cairo 1949).

Bibliography: (In addition to works mentioned in the text): BGA, i, 27; ii², 40; iii, 12, 53, 69, 83, 97, 107, 110; v, 78; vi, 153, 191; vii, 96, 313, 341;

Hamdānī (ed. D. H. Müller) 47, 182, 218; Yāḳūt, *Mushtarik* (ed. Wüstenfeld) *passim*; Bakrī, *Muʿdjam*, ii, 355-7 (ed. al-Saḳḳā', Cairo 1947); *Ḥudūd al-ʿĀlam* (transl. Minorsky) 81, 148, 414; Abu 'l-Fidā' (ed. Reinaud) 82; Dimashḳī, *Cosmogr.* (ed. Mehren) 216; *Aghānī*², ix, 25, Cairo 1936; Samʿānī, *Ansāb*, fol. 119 a, b; Wüstenfeld, *Das Gebiet von Medina*, 12 f.; Sprenger, *Geographie des alten Arabien*, 38; Ritter, *Erdkunde*, xii, 181-3.

(A. DIETRICH)

DJARĀD, locusts. The word is a collective noun, the nom. unit. being *djarāda*, which is applied to the male and the female alike. No cognate synonym seems to exist in the other Semitic languages. For the different stages of the locust's development the Arabic language possesses special names (such as *sirwa, dabā, ghawghā', khayfān*, etc.) which, however, are variously defined by different authorities.

Being found in abundance in the homeland of the Arabs, locusts were often mentioned and described in ancient Arabic poetry and proverbs. In the Ḳur'ān they figure in the enumeration of the Plagues of Egypt (VII, 133) and in a simile describing the resurrected on the day of judgement (LIV, 7). According to some *ḥadīth*s they are lawful as human food.

In Arabic zoological, pharmacological and lexicological works numerous kinds are mentioned, part of which, according to some authors, differ in colour (green, red, tawny [*aṣfar*], white). Where it is stated that the male is tawny and the female black, a specific variety is obviously spoken of. Some locusts fly and some leap. Some have a big and some a small body. They have no fixed habitat but wander about from place to place following a leader. The males have a lighter body and therefore are better able to fly. Locusts have six feet, the tips of which (or: the tips of the two hindlegs) are like saws. Their eyes are immobile. Next to fish they lay the largest number of eggs of all oviparous animals. The young hatch in less than a week. Several authors state that, for laying eggs, the female seeks rocky ground which cannot be broken even with sharp tools, strikes that ground with her tail (ovipositor) and thus makes a crevice into which she lays the eggs. Other sources give a different and more detailed description: In spring, the females seek out good, soft soil, dig holes with their tails, in which they conceal the eggs, fly away and perish of cold or are killed by birds; in spring of the following year, these buried eggs open, the young hatch, feed on all they can find and, when they are big, fly to another country where they in their turn lay eggs. Locusts eat dung and the young of hornets and of similar animals; they themselves are eaten by sparrows, crows, snakes and scorpions. No animal causes greater harm to the means of human sustenance since they eat all that they come across. Their saliva is a deadly poison to plants. Some devices to keep them away from crops are mentioned in the sources.

In the opinion of the ancient Arabs, who used to eat them, locusts yield a delicious food tasting like the meat of scorpions; and Djāḥiẓ wondered why certain people did not like it. Yet eating it was believed to cause epilepsy (*ṣarʿ*). Locusts are eaten to this day by the Bedouin; methods of preparation in Hess, 124.

Medicinal uses of the locust and its significance when occurring in dreams are dealt with in pertinent works.

Three writings, each entitled *Kitāb al-Djarād* (probably little lexical treatises), none of which is extant, are attributed to the following authors (*Fihrist*, 56, 59, 83): 1) Abū Naṣr Aḥmad b. Ḥātim (al-Bāhilī [*q.v.*]); 2) Abū Ḥātim al-Sidjistānī [*q.v.*]; 3) al-Akhfash al-Aṣghar [*q.v.*].

Bibliography: ʿAbd al-Ghanī al-Nābulusī, *Taʿṭīr al-anām*, Cairo 1354, i, 126 f.; Damīrī, s.v. (transl. Jayakar, i, 407 ff.); Dā'ūd al-Anṭākī, *Tadhkira*, Cairo 1324, i, 96; Djāḥiẓ, *Ḥayawān*², index; J. J. Hess, *ZATW*, xxxv (1915), 123 f.; Ibn al-Bayṭār, *Djāmiʿ*, Būlāḳ 1291, i, 161; Ibn Ḳutayba, *ʿUyūn al-akhbār*, Cairo 1925-30, ii, 100 f. (transl. Kopf, 75, 77); Ibn Sīda, *Mukhaṣṣaṣ*, viii, 172 ff.; Ibshīhi, *Mustaṭraf*, bāb 62, s.v.; *Rasā'il Ikhwān al-Ṣafā'*, Bombay 1305, ii, 202 (= Dieterici, *Thier und Mensch*, 84); Ḳazwīnī (Wüstenfeld), i, 430 f. (transl. Wiedemann, *Beitr. z. Gesch. d. Naturw.*, liii, 252, 271); al-Mustawfī al-Ḳazwīnī (Stephenson), 37, 67; A. Malouf, *Arabic zool. dict.*, Cairo 1932, 152; Nuwayrī, *Nihāyat al-arab*, x, 292 ff.

(L. KOPF)

(ii). The locust, more commonly known as grasshopper, exists in various harmless forms in almost all climatic regions, but in its gregarious destructive form it is particularly and lamentably well-known. Invasions of locusts are a phenomenon not peculiar to the Muslim world, since they occur from China to America and from the U.S.S.R. to South Africa, but almost the entire Muslim world lies within the affected area, and in a region where invasions are especially frequent and severe. There is no need to give an account here of a well-known phenomenon which from the Bible to our own times has been described by many writers. Contemporary biologists have established that in their gregarious forms locusts are the same as in their solitary, peaceful forms: unfavourable climatic conditions simply modify the nature of their reproduction and mode of life. Young locusts then take flight in dense masses numbering millions which darken the sky like a vast cloud; the sound of the rasping of their legs and wings is intensified; when there is a drop in temperature, as for example in the evening, they suddenly settle on the ground and in a few moments every scrap of vegetation is destroyed, sometimes over an area of several square kilometres. As a result the local population suffers an economic catastrophe, except only that the locusts themselves, if they can be killed, provide some food.

From time to time chronicles mention certain particular invasions of locusts, but generally without giving details, and the information to be gathered from these references is, it seems, too haphazard and localized to allow any deductions to be made in respect of possible modifications in the habits of the locusts, the periodicity of their invasions or the area of their migrations. Today there are several migratory species, the two that chiefly concern us being the Desert Locust (Schistocerca gregaria, mainly in East Africa and Asia) and the Migratory Locust (Locusta migratoria, all other parts of Africa). Attempts have always been made to prevent these invasions; and although modern techniques have to some extent increased the effectiveness of control, they have not in fact introduced any new methods for a long time nor, as yet, have they overcome the scourge. Naturally, the local inhabitants have destroyed the eggs whenever they have found them, as a preventive step. When an invasion takes place, they try to stop the locusts advancing, or to kill them by digging pits, spraying poison, using wheeled screens and flame-throwers etc., (poison and fire already envisaged by Ibn Waḥshiyya) although the destruction inflicted does not prevent terrible damage being done. Resistance can only be successful if immediate notice of the locusts' flight from their outbreak areas is sent, together with details of their route; and it is obvious that particular efforts must be made to discover the places where egg-masses are deposited and to destroy eggs and young on the spot, and perhaps later to make these areas ecologically unsuitable as breeding-grounds. This is what the international organizations are now trying to do, so far without success; and they have suffered from the vicissitudes of African politics, particularly the Organisation Internationale contre le Criquet Migrateur which is chiefly concerned with the breeding grounds on the Niger, and the Anti-Locust Research Centre for East Africa and West Asia, with its headquarters in Nairobi. Partial successes have been gained, for example in South Africa, and it is to be hoped that, so long as the state of international relations does not once again lead to a postponement of effort, it may at last be possible to put an end to one of the strangest and most fearful of the scourges of nature ever known, particularly in the climatic zones inhabited by the Muslim peoples.

Bibliography: It seems difficult to include a bibliography, since in essence it consists of semi-official publications of the various regional administrations concerned. For biological questions the pioneer works are those of P. B. Uvarov, *e.g.*, *Locusts and Grasshoppers*, 1928; for the geographical aspect the synthesis, dated, however, 1935, by E. W. Schleich, *Die geographische Verbreitung der Wanderheuschrecken*; for anti-locust control see in particular the periodical *Locusta*, from 1954.

(Cl. Cahen)

DJARĀDJIMA (Mardaïtes). This name, the singular of which is Djurdjumānī (cf. *Aghānī*[1], v, 158, *Aghānī*[2], v, 150, in a poem of Aʿshā Hamdān), according to Yāḳūt, ii, 55 denotes the inhabitants of the town of Djurdjūma, situated in the Amanus (Lukkām), and of the marshy districts north of Antioch between Bayās and Būḳā. This word could also be connected with Gurgum, the old name of a legendary province in the region of Marʿash, on which see Dussaud, *Topogr. hist. de la Syrie*, 285, 469. On the other hand Father Lammens recorded a village called Djordjūm near the road between Aleppo and Alexandretta and the springs of Ḥammām (Ḥammām Shaykh ʿĪsā?).

As inhabitants of the Arabo-Byzantine border country, the Djarādjima played an important part during the early days of Islam in the wars between Arabs and Byzantines, and they were known to Byzantine historians by the name Mardaïtes (see below). Somewhat lukewarm Christians, though whether Monophysite or Monothelite is not known, and dependants of the "patriarchate of Antioch", they enjoyed a semi-independence vis-à-vis the Byzantines to whom they supplied soldiers and irregular troops. The Arabs, after taking Antioch, sent an expedition against them commanded by Ḥabīb b. Maslama al-Fihrī. According to al-Balādhurī and Ibn al-Athīr, the Djarādjima agreed to serve the Arabs as scouts and spies, to guard the Amanian Gates and, along with the Arabs, to garrison the small forts commanding the road into and out of Syria. Wellhausen has, however, questioned whether they ever played this rôle before the time of Walīd I, after 89/708 (see below). They were given exemption from *djizya* and had the right to a share of the booty when they took part in military operations. But their loyalty was intermittent, and they did not hesitate to betray the Arabs and pass information to the Byzantines. The instability of the frontier and the difficulty of access to their country made it impossible for the Arabs to impose their authority over them.

The Byzantine historian Theophanes, like Michael the Syrian and Bar Hebraeus, states that during the reign of Muʿāwiya, the emperor Constantine Pogonatus (641-68) sent the Mardaïtes (Djarādjima) against Syria. Suported by Byzantine troops and under the command of Greek officers, their forces occupied the whole stretch of territory from the Black Mountain (the Amanus) to the Holy City (Jerusalem) and took control of all the mountains in the Lebanon. Many runaway slaves, no doubt Greek in origin, joined the Djarādjima, as did a number of the inhabitants of the mountain districts. In a short time their forces numbered several thousand men. According to Father Lammens, this operation is said to have started in about 46/666. To put a stop to this dangerous development, Muʿāwiya began negotiations with the emperor and, after lengthy discussions, accepted a severe peace treaty (annual tribute of 3,000 gold pieces, liberation of 8,000 prisoners and handing over of 50 thoroughbred horses). This treaty was perhaps accompanied by a promise that the emperor would abandon the Mardaïtes and withdraw from them all help in the form of men, arms and money. It is not known if the emperor intervened with the Mardaïtes in the Lebanon who in any case, as Michael the Syrian testifies, suffered partial defeats at the hands of Muʿāwiya and were further discomfited in about 49 or 50 by the settlement of the Zuṭṭ [*q.v.*] in the Antioch region and further north in the country of the Djarādjima (al-Balādhurī).

It is curious that the account given by Theophanes is not confirmed by the Arab historians who do not connect the peace treaty, probably concluded in 58 or 59/678-9 shortly before Muʿāwiya's death, with the question of the Djarādjima whom they do not mention at that period. Wellhausen has accordingly raised doubts regarding the account given by Theophanes, suggesting that he had brought the Mardaïtes into Muʿāwiya's treaty as a result of confusing it with the treaty made by ʿAbd al-Malik and the history of the Djarādjima in his time, which we shall deal with later; while Father Lammens thinks, on the contrary, that the Arab historians have not preserved any record of this incident because they have confused it with events at the time of ʿAbd al-Malik. However al-Balādhurī, when speaking of the Djarādjima at the time of ʿAbd al-Malik, makes a very clear reference to a treaty concluded with them by Muʿāwiya, who gave them money and in return took hostages whom he kept at Baʿalbekk. But the writer places this incident at the time of Muʿāwiya's war against "the people of ʿIrāḳ". That would mean the war against ʿAlī, that is to say at an earlier period. The uncertainty remains.

In the time of ʿAbd al-Malik, in 69-70/688-9, taking advantage of the fact that the caliph was not only engaged in a difficult war with the anti-caliph Ibn al-Zubayr but also preoccupied with the revolt of the Umayyad ʿAmr b. Saʿīd al-Ashdaḳ whom he had left in command of Damascus, the emperor Justinian II sent the Djarādjima to attack Syria. Al-Balādhurī reports that Greek cavalry, under the command of a Byzantine officer, came into the Amanus district and then advanced as far as the Lebanon, and that this force was joined by large numbers of Djarādjima, native peasants (*anbāṭ*) and runaway slaves. To put an end to the attacks of these adventurers the caliph was compelled to sign a treaty with them, guaranteeing a weekly payment of 1,000 dinars. Then he offered the emperor to make peace on the same terms as Muʿāwiya when the latter had been engaged in the war with the people of ʿIrāḳ. Theophanes also mentions this treaty, in connexion with two particular years, 6176 (65/684) and 6178 (67-8/686), the latter possibly being a renewal. The figures given by him are not the same as for the treaty with Muʿāwiya (for 6176 : 365,000 gold pieces, 365 slaves, 365 thoroughbred horses; for 6178 : 1,000 gold pieces a day, 1 horse and 1 slave). But at the same time the emperor increased his claims, for we see in 6178 that the caliph had to surrender to the emperor half the tribute from Cyprus, Armenia and Iberia (cf. Michael the Syrian, ii, 469). For this consideration Justinian agreed to withdraw the Mardaïtes, and he recalled 12,000 of them; they settled on Byzantine territory. Theophanes reproves him for denuding the frontier in this way. But al-Balādhurī who dates the treaty 70/689 is unaware of this withdrawal and, according to Nicephorus, *Breviarium*, 36, the recall of the Mardaïtes, insofar as they were recalled, took place when Justinian broke the truce, and in order to reinforce his army. Theophanes also says under 6179 (68-9/687) that some Mardaites from the Lebanon came to rejoin the emperor's army in Armenia. Others remained in the Amanus, and there were still some there at the time of Walīd II (see below).

According to al-Balādhurī, the caliph after signing the treaty resorted to a trick to get rid of the Djarādjima. He sent one of his trusted supporters, by name Suḥaym b. al-Muhādjir, to see the Greek officer commanding them; Suḥaym succeeded in winning his confidence by pretending to take his part against the caliph. Then, using troops that had been in hiding, he made a surprise attack, killing the officer and massacring the Greeks who were with him. As for the Djarādjima, he granted them the *amān*; some went away and settled in villages in the neighbourhood of Ḥimṣ and Damascus, others went back to the Amanus. The native peasants who had made common cause with them returned to their villages and the runaway slaves returned to their masters.

Some of these adventurers entered the caliph's service. According to al-Balādhurī, one of them named Maymūn al-Djurdjumānī (known to the Byzantines as Maïouma), a former Greek slave of a member of the Umayyad family, was set free at the request of ʿAbd al-Malik who had been told of the prowess he had shown in battle in the Lebanon, and he was put in charge of a garrison at Antioch. In the time of Walīd, at the head of an army of 1,000 men who were no doubt Mardaïtes, he took part in the expedition sent by Maslama b. ʿAbd al-Malik against Tyana, where he was killed. But al-Balādhurī was certainly mistaken when he said that his death was a great sorrow to ʿAbd al-Malik, for the latter was already dead at that time. Another mistake about him occurs in al-Ṭabarī who, under 87/706, records a tradition from Wāḳidī, according to which he was said to have been killed in the ranks of the Greeks. We see from Theophanes (under 6201 (89/709-10); cf. Nicephorus, *Breviarium*, 43-4) that this is certainly a reference to a former Mardaïte fighting for the Arabs; it was precisely to avenge his death that the Arabs were said to have undertaken the expedition in the course of which they laid siege to Tyana. (For the complications of this incident see Wellhausen 436-7, according to whom the Tyana expedition lasted for two years, 88 and 89).

However the Djarādjima, in their retreats in the Amanus, and with the support of Greeks who had come from the neighbourhood of Alexandretta, continued to be a source of trouble for, in the same year 89, Maslama organized an expedition against their stronghold Djurdjūma which was captured and destroyed. But the Djarādjima were treated exceptionally : they were allowed to keep their Christian faith whilst wearing Muslim dress, without being subject to *djizya*, to receive pay and rations for themselves and their families and to take part in Muslim expeditions with the right to despoil those whom they slew; their goods and their trade were not to be subject to any discrimination from the fiscal point of view. This shows beyond doubt that their secession was feared and that they were needed. A number of them were settled in the region of Tīzīn and Laylūn in north Syria, others at Ḥimṣ and at Antioch. Many emigrated however, crossing over into imperial territory. They settled in Pamphylia in the neighbourhood of Attaleia where they were known by the name of Mardaïtes and were commanded by a catapan. It has been observed that, even today, the population of this district still shows very clear traces of its Syrian origin (see Honigmann, *Ostgrenze*, 41, following Petersen and Von Luschan, *Reisen in Lykien, Milyas und Kibyratis*, ii, 1889, 208 ff.).

We find references to those who stayed on in Muslim territory under Yazīd II in the ʿIrāḳ army (al-Djāḥiẓ, *Bayān*, i, 114), and under Hishām b. ʿAbd al-Malik in a garrison in the Amanus (al-Balādhurī, 167, ed. Cairo, 174). During the ʿAbbāsid period their privileges were confirmed for them by Wāthiḳ, but Mutawakkil ordered that they should be subject to *djizya*, though continuing to give pay to those who were employed in the frontier posts.

As we have seen, the Djarādjima are the Mardaïtes. The Syrian historians call them Gargūmayē, with the additional epithet Līphūrī or Līporē, that is to say brigands (cf. *luṣūṣ* in Ibn al-Athīr, *Nihāya*, under *ḥardjama*). The name Djarādjima is given in Ibn al-Faḳīh, 35, as denoting natives (*ʿulūdj*) of Syria, as opposed to Djarāmiḳa, natives of Djazīra, Nabaṭ, natives of Sawād and Sabābidja, natives of Sind. But we find in *Aghānī*[1], xvi, 76 (*Aghānī*[2], xvi, 73) that Djarādjima, in Syria, denotes those of Persian origin like the Abnāʾ in the Yemen, the Aḥāmira in Kūfa, the Asāwira in Baṣra and the Khaḍāmira in Djazīra. An allusion to the existence of the Djarādjima in the Amanus in the 4th/10th century will be found in H. Zayat, *Vie du Patriarche melkite d'Antioche Christophore* (d. 967) *par le protospathaire Ibrâhîm b. Yuhanna. Document inédit du Xe siècle*, in *Proche Orient Chrétien*, ii, 1952, 60, where mention is made of a monastery of the Virgin called Dayr al-Djarādjima in the Djabal al-Lukkām.

Bibliography: In addition to the authors referred to in the text of the above article, see: Masʿūdī, *Murūdj*, iv, 224-5; Balādhurī, 159-67 (Cairo ed., 166-9); Ṭabarī, ii, 796, 1185; Ibn al-Athīr, Cairo ed. 1303 H, ii, 192, iv, 118-9; idem *Nihāya* under *djardjama* and *ḥardjama*; Suyūṭī, *Taʾrīkh al-khulafāʾ* 87 (where Djurdjūma should be read instead of Djurthūma); Michael the Syrian, ed. Chabot, ii, 455 479; Bar Hebraeus, *Chronographia*, ed. Budge, 101; Theophanes, A.M. 6169, 6176, 6178, 6179, 6201 (Bonn ed., 542, 552, 555, 557, 576-7); Constantine Porphyrogenitus, ch. 21, 22 (repeated from Theophanes), and 50; Wellhausen, *Das arabische Reich*, 116 (= Eng. tr., 187), and *Die Kämpfe der Araber mit den Romäern in der Zeit der Umaijiden*, in *NGW* Gött., 1901, 216 ff., 428 ff., 436 ff.; H. Lammens, *Études sur le règne du calife omaiyade Moʿāwiya Ier*, in *MFOB*, i, 14-22; Van Gelder, *Moḫtar de valsche profeet*, Leiden 1888, 98-9; Sachau, *Zur historischen Geographie von Nordsyrien*, in *SB I Pr. Ak. W.*, 1892, 320; Schiffer, *Die Aramäer*, 92-3.

(M. Canard)

DJARASH, the ancient Gerasa, a place in Transjordan situated south-east of the Djabal ʿAdjlūn, in a well-wooded hilly district, standing on the bank of a small tributary of the Wādī 'l-Zarḳā', the Wādī 'l-Dayr or Chrysoroas of the Greeks. Founded in the Hellenistic era at a centre of natural communications, later to be followed by Roman roads, it was captured by the Jewish leader Alexander Jannaeus in about 80 B.C., but freed by Pompey; it then belonged to the towns of the Decapolis, being incorporated successively in the Roman province of Syria and the province of Arabia. Known as Antioch on the Chrysoroas, it enjoyed its greatest prosperity in the time of the Antonines, and it was then that most of the monuments whose imposing remains we admire today were built. A fortified city in the 4th century, it became the seat of a bishopric, and churches and basilicas abounded.

Conquered in 13/634 by Shuraḥbīl, it formed part of the district of al-Urdunn. In the 3rd/9th century, according to al-Yaʿḳūbī, its population was still half Greek, half Arab. But soon the town lost all its importance. No building of the Muslim period survives, nor is there any trace of the castle which Tughtakīn, *atabeg* of Damascus, had built, and which Baldwin captured and destroyed in 515/1121. According to Yāḳūt, the town was entirely in ruins at the beginning of the 7th/13th century, and through it ran various water-courses used to drive mills, while numerous villages were scattered over the nearby hills.

It was only in 1878 that the Čerkes came and settled on the deserted site of Djarash, and built the present village on the east bank of the *wādī*.

Bibliography: C. Kraeling, *Gerasa, City of Decapolis*, New Haven 1938; Balādhurī, *Futūḥ*, 116; *BGA*, indices; Yāḳūt, ii, 61; Le Strange, *Palestine*, 462; A. S. Marmardji, *Textes géographiques arabes sur la Palestine*, Paris 1951, 4, 46, 58, 106; F. M. Abel, *Géographie de la Palestine*, Paris 1938, particularly 331-2. (D. Sourdel)

DJARBA (Djerba) is the largest island of the Maghrib littoral, with an area of 514 sq. kms. It lies to the south of Tunisia in the gulf of Gabès (Little Syrtis in ancient times), an area noted for its sandbanks and tidal currents. The two peninsulas of Mehabeul and Accara reach out towards it from the Djeffara plain, but the island is separated from the mainland by the Bou Grara Sea and Strait of al-Ḳanṭara to the west, and the Adjim channel to the east. Although the channel is no more than 2 kms. wide, it can be navigated by ships drawing up to 4 metres of water. The Bou Grara Sea, in the shape of a sack, has an area of 500 sq. kms., and a depth ranging between 5 to 25 metres. Low tide forms a series of shallows in the Strait of al-Ḳanṭara. Djerba consists of a small plateau with an elevation of 15-40 metres. It attains its highest point to the south near Sedwikesh (55 m.) and slopes down towards the coastal plains, which are very wide to the west of the island. The terrain is a deposit of the quaternary age, being marine on the periphery and continental inland.

There is no source of fresh water on the island apart from the few gullies along the clayey cliff of Guellala in the south, where the water merely trickles for a few hundred yards even after the heavy rains. The precipitation is slight and sporadic, an average of 200 mm. (= 7.84 in.) falling in a season of about 40 days, and even a continually high relative humidity cannot offset this lack of rain. The underground water-level to which wells are sunk through a layer of sandy soil and a limestone crust is abundant but salty, except in the eastern interior. Deep drillings have been made to an artesian water-level in the miocene clay of the substructure, but the water is salty and virtually unusable. The inhabitants of the island have always had to collect water in tanks, private and public, and except on certain small plots, cultivation of the land has yielded a very low output. All those who throughout the centuries have attacked the island have had to contend with its shortage of water.

Like the Kerkena islands, Djerba is connected with the mainland by the wide sandbanks which surround it less than 10 m. below the surface of the sea. These banks often silt up completely. At Ṭriḳ el-Djmel, for instance, the caravans cross them on their way to the Tarbella peninsula, and nearby a road has recently been constructed over the remains of the Roman causeway to al-Ḳanṭara. There is thus a direct link for modern traffic between the mainland and the island. The effect of tidal currents on the mud and fine sand has been to create a series of channels, 'oueds', in the sandbanks. Indeed, the gulfs of Venice and Gabès are the only areas of the Mediterranean which are tidal. At Djerba there is a difference of 1 m. between high and low tide. The dangers of navigating the currents and sandbanks have always served as a defence against outside intruders. In 253 B.C., during the first Punic War, a Roman fleet ran aground at low tide off Djerba, and it was only refloated at high tide by unloading the ships. (Polybius, i, 39). In 1511, Pedro Navarro landed his troops at high tide, and had sufficient foresight to withdraw his ships with the ebb tide. But the Spanish soldiers were thrown back by the islanders, and had great difficyulty in regaining their ships which were lying four miles offshore (Leo Africanus, trans. Êpaulard, 401). It should be added that the sea abounds in fish, and certain shallows are strewn with sponges.

"Djerba, the isle of the shallows of Periplus, of the Lotus-eaters of Erasthones and other Greek writers, was called Pharis by Theophrastus, Meninx by Polybius, and possibly Phla by Herodotus. The land was well cultivated from the middle of the fourth century B.C. onwards, at which time it was certainly under the rule of Carthage" (Gsell, *Hist.*, ii, 124). As in Roman times, its economy was based mainly on the growing of olives, although in the fourth century B.C. the oil was still extracted from wild trees. Not much is known about its maritime activity during classical times apart from the fact that there were considerable fishing-grounds in the area. The for the most part shapeless remains of ancient settlements point to its economic importance at that time. Only Meninx can be accurately located, its ruins standing under the Burdj al-Ḳanṭara at the end of the Roman causeway. It is probable that Girba, from which the island's name originated, was situated near Houmt-Souk, and that Tipaza and

Haribus were in the neighbourhood of Adjim and Guellala respectively. The sack of Jerusalem in the first century A.D. resulted in a considerable influx of Jews, from whom most of the present-day Jewish population is descended. After having been part of the proconsular province, Djerba fell successively under the power of Tripolitania, the Vandals, and Byzantium. In the Byzantine age the bishop of Djerba was appointed from Tripoli. In 665, during the wars waged in Byzacene by Maʿāwiya b. Ḥudaydj, Djerba was conquered and occupied by Ruwayf b. Thābit. For the next few centuries little is known about the island, except that it came under the rule of Ḳayrawān and Mahdiyya. Its natural isolation was reinforced by the independent spirit of its inhabitants and their attachment to the Khāridjite schism, which between the 2nd/8th and 4th/10th centuries extended to places so wide apart as Djabal Nafūsa (Tripolitania) and the Mzāb (Algerian Sahara). It explains perhaps why Arab writers such as al-Bakrī and al-Idrīsī have so few kind words to spare for them, finding them ill-natured and hypocritical. Al-Bakrī remarked that they 'acted piratically on both land and sea', and al-Idrīsī pointed out that they were Berbers and could speak no other tongue. Nevertheless the island was described in the eleventh century as a mass of gardens and olive-groves, and Djerba (Girba) figured as one of its small towns.

The invasions of the Banū Hilāl in the 5th/11th century, and the fall of the Zīrid dynasty, seemed to increase the Djerbians' spirit of independence. Their piratical raids on the Tunisian coast and on the Christian fleets became more frequent. In 1115-6 ʿAlī b. Yaḥyā the Zīrid was still their master. But George of Antioch, admiral to the Norman king of Sicily Roger II, conquered and occupied the island in 1135. The capture of Mahdiyya in 1148 strengthened Norman rule, which persisted until 1160 despite an uprising in 1153 which was rapidly suppressed. They were then driven from the Tunisian coast and islands by the great Almohad conqueror ʿAbd al-Muʾmin. In 683/1284, at the beginning of the reign of the Ḥafṣid prince Abū Ḥafṣ ʿUmar, a Christian expedition easily retook the island. It was under the command of Roger of Lauria, and was sent by the king of Sicily, Peter III of Aragon. In 1289 the Christians built a fortress to guard over the Strait of al-Ḳanṭara and the Roman causeway. It was sited near the ruins of ancient Meninx, and its towers and battlements formed a square surrounded by a moat. After several uprisings, and a raid by the Tunisians in 706/1306, Frederick of Sicily sent Ramon Muntaner to reoccupy Djerba. This Catalan adventurer maintained an iron rule from 1311 until 1314, at which date the island was brought under the direct rule of Sicily. But a fresh revolt, in which the Djerbians gained the assistance of the Ḥafṣid king Abū Bakr, forced the Christians to relinquish the island after a heroic resistance in the Ḳashtīl (1334-5), Only once more were they to regain control of it. from 1383 until 1392, when the Sicilian expedition was reinforced by a Genoese fleet. In the following century, attempts by Alfonso V of Aragon to recapture the island were doomed to failure. During his second assault, in 835/1432, the sultan Abū Fāris came in person to the assistance of the Djerbians, and the Arabs built a second fortress on the island, this time near the ancient ruins of Girba in the north. It became known as al-Burdj al-Kabīr, and in time a small trading settlement named Houmt-Souk grew up round its walls.

The defiant and independant spirit of the Djerbians brought clashes with the Ḥafṣids as well as with the Christians. Not only did they turn a deaf ear to Abū Fāris's peaceful propaganda in favour of orthodoxy, but in 885/1480 they suddenly broke their association with Abū ʿUmar ʿUthmān and deliberately destroyed their only link with the mainland, the Roman causeway. Up to then it had been restored several times and kept in good condition.

Despite the plunderings, massacres and deportations resulting from Christian invasions, and the internal dissensions of the two rival sects (the Wahbiyya in the north-west and the Nakkāra in the south-east), Djerba was reputed for its wealth. The Sfaxians came from the ravaged mainland to buy oil, there was a considerable trade in dried raisins, and the vegetation included apple-trees, fig-trees and palms. Salt was supplied to the visiting merchants of Venice, and the fishing industry flourished. There were also exports of *djarbī*, the name given to the plain and coloured woollen cloths produced on the island. Goods were stored in 'fondouks', which also housed Christian merchants. The general population was dispersed among the plantations in houses 'of a square shape and very unusual in style'. In the fifteenth century the traveller Adorne recorded that 'the king raises taxes of 20,000 doubloons or ducats annually'. But successive wars and droughts brought serious famines, such as that of 711/1311, when bread was made from the sawdust of palm-trees.

In the sixteenth century, Djerba became a stake in the struggle between Spaniards and Turks for mastery of the Mediterranean. The Ḥafṣids ceded it to the latter as a base, from which the Christians were not able to dislodge them. The Spanish invasion of 1511, led by Pedro Navarro, victor in Algeria and Tripoli, ended in failure. In 1550 the island served as an operational base for Dragut, the famous corsair [see ṬŪRGHŪD ʿALĪ PASHA and the following article].

Djerba finally came under Turkish rule, and it was variously administered from Algiers, Tripoli, and Tunis. It came under the permanent control of Tunisia during the reign of Ḥammūda-Bey (1040-69/1631-59). It was to suffer under its several masters. In 976/1568, the Pasha of Tripoli imposed a crushing burden of taxation, and in 1006/1598 the island was literally laid waste by Ibrāhīm Pasha in punishment for its refusal to bow to the demands of Tripoli. The description of Djerba given by the writers of the 16th century, though more detailed than that of their predecessors, differs little from earlier accounts; the cultivation of trees and export of woollen cloths were still its principal occupations. There was a persistent shortage of corn and abundance of dromedaries and donkeys. All livestock came from the mainland. The population varied between 30-40,000, and the countryside was only sparsely inhabited. In the mid-seventeenth century Leo Africanus wrote that 'trade done with merchants from Alexandria, Turkey and Tunisia yielded a revenue of 20,000 doubloons from the salt tax and customs duties'.

The rulers of Turkish Tunisia, Deys and Beys, who were succeeded from 1117/1705 onwards by the rulers of the Ḥusaynid dynasty, appointed first *shaykhs* and then *ḳāʾids* to represent them in the outlying possession of Djerba; these important officials were recruited hereditarily from certain families. In the 10th/16th century it was the Semumeni family which ruled, and they were succeeded by the Bel Djellouds. One of them, Saʿīd, was put to death in 1151/1738 for ordering the sinking of all flat-bottomed boats in order to prevent them falling into the hands of the invading troops of Yūnus Bey, son of ʿAlī Pa<u>sh</u>a. Thereafter the Ben Ayed *ḳāʾid*s ruled the island until the last quarter of the nineteenth century.

From the early eighteenth century onwards, Mālikī orthodoxy gradually replaced the Ibāḍī schism, and Arabic began to establish itself as the most common language. Uprisings against the central power periodically brought war to the island, in particular from 1007/1599 to 1009/1601, and in 1864. In the 18th century there were also several raids by the nomadic Ur<u>gh</u>āmma and Accara tribes from the plain of <u>Dj</u>effara. In 1794 a bold adventurer from Tripoli, ʿAlī Bur<u>gh</u>ul, occupied and plundered the island for 58 days. In 1864 it was the turn of tribesmen from the Zarzis area to invade it. Plague ravaged the island in 1705-6, 1809, and 1864. Its economy was severely affected when Aḥmad Bey suppressed the slave-trade in 1846, for until then Djerba and Gabès had been the principal outlets for the slaves carried by merchant caravans which crossed the desert from eastern Sudan via <u>Gh</u>adamès and <u>Gh</u>āt. The new law forced the caravans to head for Tripoli, which was already supplied with slaves from the Fezzān route. Nevertheless, travellers of the nineteenth century describe an active and prosperous island, and so it was when, by the treaty of the Bardo Protectorate, a small French force came to garrison the Bur<u>dj</u> al-Kabīr on 28 July 1881.

The population had always been relatively large, and the period of peace ensuing after 1881 saw a great increase. Although there has been much emigration, its population in 1956 was 63,200, or 121 per sq.km. Ibn <u>Kh</u>aldūn (iii, 63) classes the Djerbians as part of the Kutāma people, although he is careful to point out that there are elements also of the Nefza, Huwwāra and other Berber tribes. In recent years there has been much immigration from the mainland, especially from southern Tunisia. Some were from the Ibāḍī tribe of Nafūsa, others were penniless shepherds given work as labourers, whilst yet others were exiles from various countries, seeking asylum in Djerba. Most of them were easily absorbed into the population. Djerbians themselves are nearly all distinguished by their short stature and flat skulls. About 50% of them speak Berber—particularly in the south-west—but they virtually all speak Arabic as well. Half the population has retained the Ibāḍī faith in its local form of 'Wahbism', but the great majority in the eastern and central parts are orthodox Muslims. In general the Wahbīs are bearded and wear the turban (*ḳa<u>sh</u>ṭa*). They lead an austere life which excludes gambling and smoking, and they only break the fast of Ramaḍān after having personally observed the crescent moon. The great number of squat and simple mosques is evidence of the former importance of their sect. They have certain traditional customs in common with orthodox Muslims, such as the ritual visit to the olive-grove, symbol of wealth and peace, on the occasion of marriage or circumcision. Another marriage custom, of Berber origin, is the *<u>dj</u>aḥfa* procession, which recalls the old Bedouin custom of the abduction of the bride. The island's Jewish inhabitants are mostly descended from immigrants of the first century, and have remained dolichocephalic. They are concentrated in the two villages of Ḥāra Kabīra and Ḥāra Ṣa<u>gh</u>īra, in the north. These villages, together with the economic and administrative centre of Houmt-Souk, which for the most part is of recent construction, are the only centres of population in an island which is characterized by the sparse distribution of its rural settlements.

Cultivation of the land is intensive only in the centre and east, where irrigation of fruit and vegetable crops from an underground water-level is effected by means of animal-driven pumps. Cereal crops are grown on only a few small fields in the south. The island contains 400,000 olive trees, most of them now too old to be productive, and 570,000 palm trees, many of which are neither fertile nor irrigated. As in Zarzis, they are extensively used in the making of fishing tackle. Land-holdings are small, being usually of 2 to 5 acres where there is irrigation, and 7 to 13 where the land is dry, but they are cultivated to an average degree of 70%. As already mentioned, there is virtually no stock-farming.

For centuries the houses have been dispersed all over the island, for the constant danger of attack precluded the islanders from living in village communities as on the mainland. Many of the farms were built on defensive lines, and the earth embankments, from which Barbary fig trees stand out like spikes, served the double purpose of enclosing the fields and guarding against attack. Because of the shortage of productive land on the island itself, the Djerbians have for centuries owned land on the nearby coastal strip, and farmed it with labour from their related tribe, the Towazins.

The old crafts have lost a lot of their former importance, but nevertheless there are still 1500 looms in use, mostly primitive machines grouped 3 or 5 to a small workshop. Their supply of wool comes from the island's 8,000 sheep, and imports which find their way from the steppes. The industry produces brightly-striped woollen cloths, and other fabrics. The art of pottery has not died out in Guellala (S.-W.), where there are some 250 kilns, and various types of vessels are shipped to all parts of the coast, as far as Tunis. Jewellery and embroidery are the domain of the Jews, and are consequently declining in importance as the Jewish elements emigrate.

The main source of wealth for Djerba lies outside the island itself. It is derived from the fishing industry (employing 11% of the adult population), coastal traffic to Sfax, Sousse and Tunis by *lūd*s (flat-bottomed sailing ships which can safely negotiate the shallows), navigating for the Mediterranean or even other shipping companies, and above all from emigration.

Emigration is exclusively by males, for a temporary period, and for commercial reasons. The Djerbians form themselves into limited partnerships and dispense with the need for banks. Wherever possible, the partnership is restricted to a particular family, and they are found predominantly in the grocery, weaving, and hosiery trades. Of the 6,000 traders who are known to be living outside Djerba, 80-90% are in Tunisia, concentrated in the Tell and Tunis areas, and a few have settled in the Constantine and in Tripolitania. The male members of the partnerships replace each other abroad according to a certain roster, which is so arranged that they spend about one third of their time with their family in Djerba. This system enables the island to support a greater population than would otherwise be possible on its meagre natural resources.

Fishing is carried out in the gulf of Gabès, mostly from 'bordigues', which are small constructions built in the sandbanks with mud and palm leaves. A speciality of their catch is the large number of octopuses and sponges which are so abundant in the waters off Djerba. The islanders also fish with rods, eel-pots and various types of nets.

The Djerbians work hard in their several occupations, and although they emigrate a good deal they remain very devoted to their island, and to their social and family ties.

Bibliography: R. Stablo, *Les Djerbiens*, Tunis 1941; S. Tlatli, *Djerba et les Djerbiens*, Tunis 1942; Y. Delmas, *L'île de Djerba*, in *Les Cahiers d'Outre-Mer*, Bordeaux 1952; S. Gsell, *Hist. ancienne de l'Afrique du Nord*, Paris, ii, 1921, iv, 1924; Bakrī, *Description de l'Afrique septentrionale*, trans. de Slane², 1911; Idrīsī, *Description de l'Afrique et de l'Espagne*, trans. Dozy and De Goeje; Ibn Khaldūn, *Histoire des Berbères*, trans. de Slane, iii, Paris 1934; Tidjānī, *Riḥla*, ed. Ḥ. Ḥ. ʿAbd al-Wahhāb, Tunis 1378/1958, index (trans. Rousseau, in *JA*, 1852); R. Brunschvig, *La Berbérie orientale sous les Ḥafṣides*, Paris, 2 vol., 1940 and 1947; idem, *Deux récits de voyage inédits d'Abdalbasit B. Halil et Adorne*, Paris 1936; F. Braudel, *La Méditerranée et le monde méditerranéen à l'époque de Philippe II*, Paris 1949; Leo Africanus, *Description de l'Afrique*, trans. Épaulard, Paris 1956; Monchicourt, *L'expédition espagnole de 1560 contre l'ile de Djerba*, Paris 1913; A. Bombaci, *Le fonti turche della battaglia delle Gerbe (1560)*, in *RSO*, 1946, 193-218; M. Seghir ben Youssef, *Mechra el Melki*, trans. V. Serre and M. Lasram, Tunis 1900; L. Ch. Feraud, *Annales tripolitaines*, Paris-Tunis 1927; Exiga dit Kayser, *Description et histoire de Djerba*, Tunis 1884; J. Servonnet and F. Lafitte, *Le golfe de Gabès en 1888*, Paris 1888; Bossoutrot, *Documents musulmans pour servir à une histoire de Djerba*, in *RT*, Tunis 1903.

(J. Despois)

DJARBA (Battle of). — In the middle of the 10th/16th century the Ottoman corsair Ṭūrghūd Raʾīs made the island of Djarba the base of his operations against the Spaniards. Although the latter had succeeded in blockading it in Rabīʿ I 958/ April 1551, he was able to escape with his fleet by cutting the causeway of al-Ḳanṭara and digging a channel which enabled him to reach the Gulf of Bū Ghrāra and thence the high seas (13 Rabīʿ II 958/20 April 1551). Shortly afterwards he seized Tripoli (Shaʿbān 958/August 1551), then put into repair the fortress of Houmt Souk (Burdj al-Kabīr; inscr. of 964/1557). In the face of the menace of these Turkish bases of Tripoli and Djarba John of Valletta, the Grand Master of Malta, and the Duke of Medina-Celi obtained in 1559, from Philip II, king of Spain, permission to send out a naval expedition. This left Malta on 10 February 1560 with 54 galleys, 36 cargo-vessels, and 11 to 12 thousand men; but, rather than attack Tripoli, it sailed on Djarba, which was occupied on 7 March. The Ottoman fleet, however, under the command of Piyāle Pasha and Ṭūrghūd Raʾīs surprised the Spanish fleet at its anchorage on 11 May, and destroyed the greater part of it. The garrison of Burdj al-Kabīr, commanded by Alvaro de Sande, was besieged from 16 May; short of water and decimated by sickness, it surrendered on 31 July 1560, and the few thousand survivors were either massacred or divided among the Ottoman galleys as oarsmen. Following their defeat the Spanish were totally driven out of southern and central Tunisia.

The famous "Tower of Skulls" (Burdj al-ruʾūs) built by the Djarbans with the bones of the dead, often mentioned by European travellers, was demolished in 1848 by order of Aḥmad Bey, bey of Tunis.

Bibliography: Ch. Monchicourt, *Episodes de la carrière de Dragut*: ii, *Le stratagème de Dragut à El-Kantara de Djerba*, in *RT*, xxv (1918), 263-73; and, especially, idem, *L'expédition espagnole de 1560 contre l'île de Djerba*, in *RT*, xx (1913), 499-519, 627-53; xxi (1914), 14-37, 136-55, 227-46, 332-53, 419-50, where there is an important bibliography of documents in archives and of various sources relevant to this expedition; İ. H. Uzunçarşılı, *Osmanlı tarihi*, ii, Ankara 1949, 372, 375-6; A. Bombacı, *Le fonti turche della battaglia delle Gerbe (1560)*, in *RSO*, xix, (1946) 193-218.

(R. Mantran)

AL-**DJARBĀʾ**, an ancient fortress in Arabia Petraea situated on the Roman road leading from Buṣrā to the Red Sea, about one mile north of Adhruḥ [*q.v.*]. Like Adhruḥ, it submitted to Muḥammad, in 9/631, on condition of payment of tribute. The distance between Adhruḥ and al-Djarbāʾ, estimated at "three days' journey", has been mentioned frequently in the *ḥadīth* as an indication of the size of the basin (*ḥawḍ* [*q.v.*]) where the Prophet will stand on the day of Judgment. The expression "between Adhruḥ and al-Djarbāʾ" has thus become proverbial to denote a considerable distance.

The place came into prominence for the second time during the Crusades, when Ṣalāh al-Dīn camped there in August 578/1182, during his expedition against Damascus.

Bibliography: Balādhurī, *Futūḥ*, 59; Ṭabarī, i, 1702; Yāḳūt, ii, 48; Bakrī, *Muʿdjam*, ed. Wüstenfeld, 83-4, 239; Le Strange, *Palestine*, index; A. S. Marmardji, *Textes géographiques arabes sur la Palestine*, Paris 1938, 183; Ch. Clermont-Ganneau, *La marche de Saladin du Caire à Damas*, in *RB*, 1906, 469-70 (following William of Tyre, xxii, 14, 15); Ibn Ḥanbal, *Musnad*, ed. Cairo 1313 H, ii, 21; Muslim, *Ṣaḥīḥ*, ed. 1330-4 H, ii, 209.

(D. Sourdel)

AL-**DJARDJARĀʾĪ**, patronymic deriving from the locality of Djardjarāyā in ʿIrāḳ (on the Tigris, south of Baghdād), borne by several viziers of the ʿAbbāsid and Fāṭimid caliphs.

1. — Muḥammad b. al-Faḍl, former secretary of al-Faḍl b. Marwān [*q.v.*], was vizier to al-Mutawakkil at the beginning of the reign, after Ibn al-Zayyāt's disgrace, but was soon discarded by reason of his negligence. Recalled to the vizierate by al-Mustaʿīn in Shaʿbān 249/September-October 863, he died soon afterwards in the year 250/864-5, aged about eighty (see Ṣafadī, *al-Wāfī*, iv, 4, ed. Dedering, no. 1878).

2. — Aḥmad b. al-Khaṣīb, son of a governor of Egypt (Ibn al-ʿImād, *Shadharāt*, a. 265), had been secretary-tutor to prince al-Muntaṣir and became vizier in Shawwāl 247/December 861 when his master was proclaimed caliph; after his death, he helped to secure al-Mustaʿīn's succession, but he incurred the hostility of the Turkish officers in Sāmarrā and was exiled to Crete in Djumādā I 248/August 862. He died in 265/879.

3. — al-ʿAbbās b. al-Ḥasan, private secretary to the vizier al-Ḳāsim b. ʿUbayd Allāh under al-Muktafī, thanks to the recommendation left by his master succeeded in taking his place after his death in Dhu 'l-Ḳaʿda 291/October 904. As vizier to al-Muktafī, he entered into close alliance with Abu 'l-Ḥasan ʿAlī b. al-Furāt whom he made his right hand man and chose as his successor; it was on the advice of this unscrupulous individual that, in Dhu 'l-Ḳaʿda 295/September 908, he had the young

Djaʿfar proclaimed caliph when he was only thirteen years old; he took the name of al-Muḳtadir and retained him as his minister. The haughty attitude of al-ʿAbbās seems to have occasioned the conspiracy of Rabīʿ I 296/December 908 which, even if it did not succeed in replacing al-Muḳtadir by Ibn al-Muʿtazz, nevertheless cost the vizier his life.

Bibliography: D. Sourdel, *Le vizirat ʿabbāside*, i, Damascus 1959, 271-5, 293, 289-90, 359-71.

4. — Abu 'l-Ḳāsim ʿAlī b. Aḥmad, a secretary of ʿIrāḳī origin who came to Fāṭimid Egypt with his brother, and held various offices in the provinces where his peculation was punished by his hands being cut off in 404/1013-4 on al-Ḥākim's orders; nevertheless he succeeded in becoming director of the *dīwān al-nafaḳāt* in 406/1015-6, and then in holding the office of *wāsita* in 412/1021-2 and of vizier in 418/1027. He was retained in the vizierate under the reigns of al-Ẓāhir and al-Mustanṣir until his death in Ramaḍān 436/March 1045.

Bibliography: Ibn Khallikān, ed. Cairo 1948, iii, 84-5; Ibn al-Ṣayrafī, *al-Ishāra ilā man nāla 'l-wizāra*, in *BIFAO*, xxv (1925), 77-9.

(D. Sourdel)

AL-DJARḤ WA 'L-TAʿDĪL, (disparaging and declaring trustworthy), a technical phrase used regarding the reliability or otherwise of traditionists and witnesses. This article deals with the former; for the latter see ʿADL. While the criticism of *ḥadīth* did not, as is often said, apply solely to the *isnād*, this formed a very important part of it. In the course of the 2nd/8th century when it was realized that many false traditions were being invented, interest in the transmitters developed, and statements regarding their qualities were made. In the 3rd/9th century books began to be written, generally in the form of lists of men with their dates, and statements regarding their credibility. We also find notes on the qualities of traditionists in the canonical *Sunan* collections of tradition, in the *Sunan* of al-Dārimī [*q.v.*], and elsewhere. In the introduction to his *Ṣaḥīḥ* Muslim found it necessary to justify the investigation of traditionists' credentials because many felt it was wrong to criticize them. Such views must have continued for a long time, for al-Ḥākim (d. 405/1014) still found it necessary to defend the practice. When books on *ʿIlm al-ḥadīth* were written (4th/10th century onwards), *al-djarḥ wa 'l-taʿdīl* formed a recognized branch of the subject.

The Companions of the Prophet were considered reliable, so *djarḥ* could not apply to them; but traditionists of later generations were subject to investigation. Views were held regarding the qualities of a reliable transmitter. He must (1) be a Muslim, (2) have sound intelligence, (3) be truthful, (4) never conceal defects in his transmission, (5) be trustworthy. In his *K. al-djarḥ wa 'l-taʿdīl*, Ibn Abī Ḥātim al-Rāzī (d. 327/939) discusses in the introduction the various classes of transmitter, and his classification served as a standard for writers of later times; *e.g.*, al-Khaṭīb al-Baghdādī (d. 463/1071) in his *Kifāya*, and Ibn al-Ṣalāḥ (d. 643/1245) in his *ʿUlūm al-ḥadīth*. He mentions in order of merit four types whose traditions may be accepted. They are (1) *thiḳa* (trustworthy), or *mutḳin* (exact); (2) *ṣadūḳ* (truthful), *maḥalluhu al-ṣidḳ* (his station is veracity), or *lā baʾs bihi* (there is no harm in him); (3) *shaykh*; (4) *ṣāliḥ al-ḥadīth* (good, or upright, in tradition). The second type is not so authoritative as the first and the third is slightly inferior to the second. The fourth contains men whose traditions may be written down for comparison with those of others. There are four classes of lower authority still: (1) *layyin al-ḥadīth* (easy-going in tradition); (2) *laysa bi-ḳawī* (not strong); (3) *ḍaʿīf al-ḥadīth* (weak in tradition); (4) *matrūk al-ḥadīth* (one whose traditions are abandoned), *dhāhib al-ḥadīth* (rejected), or *kadhdhāb* (liar). The first two deserve to have their traditions considered and compared with those of others; the third, though inferior, is not to be rejected outright, but one must find whether his traditions are supported elsewhere. The fourth is utterly rejected. A number of other terms are also applied by other writers.

But while this sounds straightforward matters were not so simple, for sometimes a transmitter called trustworthy by one authority was called weak by another. This raised a difficulty, but opinion seemed to prefer the view that when both *djarḥ* and *taʿdīl* were expressed about the same man, the *djarḥ* had more authority because those who expressed this view must have possessed information not available to others. But while those who expressed *taʿdīl* did not need to supply reasons for their view, those who expressed *djarḥ* must do so, for people differed in their idea of what constituted weakness, and it is only when the reasons are stated that one can know whether the judgment is valid. Opinions differ as to whether one authority is enough to express *djarḥ* and *taʿdīl*. Two men are required to attest the reliability of witnesses, but Ibn al-Ṣalāḥ holds that the testimony of one man is sufficient to state the reliability or otherwise of a transmitter of tradition.

Bibliography: ʿAbd al-Raḥmān b. Abī Ḥātim al-Rāzī, *K. al-Djarḥ wa 'l-taʿdīl*, 9 vols., Ḥaydarābād 1952-3; al-Ḥākim Abū ʿAbdallāh Muḥammad b. ʿAbdallāh, *Maʿrifat ʿulūm al-ḥadīth*, Cairo 1937, 52 ff., and *al-Madkhal ilā maʿrifat al-Iklīl*, ed. J. Robson, London 1953; al-Khaṭīb al-Baghdādī, *K. al-Kifāya fi ʿilm al-riwāya*, Ḥaydarābād 1357, 81 ff.; Ibn al-Ṣalāḥ, *ʿUlūm al-ḥadīth*, Aleppo 1931, 114 ff.; al-Dhahabī, *Mīzān al-iʿtidāl*, Cairo 1325, i, 2 ff.; Ibn Ḥadjar al-ʿAsḳalānī, *Lisān al-mīzān*, Ḥaydarābād 1329-31, i, 5 ff.; Abū Bakr Muḥammad b. Mūsā al-Ḥāzimī, *Shurūṭ al-aʾimmat al-khamsa*, Cairo 1357, 20-30, 38 ff.; Abu 'l-Ḥasanāt Muḥammad ʿAbd al-Ḥayy, *al-Rafʿ wa 'l-takmīl fi 'l-djarḥ wa 'l-taʿdīl*, at end of al-Dhahabī's *Mīzān*, ii; Muḥammad ʿAbd al-ʿAzīz al-Khawlī, *Miftāḥ al-sunna*, Cairo 1921, 44 ff (containing lists of writers); Aḥmad Muḥammad Shākir, *al-Bāʿith al-ḥathīth*, commentary on Ibn Kathīr's *Ikhtiṣār ʿulūm al-ḥadīth*, 2nd. edn., Cairo 1951, 101 ff.; Aḥmad Amīn, *Ḍuḥā 'l-Islām*, Cairo 1952, ii, 129 ff.; Ṣubḥī al-Ṣāliḥ, *ʿUlūm al-ḥadīth wa-muṣṭalaḥuh*, Damascus 1959, 107-9, 130-40; I. Goldziher, *Muh. St.*, ii, 141 ff., 272 ff; J. Robson, in *Bulletin of the John Rylands Library*, Manchester, xliii, 462 ff.

(J. Robson)

DJARĪB [see KAYL].

DJARĪD [see DJERĪD].

DJARĪD (Bilād al-). The Djerid or "country of palms" is a district of the Sahara situated in south-western Tunisia which includes the oases of Nefṭa, Tozeur (Tūzar), El-Oudiane (al-Udyān) and al-Ḥamma (not to be confused with al-Ḥamma of Gabès). In the Middle Ages the Djerid was more often called Ḳasṭīliya; but this name which is sometimes a synonym of Tozeur only (Ibn Ḥawḳal, 243; al-Idrīsī, 121), frequently embraces Gafsa and the Nefzāwa (Ibn Khaldūn, i, 192) along with the modern Djerid, and sometimes even the district of Gabès (Leo Africanus, 8).

Apart from al-Ḥamma which is in the north, the oases are situated at the foot of the last anticlinal fold (Drāʿ al-Djarīd) of the Atlas, between 25 and 75 metres in altitude, on the edge of an immense *sebkha* wrongly named Chott el-Djerid on maps: it is an immense plain of salty clay, absolutely sterile, 110 by 70 km.; it produces no pasturage of salsolaceous plants except along its border, to which alone the name *shoṭṭ* applies; this is the *sebkha* Takmart of Arab writers. According to tradition, the sea covered this district at quite a recent period; in fact, its altitude is about twenty metres, and it has been possible to show recently that the *sebkha* of Djerid and its eastward extension, the *sebkha* of Fedjedj, were in the Quaternary Age merely lagoons temporarily connected with the Gulf of Gabès.

The climate is essentially that of a desert: Tozeur only receives 89 mm. (3½ ins.) of rain a year, and very irregularly; mean temperatures there for January and July are 10°5 C. (50.9° F.) and 32°3C. (90.1° F.); frosts are very rare, but the temperature often exceeds 40° C . It is the typical climate of the date-palm, provided that it is given abundant irrigation. Numerous springs appear at the foot of the Drāʿ al-Djarīd, fed by a strong artesian water-level enclosed in the upper Cretaceous limestones and Pontien sandstones (Tertiary): with some artesian wells, which have been sunk fairly recently, they provide a total of about 1850 litres a second. Thus the oases of the Djerid have always had the reputation of being the finest in Tunisia.

Tozeur (Tusuros, or Blād al-Ḥaḍar), Nefṭa (Nepte) and al-Ḥamma (Aquae) were points on a forward road near the Roman and Byzantine *limes*. It is not certain that Tokyūs (El-Oudiane), referred to by al-Yaʿḳūbī in the 3rd/9th century, is of ancient origin. The Djerid was twice conquered by Arab conquerors: in 26/647 by Ibn Zuhayr and in 49/669 by ʿUḳba b. Nāfiʿ. But the Djerid was "at all times the home of separatist movements and rebellions" (G. Marçais). In the 9th century, however, Ḳasṭīliya was an Aghlabid province with a governor and, although mainly Ibāḍite, it only once revolted, in 839. There were then few Arabs in the district; the nomads were Luwātā, Zowāra and Miknāsa. The "Rûm" (of European origin) were still mentioned in the cases. The sugar-cane was cultivated there, the Ḳasṭīliyan fairs were crowded and trade in black slaves was brisk. The country remained prosperous until the middle of the 5th/11th century although it was often autonomous; its centres were in fact small principalities administered by councils of notables who were to a greater or lesser degree consulted by the heads of the most powerful families like the Banū Furḳān, and the Banū Waṭṭa of Tozeur. Tozeur was a real town, with ramparts pierced by four gates, a large mosque, crowded bazaars, baths and densely populated suburbs. The mosque of Blād al-Ḥaḍar, built between 1027 and 1030 in the traditional style of al-Ḳayrawān, did not have its *miḥrāb* ornamented with Hispano-Maghribin decoration until 1193. The system of irrigation described by Al-Bakrī is still in existence. Nefṭa was guarded by a wall and had a large population. At Tokyūs, which included "four cities enclosed by walls, so close that it was possible to hold a conversation from one to the other", various crops including olives were cultivated. The Djerid had plentiful resources, its oranges were celebrated, its sugar-cane was well known, but the date was its great product: Al-Bakrī claims that every day there left Tozeur "a thousand camels or even more, laden with this fruit". The inhabitants were reputed to be cynophagists. There were still some Ibāḍites in the 5th/11th century.

In 1053, the Ḳasṭīliya was ravaged by the Riyāḥ, the vanguard of the Banū Hilāl, commanded by ʿAbid b. Abi 'l-Rayth; it was quickly incorporated in the independent principality carved out of southern Tunisia by the governor of Gafsa, ʿAbd Allāh b. al-Rand; this principality, with its sometimes brilliant court, was to endure until the Almohad conquest (1159-60). Shortly afterwards the Djerid became one of the bases of operations of ʿAlī, and then of Yaḥyā b. Ghāniya, in their attempts to restore the Almoravid empire. Under the Ḥafṣids, in the 13th and 14th centuries, it was in fact in the hands of families who were seeking to preserve their hereditary power; among them were the Banū Yamlūl at Tozeur and the Banu 'l-Khalaf at Nefṭa, both descended from nomadic Arabs; they paid no more heed to the councils of notables than to the advice of their sovereigns, especially in the 14th century. But they were compelled to negotiate constantly with the nomads, to whom the settled population paid tribute (*ghafāra* on harvests or a payment of money); the nomads guaranteed their supplies of grain and the export of dates, stored provisions in the houses and guarded the flocks of the rich oasis inhabitants; though turbulent and dangerous, it was not in the nomads' interest to abuse their strength. These nomads, the Riyāḥ, were little by little thrust back in the course of the 6th/12th century, and in the 13th century were replaced by tribes of Sulaym origin, the Kūb and Mirdās, who migrated from the Djerid to the neighbourhood of Bône. In the 14th century the Kūb levied the *iḳṭāʿ*, whilst certain Mirdās, after acquiring property at Tozeur, gradually began to settle. But the great Ḥafṣid sovereigns of the 15th century, as a result of several expeditions, succeeded in imposing their authority over the settled as well as the nomadic population, through the help of active governors.

From the 12th century Khāridjism was in full decline, weakened by dissensions between Wahbiyya and Nekkāra; it seems to have disappeared when faced with the propaganda of a marabout who lived in about 1200, Sīdī Abū ʿAlī al-Nafṭī, whose tomb stands in the middle of the palm grove at Nefṭa. The economy was still based on cultivation of oases and on trade with nomads. Tozeur was still the capital, and was renowned for the additions which had been made to its palm grove: it had two mosques with *khuṭba* and public baths; but the trade in human excrement and the practice of cynophagy sometimes brought its inhabitants into disrepute.

From the end of the 16th century the Turks, and from 1705 the Ḥusaynid sovereigns, attempted by repeated expeditions to maintain their authority over the Djerid and to enforce the payment of taxes. As a result of the refusal of the inhabitants of Ceddada to pay taxes during the third quarter of the 17th century, their village which at that time was situated high up by the tomb of Sīdī Bū Helāl, was destroyed and a number of the inhabitants massacred by the regular troops; the survivors went down and settled by their palmtrees at El-Oudiane. The habit grew up among the Ḥusaynides of organizing a force (*meḥalla*) in winter, to come in January and February to collect taxes and, where necessary, to restore order in the tribes in the South and the oases. This practice gave rise to abuses which were denounced at the beginning of the 18th century by the traveller Moula-Ahmed (Berbruger, *Voyages dans le sud de l'Algérie*, 245-7) shortly after Yūnus, the son of ʿAlī Pas͟ha, kept the proceeds of heavy fines levied irregularly on the wealthy inhabitants of Djerid. More than once, unjustified confiscations of estates were effected for the benefit of the Bey who lost no time in reselling them. Nevertheless the *meḥalla* was successful in settling, at least for the time being, the not infrequent disputes between the settled population and the nomads, and internal feuds like the one between the inhabitants of the El Ḥādef and Zebda districts of Tozeur. The Djerid trade suffered from the abolition of slavery (1857) and the decline in trans-Sahara trade.

Since 1880, the year when the French Protectorate was established, the oases have been extended as the result of a number of borings, and many more palm-trees of the *deglat al-nūr* variety, which produces soft dates for export to Europe, have been grown. In the Djerid there are more than 1,100,000 date-palms, almost half of which are *deglat al-nūr*; but the cultivation of fruit and vegetables is not on a large scale. The luxuriance of the vegetation is in contrast to the abject poverty so wide-spread among the people, the result in part of the rapid increase in population (despite considerable emigration to Tunis), in part of the very unequal distribution of land, or division into too small units, and also the decline in handicrafts. In addition, the land is often inadequately manured and indifferently cultivated. Gardens are enclosed by banks of earth (*tabya*), thickly planted with palm-trees; a Spring festival, a nature festival of pagan origin, called *mayo*, is still celebrated there.

The richest palm-grove, where however the greatest disparity between the various proprietors is to be seen, is at Tozeur. Tozeur, with its 12,000 inhabitants, is the chief town of the Djerid and the largest market in the Tunisian Sahara; it is patronized in particular by the Ulād Sīdī ʿAbīd, nomads from the frontier region. Tozeur often has an urban appearance, with its lofty houses of brick decorated with geometrical motifs, and with new districts near the station. It has been connected by railway with Sfax since 1919. Nefṭa, with a larger population (14,600 inhabitants) is more purely rural, and suffers from an irregular water supply in summer: the Nememcha, who are Algerian nomads, are its principal customers. El-Oudiane has five villages (Degache, Zaouyat al-Arab, Zorgane, Kriz and Ceddada) which are scattered along an almost continuous palm-grove, fed by a chain of abundant springs: its trade is mostly with the Hamāma. This is true also of al-Ḥamma, a modest group of three villages (El-Nemlet, Mharet, El-Erg), situated on the north of the Drāʿ al-D̲j̲arīd, with only 2,800 inhabitants, but with a local reputation since ancient times for its hot springs. The small mountain oases of Tamerza, Midès and Chebika, near the Algerian frontier, as picturesque as they are poverty-stricken and inaccessible, are for administrative purposes grouped with the Djerid.

Bibliography: Ibn Ḥawḳal, *Description de l'Afrique*, trans. de Slane, in *JA*, 1842; Bakrī, *Description de l'Afrique septentrionale*, trans. de Slane, 2nd ed. 1913; Idrīsī, *Description de l'Afrique et de l'Espagne*, trans. Dozy and De Goeje, 1866; Ibn K͟haldūn, *Histoire des Berbères*, 2nd. ed.; ʿUmarī, *L'Afrique moins l'Egypte*, trans. Gaudefroy-Demombynes, 1927; Leo Africanus, *Description de l'Afrique*, trans. Épaulard, 1956; M. Seghir Ben Youssef, *Mechra el Melki*, trans. V. Serre and M. Lasram, Tunis 1900; V. Guérin, *Voyage archéologique dans la Régence de Tunis*, 2 vols., 1862; P. Penet, *Kairouan, Sbeitla, le Djerid*, 1912; idem, *L'hydraulique agricole de la Tunisie méridionale*, 1913; G. Castany, R. Dégallier and Ch. Domergue, *Les grands problèmes d'hydrologie en Tunisie*, 1952; G. Marçais, *Les Arabes en Berbérie*, 1913; R. Brunschwig, *La Berbérie orientale sous les Hafsides*, 2 vol., 1940-7; G. Payre, *Une fête du printemps au Jerid*, in *RT*, 1942; H. Attya, *L'organisation de l'oasis*, in *CT*, 1957. (J. Despois)

D̲J̲ARĪDA, literally "leaf", which has become the usual term in modern Arabic for a newspaper, its adoption being attributed to Fāris al-S̲h̲idyāḳ [*q.v.*]. Its synonym *ṣaḥīfa* is less used in the sing., but the plural *ṣuḥuf* is more common than *d̲j̲arāʾid*. Some interest in the European press was shown by the Ottomans as early as the 18th century and, it would seem, excerpts from European newspapers were translated for the information of the *dīwān* (Prussian despatch from Constantinople, of 1780, cited by J. W. Zinkeisen, *Geschichte des osmanischen Reiches*, vi, Gotha 1859, 290-1). This grew into a press bureau, which served the Ottoman government throughout the 19th century and after.

The first newspapers in the Middle East were in French, and were published under French official auspices. In the seventeen-nineties the French printing press in Constantinople (see MAṬBAʿA) began to produce bulletins, communiqués and other announcements put out by the French embassy. In 1795 the ambassador, Verninac, reported that he was printing every fortnight, after the arrival of the mail from Europe, a bulletin of 6 to 8 octavo pages where French nationals could find information about new laws and events of concern to them. This bulletin was distributed throughout the Levant. In the following year, under his successor Aubert Dubayet, the bulletin became a newspaper—the *Gazette française de Constantinople*, the first to appear in the Middle East. It consisted of 4 octavo pages, sometimes increased to six, and was published rather irregularly, at intervals of about a month, from the French Embassy, for a period of about two years. In September 1798, after the French expedition to Egypt, the French staff were interned and the press sequestered by the Turkish authorities. It was returned in 1802, and later used to reprint military communiqués for local distribution, but the *Gazette* did not apparently resume publication.

At the time of the Egyptian expedition, Bonaparte was accompanied by two printing-presses; one of these, privately owned, belonged to the printer Marc Aurel and only possessed Latin characters, while the other, officially owned, was placed under the direction of the orientalist J. Marcel and was equipped with French, Arabic and Greek characters. It was from the former printing-press that the first number of the *Courrier* [sic] *de l'Égypte* appeared in Cairo on 12 Fructidor VI = 29 August 1798; published every five days, it contained local news, announcements, notices etc., as well as items of European news. A month later, on 10 Vendémiaire VII = 1 October 1798, the same publisher was selling the first number of a quarterly review, *La Décade égyptienne*, which was devoted to the publication of records of the meetings of the "Institut d'Égypte" and the papers read to this learned society. When Bonaparte returned to France, Marc Aurel followed him, with the result that J. Marcel's "Imprimerie orientale et française" took on the printing of the two periodicals, with the direction of which the names of the mathematician Fourier and doctor Desgenettes, among others, were connected. The 116 numbers, each of 4 quarto pages, of the *Courrier* and the 3 volumes of the *Décade* constitute a historical source of the highest importance. In Arabic, Marcel's printing-press had mainly published proclamations, notices and communiqués, but after Kléber's assassination (16 June 1800) it also printed the first Arabic newspaper, *al-Tanbīh*, which was founded by Menou and, it seems, was only short-lived (see F. Charles-Roux, *Bonaparte, gouverneur d'Égypte*[4], Paris n.d., 138 ff.; R. Canivet, *L'imprimerie de l'expédition d'Égypte*, in *BIÉ*, 1909; Reinaud, in *JA*, 1831, 249).

It was at Ceuta, at the opposite end of the Maghrib, on 1 May 1820, that the first newspaper to be published in Morocco appeared, *El Liberal Africano*, the weekly publication of the patriotic Society of the town; it came to an end after 6 numbers on 5 June of the same year (V. Ferrando la Hoz, *Apuntes para la historia de la Imprenta en el Norte de Marruecos*, Tetuan 1949, 23).

In 1824 a French monthly, called *Le Smyrnéen*, was founded in Izmir by a Frenchman, Charles Tricon. After some initial difficulties with both the Turkish and French authorities, it was reorganized under new management, and began to appear weekly, under the name of *Le Spectateur oriental*, with four quarto pages. It circulated mainly among foreign commercial elements. In 1827 Alexandre Blacque, a lawyer from Marseilles and a well-known figure in the Levant, became part owner and effective editor of the *Spectateur*, to which he was already a regular contributor. Later renamed the *Courrier de Smyrne*, it played a lively rôle in the affairs of the time, and more than once involved its editor in trouble with the Powers by its forthright comment, notably by its advocacy of the Ottoman cause against the Greek insurgents (L. Lagarde, *Note sur les journaux français de Constantinople à l'époque révolutionnaire*, in *JA*, ccxxxvi, 1948, 271-6; idem, *Note sur les journaux français de Smyrne à l'époque de Mahmoud* II, in *JA*, 1950, 103-44; Selim Nüzhet, *Türk Gazeteciliği 1831-1931*, Istanbul 1931, 10-28—with a reproduction of a whole issue of the *Gazette*, dated 1 Floréal, year V = 20 April 1797, and of *Le Spectateur Oriental* of 21 July 1827; Ahmed Emin, *The development of modern Turkey as measured by its press*, New York 1914, 28-9; Charles White, *Three years in Constantinople*, ii, London 1845, 218-22). A Turkish account of Russian attempts to get the paper suppressed will be found in the history of Luṭfī (*Taʾrīkh-i Luṭfī*, iii, 98 ff.). Luṭfī quotes the Russian ambassador as saying "Indeed, in France and England journalists (*gazetedji*) can express themselves freely, even against their kings; so that on several occasions, in former times, wars broke out between France and England because of these journalists. Praise be to God, the divinely-guarded realms were protected from such things, until a little while ago that man turned up in Izmir and began to publish his paper. It would be well to prevent him . . ." (Luṭfī, iii, 100; cf. Emin 28).

It was at this point that Egypt was to re-appear on the scene. As early as 1821, Muḥammad ʿAlī had given instructions for the publication of a daily newspaper which was to be submitted to him each day and to contain various official, administrative and economic items of information, but it was probably (the numbers prior to 1840 have not been preserved) on 12 Djumādā I 1244/20 November 1828 that there appeared in Cairo the first number of the first real periodical in Arabic, *al-Waḳāʾiʿ al-Miṣriyya*, the organ of Muḥammad ʿAlī's Government of Egypt; at first issued weekly in Arabic, it later appeared for several months in Turkish and then finally returned to Arabic; it subsequently appeared three times weekly, with a separately published French edition, and it remained the only periodical in Egypt under Muḥammad ʿAlī's Government; from the time of the Khedive Ismāʿīl it was published daily, and in addition to orders, decrees and laws it also contained new local and foreign items, editorials and occasional illustrations. In 1881, with Muḥammad ʿAbduh [*q.v.*] as chief editor, it was the most important and widely circulated newspaper of the time.

During the British occupation it reverted to its earlier form and merely contained notices and information on affairs of state. In 1929 it still appeared in official lists.

In this as in so many other matters, the Sultan in Istanbul responded quickly to the challenge of the pasha in Cairo. In 1831 M. Blacque was summoned to Istanbul to publish the *Moniteur ottoman*, the official journal of the Ottoman government, in French. The following year, on 1 Djumādā I 1247/14 May 1832, the first issue of the Turkish *Taḳwīm-i Weḳāʾiʿ* appeared. A leading article presented the newspaper as a natural development of the imperial historiographies, with the function of making known the true nature of events and the real purport of the acts and commands of the government, in order to prevent misunderstanding and forestall uninformed criticism. A further purpose was to provide useful knowledge on commerce, science, and the arts. Unlike the *Moniteur*, which gave some space to news and comment, the *Taḳwīm* was limited to official statements. It was issued by an office called the *Taḳwīmkhāne-i ʿĀmire*, the first director of which was the Imperial Historiographer Esʿad Efendi (on whom see Babinger, *GOW*, 354-6). Five thousand copies were distributed to officials and notables, as well as to foreign embassies. The inauguration of the postal service in 1834 greatly helped its circulation. Between 1832 and 1838 about 30 issues a year were published. Thereafter it appeared about once a week, though with some interruptions. The final issue, number 4,608, was published on 4 Rabīʿ I 1341/4 November 1922, after which it was replaced as official organ of the Turkish government by the *Resmī Djerīde*, later renamed *Resmi Gazete*, of Ankara. (Luṭfī, iii, 156-60; Nüzhet, 30-5; Emin 29-32).

The first non-official newspaper published in the Turkish language was the weekly *Djerīde-i Ḥawādith*, founded in 1840 by the Englishman William Churchill. After his death in 1864 it was continued by his son. In appearance rather like the *Taḳwīm-i Weḳāʾiʿ*, it was commercial in purpose, and carried an increasing amount of advertising. It did, however, publish many articles and features, often in serial form, thus offering an apprenticeship in journalism to a number of Turkish men of letters. (On some of the contributors to the *Djerīde-i Ḥawādith* see the articles of Ibnülemīn Maḥmūd Kemāl in *Türk Taʾrīkhi Endjümeni Medjmūʿasi*, 96 and 97). The Crimean War brought new needs and opportunities. Churchill reported from the battlefront for English newspapers, and his reports were also published in Turkish in special supplements of the *Djerīde-i Ḥawādith*, giving the Turkish reader, anxious for news of the war, a new insight into the function of the press.

A second officially sponsored Turkish periodical was the *Waḳāʾiʿ-i Ṭibbiyye*, a medical monthly published for the first time in 1850, in both Turkish and French. Other journals also appeared in French, as well as in Italian, Greek, Armenian, and Judaeo-Spanish.

In 1855, the second Arabic newspaper, the *Mir'āt al-Aḥwāl*, founded by Ḥassān who was compelled to take refuge in London [see below, iii], appeared in Beirut; the same town also saw the start of *al-Sulṭāna* in 1857 and, on 1 January 1858, of the *Ḥadīḳat al-Afkār*, published in Arabic and French by Khalīl al-Khūrī; the main purpose of this publication, which had the backing of the Turkish Government, was to acquaint the numerous foreigners residing in Beirut with the Porte's views.

The year 1860 brought two important innovations: the first was the establishment of an Arabic newspaper, *al-Djawā'ib*, compared with which the earlier efforts seemed formless and inarticulate; started in Constantinople by the Lebanese Aḥmad Fāris al-Shidyāḳ in July 1860, and vigorously supported by the Turkish Government, this periodical defended the cause of Islam which had been recently embraced by its founder. The latter can be regarded as the father of newspaper Arabic, having done so much to enrich the language, while *al-Djawā'ib* was the greatest Arabic newspaper of the 19th century, on sale in Cairo, Beirut, Damascus, ʿIrāḳ and West Africa, its wide circulation depending on the care lavished upon its editing and presentation. It reached its apogee in about 1880, but after the death of Aḥmad Fāris in 1884 his son Sālim was unable to maintain the earlier standard. From 1288 to 1298/1871-81, al-Shidyāḳ printed, under the title *Kanz al-raghā'ib fī muntakhabāt al-Djawā'ib*, seven volumes made up of articles on literature, history etc. reproduced from his newspaper, and still of undeniable documentary interest. — The second innovation of 1860 was the weekly *Terdjümān-i Aḥwāl*, the first privately owned newspaper produced by a Turk. Its founder was Čapanzāde Agāh Efendi, scion of a *derebey* [*q.v.*] family, and a senior official in the Translation Office of the Sublime Porte. Associated with him as editor was the writer Ibrāhim Shināsī [*q.v.*]. Churchill responded to this competition by publishing a daily version of his paper five times a week—the *Rūznāme-i Djerīde-i Ḥawādith*, and for a while there was keen rivalry between the two. In the increasingly authoritarian mood of the time the press began to encounter difficulties, and soon the *Terdjümān* was suspended for two weeks because of an article probably written by Ziya (Ḍiyā') Pasha. This was the first time a newspaper was suppressed by the government in Turkey.

(B. Lewis & Ch. Pellat)

In the preceding section we have tried to give an account of the first attempts to establish a press throughout the Muslim world, necessarily devoting most attention to the publications directed by foreigners in the various Islamic countries, since they played a considerable part in the rise of journalism. From about 1860 there began a new period during which journalistic activity developed to the point at which it becomes necessary to relegate newspapers published in European languages to second place, despite their importance, and to trace the history of the press in the various Muslim countries separately, with due regard to the language in which publication was made.

i. — ARABIC LANGUAGE PRESS

A. — Middle East.

Egypt.—The history of the Arabic press of Egypt can be divided into four periods. The first lasts until the time of the British occupation. After *al-Waḳā'iʿ al-Miṣriyya*, it was only in 1866 that the *Wādi 'l-Nīl* appeared, founded in Cairo by ʿAbd Allāh Abu 'l-Suʿūd; in 1869, the *Nuzhat al-Afkār* was started by two Egyptians, Ibrāhīm al-Muwayliḥī and ʿUthmān Djalāl, but it was between 1876 and 1878, under the impulse of Syro-Lebanese journalists who were unable to follow their career in their own countries in freedom, that the great organs of the press came into being. At their head we must note *al-Ahrām*, founded by Salīm and Bishāra Taḳlā, and making a modest start in 1876 at Alexandria in the form of a 4-page weekly, dependent upon French cultural influence but paying close attention to the policies of the caliph in Constantinople; it was later issued daily and, maintaining its high literary standards and scrupulous presentation, was to remain until our own time as the greatest newspaper in the Arabic language. In addition to *al-Ittiḥād al-Miṣrī*, a bi-weekly founded in Alexandria in 1879 which lasted until 1892, we should mention the Cairo Coptic newspaper *al-Waṭan* (founded in about 1878, and still recorded in 1929), and the interesting attempt at nationalistic propaganda by Yaʿḳūb Ṣanūʿ, known as Abū Naḍḍāra [*q.v.*] who had to continue his activities in Paris.

The second period lasts from the British occupation to the first world war. It was in about 1885 that the Ṣarrūf-Nimr-Maḳāryos consortium was set up for a group of publications, the most important of them being the fortnightly review *al-Muḳtaṭaf*, founded in Beirut in 1877 and moving to Cairo, and *al-Muḳaṭṭam*, a daily paper with political news which was pro-British and in sympathy with reform; after 1889 it became an opponent of *al-Ahrām* which still supported the policies of Constantinople. A third party, opposed to reforms and advocating traditional Islam, was formed and, after 1890, represented by a daily newspaper, *al-Mu'ayyad*, under the remarkable and skilful direction of Shaykh ʿAlī Yūsuf. The Syro-Lebanese, who until then had had a monopoly of the press, were gradually replaced by Muslim Egyptians, mostly conservative and orthodox; *al-ʿAdāla*, founded in 1897, took over the rôle held by *al-Muʿayyad* as soon as the latter began to become more moderate and, during the last decade of the 19th century, there appeared a considerable number of newspapers also belonging to the conservative party, and of varying degrees of fanaticism. The growing nationalism was defended at first by Adīb Isḥāḳ, one of the chief editors of the daily *Miṣr* (1896), and later by Muṣṭafā Kāmil whose principal organ was *al-Liwā'*. It was during this period that another large newspaper appeared in Cairo, *al-Djarīda*, which took account of the effective domination of the British. Mention must also be made of the review of *al-Hilāl*, directed in Cairo (1892) by Djirdjī Zaydān, which has survived until our own time, and of the *Manār*, founded by Rashīd Riḍā in 1897. For that same year Washington-Serruys (XVII-XIX) lists 52 different publications in Cairo, more than half of which date from 1895 at the latest, and 6 in Alexandria, including *al-Ahrām*. In 1909 there appeared in Egypt 144 reviews and various newspapers, 90 of them in Cairo and 45 in Alexandria (see *RMM*, xii, 308).

During this second period, therefore, we see the expansion of a powerful press, still producing many non-political publications, but tending, when entering the political arena, to express the still vague aspirations of the Muslim peoples, to formulate them more precisely, and to stimulate the concentration of the divergent trends in an Arab and Muslim nationalism. In the third period of the Egyptian press, after the dismemberment of the Ottoman Empire, the general aspiration for independence took shape and gathered momentum, though not without the accompaniment of violent crises. In 1922 the "Liberal-Constitutional" Party started a weekly publication, *al-Siyāsa*, under the direction of Ḥusayn Haykal; after 1926 it was duplicated by a daily edition, and it shows signs of an Egyptian particularism. The Wafd Party in its turn owned a group of newspapers representing the opinions of Saʿd Zaghlūl and his successors: *al-Balāgh*, *Kawkab al-Shark* and *al-Miṣrī* are the most important.

During the second world war and the years following, the Egyptian press took a more active part in the political struggle which culminated in the evacuation of British troops. From October 1944 the different parties created new organs: *al-Kutla* (the Wafdist "Bloc"), *Bilādī* (Saʿdist weekly), *al-Liwāʾ al-Djadīd* (Nationalist Party weekly), to which was added a weekly review of news, *Akhbār al-Yawm*. This upsurge of newspapers does not include the rise of extensive undertakings made by the press: *Société Orientale de Publicité*, *Ahrām*, *Dār al-Hilāl*, all of whose publications cannot be listed (for the state of the Arabic press of Egypt at the end of 1944, see *COC*, No. 1, 124-6; at the end of 1946, *ibid.*, No. 4, 817, giving a detailed list).

The final period opens with the suspension of the political press as a result of the revolution of 25 July 1952. The political parties having been dissolved and replaced by a single party, the "National Union", in 1958, the press was reorganized in May 1960 and the ownership of newspapers was transferred from the hands of private individuals or companies to the National Union, with the result that the whole press was subject to a single official administration. Of the principal newspapers which continued to appear, mention may be made of *al-Ahrām*, *al-Djumhūriyya*, *al-Masāʾ*, and *al-Akhbār*. (Ed.)

The Sudan.—The Sudanese periodical press originated during the Anglo-Egyptian Condominium (1899-1955). The earliest Arabic newspaper, *al-Sūdān*, was first issued on 24 September 1903, by a Syrian editor, under the auspices of Dr. Fāris Nimr. Four or five other papers appeared during the next thirty years, the most successful being *Haḍārat al-Sūdān*, which ran from 1919 to 1938. The rise of Sudanese nationalism in the 'thirties resulted in a greatly increased output of newspapers, chiefly as organs of political comment. In 1958, out of a total of 35 papers, mostly dailies or weeklies, 5 had been founded between 1935 and 1945, 20 between 1946 and 1955, and 10 under the Republic. There has also been a succession of English and Greek journals from 1903 and 1909 respectively. Since the establishment of the military régime in November 1958, the Sudanese press has not enjoyed freedom of expression. (P. M. Holt)

Lebanon.—It was only in 1869 that the first real Arabic newspaper appeared in Beirut, *al-Bashīr*, a weekly published by the Jesuits which survived until recent times. Before that, Buṭrus al-Bustānī had founded the modest *Nafīr Sūriya* as far back as 1860, but it was from the middle of 1870 that, to interest public opinion in the cause of general education and national literature, he brought out the bi-weekly *al-Djanna* which his son Salīm continued to publish until 7 July 1886. Its vogue was such that *djanna* became synonymous with newspaper in Lebanon. Al-Bustānī also published *al-Djunayna*, which only lasted three years, and *al-Djinān*.

Not wishing to be left behind, the Muslims of Beirut in 1874 founded the weekly *Thamarāt al-Funūn* which carried on until the Young Turk revolution and then took the name of *al-Ittiḥād al-ʿUthmānī*; this newspaper was conspicuous for its poverty and the turgid prose of its pedantic conservative contributors. The same year saw the foundation of *al-Taḳaddum*, which declared itself the earnest champion of progress and the inveterate enemy of all reactionary elements in the country; Adīb Isḥāḳ was a notable contributor.

On 18 October 1877 Khalīl Sarkīs, son-in-law of Buṭrus al-Bustānī, brought out the first number of the *Lisān al-Ḥāl*, a daily and, to some extent, a rival to *al-Djanna*. The two newspapers hardly concerned themselves with politics and presented events in as colourless a form as possible, while paying particular regard to the government's opinion. The *Lisān al-Ḥāl* mainly concerned itself with scientific and economic matters, but nevertheless it fell foul of the Ottoman Government which suspended it for some months, during which Sarkīs published another newspaper, *al-Mishkāt*; but that did not stop him from resuming publication, and he became the doyen of the Lebanese press in our day.

In 1880 a new party took shape: the Maronites who opposed the encroachments of the Roman Curia founded a small newspaper *al-Miṣbāḥ*, while Protestantism was supported by the reviews *Kawkab al-Ṣubḥ al-Munīr* and *al-Nashra al-Usbūʿiyya*; the Greek Orthodox church, for its part, also had a newspaper, *al-Hadiyya*. An important addition to the press came in 1885 with the weekly *Bayrūt* which, with government support, served as a counterpoise to the *Thamarāt al-Funūn*. When in March 1888 Beirut became the chief town of the *wilāyet*, an official governmental organ was set up under the name *Bayrūt al-Rasmiyya*. At the nd of the century (see Washington-Serruys, XIX, XX), 9 periodicals were being published in Beirut and 3 elsewhere in Lebanon; for 1912, the figures are 8 dailies, 17 weeklies and 12 reviews (*RMM*, xix, 76 ff.).

In addition to the *Lisān al-Ḥāl*, various dailies date from this period as for example the *Ṣadā Lubnān* (1900), *al-Balāgh* (1910), *al-Bayraḳ* (1913) and the Zahle weekly, *Zaḥla al-Fatāt* (1910), all of which can be regarded as veterans. Later, the development of the Lebanese press continued without interruption. During the French mandate a certain number of dailies appeared, some of which have survived until our own time: *al-Aḥrār* (1923), *al-Shark* (1926), *al-Nahār* (1933), *al-Ittiḥād al-Lubnānī* (1933), *al-Rawwād* (1934), *Bayrūt* (1936), *al-Niḍāl* (1936), *al-Yawm* (1937), *Raḳīb al-Aḥwāl* (1939), and finally *al-ʿAmal* (1939), the organ of the *Katāʾib* (Phalanges).

Since 1941, and especially in the years following the second world war, a considerable number of newspapers and reviews were introduced; the situation of the Arabic press of Lebanon in 1946 was the subject of a survey in *COC*, No. 4, 809-12, which noted 29 dailies and 25 periodicals appearing in Beirut, and 16 other periodicals elsewhere in the country.

In 1956 the Lebanese press consisted of 27 dailies and 37 periodicals, figures which are explained only by the extreme complexity of the social, religious and political structure of the country, as well as by the great liberty enjoyed by the press. To these figures should be added 18 periodicals from inland districts,

2 dailies in Armenian, 2 publications in English and 10 in French, of which *L'Orient* (1924), *la Revue du Liban* (1928) and Le Jour (1934) date from the time of the mandate, and reacher circulation figures that were high for this country (up to 7,000 or 8,000 copies); *Le Commerce du Levant* (1928), on economic and financial subjects, had a wide distribution.

Syria.—It was only in 1865 and 1866 that there appeared, in Damascus and Aleppo respectively, the first newspapers to be printed in Arabic and Turkish and founded by the Ottoman Government, *Sūriya* and *al-Furāt*; the foundation of these publications was correlated with the reorganization of the Turkish administration; it was decided at the same time that the authorities of all *wilāyet*s should have a newspaper printed, and this fact explains the bilingual nature of these publications. Other instances which may be quoted are *Dimashk*, set up by the Turkish Government in 1879, and the *Mirʾāt al-Akhlāk* which appeared in 1886. An independent political weekly, *al-Shām*, came out in Damascus in 1896, whilst in Aleppo the weekly *al-Shahbāʾ* was published from 1893, and *al-Iʿtidāl* from 1879, and in Tripoli *Ṭarābulus al-Shām*, a weekly publication, from 1892.

In Syria, however, as in Lebanon, the press had a precarious existence, all the more since the government treated any independent criticism of its actions with the greatest severity. Consequently we find that a good many Syro-Lebanese journalists took refuge in Egypt. After the setting up of the French mandate, the Damascus press underwent a very extensive development and a large number of newspapers made their appearance, but for the most part circulation figures remained very low. In 1939, 9 Arabic and 2 French dailies, not counting a varying number of periodicals, appeared in Damascus alone; the number is obviously excessive since an output of this order was in no way justified by the same reasons as at Beirut; and yet this number actually increased after the second world war. In 1946, 19 dailies are recorded at Damascus, 7 at Aleppo and 1 at Ḥamāt, as well as 3 Damascus periodicals (*COC*, No. 4, 812-3). From the period of the mandate the only survivors in 1956 were *Alif Bāʾ* (1920) and *al-Ayyām* (1931), both moderate, *al-Ḳabas* (1928), *al-Akhbār* (1928) and *al-Inshāʾ* (1936), organs of the National Party; in addition to these veteran dailies about 15 others came out, representing every sort of political opinion. At the same time half a dozen periodicals also sprang up and, elsewhere in Syria, about ten other publications, the organs of the various parties. We may note that an independent Aleppo paper established in 1928 and published in French, "*L'Éclair du Nord*", in 1945 became the *Bark al-Shimāl*.

Palestine.—The development of the Arabic press in Palestine was slower and later than in Egypt, Syria, or Lebanon. Syrian and Lebanese publications no doubt circulated in Ottoman Palestine, but apart from a few mission sheets and school publications, the first Palestinian Arabic newspaper was *al-Karmal*, founded in Haifa in 1908 by Nadjīb Naṣṣār, an Orthodox Christian. It lasted until 1942. In 1911 another orthodox Christian, ʿĪsā al-ʿĪsā, started the newspaper *Falasṭīn* in Jaffa. Both papers appeared at somewhat irregular intervals, and during the first world war were suppressed by the Turkish authorities. After the war, they resumed publication, and were accompanied by many new journals, expressing Arab political reactions to the British Mandate and the policy of the Jewish national home. Among these were *Sūriya al-Djanūbiyya* (ed. ʿĀrif

al-ʿĀrif and Muḥ. Ḥasan al-Budayrī) and *Mirʾāt al-Shark* (ed. Būlus Shehāda); both were started in 1919, and were of brief duration. *Al-Ṣabāḥ* (ed. Muḥ. Kāmil al-Budayrī and Yūsuf Yāsīn), founded in 1921, became the organ of the Arab executive.

The first daily newspaper in Arabic was the old *Falasṭīn*, which began regular daily publication in 1929, and has continued to the present day in the old city of Jerusalem. Other dailies were *al-Ṣirāṭ al-Mustakīm* (founded 1925, daily from 1929, edited by Shaykh ʿAbdallāh al-Ḳalkīlī) and *al-Difāʿ* (founded 1934, ed. Ibrāhīm al-Shanṭī). Both papers were owned and edited by Muslims; the former was markedly Islamic in tone; the latter expressed strong Arab nationalist views, at first connected with the *Istiḳlāl* party, later with the groups led by the Ḥusaynīs. It is still published in Jordanian Jerusalem. The weekly *al-Waḥda*, founded in 1945, became a daily in the following year.

During the nineteen-thirties and forties there was a very rapid development of the periodical press, notably of political weeklies and fortnightlies. Modelled on the Egyptian weeklies, some of them offered their readers feature articles, film news and other lighter entertainment, sometimes with pictures, in addition to political news and comment. Two papers, the weekly *al-Ittiḥād* (founded 1944) and the fortnightly *al-Ghadd* (first published irregularly in the twenties, re-started 1945) represented communist or pro-communist views; the remainder expressed various shades of Arab nationalism and factions among the Arab leadership. The press in languages other than Arabic was mainly Jewish. The first Hebrew journal, the *Ḥavaṣeleth*, began publication in Jerusalem in 1871. Other Jewish papers, in Hebrew and other languages, followed in great numbers.

After the termination of the Palestine Mandate, the major Palestinian Arab journals continued or resumed publication in Jordan where, according to the *Middle East* for 1961, there were 7 daily newspapers in Jerusalem and Amman, and 14 periodicals, in Arabic and English. The same source cites one Arabic daily newspaper and 6 Arabic periodicals in Israel.

ʿIrāḳ.—The liberal Ottoman governor Midḥat Pasha in 1868 set up the first newspaper in ʿIrāḳ, *al-Zawrāʾ*, which appeared in Arabic and Turkish and, while supporting the government's policy, published official texts and news in general. In 1875 the government started another newspaper in Mosul, *al-Mawṣil*, and, in 1895, a third entitled *al-Baṣra*, in Basra.

Among the many newspapers which sprang up after the promulgation of the Constitution of 1908, the following may be mentioned: *Baghdād* (1908), *al-Raḳīb* (1909), *Bayn al-Nahrayn* (1909) in Arabic and Turkish, *al-Riyāḍ* (1910), *al-Ruṣāfa* (1910), and *al-Nahḍa* (1913). Under the British mandate a great number of new newspapers appeared, notably *al-Waḳāʾiʿ al-ʿIrāḳiyya*, *al-Mawṣil*, *al-ʿIrāḳ* and *al-Shark*. After the second world war the many newly established political parties owned their own organs and until the revolution of 14 July 1958 practically every town in ʿIrāḳ had a daily or weekly newspaper.

Arabia.—In the Arabian peninsula the oldest newspaper, *Ṣanʿāʾ*, dates back to 1877 and, like so many official publications under the Ottoman régime, was printed in Arabic and Turkish. It was only in 1908 that Mecca had its first newspaper, *al-Ḥidjāz*. The press is now represented by the official newspaper which appears once a week in Mecca, *Umm al-Ḳurā*, and by *al-Bilād al-Suʿūdiyya* (bi-weekly,

Mecca), *al-Ḥadjdj* (monthly, Mecca) and *al-Madīna* (weekly, Medina). In 1953 a more modern newspaper, *al-Riyāḍ*, made its appearance at Djudda but it was compelled to stop publication as a result of the hostility of the *Ikhwān* [*q.v.*].

The Colony of Aden has six Arabic publications, among which *al-Akhbār al-ʿAdaniyya* and *Fatāt al-Djazira* may be noted. In Kuwayt the most important newspaper is *al-Kuwayt al-Yawm* (1955), but it also produces a monthly review with coloured illustrations, *al-ʿAsalī*, published by the government.

Bibliography: Ph. de Ṭarrāzī, *Taʾrīkh al-ṣiḥāfa al-ʿarabiyya*, Beirut 1913-33 (4 vol.); Ibrāhīm ʿAbduh, *Taṭawwur al-ṣiḥāfa al-miṣriyya*, Cairo 1945; Ḳostāḳī al-Ḥalabī, *Taʾrīkh takwīn al-ṣuḥuf al-miṣriyya*, Alexandria n.d.; ʿAbd al-Razzāḳ al-Ḥasanī, *Taʾrīkh al-ṣiḥāfa al-ʿirāḳiyya*², Baghdād 1957; M. Samhān, *al-Ṣiḥāfa*, Cairo 1358/1939; Kamal Eldin Galal, *Entstehung und Entwicklung der Tagespresse in Ägypten*, Frankfurt am Main 1939; *al-Hilāl*, i (1892), 9-16, v (1896), 141 ff.; Washington-Serruys, *L'arabe moderne étudié dans les journaux et les pièces officielles*, Beirut 1897 (situation of the Arabic press at that date); M. Hartmann, *The Arabic press of Egypt*, London 1899; *L'Égypte indépendante 1937*, Paris 1938, 369-456; Pearson, 343-6; *RMM*, passim; *The Middle East*, passim; *Annuaire du monde Musulman*³, Paris 1929, 49-77; Margot, *La presse arabe en 1927*, Casablanca 1928.

B. — North Africa.

Paradoxical though it may appear, it was Algeria, at present the Maghrib country which is poorest in Arabic newspapers, which was the first of them to put into circulation a modest periodical, *al-Mubashshir*, from 1847 to 3 December 1926; this was an Arabic edition of the official *Moniteur* founded at Algiers on 27 January 1832 (see H. Fiori, in *RAfr.*, lxxxii (1938), 173-80; G. Sers-Gal, in *Documents algériens*, 8 December 1948). As well as official information, the *Mubashshir* carried news, historical, archaeological, and medical studies, etc. Its example was not immediately followed, and it was necessary to wait until the beginning of the 20th century for an independent press to appear, edited by Muslims indeed, but directed in many cases by Europeans who were desirous of informing and educating the Arabic-reading public; in this way *al-Nāṣiḥ* (1899), *al-Djazīrī* (1900), then *al-Iḥyāʾ* (1906), *Tilimsān* (Tlemcen), *Kawkab Ifrīḳiya* (Algiers, 17 May 1907), *al-Djazāʾir* (Algiers, 1908), *al-Fārūḳ* (Algiers, 1909), *al-Rashīdī* (Djidjelli), etc., were founded. These publications, however, had only an ephemeral life and disappeared before 1914.

The inter-war period was the second in the history of the Muslim press in Algeria. This saw the birth, on the one hand, of a series of newspapers edited in French by Muslims, such as *La Voix indigène*, *La Voix des Humbles* (1923), *L'Entente*, *La Défense*, *La Justice*, *Le Réveil de l'Islam* (Bône, 1922), etc., all intended for the expression of popular aspirations and various political tendencies; and, on the other hand, of a periodical press in Arabic, of a distinct politico-religious character. This period was, in fact, dominated by the struggle which opposed two active groups and caused heated polemics: the reformist *ʿUlamāʾ* (Oulémas), hostile to the Brotherhoods [see ṬĀʾIFA], and to the *bidāʿ* [see BIDʿA], etc., relied on *al-Shihāb* (daily, then monthly; Constantine 1924-39), then on *al-Iṣlāḥ* (Biskra 1929-42), and finally *al-Baṣāʾir* (Algiers, 27 December 1935-56); and the Marabout party, generally favourable to the Franco-Muslim entente, which had as its organs *al-Nadjāḥ* (tri-, then bi-weekly, Constantine, 1919-56) and *al-Balāgh al-Djazāʾirī* (Mostaganem, 1927-47). The Khāridjī *Wādī Mīzāb* (Algiers, 1926-38) is also worthy of mention, among about ten papers which flourished during this period.

In 1945 only *al-Balāgh al-Djazāʾirī*, *al-Baṣāʾir* (prohibited 5 April 1956), and *al-Nadjāḥ* (which ceased to appear from 1 September the same year) remained. The organ of the *ʿUlamāʾ* had been supplemented, from 15 December 1949 to 8 February 1951, by a weekly published at Constantine, *al-Shuʿla*, while the Marabout party published a monthly, *al-Dhikrā*, at Tlemcen from 15 December 1954 to August 1955. However, during this third period, Muslim predilections perceptibly changed, and some essentially political newpapers (*al-Djazāʾir al-Djadīda*, January 1946 to 14 September 1955, communist; *Ṣawt al-Djazāʾir*, from 21 November 1953, which became *Ṣawt al-Shaʿb* from 21 August 1954 to 5 November 1956: MTLD) made a timid appearance. All have now (1960) ceased to appear, or have been prohibited by the authorities; for its information the public depends on a highly developed French-language press. It must be noticed, moreover, that none of the Arabic dailies has ever held good in Algeria, and that the papers mentioned above have, in many cases, known only an irregular appearance. It should be said that they were published by amateurs, with precarious financial resources and rudimentary technical means.

In Morocco, the first newspaper was founded at Ceuta on 1 May 1820, but was in Spanish; and in this language or in French the press developed, particularly at Tangier, in the course of the 19th century. In 1889 an Arabic paper (*al-Maghrib*) appeared a few times, published by an Englishman in that town, where, at the beginning of the 20th century, many European journalists tried to reach the Muslim population by supplementing their papers with an entire or partial Arabic edition. Thus, thanks to European initiative and the collaboration of editors from Syria and Lebanon, the weeklies *al-Saʿāda* (1905), *al-Ṣabāḥ* (1906), *Lisān al-Maghrib* (1907), the Arabic supplement to *El Telegrama del Rif* (1907), and the *Istiḳlāl al-Maghrib*, Arabic edition of the bi-monthly *L'Indépendance marocaine* (1907), were able to appear at Tangier. The first Muslim newspaper was *al-Ṭāʿūn* ("The Plague", *sic*), a monthly controlled by the *sharīf* al-Kittānī (March 1908). In the same year the Moroccan government had an official newspaper published, *al-Fadjr*, edited by a Syrian Christian, which was transferred to Fez in 1909. Other weeklies also were founded at Tangier, notably *al-Ḥaḳḳ* (1911) and *al-Taraḳḳī* (1912).

After the inauguration of the Protectorate, *al-Saʿāda* was transferred to Rabat, where it became first tri-weekly, then daily; this semi-official newspaper, edited with care, beautifully printed, graced with numerous illustrations, anxious to inform its readers of events in Moroccan life, and widely circulated in all Morocco, played an undeniable educative and political rôle. In other towns the Arabic press hardly developed at all. *Al-Widād* had only a restricted number of readers; a daily, *al-Akhbār al-tilighrāfiyya*, was started at Fez, while a weekly, *al-Akhbār al-Maghribiyya*, supplemented *L'Information Marocaine* at Casablanca; at Marrakesh *al-Djanūb* had only a short life, but in the north, at Tetuan, several political newspapers met with some success (*al-Iṣlāḥ*, *al-Ittiḥād*, *Iẓhār al-Ḥakk*).

The accession of Morocco to independence (1956) saw the renewal of the Arabic press in the country, although the French-language newspapers had received authority to continue publication, at least provisionally. Three dailies were produced: the unofficial *al-ʿAhd al-Djadīd* (Rabat), supplemented since 1 September 1960 by *al-Fadjr*, which was destined to replace it, *al-ʿAlam* (Rabat), and *al-Taḥrīr* (Casablanca), these two latter being organs, with some bias, of the Istiḳlāl party. The total circulation of these three dailies was less than 25,000. The Democratic Party of Independence (PDI), which has on occasion published a weekly in French (*Démocratie*), relies on a bi-weekly, *al-Raʾy al-ʿĀmm*. The Moroccan Labour Union (UMT) and the Moroccan Union of Commerce, Industry and Handicrafts (UMCIA) own two weeklies at Casablanca, *al-Ṭalīʿa* and *al-Ittiḥād* respectively. In 1959 four other political weeklies were also published: *al-Ayyām* (Istiḳlāl, Casablanca), *al-Maghrib al-ʿArabī* (Moroccan Popular Movement, Rabat), *al-Niḍāl* (independent Liberals, Rabat), and *Ḥayāt al-Shaʿb* (communist). Finally, a monthly literary review at Marrakesh, *Risālat al-Adīb*, must be mentioned.

It is, naturally, in Tunisia that the Arabic press has reached its greatest development; the two world wars, bringing about some flexibility, would make it possible for three periods to be distinguished, but on the whole one can consider that the end of the French Protectorate and the advent of the country's independence (1955) mark the limits of two well-differentiated periods.

As early as 1861 Tunisia possessed an official newspaper, *al-Rāʾid al-Tūnusī*, and, from 1890, a daily news-sheet, *al-Zuhra*, which was to survive more than 60 years; a second daily, *al-Rushdiyya*, appeared from 1904 to 1910, and a third, *al-Nahḍa*, was founded in 1923. To these publications a crowd of periodicals of political, religious, commercial, etc., character, and of more or less ephemeral duration, was early added. Among the weeklies may be mentioned the unofficial *al-Ḥāḍira*, from 1888 to 1910, then the liberal *al-Zamān* (1930), the Pan-Islamist *al-Ṣawāb* (1904-11, 1920), the (Archaeo-) Destourian *Lisān al-Shaʿb* (1920-37). In the inter-war period a few weeklies appeared in the provinces; of a sharply marked political character, they were divided between Archaeo-Destourian (*al-ʿAṣr al-Djadīd*, Sfax 1919-25, 1936; *al-Difāʿ*, Ḳayrawān, 1937) and, especially, Neo-Destourian tendencies (at Sfax, *Ṣadā al-Umma*, 1936-7; *al-Anīs*, 1937; *al-Inshirāḥ*, 1937; *al-Kashkūl*, 1937. At Sūsa: *Fatā al-Sāḥil*, 1936-7. At Ḳayrawān: *Ṣabra*, 1937).

In 1937 G. Zawadowski (see *Bibliography*) collected 161 titles and presented a very striking diagram: from 1861 to 1903 the number of Arabic journals varied between one and six; it reached 23 in 1907, after the relaxation of security on 2 January 1904, fell to four during the first world war, to attain 32 in 1921; it fell again to eleven in 1928-9, following the measures taken for the suppression of criminal and political offences, and finally reached the figure of 51 in 1937. The same author indicates, moreover, 13 periodicals published in French by Tunisians, and, no less interesting, 73 titles of Judaeo-Arabic publications, in Arabic but in Hebrew characters, the oldest of which, *al-Mubāshir*, appeared in 1884-5. Flourishing until the first world war, this Jewish press afterwards continually declined until in 1937 there were only three miserable papers, at Tunis and at Sūsa.

The Arabic press of the capital played an important part during the years which immediately preceded the country's independence; depending on financial resources and skilled techniques, directed and partly edited by professional journalists, it became the herald of nationalism, endeavoured to bring its public round to the idea of independence, and spread the themes of anti-French propaganda in the towns and villages. Their end achieved, or on the point of being so, some papers, among the most important, went into opposition and tried to outbid the government; they had finally to cease publication, so that there remained of the former press only *al-ʿAmal*, a bi-weekly founded 1 June 1934 by the future president of the Republic, al-Ḥabīb Abū Ruḳayba (Bourguiba), and now a daily; and the communist weekly *al-Ṭalīʿa*, founded 1937. A new daily, *al-Ṣabāḥ*, has been started, while the weekly *al-Irāda*, organ of the Archaeo-Destūrians since 1934, has been replaced by *al-Istiḳlāl*. A few other nationalist periodicals such as *al-ʿAlam*, *al-Nidāʾ* and *al-Djumhūrī* appear more or less regularly. The organ of the FLN, the weekly *al-Muḳāwama al-Djazāʾiriyya*, has become *al-Mudjāhid*. Finally must be noticed a monthly cultural review, since 1 October 1955, *al-Fikr*, which young Tunisians of university education maintain at a respectable standard. Three French dailies, the oldest of which is *Dépêche tunisienne*, and one Italian, now (1960) appear at Tunis.

Worthy of mention is a political weekly *l'Action* (now *Afrique-Action*) which won some renown abroad.

Bibliography: *RMM*, i-lxii, *passim* (and particularly L. Mercier, *La presse musulmane au Maroc*, 1908, 619-30); L. Massignon, *Annuaire du Monde musulman*³, Paris 1929, 49-77, *passim*; E. Dermenghem, in *Sciences et Voyages*, xxv/4, 1935; H. Pérès, *Le mouvement réformiste en Algérie et l'influence de l'Orient, d'après la presse arabe d'Algérie*, in *Entretiens sur l'évolution des pays de civilisation arabe*, Paris 1936, 49-59; Tawfīḳ al-Madanī, *Kitāb al-Djazāʾir*, 367-72; J.-L. Miège, *Journaux et journalistes à Tanger au XIXᵉ siècle*, in *Hespéris*, 1954, 191-228; G. Zawadowski, *La presse indigène de Tunisie*, in *REI*, 1937, 357-89; Vassel, *La littérature populaire des Israélites tunisiens*, 1905-7; A. Canal, *La littérature et la presse tunisienne de l'occupation à 1900*, Paris 1924, 133-204; A. van Leeuwen, *Index des publications périodiques parus en Tunisie (1874-1954)*, in *IBLA*, xviii (1955), 153-67.

Libya.—In 1871 the first Arabo-Turkish newspaper, *Ṭarābulus al-Gharb*, was started in Tripoli; it was of an official character. It still continues to be published in Arabic and forms the chief organ of information for the Federal Kingdom. A second weekly, of a scientific and political nature, *al-Taraḳḳī* was published from 1897. Other newspapers were published during the period of Italian domination but are of only the most slender interest. Since the country became independent various newspapers have made their appearance, notably the periodicals *al-Rāʾid* and *al-Ṭalīʿa* (the organ of the Federal Union of Workers). (Ed.)

C. — Arabic-speaking Emigrants.

In the course of the last decade of the 19th and the first of the 20th centuries colonies of Arabic-speaking emigrants (*djāliya*, [*q.v.*]) sprang up in large cities of North and South America, Australia and West Africa. The main source of emigration was Lebanon and Syria, where the Arabic press was cradled and

Arabic journalism, in the proper sense, was born and nurtured. Prior to 1890 Ottoman authorities in the area permitted emigration nominally only to Egypt, but Lebanese and Syrian emigrants had found their way, even earlier, into numerous European capitals where a rash of Arabic papers and magazines made its appearance. The census of the historian of the Arabic press, Ṭarrāzī (iv, 490), for the period ending 1929 makes the number in Constantinople 49, Russia 3, Switzerland 2, Germany 7, Italy 4, France 43, Great Britain 14, Malta 8, Cyprus 5, a total of 135 of which 107 were newspapers.

The pioneer emigrant journalist was an Armenian from Aleppo, Rizḳ Allāh Ḥassūn, who founded *Mir'āt al-Aḥwāl* and later (1872) in London *Āl Sām*. First a favourite with the Ottoman authorities, Ḥassūn had to flee for his life to London. There he re-issued *Mir'āt al-Aḥwāl* in about 450 lithographed copies and used it to attack the Ottoman government.

Of the Paris publications mention should be made of *al-ʿUrwa al-Wuthḳā* issued March 1884 by the Egyptian reformer Muḥammad ʿAbduh and his celebrated friend Djamāl al-Dīn al-Afghānī. Though short lived, *al-ʿUrwa* distinguished itself in its vigorous defence of Islam and attack on the British in Egypt and India. A Beiruti deputy in the Ottoman parliament of 1876, Khalīl Ghānim, incurred the anger of the Porte for his liberal views and fled to Paris, where he started (April 1881) *al-Baṣīr*, which exposed the massacre of Armenians. Like other anti-Ottoman publications *al-Baṣīr* was banned by Turkish authorities and thus doomed to early death. With Amīn Arslān, a Lebanese Druze, Ghānim issued (1890), partly in French, *Turkiyā al-Fatāt*. Of a different character was the only known paper in West Africa, *Ifrīḳiyya al-Tidjāriyya* (commercial Africa, Dakar, 1931-5).

Most of these papers began as and remained personal sheets with the founder, editor and publisher as one person. They were more concerned with politics and literature than with news and, with no local colonies to support them, they were destined to be short lived. None survived.

The New World papers likewise began as personal sheets but the founder-editor-publisher was usually an *adīb* (literary) emigrant—not a political émigré—who sought his living by the pen. Though the rate of mortality was high, certain papers developed into real newspapers and received enough local support to give them a long lease of life. But the circulation rarely exceeded 5,000. The census of Ṭarrāzī (iv, 492; cf. *al-Hilāl*, i (1892), 12, 14) for the period ending 1929 credits North and Central America with 102 publications, of which 71 are newspapers, South America with 166, including 134 newspapers of which 3 appeared in Cuba. The pioneer in this area was Ibrāhīm ʿArbīlī, a Damascene graduate in medicine from what is now the American University of Beirut. ʿArbīlī had to secure the aid of the American embassy in Constantinople for a permit to export Arabic type from Beirut. The first number of his *Kawkab Amīrikā* was issued in New York, 15 April 1892, and bore his and his brother Nadjīb's name. One of his editorial assistants, Nadjīb Dhiyāb, a Greek Orthodox Lebanese, founded seven years later *Mir'āt al-Gharb*, still issued in New York. In February 1898 a Maronite, Naʿʿūm Mukarzal, founded in Philadelphia *al-Hudā*, which later moved to New York and is still perhaps the most widely read in America. Sectarian rivalry between these two papers spurred their early circulation. Both Dhiyāb and Mukarzal attended the Arab congress of Paris (1913) which advocated decentralization for the Arab provinces of Turkey. Other than these two papers New York had in December 1961 *al-Bayān*, founded 1911; *al-Iṣlāḥ*, 1933; *al-Rābiṭa al-Lubnāniyya*, 1957 (cf. Hitti, *Syrians*, app. F). The late birth of this paper is rather unusual. For many years after its foundation in 1912 *al-Sā'iḥ* served as an organ for a circle of literary men (*al-Rābiṭa al-Ḳalamiyya*) led by the celebrated Djabrān Khalīl Djabrān [*q.v.*] (Kahlil Gibran). So did *al-Funūn* magazine, founded 1913. A leading poet, Iliyā Abu Māḍī, published in New York *al-Samīr* from 1929 till his death in 1956. Detroit supports at present (December 1961) three newspapers.

In South America al-ʿĪd, himself a Syrian journalist in Buenos Aires, names in Rio de Janeiro (1958) 31 newspapers, of which 2 are living, and 3 magazines (391-2); in São Paulo 52 papers and magazines, of which 5 are extant (350-1); in Buenos Aires 31 newspapers, of which 6 are living, and 16 magazines (381-3); cf. al-Badawī, ii, 567-85). The pioneers were again Christian Lebanese: Naʿʿūm Labakī, co-founder in 1896 at Rio of *al-Raḳīb* and later of two other papers in São Paulo, and Shukrī al-Khūrī, co-founder in 1899 of the first paper in São Paulo and in 1906 of the longer lived and especially influential *Abu 'l-Hawl*. Of special interest in São Paulo was *al-ʿUṣba al-Andalusiyya* magazine (founded 1928), organ of a literary circle headed by the two poets Rashīd Salīm al-Khurī (al-Shaʿir al-Ḳarawī) and Shafīḳ Maʿlūf. In Buenos Aires the oldest surviving paper is *al-Salām* (1902), and of special interest is *al-Istiḳlāl* (1926) founded and still edited by a Druze.

In the struggle for existence within a steadily shrinking market of readers some editors resorted to dubious if not outright unethical journalistic practices. Others, wiser and more adventurous, made their publications bilingual or entirely in the new language of the second generation of emigrants. One pictorial monthly in Portuguese (São Paulo), one in Spanish (Mexico City) and a third in English (Hollywood) thrive on social functions. The *Lebanese American Journal* (founded 1951), and *The Caravan* (1953, which was to cease publication in 1962), are weekly newspapers. More learned was *The Syrian World* (New York, 1926-32) of Sallūm Mukarzal, who also edited Arabic papers and introduced the Arabic linotype.

The Arabic press of the diaspora was predominantly liberal but hardly ever radical, loyal to the countries of its adoption while mindful of its obligation to the countries of origin. As a liaison agent it kept alive the ties of relationship between emigrants and old folks and meanwhile interpreted the new culture and helped adjustment to it. It contributed generously to the enrichment of modern Arabic literature—prose and poetry—in vocabulary and ideas and to the enhancement of the Westernization of the Arab East.

Bibliography: al-Badawī al-Mulaththam [Yaʿḳūb al-ʿUdāt], *al-Nāṭiḳūn bi 'l-ḍād fī Amīrikā al-Djanūbiyya*, 2 pts., Beirut 1956; Philip K. Hitti, *The Syrians in America* (New York 1924); idem, *Lebanon in History*², London and New York 1962, 464-7; Yūsuf al-ʿĪd, *Djāwlāt fi 'l-ʿālam al-djadīd*, Buenos Aires 1959; The Institute of Arab American Affairs, *Arabic-speaking Americans*, ii, New York 1946; McFadden, *Daily journalism in the Arab states*, Columbus 1953; Adīb Murūwa, *al-Ṣaḥāfa al-ʿArabiyya: nash'atuhā wa-taṭawwuruhā*, Beirut 1960; Joseph Nasrallah, *L'imprimerie au*

Liban, Beirut 1948; Khalīl Ṣābāṭ, *Taʾrīkh al-ṭibāʿa fi 'l-sharḳ al-ʿArabī*, Cairo 1958; Djūrdj Ṣaydaḥ, *Adabunā wa-udabāʾunā fi 'l-mahādjir al-Amīrikiyyaʾ*, Beirut 1957; Luwīs Shaykhū (Cheikho), *al-Ādāb al-ʿArabiyya fi 'l-ḳarn al-tāsiʿ ʿasharʾ*, ii, Beirut 1926, 75; idem, in *al-Machriḳ*, i (1900), 174-80, 251-7, 355-62; Fīlīb Ṭarrāzī, *Taʾrīkh al-ṣaḥāfa al-ʿArabiyya*, i-iv, Beirut 1913-33; Djurdjī Zaydān, *Taʾrīkh ādāb al-lugha al-ʿArabiyya*, new ed. Shawḳī Ḍayf, Cairo 1950, 43-54, 63-4; Elie Safa, *L'émigration Libanaise*, Beirut 1960.

(PHILIP K. HITTI)

D.—Survey of the Arabic Language Press.

The language of the press has already been studied in the art. ʿARABIYYA, II, 4, but one cannot emphasize too strongly the part taken by the various newspapers, and particularly the Egyptian ones, in the evolution, development and enrichment of the so-called modern or contemporary Arabic which is indebted to them, far more than to actual literature, for its ability to express a multitude of new ideas, most of which have been imported from the West.

Basically, the Arabic press has made enormous progress; for a long time the only material that it had presented to the public, apart from news from abroad that was already stale, had been such information as would please the Ottoman Government or the notices provided by it; *al-Djawāʾib* alone perhaps constituted a fortunate exception. From the beginning of the century and especially since the first world war the main daily newspapers have explored a wider field, giving their readers information of every kind, concerning themselves with social, economic, literary and artistic questions, and shaping, orienting or arousing public opinion by means of commentaries which are not always dictated by the most praiseworthy objectivity. Side by side with this press, which in certain respects is comparable with the Western press and has at its disposal powerful technical and financial resources, a large staff and modern printing presses, there exists a swarm of minor publications whose preparation is entirely the work of craftsmen, when their frequency of publication does not depend upon the more or less acknowledged resources of their proprietors. Without going so far as to resort to the odious practice of blackmail to guarantee a certain edition of their newspaper, far too many journalists of the lowest category often indulge in petty polemics, crude quarrels and personal vituperation. Sanctions are frequently taken, sometimes leading to the disappearance of the paper, but they can hardly change the general demeanour of the so-called independent press. The measures taken in recent years in Egypt, even though they have unfortunately deprived journalists of their freedom, at least have the merit of having clarified the situation.

The very large daily newspapers, like the *Ahrām*, can call upon sources of information which could well be a matter of envy to many of the organs of the Western press. But this is not the case with the majority of newspapers. These do indeed receive bulletins from one or two world-wide European or American agencies, without counting the purely Arabic Middle East Agency, but in each of them one editor exploits broadcast material, while one or two colleagues are employed in collecting local news. It is rare for newspapers to keep correspondents abroad, and the proprietor generally acts as chief editor.

Newspapers of this sort almost always have a small printing press where the newspaper is composed by hand and printed on 4 or 6 pages; the circulation figures seldom exceed a few thousands, and readers are few outside the town where the newspaper is printed. Some Lebanese newspapers, however have, subscribers in America, and copies of the leading Egyptian or Lebanese dailies can be seen on newspaper stalls in the European and American capitals.

The reviews deserve especial mention. Many of these have assumed the task of spreading among the populace a useful knowledge of science, literature and history, and circulation figures reveal that they often reach a fairly wide public. The *Hilāl* (1892) needs no further praise; the *Machriḳ*, published since 1898 by the Jesuits in Beirut, enjoys an international scientific reputation. The *Muḳtabas*, founded in Damascus in 1908 by Muḥ. Kurd ʿAlī and the *Lughat al-ʿArab*, published in Baghdād by the Rev. Father Anastasius, played a cultural and scientific rôle that in our own time has been taken by the journals of the various academies of the Arab world. The different published lists also contain the titles of various reviews of juridical, economic, financial, commercial or corporate character, etc., as well as a certain number of feminist publications.

Since the experiment of Abū Naḍḍāra, satirical and humorous papers are not very numerous: in Beirut *al-Ṣaḥāfī al-tāʾih* (1920) and *al-Dabbūr* (1924), with the addition in 1943 of *al-Ṣayyād*, are still continuing, while a larger number of illustrated magazines like *al-Muṣawwar* (Cairo) are enjoying an undeniable success.   (ED.)

ii. — IRĀN

The first printing press was set up in about 1817 in Tabrīz, followed by one in Tehran; but in about 1824 lithography quickly and almost completely eclipsed printing for over half a century. From 1848 the first newspapers appeared, first in Tehran, then in Shirāz, Iṣfahān and Tabrīz; in about 1860 portraits and illustrations were introduced; the first periodical of scientific character dates from 1863; the first daily newspaper from 1898; the first humorous and satirical newspaper from 1900. In 1875 the first of the newspapers established outside Irān appeared in Constantinople; others appeared in London, Calcutta, Cairo, Paris, Bombay and Washington (Bahāʾī).

In its early period the press was literary rather than political; the opposite was true after the Constitution of 1906. The development of the press was caused by the spread of printing which little by little replaced lithography. From 1910 to 1912 it underwent various changes caused by the political turmoil in the country. Nevertheless, E. G. Browne (*The Press* . . .), completing the list drawn up in 1911 by H. L. Rabino, named 371 daily publications and periodicals in 1914 (see his summary of the development of the press, 7 ff.); many periodicals are of literary or scientific character; it is important to add that political newspapers very frequently ranked as literature: so too the numerous political poems and satirical articles in prose which, besides their literary value, also possess actual historical interest (see Browne, *op. cit.*, introd., xvi and the anthology, 167 ff.).

If the newspapers of the early period were often unofficial and poorly supplied with information, they provided a wealth of instructive articles, edited in excellent style; "they inspired a taste for reading and thus contributed to the progress of general instruction" (Rabino). As for the press which prepared for and followed the Constitution of 1906,

Browne, the eminent authority, states: "Several of these newspapers, in particular the *Ṣūr-è Isrāfīl*, the *Ḥabl ol-matīn* and the *Musāwāt* were indeed of a superior sort and serve as models of a vigorous, nervous and concise style which until then was virtually unknown" (*The Persian Revolution*, 127); later he defined his views (*Lit. History*). To the bibliography which he drew up (in *The Press*) can be added the lists of newspapers and periodicals compiled by ʿAlī Nô Rouze (Nawrūz) (1914-1925) and the *Annuaire du monde musulman* (1929). It is also worth recalling various newspapers published in French, Armenian and Chaldaean.

In 1930, in his supplement to the Persian translation of Browne's *Literary History*, Rashīd Yāsmī makes a stand against the increasing disregard for literary form in many newspapers, the result of the enforced speed of publication, and of the invasion of foreign words introduced in information and articles translated from European newspapers; he provides a list of newspapers (among which he singles out *Raʿd* "The thunder", *Īrān*, *Shafaḳ-i surkh* "The red twilight", *Iṭṭilaʿāt* "Information", *Nāhīd*) and a list of periodicals (among which he notes *Armaghān* "Gift", *Bahār* and *Nawbahār* "Spring", *Āyanda* "Future", *Īrān-i djawān* "Young Iran", *Sharḳ* "East", *Mihr* "Sun"); to these periodicals should be added those published by the Ministry of Public Instruction and the Universities (Tehran and Tabrīz) and, though it is not possible to mention them all, the literary review *Yādgār* "Memorial", the critical review *Rāhnumā-yi kitāb* "Guide to [new] books", and several scientific and technical reviews; finally he mentions some annual publications with a wealth of information as important as it is varied (*Pārs*, *Gāhnāma*). Several newspapers listed by the *Annuaire du monde musulman* have disappeared; to the list should be added, among others, *Kayhān* "The world", (Tehran), *Āzādī* "Liberty" (Mashhad) and the remarkable reviews *Farhang-i Īrān zamīn* "Iranian culture", *Madjalla-yi mūsīḳī*, *Sukhan* "The word", *Yāghmā* "Booty".

Bibliography: E. G. Browne, *The press and poetry of modern Persia*, Cambridge 1914; his list completes that given by H. J. Rabino, *La presse depuis son origine jusqu'à nos jours*, in *RMM*, 1913, xxii, 287: Fr. tr. from the original Persian mentioned by Browne, *op. cit.*, 2, n. 2; idem, *The Persian Revolution of 1905-1909*, Cambridge 1910; Ali Nô Rouze, *Registre analytique de la presse persane*, 318 items, 1919-23 (*RMM*, 1925, (lx), 35 ff.); *RMM*, general index (index vi: Presse: Bakou, Bender-Bouchir, Ourmiah, Perse procès de presse, Tauris, Téhéran, "persane"); *Annuaire du monde musulman*, 1925, 351 (general index of the Muslim press; see Chiraz, Enzéli, Hamadan, Ispahan, Kaboul, Kazwīn, Kerman, Khoī, Méched, Qandahar, Recht, Tabriz, Téhéran, Yezd); *ibid.*, ³1929, 51 (index of the press; besides the towns named above, see Kermanchah, Djélalabad, Hérat); Bogdanov, in *IC*, 1929, 126-52, for the Āfghān press); E. G. Browne, iv, (ed. 1930), 468-90; Rashīd Yāsmī, *Taʾrīkh-i adabiyāt-i Irān taʾlīf-i professor Edward Browne, wa adabiyāt-i muʿāṣir*, Tehran 1316/1938; Bahār Malik al-Shuʿarā, *Sabḳ-shināsī*, Tehran 1321/1943, iii, 344 ff.; *Taʿlīm-o tarbiyat*, Tehran 1313/35, iv, 657-64 and 721-5; *Yādgār*, Tehran 1323-4/1945 iii, 49-54 and vii, 6-17; Muḥammad Ṣadr Hashīmī, *Taʾrīkh-i djarāʾid-wa madjallāt-i Irān*, Iṣfahān 1327/1949, 2 vols. (important); Jan Rypka, *Iranische Literatur-geschichte*, Leipzig 1959, 323 ff., 346 ff., 369 ff., 459 ff., A. Towfigh, *Le rôle de la presse humoristique et satirique dans la société iranienne*, unpublished Sorbonne thesis, 1962.

(H. Massé)

iii. — Turkey

The early history or the press in Turkey is given in section i above. 1860 saw the birth of the first unofficial Turkish newspaper published by a Turk. This was the *Terdjumān-i Aḥwāl* published by Agāh Efendi, with the help of the writer and poet Shināsī and numbering Aḥmed Wefīḳ Pasha among its contributors. Polemics between this and Churchill's paper were frequent, the first occasion being a criticism in Churchill's newspaper of Shināsī's *Shāʿir Evlenmesi* ("A Poet's Marriage") which was serialized in the *Terdjumān-i Aḥwāl.*

In 1861 Shināsī, wishing for greater freedom of expression in his own newspaper, started the *Taṣwīr-i Efkār* which also carried articles by Nāmik Kemāl as from issue number 200. The *Taṣwīr-i Efkār* closed down in 1866: in all 830 issues were published, issues of the greatest importance in the history of the Turkish Press, because of the newspaper's advocacy of libertarian ideas.

1861 also saw the birth of the first purely Turkish magazine in Turkey, the *Medjmūʿa-i Funūn* of Munīf Pasha [*q.v.*; see also djemʿiyyet-i ʿilmiyye-i ʿothmāniyye], followed in 1863 by the first military publication, the *Djerīde-i ʿAskeriyye* of Aḥmed Midḥat Efendi, and then in 1865 by the first commercial magazine, the *Taḳwīm-i Tidjāret* of Ḥasan Fehmī Pasha. In the meantime, in 1864, the Government published the first Press regulations (the 1857 regulations did not mention the periodical Press as such, but applied to books and pamphlets which were to be submitted to the Council of Education, *Maʿārif Shūrāsī*, before publication). The 1864 regulations remained in force, save for a short interruption, until 1909, and provided for official warnings to the Press, for suspension and the cancellation of licences at government discretion, and also for the trial of Press offences by the *Medjlis-i Aḥkām-i ʿAdliyye* tribunal. Newspapers were also asked to submit a copy of each issue, signed by the responsible Editor, to the Press Directorate, a Government office the beginnings of which are obscure, but the existence of which in 1862 can be inferred from the fact that Saḳīzlī (from Chios) Ohannes Pasha was appointed to it. The 1864 Press regulations were inspired by the Press Law of Napoleon III and did not provide for a censorship as such. Until 1877 Press affairs were the responsibility of the Ministry of Education, although the 1864 regulations provided for the submission to the Foreign Ministry of applications for Press licences by foreigners. Mention must also be made of the "Society for original compositions and translations" (*Teʾlīf we Terdjeme Djemʿiyyeti*), attached to the Ministry of Education and entrusted with the choice and translation into Turkish of useful foreign publications. The 1864 regulations seem to have fallen into desuetude in 1867, when an order issued by ʿĀlī Pasha authorized administrative action against the Press, including suspension, where this was dictated by the public interest. The reason for this was the growth of the revolutionary Press, ushered in by ʿAlī Suʿāwī's *Mukhbir*, first published in Philippopolis (Filibe) in 1866 and closed down in the following year. The task which that newspaper set itself originally was to defend the rights of the

Muslims against foreign (Christian) encroachment and in the face of presumed official lethargy. The publication of the 1867 order led to the flight abroad of members of the "Society of New Ottomans" (*Yeñi ʿOt̲h̲mānlîlar D̲j̲emʿiyyeti*), including ʿAlī Suʿāwī, Nāmîk Kemāl, Ziya (Ḍiyāʾ) Pas̲h̲a, Agāh Efendi and others. With financial help from the Egyptian prince Muṣṭafā Fāḍil Pas̲h̲a they undertook the publication of revolutionary newspapers directed against the policy of ʿAlī Pas̲h̲a. ʿAlī Suʿāwī restarted the *Muk̲h̲bir* in 1867 in London. In 1868 it was followed in London by *Ḥürriyyet* designed by Ziya Pas̲h̲a and Nāmîk Kemāl as a weekly organ of the New Ottomans. Nāmîk Kemāl left the paper in 1869, while in the following year *Ḥürriyyet* moved to Geneva, where another 11 issues were published, making 200 in all. ʿAlī Suʿāwī had in the meantime moved to Paris, where in 1869 he published *ʿUlūm*, which was the first newspaper in Turkish to advocate Turkish nationalism. Another revolutionary sheet, *Inḳilāb*, published in 1870 in Geneva by Ḥuseyn Waṣfī Pas̲h̲a and Meḥmed Bey, is noteworthy for the fact that it attacked not the Sultan's Ministers, but Sultan ʿAbd al-ʿAzīz himself.

In the meantime there was an increase in Press activity in Turkey, particularly between 1868 and 1872; new publications included important organs of opinion like *Teraḳḳī, Baṣīret, ʿIbret* and *Ḥadīḳa* and humorous publications like *Diogène* and *K̲h̲ayālī*, whose outspokenness shows that the "provisional" order of 1867 was no longer applied. *Teraḳḳī*, which first appeared in 1868, had the first weekly supplement for women, while *Mümeyyiz*, which followed it in 1869, had the first children's supplement in the country. *Diogène* started publication in Greek and in French, appearing later in Turkish. *Ḥadīḳa* was started in 1869 by ʿĀs̲h̲ir Efendi, as a scientific publication passing in 1871 under the control of Ebū 'l-Ziyā (Abu 'l-Ḍiyāʾ) Tewfīḳ [*q.v.*] (who had collaborated earlier with *Teraḳḳī*) and in 1873 under that of S̲h̲ems al-Dīn Sāmī. *Baṣīret*, which carried articles by the Pole Karski, by Aḥmed Mid̲h̲at Efendi and also by ʿAlī Suʿāwī, can be considered as the most successful newspaper of the time, coming second in popularity after the official police sheet *Waraḳa-i Ḍabṭiyye*. *ʿIbret*, first edited unsuccessfully by Aḥmed Mid̲h̲at Efendi, passed in 1872 under the control of Nāmîk Kemāl, Ebū 'l-Ziyā Tewfīḳ and Res̲h̲ād Nūrī. In it Nāmîk Kemāl attacked the Grand Vizier Maḥmūd Nedīm Pas̲h̲a, who in consequence had him exiled to Gallipoli, suspending the newspaper for four months. Nāmîk Kemāl returned from exile and resumed editorship after his enemy's fall from favour. The newspaper suffered one more suspension and was then permanently closed down in 1873, as a result of the excitement caused by Nāmîk Kemāl's play *Waṭan weyā Silistre*, the author being exiled this time to the castle of Famagusta. In all 132 issues of *ʿIbret* appeared, and this newspaper can be considered as the best propagator of liberal ideas during the period of the *Tanẓīmāt*. The period saw the birth of many short-lived journalistic ventures of predominantly political character, as well as of some organs of more enduring importance, like the best-selling newspaper *Waḳit*, which owed its popularity to the political commentaries of Saʿīd Bey; Meḥmed Tewfīḳ Bey's *Ṣabāḥ*, first published in 1876 and noteworthy for its courage in being the first newspaper to appear with several blank columns as a protest against the censors; and finally, the high-minded *Istiḳbāl* which devoted much attention to educational matters.

Mention must also be made of the *Med̲j̲mūʿa-i Ebü 'l-Ḍiyā*, published by the prolific journalist and author Ebü 'l-Ziyā Tewfīḳ (1880), and of the first children's magazine *Eṭfāl*.

The return to absolutism under ʿAbd al-Ḥamīd II was marked administratively by the transfer of Press affairs to the Ministry of the Interior in 1877; in 1878 newspapers came under the joint censorship of the Ministries of Education, Interior and Police; in 1881 an "Inspection and Control Commission" (*End̲j̲ümen-i Teftīs̲h̲ we Muʿāyene*) was formed and charged with preventive censorship, an even higher authority, the "Commission for the Examination of Compositions" (*Tedḳīḳ-i Muʾellefāt Komisyonu*) being formed in 1897 and supplemented for religious publications in 1903 by the "Commission for religious and legal books" (*Kutub-i Dīniyye we S̲h̲erʿiyye heyʾeti*); dangerous publications outside the borders of the Empire were dealt with by the Foreign Press Directorate (*Maṭbūʿāt-i Ed̲j̲nebiyye Müdürlüg̲h̲ü*) formed in 1885. All these measures were taken in spite of the 1876 Constitution which, in article 12, guaranteed the freedom of the Press "within the bounds of the law", and in spite of the rejection by Parliament of the draconic Press Law of 1877. Press censorship under ʿAbd al-Ḥamīd II was supplemented by control of printing presses (1888) and of booksellers (1894).

All this limited the number and contents of publications, although it did not stop the development of the Turkish Press. Important dailies included Mihrān Efendi's *Ṣabāḥ*, founded in 1876 and already mentioned, which included the young and later famous journalist Ḥüseyn D̲j̲āhid Bey among its contributors; Aḥmed D̲j̲ewdet Bey's *Iḳdām* (1890), which had a semi-legal correspondent in Paris in the person of the later famous ʿAlī Kemāl Bey, and Aḥmed Mid̲h̲at Efendi's (known as "the typewriter" for his prolific writings) *Terd̲j̲ümān-i Ḥaḳīḳat*, which between 1882 and 1884 had a passing literary phase thanks to Muʿallim Nād̲j̲ī. Important periodicals included Murād Bey's political weekly *Mīzān* (1886-90 with interruptions), and above all ʿAḥmed Iḥsān Bey's *T̲h̲erwet-i Fünūn*, standard-bearer of a new literary school (Tewfīḳ Fikret, D̲j̲enāb S̲h̲ehāb al-Dīn [see D̲J̲ANĀB S̲H̲IHĀB AL-DĪN], K̲h̲ālid Ziyā (Ḍiyāʾ) etc.) in opposition to Muʿallim Nād̲j̲ī's conservatives. *T̲h̲erwet-i Fünūn* was started in 1892 and, after a period of brilliance, was reduced to dull harmlessness by official pressure.

This official repression led to a rebirth of revolutionary publications abroad: in 1880 ʿAlī S̲h̲efḳatī started *Istiḳbāl* in Geneva; in 1895 Aḥmed Rîḍā (Riḍāʾ) Bey founded the important *Mes̲h̲weret* in Turkish and French (the French side being edited by another temporary expatriate, Murād Bey of *Mīzān*). Started in Paris, *Mes̲h̲weret* was driven by official Ottoman pressure first to Switzerland and then to Belgium. The last decade of the 19th and the first years of the 20th centuries saw a host of short-lived Turkish revolutionary sheets in Paris, Switzerland, London and Egypt. They included organs of the Committee of Union and Progress, such as *ʿOt̲h̲mānlî*, published by Isḥāḳ Sukūtī and ʿAbdullāh D̲j̲ewdet; *Ḥaḳḳ* and *S̲h̲ūrā-i Ummet*, published in Cairo with the cooperation of Aḥmed Rîḍā Bey. In the same year as the latter, in 1902, Prince Ṣabāḥ al-Dīn published his newspaper *Teraḳḳī*. Another influen tial newspaper published abroad was *Terd̲j̲ümān*, which Gaspîralî Ismāʿīl (Gasprinski) founded in the Crimea in 1883.

When the Constitution was once again put into practice on 24 July 1908, the Turkish Press attained to unlimited freedom for a period of some eight or nine months. The three main newspapers of the Hamidian era (*Iḳdām*, *Ṣabāḥ* and *Terdjümān-i Ḥaḳīḳat*) were soon joined by a daily edition of *Therwet-i Fünūn*, by the *Yeñi Gazete* of ʿAbdullāh Zuhdī and Maḥmūd Ṣādiḳ and, most important, by *Ṭanīn*, published by Tewfīḳ Fikret, Ḥüseyn Kāẓim and Ḥüseyn Djāhid. In all more than two hundred newspaper licences were granted in the first few weeks of the constitutional régime, while the number of periodical publications in 1908-9 amounted to 353. This number decreased constantly in subsequent years: 130 in 1910, 124 in 1911, 70 in 1914. The fortunes of the Press were linked closely with the course of the political struggle between the Committee of Union and Progress and its opponents. In the months between the restoration of the Constitution and the "31st March incident" (13 April 1909) the Committee was opposed by *ʿOthmānlī*, the organ of the Liberal Party of Prince Ṣabāḥ al-Dīn, by *Iḳdām*, which carried articles by ʿAlī Kemāl, by *Yeñi Gazete*, *Therwet-i Fünūn* and others. It was supported by *Shūrā-i Millet*, Ebü 'l-Ziyā Tewfīḳ's *Yeñi Taṣwīr-i Efkār*, *Milliyyet*, *Ḥürriyyet* and other publications. The religious opposition was led by Derwīsh Waḥdetī's newspaper *Volkan* and by the magazine *Beyān al-Ḥaḳḳ*. After the "incident" censorship was re-imposed by the military administration, in spite of the provision in the revised constitution forbidding all pre-publication censorship. Military censorship continued until the assumption of power by the "opposition" in 1912, but was reimposed by the Union and Progress after the coup of 10 January 1913. It then lasted until the dissolution of the Empire. Military censorship rendered largely inoperative the 1909 liberal Press Law, which was in any case amended in 1913, the amendment granting wide powers to the authorities in cases where publications were deemed to endanger the security of the State. A Directorate-General of the Press was formed at the same time. Opposition newspapers tended in these conditions to be short-lived. Among the few which deserve mention one could include *Selāmet-i ʿUmūmiyye* (1910) which carried articles by ʿAbdullāh Djewdet, signed "A Kurd", and also *Teʾmīnāt*, published in 1912 by Ismāʿīl Ḥaḳḳī Pasha on behalf of the Party of Freedom and Concord (*Ḥürriyyet ve Iʾtilāf*). The years before the First War also saw the birth of some important literary and scientific magazines, like the journal of the Ottoman Historical Society (*Taʾrīkh-i ʿOthmānī Endjümeni Medjmūʿasī*) (1910), *Türk Yurdu*, the organ of the Turkish Hearths (*Türk Odjaḳlarī*), and the literary avant-garde papers *Genč Ḳalemler* and *Rubāb*. One must also point to the existence of a numerous religious periodical Press. In 1913 ʿAlī Kemāl founded the daily *Peyām*, which was to amalgamate after the war with Mihrān Efendī's *Ṣabāḥ* and, under the name of *Peyām-i Ṣabāḥ*, to be in the forefront of the opposition to Muṣṭafā Kemāl in Istanbul during the Turkish War of Independence. The last years of the 1914-18 war witnessed the first ventures of journalists who were to become famous under the Republic. It was then that Aḥmed Emīn (Yalman) and Ḥaḳḳī Ṭāriḳ (Us) started *Waḳit*, that Yūnus Nādī entered the field with *Yeñi Gün* and Sedād Sīmāvī with the humorous magazine *Diken*; it is also to those years that the important daily *Akṣham* goes back. Newspapers published in Istanbul at the end of the war included also Saʿīd Mollā's *Istanbul*, Refīʿ Djewād's *ʿAlemdār* and Meḥmed Zekeriyyā (Sertel)'s *Büyük Gazete*.

In Anatolia the nationalist movement was first defended by *Irāde-i Milliyye*, the organ of the Sivas Congress, which first appeared on 4 September 1919. A fortnight after his arrival in Ankara on 27 December 1919 Muṣṭafā Kemāl Pasha founded his organ *Ḥākimiyyet-i Milliyye*, which was renamed *Ulus* in 1928, *Halkçı* in 1955, reverting to *Ulus* in 1956. In 1920 Yūnus Nādī transferred his *Yeñi Gün* to Ankara, returning to Istanbul in 1923 to found *Djümhūriyyet* (*Cümhuriyet*), which then became the main Kemalist newspaper in the old capital. Noteworthy magazines founded or published in the years between the end of the war and the proclamation of the Republic included the Communist *Aydinlik*, the literary *Dergāh*, which carried articles by Yaʿḳūb Ḳadrī (Karaosmanoğlu) and Ziya Gökalp's *Küčük Medjmūʿa*, started in Diyarbekir (Diyār-Bakr) in 1922.

Censorship ceased with the entry of the Turkish Army into Istanbul on 7 October 1923. The 1924 Constitution re-asserted the existing constitutional assurance that the Press was free within the bounds of the law and could not be submitted to prepublication censorship. Powers of suspension were, however, assumed by the authorities the following year under the Maintenance of Order (*Taḳrīr-i Sukūn*) law which remained in force for two years. Suspension and confiscation by Government decision were also allowed by the 1932 Press Law, which was later repeatedly amended, Press offences, penalties and other provisions being several times re-defined. The Directorate-General of the Press which had been disbanded in 1931 was reformed in 1933, becoming in 1940 the "Directorate General of Press, Broadcasting and Tourism", attached to the office of the Prime Minister, and, towards the end of the Democratic Party administration (1950-60), the Ministry of Press, Broadcasting and Tourism.

The Turkish Press was faced with great difficulties in 1928 when the Arabic alphabet was replaced by the Latin alphabet. Newspapers appeared for a time printed in both alphabets. Circulations dropped and the Government had to come to the assistance of the Press with subventions which were continued for three years. The development of the Press under the Turkish Republic was greatly influenced by a small number of distinguished journalists and journalistic dynasties. They include Ahmed Emin Yalman who, after leaving *Vakit*, founded *Vatan* in 1923, *Inkilâb* in 1934, was associated with *Tan* in 1935, then restarted *Vatan* and remained in control of it until 1960 when he founded a new paper *Hürvatan*; the Nadi family who retained control until the present day of *Cümhuriyet*; the Simavi family who own the best-selling *Hürriyet*, founded by Sedad Simavi; the Sertel family who edited *Tan* until 1946 when the newspaper's left-wing views provoked official displeasure and student demonstrations, as a result of which the paper's offices were wrecked; the Ali Naʿi family, associated with *Inkilâb*, *Ikdam* and, at present, with the successful *Milliyet* etc. An important part was also played by the veteran journalist Hüseyin Cahid (Yalçın) who, after having made his peace with the Republic, resumed journalistic activity in *Yeni Sabah* (started in 1938) and then re-started *Tanin*, in whose columns he defended the Allied cause during the Second World War and the policy of the Turkish Republican People's Party after it.

Important political and social developments in the Republican period were reflected largely in political, social and literary periodicals: the People's

Houses (*Halkevleri*) organization had its organ in *Ülkü*; new ideas of social development which inspired the policy of *Étatisme*, were championed in *Kadro* (1933); a populist conception of literature took shape in the columns of *Varlık* (1933-); the revival of racialist and Pan-Turanian ideals, particularly noticiable in the years of the Second World War, was marked by the appearance of the reviews *Bozkurt*, *Çınaraltı* etc.; the vogue for extreme left-wing views at the end of the war had its counterpart in the periodical *Görüşler* (and the short-lived newspaper *Gerçek*); the influence of American news magazines led to the appearance of their Turkish equivalents, such as *Akis* (Ankara) and *Kim* (Istanbul); the influence of serious British political weeklies made itself felt in the fortnightly *Forum* (Ankara) etc.

The years after the Second World War were marked by the political struggle between the Republican People's Party and its opponents, a struggle in which the Turkish Press played a prominent part. Between 1950 and 1960 the Democratic Party administration had an organ in Ankara in the daily *Zafer*, while in Istanbul the Government cause was defended by *Havadis* and criticized by the majority of the other dailies. The Turkish Press, as a whole, played an important part in preparing the ground for the military *coup d'état* of 27 May 1960 as well as in the political struggle which has followed it. Just as important, however, as this political rôle has been the increasing professional competence of the Press: equipment and lay-out were much improved, circulations soared (reaching the 300,000 mark), the industry became highly capitalized with a growing tendency to produce mass-circulation, non-political newspapers, providing not only news, but also entertainment. This tendency can be expected to gather strength, with a consequent reduction in the number of newspapers published in the country. Journalistic history was made in 1960 when the daily *Akşam* started simultaneous publication in Istanbul and Ankara, thus opening a new line of approach to the problem of increasing circulations. In the meantime improved communications and distribution have consolidated the dominant position of the Istanbul papers in the life of the Turkish Press.

Bibliography: Selim Nüzhet Gerçek, *Türk gazeteciliği*, Istanbul 1931; Sadri Ertem, *Propaganda*, Ankara 1941; Server Iskit, *Türkiye'de matbuat rejimleri*, Ankara 1938; idem, *Türkiye'de matbuat idareleri ve politikaları*, Ankara 1943; Mustafa Nihat Özön, *Son asır Türk edebiyatı*, Istanbul 1945, 416 ff.; Ragıp Özdem, *Gazete dili* in *Tanzimat*, Istanbul 1940, 859-931; Hasan Refik Ertuğ, *Basın ve yayın tarihi*, Istanbul 1955, i, 82-88; Necmettin Deliorman, *Meşrutiyetten önce . . . hudut harici Türk gazeteciliği*, Istanbul 1943; J. Deny, *État de la presse turque en juillet 1925* in *RMM*, lxi (1925), 43-74; *Almanak*, Istanbul 1933; Hilmi Z. Ülken, *Türk düşüncesi ve dergilerimiz* in *Türk Düşüncesi*, i, 1945, 82-87.

(VEDAD GÜNYOL and ANDREW MANGO)

iv. — MUSLIM PRESS OF RUSSIA AND THE SOVIET UNION

Compared with the press of the other Islamic countries, the Muslim press of Russia is of relatively recent date, mainly on account of the hostility of the Russian authorities towards movements of cultural revival among the non-Russian peoples of the Empire.

Nevertheless, the first attempt to establish an organ in a Muslim language dates back to the beginning of the 19th century. It was due to a professor of Kazan University, Zapol'skiy, who in 1808 worked out a plan for a bilingual weekly in Russian and Tatar, but the project remained unfulfilled. In 1828, a second attempt was made, successfully this time, by a Russian official in the Military Administration of Transcaucasia, A. S. Sosnovskiy, who succeeded in publishing at Tiflis a Russian newspaper, *Tifliskie Vedomosti*, which also included an edition in Persian and, after in 1832, in Ādharī Turkish. After a few numbers this original venture came to an end, and we have to wait until 1870 to see the appearance of the first newspaper intended for Muslims, the *Türkistān Wilāyetiniñ Gazeti*, published at Tashkent in Uzbek, on behalf of the Chancellery of the General Government of Turkestan, by the Russian missionary N. P. Ostrumov. Five years later, at Baku, there appeared the Ādharī weekly *Ekinči*, edited by the author-schoolmaster Ḥasan Bey Melikov Zerdabi [*q.v.*]; and it is this little newspaper, with only 700 printed copies, that can be regarded as the true ancestor of the Muslim press in the Russian Empire. Quite soon it brought upon itself the hostility of conservative circles, and it was suspended by the Russian authorities in 1877.

The Muslim press of Russia only reached international rank with the famous *Terdjümān*, published at Baghče-Saray in 1883 by Ismāʿīl Bey Gasprinski [see GASPĪRALĪ ISMĀʿĪL], in the Crimean Tatar language strongly influenced by Ottoman Turkish. The *Terdjümān* survived until 1918. For some forty years it was the mouth-piece of the reform movement and of pan-Turkism in Russia, and for over twenty years remained the only press organ of the Muslims in Russia, since the severity of the Russian censorship over the Muslims, until 1905, prevented the rise of the national press. Until the revolution of 1905, in fact, apart from the above-mentioned newspapers there were only six organs of local significance. Four were in Ādharī Turkish : *Ḍiyāʾ* (1879), *Ḍiyā Ḳāfḳāsiyā* (1880), *Keshkül* (1884), and *Sharḳ-i rūs* (1903) at Tiflis; one in Ḳazaḳ (Ḳirghiz) : *Dālā Wilāyeti*, published in 1899 at Omsk (Siberia); and one in Ḳāzān Tatar at St. Petersburg: *Nūr*, in 1904.

After the publication of the Manifesto of 17 October 1905 granting liberty of the press to all the peoples of Russia, periodicals sprang up throughout all the regions of the Empire inhabited by Muslims, representing every sort of political opinion from right-wing conservative to left-wing socialist.

Thus, from 1905 until the revolution of February 1917, Muslims in the Russian Empire published 159 periodicals (newspapers and reviews) in the following languages : Ḳāzān Tatar, 62; Ādharī Turkish, 61; Uzbek, 17; Ḳazaḳ (Ḳirghiz), 8; Crimean Tatar, 6; Arabic, 2; Türkmen, 2; Persian, 1. The principal centres for the editing and publication of the press were Baku (59 periodicals), Ḳāzān (22), Orenburg (13), Tashkent (12), St. Petersburg (9), Astrakhan (9), Ufa (6), and Baghče-Saray (5). Periodicals and newspapers were also published at Troïtzk, Ural'sk, Tomsk, Samarḳand, Ashḳabād, Bukhārā, Samara, Ḳarasu-Bazar, Omsk, Erevan, Ḳoḳand, Gandja and Petropavlovsk.

The majority of the Muslim newspapers had only an ephemeral existence because of their very slender finances, lack of subscribers and, above all, the interference of the censorship which after 1908 again became very vigilant. Some of them, however, played a leading part in developing a national feeling among the Turkish peoples of Russia.

Among the most remarkable which were read far beyond the frontiers of the Russian Empire, we should mention the liberal organs *Waḳīt* and *Shurā* of Orenburg which, from 1906 to 1917, made themselves the disseminators of pan-Turkism in Russia; *Ḳāzān Mukhbire* (1905) and *Yulduz* (1906) in Ḳāzān; *Ḥayāt* (1904), *Irshād* (1905) and *Fuyuḍāt* (1906) in Baku; *Mollā Naṣreddīn* (1906) in Tiflis; the last-named, a satirical weekly, had a fairly wide circulation in Persian Ādharbāydjān. Other organs, of local importance and with a more restricted circulation, also exerted a lasting influence on the cultural life of the Muslims, such as the *Ḳazaḳ* of Orenburg (1913), published in Ḳazaḳ by Ahmed Baytursunov. In Turkestan alone, where the Russian authorities maintained a very close watch on the cultural development of the Muslim population, there existed no real press, all the organs which made their appearance there being swiftly banned by the censorship.

The overthrow of the monarchy in February 1917 introduced a new chapter in the history of the Muslim press in Russia. The earlier, and often apolitical, periodicals were succeeded by a 'committed' press reflecting the opinions of the various political groups of Muslim society which, after October 1918, whether from intention or force of circumstances, were to be involved in the Revolution and civil war. From February 1917 to the end of 1920, 256 periodicals made their appearance on Russian territory, spread over 53 towns and large villages. Inferior in quality to its predecessors, the press of the revolutionary period attempted to reach wider circles, both by a larger circulation and also by the use of language nearer to popular speech. Ḳāzān Tatar enjoyed unrivalled supremacy since nearly half (139 exactly) of the periodicals published during this period were in this language, Ādharī Turkish coming far behind with only 39 organs, followed by Uzbek (37), Ḳazaḳ (21), and Crimean Tatar(7). In 1917 other newspapers also appeared, in Turkish (2 at Batum), Ḳumīḳ (3 at Temir Khan Shura), in Avar, Abkhaz and Lak.

In 1921, with the victory of the Red Army in the civil war, a new era began, that of the Soviet press, distinguished from earlier periodicals by its monolithic character, its very wide circulation and, lastly, by the appearance of new languages. Under the Soviet regime, six Turkic languages, two Iranian languages and nine Ibero-Caucasian Muslim languages became literary languages. Until 1924-8 they were written in Arabic characters; between 1928 and 1930 they were given a Latin alphabet, which was replaced between 1938 and 1940 by the Cyrillic alphabet. These new languages are : Bashkir, Ḳīrghīz (formerly Ḳara-ḳīrghīz), Nogay, Ḳaraḳalpaḳ and Uyghur (Turkic languages); Kurdish and Tat (Iranian languages); Abkhaz, Kabard, Adighe, Čečen, Ingush, Abaza, Darghin, Lezg and Tabasaran (Ibero-Caucasian languages). The total number of periodicals has much increased. In 1954 in the Soviet Union there existed (counting only the dailies) : 190 newspapers in Uzbek, 171 in Ḳazaḳ, 116 in Ādharī Turkish, 107 in Ḳāzān Tatar, 72 in Ḳīrghīz, 70 in Tādjīk, 53 in Türkmen, 30 in Bashkir, 19 in Avar and Ossetic, 17 in Kabard, 13 in Ḳaraḳalpaḳ 11 in Darghin, 9 in Ḳumīḳ, 8 in Lezg, 5 in Abkhaz, 4 in Nogay, 3 in Uyghur and Lak, 2 in Tabarasan and Abaza, 1 in Adighe, 1 in Čerkes, 1 in Tat and 1 in Kurdish. Since then, new periodicals have been published in Čečen, Ingush, Crimean Tatar and Ḳaračay-balḳar.

Bibliography: No comprehensive study on the Muslim press of Russia exists, but only monographs or articles for certain regions. For the Tatar press, besides the basic work of Ismail Ramiev, *Waḳītlī Tatar Maṭbūʿātī*, Ḳāzān 1926, fragmentary information is contained in Elif-Bi, *Iz tatarskoy musul'manskoy pečati*, Ḳāzān 1908; Fedotov, *Pečatʾ Tatrespubliki*, in *Bulletin d'information du V.O.K.S.*, Moscow 1927, no. 23-5; T. Nasīrov, *Sovet vlastenin berenče ellerinda tatar vaḳītlī maṭbūʿātī*, in *Sovet Ädäbiyatī Ḳāzān*, no. 9 1956); A. Saadi, *Tatar ädäbiyatī taʾrīkhi*, Ḳāzān 1926; A. Safarov, *Z istorii tatarskoy periodičnoy presi- 1905-25*, in *Shidny Svit*, Kharkov 1928, no. 3-4 (in Ukrainian); Dj. Validov, *Očerki istorii obrazovannosti i litteraturī Tatar do revolyutsii 1917 goda*, Moscow 1933; P. Žuže, *Musul'manskaya pečat' v Rossii*, St. Petersburg 1911.

On the Caucasian Ādharī press, we have a detailed study in Jeyhun bey Hajibeyli, *The origins of the national press in Azerbaydjan*, in *The Asiatic Review*, xxvi (1930), fas. 88 and xxvii, fas. 90, and also an anonymous article *Ādherī maṭbūʿātīnīn mukhtaṣar taʾrīkhčesi*, in *Yeñi Ḳafkasiya*, Istanbul, iii/9. For the origins of the Caucasian press one may consult the article of I. Enikopolov, *Pervaya turkskaya gazeta na Kavkaze*, in *Kul'tura i pis'mennost' Vostoka*, iii, Baku 1928, as well as the monographs devoted to the newspaper *Ekinči*, the most important being *Ādharbāydjān maṭbūʿātīnīn yīllīğī-Ekinči*, Baku 1926. Several works have been devoted to the review *Mollā Naṣreddīn*, among them being A. H. M. Ahmedov, *Molla Nasreddin Žurnalīnīñ yayīlmasī ve taʾsiri ḥaḳḳīnda*, in *Izvestiya Akademii Nauk Adher. SSR*, Series of Social Sciences, i, Baku 1958 and A. Sharif, *Molla Nasreddin*, Baku 1946.

Information on the history of the press in the Crimea, with more particular reference to the *Terdjümān*, is contained in the work of Cafer Seydahmet, *Gaspıralı Ismail Bey*, Istanbul 1934, and in the study of Ahmed Özenbashlī, *Gečen devrimize tenkitli bir bakīş*, in *Oku Ishleri*, Baghče-Saray June 1925.

For the press of Turkestan, we possess an excellent monograph of Ziya Saidov, *Uzbek vakītlī maṭbūʿātī tarihige matiriyyalar*, Samarkand-Tashkent 1927. For the Turkmen press, an article of Mihaylov, *Natsional'naya pečat' Turkmenii*, in *Revolutsiya i natsional'ni nosti*, Moscow 1931, no. 4 and for the press of Daghistān, that of Sh. Magomedov, *Kumīkskaya periodičeskaya pečat' v 1917-8 godakh*, in *Trudī Instituta Istorii Partii pri Dagestanskom obkome K.P.S.S.*, ii, Mahač-Ḳala 1958.

(Ch. Quelquejay)

v. — the Muslim press in China and Japan

(*a*) China.—China has a Muslim population of some ten to twelve million persons according to the census of 1959. About two-thirds live in Sinkiang province where they constitute an overwhelming majority. The following table contains data on the geographical distribution of Chinese mosques in 1935 and on Muslim periodical publications during the period 1908-39. We may assume that an average Chinese mosque serves 200 to 250 people. In the absence of precise statistics, the table therefore indicates the distribution of the Muslim population in the mid-Thirties.

DISTRIBUTION OF MOSQUES AND MUSLIM PERIODICALS IN CHINA

Province	Number of mosques (1935)	Number of periodicals (1908-39)
Anhwei	1,515	
Chekiang	239	
Chinghai	1,031	3
Fukien	157	
Honan	2,703	4
Hopei	2,942	33
Hunan	932	2
Hupei	1,134	4
Kansu	3,891	
Kiangsi	205	
Kiangsu	2,302	24
Kwangsi	429	2
Kwangtung	201	7
Kweichow	449	
Manchuria	6,811	2
Mongolia	1,083	1
Shansi	1,931	2
Shantung	2,513	1
Shensi	3,612	3
Sinkiang	2,045	
Szechwan	2,275	1
Yünnan	3,971	6
Others		5
Total	42,371	100

A total of 100 Chinese-Muslim papers have been located. One was published abroad (1908), and for 13 the dates of origin are unknown. The remaining 86 were founded between 1913 and 1939; 18 magazines being established between 1913 and 1926. In the decade marked by the establishment of the Chinese Nationalist Government in Peking (1927) and the beginning of the Chinese-Japanese conflict (1937), the press expanded rapidly, and 63 new journals came into being—38 after the capital was moved from Peking to Nanking (1932). The outbreak of hostilities between China and Japan brought repressions and most of the papers disappeared. The five new periodicals which were issued during the next two years were actually official publications of the two combatants aimed at gaining increased Muslim support of the war effort.

The frequency of issue is known for 71 magazines: 12 appeared at least weekly; 50—monthly or semimonthly; 9—quarterly or annually. One magazine had a circulation of more than 3,000 copies; eight others ranged from 1,000 to 2,000 copies, while the remainder served local needs and ran to a few hundred copies only. Not more than six periodicals exceeded 40 pages.

Most of the publications appeared in Chinese, though a few were written partly or entirely in Japanese, Arabic, Uygur (Eastern Turkī), and English. The great majority were religious in content, while the remainder in addition dealt with historical or contemporary problems. Most of the magazines were printed and circulated in the cultural and national centres of Peiping and Nanking, and in large port cities, such as Tientsin, Shanghai, Canton, and Hongkong.

Yüeh Hua (月華), Peiping, was the leading Muslim national magazine with a circulation of 3,000. It was begun in 1929 under private subsidies and attempted to represent all factions fairly. In its columns were domestic and international news items pertaining to Islam.

T'u Chüeh (突崛), Nanking, was established in 1934. It was the most substantial Muslim organ in the capital area, and advocated the "Three People's Principles", improvement of education, domestic unification, and contacts with co-religonists abroad.

T'ien Fang Hsüeh Li Yüeh K'an (天方學理月刊), Canton, was founded in 1929. It was distributed monthly without charge, but financial support was solicited. *T'ien Fang* dealt chiefly with contemporary issues, and the editor answered readers' queries in a special column.

The Muslim communities in the large cities during the 1930's organized protest demonstrations under *Ahungs* (*Mullahs*) whenever Islam was slandered in the Chinese press. In some instances the offices and printing plants of the offending newspapers were wrecked. The Nationalist government, needing the good will of its Muslim subjects, took prompt action to prevent further insult.

During the first decade of the twentieth century, in addition to native papers, some liberal Arabic and Turkish journals advocating constitutional reform were imported from Constantinople. The need for them was gone after the revolution of 1911.

The Muslim press in China was late in developing because of low educational and economic standards and because of language difficulties. Arabic was known only to religious leaders and to a few theologically trained laymen. The *Ahungs*, on the other hand, had often only a rudimentary knowledge of the Chinese script. Most of the population were illiterate. The declining Manchu dynasty was suspicious of any particularistic or sectarian tendencies, especially in the Turkī-speaking north-west borderland. One might say that the revolution of 1911 paved the way for the Muslim press in China, while the Communist revolution of 1949 decisively ended it. Muslim publication efforts were fragmentary. Most magazines were too small or too ephemeral to have a lasting influence. In contrast to the Protestant and Catholic missions in China, the Muslims lacked a centralized organization and adequate funds.

(*b*) Japan.—Japan has very few Muslims, but Japanese interest in Islam dates from the invasion of China (1937-45) when efforts were made to win over Chinese Muslim minorities. Prior to that date Japan experienced three private attempts to publish Muslim papers. *Hsing Hui* (醒回 "Muslims Awake") was established as a quarterly by Chinese students of the Muslim College in Tokyo for distribution in China; it dates back to 1908. In 1925, I. T. Sakuma, a Japanese business man and convert to Islam, founded in Shanghai the progressive *Mu Kuang* (穆光 "Light of Islam") with articles in Chinese, Japanese, and English. He desired an Islamic revival in China, Korea, and Japan and even advocated the translation of the Ḳurʾān into Chinese; *Mu Kuang* survived only three issues. *Hui Chiao* (回教 "Islam"), a Peiping monthly devoted to social and historical problems, was published in Japanese between 1927 and 1929. The issues also contained biographies of Chinese Muslim leaders.

Following the actual occupation of Chinese territory, Japanese military authorities launched new Muslim papers, or adapted existing periodicals to their own purposes. The Japanese took over the ten-year old illustrated monthly *Chen Tsung Pao* (震宗報) after they occupied Peiping in 1937. Thereafter it assumed a strongly anti-Soviet character. The *Hsing Shih Pao* (醒時報), a non-political monthly, first appeared in Mukden, Manchuria, in 1925. It was revived by the Japanese in 1937, reporting mainly on Muslim life in Japan. Copies were distributed locally free of charge. Another monthly by the name of *Hui Chiao* (回教 "Islam") began to appear in April 1938 under the auspices of the Japanese-sponsored United Chinese Muslim Association, Peiping. This was a Japanese propaganda organ, but it was printed in Chinese. The *Hsin Min Pao* (新民報), official Chinese newspaper of the Japanese occupation authorities in Peiping, launched in October 1939 a weekly supplement, the *Tsung Chiao Chou K'an* (宗教週刊), which furnished historical and religious information on Islam.

Japanese research on Islam and Islamic peoples is scattered among numerous academic journals. Only two Japanese periodicals are entirely devoted to this topic. Both are published in Tokyo and date from 1959 and 1960 respectively. *Chû-Kintô geppô* (中近東月報 "Middle and Near East Monthly") is issued in mimeographed form by the Ministry of Foreign Affairs. The Ajia Rengô Yuko Kyokai (アシア達合好友會) publishes *Arabu* (ヤテブ "Arab") reporting on Arabs and Arab countries.

Bibliography: R. Loewenthal, *The Mohammedan press in China*, in *Collectanea Commissionis Synodalis in Sinis*, Peking, xi/9-10 (Sept.-Oct. 1938), 867-94, with 2 charts.—Reprinted in: *The religious periodical press in China*, Peking, The Synodal Commission in China, 1940, 211-49.

(RUDOLF LOEWENTHAL)

vi. — THE HAUSA PRESS

There is a regular weekly newspaper in Hausa, *Gaskiya ta fi kwabo*, printed in Zaria, which began publication in January 1939. In addition, news sheets in the main recognized Hausa dialects are also published, while the *Kano Times* includes articles in the Hausa language.

It was on Saturday 14 November 1931 that there issued from the newly built printing house at Kaduna the first number of *The Northern Provinces News*. It consisted of sixteen pages of items in three columns, printed respectively in English, in Hausa in a roman orthography, and in Arabic, together with a page of photos of stallions and agricultural subjects. The reader is told "Mallams of the Secretariat have written the Hausa and Arabic translations, and compositors sent to the Press by the Emir of Kano have set up the Arabic type". This number was produced "as a basis for discussion as to whether Residents and Native Chiefs would desire the regular issue of a News Sheet of this or a similar type in the future". The next issue was on 9 April 1932, and had the Hausa title added, *Jaridar Nigeria Ta Arewa*, together with an Arabic title. It consisted of twenty-six pages of print and three pages of pictures. The third number also included items translated into two other Northern vernaculars, Tiv and Fula (Fulani). By July 1934, when number eight appeared, the paper was of a smaller format, and was printed only in Hausa, and no longer bore titles in English and Arabic. The tenth issue, 1 June 1935, included an article by R.M. East, of the Translation Bureau, Zaria, on the subject of Hausa books and writing. The spelling included new letters, ƙ, ɗ and ɓ.

After the Translation Bureau in Zaria began publication of *Gaskiya ta fi kwabo*, it also produced a smaller news sheet *Jakadiya*, in a simpler form of the language, as well as a news sheet in Tiv. In addition, it undertook the production of a large number of cheap pamphlets in Hausa on a wide range of educational topics, from well-digging to baby care. More literary works in Hausa were produced, as well as books in other Nigerian languages, such as Igbo. The Hausa newspaper has helped to develop the written language and has set a standard for the importation into Hausa of a large number of borrowed words—mostly from English. The printing of the news also in the chief dialects is now enriching the standard language, by enabling people from all over the Hausa-speaking area to share and enjoy the different forms, expressions and idioms of this widely used and colourful language. (J. CARNOCHAN)

vii. — INDIA and PAKISTAN

viii. — EAST AFRICA

[see SUPPLEMENT].

DJARĪMA (A.), also *djurm*, a sin, fault, offence. In Ottoman usage, in the forms *djerīme* and *djereme*, it denoted fines and penalties (see DJURM). In the modern laws enacted in Muslim countries it has become a technical term for *crime* (*djurm* in Pakistan). For the corresponding Islamic concepts, see ḤADD, and for penal law in general, ʿUḲŪBA. (ED.)

DJARĪR B. ʿAṬIYYA B. AL-KHAṬAFA (HUDHAYFA) B. BADR was among the most important *hidjāʾ*-writers of the Umayyad period (the other two were his rivals al-Akhṭal and al-Farazdaḳ [*qq.v.*], and may be considered one of the greatest Islamic-Arabic poets of all time. He belonged to the clan of the Banū Kulayb b. Yarbūʿ an, a branch of the Muḍarī Tamīm who were widespread in the eastern part of central and northern Arabia. He was born in the middle of the 1st/7th century and began by entering into verbal disputes with second class writers in his own district, ostensibly because he himself had been attacked but in fact because of his naturally argumentative disposition. In 64/683-4 or shortly afterwards he began his famous forty-year-long dispute with al-Farazdaḳ, who was a foe worthy of his steel. It was caused indirectly by a long quarrel between the Banū Dhuhayl, a branch of the Banū Yarbūʿ, and the Mudjashiʿ, also Tamīmī and the tribe to which al-Farazdaḳ belonged, over the theft of a camel. After they had abused each other from a distance for some time, Djarīr went to ʿIrāḳ and met al-Farazdaḳ for the first time in Baṣra. There were such scenes that the authorities had to put a stop to the meetings—although without any lasting success.

Djarīr began his public career by writing poems

in praise of al-Ḥakam b. Ayyūb, an official of the governor of ʿIrāḳ, al-Ḥadjdjādj. Al-Ḥakam recommended him to his master who invited him to Wāsiṭ. After staying with al-Ḥadjdjādj for some time and writing a series of *ḳaṣīda*s of praise to him, Djarīr was sent with his son Muḥammad to ʿAbd al-Malik's court in Damascus. He was first rejected, then graciously received by ʿAbd al-Malik. But in the long run their relationship was not particularly good, for the caliph favoured the Taghlibī Christian al-Akhṭal ("al-Akhṭal is the poet of the Umayyads!") who took al-Farazdaḳ's part against Djarīr. Djarīr's relations with ʿAbd al-Malik's successor al-Walīd were even worse; the latter supported his favourite ʿAdī b. al-Riḳāʿ [*q.v.*] against Djarīr's attacks. In fact Djarīr and his friend Ladjʿa al-Taymī are even said to have been whipped and publicly stripped on account of some satirical lines on the court ladies. However he was on a rather better footing with ʿUmar II who, as a pious man, took no very passionate interest in either eulogies or satires, and remained courteously neutral. Nevertheless he does seem to have preferred Djarīr to his rivals. Djarīr also attempted to win the favour of the later caliphs Yazīd II and Hishām by writing poems in praise of them. Finally, in old age he retired to the Yamāma where he owned property (in Uthayfiyya). He died there when over eighty, in 110/728-9 or a little later, shortly after the death of his opponent al-Farazdaḳ. Among his numerous descendents were three sons (Bilāl, ʿIkrima and Nūḥ) who also produced poetry but did not, however, approach their father's importance.

In Djarīr's *dīwān*, collected by Muḥammad b. Ḥabīb (died 245/859), the satirical poems occupy the most space, and of them the larger number are directed against al-Farazdaḳ. The extent to which contemporaries were interested in this poetic battle is shown by a report of a quarrel which broke out among soldiers in al-Muhallab's camp during the Azraḳī war—a quarrel eventually decided (thanks to one of the Khāridjī soldiers) in Djarīr's favour. The total number of poets satirized by Djarīr is something over forty. After the satirical poems, the poems of praise form the largest category in the *dīwān*, but it also contains some fine elegies. According to his adversary al-Akhṭal, Djarīr was particularly skilled in the *nasīb* and the *tashbīh*. The Arabic literary historians and critics rightly praise Djarīr's fluent diction.

Djarīr's work does indeed show him to be a true descendent of the old Bedouin poets, with all their strong points and weaknesses. In his work and that of his rivals al-Akhṭal and al-Farazdaḳ, the old Arabic form of *ḳaṣīda*-poetry underwent "an Indian summer of undeniable loveliness' (G. E. Von Grünebaum).

There are several editions of Djarīr's *dīwān* in which the poems are sometimes arranged according to the rhyme-letters. Maḥmūd ʿAbd al-Muʾmin al-Shawāribī is the man chiefly responsible for the first of these editions (Cairo 1313); its sources are not given. The editions of Muḥammad al-Sāwī (Cairo 1353), and Karam al-Bustānī (Beirut 1379/1960) are no more worthy of critical attention. The *Naḳāʾid*, however, of Djarīr and Farazdaḳ, as collected by Abū ʿUbayda (d. ca. 210/825) and revised by others, have been published in a model edition by A. A. Bevan (Leiden 1905-12), and furnished with a glossary and indexes. Finally, the *Naḳāʿid* of Djarīr and Akhṭal have also been published, according to the recension of Abū Tammām, by the Akhṭal scholar Salḥānī (Beirut 1922). Both *Naḳāʾiḍ* also contain poems attacking other persons and their answers.

Bibliography: Djumaḥī (ed. Hell), 86-108; Ibn Ḳutayba, *al-Shiʿr*, 283; *Aghānī*[3], viii, 3-89; Marzubānī, *Muwashshaḥ*, 118-32 and *passim*, cf. Brockelmann, II, 53-5; S I, 86-7. Cf. also Rescher, *Abriss*, i, 265-74 and A. Schaade, *Djarīr* (supplement to the German edition of *EI*[1].

(A. SCHAADE-[H. GÄTJE])

DJĀRIYA [see ʿABD].

DJĀRIYA B. **ḲUDĀMA** B. ZUHAYR (or: b. Mālik b. Zuhayr) B. AL-ḤUṢAYN B. RIZĀḤ B. ASʿAD B. BUDJAYR (or: Shudjayr) B. RABĪʿA, ABŪ AYYŪB (or: Abū Ḳudāma, or: Abū Yazīd) AL-TAMĪMĪ, AL-SAʿDĪ, nicknamed "al-Muḥarriḳ", the "Burner"—was a Companion of the Prophet (about the identity of Djāriya b. Ḳudāma with Djuwayriya b. Ḳudāma see *Tahdhīb*, ii, 54, 125, and *Iṣāba*, i, 227, 276). Djāriya gained his fame as a staunch supporter of ʿAlī b. Abī Ṭālib.

According to a tradition quoted by Ibn Saʿd (*Ṭabaḳāt*, vii/1, 38) Djāriya witnessed the attempt at the assassination of ʿUmar; later, he was in Baṣra when the forces of Ṭalḥa and al-Zubayr entered the city. He harshly reproached ʿĀʾisha (al-Ṭabarī, ed. Cairo 1939, iii, 482; *al-Imāma wa 'l-Siyāsa*, ed. Cairo 1331 A.H., i, 60), and took part in the battle of the Camel with ʿAlī (although his tribe, the Saʿd, remained neutral); he was given command of the Saʿd and the Ribāb of Baṣra in the battle of Ṣiffīn and distinguished himself in this battle (Naṣr b. Muzāḥim: *Waḳʿat Ṣiffīn*, 153, 295, ed. Beirut). He seems to have approved the idea of arbitration and was among the delegation of the heads of Tamīm, who tried to mitigate al-Ashʿath and the Azd (al-Mubarrad, *al-Kāmil* (ed. Wright) 539).

Djāriya remained faithful to ʿAlī after the arbitration and supported him in his struggle against the Khawāridj: he was at the head of the troop levied with difficulty by ʿAbd Allāh b. ʿAbbās from Baṣra (37 A.H.) and despatched to fight the Khawāridj (al-Ṭabarī, iv, 58; Caetani, *Annali*, x, 85). He remained faithful when the influence of ʿAlī began to shrink and ʿAlī was deserted by his friends. After his conquest of Egypt Muʿāwiya, being aware of the peculiar situation in Baṣra, in which the differences between the tribal groups were acute and the partisans of ʿAlī not numerous, decided to wrest the city from ʿAlī. The details about these events holding ʿIrāḳ are provided by al-Balādhurī's *Ansāb al-Ashrāf* among other sources (fols. 206b-209a). Muʿāwiya sent to Baṣra (in 38 A.H.) his emissary, ʿAbd Allāh b. ʿĀmir (or b. ʿAmr) al-Ḥaḍramī, [see IBN AL-ḤAḌRAMĪ] in order to win the hearts of the Banū Tamīm in Baṣra. He gained in fact the protection of the Banū Tamīm. The deputy prefect of Baṣra Ziyād b. Abīhi was compelled to seek protection for himself with the Azd in Baṣra. ʿAlī sent his emissary, Aʿyan b. Ḍubayʿa al-Mudjāshiʿī in order to prevent the fall of the city into the hands of Muʿāwiya; he was, however, killed by a group of men said to have been Khāridjites (although the version of the participation of ʿAbd Allāh Ibn al-Ḥaḍramī seems to be plausible). Ziyād asked ʿAlī to send to Baṣra Djāriya b. Ḳudāma, who was highly respected in his tribe (Ibn Abi 'l-Ḥadīd, *Sharḥ Nahdj al-Balāgha*, i, 353). Djāriya arrived at Baṣra with a troop of 50 warriors (or 500—see al-Ṭabarī, iv, 85; or 1000 or 1500—see *Ansāb*, fol. 208b), met Ziyād b. Abīhi, rallied the followers of ʿAlī, succeeded in winning the hearts of groups of Tamīm who joined him, attacked the forces of Ibn al-Ḥaḍramī and defeated them. Ibn al-Ḥaḍramī retreated with a group of 70 followers to a fortified Sāsānid castle, belonging to a Tamīmī called Sunbīl (or Ṣunbīl). Djāriya besieged the castle, ordered wood to be placed around it and set the wood on fire. Ibn al-Ḥaḍramī and his followers were burnt alive. There are controversial traditions about the course of the encounter between Djāriya and Ibn al-Ḥaḍramī (see *Ansāb*, fol. 208b). According to a rather curious tradition (refuted by al-Balādhurī) Djāriya came to Baṣra as an emissary of Muʿāwiya together with Ibn al-Ḥaḍramī, but forsook him however in Baṣra (*Ansāb*, fol. 209a). After the victory of Djāriya, Ziyād returned to the residence of the Governor of Baṣra.

The authority of ʿAlī was thus secured in Baṣra. Ziyād b. Abīhi praised in his letter to ʿAlī the action of Djāriya and described him as the "righteous servant" (*al-ʿabd al-ṣāliḥ*). It was Djāriya who advised ʿAlī in 39 A.H. to send Ziyād to the province of Fārs to quell the rebellion of the Persians who refused to pay their taxes (al-Ṭabarī, iv, 105). According to Ibn Kathīr (cf. Ibn al-Athīr, *al-Kāmil*, iii, 165) the revolt was caused by the brutal action of burning committed by Djāriya (*al-Bidāya*, vii, 320).

Djāriya fought his last fight in the service of ʿAlī against Busr b. Abī Arṭāt [*q.v.*] in 40 A.H. When the tidings about the expedition of Busr reached ʿAlī he dispatched Djāriya with a troop of 2000 men to pursue Busr (another troop under the command of Wahb b. Masʿūd was also despatched by ʿAlī). Djāriya, following Busr, reached the Yemen (so al-Balādhurī, *Ansāb* 211b; according to al-Ṭabarī, iv, 107 he reached Nadjrān) and severely punished the partisans of Muʿāwiya. Pursuing the retreating Busr, Djāriya arrived at Mecca and was told that ʿAlī had been killed. He compelled the people of Mecca to swear allegiance to the Caliph who would be elected by the followers of ʿAlī. In Medina he compelled the people to swear allegiance to Ḥasan b. ʿAlī.

In the time of Muʿāwiya there was a reconciliation between Djāriya and Muʿāwiya. Anecdotal stories report about the talks between Djāriya and Muʿāwiya (*al-Naḳāʾiḍ*, ed. Bevan, 608; al-Balādhurī, *Ansāb*, fol. 358b; al-Djāḥiẓ, *al-Bayān*, ii, 186; al-Mubarrad, *al-Kāmil*, ed Wright, 40). According to a fairly reliable tradition in al-Balādhurī's *Ansāb* (fol. 1048b) Muʿāwiya granted Djāriya a large fee of 900 *djarīb*.

Djāriya died in Baṣra. His funeral was attended by al-Aḥnaf.

Bibliography: al-Bukhārī, *Taʾrīkh*, i/2 (ed. Ḥaydarābād 1362 A.H.) 236, 240 (N. 2309, 2325); al-Dhahabī, *Taʾrīkh*, ii, 182, 187; Ibn ʿAsākir, *Taʾrīkh*, ed. 1331 A.H., iii, 223; Wellhausen, *The Ar. kingdom*, 100; Ibn al-Kalbī, *Djamhara*, Ms. Br. Mus., fol, 82a; Ibn Durayd, *al-Ishtiḳāḳ*, (ed. ʿAbd al-Salām Hārūn), 253; al-Balādhurī, *Ansāb al-Ashrāf*, fols. 206b-209a, 211a, 366a, 358b, 1048b, 1130b; Muḥ. b. Ḥabīb, *al-Muḥabbar*, index; al-Mubarrad, *al-Kāmil*, index; Ibn al-Athīr, *al-Kāmil* (ed. Cairo 1301 A.H.), iii, 156, 165-7; Ibn Kathīr, *al-Bidāya*, vii, 316, 322, 320; Ibn Saʿd, *Ṭabaḳāt*, index; al-Yaʿḳūbī, *Taʾrīkh*, index; al-ʿAsḳalānī: *Tahdhīb al-tahdhīb*, s.v. Djāriya and Djuwayriya; al-ʿAsḳalānī, *al-Iṣāba*, s.v. Djāriya and Djuwayriya; al-Marzubānī, *Muʿdjam al-shuʿarā*, (ed. Krenkow), 306; Muir, *The Caliphate*, Edinburgh 1924, 280; Ṭāhā Ḥusayn, *ʿAlī wa banūhu*, 143-6, 150-1; al-Ṭabarī, index; a tradition of Djāriya and its parallels, see: Djāmiʿ Ibn Wahb (ed. David-Weill) 54, 106; Ibn al-Ḥadīd. *Sharḥ Nahdj al-Balāgha*, ed. 1329 A.H.

(M. J. Kister)

DJARR [see NAḤW].

DJARRĀḤ, "he who heals wounds", "surgeon"; *djirāḥa*, "the art of healing wounds , "surgery", from *djurḥ*, "injury", "wounds"—like the German "Wund , whence "Wundarzt", "Wundarznei", etc. In the time of the Arabic versions of the Greek texts on medicine, another expression corresponding exactly to *djirāḥa* made its way into Arabic medical language and was adopted by the classical authors, namely: *ʿamal bi ʾl-yad* (Ibn Sīnā) or *ʿamal al-yad* (al-Zahrāwī), "work, action performed with the hand" or "by hand" (which was only a literal translation of χειρουργία). But this last expression, perhaps for practical reasons of usage, was gradually to lose ground in the course of centuries and ultimately to be replaced by the first, which is the only one to have remained in use until today, with all its derivatives. However, it is under the title *ʿamal bi ʾl-yad* or *ʿamal al-yad*, in classical texts, that we find mentioned many expressions relating to medico-surgical techniques. From general surgery we may note such terms as *rabṭ* "ligature" (of veins), *ḳaṭʿ* "excision" (of soft diseased substance), *baṭṭ* and *batr* "incision" (for the removal of morbid matter), *kayy* "cauterization by fire (from καίειν "to burn"), with the object of surgical excision; from specialized surgery such terms as *ḳadḥ* "operation for cataract", "*reclinatio*"); from minor or simple surgery, *djabr* "reduction" of a fracture (*kasr*) or luxation (*khalʿ*); from manual practices having medical purposes, like *ḥadjm* "cupping" without or after the *sharṭ* "scarification", *faṣd* "bleeding", *kayy* itself as a revulsive or stimulating remedy, etc.

From *ʿamal* [*al-yad*] there remain in modern Arabic only the words *ʿamaliyya*, followed by the adjective *djirāḥiyya*, "operation", or "surgical operation" properly speaking, and *ʿamalī*, "operative" or "operational".

In old texts one very often comes across the forms [*ʿilādj*] *bi ʾl-ḥadīd* or *bi ʾl-āla*, the [*cura*] *cum ferro* and *cum instrumento* respectively of the Latin translators of the Middle Ages, referring specifically to surgical operations which necessitated the use of cutting instruments.

Djarrāḥ occurs for the first time in Arabic literature in translations of the 3rd/9th century, and from there the expression made its way into medical literature. As the name of a well-known family we find the word in the 4th/9th century [see Ibn al-Djarrāḥ]. However, in contradistinction to the custom of the Hellenistic-Roman period, in Islam, as in mediaeval Europe, the surgeon has always been regarded as a worker of an inferior order. It is probable that this point of view derives in essence from the Islamic aversion from any interference with the condition of the human body, and even with the bodies of animals (the prohibition of vivisection of animals). With regard to the most celebrated and distinguished doctors in Islam such as Ibn Sīnā and Ibn Zuhr, we know that they vigorously expressed their dislike of every sort of surgical treatment, which they left to the *djarrāḥ* and *mudjabbir* (bone-setter and bone-healer). In spite of that, Ibn Sīnā devoted a large part of his *Ḳānūn* to the art of surgery (*ʿilm al-djirāḥa*), and his precursor ʿAlī b. al-ʿAbbās al-Madjūsī (d. 384/994) treated surgery in great detail in the ninth book of his work *Kāmil al-ṣināʿa*, devoting no less than 110 chapters to it, and added to the tenth book a special theory of surgical therapy.

The only specialized surgical manual of any importance in Islamic medical literature seems to be *al-ʿUmda fī ṣināʿat al-djirāḥa* of Ibn al-Ḳuff

(Syria, 7th/13th century). The work which exerted the greatest influence on the West was the part on surgery by Abu 'l-Ḳāsim al-Zahrāwī (Cordova, 4th/10th century), section XXX of his *Kitāb al-Taṣrīf*. This part was translated into Latin at a very early date and was studied with great enthusiasm in the West, although close links between this work and Paul of Aegina's surgery can be noted. It is illustrated with drawings of instruments. In the works on *ḥisba* [*q.v.*] one frequently finds a section devoted to doctors, oculists and surgeons, as for example in the unpublished book of al-Shayzarī. In it the surgeon is required to be familiar with the anatomy and therapy of Galen (Djālīnūs [*q.v.*]) and to possess a well-assorted set of instruments which must include methods for checking bleeding. The work of the bone-setter (*mudjabbir*) is given special attention by al-Shayzarī: he is required to know the number and shape of all the bones as well as Paul of Aegina's chapter on bone fractures and sprains.

Throughout the Middle Ages, Arab surgery was always advanced in comparison with European surgery, and indeed it helped the latter to make great advances (it is known that Lanfranc of Milan, a famous exponent of surgery in Paris in the 13th century, had based his theories almost exclusively on the *Maḳāla fi ʿamal al-yad*, the famous treatise *De chirurgia* of Abu 'l-Ḳāsim al-Zahrāwī). But Arab surgery avoided every kind of destructive operation (amputation), even apart from prohibitions or scruples of a religious nature. Nor did it fail to contribute as well to the knowledge of the human body, replacing anatomical dissection, however, casually and in a limited way. Incidentally, *ʿilm al-tashrīḥ* "anatomy" was always regarded as an indispensable science even in the practice of specialized surgery. In this connexion one may recall the anecdote of al-Rāzī dismissing the man who was to have operated on him for cataract, but who had been unable to answer the questions on ocular anatomy previously put to him by the great doctor (Ibn Abī Uṣaybiʿa).

Bibliography: Ibn Abī Uṣaybiʿa, *ʿUyūn al-anbāʾ*, Cairo 1882, i; H. Bowen, *The life and times of ʿAlī b. ʿĪsā*, Cambridge 1928, 33-6; ʿAlī b. al-ʿAbbās al-Madjūsī, *Kāmil al-ṣināʿa*, Būlāḳ 1924, ii, 454-607; Ibn Sīnā, *Ḳānūn fi 'l-ṭibb*, Būlāḳ 1924, iii, 146-217; ʿAbd al-Raḥmān b. Naṣr b. ʿAbd Allāh al-Shayzarī, *Nihāyat al-rutba fī ṭalab al-ḥisba*, chap. 8 of manuscript 20 *ʿUlūm maʿāshiyya* of Bibl. Egypt., Cairo; Ibn al-Ḳuff, in Ibn Abī Uṣaybiʿa, ii, 273; Leclerc, *Hist. de la méd. arabe*, Paris 1876, ii, 203; idem, *La chirurgie d'Abulcasis*, Paris 1861; G. Sarton, *Introduction to the history of science*, Baltimore 1927-31, i, 681; ii, 1098; K. Sudhof, *Beiträge zur Geschichte der Chirurgie im Mittelalter*, Leipzig 1918; Aḥmad ʿĪsā Bey, *Ālāt al-ṭibb wa 'l-djirāḥa wa 'l-kiḥāla ʿind al-ʿArab* (Opening address at the Arab Academy, Damascus, with 187 drawings, 5 tables ,and explanatory notes), Cairo 1925; A. Khairallah, *Outline of Arabic contributions to medicine and allied sciences*, Beirut 1946; Goyanes Capdevila, *El ingenio técnico en la cirugía arábigo-española*, in *Actas del XV Congreso Internac. de Hist. de la Medicina*, Madrid 1956. (M. MEYERHOF-[T. SARNELLI])

AL-**DJARRĀḤ** B. **ʿABD ALLĀH** AL-ḤAKAMĪ, Abū ʿUḳba, an Umayyad general, called *Baṭal al-Islām*, 'hero of Islam', and *Fāris Ahl al-Shām*, 'cavalier of the Syrians'. He was governor of al-Baṣra for al-Walīd (Caliph 86-96/705-15) under al-Ḥadjdjādj, then governor of Khurāsān and Sidjistān for ʿUmar b. ʿAbd al-ʿAzīz, till deposed by ʿUmar after a year and five months (99-100/718-9) for harsh treatment of the new converts to Islam in Khurāsān. In 104/722-3 al-Djarrāḥ was appointed governor of Armenia with orders to attack the Khazars, who at this time were threatening the lands south of the Caucasus. Advancing from Bardhaʿa, he occupied Bāb, the frontier town (see BĀB AL-ABWĀB), near which he defeated a large Khazar force under 'Bārdjīk, the son of the Khāḳān'. Continuing his advance round the eastern end of the Caucasus, al-Djarrāḥ captured the Khazar towns of Balandjar and Wabandar, and reached the neighbourhood of Samandar, probably Ḳizlar (Kizliyar) on the Terek, before withdrawing. Some time later he was recalled, but was reappointed in 111/729-30. Next year the. Khazars appeared in force in his province and were met by al-Djarrāḥ with an army of Syrians and local levies in the plain of Ardabīl (Mardj Ardabīl). Here for several days in Ramaḍān 112/November-December 730, a great battle was fought, which ended in the total defeat of the Muslims and the death of al-Djarrāḥ. The Khazars temporarily occupied the whole of Ādharbāydjān, their cavalry raiding as far south as Mosul. The loss of al-Djarrāḥ caused widespread consternation and grief, especially among the soldiers. He is said to have been so tall a man that when he walked in the Great Mosque of Damascus, his head seemed to be suspended from the lamps.

Bibliography: al-Dhahabī, *Taʾrīkh al-Islām* (Cairo, A.H. 1367-9), iv, 237-8; al-Ṭabarī, ii, 1352-6; D. M. Dunlop, *History of the Jewish Khazars*, Princeton 1954, index; F. Gabrieli, *Il Califfato di Hishâm*, Alexandria 1935, 74 ff.

(D. M. DUNLOP)

DJARRĀḤIDS or BANU 'L-DJARRĀḤ, a family of the Yemeni tribe of Ṭayy which settled in Palestine and in the Balḳāʾ region, in the mountains of al-Sharāt as well as in the north Arabian desert where the two hills of ʿAdjāʾ and Salmā, known also as the mountains of the Banū Ṭayy, are part of their territory. This family attained some importance at the end of the 4th/10th and 5th/11th centuries, but without ever succeeding in creating a state as the Banū Kilāb tribe did at Aleppo, or in having a capital, except for a very short time at Ramla. The Banu 'l-Djarrāḥ followed a policy of vacillation between the Fāṭimids and the Byzantines, at times supporting one side and at times the other, not hesitating to flatter abjectly either of them when danger threatened, or to betray them, and only abandoning these equivocal tactics to seize the chance of plundering towns or the countryside or caravans on pilgrimage. In general they remained essentially Bedouins, with the qualities and failings of the Arabs of the desert, and their activities were far from glorious.

The first of the Banu 'l-Djarrāḥ to figure in the chronicles was named Daghfal b. al-Djarrāḥ and was an ally of the Ḳarmaṭians. At the time of his expedition against Egypt in 361/971-2, al-Djannābī [*q.v.*] left one of his officers with Daghfal at Ramla. During the second Ḳarmaṭian invasion of Egypt in 363/974, a Djarrāḥid named Ḥassān b. al-Djarrāḥ was in the Ḳarmaṭian army, and it was thanks to his defection, in return for a bribe of money by the caliph al-Muʿizz, that the Ḳarmaṭian force was routed after reaching the gates of Cairo. Daghfal and Ḥassān are possibly one and the same person.

Some years later Daghfal's son Mufarridj made his appearance, and was to remain in prominence until 404/1013-4; certain texts give his name wrongly as

Daghfal b. al-Mufarridj. At the time of the caliph al-ʿAzīz's expedition against Alptekīn, a Turk who had seized Damascus and allied himself with the Ḳarmaṭians, in the battle which took place outside Ramla in Muḥarram 367/August-September 977. Alptekīn took to flight and was found dying of thirst by Mufarridj with whom he was on friendly terms. As the caliph had promised 100,000 dinars to anyone who handed over Alptekīn to him, Mufarridj, whose allegiance at that moment is not specified in the records, had Alptekīn kept in custody at Lubnā. He then went to the caliph and, on receiving an assurance that the offer of the reward still held good, betrayed Alptekīn and took him to the caliph. Two years later we find him involved in the Ḥamdānid Abū Taghlib's venture in Palestine. For the moment he was in control of Ramla, a fact recognized by the head of an Egyptian army, al-Faḍl, whom the vizier Ibn Killīs had sent into Syria at that time against a usurper from Damascus, Ḳassām, and Abū Taghlib. Mufarridj was then on bad terms with the Banū ʿUḳayl; as they appealed to Abū Taghlib, war broke out between him and Mufarridj who was supported by Faḍl. Abū Taghlib was defeated and made prisoner by a supporter of Mufarridj. Faḍl asked the Djarrāḥid to surrender Abū Taghlib to him so that he might take him to Egypt. Fearing that the caliph might use Abū Taghlib against himself, Mufarridj killed his prisoner with his own hand.

The agreement between Mufarridj and Faḍl did not last long, and Faḍl turned against him. But Mufarridj was sufficiently adroit to persuade the caliph al-ʿAzīz to give orders to his general to leave him in peace, so allowing Mufarridj to become master of Palestine once again and to ravage the land (370/980). His exactions led the caliph to send troops against him in the following year. Being put to flight, he went off to raid a caravan of pilgrims returning from Mecca, probably at the end of 371/June 982. He was more fortunate against a second Fāṭimid force which he crushed at Ayla. He returned to Syria but was defeated and, taking the desert route, sought refuge at Ḥimṣ with Bakdjūr, the governor of the Ḥamdānid Saʿd al-Dawla, probably at the end of 982; from there he went on to Antioch where he sought protection and help from the Byzantine governor. He appears to have received nothing more than gifts and fair words. It is not certain that he returned to Syria, for after 373/983 we find him accompanying Bardas Phocas the Domesticus when he went to the rescue of Aleppo after it had been attacked by the rebel Bakdjūr. Warned by him of the imminent arrival of the Byzantine troops, Bakdjūr took to flight.

Mufarridj then seems to have rejoined Bakdjūr, for when the latter received from the caliph al-ʿAzīz the governorship of Damascus, entering office in Radjab 373/December 983, the vizier Ibn Killīs put the caliph on his guard against a possible revolt by Bakdjūr with the warning that he had Mufarridj with him, and that he was an enemy. He followed Bakdjūr when the latter, threatened by a Fāṭimid army, left Damascus for Raḳḳa in Radjab 378/October 988. In the following year we find him attacking a caravan of pilgrims in north Arabia. It is said that Ibn Killīs regarded him as a dangerous individual and that on his deathbed in 380/991 he advised his master not to spare Ibn Djarrāḥ if he fell into his power. Nevertheless the caliph pardoned him, for next year he had a gift of apparel and horses sent him and invited him to take part in the expedition against Aleppo for which the Turkish general Mangūtekīn was making extensive preparations. But we do not know if he took any part in the campaign of 382/992 or in subsequent campaigns. We find no other mention of him until 386/996, the year of al-Ḥākim's arrival.

At that period he was supporting Mangūtekīn, the governor of Damascus, in his attempt to seize power from Ibn ʿAmmār and the Kutāma, and took part in the fighting led by the Turkish general outside ʿAsḳalān against Sulaymān b. Djaʿfar b. Falāḥ. Following his usual tactics, however, he did not hesitate to desert Mangūtekīn and to cross over to Sulaymān's camp. It was one of his sons, ʿAlī, who pursued and captured Mangūtekīn when he took to flight.

In 387/997 he tried to take Ramla and laid waste the district. The new governor of Damascus, Djaysh b. Ṣamṣāma, having crushed ʿAllāḳa's revolt at Tyre, attacked and gave chase to Mufarridj who took refuge in the mountains of the Banū Ṭayy. When on the point of being captured he took part in a little comedy, sending the old women of his tribe to ask for *amān* and pardon, which were granted. And thus in 396/1005-6 we find Mufarridj sending his three sons ʿAlī, Ḥassān and Maḥmūd with a large number of Bedouins to assist al-Ḥākim's troops against the rebel Abū Rikwa. But in the following year he held up pilgrims from Baghdād north-east of the mountains of ʿAdjāʾ and Salmā, that is to say in Ṭayyī territory, and compelled them to pay tribute; as the enforced halt had made them lose time, they were obliged to turn back and to call off their pilgrimage.

Some years later, an opportunity occurred for Mufarridj to play a part of genuinely political significance. In about 402/1011-2 the Fāṭimid vizier Abu 'l-Ḳāsim al-Ḥusayn b. ʿAlī al-Maghribī fled and took refuge in Palestine at the encampment of Mufarridj's son Ḥassān who gave him his protection. The caliph having given the governorship of Damascus and the command of troops in Syria to Yārūkh, a Turk, Mufarridj's sons were unwilling to submit to his authority, representing to their father the danger to which they would be exposed from this all-powerful governor and advising him to attack Yārūkh before he arrived at Ramla. The vizier al-Maghribī also stirred up Ḥassān against Yārūkh, with the result that the Djarrāḥids laid an ambush for him on the Ghazza road, took him prisoner and, at al-Maghribī's instigation, occupied Ramla. Ḥassān, fearing that his father would yield to the pleas of the caliph to have Yārūkh set free, had him beheaded. Urged on by this same al-Maghribī, Mufarridj took a further step towards rebellion against al-Ḥākim at the beginning of 403/July 1012 when, at Ramla, he proclaimed an anti-caliph in the person of the ʿAlid Sharīf of Mecca. But al-Ḥākim knew that it was always possible to suborn the members of this family. He had already arranged for Ḥassān, who had been entrusted with the care of Djawhar's grandsons, to betray them to one of the caliph's officers who had them executed. He also succeeded in persuading Ḥassān and his father to abandon the anti-caliph who returned crestfallen to Mecca, whilst al-Maghribī fled to ʿIrāḳ.

The Djarrāḥids remained masters of Palestine for only two years and five months. During this period Mufarridj tried to win the favour of the Christians in Jerusalem, and perhaps of the Emperor also, by giving orders for, and helping with, the restoration of the Church of the Resurrection which had earlier been destroyed on al-Ḥākim's instructions.

At the beginning of 404/July-August 1013 al-

Ḥākim, changing his tactics, decided to treat the Djarrāḥids with severity and sent an army against them. ʿAlī and Maḥmūd surrendered; at that moment Mufarridj died, possibly poisoned by order of al-Ḥākim; Ḥassān who had taken to flight succeeded in obtaining a pardon from the caliph by sending his mother to beg the caliph's sister, Sitt al-Mulk, to intercede for him. The caliph pardoned him and allowed him to return to Palestine where he recovered his father's lands. Thereafter he refrained from stirring up trouble until the disappearance of al-Ḥākim. He even took part in the expedition against Aleppo organized by ʿAlī b. Aḥmad al-Ḍayf, the former governor of Afāmiya, at the same time as the Kalbids of Sinān b. Sulaymān in 406/1015-6. However he entered into closer relations with the heir presumptive to the throne, ʿAbd al-Raḥīm, brother of al-Ḥākim and governor of Damascus, who sent an envoy to him to seek an undertaking that he would support him in case of need. But Sitt al-Mulk, the regent, had ʿAbd al-Raḥīm assassinated. Ḥassān also intrigued with ʿAlī al-Ḍayf who was anxious to be sent to Palestine, and who was also put to death by Sitt al-Mulk. Ḥassān himself escaped an attempt on his life, also made on her orders.

Ḥassān's ambition was to rule Palestine. Even in al-Ḥākim's time he had concluded a pact with the Kalbid Sinān and the Kilābid Ṣāliḥ b. Mirdās, whereby Damascus was allotted to the Kalbid, Aleppo to the Kilābid and Palestine to himself. This pact was renewed in 415/1024-5. The emperor Basil refused to give them his support. Nevertheless they overcame the general sent by al-Ẓāhir, Anushtekīn al-Duzbarī, at ʿAskalān, and Ḥassān entered Ramla. With the help of Ṣāliḥ b. Mirdās, Ḥassān once again defeated Anushtekīn and continued his depredations in Syria. After Sinān's death, his nephew joined the caliph's cause; but Ṣāliḥ continued to support Ḥassān. In 420/1029, at al-Ukhuwāna near lake Tiberias, they joined battle with Anushtekīn who gained a complete victory. Ṣāliḥ was killed and Ḥassān fled to the mountains.

Like his father, Ḥassān was in touch with the Byzantine empire. In the next year, 1030, when the emperor Romanus Argyrus was preparing his expedition against the sons of Ṣāliḥ b. Mirdās of Aleppo, he offered him the support of his tribe, and the emperor received his envoys at Antioch with great cordiality, gave them a flag for their master (according to Ibn al-Athīr, it was decorated with a cross) and promised to reinstate the Djarrāḥid in his country once again. The emperor's expedition ended in disaster. Ḥassān, again with the support of the Kalbids of Rāfiʿ b. Abi 'l-Layl, started a campaign against the Fāṭimid troops in the region of Ḥawrān, but was driven back towards the desert. There, in the neighbourhood of Palmyra, he met an envoy from the emperor who persuaded him to come and settle near Byzantine territory. As a result, a group of over 20,000 people, with their herds and tents, moved towards the region of Antioch, almost certainly in the year 422/1031. Ḥassān was loaded with gifts from the emperor and his son ʿAllāf was received at court.

The Ṭayyīs pitched their camps in the neighbourhood of the Rūdj, south-east of Antioch. They were twice attacked by Anushtekīn al-Duzbarī. The names of the places mentioned in this connexion (Kasṭūn, al-Arwādj, Inab; for the identification of the last-named place, see Ibn al-Shiḥna, *al-Durr al-muntakhab*, 117; Dussaud, *Top. historique* ...., 168; *Guide bleu*, 280) show that they were not in Byzantine territory. Ḥassān gave active support to the Byzantines, not only making a successful raid on Afāmiya but also, according to the Byzantine historians, helping Theoctistus, Domesticus of the Scholae, to take the fortress of Menikos (Manīka) in the Djabal al-Rawādīf then held by Naṣr b. Musharraf. It was on this occasion, so it is recorded in Scylitzes-Cedrenus, that his son ʿAllāf (Allach to the Byzantines) was received at court and made a patrician. Ḥassān is called Pinzarach (Ibn al-Djarrāḥ) or Apelzarach (by Kekaumenos), but Scylitzes incorrectly gives him the title of amīr of Tripoli. According to these authors he was twice received at Constantinople, but Kekaumenos says that he did not always have cause to be satisfied with his visits.

Moreover we know that, at the time of the negotiations which took place between the caliph and the emperor, after the Byzantines captured the fortress of Bīkisrāʾīl in the summer of 423/1032, Ḥassān was present in person at the discussions at Constantinople. One of the conditions laid down by the emperor for the peace settlement was that the caliph should allow Ḥassān to return to his country and to resume possession of the lands he held at the time of al-Ḥākim, except for those that he had appropriated since the coming of al-Ẓāhir, in return for a promise of fidelity to the caliph. But the caliph refused.

When Anushtekīn al-Duzbarī, taking up a curious attitude, asked the emperor to send an expedition against Aleppo (which he did not enter until 429/1037-8), promising to hold it as a vassal of the empire, we note that with him was Ḥassān's son ʿAllāf (ʿAllān in Kamāl al-Dīn). In 427/1035-6, when the Numayrid Ibn Waththāb and the Marwānid Naṣr al-Dawla attacked Edessa, a Byzantine possession since 422/1031, Ḥassān came to the rescue with 5,000 Greek and Arab horsemen. There is a further mention of him in 433/1041-2 (we are then in the reign of al-Mustanṣir, al-Ẓāhir having died in 427/June 1036). It is said that at that moment he regained possession of Palestine, after al-Duzbarī had been driven from Damascus, but that the new governor of Damascus continued the war against him.

After that date we hear nothing more of Ḥassān. Much later, we come across his nephews, Ḥumayd b. Maḥmūd and Ḥāzim b. ʿAlī, during the disturbances which Badr al-Djamālī had to face in Damascus in about 458/1065-6, in the entourage of an ʿAlid sharīf, Ibn Abi 'l-Djann, who tried to seize Damascus. They must have been arrested and imprisoned in Cairo, for in 459/1066-7 the amīr Nāṣir al-Dawla b. Ḥamdān asked the caliph to free them from the Flag store where they were incarcerated.

Finally, in 501/1107-8 we find a certain Abū ʿImrān Faḍl b. Rabīʿa b. Ḥāzim b. al-Djarrāḥ coming from Baghdād to enter the service of the Saldjūḳid sultan. His equivocal behaviour in Syria —at times he was on the side of the Franks, at others on the side of the Egyptians—led the *atābek* Tughtekīn of Damascus to expel him from Syria. In Baghdād he offered to fight the Mazyadid from Ḥilla, Ṣadaḳa, and to bar the desert route to him. He went to Anbār and nothing more is heard of him.

That, it seems, is all that we know of this turbulent family who were not without significance as pawns on the chess-board of Syria in the 4th-5th/10th-11th centuries, whom the Fāṭimids alternately attacked and wooed, whom the Byzantines succeeded in using, but who seem to have created for themselves, in their own best interests, a rule of duplicity, treason and pillage.

Bibliography: Yaḥyā b. Saʿīd al-Anṭākī, *P.O.* xxiii, 403, 411-2, 476, 501-2, 504, 520 (ed. Cheikho, 207, 215, 226-7, 244-6, 253-6, 261-2, 266 ff.); Miskawayh, in *Eclipse* ...., ii, 385, 402-3; Abū Shudjāʿ, in *Eclipse* ...., iii, 185, 226-7, 233-5, 238-9; Ibn al-Ḳalānisī, 3, 19, 22, 24-5, 29, 30, 46-9, 62-4, 72-3, 93; Sibṭ Ibn al-Djawzī, in Ibn al-Ḳalānisī, 2, 96-7; Ibn al-Athīr, viii, 469; ix, 5, 48, 86-7, 145, 233-4, 260, 286 bis, 305, 343-4; x, 308 (ed. Cairo 1303, viii, 211, 219, 232; ix, 19, 24, 41-2, 71, 78 ff., 114, 128, 132, 145, 155, 173; x, 20, 155; Kamāl al-Dīn, ed. Dahhān, i, 215, 223, 228, 231, 250-1; Ibn Muyassar, 48-9; Dhahabī, in Ibn al-Ḳalānisī, 64; Ibn Taghrībirdī, Cairo, iv, 248, 252, 253, 266; Ibn Khallikān, Būlāḳ ed., i, 196 (cf. Yāḳūt, *Irshād*, x, 80-1; Ibn Khaldūn, *Berbères*, tr. i, 16, 43; S. de Sacy, *Exposé de la religion des Druzes*, i, CCLXXXVII, CCCL-CCCLIII; Wüstenfeld, *Gesch. der Fat.-Chalifen*, 122, 140, 141-2, 150, 167, 193-4, 221, 223, 224-5, 229; idem, *Die Chroniken der Stadt Mekka*, iv, 218; Tiesenhausen, *Gesch. der Oqailiden-Dynastie*, 26; V. R. Rosen, *Basil Bulgaroctonos* (in Russian), 149, 150, 157, 159, 160, 162, 321, 353, 355-7, 369, 376, 377, 379, 382-3; G. Schlumberger, *Épopée byzantine*, iii, 90-2, 128 ff., 130 ff., 196; Honigmann, *Ostgrenze*, 109-10, 114-5, 137-8; Scylitzes-Cedrenus, ed. Bonn, ii, 495-6, 502; Kekaumenos, *Strategikon*, tr. H. G. Beck, 221-2; Muḥammad ʿAbd Allāh ʿInān, *al-Ḥākim bi-Amr Allāh*, 101-2; G. Wiet, in *Hist. de la nation égyptienne*, iv: *L'Égypte arabe*, 183-5, 192-3, 194, 198, 210-1, 216-7, 221-3, 224; M. Canard, *Hist. de la dynastie des H'amdānides*, i, 570-1, 686-7, 850. (M. Canard)

DJĀRSĪF [see guercif].

al-**DJĀRŪDIYYA** (or Surḥūbiyya), a group of the early Shīʿa, listed as "Zaydī" [*q.v.*] because they accepted any Fāṭimid ʿAlid as *imām* if he were worthy and claimed the imāmate with the sword. Their chief teacher was the blind Abu 'l-Djārūd Ziyād b. al-Mundhir, who reported *ḥadīth* from Muḥammad al-Bāḳir and was nicknamed by him "Surḥūb" (blind sea-devil); other leaders were Abū Khālid Yazīd al-Wāsiṭī and Fuḍayl b. al-Zubayr al-Rassān. In contrast to other early "Zaydīs", they rejected Abū Bakr and ʿUmar, not admitting the imāmate of the less worthy when the worthier was present. They seem to have regarded supporters of a non-ʿAlid *imām* as *kāfir*. They claimed that authority was potentially equal in all Fāṭimids; some claimed that the needful knowledge came to the *imām* by nature, not by teaching. The name continued to be applied to certain Shīʿīs for a century and a half. Some of them are said to have believed that one or another ʿAlid rebel was to return as *mahdī*: either Muḥammad al-Nafs al-Zakiyya of Madīna (killed under al-Manṣūr), or Muḥammad b. al-Ḳāsim of Ṭāliḳān (killed under al-Muʿtaṣim), or Yaḥyā b. ʿUmar of Kūfa (killed under al-Mustaʿīn).

Bibliography: Abu 'l-Ḥasan b. Mūsā al-Nawbakhtī, *Firāḳ al-Shīʿa*; al-Shahrastānī; al-Ashʿarī, *Maḳālāt al-Islāmiyyīn*; Baghdādī, *Farḳ* (see indexes). Other references in Israel Friedländer, *Heterodoxies of the Shiʿites* in *JAOS*, xxix, 22. Discussion in Rudolph Strothmann, *Staatsrecht der Zaiditen*, Strassburg 1912, 28-36, 63-67. (M. G. S. Hodgson)

DJARUNDA (Spanish *Gerona*), capital of the province of the same name, one of the four capitals of the principality of Catalonia. It stands about 25 km. from the sea, and its coastline extends along the well-known Costa Brava. Situated in the outer foothills of the Pyrenees, on a small eminence surrounded by the Ter and Oñar rivers, it has at the present day about 40,000 inhabitants. By reason of its strategic situation on the eastern route between France and Spain it has throughout its history been subjected to sieges and constant attacks, from which it derives its name *Ciudad de los sitios* "the town of sieges". From a village of Iberian origin the Romans raised it to the rank of a town: it figures in the *Itinerary* of Antoninus as a halting-place on the first road to cross Catalonia. Falling in turn into the hands of the Visigoths, Arabs, Franks of the Spanish march and the Catalan-Aragonese, it became a great fortress known in the Middle Ages as *Forsa vella*. At the beginning of their occupation the Muslims, under the command of ʿAbd al-ʿAzīz, son of Mūsā b. Nuṣayr, took possession of the whole sub-Pyrenean region, including Gerona, passing through it on their way to invade the Narbonnaise. In the 2nd/8th century there was no fixed frontier on what was later the Spanish march. For this reason the inhabitants of Gerona in 169/785 entrusted their town to the authority of the Franks, under Louis the Pious, after the Amīr of Cordova ʿAbd al-Raḥmān I had been defeated in this sector. The establishment of this Frankish enclave on Spanish soil foreshadowed the conquest of more extensive territories, that is to say Barcelona, in the near future. But the Muslims were not long in reacting, and in 177/793 ʿAbd al-Malik b. Mughīth, Hishām I's general, laid siege to Gerona and, according to the Arab chroniclers, decimated the Frankish garrison and destroyed a large part of the towers and ramparts, but he was unable to capture the town by assault and went on to raid Narbonne. In 178/798 the Franks occupied the mountain region between Gerona and the upper valley of the Segre, and surrounded Barcelona which they succeeded in capturing after a long siege. Among the feudal overlords taking part in this siege was Rostaing, Count of Gerona, at the head of one of the three corps which comprised the besieging army. In 212/828, a new *ṣāʾifa* against Barcelona and Gerona failed; the Spanish march having been consolidated, the Muslims were unable to reach Gerona, even when the *ḥādjib* al-Manṣūr captured Barcelona. On the other hand, during the final period of the caliphate in Dhu 'l-Ḳaʿda 400/June 1010, a band of Catalans fought on the side of caliph Muḥammad al-Mahdī against the Berbers in the valley of the Guadiaro, not far from Ronda; they were routed and suffered casualties, among them Otón, Bishop of Gerona, at the head of his contingent from Gerona. The county of Gerona, as a dependency of the principality of Catalonia, was the scene of a meeting on 1 November 1143 at which the Order of Templars of Catalonia was admitted. In 1205 Philip Augustus of France seized it. Thereafter, as the result both of civil wars provoked by the prince of Viana and also of struggles against France, the town had to endure numerous sieges and assaults; after being razed to the ground during the war of the Spanish Succession for declaring itself in favour of the Archduke, its tribulations reached their culminating point with the heroic resistance directed by General Alvarez de Castro when, for seven months, the town stood out against Napoleon's Marshals.

Bibliography: Codera, *Narbona y Barcelona*, in *Estudios crit. hist. ar. esp.*, viii, 339-41; L.

Auzias, *Aquitaine carolingienne*, 43-53 and 59-66; Soldeville, *Hist. de Catalunya*, i, 32; *Chronique de Moissac*, ad. ann. 785; Madoz, *Diccionario geográfico*, s.v. (A. Huici Miranda)

DJĀSAK (Djāsek or Djāsik), an island in the Persian Gulf mentioned only by Yāḳūt, ii, 9) and Ḳazwīnī (*Kosmographie*, ed. Wüstenfeld, 115) among Arab geographers. From their statements, it is probably to be identified with the island of Lārak in the straits of Hormuz 35 km. SSE. of Bandar ʿAbbās [*q.v.*], and not with the large island of Ḳishm as was done by Le Strange (261). In the time of these two authors Djāsak belonged to the prince of Kis (Kish, the modern Ḳays), a small island in Lat. 26° 33′ N., Long. 54° 02′ E.

At the present time the name Djāsak (now pronounced Djāsk) is borne by the flat, low-lying promontory on the Persian side of the Gulf of ʿUmān in Lat. 25° 31′ N., 57° 36′ E. and by the adjoining village. Early in the 10th/16th century Djāsk was seized and fortified by the Portuguese and in the following century the English East India Company established a factory there. There is a landing strip for aircraft south-west of the village. The population in 1951 was 3,115.

Bibliography: in addition to the references in the text: *Marāṣid al-iṭṭilāʿ*, *Lexic. geograph.* (ed. Juynboll), ii, 235; Tomaschek, *Die Küstenfahrt Nearchs* in *Sitz.-Ber. der Wien. Akad.*, cxxi, no. viii, 37, 48; P. Schwarz, *Iran im Mittelalter nach d. arab. Geogr.*, ii, 89. On the cape and village of Djāsk, cf. Thomas Herbert, *Travels in Persia*, ed. Sir W. Foster, London, 1928, 39; Ritter, *Erdkunde*, xii, 428-30; Preece, *Journey from Shiraz to Jashk* in the *Supplem. Papers, the Royal Geographical Society*, i, 403 ff.; Sir A. T. Wilson, *The Persian Gulf*, Oxford 1928, 40, 136-8, 224; Razmārā and Nawtāsh, *Farhang-i djughrāfiyā-yi Īrān*, viii, 94. (L. Lockhart)

al-**DJAṢṢĀṢ**, Aḥmad b. ʿAlī Abū Bakr al-Rāzī, famous Ḥanafī jurist and chief representative of the *aṣḥāb al-raʾy* [*q.v.*] in his day. He was born in 917/305, went to Baghdād in 324, and there studied law under ʿAlī b. al-Ḥasan al-Karkhī. He also worked on the Ḳurʾān and *ḥadīth*, handing down the *ḥadīth*s of al-Āṣim, ʿAbd al-Bāḳī Ḳāniʿ (the teacher of the famous al-Dāraḳuṭnī [*q.v.*]), ʿAbd Allāh b. Djaʿfar al-Iṣfahānī, Ṭabarānī, and others. Following the advice of his teacher Karkhī, he went to Nīshāpūr, in order to study *uṣūl al-ḥadīth* under al-Ḥākim al-Nīsābūrī. During this time, Karkhī died, whereupon he returned to Baghdād (in 344). Later, Djaṣṣāṣ became the head of the Ḥanafīs in Baghdād. According to reports, he was twice nominated for the office of judge but he declined. He mediated between the traditionists and the lawyers. Amongst his pupils were Ḳudūrī, Abū Bakr Aḥmad b. Mūsā al-Khwārizmī, and others. He died on 7 Dhu 'l-Ḥidjdja 370/14 August 981 in Nīshāpūr.

Of his works, the following survive: *Kitāb al-Uṣūl*; his commentary on *al-Djāmiʿ al-kabīr* by Shaybānī; his commentary on *al-Mukhtaṣar fi 'l-fiḳh* by Ṭaḥāwī (which is the oldest of its commentaries); his excerpts from the *Kitāb ikhtilāf al-fuḳahāʾ* by Ṭaḥāwī, compare Schacht, *Aus den Bibliotheken*, i, no. 24; *Aḥkām al-Ḳurʾān*, ed. Kilisli Rifʿat, Istanbul 1335-38; 3 vols., Cairo 1347.

Bibliography: *Taʾrīkh Baghdād*, iv, 314, no. 2112; *al-Djawāhir al-muḍīʾa*, i, 84; Ibn Ḳutlubugha, 4, no. 11; *Shadharāt* iii, 71; Flügel, *Classen der hanefitischen Rechtsgelehrten*; Brockelmann, I², S I, 335. (O. Spies)

al-**DJASSĀSA**, "the informer", "the spy", a name which seems to have been given by Tamīm al-Dārī [*q.v.*] to the fabulous female animal which he claimed to have encountered on an island upon which he had been cast by a storm, at the same time as the Dadjdjāl [*q.v.*] who was chained there; the latter being unable to move about, the Djassāsa, which is a monster of gigantic size, brings him whatever news it has gathered. Assimilated by later exegesis with the Beast (*dābba* [*q.v.*]) mentioned in the Ḳurʾān (XXVII, 84/82), it adds considerably to the fantastic element in travellers' and geographers' tales in the classical period which place the incident on an island in the Javaga (Zābadj [*q.v.*]) to which Ibn Khurradādhbih (48) and others give the name Barṭāʾīl. (Ed.)

DJASSAWR (Jessore), principal town of a district of East Pakistan. The town has a garrison and a landing strip. Population of the district in 1951 : 1,703,000. Its name is said to derive from the Sanskrit *yashohara* "disgraced", relating to the story of Rādjā Pratāpāditya, a *zamīndār* whose rebellious attitude was crushed at the time of the Mughal emperor Djahāngīr. Under Muslim rule the region formed part of the *sarkār* of Khalīfatābād, represented now by Bāgerhāt in Khulna district, where Khān Djahān (d. 863/1459), conqueror of this region under the Bengal sultan Nāṣir al-Dīn Maḥmūd II, is buried. A number of monuments of this period remain at or near Bāgerhāt, the most important being the tomb of Khān Djahān and the Sāthgunbad, Masdjidkur, Ḳaṣba and Saylkuppa mosques. These mosques mark the appearance of a new style of Muslim architecture in Bengal which, with its dwarf angle buttresses and covered *ṣaḥn*, seems to bring together some aspects of the Dihlī style of Fīrūz Shāh Tughluḳ and those of local origin. Khān Djahān, popularly called Khāndjā ʿAlī, is today venerated as a saint; with Muḥammad Ṭāhir, alias Pīr ʿAlī, he promoted the expansion of Islam in this region. The latter personage brought into being a sect, the Pīr ʿAlī Muslims, which is widespread in the region.

Bibliography: Babu Gourdas Bysack, in *JASB*, xxxvi (1867); J. Westland, *A report on the district of Jessore*, Calcutta 1871; J. N. Sarkar, *History of Bengal*, ii, Dacca 1948; A. H. Dani, *Muslim architecture in Bengal*, Dacca 1961, 141-52. (A. H. Dani)

DJASTĀNIDS, DJUSTĀNIDS [see daylam].

DJĀSŪS, a word used to denote the spy, concurrently with *ʿayn*, observer, literally "eye", with the result that it is not always possible to distinguish between the two words and one can hardly discuss the one without speaking of the other. However, it seems that *djāsūs* is used more particularly to refer to a spy sent among the enemy. Dictionaries also give for *djāsūs* the sense of bearer of an unfavourable secret (*ṣāḥib sirr al-sharr*) as opposed to *nāmūs*, the bearer of a favourable secret (*ṣāḥib sirr al-khayr*; see *LA*, vii, 337, Ibn al-Athīr, *Nihāya*, i, 163).

The Ḳurʾān (XLIX, 12) ordains that believers should not spy upon one another. According to al-Māwardī (*Aḥkām*, tr. Fagnan, 538) it is permissible for the *muḥtasib* to make use of *tadjassus* when there is a violation of a prohibition and proof of it might be overlooked, but al-Ghazzālī (*Iḥyāʾ*, ed. 1348, ii, 285, 289) refutes this.

Espionage was practised by the authorities internally for administrative and governmental reasons, and externally for politico-military reasons. Works of the Mirror of Princes type note that sovereigns of all periods have invariably made use of spies in order to obtain information about their subjects, their ministers and officials, their entourage and even their own family (see the *Kitāb al-tādj* of the Ps. al-Djāḥiẓ, 99, tr. 124; 122, tr. 141-2 (on this passage, cf. al-Ḳalḳashandī, *Ṣubḥ*, i, 116), 167, tr. 184 ff.; *Āthār al-uwal*, of al-Ḥasan al-ʿAbbāsī, in the margin of *Taʾrīkh al-khulafāʾ* of al-Suyūṭī, 97 ff.; the *Siyāsat-nāma* of Niẓām al-Mulk, tr. Schefer, 88, 99, 103 ff.; R. Levy, *A mirror of Princes*, tr. of Ibn Ḳābūs, 135). We know that the Postal Service (*barīd*) was made responsible for this surveillance. Thus the official organization of espionage was reflected in the allegory of the *djunūd al-ḳalb* of al-Ghazzālī, in which the five senses are the spies (*djawāsīs*) who bring their information to the imagination which is, so to speak, the *ṣāḥib al-barīd* (*Iḥyāʾ*, iii, 5 and 8; cf. *Kimiyāʾ al-saʿāda*, ed. 1343, 10 and tr. H. Ritter, *Das Elixir der Glückseligkeit*, 30). There are numerous accounts relating to the use of spies of this sort, for example al-Tanūkhī, *Nishwār*, ii, 157-63, tr. 253-8 (al-Muʿtaḍid having his vizier spied on), Abū Shudjāʿ al-Rūdhrāwarī, 59 (ʿAḍud al-Dawla asking schoolmasters to seek information from the children about their fathers' activities, and to pass it on to the *ṣāḥib al-barīd*). For the spies in the Buwayhid period, sent out to search for fortunes to be confiscated, known as *suʿāt*, calumniators, and *ghammāzūn*, informers, see Miskawayh, ii, 308 (cf. ii, 83), Hilāl al-Ṣābiʾ, in *Eclipse*, iii, 438.

Politico-military espionage was used by the Prophet who had his *djawāsīs* and *ʿuyūn* against the polytheists and Abū Sufyān. There are many instances of the use of spies in war, particularly in civil wars and rebellions: al-Ṭabarī, ii, 585, 904, 947, 949 (Khāridjī affairs), ii, 1248 (Ḳutayba's conquests in central Asia); ii, 1588, 1966 (ʿAbbāsid movement); iii, 284 (affair of the ʿAlid Ibrāhīm b. ʿAbd Allāh); iii, 1174 ff. (war with Bābek: al-Afshīn wins over Bābek's spies). For the Arabo-Byzantine wars, see al-Masʿūdī, *Murūdj*, ii, 434; viii, 75 ff.; al-Ṭabarī, iii, 485 etc. We know that in Constantinople St. Basil the Younger was mistaken for an Arab spy (*BÉt.Or.*, xiii, 55); cf. the legend of al-Baṭṭāl, a spy of Hārūn al-Rashīd. The Mongols used spies disguised as *faḳīrs*, ascetics and holy men (al-Mufaḍḍal, *Hist. des sult. mamelouks*, ed. Blochet, 343, 355).

Just as military leaders are recommended to send spies among the enemy (R. Levy, *op. cit.*, 219; Ibn Djamāʿa, *Taḥrīr al-aḥkām*, in *Islamica*, vi, 402), so they are advised to exclude from their forces all those who might act as spies for the enemy (al-Māwardī, tr. 74), and the *ṣāḥib al-barīd* must watch both land and sea routes by which enemy agents might enter (al-ʿAbbāsī, *Āthār al-uwal*, 100). One of the reasons why it is recommended that non-Muslim secretaries be not employed is that they might act as spies for the Infidels (al-Ḳalḳashandī, *Ṣubḥ*, i, 61). Precautions against espionage were not otiose, for there are instances of correspondence with the enemy (Theophanes, under the year 6248: the Patriarch of Antioch writing to the Byzantines with information about the Arabs; al-Balādhurī, 192, ed. Cairo, 201: an amīr executed for having corresponded with the Greeks).

In al-Ḳalḳashandī (i, 123 ff., *Fī amr al-ʿuyūn wa 'l-djawāsīs*), we find a statement of the conditions which a good spy has to fulfil: absolute sincerity, intelligence and sagacity, cunning, experience of travel and knowledge of the countries to which he is sent, the ability to endure torture if caught in order to avoid betrayal of what he knows. The author also indicates the rules of conduct of the *ṣāḥib dīwān al-inshāʾ* (upon whom they were dependent in the time of the Mamlūks) with regard to spies: to show them sincere affection and not let them feel any suspicion on his part, to pay them liberally both before and, what is more important, after their mission, to provide for their families' needs, not to hold a grudge against them in the event of failure; spies must never know each other, or be known by the army; there must be no intermediary between them and the *ṣāḥib dīwān al-inshāʾ*, etc. This long passage ends with a warning against enemy agents and stresses the importance of winning them over to one's own cause. See also the less detailed statement by al-ʿAbbāsī, *loc. cit.*

There is also some discussion of *djawāsīs* and *ʿuyūn* in works of jurisprudence. First of all, in the rules relating to *dhimmīs*, which include a clause forbidding them to communicate to the enemy any secrets relating to poorly defended points of Muslim territory, or to guide or give shelter to their agents (see, for example, Abū Yūsuf, tr. Fagnan, 305; al-Shīrāzī, *Tanbīh*, 295; Abū Shudjāʿ, *Taḳrīb*, tr. Van den Berg, 624; al-Ṭabarī, *Ikhtilāf*, 239). Incidentally this clause occurs in the first treaties drawn up between Muslims and Christians (Ibn ʿAsākir, i, 149, l. 8, 178, l. 9. See also the typical treaty from the *Kitāb al-umm* of al-Shāfiʿī in Tritton, *The Caliphs and their non-Muslim subjects*, chap. I and A. Fattal, *Le statut légal des non-Musulmans en pays d'Islam*, 77).

In the *Kitāb al-ikhtilāf* of al-Ṭabarī (58-9, cf. 24) or in *al-Mīzān al-kubrā* of al-Shaʿrānī (ed. 1291, ii, 233 ff. and tr. Perron, 1898, 198 ff.), we find a summary of the jurists' views as to how spies working for the enemy should be treated, on which subject there is a considerable divergence of opinion. In the event of a spy being a *dhimmī*, according to al-Awzāʿī he is thus breaking the contract which binds him to the Muslims and he can be put to death; Abū Yūsuf, tr. 294, takes the same line. But al-Shāfiʿī believes that he is only subject to an exemplary punishment since there is no breach of contract. Abū Ḥanīfa also maintains that there is no breach of contract and the *dhimmī* is only liable to corporal punishment and imprisonment. According to the Mālikīs (Ibn al-Ḳāsim), there is a breach of contract and the *dhimmī* can be put to death (al-Khalīl, tr. Guidi, i, 418). The Ḥanbalīs (see, *e.g.*, Ibn Ḳudāma's commentary on *al-Muḳniʿ* in *al-Rawḍ al-murbiʿ* of al-Manṣūr al-Bahūtī, ii, 71) consider that there is a breach of contract: the criterion is the harm caused to the Muslims (for the whole question cf. Fattal, *op. cit.*, 81 ff.).

When the spy is a foreigner who has entered Muslim territory without a safe-conduct he is put to death, and if he came with a safe-conduct without commercial objectives he is simply expelled; if travelling for purposes of commerce, he is sentenced to corporal punishment and is expelled (Abū Ḥanīfa; cf. also al-Shāfiʿī, *Kitāb al-umm*, iv, 167). According to the Mālikīs, (Khalīl, i, 392), it is permitted to kill enemy spies even though they have come armed with a safe-conduct, and Abū Yūsuf (tr. 294) also recommends having them beheaded. If the spy is a Muslim guilty of corresponding with the Greeks and passing them information about the Muslims, according to al-Awzāʿī he is liable to corporal punishment, banishment and prison, unless he shows repentence; the same is true of Abū Ḥanīfa (cf. also Abū Yūsuf, tr. 294). In al-Shāfiʿī's view, since the action is not a characteristic act of *kufr*, punishment is therefore not inevitable and it rests with the *imām* to decide. Mālik also states that the case is left to the free decision of the *imām* (al-Ṭabarī, *Ikhtilāf*, 172). It is probable that, in practice, and according to circumstances, greater severity was shown.

Bibliography: in the article. See also ʿAbd al-Ḥamīd al-Kātib, *Risāla fī naṣīḥat walī ʿahd Marwān b. Muḥammad*, in *Rasāʾil al-bulaghāʾ*, ed. Kurd ʿAlī, 153. (M. Canard)

DJĀṬ, the central Indo-Aryan (Hindī and Urdū) form corresponding to the north-west Indo-Aryan (Pandjābī, Lahndā) Djaṭṭ, a tribe of the Indo-Pakistan sub-continent found particularly in the Pandjāb, Sind, Rādjāsthān and western Uttar Pradēsh. The name is of post-Sanskritic Indian origin (Middle Indo-Aryan **djaṭṭa*), and the form with short vowel is employed by the Persian translator of the *Čač-nāma* (compiled 613/1216), the author of the *Taʾrīkh-i Sind* (*Taʾrīkh-i Maʿṣūmī*) and Shāh Walī Allāh al-Dihlawī [*q.v.*] in his Persian letters. For the Arabicized form *Zuṭṭ* [*q.v.*] see *TA* and Muḥammad Ṭāhir al-Patanī, *Madjmaʿ biḥār al-anwār*, Kānpur 1283, ii, s.v. *Zuṭṭī*.

Little scientific or systematic study has been undertaken so far to determine the ethnological and anthropological strains in the Djāṭs, tall, well-built, sturdy with a dark complexion. It may be presumed that they are racially Aryans, although some writers have alluded to their Scytho-Aryan origin and to the subsequent fusion of various local tribes into the main body (cf. Pradhan, 15). In the undivided Pandjāb the Djāṭs in the districts west of the Ravī were mostly Muslims, those in the centre mostly Sikhs and those in the south-east mostly Hindūs. The non-Muslim Djāṭs of the present Pakistan regions have now all migrated to India. In the northern and western districts of Uttar Pradēsh (India) they constitute an important element of the population, and played a significant rôle in bringing about the downfall of the Mughal empire, which was unable to withstand, in the days of its decadence, their lawlessness and predatory raids on the seat of the government itself. Mostly agricultural by profession, they include Hindūs and Muslims, while many Djāṭs in the Indian Pandjāb profess Sikhism. The Hindū and Sikh Djāṭs may still interdine (and intermarry?); Muslim Djāṭs in many cases retain the old tribal and clan (*khap*) names, and although they may associate with Hindū and Sikh Djāṭs in some social and political activities at the village level in India, their Pakistan cognates have largely lost this connexion.

The Indian Hindū Djāṭs practised polygamy until the passing of the Hindū Marriage Act (1955), and a fraternal polyandry was at one time common. Female infanticide was fairly common until the end of the 19th century. Widow marriage and the levirate are still permitted. The widespread and indiscriminate exogamous marriages and liaisons reported by earlier writers seem no longer to be permitted.

The Djāṭs are proverbially stupid, awkward, and simple in money-matters, caring more for their buffaloes and sugarcane than for their fellow humans, although they are courageous and make good soldiers. On the Djāṭs in the Muslim countries of the Middle East see Zuṭṭ.

In India they fought against the Arab commander, Budayl b. Ṭahfa al-Badjalī, during his attack on the sea-port of Daybul [*q.v.*], some years prior to the invasion of Muḥammad b. al-Ḳāsim, and killed him, and again encountered the forces of Muḥammad b. al-Ḳāsim when he marched upon Daybul in 94/712. A very large number of them was captured by the Muslims, and Muḥammad b. al-Ḳāsim sent ship-loads of them to al-Ḥadjdjādj b. Yūsuf [*q.v.*]. Thereafter they seem to have taken to a settled and peaceful life both in Sind and abroad, as they figure in no further events until the times of Maḥmūd of Ghazna [*q.v.*] who had to fight a naval engagement with them on the Indus, where they troubled the victorious Sultan by attacking his rear and several times looting the baggage (see Gardīzī. *Zayn al-akhbār*, ed. M. Nazim, Berlin 1928, 87-9). The Djāṭs, thereafter, suffered a long eclipse until the reign of the Mughal emperor Shāhdjahān [*q.v.*], when in 1047/1637 they broke out into a revolt and killed the *fawdjdār* [*q.v.*] of Mathurā, Murshid Ḳulī Khān. During the reign of Awrangzīb [*q.v.*], taking advantage of his preoccupation with the Deccan wars, the Djāṭs of northern India, under their leaders Rādjā Rām and Rām Čehrā, terrorized the population and even attempted to despoil the tomb of the emperor Akbar at Sikandra. They were, however, met with stout opposition from the local commandant, Mīr Abu 'l-Faḍl (Jadunath Sarkar, *History of Aurangzib*, v, 696-7). In 1097/1686 Awrangzīb, in a bid to crush them, deputed his general Khān-i Djahān Kokaltāsh, who was, however, defeated by the Djāṭs in several engagements; this compelled the emperor to change the command, and entrust it to his grandson, Bīdār Bakht b. Muḥammad Aʿẓam. After the death of Awrangzīb, when the Mughal empire had begun to disintegrate, the Djāṭs of Bharatpūr [*q.v.*] and the surrounding territory, under their leader Sūradj Mall, terrorized the entire country lying between Agra and Dihlī. The atrocities perpetrated by them on the ill-starred inhabitants of Dihlī have been vividly described by Shāh Walī Allāh al-Dihlawī and his son Shāh ʿAbd al-ʿAzīz al-Dihlawī [*qq.v.*] in their letters. The depredations of the Djāts provoked Aḥmad Shāh Abdālī, when he attacked India, to say "Move into the territories of the accursed Jat, and in every town and district held by him slay and plunder .... Up to Agra leave not a single place standing". (cf. *Indian Antiquary*, ... 58-9 and J. N. Sarkar, *Fall of the Mughal empire*, Calcutta 1950, ii, 61, 85). In 1171/1757, during his fourth invasion of India, Abdālī marched against them but could not subdue them completely, and the Djāṭ chieftain refused to own allegiance to the Durrānī chief. The terrible defeat of the Marāṭhas at his hands in 1175/1761 at the third Battle of Pānīpat practically broke the back of the Djāṭs. Almost at the same time, a petty Djāṭ chieftain of the Pandjāb, Ālā Singh, received a number of villages from the retiring Shāh as a grant, in return for military services rendered. Later these villages formed the nucleus of the former Indian princely state of Paṭiālā. Early in the 13th/18th century Randjit Singh Djāṭ succeeded in establishing a small and shortlived Sikh kingdom in the Pandjāb. Elsewhere the Djāṭs kept quiet till the Mutiny of 1857 when, taking advantage of the general chaos at Dihlī, they indulged in loot and massacre and became a terror to the neighbouring population and the refugees. The subsequent British occupation of India subdued them. During the disturbances of 1947 they were again active in and around Alwār and Bharatpur [*qq.v.*], taking a leading part in the loot and massacre that followed the partition of India. They are still politically active in the Indian Pandjāb and Uttar Pradēsh. For their political organization, see Pradhan (in Bibliography).

In India some Djāṭs appear to have embraced Islam during or soon after the Muslim conquest of Sind; in the Pandjāb most of the Djāṭ tribes were converted either by Djalāl al-Dīn Ḥusayn Buk̲h̲ārī or by Farīd al-Dīn Gand̲j̲-S̲h̲akar [qq.v.] of Pak-pattan (see Gazetteers of Multan district and Bahawalpore); many further conversions are reported from the time of Awrangzīb.

Contrary to the popular belief that the Djāṯs are deplorably lacking in common sense and are illiterate and uncultured, they have produced a number of people who have made a name for themselves in the field of learning. A Djāṯ (Zuṭṭ) physician, who was apparently well-versed in witch-craft also, is said to have been called in to treat ʿĀʾis̲h̲a, when she fell seriously ill. (Cf. al-Buk̲h̲ārī, al-Adab al-Mufrad, Cairo 1349 A.H., 45, Urdū tr. Kitāb-i Zindagī by ʿAbd al-Ḳuddūs Hās̲h̲imī, Karachi 1960, 84, where the translator, in a note, characterizes this tradition as munkar). Abū Ḥanīfa [q.v.] was also of Zuṭṭ stock, his grandfather being known as Zūṭī, a corruption of Zuṭṭī. (Cf. Taʾrīk̲h̲ Bag̲h̲dād, xiii, 324-5). Imām al-Awzāʿī [q.v.] was of Sindhī origin and his forefathers might have belonged to those Djāṯs who fell into the hands of Muḥammad b. al-Ḳāsim and were sent as prisoners of war to ʿIrāḳ (cf. D̲h̲ahabī, Ḥuffāẓ, ii, 61). The Indian Muslim writer and biographer of the Prophet, S̲h̲iblī Nuʿmānī [q.v.] was also of Djāṯ (Rāwat) origin, a fact reflected in his self-adopted nisba Nuʿmānī, pertaining to Abū Ḥanīfa. A Pākistānī Djāṯ (Muḥammad Ẓafar Allāh K̲h̲ān) till recently (1961) served as a judge of the International Court of Justice at the Hague.

Bibliography: In addition to the authorities cited in the text: ʿAlī b. Ḥāmid b. Abī Bakr al-Kūfī, Čačnāma, Dihlī 1358/1939, index; Sayyid Muḥammad Maʿṣūm Bhakkarī, Taʾrīk̲h̲-i Sind (ed. U. M. Daudpota), Poona 1938, index; Maḥāsin al-masāʿī fī manāḳib .... al-Awzāʿī, Cairo n.d., 48; Jadunath Sarkar, Fall of the Mughal empire, Calcutta 1950-2, ii, 60, 84-5, 306-51, 353; iii, 62-91; K. R. Qanungo, History of the Jats, Calcutta 1925; G̲h̲ulām Muḥammad K̲h̲ān, Nawādir al-ḳiṣaṣ (Aḥwāl-i Djāṯ), Persian MS. Rieu, iii, 981 b; H. A. Rose, A glossary of the tribes and castes of the Punjab and the North-West Frontier Province, Lahore 1911-26, s.v. Jats; Ibn Baṭṭūṭa, index; Firis̲h̲ta, Nawal Kis̲h̲ore ed. 35; Abū Ẓafar Nadwī, Taʾrīk̲h̲-i Sindh (in Urdū), Aʿẓamgaṛh 1366/1947, 273, 275-6; D. Ibbetson, Outlines of Punjab ethnography; idem, Glossary of the tribes and castes of the Punjab and N.W. Frontier Province..., Lahore 1911-4, s.v. Jats; H. M. Elliot, Races of the North-Western Provinces; W. Crooke, Tribes and castes of the North-Western Provinces, 1896; S̲h̲āh Walī Allāh ke Siyāsī Maktūbāt (ed. K̲h̲alīḳ Aḥmad Niẓāmī), ʿAlīgaṛh (?) 1950, 48-9, 51, 60-5, 85, 88-9, 168, 196. See also ZUṬṬ.

For their tribal organization, much general information, and full bibliography, see M. C. Pradhan, Socio-political organization of the Jats of Meerut District, Ph. D. thesis, London November 1961.   (A. S. Bazmee Ansari)

DJĀWA [see DJĀBA, DJĀWI, INDONESIA, JAVA].

AL-DJAWĀD AL-IṢFAHĀNĪ, ABŪ DJAʿFAR MUḤAMMAD B. ʿALĪ (he also had the honorific name of DJĀMAL AL-DĪN), vizier of the Zangids; he had been carefully educated by his father, and at a very early age was given an official appointment in the dīwān al-ʿarḍ of the Saldjūḳid sultan Maḥmūd. Subsequently he became one of the most intimate friends of Zangī, who made him governor of Naṣībīn and al-Raḳḳa and entrusted him with general supervision of the whole empire. After Zangī's assassination he very nearly shared his master's fate, but succeeded in leading the troops to Mosul. Zangī's son, Sayf al-Dīn G̲h̲āzī, then confirmed his position. Meanwhile, Djamal al-Dīn was so greatly renowned for his charity that he was given the name al-Djawād "the noble". He particularly deserved the Muslims' gratitude for the many useful improvements he made at his own expense in the two holy cities of Medina and Mecca. However, in 558/1163 he was imprisoned in Mosul by Ḳuṭb al-Dīn Mawdūd who had in the meanwhile succeeded his brother, and he died in prison during the course of the following year. His body was taken, first to Mecca where it was carried round all the holy places, then to Medina where it was buried. Ḥayṣa-Bayṣa and ʿImād al-Dīn were among his panegyrists.

Bibliography: see especially Ibn al-Ath̲ī̲r, Atabeks, in Recueil des Historiens des Croisades, ii, 147 and 226 ff., and Ibn K̲h̲allikān, no. 714, de Slane, iii, 295; of secondary importance, Ibn al-Ḳalānisī, ed. Amedroz, 286, 307, 356, 361, with extracts from Ibn al-Azraḳ published in notes ibid.; ʿImād al-Dīn al-Iṣfahānī, Seldjoucides, ed. Houtsma, 209 ff. and in Abū S̲h̲āma, i, 134; Ibn al-Djawzī, al-Muntaẓam, ed. Ḥaydarābād, x, 209; Usāma b. Munḳid̲h̲, in H. Derenbourg, Vie d'Usāma, 298; Ibn Djubayr, ed. De Goeje, 124; Ibn al-Ath̲ī̲r, xi, 202 ff.   (Ed.)

DJAWĀD PAS̲H̲A, AḤMAD (T. Ahmed Cevad Paşa), 1851-1900, Ottoman Grand Vizier. Born in Syria, the son of the miralāy Muṣṭafā ʿĀṣim (whose family originated from Afyonkarahisar), he was educated at the Military College and completed the Staff College course in 1871. He served in the Russo-Turkish war as A.D.C. to the Commander-in-Chief Süleymān Pas̲h̲a and as chief of staff of Nadj̲ī̲b Pas̲h̲a's division. Rapidly promoted, he was appointed successively ambassador to Montenegro, with the rank of mīrliwā (1301/1884), chief of staff to the governor and military commander of Crete, S̲h̲ākir Pas̲h̲a, with the rank of ferīḳ (1306/1889), and soon afterwards vice-governor of Crete and extraordinary commissioner. His services in Crete having commended him to ʿAbd al-Ḥamīd, he was appointed Grand Vizier on 29 Muḥarram 1309/20 February 1891 and held office for over three years.

During this period, when the Ottoman Empire was disturbed particularly by the Armenian question, Djawād Pas̲h̲a tried to act justly, but he lost the favour of ʿAbd al-Ḥamīd, who was dissatisfied with his conduct of affairs. In memorials addressed to the Palace Djawād Pas̲h̲a attributed the various revolts in different parts of the Empire to the ineffectiveness of the system of government, and proposed that the influence of the Palace in the government should be reduced and the authority of the Bāb-i ʿĀlī increased: these recommendations led to his dismissal on 9 June 1895. After a period in disgrace, he was again appointed military commander of Crete (14 July 1897) and soon after, when he was already a sick man, commander of the Fifth Army in Syria. His health worsened in Syria and he was recalled to Istanbul, where he died shortly afterwards (14 Rabīʿ II 1318/11 August 1900).

Djawād Pas̲h̲a, who had from his early years devoted himself to study, was a man of learning, and knew Arabic, Persian, French, Italian and Greek. Among his works are: Maʿlūmāt-i kāfiye fī memālik-i ʿOthmāniyye, Istanbul 1289 (a textbook for military iʿdādī schools); Taʾrīk̲h̲-i ʿaskerī-i ʿOthmānī, Istanbul 1297, = État militaire ottoman ..., 1882, (on the history of the Janissaries); Riyāḍiyyenīn mebāḥith̲-i daḳīḳasī; Kimyānīn ṣanāyiʿa taṭbīḳi; Semā; Telefon.

He published a review entitled *Yādigār* and founded a rich library.

Bibliography: Memdūḥ Pas͟ha, *Aṣwāt-i ṣudūr*, Izmir 1328; ʿOt͟hmān Nūrī, *ʿAbdülḥamīd II ve dewr-i salṭanati*, Istanbul 1327; Ibnülemin Mahmud Kemal, *Osmanlı devrinde son sadrazamlar*, Istanbul 1949, x; Bursalī Ṭāhir, *ʿOt͟hmānlī Müʾellifleri*, iii, 43; *İA*, art. Cevad Paşa (M. Tayyib Gökbilgin); Babinger, 382-3. (Cavid Baysun)

DJAWĀLĪ, double plural of *d͟jālī* (through the intermediate form *d͟jāliya* which is also found, particularly in old papyri), literally "émigrés", a term which, in administrative usage, very soon served to denote the *d͟jizya* [*q.v.*]. Ancient writers believed that the word had originally been applied to the poll-tax on the *d͟himmīs* who were émigrés (driven out) from Arabia; some modern writers have thought that it could have taken on its meaning, by extension, from a term used of the tax on the Jewish community in "Exile" *d͟jālūt*: there is no trace of any such specific use. It would seem that, in order to understand the semantic development of the word, account should be taken of the distinction, going back to the Roman Empire, made between colonists attached to the soil, and consequently to an immutable fiscal community, and those men whom the efforts of the administration did not succeed in preventing from changing their place of residence and occupation, *inquilini*, φυγάδεις. Muslim fiscal practice distinguishes more and more sharply between, on the one hand, the tax due upon the land, which was immovable, from the community collectively responsible, irrespective of the actual whereabouts of each individual on the date of the assessment or payment, and, on the other, the tax due upon the person, which could only be paid by the individual in the place where he was. In the tax registers therefore an entry was made, among the theoretical inhabitants of each district, of the names of those who were "émigrés", together with their place of emigration, for the purpose of informing the authorities concerned. Since this procedure related more particularly to the *d͟jizya*, it might in consequence have led to the name *d͟jawālī* being given to this tax, meaning the individual tax paid also by the émigrés, or, to express it better, by all individuals irrespective of their place of residence. However, no text confirms the truth of this explanatory hypothesis.

Bibliography: see D͟JIZYA; more particularly Løkkegaard (index), and Fattal, 265.

(Cl. Cahen)

al-**DJAWĀLĪḲĪ** or Ibn al-D͟jawālīḳī, Abū Manṣūr Mawhūb b. Aḥmad b. Muḥ. b. al-K͟haḍir, so named according to Brockelmann, I², 332 and S I, 492. Born in Bag͟hdād in 466/1073, he died there on 15 Muḥarram 539/19 July 1144. According to Brockelmann, he belonged to an ancient family, but the *nisba al-d͟jawālīḳī* "maker, seller of sacks", Persian *gowāl(e)* "sack", arabicized *d͟juwāliḳ*, pl. *d͟jawāliḳu*, recorded in the *Muʿarrab* (48 end - 49), pl. *d͟jawālīḳu* (Sībawayhi, ii (Paris), 205, allows us to suppose a humble origin.

He was the second successor of his master al-Tibrīzī in the chair of philology at the Niẓāmiyya. A zealous Sunnī (Ḥanbalī, according to *S͟had͟harāt al-d͟hahab*, iv, 127 and al-Tanūk͟hī, in *RAAD*, xiv, 164), he was appointed in place of ʿAlī b. Abī Zayd (d. 516/1122), a too notorious S͟hīʿī who was compelled to resign.

The man was a conscientious teacher, prudent in his answers to questions and with a much admired calligraphy. His works deservedly take their place along with those of al-Tibrīzī in raising the cultural level in the Arabic language from the depths to which it had fallen in the Sald͟jūḳid period: a) the *K. al-Muʿarrab min al-kalām al-ʿad͟jamī ʿala ḥurūf al-muʿd͟jam*, to preserve the *faṣīḥ* language by collecting together words of foreign origin and recording them as such. This explanatory lexicon, which was highly thought of in its time, has proved to be very useful and made Ibn al-D͟jawālīḳī's reputation. In fact, as was said by one of his pupils (Abu 'l-Barakāt Ibn al-Anbārī, *Nuzha*, 475), "the s͟hayk͟h was a better lexicographer than grammarian". But it remains principally a creditable application of his predecessors' work: published by Ed. Sachau, from the Leiden MS, Leipzig 1867, x + 70 (notes) + 158 (Arabic text) + 23 (Index) pp. in 8°. W. Spitta filled the gaps from the two Cairo MSS (*ZDMG*, xxxiii, 208-24); an edition in Cairo (Dār al-kutub al-Miṣriyya), 1361 A. H. by Aḥmad Muḥ. S͟hākir. Glosses originated by Ibn Barrī (d. 582/1186) occur in an Escurial MS (H. Derenbourg, *Les Manuscrits arabes de l'Escurial*, ii, 772, 5). b) *K. al-Takmila fī mā yalḥan fīhi 'l-ʿāmma*, the aim of this work on incorrect expressions is evident: published by H. Derenbourg, *Morgenländ. Forsch.* (Festschrift Fleischer), Leipzig 1875, 107-66 (from a Paris MS, entitled: *K. K͟haṭaʾ al-ʿawāmm*), published again in Damascus by ʿIzz al-Dīn al-Tanūk͟hī (*RAAD*, xiv, 1936, 163-226) from the Ẓāhiriyya MS (with glosses by Ibn Barrī), under the title *Takmilat iṣlāḥ mā tag͟hliṭ fīhi 'l-ʿāmma*, This complements the works of this sort, apart from the *Durrat al-g͟hawwāṣ* by al-Ḥarīrī (al-Tanūk͟hī, *ibid.*, 167-168). c) The *S͟harḥ* of the *Adab al-kātib* by Ibn Ḳutayba, a guide for the practice of the pure Arabic language, in fact an average work; printed, Cairo, Maktabat al-Ḳudsī, 1350 A.H.

In manuscript (Köpr. 1501, Mesh. xi, 16, 50), the *K. al-Muk͟htaṣar fi 'l-naḥw*. Ibn al-Anbārī (*Nuzha*, 474) attributes to him a *K. al-ʿArūḍ* written for the caliph al-Muḳtafī. Brockelmann lists as his work a *S͟harḥ Maḳṣūrat Ibn Durayd* (S I, 492) and al-Tanūk͟hī (*loc. cit.* 166) a *K. G͟halaṭ al-ḍuʿafāʾ min al-fuḳahāʾ*. The *K. Asmāʾ k͟hayl al-ʿarab wa-fursānihā* is to be deleted from his works.

Bibliography: J. Fück, *ʿArabīya*, Paris 1955, 179; Ibn al-Anbārī, *Nuzhat al-alibbāʾ*, 473-8; Yāḳūt, *Udabāʾ*, xix, 205-7; Ibn K͟hallikān, iv, 424-6 (no. 722); Suyūṭī, *Bug͟hya*, 401; Ibn al-ʿImād, *S͟had͟harāt al-D͟hahab*, iv, 127; Ḳifṭī, *Inbāʾ al-ruwāt ʿalā anbāʾ al-nuḥāt*, iii, 335-7, see 335 note for other references. (H. Fleisch)

DJAWĀN, Mirzā Kāẓim ʿAlī, one of the pioneers of Urdū prose literature and a *muns͟hī* at Fort William College (Calcutta), originally a resident of Dihlī, migrated to Lucknow after the break-up of the cultural and social life of the Imperial capital following the invasion of Aḥmad S͟hāh Abdālī in 1174/1760, and was living in Lucknow in 1196/1782 when Ibrāhīm K͟hān K͟halīl was busy compiling his *tad͟hkira* (see *Gulzār-i Ibrāhīm*, ʿAlīgaṙh 1352/1934, 93). A writer of simple, chaste and unornamented Urdū prose and a scholar of Persian and Arabic (he revised the Urdū translation of the Ḳurʾān, undertaken partially by Amānat Allāh and others), he was also conversant with Brad͟j-bhās͟hā. He joined Fort William College on its establishment in 1800 as a teacher and settled permanently in Calcutta. He was alive in 1815 when he revised, in part, the second edition of Ḥafīẓ al-Dīn's *K͟hirad Afrūz*, an Urdū translation of Abu 'l-Faḍl's *ʿIyār-i Dānis͟h*.

In 1216/1801 he translated from a Bradj-bhāshā version Kālidāsa's Sanskrit drama *Shakuntalā* into Urdū at the instance of Dr. Gilchrist, head of the Hindustānī Department of Fort William College and one of the early patrons of Urdū literature (ed. Calcutta 1804, London 1826, Bombay 1848 and Lucknow 1875). His second literary achievement is the *bārah-māsa Dastūr-i Hind*, a long poem in Urdū, arranged according to the Hindū calendar months, describing in detail the Hindū and Muslim festivals falling in those months, composed 1802 and published at Calcutta 1812. He also attempted a translation of the *Ta'rīkh-i Firishta* comprising the chapters on the Bahmanīs [*q.v.*], and collaborated in the preparation of an anthology of the poems of Walī, Mīr, Sawdā and Sōz [*qq.v.*]. He also helped Munshī Lallūdjī Lāl, his colleague at Fort William College, in the translation of the *Siṃhāsana Dvātriṃśika*, a collection of tales of Vikramāditya, the rādjā of Udjdjayn, from the Bradj-bhāshā version (*Singhāsan Battīsī*) made by Sundar, a *kavi-rāy* of Shāhdjahān's court. He died some time after 1815.

Bibliography: Sayyid Muhammad, *Arbāb-i Nathr-i Urdū*[3], Lahore 1950, 196-207; Muḥammad Yaḥyā Tanhā, *Siyar al-Muṣannifīn*, Dihlī 1924, 119-20; Rām Bābū Saksēna, *A history of Urdu literature*[2], Allahabad 1940, 248; T. Grahame Bailey, *A history of Urdu literature*, Calcutta 1932, 82; Bēni Narāyan Djahān, *Dīwān-i Djahān* (a *tadhkira* of Urdū poets compiled in 1227/1812); *EI*[1], s.v. (A. S. Bazmee Ansari)

DJAWĀN MARDI [see futuwwa].

DJAWĀNRŪD (local Kurdish djwānrō), a district of Persian Kurdistān lying to the west of Mt. Shāhō, between Avroman (Hawermān [*q.v.*]) in the north, Shahrizūr in the west, and Zuhāb and Rawānsar in the south and east. The country is generally mountainous and thickly wooded. The valleys are well watered and very fertile, being in effect the granary of the Avroman area.

There is no river now known by this name, but Minorsky derives it from **Djāwān-rūd*, influenced by Persian *djawān* 'young'. A Kurdish tribe Djāwānī, listed by Masʿūdī (*Murūdj*, iii, 253; *Tanbīh*, 88), appears to be the same as the Djāf [*q.v.*]. Those sections of the Djāf still living in Persia are known collectively as Djāf-i Djawānrūd. The Kurd-ī Djwānrō proper occupy villages as far north as the river Sīrwān, where this becomes the frontier of ʿIrāḳ, and thus surround the Hawrāmī villages of Pāwa.

There have been a number of poets of Djawānrūd, the most famous being Mawlawī [*q.v.*].

Bibliography: V. Minorsky, *The Gūrān*, in *BSOAS*, xi, 81; C. J. Edmonds, *Kurds, Turks and Arabs*, London 1957, 141, 189, 198; ʿAlī Razmārā, *Djughrāfiyā-yi niẓāmī-yi Īrān, Kurdistān*, [Tehran] 1941; Muḥammad Mardūkh Kurdistānī, *Kitāb ta'rīkh-i Mardūkh*, 2 vols., Tehran n.d.; B. Nikitine, *Les Kurdes*, Paris 1956, 36, 55 n. 1, 204; M. Amīn Zakī, *Khulāṣat ta'rīkh al-Kurd wa-Kurdistān*, Ar. tr. Cairo 1936, 362-3. (Ed.)

al-**DJAWBARĪ** [see supplement].

DJAWDHAR, a eunuch—as is indicated by the epithet *ustādh* generally appended to his name—and slave who played an important part under the first Fāṭimid caliphs. Even in the time of the last Aghlabid he was already working in his service and, while still young, was marked out by al-Mahdī when he came to al-Raḳḳāda. By his devotion he won the favour of the caliph and his son al-Ḳā'im. During the latter's reign he became director of the Treasury and Textile Stores, but in addition was the intermediary (*safīr*) of the caliph, that is to say in charge of relations between him and the various functionaries and officers. In this capacity he was chosen as the depository of important secrets, for example al-Ḳā'im's choice of al-Manṣūr as his heir. In the time of al-Manṣūr, who was much preoccupied with the struggle against Abū Yazīd, very real power had been delegated to Djawdhar. He was given his freedom, directed the *ṭirāz* workshops and had his name marked on officially woven fabrics. Moreover he was responsible for the upkeep of the treasure, in particular the caliph's books, and for watching over the inhabitants of the palace, especially the caliph's uncles and brothers, and he was the sovereign's confidential adviser. Under al-Muʿizz who made him move from al-Mahdiyya to the new capital al-Manṣūriyya he exercised still greater responsibilities, dealing with the receipt and transmission of letters and requests addressed to the caliph, and with the transmission of the sovereign's replies and decisions. But he did more than merely transmit letters; sometimes he not only made for the caliph a résumé of incoming letters and the problems they raised, but the sovereign also made him answer them himself, merely indicating what general lines he should take in his reply.

Djawdhar's boundless devotion inspired such confidence in the caliph that he became a sort of prime minister. Holding the secret of the nomination of the heir to the throne, flattered by members of the great families from whom the governors were selected, and apparently even figuring in the Ismāʿīlī hierarchy, he ranked third in the State, coming after the heir apparent. He possessed great wealth, ships with which he imported wood from Sicily (perhaps he owed his skill in maritime commerce to his slave ancestry?), and he was in a position to make gifts of wood and money to the caliph.

Djawdhar left for Egypt at the same time as al-Muʿizz, and died on the road near al-Barḳa, still affectionately regarded by the caliph who held him in his arms shortly before he died.

Certain information about this person whom historians have ignored is to be found in his *Life* (*Sīra*), compiled by his private secretary al-Manṣūr, who was probably a slave like himself, in the time of al-ʿAzīz. This work contains biographical sections, but it is also primarily a collection of documents relating to the various affairs in which Djawdhar was involved, and includes sermons, letters and drafts made by the caliphs, and from this point of view it is very important historically. It was published in Cairo in 1954.

Bibliography: See M. Kāmil Ḥusayn and M. ʿAbd al-Hādī Shaʿīra, *Sīrat al-ustādh Djawdhar*, Cairo 1954 (Silsilat makhṭūṭāt al-Fāṭimiyyīn, 11), with a detailed introduction, and the French translation with introduction and notes by M. Canard, *Vie de l'ustādh Jaudhar*, Public. de l'Inst. d'Études Orientales de la Fac. des Lettres d'Alger, IIe série, tome xx, Algiers 1958. See also Ivanow, *Ismaili tradition concerning the rise of the Fatimids*, 263 and index, and M. Kāmil Husayn, *Fī adab Miṣr al-Fāṭimiyya*, 29, 114-6, 170, 309. (M. Canard)

DJAWF, a topographical term denoting a depressed plain, is similar in meaning to and sometimes replaced by *djaww*, as in Djawf or Djaww al-Yamāma (al-Bakrī, ll, 405) and Djawf or Djaww Tu'ām. The name *djawf* is applied to many locations: chiefly Djawf al-Sirḥān and Djawf Ibn Nāṣir (also known as Djawf without the definite article (al-

Bakrī), Djawf al-Yaman, al-Djawf, and the two Djawfs—Djawf Hamdān and Djawf Murād of the lexicographers). Djawf Ibn Nāṣir of north-west al-Yaman is a broad plain, roughly trapeziform, bounded on the north by Djabals al-Lawdh, Baraṭ, and Shaʿaf; on the west by Djabals Madhāb, Khārid Khabash, and al-ʿIshsh; on the south by Djabal Yām; and on the east by the sands of Ramlat Dahm of the south-western Rubʿ al-Khālī. Djawf Ibn Nāṣir, which lies north-west of Maʾrib [*q.v.*], was the centre of the Minaean Dynasty and abounds with archaeological sites (called locally Kharib, the plural of Khariba) which were first described by Hamdānī and later by Halévy, Ḥabshūsh, Glaser, Philby, Fakhry, Tawfīḳ, and von Wissman, and which include Maʿīn, al-Ḥazm, Barāḳish, Kamnā (Kumnā in the local dialect), al-Sawdā, and al-Bayḍā. Among the *wādī*s originating in the mountains to the west and flowing into Wādī al-Djawf and thence to the sands in the east, are Wādī al-ʿUla, Wādī al-Khārid, and Wādī Madhāb. Two canals of ancient construction, Bāhī al-Khārid (which parallels Wādī al-Khārid) and Bāhī al-Sāḳiya, are still in use to irrigate the agricultural lands of al-Ḥazm and al-Ghayl respectively, while al-Maṭimma is irrigated by the seasonal waters of Wādī Madhāb. Al-Ḥazm, the chief village of Djawf Ibn Nāṣir, is the *markaz* of the *nāḥiya* of al-Djawf and seat of the *ʿāmil*, who reports to the governor of the province in Ṣanʿāʾ. Djawf Ibn Nāṣir produces wheat, barley, grain sorghums, sesame seeds and oil, cotton, fruit, camels and sheep for export. It is the *dīra* of Dahm, a tribe tracing its ancestry to Nāṣir (whence Djawf Ibn Nāṣir) through Hamdān [*q.v.*]. Dahm's warlike reputation, which was noted by Niebuhr in 1763, has survived to the present, and raids were carried out by Dahm until the late 1940's (Thesiger). Hamdānī speaks of the bellicosity of the tribes of al-Djawf and mentions two opposing groups, Hamdān and Madhḥidj, whence Djawf Hamdān and Djawf Murād ibn Madhḥidj according to Schleifer) of the lexicographers.

Bibliography: Hamdānī, index s.v.; Yāḳūt, ii, 157 ff.; *BGA*, iii, 89; vi, 137, 249; al-Bakrī, *Muʿdjam mā istaʿdjam*, ii, 404-6, Cairo 1945; Ibn Bulayhid, *Ṣaḥīḥ al-akhbār*, iv, 167-9, Cairo 1953; M. Tawfiḳ, *Āthār Maʿīn fī Djawf al- Yaman*, Cairo 1951; A. Fakhry, *An archaeological journey to Yemen*, i, 139-52, Cairo 1952; N. Faris, *The antiquities of South Arabia*, Princeton 1938; S. Goitein (ed.) *Travels in Yemen*, Jerusalem 1941; N. Lambardi, *Divisioni amministrative del Yemen*, in *OM*, xxvii, no. 7-9; D. Müller and N. Rhodokanakis, *Eduard Glasers Reise nach Marib*, Vienna 1913; C. Niebuhr, *Description de l'Arabie*, Copenhagen 1773; H. St. J. Philby, *Sheba's Daughters*, London 1939; Thesiger, *Arabian sands*, London 1959; H. von Wissman and M. Höfner, *Beiträge zur historischen Geographie des vorislamischen Südarabien*, Mainz 1952. (M. Quint)

al-DJAWF, district and town in north central Saudi Arabia, near the southern terminus of Wādī al-Sirḥān. The district of al-Djawf (= "belly, hollow"), also known as al-Djuba, is a roughly triangular depression, with one base along the northern fringe of al-Nafud and its northern apex at al-Shuwayḥiṭiyya. It is bounded on the west by Djāl al-Djūba al-Gharbī and on the east by Djāl al-Djūba al-Sharḳī. Al-Djawf, or al-Djūba, with an area of approximately 3,850 square kms., is separated from Nadjd by the sand desert of al-Nafūd. It is administered as a district under the Saudi Arabian Amirate of the Northern Frontiers. The area is relatively well watered, has many palm groves, and is considered to have agricultural potential. The two most important settlements of al-Djawf are the towns of Sakākā, now the administrative centre, and al-Djawf. Ḳāra, al-Ṭuwayr, and Djāwa are smaller villages. The total population of the district was roughly estimated as 25,000 in 1961.

The town of al-Djawf, or Djawf ʿĀmir (29° 48.5′ N., 39° 52.1′ E., elev. c. 650 m.), has historically been the centre of al-Djūba and has been identified with the Dumetha of Ptolemy. It was known to the early Arab geographers as Dūmat al-Djandal, [*q.v.*]. The name Djawf ʿĀmir (also Djawf Al ʿĀmir, Djawf Ibn ʿĀmir) is often used to differentiate the town from the southern Djawf, Djawf Ibn Nāṣir, south-east of Wādī Nadjrān.

Muḥammad b. Muʿayḳil added al-Djawf to the Wahhābī realm of ʿAbd al-ʿAzīz b. Muḥammad b. Saʿūd in 1208/1794, when the people of the area surrendered to his combined forces from Nadjd. In c. 1853 the district was taken by Āl Rashīd of Haʾil who held it, in the face of internal rebellion and threats from the Turks, until 1909. In that year, Nūrī b. Shaʿlān, the Ruwala chief, took al-Djawf. There followed 13 years of struggle between the Ruwala and Shammar for mastery of the area, with the town changing hands several times. The *Ikhwān* levies of Ibn Saʿūd took al-Djawf in 1922 with the aid of local leaders who had adopted Wahhābī tenets. The area has since remained a part of the Saʿūdi state. Al-Djawf, now declining in importance because of the rise of the new administrative centre at Sakākā, has been a trading town of the Shammar, Ruwala, and Sharārāt. It is still known for its date market and crafts, while a planned (1961) road system and development scheme may make it an important agricultural centre.

Bibliography: ʿUthmān b. Bishr, *ʿUnwān al-madjd*, Cairo 1373, 110-11; Ḥāfiẓ Wahba, *Djarīrat al-ʿArab*[3], Cairo 1956, 45, 67; J. Euting, *Tagebuch einer Reise in Inner-Arabien*, i, 123-40; Ibn Hishām, 668, 903, 991; J. G. Lorimer, *Gazetteer of the Persian Gulf*, Calcutta 1908-15, 935-3; A. Musil, *Arabia Deserta*, New York 1927, 464-74, 520-3, 531-53 (a valuable historical discussion with many additional references); H. St. J. B. Philby, *Arabia*, London 1930; *Saudi Arabia*, London 1955; Ritter, *Erdkunde*, xii, 71, 713, 842; xiii, 343, 362, 377 ff., 389-95, 467; Yāḳūt, i, 825; ii, 157-8, 625-9; iii, 106, 277; iv, 12, 32, 76, 389, index; C. A. Nallino, *L'Arabia Saʿudiana*, Rome 1938, 68 ff., 87.

Maps: Series by the U. S. Geological Survey and Arabian American Oil Company under joint sponsorship of the Ministry of Finance and National Economy (Kingdom of Saudi Atabia) and the Department of State (U.S.A.). Jawf-Sakākah, Map I-201 B, scale 1 : 500,000 (1961). (J. Mandaville)

DJAWF KUFRA is the chief oasis of the Kufra oasis complex in the Libyan Desert and is located about 575 miles SE of Benghazi. The 2200 (1950 estimate) inhabitants of Djawf raise dates, grapes, barley, and olives. Local industry is limited to handicrafts and olive pressing. In the mid-nineteenth century, the founder of the Sanūsī Order, al-Sayyid Muḥammad b. ʿAlī al-Sanūsī, established Zāwiyat al-Ustādh at Djawf at the request of the local tribe, Zwuyya (Ziadeh 49, cf. *EI*[1], iv, 1108 which gives the tribe's name as Zāwiya) and opened the Sahara and the central Sudan to Sanūsī penetration. Djawf experienced a short period of prominence in 1895 when al-Sanūsī's son and successor, al-Sayyid Muḥammad al-Mahdī, transferred the capital of the order to Zāwiyat al-Ustā<u>dh</u>. However, the capital was soon moved to the newly constructed Zāwiyat al-Tā<u>dj</u>, also in the Kufra Oasis, and finally in 1899 was moved to the Central Sudan.

Bibliography: A. Desio, "*Cufra*", *Enciclopedia italiana*, xii, 86-8, Milan 1931-40; E. Evans-Pritchard, *The Sanusi of Cyrenaica*, Oxford 1949; R. Forbes, *The secret of the Sahara*, New York 1921; J. Wright, *Wartime exploration with the Sudan Defence Force*, in *GJ*, cv, Nos. 3-4, 100-11; N. Ziadeh, *Sanūsīyah*, Leiden 1958. (M. Quint)

<u>DJ</u>AWHAR "substance" (the Arabic word is derived from Persian *gawhar*, Pahlawī *gōr*, which has already the meaning of substance, although both in Pahlawī and in Arabic, it can mean also jewel) is the common translation of οὐσία, one of the fundamental terms of Aristotelian philosophy. "Substance" in a general sense may be said to signify the real, that which exists in reality, *al-mawdjūd bi 'l-ḥaḳīḳa*. In opposition to Plato, for whom the particular transitory things of the visible world are but appearances and reality lies in a world beyond, the world of constant, eternal ideas, for Aristotle and his followers in Islam the visible world possesses reality and consists of individuals and in its most pregnant sense "substance" is the first and most important category of Aristotle's table of categories, that which signifies the concrete individual, τόδε τι, *al-mu<u>sh</u>ār ilayhi, al-<u>sh</u>a<u>kh</u>ṣ*. In this sense it may be said that all things in the visible world, all bodies, parts of bodies, plants and animals are substances (these individual substances are sometimes called first substances, πρῶται οὐσίαι, *<u>dj</u>awāhir uwal* to distinguish them from the second substances, δεύτεραι οὐσίαι, *al-<u>dj</u>awāhir al-<u>th</u>awānī*, species and genera). However, according to Aristotle and his school every concrete individual is composed of two factors, matter and form, and although mere matter, unendowed with form, cannot exist by itself, nor form—at least in the sublunar world—can exist without matter, both possess objective reality. Matter in its pregnant sense is prime matter, the underlying entity, substratum of the forms, and is by itself absolutely undetermined. Still, as it bears or carries the forms, the universal essences, it has at least some reality and therefore the name of substance cannot be denied to it. Besides, although it is mere potentiality, it is the principle of all becoming and therefore cannot have become itself, but is eternal. Form is the essence, τὸ τί, τὸ τί ἦν εἶναι, *<u>dh</u>āt, māhiyya, ḥaḳīḳa*, the universal character of any particular and is the cause which differentiates this particular being from other particular beings of its genus through its species, for instance, every particular man is a man and his being a man, his essence, differentiates him from other living beings and is the cause—the formal cause according to Aristotle and his school—of his being a man. Although these essences, according to Aristotle, never exist by themselves, for only particular beings exist, he regards them as having a reality superior to that of the transitory beings, for they are causes—and a cause, according to him, is superior to its effect— and they are eternal and they merit therefore still more the name of substance than the particular things. But how can one regard these essences, non-existent by themselves, but eternal, as the formal causes of the transitory existents? It is here that the neoplatonizing Muslim philosophers go beyond Aristotle. According to them the fundamental and eternal source of these essences lies in the mind of God or in God's thinking them; it is God's thought which is the ultimate formal and final cause of all things. However, God's absolute Unity is not affected by his thought; in God's self-consciousness these essences are comprehended and in God, the thinker, the thinking and the object of thought are all one.

There is besides another point where the Muslim Aristotelians go beyond their master. It is one of the characteristics of Aristotle's system that reality is regarded as having degrees or, as he expresses it, that being is predicated analogically; first there is the sublunar world of transitory things, then beyond it is the heavenly eternal world of the incorruptible in which there is this mysterious substance, the active intellect, ὁ νοῦς ποιητικός, *al-ʿaḳl al-faʿʿāl*, ungenerated and immortal, the immaterial form which in combination with the passive reason activates the thoughts in human beings. Still higher are the intellects, pure immaterial forms or substances, which are the movers of the celestial sphere, and at the pinnacle is God, the most Real, substance in the truest sense. However, for Aristotle God is but the eternal mover of an eternal universe, he is not its creator, nor are the movers of the celestial spheres dependent on him in their nature or existence. But for the Muslim philosophers under the influence of the neoplatonic theory of emanation God is the eternal, constant creator of the world, co-existent and co-eternal with him. According to them the plurality of the world arises out of God's unity through the eternal and timeless emanation of a descencing chain of intermediaries, intellects and souls, immaterial substances moving the heavenly spheres and, the last of these intellects is the active intellect, the *dator formarum*, *wāhib al-ṣuwar*, which according to Avicenna, when the matters are disposed to receive them, provides them with their forms. All these immaterial substances, essences or forms have a different degree of reality and their reality increases with their nearness to God, who is an existent, a substance, an intellect and a cause, these terms taken, however, in a superior sense to what they have in all other beings, for God's very essence consists in his existence which is necessary by itself and exclusively confined to him and God's substance is the only truly independent substance on which all other substances depend.

The whole theory is highly controversial and <u>Gh</u>azālī in his *Tahāfut al-falāsifa* has seen its fundamental weakness. If the plurality in the world derives from the intermediaries, there will be primary causes besides God, if from God himself, they will be useless; if God is the supreme, eternal and constant cause of the World's existence all changes in the world will derive from him; they cannot derive from a pre-existent mattter, since here is no such pre-existence and besides, matter not endowed with form does not exist. The philosophers, indeed, tried to combine two contradictory theories: the supernaturalistic theory of a divine, eternally acting cause for all existence and the naturalistic theory of an eternal and independent matter in which lie the potentialities of all becoming.

The theory of the A<u>sh</u>ʿarī theologians, on the contrary, is frankly supernaturalistic. For them *<u>dj</u>awhar* means simply the underlying substratum of accidents; one may regard it as matter—not of matter in the Aristotelian sense of an entity possessing potentialities, but only as that which bears or carries accidents—or even as body for the substratum consists of atoms which by their aggregation compose the body. The term, however, is somewhat ambiguous, since often in Ash^carī terminology *djawhar* means atom, although the full designation for atom is *al-djawhar al-fard* or *al-djawhar al-wāḥid*. The atoms out of which the world consists have no independent existence; they rest only on the power of God who, continually, in every time-atom, creates and recreates his atomic world. And since *djawhar* has in theology a purely material meaning it is forbidden to apply the term to God.

One point, where the Muslim Aristotelians deviate from Aristotle, should be still mentioned. Although Aristotle calls the soul a substance, since it is the formal cause of the living organism, he does not regard it as having an existence separate from the body, that is independent of the body and surviving it. The Muslim philosophers regard the soul as a substance subsistent by itself, *djawhar ḳā'im binafsihi*, that is independent of the body, and they teach personal immortality. It is however somewhat difficult for them as Aristotelians to uphold this, since, according to Aristotle, matter is the *principium individuationis*—Avicenna gives this as an argument against the possibility of the pre-existence of the soul—perception and representation are localized in the body and all thinking, according to Aristotle, presupposes preliminary perception and representation and is activated by the active intellect which is one for all human beings. Their theories are therefore not always consistent or easily understood.

Bibliography: al-Ghazāli, *Tahāfut al-falāsifa* (ed. Bouyges), Beirut 1927, where the philosophers' theories are exposed and critically examined; Ibn Rushd, *Tahāfut al-tahāfut* (ed. Bouyges), Beirut 1931. (S. VAN DEN BERGH)

DJAWHAR (ii) [see SUPPLEMENT].

DJAWHAR ĀFTĀBAČĪ, the author of *Tadhkirat al-wāḳi^cāt*, valuable memoirs of the reign of Humāyūn [*q.v.*] and giving much useful information not available elsewhere, was for some years ewer-bearer (*āftābačī*) to Humāyūn and in this capacity came very close to the emperor. He enjoyed the honorific title of *mihtar* (cf. *Akbarnāma*, Bib. Ind., i, 346; the appellation *mihtar* was, however, common to all the *āftābačīs* in the service of the emperor), and was a trusted confidant of his master. Although he was neither a scholar not a writer of any high standard, history has, however, preserved Djawhar's name for the simple, unostentatious and truthful narration of events of the reign of Humāyūn and his deep loyalty to his master. In recognition of his services he was appointed in 962/1554-5 *muḥaṣṣil* (tax-collector) of the *pargana* of Haybatpur Bīnī and subsequently of the villages included in the *djāgīr* of Tātār Khān Lodī. It, however, appears that he enjoyed this office for a short while only, as the same year (cf. *Akbarnāma*, i, 346; tr. Beveridge, i, 627) he was appointed the *khazīnadār* (treasurer) of the government of the *sarkārs* of the Pandjāb and of Multān. While in Haybatpur, dominated by the Baniyās (Hindū traders and bankers), Djawhar paid off the debts which the local Afghāns owed to the Hindūs and secured the release of pawned Afghān women and children. This humanitarian act earned for him royal approbation resulting in his promotion as a provincial treasurer (*khizānčī*; cf. *Tadhkifat al-wāḳi^cāt*, fol. 132, B.M. MS. Add. 16711). Although a personal servant of Humāyūn, he was entrusted with special State assignments on critical occasions and his counsels were given due weight (cf. *Tadhkirat al-wāḳi^cāt*, faṣl 32 *passim*). As with the meagre details of his life, nothing is known about the dates of his birth and death. He survived his imperial patron but passed into eclipse after Humāyūn's sudden death in 963/1556.

His claim to fame rests chiefly on his only work, the *Tadhkirat al-wāḳi^cāt*, whose value as a very useful source-book for the reign of Humāyūn has been fully recognized. The original Persian text is still in MS. although English and Urdū translations have since appeared; (C. Stewart, *The Tezkereh al-Vakiat* .... London 1832 Calcutta 1904; Mu^cīn al-Ḥaḳḳ, *Tadhkirat al-wāḳi^cāt*, Karachi n.d.). At the request of Djawhar a recension in ornate prose was made by Ilāh-dād Fayḍī Sirhindī the author of the Persian lexicon *Madār al-Afāḍil* for presentation to Akbar (cf. Rieu, iii, 927a and Ethé 222).

Bibliography: *Tadhkirat al-wāḳi^cāt* (Urdū tr. Mu^cīn al-Ḥaḳḳ), Karachi n.d., index s.v. Djawhar; Storey, i, 536-7; Rieu, i, 246; Elliot and Dowson, *History of India* ...., v, 136-49.

(A. S. BAZMEE ANSARI)

DJAWHAR AL-ṢIḲILLĪ, general and administrator, one of the founders of the Fāṭimid Empire in North Africa and Egypt.

His name was Djawhar b. ^cAbd Allāh, also Djōhar together with the epithets of al-Ṣaḳlabī (the Slav), al-Ṣiḳillī (the Sicilian) or al-Rūmī (the Greek) and al-Kātib (the State Chancellor) or al-Ḳā'id (the General). The first two epithets cast some light on his obscure origin, the other two denote the two highest posts he occupied. His birth date is unknown, but judging by the date of his death (20 Dhu 'l-Ḳa^cda 381/28 April 991) we may guess that he was born sometime during the first decade of the 4th/10th century; he was in the prime of his activity between 340/950 and 366/975. From the parallel career of Djawdhar, well known to us, thanks to his recently published biography, we may infer that Djawhar was a freedman of the Fāṭimid house, of Slav origin. (Leo Africanus, tr. Épaulard, 19, 503 = Esclavon; on this question see I. Hrbek, *Die Slaven im Dienste der Fāṭimiden*, in *ArO*, xxi (1953), 560-71). His father ^cAbd Allāh was most probably a slave, but Djawhar appears as a freedman from the very beginning.

The first time we hear of Djawhar he was a *ghulām*, perhaps also the secretary of the third Fāṭimid Caliph al-Manṣūr. In 347/958 al-Mu^cizz decided to put all the power he possessed in a military venture to dominate the whole of North Africa, and chose for the leadership of this important campaign his secretary Djawhar, giving him in this way the opportunity to prove that he was the most talented soldier the Fāṭimids ever had.

Djawhar's campaign in the Central and Far Maghrib was perhaps the most resounding achieved by a Muslim army since that of ^cUḳba b. Nāfi^c some 284 years before, but in spite of the victories Djawhar gained, it was neither decisive nor of any lasting effect. This was due not to any fault of Djawhar, but to the difficulty of the terrain and to the greatly superior strength of the enemy. Near Ṭahart Djawhar had to measure arms with a large army of Zanātīs, supporters of the Umayyads, under Ya^clā b. Muḥammad al-Yafrānī, governor of Ṭahart and Ifkan; according only to Ibn Abī Zar^c, also of Ṭandja (Tangier). He won the day and killed Ya^clā (347/958). Instead of marching on Fez and the other Umayyad strongholds in the region, he chose to use his small forces to realize easier gains. He turned south-east, invaded the small principality of Sidjilmāsa and put its prince Muḥammad b. al-Fatḥ b. Maymūn b. Midrār to flight. Some days later this last of the Midrāris fell into the hands of Djawhar who killed him mercilessly. He spent more than a year in this region waiting for a suitable opportunity to move northwards. In the last days of Shaʿbān 349/October 960 he headed towards Fez and laid siege to it. On 20 Ramaḍān 349/13 November 960 he stormed the city, thanks to the bravery of Zīrī b. Manād al-Ṣanhādjī who was under his command. Its Umayyad governor Aḥmad b. Abī Bakr al-Djudhāmī was taken prisoner and died in prison. This great victory brought all the Maghrib al-Aḳṣā (except Ṭandja and Sabta) under Fāṭimid authority for a short time. Even the last of the Idrīsids, al-Ḥasān b. Djannūn, who contented himself with a small principality around the city of al-Baṣra under Umayyad vassalage, paid homage. To give al-Muʿizz a tangible proof of his victory he sent to him some live fish, taken from the Atlantic Ocean, in huge jars full of water. Some months later he returned victorious to al-Ḳayrawān with prisoners and rich booty.

These victories of Djawhar's opened the eyes of his master al-Muʿizz to his talents, and convinced him that with his aid he could realize the dearest Fāṭimid dream since the rise of their power: the conquest of Egypt.

Between 350/961 and 358/968-9 we have no information whatsoever about Djawhar. But in 358/968-9 he came to the fore once more as the general chosen by al-Muʿizz to lead the campaign in Egypt. Al-Muʿizz had such confidence in him that he is reported to have said: "By God, if this Djawhar were to go alone, he would conquer Egypt and we would be able to enter this land clad only in our simple clothes (*i.e.*, without armour or shield) without war and we could dwell in the ruined abodes of Ibn Ṭūlūn and build a city which would dominate the world" (*Khiṭaṭ*, i, 378). As a sign of honour al-Muʿizz bestowed on Djawhar before his depature all his royal garments and apparel except his seal and underwear. He ordered all the governors on the route to Egypt to meet him dismounted and to kiss his hand. The governor of Barḳa [*q.v.*] Aflaḥ al-Nāshib offered to pay 100,000 dinars to be spared this humiliation to his dignity, but the Caliph refused. Djōdhar, the highest dignity after the Caliph, was ordered to address Djawhar as an equal brother.

Al-Muʿizz was not disappointed in his hopes. Within four months Djawhar achieved the conquest of Egypt. He left al-Ḳayrawān in Rabīʿ II 358/February 969 and by mid-Shaʿbān of the same year/1 July 969 he was already master of al-Fusṭāṭ after a very little fighting near al-Djīza on 11 Shaʿbān/30 June. He knew how to gain the sympathies of the Egyptians and inspire their confidence in the new régime through a long pompous proclamation read in public and through the nomination of Djaʿfar b. al-Furāt as *wazīr*. As a measure of precaution, however he did not dwell in Fusṭāṭ, but passed the first night after his victory in his camp to its north. The next day he laid the foundations of a new capital Cairo (al-Ḳāhira [*q.v.*]) which was destined to be the greatest of Muslim cities after Baghdād. A year later (24 Djumādā I 359/4 April 970) he founded the famous mosque of al-Azhar [*q.v.*].

Having established Fāṭimid rule in Egypt, Djawhar stayed as sole governor of Egypt for more than four years; al-Muʿizz entered Cairo only on 17 Muḥarram 364/7 October 974. A little later he dismissed Djawhar.

During these four years Djawhar showed noteworthy capacity and foresight as administrator. Besides the sympathies of the people, which he fully gained, he succeeded in putting order in the finances of the country which were in complete chaos during the last years of the Ikhshīdids. It is known that Egypt had yielded since the time of Muʿāwiya an annual revenue of about 4 million dinars when well administered. Djawhar raised 3,400,000 dinars during the first year of his administration, almost the largest revenue of Egypt in the Fāṭimid period. Some 85 years later, the able vizier al-Yāzūrī could raise only 800,000. Djawhar had more confidence in the Maghribīs who came with him than in Egyptians, and gave them almost all the important posts. He may have been following in this respect the instructions of al-Muʿizz.

Besides his work in the administration of the new province, Djawhar had to face the menacing peril of the Ḳarmaṭians [*q.v.*], who in Dhu 'l-Ḥidjdja 358/September 969 defeated and took prisoner at Damascus his lieutenant Djaʿfar b. Fallāh, who had been placed in change of the occupation of Palestine and Syria. During this conflict with the Ḳarmaṭians and their allies, Djawhar was able to annex al-Ḥidjāz to Fāṭimid rule. By 366/976 the *khuṭba* was read in their name in Mecca and Medina.

After 368/976 we hear no more of Djawhar till his death in 20 Dhu 'l-Ḳaʿda 381/30 April 992. He is said have passed those idle years of his life between 368 and 381 in works of piety and welfare. His son al-Ḥusayn, commander-in-chief to the caliph al-Ḥākim, was killed as a result of intrigues in which he took part against the Caliph.

Bibliography: Nuʿmān (Abū Ḥanīfa b. Muḥ. al-Maghribī), *al-Madjālis wa 'l-musāyarāt* (Ms. Nat. Library, Cairo No. 26060); Ibn Ḥammād (Muḥ. b. ʿAlī, *Akhbār mulūk Banī ʿUbayd* (ed. M. Vonderheyden, Algiers-Paris 1927, 40-49; Ibn Khallikān, Cairo ed. 1948, biog. no. 130, 141, 698; Ibn Abī Zarʿ, *Ḳirṭās*, ed. Tornberg, Upsala-Paris 1843, 27-63, (tr. Beaumier, 49 122); Ibn al-Athīr, viii, *passim*, ix, 64 (tr. Fagnan, *passim*); Bakrī, *Description de l'Afrique septentrionale* s.v. Sidjilmāsa; *Kitāb mafākhir al-Barbar*, ed. Levi-Provençal, Rabat, 1934, 4-5; Yaḥya b. Saʿīd al-Antākī, *Ṣilat Kitāb Aftīshyush* (Eutychius), Beirut 1909, i, 132; Ibn al-Ḳalānisī, *Dhayl Taʾrīkh Dimashḳ*, (Beirut, 1902, 1-20; Ibn Duḳmāḳ, *Intiṣār*, Cairo 1893, iv, 10 ff.; Manṣūr al-Kātib, *Sīrat al-Ustādh Djawdhar*, ed. M. K. Ḥusayn and ʿAbd al-Hādī Shaʿīra, Cairo 1954, index (tr. M. Canard, *Vie de l'Ustādh Jaudhar*, Algiers 1958), Ibn ʿIdhārī, i, 191 ff.; Maḳrīzī, *Khiṭaṭ*, ed. Būlāḳ 1270, i, 350 ff.; idem, *Ittiʿāẓ al-ḥunafāʾ*, ed. Dj. Shayyāl, Cairo 1947, 64-87; Nāṣirī, *Istiḳṣā*, Casablanca 1954, i, 198-206; Ḥasan Ibrāhīm Ḥasan, *Taʾrīkh al-dawla al-fāṭimiyya*, Cairo 1958, index; Quatremère, *Vie du Khalife fatimite Moëzz-li-din Allāh*, in *JA*, 1836; S. Lane-Poole, *The story of Cairo*, London 1912, 119-20; G. Marçais, *Berbérie musulmane*, Paris 1946, 153-6; ʿAlī Ibrāhīm Ḥasan, *Taʾrīkh Djawhar al-Ṣiḳillī*. Cairo 1933; Ḥasan Ibrāhim Ḥasan and Ṭāhā Aḥmad Sharaf, *Al-Muʿizz li-dīn Allāh*, Cairo 1367/1948.

(H. Monés)

AL-DJAWHARĪ, Abū Naṣr Ismāʿīl (b. Naṣr?) b. Ḥammād, a celebrated Arabic lexicographer of Turkish origin, born in the town (or: in the province) of Fārāb [*q.v.*] (whence his *nisba* al-Fārābī), situated east of the Sir-Daryā. In later times, Fārāb was called Otrār or Oṭrār.

The date of his birth is unknown. For the year of his death most sources give either 393/1002-3 or 398/1007-8, while others mention 397/1006-7 or about 400/1009-10. The first date (or even earlier ones; see Rosenthal) is made doubtful by the statement of Yāḳūt that he had seen an autograph copy of al-Djawharī's *Ṣiḥāḥ* dated 396.

Al-Djawharī commenced his studies at home under his maternal uncle Abū Ibrāhīm Isḥāḳ b. Ibrāhīm al-Fārābī (Brockelmann I, 133; S I, 195 f.), the author of the *Dīwān al-adab*, an Arabic lexicon which greatly influenced al-Djawharī's own dictionary *al-Ṣiḥāḥ*. In order to complete his education he went to Baghdād where he attended the lectures of Abū Saʿīd al-Sīrāfī [*q.v.*] and Abū ʿAlī al-Fārisī (Brockelmann I, 116; S I, 175) and later travelled to the abodes of the Bedouin tribes of Muḍar and Rabīʿa (probably in Syria and ʿIrāḳ) and even to the Ḥidjāz and Nadjd (see, *e.g.*, *Ṣiḥāḥ*, s.v. *n kh s*). He thus followed the habit of earlier lexicographers who used to make linguistic investigations among the Arabs of the desert, and he seems to have been the last lexicographer of fame to maintain that tradition. After having spent a large part of his life on travel he returned to the east, stayed some time in Dāmaghān [*q.v.*] with the *Kātib* Abū ʿAlī al-Ḥasan (variant: al-Ḥusayn) b. ʿAlī and then settled in Nīsābūr, where he made a living by teaching and copying books, especially the Ḳurʾān, and also devoted himself to literary activity. His beautiful handwriting was so much admired that it was put on the same level as that of the celebrated Ibn Muḳla. He died in Nīsābūr either as the result of an accidental fall from the top of his house or of the old mosque, or else, in a fit of madness, while trying to fly with two wooden wings (or: with the two wings of a door) fastened to his body.

Besides some verses, part of which are preserved in a Berlin MS. (Ahlwardt 7589_2) or quoted by later authors (*e.g.*, al-Thaʿālibī and Yāḳūt), he wrote an introduction to syntax, *Muḳaddima fi 'l-naḥw*, and a treatise on metre, *ʿArūḍ al-waraḳa*, both of which appear to be lost. His distinction in the field of metrics, where he deviated in some respects from the system laid down by al-Khalīl [*q.v.*], is pointed out by Ibn Rashīḳ.

His fame rests on his dictionary *Tādj al-lugha wa-ṣiḥāḥ al-ʿArabiyya*, commonly known as *al-Ṣiḥāḥ* (*al-Ṣaḥāḥ* is also correct), which represents a milestone in the development of Arabic lexicography. For centuries it was the most widely used Arabic dictionary until, in more recent times, the *Ḳāmūs* of al-Fīrūzābādī [*q.v.*] took its place. In addition to outspoken statements in the sources, the important standing of al-Djawharī's lexicon is attested to by the fact that, in the centuries following its appearance, it gave rise to a huge mass of lexicographical literature, part of which has been described and characterized by Goldziher. The *Ṣiḥāḥ* was abridged, rearranged, supplemented, commented upon, and translated into Turkish and Persian; its contents, together with those of other dictionaries, were merged into new lexicographical works; the verses and *ḥadīths* quoted in it as *shawāhid* were assembled in special treatises; a versification of it was begun by Zayn al-Dīn al-Maghribī (Yāḳūt, ed. Margoliouth, vii, 292); and a considerable number of writings were devoted to criticism of its shortcomings. On the other hand, several authors made it a point to defend al-Djawharī from the attacks of his critics.

As the title suggests, the *Ṣiḥāḥ* was intended to contain only authentic lexicographical data, their authenticity, according to the notions of indigenous Arabic lexicography, being dependent upon their transmission through a continuous chain of reliable tradition (cf. Suyūṭī, *Muzhir*, i, 58). Hence, the same degree of authority was attributed to the *Ṣiḥāḥ* in lexicography as to the two *Ṣaḥīḥ*s of Bukhārī and Muslim in the science of *ḥadīth*. In both cases, however, the formal principles adopted did not make for absolute correctness, and numerous errors were detected in the *Ṣiḥāḥ* although the work as a whole was held to be highly reliable.

In his short introduction, al-Djawharī claims that he arranged his subject matter according to an entirely new scheme. His innovations, however, are mainly a combination of various principles followed by his predecessors. The arrangement of the roots under the last radical, adopted, after the model of the *Ṣiḥāḥ*, by the best known of later lexicographers, had already been introduced by al-Djawharī's teacher and uncle, al-Fārābī, in the *Dīwān al-adab*. The use of the common order of the Arabic alphabet, in contrast to the phonetical arrangement of al-Khalīl which was followed by several of al-Djawharī's forerunners and successors, had also been in vogue before the *Ṣiḥāḥ*. As to the principle of authenticity, as understood by Arabic lexicographers, al-Djawharī's older contemporary, Ibn Fāris [*q.v.*], had set the example in his *Mudjmal*.

The use of the last radical as the primary basis for the arrangement of the *Ṣiḥāḥ* has been interpreted as being due to the author's intention to help poets find rhyme words. However, Sanskrit lexicography, which seems to have influenced Arabic lexicography in some respects, occasionally used the same principle, although Sanskrit poetry has no rhyme.

At al-Djawharī's time, independent lexicological research had already come to a close. So the *Ṣiḥāḥ* contains mainly an abstract from earlier lexicographical works, in the first place the *Dīwān al-Adab* (see Krenkow), while al-Djawharī's own contributions are minimal. Being replete with grammatical discussions, the *Ṣiḥāḥ* earned its author the reputation of being the outstanding expert on grammar among lexicographers. It is reported that al-Djawharī compiled his dictionary for the *Ustādh* Abū Manṣūr ʿAbd al-Raḥīm (variant: Raḥmān) b. Muḥammad al-Bīshakī, with whom he became closely associated in Nīsābūr (cf. Yāḳūt, *Buldān*, s.v. Bīshak). In the circulation of the work an important part was taken by the author's pupil Ismāʿīl b. Muḥammad b. ʿAbdūs al-Dahhān al-Nīsābūrī, the Egyptian philologist Abū Sahl Muḥammad b. ʿAlī b. Muḥammad al-Harawī and, later on, the well known calligrapher Yāḳūt al-Mawṣilī. Variant readings in different MSS of the *Ṣiḥāḥ* are frequently pointed out by later lexicographers.

According to a tradition which has never been doubted by Western scholars, al-Djawharī did not live to finish a fair copy of his work, reaching only the middle of the letter *Ḍād*, while the rest was completed from his rough draft by his pupil Ibrāhīm b. Sahl (variant: Ṣāliḥ) al-Warrāḳ. This fact, according to tradition, is held responsible for the numerous errors which later scholars detected in the *Ṣiḥāḥ*. The account, however, may have been a mere invention, probably designed to maintain al-Djawharī's reputation as an unfailing authority. Doubts with regard to its correctness were already voiced by Yāḳūt and, more outspokenly, by Ḥadjdjī Khalīfa, since the existence of autograph copies of the complete work had come to their knowledge or else since, according to some traditions, the entire lexicon had been handed down from al-Djawharī himself. In addition, errors were found not only in the latter part of the *Ṣiḥāḥ* but also in the first which, as agreed by all, had been edited by the author himself. A similar account, probably resulting from the same tendency, exists with regard to the authorship of al-Khalīl's *Kitāb al-ʿAyn*.

The *Ṣiḥāḥ* is available in a Persian lithographed edition (1270) and two Būlāḳ prints (1282 and 1292), while a critical edition is still awaited. Of a European edition, undertaken by E. Scheidius, only the first fascicle appeared (1776; 179 pp.; see Zenker, *Bibl. Or.* i, Leipzig 1846, 5). The Turkish version of Van Kulu [*q.v.*] was the first book issued from the Müteferriḳa press in Istanbul, in 1141/1729.

Bibliography: Abu'l-Fidāʾ, *Taʾrīkh*, year 398; Brockelmann, I, 133 f.; S I, 196 f., 943 f.; S III, 1196; idem, *Ǧauharī u. d. Anordnung d. arab. Alphabets*, in *ZDMG*, xix (1915), 383 f.; M. Djawād, *Fawāʾid Lughawiyya*, in *Lughat al-ʿArab*, viii (1930), 48 ff.; Flügel, *Gramm. Schulen*, 227, 253 f.; Goldziher, *Beitr. z. Gesch. d. Sprachgelehrsamkeit b. d. Arabern II*, in *SBAk. Wien*, lxxii (1872), 587 ff.; Huart, *Les calligraphes et les miniaturistes*, 78, 83, 119; Ḥādjdjī Khalīfa, ii, 1071 ff.; idem, ed. Flügel, iv, 91 ff. and *passim* (see index, vii, 1184, no. 6859); Ibn al-Anbārī, *Nuzha*, Cairo 1294, 418 ff.; Djamʿiyyat Iḥyāʾ Maʾāthir ʿUlamāʾ al-ʿArab, Cairo, 227 ff.; Ibn al-ʿImād, *Shadharāt*, year 393; Ibn al-Ḳifṭī, *Inbāh al-ruwāh*, i, 194 ff.; Ibn Rashīḳ, *ʿUmda*, Cairo 1934, i, 114; Ibn Taghrībirdī, *Nudjūm*, year 393; Krenkow, *The beginnings of Arabic lexicography*, in *Cent. Suppl. to the JRAS*, 1924, 269; Lane, Preface, xiv, xvi f.; Naṣr al-Hūrīnī, *Muḳaddima*, at the beginning of the edition of the *Ṣiḥāḥ*, Būlāḳ 1292; F. Rosenthal, *The technique and approach of Muslim scholarship*, 21; Sarton, *Introduction to the history of science*, i, 652, 654, 689; al-Suyūṭī, *Bughya*, 195; idem, *Muzhir*, Cairo, index; Tāshköprüzāde, *Miftāḥ al-saʿāda*, i, 100 ff.; al-Thaʿālibī, *Yatīma*, iv, 289 f.; G. Weil, *Grundriss u. System d. altar. Metren*, 49; Yāḳūt, *Irshād*, ed. Margoliouth, ii, 226 ff., 266 ff., 356, v, 107, vi, 419 f., vii, 268; ed. Cairo, vi, 63 f., 151 ff., vii, 40 f., xii, 280, xviii, 34 f., xix, 313; ʿAbd Allāh Darwīsh, *al-Maʿādjim al-ʿArabiyya*, Cairo 1956, 91 ff.

(L. Kopf)

DJĀWĪ, plur. Djāwa, Muslims from the Bilād al-Djāwa. Bilād al-Djāwa was the collective name for the South-East Asian area used by the inhabitants of Mecca when C. Snouck Hurgronje visited it in 1884-5, and probably much earlier; it has remained in use. Djāwa means not only the Javanese, but also the linguistically related people from the other islands, including the Philippines, and even the linguistically non-related peoples from the South-East Asian mainland. Generally well-to-do and pious, the Djāwa were welcome guests in Mecca, especially since they were less parsimonious than the pilgrims from various other countries and therefore more apt to provide the *shaykh*s concerned with pilgrims with an easy income. Snouck Hurgronje took a particular interest in those Djāwa who came from the Netherlands Indies; to this circumstance we owe the valuable sociological treatise on the Djāwa group in Mecca in *Mekka*, ii, *Aus dem heutigen Leben*, The Hague 1889, ch. iv. The whole pattern of Djāwī life, *e.g.*, their behaviour in their unfamiliar surroundings, how they spent their time in case of a prolonged sojourn, how they reacted upon international and pan-Islamic influences, is discussed here brilliantly and in a very illuminating way. This picture, however, needs to be completed by Snouck Hurgronje's later studies of Islam in Indonesia [*q.v.*], and it is now of historical interest only owing to the considerable change in conditions both in Mecca and in South-East Asia. (C. C. Berg)

DJĀWĪD, Young Turk economist and statesman. Meḥmed Djāwīd was born in 1875 in Salonika, where his father was a merchant, and received his early education both there and in Istanbul. He graduated from the *Mülkiyye* in 1896, where he formed a lasting friendship with his classmate Hüseyin Djāhid [Yalçin], the journalist. After a brief tour of duty with the Agricultural Bank, he entered the service of the Ministry of Education, resigning in 1902 as secretary of the bureau of primary education. Back in Salonika he became director of a private elementary school, *Mekteb-i Tefeyyüz*, and joined the *ʿOthmanlî Ittiḥād we Teraḳḳī Djemʿiyyeti*, the Macedonian nucleus of the Young Turk conspiracy against the despotism of ʿAbd al-Ḥamīd II. In 1908 he became lecturer in economics and statistics at the *Mülkiyye*. During this period in Salonika and Istanbul he published several textbooks on economics (*ʿIlm-i iḳtiṣād*, 4 vols., 1905, ²1912; *Inshāʾiyyāt*, 1909; and *Mekātib-i iʿdādiyyeye makhṣūṣ ʿilm-i iḳtiṣād*, 1909, ²1913) and, together with Aḥmed Shuʿayb and Riḍa Tewfīḳ [Bölükbaşi], edited a learned journal called *ʿUlūm-u Iḳtiṣādiyye ve Idjtimāʿiyye Medjmūʿasî* (1909-11). Following the 1908 revolution he was elected a deputy for Salonika (1908-12) and Bīgha (Çanakkale, 1912-8), and became minister of finance (1910, 1913-4, 1917-8), and a member of the general assembly (*medjlis-i ʿumūmī*) of the Union and Progress (*Ittiḥād we Teraḳḳī*) party (1916-8). In the Chamber of Deputies he soon distinguished himself as an eloquent orator and a competent rapporteur of the Budget Commission. During his years as finance minister he conducted delicate negotiations in Paris and other European capitals for public loans to the Ottoman Empire. Together with a number of other ministers he resigned from the cabinet after Turkey's entry into the war, in opposition to the Germanophile policy of Enwer Pasha; later he re-entered it on the plea of Ṭalʿat Pasha. He was the only wartime Young Turk minister to retain his position in the ʿIzzet Pasha cabinet (14 October to 14 November 1918). Subsequently he went into hiding and exile to escape the wave of prosecution of Union and Progress leaders; in July 1919 an Istanbul tribunal sentenced him *in absentia* to 15 years' hard labour. In 1920 he married ʿAliyye, divorced wife of Burhān al-Dīn, son of the late ʿAbd al-Ḥamīd II.

Djāwīd returned to Istanbul in 1922, where he acted as representative of the Ottoman creditors of the *Dette publique ottomane*. According to Halide Edib, *The Turkish Ordeal*, London 1928, 74, Mustafa Kemal rejected Djāwīd's suggestion that he be allowed to join the Anatolian movement. In 1923 he served as an adviser to the Turkish delegation to the Lausanne peace conference. He was arrested following the 1926 assassination attempt on Mustafa Kemal [Atatürk], and tried before the special Independence tribunal in Izmir (6 July) and Ankara (10 August) on charges of having conspired to resuscitate the Union and Progress movement and thereby to subvert the regime. Much of the questioning turned around a meeting of former Union and Progress leaders held in Djāwīd's house in Instabul on 16 April 1923; yet no specific or overt acts of high treason were alleged or proved against him. Together with three other ex-Unionist leaders he was sentenced to death and executed by hanging in the Djebedji quarter of Ankara on 26 August 1926.

Bibliography: Djāwīd, Memoirs, *Tanin*, 30 August 1943 to 22 December 1946; *Türk Ansiklopedisi*, x, 37-8; Ibrahim Alâettin Gövsa, *Türk meşhurlar ansiklopedisi*, Istanbul 1946, 79; Ali Çankaya, *Mülkiye ve mülkiyeliler*, Ankara 1954, ii, 332 f.; Ali Fuat Türkgeldi, *Görüp işittiklerim*[2], Ankara 1951, 117; *Harp kabinelerinin isticvabı*, Istanbul: Vakıt Matbaası, 1933; Kandemir, *İzmir suikastının içyüzü* (Ekicigil Tarih Yayınları), Ankara 1955, ii, 29-49.

(Dankwart A. Rustow)

DJĀWĪDĀN [see supplement].

DJAWKĀN [see čawgān].

al-**DJAWLĀN**, a district in southern Syria bounded on the west by the Jordan, on the north by the spurs of Hermon, on the east by the Nahr al-ʿAllān and on the south by the Yarmūk. The northern part lies at a certain altitude and presents the appearance of a wild, hilly region, covered with blocks of lava and oak forests which were once magnificent but are now extremely impoverished. The southern part is fairly low-lying and differs but little from the plain of Ḥawrān, with a soil of volcanic detritus, more even and of greater fertility.

The territory of Djawlān corresponds with the ancient Gaulanitis of the Hellenistic period, which probably took its name from the town of Golan mentioned in the Old Testament. But it appears to have dwindled with time. At one period, continuing into the early days of Islam, this province included the country lying to the east of Nahr al-ʿAllān, which can be inferred from the existence of places called Djābiyat al-Djawlān and Saḥm al-Djawlān beyond that boundary. It was the latter village, which still keeps the same name, that Schumacher thought to be identified with the ancient Ǧōlān. A distinction may have been made later, from the 7th/13th century, between Djawlān and Djaydūr where Yāḳūt places al-Djābiya [*q.v.*].

Djawlān, which during the Byzantine period belonged to Palestina Secunda and which had then been one of the centres of power of the Ghassānids (Nābigha, ed. Derenbourg, iv, 4; xxiv, 25, 29; Ḥassān b. Thābit, ed. Hirschfeld, index) was conquered by Shuraḥbīl when he occupied Urdunn, but was later restored to the province of Damascus (al-Ṭabarī, iii, 84) and, according to al-Muḳaddasī, formed one of its six districts. Its capital was originally Bāniyās [*q.v.*] which still held that position in the Mamlūk period but which in modern times was replaced by Ḳunaytra, situated on the important road between Damascus and Tiberias. The population, which previously consisted mostly of Banū Murra, now forms an ethnic and linguistic mosaic in which Druzes and *mutāwila* Shīʿis who have settled at the foot of Hermon live side by side with Čerkes and Turkoman colonies and various nomadic tribes who are turning to a sedentary life. It has always been praised for the richness of its agricultural produce which served to supply Damascus and today still forms the main resource of the region.

Bibliography: Balādhurī, *Futūḥ*, 116; *BGA*, indices; Schumacher, *Across the Jordan*, London 1886, 91-9; idem, *Der Dscholan*, in *ZDPV*, xi (1886), 165-368, and xxii (1899), 178-88; R. Dussaud, *Topographie historique de la Syrie*, Paris 1927, particularly 343-4 and 381 ff.; F. M. Abel, *Géographie de la Palestine*, Paris 1938, 338-9; J. Cantineau, *Les parlers arabes du Horân*, Paris 1946, 4.

(D. Sourdel)

DJAWNPUR (Jaunpur), city on the Gumtī in Uttar Pradesh, north India, lat. 25° 48′ N., long. 82° 42′ E., and the surrounding district. The city was founded in 760/1359 by Fīrūz Shāh Tughluḳ [*q.v.*], near the ancient Manāyč reduced by Maḥmūd of Ghazni in 409/1018 and renamed Ẓafarābād by Ẓafar Khān, its governor under Ghiyāth al-Dīn Tughluḳ after 721/1321. Muslim historians derive the name Djawnpur from Djawna Shāh, Muḥammad b. Tughluḳ's title before his accession; but Djamanpur is known as a by-form of the name (? connexion with Djawn = Djamnā, [*q.v.*]; Skt. *Yamunendrapura* has been suggested as the etymon), and this origin cannot be regarded as established.

In the confused conditions at the beginning of the reign of Nāṣir al-Dīn Maḥmūd Tughluḳ [see dihlī sultanate] the disaffected Hindūs of the eastern provinces rejected all obedience to Dihlī. The eunuch Malik Sarwar, Khʷādja Djahān, persuaded Maḥmūd to grant him the title of Sulṭān al-Sharḳ and send him to crush the rebellion in 796/1394; having brought under control Koyl, Eṭāwā and Kanawdj he occupied Djawnpur, and there established himself as independent ruler of a kingdom extending over Awadh, west to Koyl and east into Tirhut and Bihār; to these lands were later added the Čunār district of Uṛīsā (857/1453) and Rohilkhanḍ (870/1466). For the history of this kingdom see sharḳids. In 884/1479 Bahlōl, the first Lōdī sultan of Dihlī, defeated the last Sharḳī sultan, Ḥusayn, and established his son Bārbak as ruler over Djawnpur with permission to use the royal title and to issue coin. After Sikandar overcame his brother Bārbak as sultan of Dihlī in 894/1489 Djawnpur was absorbed in the Dihlī empire.

In 933/1526-7 Djawnpur was taken for his father Bābur by Humāyūn, and a governor was appointed; but the growth of the power of Shīr Khān (Shīr Shāh Sūrī, [*q.v.*]) and the disaffection of the Afghān faction on the death of Djunayd Birlās, the governor, compelled Humāyūn to march again on Djawnpur in 943/1536, with success; but Humāyūn's long absence from Dihlī lost him his hold on the eastern provinces, and even before his great victory of Muḥarram 947/May 1540 Shīr Shāh was in command, with his son ʿĀdil Khān installed as viceroy in Djawnpur. The importance of Djawnpur declined with the rise of Čunār, and not until the rebellion (970/1563 onwards) of ʿAlī Ḳulī Khān, governor since 965/1558, does it again come into prominence; ʿAlī's final defeat in Dhu 'l Ḥidjdja 974/June 1567 led to Akbar's temporary residence there and the governorship of Khān-i Khānān Muḥammad Munʿim Khān. After the foundation of Allāhābād [*q.v.*] the importance of Djawnpur waned; it passed into the possession of the Nawwābs of Awadh in the early 12th/18th century, and into British hands in 1775.

Djawnpur was long celebrated for its learning, "the Shirāz of Hind", from its foundation by Fīrūz certainly until the time of Shīr Shāh; some of its rulers—notably Ibrāhīm and Ḥusayn—were cultured connoisseurs of more than mere scholastic learning; Ḳurʾān schools still exist within the precincts of the mosques.

Monuments. The fort of Fīrūz Shāh, an irregular quadrilateral on the north bank of the Gumtī, is of high stone walls built largely from local temple spoil, with a single gateway protected by tapering semicircular bastions; other bastions were destroyed in 1859 by the British, as were some of the

Čihil Satūn (destroyed 1858).
(Markham Kittoe, *Illustrations of Indian architecture from the Muhammadan conquest* ..., Calcutta 1838)

D̲j̲āmiʿ masd̲j̲id.
(T. and W. Daniell, *Oriental scenery*, 3rd series, London 1801-3: "A mosque at Juanpore")

internal buildings, including the palace built by Fīrūz Shāh's governor, the Čihil Sutūn (Plate I). The fort mosque of the same governor, Ibrāhīm Nā'ib Bārbak, still stands: the side *līwān*s are low, trabeate, supported on rows of pillars from Hindū temples set up at random; there are many additions of later periods (illustration in Kittoe, see *Bibl.*); a detached *mīnār* in the court-yard, some 12 m. high, has a fine Arabic inscription giving its date as Dhu 'l-Ḳa'da 778/March-April 1377. A small detached pillar within the fort proclaims an edict of Āṣaf al-Dawla of Awadh on the continuance of the daily stipend to indigent sayyids (*sādāt bī-nawā*) from the revenues of Djawnpur (1180/1766).

The Aṭalā mosque, whose foundations were prepared on the site of the Hindū temple to Aṭalā Devī by Fīrūz Shāh Tughluḳ, was not built until 810/1408 under Ibrāhīm Sharḳī; its main feature, the central bay of the west *līwān* covered by a large dome which is concealed from the court-yard by a tall pyramidal gateway resembling the Egyptian propylon, is the special characteristic of the Djawnpur style under the Sharḳī sultans. The Aṭalā mosque is the largest (78.7 m. square) and most ornate: the *līwān*s on north, east and south are composed of five pillared aisles in two storeys, the two outer aisles at ground level being formed into a range of pillared cells facing the streets; in the middle of each side is an archway, with a smaller propylon on the outside, and with domes over the north and south gates; a dome covers the central bay of each *līwān* on the north and south of the main dome, each with its propylon facing the court-yard. Within each propylon is a large arched recess, with a fringe of stylized spear-heads similar to those of the Khaldjī buildings at Dihlī [*q.v.*], in which are pierced arched openings in front of the dome, and the main entrances beneath. The main propylon is 22.9 m. high, the dome behind being only 19.5 m., and 16.8 m. wide at its base. The dome is supported on a sixteen-sided arched triforium, on corner brackets over an octagon with pierced windows, supported on squinch arches. The *ḳibla* wall is relieved on its exterior by square projections behind each dome, the corners of each supported by a tapering buttress; larger tapering buttresses support the main angles of the wall. There are no *mīnār*s, the top storeys of the propylon serving for the *mu'adhdhin*.

The masdjid Khāliṣ Mukhliṣ, built by two governors of Ibrāhīm, is of the same period, only the central propylon and dome and western *līwān*s remaining, all massive and without ornament. Of the contemporary Djhandjharī (*djhandjhar* "perforated") mosque only the screen of the central propylon remains, filled with the finest stone tracery in Djawnpur. The Lāl darwāza ("red gate"; near the gate of a former palace) mosque in the north-west of the city, the smallest of the Djawnpur mosques, was built c. 851/1447, the sole surviving monument of the reign of Maḥmūd Sharḳī, has a single central dome and propylon with tall trabeate transepts, and *zanāna* galleries on a mezzanine floor flanking the central bay. The foundation of the Djāmi' masdjid (Plate II) was laid in 842/1438, but it was not finished until the reign of Ḥusayn. The mosque stands on a raised terrace 5 to 6 m. above street level, with a single propylon in the west *līwān*, the transepts covered by fine barrel-vaults, and the façade entirely arcuate. These are the only remains of the Sharḳīs standing at Djawnpur, the rest having been demolished by Sikandar Lōdī; all are of stone, largely pillaged from Hindū or Buddhist temples, and cement, the work of Hindū craftsmen. Echoes of the characteristic style of the capital occur in other places within the quondam Djawnpur kingdom, in the Aṙha'ī Kangura masdjid at Banāras (Benares), and in the Djāmi' masdjids at Eṭāwā and Kanawdj [*qq.v.*].

By far the most significant monument of Mughal times is the great bridge of Mun'im Khān, begun 972/1564 and finished 976/1568. Built by Afghān workmen under a Kābul architect, Afḍal 'Alī, it consists of ten spans of arches—the four central ones of wider span than those at each end—the very massive piers of which carry pillared and screened pavilions at road level, partly projecting over the water on brackets; a further five spans carry the road over a smaller branch of the Gumtī.

In the old town of Ẓafarābād, 6.5 km. south-east of Djawnpur, is the mosque of one Shaykh Bārha, converted c. 711/1311 from Buddhist temple remains, entirely trabeate though originally with a large central arch between two piers which was probably the prototype of the propylons of the Djawnpur mosques. There are also many tombs, the most noteworthy being those of Makhdūm Ṣāḥib Čirāgh-i Hind (781/1389) and Sayyid Murtaḍā in the *dargāh-i shahād*, the burial ground of the martyrs who fell in the invasion of Shihāb al-Dīn Shūrī in 590/1194.

Bibliography: Khayr al-Dīn Muḥammad Ilāhābādī, *Djawnpūr-nāma*, ed. Djawnpur n.d., a late 18th century work which makes much use of the *Ta'rīkh-i Firishta* and Baranī's *Ta'rīkh-i Fīrūz Shāhī*, but is not entirely derivative; Eng.tr. R. W. Pogson, Calcutta 1814; for the monuments: A. Cunningham, *ASI* xi, Calcutta 1880, 102-26; A. Führer, *The Sharqi architecture of Jaunpur* (architectural drawings by E. W. Smith), *ASI*, NIS xi, Calcutta 1889: text very turgid; J. Fergusson, *History of Indian and eastern architecture*, London 1876, 522 ff. Illustrations of some buildings not available elsewhere in Markham Kittoe, *Illustrations of Indian architecture from the Muhammadan conquest* ..., Calcutta 1838. A new monograph on Djawnpur is badly needed.

(J. Burton-Page)

AL-DJAWNPŪRĪ, Sayyid Muḥammad al-Kāẓimī al-Ḥusaynī b. Sayyid Khān alias Baḍḍh Uwaysī (cf. *Ā'īn-i Akbarī*, Bibl. Ind., ii, 241) and Bībī Āḳā Malik, the pseudo-Mahdī [*q.v.*], was born at Djawnpur [*q.v.*] on Monday, 14 Djumādā I 847/10 September 1443. None of the contemporary sources mentions the names of his parents as 'Abd Allāh and Āmina, as claimed by the Mahdawī sources (*e.g.*, *Sirādj al-Abṣār*, see Bibliography), in an obvious attempt to identify them with the names of the Prophet's parents so that the prediction made in the *aḥādīth al-Mahdī* (cf. Ibn Taymiyya, *Minhādj al-Sunna*, Cairo 1321/1903, ii, 133) might fit his case. The *Tuḥfat al-kirām* of 'Alī Shīr Ḳāni' and the *Djawnpūrnāma* of Khayr al-Dīn Ilāhābādī, which mention these names, are much later compilations and therefore not reliable.

A precocious child, gifted with an extraordinary memory, he committed the Ḳur'ān to memory at the early age of seven and received the title, according to Mahdawī sources, of Asad al-'Ulamā' at the age of twelve from his teacher Shaykh Dāniyāl Čishtī. At the age of forty he left Djawnpur for Mecca and, after visiting a number of places *en route* such as Dānāpur, Kālpī, Čandērī, Djāpānīr, Māndū, Burhānpur, Dawlatābād, Aḥmadnagar and Bīdar, reached there in 901/1495. During his stay at Mecca, one day while performing the *ṭawāf*, [*q.v.*], he suddenly announced that he was the promised

Mahdī. He was not taken seriously by the Meccan *ʿulamāʾ*, who simply ignored his claim. He returned to Gudjarāt the following year. While at Aḥmadābād he came into conflict for the first time in 903/1497 with orthodox *ʿulamāʾ*, who challenged his assertion that God could be seen with physical eyes. Finding the atmosphere hostile, he left Aḥmadābād and in 905/1499 reasserted his claim to being the Mahdī at a small place called Baṙhlī near Paṫan.

The same year he wrote to some of the independent rulers about his mission inviting them either to accept him as the Mahdī or condemn him to death if he was proved to be an impostor. Of these, according to Mahdawī sources, Ghiyāth al-Dīn Khaldjī of Mālwa, Maḥmūd Bēgṙā of Gudjarāt, Aḥmad Niẓām Shāh of Aḥmadnagar, Shāh Bēg of Ḳandahār and Mīr Dhu' l-Nūn of Farāh accepted his claim. This, however, failed to impress the *ʿulamāʾ*, and the majority of the people continued to regard him as an impostor. The *ʿulamāʾ*, finding his influence growing among the masses and unable to counteract or stem it, demanded his banishment. Hounded from place to place and unable to convince the leading *ʿulamāʾ* of the validity of his claim, he ultimately came to Farāh [*q.v.*] in Khurāsān and died there on Thursday 19 Dhu 'l-Ḳaʿda 910/23 April 1505. Monday, as claimed by the Mahdawī sources to be the day on which he died in order to make it tally with the day of his birth, is definitely to be discarded, as Dhu 'l-Ḳaʿda 910 began on a Sunday. His shrine in Farāh is still visited by his followers who are mainly concentrated in certain places in South India.

After his death he was succeeded in his spiritual heritage, in imitation of the Prophet, by a number of his *Khulafāʾ*, the first being his son Sayyid Maḥmūd. By this time the Mahdawīs had established a number of centres called *dāʾira*s, mostly in Gudjarāt, where they lived a communal life, dealing only among themselves and shunning the rest of the population who were regarded as unbelievers. Their growing popularity was interpreted as a danger to the State and society, leading to the persecution of the Mahdawīs. They were accused of heresy and their leader, Sayyid Maḥmūd, was put into prison where he died in 918/1512, unable to bear the rigours of incarceration. His successor, Khʷānd Mīr, faced still harder times when the *ʿulamāʾ* of Gudjarāt declared it permissible to kill a Mahdawī. Consequently a pitched battle was fought between the Mahdawīs and the Gudjarāt troops at Sadrāsan in Shawwāl 930/August 1524 in which Khʷānd Mīr, along with a large number of his followers, was killed. In spite of these reverses and the mounting opposition of the *ʿulamāʾ* and the masses, the movement did not completely die out. Among historical personalities who suffered in the cause of the movement are Shaykh ʿAbd Allāh Niyāzī, who flourished during the reign of Islām Shāh Sūr, his disciple, Shaykh ʿAlāʾī and Miyāṇ Musṭafā Gudjarātī, a very learned man of his times who ably argued his case with the *ʿulamāʾ* of the Court of Akbar but failed to convince them. After his death in 983/1575-6, while on his way from Fatḥpur Sīkrī to Gudjarāt, the movement withered and collapsed.

The piety, learning and sincerity of Sayyid Muḥammad convinced even a severe critic like ʿAbd al-Ḳādir al-Badāʾūnī, who regards him as one of the greatest of the *awliyāʾ*. Like most of the *ṣūfī shaykh*s who lay stress on the renunciation of the world (*tark al-dunyā*), seclusion from the people (*ʿuzla ʿan al-khalḳ*), *tawakkul*, associating with righteous people, Sayyid Muḥammad bade his followers to remain constantly absorbed in *dhikr*, which he raised to the level of an article of faith with them. Great importance was also attached to *hidjra* and here again the founder himself set the example in imitation of the *Hidjra* of the Prophet. Although the Mahdawīs abjured politics, their activities compelled the authorities to act. Consequently, ʿAbd Allāh Niyāzī, his piety notwithstanding, was severely punished, and Shaykh ʿAlāʾī, his disciple, lost his life. *Sawiyat*, which the Mahdawīs interpret as the equal distribution of wealth, material possessions and whatever comes to or is acquired by the community, among its members living within a particular *dāʾira*, is the cardinal point of the teachings of Sayyid Muḥammad, who also denounced capitalism, stockpiling and hoarding as utterly un-Islamic. The failure of the movement, on a deeper analysis, can be attributed to the aloofness of its adherents from the main body of the Muslims, their insistence on the recognition of the founder as the promised Mahdī and the consequent opposition of the *ʿulamāʾ* and the State. Lack of capable leadership in the North and the subsequent involvement of its adherents in politics in the Deccan hastened the decline of the movement which had, in its heyday, fired the Indian Muslim community with a new zeal and religious fervour. At the present day pockets of Mahdawīs exist in the former Ḥaydarābād State (India), Mysore, Djaypur and Gudjarāt. In Pakistan, at Shahdādpūr in Sind, they have established a *dāʾira* after their migration from India.

ʿAlī al-Muttaḳī (d. 975/1567), the author of *Kanz al-ʿummāl* and ʿAlī al-Ḳārī (d. 1016/1607) took serious notice of the movement and wrote *al-Burhān fī ʿalāmāt Mahdī ākhir al-zamān* and *Risālat al-Mahdī* respectively in which they forcefully rebutted the claim of Sayyid Muḥammad to being the promised Mahdī. ʿAlī al-Muttaḳī followed *al-Burhān* by his *Risālat al-radd*, which aroused considerable opposition among the Mahdawīs and has been the subject of criticism in a number of Mahdawī works in vindication of their faith. Asʿad al-Makkī (see Raḥmān ʿAlī, *Tadhkira-i ʿulamāʾ-i Hind*, 178) also wrote his *Shuhub muḥriḳa* on the same subject. An Indian writer, Abū Ridjāʾ Muḥammad Zamān Khān of Shāhdjahānpūr, who strongly criticized the Mahdawīs and the founder of the movement, fell in 1872 to the knife of an assassin for his polemic work *Hadya Mahdawiyya* (ed. Baroda 1287/1870, Kānpur 1293/1876).

Bibliography: ʿAbd al-Ḳādir al-Badāʾūnī, *Muntakhab al-tawārīkh* (Bib. Ind.), ii 319; idem, *Nadjāt al-rashīd* (MS. Asafiyya no. 1564), a near-contemporary and very detailed account of Sayyid Muḥammad and his movement; Abu 'l-Faḍl, *Āʾīn-i Akbarī* (Bib. Ind.) ii 241, English translation, H. Blochmann, Calcutta 1873, Intro. iv-v; Sikandar Mandjhū b. Muḥammad, *Mirʾat-i Sikandarī* (Eng. trans. Fazlullah Lutfullah Faridi), 90-1; ʿAlī Shīr Ḳāniʿ, *Tuḥfat al-kirām*, Lucknow 1304/1886-7, ii, 22 ff.; Ashraf ʿAlī Pālanpūrī, *Siyar-i Masʿūd*, Murādābād 1315/1897-8, 7 ff.; ʿAbd al-Malik al-Sadjāwandī, *Sirādj al-abṣār* (with a voluminous introduction and Urdū translation by S. Musṭafā Tashrīf Allāhī), Ḥaydarābād (Dn.) 1365 (this work contains, in the beginning, a very comprehensive and detailed bibliography); Shāh ʿAbd al-Raḥmān, *Mawlūd* (MS. in Persian); Sayyid Yūsuf, *Maṭlaʿ al-wilāyat* (MS.); Shāh Burhān al-Dīn, *Shawāhid al-wilāyat*, Ḥaydarābād 1379 (a first-hand complete biography of the

Sayyid, very rich in detail); Walī b. Yūsuf, *Inṣāf nāma*, Ḥaydarābād 1367; ʿAbd al-Rashīd, *Naḳliyyāt*, Ḥaydarābād 1369; S. Athar ʿAbbās Rizvī in *Medieval India*, ʿAlīgaṙh 1954 ("*The Mahdavi movement in India*"); Abu 'l-Kalām Āzād, *Tadhkira*[3], Lahore 1960, 39-44, 52 ff.; Khayr al-Dīn Muḥammad Ilāhābādī, *Djawnpūrnāma*, Djawnpur 1878; D. S. Margoliouth, *On Mahdis and Mahdism*, London 1916; Maḥmūd Shīrānī in *Oriental College Magazine*, Lahore, Nov. 1940; Muḥammad Maʿṣūm Bhakkarī, *Taʾrīkh-i Sind*, Poona 1938, index; ʿAbd al-Ḥaḳḳ Muḥaddith Dihlawī, *Akhbār al-akhyār*, s.v. Muḥammad b. Yūsuf; idem, *Zād al-muttaḳīn* (MS.); Samsām al-Dawla Shāh Nawāz Khān, *Maʾāthir al-umarāʾ*, (Bib. Ind.) i, 124 ff.; I. Goldziher, *Vorlesungen*[2], 364; idem, *Ghair Mahdi* in *ERE*, vi, 189; *Bombay Gazetteer*, Bombay 1899, ix/2, 62; Djaʿfar Sharīf, *Qanoon-e-Islam*[2], Oxford 1921, 208-9; Sayyid Walī, *Sawāniḥ Mahdī Mawʿūd* (not available to me); Miyān Muṣṭafā Gudjarātī, *Makātīb* (MS.); Sayyid Shah Muḥammad, *Khatm al-hudā subul al-sawā*, Bangalore 1291; ʿAbd al-Ḥayy Lakhnawī, *Nuzhat al-khawāṭir*, iv, Ḥaydarābād, s.v. Muḥammad b. Yūsuf; apparently follows the notice in *Akhbār al-akhyār* where the copyist seems to have read Yūsuf for Sayyid Khān written in *shikasta* style; Muḥammad Sulaymān, *Khātam-i Sulaymānī* (still in MS.); ʿAbd Allāh Muḥammad b. ʿUmar al-Makkī, *Ẓafar al-wālih bi Muẓaffar wa ālih*, (ed. Denison Ross), 35-6; ʿAbd al-Ḳādir b. Aḥmad, *Maʿdan al-djawāhir*, Ḥaydarābād 1304, 98 ff., 161; Firishta, *Gulshan-i Ibrāhīmī*, Kānpur 1874, ii, 150; Khʷānd Mīr, *ʿAḳīda-i sharīfa* (MS.), an important Mahdawī source as it is the work of the son-in-law of Sayyid Muḥammad; ʿAbd al-Ghanī Rāmpūrī, *Madhāhib al-Islām*, Kānpur 1924, 713 ff.; Raḥmān ʿAlī, *Tadhkira-i ʿulamāʾ-i Hind*, Lucknow 1332/1914, 197-201; ʿAlī al-Muttaḳī, *al-Burhān fī ʿalāmāt Mahdī ākhir al-zāman*, (MS.) Asafiyya no. 968); idem, *Risālat al-Radd* (MS.) extensively quoted in *Sirādj al-abṣār*; ʿAli al-Ḳāri, *Risālat al-Mahdī* (MS. Saʾīdiyya, Ḥaydarābād (*ʿaḳāʾid wa kalām* no. 65); idem, *Mirḳāt* (ed. Cairo), v, 183 ff; Niẓām al-Dīn Aḥmad Bakhshī, *Ṭabaḳāt-i Akbarī* (Bib. Ind.), index; W. A. Erskine, *A history of India under the first two sovereigns of the House of Taimur*, London 1854, ii, 475 ff.; *Beloochistan Gazetteer* (s.v. *Zikris*); Sayyid Gulāb Miyāṇ, *Taʾrīkh-i Pālanpūr*; Sayyid ʿĪsā, *Maʿāriḍ al-riwāyāt*, Bangalore 1283; idem, *Shubhāt al-fatāwā*, Bangalore 1283 (both in refutation of *Risālat al-Radd*); anon., *Ḥālāt-i Sayyid Muḥammad-i Djawnpūrī*, MS. Asafiyya, ii, no. 34; anon., *Intikhāb-i tawārīkh al-Aghyār*, MS. Peshāwar no, 1549. See also MAHDAWĪ, MAHDĪ.

(A. S. BAZMEE ANSARI)

AL-**DJAWWĀNĪ**, ABŪ ʿALĪ MUḤAMMAD B. ASʿAD, Arab genealogist and historian, b. 525/1131, d. 588/1192. The Djawwānī family claimed ʿAlid descent through a son of ʿUbayd Allāh b. al-Ḥusayn b. ʿAlī b. al-Ḥusayn b. ʿAlī b. Abī Ṭālib. This pedigree was well established at least as early as the first half of the 4th/10th century when Abu 'l-Faradj al-Iṣfahānī (*Maḳātil al-Ṭālibiyyīn*, Cairo 1368/1949, 193, 435, 438) reported historical information received by him personally from ʿAlī b. Ibrāhīm al-Djawwānī, himself a genealogist and the eighth lineal ancestor of our Djawwānī. The latter was born and educated in Egypt. He taught *ḥadīth* there as well as in Damascus and Aleppo. At one time, he was appointed ʿAlid Chief of Egypt, apparently by Shīrkūh or Ṣalāḥ al-Dīn in the late 1160s. It seems that he did not hold this position very long. His main love and occupation were his genealogical and historical studies. They may have compensated him for the pain he must have felt in witnessing the decay of the power of the Fāṭimids whose fame, it seems, had attracted his family to Egypt. However, he continued to enjoy the favor of the Ayyūbids to whom he dedicated some of his works. Ṣalāḥ al-Dīn is said to have granted al-Djawwāniyya, the estate near Medina after which his family was named, to him as a fief.

A list of his works from al-Maḳrīzī's *Muḳaffā* mentions eighteen titles, some of them large works. They deal with ʿAlid genealogy, including a history of the Djawwānī family, a study of his father's pedigree, and works on Ṭālibid biographies, Ṭālibid genealogists, the Banu 'l-Arḳaṭ, and the Idrīsids. He also wrote genealogical and historical works of a more general nature, among them works on the praiseworthy qualities of the *ʿashara* (*al-mubashshara*, [*q.v.*]), on those who, like al-ʿĀdil, had the *kunya* Abū Bakr, and on Arabic tribes (*al-Djawhar al-maknūn fī dhikr al-ḳabāʾil wa 'l-buṭūn*). The last work, as well as a topographical work on Egypt (*al-Nuḳaṭ ʿala 'l-khiṭaṭ*) and a monograph on the sanctuary of Sayyida Nafīsa, are also known from quotations in al-Maḳrīzī's *Khiṭaṭ* (the *Djawhar* is also cited in Ibn al-ʿAdīm's *Bughya*). These quotations tend to confirm al-Djawwānī's considerable stature as a scholar, although even in his case orthodox scholars could not entirely suppress their customary suspicion of the veracity of Shīʿī genealogists.

Manuscripts of only two works by al-Djawwānī appear to have been signalized so far. One of them, on the genealogy and history of the Prophet and the people in his life, is dedicated to al-Ḳāḍī al-Fāḍil and entitled *al-Tuḥfa al-sharīfa* (Berlin 9511, Paris 2010, 4798, Topkapusaray Ahmet III, 2759, Cairo[2], v, 129 f., Sohag 315 taʾrīkh). The other, on tribal genealogy, is called *al-Tuḥfa al-ẓarīfa* or *Uṣūl al-aḥsāb wa-fuṣūl al-ansāb* (Paris 4798, Cairo[2], v, 30 f.). Al-Maḳrīzī's list does not include any exactly corresponding titles, but the second work may correspond either to *Tādj al-ansāb wa-minhādj al-ṣawāb* or to *Tadhkirat uli 'l-albāb li-uṣūl al-ansāb*.

Bibliography: Ibn al-Ṣābūnī, *Takmilat Ikmāl al-ikmāl*, Baghdād 1377/1957, 83, 99-104, 189, 299. The editor, Muṣṭafā Djawād, adds detailed information on other sources, to wit: al-ʿImād al-Iṣfahānī, *Kharīda* (on Egyptian poets), Cairo, n.d. (1951), 117 ff.; al-Ḳifṭī, *al-Muḥammadūn min al-shuʿarāʾ*, and *Inbāh*; Yāḳūt, ii, 137; al-Dhahabī, *Taʾrīkh al-Islām*, *anno* 588; al-Ṣafadī, *Wāfī*, ii, 202; Ibn Ḥadjar, *Lisān*, v, 74 ff. (containing references to other sources at present unavailable); Ibn ʿInaba (ʿUtba), *ʿUmdat al-ṭālib*, 212, 285. Cf., further, C. H. Becker, *Beiträge zur Geschichte Ägyptens*, Strasburg, 1902, 26 ff.; Brockelmann, I, 451 f., S I, 626; *Fihrist al-makhṭūṭāt al-muṣawwara*, ii/1, Cairo n.d. (1954), 83.

(F. ROSENTHAL)

AL-**DJAWZĀʾ** [see NUDJŪM].

AL-**DJAWZAHAR** or AL-DJAWZAHR, technical term occurring in Arabic and Persian astrological and astronomical texts.

1. It indicates primarily the two lunar nodes, *al-ʿuḳdatāni*, *i.e.*, the two diametrically opposite points of intersection between the moon's orbit and the ecliptic: the ascending node or "head", *raʾs*, and the descending node or "tail", *dhanab* (*scil.* of the

dragon, *al-tinnīn*). In many cases it refers only to the "head"; in some mss. a special word, *nawbahr*, is used for the "tail" [see below].

The word Djawzahar, though explained differently in the *Mafātīḥ al-ʿulūm*, clearly derives from the Avestan *gao-čithra* (= Pahlawī *gočihr* = mod. Persian *gawzahr*), an (adjectival) epithet of the Moon meaning "forming the origin of the bull" (Bartholomae) or rather "preserving the *sperma bovis*". In the *Bundahishn*, *gočihr*, together with the tailed (*dumbōmand*) *mūsh-parīk*, on one occasion appears as an antagonist of the sun and the moon, while, on another, it is said to have "placed itself in the centre of the heaven, in the shape of a serpent (*mār*, 'draco')".

The complicated semasiological development of the word and its various functions in mythology and early astrology can be understood only when seen in connexion with the myth of the eclipse monster (dragon), of wide distribution all over the Eurasian continent, and in particular the Indian Rāhu myth: There the demon Rāhu, immortalized by the forbidden *amṛta* drink, from which he had sipped, is beheaded by Vishnu; but his two parts, the head (Rāhu) and the tail (thenceforth called Ketu), having become stellified, incessantly try to devour the Sun and the Moon so as to take revenge for their having denounced Rāhu's crime to Vishnu. Thus Rāhu and Ketu are both identified with the eclipse monster, but the latter also appears at irregular intervals in the shape of a comet (*dhūmaketu*, "smoke-*ketu*"; see also art. KAYD, under which name the cometary aspect of the Indian *Ketu* has survived in Islamic astrology).

In the later, "scientific" (*i.e.*, computing) phase of astrology, in India, Rāhu was identified with the ascending, and Ketu, with the descending, node, in view of the fact that eclipses can occur only when the two luminaries stand sufficiently near the nodes. In Arabic it is undoubtedly owing above all to Indian influence that the Gr. terms ὁ ἀναβιβάζων and ὁ καταβιβάζων (scil. σύνδεσμος) as found in the Almagest were replaced by *al-raʾs* and *al-dhanab*; in particular, the synonym of *al-dhanab*: *nawbahr*, "the new part", clearly betrays its relationship with Ketu. As for the eclipse monster, the Djawzahar, it is regarded as a giant serpent or dragon (*tinnīn*); for its representation in Near Eastern art, see Hartner, *opp. cit.* below; for its appearance in Western art, see also Kühnel, *op. cit.* below. As indicated above, the *Bundahishn* identifies the *gočihr* with the constellation of the Dragon, which stands in fact "in the centre of the heaven", near the pole of the ecliptic; but in the same context it is said that it "retrogrades in such a way that after 10 years the head takes the place of the tail, and the tail that of the head". This applies of course not to the immovable constellation but to the Djawzahar joining the two nodes, because these make indeed a complete retrograde revolution in the course of 18.6 years (of which one-half is approximately 10). The circumstance that the nodes have a constant motion, again, gave rise to the astrologers' conceiving of, and treating them as invisible planets ("pseudo-planets"): they attributed to them "exaltations" (*ashrāf*), viz. Gemini to the head, and Sagittarius to the tail, and counted them among the maleficent stars. In European horoscopes, the Djawzahar is always called *Caput et Cauda* (Draconis), and Latin transliterations of the term itself, though sometimes occurring, have not become common. Ephemerides for the Djawzahar are contained in all astronomical tables; they serve of course not only astrological but also astronomical purposes because they are needed for the computation of solar and lunar eclipses.

2. The following two meanings, encountered mostly in texts dating from the 11th century A.D. or later, are obviously secondary: (a) al-Djawzahar = the *circulus pareclipticus* [see article ʿILM AL-HAYʾA, section on "Theory of planetary motion"] of the moon, Ar. *al-mumaththal bi-falak al-burūdj* = ὁ ὁμόκεντρος τῷ κόσμῳ κύκλος (Alm.), or in Ibn al-Haytham's theory of *solid* spheres, the spherical shell concentric with the earth, within which the excentric sphere (*al-falak al-māʾil*, "*sphaera deflectens*") is comprised. (b) al-Djawzahar = the nodes of the orbit of any of the five planets.

Bibliography: W. Hartner, *The pseudo-planetary nodes of the moon's orbit in Hindu and Islamic iconographies*, in *Ars Islamica*, idem, v/2, Ann Arbor 1938; idem, *Zur astrologischen Symbolik des "Wade Cup"*, in *Aus der Welt der islamischen Kunst*, Festschrift für Ernst Kühnel, Berlin 1959; E. Kühnel, *Drachenportale*, in *Zeitschrift für Kunstwissenschaft*, iv, 1/2, Berlin 1950; Albattānī, *Opus Astronomicum*, i, 250; *Mafātīḥ al-ʿulūm* (ed. van Vloten), 220; *Dictionary of technical terms*, etc. (ed. Sprenger) s.v. Djawzahar and Dhanab; *Tabulae long. ac latit. stellar, fixar. ex observat. Ulugh Beighi* (ed. Th. Hyde, Oxford 1665), p. 14 of the commentary.

(W. HARTNER)

DJĀYASĪ [see MALIK MUḤAMMAD DJĀYASĪ].

DJAYB-I HUMĀYŪN, the privy purse of the Ottoman Sultans. Under the authority of the privy secretary (*Sirr kātibi*), it provided for the immediate needs and expenses of the sovereign. Its regular revenues consisted of the tribute from Egypt (see IRSĀLIYYE), the income from the imperial domains (see KHĀṢṢ), and the proceeds from gardens, orchards, forests etc. belonging to or attached to the imperial palaces. Irregular revenues included the fees paid by newly appointed rulers of Moldavia, Wallachia, Transylvania and, for a while, Ragusa, the Sultan's share of war-booty, and the proceeds of confiscations (see MUṢĀDARA).

Bibliography: İsmail Hakkı Uzunçarşılı, *Osmanlı devletinin saray teşkilâtı*, Ankara 1945, 77-8; idem, *Osmanlı devletinin merkez ve bahriye teşkilâtı*, Ankara 1948, 363-4; Pakalın, i, 265-6; Midhat Sertoğlu, *Resimli Osmanlı tarihi ansiklopedisi*, Istanbul 1958, 55. See further KHAZĪNE.

(ED.)

DJAYḤĀN, (modern Turkish Ceyhan), the name by which the Arabs denote the ancient Pyramus, one of the two rivers which cross Cilicia and flow into the Mediterranean, the other and more westerly river being the Sayḥān, the ancient Saros. The names Djayḥān and Sayḥān appear to have been given by the Arabs to these rivers which separate them from Greek territory, on the analogy of the Djayḥūn and Sayḥūn in central Asia, rivers which separate them from Turkish territory, and which owe their names to a corruption of the names of biblical rivers (Genesis, ii, 11, 13), unless they are an arbitrary translation of the Greek names (cf. Nöldeke, in *ZDMG*, xliv, 700 and the articles ĀMŪ DARYĀ, SAYḤĀN, SIR DARYĀ).

The Djayḥān rises a little to the north-east of Elbistan, in the mountains which divide it from the valley of the Tohma Suyu, a tributary of the Euphrates. Its upper part is the Söğütlü Suyu. Near Elbistan it is swollen by numerous secondary streams, one of the most important being the Hurman Suyu.

Below its confluence with the Göksün Çayı, south of Afshīn (the old Yarpuz-ʿArbasūs-Arabissos), it flows southwards towards Marʿash. On the outskirts of this town it is joined by the Ak Sū (Nahr Ḥūrīth of Suhrāb) which comes from the north-east and flows past al-Ḥadath. It then turns south-west, passing to the west of the Anti-Taurus, and reaches the edge of the Cilician plain after receiving tributaries from the region of Sīs (now Kozan). It makes its way to Missis (al-Maṣṣīṣa) where the main Adana road crosses it by an ancient stone bridge. The mouth of the Djayḥān into the Mediterranean has moved several times owing to the delta formed by alluvial deposits. At the present time, after bending sharply to the east, it comes into the sea in a bay lying to the west of Yumurtalık (the old Āyās). Abu 'l-Fidāʾ compares it in importance with the Euphrates.

The region of the lower and middle Djayḥān formed part of the *thughūr* (frontier districts). The name of the river consequently occurs more than once in poets of the Ḥamdānid period, al-Mutanabbī, Abū Firās and al-Sarī [for its history, see CILICIA]. In the Mamlūk period this region was conquered by Malik Nāṣir Muḥammad and was known as *al-Futūḥāt al-djāhāniyya*, following the Armenian corruption Djahān from Djayḥān.

The name Djayḥān is sometimes used to signify the region rather than the river. This is so in Yaḥyā b. Saʿīd al-Anṭākī (cf. Stephanus of Taron, tr. Gelzer and Burckhardt, 140).

Bibliography: *BGA*, i, 63-4; ii, 122, 246; iii, 19, 22, 137; vi, 177; vii, 91, 362; viii, 58; Suhrāb, ed. v. Mžik, 143; Masʿūdī, *Murūdj*, ii, 359; vi, 273; Yāḳūt, ii, 170; Abu 'l-Fidāʾ, ed. Reinaud, 50 (tr. ii, 62-3); Dimashḳī, ed. Mehren, 107; Ibn Faḍl Allāh al-ʿUmarī, *Taʿrīf*, Cairo 1312, 56, 183; al-ʿUmarī's *Bericht über Anatolien*, ed. Taeschner, 6, 30; Ibn al-Shihna, *al-Durr al-muntakhab*, 180; Maḳrīzī, *Sulūk*, i, 617, 632, 838, 869; Abu 'l-Maḥāsin, *Nudjūm*, ed. Cairo, vii, 168 and index; Ḳalḳashandī, *Ṣubḥ*, iv, 76, 82, 123, 133, 134, 136; xiv, 145; Mufaḍḍal, *Hist. des sult. mamelouks*, ed. and tr. Blochet, 229; Quatremère, *Hist. des sult. mamelouks*, ii/1, 260; Ḥādjdjī Khalīfa, *Djihānnümā*, 598, 601; von Kremer, *Gesch. des nördl. Syriens*, 19; R. Hartmann, *Pol. Geogr. des Mamlūkenreichs*, in *ZDMG*, lxx (1916), 32; Tomaschek, *Zur hist. Topographie von Kleinasien in Mittelalter*, in *SBAk. Wien*, cxxiv (1891), 86; idem, *Hist.-Topographisches vom oberen Euphrat und aus Ost-Kappadokien*, in *Kiepert Festschrift* (1898), 145; Ritter, *Erdkunde*, xix, 6-119; Schaffer, *Cilicia*, 18 ff.; Le Strange, 131, 132 and cf. 434; Rosen, *Basil Bulgaroctonos*, 2, 23 (= Yaḥyā b. Saʿīd, *PO*, xxiii, 165, 214), 85, 193; Gaudefroy-Demombynes, *La Syrie du Nord à l'époque des Mamelouks*, 8, 18, 88, 98-101; Honigmann, *Ostgrenze*, 63, 84-5, 87, 103, 153; Cahen, *La Syrie du Nord* ..., 150; Canard, *Sayf al-Daula, Recueil de textes*, 44-6, 91, 98, 103, 104, 114, 141, 393; idem, *Hist. de la dynastie des H'amdānides*, i, 270 ff., 279 ff., 764, 775 and *passim*; *IA*, art. Ceyhan (Besim Darkot).

(M. CANARD)

AL-**DJAYHĀNĪ** [see SUPPLEMENT].

DJAYḤŪN [see AMU DARYĀ].

DJAYN, The Djayn (Jain) community (followers of Mahāvīra, called the Jina) was much more widely distributed over the Indian sub-continent at the time of the Muslim conquest than in later times, as is shown by the re-utilization of Djayn material in early Islamic building. Although they were fairly widespread in the Deccan, their particular stronghold was peninsular Gudjarāt. Allusions to the Djayns in earlier histories have probably been obscured by their being not distinguished from their Hindū neighbours and described with them as "unbelievers" and "idolators"; but their chief social characteristic, an exaggerated reverence for the sanctity of all animal life, was certainly known to and exploited by the Muslims, as the account of the Portuguese traveller Duarte Barbosa, who visited Gudjarāt early in the 10th/16th century, shows: the Muslims would take fowls and other birds and offer to kill them in the presence of devout Djayns, or threaten to kill themselves, or visit them as rat- or snake-catchers, and would be paid large sums of money not to do these things. They were, however, tolerated by the Muslims, since they were of economic importance as the money-lending community (cf. *The book of Duarte Barbosa*, ed. and tr. M. Longworth Dames, Hakluyt Socy., i, 111-2).

Religious contact with the Djayns was made by the Mughal emperor Akbar in 990/1582, who invited first Hīravidjaya and later the great Bhānučandra to the Mughal court, and whose personal beliefs and habits seem to have been much influenced by the Djayn leaders (Badāʾunī, *Muntakhab al-tawārīkh*, tr. Lowe, ii, 331, speaks with disgust of Akbar's orders prohibiting the slaughter of animals on certain days—adding that disobedience was visited with capital punishment!). Many of Akbar's *farmān*s in favour of the Djayns were confirmed by his successor Djahāngīr, on whom however the personal influence was never profound and who ended by condemning their character and morals (cf. *Tūzuk-i Djahāngīrī*, ed. trans. Rogers and Beveridge, i, 437-8).

Bibliography: For Mughal *farmān*s in favour of the Djayns see particularly M.S. Commissariat, *Imperial Mughal farmans in Gujarat*, in *Journal Univ. Bombay*, ix/1, 1940; cf. also *Akbar-nāma*, tr. Beveridge, iii, 1061-3. For Djayn sources on the relationship between Bhānučandra and Akbar and Djahāngīr see *Bhānučandra-čarita*, ed. and Gudj. trans. Mohanlāl M. Desai, Ahmedabad 1941; some *farmān*s corroborated in Djayn inscriptions especially in *Epigraphia indica*, ii, and in A. Guerinot, *Répertoire d'épigraphie jaina*, Paris 1908. See also Kamta Prasad Jain, *Jainism under the Muslim rule*, in *New Indian Antiquary*, i, 516-21; Kalipada Mitra, *Jain influence at Mughul court*, in *Proc. 3rd Ind. Hist. Cong*, 1939, 1061-72; idem, *Historical references in Jain poems*, in *Proc. 6th Ind. Hist. Cong.*, 1943, 344-7; idem, *Jahangir's relations with the Jains*, in *IHQ*, xxi (1945), 44-8.

(J. BURTON-PAGE)

DJAYPUR, formerly a princely state in India, now a part of the Indian Union, lying between 25° 41′ and 28° 34′ N. and 74° 13′ E., with an area of 15,579 sq. miles and a population of 1,650,000 in 1951. The ruling dynasty claimed descent from a son of Rāma, the legendary king of Ayōdhyā and the hero of the Sanskrit epic Rāmāyaṇa by Valmīki, in spite of the fact that the ex-ruler was also the head of the Kačhwāha clan of Rādjpūts. The first ruler of the country, then known as Dhundhār, was a descendant of the Kačhwāha chief of Gwāliyār, who had received the district of Daosa in about 522/1128 as a gift from his father-in-law. Daosa thus became the first capital of the newly acquired territory. The present city of Djaypur, which gave its name to the entire state was, however, founded by Rādjā Djay Singh II, better known to history as Djay Singh Sawāʾī, in 1141/1728. Abandoning Ambēr, the former capital, he made the new city the seat of his government. The city was planned on the model of Aḥmadābād [*q.v.*] with broad boulevards and spacious bazars. Even craftsman skilled in various trades were sent for from that place, but the founder of Djaypur did not succeed in making the new city as prosperous as its model (ʿAbd al-Ḥayy Lakhnawī, *Yād-i Ayyān*, ʿAlīgaṙh 1337, 30-1, in which the city is called Djaynagar). The title *Sawāʾī*, conferred on him by the Mughal emperor, and meaning $1^1/_4$, is not only indicative of the respect that he enjoyed at the Mughal Court but is also a tribute to his personal qualities as the scion of an illustrious ruling family. This ruler who ascended the *gaddī* of Ambēr in 1111/1699 and died in 1156/1743 was a remarkable and accomplished person. He made good use of his scientific knowledge and skill in constructing observatories at Djaypur, Dihlī, Banāras, Mathurā and Udjdjayn (see G. R. Kaye, *A guide to the old observatories at Delhi, Jaipur, Ujjain and Benares*, Calcutta 1920). The sun-clock, mounted on a triangular tower in the Dihlī observatory, gives accurate time even to this day. He also reconstructed the astronomical tables known after the reigning Mughal emperor of Dihlī, Muḥammad Shāh, as the Zīdj Muḥammad Shāhī. More illustrious and better known to history is, however, Djay Singh I who enjoyed a *manṣab* of 6,000 and the imperial title of Mīrzā Rādja, conferred on him by Awrangzīb. Soon after Djay Singh's death in 1156/1743 the Djāṫs of Bharatpur [*q.v.*] succeeded in wresting, following a number of sharp encounters, a part of the state; the defection of the chief of Māčērī (now Alwar) about 1205/1790 further reduced the area of the State. By the end of the century Djaypur was in confusion, torn by internal strife and the extortions of the depredatory Marāṫhās. A treaty concluded in 1218/1803 with the East India Company, was dissolved only two years later. Another treaty was concluded in 1234/1818 putting a stop to the molestation of the Marāṫhās.

On the outbreak of a rebellion in 1820, during the infancy of Djay Singh III, a British Officer was posted in the state. In 1835 another rising took place resulting in the murder of a British political officer and injuries to the Agent to the Governor-General. Repression naturally followed resulting in the tightening of the administration and reduction in the state troops.

The Djaypur Records Office has a rich and rare collection of historical documents, including a large mass of *akhbārāt*, the daily news-sheets pertaining mostly to the reign of Awrangzīb. Two unique works of Amīr Khusraw [*q.v.*], the *Khazāʾin al-futūḥ* (ed. Waḥīd Mīrzā, Calcutta 1952) and *Inshāʾ-yi Khusraw* are preserved in the State Library.

Bibliography: C. U. Aitchison, *A collection of treaties, engagements and sanads relating to India*, New Delhi 1940, s.v.; J. C. Brooke, *Political history of the state of Jeypore*, London 1868; T. H. Hendley, *Handbook of the Jeypore courts at the London Indo-Colonial exhibition*, London 1886; idem, *Medico-topographical account of Jeypore*, London 1895; V. P. Menon, *The story of the integration of the Indian states*, Calcutta 1956, index; *Rajputana Gazetteer*, ii, 1879; Ardjumand Muḥammad Khān Salīm, *Taʾrīkh-i Djaypūr* (*or Jaipur Guide*), Lahore 1904; R. N. Chowdhuri, *A glimpse of Jaipur a century ago*, in *Proc. 14th Ind. Hist. Cong*, 1951, 355-62; *Imperial Gazetteer of India*, Oxford 1908, xiii 382-402.

(A. S. Bazmee Ansari)

DJAYSH, one of the common Arabic terms (with *djund* and *ʿaskar*) for the army.

i. — Classical.

Except possibly in the Yaman, pre-Islamic Arabia, although living under permanent conditions of minor warfare, knew no armies in the proper meaning of the term apart from those of foreign occupation. Conflicts between tribes brought into action virtually all able-bodied men, but without any military organization, and combats were very often settled by individual feats of arms. The embryo of an army may be said to have appeared with Islam in the expeditions led or prepared by the Prophet, although the *djihād* at this stage was the duty of all able-bodied Muslims. One cannot speak of a real army until the beginning of the Conquests, when there first appeared a division between the combatant and non-combatant sections of the Muslim people. Even though in principle all able-bodied Muslims could be summoned to the *djihād*, in practice the tribes had only to supply a certain percentage of their menfolk, and the numbers were usually more or less made up by volunteers. Their installation in the conquered countries separated these men, if not from their families who usually accompanied them, at any rate from the other members of their tribe and from their traditional way of life. They did not form an army *stricto sensu*, inasmuch as that, in the intervals between campaigns, they followed other activities if they wanted to and, with few exceptions, were not shut up in barracks away from their families; but in any case they were a section of the people permanently obliged to respond to the call of war, and deriving their main livelihood from this. In relation to the conquered, they considered themselves from the start not entirely as a conquering people but rather as an army of occupation. Superior to their adversaries because of their mobility, their being used to a rough mode of life, and a consecrated enthusiasm which was reinforced by the appeal of booty and confirmed by victory, they lacked all knowledge of strategy, their arms remained rudimentary, and their successes were more than half due to the weakness of the enemy empires, the disaffection of the peoples of which these were made up, and to the recruitment of foreign mercenaries as part of the troops which these empires employed. It is perhaps imprudent to try to reckon the manpower which the conquerors were actually able to mobilize: probably round about fifty thousand men under ʿUmar, and double this at the time of the greatest extension of the Umayyad empire.

Except to a certain degree in Syria, the Arab troops were not installed in the settlements of the natives, but rather in camps which ultimately became new cities, the *amṣār* (see misr). Thus there came into being Baṣra and Kūfa in ʿIrāḳ, Fusṭāṭ in Egypt, somewhat later Ḳayrawān in Ifrīḳiya, and so on. Their organization was a compromise between new necessities and tribal heritage: the whole army was a mixture of men of various tribes, but in the lower ranks of the army as in the towns, the soldiers remained grouped in communities of tribal origin. Originally they had no other income but the profits of victory which rapidly became considerable, and were regulated by the rules relating to the *ghānima* [*q.v.*]. When immense territories were added to the spoils reaped on the battlefield, there were differences of interest between those who would have liked to have seen them entirely divided up, and those around the growing Caliphate who succeeded in imposing the doctrine that they belonged to the Islamic community collectively, both present and future, which meant in fact allowing the original owners to keep them against payment of taxes, which in turn served to provide the money for regular army pay (see ʿARĪF, ʿAṬĀʾ, and DĪWĀN). In Syria, and later in the Islamic west, the coordinated provincial-military organization of the *djund* [*q.v.*] was brought into being, an organization no precise equivalent of which ever appeared in the vast area of expansion in the east (ʿIrāḳ-Īrān).

Needless to say, this first, primitive army was entirely Arab-Muslim; in the former Byzantine provinces at any rate, this was all the easier to ensure, as the native populations had long since lost the habit of following the profession of arms. Nevertheless, soon enough, the Arab chiefs began to bring their *mawālī* [*q.v.*] with them in a subordinate rank, while on the other hand, certain warlike border peoples (in Central Asia, northern Īrān and Armenia, and in the Syrian Amanus), without embracing Islam, were associated with the military operations of the Muslims as auxiliaries exempt from taxes; only a little later the Berbers, superficially converted to the new religion, were to form the greater part of the army that set out to conquer Spain.

Fairly soon, a special corps under the name of *shurṭa* [*q.v.*] was constituted which, more closely linked to the Caliph or the Governor, was basically concerned less with war than with the maintenance of internal order, and little by little became a kind of police force (see also AḤDĀTH).

From the time of the Umayyads onward, the conditions of military organization were very con-considerably modified. War, because of growing resistance and lengthening lines of communication, ceased to be as profitable as before. The result was that pay, which was not very high, now became the main source of income of the troops, if not of their commanders, and they therefore became all the more demanding. On the other hand, a new cleavage appeared between the reserve troops stationed at Baṣra, Kūfa, etc., living an increasingly civilian life, and the frontier elements who no longer came back but continued to live on the borders of Asia Minor, Central Asia, the Maghrib or Spain. Finally, the nature of military operations changed and demanded war-materials and methods adapted from those of their enemies, an adaptation for which the Arabs were not always very well prepared. Tradition credits tactical reform to the last of the Umayyads, Marwān II, who had had long experience of war in Armenia; but on the whole, the army had not been substantially re-organized when the dynasty was overthrown by the ʿAbbāsids.

These owed their success from the military point of view to the new army organized by Abū Muslim [*q.v.*] from among the people of Khurāsān. For nearly a century, this army was the backbone of the new régime, and at first, the Khurāsānīs alone formed the troops quartered near the Caliph and in the great political centres. There were thus for a certain time two armies side by side. Of prime importance from the social point of view, the intervention of the Khurāsānīs was no less so from the military standpoint. Īrān, and more especially Khurāsān, had, in this respect, their own traditions which the Arab occupation had not succeeded in effacing. In archery, in siege warfare, in the use of "naphtha" (Greek fire), they possessed skills with which the Arabs could not compete, and thus brought to the ʿAbbāsids an element of technical reform which had been missing in the Umayyad army. On the other hand, the Arabs divided their lives between civilian life and that of the camps, still closely linked to the quarrels of the tribes and the clans; the Khurāsānīs, however, formed a more clearly defined corps of professional mercenaries linked to the person of the sovereign. Actually, despite some brilliant exceptions, it was less in external warfare than in the repression of internal revolts that they were mainly employed. The Arabs themselves henceforth belonged to two categories: there were those who lived far away from the zones of military activity, who were above all the cause of disorders, and whom in Egypt the Caliph al-Muʿtaṣim was for this reason to delete entirely from the registers of the *dīwān*; and there were the frontiersmen who could not be demilitarized in the same way, but who organized themselves according to the autonomous new world of the *ghāzīs* and *murābiṭ(ūn)*, cutting themselves off from the regular army proper. The result socially was that the Arabs for the most part no longer formed the breeding-ground of the aristocracy and were lucky indeed if they did not relapse into a miserable Bedouin way of life.

Whoever its members were, the regular army was distinguished from other more ephemeral bodies of combatants, in that they alone appeared on the registers of the *dīwān* as having a right to a permanent wage and a status which made a kind of state corporation out of them. The others, who were various kinds of free corps of "volunteers" (*muttawiʿa*), not only received less pay but, what is more important, only received it for the duration of the campaign for which their presence was required, and were not considered as professionals. As for the *ghāzīs*, they lived on the combined profits of their non-military activities in the intervals between campaigns, on booty during them, and on pious foundations which the Muslims of the interior created in increasing numbers in their favour as a substitute for waging the *djihād*. They also did not appear in the ordinary registers of the *djaysh* and were clearly not professionals.

In its turn, the Khurāsānī army did not survive the first ʿAbbāsid century. When the Caliph al-Maʾmūn bestowed the autonomous government of Khurāsān on the family of the Ṭāhirids, these tended to keep for themselves a large part of the Khurāsānī recruitment. Furthermore, if the ʿAbbāsid dynasty had owed its power to the Khurāsānīs, and more recently, in particular, al-Maʾmūn had owed his victory over his brother, al-Amīn, to them, they themselves were fully aware of this, and in Baghdād itself, where the Ṭāhirids were responsible for keeping order, they came in the end to be resented as somewhat burdensome protectors. Al-Muʿtaṣim, the same who had suppressed the regular Arab army in Egypt, also took the initiative in replacing the Khurāsānīs by Turks. Actually, it was at first mainly the Turks established within the frontiers of Islam who were referred to as such, above all the people of Farghāna whose social conditions resembled those of the Khurāsānīs; but soon young people born outside Islam and brought there as slaves (*mamlūk* in this case rather than *ʿabd*) from Central Asia or what are now the Russian steppes by warriors or merchants, were to be recruited as Turks. The Turks, who were above all excellent horsemen, not only had an apparently justified reputation for military, physical and moral courage, as is witnessed by a well-known short treatise of al-Djāḥiẓ, but it was thought that they, linked to the person of their master by ties of slavery, acquired young enough to be formed in character by him, and being strangers to the aspirations and rivalries of the indigenous peoples, would form a still more reliable army for the sovereign than had the first Khurāsānīs. In fact, experience was to prove that, having the sovereign in their power, they were to be far less tolerable and far more devoted to their own generals than to the Caliph (who, after al-Muʿtaṣim, never again commanded them directly). Nevertheless, because of their technical qualifications, because of the care bestowed by the Turkish chieftains on maintaining recruitment, and even because the acquisition of new slaves was the easiest remedy against the lack of discipline of the old ones (although in the long run, of course, it merely perpetuated the evil), it seemed no longer possible, right up to modern times, for oriental Muslim states to do without a Turkish army, and all of them, one after another, were to adopt one. At best, in the orient, they were counter-balanced by the calling in of other elements, rough, indigenous mountain people, skilled in fighting on foot in the mountains, such as the Daylamīs, or horsemen like the Kurds, or locally negroes (in Arabia) or Hindūs (army of the Ghaznavids). In Egypt, the Fāṭimids, who conquered it with Berber contingents, reinforced as in Ifrīḳiya with negroes, Slavs and Rūmīs, themselves later tried to neutralize these by introducing Turks, whom in turn they sought to replace by Armenians under chiefs who could hardly be claimed as Muslims, and finally gave back some part in army affairs to the Arabs. The breaking up of the ʿAbbāsid empire also gave the opportunity of a military career to the Arabs of Mesopotamia and Syria, who gave support to the Ḥamdānid [*q.v.*], Mirdāsid [*q.v.*], ʿUkaylid [*q.v.*] and other principalities. The Būyids in western Īrān owed their specific strength to the Daylamīs, but the need for cavalry compelled them nevertheless to reinforce them from the start with Turks. But the racial differences of the contingents, which language and technical differences hindered from mixing easily together, were the cause of disorders, because they were jealous of each other, quarrelled over their share of the state revenues, and espoused the disagreements of their leaders; they made the streets of Baghdād and Cairo run with blood when they were not occupied in promoting their respective generals to power. Even when, later on under the Saldjūḳids, a Turkish people and no longer only an army were to instal themselves in former Islamic territory, the structure of the army was not permanently affected: in the beginning, the Turkoman element, nomadic and natural warriors like the first Arabs, assured them victory; but the new masters of the Muslim east re-organized their army in the traditional manner with Turco-Muslim forces recruited from slaves, and the Turkomans were only able to use their warlike qualities as *ghāzīs* in the outer battlefields of Asia Minor, which they had taken from the Byzantines. The successors of the Saldjūḳids added a new element by introducing, among their Turks, some Kurds, from whom the Āyyūbid dynasty was to rise; but the Ayyūbids, masters of Egypt which they had taken from the Fāṭimids, had themselves an army which became increasingly Turkish in content. The Saldjūḳids of Asia Minor added Armenian mercenaries, Franks, etc., to their ranks in the Byzantine manner, and the Mongol conquerors brought Georgians into theirs. As for the Arabs, the Turkish conquest, combining as it did the old half-Bedouin country of the "fertile crescent" with the Asiatic part of the Byzantine empire which had been the stage of their occasional efforts as *ghāzīs*, eliminated them finally and completely (except in some corners of Arabia) from any part whatsoever in military life.

The evolution which has just been described was not peculiar to the Muslim world. Following the example of the former Roman empire, Byzantium in Islamic times left the running of its wars more and more to mercenaries, of whom a great number were Turkish. Recruitment of slaves proper was unknown to it, but this omission probably made only a limited difference in practice. It was uncommon for the mercenaries to return to their country of origin and they were bound by oath to the emperor. On the Muslim side it must be emphasized that the *mamlūk* in the army of a sovereign, whose agent of power he was, could not be compared with a private, domestic slave. Like the mercenary, he received a salary, he had considerable freedom of action outside his military duties, if he rose in rank he could be set free and the most successful could even rise to govern provinces and rule over free men.

It has already been indicated that the development outlined here was affected by technical as well as social factors. There is no need to give here the full account of armaments and military art (difficult enough in any case because of the lack of earlier studies of these subjects) which will be attempted in the articles ḤARB and SILĀḤ (see in the meantime the names of the various arms); this much, however, must be said—that the dominant characteristic of the development of warfare was the growing rôle of heavy cavalry. This was also the situation in Europe, but, because of the oriental tactical preference for mobility, they never went quite as far as the Europeans in the matter of sheer weight of equipment. From the time of the Arab conquests up to the appearance of fire-arms, armament changed little in nature, but it could change in bulk and above al lin the relative propor tions of the various arms, and technical progress, albeit of a secondary kind, could exercise some influence on the art of combat and the fortunes of war. The struggle against the Crusaders before the time of the Mongols possibly played a locally stimulating part in this respect.

Amongst the ancient Arabs the principal arms were the sword (*sayf*) and the javelin (*rumḥ*), as well as the lance (*ḥarba*) used by the infantry; the bow was not unknown, but little used on horseback; it served more as a weapon in hunting than in warfare, where it did not lend itself well to single combats of the traditional type. Here lay a difference between the Arabs on the one hand, and the Persians and Turks on the other: among the Persians the exercise of drawing a bow, which might be of any shape or size, was a living tradition among the whole population; the Turks excelled in the rapid shooting from horseback of a hail of arrows (*nāvak*) in all directions, thus sowing disorder in the ranks of their enemies. The cross-bow (*djarkh*), often included also with the ordinary bow under the same name (*ḳaws*), followed by a qualifying expression, seems to have been known in the orient since the 3rd/9th century. ʿAbbāsid and later cavalry made much use of the bow, but still also of the javelin, and the lance, too, now became a cavalry weapon; the infantry used the cross-bow while remaining faithful also to the sword which was was much improved by the quality of the so-called "Damascus" steel—in reality an Indian technique; amongst other weapons, the club (*ʿamūd*, Persian *gurz*) was still employed as well as the knife (*sikkīn*). In defence, Arabs used the shield (*daraḳa*), the cuirass (*tirs*), various types of coats of mail (*durʿ*, *zarad*, *djawshan*), and the helmet; they nevertheless avoided armour that was too heavy, and the large shield does not seem to have been in current usage before the Crusades, the period when this size in shields became fashionable. The cavalryman was almost always mounted on a horse which was also protected by armour; in the armies of eastern Īrān, the Indian elephant was used in some heavy corps; the camel, however, was only used for transport. The fully equipped horseman was given various names, one of which among the Ayyūbids was *ṭawāshī*, a meaning which should be carefully distinguished from its other possible meaning of "eunuch". The soldiers had to maintain their arms as well as their animals but, except in very early times, they were given to them in the first place and renewed in case of need; most of them came from state workshops which, in Egypt, held an almost complete monopoly in their manufacture. *A fortiori*, the state workshops alone dealt in engines worked by teams, that is to say, above all, siege artillery whose use developed increasingly: the heavy-beamed mangonels (*mandjanīḳ*), light ballistas, (*ʿarrāda*, [*q.v.*]), battering-rams (*dabbāba*), etc. The Muslims did not take very long to pierce the secret of *nafṭ* or "Greek fire", which land as well as naval forces used; archaeology has found the pots from which it was hurled. It was to an army possessing all this equipment that the term *ʿaskar* (Persian *lashkar*) was more particularly applied. When on campaign they settled themselves in camps and based themselves on fortresses, *ḥiṣn* [*q.v.*] or *ḳalʿa*, the attacking of which, from the opposing point of view, was one of the most important forms of warfare (see ḤIṢĀR). Finally, mention may be made of the importance, at the beginning of a battle, of the trumpet and other resounding instruments.

We know little of how young soldiers (*ghulām*, pl. *ghilmān*) of the ʿAbbāsid army were trained, and what Niẓām al-Mulk says about the Ghaznavid army must be treated with some reserve; for precise information we must wait until the time of the Mamlūks [*q.v.*]. Occasionally billeted on the people, the troops were far more usually gathered together in barracks or camps, one group of them, the *ḥudjariyya*, near the palace of the sovereign, whether Caliph or otherwise entitled. The brawls which nevertheless frequently broke out between them and the population were one of the causes of the temporary emigration of the Caliphate to Samarra from the time of al-Muʿtaṣim. The *shurṭa*, however, was no longer recruited from amongst themselves, and tended to be replaced by local elements which were sometimes opposed to them. But the Saldjūḳid conquest re-created unity by increasing the numbers of heads of garrisons (*shiḥna*), and giving them the duties of the *shurṭa* which was generally abolished. The army did its military training in open spaces situated on the outskirts of cities.

The army of a large state was divided into regiments which generally corresponded both with a division into ethnic groups and a division according to technical functions, complemented by detachments of sappers. There was also a division according to recruitment under famous generals or during certain reigns. The soldiers who had been part of a general's army continued to form a group solidary until death, and those who had been recruited by one prince kept themselves apart from those younger ones who had been recruited by his successor; hence there were differences and jealousies, with each prince favouring his own. In the lower ranks there were units which might be of ten or a hundred, etc., but these numbers seem fluid. The head of an army, often called *ḳāʾid* in the early days of Islam, and even later than this in the Islamic west, now began to call himself *amīr* [*q.v.*], a title which ultimately included the rule over a province linked to the command of an army. Where there was a commander-in-chief he called himself *amīr al-umarāʾ*; but the title of *amīr* was in the end to become devalued and to finish as a title for all officers, and consequently *amīr al-umarāʾ* fell to being the title of any general. In the Saldjūḳid period, etc., the man who represented the military authority of the sovereign when he himself did not exercise it over the body of the army, was the Grand Chamberlain, *ḥādjib*, who was first and foremost head of the guard. In Īrān, the commander of an army was called *sālār*, the commander-in-chief, *ispāhsālār* or *sar-i lashkar*; among the Turks, the practical equivalent of *amīr* was *beg*, while *amīr al-umarāʾ* was *beglerbeg* or *subashī*.

While there was no uniform in the modern sense, each regiment had its own regulation dress. We can picture for example, that of the Ghaznawid guard since the archaeological discoveries at Lashkar-i Bāzār. The different corps had their flags (*rāya*), and the general or sovereign his own (*liwāʾ*), flying near the tent from which he commanded the battle and forming a rallying point. If there were no true medical services, at least there were transports of arms and food, for which purpose the camel was invaluable. Women often accompanied the army and in case of defeat, formed part of the spoils. A *ḳāḍī*, "readers" of the Ḳurʾān and preachers, sometimes doctors as well, were likewise attached to the army.

The chief preoccupation, whether of the soldiers or of the power they served, was the provision for their pay (*rizḳ*, *khubz*), which went with the supervision of the strength of the establishment and its maintenance. These services were dependent on the section of the *dīwān al-djaysh* called *ʿarḍ*, which was so important that in the Īrānian states the head of military administration was called *ʿāriḍ*. This supervision was based on an extremely exact registration of the men, and of the animals branded with the mark of the prince. It was exercised by means of periodic and very strict parades (*ʿarḍ*) which were taken if possible by the prince or at least in his presence, and at the end of which the men were given their pay [see DAFTAR].

The total amount of pay was very variable, as was its nature and the intervals at which it was paid, which might be monthly or yearly, while the situation of temporary soldiers was a further confusing factor. In general, money payments and payments in kind which could be dealt with in accounts together with the former were combined. As far as we can believe the scattered and inaccurate data which are all we have, it seems that up to about the 4th/10th century, the pay of a foot-soldier in the Caliphate varied between 500 and 1,000 dirhams a year, that is, about two to three times the earnings of a Baghdād journeyman; the cavalry earned double this and the commanders naturally more again. To this must be added payments in kind, gifts from sovereigns on their succession to the throne, gratuities on the occasions of feasts, battles, etc., not to mention those which the troops' growing lack of discipline enabled them to appropriate, or the booty taken after victories or perhaps rather in the permitted period of pillage which followed them. In addition, the state budget had to support the cost of manufacturing arms, the upkeep of armouries, fortresses, roads of military importance, transports, animals, etc. At $14^1/_3$ dirhams to the dīnār, the legal rate of exchange in ʿAbbāsid times, the manufacture of arms, etc., may be estimated to have cost some five million dīnārs, quite apart from the expense of an army of 50,000 men, whose overall budget at the zenith of the empire we know to have been in the neighbourhood of fourteen million dīnārs. The two together presumably accounted for half the income of the state; a heavy burden, bringing with it heavy taxation, discontent and, in a vicious circle, revolts provoked by this discontent which lessened the chances of a decrease in taxes since military effort had then to be intensified and an ever-growing proportion of the budget be taken up by the demands of the army. Moreover, even when it had sufficient available funds on account, the Treasury did not always possess the liquid assets needed for the payment of the army at the time promised, and when this happened another vicious circle appeared, and the complaints of those concerned over the delays could only be appeased by means of increases which compromised the future even more. More and more often, the caliphs had to cede the government of provinces to generals on condition that henceforward they and not the state would pay their own army. It is hardly necessary to recall the way in which this development led to the formation of autonomous principalities, but all the same it did not solve the problem of finding by one means or another the resources needed for the upkeep of the whole army.

This was why very soon it was necessary to reorganize the system of payment completely by means of the spread and transformation of the system of *iḳṭāʿ* ([*q.v.*]; see also ḌAYʿA) which, to express it briefly, allowed the army to tax a village or a district and thus take directly from the source the sums which were due to them. It is not possible to dwell here on the alterations in the administrative order which resulted from this development, but it is worth remarking that the value of the *iḳṭāʿ* seems to have been considerably greater than that of their former pay (500-1,000 dīnārs). This indicates clearly the growing social and political importance of the army and fits in with the fact that on his *iḳṭāʿ* the cavalryman had to provide for some few retainers as well as to maintain an increasingly large amount of gear and secure the whole of his supplies in kind. It must be kept in mind, too, that in the district allocated to him, the *muḳṭāʿ* had now to take over the expenses which had formerly been the business of the state, so that the income of the *iḳṭāʿ* was not solely given up to covering the simple pay of earlier times. Such very varied applications of *iḳṭāʿ* were tried out under different states and in different periods, that only a brief enumeration of them is possible here. The system of *iḳṭāʿ* could be used for the whole army or for only a part of it; it could free the *muḳṭāʿ* or not from the obligation of paying the tithe, *zakāt*; it could be temporary and exchangeable or definitive and hereditary; it could be individual, that is to say formulated to assure the upkeep of each cavalryman and his few retainers or general, that is to say very much broader and put into the charge of an officer on condition of his being responsible for the supplies and upkeep of a whole contingent, a situation which, due allowances being made, amounts more or less to the grant of a whole district (for which see above). Finally, the *iḳṭāʿ* could to all intents and purposes free the *muḳṭāʿ* of all narrow governmental control within the extent of the jurisdiction assigned to him or, on the contrary, leave him under detailed supervision and subject to the intervention of the state administration. This was the situation in Egypt, and from it developed the organization of the Mamlūks [*q.v.*]. It is possible that in Syria certain mutual influences occurred between the Muslim *iḳṭāʿ* and the fief of the Latins installed there following the Crusades.

Leaving aside differences of time and place, it can be seen that in almost every country of the Muslim east (rather less so in the west), the army has played an important and special part. Guardian of real power and of growing fortunes based on landed property, it constituted more and more the true aristrocracy superimposed upon the ancient native rural and urban aristocracies. By the manner of their recruitment almost foreigners to the native population, which in consequence paid little attention to their internal conflicts and changes of domination, the army imposed on this native population something of the régime of a military occupation which, nevertheless, was only upheld by the mutual support given to one another by the army and the orthodox religious framework of the régime which depended on it. This was a development whose scope, overflowing by far the domain of military matters proper, can in conclusion be no more than indicated here.

Bibliography: Most of the important information is to be found in the chronicles. However, ideas concerning certain aspects or problems of the army are to be found more explicitly discussed, from the first century of the ʿAbbāsids on, in treatises such as the *Risālat al-ṣaḥāba* of Ibn al-Muḳaffaʿ and the *Risāla fī manāḳib al-Turk wa ʿāmmat dj̲und al-K̲h̲ilāfa* of al-Dj̲āḥiẓ (ed. Van Vloten 1903); and in some works on finance, certain chapters deal specifically with military administration, for example, the *K. al-K̲h̲arādj̲* of Abū Yūsuf and especially, the general treatise on institutions with the same title by Ḳudāma written at the beginning of the 4th/10th century; then in the 6th/12th century, the *Minhādj̲* of Mak̲h̲zūmī for Egypt which enables us to complete the retrospective accounts in the *K̲h̲iṭaṭ* of Maḳrīzī (i, 94 ff.) and, in Persian, the *Siyāsatnāma* of Niẓām al-Mulk (Saldj̲ūḳids), the *Adab al-mulūk* of Fak̲h̲r-i Mudabbir Mubārak-s̲h̲āh (representing the military tradition of the G̲h̲aznawids and G̲h̲ūrids, still unpublished), the *Dastūr al-kātib* of Hindūs̲h̲āh Nak̲h̲dj̲awānī (representing the military tradition of the Mongols of Persia), etc. On the other hand, according to the evidence of the *Fihrist*, there existed early enough a technical literature in Arabic concerned with the military arts and engines of war, which drew its inspiration from Greek and Īrānian antiquity; however, no example of this has been preserved prior to the Ayyūbid period which produced the *Tadhkira fī 'l-ḥiyal al-ḥarbiyya* of al-Harawī, ed. and French trans. J. Sourdel-Thomine in *BEO*, xvii (1962), the *Treatise on swords* attributed to Kindī, analysed by J. v. Hammer-Purgstall in *JA*, v/3 (1854) and published by ʿAbd al-Raḥmān Zakī in *Rev. Fac. Lettres Univ. Fuad I* xiv/2 (1952), and especially, the *Traité d'armurerie* put together for Ṣalāḥ al-Dīn by Marḍā or Marḍī Ṭarsūsī, ed. Cl. Cahen in *BEO*, xii (1947), a type of literature which was to be developed further in the time of the Mamlūks. On the Persian side should be mentioned the *K. al-ḥarb wa 'l-s̲h̲adj̲āʿa* (G̲h̲aznawid), published by I. and M. Sh̲āfiʿ in *IC*, 1946. Earlier information about the Muslims' manner of fighting has been preserved in Byzantine literature, especially in the *Taktikon* of Leon VI and the *Strategikon* of Kekaumenos, as well as in Armenian chronicles.

No general and thorough modern work exists on the Muslim army in the "classical" centuries. The account of A. v. Kremer in his *Kulturgeschichte des Islams*, i, remains useful; it should be complemented on several points by the corresponding chapters of R. Levy in his *Social structure of Islam*, by ʿA. Ibrāhīm Ḥasan and Ḥ. Ibr. Ḥasan in *al-Nuẓum al-Islāmiyya*, and by A. v. Pawlikowski-Cholewa in *Die Heere des Morgenlandes*, 1940; better, but more limited geographically, is the chapter, p. 485-508, of B. Spuler in his *Iran in frühosmanischer Zeit*; see also M. F. G̲h̲āzī, *Remarques sur l'armée chez les Arabes*, in *Ibla*, 1960. The following are monographs dealing with shorter periods: for pre-Islamic Arabia, F. W. Schwarzlose, *Die Waffen der alten Araber*, 1886, which should be complemented by the studies on pre-Islamic Arab society of H. Lammens, B. Farès, etc.; for the period of the conquests, the considerations of Caetani in his *Annali*, iv, and the dissertation of L. Beckmann, *Die musl. Heere der Eroberungszeit*, Hamburg 1952; for the Umayyads, N. Fries, *Das Heereswesen der Araber zur Zeit der Omayyaden nach Tabari*, 1921, and A. E. Kubbel, *Sur certains traits du système militaire omayyade*, in *Palestinskiy Sbornik*, iii, 66 (1958) (in Russian, with an analysis in French by M. Canard, in *Arabica*, 1960, 219-21); for the ʿAbbāsids, W. Hoenerbach, *Zur Heeresverwaltung der Abbasiden, Studie über Qudama*, in *Isl.*, xxix (1950); and for some later states, the two important studies by C. E. Bosworth, *Ghaznavid military organization*, in *Isl.*, xxxvi (1960), and H. A. R. Gibb, *The armies of Saladin*, in *Cahiers d'Histoire Égyptienne*, iii (1951); see also the chapter on military matters in B. Spuler's *Mongolen*², 1955. For the political and social aspects, see Cl. Cahen, *The body politic*, in *Unity and variety in Muslim civilization*, ed. G. E. Von Grünebaum, 1955.

From a more technical point of view, K. A. C. Creswell's *Arms and Armour*, 1956, gives considerable space to examples from the museums, for the most part of a later period than that which has been dealt with here; important is K. Huuri, *Zur Geschichte des mittelalterlichen Geschützwesens aus orientalischen Quellen*, Helsinki 1941, which compares all the "oriental" societies; also A. Zeki Velidi, *Die Schwerter der Germanen* (in fact, this speaks mainly of the Muslim world), in *ZDMG*, xc (1936), not used by A. Mazahéri, *Le sabre contre l'épée*, in *Annales ESC*, xiii (1958); cf. Cl. Cahen's notes to his editon quoted *supra*. For Greek fire, there is now a general review of the use of this in all countries by J. R. Partington, *A history of Greek Fire and gunpowder*, Cambridge 1960 (cf. D. Ayalon, *A reply to Prof. J. R. Partington*, in *Arabica*, 1963). For the *iḳṭāʿ*, see Cl. Cahen, in *Annales ESC*, 1953. For the sake of comparison, it is worth reading R. C. Smail, *Crusading warfare*, Cambridge 1956.　　　　　(CL. CAHEN)

ii. — MAMLŪK [see MAMLŪKS].

iii. — MUSLIM WEST

The word *djaysh* in north-west Africa has two further special meanings.

1. *Djīsh*, plur. *Djyūsh* means in the south of Algeria and Morocco **an armed band** to go out on a *ghazw* (ambush for purposes of plunder or of a holy war) against a caravan or a body of troops. When the *djīsh* consisted of several hundred men, it was called a *ḥarka*. The *Djyūsh* carried on their operation from the northern Sūdān or the Niger valley throughout the Sahara and the south of Algeria and Morocco. They were composed sometimes of Tuāregs but more often of Berbers from the southern slopes of the High Atlas. The latter assembled on the al-Mayder plateau in the valley of the Wēd G̲h̲eris.

When the formation of a *djīsh* was decided upon, the Tuāreg who were to belong to it bound themselves together by an oath before setting out. Among the Awlād Djarīr on the borders of Algeria and Morocco, two mounted marabouts were placed opposite one another. Between these two men of religion ran those intended for the foray, with a branch of the *retem* (Sahara broom) in their hands which they would throw into the air. Each *djīsh* took with him some one to bring him luck, usually a marabout or a warrior who had already taken a successful part in several similar enterprises.

In the sandy plains of the Sahara or in the sand hills the members of the *djīsh* walked in Indian file so that the enemy could not estimate their number from their tracks. They also made all sorts of deviations. When they came to the place chosen for the ambush, they lay in wait. The attack was usually made by night or in the grey of morning, a fierce onslaught, a hail of shot mingled with the shrill wild yells of people shrieking like demons, while the rifles poured forth bullets. All the forces of the attacking party were concentrated on the first onslaught. The terrified animals could no longer be controlled and often stampeded in all directions. Then began the second part of the fight, in which the best horsemen of the *djīsh* played the principal part in driving their dismounted opponents into the desert to die. It was mainly to put down the *djyūsh* that the French military authorities instituted the corps of *Méharistes Sahariens*, who have succeeded in restoring order.

Bibliography: D. Albert, *Une Razzia au Sahel*, in *Bull. Soc. Géog. d'Alger*, 1900, 126 ff.; M. Benhazera, *Six mois chez les Touaregs du Hoggar*, Algiers 1908, 55 ff.; Augustin Bernard, *Les confins algéro-marocains*, Paris 1911, 95, 96; M. Bernard, *Notes sur l'O. Gheris*, in *Bull. Soc. Géog. d'Oran*, xxx, 373; Deschamps, *Le Méhariste saharien*, in *Bull. Soc. Géog. d'Oran*, xxix, *passim* and more particularly 283 ff.; A. Durand, *Notes sur les Touaregs*, in *Bull. Soc. Géog. d'Alger*, 1904, 691 ff.

2. *Djīsh*, or according to the pronunciation in western Morocco *gīsh*, a kind of feudal organization in the Moroccan Army.

Historical. The *djīsh* dates from the beginnings of the reigning dynasty. Previously the various dynasties of North Africa had succeeded to power with the help of groups of the people whose political and religious interests were their own. Revolutions not only overthrew the ruling families but forced them to maintain their power by force of arms and to spill their blood on countless battlefields. The great families, tribes and clans, who had accompanied the first ruler, became extinct. Lest they should become dependent on Berber clans, who could not be relied on to be faithful to a dynasty they had not created, the sultans had to surround themselves with foreign mercenaries, who had no connexion with the

Atlas territory. The older North African dynasties enlisted Christians, Kurds, Persians and negroes. Under the Banū Waṭṭās, however, the Kurd, Christian and negro guards were abolished and replaced by a guard composed solely of Arabs (*al-shurṭa*). This was composed mainly of the elements which had been introduced to west Morocco by the Almohad ruler Yaʿḳūb al-Manṣūr (Dwī Ḥassān, Shabanat, Kholoṭ etc.) or of Maʿāḳil Arabs from the Tlemcen country (Swīd, Banū ʿĀmir, Ṣbāyḥ, Riyyāḥ, etc.). The latter were quartered in the environs of Fās (Fez) and formed the corps of Sherāga (Orientals). The attacks of the Christians in the 9th/15th century forced the ruler of Fās to place garrisons in the strongholds on the coast called *makhzen* (garrison placed in a stronghold), which was very soon to be transferred to the whole feudal organization of Morocco. But this *makhzen* succumbed to the attacks of the Portuguese and Spaniards, the rebellious Berbers and those of a new Maʿāḳil *makhzen*, which had been formed by the Saʿdid Sharīfs of Sūs (1545).

When the Saʿdids had become lords of the kingdom of Fās, they quartered the Arabs of their *djīsh* in the garrisons of Fās, under the name of *Ahl Sūs*; they were soon afterwards transferred to the fortresses of the Gharb as a defence against the Kholoṭ Arabs of the former Marīnid *djīsh*. They later united the remnants of the *djīsh* of the Banū Waṭṭās (Shabana, Zirāra, Awlād Mṭāʿā, Awlād Djerrār) with their own and placed them in the garrisons of Tadla and Marrākūsh. The Sherāga were also enlisted and remained in garrison in the neighbourhood of Fās. The Saʿdid army, the *djīsh*, was thus created. As in the time of the Banū Waṭṭās, it consisted of military cantonments of members of the *makhzen* who were at the call of their sovereign throughout their lives. They lived on estates which formed a kind of fief and were free from taxation. The highest officials rose from their ranks.

But the Saʿdid court became influenced by the Turks in the adjoining lands. In addition to the corps of *djīsh*, the Sharīfs wished to have a corps drilled in the European fashion by Turkish instructors. The nucleus of this corps, consisting of Andalusian Moors, renegades and for the greater part of Sudan negroes, was only of any real value in the reign of Sultan Aḥmad al-Dhahabī (al-Manṣūr). While this dynasty was breaking up in the civil wars caused by rival claimants for the throne, Sultan ʿAbd Allāh b. Shaykh wished to have a body of faithful troops upon whom he could implicitly rely and gave the Sherāga most of the lands which they had previously held only in fief.

When Mawlāy al-Rashīd seized the throne in 1665, and with the help of Arabs and Berbers from the Udjda country founded the dynasty of ʿAlid Sharīfs, he amalgamated his retainers with the Sherāga of Fās. His successor Mawlāy Ismāʿīl gave the *djīsh* its character. His mother belonged to the Arab tribe of Mghāfra, a division of the Udāya. He invited this tribe to come from the other end of Sūs and settled them as a *makhzen* tribe near the lands of the Sherāga of Fās. He reorganized the negro contingent the members of which he had sought out with the help of the Saʿdid Sultan Aḥmad al-Manṣūr's registers. They had to swear an oath of fealty on the Imām al-Bukhārī's book; whence their name *ʿAbīd al-Bukhārī* (slaves of Bukhārī, plur. Bwākher). The *djīsh* further consisted of the Sherāga (Awlād Djamaʿ, Hawwāra, Banū ʿĀmir, Banū Snūs, Sedjʿa, Aḥlāf, Swīd, etc.), the Sherārda (Shabana, Zirāra, Awlād Djerār, Ahl Sūs, Awlād Mṭāʿ, etc.), the Udāya (the Udāya proper, Mgafra etc.) and Bwākher. These were the four *makhzen*-tribes and together formed the *djīsh*. Henceforth the history of the *djīsh* is that of the domestic history of Morocco; indeed it may be said that their history is that of the revolutions of Morocco. In the reigns of Mūlāy Ismāʿīl's successors, it was the *djīsh* that decided the fate of the rulers. The four great tribes acted as suited their individual interests. From 1726 to 1757, in the brief space of 31 years, 14 Sultans were enthroned, and deposed or slain by them, in consideration of the presents (*munā*) they received. In 1757 on the death of the Sultan ʿAbd Allāh b. Ismāʿīl, who had himself been seven times deposed and restored again, his son Muḥammad succeeded him. Under his iron rule, the *djīsh* tribes were kept under control. He broke the power of the Bwākher by dividing them up and sending them to garrison the various seaports. To counteract the influence of the Sherārda of Tadla and the plain of Marrākush, he enlisted sections of the tribes of this plain in the *makhzen*—Mnābeha, Rḥāmna, ʿAbda, Aḥmar and Harbil. Each of these tribes had to send two ḳāʾids and their retainers to the *djīsh*. These detachments were released from their tribes, entered the *makhzen* of Marrākush, to which they belonged, received the pay of other troops and were freed from taxes (*nayba*).

Under Sultan Yazīd, son of Muḥammad, insubordination again broke out, favoured by the weak character of the ruler. He was assassinated and the struggles for the throne of Morocco began again, which became the plaything of the *djīsh* tribes. Finally, about 1791, Mawlāy Slīmān succeeded in winning his way to the throne and overthrowing his rival Mawlāy Hishām, who had been chosen in Marrākush. While he was on a campaign against the Berbers in the south, the Sherārda aroused a great rebellion against him. The Udāya took his side against the rebels and seized the opportunity to plunder Fās. Mawlāy Slīmān was victorious but on his death his successor Mawlāy ʿAbd al-Raḥmān was proclaimed sultan by the Udāya in 1822. The latter was almost overthrown by another rising of the Sherārda and had as a rule to reside in Marrākush, the better to be able to control the tribes. But events in the north of his kingdom, a rising of the Udāya, the conquest of Algeria by the French and the wars of his representative ʿAbd al-Ḳādir against them, forced him to retire to Fās. He wished to take the field in person against the French. But after his defeat at Isly, he recognized how unequal to European armies his *djīsh* was, and resolved to have an army modelled on those of Europe. His successor Muḥammad carried out this plan by his edict of 22 Radjab 1277/18 July 1861. The organization of the new army was after many experiments finally entrusted to a body of French officers.

State of the Djīsh since the French Protectorate. The *djīsh* still consisted of the Sherāga, Sherārda, Udāya and Bwākher with the half *makhzen*-tribes of the plain of Marrākush (ʿAbda etc.). The tribes still had only the use of the lands occupied by them, except the Sherāga, who obtained the cession of most of their lands, and the Bwākher, almost all of whom had land around Meknès (Miknāsa). The *djīsh*-tribes were divided into regiments of 500 men (*rḥa*). At the head of each *rḥa* was a *Ḳāʾid rḥa*, a kind of colonel. Below him were five *ḳāʾid al-mya*, commanders of 100 men, each of whom had 5 *muḳaddams* below them, who were subordinate officers commanding 20 men. The private soldier of the *djīsh* was called *mkhāznī*.

The members of the *djīsh* could attain to the highest positions in the *makhzan*. The Bwākher retained a special privilege; from their ranks alone were drawn the *Shwirdet*, pages of a kind, who were employed in the palaces of the sovereign. The Udāya had the right to call themselves "Uncles of the Sultan". The tribes belonging to the *djīsh* were each commanded by a Pasha, except the Sherārda and Udāya, who were divided into garrisons, each of which was commanded by a Ḳāʾid. The Pasha of the Bwākhīr was also Pasha of Meknès, and the Pasha of the Ahl Sūs was also Pasha of Fās Djadīd. All officers were supposed to live in their garrison towns but in time of peace they did not strictly observe this rule. Their military duties were not taken very seriously and most of them lived on their estates. The administration of the affairs of the tribe was in the hands of the *shaykh*, the oldest of the *ḳāʾid rḥa*.

When the Sultan required troops each *makhzen*-tribe sent a detachment corresponding to the number of its *rḥa*. This held for the Sherāga, Sherārda and Udāya, all of which consisted of too many families for them to belong in a body to the *djīsh*. The families who were to be detached were chosen by drawing lots. The others were free, though they paid no taxes and tilled the lands granted them for the time. They formed the reserve of the *djīsh*, from which the Sultan drew the corps of *msakhkhrīn* (muleteers, army service corps) for the *ʿasker* (regular army) and for the artillery. Each member of the *djīsh* called to the colours received in his garrison an allowance of rations (*mūna*) and a monthly pay (*rāteb*).

The Bwākher, who numbered only 4000 men at the time in question, and the Ahl Sūs, were all soldiers. A special register was kept of them. They all received the *mūna* and the *rāṭeb* and their widows also received pensions.

Positions in the *djīsh* often descended from father to son and their holders thus formed a permanent element in the *makhzen* caste.

Although the creation of a standing army on the European model, the *ʿasker*, lessened the influence and political importance of the most prominent members of the *djīsh*, it by no means destroyed its military value. The fact that they were peerless horsemen was largely due to the *laʿb al-bārūd* [*q.v.*] "powder-game", in which the *djīsh* excelled. The field artillery of the standing army was also recruited from them. Trained by the officers of the French military mission, this artillery acquitted itself excellently.

As we have already seen, the *djīsh* was divided into *rḥa* and these were commanded by a *ḳāʾid*, below whom were five *ḳāʾid mya* with their *muḳaddams*. The standing army on the other hand was divided into *ṭābōrs* (battalions or regiments) of varying strengths; these were commanded by a *ḳāʾid rḥa* who had a *khalīfa* and a corresponding number of *ḳāʾid mya* below him.

Distribution, Armament and Dress. The *djīsh*-troops were unequally distributed among the four imperial cities Fās, Meknès, Rabāṭ and Marrākush, the two seaports Tangier and Larash, and a few small garrisons in the Gharb (west), and the east and south of Morocco. In these places the *djīsh* and their people lived by themselves and hardly mixed with the local populations by whom they were feared.

These horsemen were armed with the Winchester rifle, which supplanted the long flintlock; they also carried the *sekkīn*, a sword with an almost straight blade, a horn handle and a wooden sheath covered with red leather. They also carried the *kummiyya* and the *khandjar*, engraved daggers with very curved blades. Their horses as a rule, were good, but the harness as usual among the Arabs was very poor.

They wore a cloth kaftan of some loud colour over which they put a white *faradjiyya*, the whole being held together by a leather girdle with silk embroidery. Their red *sheshiyya* was conical in shape and wound round by a turban of white muslin. Soft slippers of yellow leather with long spikes instead of spurs completed this picturesque outfit.

Bibliography: al-Salāwī, *Kitāb al-Istiḳṣā*, Cairo 1312, *passim*, especially iii and iv; Cour, *Établissement des dynasties des Chérifs*, Paris 1904, *passim*; E. Aubin, *Le Maroc d'aujourd'hui*, Paris 1905, 172 ff.; Weisgerber, *Trois mois de campagne au Maroc*, Paris 1904, 82 ff.; Massignon, *Le Maroc dans les premières Années du XVIe Siècle*, Algiers 1906, 172 ff.; Houdas, *Le Maroc de 1631 à 1812*, Paris 1886, *passim*. (A. Cour)

iv. — Modern period

The history of Islamic armies in modern times is, in its most significant aspect, the history of their reform and westernization. The progress of the sciences in Europe enabled European Powers to wage war with increasing efficiency and their threat to the Islamic domain became progressively more difficult to contain. But it is only towards the end of the eighteenth century that Islamic rulers came to appreciate the threat in its full extent and began to take measures to cope with it. It is true that European techniques of war had been introduced here and there before that time, but the attempts were neither systematic nor long-lived. In the Crete campaign of 1644-69 the Ottoman Government employed English and Dutch instructors to train their sappers. At the end of the seventeenth century, the foundries for the manufacture of cannon were being supervised by a Venetian ex-officer of artillery named Sardi who had turned Muslim. In 1731, the French Count de Bonneval (1675-1747) who had adopted Islam and taken the name of Aḥmad (see AḤMAD PASHA BONNEVAL), was given the task of reforming the Corps of Bombardiers. He recruited and trained some 300 Bombardiers and opened a school of geometry. The innovation did not survive opposition by the Janissaries. In the 1770s, the Baron de Tott, a French Officer of Hungarian extraction who had gone to Turkey with Vergenne's Embassy, and had then been employed by Choiseul on an embassy to the Crimean Tatars, was employed to form a corps of artillery on modern lines. He formed a corps of 600 *sürʿatči*s and built a foundry for cannon. He also introduced the use of the bayonet and set up a mathematical school for the navy. His work was continued, after his return to France in 1775, by a Scotsman called Campbell who had adopted Islam and was known as Ingiliz Muṣṭafā. When the Russians annexed the Crimea in 1783, westernization of the Ottoman army gained impetus, and the French Government, fearing the extension of Russian power further, lent officers headed by General Lafitte for technical instruction and training in military engineering and the art of fortification.

But it was not until the reign of Selīm III (1203-22/1787-1807) that a sustained attempt was made to transform the old-style army into an instrument fit for modern conditions. In 1792 and 1793, as part of his attempt to reform the civil and military institutions of the Empire, and to set up a new system, a *Niẓām-i djadīd*, he issued regulations for a new model army, which itself came to be known by this very title. The advantages to be derived from a new model army may be gathered from a treatise published in translation in an appendix to W. Wilkinson, *An account of the principalities of Wallachia and Moldavia* ..., London 1820. The treatise, which the author states to be a translation from a Turkish Ms, dating from 1804, when the Sultan was concerned to extend his military reforms, purports to be "An explanation of the Nizam-y-Gedid institution", and to have been written on the Sultan's orders by "Tshelebi-Effendi, one of the Chief dignitaries of the Ottoman Empire, Counsellor, Minister of State etc. [= Čelebi Muṣṭafā Re<u>sh</u>īd Efendi, known as Köse Ked<u>kh</u>udā]". It is a long defence of the Sultan's policy setting out the evils of the old system and the reason for the superiority of European armies which it explains thus: "... their regular troops keep in a compact body, pressing their feet together that their order of battle may not be broken; and their cannon being polished like one of Marcovich's watches [Markwick Markham, a London watchmaker in great esteem with the Turks] they load twelve times in a minute and make the bullets rain like musket balls". The advantages of the *Niẓām-i <u>dj</u>adīd*, according to the author, are that the wearing of a distinctive uniform makes desertion more difficult, that the troops, drawn up in lines with the rear ranks parallel with the front, are easy to manœuvre, that discipline is easier to enforce, and that defeats are not turned into routs. A British Admiralty handbook of 1920 summed up and contrasted, after a century or so of reform, the methods and aims of the old and the new model armies: "The chief features of the new methods were the systematic training of the soldiers in drill movements and in the handling of weapons; (2) their organization in symmetrical units (regiments etc.). The undrilled forces of the older armies fought to a large extent as individuals, and the military units, so far as they existed, lacked cohesion and discipline, and therefore full effectiveness in attack and defence. Under the new system the commanders exercised more control in battle and could better calculate the numbers of their troops and thus dispose them more accurately to plan [whilst in the old style armies units were not of uniform size, even approximately]. Under the reformed system an army in battle order was arranged in two or three successive lines, the rear line acting in support and as reserves and each unit being of uniform depth. The ancient crescent movement of the front line was replaced by movement in straight lines". (Geographical Section of the Naval Intelligence Division, Naval Staff, Admiralty, *A handbook of Syria*, 1920, 163). From all this it may be concluded that the objects of military reforms were threefold: the acquisition and manufacture of modern weapons, the inculcation of technical knowledge in the appropriate sections of the army such as sappers and artillerymen, and the creation of a disciplined body of troops easily manœuvrable by their commanders. The second requisite has always been, in the modern period, more difficult to attain than the first, and the third infinitely more so than the second.

Selīm III took up and amplified previous attempts at modernization. He introduced reforms in the artillery, tightened discipline, and increased the pay for privates from 20 to 40 aspers per day. The corps was put under the command of a *topči ba<u>sh</u>ī* who was made a pa<u>sh</u>a of two tails, but administration, supplies and finances were separated from operational command and entrusted to a *nāẓir*. In 1796, following earlier negotiations, the Ambassador of the French Republic Aubert-Dubayet brought with him to Istanbul a number of officers who were assigned to train the *Niẓām-i <u>dj</u>adīd*. The new corps, composed of voluntary recruits, consisted of *topčis*, *sipāhīs* and infantry. The recruits were drilled in the European fashion and taught how to manœuvre in a body on the battlefield. Seeking to avoid undue contact with the Janissaries who looked askance at these innovations, the Sultan housed the *Niẓām* in barracks outside Istanbul. When the French, in Bonaparte's Egyptian expedition, marched into Palestine in 1798, the new corps, which amounted by then to three or four thousand gunners and musketeers, was employed to help with the defence of Acre and gave a good account of itself. This raised its reputation particularly with the people of Istanbul and encouraged the Sultan to take a further step. He now desired to recruit troops for the *Niẓām* by conscription both from among the Janissaries and the general population. This new departure had the support of the Mufti, Welizāde Meḥmed Emīn, and other high religious dignitaries who were convinced of the necessity of reform. It is presumably in aid of this policy that the treatise of "Tshelebi-Effendi" mentioned above was written. The Sultan promulgated a *<u>kh</u>aṭṭ* on these lines in 1805, but strong opposition was soon apparent. The reading of the *<u>kh</u>aṭṭ* was interrupted by a riot in Edirne, and one *ḳāḍī* reading its text in Rodosto was actually killed. The Janissaries broke out in revolt in Rumelia and the authorities dared not have the *<u>kh</u>aṭṭ* read in Istanbul. A regiment of *Niẓām* sent from Anatolia against the rebellious Janissaries was decisively defeated. The Sultan had to appoint the A<u>gh</u>a of the Janissaries as Grand Vizier, to return the *Niẓām* to Anatolia, and abandon for the time being the extension of reforms. But he does not seem to have given them up altogether for in 1806 an attempt was made to recruit for the *Niẓām* in Ḳaramān whose Wālī, ʿAbd al-Raḥmān Pa<u>sh</u>a, had shown energy and loyalty in carrying out the Sultan's policy, and in 1807 auxiliary levies, Yamaks, were ordered to put on the *Niẓām* uniform. This precipitated a revolt, and the Yamaks marched on Istanbul and were soon the masters there. The Sultan attempted to save his throne by decreeing the abolition of the *Niẓām*, but he was deposed by virtue of a *fatwā* which ruled that his actions and enactments were contrary to religion. The Janissaries burnt down the barracks of the *Niẓām*.

Bayraḳdār Muṣṭafā Pa<u>sh</u>a, who shortly thereafter procured the deposition of Selīm's successor Muṣṭafā IV and the enthronement of Maḥmūd II, attempted in 1808 to carry on with Selīm's schemes, by recruiting troops for the new model army which he sought to disguise by giving its members the traditional title of *Sagbāns* [*q.v.*], but his ruin and death at the hands of the Janissaries ended attempts at reform for the time being. It was not until eighteen years afterwards, in 1826, that Sultan Maḥmūd II (1808-39) was enabled, by a shrewd and lucky stroke, to end the power of the Janissaries and endow the Empire with a modern army. In 1826, having secured the support of the Mufti and the principal Janissary officers at a council held on 24-5 May 1826, the Sultan promulgated a *<u>kh</u>aṭṭ* which, while speaking of restoring the traditional practices of the Empire, in effect proposed the continuation of Selīm's reforms. A new force was to be formed by each Janissary battalion stationed in Constantinople providing 150 men from its ranks; 5,000 men in all were to be enrolled. The *khaṭṭ* provided for regular payment of salaries, for promotion by seniority, for the orderly provision of leave and pensions and for the abolition of the sale of military offices. The troops were to be armed with rifles and swords and to be trained by Muslim and not European officers. In spite of the ostensible agreement of their chiefs, the Janissaries revolted against the innovation. They proclaimed rebellion on 15 June, but the Sultan was ready for them and the mutiny was crushed. On 17 June the order of the Janissaries was abolished and shortly thereafter the *Sipāhīs*, the *Silihdārs*, the *Ghurabā* and the *ʿUlūfedjis* likewise.

No time was lost in proclaiming the formation of a new army which, to emphasize the ostensibly Islamic and traditional character of his reforms, the Sultan called the *ʿAsākir-i Manṣūre-i Muḥammediyye*. The new military code, published towards the end of 1826, divided the army into 8 sections and put at its head the *Serʿasker* [*q.v.*] who combined the functions of commander-in-chief and minister of war, and, under the Sultan, controlled the whole, except that a Grand Master of the Artillery (*Ṭopkhāna Nāẓiri*) was made responsible directly to the Sultan for the artillery, the engineers and munitions (see further BĀB-I SERʿASKERI). This division of functions between the Commander-in-chief and the Grand Master of the Artillery remained until 1909. The new army was to consist of 12,000 troops serving for twelve years; but the term of service was at times extended, as appears from a letter of Helmut v. Moltke of 1838, where he speaks of a term of service of 15 years.

In the following decades the army was considerably enlarged and its administration rationalized. By a law of 1843 army service was fixed at five years. In 1869 service was reduced to four years, in 1886 to three. In the Army Law of 1886, Ottoman subjects were made liable to service in the army for nine years from the age of twenty; they were then to be transferred to the reserve (*redīf*) for a further nine years and to the territorial army (*mustaḥfiẓ*) for a further two. The Law of 1843 provided for five army corps: the Imperial Guard, and the army corps of Istanbul, Rumelia, Anatolia and Arabistan. In 1848 a sixth army corps, with headquarters at Baghdād, was created. The army ranks were graded in the European fashion (a list of Ottoman army ranks with their equivalents in the British Army is conveniently found in Captain M. C. P. Ward, R.A., *Handbook of the Turkish army*, London 1900). The 12,000 of Sultan Maḥmūd's army were quickly increased. By the eighteen-forties the Ottoman armies had some 150,000 members, and this seems to have remained its peace-time strength thereafter. Until the promulgation of the *Khaṭṭ-i humāyūn* of 1856 the army was exclusively drawn from the Muslim population of the Empire. The *Khaṭṭ*, envisaging equality of rights and duties for all the Sultan's subjects, laid it down that henceforth military service would be borne by all, the poll-tax payable by the *dhimmīs* being abolished. This intention remained a dead letter, for until 1909, the non-Muslim subjects of the Sultan were exempt from military service against payment of a *badal* [*q.v.*], and such exemption seems to have tallied with the consensus of both the Muslim and the non-Muslim communities. The law of 1909 which abolished exemption for non-Muslims also abolished the privileged exemption from military service of the inhabitants of Istanbul.

This latter exemption gives an indication of the kind of difficulty which stood in the way of uniform military administration. The heterogeneous character of the Empire, the multiplicity of its religions and sects, the survival of ancient privileges and the creation of new ones during the nineteenth century militated against uniformity. The law of 1886 which mentions the exemption of the inhabitants of Istanbul also lays down that inhabitants of the *sandjaḳ* of the Lebanon and of Samos would also be exempt. Also the law was not to be applied in Scutari (except for Durazzo), in the Yemen, the Ḥidjāz, Nadjd, Tripoli and Benghazi. These anomalies are a fair indication of the resistance which uniform European-style administration aroused.

The training and management of a conscript army and its performance in war depend on the existence of efficient health, supply and financial services, and on the orderly keeping of records. It was of course the case that such services had to be created at the same time as the army was being recruited and expanded, and it is to be expected that in time of emergency, particularly in the beginning, they would fall short of the need. In 1842, for instance, soldiers slept in their clothes and wore a heterogeneous collection of uniforms. Furthermore, the new model army depended heavily for training on a miscellany of foreign officers, French, English, Prussian, Austrian, who, as Christians, were treated with scant respect by the rank and file. Leadership at the top may have been energetic and knowledgeable, but subalterns and non-commissioned officers were scarce and inexperienced. This was the judgment of one observer in 1828 (C. Macfarlane, *Constantinople in 1828 ...*, London 1829, 26). The judgement is echoed by the Maréchal de St.-Arnaud in 1854 who wrote that in the Turkish Army there were two things only: a commander-in-chief and soldiers and that there were no intermediary points, no officers, and even less non-commissioned officers (E. Engelhardt, *La Turquie et le Tanzimat*, Paris 1882, i, 116). In Helmut v. Moltke's judgment the advantages of European drill were lost by reason of the impersonality and mass character of the conscript army. The cavalry, he wrote, "learned to ride in masses, but they lost the impetuosity of the wild Turkish charge; and with their endurance of new customs, the old fanatical inspiration vanished. What was good in barbarian warfare was lost without gaining much benefit from the resources of civilization; popular prejudices were shaken, but the national spirit was destroyed at the same time, and the only change for the better was that the troops obeyed the orders of their leaders more than before". (*The Russians in Bulgaria and Rumelia ...*, London 1854, 269.) The deficiency of officers was gradually made good. Maḥmūd II sent military and naval cadets to European colleges in 1827, and in 1834 the military college at Pangaltï (see ḤARBIYE) was opened. The following decades saw a steady increase in and accumulation of modern military knowledge, but it was not until the educational reforms of Sultan ʿAbd al-Ḥamīd II that a notable extension of military education came about. The creation of this modern military *élite*, conscious of its superior knowledge and open, by virtue of its training, to European ideologies, was to have momentous consequences in the political history of the Empire and its successor states.

Contemporary with the Ottoman army reforms were those carried out by Muḥammad ʿAlī, the Wālī of Egypt. Shortly after the consolidation of his power in the country, Muḥammad ʿAlī determined on forming an efficient army. In 1815, after his return from the Ḥidjāz expedition, Muḥammad ʿAlī introduced European drill in his forces. The enterprise aroused great discontent and a mutiny broke out in Cairo; Muḥammad ʿAlī had to postpone his plans for the time being. In 1819 he obtained the services of Colonel Joseph Sève, a retired Napoleonic officer (who later embraced Islam and became known as Sulaymān Pasha [*q.v.*]) to direct training in a new military school which he established at Aswān, away from Cairo. The trainees were Sudanese slaves and 300 of Muḥammad ʿAlī's mamlūks. Sève encountered the same difficulties which European officers met in the Ottoman Empire: insubordination owing to contempt for the European Christian, and utter unfamiliarity with European techniques and drill. To start with, Muḥammad ʿAlī attempted to recruit Sudanese slaves for the rank-and-file, but their rate of mortality was extremely high: of the 24,000 slaves collected up to 1824 only some 3,000 were still alive by then. This method was abandoned and Muḥammad ʿAlī began recruiting from among the Egyptian peasantry. The *mudīr*s of the provinces were ordered each to provide a fixed quota of recruits. Press-gangs were first used to round up the recruits, an attempt was then made to substitute choice by lot (*ḳarʿa*) for the more forcible method, but neither force not persuasion could overcome the peasant's repugnance for military service: resistance, flight, self-mutilation were his unavailing resort; recruitment by lot proving even more unsatisfactory, the press-gang was once again employed. After the Morea campaign, Muḥammad ʿAlī, seconded by his son Ibrāhīm, increased the facilities for the training of officers; an infantry school, a cavalry school and an artillery school, all directed by Europeans, were established, and the French military code was translated and adapted for use in the army. He entrusted the administration of the army to a *nāẓir al-djihādiyya*, whose labours were to be guided and supervised by a council of officials, *dīwān al-djihādiyya*. By 1831 a disciplined force consisting of 20 regiments of infantry and 10 of cavalry was ready to take the field against the Ottoman Army in the Levant. At the end of the Levant campaigns in 1841 it was estimated that some 100,000 troops, including irregulars, were at the disposal of the Wālī of Egypt.

As part of the settlement between Muḥammad ʿAlī and the Ottoman Empire following his withdrawal from the Levant, the Egyptian Army was reduced to 18,000 troops, by a *fermān* of 13 February 1841. This figure was, however, informally increased by vizieral letters under the khedivate of ʿAbbās I and Saʿīd, the informal arrangement being confirmed by a *fermān* of 27 May 1866 issued to Ismāʿīl. This Khedive later succeeded in removing the limit on the number of Egyptian troops, a *fermān* to this effect being issued to him on 8 June 1873. But following his deposition, and consequent on the disturbed and enfeebled state of Egypt, the Ottoman Government was able to withdraw this concession on the accession of Tawfīḳ, and a *fermān* of 7 August 1879 once again limited the number of Egyptian troops to 18,000.

The second year of Tawfīḳ's khedivate saw the promulgation of a law (of 31 July 1880) which laid down that all Ottoman subjects in Egypt regardless of religion were liable, from the age of 19, to four years' active military service, followed by five years in the *redīf* and a further six in the territorial reserve. The recruits were to be chosen by lot from among those liable to conscription. It seems that this law contributed to the discontent which led to the ʿUrābī movement, since ʿUrābī and his friends argued that four years active service were not enough to gain promotion from the ranks; they therefore considered this law as directed by the Turkish element in the Army against the Egyptian element. An indication of their feelings on this matter is the law of 22 September 1881, which they forced the Khedive to promulgate, and which made promotion regular and mandatory once the prescribed periods of service, and examinations, were passed.

Following the collapse of ʿUrābī's movement and the British occupation of Egypt, the Khedive, by a decree of 17 September 1882, disbanded the Egyptian Army prior to its reorganization. A Khedivial rescript of December 1882 provided for a new army to be formed limited to 10,000 men. This army was intended for internal purposes, its general officers were British and its methods of training and organization followed the British model. Khedivial decrees promulgated in 1886 reiterated the provisions of the Law of 1880 and further allowed exemption on payment of a *badal* (a decree of 22 April 1895 disallowed exemption by payment of *badal* after the holding of the annual recruitment ballot). At the reconquest of the Sudan in 1898, the Army was increased to some 30,000 troops, but numbers thereafter reverted to 10,000-15,000 men until the signature of the Anglo-Egyptian Treaty of 1936.

The attempts to reform military institutions in Persia during the nineteenth century were neither as sustained nor as systematic as in Egypt and the Ottoman Empire. Persia was drawn into European politics during the Napoleonic period, and both France and Britain attempted to acquire exclusive influence in the country. The French sent a mission to train Persian troops in 1807-8, as did the British in 1810. Thereafter a succession of foreign officers, Russian, French and Italian, attempted to introduce European drill and techniques, but their impact was neither profound nor lasting. In 1842 a modified form of conscription was introduced. The cultivated land was surveyed and divided into units, each unit (the amount of land which could be tilled by one plough) being liable to provide a soldier together with a monetary contribution, part of which went to provide for the conscript's family and part to the Government, to defray the expenses of the soldiers. The division of the country into British and Russian zones of influence following the Anglo-Russian Agreement of 1907, and the events of the First World War, prevented the Persian Government from exercising effective control over its armed forces, and it was not until after the *coup d'état* of 1921 that Riḍā (Rizā) Shāh, who then became commander-in-chief, was able to organize the Persian army on the European model. A Conscription Act passed in 1925 provided for universal military service for a period of 2 years. A military college was also set up in Tehrān.

The successor Arab States which were set up after the defeat of the Ottoman Empire in the First World War had, under the mandatory régime, small volunteer forces organized and trained by the mandatory governments whose methods of training and organization tended to influence later practices. On attaining full independence these states speedily introduced universal conscription, the administration of which was not always easy. The Government of ʿIrāḳ, the first to do so (by Law No. 9 of 1934), encountered armed resistance to conscription among the Euphrates tribes and the Yazīdīs of Djabal Sindjār. A table of equivalent ranks in the armies of Arab states is conveniently set out in ʿAbdallāh al-Tall, *Kārithat Filasṭīn*, Cairo 1959, p. x.

Bibliography: ʿAbd al Raḥmān al-Rāfiʿī, *ʿAsr Ismāʿīl*, i, Cairo 1932; *Actes diplomatiques et Firmans impériaux relatifs à l'Égypte*, Cairo 1886; Aḥmad ʿUrābī, *Kashf al-sitār ʿan sirr al-asrār*, Cairo n.d.; Aristachi Bey, *Législation ottomane*, Istanbul 1875; A. Bilioti and Ahmed Sedad, *Législation ottomane depuis le retour de la constitution* . . ., i, Paris 1912; A.-B. Clot Bey, *Aperçu général sur l'Égypte*, 2 vols., Paris 1840; G. N. Curzon, *Persia and the Persian question*, 2 vols., London 1892; Ahmed Djevad, *État militaire ottoman*, i, Istanbul 1882; H. Dodwell, *The founder of modern Egypt*, Cambridge 1931; Egypt, *Dekretāt wa taḳrirāt* . . ., Bulāḳ 1881 . . .; *Egyptian Government Almanac* (annual); E. Engelhardt, *La Turquie et le Tanzimat*, 2 vols., Paris 1882-4; Gibb-Bowen, i/1; *Iraq directory*, Baghdād 1935; Iraq, Ministry of Defence, *English-Arabic military dictionary*, Baghdād n.d.; Ismāʿīl Sarhank, *Haḳāʾiḳ al-akhbār ʿan duwal al-biḥār*, 2 vols., Bulāḳ 1314-41; Juchereau de St.-Denis, *Histoire de l'Empire ottoman*, 2 vols., Paris 1844; L. Lamouche, *L'organisation militaire de l'empire ottoman*, Paris 1895; B. Lewis, *The emergence of modern Turkey*, London 1961; C. Macfarlane, *Constantinople in 1828* . . ., London 1829; Maḥmūd Shewket, *ʿOthmanlî teshkīlāt we ḳiyāfet-i ʿaskeriyyesi*, 2 vols., Istanbul 1325; H. v. Moltke, *Briefe über Zustände und Begebenheiten in der Türkei aus den Jahren 1835 bis 1839*[3], Berlin 1877; Muḥammad Esʿad, *Üss-i ẓafer*, Istanbul 1243 (tr. Caussin de Perceval, *Précis historique de la destruction du corps des Janissaires*, Paris 1833); H. W. V. Temperley, *England and the Near East* . . ., Cambridge 1936; Baron F. de Tott, *Mémoires*, 4 vols., Amsterdam 1784; A. Vingtrinier, *Soliman-Pacha*, Paris 1886; A. Ubicini, *Lettres sur la Turquie*, 2 vols., Paris 1853-4; M. C. P. Ward, *Handbook of the Turkish army*, London 1900; M. Weygand, *Histoire militaire de Mohamed Ali et de ses fils*, 2 vols., Paris 1936; W. Wilkinson, *An account of the principalities of Wallachia and Moldavia* . . ., London 1820; A. T. Wilson, *Persia*, London 1932; G. Young, *Corps de droit ottoman*, Oxford 1905; H. Zboiński, *L'Armée ottomane* . . ., Paris 1877. (E. Kedourie)

al-**DJAYṬĀLĪ** (also al-Djīṭālī, var. al-Djiṭālī), Abū Ṭāhir Ismāʿīl b. Mūsā, celebrated Ibāḍite scholar who was a native of Īdjayṭāl (also Īdjīṭāl or Djiṭāl), an ancient village of the Djabal Nafūsa still there today and now called Idjeyṭal or Djeyṭal. The date of his birth is unknown. However, we know that he was a pupil of the *shaykh* ʿĪsā b. Mūsā al-Ṭarmīsī, who lived in the second half of the 7th/13th century. For some time he taught at Mazghūra (today Mezghūra or Timezghūra) in the eastern part of the Djabal Nafūsa not far from Īdjeyṭal. He also lived for nine years at the village of Forsaṭā situated in the western part of the Djabal Nafūsa. It seems that at this period he was occupied with trade. It is said that he once went to Tripoli with some slaves he wished to sell there. Thrown into prison by the *ḳāḍī* and the *amīr* of this town who wished to confiscate his goods, he was freed by the intervention of Ibn Makkī, governor of Gabès, to whom he had addressed a poem full of eulogies. Set at liberty, he retired to Djarba, which at this time was under the authority of the governor of Gabès. He died there, according to al-Shammākhī, in 750/1349-50, or according to Abū Rās in 730/1329-30, and he was buried in the cemetery of the great Ibāḍite-Wahbite mosque on this island.

He was the author of many treatises, especially concerning dogma and the law, which, according to the opinion of later Ibāḍite scholars, revived their sect: 1) *Ḳawāʿid al-Islām* on the fundamental tenets of Islam, of which there is a lithographed Cairo edition with a commentary by Abū ʿAbd Allāh Muḥammad b. Abī Sitta al-Kusbī (10th/16th century); 2) *Al-Ḳanāṭir* (or *Ḳanāṭir al-khayrāt*), a kind of religious and moral encyclopaedia in several volumes, lithographed at Cairo; 3) *Sharḥ al-Nūniyya* (also *Sharḥ al-Ḳaṣīda 'l-Nūniyya* or *Sharḥ al-Uṣūl al-dīniyya mushtamil*^{an} *ʿala talkhīṣ maʿānī 'l-ḳaṣīda 'l-nūniyya*, a three-volume commentary on the poem rhyming in *nūn* on the principles of religion composed by Abū Naṣr Fatḥ b. Nūḥ al-Malūshāʾī; 4) *Kitāb fi 'l-ḥisāb wa-ḳism al-farāʾiḍ* or simply *Kitāb al-Farāʾiḍ*, a treatise on the calculation and division of inheritances based on a compilation by Abu 'l-ʿAbbās Aḥmad b. Saʿīd al-Dardjīnī (7th/13th century, printed edition); 5) *Adjwibat al-aʾimma*, a collection of legal opinions originating with imāms of the Ibāḍite sect (in three parts); 6) *Kitāb al-Ḥadjdj wa 'l-manāsik*, a book on the pilgrimage and the ritual practices attaching to it; 7) a collection of epistles (*mā djamaʿa min al-rasāʾil*); 8) poems (*ḳaṣāʾid*), probably religious; 9) *Maḳāyīs al-djurūḥ wa'stikhrādj al-madjhūlāt*, on *fiḳh*, lithographed edition appended to the *K. al-Farāʾiḍ*; 10) *Tardjamat al-ʿaḳīda al-ḳanāṭir*; 11) *Kitāb al-Mirṣād*. Several manuscripts of these works are to be found in the libraries of the Mzab.

Bibliography: Al-Shammākhī, *Kitāb al-Siyar*, Cairo 1301/1883-4, 460-1, 556-9; Abū Rās, *Taʾrīkh Djazirat Djerba*, ed. and tr. Exiga, Tunis 1884, 8 (of the Ar. text); E. Masqueray, *Chronique d'Abou Zakaria*, Algiers 1878, 141 *n.*; A. de C. Motylinski, *Bibliographie du Mzab. Les livres de la secte abadhite*, in *Bulletin de Correspondance Africaine* iii (1885), 23; idem, *Le Djebel Nefousa*, Paris 1898-9, 94-6; R. Basset, *Les Sanctuaires du Djebel Nefousa*, in *JAs.* 1899 (July-August), 89-90; T. Lewicki, *Études ibāḍites nord-africaines*, i, Warsaw 1955, 33-4 and *passim*; J. Schacht, *Bibliothèques et manuscrits abadhites*, in *RAfr.*, c, nos. 446-8 (1956), 388, 391, 395. (T. Lewicki)

DJAYYĀN (Spanish Jaén), capital of the Andalusian province of the same name, situated on the slopes of the rocky hill of Santa Catalina, on the summit of which the Muslims built a fortress which was considered to be impregnable; they also encircled the town with a wall. At the present time the town has a population of about 70,000. It stands in the centre of a fertile plain in which al-Idrīsī noted as many as 3,000 villages devoted to agriculture, and in particular to the breeding of silk-worms which is also the speciality of the *iḳlīm* of the Alpujarras, of which Jaén is the capital. On the other hand, he does not mention the cultivation of olive-trees, now the chief source of wealth. Ibn Ḥawḳal speaks of it as one of the ancient cities of Spain under the name Auringis, conquered by Scipio during the second Punic war, after Hasdrubal's defeat nearby. At the time of the Arab conquest of the Peninsula, the *djund* of Kinisrīn settled there; on his arrival in al-Andalus, ʿAbd al-Raḥmān I came in touch with it. In 210/825 ʿAbd al-Raḥmān II ordered the *fata* Maysara, governor of Jaén, to build the great mosque with five naves supported by marble pillars, which dominated the whole view of the city. At the end of the reign of the *amīr* Muḥammad, the revolt of

ʿUmar b. Ḥafsūn broke out and the district of Jaén was the scene of struggles and frequent uprisings until the rebel was crushed at Poley in Ṣafar 278/May 891. The town took the side of the *amīr* of Cordova but, in the following year, it was recaptured by the rebel and remained under his domination until 290/903. On the fall of the Caliphate the Banū Birzāl and the Banū Ifrān settled there as the result of a grant made by Sulaymān al-Mustaʿīn. Later the town was taken by Habbūs b. Māksan, lord of Granada. The Almoravids occupied it without resistance, and it was from this town that Tamīm b. Yūsuf set out, in 501/1108, for the Uclés campaign. The Almohads entered the town in 543/1149, but the king of Murcia Ibn Mardanīsh annexed it in 554/1159 and handed it over to his father-in-law Ibn Hamus̲h̲k. The *sayyid*s Yūsuf and ʿUt̲h̲mān laid siege to it in the summer of 557/1162 but failed to capture it; and Ibn Mardanīs̲h̲, irritated by the defection of his father-in-law who had given the town to the Almohads in 564/1169, also failed. When starting the campaign for al-ʿIḳāb (Las Navas de Tolosa), al-Nāṣir set up his head-quarters at Jaén. The *sayyid* ʿAbd Allāh al-Bayāsī, governor of Jaén, rebelled against the caliph al-ʿĀdil, and allied himself with Ferdinand III of Castile, who laid siege to the town with great vigour, but was compelled to withdraw with heavy losses, in revenge for which he devastated the whole district. It was only in 644/1246 that he finally succeeded in incorporating the town in the kingdom of Castile. During the 7th/13th and 8th/14th centuries the town was subjected to constant attacks by the Banū Marīn and the Naṣrids of Granada and, thanks to its powerfully-built castle, became the defensive bastion of Castile. Al-Idrīsī, and Ibn ʿAbd al-Munʿim who copied him, noted the variety and wealth of springs, both hot and cold, within the town; some of these springs existed before the Arab period, such as *Ḥammām al-t̲h̲awr* "the hot springs of the bull", where there was a marble statue of a bull, and the large spring covered with very ancient vaulting, from which the water flowed out into a large pool. Today, the cathedral square is embellished with a monumental fountain. Among the famous natives of Jaén in the Muslim period can be mentioned the poet Yaḥyā al-G̲h̲azāl "the gazelle", who was sent to Constantinople by ʿAbd al-Raḥmān II as his ambassador to the emperor Theophilus; the philologist Abū D̲h̲arr Muṣʿab, *ḳāḍī* of his native town in 509/1115-6, and referred to in *al-Rawḍ al-miʿṭar* in various poems; Abū Muḥammad b. D̲j̲iyār al-D̲j̲ayyānī, tax-collector in Fez under the Almoravids, who betrayed the governor prince Yaḥyā Ibn al-Ṣahrawiyā, great-grandson of Yūsuf b. Tas̲h̲fīn, handed it over in 540/1146 to ʿAbd al-Muʾmin and thereafter enjoyed great influence under his government.

Bibliography: Idrisi, *Descrip.*, 202 of text and 248 of trans.; Ibn ʿAbd al-Munʿim, *al-Rawḍ al-miʿṭar*, ed. Lévi-Provençal, 70-1 of text and 88-9 of trans.; Ibn ʿId̲h̲ārī, *al-Bayān al-mug̲h̲rib*, ii, 86; trans., 137; Codera, *Bibl. Arabico-Hispana*, v; Ind. Madoz. *Diccionario geográfico*, ix, 563-4; *Rawḍ al-ḳirtas*, 183.

(A. Huici Miranda)

D̲J̲AYYĀS̲H̲ b. Nad̲j̲āḥ [see Nad̲j̲āḥ, Bā].

D̲J̲AYZĀN, the name of a wadi, a port, and a *muḳāṭaʿa* (district or province) on the Red Sea in south-western Saudi Arabia. The classical form, D̲j̲āzān, is still often used, especially by writers from the province itself. Variant pronunciations are D̲j̲ē-, D̲j̲ī-, D̲j̲ō-, and rarely Zē- (among the tribe of the Masāriḥa). The form Qīzān, which occurs on many maps, is spurious; it is said to be the plural of *ḳawz* (sand hill), whereas the plural of this word is actually *aḳwāz*.

The name appears to have belonged originally to the wadi, which rises in D̲j̲abal Rāziḥ and the territory of K̲h̲awlān in the Yaman, flows south of D̲j̲abal al-ʿUrr, and then turns south-westwards to empty into the Red Sea at the modern port (lat. 16° 53′ N, long. 42° 33′ E). A detailed list of tributaries is given in al-ʿUḳaylī, i, 33-5, along with the names of 13 small dams (*ʿaḳm*, pl. *ʿuḳūm*). The *sayl*s, with a volume of water reaching 500,000 gal. a second and waves over 10 m. high, make the lower reaches one of the most productive agricultural regions in Arabia, but without proper flood control much of the water is wasted. The principal crops are millets (*d̲h̲ura* and *duk̲h̲n*) and sesame; other grains, cotton, and indigo are also grown. The soil is so rich that fertilizers are not needed, and four plantings a year can be raised. In 1380/1961 the Saudi Arabian Government, with technical and financial assistance from the United Nations, was implementing a scheme for erecting a large dam across the wadi, modernizing the irrigation system, and building good roads to link the port with its immediate hinterland.

Two channels, one of which is known as the Pearly Gates, lead from the open sea past the Farasān Bank to D̲j̲ayzān port. The approach is beset with shoals, and large vessels must anchor a mile or more offshore. A haven for dhows lies inside the reefs. The town is built beside hills, the highest rising c. 60 m. Probably salt domes in origin, the hills are now capped with forts. There is no other elevated ground in the vicinity, and on the landward side the town is encircled by a salt flat. Round grass huts with conical roofs of African design prevail, but there are also a number of masonry houses, along with a new hotel, hospital, customs house, and school, all of modernistic aspect.

The climate is trying, with very high temperatures and humidity and fierce sand storms in summer, and the water supply is poor, the only sweet wells lying some distance out of town. Many inhabitants are stricken with malaria during the monsoon rains.

Pearling was once the occupation for which D̲j̲ayzān enjoyed special fame. On the outskirts of the town a salt mine is exploited commercially; the open face of the salt is c. 5 m. thick.

D̲j̲ayzān province, sometimes called Tihāmat ʿAsīr [see ʿAsīr and the accompanying map], embraces, in addition to the lowlands, the mountains west of the continental divide on the crest of which stands Abhā. Among the mountains belonging to D̲j̲ayzān are those of al-Ḳahr, Harūb, al-Rayt̲h̲, Banū Mālik, and Fayfā, all of which are 50 km. or more from the coast. The port of al-Ḳaḥma, cut off from the rest of the province by a lava field, its neighbour al-S̲h̲uḳayḳ, and the Farasān Islands [*q.v.*] are the only places in the province where the date palm grows; elsewhere the *dawm* palm flourishes. Some of the numerous livestock are regularly exported to the Ḥid̲j̲āz. The grazing grounds of the nomads are called *mayr*.

The chief tribe of the region in early Islamic times was Ḥakam b. Saʿd al-ʿAs̲h̲īra [*q.v.*] of the Southern Arabian stock of Kahlān, with Banū ʿAbd al-D̲j̲add as the ruling family. The tribe's capital was the city of al-K̲h̲aṣūf, the site of which appears to be no longer known, and its port was al-S̲h̲ard̲j̲a, the ruins of which lie near al-Muwassam just north of the present Yemen border. Other tribes in the lowlands were Kināna, al-Azd, and Khawlān. It has been suggested that Ghassān [q.v.] once lived in this part of Arabia.

A comprehensive list of the modern tribes is provided by al-ʿUḳaylī, i, 83-93, including 12 tribes in the lower wadi with Djayzān port as their headquarters and 17 in the upper wadi centered on Abu ʿArīsh [q.v.]. Among the more important ones are the Masāriḥa near Abū ʿArīsh, the Djaʿāfira along the coast of Ṣabyā [q.v.], and Banū Shuʿba with their capital at al-Darb (or Darb Banī Shuʿba, incorrectly shown on the map in *EI*², i, 708 simply as Darb). The province contains a noteworthy linguistic boundary: in Djayzān port and Abū ʿArīsh and to the south the old form *am* for the definite article is still common, while in Ṣabyā and Baysh and to the north it gives way to *al*.

The information given here on the history of the province supplements the account in the article ʿASĪR.

The name Djayzān (Djāzān) occurs in a *ḥadīth* attributed to the Prophet, in which it is bracketed with Ḍamad, the name of the wadi immediately to the north. Djayzān when mentioned in the early geographers apparently refers to the wadi only, and not to a town.

The dates 373-93/c. 983-1003 are suggested by al-ʿUḳaylī for the rule of Sulaymān b. Ṭarf (or Ṭaraf), the lord of ʿAththar (or ʿAthr) on the coast of Baysh, but these dates are not certain. Possibly al-Ḥusayn b. Salāma (d. 402/1011-2), the Ziyādid vizier who improved the pilgrim road to Mecca, was the one who broke Sulaymān's power and brought al-Mikhlāf al-Sulaymānī back under Ziyādid rule.

Ḥusayn al-Hamdānī, 101-3, presents new evidence to show that ʿAlī b. Muḥammad al-Ṣulayḥī was killed in 459/1067, not in 473/1081 (cf. *EI*¹, iv, 516). If this is correct, ʿAlī's victory in the battle of al-Zarāʾib could not have taken place in 460/1068; Ḥusayn al-Ḥamdānī, 83, dates it in 450/1058.

The time of the establishment of the Sulaymānid *sharīfs* in the Mikhlāf is undetermined. One source states that Dāʾūd b. Sulaymān, great-grandson of Mūsā al-Djūn, was the first of the line to migrate from the Ḥidjāz to the Mikhlāf, in the days of the Rassid al-Hādī Yaḥyā (d. 298/910). However, the Sulaymānids do not appear to have transferred the core of their power to the Mikhlāf until after the final defeat in Mecca, c. 462/1070, of their leader Ḥamza b. Wahhās at the hands of the Hāshimid Abū Hāshim Muḥammad. Ḥamza's son Yaḥyā and grandson Ghānim both held authority in the Mikhlāf. The Sulaymānids from Ghānim on are often called Ghānimids (al-Ghawānim), a name which has the advantage of avoiding confusion with Sulaymān b. Ṭarf. Wahhās b. Ghānim was the Ghānimid killed in battle near Ḥaraḍ by the Mahdid ʿAbd al-Nabī b. ʿAlī in 560/1164.

Under the Ziyādids, the Nadjāḥids, and the Mahdids, parts of the Mikhlāf, if not the whole region, were at times brought under the nominal or real suzerainty of Zabīd, the capital of all these dynasties (204-569/819-1174). For example, Surūr, who as vizier was the power behind the Nadjāḥid throne, 529-51/c. 1135-56, secured the Mikhlāf as a fief for himself. From time to time the Zaydī Imāms, often reigning in Ṣaʿda in the highlands almost due east of Djayzān, intervened in the affairs of the Mikhlāf.

Under the Ayyūbids the Ghānimids in the Mikhlāf were called the Shuṭūṭ, the meaning of which sobriquet is not given. Two sons of Ḳāsim b. Ghānim in succession revolted against Ayyūbid rule but were overcome.

The Rasūlid al-Malik al-Ashraf ʿUmar b. Yūsuf (d. 696/1296) in his *Ṭurfat al-aṣḥāb* names Hāshim b. Wahhās, a great-great-grandson of Ghānim b. Yaḥyā, as lord of Djayzān in his time. Other Ghānimids were lords of Baysh and Bāghita, while members of collateral branches ruled in lower and upper Ḍamad, Ṣabyā, and al-Luʾluʾa (al-Shuḳayḳ).

In the early 9th/15th century a new branch of Ghānimids appeared, the Ḳuṭbids, the issue of Ḳuṭb al-Dīn Abū Bakr b. Muḥammad, who chose as their capital Darb al-Nadjā, the ruins of which are still to be seen near Abū ʿArīsh. The Ḳuṭbids were usually subject to the Rasūlids and later the Ṭāhirids. In 882/1477 or 884 the Sharīf of Mecca, Muḥammad b. Barakāt I, raided the Mikhlāf and carried off much loot, including precious books. The connexion of Barakāt II's brother and rival, Aḥmad Djayzān (or al-Djayzānī, d. 909/1503-4), with the Mikhlāf is not clear. He may have lived with his Ghānimid relatives there for a time and secured support from them. One of his descendants was ʿAbd al-Malik al-Djayzānī. Some of the descendants of the Sharīf al-Ḥasan b. Muḥammad Abū Numayy (d. 1010/1601) were also known as Dhawū Djayzān.

Visiting Djayzān in 909/1503, Varthema found 45 vessels from different countries in the port. Writing in the late 9th/15th century, the master pilot Shihāb al-Dīn Aḥmad b. Mādjid [q.v.] gives instructions for entering Djayzān (Djāzān) port. He mentions both the Mikhlāf and the port of al-Shardja. As an authority on this part of the Red Sea he cites the famous captain ʿUthmān al-Djāzānī.

During the first half of the 10th/16th century, Djayzān was attacked on three different occasions by Ḳays b. Muḥammad al-Ḥirāmī, the lord of Ḥaly Ibn Yaʿḳūb [q.v.].

In 946/1539 an Ottoman Mudīr was assigned to the Mikhlāf with headquarters at Abū ʿArīsh. About this time the district was occupied briefly by the Sharīf Muḥammad Abū Numayy. In the 11th/17th century the influence of the Zaydī Imāms grew stronger. In 1102/1690 Aḥmad b. Ghālib, who had made himself master of Mecca for several years despite the fact that he did not belong to any of the three principal clans of Sharīfs (Dhawū Barakāt, Dhawū ʿAbd Allāh, and Dhawū Zayd), was appointed governor of the Mikhlāf by the Zaydī Imām of Ṣanʿāʾ to whom he appealed for favour after his expulsion from Mecca. The first Khayrātid master of the Mikhlāf, Aḥmad b. Muḥammad, also began his career in 1141/1728-9 as governor there for the Zaydīs. Aḥmad's grandfather Khayrāt, on coming from Mecca to Abū ʿArīsh, had been assigned a stipend from the revenues of Djayzān port by the Zaydī Imām al-Mutawakkil Ismāʿīl b. al-Ḳāsim (d. 1087/1676).

In the mid-12th/18th century the warlike tribe of Yām of Nadjrān penetrated into the Mikhlāf under its new leaders, the Makramid [q.v.] *dāʿīs* of the Ismāʿīlī persuasion.

Niebuhr in 1176/1762-3 found the second Khayrātid, Muḥammad b. Aḥmad, an independent ruler over the extensive district of Abū ʿArīsh, which included Djayzān port.

Although the Wahhābīs were never very active in the Red Sea, in 1809 ships of theirs entered Djayzān port and seized coffee and other goods. About a year later the port was taken by Wahhābī *mudjāhidūn* of the tribe of Ridjāl Almaʿ. The Khayrātid Sharīf Ḥamūd Abū Mismār was instrumental in bringing about the capture by Muḥammad ʿAlī Pas̲h̲a's forces of the Wahhābī highland chieftain, Ṭāmī b. S̲h̲uʿayb al-Rufaydī, who recited the Ḳurʾān as he was paraded through the streets of Cairo in a scene described by al-D̲j̲abartī, iv, 219-20.

Combes and Tamisier, visiting D̲j̲ayzān in 1835, observed that the commerce of the port had greatly declined as a consequence of Muḥammad ʿAlī's monopolistic practices. Senna and coffee were sent from the mountains to Cairo.

The most powerful of the K̲h̲ayrātids who came after Ḥamūd was his grandnephew al-Ḥusayn b. ʿAlī (regn. 1840-8), who held Tihāma as far south as Mocha and even occupied for a time Taʿizz and other places in the mountains of al-Yaman al-Asfal. Beaten in battle by the Zaydī al-Mutawakkil Muḥammad b. Yaḥyā, al-Ḥusayn abdicated. Under Ottoman rule two of al-Ḥusayn's sons served short terms as Ḳaʾimaḳāms in Abū ʿArīs̲h̲.

The last K̲h̲ayrātid, a nephew of al-Ḥusayn b. ʿAlī, revolted against the Turks and ruled independently and oppressively for a brief span. His name is given by al-ʿUḳaylī as al-Ḥusayn b. Muḥammad, whereas *Nayl al-waṭar*, i, 356, calls him al-Ḥasan.

Having supplanted the Turks in the Mik̲h̲lāf in 1909, Muḥammad b. ʿAlī al-Idrīsī defeated them two years later at al-Ḥafāʾir, close to D̲j̲ayzān port. The capital was moved by al-Idrīsī from Abū ʿArīs̲h̲ to Ṣabyā.

Under Saudi Arabian administration the capital has been transferred to D̲j̲ayzān port. The fullest description of the port and province in recent times is given by Philby, who was there in 1936.

Bibliography: To the works given under ʿASĪR should be added Aḥmad b. Mād̲j̲id in G. Ferrand, *Instructions nautiques*, i, Paris 1921-3; Daḥlān, *al-D̲j̲adāwil al-marḍiyya*, Cairo 1306; al-D̲j̲abartī, *ʿAd̲j̲āʾib*, Cairo 1297; ʿAbd Allāh b. ʿAbd al-Karīm al-D̲j̲irāfī, *al-Muḳtaṭaf min taʾrīk̲h̲ al-Yaman*, Cairo 1370; Ḥusayn b. Fayḍ Allāh al-Hamdānī, *al-Ṣulayḥiyyūn*, Cairo n.d.; al-S̲h̲awkānī, *al-Badr al-ṭāliʿ*, Cairo 1348; Muḥammad b. Aḥmad ʿĪsā al-ʿUḳaylī, *Min taʾrīk̲h̲ al-Mik̲h̲lāf al-Sulaymānī*, i [ii not yet published], al-Riyāḍ 1378; Zabāra, *Nas̲h̲r al-ʿurf li-nubalāʾ al-Yaman baʿd al-alf*, Cairo 1359; E. Combes and M. Tamisier, *Voyage en Abyssinie*, Paris 1838; C. Niebuhr, *Beschreibung von Arabien*, Copenhagen 1772; Ch. Schefer, *Les Voyages de Ludovico di Varthemo*, Paris 1888; F. Wüstenfeld, *Jemen im XI. (XVII.) Jahrhundert*, Göttingen 1884; numerous articles in the Saudi Arabian press and periodicals, particularly *al-Yamāma* of al-Riyāḍ and *al-Manhal* of Mecca. (G. RENTZ)

D̲J̲AZĀʾ (AR.), recompense, both in a good and in a bad sense, especially with reference to the next world; *t̲h̲awāb* (Ar.) means the same but usually only in a good sense. Opinions differed on its nature, duration, the recipients, and how men knew of it. The Muʿtazila held that God must reward goodness and punish wickedness; reason shows this though some held that the eternal duration of recompense was known only by revelation. The opposing view was that God is not a subject for argument; if He sends all to the fire, it is His justice, and if He takes all into paradise, it is His mercy. The Muʿtazila of Baṣra said that God must reward goodness but may forgive all sinners. Ibn Karrām taught that revelation told that reward may be merited. Some said that reward should be eternal because it is greater than man's merit but not punishment because of God's mercy, though wilful disobedience to Him deserves an eternity of penalty. The common view was that no believer would be kept in the fire for ever; God would at last deliver him. Most Muʿtazila and the K̲h̲awārid̲j̲ said that great sins sent the sinner to the fire for ever but D̲j̲āḥiẓ said that this was the fate of obstinate unbelievers only and that the fire drew such to itself by its nature, God did not send them. Kaʿbī said that venial sins would not be punished in the fire but that they might add up to great. Murdār said that even venial sins sent to the fire for ever. Some argued that, if the penalty were limited, so should the reward be, for man's acts are limited. Another view was utilitarian; if God's threats were to be efficacious, they should be as wide as possible but, if encouragement were needed, the limitation of punishment should be stressed. The general view was that all infants would go to paradise though some made their lot depend on the religion of the parents.

Bis̲h̲r b. Muʿtamir [*q.v.*] said that God can punish infants without being unjust. Some held that believing *d̲j̲inn* would be in paradise but others thought there would be no resurrection for them, either because there was no resurrection except as a reward or no reward except after responsibility and on either ground *d̲j̲inn* were excluded. Some said that useful animals would be in paradise but in more beautiful forms to delight the blessed while noxious beasts and insects would be in the fire, helping to torment the wicked but feeling no pain themselves. Paradise is a reward for merit or bounty to those without it, infants and madmen. The nature of recompense was in dispute, whether spiritual, corporeal or both; Naẓẓām argued that bodies were needed if the blessed were to eat and drink. He also said that there were no rewards in this world as blessings were only for encouragement; he also said that God cannot lessen the joys of paradise nor the pains of the fire. D̲j̲ubbāʾī taught that the torments in hell were not profitable to any but were the result of wisdom and justice. A saint, seen in a dream, said that friends were eating and drinking before the throne but God knew that he cared for none of these things so granted him to look on His face. It was one of the charges against the philosophers that they taught only a resurrection of the spirit. Kaʿbī said that if the hand of a thief were cut off and he died an unbeliever, it was given to one who had lost a hand but died a believer or was given to some other believer. The next world is *dār al-d̲j̲azāʾ*.

Bibliography: S̲h̲āhrastānī, *Nihāyat al-iḳdām chap.* 17; Ibrāhīm al-Ṣaffār, *Talk̲h̲īṣ al-adilla* (B. M. Add. 27526) f. 92 ff.; A. S. Tritton, *Muslim theology*, London 1947; G. Vajda, in *Stud. Isl.*, xi, 29 ff. gives quotations from Dāwūd b. Marwān b. Muḳammiṣ which reproduce ideas of the Muʿtazila. (A. S. TRITTON)

ii.—OTTOMAN PENAL LAW

In Ottoman usage, *d̲j̲azāʾ* means punishment and *ḳānūn-i d̲j̲azāʾī* (cezâi) a penal code.

The oldest Ottoman penal code so far discovered forms part of the *ḳānūn-nāme* of Meḥemmed II published by Kraelitz (*MOG*, i, 1921, 13-48). It deals chiefly with those criminal offences that are to be punished by strokes and fines. Soon it was enlarged by an additional chapter, a *siyāsetnāme* [*q.v.*] (see *Belleten*, vi, 1942, 37-44), which prescribes capital or severe corporal punishment (*siyāset*) and regulates criminal procedure. This enlarged code constitutes the first part of the so-called *Ḳānūnnāme* of Süleymān I (*TOEM*, 1329, suppl.) which in its major parts, however, seems to have been compiled already under Bāyezīd II. A third criminal code came into existence in Süleymān I's time. This *ḳānūnnāme*, which will be published soon, covers many additional fields and is differently organized. A fourth, most comprehensive but rather inconcise version, was compiled privately by a clerk of a *s͟harīʿa* court in the 11th/17th century. In addition, there exist a number of intermediary and secondary types.

Criminal regulations are also found in individual *fermān*s and *yasaḳnāme*s (*e.g.*, Babinger, *Sult. Urkunden*, Munich 1956) and in the *ḳānūnnāme*s concerning the organization of the State, the market police, the artisans, and the various military forces. The numerous provincial *ḳānūnnāme*s contain relatively few penal regulations, since in principle the same criminal law was in force in all parts of the Ottoman Empire. In some Muslim countries conquered in the early 10th/16th century the Ottomans at first confirmed existing secular, including criminal, law, such as the D͟hu 'l-Ḳadr codes (Barkan, *Kanunlar*, 119-29). After a short time, however, they introduced their own penal code, proclaiming their wish to abrogate many *bidaʿ* of the previous rulers and alleviate the plight of the population by reducing penalties and abolishing abuses in criminal procedure.

In Ottoman criminal codes wide use is made of *taʿzīr*, *i.e.*, discretionary punishment by the *ḳāḍī* in the form of corporal chastisement, generally the bastinado [see FALAḲA]. For many offences the penalty is a fine (*ḳînlîḳ*, *d͟jerīme*), with or without *taʿzīr* and often in addition to damages. Fines are laid down either as fixed amounts of money (mostly graded in accordance with the financial circumstances of the offender) or set in a certain ratio to the number of strokes inflicted on the criminal. In many instances slaves and non-Muslims pay half the fine of a free Muslim, but in the case of the non-Muslims this privilege is partly cancelled out by their being graded differently. The fines constituted a considerable income for the fief-holders and/or governors (or their subordinates); in later periods *ḳāḍī*s often exacted fines for themselves. Many offenders were also condemned to be ignominiously led through the town and exposed to to public scorn (*tes͟hhīr*). Imprisonment and banishment are rarer penalties; sending to the galleys, though not mentioned in the *ḳānūn*, was quite common. The form of capital punishment referred to specifically in the criminal codes is hanging; historians and travellers also report impaling, beheading, ganching, strangling, etc. Other severe penalties mentioned in *ḳānūnnāme*s are emasculation, the cutting off of a hand or the nose, the branding of the forehead, etc.

The *ḳānūn*, though pretending merely to complete the *s͟harīʿa*, diverges from its criminal law in a number of important points. On the one hand, it commutes certain *ḥadd* penalties or seems to assume that they are commonly commuted to lighter punishment. On the other hand, it extends the range of many penal regulations of the *s͟harīʿa* and adds a great many delicts not covered by it. With a view to serving, above all, the interests of the State and ensuring public peace and order, many more crimes are made punishable by death (*siyāseten ḳatl*); many of the penalties are evidently meant to be preventive or intimidating. The monetary fines and some of the corporal penalties laid down in the *ḳānūn* are unknown to religious law. The treatment of attempt, complicity and repeated offences also differs from the *s͟harīʿa*. Most important, the *ḳānūn* frees criminal procedure from the latter's limitation and strict regulations. Similar to the earlier *maẓālim* (*s͟hurṭa*, *ḥād͟jib*) and *muḥtasib* jurisdiction in other Muslim countries, the Ottoman *ḳānūn* accepts evidence that is not admissible according to the *s͟harīʿa* and proof regarded by it as insufficient. Admission of guilt may be obtained by torture; suspicion and the criminal past of the accused are taken into decisive consideration. In several later *ḳānūnnāme* manuscripts, marginal notes, mostly ascribed to the *Nis͟hānd͟jî*, abolish some regulations of the criminal code because of their inconsistency with the *s͟harīʿa*.

The Ottomans tried to eliminate the traditional dualism of *ḳāḍī* and *maẓālim* jurisdiction by making the *ḳāḍī* administer both *s͟harīʿa* and *ḳānūn*. Ordinary citizens were generally to be punished by the governors, *subas͟hî*s, *voyvoda*s, etc. only after a trial by a *ḳāḍī*, but in reality this rule was constantly violated. The clash between the authority of the *ḳāḍī* and the governor in the administration of criminal justice remained a major problem throughout Ottoman history. Certain classes of the population (soldiers and other *ḳapî ḳullarî*, *tīmār*-holders, *s͟herīf*s, *ʿulemāʾ*, foreigners, etc.) were in many cases subject to special penal regulations and tried by separate tribunals. Trade delicts and certain religious and moral misdemeanours were dealt with by the *muḥtasib* [*q.v.*].

The Ottoman penal codes were not conceived merely as laws for the protection of society from the criminals but to a large extent also as a means of protecting the people from oppressive officials and fief-holders. Sulṭān Süleymān I ordered that a bound copy of the penal and feudal *ḳānūnnāme* be sent to every law-court, but to what extent its criminal regulations were actually enforced is not known. From the 11th/17th century, in any case, the *ḳānūn* for various reasons began to lose its practical importance. Criminal justice was henceforth based exclusively on the *s͟harīʿa* as administered by increasingly corrupt *ḳāḍī*s or the arbitrary will of oppressive governors and their subordinates. Ottoman criminal justice, praised by European observers in earlier periods for its efficiency, degenerated completely.

Modern reform of Ottoman penal law began under Maḥmūd II. After the destruction of the Janissaries (1826), governors were forbidden to inflict the death penalty without the formal sentence of a *ḳāḍī*. A new penal code, published in 1840 in the spirit of the Gülk͟hāne Charter, still largely aims at curbing tyrannic officials. Penalties are reduced and procedure is to become more regular; every capital punishment has to be confirmed by the Sultan. This primitive and very deficient law was somewhat improved by the code of 1851, only to be replaced in 1858 by a completely different, secular and comprehensive penal code which followed French law and, with many amendments, remained in force until 1926.

Bibliography: D'Ohsson, *Tableau général*, iii, 1820, 236-81, 362-3; B. Djurdjev and others, *Kanuni*, Sarajevo 1957, 160-68; H. Hadžibegić, in *Glasnik*, N.S., iv-v (1949-50); J. Schacht, in *Isl.*, xx (1932), 211-2; xxii (1934-5), 226-31; C. Üçok, in *Ank. Huk. Fak. Derg.*, iv (1947), 52-73; H. Inalcık, in *Siy. Bilgiler Fak. Derg.*, Ankara, xiii (1958), no. 2; *Tanzimat*, i, Istanbul 1940, 176-80, 221-32; U. Heyd, *Studies in Old Ottoman criminal law* (with text of codes) (in preparation).

(U. HEYD)

AL-**D͟JAZĀʾIR** is the name given to the islets just off the north-west coast of Algiers Bay, and which now constitute the Admiralty of the town. The Arabs applied the name of the islets to the town, which was founded in the 4th/10th century on the mainland opposite them. Under the Turks it became the capital of Algeria, and has remained so ever since. It was the French who transformed its Arab name into "Alger" (Algiers). It lies at a latitude of 36° 47′ N., and a longtitude of 3° 4′ E. (Greenwich) In the census of 1954 a municipal population of 355,000 was recorded, of whom 162,000 were Muslims; in 1959, the population of Greater Algiers (city and adjacent communes) stood at 805,000, of whom 456,000 were Muslims.

The discovery in 1940 of an important collection of Punic coins, of lead and bronze, found in the district neighbouring the port (J. Cantineau & L. Leschi, *Monnaies puniques d'Alger*, in *Comptes Rendus Ac. Inscr. et Belles Lettres*, 1941, 263-77), is ample proof of the existence of a Phoenician warehouse, probably on the islets, with the name Ikosim (the isle of owls, or thorns).

The Latin form of the name, Icosium, was given to the Roman settlement on the mainland. It is not known at which date this was founded, but it was not an important settlement, although it was the seat of a bishopric. We find no more reference to it in historical documents after the fifth century. According to al-Bakrī (*Desc. de l'Afr. sept.*, 66, *tr.*, 156), its ruins existed until the 4th/10th century, when the Muslim town was founded by Buluggīn b. Zīrī.

Its name then became Djazāʾir Banī Mazghanna, after a Ṣanhādjian tribe which lived in the region at that time. It remained a town and port of little importance up to the early 10th/16th century, and was tied to the vicissitudes of the central Maghrib. It should nevertheless be mentioned that at the beginning of the 6th/12th century the Almoravids erected a large mosque in Algiers, and that from about 771/1370 onwards, under the protection of the Thaʿāliba Arabs in the Mitidja area, it gradually asserted its claim to be an independent town. In the 9th/15th century its protector was a holy figure, Sīdī ʿAbd al-Raḥmān al-Thaʿālibī, and since that time he has been the patron saint of the city. The mediaeval population of Algiers consisted in part of refugees who had fled from the Christian reconquest of Andalusia, and many of them established themselves as corsairs in Algiers.

In 1510 the Spanish imposed a levy on the city and occupied the islets, in order to suppress the corsairs. When it was realised that this would seriously impair their prosperity, the inhabitants and their leader, Salīm al-Tūmī, sought for an ally to help rid them of the Spanish yoke. When they summoned to their aid the Turkish corsair, ʿArūdj [*q.v.*], who at that time ruled over Djidjelli, he did not succeed in expelling the Spaniards, but seized the town himself and established it as his principal base of operations. The Spaniards attempted to recapture Algiers in 1516 and 1519, but met both times with failure. After the death of ʿArūdj in 924/1518, his brother Khayr al-Dīn assumed power, but was not able to maintain control over Algiers, and fell back to Djidjelli, 926-31/1520-5. Then in 1525 Algiers once more sent out an appeal for assistance, and on 27 May 1529 he succeeded in capturing the fortress (Peñon) which the Spaniards had built on the largest of the islets. The Peñon was pulled down, and the materials served to construct the breakwater which henceforth connected the islets with the mainland. Such was the origin of the port of Algiers.

Meanwhile, Khayr al-Dīn had bequeathed his conquest to the Ottoman Empire, which was thus in possession of an important naval base in the western Mediterranean. It is therefore in no way surprising that Charles V attempted to capture Algiers in 1541. On October 23 his forces landed on the shores of the Bay of Algiers, and after crossing the Wādī Harrāsh, they set up camp on a hill overlooking the town, now known as the Fort l'Empereur but at that time called Kudyat al-Ṣabūn. But during the night of 24-5 October the weather quickly deteriorated, and half the landing fleet was lost in the consequent storm. Defeated as much by the elements as by the Turks, Charles V had to abandon much material and withdraw from Algiers, leaving it with a legend of invincibility which remained intact until 1830.

Charles V's expedition served as a warning signal to the Turks, and they proceeded to extend and perfect the fortifications, especially on the seaward side, until Algiers literally was a stronghold. Moreover, it had become the capital of a considerable Turkish province, enjoying a *de facto* independence of Constantinople, and was the operating base for many corsairs. All these factors contributed to its great economic and social development, beginning in the 16th century.

Very little is known of the town before the Turkish period. It is probable that the original city-wall extended as far as the Turkish wall, but that the density of building within it was much smaller. The Turkish wall, 3,100 m. long, was continuous, even on the coastal side, and was equipped with towers and a moat. Five gates gave access to the city: the Fishery gate and the Fleet gate on the harbour side, Bāb al-Wād to the north, Bab ʿAzzūn to the south, and Bāb Djadīd to the south-west. Various other fortifications reinforced the protection offered by the city-wall: the Ḳaṣba, which in 1816 became the residence of the Dey of Algiers, was built in 1556 to replace a Berber stronghold on the summit of the triangle which the town then formed; the Fort l'Empereur, built on the site of Charles V's camp; several forts and gun emplacements between the Bāb al-Wād and Bāb ʿAzzūn gates along the sea-front, and on the former islets which guarded the port.

The Turks built a palace called the 'Djanīna' (small garden) inside the town, and the former archbishop's palace was at one time part of it. It was used as the Regent's residence until 1816. In the lower part of the town, near the port, several Turkish dignitaries and wealthy privateers built themselves luxurious dwellings. The interior decorating, depending on the owner's taste and his 'catch' on the high seas, was often of European origin (Venetian crystal, Dutch porcelain, etc.). Many mosques were built, the best-known of which is the Djāmiʿ Djadīd (also called the 'Fishery Mosque') in Government Square (1660). There were also a number of barracks and prisons in the town, but virtually nothing remains of them.

We have at hand only rough estimates of the population at various times. Haëdo put it at 60,000 at the end of the 16th century. According to P. Dan, it was 100,000 in 1634, whereas Venture de Paradis counted only 50,000 inhabitants at the end of the 18th century, and 30,000 in 1830. It was always a very mixed population; there were the Turks, mainly members of the army and administration (numbering 4,000 in 1830); the Kulughlis (Turkish Kul-oghlu, cf. the Awlād al-Nās in Egypt), offspring of Turks and the indigenous women of that region, and held in disdain by the Turks; old families with long roots in the past, often of Andalusian or Moorish origin, forming the bulk of the commercial and artisan classes; the numerous Kabyles, forming the labouring class; Saharans from Biskra and the Mzāb; Jews (4,000 in 1830), the richest of whom had come from Leghorn in the 18th century, and enjoyed the privileges of Europeans; some European business-men and consuls; finally, those taken prisoner from the Christians, numbering as many as 25,000 in 1634 (P. Dan). It is clear that the population was just as much Mediterranean as North African.

As far as is known, the town of Algiers was placed directly under the authority of the head of government. The judicial system was administered by two Ḳāḍīs, one from the Hanafī school for the Turks, the other from the Mālikī school for the Arabs. They worked together with a tribunal of rabbis and consuls representing the Jewish and Christian minorities. The police-force was staffed by *s͟hāws͟h*s (Turkish *čāʾūs͟h* [*q.v.*]) under the command of a *bās͟h s͟hāws͟h*. There was one force to deal with the Turks, and another to deal with the Moors. To complete the administration, there was a chief of municipal services (*s͟hayk͟h al-balad*), and a *mizwār*, more or less the equivalent of the *muḥtasib* in Moroccan cities. The Jewish community had its own institutions, and Europeans enjoyed the protection of their respective consuls.

Privateering was the great industry of the Turkish era. After having taken the form of a holy war or of a conflict between the Ottoman Empire and the Austro-Spanish Empire of Charles V and Philip II, it became a profitable business and therefore the chief occupation of the inhabitants. All sections of the population drew benefit from it—the government, which received part of the takings, private individuals, who formed companies to arm the ships, and the general populace, who gained from the generosity of the privateers and wealthy ship-owners. It also led to an influx of adventurers, usually of European or Mediterranean origin, who 'took to the turban' to give vent to their spirit of adventure and taste for plunder, or simply to avoid falling into the hands of slave-traders. It has been estimated that there were 8,000 renegades in Algiers in 1634.

Such piracy often provoked reprisals from the European powers. They generally took the form of naval bombardments of Algiers, some of which caused serious damage. The Spaniards bombarded it in 1567, 1775 (the ensuing landing did not succeed) and 1783, the Danes in 1770. The main attacks came from France (1661, 1665, 1682, 1683, 1688) and England (1622, 1655, 1672). After having been largely suppressed by the end of the 18th century, privateering experienced a revival during the wars of the French Revolution and the First Empire, and the British consequently carried out further shellings in 1816 and 1825.

The French invasion of 1830 had been prepared in 1808 by Major Boutin, an engineering officer sent by Napoleon to make a first-hand report of the conditions necessary to carry out such an operation successfully. The general lines of his plan were used by those who prepared the expedition of 1830; the French forces landed on the shore of the Sīdī Farrūs͟h peninsula, to the west of the town, on 14 June, and by the 29th they had reached the defences of the Fort l'Empereur. It was captured on 4 July, and on the following day the town itself surrendered, without having suffered much damage.

For many years the French lived within the existing urban boundaries, although they did burst out at one or two points. But as the town's population increased, it overflowed northwards (Bāb al-Wād quarter) and southwards (Bāb ʿAzzūn quarter). Today the metropolis extends to the suburban districts of Saint-Eugène (N), Hussein Dey (S.-E.), Birmandreis (Biʾr Murād Raʾīs) (S), El-Biar (S.-W.) and almost as far as Bouzaréa (W). Its growth remains uninterrupted, and is gradually spoiling the open spaces and gardens which formerly surrounded the town.

The port has undergone a considerable expansion in recent years, and in 1955 it registered the movement of 9387 ships and 500,000 passengers. The airport of Maison-Blanche (25 kms. E. of the town) meets all the requirements of modern international air services.

The organization of local authorities has been modified since April 1959. The city, divided into arrondissements on the French pattern, together with the neighbouring communes, forms the single municipality of Greater Algiers.

After the Anglo-American landings of 8 November 1942, Algiers became the provisional capital of France until Paris was liberated in August 1944. Since the beginning of the Algerian revolution on 1 November 1954, Algiers itself has been the scene of political events of far-reaching importance, particularly those of 6 February 1956, 13 May 1958 and 24 January 1960 and the following days. Since 1 July 1962 it has become the capital of independent Algeria.

Bibliography: *Corpus Inscr. Latin.*, VIIIb, xv (Icosium) and Supplement; G. Colin, *Corpus des inscriptions arabes et turques de l'Algérie*, i, *Département d'Alger*, Paris 1901; Ibn Ḥawḳal, tr. de Slane, in *JA*, Feb. 1842, 183; Bakrī, *Descr. de l'Afr. sept.*, 66, tr. de Slane, 156-7; Idrīsī, *Extraits*, éd. H. Pérès, 62; ʿAbdarī, *Notices et extraits du voyage d'El-Abderi*, tr. Cherbonneau, in *JA*, 1854, ii; Leo Africanus, *Descr. de l'Afrique*, tr. Épaulard, ii, 347-50; D. Haëdo, *Topographia e historia general de Argel*, Valladolid 1612, French trans. Monnereau and Berbrugger, in *R.Afr.*, 1870-1; *Histoire des rois d'Alger*, French trans. H. de Grammont, in *R.Afr.*, 1880-81; P. Dan, *Histoire de Barbarie et de ses corsaires*, Paris 1637, 94-138; Venture de Paradis, *Alger au XVIIIe siècle*, éd. Fagnan, Algiers 1898; Boutin, *Reconnaissance de la ville, des forts et batteries d'Alger*, in Nettement, *Hist. de la conquête d'Alger*, Paris 1879, 574-99; H. de Grammont, *Histoire d'Alger sous la domination turque*, Paris 1887; S. Lane-Poole, *The Barbary Corsairs*, London 1890; A. Devoulx, *Les édifices religieux d'Alger*, in *R.Afr.* vi-xiii; H. Klein, *Feuillets d'El-Djezaïr*, Algiers 1937; Lespès, *Alger*, Paris 1930; G. Esquer, *Les commencements d'un Empire. La prise d'Alger*, Paris 1929; idem, *Alger et sa région*, Paris 1949; Laye, *Le port d'Alger*, Algiers 1951; *Documents Algériens*, economic series, no. 82-3; cultural series, no. 55-6 et 62.

(R. LE TOURNEAU)

DJAZĀʾIR-I BAḤR-I SAFĪD, the name given to an *eyālet* of the Ottoman empire, often called simply DJAZĀʾIR and usually known to Europeans as the Vilayet of the Archipelago. It originated as the area under the administration of the Ḳapudan Pas͟ha, the *sandjaḳ beyleri* being known as *deryā beyleri* [see DARYĀ-BEGI] and serving with the fleet instead of with the army. At its greatest extent, in the 11th/17th century, it comprised most of the islands of the Aegean Sea, coast districts of Asia Minor and Greece, and for a time Cyprus, but never Crete. At first the Ḳapudan Pas͟ha, an official of two *ṭug͟h*s, governed the *sandjaḳ* of Gallipoli (Gelibolu) with the *ḳaḍāʾ*s of Galata and Izmid. Khayr al-Dīn Barbarossa, who submitted to the Sultan in 940/1533, and his successors were *wazīr*s of three *ṭugh*s and members of the *dīwān-i humāyūn*. He already governed Algeria and Mahdiyya. His *eyālet* was extended to incorporate the *sandjaḳ*s of Ḳodja-eli, Ṣughla and Bīgha in Asia, and Negropont (Eghriboz, Euboea), Lepanto (Aynabakhtī), Ḳarlī-eli, Mitylene (Midilli), and Mistra (Mizistre) in Europe. Rhodes (Rodos) was added after his death and about 1027/1618 Chios (Sakīz), Naxos (Naksha) and Andros (Andīra). In 1052/1642 Algiers became virtually independent. Cyprus was added to the *eyālet* about 1080/1670 but was detached again in 1115/1703 when it became a *khāṣṣ* of the Grand Vizier. It reverted to the Ḳapudan Pasha in 1199/1785. Mistra and Ḳarlī-eli were attached to the *eyālet* of the Morea by Merzifonlū Ḳara Muṣṭafā Pasha, and by the time that the Tanẓīmāt abolished the jurisdiction of the Ḳapudan Pasha the eyālet consisted of the six *sandjaḳ*s of Bīgha from which it was governed, Rhodes, Chios, Mitylene, Lemnos (Limni) and Cyprus. In 1876, after the transfer of Bīgha to the eyalet of Khudāvendigar, the centre was moved to Chios and later, in the course of further reorganizations, to Rhodes. Cyprus was occupied by Britain in 1878; Rhodes and the Dodecanese islands passed to Italy after the war of 1911-2, and were incorporated in the Greek kingdom after the second world war; the remaining islands were occupied by Greece during the Balkan war, and the 'eyalet of the islands' ceased to exist. The islands of Imroz (Imbros) and Bozdja-Ada (Tenedos) [*qq.v.*] were returned to Turkey by the treaty of Lausanne, 1923.

Bibliography: Sāmī Frasherī, *Ḳāmūs al-aʿlām*, iii, 1794-5; I. H. Uzunçarşılı, *Osmanlı devletinin merkez ve bahriye teşkilâtı*, Ankara 1948, 420-2; further information will be found in the articles on the various islands, placed under their Turkish names. (C. F. BECKINGHAM)

AL-**DJAZĀʾIR** AL-**KHĀLIDA**, 'the Eternal Islands', the Arabic equivalent of Gk. αἱ τῶν Μακάρων νῆσοι, Lat. Fortunatae Insulae, as applied to certain islands off the W. African coast, apparently the Canaries. The 'Fortunate Islands', Djazāʾir al-Saʿādāt (also Djazāʾir al-Suʿadāʾ), are sometimes distinguished from, more usually identified with, the Eternal Islands. As these names indicate, the early Arab geographers acquired their knowledge of the Atlantic islands from Classical, *i.e.*, Greek, sources, and their accounts share the vagueness of reference of the originals. Thus, as well as the Canaries, the Madeira group and the Azores, even the Cape Verde Islands, may occasionally be intended (cf. Reinaud, *Taḳwīm*, i, ccxxxv). The islands are described as possessing rich natural fertility and a mild climate throughout the year. They are inhabited, six or seven in number, lying in the Circumambient Ocean (al-Baḥr al-Muḥīṭ) at the farthest point to the west. According to al-Bīrūnī (cited Yāḳūt, *Buldān*, ii, 70), they are 200 *farsakh*s out to sea, while in other accounts (Maḳḳarī, *Nafḥ al-ṭīb*, i, 104, see also below) they can be seen from shore on a clear day. Following Ptolemy, Arab geographers made the prime meridian pass through the Eternal Islands. The Spaniard Bakrī (d. 487/1094) has fresh knowledge, or at least a new source, for he names the islands Furṭunātash, certainly from Latin (cf. Pons Boigues, *Historiadores*, 163), and al-Idrīsī (*circa* 1154) gives the names of two of the six islands: Masfahān, for the volcanic peak of which he cites a description, evidently Teneriffe, and Lamghūsh (?). Al-Idrīsī also knows that in the time of the Almoravid ʿAlī b. Yūsuf b. Tāshifīn (500-37/1106-43) an expedition was planned, though it never took place, to an island opposite Āsafī (Safi, Morocco), the smoke of which could be seen on a clear day. Al-Dimishḳī (d. 727/1327) has the story of a successful voyage to certain islands 10° west of al-Andalus (ed. Mehren, 135), which should be taken with accounts of the exploits of Khashkhāsh and the Adventurers (al-Mugharrirūn) (see AL-BAḤR AL-MUḤĪṬ). These stories afford perhaps the only indications of direct contact in early times between the lands of Islam and the Atlantic islands. On the other hand, Ibn Khaldūn (*Muḳaddima*, ed. Būlāḳ-Beirut, 53-4) mentions a Christian expedition to the Eternal Islands, which seems to refer to Portuguese activity in the Canaries in 1341 (cf. R. Hennig, *Terrae Incognitae*, Leiden 1936-9, iii, 138, 206 ff.).

Bibliography: C. A. Nallino, *Al-Ḫuwârizmî e il suo rifacimento della Geografia di Tolomeo, Memorie d. R. Accad. d. Lincei, class. sci. morali.*, Ser. quint., ii/1a (Rome, 1896), 24-5 (reprinted in *Raccolta di scritti*, v. 490 ff.); *Al-Battani sive Albatenii Opus Astronomicum*, ed. Nallino, 25-8, transl. 17-20; al-Bakrī, *Description de l'Afrique septentrionale*, ed. De Slane, 109; al-Idrīsī, *Description de l'Afrique et de l'Espagne*, ed. R. Dozy and M. J. de Goeje, 2, 28, 55, transl. 1, 33-34, 63; F. Rosenthal, *The Muqaddimah*, London 1958, i, 117. (D. M. DUNLOP)

AL **DJAZARĪ**, the historian Shams al-Dīn Abū ʿAbd Allāh Muḥammad b. Madjd al-Dīn Abī Isḥāḳ Ibrāhīm b. Abī Bakr b. Ibrāhīm b. ʿAbd al-ʿAzīz al-Djazarī al-Dimashḳī (not to be confused with his compatriot Abu 'l-Khayr Shams al-Dīn Muḥammad b. Muḥammad . . . , better known as Ibn al-Djazarī [*q.v.*], the author of *Ḥiṣn Ḥaṣīn* and a contemporary of Tīmūr), was born at Damascus on 10 Rabīʿ I 658/25 February 1260. He studied with a number of teachers including al-Fakhr ʿAlī al-Bukhārī, Ibrāhīm b. Aḥmad b. Kāmil al-Taḳī al-Wāsiṭī, Ibn al-Mudjāwir and al-Dimyāṭī [*q.v.*]. Hard of hearing, he was a good conversationalist, pure of heart, sincere and upright; he liked the company of virtuous people, towards whom he showed great magnanimity. His fame chiefly rests on his historical work styled *al-Taʾrīkh al-musammā bi-ḥawādith al-zamān wa-anbāʾih wa-wafayāt al-akābir wa 'l-aʿyān min abnāʾih*, better known by the shorter and simpler title of *Taʾrīkh al-Djazarī*. It is a large work of which only the last volume is preserved both in the library of Köprülüzāde at Istanbul and in the Dār al-Kutub al-Miṣriyya. Several other copies are also to be found in European libraries; a detailed analysis of the Paris fragment was published by J. Sauvaget in 1951. The remaining portion, however, still awaits an editor. It is patterned more or less on the lines of al-Dhahabī's *Taʾrīkh al-Islām*, arranged as a diary of events (annals). The latter's work is apparently a continuation of al-Djazarī's. The Istanbul MS. has a detailed biography of the author appended to it in the hand of his friend and admirer the historian al-Ḳāsim b. Muḥammad al-Birzālī [*q.v.*] who also compiled for him a *Mashyakha* (*Mashīkha*) comprising the biographies of ten of his *shaykh*s. The extant portion of his work is in three volumes and comprises the events of thirteen years from 726/1326 onwards until his death in 739/1338.

He was rated very highly as a historian, and his work would have proved a mine of information had the whole of it survived. Al-Dhahabī and al-Birzālī have both utilized it and extensively quoted from it. Al-Dhahabī, however, is of the opinion that facts have been mixed up with fiction (*al-ʿadjaʾib wa 'l-gharāʾib*) in this work. Al-Djazarī died at Wāsiṭ on 12 Rabīʿ I 739/29 September 1338.

Bibliography: Ibn Ḥadjar al-ʿAskalānī, *al-Durar al-kāmina*, iii, 301; al-Ḥusaynī al-Dimashḳī, *Dhayl Tadhkirat al-ḥuffāẓ*, Damascus 1347 A.H., 22; idem, *al-Tanbīh wa 'l-īḳāẓ*, Damascus 1347 A.H., 8-9; Ibn Kathīr, *al-Bidāya wa 'l-nihāya*, xiv, 186 (where his *nisba* is wrongly printed as al-Djawzī); Maḳrīzī, *Sulūk*, 2, 471; Muḥammad b. Rafīʿ al-Sulamī, *Taʾrīkh ʿulamāʾ Baghdād*, Baghdād 1357/1938, 212-3; *Fihris Dār al-Kutub al-Miṣriyya*, 80a-b; al-Ziriklī, *al-Aʿlām*, vi, 189a-b; Cl. Cahen, *La Syrie du Nord . . .*, Paris 1940, 80; idem, *Chroniques des derniers Fatimides*, in *BIFAO*, 1937, 8-9; Brockelmann, S II, 45 (also see S II, 33 where Brockelmann confuses the author's name and the year of his death).

(A. S. BAZMEE ANSARI)

DJAZĪRA (Ar.), pl. *djazāʾir*, a term which signifies essentially an island and secondarily a peninsula (for example *Djazīrat al-Andalus*, Spain; *Djazīrat al-ʿArab* [see AL-ʿARAB, DJAZĪRAT-]). By extension, this same word is applied also to territories situated between great rivers (see following article) or separated from the rest of a continent by an expanse of desert; it also designates a maritime country (see Asín Palacios, *Abenházam de Cordoba*, Madrid 1927-32, i, 291 n. 347) and, with or without a following *al-nakhl*, an oasis (see Dozy, *Suppl.*, s.v.). Finally, with the Ismāʿīlīs *djazīra* is the name of a propaganda district; see S. de Sacy, *Exposé de la religion des Druzes*, cxiv; W. Ivanow, *The organization of the Fatimid propaganda*, in *JBBRAS*, xv (1939), 10, and *Ismaili tradition concerning the rise of the Fatimids*, 20-1. See also DĀʿĪ. (ED.)

AL-**DJAZĪRA**, DJAZĪRAT AḲŪR or IḲLĪM AḲŪR (for Aḳūr or Athūr see Yāḳūt, i, 119, 340; ii, 72) is the name used by Arab geographers to denote the northern part of the territory situated between the Tigris and the Euphrates. But the Djazīra also includes the regions and towns which are across the upper Tigris in the north (Mayyāfāriḳīn, Arzan, Siʿirt) and which lie to the east of the middle stretch of the river (Bāʿaynāthā, the Khābūr al-Ḥasaniyya, the two Zāb). In the same way, a strip of land lying to the west, along the right bank of the Euphrates, in the neighbourhood of the Euphrates Route, is also considered to belong to the Djazīra.

The Djazīra is a fairly low-lying plateau which includes certain groups of mountains, the Ḳaradjā Dāgh between Āmid and the Euphrates, the Ṭūr ʿAbdīn between Mārdīn and Djazīrat Ibn ʿUmar, the Djabal ʿAbd al-ʿAzīz between the Balīkh and the Khābūr, the Djabal Sindjār between the Khābūr and the Tigris, and the Djabal Makḥūl south of Mosul. In these mountains rise various streams, and in particular the tributaries of the left bank of the Euphrates, that is to say the Balīkh which comes from the district of Ḥarrān, and the Khābūr which comes from Raʾs ʿAyn with its tributary the Hirmās which rises in the Ṭūr ʿAbdin. In the Djabal Sindjār are the sources of the Nahr Tharthār which flows into the desert and disappears.

The Djazīra is bounded on the west by Syria, on the north-west by the region of the Mesopotamian *thughūr*, on the north and north-east by Armenia, on the east by Ādharbāydjān and on the south by ʿIrāḳ which begins at a line from Anbār to Takrīt. It consists of three districts (*kūra*), the Diyār Rabīʿa in the east, the Diyār Muḍar in the west, the Diyār Bakr in the north, called after the names of tribes who inhabited them in the pre-Islamic period and at the beginning of the Islamic period. But even in ancient times there were already Arabs in the Djazīra and one of its districts, that of Nisibis (Nāṣibīn) was called Arvastān by the Persians and Bēth Arabāyā by the Aramaeans. Apart from the Arabs, the Djazīra contained considerable Aramaean elements, especially in the Ṭūr ʿAbdīn, and a number of localities bear Aramaean names, and there were Kurds in the Mosul region and Armenians to the north of the upper Tigris.

The Djazīra is of great importance historically, being astride the lines of communication between ʿIrāḳ and Anatolia (it is crossed by the Baghdād railway), ʿIrāḳ and Syria on the vast curve of the so-called Fertile Crescent, and between the Armeno-Iranian regions and Syria on the one side and ʿIrāḳ on the other. It contained many market-towns and cities on the banks of the two rivers and on their tributaries in the Ṭūr ʿAbdīn and along the Mawṣil-Raḳḳa road. In the Romano-Byzantine period it was divided between Persia and Rome-Byzantium. At the time of the Arab conquest, Byzantium held the region extending from Raʾs ʿAyn to the Euphrates and the plain to the south of the Ṭūr ʿAbdīn. The frontier lay between Nisibis and Dārā, at the fort of Sardja (Yāḳūt, ii, 516; iii, 70; Abū Yūsuf Yaʿḳūb, *K. al-kharādj*, ed. 1302, 22, tr. Fagnan, 62). After the conquest of Syria the Byzantine garrisons were isolated, only being able to communicate with the Empire through Armenia. ʿIyāḍ b. Ghanm therefore encountered no resistance; the western part was conquered between 18/639 and 20/641, and the eastern part in 20/641 by troops coming from ʿIrāḳ (al-Balādhurī, 171 ff., ed. Cairo, 179 ff.).

In the Umayyad period the Djazīra was the scene of strife between the Syrians and the ʿIrāḳī Shīʿīs: Sulaymān b. Ṣurad, supported by the Ḳaysī Zufar b. al-Ḥarīth, was killed in 65/685 in a battle near Raʾs ʿAyn against a lieutenant of ʿUbayd Allāh b. Ziyād; after Mukhtār's victory over the Syrians in 67/686 on a tributary of the Zāb, the victors occupied Nisibis, Dārā and Sindjār (see al-Ṭabarī and Ibn al-Athīr under the years indicated). ʿAbd al-Malik, before being able to go on to defeat Muṣʿab b. al-Zubayr at Dayr al-Djāthalīḳ in ʿIrāḳ in 72/691, first had to conquer the Djazīra. It was also in the Djazīra that the fighting between the Ḳaysīs and Taghlabīs took place before and after this date (cf. al-Ṭabarī and Wellhausen, *Das arabische Reich*, 126 ff.; Eng. tr. 202 ff.). In like manner numerous Khāridjī revolts started in the Djazīra at the time of al-Ḥadjdjādj, and later in the reigns of the last Umayyads when the Khāridjīs of Djazīra all but succeeded in seizing power (see Wellhausen, *Oppositionsparteien*, 41 ff.) It was in the Djazīra, at Ḥarrān, that the last Umayyad, Marwān II, had his capital.

At the time when Muʿāwiya was governor of Syria the Djazīra was joined with it under a single administration. It later became a separate province comprising the three districts, responsibility for it being sometimes held by members of the Umayyad family, such as Muḥammad b. Marwān and Maslama b. ʿAbd al-Malik who were at the same time governors of the neighbouring province of Armenia. Mosul was separate, and it was only under Marwān II that it became the capital of the Djazīra.

The Djazīra did not submit to the ʿAbbāsids without resistance, and there were even grave incidents at Mosul where Muḥammad b. Ṣūl, and then Yaḥyā, brother of the first ʿAbbāsid caliph, had been sent (see Ibn al-Athīr, *anno* 132, ed. 1303 A.H., 163 and 166-7). It was the scene of the rebellion of ʿAbd Allāh b. ʿAlī, al-Manṣūr's uncle; later, under al-Maʾmūn, Naṣr b. Shabath's revolt swept through the Djazīra and was with difficulty crushed by ʿAbd Allāh b. Ṭāhir, governor of Syria and the Djazīra, in 209/821. In the reign of al-Muʿtaṣim, a Kurdish revolt to the north of Mosul was put down with difficulty. Khāridjī revolts broke out again in the Djazīra, particularly after al-Mahdī's reign. The province was known as a Khāridjī stronghold, and al-Djāḥiẓ was able to say: *ammā 'l-Djazīra faḥarūriyya shāriyya wa-khāridja mārika* (*Fī manākib al-Turk*, ed. 1324, 10; cf. on the Khāridjīs in the Djazīra, *Ḥudūd al-ʿālam*, tr. Minorsky, 140). In Hārūn al-Rashīd's time there took place the rebellion of the Taghlabī Khāridjī al-Walīd b. Ṭarīf (see Ibn al-Athīr, vi, 47). Violent Khāridjī outbreaks occurred in the second half of the 3rd/9th century with Musāwir, and later with Hārūn al-Shārī [see the references given in DIYĀR RABĪʿA]. The caliph al-Muʿtaḍid put an end to these revolts (same references).

In the ʿAbbāsid period Mosul was at times separated from the administration of the Djazīra, at other times the province was included in a larger grouping. Armenia, the neighbouring province, was often linked with it or on occasion united merely with the Diyār Bakr [see DIYĀR BAKR]. Among the governors of the Djazīra worthy of note, we may mention Ṭāhir b. al-Ḥusayn and, later, his son ʿAbd Allāh b. Ṭāhir in al-Muʾmūn's reign. In the second part of the 3rd/9th century the Djazīra for a time escaped from the central authority and became a dependency of the Ṭūlūnid ruler of Egypt, with Isḥāḳ b. Kundādjīḳ, then Muḥammad b. Abi 'l-Sādj, and then Isḥāḳ's son. But it was recovered by the caliph al-Muʿtaḍid after 279/892.

The Djazīra is the home of the Ḥamdānid family who, after various wanderings (their ancestor Ḥamdān was himself a Khāridjī), extended their power over the entire province which was divided between the two Ḥamdānid amīrates of Mosul and Aleppo which, though recognizing the nominal authority of the caliph, were almost independent. It then passed under the domination of the Buwayhids of Baghdād after the conquest by ʿAḍud al-Dawla in 367/977. Then, as a result of the increasing weakness of the Buwayhids, it was divided between the Marwānids in the north (Diyār Bakr) and the ʿUḳaylids (Mosul), one of whose princes, Ḳirwāsh b. Muḳallad, in 401/1010-1 recognized Fāṭimid suzerainty. The Saldjūḳids put an end to these two dynasties.

The Djazīra was a relatively rich and fertile province, plentifully supplied with water by its rivers, and the steppes with their abundant pastures were not short of wells. The triangle enclosed by the Armenian mountains, the Djabal ʿAbd al-ʿAzīz and the Djabal Sindjār, was an immense cultivated area, and there were also large areas of cultivation along the Balīkh and the Khābūr. Horses and sheep, cereals (Mosul supplied Baghdād and Sāmarrā with flour—see al-Ṣūlī, *Akhbār al-Rāḍī*, 76, 109, tr. 133, 177—and the floating mills of Mosul and Balad were famous), rice (Nisibis), olive-oil (al-Raḳḳa, Mārdīn), butter, cheese, sugar-cane (Sindjār), fowls, fresh and dried fruit, raisins, chestnuts (Nisibis), jam (*ḳubbayṭ*), honey, dried meat (*namaksūd*), charcoal, cotton (Ḥarrān and the Khābūr valley) etc.—these, among other things, were the agricultural products of the Djazīra specially mentioned by al-Muḳaddasī and Ibn Ḥawḳal. Among the products of local industrial crafts are mentioned: soap, tar, iron, buckets, knives, arrows, chains, straps, scales (Ḥarrān and Nisibis), linen and woollen fabrics (Āmid), fullers' hammers. Aided by shipping on the Tigris and Euphrates, commerce flourished there. Djazīrat Ibn ʿUmar was the port of shipment for goods from Armenia and the Greek countries, and Bālis for goods from Syria.

It is therefore not surprising that the authority established in Baghdād always tended to keep the Djazīra either directly or indirectly under its domination, which explains the policy of al-Muʿtaḍid, and of the central authority in Baghdād in the Ḥamdānid period. It is difficult to form an exact idea of the revenues of the Djazīra. The amounts vary greatly, and if one compares the figures given by Ḳudāma with those for the 306 budget, given in von Kremer, *Über das Einnahmebudget des Abbasiden-Reiches vom Jahre 306 H*, and with the figures of tribute paid by, or demanded from, the Ḥamdānid amīr of Mosul, we notice a large fall in the contribution. According to Ḳudāma, the Diyār Muḍar had a revenue of 6 million dirhams, the Diyār Rabīʿa 9,635,000, Mosul 6,300,000. However, in 332/944 the Ḥamdānid Nāṣir al-Dawla agreed to pay for the Diyār Rabīʿa and part of the Diyār Muḍar 3,600,000 dirhams, in 337 the Buwayhid demanded 8 million dirhams from him but settled for 3 million, and it seems that he never paid more than 2 million. Even if payments made in kind are added, it is little enough. But for the central authority it was not to be despised.

For the subsequent history of the Djazīra, see DIYĀR BAKR, DIYĀR RABĪʿA, and DIYĀR MUḌAR.

Bibliography: Le Strange, 86-114 where references to the Arab geographers are given; in addition, the anonymous *Ḥudūd al-ʿālam*, tr. Minorsky, see index; E. Herzfeld, *Über die historische Geographie von Mesopotamien* (*Pet. Mitt.*, 1909, xii); F. Sarre and E. Herzfeld, *Archäologische Reise im Euphrat- und Tigris-Gebiet* (*Forschungen zur islamischen Kunst*), 3 vols. 1911-20; Von Oppenheim, *Vom Mittelmeer zum Persischen Golf*, 2 vols. 1899-1900; Banse, *Die Türkei*, 238 ff.; A. Poidebard, *Les routes anciennes de Haute Djezireh*, in *Syria*, viii (1927); idem, *Mission archéologique en Haute Djezireh*, in *Syria*, xi (1930); Maḥmūd Alūsī, *Bulūgh al-ʿArab*, i, 217 ff.; Dussaud, *Topographie historique*, deals with the towns on the middle Euphrates and in the Khābūr basin, 447 ff., 481 ff.; M. Canard, *Hist. de la dynastie des H'amdânides*, i, 75-143, 291-302, 308-11, 334 ff., 377-407, 418, 520 ff., 526-31 and passim.

(M. CANARD)

AL-**DJAZĪRA** AL-**KHAḌRĀ'**, Spanish ALGECIRAS. The town takes its Arabic name from the Isla Verde which lies opposite, in the bay between the Punta del Carnero and the Punta de Europa. It is also called Djazīrat Umm Ḥakīm, from the name of a woman with whom Ṭāriḳ b. Ziyād, when freed by Mūsā b. Nuṣayr, entered the peninsula and to whom he left it as a bequest. It was here that Julia Traducta must have been founded by a number of colonists brought from Arcila and Tangier; and it was here that the Syrian leaders were held the hostages given by Baldj in 124/740 when he crossed from Ceuta to the peninsula to suppress the Berbers' revolt. The town also had the hybrid Latino-Punic name of Julia Ioza which is the equivalent of Julia Traducta.

In the time of the Romans the present Algeciras was called Ad Portum Album, and in Christian sources there are references to two places with the name Algeciras, one on the island which was later deserted, the other on the mainland which kept its name and importance since its harbour and bay have from remotest antiquity provided a safe anchorage, even in winter, and it is the starting point for the crossing to Ceuta, a distance of only 18 miles. The Almohads almost always preferred to cross by the Tarifa-Alcazarseguir route, which is 12 miles across; and the Marīnids followed their example.

The town is situated on a hill dominating the sea, and its walls go right down to the sea-shore; the citadel, built of stone, rises sharply above the ravine that lies alongside the town, to the East.

Through the town runs a river, the Wādi 'l-ʿAsal —river of honey—which has kept this name in Spanish; its banks are covered with orchards and gardens. To the south-east, not far from the gate to the sea, was the Mosque of Banners where the standard-bearers met before the invasion, whilst the Berber contingents sent by Ṭāriḳ came by Gibraltar. It was opposite this same mosque that the Normans (al-Madjūs [*q.v.*]) drew up their forces in 245/859-60, when they seized and burnt it. ʿAbd al-Raḥmān III built an arsenal there for his squadrons and it was from this port that his generals undertook expeditions against the Idrīsids of Morocco. On the fall of the caliphate the Berbers pillaged it in 401/1011 and from 427 to 448/1035-56, the Hammūdids Muḥammad and al-Ḳāsim established themselves there as caliphs before it was annexed to Seville.

In 479/1086, al-Muʿtamid delivered it to Yūsuf b. Tāshfīn who went into al-Andalus to rout Alfonso VI at al-Zallāḳa. Yūsuf lost no time in fortifying the town and repairing the weak points in the walls; he had the town entirely surrounded by a moat, laid in stocks of arms and food, and installed a picked garrison of his best soldiers. On his second crossing he again disembarked at Algeciras, setting out from there to lay siege to Aledo. The Almohads occupied the town in 541/1146, and the Castilians laid waste its territory and that of Ronda in 569/1173 and 578/1182. In 629/1231-2 Algeciras recognized Ibn Hūd. Alfonso the Learned blockaded Algeciras by sea in the summer of 677/1278, and the Christian army camped there in March 1279; on 10 Rabīʿ I/21 July the Castilian squadron was routed by the Marīnids; Algeciras was taken by assault and its defenders put to the sword. In his four Andalusian campaigns Abū Yūsuf made Algeciras the base of his operations and built nearby the royal palace of al-Binya, on the lines of the palace he had built at Fez with Fās al-djadīda; he died there in Muḥarram 685/March 1286. On the same day his son Yaʿḳūb was proclaimed king in this same palace of al-Binya. Abu 'l-Ḥasan ʿAlī returned to the Marīnid tradition of a *djihād* in al-Andalus and, in 741/1340, after defeating admiral Tenorio's squadron in Algeciras bay, he disembarked there and set out to lay siege to Tarifa nearby; after being defeated on the Salado on 7 Djumādā I 741/29 October 1340, he returned to Algeciras where he had left his harem, and from there went back to Morocco. With him the Marīnids' intervention in al-Andalus came to an end; two years later Alfonso XI laid siege to his great naval base and, after twenty months of fierce fighting, succeeded in taking it. In 771/1369 the sultan of Granada recaptured it and completely destroyed it. The territory was annexed to that of Gibraltar and it was not separated administratively from San Roque until 1755. Later, it developed rapidly in the 18th and 19th centuries and, in 1905, an international conference on the question of Morocco was held there.

Bibliography: Idrīsī, *Descript.*, 176-7 in the text, 212-3 in the trans.; Ibn ʿAbd al-Munʿim al-Ḥimyarī, *al-Rawḍ al-miʿṭār*, ed. Lévi-Provençal, 73-5 in the text, 91-4 in the trans.; Ibn ʿIdhārī, *Bayān*, ii, 99 in the ṭext and 158 in the trans.; *Mémoirs of ʿAbd Allāh b. Zīrī King of Granada*, in *al-Andalus*, ii/2, 399 in the text and iv/1, 72 in the trans.; A. Huici, *Les grandes batallas de la reconquista*, 399 ff.; *Crónica de Alfonso XI*, in *Biblioteca de Autores españoles*, lxvi, 339 ff.; Carlos da Silva, *Crónica dos sete reis*, ii, 317 ff.; Ibn Abī Zar, *Rawḍ al-ḳirṭās*, Fās ed., 191 ff. in the text and 302 ff. in the Huici trans.

(A. Huici Miranda)

DJAZĪRAT IBN ʿUMAR [see IBN ʿUMAR, DJAZĪRAT-].

DJAZĪRAT ḲAYS [see ḲAYS, DJAZĪRAT].

DJAZĪRAT SHARĪK, Name given by the Arabs to the small peninsula thrusting from the eastern coast of Tunisia between the two gulfs of La Goulette (Ḥalḳ al-wādī) and al-Ḥammāmāt. As a physical continuation of the Tunisian Dorsal range, its surface is rather hilly and cut by ravines, but in its east and west and particularly its northern part are wide plains famous since Roman times for their wheat and olives. Its area is about 600 square kilometres. Its farthest point in the north (Cap Bon, or Raʾs Maddār, currently called al-Dakhal) is the nearest point of Africa to Sicily. The peninsula is actually a part of the province (*wilāya*) of Grombalia (Ḳurunbāliya). Its western and northern parts form a subdivision (*délégation, muʿtamadiyya*) of that province called Kilibia (Iḳlībiya). There are some middle-sized and small towns, such as Grombalia (capital of the province), Korbes (Ḳurbus), Sulaymān, Manzil Bū Zalfā, and Tazeghzān; fishing-ports, such as Iḳlībiya, Manzil Tamīm, Ḳurba, Banī Khiyār, and two fairly important ports: Nabeul (Nābil) and al-Ḥammāmāt. Communications are assured by railways between Nābil, al-Ḥammāmāt, Manzil Tamīm, and Tunis.

Sharīk al-ʿAbsī, after whom the peninsula was named, was one of the officers of the Arab army which conquered Ifrīḳiya under ʿAbd Allāh b. Saʿd b. Abī Sarḥ in 27-8/647-9. After the victory of Subayṭila (Sbeitla, Suffitulum), ʿAbd Allāh b. Saʿd sent Sharīk to occupy the peninsula and nominated him its governor. ʿAbd Allāh b. Saʿd evacuated Ifrīḳiya before the end of 28/649 and the Byzantines were able to reconquer the peninsula from their stronghold of Carthage (Ḳarṭādjanna). Some 32 years later Abu 'l-Muhādjir Dīnār, leader of the Arab troops in Ifrīḳiya between 55/674 and 62/681, was able to conquer Carthage and consequently assure permanent Muslim domination of this important bridgehead to Sicily.

Owing to its strategic importance, Djazīrat Sharīk was always a target for all those contemplating the conquest of Ifrīḳiya from the sea, and hence for long periods of its history it was a battlefield between Ifrīḳiya and its attackers. The Normans dominated it after their conquest of al-Mahdiyya in 543/1148 and held it till 555/1160, when the Almohads under ʿAbd al-Muʾmin b. ʿAlī expelled them and annexed Ifrīḳiya to their Empire). Later, during the 10th/16th century, Djazīrat Sharīk, like the rest of

Tunisia, was one of the battlefields in the war between the Spaniards and the Ottomans in their fierce dispute for the hegemony of the Mediterranean [see TUNISIA].

Two other aspects are characteristic of the history of Djazīrat Sharīk during the middle ages: the first is that its hilly terrain offered refuge for rebels against the governors of Ifrīḳiya, especially under the Fāṭimids, when a group of the Nakkāriyya (a branch of the Khawāridj) allies of Abū Yazīd [q.v.] caused much trouble to al-Ḳāʾim; later, during the second half of the 6th/12th century, the Banū Ghāniya [q.v.] invaded Djazīrat Sharīk, and committed atrocities against its inhabitants. The second aspect is that its coasts, as well as those of the adjacent islands of Ḳawṣara (Pantelleria), Ḳirḳinnā and Djarba were from the beginning of the 8th/14th century suitable lairs for pirates (ghuzāt al-baḥr), which brought against Ifrīḳiya the wrath of the Normans, the Pisans, the Genoese, the Venetians, the Spaniards, and almost all Europe, and were the cause of disastrous attacks on their part.

Djazīrat Sharīk was described by at least four of the leading Muslim geographers and travellers in the middle ages, namely al-Bakrī, al-Tidjānī, al-Idrīsī and Yāḳūt. All, except al-Tidjānī, agree that the peninsula was flourishing and rich. Al-Idrīsī calls it Djazīrat Bashshū, after its then biggest town Manzil Bashshū. Al-Tidjānī, who visited it in 706/ 1306-7, gives in his *Riḥla* the most detailed description we possess, including a sad picture of the peninsula as a result of the devastations of the Banū Hilāl and the Banū Ghāniya [q.v.]. A branch of the Hilāliyya, the Banū Dalādj, were masters of Djazīrat Sharīk in his days. He mentions only three towns: Manzil Bashshū, Ṣilṭān and al-Fallāḥīn.

Bibliography: Bakrī, *Ṣifat Ifrīḳiya*, ed. De Slane, Algiers 1911, 39-40; Yāḳūt, iii, 99-100; Idrīsī, *Maghrib*, 118-25; Tidjānī, *Riḥla*, ed. H.H. ʿAbd al-Wahhāb, Tunis 1958, 11-23; H. Monés, *Fatḥ al-ʿArab li ʾl-Maghrib*, Cairo 1947, 173-4; R. Brunschvig, *Ḥafṣides*, i, 239-78; P. Hubac, *Tunisie*, Paris 1948, 9-18.   (H. MONÉS)

DJAZĪRAT SHUḲR, Spanish Alcira, called by the Muslims the island of the Júcar, since it is situated between two channels of the river Júcar, in Latin Sucro, one of which is now dry. 37 km. from Valencia, it has a population of about 30,000 and stands at the centre of a natural region known as the Ribera which includes the lower part of the Júcar valley, from Játiva to Catarroja and from the sea to the valley of Cárcer. The fertile alluvial plain is one of the richest in the Peninsula. It is watered by the royal irrigation canal of the Júcar which was constructed by James I the Conqueror in the second half of the 13th century, built up on the site of earlier irrigation works which go back not merely to the Arab period but to the Visigothic and Hispano-Roman periods. Orange-trees, rice and horticulture have brought prosperity. Al-Idrīsī praised it for its fertility and the distinction of its inhabitants; he said that in his time it was possible to reach it only by boat in winter, and by a ford in summer, but in 622/1225, according to al-Muʿdjib, it had a bridge. It must have been inhabited even in prehistoric times, to judge by excavations made on its boundaries, on the mountain of Solá. Its identity with Sucro or Sicania Iberica is open to question, and in the Roman period it must have been fortified, as a stopping place on the Via Augusta, to judge by the commemorative tablets found there.

During the Arab period and until comparatively recent times, timber felled in the great pine-forests of Cuenca was transported on the river Cabriel and, after being taken across the Júcar was brought through Alcira to Cullera, with Denia as its final destination for ship-building and Valencia for building.

Throughout the amīrate and Umayyad caliphate its history was uneventful; it was a dependency of Murcia or of Valencia at the time when the first kingdoms of Taifas were created, until the Cid took possession of it when conquering Valencia and its territories. Ibn ʿĀʾisha, the son of Yūsuf b. Tashfīn, reconquered it and then routed and wiped out a division of the Cid's army. In 519/1125 Alfonso I the Warrior, when undertaking his celebrated expedition into Andalusia, tried to seize it; but after several days he was repulsed, and withdrew with heavy losses. In 523/1129 he once again invaded the region, and between Alcira and Cullera he routed another Almoravid army, thereby opening up the way.

When the Almoravids of al-Andalus disappeared and the second period of the kingdoms of Taifas started, Saʿd b. Mardanīsh succeeded in making himself master of Murcia and Valencia, and appointed as governor of Alcira a noble inhabitant of the town, Aḥmad b. Muḥammad b. Djaʿfar b. Sufyān. The latter, after seeing Ibn Mardanīsh reinforce the Christian garrison of Valencia and, to make way for them, turn out a number of Muslims from their homes, and fearing that he too would be turned out in the same way, rebelled and joined the Almohads, as Ibn Hamushk had done at Jaén and ʿAbd Allāh b. Saʿd at Almería.

Believing that he could recapture the town and so set an example, Ibn Mardanīsh laid siege to Alcira in the middle of Shawwāl 566/June 1171, helped by his brother Abu ʾl-Ḥadjdjādj Yūsuf, amīr of Valencia; the siege lasted for two months until the middle of Dhu ʾl-Ḥidjdja/August. The caliph, who had been in Cordova since July, and the sayyid Abū Ḥafṣ ʿUmar, who was besieging Murcia, came to the help of the inhabitants of Alcira; but they saw that they were being more and more closely confined, and appealed to Abū Ayyūt Muḥammad b. Hilāl, the friend and colleague of Ibn Baṣīt during the relief of Almería. Ibn Mardanīsh, unable to force the town, had to withdraw.

Under the Almohads the town enjoyed a period of comparative calm, but was soon threatened by the advance of the Christians; and two celebrated poets, Ibn Khafādja and Abu ʾl-Muṭarrif Ibn ʿAmīra, sensing that its loss was imminent, wrote with nostalgia of its charms and the beauty of its surroundings. At the end of 1242 James I the Conqueror captured the town.

Bibliography: Ibn ʿAbd al-Munʿim al-Ḥimyarī, *al-Rawḍ al-miʿṭār*, ed. Lévi-Provençal, 102-3 of text and 126-7 of trans.; Ibn al-Abbār, *al-Ḥullā*, ed. Dozy, 236-7; Idrīsī, *Descript.*, 192, 195 of text and 233, 237 of trans.; *Dict. geográfico de España*, i, 515 ff.; Ribera, *Topografía de Alcira Arabe*, in *El Archivo*, ii, 54.

(A. HUICI MIRANDA)

DJAZM [see NAḤW].

AL-DJAZR WA ʾL-MADD [see MADD].

DJAZŪLA, Arabic name of a small ancient Berber tribe in south-western Morocco, doubtless related to the Ṣanhādja group [q.v.]. In association with the Lamta [q.v.], their kinsmen, they led a nomadic life south of the Anti-Atlas. But, at quite an early date, some of them began to settle in the western part of this mountain (Djabal Hankīsa); their chief settlement was at Tāghdjīzat, now known as Tāghdjīdjt, 80 km. south-south-east of Tīznīt.

It was among them that ʿAbd Allāh b. Yāsīn was born, the originator of the religious and political movement of the Murābiṭūn [*q.v.*]. The Djazūla took an important part in it and some of them settled in the Moroccan plains.

At the time of the first reverses of the Almoravids in the Sūs, the Djazūla rallied round the Almohads (533/1138) and provided them with contingents. But the loyalty of the latter at Tlemcen, when faced by their kinsmen the Almoravids, was so suspect that the Almohads treacherously massacred them (539/1144). As a result, they gave a welcome to several persons who had revolted against the Almohads and were severely punished.

Later, for almost a century the Djazūla were subjugated by the Banū Yaddar of Sūs. The latter having introduced Arab Bedouin from the group of the Maʿḳil as allies, the Djazūla in the end united with one of their tribes, the Dhawū-Ḥassān. At the beginning of the 16th century, Leo Africanus described them as impoverished and bellicose villagers; it was from among them that the first Saʿdid princes recruited their harquebusiers.

During the decline of the Saʿdid dynasty, the Djazūla's country was governed by the Djaʿfarid (?) Shurafāʾ of the tribe of the Samlāla, with Īlīgh as capital. Their domination lasted for about fifty years until 1080/1670; it extended over the Sūs and, for the time being, over Darʿa and Sidjilmāsa (period of Abū Ḥassūn, surnamed Abū Dumayʿa).

At the beginning of the 19th century a new principality appeared, still with Īlīgh as its centre, founded by a sharīf of the Samlāla; it was to be maintained until towards the end of the 19th century. Under the name of the "kingdom of Sīdī Hāshem, or Hīshem", it enjoyed among European travellers and cartographers a notoriety not attested by the Arab historians of Morocco.

Today the name Djazūla is no longer used except for one of the two ethno-political clans (*laff*) between whom the tribes of the Anti-Atlas district were divided. The former Djazūla are now the confederation of the Waltīta (Berb. Idā Ultīt); the centre of this district is the Tāzarwālt.

In addition to ʿAbd Allāh b. Yāsīn and the two personages who form the subject of the following articles, the Djazūla have produced two other men of distinction: the great saint Aḥmad b. Mūsā al-Samlālī (d. 971/1563), popularly known by the name Sīdī Ḥmād u-Mūsā [*q.v.*], and Muḥammad b. Aḥmad al-Ḥuḍīgī [*q.v.*] (d. 1197/1782), author of a collection of biographies of local saints.

The Arabic orthography *Djazūla* (sometimes *Djuzūla*) corresponds with the Berber plurals *awgūzūlen* (archaic) and *igzūlen*. Some have tried to identify them with the ancient Getuli.

Bibliography: The ancient Arab historians and geographers, in the indexes (in particular those quoted in the bibl. to the article AL-SŪS AL-AḲṢĀ); Leo Africanus, trans. Épaulard, i, 94, 115; Marmol, *L'Afrique*, trans. d'Ablancourt, ii, 42, 75; Justinard, *Notes sur l'histoire du Sous*, in Archives Marocaines, xxix (1933), 59 and *passim*; also in *Hespéris*, v (1925), 265 and vi (1926), 351; Ch. de Foucauld, *Reconnaissance au Maroc*, 318.

(G. S. COLIN)

AL-**DJAZŪLĪ**, ABŪ ʿABD ALLĀH MUḤAMMAD B. SULAYMĀN B. ABĪ BAKR AL-DJAZŪLĪ AL-SAMLĀLĪ, although both his father's name and, still more, his grandfather's are in dispute, according to his biographers and associates was descended from the Prophet, like all founders of religious orders. He was born and bred in the Berber tribe of Djazūla in Moroccan Sūs [*q.v.*].

After having studied for a time in his native country he went to Fās and entered the madrasat al-ṣaffārīn where one can still see the room he occupied. Hardly had he returned to his tribe when he was compelled to go back to north Morocco, after charging himself with a crime he did not commit in order to avoid bloodshed. He went to Tangier, then he sailed for the East, spending forty years (?) there partly at Mecca and Medina, partly at Jerusalem. He returned to Fās, and it was during this second stay that, with the help of books from the library of al-Ḳarawiyyīn, he wrote his *Dalāʾil al-khayrāt*. He was then initiated into the order of the Shādhiliyya, then he withdrew into a *khalwa* to worship the Eternal for fourteen years. On leaving his retreat he went to live at Asfī (Safī) where he soon had so great a number of proselytes that the governor of the town felt obliged to expel him. Al-Djazūlī thereupon invoked the help of God against the town which, as a result, was for forty years in the hands of the Christians (Portuguese). It even appears that this governor, thinking him to be the awaited Fāṭimid (the Mahdī), is said to have poisoned him, and the Shaykh died in prayer at Āfūghāl in Dhu 'l-Ḳaʿda 869/25 June-24 July 1465, or 16 Rabīʿ I 870, 872 or even 875.

One of his disciples, ʿUmar b. Sulaymān al-Shayẓamī, known as al-Sayyāf, who as a result claimed to be a prophet himself, conceived the idea of avenging al-Djazūlī. He had the body of his master placed on a bier and raised the standard of revolt. For twenty years he burned and sacked the district of Sūs, accompanied by the body of his master; every evening he laid it out in a place he called *al-ribāṭ*, surrounded by a guard and illuminated all night long by a wick the size of a man's body which stood in a sort of bushel measure full of oil. ʿUmar al-Sayyāf was killed in 890/1485-6. Al-Djazūlī was then buried in the locality of Ḥāḥa, at a place called Āfghāl or Āfūghāl. Seventy-seven years later, on the orders of Sultan Abu 'l-ʿAbbās Aḥmad known as al-Aʿradj, at the time of his entry into Marrākush, and for what were perhaps political motives, his body was exhumed together with that of the Sultan's father who had been buried beside al-Djazūlī. Wrapped in shrouds, they were taken to Marrākush where they were both finally buried side by side, in the place known as Riyāḍ al-ʿArūs where his mausoleum stands. It seems that when the *shaykh* was exhumed from his first tomb, his body had suffered no change and it would have been thought that he had just died. Popularly known by the name of Sīdī Ben Slīmān, he became one of the patron saints (*sabʿatu ridjāl*) of Marrakush.

There grew up in Morocco a sort of religious brotherhood called the Aṣḥāb al-Dalīl, whose essential function was the recital of the celebrated collection of prayers. This book of prayers is often carried as a talisman, hanging over the shoulder in an embroidered leather or silver case (*tahlīl*).

Apart from his immense knowledge of Ṣūfism al-Djazūlī was also a jurisconsult and knew by heart the *Mudawwana* and *al-Mukhtaṣar al-farʿī* of Ibn al-Ḥādjib.

Of his numerous Ṣūfī works only the following are

now known: 1.—*Dalāʾil al-khayrāt wa-shawārik al-anwār fī dhikr al-ṣalāt ʿala 'l-nabī al-mukhtār*, a collection of prayers for the Prophet, description of his tomb, his names, etc., published several times in Cairo and Constantinople, and in St. Petersburg in 1842; 2.—*Ḥizb al-falāḥ*, a prayer, exists in MS. in Berlin 3886, Gotha 820, Leiden 22003; and 3.—*Ḥizb al-Djazūlī*, now called *Ḥizb subḥān al-dāʾim lā yazūl*, which is found among the Shādhilīs, is in the vernacular.

Al-Djazūlī founded a Shādhilī sect called al-Djazūliyya whose adherents are required without fail to recite the *basmala* 14,000 times and the *Dalāʾil al-khayrāt* twice a day, the *Dalāʾil* once and a quarter of the Ḳurʾān every night.

Bibliography: Ibn al-Ḳāḍī, *Djadhwat al-iḳtibās*, Fās 1309, 135; Aḥmad Bābā, *Nayl al-ibtihādj*, Fās 1317, 339; idem, *Kifāyat al-muḥtādj*, MS. in the Médersa at Algiers, fol. 174 v°; Muḥammad al-Mahdi al-Fāsī, *Mumtiʿ al-asmāʿ fī dhikr al-Djazūlī wa 'l-tabbāʿ wa-mā lahumā min al-atbāʿ*, Fās 1313, 2-33; Ḳādirī, *al-Ishrāf ʿalā nasab al-aḳṭāb al-arbaʿa al-ashrāf*, Fās 1309; Abū Ḥāmid, *Mirʾāt al-maḥāsin min akhbār Abī 'l-Maḥāsin*, MS. in Bibl. nat. Algiers, 1717, fol. 141; Wafrānī, *Nuzhat al-ḥādī* (ed. Houdas), Paris 1888, Ar. text, 18; Nāṣirī, *al-Istiḳṣā*, Cairo 1312, ii, 161, iii, 7; Brockelmann, II, 252, S II 359; Leo Africanus, *Descr. de l'Afrique*, trans. Épaulard, i, 82; De Castries, *Les sept patrons de Merrakech*, in *Hespéris*, 1924, 272. (M. Ben Cheneb)

AL-**DJAZŪLĪ**, Abū Mūsā ʿĪsā b. ʿAbd al-ʿAzīz b. Yalalbakht b. ʿĪsā b. Yūmarīlī, a member of the Berber tribe of Djazūla, a section of the Yazdakten in southern Morocco, is chiefly known for his short Introduction to the study of Arabic grammar, *Muḳaddima*, entitled *al-Ḳānūn*.

After studying at Marrākush he went to the East to make the pilgrimage to Mecca and Medina. In Cairo he attended classes given by the celebrated lexicologist Abū Muḥammad ʿAbd Allāh b. Barrī; and some have even said that the Introduction merely reproduces his teacher's lectures on *al-Djumal* by al-Zadjdjādjī, adding by way of proof that al-Djazūlī himself admitted that he was not the author. In Cairo he also studied the *Ṣaḥīḥ* by al-Bukhārī with Abū Muḥammad b. ʿUbayd Allāh. While in Cairo he endured the greatest privations and, to raise some money to meet his needs and to be able to complete his studies, he was on several occasions compelled to take on the duties of *imām* in a mosque in the suburbs, refusing to go into a *madrasa*.

On returning from the East, and still in the grip of poverty, he stopped at Bougie for a time, which he spent teaching grammar.

In 543/1148-9 he was in Algiers where he taught his *Ḳānūn* to Abū ʿAbd Allāh b. Muḥammad b. Ḳāsim b. Mandās, a grammarian and native of Āshīr. Crossing into Spain, he stayed for some time in Almeria where he taught grammar. It was in this town that he pawned his copy of the *Uṣūl* by Ibn al-Sarrādj which he had studied with Ibn Barrī and which was in his own handwriting. His creditor to whom this work was given as security disclosed his plight to Abu 'l-ʿAbbās al-Maghribī, at that time the greatest ascetic in the land, and he in his turn approached the Almohad sultan on his behalf. The latter entrusted al-Djazūlī with the *khuṭba* at the great mosque at Marrākush. He died at Azammūr in 606 or 607 or 610, or else in 616 according to Ibn Ḳunfudh in his *Wafayāt*.

Of his disciples two in particular are noteworthy, Zayn al-Dīn Abu 'l-Ḥusayn Yaḥyā b. ʿAbd al-Muʿṭī (or more simply Ibn Muʿṭī) b. ʿAbd al-Raḥmān al-Zawāwī, the first grammarian to compose an *Alfiyya*, and Abū ʿAlī ʿUmar b. Muḥammad b. ʿUmar b. ʿAbd Allāh al-Azdī al-Shalūbīnī who edited his master's *Ḳānūn* with commentaries, copies of which survive at the Escurial (Cat. Serenbourg; no. 2, 36, 190).

Al-Djazūlī composed the following works: 1.—Commentary on *Bānat Suʿād* by Kaʿb b. Zuhayr, published by M. R. Basset in Algiers in 1910; 2.—*al-Kānūn*, also called *al-Muḳaddima al-Djazūliyya*; 3.—Commentary on the preceding work; 4.—*Amālī fī 'l-naḥw* (dictations on grammar); 5.—An abridged version of the commentary by Abu 'l-Fatḥ ʿUthmān b. Djinnī on the *dīwān* by al-Mutanabbī; 6.—Commentary on the *Uṣūl* by Ibn al-Sarrādj (grammar).

Bibliography: Ibn al-Abbār, *Takmila* (ed. Codera), Madrid 1889, no. 1932; Ibn Khallikān, ed. de Slane, 486, (Cairo 1310, i, 94); Suyūṭī, *Bughyat al-waʿāt*, Cairo 1326, 369; Ghubrīnī, *ʿUnwān al-dirāya*, Algiers 1911, 231; Ibn Ḳunfudh, *Wafayāt*; Aḥmad b. ʿAlī al-Daladjī, *al-Falāka wa 'l-maflūkūn*, Cairo 1322, 91; Brockelmann, I, 308, S I 541-2. (M. Ben Cheneb)

DJAZZĀR PASHA [see SUPPLEMENT].

DJEBEDJI [see SUPPLEMENT].

DJEBELI, also DJEBELÜ, in the Ottoman empire an auxiliary soldier equipped by those to whom the state assigned a source of income such as *tīmār*, *čiftlik*, *waḳf* etc. The word *djebeli* is made by adding the suffix *-li* or *-lü* to the word djebe, arms (cf. *Mogolların gizli tarihi*, tr. A. Temir, Ankara 1948, 75; in the Ottoman army the *djebedji-bashî* was the superintendent of the arms store at the Porte, see I. H. Uzunçarşılı, *Kapîkulu ocaklarî*, ii, Ankara 1944, 3-31).

In the 15th century the arms of a *djebeli* consisted mainly of a lance, bow and arrow, a sword, and a shield (cf. *Kānūnnāme Sultan Meḥmeds des Eroberers*, ed. F. Kraelitz-Greifenhorst, *MOG*, i, 28; B. de La Broquière, *Voyage d'outremer*, ed. Ch. Schefer, Paris 1892, 221, 269, 270). Soldiers equipped with such arms and sent to the Sultan's army from various organizations in the provinces such as *yaya müsellem*, *tatar*, *yürük* etc. were designated under the general term of *djebeli* or *eshkündji* [*q.v.*]. Certain *waḳf*s and *mülk*s also were required to send such *djebeli*s for the Sultan's army (see for example, *Vakıflar Dergisi*, ii, 318 doc. 49; ʿAynī ʿAlī, *Ḳawānīn-i Āl-i ʿOsmān . .*, Istanbul 1280 H., 75). In the Ottoman *tīmār* [*q.v.*] the *djebeli* was a cavalryman equipped with the same kind of arms. According to a *tīmār* register of 835/1431 (*Sūret-i defter-i sancāk-i Arvanid*, ed. H. Inalcık, Ankara 1954) the holders of the smallest *tīmār*s between 750-1500 *akče*s were *djebeli*s themselves. Those between 1500-2000 approximately were *djebeli*s themselves but in addition were to bring with them an *oghlan*, or *ghulâm*, page. Those above 2000 were called *bürüme*, "one with a coat of mail". These and the *beg*s who usually held *tīmār*s of more than 20,000 *akče*s were to furnish *djebeli*s for a certain portion of their *tīmār*s (for the number of *djebeli*s in proportion to the *tīmār*s see the table in *Süleymān's Ḳānūnnāme*; M. ʿĀrif's edition in *TOEM* is unreliable in this part).

If the heir to a *tīmār* was too young to join the army in person he had to send a *djebeli* instead (see *Ḳānūnnāme*, Bib. Nationale, Paris, MS. turc 41). To "show one's djebelis" meant a military parade and inspection (cf. ʿĀshıḳpashazāde, *Taʾrīkh*, ed. ʿĀlī, Istanbul 1332, 135). Most of the *djebelis* in the *tīmār* system were of slave origin.

(HALİL İNALCIK)

DJEDDA [see DJUDDA].

DJEK [see SHAHDĀGH].

DJELALI [see SUPPLEMENT, s.v. DJALĀLĪ].

DJEM, son of Sultan Meḥemmed II, was born on 27 Ṣafar 864/22 December 1459 in Edirne (cf. *Wāḳiʿāt-i Sulṭān Djem*, 1). His mother, Čiček Khātūn, was one of the *djāriyes* in Meḥemmed II's harem. She may have been connected with the Serbian royal house (cf. Thuasne, *Djem-Sultan*, Paris 1892, 2). Her brother, ʿAlī Beg, was with Djem in Rhodes in 887/1482 (*Wāḳiʿāt*, 7).

Djem was sent to the sandjaḳ of Ḳastamoni as its governor with his two *lalas* in the first ten days (*awāʾil*) of Radjab 873/15-25 January 1469 (*Wāḳiʿāt*, 1; according to Kemāl Pashazāde, *Tevârih-i Âl-i Osman*, ed. Ş. Turan, Ankara 1954, 316, 412, he was sent to Magnisa). There, in these early years, he showed a keen interest in Persian literature (cf. I. H. Ertaylan, *Cem Sultan*, Istanbul 1951, 11-4). He came back to Istanbul for his circumcision in 875/1470-1 (cf. Kemāl Pashazāde, 316) and to Edirne (cf. *Speculum*, xxxv/3, 424) to safeguard Rūmeli during Meḥemmed II's expedition against Uzun Ḥasan in 878/1473. A reliable source (Angiolello, cited in Thuasne, 8) relates that having no news from his father for more than forty days, his two *lalas* made Djem decide to take the *bayʿa* [*q.v.*] of high officials. On his return Meḥemmed II, though he forgave the young prince, executed the two *lalas*, Ḳara-Süleymān and Nasūḥ (cf. his letter to Djem in Ferīdūn, *Munsheʾāt*, i, 283). In the middle of Shaʿbān 879/20-30 December 1474 (*Wāḳiʿāt*, 1) Djem succeeded his deceased brother Muṣṭafā as governor of Ḳaramān in Konya. Ḳaramānī Meḥemmed Pasha, grand vizier from 881/1476 to 886/1481, favoured Djem (cf. *Al-Shaḳāʾiḳ al-Nuʿmāniyya*, tr. Madjdī. Istanbul 1269, 285; Th. Spandouyn Cantacasin, *Petit traicté de l'origine des Turcqz*, ed. Ch. Schefer, Paris 1896, 43). But Bāyezīd, his elder brother, had become virtually the leader of all the opponents to Ḳaramānī and his financial policy which had been especially ruinous for the holders of *waḳfs* and *mulks* in the empire (cf. art. Meḥmed II, in *İA*). Meḥemmed II himself had serious complaints against Bāyezīd in the last years of his reign (see the documents in Ertaylan, 51, 53).

When Meḥemmed II died on 4 Rabīʿ I 886/3 May 1481 Ḳaramānī's enemies, supported by the Janissaries, eliminated him, invited Bāyezīd to the throne and took all measures to block the way for Djem (cf. documents in I. H. Ertaylan, 82, 84). When Bāyezīd was in Istanbul Djem came to capture Bursa (Rabīʿ I 886/May 1481). Here he had the *khuṭba* read and coins struck in his name (Neshrī, *Djihānnumā*, ed. F. Taeschner, i, Leipzig 1951, 220; the silver coin described by H. Edhem, *Meskūkāt-i ʿOthmāniyye*, i, Istanbul 1334, No. 447). He cooperated with the Ḳaramānids (cf. document in I. H. Ertaylan, 97). His proposal for dividing the empire was declined by Bāyezīd (Neshrī, 22-3). Defeated by the regular forces of the empire under Bāyezīd at Yenishehir on 22 Rabīʿ II 886/20 June 1481 (cf. *Wāḳiʿāt*, 2; Neshrī, 221, Ferīdūn, *Munsheʾāt al-Salāṭīn*, i, Istanbul 1274, 290), Djem fled to Konya (he arrived on 27 Rabīʿ II 886/25 June 1481) and took refuge in Tarsus, a town under the Mamlūks (12 Djumādā I 886/9 July 1481). He arrived in the Mamlūk capital on 1 Shaʿbān 886/25 September 1481 and was received by Sultan Ḳāyitbāy as a prince (*Wāḳiʿāt*, 4; Ibn Iyās, *Badāʾiʿ al-zuhūr* . ., ii, Bulāḳ 1311, 208). When he made the pilgrimage and returned to Cairo (1 Muḥarram 887/20 February 1482) Ḳāsim Beg, the Ḳaramānid pretender (see ḲARAMĀN-OGHLU) and Meḥemmed, sandjaḳ-beg of Ankara, urged him to return to Anatolia. Despite the objection of the Mamlūk amīrs, Sultan Ḳāyitbāy permitted him to leave Egypt for Anatolia (Ibn Iyās, ii, 213; *Wāḳiʿāt*, 5; document in Ertaylan, 121). Djem was in Aleppo on 17 Rabīʿ I 887/6 May 1482; Ḳāsim and Meḥemmed joined him in Mamlūk territory. While Djem and Ḳāsim came to lay siege to Konya, Meḥemmed Beg, who had moved towards Ankara, was defeated and killed in Čubuḳ-Owa. They gave up the siege of Konya and went to capture Ankara, but, at the news of the advance of an army under Bāyezīd II himself, hastily retreated. Djem, changing his original plan of going to Īrān, fled to Tash-eli in Ḳaramān (29 Rabīʿ II 887/17 June 1482). There he entered into negotiations with Bāyezīd II who always rejected his demand for the assignment to him of at least a part of the Ottoman territories. He only promised a yearly allowance of one million *akčes* provided that he would retire to Jerusalem (cf. *Wāḳiʿāt*, 5 and his letters in Ferīdūn, i, 291-2; Djem's original letter in Ertaylan, 127). Ḳāsim, who never gave up the idea of restoring his principality of Ḳaramān, made Djem decide to pass over to Rūm-eli by sea. With this in mind Djem made an agreement with P. d'Aubusson, Grand Master of the Knights of St. John in Rhodes. While governor of Ḳaramān in his father's time Djem had had close relations with P. d'Aubusson (cf. Thuasne, 11-7). The agreement of safe-conduct (text in Thuasne, 60, cf. *Wāḳiʿāt*, 7) dated 24 Djumādā I 887/10 July 1482 provided that Djem could enter, stay and leave Rhodes as he pleased. He arrived at the island on 13 Djumādā II 887/30 July 1482 (*Wāḳiʿāt*, 7). P. d'Aubusson wrote to the Pope that Djem should be used as an instrument to destroy the Ottoman empire (Thuasne, 68) while Djem hoped that he could at least reach an agreement to partition the empire with his brother. In Shaʿbān 887/September 1482 Bāyezīd agreed to a peace treaty with the knights favourable to the Order and at the same time his ambassador to the Grand Master made a separate agreement about Djem who was to be detained by the Knights so as not to cause any concern to Bāyezīd (Thuasne, 85; document in Ertaylan, 152). In return he was to pay 45 thousand Venetian gold ducats annually to meet Djem's expenses (24 Shawwāl 887/6 December 1482) (Thuasne, 86; for the negotiations now see the documents in Ertaylan, 156-61). It was understood that the Grand Master had Djem's mandate on this matter (cf. Thuasne, 80, 86 and Bāyezīd's letter to the French King in Ertaylan, 186). With the promise of sending him to Hungary via France (cf. *Wāḳiʿāt*, 8) d'Aubusson interned him in the Order's places in France for seven years (his departure from Rhodes was on 17 Radjab 887/1 September 1482). Bāyezīd II had asked Venice to intercept him on the sea if he should leave Rhodes (see documents in Ertaylan, 142-3, 188). Actually the Venetians must have attempted to seize him on his way to France (doc. in Ertaylan, 158-9; in *Wāḳiʿāt*, 8, Neapolitan ships). Worried lest Djem should proceed to Hungary, Bāyezīd sent envoys and spies to the West to prevent it (see documents in Ertaylan, 186, 189, 192, 193, 203). His envoy to the French King, Ḥüseyn Beg, was sent to assure Djem's detention there (*Wāḳiʿāt*, 12; Thuasne, 110).

As Djem was a valuable hostage bringing political prestige as well as money the rulers of the time were most anxious to have him and the Kinghts had to be always on guard. In 892/1487 they imprisoned him in the *Grosse Tour* or *Tour de Zizim*, a fort especially built to intern him near Bourgneuf (*Wāḳiʿāt*, 16; Thuasne, 157). Sultan Ḳāyitbāy who had been at war against the Ottomans since 890/1485 and Matthias Corvinus, Hungarian King, maintained active diplomatic relations with the Knights and the Pope to get Djem (for Ḳāyitbāy's ambassadors in Europe see Thuasne, 174, 199, 337). Djem's early attempt to get into contact with Matthias Corvinus had failed (cf. *Wāḳiʿāt*, 11, in Muḥarram 888/February 1483).

When Djem was interned in France Bāyezīd II put to death Gedük Aḥmed Pasha, the strong man of the empire, and Djem's son, Oghuz-khān, who was then only three years old (Shawwāl 887/December 1482) (documents in Ertaylan, 167-8).

Finally the Knights and the Pope Innocent VIII thought it necessary "for the general good of Christendom" to transfer Djem to Rome, where he arrived on 1 Rabīʿ II 894/4 March 1489. He met the Pope in a royal reception ten days later (description of the reception in *Wāḳiʿāt*, 21-2; Thuasne, 232) and in their private talk Djem complained that the Knights had violated their agreement to lead him to Rūm-eli and treated him as a prisoner. He wanted the Pope to send him back to his family in Egypt asserting that he would never cooperate with the Hungarians against his co-religionists (*Wāḳiʿāt*, 21-3).

Djem's presence in Rome increased the international prestige and activities of the Pope who now planned a Crusade against the Ottomans for which, he said in the letters to the Christian rulers, the conditions were most propitious (Thuasne, 241, 260, 265).

Bāyezīd was most worried by Djem's transference to Rome and he protested against it as a breach of the pact on the part of the Knights. Actually Matthias Corvinus was now pressing the Pope and the Egyptian Sultan was offering 150-200 thousand ducats to have Djem. On 17 Muḥarram 896/30 November 1490 Bāyezīd's ambassador, Ḳapîdjî-bashî Muṣṭafā Beg, came to Rome with a letter assuring the Pope of his friendship and asking him to stand by the agreement made with the Knights. He had brought with him 120 thousand ducats representing three years' pension for Djem which was to be delivered after Muṣṭafā's seeing him alive. Muṣṭafā saw him and delivered him a letter and presents from Bāyezīd. (*Wāḳiʿāt*, 23-4). On 23 Shaʿbān 898/9 June 1493 another ambassador of Bāyezīd came to Rome to renew the agreement about Djem with Alexander VI, successor of Innocent VIII, and delivered 150 thousand ducats as Djem's pension (Thuasne, 314). The Pope gave guarantees about Djem, and, on the other hand he assured the Christian powers that with Djem in his hands he could neutralize the Ottomans in their plans against Christendom. Soon afterwards he could even expect support from Bāyezīd II against Charles VIII of France who was about to invade Italy. The French King came to Rome in 899/1494 and compelled the Pope to hand Djem over to him for his plans of crusade (1 Djumādā I 900/27 January 1495) (*Wāḳiʿāt*, 30). He was taken by the king in his expedition against Naples. On the way he fell ill and died in Naples on the night of 29 Djumādā I 900/25 February 1495. Rumours spread that the Pope had poisoned him (Thuasne, 365-76; Saʿd al-Dīn, *tādj al-tewārīkh*, ii, 37; but in *Wāḳiʿāt*, 30-5, the latter's source, there is no hint at Djem being poisoned; Saʿd al-Dīn must have taken this from Idrīs Bidlīsī's *Hasht Behisht*. Bāyezīd took the place of the Pope in the story in some Ottoman chronicles, see ʿĀlī, *Kunh al-akhbār*, MS.). Djem left a testament (*Wāḳiʿāt*, 32) in which he expressed the wish that his death be made public so that the "infidels" could not use his name in their plans of crusade, that Bāyezīd should have his corpse taken to the Ottoman land, that all his debts be paid, and that his mother, daughter and other kin and servants receive proper care from the Sultan Bāyezīd.

Bāyezīd learned of Djem's death through the Venetians on 24 Radjab 900/20 April 1495. He made it known throughout the empire by public prayers for Djem's soul (Ferīdūn, i, 294), and brought back his corpse, which was embalmed and put in a lead coffin (*Wāḳiʿāt*, 32), from Naples only in Ramaḍān 904/April 1499. Buried at last in the mausoleum of Muṣṭafā, his elder brother, in Bursa (cf. I. Baykal, *Bursa ve Anıtları*, Bursa 1950, 40), Djem's corpse, too, had been subject of high politics (cf. Thuasne, 378-87).

Djem's will was fulfilled by Bāyezīd II (an official record shows that his daughter Gawhar Malik Sulṭān was honored by the Sultan with presents in Ramaḍān 909/February 1504, cf. T. Gökbilgin, *Edirne ve Paşa Livası*, Istanbul 1952, 474). His son Murād, however, who took refuge in Rhodes, was captured during the conquest of the Island and executed with his son on 8 Ṣafar 929/27 December 1522. Murād's wife and two daughters were sent to Istanbul (Ferīdūn, i, 539; Thuasne, 389).

Djem, whose poems were collected in two *dīwān*s, one in Persian (ed. in part by I. H. Ertaylan, *Cem Sultan*) the other in Turkish (ed. by I. H. Ertaylan, *Cem Sultan*) was considered as a distinguished poet (cf. Laṭīfī, *Tedhkire*, Istanbul 1314, 64). He is also the author of a *Fāl-i reyhān-i Sulṭān Djem* (ed. by I. H. Ertaylan, *Fālnāme*, Istanbul 1951).

Bibliography: Documents connected with Djem and his own letters that are preserved in the archives of Tokapî Sarayî Müzesi, Istanbul, have recently been published in fascimile by I. H. Ertaylan (*Sultan Cem*, Istanbul 1951). These original documents as well as the correspondence of Djem in Ferīdūn (*Munsheʾāt al-Salāṭīn*, i, Istanbul 1274, 290-4) have not yet been studied properly. They are mostly undated. The *tahrīr defter*s of Konya and Ḳaramān contain a number of documents given in the name of Djem (Başvekâlet Arşivi, Istanbul, tapu def. No. 119, 392, 63, 32, 40, 58, 809). The *Wāḳiʿāt-i Sulṭān Djem* (ed. M. ʿArif, Istanbul 1330 H.) was written or dictated by one of the closest men to Djem, Ḥaydar (cf. M. Ârif's introduction) Ayās or Sinān, who had been with him from his childhood until his death. Saʿd al-Dīn (*Tādj al-tewārīkh*, i, Istanbul 1280, 8-40) reproduced it with a few additions from other sources. *Ghurbetnāme* (Ist. Universite Kütüphanesi, Hāliș Efendi Kitapları) is an incomplete copy of the *Wāḳiʿāt*. The collections of poems of ʿAynī-i Tirmīdhī (Konya Müzesi Kütüphanesi 2420/16), of Ḥamīdī (ed. I. H. Ertaylan) and of Ḳabūlī (ed. I. H. Ertaylan) contain contemporary information on Djem's life in Anatolia. Donado Da Lezze, *Historia turchesca*, ed. I. Ursu, Bucarest 1911; L. Thuasne, *Djem-Sultan, étude sur la question d'Orient à la fin du XVe siècle*, Paris 1892; Ḥasan b. Maḥmūd Bayātī, *Djām-i Djemāyīn*, Istanbul 1331 H.; Aḥmad Sayyid al-Darrādj,

Djem Sulṭān wa 'l-diblūmāsiyya al-duwaliyya, in *al-Madjalla al-taʾrīkhiyya al-miṣriyya*, viii, (1959), 201-42; *İA*, art. Cem (Cavid Baysun).

(Halil İnalcik)

DJEMĀL PASHA (Cemal Paşa), Young Turk soldier and statesman. Aḥmed Djemāl was born in Istanbul in 1872. He graduated from the *erkān-i ḥarbiyye mektebi* in 1895, was commissioned as a captain in the general staff, and posted to the Third Army in Salonika. There he joined the Macedonian nucleus of the Young Turk conspiracy, the *ʿOthmānlī Ittiḥād we Terakkī Djemʿiyyeti* (known in Europe as the Committee of Union and Progress), using his assignment as inspector of railways in Macedonia to help spread and consolidate the Committee's organization. Following the 1908 revolution he became a member of the *Ittiḥād we Terakkī*'s executive committee (*merkez-i ʿumūmī*). He participated energetically in the suppression of the 1909 counter-revolution (the *Otuz-bir Mart Wakʿasî*) and became military governor (*muḥāfiẓ*) of Üsküdar (Asiatic Istanbul). Later that year he was appointed *wālī* of Adana and, in 1911, of Baghdād. In 1912 he took command of the Konya reserve division and, in the First Balkan War, fought at Vize, was defeated at Pînar Ḥiṣār, and later took over the inspectorate of the Čataldja front.

Following the *Ittiḥād we Terakkī*'s *coup d'état* of 23 January 1913 (known as the Sublime Porte Incident or *Bāb-î ʿĀlī Wakʿasî*), Djemāl Pasha became military governor and *wālī* of Istanbul. He strongly supported the Unionists' plans for recapturing Edirne in the Second Balkan campaign and, by his forceful measures in rounding up and deporting opposition leaders in the capital, contributed decisively to the consolidation of the new régime; he could not, however, prevent the assassination, in June 1913, of the *ṣadr aʿẓam*, Maḥmūd Shewket Pasha. From this period onward and until the end of the World War, Djemal was widely considered, together with Enwer and Ṭalʿat Pashas, to be part of the informal dictatorial triumvirate ruling the Ottoman Empire. He was promoted to Lieutenant-General, in December 1913 entered the cabinet as minister of works and, in February 1914, was transferred to the navy office, where he worked hard to improve the equipment and training of the fleet. His efforts, during a trip to Paris in July 1914, to bring about a closer understanding between the Ottoman Empire and France bore no fruit and he later supported, somewhat reluctantly, Enwer's policy of alliance with Germany.

In August 1914 Djemāl Pasha was given command of the Second Army (then stationed on the Aegean coast), and from November 1914 until December 1917 he was commander of the Fourth Army, with headquarters in Damascus, as well as military governor of the Syrian Provinces (including Palestine and the Ḥidjāz). Throughout this period, and until October 1918, he retained the navy portfolio, which put him in the anomalous position of being both the colleague and subordinate of Enwer Pasha (as minister of war and deputy commander-in-chief). Djemāl Pasha's initial assignment on the Syrian front was to prepare an attack on the Sinai peninsula and the Suez canal. But several successive forays towards the canal (in February 1915, and in April and July 1916) brought no decisive advance, and Ottoman hopes for an anti-British uprising in Egypt in response to the Ottoman proclamation of *djihād* were disappointed. During the early war years, Djemāl undertook a large programme of public works in the Syrian provinces and took an active interest in the archaeology of the region. But there were indications of political disaffection among the local Arab leaders, and to these Djemāl reacted with characteristic severity. Eleven prominent Arabs were hanged after a summary trial in August 1915, and 21 more, including a member of the Ottoman senate (*medjlis-i aʿyān*), in May 1916—this time without formal trial. A month later, the revolt in the Ḥidjāz under the Sharīf Ḥusayn (with which some of the executed Syrians had been connected) greatly weakened the Fourth Army's position. Early in 1917 the British began their attack on Palestine, and when Djemāl was recalled from the Syrian front at the end of the year, his forces were retreating before Allenby's advance.

Djemāl resigned as minister of navy along with the rest of the Ṭalʿat Pasha cabinet. On 2 November 1918 he fled with Enwer and Ṭalʿat, going first to Berlin and then to Switzerland. (In the meantime his case was tried before an Istanbul court-martial, and he was ordered to be expelled from the army and was later sentenced to death *in absentia*). While in Europe, Djemāl took service with Amīr Amān Allāh of Afghānistān and upon the mediation of Karl Radek, travelled to Russia, where he secured the support of Chicherin, Soviet commissar of foreign affairs, for his mission of modernizing the Afghān army. While in Moscow, he offered his support to the Turkish nationalist movement under Muṣṭafā Kemāl (Atatürk), with whom he carried on an intermittent correspondence by letter and telegram beginning in June 1920; together with Enwer's uncle Khalīl Pasha (Halil Kut), he facilitated the diplomatic contacts between the Bolshevik and Kemalist régimes which culminated in the Treaty of Moscow of 1921. In the summer of 1920 Djemāl stopped in Ṭāshkent, where he recruited a group of interned Ottoman officers for his mission, and proceeded to Afghānistān to assume his post as inspector-general of the army. He returned to Moscow in September 1921 for further negotiations with the Bolsheviks, with Kemāl, and with Enwer Pasha (whom he tried to dissuade from his activities against Kemāl and from his adventurous plans in Uzbekistān). On his way back to Afghānistān, Djemāl was shot to death in Tbilisi (Tiflis) on 21 July 1922 by two Armenians, Kerekin Lalayan and Sergo Vartayan—his death apparently being part of the same assassination campaign to which Ṭalʿat and Saʿīd Ḥalīm Pashas had earlier fallen victim. He was buried in Tbilisi and later reburied in Erzurum.

Bibliography: *Türk Ansiklopedisi*, x, 141 f.; Ibrahim Alâettin Gövsa, *Türk meşhurları ansiklopedisi*, Istanbul [1946], 82; *Millī Newsāl* 132, 314 f.; Djemāl's memoirs (*Khāṭîrāt* 1913-1922, Dersеʿādet 1922, and modernized and annotated edition, *Hatiralar*, ed. Behcet Cemal (his son), Istanbul 1959; translations: *Erinnerungen eines türkischen Staatsmannes*, Munich 1922, and *Memories of a Turkish Statesman 1913-1919*, London, n.d.) are largely an apologia for his conduct in Syria, as is the "red book" *La vérité sur la question syrienne*, Istanbul 1916, issued by the Fourth Army; for the Arab point of view, see especially George Antonius, *The Arab Awakening*, London 1938, 150-52, 185-90, 202-3. On the war years in Syria much information will he found in the memoirs of his chief of staff Ali Fuad Erden, *Birinci Dünya Harbinde Suriye hâtıraları*, i, Istanbul 1954. The most detailed and reliable account of Djemāl's last three years is provided by his comrade-in-arms of his Syrian days, Ali Fuat Cebesoy, *Moskova hâtıraları*, Istanbul 1955, 48-50, 57-8, 274-99. Djemāl's archaeological interests are reflected in his book *Alte Denkmäler aus Syrien, Palästina, und West-Arabien*, Berlin 1918. (D. A. Rustow)

DJEMALĪ EFENDI [see djamālī efendi].

DJEMʿIYYET-I ʿILMIYYE-I ʿOTHMĀNIYYE, the Ottoman Scientific Society, was founded in Istanbul in 1861 by Munīf Pasha [*q.v.*]. Modelled on the Royal Society of England, and perhaps inspired by the reopening of the *Institut d'Égypte* [*q.v.*] in Alexandria in 1859, it consisted of a group of Turkish officials, dignitaries and scholars, some of them educated in Europe. It was the third such learned society to appear in 19th century Turkey, having been preceded by the *Endjümen-i Dānish* in 1851 (see andjuman), and by the 'learned society of Beshiktash' in the time of Maḥmūd II (see Djewdet, *Taʾrīkh*², xii, 184; Luṭfī, 168-9,; Djewād, 69, n. 1.; Mardin, 229 ff.). The Ottoman Scientific Society arranged public lectures and courses on premises assigned to it by the government, where there was also a reading-room with a small library. Its most important achievement, however, was the publication of the *Medjmūʿa-i Fünūn*, the first scientific periodical in Turkish, published monthly and circulated with official support. Besides the natural sciences, history and geography, politics, economics and philosophy figured largely in the pages of the journal, which introduced its readers to classical and European achievements and writings in these fields, and to the scientific, non-dogmatic study of scientific and philosophical problems. Its rôle in Turkey has been likened by Ahmed Hamdi Tanpınar to that of the *Grande Encyclopédie* in 18th century France. It was of brief duration. During the cholera epidemic of 1865 the journal was compelled to cease publication, and after a brief resumption some years later was finally suppressed in 1882 by Sultan ʿAbd al-Ḥamīd II.

Bibliography: Maḥmūd Djewād, *Maʿārif-i ʿUmūmiyye Neẓāreti taʾrīkhče-i teshkīlāt we idjrāʾātī*, Istanbul 1339, 69-72; Schlechta-Wssehrd, *Ueber den neugestifteten türkischen Gelehrten-Verein*, in *ZDMG*, xvii (1863), 682-4; cf. *ibid.* 711-4; Ali Fuad, *Münif Paşa*, in *Türk tarih encümeni mecmuası*, n.s. i/4, 1930, 5-6; A. H. Tanpınar, *XIX asır Türk edebiyatı tarihi*², Istanbul 1956, 151-4; A. Adnan-Adivar, *Interaction of Islamic and western thought in Turkey*, apud T. Cuyler Young, (ed.), *Near eastern culture and society*, Princeton 1951, 124-5; B. Lewis, *The emergence of modern Turkey*, London 1961, 431-2; V. A. Gordlevsky, *Izbrannîe Sočineniya*, ii, Moscow 1961, 366-8; Ş. Mardin, *The genesis of Young Ottoman political thought*, Princeton 1962, 238-40. (B. Lewis)

DJEMSHĪD [see djamshīd].

DJENDERELI [see djandarlī].

DJENNÉ [see dienné].

DJERBA [see djarba].

DJERĪD. the wooden dart or javelin used in the game of Djerīd, *i.e.*, Djerīd Oyunu in Turkish and, in the Arabic of Egypt, Laʿb al-Djerīd—a game which was popular and widespread in the Ottoman empire of the 10th/16th-13th/19th centuries. The actual form of the djerīd or wooden javelin varied somewhat in the different parts of the empire; its length, moreover, seems to have ranged in general between $^3/_4$ and $1^1/_2$ metres (von Oppenheim, 598-9). The djerīd, in Egypt, consisted of a palm branch stripped bare of its leaves, such being indeed the original sense of the Arabic word *djarīd*. At the court of the Ottoman Sultan in Istanbul the game of Djerīd was much in evidence and never more so than in the second half of the 11th/17th century. It afforded to the pages of the Sultan and to the other personnel of the court an admirable opportunity to show their physical prowess and dexterity. The Djerīd Oyunu was in fact a mock battle in the course of which horsemen threw darts at one another, each participant in the game being now the pursuer and now the pursued. Some of the sources declare that the Djerīd horsemen sought, during their mounted evolutions, to gain possession of the darts thrown earlier in the game and carried for this purpose thin canes curved at one end (Hobhouse, 634). At Istanbul large numbers of the court personnel often engaged in the Djerīd Oyunu—indeed rival "factions" existed under the names of Lahanadjī (cabbage men) and Bamyadjī (gumbo men). The game of Djerīd demanded a high degree of skill in horsemanship and in the throwing of the javelin or dart (Guer, *Mœurs et usages des Turcs*, ii, 252 gives an interesting account of the methods followed in order to acquire proficiency in this latter art.). It meant also for the participants a considerable risk of serious wounds and even of death, since the head was a common target of attack. The Djerīd Oyunu was abolished at Istanbul in the reign of Sultan Maḥmūd II (1223-55/1808-39) after the suppression of the Janissaries in 1241/1826, but it survived long thereafter in the provinces as a game popular amongst the mass of the people.

Bibliography: Ḥāfiẓ Khiḍr Elyās, *Taʾrīkh-i enderūn*, Istanbul A.H. 1276, 6, 111 ff., 389 ff.; ʿAṭā, *Taʾrīkh*, Istanbul A.H. 1291, 31 ff., 127 ff., 177 ff.; S. Gerlach, *Tage-buch*, Frankfurt am Main 1674, 312 (according to von Oppenheim, 599, the oldest Western account of the Djerīd Oyunu); La Boullaye Le Gouz, *Voyages et observations*, Paris 1657, 291; J.-B. Tavernier, *Nouvelle relation de l'intérieur du Sérrail du Grand Seigneur*, Paris 1675, 69-71; G. Bremond, *Descrittioni esatte dell'Egitto .... tradotta dal Francese dal Sig. Angelo Riccardi Ceri*, Rome 1680, lib. ii, cap. 29; *Reizen van Cornelis de Bruyn, door .... Klein Asia .... Aegypten, Syrien en Palestina*, Delft 1698, 136 ff.; J. A. Guer, *Mœurs et usages des Turcs*, Paris 1747, ii, 218, 252; C. F. de Volney, *Voyage en Syrie et en Égypte, pendant les années 1783, 1784 et 1785*, Paris 1787, i, 160-2; G. A. Olivier, *Voyage dans l'empire Othoman, l'Égypte et la Perse*, Paris 1801-7, i, 52-3; W. Wittman, *Travels in Turkey, Asia Minor, Syria and .... Egypt during the years 1799, 1800, and 1801*, London 1803, 35, 125, 208-9; J. C. Hobhouse, *A journey through Albania and other provinces of Turkey in Europe and Asia, to Constantinople, during the years 1809 and 1810*, London 1813, 633-5; J. B. Schels, *Militär = Verfassung des türkischen Reiches. Im Jahre 1810 .... dargestellt* (= *Oesterreichische militärische Zeitschrift*, Zweyte Auflage der Jahrgänge 1811 und 1812, Zweyter Band, Vienna 1820, 207-350), 279-81; J. J. Morier, *Ayesha, The Maid of Kars* (Standard Authors, no. 100), 133 ff. (a detailed description of the Djerīd Oyunu); *Journal et correspondance de Gédoyn "Le Turc"*, ed. A. Boppe, Paris 1909, 126; E. W. Lane, *Manners and customs of the modern Egyptians*, London 1895, 362-3 (an account of the Djerīd game as played amongst the peasants of Upper Egypt); M. von Oppenheim, *Der Djerīd und das Djerīd-Spiel*, in *Islamica*, ii/4, Leipzig 1927, 590-617; B. Miller, *The curriculum of the palace school of the Turkish sultans*, in *MacDonald Presentation Volume*, Princeton, New Jersey 1933, 303-24 (Djerīd = ibid. 321-3) and also *The palace school of Muhammad the Conqueror* (Harvard Historical Monographs, XVII), Cambridge, Mass., 1941, 120-3; N. M. Penzer, *The ḥarēm*, London 1936, 69-70; Halim Baki Kunter, *Eski Türk sporları üzerine araştırmalar*, Istanbul 1938, 47 ff.; Eremiya Çelebi Kömürcüyan, *Istanbul tarihi. XVII.asırda Istanbul*, ed. H. D. Andreasyan Istanbul Üniversitesi Edebiyat Fakültesi Yayınları, no. 506), Istanbul 1952, 98 ff.; Metin And, *Kırk gün kırk gece*, Istanbul 1959, 192-3 (quoting from the *Sūrnāme* of Ḥuseyn Wehbī (d. 1148-9/1736): cf. Metin And, *op. cit.*, 199). (V. J. Parry)

DJEWDET, ʿAbd Allāh (Abdullah Cevdet) Turkish poet, translator, politician, free-thinker and publicist. He was born of the Kurdish family of the ʿUmar Oghullarī, at ʿArabgīr, on 3 Djumādā II 1286/9 September 1869. Having completed his studies at the military school at Maʿmūret el-ʿAzīz (Elâzığ), he came to Istanbul about the age of 15 to attend the Army Medical School. There, in May 1889, he became a founder-member of the Ottoman Society for Union and Progress.

By 1891 he had published four small volumes of poetry, the second of which opened with the well-known *Naʿt-i Sherīf* in praise of the Prophet, which more than once during his stormy career swayed officialdom in his favour. In 1892 he underwent a brief spell of imprisonment for his political activities, and in 1896 was exiled to Tripoli. Becoming involved with the local branch of Union and Progress he was again imprisoned, but after his release succeeded in escaping from Tripoli and making his way to Geneva (September 1897), where he worked for the Young Turk fortnightly *ʿOthmānlī*. In 1899 he was induced to accept the post of medical officer to the embassy in Vienna: by thus taking service under ʿAbd al-Ḥamīd he debarred himself for life from attaining office under the Young Turks.

Yet so far was he from abandoning his revolutionary activities that in September 1903 he was dismissed from his post and forced to leave Austria. Returning to Geneva, he put all he possessed into founding the *Imprimerie Internationale*, which on 1 September 1904 produced the first number of *Idjtihād*, a periodical devoted to the cause of political, intellectual, religious and social liberty, which Djewdet was to edit, albeit with interruptions, for almost 30 years. In the same year he began publication of the series known as *Kütübkhāne-i idjtihād*, in which many of his own works appeared and which he controlled until his death.

Among his works published about this time were *Ḳafḳasyadaki Müslümanlara Beyānnāme*, an appeal to the Muslims of the Caucasus to fight against Russian absolutism, and translations of Byron's *Prisoner of Chillon* and Alfieri's *Del principe e delle lettere*.

Within a few months the Turkish ambassador in Paris brought about Djewdet's expulsion from Switzerland. After a short stay in France, during which the Ottoman government sentenced him, in his absence, to life-imprisonment, loss of civil rights and confiscation of his property, he moved on to Cairo (late 1905), where he remained till mid-1911, working as an oculist while continuing his political and publishing activities. He joined the Young Turk Decentralist party and maintained an incessant output of pamphlets against the Sultan and, for a short while only, against the Ottoman house in general. Regarding ʿAbd al-Ḥamīd as an incorrigible despot, he was not impressed by his acceptance of the Constitution in 1908, but in this matter Djewdet's was a lone voice.

In July 1909, after the Sultan's abdication, *Idjtihād* ceased publication in Cairo, reappearing in June 1911 in Istanbul, where Djewdet had taken up residence. But his troubles did not end with the abdication. In February 1910 the Young Turk cabinet of Ibrāhīm Ḥaḳḳī Pasha banned 'the *History of Islām* by ʿAbd Allāh Djewdet Bey, which is directed against the Muslim faith', though it was Dozy's original and not Djewdet's preface to his translation of it which most offended the authorities. He was imprisoned for a month in the winter of 1912, after the Turkish defeats in the Balkan war. His attacks on the official theologians in the pages of *Idjtihād* led to its temporary suspension in 1913 and to a compulsory change in its title on three occasions in 1914. Djewdet's opposition to Turkish participation in the First World War caused the periodical to be suppressed again, from 13 February 1915 to 1 November 1918. Meanwhile he published several non-political works, among them his edition and translation of the *Rubāʿiyyāt-i Khayyām*.

During the grand-vizierate of Dāmad Ferīd Pasha he twice served as director-general of public health. But he again brought himself into conflict with the authorities by an article which he wrote in favour of Bahāʾism; in April 1922 he was sentenced to 2 years' imprisonment for blasphemy (*enbiyāya ṭaʿn*), but the legal argument dragged on till December 1926. In the result he was discharged and the crime itself was dropped from the new Turkish code. He died on 29 November 1932, working to the end.

His published works, original and translated, number over 60. Among his translations are six of Shakespeare's plays: although all but *Anṭuān we Kleʾopātrā* suffer through being made from French versions, they are by no means without merit. He deserves great credit also for making the modern study of psychology known to his compatriots.

The long article on djewdet by K. Süssheim in *EI*¹ (Suppl.), on which the present article is based, gives a complete list of his works and a bibliography, to which may be added: Enver Behnan Şapolyo, *Ziya Gökalp, İttihat ve Terakki ve Meşrutiyet tarihi*, Istanbul 1943, 30, 49-50, 70; Ahmed Bedevî Kuran, *İnkılâp tarihimiz ve Jön Türkler*, Istanbul 1945; idem, *İnkılâp tarihimiz ve İttihad ve Terakki*, Istanbul 1948; E. E. Ramsaur, Jr., *The young Turks*, Princeton 1957; B. Lewis, *The emergence of modern Turkey*, London 1961. (G. L. Lewis)

DJEWDET PASHA [see aḥmad djewdet pasha].

DJEZĀʾIRLI GHĀZĪ ḤASAN PASHA, one of the most famous *ḳapudan pasha*s (Grand Admirals) of the Turkish navy. He was born in Tekfurdaghī (Rodosto) on the Sea of Marmora, where he is said to have been a slave in the service of a Muslim merchant; on being set free, he took part as a janissary in the campaign against Austria in 1737-39. At the end of the war he went to Algiers where he was received by the Deys and in the end was appointed beg of Tlemcen. Some time afterwards, to escape from the persecution of the Dey of Algiers, he took refuge in Spain. In 1760 he returned to Constantinople and was put in command of a warship by Sultan Muṣṭafā III. In 1180/1766-7 he obtained command of the *ḳapudana* (admiral's flag-ship) and in 1770 took part in the naval war against Russia in the Mediterranean. At the nava

battle of Česh̲me [q.v.] the k̲apudana of which he was
in command caught fire while an attempt was being
made to board the Russian flag-ship, and both
ships blew up; Ḥasan Beg, although wounded,
swam to safety. He then reached the Dardanelles
and from there embarked on a daring manœuvre,
as a result of which he succeeded in capturing from
the Russians the island of Lemnos which they had
previously occupied (10 October 1770). For this
brilliant feat he was awarded the title of G̲h̲āzī and
the position of k̲apudanpas̲h̲a. In 1773 and 1774 he
took part, as ser'asker of Rusčuk, in the continental
war against Russia; after the signature of the
Treaty of Kaynardja (17 July 1774) he once again
held the office of k̲apudanpas̲h̲a. During the following
years (1775 and 1776) he brought to an end the
domination of S̲h̲ayk̲h̲ Ẓāhir al-'Umar [q.v.] and his
sons over 'Akkā; in 1778, when disputes with Russia
over the Crimea gave rise to fears of a new war, he
conducted a naval demonstration in the Black Sea;
but in fact it entirely failed to achieve its purpose
and resulted in the loss of several large ships which
ran aground or were involved in various accidents.
In 1779 he was sent to the Morea and drove out the
hordes of Albanians who had settled there after the
withdrawal of the Russian fleet. He was made
responsible for governing the Morea while continuing
to hold the position of k̲apudanpas̲h̲a; and in 1780
he crushed the revolt of the Maïnots. In the years
that followed he took an important part in the
government of his country. On three separate
occasions (in 1781, 1785 and 1786), though for short
periods only, he was entrusted with the Grand
Vizierate in the capacity of k̲ā'immak̲ām. His second
tenure of the Grand Vizierate followed the fall of
his rival K̲h̲alīl Ḥāmid Pas̲h̲a (31 March 1785) whom
he had denounced to Sulṭān 'Abd al-Ḥamīd I as the
instigator of a plot to depose the sultan and replace
him by the crown prince Selīm. At the same time he
carried out a reorganization of the navy, built the
first barracks for the crews of the fleet (1784) and
organized the upkeep of the forts on the Bosphorus,
at the entry into Black Sea. In the years 1786 and
1787 he was given the task of restoring the Porte's
control over Egypt which, under the Mamlūk begs
Murād and Ibrāhīm, had become virtually independent. Though with only inadequate forces, he
advanced to Cairo, set at liberty Yegen Meḥmed
Pas̲h̲a who was imprisoned there (8 August 1786)
and routed the rebel begs; but in the autumn of
1787, while still engaged in restoring order in Egypt,
he was recalled on account of the threat of war with
Russia. When hostilities broke out, he was ordered
to relieve the siege of Oczakov; with this aim, he
engaged in several naval battles with the Russians
in June 1788, in the vicinity, but in each case
without success; he did contrive to send troops and
supplies of food into the town, but he was unable
to force the Russians to raise the siege. After losing
several ships in a storm, he returned to Constantinople at the beginning of December 1788. On
7 April 1789 his patron Sultan 'Abd al-Ḥamīd died.
The new sultan, Selīm III, dismissed Djezā'irli
Ḥasan Pas̲h̲a from the office of k̲apudanpas̲h̲a and
appointed him ser'asker of Ismā'īl. After the Grand
Vizier had suffered a severe defeat near Martines̲h̲ti
(22 September), Ḥasan Pas̲h̲a who had just driven
back a Russian army from the fortress of Ismā'īl
received the seal of office as Grand Vizier and Commander-in-chief of the forces (end of November).
He spent the winter at S̲h̲umla and there carried
on negotiations with Prince Potemkin. Some days

after giving orders to leave winter-quarters he
fell ill and on 14 Radjab 1204/30 March 1790 he
died, perhaps poisoned by order of the Sultan. He
was buried in the Bektas̲h̲i convent which he had
himself built outside the gates of S̲h̲umla.

Djezā'irli G̲h̲āzī Ḥasan Pas̲h̲a was distinguished
in a quite remarkable way from other commanders
of his time by his personal bravery: his missions
to Syria, the Morea and Egypt show not only his
military skill but also a political clear-sightedness
which was rare at that period. Although his two
expeditions in the Black Sea in 1778 and 1788 failed
on all counts, he at least had the merit of rebuilding
the fleet which had been destroyed at the battle
of Česh̲me and of inaugurating the work of reorganizing the Turkish navy with the help of European
technicians, a task which was to be continued by
Küčük Ḥuseyn Pas̲h̲a [q.v.]. His complicity in the
fall and death of K̲h̲alīl Ḥāmid Pas̲h̲a, though a
proof of his own fidelity to his master, was nevertheless a dastardly action which delayed the revival
of the Empire.

Bibliography: Aḥmed Djāwid, Ḥadīkat al-
wuzarā', App. II, 41 ff.; Aywānsarāyī Ḥüseyn,
Ḥadīkat al-djawāmi', ii, 28 ff.; Djewdet, Ta'rīkh²,
i-v; G̲h̲azawāt-i G̲h̲āzī Ḥasan Pas̲h̲a, MS. Süleymaniye Kütüph. Es'ad Ef. no. 2419 (for other
MSS.: Agâh Sırrı Levend, Gazavāt-nāmeler, Ankara
1956, 153 ff.) see also Ercümend Kuran, Gazavat-i
Cezayirli Gazi Hasan Paşa'ya dair in TD, xi,
1960, 95 ff.; Hammer-Purgstall, viii; idem, Staatsverfassung . . ., ii, 350 ff.; Zinkeisen, vi; W. Eton,
A Survey of the Turkish Empire³, London 1801,
79 ff.; I. H. Uzunçarşılı, Cezayirli Gazi Hasan
Paşa'ya dair, TM, 1940-42,17 ff.; idem, Osmanlı
Tarihi, Ankara 1959, iv/2, 446 ff.; İA, s.v. (by
Uzunçarşılı). (J. H. MORDTMANN-[E. KURAN])

DJIBĀL, plural of the Arabic djabal (mountain
or hill), a name given by the Arabs to the region
formerly known as Māh (Māda, Media), which they
also called 'Irāk̲ 'Adjamī, to distinguish it from
Arabian 'Irāk̲, i.e., Lower Mesopotamia. The province came by its name of Djibāl because it is,
except in its north-eastern portion, extremely
mountainous. It was bounded in the east by the
great desert of K̲h̲urāsān, on the south-east by
Fārs, on the south by K̲h̲ūzistān, on the west and
south-west by Arabian 'Irāk̲, on the north-west by
Ād̲h̲arbāydjān and on the north by the Alburz
range. The boundaries were never well defined and
therefore underwent frequent changes. According to
Iṣṭak̲h̲rī (203) and Ibn Ḥawk̲al (267) there were
antimony mines at Iṣfahān. Owing to the altitude,
the climate is in general cold and there is much
snow in winter.

Bibliography: Yāk̲ūt, ii, 15 (= Barbier de
Meynard, Dict. de la Perse, 151); A. F. Mehren,
Manuel de la cosmographie, 248; Muk̲addasī, 384;
General Sir A. Houtum-Schindler, Eastern Persian
Irak (Royal Geographical Society publication,
London 1896); Le Strange, 185 ff.
(L. LOCKHART)

AL-DJIBĀL, name formerly given by Arab
authors to that portion of Arabia Petrea
situated directly south of the Wādī al-Ḥaṣā, an
affluent of the southern extremity of the Dead Sea,
which from its lofty summits (rising to 1400 or
1600 m.) dominates the depression of the Wādī al-
'Araba [q.v.], the southern prolongation of the Jordan
Fault. This important mountain system, continued
afterwards by that of al-S̲h̲arāt [q.v.] with which
it is often confused, thus corresponds to the broken

border of the steppe desert, in a region where the Transjordan plateau perceptibly rises. Its tortuous relief, which makes it appear almost like a wall coloured with granites and porphyries on the east of Palestine, opens however by deep gashes on to the basin of the Dead Sea which receives most of the water of its streams, and for long supported by exports of bitumen the traffic of its commercial routes. It was always a region of communication, the strategic importance of which was plain at the time of the defence of the Roman *limes* against the invasions of the nomads, and at the time of the struggles between the Franks of Palestine (fortress of Montreal or al-Shawbak built by Baldwin I in 1115) and the Muslim principalities of Egypt and Syria. But it was also, until the first centuries of Islam, a cultivated region where the relatively abundant springs permitted the development of small centres of settled population, still attested by numerous ruins although these have been little studied.

In the Hellenic period this ancient land of eastern Edom, separated from the country of Moab by the traditional frontier of the Wādī al-Ḥasā already mentioned, had seen the growth of Nabataean power, the apogee of which must have marked the first period of Arab penetration to the borders of Palestine. We know that some sites of Gebalene like Boṣra, the former Mibṣar identified with the present-day village of Buṣayra to the south of al-Ṭafīla, are reckoned among the localities of the caravan kingdom of Petra. The same territory thereafter became part of the province of Arabia, the frontier marches which Trajan had substituted, in 106, for the Nabataean kingdom and which must then have gradually lost, to Palmyra's advantage, its monopoly of wealth of merchant origin. In 295 new administrative changes rejoined Gebalene to Palestine, an enormous province which was divided first into two and later into three departments in the second half of the 4th century. It was thus to the Third or Salutary Palestine that belonged, according to the Byzantine lists, the towns of Metrocomia (al-Ṭafīla), Mamopsora (Buṣayra), Arindela (al-ʿArandal) and the military post of Rabatha (the former Reḥoboth near the Wādī al-Riḥāb), all townships whose location can today only be established with difficulty, but whose importance seems to have been maintained at the very beginning of Muslim domination.

In fact the names of ʿArandal (Arindela), provided by al-Yaʿḳūbī, and of Ruwāth (Robatha), given by Ibn Ḥawḳal (113), are generally found in the early Arab geographers mentioning the capital of the canton of al-Djibāl (according to the authors a canton of the djund of Damascus or of the djund of Filasṭīn) and distinguishing this district from Maʾāb (capital: Zughār) and from al-Sharāt (capital: Adhruḥ). Such a distinction, which Ibn Khurradādhbih also observes in his enumeration of the Syrian cantons, was not long in becoming blurred, doubtless because of the impoverishment and the progressive abandonment by its population of a region which had however been conquered without a struggle by Yazīd b. Abī Sufyān and would have been able to continue to live on its former prosperity. Even al-Maḳdisī (145) knows only al-Sharāt, to which he attributes Zughār as its capital and cites Maʿān and Adhruḥ as its principal towns, and Yāḳūt does likewise, locating the village of ʿArandal there. The term al-Djibāl had then fallen into desuetude, and in the Mamlūk period writers, such as al-Ḳalḳashandī and al-ʿUmarī, only mention, in the *niyāba* of al-Karak, the *wilāya*s of al-Shawbak, Zughār and Maʿān, extending over all the southern part of the province of Syria.

Bibliography: F. M. Abel, *Géographie de la Palestine*, Paris 1933-8, i, 15-6, 18, 69, 157, 283; ii, *passim*, esp. 287 (Boṣra), 386 (Mibṣar), 434 Reḥoboth), 479 (Thaiman/Teimân); Le Strange, *Palestine*, 28, 32, 35, 395; A. S. Marmardji, *Textes géographiques*, Paris 1953, 43, 105; M. Gaudefroy-Demombynes, *La Syrie à l'époque des Mamelouks*, Paris 1923, 129-34; A. Musil, *Arabia Petraea*, Vienna 1907, ii; Brünnow and Domaszewski, *Die Provincia Arabia*, Strasbourg 1904-9, i; Balādhurī, *Futūḥ*, 126; *BGA*, indexes; Yaʿḳūbī-Wiet, 174-5; Yāḳūt, iii, 657 (ʿArandal).

(J. Sourdel-Thomine)

DJIBĀYA [see ʿĀMIL, BAYT AL-MĀL, ḌARĪBA, DJAHBADH, KHARĀDJ, etc.].

DJIBRĪL [see DJABRĀʾĪL].

DJIBŪTĪ (modern orth. Djibouti), a town and port on the African coast of the Gulf of Aden, at the mouth of the Gulf of Tadjoura. The promontory, composed of four small madrepore reefs upon which the town is built, was called Ras Djabūtī or Gabūtī, probably an Arabicized form of Gabod (in ʿAfar: "the plateaux in wicker-work"), a name still used for part of the coast nearby. The territory of Djibūtī was given to France in March 1885 by local notables of the ʿĪse, a Somali-speaking tribe who had taken the place of the ʿAfar in that region during the 19th century and enjoyed independent status.

The town and port were built up from nothing by France. The former was founded by governor Lagarde on 6 March 1888. In 1896 it officially replaced Obok as chief town of the French establishments in the Gulf of Aden. In 1897 work was started on the Franco-Ethiopian railway (completed in 1917) which connects Djibūtī with Addis Ababa, the capital of Ethiopia (784 m.). The port very soon supplanted Zaylāʿ and Tadjoura as the outlet for southern Ethiopia: possessing several deep-water docks, it is one of the leading ports on the east coast of Africa.

The population of Djibūtī consists of 32,000 inhabitants, 28,000 of whom are Muslim. About two-thirds of the latter are Somalis (ʿĪse, Gadabbūrsi, Habar-Awwal and other Isāḳ, and some Dārōd), mostly immigrants from the former Somaliland or Ethiopia; a quarter are of foreign extraction. In addition, there are about 5,000 Arabs, 2,000 of whom are of foreign extraction, from the Yemen and Aden Territory, and who hold an important position in commerce; about 3,000 ʿAfar, and a small number of Indian, Ethiopian and Sudanese Muslims. Arabic is the common language of the majority.

For the territory known as French Somali Coast the Ḳāḍī of Djibūtī, traditionally of Arab origin, is the leading religious personage. A very great majority of the population belongs to the Shāfiʿī school; almost the only exception are some Zaydī Arabs. With the ʿAfar and the Somali, custom (*ʿāda* and *ḥēr*, respectively) frequently takes precedence over the *sharīʿa*. The religious order most widespread in Djibūtī and throughout the region is the Ḳādiriyya; the next, though only in Djibūtī, is the Aḥmadiyya which predominates in the Somali tribe of the Habar-Djaʿlo. In addition to ʿAbd al-Ḳādir al-Djīlānī, whose *maḳāmāt* are numerous, various saints of either foreign or local origin are venerated almost everywhere; in the ʿAfar country the (false) tomb of a certain shaykh Abū Yazīd, who is said to be Abū Yazīd al-Bisṭāmī [*q.v.*] dominates the Goda mountain. Besides the veneration of local inhabitants, pilgrims from the Arab and Somali regions sometimes visit it. In Djibūtī there are eight large mosques (*djāmi*ʿ) of masonry, and several other smaller ones of lighter construction. Several Somali tribes or tribal groups (ʿĪse, Izāḳ, Dārōd) have dedicated small mosques or oratories in the town to their eponymous ancestors.

Since 1957, through the application of the law of 23 June 1956, Djibūtī, an over-seas territory of the French Republic, is administered, under the tutelage of a Governor representing metropolitan France, by a Council of Government, and possesses a Territorial Assembly elected by universal suffrage.

Bibliography: S. Vignéras, *Une mission française en Abyssinie*, Paris 1897; Angoulvant and Vignéras, *Djibouti, Mer Rouge, Abyssinie*, Paris 1902; Martineau, *La Côte Francaise des Somalis*, Paris 1931; Jourdain and Dupont, *D'Obock à Djibouti*, Paris 1933; Aubert de la Rüe, *La Somalie française*, Paris 1939; Deschamps, Decary, Ménard, *Côte des Somalis, Réunion, Inde*, Paris 1948; Trimingham, *Islam in Ethiopia*, London 1952; articles in *Tropiques* (*Revue des Troupes Coloniales*), Paris May 1955; *Cahiers de l'Afrique et l'Asie*, v, *Mer Rouge, Afrique Orientale* (Albospeyre, etc.), Paris 1959. (E. CHÉDEVILLE)

AL-**DJIDD** WA 'L-**HAZL** "seriousness and joking", a common combination of antithetical terms which have a certain resonance in Muslim ethics and the Arabic literary genre known as *adab*. Although only the second of these words occurs in the Ḳur'ān, without implication of any kind, while its antonym *djidd* and its synonym *muzāḥ* do not appear there at all, and although the Ḳur'ān does not explicitly prescribe either serious behaviour or the avoidance of jocularity, Islam without necessarily inspiring sadness and tears in spite of its pessimistic view of this world here below, at least invites Believers seriously to consider the divine promises and threats and, during their life on earth, to prepare for the eternal life which awaits them. Thus, in contrast to the levity and carefree attitude of the heathen who, not believing in the immortality of the soul and the resurrection, are inclined to enjoy all worldly pleasures with impunity, in Islam there is found a gravity dictated by the constant anxiety to deserve the divine reward; if, furthermore, *ḥilm* [*q.v.*] is a fundamental basis of Islamic ethics, it implies in particular a dignity of attitude which excludes any possibility of giving way to laughter and joking. The recollection of the ridicule suffered not only by the first Muslims but also by God's earliest messengers inspires a distaste for mockery which moreover is forbidden by the Ḳur'ān (XLIX, II), and even mere laughter, which is itself disapproved of; it is indeed God "who causes to laugh and causes to weep" (LIII, 44), but they will weep much in the other world who in this world have laughed a little (IX, 83/82); laughter is the behaviour of the enemies of God (cf. XXIII, 112/11; XLIII, 46/47; LIII, 60; LXXXIII, 29); however, the Believers will be rewarded in the hereafter, they will laugh and their faces will be bright and joyful (LXXX, 38-9).

Conscious of the nobility and dignity of his religion, of the gravity of his most ordinary actions and the moderation which he must observe in all things the Muslim, when he does not consider himself compelled to shed countless tears [see BAKKĀ'], accordingly feels that he must be essentially serious and must reject any conduct incompatible with the impassivity which *ḥilm* requires, above all laughter and jocularity. This feeling, based upon a narrow interpretation of Ḳur'ānic ethics, finds an additional justification in a certain number of *ḥadīth*s and memorable sayings which somewhat later authors of ethical works or popular encyclopaedias unfailingly collect together in special paragraphs. Thus al-Ghazālī (*Iḥyā'*, book xxiv) declares jocularity to be forbidden and blameworthy, and quotes various *ḥadīth*s in support of his assertion, not, however, without tolerating a moderate joke; al-Ibshīhī (*Mustaṭraf*, ii, 308), immediately after the chapter concerning the prohibition of wine, devotes a paragraph to the forbidding of the joke, but does not fail to quote the favourable traditions at greater length and to repeat a certain number of droll anecdotes.

Indeed, the defenders of the joke are not short of arguments; the basic ideas which would serve to justify complete condemnation are in fact contradicted by certain *ḥadīth*s and reflections of wise Muslims, and it is easy to invoke the help of the Prophet himself who joked in various circumstances, as well as the pious forbears who hardly seem to have observed literally the Ḳur'ānic provisions against laughter and jocularity. The instance of the great *fuḳahā'* of Medina is readily taken as a precedent, and one cannot forget the curious but explicable fact, from the 1st/8th century in the Holy Cities, especially Medina, of the rise of an actual school of humourists whose profession it was to bring laughter and who helped to raise the amusing anecdote, the *nādira* [*q.v.*], to the rank of a literary form. ʿIrāḳ was not unaffected by this movement, and it is only necessary to glance through the *Fihrist* (Cairo ed., 201 ff., 435) to get an idea of the wealth of collections of anecdotes, either signed or anonymous, in circulation as early as the time of Ibn al-Nadīm; it is very probable that, insofar as they have a historical existence—and it is known that some of them did indeed exist—these entertainers and their aristocratic clients were scarcely embarrassed by prohibitions which others considered absolute. Collections of this kind, which certainly enjoyed a great vogue, have for the most part disappeared—like the imaginative writings, the richness of which is shown by the *Fihrist*—probably as the result of puritanical reaction, but they have been partly absorbed in more recent collections, and the literature of *adab* has preserved extracts from them which testify to the enduring though unacknowledged taste of Arab readers for the anecdote that is piquant, not to say obscene and indecent.

Apart from its moral aspect properly speaking, the comic element in fact raises a literary problem which al-Djāḥiẓ appears, once again, to have been the first to define clearly. Inheriting a religious and literary tradition of long standing, he was shocked by the needlessly stiff attitude of some of his contemporaries, and from the start he set out to justify laughter, which he associated with life, and jocularity, stressing its advantages so long as it was not exaggerated, and showing that Islam was a liberal religion which in no way enforced reserve and severity; from there he went on to attack the boredom bred by most writings which, in his opinion, were too serious, and he suggested a leavening of a little *hazl* in even the most severe speculations; at times he did not hesitate to interrupt a learned argument to quote some anecdotes, at the risk of discrediting the rest of his work, but he succeeded in harmoniously blending together the serious and the comic in several of his writings, among which the *Kitāb al-Tarbīʿ wa'l-tadwīr* is unquestionably the most perfect example; in a word, he wished the literary form of *adab* to instruct while it amused. On this point he seems to have been partially successful for he has many imitators in both West and East. Going still further he put into practice, although unknowingly, the motto *castigat ridendo mores*, and wrote the *Kitāb al-Bukhalā'* in which he used laughter as an element in a moralizing design; in this case, however, his success is more questionable, and Ibn al-Djawzī appears to be more or less the only other writer who tried to use laughter freely for a similar purpose (*Akhbār al-ḥamḳā wa 'l-mughaffalīn*, Damascus 1345, 2-3). In general, comic writings and even contemporary theatrical comedies (a comedy is called *hazliyya*) are never looked on as more than an agreeable diversion, without any moral significance. (CH. PELLAT)

DJIDDA [see DJUDDA].

DJIDJELLI (Gegel in Leo Africanus; Zizeri, Zigeri-Gigerry, Gigeri in western writers), a coastal town in Algeria, 70 km. west of Bougie and 50 km. east of Collo. Geographical position 36° 49′ 54″ N.-5° 44′ 38″ E. Population 21,200 inhabitants (1955).

The ancient town of Djidjelli stood high up, where the citadel still stands, on a rocky peninsula which juts out between two bays, one to the west, small and very sheltered, the other lying to the east in a deep basin divided from the open sea by a line of reefs. The present town was built after the destruction of the Turkish town by an earthquake in 1856, and lies along the sea near to the large easterly bay. The port gains a certain importance from the export of cork which comes from the forests of the Little Kabylia.

Djidjelli is of very ancient origin. The Phoenicians in fact established a trading post at this spot, named Idgil, which later passed into the hands of the Carthaginians. During the Roman period the colony of Idgilgili was included in Mauretania Caesariensis, eventually being restored to Setifian Mauretania in the time of Diocletian. It was the seat of a bishopric. It passed successively under the domination of the Vandals and Byzantines. When the Arabs became masters of the Maghrib, Djidjelli no doubt retained its independence. Ibn Khaldūn tells us, in effect, that for the early centuries of the Hidjra it was in the hands of the Berber tribe of the Kutāma, who inhabited the nearby mountains (Ibn Khaldūn, *Hist. des Berbères*, tr. de Slane, i, 198). It seems, however, to have been ravaged and in some measure depopulated, since al-Bakrī describes it as a town "now inhabited" (*Description de l'Afrique septentrionale*, tr. de Slane, 193). According to this geographer, some remains of ancient monuments still survived. The inhabitants exported copper ore from the surrounding mountains to Ifrīḳiya and to other even remoter regions (al-Idrīsī, IIIe climat, tr. De Goeje, 114). The Ḥammādids who had incorporated it in their kingdom had a castle built there.

Like various other places on the coast of Africa, Djidjelli passed into the hands of the Christians in the 6th/12th century. In 537/1143 George of Antioch, an admiral of Roger II of Sicily, seized the town and the castle. This situation remained unchanged until the overthrow of the Ḥammādid dynasty by ʿAbd al-Muʾmin (547/1152). The Christians were then compelled by this prince to evacuate Djidjelli.

After the break-up of the Almohad empire, Djidjelli fell to the Ḥafṣids and on several occasions was the subjects of disputes between the kings of Bougie and Tunis. Taking advantage of these quarrels, the inhabitants succeeded in making themselves practically independent of both parties (Leo Africanus, ed. Épaulard, 362). They made their living by exporting barley, flax, hemp, nuts and figs which they sent to Tunis, Egypt and even to towns in Italy. The port there was crowded with Christian shipping from Naples, Pisa, Catalonia and Genoa. Genoese merchants were even given favoured treatment there. The commercial importance of Djidjelli declined however in the 9th/15th century owing to the increase in piracy.

At the beginning of the 10th/16th century the Genoese, alarmed by the Spanish occupation of Bougie [see BIDJĀYA], had Djidjelli occupied by a fleet commanded by Andreas Doria. But in the following year ʿArūdj, who had been called in by the inhabitants, seized the Genoese fortress with the help of the Kabyle chief Aḥmad b. al-Ḳāḍī and settled in Djidjelli. It was from there that he set out in 918/1512 to lay siege to Bougie and, in 922/1516, to take Algiers [see ʿARŪDJ]. It was also there that Khayr al-Dīn came to seek refuge when defeated by the Kabyles, while his enemies ravaged Mitīdja and made themselves masters of Algiers. He lived there from 926/1520 until 934/1527, making it the base for his fleet, and even thought of choosing Djidjelli as his capital. He gave up the idea after the capture of the Peñon at Algiers [see KHAYR AL-DĪN], but granted exemption from all taxes in kind to the people of Djidjelli, for themselves and their descendants, as a reward for their fidelity.

Throughout the 16th century and the first half of the 17th, the Djidjelli seafarers continued their privateering, thus provoking reprisals from the Christian Powers. In 1020/1611 a Spanish fleet commanded by the marquis of Santa Cruz came and burnt the town. In 1074/1663 the French Government, on the advice of Admiral Duquesne and the engineer Clerville, considered setting up in Djidjelli a permanent base for the warships engaged in combating the Barbary corsairs. In the following year, a squadron under the orders of the duke of Beaufort disembarked at Djidjelli an expeditionary corps of 8,000 men commanded by the count of Gadagne. The French troops took possession of the town, almost without striking a blow, on 23 July 1664, and constructed entrenchments and fortifications at some distance from the shore. But, paralysed by the quarrels between their two leaders, they remained inactive in their positions and allowed the Algerians to bring up an army and to establish powerful batteries. Pulverized by the fire of the enemy's artillery, they were compelled to evacuate the town on 31 October 1664 and with great difficulty they re-embarked, with the loss of 2,000 men.

As a guarantee against further attacks, the Turks then established a permanent garrison in the town. It was, however, much too small to overawe the Kabyle tribes, and it remained penned in the citadel in a state of almost perpetual siege. The deys were only able to negotiate with the local inhabitants, from whom they had to obtain the wood required for ship-building, through the intermediary of marabouts belonging to one of the branches of the family of the Moḳrānī. One of them, al-Ḥādjdj ʿAbd al-Ḳādir, was appointed marabout of Djidjelli in 1168/1755, and the office was inherited by his descendants. At this period Djidjelli seems to have regained some of its commercial activity.

This relative prosperity was compromised by the Kabyle insurrection of 1803. The marabout Bū

Dali (al-Ḥādjdj Muḥammad b. al-Ḥarsh) attacked the town, and the Turkish garrison fled. Bū Dali proclaimed himself sultan and entrusted the government of Djidjelli to one of his supporters with the title of *agha*. Sent with a squadron to punish the rebels, the raʾīs Ḥamīdu bombarded the town, without result (1805). But shortly afterwards, having been maltreated by the Kabyles, the inhabitants made their submission to the dey who set up a new garrison in the town.

The fall of the Turkish Government in 1830 gave the people of Djidjelli their independence which they kept until 1839, when the sack of a French trading-post made Marshal Valée, the Governor-General of Algeria, decide to have the town occupied, on 13 May 1839. But the garrison, having no communications with the hinterland, remained besieged by the Kabyles until the moment when an expedition led by general Saint-Armand brought the tribes of the Little Kabylia to submission (1851).

Bibliography: Féraud, *Histoire des villes de la province de Constantine, Gigelli*, Constantine 1870; Watbled, *Expédition du duc de Beaufort contre Gigelli*, in *RA*, 1873; Montchicourt, *L'expédition de Djidjelli (1664)*, in *Revue maritime*, 1898; P. Marçais, *Textes arabes de Djidjelli*, Paris 1954; idem, *Le parler arabe de Djidjelli (Nord Constantinois, Algérie)*, Paris 1956; A. Retout, *Histoire de Djidjelli*, Algiers 1927; *Guide Bleu*, Paris 1955. (G. Yver*)

DJIHĀD etymologically signifies an effort directed towards a determined objective. (Cf. *idjtihād*: the work of the scholar-jurists in seeking the solution of legal problems; *mudjāhada* or, again, *djihād*: an effort directed upon oneself for the attainment of moral and religious perfection. Certain writers, particularly among those of Shīʿite persuasion, qualify this *djihād* as "spiritual *djihād*" and as "the greater *djihād*", in opposition to the *djihād* which is our present concern and which is called "physical *djihād*" or "the lesser *djihād*". It is, however, very much more usual for the term *djihād* to denote this latter form of "effort").

In law, according to general doctrine and in historical tradition, the *djihād* consists of military action with the object of the expansion of Islam and, if need be, of its defence.

The notion stems from the fundamental principle of the universality of Islam: this religion, along with the temporal power which it implies, ought to embrace to whole universe, if necessary by force. The principle, however, must be partially combined with another which tolerates the existence, within the Islamic community itself, of the adherents of "the religions with holy books", *i.e.*, Christians, Jews and *Madjūs* [*q.v.*]. As far as these latter are concerned the *djihād* ceases as soon as they agree to submit to the political authority of Islam and to pay the poll tax (*djizya* [*q.v.*]) and the land tax (*kharādj* [*q.v.*]). As long as the question could still, in fact, be posed, a controversy existed—generally resolved by a negative answer—on the question as to whether the Christians and Jews of the Arabian peninsula were entitled to such treatment as of right. To the non-scriptuaries, in particular the idolaters, this half measure has no application according to the opinion of the majority: their conversion to Islam is obligatory under pain of being put to death or reduced into slavery.

In principle, the *djihād* is the one form of war which is permissible in Islam, for, in theory, Islam must constitute a single community organized under a single authority and any armed conflict between Muslims is prohibited.

Following, however, the disintegration of Muslim unity and the appearance, beginning in the middle of the 2nd/8th century, of an ever increasing number of independent States, the question arose as to how the wars which sprang up between them were to be classified. They were never included within the strict notion of *djihād*—even in the case of wars between states of different religious persuasion—at least according to the general Sunnī doctrine; and it is only by an abuse of language that this term is sometimes applied to them, while those authors who seek for a precise terminology label them only as *ḳitāl* or *muḳātala* (conflict, war). There is even hesitation in referring to the struggle against the renegade groups in Islam as *djihād*. The viewpoint of Shīʿite doctrine is not the same, for, according to the Shīʿa, a refusal to subscribe to their teaching is equivalent to unbelief (*kufr*). The same holds good, *a fortiori*, for the Khāridjite doctrine [see further TAKFĪR].

The *djihād* is a duty. This precept is laid down in all the sources. It is true that there are to be found in the Ḳurʾān divergent, and even contradictory, texts. These are classified by the doctrine, apart from certain variations of detail, into four successive categories: those which enjoin pardon for offences and encourage the invitation to Islam by peaceful persuasion; those which enjoin fighting to ward off agression; those which enjoin the initiative in attack, provided it is not within the four sacred months; and those which enjoin the initiative in attack absolutely, at all times and in all places. In sum, these differences correspond to the stages in the development of Muḥammad's thought and to the modifications of policy resulting from particular circumstances; the Meccan period during which Muḥammad, in general, confines himself to moral and religious teaching, and the Medina period when, having become the leader of a politico-religious community, he is able to undertake, spontaneously, the struggle against those who do not wish to join this community or submit to his authority. The doctrine holds that the later texts abrogate the former contradictory texts (the theory of *naskh* [*q.v.*]), to such effect that only those of the last category remain indubitably valid; and, accordingly, the rule on the subject may be formulated in these absolute terms: "the fight (*djihād*) is obligatory even when they (the unbelievers) have not themselves started it".

In two isolated opinions, however, attempts were made to temper the rule in some respects. According to one of these views, attributed to ʿAṭā (d. 114/732-3), the ancient prohibition against fighting during the sacred months remains valid; while according to the other, attributed to Sufyān al-Thawrī (born 97/715), the *djihād* is obligatory only in defence; it is simply recommended (*li 'l-nadb*) in attack. According to a view held by modern orientalist scholarship, Muḥammad's conception of the *djihād* as attack applied only in relation to the peoples of Arabia; its general application was the result of the *idjmāʿ* (general consensus of opinion) of the immediately succeeding generations. At root, of course, this involves the problem as to whether Muḥammad had conceived of Islam as universal or not.

The opinion of al-Thawrī appears to have been adopted by al-Djāḥiẓ. The heterodox movement of the Aḥmadiyya [*q.v.*], beginning towards the end of the 19th century, would go further than al-

T͟hawrī inasmuch as it refuses to recognize the legitimacy of the *d͟jihād* even as a recommended activity. Cf., in the same sense, the doctrine of Bābism (see BĀB).

According to the general doctine of the S͟hīʿa, due account taken of their dogma concerning "the absence of the Imām", who alone has the necessary competence to order war, the practice of the *d͟jihād* is necessarily suspended until the re-appearence of the Imām or the *ad hoc* appointment of a vicar designated by him for this task. The Zaydī sect, however, which does not recognize this dogma, follows the same teaching as that of the Sunnī doctrine.

Characteristics of the duty of *d͟jihād*. The *d͟jihād* is not an end in itself but a means which, in itself, is an evil (*fasād*), but which becomes legitimate and necessary by reason of the objective towards which it is directed: to rid the world of a greater evil; it is "good" from the fact that its purpose is "good" (*ḥasan li-ḥusn g͟hayrih*).

A religious duty. The *d͟jihād* has the effect of extending the sway of the faith; it is prescribed by God and his Prophet; the Muslim dedicates himself to the *d͟jihād* in the same way that, in Christianity, the monk dedicates himself to the service of God; in the same vein it is said in different *ḥadīt͟h*s that "the *d͟jihād* is the monasticism of Islam"; the *d͟jihād* is "an act of pure devotion"; it is "one of the gates to Paradise"; rich heavenly rewards are guaranteed for those who devote themselves to it; those who fall in the *d͟jihād* are the martyrs of the faith, etc. A substantial part of the doctrine reckons the *d͟jihād* among the very "pillars" (*arkan*) of the religion, along with prayer and fasting etc. It is a duty which falls upon every Muslim who is male, free and able-bodied. It is generally considered that non-Muslims may be called upon to assist the Muslims in the *d͟jihād*.

A "collective" obligation (*farḍ kifāya*) in contrast to *farḍ ʿayn*. The *farḍ kifāya* is that duty which is imposed upon the community considered as a whole and which only becomes obligatory for each individual in particular to the extent that his intervention is necessary for the realization of the purpose envisaged by the law. Thus, as soon as there exists a group of Muslims whose number is sufficient to fulfil the needs of a particular conflict, the obligation of the *d͟jihād* no longer rests on the others. The general teaching is that the duty of *d͟jihād* falls, in the first place, individually as a *farḍ ʿayn*, upon those who live in the territory nearest to the enemy, and that the same holds good in the case of the inhabitants of a town which is besieged. In the organized State, however, the appreciation of the precise moment at which the *d͟jihād* is transformed into an *ʿayn* obligation is a matter for the discretion of the sovereign; so that, in the case of general mobilization, the *d͟jihād* loses, for all the members of the community, its character of *farḍ kifāya*, and becomes, instead, *farḍ ʿayn*.

All this implies, however, that for those who hold the reins of authority and, in particular, the sovereign, the *d͟jihād* is always an individual duty, since their own personal action is necessary in every case. Where there are several independent Muslim states, the duty will fall upon the ruler of the state which is nearest to the enemy.

Further, the duty of the *d͟jihād* is relative and contingent in this dual sense that, on the one hand, it only comes into being when the circumstances are favourable and of such a nature as to offer some hope of a victorious outcome, and, on the other hand, the fulfilment of the duty may be renounced in consideration of the payment by the enemy of goods reaching a certain value, if such policy appears to be in conformity with the interests of the moment.

Its subsidiary character. Since the *d͟jihād* is nothing more than a means to effect conversion to Islam or submission to its authority, there is only occasion to undertake it in circumstances where the people against whom it is directed have first been invited to join Islam. Discussion turned on the question as to whether it was necessary, on this ground, to address a formal invitation to the enemy. The general doctrine holds that since Islam is sufficiently widespread in the world, all peoples are presumed to know that they have been invited to join it. It is observed, however, that it would be desirable to repeat the invitation, except in cases where there is ground for apprehension that the enemy, thus forewarned, would profit from such a delay by better organizing his defences and, in this way, compromising the successful outcome of the *d͟jihād*.

Its perpetual character. The duty of the *d͟jihād* exists as long as the universal domination of Islam has not been attained. "Until the day of the resurrection", and "until the end of the world" say the maxims. Peace with non-Muslim nations is, therefore, a provisional state of affairs only; the chance of circumstances alone can justify it temporarily. Furthermore there can be no question of genuine peace treaties with these nations; only truces, whose duration ought not, in principle, to exceed ten years, are authorized. But even such truces are precarious, inasmuch as they can, before they expire, be repudiated unilaterally should it appear more profitable for Islam to resume the conflict. It is, however, recognized that such repudiation should be brought to the notice of the infidel party, and that he should be afforded sufficient opportunity to be able to disseminate the news of it throughout the whole of his territory [see ṢULḤ].

Its defensive as well as offensive character. The *d͟jihād* has principally an offensive character; but it is equally a *d͟jihād* when it is a case of defending Islam against aggression. This indeed, is the essential purpose of the *ribāṭ* [*q.v.*] undertaken by isolated groups or individuals settled on the frontiers of Islam. The *ribāṭ* is a particularly meritorious act.

Finally, there is at the present time a thesis, of a wholly apologetic character, according to which Islam relies for its expansion exclusively upon persuasion and other peaceful means, and the *d͟jihād* is only authorized in cases of "self defence" and of "support owed to a defenceless ally or brother". Disregarding entirely the previous doctrine and historical tradition, as well as the texts of the Ḳurʾān and the *sunna* on the basis of which it was formulated, but claiming, even so, to remain within the bounds of strict orthodoxy, this thesis takes into account only those early texts which state the contrary (v. *supra*).

Bibliography: Dāmād Ef., *Mad͟jmaʿ al-anhur*, ed. Aḥmad b. ʿUt͟hmān, 1328/1910, i, 636 ff.; Dardīr, *al-S͟harḥ al-ṣag͟hīr*, with the gloss of Ṣāwī, i, 398 ff.; D͟jāḥiẓ, *Rasāʾil*, ed. Sandūbī, Cairo 1933, 57: Farrāʾ, *Aḥkām sulṭāniyya*, Cairo, 25 ff.; Goldziher, *Schīʿitisches*, in *ZDMG*, lxiv, 531 ff.; Addison, *The Ahmadiya movement*, in *Harvard Theological Review*, xxii, 1 ff.; Ibn ʿAbidīn,

Radd al-muḥtār, Istanbul 1314/1905, iii, 315 ff.; Ibn ʿAbd al-Raḥmān, *Raḥmat al-umma fī 'khtlāf al-aʾimma*, Cairo, 294; Ibn Djumāʿa, *Taḥrīr al-aḥkām*, ed. Kofler, (in *Islamica*, 1934), 349 ff.; Ibn Ḳudāma, *Mughnī*, 3rd. ed. Rashīd Riḍā, Cairo 1367/1947, viii, 345 ff.; Ibn Taymiyya, *al-Siyāsa al-sharʿiyya*, Cairo 1322/1904, 156 ff.; Marāghī, *al-Tashrīʿ al-islāmī*, Cairo, 24 ff.; Māwardī, *Aḥkam sulṭāniyya*, Cairo, 30 ff.; Querry, *Recueil de lois concernant les musulmans chiites*, Paris 1871, i, 321; Rashīd Riḍā, *Khilāfa*, Cairo 1341/1922, 29, 51; Sarakhsī, *Mabsūṭ*, Cairo, x, 35; Shāfiʿī, *Kitāb al-umm*, Cairo 1903, with the Muzanī gloss, v, 180 ff.; Gaudefroy-Demombynes, *Mahomet*, Paris 1957, 578 ff.; Draz, *Le droit international publié et l'Islam*, in *Revue égyptienne de droit international public*, 1949, 17 ff.; Haneberg, *Das muslimische Kriegsrecht* (Abh. der kgl. Bayer. Akad. der Wissensch., 1870, philos.-philol. cl., xii. Bd., II. Abt.), 219 ff.; Juynboll, *Handbuch* 57, 335 ff.; Milliot, *Introd. à l'étude du droit musulman*, Paris 1953, 22, 34; Ṣaʿīdī, *al-Siyāsa al-islāmiyya*, Cairo; Sanhoury, *Le Califat*, thesis, Lyon 1925, 146; Strothmann, *Das Staatsrecht der Zaiditen*, Strasbourg 1922, 42 ff.; Muh. Shadīd, *al-Djihād fi 'l-Islām*, 1960; *İA*, art. Cihâd (Halim Sabit Şibay).

(E. Tyan)

DJIHĀNGĪR [see djahāngīr].

DJILD. The use of leather (*djild, adīm*) as a writing material is well known in the Near East. In Egypt it was used already in the Middle Kingdom; leather manuscripts are known from the empire of Meroe and Nubia to the south of Egypt, from Palestine and Persia. In the latter country the βασιλικαὶ διφθέραι—the Royal archives consisting of leather documents—were known to Ctesias (*apud* Diodorus Siculus, ii, 32, cf. daftar), and when the Persians conquered Egypt for a short time at the beginning of the 7th century A.D., they continued to write on leather here. The leather pieces found in Egypt and preserved in several European collections testify to this fact. When the Persians conquered Southern Arabia soon after 570 A.D., they greatly encouraged the leather industry there; the South-Arabian leather was famous as a writing material of special delicacy and smoothness. But even before the Persian occupation of the Yaman, leather was known there as a writing material. The debenture of a Ḥimyarite to the grandfather of the Prophet Muḥammad, ʿAbd al-Muṭṭalib b. Hāshim, which was preserved in the treasury of the Caliph al-Maʾmūn, was written on a piece of leather. Leather was thus well known to the Arabs even before Islam, and poets like al-Muraḳḳish the Elder and Labīd quote instances to this effect. Arabs even knew how to colour skins yellow with saffron, and later invented, in al-Kūfa, an improvement on the treatment of skins, *viz.*, they replaced quick-lime (which made the skins very dry) by dates, so that the skins became soft. We are told of numerous cases when the Prophet Muḥammad wrote (or had written) on leather—*e.g.*, gifts of lands and wells—and even pieces of the Revelation were written on it. His immediate successors, *e.g.*, ʿAlī, followed this example. As a peculiarity it may be mentioned that the Caliph ʿUthmān is credited with a Ḳurʾān, written on ostrich-skin and preserved in the ʿĀrif Ḥikmet Library in Medina (cf. *ZDMG*, xc, 1956, 102). During the Umayyad period leather was used among the Arabs as writing material; for example the poet Dhu 'l-Rumma (d. 117/735-6) mentions it in one of his *Ḳaṣīdas* (*Aghānī*, xvi, 111). A letter on leather, addressed in Arabic by the Soghdian ruler Diwashtī to the governor Djarrāḥ b. ʿAbd Allāh about 100/719, was discovered in 1932 in Zarafshān in Central Asia (cf. I. Yu. Krachkovsky, *Among Arabic manuscripts*, Leiden 1953, 142). This document was not a unique piece, for the book-collection of Muḥammad b. al-Ḥusayn, mentioned in Ibn al-Nadīm's *Fihrist* (40, 54), contained also leather pieces along with papers and papyri. Various documents on leather are preserved in different papyrus-collections; the oldest piece, a debenture in respect of a nuptial gift, dated 233/847, is in the possession of the Egyptian National Library in Cairo (Cat. Taʾrīkh, n° 1871), the youngest, dated 722 A.H., of the State Museum in Berlin. Special mention must be made of Ḳurʾān-manuscripts written on antelope-skins, to which al-Bīrūnī refers in his *Taʾrīkh al-Hind* (81).

A special kind of leather is parchment (*djild, warak, ḳirṭās, raḳḳ, riḳḳ*), refined from skins of sheep, goats and calves. It was known in Arabia already in the fifth century A.D., since the Himyarite poet Ḳudam b. Ḳādim mentions it in his poem, and Labīd speaks of "talking parchment" (*ṭirs nāṭiḳ*). *Ṭirs* means parchment from which the original text had been washed off and which then was written on again; such a *ṭirs*, bearing a Latin biblical fragment of the fifth century A.D. on one side and an Arabic legal text of the 1st/7th century running across the Latin text on the other, is preserved in Florence. Such palimpsests are still rare. Parchment was used—among other materials—to write parts of the Revelation, and such scraps were found in the legacy of the Prophet. The use of parchment for sacred books was specific for the Hebrews, and the parchment *Thora*-rolls were well known to the Arabs (cf. Bakrī, *Muʿdjam*, ii, 511, who quotes a verse of Djarīr (d. 110/728)). Also the Prophet Muḥammad used parchment on several occasions, and *raḳḳ* as well as *ḳirṭās* is mentioned in the Ḳurʾān (VI, 7, LII, 3). The collection of the Holy Book of Islam, arranged by Zayd b. Thābit, is also said to have been written on parchment (A. Sprenger, *Das Leben und die Lehre des Muhammad*, iii, p. xl). In the early Umayyad period parchment was preferred as a writing material along with papyri in Syria; in Egypt it was especially used for Ḳurʾān-codices—as also in other Islamic countries—but only exceptionally for secular literary texts. In North Africa a depository of the Sidi ʿUḳba Mosque in al-Ḳayrawān furnished lately some hundreds of literary parchment manuscripts. In ʿIrāḳ parchment was predominantly used in the chanceries until the Barmakid al-Faḍl b. Yaḥyā b. Khālid replaced it by paper. A special precious kind of parchment was made of gazelle-skins. This gazelle-parchment was expensive but nevertheless mentioned several times in papyri, *e.g.*, also in a magical text. The Egyptian National Library possesses several Ḳurʾān manuscripts written on gazelle-parchment (cf. *Fihrist al-kutub al-ʿarabiyya al-maḥfūẓa bi 'l-kutubkhāna al-Khedīwiyya*, i, Cairo 1892-93, 2). In Egypt parchment, made of skins of sheep, goats and calves, plays a very minor rôle in comparison with papyrus. The oldest parchment document hitherto known is dated 168/784; it formed part of the collection of the late German consul Todros Muhareb in Luxor. A specially precious kind of parchment was purple-coloured, well known from early Latin mediaeval manuscripts. The collection of F. Martin contained a beautiful blue-coloured parchment with exquisite Kūfic script in gold, originally belonging to a

Ķur'ān manuscript from the Mosque at Meshhed (Persia).

Bibliography: A. Grohmann, *Corpus Papyrorum Raineri Archiducis Austriae*, III series *Arabica* i/1, Vienna 1924, 51-8; *From the World of Arabic Papyri*, Royal Society of Historical Studies, Cairo 1952, 44-9, 237; *Einführung und Chrestomathie zur arabischen Papyruskunde*, i, Prague 1954, Monografie Archivu Orientálního XIII, 71-72.

(A. GROHMANN)

AL-**DJILDAĶĪ** [see SUPPLEMENT].

AL-**DJĪLĪ** [see ʿABD AL-ĶĀDIR AL-DJĪLĀNĪ].

DJILLIĶ, the name of a pre-Islamic site famous for its abundant water and shady gardens, and often celebrated by Damascene poets who discovered this name in Ḥassān b. Thābit. It was there that the Ghassānid princes of the Djafnid branch venerated the tomb of one of their ancestors, and that they built what was, with the exception of Djābiya [*q.v.*], the most renowned of their dwellings. It was also no doubt the principal, if not permanent, place of encampment for their troops. About twelve kilometres south of Damascus, the place became a *bādiya* [see ḤĪRA] to which Yazīd b. Muʿāwiya loved to go. When praising the beauties of this resort, the poet ʿArķala al-Dimashķī called it "the languorous pupil of the eye of the world".

The identification of this site is somewhat vague in the writings of Arab authors: according to some, it is a village in the Ghūṭa, where there is a statue of a woman from which a spring gushes forth; for others, the name covers the whole group of districts of Damascus together with the Ghūṭa. Finally, some writers, among whom are the mediaeval geographer al-Dimashķī and the polygraph al-Ķalķashandī, who is the only one to use the spelling Djillāķ, attribute the name to Damascus itself; thus for instance Quatremère in his *Histoire des Sultans Mamelouks* always translates Djilliķ by Damascus. Yāķūt placed Djilliķ in the Ghūṭa, by which term we must understand all the cultivated land in the territory of Damascus, the southern boundary of which for administrative purposes was on the Djabal Kiswa. From the different texts at our disposal we can deduce the following topographical data: Djilliķ was situated to the south-east of Mount Hermon for, when coming from the south, one could see the "snow mountain" behind the town; it was not far distant from Boṣrā [*q.v.*]; through it passed the road from the Balķā', as well as the road from Damascus to Cairo, crossing the hills at Djilliķ by the pass of the ʿ*aķāba* of al-Shaḥūra.

Relying on these facts, R. Dussaud has shown that Djilliķ must be distinguished from Damascus and identified with Kiswa. These conclusions, although accepted by R. Devreesse, were not shared by H. Lammens who tried to fix the place in the south of Syria and, despite the philological difficulties of the change in the last syllable, identified it with Djillīn in southern Ḥawrān. In support of his theory Lammens quoted as evidence a gloss from De Goeje. The identification of Djilliķ with Kiswa is supported by the fact that on two occasions, in 12/633 and 15/636, the Byzantines when fighting against the Muslim conquerors pitched camp at Djilliķ; now the only place south of Damascus where a strategic position for the defence of the town is to be found, and where, on many occasions throughout the centuries, armies have regrouped at the natural barrier (the *thaniyya* of al-Ṭabarī) formed by the Nahr al-Aʿwadj is precisely at Kiswa [*q.v.*].

We do not know at what date the name Djilliķ disappeared from Syrian toponomy. At the end of the Umayyad period it was still sufficiently alive for the Syrian conquerors of Spain to give the name to a spot renowned for its abundant supplies of water, not far from Sarragossa.

Bibliography: Ṭabarī, i, 2081, 2107; Ḥassān b. Thābit, *Dīwān*, ed. Hirschfeld, xiii, 4; Yāķūt, ii, 104-6 (Beirut ed., 154-5); De Goeje, *Mémoire sur la conquête de la Syrie*², Leyden 1900, 55-6; A. F. Mehren, *Syrien og Palestina*, Copenhagen 1862, 37-8; Le Strange, *Palestine*, 258, 265, 424, 488; Ibn Baṭṭūṭa, i, 157, 192, 196; ʿImād al-Dīn al-Iṣfahānī, *Kharīdat al-ķaṣr*, ii, ed. Sh. Fayṣal, 1959, 113, 338, 339; M. Kurd ʿAlī, *Ghūṭat Dimashķ*, 1949, index; Quatremère, *Histoire des Sultans Mamelouks*, Paris 1837-45, ii², 161 n. 19; Caetani, *Annali*, ii, 1224-5; iii, 517; H. Lammens, *Moʿawiya Ier*, Beirut 1908, 379 n. 10, 442; R. Dussaud, *Mission dans les régions désertiques de la Syrie Moyenne* (1903), 441-3 (39-41); idem, *La pénétration des Arabes en Syrie*, *BAH*, lix, 1955, 70; idem, *Topographie historique de la Syrie*, *BAH*, iv, 1927, 317, 320; M. Gaudefroy-Demombynes, *La Syrie à l'époque des Mamelouks*, *BAH*, iii, 1923, 32, 49; R. Devreesse, *Arabes Perses et Arabes Romains*, in *Vivre et penser*, II series, 1942, 301.

(N. ELISSÉEFF)

DJILLĪĶIYYA, Galicia, the north-west region of the Iberian peninsula, which now includes the four Spanish provinces of La Coruña, Lugo, Pontevedra and Orense. Arab geographers thought of al-Andalus as a triangle, one of the angles being fixed on the sea-coast at the end of the Cantabrian *cordillera*; there they placed an image or monument which can be identified with the Tower of Hercules —situated on the promontory where the town of La Coruña stands—which, from Roman times, has served as a lighthouse. As Arab rule lasted for only a short time in this part, historians were not very familiar with its boundaries or topography. They made no distinction between Galicia and Asturias, and gave no clear definition of the eastern frontier, even putting it as far away as the country of the Vascones. They placed the Rock of Galicia and the mountain of Pelayo—Covadonga—in the sea. For al-Idrīsī, the church of St. James of Compostella stood on a promontory in the Atlantic, and *al-Rawḍ al-miʿṭār* speaks of the lighthouse castle—the Tower of Hercules?—as being near Lugo, on the third angle of the triangle and near the church of St. James. In order to indicate the frontiers of Galicia they relied on the state of the country as they knew it at the time they were writing or as described by their sources, without taking their date into account. In this way they placed the south-west frontier in the Algarve, the old name of what is now Portugal, and gave Braga as the frontier, while at other times they spoke of the town of Viseo as the centre of Portuguese Galicia which extended to the Mondego.

At the time when it was conquered, Lugo was looked upon as the capital and the whole of Galicia was occupied by the Berbers who, after being defeated by the Arabs and made desperate by famine, fled to Morocco, leaving Alfonso I to extend the territories of the Djillīķiyya as far as the Duero. A state of war existed permanently between Galicia and Cordova, and military expeditions were halted only when the belligerents were compelled by disputes and internal difficulties to refrain from war. Al-Bakrī, an Andalusian, writing in the middle of the 5th/11th century, is the Arab writer who indicates most precisely the limits and divisions of the Djillīḳiyya at his own time, that is to say when the kingdom of the Taifas was at its height. In the Ḳayrawān manuscript which the editor of *al-Rawḍ al-miʿṭār* cannot have known, he tells us that the ancients had already divided Galicia into four regions: the first lies to the west, curving round towards the north. Its inhabitants are Galicians and its territory is Galicia, properly speaking, reaching as far north as the town of Braga; the second is the region of Asturias which, according to him, takes its name from the river Ashtru, an unknown name which cannot be identified phonetically with the Nalón, the principal river in Asturias; the third zone is south-west Galicia, and its inhabitants, owning only the small enclave between Braga and Oporto, took from the latter town the name "Portuguese"; the fourth zone, situated in the south-east, was called Castile and included two sub-divisions, Upper Castile corresponding with the kingdom of Leon and Lower Castile, at that time with fortresses at Grañon in the province of Logroño, 25 km. from Najera, Alcocero on the Oca 30 km. from the same town, and lastly Burgos *caput Castellae.* Al-Bakrī was familiar with Constantine's division of the Peninsula into six zones; in the second of these zones, the centre of which was Braga and which included the region of the Galicians and Celts, he names Oporto, Tuy, Orense, Lugo, Britania—now Santa Maria de Bretonia, in the *partido judicial* of Mondoñedo—Astorga, in the province of Leon, St. James of Compostella—which can only be the town of the Golden Church (*Kanīsat al-dhahab*), although al-Bakrī makes them two distinct towns—and lastly Iria—now Padrón in the province of La Coruña—Bataca, an unidentified name, and Sarria, 35 km. south of Lugo. Ibn ʿAbd al-Munʿim, following al-Bakrī, describes Galicia as a country with flat, sandy ground while the inhabitants are depicted as unscrupulous warriors, highly primitive in their customs. On the other hand al-Maḳḳarī praises them for their beauty and remarks upon the good qualities of captives; but all are agreed in thinking their reckless courage equal or even superior to that of the Franks, and in striking contrast to the character of the Visigoths and Hispano-Romans before the Muslim invasion.

Under the one name Djillīḳiyya Arab historians include the kingdoms of Asturias and Leon; in their view, the kings of both are Galician, and the towns Galician also, Oviedo and Leon like Zamora and Astorga. Military expeditions by the Caliphate did not succeed in reestablishing a firm hold upon the territories south of the Duero which had been lost; and although ʿAbd al-Raḥmān III and *al-ḥādjib* al-Manṣūr were successful in imposing their authority over the kings of Asturias and Leon and making them their vassals, the victorious campaigns of the latter, which reached their apogee with the capture and sack of St. James of Compostella, completed the wide ring of devastating raids into the territories of the Great Djillīḳiyya; and very soon afterwards, when the Umayyad caliphate crumbled, it was these kingdoms, springing from the nucleus of Galicia, which carried the war into the Muslim territories and, under Alfonso VI, even captured Toledo.

Bibliography: Ibn ʿAbd al-Munʿim al-Ḥimyarī, *al-Rawḍ al-miʿṭār*, ed. in part Lévi-Provençal, 28, 66 and 185 in text, 35, 83, 223 and 248 in the trans.; Ibn ʿIdhārī, Bayān, ii, *passim*; Maḳḳarī, *Analectes*, i, *passim*; Dozy, *Recherches*³, i, 89 ff.

(A. Huici Miranda)

DJILWA, the ceremony of raising the bride's veil, and the present made by the husband to the wife on this occasion.

According to al-Djurdjānī who bases himself on Muḥyi 'l-Dīn al-ʿArabī (*Definitiones*, ed. Flügel, 80, 294), *djilwa* is the name of the state in which the mystic is on coming out of the *khalwa*: filled with the emanations of divine attributes, his own personality has disappeared and mingles with the being of God (cf. Guys, *Un derviche Algérien*, 203).

One of the two sacred books of the Yazīdīs is called *Kitāb al-Djilwa* [*q.v.*].

(Cl. Huart)

DJILWATIYYA (Turkish Djelwetiyye), the name of a *ṭarīḳa* founded by Sheykh ʿAzīz Maḥmūd Hudāʾī of Üsküdar (Scutari, nr. Istanbul). The name is said to come from *djalwa* (leaving one's native country, emigrating), which, as a *ṣūfī* term, denotes a creature's emergence from solitary withdrawal (*khalwa*) through contemplation of God's attributes and its annihilation in God's Being (Sayyīd Sharīf, *Taʿrīfāt*, 3). An alternative or simultaneous derivation from *djilwa* [*q,v.*], can also be put forward. The Djilwatiyya were a purely Sunnī *ṭarīḳa*, based on the *dhikr* [*q.v.*] of seven of the names (*asmāʾ*) of God, known as "essential" or "root-names" (*uṣūl-i asmāʾ*) to which five "branch-names" *furūʿ-i asmāʾ*) were added (*i.e.*, *Wahhāb*, *Fattāḥ*, *Wāḥid*, *Aḥad* and *Ṣamad*). The *sheykh* of the *ṭarīḳa* prescribed to individual dervishes those names which they had to recite, a prescription which might be varied on the basis of dreams reported by the dervishes. Other devotional practices of the *ṭarīḳa* included various supererogatory prayers and fasts. Djilwatīs wore green turbans (*tādj*) made of 13 strips of material which were meant to symbolize the 12 names of God and their transcendent unity (Ismāʿīl Ḥaḳḳī, *Silsilanāme-i Djilwatiyye*, 1291 AH, 87). The centre (*pīr maḳāmī*) of the *ṭarīḳa* was in the *tekke* in Üsküdar where Maḥmūd Hudāʾī was buried. A second famous centre was the *tekke* in Bursa of Ismāʿīl Ḥaḳḳī, the historian of the order and the author of the Turkish commentary *Rūḥ al-bayān* and of other treatises.

According to Ismāʿīl Ḥaḳḳī (*Silsilanāme*, 63) the practice of the *dhikr* of seven names derives from Sheykh Ibrāhīm Zāhid Gīlānī (690/1291) through his pupil *Shaykh* Abū Isḥāḳ Ṣafī al-Dīn Ardabīlī (735/1334-5). It was also the former who devised the practice (*mashrab*) of *djalwa*, as opposed to that of *khalwa*. Ismāʿīl Ḥaḳḳī adds that a Djilwatī who stops short at the withdrawal of *khalwa* should really be considered a Khalwatī, just as a Khalwatī who has tasted the joy of *djalwa* (or *djilwa*) is really a Djilwatī (*op. cit.*, 64).

In any case the Djilwatiyya were an off-shoot of the Bayrāmiyya, although the spiritual filiation of Maḥmūd Hudāʾī to Ḥādjdjī Bayrām is uncertain in places. In his treatise entitled *Wāḳiʿāt*, Hudāʾī names as his *sheykh* Muḥyī al-Dīn Uftāde, who died in Bursa in 988/1580-1. The latter was, according to Ismāʿīl Ḥaḳḳī, the *khalīfa* of Kötürüm (or Paralytic) Khiḍr Dede, also of Bursa, who was in turn a follower of Ḥādjdjī Bayrām (*op. cit.*, 76). Another tradition (Ḥarīrīzāde Kamāl al-Dīn, *Tibyān wasāʾil al-ḥaḳāʾiḳ fī bayān salāsil al-ṭarāʾiḳ*, Fātiḥ Lib., Ibrāhīm Efendī Collection, Nos. 430-2, i, 227b, 246a), the spiritual genealogy is from Ḥādjdjī Bayrām to Aḳ Shams al-Dīn to Ḥamd Allāh Čelebi to Uftāde.

According to ʿAṭāʾī (*Shaḳāʾiḳ-i nuʿmāniyye dheyli*, 64 ff., 358 ff., 760 ff.), Hudāʾī was born at

Seferī-Ḥiṣār. Meḥmed Gülshen Efendi (*Kulliyāt-i Ḥaḍrat-i Hudā'ī*, 1338-40 A.H.) varies this to Sivri-Ḥiṣār and gives the date of birth as 950/1543-4, while both the *Silsilanāme* and *Tibyān* agree on Koč-Ḥiṣār of Ḳonya, the latter bringing the date of birth forward to 948/1541-2. Hudā'ī studied in Istanbul before becoming an instructor (*mu'īd*) at the *madrasa* of Sultan Selīm in Edirne, from where he went to Syria and Egypt as assistant *ḳāḍī* (*nā'ib*). In Egypt he attached himself to one Karīm al-Dīn Khalwatī, becoming himself a Khalwatī. He went next to Bursa where he was appointed *mudarris* at the Farhādiyya *madrasa* and *nā'ib* at the Court of the Old Mosque (Djāmi'-i 'Atīḳ). Tradition has it that it was at this time that he saw in a dream a vision of some people whom he considered righteous tormented in hell, and others in heaven whom he had thought sinners. He thereupon made his submission to Sheykh Uftāde. The *Tibyān* and the *Kulliyāt* give the date of the conversion as 985/1577, the latter giving another version of the story, according to which Hudā'ī first served Uftāde for some three years and was then sent as the latter's *khalīfa* to Sivri Ḥiṣār (*op. cit.*, 4 ff.). Going later to Istanbul, Hudā'ī first settled in two rooms which he had built of stone next to the *masdjid* of Muṣallā in Čamlīdja, moving on first to a room near the mosque of Rūm (the Greek) Meḥmed Pasha and then to the present Djilwatiyya mosque and *tekke* which was built between 997/1589 and 1003/1595. He also preached and taught in other mosques, chief among them the Conqueror's mosque (Fātiḥ Djāmi'i), where, according to Pečewī (*Ta'rīkh*, 1283 AH, ii, 36, 357) he was appointed preacher at the instigation of Ṣun' Allāh, the *ḳaḍ'asker* of Rumeli. This, Pečewī says, was the beginning of his fame. He enjoyed the favour and the respect of the Sultan Aḥmed I, owing these, according to the *Silsilanāme*, to a miraculous interpretation of the Sultan's dream. This royal favour is corroborated by the respectful references to Hudā'ī in both Pečewī and Na'īmā (*Rawḍat al-Ḥusayn fī khulāṣat akhbār al-khāfiḳayn*, 1280 AH, i, 112 ff., 357; ii, 154, 158). Na'īmā reports, for example, that he was asked to wash the dead Sultan's body, but that he excused himself on the grounds of old age, entrusting the duty to his *khalīfa* Sha'bān Dede (ii, 154). Hudā'ī per-formed the pilgrimage three times. He died in 1038/1628.

Na'īmā describes Hudā'ī as an eloquent and soft-spoken man. The *dhayl* (continuation) of the *Shaḳā'iḳ* (i, 64) reports that he let his hair grow long, a habit which was imitated by his followers. Hudā'ī wrote 18 works in Arabic and 12 in Turkish. These are to be found in the Selīm Āghā Library in Üsküdar (for titles of lost works see *Kulliyāt*, 607 note). Most of them are short treatises, including an unfinished Arabic commentary on the *Ḳur'ān* entitled *Madjālis*. His printed *Kulliyāt* includes a *dīwān*, as well as an Arabic treatise entitled *Risāla fī Ṭarīḳāt al-Muḥammadiyya*, a Turkish *Ṭarīḳatnāme* and a Turkish rhymed treatise, entitled *Nadjāt al-gharīḳ* (Salvation of the Drowned). His most important work is undoubtedly the *Wāḳi'āt* or collected sayings (in Arabic rendering) of Sheykh Uftāde (MS in the author's hand, No. 574 in the Selīm Āghā Library). Apart from its mystical interest, this contains many important historical references to contemporary men and events. Meḥmed Gülshen Efendi in his edition of the *Kulliyāt* dates many of the devotional poems, one of which commemorates the death of Murād III (p. 79), adding that many of them were set to music, some by Hudā'ī himself. Some of the poems are syllabic in metre and are strongly influenced by Yūnus Emre. They show Hudā'ī as an orthodox Sunnī *shaykh*, an ascetic (*zāhid*) within the limits of the *sharī'a*, hostile to exalted and more-or-less free-thinking *ṣūfīs*. He even petitioned the Sultan against Badr al-Dīn, the son of the *ḳāḍī* of Simavna, and his followers, among whom he seems to have been numbered for a time (M. Sharaf al-Dīn (Şerefeddin), *Simavnaḳāḍīsi-oghlu Sheykh Badr al-Dīn*, Istanbul 1927, 72 ff.).

The Djilwatiyya had an off-shoot in the Hāshimiyya, founded by Hāshim Baba (d. 1773), a Djilwati *sheykh* who was simultaneously a Malāmī (even laying claim to the title of "Pole" or *ḳuṭub*) and also a Bektashī (among whom he was known as *Baba* or *Dede* and whom also he tried to split by devising an amended ritual).

Bibliography: in the article.

(ABDÜLBÂKÎ GÖLPINARLI)

DJĪM, 5th letter of the Arabic alphabet, transcribed *dj*; numerical value 3, so agreeing, like *dāl*, with the order of the letters of the Syriac (and Canaanite) alphabet [see ABDJAD]. It represents a *g* (occlusive, postpalatal[1], voiced) in the ancient Semitic (and in common Semitic).

In Arabic, this articulation has evolved: the point of articulation has been carried forward, in an unconditioned way[2], to the middle and prepalatal region, as a consequence of which it readily developed elements of palatalization (g^y and d^y) and affrication (*dj*). A simplification of the articulation into a spirant became possible, through the dropping of the first occlusive phase in the affricated (*dj* > *j* where *j* represents a voiced palatal fricative, as French *j*), through the weakening and disappearance of the occlusive element in the palatalized consonant ($d^y > y$). This course of evolution can be written out as follows:

$$g > g^y > d^y \left\{ \begin{array}{l} d^y > y \\ d^y > \underline{dj} > j \end{array} \right.$$

It is probable that the sound *g* of the Semitic *djīm* began at a very early time to evolve in the field which we are now considering. In any event, from the traditional pronunciation of the readers of the Ḳur'ān, from the basic ideas of the Arab grammarians regarding its articulation, and from the modifications in it conditioned by the proximity of other sounds which they have noted (assimilations and dissimilations), one can justifiably conclude that,

1) *g* is defined as: occlusive, postpalatal, voiced; but *g* and *k* (the corresponding unvoiced) are the consonants most influenced, as regards the point of articulation, by the adjacent vowel; they are brought forward to the mediopalatal region with a palatal vowel, and carried back to the velar region with a velar vowel; *postpalatal* signifies a medial position: that of *g*, *k*, articulated with a vowel *a*.

2) It would be better to say: for reasons unknown. A. Martinet has tried precisely to discover the causes of this displacement by structural methods, in his study *La palatisation "spontanée" de* g *en arabe*, in *BSL*, liv/1, 90-102; he has brought out the structural conditioning of the evolutionary processes, by starting from the concept that Arabic emphatics are derived from glottalized consonants. His analysis is original and instructive, but in its turn also is conditioned by the basic hypothesis described above.

from the dawn of the classical period, the occluded *g* in *djīm* was opened through palatalization, affrication or even complete spirantization, at least in certain dialects. Naturally, differences analogous to those existing today in spoken languages, concerning the pronunciation of *djīm*, must have existed between the various ancient languages; some of them had no doubt gone much further than others in evolving towards spirantization. Besides, this process of evolution is still continuing today, as we can see: in Jerusalem, for example, a European observer (Dr. Rosen) has noticed that the affricated *dj* which as a child he used to hear as the pronunciation of *djīm* has now, in the pronunciation of the present time, become a palato-alveolar *j* (see E. Littmann, *Neuarabische Volkspoesie*, 3 n. 1). In certain languages in which the current pronunciation of *djīm* is now *j*, dissimilations in *d* or *g* can only be explained as fixed survivals of a former condition, at a comparatively recent stage in the development of this consonant (cf. Brockelmann, *Grundriss*, i, 235-6).

Arab grammarians looked upon *djīm* as a *shadīda*, and therefore an occlusive, which excludes an affricated (*dj*) or spirant (*j*); and as a *madjhūra*, which means *voiced* (Sībawayhi, ii (Paris), 453 and 454; al-Zamakhsharī, *Muf.*, 2nd ed. Broch. § 734; etc.). As regards the *makhradj*, al-Khalīl's *shadjriyya* (*Muf.*, *ibid.*) is difficult to interpret, but the description given by Sībawayhi (ii, 453 l. 7-8) indicates clearly that the active organ of articulation is the middle of the tongue (that is to say, the front) and the middle of the upper palate. Elsewhere they rejected (Sībawayhi, ii, 452; etc.) the articulation of *djīm* like *kāf* (usual in Baghdād and in the Yemen) and of *djīm* like *shīn*, that is to say like *g* for the first and *j* for the second, which is a quite justifiable interpretation (as in J. Cantineau, *Cours*, 72 and others); d^y (palatalized *d*) being excluded by the designation of the front (and not the tip) of the tongue, there only remains g^y [1]. Arab grammarians appear indeed to consider this to be the only correct pronunciation of *djīm*. This articulation fulfils the required conditions and in addition easily conforms with the passage of *yā'* to *djīm* practised in certain tribes (Rabin, chart 19). In the traditional reading of Arabic the pronunciation *dj* (affricated, prepalatal, voiced) is generally adopted.

As regards the modern dialects, it is possible to draw up a table tracing the pronunciation of *djīm* in general lines as follows:

1. Retention of the original pronunciation *g*: this seems to have been known in Aden in the Middle Ages (according to al-Muḳaddasī, 96 *l.* 14). It is found today in Muscat, in Yemeni dialects and in various Bedouin-dialects in central Arabia. In Dathīna (south-west Arabia) it is found in the conjugation of verbs with *djīm* as first radical, when it forms a syllable with the prefixes (e.g.: *yigzaʿ*). In Ḍofār (south-east Arabia) this pronunciation no longer exists save in the recitation of poetry, that is to say it has an archaic and quasi-artificial character. This pronunciation is also the manner of articulation proper to the dialects of Lower Egypt, and of Cairo in particular. Finally, in most of the dialects of north Morocco and also in Nédroma (Algeria), *g* is by dissimilation the pronunciation of *djīm* when used in conjunction with a sibilant or palato-alveolar.

2. Pronunciation of *djīm* as g^y or d^y: this is the pronunciation found in the majority of Bedouin-dialects in north, central and south Arabia. It is also the pronunciation used by the fellaheen and Bedouins of Upper Egypt. It occasionally occurs in Ḍofār.

3. Pronunciation of *djīm* as *y*: today this occurs widely in the lower Euphrates region. It is the most widely used pronunciation in Ḍofār. It is common but not regularly used in various dialects in south-west Arabia. It is attested in a certain number of north Arabian tribes (notably the Sardīye and the Sirḥān) and in the Djōf; for further particulars see J. Cantineau, *Cours*, 74. In the other Arabic dialects only a few sporadic examples can be given.

4. Pronunciation of *djīm* as *dj*: this pronunciation is already attested in ʿIrāḳ in the golden age of classical literature (according to Brockelmann's interpretation, in *ZA*, xiii (1898), 126 and *Grundriss*, i, 122). It is found in certain places in central Arabia, it is the form most widely used in the Yemen, it is current in Mecca, in ʿIrāḳ, among the Muslims in Jerusalem, in Aleppo, and is most widely used in country districts in Palestine, Jordan and Syria; in the Syrian desert it is regularly used among the tribes of nomad-shepherds. In north Africa it is in almost general use in both rural and urban dialects in north Algeria (for more precise details see J. Cantineau, *Cours*, 75); it has remained in use in Tangier and perhaps in certain places in north Morocco, in cases of gemination (*ḳudjdja* "lock of hair", but pl. *ḳ^{u}jej*).

5. Pronunciation of *djīm* as *j*: in Syria, Palestine and Jordan this is the town-dwellers' pronunciation: Damascus, Nablus, Jaffa, Jerusalem (Christians), etc. It is the pronunciation of the whole of the Lebanon (except to the north of the Beḳāʿ: *dj*), the Anti-Lebanon and the Djabal al-Drūz. In North Africa it is found in Tunisian, Tripolitanian, Moroccan and south Algerian dialects; it is found in certain places in northern Algeria. Probably it was the usual pronunciation of *djīm* in the Arabic dialect of Granada.

6. Pronunciation of *djīm* as *z*: it must, finally, be noted that in the towns of north Africa one can observe a tendency in certain individuals to open the palato-alveolar *j* into a sibilant *z*. This tendency appears to be limited to certain social groups (Jews) or to certain social classes (lower-class people in north Morocco), and is not sufficiently generalized to make it possible to refer to anything more than individual pronunciations.

All the pronunciations of *djīm* given above are voiced. Some unvoiced pronunciations are known, and are extremely local: *č* in Palmyra and in some villages in the Anti-Lebanon, *ts* in Sukhne (between Palmyra and the Euphrates).

In classical Arabic *djīm* is subject to certain conditioned modifications (accommodations, assimilations), see J. Cantineau, *Cours*, 72-3; (for the various modifications in modern dialects, see *ibid.*, 76-9). For the phonological oppositions of the phoneme *djīm*, see idem, *Esquisse*, *BSLP*, cxxvi, 102, 18; for the incompatibilities, see *ibid.* 135.

Bibliography: K. Vollers, *The Arabic sounds*, in *Proc. IXth Orient. Congress*, London 1892, ii, 143 and *Volkssprache und Schriftsprache im alten Arabien*, Strasbourg 1906, 10-11; C. Brockelmann, *Grundriss*, i, 122-3 and references; A. Krimsky, in *Machriq*, i, 1898, 487-93; A. Schaade, *Sībawaihi's Lautlehre*, Leiden 1911, 72-4; de Landberg, *Études sur les dialectes de l'Arabie Méridionale*, i, 539, ii, 353 n. 4, 806 n. 1; idem *Glossaire Dathînois*, i, 256-7; A. Socin, *Diwan aus Centralarabien*, iii, § 161; N. Rhodokanakis, *Der vulgärarabische*

1) An occlusive dorsal mediopalatal with palatalization.

Dialekt im Ḍofâr, i, p. viii, ii, 78-9; J. Cantineau, *Cours de Phonétique arabe*, Algiers 1941, 71-9; M. Bravmann, *Materialien und Untersuchungen zu den phonetischen Lehren der Araber*, Göttingen 1934, 48-9; C. Rabin, *Ancient West-Arabian*, London 1951, 31, 126.

(W. Marçais-[H. Fleisch])

ii.—LANGUAGES OTHER THAN ARABIC

In Persian the letter *djīm* represents a voiced palatal affricate, which has a voiceless counterpart *č* (*čīm*). The voiced velar occlusive is represented always by *gâf*, although in Arabic loanwords from Iranian *djīm* frequently represents this Iranian *g* (*e.g.*, *djāmūs* "buffalo", P. **gāw-mēsh*). The letter *čīm* is formed on the model of *djīm*, with three *nuḳṭa*s instead of one.

In Ottoman Turkish, *djīm* and *čīm* are written as in Persian and with the same values, except that in some morphophonemically conditioned situations the voiced/voiceless opposition disappears. In the modern Turkish orthography *djīm and čīm* are replaced in general by *c* and *ç* respectively with, however, account taken of phonetic values; hence *ç* can on occasion represent original *djīm*.

In Urdū *dj̱* (*djīm*) and *č* (*čè*, *čīm*) are palatal affricates as in Persian, frequently but not invariably uttered with dorsal contact with the tongue-tip behind the lower teeth. Among less educated speakers, especially in areas in India away from the main centres of Muslim culture, *dj̱* is also the pronunciation of the four *z* sounds (*dẖāl* [zāl], *ḍād* [zād, zwād], *ẓāʾ* [zwē, zoē], as well as *zāʾ* [zē]), which results in occasional false back-formations, *e.g.*, *mawzūd* for *mawdj̱ūd*. Both *dj̱* and *č* occur with aspiration, written with *djīm* or *čè* with the "butterfly" (*dūčashmī*) form of *hā*.

In Sindhī there occurs beside *dj̱* and *dj̱h* the voiced palatal *implosive* affricate, written with two *nuḳṭa*s arranged vertically, ڄ . Other modifications of *djīm/čīm* are the aspirated *čh* (ڇ), and the palatal nasal, *ñ*, with two *nuḳṭa*s placed horizontally, ڃ.

In Pashtō beside *dj̱* and *č* occur the dental affricates *dz* and *ts*, both, however, written with the sign څ.

Bibliography: see Bibliography to DĀL, ii.

(J. Burton-Page)

DJIMAT (Malay), an amulet, more particularly a written amulet. The word is of Arabic origin = *ʿazīma*. [see ḤAMĀʾIL]   (Ed.)

DJIMMĀ, known also as Djimmā Kāḳā, "Djimmā of the confederacy", and Djimmā Abbā Djifār, from the name of its most famous king. This state lies in the angle formed by the Omo and Godjeb rivers in south-west Ethiopia, and was inhabited by Sidamā (Hamites) of the same stock as the neighbouring kingdom of Kafa; the south-east corner of Djimmā, called Garo, was inhabited by the Bosha, who are mentioned in an epinikion of Yeshaḳ of Ethiopia (1412-27) together with the neighbouring state of Enāryā, later known as Limmu and Limmu-Enāryā (I. Guidi, *Le canzoni geez-amariña*, in *Rend. Lin.*, ii, 1889,). The Bosha were among the pagans forcibly converted to Christianity by Sarṣa Dengel of Ethiopia about 1586. When the Galla invaded Ethiopia they reached this region about the middle of the 16th century, and began to found small monarchies in the Gibē region, the first of which was Enāryā, where a Galla dynasty was founded about 1550-70. In Djimmā six tribes of the Djimmā group formed the basis of the Galla state,

whence the name Djimmā Ḳāḳā. Nominally Christian under Ethiopian rule, which ended about 1632, and pagan under the Galla founders of the new dynasty, a Muslim element soon entered, but died out together with Christianity during the 18th century. A monarchy is repugnant to the Galla, and its development was due to the influence of Islam. In Djimmā alone of the five Galla monarchies was the kingship allowed to survive after the Ethiopian conquest between 1891 and 1900. The language spoken here is Galla, and there has been a blending of Galla and Islamic institutions. The king has both a Galla war-name, *e.g.*, Abbā Djifār, "owner of a dappled horse", and a Muslim name, Muḥammad b. Dāʾūd. The kingship was hereditary, passing to a brother if there was no son. Owing to the influence of the monarchy, which was inconsistent with the Galla ideal of a tribal ruler who held office for only eight years, the Galla *gada*-system became much curtailed, and eventually the *gada*-grades were reduced from five to two. Islam was re-introduced early in the 19th century, and by the last quarter of the century Djimmā had become a centre of Islamic learning in western Ethiopia, though it caused no real anxiety to the kings of Ethiopia; nevertheless this did prevent Menilek II from annexing Djimmā to his kingdom along with the rest of the tributary states that lay round Ethiopia. From the time of the re-introduction of Islam till the end of the century the names of eight kings are preserved, the best known being Sanna Abbā Djifār I; the last king was also called Abbā Djifār. The trade route from Kafa to the coast lay through Djimmā; since it was a fertile land, the presence of traders from outside encouraged the development of agriculture; wheat, coffee, cotton, and aromatics were its chief products. It was also a centre of the slave-trade. Under Ethiopian rule the kingship was allowed to remain, the king being a vassal of the king of Ethiopia.

Bibliography: Cecchi, *Da Zeila alle frontiere del Caffa*, 1885, ii; E. Cerulli, *Etiopia occidentale*, 1932-3, i, 87-91, and ii chap. xii; Beckingham and Huntingford, *Some records of Ethiopia*, 1954, lxi-lxii, lxxxii-lxxxiv; Huntingford, *The Galla of Ethiopia*, 1955, 53, 56-7, and map opp. 14.

(G. W. B. Huntingford)

DJINĀḤ (Indian-Pākistānī equivalent of Djanāḥ; English spelling: Jinnah), Muḥammad ʿAlī. Muḥammad ʿAlī Djināḥ, known by his fellow-countrymen as the Ḳāʾid-i Aʿẓam, was the founder of the state of Pākistān. He organized and led the Pākistān movement and became the first Governor-General of the new state.

It is generally accepted that he was born on 25 December 1876, though some records give dates in 1875 and 1874. His father was a moderately wealthy merchant, a member of a Khōdja family living in Karachi. His early education took place in Bombay and later at the Sindh Madrasat al-Islām and the Missionary Society High School in Karachi. After matriculation he was sent to England in 1892 where he qualified for the bar (Lincoln's Inn) in 1896.

While in London, during the final days of Gladstonian liberalism, he showed a keen interest in public life, as an admirer and supporter of Dādābhāʾī Nawrōdjī, the first Indian to be elected to the House of Commons. At this stage also he assumed the outward appearance of an Englishman. Until the last year of his life he normally wore immaculate English clothes and he used a monocle. All his important speeches were delivered in English and even his broadcast on 3 June 1947 on the acceptance of the partition scheme was translated into Urdū by others. In short, he had become "Mr. Jinnah".

He returned to India in 1896 and in the following year began to practise law in Bombay. After several lean years he became quite rapidly a leading member of the Bombay bar. His mind was always that of the lawyer. His speech aimed at precision rather than eloquence. He had little patience with those who used words as symbols to awaken emotions. He addressed himself to the British government or to the educated Indian minority. When he spoke to the masses it was in English and in the same terms he employed in writing a brief. If the masses responded it was to the man's intensity and uprightness, not to the warmth of his words.

D̲j̲ināḥ's first venture into Indian politics was as a member of the Indian National Congress. He attended the 1906 session as private secretary to Nawrōd̲j̲ī who was then Congress President. Three years later, in January 1910, he took his place as a member of the first Imperial legislative Council. He was elected to represent the Muslims of Bombay, and he was the first non-official member to secure adoption of a legislative Act, in this case an Act validating Muslim *waḳfs*.

In 1913, while remaining an influential figure in the Congress, D̲j̲ināḥ joined the Muslim League. He was to serve, said Gokhale, as the "ambassador of Hindū-Muslim unity". He took the leading rôle in negotiating the "Lucknow Pact" whereby the Congress and the Muslim League agreed on a scheme of constitutional reform containing guarantees for the rights of the Muslim community. D̲j̲ināḥ presided over the 1916 session of the League which approved these proposals.

The years after 1918 brought a wave of radicalism and violence into Indian politics. D̲j̲ināḥ, with his repeated emphasis on what he called "constitutional lines" felt himself being supplanted by the extremists. In 1919 he resigned from the Legislative Council in protest against the extension of repressive police authority. The following year he parted from the Congress on the issue of non-cooperation. In addition to his break with the Congress, D̲j̲ināḥ found himself separated from many of his fellow Muslims who were ardent supporters of the K̲h̲ilāfat movement. The Muslim League declined in importance and was internally divided.

D̲j̲ināḥ was married for the first time as a child, before he left for England in 1892, but his wife died whilst he was away. His second marriage, to the daughter of a rich Pārsī, took place in 1918. It was not a success and they had separated before her death ten years later. Throughout most of his life his sister Fāṭima looked after his domestic needs.

Between 1920 and 1930 D̲j̲ināḥ played a part in Indian public life but he cannot be said to have been a leading figure and certainly not the sole or principal spokesman for the Indian Muslims. He was elected to the new Central Assembly and was a delegate to the first two Round Table Conferences (1930-1). At this stage he began to practise at the Privy Council bar and established a home in London, paying only intermittent visits to India.

His final return took place in 1935, after the enactment of the new constitutional provisions of the Government of India Act. Almost at once he began to move toward control of the Muslim League and its development as the main instrument of Muslim nationalism. In 1936 be became President of the Parliamentary Board of the League, the committee that took charge of the election campaign. Their object was a programme of mass contact but they were not markedly successful as was shown by the poor electoral record of the League in 1937. The Congress, which had done well, now assumed power in the majority of the Provinces and seemed to have established a claim to be the sole heir to British authority. D̲j̲ināḥ, now President of the League, moved to dispute this claim, stating that no further constitutional steps could be taken without the consent of the Muslim nation, represented by the League.

D̲j̲ināḥ's first line of argument was that the Muslims could not expect full justice in a political society with a Hindū majority. The League gave much attention to Muslim grievances against Congress provincial ministries. In 1939, after the outbreak of war, the Congress governments resigned. D̲j̲ināḥ, giving cautious support to the war effort, was able to strengthen his organization and to bring about, during the war years, League participation in the government of several provinces.

The second main argument was now launched. It consisted in the assertion that a separate state for the Muslims of India was possible and necessary. Muḥammad Iḳbāl had suggested such a scheme in 1930 but it was not adopted as a political programme until the meeting of the Muslim League at Lahore in March, 1940. This was the Pākistān Resolution.

It was not yet clear whether D̲j̲ināḥ could validly claim to speak for Muslim opinion. In Bengal, the Pand̲j̲āb, Sindh and the North-West Frontier Province, all Muslim-majority areas, the League was unable to exercise effective and continuous control. However, in the elections of 1946 the League won almost all the Muslim seats and D̲j̲ināḥ's position as spokesman for the overwhelming majority could not be denied.

He participated actively in the negotiations leading to the partition scheme, insisting always that the Muslims must be allowed to choose a separate state. In June 1947 his object was accomplished and the state of Pākistān came into existence at midnight on 14-15 August 1947. He took office as Governor-General and President of the Constituent Assembly. His first efforts were directed to ending communal bloodshed and hatred. He was, by this time, seventy years old and his health was showing signs of collapse. Nevertheless he presided over the establishment of the machinery of government and was in effective control of policy. During 1948 he became progressively weaker and on 11 September he died.

He was a man who changed the course of history, for, while there was Muslim national feeling before D̲j̲ināḥ, he gave it self-confidence and organization. He was a man of rigid integrity, perhaps hard to love but made for admiration. He was a nationalist who seemed at times to be more English than Indian; he was a Muslim who made few references to God or the Prophet or the Ḳurʾān. He was not a deeply religious man. To him the Muslim heritage was a civilization, a culture and a national identy. And he founded a state just as surely as had Bābur.

Bibliography: H. Bolitho, *Jinnah*, London 1954; Matlubul Hasan Sayid, *Mohammad Ali Jinnah*, Lahore 1953; Jamilud Din Ahmad (ed.), *Speeches and writings of Mr. Jinnah*, 2 vols., Lahore 1942 and 1947. (K. Callard)

D̲J̲INĀS [see TAD̲J̲NĪS].

D̲J̲IND̲J̲I K̲H̲ʷĀD̲J̲A [see ḤUSAYN D̲J̲IND̲J̲I].

D̲J̲INN, according to the Muslim conception bodies (*ad̲j̲sām*) composed of vapour or flame, intelligent, imperceptible to our senses, capable of appearing under different forms and of carrying out heavy labours (al-Bayḍāwī, Comm. to Ḳur'ān, LXXII, 1; al-Damīrī, *Ḥayawān*, *s.v.* *d̲j̲inn*). They were created of smokeless flame (Ḳur'ān, LV, 14) while mankind and the angels, the other two classes of intelligent beings, were created of clay and light. They are capable of salvation; Muḥammad was sent to them as well as to mankind; some will enter Paradise while others will be cast into the fire of hell. Their relation to Iblīs the S̲h̲ayṭān, and to the S̲h̲ayṭāns in general, is obscure. In the Ḳur'ān, XVIII, 48, Iblīs is said to be a *d̲j̲inn*; but according to the Ḳur'ān, II, 32, he is said to be an angel. In consequence there is much confusion, and many legends and hypotheses have grown up on this subject; on the last passage quoted, see al-Bayḍāwī and al-Rāzī, *Mafātīḥ*, Cairo 1307, i, 288 ff. The Arab lexicographers try to make the word *d̲j̲inn* derive from *id̲j̲tinān*, "to be hidden, concealed" (see Lane, *s.v.* *d̲j̲inn* and al-Bayḍāwī, on II, 7). But this etymology is very difficult, and the possibility of explanation through borrowing from Latin (*genius*) is not entirely excluded. The expression "naturalem deum uniuscuiusque loci" (Serv. Verg. G., i, 302) exactly expresses the formal localization of the *d̲j̲inn* (cf., *e.g.*, Nöldeke, *Muʿallaḳāt*, i, 74, 78 and ii, 65, 89) as well as their standing as semi-divinities in old Arabia (Robertson Smith, *Rel. of Semites*², 121; Ger. tr. (Stübe), 84 ff.). In the singular one says "*d̲j̲innī*"; *d̲j̲ānn* is also used as the equivalent of the form *d̲j̲inn* (but cf. Lane, *Lexicon*, 492c); *g̲h̲ūl*, *ʿifrīt*, *siʿlāt* are classes of the *d̲j̲inn*. For an Ethiopic point of contact with *d̲j̲ānn* see Nöldeke, *Neue Beiträge*, 63.

Consideration of the *d̲j̲inn* divides naturally under three heads, though these necessarily shade into one another.

I. The *d̲j̲inn* in pre-Islamic Arabia were the nymphs and satyrs of the desert, and represented the side of the life of nature still unsubdued and hostile to man. For this aspect, see Robertson Smith, *loc. cit.*; Nöldeke in *ERE*, i, 669 ff.; Wellhausen, *Reste*; van Vloten, *Dämonen . . . bei d. alt. Arabern*, in *WZKM.*, vii and viii (the author uses materials in al-D̲j̲āḥiẓ, *Ḥayawān*). But in the time of Muḥammad *d̲j̲inn* were already passing over into vague, impersonal gods. The Arabs of Mecca asserted the existence of a kinship (*nasab*) between them and Allāh (Ḳur'ān, XXXVII, 158), made them companions of Allāh (VI, 100), offered sacrifices to them (VI, 128), and sought aid of them (LXXII, 6).

II. In official Islam the existence of the *d̲j̲inn* was completely accepted, as it is to this day, and the full consequences implied by their existence were worked out. Their legal status in all respects was discussed and fixed, and the possible relations between them and mankind, especially in questions of marriage and property, were examined. Stories of the loves of *d̲j̲inn* and human beings were evidently of perennial interest. The *Fihrist* gives the titles of sixteen of these (308) and they appear in all the collections of short tales (cf., *e.g.*, Dāwūd al-Anṭākī, *Tazyīn al-aswāḳ*, Cairo 1308, 181 ff.; al-Sarrād̲j̲, *Maṣāriʿ al-ʿus̲h̲s̲h̲āḳ*, Istanbul 1301, 286 ff.). There are many stories, too, of relations between saints and *d̲j̲inn*; cf. D. B. Macdonald, *Religious attitude and life in Islam*, 144 ff. A good summary of the question is given in Badr al-Dīn al-S̲h̲iblī (d. 769/1368), *Ākām al-mard̲j̲ān fī aḥkām al-d̲j̲ān* (Cairo 1326); see also Nöldeke's review in *ZDMG*, lxiv, 439 ff. Few even of the Muʿtazila ventured to doubt the existence of *d̲j̲inn*, and only constructed different theories of their nature and their influence on the material world. The earlier philosophers, even al-Fārābī, tried to avoid the question by ambiguous definitions. But Ibn Sīnā, in defining the word, asserted flatly that there was no reality behind it. The later believing philosophers used subterfuges, partly exegetical and partly metaphysical. Ibn K̲h̲aldūn, for example, reckoned all references to the *d̲j̲inn* among the so-called *mutas̲h̲ābih* passages of the Ḳur'ān, the knowledge of which Allah has reserved to himself (Ḳur'ān, III, 5). These different attitudes are excellently treated in the *Dict. of techn. terms*, i, 261 ff.; cf. also al-Rāzī, *Mafātīḥ*, lxxii.

III. The *d̲j̲inn* in folk-lore. The transition to this division comes most naturally through the use of the *d̲j̲inn* in magic. Muslim theology has always admitted the fact of such a use, though judging its legality varyingly. The *Fihrist* traces both the approved and the disapproved kinds back to ancient times, and gives Greek, Ḥarrānian, Chaldean and Hindū sources. At the present day, books treating of the binding of *d̲j̲inn* to talismanic service are an important part of the literature of the people. All know and read them, and the professional magician has no secrets left. In popular stories too, as opposed to the tales of the professed littérateur, the *d̲j̲inn* play a large part. It is so throughout the *Thousand and One Nights*, but especially in that class of popular religious novels of which Weil published two in his Translation of the *Nights*, namely the second version of "D̲j̲ūd̲h̲ar the Fisherman" and the story entitled "ʿAlī and Ẓāhir of Damascus". In the *Thousand and One Nights*, particularly in the first part, the *d̲j̲innī* generally turns against any human being out of spite to get the better of him; roaming the world at night (Night No. 76), the *d̲j̲innī* (or fairy, *parī*) transports a man for immense distances, to make him lose his way; he turns him into an animal (a monkey, in No. 48, a dog, in No. 5 and 66); but on the other hand he sometimes restores his human form (No. 5 and 34); he protects the man undeservedly duped by one of his fellows (No. 47); he teaches man how to free someone possessed by another *d̲j̲innī*, by means of exorcism (*ibid.*); moreover, *d̲j̲inn* and fairies sometimes join together to do good (No. 78); on the other hand, man can defend himself and by his cunning has the *d̲j̲innī* at his mercy (like the fisherman who imprisons him in a jar, No. 11); and sometimes a man harms *d̲j̲inn* unintentionally (a man eating dates throws away a stone which kills one of their children, No. 1). Still nearer to the ideas of the masses are the fairy stories collected orally by Artin, Østrup, Spitta, Stumme, etc. In these stories the folk-lore elements of the different races overcome the common Muslim atmosphere. The inspiration of these tales is more characteristic of the peoples of North Africa, as well as of the Egyptians, Syrians, Persians and Turks rather than of Arabia or Islam. Besides this there are the popular beliefs and usages, so far very incompletely gathered. Throughout this field also there are points of contact with the official Islamic view. Thus, in Egyptian popular belief, a man who dies by violence becomes an *ʿifrīt* and haunts the place of his death (Willmore, *Spoken Arabic of Egypt*, 371, 374), while in the Islam of the schools a man who dies in deadly sin may be transformed into a *d̲j̲innī* in the world of al-Barzak̲h̲ (*Dict. of techn. terms*, i, 265). Willmore has other details on the *d̲j̲inn* in Egypt. For South Arabia see ʿAbdullah Mansur, *The land of Uz*, 22, 26, 203, 316-20. See also R. C. Thomson in *Proc. of Soc. of*

Bibl. Arch., xxviii, 83 ff.; Sayce, in *Folk-lore*, 1900, ii, 338 ff.; Lydia Einszler, in *ZDPV*, x, 170 ff.; H. H. Spoer, in *Folk-lore*, xviii, 54 ff.; D. B. Macdonald, *Aspects of Islam*, 326 ff. But much still remains to be done.

D̲j̲inn are most commonly spoken of by allusion (*hāduk al-nās*, "those people there", North Africa) or by antiphrasis, like the Eumenides (*az mā bihtarān*, "those better than ourselves", Īrān).

Bibliography: Damīrī, *Ḥayawān*, for the words *d̲j̲inn*, *siʿlāt*, *ʿifrīt*, *g̲h̲ūl* (cf. also the translation of Jayakar, London and Bombay 1906-8); Ḳazwīnī, *ʿAd̲j̲āʾib*, ed. Wüstenfeld, 368 ff.; R. Basset, *Mille et un contes, récits et légendes arabes*, i, 59, 74, 90, 123, 151, 159, 174, 175, 180; Goldziher, *Arabische Philologie*, i, index; idem, *Vorlesungen*, 68, 78 ff.; Macdonald, *Religious attitude and life in Islam*, chap. V and X and index; Lane, *Arabian Nights*, Introd. n. 21 and chap. I, No. 15 and 24. For Egypt: Lane, *Manners and customs of the modern Egyptians*, 1836 (vol. i, chap. X; superstitions, and index, *s.v. ginn*); Aḥmad Amīn, *Ḳāmūs al-ʿādāt . . . al-miṣriyya*, 141 ff. For the Yemen: two *d̲j̲inn*, the *ʿudrūṭ* and the *dubb*, are described in R. B. Serjeant, *Two Yemenite d̲j̲inn*, in *BSOAS*, xiii/1 (1949), 4-6, with further bibliography. For North Africa: E. Doutté, *Magie et religion* (passim); Dermenghem, *Le culte des saints dans l'Islam maghrébin*, 96 ff.; Desparmet, *Le mal magique*, in *Publ. Fac. Lettres Alger*, lxiii (1932); Legey, *Essai sur la folklore marocain* (index, *s.v.* génies); E. Westermarck, *Ritual and belief in Morocco* (index: *s.v. jenn, jinn, jnūn*); H. Basset, *Le culte des grottes au Maroc*; idem, *Essai sur la littérature des Berbères*, 101 ff.; M. L. Dubouloz-Laffin, *Le Bou-Mergoud, folklore tunisien* (Ist part); W. Marçais, *Textes arabes de Takroûna*, index *s.v. Djinns*; P. Bourgeois, *L'univers de l'écolier marocain*, Rabat 1959, 23-43. For Īrān: A. Christensen, *Essai sur la démonologie iranienne*, 71: *dīw* and *d̲j̲inn*; H. Massé, *Croyances et coutumes persanes* (index III: *d̲j̲inn*). (D. B. Macdonald-[H. Massé])

In Turkish folklore. Of the words used to denote these, *cin* (d̲j̲in) is the most common; *ecinni* (ed̲j̲inni) is a variation of it. The word *in*, used only in the form *in-cin*, has in certain instances the same sense as *d̲j̲inn*; it is a corruption of *ins*, from the group *ins wa d̲j̲inn* (= "men and d̲j̲inn"), which occurs frequently in the Ḳurʾān. In everyday speech as well as in stories of fantastic adventures and tales of the supernatural, the word *peri* is often taken as a synonym of *d̲j̲inn*; the two terms are often confused even in traditions, nevertheless the former really belongs to the realm of supernatural tales where the word *d̲j̲inn* is less common. In parts of eastern Anatolia (at Tokat and Erzurum, for example: for the latter locality, see Sami Akalın, *Erzurum bilmeceleri*, Istanbul 1954, glossary) the word *mekir* is used to denote a supernatural being with all the characteristics of a *d̲j̲inn*. At times when one is anxious to avoid any harm being done by them, the word *d̲j̲inn*, by a linguistic taboo, is replaced by expressions such as *iyi saatte olsunlar* ("may they be at an auspicious moment", meaning: "beings who, I hope, are in good humour and well-disposed towards us"). It is believed that there are Muslim *d̲j̲inn* and heathen *d̲j̲inn*; the latter are considered to be the more wicked and difficult to control.

They are thought of as beings of both sexes, and living collectively. They have their chief or, as he is usually called, *pādis̲h̲āh*. All their activities take place at night and come to an end with the first cock-crow or the first call to morning prayer. Traditions, tales and supernatural stories of all kinds name the places where they live or which they frequent and where they choose to meet for their amusement (always at night); — mills, *ḥammām*s (public baths), ruins, derelict houses, cemeteries, certain inns (particularly when deserted and falling into ruin), certain places in the country, especially at the foot of big trees. Certain private houses are reputed to be haunted by *d̲j̲inn*, and similarly "guest rooms" in villages. In Istanbul, according to local tradition, there are a number of places inside and outside the town which are reputed to be inhabited by these supernatural beings; and the home of the King of the sea-*d̲j̲inn* is said to be off Leander's Tower, in the Bosphorus. One legend explains why even a mosque, at Dimetoḳa (in Rumelia) is frequented by *d̲j̲inn* at night. Even in daytime precautions have to be taken with regard to certain places such as water-closets, remote corners where rubbish is piled or where dirty water overflows, at the foot of trees, quiet dirty corners on river-banks, the base of walls above the gutter, enclosed dark places in houses (like lumber-rooms) etc.

D̲j̲inn appear to men in many different forms, most often in the guise of animals, such as; — a black cat (without any light markings), a goat (kid, or he-goat), a black dog, a duck, a hen with chickens, a buffalo, a fox; or else in human shape; either as men of ordinary size or dwarfs, and sometimes as men of gigantic stature (many who claim to have seen them describe them as quite white, thin, and as tall as a minaret or a telegraph pole); they also appear with the features of a baby wrapped in its swaddling-clothes. In the magic arts of the negroes in Turkey, the snake is regarded as the animal in which *d̲j̲inn* are incorporated. Wolves and birds are the only other living creatures to whose attacks *d̲j̲inn* are vulnerable.

Their behaviour towards human beings is of three sorts: if people understand how to refrain from irritating them, they do no harm: they are indifferent or, at times, are satisfied if they tease people by playing various harmless tricks; to those whose actions deserve some reward they bring great benefits; the imprudent and insolent they punish by inflicting illnesses or infirmities. Some tales, and in particular some legendary stories, give accounts of happenings at certain places, in which persons who have suffered strange treatment by these supernatural beings are mentioned by name (for stories of this type see Eberhard-Boratav, *Typen türkischer Volksmärchen*, Wiesbaden 1953, types no. 67, 67 III, 67 V, 118 and the words: *Geister, Peri, Teufel* in the index; Melahat Sabri, *Cinler* in *Halk Bilgisi Haberleri*, iii, 143-51; the same article is repeated intact in M. Halit Bayrı, *Istanbul folkloru*, Istanbul 1947, 176-181; A. Caferoğlu, *Orta Anadolu ağızlarından derlemeler*, Istanbul 1948, 209-210). Among these supernatural stories there are some which tell how men can make requests, either on their own initiative or with the help of an "initiate", to the King of the D̲j̲inn while he is taking counsel. A characteristic feature of the rewards granted by *d̲j̲inn* to those they favour is that they are given in the form of onion and garlic peel, the former being subsequently changed into gold pieces, the latter into silver.

The illnesses which they inflict are of various kinds: hemiplegia, different forms of paralysis and twisted limbs are the most usual. They sometimes interfere in family life and wreck marriages; such incidents are due to the young man or woman having irritated a *djinn* in some way, or else because one or other of them is loved—and indeed "regarded as a spouse"—by one of these supernatural beings, either by a male or female *djinn* according to the circumstances.

Methods of avoiding *djinn* and their misdeeds can be put into two categories: precautionary measures which anyone can take of his own initiative, and measures to be taken in cases requiring recourse to a specialist. Some of the precautions to be taken in order not to irritate *djinn* are as follows: — so far as one can, to avoid the places they frequent, never to "profane" those places (by soiling, spitting, urinating etc.), always to say a *besmele* (*bism-illāh*) or a *destūr* (this word means "with your permission") before each action and before moving anything, never to forget to say these words, *e.g.*, each time any object or article of clothing is put away in a chest or when any provisions are put in store etc., so that the *djinn* may not consume them.

In serious cases of illnesses or infirmities thought to have been incurred through *djinn*, recourse is made to specialists, who are *khodja* or *shaykh*s or even simple people without any religious title who however are initiates of the *djinn*; they are called *huddamlı*, "masters—or patrons—of servants", the *djinn* being considered as servants or slaves entirely subject to them. The procedure for exorcising takes various forms, but the principle is invariable: the sorcerer (who is also given such names as *cindar* [djindār] or *cinci* [djindjī], signifying the captor of a *djinn*), invokes the *djinns* or *djinn* thought to be responsible for the trouble, or to be able to reveal it; when he succeeds in calling up the guilty *djinn*, he negotiates with him, either with apologies or with threats, to free and cure the victim. Some of these exorcisms are carried out in the absence of the victims; others require their presence—as is the case in the magic arts of the Turkish negroes (natives of Africa) who, before 1920, and especially in big towns like Istanbul and Izmir, set up corporations of exorcisors under the *godyas*, their spiritual leaders; the efficacity of their magic cures was acknowledged by the white population also. (On this subject see: A. Bombaci, *Pratiche magiche africane*, in *Folklore*, iii, no. 3-4, 1949, Naples, 3-11; P. N. Boratav, *The Negro in the Turkish folklore*, in *Journal of American Folklore*, lxiv (1951), no. 251, 83-8; P. N. Boratav, *Les Noirs dans le folklore turc et le folklore des Noirs de Turquie*, in *Journal de la Société des Africanistes*, xxviii (1958), 7-23).

Bibliography: In addition to the works quoted in the text of the article, the author has made use of materials resulting from his own research, together with the texts of tales, legends and fantastic stories in his collection of manuscripts. The lack of any single comprehensive work on this subject is a gap in Turkish folklore studies.

(P. N. Boratav)

India: In India one encounters three distinct concepts of *djinn*—traditional or orthodox, based on literal interpretations of the Ḳur'ānic verses; superstitious, as revealed in the popular superstitions; and rationalistic, as attempted by Sir Sayyid Aḥmad Khān and others of his school of thought.

(*a*) In traditional or orthodox accounts the *djinn* is represented as a creature created from fire, unlike man who has been created from clay. The *djinns* are invisible and aery (*Lughāt al-Ḳur'ān*, ʿAbd al-Rashīd Nuʿmānī, ii, 254-6). Almost all the Indian scholars on exegesis have held this view. ʿInāyat ʿAlī mentions four types of *djinn*: (i) aerial creatures, without any physical form, (ii) snake-like creatures, (iii) those who shall be subjected to the same process of divine dispensation on the Day of Judgment as human beings, and (iv) creatures with beast-like features (*Miṣbāḥ al-furḳān fī lughāt al-Ḳur'ān*, Dihlī 1357 A.H., 85). Some jurists have, despite their belief in the supernatural character of the *djinns*, considered them so real as to deal with hypothetical problems arising out of human marriages with *djinns*.

(*b*) It is popularly held that the *djinns* are invisible creatures with great supernatural powers and with an organization presided over by a king. Even in the educated circles of Muslim society, this concept was common in the middle ages. During the time of Iletmish, an area in the vicinity of the Ḥawḍ-i Shamsī of Dihlī had the reputation of being the abode of *djinns* (*Miftāḥ al-ṭālibīn*, Ms personal collection). Djamālī [*q.v.*] refers to a guest house which was constructed by Iletmish (607-33/1210-35) and was known as *Dār al-Djinn* because it was thought to be frequented by the *djinns*. A *Shaykh al-Islām* of Dihlī, Sayyid Nadjm al-Dīn Ṣughra, accommodated Shaykh Djalāl al-Dīn Tabrīzī in this house in order to test his spiritual powers. The Shaykh sent his servant to place a copy of the Ḳur'ān in the house before he himself occupied it (*Siyar al-ʿArifīn*, Dihlī 1311 A.H., 165, 166). This has given birth to a superstition that before a new house is occupied, a copy of the Ḳur'ān should be placed therein in order to expel the *djinns*. Since it was believed that the *djinns* could do harm to human beings and also cause serious ailments, many religious writers deal with incantations and litanies to counteract their evil effects. Shāh Walī Allāh (d. 1763) suggests methods to expel *djinn* from houses (*Ḳawl al-Djamīl*, Kānpur 1291 A.H., 96, 97).

(*c*) An attempt to rationalize the concept of *djinn* by divesting it of all supernatural and superstitious elements was made by Sayyid Aḥmad Khān. He held the view that by the word *djinn* the Ḳur'ān meant Bedouins and other uncivilized and uncultured people. To him the expression *djinn wa 'l-ins* which occurs fourteen times in the *Ḳur'ān* meant 'the uncultured and the cultured people'. The different contexts in which the word *djinn* is used in the Ḳur'ān have been explained by him as references to different qualities and characteristics of these 'people' (*Tafsir al-Ḳur'ān*, iii, ʿAlīgaṙh 1885, 79-89); this point of view was subjected to criticism by the *ʿulamā'*.

Bibliography: In addition to references above and the different *tafsīr*s written by Indo-Muslim scholars: Mawlānā Muḥammad Zaman, *Bustān al-Djinn*, Madrās 1277 A.H.; Ṣādiḳ ʿAlī, *Māhiyyat al-malāk wa 'l-djinn wa 'l-insān ʿalā mā thabata min al-tadabbur fī āyāt al-Ḳur'ān*, Rawalpindi 1899; Aslam Djayrādjpurī, *Taʿlīmāt al-Ḳur'ān*, Dihlī 1934, 37-8; Mawlawī Abū Muḥammad ʿAbd al-Ḥaḳḳ Ḥaḳḳānī, *al-Bayān fī ʿulūm al-Ḳur'ān*, Dihlī 1324, 119-28.

(K. A. Nizami)

Indonesia. The Arabic *djinn* is generally known to Indonesian Muslims from Arabic literature and its offshoots. The word *djinn* passed into various Indonesian languages (Malay, Gayō etc. *djin*, Javanese *djin* or *djim*, Minangkabau *djihin*, Acheh *djén* etc.) and even into the literary language of a non-Muslim people such as the Batak (*odjim*). Malays use it as a polite equivalent or euphemism for *hantu* (evil spirit); in some languages (*e.g.*, Gayō) it is used as a general name for all kinds of indigenous spirits. (P. Voorhoeve)

DJINS, γένος, genus, is the first of the five predicables *al-alfāẓ al-khamsa* (genus, species, difference, property, accident) as given by Porphyry in his Introduction (Isagoge) to Aristotle's Logic—introduction which is incorporated by the Muslim philosophers in Aristotle's Organon—and its logical sense (for also its common sense of "race", "stock", "kin", is mentioned by Aristotle, Porphyry and the Arab commentators) is said to be that which is predicated of many things differing in species in answer to what a thing is, *e.g.*, animal. These predicables are also called *al-maʿānī al-thāniya*, "*intentiones secundae*" in scholastic terminology, to distinguish them from *al-maʿānī al-ūlā*, "*intentiones primae*". According to the later Greek and to the Muslim commentators the first intentions refer to the particular things, the second intentions refer to the ten categories which are themselves the highest genera of particular things and to which the Muslim philosophers give the name of the *al-adjnās al-ʿashara*, the ten genera.

As to the problem of the objective reality of the genera, species and, generally speaking, of universals, it is not discussed as much in Muslim philosophy as in Scholasticism, although it is one of the fundamental problems in Aristotilean philosophy and constitutes one of its fundamental difficulties (cf. for this and the following the article DJAWHAR). There are three possible views, the realist view that universals exist objectively, the conceptualist view that they are but abstractions of the mind without a corresponding reality, the nominalist view that they are but names without any reality. Now Aristotle holds at the same time the conflicting realistic and conceptualist views. On the one hand he holds the immanent realistic view that universals form a constitutive part in individuals, Socrates, *e.g.*, is a man because the specific, the universal form of man is realized in him, on the other hand he holds that universals are but entities in the mind and acquired by abstraction. The Muslim philosophers tend to the view that the specific forms are individualized through their realization in the individual, a theory already held by Alexander of Aphrodisias (an individual specific form, however, is a *contradictio in adjecto* and they express Aristotle's conceptualist view by the maxim, often quoted in scholastic philosophy, *intellectus in formis agit universalitatem*, it is the mind that gives the forms their universality. On the other hand they go beyond Aristotle in their neoplatonizing transcendent realism and they hold that the universal forms emanate from eternity out of the mind of God, the supramundane intellects and the *dator formarum*, and we find in a passage in Avicenna's Introduction, *al-Madkhal*, to the Logic of his *Shifāʾ*, Cairo 1952, 65, a threefold distinction *djins ṭabīʿī*, natural genus, *djins ʿaḳlī*, mental genus, *djins manṭiḳī*, logical genus, the first exists before the many, *ḳabl al-kathra* (*ante res*, as the Latins have it) that is in the active intellect, the second in the many, *fi 'l-kathra* (*in rebus*) that is in the particular things, the third *baʿd al-kathra* (*post res*) that is in the human mind. In this passage Avicenna takes the curious view that genera in their own nature are neither universal nor individual; if *e.g.*, "animal" by itself were universal, there could not be several animals; if it were indivudual, there could not be the universal "animal", individuality and universality are therefore accidents added to it, the former in the exterior world, the latter in minds (this passage has been discussed by I. Madkour in his introduction to *al-Madkhal* 63, and his *L'Organon d'Aristote dans le monde arabe*, Paris 1934, 151).

Although Averroës often polemizes against the transcendent realism in Avicenna's theory of the *dator formarum*, he holds fundamentally the same position and he says *e.g.*: "Just as artifical products can only be understood by him who has not made them, because they take their origin in an intellect that is in the form which is in the soul of the artisan, so the products of nature prove the existence of supermundane Forms which are the causes that the sensible substances are potentially intelligible". And he adds: "This is the theory to which the partisans of the Ideas tended, but which they could not attain" (cf. my *Die Epitome der Metaphysik des Averroës*, Leiden 1924, 42).

The Muslim theologians, generally speaking, are nominalists. They argue against the conceptualist side of the philosophers' view by asking: "how can knowledge give any truth, if reality is individual and knowledge universal, since truth is the conformity of thought with reality?" The theologians do not admit the objective reality of forms, all reality is individual, universals exist only in minds, they are *ṣifāt nafsiyya*, spiritual qualities which, however, are not wholly real, but something intermediate between reality and unreality, or unreal, that is to say they are *ḥālāt*, *modi*, or *maʿānī* (the Stoic λεκτά or σημαινόμενα, *maʿnā* in this sense is the literal translation of σημαινόμενον, meaning, something meant, cf. Lane, s.v.). We find also the absolute denial of universals. Since for their sensualism thinking is nothing but the possession of representations and you cannot represent a universal *e.g.*, "a horse", but only a particular, *e.g.*, a definite horse, the universals are totally denied by then, (cf. Ghazzālī, *Tahāfut al-Falāsifa* (ed. Bouyges, Beirut 1927, 330).

Bibliography: The works quoted in the text and my translation (with notes) of Ibn Rushd *Tahāfut al-Tahāfut* (*the Incoherence of the Incoherence*), Oxford 1954. (S. van den Bergh)

DJINS is the Arabic word in use at the present time to denote "sex", the adjective *djinsī* corresponding to "sexual" and the abstract *djinsiyya* to "sexuality" as well as "nationality". The juridical aspect of sexual relations has already been examined in the article BĀH, and is to be the subject of further articles, NIKĀḤ and ZINĀ; the present review will be limited to general considerations on the sexual life of the Muslims and the place that it occupies in literature.

Pre-Islamic poetry, in so far as it is authentic, indicates that a certain laxity of behaviour was prevalent among the Arabs of the desert (Lammens, *Le berceau de l'Islam*, 276 ff.), and the "réunions galantes" of the contemporary Touaregs, described by Father de Foucauld (in his *Dictionnaire touareg-français*, Paris 1952, ii, 559 ff., s.v. *ahāl*), probably are not far removed from pre-Islamic practices. The *nasīb* of the classical *ḳaṣīda*, markedly erotic in character, is no doubt an indication of the existence of temporary unions in the encampments; in any case, its position at the head of the poem is evidence of the importance which the ancient Arabs attached to love, and especially sensual love, particularly since a number of lines of verse as realistic as those of Imruʾ al-Ḳays have probably been deleted, through puritanical reaction, from the ancient poems collected in the 2nd and 3rd/8th and

9th centuries; a further indication of this interest is shown by the richness of the vocabulary relating to the sexual organs, which is no doubt mainly due to the use of slang terms, as is confirmed at the present time by an unpublished study by Dr. Mathieu on the prostitutes of Casablanca. Incidentally we know that prostitution (*bighā*ʾ), which is to be discussed in the article ZINĀ, was already in existence and that prostitutes were distinguished by a special emblem which floated over their tents (see Caussin de Perceval, *Essai*).

It does not seem that Islam has in practice made many changes from the earlier state of affairs. Certainly the Ḳurʾān, in several verses (IV, 30; XVII, 34; XXIII, 5-7, 35; XXIV, 31, 33; LXX, 29-31), enjoins chastity, but only outside the bonds of marriage or concubinage (see S. H. al-Shamma, *The ethical system underlying the Qurʾān*, Tübingen 1959, 95 ff. and bibliography); it condemns prostitution (XXIV, 33) and, above all, fornication [see ZINĀ], but the conditions laid down by the *fuḳahā*ʾ for the legal proof of *zinā* are such that it more often than not escapes punishment. Marriage, as conceived by the Ḳurʾān, has a two-fold object: it is intended to allow the male, who is largely favoured since it is he who benefits from the privileges of polygamy and repudiation (while women are in certain cases even deprived of the right of giving their consent), to satisfy his sexual needs lawfully, and to ensure the perpetuation of the race. That is why celibacy is in no way recommended, and it is even recommended to give the celibate in marriage (XXIV, 32). The Ḳurʾān is realistic where it deals with sexual pleasures which it authorizes and the enjoyment of which it encourages, on the sole condition that Believers should make use of one of the two means at their disposal, marriage and concubinage [see ʿABD]. The celebrated verse (II, 223; see also 183, 222) "Your women are a field for you. Come to your field as you will" may be compared with some of the sūras, such as that of Joseph (XII), or verses such as those which describe the delights of paradise and, above all, the houris (LV, 56, 70, etc.). The Prophet himself is cited as an example of ardent sensuality, and tradition has preserved a certain number of *ḥadīth*s which strongly favour satisfaction of the sexual instinct; G.-H. Bousquet (*Éthique sexuelle*, 41) notes that the 25th of the *Forty ḥadīth*s of al-Nawawī contains this statement by the Prophet: "Each time that you satisfy the flesh, you do a deed of charity"; al-Ghazālī (*Le livre des bons usages en matière de mariage*, trans. L. Bercher and G.-H. Bousquet, Paris-Oxford 1953, 40 ff.) sees only three disadvantages in marriage (the impossibility of lawfully gaining the necessities of life, the difficulty for the husband of meeting all his obligations to his wives, and neglect of religion), while he has no difficulty in celebrating its virtues. It should, however, be noted that sexual relations, though greatly facilitated by Islamic legislation, not only are not absolutely free, but even within their lawful sphere place the partners in a state of major impurity which only the greater ablution (*ghusl*) can remove; in this a certain ambiguity of attitude manifests itself.

Pederasty [see LIWĀṬ] is explicity condemned by the Ḳurʾān (VII, 78, 79) which on the other hand makes no reference to sapphism (*saḥḳ, siḥāḳ, tasāḥuḳ*), to bestiality (*waḥshiyya*) which the jurists rank with *zinā* without, however, considering that it entails the penalty of death, nor finally to onanism (*istimnā*ʾ; *nikāḥ al-yad*; *djald ʿUmayra*), regarding which the jurists' opinions do not agree (see al-Ghazālī, *op. cit.*, 119, n. 47) but which is often considered as more reprehensible than sodomy and bestiality (see Bousquet, *Éthique sexuelle*, 57).

The freedom with which the Ḳurʾān and the Prophet discuss these delicate questions ensured that the early Muslims felt no shame in speaking of them in the most direct terms, as is especially shown by juridical literature in its treatment of particular cases. Traditions relating to the early years of Islam are full of details about the importance then attached to sexual life, and in this respect the *Kitāb al-Aghānī* is a mine of information for the historian; it abounds with precise particulars about relations between the sexes in the holy cities, and about the tastes of the women of the aristocracy who often lived lives of the greatest freedom, entirely preoccupied with their pleasures, in surroundings where the flourishing arts of poetry and music invited frivolity (see GHAZAL]. It is impossible in this brief account to mention all the anecdotes which cast a harsh light on the preoccupations of this leisurely society, and of certain caliphs too, but it will be recalled that temporary marriage [see MUTʿA] which the Ḳurʾān had not suppressed (although Sunnī Islam finally rejected it) allowed transitory unions at small cost and, along with female musicians and singers, true professionals of love gained lasting reputations; for example the woman of Medina, by name Ḥubbā, of whom al-Djāḥiẓ (*Djawārī*, 64, 65; *Ḥayawān*, ii, 200; vi, 61, 75) relates that she gave her son advice which seems to us shocking, and that she taught the women of Medina every sort of erotic refinement.

Under the ʿAbbāsids we see the development of a refined society, of luxury and pleasures (on the old Persian practice of incest, see particularly al-Djāḥiẓ, *K. al-Bukhalā*ʾ, ed. Ḥādjirī, 3-4). We have little information about the sexual life of the lower orders of Muslims, among whom there was apparently a certain degree of laxity, but it seems clear that if the members of the aristocracy and bourgeoisie married free women who gave them children, they went elsewhere in search of sensual pleasures; this is the reign of the *ḳiyān* [see ḲAYNA], so magnificently described by al-Djāḥiẓ, bringing with them an atmosphere of distinguished sensuality. Although during the pre-Islamic period and in the early days of Islam men's tastes had favoured women of ample proportions, it was now slenderness of figure that they sought, and literature provides many examples of the dubious taste shown with regard to *ghulāmiyyāt* who adopted the appearance of boys. The pronounced liking for ephebes (*ghulām* [*q.v.*]), whose praises were so often sung by poets such as Abū Nuwās, is a recurring characteristic (see A. Mez, *Renaissance*, 337 ff.; English trans., 358 ff.; Spanish trans., 427 ff.). A text such as the one by al-Djāḥiẓ entitled *Mufākharat al-djawārī wa 'l-ghilmān*, despite the obscenity of certain passages, is in this respect extremely instructive. The literary sources abound with anecdotes which refer to sexual abnormalities such as bestiality (al-Djāḥiẓ, *K. al-Bighāl*, (53, § 73, 67, § 100) and sapphism. Prostitution, controlled, existed almost everywhere (Mez, *op. cit.*, 432). In the account of Bashshār given in the *Aghānī*, the most striking detail is the number of successes with women that this poet achieved, but it would be wrong to generalize too hastily and to conclude that debauchery had invaded the whole of society. The heroes of the anecdotes which are related to us almost all belong to the same class of libertines, whilst persons of rectitude, especially the Ḥanbalīs, protested vigorously against public immorality.

On this question, an anecdote attributed to al-Aṣmaʿī [*q.v.*] seems to show to what an extent certain Bedouins had succeeded in keeping their sober habits; the philologist having asked a Bedouin to give him a definition of love (*ʿishḳ*), the latter replied: "a glance after a glance and, if it be possible, a kiss after a kiss; this is the entrance to Paradise". The Bedouin's reply astonished al-Aṣmaʿī who, when asked in his turn to give his own definition, drew this remark from his interlocutor: "But you are not in love! You are merely seeking to have a child!" (al-Washshāʾ, *Muwashshā*, 77).

Throughout the following centuries, interest in sexual matters continued, as can be seen from the copious literature devoted to these subjects. In this connexion we should note that, if writers and poets of restraint do exist in Arabic literature, many others practise complete freedom of language; the restrictions on the circulation of unexpurgated translations of the *Arabian Nights* are well known, and *Das Buch der wunderbaren Erzählungen und seltsamen Geschichten* edited by H. Wehr, Damascus-Wiesbaden 1956, again confirms the general tendency towards indecency, towards *sukhf*, later successfully cultivated by the poet Ibn al-Ḥadjdjādj and many others.

To meet the sort of demand that requires that serious matter should be interspersed with amusing passages, works of *adab* literature frequently contain smutty anecdotes, and even popular encyclopaedias indulge in scabrous sections; there is no reason to be shocked by thus, for the prudishness displayed by some is often no more than hypocrisy, as al-Djāḥiẓ points out, who, in his introduction to the *Mufākharat al-djawārī wa 'l-ghilmān*, after making fun of the Tartuffes who are too easily offended, recalls that the virtuous ancestors were in no whit so prudish and states that the words of the Arabic language were made to be used, even though they may seem shocking. The short work just referred to is particularly scabrous, dealing plainly with one aspect of sexual life and at the same time providing a sort of anthology of love, normal and abnormal; the author verges on obscenity without any sort of restraint.

Earlier works dealing with sexual life seem to have been quite numerous already, if we can judge by the references that Djāḥiẓ makes to the *Kutub al-bāh*, of Indian origin, saying that these works are in no sense pornographic and that the Indians regarded them as manuals of sexual education with which they taught theirc hildren (*K. al-Ḥayawān*, index); no doubt he is here alluding to the *Kāmasūtra*, of which, however, no Arabic translation has survived. Other and later works also appear to have been inspired by the Indian tradition, in particular the *K. al-Alfiyya* which the *Fihrist* quotes, while Ḥādjdjī Khalīfa (see index) says that it was written by a certain al-Ḥakīm al-Azraḳ for the master of Nīsābūr, Tughān Shāh (569-81/1174-85), and embellished with suggestive illustrations. In its development, *adab* literature soon spread to sexual questions also, and two authors of the 3rd/9th century seem to have specialized in this type of writing. The first, Abu 'l-ʿAnbas al-Ṣaymarī (d. 275/888 [see AL-ṢAYMARĪ]), who had, however, been a *ḳāḍī* and to whom are attributed books on astrology still preserved in mss., is the author of some forty works which include one treatise on onanism (*K. al-Khaḍkhaḍa fī djald ʿUmayra*) and one on sapphism (*K. al-Saḥḥāḳāt wa 'l-baghghāʾīn*). The second is a certain Muḥammad b. Ḥassān al-Namalī to whom the *Fihrist* (217) devotes a passage, reproduced in full by Yāḳūt (*Udabāʾ*, xviii, 119), and entirely taken up with the enumeration of titles relating to sexual questions, in particular a large work *K. Bardjān wa-ḥubāḥib* in which the author makes a special study of the best ways to fascinate women. The *Fihrist* (436) lists the titles of 12 works "on the Persian, Indian, Byzantine and Arab *bāh*", none of which appear to have survived, but it is probable that some of them were serious in purpose: a study of the harmony between men and women in relation to their physical characters, female physiology, the mystery of generation, sexual medicine and hygiene, etc.

Subsequently, the literature that can be described as erotologic *adab* developed quite considerably; to modern eyes it may appear obscene in character, though it was not so regarded by its readers, since whole chapters characteristically combine verses from the Ḳurʾān and *ḥadīth*s of the Prophet with obscene anecdotes or poems, while others on the contrary are merely inspired by the wish to popularize certain notions about medicine and hygiene. Ṣ. al-Munadjdjid (*Ḥayāt djinsiyya*, 107 ff.) reproduces a list of the contents of several of these works which are mostly unpublished; we will name them briefly, noting the characteristics of the authors to whom several are, rightly or wrongly, attributed: *Djawāmiʿ al-ladhdha* of Abu 'l-Ḥasan ʿAlī b. Naṣr al-Kātib who took his documentation from earlier texts, now lost, particularly the *K. Bardjān wa-ḥubāḥib* referred to above; in character it is at once lexicographical, juridical, medical, psychological and magical, and deals especially with aphrodisiacs. —*Nuzhat al-aṣḥāb fī muʿāsharat al-aḥbāb* of the doctor al-Samawʾal b. Yaḥyā al-Maghribī al-Isrāʾīlī (d. 570/1174, see Brockelmann, I, 892), composed for the Artuḳid ʿImād al-dīn Abū Bakr; it is an *adab* work of somewhat composite nature, medical ideas appearings side by side with advice on buying slaves or behaviour in society. *Nuzhat al-albāb fī-mā lā yūdjad fī kitāb* of Aḥmad b. Yūsuf al-Tīfāshī (d. 651/1253 [see AL-TĪDJĀNĪ]) is mainly devoted to prostitution and sexual anomalies.—*Kitāb al-Bāhiyya wa 'l-tarākīb al-sulṭāniyya* of Naṣīr al-Dīn Ṭūsī (d. 672/1274 [see ṬŪSĪ]), a medical work with some chapters on sexuality.—*Nuzhat al-nufūs wa-daftar al-ʿilm wa-rawḍat al-ʿarūs*, an anonymous *urdjūza* of 10,000 lines of verse on the virtues of marriage, the terminology of the subject, aphrodisiacs, physiognomy and its use in love.—*Tuḥfat al-ʿarūs wa-rawḍat al-nufūs* of Muḥammad b. Aḥmad al Tidjānī (d. after 709/1309 [see AL-TĪDJĀNĪ]), which contains above all the canon of female beauty; this very popular work was printed at Cairo in 1301.—*Rudjūʿ al-shaykh ilā ṣibāh fi 'l-ḳuwwa ʿalā 'l-bāh*, attributed to Ibn Kemāl Pasha (d. 941/1535 [see KEMĀL-PASHAZĀDE]), a compilation of earlier works, medical and hygienic in character but at the same time markedly erotic; this work was printed several times at Cairo and Bombay, and enjoyed great popularity. To this list must be added *al-Rawḍ al-ʿāṭir fī nuzhat al-khāṭir*, composed ca. 813/1910 by Muḥammad al-Nafzāwī on the request of a minister of the Ḥafṣid Abū Fāris, and which offers "the advantage of informing us of the ideas then current, at certain levels, on the subject of women and love" (R. Brunschvig, *Ḥafṣides*, ii, 372-3); this has been the object of numerous editions and a Fr. trans. (Algiers 1876, Paris 1904, 1912).

Systematic search through catalogues of manuscripts would certainly provide a richer harvest, but the particulars given above should prove sufficient.

Bibliography: In the text. Two fundamental studies have been devoted to the subject discussed in this article; the first, by G.-H. Bousquet, *La morale de l'Islam et son éthique sexuelle*, Paris 1953, is the work of a jurist and sociologist who does not neglect practical reality; the second, by Ṣalāḥ al-Dīn al-Munadjdjid, *al-Ḥayāt al-djinsiyya ʿind al ʿArab*, Beirut 1958, is an excellent exposé based essentially on literary sources; another work by the same author, *Djamāl al-marʾa ʿind al-ʿArab*, Beirut 1957, is also rewarding. Since then two works have appeared but have remained unavailable to me: M. ʿAbd al-Wāḥid, *al-Islām wa'l-mushkila al-djinsiyya*, Cairo 1380/1961, and Y. el-Masri, *Le drame sexuel de la femme dans l'Orient arabe*, 1962. (CH. PELLAT)

DJIRDJA [see GIRGA].

DJIRDJENT (in Arabic *Dj.r.dj.n.t* and *K.r.k.nt.*; we know of a *nisba* of Kirkintī, borne by a mystic of Sicilian origin, in the 4th/10th century), Agrigentum. Far removed from its ancient splendour, the town fell into the hands of the Arabs in 214/829 and was destroyed, or more probably dismantled, in the following year for fear that the Byzantines would return. It rose again, however, under Arab rule, and was frequently involved in hostilities with Palermo, which resulted in the bloody struggles of the first half of the 4th/10th century: in the years 325-9/937-41 in particular the people of Agrigentum rose against the Fāṭimid authorities, whose representative in Sicily was the governor Sālim b. Rāshid until he was succeeded by the general Khalīl b. Isḥāḳ, sent by the caliph of of Mahdiyya, al-Ḳāʾim. The general reduced Djirdjent to a state of obedience to the Fāṭimids and carried off several notables as prisoners to Africa; he had them drowned during the crossing by sinking the ship in which they were travelling. Djirdjent then came under the rule of the Kalbid *amīr*s of Sicily, and when in about 431/1040 their power collapsed, it was taken into the territories of the *amīr* of Castrogiovanni Ibn al-Ḥawwās who had a palace at Djirdjent. In the general anarchy which preceded the arrival of the Normans, the town was occupied first by the Zīrid prince Ayyūb b. Tamīm, and then by a Ḥammūdid *sharīf* from Spain. The Normans under Roger captured the town from the *sharīf* on 25 July 1087, and thereafter it formed part of the Norman state of Sicily. Al-Idrīsī speaks of Djirdjent as a flourishing town with very rich markets, beautiful buildings and imposing ancient remains (this certainly refers to the Greek temples). Today nothing survives from the Muslim period apart from the name "Porta Bibirria" (Bāb al-Riyāḥ, Gate of the Winds) which is still current. The Biblioteca Lucchesiana there possesses a few dozen Arabic manuscripts.

Bibliography: M. Amari, *Storia dei Musulmani di Sicilia* and *Biblioteca Arabo-Sicula*, index; Idrīsī, *L'Italia nel libro del re Ruggero*, ed. Amari and Schiaparelli, Rome 1883, 31-2 in the text, 36 in the trans. (F. GABRIELI)

DJIRDJĪ ZAYDĀN [see ZAYDĀN].

DJIRDJĪS, St. George. Islam honours this Christian martyr as a symbol of resurrection and renovation; his festival marks the return of spring.

The legend of St. George had become syncretic long before the days of Islam, for we can recognize in St. George overthrowing the dragon a continuation of Bellerophon slaying the Chimaera. Bellerophon himself was symbolic of the Sun scattering the darkness, or of spring driving away the mists and fogs of winter.

According to Muslim legend, Djirdjīs lived in Palestine in the time of the disciples, and was martyred at Mosul under the ruler Dādān—presumably Diocletian; during his execution the saint died and was resurrected three times. The legend is found in a considerably developed form in the Persian version of Ṭabarī and always with the same motif: it is simply a series of deaths and resurrections. The saint makes the dead rise from the tombs; he makes trees sprout and pillars bear flowers; in one of his martyrdoms, the sky becomes dark and the sun only appears again after he has returned to life.

In the end St. George converts the wife of the monarch persecuting him; she is put to death; the saint then begs God to allow him to die, and his prayer is granted.

In the town of Mosul a *mashhad* of Nabī Djirdjīs is still known, already noticed in the 6th/12th century by al-Harawī (*K. al-Ziyārāt*, ed. Sourdel-Thomine, Damascus 1953, 69; trans. Damascus 1957, 154), and which corresponds to a former Chaldaean church (F. Sarre and E. Herzfeld, *Archaeologische Reise im Euphrat und Tigris Gebiet*, Berlin 1911-22, ii, 236-8; A. Sioufi, *Les antiquités et monuments de Mossoul*, Mosul 1940, 17-23; J. M. Fiey, *Mossoul chrétienne*, Beirut 1959, 118-20).

In Islam St. George is frequently confused with the prophets Khiḍr and Elias [see KHIḌR and KHIḌRELLEZ].

Bibliography: Ṭabarī, index; Ṭabarī, *Chronicle*, tr. Zotenberg, Paris 1869, ii, 54-66; Ibn Ḳutayba, *Maʿārif*, ed. ʿUkāsha, index; Thaʿlabī, *Ḳiṣaṣ al-anbiyā*, Cairo 1282, 466 ff.; Sāmī, *Ḳāmūs al-aʿlām*, iii, 1778. (B. CARRA DE VAUX *)

DJIRM [see DJISM].

DJĪRUFT, a fertile, high lying district of Kirmān with a city of the same name south-west of Bam and separated from it by the Bāridjān Mountains. There is no record of the city in pre-Islamic times and the first mention of the city is when Djīruft was captured by Mudjāshiʿ b. Masʿūd in 35/655 (al-Balādhurī, *Futūḥ*, 391). Thereafter the city is mentioned many times, especially in the Arabic geographies.

The Khāridjites were active in Djīruft but nothing is known of the history of the city. The geographer al-Muḳaddasī (461) praises the district highly in describing the fertility of its land and its beauty. The Ṣaffārid Yaʿḳūb and his brother ʿAmr are said to have embellished Djīruft with buildings (Sykes, ii, 16). The city suffered much from the anarchy of the Mongol and post-Ilkhānid periods but it continued to exist in the Tīmūrid period after which Djīruft disappears from the sources, although the district or *shahristān* retains the name to the present day.

The site of the old city of Djīruft is unknown but it must be near the present town of Sabzāwārān, and some nearby ruins (Le Strange, 314) may be those of the old city.

Bibliography: Le Strange, 314; Schwarz, *Iran*, iii, 240; P. Sykes, *A history of Persia*, London 1930, ii, 16. (R. N. FRYE)

DJISM (A.), body. In philosophical language the body (σῶμα) is distinguished from the incorporeal (ἀσώματον), God, spirit, soul, etc. In so far as speculation among the Muslims was influenced by Neo-Platonism two features were emphasized: 1. the incorporeal is in its nature simple and indivisible, the body on the other hand is composite and divisible; 2. the incorporeal is in spite of its negative character the original, the causing principle, while the body is a product of the incorporeal.

The more or less naive anthropomorphism of early Islam, *i.e.*, the conception of God after the analogy of the human form, is not to be considered here. On it one may consult I. Goldziher, *Vorlesungen über den Islām*, 1910, 107 f., 120 f., and A. J. Wensinck, *The Muslim Creed*, 1932, 66 f. But from the usual *tadjsīm* or *tashbīh* we must distinguish the teaching of certain philosophers who called God a body; this is to some extent a question of terminology. According to al-Ashʿarī (*Maḳālāt*, ed. Ritter, i, 31 f., 44 f., 59 f., 207 f., ii, 301 f.), the Shīʿī theologian Hishām b. al-Ḥakam (first half of the 3rd/9th century) was the most important champion of the view that God is a body. He would not however (cf. 208 and 304) compare Him with worldly bodies but only describe Him in an allegorical sense as an existing being, existing through Himself. His description of God (p. 207) is thus to be interpreted: God is in a space which is above space; the dimensions of His body are such that His breadth is not distinguished from His depth and His colour is similar to His taste and smell; He is a streaming light, a pure metal shedding light on all sides like a round pearl. If we add that the qualities of bodies are also called bodies by Hishām and others, then we must conclude with S. Horovitz (*Über den Einfluss der griechischen Philosophie*, 1919, 38 f.) that here Stoic terminology is present but with foreign additions. The doctrine that God is light etc. is not a Stoic theory.

After a long fight among the theological schools the incorporeality of God was recognized by Islam. Only the doctrine of the spirituality of the soul of man, held by many theologians, notably Ghazālī, did not find general recognition [cf. NAFS]. Ibn Ḥazm, for example (*Kitāb al-Faṣl*, 80 ff.), calls the individual *nafs* a *djism*, because it is distinguished from the souls of other individuals, because it has knowledge about much that another does not know, and so on.

A remarkable doctrine about the body had already appeared before Ashʿarī and then developed in his school, namely a theological atomism. Regarded from the philosophical side, the atomists and their opponents have at least one hypothesis in common: the body is composed of the incorporeal. But how? According to the view of the atomist theologians, the body is composed of the smallest particles (atoms) which cannot be further subdivided, incorporeal themselves and not perceptible. They then fall out over the question how many atoms are required to make a body, in a way which reminds one of the old problem of how many grains of corn make a heap. A survey of this speculative atomism, the origins of which have not yet been fully explained, is given by D. B. Macdonald, *Continuous re-creation and atomic time in Muslim scholastic theology* (in *Isis*, no. 30, ix/2, 1927, 326 ff.).

The philosophers, on the other hand, say with Aristotle and his school that the body is composed of matter and form (*hayūlā* or *mādda* and *ṣūra*). Both are in themselves incorporeal, indivisible and imperceptible, but their combination, the body, is divisible because the body is a continuous magnitude. This is really a philosophically diluted cosmogonic conception, the birth of the body from a male active principle (form) and a female receptive principle (matter). For Aristotle, who taught the eternity of a world order coming from God, the idea had hardly any importance; still less had it for the Stoics, who taught that matter and form are in reality eternally combined and can only be separated in imagination (Arab. *fi 'l-dhihn, fi 'l-wahm*). But for the Neo-Platonists it became a gigantic problem, to derive the material, corporeal world from the incorporeal; it became still more difficult for the Muslim philosophers to effect a reconciliation with the absolute doctrine of creation.

Aristotle gives the following definition (cf. *De coelo*, i, I, 268ª, 7 f., and *Metaph.*, v, 13, 1020ª, 7): a body is that which has three dimensions (dimension = διάστασις, διάστημα, Arab *buʿd, imtidād*) and is a continuous, therefore always divisible, quantity (ποσὸν συνεχές, *kam muttaṣil*).

A wordy dispute arose over this; the question was which is the most essential, the dimension or the magnitude, and how the magnitude is to be conceived (as incorporeal form). When the Neo-Platonists wish to "explain" something they make an abstract out of the concrete: ποσόν becomes ποσότης, *kam* becomes *kamiyya*, magnitude becomes quantity and *djism djismiyya* (corporeality). The following answer is then given to the question how a body comes into being: through corporeality (= corporeal idea of form) being assumed by matter (also incorporeal by definition). When the absolute body or second matter is thus brought into existence, the dimensions and other qualities of the concrete bodies come into existence; the gap between in corporeal and corporeal is thus bridged.

As regards matter, this doctrine comes from the Enneads (ii, 4); the formulation, that corporeality is the first form of the body (σωματικὸν εἶδος) is found in the Neo-Platonist expositor Simplicius (4th century) in his commentary on Aristotle's Physics (ed. Diels, 227 ff.). Hence in Arabic the expression *ṣūra djismiyya* and in Latin *forma corporeitatis*; because the body according to Aristotle is one of the five continuous magnitudes (like line, surface, space and time) one talks of continuity (*ittiṣāl*) as the form of the body.

The Ikhwān al-Ṣafā, Ibn Sīnā and al-Ghazālī adopted these subtleties, although in different proportions. The Ikhwān al-Ṣafā place corporeality or absolute body (*djism muṭlaḳ*) last in the series of emanations [cf. FAYḌ].

Ibn Sīnā, who also distinguishes two matters, although he knows that *mādda* is the translation of the Greek ὕλη (*hayūlā*) and he regularly uses it synonymously, regards as the first form of existence of the body continuous quantity, in which the power is according to the dimensions, in other words, the dimensions are added like attributes or accidents (cf. *ḥudūd* in *Tisʿ Rasāʾil*, 58, 60 [thereon al-Ghazālī, *Miʿyār al-ʿilm*, 180]; *Ishārat*, ed. Forget, 90 ff.).

Ibn Rushd disputes (*Metaphysics*, Cairo ed., 37 ff.), as so often, the teachings of his predecessor without quite clearing up the problem.

When the Neo-Platonizing philosophers and theologians talk of the body, it should always be asked what they mean by it: the divine original (= idea of the body) or its purest, unalterable copies in the heavenly spheres and constellations, or lastly the sublunar elementary bodies with their qualities, changes and combinations. This is the first step to comprehension, so far as this is possible.

The distinction between the heavenly bodies and earthly bodies influenced by them was very important for the natural philosophy of the period. The latter were composed of the four relatively simple bodies (elements, in Aristotle ἁπλᾶ σώματα: Arab. *al-basāʾiṭ*). In the higher sense the heavenly bodies were simple; to describe them the term *djirm* (plur. *adjrām*) was often used, which otherwise is synonymous with *djism*. It is to be noted that the *Theology of Aristotle* (ed. Dieterici, 32, 40 f.) understands by

Djirmiyyūn those philosophers who as followers of Pythagoras teach that the soul of man is the harmony of its body (*iʾtilāf, ittifāḳ, ittiḥād*). This was a theory particularly common among physicians.

Generally popular also was the distinction taken from Aristotle between the physical and the mathematical body (*dj. ṭabīʿī* and *dj. taʿlīmī* = *dj. al-handasa*). The geometricians are said to regard dimensions as ideal figures, abstracted from the many qualities possessed by natural bodies, with which the physicists deal.

Djirm, badan and *djasad* are used as synonyms of *djism*; the two last are usually applied to the human body, *badan* often only to the torso. While *badan* is also used for the bodies of animals, *djasad* is rather reserved for the bodies of higher beings (angels etc.). *Djamād* is an inorganic body, but *adjsād* is used particularly for minerals. It may also be mentioned that *haykal* (plur. *hayākil*) means with the gnostics and mystics the physical word as whole as well as the planets, because the world-soul and the spirits of the stars dwell in them like the soul of man in its body (cf. AL-ṢĀBIʾA; Nicholson, *Studies in Islamic mysticism*, 110; cf. *Theology of Aristotle*, 167).

Bibliography: P. Duhem, *Le système du Monde*, iv, 541 ff.; S. v. d. Bergh, *Die Epitome des Averroes*, Leiden 1924, 63 ff.; H. A. Wolfson, *Crescas' critique of Aristotle*, 278 ff.; S. Pines, *Beiträge zur islamischen Atomenlehre*, Berlin 1936, 4; L. Gauthier, *Ibn Rochd, Averroès*, Paris 1948, 71.

See also ʿĀLAM and MĀDDA. (TJ. DE BOER*)

DJISR, pl. *djusūr* (Ar., cf. Fränkel, *Aram. Fremdwörter im Arabischen*, 285), "bridge", is more particularly, though by no means exclusively, a bridge of boats in opposition to *ḳanṭara* [*q.v.*], an arched bridge of stone.

An incident in the history of the conquest of Babylonia has become celebrated among the Arab historians as *yawm al-djisr* "the day of [the fight at] the bridge": in 13/634 Abū ʿUbayd al-Thaḳafī was defeated and slain in battle against the Persians at a bridge across the Euphrates near Ḥīra; cf. Wellhausen, *Skizzen und Vorarbeiten*, vi, 68 ff., 73; Caetani, iii, 145 ff. (ED.)

DJISR BANĀT YAʿḲŪB, the "bridge of the daughters of Jacob", name of a bridge over the Upper Jordan, above the sea of Galilee and to the south of the former marshy depression of the lake of al-Ḥūla, now dry. At this point, which was that of an old ford known at the time of the Crusades under the name of the "ford of Yaʿḳūb" (*Vadum Jacob* of William of Tyre) or "ford of lamentations" (*makhādat al-aḥzān* of Ibn al-Athīr and Yāḳūt), the *Via maris* from Damascus to Ṣafad and ʿAkkā crossed the river, following a trade route which was especially frequented in Mamlūk times and which coincided also with a *barīd* route. From this time dates the improvement of the crossing by the erection of a bridge of basalt of three arches, traces of which are still visible, and the construction nearby of a caravanserai, before 848/1444, by a Damascene merchant, who marked along with his foundations the route from Syria to Egypt (al-Nuʿaymī, *al-Dāris*, ed. Dj. al-Ḥasanī, ii, Damascus 1951, 290; cf. H. Sauvaire, in *JA*, 1895, ii, 262). Travellers and geographers, oriental and western alike, only rarely omit mention of this stage, sometimes under the designation, also frequent, of Djisr Yaʿḳūb or *Pons Jacob*.

The strategic importance of this crossing, again emphasized in 1799 when it marked the extreme point of the advance of French troops, was especially marked in the 6th/12th century when Franks and Muslims contested it furiously: Baldwin III was defeated here by Nūr al-Dīn in 552/1157; Baldwin IV built here in 573/1178 a fortress entrusted to the Templars, the Castellet of the ford of Jacob, whose ruins still remain on a knoll on the west bank 500 m. south of the bridge; this stronghold was taken and destroyed by Ṣalāḥ al-Dīn a year later, in 575/1179.

The favour enjoyed by the Biblical reminiscences centred on this locality even in the middle ages, and which seem to have resulted from a transfer to the Jordan of the tradition of Jacob's crossing of the Jabbok (now Nahr al-Zarḳā), according to *Genesis*, xxxii, 22, is attested by the toponymy of the region and by the mentions in Arabic authors of the 6th/12th century of a *mashhad Yaʿḳūbī*, then a place of pilgrimage, and of a "castle of Jacob" (*ḳaṣr Yaʿḳūb*) or "house of lamentations" (*bayt al-aḥzān*); the latter name refers to the lamentations of Jacob for the death of his son Joseph (recalled not far from there, at the place called Djubb Yūsuf or Khān Djubb Yūsuf, by the pit in which he is said to have been cast by his brothers). At the present day there further exists the "grotto of the daughters of Jacob" (*maghārat banāt Yaʿḳūb*), a sanctuary whose name explains that of the bridge, and whose history is fixed by an inscription of the 9th/15th century (L. A. Mayer, *Satura epigraphica arabica*, in *QDAP*, ii (1932), 127-31).

Bibliography: R. Dussaud, *Topographie historique de la Syrie*, Paris 1927, 314; F. M. Abel, *Géographie de la Palestine*, Paris 1933-8, i, 162, 480, 486; ii, 226; Le Strange, *Palestine*, 53; A. S. Marmardji, *Textes géographiques*, Paris 1951, 7; M. Gaudefroy-Demombynes, *La Syrie à l'époque des Mamelouks*, Paris 1923, 246; R. Hartmann, *Die Strasse von Damaskus nach Kairo*, in *ZDMG*, lxiv, 694-700; William of Tyre, xxi, 26; Ibn al-Athīr, xi, 301; *RHC Or.*, i, 636; iv, 194, 203 ff.; Harawī, *K. al-ziyārāt*, ed. Sourdel-Thomine, Damascus 1953, 20 (Fr. tr. idem, Damascus 1957, 51 and note); Yāḳūt, i, 775; Dimashḳī, ed. Mehren, 107; R. Grousset, *Hist. des Croisades*, Paris 1934-6, index s.v. *Jisr Banât Yaqūb* and *Gué de Jacob*). (J. SOURDEL-THOMINE)

DJISR AL-ḤADĪD, "iron bridge", name of a bridge over the Orontes in the lower part of its course, at the point where the river, emerging from the valleys of the calcareous plateau and widening towards the depression of al-ʿAmḳ [*q.v.*], turns sharply westwards without being lost in that marshy depression whose waters it partly drains to the sea. The fame of this toponym, frequently mentioned in mediaeval documents but of obscure origin (perhaps local legend), is explained by the strategic and commercial importance of this stage, through which, in antiquity and in the middle ages, has always passed the route joining Antioch to Chalcis (Ḳinnasrīn) and then Aleppo (a route frequently taken, at the time of Antioch's prosperity, by the caravan traffic descending from the col of Baylān [*q.v.*]). The bridge itself, defended by strong towers and fortified on various occasions (notably in 1161 by Baldwin IV), is known to have played a part of prime importance in the wars between Arabs and Byzantines as early as the 4th/10th century, later in the history of the principality of Antioch after its storm by the Franks of the first crusade. The present bridge retains no trace of the building of this period. In the neighbourhood is a raised site which doubtless marks the position of the ancient Gephyra.

Bibliography: J. Weulersse, *L'Oronte*, Tours 1940, *passim*; R. Dussaud, *Topographie historique de la Syrie*, Paris 1927, 170, 171-2, 434; M. van Berchem and E. Fatio, *Voyage en Syrie*, Cairo 1913-5, 238-9; Cl. Cahen, *La Syrie du nord*, Paris 1940, part. 134 and index; Abu 'l-Fidā', *Taḳwīm*, 49; Le Strange, *Palestine*, 60; M. Gaudefroy-Demombynes, *La Syrie à l'époque des Mamelouks*, Paris 1923, 17. (J. Sourdel-Thomine)

DJISR AL-SHUGHR or Djisr al-Shughūr, the modern name of a place in north Syria, the site of a bridge over the Orontes which has always been an important centre of communications in an area that is mountainous and difficult to traverse. It was in fact at this spot that the most direct route from the Syrian coast to the steppes in the interior and the Euphrates, passing over the Djabal Nuṣayri and the Limestone Massif, crossed the line of communications that ran north-south and followed the Orontes between Apamea/Ḳalʿat al-Muḍīḳ and Antioch/Antāḳiya. Of these two routes the second is today abandoned, its traffic having gradually declined during the Middle Ages, while swamps spread over the once fertile and cultivated plain of al-Ghāb [*q.v.*]. But the valley of the Nahr al-Kabīr and the depression of al-Rūdj are still partly followed by the modern road from al-Lādhikiya to Ḥalab, crossing the Orontes by this bridge which has been so often rebuilt and altered, and across which the old trade route used to run, linking the coastal town of Laodicaea with Chalcis/Ḳinnasrīn and Berea/Ḥalab, in one direction, and with al-Bāra [*q.v.*] and Arra/Maʿarrat al-Nuʿmān in the other.

There have long been attempts to identify this spot with the Seleucia ad Belum of Ptolemy, or Niaccuba (corruption of Seleucobelus) of the *Itinerary of Antoninus*, which in ancient times commanded one of the routes leading from the Limestone Massif. But the identification of this bridge with the one at Kashfahān, so often mentioned in the fighting at the time of the Crusades, has given rise to much discussion which has served to emphasize the utter lack of precision in the descriptions given by Arab authors, and also the modern aspect of the present village. Only a caravanserai and a mosque of the Ottoman period testify to the fact that it was once a halting-place for pilgrims of the ḥadjdj coming from Anatolia and crossing Syria by the ancient road along the Orontes valley, and it is difficult to place at a date earlier than the Mamlūk period (defaced inscription) the bridge with its assortment of materials and the sharp elbow projecting upstream. There seems however to be a convincing case, and on this point we follow R. Dussaud in his refutation of Max van Berchem's suggestion, for distinguishing the site of the cross-roads, the Kashfahān of the Crusades, and Shughr in the *Voyage* of the Mamlūk sultan Ḳāytbāy, from the site of the twin castles of al-Shughr and Baḳās which stood in the same valley, but 6 km. to the north-west, and constituted one of the eastern defences of the Frankish principality of Antioch.

It is this fortress, whose ruins still crown a ridge of rock of which the central part has collapsed (hence the need to build two separate fortications) and dominate the village of Shughr al-Ḳadīm amidst its gardens, which was conquered by Ṣalāḥ al-Dīn in the course of the celebrated campaign of 584/1188, during which he first halted at Tall Kashfahān. Later, this fortress formed part of the domains of the Ayyūbid al-Malik al-Ẓāhir Ghāzī and, after being captured by the Mongols, it became during the Mamlūk period the centre of a military district ranking as one of the *niyāba*s of the province of Aleppo. Its decline, from the time when it lost all its strategic importance, finally explains the subsequent rise of the modern Djisr al-Shughūr and the return of a settled population to the neighbourhood of the bridge where, in the time of Abu 'l-Fidā', there had only been a weekly market (crowded, however), and where caravanserais for foreign merchants were then built (the sovereign of Aleppo promised to put up a *fondaco* for the Venetians).

Bibliography: J. Weulersse, *L'Oronte*, Tours 1940, *passim*; R. Dussaud, *Topographie historique de la Syrie*, Paris 1927, 155-64, 180; G. Tchalenko, *Villages antiques de la Syrie du nord*, Paris 1953-8, index s.v. *Ğisr al-Šuğūr*; M. van Berchem and E. Fatio, *Voyage en Syrie*, Cairo 1913-5, 251-64; Cl. Cahen, *La Syrie du Nord*, Paris 1940, index under *Djisr ach-Choughour*, *Tell Kachfahān* and *Choughr-Bakas*; Le Strange, 80, 537, 543; M. Gaudefroy-Demombynes, *La Syrie à l'époque des Mamelouks*, Paris 1923, 89, 216; Yāḳūt, i, 704, 869; iii, 303; Abu 'l-Fidā', *Taḳwīm*, 261; Ibn Baṭṭūṭa, i, 165; J. Sauvaget, *Les caravansérails syriens du hadjdj de Constantinople*, in *Ars Islamica*, iv (1937), 108-9; W. Heyd, *Histoire du commerce du Levant*, Amsterdam 1959, i, 377.

(J. Sourdel-Thomine)

DJIṢṢ (A.), plaster.—Muslim builders have generally shown themselves unanxious to use carefully chosen and worked materials in their constructions. Frequently walls, apparently hurriedly built, are composed of rubble (undressed stones) or even of pisé (compacted earth and lime) or mud-brick. This mediocre skeleton, however, is clad by facings which disguise its poverty and give it the illusion of richness. Just as the Byzantine builders decorated church sanctuaries and rooms in princely dwellings with marble plaques and mocaics with a gold ground, those of Persia, Egypt, or the Maghrib have covered the façades and interiors of their mosques and palaces with incised fayence or with sculptured and coloured plasters, and the windows themselves are adorned with perforated plaster *claustra*, their voids filled with coloured panes.

Plaster and stucco (made of a mixture of lime and marble or powdered eggshell, or else of pure gypsum and dissolved glue) are both of especial interest as the facings of exteriors and interiors. The plaster is carefully smoothed and decorated with paint, or, when it has been applied more or less thickly on the wall, sculptured by an iron tool whence the name of *naḳsh ḥadīda* given in North Africa to work of this genre. In his book *L'Alhambra de Grenade*, 5, Henri Saladin has provided the following technical account [here translated]: 'On a wall coated with plaster the craftsman would trace the intended design with a dry-point; then, with the help of chisels and burins, he would cut in the fresh plaster the ornaments which he had outlined. This prodecure necessitated the use of a slow setting plaster, which could be obtained by the addition of gum or salt to the plaster, as the Tunisian craftsman do today. Later this method was replaced by moulding, but this gives less delicacy. Mouldings of the Arab period may still be seen at the Alhambra. An examination of the ornamentation of the convent at S. Francisco, an old Arab palace . . . reveals the manner in which plaster was retained against wooden surfaces: at one place where the plaster has fallen the wooden backing can be seen, pierced by nails joined one to another by a network of string'. One should add that besides the sculpture obtained by cutting away the field between the decorative elements one does also find moulded or impressed reliefs—particularly border mountings—level with and adhering to the groundwork, which has been cut back for this purpose.

The important rôle played by decoration of this genre in the Islamic art of the 8th/14th century, which saw the erection of the most notable parts of the Alhambra, is attested by a passage of Ibn Khaldūn, who considers it as a branch of architecture (*Muḳaddima*, ii, 321; Rosenthal, ii, 360-1): he remarks that the work is executed by iron tools (*bi mathāḳib al-ḥadīd*) in the still wet plaster. However, it goes without saying that plaster as an element of decoration is much earlier than the blossoming of Hispano-Moorish art. To what period should one assign its adoption by the Muslims, and to what influence can it be attributed?

Hellenistic art, one of the essential sources of the Muslim arabesque, was not ignorant of stucco relief, which was often delicately modelled. It must not be supposed, however, that Islam has inherited the art of the Roman or Byzantine workers in gypsum plaster, for Islamic moulded-plaster decoration is very different, both as a technique and as a style. It is apparently towards Sasanian art that the search for its origin must be directed. The Syrian castle of Ḳaṣr al-Ḥayr, founded by the Umayyad Hishām in 110/728, in the ornamentation of which Sasanian motifs preponderate, presents some panels which are indicative of this origin. A compact floral decor, wholly filling the geometrical frames which divide the panels, is treated without relief but by cutting out the plaster perpendicularly or obliquely to the surface plane. This sunken two-dimensional scupture, in which there is no projection, is already that of the Muslim works in plaster of the succeeding centuries. It flourishes in the 3rd/9th century at Sāmarrā and, mixed with Hellenistic elements, gives rise to the linear undercut decoration of the ʿAbbāsid palaces. This was transmitted, with many another fashion, from ʿIrāḳ to the Egypt of the Ṭūlūnids. From Egypt it reached North Africa, where it found a favourable soil. An extension towards the Sahara among the Khāridjites, who had taken refuge at Sedrāta near Wargla, must be mentioned. The plaster there, which mixed with sand is very durable, is used, under the name of *timshent*, for incised decorative facings, where the African Christian inheritance appears side by side with Mesopotamian reminiscences. However, it is especially in the Maghrib and in Spain that sculptured plaster attains its greatest beauty. The 6th/12th century saw the birth in Marrakesh, Fez, and Tlemcen, of facings with a floral decoration where the sculptor has given to this plastic decoration a richness of forms, a firmness yet a flexibility of composition, a vigour in relief (*e.g.*, the Almoravid domes of the *mīḍāt* at Marrakesh and of the Ḳarawiyyin of Fez, the Almohad capitals of the Kutubiyya etc.) which greatly transcend the usual frontiers of the arabesque. The rôle played by sculptured plaster in Hispano-Moorish art in the 13th and 14th centuries is well known. It was to be maintained in Spain in the *mudéjar* monuments, and to survive in the later Tunisia and Morocco, attesting less the decorative invention of the artists than their fidelity to tradition and their manual skill. (G. MARÇAIS)

DJĪTAL [see SIKKA, WAZN].

AL-**DJIWĀʾ** (also Līwā, probably derived from the local pronunciation of *dj* as *y*, resulting in al-yiwāʾ > līwā) a district of many tiny oases in the heavy sands of south-central al-Ẓafra, the large, almost completely sand-covered region extending southward from the Persian Gulf between Sabkhat Maṭṭī in the west almost to Long. 55° E. The oases nestle in the hollows and passage ways of the northernmost sand mountains of al-Baṭīn, with the greatest number lying between Lat. 23° N. and Lat. 23° 15′ N. The eastern third of the oases, which are smaller and less frequented than the others, bear to the south-east below Lat. 23° N.

The water of al-Djiwāʾ, which lies only a few feet below the surface, supports numerous small groves of date palms growing on the sheltered side of great dunes. In many places the owners live above their gardens on the dunes themselves, where there is a chance of catching a cooling breeze. The ruins of several forts are scattered throughout the district, but today the inhabitants live only in palm-thatch huts. All but a few of the oases are uninhabited except during the summer when the date groves require attention. During the rest of the year most of the owners are in the desert with their herds or along the coast of the Persian Gulf. Among the settlements usually inhabited the year round are al-Māriya, Ḳaṭūf, Shidḳ al-Kalb, al-Kayya, al-Ḳarmida, Shāh, and Tharwāniyya.

The people of al-Djiwāʾ belong, in roughly descending order of numbers, to the tribes of al-Manāṣīr, al-Mazārīʿ, al-Hawāmil, al-Maḥāriba, al-Ḳubaysāt, Āl Bū Falāḥ, al-Marar, and Āl Bū Muhayr. All but al-Manāṣīr belong to the conglomeration usually referred to as Banī Yās [*q.v.*]. Sand-dwelling tribesmen, such as members of Āl Rāshid and al-ʿAwāmir, some of whom even own a few palms, are frequent visitors. A few residents of al-Djiwāʾ own pearling boats, and every year some of the men journey north to the Persian Gulf to seek their fortunes on the pearling banks. Their number declines, however, as more find employment with the oil companies operating in various parts of Arabia.

Al-Djiwāʾ lies within the more than 70,000 sq. km. of territory in dispute between Saudi Arabia and Abū Ẓaby. During the abortive arbitration of this dispute in 1954-5 (see AL-BURAYMĪ), both sides contended that they had historical rights to sovereignty over al-Djiwāʾ and that they had exercised jurisdiction by collecting *zakāt* (Saudi Arabia on camels and Abū Ẓaby on dates) and by maintaining law and order. Abū Ẓaby claimed the traditional loyalty of all the inhabitants of al-Djiwāʾ, while Saudi Arabia maintained that the preponderance, including all of al-Manāṣīr and al-Mazārīʿ, were loyal Saudis.

Al-Djiwāʾ was unknown to the Western world until 1324/1906 when the acting British Political Resident in the Persian Gulf, P. Z. Cox, learned of its existence from a former inhabitant.

Bibliography: Admiralty, *A handbook of Arabia*, London 1916-17; R. Bagnold in *GJ*, cxvii, 1951; H. Hazard, *Saudi Arabia*, New Haven 1956; F. Hunter in *GJ*, liv, 1919; J. Lorimer, *Gazetteer of the Persian Gulf, ʾOmān, and Central Arabia*, Calcutta 1908-15 (in vol. ii see DHAFRAH); Saudi Arabia, *Memorial of the Government of Saudi Arabia* [al-Buraymī Arbitration], 1955; W. Thesiger, *Arabian Sands*, London 1959; idem, in *GJ*, cxi, cxiii, cxvi, 1948, 1949, 1950; United Kingdom, *Arbitration concerning Buraimi and the Common Frontier between Abu Dhabi and Saudi Arabia*, 1955. The only detailed material on the district in Arabic is to be found in the Arabic versions of the Saudi Arabian and United Kingdom arbitration memorials cited above. (W. E. MULLIGAN)

DJĪWAN, the ʿurf of Mullā Aḥmad b. Abī Saʿīd b. ʿUbayd Allāh b. ʿAbd al-Razzāḳ b. Maḵẖdūm Ḵẖassa-i Ḵẖudā al-Ḥanafī al-Ṣāliḥī (he claimed descent from the Prophet Ṣāliḥ) was born at Amēt̲ẖī, near Lucknow, in 1047/1637, as he was 21 (?) lunar years old in 1069/1658 when he completed his *al-Tafsīr al-Aḥmadī* (cf. *Ḥadā᾽iḳ al-Ḥanafiyya*, 436). The same source, however, states that he was 83 years of age at the time of his death in 1130/1717. Gifted with an extraordinary memory, he learnt the Ḳur᾽ān by heart at the age of seven. Studying in his early years first with Muḥammad Ṣādiḳ al-Sitarkhī, he completed his education in rational and traditional sciences at the age of sixteen with Luṭf Allāh Kōrā-Djahānābādī. Contrary to the official histories such as the *ʿĀlamgīr-nāma* and the *Ma᾽āt̲ẖir-i ʿĀlamgīrī*, all his biographers unanimously agree that he was appointed as one of his 'teachers' by Awrangzīb who greatly respected and honoured him. This must have happened between 1064/1653 and 1068/1657, the year Awrangzīb ascended the throne. Most probably the emperor, on his accession, read certain books with the youthful Mullā. Shāh ʿĀlam I, the son and successor of Awrangzīb, like his father, also held him in great esteem. The Mullā must have attained high proficiency in *fiḳh* as, at the comparatively young age of 21, he compiled his Arabic *Tafsīr* dealing with those *aḥkām s̲ẖarʿiyya* that are deducible only from the Ḳur᾽ān. After completing his education, he began to teach at his home-town. He left for Adjmēr and Dihlī in 1087/1676, where he stayed for a considerable time teaching and preaching. In 1102/1690 he left on a visit to Mecca and Medina for the first time and after a stay of five years there returned to India in 1107/1695. He then joined the imperial service and spent some six years with the armies of Awrangzīb who was then engaged in fighting against the Deccan kingdoms. In 1112/1700 he left for the second time for al-Ḥidjāz and after twice performing the *ḥadjdj* and *ziyāra* returned to Amēt̲ẖī in 1116/1704. After a short stay of two years, during which he received the Ṣūfī *k̲ẖirḳa* from the S̲ẖayk̲ẖ Yāsīn b. ʿAbd al-Razzāḳ al-Ḳādirī, he repaired to Dihlī with a large number of pupils. He was received in audience at Adjmēr by S̲ẖāh ʿĀlam I (1119-24/1707-12) who took him to Lahore. He returned to Dihlī on the death of S̲ẖāh ʿĀlam and engaged himself again in his favourite profession of teaching. He had also established a *madrasa* in his home-town Amēt̲ẖī. A detailed account of this institution appears in the Urdū work *Ta᾽rīk̲ẖ ḳasaba-i Amēt̲ẖī* by K̲ẖādim Ḥusayn (ed.? date ?). He died in his *zāwiya* in the Djāmiʿ masdjid of Dihlī in 1130/1717 but his dead body was later disinterred and taken to his home-town for final burial.

He is the author of: (i) *al-Tafsīrāt al-Aḥmadiyya fī bayān al-āyāt al-s̲ẖarʿiyya*, compiled in five years 1064-9/1653-8 while he was still a student (ed. Calcutta, 1263 A.H.); (ii) *Nūr al-anwār*, a commentary on al-Nasafī's *Manār al-anwār* on the principles of jurisprudence, written at the request of certain students of Medina in a short period of two months; also frequently printed; (iii) *al-Sawāniḥ*, on the lines of Djāmī's [*q.v.*] *al-Lawā᾽iḥ* written in the Ḥidjāz during his second visit in 1112/1700;

(iv) *Manāḳib al-awliyā᾽*, biographies of saints and *mas̲ẖāyik̲ẖ* which he compiled in his old age at his home-town. The work contains a supplement by his son ʿAbd al-Ḳādir and a detailed autobiographical note (for an extract see *Nuzhat al-k̲ẖawāṭir*, vi, 21); (v) *Ādāb-i Aḥmadī*, on ṣūfism and mystic stations, compiled in his younger days.

Bibliography: Āzād Bilgrāmī, *Subḥat al-mardjān*, Bombay 1303/1885, 79; idem, *Ma᾽āt̲ẖir al-kirām*, Agra 1328/1910, 216-7; Raḥmān ʿAlī, *Tad̲ẖkira-i ʿulamā᾽-i Hind²*, Cawnpore 1914, 45; Faḳīr Muḥammad, *Ḥadā᾽iḳ al-Ḥanafiyya³*, Lucknow 1324/1906, 436; Ṣiddīḳ Ḥasan K̲ẖān, *Abdjad al-ʿulūm*, Bhopāl 1295 A.H., 907; ʿAbd al-Ḥayy Lakhnawī, *Nuzhat al-k̲ẖawāṭir*, Ḥaydarābād 1376/1957, vi, 19-21 (contains the most detailed and authentic notice); ʿAbd al-Awwal Djawnpūrī, *Mufīd al-Muftī*, 113; S̲ẖāh Nawāz K̲ẖān, *Ma᾽āt̲ẖir al-umarā᾽*, Bibl. Ind., iii, 794; M. G. Zubaid Ahmad, *Contribution of India to Arabic literature*, Allāhābād 1946, index; Brockelmann, S II 264, 612; K̲ẖādim Ḥusayn, *Ta᾽rīk̲ẖ ḳasaba-i Amēt̲ẖī*, n.p. n.d.; Sarkis, *Muʿdjam al-maṭbūʿāt al-ʿArabiyya*, ii, col. 1164-5; Muḥammad b. Muʿtamad K̲ẖān, *Ta᾽rīk̲ẖ-i Muḥammadī* (Ethé 2834), contains a short but useful notice in Arabic; K̲ẖādim Ḥusayn, *Ṣubḥ-i Bahār* (MS. in Urdū).
(A. S. BAZMEE ANSARI)

DJIWĀR, "protection" and "neighbourhood", noun of action of the 3rd form to which only the second meaning corresponds, as in the grammatical term *djarr al-djiwār* "attraction of the indirect case" (syn. *djarr al-mudjāwara*, cf. Wright, *Gr. Ar. Lang.³*, 1955, ii, 234 B). *Djiwār* "protection" corresponds to the 4th form *adjāra*, and particularly to the substantive *djār* "one protected, client" coinciding with the Hebrew *gēr* "one protected by the clan or community". Nöldeke in his study of the *Aḍḍād* noted the identity of the institution "in the same juridical sense" (im wesentlich demselben rechtlichen Sinne, *Neue Beiträge zur sem. Sprachw.*, Strasbourg 1910, 38). The religious suggestion of "protection of a holy place", so frequent in Arabic, strangely recurs in the Hebrew *gēr* and especially in the Phoenician equivalent which, in numerous proper names, denotes one protected by a sanctuary or divinity, as well as in a text of Ras S̲ẖamra kindly brought to our attention by M. Ch. Virolleau, the eminent pioneer in this field of study: "gr already figures in the 14th century B.C. in a poem containing the expression *gr bt il* which I translated in 1936, in my *Légende de Danel*, 165, as 'l'hôte de la maison de Dieu' ... Cyrus H. Gordon, *Ugar. Manual glossary* no. 357, rendered it by 'a person taking asylum in a temple' ". The evident relationship of the term to the religious vocabulary is further emphasized by the later evolution of the Hebrew *gēr* in the well-known sense of "converted to Judaism". Nöldeke's remark (*loc. cit.*) giving precedence to the sense of "one protected" presupposes, in accordance with a well-known law, a term of socio-religious significance, owing its survival to the importance of the institution in nomadic customary law. Despite the Arab lexicographers, and also Gesenius, who wish to derive from a primitive meaning "to deviate", the meaning "to stay in the house of a host", it may be a question of the almost universal semantic link between "foreigner, enemy" (cf. Latin *hostis*) and "guest, client", for the root *gwr* in both languages also has the sense of hostility, injustice. Gesenius compares the Akkadian *gēru*, but it is rather *gâr*, "enemy", which would agree with the suggested etymology.

Bibliography: Gesenius-Buhl, *Hebr. aram. Hdwörterbuch*, 16 ed. Leipzig 1915, 134-5; also quotes an Egyptian proper noun and Coptic *ğoile*, "foreigner", Aramaic *giyyūra* from which the Septuagint took a Greek γειώρας on which see Nöldeke, *op. cit.*, 37. On the old sense of *gēr*, cf. A. Lods, *Israel des origines au VIII siècle*, 229, and for the later evolution, *JE*, art. Proselyte, and Vigouroux, *Dict. de la Bible*, Paris 1912, v, 758. The Akkadian *gāru* is noted in the index of J. J. Stamm, *Die Akkadische Namengebung*, Leipzig 1959, with reference to p. 179.

(J. Lecerf)

DJĪZA [see al-Ḳāhira].

DJĪZĀN [see Djayzān].

al-**DJĪZĪ**, Abū Muḥammad al-Rabīʿ b. Sulaymān b. Dāwūd al-Azdī al-Aʿradj (died in Djīza, Egypt, in Dhu'l-Ḥidjdja 256 or 257/870 or 871), an eminent follower of al-Shāfiʿī and most probably a direct disciple of his. Like a good number of early Shāfiʿīs he was originally a Mālikī and disciple of ʿAbd Allāh b. ʿAbd al-Ḥakam. After his adherence to Shāfiʿism he devoted himself to making an accurate compilation of *Kitāb al-Umm*. Together with that of al-Buwayṭī, his version of this master work of Shāfiʿism is the most trustworthy. It may be considered as representing the second phase of Shāfiʿī jurisprudence known as the Egyptian. His compilation was rewritten at a later date with insertions of another Rabīʿ (Abu Muḥammad b. Sulaymān al-Murādī, d. 270/883). It is difficult to distinguish in *Kitāb al-Umm* things attributed to our Rabīʿ from those of the other. Zakī Mubārak, in his study of *Kitāb al-Umm* has tried to find characteristics of both, but his reasoning is not convincing. Al-Rabīʿ al-Djīzī counts among his disciples Abū Dāwūd and al-Nasāʾī. Ibn Khallikān illustrates him as a most virtuous and modest man.

Bibliography: Al-Subkī, *Ṭabaḳāt*, Cairo, i, 53; Ibn Khallikān, *Wafayāt*, Cairo 1948, i, 53, no. 220; Ibn al-Zayyāt, *Al-Kawākib al-sayyāra fī tartīb al-ziyāra*, Cairo, 151; Zakī Mubārak, *Taḥḳīḳ nasab Kitāb al-Umm*, Cairo 1932, 73; M. K. Ḥusayn, *Adab Miṣr al-Islāmiyya*, Cairo, 58, 95 (note).

(H. Monés)

DJIZYA (i)—the poll-tax which, in traditional Muslim law, is levied on non-Muslims in Muslim states. The history of the origins of the *djizya* is extremely complex, for three different reasons: first, the writers who, in the ʿAbbāsid period, tried to collect the available materials relating to the operation of the *djizya* and the *kharādj* found themselves confronted by texts in which these words were used with different meanings, at times in a wide sense, at others in a technical way and even then varying, so that in order to be able to complete a reasonable picture they tended to interpret them according to the meaning which had become current and best defined in their own time; secondly, it is a fact for which due allowance is not made that the system which sprang from the Arab conquest was not uniform, but resulted from a series of individual, and not identical, agreements or decisions; finally, this system followed after, but did not overthrow, earlier systems which themselves differed one from another and which, moreover, in the period immediately before Islam, are imperfectly understood and a subject of controversy. In these conditions, the account that follows can do no more than serve as a provisional guide.

The word *djizya*, which is perhaps connected with an Aramaic original, occurs in the Ḳurʾān, IX, 29 where, even at that time, it is applied to the dues demanded from Christians and Jews, but probably in the somewhat loose sense, corresponding with the root, of "compensation" (for non-adoption of Islam), and in any case as collective tribute, not differentiated from other forms of taxation, and the nature of its content being left uncertain (the examples given in the works on the biography of the Prophet are very variable; tribute was adapted to the individual conditions of each group concerned). It is possible that, *mutatis mutandis*, precedents can be found in pre-Islamic Arabia outside the religious sphere, in the conditions of submission of inhabited oases to more powerful tribal groups, in return for protection; but as a result of their conquests the Arabs, heirs of the Byzantine and Sāsānid régimes, were to be faced with new practical problems.

Naturally there was no hesitation over the fact that the *dhimmīs* [*q.v.*] had to pay the Muslim community a tax which, from the point of view of the conqueror, was material proof of their subjection, just as for the inhabitants it was a concrete continuation of the taxes paid to earlier regimes. This tax could be of three sorts, according to whether it was levied on individuals as such, or on the land, or was a collective tribute unrelated to any kind of assessment. In the ʿAbbāsid period, the texts show us a clear theoretical distinction between two taxes, on the one hand a tax on land, the *kharādj*, which except only in particular instances could not be suppressed since the land had been conquered once for all for the benefit of the permanent Muslim community, and a tax on persons, the *djizya*, which, for its part, came to an end if the taxpayer became Muslim. But it is far from being the case that such a distinction was always made, either in law or in fact, in the first century of Islam, and the problem is simply to determine what was the primitive practice, and how the ultimate stable system was gradually attained.

Starting from the indisputable fact that in the very early texts the words *djizya* and *kharādj* are constantly taken either in the wide sense of collective tribute or else in apparently narrower but interchangeable senses (*kharādj* on the head, *djizya* on land, as well as *vice versa*), Wellhausen, and then Becker and Caetani etc., built up a system according to which the Arabs, at the time of the conquest, are alleged to have levied collective tribute on the defeated, without taking the trouble to distinguish between the different possible sources of tax, and it was only the multiplicity of conversions which, at the very end of the Umayyad rule, led, particularly in Khurāsān, to a distinction in the total revenues being made between two taxes, the one on the person, ceasing with the status of *dhimmī*, the other on land which remained subject to the obligations placed upon it by the conquest. This theory, apart from the prejudicial question that it contradicts the opinion of all classical jurists, in fact comes up against numerous difficulties and recently has been severely breached, especially by Løkkegaard and even more by Dennett whose conclusions, in their general lines and inspiration, no longer seem to be refutable, although even they do not answer all the problems which they in their turn raise. They have demonstrated completely that the texts often make an effective distinction between the tax on land and the tax on the person, even if the term denoting them is variable, and have stressed the improbability that a reform which covered the whole empire should have started in the remote province of Khurāsān during the final anarchic years of the Umayyad dynasty, and (especially Dennett in a closely reasoned analysis of the situation region by region) that one could not speak of a uniform system immediately after the conquest, since neither the earlier institutions nor the conditions of occupation had been everywhere the same.

The Sāsānid empire had possessed a fiscal system which distinguished between a general tax on land and a poll-tax, at rates varying according to the degree of wealth, but from which the aristocracy were exempt. The Roman-Byzantine empire had a more complex system about which we still remain uncertain on many points. A personal tax did exist, but was scarcely used, except only for colonists and non-Christians. The general tax made no distinction; in the case of a small property fiscally subject to the direct administration of the State, it was apparently levied on agricultural cultivation, on the basis of a unit of measurement or *jugum*; on the other hand, in large estates enjoying a certain autonomy it appeared to be more practical to base the calculation on the number of persons working; but if the tax was in this way proportional to the size of the population, it was still in no way a specific poll-tax since it was not added to another tax which was apparently based on the land. This precise point must be kept clearly in mind if we wish to understand the subsequent developments.

Now in some instances the conquest was effected purely by force, in which case the system established was at the conqueror's discretion, at other times as the result of a treaty of capitulation, and in this case, when the native population kept its fiscal autonomy, a particular fiscal system might be merely stipulated, or else a certain sum might be fixed in advance as tribute to be paid, with allowances being made for considerations of assessment. In ʿIrāḳ, the province to which most of the ʿAbbāsid jurists refer, the conquest was in general effected by force, or at least with the abandonment of the Sāsānid administrative services; with the help of native subordinates the Arabs controlled the institution and collection of taxes which followed the tradition, that is to say a poll-tax was still distinct from a land tax, though its rate was probably increased (1, 2, 4 dīnārs = 12, 24, 48 dirhams), but the grading of wealth was maintained. To remain exempt from this poll-tax, the members of the aristocracy declared their allegiance to the Muslim faith; one cannot say if at the same time they were freed from the land tax, though subject to it in the modified form of the tithe levied on Muslims' property.—In most of the towns of Syria and Upper Mesopotamia, the Arab occupation was carried out by means of treaties which distinguished them from the large autonomous estates of the previous régime; although temporary agreements at the very beginning had established collective tribute, the system which was set up was one of autonomous control, but with the tax defined by the conqueror and usually calculated (as at Ḥīra in ʿIrāḳ) on the basis of a fixed contribution (generally 1 dīnār) per head, and thus a tax proportional to the population, as was the case before on the large estates; the same method of calculation may have continued on the large estates, but under the direct control of the conqueror, since most of the great Byzantine landowners had disappeared, and with the addition of the poll-tax on the colonists (?); incidentally the conquerors often found it advantageous at that time to accept the peasants' payments in kind. In Egypt most of the Christian communities were taxed under a system which united payments in kind, a land tax of 1 dīnār per *faddān* (unit of cultivated land) and a specific poll-tax of 2 dīnārs per head, this last figure, however, being based on the calculation of the sum which the community had to pay, on the condition that the total amount would eventually be divided among the inhabitants in the most equitable proportions (as papyri show); contrary to previous belief, this poll-tax must in practice have constituted for the mass of the inhabitants a burden almost as heavy as the land tax. Finally, in the greater part of Īrān and central Asia, as well as in some places in Cyrenaica, the system established was of fixed tribute to be paid by the local rulers who were maintained in office, with no interference from the conquerors either in declaring or collecting the tax; in K͟hurāsān in particular, taxpayers continued to be charged on the basis of the Sāsānid dual system of land tax and poll-tax, apart from any questions of conversion or non-conversion to the new religion. Whatever uncertainties remain in particular systems (especially in Syria, it seems), it will be seen that, in general, the duality of land tax and poll-tax existed at the taxpayer's level, under various conditions, for the greater part of the peasant populations, while on the other hand a system of unitary contribution prevailed throughout most of the Syrian towns and in Upper Mesopotamia; the conquerors, particularly in the East, held aloof from these distinctions so long as the tribute was paid.

However, difficulties very soon appeared. In Egypt monks were exempt from poll-tax; the Copts, who since Roman times had been past masters of tax evasion, noted that the taxpayer could escape payment of poll-tax if he left the district where he was enrolled or, better still, if he entered a monastery. It therefore became necessary to make all monks in their turn subject to poll-tax (a much more probable explanation than the alternative upon which one is driven back if one accepts that the poll-tax was absent at the beginning of the Muslim régime: since it was later found applied to monks, the argument runs that it made its original appearance in the form of a tax on the monks). It was necessary to apply for authorization for removal, and to mark taxpayers with an indelible stamp, hence all those passports, seals etc. of which archaeologists have provided us with so many unimpeachable examples. Phenomena of the same sort must have existed in many places, and are for example recorded in Upper Mesopotamia and also in ʿIrāḳ.

There, however, matters are presented to us somewhat differently. In ʿIrāḳ, in fact, evasion of taxes took the form of conversion to Islam, the convert believing that his new status would free him from the whole fiscal complex levied on the non-Muslim, that is to say the land-tax and the poll-tax. In reality what happened at the beginning —and the Muslim administration did not look upon it amiss—was that the convert abandoned his land, with no thought of it ceasing to be subject to the *k͟harād͟j*, to a non-convert who guaranteed its cultivation and fiscal capacity. The thing was possible so long as it happened infrequently and the treasury had little to fear, for the new régime had inherited from its predecessors, both Byzantine and Sāsānid, the idea of the joint liability of each locality in regard to taxation, and those who remained therefore paid for those who had left and whose land they exploited. However, by the time when the terrible governor al-Ḥad͟jd͟jād͟j came to ʿIrāḳ the matter had already assumed dangerous proportions as regards the development of land, and hence also threatened the treasury. He then took the draconic decision to send back the peasants to the land, to subject them to taxation again, including poll-tax, and, in practice, to forbid them to be converted to Islam.—A similar problem arose in Khurāsān; but there it was the native aristocracy who persecuted the peasantry who were guilty of conversion to Islam: since every conversion risked increasing the burden of taxes on non-Muslims and compelling the aristocracy to make good from their own pockets any short-comings in payments, they tried wherever they could to impose still heavier taxes upon the Muslims, at least the poorer ones, rather than on the non-Muslims: inequality in reverse ....

It is clear that these repressions also could not last. It was somehow inadmissible, in a Muslim State, virtually to penalize entry into Islam. The pious ʿUmar b. ʿAbd al-ʿAzīz is credited with an attitude of absolute reaction to the policy, and he is said to have gone so far as to encourage conversions by the remission of the whole complex of taxes levied on non-Muslims. The most authoritative texts recently discovered or interpreted do not confirm such a Utopian outlook (H. A. R. Gibb, *The fiscal rescript of Umar II*, in *Arabica*, ii, (1955)). It seems that, under the influence of the jurists who elaborated the doctrine of *fay*ʾ [*q.v.*], there was a move towards the idea of dissociating from the complex of taxes imposed on the non-Muslims the *kharādj*, which from this time on was regarded rather as being levied specifically on land and not on the person, and hence was compatible with the status of Muslim: the poll-tax, as such, was to disappear, but the treasury did not necessarily suffer nor did the taxpayer gain as a result, since the convert had to pay the *zakāt* on his income. It was a system of this sort that, at a later date, Naṣr b. Ṣayyār, the last great Umayyad Governor, tried to introduce in Khurāsān; he is thus at the rear of the movement, and not in the vanguard. In a country like Syria a more delicate adaptation must have been necessary, and appears to have been undertaken from the time of Yazīd and ʿAbd al-Malik (Abū Yūsuf, 24; cf. Løkkegaard, 133), to give a truly personal character to the traditional poll-tax, in addition to a tax on land. In any case, from the moment when the poll-tax had been differentiated from the land-tax in the assessment, the same could also be done in the collection, and the collective responsiblity of places in respect of taxation would cease to operate in this matter. In Egypt particularly, we know that movement of persons became legal, provided that a record of them was kept and that the whereabouts of those concerned was known (see Cl. Cahen, *Impôts du Fayyum*, quoted below, 21). Thus the term which customarily denoted "fugitives"—in Greek φυγάδες —the *djawālī* (plur. of *djāliya*), in administration came to be taken, without further addition, as a synonym of *djizya* in the sense of poll-tax. Naturally, this fiscal arrangement did not solve the economic problem of peasant emigration, and there were further instances of the enforced return of peasants to their fields (see Cl. Cahen, *Fiscalité*, etc. in *Arabica*, i (1954), 146-7); but, in proportion as the rural communities were now able to become Muslim, the problem no longer affected the *djizya*, and it is probable that it was less grave in the solidly-based Christian communities which remained faithful to their creed (Lebanon, Upper Mesopotamia, Egypt itself) and where collective responsibilty was to act against emigration (ibid., 151). Other factors may have counted in favour of attachment to the land, and against emigration to towns, which cannot be discussed here; it seems in any case that, in the centuries that followed, the problem was no longer expressed in the terms in which the sons of the Arab conquerors had known it.

The ʿAbbāsid period thus witnessed the specialization of terminology, as of institutions, at least in technical writings and works of *fiḳh* (the latter treat of it as an appendage to the *djihād*); and whilst the *kharādj* no longer denotes anything more than land-tax, *djizya* is henceforth applied only to the poll-tax on *dhimmīs*. The latter incidentally lost its financial importance everywhere when the non-Muslim communities ceased to be numerically superior. Even when thus diminished, it does not appear to have become uniform. Syria-Palestine and Egypt kept their own system until the 18th century (see Gibb-Bowen, i/2, 254 and Nābulusī in Cl. Cahen, *Impôts du Fayyum*, in *Arabica*, iii (1956), 21-2), despite the assertions of theorists (including Balādhurī but, characteristically, excluding Mālik and Shāfiʿī), while the hierarchized tax system attributed to ʿUmar continued to be practised in the East and from there later passed into the non-Arab provinces of the Ottoman Empire. The numerical importance to it of the *dhimmīs*, as earlier in Saldjūḳid Asia Minor (for this point see in particular Kerimüddin Aksarayī, *Müsâmeret ül-ahbar*, ed. O. Turan, 153, with analysis of F. Işıltan, 1943, 81), once again confers considerable importance on the *djizya*, although the word often bestowed on it is *kharādj* (the land-tax at that time bearing other names; see below).

A certain number of rules formulated during the ʿAbbāsid period appear to be generally valid from that time onwards. *Djizya* is only levied on those who are male, adult, free, capable and able-bodied, so that children, old men, women, invalids, slaves, beggars, the sick and the mentally deranged are excluded. Foreigners are exempt from it on condition that they do not settle permanently in the country. Inhabitants of frontier districts who at certain times could be enrolled in military expeditions even if not Muslim (Mardaïtes, Armenians, etc.), were released from *djizya* for the year in question.

A personal fixed contribution, the *djizya* was levied by lunar years (generally just before or just after the beginning of the year; sometimes in Ramaḍān under the Mamlūks), unlike taxes connected with agriculture; it could thus be dissociated from them in tax-farming and *iḳṭāʿ* concessions. Money was stipulated, and normally payment had to be made in it, but payment in kind was admissible, under an officially determined scale of equivalent values. According to the Ḳurʾānic text, one must give *al-djizyat*^{a} *ʿan yad*^{in}, which has since been interpreted, perhaps wrongly, to mean "by hand" and personally (on this point see F. Rosenthal, *Some minor problems in the Qur'ân*, in *The Joshua Starr Memorial Volume*, New York 1953, 68-72, and Cl. Cahen, *Coran IX-29 ...*, in *Arabica*, ix (1962), 76-9); administratively, this meaning suggests the need to count the non-Muslim population, hence for instance the forbidding of all village notables to accept a lump payment of *djizya* from their subordinates. Furthermore it was desired to have confirmation given to every individual concerned of his status as a subject of Islam or, more accurately, as a member of an inferior social class; it is apparently in this way that we must interpret the Ḳurʾānic formula (which follows the one given above) *wa-hum ṣāghirūn* (sometimes glossed as *aḳarrū bi 'l-ṣaghār*), in connexion with the well-known instances of notables or Arabs refusing, although Christians, to pay the "*djizya* of the *ʿulūdj*", rather than as implying the necessity for a humiliating procedure, which later rigorists claimed to find in it. Actual censuses were apparently undertaken, especially at the time of the differentiation between *djizya* and *kharādj* (by ʿAbd al-Malik in Syria, Yazīd II in Egypt, etc.), and, reciprocally, the evaluation at 130,000 dīnārs of the total return from *djizya* in Egypt at the time of Saladin, for example, at the average rate of 2 dīnārs, allows us to estimate the Christian population then in the country at about 65,000 heads of families.

In principle, the *djizya*, like the *zakāt*, had to be used for pensions, salaries and charities. But under this pretext it was often paid into the Prince's *khāṣṣ*, "private" treasury. Mālik and al-Shāfiʿī admit that the rate of tax could be increased; with or without doctrinal justification, arbitrary demands appeared at times during the economically difficult and religiously strict period of the Mamlūks; however, we must take count of the fact that the growing scarcity of gold and the devaluation of the dirham had often brought the *djizya* to a level lower than was stipulated by doctrine; moreover the monks, or at least those in poor monasteries, found a way to reduce their returns.

In the territories directly controlled by the Mongols, before their conversion to Islam, the original fiscal system abolished the poll-tax on non-Muslims; when they adopted the Muslim religion, zealous agents sought to make the Christians pay all the arrears (forty years . . .) (al-Djazarī, *Chronique*, ed. Sauvaget, 48, Nr 307).—In Sicily, after the Norman conquest, the poll-tax on Muslims and Jews was called *djizya*.

The *djizya* has naturally disappeared from modern Muslim States as a result of the growing equality of religions, the introduction of military service and the organization of new fiscal systems.

Bibliography: Almost the whole bibliography of sources, al-Balādhurī, Abū Yūsuf, al-Māwardī and other chroniclers, recorders of traditions, jurists, etc., is to be found collected together in Caetani, quoted *infra*; to it should be added Abū ʿUbayd b. Sallām, *K. al-Amwāl*, and, for the *K. al-Kharādj* of Yaḥyā b. Adam, the annotated English translation by A. Ben Shemesh, 1958; for papyri see, besides Becker and Grohmann quoted *infra*, C. Becker, *Papyri Schott-Rheinhardt*, 1906, and H. I. Bell, *Greek papyri in the British Museum*, iv, 1910, as well as R. Rémondon, *Les papyrus d'Apollonos Ano*, 1953, and C. J. Kraemer, *Excavations at Nessana*, iii, *Non-literary papyri*, 1958.

It is not possible here to give the very extensive bibliography of works relating to poll-tax and the associated problems in the Roman-Byzantine Empire; the latest restatements will be found in the bibliography of R. Palanque's edition of the posthumous *Histoire du Bas-Empire* of E. Stein, i, 1959, and in Karayannopoulos, *Das Finanzwesen des frühbyzantinischen Staates*, 1958; the outstanding works are still those of Piganiol, F. Lot and E. Deléage; for Egypt, A. Ch. Johnson and L. C. West, *Byzantine Egypt*, 1949.

For the Muslim world, J. Wellhausen, *Das arabische Reich*, 172 ff., Eng. tr. 276 ff.; C. Becker, *Beiträge zur Geschichte Aegyptens*, 81 ff. (in the 2nd fascicule); idem, *Islamstudien*, i, 1924; Caetani, *Annali*, v, 280-532; A. Grohmann, *Probleme der arabischen Papyrusforschung*, in *ArO*, 1933, 276 ff. and 1934, 125 ff.; Fr. Løkkegaard, *Islamic taxation*, ch. VI; D. C. Dennett, *Conversion and the poll-tax in early Islam*, 1951; A. Fattal, *Le statut légal des non-musulmans en pays d'Islam*, 1958, ch. VII, more detailed than Tritton, *The Caliphs and their non-Muslim subjects*, 1930; M. Ḍiyā al-Dīn al-Raʾīs (Rayes), *al-Kharādj fī al-dawla al-islāmiyya* (a history of Muslim state-finances), Cairo 1957, especially 107 ff.; Mez, *Renaissance*, ch. IV and VIII. Among specialized studies, Ḥabīb Zayyāt, *al-Djizya* in *al-Machriq*, xli (1947), 2; Finocchiaro-Sartorio, *Gizyah e Kharaj nella Sicilia*, in *Archivio giuridico*, lxxxi (1908). (CL. CAHEN)

ii.—Ottoman

The word *kharādj* was used for preference instead of *djizya* by the 10th/16th century, later *djizye* or *djizye-i sherʿī*. (cf. indexes in R. Anhegger-H. Inalcık, *Ḳānūnnāme-i Sulṭānī* . . ., Ankara 1956; Tayyib Gökbilgin, *Paşa Livası*, Istanbul 1952; F. Kraelitz, *Os. Urkunden in türkischer Sprache*, Vienna 1922; Ö. L. Barkan, *Kanunlar*, Istanbul 1943). *Bash-kharadjī* for *djizya* was occasionally found in the documents (cf. T. Gökbilgin, 158, and B. Lewis, in *BSOAS*, xiv (1952), 553, 559) to distinguish it from land-*kharādj*. For the collector of *djizya*, *kharādjī* or *kharādjdjī* is used in the first period, *djizyedār* later.

The payment of *djizya* was sometimes dependent on the land possessed: anyone, Muslim or non-Muslim, who possessed a *bashtina*, land recorded under the possession of a *dhimmī* (cf. ČIFTLIK), was to pay *djizya* (cf. the regulation of Ohri dated 1022/1613 in Ö.L. Barkan, 295; that of Avlonya in *Sûret-i Defter-i Sancak-i Arvanid*, ed. H. Inalcık, Ankara 1954, 124). The reason given for this was the treasury's concern to protect the *djizya* revenues.

Following a conservative policy in the conquered lands, the Ottomans identified certain pre-Ottoman poll-taxes with *djizya*. Upon the request of their new subjects in Hungary (Barkan, 304) they accepted for *djizya* the old tax of one *flori*, gold, paid per family to the Hungarian kings before the conquest (cf. Barkan, 303, 320). Previously in the Balkans the Ottomans, however, had introduced a native poll-tax, probably of the same origin as the Hungarian one *flori* tax, in their own taxation only as an *ʿurfī* poll-tax under the name of *ispendje* (cf. H. Inalcık, *Osmanlılarda raiyyet rüsûmu*, in *Belleten*, xcii, 602-8). They ruled that anyone subject to *djizya* was to pay *ispendje* (*Belleten*, xcii, 602). But the latter was ordinarily included in *tīmārs* [*q.v.*]. It can be supposed that the Ottomans, like the first Muslim conquerors of Egypt and Syria, found in the Balkans and Hungary a poll-tax of one gold piece, probably from a common Roman origin (cf. F. Løkkegaard, *Islamic taxation*, Copehagen 1950, 134-5). Sanctioned by *naṣṣ* and *idjtihād* as asserted in the firmans, *djizya* was for the Ottomans a religious tax the collection and spending of which had to receive special care. It was collected as a rule directly for the state treasury by the Sultan's own *kuls* [*q.v.*]. It was exceptional to grant *djizya* revenues as *tīmār* or *mülk*. Also it was farmed out only in special cases (cf. Anhegger-Inalcık, 39). As a *sharʿī* tax belonging to the *bayt māl al-muslimīn* its administration was put under the supervision of the *ḳāḍīs* and not infrequently its actual collection was made by them (cf. Gökbilgin, 158).

The *djizya* revenues were spent usually for military purposes or assigned to the regular pay of a military unit as *odjaklïk*. Mahmūd II raised the rates of *djizya* and assigned it to the upkeep of his reformed army of *ʿasākir-i manṣūra*, claiming this as a religious use for *ghazā* (cf. Hadžibegić, *Džizja ili harač*, in *Prilozi*, v (1954-5), doc. 19, 78-9). Exemption from *djizya* was usually made in return for military services as was the case with the *voynuk*s, *martolos* and *eflak*s.

When a conquered land was to be organized as an Ottoman province a census of people subject to *djizya* was made by the *ḳāḍī* appointed there, and a book called *defter-i djizya-i gabrān* was drawn up (for an example made after the conquest see the *defter* of Buda and Pest in L. Fekete, *Die Siyāqatschrift in der türkischen Finanzverwaltung*, Budapest 1955, i, doc. 8, 20, pp. 176-98, 350-5; ii, facsimiles, Tables XI, XXXVI). Referred to also as *aṣl defter*, original *defter*, this book was made in two copies, one for the central treasury, the other for the provincial administration. The census was to be renewed. But, as we read in the *nishān* of 22 Djumādā II 1102/23 March 1691 such censuses were not renewed for long periods and as a result of deaths and births, flights and conversions the books did not reflect the actual situation. In the reign of Meḥemmed II half of the *djizya* due from the fugitives of a village was to be made good by its *tīmār*-holder and the other half by the remaining *djizya*-payers (R. Anhegger-H. Inalcık, 76). But with the collapse of the *tīmār* system in the late 10th/16th century the whole burden fell upon the latter. Finally by the reform of 1102/1691 each *djizya* payer was made responsible only for his own personal *djizya* and a paper, *kāghïd* or *waraḳ*, was delivered to certify its payment. On the other hand the fugitives were pursued, (*ibid.*) or, sometimes, the authorities would try to bring them back by promising a reduction in the rate of *djizya*, as was done to repopulate the deserted villages in the province of Manastir (Monastir) in 1117/1705.

As a rule every third year, called *new-yāfte* (*Naw-Yāfta*) *yïlï* a general inspection was made to cross out the dead, *mürde* (*murda*) and to add *new-yāfte* (*naw-yāfta*), those who were omitted from the *defter* for one reason or another, among them the *bāligh*, adolescents who by the time of the inspection had become legally fit to pay *djizya*. But the inspectors were instructed to carry out this operation so as not to reduce the number of *djizya*-payers. Strangers and passers-by found in a district were subject to the payment of *djizya* on the spot, as ordered in the firmans issued after the reform of 1102/1691 (cf. Hadžibegić, doc. 5, in vol. iii-iv, 111).

It seems that *ruhbān*, clerics, and *keshīsh*, monks, were exempted from *djizya* in the first period (for exemption from *djizya* of a *metropolit* in the time of Meḥemmed II see Anhegger-Inalcık, 66). But in the reform *nishān* of 1102/1691 all clerics except those who had really a disability were subjected to *djizya*. In 1103/1692 the *ruhbān* sent a petition to the Sultan stating a *sharʿī* opinion about the exemption of those *ruhbān* who were in retirement and not earning their own living (cf. *Al-Durar*, 213; Mewḳūfātī, i, 351), but it was rejected on the basis of the different opinion of Imām Yūsuf. By 1255/1839 the monks of the Mount Athos were exempted from all taxes but *djizya*.

However, in accordance with the precise command of the *sharīʿa*, the Ottoman government always exempted from *djizya* children, women, disabled and blind men, and the unemployed poor. Only the widows (*bīve*) possessing the land of their deceased husbands were liable for *djizya*.

The treatises of *fiḳh* (*Al-Durar*, 212; Mewḳūfātī, i, 350) distinguished two kinds of *djizya*, that fixed by *ṣulh*, agreement, the amount of which could not be altered, and that levied from individuals, *al-djizya ʿala 'l-ruʾūs*. The former, called in Ottoman official terminology *djizya ber wedjh-i maḳṭūʿ* or simply *maḳṭūʿ*, was extensively applied and found two different fields of application in the Ottoman empire: (*a*) The submission as a vassal of a Christian prince always implied the payment of an agreed yearly tribute however small the amount might be. Then the Sultan considered the non-Muslims under the prince as the Sultan's own *kharādj*-paying subjects (see BOGHDAN, RAGUSA) and the yearly tribute which was usually paid in gold pieces as a *kharādj-i maḳṭūʿ* (see DĀR AL-ʿAHD); (*b*) In some cases the *dhimmī*s under the Sultan's direct rule were permitted to pay their *djizya* in a fixed sum, *ber wedjh-i maḳṭūʿ*, as a community. The *dhimmī raʿāyā* applied for it mostly to escape the abuses of the *djizya*-collectors and their request was accepted by the government often to insure its payment, for otherwise they often threatened to abandon their villages and run away. On the other hand the Albanian mountain tribes of Klementi living in five villages were permitted to pay a nominal *fixed* sum of one thousand *akče* for their *djizya* in 902/1497, and in return they promised to guard the highway passing through their area. Also in Ḳurvelesh, Albania, seventeen villages in rebellion agreed to submit on condition that they paid their *djizya ber wedjh-i maḳṭūʿ* at a fixed sum of 3301 esedī ghurūsh in 1106/1695. In these examples we see the government being rather forced to come to an agreement with its *dhimmī* subjects. Sometimes the *maḳṭūʿ* was agreed upon between the *djizya*-collectors and the *ḳodja-bashï*s, Christian notables, who thus being able to distribute the *djizya* in their communities themselves expected to have some advantages such as to alleviate their own share, as actually stated in a document. But this practice was denounced by the government.

The *maḳṭūʿ* system gave the Jewish community of Ṣafad the opportunity to save their clerics from paying *djizya* (B. Lewis, *Notes and documents from the Turkish Archives*, Jerusalem 1952, 11; U. Heyd, *Ottoman documents on Palestine*, Oxford 1960, 121; cf. idem on the Djizya-registers for Palestine in *Jerusalem*, iv (1952), 173-84 (in Hebrew, with Turkish documents).

Considering its basic character of a poll-tax, however, the government often insisted on its payment individually. On the other hand the *maḳṭūʿ*, fixed sum of *djizya* for a group, might become too onerous when the number in such a group for one reason or another decreased. In such cases a new census was often asked for, to reduce the amount or to return to the payment by individuals.

The *maḳṭūʿ* system in *djizya*, however, came to be more and more extensively applied in the period of decline during which the central government had increasingly lost the control of tax collection in the provinces. The *ḳodja-bashï*s, *čorbadjï*s and *knez* then took over, as the *aʿyān* among the Muslim population, the collection of taxes within their communities, and this prepared their rise as a local aristocracy in the Balkans in the 12th/18th century. In the belief that the *maḳṭūʿ* system was favourable for the *raʿāyā* the initiators of the *tanẓīmāt* [*q.v.*] generalized the system (the circular of 25 Muḥarram 1257/17 March 1841 in Mühimme no. 13663 Maliye Yeni

Seri, Başvekâlet Archives) and even sanctioned it by a *fatwā* [*q.v.*].

It was the Sultan's responsibility to declare every new year the rates of *djizya* to be collected on the basis of a *fatwā* given by the Shaykh al-Islām who determined it according to the *sharʿī* scale. In Ottoman terminology the grades were *aʿlā*, *awsaṭ* and *adnā* corresponding to *ẓāhir al-ghināʾ mukthir*, wealthy, *mutawassiṭ al-ḥāl*, medium status, and *faḳīr muʿtamal*, working poor man, who were to pay, 48, 24 and 12 *dirham-i sharʿī* (see DIRHAM) of pure silver, or four, two and one dīnār gold pieces respectively. In a document of 6 Djumādā II 896/16 April 1491 (Gökbilgin, 159) we find *djizya* applied according to the *sharʿī* scale. But in a firman of 880/1475 the collector was instructed to accept payments over fixed rates (Anhegger-Inalcık, 78).

Payment could be made in silver and gold coins in circulation, and rarely the rates were also shown in current copper coins. In Radjab 1101/April 1690 the rate for the lowest grade was fixed as one Egyptian gold piece, *sharīfī altun*, or 2¼ esedī (Dutch) ghurūsh, or 90 para or 1170 copper manghīr. But payments were mostly made in silver *akče* [*q.v.*] until the late 10th/16th century, and in *ghurūsh* or *para* in later periods. The recurrent debasements and depreciations in coinage (cf. H. İnalcık, in *Belleten*, loc., 676-84; Hadžibegić, in *Prilozi*, v, 51-6) made it necessary for the Ottoman government to declare in the firmans of *djizya*-collection every year (cf. examples in Hadžibegić, doc. nos. 1, 2, 4, 5, 6, 10, 12, 14, 19, 22, 25) a schedule of the official rates of the coins in circulation. But disparities between the official and current rates often gave rise to disputes between the tax-payers and collectors, and the treasury sometimes preferred to accept only gold pieces. At other times, on their own initiative, the collectors forced the tax-payers to pay only in gold with the intention of exchanging this later for their own profit. To prevent this the Sultan often had to send special orders to the collectors to accept silver coins too (the *Aḥkām defterleri* in the Başvekâlet archives, Istanbul, are indeed full of such orders). The rates of *djizya* in the Ottoman silver coinage went up from 1102/1691 to 1249/1834 as shown in the following table (Hadžibegić, in *Prilozi*, v, 102).

(in esedī ghurūsh)

Year	*aʿlā*	*awsaṭ*	*adnā*
1102/1691	9	4½	2¼
1108/1696	10	5	2¼
1156/1744	11	5½	2¾
1218/1804	12	6	3
1231/1816	16	8	4
1239/1824	24	12	6
1242/1827	36	18	9
1244/1829	48	24	12
1249/1834	60	30	15

Maḥmūd II emphasized in his firmans that the increases, *ḍamāʾim*, were not newly assessed taxes, *muḥdathāt*, but simply the result of a necessary adjustment of the fixed *sharʿī* quantities of silver to be paid as *djizya* in the currency of the day (cf. Hadžibegić, v, 69, 79). But these increases, even if they were not real in value, gave rise to widespread discontent among the *dhimmī*s in the Ottoman empire.

It must be remembered that until the introduction of radical changes in the Ottoman finances in the 11th/17th century, *djizya* was levied in some large areas of the empire only at one single fixed rate (cf. the Sandjaḳ regulations in Barkan, 83,201, 226, 316): for the *dhimmī*s subject to *djizya* of all classes 25 *aḳče* in the province of Yeni-il in Süleyman's time, 40 *aḳče* in 991/1583, 35 *aḳče* in some areas and 55 in others in the province of Bitlis 30 in the island of Tashoz, 46 in the province of Mosul in the 10th/16th century. It was 80 *aḳče* in the lands conquered from the Mamlūks, namely in the provinces of Adana, Damascus, Ṣafad; the rates here, except for the latter, were less than the normal lowest rate (one gold piece was 60-70 *aḳče* during this period). The reason given for this special treatment in the provinces of Eastern Anatolia was the poverty due to the physical conditions of the area. As for the islands, similar conditions together with the special defence responsibilities imposed on the population accounted for it. The *dhimmī*s of the island of Imbros were even exempted altogether from *djizya* (Barkan, 237). The single rate of 80 *aḳče* in Syria and Palestine appears to be a survival from the last phase of the Mamlūk period during which *djizya* was for all classes one gold piece plus a fraction to cover collection costs (B. Lewis, *Notes*, 11). Being considered too low as compared to the *sharʿī* rates, these fixed single rates of assessment were raised on the accession of a new Sultan to the throne (on Selīm II's accession an increase of ten *aḳče* was made; cf. Barkan, 318).

The assessment of *djizya* was made per family in Hungary, Palestine in the 10th/16th century (cf. B. Lewis, *Notes*, 10; idem, *Studies in the Ottoman Archives*, in *BSOAS*, xvi/3 (1954), 484-5), in the province of Salonika, and many other places in the Balkans (cf. Gökbilgin, 155-7) before the reform *nishān* of 1102/1691.

Also in the early period there were certain groups exempted from *djizya*. It was true, in principle, that the exemption from *djizya* was considered as a waste of a revenue belonging to the *bayt māl al-muslimīn*; hence it was made only exceptionally and, if done, in return for military services. Thus the *dhimmī* population of a crucial fortress (cf. Barkan, 204; but in 835/1431 the population of Akčaḥiṣār, Albania, was exempted from all taxation but *djizya*, cf. *Sûret-i Defter-i Sancak-i Arvanid*, 104), *dhimmī*s in charge of guarding a mountain pass (cf. H. Inalcık, *Fatih devri*, i, Ankara 1954, doc. 1), relatives of the children levied for the Janissaries, *dhimmī*s supplying sulphur for the powder factories in Salonika (defter, K. Kepeci tasnifi no. 3510, Basvekâlet archives) were exempted from *djizya*. The Christian soldiers who formed part of the Ottoman fighting army in the 9th/15th century, namely Christian tīmār holders, *voynuḳ*s [*q.v.*], *martolos* [*q.v.*] and *eflaḳ*s, enjoyed total exemption from *djizya* (H. Inalcık, *Fatih devri*, i, 176-9). The sons and brothers of *voynuḳ*s were subjected only to a *bedel-i djizya*, substitute of *djizya*, at a fixed rate of 30 *aḳče* which was about half of the lowest rate of *djizya* by 922/1516 (Barkan, 396, 398). When these groups lost their military use in the 10th/16th century they were mostly made *dhimmī raʿāyā* and subjected to *djizya*. Those maintained were subjected to a fixed low rate.

At all times the Ottoman government granted partial exemption from *djizya* to the *dhimmī*s of a particular position. Those living in the provinces in the borderland, *i.e.*, Serbia, Bosnia, Herzegovina, Montenegro, paid *djizya* only at the lowest rate, *adnā*, and in time of war the *dhimmī*s living nearest to the fields of operation and on the military routes paid it as half (cf. Hadžibegić, in *Prilozi*, iii, doc. 2,

101; v, V, 102). The *dhimmīs* having to abandon their homes because of enemy invasion were exempted from *djizya* for a certain period.

The *dhimmī* miners in some regions paid it at a very low rate (only six *akče* in Silistre in the mid-16th century, cf. H. İnalcık, *Osmanlılarda raiyyet rüsûmu*, in *Belleten*, xcii, 608, note 173). As late as 1170/1757 the *dhimmīs* of 21 villages in Chios who were engaged in the production of mastic paid it all equally at the lowest rate.

Under the capitulations the *dhimmī terdjumāns*, dragomans, attached to the foreign embassies, enjoyed exemption from *djizya*. But many *dhimmīs* had managed to obtain *berāts* of *terdjumān* by dubious ways to escape paying *djizya* (see BERĀTLĪ).

If a *musta'min* (see ĀMĀN) prolonged his stay in the Ottoman dominions longer than one year he was treated as a *dhimmī*, subjected to *djizya*, and could not leave the country for the *Dār al-ḥarb* [*q.v.*] (cf. *Al-Durar*, 207). Though we find in the records, *sidjillāt*, of the ķāḍī of Bursa cases testifying the application of this rule, some ways must have been found to allow foreign merchants to stay as *musta'min* for longer periods in the great commercial centres even as early as the 9th/15th century (cf. documents in *Belleten*, xciii, 67-96). Later on under the capitulations the Ottoman government became more and more tolerant on this matter (cf. the capitulation of 1153/1740 to France, article 63). The Armenians of Persia, *Arāmīne-i ʿAdjem*, visiting the Ottomans lands usually as merchants, were also subject to *djizya* (the *nishān* of 1102/1691, and Hadžibegić, doc. 4, 10, pp. 107, 125).

The *nishān* of 1102/1691 provided that *djizya* was to be levied per head by all the *dhimmīs* subject to *djizya* on the basis of the *Sharʿī* scale, thus abolishing the *maķtuʿ* system and exemptions (cf. Fîndîķlîlî Meḥmed Agha, *Silāḥdār ta'rīkhi*, i, ed. A. Refîķ, Istanbul 1928, 559). But many old practices and exemptions survived, and only in 1255/1839 with the proclamation of equality in payment of taxes all such exemptions and privileges were abolished.

Djizya-payers had always to pay two additional dues, *maʿīshat* or *maʿāsh* for the living expenses of the collector and *resm-i kitābet* (also called *resm-i ḥesāb*, *udjrat-i kitābet*, *khardj-i muḥāsebe* or *ķalemiyye*) for the services of the central department of *djizya* (cf. Hadžibegić, iii, 112). Actually these were well established dues found with all the departments of the Ottoman finances. In the firman of 880/1475 on the collection of *djizya* (Anhegger-Inalcık, 77-8) we find a due of two *akče* per family called *resm-i kitābet* and a one *akče* due levied formerly by the *il-ketkhudās*. In the 10th/16th century the collector and the scribe accompanying him each took one *akče* for themselves (Barkan, 180; in Hungary, in addition, one *akče resm-i khāne*, Barkan, 316). In 1102/1691 *maʿīshat* was 12, 6 and 3 para for *aʿlā*, *awsaṭ* and *adnā* respectively and one *para* was paid for *udjrat-i kitābet* by all alike. Four years later a new due, *maʿīshat* for the ķāḍīs, was added, which was 9, 4 and 1½ para for *aʿlā*, *awsaṭ* and *adnā* respectively. In 1106/1694, to prevent the abuses in collection of these dues, it was made clear that the collectors were to levy these not for their own account but for the treasury, and the remunerations were to be paid to them by the treasury from the *djizya*-revenues at the central department of *djizya* (Hadžibegić, iii-iv, doc. 4, 5, 10, 11, pp. 107, 112, 125, 131). The total sum of these legal dues amounted to 1/25 of the *djizya* itself and their rates were raised following the increases in *djizya*. From the same firmans we learn that the collectors were illegally subjecting the *djizya* payers to some exactions under the names *dhakhīra*, *kātibiyya*, *ṣarrāfiyya*, *ķoldju akčesi*, *khardj-i maḥkeme* (Hadžibegić, iii-iv, 113, 127), *mum-akčesi buyruldu awā'idi* and others. With the proclamation of the *Tanẓīmāt* in 1255/1839 collectors with a salary from the treasury were appointed and were allowed to take from the tax-payers only a minimum of provisions for themselves and their animals (Hadžibegić, *Prilozi*, v, doc. 25, 93). But the heaviest burden on the *djizya*-payers was the obligation to make good the *djizya* of the fugitive *dhimmīs*, *gurīkhta* (in Turkish *gürikhte*) and the dead, *murda* (in Turkish *mürde*), which sometimes caused the depopulation and ruin of a whole village. As disclosed in the *nishān* of 1102/1691, in some villages the surviving quarter of the previous population was forced to pay the *djizya* of the missing three quarters too. On the other hand the collectors in cooperation with the local ķāḍīs sometimes tried, without official permission, to collect *djizya* from the *new-yāfte* (*naw-yāfta*), those not yet recorded as *djizya* payers in the official *defters*. They also collected *bedel-akčesi*, a lump sum for those names in the *defter* under which no one could be identified. The government always struggled to prevent such abuse and ended by assessing a fixed new tax, called *gürikhte*, to be levied equally on each *djizya* payer. This appears in the *djizya* accounts of 1102/1691 and it was then 40 *akče* per head, a sum about one-eight of the *djizya* itself. Also we find a similar tax called *nev-yāfte akčesi* even at an earlier period. These proved to be only new burdens for the *raʿāyā* since the collectors continued their exactions according to the established customs. When in 1102/1691 the method of collecting *djizya* by distributing personal certificates of payment was established, the collectors, in an effort to use all the certificates delivered to them by the treasury, forced people not subject to *djizya* to accept them, or imposed certificates of higher rates to those subject to low rates. Some of the collectors were denounced as having accepted bribery from the wealthy to save them from the certificates of high rate and then forced the poor to accept them. To all this must be added the common complaint about the *raʿāyā* having to provide the needs of the collectors' large suite of *ķoldjīs*, guardians, and many other exactions which were common in the collection of taxes in the period of decline. The collectors acted apparently even more harshly towards *djizya*-payers, since the firmans commanded, on the basis of the *sharīʿa*, that the *dhimmīs* were to pay *djizya* in complete humiliation, *dhull wa ṣaghār* (cf. Hadžibegić, doc. 5, 10, pp. 112, 126). All this was no doubt mainly responsible for the discontented *raʿāyās* cooperating with foreign invaders from the late 11th/17th century on. The reform measures taken in 1102/1691 and later did not improve the situation, and it can be safely said that the abolition of the exemptions, especially those of clerics under the new system, ended by turning some influential groups among non-Muslims against Ottoman rule.

Bibliography: The Ottoman state followed the Ḥanafī school in the application of *djizya*; *Al-Durar fī sharḥ al-ghurar al-aḥkām* by Molla Khüsrew (Istanbul 1258, 195-216) and later Mewķūfātī's translation of the *Multaķā al-abḥur* (Istanbul 1318, 349-51) became the principal authorities for the Ottoman ʿulemā' and administrators on these matters. For a statement of the *sharʿī* principles in an official Ottoman regulation see Ö. L. Barkan, *Kanunlar*, 351. The earliest firman on the levy of *dj̲izya* that has come down to us is dated 880/1475-6 in R. Anhegger-H. İnalcık, *Ḳānūnnāme-i Sulṭānī ber mūceb-i ʿörf-i Osmānī*, Ankara 1956, 76-8; facsimile in F. Babinger, *Sultanische Urkunden zur Geschichte der osmanischen Wirtschaft und Staatsverwaltung am Ausgang der Herrschaft Mehmeds II, des Eroberers*, i, Munich 1956, 270-80; French summary in N. Beldiceanu, *Les actes des premiers Sultans*, Paris-The Hague 1960, 148-50; H. Hadžibegić in his fundamental article on *dj̲izya* in the Ottoman empire *Džizja ili harač*, in *Prilozi*, iii-iv, 55-135; v, 43-102, published twenty-seven documents from the *sidj̲illāt* of the ḳāḍīs of Bosnia and Macedonia. Two *berāt*s dated 5 Ramaḍān 1111/24 February 1700 and 1 S̲h̲aʿbān 1121/6 October 1709 published by B. C. Nedkof in *Sammlung orientalischer Arbeiten*, xi, Leipzig 1942 and reproduced in *Belleten*, xxxii, 641-9, are transcribed with some errors.

The *cizye muhasebe defterleri, mâliye ahkâm defterleri* and *mukataât defterleri* in the collections of Mâliye, Kâmil Kepeci and Yeni Seri, the Başvekâlet archives, Istanbul, constitute an inexhaustible source on the subject. The oldest *defter*s in these series are a *defter-i muḳāṭaʿāt* of Meḥemmed II's time, Yeni seri, nos. 176, 6222 and 7387, a *defter-i tawzīʿ-i dj̲izya-i gabrān-i wilāyat-i Rumeli wa Anadolu*, dated 958/1551, K. Kepeci, no. 3523 and a *defter-i aḥkām-i māliyye*, dated 973/1565 Mâliye Yeni Seri, no. 2775. The collection of *daftar-i muḥāsebe-i dj̲izya*, the most comprehensive source on *dj̲izya*, start in 1101/1690, K. Kepeci nos. 3508-3799. (Halil İnalcik)

iii.—India

The question of the levy of *dj̲izya* in India has provoked more emotion than scientific study, it being assumed that practice in India was closely modelled on the teachings of *fiḳh*, or the precepts of Indo-Muslim scholars, or the policies of the Ottomans. The view taken here that *dj̲izya* was not normally levied under the Dihlī Sultanate in the sense of a discriminatory religious tax may be contested; the evidence for this view is set out below.

The earliest extant source for the Arab conquest of Sind, Balād̲h̲urī, *Futūḥ*, 439, speaks of Muḥammad b. Ḳāsim levying *k̲h̲arādj̲* as tribute upon the conquered. The *Čač-nāma*, said to be a Persian translation (c. 613/1216-7) of an early Arabic account of the conquest, speaks (India Office Library MS 435, 268) of the Sindhīs being allowed the status of *d̲h̲immī* and of a graduated poll-tax being laid upon the people of Brāhmanābād, the three classes paying at the canonical rates of 48, 24 and 12 *dirhams* respectively (MS. 261-262). This account, however, would seem more a reflection of later tradition than of events in 94/712 which antedate the differentiation between *k̲h̲arādj̲* as land-tax and *dj̲izya* as poll-tax under the late Umayyads which became the basis of *fiḳh* teaching.

Under the Dihlī sultanate [*q.v.*], political conditions —the continued presence of armed Hindū chiefs in rural areas, the particularism of the period 801/1398-9 to 932/1526—do not appear apt for the imposition of a novel discriminatory tax by a minority upon a majority. Ḳāḍī Minhādj̲ al-Sirādj̲ Dj̲ūzdj̲ānī does not refer to *dj̲izya* being levied in the period to 658/1260. Amīr K̲h̲usraw, *Ḳirān al-saʿdayn*, ʿAlīgaṙh lith, 1918, 35, uses *dj̲izya* to mean tribute from Hindū kings. References in the K̲h̲aldj̲ī and early Tug̲h̲luḳ period couple *dj̲izya* indiscriminately with *k̲h̲arādj̲* to mean tribute or land revenue (*e.g.*, Ḍiyāʾ al-Dīn Baranī, *Taʾrīk̲h̲-i Fīrūz S̲h̲āhī*, *Bib. Ind.*, 291, 574; Baranī states also (*Fatāwa-yi Dj̲ahāndārī*, India Office Library MS 1149, fol. 119a) that Hindū *Rāys* and *Rānās* levied *k̲h̲arādj̲* and *dj̲izya* from their own Hindū subjects). An anecdote in Amīr Ḥasan Sidj̲zī's *Fawāʾid al-Fuwād* (707/1307-722/1322) speaks (Dihlī lith. 1865, 76) of a Muslim *darwis̲h̲* being required to pay *dj̲izya*, in a context showing that tax in general is meant.

There are, however, for the reign of Fīrūz S̲h̲āh Tug̲h̲luḳ, a number of references, principally in works of the *manāḳib* idiom, stating that that Sultan levied *dj̲izya*. The anonymous *Sīrat-i Fīrūz S̲h̲āhī*, (772/1370-1), (India Office Library Roto 34 of Bankīpur MS, fol. 61b), claims that Fīrūz S̲h̲āh Tug̲h̲luḳ ordered that only canonical taxes should be collected, a claim repeated in the *Futūḥāt-i Fīrūz S̲h̲āhī*, ed. Shaykh Abdur Rashid, ʿAlīgaṙh 1954, 6. S̲h̲ams al-Dīn Sirādj̲ ʿAfīf, *Taʾrīk̲h̲-i Fīrūz S̲h̲āhī*, states (*Bib. Ind.* ed. 382-4) that Fīrūz, having obtained a *fatwā* that *dj̲izya* should be levied from the Brāhmans, ordered it to be levied, but reduced its incidence, after protest from the Brāhmans of Dihlī and petition from other Hindūs, from the three rates of 40, 20 and 10 *tanka*s to 10 *tanka*s of 50 *dj̲ītal*s. The contemporary collection of ornamental epistles, *Ins̲h̲ā-yi Mahrū* (ed. Shaykh Abdur Rashid, ʿAlīgaṙh n.d.), also mentions (41, 53-4) the levy of *dj̲izya*, although the latter context suggests it was not distinguished from land revenue.

In the Sayyid and Lodī period nothing is heard of the levy of *dj̲izya*. From the manner in which the historians of Akbar's reign report its abolition by him, even the references to it in the Tug̲h̲luḳ period may be largely panegyrical There is indeed no agreement on the date at which the abolition took place. Abu 'l-Faḍl in the *Akbar-nāma* (*Bib. Ind.*, ii, 203), places it in 971/1564, Badāʾūnī in 987/1579 (*Muntak̲h̲ab al-tawārīk̲h̲*, *Bib. Ind.*, ii, 276). The latter, who is otherwise quick to condemn Akbar for any deviation from orthodoxy, mentions the event without comment. Niẓām al-Dīn Aḥmad does not refer to *dj̲izya* but mentions an abolition of *zakāt* in 989/1581.

Following a number of orthodox measures discriminating against non-Muslims, Awrangzīb imposed *dj̲izya* in 1090/1679, the *Mirʾāt-i Aḥmadī* states (i, 296-8), after a petition by *ʿulamāʾ* and *fuḳahāʾ*. Financial stringency as well as Awrangzīb's personal inclination doubtless helped to prompt the decision, although this would not, of course, explain the discriminatory character of the tax. Īsar Dās, *Futūḥāt-i ʿĀlamgīrī*, (British Museum Add. 23884, fol. 74a-74b), states that government servants were exempted and that there were three rates of tax—owners of property worth 2,500 rupees were assessed at 16 rupees, those worth 250 rupees at 6 rupees 8 annas, and those worth 52 rupees were assessed at 3 rupees and 4 annas, the blind, the paralysed, and the indigent being exempt. Its introduction encountered popular and court opposition at Dihlī, which was, however, overborne. The *Mirʾāt-i Aḥmadī* states that *dj̲izya* brought in 500,000 rupees in the province of Gudj̲arāt.

Dj̲izya did not long survive the death of Awrangzīb in 1118/1707. Bahādur S̲h̲āh, Dj̲ahāndār S̲h̲āh, Farruk̲h̲siyar and Muḥammad S̲h̲āh are all said to have abolished it, although Farruk̲h̲siyar had at one time struck a *dirham s̲h̲arʿī* to facilitate payment of the *dj̲izya* at the canonical rates (see dār al-ḍarb, iii). Niẓām al-Mulk Āsaf Ḏjāh attempted to revive it in 1135/1723, and Muḥammad Shāh nominally restored it in 1137/1725, but this restitution was never carried into effect.

Bibliography: In addition to references above, see: ʿAlī Muḥammad Ḵẖān, Mirʾāt-i Aḥmadī, i, Baroda 1928, 296-298; Muḥammad Saḳī Mustaʿidd Ḵẖān, Maʾāthir-i ʿĀlamgīrī, Calcutta 1870-3, 174; Ḵẖāfī Ḵẖān, Muntakhab al-lubāb, Calcutta 1860-74, index s.v. ḏjizya; N. Manucci, Storia do Mogor, ed. and trans. W. Irvine, iii, London 1907, 288-9; S. R. Sharma, Religious policy of the Mughal emperors, Calcutta 1940, index s.v. jizya; W. Irvine, Later Mughals, two vols., Calcutta 1921-2, index s.v. jizya; Satish Chandra, Jizyah in the post-Aurangzeb period, in Proc. 9th Indian History Congress, 1946, 320-6. (P. HARDY)

DJŌDHPUR or MĀRWĀṚ was the largest of the former Indian States in the Rajputana Agency with an area of 36,120 sq.m. and a population of 2,555,904 (1941 Census). There appears to be no evidence to support the Rādjpūt legend that the state of Ḏjōdhpur was founded by the Rādjpūts of Kanawḏj after their defeat by Muḥammad of Ghūr in 590/1194. Siyāhḏjī, the founder of the Rāthōr dynasty of Ḏjōdhpur, was probably descended from Rāthōr rādjās whose inscriptions are found in Ḏjōdhpur as early as the tenth century. The city of Ḏjōdhpur dates back to 1459. Rāw Māldew of Ḏjōdhpur, who refused to grant asylum to Humāyūn, was defeated by Shīr Shāh and by Akbar whose tributary he became. From this time the rulers of Ḏjōdhpur were closely connected with the Mughal emperors of Dihlī, giving their daughters in marriage to the imperial family and serving in the Mughal armies. The most famous Rādjpūt in the service of the Mughal emperors was Mahārādjā Ḏjaswant Singh (1048-89/1638-73). Because of Awrangzīb's orthodox religious policy war broke out in 1090/1679. Ḏjōdhpur was sacked, but guerilla warfare continued for many years. The Sayyid brothers forced the ruler of Ḏjōdhpur to give a daughter in marriage to the Emperor Farrukhsiyar. With the decline of Mughal power Ḏjōdhpur was overrun by Marāthās and by the forces of Amīr Ḵẖān the Paṭhān freebooter. It came under British protection in 1818. Mahārādjā Takht Sing who was loyal to the British in 1857 was guaranteed the right of adoption in 1862. The history of the State under British protection is uninteresting. In 1949 Ḏjōdhpur was merged into the new Indian State of Rādjāsthān.

Bibliography: C. U. Aitchison, Treaties, Engagements and Sanads, iii, Calcutta 1909; Annual reports on the political administration of Rajpootana (Selections from the Records of the Government of India. Foreign Department), Calcutta 1867 ff.; Imperial Gazetteer of India (1908) s.v. Jodhpur; J. Tod, Annals and antiquities of Rajasthan, 2 vols., London.

(C. COLLIN DAVIES)

DJOLOF (DIOLOF) is the name of a kingdom which was set up on what is now Senegalese territory from the 13th to the 16th centuries. At the height of its power this kingdom included Walo, Cayor, Baol, Sine, Salūm and Dimar, as well as part of Bambūk. The inhabitants and their language are called Wolof (modern spelling: Ouolof).

Physical features.—Djolof, which now designates merely one region of the Republic of Senegal, lies between 14°-16° N., and 16°-18° W. On the north it is bounded by Walo, Dimar and Fūta Toro, on the

east by Fūta Damga and Ferlo, on the south by Niani-Ouli and Baol, and on the west by Cayor and N'Diambour.

The Nounoum runs across Djolof from south-east to north-west, a river which is permanent only in its lower reaches where, from downstream, it receives the outflow from lake Guiers. It is one of the least fertile regions of Senegal; it can count on only 500 mm. of rain during the four months of the rainy season (July to October), called navète, a period of violent storms alternating with dry tornadoes. A transition period which is already dry, the lollé, though sometimes marked by a little rain (heug), then follows, corresponding with the ground-nut season (November to January). It is then that water-melons (beref) are cultivated, being harvested at the end of the dry season (nor). The harmattan blows violently in February and March, while in May and June, during the tiorom, the drought is alleviated and vegetation begins to grow green again.

History.—The history of Djolof is not fully known. Legend relates that in about 595/1200, a pious Muslim of the Prophet's family, by name Būbakar (Abū Bakr) b. ʿUmar, also called Abū Dardāy, came from Mecca to settle in Senegal, and converted the country to Islam. Apparently it was only in the 15th century that one of his presumed descendants, Ndiadiane Diaye, freed Djolof from the domination of Tekrūr and annexed Walo, Baol, Sine and Salūm in turn. The sovereigns bore the title of Bour ba Djolof. Quarrels that broke out between the various Ouolof communities led to the secession of the Lebou who crossed Cayor and went to settle on the peninsula of Cap Vert under the suzerainty of the damel. In the 16th century a certain Koumbi Guielem, with the help of the Lebou, started a revolt against Bour Biram Diem Koumba who crushed it, but was unable to prevent the chiefs of Cayor and Baol from seceding. In the middle of the 16th century, Leleful Fack was unable to withstand a further revolt, led by a certain Amani Goné Sohel who was the true founder of the kingdom of Cayor, with M'Bour as its capital.

Probably as a result of the profoundly democratic temperament of the Ouolofs, there is not a single sovereign from this period whose name is outstanding. But the linguistic and cultural mark had been set, and was later confirmed during the colonial period.

Djolof, being situated inland, was affected by European colonization only at a late date. In the 16th century Islam had only superficially penetrated to this region where the pagan practices of the Ouolofs scandalized the pious Muslims. However, the progressive Islamization of the inhabitants was noted as early as 1445 by Ca da Mosto.

After settling on the coast from 1683, the French explored the interior. In 1682 Lemaire gave information about the Ouolofs, while three years later La Courbe sent his agents to make a treaty with the Bour ba Guiolof. From 1749 to 1753, Djolof was visited by the French naturalist Michel Adanson. A century later it served as a place of refuge for rebels during the campaigns conducted against Lat Dior, damel of Cayor. In 1871 the Tīdjānī chief Aḥmadu Sheykhu invaded Djolof and Cayor, but was routed by an expeditionary force and killed in 1875.

In 1889, a force under the command of Colonel Dodds put the bour ba Djolof to flight. The latter's brother acknowledged the French Protectorate on 3 May 1890. Henceforth Djolof shared in the development of Senegal and, in 1931, a branch line of the

Dakar-Saint Louis railway reached Linguère in the heart of the Djolof country. At the present time the region is almost entirely Islamized. In every village can be found a place reserved for communal prayer (*diāma*) and one or more marabouts. The Muslim Ouolofs are very strict in praying and fasting; the name *tabaski* (Touareg *tafaski*, from *pascha*) which they give to *al-ʿīd al-kabīr* is evidence of their partial conversion by the Berbers; they are very ready to become members of a religious confraternity, usually the Ḳādiriyya. It was from Djolof that Aḥmadu Bamba, founder of the Murīd sect, recruited his followers. This Murīdism (in a peasant form) is regarded as a "Ouolofisation" of Islam.

Society.—According to tradition, the first villages are said to have been formed by gifts of land by the Burba Djolof to warriors who had distinguished themselves in expeditions. As in most of the Ouolof country, society is divided into endogamous groups which no-one can leave or join. The freemen (*gor*) are descendants of the founder of the village or marabout: artisans, cobblers (*wudé*), blacksmiths (*teugne*), wood-workers (*laobé*), sorcerers (*gueveul*). The caste of the unfree (or *diame*) seems to have disappeared.

The place of habitation is the village (*deuk*), formed of squares which house the scattered family. Although the ground-nut has noticeably improved living conditions, Djolof is one of the most barren regions of Senegal, and hence the temporary emigration of the men to the towns.

Bibliography: Adam, *Le Djolof et le Ferlo*, in *Annales de Géographie*, 1915; Ancelle, *Les explorations du Sénégal*, Paris 1887; Dr. Anfreville de la Salle, *Notre vieux Sénégal*, Paris 1909; Angrand, *Manuel français-Ouolof*, Dakar 1942 (bibliography); J. Audiger, *Les Ouolof du Bas Ferlo*, in *Les Cahiers d'Outre-Mer*, Bordeaux, April-June 1961, 157-81; Béranger-Féraud, *Les peuplades de Sénégambie*, Paris 1879; *Histoire militaire de l'Afrique occidentale française*, Paris 1931; Carrère and Holle, *De la Sénégambie française*, Paris 1855; Chevalier, *Monographie de l'arachide*, Paris 1936; *Coutumiers juridiques de l'A.O.F.*, i; Faidherbe, *Notice sur la colonie du Sénégal et sur les pays qui sont en relation avec elle*, Saint Louis 1868; idem, *Le Sénégal*, Paris 1889; Gaden, *Légendes et coutumes sénégalaises d'après Yoro Diao*, Paris 1912; Geismar, *Coutumes civiles des races du Sénégal*, Saint Louis 1931; Hardy, *La mise en valeur du Sénégal de 1816 à 1854*, Paris 1921; Mgr. Kobès, *Dictionnaire ouolof-français revu par le P. Abiven*, Dakar 1923; Labouret, *Paysans de l'Afrique occidentale*, Paris 1941; Marty, *Étude sur l'Islam au Sénégal*, Paris 1917; Olivier, *Le Sénégal*, Paris 1906; Papy and Pélissier, *Problèmes agricoles au Sénégal*, Saint Louis 1952; Séré de Rivières, *Sénégal-Dakar*, Paris 1953; Villard, *Histoire du Sénégal*, Dakar 1943.

(R. CORNEVIN)

DJUBAYL, a small port in Lebanon situated between Bayrūt and Tripoli on the site of the ancient Byblos (or Gebal in the Old Testament), formerly a centre at once maritime, commercial and religious, closely connected with Egypt since the 4th millennium B.C., and as celebrated for the worship of Adonis, of a syncretistic nature, as for its specialization in woodwork and products from the forests on the mountains nearby. If Byblos remained truly prosperous in the Roman period and later became the seat of a bishopric, it appears to have greatly declined by the time when it was conquered by the Muslims, and when Muʿāwiya established a colony of Persians there, as in the neighbouring territories. Djubayl, which was attached to the *djund* of Damascus, kept a small garrison until the 5th/11th century. At that period, when the Fāṭimids had extended their domination over the Syrian coast, it was under the direct dependency of the Shīʿī ḳāḍīs of Tripoli, the Banū ʿAmmār. According to the traveller Nāṣir-i Khusraw who passed through it in 438/1047 the town, triangular in shape and surrounded by high walls, stood by the sea, whilst the surrounding plain, at the foot of Mount Lebanon, was covered with date-palms.

Captured in 496-1103 by Raymond de Saint Gilles, Count of Tripoli, it became a feudal domain under the name Gibelet, and was given to a family of Genoese origin who were known as the "lords of Gibelet"; it remained in the hands of the Crusaders until reconquered by Saladin in 583/1187. Archaeological traces of the Frankish period can be seen in the castle which stands on a hill at the north-east angle of the enceinte, no doubt on the site of an earlier Muslim fortress, and in the church of St. John, most of which was later rebuilt, though the baptistery, a masterpiece of Romanesque art, has survived intact.

At one time reoccupied by the Franks, to whom the Kurdish garrison put there by Ṣalāḥ al-Dīn had surrendered in 593/1197, the town was reconquered in 665/1266-7 by Baybars who restored the fortifications, and later made it part of the Mamlūk district of Bayrūt. Then, at the end of the 9th/15th century, it fell into the hands of the Banū Ḥamāda, a family of Mutawālīs dominating Upper Lebanon, and remained in their power until the 12th/18th century. The importance of its port had by then greatly diminished, its place being taken by Djūniya, a rival port from ancient times which had long been in control of the local coastal shipping.

At the present day Djubayl is merely a small village of about 1,500 inhabitants, almost all Maronite, and it is chiefly known for the ruins of the Phoenician town which have been methodically excavated since 1921 by the French mission under the direction of M. Montet and M. Dunand respectively.

Bibliography: Pauly-Wissowa, s. v. *Byblos*; R. Dussaud, *Topographie historique de la Syrie*, Paris 1927, 63-9; M. van Berchem and E. Fatio, *Voyage en Syrie*, Cairo 1913-5, 105-13; *Guide Bleu, Syrie-Palestine*, Paris 1932, 38-45; Le Strange, *Palestine*, 32, 464-5; M. Gaudefroy-Demombynes, *La Syrie à l'époque des Mamelouks*, Paris 1923, cv and 74; R. Grousset, *Histoire des Croisades*, index, esp. i, 141 and iii, 147; Ibn Khurradādhbih, 77 and 255; Ibn al-Faḳīh, 105; Yaʿḳūbī, *Buldān*, 328; Yaʿḳūbī-Wiet, 178; Nāṣir-i Khusraw, ed. Schefer, 43; Ibn Shaddād, *al-Aʿlāḳ al-khaṭīra*, 2nd part, ms. Leyden 800, f° 98b; Yāḳūt, ii, 32; *Marāṣid*, 1, 240.

(D. SOURDEL)

AL-**DJUBAYL**, a Saʿūdī Arabian port on the Persian Gulf, located at 27° 00′ N., 49° 39′ E.; also known as ʿAynayn. Al-Djubayl al-Baḥrī, a rocky islet several hundred metres offshore, is the most prominent landmark of the site; al-Djabal al-Barrī is a hill about 12 km. to the south of the town. Al-Djubayl is located at the start of the Darb al-Kunhurī, a caravan trail and motor track leading to al-Riyaḍ. Members of the tribe of Āl Bū ʿAynayn assert that the site was settled by their ancestor Khuwaylid b. ʿAbd Allāh b. Dārim of Banī Tamīm and took the name ʿAynayn from its two flowing springs; it is also said to have been once occupied by the tribe of ʿAbd al-Ḳays. In the early Islamic period ʿAynayn was noted for its plentiful date palms and for a poet, Khulayd ʿAynayn, who is chiefly remembered for exchanging lampoons with the famous Umayyad satirist Djarīr b. ʿAṭiyya. The site was later abandoned. The present town was populated about 1330/1911-2 by members of Āl Bū ʿAynayn who emigrated from Ḳaṭar, with the permission of the Turkish authorities, as the result of a local dispute. The settlers were Mālikī Sunnīs engaged in pearl fishing and other seafaring occupations. Al-Djubayl came under Saʿūdī rule during the conquest of al-Ḥasā by ʿAbd al-ʿAzīz Āl Saʿūd in 1331/1913. The town was formally acknowledged to be Saʿūdī territory in the treaty of 1334/1915 by which Britain recognized the independence of ʿAbd al-ʿAzīz. During the consolidation of the Saʿūdī Kingdom, al-Djubayl became a port of entry for goods destined for Central Arabia. Its significance has since diminished as the result of the decline in the Persian Gulf pearling trade and of the development of modern communication routes through the port, rail, and road centre of al-Dammām [*q.v.*]. The population of al-Djubayl was estimated in 1960 at 4,200.

Bibliography: *LA*, xiii, Beirut 1955, 308; al-Bakrī, *Muʿdjam mā istaʿdjam*, iii, Cairo 1949, 986; al-Fayrūzābādī, *al-Ḳamūs al-muḥīṭ*, iv, Cairo 1344/1925, 252; J. G. Lorimer, *Gazetteer of the Persian Gulf, ʿOman, and Central Arabia*, Calcutta 1908-15. (H. W. ALTER)

AL-**DJUBAYLA,** a small town of 50-60 dwellings located in Nadjd at 24° 54′ N, 46° 28′ E, on the left bank of Wādī Ḥanīfa between al-ʿUyayna and al-Dirʿiyya. Yāḳūt mentions a place called al-Djubayla as the chief town of Banū ʿĀmir of ʿAbd al-Ḳays, but there is no evidence definitely linking this place with the present town. According to Ibn Bulayhid and local tradition, the site of ʿAḳrabāʾ [*q.v.*] is near the present town. Mounds on the right bank of Wādī Ḥanīfa, called locally Ḳubūr al-Ṣaḥāba, are believed to be the graves of Companions fallen in the battle of ʿAḳrabāʾ, and ʿAḳrabāʾ is the name of the garden area of al-Djubayla, a small *rawḍa* about one kilometre east of the town, which is said to be the actual site of the gardens in which the battle took place.

Ibn Bishr relates that in 850/1446 al-Djubayla belonged to Āl Yazīd, whom Mūsā b. Rabīʿa b. Māniʿ al-Muraydī, an ancestor of Āl Saʿūd, attacked and virtually exterminated shortly thereafter. Āl Dughaythir of al-Dirʿiyya claim descent from the survivors of Āl Yazīd, who were a branch of the Banū Ḥanīfa (Ḥanīf b. Ludjaym of Bakr ibn Wāʾil), the supporters of Musaylima al-Kadhdhāb at the battle of ʿAḳrabāʾ and the tribe which gave its name to Wādī Ḥanīfa. The battle site of ʿAḳrabāʾ was in ancient al-Yamāma, which is believed to have extended as far north as the present town of al-Djubayla and its garden of ʿAḳrabāʾ. However, in many cases the identification of ancient places by modern usage remains inconclusive.

Both al-Djubayla and ʿAḳrabāʾ are mentioned several times by Ibn Bishr as the scene of clashes between the growing power of Āl Saʿūd and the influential lords of Banū Khālid from al-Ḥasā (al-Aḥsāʾ) between 1133/1721 and 1172/1758-59.

In 1153/1740 the young reformer, Shaykh Muḥammad b. ʿAbd al-Wahhāb, then virtually unknown outside of al-ʿUyayna, destroyed the alleged tomb of Zayd b. al-Khaṭṭāb, the eldest brother of the Caliph ʿUmar and one of the Companions who fell at ʿAḳrabāʾ, as a step towards the obliteration of false worship in Nadjd. Today the site of the tomb is forgotten.

Al-Djubayla lies at the juncture of two roads from al-Riyāḍ to al-Ḥidjāz; one road winding across the rolling rocky country between the east bank of Wādī Ḥanīfa and al-Riyāḍ, and a second road which is paved as far as al-Dirʿiyya [*q.v.*] and then follows the bed of Wādī Ḥanīfa to al-Djubayla. These roads give the town access to al-Riyāḍ for the sale of crops raised in the garden of ʿAḳrabāʾ and a small steady income from trans-peninsular motor traffic. In 1961 a new road was completed which provides a paved all-weather route from al-Riyāḍ to the Tuwayḳ escarpment at Shaʿīb Luḥā (sometimes shown on maps as al-Ha) south-south-east of al-Riyāḍ, whence it proceeds north-west, parallel to the escarpment, as far as Marāh where it rejoins Darb al-Ḥidjāz, eliminating completely the difficult stretch of road between al-Djubayla and the pass of al-Ḥaysiyya at the head of Wādī Ḥanīfa.

Bibliography: Ibn Bishr; Ibn Bulayhid; Philby, *Saʾudi Arabia*, London 1955; Yāḳūt. (R. L. HEADLEY)

DJUBBA [see LIBĀS].

AL-**DJUBBĀʾĪ,** ABŪ ʿALĪ MUḤAMMAD B. ʿABD AL-WAHHĀB, one of the most celebrated of the Muʿtazila [*q.v.*]. Born at Djubbā in Khūzistān, he attended the school at Baṣra of Abū Yaʿḳūb Yūsuf al-Shaḥḥām who at that time occupied the chair of Abu ʾl-Hudhayl al-ʿAllāf. He succeeded al-Shaḥḥām, and it can be said that he was able to add a final brilliance to the tradition of the masters, while at times he refreshed it and opened the way to new solutions. He died in 303/915-6.

He thus holds a place in the line of the Baṣra Muʿtazila who, especially over the question of human actions, differ from the Baghdād Muʿtazila. In Baṣra itself, he was particularly at variance with al-Naẓẓām (whom he opposed) and al-Djāḥiẓ, but he also differed from the two lines of thought of al-Aṣamm and ʿAbbād although these were closer to his own. The two last-mentioned both combined the influence of Muʿammar with the tradition of Abu ʾl-Hudhayl; and the two former added to the Baṣra teaching influences deriving from Baghdād (school of al-Murdār).

Al-Djubbāʾī had two pupils who later became celebrated: his son Abū Hāshim (cf. below), and Abu ʾl-Ḥasan al-Ashʿarī [*q.v.*] who, after breaking away, was to devote himself to refuting Muʿtazilism and to become the "founder" of the so-called school of the *Ashʿariyya* [*q.v.*]. The traditions of the *ʿilm al-kalām* take pleasure in recounting the dialogue reputed to have brought al-Ashʿarī and his teacher into conflict on the subject of the fate of the "three brothers"—one pious, one impious and one who died *infans*. In this issue was posed the problem of the rational justification of the divine Decree. Al-Djubbāʾī, it is said, was unable to reply, and al-Ashʿarī left him. W. Montgomery Watt has reminded us that the wish to "justify" absolutely the divine Decree in respect of every human destiny seems to derive perhaps from the Baghdād Muʿtazila rather than from the Baṣra school (*Free will and predestination in early Islam*, 137).

However that may be, no complete work of al-Djubbāʾī has survived until the present time. We know that he left a *Kitāb al-uṣūl*, to the refutation of which al-Ashʿarī devoted several treatises (cf. in the bibliography of McCarthy, *Lumaʿ*, Appendix iii, nos. 16, 61, 65, 78), and various polemical works against Ibn al-Rāwandī and al-Naẓẓām. But one of the best available sources allowing us to evaluate his tendencies is still the *Maḳālāt al-Islāmiyyīn* of al-Ashʿarī (see particularly Cairo ed., ii, 181-5, 196, 199-201, 243, etc.).

The teaching given by al-Djubbāʾī followed after the reaction by caliph Mutawakkil which dates from 235/850. Muʿtazilism is no longer the official doctrine. Certain tendencies of al-Djubbāʾī are linked with the best traditions of the school, others already proclaim the solutions of the Ashʿarī *kalām*. On the one hand, he maintains the validity of *ʿaḳl* (reason) as a criterion, and he continues to affirm the identity of the divine attributes and the divine essence; on the other hand, however, he tends to introduce once again the mystery of the divine Will and its action upon the world.—Two examples: (1) those of the Baghdād Muʿtazila, followed with certain modifications by al-Shaḥḥām, who adopted the idea of "acquisition" (*kasb, iktisāb*), applied it only to involuntary human actions, God being, in their view, in no way the "cause" of free human actions; for al-Djubbāʾī, on the contrary, God retains Supreme Power even over the actions which man performs freely. But, unlike the later Ashʿarī solution, he refuses to apply the theory of the *kasb* to free actions; and he calls man the "creator" (*khāliḳ*) of his actions, in the sense that man acts, or his actions proceed from him, with a determination (*ḳadar*) which comes from God.—(2) ʿAbbād objected to any association of God with evil, and for example refused to speak of *sharr* or *ḳabḥ* as sickness or weakness; according to al-Djubbāʾī, they can be called "evils", provided that this term is taken metaphorically. Similarly, he offers personal solutions to the problem of "divine aid" (*tawfīḳ*) and "divine favour" (*luṭf*), which do not destroy the voluntary character of the action. What is more, foreshadowing certain Ashʿarī theories, he breaks away from the Muʿtazila tradition of allotting merit and demerit according to an exact, rational criterion, and maintains that God grants to whom He will His favour or good-will gratuitously (the problem of *tafaḍḍul*).

Al-Djubbāʾī was no doubt one of the Muʿtazila whom al-Ashʿarī took the greatest pains to refute, all the more since he knew him better; but this did not happen without his influence being felt, and we have already noted al-Djubbāʾī putting forward certain Ashʿarite arguments. This complex relationship between al-Ashʿarī and his former teacher helps, we feel, to explain the paradox of Ashʿarism in its infancy: claiming kinship with the "Ancients", particularly Ibn Ḥanbal, but rejected, no less than Muʿtazilism, by contemporary Ḥanbalites.

Abū Hāshim ʿAbd al-Salām, son of al-Djubbāʾī, d. 321/933. He was a contemporary of al-Ashʿarī, and one of the very last Muʿtazila to exercise a direct influence on Sunnī thought. He conducted a school, his disciples being called *bahshamiyya*, or even, by their enemies, *dhammiyya* [*q v.*] (mentioned in al-Baghdādī). The Muʿtazilī influence, though opposed by the official Sunnism, continued to affect the Shīʿa, and Ibn ʿAbbād al-Ṭālaḳānī (326-85/938-95), vizier of the Būyid princes Muʾayyid al-Dawla and Fakhr al-Dawla, recognized Abū Hāshim as his master.

The works of Abū Hāshim have not survived, and we know almost nothing of the author himself except from later polemical works. He was known chiefly for his theories of "modes" (*aḥwāl*), a sort of conceptualism which was to exert great influence on the *falsafa* on the one hand, and on the later *kalām* on the other. It was on the question of the relationship between the divine attributes and the divine essence that the problem was raised. Anxiety to safeguard the absolute Unity of God led the Muʿtazila, and even al-Djubbāʾī, to "extenuate" (*taʿṭīl*) the reality of the attributes to the point of turning them into simple denominations. Abū Hāshim made use of the grammatical notion of *ḥāl*, "state" of the verb in relation to the agent, to define the degree of reality of mental concepts, and thence the degree of reality of the divine attributes. According to an observation of L. Massignon (*Passion d'al-Ḥallādj*, 556), he compares "les modes [*aḥwāl*] d'inhérence des attributs divins en Dieu avec les modalités [*id.*] d'insertion des concepts en notre esprit". Now, as Fakhr al-Din al-Rāzī was to say (*Muḥaṣṣal*, 38), the *ḥāl* is the "state" established in our mind by the meaning according to which the idea is received, and it is intermediate "between existence and non-existence".

From the human concept to the divine attribute there is thus, for Abū Hāshim, a constant interplay between the logical (and noetic) and the metaphysical. Just as the *kasb* of al-Shaḥḥām (rejected by al-Djubbāʾī) was later taken up and transformed by the Ashʿarīs, so the *ḥāl* of Abū Hāshim was later adopted in terms of their own perspectives by al-Ashʿarī, no doubt by Bāḳillānī, and certainly by Djuwaynī, master of al-Ghazzālī in *kalām*. What is more, it is not inopportune to turn to Abū Hāshim's theses to explain the semi-conceptualism of Ibn Sīnā and his commentator the Shīʿī Naṣīr al-Dīn al-Ṭūsī.—Al-Djubbāʾī and his son thus exerted on Muslim thought an influence which far surpassed the direct rôle of Baṣra Muʿtazilism, considered as an independent school.

Bibliography: Houtsma, *Zum Kitāb al-Fihrist*, in *WZKM*, iv, 224; Ibn Khallikān, nr 393, 618; Arnold, *al-Muʿtazilah*, 45 ff.; Shahrastānī, *Milal* (ed. Cureton), 54 ff.; Baghdādī, *Farḳ*, 167; Steiner, *Die Muʿtaziliten*, 82 ff.; Horten, *Die Modustheorie des Abū Hāshim*, in *ZDMG*, lxiii, 308 ff.; idem, *Die philosophische Systeme der spekulativ. Theologen im Islām*, 352 ff., 403 ff. (and ref.); Abu 'l-Ḥasan al-Ashʿarī, *Kitāb al-Lumaʿ*, ed. and English tr. R. J. McCarthy, Beirut 1953, 29-30/41-2 and ref. in art.; idem, *Maḳālat al-Islāmiyyīn*, ref. in art.; Fakhr al-Dīn al-Rāzī, *Muḥaṣṣal*, Cairo n.d., 38; Ibrāhīm Bādjūrī, *Ḥāshiya . . . ʿalā Djawharat al-tawḥīd*, Cairo 1352/1934, 64; L. Massignon, *Passion d'al-Ḥallādj*, Paris 1922, s.vv. *Djubbāʾī* and *Abū Hāshim*; L. Gardet and M. M. Anawati, *Introduction à la théologie musulmane*, Paris 1948, index; W. Montgomery Watt, *Free will and predestination in early Islam*, London 1948, 83-7, 136-7.

(L. GARDET)

DJUBŪR, a large and predominantly sedentary Sunnī tribe of central and northern ʿIrāḳ. A considerable community so named occupies land and villages in the Khāliṣ *ḳaḍā* of the Diyālā *liwāʾ*, and another on canals drawing from the Ḥilla branch (right bank) of the Euphrates, below Ḥilla. Minor sections calling themselves Djubūr are also found elsewhere in central ʿIrāḳ. But the largest body lives in riverain villages on the Lesser Zāb between Altun Köprü and the Tigris, and on the latter river between points south of Mosul and north of Takrīt. The former of these branches have habitually quarrelled with the ʿUbayd of the Ḥawīdja west of Kirkūk and the Dizāʾī in the plain between the two Zābs; the latter have a long history of bad relations with the S̲h̲ammar (D̲j̲arbā) of the D̲j̲azīra. All alike were in frequent collision with the Turkish Government in the 13th/19th and earlier centuries. As with most settled ʿIrāk tribes, however, disorder and disobedience are now less in evidence than ever before.

The D̲j̲ubūr have limited sheep-grazing sections, who take their flocks into the steppe each winter; but the great majority are cultivators on the flow canals of the Khāliṣ or the Ḥilla river, or on the water-lift lands of the Zāb and Tigris where mechanical pump-irrigation and some flow-irrigation have greatly developed. Many from the latter districts work for the oil company whose pipelines from Kirkūk oilfields cross or skirt their territory.

The various D̲j̲ubūr sections have little cohesion, and have produced no unifying leader for generations. They consist of many unconnected elements with little bond save their name. The usual legend of noble origins in Nad̲j̲d, and entry into ʿIrāk via the Wādī Ḥawrān as conquering immigrants, does not contain any assessable historical basis.

(S. H. LONGRIGG)

DJUČI or rather D̲j̲oči (ca. 580-624/1184-1227), the eldest son of Čingiz-Khān [q.v.] and the ancestor of the Khāns of the Golden Horde, Krîm, Tiumen, Bukhārā and Khīwa. A depalatalized, perhaps Turkish form of his name, Toshî or Doshî, is represented by the Tūshî of D̲j̲uwaynī and D̲j̲ūzd̲j̲ānī, the Tosucchan (i.e., Toshî Khān) of Carpini and the Dūshî of Nasawī. The historical data on this progenitor of so many dynasties are sparse and contradictory. His very paternity is uncertain. It is implied in the *Secret history of the Mongols* that his real father was Čilger Bökö of the Merkit, by whose tribe his mother Börte Fud̲j̲in was carried off into captivity shortly after her marriage to Čingiz-Khān. On the other hand Rashīd al-Dīn, who reproduces the *Altan Debter*, the official chronicle of the imperial family, specifically states that Börte was already pregnant at the time of her capture. Contrary to the *Secret history* she was not, according to Rashīd al-Dīn, rescued by a joint expedition of Čingiz-Khān, D̲j̲amuka and Ong-Khān but was handed over by the Merkit to the last named, with whose tribe, the Kereyt, they were then at peace. Delivered up by Ong-Khān to an emissary of Čingiz-Khān Börte gave birth to D̲j̲oči in the course of the homeward journey; and the circumstances of his birth are in some way reflected in his name, apparently the Mongol word *d̲j̲oči* "guest". D̲j̲oči is first mentioned in the *Secret history*, under the year 1207, as being sent on a campaign against the Oyrat and other forest peoples along the western shores of Lake Baykal: after conquering these peoples he advanced in a westerly direction to receive the submission of the Kîrghîz tribes in the region of the Upper Yenisey. Rashīd al-Dīn, whilst recording the submission of the Kîrghîz in 1207, makes no mention of D̲j̲oči in this connection, though he refers to him as having suppressed a revolt of that people in the winter of 1218-19. D̲j̲oči took part in his father's campaigns against the Chin rulers of Northern China, being active with his brothers Čaghatay and Ögedey in Shan-hsi (1211) and Chih-li, Ho-nan and Shan-hsi (1213). He likewise took part, in 1216 or 1217, in a campaign against the remnants of the Merkit which resulted in their defeat and annihilation in what is to-day the Kustanai region of Northern Kazakhstān. A clash with Sultan Muḥammad Khʷārizm-S̲h̲āh [q.v.] as the Mongols were returning eastwards from this campaign formed the prelude to the hostilities which broke out in 1219. Upon the arrival of Čingiz-Khān's forces before Otrar, probably in September of that year, D̲j̲oči was dispatched upon an expedition down the Sîr-Daryā. The details of this expedition, which is passed over in silence by the contemporary Muslim sources, are given by D̲j̲uwaynī, who refers to D̲j̲oči as Ulush-Idi, a title which Rashīd al-Dīn, in reproducing D̲j̲uwaynī's account, takes to be the name of a general in joint command. Advancing down the Sîr-Daryā D̲j̲oči captured Sughnak, Özkend, Barčin and Ashnās. It had been his intention not to attack D̲j̲and but to rest his troops in the Kara-Kum steppe to the north-east of the Aral Sea in what is now Central Kazakhstan. However a report on the conditions prevailing in D̲j̲and caused him to change the direction of his march and lay siege to the town, which surrendered in April or May, 1220. D̲j̲oči now proceeded to the Kara-Kum steppe and seems to have remained in this region or in the D̲j̲and area until the end of the year, when he was ordered by Čingiz-Khān to join Čaghatay and Ögedey in the siege of Gurgānd̲j̲ [q.v.]. The siege operations appear to have been hampered by a quarrel between D̲j̲oči and Čaghatay: upon the fall of the town in Ṣafar 618/March-April 1220 it became part of D̲j̲oči's *yurt* or appanage, which now extended from the region of Kayalîgh [q.v.] to the eastern banks of the Volga, comprising within its limits almost the whole of the present-day Kazakhstan. From Gurgānd̲j̲ D̲j̲oči withdrew northwards into this enormous territory, there to remain till the spring of . . ./1223, when he joined his father and brothers in the Kulan-Bashi steppe between the present-day Čimkent and D̲j̲ambul in Southern Kazakhstan, driving before him, for the purposes of a *battue*, great herds of wild asses: he brought also with him, as a present for Čingiz-Khān, 20,000 grey horses. After the *battue* the princes passed the remainder of the summer in Kulan-Bashi and D̲j̲oči then returned to his own territories, where he remained for the rest of his life, apparently on bad terms with his father, whom he predeceased by several months. Upon his death his *yurt* was divided between his eldest son Orda and his second son Batu [q.v.], the founders respectively of the White Horde and the Kipčak Khānate or Golden Horde.

Bibliography: As in the article ČINGIZ-KHĀN with the following additions: Barthold, *Turkestan*; Pelliot, *Notes sur l'histoire de la Horde d'Or*, Paris 1950; J. A. Boyle, *On the titles given in Juvainī to certain Mongolian princes*, in *HJAS*, xix (1956). (J. A. BOYLE)

DJUDĀLA [see GUDĀLA].

DJUDDA, pronounced D̲j̲idda locally, a Saudi Arabian port on the Red Sea at 21° 29′ N., 39° 11′ E. Its climate is notoriously poor. The town, flanked by a lagoon on the north-west and salt flats on the south-east, faces a bay on the west which is so encumbered by reefs that it can only be entered through narrow channels. By paved road, D̲j̲udda is 72 km. from Mecca and 419 km. from Medina.

Most Arab geographers and scholars maintain that D̲j̲udda, signifying a road (Lane; al-Bakrī, ii, 371) is the correct spelling of the name of the town, rather than D̲j̲idda or D̲j̲adda (grandmother) as claimed by Gautier, Philby (*Heart*, i, 221) and others (cf. Yāḳūt, ii, 41; Hitti; Wahba) on account of the existence (until 1928), of the "tomb of Eve" not far from the city (for description and photographs, see E. F. Gautier, *Mœurs et coutumes des Musulmans*, Paris 1931, 64-6). The town dates from pre-Islamic times. Hishām b. Muḥammad al-Kalbī in *al-Aṣnām* claims that ʿAmr b. Luhayy of the Khuzāʿa introduced idols from Djudda into Mecca several centuries before Islam (cf. al-Anṣārī, in bibliography). According to Yāḳūt, Djudda b. Ḥazm b. Rabbān b. Ḥulwān of the Ḳuḍāʿa took his name from the town which was part of the territory of the Ḳuḍāʿa [*q.v.*]. The foundations of Djudda's importance were laid in 26/646 by the Caliph ʿUthmān, who chose it as the port of Mecca in place of the older port of al-Shuʿayba a little to the south (al-Batanūnī, 6; Nallino, 155). As the focus of the Muslim world, Mecca became a great importing centre, its supplies coming from Egypt and India via Djudda.

By the 4th/10th century Djudda was a prosperous commercial town and its customs were a considerable source of revenue to the rulers of al-Ḥidjāz (Muḳaddasī, 79, 104). In addition, taxes were levied on pilgrims at Djudda, for it was here that those who came by sea landed on Arabian soil. Nāṣir-i Khusraw (ed. Schefer, 65; 181-3 of the translation) describes the city in the 5th/11th century as an unwalled town, with a male population estimated at 5,000, governed by a slave of the *sharīf* of Mecca, whose chief duty was the collection of the revenues. A century later Ibn Djubayr (ed. De Goeje, 75 ff.) gives a picture of the town with its reed huts, stone *khāns*, and mosques, and he praises Ṣalāḥ al-Dīn for having abolished the taxes levied by the *sharīfs*.

With the decline of the ʿAbbāsid Caliphate, much of the trade formerly going to al-Baṣra was diverted to Djudda, where ships from Egypt, carrying gold, metals, and woollens from Europe, met those from India carrying spices, dyes, rice, sugar, tea, grain, and precious stones. Djudda exacted about ten per cent *ad valorem* on these goods. After 828/1425 the Mamlūk Sultans of Egypt, whose cupidity had been aroused by Djudda's prosperity, took the collection of customs at Djudda into their own hands (although they shared it with the *sharīfs* from time to time), thus making Djudda politically as well as economically dependent on Egypt (Ibn Taghrībirdī, iv, 21, 41; v, 79).

The coming of the Portuguese to eastern waters, and their attacks on Muslim shipping from 1502 onward, brought a new threat to Djudda, which the Mamlūks and after them the Ottomans made determined efforts to meet. Ḥusayn al-Kurdī, the Governor of Djudda, appointed by the Mamlūk Sultan Ḳānṣūh al-Ghūrī, built a formidable wall around the town in 917/1511 (al-Batanūnī erroneously states that it was in 915/1509) and made Djudda a base for attacks against the Portuguese fleet. Lopo Soares de Albergaria sailed to the Djudda harbour in 923/1517 in pursuit of the Mamlūk fleet commanded by Salmān Reʾīs but declined to attack the city because of its powerful fortifications (Danvers, *The Portuguese in India*, 1894, 335). In 945/1538 the Ottoman naval expedition, on its way to India, called there, and collected masts and guns (Hammer-Purgstall, *GOR*², ii, 156-8; Uzunçarşılı, *Osm. Tar.*, ii, 379 ff., 538; Fevzi Kurtoğlu in *Belleten*, iv, (1940), 53-87; Stribling, 89-90). In 948/1541 the Portuguese made their last unsuccessful attempt to take the city, which was defended by the Sharīf Abū Numayy. The Sultan Süleymān repaid him for his successful resistance by granting him half of the fees collected at Djudda (Daḥlān, 53). The trade of the Red Sea did not, as was at one time thought, end with the Portuguese circumnavigation of Africa, but continued under Ottoman protection, right through the 10th/16th century. Ottoman sources of this period refer to the regular appearance at Djudda of ships from India, and a Venetian consul in Cairo, in May 1565, speaks of the arrival of 20,000 quintals of pepper at Djudda. It was not until the late 16th and early 17th centuries that the transit trade through the Red Sea began to come to an end (F. Braudel, *La Méditerranée et le monde méditerranéen à l'époque de Philippe II*, Paris 1949, 423-37; Halil İnalcık, in *Belleten*, xv, (1951), 662 ff.).

Little of importance occurred in the history of Djudda during the 11th/17th and 12th/18th centuries. Al-Ḥidjāz, under the suzerainty of the Sultan, was ruled locally by the Ḥasanid family of the *sharīfs*, who intrigued to their own advantage against the declining power of the Turks (Daḥlān, al-Djabartī). The town of Djudda was a sandjaḳ, for a while the centre of the *eyālet* of Ḥabesh, later part of the *wilāyet* of Ḥidjāz. According to Ottoman sources, the Grand Vizier Ḳara Muṣṭafā Pasha (held office 1087/1676-1094/1683) endowed Djudda with a mosque, khān, ḥammām, and water supply.

During the 13th/19th century, Djudda passed through a number of vicissitudes. In 1217/1803 the Wahhābīs [*q.v.*] besieged the *sharīf* Ghālib in Djudda but were unable to take the town, which began to boast of itself as a Gibraltar (Ibn Bishr, i, 122). Ghālib later surrendered and Djudda was subject to the rule of the Wahhābīs until 1226/1811, when Muḥammad ʿAlī restored nominal Ottoman sovereignty. In 1229/1814 Burkhardt described Djudda as a town with 12,000 to 15,000 inhabitants, among whom indigenous elements were scantily represented, while strangers from the Yemen and Ḥaḍramawt appeared to be numerous. Both Burton (i, 179) and al-Batanūnī (6) mention the coral and mother-of-pearl taken from the Red Sea at Djudda and made into prayer beads at Mecca and crucifixes at Jerusalem. In 1256/1840 Egyptian rule was replaced by the direct rule of the Porte, represented by a *wālī* in Djudda.

On 3 Dhu 'l-Ḳaʿda 1274/15 June 1858 Djudda was the scene of a massacre, instigated, it is thought, by a former Djudda police chief, and several dissatisfied Djudda merchants, in which about 25 Christians were killed, including the British and French Consuls and a group of wealthy Greek merchants. The British steamship *Cyclops*, anchored in the harbour, bombarded the city for two days and restored order without much damage (Isabel Burton, ii, 513 ff.).

Djudda was the first Ḥidjāzī city to fall into sharīfian hands after Sharīf al-Ḥusayn's proclamation of Arab independence in 1334/1916 (Naṣīf, 50). The Turks surrendered the city on 15 Shaʿbān/17 June after a combined land attack by Sharīf al-Ḥusayn's army and a six-day bombardment by the British navy. The port then became the major supply depot for the sharīfian forces operating behind Turkish lines during the Arab revolt.

Under the short-lived Kingdom of al-Ḥidjāz, Djudda was a focal point in the struggle between the Wahhābīs and the *sharīfs* for control of al-Ḥidjāz. After the Saʿūdī occupation of Mecca in Rabīʿ I 1343/October 1924, Djudda became the capital of the government of ʿAlī b. al-Ḥusayn. The city was under siege by the Wahhābī forces, situated in the coastal hills ten miles from the town, for almost an entire year from Djumādā II 1343/January 1925 until its submission in Djumādā II 1344/December 1925. Defence of the city was hindered by the inadequacy of the sharīfian army, estimated by

Philby (*Forty Years*, 114) at 1,000 regulars augmented by Bedouin recruits, and by internal divisions among the citizens, a party of whom, led by the Ḳāʾimmaḳām, favoured negotiation with the Saʿūdīs and the deposition of ʿAlī (Naṣīf, 156 ff. Details of the town's history during this year are contained in the newspaper *Barīd al-Ḥidjāz*, ed. Muḥammad Naṣīf). In Dhu 'l-Ḳaʿda 1345/May 1927 ʿAbd al-ʿAzīz Ibn Saʿūd and Gilbert Clayton met in Djudda and concluded the Treaty of Djudda in which Britain recognized the "complete and absolute" independence of Āl Saʿūd's territories.

Nallino, describing the town in 1938, mentions the site of the tomb of Eve, quietly demolished by the Saʿūdis in 1928, the so-called European cemetery, which is thought to date from 1235/1820 and which contains the remains of some Jews and Asiatics, and the villages beyond the wall. These included al-Hindawiyya to the south, al-Nuzla to the south-west, al-Baghdādiyya and al-Ruways to the north, and Nākatū, a reed hut settlement inhabited by Takārīr (sing. Takrūrī) [*q.v.*], all of which have become part of the enlarged city.

The city now has a population variously estimated at 106,000 to 160,000; it is governed by a Ḳāʾimmaḳām (the only local governor in Saudi Arabia who still retains the Turkish title), who is under the administrative authority of the Governor of Mecca. The town has an elected Municipal Council. Since World War II, Djudda has experienced a commercial boom. Its wall was demolished in 1946-7, and the town expanded in three directions: east along the road to Mecca, north along the road to Medina, and south along the pier road. Many of the traditional coral block houses with their latticed balconies have been razed in the old section of the town to make room for modern office buildings. Djudda is known for the cosmopolitan character of its populace: Bukhārīs, Yamanīs, Ḥaḍramīs, and some tribal communities, notably Ḥarb, still live in separate quarters of the town.

Djudda has numerous light industries including a cement plant and several marble cutting works. A new water system completed in 1948 supplies the town with over 2,500,000 gallons of water a day, most of which is piped in from wells in Wādī Fāṭima. A modern port at the southern end of the city, equipped with a two-berth pier 1,300 feet long, handles over 800,000 tons of cargo a year. Djudda is the official air and sea port of entry for pilgrims on their way to Mecca, over 147,000 of whom landed in Djudda during 1381/1961. The city has a quarantine station, with a hospital and an observation clinic, and two Pilgrim Towns, one attached to the pier and the other attached to the airport, all built since 1950, to handle the pilgrims.

Bibliography: al-Bakrī, *Muʿdjam mā istaʿdjam*, Cairo 1945-51; Yāḳūt; Aḥmad b. Zaynī Daḥlān, *Khulāṣat al-kalām*, Cairo 1887; ʿUthmān b. Bishr, *ʿUnwān al-madjd*, Mecca 1349; Ḥusayn b. Muḥammad Naṣīf, *Māḍī al-Ḥidjāz wa-ḥāḍiruh*, 1349; Muḥammad Labīb al-Batanūnī, *al-Riḥla al-Ḥidjāziyya*, Cairo 1329; Ḥāfiẓ Wahba, *Khamsūn ʿām fī Djazīrat al-ʿArab*, Cairo 1960; Fuʾād Ḥamza, *Ḳalb Djazīrat al-ʿArab*, Cairo 1352; al-Djabartī, *ʿAdjāʾib al-āthār*, Cairo 1904; Muḥammad b. Bulayhid, *Ṣaḥīḥ al-akhbār*, Cairo 1951-3; Ibn Taghrībirdī; Ritter, *Erdkunde*, xiii, 6-33; von Maltzan, *Wallfahrt nach Mekka*, i, 213-323; idem, *Reise nach Südarabien*, 46 ff.; British Admiralty, *Western Arabia and the Red Sea*, 1946; C. A. Nallino, *Scritti*, i; Isabel Burton, *The life of Captain Sir Richard Burton*, 1893, ii, 513 ff.; Hopper; *Jiddah*, in *Lands East*, Feb. 1956; H. St. J. Philby, *Forty years in the wilderness*, 1957; idem, *Arabian jubilee*, 1952; idem, *Saʿudi Arabia*, 1955; idem, *Arabian Days*, 1948; Snouck Hurgronje, *Mekka*, ii, 1888; idem, in *Bijdragen tot de taal-, land- en volkenkunde van Nederlandsch-Indië*, 5th series, ii, 381 ff., 399 ff.; idem, in *Verhandl. der Gesell. für Erdkunde*, xiv, 141; ʿAbd al-Ḳuddūs al-Anṣārī, *Djudda ʿabr al-taʾrīkh* in *al-Manhal*, Djudda Jan/Feb. 1962.—For the Ottoman period see Ferīdūn, *Munshaʾāt al-salāṭīn*, Istanbul 1265, ii, 6 ff.; Ewliyā Čelebi, *Seyāḥatnāme*, ix, 794 ff.; Ḥādjdjī Khalīfa, *Djihānnümā*, 519; I. H. Uzunçarşılı, *Osmanlı tarihi*, iii/2, Ankara 1934, 44-5; G. W. F. Stripling, *The Ottoman Empire and the Arabs 1511-1874*, Urbana 1942, index.

(R. Hartmann-[Phebe Ann Marr])

DJUDHĀM, an Arab tribe which in Umayyad times claimed descent from Kahlān b. Sabaʾ of Yemen and relationship with Lakhm and ʿĀmila; this certainly corresponded with the prevailing political alliances. However, the North Arab tribes claimed that Djudhām, Ḳuḍāʿa and Lakhm were originally of Nizār but had later assumed Yemenī descent. Djudhām were among the nomads who had settled in pre-Islamic times on the borders of Byzantine Syria and Palestine; they held places like Madyan, ʿAmmān, Maʿān and Adhruḥ, and ranged as far south as Tabūk and the Wādī 'l-Ḳurā. The Judaized tribe of al-Naḍīr in Medina allegedly arose from them. From their Byzantine contacts, part of Djudhām were superficially Christian, but Ibn al-Kalbī includes them among the "people of Syria" who worshipped the idol al-Uḳayṣir.

When Muḥammad was expanding northwards, Djudhām barred his way at Muʾta. One clan, that of al-Ḍubayb, had become Muslim, but punitive expeditions under Zayd b. Ḥāritha and ʿAmr b. al-ʿĀṣ were necessary. Djudhām were among the Arab allies (*Mustaʿriba*) of the Emperor Heraclius, and fought for him at the Yarmūk in 15/636; later, they became Muslims and took part in the conquest of Syria. Under the Umayyads, they formed the greater part of the Djund of Filasṭīn, and together with Kalb, were the mainstay of the Yemenī party in the tribal warfare in Syria. On the death in 64/684 of Muʿāwiya b. Yazīd, their chief Rawḥ b. Zinbāʿ proposed the succession of Marwān b. al-Ḥakam as Caliph, and their connexions with the Marwānids remained close until the fall of that dynasty.

Bibliography: Ibn Hishām, 975-9, tr. Guillaume, 662-4; Ibn Saʿd, i/2, 83 (= Wellhausen, *Skizzen*, iv/3, no. 140), ii/1, 93; Wāḳidī (Wellhausen), 235-6; Yaʿḳūbī, *Historiae*, i, 229, 264, ii, 299; Ṭabarī, i, 1555-6, 1604-5, 1611, 1740-1, 2347-8, ii, 468; Ibn al-Kalbī, *The book of idols*, tr. N. A. Faris, Princeton 1952, 33-4, 42-3; Hamdānī, *Djazīra*, 129; Ibn Durayd, *Ishtiḳāḳ* (Wüstenfeld), 225; Wüstenfeld, *Register zu den genealogischen Tabellen*, 186; O. Blau, *Arabien im sechsten Jahrhundert*, in *ZDMG*, xxiii, 1869, 572-3.

(C. E. Bosworth)

DJŪDĪ, Djabal Djūdī or Djūdī Dagh, a lofty mountain mass in the district of Bohtān, about 25 miles N.E. of Djazīrat Ibn ʿUmar, in 37° 30′ N. Djūdī owes its fame to the Mesopotamian tradition, which identifies it, and not Mount Ararat, with the mountain on which Noah's ark rested. It is practically certain from a large number of Armenian and other writers that, down to the 10th century, Mt. Ararat was in no way connected with the Flood. Ancient Armenian tradition certainly knows nothing of a mountain on which the ark rested; and when one is mentioned in later Armenian literature, this is clearly due to the gradually increasing influence of the Bible, which makes the ark rest on the mountains (or a mountain) of Ararat. The highest and best known mountain there is Masik (Masis), therefore Noah must have been stranded on it; the next stage in the growth of the Armenian tradition is due to Europeans, who transferred Ararat (Armen. Ayraraṭ), the name of a district, to Masik, through an incorrect interpretation of Genesis, viii, 4.

The tradition that Masik was the mountain on which the ark rested only begins to find a place in Armenian literature in the 11th and 12th centuries. Older exegesis identified the mountain now called Djabal Djūdī, or according to Christian authorities, the mountains of Gordyene (Syr. *Ḳardū*, Armen. *Kordukh*) as the apobaterion of Noah. This localization of the ark's resting-place, which is found even in the Targums, is certainly based on Babylonian tradition, and arose out of the Babylonian Berossus. Besides, the mountain Niṣir which appears in the Flood-legend in the cuneiform inscriptions might well be located in Gordyene (in the widest application of the name). The ancient Jewish-Babylonian tradition was adopted by the Christians and the Arabs learned it from them, when their conquests carried them into Bohtān in 20/640. "They simply transferred the name Djūdī, which the Ḳur'ān (Sūra XI, 46) mentions as the landing-place of Noah, to Mount Ḳardū which had, from the remotest times, been regarded as the apobaterion". Thus writes Nöldeke in the *Festschr. für Kiepert* (1898), 77, and he is clearly right. But the Ḳur'ān meant Djūdī in Arabia (Ḥamāsa, 564 = Yāḳūt, ii, 270, 11 = *Mushtarik*, 111), which was probably considered the highest mountain of all. It is also possible that the Ḳur'ān in its localization of the mount on which the ark rested had taken over some older tradition current in Arabia. For this view we might quote a remark of the apologist Theophylus (*ad Autolycum*, lib. iii, c. 19) who mentions that, even in his time, the remains of the ark were to be seen on the mountains of Arabia. The transference of the name Djūdī from Arabia to Mesopotamia by the Arabs must have taken place fairly early, as has been mentioned, probably as early as the time of the Arab invasion; even in the older poets, for example, Ibn Ḳays al-Ruḳayyāt (ed. Rhodokanakis, cf. Nöldeke, *WZKM*, xvii, 91) and Umayya b. Abi 'l-Ṣalt (ed. Schulthess, *Beitr. z. Assyr.*, viii, no. 3, 5) Djabal Djūdī is no longer the Arabian, but the Mesopotamian mountain. The transference of the name Djūdī to the Ḳardū chain and the rapid acceptance of the new name may probably have been favoured by the circumstance that the land south of Bohtān, towards Assyria, had often in the Assyrian period formed part of the district of Gutium, the land of the Gutī (Ḳutū) nomads, and this, the name of a people and district, had not quite disappeared in the early years of Islam. On the geographical term Gutium, which is known to have existed even in the early Babylonian period, see Scheil, *Compt.-rendus de l'Académie des Inscript. et Bell. Lettres*, 1911, 378 ff., 606 ff.

If we assume, as is obvious, that the term Ararat (Assyr. Urarṭu) at one time also included an area to the south of Lake Van (cf. the mountain name Ararṭi in the Gordyene cuneiform inscription; see also Šanda, in the bibliography) then Masik (Great Ararat) and Djebel Djūdī, both traditional resting-places of the Ark, might each be called Mount Ararat in conformity to the Biblical account.

Like the whole country round Ararat, the neighbourhood of Djabal Djūdī is to this day full of memorials and legends which refer to the Flood and the life of Noah after leaving the ark. Thus for example at the foot of the mountain is the village of Ḳaryat Thamānīn = "the village of the 80 (Syr. *Thᵉmānīn*; Armen. *Tᶜmān* = 8; now: Bētmānīn)" where legend says the people saved in the ark first settled; cf. Hübschmann, xvi, 333-4. The Arab geographers also mention a monastery on Djūdī in their time, Dayr al-Djūdī; on this cf. Shābushtī, *Kitāb al-Diyārāt* (J. Heer, *Quellen*, 1898, 96; Sachau, *Vom Klosterbuch*, Berlin 1919, 20, no. 49) = Yāḳūt, ii, 653. The ruined sanctuary (known today as *Safīnat Nabī Nūḥ*) is venerated by Muslims, Jews and Christians (G. L. Bell, *Amurath*², 293).

We might further mention that Layard and subsequently (1904) L. W. King discovered rock-sculptures and inscriptions of Sennacherib in the Djabal Djūdī; King therefore proposes to identify this mountain with the Nipur of the Sanherib texts. Cf. Layard, *Niniveh u. Babylon*, 621; King in the *Journ. of Hellenic Stud.*, 1911, xxx, 328².

Bibliography: Harawī, *Ziyārat*, 68-9 (French transl. 152-3); Masᶜūdī, *Murūdj*, index; Yāḳūt, ii, 653; *Marāṣid al-iṭṭilāᶜ* (ed. Wüstenfeld), v, 111; Ibn Baṭṭūṭa, ii, 139; Ḳazwīnī, *Kosmographie* (ed. Wüstenfeld), i, 156); Le Strange, 94; Tuch, in *ZDMG*, i, 59 ff.; G. Hoffmann, *Auszüge aus syr. Akten persisch. Märtyrer*, 174 ff., 213 ff.; M. Hartmann, *Bohtan*, in *Mitt. der Vorderas. Ges.*, i, 121 ff., ii, 27, 67 (and index); H. Hübschmann, in *Indo-germ. Forsch.*, xvi, 316, 334, 371, 384¹; Ritter, *Erdkunde*, xi, 156, 449; Petermann, *Reisen im Orient*, 1886, 106 ff.; G. L. Bell, *Amurath to Amurath*², London 1924, 291-5. *Ḥudūd al-ᶜālam*, 203; M. Canard, *H'amdânides*, 112. On the Christian and Muslim legends of the Ark and their association with Ararat and Djūdī, cf. in particular G. Weil, *Bibl. Legenden der Muselmänner*, 1845, 45; Grünbaum, in *ZDMG*, xxxi, 301 ff.; M. Streck, in *ZA*, xv, 272 ff.; Fr. Murad, *Ararat u. Masis*, Heidelberg 1901; S. Weber, in *Tübinger Theolog. Quartalschr.* 83 (1901), 321 ff.; A. Sanda, in *MVAG*, vii (1902), 30 ff.; Dölmer, in *Bibl. Zeitschr.*, i, (1903), 349 ff. (cf. a contrary view in Šanda, *loc. cit.*, ii, 113 ff.); J. Marquart, *Streifzüge*, 1903, 286 ff.; H. Hübschmann, *loc. cit.*, xvi, 206, 278-83, 364, 370, 398, 451; H. Hilprecht, *The earliest version of the Deluge story*, Philadelphia 1910, 30-2; B. Nikitine, *Les Kurdes*, Paris 1956, 26-7, 153.

(M. Streck*)

DJŪDĪ AL-MAWRŪRĪ, eminent Andalusian grammarian. His complete name is Djūdī b. ᶜUthmān al-ᶜAbsī al-Mawrūrī (of Morón). Born in Toledo, he later went to Granada where he specialized in grammatical studies. He made a long voyage to the East where he studied with leading representatives of the school of Kūfa, such as al-Ru'āsī, al-Farrā' and al-Kisā'ī. Returning to Spain he brought with him the book of al-Kisā'ī and set up to teach it. This is considered a marked event in the history of grammatical studies in Spain, because all such studies in that part of the Muslim world had hitherto been based on the principles of the school of Baṣra, particularly the book of Sībawayh. In spite of the predominance of the Baṣrans, the Kūfans found their way and gained disciples. The two schools were later on reconciled in Spain, thanks to the work of the most active of the grammarians of Muslim Spain, al-Rabāḥī [*q.v.*]. Dj̲ūdī was successful in his work. His *ḥalaḳa* in the Mosque of Cordova was famous. Umayyad amīrs chose him to teach their sons. Ibn al-Abbār attributes to him a book called *Munbih al-ḥidj̲āra*, a title which suggests an agreeable sense of humour. He died in 198/813.

Bibliography: al-Zubaydī, *Tabaḳāt al-lug̲h̲awiyyīn wa 'l-nuḥāt* (ed. Abu 'l-Faḍl Ibrāhīm), Cairo 1958, Index; al-Suyūṭī, *Bug̲h̲yat al-wuʿāt*, Cairo 1326, i, 213-214; Ibn al-Abbar, *Takmila* (Madrid 1886) i, 8 no. 7; Ibn K̲h̲ayr, *Fahrasa* (ed. F. Codera and J. Ribera), Madrid 1893, 305 ff.; A. González Palencia, *Historia de la literatura Arabigo-española*, Madrid 1945, 136 and its enlarged Arabic version entitled *Taʾrīk̲h̲ al-fikr al-Andalusī* by H. Monés, Cairo 1948, index; M. A. Makki, *Estudio sobre las aportaciones orientales en la España musulmana* (unpublished thesis) 387-390. (HUSSAIN MONÉS)

AL-**DJ̲UFRA**, a depression in the Libyan desert situated on the 29th parallel, between the district of Sirte and the Fezzān. The word denotes the three oases of Waddān, Hōn and Sokna, and also the depression (170-280 m.) in which they are situated between the Dj̲. Waddān and the gloomy volcanic massif of the Dj̲. al-Sōdā (803 m.). The historical significance of Dj̲ufra is explained by the abundance of the underground water-supply throughout the depression, and also by its position at the meeting-point of three traditional routes which were once much frequented and which lead respectively from Tripoli via Bū-Nedj̲em, from the Sudan via the Fezzān, and from Egypt via Dj̲alo and Awdj̲īla.

When the Arab conqueror ʿUḳba b. Nāfiʿ imposed his authority in 47/667 upon the local prince, the latter was called the Waddān, after the name of his principal oasis. It was inhabited by Mazāta Berbers. It was for a time Ibāḍite and belonged to the district of Surt. In the 5th/11th century the settlement at Waddān consisted of two hostile quarters inhabited, according to al-Bakrī (29-30), by Sehmids and natives of the Ḥaḍramawt; but there was only one large mosque, and there a number of scholars. Most authors speak highly of the quality of the local dates. This remote oasis served as a hiding-place for the Armenian adventurer Karakouch who was traced there, captured and put to death by the Almoravid Ibn G̲h̲āniya (1195). We know almost nothing about the region during the centuries that followed, either in respect of its trade, or at what period Sokna took the place of Waddān as leading town of the district, or when the district took the name of Dj̲ufra. It was comparatively independent, being partly isolated by the powerful and dreaded tribe the Ūlād-Slīmān (of the Debbāb), nomads who were partly exterminated by the Turks after the revolt of their chieftain ʿAbd al-Dj̲alil in 1842; at that the Dj̲ufra was a *ḳaḍāʾ* dependent upon the *sandj̲aḳ* of the Fezzān. Of the 19th century European travellers, only Rohlfs has left us detailed information (chapters VI and VII). The district was occupied by the Italians in February 1928 and abandoned by them in 1943.

The population consists of about 5,000 inhabitants, most of them settled. A copious supply of water not far below the surface enables date-palms to bear crops, provided that they are cross-fertilized; there are known to be about 90,000 date-palms of which 15 to 20,000 are infertile. The best crops of dates are produced in gardens irrigated from wells worked by animals; the cultivation of other crops is of secondary importance, and this is true also of the breeding of camels and sheep which for grazing go as far as the ravines of the Dj̲. al-Sūda.

Waddān, the most easterly and no doubt the oldest of the settlements, still stands on its mound, encircling the ruins of its old castle; but the greater part of the population lives in an ancient town which lies to the north. In 1936 there were 1,700 inhabitants; half of them claim to be *s̲h̲urfa*, and a quarter of the rest are semi-nomadic. To the west, the houses of Sokna huddle round the old castle, within crumbling ramparts pierced by eight gates: the Turks made this the leading town of the district, and their garrison occupied a small fort to the north. Half of the 1,200 inhabitants still speak Berber and live in a separate quarter, and from two to three hundred are semi-nomadic Riyāḥ. Hōn, in the centre, is a settlement of recent date, 4 km. to the north of a ruined village. The Italians made it the leading town. The 1,800 inhabitants, several groups of whom are said to be Berber, live in a compact and crowded rectangular area of houses; the market-place and the Italian buildings lie to the south.

Bibliography: G. Rohlfs, *Kufra. Reise von Tripolis nach der Oase Kufra*, Leipzig 1881; E. Scarin, *la Giofra e Zella*, in *Rivista geografica italiana*, 1937; Bakrī, *Description de l'Afrique*, trans. de Slane, 2nd. ed. 1913; Idrīsī, *Description de l'Afrique et de l'Espagne*, trans. Dozy and De Goeje, 1866; Fagnan, *Extraits inédits relatifs au Maghreb*, Algiers 1924; E. de Agostini, *Le popolazioni della Tripolitania*, Tripoli 1917. (J. DESPOIS)

DJ̲UG̲H̲RĀFIYĀ, Geography.

(I) The term *dj̲ug̲h̲rāfiyā* and the Arabs' conception of geography

The term *dj̲ug̲h̲rāfiyā* (or *dj̲ig̲h̲rāfiyā*, *dj̲āōg̲h̲rāfiyā*, etc.), the title of the works of Marinos of Tyre (c. 70-130) and Claudius Ptolemy (c.A.D. 90-168) was translated into Arabic as *Ṣūrat al-arḍ* which was used by some Arab geographers as the title of their works. Al-Masʿūdī (d. 345/956) explained the term as *ḳaṭʿ al-arḍ*, 'survey of the Earth'. However, it was used for the first time in the *Rasāʾil Ik̲h̲wān al-Ṣafāʾ* in the sense of 'map of the world and the climes'. The Arabs did not conceive of geography as a well-defined and delimited science with a specific connotation and subject-matter in the modern sense. The Arabic geographical literature was distributed over a number of disciplines, and separate monographs on various aspects of geography were produced under such headings as *Kitāb al-Buldān*, *Ṣūrat al-arḍ*, *al-Masālik wa 'l-mamālik*, *ʿIlm al-ṭuruḳ*, etc. Al-Bīrūnī considered *al-Masālik* as the science which dealt with fixing the geographical position of places. Al-Muḳaddasī came nearest to dealing with most aspects of geography in his work *Aḥsan al-taḳāsīm fī maʿrifat al-aḳālīm*. The present use of the term *dj̲ug̲h̲rāfiya* for geography in Arabic is a comparatively modern practice.

(II) Pre-Islamic and Early Islamic Periods

In pre-Islamic times the Arabs' knowledge of geography was confined to certain traditional and ancient geographical notions or to place-names of Arabia and the adjacent lands. The three main sources where these are preserved are: the Ḳurʾān, the Prophetic Tradition (*ḥadīth*) and ancient Arabic poetry. Many of these notions must have originated from Babylonia in ancient times or were based on Jewish and Christian traditions and indigenous Arab sources.

The geographical concepts or information contained in ancient Arabic poetry reflect the level of understanding of the pre-Islamic Arabs of geographical phenomena and the limits of their knowledge. The Ḳurʾān preserves traces of some geographical and cosmographical ideas which resemble ancient Babylonian, Iranian and Greek concepts and the Jewish and Christian Biblical traditions. Verses like 'the heavens and the earth were joined together before we clove them asunder' (XXI, 30); 'God is He Who created seven Firmaments and of the earth a similar number' (LXV, 12); 'God is He who raised the heavens without any pillars' (XIII, 2); 'And we have made the heavens as a canopy well guarded' (XXI, 32); 'He withholds the sky from falling on the earth except by His leave' (XXII, 65); and verses that describe the earth as being spread out and the mountains set thereon firm so that it may not shake, all form a picture which resembles the ancient Babylonian concept of the universe in which the Earth was a disc-shaped body surrounded by water and then by another belt of mountains upon which the Firmament rested. There was water under the Earth as well as above it. Again, concepts like that of 'the Sun setting in a spring of murky water' (XVIII, 86) referring to the Atlantic, and of the earth's being flat must have had their origin in Greek geography. The concept of the two seas, one of sweet water and the other saline (XXV, 53), referring to the Mediterranean and the Arabian Sea, and that of *al-barzakh*, 'the barrier' between them (a by-form of *farsakh* 'parasang', from Pahlavi *frasang*) were most probably of Iranian origin. Besides, certain terms in the Ḳurʾān, *e.g.*, *burūdj* (= Gr. Πύργος, Latin *burgus*), *baladun* or *baladatun* (a Semitic borrowing from the Latin *palatium*: Gr. Παλάτιον), *ḳarya* (> Syriac *ḳrītha*ʾ, a town or village), indicate the non-Arab origin of the concepts with which these terms are associated in the Ḳurʾān.

There are some traditions attributed to ʿAlī b. Abī Ṭālib (d. 40/660), Ibn ʿAbbās (d. 66-9/686-8), ʿAbd Allāh b. ʿAmr b. al-ʿĀṣ and others, which deal with cosmogony, geography and other related questions, but it seems that these traditions which reflect the ancient geographical notions of the Arabs were concocted in a later period to counteract the scientific geographical knowledge that was becoming popular among the Arabs of the period, although they were presented as authentic knowledge by some geographers in their works. Though scientific knowledge advanced, some of the traditions exercised deep influence on Arab geographical thought and cartography, *e.g.*, the tradition according to which the shape of the land-mass was compared to a big bird whose head was China, right wing India, left wing al-Khazar, chest Mecca, Ḥidjāz, Syria, ʿIrāḳ and Egypt and tail North Africa (Ibn al-Faḳīh, 3-4) became the basis of the geographical writings of the Balkhī School. It is not unlikely that this concept had its origin in some ancient Iranian maps observed by the Arabs.

The political expansion of the Arabs, after the rise of Islam, into Africa and Asia, afforded them opportunities to collect information and to observe and record their experiences of the various countries that had come under their sway or were adjacent to the Arab Empire. Whether such information was gathered for military expeditions or for other purposes, it is very likely that it was also utilized in the topographical works that were produced during the early ʿAbbāsid period.

(III) The Transmission of Indian, Iranian and Greek Geographical Knowledge to the Arabs

It was not until the beginning of the ʿAbbāsid rule and the establishment of Baghdād as the capital of the empire that the Arabs began acquainting themselves with scientific geography in the true sense. The conquest of Īrān, Egypt and Sind gave the Arabs the opportunity to gain first hand knowledge of the scientific and cultural achievements of the peoples of these ancient cradles of civilization, as well as giving them ownership of, or easy access to their centres of learning, laboratories and observatories. But the process of acquiring and assimilating foreign knowledge did not begin until the time of the Caliph Abū Djaʿfar al-Manṣūr (135-58/753-75), the founder of Baghdād. He took a keen interest in the translation of scientific works into Arabic, which activity lasted for nearly two hundred years in the Islamic world. The Barmakid [*q.v.*] *wazīr*s also played an important role in the promotion of scientific activity at the court. Quite often the translators were themselves eminent scientists whose efforts enriched the Arabic language with Indian, Iranian and Greek geographical, astronomical and philosophical knowledge.

Indian Influences. Indian geographical and astronomical knowledge passed on to the Arabs through the first translation into Arabic of the Sanskrit treatise *Sūrya-siddhānta* (not *Brahmasphuṭasiddhānta* as believed by some scholars) during the reign of al-Manṣūr. The work showed some earlier Greek influences (see A. B. Keith, *History of Sanskrit literature*, 517-21), but once translated into Arabic it became the main source of the Arabs' knowledge of Indian astronomy and geography, and formed the basis of many works that were produced during this period, *e.g.*, *Kitāb al-Zīdj* by Ibrāhīm b. Ḥabīb al-Fazārī (wrote after 170/786), *al-Sind Hind al-saghīr* by Muḥammad b. Mūsā al-Khwārizmī (d. after 232/847), *al-Sind Hind* by Ḥabash b. ʿAbd Allāh al-Marwazī al-Baghdādī (second half of the 3rd/9th century) and others.

Among other Sanskrit works translated into Arabic during this period were: *Āryabhaṭīya* (Ar.: *Ardjabhad*) by Āryabhaṭa of Kusumapura (b.A.D. 476) who wrote in A.D. 499; then, *Khanḍakhādyaka* of Brahmagupta son of Djishnu of Bhillamāla (near Multān). He was born in A.D. 598 and wrote this work in A.D. 665. It was a practical treatise giving material in a convenient form for astronomical calculations, but this was based on a lost work of Āryabhaṭa, who again agreed with the *Sūrya-siddhānta*. The Sanskrit literature translated into Arabic belonged mainly to the Gupta period.

The influence of Indian astronomy on Arab thought was much deeper than that of Indian geography, and although Greek and Iranian ideas had a deeper and more lasting effect, Indian geographical concepts and methods were well known. Indians were compared to the Greeks in their talent and achievements in the field of geography, but the Greeks were considered more accomplished in this field (al-Bīrūnī, *al-Ḳānūn*, 536).

Among the various geographical concepts with which the Arab scientists became acquainted were: the view of Āryabhaṭa that the daily rotation of the heavens is only apparent, being caused by the rotation of the earth on its own axis; that the proportion of water and land on the surface of the Earth was half and half; that the land-mass, which was compared to a tortoise, was surrounded by water on all sides, and was shaped like a dome whose highest point had Mount Meru (an imaginary mountain) on it directly under the North Pole; the northern hemisphere was the inhabited part of the Earth and its four limits were Djamakūt in the East, Rūm in the West, Lankā (Ceylon) which is the Cupola and Sīdpūr, and the division of the inhabited part of the Earth into nine parts. The Indians calculated their longitudes from Ceylon and believed that this prime meridian passed through Udjdjayn [*q.v.*] (Ujjain). The Arabs took over the idea of Ceylon's being the Cupola of the Earth, but later believed that Udjdjayn was the Cupola, mistakenly thinking that the Indians calculated longitudes from that point.

Iranian Influences. There is sufficient evidence in Arabic geographical literature to point to Iranian influences on Arab geography and cartography, but the actual process of the transmission of Īrān's knowledge to the Arabs has not been worked out in detail. J. H. Kramers correctly points out that during the 9th century Greek influence was supreme in Arab geography, but from the end of the 9th century the influence was more from the east than from the west, and it was from Īrān that these influences mainly came, for most of the authors came from the Iranian provinces (*Analecta Orientalia*, i, 147-8). Djundaysābūr was still a great centre of learning and research and there is little doubt that the Arabs were acquainted with some of the Pahlavi works on astronomy, geography, history and other subjects which were extant in some parts of Īrān during this period. Some of these works were translated into Arabic and formed the basis of the Arabic works on the subject. Al-Masʿūdī ascribes to Ḥabash b. ʿAbd Allāh al-Marwazī al-Baghdādī an astronomical treatise *Zīdj al-Shāh* which was based on the Persian style. He also recorded a Persian work entitled *Kāh-nāma* which dealt with the various grades of kings and formed a part of the larger work entitled *Āʾīn-nāma*, '*Book of Customs*'. Again, he mentions having seen at Iṣṭakhr in 302/915 a work that dealt with the various sciences of the Iranians, their histories, monuments, etc. and other information that was not found either in *Khudāʾī-nāma*, *Āʾīn-nāma* or *Kāh-nāma*. This work was discovered among the treasures of the Persian kings and was translated from Persian into Arabic for Hishām b. ʿAbd al-Malik b. Marwān (105-25/724-43). It is not unlikely that works of this nature formed part of the sources of the Arabs' knowledge on the geography and topography of Īrān and on the limits of the Sāsānian Empire, its administrative divisions and other details.

Among the various Iranian geographical concepts and traditions followed by Arab geographers, the concept of the Seven *Kishwars* (*Haft Iḳlīm*) was the most important. In this system the world was divided into seven equal geometric circles, each representing a *kishwar*, in such a manner that the fourth circle was drawn in the centre with the remaining six around it, and included Īrānshahr of which the most central district was al-Sawād. The Arab geographers continued to be influenced by this system for a long time, and in spite of the view of al-Bīrūnī that it had no scientific or physical basis and that the Greek division of the Climes was more scientific, the Greek division of the world into three or four continents never appealed to them. The concept of the two main seas, namely, the Baḥr al-Rūm and the Baḥr Fārs (the Mediterranean and the Indian Ocean) which entered the land from the Baḥr al-Muḥīṭ (the Encircling Ocean), one from the north-west, *i.e.*, the Atlantic and the other from the east, *i.e.*, the Pacific, but were separated by al-Barzakh ('the Barrier', *i.e.*, the Isthmus of Suez), also dominated Arab geography and cartography for several centuries. As pointed out by J. H. Kramers, although it is very probable that the notion rests in the last resort on Ptolemy, the fact that the Indian Ocean is most often called Baḥr Fārs, seems to prove that this sea, at least, formed part of the original geographic sketch of the Persians. As to the origin of this sketch itself we find ourselves in uncertainty (*Analecta Orientalia*, i, 153).

Persian traditions deeply influenced Arab maritime literature and navigation also, as is evident from the use of words of Persian origin in the nautical vocabulary of the Arabs, *e.g.*, *bandar* (port), *nākhudā* (shipmaster), *rahmānī* (book of nautical instructions), *daftar* (sailing instructions), etc. Certain Persian names like *khann* (rhumb), *ḳuṭb al-djāh* (pole), etc., also indicate Persian influences on the Arab windrose. Such examples can be multiplied. Persian influences are apparent in Arab cartography as well, an indication of which is found in the use of terms of Persian origin, *e.g.*, *ṭaylasān*, *shābūra*, *ḳuwāra*, etc., to describe certain formations of coasts. These terms, originally indicating certain garments, were used right down to the 7th/13th century. They also point to the existence of maps in ancient Īrān (J. H. Kramers, *op. cit.* 148-9). As for the 'Indian map which is at al-Ḳawādhiyān' (Ibn Ḥawḳal, ed. Kramers, 2) Kramers pointed out that al-Ḳawādhiyān must contain here an allusion to more primitive maps of the Balkhī-Iṣṭakhrī series, because the maps of Ibn Ḥawḳal are partly in conformity with this series and partly different (Kramers, *op. cit.*, 155). A correct identification of these maps or their discovery would certainly help to solve the problem of the origin of the maps of the Balkhī school. Here it may be pointed out that if we read Ibn Ḥawḳal's text as 'the geometrical map at al-Ḳawādhiyān' (a town near Tirmidh in Central Asia), then he must have been referring to some map that was there and was used by geographers as a basis for cartography. It is quite likely that it was based on the Persian *kishwar* system, for al-Bīrūnī remarks that the term *kishwar* was derived from 'the line' (*al-khaṭṭ*) which really indicated that these divisions were as distinct from each other as anything that was drawn in lines would be (*Ṣifat*, ed. Togan, 61).

Greek Influences. More positive data are available on how Greek geographical and astronomical knowledge passed on to the Arabs in the mediaeval period. The process began with the translations of the works of Claudius Ptolemy and other Greek astronomers and philosophers into Arabic either directly or through the medium of Syriac.

Ptolemy's *Geography* was translated several times during the ʿAbbāsid period, but what we possess is the adaptation of Ptolemy's work by Muḥammad b. Mūsā al-Khʷārizmī (d. after 232/847) with contemporary data and knowledge acquired by the Arabs incorporated into it. Ibn Khurradādhbih mentions having consulted and translated Ptolemy's work (perhaps it was in the original Greek or in Syriac translation) and al-Masʿūdī also consulted a copy of the *Geography* and also the world map by Ptolemy. It seems that some of these translations had become corrupt, and foreign material was interpolated into them which did not belong to the original work, *e.g.*, the copy consulted by Ibn Ḥawḳal (ed. Kramers, 13). Among other works of Ptolemy translated into Arabic and utilized by Arab geographers were: *Almagest* (Ar.: *Almadjisṭī*); *Tetrabiblon* (Ar.: *al-Maḳālāt al-arbaʿa*); *Apparitions of fixed stars*, etc. (Ar.: *Kitāb al-Anwāʾ*).

Among other works translated into Arabic were: the *Geography* of Marinos of Tyre (c. A.D. 70-130) consulted by al-Masʿūdī who also consulted the world map by Marinos; the *Timaeus* (Ar.: *Ṭaymāʾūs*) of Plato; the *Meteorology* (Ar.: *al-Āthār al-ʿulwiyya*), *De caelo* (Ar.: *al-Samāʾ wa 'l-ʿālam*) and *Metaphysics* (Ar.: *Mā baʿd al-ṭabīʿa*) of Aristotle.

The works of these writers and of several other Greek astronomers and philosophers, when rendered into Arabic, provided material in the form of concepts, theories and results of astronomical observations which ultimately helped Arab geography to evolve on a scientific basis. Persian influences were no doubt marked in regional and descriptive geography as well as in cartography, but Greek influence dominated practically the whole canvas of Arab geography. Even in fields where it may be said that there was a kind of competition between Persian and Greek ideas or methodology, *e.g.*, between the Persian *kishwar* system and the Greek system of Climes, the Greek were more acceptable and remained popular. The Greek basis of Arab geography was most prominent in mathematical, physical, human and bio-geography. The Greek impact had a very lasting influence, for it remained the basis of Arab geography as late as the 19th century (traces found in 19th century Persian and even Urdū works on geography written in India), even though on European minds Ptolemaic influence had decreased much earlier. It cannot, however, be denied that throughout this period there was an undercurrent of conflict between the theoretical concepts of the Greek masters on the one hand and the practice and observation of the merchants and sailors of this period on the other. Al-Masʿūdī refers to it in the case of the Ptolemaic theory of the existence of an unknown land in the southern hemisphere. On the other hand Ibn Ḥawḳal considered Ptolemy almost infallible. The fact was that Greek information when transmitted to the Arabs was already outdated by about five centuries, and so difficulty arose when Arab geographers tried to incorporate fresh and contemporary information acquired by them into the Ptolemaic frame-work and to corroborate it with Greek data. The result was confusion and often misrepresentation of facts in geographical literature and cartography, as is evident from the works of geographers like al-Idrīsī.

(IV) The Classical Period (3rd-5th/9th-11th centuries)

(a) The Period of al-Maʾmūn (197-218/813-33):

Over half a century of Arab familiarity with, and study of Indian, Iranian and Greek geographical science, from the time of the Caliph al-Manṣūr (136-57/754-74) up to the time of al-Maʾmūn, resulted in completely revolutionizing Arab geographical thought. Such concepts as that the Earth was round and not flat, and that it occupied the central position in the Universe, were introduced to them for the first time properly and systematically. Henceforth, the Ḳurʾānic verses dealing with cosmogony, geography, etc. and the Traditions were utilized only to give religious sanction to geographical works or to exhort the believers to study geography and astronomy. Thus, by the beginning of the 3rd/9th century the real basis was laid for the production of geographical literature in Arabic and the first positive step in this regard was taken by the Caliph al-Maʾmūn, who successfully surrounded himself with a band of scientists and scholars and patronized their academic activities. Whether al-Maʾmūn's interest in astronomy and geography was genuine and academic, or whether it was political is not certain. During his reign, however, some very important contributions were made towards the advancement of geography: the measurement of an arc of a meridian was carried out (the mean result gave $56^2/_3$ Arabic miles as the length of a degree of longitude, a remarkably accurate value); the astronomical tables called *al-Zīdj al-mumtaḥan* (*The verified tables*) were prepared by the collective efforts of the astronomers; lastly, a World Map called *al-Ṣūra al-Maʾmūniyya* was prepared, which was considered superior to the maps of Ptolemy and Marinos of Tyre by al-Masʿūdī who had consulted and compared all three (*Tanbīh*, ed. De Goeje, 33). It was most probably based on the Greek system of climes.

(b) The Astronomers and Philosophers:

The Arab astronomers and philosophers made equally important contributions to mathematical and physical geography through their observations and theoretical discussions. From the time of the introduction of Greek philosophy and astronomy in the second half of the 2nd/8th century up to the first half of the 5th/11th century a galaxy of philosophers and astronomers worked on various problems of mathematical, astronomical and physical geography. The works of the Greek scientists had already provided enough basis and material for this. Thus the results of the experiments, observations and theoretical discussions of the Arab scientists were recorded in their more general works on astronomy and philosophy or in monographs on special subjects like tides, mountains, etc. The contemporary and later writers on general geography in Arabic often, though not always, reproduced these results in their works and sometimes discussed them. Some of these writers reproduced various current theories, Greek or otherwise, about a problem in the introductory parts of their works. Thus a tradition was established of writing on mathematical, physical and human geography in the beginning of any work dealing with geography. This is noticeable, for example, in the works of Ibn Rusta, al-Yaʿḳūbī, al-Masʿūdī, Ibn Ḥawḳal, etc.

Among the outstanding Arab philosophers and astronomers whose works were utilized and theories discussed by Arab geographers were: Yaʿḳūb b. Isḥāḳ al-Kindī (d. 260/874), to whom two works on geography are attributed, (1) *Rasm al-maʿmūr min al-arḍ* and (2) *Risāla fi 'l-biḥār wa 'l-madd wa 'l-djazr*. One of al-Kindī's pupils, Aḥmad b. Muḥammad b. al-Ṭayyib al-Sarakhsī (d. 286/899), is also said to have written two works, (1) *al-Masālik wa 'l-mamālik* and (2) *Risāla fi 'l-biḥār wa 'l-miyāh wa 'l-djibāl*. Neither the works of al-Kindī nor those of al-Sarakhsī are extant, and what we know of their geographical views are from other sources which used them. It seems that the two authors utilized the works of Ptolemy and other Greek writers, as we find in al-Masʿūdī that their works did contain Ptolemaic information on physical and mathematical geography and on oceanography. Al-Kindī's work *Rasm al-maʿmūr min al-arḍ* may have been a version of Ptolemy's *Geography* as the title of the work itself suggests; al-Masʿūdī consulted a work of Ptolemy's entitled *Maskūn al-arḍ* and a world map called *Ṣūrat maʿmūr al-arḍ* (al-Masʿūdī, *Murūdj*, i, 275-7; *Tanbīh*, 25, 30, 51).

Among other philosophers and astronomers whose writings served as a source of information on mathematical and physical geography were: al-Fazārī (second half of the 2nd/8th century); Aḥmad b. Muḥammad b. Kat̲h̲īr al-Farg̲h̲ānī (d. after 247/861) author of *al-Fuṣūl al-t̲h̲alāt̲h̲īn* (al-Masʿūdī, *Murūdj*, iii, 443; *Tanbīh*, 199) and *al-Mudk̲h̲il ilā ʿilm hayʾat al-aflāk*; Abū Maʿs̲h̲ar Djaʿfar b. Muḥammad al-Balk̲h̲ī (d. 273/886), author of *al-Mudk̲h̲il al-kabīr ilā ʿilm al-nudjūm*; al-Masʿūdī consulted another work by him entitled *Kitāb al-ulūf fi'l-hayākil wa 'l-bunyān al-ʿaẓīm*; then Abū ʿAbd Allāh Muḥammad b. Djābir al-Battānī (d. 317/929) and others. The fourth *Risāla* of the *Rasāʾil Ik̲h̲wān al-Ṣafā* deals with *Djug̲h̲rāfiyā*. Written in about 370/980, it simply deals with elementary knowledge about mathematical and physical geography based on Greek geography, since the main purpose of the writers was to guide the reader to achieve union with God through wisdom.

(c) General Geographical Literature:

By the 3rd/9th century a considerable amount of geographical literature had been produced in various forms in the Arabic language, and it appears that the Arabs had at their disposal some Pahlavi works, or translations thereof, dealing with the Sāsānian Empire, its geography, topography, postal routes and details essential for administrative purposes. These works must have become available to those interested in geography and topography. It is not surprising, therefore, to find that early writers like Ibn K̲h̲urradād̲h̲bih, Ḳudāma and others were heads of postal departments or government secretaries, besides being men of learning. During the 3rd/9th century, therefore, a number of works were produced that were given the generic title *al-Masālik wa 'l-mamālik*. In all probability the first work bearing this title was that of Ibn K̲h̲urradād̲h̲bih. The first draft of his work was prepared in 231/846 and the second in 272/885; it became the basis and model for writers on general geography and was highly praised by almost all geographers who utilized it. He was the Director of the Post and Intelligence Department and was a man of learning and erudition. What prompted him to write a geographical treatise may be explained from his own statement that it was in fulfilment of the desire of the Caliph, for whom he also translated the work of Ptolemy (from Greek or Syriac) into Arabic (Ibn K̲h̲urradād̲h̲bih, 3). However, the desire of the Caliph may itself have arisen from the practical needs of the government. We find that Ḳudāma b. Djaʿfar al-Kātib considered the 'science of roads' (*ʿilm al-ṭuruḳ*) not only useful for general guidance in the *Dīwān*, but also essential for the Caliph who might need it for his travels or for despatching his armies (185).

The geographical works produced during the 3rd/9th and 4th/10th centuries may be divided into two broad categories: (1) works dealing with the world as a whole but treating the ʿAbbāsid Empire (*Mamlakat al-Islām*) in greater detail. They attempted to give all such secular information as could not find a place in the general Islamic literature, and hence this category is called 'the secular geographical literature of the period'. The writers described the topography and the road-system of the ʿAbbāsid Empire and covered mathematical, astronomical, physical, human and economic geography. Among the representatives of this class of geographers were: Ibn K̲h̲urradād̲h̲bih, al-Yaʿḳūbī, Ibn al-Faḳīh, Ḳudāma and al-Masʿūdī. Since ʿIrāḳ was the most important centre of geographical learning at this time and many of the geographers belonged to it, we may for the sake of convenience use the term ʿIrāḳī School for them. Within this School, however, two groups of writers may be discerned: those who present the material following the four directions, *viz.*, north, south, east and west, and tend to consider Bag̲h̲dād as the centre of the world, and those who arrange it according to various *Iḳlīm*s (regions) and for the most part treat Mecca as the centre. (2) To the second category of works belong the writings of al-Iṣṭak̲h̲rī, Ibn Ḥawḳal and al-Muḳaddasī, for whom the term Balk̲h̲ī School has been used, as they followed Abū Zayd al-Balk̲h̲ī (see below). They confined their accounts to the world of Islam, describing each province as a separate *Iḳlīm*, and hardly touching upon non-Islamic lands except the frontier regions.

(i) The ʿIrāḳī School. The works of Ibn K̲h̲urradād̲h̲bih, al-Yaʿḳūbī and al-Masʿūdī are distinguished from the writings of other geographers of this School by two special features: first, they follow the Iranian *kis̲h̲war* system, and second, they equate ʿIrāḳ with Īrāns̲h̲ahr and begin their descriptions with it, thus placing ʿIrāḳ in a central position in Arab regional and descriptive geography. According to al-Bīrūnī the Seven *kis̲h̲war*s were represented by seven equal circles. The central *kis̲h̲war* was Īrāns̲h̲ahr which included K̲h̲urāsān, Fārs, Djibāl and ʿIrāḳ. He considered that these divisions were arbitrary and had been made primarily for political and administrative reasons. In ancient times the great kings lived in Īrāns̲h̲ahr, and it was necessary for them to live in the central zone so that they would be equidistant from other kingdoms and therefore find it easy to deal with matters. Such a division had no relation either to the physical systems or to astronomical laws, but was based on political changes or ethnological differences (*Ṣifa*, ed. Togan, 5, 60-62). With the foundation of Bag̲h̲dād as the capital of the ʿAbbāsid Empire, ʿIrāḳ naturally occupied a central and politically important position in the world of Islam. Ibn K̲h̲urradād̲h̲bih equated ʿIrāḳ with Īrāns̲h̲ahr and the district of al-Sawād which was called *dil-i Īrāns̲h̲ahr* in ancient times occupied the central position in his system of geography, and he begins his account with its description. Similarly, al-Yaʿḳūbī considered ʿIrāḳ as the centre of the world and 'the navel of the earth' (*surrat al-arḍ*), but for him Bag̲h̲dād was the centre of ʿIrāḳ, for it was not only the greatest city of the world unparalleled in its glory, but it was also the seat of government of the Banū Hās̲h̲im. Because it occupied a central position in the world, ʿIrāḳ had a moderate climate, its inhabitants were handsome and intelligent and possessed high morals. But in his system of geography Bag̲h̲dād is grouped with Sāmarrā, and the description begins with these two towns. A similar note of the superiority of ʿIrāḳ is struck by the historian and geographer al-Masʿūdī, who thought of Bag̲h̲dād as the best city in the world (*Tanbīh*, 34; cf. Ibn al-Faḳīh, 195 ff.).

As against these writers, Ḳudāma, Ibn Rusta and

Ibn al-Faḳīh display no enthusiasm for ʿIrāḳ or Īrānshahr. In their system Mecca and Arabia are given precedence. In Ḳudāma Mecca is given absolute precedence and all roads leading to Mecca are described before an account of roads leading out of Baghdād is given. He did give importance to ʿIrāḳ, but as the capital province of the *Mamlakat al-Islām*. Thus he considered it important, but only from a political and administrative point of view. In his system of geography, therefore, there is a slight shift of emphasis from the Iranian concept to what might be termed an 'Islamic approach' to geography. A similar tendency is also noticeable in Ibn Rusta (beginning of 4th/10th century) who departed completely from the Iranian traditions and assigned to Mecca and Medina the foremost place in his arrangement of geographical material. In his description of the Seven *Iḳlīm*s he prefers to describe them according to the Greek pattern and not according to the *kishwar* system. In the geographical work of Ibn al-Faḳīh also, the description of Mecca takes precedence, but a considerable portion of the work is devoted to Fārs, Khurāsān, etc. and the *Iḳlīm*s are described according to the *kishwar* system.

An important feature of the works of Ibn Khurradādhbih, al-Yaʿḳūbī and Ḳudāma is that the material in them is arranged and described following the four directions, namely, east, west, north and south according to the division of the world into four quarters. Such a method of description must have had its origin in some Iranian geographical tradition, and the Arab geographers must have had some pattern before them to copy. According to al-Masʿūdī the Persians and the Nabataeans divided the inhabited part of the world into four parts, *viz.*, Khurāsān (east), Bākhtar (north), Khurbarān (west) and Nīmrūz (south) (*Tanbīh*, 31; cf. al-Yaʿḳūbī, 268). However, Ḳudāma points out the arbitrariness of such a division. For him the terms east, west, north and south had only a relative value. In Ibn Rusta and Ibn al-Faḳīh, the arrangement is by regions.

Ibn Khurradādhbih, who may be called the father of geography, laid down the pattern and style for writing geography in the Arabic language. But, as J. H. Kramers pointed out, he was not an inventor of this style or pattern. He must have had some pattern or sample of an earlier work on the subject before him. There is a great likelihood that an Arabic translation of some earlier Pahlavi work on ancient Īrān was accessible to him. His work covers not only the *Mamlakat al-Islām*, but describes its frontiers and kingdoms and the peoples bordering on them. He was well acquainted with Ptolemy's work as is evident from his description of the limits of inhabited parts of the world and from the description of the Greek conception of the continents, namely, *Arūfā, Lūbya, Ityūfiyā* and *Isḳūtiyā*.

Aḥmad b. Abī Yaʿḳūb b. Wāḍiḥ al-Kātib al-Yaʿḳūbī (d. 284/897) claims to have travelled a great deal. He emphasized the fact of having obtained information from the inhabitants of the regions concerned, and of having verified it from trustworthy persons (232-3). His object in writing the book was to describe the routes leading to the frontiers of the Empire and the territories adjacent to them. It is for this reason that he dealt in a separate monograph with the history and geography of Rūm (the Byzantine Empire), and devoted another work to the conquest of Ifrīḳiya (North Africa). Al-Yaʿḳūbī's work deals mainly with topography and itineraries, and his arrangement of the material is similar to that of Ibn Khurradādhbih.

Ḳudāma b. Djaʿfar al-Kātib (4th/10th century) devoted the eleventh chapter of his work *Kitāb al-kharādj wa ṣanʿat al-kitāb* to a description of the postal stations and routes of the ʿAbbāsid Empire. The main objective of his work was to describe the *Mamlakat al-Islām* and its frontiers, especially the frontiers with the Byzantine empire (Rūm) which he considered the greatest enemy of Islam (252). In his geography the 'Islamic approach' is perceptible, but a political attitude like the defence of the frontiers is also discernible. His work also covers descriptions of peoples and kingdoms surrounding the *Mamlaka*. He deals with general and physical geography and seems to have borrowed information on regional and descriptive geography from the Greek sources.

Ibn Rusta's work (beginning of 4th/10th century) entitled *al-Aʿlāḳ al-nafīsa* resembles that of Ḳudāma in that it describes Mecca and Medina in the very beginning of the portion dealing with regional geography. The main purpose of the work, however, seems to have been to provide general information about the world as a whole, and hence one finds in it, besides a description of the Islamic lands, descriptions on a regional basis of several countries lying outside the limits of Islam. He dealt with mathematical geography in a systematic and exhaustive way and collected varied theories and opinions about various problems (23-4). He presents material on general and physical geography and describes the *Iḳlīm*s after the Greeks. Considering the variety of information accumulated in it, his work may be described as a 'small encyclopaedia of historical and geographical knowledge'.

Like Ibn Rusta, Ibn al-Faḳīh al-Hamadhānī also arranged his geographical material on a regional basis in his *Kitāb al-Buldān* (written c. 290/903). The description of Mecca takes precedence over other places, and the general arrangement of the subject-matter resembles that of al-Iṣṭakhrī and Ibn Ḥawḳal. He incorporated the account of the merchant Sulaymān on India and China, but the special feature of his work is that, along with trustworthy and authentic information, it records long pieces of verse, various traditions and information of a legendary character. The work is poor in the treatment of general and mathematical geography.

Abu 'l-Ḥasan ʿAlī b. al-Ḥusayn al-Masʿūdī (d. 345/956), the celebrated historian, combined the qualities of an experienced traveller with those of a geographer of high distinction. Unfortunately his own account of his travels (*Kitāb al-Ḳaḍāyā wa 'l-tadjārib*) is not extant, but an approximate idea of his travels can be formed from his extant works, namely, *Murūdj al-dhahab wa maʿādin al-djawhar* and *al-Tanbīh wa 'l-ishrāf* (the work entitled *Akhbār al-zamān*, etc. ed. ʿAbd Allāh al-Ṣāwī, Cairo 1938, and a MS of the Maulana Azad Library, Muslim University, ʿAlīgaṛh (Qutbuddin Collection, MS No. 36/1) entitled *Kitāb ʿAdjāʾib al-dunyā* (in the colophon *Kitāb al-ʿAdjāʾib*) are both wrongly attributed to al-Masʿūdī and have nothing to do with his great work *Kitāb Akhbār al-zamān* which is lost). Al-Masʿūdī regarded geography as a part of history, which explains the fact that his works deal with geography as an introduction to history. He drew upon the earlier geographical writings in Arabic as well as upon contemporary travel accounts and maritime literature. This he reinforced by the information collected by himself during his travels or from people whom he met. He does not give any systematic topographical account of the ʿAbbāsid Empire or deal with routes of the kingdom or postal stations, but he presents an excellent survey of contemporary Arab knowledge on mathematical and physical geography. However, al-Masʿūdī's main contribution was in the field of human and general geography. He advanced geographical science by challenging certain theories and concepts of Arab geographers which he found baseless in the light of his own experience and observation. He did not hesitate even to question the age-old theories of the Greek masters like Ptolemy, *e.g.*, the existence of land in the southern hemisphere. In the field of human and physical geography he emphasized the influence of the environment and other geographical factors on the physique and character of animals, plants and human beings. Al-Masʿūdī was also influenced by Iranian geographical traditions, *e.g.*, the Seven *kishwar* system, considering ʿIrāḳ as the central and the best *iḳlīm* in the world and Baghdād as the best city, etc.

An outstanding geographer of this period whose influence on the development of Arab geography was as varied and deep as that of Ibn Khurradādhbih was the Sāmānid *wazīr* Abū ʿAbd Allāh Muḥammad b. Aḥmad al-Djayhānī (earlier part of the 4th/10th century). Unfortunately, his work *Kitāb al-Masālik wa 'l-mamālik* (the Kābul MS has nothing to do with the great work of Djayhānī, see V. Minorsky, *A false Jayhānī*, in *BSOAS*, xiii, 1949-50, 89-96) has not come down to us; but it is quite likely that al-Djayhānī used the original text of Ibn Khurradādhbih's *Kitāb al-Masālik*. Being in the privileged position of a *wazīr* and writing in Bukhārā he 'could extend the field of his investigation much deeper into central Asia and the Far East than was possible for his Arab contemporaries' (Minorsky, *Marvazī*, etc. 6-7, London 1942). He collected first-hand information from different sources, hence the importance of his work. A large number of later Arab geographers utilized al-Djayhānī's work which, in the opinion of al-Masʿūdī, was 'interesting because of its novel information and interesting stories'.

The anonymous *Ḥudūd al-ʿālam*, written in Persian in 372/982 is one of the earliest works in Persian on world geography. The author utilized numerous earlier Arabic authorities on the subject and he had undoubtedly a copy of the work of al-Iṣṭakhrī before him. There is a tendency in the work towards completeness and numerical exactitude. Besides, the author is independent of other geographers in his geographical generalizations and terminology. The originality of the author lies in his conception of the division of the inhabited world into 'parts of the world' and separate 'countries' (see Barthold, Preface to *Ḥudūd al-ʿālam*, 21-33). The work appeared in an English translation with an excellent commentary by V. Minorsky (London 1937), one of the most exhaustive ever written on any Persian or Arabic geographical work in modern times.

(ii) The Balkhī School. To the second main category of writers on general geography belonged al-Iṣṭakhrī, Ibn Ḥawḳal and al-Muḳaddasī as well as Abū Zayd Aḥmad b. Sahl al-Balkhī (d. 322/934) after whom this School is named. Al-Balkhī wrote his geographical work *Ṣuwar al-aḳālīm* (primarily a commentary on maps) in 308/920 or a little later. He spent some eight years in ʿIrāḳ and had studied under al-Kindī. He had travelled widely before his return to his native place and had acquired a high reputation for knowledge and erudition. However, probably in the later part of his life he held orthodox views and wrote several treatises which were highly appreciated in orthodox circles. Although the text of al-Balkhī's geographical work has not yet been separately established, and the MSS, at one time attributed to al-Balkhī, have now been proved to be of al-Iṣṭakhrī, the view of De Goeje still seems to hold good that the work of al-Iṣṭakhrī represents a second and greatly enlarged edition of al-Balkhī's work, compiled between 318/930 and 321/933, in al-Balkhī's lifetime.

The geographers of the Balkhī School gave a positive Islamic colouring to Arab geography. In addition to restricting themselves mainly to Islamic lands, they laid emphasis on such geographical concepts as found concurrence in the Ḳurʾān or were based on the traditions and sayings of the Companions of the Prophet and others, *e.g.*, they compared the land-mass with a big bird (see above). This was in conformity with a tradition attributed to ʿAbd Allāh b. ʿAmr b. al-ʿĀṣ (Ibn al-Faḳīh, 3-4). Again, the land-mass, round in shape, was encompassed by the 'Encircling Ocean' like a neck-ring, and from this Ocean the two 'gulfs' (the Mediterranean and the Indian Ocean) flowed inwards without joining each other, being separated by al-Barzakh [*q.v.*], the 'barrier' at al-Ḳulzum, a concept found in the Ḳurʾān (see above). Again, unlike some geographers of the ʿIrāḳī School, the geographers of the Balkhī School assigned to Arabia the central place in the world, for it had Mecca and the Kaʿba in it. These new trends in the methodology and treatment of the subject-matter became the dominant feature of the geographers of this School, and must in all probability have been a culmination of the early process wherein Mecca was given precedence over ʿIrāḳ by one group of geographers. The prime object of these later geographers was to describe exclusively the *bilād al-Islām* which they divided into twenty *iḳlīms*, except that they discussed the non-Islamic lands in general in their introductory notes. The basis of the division of these 'provinces' was neither the Iranian *kishwar* system nor the Greek system of Climes. It was territorial and purely physical. This was a positive advancement on previous methods and in a way 'modern'. As pointed out by Ibn Ḥawḳal (2-3) he did not follow the pattern of the 'seven *iḳlīms*' (of the map at al-Ḳawādhiyān, see above), for although it was correct, it was full of confusion, with some overlapping of the boundaries of the 'provinces'. Hence he drew a separate map for each section describing the position of each 'province', its boundaries and other geographical information. An important contribution made by these geographers was that they systematized and enlarged the scope of geography by including in it new topics with a view to making it more useful and interesting, for they believed that a much wider range of people were interested in it, like the kings, the people of *muruwwa* and the leading sections of all classes (Ibn Ḥawḳal, 3). In cartography, besides drawing the regional maps on a more scientific basis, they may be said to have introduced the element of perspective. They drew a round map of the world showing the various 'regions' of the *bilād al-Islām* and other non-Islamic 'regions' of the world. The aim was to bring them in proper perspective and to show the relative position and size of each. But since it did not represent the true size and shape (round, square or triangular) of the respective *iḳlīms*, they mapped each in a magnified form. Their drawing these on a purely physical basis was probably the first experiment of its kind in Arab cartography. The maps of al-Iṣṭakhrī and Ibn Ḥawḳal are, in this respect, superior to those of al-Idrīsī, who divided the seven latitudinal Climes into ten longitudinal sections each and drew a map for each section separately with the result that these sectional maps do not represent geographical units but geometrical divisions. Al-Iṣṭakhrī, Ibn Ḥawḳal and al-Muḳaddasī present for the first time the concept of a country as defined in geographical terms, and even go so far as to delimit the boundaries of each, just as they define the boundaries of the four main kingdoms of the world.

Abū Isḥāḳ Ibrāhīm b. Muḥammad al-Fārisī al-Iṣṭakhrī (first half of the 4th/10th century) seems to have been mainly responsible for spreading the ideas of the Balkhī School. Little is known of his life, but he travelled a good deal and incorporated the experiences of his travels in his work *al-Masālik wa 'l-mamālik* (a new edition of this work has appeared recently, ed. by M. Djābir ʿAbd al-ʿĀl al-Ḥīnī, Cairo 1961). There is little doubt that the work was based on that of Abū Zayd al-Balkhī. Al-Iṣṭakhrī's work served as an authentic source of information for the geographers of this School. It was translated into Persian and became the basis of many Persian works on geography.

Abu 'l-Ḳāsim Muḥammad b. Ḥawḳal, a native of Baghdād, completed his geography entitled *Kitāb Ṣūrat al-arḍ* (2nd ed. J. H. Kramers, Leiden 1938) in c. 366/977. From his childhood, Ibn Ḥawḳal was interested in geography and had travelled widely between 331/943 and 357/968. He was so devoted to geography that the works of al-Djayhānī, Ibn Khurradādhbih and Ḳudāma never parted from him during his travels. About the first two he says that they so engaged him that he was unable to devote any attention either to the other useful sciences or to the Traditions. However, what prompted him to write his work was that he found none of the existing works on the subject satisfactory. He claims to have improved the work of al-Iṣṭakhrī whom he had met. However, the claims of Ibn Ḥawḳal may not be accepted unequivocally, for the similarity between the works of the two geographers itself suggests that Ibn Ḥawḳal must have been considerably indebted to al-Iṣṭakhrī. There is little doubt, however, that he ranks among the most outstanding geographers of the period, for in cartography he shows independence and individuality and does not follow others slavishly. Besides, he incorporated new information based on his travels or acquired from hearsay. He remained an authentic source of information for the succeeding geographers for several centuries to come.

Abū ʿAbd Allāh Muḥammad b. Aḥmad al-Muḳaddasī (d. 390/1000), the author of *Aḥsan al-taḳāsīm fī maʿrifat al-aḳālīm* was a very original and scientific geographer of his time. He rightly claims to have put Arab geography on a new foundation and given it a new meaning and wider scope. Since he considered the subject useful to many sections of society, as also to the followers of various vocations, he widened its scope, including in it a variety of subjects ranging from physical features of the *iḳlīm* (region) under discussion to mines, languages and races of the peoples, customs and habits, religions and sects, character, weights and measures and the territorial divisions, routes and distances. He believed that it was not a science that was acquired through conjecture (*ḳiyās*), but through direct observation and first-hand information. Hence he laid his main emphasis on what was actually observed and was reasonable. From the earlier writers he borrowed what was most essential 'without stealing from them'. Thus, according to the nature of the sources of information, his work may be divided into three parts: what he observed himself; what he heard from trustworthy people; and what he found in written works on the subject. Al-Muḳaddasī is one of the few Arab geographers who discusses geographical terminology and specific connotations of certain phrases and words used, besides giving a synopsis and an index of the *iḳlīms*, districts, etc., in the introduction of his work for the benefit of those who want to get an idea of the contents quickly or wish to use it as a traveller's guide. Unlike Iṣṭakhrī and Ibn Ḥawḳal, al-Muḳaddasī divided the *Mamlakat al-Islām* into fourteen *iḳlīms* (seven *ʿarab* and seven *ʿadjam*) perhaps to conform to the belief that there were seven climes north of the Equator and seven others to its south, an idea attributed to Hermes, the legendary figure known to the Arabs as an ancient philosopher of Egypt. In this respect he differed from Abū Zayd al-Balkhī and al-Djayhānī, whom he however considered *Imāms* (here authorities). An important feature of his work is that like a *mufassir* he discusses at length certain questions relating to general geography, *e.g.*, the number of the seas, etc., in order to bring them into conformity with the Ḳurʾānic verses relating to them.

(d) Trade and exploration: the maritime literature:

An important aspect of the development of Arabic geographical literature of this period was the production of the maritime literature and travel accounts, which enriched the Arabs' knowledge of regional and descriptive geography. This became possible firstly, because of the political expansion of the Muslims and the religious affinity felt by them towards one another irrespective of nationality or race, and secondly, because of the phenomenal increase in the commercial activities of the Arab merchants. Incentive to travel and exploration was provided by several factors, *viz.*, pilgrimage to Mecca, missionary zeal, deputation as envoys, official expeditions, trade and commerce, and, last but not least, the mariners' profession.

From very ancient times the Arabs played the rôle of intermediaries in trade between the East (India, China, etc.) on the one hand and the West (Egypt, Syria, Rome, etc.) on the other. But with the foundation of Baghdād as the capital of the ʿAbbāsid Empire and the development of the ports of Baṣra and Sīrāf, the actual and personal participation of the Arabs now extended as far as China in the east and Sofala on the east coast of Africa. They had learned and mastered the art of navigation from the Persians, and by the 3rd/9th century Arab navigators had become quite familiar with the monsoon and trade winds, and their boats sailed not only along the coasts but direct to India from Arabia. They had become intimate with the various stretches of the sea between the Persian Gulf and the Sea of China, which they divided into the Seven Seas giving each a specific name. Again, they sailed from Aden to East Africa as far south as Sofala and freely sailed on the Red Sea, the Mediterranean, the Black Sea and the Caspian and also on a number of navigable rivers including the Nile and the Indus. Although their boats were small as compared to those of the Chinese, and the Indian Ocean was infested with whales, they performed long and hazardous voyages with courage and fortitude. They used sea-charts (*rahmānīs* and *dafātir*). Al-Masʿūdī (*Murūdj*, i, 233-4) records names of certain captains of boats whom he knew and expert sailors of the Indian Ocean; similarly, al-Muḳaddasī (10-11) gives the name of an expert merchant-sailor whom he consulted on the question of the shape of the Indian Ocean. Aḥmad b. Mādjid ([*q.v.*], see also below) speaks of an old *rahmānī* composed by Muḥammad b. Shādān, Sahl b. Abbān and Layth b. Kahlān (lived in the later part of the 3rd/9th century), but he considered them much below the standard (see Hourani, *Arab seafaring*, 107-8). Since none of these charts is extant, it is not possible to make a correct assessment of the contribution made by these early Arab navigators to nautical geography.

With the development of Arab navigation, Arab trade also expanded. With a strong political power in the Middle East and a developing economy at home, the Arabs acquired considerable importance as traders in the East. The sphere of their trade not only widened, but became more intensive. They even traded by barter with the primitive tribes of the Andaman and Nicobar Islands, whose languages they did not understand. Arab trade with China declined from about the end of the 3rd/9th century, for it is said that in the peasant rebellion under Huang Ch'ao (A.D. 878) large numbers of foreigners were massacred in China. From this time onwards Arab boats went only as far as Kala, a port on the western coast of the Malay Peninsula, no longer existing.

The Arabs' urge to explore new lands was mainly prompted by a desire for trade and rarely for the sake of exploration. Although some instances of early Arab adventures and exploration are recorded, many of these seem to have been 'wonder tales' (*e.g.*, the interpreter Sallām's account of his trip to the wall of Gog and Magog under the orders of the Caliph Wāthiḳ (227-32/842-7), see Minorsky, *Ḥudūd al-ʿālam*, 225). The story of a certain young man of Cordova (Spain) who sailed with a group of young friends on the Atlantic Ocean and then returned after some time, laden with booty, may have had some historical truth in it (al-Masʿūdī, i, 258-9). On the whole the Arabs of this period did not make any substantial contribution to or improve upon the knowledge acquired from the Greeks. There is no doubt however that in regard to certain regions, *viz.*, North and East Africa, West Asia, Middle Asia, India and a few other countries, their information was much more authentic and intimate.

The fact that the Arabs did not explore the regions unknown to them, even those of which they had a theoretical knowledge, may be explained by several factors: wherever the trade incentive was satisfied, they did not proceed beyond that point; secondly, certain notions or preconceived ideas continuously dominated their thought and dissuaded them from taking a bold step, *e.g.*, the Atlantic was a Sea of Darkness and a Muddy Spring (*al-ʿayn al-ḥamiʾa*). For the same reason they did not sail further south along the east coast of Africa, for they believed that there were high tidal waves and sea commotion there, although al-Bīrūnī, on the basis of certain evidence discovered in the 3rd/9th century, namely, the discovery in the Mediterranean of planks from boats of the Indian Ocean (see above), had conceived that the Indian Ocean was connected with the Atlantic by means of narrow passages south of the sources of the Nile (*Ṣifa*, 3-4). Lastly, the fear of encountering aboriginal tribes and cannibals of the East Indies must have prevented the Arabs from sailing further east.

Among the travel accounts of this period that have survived, one of the earliest is that attributed to the merchant Sulaymān, who performed several voyages to India and China and described his impressions of the lands and the peoples in the travelogue *Akhbār al-Ṣīn wa 'l-Hind* (235/850). The work is a testimony of the keen but academic interest taken by Arab merchants in conveying to the Arabic-reading peoples of the time unique and interesting information about the distant lands of the East. This account was first published in 302/916 by Abū Zayd al-Ḥasan of Sīrāf along with other accounts collected and verified by him in a work entitled *Silsilat al-tawārīkh*. Abū Zayd was apparently a well-to-do person, and although he had not himself travelled, he was keenly interested in gathering information from travellers and merchants and in recording it. He met al-Masʿūdī at least twice and exchanged much information with him. Al-Masʿūdī, who represented the finest spirit of exploration of his time, had travelled very widely and sailed on many seas including the Caspian and the Mediterranean. He must have discussed with Abū Zayd the discovery near Crete of the planks of a boat belonging to the Arabian Sea. This was a unique phenomenon for it was believed that the Arabian Sea had no connexion with the Mediterranean. Al-Masʿūdī came to the conclusion that the only possibility was that these planks may have flowed towards the East into the Eastern Sea (the Pacific) and then northwards and finally, through the *khalīdj* (an imaginary channel flowing down from the northern Encircling Ocean into the Black Sea) into the Mediterranean (*Murūdj*, i, 365-6). The fact that they both recorded this unique discovery is evidence of their concern about geographical problems. It also shows that interest in geography was dynamic during this period, and had not become static as in the later period.

An interesting writer of this period was Buzurg b. Shahriyār, the captain of Rāmhurmuz (299-399/912-1009) who compiled a book of maritime tales, entitled *Kitāb ʿAdjāʾib al-Hind* in about 342/953. The book relates a number of very amusing and very strange stories concerning the adventures of the sailors in the Islands of the East Indies and other parts of the Indian Ocean. These were apparently composed for the general reader, and though mostly fantastic, they cannot be completely brushed aside as untrue and ignored in any serious study of Arab geography and exploration. It seems that during this period there was a great demand for wonderful and amusing tales, which fact is borne out by the existence of several MSS in Arabic dealing with *ʿadjāʾib* literature.

This period was on the whole marked by a spirit of enquiry and investigation and exploration among the Arabs. But the maritime literature, most of which seems to have perished, posed itself against the theoretical knowledge derived from the Greek and other sources. Hence at times there was a contradiction between theory and practice, and this was the fundamental problem with which the Arab geographers and travellers were faced. It was this conflict between theory and practice that finally determined the course of the development of Arab geography in the later period. When the 'practicalists' gave way to the theoreticians, the decline of Arab geography became certain. Why the word of the sailor, the traveller and the merchant was not given due credence is difficult to explain, but a large amount of maritime literature must have perished through either neglect or animosity.

(e) Al-Bīrūnī and his contemporaries:

The 5th/11th century may be taken as the apogee of the progress of Arab geography. The geographical knowledge of the Arabs, both as derived from the Greeks and others and as advanced by themselves through research, observation and travel, had, by this period, reached a very high level of development. Besides, geographical literature had acquired a special place in Arabic literature, and various forms and methods of presenting geographical material had been standardized and adopted. The importance of al-Bīrūnī's contribution to Arab geography is two-fold: firstly, he presented a critical summary of the total geographical knowledge up to his own time, and since he was as well-versed in Greek, Indian and Iranian contributions to geography and in that of the Arabs, he made a comparative study of the subject. He pointed out that the Greeks were more accomplished than the Indians, thereby implying that the methods and techniques of the former should be adopted. But he was not dogmatic, and held some important views that were not in conformity with Greek ideas. Secondly, as an astronomer he not only calculated the geographical positions of several towns, but measured the length of a degree of latitude, thus performing one of the three important geodetic operations in the history of Arab astronomy. He made some remarkable theoretical advances in general, physical and human geography. On the basis of the above-mentioned discovery in the Mediterranean of the planks of an Arabian Sea boat a hundred years earlier, he conceived the theoretical possibility of the existence of channels connecting the Indian Ocean with the Atlantic, south of the Mountains of the Moon and the Sources of the Nile. But these were difficult to cross because of high tides and strong winds. He argued that just as towards the east, the Indian Ocean had penetrated the northern continent (Asia) and had opened up channels, similarly, to balance them, the continent has penetrated the Indian Ocean towards the west; the sea there is connected through channels with the Atlantic. Thus, although theoretically he laid down the possibility of circumnavigating the South African coast, in practice it was never accomplished by the Muslims. The idea, however, persisted until the time of the arrival of the Portuguese, when it was hinted by al-Nahrwālī that the Portuguese might have taken this route. Al-Bīrūnī conceived that the land-mass was surrounded by water, that the centre of 'Earth's weight' shifted and caused physical changes on its surface, *e.g.*, fertile lands turned barren, water turned into land and *vice versa*. He described very clearly various concepts and the limits of the inhabited parts of the earth of his time, for which he seems to have had recourse to some contemporary sources which were not available to the earlier geographers. He made an original contribution to regional geography by describing India in detail.

Among the astronomers of the 5th/11th century one who deserves mention was Ibn Yūnus, Abu 'l-Ḥasan ʿAlī b. ʿAbd al-Raḥmān (d. 399/1009). While al-Bīrūnī was working in India and other places, Ibn Yūnus made valuable observations in the observatory on the Mt. al-Muḳaṭṭam in Egypt under the patronage of the Fāṭimid caliphs al-ʿAzīz and al-Ḥakīm. The results of his observations recorded in the *al-Zīdj al-kabīr al-Ḥākimī* became an important source of up-to-date astronomical and geographical knowledge for the scientists of the Islamic East.

Among the geographers and travellers contemporary to al-Bīrūnī there was the Ismāʿīlī poet-traveller Nāṣir-i Khusraw (d. 452/1060 or 453/1061) whose travel account entitled *Safar-nāma* written in Persian covers the author's personal experiences in and descriptions of Mecca and Egypt.

Abū ʿUbayd ʿAbd Allāh b. ʿAbd al-Azīz al-Bakrī (d. 487/1094) was the best representative of lexicography of the period in as far as place-names were concerned. His geographical dictionary *Muʿdjam mā 'staʿdjam min asmāʾ al-bilād wa 'l-mawāḍiʿ* is an excellent literary-cum-geographical work. It discusses the orthography of place-names of the Arabian peninsula mainly, furnishing literary evidence from Arabic literature, ancient Arabian poetry, *Ḥadīth*, ancient traditions, etc. His second geographical treatise *Kitāb al-masālik wa 'l-mamālik* has not survived in its entirety. Al-Bakrī was, however, more a litterateur than a geographer [see ABŪ ʿUBAYD AL-BAKRĪ].

(V) The period of consolidation (6th/12th-10th/16th centuries)

From the 6th/12th to the 10th/16th century Arab geography displayed continuous signs of decline. The process was chequered and with some exceptions like the works of al-Idrīsī and Abu 'l-Fidāʾ the general standard of works produced was low compared to those of the earlier period. The scientific and critical attitude towards the subject and emphasis on authenticity of information that was the mark of the earlier writers gave place to mere recapitulations and *résumés* of the traditional and theoretical knowledge found in the works of earlier writers. This was, in a way, the period of consolidation of geographical knowledge, and the literature may be divided into eight broad categories:

(a) world geographical accounts;
(b) cosmological works;
(c) the *ziyārāt* literature;
(d) *muʿdjam* literature or geographical dictionaries;
(e) travel accounts;
(f) maritime literature;
(g) astronomical literature;
(h) regional geographical literature.

(a) World geographical accounts:

The tradition of describing the world as a whole as practised by the geographers of the classical period continued to be followed by some geographers of this period, but works dealing exclusively with the world of Islam had become rare, for the ʿAbbāsid Empire had itself disintegrated. The pattern of description and arrangement was also different from the earlier works. There was a tendency towards rapprochement between astronomical and descriptive geography in these works, and Greek influence was still prominent in some works, while Persian influence had comparatively diminished probably because of the production of geographical literature in Persian as well. But geographical activity had expanded and places like Syria, Sicily and Spain had become important centres of geographical learning, and some very important works were produced there.

Among the important works on world geography and astronomy produced during this period we may mention *Muntahā al-idrāk fī taḳsīm al-aflāk* by

Muḥammad b. Aḥmad al-Kharaḳī (d. 533/1138-9); *Kitāb al-Djughrāfiyā* by Muḥammad b. Abū Bakr al-Zuhrī of Granada (lived towards 531/1137); *Nuzhat al-mushtāḳ fi 'khtirāḳ al-āfāḳ* by al-Sharīf al-Idrīsī (d. 56/1166); *Kitāb al-Djughrāfiyā fi 'l-aḳālīm al-sabʿa* by Ibn Saʿīd (d. 672/1274); and *Taḳwīm al-buldān* by Abu 'l-Fidā (d. 731/1331).

Al-Zuhrī's work was based on the Greek system of *iḳlīms* and represented the trend of rapprochement between astronomical and descriptive geography. The work of al-Idrīsī, which also represents this tendency, is a fine example of Arab-Norman co-operation in geographical activities. It was produced at Palermo under the patronage of the Norman king Roger II. Al-Idrīsī, who was a prince, and belonged to the Ḥammūdid dynasty, was neither a renowned traveller nor a trained geographer before he joined the court of Roger. The aim of Roger in calling him to his court seems to have been to utilize his personality for his own political objectives. There is little doubt, however, that Roger was interested in geography and he was able to collect a team of astronomers and geographers in his court. As a result of their efforts, for the first time in the history of Arab cartography, seventy regional maps based on the Ptolemaic system of climes were drawn, and a large silver map of the world constructed. The total geographical information acquired from contemporary as well as earlier Greek or Arab sources was classified according to the relevant sections each of which formed a description of one of these maps. The work was an important contribution to physical and descriptive geography. The work of Ibn Saʿīd was based on the clime-system. It also gives the latitudes and longitudes of many places which facilitates their reconstruction into a map. By this time Syria had become an important centre of geographical activities. Abu 'l-Fidāʾ, the Syrian prince, historian and geographer, completed his important compendium on world geography in 721/1321. The work gives latitudes and longitudes of places and treats the subject-mattei on a regional basis. It is arranged in a systematic way and covers descriptive, astronomical and human geography. The author seems to have utilized some contemporary sources, for we find some new information which is not available in earlier works.

(b) Cosmological works:

During this period several works were produced which dealt not only with geography but also with cosmology, cosmogony, astrology and such other topics. The main purpose of these works seems to have been to present in a consolidated and systematic form world knowledge for the benefit of the average reader. No doubt the authors utilized earlier Arabic sources, but on the whole the material is presented uncritically, and there is hardly any question of investigation or research, and the zeal of enquiry is totally lacking. The tendency to produce such works was mainly due to the decline in education and learning which affected the progress of geographical knowledge.

The following are some of the works that belong to this category: *Tuḥfat al-albāb* (or *al-aḥbāb*) *wa nukhbat al-ʿadjāʾib* by Abū Ḥāmid al-Gharnāṭī (d. 565/1169-70); *ʿAdjāʾib al-buldān* and *Āthār al-bilād* by al-Ḳazwīnī (d. 682/1283); *Nukhbat al-dahr fī ʿadjāʾib al-barr wa 'l-baḥr* by al-Dimashḳī (d. 727/1327); *Kharīdat al-ʿadjāʾib wa farīdat al-gharāʾib* by Ibn al-Wardī (d. 861/1457).

(c) The *ziyārāt* literature:

A special feature of this period was that a number of works dealing with the towns and places of religious significance or places of pilgrimage were produced. These were not purely descriptive or topographical works. They dealt with the holy spots of Islam, tombs of saints, the *takyas* of the ṣūfīs and *ribāṭs* along with educational institutions (*madrasas*) specializing in various schools of the Sharīʿa and other such topics. One finds in them detailed accounts of place-names in various towns like Mecca, Damascus, etc. On the whole such works were meant to be religious guides for pilgrims and devotees, and represent the period of religious reaction in Islam. Among the representative works of this type of literature are: *Ishārāt ilā maʿrifat al-ziyārāt* by al-Harawī (d. 611/1214); *al-Dāris fī taʾrīkh al-madāris* by ʿAbd al-Ḳādir Muḥammad al-Nuʿaymī (d. 648/1520); in the Maulana Azad Library, ʿAlīgaṛh Muslim University, there exists a MS (Shērwānī Collection, MS No. 27/34) which, in all probability, is an abridgment of al-Nuʿaymī's original work, written 50 years after his death.

(d) *Muʿdjam* literature or Geographical dictionaries:

The traditions of geographical studies developed in Syria bore many fruitful results. Besides the Compendium of Abu 'l-Fidāʾ and the *ziyārāt* literature, Yāḳūt al-Ḥamawī (d. 626/1229) produced one of the most useful works in Arabic geographical literature, namely, *Muʿdjam al-buldān*. Completed in 621/1224, this geographical dictionary of place-names, which includes other historical and sociological data, was in keeping with the literary and scientific traditions of the earlier period, and represents the consummation of geographical knowledge of the time. As a reference book it is indispensible even to-day for the student of Arab historical geography. The fact that Yāḳūt crowned the work with an introduction on Arab geographical theories and concepts and physical and mathematical geography shows the depth of knowledge of the author. The work also represents that period of Arab geographical development when scholars thought in terms of compiling geographical dictionaries, which would not have been possible without the vast amount of geographical literature that had already come into existence by this time and without the geographical tradition that was present in Syria. Another important work of Yāḳūt is the *Kitāb al-Mushtarik waḍʿan wa'l-mukhtalif ṣaḳʿan*, composed in 623/1226.

(e) Travel accounts:

During this period the Arabs' knowledge of regional and descriptive geography was considerably enriched by the production of travel literature in Arabic on a large scale. Besides the usual incentives for travel like the pilgrimage to Mecca or missionary zeal, the extension of Muslim political and religious influences, especially in the East, had opened up for Muslims new vistas of travel and more opportunities for earning a livelihood.

Among the outstanding travel accounts may be included the work of al-Māzinī (d. 564/1169); the *Riḥla* of Ibn Djubayr (d. 614/1217); *Taʾrīkh al-Mustanṣir* (written in c. 627/1230) by Ibn Mudjāwir; then the *Riḥlas* of al-Nabātī (d. 636/1239), al-ʿAbdārī (d. 688/1289), al-Ṭayyibī (698/1299) and al-Tidjānī (708/1308) and others. Whereas these accounts are of great importance for the Middle East,

North Africa and parts of Europe, for they furnish contemporary and often important information, the work of Ibn Baṭṭūṭa [*q.v.*] (d. 779/1377) entitled *Tuḥfat al-nuẓẓār* remains the most important mediaeval travel account in Arabic for the lands of India, South-East Asia and other countries of Asia and North Africa.

(f) Maritime literature:

During the period under consideration Arab maritime activities were confined to the Mediterranean and the Arabian Seas. In the Mediterranean the Arab navies, using the term in a broader sense, could never really become all-powerful. They were always busy in sea-wars with the Christian navies and sometimes as many as a hundred men-of-war were employed in the forays. Again, although the Arab navigators were quite familiar with the Mediterranean, sailing on the Atlantic was still dreaded, and there is only one instance of Arab adventure, namely, that of Ibn Fāṭima (648/1250). From the account of his voyage preserved in Ibn Saʿīd it appears that he had reached as far as White mountain (identified with Cape Branco) along the West African coast. On the whole it is difficult to assess the amount of the contribution made by the Arabs of this Sea to nautical geography, for very little is known of their accounts. But with the rise of the Ottoman power in Asia Minor, the Ottoman Navy ultimately became very powerful in the Mediterranean (see VI below).

In the Indian Ocean, however, the Arab navigators maintained their importance until the arrival of the Portuguese. It was S̲h̲ihāb al-Dīn Aḥmad b. Mād̲j̲id (the date of his birth or death is not known) who piloted the boat of Vasco da Gama from Malindi on the east coast of Africa to Calicut in India in 1498. This incident indeed marks the turning point in the history of Arab navigation and trade in the East. The advent of the Portuguese had an adverse effect on the trade and commerce of the Arabs. Their maritime strength was destroyed and their trade systematically ruined by the Portuguese.

Ibn Mād̲j̲id, who spent more than fifty years of his life on the high seas, may be considered as one of the greatest Arab navigators of all times. He wrote thirty nautical texts and was one of the most important Arab writers on oceanography, navigation, etc. His contributions bring him in line with the leading scientists of the period. His most important contribution is the work *Kitāb al-Fawāʾid fī uṣūl ʿilm al-baḥr wa 'l-ḳawāʿid*.

Sulaymān b. Aḥmad al-Mahrī, a younger contemporary of Ibn Mād̲j̲id, was another important navigator of this period. He was also author of five nautical works written in the first half of the 10th/16th century. Among these may be mentioned of special importance: *al-ʿUmda al-mahriyya fī ḍabt al-ʿulūm al-baḥriyya* compiled in 917/1511-2 and *Kitāb S̲h̲arḥ tuḥfat al-fuḥūl fī tamhīd al-uṣūl*.

The works of Ibn Mād̲j̲id and Sulaymān al-Mahrī represent the height of the Arabs' knowledge of nautical geography. These navigators used excellent sea-charts, which are supposed to have had the lines of the meridian and parallels drawn on them. They also used many fine instruments and made full use of astronomical knowledge for navigation. There is little doubt that their knowledge of the seas was considerably advanced, especially of the Indian Ocean, for in their works they describe in details the coastlines, routes, etc. of the countries they visited. They were familiar with the numerous islands of the East Indies.

(g) Astronomical literature:

During this period some very important works were produced on astronomy, and one of the most outstanding astronomers of this period was the Tīmūrid prince-mathematician Ulug̲h̲ Beg (d. 853/1449). But with the death of Ulug̲h̲ Beg Muslim astronomical literature may be said to have come to an end, for this was the last scientific effort on the part of a Muslim prince, before the period of decline in Islamic society set in, to revise the data of Ptolemy and to perform independent astronomical observations. The results of Ulug̲h̲ Beg's observations in which his collaborators also participated were included in the *Zīd̲j̲-i d̲j̲adīd-i Sulṭānī*.

(h) Regional geographical literature:

Between the 7th/13th and the 10th/16th centuries a large amount of geographical literature, both in Arabic and Persian, came into existence on a regional or 'national' basis. Although no outstanding contributions were made by the geographers of this period, regional geographical knowledge was enriched by the efforts of several historians and geographers. Geographical traditions of the classical period were kept up, but there was no originality in thought or practice. In astronomical, physical or human geography no substantial advances were made. The production of literature on regional geography during this period was closely connected with the extension of Islam and Muslim political power in the East, and due to the attention paid by Muslim potentates to historiography and geography mainly for political purposes.

In ʿIrāḳ and Mesopotamia, the old centre of geographical activity, little was produced in geographical literature; *Meārath̲ Kudsh̲ē* by Bar Hebraeus (d. 685/1286) showed much influence of Islamic tradition and has a semi-circular world map. In Egypt and Syria the *k̲h̲iṭaṭ*-literature was produced under the Ayyūbids and the Mamlūks. Interest in the *ʿad̲j̲āʾib* literature and ancient Egypt from the time of the Ayyūbids resulted in the production of and collection of some fantastic accounts and stories about ancient Egyptian kings (!) and other tales of common interest. However, some new and fresh information on the Muslim states of the East, India and other countries, was also incorporated in these accounts. Authors who wrote on such subjects were Ibrāhīm b. Waṣīf S̲h̲āh (wrote in 605/1209); Nuwayrī (d. 629/1332); Maḳrīzī (d. 845/1441-2); Ibn Faḍl Allāh al-ʿUmarī (d. 749/1348); al-Ḳalḳas̲h̲andī (d. 821/1418) and others. In North Africa, al-Ḥasan b. ʿAlī al-Marrākus̲h̲ī wrote *D̲j̲āmiʿ al-mabādī wa 'l-g̲h̲āyāt* which gives latitudes and longitudes partly compiled by the author. Ibn K̲h̲aldūn's *Muḳaddima* contains a chapter on geography, representing the tradition of some Arab historians of describing the world as a prelude to history.

In Īrān, Central Asia and India some historical works in Persian dealt with regional and descriptive geography, and some monographs on world geography were also produced. The geographical works were mainly based on earlier Arabic authorities; additional contemporary information was included in general histories and accounts of conquests. Among the important works we may mention: Ibn al-Balk̲h̲ī, *Fārs-nāma*, written in the beginning of the 6th/12th century; Ḥamdallāh al-Mustawfī (d. 740/1340), *Nuzhat al-ḳulūb*; Muḥammad b. Nad̲j̲īb Bakrān (wrote for the Khwārizm-shāh Muḥammad, 596-617/1200-20), *Djihān-nāma*, which contains some 'interesting information on the geography of Transoxania'; ʿAbd al-Razzāḳ al-Samarḳandī (d. 887/1482), *Maṭlaʿ al-saʿdayn*; Amīn Aḥmad Rāzī, *Haft iḳlīm*, written in 1002/1594, a biographical work, but contains much valuable geographical information.

Bibliography: Arabic geographical literature is too vast to allow any brief survey here. Hence only a select bibliography is given below:

1. Texts, translations and commentaries: Abū Dulaf Misʿar b. al-Muhalhil, *al-Risāla al-thāniya*, ed. V. Minorsky, Cairo 1955; al-Bīrūnī, *Kitāb al-Ḳānūn al-Masʿūdī*, published by the Dāʾirat al-Maʿārif, Ḥaydarābād (India), 2 vols., 1955; idem, *Bīrūnī's picture of the world* (*Ṣifat al-maʿmūra ʿalā al-Bīrūnī*), ed. A. Zeki Velidi Togan, *Memoir ASI*, liii, New Delhi 1941 (the work contains texts pertaining to geography selected from al-Bīrūnī's: 1. *al-Ḳānūn al-Masʿūdī*, 2. *Taḥdīd nihāyāt al-amākin li-taṣḥīḥ masāfāt al-masākin*, 3. *al-Djamāhir fī maʿrifat al-djawāhir*, and 4. *al-Ṣaydana*); Ḥamdallāh Mustawfī, *Nuzhat al-ḳulūb*, ed. Muḥammad Dabīr Siyāghī, Tehrān 1958; al-Hamdānī, *Kitāb Ṣifat Djazīrat al-ʿArab*, ed. Muḥammad b. Balhīd al-Nadjdī, Cairo 1953; al-Harawī, ʿAlī b. Abī Bakr, *al-Ishārāt ilā maʿrifat al-ziyārāt*, ed. and French transl. J. Sourdel-Thomine, Damascus 1953-7; *Ḥudūd al-ʿālam*; Ibn Baṭṭūṭa (Eng. tr. H. A. R. Gibb, i- , Cambridge 1958-); Ibn Faḍlān, *Risāla*, second edition of the translation and commentary by A. P. Kovalevsky 1955 (transl. Canard, in *AIEO Alger*, xvi, 1958); Ibn Ḥawḳal; Ibn Khaldūn-Rosenthal; Ibn Mādjid, *Three unknown nautical instructions on the Indian Ocean*, published by T. A. Shumovsky, Moscow 1957; al-Idrīsī, *Polska i kraje sasiedni w świetle "Ksiegi Rogera", geografa arabskiego z XII w. al-Idrīsīʾego*, cześć i, Kraków, 1945; cześć ii, Warsaw 1954; al-Idrīsī, *India and the neighbouring territories in the Kitāb Nuzhat al-mushtāḳ fi 'khtirāḳ al-āfāḳ of al-Sharīf al-Idrīsī*, tr. and commentary by S. Maqbul Ahmad, Leiden 1960; al-Idrīsī, *India and the neighbouring territories as described by the Sharīf al-Idrīsī*, ʿAlīgaṙh 1954; al-Iṣṭakhrī, *al-Masālik wa 'l-mamālik*, ed. M. Djābir ʿAbd al-ʿĀl al-Ḥīnī, Cairo 1961; T. Lewicki, *Zrodla arabskie de dziejow stowianszczyzny*, i, Wroclaw, Cracow 1956; Muḥammad b. Nadjīb Bakrān, *Djihān-nāma*, reproduced with translation by Y. Borshčevsky 1960; al-Nuʿaymī, ʿAbd al-Ḳādir, *al-Dāris fī taʾrīkh al-madāris*, 2 vols., Damascus 1948-51; Marwazī, *Sharaf al-Zamān Ṭāhir Marvazī on China, the Turks and India*, text, tr. and commentary by V. Minorsky, London 1942; *Akhbār al-Ṣīn wa 'l-Hind, Relation de la Chine et de l'Inde, rédigée en 851*, text, French tr. and Notes by Jean Sauvaget, Paris 1948; Yāḳūt, *The Introductory chapters of Yāqūt's Muʿjam al-buldān*, tr. and annotated by Wadie Jwaideh, Leiden 1959; R. Blachère and H. Darmaun, *Extraits des principaux géographes arabes du moyen âge* [2], Paris 1957.

2. General Works: Nafis Ahmad, *Muslim contribution to geography*, Lahore 1947; Barthold, *Turkestan*; G. F. Hourani, *Arab seafaring*, Princeton 1951; Hādī Hasan, *A history of Persian navigation*, London 1928; G. H. T. Kimble, *Geography in the middle ages*, London 1938; J. H. Kramers, *Geography and Commerce* in *The legacy of Islam*, ed. T. Arnold and A. Guillaume, London 1943; *Analecta Orientalia, posthumous writings and selected minor works of J. H. Kramers*, Leiden 1954; I. Y. Kračkovskiy, *Arabskaya geografičeskaya literatura* (vol. iv of his collected works), Moscow 1957; *Al-Masʿūdī commemoration volume*, ed. S. Maqbul Ahmad and A. Rahman, ʿAlīgaṙh 1960; S. Muzaffar Ali, *Arab geography*, ʿAlīgaṙh 1960 (being the tr. of Section IIof M. Reinaud's *Introduction générale à la géographie des Orientaux*).

3. Articles: Ziauddin Alavi, *Physical geography of the Arabs in the Xth Century A.D.*, in *Indian Geographical Journal*, xxii/2, Madras 1947; idem, *Arab geography in the 9th and 10th centuries A.D.*, in *Muslim University Journal*, ʿAlīgaṙh 1948; Leo Bagrow, *The Vasco Gama's Pilot*, in *Studi Colombiani*, Genoa 1951; S. Q. Fāṭimī, *In quest of Kalah*, in *Journal Southeast Asian History*, i/2, September 1960; V. Minorsky, *A False Jayhānī*, in *BSOAS*, xiii, 1949-50, 89-96; S. Maqbul Ahmad, *Al-Masʿūdī's contribution to mediaeval Arab geography*, in *IC*, xxvii/2, 1953; *IC*, xxviii/1, 1954; idem. *Travels of Abu 'l-Ḥasan ʿAlī b. al-Ḥusayn al-Masʿūdī*, in *IC*, xxviii/4, 1954; C. Schoy, *Geography of the Muslims of the Middle Ages*, in *Geographical Review* (American Geographical Society), xiv, 1924, 257-69. Other articles in Pearson, pp. 269-79; idem, *Supplement 1956-60*, pp. 82-5.

(S. Maqbul Ahmad)

VI. The Ottoman geographers

The Ottoman Turks do not seem to have begun to write geographical works until the middle of the 9th/14th century. The first of these were small cosmographies in the style of *Books of Marvels*, which treat of the wonders of Creation. The best known of these works is probably the "Well-preserved Pearl" (*Dürr-i meknūn*) by Yazīdjī-oghlu Aḥmed Bīdjān (d. ca. 860/1456) [*q.v.*], the brother of the early Ottoman poet Yazīdjī-oghlu Meḥemmed (died 855/1451. The same Aḥmed Bīdjān was also the first to make a translation of extracts from an Arabic cosmographical work, the *ʿAdjāʾib al-makhlūḳāt* of Ḳazwīnī (1203-1283), under the same title, in which the stress likewise is less upon scientific knowledge than upon the wonders of Creation (see Rieu, *Catal. of Turkish Mss. in the Brit. Mus.*, 106 ff.).

Ḳazwīnī's *ʿAdjāʾib al-makhlūḳāt* was translated several times into Turkish (Brockelmann, S I, 882, indicates four Turkish translations of the work). Likewise under the same title there were in circulation Turkish translations of Ibn al-Wardī's (d. 1457) *Kharīdat al-ʿadjāʾib* (indicated in *Beiträge zur historischen Geographie .... vornehmlich des Orients*, ed. Hans Mžik, *Festband Eugen Oberhummer*, Leipzig and Vienna 1929, 86 ff.), among them one with some contemporary additions by a man of the early Ottoman period called ʿAlī b. ʿAbd al-Raḥmān (see my articles *Der Bericht des arabischen Geographen Ibn al-Wardī über Konstantinopel* in *Festband Eugen Oberhummer*, 84-91, and *Ein altosmanischer Bericht über das vorosmanische Konstantinopel* in *AION*, N.S., i, 1940, 181-9). Further, after Sipāhīzāde Meḥemmed b. ʿAlī (d. 997/1588) had produced a new Arabic edition of Abu 'l-Fidā's *Taḳwīm al-buldān* under the title *Awḍaḥ al-masālik ilā maʿrifat al-buldān wa'l-mamālik* with the material arranged in alphabetical order and supplemented (Brockelmann, II, 46), he translated extracts of the work into Turkish under the same title (Brockelmann, S II, 44).

One of the last of the translations from earlier geographical works is the "Views of the Worlds" (*Menāẓir al-ʿawālim*) by Meḥmed b. ʿÖmer (not ʿOthmān), b. Bāyezīd al-ʿĀshiḳ (b. 964/1555, date of death unknown; the book was completed 1006/1598). It consists of two parts, of which the first treats the "world above", that is, heaven, its inhabitants and the celestial bodies, and, in appendix, a part of the "world below", that is, hell and its inhabitants. Apart from astronomy, which indeed is only summarily included, this section consists almost exclusively of theology and mythology. But this first part is actually only an introduction. The bulk of the work is contained in the second part, which describes the "world below", that is, the earth and its inhabitants. It contains first a universal geography, that is, a little general knowledge of the earth, followed by separate descriptions arranged in the mediaeval manner according to natural objects: oceans, islands, swamps and lakes, rivers, springs, warm springs, mountains and finally, comprising the main section of the descriptive geography, cities. In this section all of the geographical material is arranged according to the seven climates of Ptolemy, the "actual climates" (*aḳālīm-i ḥaḳīḳiyye*). Within this framework the localities represented are arranged according to the 28 "traditional climates" (*aḳālīm-i ʿurfiyye*) or regions, a principle which ʿĀshiḳ had borrowed from the work of Abu 'l-Fidāʾ, with result that some of the cities treated, according to their location, appear in more than one of the *aḳālīm-i ḥaḳīḳiyye*, the applications of the two principles thus overlapping. Under each heading ʿĀshiḳ indicates in order the reports of his authorities translated into Turkish, of the mediaeval Arabic and Persian writers such as Ibn Khurradādhbih, Ibn al-Djawzī, Yāḳūt, Ḳazwīnī, Ḥamdullāh Mustawfī and Ibn al-Wardī, each with a precise indication of the source. ʿĀshiḳ supplements these with his own reports, especially for Anatolia, Rumelia and Hungary, also with precise indication that this particular information derived from the "writer" (*rāḳim al-ḥurūf*), with the date of his visit to the city in question, thus affording a chronological sequence of his travels.

The geography is followed by a universal descriptive natural science, that is, the solid, liquid and gaseous minerals, scents, metals, plants, animals and man. The work in its totality is a broadly sketched compendium of traditional geography and natural science.

Belonging in a wider sense to the translations of geographical literature is the manual of astronomy and mathematics written in Persian by ʿAlī Ḳushdji (d. 879/1474), formerly director of Ulugh Beg's observatory in Samarḳand and later the court astronomer of Meḥemmed II, which was several times translated into Turkish (see *ZDMG*, lxxvii, 1923, 40 note 2). To this category also belongs the "China Book" (*Khitāy-nāma*) written originally in Persian by Sayyid ʿAlī Akbar Khitāʾī in 1516, in which the author describes his journey to China in 912-4/1506-8 and his stay of three years there, and which he dedicated to Selīm I. Under Murād III, probably in 990/1582, it was translated into Turkish (see P. Kahle in *AO*, xii, 91 ff, and *Opera Minora* 322-3).

In the fields of marine geography and navigation the Ottoman Turks produced original works. In this respect special mention should to made of the work of Pīrī Muḥyi 'l-Dīn Reʾīs (d. 962/1554), a nephew of the famous naval hero Kemāl Reʾīs who knew every corner of the Mediterranean. In 919/1513 he produced a map of the world in two parts, of which only the western part has been preserved, which he presented to Sultan Selīm I in Cairo (923/1517). For that portion of his work treating the west Pīrī Reʾīs used as sources maps containing the Portuguese discoveries up to 1508, as well as a map, since lost, containing the discoveries made by Christopher Columbus during his third voyage (1498). He had got the latter from a Spanish sailor who had gone with Columbus to America three times and who in 1501 at Valencia had been made a Turkish prisoner by Pīrī Reʾīs's uncle Kemāl Reʾīs (see P. Kahle, *Die verschollene Columbus-Karte vom Jahre 1498 in einer türkischen Weltkarte von 1513*, Berlin-Leipzig 1933; idem, *A lost map of Columbus*, in *Opera Minora*, Leiden 1956, 247-65; Ibrahim Hakkı, *Eski Harıtalar*, Istanbul 1936; Afet, *Un Amiral Géographe turc du XVIe siècle, Piri Reïs, auteur de la plus ancienne carte de l'Amérique* in *Belleten*, i (1937), 333-49; Sadi Selen, *Die Nord-Amerika-Karte des Piri Reïs (1528)*, ibid. 519-23).

Pīrī Reʾīs then wrote a nautical handbook of the Mediterranean, the *Baḥriyye*, containing 129 chapters each provided with a map in which he gives an exact description of the Mediterranean and all its parts. His models are Italian portulans and other navigational handbooks, the major part of which have disappeared. He first dedicated the work to Sultan Selīm I in 927/1521. After the latter's death he prepared a second edition with many additional maps, a modified text, and a poetical introduction of some 1200 verses in Turkish on the lore of the sea and the sailor, which he presented in 932/1525-26 to Sultan Süleymān by means of the Grand Vizier Ibrāhīm Pasha (see P. Kahle, *Piri Reʾīs und seine Baḥrīye* in *Beiträge zur historischen Geographie ..., Festband E. Oberhummer*, Leipzig-Vienna 1929, 60-76; idem, *Baḥriyya, das türkische Segelhandbuch für das Mittelländische Meer vom Jahre 1521*, the first part of an unfinished edition, Berlin-Leipzig 1926; the complete work in facsimile, *Kitabi Bahriye*, Istanbul 1935).

A similar work of marine geography and navigation on the Indian Ocean was written in 961/1554 by Seyyidī ʿAlī Reʾīs b. Ḥüseyn, known as Kātib-i Rūmī (died 970/1562), entitled "The Ocean" (*al-Muḥīṭ*). ʿAlī Reʾīs made use of the experience of South Arabian sailors who had served as guides for Vasco de Gama on his voyage to Calicut, and also translated parts of Suleymān al-Mahrī's *al-ʿUmda al-Mahriyya* into Turkish in his work (see W. Tomaschek and M. Bittner, *Die topographischen Kapitel des indischen Seespiegels Mohit*, Vienna 1897; for the Arabic precursors see Gabriel Ferrand, *Relations de Voyages et textes géographiques ...*, ii, Paris 1914).

Yet another work of marine geography from a later period is the "Book of the Black and White Seas" (*Kitāb Baḥr al-aswad wa 'l-abyaḍ*) written by Seyyid Nūḥ during the reign of Meḥemmed IV (see F. Babinger, *Seyyid Nūḥ and his Turkish sailing handbook* in *Imago Mundi*, xii (1955), 180-2).

A kind of terrestrial counterpart to these works of marine geography is the "Collection of Stations" (*Medjmūʿ-i menāzil*), an illustrated book by Naṣūḥ al-Maṭrāḳī (dates unknown) in which he describes briefly and depicts separately the stages of Sultan Süleymān Ḳānūnī's first Persian expedition (940-2/1534-5). It exists only in a single manuscript, in all probability the dedication copy for the sultan, in the University Library in Istanbul, and constitutes an important source for the military routes used by the sultans for their eastern expeditions (see Albert

Gabriel, *Les étapes d'une campagne dans les deux Irak d'après un manuscrit turc du XVIe siècle* in *Syria* (1928), 328-41; Franz Taeschner, *The itinerary of the first Persian campaign of Sultan Suleyman 1534-36, according to Naṣūḥ al-Maṭrāḳī* in *Imago Mundi* xiii (1956), 53-5; idem, *Das Itinerar des ersten Persienfeldzuges des Sultans Süleyman Kanuni nach Matrakçi Nasuh*, in *ZMDG*, 1961).

The campaign itineraries of sultans Selīm I and Süleymān I, as well as those of Murād IV are contained, moreover, in the collection of documents called *Münshe'āt al-Selāṭīn* of Ferīdūn Aḥmed Beg (d. 991/1583), or his continuator (only the two volume second edition of the *Münshe'āt* contains the itineraries, Istanbul 1274-75/1857-59; the itineraries there are enumerated in F. Taeschner, *Das anatolische Wegenetz nach osmanischen Quellen*, i, Leipzig 1924, 20).

The most important comprehensive geographical work, constituting at the same time the transition in Turkey from the mediaeval oriental to the modern European point of view, is the "View of the World" (*Djihānnümā*) of the famous scholar Muṣṭafā b. ʿAbdallāh, known as Kātib Čelebi [*q.v.*] or Ḥadjdjī Khalīfa (1017-67/1609-57). The work has a complicated history. Kâtib Čelebi began it twice and twice it remained uncompleted. In 1058/1648 he had begun it as cosmography in the medieval style of such works as the one mentioned above of Meḥmed ʿĀshiḳ, which he used and acknowledged. After he had described oceans, rivers and lakes, he started on lands, of which the western came first, Muslim Spain and North Africa. The lands of the Ottoman Empire were to follow as the main section, which he began with the three imperial capitals, Bursa, Edirne and Constantinople, followed by the provinces of the European half of the empire, Rumelia, Bosnia and Hungary (from a manuscript of this version in Vienna, J. von Hammer translated *Rumeli und Bosna*, Vienna 1812; see F. Taeschner, *Die Vorlage von Hammers "Rumeli und Bosna"* in *MOG*, i (1923-25), 308-10).

When Kātib Čelebī had reached the heading Hatván in writing the description of Hungary he came across a copy of the *Atlas Minor* of Gerhard Mercator, edited by Jodocus Hondius in 1621 at Arnheim. He abandoned the *Djihānnümā* and from 1064/1654 on, with the help of a French renegade, Meḥmed Efendi Ikhlāṣī, he worked at a translation of the atlas, to which he gave the title *Lewāmiʿ al-nūr fī ẓulumāt-i Aṭlās Minūr*.

When this work was two-thirds finished Kâtib Čelebi began again to write his *Djihānnümā*, according to a new plan based on the western model. This time however he began in east Asia for which he used, in addition to European, Oriental sources as well, such as the *Khitāy-nāme* of ʿAlī Akbar; these preponderated the further west he moved. When he had progressed in his description from east to west as far as Armenia (Eyālet of Vān), death hastened on by an accident stayed his hand (1067/1657). Thus the second version of his work also remained unfinished.

Yet another European work was to provide the impulse for the continuation of the *Djihānnümā* and eventually its completion. On 14 August 1668 the Dutch envoy Colier presented to Sultan Meḥemmed IV in Edirne on behalf of his government a copy of the Latin edition in eleven volumes of Blaeu's *Atlas Maior sive Cosmographia Blaviana* (1662). A few years later, in 1086/1675, the Sultan had this work translated into Turkish by Abū Bakr b. Bahrām al-Dimashḳī (d. 1102/1691). Abū Bakr published his translation under the title *Nuṣrat al-Islām wa 'l-surūr fī taḳrīr-i Aṭlas Māyūr*, and based on it, with the further use of other, especially, Oriental sources, produced a "Major Geography" (*Djughrāfiyā-yi kebīr*) (see P. Kahle, *The Geography of Abu Bekr Ibn Behram ad-Dimashki*: Ms. A.S. 575 of the Chester Beatty Collection).

When later, in 1140/1728, the Hungarian renegade Ibrāhīm Müteferriḳa established the first printing-press in Istanbul, the *Djihānnümā* of Kātib Čelebi became the eleventh product (in 1145/1732) in the new Turkish art of printing. As a basis for this edition Ibrāhīm used the second version of the work, that is, the description of Asia begun by Kātib Čelebi, and supplemented this with the corresponding portions ("insertions", *lāḥiḳa*) from the work of Abū Bakr, so that the printed edition included the complete description of Asia. In the introductory chapters containing astronomical, mathematical and geographical data, he brought the work up to date by means of series of "printer's addenda" (*tadhyīl al-ṭābiʿ*) (see F. Taeschner, *Zur Geschichte des Djihānnumā* in *MSOS* ii, 29 (1926), 99-111; idem., *Das Hauptwerk der geographischen Literatur der Osmanen, Kâtib Çelebis Gihannüma* in *Imago Mundi* 1935, 44-7; *Kâtip Čelebi, Hayatı ve eserleri hakkında incelemeler*, Ankara 1957: on the *Djihānnümā* the essay by Hamit Sadi Selen, 121-36).

In 1153/1740 one Shehrīzāde Aḥmed b. Müdhehhib Saʿīd (d. 1178/1764-5) undertook a further continuation of Kātib Čelebi's *Djihānnümā* with the title *Rawḍat al-anfus*. But the work was never printed owing on the one hand to the death of Ibrāhīm Müteferriḳa (1157/1744) after which the press was silenced and, on the other hand, to the influx of original European literature in the face of which Turkish productions in the geographical field lost in originality and thereby in interest.

Concerning travel descriptions those of ʿAlī Akbar from China and his sojourn there have been mentioned. Worthy also of indication is the brief description by Seyyidī ʿAlī Re'īs of his journey to India and, after the unsuccessful Ottoman naval expedition against the Portuguese in the Indian Ocean, his fortunate return to the sultan's court in Edirne. These are contained in the tiny book *Mir'āt al-mamālik* (completed 964/1557 and printed Istanbul 1313; Eng. tr., A. Vambéry, *Travels and adventures of the Turkish Admiral Sidi Ali Reïs .... during the years 1553-1556*, London 1899).

The major work, however, in the field of travel description is the great, ten-volume "Travel Book" (*Seyāḥatnāme*) or "History of the Traveller" (*Ta'rīkh-i seyyāḥ*) of Ewliyā b. Derwīsh Meḥemmed Ẓillī, usually known as Ewliyā Čelebi [*q.v.*]. It is a unique work in the entire literature of the Islamic peoples. For forty years (1631-1670) Ewliyā Čelebi travelled in every direction throughout the Ottoman Empire and its neighbouring lands, largely as field chaplain in the retinues of dignitaries, governors and ambassadors, as well as with divisions of the army. His work is thus a kind of memoir and contains in addition to a knowledge of the lands which he visited many insights into the higher politics of his period. Besides his own experiences he has mingled the results of his reading and the manifold products of his lively imagination in the work. Through his contacts with political personalities and his participation in their destinies, Ewliyā Čelebi's book has become an important record for the history of his times.

A stimulation to travel description was provided by the annual pilgrimage to Mecca. There are indeed, especially from the 18th century, a series of texts which describe the journey from Üsküdar, the point of departure on the Asiatic coast of the Bosphorus for pilgrims to Mecca, and the ceremonies accomplished in Mecca. Most of the pilgrims limited their descriptions to the latter and touched only in passing the voyage itself. Some, however, did describe the journey and for that reason are of importance from the point of view of geography. The most detailed of these is "The ceremonies of the pilgrimage" (*Manāsik al-ḥadjdj*) by Meḥemmed Edīb (1193/1779) (printed in Istanbul 1232/1816-17; Fr. tr. by M. Bianchi, *Itinéraire de Constantinople à la Mecque* in *Recueil des Voyages et des Mémoires publiés par la Société de Géographie*, ii, Paris 1825, in which the work is wrongly dated 1093/1682 instead of 1193/1779).

To travel literature in a certain sense belong also the reports from the ambassadors of the Porte to European courts (*Sefāretnāme*). These belong at the same time to the category of historical literature, for which reason they are generally included by the historiographers of the Empire in their works (enumerated by me in *ZDMG*, lxxvii (1923), 75-8; more completely by Faik Reşit Unat in *Tarih Vesikaları*, reprinted in *Resimli Tarih Mecmuası*, 8 August 1950) (see further ELČI).

A brief word may also be said concerning cartography. Pīrī Reʾīs's world map of 1513, originally in two parts, has already been described above. In his sailing manual for the Mediterranean (the *Baḥriyye*), Pīrī Reʾīs included in each chapter, after the fashion of the Italian portulans and probably based on them, a map representing the region of the Mediterranean treated in the respective chapter. The late editor of the periodical *Imago Mundi*, Leo Bagrov, had in his possession such a map of the entire Mediterranean with parallel meridians, based on a mistaken planispheric concept.

The manuscripts of the first version of Kātib Čelebi's *Djihānnümā* have in the margins finely sketched maps of the *Liwā* (*Sandjak*) in question. The 1145/1732 printing of the *Djihānnümā* is provided with full-page maps, obviously in the style of contemporary European cartography, but with inverse orientation (north at the bottom). From the workshop of the printer Ibrāhīm Müteferriḳa came as well a manuscript map of the Near and Middle East, now preserved in the Austrian Military Archives, dated either 1139/1726-7 or 1141/1728-9 (see F. Taeschner, *Das anatolische Wegenetz nach osmanischen Quellen*, ii, Leipzig 1926, 62 ff.).

In conclusion brief reference may be made to the world map known as that of Ḥadjdjī Aḥmed of Tunis, dated 967/1559, in the Marciana in Venice. At one time believed to be of Muslim origin, this has now been shown to be of European manufacture, prepared for the Muslim market (V. L. Ménage, *'The Map of Hajji Ahmed' and its makers*, in *BSOAS*, xxi, 1958, 271-314; see also George Kish, *The suppressed Turkish map of 1560*, Ann Arbor (William L. Clements library, 1957 [includes facsimile]).

Bibliography: in the article, and general: F. Taeschner, *Die geographische Literatur der Osmanen*, in *ZDMG*, lxxvii (1923), 31-80; F. Babinger, *Die Geschichtsschreiber der Osmanen und ihre Werke*, Leipzig 1927, in which the geographical writers are also discussed; Abdülhak Adnan-Adıvar, *Osmanlı Türklerinde Ilim*, Istanbul 1943; idem, *La science chez les Turcs Ottomans*, Paris 1939.

(FR. TAESCHNER)

DJUḤĀ (جحا or جحى), the nickname of a personage whom popular imagination made the hero of a few hundred jests, anecdotes and amusing stories. The oldest literary instance of this name goes back to the first half of the 3rd/9th century, in al-Djāḥiẓ, who numbers Djuḥā among others renowned for their follies (*Risāla fi 'l-Ḥakamayn*, ed. Pellat, in *Machriq*, 1958, 431), and attributes to him futile schemes and an extraordinary tendency to make mistakes and blunders; the same author also quotes (*K. al-Bighāl*, ed. Pellat, Cairo 1955, 36) a story borrowed from Abu 'l-Ḥasan [al-Madāʾinī?] in which Djuḥā gives an unexpected but witty retort to a Ḥimṣī (the inhabitants of Ḥimṣ were considered particularly dull-witted; see R. Basset, *1001 Contes*, i, 427-8, 451-2). Already a by-word by the time of al-Djāḥiẓ, Djuḥā soon became the central figure in a number of stories which were to form the anonymous miscellany called *K. Nawādir Djuḥā*, mentioned by the *Fihrist* (written in 377/987-8) in the following century (i, 313; Cairo ed., 435), from which later writers, notably al-Ābī (d. 422/1030) in *Nathr al-durar* (*MS* Dār al-kutub) and al-Maydānī (d. 518/1124) were to borrow material. In recording the term *aḥmaḳ min Djuḥā*, the latter quotes three anecdotes and adds that Djuḥā was a member of the Banū Fazāra bearing the *kunya* of Abu 'l-Ghuṣn; this is also mentioned in other works: the *Nathr al-durar*, the *Ṣaḥāḥ* (s.v.) by al-Djawharī (d. ca. 400/1009), the *Akhbār al-ḥamḳā wa -'l-mughaffalīn* (Damascus [1926]) by Ibn al-Djawzī (d. 597/1200), the *ʿUyūn al-tawārīkh* (Paris *MS*. 1588, s.a. 160) by Ibn Shākir al-Kutubī (d. 764/1363), the *Ḥayāt al-ḥayawān* (s.v. *dādjin*) by al-Damīrī (d. 808/1405), the *Ḳāmūs* (sub *D.DJ.N.*, *DJ.Ḥ.W.*, *GH.Ṣ.N.*), the *Lisān* (sub *GH.Ṣ.N.*), the *Muḍḥik al-ʿabūs* (anonymous *MS*. Dār al-kutub, 5102 *adab*.). As for his name, it varies according to the source: Nūḥ, Dudjayn/al-Dudjayn b. Thābit (or b. al-Ḥārith), finally ʿAbd Allāh. None of them calls into question his historical existence: the *Nathr al-durar* makes him live more than a hundred years, and die at Kūfa in the reign of Abū Djaʿfar al-Manṣūr (136-58/754-75), and refers to a text, now lost, by al-Djāḥiẓ in which moreover was quoted a poem by ʿUmar b. Abī Rabīʿa (d. 93/712?) containing an allusion to Djuḥā (but this poem does not appear in the *Dīwān* of the poet); for his part, Ibn al-Djawzī, who undertakes the defence, asserts that he was simply scatter-brained (*mughaffal*) and that it was his neighbours, at whom he jested, who made up at his expense the stories which we know; he quotes among his contemporaries Makkī b. Ibrāhīm (116-214 or 215/734-830 or 831; see *Tahdhīb al-Tahdhīb*, s.v.; the passage from Ibn al-Djawzī was taken up by the author of the *Nuzhat al-udabāʾ*; but the translation given in *Fourberies* [see Bibliography], 4-5, should be corrected), and some anecdotes actually connecting him with certain personnages of the first half of the 2nd/8th century, particularly Abū Muslim and al-Mahdī.

The biographers make mention of a traditionist of weak reputation, Abu 'l-Ghuṣn Dudjayn b. Thābit al-Yarbūʿī al-Baṣrī, whose mother was a slave of the mother of Anas b. Mālik [*q.v.*]; this *tābiʿī*, who collected traditions from Anas, Aslam (*mawlā* of ʿUmar), Hishām b. ʿUrwa, and handed them down to Ibn al-Mubārak, Wakīʿ, and even al-Aṣmaʿī, is said to have been called Djuḥā, so that he is sometimes confused with our hero. Ibn Ḥadjar al-ʿAsḳalānī (d. 852/1449) rejects such an identification (*Lisān al-mīzān*, s.v. Dudjayn), but an earlier and clearer passage from al-Kutubī (*op. cit.*) hints at the solution to this problem: it says in effect that Dudjayn, surnamed Djuḥā, died in 160/777 but adds, according to Ibn Ḥibbān, that two men, one the traditionist [of Baṣra] Dudjayn, and the other Nūḥ = Djuḥā [established at Kūfa], have been confused because both died in 160. This coincidence is, to say the least, strange, and it is not impossible that the traditionist of Baṣra was a victim of the spite of the inhabitants of Kūfa, but, until we are better informed, there is no reason to doubt the historic existence of Djuḥā, who might, moreover, have been called Abu 'l-Ghuṣn Nūḥ al-Fazārī. Some Shīʿī authors regard Djuḥā as a Shīʿī and consider him as a traditionist together with Abū Nuwās and Buhlūl [*qq.v.*]; as a matter of fact, al-Astarabādhī, *Minhādj al-maḳāl*, Tehran 1888, 258, mentions a *Musnad Abī Nuwās wa-Djuḥā wa-Buhlūl . . . wa-mā rawaw min al-ḥadīth*, which was in the hand of Abū Fāris Shudjāʿ al-Arradjānī, d. 320/932 (cf. J. M. Abd-El-Jalil, *Brève histoire de la litt. ar.*, Paris 1943, 169).

Al-Suyūṭī (d. 911/1505), who must have had at his disposal sources inaccessible to us, saw in Djuḥā (in *Ḳāmūs*) an open-hearted *tābiʿī* and declared that most of the stories of which he is the hero are without foundation; this proves that the character was well known in Egypt, but throws no light at all on the problem which now presents itself; which is, that at an undetermined date towards the end of the Middle Ages there appeared among the Turks another symbolic figure who, under the name of Naṣr al-Dīn Khōdja [*q.v.*], partially and at least locally took the place of Djuḥā. Indeed the first Arabic edition of the collection of anecdotes published in lithograph about 1880 at Būlāḳ bore the unexpected title of *Nawādir al-Khūdjā Naṣr al-Dīn al-mulaḳḳab bi-Djuḥā al-Rūmī*, and the Egyptians again turned Naṣr al-Dīn and Djuḥā into one and the same person.

For R. Basset (in *Fourberies*, see *Bibliography*), this confusion arises from the fact that the primitive *K. Nawādir Djuḥā* was translated into Turkish in the 9th/15th or 10th/16th century, and that this Turkish version, adapted and amplified, was in turn translated into Arabic in the 11th/17th century; if this latter assertion corresponds with reality, the first is not entirely accepted, and there is every reason for believing, with Christensen (see below), that the "follies" of Naṣr al-Dīn were an independent collection into which were incorporated the stories of Djuḥā which had been handed down orally. This problem, already complex enough, will be examined in the article NAṢR AL-DĪN. We should however note here that the introduction of the figure of Djuḥā among the Turks may have been accomplished through the intermediary of Persia, where A. Christensen (*Júḥi in the Persian Literature*, in *A Volume . . . presented to E. G. Browne*, Cambridge 1922, 129-36) discovered some early evidence of Djuḥā (Djuḥī/ Djūḥī), notably in the *Mathnawī* of Djalāl al-Dīn Rūmī (d. 672/1273) and the *Bihāristān* of Djāmī (d. 898/1492).

The method advocated by Christensen, consisting in the search for stories about Djuḥā in literature prior to the presumed appearance of Naṣr al-Dīn, was recently applied independently and successfully by ʿAbd al-Sattār Aḥmad Farrādj, in his *Akhbār Djuḥā* (Cairo n.d. [1954]). Taking advantage of the article NAṢR AL-DĪN in the *EI*¹ (by F. Bajraktarevič), he took as his starting point R. Basset's thesis, without, however, referring to the works of that distinguished orientalist, and attempted partially to restore the original *K. Nawādir Djuḥā*, by a searching analysis of early literary works in Arabic; he thus discovered about 166 anecdotes of which two-thirds (107) appeared in the edition of the collection of *Nawādir Djuḥā*; of the other 241 anecdotes of this latter collection (which he had not immediately eliminated on account of their manifestly recent insertion), he counted 217 for which he could discover no early evidence, 17 in which Tīmūr Lang (8th/14th century) appeared, and finally 7 which contained Turkish words. From these figures, which are by no means final, two provisional conclusions may be drawn: the first, that the proportion of anecdotes attested at an early date is comparatively considerable (40%), and the second, that the additions of undoubted Turkish origin are rather few (6%). These proportions are given here only as an indication, for the published collection which served as a basis for the calculation is very far from containing all the stories in circulation under the name of Djuḥā which in fact belong largely to the world's folk-lore. Farrādj moreover has not examined all the works, as a matter of fact the more recent, which contain further stories about Djuḥā, whether or not the name appears therein, in particular Ibn Ḥidjdja (d. 837/1434), *Thamarāt al-awrāḳ*, Būlāḳ 1300; al-Ibshīhī (d. after 805/1446), *Mustaṭraf*, Cairo n.d.; al-Ḳalyūbī, *Nawādir*, Cairo 1302 (see O. Rescher, *Die Geschichten und Anekdoten aus Qaljûbi's Nawâdir*, Stuttgart 1920); al-Balawī, *K. Alif bāʾ*, Cairo 1287; *Nuzhat al-udabāʾ*, B.N. Paris MSS 6008, 6710.

The jests of Djuḥā are known outside the Muslim world (see NAṢR AL-DĪN), and on the east coast of Africa they are attributed to Abū Nuwās [*q.v.*] but the character is popular in Nubia (Djawha), in Malta (Djahan), in Sicily and in Italy (Giufà or Giucca) and, with greater reason, in North Africa, where he was certainly introduced at an early period (al-Ḥuṣrī [d. 413/1022], *Djamʿ al-Djawāhir*, Cairo 1953, 82, knows that a wit of the 3rd/9th century, Abu 'l-ʿAbar, wore a ring on which was engraved "Djuḥā died on [a] Wednesday"; in the 11th/17th century Yūsuf b. al-Wakīl al-Mīlawī wrote an *Irshād man naḥā ilā nawādir Djuḥā*, see L. Nemoy, *Ar. MSS in the Yale Univ. Lib.*, New Haven 1956, no. 1203). Some vestiges certainly remain, in Arabic or Berber, of the primitive Arabic version, amplified doubtless by folk-lore elements from other sources. A. Mouliéras (see *Bibliography*) has succeeded in mustering 60 "fourberies" in Kabyle, and some of them can be found in several studies of Berber dialectology (H. Stumme, *Märchen der Berbern von Tamazratt*, Leipzig 1900, 39-40; R. Basset, *Zenatia du Mzab*, Paris 1892, 102, 109; idem, *Recueil de textes . . . .* Algiers 1887, 38; idem, *Manuel Kabyle*, Paris 1887, 37*; B. Ben Sedira, *Cours de langue kabyle*, Algiers 1887, *passim*; S. Biarnay, *Dial. berbère des Bet't'ioua du Vieil Arzeu*, Algiers 1911, 130; E. Laoust, *Dial. berbère du Chenoua*, Paris 1912, 185, 190). The personality of the Berber Djuḥā formed the subject of a rather detailed analysis by H. Basset, *Essai sur la littérature des Berbères*, Algiers 1920, 170 ff., which for the greater part holds good for the Arab Djuḥā. In dialectal Arabic, most manuals reproduce some anecdotes (see especially F. Mornand, *La vie arabe*, Paris 1856, 115-24; F. Pharaon, *Spahis et Turcos*, Paris 1864, 174-210; Abderrahman Mohammed, *Enseignement de l'arabe parlé*. . ., Algiers ²1913, 1-28; Allaoua ben Yahia, *Recueil de thèmes et versions*, Mostaganem 1890, 1-66, *passim*; L. Machuel, *Méthode pour l'étude de l'arabe parlé*, Algiers ⁵1900, 210 ff;.

references in H. Pérès, *L'arabe dialectal algérien et saharien, bibliographie* ..., Algiers 1958, 111). For Morocco, there is a series in G. S. Colin, *Chrestomathie marocaine*, Paris² 1955, 87-114, and *Recueil de textes en arabe marocain*, Paris 1937, 15-26. The Moroccans claim that the authentic Djuḥā (Žḥa) was originally from Fās, where a road bears his name (L. Brunot, *Textes arabes de Rabat*, Paris 1931, 118); as opposed to this Žḥa 'l-Fāsi, malicious and humorous, there are some secondary characters, also called Žḥa, but who symbolize the gullible provincial. The Moroccans make a sharp distinction between their national and multiform Žḥa and the "Egyptian" Djuḥā (Goḥa), confused in the printed collection with Naṣr al-Dīn.

The Goḥa who was the hero of a tale by A. Adès and A. Josipovici, *Le livre de Goha le simple*, Paris n.d. [ca. 1916] has just (1959) made his appearance in the cinema in a film in two versions, Arabic and French, based on the above-mentioned novel and entitled *Goha* (although pronounced Žḥa by the Tunisian actors).

There the popular figure of Djuḥā can hardly be rediscovered. Of him al-Suyūṭī (in *Ḳāmūs*) said: "No-one should laugh at him on hearing of the amusing stories told against him; on the contrary it is fitting that everyone should ask God to allow him to profit from the *barakāt* of Djuḥā [as a *tābiʿī*]"; he was a little ingenuous, simple and sometimes clumsy, but at times singularly clever, later on, he appeared in many different aspects: rarely completely stupid, he was more often, under a foolish exterior, supremely cunning; he sometimes assumed the demeanour of a simpleton only to hoax his fellows or to gull them and live at their expense, for parasitism was his life; his sham silliness was prompted by interest and his intentions were rarely honest. Fertile in expedients, capable, through his knack of doing the right thing, of extricating himself from the most delicate situations, he reminds us less of Gribouille than of Panurge and, by his "espiègleries", of Eulenspiegel.

It is indeed strange that folklore has retained the name of Djuḥā from among so many figures who were at an early period proverbial among the Arabs and who are now forgotten; that it has gathered round his name a great part of the little stories of which they were the heroes, and that it has preferred him to all the professional humorists (see F. Rosenthal, *Humour in early Islam*, Leiden 1956) who flourished in the 2nd/8th and 3rd/9th centuries and vied with each other in inventing droll stories [see NĀDIRA].

Bibliography: The first Arab edition of the *Nawādir* was followed in 1299/1883 by the *Nawādir Djuḥā*, then by the *Ḳiṣṣat Djuḥā*, Beirut 1890, and by a series of popular editions in booklet form. A translation of the Turkish collection was elaborated by Ḥikmat Sharīf al-Ṭarābulusī who published it under the title *Nawādir Djuḥā al-kubrā*, Cairo n.d.; also to be noted are Ḥasan Ḥusnī Aḥmad, *Djuḥā, taʾrīkhuh, nawādiruh, ḥikāyātuh, ʿilmuh, khawāṭiruh, falsafatuh*, Cairo 1950; ʿAṭāʾ Allāh Tarzī Pasha, *Djuḥā al-ḳāḍī*, in *al-Risāla*, no. 993 (4 July, 1952). R. Basset has explained his thesis in an introduction to A. Mouliéras, *Les fourberies de Si Djeh'a*, Paris 1892, 1-79 and 183-7, which comprises a comparative and abundantly annotated table of the three versions, Turkish, Arabic and Berber; there are also some studies by the same author, published in the *Revue des traditions populaires*, as well as *1001 Contes, récits et légendes arabes*, Paris 1924, i, *passim*, where some stories are translated. For translations, see Galland, *Les paroles remarquables, les bons mots et les maximes des Orientaux*, Paris 1694, the works cited by R. Basset, in *Fourberies*, 12, and especially A. Wesselski, *Der Hodscha Nasreddin*, Weimar 1911, 2 vols. and T. Garcia-Figueras, *Cuentos de Ÿeha* ..., Jerez 1934. —see also the Bibliography of the article NAṢR AL-DĪN. (CH. PELLAT)

DJUHAYNA [see Supplement].

DJULAMARG [see ÇÖLEMERIK].

AL-**DJULANDĀ** (also AL-DJULUNDĀ, according to *TA* and *al-Iṣāba*) B. **MASʿŪD** B. **DJAʿFAR** B. AL-**DJULANDĀ** was the chief of the Ibāḍī Azd in ʿUmān. During the caliphate of the Umayyad Marwān II al-Djulandā supported the claims of ʿAbd Allāh b. Yaḥyā, known as Ṭālib al-Ḥaḳḳ, who was defeated and killed in 129/747. When the ʿAbbāsids came to power the Ibāḍīs tried to assert their independence in ʿUmān and elected al-Djulandā as their first imām, but in the year 134/752 al-Saffāḥ sent an expedition under Khāzim b. Khuzayma al-Tamīmī against the Khāridjīs in the ʿUmān region. He first drove the Sufrīs out of Djazīrat Ibn Kāwān (Ḳishm [*q.v.*]); they took refuge in ʿUmān where they were routed by al-Djulandā, so that when Khāzim crossed to ʿUmān he had only the Ibāḍīs to subdue. They refused to pay homage to al-Saffāḥ and resisted successfully until Khāzim adopted the stratagem of setting fire to their hutments, thus causing them to abandon their positions and rush to save their women and children. In their panic they were cut down with an estimated loss of 10,000 men, including al-Djulandā.

Bibliography: Ṭabarī, iii, 1, 77-8; Ibn al-Athīr, v, 346-7; Masʿūdī, vi, 66-7; Yaʿḳūbī, ii, 405 (ed. Beirut 1960, ii, 339); Ibn Kathīr, x, 57; al-Sālimī, *Tuḥfat al-aʿyān* (1332), i, 66-72; Salīl Ibn Razīḳ, *Imams and Sayyids of 'Oman* (tr. G. P. Badger), 7-8; Sirḥān b. Saʿīd b. Sirḥān, *Kashf al-ghumma* (tr. E. C. Ross as *Annals of Oman*), Calcutta 1874, 12. (W. ʿARAFAT)

DJULFA (i) [see Supplement]. (ii) [see IṢFAHĀN].

DJULŪS [see KHILĀFA, SULṬĀN, TAḲLĪD-I SAYF, TAʾRĪKH].

DJUMʿA (Yawm al-), the weekly day of communal worship in Islam. The only reference to it in the Ḳurʾān, LXII, 9-11, clearly indicates that the term is pre-Islamic, for v. 9 says: "When you are called to prayer *on the day of* the assembly", and not "to the Prayer of the Assembly". The decisive proof for the correctness of this interpretation is the fact that Ibn Ubayy read *yawm al-ʿarūba al-kubrā* for *yawm al-djumʿa*, the former being another pre-Islamic name for Friday, meaning eve of the Sabbath, cf. A. Jeffery, *Text of the Qurʾān*, 1937, 170; R. Blachère, *Le Coran*, 1950, 825.

The expression *yawm al-djumʿa*, "the day when people come together", an exact equivalent of Hebrew (and Aramaic) *yōm hak-kenīsa*, designated the market day, which was held in the oasis of al-Madīna on Friday, "when the Jews bought their provisions for the Sabbath", cf. Kāshānī, *Badāʾiʿ al-ṣanāʾiʿ*, Cairo 1327/8, i, 268 and Ibn Saʿd iii, 1, 83, where *tdjhz* (*tadjahhazu*) is to be read for *ydjhr*, as in Kāshānī. It is natural that the day preceding the weekly holiday of the Jews should have been chosen as the market day in a place like Medina, which had a large Jewish population. Similarly, in Islam, Thursday served as a weekly market day all over Arabia, cf. H.St. J. Philby, *Arabian Highlands*, 1952, 36, 130, 233, 274-5, 387, 485-7, 597. Friday as market day is well attested in pre-Islamic Jewish literature, cf. S. Krauss, *Talmudische Archaeologie*, Leipzig 1911, ii, 690, note 340.

According to the unanimous testimony of the ancient Muslim sources, no Friday service was held in Mecca, cf., *e.g.*, al-Ṭabarī, i, 1256. However, even before Muḥammad arrived in Medina, the Muslims convened there for public worship, but it was Muḥammad who ordered that it should be observed regularly on "the day when the Jews prepared for their Sabbath", cf. Ibn Saʿd, quoted above, and parallel sources. The Jewish and Christian institutions of a weekly day of public worship might have served as an example in general, as suggested by al-Ḳasṭallānī, ii, 176. However, the reference to the Jews in the ancient account of the inauguration of the Friday service betrays no particular dependence on Judaism, nor a polemical tendency against the older religions —two assumptions in vogue in modern research on the subject, cf. D. S. Margoliouth, *Mohammed*, 1905, 248-9, M. Gaudefroy-Demombynes, *Mahomet* 1957, 522, and the works of Wensinck, Buhl and Watt quoted in the bibliography. It was Muḥammad's practical wisdom, which decided for Friday, as in any case on that day the people of the widely dispersed oasis dwellings of Medina gathered regularly for their weekly market.

This origin of the Friday service explains one of its most puzzling aspects: It is held at noon, a very inconvenient time in a hot climate. The market is dissolved early in the afternoon, see, for Arabia, *e.g.*, Philby, *Arabian Highlands* 234. In classical times, ἀγορῆς διάλυσις, the breaking up of the market, was a term designating the early afternoon, Liddell and Scott s.v. Thus noon was the reasonable time for the public prayer.

The admonition of the Ḳurʾān, not to leave the prayer and to run after business and amusement, LXII, 11, is to be understood against this background. The people of Medina were farmers, not business men; but Friday was their market day, on which also, as everywhere at fairs, amusements were provided.

The main feature of the Friday service is the *khuṭba* [*q.v.*], a sermon, the preacher of which holds in his hand a rod or sword or lance. These were originally, as C. H. Becker has pointed out, the insignia of the pre-Islamic judges. Market days provide a natural opportunity for people gathered there to settle their law suits. Philby describes the sitting of the judges on the weekly markets and the same custom prevailed in the Greek world and on the *yōm hak-kenīsa* of the ancient Jews. The ancient epithet *yawm al-ḥarba* "the Day of the Lance", see *TA*, i, 206, s.v. *ḥrb*, may have had its origin in this aspect of the *yawm al-djumʿa*. However, the biographies of the Prophet do not seem to stress that he preferred Friday over other days for sitting as a judge.

From its very inception the Friday service had a political connotation. In early Islam it was a proof that the participants had joined the Muslim community; later on, it implied a manifestation of allegiance to the caliph or governor who conducted the service, or whose name was mentioned in the sermon. This religio-political background explains why attendance at the Friday service—as opposed to the daily prayer—is a duty incumbent on all male, adult, free, resident Muslims; why, according to the Shāfiʿīs and many others, it should, if feasible, be held only in one mosque (the *djāmiʿ*) in each town; and why it required a minimum attendance of 40 according to the Shāfiʿis, or at least a sizeable number according to others.

The fully developed Friday ceremonial consists of an *adhān*, which is proclaimed inside the mosque, a *khuṭba*, which is said in two sections, during which the preacher is standing up, interrupted by an interval, during which he is required to sit down, and a *ṣalāt*, consisting of two *rakʿas*, which follows the sermon. Usually, a *ṣalāt* of two *rakʿas* is performed also before the *khuṭba*. According to C. H. Becker, some of these features follow the pattern of the mass in the ancient Oriental churches.

The *yawm al-djumʿa* is not a day of rest. According to Mālik, the *aṣḥāb* disapproved of the practice of some Muslims who refrained from doing work on Friday in imitation of the Jewish and Christian weekly holidays (al-Ṭarṭūshī, *K. al-Ḥawādith*, Tunis 1959, 133). In general, the Sabbath institution is foreign to Islam (for a socio-economic explanation of this difference between Islam and the older religions cf. S. D. Goitein, *Jews and Arabs*, New York 1955, 39-40). Still we have reports about government offices and schools being closed on Fridays in ʿAbbāsid times, and a query addressed to Maimonides around 1200 speaks about Jewish and Muslim partners in a jewellery workshop, who replaced one another on Fridays and Saturdays (cf. Moshe ben Maimon, *Responsa*, Jerusalem 1934, 62). In modern times most Muslim states have made Friday an official day of rest. Turkey has chosen Sunday, while in Pakistān Friday is a half-holiday, Sunday a full day of rest.

As a holiday, Friday is honoured by special food —already referred to in the *Ḥadīth*—and better clothing. The night preceding it is set aside for the fulfilment of matrimonial duties, to be followed on Friday morning by a bath, as well as perfuming.

The Sabbath should be a foretaste of the world to come, where the righteous are granted the beatific vision of God. This idea, prevailing in ancient Judaism, was enormously expanded—or perhaps developed independently—by Islamic mysticism and religious folklore. In Heaven, Friday is called *yawm al-mazīd*, the day of Allāh's special bounty (cf. Sūra L, 35). On it, Allāh sends to each of the pious Muslims in Paradise an apple. When they take the apple in their hands, it splits in two, and out steps a beautiful maid with a sealed letter containing a personal invitation from Allāh. Soon the general move of those who are thus invited begins. The men on horseback, the women in litters, the men led by Muḥammad, who is accompanied by Adam, Moses and Jesus, the women led by Fāṭima and other women saints, all move towards the Holy Enclosure, where a gorgeous meal, described with glowing details, awaits them. At its conclusion the pious call on Allāh asking Him to show them His face. Allāh lifts His veil and reveals Himself to them (cf. al-Ṭabarī, *Tafsīr*, 1326, xxvi, 108; Abū Ṭālib al-Makkī, *Ḳūt al-ḳulūb*, i, 72; Abu 'l-Layth al-Samarḳandī, *Ḳurrat al-ʿuyūn*, 130-1 and the extensive literature quoted in S. D. Goitein, *Beholding God on Friday*, in *IC*, xxxiv, 1960, pp. 63-8).

Bibliography: in addition to that indicated in the article: The chapters on *Djumʿa* in the collections of *Ḥadīth* and *Fiḳh*; Dimishḳī, *Raḥmat al-umma fī-'khtilāf al-aʾimma*, Būlāḳ 1300, 29 ff.; C. H. Becker, *Zur Geschichte des islamischen Kultus* in *Isl.*, iii, 1912: now in *Islamstudien*, Leipzig 1923, i, 472-500); idem, *Die Kanzel im Kultus des alten Islam* in *Nöldeke-Festschrift*, 1906, i, 331-51: now in *Islamstudien*, i, 450-71); I.

Goldziher, *Die Sabbath-institution im Islam* (*Gedenkbuch für David Kaufmann*, 86-105); Fr. tr. Bousquet, in *Arabica*, vii (1960), 237-40; idem, *Islamisme et Parsisme* (*RHR*, xliii, 1901, 27 ff.); idem, *Muh. Stud.*, ii, 40-4; idem, *ZDMG*, xlix, 1895, 315; E. W. Lane, *Manners and customs of the modern Egyptians*, chap. iii; A. J. Wensinck, *Mohammed en de Joden te Medina*, 1908, 110 ff. (Fr. tr. in *RAfr.*, 1954); Frants Buhl, *Das Leben Muhammeds*, Leipzig 1930, 214-5; W. Montgomery Watt, *Muhammad at Medina*, Oxford 1956, 198; Muhammad Hamidullah, *Le prophète de l'Islam*, Paris 1959, 115, 681; S. D. Goitein, *Le culte du Vendredi musulman; son arrière-plan social et économique*, in *Annales, Économies, Sociétés, Civilisations*, 1958, 488-500; idem, *The origin and nature of the Muslim Friday worship*, in *MW* 1959, 183-95.

(S. D. Goitein)

DJUMĀDĀ [see TAʾRĪKH].

AL-**DJUMAḤĪ** [see IBN SALLĀM].

DJUMBLĀṬ [see DJANBULĀṬ].

DJUMHŪRIYYA, in Turkish *djümhūriyyet*, republic, also republicanism, a term coined in Turkey in the late 18th century from the Arabic *djumhūr*, meaning the crowd, mass, or generality of the people, and first used in connexion with the first French Republic. In classical Arabic, as for example in Arabic versions and discussions of Greek political writings, the usual equivalent of the Greek πολιτεία or Latin *res publica*, *i.e.*, polity or commonweal, was *madīna*; thus, the 'democratic polity' of Plato's classification is called, by Fārābī and others, *madīna djamāʿiyya* (Fārābī, *Arāʾ ahl al-madīna al-fāḍila*, ed. Dieterici, Leiden 1895, 62; E. I. J. Rosenthal, *Political thought in medieval Islam*, Cambridge 1938, 136, 278; F. Rosenthal, *The Muslim concept of freedom*, Leiden 1960, 100-1). According to the law as stated by the Sunnī jurists, the Islamic polity itself was to be headed by a non-hereditary, elective sovereign, subject to and not above the law (see KHILĀFA). This principle has led some 19th and 20th century writers to describe the Islamic doctrine of the Caliphate as republican (*e.g.*, Nāmîk Kemāl in *Ḥürriyyet*, 14 September 1868, cited by Şerif Mardin, *The genesis of Young Ottoman political thought*, Princeton 1962, 296-7; Agaoghlu Aḥmed, in *Khilāfet we millī ḥākimiyyet*, Ankara 1339 [= 1923], 22 ff.; Rashīd Riḍā, *Al-Khilāfa*, Cairo 1341, 5, tr. in H. Z. Nuseibeh, *The ideas of Arab nationalism*, Cornell 1956, 125). Others, perhaps under the influence of recent developments in the use of the term, have gone further, and described the government of the patriarchal caliphs as a republic. In the more technical sense of a state in which the head holds his place by the choice of a defined electorate exercised through prescribed legal processes, the term republic seems to have no precise equivalent in classical Islamic usage. Such states existed and were encountered in Europe, in Ragusa, Venice and other Italian city republics. Arabic seems to have used no special term for them; thus Ḳalḳashandī, speaking of the government of Genoa, calls them a *djamāʿa mutafāwitū 'l-marātib*; for Venice he speaks only of the Doge (*Ṣubḥ*, viii, 46-8). Turkish used *djumhūr*. Perhaps this was the word chosen by the dragomans of the Porte as equivalent, for official usage, to the Latin *res publica*. Thus, Venedik Djumhūru was the formal translation of 'Republic of Venice'. Even so, the word *djumhūr* was comparatively rare in the sense of republic; more commonly the Turks, in their letters to Venice and their discussions of Venetian affairs, preferred to speak of the Doge (Venedik Dozhu) or Signoria (Venedik Beyleri) rather than of the Republic.

The word *djumhūr* took on new life after the French Revolution, when it was used in Turkish to denote the French Republic as well as other republics —some of them on the borders of Turkey—that were formed on the French model. In Egypt, some of the translators attached to General Bonaparte's expedition, groping for an Arabic equivalent for republic, chose *mashyakha* (cf. J. F. Ruphy, *Dictionnaire abrégé français-arabe*, Paris, an X [1802], 185). This term is recorded by some subsequent Arabic lexicographers, and was used of the French Republic by Ḥaydar al-Shihābī (d. 1835: *Lubnān fī ʿahd al-umarāʾ al-Shihābiyyīn* Beirut 1933, ii, 218-9 etc.) and others. It was not, however, confirmed by subsequent usage. The documents of the French occupation of Egypt, as cited by Ḥaydar himself (ii, 222-4) and by Niḳūlā al-Turk (cited *op. cit.* 213 n. 1) and al-Djabartī (*ʿAdjāʾib*, iii, 5, etc.; *Maẓhar al-taḳdīs*, ed. Cairo n.d. i, 37) prefer the Ottoman term *djumhūr*, and speak of *al-Djumhūr al-Faransāwī*.

The modern word *djumhūriyya*—which is simply *djumhūr* with an abstract ending—was coined, like many other Islamic neologisms, in Turkey, the first Islamic state to encounter the ideas, institutions, and problems of the modern world, and to seek and find new terms to denote them. It was at first used as an abstract noun denoting a principle or form of government. and meaning republicanism rather than republic, the usual term for which was still *djumhūr* (see for example ʿĀṭif Efendi's memorandum of 1798, in Djewdet, *Taʾrīkh*², vi, 395, speaking of 'equality and republicanism'—*müsāwāt we-djümhūriyyet*; the documents on the Septinsular republic (*Djezāʾir-i Sebʿa-i Müdjtemiʿa Djümhūru*) of 1799 published by İ. H. Uzunçarşılı in *Belleten*, i, 1937, 633,—*djümhūriyyet wedjhile idjtimāʿ*; the despatches of Ḥālet Efendi from Paris in E. Z. Karal, *Halet Efendinin Paris Büyük Elçiliği* (*1802-06*), Istanbul 1940, 35; cf. ʿĀṣim, *Taʾrīkh*, i, 61-2, 78-9, and the Turkish translation of Botta's *Storia d'Italia*, Cairo 1249/1834, repr. Istanbul 1293/1876, passim. Shaykh Rifāʿa Rāfiʿ al-Tahtāwī (*Talkhīṣ al-ibrīz*), Būlāḳ 1834, Ch. 5 = Cairo ed. 1958, 252-3) uses *djumhūriyya* in both senses). From Turkey the term spread to the Arabs, Persians, Indians, and other peoples, and was used in the new political literature inspired by western liberal and constitutional ideas. In the 19th century republic and democracy were still regarded as broadly synonymous terms, and the same words were often used for both. It is instructive to trace the renderings of the terms democracy and republic in the 19th century dictionaries from English or French into Arabic, Turkish etc. Bocthor (1828) translates the two terms by *Ḳiyām al-djumhūr bi 'l-ḥukm* and *djumhūr* or *mashyakha*; Handjeri (1840) by *ḥukūmat al-djumhūr al-nās* [*sic*] and *djumhūr*; Redhouse (1860) translates democracy as *djümhūr* or *djümhūriyyet uṣūlu*, republic as *djümhūr*, and republicanism as *djümhūriyyet*. Zenker (1866) and Sami Frasheri (1883) already identify *djümhūriyyet* with republic. In Urdū the same word, with a minor variation, has served both for democracy (*djumhūriyyat*) and republic (*djumhūriyya*).

Republican ideas are rarely expressed in the writings of the 19th century Muslim liberals, even the most radical of whom seem to have thought in terms of a constitutional monarchy rather than a republic. Even where the terms *djumhūrī* and *djumhūriyya* do occur, they often connote popular and representative rather than republican government (see for example the instructive comments of ʿAlī Suʿāwī in 1876 on the 'true meaning' of *djumhūr*, cited in M. C. Kuntay, *Ali Suavi*, Istanbul 1946, 95, tr. in Ş. Mardin, *op. cit.*, 382-3. It is probably in this sense that the term is used of the Lebanese peasant rebels led by Ṭanyūs S̲h̲āhīn: see Yūsuf Ibrāhīm Yazkak, *Thawra wa-fitna fī Lubnān*, Damascus 1938, 87; Eng. trans. M. H. Kerr, *Lebanon in the last years of feudalism.*., Beirut 1959, 53; cf. Raʾīf al-K̲h̲ūrī, *Al-fikr al-ʿarabī al-ḥadīth*, Beirut 1943, 94). During the 20th century, however, republicanism developed rapidly. The first republics to be established were in the Muslim territories of the Russian Empire, when the temporary relaxation of pressure from the centre after the revolutions of 1917 allowed an interval of local experimentation. In May 1918, after the dissolution of the short-lived Transcaucasian Federation, the Ād̲h̲arbāyd̲j̲ānī members of the former Transcaucasian parliament, together with the Muslim National Council, declared Ād̲h̲arbāyd̲j̲ān an independent republic—the first Muslim republic in modern times. In April 1920 it was conquered by the Red Army, and a Soviet Republic formed. The same pattern was followed by the Bashkirs and other Turkic peoples of the Russian Empire, who set up their own national republics, all of which were in due course taken over and reconstituted by the Communists, and incorporated, in one form or another, in the U.S.S.R.

The first Muslim republic to be established outside the Russian Empire seems to have been the Tripolitanian Republic, proclaimed in November 1918 by Sulaymān Pas̲h̲a al-Bārūnī [*q.v.*] (documents in ʿA. K. G̲h̲arāʾiba, *Dirāsāt fī taʾrīkh Ifrīḳiya al-ʿArabiyya*, Damascus 1960, 105 ff.), and later incorporated in the Italian colony of Libya. The first independent republic to remain both independent and a republic was that of Turkey, proclaimed on 29 October 1923 (for texts and debates see A. S. Gözübüyük and S. Kili, *Türk Anayasa metinleri*, Ankara 1957, 95 f.; K. Arıburnu, *Millî Mücadele ve inkılâplarla ilgili kanunlar*, i, Ankara 1957, 32 ff.; cf. E. Smith, *Debates on the Turkish constitution of 1924*, in *Ankara Üniv. Siyasat Bilg. Fak. Derg.*, xiii (1958), 82-105). In Syria-Lebanon republican ideas were current in some circles at an earlier date, and the forms of government set up by the French as mandatory power were generally republican in tendency. The republics were not, however, formally constituted until some years later; Greater Lebanon was proclaimed a republic on 23 May 1926, Syria on 22 May 1930.

The ending of West European colonial rule in Islamic lands after the second World War brought several new republics into being. The republic of Indonesia was proclaimed in August 1945; Pakistan, independent since 1947, introduced a new theme by declaring an 'Islamic Republic' in November 1953. In Africa, the Sudan became a republic on attaining independence in January 1956; Tunisia, already independent, abolished the monarchy and proclaimed a republic in May 1959. Among the older Arab states in the Middle East two new republics were established after the revolutionary overthrow of the existing monarchical régimes—in Egypt in June 1953, in ʿIrāḳ in July 1958. A union of Egypt and Syria, called the United Arab Republic (*al-Djumhūriyya al-ʿArabiyya al-Muttaḥida*) was formed in February 1958 and dissolved in September 1961. The name United Arab Republic has been retained by Egypt. An anti-monarchist revolution began in the Yemen in September 1962. At the present time the majority of Muslim states are called republics, though the common designation covers a wide variety of political realities.

Bibliography: given in the article. On the idea of freedom see ḤURRIYYA; on political thought in general, see SIYĀSA; on constitutions see DUSTŪR; on parliamentary government, see MAD̲J̲LIS; on revolutionary and insurrectionary movements, see INḲILĀB and T̲H̲AWRA; on military rule, see NIẒĀM ʿASKARĪ; on socialism, see IS̲H̲TIRĀKIYYA; on the case-histories, see the articles on the individual countries. (B. LEWIS)

DJŪMHŪRIYYET K̲H̲ALḲ FÍRḲASÍ (modern Turkish *Cümhuriyet Halk Partisi*, Republican People's Party), the oldest political party in the Turkish Republic, was organized by Mustafa Kemal [Atatürk] in Ankara on 11 September 1339/1923. It was successor to the Society for the Defence of Rights of Anatolia and Rumelia (*Anadolu ve Rumeli Müdāfaʿa-i Ḥuḳūḳ Djemʿiyyeti*) the organization formed by Kemal in 1919 as the political instrument to fight the War of Independence. The party's original name was *K̲h̲alḳ Fírḳasí*. On 10 November 1340/1924 the name was changed to *Djümhūriyyet K̲h̲alḳ Fírḳasí*, and at the 4th National Congress in 1935, in connexion with the language modernization programme, became the *Cümhuriyet Halk Partisi* (*CHP*).

Few exact membership figures for the party are available. Membership in 1948 was estimated at 1,898,000, or about 10% of the population.

The party is organized vertically beginning with the branch (*ocak*) in villages, localities and subdivisions of towns and cities. The number of these local branches was estimated in 1950 to be about 23,000. The organization continues at the county (*nahiye*), district (*kaza*), and province (*vilâyet*) levels, and culminates in the national organization with head-quarters in Ankara. The party is headed by a General Chairman (*Genel Başkan*), a post occupied from 1923 to 1938 by Atatürk, and since that time by İsmet İnönü. In 1927 Atatürk was made "unchanging" (*değişmez*) General Chairman, and after his death the Special National Congress of 1939 proclaimed him "eternal" (*ebedi*) General Chairman. Most of the actual work of the party, however, is directed by the General Secretary. General Secretaries have included Recep Peker (1923-5 and 1931-6); Şükrü Kaya (1936-8); Refik Saydam (1938-9); Dr. Fikri Tuzer (1939-42); Memduh Şevket Esendal (1942-5); Nafi Atuf Kansu (1945-7); Tevfik Fikret Sılay (1947-50); Kasım Gülek (1950-9); Ismail Rüştü Aksal (1959-62); and Kemal Satir (1962 —). The National Congress meets periodically to make general policy and elect a 40-member Executive Committee. Fifteen regular Congresses were held between 1919 and 1961. The Sivas Congress of the Defence of Rights Society in 1919 is generally called the first Congress of the party. In addition there were special Congresses in 1939 and 1946. The 2nd National Congress in 1927 was the occasion of Atatürk's Six-Day Speech (*Büyük Nutuk*).

Party organization has vacillated from time to time between tendencies toward more or less centralization. In the 1920's the national organization controlled its branches tightly through a network of Inspectors and sub-Inspectors. In 1930 maximum authority and responsibility were given to local and provincial party officials. The period of greatest centralization was between 1936 and 1939 when the Interior Minister was concurrently CHP General Secretary, and governors of the provinces were also

CHP chairmen in their provinces. Since 1950 law as well as political expediency has resulted in considerable decentralization, though policy and party discipline remain in the hands of the national organization.

From 1923 to 1946 the CHP was the sole party in the Grand National Assembly, except for two occasions when opposition was permitted but then eliminated after short periods. The oppositions were the Republican Progressive Party (*Teraḳḳiperver Djümhūriyyet Fîrḳasî*) of 1924, composed of a group of prominent conservatives who split off from the CHP when Atatürk began his personal direction and domination. The Progressive Party was closed by the government in 1925 in reaction to a resurgence of conservative sentiment in the country. In 1930 another attempt at opposition took place when Atatürk persuaded several close friends to form the Free Party (*Serbest Fırka*), but this party also was dissolved after three months when it became the rallying ground for counter-revolutionary groups. Neither of these parties contested a general election. After the failure of the Free Party Atatürk introduced several "independent deputies" into the 1931 and 1935 Assemblies. They were to criticize and to be free of party discipline, but not to organize as an opposition or oppose basic aspects of the CHP program. By 1939, these independents were limited to a token representation of non-Muslim minorities. In addition the 1939 party Congress decided on the formation of an Independent Group of 21 members selected from among the already-elected CHP deputies. In the 7th Assembly in 1943 the size of the Independent Group was increased to 25. The Independent Group was abolished by the Special National Congress of 1946 when it was decided to permit opposition parties. Following the 1946 election a group of 35 young CHP deputies (the *Otuzbeşler*) rebelled against the policies of the Prime Minister Recep Peker, but did not leave the party.

In 1945 opposition parties were again allowed, and four CHP deputies, Celal Bayar, Adnan Menderes, Refik Koraltan and Fuat Köprülü formed the *Demokrat Parti* [*q.v.*]. In 1946 an election was held before the Democrats had time to organize in more than a few provinces, and the CHP retained a heavy majority. In 1950, however, the Democratic Party won a majority, and the CHP went into opposition. In the 1954 election the CHP strength was reduced to 21, but in 1957 it again increased to 178. Following the overthrow of the Menderes government by the army in 1960, three opposition parties arose to compete with the CHP in the 1961 election, in which the CHP received 36.7% of the vote and returned 173 members to the 450-man Assembly, and 36 to the newly-created 150-man Senate of the Republic. The CHP leader Ismet Inönü was appointed to head a coalition cabinet. The CHP's Assembly strength after each election since 1923 has been as follows:

Assembly 2 (1923):	all CHP.
Assembly 3 (1927):	all CHP.
Assembly 4 (1931):	CHP 290, Independents 8.
Assembly 5 (1935):	CHP 390, Independents 9.
Assembly 6 (1939):	CHP 404, Indep. Group 21, Independents 4.
Assembly 7 (1943):	CHP 416, Indep. Group 25, Independents 4.
Assembly 8 (1946):	CHP 397, others 68.
Assembly 9 (1950):	CHP 67, others 420.
Assembly 10 (1954):	CHP 31, others 510.
Assembly 11 (1957):	CHP 178, others 432.
Assembly 12 (1961):	Assembly: CHP 173, others 277; Senate: CHP 36, others 114.

The Nine Principles (*Dokuz ʿUmde*) proclaimed by the Defence of Rights Society in April 1923 were adopted by the CHP that September as its first programme. Its points proclaimed that sovereignty belongs unconditionally to the nation, that full authority is granted to the Grand National Assembly, and outlined political, social, and economic reforms to be undertaken. When Atatürk brought into the open his plans for rapid and radical transformation of the Turkish nation, the programme was expanded to include the principles which in 1931 became the Six Arrows (*Altı Ok*), Republicanism, Nationalism, Secularism (*Lâiklık*), Populism (*Halkçılık*), Étatism (*Devletçılık*), and Revolutionism (*İnkilâpcılık*). In 1938 the Six Arrows were incorporated into Article 2 of the Constitution, and all except Étatism and Revolutionism were carried over into the Constitution of the 2nd Republic in 1961. Secularism has been one of the points of greatest emphasis in the CHP program, and was one of Atatürk's major interests. Its implications of rapid and radical change in the lives of the great majority of Turks have made specific policies for its application a major area of controversy among Turkish political parties, though all accept the secularization of political life as a principle. Revolutionism has been taken to mean various things from an acceptance of the Atatürk reforms to a spirit of continuous rapid and radical change until westernization is complete. Populism at the least means equality of all citizens before the law, and usually is taken to include the principle of majority democracy as well. One of the principles which most distinguishes the CHP from other parties is étatism, *i.e.*, a major rôle for the state in economic development. Most authorities agree that it was necessary in the 1920's and 1930's, but all of Turkey's other political parties contend that it is no longer needed today. The six principles remain at the head of the CHP programme, but since the beginning of the multiparty period in 1946 there have been tendencies to modify the more extreme policies for their implementation.

In 1931 the CHP abolished the *Türkocaği* national cultural organization and instead began creation of a series of People's Houses (*Halkevleri*) and People's Rooms (*Halkodaları*) throughout the nation to serve as centres of education and community activity. Their programmes included practical education in agricultural, home-making, and literacy skills; political education in the principles of secular, Republican politics; sports activities, cinemas, concerts, lectures, and libraries; and attempts to strengthen physical and social-psychological links between urban and village populations. In 1950 there existed 478 *Halkevleri* and 4,322 *Halkodaları*. Wholly owned by CHP, the *Halkevleri* became involved in political controversy during the multiparty period after 1946, and were closed by the Democratic Party régime.

The CHP has published the proceedings of most of its Congresses, as well as numerous reports of programmes and activities. In the 1930's the *Halkevleri* published a regular monthly magazine *Ülkü*, and local *Halkevi* publications abounded. The CHP central office today includes a Research Bureau which publishes analyses of political, social and economic problems. The party has published its own daily newspaper in Ankara since 1920 under the name *Ḥākimiyyet-i Milliyye* ("National Sovereignty"), and later as *Ulus* ("The Nation").

Bibliography: Tarik Z. Tunaya, *Türkiye'de siyasî partiler*, Istanbul 1952, 540-605; *Türkiye'de siyasî dernekler* (vol. ii only), Ankara 1951; Kemal H. Karpat, *Turkey's politics*, Princeton, N. J., 1959, 393-408; Bernard Lewis, *The emergence of modern Turkey*², London 1962, *passim*; Donald E. Webster, *The Turkey of Ataturk*, Philadelphia 1939; *CHP Büyük Kurultayı Zabıtları*, 1927, 1931, 1935, 1939, 1943, 1947; *CHP X* [XV, XXV] *Yıl Kitapları*, 1933 [1938, 1948]; Mustafa Kemal [Atatürk], *Nutuk*, *passim*; *Atatürk'ün söylev ve demeçleri*, i, Istanbul 1945; *Inönü'nün söylev ve demeçleri*, i, Istanbul 1946.

(Walter F. Weiker)

DJUMLA [see naḥw]

DJŪNĀGAŔH, a city and (formerly) a princely State in India lying between 22° 44′ and 21° 53′ N. and 70° and 72° E., with an area of 3,337 sq. miles and a population of 670,719 in 1941, of whom some 20% were Muslims. While otherwise contiguous with the Indian mainland, it is bounded on the west and south-west by the Arabian sea with the flourishing port of Vērāval, 300 nautical miles from Karachi (Pakistan). It is dotted with a group of the sacred Girnār hills, housing a number of Djayn and Hindū temples of great antiquity. The edicts of Aśoka are found inscribed on a rock in the gorge between the town of Djūnāgaŕh and the Girnār hills, pointing out unmistakably to the area being in ancient times thriving centre of Buddhism and forming a part of the Mawryan empire. The dense Gir forests are the only abodes of lions outside Africa; hence a favourite hunting ground for the nobility and native chiefs. The State also enshines within its boundaries the temple of Sōmnāth, sacked and destroyed by Sultan Maḥmūd of Ghazna [*q.v.*].

The Mawryas were followed by the Bactrians and the Greeks with their seat of government at Djūnāgaŕh (< Yavanagaḋha or Yavananagara, as is proved by the discovery of some Greek coins of Apollodotus at Bhadardaw). These foreigners in their turn were subjugated and expelled by the local Rādjpūt chiefs who were still ruling the territory when Maḥmūd of Ghazna invaded Sōmnāth Paṫan in 416/1025, conquered the place, ruined the temple and destroyed the idol of Sōmnāth. The victorious Sultan retreated to Ghazna leaving the place in the charge of a Muslim *fawdjdār* [*q.v.*], who was thereafter turned out by the Wādjā Rādjpūts of the area. Ḳuṭb al-Dīn Aybak [*q.v.*] marched on Sōraṫh (Skt. Sawrāshṫra = Kāṫhiyāwāŕ including Djūnāgaŕh) after conquering Anhilwāŕā [*q.v.*] in 593/1194, but it was no more than a plundering raid. Although during the next hundred years no Muslim ruler invaded the territory, it continued to be visited by Muslims from the North some of whom settled in the area. The Māʾī Gaḋīčī inscription dated 685/1284, discovered at Djūnāgaŕh, reveals that the place was the headquarters of a Muslim *ṣadr* (agent?), who supervised the departure of Muslim pilgrims to Mecca via the port of Balāwal. In 697/1297 Almās Bēg Ulugh Khān, a brother of ʿAlāʾ al-Dīn Khaldjī, invaded Sōraṫh, wrested Sōmnāth from the Rādjpūts, and in a fit of fanaticism razed the already ruined temple to the ground. He, however, did not interfere with the Čawdāsamā Rādjpūts who were in control of Djūnāgaŕh. The historic temple seems to have been soon rebuilt, as it attracted the attention of Muḥammad b. Tughluḳ [*q.v.*] who in 751/1350 invaded the territory and captured the fort of Djūnāgaŕh which then became a dependency of the *ṣūba* of Gudjarāt. During the reign of Fīrūz Shāh Tughluḳ (752-89/1351-88), Shams al-Dīn Abū Ridjāʾ, *nāʾib* of the *nāẓim* of Gudjarāt, established a *thāna* (post) in Djūnāgaŕh. It, however, appears that the local chiefs were not completely reconciled to the change as Ẓafar Khān, the *nāẓim* of Gudjarāt, who later proclaimed his independence in 810/1407, twice marched on Sōmnāth in 797/1394 and 804/1401 in order to punish the refractory Rādjpūts, who continued to chafe under foreign rule until 871/1467 when the last ruler of the Čawdāsamā dynasty was defeated and ousted by Maḥmūd Bēgaŕā (863-917/1459-1511) of Gudjarāt, who annexed Djūnāgaŕh to his territory. Maḥmūd Bēgaŕā had to mount another two punitive expeditions in 872/1468 and 874/1469-70 to suppress the revolt of the deposed Rādjpūt ruler who regained much of his lost possessions. After a year of bitter fighting the Sultan was able to recover the fort of Djūnāgaŕh, terminating Hindū rule once and for all. The city was renamed Muṣṭafābād and Sayyids, *ʿulamāʾ*, *ḳāḍī*s and other notables mainly from Aḥmadābād were invited to settle in the town. The ancient citadel called Ūparkōṫ was repaired and well-to-do people were persuaded to build large houses, mosques, public buildings, etc., thus adding to the glory of the town. The citadel-town of Ūparkōṫ continued to be called Djūnāgaŕh while the new town lower down was named Muṣṭafābād, although this name was never popularly adopted.

The *sarkār* of Djūnāgaŕh remained in the possession of the Sultans of Gudjarāt till 999/1590 when it was conquered and annexed to the Mughal empire by the victorious armies of ʿAbd al-Raḥīm Khān-i Khānān [*q.v.*]. As a part of the *ṣūba* of Gudjarāt it was controlled by *fawdjdār*s appointed by the *nāẓim*. One such *nāʾib fawdjār* Shīr Khān Bābī, a man of Afghan stock, whose ancestors had migrated from the Ḳalāt-Ḳandahār region to the plains of Hindustān in search of employment during the beginning of Mughal rule, taking advantage of the enfeeblement of the central authority, expelled the local *fawdjdār* Mīr Dūst ʿAlī and founded his independent dynasty in 1150/1737-8. A shrewd military commander, he successfully kept at bay the marauding bands of the Marāṫhās, who in the glow of easy victories wanted to overrun the whole of Kāṫhiyāwāŕ. During his rule of 20 years, marred by minor clashes with the Marāṫhās, he consolidated his position and firmly established his rule. On his death in 1172/1758 he was succeeded by his son, Muḥammad Mahābat Khān I, whose very first year of rule was marred by an abortive dynastic conspiracy to depose him. After a brief rule of 12 years he died in 1184/1770 and was succeeded by his minor son, Muḥammad Ḥāmid Khān, all other rival claimants having fully recognized the title of the Shīr Khān family to the rulership of the new principality.

After an otherwise inconspicuous rule of 27 years, which witnessed the murder of the Dīwān Amar-djī father of Rančōŕ-djī (see *Bibl.*), he died in 1226/1811. The East India Company entered into an engagement with the ruler of Djūnāgaŕh for the first time in 1222/1807. A year earlier, a settlement had been arrived at between Djūnāgaŕh and the vassal states of Manāwādār and Mangrōl and other *taʿluka*s, recognizing the overlordship of Djūnāgaŕh, regarding the amounts of *zorṭalbī* (tribute exacted by force), a relic of Muslim supremacy, due from the feudatory states etc., with the active intervention of the British Resident at Baroda. This incident, small in itself, throws ample light on the growing influence of the British in the internal affairs of even as remote a part of the country as Kāthiyāwāŕ, long before the final eclipse of the Mug͟hal rule in 1857. In 1821 the ruler of D̲j̲ūnāgaŕh recognized the paramountcy of the East India Company, who undertook to collect *zōrṭalbī* on behalf of the ruler and pay it into his treasury. He died in 1840 and was succeeded by a minor son.

Among the later rulers, Muḥammad Rasūl K̲h̲ān (1892-1911) deserves special mention as a progressive and enlightened chief. It was during his rule that a colege, a library and museum, a modern hospital a water-works and an orphanage were established. Steps were also taken for the protection and preservation of the historic edicts of Aśoka and the temple of Sōmnāth was repaired at considerable expense to the State. On his death in 1911, his son Muḥammad Mahābat K̲h̲ān being a minor, the administration of the State was taken over by the Government of India. On his attaining the age of maturity the prince, the ninth in succession and the last *de facto* ruler of D̲j̲ūnāgaŕh, was invested with full powers in 1920. According to the Attachment Scheme, introduced by the Government of India in 1943, the feudatory estates of Sardārgaŕh and Bānṫwah and many other *taʿluka*s were attached to D̲j̲ūnāgarh with a view to ensuring better administration. On the lapse of British paramountcy in August 1947 the State acceded to Pakistan. This was, however, disputed by the Government of India, and on the refusal of the ruler to retract his decision the State was occupied in November of the same year by Indian troops. The ruler, along with his family, took refuge in Pakistan (Karachi) where he died in 1960. The accession and possession of D̲j̲ūnāgaŕh are still (1962) the subject-matter of a dispute between India and Pakistan, which figures on the agenda of the Security Council of the United Nations.

The chief city of the State, D̲j̲ūnāgaŕh, is one of the most picturesque towns in India. Its ancient citadel, the Ūparkōṫ, is one of the strongest mountain fastnesses in the sub-continent. It has two large-size cannon dating back to the times of the Turkish Sultan Suleymān the Magnificent, brought to D̲j̲ūnāgaŕh by gunners of foreign origin who were in the employ of the ruler. The town has a number of stately buildings, including the mausolea of the former rulers, their wives and the Minister S̲h̲ayk̲h̲ Bahāʾ al-Dīn, which are fine specimens of a style of architecture similar to that of the Deccan, the dominant feature of which, however, is the flanking minaret with an exterior winding stair-case, after the style of the minaret of the mosque of Ibn Ṭūlūn, found nowhere else in the subcontinent.

Bibliography: Rančōŕ-d̲j̲ī Amar-d̲j̲ī, *Taʾrīk̲h̲-i Sōraṫh* or *Waḳāʾiʿ-i Sōraṫh*, Persian text still in manuscript, Eng. transl. Bombay 1882 (one of the earliest histories of D̲j̲ūnāgaŕh by a native of the State, who like his father and brother was Dīwān of D̲j̲ūnāgaŕh. Many statements of the author are, however, not free from bias, as he suspected that in the murder of his father Dīwān Amar-d̲j̲ī the ruler of the State was indirectly involved); ʿAlī Muḥammad K̲h̲ān, *Mirʾāt-i Aḥmadī*, (ed. Nawab Ali), Baroda 1928, i, 177-9; Sikandar b. Mand̲j̲hū, *Mirʾāt-i Sikandarī*, Bombay 1308/1890, 71 ff., 87 ff., 114; G̲h̲ulām Muḥammad, *Taʾrīk̲h̲ Mirʾāt-i Muṣṭafābād*, Bombay 1931 (a detailed court-chronicle of D̲j̲ūnāgaŕh, hence suffers from all those defects which are common to all court-historians); *Imp. Gaz. of India*, Oxford 1908, xiv, 236-9; *Gazetteer of the Bombay Presidency (Kathiawar)*, Bombay 1884, viii, 462 ff.; C. U. Aitchison, *Collection of Treaties, Sanads etc.*, vi, 90 ff., 168 ff.; J. Burgess, *Report on the Antiquities of Kâṭhiâwâḍ and Kachh* (*Archaeological Survey of Western India*), ii and xvi, 242 ff.; Niẓām al-Dīn Aḥmad, *Ṭabaḳāt-i Akbarī*, Eng. transl. Bibl. Ind., index; H. Wilberforce-Bell, *The history of Kâṭhiâwâḍ*, London 1916, 147, 156, 160-4, 192, 194; *Bombay Government Selections* no. 39; Col. Walker, *Statistical account of Junagadh*, Bombay 1808; J. W. Watson, *A history of Gujarat* (not available to me); V. P. Menon, *The story of the integration of the Indian States*, Calcutta 1956, 124-50 and index; *Memoranda on the Indian States*, Delhi 1940; *Indian Antiquary*, iv, 74 ff.; Anon., *Ṣaḥīfa-i Zarīn*, Lucknow 1902, i, 130 ff.; Anon., *Who's Who in India*, (Coronation ed.), Lucknow 1911, ii/vii, 7-8; *Cambridge History of India*, iii, 59, 64ff., 70, 340; Commissariat, *History of Gujarat*, Bombay 1938. (A. S. Bazmee Ansari)

DJUNAYD, s̲h̲ayk̲h̲, the 4th Ṣafawid *s̲h̲ayk̲h̲* in line of descent from S̲h̲ayk̲h̲ Ṣafī al-Dīn Isḥāḳ, the founder of the Ṣafawid *ṭarīḳa*, succeeded his father Ibrāhīm as head of the Ṣafawid order at Ardabīl in 851/1447-8; the date of his birth is not known. D̲j̲unayd for the first time organized the Ṣafawid *murīd*s on a military footing and, unlike his predecessors, clearly aimed at temporal power as well as religious authority. His political ambitions at once brought him into conflict with D̲j̲ahāns̲h̲āh [*q.v.*], the Ḳara-Ḳoyunlu ruler of Ād̲h̲arbāyd̲j̲ān, who ordered him to disband his forces and leave Ḳara-Ḳoyunlu territory; if he failed to comply, Ardabīl would be destroyed. D̲j̲unayd fled to Asia Minor, but the Grand Vizier K̲h̲alīl Pas̲h̲a dissuaded Sultan Murād II from granting him asylum in Ottoman territory. After staying successively in Ḳaramān, with the Warsāḳ tribe in Cilicia, and at D̲j̲abal Arsūs in Syria, D̲j̲unayd was forced to flee northwards (Sultan Čaḳmaḳ [*q.v.*] had ordered the governor of Aleppo to seize him; this must have occurred before 857/1453, the year of Čaḳmaḳ's death), and went to D̲j̲ānīḳ [*q.v.*] on the Black Sea. After an unsuccessful attempt to capture Trebizond (860-1/1456), D̲j̲unayd went to Ḥiṣn Kayfā in Diyār Bakr and thence to Āmid, where he spent three years (861-3/end of 1456 to 1459) with the Aḳ-Ḳoyunlu ruler Uzun Ḥasan [*q.v.*]. In 862-3/1458, or early 1459, D̲j̲unayd married Uzun Ḥasan's sister K̲h̲adīd̲j̲a Begam. The advantages of a political alliance outweighed the religious antipathy between the S̲h̲īʿī Ṣafawiyya and the Sunnī Aḳ-Ḳoyunlu; each saw the other as a useful ally against the Ḳara-Ḳoyunlu who, doctrinally, were much closer to the Ṣafawiyya.

In 863/1459 D̲j̲unayd left Diyār Bakr and attempted to recover Ardabīl; threatened by superior Ḳara-Ḳoyunlu forces, he decided on an expedition against the Circassians (autumn 1459). While crossing the territory of the S̲h̲īrwāns̲h̲āh K̲h̲alīl Allāh b. S̲h̲ayk̲h̲ Ibrāhīm, he was attacked and killed near Ṭabarsarān on the banks of the river Kur on 11 D̲j̲umādā I 864/4 March 1460.

Bibliography: The Persian and Turkish manuscript sources listed in W. Hinz, *Irans Aufstieg zum Nationalstaat im fünfzehnten Jahrhundert*, Berlin and Leipzig 1936, which contains the best and fullest account of D̲j̲unayd's life. For a discussion of the question whether D̲j̲unayd was the first Ṣafawid *s̲h̲ayk̲h̲* to adopt the title *sulṭān*, see R. M. Savory, *The development of the early Ṣafawid state under Ismaʿīl and Ṭahmāsp*, unpublished University of London thesis, 1958, 54-5. (R. M. Savory)

DJUNAYD, last of the *amīrs* of the family of the Aydı̊n-oghlu [*q.v.*]. Djunayd who is given in the Ottoman sources the surname of Izmir-oghlu, succeeded for nearly a quarter of a century in prolonging the existence of the Aydı̊n amirate through intrigues as clever as they were bold and by turning to account the dynastic wars between the sons of Bāyezīd I. The recent researches by Himmet Akın, whose efforts were directed mainly towards documents in Turkish archives, have helped to enrich the insufficient information from sources, and to shed light on the origins of this figure who has been unjustly called an adventurer. The son of Ibrāhīm Bahādur, Amīr of Bodemya, and grandson of Meḥmed Beg, founder of the Aydı̊n amirate, Djunayd appears in history after the departure from Anatolia of Tīmūr-Lang. In 804/1402 Tīmūr had restored the Aydı̊n amīrate annexed in 792/1390 by Bāyezīd I, and returned it to the sons of ʿĪsā b. Meḥmed, Mūsā, then Umūr II. Djunayd and his brother Ḥasan Agha, who had been the *ḳara-ṣubashı̊* of the upper fortress of Izmir (the fortress of the port, occupied since 744/1344 by the Knights of Rhodes, had been retaken in 804/1402 by Tīmūr) during Ottoman rule, contended for power with their cousins and obtained respectively Izmir and Ayasoluḳ. But upon the death of Mūsā in 805/1403, Umūr II sought the aid of his kinsman Menteshe-oghlu Ilyās Beg, who helped him to reconquer Ayasoluḳ and imprisoned Ḥasan Agha in Marmaris. Djunayd succeeded in arranging the escape of his brother who was brought to Izmir by boat, and then, thanks to the intervention of the former governor of the province of Aydı̊n, Süleymān Čelebī, who was proclaimed Sultan at Edirne he regained Ayasoluḳ and made peace with Umūr II whose daughter he married. On the death of his father-in-law in 807/1405, he alone governed the amīrate to which he had added Alashehir, Ṣāliḥli and Nif. In the same year ʿĪsā Čelebī, whom Süleymān supported, came to Izmir to seek the help of Djunayd against his brother Meḥmed; Djunayd brought into the war his neighbours, the amīrs of Ṣarukhan, Menteshe, Teke and Germiyān, but in spite of their greater numbers, the allies were defeated by Meḥmed; ʿĪsā fled, while Djunayd asked for pardon and safeguarded his authority by submitting to the victor. The following year Süleymān led a campaign in Anatolia; Djunayd, allied with the Amīrs of Ḳaraman and of Germiyān, made preparations for resistance; but, fearing betrayal by this allies, he deserted their side to ask pardon of the sultan; Süleymān, who now mistrusted him, took him into Rumelia and made him governor of Ochrida. In 814/1411, however, Süleymān was killed in fighting his brother Mūsā, and Djunayd profited from the troubles of the interregnum and returned to Izmir, expelled the governor of Ayasoluḳ, appointed by Süleymān and reconquered his former amīrate. But when Meḥemmed I had triumphed over Mūsā and consolidated his power in Rumelia, he turned against Djunayd and took the fortresses of Kyma, Ḳayadjı̊k and Nif; then he besieged Izmir which had to surrender after ten days. Once more Djunayd asked pardon and won it; according to Turkish sources, the sultan granted him the region of Izmir after making him renounce the right to pronounce the *khuṭba* and to mint money. The Sultan, however, had to alter his decision for, according to Dukas' testimony, towards 818/1415 Djunayd was sent to Rumelia and made governor of Nicopolis, while the province of Aydı̊n was given to Alexander, son of Shishman, of the royal family of Bulgaria, who was killed in 819/1416 during the revolt of Börklüdje Muṣṭafā. Djunayd, meanwhile, in his Danubian province, did not hesitate to get into contact with the pretender whom the Turkish historians call Muṣṭafā Düzme [*q.v.*] and who was, according to Neshrī and the Byzantine historians, the son of Bāyezīd I who had disappeared in the battle of Ankara. After seeking the aid of Byzantium and Venice, Muṣṭafā had taken refuge with the prince of Wallachia, with the support of some Begs of Rumelia; he made Djunayd his vizier. In 819/1416, profiting from the troubles aroused in Anatolia by the religious propaganda of Shaykh Bedreddin (Badr al-Dīn) and Börklüdje Muṣṭafā, and supported in part by Byzantium and Venice, Muṣṭafā laid claim to the throne. But Meḥemmed I, returning from Anatolia, concluded a treaty with Venice; Muṣṭafā and Djunayd took refuge in Salonika where the Byzantine governor refused to deliver the fugitives to the Sultan who blockaded the town. Meḥemmed I undertook to pay an annual allowance for the custody of the prisoners; Muṣṭafā was interned on the isle of Lemnos, and Djunayd in the monastery of Pammakaristos, at Constantinople. But in 824/1421, on the death of Meḥemmed, the emperor restored the prisoners to liberty. With the support of Byzantium, Muṣṭafā had himself proclaimed sultan at Edirne and won to his cause all the Begs of Rumelia. In spite, however, of his promise to the Emperor, he refused to restore to him Gelibolu, taken with his assistance, and Byzantium turned against him. The meeting with Murād II took place at Ulubād (Lopadion) in 825/1422; by trickery, Murād induced the defection of the Rumelian Begs and promised to Djunayd the restitution of his former territory, if he abandoned the pretender's cause; Djunayd fled in the night and returned to Izmir where the population welcomed him with open arms. But not content with the region of Izmir, he expelled from Ayasoluḳ the son of Umūr II, Muṣṭafā, who was subject to the Ottomans, and gradually reconquered the former amīrate of Aydı̊n. In 827/1424 Murād II turned against Djunayd; meaning to limit the possessions of the latter to the region of Izmir, he named as governor of the province of Aydı̊n a renegade Greek, Khalīl Yakhshı̊, who recaptured the towns of Ayasoluḳ and of Tire. But Djunayd did not stop raiding the Ottoman territories, and seized the sister of the new governor. Murād II sent against him a new army under the command of the son of Timurṭash, Orudj, *beğler-beği* of Anatolia; the region of Izmir was conquered, and Djunayd had to take refuge in the fortress of Ipsili, situated on the coast opposite Samos; he put to death his prisoner, the sister of Yakhshı̊. From Ipsili, Djunayd sent a petition to Venice, asking help for himself and for the son of Muṣṭafā, brother of the Sultan Meḥemmed, who was with him; but Venice did not respond to this appeal. Meanwhile, Orudj having died, his post was given to Ḥamza, a forceful man. In 828/1425 there was a new appeal from Djunayd to Venice and a request for assistance to the amīr of Ḳaraman, who did not reply. Djunayd's army, under the command of his son Ḳurt Ḥasan, was defeated in the plain of Aḳ Ḥiṣār (Thyatira), and Ḳurt Ḥasan was taken prisoner. On the other side, with the help of some Genoese from Phocea, Ipsili was attacked from the sea. Blockaded on two sides, Djunayd had to surrender; but although he had obtained a safeguard for his life, Yakhshı̊, to avenge his sister, put him to death, as well as Ḳurt Ḥasan and all the other members of his family. Such was the end of the Aydîn-oghullarî.

Bibliography: Dukas, Bonn ed., 79-89, 96-7, 103-21, 134, 139-56, 164-76, 189-96; Chalkokondyles, Bonn ed. 204, 223-6; ʿĀshîḳpashazāde, ed. ʿĀlī, Istanbul 1332, 96, 107-9; Neshrī, edd. Unat and Köymen, ii, Ankara 1957, 445-51, 497-9, 555, 557-63, 583-7; Saʿd al-Dīn, i, Istanbul 1279, 232-6, 261-5, 306-15, 323-7; ʿĀlī, *Künh al-akhbār*, v, Istanbul 1285, 156, 167-8, 198-9, 203; N. Iorga, *Geschichte des osmanischen Reiches*, i, Gotha 1908, 366-7, 369-74, 379-80, 384-6; Himmet Akın, *Aydın oğulları tarihi hakkında bir araştırma*, Istanbul 1946, 63-82, 113, 122-3, 141, 147, 159, 174, 185, 202; I. H. Danişmend, *Izahlı Osmanlı tarihi kronolojisi*, i, Istanbul 1947, 152-4, 156, 157, 165-6, 171, 176, 181, 185-6, 191-3.

(I. Mélikoff)

AL-DJUNAYD, Abu 'l-Ḳāsim b. Muḥammad b. al-Djunayd al-Khazzāz al-Ḳawārīrī al-Nihāwandī, the celebrated Ṣūfī, nephew and disciple of Sarī al-Saḳaṭī, a native of Baghdād, studied law under Abū Thawr, and associated with Ḥārith al-Muḥāsibī [*q.v.*], with whom indeed he is said to have discussed during walks all kinds of questions relating to mysticism, Muḥāsibī giving his replies *extempore* and later writing them up in the form of books (Abū Nuʿaym, *Ḥilyat al-awliyāʾ*, Leyden MS, fol. 284a). He died in 298/910. With Muḥāsibī he is to be accounted the greatest orthodox exponent of the "Sober" type of Ṣūfism, and the titles which later writers bestowed on him—*sayyid al-ṭāʾifa* ("Lord of the Sect"), *ṭāʾūs al-fuḳarāʾ* ("Peacock of the Dervishes"), *shaykh al-mashāyikh* ("Director of the Directors")—indicate in what esteem he was held. The *Fihrist* (186) mentions his *Rasāʾil*, which have in large measure survived, in a unique but fragmentary MS (see Brockelmann, S I, 354-5). These consist of letters to private persons (examples are quoted by Sarrādj, *Kitāb al-lumaʿ*, 239-43), and short tractates on mystical themes: some of the latter are cast in the form of commentaries on Ḳurʾānic passages. His style is involved to the point of obscurity, and his influence on Ḥallādj [*q.v.*] is manifest. He mentions in one of his letters that a former communication of his had been opened and read in the course of transit: doubtless by some zealot desirous of finding cause for impugning his orthodoxy; and to this ever-present danger must in part be attributed the deliberate preciosity which marks the writings of all the mystics of Djunayd's period. Djunayd reiterates the theme, first clearly reasoned by him, that since all things have their origin in God they must finally return, after their dispersion (*tafrīḳ*), to live again in Him (*djamʿ*): and this the mystic achieves in the state of passing-away (*fanāʾ*). Of the mystic union he writes "For at that time thou wilt be addressed, thyself addressing; questioned concerning thy tidings, thyself questioning; with abundant flow of benefits, and interchange of attestations; with constant increase of faith, and uninterrupted favours" (*Rasāʾil*, fol. 3a-b). Of his own mystical experience he says "This that I say comes from the continuance of calamity and the consequence of misery, from a heart that is stirred from its foundations, and is tormented with its ceaseless conflagrations, by itself within itself: admitting no perception, no speech, no sense, no feeling, no repose, no effort, no familiar image; but constant in the calamity of its ceaseless torment, unimaginable, indescribable, unlimited, unbearable in its fierce onslaughts" (fol. 1a). Eschewing those extravagances of language which on the lips of such inebriates as Abū Yazīd al-Bisṭāmī and Ḥallādj alarmed and alienated the orthodox, Djunayd by his clear perception and absolute self-control laid the foundations on which the later systems of Ṣūfism were built.

Bibliography: in addition to references in the text: A. H. Abdel-Kader, *The life, personality and writings of al-Junayd*, GMS, NS XXII, London 1962 (with text and translation of the Istanbul ms of the *Rasāʾil*). (A. J. Arberry)

AL-DJUNAYD B. ʿABD ALLĀH, al-Murrī, one of the governors and generals of the Umayyad caliph Hishām who in 105/724 appointed him governor of the Muslim possessions in India (Sind, and Multān in the south Pandjāb), conquered some years earlier in 92-4/711-3 by Muḥammad b. al-Ḳāsim. ʿUmar II had recognized Djūshaba b. Dhābir, the Indian king who had embraced Islam, as sovereign of these territories. Al-Djunayd evidently had doubts about this man's loyalty for he attacked him, took him prisoner and put him to death; by subterfuge he also contrived the assassination of Ibn Dhābir's brother who was anxious to go to ʿIrāḳ to protest against what he considered to be perfidious behaviour. Al-Djunayd remained governor of Sind until 110/728-9, and during his tenure of office made several expeditions (*e.g.*, against the king of al-Kīrādj who was compelled to flee) and occupied various towns whose names are recorded in Arabic sources. Since the Muslim conquest of territories outside Sind only took place from the second half of the 4th/10th century, it should be noted here that from the time of al-Djunayd the Muslim invasions in the south penetrated into Gudjarāt, and in the east as far as the plateau of Mālwā in central India. Other expeditions in the north, according to Arabic sources, enabled al-Djunayd to reach the country of the Ghuzz, and also a dependency of China where he captured a town and a castle.

In 110/729 al-Djunayd was dismissed from his post, and after his fall a revolt compelled his successor to give up Sind. However, he had not forfeited the caliph's esteem for he was appointed governor of Khurāsān by him in 111/729-30 (according to al-Balādhurī, in 112); his military skill was relied on to restore the situation in Transoxiana which had become precarious through attacks by the Turks, and Ashras b. ʿAbd Allāh al-Sulamī, the former governor of the Khurāsān, was at war with them. Al-Djunayd hastened to give help, joined forces with Ashras at al-Bukhārā and fought a number of battles with the Turks, finally crushing them at Zarmān, not far from Samarḳand. On his return to Khurāsān (where he selected his lieutenants from among the Muḍar), he invaded Ṭukhāristān, but was soon forced to return to Transoxiana, summoned to the aid of the prefect of Samarḳand, Sawra b. Ḥurr al-Tamīmī, in face of the threats of the Turkish *khāḳān*. Al-Djunayd hurriedly crossed the Oxus. From Kiss he had a choice of routes to Samarḳand, either through the steppes or across the mountains; he decided to take the latter, but when he reached al-Shiʿb (= the Gorge) he was attacked by the people of Ṣughd, Shāsh and Farghāna. The battle, in which a great number of Muslims perished, has remained famous in the history of Islam under the name Waḳʿat al-Shiʿb. However, it was not a complete disaster: al-Djunayd sent a message to Sawra ordering him to leave Samarḳand and come to his aid, and Sawra obeyed, although he realized the full extent of the danger to which he was exposing himself. As was foreseen, he was attacked by the Turks and fell in the mêlée; his troops were wiped out. But al-Djunayd succeeded in disengaging from the enemy and entering Samarḳand. For the next four months he stayed in Ṣughd, and as Bukhārā, defended by Ḳaṭan b. Ḳutayba, was being besieged by the Turks and was in great danger he organized an expedition to free it. He defeated the Turks near al-Ṭawāwīs (Ramaḍān 112/730 or 113/731), and afterwards made his entry into Bukhārā. Transoxiana had been occupied only about twenty years earlier by Ḳutayba b. Muslim, and the conquest was far from being final; the instability of the situation can be gathered from the fact that Hishām had to send from al-Baṣra and al-Kūfa 20,000 men who rejoined al-Djunayd on the way and were later left at Samarḳand. At the beginning of the year 116/734 al-Djunayd was recalled, having incurred the caliph's displeasure by his marriage to al-Fāḍila, a daughter of the rebel Yazīd b. al-Muhallab. He died at Marw from a severe attack of dropsy even before his successor ʿĀṣim b. ʿAbd Allāh al-Hilālī arrived in Khurāsān. The latter could persecute only al-Djunayd's relatives and employees.

The report according to which al-Djunayd, after being dismissed from the office of governor of Sind, supported the anti-Umayyad movement fostered by Bukayr b. Māhān in Sind, seems to be absurd in view of the fact that he was almost immediately appointed governor of Khurāsān, and that he even had the leaders of this movement arrested there. The information which al-Dīnawarī (387 ff.) gives in this respect is suspect for it is wrong chronologically, as is also the information about the deposition of Asad b. ʿAbd Allāh (337).

Al-Djunayd must have been a general of exceptional qualities, and it was probably to his merits that the Muslims were indebted for the stability of their authority in Transoxiana during a very strong Turkish counter-movement. It is more difficult to judge his qualities as an administrator since on this point we have only one detail at our disposal: al-Djunayd left in the *Bayt al-māl* of Sind 18 million *ṭaṭarī* dirhams (1 *ṭaṭarī* dirham = 1$^1/_2$ dirhams of fine silver; see the glossary to al-Balādhurī and Dozy, *Suppl.*), and his successor sent the whole sum to the caliph.

Bibliography: Ṭabarī, ii, 1467, 1527-30, 1532-59, 1563, 1564-5; Balādhurī, 442-3; Yaʿḳūbī, *Hist.*, ed. Houtsma, ii, 379-80; Dīnawarī, 337-8; Ibn al-Djawzī, *Muntaẓam*, ms. Aya Sofya 3095, f° 21 v°, ms. Bodl. Pococke 255, f°s 90 v°-91 r°; Sibt Ibn al-Djawzī, *Mirʾāt*, ms. Bodl. Pococke 371, f°s 110 v°-111 r°, 115 v°-117 v°, 123 v°, 124 v°-126 v°, ms. Br. M. Add. 23277 f°s 168 r°, 171 r°-172 r°, 175 v°-176 r°-177 r°; Ibn al-Athīr, iv, 466; v, 93, 101, 115-7, 120-8, 134-5; Ibn Khaldūn, iii, 88, 91; other references in Caetani, *Chronographia Islamica*, for the years 105, 107, 110-6.

(L. VECCIA VAGLIERI)

DJUND, a Ḳurʾānic word of Iranian origin denoting an armed troop. In the Umayyad period the term applies especially to military settlements and districts in which were quartered Arab soldiers who could be mobilized for seasonal campaigns or for more protracted expeditions. Quite naturally it also denotes the corresponding army corps. According to the chroniclers, the caliph Abū Bakr is said to have set up four *djunds* in Syria, of Ḥims, Damascus, Jordan (al-Urdunn, around Tiberias) and Palestine (around Jerusalem and ʿAsḳalān and, afterwards, al-Ramla). Later, the *djund* of Ḳinnasrīn is said to have been detached from this organization by the Umayyad caliph Yazīd I, and the fortified towns known as *al-ʿAwāṣim* [*q.v.*] by the ʿAbbāsid caliph Harūn al-Rashīd. The term *djund*, in practice restricted to the military areas in Syria which were to correspond approximately to the old Byzantine divisions, did not apply to the military settlements in ʿIrāḳ or Egypt. The army corps thus established consisted exclusively of Arabs drawing regular pay (*ʿaṭāʾ* [*q.v.*]), the sum required for this purpose being normally provided by the proceeds of the land-tax on the corresponding district, but the troops seem to have benefited also in the majority of cases from grants of property, though we still do not know the exact conditions under which such grants were made and enjoyed. These regular troops were generally accompanied by detachments of retainers or *shākiriyya*, and in addition there were often volunteers (*mutaṭawwiʿa* [*q.v.*]), who received no pay (Ṭabarī, i, 2090, 2807; Balādhurī, *Futūḥ*, 166).

In the ʿAbbāsid period the term *djund* continued to apply to Syrian administrative districts (Ṭabarī, iii, 1134) which survived until the time of the Mamlūks, but the *dīwān al-djund*, which can be proved to have been still in existence under al-Mutawakkil (Yaʿḳūbī, *Buldān*, 267, and Yaʿḳūbī-Wiet, 61), administered the non-Arab contingents. (Ṭabari, iii, 1507, 1685). The word *djund* in fact little by little took on a wider meaning, namely the armed forces (Ṭabarī, iii, 654, 815, 1369, 1479, 1736) while for the geographers of the 3rd/9th and 4th/10th centuries the *adjnād*, the equivalents of *amṣār*, denoted the large towns.

The Umayyad organization of the *djund* seems to have been partly imitated in the province of al-Andalus. From 125/742 Arab, Syrian and Egyptian contingents received grants of land in nine districts (*kūras*), called *mudjannada*, in the Iberian peninsula [see AL-ANDALUS, iii]. To the members of these *djunds* there were added, as in the East, enlisted volunteers (*ḥushūd*) who were all grouped together under the same denomination in the 4th/10th century and were distinct from the foreign mercenaries (*ḥasham*) who gradually eliminated the old army. In Aghlabid Ifrīḳiya the word *djund*, which at first denoted Arab contingents brought by the conquerors and successive governors, came ultimately to signify the personal guard, the nucleus of the new permanent army. Under the various dynasties connected with the Maghrib, the term *djund* kept a restricted sense which is often difficult to define, rarely applying to the whole army. Similarly, with the Mamlūks the word *djund* is sometimes applied to a category of soldiers in the sultan's service, but distinct from the personal guard [see ḤALḲA].

Bibliography: Balādhurī, *Futūḥ*, 131-2, 144, 166; Yaʿḳūbī, *Buldān*, 324-9 (Yaʿḳūbī-Wiet, 169-83); Ibn al-Faḳīh, 109; Ibn Rusta, 107-8 (Ibn Rusta-Wiet, 119-20); Ḳudāma, *K. al-Kharādj*, *BGA*, vi, 246,247, 251; Yāḳūt, i, 136; Muḳaddasī, 415, 416; Ṭabarī, i, 2090; iii, 1134; Abu 'l-Fidāʾ, *Taḳwīm*, ii/2, 2-3; Le Strange, *Palestine*, 24-30; M. Gaudefroy-Demombynes, *La Syrie à l'époque des Mamelouks*, Paris 1923, XXXIII, CIV, 29-31; E. Herzfeld, *Geschichte der Stadt Samarra*, Hamburg 1949, 98, 99 n. 1 (on the origin of the word *djund*); R. Levy, *The social structure of Islam*, Cambridge 1957, 407-27; A. Vonderheyden, *La Berbérie orientale sous la dynastie des Banu 'l-Arlab*, Paris 1927, 69, 80-6; R. Brunschvig, *La Berbérie orientale sous les Hafsides*, ii, Paris 1947, 82, 88; J. F. P. Hopkins, *Medieval Muslim government in Barbary*, London 1958, 71-84; E. Lévi-Provençal, *Hist. Esp. Mus.*, iii, 66-72; D. Ayalon, *Studies on the structure of the Mamluk army*, in *BSOAS*, xv (1953), 448-59. On military organization in general, see DJAYSH. (D. SOURDEL)

DJUNDAYSĀBŪR [see GONDĒSHĀPŪR].

DJUNDĪ [see ḤALḲA].

DJUNNAR, town in the Indian State of Bombay, 56 m. north of Poona. Its proximity to the Nānā Pass made it an important trade centre linking the Deccan with the west coast. The fort of Djunnar was built by Malik al-Tudjdjār in 840/1436. The district around Djunnar was one of the *ṭarafs* or provinces of the Bahmanī kingdom of the Deccan during the administration of Maḥmūd Gāwān [*q.v.*]. It later formed part of the Sultanate of Aḥmadnagar. In 1067/1657 the town was plundered by Shiwadjī, the Marāṭhā leader, who was born in the neighbouring hill-fort of Shiwnēr. The surrounding hills are famous for their Buddhist caves. These are described in great detail in the *Gazetteer of the Bombay Presidency*, xviii (Part iii), 140-231.

(C. COLLIN DAVIES)

DJŪR [see FĪRŪZĀBĀD].

DJUR'AT, *takhalluṣ* of Ḳalandar Bakhsh, an Urdū poet of Indian origin, whose real name was Yaḥyā Amān, son of Ḥāfiẓ Amān, one of whose ancestors Rāy Amān, after whom a street in Old Dihlī is still known, suffered at the hands of Nādir Shāh's troops during the sack of Dihlī in 1152/1739. The title of Amān or Mān was conferred on the ancestors of Djur'at, according to Mīrzā ʿAlī Luṭf (*Gulshan-i Hind*, 73), by the Emperor Akbar. Born at Dihlī, Djur'at was brought up at Fayḍābād and later joined the service of Nawwāb Muḥabbat Khān of Bareilly, a son of Ḥāfiẓ Raḥmat Khān Rohilla [*q.v.*] at an early age. In 1215/1800 he went to Lucknow and ingratiated himself with prince Sulaymān Shukōh, a son of Shāh ʿĀlam II [*q.v.*], titular emperor of Dihlī. The 'court' of Sulaymān Shukōh had become the refuge, after the sack of Imperial Dihlī, of great poets and writers like Muṣḥafī and Inshā' Allāh Khān [*qq.v.*], included among his stipendiaries. Ten years later Djur'at died in that city in 1225/1810.

A pupil of Djaʿfar ʿAlī Khān Ḥasrat, a poet of some note, he was a skilled musician and played on the guitar with dexterity. He was also a good astrologer and well-groomed in social etiquette, qualities which made him extremely popular with people of high rank. On account of cataract, which afflicted him in the prime of life, he lost his eyesight; others say he feigned blindness in order to further his amours. Essentially a *bon viveur*, Djur'at was a lyrical and especially an erotic poet. Author of more than 100,000 lines (Aḥad ʿAlī Yakta: *Dastūr al-faṣāḥāt*, Rampur 1943, 98 ff.), mostly passionate *ghazals*, he wrote some voluptuous *mathnawīs* also, of which one, entitled *Ḥusn wa ʿishḳ*, deserves mention. The well-known Urdū poet Mīr [*q.v.*] spoke slightingly of Djur'at whose compositions he described as mere *bon mots*, of the 'kissing and hugging type'. Mīr's verdict has been characterized as wholly unjustified as he failed to appreciate the social and political conditions of Djur'at's times and the Lucknow of his days, where Mīr was comparatively a stranger. It was Djur'at, who for the first time in Urdū poetry, addressed his *ghazals* to women, contrary to the time-dishonoured practice of showering praises on young, handsome boys and *amrads*. His *dīwān* was published in the now defunct *Urdū-i Muʿallā* (ed. Ḥasrat Mohāhī), Kanpur, October-December, 1927.

Bibliography: All the relevant *tadhkiras* of Urdu poets (enumerated in *Dastūr al-faṣāḥat*, 99 n.); Muḥammad Ḥusayn Āzād, *Āb-i ḥayāt*, s.v. Djur'at; Ram Babu Saksena, *History of Urdu literature*, Allāhābād 1940, 88-90; T. Grahame Bailey, *History of Urdu literature*, London 1932, 55-6; Abu 'l-Layth Ṣiddīḳī, *Djur'at unkā ʿahad awr ʿishḳiyya shāʿirī*, Karachi 1952 (the first critical study of Djur'at).

(A. S. BAZMEE ANSARI)

DJURAYDJ, a saint whose story is said to have been related by the Prophet himself and has therefore found a place in the *ḥadīth*. The various versions differ in details one from another, but one motif is common to them all, that the saint is accused by a woman, who had had a child by another man, of being its father; but the child itself, on being asked by the saint, declares the real father's name and thus clears the saint from suspicion. "Djuraydj" is the Arabic reproduction of Gregorius, and one version rightly states that he lived in the prophetless period (*fatra* [*q.v.*]) between Jesus and Muḥammad. There is a similar episode in the biographies of Gregorius Thaumaturgus, and it may be assumed as probable that the story became known among Muslims through the Christian tradition until finally it was accepted in the *ḥadīth*.

Bibliography: Bukhārī, *Saḥīḥ al-ʿamal fi 'l-ṣalāt*, Bāb 7, *Maẓālim*, Bāb 35; Muslim (Cairo 1283), v, 277; Maḳdisī, *al-Bad' wa 'l-ta'rīkh*, ed. Huart, Ar. text 135; Samarḳandī, *Tanbīh*, ed. Cairo 1309, 221; Migne, *Patrologia graeca*, xlvi, 901 ff.; *Acta martyrum et sanctorum*, ed. Bedjan, vi, 101 ff.; Horovitz, *Spuren griechischer Mimen*, 78-83. (J. HOROVITZ)

DJURBADHĀḲĀN [see GULPĀYAGĀN].

DJURDJĀN [see GURGĀN].

AL-**DJURDJĀNĪ**, ʿABD AL-ḲĀHIR [see Supplement].

AL-**DJURDJĀNĪ**, ʿALĪ B. MUḤAMMAD, called al-Sayyid al-Sharīf, was born in 740/1339 at Tādjū near Astarābādh; in 766/1365 he went to Harāt to study under Ḳuṭb al-Dīn Muḥammad al-Rāzī al-Taḥtānī, but the old man advised him to go to his pupil Mubārakshāh in Egypt; however he stayed in Harāt and went in 770/1368 to Ḳaramān to hear Muḥammad al-Aḳṣarā'ī who died before his arrival (al-Aḳṣarā'ī died in 773/1371: *al-Durar al-kāmina* iv, 207). He studied under Muḥammad al-Fanārī and went with him to Egypt where he heard Mubārakshāh and Akmal al-Dīn Muḥammad b. Maḥmūd, staying four years in Saʿīd al-Suʿadā'; he visited Constantinople in 776/1374 and then went to Shīrāz where he was appointed teacher by Shāh Shudjāʿ 779/1377. When Tīmūr captured the town, he took him to Samarḳand where he had discussions with Saʿd al-Dīn al-Taftazānī [*q.v.*]; opinions differed as to who was the victor. On Tīmūr's death he went back to Shīrāz where he died 816/1413. The usual tales are told of his brilliance as a student. He wrote on many subjects, on grammar and logic in Persian. He belonged to an age which wrote commentaries on earlier works; as a theologian he allowed a large place to philosophy, thus half his commentary on al-*Mawāḳif* of al-Īdjī [*q.v.*], is given up to it. On law, he wrote a commentary on al-*Farā'iḍ al-sirādjiyya* of al-Sadjāwandī; on language, glosses on al-*Muṭawwal* a commentary by al-Taftazānī on *Talkhīṣ al-miftāḥ* by al-Sakkākī; on logic, glosses on a commentary by al-Rāzī al-Taḥtānī on *al-Risāla* *al-shamsiyya fi 'l-ḳawāʿid al-manṭiḳiyya* by al-Kātibī. In his *Taʿrīfāt* he was not afraid to be simple.

His son, Nūr al-Dīn Muḥammad, translated his father's Persian logic into Arabic, wrote on logic, also a commentary on his father's book on tradition and a *Risāla fi 'l-radd ʿalā 'l-rawāfiḍ*. Nothing is known of his biography except the date of his death in 838/1434.

Bibliography: al-Sakhāwī, *al-Ḍawʾ al-lāmiʿ*, v, 328; al-Shawkānī, *al-Badr al-ṭāliʿ*, i, 488; Muḥammad Bāḳir, *Rawḍat al-djannāt*, 497; al-Lakhnawī al-Hindī, *al-Fawāʾid al-bahiyya*, 125; Khwāndamīr, *Ḥabīb al-siyar*, iii/3, 89, 147; Brockelmann, II, 216, S II, 305; Browne, iii, 355; Storey, i, 36. (A. S. Tritton)

DJURDJĀNĪ, FAKHR AL-**DĪN** [see GURGĀNĪ].

AL-**DJURDJĀNĪ, ISMĀʿĪL** B. AL-**ḤUSAYN** ZAYN AL-DĪN ABU 'L-FAḌĀʾIL AL-ḤUSAYNĪ, often called al-Sayyid Ismāʿīl, a noble and celebrated physician who wrote in Persian and in Arabic. He went to live in Khwārizm in 504/1110 and became attached to the Khwārizmshāhs Ḳuṭb al-Dīn Muḥammad (490/1097-521/1127), to whom he dedicated his *Dhakhīra*, and Atsïz b. Muḥammad (521/1127-551/1156), who commissioned him to write a shorter compendium, *al-Khuffī al-ʿAlāʾī*, so called because its two volumes were small enough to be taken by the prince on his journeys in his boots (*khuff*). He later moved to Marw, the capital of the rival sultan Sandjar b. Malikshāh, and died there in 531/1136. His *Dhakhīra-i Khwārizmshāhī*, probably the first medical Encyclopaedia written in Persian and containing about 450,000 words, is one of the most important works of its kind; it also exists in an Arabic version, and was translated into Turkish and (in an abbreviated form) into Hebrew. Apart from the *Dhakhīra* and the *Khuffī*, al-Djurdjānī wrote about a dozen other works, some of them substantial, mainly on medicine and philosophy. Most of his literary output, which was highly regarded already by his contemporaries, has been preserved in manuscripts. A short treatise on the vanity of this world, *al-Risāla al-munabbiha* (in Arabic), was incorporated by Bayhaḳī in his biography.

Bibliography: Ẓahīr al-Dīn ʿAlī b. Zayd al-Bayhaḳī, *Taʾrīkh ḥukamāʾ al-Islām*, Damascus 1946, 172 ff.; idem, *Tatimmat Ṣiwān al-ḥikma*, ed. M. Shafīʿ, Lahore 1935, i, 172 ff. (text), 216 ff. (bibliographical notes); M. Meyerhof, in *Osiris*, viii, 1948, 203 f. (digest of the preceding, with additional bibliography); Niẓāmī-i ʿArūḍī, *Čahār maḳāla*, ed. Mīrzā Muḥammad, 1910, 70 f. (text), 233, 236 ff. (notes); transl. E. G. Browne, 1921, 78 ff. (transl.), 158 f. (notes); Ibn Abī Uṣaybiʿa, *ʿUyūn al-anbāʾ*, ii, 31; A. Fonahn, *Zur Quellenkunde der persischen Medizin*, 1910, 13 ff.; E. G. Browne, *Arabian medicine*, 98 ff.; Abbas Naficy, *La Médecine en Perse*, 1933, 41-48 (biography), 65-124 (summary of the first four "books", on the theoretical foundations of medicine, of the *Dhakhīra*); G. Sarton, *Introduction to the history of science*, ii, 1931, 234 f.; C. Elgood, *A medical history of Persia*, 1951, 214 ff. and index; Brockelmann I, 641; S I, 889 f. (J. Schacht)

AL-**DJURDJĀNĪ, NŪR** AL-**DĪN** [see AL-DJURDJĀNĪ, ʿALĪ B. MUḤAMMAD].

AL-**DJURDJĀNIYYA** [see GURGANDJ].

DJURDJURA, a scarped chain of mountains 60 km. long in the Tellian Atlas of Algeria, enclosing and dominating the wide depression of the *wādī* Sahel-Soummam, and the principal Kabyle massif in the West, known as Greater Kabylia or Kabylia of Djurdjura. It consists of four ridges running roughly E.-W., almost everywhere exceeding 1,500 m. (4,921 ft.) in altitude and with the Dj. Haïzer reaching 2,133 m. (6,998 ft.), the Akouker 2,305 m. (7,562 ft.) and the Tamgout (Berber for summit) of Lalla Khadīdja 2,308 m. (7,572 ft.). Massive limestone deposits of the Lias and, in the West, of the Eocene, sharply inclined and faulted, give the appearance of Sierras, with such characteristic features as eroded rocky plateaux, vertical shafts leading to caverns, and swallow-holes (the one at Boussouil is over 360 m. [1181 ft.] deep).

Standing 50 km. from the Mediterranean, the Djurdjura has a very heavy rainfall (1200 to 1800 mm. [47.24 to 70.86 ins.]) and is under snow for from one to three months. For this reason it is the source of vigorous springs which are utilized by numerous villages on both sides of the range, as well as by various hydro-electric power-stations. The white mountain-tops tower above ancient but decayed forests of cedars and the remnants of groves of evergreen oaks, the home of colonies of Barbary apes. Grasslands provide summer pasturage for the small flocks from nearby villages. The altitude, the picturesque scenery and in addition the snow attract summer visitors and skiers in winter.

The villages, in which only the Kabyles speak Berber, are situated not higher than 1150 m. (3,772 ft.) on the north side and 1,350 m. (4,429 ft.) on the south side. The mountain range is thus inhabited. The altitude of the passes (*tizi*), 1,636 m. (5,367 ft.) at the Tizi n-Kouilal and 1,760 m. (5,774 ft.) at Tizi n-Tighourda, proves an effective barrier as regards both weather and inhabitants. Together with the wide belt of forest stretching eastward from the high ground of Sebaou and reaching as far as the sea, the range cuts off and isolates a Kabylia of irregular form, at the centre of which is Tizi Ouzou, and also a long depression, the *wādī* Sahel-Soummam, which again is Kabyle but exposed to the direct influence of Algiers and Bougie.

Bibliography: A. Belin, J. Flandrin, M. Fourastier, S. Rahmani, M. Rémond and R. de Peyerimhoff, *Guide de la montagne algérienne. Djurdjura*, Algiers 1947. See also KABYLIA. (J. Despois)

DJURHUM or **DJURHAM**, an ancient Arab tribe reckoned to the *ʿArab al-ʿĀriba* (see art. ʿARAB, DJAZĪRAT AL-, vi). According to later standard Arab tradition, Djurhum was descended from Yaḳṭān (Ḳaḥṭān). The tribe migrated from the Yaman to Mecca. After a protracted struggle with another tribe Ḳatūra (also referred to as ʿAmālīḳ), led by al-Sumaydiʿ, Djurhum under their chief (called Muḍāḍ b. ʿAmr, al-Ḥārith b. Muḍāḍ, etc.) gained control of the Kaʿba. This they retained till driven out by Bakr b. ʿAbd Manāt of Khuzāʿa. The above is doubtless the pre-Islamic form of the tradition, and it presumably has some historical basis. This older account, however, has been transformed by the introduction of Ḳurʾānic material about Ismāʿīl (Ishmael), who is said to have been given protection along with his mother by Djurhum and to have married a woman of the tribe. The Ḳurʾānic material, and the need for sufficient generations back to Ismāʿīl (by Biblical chronology) has encouraged the suggestion that Djurhum flourished in the distant past and was extinct by Islamic times. Careful study of references, however, especially those in early poems, shows that Djurhum had been at

Mecca in the comparatively recent past (cf. Th. Nöldeke, *Fünf Mo*ʿ*allaqāt*, iii, 26 f.; S. Krauss, in *ZDMG*, xli, 717; also *ZDMG*, lxx, 352; al-Ḥassān b. Thābit, *Dīwān*, ed. Hirschfeld, 43 f. [= Ibn Hishām, 251]). This is further confirmed by the mention of Γόραμα and Γοραμῆνοι by the Greek writer Stephanus Byzantinus (London 1688, 276), and by the occurrence of an ʿAbd al-Masīḥ among the chiefs of Djurhum (cf. E. Pococke, *Specimen*, 79 f.). Al-Azraḳī (ed. Wüstenfeld, i, 54) speaks of a remnant in his day, and the *nisba* Djurhumī occurs. Al-Ṭabarī (i, 749) states that Banū Liḥyān are descended from Djurhum, but the basis of this is unknown.

Bibliography: Ibn Hishām, 71-74; Ṭabarī, i, 219, 283, 749, 768, 904, 1088, 1131-4; al-Azraḳī (*Chroniken der Stadt Mekka*, ed. Wüstenfeld, i), 44-56; Masʿūdī, *Murūdj*, iii, 95-103; idem, *Tanbīh* (*BGA*, viii), 80, 82, 184 f., 202; Ibn Ḥabīb, *Muḥabbar*, 311, 314, 395; Caussin de Perceval, *Histoire des Arabes avant l'Islamisme*, i, 33 f., 168, 177, 194-201, 218; Buhl, *Muhammed*, 106 n.; al-Aʿshā, *Dīwān*, 15, 44.

(W. Montgomery Watt)

DJURM (fine) (in the Ottoman Empire).

Though fines are unknown to the criminal law of the *sharīʿa*, some *fuḳahā*ʾ admitted of monetary penalties in certain cases (see *e.g.*, Dede Efendi, *Siyāsetnāme*, at end). The Ottoman *ḳānūnnāmes* ([*q.v.*]; see also djazaʾ), while pretending merely to apply and complete the *sharīʿa*, prescribed fines (*djürm*, *djerīme* or *djereme*, *ḳinlïḳ*, *gharāmet*) for a large number of offences. These even included crimes liable to *ḥudūd* [*q.v.*] penalties, such as adultery, theft, the drinking of wine, etc. Generally fines were imposed in addition to corporal chastisement (*taʿzīr*, [*q.v.*]) and sometimes in addition to to blood-money (*diyet*) or damages (*tazmīn*).

The fines were of three kinds: (*a*) a certain amount (one aḳče, more rarely half an aḳče or less) for each stroke inflicted on the offender; (*b*) a certain number of aḳče for each dirhem lacking in the weight of a price-controlled commodity; or (*c*) as usual in the Dhu 'l-Ḳadr codes (Barkan, *Kanunlar*, 120-9) and many Ottoman provincial *ḳānūnnāmes* where no *taʿzīr* is mentioned, a fixed amount of money. The fines of the third group were, similarly to the poll-tax (*djizya*), mostly graduated in accordance with the financial circumstances of the offender—rich, medium, poor (and very poor), the ratio being 4 : 3 : 2, 8 (6) : 4 : 2 : 1, etc. They varied between 10 and 400 aḳče, but a fifteenth century *fermān* (Anhegger-Inalcık, *Ḳānūnnāme-i Sulṭānī*, 58) and *ḳānūnnāme* (*TOEM*, 1330, Suppl., 28) prescribed higher fines. In many cases non-Muslims were to pay only half the fine imposed on Muslims (*MOG*, i, 29; Barkan, 81), but this privilege was partly cancelled out by discrimination in the way they were graduated. For certain offences slaves paid half the fine of a free Muslim, while in Egypt fellahs were subject to double the fine collected in the old Ottoman dominions (Barkan, 362). No fines were to be exacted from criminals sentenced to retaliation (*ḳiṣāṣ*) or to capital or severe corporal punishment (*siyāset*).

Fiscally the fines formed part of the *rüsūm-i ʿurfiyye* and were sometimes included in the *bād-i hawā* [*q.v*]. After the offender had been duly convicted by a *ḳāḍī*, the fine was exacted by the organs of the executive power (*ehl-i ʿurf*). Peasants on most of the "free" (*serbest*) lands had to pay fines to their "landowners" (*ṣāḥib-i arḍ*), *i.e.*, the Sultan, members of his family, *beylerbeyis*, *sandjaḳbeyis*, *zaʿīms* and other high officers, or to their agents, (*ʿāmils*, *emīns*, *voyvodas*, *mütesellims*, etc.). On lands that were not "free", *i.e.*, most of the smaller *tīmārs*, half the fines usually went to the fief-holder and the other half to the local governor and/or his subordinate (*subashï*). Fines from people on *waḳf* lands were due to the *waḳf* or, as in the case of offenders on privately owned land, to the Sultan's Treasury. In towns they generally belonged to the *subashï*, *ʿasesbashï* or *muḥtasib* [*q.v.*]. Egyptian fellahs paid to their *kāshifs*, Kurds to their *beys*. Special regulations also applied to soldiers, nomads, gypsies, foreigners and others who were subject to separate jurisdiction. No fines were imposed on fief-holders and holders of a *berāt* [*q.v.*].

In the cadastral registers the annual revenue from the fines of a certain district (*niyābet*, [*resm-i*] *djürm we djināyet*) was often entered as a fixed sum and those entitled to it used to lease out its collection. Many *fermāns* and *ʿadāletnāmes* contain strict orders to prevent illegal or excessive fining. From the 10th/16th century, however, such abuses greatly increased. The officials more and more ignored the prescribed amounts of fines which, despite the considerable depreciation of the Ottoman currency, had remained unchanged. On the other hand, many offenders punishable with fines (and *taʿzīr*) were henceforth sent to the galleys or forced labour. In the early 12th/18th century several provincial *ḳānūnnāmes* (Barkan, 333, 338, 354) abolished the fines, together with all other *rüsūm-i ʿurfiyye*, as impositions contrary to the *sharīʿa*. In the first two modern Ottoman penal codes (1840, 1851) no mention is made of fines; in the latter (iii, 10) they are even expressly forbidden. The last Ottoman criminal code (1858) prescribes a great many fines (*djezā-yi naḳdī*), now however in accordance with the French legal conception.

Bibliography: *Ḳānūn-i Pādishāhī-i Sulṭān Meḥemmed bin Murād* in *MOG*, i, Vienna 1921, 19-48; *Ḳānūnnāme-i āl-i ʿOthmān* in *TOEM*, 1329, Suppl., 1-10, 38, 45, 47, 49, 62-8; 1330, Suppl., 28; Aḥmed Luṭfī, *Mirʾāt-i ʿadālet*, Istanbul 1304, 47-57, 78-89, 127-76; Hammer-Purgstall, *Staatsverfassung*, i, 143-52 (incomplete and often faulty transl. of criminal code); Ö. L. Barkan, *Osm. imparatorluğunda ziraî ekonominin . . . esasları*, i, *Kanunlar*, Istanbul 1943, index; ʿOthmān Nūrī, *Medjelle-i umūr-i belediyye*, Istanbul 1338/1922, 409-18; M. Ç. Uluçay, *XVII. Asırda Saruhan'da eşkiyalık*, Istanbul 1944, 164; H. İnalcık, *Sûret-i defter-i Sancak-i Arvanid*, Ankara 1954, XXVII-XXVIII, XXXII; J. Schacht, in *Isl.*, xx, 211-2; G. Üçok, in *Ankara Üniv. Hukuk Fak. Dergisi*, iv (1947), 48-73; U. Heyd, *Studies in old Ottoman criminal law* (in preparation). (U. Heyd)

DJURZ, DJURZĀN [see gurdjistān].

DJUSTĀNIDS, DJASTĀNIDS [see daylam].

DJUWAYN, name of several localities in Īrān.

1. A village in Ardashīr Khurra, five *farsakh* from Shīrāz on the road to Arradjān, usually called Djuwaym, the modern Goyum, cf. Le Strange, 253; P. Schwarz, *Iran im Mittelalter*, 44, 173, 179 (not to be confused with Djuwaym Abī Aḥmad in the province of Dārābdjird, the modern Djuyum, see Le Strange, 254; Schwarz, 102, 201).

2. Djuwayn (also written Gūyān), a district in the Nīshāpūr country, on the caravan route from Bisṭām, between Djādjarm and Bayhaḳ (Sabzewār). The district, whose capital is given as Āzādhwār, later Fariyūmad (see *JRAS*, 1902, 735) contained 189 villages according to Yāḳūt, ii, 164-6, whose

information is taken from Abu 'l-Ḳāsim al-Bayhaḳī; they were all in the northern half, while the southern half was unsettled; cf. Le Strange, 391 ff. The plain of Djuwayn, enclosed on the north and south by ranges of hills, still forms a district of Sabzewār with about 65 townships, which lie along the river Djuwayn in a long series. In the middle of the valley, near the village of Āzādhwār, lie the ruins of the ancient capital. The modern centre is Djugatay (Čaghatāy) which is situated to the south-east of it, at the foot of the hills on the south; cf. McGregor, *Khorasan*, ii, 145, 225; C. E. Yate, *Khurasan and Sistan*, 389 ff.

3. Djuwayn or Guwayn, a fortified place in Sidjistān, 3 to 5 km. north-east of Lāsh on the Farāhrūd, appears under its modern name in ancient (see Marquart, *Ērānšahr*, 198: Γαβηνὴ πόλις, emendation on Isidorus of Charax) and mediaeval itineraries (Iṣṭakhrī, 248; Ibn Ḥawḳal, 304). The importance of the sister towns of Lāsh and Djuwayn still rests on the fact that the roads from Ḳandahār and Harāt from the Afghān side, and those from Mashhad, Yazd and Nāṣirābād on the Persian side, meet here. The Arab geographers say that Djuwayn on the road from Harāt to Zarandj was a Khāridjī stronghold (Muḳaddasī, 306; Ibn Rusta, 174). It was sacked by Yaḳūtī, the Ghuzz leader, in 447/1055-6 (*Taʾrīkh-i Sistān*, ed. Bahār, 376-7).

Djuwayn, built on a slight elevation in the centre of a fertile plain covered with ruins, and surrounded by a quadrangular wall of clay, forms a striking contrast to the rocky stronghold of Lāsh; it appears to have considerably declined in the second half of the 19th century. Cf. Le Strange, 341 ff.; Euan Smith in *Eastern Persia*, i, 319 ff.; A. C. Yate, *England and Russia face to face in Asia*, 99 ff.

(R. Hartmann)

AL-**DJUWAYNĪ**, ʿAbd Allāh b. Yūsuf Abu Muḥammad, a Shāfiʿī scholar, father of ʿAbd al-Malik [see the following art.], lived for most of his life in Nīsābūr, and died there in 438/1047. As an author, he was mainly concerned with the literary form of *furūḳ*, on which see Schacht, in *Islamica*, ii/4, 1927, 505 ff.

Bibliography: al-Subkī, *Ṭabaḳāt*, iii, 208-19; W. Wüstenfeld, *Der Imâm el-Schâfiʿi*, etc., no. 365 (a), 248 ff.; Brockelmann, I, 482; S I, 667.

(J. Schacht)

AL-**DJUWAYNĪ**, Abu 'l-Maʿālī ʿAbd al-Malik, son of the preceding, celebrated under his title of Imām al-Ḥaramayn, born 18 Muḥarram 419/17 February 1028 at Bushtanikān, a village on the outskirts of Nīsābūr; after his father's death, he continued the latter's teaching even before he was twenty years old. He was connected with the school of *ʿilm al-kalām* inaugurated by Abu 'l-Ḥasan al-Ashʿarī at the beginning of the 4th/10th century. But ʿAmīd al-Mulk al-Kundurī, vizier of the Saldjūḳ Tughrul Beg, declared himself against this "innovation", and had the Ashʿarīs, as well as the Rawāfiḍ, denounced from the pulpits. Al-Djuwaynī, like Abu 'l-Ḳāsim al-Ḳushayrī, immediately left his country and went to Baghdād; then, in 450/1058, he reached the Ḥidjāz where he taught at Mecca and at Medina for four years: hence his honorary name of "Imām of the two holy Cities". But when the vizier Niẓām al-Mulk came to power in the Saldjūḳ empire, he favoured the Ashʿarīs and invited the emigrants to return home. Al-Djuwaynī was among those who returned to Nīsābūr (the information in *ZDMG*, xli, 63 is not quite exact), and Niẓām al-Mulk actually founded in this town a special *madrasa* for him, which was called Niẓāmiyya like the similar establishment in Baghdād. Al-Djuwaynī taught there to the end of his days (we know that al-Ghazālī held a chair there for some time towards the end of his life, from 499/1105 onwards). Al-Djuwaynī died in the village of his birth—where he had gone in the hope of recovering from an illness—on 25 Rabīʿ II 478/20 August 1085. In his *Ṭabaḳāt al-Shāfiʿiyya*, al-Subkī devoted to him a long laudatory study, and declared (*Tab.*, ii, 77, 20) that the abundance of his literary production could be explained only by a miracle.

Al-Djuwaynī's researches were divided between the *fiḳh* (more precisely the *uṣūl al-fiḳh*) and the *ʿilm al-kalām*.—Fiḳh: His principal treatise, *K. al-Waraḳāt fī uṣūl al-fiḳh*, continued being commented upon until the 11th/17th century. His methodology is best expressed in the *K. al-Burhān fī uṣūl al-fiḳh*, where he was probably the first to wish to establish a juridical method on an Ashʿarī basis. In his *Ṭabaḳāt* (iii, 264), al-Subkī remarked the difficulty of the work and called it *laghz al-umma* ("the enigma of the Community"). He also drew attention to the reservations entered by al-Djuwaynī with regard to al-Ashʿarī and Mālik, reservations which would have prevented this juridical work from becoming very popular, espe cially among the Mālikīs.

ʿIlm al-Kalām: it is in the rôle of doctor in *kalām* that al-Djuwaynī made his deepest impression on Muslim thought; and to him goes the glory of being the teacher of Abū Ḥāmid al-Ghazālī in this discipline. Unfortunately, his great work, the *Shāmil*, has not been published. One manuscript (incomplete) is to be found in the National Library in Cairo (*ʿilm al-kalām*, no. 1290), copied from a manuscript in the Köprülü library; another copy, with extracts from al-Nasafī added, belonged to Dr. al-Khudayri in Cairo. These manuscripts have been studied by G. C. Anawati (cf. *Introduction à la théologie musulmane*, Paris 1948, 181-5). On the other hand, the compendium *K. al-Irshād ilā ḳawāṭiʿ al-adilla fī uṣūl al-iʿtiḳād* has been edited, and often studied and quoted. There are two modern editions: (1) by J.-D. Luciani, Paris 1938, with a French tr. (left unfinished by the death of the editor-translator); (2) by M. Y. Mūsā and A. ʿAbd al-Munʿim ʿAbd al-Ḥamīd, Cairo 1950, which is the best critical edition.

Al-Djuwaynī is important because he wrote in the intermediate period between the old Ashʿarism and the school which Ibn Khaldūn was to call "modern". This is marked by (1) a systematical enquiry, influenced—not without the introduction of new schemes—by that of the Muʿtazila (whose theories are rejected); (2) the emphasis laid, in the theory of knowledge, and with regard to the divine attributes, on the idea of "modes" (*aḥwāl*), thus taken over from the semi-conceptualist line initiated by the Muʿtazilī Abū Hāshim; (3) the importance attributed to rational methods, and the use of "reasoning by three terms" in the Aristotelian way: *e.g.*, the proof of the existence of God, which is nevertheless *a novitate* (rather than *a contingentia*) *mundi*. The Aristotelian syllogisms moreover remain affected by the inference "from two terms" (*istidlāl*), cf. Gardet-Anawati, *Intr. à la théol. musulmane*, 360-1.—The solutions to the principal problems are for the most part faithful to the Ashʿarī tradition. Methodological trends proper to al-Djuwaynī exist, but they show themselves mainly in the presentation of the problems, the conduct of the discussions, and the importance accorded to the channels (*asbāb*) by which conclusions are reached. In *kalām* as in *fiḳh*, it was above all the question of the *uṣūl* that interested the Imām al-Ḥaramayn.

Bibliography: in addition to the references in the article: Ibn Khallikān, Cairo no. 351; Subkī, *Ṭabaḳāt*, ii, 7071; iii, 249-82; Ibn al-Athīr, (ed. Tornberg), x, 77 (ann. 485); Ibn Taghribirdī, 771; Wüstenfeld, *Die Akademien der Araber*, no. 38; idem, *Shāfiʿiten*, no. 365; Schreiner, in *Grätz' Monatsschrift*, xxv, 314 ff.; Brockelmann, I, 388.

(C. Brockelmann-[L. Gardet])

DJUWAYNĪ, ʿAlāʾ al-Dīn ʿAṭā-Malik b. Muḥammad (623/1226-681/1283), a Persian governor and historian, author of the *Taʾrīkh-i djahān-gushāy*, a work which is almost our only source on the details of his life. His family belonged to Āzādwār, then the chief town of Djuwayn ([*q.v.*], No. 2). According to Ibn al-Ṭiḳṭaḳā (*al-Fakhrī*, ed. Ahlwardt, 209) they claimed descent from Faḍl b. Rabīʿ, the vizier of Hārūn al-Rashīd. ʿAlāʾ al-Dīn's great-grandfather, Bahāʾ al-Dīn Muḥammad b. ʿAlī, had waited on the Khwārazm-Shāh Tekish [*q.v.*] when in 588/1192 he passed through Āzādwār on his way to attack Toghril II [*q.v.*], the last Saldjuḳ ruler of ʿIrāḳ-i ʿAdjam. His grandfather, Shams al-Dīn Muḥammad b. Muḥammad, was in the service of Sultan Muḥammad Khwārazm-Shāh [*q.v.*], whom he accompanied on his flight from Balkh to Nīshāpūr. At the end of his life the Sulṭān appointed him *Ṣāḥib Dīwān*, a post which he continued to hold under Sultan Djalāl al-Dīn: he died during the latter's siege of Akhlāṭ, *i.e.*, at some time between Shawwāl 626/August 1229 and Djumādā I 627/April 1230. His son, Bahāʾ al-Dīn, ʿAlāʾ al-Dīn's father, is first heard of *ca.* 630/1232-3 in Nīshāpūr. Two of Djalāl al-Dīn's officers, Yaghan-Sonḳur and Ḳarača, had been active in this area, and Čīn-Temür, the Mongol governor of Khurāsān and Māzandarān, sent an army to dislodge them. Upon the approach of the Mongol forces Bahāʾ al-Dīn together with some of the chief notables of the town fled to Ṭūs, where they sought refuge in a castle amidst the ruins of the city. The governor of the castle handed them over to the Mongols, by whom, however, they were kindly received: Bahāʾ al-Dīn was admitted into the conquerors' service and held the office of *Ṣāḥib Dīwān* not only under Čīn-Temür but under his successors Körgüz and Arghun Aḳa. In 633/1235-6 he accompanied Körgüz upon a mission to the Great Khan Ögedey, from whom he received a *payza* or "tablet of authority" and a *yarlīgh* or rescript confirming his appointment as *Ṣāḥib Dīwān*. On several occasions he was left in absolute control of the occupied territories in Western Asia while the governor was absent in Mongolia. In 651/1253, being then in his 60th year, it was his wish to retire from the public service, but to this the Mongols would not agree, and he died during the same year in the Iṣfahān region, whither he had been sent to carry out fiscal reforms.

ʿAlāʾ al-Dīn tells of himself that while still a youth he chose, against his father's wishes, to take a position in the *dīwān*. He twice visited Mongolia in the suite of Arghun Aḳa, first in 647-9/1249-51 and then in 649-51/1251-3: upon the arrival of Hülegü in Khurāsān early in 654/1256, he was attached to his service and accompanied him on his campaigns against the Ismāʿīlīs of Alamūt and the Baghdād Caliphate. It was ʿAlāʾ al-Dīn who drew up the terms of surrender of the last Ismāʿīlī Grand Master Rukn al-Dīn Khur-Shāh, and it was through his initiative that the famous library of Alamūt was saved from destruction. In 657/1259, a year after the capture of Baghdād, he was appointed governor of ʿIrāḳ-i ʿArab and Khūzistān, a post which he continued to hold for more than 20 years, though under Abaḳa, Hülegü's son and successor, he was nominally subordinate to the Mongol Sughunčaḳ. During his tenure of office he did much to improve the lot of the peasantry and it was said, with some exaggeration, that he restored these provinces to greater prosperity than they had enjoyed under the Caliphate: at the expense of 10,000 dīnārs of gold he caused a canal to be dug from Anbār on the Euphrates to Kūfa and Nadjaf and founded 150 villages along its banks.

During the reign of Abaḳa both ʿAlāʾ al-Dīn and his brother Shams al-Dīn [see below] the *Ṣāḥib Dīwān* were much exposed to hostile attacks, of which the consequences were more serious for the former than the latter. In the late autumn of 680/1281 he was arrested, at the instigation of a personal enemy, on the charge of embezzling from the Treasury the enormous sum of 2,500,000 dīnārs. On 4 Ramaḍān 680/17 December 1281, thanks to the intervention of certain members of the Il-Khān's family, he was released from custody, only to be almost immediately re-arrested on a charge of maintaining a correspondence with the Mamlūk rulers of Egypt. His arrival in Hamadān to answer this charge coincided with the Il-Khān's death and he was retained in custody until the election of Abaḳa's successor Tegüder or Aḥmad (1282-4), a convert to Islam, who at once gave orders for ʿAlāʾ al-Dīn's release and reinstatement as governor. He did not long survive his rehabilitation. Tegüder's nephew, the future Il-Khān Arghun (1284-91), arrived in Baghdād in the winter of 681/1282-3 and reviving the old charge of embezzlement began to arrest the governor's agents and put them to the torture. News of these proceedings reaching ʿAlāʾ al-Dīn in Arrān, where he then was, he had an apoplectic stroke and died on 4 Dhu 'l-Ḥidjdja 681/5 March 1283.

ʿAlāʾ al-Dīn's references to the defects in his literary education must certainly be put down to conventional modesty; he is praised by his contemporaries as a highly cultured man and a patron of poets and scholars; and his history was held up as an unrivalled model of style. The work is divided into three main sections: I. History of the Mongols and their conquests down to the events following the death of the Great Khan Güyük, including the history of the descendants of Djoči and Čaghatay; II. History of the dynasty of the Khwārazm-Shāhs, based in part on previous works such as the *Mashārib al-tadjārib* of Abu 'l-Ḥasan Bayhaḳī and the *Djawāmiʿ al-ʿulūm* of Fakhr al-Dīn al-Rāzī, and a history of the Mongol governors of Khurāsān down to the year 656/1258; III. Continuation of the history of the Mongols to the overthrow of the Ismāʿīlīs, with an account of the sect, based chiefly on works found in Alamūt such as the *Sargudhasht-i Sayyidnā*; other works now lost are also quoted such as the *Taʾrīkh-i Djīl wa Daylam* and the *Taʾrīkh-i Sallāmī* (written for the Būyid Fakhr al-Dawla). The *Taʾrīkh-i djahān-gushāy*, which has considerably influenced historical tradition in the East, is for us also a historical authority of the first rank. The author was the only Persian historian to travel to Mongolia and describe the countries of Eastern Asia at first hand; it is to his work and the *Journal* of William of Rubruck that we owe practically all we know of the buildings in the Mongol capital of Ḳara-Ḳorum. The accounts of Čingiz-Khān's conquests are given nowhere else in such detail; many episodes, such as the battles on the Sîr-Daryā above and below Otrar and the celebrated siege of Khudjand are known to us only from the *Taʾrīkh-i djahān-gushāy*. Unfortunately Djuwaynī gives us in these cases not the first-hand impressions of a contemporary, but the opinions of the next generation, so that the details of his narrative, particularly the statements on the numbers of the combatants and the slain have to be taken with great caution; *cf.* for example, the fact, pointed out long ago by d'Ohsson (i, 232 ff.), that the citadel of Bukhārā according to Djuwaynī was defended by 30,000 men, all of whom were slain upon its capture, while Ibn al-Athīr (xii, 239), on the authority of an eye-witness, says the garrison consisted only of 400 horse. Again we find in Djuwaynī two versions of the struggle between the Ḳara-Khitay and Muḥammad Khʷārazm-Shāh, based apparently on different sources (written or oral). It was only by later compilers like Mīrkhʷānd that these contradictory accounts were woven into a uniform narrative, not, of course, in accordance with the standards of modern criticism; European scholars, to whom such compilations were much more accessible than the original authorities, have been frequently led astray by them.

Djuwaynī began work on his history during his residence in Mongolia in 650/1252-3; he was still working on it in 658/1260, for he refers to the state of Mā warāʾ al-Nahr in 658/1259-60 (Ḳazwīnī's text, i, 75, tr. Boyle, i, 96) and also to a Georgian rising that took place in the autumn of that year (text, ii, 261; tr., ii, 525); but there are no references to subsequent events, nor indeed to the operations against the Caliphate 655-6/1257-8), and there are many indications that the history was left in a state of incompletion.

Towards the end of his life he composed in Persian (not in Arabic as stated by Quatremère and repeated by Barthold in *EI*[1]) two treatises describing the misfortunes which had befallen him under Abaḳa, the first named *Tasliyat al-ikhwān* and the second bearing no special title: extracts from these short works have been published in the Persian introduction to Ḳazwīnī's edition of the *Taʾrīkh-i djahān-gushāy*.

Bibliography: The text of Djuwaynī's history is available in the edition of Mīrzā Muḥammad Ḳazwīnī: *The Taʾrikh-i-jahán-gushá* of *ʿAláʾu ʾd-Din ʿAtá-Malik-i-Juwayni*, 3 vols., (*GMS*, Old Series, xvi/1, 2, 3), London 1912, 1916 and 1937; and in the translation of J. A. Boyle, *The history of the world-conqueror*, 2 vols., Manchester 1958. On Djuwaynī as a stylist see Bahār, *Sabk-Shināsī* iii, 51-100. (W. Barthold-[J. A. Boyle])

DJUWAYNĪ, Shams al-Dīn Muḥammad b. Muḥammad, Persian statesman known as "*Ṣāḥib Dīwān*", brother of the historian ʿAlāʾ al-Dīn Djuwaynī (difference in their respective ages unknown), was made Chief Minister in 661/1262-3 by the Ilkhān Hülegü [*q.v.*], according to Rashīd al-Dīn, ed. Quatremère, i, 302 ff., 402. Nothing is known about his youth, and his brother does not mention him in his historical work. He became *Ṣāḥib* (-*i*) *Dīwān* (approximately equivalent to Finance Minister), and also held this post under Abaḳa (664-81/1265-82); with the help of devoted officials he extended his influence throughout the whole state of the Ilkhāns. His reputation grew steadily, especially among his fellow-Muslims, whom he protected from many a despotic act on the part of their heathen overlords. His fortune grew simultaneously, especially with regard to landed property, from which, it is reckoned, he finally had a daily income of one *tūmān* (Waṣṣāf, ed. Bombay, i, 56; although Rashīd al-Dīn speaks of only one-tenth of this sum). Thus in 676/1277 Djuwaynī emerged as the fitting personality to strengthen the weakened position of the Mongols in Anatolia. He also succeeded in establishing himself with the Ḳaraman Oghullarî, installing his son Sharaf al-Dīn Hārūn as governor there (transferred to Baghdād 682/1283 and put to death there 685/1286), and then returned home to Īrān. In the meantime one of his opponents, Madjd al-Mulk Yazdī, had come to the fore and was created State Controller (*Mushrif al-mamālik*); all decrees had to bear his signature alongside Djuwaynī's (Waṣṣāf, ed. Bombay, i, 95). From now on Abaḳa withdrew his favour more and more from Djuwaynī; it has been supposed (Köprülü in *IA*) that the contrast between the anti-Islamic ruler with his policy of western alliance and the strictly Muslim Djuwaynī may have contributed to this. In this difficult situation Djuwaynī also met with a stroke of fate in the death of his (eldest?) son, the admittedly very harsh governor of Iṣfahān, Bahāʾ al-Dīn Muḥammad, in Shaʿbān 678/December 1279 (cf. Waṣṣāf, i, 60-6). Only Abaḳa's death (Muḥarram 681/April 1282) gave Djuwaynī the chance of ridding himself of Yazdī (put to death Djumādā I 681/August 1282). Djuwaynī was once again the sole leading minister and stood in high favour with the new Ilkhān Aḥmad, who was the first Muslim in this position—the more so since he had helped him towards a temporary victory over the pretender to the throne, Arghun, son of Abaḳa. He made use of this time to bring about an agreement with Egypt (682/1283), and thus to terminate for the time being the struggles which, hitherto, had been religious in nature. When Arghun finally succeeded in establishing himself (683/1284) Djuwaynī at first attempted to flee to India, but later decided to ask the new Ilkhān for pardon. He offered a ransom for himself and his family but, as he was able to raise only 400,000 *dirham* out of the 2000 *tūmān* demanded, he was cruelly put to death on 4 Shaʿbān 683/16 October 1284 near the village of Ah(a)r between Ḳazwīn and Zandjān. Several of his sons also met with the same fate, although information about this is self-contradictory in detail.

Like his brother, Djuwaynī patronized theology, science and art to the best of his ability, and gave a large proportion of his income to this end (Ḥamd Allāh Mustawfī, *Taʾrīkh-i guzīda*, i, 584). A number of learned men such as Naṣīr al-Dīn Ṭūsī [*q.v.*], and theologians have dedicated their works to him or to one of his sons, and poets have composed *ḳaṣīdas* to him (*e.g.*, Saʿdī, Ṣaḥibiyya). Djuwaynī himself wrote Arabic and Persian poetry with great command of language which (with reservations about Arabic: Waṣṣāf, i, 58) was also recognized by his contemporaries (several published in the Tehrān periodical *Armaghān*, v, 284 ff.; xiii, 379 ff.). Besides these some of his writings from government offices have been preserved in collections (*munshaʾāt*).

Bibliography: M. Fuat Köprülü in *İA*, iii, 255-9; Spuler, *Mongolen*², Berlin 1955, index (here references to the original sources are also to be found). (B. Spuler)

DJUZʾ, pl. adjzāʾ, (i) a "foot" in prosody [see ʿarūḍ]. (ii) a division of the Ḳurʾān for purposes of recitation [see ḳurʾān].

DJUZʾ (pl. *adjzāʾ*), part, particle, term used in the technical language of *kalām* and of *falsafa* to describe the (philosophical) atom in the sense of the ultimate (substantial) part, that cannot be divided further, *al-djuzʾ alladhī lā yatadjazzaʾ* (cf. al-Djurdjānī, *Taʿrīfāt*, ed. Flügel, Leipzig 1845, 78); *al-djuzʾ al-wāḥid* is sometimes used. Synonym: "elementary and indivisible matter": *djawhar fard*; *al-djawhar al-wāḥid alladhī lā yanḳasim*.—For other definitions of vocabulary see DHARRA.

Atomistic conceptions of the world (philosophical atomism) existed very early in Islam, sometimes along heterodox lines, sometimes fully accepted by official teaching. Thus we have the atomism of Muḥammad b. Zakariyyā al-Rāzī [*q.v.*], and of numerous trends from the *ʿilm al-kalām*. One of the first elaborations, as Horten has shown, was that of the Muʿtazilī Abu 'l-Hudhayl (contested by al-Naẓẓām and the Ismāʿīlī Abū Ḥātim al-Rāzī).—Al-Bāḳillāni and his school inherited this atomism, modified it along Ashʿarī principles, formed from it a strict occasionalism, and organized it into a natural philosophy which has become famous. Many Ashʿarīs were faithful to it, in a rigid form in various manuals and later commentaries (al-Laḳānī, al-Sanūsī of Tlemcen, al-Bādjūrī, etc.)—sometimes in a mitigated form, *e.g.*, al-Īdjī and his commentator al-Djurdjānī (there is a similar tendency in the Māturīdī al-Nasafī, and in al-Taftāzānī). It may be said on the other hand that the atomism of the old *kalām*, hardly mentioned and made much more flexible by al-Ghazālī, was practically abandoned by Fakhr al-Dīn al-Rāzī, whilst al-Shahrastānī attempted an intermediate solution (see below). It would therefore be inaccurate to join together, as has sometimes happened, occasionalist atomism and Ashʿarī solutions.

This atomism of the *kalām* certainly derives from Greek sources, Democritus and Epicurus, but transforming them; and still more perhaps from Indian sources (see S. Pines, *Beiträge zur islamischen Atomenlehre*, Berlin 1936, 102-23). It was known to Maimonides, explained and refuted in the "Guide to the Perplexed", but in a somewhat more rigid form. Thomas Aquinas made a similar refutation in the *Summa contra Gentiles*, and made it familiar to the Latin Middle Ages. A detailed statement of the atomist theses of Abu 'l-Hudhayl, and especially the Ashʿarī theses, would take a long time and belongs rather to the history of *kalām* [*q.v.*]. There is a suggestive summary in L. Massignon, *Passion d'al-Ḥallādj*, Paris 1922, 550-3. In brief: only the atom is substance, and material substance, tangible or tenuous; all the rest is of the order of "accidental" (*ʿaraḍ*); no accidental lasts longer than an instant (*ān, waḳt*); no accidental can be superadded to another, it can only reside in the substance-atom and cannot pass from one subject to another; each accidental is thus created directly by God; in consequence, all transitive action between two bodies is impossible; therefore, there can be no effective secondary causes (*asbāb*). We can see the link between atomism and the Ashʿarī negation of secondary causes.

To conclude, here is an enumeration that al-Djurdjānī gives, following al-Īdjī, in the chapter where he treats of the nature of simple bodies (*Sharḥ al-Mawāḳif*, Cairo ed. 1325/1907, vii, 5 ff.). He notes five possible theories, and centres them all on atoms, *al-adjzaʾ*: (1) atoms exist *in esse* (*bi 'l-fiʿl*), are determined and indivisible: these are atoms in al-Bāḳillānī's sense; (2) al-Naẓẓām's thesis (corrected by S. Pines, id., v. Index): atoms exist *in esse* but are not determined—a thesis that al-Djurdjānī compares to Galen and Xenocrates (?); (3) contrary thesis of al-Shahrastānī (this time closer to Plato (?): atoms are determined, which rules out hylomorphism, but they only exist *in posse* (*bi 'l-ḳuwwa*); (4) thesis of the *falāsifa*: atoms are not determined and exist only *in posse*, extent is absolutely continuous,—hylomorphism is thus the principle of explanation; (5) to these four theses collected by al-Īdjī, al-Djurdjānī adds a fifth which he attributes to Democritus; the simple body is composed of "little bodies" which cannot be divided in fact, but can in spirit, by hypothesis. From an historical point of view, need it be said, this summary requires revision. It is nevertheless an indication of the efforts of al-Īdjī and al-Djurdjani to give an account of all the theories—including the hylomorphism of the *falsafa*—in terms of atoms.

Bibliography: in the article. The fundamental work remains that of S. Pines, where essential references to Arabic texts and works in European languages are given. See in particular the article by O. Pretzl, *Die frühislamische Atomenlehre*, in *Isl.*, 1931, 117-30. Also Gardet-Anawati, *Introduction à la théologie musulmane*, Paris 1948, see index I, "Atomisme". (L. GARDET)

DJŪZDJĀN, Persian GŪZGĀN, the older name of a district in Afghān Turkestan between Murghāb and the Āmū Daryā. Its boundaries were not well defined, particularly in the west, but it certainly included the country containing the modern towns of Maymana, Andkhūy, Shibargān and Sar-i Pul. Lying on the boundary between the outskirts of the Iranian highlands and the steppes of the north, Djūzdjān probably always supported nomad tribes as it does at the present day in addition to the permanent settlements in its fertile valleys (cf. Ibn Ḥawḳal, 322 ff.; Ḥādjdjī Khalīfa, *Djihān-numā*, ed. 1145 A.H., 316). The principal wealth of the land lay in its flocks (camels: Ibn Ḥawḳal, *loc. cit.*; Vámbéry, *Reise in Mittelasien*², 213; horses: Marquart, *Ērānšahr*, 138, 147; Vámbéry, 222; sheep: Vámbéry, 213; Yate, *Northern Afghanistan*, 344; cf. Iṣṭakhrī, 271; Ibn Ḥawḳal, 322). Although the way from the highlands of Īrān to Mā warāʾ al-Nahr lay through Djūzdjān, it was used not so much for friendly intercourse as as a military road for armies passing through it.

The district, which in the beginning of the 1st/7th century was attached to Ṭukhāristān (see Marquart, *op. cit.*, 67), was conquered on the occasion of the campaign of al-Aḥnaf b. Ḳays in 33/653-4 by his lieutenant al-Aḳraʿ. The marches suffered not only from the wars with the Turks but also from domestic differences within Islam. In the year 119/737 the Khāḳān was defeated by Asad b. ʿAbd Allāh al-Ḳasrī near the capital of Djūzdjān (Shubūrḳān). In 125/743 the ʿAlid Yaḥyā b. Zayd, whose tomb was revered long afterward (cf. Wellhausen, *Arab. Reich*, 311), fell in battle here against the Umayyads. During the ʿAbbāsid period the governor's residence was in Anbār (probably the Djūzdjānān of Nāṣir-i Khusraw, 2, possibly the modern Sar-i Pul); the native ruling house of Gūzgān-Khudhā, the Afrīghūn dynasty, continued however to survive, and had its capital in Kundurm (cf. Iṣṭakhrī, 270; Ibn Ḥawḳal, 321 ff.; Yaʿḳūbī, 287). Shubūrḳān occasionally appears as the political centre of Djūzdjān, while Muḳaddasī (297) and Yāḳūt (ii, 149 ff.) mention al-Yahūdiyya (= Maymana [*q.v.*]) as the capital. The ancient name Djūzdjān appears gradually to have fallen into disuse, to survive in literature only for some time longer. The various towns in it continue to be repeatedly mentioned as the scenes of hostile attacks; only the invasions of Čingiz Khān and Tīmūr can be mentioned here. Nothing shows the importance of the district more clearly than the fact that a number of towns have survived all these vicissitudes until the present day.

In modern times a number of petty Uzbeg Khānates (Akče, Andkhūy, Shibargān, Sar-i Pul, Maymana) have been established in the ancient Djūzdjān, but they were much harassed by raids of their more powerful neighbours such as the invasions of the Turkoman nomads. Since the time of Dūst Muḥammad these Khānates have gradually been incorporated in Afghān Turkestān; Maymana alone retains a vestige of independence under Afghān suzerainty.

Bibliography: Marquart, *Ērānšahr*, 78, 80 ff., 86 ff.; S. de Sacy in *Annales et voyages*, xx (1813), 172 ff.; Le Strange, 423 ff.; Vambéry, *Reise in Mittelasien*², 211 ff.; C. E. Yate, *Northern Afghanistan*, 334-52. (R. Hartmann)

al-**DJŪZDJĀNĪ**, Abū ʿAmr (not ʿUmar as stated by Storey, i, 68) Minhādj al-Dīn ʿUthmān b. Sirādj al-Dīn Muḥammad al-Djūzdjānī, commonly known as Minhādj-i Sirādj, the premier historian of the Slave dynasty of India, was born at Fīrūzkūh [*q.v.*] in the royal palace in 589/1193, as, on his own showing, he was 18 years of age in 607/1210-1 when Malik Rukn al-Dīn Maḥmūd was slain at Fīrūzkūh. His father, Sirādj al-Dīn, a leading scholar and jurist of his day, and a courtier of Sultan Ghiyāth al-Dīn, ruler of Fīrūzkūh, was appointed *ḳāḍī* of the army stationed in India by the Ghūrī sultan Muʿizz al-Dīn Muḥammad b. Sām, also known as Shihāb al-Dīn, in c. 582/1186. He seems to have returned to Ghazna and was subsequently summoned from Fīrūzkūh to Bāmiyān by Bahāʾ al-Dīn Sām b. Shams al-Dīn Muḥammad who appointed him the *ḳāḍī* and *khaṭīb* of his kingdom. Being a state dignitary his father was held in great esteem by the members of the royal family. Minhādj al-Dīn consequently passed his childhood in the *harīm* of the princess Māh-i Mulk, a daughter of Ghiyāth al-Dīn Muḥammad b. Sām, sultan of Ghūr and Fīrūzkūh (558-99/1162-1202). In 622/1225 at the age of 33 he was sent as an envoy to the court of Malik Tādj al-Dīn Yināltigīn (incorrect form: Niyāltigīn, see V. Minorsky in *BSOS*, viii/1 (1935), 257), at Nīmrūz. He was sent on a similar mission again in the following year.

The same year, *i.e.*, 623-4/1226-7, he left for India, most probably at the invitation of Nāṣir al-Dīn Ḳabāča, ruler of Uč̣h, where he was appointed, in view of his erudition and vast learning, principal of the Madrasa-i Fīrūzī, one of the earliest educational institutions in India established by the Muslims. On the overthrow of Ḳabāča by the Slave sultan of Dihlī, Shams al-Dīn Iletmish, in 625/1228, Minhādj changed his loyalty and accompanied the conqueror to Dihlī, where he held, under him, high legal and judicial offices, including that of the Chief Justice of the realm. A great orator and an accomplished scholar, his discourses and lectures were attended even by the highest nobles and the grandees of the Sultanate. In 639/1241-2 he was made *ḳāḍī al-ḳuḍāt* by the Slave king Muʿizz al-Dīn Bahrām Shāh (reigned: 637-9/1239-41). Disturbed by the prevailing political instability and confusion at Dihlī, al-Djūzdjānī decided to try his luck at the court of Lakhnawtī, the stronghold of Muslim occupation in Bengal. However, he did not find conditions very congenial there, and after a stay of two years returned to Dihlī in 642/1244-5.

He was once more the recipient of royal favours and held the double appointment of the *ḳāḍī* of Gwāliyar and the principal of the Madrasa-i Nāṣiriyya, a college named after the sultan Nāṣir al-Dīn Maḥmūd Shāh, son of Iletmish, who reigned from 644-64/1246-65.

The same Sultan, greatly impressed with his vast and varied knowledge of Islamic jurisprudence and the dispensation of justice, appointed him once again the Chief Judge of the realm. He, however, fell a prey to the machinations of a court clique, headed by ʿImād al-Dīn Rīhān, Wakīl-i Dar, who compassed his ruin, and he fell from grace in 651/1253, after having been in office for two years only. He was reinstated in 652/1254 and soon afterwards the title of *Ṣadr-i Djahān* was conferred on him. The next year he was re-appointed Chief Judge of the realm, through the good offices of his patron Ulugh Khān-i Aʿẓam, the powerful minister of Sultan Nāṣir al-Dīn. He was alive uutil at least 658/1259-60 when he completed *ṭabaḳa* 22 of his work. He seems to have died some time during the reign of Sultan Ghiyāth al-Dīn Balban (664/1265-686/1287), full of years and honours, and was, in all probability, buried at Dihlī.

His fame chiefly rests on his *magnum opus*, the *Ṭabaḳāt-i Nāṣiri*, written mainly during the years 657-8/1259-60, after his retirement from active life, and dedicated to Sultan Nāṣir al-Dīn Maḥmūd. It is the main source of information for the early Sultanate period, the author having utilized some of the works which are now no more extant. Among its notable omissions is the total lack of mention of the embassy of Raḍī al-Dīn Ḥasan b. Muḥammad al-Ṣāghānī [*q.v.*], who was sent by the ʿAbbāsid Caliph al-Nāṣir li-Dīn Allāh as a special envoy to the court of Iletmish in 616/1219-20 (see *TA* under the root *K.N.DJ* and the Urdū monthly *Maʿārif*, Aʿẓamgaṙh, June 1959). A Ṣūfī and a poet given to *wadjd* and *samāʿ*, he has been mentioned by ʿAbd al-Ḥaḳḳ Muḥaddith in his *Akhbār al-akhyār* (see Bibliography), where one *rubāʿī* of Minhādj has been quoted. Some other *tadhkiras* of Indian Persian poets (see Ḥabībī in the Bibl.) also mention him, but his poetry and other achievements have been overshadowed by his historical talents.

Bibliography: H. G. Raverty, Eng. trans. of *Ṭabaḳāt-i Nāṣiri*, London 1881, ii, xix-xxxi (mainly gleaned from the *Ṭabaḳāt* itself); *Ṭabaqāt-e-Nāṣīri* (ed. Āqā-ye ʿAbd-ul-Ḥayy Ḥabībī Afghānī), Lahore 1954, ii, 724-72 (mostly based on the *Ṭabaḳāt*, but contains numerous other references); ʿAbd al-Ḥaḳḳ Muḥaddith al-Dihlawī, *Akhbār al-akhyār*, Meerut 1278/1861, 80; H. G. Raverty in *JASB*, li, 1882, 76; Rieu, i, 72; *Catalogue of Persian MSS. in the Bankipur Library*, vi, 451; Elliot and Dowson, *History of India as told by its own Historians*, ii, 259 ff.; ʿAbbās Iḳbāl, *Taʾrīkh-i istīlāʾ-yi Mughūl*, Tehran, 483; Ḥakīm ʿAbd al-Ḥayy Lakhnawī, *Nuzhat al-khawāṭir*, Ḥaydarābād 1366/1947, i, 174-8; *Aligarh Magazine* (in Urdū) vol. xiii/1 (Jan. 1934), article by Zakariyya Fayyāḍī; ʿAbd al-Ḥaḳḳ Muḥaddith, *Tadhkira-i muṣannifīn-i Dihlī*, 7; Storey, i, 68-70; there are also casual references in *Fawāʾid al- fuʾād* by Amir Hasan Sidjzī; Barthold, *Turkestan*², 38 and index. (A. S. Bazmee Ansari)

DOʾĀB, (Pers.) 'two-waters', corresponding to the Greek μεσοποταμία, is in the Indo-Pākistān sub-continent generally applied to the land lying between two confluent rivers, and more particularly to the fertile plain between the Djamnā and the Ganges in Uttar Pradesh. The long tongues of land between the five rivers of the Pandjāb are also known as *doʾābs*. Between the Satladj and the

Beʾās lies the Bist *doʾāb*; between the Beʾās and the Rāwī, the Bārī *doʾāb*; between the Rāwī and the Čenāb, the Rečnā *doʾāb*; between the Čenāb and the Djhelam, the Čadj or Dječ *doʾāb*; and between the Djhelam and the Indus, the Sind Sāgar *doʾāb*. The names for these *doʾāb*s are said to have been invented by the emperor Akbar (*Āʾīn-i Akbarī*, trs. H. S. Jarrett, ii, 311 ff.). The most famous *doʾāb* in Southern India is the Rāyčūr *doʾāb* between the Kistna (Krishna) and the Tungabhadra rivers which formed a fluctuating frontier between the Hindū kingdom of Vidjayanagara and the Muslim states of the Deccan. (C. COLLIN DAVIES)

DŌʿĀN [see DAWʿĀN].

DOBRUDJA, the plateau between the Danube and the Lom river in the North, the Black Sea in the East and the Prowadijska river or the Balkan range in the South. Deli Orman in this area is distinguished from the steppe region, Dobrudja-Kîrî, in the East which is considered as the Dobrudja proper. Called Scythia Minor in the Graeco-Roman period, it was included in the Byzantine province of Paristrion (Bardjān in Idrīsī's world map) in 361/972. In Bulgarian Karvunska Chora, it was 'the land of Karbona' in the mediaeval Italian maps. Its modern name came from Dobrudja-eli (as Aydîn from Aydîn-eli) which in Turkish meant the land of Dobrudja, Dobrotič (as Karlofdja from Karlowitz) (cf. *Susmanos-eli* in Neshrī, *Ğihānnümā*, ed. Fr. Taeschner, Leipzig 1951, 66). Yanko or Ivanko, son of Dobrotič, was mentioned as Dobrudja-oghlu in Neshrī (66, 68).

From the early 5th century A.D. until the 13th/19th century Dobrudja became, primarily for the peoples of Turkic origin coming from the Eurasian steppes, a natural route leading to the invasion of the Balkans or a refuge for those pushed by their rivals beyond the Danube. Thus in the footsteps of the Huns (408 A.D.) came Avars (in 534 and especially in 587 A.D.), Bulghars (especially in 59/679) with their capital in Preslav, southern Dobrudja, Pečeneks (440/1048), Uz (456/1064) and Ḳîpčaḳs (Cumans) (484/1091). Among those the Ḳîpčaḳs appeared to play politically and ethnically the most important part in the history of Dobrudja until the advent of the Ottoman Turks. T. Kowalski finds (*Les Turcs et la langue turque de la Bulgarie du Nord-Est*, in *Ac. Pol. Mém. de la commission orientaliste*, xvi, Cracow 1933, 28) linguistic remains of these early Turkish invasions from the North in the Gagauz Turkish (cf. GAGAUZ). The name Deli Orman comes from the Cuman Teli Orman (cf. G. Moravcsik, *Byzantinoturcica*, ii, Berlin 1958, 305-6). The Cumans in the Balkans were mostly Christianized, and, mingled with the native Wallachs and Slavs, they continued to play the rôle of a ruling military class among them (cf. L. Rásonyi-Nagy, *Valacho-turcica*, Berlin-Leipzig 1927, 68-96; P. Nikov, *The Second Bulgarian Kingdom*, Sofia 1937, in Bulgarian). Furthermore the Mongol invasion of the Dasht-i Ḳîpčaḳ in 620/1223 and the foundation of the Khānate of the Golden Horde in 635/1238 caused large groups of Cumans to flee to the West (cf. B. Spuler, *Die Goldene Horde*, Leipzig 1945, 19-20). As to the bulk of the Ḳîpçaḳs who remained in the Dasht under Mongol rule, they mostly adopted Islam and were to play a significant part under the name of Tatar in Dobrudja's history in the following periods. With their support Noghay [*q.v.*] established his overlordship on the Bulgarian kingdom by 681/1282, where the king and many of his boyars were of Cuman origin. The lower Danube with Sakdjî (Isaccea) was reported in the Arabic sources (Baybars, *Zubdat al-fikra*, in W. de Tiesenhausen, *Altin-ordu devleti tarihine ait metinler*, Turkish trans. I. H. Izmirli, Istanbul 1941, 221; Nuwayrī, *ibid.*, 282) as one of the headquarters of Noghay. He was, Z. V. Togan thinks (*Umumî Türk tarihine giriş*, Istanbul 1946, 256, 325), acting against the Byzantines under the influence of the *ghazā* preachings of Ṣaru Ṣaltuḳ, who was active in Sakdjî and the Crimea during this period. After the suppression of Noghay by Tokhtu, Khān of the Golden Horde (autumn 698/1299), Tukal Bogha, his son, was placed in the lower Danube and Sakdjî and Noghay's son Čeke came into Bulgaria to seize the throne for a short time (cf. Baybars and Nuwayrī, *ibid.*).

As for the Anatolian Turks who were said to come with Ṣaru Ṣaltuḳ in Dobrudja in this period, we are now in a position to assert after P. Wittek's comparative study of the original Turkish account of Yazîdjîoghlu ʿAlī with the Byzantine sources (*Yazîjîoghlu ʿAli on the Christian Turks of Dobruja*, in *BSOAS*, xiv (1952), 639-68) that these came actually to settle in Dobrudja after 662/1263-4 with Sultan ʿIzz al-Dīn Kaykāūs who was then a refugee in Byzantium. Michael VIII Palaeologus gave permission to Kaykāūs's followers in Anatolia to come to settle in Dobrudja, then a no-man's-land between the Golden Horde, Bulgaria and the Byzantine empire (the arguments of P. Mutafčiev, *Die angebliche Einwanderung von Seldschuk-Türken in die Dobrudscha im XIII. Jahrh.*, in *Bulg. Acad. Sci. Lett.*, lxvi/1, 2, are not valid after Wittek's study; cf. also H. von Duda, *Zeitgenössische islamische Quellen und das Oguznāme des Jazygyoglu ʿAli...*, *ibid.* 131-45; see also Adnan S. Erzi, in *İA*, v/2, 716). These Muslim Turks from Anatolia, mostly nomads, formed there "two or three towns and 30-40 *oba*, clans" (Yazîdjîoghlu in Wittek, 648; von Duda, 144). Abu 'l-Fidāʾ's note about the majority of the population of 'Ṣakdjī' being Muslims (*Géographie*, ed. Reinaud and de Slane, Paris 1840, 34) apparently referred to them rather than the Tatars settled under Noghay. With his headquarters in Sakdjî Noghay, then converted to Islam, must have become after Berke Khān's death (665/1267, cf. Spuler, 51) the protector of the Anatolian Turks in Dobrudja (cf. Z. V. Togan, *ibid.*). It is interesting to note that the emigration of them back to Anatolia about 706/1307 followed the death of Noghay and the arrival of Tukal Bogha, apparently a pagan like his father Tokhtu Khān. In 699/1300 Noghay's son Čeke too was killed by Svetoslav in Bulgaria. Yazîdjîoghlu noted (Wittek, 651) that these Turks decided to emigrate because the Bulgarian princes had risen up and occupied the larger part of Rumeli. Those who remained, he added, became Christians. These people of Kaykāūs were, as Wittek demonstrated after Balasčev, named *Ghaghauz* after their lord Kaykāūs (cf. Wittek, *ibid.*, 668). But in 732/1332 Baba Ṣaltuḳ (later Baba-dagh) was, Ibn Baṭṭūṭa reported (*Voyages*, ii, 416; English trans. Gibb, ii, Cambridge 1959, 499), an important town possessed by the 'Turks'.

By 766/1365 an independent despotate under a Christianized Turkish family rose in the part of Dobrudja where the Gagauz always lived (in the Ottoman *defter* of 1006/1598, Tapu Kadastro Um. Md, Ankara, no. 399, some Christians in the area still bore Turkish names such as Arslan, Ḳaragöz). Balîk (758/1357) (also Balica; the name is a Cuman name, cf. Rásonyi, *ibid.*; Iorga identified it with Rumanian Baliţa: *Notes d'un historien*, in *Acad.*

Roum. Bull. Sec. His. ii-iv (1913), 97. Čolpan, an important man under the son of Dobrotič, bore an Anatolian Turkish name) and especially his energetic brother Dobrotič (the name is undoubtedly of Slav origin) founded in the area from the delta of the Danube down to the Emine promontory south of Varna a despotate independent of Byzantium and Bulgaria. Its capital was at Kalliakra by 767/1366 (Iorga, *Dobrotisch*, in *Ac. Roum. Bull. de la Sec. His.* ii-iv, 1914, 295) and Varna by 790/1388 (Neshrī, 68). Apparently he profited from the Ottoman onslaught in Byzantine Thrace and Shishman's Bulgaria between 762-73/1361-71. From 763/1362 to 767/1366 his and the Ottomans' enemies were the same (cf. Iorga, *Dobrotisch*, 295). Allied with Venice, Dobrotič challenged the Genoese in the Black Sea. For Venice the wheat export of Dobrudja was then vitally important (cf. F. Thiriet, *Régestes des déliberations du Sénat de Venise concernant la Romanie*, i, 1958, documents nos. 545, 575, 576, 653, 671, 689). The land over which he ruled was named after him 'the Land of Dobrotič', *terra Dobroticii* (in 758/1357, *Acta Patr. Const.*, i, 367) or Dobrudja-eli in Turkish (Yazîdjîoghlu in Wittek, 649). His son Ivanko or rather Yanko (*Ioanchos*) was an Ottoman vassal by 790/1388 (Neshrī, 66, 68). It is most likely that Dobrotič too had accepted Ottoman suzerainty as had Shishman since 773/1371. Under Yanko Dobrudja experienced the first Ottoman conquest.

In the winter of 790/1388 Murād I hastily sent an army under ʿAlī Pasha against Shishman and Yanko who had refused to join as his vassals the Ottoman army against Serbia. ʿAlī passed the Balkan range through the pass of Nadir, captured Provadija (Pravadi), Shumla (Shumnu), Eski-Istanbulluk (ancient Preslav), Madera, and proceeded toward Trnovo (see BULGARIA). Then Yakhshi, son of Timurtash, was ordered to subdue the land of Dobrudja. According to a Turkish source (Neshrī, 66-70, reproduces an old and detailed account of this expedition. Rūḥī gives the same account with omissions. Fr. Babinger, *Beiträge zur Frühgeschichte der Türkenherrschaft in Rumelien*, München 1944, 30, confused the expeditions of 790/1388 and 795/1393) two men from Varna came and said that the notables of the city had decided to seize the Tekvur, son of Dobrudja, and surrender the fortress to the Pasha. But the fortress did not surrender when Yakhshi came (Neshrī, 68). The Ottomans, busy elsewhere, left Bulgaria to come back only in 795/1393. In the meantime Dobrudja and Silistre (Durostor) were occupied by Mirčea, a Wallachian prince. In his treaty with Poland in 791/1389 and in its renewal in 793/1391 he called himself 'the Lord of Silistre and Despot of the Land of Dobrotič' (*despotus terrarum Dobrodicii*) (N. Iorga, *Hist. des Roumains*, iii, Bucarest 1937, 339). The 'Turkish Towns' mentioned among his possessions (Iorga, *Dobrotisch*, 298) might be Sakdjî and other towns founded by the 'people of Kaykāūs'. From there Mirčea attacked the aḳîndjîs at the Ottoman *udj* of Karîn-ovasî (Karnobad) who were a constant threat to his new possessions (cf. A. Decei, *L'expédition de Mirčea I contre les akindji de Karinovasi*, in *Rev. des Ét. Roumaines*, Paris 1953, 130-51). It was this bold attack that made Bāyezīd I come to consolidate Ottoman rule in Bulgaria (see BĀYAZĪD I). Dobrudja and Silistre were taken under direct Ottoman rule during the operations in 795/1393. Then Dobrudja was made an important *udj* [*q.v.*] for aḳîndjîs, and preserved this character throughout its history, attracting warlike elements as well as dissidents and sectarians. Mirčea profited from the Ottoman disaster at Ankara in 805/1402 to take back Silistre and the northern Dobrudja (Iorga, *Hist. des Roumains*, iii, 385). Süleymān, Bāyezīd's successor in Rumeli, appears then to have recognized the fact. But soon the aḳîndjîs renewed their raids against Mirčea (Neshrī, 130; P. Ş. Nāstrul, *Une victoire de Voyvode Mirčea*, in *Studia et Acta Orientalia*, i, Bucarest 1958, 242). To free himself of them Mirčea invited and gave his support to Mūsā Čelebī, Süleymān's brother and rival (Neshrī, 130; P. P. Panaitescu, *Mirčea čel Bătran*, Bucarest 1943, 214). The aḳîndjîs joined Mūsā [*q.v.*] against Süleymān, and left Mirčea alone. In 819/1416 he supported Muṣṭafā, another pretender, and Shaykh Badr al-Dīn [*q.v.*] against Meḥemmed I [*q.v.*] in Dobrudja and Deli Orman. The *ṭovidjas*, aḳîndjî leaders, Ṣūfī dervishes who were in this *udj* area in great numbers joined them (cf. Ş. Yaltkaya, *Şeyh Bedreddin'e dair bir kitap*, in *TM*, iii, 251; Orudj, ed. Fr. Babinger, 45, 111). Though in their official titles Mirčea and Mihai, his successor, always mentioned 'the two sides of the Danube' among their possessions it was apparent that Dobrudja and Silistre were then actually in the hands of the akîndjîs, who in their antipathy toward Meḥemmed I must have continued their friendly relations with the Wallachian voyvodas. Mirčea's death (Dhu 'l-Ḥidjdja 820/ January 1418) and the ensuing confusion provided the Sultan with the opportunity to establish his control in Dobrudja in 822/1419. After he subdued his rivals in Anatolia, the Djāndārids and then the Ḳaramānids (see ḲARAMĀN OGHLU), Meḥemmed I organized a large-scale expedition against Wallachia in which both Anatolian principalities sent auxiliary forces. An Ottoman fleet participated in the operations. In the summer of 822/1419 he crossed the Danube, captured and fortified Yergögü (Giurgiu) and attempted to take Kilia while the raiders devastated the enemy's country. Mihai first took refuge in Argesh and then perished in an skirmish. Before his return the Sultan strengthened Sakdjî and Yeni-Sale against future attacks of the Wallachians. No mention is made of Silistre during this expedition. Dan I, the new Voyvoda, recognized Ottoman suzerainty, though the Emperor Sigismond had started southwards with the intention of invading the Dobrudja. He was delayed by the Ottoman action against Severin (autumn 822/1419). (Iorga, *GOR*, i, 375, and *Hist. des Roumains*, iii, 401-2, dates this expedition 820/1417. In this year Meḥemmed I was at war against the Ḳaramān oghlu in Anatolia, cf. Ibn Ḥadjar, text in Ş. Inalcık, *Ibn Hacer'de Osmanlılara dair haberler*, *AÜDTCF Dergisi*, vi/5, 525. Following Neshrī's confused chronology, Uzunçarşılı, *Osmanlı tarihi*, i, new ed. Ankara 1961, 356; and A. Decei, *IA*, iii, 635, adopted 819/1416 as the date of the expedition against Wallachia. For our dating see further O. Turan, *Tarihi takvimler*, Ankara 1954, 20, 56; Atsız, *Osmanlı tarihine ait takvimler*, Istanbul 1961, 20; Ibn Ḥadjar, *ibid.*, the years 821/1418 and 822/1419; and a letter of Meḥemmed I to the Mamlūk Sultan in Ferīdūn, *Munshaʾāt al-salāṭīn*, i, 164-5). The Wallachians under Dan attempted to take Silistre during the period of the renewed civil war in the Ottoman empire in 825/1422 (Iorga, *Hist. des Roumains*, iv, 20; Neshrī, 154; ʿĀshîkpashazāde, ed. ʿĀlī, 105). Against him Fīrūz (Feriz) Beg was appointed in this *udj* to organize counter-raids.

Firmly established in Dobrudja since Meḥemmed I's expedition in 822/1419, the Ottomans used it as a base to extend their control on the other side of the Danube. The imperial army under Meḥemmed II invaded Boghdan [*q.v.*] in 881/1476, passing through Dobrudja (see MEḤEMMED II), Bāyezīd II using the same route took Kilia and Aḳkermān in 889/1484. During this expedition he built the great mosque and the *zāwiya* of Ṣaru Ṣaltuḳ in Baba Ḳaṣabasî (Baba-dagh) and endowed them with all the tax revenues of the town and surrounding villages (for these endowments a *waḳf defteri* exists in the *Tapu ve Kadastro Um. Md.*, Ankara, no. 397). In his expedition against Boghdan in 945/1538 Süleymān I too showed the same interest in this pre-Ottoman Islamic centre (cf. Ferīdūn, i, 602-3).

According to the *defter*s (see DAFTAR-I KHĀḲĀNĪ) of the 10th/16th century (in the *Başvekâlet* Archives Istanbul, Tapu nos. 65, 542, 688, 304, 483, 732, and, in *Tapu ve Kadastro Um. Md.* Ankara, nos. 397, 398, 399) the sandjaḳ of Silistre and Aḳkermān comprised the *ḳaḍā*s of Aḳkermān, Djankermān, Kili, Bender, Ibrail, Silistre, Ḥîrsova, Tekfurgölü and the nāḥiyes of Varna, Pravadi, Yanbolu, Ahyolu, Rusi-Ḳaṣrî, Karin-ābād and Aydos. Balčık, Kavarna and Kaligra were included in the nāḥiye of Varna. The Ottomans applied in Dobrudja typical Ottoman laws and regulations with special provisions for such groups as *eshkündji*s, *müsellem*s, *Djebelü-Tatar*s, *Matrak-Tatarlarî*, *djānbāz* (cf. the *ḳānūnnāme*s in Ö. L. Barkan, *Kanunlar*, 272-89).

The following is a table drawn up according to the defters of 1006/1597 (*Tapu ve Kadastro Um. Md.*, Ankara, nos. 397, 398, 399).

Dasht-i Ḳîpčaḳ in autumn 797/1395. Their leader Aḳtaw was a general of Tokhtamîsh Khān (cf. Niẓām al-Dīn Shāmī, *Ẓafarnāma*, Turkish trans. N. Lugal, Ankara 1949, 194). Bāyezīd I took them into his own service with the same status as the *Yürük* [*q.v.*] (Ö. L. Barkan, in *Iktisad Fak. Mec.*, xv, 211-3). From Budjaḳ [*q.v.*] and the Crimea Tatar refugees continued to come into Dobrudja in later periods (especially in 918/1512 and 920/1514, cf. Müstecib H. Fazıl, *Dobruca ve Türkler*, Köstence 1940, 36). In 1007/1599 Baldasarius Waltheri reported that in the plain of Dobrudja lived 6000 Tatar families, Dobrudja Tatarlarî, who provided an auxiliary force to the Ottoman army under a Crimean prince (Müstecib H. Fazıl, *ibid.*, 37).

In the regions of Tekfur-gölü, Ḥîrsova, Silistre and Varna also lived the *Yürük* [*q.v.*] groups: those of *Ḳodjadjîk* 44 odjaḳ, each odjaḳ being regularly 30 men, *Nal-döken* 34 odjaḳ, *Tañrî-dagh* about 95 odjaḳ by 1009/1600 (cf. T. Gökbilgin, *ibid.*, 56, 70, 76, 212-30). Each odjaḳ furnished five fighters for the army.

Turkish Muslims made up, in the countryside too, the majority of the population. The study of personal names and village names (the above mentioned defters are *mufaṣṣal defter*s in which the names of the heads of the households are recorded) shows that an overwhelming majority of the villages were the new ones founded by the Turkish Muslim immigrants from Anatolia. We know that the Ottoman state made from the early conquest onwards forced settlements of Anatolian Turks in this important *udj* area (cf. Barkan, *Kanunlar*, 273, 274,

Town	Number of Muslim districts	Number of non-Muslim districts	Tax revenue
Silistre	16	8 1 Jewish 1 Gypsy	215,429
Isaḳdjî (Isaḳča, Saḳdjî)	1	6	187,995
Mačin	—	4	83,113
Baba (Baba-dagh)	16	2	107,350 (Waḳf)
Ḥîrsova	2	—	50,000
Tekfur-gölü	1	1 56 families of tuzdju	34,477
Balčîḳ	12	3	—
Ḳavarna	—	4	32,666
Pazardjîḳ	16	1	20,000
Kaligra (Kalliakra)	1 (dervishes in the zāwiya)	1	12,110

As separate small communities gypsies lived in all these towns. They were mostly Christians. Only in Silistre 21 Jewish families were recorded. Here is a table of the ports in Dobrudja with their revenues from the dues on fish, salt, mills and the customs dues:

Silistre: 566,666, Tulča, Isaḳdjî and Mačin together: 561, 675. Varna, Balčîk, Kaligra, Mangalya, Köstendje, Ḳara-Ḥarmanlîḳ, Ḳamčî-suyu, Galata, Baba-gölü and Yeni-Sale together: 281,004.

In 32 villages of the *ḳaḍā* of Ḥîrsova and in 9 villages of that of Tekfur-gölü lived *Tatarān-i Djebelüyān* (*Djebelü Tatarlar*) with the obligation to equip at their own expense 360 *djebelü*s for the army, and in return they were exempted from the *ʿawāriḍ* [*q.v.*] taxes. The Tatars of Aḳtaw who were settled around Tekfur-gölü, Pravadi, Varna, Yanbolu and Filibe (T. Gökbilgin, *Rumeli'de Yürükler, Tatarlar ve Evlâd-i Fâtihân*, Istanbul 1957, 26, 87, 88) had immigrated into Rumeli when Tīmūr invaded the

and *Iktisad Fak. Mec.*, xv, 227). A great number of the villages bore a personal name ending with the word *ḳuyu*, well (Aḳîndjî Ḳuyusu, Ḳara Bali Ḳuyusu, Avunduḳ Ḳuyusu etc.). A large number of them revealed a tribal origin with the word *djemāʿat* (for example Ḳarye-i Eyerdji Khayr al-Dīn Pînarî, djemāʿat-i Seyyid Khîzîr, Ḳarye-i Ḳartallu Muṣṭafā ʿan djemāʿat-i Ṣaliḥ Ṭovidja etc.). Apparently few villages with a mixed population of Muslims and Christians were pre-Ottoman. In the northern Dobrudja there existed large villages of exclusively Christian population (Mačin, Ḳara-Ḥarmanlîḳ, Esterbend etc.). Some names indicated their Romanian origin (Radul, Yanko, Mihne etc.). Most of the Christian villages enjoyed exemption from *ʿawāriḍ* taxes in return for their services to repair the bridges and roads, or for their work in the salt production.

The repopulation and prosperity of Dobrudja under the Ottomans were primarily due to the fact that they considered it as an important *udj* area, and the Anatolian immigrants were encouraged to engage in agriculture by the increasing demand for and easy transportation of the wheat production of Dobrudja for Istanbul. From Ḳara-Ḥarmanlîḳ, Köstendje, Mangalya, Balčîk and Kaligra a large quantity of wheat and fish was exported regularly to the Ottoman metropolis. At these ports the state had built special storehouses for wheat. Muslims paid two per cent and *dhimmīs* four per cent as customs due on their export. The ports of Silistre, Tulča, Isakdjî, Mačin, Ḥîrsova exported, in addition, Wallachian timber, salt, felt of Brashow and slaves for Istanbul and Rumeli (The *ḳānūnnāmes* of the ports of Dobrudja in the above-mentioned defters are not yet published; also see ʿOthmān Nūrī, *Medjelle-i Umūr-i Belediyye*, Istanbul 1338, 781, and *Tarih Vesikaları*, v, 333). The towns of Ḥadjîoghlu Pazardjîk, Mangalya and Baba with their weekly fairs were important trade centres for the whole region (cf. Ewliyā Čelebi, *Seyāḥatnāme*, iii, Istanbul 1314, 329-71).

From 983/1575 onwards Cossack attacks became a constant threat to Dobrudja. In 995/1587 they burned down Baba (Babadagh). In 1003/1595 Mihai, the rebellious Voyvoda of Wallachia, supported by the Cossacks, renewed Mirčea's attacks on the Ottoman cities and fortresses in Dobrudja and caused a mass emigration (cf. A. Decei, in *İA*, iii, 637). The continuing Cossack threat made the Ottoman government decide to create a new *eyālet* including the sandjaḳs of the Eastern Black Sea with Silistre and Özü as its capitals (cf. ʿAynī ʿAlī, *Ḳawānīn-i Āl-i ʿOthmān . . .*, Istanbul 1280, 13).

The Dobrudja was invaded by the Russian armies for the first time in 1185/1771. Babadagh, general headquarters of the Ottoman armies, fell in 1185/1771, and, when in 1188/1774 Ḥadjioghlu Pazardjîḳ, the new headquarters, also fell the Ottomans demanded a cease-fire. The Dobrudja became again a battlefield between the Ottoman and Russian armies in 1224/1809, 1244/1829 and 1271/1855. The Russian invasion of 1244/1829 proved especially ruinous for the Dobrudja, causing a mass emigration of the Turkish-Tatar population. Whole towns and villages were deserted. The population of the Dobrudja after this war was estimated at only 40,000 (Müstecib H. Fazıl, *op. cit.*, 75; E. Z. Karal, *Os. Imp. ilk nüfus sayımı*, Ankara 1943). Appreciating its strategical importance the Ottoman government took special measures to repopulate the Dobrudja by improving agriculture and bringing in settlers. In Muḥarram 1253/April 1837 Maḥmūd II (cf. H. Inalcık, *Tanzimat ve Bulgar Meselesi*, Ankara 1943, 27-8) and in spring 1262/1846 Sultan ʿAbd al-Medjīd (*Seyāḥatnāme-i Hümāyūn*, 11-5) visited the area. In 1266/1850 an expert was sent to explore the agricultural possibilities there (I. I. de la Brad, *Excursion agricole dans la plaine de la Dobroudja*, Const. 1850). At this date in the *ḳaḍās* of Tulča, Isaḳča, Mačin, Ḥîrsova, Babadagh, Köstendje, Mangalya, Pazardjîk, Balčîk and Silistre were 4800 Turkish, 3656 Romanian, 2225 Tatar, 2214 Bulgarian, 1092 Cossack, 747 Lipovani, 300 Greek, 212 Gypsy, 145 Arab, 126 Armenian, 119 Jewish and 59 German families. After the Crimean war in the period between 1270/1854 and 1283/1866 the Tatar immigrants from the Crimea who were settled in the Dobrudja were estimated at dabout 100,000 (F. Bianconi quoted in M. H. Fazıl, 90-1). When in 1281/1864 the *wilāyet* of Tuna was created the *sandjaḳs* or *liwās* of Tulča and Varna with a total population of 173,250 made a part of it. The former included the *ḳaḍās* of Balčîk, Pazardjîk, Pravadi, and Mangalya, the latter those of Baba, Ḥîrsova, Sünne, Köstendje, Mačin and Medjidiye (Karasu) (*Sālnāme*, 1294; cf. N. V. Michoff, *La population de la Turquie et de la Bulgarie au XVIIIe et au XIXe siècles*, i, Sofia 1929).

The Turco-Russian war of 1877-8 caused about 90,000 Turks and Tatars to emigrate from the Dobrudja to Turkey and Bulgaria and most of them never returned. By the treaty of Berlin signed on 13 July 1878 (Art. 46), the sandjaḳ of Tulča and the Southern Dobrudja from the east of Silistre to the south of Mangalya were annexed to Romania. The rest of the Dobrudja made the part of the Prin cipality of Bulgaria under Ottoman suzerainty (Art. 1-2). Under the Romanian administration emigrations of Muslim population into Turkey continued especially in 1300/1883 when these were subjected to compulsory military service and in 1317/1899 during the famine in the Dobrudja (M. H. Fazıl, 109-10). In 1328/1910 in the Romanian Dobrudja only thirty per cent of a population of 210,000 and in the Bulgarian Dobrudja forty per cent of a population of 257,000 were Muslim Turks and Tatars.

Bibliography: The *Başvekalet* Archives, Istanbul, *Tapu Defterleri*, nos. 304, 483, 732; *Tapu ve Kadastro Um. Md.*, Ankara, *Ḳuyūd-i Ḳadīme*, nos. 397, 398, 399; I. Bromberg, *Toponymical and historical miscellanies on mediaeval Dobrudja, Bessarabia and Moldo-Wallachia*, in *Byzantion*, xii, 151-207, 459-475; xiii, 9-72; N. Bănescu, *La question du Paristrion*, in *Byzantion*, viii (1933); P. Mutafčiev, *Dobrudja*, Sofia 1947 (in Bulgarian); *La Dobrudja*, ed. Acad. Roumaine, Bucarest 1938; Müstecib H. Fazıl (Ülküsal), *Dobruca ve Türkler*, Köstence 1940; C. Jireček, *Geschichte der Bulgaren*, Prague 1876; N. Iorga, *Hist. des Roumains*, i-x, Bucarest 1936-9; P. Wittek, *Yazîjîoghlu ʿAli on the Christian Turks of the Dobruja*, in *BSOAS*, xiv (1952), 639-68; A. I. Manof, *Gagauzlar*, Turkish trans. by T. Acaroğlu, Ankara 1940; N. Iorga, *La politique vénitienne dans les eaux de la mer noire*, in *Acad. Roumaine, Bull. sect. hist.*, ii-iv (1914), 289-307; idem, *Dobrotich, Dobrotič, Dobrotici*, in *Rev. hist. du Sud-Est Européen*, v (1928); *Documente privind Istoria Romîniei, A. Moldova*, i, Bucarest 1954 (the text of the treaty between Ivanco and the Genoese, 296-301); G. I. Brătianu, *Recherches sur Vicina et Cetătea Alba*, Bucarest 1935; Ewliyā Čelebi, *Seyāḥatnāme*, iii, Istanbul 1314 H., 335-75; *Analele Dobrogei*, publ. in Constanta since 1920; *İA*, art. Dobruca (Aurel Decei). See also BABADAGHÎ, DELI ORMAN, GAGAUZ, ṢARÎ ṢALTÎḲ (Ṣaru Ṣaltuḳ).

(HALIL INALCIK)

ḌOFĀR [see ẓAFĀR].

DOG [see KALB].

DÖGER, name of an Oghuz tribe (*boy*). They are mentioned in the *Oghuz-nāme* (the account of the life of the Oghuz people before they embraced Islam, see F. Sümer, *Oğuzlar'a ait destanî mahiyette eserler*, in *Ank. Ün. DTCFD*, xvii/3-4), where it is said that some prominent beys of the Oghuz rulers belonged to this tribe. According to the Syrian historian Shams al-Dīn Muḥammad al-Djazarī (658/1260-739/1338), the Artuk [*q.v.*] dynasty, ruling the Mardin-Diyārbekir region, belonged to the Döger tribe (F. Sümer, *op. cit.*, 405, n. 171), which must therefore have taken part in the conquests of the Selčuks. In the second half of the 8th/13th century an important branch of the Döger was living south of Urfa (Edessa) and around Dja'bar; their leader was, in 773/1371-2, a bey named Sālim.

Sālim played a part in the events of North Syrian history and died towards the end of the century. Three sons of his are known. Dimashk Khodja, probably the eldest, was in 801/1398 appointed *nā'ib* of Dja'bar by the Mamlūk Sultan; profiting from the anarchy left by Tīmūr's invasion, he brought under his control also Rakka, Sarūdj, Harrān, Urfa and Siverek, but was killed in battle with the famous Arab *amīr* Nu'ayr (Muhammad b. Muhannā) and his head was sent to Cairo (806/1404). He was succeeded by his brother Gökče Mūsā, who, like Dimashk, was hostile to the Ak-koyunlu and friendly with the Kara-koyunlu: in 807/1405 he entertained at Dja'bar the Kara-koyunlu ruler Kara Yūsuf, who was travelling home from Syria; he assisted the Kara-koyunlu in various campaigns, helping Kara Yūsuf's son Iskender to defeat Kara Yülük 'Othmān Beg in the battle fought at Sheykh-kendi (between Mardin and Naṣībīn) in 824/1421. In 840/1436 he defeated Kara Yülük's grandson, 'Alī Beg-oghlu Djihāngīr, and sent him prisoner to Cairo, but died in the same year. Thereafter, under pressure from the Ak-koyunlu, the Döger lost even Dja'bar. In Gökče Mūsā's lifetime his younger brother Hasan Beg had entered the service of the Mamlūk Sultan and became *nā'ib* of 'Adjlūn; Hasan's son Amīrza was *nā'ib* of Karak in 890/1485.

Apart from Sālim's family, other beys of the Döger—Yār 'Alī, Muhammad and Katî—are found in Syria as leaders of Döger clans among the Turkmens of Haleb; Katî was in 857/1453 *nā'ib* of Buhayra for the Mamlūks. In the time of Süleymān I, the Döger of Syria were divided in three clans (*oymak*) in the regions of Haleb, Hamā and Dimashk. The *tapu* registers show two small groups in Jerusalem residing in the Bāb al-'Āmūd and Banū Zayd quarters (cf. B. Lewis in *BSOAS*, xvi/3 (1954), 479). Other clans were found around Diyārbekir, among the Boz-Ulus (one remnant of the Ak-koyunlu confederacy), at Karkūk, and even among the Turkish tribes in Persia. In the 10th/16th century the name Döger was found in many toponyms, few of which have survived.

Bibliography: F. Sümer, *Dögerlere dâir*, in *Türkiyat Mecmuası*, x, 1953, 139-158; Cl. Cahen, *Contribution à l'histoire du Diyâr Bakr au quatorzième siècle*, in *JA*, ccxliii, 1955, 81; Abū Bakr-i Ṭihrānī, *Kitāb-i Diyārbakriyya*, ed. N. Lugal and F. Sümer, Ankara (TTK) 1962, 53, nn. 5-7; 123, n. 1.

(F. SÜMER)

DOGHANDJÎ, Turkish term for falconer, from *doghan*, falcon (*toghan* in Kîpčak Turkish, cf. *al-Tuhfa al-zakiyya fi 'l-lugha al-Turkiyya*, ed. B. Atalay, Istanbul 1945, 260), and in general use any kind of bird of prey. *Bāzdār*, from Persian, was also frequently used for the *doghandjî*.

In the Ottoman empire the term *doghandjî* in the same sense as in later periods was found as early as the 8th/14th century (cf. P. Wittek, *Zu einigen frühosmanischen Urkunden*, in *WZKM*, liv (1957), 240; lvii (1961), 103; for *doghandjî čiftligi* see H. Inalcık, *Sûret-i defter-i sancak-i Arvanid*, Ankara 1954, 106).

Hawking, a favourite traditional sport at the Ottoman court, gave rise to a vast organization in the empire. There were *doghandjî*s at the Enderūn and the Bīrūn [*qq.v.*], and in the provinces. The *doghandjî*s at the Enderūn, under a *doghandjî-bashî*, were found in the different *oda*s (chambers). They accompanied the Sultan in his hawking parties. Their number varied according to the reigning Sultan's care for the sport (nine in 883/1478, forty in the early 17th century, cf. İ. H. Uzunçarşılı, *Osmanlı devletinin saray teşkilâtı*, Ankara 1945, 421-2).

At the Bīrūn the *doghandjî*s, generally called *shikār khalkî*, made three different *djemā'at*, groups, divided into *bölük*s, *čakîrdjîyān*, *shāhîndjiyān* and *atmadjadjiyān*, those taking care of *čakîr*s, merlins and falcons, of *shāhîn*, peregrine falcons, and of *atmadja*, sparrow-hawks. They were under a *čakîrdjî-bashî*, a *shāhîndji-bashî* and an *atmadjadjî-bashî* respectively. The *čakîrdjî-bashî* [*q.v.*] was the head of the whole organization, and in this capacity was usually called *mīr-i shikār*. In the hierarchy of aghas at the Bīrūn he stood in the fourth grade, the first being *yeničeri-aghasî* (cf. *Kānūnnāme-i Āl-i 'Othmān*, ed. M. 'Ārif, in *TOEM*, 1330 H., appendix, 12). When promoted, the *čakîrdjî-bashî* was made *sandjak-begi* under Mehemmed II (*ibid.*, 15), and beglerbegi in the 11th/17th century. The *shāhîndji-bashî* was then made *čakîrdjî-bashî*, and the *doghandjî-bashî* from the Enderūn *shāhîndji-bashî*. The *doghandjî*s at the court all received *'ulūfe*, salary (cf. Ö. L. Barkan, *H. 933-934 malî yılına ait bir bütçe örneği*, in *İst. Üniv. Iktisat Fakültesi Mecmuası*, xv (1953-4), 300; 'Aynī 'Alī, *Kawānîn-i Āl-i 'Othmān* . . ., Istanbul 1280, 95).

In the provinces there existed a similar organization. In the sandjaks [*q.v.*] where birds of prey were found, there were *doghandjî*s or *bāzdārān*, *čakîrdjî*s, *shāhîndji*s and *atmadjadjî*s under a *doghandjî-bashî*. Their number with their dependents reached 2171 persons in Anatolia and 1520 in Rumeli in 972/1564 (*Defter-i bāzdārān-i wilāyet-i Rumeli we Anadolu we ghayruh*, in Belediye Kütüphanesi, Istanbul, Cevdet Kitapları, O 60. This important source gives in *idjmāl*, summary, the number of *doghandjî*s and the copies of the *hükm*s, decrees, on them). They formed large groups especially in the sandjaks of Gallipoli (642), Vidin (706), Menteshe (503), Mar'ash (770) and Kars (537). The local *doghandjî-bashî*s were appointed by the *čakîrdjî-bashî* and were given *tîmār*s [*q.v.*]. Under each *doghandjî-bashî* there were two *khāṣṣa kushbāz*, *gürenčdji* (apparently from *güre*, wild) and *götürüdjü*, who also held *tîmār*s and were in charge of training and taking to the court the birds of prey caught in their areas.

Under the *doghandjî-bashî*s there were a group of *doghandjî*s living in the villages who were originally *re'āyā* [*q.v.*], Christian and Muslim, to provide birds of prey. They were assigned to this service by the Sultan's diploma, *doghandjî berātî*, which granted the possession for cultivation of a piece of land called *doghandjî čiftligi* or *doghandjî bashtinasî* (see ČIFTLIK) with the exemption from *'ushr*, *čift-resmi* [*q.v.*] and *'awāriḍ* [*q.v.*] taxes. They paid the *bād-i hawā* [*q.v.*] taxes to their *doghandjî-bashî* or to the Sultan's collectors directly. If they cultivated any land outside their *čiftlik*s they had to pay in addition the regular *re'āyā* taxes for it to the land-holder. Their sons had the right of inheritance on the *čiftlik*s and, in their turn, became *doghandjî*s (for all these cf. Ö. L. Barkan, *Kanunlar*, Istanbul 1943, 20, 272, 274, 280, 331). But in the 10th/16th century the *re'āyā* who were made *doghandjî*s only one generation before were not granted these exemptions.

The *doghandjî*s of *re'āyā* origin were divided into different groups according to the kind of bird of prey they were to catch or train as *bāzdār*s, *čakîrdjî*s, *shāhîndji*s or *atmadjadjî*s. Also according to their functions they were divided into *ṣayyād*s, hunters, and *yuwadjî*s, nest-tenders. The latter were in their turn divided into *ḳayadjis* and *dīdebāns*, *i.e.*, those who discovered the nests in the mountains and guarded them, and *tülekdjis*, those taking care of the nestlings. When the *ṣayyāds* or *yuwādjīs* delivered the birds to the local *doghandjî-bashî* they were given a *mühürlü tedhkire*, certificate of delivery. Then at a certain time of the year the *doghandjî-bashî* and *khāṣṣa doghandjîs* took the birds to Istanbul to deliver to the *čakîrdjî-bashî*. Anybody who took a bird of prey from the guarded places or through a *ṣayyād* had to pay a fine of 500 *akče* to the treasury. The ordinary *reʿāyā* and *ʿaskerī* were forbidden to hunt birds of prey.

From the 11th/17th century onward, the *doghandjî* organization in the provinces was neglected, and, in most places, abolished. The *doghandjîs* were returned to the status of simple *reʿāyā* with the abolition of their exemptions. But the organization in general survived until Rabīʿ II 1246/September-October 1830 when Maḥmūd II abolished it altogether.

(HALIL İNALCIK)

DOLMA BAGHČE [see ISTANBUL].

DONANMA, 'a decking-out, an adorning', Turkish verbal noun derived ultimately from *ton*, 'clothes'. The word is used in Ottoman Turkish in two restricted meanings:

(1) 'fleet of ships, navy' (presumably a calque of Ital. 'armata'), for which see art. BAḤRIYYA, iii (adding to bibliography H. and R. Kahane and A. Tietze, *The Lingua Franca in the Levant*, Urbana 1958, 1-45).

(2) 'decoration of the streets of a city' (synonyms: *shenlik, shehr-āyīn*) for a Muslim festival or on a secular occasion of public rejoicing such as a victory, an accession, a royal birth, circumcision or wedding; and, more particularly, the illumination of the city by night (*ḳandīl donanmasî*) and the firework-displays which formed part of these celebrations. The most elaborate of these public feasts was that given by Murād III in 990/1582 for the circumcision of his son, the future Meḥemmed III.

Bibliography: For full descriptions, with extensive quotations from Turkish and European sources, see Metin And, *Kırk gün kırk gece*, Istanbul 1959. (V. L. MÉNAGE)

DONBOLÎ [see KURDS].

DONGOLA (Arabic, Dunḳula, Dunḳulā; obsolete forms, Dumḳula, Damḳala), the name of two towns in Nubia; more generally, the riverain territory dependent on these towns. All lie within the present Republic of the Sudan. The arabized Nubians of Dongola are called Danāḳla, a regional, not a tribal, designation.

(1) Old Dongola (Dunḳula al-ʿadjūz), on the right bank of the Nile, is on the site of a pre-Islamic town, the capital of the Christian kingdom of al-Maḳurra. It was besieged by an army under ʿAbd Allāh b. Saʿd b. Abī Sarḥ [*q.v.*] in 31/652, but the Muslims withdrew after concluding a convention (*baḳt*, [*q.v.*]) which regulated relations between Nubia and Egypt for some six centuries. Mediaeval Dongola is described as a walled city with many churches, large houses and wide streets. The royal palace with domes of red brick was constructed in 392/1002. With the collapse of Christian Nubia, Dongola became a Muslim town; the mosque, formerly a church, has an Arabic inscription dated 16 Rabīʿ I 717/29 May 1317. With the establishment of Fundj [*q.v.*] hegemony over Nubia in the 10th/16th century, Dongola reappears as the seat of a vassal king (*makk*). His authority extended as far north as the Third Cataract, the border between the Fundj dominions and the Barābra [*q.v.*], who recognized Ottoman suzerainty. After the rise of the Shayḳiyya confederacy in the late 11th/17th century, the principal north-south trade-routes tended to avoid the Dongola region. In its last days, the territory was the prey of both the Shayḳiyya and of the Mamlūk refugees in New Dongola. The petty rulers therefore welcomed the Turco-Egyptian forces of Ismāʿīl Kāmil Pasha, who suppressed both these predatory military aristocracies (1236/1820).

(2) New Dongola (al-ʿUrdī, *i.e.*, Ordu, "The Camp"), now the principal town of the region, arose on the site of the settlement of the Mamlūks who escaped from the proscription by Muḥammad ʿAlī Pasha in 1226/1811. After their expulsion, New Dongola became the seat of a *kāshif* (later *mudīr*, governor) and the capital of the province of Dongola. Between 1886 and 1896 the province was ruled by Mahdist military governors (*ʿummāl*, sing. *ʿāmil*). Kitchener's Dongola campaign of 1896 effected the reconquest of the province. It has now lost its separate identity as, during the Condominium, it was fused with Wādī Ḥalfā and Berber [*q.v.*] to form the Northern Province.

Bibliography: The scattered and rather slight references in mediaeval sources are listed in Maspero-Wiet, *Matériaux*, 94. To these may be added O. G. S. Crawford, *The Fung kingdom of Sennar*, Gloucester 1951, especially 33-6. Old Dongola in 1698 was described by Ch. J. Poncet, *A voyage to Ethiopia*, London 1709; reprinted by Sir William Foster (ed.), *The Red Sea and adjacent countries at the close of the seventeenth century*, (Hakluyt Society, Second Series, no. C); London 1949, 99-100. It was described in 1821 by L. M. A. Linant de Bellefonds, *Journal d'un voyage à Méroé*, (ed. M. Shinnie), Khartoum 1958, 32-4. The official correspondence of the Mahdist period is preserved in the Sudan Government Archives in Khartoum. (P. M. HOLT)

DÖNME (Turkish: convert) name of a sect in Turkey formed by Jews upon their conversion to Islam late in the 11th/17th century in emulation of Shabbetai Ṣebi whom they considered the Messiah.

The sect emerged out of mystic speculations justifying the conversion of Jews to Islam as a link in the chain of Messianic events, and served as a means to consolidate those who wished to emulate and remain faithful to the converted Messiah, even after his death. It attempted, in the spirit of the Messiah, to maintain secretly within Islam as much as possible of Judaism, its lore and rites, with sabbatian-messianic modifications. In the course of time the original concepts of the stormy period of messianism and conversion were largely blurred and forgotten, and the life of the group expressed itself in ritual pecularities, social welfare activity, and basic devotion to the memory of the Messiah in expectation of his reincarnation or second advent, with subsequent dissensions concerning rightful succession to leadership.

Thus, intermarriage with Muslims was avoided; the fast-day commemoration of the destruction of the Temple (9th of Āb) became a day of rejoicing as the birthday of the Messiah; some knowledge of Hebrew was maintained; outward conformity with Islamic rites was encouraged while, in secret, Hebrew names were preserved and separate marriage and funeral rites were held.

The group conversion took place, it seems, in Salonika in 1094/1683. Salonika became the the centre but there were branches in Edirne, İzmir, later Istanbul, and in Albania.

Inner squabbles, mostly engendered by various pretenders to Messianic succession and leadership, brought about the split into three sub-sects (the names vary: the recent being *Hamdibeyler*, *Karakaş*, *Kapancılar*) all refusing intermarriage. This division may have been not unrelated to social divisions, and expressed itself in peculiarities of hairstyle and garb. The *Dönme* lived in separate quarters.

The sect considered itself the community of the believers (*ma'amīnīm*). It maintained strict secrecy. After the initial period, its literary output appears to have shrunk to poems and prayers in Hebrew, Aramaic, Judaeo-Spanish, and Turkish. Paucity of sources and secretiveness combine to make the study of the sect difficult, and its history obscure.

Around 1700, there were a few hundred families belonging to the central Salonika group. About 1900, the number of that group was estimated at 10,000. They were represented in trade, crafts, and the civil service.

Toward the end of the 19th century, a growing new layer of westernized young people came to the fore as teachers, doctors, lawyers, journalists, and these took part in Turkish public life, sometimes with considerable success. Most spectacular was the rise of Djāwid Bey [*q.v.*] in the Young Turkish régime following the revolution of 1908.

On the whole the Muslims were indifferent to the sect's existence, but from time to time there was a spurt of inquiry or persecution (*e.g.*, in 1720, 1859, and 1875). Imputing *Dönme* origin to undesirables was not unknown.

A new phase began for the *Dönme* when, with the Graeco-Turkish exchange of population, the Salonika *Dönme* were forced to quit their ancestral town and to move into the Turkish Republic (1923-24). They settled mostly in Istanbul, smaller groups settling also in other cities. This change of domicile, the dispersal that followed, the loss of contact with the solid Jewish atmospere of Salonika, the influence of the secular Turkish national school—all contributed to a growing loss of cohesion and indifference among the younger generation of the *Dönme* although group existence, especially in the area of social welfare, continued. The arrival in Istanbul of several thousand *Dönme* stimulated a discussion of sectarian segregation *versus* national assimilation in the Turkish press in 1924-5. Intermarriage with Muslims is slowly spreading and complete integration into modern Turkish society, despite setbacks, is on the increase.

Bibliography: Accounts will be found in the general works on Jewish history by H. Graetz, S. Dubnow, S. W. Baron. G. Scholem's capital researches on Jewish mysticism are summarized in the sketch included in *The Jewish people*, i, New York 1948; idem, *Main trends in Jewish mysticism*, New York 1941, esp. 287-236; idem, *Shabbetai Ṣebī* (Hebrew), 2 vols., Tel Aviv 1957; idem, articles in *Zion* vi, *Kiryat Sepher* xviii-xix; idem, *Die kryptojüdische Sekte der Dönme (Sabbatianer) in der Türkei*, in *Numen*, vii (1960), 93-122; Cf. s.v. in *Encyclopaedia Hebraica* (xi, 1959, I. Ben Zvi), and *İA* iii, 646 ff.; I. Ben Zvi, *The exiled and the redeemed*, Philadelphia 1957; A. Danon, in *REJ* 1897; L. Sciaky, *Farewell to Salonica*, New York 1946, Ch. 9; A. Struck, in *Globus* 1902; A. Galante, *Nouveaux documents sur Sabbetai Sevi*, Istanbul 1935; E. E. Ramsaur Jr., *The Young Turks*, Princeton 1957, 96 ff., 108 n. Turkish reactions are reflected in A. Gövsa, *Sabatay Sevi*, Istanbul, n.d., and W. Gordlevsky's paper in *Islamica*, ii, 1926. *Dönme* texts have been published by M. Atias, I. Ben Zvi, R. Molho, G. Scholem; cf. *Sefunot*, iii, Jerusalem 1960.

(M. Perlmann)

DÖNÜM [see miṣāḥa].

DŌST MUḤAMMAD [see dūst muḥammad].

DOUAR [see dawār].

DOWRY [see mahr].

DRAA [see darʿa].

DRAČ (Dīrač, Durač), Slavonic and hence Ottoman name for the classical Dyrrhachium (med. Latin Duracium, Ital. Durazzo, Alb. Durrës), the principal port of modern Albania (41° 18′ N., 19° 26′ E.). The classical town was founded (c. 625 B.C.) under the name Epidamnus at the southern end of a narrow rocky peninsula (once an island) running parallel to the mainland coast, to which it was connected in antiquity at the North by a sand-spit and at the South by a bridge; the lagoon so enclosed has progressively contracted over the centuries. In Roman times, now known (perhaps after the Illyrian name of the peninsula) as Dyrrhachium, to its commercial prosperity was added immense strategic importance as the starting-point of the Via Egnatia, the continuation, after the short and easy sea-crossing from Brundisium, of the Via Appia, and the principal military road between Italy and the East. Hence in Byzantine times too Dyrrhachium was strongly fortified as the Western gateway to the Empire.

After falling to Venice at the partition of 1205, Dyrrhachium changed masters repeatedly, to be ceded to Venice in 1392 by the native Thopia dynasty, who were no longer able to protect it against the Ottomans. The Venetians rebuilt the walls on a narrower circuit and made vigorous but fruitless attempts to scour the lagoon, in order to arrest the silting of the harbour and the spread of malaria. During Meḥemmed II's Albanian campaign of 1467, Durazzo, practically deserted by its terrified inhabitants, escaped a determined assault (see F. Babinger, *Mahomet II le Conquérant et son temps*, Paris 1954, 311-3); the end came only in 1501 (17 August), when, the governor being temporarily absent, Durazzo fell to a night-attack by ʿĪsā Beg-oghlu Meḥemmed Beg, sandjaḳ-bey of the nearby Elbasan (Saʿd al-Dīn, ii, 113-4, following the contemporary account of Idrīs Bidlīsī). Thereafter Durazzo was administered as a *ḳaḍā* of Elbasan [*q.v.*]; its walls were reconstructed to enclose a still smaller area (600 m. × 250 m.) in the South-East corner of the antique city, leaving the ancient acropolis outside the enceinte.

Under the Ottomans practically nothing of Durazzo's old importance remained. Ewliyā (1670) describes a small town of 150 houses with only one mosque; it had still (as in mediaeval times) a considerable salt industry and a not insignificant trade, and was administered as a *voyvodalık* under an *emīn* (who, with the *ḳāḍī*, resided at the more salubrious Kavaya, 20 kms. to, the South-East).

Durazzo's modern prosperity began shortly before the Second World War, with the construction by Italy of a first-class harbour; now linked by rail with Tirana and Elbasan, it has developed considerably both as a port and as a holiday-resort (pop. 30,000).

Bibliography: Pauly-Wissowa, s.v. Dyrrhachion (Philippson); K. Jireček, *Die Lage und Vergangenheit der Stadt Durazzo in Albanien*, in L. von Thallóczy, *Illyrisch-Albanische Forschungen*, i, 1916, 152-7; L. Heuzey, *Mission archéologique de Macédoine*, Paris 1876, 349-92 and plan; Ewliyā Čelebi, *Seyāḥatnāme*, viii, 710-2 = F. Babinger's abridged trans. and comm., *MSOS*, xxxiii (1930) 166 (with further references); H. Hecquard, *Histoire et description de la Haute Albanie ou Guégarie*, Paris 1858, 258-63; Baedeker's *Dalmatien und die Adria*, 1929, 235-6 (F. Babinger); *Enc. It.*, s.v. Durazzo; S. Skendi (ed.), *Albania*, London 1957; *Guide d'Albanie* (Albturist), Tirana 1958, 166-73; art. ARNAWUTLUḲ above.

(V. L. MÉNAGE)

DRAGUT [see TURG͟HUD ʿALĪ PAS͟HA].

DRAMA [see MASRAḤIYYA].

DREAMS [see TAʿBĪR AL-RUʾYĀ].

DRESS [see LIBĀS].

DRUZES [see DURŪZ].

DUʿĀʾ, appeal, invocation (addressed to God) either on behalf of another or for oneself (*li* . . .), or else against someone (*ʿalā* . . .); hence: prayer of invocation, calling either for blessing, or for imprecation and cursing, connected with the Semitic idea of the effective value of the spoken word. Cf. Ḳurʾān XVII, 11: "Man prays for evil as he prays for good".—*Duʿāʾ* therefore will have the general sense of personal prayer addressed to God, and can often be translated as "prayer of request".

I.—The scope and practice of *duʿāʾ*.

1. In the Ḳurʾān, *duʿāʾ* always keeps its original meaning of invocation, appeal. Man "appeals" for good fortune (XLI, 49), and "when misfortune visits him, he is filled with unceasing prayer (*duʿāʾ*)" (ibid., 51). To practise *duʿāʾ* is to raise one's supplications to God; *duʿāʾ* here assumes the general meaning of "prayer", of two categories in particular: (a) prayer (and especially prayer of request) made by the pre-Islamic worthy men and prophets; (b) the vain prayer of the infidels. In the first case, God is He who hears, who answers the *duʿāʾ*: it was so for Abraham (XIV, 39-40; XIX, 48) and for Zachariah (III, 38). In the second case, "the prayer of the infidels is but vanity" (XIII, 14; cf. XLVI, 5); and the false gods hear no part of the prayer addressed to them (XXXV, 14), etc.—Some shades of meaning should be distinguished: thus, in verse XXV, 77 (addressed to the opponents), *duʿāʾ* evokes any relationship of man to God; "Say: my Lord will not become anxious save through your prayer"; whilst XIX, 40, repeating a saying of Abraham, distinguishes between *ṣalāt*, a ritual and liturgical prayer to be "performed", and *duʿāʾ*, prayer, personal invocation: "Lord, make of me one who performs the *ṣalāt* (and let it be so) for my posterity, O Lord, and accept my prayer (*duʿāʾ*)".

2. There are numerous *ḥadīt͟h*s which speak of *duʿāʾ*. Traditionists and jurists define its significance, the principal ones being reproduced by al-G͟hazālī, *Iḥyāʾ ʿulūm al-dīn* (Cairo 1352), i, 274-8.— Tradition attributed to ʿAlī: "my followers are those who have taken the earth as their carpet, water as their perfume, prayer (*duʿāʾ*) as their adornment".

Duʿāʾ must be clearly distinguished from *ṣalāt* [*q.v.*], ritual or liturgical prayer. But it would be inaccurate to express it as a contrast between *ṣalāt*, vocal fixed prayer, and *duʿāʾ*, mental prayer or orison. Ibn Taymiyya (*Fatāwā*, Cairo 1326, i, 197) proposes this scale of values: "the *ṣalāt* constitutes a form (*d͟jins*) which is superior to Ḳurʾānic recitation (*ḳirāʾa*); recitation in itself is superior to *d͟hikr*, and *d͟hikr* to individual invocation (*duʿāʾ*)" (from the trans. of Laoust, *Essai sur les doctrines sociales et politiques de Taḳī-d-Dīn Aḥmad b. Taimīya*, Cairo 1939, 328-9). A critical enumeration frequently mentions *ṣalāt*, *d͟hikr* [*q.v.*] (incessant repetition, ejaculatory prayer), *ḥizb* and *wird* (supererogatory "liturgies"), *duʿāʾ*. Inward prayer would be suggested rather by *d͟hikr* and *fikr* (meditation), *duʿāʾ* always connoting the idea of a formulated request, of an invocation either beneficent or imprecatory.

3. The request addressed to God in the *duʿāʾ* can be greatly varied according to the circumstances. It is in this sense that it is legitimate to translate it (cf. translation from Laoust above) as "personal invocation"; it can also assume a communal value and aspect. The choice of words is free, but Ḳurʾānic texts or traditional prayers already in existence will often be used.

Treatises which recommend *duʿāʾ*, and especially the Ṣūfī treatises, like to define the conditions which must accompany it and the rules of its *adab*. Both of these seek to provide a maximum guarantee of its being received by God. A brief summary (al-Bād͟jūrī, *Ḥāshiya* . . . *ʿalā D͟jawharat al-tawḥīd*, Cairo 1353/1934, 90-1) gives them as follows. (a) *Conditions*: to eat only food that is legally permitted; to pray, feeling convinced that the prayer will be answered; not to be distracted during prayer; that the object of the request should not lead to any sinful act, or give rise to enmity between those of the same blood, or harm Muslims' rights; and finally, not to ask for anything impossible, for that would be a lack of respect towards God. (b) *Adab* (how to pray): to choose the best times, and al-Bād͟jūrī suggests during the *sud͟jūd*, when one is prostrate, or while standing upright (*iḳāma*), or during the summons to prayer (*ad͟hān*); to precede the *duʿāʾ* with ablutions and the *ṣalāt* on the one hand, and on the other with a confession of faults and an act of repentence; to turn towards the *ḳibla*; to raise the hands towards heaven (*rafʿ al-yadayn*); to pronounce the "divine praise" (*al-ḥamdu li'llāh*) and the "blessing on the Prophet" at the beginning, in the middle and at the end of the *duʿāʾ*.

These detailed recommendations are in some measure "advisory". In some cases, however, when the object of the *duʿāʾ* concerns the common good of the Community, it assumes a ritual, set form recognized by all; in these circumstances it makes use of the procedure for *ṣalāt*. The most notable example is that of the *istisḳāʾ* ("prayer for rain"): for this, the *duʿāʾ* must be preceded by a ritual prayer of two *rakʿa*s [*q.v.*], two *k͟huṭba*s ("sermons"), and the rite (sympathetic magic) of the "turning of the cloak". The "prayer for the dead" made communally (frequently during the "sessions" of the brotherhoods) also obeys various regulations.

These conditions and rules for the *duʿāʾ* are intended to surround it with guarantees of efficacy. And we see that to the power of the word there are added the effective forces of legal purity and of gesture. This last point provides matter for discussion. Texts which widely recommend the practice of *duʿāʾ* speak constantly of ablution and the *rafʿ al-yadayn*; in doing so they rely on *ḥadīt͟h*: before raising his hands in the *duʿāʾ* the Prophet had performed the ablution of *wuḍūʾ* (al-Buk͟hārī, *Mag͟hazī*, ii, 55). But al-Nasāʾī and Ibn Ḥanbal (ii, 243) only accept the raising of the hands in the *duʿāʾ* of the "prayer for rain".

4. Islamic devotional trends insist on the *duʿāʾ* being regarded as a prayer of request for well-being, especially the public weal of the Muslim community, and the personal spiritual well-being of oneself and others. Beautiful *duʿāʾ* texts are not rare in S͟hīʿī works of piety. The popular pietism of the

Ḥanbalīs often mentions it. It is to be seen mingled with the liturgies of *ḥizb* and *wird* in the handbooks of the religious brotherhoods. It is, then, much less an appeal of invocation (and of imprecation, especially) than an appeal trusting in divine Mercy. It is in this way that the utterance of the divine Names can turn either to the metrical repetition of the *dhikr* or to a form of *duʿāʾ* which links its request with the evocation of each Name and each attribute, and thereby defines it; in this connexion, see the monograph written in the last century by Muḥammad ʿAlī Khān al-Bukhārī, *Kitāb minḥat al-sarrāʾ fī sharḥ al-duʿāʾ* (ed. Ḥaydarābād, 1337). The *duʿāʾ* becomes an equivalent of the spiritual impulse towards God.

II.—Questions raised in *kalām* and *falsafa*.

The incantation value and the effectiveness of word and gesture was no doubt the first consideration in the idea of *duʿāʾ*, and derived from a Semitic understanding of the relation of man to what is holy. But the Hellenistic influence which moulded Muslim thought encouraged *falsafa* on one hand, and the *ʿilm al-kalām* ("theology" or, more accurately defensive apology) on the other, to raise the question of the prayer of request and of its efficacity before the Almighty and the Decree of God.

The reply varies according to the school and the writer. Here are three typical examples. (A summary of the principles of *kalām* is given by al-Bādjūrī, *loc. cit.*, among others).

(a). The Muʿtazila deny the usefulness of the prayer of request; in their eyes it would be derogatory to the pure divine transcendence. Man, in fact, being the "creator of his own actions" has no need to ask God to make his enterprises favourable. Human actions themselves bear the weight of their own consequences. Thus when God, in the Ḳurʾān, tells His servants to invoke Him, it is the attitude of adoration that He is demanding; and when He promises to hear their prayers, it is the just reward for a rationally good action that He is guaranteeing.

(b). On the other hand the Ashʿarī *kalām*, centred upon the absolute and free will of God, was to restore its traditional value to *duʿāʾ*. The "prayer for the dead" (*al-ṣalāt ʿalā 'l-mayyit*, or *al-djināza*) has the value of a *duʿāʾ* asking God for mercy, if such be His will. Moreover, the imprecatory aspect of *duʿāʾ* is not forgotten. The invocation is harmful to those one curses, if the cause is just. "The *duʿāʾ* of one suffering an injustice is answered (says a *ḥadīth* of Anas), even if it be an infidel". Sometimes the prayer will be answered exactly as it has been formulated and at once, sometimes after a delay for a reason known to God; and sometimes God will grant something different from what was asked, in view of a greater benefit.

The acknowledged virtue of *duʿāʾ* clearly proves that the Ashʿarī denial of free human choice and secondary causes, and the total surrender required with regard to the divine will, in no way constitutes, strictly speaking, a "fatalistic" attitude. Incidentally the Ashʿarī manuals pose very clearly the problem of reconciling effective *duʿāʾ* with absolute divine predetermination (*ḳaḍāʾ*) or immutable decree (*ḳadar*).

The usual reply makes a distinction between "fixed" predetermination (*ḳaḍāʾ*) and "suspended" (conditional) predetermination. In the latter case, whether some event will happen or not is decided by God considering the actual fact of the *duʿāʾ* which thus, in its turn, enters into the conditions determined by divine decree. In the case of "fixed" predetermination, the prayer of request can change nothing in God's will—He will, however, grant His favour to one who implores Him. And this favour will indeed bear on the actual objectof the request, the circumstances of granting the prayer then being taken in a "suspended decree".

(c). Following quite different principles but a similar approach, the *falāsifa* logically include the *duʿāʾ* in their universal determinism. The subject is treated on several occasions by Ibn Sīnā (*e.g.*, *Nadjāt*, 2nd ed. Cairo 1357/1938, 299-303; *Maʿnā al-ziyāra* and *Risāla fī māhiyyat al-ṣalāt*, ed. A. F. Mehren, Leiden 1894). The effective prayer of request is a result of the co-operation of terrestrial dispositions and celestial causes. The invocation by the *duʿāʾ* comes as a psychical influx which acts physically upon the phantasms of the celestial Spheres according to all the laws of the macrocosm, as inevitably as man's imagination acts upon his own body. Furthermore, it is these celestial Spheres which in reality gave men the suggestion to pray, this suggestion in turn taking its place in the universal chain of causes. And it can then be said, as a result in fact of the interplay of causes, that the prayer is answered. The *duʿāʾ*, according to Avicenna, puts man into direct relationship with the celestial Spheres alone. That is why "those prayers particularly which beg for rain and other such things" are found to possess "very great usefulness" (*Nadjāt*, 301; cf. L. Gardet, *La pensée religieuse d'Avicenne*, Paris 1951, 135-7).

These various attempts to provide a rational justification of *duʿāʾ* testify to its importance in the religious life of Islam. But we must observe that the cosmological interpretation of an Ibn Sīnā does not in any way spring from the most current vision of the world. For the pious Muslim by and large, *duʿāʾ* effects a relationship between the man at prayer and not the celestial spheres, but God, integrating and often sublimating the familiar conception of the power of the name (*ism*) over the one named (*musammā*).

Bibliography: in the article. (L. Gardet)

DUALISM [see KHURRAMIYYA, THANAWIYYA, ZINDĪḲ].

DUBAYS [see MAZYADĪS].

DUBAYTĪ [see RUBĀʿĪ].

DUBAYY (commonly spelled Dubai), a port (25° 16′ N., 55° 18′ E.) and shaykhdom on the Trucial Coast of Arabia. The town lies at the head of a winding creek (*khawr*) extending some eight miles inland; ferries ply between Dayra, the market quarter on the north-east bank, and al-Shandagha and Dubayy proper, quarters on the south-west bank. The population of the town, about 47,000, is predominantly Arab with some Iranians, Indians, and Balūčīs (Hay, 114). The Arab inhabitants of the principality comprise members of al-Sūdān, al-Marar, al-Mazārīʿ, Āl Bū Muhayr, al-Hawāmil, al-Ḳumzān, al-Maḥāriba, al-Sabāyis, and Āl Bū Falāḥ, tribal groups considered components of Banī Yās in the Persian Gulf area, as well as members of al-Manāṣīr, primarily a Bedouin tribe. The ruling family, Āl Bū Falāsā, are members of al-Rawāshid and, like the majority of the inhabitants, are Mālikīs.

The frontiers of the shaykhdom are not completely defined. The land boundary between the shaykhdoms of Dubayy and Abū Ẓaby has a coastal terminus between al-Djabal al-ʿĀlī (sometimes called al-Djubayl) and Khawr Ghanāḍa; the land boundary between the shaykhdoms of Dubayy and al-Shāriḳa terminates just north-east of Dayra. Two small coastal villages, Umm al-Suḳaym and Djumayra, and the larger village of Ḥadjarayn, about 50 miles inland in Wādī Ḥattā and separated from the rest of the principality's territory, acknowledge the overlordship of the Ruler of Dubayy. Some date cultivation is practised, but water is scarce.

Little is known about Dubayy before 1213-4/1799 when it is first mentioned in available sources (Lorimer). Dubayy was considered a dependency of Abū Ẓaby during the first third of the 19th century, with the exception of a period of several years after 1241/1825 when Shaykh Sulṭān b. Ṣaḳr of al-Ḳawāsim, Ruler of al-Shāriḳa, increased his influence over Dubayy by marrying a sister of its governor, Muḥammad b. Hazzāʿ b. Zaʿal (India, *Selections*, xxiv, 317).

Dubayy became an independent principality in 1249/1833 when about 800 members of Āl Bū Falāsā, under the leadership of Maktūm b. Baṭī b. Suhayl, left Abū Ẓaby and took control of the settlement of Dubayy (al-Sālimī, 31). Rivalry between al-Ḳawāsim and Banī Yās for control of the shaykhdom continued throughout the 19th and early 20th centuries, but Dubayy preserved its independence by aligning itself sometimes with al-Shāriḳa, sometimes with Abū Ẓaby, and on occasion with the smaller shaykhdoms of ʿAdjmān and Umm al-Ḳaywayn. Dubayy increased in population and wealth, derived primarily from pearl fishing and entrepôt trade.

Like other Trucial States, Dubayy signed the General Treaty of Peace with Britain in 1235/1820 and the temporary Maritime Truce (later made perpetual) in 1251/1835 (see ABŪ ẒABY). In 1309/1892 the Ruler of Dubayy agreed not to establish relations with any foreign country except Britain without British consent, and in 1340/1922 he agreed not to grant rights to any oil found in his territory except to a person appointed by the British Government. The British Petroleum Exploration Company, Limited (formerly D'Arcy Exploration Company, Limited) holds a two-thirds interest, and Compagnie Française des Pétroles holds one-third interest in an offshore oil concession, while Petroleum Development (Trucial Coast), Limited, an Iraq Petroleum Company affiliate, holds an onshore concession. Until 1381/1961, no oil had been discovered.

The silting up of al-Shāriḳa creek and the decline of Linga [*q.v.*] have contributed to the recent prosperity of Dubayy. It exports pearls (a declining industry) and dried fish; it imports foodstuffs, textiles, and light machinery. A coastal route connects Dubayy with al-Shāriḳa, nine miles to the north, and with Abū Ẓaby town, about 80 miles to the south; desert tracks lead inland to al-Buraymī and to Muscat.

The administrative agencies of the shaykhdom have recently expanded and now include a Municipal Council, a Customs Administration, Courts, and Departments of Education, Health, Land Registration, and Water Supply. The town has a hospital, four schools for boys and two for girls, telegraph and telephone communications, regular mail service, and a small airport. The headquarters of the British Political Agent for all of the Trucial States except Abū Ẓaby was transferred from al-Shāriḳa to Dubayy in 1374/1954. The present (1962) Ruler of Dubayy is Shaykh Rāshid b. Saʿīd b. Maktūm.

Bibliography: *al-ʿArabī*, no. 22, Kuwait, Sept. 1960; Muḥammad al-Sālimī, *Nahḍat al-aʿyān bi-ḥurriyyat ʿUmān*, Cairo 1380/1961; Admiralty, *A handbook of Arabia*, London 1916-7; C. Aitchison, ed., *A collection of treaties, engagements and sanads*, xi, Delhi 1933; India, *Selections from the records of the Bombay government*, n.s., xxiv, Bombay 1856; Rupert Hay, *The Persian Gulf states*, Washington 1959; J. Lorimer, *Gazetteer of the Persian Gulf, ʿOmān and Central Arabia*, Calcutta 1908-15; Saudi Arabia, *Memorial of the government of Saudi Arabia* [al-Buraymī Arbitration], 1955; Reference Division, Central Office of Information, *The Arab states of the Persian Gulf and south-east Arabia*, London 1959; United Kingdom, *Arbitration concerning Buraimi and the common frontier between Abu Dhabi and Saudi Arabia*, 1955. (PHEBE MARR)

AL-**DUBB** [see NUDJŪM].

DUBDŪ (modern spelling Debdou; usual pron.: Dəbdu, ethn. *dəbdūbī*, pl. *dbādba*), a small town in eastern Morocco, at an altitude of 1,100 m., "at the foot of the right flank of the valley" of the Oued Dubdū "which rises in a perpendicular cliff to a height of 80 m. above the valley"; on a plateau nearby stands the fortress (*ḳaṣba* [*ḳaṣaba*]) protected by a fosse on the side facing the mountain; on the left side of the valley lies a suburb named Mṣəllā. A dependency of the *ʿamāla* (under the administration of the French Protectorate in the region) of Oujda, it is the centre of the tribe of the Ahl Dubdū (numbering 6,599 in 1936), but its own population consists of Arabized Berbers, of Arabs and of Jews who, though becoming less and less numerous, still form the majority (in 1936, 917 out of 1,751 inhabitants); the Jews, who live in the central quarter (*məllāḥ*) of the township, are in some cases of Berber origin, and in others are the descendants of Andalusian Jews who emigrated at the time of the Reconquest. This Jewish community of traders and artisans, not to mention agricultural workers, has been reduced since the establishment of the French Protectorate as many of its members have swarmed away to newly created centres in eastern Morocco (Missour in particular), though not without preserving firm links with their native town.

Situated on the route to Taza taken by Saharan tribes, Debdou (where a market is held on Thursdays) has always been a commercial centre of some importance; the fertility of the surrounding districts (vines, fruit trees, wheat, barley, etc.) also make it an agricultural centre.

It is certain that Debdou is a very ancient foundation; and since the 7th/13th century it has never ceased to play a part in the history of Morocco, as it occupies a strategic position between Fās and Tlemcen and was consequently a perpetual source of strife in dynastic struggles. At the time of the partition carried out by ʿAbd al-Haḳḳ (592-614/1197-1218) between the Marīnid tribes, it fell to the lot of the Berber Banū Urtajjən who, given the task of protecting Fās from the designs of the ʿAbd al-Wādids [*q.v.*] of Tlemcen, made it the capital of their fief; it was rewarded by being sacked, in 766/1364-5, by the king of Tlemcen. However in about 833/1430 a chieftain of the Banū Urtajjən succeeded in setting up a small principality at Debdou; its rulers remained independent of the Waṭṭāsids and even conceived the project, in 904/1499, of capturing Taza; the little state of Debdou only disappeared in the reign of the second Saʿdid sovereign, al-Ghālib bi'llāh, who in 970/1563 placed his territory under the authority of a pasha. From this point the history of the town, which is somewhat obscure, was reduced to the level of local conflicts between Arabs and

Berbers. Nevertheless, in the 19th century Debdou still possessed an autonomous administration; the Muslim population were dependents of the *ʿāmil* of Taza who every year sent his *khalīfa* to receive taxes, while the Jews sent their tribute to the pasha of Fās al-Djadīd. At the end of the century after the coming of Mawlāy ʿAbd al-ʿAzīz (1894) and during the revolt of the pretender Bū Ḥmāra [*q.v.*], a Berber named Bū Ḥaṣīra tried to make himself independent, but in 1904 the town and district gave their support to Bū Ḥmāra at the instigation of a Jew named Dūdū b. Ḥayda who was appointed *ḳāʾid* of Debdou, and took advantage of his position to inflict reprisals on his enemies, the Jews of Andalusian origin. Peace was restored by the French occupation which was decided upon in 1911 as a result of the murder of a Frenchman.

Throughout the last centuries, Arab influence and the Arabic language have been dominant to such a degree that Berber is no longer used except in the surrounding mountains. The dialect of the Jews presents some interesting features (see Ch. Pellat, *Nemrod et Abraham, dans le parler arabe des Juifs de Debdou*, in *Hespéris*, 1952, 1-25).

Bibliography: Ibn Khaldūn, *ʿIbar*, tr. de Slane, index; Yaḥyā Ibn Khaldūn, *Bughyat al-ruwwād*, ed. tr. A. Bel, Algiers 1903-13, index s.v.; Leo Africanus, tr. Épaulard, i, 299-302; Ch. de Foucauld, *Reconnaissance au Maroc*, 248 ff.; Marmol, *L'Afrique*, ii, 296; L. Massignon, *Le Maroc dans les premières années du XVIème siècle*, Algiers 1906, passim; La Martinière and Lacroix, *Documents pour servir à l'étude du Nord-ouest africain*, i, 122 ff.; A. Bernard, *Les Confins algéro-marocains*, 28 ff.; Nehlil, *Notice sur les tribus de la région de Debdou*; N. Slousch, *Les Juifs de Debdou*, in *RMM*, xxii (1913) 221-69; L. Gentil, *L'amalat d'Oudjda*, in *La Géographie*, 1911, 11-38, 332-56; Desnottes and Célérier, *La vallée de Debdou*, *ibid.*, 1928, 337-57; L. Voinot, *De Taourirt à la Moulouya et à Debdou*, *ibid.*, 1912, 21-33; idem, *Pèlerinages judéo-musulmans du Maroc*, Paris 1948, 9, 10, 32-4, 76, 93, 96, 97; *EI*[1], art. by A. Cour (which has been considerably abridged). (Ed.)

DUBROVNIK [see RAGUSA].

DŪD AL-ḲAZZ [see ḤARĪR].

DUDJAYL [see KĀRŪN].

DUFF (DAFF, the modern pronunciation, may be traced back to Abū ʿUbayda [d. ca. 210/825]) generic name for any instrument of the tambourine family, although sometimes it is the name for a special type. Islamic tradition says that it was invented by Tubal b. Lamak Masʿūdī, *Murūdj*, viii, 88) whilst other gossip avers that it was first played on the nuptial night of Sulaymān and Bilḳīs (Ewliyā Čelebi, i/2, 226). Al-Mufaḍḍal b. Salama (d. 307-8/920) says that it was of Arab origin (fol. 20) and Ibn Iyās (d. ca. 930/1524) says in his *Badāʾiʿ al-zuhūr* that it was the *duff* that was played by the Israelites before the Golden Calf. Certainly the name can be equated with the Hebrew *toph* and perhaps with the Assyrian *adapa*. Saʿadya the Jew (d. 312/924) translates *toph* by *duff*. We see both the round and the rectangular instrument in ancient Semitic art (Rawlinson, *Five great monarchies*, i, 535; Perrot-Chipiez, *Hist. de l'art*, iii, 451; Heuzey, *Figurines antiques*, pl. vi, 4), and in ancient Egypt (Wilkinson, *Manners and customs of the ancient Egyptians*, i, 443, fig. 220).

The tambourine of Islamic peoples may be divided into seven distinct types: 1. The rectangular form; 2. The simple round form; 3. The round form with snares; 4. The round form with jingling plates; 5. The round form with jingling rings; 6. The round form with small bells; 7. The round form with both snares and jingling implements.

1. The rectangular tambourine of modern times has two heads or skins with "snares" (*awtār*) stretched across the inside of the head or heads. We know from al-Muṭarrizī (d. 610/1213) that the name *duff* was given both to a rectangular and to a round tambourine. As early as the 6th century A.D. we read of the *duff* in the poet Djābir b. Ḥuyayy and this was probably the rectangular instrument. The author of the *Kashf al-humūm* says that the pre-Islamic tambourine (*ṭār djāhilī*) was different from the round Egyptian tambourine (*duff miṣrī*) of his day (fol. 193). Tuways, the first great musician in the days of Islam, played the *duff murabbaʿ* or square tambourine (*Aghānī*, iv, 170). He belonged to the *mukhannathūn* and it was perhaps on that account that the rectangular tambourine was forbidden whilst the round form was allowed (al-Muṭarrizī). At the same time the rectangular instrument was favoured by the *élite* of Medina in the first century of Islam (al-Mufaḍḍal b. Salama, fol. 11). We know also that the Syrians used this type of instrument since it is called *rᵉbhīʿa* (rectangular) in the Syriac version of the O.T. (*Exodus*, xv, 20; *Judith*, iii, 7). To-day this form has fallen into desuetude in Arabia, Syria, Egypt and Persia, but may be found in the Maghrib. For designs see Christianowitsch, 32, pl. 11 where it is called a *daff*, and Höst, 262, Tab., xxxi, 11, where it is called a *bandayr*. Actual specimens are to be found at Brussels, Nrs. 339, 340 (Mahillon, i, 400) and at New York, Nrs. 392, 1316 (*Catalogue*, ii, 82; iv, 50).

2. The simple round form. This was also called the *duff* (al-Muṭarrizī) and it is said that this type, without jingling plates or bells, was considered "lawful" (Ewliyā Čelebi, i/2, 226). Probably, this was the *mazhar* or *mizhar* of pre-Islamic and early Islamic times. It is true that Arabic lexicographers say that the *mizhar* was a lute (*ʿūd*), a definition borne out by Arabic writers on music (*ʿIḳd al-farīd*, iii, 186; al-Mufaḍḍal b. Salama, fol. 27; *Kitāb al-Imtāʿ wa 'l-intifāʿ*, fol. 13ᵛ; Masʿūdī, *Murūdj*, viii, 93), but it is extremely doubtful that the *mizhar* or *mazhar* was a lute. The mistake probably arose with an early lexicographer saying that "the *mizhar* was a musical instrument (see the *Miṣbāḥ* of al-Fayyūmī) like the *ʿūd* (lute)" meaning "like the *ʿūd* is a musical instrument". In the 11th century *Glossarium Latino-Arabicum* the *mazhar* (562) or *mizhar* (508) equates with *tinfanum* (= *tympanum*). The type is still to be found under this name in Turkey (Lavignac, 3023) and in Palestine (*ZDPV*, l, 64, plate 8). The *mazhar* of Egypt has jingling rings attached to it.

3. The round form with "snares". This is similar to the preceding but with the addition of "snares" stretched across the inside of the head. We cannot be sure of its name in the early days of Islam but probably it was the *ghirbāl*, so-called because it was round like a sieve. Al-Ṣaghānī (d. ca. 660/1261-2) says that this was the tambourine which was referred to by Muḥammad when he said: "Publish ye the marriage, and beat for it the tambourine (*ghirbāl*)". Other accounts of this *ḥadīth* call this instrument the *duff*. In Algeria of modern times this type of instrument is known as the *bandayr* or *bandīr*, a name borrowed, seemingly, from the Gothic *pandero*, one of the instruments of pre-Moorish Spain mentioned by Isidore of Seville. The *bandayr* is

generally larger than the other types such as the *duff*, *mazhar* and *ṭār*, although in the *Kas͟hf al-humūm* we read that tambourines were made in various sizes 'from the large *ṭār* (*ṭār kabīr*) to the small *g͟hirbāl* (*g͟hirbāl daḳīḳ*)". For the Egyptian instrument see Villoteau (988), and for the Algerian see Christianowitsch (31, pl. 9), Delphin et Guin (37) and Lavignac (2931). In Morocco, according to Höst (261, pl. xxxi, 6), it was called the *ḍīf* (ضيف). Actual specimens may be found at Brussels, Nrs. 308, 309 (Mahillon, i, 393, 400) and at New York, Nr. 452 (*Catalogue*, iii, 50).

4. The round form with jingling plates. This is similar to No. 2 but with the addition of several pairs of jingling plates (*ṣunūd͟j*) fixed in openings in the shell or body of the instrument. This is the *ṭār*. Although the author of the *Kas͟hf al-humūm* makes the name older than that of the *duff*, yet we have no substantial proof of this. We find the *ṭār* in the Yemen in the 6th/12th century (Kay, *Yaman*, 54) and in the 7th/13th century *Vocabulista in Arabico* it is given as *ṭarr* (= *tinpanum*). The Persian instrument is depicted by Kaempfer under the name of *daf* (741, fig. 7) and Niebuhr shows an Arabian example which he calls the *duff* (i, pl. 26). Höst (261, pl. xxxi) gives a design of a Moroccan instrument in the 12th/18th century under *tirr* (تِرّ). In Algeria it is called the *ṭār* (Delphin et Guin, 42; cf. *Tad͟hkirat al-nisyān*, 93; Lavignac, 2844), and a design is given by Christianowitsch (pl. 10). The Egyptian *ṭār* is described and delineated by Villoteau (i, 988) and Lane (chap. xviii), whilst actual examples may be seen at Brussels, Nrs. 312-5 (Mahillon, i, 394-5) and New York, Nrs. 455, 1319, 1359 (*Catalogue*, iii, 51). In Egypt the smaller types were given the name of *riḳḳ* (Villoteau, i, 989), by no means a modern name (*Kas͟hf al-humūm*, fol. 193). There are examples at Brussels, Nrs. 316, 317 (Mahillon, i, 395).

5. The round form with jingling rings. This is a similar instrument to the preceding but with jingling rings (*d͟jalād͟jil*) fixed in the shell or body instead of jingling plates. In Egypt, in the time of Villoteau (i, 988), it was known as the *mazhar*, but in Persia, a century earlier, Kaempfer calls it the *dāʾira* (741, 8).

6. The round form with small bells. This is the same instrument as the preceding in regard to shape but the jingling apparatus, instead of being fixed in spaces in the shell or body, is attached to the inside of the shell or body. These small bells (*ad͟jirās*), often globular in shape like sonnettes, are sometimes attached to a metal or wooden rod fixed across the inside of the head. This instrument is popular in Persia and Central Asia where it is generally known as the *dāʾira*. An 11th/17th century instrument is shown by Kaempfer (742, 8). For a modern instrument see Lavignac (3076). Apparently *dāʾira* and *duff* became generic names for all types of the tambourine although the former must have been reserved for a round type.

7. The round form with both snares and jingling implements. In the Mag͟hrib this instrument is called the *s͟haks͟hāk* (Delphin and Guin, 38, 65; Lavignac, 2932, 2944). In some parts, however, this type is called the *ṭabīla*. In Egypt, according to Villoteau, it was the *bandayr*.

If the drum (*ṭabl*) sounds the martial note of Islam, as Doughty once said, the tambourine sounds the social note. It is true that in the *d͟jāhiliyya* the tambourine was in the hands of the matrons and singing-girls (*ḳaynāt*) during the battle, sometimes in company with the reed-pipe (*mizmār*) as with the Jewish tribes (*Ag͟hānī*, ii, 172), but it was also the one outstanding instrument of social life (al-Suyūṭī, *Muzhir*, ii, 236) as many a *ḥadīt͟h* testifies. In artistic music the tambourine has ever been the most important instrument for maintaining the rhythm (*īḳāʿāt*, *uṣūl*, *ḍurūb*).

The *duff* became the Persian *daff* or *dap*, the Kurdish *dafik*, the Albanian and Bosnian *def*, and the Spanish and Portuguese *adufe*. The *dāʾira* is the Caucasian *dahare*, the Serbian and Albanian *daire*, and the *dārā* of India. The *ṭār* survives in the Polish *tur* and the Swahili *atari*. The tambourine was popularized in Europe by the Moors of Spain and was, for a long time, known as the *tambour de Basque*, the latter region being one of the gateways for the infiltration of Moorish civilization. It fell into desuetude in Europe about the 15th century but was revived again in the 17th century when Europe adopted it as part of the Turkish or Janissary music craze.

Bibliography: Farmer, *History of Arabian music to the xiiith century*, 1929; idem, *Studies in oriental musical instruments*, 1931; Sachs, *Reallexikon der Musikinstrumente*, 1913; Fétis, *Histoire générale de la musique*, 1869-76; Christianowitsch, *Esquisse historique de la musique arabe*, 1863; Delphin and Guin, *Notes sur la poésie et la musique arabes dans le Maghreb algérien*, 1886; Advielle, *La musique chez les Persans en 1885*, 1885; Höst, *Nachrichten von Marokos und Fes*, 1787; Kaempfer, *Amoenitatum exoticarum* . . ., 1712; al-Mufaḍḍal b. Salama, *Kitāb al-Malāhī*, Cairo MS., f. dj. 533; *Kas͟hf al-humūm*, Cairo MS., f. dj. 1; *Ag͟hānī*, Būlāḳ ed.; Mahillon, *Catalogue . . . du Musée Instrumental du Conservatoire Royal de Musique*, 2nd ed.; *Catalogue of the Crosby Brown collection of musical instruments*, New York; Ewliyā Čelebi, *Narrative of Travels . . . . by Evliya Efendi*, tr. J. von Hammer, 1834; Ibn ʿAbd Rabbihi, *al-ʿIḳd al-farīd*, Cairo 1887-8; *Kitāb al-Imtāʿ wa 'l-intifāʿ*, Madrid MS., Nr. 603; G. Toderini, *Letteratura turchesca*, Venice 1787; Lavignac, *Encyclopédie de la musique*, v, 1922; Villoteau, in *Description de l'Égypte*, i, (Folio ed.); *Glossarium Latino-Arabicum*, ed. Seybold; Niebuhr, *Voyage en Arabie*, 1776; Fitrat, *Uzbek ḳilassiḳ mūsiḳāsī*, Tas͟hkent 1927; Mironov, *Pesni Fergani Bukharī i khivī*, Tas͟hkent 1931; Belaiev, *Musīkalnīe instrumentī uzbekistana*, Moscow 1933; Kāmil al-K͟hulaʿī, *Kitāb al-Musīḳī al-s͟harḳī*, Cairo 1322.

(H. G. Farmer)

DŪG͟HLĀT, occasionally Dūḳlāt, a Mongol tribe whose name, according to Abu 'l-G͟hāzī (ed. Desmaisons, St. Petersburg 1871, i, 65), derives from the plural of the Mongol word dog͟holong (-lang) "lame". The tribe appears to have played no part in the early period of the Mongol Empire, though it is supposed always to have supported Čingiz K͟hān (Ras͟hīd al-Dīn, ed. Berezin in *Trudī vost. otd. Imp. Russk. Ark͟heol. obshčestva*, vii, 275, xiii/text 47, 52; tr. L. A. Khetagurov, Moscow-Leningrad 1952, i/1, 193). At that time the tribe apparently emigrated in its entirety out of Mongolia; there is at least no Mongol tribe of that name today.

The Dūg͟hlāt did not attain political significance until after the disintegration of the Ilk͟hān Empire [*q.v.*], from which time Muḥammad Ḥaydar Dūg͟hlāt (Ḥaydar Mīrzā, [*q.v.*]), a member of the tribe, provides information about them in his *Taʾrīk͟h-i*

Ras͟hīdī (ed. N. Elias and E. Denison Ross, London 1895). But his information is not everywhere reliable and, in the few places where the tribe is mentioned in other sources, contradicts these. According to Ḥaydar a member of the Dūg͟hlāt, Tūlik or perhaps his younger brother Būlād͟jī (the form Pūlādčī printed in the edition of Abu 'l-G͟hāzī, 56 ff., does not appear in the manuscripts), is supposed in 748/1347-8 to have placed K͟hān Tug͟hluḳ Temür on the throne at Aḳsū in the Tarim Basin. The latter in turn is supposed to have expressed his gratitude to the Dūg͟hlāt by granting them "nine powers" and thus to have stabilized their power in the Tarim Basin. Ḥaydar Dūg͟hlāt claims to have seen this document "in the Mongol language and script" in his childhood, but says that it was lost during the reign of S͟haybānī K͟hān, d. 916/1510 [*q.v.*] (*Taʾrīk͟h-i Ras͟hīdī*, 54 f., 305). But the inaccurate chronology of this historian in the pertinent notices tends to provoke strong doubt as to the genuineness of the document. Between 769/1368 and 794/1392 (?) power in Mog͟holistān (as eastern interior Asia starting at about Semiryečʹe was at that time called) was wielded by Ḳamar al-Dīn Dūg͟hlāt (S͟haraf al-Dīn Yazdī, *Ẓafar-nāma*, ed. Bibl. Ind., Calcutta 1887-8, i, 78 ff.), a brother of Būlād͟jī according to the *Taʾrīk͟h-i Ras͟hīdī*. After an early period of co-operation with Tīmūr [*q.v.*], he was forced by the latter, after a long struggle, to flee across the Irtīs͟h into the Altai (Yazdī, i, 494 ff.). Two of his brothers remained in the service of Tīmūr (Yazdī, i, 104 ff., 650), whose sister was married to a member of the Dūg͟hlāt.

After 1392 Ḳamar al-Dīn's nephew (?) K͟hudāydād, nominally major domo, was in fact the ruler of Mog͟holistān. The Čingizid [*q.v.*] k͟hāns whom he put on the throne were nothing but puppets. K͟hudāydād demonstrated his readiness to reach a settlement with the Tīmūrids [*q.v.*], ostensibly owing to their common Islamic faith, and met in 828/1425 Ulug͟h Beg [*q.v.*] without battle in Semiryečʹe (ʿAbd al-Razzāḳ Samarḳandī, *Maṭlaʿ al-saʿdayn*, Ms. Leningrad, 157, fol. 230). In view of this agreement the k͟hāns of Mog͟holistān had to accept the division of their land among the brothers and sons of K͟hudāydād (*Taʾrīk͟h-i Ras͟hīdī* 100). His eldest son Muḥammad S͟hāh was appointed tribal chief (Ulus Begi) by K͟hān Waʾīs (ca. 1418-29) and took up residence in Semiryečʹe (*Taʾrīk͟h-i Ras͟hīdī* 78). His younger son was driven out of the western Tarim Basin by the Tīmūrids (1416? Samarḳandī in *Notices et extraits* xiv, i, 296) and died even before his father did. His son Sayyid ʿAlī finally retook Kās͟hg͟har and ruled there for 24 years (died 862/1457-8, according to his tomb in Kās͟hg͟har; see *Taʾrīk͟h-i Ras͟hīdī* 87, 99). He was succeeded by his two sons Sāniz Mīrzā (until 869/1464-5) and Muḥammad Ḥaydar (until 885/1480), both of whom performed great services in the development of the region. Then Abū Bakr Mīrzā, the son of Sāniz, drove his uncle and K͟hān Yūnus of Mog͟holistān out of the western Tarim Basin, after which he took up residence in Yarkend and defended himself in 904-5/1499 against an attack by the k͟hāns of Mog͟holistān. Not until 920/1514 was he eliminated by Saʿīd K͟hān (*Taʾrīk͟h-i Ras͟hīdī* 293).

In addition to the principal line other branches of the Dūg͟hlāt repeatedly established small principalities, occasionally at war with the former. Muḥammad Ḥaydar for example, the grandfather of the historian Muḥammad Ḥaydar, fought in alliance with the Čingizid Yūnus and with the Tīmūrid Aḥmad Mīrzā against Abū Bakr Mīrzā (see above). His sons Muḥammad Ḥusain and Sayyid Muḥammad Mīrzā vacillated continuously between the two dynasties and were even from time to time in the service of the Uzbeks. The former was finally killed in Herāt at the command of S͟haybānī [*q v.*] in 914/1508-9. His brother fell victim in 1533 to the hatred of K͟hān ʿAbd al-Ras͟hīd of Mog͟holistān, who had come to power in the same year (*Taʾrīk͟h-i Ras͟hīdī* 106 ff., 305, 450). Muḥammad Ḥusayn's son, the historian Muḥammad Ḥaydar Mīrzā, left in 1541 his position as governor of Ladakh in the service of the ruler of the Tarim Basin to proclaim his independence in Kas͟hmīr (see ḤAYDAR MĪRZĀ).

With the elimination of this line and the end of Abū Bakr's (see above) rule in 920/1514, the independence of the Dūg͟hlāt in the Tarim Basin came to an end. They continued to support the Čingizids there and wielded considerable power into the 17th century.

A tributary of the "Great Horde" of Ḳazak͟hs between the Ili and the Jaxartes bore the name Dulat into the 20th century, obviously derived from Dūg͟hlāt. At the end of the 19th century, they included almost 40,000 tents (see N. Aristov, *Zamětki ob ėtničeskom sostavě Tyurkskik͟h plemën i narodnostey*, St. Petersburg 1897, 77).

Bibliography: the sources are mentioned above. Studies include W. Barthold, *Zwölf Vorlesungen über die Geschichte der Türken Mittelasiens*, Berlin 1935, 209-14 (French tr. Paris 1945); idem, *Four studies on the history of Central Asia*, tr. V. Minorsky, i, 1956, 54; R. Grousset, *L'Empire des steppes*, Paris 1939, index; P. P. Ivanov, *Očerki po istorii Sredney Azii* (Outlines of the history of Central Asia), Moscow 1958, i and ii; B. Spuler, in *Handbuch der Orientalistik*, volume v, 5, index. The last two works named contain further detailed bibliography.

(W. BARTHOLD-[B. SPULER])

ḌUḤĀ (AR.), "forenoon", the hour of one of the prayers [see ṢALĀT].

DUKAYN AL-RĀD͟JIZ, the name of two poets who were confused by Ibn Ḳutayba (*S͟hiʿr*, S͟hākir ed. 592-95) and the authors who copied or utilized him: Ibn ʿAbd Rabbih, *ʿIḳd*, 1346/1928 ed., 202-3; *Ag͟hānī*, viii, 155—Beirut ed., ix, 252-3; C. A. Nallino, *Litt.*, (with a note of correction by M. Nallino).

1. — Dukayn b. Rad͟jāʾ al-Fuḳaymī (d. 105/723-24); a panegyric in *rad͟jaz* composed by him on Muṣʿab b. al-Zubayr, and an *urd͟jūza* upon his horse who won a race organized by al-Walīd b. ʿAbd al-Malik (see Yāḳūt, xi, 113-17; Ibn ʿAsākir, v, 274-9), have been preserved.

2. — Dukayn b. Saʿīd al-Dārimī (d. 109/727-28) to whom Ibn Ḳutayba actually dedicated his article entitled Dukayn al-Rād͟jiz; see also Ibn ʿAsākir, *ibid.*; Yāḳūt, xi, 117-19. He wrote a panegyric on ʿUmar b. ʿAbd al-ʿAzīz when the latter was made governor of Medina (87/706), which brought him a rich present, formal promises and perhaps the intimacy of ʿUmar. After the latter had risen to the Caliphate (99/717), Dukayn went to visit him, reminded him of their covenant and received a new gift. This Dukayn is said to have written the line: "When a man has not sullied his honour with vile deeds, whatever garment he wears is fine", which appears, however, at the beginning of the famous *Lāmiyya* by al-Samawʾal (F. Bustānī, *al-Mad͟jānī al-ḥadīt͟ha*, i, 345).

This poet should not be confused with Dukayn

b. Saʿīd (Saʿd) al-Khathʿamī (al-Muzanī), Companion of the Prophet (see Ibn Ḥadjar, *Iṣāba*, no. 2401).

Bibliography: in the text. (CH. PELLAT)

DUKHĀN [see TÜTÜN].

DUKKĀLA, a confederation of Moroccan tribes which constituted an autonomous administrative region during the French Protectorate. When Morocco attained independence, it was attached to the province of Casablanca, and now forms no more than the al-Djadīda circle (Mazagan). Some sections of the Gharb tribe also have this name.

Al-Bakrī does not mention the Dukkāla, but al-Idrīsī, together with Ibn Khaldūn (*ʿIbar*) and Leo Africanus later, attribute an extensive area to the confederation, comprising roughly the triangle within the rivers Umm al-rabīʿ and Tensift, and the Atlantic coast. The name Dukkāla, moreover, was given to one of the gates of Marrakesh from the early 12th century onwards. Tradition has it that there were 6 tribes in the confederation, the Ragrāga, Hazmīra, Banū Dghūgh, Banū Māgir, Mushtarayya, and Ṣinhādja tribes. The above list explains a contradiction already pointed out by Ibn Khaldūn, whereby the Dukkāla are sometimes considered part of the Maṣāmida [*q.v.*] (the first five tribes certainly were), and at other times part of the Ṣinhādja [*q.v.*]. Both were of Berber descent. Their relationship with another Berber group which is now extinct, the Tāmasnā, is difficult to define. The confederation was not spared the serious events which, under the Almohads, followed the introduction of Arab tribes into Morocco, and later the Ḥāḥa and the Banū Maʿḳil tribes were driven back onto their territory. In the south only the Ragrāga tribe remained intact, after having played an important role historically. The legend of its seven saints found a place in all religious chronicles; on receiving news of the Islamic revelation, all seven went to Mecca and spoke, in Berber, with the Prophet. Their tombs in the Djabal al-Ḥadīd are objects of veneration to the present day. The name Dukkāla no longer has any ethnic significance today; it denotes Arab tribes, or tribes completely under Arab influence. The tribes are sedentary, and although some of them still inhabit tents, it is for practical reasons and not in order to pursue a nomadic existence. The wind blows fair for the economic future of the region if developments based on the Imfout dam, completed in 1950, go according to plan. On relations between the Dukkāla and the Portuguese, see the articles ASFĪ, AZAMMŪR and above all AL-DJADĪDA.

Bibliography: The essential information is given by M. Michaux-Bellaire, *Reg. des Dukkala*, I, in *Villes et Tribus du Maroc*, x, Paris 1932; see also P. Lancre, *Rep. alph. des Conf. de tribus, des tribus de la zone franç. de l'emp. chér.*, Casablanca 1939; H. Terrasse, *Histoire du Maroc*; Ibn Zaydān, *Itḥāf aʿlām al-nās* (5 vols. published 1929-33) and Muḥammad b. Aḥmad al-Kanūnī, *Āsafī ....*, Cairo 1353/1934. (G. DEVERDUN)

DŪLĀB [see NĀʿŪRA].

DULAFIDS, an important tribe in the 3rd/9th century whose holdings formed a special district of their own known as al-Īghārayn (the two fiefs) in al-Djibāl, east of Nihāwand between Hamadān and Iṣfahān. ʿĪsā b. Idrīs laid the basis for the Dulafid fortune by engaging in highway robbery to such an extent that he was able to retire and erect a stronghold at al-Karadj, which his son and successor, al-Ḳāsim b. ʿĪsā al-Idjlī, known as Abū Dulaf, employed as the foundation for the Dulafid dynasty.

Abū Dulaf was a Shīʿī, a highly educated man, a lauded poet, a great general and a competent leader whose integrity was such that although he was a fervent pro-ʿAlid and had led troops against al-Maʾmūn, the latter pardoned him and accepted him at court. (Cf. AL-ḲĀSIM). With his troops he played an active rôle in subduing the revolt of Bābak al-Khurramī (222/836-7) [*q.v.*], and his descendants, known as the Dulafids, served under and on the side of the reigning Caliphs, taking part as loyal supporters in many military enterprises of the Caliphate. Abū Dulaf and his grandson, Aḥmad, especially distinguished themselves as generals under the Caliphs al-Muʿtaṣim and al-Muʿtaḍid respectively. Theirs was an almost completely independent dynasty which existed for some seventy years; their fief was given in perpetuity and the Dulafids paid a fixed yearly tribute to the Caliphs with no other taxes levied. They also coined their own money.

The Dulafid capital, al-Karadj, was a long town built on a height, an important site in the midst of fertile lands which averaged an annual yield amounting to 3,100,000 dirhams. Abū Dulaf had extended the town to an area covering about two leagues with well-built houses of clay brick, two markets and numerous baths.

Upon the death of Abū Dulaf in 225/839-40 the principality was governed in turn by his direct descendants commencing with his son, ʿAbd al-ʿAzīz who, in 252/866 under the Caliph al-Muʿtaḍid, was also governor of al-Rayy (d. 260/873-4), and followed successively by his grandsons, Dulaf (d. 265/878-9), Aḥmad (d. 280/893-4), ʿUmar (d. 283/896-7), and al-Ḥārith, known as Abū Layla, all of whom were loyal to the existing Caliphate.

Al-Ḥārith was accidentally killed in battle in 284/897-8 when, according to Masʿūdī, his horse was felled under him causing the unsheathed sword he was carrying on his shoulder to plunge into him and mortally wound him. With his death the power of the Dulafids and their dynasty came to an end and their lands reverted to the control of the central government.

Bibliography: Ṭabarī, iii; Masʿūdī, *Murūdj*, indexes, s.v.; Schwarz, *Iran*, v, 573 ff.; Le Strange, 197-8; Ibn Khallikān, tr. de Slane, ii, 502-7; Meynard, *Dictionnaire géographique*, 478-9; Yāḳūt, ii, 832; Ibn Khurradādhbih, 244; Zambaur, 199, 44; Ritter, *Die Geheimnisse der Wortkunst* (*Asrār al-Balāgha*) *des Abdalqāhir al-Curcānī*, Bibl. Isl., xix, 1959, note on p. 34. (E. MARIN)

DULAYM, a large Sunnī tribe in ʿIrāḳ, living on the Euphrates from a point just below Fallūdja to al-Ḳāʾim. They claim origins at Dulaymiyyāt in Nadjd five centuries ago, but these are doubtless mythical and in fact the tribe represents a wide variety of mixed tribal fragments and tribeless peasantry. A few sections are nomadic in the Djazīra, moving to the river only from April to September; but the great majority live, at the humble level of ʿIrāḳī peasantry, by cultivating by water-lift or flow-canal (notably the Ṣaḳlāwiyya) from the Euphrates, and entrust their sheep and camels to specialized grazing parties or sections of their own sub-tribes. The populations of ʿĀna, Rāwa, Ḥadītha and Fallūdja contain certain elements of settled Dulaym. The tribe itself is divided into many sub-tribes and sections, cohesion among which depends upon the personality and inter-relations of the leading shaykhs. Numbers work for the oil company whose pipelines from Kirkūk cross their territory in the Ḥadītha neighbourhood, and others at the Hīt bitumen deposits. The tribe has a record of bad relations with the Shammar of the Djazīra, and of friendliness with the ʿAnaza in the Syrian desert; but tribal disorder has been slight and rare since 1340/1921, and the Dulaym, thanks largely to leadership by two or more outstanding shaykhs (notably ʿAlī Sulaymān) are among the better behaved major tribes of ʿIrāḳ. In Turkish times their frequent aggressions against travellers on the Baghdād-Aleppo trunk road called for punitive action by Government, notably by Nāẓim Pasha in 1910, and for the building of a line of military posts and khāns in the 12th/19th century. The tribal area was occupied by the British in 1917, and insurgent action in the turbulent year 1920 was limited to one section of the tribe. Since then, settlement and prosperity have increased.

The tribe has given its name to the Dulaym *liwā*ʾ (province) of ʿIrāḳ (population in 1947, 193,000) which, with headquarters at Ramādī, contains the *ḳaḍā*ʾs of ʿĀna, Fallūdja and Ramādī.

(S. H. LONGRIGG)

DULDUL, the name of the grey mule of the Prophet, which had been given to him by the Muḳawḳis [*q.v.*], at the same time as the ass called Yaʿfūr/ʿUfayr. After serving as his mount during his campaigns, she survived him and died at Yanbuʿ so old and toothless that in order to feed her the barley had to be put into her mouth. According to the Shīʿī tradition, ʿAlī rode upon her at the battle of the Camel [see AL-DJAMAL] and at Ṣiffīn. As *Duldul* in Arabic means a porcupine, it is possible that she derived her name from her gait, but this is far from certain. For the names of the horses of the Prophet, see G. Levi Della Vida, *Les "livres des chevaux"*, Leiden 1928, 8, 51; for his she-camels al-ʿAḍbāʾ and al-Ḳaṣwāʾ, see al-Djāḥiẓ, *Ḥayawān*, index.

Bibliography: Djāḥiẓ, *Bighāl*, ed. Pellat, Cairo 1955, 21; Muḥ. b. Ḥabīb, *Muḥabbar*, 76; Ṭabarī, i, 1783; Masʿūdī, *Murūdj*, iv, 317, 356, 369; Ibn al-Athīr, ii, 238; Nawawī, 46; Damīrī, s.v.: *TA* s.v.; *LA*, s.v. (CL. HUART-[CH. PELLAT])

AL-**DULFĪN** [see NUDJŪM].

DULŪK, the name given by the Arab authors to a locality situated, on the borders of Anatolia and Syria, in the upper valley of the Nahr Karzīn, at the foot of the Anti-Taurus (Kurd Dagh), north-west of ʿAyntāb. It was the ancient Doliche, famous for the cult of a Semitic divinity who in the Graeco-Roman period received the name of Zeus Dolichenos. Being at the intersection of the routes from Germanicia, Nicopolis and Zeugma, it had been conquered by ʿIyāḍ b. Ghānim and became one of the fortresses which since the earliest days of Islam had defended the frontier against the Byzantines (cf. the verse of ʿAdī b. al-Rikāʿ in Yāḳūt, ii, 583, and Nöldeke's remark in *ZDMG*, xliv, 700); it belonged to the *djund* of Ḳinnasrīn before being incorporated in the district of the ʿAwāṣim [*q.v.*] organized by Hārūn al-Rashīd. Dulūk also played a part in the Ḥamdānid-Byzantine wars at the time of Sayf al-Dawla and Abū Firās, and was conquered by the Byzantines in 351/962 (Ibn al-Athīr, viii, 404), the year in which Abū Firās [*q.v.*] was captured. The citadel at this time was supplied with water by an important aqueduct, and it was surrounded by rich orchards. Having become during the Crusades the seat of a bishop of the province of Edessa (under the name of Tulupe), it was the theatre for numerous engagements, and when, in 549/1155, the troops of Nūr al-Dīn regained possession of it, shortly after ʿAyntāb [*q.v.*], Dulūk had much declined; its fortress was ruined and there remained no more than a mediocre village.

The old name is preserved in that of the village of Dülük köy, a Turkish village near the Syrian border, and in that of Tell Dülük situated to the south of this locality where there is now a monument erected for a *wālī*.

Bibliography: Fr. Cumont, *Études syriennes*, Paris 1917 173-7; idem, *Syria*, i (1920), 189; P. Merlat, *Jupiter Dolichenus*, Paris 1960, 1-5; R. Dussaud, *Topographie historique de la Syrie*, Paris 1927, 472; M. Canard, *Histoire de la dynastie des H'amdanides*, i, Algiers 1951, 232; Cl. Cahen, *La Syrie du nord à l'époque des Croisades*, Paris 1940, index, esp. 115, 320; R. Grousset, *Histoire des Croisades*, 3 vols. Paris 1934-6, index; Le Strange, *Palestine* 36, 386-7, 438; Balādhurī, *Futūḥ*, 132; Ibn Khurradādhbih, 75, 97; Ḳudāma, 254; Yaʿḳūbī-Wiet 230; Yāḳūt, iii, 742, 759; Ibn al-Shiḥna, *al-Durr al-muntakhab*, 224; Ibn al-ʿAdīm, *Taʾrīkh Ḥalab*, ed. S. Dahan, index; Ibn al-Athīr, index; Ibn Wāṣil, *Mufarridj al-kurūb*, ed. Shayyāl, i, 125; Abū Shāma, *K. al-Rawḍatayn*, Cairo, i, 76, (= ed. Hilmy Ahmad, i/1, Cairo 1956, 192-3). (D. SOURDEL)

DŪMAT AL-DJANDAL, an oasis at the head of the Wādī Sirḥān which runs from south-east to north-west, linking central Arabia on one side and the mountains of Ḥawrān and Syria on the other; it is thus situated on the most direct route between Medina and Damascus, being about 15 days' journey on foot from the former and about 7 days or rather more from the latter. The oasis is in a *ghāʾiṭ* "depression" or *khabt* "vast low-lying area", the length of which, according to Yāḳūt, is 5 parasangs or, in modern terms, according to Ḥāfiẓ Wahba, 3 miles, the width half a mile and the depth 500 feet below the level of the desert surrounding it. The morphology of the region has brought about a change in the name of the oasis which, at least since the last century, has become al-Djawf (el-Djōf), "vast depression", "round basin", "flat, spongy floor of a valley or region in which water collects". Yāḳūt, who describes the locality at some length, is unaware of this change in the name.

Dūma (the spelling Dawma is not acceptable) is perhaps an Aramaic word; according to the ancient Arab scholars Ibn al-Kalbī and al-Zadjdjādjī, this term derives from the name of one of the sons of Ismāʿīl (Dūm or Dūmān or Dūmāʾ): incidentally the name Dūmāh also occurs in the Bible (*Genesis*, xxv, 14; *Chronicles*, i, 30) as the name of an Ishmaelite tribe. The Arab writers say that, as the Tihāma no longer provided sufficient grazing for the too numerous Ismāʿīl clan, the son mentioned above emigrated to this region which took its name Dūma from him, and there he built a fortress. In fact, a fortress was already in existence before Islam at Dūmat al-Djandal, and its name Mārid is mentioned in an ancient proverb deriving from a phrase said to have been uttered by al-Zabbāʾ (*tamarrada Mārid wa ʿazza al-Ablaḳ*). The remains of an ancient fortress still survived in the last century, and Euting made a sketch of them in 1883. The fortress was built of stone and in addition there stood around it a wall also of stone; it was on account of these constructions that Dūma was given the additional epithet al-Djandal, a common noun signifying "stone". In the pre-Islamic period the idol Wadd was worshipped there.

Yāḳūt and other Arab geographers tell us that three places bore the name Dūma, one near Damascus (where there is still a Dūma), another near al-Ḥīra, and the one with which we are concerned, in northern Arabia. This identity of names has given rise to confusion in certain Arab historical sources; and there has been a tendency to ascribe to Dūmat al-Djandal events which took place in the other localities.

The inhabitants of Dūmat al-Djandal were the Banū Kināna, for the greater part of this sub-tribe of the Banū Kalb had, before Islam, spread into the desert of al-Samāwa in northern Arabia, from the plain of Dūmat al-Djandal in the north as far as the two mountains of the Ṭayy (Adja' and Salmā) in the south. This territory had been allotted to them as their pasturages at a general assembly of the Kalb, held in order to put an end to a civil war between two groups (F. Wüstenfeld, *Register*, *s.v.* Kalb b. Wabara; cf. al-Bakrī, *Muʿdjam*, 33 ff.). But in the oasis itself a certain number of the ʿIbād of al-Ḥīra had settled (in Balādhurī, the name appears as "ʿIbād al-Kūfa", but De Goeje corrected it to ʿIbād al-Ḥīra), that is to say a certain number of Christians who lived in that town and who were distinct from the Tanūkh, nomads from the surrounding districts. It may be conjectured that these ʿIbād in the oasis practised trade as well as agriculture, for Dūmat al-Djandal was one of the principal markets of northern Arabia.

Dūmat al-Djandal enjoys a certain fame in the annals of ancient Islam, particularly on account of the three expeditions undertaken by Muḥammad to conquer it; the first, in 5/626, led by the Prophet himself, achieved no results since the inhabitants of the oasis scattered before he arrived; the second, in 6/627-8, commanded by ʿAbd al-Raḥmān b. ʿAwf, brought about the conversion to Islam of the chief al-Aṣbagh (in some sources al-Aṣya, probably an error) b. ʿAmr al-Kalbī; the third was organized by Muḥammad at Tabūk and entrusted to Khālid b. al-Walīd. The latter took possession of the town in the oasis, levied a heavy war indemnity on the population and compelled the chief Ukaydir b. ʿAbd al-Malik al-Kindī al-Sakūnī [*q.v.*] to go to Medina to conclude a treaty with the Prophet; the text of the treaty still survives, possibly with interpolations (al-Balādhurī, *Futūḥ*, 61 ff.; Ibn Saʿd, i, 2, 36 ff.; Yāḳūt, ii, 627; see also M. Ḥamīdallāh, *Wathā'iḳ*, Nr. 191; Wellhausen, *Skizzen und Vorarbeiten*, iv, 133, n. 3, 404 n. 1; Caetani, *Annali*, 9 A.H. and 45, note 3). The difference in the names of the chiefs with whom the Muslims had to deal in 6 and 9, the difference in origin of these chiefs, one Kalbī the other Kindī, the diversity of certain details in traditions relating to Ukaydir, led De Goeje to raise questions and Caetani to express doubts which appear to be excessive. In reality, various difficulties can be overcome if one distinguishes the Kalb, nomads inhabiting a vast area and having their own chiefs, from the population of the oasis which was sedentary and composed of agricultural workers, merchants and artisans, and had immigrated even before Muḥammad's expeditions, as moreover al-Masʿūdī confirms (*Tanbīh*, 248). In the account relating to Ukaydir it should be noted that, according to al-Balādhurī (*Futūḥ*, 62) and Yāḳūt (ii, 626 ff.), Ukaydir is said to have called his dwelling in ʿIrāḳ Dūma, in remembrance of Dūmat al-Djandal, after leaving the oasis; another tradition also preserved by al-Balādhurī (*ibid.*, 63) and Yāḳūt (ii, 627) relates on the contrary that Ukaydir called the Arabian oasis Dūmat al-Djandal in order to distinguish it from the Dūma near al-Ḥīra from which he came, but the first tradition appears to be the more probable, since there are grounds for maintaining that the name Dūma borne by the oasis is an ancient one.

References to Dūmat al-Djandal occur in certain sources in connexion with the celebrated crossing of the desert made by Khālid b. al-Walīd in 12/633. Having been asked to rejoin the Muslim forces in Syria as soon as possible since they were in danger, Khālid set out, and is said to have attacked Dūmat al-Djandal and killed Ukaydir. De Goeje (*op. cit.*, 15 ff.) considers al-Djandal here to be an interpolation, and supposes that the Dūma referred to by the sources is Dūma of al-Ḥīra; it seems impossible that Khālid could have made such a detour which would have taken him so far out of his way while delaying the accomplishment of his mission. De Goeje's argument is very logical, and it has been accepted by Mednikov (*Palestina*, i, 435 ff.) and Caetani, so that the murder of Ukaydir, if murder it was, would have taken place in ʿIrāḳ. Let us also add that ʿAmr b. al-ʿĀṣ was ordered during the *ridda* to fight the Kalbī Wadīʿa who had revolted with some of the Kalb and entrenched himself at Dūmat al-Djandal, whilst al-Aṣbagh's son had remained faithful to Islam (al-Ṭabarī, i, 1872, 1880); it was perhaps ʿAmr who conquered Dūmat al-Djandal, but it is also possible to attribute this feat to ʿIyāḍ b. Ghanm; in fact, the story goes that an expedition under his command set out from Medina with this objective but ran into difficulties, but it is also related that ʿIyāḍ was governing the oasis in 13/634 (al-Ṭabarī, i, 2136). In the same way, it was at neither Dūmat al-Djandal nor Dūma near al-Ḥīra, but at Dūma near Damascus that, according to De Goeje (*ibid.*, 16 ff.), the fair Laylā, the daughter of al-Djūdī al-Ghassānī and loved by ʿAbd al-Raḥmān b. Abī Bakr, fell into the hands of the Muslims.

On another occasion in the history of Islam, at the time of an incident of great importance, the mention of Dūmat al-Djandal has given rise to argument: the oasis was said to have been chosen at Siffin as the meeting-place for the arbitrators Abū Mūsā al-Ashʿarī [*q.v.*] and ʿAmr b. al-ʿĀṣ [*q.v.*] after their investigation of the dispute between ʿAlī and Muʿāwiya, and it was there that they were to announce their verdict; but some sources place the meeting at Adhruḥ [*q.v.*], and it has been explained *supra*, s.v. ʿALĪ B. ABĪ ṬĀLIB, that in fact there were two meetings, on different dates, one at Dūmat al-Djandal and the other some months later and in very different circumstances, at Adhruḥ (this point being established, the sequence of events becomes clear and the highly complicated question of their chronology becomes soluble). One of the actions which Muʿāwiya took to harass ʿAlī was to dispatch a force to Dūmat al-Djandal in 39/660; ʿAlī succeeded in driving it out, but the inhabitants of the oasis refused to recognize either his authority or Muʿāwiya's. When the centre of the Muslim empire was set up in Syria, under the Umayyads, and in ʿIrāḳ, under the ʿAbbāsids, Dūmat al-Djandal lost all its importance; from then onwards it was no more than an oasis in Arabia inhabited by a poor sparse population of agricultural workers, since trade henceforth followed other routes; the Arab geographers in fact do no more than relate the historical events described above and quote from the verses of ancient poets.

We know that during the last centuries of Ottoman domination in northern Arabia anarchy was general and the situation only improved when the Wahhābis imposed their authority over the country. They also took possession of Dūmat al-Djandal which belonged to them until the time of Ṭalāl, *amīr* of Shammar, of the Āl Rashīd, for in 1855 it became a dependency of Ḥāyil. In 1909 it was occupied by Nūrī Ibn Shaʿlān, chief of the Ruwalā tribes, in 1920 the *amīr* of Shammar recovered possession of it, and finally ʿAbd al-ʿAzīz Ibn Saʿūd, when he overthrew the amīrate of Shammar, added it to his domains (1921). Immediately afterwards, Transjordania attempted to move her frontier southwards to Nafūd, but Ibn Saʿūd held firm and at the Congress of al-Kuwayt (1923-4) the question was not resolved. Ibn Saʿūd also made incursions into Transjordania, within the framework of his much wider activities against the Ḥidjāz and ʿIrāḳ. The frontier was established by the Ḥadda Agreement between Ibn Saʿūd and Sir G. Clayton (2 November 1925), and the Wādī Sirḥān along with al-Djawf [*q.v.*] and Ḳurayyāt al-Milḥ thenceforward became part of Nadjd (*OM*, i-viii (1922-8), index).

The nomadic or semi-nomadic tribes who inhabit the region between Taymāʾ in the south as far as Kerak in the north, Nafūd and Wādī Sirḥān in the east are grouped under the collective name of al-Ḥuwayṭāt [*q.v.*]. During the last century several European travellers visited the oasis; an account of their explorations will be found in Hogarth.

Bibliography: Wāḳidī, ed. Wellhausen, 174 ff., 236 ff., 391, 403 ff.; Ibn Hishām, ed. Wüstenfeld, 668, 903 (and ii, 205), 991; Ibn Saʿd, i/2, 36 ff., ii/1, 119 ff.; Balādhurī, *Futūḥ*, 61-3, 111; Ṭabarī, i, 1462 ff., 1556, 1702 ff., 1872, 1880, 2065, 2077, 2136 and index *s.v.* Dūmat al-Djandal and Ukaydir; Masʿūdī, *Tanbīh*; *BGA*, vol. viii, 248, 253, 272, 296; Ibn al-Athīr, ii, 135 ff., 160, 214 ff., 303 and index; Yāḳūt, i, 152, 825; ii, 625-9, 852; iii, 106; iv, 76, 389, 913; idem, *Mushtarik*, ed. Wüstenfeld, 186 ff., 338; Bakrī, *Muʿdjam*, ed. Wüstenfeld, 352 ff.; Ibn al-Athīr, *Usd al-ghāba*, *s.v.* Ukaydir; Caetani, *Annali*, 4 a.H., § I, Nr 7, 5 a.H., §§ 4, 77-8, 6 a.H., § 16, 9 a.H., §§ 24, 36, 45-8, 12 a.H., §§ 170, 180-2, 219-20, 232-4, 38 a.H., §§ 28, 38; L. Veccia Vaglieri, *Il conflitto ʿAlī-Muʿāwiya e la secessione khārigita riesaminati alla luce di fonti ibāḍite*, in *AIUON*, 1952, 49-50, 52, 53, 82-7; J. Wellhausen, *Skizzen und Vorarbeiten*, iv, 133 note 3, 404 note I; M. J. de Goeje, *Mémoire sur la conquête de la Syrie* (in his *Mémoires d'histoire et de géographie orientales*), 2nd ed., 10-5; D. G. Hogarth, *The penetration of Arabia*, London 1904, index. (L. Veccia Vaglieri)

DUNAYSIR, mediaeval ruined town of Upper Mesopotamia (within the borders of modern Turkey), situated 20 km. south-west of Mārdīn on a tributary of the Khābūr, the site of which is today marked by the Kurdish village of Koč Ḥiṣār, the *Kosar* of the western chroniclers. A fortress of former times, generally identified with the *Adenystrai* of Dio Cassius, Dunaysir is not noted as an important place in the early years of Islam, and was subsequently never a fortress. Not until the 4th/10th century does its name appear, in a ms. of Ibn Ḥawḳal, as the site of a market. Later, at the beginning of the 7th/13th century, the town of Dunaysir had become a caravan, agricultural and intellectual centre, whose prosperity is reflected in the monuments erected at this time by order of the Artuḳid princes: mosques and *madrasa*, traces of which still remain. Spread over a wide plain, without a wall, beside a watercourse crossed by a stone bridge, it was, says Ibn Djubayr, "surrounded by flower and vegetable gardens", and was a centre of attraction for all inhabitants of the neighbouring regions. A popular fair was held there from Friday to Sunday. Later, Dunaysir declined and became a direct dependency of Mārdīn.

Bibliography: Pauly-Wissowa, s.v. Adenystrai; R. Dussaud, *Topographie historique de la Syrie*, Paris 1927, 493; Le Strange, 96; A. Gabriel, *Voyages archéologiques dans la Turquie orientale*, Paris 1940, 45-53; Ibn Ḥawḳal, in *BGA* ii, 151 n. b; Ibn Djubayr, *Riḥla*, ed. De Goeje, 240-2, tr. Gaudefroy-Demombynes, 277-8; Yaḳut, ii, 612. On the dictionary of the literati of Dunaysir, see Brockelmann, I, 406 (333), S I, 569. (D. Sourdel)

DUNBĀWAND [see damāwand].

DUNGHUZLUM [see deñizli].

DUNḲULA [see dongola].

DUNYĀ (Ar.), the feminine of the elative adjective meaning 'nearer, nearest', is used in the Ḳurʾān, often combined with 'life' to mean this world. It had more or less this sense before Islam (Noeldeke, *Muʿallaḳāt des ʿAmr und des Ḥārith*, 49). The heaven of the *dunyā* is the lowest of the seven; *dunyā* is what is contained in the succession of night and day, is overshadowed by the sky and upheld by the earth, is all that the eye can see, the world of the seen (*shahāda*). In the realm of the spirit it includes all that Christians mean by the world and the flesh and it denotes the lot of man, whatever befalls him before death and does not continue with him afterwards. The interests of this world may oppose those of the next so a man may have to deny himself or use temperately part of his *dunyā*, money, food, drink, clothing, houseroom and, some say, life itself. One authority says that love of women is not love of the *dunyā*. Another definition is: every pleasure or desire, even speech with friends, so long as they are not aimed at the service of God. Denial of the *dunyā* means putting less trust in what is in your own power than in what is in the hand of God. All this is only a development of what is said in the Ḳurʾān: Those who buy this world at the price of the hereafter (*sūra* II, 80/86) and, The hereafter is better (*sūra* LXXXVII, 16). The truly religious man will have no desires (Muḥammad b. Muḥammad b. al-Zayyāt, *al-Kawākib al-sayyāra*, 130), and an extreme statement is ascribed to the prophet: Grant to one who loves me and obeys me little wealth and few children and to one who hates me and does not obey me much wealth and many children. At the judgement the *dunyā* will appear as a horrid old hag and will be cast into the fire (Ghazzālī, *Iḥyāʾ ʿulūm al-Dīn* (1312 A.H.), 3, 54, 148) an idea which contradicts the fundamental thought of Islam.

Without going into legal details, the *dunyā* consists of things allowed and things forbidden. Good Muslims avoided what was forbidden but many carried scruple to excess, *e.g.*, by refusing to eat the food of one who might have made some money by sharp practice in trade or by acting as a government servant. Asceticism was often considered good in itself and some went so far as to say: Entrust your affairs to God and take your rest.

Bibliography: see Ākhira, and in addition: Ibshīhī, *al-Mustaṭraf*, last chapter. (A. S. Tritton)

DURAYD b. al-ṢIMMA, ancient Arabic poet and leader of the Banū Djusham b. Muʿāwiya, one of the most powerful Bedouin opponents of Muḥammad, born ca. 530. He is a prominent figure of Arabic pre-Islamic antiquity; to later generations, he was the embodiment of ancient paganism which fought stubbornly against Islam.

His father was Muʿāwiya b. al-Ḥāri**th**, called al-Ṣimma, leader of the Banū **Dj**u**sh**am b. Muʿāwiya, who belonged to the group of the Hawāzin tribes, and lived between Mecca and Ṭāʾif. Despite the similarity in their religion, and their economic, political and social ties, there was an ancient rivalry between these two places, which also concerned the Bedouin tribes who lived between Mecca and Ṭāʾif. This antagonism was caused by the contrast between the urban Ḳuray**sh**, and the predominantly nomadic Hawāzin, the difference of their cultural standing, and their different economic and political conditions. This period of the Ḥi**dj**āz was characterized by the resultant battles. These disturbances are known as the battles of al-Fi**dj**ār.

Durayd b. al-Ṣimma did not take part in these battles for personal reasons arising from his links with the Kināna tribes, although he himself had fought earlier on against the Kināna, and although his father had played an important part in the Fi**dj**ār war.

He did, on the other hand, play an important part in the battles between Hawāzin and **Gh**aṭafān, where he lost his two brothers ʿAbd al-Ya**gh**ū**th** and ʿAbd Allāh. It was particularly the death of ʿAbd Allāh which resulted in the renewed enmity and battles, in which the tribe of the Banū **Dj**u**sh**am again played a prominent part. It was the duty of Durayd b. al-Ṣimma to avenge his brother's death, and he fulfilled this duty in numerous raids against the **Gh**aṭafān.

Friendly ties linked him with Banū Sulaym. He also asked for the hand of the young poetess al-**Kh**ansāʾ in marriage, but she refused him because of his advanced years, although her relatives would have wished to retain the favour of this influential chief. The al-**Kh**ansāʾ episode did not, however, endanger his friendship with her brothers Muʿāwiya and Ṣa**kh**r.

Even in the time when Muḥammad began to spread his teaching among the Bedouin, the old Durayd b. al-Ṣimma played a prominent part. It would even appear that he was responsible for the opposition which the Hawāzin tribes offered the new faith, and that he was also the tool of the intentions of the **Th**aḳīf tribe from Ṭāʾif. Perhaps he was the instigator of the alliance—which never materialized—between the Hawāzin and the Ḳuray**sh**.

After Muḥammad had left for his last battle against Mecca, the Hawāzin, the **Th**aḳīf, and his *khalīfa*s under Mālik b. ʿAwf of the tribe of Naṣr in Ḥunayn, rose in opposition to Muḥammad. The aged Durayd b. al-Ṣimma was brought on a litter, to give the benefit of his experience of battle to the tribes. Just before the battle he had an argument with Mālik b. ʿAwf, concerning the accomodation of women, children, and the cattle of the tribe, all of whom he wanted to get away from the battle-field.

After the defeat of Mecca, Muḥammad went against the Hawāzin. The armies met in Ḥunayn. After an initial success, the Bedouin were beaten and scattered. The faithful gained great booty. Durayd b. al-Ṣimma met with a tragic death in this battle, at the hand of Rabīʿa b. Rufayʿ, of the formerly allied tribe of Sulaym. He died at a great age, about 100 years old.

Al-Aghānī, ix, 2 summarizes the significance of Durayd b. al-Ṣimma by stating that he was a brave *fāris*, a *shāʿir faḥl*. Muḥammad b. Sallām placed him first among those who were considered *shuʿarāʾ* and *fuḥalāʾ*. According to the Arabs, he was the greatest *fāris* poet. Al-Aṣmaʿī in *Fuḥūlat al-shuʿarāʾ*, in *ZDMG* 65, 498, line 20, also regards him highly.

In his poems, which may be regarded as typically Bedouin, battle descriptions, expressions of love and friendship, lament, and praise can be found. He has all the advantages and shortcomings of an embodiment of all that is typical of the Arab.

The metres he used most frequently are *wāfir* and *ṭawīl*, and also *basīṭ*, *mutaḳārib*, *radjaz*, *kāmil* and *ramal*.

Bibliography: *Aghānī*, ix, 2-20, and also see Tables 332; Ibn Ḳutayba, *K. al-Shiʿr*, 197, 219, 470-3; *Khizānat*, i, 125, ii, 121, 324, iii, 166, iv, 148, 444-7, 513, 516; There are also verses in: Bakrī, *Muʿdjam*, *Sīrat ʿAntar*, *ʿIḳd*, *Aṣmaʿiyyāt*, *Kāmil*, *Ḥamāsa* of *Buḥturī* and *Abū Tammām*, *LA*, *TA* and others.

Editions: R. Růžička, *Duraid ben aṣ-Ṣimma, obraz středního Hidžázu na úsvitě islamu*, Prague 1925-1930, part 3, vol. 2 in *Rozpravy České akademie věd a umění*, Kl. III, no. 61, 67. Contents cf. *ArO*, xix, 1951, nos. 1-2, 99-100.

(K. PETRÁČEK)

DURAZZO. [see DRAČ].

DŪRBĀSH (Persian, lit. "be distant"), the mace or club used as an emblem of military dignity; in Persian and Turkish usage the *dūrbāsh* can also be the functionary who carries the mace [see ČĀʾŪSH, SARHANG]. The *čūbdār*s described by Niẓām al-Mulk, *Siyāsat-nāme*, ch. xxxix, who seem to have been similar functionaries, carried gold and silver staffs; ʿAwfī, *Djāmiʿ al-ḥikāyāt* (passage cited by M. Fuad Köprülü, *Bizans müesseselerin Osmanlı müesseselerine tesiri hakkında bazı mülâhazalar*, in *Türk Hukuk ve Iktisat Tarihi Mecmuası*, Istanbul 1931, 213; Ital. tr., *Alcune osservazioni* ...., Rome 1953, 57) describes the *dūrbāsh* as wearing silver belts and carrying maces encrusted with gems; Köprülü, *loc. cit.*, attributes the use of the jewelled mace, found also with the **Gh**aznawids and indeed with the Sāmānids, to an inheritance from the Sāsānid court.

In Muslim India the word is applied to the mace rather than to the functionary. The earliest mention of it appears to be in Amīr **Kh**usraw, *Nuh sipihr*, ii, where the author speaks of the rā**dj**ā of Warangal delivering the *dūrbāsh* he had received from the former sultan to **Kh**usraw **Kh**ān, general of Ḳuṭb al-Dīn Mubārak **Sh**āh, for its replacement by a *dūrbāsh* from the reigning sultan in ca. 718/1318 (the word here is mistranslated "canopy" in Elliot and Dowson, *History of India* ...., iii, 561); cf. Amīr **Kh**usraw, *Ḳirān al-saʿdayn*, lith. ʿAlīgaṛh, 78-9. According to Ḍiyāʾ al-Dīn Baranī, *Taʾrīkh-i Fīrūz Shāhī*, Bibl. Ind., 136, men would run "before the stirrups of kings" with the *dūrbāsh* on their shoulders. Yaḥyā b. Aḥmad Sirhindī, *Taʾrīkh-i Mubārak Shāhī*, speaks of it as a two-branched ornamented baton (cf. *Ghiyāth al-lughāt*, s.v.; *Farhang-i andjuman ārā-i Nāṣirī*, s.v.), and the *Muʾayyad al-fuḍalāʾ* as spears (*nīzahā*) which are borne before emperors and kings (ms Mullā Fīrūz Library, s.v.). Its use in Mu**gh**al times is confirmed by the European travellers; Manucci, *Storia di Mogor*, i, 220, describes the use of the *dūrbāsh* in the escort of **Sh**āh**dj**ahan's daughter **Dj**ahānārā, in which 'menservants held sticks of gold or silver in their hands and called out "Out of the way!" '. These menservants are called *gurzbardār*s by the travellers Tavernier and Bernier.

Bibliography: in addition to the references in the text: Redhouse, Brit. Mus. MS Or. 2965, vii, 778-9 (detailed notice with several quotations). For rods, staffs, etc., see ʿANAZA, i; ʿAṢĀʾ; ḲAḌĪB; ṢAWLADJĀN. (J. BURTON-PAGE)

AL-**DURR**, the pearl. The ancient legend of its origin is found at great length in the Arabic authors, first in the *Petrology* (*Steinbuch*, ed. Ruska) of Aristotle, then with variants in the *Rasāʾil Ikhwān al-Ṣafāʾ* and the later cosmographers. According to it, the *asṭūrūs* (ʾοστρεῖον) rises from the depths of the sea frequented by ships and goes out to the ocean. The winds there set up a shower of spray and the shells open to receive drops from this; when it has collected a few drops it goes to a secluded spot and exposes the drops morning and evening to the breeze and the gentle heat of the sun until they ripen. It then returns to the depths of the sea where it takes root on the sea-bed and becomes a plant. If the sun or the air reach it at midday or in the night the pearls are destroyed; they are also ruined if they stay too long at the bottom of the sea, just as over-ripe dates lose their beauty and flavour.

Scattered among these fables we find a few real facts and critical observations, for example the statement that the shells, though rough and unclean outside, are smooth and brilliant within, or that the substance composing the pearl is identical with that which lines the interior of the shell, which points to its being produced from the latter. We also find a comparison with the hen's egg or with the child in its mother's womb. Of particular interest is the statement that there is a worm in the pearl, since it is now established that pearls are formed by the oyster when parasitic worms are present.

Masʿūdī gives us the earliest account of the provenance of pearls in various parts of the Indian Ocean and of the pearl-fisheries in the Persian Gulf; in the *Murūdj* he refers to an earlier work of his in which he appears to have drawn upon Yaḥyā b. Māsawayh's book on stones, which was extracted from Tīfāshī. According to him the only pearl-fisheries are on the coast of the sea of Ḥabash at Khārak in the Persian Gulf, at Ḳaṭar, ʿUmān and Sarandīb. The divers live on fish and dates; a slit is made in their necks below the ear through which they can breathe, for they close the nostrils by clasping a piece of tortoiseshell on the nose (or, according to Yaḥyā b. Māsawayh, they place a long reed in the nose and breathe through this). They can remain half an hour below the water. They put cotton-wool steeped in oil in their ears; when under the water they squeeze some of it out so that it becomes quite bright. They paint their legs with a black substance lest they should be devoured by underwater monsters. While under the water they communicate with each other by a kind of barking sound. Ibn Baṭṭūṭa also relates some of these fables, but on the whole his account of the pearl-fisheries is based on his personal observations at Sīrāf. There the Banū Siʾāf dive for pearls in a calm bay. In the months of April and May many boats assemble here with divers and Persian merchants. The diver places the clamp on his nose, ties a rope round himself, and remains one to two hours (!) under water. He finds shells firmly attached between small stones, pulls them off by hand or cuts them off with a special knife, and puts them in a leather bag which he carries hanging round his neck. When he can remain below no longer he shakes the rope; the man in the boat on seeing this pulls him up, takes the shells, opens them, and collects the pearls. The sultan receives five of each haul and the merchants sell the others, but the divers themselves have little profit as they are always in debt to the merchants for advances made to them.

The pearl is the jewel par excellence and is distinguished above other jewels by the fact that it is *ḥaywānī* and not *turābī*. Tīfāshī gives a very full account of the perfections and defects of pearls, etc., while al-Dimashḳī explains how mother-of-pearl (*ʿirḳ al-luʾluʾ* [*q.v.*]) is obtained from the layers composing the pearl shell. Valuable medicinal qualities are of course ascribed to the pearl. They are believed to be particularly effective in cases of palpitation of the heart or in melancholia, they strengthen the nerves, cure headaches, and, if dissolved in water and rubbed on the affected part, mitigate leprosy. They are dissolved with citron juice and vinegar.

The pearl has been prized by Muslim rulers for its value (a brief note on the classification and values of pearls in the Mughal emperor Akbar's treasury in *Āʾīn-i Akbarī*, i, Āʾīn 3) and as a symbol of purity. The name "pearl mosque" (*motī masdjid*) is frequently given in Muslim India to pure white mosques of marble or polished stucco. The ancient Hindū legend of the origin of pearls, that when the sun is in Arcturus (Skt. *svāti*), in October, the rain then falling drops into the open shells and so forms pearls, appears in several Indian Muslim works.

For the rôle of the pearl in book-titles, in poetry and in rhetoric see futher LUʾLUʾ.

Bibliography: *Das Steinbuch des Aristoteles*, ed. Ruska, 64, 96, 130; *Rasāʾil Ikhwān al-Ṣafāʾ* ed. Bombay, ii, 75; Masʿūdī, *Murūdj*, i, 328; Idrīsī-Jaubert, i, 157, 377; Ibn Baṭṭūṭa, ii, 244 ff.; Ḳazwīnī, *ʿAdjāʾib al-makhlūḳāt*, ed. Wüstenfeld, i, 115, 223; al-Dimashḳī, *Kosmographie*, ed. Mehren, 77 etc.; Tīfāshī, *Azhār al-afkār*, tr. Raineri Biscia, 6; Ibn al-Bayṭār, in Leclerc, *Notices et extr.*, xxvi/1, 248; Clément-Mullet, *Essai sur la min. arabe*, in *JA*, VIth ser. xi (1868), 16; M. Mokri, *La pêche des perles dans le golfe Persique*, in *JA*, ccxlviii/3 (1960), 381-97, with bibliography; idem, *Le symbole de la perle dans le folklore persan*, ibid. fasc. 4, 463-81. On trade see TIDJĀRA. (J. RUSKA*)

DURRĀNĪ, an Afghān tribe known as Abdālī until their name was changed by Aḥmed Shāh Durrānī. (See ABDĀLĪ, AḤMAD SHĀH, AFGHĀNISTĀN). The tribe was moved from Harāt and granted lands in the region of Ḳandahār by Nādir Shāh. At this time they were pastoral nomads but in the later 12th/18th century they began to take up agriculture. Their large financial and economic privileges were continued and extended in the reigns of Aḥmad Shāh and Tīmūr Shāh, when the Durrānī tribe formed the main political and military support of the monarchy. During this period they extended their landholdings in the districts more distant from the town of Ḳandahār, *e.g.*, Zamīndāwar, Nīsh, Tirīn, forcing the original cultivators (Tadjiks, Hazāras, Pārsīwāns, Balōčīs, Kākaṙs, etc.) to work as tenants or labourers, as they continued to do in the regions nearer Ḳandahār. Towards the end of the 18th century, however, and particularly after the transfer of the capital from Ḳandahār to Kābul and the cessation of Afghān expansion, the central government began to reduce the power of the Durrānī chiefs and to increase its revenue by preventing the evasion of liabilities by the Durrānīs. Durrānī resistance to this policy was a contributory cause of the civil wars of the later 18th and early 19th centuries, in which the Durrānīs suffered considerably. Under the Bārakzay Sardārs of Ḳandahār 1233-4/1818 to 1255/1839 and 1259/1843 to 1272/1855 the power of the Durrānī chiefs was further eroded by their virtual exclusion from administration and military employment, and by steadily increasing taxation and the government control of water distribution. This policy was continued after the incorporation of Ḳandahār into the Kabul dominions. Its success always varied inversely to the distance from Ḳandahār.

There is no recent information available about Durrānī clan divisions and it is supposed that these have tended to be obliterated with settlement. There is information about the important period down to the mid-19th century. According to Elphinstone the tribe was nominally divided into two branches (Zīrak and Pandjpāw), although from an early period this division had lost all importance except to indicate the descent of the clans. The clans of the Zīrak branch were the more powerful and wealthy. The Zīrak branch included three important clans, those of Popalzāy, ʿAlīkozāy and Bārakzāy. The Ačakzāys of the northern slopes of the Khʷādja Amrān range in the Quetta-Pishīn district of West Pakistan are a branch of the Bārakzāys, supposedly separated by Aḥmad Shāh. According to Elphinstone the Pandjpāw clans were those of Nūrzāy, ʿAlīzāy, Isḥākzāy, Khugānī, and Makū. There is little information about the last two although they still appeared as distinct entities on the Ḳandahār tax returns as late as 1857. The other Pandjpāw clans lived principally in the more westerly areas—the ʿAlīzāys in the fertile province of Zamīndāwar, where they settled in the early 19th century, the Isḥāḳzāys in Garmsīr on the lower Halmand and the Nūrzāys, who continued to live as nomads later than other clans, in various areas north of Ḳandahār (Nīsh, Tirīn), in Garmsīr and westwards towards Farāh and Harāt. The Zīrak clans lived nearer Ḳandahār, although they tended to spread out to other areas as well, *e.g.*, the Bārakzāys who originally settled in the Arghasān valley, south of Ḳandahār, also were found on the Halmand, and the Popalzāys of the lower Tarnak and Arghasān valleys also moved into Tirīn and the other districts in the hills north of Ḳandahār. The ʿAlīkozāys lived in the Tarnak valley as far as Djaldak on the borders of the Ghilzāy country and also were found westwards as far as the Halmand. The various clans were divided into sub-groups, *e.g.*, the Popalzāys included the royal family of the Sadōzāys and possibly also the Bāmazāys. These sub-groups, like some of the clans themselves, sometimes decayed or amalgamated to form new groups.

Bibliography: See AFGHĀNISTĀN. Also *Wāḳiʿāt-i Durrānī*, Kānpur 1292; M. Elphinstone, *Caubool*, London 1839; B. Dorn, *History of the Afghans*, London 1836; C. M. Macgregor, *Central Asia*, ii, *Afghanistan*, Calcutta 1871, esp. Appendix III; H. Rawlinson, *Report on the Dooranees* ...; Yu. V. Gankovski, *Imperiya Durrani*, Moscow 1958.

(M. E. YAPP)

DÜRRĪZĀDE, the patronymic of a famous family of Ottoman *ʿulemāʾ* of the 18th-19th centuries, five members of which attained the office of *Shaykh al-Islām* [*q.v.*] on no less than nine different occasions between the years 1734 and 1815. Only these latter can be dealt with here, and details must be confined to the periods of their *meshīkhat* which, unless otherwise stated, was reached by the normal progress through the offices of *ḳāḍī* of Istanbul, *ḳāḍī 'l-ʿasker* of Anadolu and *ḳāḍī 'l-ʿasker* of Rūmeli.

1. DÜRRĪ MEḤMED EFENDI. The son of a certain Ilyās, his date and place of birth are unknown. (The statement in the *Sidjill-i ʿOthmānī* that he was a native of Ankara probably derives from a misreading of the *Dewḥa*). While *ḳāḍi 'l-ʿasker* of Rūmeli for the second time, he was appointed *Shaykh al-Islām* on 3 Djumādā II 1147/31 October 1734 on the death of the incumbent Isḥāḳ Efendi. In Shawwāl 1148/February-March 1736 he was stricken with apoplexy, which in Dhu 'l-Ḥidjdja/April-May of the same year compelled him to retire from office. He died at his home in Üsküdar in 1149/1736-7 and was buried in the cemetery of Ḳaradja Aḥmed. (Ṣubḥī, 63b, 71b).

2. DÜRRĪZĀDE MUṢṬAFĀ EFENDI. The son of the above by the daughter of the former *ḳāḍi 'l-ʿasker* ʿAbd al-Ḳādir Efendi, he was born in 1114/1702-3. After having been *ḳāḍi 'l-ʿasker* of Rūmeli twice, he was appointed *Shaykh al-Islām* on 21 Shawwāl 1169/19 July 1756, but on 28 Djumādā I of the following year (18 February 1757) he was dismissed from office and exiled to Gallipoli. His second occupancy of this office came on 5 Shawwāl 1175/29 April 1762 and lasted until 24 Dhu 'l-Ḳaʿda 1180/23 April 1767; and on 15 Dhu 'l-Ḥidjdja 1187/27 February 1774 he was appointed for a third time. Infirm with old age, he retired on 22 Radjab 1188/28 September 1774 and died the same year on 7 Dhu 'l-Ḥidjdja/8 February 1775. He was married to the daughter of the former *Shaykh al-Islām* Pashmaḳčīzāde ʿAbd Allāh Efendi of a family claiming descent from the Prophet, and his sons by her all enjoy the title of *seyyid*. In 1179/1765-6 he restored the mosque at Yeñi Ḳapī (*Ḥadīḳat ül-djewāmiʿ*, i, 237), and would also appear to have founded a family burial ground outside Edirne Ḳapīsī in the vicinity of the fountain of Laʿlīzāde. A work on *fiḳh* entitled *Dürre-i beyḍā* is ascribed to him (*ʿOthmānlī müellifleri*, i, 308), and his translation of a short Arabic tract is to be found in a manuscript *medjmūʿa* in Topkapı, Emanet Hazinesi, no. 1308. (Wāṣīf, i, 83a, 91a, 210b, 290a; ii, 285a; Djewdet, i, 72, 78).

3. DÜRRĪZĀDE SEYYID MEḤMED ʿAṬĀʾ ALLĀH EFENDI. The second son of the above, he was born in 1142/1729-30. After having twice occupied the post of *ḳāḍi 'l-ʿasker* of Rūmeli, on 17 Djumādā II 1197/20 May 1783 he was appointed *Shaykh al-Islām* and he retained this office until 20 Djumādā I 1199/31 March 1785 when, suspected of complicity with the Grand Vizier Khalīl Ḥāmid Pasha in a conspiracy to depose Sultan ʿAbd al-Ḥamīd I, he was dismissed and sent to Gallipoli with orders to go on the pilgrimage. However, he died here of some dropsical affliction soon after his arrival, and the news of his death reached Istanbul on 6 Radjab 1199/15 May 1785. (Djewdet, ii, 71, 309, 317; İ. H. Uzunçarşılı, in *TM*, v (1935), 251, refers to a rumour that he was poisoned).

4. DÜRRĪZĀDE SEYYID MEḤMED ʿĀRIF EFENDI. The younger brother of the above, he was born in 1153/1740-1 and reached the post of *ḳāḍi 'l-ʿasker* of Rūmeli on 26 Ramaḍān 1198/13 August 1784. On 17 Shawwāl 1199/23 August 1785 he was appointed *Shaykh al-Islām*, but was dismissed from office on 10 Rabīʿ II 1200/10 February 1786 because of his political activities, and after being ordered to go on pilgrimage, he was forced to live in exile in Kütahya. He was permitted to return to Istanbul in 1205/1790-1 when his enemy the *Shaykh al-Islām* Ḥamīdīzāde Muṣṭafā Efendi was discharged from office, and on 22 Dhu 'l-Ḳaʿda 1206/12 July 1792 he was again appointed to the *meshīkhat*. Being held in some way responsible for the state of unpreparedness of Egypt when Napoleon launched his invasion, he was replaced in office on 18 Rabīʿ I 1213/30 August 1798,

and after a few months' exile in Bursa, he returned to Istanbul where he died on 20 Djumādā I 1215/9 October 1800 and was buried at Eğri Kapı. A collection of his *fetwā*s exists in Topkapı Sarayı, Yeniler, no. 4403; and no. 4783 in the same library is a notebook he kept of appointments and dismissals of the *ʿulemāʾ* for the years 1209-13 (Djewdet, ii, 292, 331, 347; iv, 456; v, 181; vii, 57, 68, 174).

5. Dürrīzāde Seyyid ʿAbd Allāh Efendi. The son of the latter, the date of his birth is not recorded. While *naḳīb ül-es̲h̲rāf* and a nominee (*pāyeli*) for the post of *ḳādi 'l-ʿasker* of Rūmeli, on 3 S̲h̲awwāl 1223/22 November 1808 he was appointed *S̲h̲ayk̲h̲ al-Islām*, remaining in office until 22 S̲h̲aʿban 1225/22 September 1810. His second term in the *mes̲h̲īk̲h̲at* began on 30 Djumādā I 1227/12 June 1812 and lasted until 10 Rabīʿ II 1230/22 March 1815. He died on 3 Djumādā I 1244/11 November 1828 and was buried near his great-grandfather in the cemetery of Ḳaradja Aḥmed (S̲h̲ānīzāde, i, 146, 399; ii, 114, 239; Luṭfī Efendi, ii, 153; K̲h̲iḍr Ilyās, 8).

Bibliography: Details of about forty members of this family who attained positions of varying importance in the learned profession can be traced through the following references to the *Sidjill-i ʿOt̲h̲mānī*, though the caution must be given that no detail, and in particular dates, can be accepted without verification from another source: i, 336, 399; ii, 338, 396; iii, 146, 242, 267, 363, 396, 476; iv, 75, 444, 586 (Nūr Allāh Efendi), 627. Müstaḳīmzāde Süleymān Saʿd al-Dīn Efendi (with the continuations of Münīb Efendi and Rifʿat Efendi), *Dewḥat ül-mes̲h̲āʾik̲h̲*, litho., Istanbul n.d., 91 (text corrupt), 100, 108, 109, 122. Specimens of the *fetwā*s issued by all the individuals mentioned in the article can be found in the *ʿIlmiyye Sālnāmesi*, Istanbul 1334, 515, 529, 551, 553, 575; I. H. Danişmend, *Izahlı Osmanlı tarihi kronolojisi*, iv, Istanbul 1961, *index*; İ. H. Uzunçarşılı, *Osmanlı tarihi*, iv/2, Ankara 1959, 472, 484, 501, 502; F. E. Karatay, *Topkapı Sarayı Müzesi Kütüphanesi Türkçe yazmalar kataloğu*, 2 vols., Istanbul 1961. The works mentioned in the article are: Meḥmed Ṣubḥī Efendi, *Taʾrīk̲h̲*, Istanbul 1198; Aḥmed Wāṣīf Efendi, *Taʾrīk̲h̲*, 2 vols., Istanbul 1219; Aḥmed Djewdet Pas̲h̲a, *Taʾrīk̲h̲*, 12 vols., Istanbul 1270-1301; Ayvansarāyī Ḥāfiẓ Ḥüseyn Efendi, *Ḥadīḳat ül-djewāmiʿ*, 2 vols., Istanbul 1281; Meḥmed ʿAṭāʾ Allāh S̲h̲ānīzāde, *Taʾrīk̲h̲*, 4 vols., Istanbul 1290-1; Aḥmed Luṭfī Efendi, *Taʾrīk̲h̲*, 8 vols., Istanbul 1290-1306; K̲h̲iḍr Ilyās Efendi, *Waḳāʾiʿ-i leṭāʾif-i Enderūn*, Istanbul 1276.

(J. R. Walsh)

DÜRRĪZĀDE ʿAbd Allāh Bey or Efendi (1869-1923), one of the last *S̲h̲ayk̲h̲ al-Islām*s of the Ottoman Empire, known for his *fetwā*s condemning the Turkish nationalist movement under Muṣṭafā Kemāl (Atatürk). He was born into a wealthy family claiming the title of *seyyid*, most of whose male members belonged to the *ʿilmiyye* class, and five of whom had previously served as *S̲h̲ayk̲h̲ al-Islām* [see preceding article]. The son of the last there mentioned, ʿAbd Allāh, was Dürrīzāde Meḥmed Efendi, who rose to the rank of Ḳadīʿasker of Rumeli, and was the father of the ʿAbd Allāh with whom this article is concerned.

ʿAbd Allāh attended secular elementary and intermediate schools, then studied at the Fātiḥ *medrese*, receiving his *idjāzet* from Eginli K̲h̲odja Ibrāhīm Haḳḳī Efendi (d. 1894), at the time under-secretary (*müstes̲h̲ār*) of the Mes̲h̲īk̲h̲at. He received his first appoinment as *müderris* (*ibtidāʾ-i k̲h̲āridj*) in 1883, and joined the Mes̲h̲īk̲h̲at in 1886, where by 1893 he rose to the rank of *müderris* of the Süleymāniyye. In 1897 he left the *ʿilmiyye* service to rejoin it in 1901 as member of the council for S̲h̲arʿī studies (*Medjlis-i Tedḳīḳat-i S̲h̲erʿiyye*), and later as ḳāḍīʿasker of Anatolia. Dismissed after the 1908 revolution, he became an opponent of the Ittiḥād we Teraḳḳī [*q.v.*] movement and devoted himself to civilian pursuits (from which period he became known as «Bey»). After the armistice of 1918 he was placed in charge of a comittee examining religious publications, became under-secretary at the Mes̲h̲ik̲h̲at on 1 February 1920, and *S̲h̲ayk̲h̲ al-Islām* in the third cabinet of Dāmād Ferīd [*q.v.*] on 3 April, less than three weeks after the reinforced Allied occupation of Istanbul. In this office he signed on 11 April 1920 four *fetwās*, of which the main one referred to the Kemālists as «certain civil persons [who] have allied and united and chosen for themselves leaders . . ., with fraud . . . are deceiving . . . the loyal Imperial subjects and without authority are rising up to enlist soldiers from the populace; and to this end are imposing, in contravention of the sacred law and against high orders, certain dues and taxes ostensibly on the pretext of feeding and equipping these soldiers but really by reason of [their own] greed for worldly goods . . .». Among many other specific accusations it charged these same persons with «treason» and with being «rebels» (*bug̲h̲āt*, *bāg̲h̲īler*), who in accordance with religious law were to be killed (*ḳatl ū ḳitālleri mes̲h̲rūʿ we farḍ olur*) one at a time or in groups. The briefer subsidiary *fetwā*s obliged Muslims to heed the sultan's call to arms against the rebels and threatened eternal punishment for deserters from any such army and earthly penalties for those disobeying orders in this fight against the rebels.

For a brief period ʿAbd Allāh also became acting Minister of Education and, during Dāmād Ferīd's attendance at the Paris Peace Conference, acting Grand Vizier (*ṣadr aʿẓam wekīli*). He was dropped from the cabinet upon its reorganization on 30 July 1920. At the time of the final nationalist victory in September 1922 he left Turkey for Rhodes and then Italy. On 23 March 1923 he left for Mecca where he died on 30 April in the act of performing the pilgrim's prayers at the Kaʿba. Although he died before the signature of the Treaty of Lausanne he was placed on the list of 150 persons (*Yüzellilikler*) excluded from its amnesty provisions.

Bibliography: *Sidjill-i ʿOt̲h̲mānī*, iv, 691; Mehmet Zeki Pakalın in *İslam Türk ansiklopedisi*, ii, 246-7, and in *Sidjill-i ʿOt̲h̲mānī d̲h̲eyli* (in the ms collection of Türk Tarih Kurumu); Ismail Hâmi Danişment, *İzahlı Osmanlı kronolojisi*, iv (1955), 536 ff.; Galip Kemali Söylemezoğlu, *Başımıza gelenler*, Istanbul 1939, 219 ff. For the original text of the *fetwā*s see *Taḳwīm-i Weḳāyiʿ* no. 3834 of 11 April 1336.

(Faik Reşit Unat and Dankwart A. Rustow)

al-**DURŪʿ** (Dirʿī), a large G̲h̲āfirī tribe, mainly nomadic and Ibāḍī, of the foothills and steppes of ʿUmān in south-eastern Arabia. From Wādī al-Ṣafā and areas of the G̲h̲āfirī Āl Bū S̲h̲āmis (of Nuʿaym) and Banī Ḳitab in al-Ẓāhira, their *dīra* extends south-east across the plain (Sayḥ al-Durūʿ) to Wādī Ḥalfīn and the territory of the Hināwī tribe of Āl Wahība. From Ḥamrāʾ al-Durūʿ and other outliers of the mountains of Inner ʿUmān (among which, centering around ʿIzz and Adam, is found the north-west enclave of the G̲h̲āfirī al-Djanaba), it extends south to the broken district of al-Ḥuḳuf (al-Ḥiḳf?) and the barren area of Djiddat al-Ḥarāsīs, and south-west to the sands of the Rubʿ al-Khālī [*q.v.*], the low borderland of which (al-Waṭāʾ) includes the *sabkhas* and quicksands of Umm al-Samīm [*q.v.*].

The main tribal centre, *ca.* 15 km. south of ʿIbrī, is the village of Tanʿam. This is the summering place (*maḳīẓ*, pl. *maḳāyiẓ*) of the shaykhly clan, al-Maḥāmīd, and of al-Maḳārida, of whom about 100 settled men care for the date gardens. Al-Maḥāmīd and al-Dabābina have gardens also in al-Sulayf, north-east of Tanʿam and south-east of ʿIbrī, and al-Maḥāmīd also at ʿIbrī. Other groups summer around their gardens at al-Maʿmūr (Maʿmūr of al-Durūʿ), al-Ḥabbī, Fill, Madrī, Bisāh, Yabrīn, Ṭaymisa, and Adam.

Although ʿIbrī is their main trading centre, al-Durūʿ also visit other inland markets including those at Nazwā, Bahlāʾ, and Adam, and occasionally travel as far as Dubayy on the Persian Gulf and al-Khābūra and Muscat on the Gulf of ʿUmān. Their chief vendibles are the following: animals—camels, goats, and sheep; handicrafts—ropes and cordage, mats (*simma*, pl. *samīm*), baskets, etc., made from fibre of the palmetto-like *saʿf* (in ʿUmān called *ghaḍaf*), and sheep's wool rugs, over the quality of which al-Durūʿ vie with Āl Ḥikmān; wood products—charcoal (*ṣakhkhām*), burned mainly of *samr* and *ghāf* from thickets growing along the numerous *wādīs* which traverse the steppe southwestward and southward; minerals—sulphur, from Ḳārat al-Kibrīt, for treating animal mange and for making gunpowder, and salt, from Ḳārat al-Kibrīt, Ḳārat al-Milḥ, and two *mamlaḥas* which lie in *sabkhas* on the eastern margin of Umm al-Samīm.

Of famous ʿUmānī camels al-Durūʿ raise three prize breeds: Banāt ʿUṣayfir, Banāt Khabār, and Banāt Ḥumra. The salt mines are exploited under general supervision of the *shaykhs*, but are not their property. The best salt comes from Ḳārat al-Kibrīt, which is also called Ḳārat al-ʿUraysha. At the sources of the coarser and less pure salt bordering Umm al-Samīm, (where the mining is safer and without the fatalities which occur at the two *ḳāras*), the salt is cut out in blocks, four to a camel-load, the gain from which ranges from one to four Maria Theresa dollars. The price is highest in summer, when mining is very difficult because of the heat and the distance from water, the nearest perennial sources—Muwayh al-Rāka and al-ʿUbayla,—being over a day away by camel.

Because al-Durūʿ ordinarily shun the vast sand desert of the Rubʿ al-Khālī, they have little reason for risking travel across Umm al-Samīm, in the quicksands of which, according to popular accounts, unwary travellers, shepherds, and raiders, and their animals, have been swallowed up. Members of the section of ʿIyāl Kharaṣ of al-Maḥāmīd are said to know safe paths leading north and south of the inner morass, but they themselves rarely cross.

Despite their commercial exploitation of what nature affords them, al-Durūʿ have no professional merchants and are a truly nomadic tribe. They have a reputation for bold and wide raiding, and active participation in tribal wars.

The majority of al-Durūʿ are Ibāḍīs, but the large division of al-Maḳārida and most of the small but ruling clan of al-Maḥāmīd are said to be Sunnīs.

The origin of the tribe is unknown. The similarity in name with Āl Dirʿ, relatives of Āl Saʿūd who formerly lived in Wādī Ḥanīfa and gave their name to the first Saʿūdī capital of al-Dirʿiyya, is probably without significance. A popular tradition of the south says that al-Durūʿ have the same origin as the tribe of al-Manāhīl—from Banī (or Ahl) al-Ẓanna. The frequency of naming from the mother—*fulān b. fulāna*—may be an indication of southern origin.

Of other groups living in the territory of al-Durūʿ the most interesting is that composed of some 40 men of al-ʿIfār [*q.v.*], a tribe originally from the area of Ḥabarūt in western Ẓufār, where the majority still live. Al-ʿIfār are Sunnīs and Hināwīs, but have the privilege of giving safe escort to strangers in Dirʿī and other Ghāfirī areas. Their leaders are accorded considerable respect. Āl (or ʿIyāl) Khumayyis, ranging in Wādī Sayfam and neighbouring valleys between Ḥamrāʾ al-Durūʿ and al-Djabal al-Akhḍar and numbering several hundred males, are said to be of Dirʿī origin, but are now regarded as a separate tribe. Other groups stemming from al-Durūʿ live in al-Sharḳiyya and al-Bāṭina.

The paramount shaykh is called *al-tamīma*. Chiefs of divisions or sections other than those of al-Maḥāmīd may be given the title of *shaykh*, but the usual title is *rashīd* (pl. *rushadāʾ*).

Bibliography: J. G. Lorimer, *Gazetteer of the Persian Gulf, ʿOmān, and Central Arabia*, ii, Calcutta 1908-15; Admiralty, *A Handbook of Arabia*, ii, London 1916-17; S. B. Miles, *The Countries and Tribes of the Persian Gulf*, ii, London 1919; Wilfred Thesiger, *Across the Empty Quarter*, in *GJ*, cxi, 1-3 (pub. July), 1948, 1-21; idem, *Desert Borderlands of Oman*, in *GJ*, cxvi, 4-6, 1950, 137-71; idem, *Arabian Sands*, London and New York 1959; Arabian American Oil Company, Relations Department, Research Division, *Oman and the southern shore of the Persian Gulf*, Cairo 1952 (in English and Arabic).

(C. D. Matthews)

DURŪZ (Druzes), sing. *Durzī*, a Syrian people professing an initiatory faith derived from the Ismāʿīliyya [*q.v.*]. They call themselves *Muwaḥḥidūn*, "unitarians", and number (in the mid-twentieth century) almost 200,000, living in various parts of Syria, especially in the mountains of the Lebanon, Anti-Lebanon, and Ḥawrān, chiefly as cultivators and landlords.

The faith originated in the closing years of the reign of al-Ḥākim [*q.v.*], Fāṭimid Caliph of Egypt (386-411/996-1021). According to the Ismāʿīlī Shīʿī faith then officially received in Egypt, al-Ḥākim, as *imām*, was the divinely appointed and authoritative guardian of Islam, holding a position among men which answered to that of the cosmic principle *al-ʿaḳl al-faʿʿāl*, the active intellect, and unquestionable head of the Ismāʿīlī religious hierarchy. Al-Ḥākim proved an eccentric ruler both in his personal life and in his religious policy, which flouted alternately the feelings of Ismāʿīlīs and Sunnīs alike. In his last years he seems to have wished to be regarded as a divine figure, above any rank which official Ismāʿīlism could accord him. A number of Ismāʿīlīs were in fact inclined so to regard him and, evidently with his private permission, set about organizing a following in the expectation of a public acknowledgement of the position.

The first of these men to catch the public eye was al-Darazī [*q.v.*], a non-Arab (like several of the leaders); the whole movement was called al-Daraziyya (or al-Durziyya) on his account. He seems to have interpreted the mood of the Ḥākim-cult circles in terms of a recurrent Ismāʿīlī heterodox attitude which exalted the *taʾwīl* (inner truth) and its representative, the *imām*, over the *tanzīl* (outward revelation) and its representative, the Prophet; so giving the current *imām*, al-Ḥākim, a supernatural status as embodiment of *al-ʿaḳl al-kullī*, the highest cosmic intellect. But his public activity (408/1017-8) caused disturbances and forced al-Ḥākim to be more cautious. In 410, however, al-Ḥākim gave his support to another leader, Ḥamza b. ʿAlī [*q.v.*] of Sūzan in Īrān, who gave to the Ḥākim cult its definitive Druze form.

Ḥamza had begun his mission in 408/1017 (the first year of the Druze era—the second being 410, when the public mission was renewed) and claimed to have been the only authorized spokesman for al-Ḥākim from the first. In 410, after al-Darazī's death, he tried to rally the whole movement under himself. His doctrine was evidently more original than al-Darazī's. It was, like Ismāʿīlī doctrine generally, a doctrine of cosmic emanation from the One and of return to the One through human gnosis. But it was unique in its special emphasis on the immediate presence of the cosmic One and made correspondingly rather less of the subordinate emanations. Hence Ḥamza called his own followers "unitarians" par excellence.

For Ḥamza, al-Ḥākim was no longer merely *imām*, however highly exalted. Ḥamza himself was the *imām*, the human guide, and therefore *al-ʿaḳl al-kullī*, the first cosmic principle; while al-Ḥākim was the embodiment of the ultimate One, the Godhead who created the Intellect itself and was accordingly Himself beyond name or office, beyond even good or evil. Compared to Him, ʿAlī and the Ismāʿīlī *imāms* as such were secondary figures (though, since the One is ever present even when unrevealed, some of the latter, together with several obscure figures from earlier times, had also been embodiments of the One in their time). In al-Ḥākim, the One was uniquely present openly in history. The contrasting extravagances of his life expressed the workings of the ultimately Powerful, Whose acts could not be called to account, though they always revealed a meaning to His *imām*, the *ʿaḳl*, the cosmic intellect, Ḥamza. Al-Ḥākim was the present *maḳām*, locus, of the Creator; only in knowledge of Him could men purify themselves. Accordingly, Ḥamza's teaching was no longer strictly an extremist Ismāʿīlism, though it made use of extremist Ismāʿīlī conceptions and language; it claimed to be an independent religion superseding both the Sunnī *tanzīl* and the Ismāʿīlī *taʾwīl*.

Ḥamza evidently looked to al-Ḥākim to introduce, by his caliphal power, the messianic culmination of history, forcing all men to discard the various symbolisms of the old revealed religions, including Ismāʿīlism, and to worship the One alone, revealed clearly in al-Ḥākim. In preparation for al-Ḥākim's decisive move, Ḥamza, as *imām*, built up his own organization within the Ḥākim-cult circles to spread the true doctrine. Like al-Ḥākim and Ḥamza himself, the members of this organization embodied cosmic principles. There were five great *ḥudūd*, cosmic ranks, adopted in a modified form from Ismāʿīlī lore: the *ʿAḳl* (Ḥamza—identical with S̲h̲aṭnīl, the "true Adam" during the current historical cycle, during which the One is also known as al-Bār); the *Nafs al-Kulliyya*, Universal Soul (Ismāʿīl b. Muḥammad al-Tamīmī); the *Kalima*, the Word (Muḥammad b. Wahb al-Ḳuras̲h̲ī); the Right Wing or the *Sābiḳ*, the Preceder, in Ismāʿīlism identified with the *ʿaḳl* but here demoted (Salāma b. ʿAbd al-Wahhāb); and the Left Wing or the *Tālī*, the Follower, in Ismāʿīlism identified with the *nafs* (Abu 'l-Ḥasan ʿAlī b. Aḥmad al-Samūkī, called Bahāʾ al-Dīn al-Muḳtanā). Below these five ranks were a number of *dāʿīs*, missionaries; *maʾd̲h̲ūns*, licensed to preach; and *mukāsirs*, persuaders—embodying respectively the cosmic *d̲j̲idd*, effort; *fatḥ*, opening; and *k̲h̲ayāl*, fantasy. Subordinated to these were the common believers. (In all these ranks what was regarded was not the individual person, the embodiment, but the undying principle of which the embodiment was merely the current veil; in the ordinary person this implied an eternally reincarnated soul). To one or another of these ranks were attributed most of the titles or concepts that figured in the complex Ismāʿīlī system. Despite this hierarchy, however, the immediate presence of the One was kept primary and remained so in later Druzism.

Ranged in opposition to these true *ḥudūd*, and equally the creatures of al-Ḥākim as the ultimate One, were a series of false *ḥudūd*, accounting for the dark side of the cosmos, and embodied likewise in men of al-Ḥākim's time—for instance, in al-Ḥākim's Ismāʿīlī officials, teachers of the misleading doctrines of the old faiths. The eschatological drama was seen as the conflict between Ḥamza as *Ḳāʾim al-zamān*, Master of the Time, with his true *ḥudūd*, who would at last be openly supported by al-Ḥākim, and these false teachers whom al-Ḥākim would openly abandon. The followers of the Ḥākim-cult, whether under al-Darazī or under Ḥamza, seem to have been eager to precipitate events by proclaiming abroad the abolition of all the old faiths, including the *s̲h̲arīʿa* law of Islam and its Ismāʿīlī *bāṭin* interpretation. Despite Ḥamza's relative cautiousness, insults to the established faith were offered publicly, with al-Ḥākim's tacit support, and riots ensued. The innovators, who regarded themselves as emancipated from the *s̲h̲arīʿa*, were accused of every sort of gross immorality. The Ḥākim cult seems to have contributed heavily to the growing political crisis of al-Ḥākim's last years.

When al-Ḥākim disappeared, late in 411/1021, Ḥamza announced that he had withdrawn to test his adherents and would soon return to manifest his full power, placing the sword of victory in Ḥamza's own hands. Soon after, at the end of 411, Ḥamza himself withdrew, to return with al-Ḥākim. The faith then entered into a period corresponding to the little *g̲h̲ayba* of the Twelver S̲h̲īʿīs, with the *Tālī*, Bahāʾ al-Dīn al-Muḳtanā [*q.v.*], as link between the absent Ḥamza and the faithful.

After al-Ḥākim's disappearance, the Ḥākim cult seems to have gradually ceased activity in Egypt, but to have afforded the ideology for a wave of peasant revolts in Syria. There proselytizing was pursued actively by a number of missionaries, some of whose names have been preserved; the movement gained control of some mountainous areas, where they are said to have torn down the mosques and established their own new system of law. Presumably they dispossessed the old landlords in favour of a free peasantry. In 423/1032 the *amīr* of Antioch, aided by the *amīr* of Aleppo, suppressed a group in the D̲j̲abal al-Summāḳ which included peasants who had gathered there from the vicinity of Aleppo.

In the midst of the turmoil, al-Muḳtanā at Alexandria (who had been appointed *Tālī* only at the last minute, in 411) tried to maintain Ḥamza's authority and his own. He was evidently in touch with the absent Ḥamza and was preparing for his momentary advent from the Yemen. He encouraged the rebels in the D̲j̲abal al-Summāḳ after their defeat. His many pastoral letters—some directed not only to Syria but to contacts and converts in all

Ismāʿīlī communities, as far away as Sind—served meanwhile to lay down Druze orthodoxy. He had to struggle against more than one claimant to leadership, of whom Ibn al-Kurdī, aided by one Sikkīn, seems to have been the most prominent; some of these seem to have encouraged a wide moral licence which he condemned. But with the years the general movement faded away and the Syrian peasant revolt seemed hopelessly torn by dissension; at last al-Muḳtanā discharged all his *dāʿīs* and, sometime after 425/1034, himself withdrew from the faithful, as had Ḥamza; though he continued to send out letters as late as 434/1042-3.

Despite al-Muḳtanā's discouragement, his work became the basis of such of the movement as did survive. Later Druzes have supposed it was al-Muḳtanā himself who compiled one hundred and eleven letters, many of them his own, some of them by Ḥamza and by Ismāʿīl al-Tamīmī, and certain pieces by al-Ḥākim, into a canon which has since served as Druze scripture, called *Rasāʾil al-Ḥikma*, the Book of Wisdom. From the time of al-Muḳtana's withdrawal began a period, lasting to the present among the Syrian Druzes, of passive expectation of Ḥamza's and al-Ḥākim's return, which has corresponded to the greater *gh̲ayba* of the Twelver S̲h̲īʿīs. Ḥamza's hierarchical organization, including the *dāʿīs* and lesser ranks, fell into disuse and the scriptural canon has served as guide in place of the absent *ḥudūd*. Though al-Muḳtanā had insisted on continuing proselytizing as long as possible, on his withdrawal it ceased and it was taught that thenceforth no further conversion to the unitarian truth could be accepted. (To this ban there have been a few exceptions). The Druzes became a closed community, keeping their doctrines secret, frowning on intermarriage and permitting neither conversion nor apostasy, and governing themselves as far as possible in such mountain fastnesses as they had seized, notably in the Wādī Taym Allāh by Mount Hermon. These converts from the Syrian peasantry, led—according to tradition—by certain families from old Arabian tribes, formed in time a homogeneous people with distinctive physical features and social customs, dominated by their own aristocracy of ruling families. The aristocratic families have been noted equally for their habits of lawless raiding, for their uncompromising hospitality, and for their strict moral discipline which spared, for instance, the women of those they plundered and which was merciless toward unchastity in Druze women. (There is little foundation for the long series of Western speculations which assigned to the Druzes one or another exotic racial source, such as Persia or France).

During this long period of autonomous closed group life there appeared a new system of religious practice strongly contrasting to the hierarchism which had disappeared. We know of a number of writers on the gnostic cosmology and cyclical sacred history implied already by Ḥamza, and commentators on the scriptural canon, but it is not known just when the new system took full form, though this was presumably at least by the time of the great Druze moralist (whose tomb is revered by both Druzes and Christians), ʿAbd Allāh al-Tanūk̲h̲ī [see AL-TANŪK̲H̲Ī, ʿABD ALLĀH], d. 885/1480. By this system the Druze community has been divided into *ʿuḳḳāl* (sing. *ʿāḳil*), "sages" initiated into the truths of the faith, and *d̲j̲uhhāl* (sing. *d̲j̲āhil*), "ignorant", not initiated and yet members of the community. (Those aristocratic notables who are not initiated may be distinguished from the ordinary *d̲j̲uhhāl* in their character of *amīr*). Any adult Druze (man or woman) can be initiated if found worthy after considerable trial, but must thereafter lead a soberly religious life, uttering regular daily prayers, abstaining from all stimulants, from lying, from stealing, from revenge (including raiding in feuds), and so on. The *ʿuḳḳāl* are distinguished by a special dress with white turbans. As long as one is still a *d̲j̲āhil*, he is permitted more personal indulgences, within the code of honour of the Druze community, but he cannot look to spiritual growth; however, if he fails to be initiated in a given lifetime he can expect a renewed opportunity in a future birth.

The more pious or learned of the *ʿuḳḳāl* are accorded special authority in the community as *s̲h̲ayk̲h̲*s. In addition to what is required of the ordinary *ʿuḳḳāl*, they must be very circumspect morally, not making use of goods of a dubious source, avoiding any excess in their daily behaviour, keeping themselves on good terms with all, and ready to make peace wherever there is a quarrel. In each Druze district some one of these *s̲h̲ayk̲h̲*s, normally chosen from a given family, is recognized as holding the highest religious authority, as *raʾīs*. The *s̲h̲ayk̲h̲*s are trained in a special school; they spend much time in copying religious works and especially the scriptural canon, and the more zealous commonly have gone on spiritual retreats in *k̲h̲alwa*s, houses of religious retirement, built in unfrequented spots; some have even devoted their whole lives to such retirement. Preferably any *ʿāḳil* should support himself with his hands, but the *s̲h̲ayk̲h̲*s are a fit object of alms by the *d̲j̲uhhāl*, nevertheless. They are expected to offer spiritual guidance to their *d̲j̲āhil* neighbours, presiding at such occasions as weddings and funerals.

All the *ʿuḳḳāl* attend at least some of the *mad̲j̲lis* services, held on the eve of Friday in starkly simple houses of worship, though *d̲j̲uhhāl* have been admitted to the least secret of these, when moral homilies are read in classical Arabic. The *ʿuḳḳāl* alone are permitted to read the more secret books of the faith and to participate in, or even know about, its secret ritual—which the Druzes have allowed the outside world to suppose involves a metallic figure of a calf in some way, whether as representing the human aspect of al-Ḥākim or possibly the animality of Ḥamza's enemies. (The neighbours of the Druzes have not been slow to accuse them of licentious orgies at their secret services).

Ḥamza and al-Muḳtanā prescribed a sevenfold set of commandments, replacing the Muslim "pillars of the faith", which have become the basis of the moral discipline of the *ʿuḳḳāl* and to some degree of all Druzes. They must above all speak truth among the faithful (or at least keep silent, but never misrepresent), a commandment which includes truth in the theological sense; but lying to unbelievers is permitted in defence of themselves or of the faith. This first commandment covers also any act, such as stealing, which must entail lying. The second commandment is to defend and help one another, and seems to imply carrying arms for the purpose. The other commandments are to renounce all former religions; to dissociate themselves from unbelievers; to recognize the unity of Our Lord (Mawlānā, the general title given al-Ḥākim as the One) in all ages; to be content with whatever he does; and to submit to His orders, particularly as transmitted through his *ḥudūd*. Ḥamza prescribed, in addition, special rules of justice and of personal status to replace the sharīʿa, notably insisting on equality of treatment between husband and wife in marriage; thus divorce was penalized in either partner unless for good cause.

The faith of the *djuhhāl* is placed under the general guidance of the *ʿukkāl*, but it is strongly affected by the principle of religious dissimulation—that to protect the secrecy of his faith, a Druze must affect to accept the faith of those in power about him; that is, normally, Sunnī Islām. Druzes have accepted the Ḥanafī legal system, though with modifications such as permission of more unlimited bequests and placing of limitations on divorce. They celebrate the *ʿīd*—though not the Ḥadjdj nor the Ramaḍān fast; many families use circumcision (or baptism), but attach no religious meaning thereto; at funerals they may use Islamic formulas but the key feature is the blessing of the *shaykh*s. Like Syrians of other faiths, they visit the shrines of Khiḍr [*q.v.*] and the tombs of the prophets and saints. Nevertheless, even the *djuhhāl* know, and may freely speak of, the principle of their unitarianism. They possess a developed doctrine of creation and eschatology, which is founded in the teachings of the *ʿukkāl*. The number of souls in existence is fixed, all souls being reincarnated immediately upon death (unless, having reached perfection, they ascend to the stars); those which believed in Ḥamza's time are always reincarnated as Druzes, either in Syria or in a supposed Druze community in China. The variety of incarnations each soul passes through gives a thorough moral testing. (Some of the *djuhhāl* believe in reincarnation of the wicked in lower animals). In the end, when al-Ḥākim and Ḥamza reappear to conquer and establish justice in the whole world, those Druzes who have shown up well will be the rulers of all mankind. The best will then dwell nearest to God—a notion which the *ʿukkāl* understand, like much else, in a spiritual sense.

Bibliography: The Druze canon is available in numerous manuscripts in European, American, and Syrian libraries, as are many other Druze writings. A description and some translation of the canon is included in the fundamental work of Silvestre de Sacy, *Exposé de la religion des Druzes*, 2 vols., Paris 1838 (partial translation, Philipp Wolff, *Die Drusen und ihre Vorläufer*, Leipzig 1845); see also his *Mémoire sur l'origine du culte que les Druzes rendent à la figure d'un veau* in *Mémoires de l'institut royal, classe d'histoire*, iii, 1818, 74 ff. Some Druze pieces are printed and annotated in Silvestre de Sacy's *Chrestomathie arabe*, ii, Paris 1826. Other Druze writings are printed in Christian Seybold, *Die Drusenschrift: Kitāb Alnoqaṭ Waldawāir* (and N.-L. Kirchhain, *Das Buch der Punkte und Kreise*), Leipzig 1902; in Henri Guys, *Théogonie des Druzes*, Paris 1863; in Martin Sprengling, *The Berlin Druze lexicon* in *American Journal of Semitic Languages*, lvi (1939), 388-414, and lvii (1940), 75 ff. (which includes an excellent study of Druze cosmology); in Rudolph Strothmann, *Drusen-Antwort auf Nuṣairī Angriff*, in *Isl.*, xxv (1939), 269-81; in Ernst von Döbeln, *Ein Traktat aus den Schriften der Drusen*, in *Monde Oriental*, iii (1909), 89-126; in J. Khalil and L. Ronzevalle, *al-Risalāt al-Qusṭanṭīniyya*, *MFOB*, iii, Beirut, 1909, 493-534. A common Druze "catechism" has been variously published and translated; see Eichhorn, *Repertorium für morgenländische und biblische Literatur*, xii (1783), or Regnault, *Catéchisme à l'usage des Druses djahels*, in *Bull. de la Société de Géographie* (Paris), vii (1827), 22-30. The most important general study, apart from those mentioned above, is Narcisse Bouron, *Les Druzes, histoire du Liban et de la Montagne haouranaise*, Paris 1930. Useful is Ḥannā Abū-Rāshid, *Djabal al-Durūz*, Cairo 1925. Henri Guys, *La Nation druze, son histoire, sa religion, ses mœurs, et son état politique*, Paris 1863, is often incautious. Of the many travellers who have written of them, the best is Max von Oppenheim, *Vom Mittelmeer zum Persischen Golf*, Berlin 1899, i, 110 ff. Also interesting is W. B. Seabrook, *Adventures in Arabia*, New York 1927, chap. ix. On modern Druze legal status see F. van den Steen de Jehay, *De la situation légale des sujets ottomans non-musulmans*, Brussels 1906, and J. N. D. Anderson, *Personal law of the Druze community* in *WI* (1952), 1 ff., 83 ff. Especially for listings of manuscripts, see Hans Wehr, *Zu den Schriften Ḥamzas im Drusenkanon* in *ZDMG*, xcvi (1942), 187-207; also A. F. L. Beeston, *An ancient Druze manuscript* in *Bodleian Library Record*, v/6 (October 1956). For further references, especially to travellers' writings, see bibliography in Bouron, and footnotes in Philip K. Hitti, *The origins of the Druze people and religion*, New York 1928 (includes also some translated fragments); omitted from these two are F. Tournebize, *Les Druzes* in *Etudes des pères de la Compagnie de Jésus*, 5 October 1897; B. J. Taylor, *La Syrie, la Palestine, et la Judée*, Paris 1855, 35-40, 76-83; Henri Aucapitaine, *Etude sur les Druzes* in *Nouvelles Annales des Voyages*, VIme série, February 1862; *Magasin pittoresque*, 1841, 367, and 1861, 226. For chroniclers on the earliest period, see Silvestre de Sacy, *Exposé* (Nuwayrī, *Nihāyat al-Arab*; Md. Djaʿfarī, *Anhadj al-ṭarāʾiḳ*; Severus of Ushmūnayn, *Life of Patriarch Zechariah*; Abu 'l-Maḥāsin Ibn Taghrībirdī, *al-Nudjūm al-zāhira* [based on Sibṭ Ibn al-Djawzī, *Mirʾāt al-zamān*]; and Djurdjus al-Makīn, *Taʾrīkh al-Muslimīn*). The latter is based on Yaḥyā al-Anṭākī, continuation of Eutychius, *Scriptores Arabici*, text, ser. III, vii/2, ed. L. Cheikho, B. Carra de Vaux, H. Zayyat, Beirut 1909, 220 ff.; see also Ibn al-ʿAdīm, *Taʾrīkh Ḥalab*, s.a. 423; M. G. S. Hodgson, *Al-Darazî and Ḥamza in the origin of the Druze religion*, in *JAOS*, lxxxii (1962), 5-20.

(M. G. S. Hodgson)

(ii) — Ottoman Period

When the Ottoman and the Mamlūk armies met in battle at Mardj Dābiḳ in 922/1516, the Druzes fought on both sides. The Buḥturids from the west of the country fought on the side of the Mamlūks, while the Maʿnids of Shūf supported the Ottomans by allying themselves to Ghazālī, the *nāʾib* of Damascus. Under the Ottomans, the Druzes were governed by local dynasties, of which the Āl Tanūkh, the Maʿnids and the Shihābids, and particularly the last two (for whose genealogy see Zambaur, i, 108 ff.) were the most important. At the battle of Mardj Dābiḳ the Maʿnids were led by the Amīr Fakhr al-Dīn I, who at the crucial point changed sides, abandoning the Mamlūk Ḳānsūh al-Ghūrī and going over to Sultan Selīm I in Damascus. The Sultan rewarded him with overlordship over the amīrs of Mount Lebanon, the Āl Tanūkh dynasty being confined to Ṣaydā and Ṣūr (Blau, *Zur Geschichte Syriens*, in *ZDMG*, viii (1854), 480 ff.). In 951/1544 Maʿnid rule passed to Fakhr al-Dīn's son Ḳorḳmaz. Druze attacks against the Ottomans led in 992/1584 to a punitive expedition by Ibrāhīm Pasha, the *wālī* of Egypt. The son of Ḳorḳmaz, the Amīr Fakhr al-Dīn

II [*q.v.*] challenged the *wālī* of Tripoli, Sayf-og͟hlu Yūsuf Pas͟ha. He had some initial successes, but was eventually forced to withdraw to the Mountain, after the defeat of the rebels in 1016/1607 in the battle between Kuyud͟ju Murād Pas͟ha and D͟jānbulāt-og͟hlu, the importance of whose family among the Druzes dates from this time. The Druze alliance dissolved as a result of the expeditions led by land by the *wālī* of Damascus, Ḥāfiẓ Pas͟ha, and by sea by the Ḳapudan Pas͟ha Öküz ("The Bull") Meḥmed Pas͟ha between 1018/1609 and 1022/1613. Fak͟hr al-Dīn allied himself to Florence in 1017/1608 and on 30 Rad͟jab 1022/15 September 1613 he went to Italy to seek help under the alliance, returning to the D͟jabal in 1027/1618. Maʿnid rule was preserved during his absence, particularly as his spies in Istanbul and Damascus gave preliminary warning of any Ottoman military measures. Although the Ottoman Sultan, by a *fermān* issued in 1034/1625, recognized Fak͟hr al-Dīn as *Amīr* of the Druzes from Aleppo to Jerusalem (Ḥaydar, i, 715), the latter was subjected to constant pressure from Küčük Aḥmed Pas͟ha, who had been appointed *wālī* of Damascus by Murād IV. In 1044/1634 the Druzes were decisively defeated at Mag͟hārat D͟jarzīn, the Amīr and three of his children being carried off prisoner to Istanbul, where all but Ḥusayn Bey were executed.

The death of Fak͟hr al-Dīn marked the end of Maʿnid ascendancy. It was followed by Ḳaysī-Yamanī dissension. Fak͟hr al-Dīn, like the ruling branch of the Āl Tanūk͟h before the Maʿnid ascendancy, belonged to the Yamanī clan (known as *aḳlî*, "white" by the Ottomans, the Ḳaysīs being known as "red", *ḳîzîllî*, cf. Fîndîḳlîlî Meḥmed Āg͟hā, *Taʾrīk͟h*, Istanbul 1928, i, 215; C.-F. Volney, i, 414, note 1). Amīr Malḥam, who succeeded him in 1045/1635, represented the Ḳaysī clan and was opposed by the Amīr ʿAlī ʿAlam al-Dīn on behalf of the Yamanīs. Dissension gave openings for Ottoman intervention, as in 1061/1651 by the *wālī* of Tripoli, Ḥasan Pas͟ha. In 1064/1654 Amīr Malḥam extended his rule to Ṣafad, by agreement with the *wālī* of Damascus. Malḥam died in 1069/1659 and was succeeded in the D͟jabal by his son Amīr Aḥmad, the last Maʿnid ruler, who died in 1108/1697 and was succeeded by S͟hihābids of the Ḳaysī clan. The latter had been protected by Amīr Aḥmad, who had refused to give them up to the *wālī* of Damascus, Köprülü Fāḍil Aḥmed Pas͟ha, in 1070/1660. The *wālī* of Damascus, helped by the *wālī* of Tripoli, thereupon defeated the joint Maʿnid-S͟hihābid forces at Kasrawān. The two dynasties later fell out, however, with the Maʿnids winning a short-lived victory at al-Fulful in 1076/1666 (Ibn Sabāṭa, Ṣāliḥ b. Yaḥyā, appendix, 237). After the death of Amīr Aḥmad, however, it was the S͟hihābid *amīr* of Rās͟hēyā, Bas͟hīr b. Ḥusayn, who was chosen overlord of the D͟jabal with the agreement of the Ottomans. The Yamanīs tried unsuccessfully to undo Ḳaysī ascendancy: from the court in Istanbul Ḥusayn, the son of Fak͟hr al-Dīn II, managed, for example, to relegate Bas͟hīr to the position of regent to the 12-year old Ḥaydar, of the family of the *amīrs* of Ḥaṣbēyā, whose local supporters later poisoned Bas͟hīr. But when Ḥaydar became Amīr in his own right he crushed the Yamanīs at the battle of ʿAyn-Dārā which changed the whole feudal picture of the D͟jabal. Thereafter under the overlordship of the S͟hihābīs, who tried to prevent Druze-Maronite struggles, the D͟jānbulāts reigned over S͟hūf, Abu 'l-Lamaʿ held Matn, while at S͟huwayfāt the Arslan family of the Yamanī clan had to share their rule with Talmūḳ Yamanīs. In holding together the D͟jabal, the S͟hihābīs had to rely on the support of Ottoman *wālīs*, whose intervention led to the increase in the number of local *s͟hayk͟hs*, who in turn exterted pressure on the *amīr*. Thus, while the *s͟hayk͟hs* paid tribute to the *amīr*, it was they who decided in council whether to keep the peace or wage war. Amīr Ḥaydar died in 1144/1732 in the S͟hihābī capital at Dayr al-Ḳamar, having in 1141/1729 abdicated in favour of his son Malḥam. Under the latter's rule which lasted until 1167/1754, the port of Bayrūt regained the importance which it had enjoyed under Fak͟hr al-Dīn and became the second S͟hihābī centre after Dayr al-Ḳamar. Many of Malḥam's children were converted to Roman Catholicism, Christianity in general gaining ground in the D͟jabal. Malḥam and his successors generally tried to maintain a balance between local Muslims and Christians. Thus, when in 1171/1758 Greek pirates flying the Russian flag attacked Bayrūt and when local Muslims retaliated by attacking the Franciscan monastery in the town, two of the Muslim leaders were hanged at the Amīr's orders.

Malḥam was succeeded by his brothers Aḥmad (the father of the historian Aḥmad al-S͟hihābī) and Manṣūr, although Nuʿmān Pas͟ha, the Ottoman *wālī* of Ṣaydā, appointed to the amīrate Ḳāsim b. ʿUmar, who, however, had to content himself with the area round Ḥazīr. Ḳāsim died a Christian in 1182/1768, his son Bas͟hīr II also making no secret of his Christian beliefs (Blau, *op. cit.*, 496; Lammens, *La Syrie*, Beirut 1921, ii, 100 ff.). These conversions did not, of course, prevent the majority of Druzes from retaining their faith, a fact which sowed the seed of future trouble. Manṣūr was dismissed in 1184/1770 by Derwīs͟h Pas͟ha, the *wālī* of Ṣaydā, and replaced by Amīr Yūsuf. In 1185/1771 when the Russian fleet commanded by Alexei Orlov was encouraged by Ẓāhir al-ʿUmar, the rebel ruler of Ṣafad and Acre, to bombard Bayrūt, Mansūr sued for peace against payment of 25,000 piastres, while Amīr Yūsuf asked for Ottoman reinforcements, whereupon ʿUt͟hmān Pas͟ha, the *wālī* of Damascus, despatched D͟jazzār Aḥmad Pas͟ha who occupied Bayrūt in the name of Amīr Yūsuf. The latter succeeded, however, in ejecting this unwelcome deputy from Bayrūt in 1187/1773 after a four-month siege, in which he was helped by the Russian fleet which he summoned from Cyprus. Nevertheless, D͟jazzār Aḥmad Pas͟ha continued to exert pressure from Acre and Ṣaydā on the S͟hihābīs of the D͟jabal. Payment of a tribute and loyalty to the Ottoman cause in the face of the Napoleonic expedition from Egypt, did not shield Bas͟hīr II from this pressure. Even although Yūsuf Ḍiyā Pas͟ha, the commander of the Ottoman forces against Napoleon, confirmed Bas͟hīr as ruler of the D͟jabal, D͟jazzār Aḥmad Pas͟ha had him expelled by forces commanded by Ḥusayn and Saʿd al-Dīn, the sons of the Amīr Yūsuf, whom he wanted to appoint in his place. Bas͟hīr sought refuge with the British admiral Sidney Smith, who took him in his flagship to al-ʿArīs͟h, returning later to the D͟jabal, D͟jazzār Aḥmad Pas͟ha contenting himself this time with keeping one of Bas͟hīr's sons as a hostage. Pressure on the Druzes decreased in 1804 with the death of D͟jazzār Pas͟ha. In 1810 when the Wahhābīs threatened Damascus, the *wālī* Yūsuf Pas͟ha asked the help of Süleymān Pas͟ha, the *sand͟jaḳ-beyi* of Acre, who in turn summoned the Druzes to Damascus. The Druzes forced the departure of Yūsuf Pas͟ha and were only with difficulty compelled to retire into the

Ḥawrān by Süleymān Pas͟ha's successor, ʿAbd Allāh Pas͟ha. Bas͟hīr's absence from the D̲j̲abal had, however, caused so much resentment that the *wālī* of Damascus and ʿAbd Allāh Pas͟ha were forced to allow the *s͟hayk͟hs* to summon him back to the Lebanon. Bas͟hīr thereafter sided with ʿAbd Allāh Pas͟ha, in his revolt against the Ottomans in Acre, whereupon his rival S͟hayk͟h D̲j̲ānbulāṭ had ʿAbbās al-S͟hihābī proclaimed *amīr*, while Bas͟hīr and his sons had to seek refuge with Muḥammad ʿAlī in Egypt. Before long, however, Bas͟hīr was back, defeated D̲j̲ānbulāṭ at the battle of Muk͟htāra in 1825 and had him executed. In the following year, an attack on Bayrūt by the fleet of the Greek insurgents led once again to a *pogrom* of local Christians, many of whom emigrated to the D̲j̲abal. Muslim feeling against Bas͟hīr was also inflamed by the permission given to Melkite Christians to settle in the D̲j̲abal. In 1830 Bas͟hīr once again helped ʿAbd Allāh Pas͟ha, this time to suppress a revolt in Nablūs. He then sided with Muḥammad ʿAlī against the Ottomans and helped the conquests of Ibrāhīm Pas͟ha.

(M. C. Şihabeddin Tekindağ)

After the Kütahya agreement of 1833 Bas͟hīr did his best to help the Egyptians, securing in return a wide autonomy for the Lebanon. Egyptian rule was at first welcomed, particularly as certain impositions on non-Muslims were abolished, but difficulties arose when Ibrāhīm Pas͟ha tried to confiscate firearms and to call up Druzes. In 1835 Ibrāhīm Pas͟ha introduced troops into Dayr al-Ḳamar and tried to collect the arms of local Christians but preferred later to suspend his measures in so far as they affected the Druzes. Nevertheless a Druze revolt broke out in 1837 when an attempt was made to call up Druzes in the Ḥawran, who retaliated by assassinating Ibrāhīm Pas͟ha's emissaries. The Ottoman Government tried to stir up the Druzes and to supply arms to them, Ibrāhīm Pas͟ha retaliating by stirring up the Kurds and by closing Syrian ports to Ottoman shipping. A Druze revolt broke out in Lad̲j̲ā, but from his palace in Bayt al-Dīn, from where he exercised wide influence over the Maronites, Bas͟hīr succeeded in preventing its spreading from the Ḥawrān to the Lebanon, believing as he did that thanks to French support the Egyptians would be finally victorious. A general revolt in the Lebanon, including this time the Maronites, broke out again, however, when Ibrāhīm Pas͟ha made another attempt to call in arms and Egyptian forces in Bayrūt found their communications cut. On 14 August 1840 the British naval commander Sir Charles Napier established contact with the rebels, who were supplied with arms after the joint bombardment of Bayrūt the following month by British, Austrian and Ottoman ships. After vainly waiting for help from Ibrāhīm Pas͟ha in Dayr al-Ḳamar, Bas͟hīr submitted to the Sultan, whose troops were in the process of reconquering Syria as a result of the London agreement. Bas͟hīr's personal security was guaranteed, but he was nevertheless deposed in favour of a relative, Bas͟hīr Ḳāsim Malḥam. The Egyptian occupation on the one hand disorganized the feudal structure of the D̲j̲abal and, on the other, sharpened antagonism between the Druzes and the Maronites. Bas͟hīr Ḳāsim's rule lasted for approximately one year and was underpinned by the *Mus͟hīr* of Ṣaydā, Selīm Pas͟ha, whose seat of government was transferred to Bayrūt and who formed a mixed council of the various communities to advise the *amīr*. Taxation reform (the Egyptians had raised the taxation of the D̲j̲abal from 3,650 to 6,500 purses and this was then reduced to 3,500 purses) and the question of compensation led to communal friction, which erupted at Baʿḳlīn, after which many houses and shops were set on fire at Dayr al-Ḳamar. Relative peace was restored after the Druze adventurer S͟hibāl al-ʿUryān, who was in the service of the *wālī* of Damascus, was forced to return to that city from Zaḥla. These events caused much stir abroad and led to foreign complaints against the Ottoman administration. The Ottomans thereupon deposed Bas͟hīr Ḳāsim, and entrusted the administration of the D̲j̲abal directly to the *serʿasker* Muṣṭafā Nūrī Pas͟ha, who in turn appointed to the amīrate one of his infantry commanders, the *mīrliwā* ʿÖmer Pas͟ha. Continued foreign displeasure led to the despatch to Bayrūt of Selīm Bey as an investigator in 1842, but the latter's report that the situation was satisfactory and that the appointment of either a Druze or a Maronite *amīr* was impossible, was disbelieved by foreign ambassadors at the Porte. Meanwhile new incidents were reported, whereupon Esʿad Muk͟hliṣ Pas͟ha was appointed *mus͟hīr* of Ṣaydā, and after his arrival at Bayrūt the *serʿasker*'s mission was declared completed. Esʿad Pas͟ha appointed two *ḳāʾim-maḳāms*, the Maronite Ḥaydar from Bayt Abi 'l-Lāmiʿ and the Druze Mīr Aḥmad from Bayt Arslān, and detached the northern districts of D̲j̲ubayl from the D̲j̲abal, placing them under Tripoli. More serious troubles broke out in 1845, when Esʿad Pas͟ha was succeeded by the *wālī* of Aleppo, Wed̲j̲īhī Pas͟ha. Bloody incidents included an attack by the Maronites on the Druzes of Matn as well as Druze attacks on the monasteries of Ābī and Sulīmā which were set on fire. Accusations and counter-accusations followed, the French accusing Wed̲j̲īhī Pas͟ha of being pro-Druze, while the French themselves were being accused of stirring up the Maronites. Another mission was then undertaken by the Foreign Minister S͟hekīb Efendi, who started by demanding that all arms should be handed in, an order which led to resistance and further complications. A further emissary, the *ferīḳ* (divisional general) Emīn Pas͟ha was sent to Bayrūt in January 1846. He helped S͟hekīb Efendī in his work of reorganization, returning with him in June 1846. S͟hekīb Efendi's reforms provided for the retention of the two *ḳāʾim-maḳāms*, advised by mixed councils, special deputies (*wekīl*) being elected in villages having a mixed population. The two *ḳāʾim-maḳāms* were to receive a salary of 12,500 piastres a month each, and to be appointed and dismissed directly by the Sultan on the advice of the *mus͟hīr* of Ṣaydā. The councils were given judicial as well as administrative and financial powers. Stability was thus established at the beginning of 1847, even although the failure to expel some trouble-making Druze leaders created difficulties. Taxes were apportioned between the two communities, the Maronites being asked to pay 1994 and the Druzes 1506 purses.

Peace was preserved until the *k͟haṭṭ-i humāyūn* of 1856, which by its promise of concessions to non-Muslim subjects led to a more generalized Christian-Muslim rivalry. The first signs of trouble appeared in 1859. In the following year the Druzes and the Maronites clashed openly, whereupon K͟hurs͟hīd Pas͟ha sent troops to the border between the two *ḳaḍās*. This did not prevent the major outbreak of 1860: in May the Druzes attacked and set fire to villages in Matn; in June they were joined by Druzes from the Ḥawrān, led by Ismāʿīl Aṭras͟h (the D̲j̲abal Druzes being led mainly by Saʿīd D̲j̲ānbulāṭ and Khaṭṭār Aḥmad). While the General Council of the province (*Medjlis-i ʿUmūmī*) rejected the *wālī*'s suggestion to send troops, the Druzes overpowered the defenders of Government House at Ḥāṣbēyā, massacring the local Christians: similar outrages were perpetrated at Rāshēyā, Baʿalbak (where local government was overthrown by the Ḥarkūbīn family), Zaḥla and Dayr al-Ḳamar. To crush the insurrection the Ottoman Government dispatched the Foreign Minister Fuʾād Pasha, arming him with emergency powers. His arrival coincided with a massacre of Christians in Damascus by the local mob, reinforced by Druzes and Bedouins. In the meantime Khurshīd Pasha had secured an armistice between Druzes and Maronites, of which Fuʾād Pasha did not approve, on the grounds that it compromised future judicial proceedings, but which he feared to denounce as bloodshed might then be renewed. France intervened directly by landing 5,000 troops and by suggesting the total expulsion of the Druzes from the Djabal. This Fuʾād Pasha succeeded in avoiding by taking firm action against guilty Druze leaders, pursuing and apprehending them, and finally putting them on trial at a court-martial at Mukhtāra, where some of them were sentenced to death. He also took severe punitive action in Damascus and had the *wālī* Aḥmed Pasha sent under escort for trial in Istanbul, Khurshīd Pasha having also been dismissed from Bayrūt. These measures made possible the evacuation of French troops from the Djabal. Under the agreement signed on 9 June 1861, the Djabal was completely detached from the *wilāyet*s of Bayrūt and of Damascus and placed under a Christian *mutaṣarrif*, who was, however, to come from outside the district. The *mutaṣarrif* was to be advised by an agent (*wekīl*) from each community. Administrative councils were also formed at the centre and in seven newly formed *ḳaḍā*s; a mixed police force was also constituted. At the instance of foreign embassies, an Armenian Catholic, Dāwūd Pasha, was appointed *mutaṣarrif*, a post which he retained for five years and in which he was succeeded by a Christian Arab, Franko Pasha. Dāwūd Pasha had many schools opened in Druze as well as in Maronite villages, and the Druzes continued to prosper under his successor. Disorder continued to prevail, however, among the Druzes of the Ḥawrān who were joined by refugees from the Lebanon, so that Djabal Ḥawrān began to be known as Djabal Durūz. Here Druzes came under the ascendancy of the Aṭrash family, as a result of the leading role played by Ismāʿīl al-Aṭrash in the events of 1860. Ismāʿīl's son Ibrāhīm raided Suwayda, the capital of the Djabal Ḥawrān, in 1879. When the *wālī* of Damascus led a punitive expedition against him, the Druzes put up a stiff resistance until an armistice was concluded in 1880. There was more trouble when Ibrāhīm's son Shiblī was imprisoned at Darʿa by the Ottoman authorities, as a result of incidents which were largely economic and social in origin. The Druzes rose up again and Shiblī had to be freed. Shiblī was once again arrested and once again freed by a Druze insurrection in 1893, when in alliance with the Banī Fadjr he led his followers against the Ruwāla tribe. During these troubles many Druze families were banished to Anatolia, but they were later allowed to return, while, at the same time, projects to call up the Druzes for military service were dropped.

In the meantime the Druzes in the Lebanon remained peaceful until 1897 when they complained that Maronite pressure was constantly increasing and when they demanded the formation of a separate *ḳaḍā* for the 10,000 Druzes of Matn, in case the Maronites succeeded in detaching four communes (*nāḥiya*) from the only one existing Muslim *ḳaḍā* at Shūf. After the Young Turkish Revolution of 1908 operations against the Druzes were entrusted to Sāmī Pasha, who proclaimed martial law and then summoned the Druze leaders to Damascus where he had many of them executed. Druze resistance continued, nevertheless, until 1911. Druze demands became irrelevant when, after the beginning of the First World War, the capitulations, and with them Lebanese autonomy, were abolished and Ismāʿīl Ḥaḳḳī Bey was appointed independent mutaṣarrif. During the war, Djemāl Pasha kept some Druze leaders as "guests" in Jerusalem. Also during the war, the Druze leader, Yaḥyā al-Aṭrash, whom Djemāl Pasha accused of complicity with the French (*Khāṭirāt*, Istanbul 1339, 179), died and was succeeded by his son Selīm. Djemāl Pasha praised the services of two members of the Aṭrash family, Nasīb and ʿAbd al-Ghaffār, but a third member, Sulṭān, whose father had been executed by Sāmī Pasha, was opposed to the Ottomans and was the first Druze leader to enter Damascus with the Allied troops on 2 October 1918.

(M. Tayyib Gökbilgin)

DUSHMANZIYĀR [see KĀKAWAYHIDS].

DŪST MUḤAMMAD, the real founder of Bārakzāy rule in Afghānistān, was the 20th son of Pāyinda Khān, chief of the Bārakzāy clan under Tīmūr Shāh. After the execution of Pāyinda Khān in the reign of Zamān Shāh, Dūst Muḥammad was brought up by his Ḳizilbash mother's relatives until he came under the care of the eldest brother, Fatḥ Khān, who held considerable influence under Maḥmūd Shāh. In the second reign of Maḥmūd, Dūst Muḥammad held prominent offices including that of governor of Kūhistān, and he led successful expeditions to suppress rebellions in Kashmīr and Harāt (1816). Following the Harāt expedition Dūst Muḥammad fell into disgrace (allegedly for insulting the wife of a Sadōzāy prince) and he fled to Kashmīr. Whether in revenge for this action or through jealousy of his power, Maḥmūd Shāh and his son Kāmrān then blinded and killed Fatḥ Khān. Dūst Muḥammad raised a force in Kashmīr and captured Kābul, putting up Shāhzāda Sulṭān ʿAlī as nominal ruler. He foiled an attempt by Maḥmūd to dispossess him but he was forced to surrender Kābul to his eldest surviving brother, Muḥammad Aʿẓam Khān, formerly governor of Kashmīr, and he himself became ruler of Ghazna. However, he continued to aspire to power in Kābul, and after the death of Aʿẓam in 1238-9/1823 he defeated his son and successor Ḥabīb Allāh Khān, but Kābul fell to another brother, Sulṭān Muḥammad Khān of Peshāwar. But Dūst Muḥammad retained the support of the Ḳizilbash element in Kābul and eventually Sulṭān Muḥammad gave up the attempt to maintain himself there and in 1241-2/1826 Dūst Muḥammad became ruler. He took the title of Amīr in 1250/1834.

Once established in Kābul Dūst Muḥammad began to extend his power over other areas of Afghānistān, replacing the existing rulers with his own sons. He failed to recover Peshāwar from the Sikhs in 1250/1835 and 1253/1837 and failed to hold it in 1265/1848-9 after it was made over to him as the price of his support for the Sikhs in the second Anglo-Sikh war. Elsewhere he was markedly successful. Before his expulsion from Kābul in 1255/

1839 by the forces of Shāh Shudjāʿ and the English East India Campany he had extended his power over Djalālābād and Ghazna and by his defeat of Murād Beg of Kunduz in 1254/1838-9 into the area north of the Hindū-kush. Within his dominions he consolidated his authority in Kūhistān, Kunar and among the Hazāra tribes. After his restoration in 1259/1843 he continued this policy. In the north he extended his power over Balkh and Khulm (1266-7/1850), Shibarghān (1271/1854), Maymana and Andkhuy (1271/1855) and Kunduz (1276/1859), although his authority was not entirely unquestioned. In the West he took Ḳandahār (1272/1855) and Harāt (1279/1863). At the same time he increased his power at the expense of the tribal chiefs, principally by developing a regular army to replace the feudal militia, which had been the basis of the Durrānī [*q.v.*] monarchy, and diverting to the support of this army the revenues which had formerly been appropriated by the tribal chiefs. He destroyed the power of the Ghalzāys, murdered, imprisoned or exiled certain prominent tribal chiefs, and held both the Ḳizilbash and the Sunnī elements, who had formerly made Kābul governments so unstable, under firm control. The weakness of his system was that it depended on the continuing co-operation of his sons, whom he employed as governors, a condition which was not met after his death. None the less he established the geographical outlines of modern Afghānistān and laid the foundations of its internal consolidation. More than anyone else he deserves the title of the founder of Afghānistān.

Dūst Muḥammad died in 1279/9 June 1863. He had numerous sons, the most important of whom were the following: Muḥammad Afḍal Khān, Muḥammad Aʿẓam Khān and Walī Muḥammad Khān, who were all sons of a Bangash wife from Kurram, and Muḥammad Akbar Khān, (d. 1848, *wazīr* 1843-8, and the leading figure in the disturbances of 1841-2), Ghulām Haydar Khān (d. 1274/1858), Shīr ʿAlī Khān (the future *amīr*), Muḥammad Amīn Khān and Muḥammad Sharīf Khān, who were all sons of a Popalzāy wife. It is noteworthy that in choosing a successor Dūst Muḥammad ignored his older sons and chose Akbar, Ghulām Ḥaydar and Shīr ʿAlī in that order, they being the sons of a nobler born wife.

Bibliography: See AFGHĀNISTĀN. Also C. M. Macgregor (ed.), *Central Asia, ii, Afghanistan*, Calcutta 1871; Hamid al-Din, *Dost Muhammad and the second Sikh war*, in *J. Pak. Hist. Soc.*, ii (Oct. 1954), 280-6; D. M. Chopra, *Dost Muhammad in India*, in *Proc. I.H.R.C.*, xix (1943), 82-6; B. Saigal, *Lord Elgin I and Afghanistan*, in *J.I.H.*, xxxii (1954), 61-81; M. E. Yapp, *Disturbances in Eastern Afghanistan 1839-42*, in *BSOAS*, xxv/3 (1962), 499-523; H. B. Lumsden, *Mission to Kandahar*, Calcutta 1860. (M. E. YAPP)

DUSTŪR, in modern Arabic constitution. A word of Persian origin, it seems originally to have meant a person exercising authority, whether religious or political, and was later specialized to designate members of the Zoroastrian priesthood. It occurs in *Kalīla wa-Dimna* in the sense of "counsellor", and recurs with the same sense, at a much later date, in the phrase *Dustūr-i mükerrem*, one of the honorific titles of the Grand Vizier in the Ottoman Empire. More commonly, *dustūr* was used in the sense of "rule" or "regulation", and in particular the code of rules and conduct of the guilds and corporations (see FUTUWWA and ṢINF). Borrowed at an early date by Arabic, it acquired in that language a variety of meanings, notably "army pay-list", "model or formulary", "leave", and also, addressed to a human being or to invisible *djinn* [*q.v.*], "permission" (see further Dozy s.v.).

In modern Arabic, by a development from the general meaning of "rule", it has come to mean constitution or constitutional charter, and is now used in this sense in the Arab countries, though not elsewhere, to the exclusion of all other terms. The following articles deal with the development of constitutional law and government in various parts of the Islamic world.

i. — TUNISIA

Until the middle of the 19th century, the despotism of the Bey (*bāy* [*q.v.*]) was tempered only by the momentary power of some members of his entourage who governed as they pleased. The foreign consuls, alarmed by the dangers of the situation, accordingly advised Muḥammad Bey [*q.v.*] to be guided by the provisions of the *khaṭṭ-i humāyūn* [*q.v.*] which had been promulgated in Turkey on 18 February 1856, granting certain guarantees to non-Muslim subjects of the Empire; but the Bey turned a deaf ear, and a grave incident was needed to precipitate the course of events. It was in fact the summary execution in 1857 of a Jewish carter who, after knocking down a Muslim child, was said to have hurled insults and blasphemies at the crowd that was threatening him with violence, that aroused the anxiety of the European Powers and made them decide to instruct their consuls to make representations to the Tunisian Government. It was in this way that Muḥammad Bey was led to make a formal announcement, on 9 September 1857, of the principles of the Fundamental Pact (*ʿAhd al-amān*; see L. Bercher, *En marge du pacte fondamental*, in *RT*, 1939, 67-86) which repeated in part the *khaṭṭ-i sharīf* of Gülkhāne (26 Shaʿbān 1255/3 November 1839; see B. Lewis, *The emergence of modern Turkey*, London 1961, 104-5 and bibl. cited there) and guaranteed complete security to all inhabitants of whatever religion, nationality and race; the equality of all before the law and taxation, as well as freedom to trade and work, were recognized. At the same date the Bey announced his intention of granting the country a constitution. Some partial reforms were actually introduced (notably the setting up of a municipal council [see BALADIYYA]), and preparatory work was in fact started on a draft constitution in which the French Consul, Léon Roches, took part. On 17th September 1860 Muḥammad al-Ṣādiḳ [*q.v.*], who had succeeded his brother Muḥammad on 24 September 1859, himself gave a copy of the constitution drafted in French to Napoleon III in Algiers, and received the Emperor's approval. The constitution, consisting of 13 headings and 114 articles, was promulgated in January 1861 and put into force on 26 April of the same year.

By the terms of this constitution, the hereditary Bey was supreme head of the State and of religion, but he no longer controlled the revenues of the State and was allotted a civil list; moreover he was responsible, as were the ministers whom he had to have at his side, to the Grand Council which consisted of 60 councillors nominated for five years and chosen by the Tunisian Government from the ministers, high officials, senior officers and notables. "The agreement of the Grand Council is indispensable for all the procedures listed below: making new laws; changing a law . . . .; increasing or cutting down . . . expenditure . . .; enlarging the army, its equipment or that of the navy; . . . . interpreting the law". Thus the Grand Council participated in the preparation of laws which were made valid by the Bey and his ministers. The executive power reverted to the Bey and his ministers, whilst the independence of the judicial power in respect of the legislature and the executives was recognized. The *ḳāʾid*s continued to preside over police courts for the trial of minor offences, courts of first instance were set up and the court of the *s̲h̲arʿ* [*q.v.*] continued to function for all questions within its competence. A court of appeal was to sit in Tunis and the Grand Council was to act as Supreme Court of Appeal. Finally, the provisions of the Fundamental Pact with regard to the rights of Tunisian and foreign subjects were confirmed and completed.

The establishment of the French Protectorate suspended the operation of the Constitution of 1861. From the earliest years of the 20th century a number of Young Tunisians, the spiritual heirs of the general K̲h̲ayr al-Dīn [*q.v.*], endeavoured to raise the material, moral and intellectual level of their compatriots, and founded various associations [see D̲J̲AMʿIYYA, iv] of a more or less political character. In 1907 was created a Consultative Conference, considered inadequate, and from that time the idea of demanding the grant of a Constitution was in germination. After the war, on 4 June 1920, the Tunisian Liberal Constitutional Party (*al-Ḥizb al-Ḥurr al-Dustūrī al-Tūnusī*) was founded, more commonly known as the Destour Party. The *vade-mecum* of Tunisian nationalism at that time was a collective work, *La Tunisie martyre*, which called for: the election of a deliberative assembly composed of Tunisian and French members elected by universal suffrage; the formation of a government responsible to this assembly; the absolute separation of powers; the access of Tunisians to all administrative posts; the election of municipal councils by universal suffrage; the respect of public liberties. In 1922 the authorities of the Protectorate set up the Great Council, an arbitral commission, councils of caïdat and regional councils [see TUNISIA]; but the conservative class of the nation, who would have been satisfied with gradual reforms, lost ground to a new petty bourgeoisie, on the whole of French and Arab culture, which tried to reach the public in greater depth; a split, the beginnings of which had been apparent in the Destour Party since 1932, came about on 1 March 1934 with the creation of the Neo-Destour (as opposed to the Archaeo-Destour) Party, which called for full and complete independence and organized mass demonstrations to achieve it. The leaders of this movement were exiled, and the second world war silenced the demands for independence. They were renewed immediately after the restoration of peace, and independence was granted to Tunisia by France on 20 March 1956; this was a triumph for the president of the Neo-Destour Party, M. Habib Bourguiba (al-Ḥabīb Abū Ruḳayba), the future President of the Tunisian Republic. (Bibliography on the nationalist movements is copious but scattered among many papers, periodicals, bulletins, etc.; in particular *REI*, *passim*; *OM*, *passim*; also Ch. Khairallah, *Essai d'histoire et de synthèse des mouvements nationalistes tunisiens*, Tunis n.d.; H. Bourguiba, *La Tunisie et la France*, Paris 1954; F. Garas, *Bourguiba et la naissance d'une nation*, Paris 1956; P. E. A. Romeril, *Tunisian nationalism, a bibliographical outline*, in *MEJ*, xiv (1960), 206-15; N. A. Ziadeh, *Origins of nationalism in Tunisia*, Beirut 1962). As early as 29 December 1955 the Bey promulgated a decree permitting the establishment of a National Constituent Assembly, which was elected on 25 March 1956 and drafted a new constitution, promulgated on 25 D̲h̲u 'l-Ḳaʿda 1378/1 June 1959, with 10 headings and 64 articles.

It is laid down in the preamble to this Constitution that the Tunisian peoples, who "have freed themselves from foreign domination thanks to their powerful cohesion and to the struggle they have sustained against tyranny, exploitation and reaction", proclaim that "the republican régime represents the best guarantee of human rights ... and the most efficacious means of ensuring the prosperity of the nation". Part I provides that Tunisia is a Republic whose religion is Islam, that it forms a part of the Greater Mag̲h̲rib, that its motto is "Liberty, Order, Justice", and that sovereignty belongs to the people. The Tunisian Republic guarantees the dignity of the individual and freedom of conscience, and protects freedom of worship provided that public order is not disturbed (art. 5). All citizens are equal before the law and for purposes of taxation, and enjoy full rights which can be limited only by law (arts. 6-7). Freedom of opinion, of expression, of the press, of publication, of assembly and of association are guaranteed, as well as trade union rights (art. 8). Inviolability of domicile, secrecy of the mails and freedom of movement are assured (arts. 9-10); right of property is guaranteed (art. 14). Part II treats of the legislative power exercised by the National Assembly which is elected for 5 years by universal suffrage, at the same time as the President of the Republic. The right to initiate legislature belongs to the President or to the President and the members of the Assembly (art. 28); the President may enact, in the interval between two ordinary annual sessions of the Assembly, decrees, which must be submitted for ratification by the deputies in the course of the following session (art. 31); in addition, in the case of imminent danger the President may enforce exceptional measures and report them to the Assembly (art. 32). The State budget is voted by the Assembly (art. 35).

Part III is devoted to the executive power exercised by the President of the Republic, who must be a Muslim, aged at least 40 years, of Tunisian father and grandfather and in possession of full civic rights (arts. 37-9). He is elected for 5 years by direct and secret universal suffrage, and is not eligible for re-election for more than three consecutive terms (art. 40). He promulgates the laws and ensures their publication within 15 days in the official newspaper, during which time he has the power of referring a bill back for a second reading before the Assembly; if the bill then receives a two-thirds majority the law is promulgated within a fresh period of 15 days (art. 44). The President decides government policy, and selects the members of the government who are to be responsible to him (art. 43). He nominates holders of civil and military office and is the supreme chief of the armed forces (arts. 45-6). The rest of the chapter deals with foreign relations, the making of treaties, the granting of pardons, and the vacancy of the Presidency.

Part IV, very short, relates to the judicial power. The Constitution assures the independence of the judiciary (art. 53) and sets up a Higher Judicial Council which supervises the application of the guarantees granted to judges (art. 55). Part V institutes a Supreme Court which is to meet to try a charge of high treason brought against a member of the government. Parts VI, VII and VIII treat of the Council of State, which is at once an administrative jurisdiction and an Audit Office, the Economic and Social Council, and municipal and regional councils. Finally Parts IX and X provide for the conditions for amending the Constitution, initiative for which belongs to the President or to one-third of the members of the Assembly, as well as of interim provisions.

Bibliography: The 1861 Constitution is analysed and studied in E. Fitoussi and A. Benazet, *L'État tunisien et le protectorat français*, Paris 1931, i, 52-117; see also J. Ganiage, *Les origines du protectorat français en Tunisie (1861-81)*, Paris 1959, 69 ff. (with bibl.); the Journal of Ibn Abi 'l-Ḍiyāf who took part in drafting the Constitution is at present being edited and translated. Constitution of 1959: *ʿAmal*, 29 May 1959; *ʿAlam*, 1 June 1959; *OM*, 1959, 411-5; *MEJ*, xiii (1959), 443-8. (Ed.)

ii. — Turkey

The word *düstūr* (modern Turkish form *düstur*) is used in Turkish in the general senses of principle, precedent, code or register of rules. It was applied in particular to the great series of volumes, containing the texts of new laws, published in Istanbul (and later Ankara) from 1279/1863 onwards. (An earlier volume of new laws, not under this name, had already been issued in 1267/1851.) Three series (*tertīb*) of the *Düstūr* were published, the first covering the years 1839-1908, the second 1908-22, and the third containing the laws of the nationalist régime in Ankara and, after it, of the Turkish Republic, from 1920 onwards (see G. Jäschke, *Türkische Gesetzsammlungen*, in *WI*, N.S. iii (1954) 225-34).

Düstūr has not been used in Turkish with its modern Arabic meaning of constitution, for which the normal terms are *ḳānūn-i esāsī* (basic law) and *meshrūṭiyyet* (conditionality, conditionedness). The former term is applied to the constitution itself, and was replaced during the linguistic reforms in the Republic by *Anayasa*; the latter denotes constitutional government. In what follows a brief sketch is given of constitutional development in Turkey during the 19th and 20th centuries.

The *Sened-i Ittifāḳ*

The modern constitutional history of Turkey is usually dated from the year 1808 when, shortly after the accession of Maḥmūd II, the Grand Vizier Bayraḳdār Muṣṭafā Pasha [*q.v.*] convened a meeting in Istanbul, to which he invited a number of the local rulers and dynasts (see Aʿyān and derebey) who at that time enjoyed virtual autonomy in most of the provinces of the Empire. A number of the leading *aʿyān* and *derebey*s, from both Rumelia and Anatolia, came with large retinues and military forces (Ismāʿīl Bey of Serez is said to have come with 12,000 men, Ḳalyondju Muṣṭafā, of Biledjik, with 5000, and others with considerable but unspecified numbers), and camped at various places outside the city; others, though not attending in person, sent agents to represent them. After an interval of discussions and negotiations to prepare the ground, a general consultative meeting (*endjümen-i meshweret-i ʿumūmiyye*) was held, at which the Grand Vizier presided; also present were the *Shaykh al-Islām*, the aghas of the Janissaries and of the sipāhīs, and other dignitaries of the central government, as well as the invited *aʿyān*. The Grand Vizier made a speech in which he described the weaknesses of the Ottoman state and army and set forth a programme of reform. His proposals were unanimously approved, and the meeting resolved that a "deed of agreement" (*sened-i ittifāḳ*) should be drafted, signed and sealed, expressing the points of agreement reached between the parties. Contacts between officials, *aʿyān* and the Sultan followed, and on 17 Shaʿbān 1223/7 October 1807 the final draft of the *sened-i ittifāḳ*, bearing the signatures and seals of the Grand Vizier, the *Shaykh al-Islām*, and other dignitaries, and of the leading *aʿyān*, was sent to the Sultan for ratification. Maḥmūd II, despite his strong objections to the document, found himself obliged to ratify and authenticate it with his imperial signature.

The *sened-i ittifāḳ* consists of a preamble, seven articles, and a conclusion. The preamble, after describing the decline of Ottoman power and the weakness of the Ottoman state, explains that the following articles represent the unanimous agreement of the signatories, reached after several meetings, on the need to strengthen the empire and the faith and on the means of accomplishing this.

Article one begins with what might be called a pledge of homage to the Sultan by the *aʿyān*, who together with the officers of the central government, undertake not to oppose or resist the Sultan, and to come to his help if others oppose him. The signatories pledge themselves collectively to enforce this against offenders, including other parties who have not signed the document. They accept these obligations for themselves during their lifetimes, and for their sons and heirs after them.

Article two is concerned with military matters. Since the main purpose of the meeting and agreements was to restore the military power of the Empire, the signatories undertake to cooperate in the recruitment of troops, and to come to the Sultan's help when required, against both foreign and domestic enemies. They accept joint responsibility for dealing with offenders.

Article three is financial, and records the promise of the signatories to respect and observe the rules and regulations laid down by the government in financial matters. They undertake to show solicitude in collecting and remitting sums due to the government, and to refrain from abuses, for the punishment of which they accept joint responsibility.

Article four establishes the authority and responsibility of the Grand Vizier. The signatories recognize the Grand Vizier as absolute representative (*wekālet-i muṭlaḳa*) of the Sultan, and promise to obey his orders in all matters, as if they came from the Sultan. Other functionaries are to keep within the limits of their own offices and jurisdictions. If they exceed them, the signatories collectively will stand forth as accusers. Similarly, if the Grand Vizier himself acts against the laws of the Empire (*khilāf-i ḳānūn*) or violates this agreement, takes bribes, practises extortion, or commits acts harmful or likely to be harmful to the state (*dewlet-i ʿaliyyeye . . muḍirr*), then all the signatories conjointly will stand forth as accusers, and secure the removal of such abuses.

Article five regulates the relations of the *aʿyān* with one another and with the officials of the central government, on a basis of mutual guarantees. If any of the signatories violates the agreement, the rest will be collectively responsible for his punishment. The article guarantees the *aʿyān* in possession of their lands, and confirms the rights of succession of their heirs, who are also to be bound by the agreement. The same guarantees are extended by the *aʿyān* to the lesser *aʿyān* under their jurisdiction; this appears to involve a kind of sub-infeudation. The *aʿyān* undertake not to attack each other's lands, not to oppress their subjects, and in general to deal justly with the government, the people, and with one another.

Article six deals with the contingency of a further outbreak of disorder in the capital, whether due to a Janissary meeting or other causes. In such an event, the *aʿyān* promise to come at once to Istanbul with their forces, to restore order and the authority of the central government.

Article seven is concerned with the protection of the subjects from extortion and oppression. The *aʿyān* undertake to deal justly with their subjects, and to observe and report on one another.

The significance of the *sened-i ittifāḳ* has been variously assessed. Turkish constitutional historians have seen in it a kind of Magna Carta, an attempt by a baronage and gentry to exact from the Sultan a recognition of their rights and privileges, and thus to limit the authority of the sovereign power. Şerif Mardin takes a diametrically opposite view; according to him, the agreement was planned by officials of central government, for whom the Grand Vizier was no more than a "military figurehead"; it "was aimed at curbing the powers of the local dynasties . . and . . was one of the first steps towards the transformation of the Ottoman Empire into a modern centralized state". The recognition of the independence of the *aʿyān* was merely "a temporary compromise due to the weakness of the central powers" (Mardin, 146-8).

From the historical evidence it would seem clear that the pact was freely negotiated between the Grand Vizier and other dignitaries of the central government on the one hand, and the leading *aʿyān* on the other. Neither side imposed its will on the other, and indeed it is difficult to see how the *aʿyān* could have been compelled, in view of the impressive armed forces that they had brought with them. D̲j̲ewdet remarks that the meeting and agreement were made possible because the *aʿyān* trusted Bayraḳdār Muṣṭafā Pas̲h̲a—though apparently not far enough to come to Istanbul without armies, or to move into the city when they had got there.

One party to the agreement is known to have objected to it—the Sultan, who saw in it a derogation of his sovereignty. According to D̲j̲ewdet he signed it unwillingly, and with the intention of annulling it at the first opportunity. He nourished resentment against the *aʿyān* and even against the drafter of the document, the *Beylikd̲j̲i* ʿIzzet Bey, whom he later found occasion to condemn to death (D̲j̲ewdet, ix, 7-8).

Whatever the historical balance of forces that produced it, the constitutional significance of the *sened-i ittifāḳ* lies in its character as a negotiated contract—an agreement between the Sultan and groups of his servants and subjects, in which the latter appear as independent contracting parties, receiving as well as conceding certain rights and privileges (cf. the comments of D̲j̲ewdet, ix, 6 on the infringement of the Sultan's absolute prerogative). The effective agreement is between the Grand Vizierate and the *aʿyān*; the Sultan merely ratifies it, and is clearly expected to reign rather than to rule.

(The text of the *sened-i ittifāḳ* will be found in S̲h̲ānīzāde, *Taʾrīk̲h̲*, i, 66-78, and D̲j̲ewdet, *Taʾrīk̲h̲*[2], ix, 278-83. For accounts of the events leading to it, see S̲h̲ānīzāde, i, 61 ff.; D̲j̲ewdet, ix, 2 ff.; A. de Juchereau de Saint-Denys, *Révolutions de Constantinople en 1807 et 1808*, ii, Paris 1819, 200 ff.; J. W. Zinkeisen, *Gesch. des osm. Reiches in Europa*, vii, Gotha 1863, 564 ff.; O. von Schlechta Wssehrd, *Die Revolutionen in Constantinopel in den Jahren 1807 und 1808*, in *SBAk. Wien* (1882), 184-8. For studies and views of the pact see I. H. Uzunçarşılı, . . . *Alemdar Mustafa Paşa*, Istanbul 1942, 138-44; A. F. Miller, *Mustafa Pasha Bayraktar*, Moscow 1947, 283-91; A. Selçuk Özçelik, *Sened-i Ittifak*, in *Istanbul Üniv. Hukuk Fak. Mec.*, xxiv (1959), 1-12; T. Z. Tunaya, *Türkiyenin siyasî hayatında batılılaşma hareketleri*, Istanbul 1960, 25-6; Ş. Mardin, *The genesis of Young Ottoman thought*, Princeton, 145-8, as well as the general works on constitutional history and law listed below.)

The approach to constitutional government

The 'Deed of Agreement' was short-lived. Almost immediately after its signature the Grand Vizier Bayraḳdār Muṣṭafā Pas̲h̲a was overthrown and killed, and in the years that followed Sultan Maḥmūd II subjugated the *aʿyān* and brought what remained of the Empire under the effective countrol of the central government. The great reforming edicts of 1839 and 1856 have sometimes been described as 'constitutional charters', in that they lay down such general principles as the security of life, honour and property of the subject, fair and public trial of persons accused of crimes, and equality before the law of all Ottoman subjects irrespective of religion. Some of the other reforms of this period may also be said to have a quasi-constitutional character, such as the councils set up by Maḥmūd II and his successors (see MAD̲J̲LIS and TANẒĪMĀT) and especially the Council of State (*S̲h̲ūrā-yi Dēwlet*), founded in 1868. Modelled on the French *Conseil d'État*, this was a court of review in administrative cases; it also had certain consultative functions, and was supposed to prepare the drafts of new laws. Though its members were all appointed and not elected, it has been described as "a kind of rudimentary chamber of deputies". In 1845 the government actually experimented—unsuccessfully —with an assembly of provincial notables in the capital (Luṭfī, *Taʾrīk̲h̲*, viii, 15-17; Ed. Engelhardt, *La Turquie et le Tanzimat*, i, Paris 1882, 76; Lewis, *Emergence*, 110-1); the provincial reorganization law of 1864 provides for elected councils in the provinces.

Despite these developments, the general effect of the Westernization of the apparatus of government was to increase, rather than to limit, the autocratic authority of the central power. The old and well-tried checks on the Sultan's despotism—the entrenched intermediate powers of the army, the *ʿulemāʾ* and the notables—were one by one abrogated or enfeebled, leaving the reinforced sovereign power with nothing but the paper shackles of its own edicts to restrain it; the new laws were too little understood, too feebly supported, too ineptly applied, to have much effect.

The growing autocracy of the state—at times of the Sultan, at others of the ministers acting in his name—did not pass unnoticed. Towards the middle of the 19th century a libertarian movement of political thought began to gain ground (see ḤURRIYYA, ii), deriving its inspiration from European liberal and constitutional ideas, which Muslim writers tried to identify with the older Islamic doctrine of consultation (by the ruler of his counsellors—see MAS̲H̲WARA). In 1839 a Turkish translation appeared of the account by the Egyptian S̲h̲ayk̲h̲ Rāfiʿ Rifāʿa al-Ṭahṭāwī [*q.v.*] of his stay in Paris; this included an annotated translation of the French constitution, with an explanation of the merits of constitutional government. Constitutionalism did not, however, become a political force in Turkey until the eighteen-sixties, when its development was stimulated by a series of external events. The Tunisian constitution of 1861 (see above) brought the first precedent of a constitution in a Muslim state; the Egyptian legislative assembly of 1866 and the Rumanian constitution of the same year provided examples nearer home. Muṣṭafā Fāḍil Pas̲h̲a [*q.v.*], the brother of the Khedive Ismāʿīl of Egypt, and later the Khedive Ismāʿīl himself, gave encouragement to members of the group of liberal patriots known as the Young Ottomans (see YEÑI ʿOTHMĀNLĪLAR), some of whom campaigned actively for the introduction of a constitutional régime in Turkey. At first they were strongly opposed by the government, and driven into exile; the Grand Vizier ʿĀlī Pas̲h̲a himself wrote refuting the arguments in favour of such a change (Mardin, 19-20). The death of ʿĀlī Pasha in September 1871, however, and the growing influence of Midḥat Pas̲h̲a [*q.v.*] brought a change in attitude at the centre, while the mounting pressure of external events made a concession to liberal opinion seem desirable. In May 1876 the British Ambassador Sir Henry Elliott reported that "the word 'constitution' was in every mouth". As early as the winter of 1875, Midḥat Pasha told Sir Henry that the object of his group was to install a constitutional regime, with ministers responsible to "a national popular assembly" (Sir Henry Elliott, *Some revolutions and other diplomatic experiences*, London 1922, 228, 231-2). The stages by which the constitution was prepared are still imperfectly known. The first steps seem to have been taken soon after the accession of Murād V, when exploratory discussions were held. The sickness and deposition of Murād delayed matters, but work was resumed after the accession of ʿAbd al-Ḥamīd II, who had promised Midḥat his support for the constitutional cause. A new constitutional commission, this time led by Midḥat himself, was appointed on 19 Ramaḍān 1293/8 October 1876 N.S. It consisted initially of the chairman and 22 members, including a number of civil and military pas̲h̲as, a contingent of *ʿulemāʾ*, most if not all of them in government service, and some high officials, several of them Christian. Other persons, including some of the Young Ottomans, were later added to the commission or to its drafting subcommittee. After some delays, and disagreements between the members and with the Sultan, a compromise text was finally adopted, and promulgated by the Sultan. Midḥat Pas̲h̲a, as president of the Council of State, as chairman of the commission, and, since 20 December 1876, as Grand Vizier, had played a predominant rôle in securing this result. (On the preparation and adoption of the constitution, see Bekir Sıtkı Baykal, *93 Meşrutiyeti*, in *Belleten*, vi/21-2 (1942), 45-83; documents in idem, *Birinci Meşrutiyete dair belgeler*, in *Belleten*, xxiv/96 (1960), 601-36; Mithat Cemal Kuntay, *Namık Kemal*, ii/2, Istanbul 1956, 55 ff.; Yu. A. Petrosian, "*Novïe Osmanî*" *i borba za Konstitutsiyu 1876 g. v Turtsii*, Moscow 1958; Ş. Mardin, *The genesis* . ., 70-8.)

The Constitution of 1876

The first Ottoman constitution (*ḳānūn-i esāsī*) was promulgated by Sultan ʿAbd al-Ḥamīd on 7 D̲h̲u 'l-Ḥid̲j̲d̲j̲a 1293/23 December 1876 N.S. In form rather more than in content it was a constitutional enactment in the Western style, consisting of twelve sections with 119 articles, and accompanied by an Imperial Rescript (*K̲h̲aṭṭ-i humāyūn*) of promulgation serving as a preamble. In framing their text, the Ottoman draftsmen seem to have been greatly influenced by the Belgian constitution of 1831, both directly and through the Prussian constitutional edict of 1850 which, while owing much to its Belgian model, adapted it in a number of respects to the more authoritarian traditions of Prussia. While the Belgian constitution was promulgated by a constituent assembly representing the sovereign people, the Prussian derived from the goodwill of the king, whose ultimate sovereignty was in no way thereby diminished. The Ottoman constitution also derives from the will of the sovereign who voluntarily renounces the exclusive exercise of some—though by no means all—of his prerogatives, and retains all residual powers. Again like the Prussian constitution, the Ottoman constitution gives perfunctory recognition to the principle of the separation of powers, but unlike the Belgian constitution does not apply it very rigorously.

The first section (articles 1-7) is headed "The Ottoman Empire" (*Memālik-i Dewlet-i ʿOt̲h̲māniyye*); it defines the Empire, names its capital, and lays down the rights and privileges of the Sultan and the imperial dynasty. The Ottoman Sultanate, with which is united the supreme Islamic Caliphate (*k̲h̲ilāfet-i kubrā-yi islāmiyye*) belongs in accordance with ancient custom to the eldest member of the Ottoman dynasty (art. 3). The Sultan, as Caliph, is protector of the Islamic religion (*dīn-i islāmīñ ḥāmīsi*) (art. 4. On the Ottoman claim to the Caliphate see KHILĀFA). The Sultan's person is sacrosanct (*muḳaddes*) and he is not responsible (*g̲h̲ayr-i mesʾūl*) (art. 5). Article 7 enumerates some of the Sultan's prerogatives, in a form of words clearly indicating that the list is not intended as a complete definition, and that there is no renunciation of residual powers (. . *ḥuḳūḳ-i muḳaddese-i Pādis̲h̲āhī d̲j̲ümlesindendir*; in the official French translation "S.M. le Sultan compte au nombre de ses droits souverains les prérogatives suivantes . ."). These include, together with such traditional Islamic rights as the striking of coins and mention in the Friday prayer, the appointment and dismissal of ministers, the making of war and peace, the execution (*id̲j̲rā*) of *s̲h̲arīʿa* and state law (*aḥkām-i s̲h̲erʿiyye we ḳānūniyye*), the regulation (*niẓāmnāmeleriñ tanẓīmi*) of public administration, the convocation and prorogation of parliament and, if he thinks it necessary (*lada 'l-iḳtiḍāʾ*—in the official French version "s'il le juge nécessaire") the dissolution of the Chamber of Deputies, on condition that new elections be held (*aʿdāsî yeñiden intik̲h̲āb olunmak s̲h̲arṭîle*).

The second section (articles 8-26) deals with the public rights (*ḥuḳūḳ-i ʿumūmiyye*) of Ottoman subjects (*tebaʿa*). It defines Ottoman nationality, and affirms the equality of all Ottomans, irrespective of religion, before the law. Though Islam is the state religion, the free exercise of other religions is protected. Article 10 lays down that personal freedom is inviolable (*ḥürriyyet-i s̲h̲ak̲h̲ṣiyye her türlü taʿarruḍdan maṣūndur*), and subsequent articles deal with freedom of worship, the press, association, education etc., together with freedom from arbitrary intrusion, extortion, arrest, or other unlawful violations of person, residence, or property.

The remaining sections deal with the ministers (articles 27-38), officials (39-41), parliament (42-59), the Senate (60-64), the Chamber of Deputies (65-80), the judiciary (81-91), the high courts (92-95), finance (96-107), and provincial administration (108-112). A final section of "miscellaneous provisions" (*mewādd-i s̲h̲ettā*) includes the notorious article 113, giving the imperial government the right to proclaim martial law on the occurrence or expectation of disorders, and giving the Sultan the exclusive right, after reliable police investigations, to deport persons harmful to the state from Ottoman territory.

The executive power belongs to the Sultan, and is exercised in part through a council of ministers (*medjlis-i wükelā*), presided over by the Grand Vizier, and including the S̲h̲ayk̲h̲ al-Islām. These two dignitaries are chosen and appointed by the Sultan; the appointment of other ministers is effected by imperial order (*irāde-i s̲h̲āhāne*). The ministers are individually but not collectively responsible—and to the Sultan. If a government bill is rejected by the Chamber of Deputies, the Sultan can, at his discretion, either change the cabinet or dissolve the Chamber and order new elections.

The legislative power also belongs to the Sultan, but its exercise is shared, on a rather restricted basis, with a Parliament (*medjlis-i ʿumūmī*). This consists of a Senate (*heyʾet-i aʿyān*), nominated directly for life by the Sultan, and of a Chamber of Deputies (*heyʾet-i mebʿūt̲h̲ān*), elected for four years on the ratio of one deputy for every 50,000 male Ottoman subjects. The Senate must not exceed one third of the numbers of the elected Deputies. The manner of election was fixed by an *irāde* of 28 October 1876, on a basis of restricted franchise and indirect elections. The power to initiate legislation in Parliament belongs to the government; proposals from either chamber must first be submitted through the Grand Vizier to the Sultan, who may, if he thinks fit, instruct the Council of State to draft a bill. To become law, a bill must be passed by both Chambers, and receive the Sultan's assent. Bills rejected by either chamber cannot be reconsidered in the same session.

The judicial power is exercised through two systems of judiciary, the first (*s̲h̲erʿī*) concerned with the Holy Law of Islam, the second (*niẓāmī*; in the official French translation rendered "civil") with the new laws made by the state. Judges are appointed by *berāt*; they are irremovable (*lā yaʿtazil*) but can resign, or be revoked after a judicial conviction. Article 86 guarantees the freedom of the courts from "any kind of interference".

The effective life of the 1876 constitution was of short duration. The first Ottoman parliament met on 4 Rabīʿ I 1294/19 March 1877 N.S. [= 7 March O.S.], with a Senate of 25 and a Chamber of 120 deputies. Its fifty-sixth and last meeting was held on 16 D̲j̲umādā II 1294/28 June 1877 N.S. [= 16 June O.S.]. After further elections, a second Parliament assembled on 13 D̲h̲u 'l-Ḥid̲j̲d̲j̲a 1294/13 December 1877 N.S. [= 1 December O.S.], and soon showed unexpected vigour. On 13 February 1878 the deputies went so far as to demand that three ministers, against whom specific charges had been brought, should appear in the chamber to defend themselves (cf. article 38 of the constitution). The next day the Sultan dissolved the Chamber, and ordered the Deputies to return to their constituencies. In the words of the Proclamation "Since present circumstances are unfavourable to the full discharge of the duties of parliament, and since, according to the constitution, the limitation or curtailment of the period of session of the said parliament in accordance with the needs of the time form part of the sacred Imperial prerogatives, therefore, in accordance with the said law, a high Imperial order has been issued ... that the present sessions of the Senate and Chamber, due to end at the beginning of March ... be closed as from today". Parliament had sat for two sessions, of about five months in all. It did not meet again for thirty years.

The Young Turk period

The Young Turk Revolution of 1908 ushered in what is known to Turkish historians as the 'second constitutional régime' (*ikinci meşrutiyet*). The Constitution had never actually been abrogated—it was indeed regularly reprinted in the imperial year books (*sālnāme*) right through the reign of ʿAbd al-Ḥamīd II; it was, however, tacitly suspended. On 21 July 1908 the Young Turk leaders in Rumelia sent a telegram to the Sultan demanding the immediate restoration of the constitution, and after a brief interlude of hesitation the Sultan gave way. A Rescript (*k̲h̲aṭṭ-i humāyūn*), dated 4 Rad̲j̲ab 1326/ 19 July 1908 O.S. [= 1 August N.S.], and addressed to the Grand Vizier Saʿīd Pas̲h̲a, declared that the country was ready for constitutional government, and that all the provisions of the constitution were effective and in force (.. *kāffe-i aḥkāmī merʿī ül-idjrā* ..). In addition, the Rescript added a number of new provisions, extending the personal liberty of the subject. These prohibit arrest and search except by proper legal procedures, abolish all special and extraordinary courts, and guarantee the security of the mails and the freedom of the press. Article 113, giving the Sultan the right to deport persons dangerous to the state, was unaffected by the Rescript, but was abolished in the following year. Another important change gave the Grand Vizier the right to appoint all ministers other than the Ministers of War and of the Navy who, like the S̲h̲ayk̲h̲ al-Islām, were to be appointed by the Sultan. The acceptance of these restrictions led to the fall of Saʿīd Pas̲h̲a; his successor, Kāmil Pas̲h̲a, secured a new Rescript reserving the nomination of *all* ministers, other than the S̲h̲ayk̲h̲ al-Islām, to the Grand Vizier.

After the opening of Parliament on 17 December 1908 further constitutional reforms were considered, and a constitutional commission formed to draft proposals. These consisted of a series of amendments to the existing text, modifying some articles, remaking or replacing others. The amendments became law on 21 August 1909, and amounted to a major constitutional reform. Their general effect was to strengthen Parliament and weaken the Throne. Both the Sultan and his nominee, the Grand Vizier, were shorn of much of their authority; and for the first time, the collective responsibility of the cabinet was clearly laid down. The sovereignty of parliament was vigorously affirmed.

These changes were adopted when the Committee of Union and Progress (see ITTIḤĀD WE-TERAḲḲI) were firmly in control of both houses of parliament, but still feared the palace. The weakness of the executive resulting from the reforms soon, however, proved inconvenient for the Unionists themselves, once they were in control of it. In 1911 the government submitted proposals for constitutional changes, increasing the Sultan's authority over parliament. These were vigorously challenged by the opposition in parliament, on the ground that their purpose was to strengthen, not the Sultan, but the Committee of Union and Progress; and in the parliamentary and constitutional crisis that followed parliament was dissolved. It was not until 28 May 1914, when the country was in effect ruled by a Unionist dictatorship, that a new set of constitutional amendments finally became law. Later amendments, in January 1915, March 1916 and April 1918, further increased the power of the Sultan, who was now able to convene, prorogue, prolong or dismiss parliament almost at discretion.

The electoral law, the preparation of which was envisaged in the constitution, was drafted and debated in 1877, but did not become law until after the 1908 revolution. It improved and extended the framework of the *irāde* of 1876, but retained the limited franchise and the system of indirect elections through electoral colleges. Elections under this law were held in 1908, 1912, 1914 and 1919. All but that of 1914 were contested by more than one party; none resulted in a transfer of power. In January 1920 the last Ottoman parliament, elected in the sixth and last general election in the Ottoman Empire, assembled in Istanbul. On 18 March the Chamber prorogued itself; on 11 April it was dissolved by the Sultan. Twelve days later the Grand National Assembly of Turkey held its opening session in Ankara.

(The Turkish text of the 1876 constitution was printed in the *Düstūr*, 1st series, iv, 2-20, and reprinted in the *sālnāme*s of the Empire; later amendments in *Düstūr*, 2nd series, i, 11 ff., 638 ff.; vi, 749; vii, 224 etc.; modern Turkish transcriptions in Gözübüyük and Kili (work cited in bibliography), 23 ff.; official French translation in G. Aristarchi, *Legislation ottomane*, v (*Appendice* .. by D. Nicolaides), Constantinople 1878, 1-25; cf. A. Ubicini, *La constitution ottomane du 7 zilhidjé 1293*, Constantinople 1877; an annotated German version of the constitution, amendments and electoral law in F. von Kraelitz-Greifenhorst, *Die Verfassungsgesetze des Osmanischen Reiches*, Vienna 1919; an English translation of the constitution in E. Hertslet, *The map of Europe* . ., iv, London 1891, 2531-40; amendments in H. F. Wright, *The Constitutions of the states at war 1914-1918*, Washington 1919, 589-605. For studies of the constitution and its application see G. Jäschke, *Die Entwicklung des osmanischen Verfassungstaates von den Anfängen bis zur Gegenwart*, in *WI*, v (1917), 5-56; idem, *Die rechtliche Bedeutung der in den Jahren 1909-1916 vollzogenen Abänderungen des türkischen Staatsgrundgesetzes*, in *WI*, v (1918), 97-152. See also W. Albrecht, *Grundriss des osmanischen Staatsrechts*, Berlin 1905.

The Republic and its antecedents

Almost from the beginning, the Grand National Assembly (*Büyük Millet Medjlisi*) convened in Ankara by the nationalists was concerned with constitutional problems. Its first formally constitutional enactment was the "Law of Fundamental Organizations" (*Teshkīlāt-i esāsiyye ḳānūnu*) of 20 January 1921—in effect the provisional constitution of the new Turkish state that was emerging (*Düstūr*, 3rd series, i, 196; Gözübüyük and Kili, 85-7). The first article proclaims the revolutionary principle that "sovereignty belongs unconditionally to the nation" (*ḥākimiyyet bilā ḳaydü sharṭ milletiñdir*), and that "the system of administration rests on the principle that the nation personally and effectively (*bi 'l-dhāt we bi 'l-fiʿl*) directs its own destinies". The second article declares that "executive power and legislative authority are vested and expressed in the Grand National Assembly, which is the only and real representative of the nation". The third article lays down that "the state of Turkey (*Türkiye dewleti*) is administered by the Grand National Assembly, and its government bears the name of 'the government of the Grand National Assembly'." The remaining articles are concerned with the holding of elections and the conduct of government business (text in *Düstūr*, 3rd series, i, 196; Gözübüyük and Kili, 85-7; English version in D. E. Webster, *The Turkey of Atatürk*, Philadelphia 1939, 97-8). This enactment, with its equally revolutionary references to "the sovereignty of the nation" and "the state of Turkey", marked the first decisive step in the series of legal and constitutional changes that regulated the transformation of Turkey from an Islamic Empire to a secular national state. The next was a resolution adopted by the Assembly on 1 November 1922, after the final victory of the nationalists. It contained only two articles: the first declared that "the Turkish people consider that the form of government in Istanbul resting on the sovereignty of an individual [the Sultanate] had ceased to exist on 16 March 1920 [*i.e.*, two and a half years previously, the day of the British military occupation of Istanbul] and had passed forever into history." The second recognized that the Caliphate belonged to the Ottoman house, but reserved to the Assembly the right to choose and appoint the most suitable Ottoman prince. This attempt to separate the Caliphate from the Sultanate proved a failure, and on 3 March 1924 the Caliphate was abolished and the last Caliph sent into exile.

Meanwhile, however, another radical change had been accomplished. On 29 October 1923, after hours of debate, the Assembly passed a group of six amendments to the constitutional enactment of 1921. Their purpose, said Muṣṭafā Kemāl, was to remove ambiguities and inconsistencies in the political system of the country. The amendments, prepared the previous night, declared that "the form of government of the state of Turkey is a Republic . . the President (*reʾīs-i djumhūr*) is elected by the Grand National Assembly in plenary session from among its own members . . . the President is head of the state . . . and appoints the Prime Minister . .". The new order was confirmed in the republican constitution, adopted by the Assembly on 20 April 1924 (on republican ideas in Islam see DJUMHŪRIYYA).

The republican constitution retains elements of the enactment of 1921 and even of the reformed Ottoman constitution, but introduces a great deal that is new. The constitution is promulgated by the Assembly, which can amend it by a two-thirds majority (art. 102). The only entrenched clause is article 1, stating that "the Turkish state is a Republic". "No amendment or modification" of this article "can be proposed in any form whatsoever". No article of the constitution can be disregarded or suspended for any reason or under any pretext, and no law may contain provisions contrary to the constitution (Art. 103; the constitution, however, provides no special machinery for testing the constitutionality of laws).

Both the legislative authority and the executive power are vested in the Assembly, representing the sovereign people. The Assembly exercises its legislative power directly, its executive authority through the person of the President, whom it elects, and through a Council of Ministers (articles 4-7). Article 7 also gives the Assembly the right—which it never exercised—to dismiss the Council of Ministers. Judicial authority is exercised by independent courts (art. 8). The Assembly consists of a single chamber, elected once every four years. The Assembly can, however, by a majority vote, decide to hold new elections before the expiration of its term (articles 13, 25). The President of the Republic is elected by the Assembly, by secret ballot and absolute majority, for the duration of one parliament. He is to promulgate laws passed by the Assembly within ten days but may refer them back, within the same period, with a statement of his reasons for doing so.

This right does not extend to the constitutional law or to budgetary laws. If the Assembly again passes a law which has been referred back, the President is obliged to promulgate it. He is responsible to the Assembly in case of high treason, but responsibility arising from decrees promulgated by the President devolves on the Prime Minister and the minister signing the decree (article 41). The Council of Ministers is collectively responsible for the general policy of the government, but each minister is individually responsible for executive matters falling within his jurisdiction, and for the acts of his subordinates (article 46). The Prime Minister is chosen by the President, the other ministers by the Prime Minister. The remaining sections deal with the judiciary, which is free and independent, with "the public rights of the Turks", and with "miscellaneous matters", including provincial administration, officials, finance, and rules relating to the constitution.

The constitution was twice amended in matters of substance before its final abrogation. The first was in April 1928, when article 2 was amended by the deletion of the words "The religion of the Turkish state is Islam", with consequential changes in some other articles, to remove references to religion or holy law. The second was in February 1937, when article 2 was again amended, by the inclusion of the six principles of the Republican People's Party, declaring that the Turkish state is "republican, nationalist, populist, étatist, secular and reformist". Some other small changes were made at the same time. The replacement of the text of the constitution by a 'pure' Turkish version in 1945, and the abandonment of the latter in 1952, are of purely linguistic interest.

General elections under the Law of Fundamental Organizations and the republican constitution were held in 1923, 1927, 1931, 1935, 1939, 1943, 1946, 1950, 1954 and 1957. Of these, only the last four were contested by more than one party; only one, that of 1950, resulted in an opposition victory and a transfer of power, bringing the Democrat Party to power. The political development of Turkey after 1945 gave reality to much that had previously been theoretical in the constitution. While the constitution itself was not touched, changes in the law of associations, the penal code, and the electoral law, accompanied by changes in administrative practice, made possible the creation and functioning of an effective constitutional opposition, which in 1950 became the government. The second electoral victory of the Democrat Party in 1954 was followed by a deterioration. Already before the election, on 7 May 1954, a new Press law was passed, providing heavy penalties for libel against official persons, and for the publication of "false news or information or documents of such a nature as adversely to affect the political or financial prestige of the State or cause a disturbance of the public order". It was no defence to a charge brought under this law to prove the statements were true. After the election two new laws, of 21 June and 5 July, gave the government powers to retire judges after twenty five years' service, and to retire all officials other than judges and members of the armed forces after a period of suspension. At the same time, on 30 June, the electoral law was amended. On 27 June 1956 an amendment to the law of meetings and associations was carried against vigorous opposition in the chamber, placing severe restrictions on the holding of public meetings and demonstrations. In April 1960, during a period of mounting political tension, a parliamentary committee of the government party was formed to investigate the opposition, with legal authority. On 27 May the government was overthrown by a military *coup d'état.*

(On the period of transition from the Ottoman to the Turkish constitutions, see G. Jäschke, *Die ersten Verfassungsentwürfe der Ankara-Türkei*, in *MSOS*, xlii/II (1939), 57-80; idem, *Wie lange galt die osmanische Verfassung?*, in *WI*, N.S. v (1957), 118-9; idem, *Auf dem Wege zur türkischen Republik*, in *WI*, N.S. v (1958), 206-18; idem, *Die Entwicklung der türkischen Verfassung 1924 bis 1937*, in *Orient-Nachrichten*, iii/9-10 (1937), 122-3; T. Z. Tunaya, *Osmanlı Imparatorluğundan Türkiye Büyük Millet Meclisi hükûmeti rejimine geçiş*, in *Prof. M. R. Seviğ'e Armağan*, Istanbul 1956; idem, *Türkiye Büyük [Millet] Meclisi hükûmeti'nin kuruluşu ve siyasî karakteri*, in *Istanbul Üniv. Huk. Fak. Mec.*, xxiv (1958). For the text of the 1924 constitution, see *Düstūr*, 3rd series, v, 576-85, amendments of 1928, *Düstür*, ix, 142, of 1937, xviii, 307 ff. and xix, 37 ff., of 1945, xxvi, 170 ff.; transcription in Gözübüyük and Kili, 101-23 (with amendments); English translation, with amendments to 1937, in D. E. Webster, *The Turkey of Atatürk*, 297-306, also in Helen M. Davis, *Constitutions, Electoral laws ... of the states in the Near and Middle East*[2], Durham N.C. 1953, and, with useful notes, in G. L. Lewis, *Turkey*, London 1955, 197-210. The reports of the parliamentary debates on the constitution were published by A. Ş. Gözübüyük and Z. Sezgin, *1924 anayasası hakkındaki meclis görüşmeleri*, Ankara 1957; documents and debates will also be found in K. Arıburnu, *Millî mücadele ve inkılâplarla ilgili kanunlar*, i, Ankara 1957; cf. E. C. Smith, *Debates on the Turkish Constitution of 1924*, in *Ankara Üniv. Siyasal Bilgiler Fak. Derg.*, xiii (1958), 82-105. On the constitution and its antecedents see further E. Pritsch, *Die türkische Verfassung vom 20 April 1924*, in *MSOS*, xxvi-xxvii/II (1924), 164-251; for a lexical study of the 'pure' Turkish text of 1945, M. Colombe, *Le nouveau texte de la constitution turque*, in *COC*, iv (1946), 771-808; on the two main parties operating in this period see DEMOKRAT PARTİ and DJÜMHŪRIYYET KHALḲ FİRḲASİ).

The second Republic

At the beginning of June 1960 the National Unity Committee which had taken over the government of the country a few days previously resolved, as a matter of urgency, to set up a provisional constitution for the transitional period until a new constitution was established. The new law, prepared with the help of a small group of jurists, was published on 12 June, and entitled "Provisional law for the abolition and amendment of certain articles of constitutional law no. 491 of 20 April 1924" (translation in *COC*, xliii (1960), 266-70). The law begins with a general statement giving the legal and constitutional justification for the army's action in overthrowing the previous régime, which had "violated the constitution ... suppressed individual rights and liberties ... made it impossible for the opposition to function ... and established the dictatorship of a single party". The Turkish army, in conformity with its duty to "safeguard and protect the Turkish homeland and the Turkish Republic established by the constitution", as entrusted to it by article 34 of the army internal service code, took action, in the name of the Turkish nation, to carry out this sacred lawful duty against the former administration ... and to reestablish a state of legality. The army therefore dissolved the Assembly and entrusted power, provisionally, to the National Unity Comittee.

The law itself consists of 4 sections, with 27 articles. The first of these lays down that the committee "exercises sovereignty in the name of the Turkish nation until the day when it shall transfer power to the Grand National Assembly of Turkey, resulting from general elections to be held as soon as possible after the approval of the new constitution and the new electoral law in conformity with democratic rules". When this happens, the Committee will "lose its juridical existence and be automatically dissolved" (article 8). Until then all the rights and powers given by the constitution to the Assembly will be exercised by the Committee. The Committee will exercise the legislative power directly, the executive power through a council of ministers appointed by the head of state and approved by the Committee (article 3). Article 6 establishes a high court of justice to try the men of the old régime. Article 9 defines the membership of the Committee; article 17 lays down that the chairman of the Committee is at the same time head of state and Prime Minister. The provisional laws adopted by the Committee will remain in force as long as they are not repealed by the Assembly created in accordance with the new constitution (article 17).

The first step towards the new, permanent constitution envisaged in this law was taken immediately after the *coup d'état*. On 28th May Gen. Gürsel, chairman of the Committee, announced in his first press conference that he had appointed a commission of constitutional lawyers to prepare a new constitution. It would provide for a bi-cameral legislature and a constitutional court. On 18 October the commission, after some differences and the dismissal and replacement of two of its members, presented a draft constitution to the National Unity Committee. It was decided not to publish the text, but to refer it to a Constituent Assembly (*Kurucu Meclis*). A committee headed by Prof. Turhan Feyzioğlu was given the task of drafting a constitution for such an Assembly. Their draft was completed on 21 November and finally adopted by the National Unity Committee, after some emendation, on 14 December. It provided for a constituent assembly of two chambers, one of them the National Unity Committee, the other a chamber of representatives (*temsilciler meclisi*) "which will represent the Turkish people in the broadest sense of the word" (article 1). It was to consist of 272 members, some nominated and some elected by various interests and bodies. Elections and nominations took place in December and early January, and the Constituent Assembly met on 6 January 1961. Its members included persons nominated by the head of state and the National Unity Committee, representatives of the provinces, of the Republican People's Party and the Republican National Peasant Party, as well as of such bodies and professions as the universities, the bar, the press, secondary school teachers, trade-unions, trade associations, chambers of commerce and industry, ex-servicemen's organizations, and youth. The ministers in the provisional government were members *ex officio*.

On 9 January the Constituent Assembly elected two committees, one, of 20 members, to deal with the constitution, the other with the electoral law. On 9 March the constitutional commission presented its draft, which was then considered by both the Chamber of Representatives and the National Unity Committee. The latter proposed some changes, and a mixed committee was set up to reconcile their views. It completed its work on 26 May, and on the following day, the first anniversary of the revolution, Gen. Gürsel announced that the draft had been accepted by an overwhelming majority of the Assembly. The text was published in the official gazette of 31 May. On 28 March, the Assembly had already passed a law requiring that the draft constitution be submitted to the nation by a referendum, conducted along lines specified in the law. The referendum was held on 9 July, and resulted in the acceptance of the new constitution; 61% of the voters voted yes, 39% voted no, and some $2^1/_2$ million, out of a total qualified electorate of $12^3/_4$ million, abstained.

The constitution provides for a Grand National Assembly of two chambers, the Senate and National Assembly. The former consists of 15 members nominated by the President, and 150 members elected for a term of six years, one third every two years, by a straight majority vote. The National Assembly, of 450 members, is to be elected every four years by a system of proportional representation. The President is elected by the Grand National Assembly in plenary session from among its own members, by a two-thirds majority, for a term of seven years. He appoints the Prime Minister, who chooses the other ministers. The government is responsible to the Grand National Assembly. A noteworthy innovation is the establishment of a constitutional court (articles 145-52), to review the legality of legislation, with power also to act as a high council for the impeachment of Presidents, ministers and certain high officials "for offences connected with their duties". The constitution contains explicit guarantees of freedom of thought, expression, association and publication, immunity of domicile, and other democratic liberties (section 2, articles 14-34). In addition, it contains a section on social and economic rights, with provision both for the right of the State to plan economic development so as to achieve social justice, and the right of the individual to the ownership and inheritance of property, and to freedom of work and enterprise (section 3, articles 35-53). The right to strike is in principle recognized, within limits to be determined by subsequent legislation. Other clauses in the constitution seek to safeguard the secularist Kemalist reforms from reaction, and the democratic basis of government from a new dictatorship. The constitution was promulgated as law no. 334 of 9 July, in the official gazette of 20 July 1961, and entered into effect immediately. (An official English translation of the constitution was published in Ankara in 1962 and reprinted in *OM*, xliii/1 (1963), 1-28, and in *MEJ*, xvi (1962), 215-38, with a commentary by K. K. Key; for an analysis of the constitution, see Ismet Giritli, *Some aspects of the new Turkish constitution*, ibid., 1-17; on the constituent assembly see R. Devereux, *Turkey and the corporative state*, in *SAIS Review*, (Spring 1962), 16-24. A useful summary of constitutional developments in 1960 will be found in *Middle East Record*, *i*, *1960*, London [1962], 452-4. See also surveys of events in *COC*, *OM*, etc.

Bibliography: in addition to references in the article: Ali Fuad Başgil and others, *Turquie* (vol. vii of *La vie juridique des peuples*, edd. H. Lévy-Ullmann and B. Mirkine-Guetzévitch), Paris 1939; Sıddık Sami Onar, *Idare hukukunun umumî esasları*, Istanbul 1952; Recai G. Okandan, *Umumî âmme hukukumuzun ana hatları*, Istanbul 1948; Ali Fuad Başgil, *Türkiye siyasî rejimi ve anayasa prensipleri*, i/1, Istanbul 1957; *IA*, article Kanun-i Esâsî, by Hüseyin Nail Kubalı (where further references are given); G. Franco, *Développements constitutionnels en Turquie*, Paris 1925; A. Mary-Rousselière, *La Turquie constitutionnelle*, Rennes 1935; T. Z. Tunaya, *Türkiyede siyasî partiler, 1859-1952* (on political parties), Istanbul 1952; K. H. Karpat, *Turkey's politics. The transition to a multi-party system*, Princeton 1959; B. Lewis, *The emergence of modern Turkey*², London 1962. Documents in A. Şeref Gözübüyük and Suna Kili, *Türk anayasa metinleri*, Ankara 1957. Further references in *Bibliografiya Turtsii (1917-1958)*, Moscow 1959, 123-4; Pearson, 138-141; idem, *Supplement 1956-1960*, 45-7.

(B. Lewis)

iii. — Egypt

Exposed to European influence earlier than other Arab lands, Egypt followed an independent course of constitutional development, although her constitutional experiments were by no means entirely unrelated to those of the Ottoman Empire. The first elaborate constitutional charter, it is true, was not promulgated until 1882, but a number of constitutional instruments, providing either for the establishment of representative assemblies or responsible cabinets, had been issued since the beginning of the nineteenth century. Bonaparte, after his capture of Cairo in 1798, issued several orders establishing *dīwān*s (councils), composed of Egyptian and French members. The significance of those *dīwān*s, though they were purely consultative in nature, lies in the recognition of the principle that the people's representatives should be consulted on public affairs. Muḥammad ʿAlī (1805-48) revived Bonaparte's *dīwān* in 1829 in the form of a *Madjlis al-Mashwara*, a consultative council which assisted him in the administration of the country. These councils, lacking the support of public opinion, were of brief duration.

It was not until the reign of the Khedive Ismāʿīl that further constitutional instruments were issued. One of them (1860) created a council of representatives, called *Madjlis Shūrā al-Nuwwāb*; another (1878) established a responsible Cabinet, called *Madjlis al-Nuẓẓār*. Ismāʿīl's immediate purpose in issuing such decrees was not necessarily to introduce constitutional reform, but to resolve financial difficulties, which could lead to foreign intervention and with it to the curbing of the Khedive's powers. On 22 October 1866 Ismāʿīl issued two decrees creating a representative assembly composed of 75 members, elected for a three-year term, called *Madjlis Shūrā al-Nuwwāb* (Chamber of Deputies). One of them embodied a fundamental law (*lāʾiḥa asāsiyya*) made up of 18 articles stating the functions of the Chamber and the procedure for electing it. The other, made up of 61 articles, called the law of internal regulations (*lāʾiḥa niẓāmiyya*, or *niẓāmnāme*), providing rules for the debates and internal procedure of the Chamber. The Khedive retained complete control over the Chamber by his final approval of its decisions. The meetings of the Chamber began on 25 November 1866, but it was suspended in 1879. It resumed its activities during the ʿUrābī Revolt and played a significant role in drawing up an elaborate constitutional instrument. The Chamber, however, proved ineffective and its functions merely consultative, since its resolutions were not binding on the Government.

On 28 August 1878 Ismāʿīl issued another decree dealing with the establishment of a Council of Ministers (*Madjlis al-Nuẓẓār*), by virtue of which he entrusted power in its hands. This executive body, the first in the history of modern Egypt, was responsible, relieving the Khedive of responsibility, with the consequential limitation of his absolute powers. However, the decree was revised by Tawfīḳ Pasha, who succeeded Ismāʿīl in 1879, making the Cabinet responsible to him. Tawfīḳ often held the meetings of the Cabinet under his chairmanship.

Before Tawfīḳ could bring the Cabinet under his full control and abolish the Chamber of Deputies, the latter took the drastic step of drawing up an elaborate constitutional charter. It was during the ʿUrābī revolt that this Chamber, meeting as a National Constituent Assembly in 1882, prepared and promulgated Egypt's first written constitution, called *al-Lāʾiḥa al-Asāsiyya*. The Chamber began to discuss the draft in January 1882; it was promulgated on 7 February 1882.

The Constitution of 1882 provided for the establishment of a parliamentary system and a responsible Cabinet, appointed by the Khedive. The Chamber of Deputies was to be an elective body for a period of five years, its meetings open to the public, and its members inviolable. Its President was to be appointed by the Khedive, chosen from three candidates nominated by the Chamber. The Chamber was to have the right to interrogate the Ministers, ask questions of information, and supervise "the acts of all public functionaries during the session, and through the President of the Chamber they may report to the Ministers concerning all abuses, irregularities or negligences charged against a public official in the exercise of his functions" (Article 20). Legislation could be initiated either by the Cabinet or the Chamber and had to be confirmed and issued by the Khedive. No new taxes were to be imposed without the approval of the Chamber. The budget was to be presented to the Chamber for discussion and approval, except for matters relating to the annual tribute to the Porte and the Public Debt. No treaty or contract between the Government and a foreign country was to be binding until approved by the Chamber, save those relating to matters where sums of money had already been approved in the budget. The Chamber of Deputies was dissolved after the collapse of the ʿUrābī Revolt and the constitution of 1882 was abrogated.

In 1883, a year after the British occupation, Tawfīḳ Pāsha issued an Organic Law reorganizing Egypt's constitutional framework which lasted from the British occupation to World War I. This law provided for the establishment of the following bodies:

First, a Provincial Council, composed of from 3 to 8 members, according to the size of the province, established in each province (*mudīriyya*), presided over by the *mudīr*. The functions of the Council were to deal with purely local matters. The total number of the Provincial Councillors was 70.

Secondly, the Legislative Council, composed of 30 members. Of these, 14 (including the President) were appointed by the Government and 16 elected by the provincial councils from among their members. No law or decree relating to general administrative matters was to be issued without prior submission to the Council, but the Government was under no obligation to carry out the resolutions of the Council. However, if the Council's resolutions were not carried out, the reasons for rejection had to be communicated to the Council. The budget was to be submitted to the Council for discussion, but the Government was not obliged to adopt the views of the Council, nor could the Council discuss any financial matters touching on Egypt's obligations under an international agreement.

Thirdly, the Legislative Assembly, composed of 82 members, included the six Ministers, the 30 members of the Legislative Council, and 46 delegates elected by the people. Candidates eligible for election had to be not less than 30 years old, able to read and write, and paying direct taxes of not less than 30 Egyptian pounds a year. No new direct taxes could be imposed by the Government without the approval of the Assembly. Moreover, the Assembly was consulted on every public loan and on all public matters relating to canals, railways, lands and land taxes. It also expressed an opinion on other financial, economic and administrative matters. As in the case of the Legislative Council, the Government was under no obligation to adopt the Assembly's views on any question discussed, for the functions of the Legislative Assembly were purely consultative; but the reasons for not adopting them had to be stated. The Assembly met at least once in two years and its meetings were not open to the public. An electoral law was issued on 1 May 1883 and the first elections for the Legislative Assembly were held in November 1883. The Assembly continued to function until World War I.

In 1913, the Assembly's functions and powers were increased under a new law issued in 1913, revising the Organic Law of 1883. The new Legislative Assembly replaced both the Legislative Council and Assembly. This Assembly, composed of 17 nominated members and 66 elected by indirect suffrage, had the power to veto proposals for the increase of direct taxes, but in all other matters its functions remained consultative and deliberative. Its proceedings were open to the public, since criticism had been levelled at its predecessor for holding closed sessions. It could delay legislation, compel Ministers to justify their proposals, interrogate them and call for information. The Legislative Assembly was intended to represent more closely the mass of the Egyptian people, but it could hardly satisfy the political aspirations of the small educated class. It met for a short period during 1914 until its sessions were suspended in 1915, never to be resumed again.

After World War I, Egypt passed quickly from a dependent to an independent status, having achieved remarkable political and social progress. The British occupation was terminated and the country was declared independent on 28 February 1922, subject to four reserved points (relating to the defence of Egypt, security of British imperial communications, protection of foreigners, and the Sudan). The Sultan of Egypt assumed the title of King on 15 March 1922, and a constitutional committee, composed of 32 members, was appointed on 3 April 1922 to draw up a draft constitution. The constitution, though communicated by the Committee to the Government on 21 October 1922, was not promulgated until 19 April 1923. Based on Belgian and Ottoman models, it provided for a monarchy endowed with many powers, which reflected the traditional pattern of administration. The King not only enjoyed the right of selecting and appointing the Prime Minister (and upon the latter's recommendation, the ministers), but also the right to dismiss the Cabinet and dissolve Parliament. He also appointed the President of the Senate and half of the Senators, presumably upon the recommendation of the Cabinet. The Cabinet was fully responsible, for its members were derived from both houses of Parliament and were collectively responsible to the Lower House. Its life was formally dependent on a vote of confidence of the Lower House, but the King could dismiss it by a decree at any moment. Legislative power was vested in Parliament and the King. The Lower House was an elected body on the basis of universal manhood suffrage, but the Senate was half elected and half appointed. Legislation could be initiated in either House, but it had to be confirmed by the King. The latter had the power to return draft laws for reconsideration by Parliament.

From the establishment of the Sultanate (1914) to the Declaration of Independence (1922), Egypt had 8 cabinets; and from the Declaration of Independence to the end of the monarchy, Egypt had 32 cabinets. Thus the average life of a cabinet was less than one year. Parliament met on the whole regularly since the first general election of 1924, although in almost all cases the Lower House was dissolved before it completed its regular term of four years. There had been ten general elections held from 1924 to 1952. These were the elections of 1924, 1925, 1926, 1929, 1931, 1936, 1938, 1942, 1945 and 1950. Only the ninth Parliament completed its term of four years, while the second held only a single meeting.

The constitution of 1923 was partially suspended by a royal decree in 1928 and replaced by another on 22 October 1930. The new constitution made no important change in the structure of government, but restricted the powers of Parliament, especially its right to withdraw confidence in the cabinet, and increased the powers of the executive. It also provided for elections in two stages, regulated by a new Electoral Law issued in 1930. These restrictions prompted opposition parties to attack the new constitution and boycott elections. However, the Government firmly enforced the provisions of the new constitution until 1936.

In 1936 a national coalition government was formed and a treaty of alliance between Britain and Egypt was signed. The nationalists had already demanded the restoration of the constitution of 1923 as a condition for their participation in the treaty negotiation, and the King formally restored it on 22 December 1935. It remained in force until it was abolished by the Revolutionary Government on 10 December 1952. Before the intervention of the army in politics, the parliamentary system had deteriorated, because of the intense competition among political parties, the rise of rival ideological groups, and the failure of the ruling class to make concessions to the rapidly increasing oppressed masses. The inability of civil government to maintain public order invited the army to intervene and put an end to internal conflict and instability.

The Revolutionary Government appointed a constitutional committee, composed of fifty members of various shades of opinion, to draft a new constitution. The new draft constitution, reputed to have included a progressive and truly parliamentary system, was never officially promulgated. Instead a provisional constitutional charter was issued on 10 February 1953, entrusting virtually full power to a Revolutionary Council, to be exercised by its chief, who presided over the Council of Ministers. The monarchy was maintained, but owing to the minority of the deposed King Fārūḳ's successor, its powers were exercised by a Council of Regency. On 18 June 1953 the monarchy was abolished and a republic, headed by Muḥammad Nad̲j̲īb (Neguib), was proclaimed. It was not until 16 January 1956 that a new constitutional charter, which proved to be of short duration, was issued, entrusting full executive powers to the hands of President Djamāl ʿAbd al-Nāṣir. This constitution, embodying several innovations, declared Egypt to be an Arab nation, and introduced the presidential system, replacing the parliamentary form of government. The President was elected by a plebiscite. He possessed the power to appoint a Cabinet responsible to him and to nominate the members of Parliament, subject to the approval of the nation by a popular plebiscite. The constitution was confirmed by a plebiscite on 23 June 1956.

The union between Syria and Egypt in 1958 called for another change in the constitutional framework of the two countries. This union, regarded as the first step toward a more complete Arab unity, was called the United Arab Republic. A provisional constitution of 73 articles was issued on 5 March 1958, providing for a central executive and a central legislature; but all essential local affairs remained in the hands of local executive councils. Before agreement could be reached on its internal constitutional structure, the union was dissolved in October 1961, following Syria's secession.

The name of the United Arab Republic, though applied only to Egypt, was not changed; but Egypt's rulers began to concentrate on the internal social and economic reorganization of the country on a socialistic basis. A National Charter, embodying the principles of nationalism and socialism, became the subject of discussion in a National Convention held during the autumn of 1962; but no new constitutional instrument has yet been issued. After the dissolution of the Union with Syria President ʿAbd al-Nāṣir made several references to the constitution of 1956, which indicated that this constitution was still in force, pending the promulgation of a new constitution. Egypt's rulers are inclined to defer the formulation of a new constitution, pending the emergence of new patterns of government, hoping that the emerging constitutional structure will conform to Arab aspirations to unity. (For the United Arab States, see below, xviii).

Bibliography: A. Giannini, *La costituzione egiziana*, in *OM*, iii (1923), 1-22; G. Douin, *Histoire du règne du Khédive Ismaïl*, Rome 1933-41; ʿAbd al-Raḥmān al-Rāfiʿī, *ʿAṣr Ismāʿīl*², Cairo 1948, 2 vols; idem, *al-Thawra al-ʿUrābiyya*², Cairo 1949; idem, *Fī aʿḳāb al-thawra al-Miṣriyya*, Cairo 1947-51, 3 vols.; W. S. Blunt, *Secret history of the English occupation of Egypt*, London 1907; M. Rashīd Riḍā, *Taʾrīkh al-ustādh al-imām*, Cairo 1931, ii; M. Sadek, *La constitution de l'Égypte*, Paris 1908; White Ibrahim, *La constitution égyptienne du 19 Avril 1923*, Paris 1924; idem, *La nouvelle constitution de l'Égypte*, Paris 1925; Amin Osman, *Le mouvement constitutionnel en Égypte et la constitution de 1923*, Paris 1924; Sir William Hayter, *Recent constitutional development in Egypt*, Cambridge 1925; El-Sayed Sabry, *Le pouvoir législatif et le pouvoir exécutif en Égypte, étude critique de la constitution du 19 Avril 1923*, Paris 1930; Hilmy Makram, *Problèmes soulevés par la constitution égyptienne*, Dijon 1927; V. A. O'Rourke, *The juristic status of Egypt*, Baltimore 1935; Diaeddine Saleh, *Les pouvoirs du roi dans la constitution égyptienne, étude de droit comparé*, Paris 1939; J. M. Landau, *Parliaments and parties in Egypt*, Tel-Aviv 1953; M. Colombe, *L'évolution de l'Égypte, 1924-1950*, Paris 1951; C. F. Jones, *The new Egyptian constitution*, in *MEJ*, x (1956), 300-6; R. Monaco, *La nuova costituzione egiziana*, in *OM*, xxxvi (1956), 281-8.

(M. Khadduri)

iv. — Īrān

The Persian constitutional movement of the early 20th century was the result of a process which had been going on in Persia, largely silently, throughout the 19th century. Up to this time the basic theories of the state and of life generally were set in the frame of Islam. The intrusion of the West into Persia in the 19th century perhaps more than any other single event led Persian thinkers to question the old theories and bases of the state and to seek some new or additional base for it. The disastrous wars with Russia in the early part of the century concluded by the Treaty of Turkomānčay in 1828 convinced Persians of the need for reform, military and otherwise. Further it was through the various military missions which came to Persia from 1807 onwards that Persians had first become acquainted with modern military and scientific techniques and with the political changes which were taking place in Europe. Mīrzā Ṣāliḥ, the first Persian known to have written an account of British parliamentary institutions, was sent to England in 1815 in pursuance of plans for military reform. He also visited Turkey and Russia. Writing in his diary of the *tanẓīmāt* he castigates obscurantist mullas who opposed them. He gives in his diary what is probably the first account by a Persian of the French revolution. Diplomatic travel also played an important rôle in the dissemination of knowledge of western institutions. Abu 'l-Ḥasan Shīrāzī, who was sent on a mission to England by Fatḥ ʿAlī Shāh, wrote in his *Ḥayrat-nāma* an account of the justice and security which he found in England, comparing it with the tyranny which prevailed in his own country. Nāṣir al-Dīn himself made three journeys to Europe, the first in 1873. The Persian merchant communities, both inside and outside Persia, were another important channel through which modern ideas spread. The Persian press published by members of the Persian communities in Istanbul, Calcutta and elsewhere also did much in the latter part of the 19th century to encourage reform.

The first attempts at administrative, as distinct from military, reform were made by Mīrzā Taḳī Khān Amīr Niẓām, the first prime minister of Nāṣir al-Dīn, but proved largely abortive. He, too, had visited Russia and Turkey and seen the *tanẓīmāt* in operation. The next minister to attempt fundamental reforms was Mīrzā Ḥusayn Khān Sipahsālār Mushīr al-Dawla, who had studied in France, and served in Tiflis, Bombay, and Turkey, where he was Persian minister from 1859 to 1871. He subsequently held various offices in Persia, including that of prime minister. While in Turkey he wrote numerous letters, official and otherwise, in which he discussed, *inter alia*, European politics, civilization, education, the need for reform in Persia, the desirability of a popular assembly, freedom, the rights of the people, and equality before the law. He maintained that foreign intervention in a country was brought about by the backwardness of that country. The main object of both Amīr Niẓām and Mushīr al-Dawla in their advocacy of reform and modernization was to prevent foreign intervention; and in this they were the precursors of the constitutional movement, which, though it was provoked in the first instance by the tyranny and injustice of the régime, was directed also against the encroachment of foreign powers and the disposal of Persian assets to foreigners.

Pleas for reform were put forward by various writers in the latter half of the 19th century. The most important figure among them in the intellectual awakening of Persia was, perhaps, Malkam K͟hān Nāẓim al-Dawla, a Persian Armenian of D̲julfā (Iṣfahān), educated in Paris, who became minister to the Court of St. James in 1872. He profoundly believed in the need for Persia to westernize and repeatedly emphasised the need for the supremacy of the law. In an essay entitled *Daftar-i tanẓīmāt*, apparently written between 1858 and 1860, he drew attention to the internal woes of Persia, the threat of encroachments upon Persia from St. Petersburg and Calcutta, and the technical advances being made in Europe. He pointed out that the progress which had been made in Europe and the orderly regulation of affairs which prevailed there were not contrary to the *s͟harīʿa*. After discussing various types of government and stating (perhaps in order not to frighten Nāṣir al-Dīn S͟hāh) that constitutional government was in no way suitable to Persia, he examines how an orderly regulation of affairs could be established under an absolute monarchy, advocates the separation of the "executive" and the "legislature", and lays down a series of *tanẓīmāt* for the administration of the kingdom. In later essays written after 1882, and especially in the Persian paper *Ḳānūn*, which he founded in London in 1890, Malkam K͟hān advocates constitutional monarchy for Persia and a national consultative assembly.

Towards the end of the reign of Nāṣir al-Dīn, and under his successor, Muẓaffar al-Dīn, internal conditions in Persia and her position vis-à-vis foreign powers, rapidly deteriorated. The financial state of the government became ever more acute. The abortive Reuter concession was granted in 1872 and subsequently cancelled under pressure from Russia. A secret railway agreement was made in 1887 and followed by the Russo-Persian agreement of 1890, which placed a prohibition on railway construction in Persia for ten years. Popular discontent at misgovernment, the growth of foreign influence, and the squandering of Persia's assets grew; it received open expression in 1890. The occasion was the grant of a monopoly for the sale and export of Persian tobacco and control over its production by a British subject, Major Gerald Talbot. Russian opposition to the Tobacco Régie was immediate, and was soon followed by a movement of popular protest. This was a dual movement, directed on the one hand against internal corruption and misgovernment and on the other against foreign influence; it rapidly became nationalist and Islamic. It owed a good deal to the support of Mīrzā Malkam K͟hān, who at that time was in London, and D̲jamāl al-Dīn Afg͟hānī [*q.v.*] and was led by the religious classes. Although it was merely a movement of protest and had no positive programme of reform, nevertheless, it was important in that it showed the religious classes and the people their power once they united; and was, in some measure, a forerunner of the constitutional movement. It was successful in its object; and in January 1892 the tobacco monopoly was rescinded. This victory against the government was not, however, followed by any material lessening of the pressure to which the people were subjected or limitation on the arbitrary rule of the Shah. Those who advocated modernization had still to work cautiously.

The next phase in the struggle against the despotism was marked by the spread of secret or semi-secret societies, which began to be formed by those who were dissatisfied with the existing state of affairs (see D̲JAMʿIYYA. Persia). Their purpose was to spread the new learning and awaken the people to the evils of the despotism and the benefits of freedom. After the assassination of Nāṣir al-Dīn in 1896 they became more active. Discontent continued to be rife and was heightened by the growing intervention of Russia and the contraction of foreign loans, including one from the Imperial Bank of Persia in 1892 to pay the Tobacco Corporation compensation for the cancellation of their monopoly, and Russian loans in 1900 and 1902. In January 1904 ʿAyn al-Dawla became prime minister. By the end of 1905 conditions were felt to be intolerable. The Shah was in the hands of a corrupt ring of courtiers. He had had recourse to foreign loans, the proceeds of which he had spent on foreign travel and his court. The annual deficit grew. Oppression of every sort was carried out and countenanced by the Prime Minister. Finally discontent came to a head on 19 Ṣafar 1323/26 April 1905 when a group of merchants took *bast* in S͟hāh ʿAbd al-ʿAẓīm, the immediate cause being dissatisfaction with the Belgian Director of Customs Administration, M. Naus. Muḥammad ʿAlī, who was acting as regent during the absence of his father, Muẓaffar al-Dīn, in Europe, promised that Naus would be dismissed on the Shah's return; and the *bastī*s dispersed. Shortly afterwards, on 3 Rabīʿ I 1323/8 May 1905, an open address to the prime minister, ʿAyn al-Dawla, who was extremely unpopular, was published by one of the leading secret societies. The address, after calling his attention to the decay and disorder of the country's affairs and protesting at the lack of security and the corruption of officials, demanded (i) a code of justice and the creation of a ministry of justice, (ii) a land survey, the delimitation and registration of estates, (iii) a fair adjustment of taxation, (iv) a reform of the army, (v) the laying down of principles for the choice of governors and their rights and the rights of those they governed, (vi) the reform and encouragement of internal trade, (vii) a cleaning up of the customs administration, (viii) an improvement in the supply of foodstuffs and goods, (ix) the adoption of general principles for the foundation of technical schools and the setting up of factories and concerns for the exploitation of minerals, (x) a clarification of the duty of the Ministry of Foreign Affairs, (xi) a reform in the payment of salaries and pensions by the government, and (xii) a limitation of the powers of ministers, ministries, and *mullā*s according to the *s͟harīʿa*. Various events meanwhile fanned the growing discontent. Eventually a large number of *mullā*s, merchants, and members of the craft guilds took *bast* in S͟hāh ʿAbd al-ʿAẓīm; and finally Muẓaffar al-Dīn acceded to their demands, which included the dismissal of the governor of Tehrān and M. Naus from the Customs, and the setting up of a Ministry of Justice. In D̲hu 'l-Ḳaʿda, 1323/January, 1906, he issued an autograph letter (*dast k͟haṭṭ*), to ʿAyn al-Dawla, giving orders for the setting up of an *ʿadālat k͟hāna-i dawlatī* for the execution of the decrees of the *s͟harīʿa* throughout Persia in such a way that all the subjects of the country should be regarded as equal before the law. With this in mind a code (*kitābča*) in accordance with the *s͟harīʿa* was to be drawn up and put into operation throughout the country. This temporarily satisfied the *bastī*s in

Shāh ʿAbd al-ʿAẓīm; and they returned to the city. No steps, however, were taken to implement the promises given; these had in effect amounted to a promise of equality before the law for the different classes but had in no way limited the absolute power of the Shah. Towards the end of April a petition was presented to the Shah praying him to give effect to his promises. This proved fruitless as also did remonstrances to ʿAyn al-Dawla. Public opinion, stirred up by denunciations of the despotism and tyranny from the *minbar*s of the mosques by Āḳā Sayyid Djamāl and others, and the efforts of secret and semi-secret societies, which attacked the despotism and endeavoured to spread modernist ideas, became increasingly roused. ʿAyn al-Dawla expelled Āḳā Sayyid Djamāl and another preacher, Shaykh Muḥammad, from the city. In the riots which attended the attempted removal of the latter on 28 Rabīʿ II 1324/21 June 1906 a *sayyid* was killed. Further riots ensued and after some days a large number of the religious classes, merchants, artisans and others took refuge in Ḳumm, this exodus being known as the *hidjrat-i kubrā*, 'the great exodus'. Meanwhile the *bāzār*s were closed and about 19 July a number of merchants, members of the guilds, and others took refuge in the British Legation. Their numbers rapidly increased and by the beginning of August had reached 12,000 or 14,000. They demanded the dismissal of ʿAyn al-Dawla, the promulgation of a code of laws, and the recall of the religious leaders from Ḳumm. The Shah did not yield to their demands until the end of the month, when he dismissed ʿAyn al-Dawla.

On 14 Djumādā II/5 August, an imperial rescript was issued to the new *ṣadr-i aʿẓam* ordering the setting up of a national consultative assembly (*madjlis-i shawrā-yi millī*), composed of representatives of the princes, *ʿulamāʾ*, members of the Ḳādjār family, notables, landowners, merchants, and members of the guilds, to consult on matters of state, to give help to the council of ministers in the reforms "which would be made for the happiness of Persia", and, "in complete security and confidence, to submit through the *ṣadr-i aʿẓam* to the Shah their views on the wellbeing of the state and nation, the public welfare, and the needs of all the people of the country, so that these might be embellished by the royal signature and duly put into operation". Regulations for the assembly were to be prepared and signed by the elected representatives and ratified by the Shah, and "by the help of God Most High, the aforesaid consultative assembly, which is the guardian of our justice, will be opened and begin the necessary reforms in the affairs of the kingdom and the execution of the laws of the holy *sharīʿa*". By this time, however, the popular party had been further provoked by the intransigence of the Shah and the court party. Profoundly mistrustful, they demanded a guarantee of the Shah's good faith. Accordingly a second rescript addressed to the *ṣadr-i aʿẓam*, supplementing the rescript of 14 Djumādā II, was issued. This stated: "In completion of our earlier autograph, dated 14 Djumādā II 1324, in which we explicitly ordered and commanded the founding of an assembly of elected representatives of the peoples, in order that the generality of people and [all] the individuals of the nation shall be aware of our full royal care, we again command and lay down that you should set up the aforesaid assembly in accordance with the description explicitly laid down in the former autograph, and, after the election of the members of the assembly, you should draw up the sections and provisions of the regulations of the Islamic consultative assembly in accordance with the approval and signature of the elected representatives, as is worthy of the nation and country and the laws of the holy *sharīʿa*, so that having been submitted to us and adorned by our auspicious signature and in accordance with the aforementioned regulations, this holy intention may take shape and be put into operation". On the issue of this rescript the *bastī*s returned from Ḳumm and the British Legation respectively.

After the official opening of "the House of Parliament" on 28 Djumādā II 1324/19 August 1906 disputes arose between the popular party and the *ṣadr-i aʿẓam* over the ordinances for the assembly which the latter had drawn up. The *bāzār*s were again closed and the people once more prepared to take *bast*. The Shah gave way and on 17 September accepted the proposed ordinance as to the constitution of the assembly, which was to consist of 156 members, 60 from Tehrān and 96 from the provinces, elections to take place every two years and the deputies to be inviolable. The immunity of the deputies was subsequently affirmed in article 12 of the Fundamental Law. The voting in Tehrān was to be direct, in the provinces by colleges of electors. Elections began and on 18 Shaʿbān 1324/7 October 1906 the assembly was opened by Muẓaffar al-Dīn without waiting for the arrival of the provincial deputies. The assembly proceeded to elect the president of the assembly and other officers, and passed on 18 October rules of procedure. On 23 November a proposal for an Anglo-Russian loan was submitted to it by the Minister of Finance; this was rejected and an alternative plan for an internal loan approved a week later. A committee was meanwhile set up to draft the Fundamental Law of the constitution (*ḳānūn-i asāsī*). This was ready by the end of October; but the Shah procrastinated and did not sign it until 14 Dhu 'l-Ḳaʿda 1324/30 December 1906. Subsequently a supplementary Fundamental Law (*Mutammim-i Ḳānūn-i Asāsī*) was passed by the Assembly and ratified on 29 Shaʿbān 1325/7 October 1907 by Muḥammad ʿAlī Shāh, who had meanwhile succeeded Muẓaffar al-Dīn. The Fundamental Law consists of fifty-one articles relating to the constitution and duties of the National Consultative Assembly and the Senate. The Supplementary Fundamental Law contains 107 articles concerning the rights of the Persian people, the powers of the realm, the rights of members of the assembly, the rights of the Persian throne, the powers of ministers, tribunals of justice, public finance, and the army.

Muẓaffar al-Dīn died in January 1907, and with his death the first phase of the constitutional revolution came to an end. The movement, which had begun as a popular demonstration against the deplorable state of the administration and country, foreign loans and concessions which were thought to be leading or contributing to national bankruptcy and foreign control, had thus ended in the grant of a constitution and the setting up of a National Consultative Assembly, a result which had been achieved virtually without bloodshed. It had been a sense of intolerable injustice or tyranny (*ẓulm*) which had eventually provoked the nationalists to action and the aims of the movement had never been clearly formulated. The general aim was simply the establishment of the rule of justice (*ʿadālat*), which, in the tradition of mediaeval Islam, they saw to be the basis of good government, rather than the establishment of constitutional government and representative institutions. The second phase of the constitutional revolution began with the accession on 8 January 1907 of Muḥammad ʿAlī, who, with his ministers, was from the first bitterly opposed to the constitution. Neither the Assembly nor the ministers had had any experience of constitutional government; they were, moreover, hampered in their conduct of affairs by lack of money and military forces and by the Shah's intrigues against the constitution. The Assembly was determined to prevent fresh foreign loans, and to get rid of the Belgians from the Customs. In these aims it was successful. It also passed various measures of financial reform; and a law for the resumption by the state of all land held as *tiyūl* [*q.v.*]. Numerous political societies or *andjumans* had meanwhile been formed in Tehrān and the provinces to defend the constitution. On 2 May 1907 Mīrzā ʿAlī Aṣg̲h̲ar K̲h̲ān Amīn al-Sulṭān was appointed Prime Minister and with his appointment the struggle between the Shah and the nationalists was intensified. Disorders, in many cases instigated and fomented by the Shah and the court party, broke out in the provinces. Turkey invaded north-west Persia in August. Russia was suspected, not without reason, of aiding and abetting the Shah against the National Assembly. The belief grew that there was secret collusion between the Shah, Amīn al-Sulṭān, and the Russians to sell the country to Russia. This second phase of the constitutional revolution was to a greater extent than the first phase anti-foreign in the sense that it was primarily concerned to check the growth of foreign control in Persia, especially Russian. On 31 August Amīn al-Sulṭān was murdered by a member of one of the popular *andjumans*. On the same day the Anglo-Russian Convention was signed, which, when it was communicated to the Assembly a month later, aroused profound misgiving. Meanwhile the authority of the central government in the provinces had been reduced to almost nothing. Provincial councils (*andjumanhā-yi ayālatī wa wilāyatī*) had sprung up in many parts of the country; these had destroyed the moral authority of the old régime, and the framework of such elementary administration as had once existed had virtually disappeared. On 7 October 1907 the Shah promulgated the Supplementary Fundamental Law (see below); and on 12 November he visited the Assembly and swore loyalty to the constitution for the fourth time. Nevertheless on 15 December he attempted a *coup d'état*, arresting the prime minister Nāṣir al-Mulk and other ministers. The popular *andjumans* both in the capital and in the provinces rallied to the defence of the Assembly. The Shah was momentarily worsted, but the truce was temporary and hope of reconciliation between the Shah and the nationalists was finally dashed by an attempt made on the Shah's life in February 1908. In the following months tension increased and eventually on 23 June fighting broke out between the royalist forces and the nationalists. The assembly and the neighbourhood were cleared by the Shah's forces. Thirty of the most prominent nationalist leaders were arrested and two of them strangled without trial the following day, 24 June 1908; on 27 June the Shah declared the Assembly dissolved and the constitution abolished as being contrary to Islamic law. Thus ended the second phase of the constitutional revolution, with the temporary closure of the Assembly.

Fighting broke out simultaneously in Tabrīz which, after Tehrān, had been the main centre of the nationalist movement, and the Shah's forces were expelled. Resistance lasted until April 1909 when the siege was raised by the entry of Russian troops to protect foreign life and property. The action of Tabrīz gave the nationalists time to reorganize their forces; and eventually in 1909 a Bak̲h̲tiyārī force under Sardār Asʿad and another force from Ras̲h̲t under the Sipahdār-i Aʿẓam, Muḥammad Wālī K̲h̲ān, advanced on Tehrān which they entered in July. The Shah fled and took refuge in the Russian Legation. A council was then held which voted his deposition and the succession of his son, Sulṭān Aḥmad, a minor, with a regency. On 9 September the ex-Shah left for Kiev. Elections were subsequently held and on 2 D̲h̲u 'l-Ḳaʿda 1327/5 December 1909 the second legislative session of the National Assembly was opened. The tasks facing the new assembly were such as might have daunted a more experienced body than they. The treasury was empty; the provincial administration was in a state of chaos; and Russian intervention threatened. Cabinet crises were frequent and the Assembly, divided into numerous small groups, was split by dissension. Russian troops, which had been introduced into Northern Persia ostensibly for a temporary occupation to defend foreign life and property, were not withdrawn. The anti-Russian feeling engendered among the nationalists by this and other actions produced a state of friction with Russia which culminated in 1911. In 1910 a proposal for a joint Russo-British loan to Persia was rejected on the grounds that its terms were incompatible with Persian independence. The possibility of the engagement of foreign advisers to reorganize the administration was meanwhile under consideration by Persia; and in 1911 Americans were engaged for the finances and Swedes for the police and gendarmerie. Russia was from the outset displeased at the invitation to the Americans. In May 1911 Mr. Morgan Shuster, an American citizen, engaged on a private contract with Persia as Treasurer-General, reached Tehrān, with a small staff. On 13 June the Assembly passed a law giving him very wide powers. On 17 June the ex-Shah suddenly landed on Persian soil in an abortive attempt to regain the throne. Simultaneously his brother, Sālār al-Dawla, raised the standard of revolt in Kurdistān. Friction meanwhile increased with Russia over the Treasurer-General's independent attitude in working for Persian financial reform and refusal to consult Russian wishes. Finally Russia seized on an incident arising from the confiscation of the estates of S̲h̲uʿāʿ al-Salṭana, a younger brother of the ex-Shah, as a punishment for the part he had taken in the latter's rebellion, to demand an apology from the Persian Government; this was followed by a 48 hours' ultimatum on 25 November to dismiss Shuster and Lecoffre, an Englishman of French extraction serving in the Ministry of Finance, from Persian government service, to engage no foreigners without the consent of Russia and Great Britain, and to defray the cost of the military expedition which Russia had sent to Enzelī to enforce this ultimatum. In the event of non-compliance Persia was threatened with an advance of Russian troops from Ras̲h̲t and an increase in the indemnity. British diplomatic protests at St. Petersburg were overridden and Russia persisted in her demands. The Assembly refused to comply. Russian troops advanced to Ḳazwīn. Skirmishes took place between Persians and Russian troops in Ras̲h̲t, Enzelī and Tabrīz. Anti-Russian feeling ran high in Tehrān; and finally to avoid disasters by impotent resistance to Russia, the regent, Nāṣir al-

Mulk, and the cabinet forcibly dissolved the obdurate assembly on 3 Muḥarram 1330/24 December 1911. On the following day Shuster was dismissed. The third and final phase of the constitutional revolution thus ended leaving Persia once more in a state of virtual chaos. The constitution remained suspended until 7 July 1914, when the third legislative session was opened.

The later history of the National Consultative Assembly was not dominated, as it had been during the period of the revolution, by the struggle between the despotism and the nationalists. It became accepted as part of the institutions of the country, even if in the Pahlawī period its power was restricted. During the Great War of 1914-8 Persia was a cockpit for the intrigues and operations of the belligerent powers. The resentment entertained by the Persians against Russia and Great Britain as her ally was fanned by German intrigue and the majority of the deputies of the assembly were either neutral or pro-Central Powers. On 15 November 1915 when Russian troops advanced from Ḳazwīn the Assembly broke up, and most of the members evacuated Tehrān with the Turks and Germans and left for Ḳumm. The constitution was, thus, again suspended; the fourth legislative assembly was not convened until 1921; since when, apart from a brief period in 1953 when Dr. Muṣaddiḳ dissolved the assembly, successive assemblies have sat until 1961, when the reigning Shah, Muḥammad Riḍā Pahlawī, dissolved the Assembly and Senate by decree.

The nationalist movement had been supported by many of the leading members of the religious classes; and in the writing of many of those who had advocated reform, and 'the rule of law', the 'law' had been equated with Islam. Deference to this point of view is found in the preamble to the Fundamental Law, which states that the purpose of the National Council to be set up under the *farmān* of 14 Djumādā II 1324/5 August 1906 was "to promote the progress and happiness of our kingdom and people, strengthen the foundations of our government, and give effect to the enactments of the sacred law of His Holiness the Prophet". Article 1 of the Supplementary Fundamental Law further lays down that the official religion of Persia is Islam of the Ithnā ʿasharī sect, which faith the Shah must profess. Article 2 states that "At no time must any legal enactment of the sacred National Consultative Assembly, established by the favour and assistance of His Holiness the Imām of the Age (may God hasten His glad advent), the favour of His Majesty the Shahinshah of Islam (may God immortalize his reign), the care of the Proofs of Islam (may God multiply the likes of them), and the whole people of the Persian nation, be at variance with the sacred principles of Islam, or the laws established by His Holiness the Best of Mankind (on Whom and on Whose household be the blessings of God and His peace)". The same article lays down that a committee of not less than five *mudjtahids* shall be set up "so that they may carefully discuss and consider all matters proposed in the Assembly, and reject and repudiate, wholly or in part, any such proposal which is at variance with the sacred laws of Islam, so that it shall not obtain the title of legality. In such matters the decision of this committee of *ʿulamāʾ* shall be followed and obeyed, and this article shall continue unchanged until the appearance of His Holiness the Proof of the Age (may God hasten His glad advent)". This article became inoperative during the reign of Riḍā Shāh, and up to the time of writing has not been revived. Article 27 of the Supplementary Fundamental Laws states that the judicial power "belongs to the *sharʿī* courts in matters pertaining to the *sharīʿa* (*sharʿiyyāt*) and to civil courts (*maḥākim-i ʿadliyya*) in matters pertaining to customary law (*ʿurfiyyāt*)". This, while contrary to the conception of Islam, was a recognition of existing practice.

The drafters of the constitution, although they made concessions to Islam, were also considerably influenced by the example of Belgian Constitutional Law and French law; and the conceptions underlying the constitution were in many respects fundamentally new to Persia. Thus, Article 26 of the Supplementary Fundamental Law states "that the powers of the realm are all derived from the people"; and the Fundamental Law regulates the employment of those powers. Similarly Article 35 states "sovereignty is a trust, as a divine gift, confided by the people to the Shah" which implies a radical change in the conception of the ruler. The main concern of the drafters was probably to limit the arbitrary nature of the Shah's rule and to give the people some defence against the arbitrary actions of government officials. A number of the articles of the Fundamental Law clearly derive from the unhappy experiences of Persia in the late 19th and early 20th centuries, when the reigning Shah recklessly contracted foreign loans and gave concessions to foreign concerns. Article 24 states "the conclusion of treaties and covenants, the granting of commercial, industrial, agricultural and other concessions, irrespective of whether they be to Persian or foreign subjects, shall be subject to the approval of the National Consultative Assembly, with the exception of treaties, which for reasons of state and the public advantage, must be kept secret". Similarly Article 22 lays down that "any proposal to transfer or sell any portion of the [national] resources, or of the control exercised by the Government or the Throne, or to effect any change in the boundaries and frontiers of the kingdom, shall be subject to the approval of the National Consultative Assembly". Further Article 23 states that "without the approval of the National Consultative Assembly, no concession for the formation of any public company of any sort shall, under any plea soever, be granted by the state". The Assembly has shown itself jealous of the rights accorded to it under these articles, as is shown by its refusal to ratify the oil agreement concluded by Prime Minister Ḳawām and the Russian government in 1949. Articles 25 and 26 respectively lay down that state loans under whatever title, internal or external, and the construction of railroads and roads depend upon the approval of the Assembly. The latter of these two articles was included, presumably because of the experience of the Russo-Persian railway agreement of 12 November 1890, by which the Persian Government engaged for the space of ten years "neither itself to construct a railway in Persian territory, nor to permit nor grant a concession for the construction of railways to a company or other persons". Article 27 of the Supplementary Fundamental Law states that the legislative power is derived from the Shah, the National Consultative Assembly and the Senate, each of which has the right to introduce laws "provided that the continuance thereof be dependent on their not being at variance with the standards of the *sharīʿa*, and on their approval by the two Assemblies (*i.e.*, the National Consultative Assembly and the Senate), and the royal ratification; but the enactment and approval of laws concerning the revenue and expenditure of the kingdom are among the special functions of the National Consultative Assembly". The executive power, which belongs to the Shah, "is carried out by the ministers and officials of the state in the name of His Imperial Majesty in such manner as the law defines". Article 28, reflecting the influence of Montesquieu, lays down that these three powers shall always be separate from one another, a principle which has been much cherished by Persian constitutionalists. Article 39 states that no Shah can ascend the throne unless, before his coronation, he appeared before the Assembly in the presence of its members and those of the Senate and the Council of Ministers and undertook by oath to defend the independence of Persia, the frontiers of the kingdom, and the rights of the people, to observe the Fundamental Law and promote S͟hīʿism of the D͟jaʿfarī rite. Similarly, by Article 40, a regent cannot enter upon his functions unless he repeats the above oath. Article 44 lays down that "the person of the Shah is exempted from responsibility and in all matters the ministers are responsible to the National Consultative Assembly and the Senate". The appointment and dismissal of ministers, however, lies with the Shah (Art. 46); but not of other officials save where this is explicitly provided by the law (Art. 48). Article 49 states that the issue of decrees and orders for giving effect to the laws is the Shah's right, provided that he shall under no circumstances postpone or suspend the carrying out of such laws. The supreme command of all military forces is vested in the Shah (Art. 50); as also is the declaration of war and conclusion of peace (Art. 51). Article 27 of the Supplementary Fundamental Law and Articles 15, 17 and 47 of the Fundamental Law mention the ratification of laws by the Shah, but he is not explicitly given the right of veto by the constitution. At a joint meeting of the National Consultative Assembly and Senate convened under the additional Article of 1949 (see below) to emend the constitution, Article 49 of the Supplementary Fundamental Law was supplemented to the effect that the Shah, should he consider it necessary that any financial bill having been passed by the National Consultative Assembly should be revised, can refer it back to that body for revision; but if it confirms its former decision by a majority of at least three-quarters of those present in the capital, he must grant his assent. Judges and the public prosecutor are appointed by royal decree (Arts. 80 and 83 of the Supplementary Fundamental Law); but by Article 81 judges are declared irremovable save with their own consent. The Shah was also given certain rights with regard to the Senate, which was to consist of sixty members, to "be chosen from amongst well-informed, discerning, pious, and respected persons of the realm". Thirty were to be nominated by the Shah, fifteen from Tehrān and fifteen from the provinces; and fifteen were to be elected from Tehrān and fifteen from the provinces (Art. 45). Its sessions were to be "complementary to the sessions of the National Consultative Assembly" (Art. 43 of the Fundamental Law). Partly, perhaps, because it was felt that the principle of nomination was undemocratic the Senate was, in fact, never convened until 1950.

In 1921 Riḍā K͟hān (later Riḍā S͟hāh Pahlawī) became Minister of War and shortly afterwards the *de facto* ruler of the country. In 1925 a constituent assembly (*mad͟jlis-i muʾassisān*) was convened. On 31 October it declared the rule of the Ḳād͟jār dynasty terminated and that another Constituent Assembly was to be convened, to make the necessary changes in the laws; and on December 12 a single act suppressed Articles 36 (which had vested the monarchy in Muḥammad ʿAlī S͟hāh and his heirs), 37, and 38 of the Supplementary Fundamental Law, substituting for these three others. The new Article 36 entrusted the sovereignty of Persia to Riḍā S͟hāh Pahlawī and his male descendants. Article 37 states "the heir apparent shall be the eldest son of the Shah whose mother shall be of Persian origin. If the Shah has no male issue the heir apparent shall be proposed by him and approved by the National Consultative Assembly provided the said heir shall not belong to the Ḳād͟jār family. But whenever a son is born to the Shah he will become heir apparent by right". Meanwhile a marriage was about to be arranged between the heir apparent and Princess Fawziyya of Egypt. Presumably with a view to the possibility of issue by this marriage the law of 14 Ābān 1317 defined the expression "of Persian origin" to include a child born of a mother who before the marriage contract with the Shah or the heir apparent should, in accordance with the high interests of the country, on the proposal of the government and the approval by the National Consultative Assembly, have been given, by a *farmān* of the reigning Shah, the quality (*ṣifat*) of a Persian". Princess Fawziyya was in due course declared an honorary Persian. The new Article 38 provided for a regency but excluded members of the Ḳād͟jār family from holding this office.

No further changes were made in the Constitution by Riḍā S͟hāh, who kept the National Consultative Assembly in being but reduced it to a mere cypher. In the early years after the Second World War Muḥammad Riḍā S͟hāh, who had succeeded to the throne in 1941, and his advisers apparently believed that the National Consultative Assembly had become too powerful *vis-à-vis* the executive. In any case, it was decided to convene, for the first time, the Senate and to make certain changes in the Constitution. A Constituent Assembly was duly convened on 21 April 1949. An additional article (*aṣl-i ilḥāḳī*) made provision in certain cases for revision of the Fundamental Law. The drafters of the Fundamental Law and Supplementary Fundamental Law had presumably included no provision of this sort in the Law (except Article 21 of the Fundamental Law, which permits the modification or abrogation of any article regulating the functions of the ministries with the approval of the Assembly), not because they were unaware of the fact that most western constitutions contained such provisions, but because they did not wish to give any opportunity to the court party to alter the constitution. Article 48 of the Fundamental Law, which gave the Senate the right in certain circumstances to dissolve the National Consultative Assembly, as emended by the Constituent Assembly of April 1949 enables the Shah to dissolve the two chambers separately or together, subject to his stating the reason and simultaneously ordering new elections so that the new chamber or chambers may convene within a period of three months; dissolution may not be ordered twice for the same reason. On 9 May 1961 the Shah used the powers thus granted to him and dissolved the National Consultative Assembly.

On 8 May 1957 a joint meeting of the National Assembly and Senate was convened under the additional Article of 1949 to emend the constitution, and in due course Article 4 of the Fundamental Law was revised, raising the number of deputies to the maximum figure of 200; Article 5 was emended, *inter alia*, to extend the legislative term of the National Consultative Assembly from two years to four. Article 7 concerning the quorum for debates and voting was also emended. Lastly Article 49 of the Supplementary Fundamental Law was supplemented as stated above.

Article 46 of the Fundamental Law lays down that after the constitution of the Senate all proposals must be approved by both Assemblies. Article 34 of the Supplementary Fundamental Law, however, states that "the deliberations of the Senate are ineffective when the National Consultative Assembly is not in session". Proposals may originate in either assembly, except that financial matters "belonged exclusively to the National Consultative Assembly. The decision of the Assembly in respect to the aforesaid proposals, shall be made known to the Senate, so that it in turn may communicate its observations to the National Consultative Assembly, but the latter, after due discussion, is free to accept or reject these observations of the Senate". The responsibility of the National Consultative Assembly for financial matters is reaffirmed by Article 27 of the Supplementary Fundamental Law, which, as stated above, lays down that the enactment and approval of laws concerning the revenue and expenditure of the kingdom are among the special functions of the National Consultative Assembly. Article 27 also lays down that "the explanation and interpretation of the laws is among the special duties of the National Consultative Assembly". The debates of the Assembly are normally public (Art. 13 of the Fundamental Law); though Article 34 makes provision for secret sessions. Bills other than those on financial matters, which originate with the government, must first be laid before the Senate by the responsible ministers or the Prime Minister, and after acceptance there by a majority of votes must then be approved by the National Consultative Assembly; when any measure is proposed by a member of the Assembly it can only be discussed when at least fifteen members shall approve the discussion (Art. 39 of the Fundamental Law); Article 13 of the Rules of Procedure of the National Consultative Assembly and Article 82 of the Rules of Procedure of the Senate lay down that Bills which originate in the Senate or the National Consultative Assembly must be signed by at least fifteen members, except that in certain cases a bill signed by less than fifteen Senators may be voted on after reference to a committee. By Articles 1, 2 and 3 of the Civil Code bills passed by the two houses are published within three days of receiving the royal assent in the Official Gazette and become law ten days thereafter in Tehrān and ten days plus one day for every six *farsakh*s in the provinces, unless special arrangements are laid down in the law itself.

One of the most important functions of the National Consultative Assembly is the fixing and approving of the budget, which power it is accorded by Articles 18 of the Fundamental Law and 96 of the Supplementary Fundamental Law. The Minister of Finance according to Articles 12-17 of the Law for the General Finances (*Ḳānūn-i muḥāsabāt-i ʿumūmī*) of 10 Isfand 1312/1 March 1934 must submit this to the Assembly annually by 1 Day (23-4 December) and they must pass the budget by 15 Isfand (6-7 March). During and after the Second World War this provision was often contravened in that the Assembly refused to pass the budget as a whole and merely authorized the payment of a proportion of the budget at intervals throughout the financial year. Under Articles 101 and 102 of the Supplementary Fundamental Law the National Consultative Assembly is given power to appoint a Financial Commission which shall be "appointed to inspect and analyse the accounts of the Department of Finance and to liquidate the accounts of all debtors and creditors of the Treasury. It is especially deputed to see that no item of expenditure fixed in the Budget exceeds the amount specified, or is changed or altered, and that each item is expended in the proper manner. It shall likewise inspect and analyse the different accounts of all the departments of state, collect the documentary proofs of the expenditure indicated in such accounts, and submit to the National Consultative Assembly a complete statement of the accounts of the kingdom, accompanied by its own observations". Article 94 further states that "no tax shall be established save in accordance with the law;" and Article 99 that "Save in such cases as are explicitly excepted by the law, nothing can on any pretext be demanded from the people save under the categories of state, provincial and municipal taxes". These provisions reflect the anxiety of the drafters of the Constitution to bring order into the financial affairs of the country and to relieve the population of the burden of extraordinary and irregular levies to which they had formerly been subject.

Article 33 of the Supplementary Fundamental Law gives both Assemblies the right to investigate and examine every affair of state. Ministers may be questioned by members of both houses, provided that the speaker gives the responsible minister prior information of the question; an answer must be given within one week. The government and individual ministers may be interpellated by members of both houses, provided a written request is made to the speaker. Article 67 of the Supplementary Fundamental Law states "If the National Consultative Assembly or the Senate shall, by an absolute majority, declare itself dissatisfied with the cabinet, or with one particular minister, that cabinet or minister shall resign their or his ministerial functions".

Ministers may not accept a salaried office other than their own (Art. 68 of the Supplementary Fundamental Law). Their number is to be laid down by law according to the requirement of the time (Art. 62). No one may become a minister unless he is a Muslim by religion, a Persian by birth, and a Persian subject (Art. 58). Sons, brothers, and uncles of the Shah may not become ministers (Art. 59). Ministers are responsible, individually and collectively, to the National Consultative Assembly and the Senate (Article 61) and may be called to account or brought to trial by them (Art. 29 of the Fundamental Law and Arts. 65 and 69 of the Supplementary Fundamental Law). Article 64 states that Ministers cannot divest themselves of their responsibility by pleading verbal or written orders from the Shah. A tendency to do so nevertheless emerged during the reign of Riḍā Shāh and has again appeared in recent years. The internal organization of the Assembly is not based on political parties; the deputies are divided into groups or "fractions". Moreover, since the government is not composed of members of the Assembly there is no clear-cut division into a pro-government party and an opposition. In the second and third legislative sessions the majority of deputies belonged either to the Iʿtidāliyyūn Party or the Democrat Party. An attempt was made in the abortive elections of 1960 to conduct them on a two-party basis, two parties having been formed under the inspiration of the court, the *Millī* and the *Mardum* parties, whose functions were to be respectively that of His Majesty's Government and His Majesty's Opposition. The experiment was not successful.

The regulations governing the election to the first National Assembly were laid down in the Electoral Law of 20 Radjab 1324/9 September 1906. The electors were divided into six classes: (i) princes and the Ḳādjār tribe, (ii) notables (*aʿyān wa ashrāf*), (iii) *ʿulamāʾ* and students of the religious schools, (iv) merchants, (v) landowners and peasants, and (vi) members of the trade-guilds. Each elector had one vote and could vote in one class only, but the classes were not compelled to elect a deputy from their own class or guild. The persons so elected then assembled in the chief town of the province and elected members for the National Consultative Assembly according to the number specified in the law for each province. In Tehrān elections were direct, the number of deputies to be as follows: Princes and members of the Ḳādjār family, four; *ʿulamāʾ* and students of religious schools, four; merchants, ten; landowners and peasants, ten; and trade-guilds, thirty-two. Women were debarred from being elected and from voting. The minimum age of an elector, who had to be a Persian subject, was to be twenty-five years; and certain minimum property qualifications were also laid down. Deputies were to be elected for two years. Those elected had, *inter alia*, also to be Persian subjects of Persian extraction; be able to read and write Persian; be locally known; not be in government employ; and their age not less than thirty or more than seventy. The law also set up temporary councils to supervise the elections, and laid down regulations for the conduct of the elections, which were to be carried out in each locality on a date specified by the local governor.

This law was superseded by the Electoral Law of 12 Djumādā II 1327/1 July 1909. This fixed the number of deputies at 120; and provided for one representative each of the Shāhsavan, Ḳashḳāʾī, Khamsa (of Fārs), Turkomān, and Bakhtiyārī tribes, and the Armenians, Chaldeans (Nestorian Christians), Zoroastrians, and Jews. The minimum age of electors was reduced to twenty but a property qualification was introduced. Voting was to be secret. Elections were to be in two stages. A necessary qualification for election, except in the case of deputies representing the Christian, Zoroastrian or Jewish communities, was profession of Islam. Princes, *i.e.*, the sons, brothers and uncles of the reigning Shah, were debarred from being deputies. This law was in due course superseded by the Law of 28 Shawwāl 1329/21 November 1911, which fixed the number of deputies at 136, to be elected from eighty-two electoral districts, some of which were, therefore, plural constituencies. This law abolished the property qualification for electors but laid down that they must be local persons or have lived for at least the six months preceding the election in the district in which they would vote. All elections were to be direct. This law forms the basis of later electoral laws, one of which, that of 10 Mihr 1313/2 October 1934, abolished the special tribal constituencies. Further an amendment to Article 4 of the Constitution made in 1957 raised the number of deputies to two hundred (see above). Five months before the legislative period of the National Consultative Assembly comes to an end a *farmān* is issued by the Shah for new elections, after which preliminary measures for the holding of elections including the setting up of supervisory councils in the electoral districts are taken.

The law for the execution of the regulations for the election of the Senate passed by the National Consultative Assembly on 14 Urdībihisht 1328/4 May 1949 laid down *inter alia* that senators were to be elected "by two degrees" by male suffrage. The term of the Senate was fixed by this law at six years (whereas Article 50 of the Fundamental Law had fixed it at two years). The Senate is opened by the Shah as soon as two thirds of the members have assembled in Tehrān. On 23 October 1952 a bill was passed limiting the Senate's term to two years. According to this bill electors must be at least twenty-five years old and have lived in or have dwelt for at least the preceding six months in the constituency where they vote. Members of the armed forces may not vote. Senators must be at least forty years old; they must be Muslims, and live in or be known in the district for which they are elected. They must be chosen from (i) the religious classes of the first rank; (ii) persons who have been deputies for at least three legislative sessions; (iii) persons who have the position of minister, ambassador, governor-general, public prosecutor, head of a tribunal of the Court of Cassation, or had at least twenty years' service in the Ministry of Justice; (iv) retired officers of the rank of field-marshal (*sipahbud*), general (*sarlashkar*), or major-general (*sartīp*); (v) university professors who have held such office for at least ten years; (vi) landowners and merchants who pay at least 500,000 rs. in direct taxes; and (vii) certain classes of attorneys. Senators are precluded from accepting government appointments and must resign if they accept such offices.

The Supplementary Fundamental Law in Articles 90-93 makes provision for the establishment of provincial councils (*andjuman-i ayālatī wa wilāyatī*) to be elected by the people to "exercise complete supervision over all reforms connected with the public interest, always provided that they observe the limitations prescribed by the law". In the early period of the constitution provincial councils were set up in many areas but the practice fell into abeyance after the restoration of the constitution in 1909. Since the Second World War there has been from time to time talk of the setting up of some form of provincial councils.

Those who had prepared the way for constitutional reform in their published works and in the discussions of the secret societies which preceded the constitutional revolution had emphasized the need for equality before the law. This was provided for in the section of the Supplementary Fundamental Law which concerns the rights of the people (Arts. 8-25). Article 8 lays down that the people shall enjoy equal rights before the law. Article 9 that "All individuals are protected and safeguarded in respect to their lives, property, homes, and honour, from every kind of interference, and none shall molest them save in such way as the laws of the land shall determine". Article 10 lays down that "No one can be summarily arrested, save *flagrante delicto* in the commission of some crime or misdemeanour, except on the written authority of the president of a tribunal of justice given in conformity with the law. Even in such case the accused must immediately, or at latest in the course of the next twenty-four hours, be informed and notified of the nature of his offence". Further, Article 14 provides that "No Persian can be exiled from the country, or prevented from residing in any part thereof, save in such cases as the law may explicitly determine". It was, perhaps, a major advance that such principles should be clearly formulated and written into the constitution, even though, like various other provisions of the constitution, they should be from time to time ignored.

Bibliography: E. G. Browne, *The Persian Revolution of 1905-9*, Cambridge 1910; idem, *The Persian constitutional movement*, in *Proc. Brit. Acad.*, viii; L. Lockhart, *The constitutional laws of Persia*, in *MEJ*, 1959; A. K. S. Lambton, *Secret societies and the Persian revolution*, in *St. Antony's Papers*, iv, 1958; *Persian political societies 1906-11*, in *St. Antony's Papers*, xvi, 1963; N. R. Keddie, *Religion and irreligion in early Iranian nationalism*, in *Comparative Studies in Society and History*, iv/3 April 1962; W. Morgan Shuster, *The strangling of Persia*, London 1912; E. Aubin, *La Perse d'aujourd'hui*, Paris 1908; Kāẓimzāda, *Ḥuḳūḳ-i Asāsī*, Tehrān 1952-3; Nāẓim al-Islām Kirmānī, *Taʾrīkh-i bīdārī-i Īrāniyān*, Tehrān n.d.; Firaydūn Ādamiyyat, *Fikr-i Āzādī*, Tehrān 1961; Sayyid Ḥasan Taḳīzāda, *Taʾrīkh-i awāʾil-i inḳilāb wa mashrūṭiyyat*, Tehrān 1959; *Taʾrīkh-i madjlis-i millī-i Īrān*, supplement no. 5 to *Kāwa*, Berlin 1919-20; Maḥmūd Farhād Muʿtamid, *Taʾrīkh-i siyāsī-i dawra-i ṣadārat-i Mīrzā Ḥusayn Khān Mushīr al-Dawla*, Tehrān 1947; Muḥammad Muḥīṭ Ṭabāṭabāʾī, *Madjmūʿa-i āthār-i Mīrzā Malkam Khān*, Tehrān 1948-9; Mīrzā Muḥammad Khān Madjd al-Mulk, *Risāla-i Madjdiyya*, Tehrān 1942; Āḳā Mīrzā Āḳā Furṣat, *Maḳālāt-i ʿilmī wa siyāsī*, Tehrān n.d.; Mushīr al-Dawla, *Yak kalima*, Rasht 1909; Shaykh Muḥammad Ḥusayn Nāʾīnī, *Tanbīh al-umma wa tanzīh al-milla dar asās wa uṣūl-i mashrūṭiyyat yā ḥukūmat*, ed. Sayyid Maḥmūd Tāliḳānī, Tehrān n.d.; Mīrzā Ṣāliḥ, [Narrative of a journey to England from A. H. 1230 to 1235], B.M., Add. 24,034; Mīrzā Khānlar Khān Iʿtiṣām al-Mulk, *Dimokrāsī-i Inglistān* in *Sukhan*, Bahman 1323/1944; Malik al-Shuʿarā Bahār, *Taʾrīkh-i mukhtaṣar-i aḥzāb-i siyāsī*, Tehrān 1944-5; Aḥmad Kasrawī, *Taʾrīkh-i mashrūṭa-i Īrān*, Tehrān; idem, *Taʾrīkh-i hidjdahsāla-i Ādharbāydjān*, 6 vols., Tehrān 1933-41; Mahdī Malikzāda, *Taʾrīkh-i inḳilāb-i mashrūṭiyyat-i Īrān*, 7 vols., Tehrān 1949-53; idem, *Zindagī-i Malik al-Mutakallimīn*, Tehrān 1946; Ismāʿīl Amīr Khīzī, *Ḳiyām-i Ādharbāydjān wa Sattār Khān*, Tabrīz 1960; Nūrullāh Dānishvar ʿAlawī, *Taʾrīkh-i mashrūṭiyyat-i Īrān wa djunbish-i waṭan-parastān-i Iṣfahān wa Bakhtiyārī*, Tehrān 1956; Karīm Ṭāhirzāda Bihzād, *Ḳiyām-i Ādharbāydjān dar inḳilāb-i mashrūṭiyyat-i Īrān*, Tehrān n.d.; ʿAlī Dīwsālār, *Yāddāshthā-yi taʾrīkhī rādjiʿ ba fatḥ-i Tehrān wa urdū-yi barḳ*, Tehrān 1957; Yaḥyā Dawlatābādī, *Ḥayāt-i Yaḥyā*, 3 vols., Tehrān n.d.; ʿAbd Allāh Mustawfī, *Sharḥ-i zindagī-i man*, 3 vols., Tehrān 1945-6; Abu 'l-Ḥasan Buzurg Umīd, *Az māst kih bar māst*, Tehrān 1955; Khān Malik Sāsān, *Siyāsatgarān-i dawra-i Ḳādjār*, Tehrān 1960; Ḥusayn Samīʿī (Adīb al-Salṭana), *Awwalīn ḳiyām-i muḳaddas-i millī dar djang-i bayn al-milalī-i awwal*, Tehrān 1954; M. Khodayar-Mohebbi, *L'influence religieuse sur le droit constitutionnel de l'Iran*, Sorbonne thesis 1957 (unpublished).

(A. K. S. LAMBTON)

v. — AFGHĀNISTĀN

The independence of Afghānistān having been recognized by the Treaty of Rāwalpindi (8 August 1919), Amān Allāh concluded agreements with his neighbours and other powers confirming the international status of his country, in the intention of endowing the state with stable and modern institutions, in the first place a Constitution. The first step in this direction was, in 1921, the Law of Fundamental Organizations (*niẓām-nāma-i tashkīlāt-i asāsiyya-i Afghānistān*), which established the general organization of the State (see L. Bouvat, *apud* J. Castagné, *Notes sur la politique extérieure de l'Afghanistan*, in *RMM*, lviii (1921), 26 ff.) and was to serve as the basis of the Fundamental Law which, drawn up under the inspiration of the Turk Ḳadrī Bey, former chief of police in Istanbul who had settled in Kābul in 1921 and died there in 1924, was unanimously approved by the members of a *Lōya Djirga* (Popular Assembly) of the eastern provinces and by the ministers in April 1923; articles 2, 9 and 24 were revised in June-July 1924 by another *Lōya Djirga* including representatives of the entire country.

Drawn up no doubt in Pashto, but published in Persian, this Fundamental Law (*niẓām-nāma-i asāsī-yi dawlat-i ʿaliyya-i Afghānistān*) comprises 73 articles divided as follows: general principles (arts. 1-7), rights of citizens (arts. 8-24), provisions relating to ministers (arts. 25-35) and officials (arts. 36-8), to councils (arts. 39-49), tribunals (arts. 50-5), to the Supreme Court (arts. 56-7), to finance (arts. 58-62), to provincial administration (arts. 63-7), and miscellaneous (arts. 68-73).

Article 1 affirms the independence and unity of the national territory, whose capital is Kābul, according to art. 3 which also provides that all the inhabitants of the country are equal before the government without distinction of religion and sect (art. 8); art. 2 specifies, however, that the religion of Afghānistān is Islam, and that only "the other religions of Hindus and of Jews" living within the territory are protected on condition that public order be not disturbed; it is interesting to note that the *Lōya Djirga*, composed of *ʿulamāʾ*, *sayyid*s and *shaykh*s and convened in June-July 1924, brought in an amendment to this article providing that the official system should be that of the Ḥanafī school, and, moreover, that Hindus and Jews were compelled to pay the *djizya* [*q.v.*] and to wear the distinguishing emblems (*ʿalāmāt-i mumayyiza*) of *dhimmī*s. Slavery was abolished and individual liberty guaranteed to all citizens (arts. 9-10), the amendment of 1924 adding, however, that they were restricted concerning religious matters. All Afghāns are equal before the *sharīʿa* and the laws of the State (arts. 16-8); torture and similar punishments were abolished, and none could be subjected to a punishment not provided for in the *sharīʿa* or in laws enacted in conformity with the provisions of the latter (art. 24, modified). Freedom of the press (art. 11) is subject to regulation and limited for the foreign press, while freedom of association (art. 12) is recognized only for business, industrial and agricultural concerns. Freedom of education is guaranteed to Afghāns (arts. 14-5), and compulsory elementary education is provided for (art. 68), but foreigners are not authorized to open schools, although systems of instruction connected with the beliefs and rites of the non-Muslim subjects (*dhimmī*s) or protected foreigners (*mustaʾmin*) may be tolerated. Right of ownership (art. 19) and the inviolability of domicile (art. 20) are guaranteed, as well as the secrecy of the mails (art. 73), but the wording of this article could be interpreted restrictively. Citizens may make a complaint against any infringement of the *sharīʿa* or of the laws committed by an official or another person, and may in this case even appeal to the sovereign (art. 13).

H.M. the *Pādshāh* (also called *amīr*, etc.) is the servant and protector of Islam and the sovereign of all subjects of Afghānistān (art. 5); in consideration of his services, a hereditary monarchy is created, the nation agreeing to raise to the sultanate his male heirs in the male line (art. 4). The sovereign's prerogatives are as follows: his name is mentioned in the Friday *khuṭba*, the coinage bears his portrait, he confers decorations, approves laws and announces their effective date, nominates and dismisses ministers, nominates to public office, is responsible for the exercise of the laws, commands the armed forces, declares war and concludes peace, and signs all treaties; he possesses the right of amnesty and pardon (art. 7).

The ministers are responsible to the sovereign (art. 31) and may be arraigned before the Supreme Court (arts. 33-4). They give a public account, at the audience which takes place before the independence festival, of work accomplished during the year (arts. 25-7).

For the details of ministerial organization the Fundamental Law refers to the Law of Fundamental Organizations, which provided for ten ministries including a Council of State and two autonomous administrations (Posts and Telegraphs, and Public Health); the Council of State is in charge of reform, services to the state, and tribunals.

The Fundamental Law makes no provisions for a parliament, but for a Consultative Council of State (*hayʾat-i shūrā-i dawlat*) at Kābul and Councils of Consultation (*madjlis-i mashwara* or *mushāwara*) with representatives of the government in the provinces, at all stages up to district level (art. 39); these latter Councils consist of officials set up by the Law of Fundamental Organizations and elected members in equal number, while the Council with its headquarters at Kābul is composed half of members nominated by the sovereign, the other half being also elected by the people (arts. 40-1). Art. 42 stipulates the functions of these councils: matters submitted to the government representatives are examined and, if necessary, transmitted to the ministry concerned; if the government representatives do not reply, the Councils of Consultation may apply to the Consultative Council who examine the matters and transmit them, with their comments, to the competent ministry.

Laws, in the drafting of which it is necessary to take into consideration the practices, needs and provisions of the *sharīʿa*, are examined by the Consultative Council, sent to the Council of Ministers, and put in operation after they have received the approval of the ministers and the sovereign (art. 46). The Consultative Council studies the budget prepared by the Finance Ministry, as well as foreign contracts and obligations (arts. 48-9).

As regards the judiciary power, the Fundamental Law confines itself to establishing certain guarantees (publicity of proceedings, the rights of the defence, the independence of the judges who are not to allow proceedings to be delayed, arts. 50-3), the competence of tribunals (art. 54) being established by the Law of Fundamental Organizations, which provides for: justices of the peace, tribunals of first instance, courts of appeal and a Court of Cassation. Extraordinary jurisdictions are forbidden (art. 55), but a Supreme Court is instituted for the trial of ministers (arts. 56-7).

Provisions relating to finance (arts. 58-62) and the institution of an Audit Office (art. 61) are followed by details on the administration of the provinces (arts. 63-7). The following articles treat of the revision of the Fundamental Law, which must receive two-thirds of the votes in the National Consultative Council (art. 70), and of the interpretation and drafting of laws (art. 71).

It is obvious that the constitutional work undertaken under the reign of Amān Allāh represented a considerable progress towards the modernization and democratization of the country. The people began to participate modestly in political life by the election of representatives to various councils, whose role was, it is true, merely consultative; on the legislative and executive sides the government and the sovereign exercised a preponderant power, and the judiciary itself, although more independent, was not free from governmental authority, since the Court of Appeal was presided over by the minister of justice and the chief *ḳāḍī* was an *ex officio* member of it. One may notice that this Constitution is not exactly a slavish imitation of western models, and has a certain originality; there is, indeed, no provision for assuring the Islamic nature of the laws, but the duty of conforming to the *sharīʿa* is underlined at several places, and the provisions concerning the Ḥanafī practice are striking; even more striking is the xenophobia and the sort of rigorism which appear in the retention of the *djizya* and the wearing of the *zunnār* imposed on some non-Muslims resident on Afghān territory.

To what extent this Constitution was applied is not exactly known, since many incidents followed in the country's internal affairs. In the summer of 1928 after Amān Allāh's return from a visit to Europe Afghānistān was troubled by a serious movement of revolt on the part of tribes instigated by *mullā*s hostile to certain forms of westernization, though not, indeed, to the provisions of the Constitution. The revolt soon spread to the eastern and northern provinces, and Kābul fell into the hands of Bačča-i Saḳaw who proclaimed himself *amīr* and took the name of Ḥabīb Allāh. Amān Allāh having given up resistance and his throne, Nādir Khān, who was related to the royal family, continued the struggle against the usurper and succeeded in recapturing Kābul in October 1929; proclaimed sovereign under the title of Nādir Shāh, he made great efforts to govern the country with wisdom and prudence and, two years later, on 31 October 1931, promulgated a new Constitution (in Pashtō and in Persian: *uṣūl-i asāsī-yi dawlat-i ʿaliyya-i Afghānistān*), which reiterated the greater part of the provisions of the Fundamental Law of 1923, but differed substantially from it by the creation of a Senate (*madjlis-i aʿyān*) and the definitive institution of a National Consultative Assembly (*madjlis-i shūrā-yi millī*), already created by a *Djirga* in August-September 1928, confirmed by another *Djirga* in 1930, and inaugurated by the Shāh in October 1930.

The new Constitution comprises 110 articles (instead of 73) arranged in the following way: general provisions (arts. 1-4), rights and duties of the sovereign (arts. 5-8), rights of citizens (arts. 9-26), organization of the National Consultative Assembly (arts. 27-66), of the Senate (arts. 67-70), of the Councils of Consultation in the provinces (arts. 71-2), rights and duties of ministers (arts. 73-83), and of officials (arts. 84-6), tribunals (arts. 87-94), the Supreme Court (arts. 95-6), finance (arts. 97-101), provincial administration (arts. 102-5), the army (arts. 106-8), and miscellaneous provisions (arts. 109-10).

On the whole the Constitutional matters are

better arranged than in the Fundamental Law of 1923, but many articles are retained almost entirely. The general provisions differ little; however, art. 1 (old art. 2) imposes the obligation on the sovereign to follow the Ḥanafī school, and no longer speaks of *djizya* and the distinguishing emblems of *dhimmīs*. The wording of art. 5 (old art. 4) is slightly modified: the monarchy is hereditary in the family of Nādir Shāh, and it is he who nominates his successor; he must now take the oath (art. 6) according to a solemn formula, and a civil list is allotted to him (art. 8). Art. 23 (old art. 11) is more liberal towards the foreign press, although art. 21 (old art. 14) provides that the teaching only of Islamic sciences is free.

The National Consultative Assembly is composed of 106 deputies elected for three years; they must take an oath and enjoy parliamentary immunity. The Assembly is charged with approving laws and regulations, financial laws, grants and concessions of all kinds, the construction of railways, etc. Members of the Senate (arts. 67-70) are nominated by the sovereign; they are a counterbalance to the Assembly in the approval of laws either before or after that body; this Senate was inaugurated in November 1931. The Councils of Consultation persist in the provinces, but they are now elected (art. 71). Provisions regarding ministers are slightly different (arts. 73-83) in that they are chosen by the prime minister with the sovereign's approval, and are responsible to the Assembly and not to the Shāh; in addition, they no longer have to give public reports on their work. On the judicial side a distinction is made between civil tribunals (*maḥākim-i ʿadliyya*) and religious tribunals (*maḥākim-i sharʿiyya*). The Audit Office (art. 100, old art. 61) is not expressly provided for; on the other hand three articles (106-8) are devoted to the army; it is there laid down that foreigners are not admitted to it except in the capacities of surgeons or instructors.

In general the second Afghān Constitution marks a noticeable progress from the former; it appears not only more liberal but also more democratic in that the people have their elected representatives in the assemblies which, indeed, have especially a consultative part to play but participate more intimately in the political life of the nation.

Bibliography: Constitution of 1923: résumé in *OM*, iv (1924), 196-9; A. Giannini, *La costituzione afghāna*, in *OM*, xi/6 (1931), 265-74 with Ital. trans. of text, *ibid.* 276-83; idem, *Le costituzioni degli Stati del Vicino Oriente*, Rome 1931, 13-41; Joseph Schwager, *Die Entwicklung Afghanistans als Staat und seine zwischenstaatlichen Beziehungen*, Leipzig 1932 (text and commentary). — Constitution of 1930: E. Rossi, *La costituzione afghana del 31 octobre 1930*, in *OM*, xiii/1 (1933), 1-6 with Ital. trans. of the text, *ibid.* 7-15, electoral law 15-9, and résumé of the regulations of the Assembly 19-20; Engl. trans. in Muḥammad b. Aḥmad, *Constitutions of Eastern countries*, in *Select constitutions of the world*[2], Karachi 1951, i, 48-59; Fr. trans. in Documentation Française, *L'Afghanistan moderne*, no. 1112, 3-39.—See also S. Beck, *Das afghanische Strafgesetzbuch vom Jahre 1924 mit dem Zusatz vom Jahre 1925*, in *WI*, xi (1928), 67-157; L. Massignon, *Annuaire du monde musulman*[4], Paris 1955; for information on constitutional developments, D. N. Wilber (ed.), *Afghanistan*. Human Relations Area Files, New Haven (Conn.) 1956. See also the bibl. given by A. Giannini and by E. Rossi, and the art. AFGHĀNISTĀN. (ED.)

vi. — ʿIRĀḲ

Next to Egypt, ʿIrāḳ may be regarded as the first Arab state to be organized along modern constitutional lines after World War I. Her parliamentary system was consciously modelled, at least in form, after the British system. The draft constitution was prepared (1922-3) by a mixed committee of ʿIrāḳī and British members, drawing its provisions from the constitutions of the Ottoman Empire, Australia, New Zealand and others. The draft was submitted to a Constituent Assembly for approval and, with some minor modifications, was passed and promulgated on 21 March 1925. It was formally called the Organic Law (*al-Ḳānūn al-Asāsī*) of ʿIrāḳ.

The constitution provided for a monarchical system, although the monarchy was instituted before the constitution was drafted. The King was not responsible. He enjoyed wide powers, such as the selection and dismissal of the Prime Minister (the latter power was given to him in the amendment of 1943), he confirmed laws, ordered their promulgation, and supervised their execution. He could also proclaim martial law, order general elections, appoint senators and diplomatic representatives, and convoke Parliament, presumably upon the recommendation of the Cabinet. When Parliament was not in session the King issued decrees with the concurrence of the Cabinet for the maintenance of public order and the expenditure of public money not provided by the budget. These decrees had the force of laws, provided they were not contrary to the provisions of the constitution, and were laid before Parliament at its first session

The Cabinet was made up of the Prime Minister and a number of other ministers (the number was not to exceed seven before the amendment of 1943). All members of the Cabinet were members of Parliament (if a person appointed minister was not already a member of Parliament, he either had to become a member of Parliament within six months or resign). The Cabinet was responsible to the Lower House; if that House passed a vote of no confidence in it, it had to resign.

Legislative power was vested in Parliament and the King. Parliament was composed of two houses—an appointed Senate (*Madjlis al-Aʿyān*) whose membership should not exceed one-fourth of the total number of the Lower House, and an elected Chamber of Deputies (*Madjlis al-Nuwwāb*). The term of the Lower House was four years, including four ordinary sessions, the duration of each session being six months. Legislation was initiated in Parliament or proposed by the Government (in the case of the annual budget, it was always proposed by the Government). Draft laws, when passed by both Houses, became laws only after being confirmed by the King. The King could confirm or reject legislation, stating reasons for so doing, within a period of three months. Members of Parliament were immune and had the right to interrogate Ministers and ask for information. The meetings of Parliament were open to the public, unless sessions in camera were decided upon by the Government or the members of Parliament (on a request by four senators or ten deputies).

From the establishment of the ʿIrāḳī government in 1921 to the abolition of the monarchy in 1958, ʿIrāḳ had 62 cabinets, including a provisional government in 1920 and the present (April 1963) cabinet. Parliament has met regularly since the general election of 1925. There had been some fifteen general elections held till the abolition of the Parliamentary system.

The revolution of 14 July 1958, produced by a growing dissatisfaction with the monarchy and the Parliamentary system, abrogated the Constitution of 1925. The newly established Council of Sovereignty, composed of three members, issued a decree establishing a republican regime for ʿIrāḳ and promising the calling of a constituent assembly to draw up a new constitution for the country. In the meantime there is no parliament. Decrees, having the force of laws, are issued by the Cabinet and approved by the Council of Sovereignty. (On the Arab Union, see below, xviii).

Bibliography: N. G. Davison, *The Constitution of Iraq*, in *Journal of Comparative Legislation and International Law*, 3rd series, vii (1925), 41-52; C. H. Hooper, *The Constitutional Law of Iraq*, Baghdad 1929; A. Giannini, *La costituzione dell'Iraq*, in *OM*, x (1930), 525-46; P. W. Ireland, *Iraq*, London 1937; S. H. Longrigg, *Iraq: 1900-1950*, London 1953; Muhammad ʿAzīz, *al-Niẓām al-siyāsī fi 'l-ʿIrāḳ*, Baghdad 1954; M. Khadduri, *Independent Iraq*², London 1958; G. Grassmuck, *The electoral process in Iraq, 1952-1958*, in *MEJ*, xiv (1960), 397-415; ʿAbd al-Razzāḳ al-Ḥasanī, *Taʾrīkh al-wizārāt al-ʿirāḳiyya*, i-x, Ṣaydā 1933-61.

(M. Khadduri)

vii. — Saʿūdī Arabia

As early as 31 August 1926 the kingdom of the Ḥidjāz provided itself with a "Constitution" comprising 9 sections and 79 articles, but this has few points in common with the constitutions of Arab countries studied in this article. By virtue of this text the Arab State of the Ḥidjāz was "a constitutional Muslim monarchy" (art. 2) in which "all the administration is in the hands of H.M. King ʿAbd al-ʿAzīz I", but the latter is "bound by the laws of the *sharīʿa*" (art. 5). The judicial norms must conform to the Book of God, to the *Sunna* of His Prophet, and the conduct of the Companions and of the early pious generations (art. 6). The king employs at his own expense a viceroy (*nāʾib ʿāmm*) and as many directors and service chiefs as he judges necessary (art. 7). The viceroy represents the supreme authority and is responsible to the king (art. 8). Section III deals with the affairs of the kingdom, which are divided into 6 groups: *sharīʿa* affairs, internal affairs, foreign affairs, financial affairs, public instruction, military affairs (art. 9). *Sharīʿa* affairs include everything which pertains to religious jurisdiction (*al-ḳaḍāʾ al-sharʿī*), the two Holy Cities, *waḳf*s, mosques and all religious establishments (art. 10). As regards internal affairs, art. 14 provides for a commission for the control of the pilgrimage. Arts. 17 ff., on foreign affairs, were modified on 19 December 1930 when the directorate of foreign affairs was transformed into a ministry. Section IV institutes a consultative council (*madjlis shūrā*) nominated by the king (arts. 28 ff.), the administrative councils of Djudda and Medina (art. 32 ff.) which comprise officials and notables nominated by the king, village and tribal councils (art. 41 ff.). A department of audit is provided for (art. 43) as well as a general inspectorate of officials (art. 46 ff.). Section VII deals with employees of the State, section VIII with municipal councils, and the last section with administrative committees of municipalities.

A royal decree of 29 January 1927 raised Nadjd to the status of a kingdom and unified it with the Ḥidjāz. A further royal decree of 18 September 1932 created the kingdom of Saʿūdī Arabia, changing nothing in the previous administration, although art. 6 of this decree provides that the council of ministers shall immediately draft a new constitution; it seems, however, that this provision has remained a dead letter.

In practice the king retained direct control over religious, military and diplomatic affairs, and partially delegated some of his powers to members of his family or his entourage. The consultative council remained purely theoretical, although the assembly of tribal chiefs met yearly at al-Riyāḍ. On 9 October 1953 king ʿAbd al-ʿAzīz Ibn Saʿūd instituted for the first time a true council of ministers presided over by the *amīr* Saʿūd, who ascended the throne on 9 November, after the death of his father. At the time of the first meeting of the council of ministers, 8 March 1954, the king expressed the wish that "the government would manage the affairs of the country taking account of the Ḳurʾānic teachings", and on the following 17 March two royal edicts established the status of this council of ministers and of connected offices; no movement developed towards the drafting of a constitution of a modern type. However, on 30 December 1960, prince Ṭalāl declared that the government of Saʿūdī Arabia had the intention of providing the country with a Constitution and of creating a National Assembly, and two days later Mecca Radio announced that King Saʿūd had promulgated a constitution comprising a preamble and 200 articles; a text was put out by wireless and the press, but on 28 December a communiqué categorically denied this information.

Bibliography: C. A. Nallino, *Raccolta di scritti*, i, Rome 1939, 233-46; Documentation française, *Notes et études documentaires*, no. 1529 of 10 September 1951; J. E. Godchot, *Les constitutions du Proche et du Moyen-Orient*, Paris 1957, 28-42; Helen M. Davis, *Constitutions, etc.*, 248-58; A. Giannini, *Le constituzioni degli Stati del vicino Oriente*, Rome 1931, 130-5; *COC*, *OM*, *MEJ*, *MEA*, etc., of the relevant years.

viii. — Yemen

The Imamate of the Yemen produced no written constitution; there exist, however, a number of texts regulating the powers of the *Imām* and the succession to the throne. The *imām* was to be elected by the *ʿulamāʾ* summoned to a consultative assembly, the *Madjlis*, before whom the sovereign was to take the oath. The latter, as spiritual head of the country, was to hold absolute power, but with the aid of a prime minister and other ministers belonging to his family. After the revolution of September 1962, a constitutional document was issued by the revolutionary council (*madjlis al-thawra*) setting forth the aims of the revolution and laying down general principles of government. The former begin with the restoration of the 'true *Sharīʿa*', the abolition of communal discrimination and the equality of all Yemenites before the law, the removal of conflicts between Zaydīs and Shāfiʿīs, followed by a series of national, political and social objectives. The principles, in addition to the usual constitutional assurances, include the statements that the Yemenite people is the source of all authority (art. 3) and that all laws derive their validity from the *Sharīʿa* of Islam, which is the official religion of the state (art. 6). The text of the document was published in *Fatāt al-Djazīra*, Aden, issue of 8 November 1962. (Ed.)

ix. — Syria and Lebanon

Like ʿIrāḳ, Syria and Lebanon began their constitutional life after their separation from the Ottoman Empire after World War I, although some of their leaders had taken an active part in Ottoman constitutional experiments. The first constitutional step undertaken by Syria took place after the capture of Damascus by Amīr Fayṣal in 1918 with the avowed intention of establishing an Arab constitutional state. Fayṣal called a Syrian Congress in 1920, representing the whole of geographical Syria (later known as Greater Syria), including Lebanon and Palestine, on the basis of the Ottoman Electoral Law. This Congress, functioning as a legislative and a constituent assembly, laid down a draft constitution of 148 articles which, though no formal vote was taken, had been accepted in principle. The Congress was still considering the draft when the French army entered Damascus and it adjourned on 19 July 1920, never to meet again.

The constitution provided for a limited monarchy, a bi-cameral legislature, and a responsible Cabinet. Syria (*i.e.*, Greater Syria) was to be an indivisible political entity, but its boundaries were left undefined. The Syrian Government was to be an Arab Government, its capital Damascus, and its religion Islam. The constitution included a Bill of Rights guaranteeing civil liberties and freedom of thought and of religion. Both the Senate and the Chamber of Deputies were to be elected bodies: the deputies by secret ballot in two degrees, and the Senators by the Chamber of Deputies of each province. The administration of the country was to be on a decentralized basis; each province was to have its own local administration with a single legislative body called the Chamber of Deputies. The judiciary was to be independent, with a High Court appointed by the King as the supreme judicial organ.

Syria remained under direct French control from 1920 to 1930 before another constitutional step was taken. While Syria was still in the midst of the revolt of 1925-7, the French came to an understanding with Lebanon and promulgated a constitution in 1926, thus providing a constitutional model for Syria.

Lebanon

The Lebanese constitution provided for a republican régime—the first to be proclaimed in the Arab East in modern times—and a bi-cameral Parliament, to be elected by a two-stage universal manhood suffrage. The Cabinet was to be individually and collectively responsible to Parliament. The President, elected by the two Houses of Parliament in a joint session, was given the right to appoint the Prime Minister and, with a vote of three-quarters of the Senate, to dissolve the Chamber of Deputies. This elaborate structure for a small state called for a revision in 1927, which increased the powers of the President, especially in expediting financial bills; it abolished the Senate and established a unicameral Parliament. The Chamber of Deputies, whose membership was 30, was increased by 15, appointed by the President. The members of the Cabinet were chosen from Parliament, and the members remained individually and collectively responsible to Parliament.

This constitution, continuing to function during the Mandate period, was suspended when war broke out in 1939. It was restored in 1943, when the independence of the country was formally declared, and was purged of the Mandate clauses by an act of Parliament on 8 November 1943. This precipitated a crisis with the French authorities, who maintained that the amendment of the constitution had been carried out before the Mandate was formally terminated, but France finally agreed to the amendment and the Mandate system itself was formally terminated in 1946 at a meeting of the Council of the League of Nations in Geneva.

Syria

The successful step taken in drawing up a constitutional framework for Lebanon prompted the Syrians to come to an understanding with the French on the need for establishing a constitutional government. Elections for a Constituent Assembly were held in 1928. A drafting committee of 27 members was appointed and a draft constitution was ready in August before the Assembly. The draft stipulated that Syria within its "natural boundaries" (*i.e.*, Greater Syria) would be an indivisible political unit and an independent sovereign state, its form of government republican, and the religion of its head Islam. The constitution also provided for a Bill of Rights, in which the principles of liberty, equality, private property, etc. were guaranteed. The head of the executive power was the President of the Republic, elected by Parliament for a period of five years, but he was not eligible for re-election until the lapse of five years from the expiration of his term. The President selected the Prime Minister and appointed the Ministers upon the latter's recommendation. The President was not responsible, since his decisions were countersigned by the Prime Minister and the Ministers concerned. The Cabinet was composed of not more than seven members responsible to Parliament. The Ministers were not all members of Parliament, but they could attend and take part in discussion. Parliament was made up of one House (*Madjlis*, or Chamber of Deputies), which was freely elected every four years. Every male Syrian who had attained his twentieth year was eligible to vote. The constitution provided also for a High Court composed of 15 members chosen from Parliament and from the judges of the courts. The constitution was ordinarily amended by two-thirds of Parliament upon the request of either the Government or Parliament. The draft constitution, ignoring the terms of the Mandate, promted France to inform the Constituent Assembly that certain articles, such as the one dealing with the "natural boundaries" of Syria, which included Lebanon, and others which contradicted France's international obligations, must be revised. Upon the Assembly's refusal, the French dissolved the Assembly in 1928 and promulgated the Constitution in 1930, having revised the articles to which they had objected The Syrians, tacitly accepting the situation, participated in the elections for Parliament in 1932. The first President of the Republic was elected in 1933. However, the Syrians and the French could not agree on a treaty regulating the relations between France and Syria after independence. Thus, when the war broke out in 1939, the French suspended the Constitution and governed the country through a "Council of Directors".

The circumstances of World War II gave Syria an opportunity to achieve independence and resume constitutional life. In 1941, Syria and Lebanon were declared independent and elections for the resumption of parliamentary life were held in 1943, although the legal termination of the Mandate did not take place until 1946. The constitution of 1930, revised by deleting the articles referring to the Mandate, was restored and a new President was elected. This constitution remained in force until 1948, when a military coup d'état was led by Ḥusnī al-Zaʿīm, who overthrew the Government and suspended the constitution. A new draft constitution, reputed to embody progressive principles, was not promulgated, since Zaʿīm himself was overthrown by the army in August 1949. Elections for a Constituent Assembly were held in a relatively free atmosphere, although the army remained in control of authority. The assembly issued a new draft constitution, prepared by a committee of 33 members under the chairmanship of Nāẓim al-Ḳudsī, on 5 September 1950, and promulgated on the same day by the President of the Republic.

The Constitution of 1950 made no fundamental changes in the form or structure of the government as it existed in the constitution of 1930. Its innovations were to be found in the general articles expressing the hopes of the Syrian people. Syria was declared to be "an indivisible political unity" and to form "a part of the Arab nation". The Bill of Rights, composed of 28 articles, defined in detail the fundamental principles of freedom and the social and economic rights of the citizens. The articles relating to land stated that "a maximum limit for land ownership shall be prescribed by law", but no such law was ever issued until Syria was united with Egypt in 1958. The constitution also provided that "the state shall distribute state lands to peasants to whom land is not available sufficient for their support, against small rents to be repaid in instalments" (Article 22). Labour was regarded as "the most basic factor in social life" and "the right of all citizens". "The state shall provide work to citizens and shall guarantee it by directing and promoting the national economy" (Article 26). Education was also declared a right of every citizen. Elementary education was compulsory and free in all government schools. Secondary and professional education, though not compulsory, was also free in all government schools. Military service was compulsory, and the family, regarded as the basis of society, was to be protected by the state. The state was also to encourage marriage and endeavour to remove the material and social obstacles which hinder it. These principles, then regarded as the most progressive in Arab lands, were overshadowed by Egypt's more radical socialistic measures when Syria joined Egypt in a union in 1958. However, before Syria joined that union, she had yet to experiment with a new constitutional charter, issued under the Shishaklī regime in 1954, by virtue of which the presidential system of government was introduced for the first time in Arab lands. This short-lived constitution was abrogated soon after the collapse of the Shishaklī regime and the Constitution of 1950 was restored. The latter constitution may well be regarded as still (1963) in force after Syria's secession from the United Arab Republic, as Syria's rulers seem to have implied in several public declarations, pending the promulgation of a revised version or perhaps a completely new constitutional charter. (See below, xviii).

Bibliography: A. Giannini, *La costituzione della Siria e del Libano*, in *OM*, x (1930), 589-615; Philippe David, *Un gouvernement arabe à Damas*, Paris 1923; A. J. Toynbee, *Survey of international affairs, 1930*, London 1931, 304-14; A. Hourani, *Syria and Lebanon*, London 1946; P. Rondot, *Les institutions politiques du Liban*, Paris 1947; N. A. Ziadeh, *Syria and Lebanon*, London 1957; S. H. Longrigg, *Syria and Lebanon under French Mandate*, London 1958; M. Khadduri, *The Franco-Lebanese Dispute and the crisis of November, 1943*, in *American Journal of International Law*, xxxviii (1944), 601-20; Wadjīh al-Ḥaffār, *al-Dustūr wa 'l-ḥukm*, Damascus 1948; ʿAbd al-Wahhāb Ḥawmad, *Ḥawl al-dustūr al-djadīd*, Damascus 1950; M. Khadduri, *Constitutional development in Syria*, in *MEJ*, v (1951), 137-60; N. A. Ziadeh, *The Lebanese elections*, in *MEJ*, xiv (1960), 367-81; J. M. Landau, *Elections in Lebanon*, in *Western Political Quarterly*, xiv (1961), 120-47; Documentation française, *Notes et études documentaires*, no. 1413 of 20 Dec. 1950 and no. 1785 of 22 Sept. 1953. (M. Khadduri)

x. — Jordan

Even before his country became independent, Amīr ʿAbd Allāh of Transjordan promulgated a constitution (*ḳānūn asāsī*) on 16 April 1928, providing for a Legislative Assembly (*Madjlis Tashrīʿī*) and an Executive Council responsible to him. This constitutional charter, though giving the Amīr extensive powers, became the basis of the new constitutional framework when Transjordan became independent. On 15 May 1946 Amīr ʿAbd Allāh was proclaimed King of the Hāshimite Kingdom of Transjordan, and the constitution of 1928, revised to fit the new independent life of the country in 1946, was replaced by a new constitution on 1 February 1947. This constitution provided for a bi-cameral Parliament and a responsible Cabinet, but the King retained extensive powers, including a veto over legislation. The incorporation of Arab Palestine with Transjordan called for another constitutional change, first in the formal act of incorporation, creating the Hāshimite Kingdom of Jordan, on 24 April 1950; and then the revision of the constitution, following King ʿAbd Allāh's assassination in 1952. The new constitution provided clearly for the responsibility of the Cabinet to the Chamber of Deputies, the establishment of a Supreme Court, the responsibility of the State for the protection of the right of workers, and compulsory education in primary schools. This constitution was revised several times later, liberalizing its provisions; but in practice the King continued to exercise effective control over the Cabinet and Parliament.

Bibliography: A. Giannini, *La costituzione della Transgiordania*, in *OM*, xi (1931), 117-31; P. R. Graves (tr.), *Memoirs of King Abdullah*, London 1950; Ann Dearden, *Jordan*, London 1958; R. Patai, *The Kingdom of Jordan*, Princeton 1958; Munīb al-Māḍī and Sulaymān Mūsā, *Taʾrīkh al-Urdun*, ʿAmmān 1959; Documentation française, *Notes et études documentaires*, no. 1613 of 14 May 1952. (M. Khadduri)

xi. — Indonesia

Little progress towards self-government had been made in Indonesia (or the Netherlands East Indies as it then was) before the Japanese invasion in 1942. In 1918 an advisory *Volksraad* (People's Council) had its first meeting, having been mooted in 1916. It was intended as a safety valve for Indonesian nationalism which had been gaining strength rapidly, especially in view of the special circumstances of the war in Europe, which tied down so much Dutch military power. However, the existence of appointed as well as elected members, the extremely limited franchise and the indirectness of the elections guaranteed that the Europeans formed a majority. In any case, its powers were restricted to the giving to the Government, in the person of the Governor-General, of advice which he could ignore.

Reforms in the composition and powers of the *Volksraad* in 1920, 1922, 1925 and 1927 did little to transform the body into an effective legislature. After 1927 it had co-legislative powers with the Governor-General, but he retained a veto. The system of election remained indirect, and the franchise narrow.

When the Japanese sensed that their defeat was inevitable they acted to hasten Indonesian independence. On 1 March 1945 they appointed a joint committee, the majority on which was Indonesian, to discuss plans for independence. Meetings held from 28 May to 1 June and from 10 to 17 July reached general agreement on the basic political principles which should guide the future Indonesian nation. Sukarno, a prominent nationalist leader since the 1920s, and subsequently Indonesia's first President, played a major part in the discussions. It was his speech on 1 June, expounding his *Panča šīla* ("five foundations", five basic principles) which made possible a workable measure of compromise between those who wanted a theocratic Islamic state (the Indonesian population is 90% Muslim) and those who, though nominally Muslim themselves, feared extreme Muslim orthodoxy. It is significant that over 90% of the *élite* from whom the leaders of the national movement were drawn had had western as opposed to strictly Islamic educations (Soelaeman Soemardi, *Some aspects of the social origins of the Indonesian political decision-makers*, in *Trans. 3rd World Congr. Sociology*, London 1956).

Sukarno's *panča šīla* were: nationalism (*kebangsaan*); internationalism, or humanitarianism (*perikemanusiaan*); democracy, or representation (*kerakjatan*); social justice (*keadilan sosial*); and faith in one God (*ke-Tuhanan*, or *pengakuan ke-Tuhanan Jang Maha-Esa*). His exposition of the principles was subtle and persuasive, reassuring, for example, the strongest supporters of the concept of an Islamic state that their best guarantee of influence was by working through the elective and democratic institutions which were going to be formed. (The text of the speech is to be found in Kemenkerian Penerangan, *Lahirnya Pantjasila*, 2nd Engl. edn. Djakarta 1952). The Djakarta Charter, signed by nine leading nationalists on 22 June 1945, is identical in wording with the Preamble to the 1945 Constitution, with the exception of the words italicized in the following extract: "The Republic is founded upon the belief in God, *with the obligation for those professing the Islamic faith to abide by the laws of Islam, in accordance with the principle of* a righteous and moral humanity . . .". Even this gesture towards Islam had dropped out when the 1945 Constitution appeared.

On 7 August 1945, the Japanese authorized the establishment of an all-Indonesian Independence Preparatory Committee (*Panitya Persiapan Kemerdekaan Indonesia—PPKI*), with Sukarno as Chairman and Hatta as Vice-Chairman, and entrusted with the task of arranging to take over government. When the Japanese surrendered a week later, Sukarno and Hatta proclaimed independence within three days, on 17 August 1945.

At the first meeting of the *PPKI*, on 18 August, Sukarno was elected President and Hatta Vice-President, in accordance with Article III of the Transitional Provisions appended to the 1945 Constitution, and they, with five others, completed work, begun during the last weeks of the Japanese occupation, on this document. Although considered at the time as provisional, it in fact remained in force until the end of 1949, though not without modification, and was restored in the middle of 1959.

The Preamble paraphrases the *panča šīla*, the concluding part reading: "We believe in an all-embracing God; in righteous and moral humanity; in the unity of Indonesia. We believe in democracy, wisely guided and led by close contact with the people through consultation, so that there shall result social justice for the whole Indonesian people".

Art. 1 lays down that Indonesia is a unitary state with a republican form of government. Sovereignty lies with the people, and is exercised through a People's Consultative Assembly (*Madjelis Permusjawaratan Rakjat*). Art. 2 stipulates that the Consultative Assembly is to consist of the members of the Chamber of Representatives (*Dewan Perwakilan Rakjat*), together with representatives of regions and groups. It is to meet at least once every five years, and to take its decisions by simple majority vote. Art. 3 entrusts it with the responsibility for enacting the permanent constitution and the main guiding lines of state policy. Art. 4 gives the President the power of Government, to be exercised in accordance with the provisions of the Constitution, and a Vice-President to assist him, and art. 5 empowers him to enact laws in agreement with (*persetudjuan dengan*) the Chamber of Representatives, and to issue ordinances for the proper execution of laws. Art. 6 stipulates that the President is to be an autochthonous Indonesian, and that he and the Vice-President should be elected by the People's Consultative Assembly by a majority vote; art. 7 lays down his term of office at five years, with the possibility of re-election; art. 10 gives him supreme command of the armed forces; art. 11 empowers him to declare war, conclude peace, and to make treaties with foreign powers, all with the sanction of the Chamber of Representatives, while art. 12 gives him the right of proclaiming a state of emergency, the conditions and consequences of which are to be regulated by law.

Art. 16 provides for a Supreme Advisory Council (*Dewan Pertimbangan Agung*), which is obliged to answer questions submitted by the President, and has the right to make proposals to the Government. Art. 17 provides for Ministers of State, whose function it is to take charge of Government Departments, and who are appointed and dismissed by the President.

Arts. 19-22 govern the Chamber of Representatives. It is to assemble at least once a year, and its sanction is required for all laws. If a bill fails to receive this sanction, it is not to be submitted again during the same session. Members of the Chamber have the right to initiate laws; if the President does not ratify these, they are not to be submitted again during the same session of the Chamber. Presidential ordinances during states of emergency require the sanction of the Chamber of Representatives in its next session, and if this is not obtained, the ordinances lapse. Art. 23 governs the financial arrangements. The annual budget is regulated by law. Arts. 24-8 govern the judicature, and guarantee the basic human rights—freedom of speech, equality before the law, and the right to work. The remaining arts. deal with religion, national defence, social welfare, the flag and language, and amendments to the Constitution. The last is effected by a two-thirds majority of the People's Consultative Assembly when at least two-thirds of its members are in attendance (art. 37).

Four transitional and two additional provisions complete the document. Of these, nos. 2 and 4 of the transitional provisions provide for the perpetuation of arrangements existing at the time the Constitution was drafted until the new ones proposed in it could be brought into being, and arrange for the President, assisted by a National Committee (*Komite Nasional Indonesia Pusat—KNIP*), to exercise the powers of the People's Consultative Assembly, the Chamber of Representatives, and the Supreme Advisory Council until such time as they can be established.

The Constitution reflects a variety of influences. The American Presidential system has obviously been more attractive than the western European parliamentary system, even though the former operates in a federal nation and the latter mainly in unitary ones. Despite the determination of the nationalists to owe as little as possible to the Dutch, several features of the 1945 Constitution are reminiscent of the Constitution of the Kingdom of the Netherlands. The Supreme Advisory Council, for example, is not unlike the Dutch Council of State. The President and the Chamber of Representatives exercise legislative power under the Indonesian Constitution, the King and the States-General under the Dutch. Other influences suggested by commentators include that of the draft Chinese Constitution of 1936 (M. Yamin, *Proklamasi dan Konstitusi Republik Indonesia*, Djakarta and Amsterdam 1952, 139), the constitution of the former Netherlands Indies (J. H. A. Logemann, *Het Staatsrecht van Indonesië*, 's-Gravenhage and Bandung 1954, 34), and the Chinese Organic Law of 1931 (H. Feith, *The decline of constitutional democracy in Indonesia*, Ithaca, N.Y., 1962, 43).

The first Cabinet under the Constitution was appointed by President Sukarno on 31 August 1945. The chosen ministers were responsible to the President and not to the *KNIP*, which had been formed on 29 August. It consisted of the members of the dissolved *PPKI*, plus a further selection of outstanding nationalist leaders, and representatives of the main economic, ethnic, religious and social groups in Indonesia. Its functions were advisory, not legislative.

However, following a meeting of the *KNIP* on 16 October 1945, the Vice-President, Hatta, announced that, pending the formation of the Consultative Assembly and the Chamber of Representatives, the *KNIP* itself was to be vested with legislative powers, and was to participate in the working out of the general orientation of state policy. The functions of the *KNIP* were normally to be assumed by a smaller component of it, known as the Working Committee, whose size permitted of more rapid decision taking. The term "Working Committee" seems to have been taken from the Indian National Congress (G. McT. Kahin (ed.), *Major governments of Asia*, Ithaca, N.Y., 1958, 504 n. 6).

At the instigation of the Working Committee, the President decreed on 14 November 1945 that Ministers should in future be responsible to the *KNIP*. Since the Working Committee met a good deal more frequently than the parent body, in effect Ministers were now responsible to it. The old Cabinet was dismissed, and a new one, under Sjahrir as Premier, formed.

The change was the result of unease, in the first months of the new state, on the part of those nationalists who had served with the anti-Japanese underground, at the power and influence of nationalists who had worked with the Japanese during the war. Sjahrir was a spokesman for this group of ex-resistance nationalists. The consequence of the change was to substitute for a Presidential system a western European type parliamentary one. It is noteworthy that 94% of the cabinet ministers in Indonesia from 1945 to 1955 had been educated in Western schools and universities (Soemardi, *op. cit.*).

In the following four years the President assumed emergency powers on three occasions (29 June to 2 October 1946; 27 June to 3 July 1947; 15 September to 15 December 1948), for the terms of which he exercised full personal control. On the third occasion, however, he did so, not on his own decree, but after an Act passed with the concurrence of the Working Committee and countersigned by the Ministers of Defence, Internal Affairs, and Justice.

Apart from the period before the modification of the Constitution in November 1945, there were two other Presidential Cabinets (29 January 1948 to 4 August 1949; and 4 August to 20 December 1949). In these, the Vice-President was premier, composition was not based on party political bargaining, and "... it was generally considered that a Cabinet so established could not be forced to resign by the Working Committee" (A. K. Pringgodigdo, *The office of President in Indonesia as defined in the three constitutions in theory and practice*, Ithaca, N.Y., 1957, 17).

At the time the *KNIP* was formed, the *PPKI* also decided on the formation of an Indonesian National Party (*Partai National Indonesia*), which was to be the sole Indonesian political organization. However, government announcements of 3 and 14 November 1945 made it clear that all trends of democratic opinion were entitled to political existence and organized expression. Once again the defeat and discrediting of the former Axis powers was probably a consideration.

There were two abortive agreements with the Dutch before Indonesia's independence was finally recognized. The Linggadjati Agreement (signed 25 March 1947) granted the Republic of Indonesia *de facto* recognition in Java, Madura and Sumatra, and provided for a "United States of Indonesia" to be formed with Dutch co-operation. The Renville Agreement (17 January 1948), which was concluded at the instigation of the United Nations, gave the Dutch the temporary right to hold the territory they had seized in the interim, on condition that they would hold plebiscites in these areas to determine the wishes of the inhabitants. The Dutch realized that the overwhelming majority of the people under them would opt for the Republic of Indonesia, so they ignored this condition, and instead set about fostering local states like the ones they had created and sustained in Borneo and the eastern islands. Throughout this period the Dutch worked unceasingly to create a viable federal structure in the areas they controlled, in contrast with their pre-war policy of maintaining a unitary structure in their colony, and rejecting federal proposals (see A. A. Schiller, *The formation of federal Indonesia, 1945-49*, The Hague-Bandung 1955, 14-25 *et passim*).

In mid-1949 delegates of the Dutch-fostered federal states and of the Republic of Indonesia met at an Inter-Indonesia Conference (*Konperensi Inter-Indonesia*), to begin planning the institutions of the state which would take over from the Dutch. In general the proposals which emerged from this, and from the work of a technical committee set up to complete a draft constitution, were embodied in the 1949 draft Constitution of the Republic of the United States of Indonesia (*RUSI*). This was issued as an Annex to the agreements reached during the Round Table Conference at the Hague (23 August to 2 November 1949), granting Indonesia "unconditionally and irrevocably" sovereignty over the whole territory of the former Netherlands East Indies. The Constitution was entirely the work of the two Indonesian factions, republican and federalist, but the Dutch expressed their approval. It was an unbalanced, and, as it was to transpire almost at once, an unworkable structure that the new Constitution envisaged. Since Indonesia had won unconditional independence, it was not of course in any way binding on her.

The main provisions were as follows. There was to be a President, who would act as Head of State, and had to be "an Indonesian" (art. 69). The President was "inviolable" and his Ministers responsible, jointly for the entire Government policy, and each individually for his part of it (art. 118). The Government consisted of the President and his Ministers by the provisions of art. 68. All Presidential decrees, with the exception of those nominating three cabinet formateurs, required the counter-signature of the relevant Minister or Ministers or formateurs (arts. 74 and 119). The President remained in supreme command of the armed forces, but if necessary these were to be placed under the command of a Commander-in-Chief (art. 182). There was no provision for a Vice-President, but the Cabinet had to include a Prime Minister (art. 74).

There was to be a bicameral legislature. The Senate was to have two representatives, appointed by their respective governments, from each of the 16 component states, while there were to be 150 members of the House of Representatives (or more if that number did not include at least the minimum numbers of representatives of minority ethnic groups stipulated) (arts. 80, 81, 100). The first House of Representatives was to be appointed (arts. 109-10), but elections were to be held within a year for an elected House (art. 111). The first House had no power to force the resignation of the Cabinet or individual Ministers (art. 122).

Legislation could originate from the Government, the Senate, or the House of Representatives (art. 128). Provision was made for amendment, delay, questioning, and Ministerial intervention (arts. 105, 120, 128, 129, 132, 134, 136, 138). Emergency laws with the same force as normal legislation could be enacted by the President alone (art. 139), but these had to be submitted to the Chamber within one month of enactment, and if rejected automatically lapsed (art. 140). The Constitution could be amended by two-thirds majorities in both chambers (art. 190).

This Constitution was in operation only from 27 December 1949 to 17 August 1950. Its defects were obvious. The state of Riau, with about 100,000 inhabitants, had the same Senate representation as the Republic of Indonesia, with 300 times the population. In the House of Representatives the Republic had fewer seats than she would have been entitled to if members had been allocated in proportion to population. Nationalists, especially from the Republic, saw it as an attempt by the Dutch to perpetuate their hegemony by tactics of divide and rule.

Sukarno was elected President by the delegates of the 16 component states, in accordance with art. 69, on 16 December 1949, and on 20 December the new Cabinet was sworn in, with Hatta as Prime Minister. In the following months the federal system rapidly fell into decay as member state after member state opted to merge with the Republic of Indonesia. The momentum of the movement was sustained by the known unitary preferences of the President, the Prime Minister, the majority of the Cabinet, and many leaders even of the "federalist" states.

On 19 May 1950, leaders of the Federal Government (acting for the only two remaining Dutch-sponsored states) and leaders of the Republic of Indonesia agreed on the essentials of a new unitary state to replace the existing structure. It was also agreed that Sukarno should be President of the new state. The House of Representatives of *RUSI* and the Working Committee of *KNIP* were to draw up a new Constitution, on the basis of the 1949 document, but incorporating the basic provisions of the Constitution of 1945. For the following two months delegates worked on the detail of a new provisional Constitution, a task completed by 20 July 1950. Once ratified by the respective legislatures, this document was signed for the two parties on 15 August, and came into operation on the fifth anniversary of the proclamation of independence in 1945, 17 August.

It differed in important respects from the federal Constitution which had preceded it. It was unicameral, sovereignty being exercised by the Government and the Chamber of Representatives (art. 1). There was to be a Vice-President, appointed on the first occasion by the President on the recommendation of the Chamber of Representatives (art. 45). The President was specifically given the power to dissolve the Chamber of Representatives (art. 84), which he had lacked under the 1949 dispensations, but this power was circumscribed by the additional provision that his decree of dissolution had also to order the holding of elections for a new Chamber within 30 days. The Presidential supreme authority over the armed forces, reiterated in art. 127, was limited by art. 85 which made it imperative for military decrees to be counter-signed by the responsible Minister.

The Chamber of Representatives in the first place was to be made up of the *RUSI* House and Senate, plus the members of the Working Comittee of *KNIP* and the Supreme Advisory Council (art. 77). Subsequently, at general elections, there was to be one representative for each 300,000 Indonesians (arts. 56-7), and the provisions allowing for a minimum representation of minority ethnic groups (nine Chinese, six Europeans, three Arabs) were retained from the 1949 document.

Generally speaking, the provisions governing the legislative procedure were very much as in the Constitution of 1949, with the necessary modifications to allow for the disappearance of the Senate (arts. 64, 89-92, 94-5). The Chamber of Representatives was not specifically barred from forcing the Cabinet or any member of it to resign. This was generally taken as tacit under-writing of full Cabinet responsibility in the western European manner. The usual guarantees of individual liberties and welfare were incorporated. The Preamble, as with that of 1949, echoed Sukarno's *panča šila*.

The 1950 Constitution was, as originally envisaged, intended to be simply provisional, like its predecessors, pending the election of a Constituent Assembly to devise the permanent Constitution. But in fact it remained in operation until suspended in 1959.

An important source of operational friction lay in the disproportion between the duties of the President according to the Constitution and the personality, calibre and standing of its holder. As Head of State, Sukarno was theoretically confined to the kinds of activities open to a constitutional monarch in western Europe. But he was also undisputed leader of a long and arduous national revolution, invested thereby with tremendous prestige and capable of quite unique command of the loyalty of the mass of the people. It was impossible to keep him out of the political process to the extent that the Constitution assumed. His frequent policy speeches, critical of other parts of the state machine, were often taken as governmental pronouncements, and could seriously embarrass the Cabinet, who need not have been apprised in advance of their contents. If conflict developed between Cabinet and President it was the Cabinet that had to go. The President was in permanent occupation, inviolable by the terms of the Constitution (art. 83), had the power to dissolve the Chamber of Representatives, and was secure in the knowledge that nowhere in the Constitution (unlike that of 1949) was there any definition of "government".

Another serious impediment to the smooth working of the institutions devised was the increasing development of personal strains among the *dramatis personae*. The 1945-9 Government had functioned as well as it had done partly because of the intense pressure to which it was unremittingly subjected. Personal differences were secondary to the overall objective of independence. With the unifying factor of Dutch persecution gone, divergences of viewpoint and incompatibilities revealed themselves.

Another weakness lay in the great number and frequent irresponsibility of the political parties. Before the elections of 1955, of the 236 seats in the Chamber of Representatives, no party ever held more than 52. Party discipline was almost completely lacking. The views of party members in a Cabinet and their colleagues in the national organization often diverged. Parties not represented in the Cabinet did not function as a restrained, constructive, responsibie opposition, but in their actions suggested that habits of obstruction acquired in the long and bitter fight against the Dutch had become ingrained. The Cabinet time and again found itself under the necessity of acting by emergency decree in order to clear arrears of legislation over the heads of the Chamber (which had, of course, to ratify in its next session, but this it usually did).

In this kind of situation, a great deal depended on personalities, their mutual compatibility, and in particular their relations with the one permanent feature of the political landscape—President Sukarno. No cabinet lasted longer than two years, and most a good deal less than that.

It is noteworthy that in his speeches and writings over many years Sukarno had made plain that his view of democracy did not coincide with western parliamentary, or even with American presidential, democracy. In 1949, Sukarno was talking about "Eastern democracy . . . Indonesian democracy . . . a democracy with leadership" (cited in Feith, *op. cit.*, 38-9). On 10 November 1956, when he saw that not even the elections of the previous year had produced a stable Chamber of Representatives, he first broached his concept of "guided democracy". Early the following year, on 21 February 1957, he made public in greater detail his proposals for radically reforming Indonesian political institutions.

However, Sukarno's major concern in mooting guided democracy was that western democracy, with its counting of heads and statistical majorities, was not in accordance with traditional Indonesian patterns of decision making, expressed in the terms *musjawarah* (deliberation, discussion), *mufakat* (agreement, deliberation), and *gotong rojong* (mutual aid, co-operation). The first implies that the leader should act only after consultation with those led, and that his leadership should consist of guidance rather than dictation. The second has the connotation of decision reached not through majority, but by final arrival at the general will, the greatest attainable degree of consensus. The third emphasizes the co-operative aspects of economic and social life, and is implicitly critical of arrangements which encourage or condone the clash of vested interests, the spirit of competition, and the thrust of individualism.

Sukarno's political role, so circumscribed by the *letter* of the 1950 Constitution, as compared with that of 1945, grew progressively more significant and direct. The essence of his proposals was that the Cabinet should represent a broad cross-section of the parties, including the communists, and that it should work with a National Council, which would include key ministers, and representatives of different interest groups in Indonesian society—trade unions, youth movements, religions, artists, farmers and peasants, journalists, women, veterans of the revolution, foreign-born citizens, Indonesian business circles, the armed forces, and the outer islands. It would be the task of the National Council to advise the President and the Cabinet and to make recommendations.

His suggestions met with resistance, and regional rebellions, which had since Independence fitfully erupted and subsided, now flared. A state of War and Siege was declared, giving recognition to the exercise of civil authority by regional military commanders. As Sukarno was unable to find a politician who could form a Cabinet on his principles, he himself stepped in and established a "National Caretaker Cabinet" under a respected non-party man, Dr. Djuanda Kartawidjaja. Two of the members of the Cabinet were reputed to be sympathetic to the Indonesian Communist Party (*PKI*). The National Council, nominated by the President, further strengthened his hand. Although Djuanda told the Chamber of Representatives that the Cabinet, as before, would continue to be responsible to it, clearly a major change in the role and power of the Presidency had taken place.

In 1958 a revolt in Sumatra offered the most serious challenge yet to Sukarno, and an alternative Cabinet and Government were formed. The legitimate Government succeeded in crushing this revolt, and in the process effectively cleared its path of the individuals and parties hostile to it who had been unwise enough to become implicated. The Army, under the leadership of General Nasution, confirmed its growing authority and influence. The *PKI*, on the other hand, had shown in regional elections in Java that its strength, too, was increasing.

Sukarno now favoured a return to the Constitution of 1945, with its basically presidential pattern. After considerable discussion and pressure, the Cabinet accepted his demand in December 1958. When the elected Consultative Assembly, whose function was the enactment of a permanent Constitution to replace that of 1950, failed to endorse the return to that of 1945, it was dissolved. The President re-introduced the 1945 Constitution by decree on 5 July 1959.

In March 1960 the elected Chamber of Representatives was dissolved, and an appointed *gotong rojong* (mutual co-operation) one took its place. President Sukarno formed a new Cabinet, with a Chief Minister, Dr. Djuanda, but he himself added the Premiership to his other roles as President, Supreme Commander of the Armed Forces, Chairman of the Supreme Advisory Council (the name by which the National Council came to be styled), and Chairman of the National Planning Council. Parties which could not accept the new circumstances were banned. Civil servants were forbidden to join political parties. The formation of a National Front was announced.

The present (February 1963) Indonesian Constitution is, therefore, the one with which Indonesia embarked in August 1945. The personal primacy of Sukarno has been recognized and endorsed by making of the Presidency the key political institution, wielding executive and legislative power, the former with the assistance of Ministers appointed by and responsible to the President, the latter with the consent of the Chamber of Representatives. The President and Vice-President are responsible to the Consultative Assembly, which elects them, and in which resides the sovereignty of the people. Functional group elements are included in the Chamber of Representatives, the Consultative Assembly, and the Supreme Advisory Council. Ten political parties, including the *PKI*, have been accorded recognition. General elections, due to be held in 1962, were postponed until "after the return of Irian Barat". These would be the first elections under the 1945 Constitution.

Bibliography: in addition to references in the text: G. McT. Kahin, *Nationalism and revolution in Indonesia*, Ithaca, N.Y., 1952; J. H. A. Logemann, *Nieuwe Gegevens over het Ontstaan van de Indonesische Grondwet van 1945* (*Mededelingen der Koninklijke Nederlandse Akademie Wetenschappen, Afd.Letterkunde* Nieuwe Reeks, xxv/14 (1962), 691-712; R. Abdulgani, *Indonesia's national council: the first year*, in *Far Eastern Survey*, xxvii (July 1958), 97-104; M. Yamin (ed.), *Naskah Persiapan Undang-Undang Dasar 1945*, Djakarta 1959; B. R. O'G. Anderson, *Some aspects of Indonesian politics under the Japanese occupation, 1944-1945*, Ithaca, N.Y., 1961; *Partij en parlement; markante punten in de ontwikkeling van de democratie in Indonesië*, in *Indonesisch Bulletin* iv/3 (March 1953), Indonesische Voorlichtingsdienst, 's-Gravenhage; *Het Parlement van de Republiek Indonesia en zijn geschiedenis* in *Indonesisch Bulletin*, iii/3 (February 1952); Soekarno, *Susunan Negara Kita*, Amsterdam 1951; F. M. Pareja, *L'evoluzione politica dell'Indonesia*, in *OM*, xxxv/12 (December 1955) and xxxvii (January 1956); C. A. O. Van Nieuwenhuijze, *Aspects of Islam in Post-Colonial Indonesia*, The Hague-Bandung 1958; text of the Constitution in *OM*, xl/9 (Sept. 1960), 552-5. (J. A. M. Caldwell)

xii. — Libya

Libya proved to be the first North African country west of Egypt to be emancipated from foreign control and organized, despite her relative backwardness, as a modern constitutional state following World War II.

On 21 November 1949, the General Assembly of the United Nations passed a resolution declaring Libya, comprising the three provinces of Cyrenaica, Tripolitania and Fazzan, to be established as a united and independent state. The resolution provided likewise that Libya should have a constitution to be laid down by her people's representatives, meeting in a national assembly. The General Assembly appointed a United Nations Commissioner, Adrian Pelt, to advise Libya's national assembly in the drawing up of her constitution.

The national assembly met on 25 November 1950 and appointed a constitutional committee composed of 18 members (each province was represented by six members). The actual drafting was entrusted to a working group of six. The national assembly began its debate over the draft as soon as the constitutional committee had completed the first chapter. The assembly formally completed its work on 7 October 1951 and the constitution was promulgated on that day. A draft electoral law, based on several Arab electoral laws, was submitted to the assembly on 21 October and was adopted on 6 November 1951.

The Libyan Constitution provided the innovation of a federal system by virtue of which the three provinces of Cyrenaica, Tripolitania, and Fazzan agreed to join in a union under a single monarchy entrusted to King Idrīs I. This union proved to be a happy compromise, capable of development into a more intimate unity, as the amendment of 1962 demonstrated. Under the federal system, Libya possessed one national (federal) government and three state (provincial) governments. The powers of the national government, such as foreign affairs, defence, and matters relating jointly to the three provinces, were specifically stated; the residuary powers remained in the provinces. The national government is composed of a bi-cameral parliament, a Cabinet responsible to the Lower House, a supreme court to decide the constitutionality of laws, and a federal administrative system. Each state (provincial) government was composed of a *wālī* (governor), an executive council, a legislative assembly, provincial courts, and a provincial administrative system. The *wālī* was responsible to the King and the chief of the executive council was responsible to the provincial legislative assembly. The first amendment to the constitution, enacted in 1962, simplified this elaborate system of government by making the *wālī* responsible to the federal government and abolishing the head of the provincial executive council, making the council responsible to the *wālī*. The progress achieved under the Libyan federal system justified the steps undertaken by the national assembly to provide such an elaborate constitutional framework, without which the three provinces would, perhaps, have been unable to unite into one state, governed by one monarchical system. This system has proved to be fairly stable, for Libya has had only one sovereign since 1951, six Cabinets, and three Parliaments (1952, 1956, 1960). The Lower House proved to be quite vocal in its criticism of governmental measures and was capable of withdrawing confidence in one of the governments (1960), although Libya's parliamentary system, in the absence of a party system, was on the whole subservient to the executive.

Bibliography: United Nations, *Annual Report of the United Nations Commissioner in Libya*, New York 1950; idem, *Second Annual Report of the United Nations Commissioner in Libya*, Paris 1951; idem, *Supplementary Report to the Second Report of the United Nations Commissioner in Libya*, Paris 1952; Documentation française: *Notes et études documentaires*, no. 1606 of 28 April 1952; Government of Libya, *Proceedings of the National Assembly*, Cairo n.d.; I. R. Khalidi, *Constitutional development in Libya*, Beirut 1956; M. Khadduri, *Modern Libya: a study in political development*, Baltimore 1963, Chapters 6, 7, and 11; constitutional texts in Niḳūlā Ziyāda, *Muḥāḍarāt fī ta'rīkh Lībyā*, Cairo 1958, 193-266.

(M. KHADDURI)

xiii. — SŪDĀN

The convention of 19 January 1899 between Great Britain and Egypt, confirmed by the treaty of 26 August 1936, made the Sudan an Anglo-Egyptian condominium, but the British authorities tended, after the second world war, to lead the country towards autonomy and independence. Negotiations between Britain and Egypt were broken off on 27 January 1947, the Egyptian government making known its desire to submit "the cause of the Nile Valley in its entirety" to the Security Council.

From 1944, however, a Consultative Council of the Northern Sudan comprising 8 members nominated by the governor-general and 18 elected by the provincial councils established in the same year had been instituted. On 9 March 1948 the Consultative Council of the Northern Sudan had adopted an organic law providing for the creation of an Executive Council and a Legislative Assembly; this text, promulgated on 19 June by the governor-general, aroused protests from Egypt and the Sudanese protagonists of the unity of the Nile Valley, who refused to take part, on 15 November 1948, in the elections to the Legislative Assembly; the latter was to have included 52 elected members (for the North), 13 appointed by the provincial councils of the South, and 10 nominated by the governor-general.

In March 1951, at the request of the Assembly which had been constituted, the governor-general charged a commission of 13 members, all Sudanese, with the drafting of a Constitution, which was adopted by the Assembly on 23 April 1952 under the name of "Ordinance on Autonomy". This text was composed of a preamble and 11 chapters containing 103 articles. Chapter III deals with the governor-general and the executive, Chapter V institutes a Senate and a Chamber of Deputies; legislation is dealt with in Chap. VI, finance in Chap. VII; the following deals with the Controller-general, Chap. IX with the judicial power; a judicature administering the *sharīʿa* (art. 79) is maintained under the presidency of the Chief *ḳāḍī*; conflicts of jurisdiction are decided by a court of jurisdiction of which the Chief *ḳāḍī* and a judge of the High Court of the *sharīʿa* are members (art. 80). Chap. X creates a commission of public administration, while the last section deals with interim provisions.

This text should have become effective on 9 November 1952, but the Egyptian revolution had broken out in the meantime; on 29 October the Egyptian government had, however, published a memorandum recognizing the right of the Sudanese to self-determination, and finally the ordinance on autonomy was promulgated on 21 March 1953 after the signature of the Anglo-Egyptian agreements of 12 February envisaging amendments to be added. The Chamber of Deputies was to consist of 97 elected members, and the Senate of 30 elected and 20 appointed members; elections were therefore arranged for November-December 1953, and on 6 January 1954 the Chamber elected the president of the council who formed the first government.

After a period of transition, independence was officially proclaimed before the Senate and the Chamber of Deputies in joint plenary session on 1 January 1956. On the same date a provisional Constitution was brought into operation comprising 11 chapters and 121 articles; it largely repeats the Ordinance on Autonomy, but Chap. III is completely modified, since it now provides for the election by parliament of a supreme commission of 5 persons which is to be the highest authority in the State (art. 10-1). Chap. IV deals with the executive power of the Prime Minister, appointed by the supreme commission, which also appoints ministers. The Council of Ministers is responsible to parliament (art. 27). The legislative body (Chap. V) continues to consist of the Senate (20 members appointed by the supreme commission, 30 elected) and the Chamber of Representatives. Chap. VI deals with legislative procedure, the following chapter with finance, property, contracts and lawsuits. Chap. VIII provides for the appointment of a Controller-general of accounts by the supreme commission. Chap. IX deals with the judicial power, comprising a civil division and a *sharīʿa* division presided over by the chief *ḳāḍī* (art. 93). Art. 95 provides that the *sharīʿa* division shall consist of tribunals and shall exercise the powers provided by the ordinance of 1902 on tribunals of Sudanese Muslim law, and by modificatory laws. Chap. X treats of public offices, and the last chapter contains interim provisions.

On 22 May 1958 both chambers of parliament joined in a Constituent Assembly to examine the definitive form of the Constitution, and in spite of the opposition of the Southerners, appointed 40 members charged with preparing a new draft. The text presented did not obtain the approval of the Southerners since it provided for a unitary and not a federal State, and also because it provided that Islam should be the state religion and Arabic the official language. Finally the Constituent Assembly voted for a motion recommending that the constitutional committee should take note of the demands of the Southerners. It had however, no time to bring its deliberations to a satisfactory conclusion, since on 17 November 1958 a *coup d'état* put the government of the country in the hands of the army. The following day the high command of the armed forces published decrees by the terms of which the Sudan was a democratic republic whose supreme constitutional organ was the high command which delegated its legislative, executive and judiciary powers to General ʿAbbūd. The constitution is suspended.

Bibliography: See the accounts of the events of the dates indicated in *COC*, *OM*, *MEJ*, *MEA*, etc.; J. E. Godchot, *Les constitutions du Proche et du Moyen Orient*, Paris 1957, 345-72, and bibl. cited; P. M. Holt, *A modern history of the Sudan*, London 1961.

(ED.)

xiv. — PĀKISTĀN

Pakistan, on coming into existence on 15 August 1947, was governed by the Government of India Act 1935, as amended by the Indian Independence Act 1947, which repealed all provisions of the former statute authorizing control from England and the reserved powers of the Governors and Governor-General. The Constituent Assembly, summoned in July 1947, was not only to make new constitutional laws but also to exercise the powers of the Federal Legislature under the Act of 1935. Pakistan commenced as a federal state; in addition to the former British Indian territory, within the territory of Pakistan were the princely states of Bahawalpur and Khairpur (Bahāwalpūr, Khayrpūr [*qq.v.*]), the Balūčistān states, and the N.W. Frontier states. The Independence Act had broken the link between these states and the Crown but they executed instruments of accession to Pakistan, surrendering powers over defence, foreign affairs and communications.

Legislative subject-matter was distributed between the centre and the Governor's provinces by three lists, one enumerating matters within the exclusive competence of the Constituent Assembly, another matters exclusively assigned to the provincial legislatures, and a third matters over which power was concurrent, though central legislation would prevail in case of repugnancy, unless assented to by the Governor-General. Administrative power generally covered the same field as legislative power, though most matters on the concurrent list were within the provincial power and the centre could direct a province to act as the instrumentality for execution of its laws and to take prescribed steps for the construction and maintenance of communications. Distribution of powers between the centre and the states was determined by their instruments of accession.

At the centre the Governor-General, though appointed by the Crown, was nominated by the Government. The Governor-General appointed the Provincial Governors. Ministers were appointed by the Governor-General and Governors; they could hold office for 10 months without being members of the appropriate Assembly. The Governor-General and the Governors could legislate by Ordinance when the appropriate legislature was not in session. The Governor-General could proclaim an emergency, if faced with a threat of war, rebellion, or mass-movement of population, which would have the effect of extending the federal power to all provincial matters; he could also, if he thought the security of Pakistan in danger or the provincial constitution could not be worked, direct the Governor to assume, as his deputy, all the executive and legislative powers of the Province.

The High Court at Lahore, the Chief Court at Karachi and the Judicial Commissioner in N. W. Frontier and Balūčistān were, when Pakistan became independent, the highest tribunals in the provinces in which they were situated. A High Court at Dacca (Dhākā) for East Bengal and a new Federal Court were created. To the powers of the latter under the Government of India Act 1935 were transferred the appellate jurisdiction of the Privy Council by statutes passed in 1949 and 1950.

In 1952 a draft constitution was presented to the Constituent Assembly but discussion was postponed until September 1953 in the hope of reconciling conflicting views regarding it.

Before this constitution could be finalized, the Governor-General dismissed the Constituent Assembly on 25 October 1954 and litigation followed, resulting in this action being upheld. A fresh Constituent Assembly was summoned and first met on 5 July 1955. On 30 September it enacted the Establishment of West Pakistan Act which came into force on 14 October, integrating the territories of the west wing into a single province and amalgamating the High Court of Lahore, the Chief Court of Sind and the judicial commissioners in N. W. Frontier and Balūčistān into a single High Court.

The Constitution of the Islamic Republic of Pakistan came into force on 2 March 1956. It was federal, in so far as relations between the centre and the two provinces were concerned. Legislative and administrative powers were distributed as before, save that the provincial power was to some degree enhanced by the transfer of some powers to the provincial list and by giving the provinces power over matters not enumerated in any list. The centre had exclusive power to impose certain taxes. All other taxing powers were assigned to the provinces, which were also entitled to a share in the proceeds of income tax, purchase tax and some export and excise duties, all imposed by the centre. Grants to provinces were also contemplated. These and the provincial shares in distributable taxes were appropriated on the advice of a National Finance Commission, consisting of the finance ministers of the Federation and the Provinces sitting with other members appointed by the President in consultation with the Governors.

The head of the state was styled "President"; he was to be elected by the members of the central and provincial legislatures; it was necessary that he should be a Muslim and not less than 40 years of age. His term of office was five years and he could not be elected more than twice. He was liable to impeachment by a resolution supported by three-quarters of the members of the National Assembly. The Constitution contemplated that he would generally act on the advice of his ministers. He was obliged to appoint as Prime Minister the person most likely to command the confidence of a majority of the members of the National Assembly. Though he held office at the pleasure of the President, he could not be dismissed unless the President was satisfied that he had lost that confidence. Other ministers were appointed and removed by the President, but any minister who for six consecutive months was not a member of the National Assembly ceased to be a minister. The Prime Minister was obliged to communicate to the President all administrative decisions of the minister, all proposals for legislation and any further information called for by the President, who could insist on a decision by an individual minister being reviewed by the whole cabinet. The purpose was to ensure collective responsibility of the ministers to the National Assembly.

All legislatures were unicameral. The National Assembly was composed of 150 members from each wing and, for the first ten years, five seats in each wing were to be reserved for women. A candidate for election had to be 25 or older and qualified for the franchise, *i.e.*, he had to be a citizen of Pakistan, of sound mind, not subject to any disqualification and resident in the constituency for which he was enrolled. The National Assembly had a maximum life of five years; it was summoned, prorogued and dismissed by the President; two sessions in each year with a maximum of six months between sessions were obligatory. The Assembly elected a speaker and deputy speaker and was empowered to make its own rules of procedure. Ordinary legislation was passed by a simple majority, bills being presented to the President, who could assent, veto or return a bill for reconsideration. The veto could be overruled by a two-thirds majority and the President was obliged to assent to a reconsidered bill, passed by a simple majority, with or without amendment. The initiative in all financial matters was vested in the Executive. No bill or amendment dealing with taxation or appropriation or involving expenditure from the revenues of the Federation could be moved except on the President's recommendation.

The President could legislate by Ordinance in emergencies, if the National Assembly was not in session; such legislation was subject to the same constitutional limitations as Acts of the National Assembly but would expire six weeks after the commencement of the next session of the National Assembly or earlier if disapproved by the National Assembly.

The powers to declare a national emergency and suspend a provincial constitution were retained but proclamations for that purpose had to be approved by the National Assembly. A new emergency power was created, to proclaim a financial emergency if the President was satisfied that financial stability was endangered; this also required the approval of the National Assembly. The effect of the first two powers was the same as before. The effect of the third was to empower the centre to control financial business in the Provinces.

The pattern of the central executive and legislature was reproduced in the Provinces with slight differences. The Governor occupied a position comparable to the President but was appointed by the President, holding office at his pleasure but normally continuing for five years. It was essential that he should have attained the age of 40 but not that he should be a Muslim. Corresponding to the Prime Minister was a Chief Minister. Each Provincial Assembly had 300 members with 10 extra seats for women for the first 10 years. Nobody could be a member of the National Assembly and a Provincial Assembly.

There was no distribution of judicial power. The Federal Court became the Supreme Court. It had original jurisdiction in disputes between Provinces and between the Federation and a Province. Appeals lay from the High Courts on constitutional matters, in civil cases involving property worth Rs. 15,000 or certified to involve an important legal point and in criminal cases where a sentence of death or transportation for life had been passed in appeal from an acquittal to a High Court or by a High Court in the exercise of its extraordinary original jurisdiction, or when a High Court certified it fit for appeal, or from commitments for contempt. The Supreme Court could also grant special leave to appeal from any order of any judicial or quasi-judicial tribunal other than a court martial. It also had an advisory jurisdiction to give an opinion on any point of law referred to it by the President. The High Courts' previous powers and jurisdiction were continued and they were empowered to issue writs for the protection of a Fundamental Right and "for any other purpose", which, as interpreted, meant in any matter where justice called for action and the petitioner had no adequate alternative remedy. The Supreme Court was also empowered to issue writs but only to protect a Fundamental Right. A Supreme Court Judge was only removable on an address supported by two-thirds of the members voting in the National Assembly; a High Court Judge could be removed on a report of the Supreme Court after enquiry.

A feature of the 1956 Constitution was its chapter on Fundamental Rights, which included a guaranteed legal remedy against any law infringing a Fundamental Right. This chapter demanded equality before the law and prohibited discrimination in respect of access to places of public resort and in appointment to government service on grounds of religion, caste, sex, place of birth or residence. No person could be deprived of life or liberty save by authority of law, and punishment under a retroactive law was forbidden. A person arrested on a criminal charge had a right to be informed of the grounds of his arrest, a right to production before a magistrate within 24 hours and a right to consult and be defended by a pleader of his own choice. A person preventively detained had a right to the grounds of detention, a right to make a representation and, in case of prolonged detention, a right of recourse to an advisory board. Citizens were, subject to conditions, entitled to freedom of speech, assembly, association, movement, residence, religion and freedom to follow a profession and deal with property. Expropriation of agricultural land or any interest in a commercial undertaking, except for public purposes, under a statute providing fair compensation, was forbidden. Religious denominations could maintain religious institutions and provide religious instruction in their educational institutions. No person could be denied admission to an educational institution on grounds of race, religion, caste or place of birth but no student could be obliged to participate in activities connected with any religion but his own.

There was also a chapter of Directive Principles, not enforceable in the courts, but intended to be followed by the executives and legislatures. They enjoined the promotion of social uplift and the promotion of economic well-being. Steps were to be taken to strengthen the bonds between Muslim countries, to promote international peace, to enable Muslims to lead their lives in accordance with Islamic principles, to see that Islamic institutions were properly managed, and to provide facilities for instruction in the religion of Islam.

Another chapter forbade the enactment of any law repugnant to the injuctions of Islam and the revision of the existing law to bring it into conformity with those injunctions. To effect these purposes a Commission was to be appointed to define the injunctions of Islam and to recommend measures for their enforcement, but an Act of the National Assembly would be necessary to implement any recommendation made. Nothing effective appears to have been accomplished in the exercise of these functions.

On 7 October 1958 the Constitution of 1956 was abrogated by the President, who placed the country under martial law. All legislatures were dismissed and political parties dissolved. The President exercised the federal executive and legislative functions, assisted by ministers appointed by him and responsible to him alone. Provincial Governors exercised the powers they would have had under the Constitution of 1956 on the suspension of a provincial constitution, but subject to control by the Martial Law Authorities. At first the distribution of powers was continued but in 1959 all matters on the provincial list were transferred to the concurrent list. The statute law previously in force was continued and protected from attack as repugnant to a Fundamental Right. The acts of the Martial Law Authorities were protected from review by the courts, whose powers, except to the extent indicated, remained intact.

It was not intended that the Martial Law experience was to continue indefinitely. In 1959 the Basic Democracies Order was promulgated, creating a hierarchy of local government boards, town and union committees, district committees and divisional councils. In the lowest tier at least two-thirds of the members were elected by persons formerly entitled to vote at elections to the legislatures, but the Sub-divisional Officer was chairman of the *thānā* or *taḥṣīl* committee, and in the higher tiers the elected element would be diluted.

In January 1960 the members of local councils elected under the Basic Democracies Order were required to declare by secret ballot whether or not they had confidence in the President. If the majority showed confidence, the President would take steps for the promulgation of a new constitution under which he would be deemed to have been elected President for the first term.

The election having gone in the President's favour, he appointed a commission to make recommendations for the new Constitution. It was promulgated on 1 March 1962. There are at the centre the President, Ministers and a National Assembly and a Governor, Ministers and a Provincial Assembly in each province but it would be difficult to maintain that the Constitution is federal in fact. There is a list of central subjects. All other matters are within the provincial power, but the National Assembly may encroach on the provincial field on the grounds that the security of Pakistan demands it or that uniformity is necessary throughout Pakistan. It is no longer possible to impugn a law as *ultra vires* the enacting legislature, and the rule that, in case of conflict, a central law prevails over a provincial law is of universal application.

After the expiry of Field-Marshal Ayyūb Khān's term of office, the President, who must be a Muslim and have attained 35 years, will be elected by an Electoral College, composed of one Elector chosen by each electoral unit, of which there are 40,000 in each Province. The President's term is five years; he is liable to be impeached for violation of the Constitution or gross misconduct, or removed for incapacity, by a resolution supported by three-quarters of all members of the National Assembly. But any such motion is discouraged by the threat that, if half the members do not support the resolution, those who gave notice of the motion will cease to be members of the Assembly.

The executive capital is Islāmābād and the legislative capital Dacca (Dhākā). Presidential government replaces parliamentary government, for the President appoints the Ministers, and may remove them without assigning reasons; they cease to hold office on a change of President. The original intention was that they should not be members of the National Assembly, but this is no longer compulsory.

The National Assembly, elected by members of the Electoral College, will consist of 156 members, half from each wing, from which three seats will be reserved for women. It has a maximum life of 5 years. It can be summoned not only by the President but also by the Speaker at the request of one-third of all the members. If summoned by the President, it is prorogued by the President; if the Speaker summons it, he prorogues.

The President dismisses the National Assembly, but he may not do so if the unexpired portion of its term is less than 120 days or before a vote on a motion to impeach or remove him. The President ceases to hold office 126 days after the dissolution of the Assembly, unless his successor has earlier entered on his office. In case of disagreement between the President and the National Assembly, the President may refer the matter to the Electoral College. As under the 1956 Constitution, the President may assent to or veto a Bill or return it for reconsideration; if he takes either the second or third course and the Bill is again passed by a two-thirds majority of all members, he may refer the matter to the Electoral College, where he may be overruled by a simple majority of the total membership.

The President retains the power to legislate by Ordinance when the National Assembly is not in session. If the Ordinance is approved by the National Assembly, it is deemed to become an Act of the Assembly; in any other case it expires 180 days after promulgation or 42 days after the Assembly next meets, whichever is less. The President is also empowered to issue a proclamation of general emergency in the same circumstance as previously and it must be laid before the Assembly, which has no power to disapprove. While this proclamation is in force, the President may legislate by Ordinance, whether the Assembly is sitting or not. The Ordinance, must be laid before the Assembly, which has no power to disapprove. If it approves, the Ordinance is deemed to be an Act of the Assembly; in any other case it ceases to have affect when the President withdraws the proclamation.

Under the 1956 Constitution the power of the National Assembly to refuse demands for grants, except to meet expenditure charged on the revenues of Pakistan, was a powerful instrument whereby the legislature could control the executive, but under the 1962 Constitution the Assembly cannot refuse a demand for recurring expenditure, including an increase up to 10% of the expenditure incurred in the previous year.

As before, the pattern of the executive and legislature in a province is similar to that at the centre, but the Governor is appointed by the President and is subject to his directions; he may be removed at any time without reasons being assigned. Provincial ministers hold office at the Governor's pleasure but cannot be removed without the President's concurrence.

Each Provincial Assembly, elected by members of the Electoral College, consists of 150 members, five seats being reserved for women. Its maximum term is five years. In case of conflict with the Governor, he or the Speaker may request a reference to the National Assembly; if the National Assembly decides in favour of the Governor, then and only then can the Governor dismiss the Provincial Assembly. The Governor's powers to legislate by Ordinance can only be exercised when the Provincial Assembly is not in session and, *mutatis mutandis*, resemble the powers of the President.

The Supreme Court no longer has powers to issue writs, and its appellate jurisdiction is limited to appeals from a High Court; while it still may grant special leave to appeal, an appeal only lies as of right against a sentence of death or transportation for life imposed by a High Court, a committal for contempt by such court, or on its certificate that a substantial question of constitutional law is involved. The High Courts have also lost their writ jurisdiction, but, where there is no adequate remedy, they may declare an act of a public authority illegal and direct such authority to act in conformity with law. A High Court may also satisfy itself as to the legality of the custody in which any person is held and the right of an incumbent to hold public office.

The old Fundamental Rights, revised and restated, appear in the guise of Principles of Law Making and the Directive Principles as Principles of Policy, but they are only binding on the consciences of legislators and public officials; no law can be impugned as violative of the Principles of

Law Making and no official act can be declared invalid as violating a Principle of Policy.

One Principle of Law Making is that no law shall be repugnant to Islam, and it is provided that any legislature, the President or a Governor may refer a proposed law to the Advisory Council of Islamic Ideology for opinion as to whether it violates any of the Principles. The members of this Council are appointed by the President, having regard to their understanding and appreciation of Islam and the economic, legal and administrative problems of Pakistan; they hold office for three years. Apart from the function indicated above, they may make recommendations to the Governments on means of encouraging Muslims to live in accordance with Islamic principles. When a question of repugnancy of a proposed law to a Principle of Law Making is referred to the Council by the President or a Governor, he must inform the Assembly of the date on which the advice is expected, but, if the Assembly, the President or the Governor thinks immediate action necessary in the public interest, the law may be enacted before the advice is furnished.

Bibliography: K. Callard, *Pakistan, a political study*, London 1957; *Report of the Constitution Commission, Pakistan*, Karachi 1962; A. K. Brohi, *Fundamental Law of Pakistan*, Karachi 1958; A. Gledhill, *Pakistan : the development of its laws and constitution*, London 1957; K. J. Newman, *Essays on the Constitution of Pakistan*, Dacca [1956], gives a survey of the constitutional movement, the text of the draft and the text adopted in 1956, with authoritative comments and an extensive bibliography; see also A. Chapy, *L'Islam dans la Constitution du Pakistan*, in *Orient*, iii (July 1957), 120-7. On the Constitution of 1962, see A. Guimbretière, *La nouvelle Constitution du Pakistan*, in *Orient*, xxiv (1962/4), 29-47 and the bibl. there given. Text of the new Constitution: *The Constitution of the Republic of Pakistan*, Karachi 1962, 134 pp.

(A. Gledhill)

xv. — Mauretania

On 28 September 1958 the Mauretanian people approved the French draft Constitution submitted to referendum, and chose adherence to the *Communauté*; on 28 November of the same year the Territorial Assembly opted for the status of Member State of the *Communauté*, proclaimed the Islamic Republic of Mauretania, and transformed itself into a Constituent Assembly. A committee prepared a draft which was adopted by the Assembly on 22 March 1959. This first Constitution comprised a preamble and 9 chapters, containing 53 articles. In the preamble the Mauretanian people proclaims its attachment to its religion, its traditions, to the rights of man and the principles of democracy. Art. 2 declares that Islam is the religion of the Mauretanian people, but guarantees to everyone freedom of conscience. National sovereignty belongs to the people, who exercise it through their representatives and by way of referendum. Chap. II treats of the government, which is composed of the Prime Minister and other ministers. The Prime Minister decides and carries out the policy of the State, exercises the power of making regulations, ensures the execution of the laws, appoints to offices of the state, negotiates and concludes agreements with the *Communauté* (art. 12), appoints the members of the government and dismisses them (art. 13). Before entering into office members of the government must take an oath according to a formula designed only for Muslims. Chap. III relates to the National Assembly, which holds the legislative power (art. 17) and is elected for five years (art. 18). The deputies enjoy parliamentary immunity (art. 19) and take the oath in a prescribed form, although the text only defines these forms in the case of Muslim deputies (art. 21). Chapter IV deals with the relations between the government and the Assembly; chap. V treats of the constitutional commission, chap. VI with justice: provisionally, the control of justice is in the domain of the competence of the *Communauté* (art. 43), but the civil courts of Muslim law are to conduct enquiries and dispense justice according to this law in all civil and commercial matters. The organization of these courts is to be determined by law. Laws shall be introduced to codify the rules of Muslim law applicable in the Islamic Republic of Mauretania (art. 44). A High Court is provided for by art. 45. Chap. VII deals with territorial entities, which are the district and the parish; chap. VIII provides for the procedure to be followed for the revision of the Constitution, and chap. IX contains interim provisions.

The National Assembly elected on 17 May 1959 took office and prepared a new constitutional text necessitated by the accession of Mauretania to independence. This text was promulgated on 20 May 1961. It consists of a preamble and nine chapters including 61 articles. In comparison with the Constitution of 22 March 1959 it presents noticeable differences especially in the new provisions which relate to the President of the Republic, who is endowed with very extensive powers. He must be of the Muslim religion (art. 10); elected for five years by direct universal suffrage (art. 13), he takes the oath before the National Assembly in a prescribed form (art. 16). As holder of the executive power (art. 12) he decides the general policies of the nation and selects the ministers, who are responsible to him (art. 17); he possesses, moreover, the power of enacting regulations (art. 18), commands the armed forces (art. 20), signs and ratifies treaties (art. 22), and exercises the right of pardon (art. 23). In case of imminent danger he takes the exceptional steps required by the circumstances (art. 25). It is he also who declares a state of war or a state of emergency (art. 42).

Chap. III is devoted to the National Assembly, elected for five years and invested with the legislative power (arts. 26-7). Deputies enjoy parliamentary immunity (art. 29). Chap. IV deals with the relations between the President of the Republic and the Assembly, especially on matters which fall within the orbit of the law (art. 33) and those which refer to the power of regulation (art. 35). The President of the Republic may, with the authority of the Assembly, take measures by decree which are normally within the purview of the law (art. 36). The initiation of laws belongs to the President of the Republic and the members of the Assembly (art. 37). The President promulgates the laws and arranges for their publication in the Official Gazette within 15 days, during which time he has the power to refer back the draft or the proposal to the Assembly for a second reading. According to chap. V, international treaties and agreements can only be ratified by virtue of a law (art. 44). Chap. VI establishes the independence of the judiciary (art. 47), which dispenses justice in the name of the people. The superior council of the magistracy assists the president of the Republic (art. 50). The Supreme Court receives the declarations of candidates for the presidency of the Republic (art. 13), declares when the Presidency is vacant (art. 24), and decides in case of dispute on the regularity of the election of deputies (art. 28), and scrutinizes the constitutionality of laws (arts. 41, 45); it also scrutinizes the correct functioning of the referendum and publishes its results. Its other powers, its composition, its rules of procedure and the procedure which are applicable before it are fixed by law (art. 51). In the case of high treason the President of the Republic and the ministers may be impeached by the National Assembly and sent before the High Court. Chapter VII concerns parishes, administered by elected councils. The following chapter provides for the procedure of revising the Constitution, and the last contains interim provisions.

Bibliography: Documentation française, *Notes et études documentaires*, no. 2687 of 29 July 1960. (CH. PELLAT)

xvi. — KUWAYT

On 16 November 1962 the *amīr* of Kuwayt published the first Constitution of the amīrate, voted by a Constituent Assembly who had spent the previous two months examining a draft prepared by specialists. Discussion had been lively, and many articles had been accepted only after long discussion. The discussion which holds most interest for Islamic scholars is that which arose on art. 2, which provides that "the State religion is Islam, and the *sharīʿa* an essential source of legislation"; some members wished to say *the* essential source, and their opponents had to struggle to make them admit the impossibility of applying Islamic law to the letter (which for example provides that the thief is to have his hands cut off) and its incompatability with the needs of a modern State as regards banks, insurance and other financial institutions.

This Constitution thus declares in its first articles that Kuwayt is an independent and sovereign Arab State, that its people are part of the Arab nation, that Islam is the State religion and that the *sharīʿa* is an essential source of legislation, but that all religions are protected provided that they do not disturb public order and morals. Art. 6, which declared that "property, capital and labour are fundamental elements of the social structure of the State" also gave rise to an acrimonious discussion, and the individual right of ownership was finally guaranteed. The nation is the source of all power, and the head of the State is a prince descended from the *amīr* Mubārak Āl Ṣabbāḥ. Freedom of opinion and expression is recognized completely. Art. 31, which stipulates that "no one may be arrested, imprisoned, subjected to search or to house arrest, deprived of his right to choose his residence or to move about freely, except in conformity with the law, and no one may be subjected to torture or any treatment contrary to human dignity", was also fiercely debated, some wishing to allow torture in order to protect society. Art. 43 recognizes the right of citizens to join parties and allows the formation of trade unions. The State aids aged and sick citizens and those incapable of work.

Arts. 54-8, dealing with the head of State, provide for an intermediate stage between presidential rule and parliamentary rule. The *amīr* exercises executive power through the intermediacy of his ministers; with the approval of a third of its members he may dissolve the National Assembly, which is invested with the legislative power. (ED.)

xvii. — MOROCCO

The latest of the Constitutions of Muslim countries to come into being is that of Morocco, made public by the king on 18 November 1962 and approved by referendum on 7 December of the same year. It represented the fruition of the "Charter of Public Liberties" which, promulgated on 8 May 1958 by king Muḥammad V, announced the setting up of a constitutional monarchy, and of the "Fundamental Law" issued on 2 June 1961 by his son and successor Ḥasan II, which prepared the way for the promulgation of a Constitution. This consists of a preamble and twelve sections divided into 110 articles.

The preamble declares that the Kingdom of Morocco is a Muslim State the language of which is Arabic, that it constitutes a part of the Great Maghrib, and is an African State.

Section I defines Morocco as "a constitutional, democratic and social monarchy" in which "sovereignty belongs to the nation, which exercises it directly by referendum and indirectly through the medium of constitutional institutions", *i.e.*, the King, Parliament and the government. Article 3 envisages the existence of political parties and declares that "there cannot be a sole party in Morocco". The equality of all Moroccans before the law is assured (art. 5), as well as freedom of worship for all, Islam being, however, the State religion (art. 6). The Constitution accords equal political rights to men and women (art. 8), and guarantees to all citizens freedom of movement, opinion, expression, association, meeting, membership of a trade union and a political party (art. 9) as well as the basic rights, including the right to strike and the right to own property (arts. 14-5).

Section II, devoted to the King, accords him a preponderant place and lays down that his person is inviolable and sacrosanct (art. 23); as the "symbol of the unity of the nation" he bears the title of *amīr al-muʾminīn* and is the guardian of Islam and of the Constitution (art. 19). Succession to the crown is assured to "male descendents in the direct line and by primogeniture" (art. 20); the King presides over all councils of State (arts. 25, 32, 33, 86, 96), appoints to civil and military offices, commands the armed forces (art. 30), accredits ambassadors and ratifies treaties (art. 31), has the right to pardon (art. 34) and possesses four essential prerogatives: he appoints and dismisses the Prime Minister and members of the government (art. 24), has the right to submit to a referendum any bill or draft law after discussion in parliament (arts. 26, 72-4), can dissolve the chamber of representatives (arts. 27, 77, 79), and finally, in case of grave danger, has the right to proclaim a state of emergency (art. 35).

Section III deals with Parliament, which consists of the Chamber of Representatives, elected for four years by direct universal suffrage (art. 44), and the Chamber of Councillors, elected for six years and renewable by halves every three years; two-thirds of this chamber consist of members elected, in each prefecture and province, by a college composed of members of the prefectoral and provincial assemblies and of communal councils, the remaining third being elected by the chambers of agriculture, commerce, industry and handicrafts, and by the trade unions (art. 45). The list of matters reserved for parliamentary legislation is relatively restricted (art. 48), while the range of administrative regulation is extensive (art. 49). The right to initiate laws belongs to the prime minister and to members of parliament (art. 55).

Section IV deals with the government, which is responsible to the King and to the Chamber of Representatives (art. 65); it is responsible for the execution of laws, controls the administration (art. 66), and exercises a regulatory power over matters which are not the concern of the law (art. 68).

Section V regulates the relations between King and Parliament and between the latter and the government. The Chamber of Representatives can overthrow the government either by a motion of no confidence (art. 80) or by a vote of censure (art. 81).

Section VI lays down the principle of the independence of the judicial power and sets up a High Council of Judiciary. According to the provisions of Section VII members of the government can be impeached by the Chamber of Representatives and sent before the High Court of Justice. Section VIII deals with provincial and local government, and Section IX with the Higher Council for national development and planning. Section X treats of the constitutional chamber and the Supreme Court. Section XI provides for the possibility of revising the Constitution, but art. 108 declares that "the monarchic form of the State and the provisions relating to the Muslim religion cannot be the object of any constitutional revision". Finally, Section XII contains transitional provisions.

Bibliography: *La Pensée*, Rabat, i/2 (1962); Italian version in *OM*, xlii/12 (1962), 909-16.

(Ch. Pellat)

xviii. — Federal constitutions

The year 1958 was marked by three attempts to create unions or federations of Arab states: on 1 February, the United Arab Republic (*al-Djumhūriyya al-ʿarabiyya al-muttaḥida*) of Egypt and Syria; on 8 March, the United Arab States (*al-Duwal al-ʿarabiyya al-muttaḥida*), of the United Arab Republic (but more particularly the former Egypt) and the Yemen; on 14 February, the Arab Union (*al-Ittiḥād al-ʿarabī*), of ʿIrāḳ and Jordan. All three were ephemeral, but they lasted a sufficiently long time for them to provide themselves with federal constitutions, drafted within a remarkably short time.

Reference has already been made (*supra*, iii, Egypt) to the constitution of the UAR, to which a little must be added here. As early as 5 February 1958 detailed provisions on the future status of the new republic were presented to the Syrian Chamber of Deputies and the National Assembly of Egypt by the heads of the two states; on 21 February the populations of both countries were asked to approve by referendum the creation of the UAR and the choice of Djamāl ʿAbd al-Nāṣir as President of this republic: about 99.99% of the voters replied in the affirmative to both questions; on 5 March the provisional Constitution of the UAR was promulgated, providing for an executive council in each of the two provinces and a central government, in addition to the already elected President. This Constitution reproduced almost verbatim in its 73 articles the essential provisions of the Egyptian Constitution of 16 January 1956. It differed from the latter, however, by not declaring that Islam was the State religion and that Arabic was the official language, and moreover did not specify whether sovereignty belonged to the nation. Certain articles also were modified in a sense generally favourable to the executive power; thus, the representatives to the legislative assembly were not elected by universal suffrage, but nominated by the president of the republic; the rights of the latter concerning the dissolution of the assembly were more extensive than in the Egyptian constitution; the Chief of State not only retained the right of direct government 'in case of necessity' by decrees 'having the force of law', but all the restrictive conditions imposed on him in this respect in the Egyptian constitution disappeared in this provisional constitution; the President was not even obliged, when proclaiming a state of emergency, to refer this to the Assembly. The remaining provisions were in general similar at all points to those of the Egyptian constitution. The Syrian coup d'état of 28 September 1961 made an end of the Union and abolished the federal constitution on 29 September.

The very day after the proclamation of the UAR at Cairo, delegates of Egypt and the Yemen began talks which culminated, on 8 March, in the signature at Damascus of the charter of the United Arab States by the president of the UAR and the crown prince of the Yemen, the *amīr* Sayf al-Islām Badr. By the terms of this charter, which consisted of 32 articles divided into three chapters, each State was to preserve its international personality and its own government; no reference was made to the religion or language of the union. All citizens were to be equal and have equal right of work; they were guaranteed freedom of movement. The unification and co-ordination of external policies, of diplomatic representation, of the armed forces, of economic activities, of the currency and of education were treated in chapter I. A supreme council, composed of the heads of member States, was to be assisted by a Council of the Union composed of an equal number of representatives of the member States. Presidency of this Council of the Union was to be assumed for a year at a time by the member States in turn. The supreme Council was charged with establishing the higher policy of the Union in matters of defence, economy and culture; it was to promulgate the laws, appoint the commander in chief of the armed forces, and draw up the budget of the union; the Council of the Union was to be its permanent organ; it would establish the annual programme, which it would submit for ratification to the Supreme Council. A council of defence, an economic council and a cultural council were also instituted. Chapter III contained general and provisional regulations on the seat of the Council of the Union, the entry into force of the laws, the suppression of diplomatic representation between the member States, and customs regulations. The federation having been broken on 26 December 1961, the constitution lapsed on that date.

As an answer to these regroupings within the Arab world the Hāshimite sovereigns Fayṣal of ʿIrāḳ and Ḥusayn of Jordan announced, on 14 February 1958, the creation of a union between their kingdoms, and on 19 March following, the Constitution of the Arab Union, drawn up by a mixed ʿIrāḳī-Jordanian commission, was promulgated simultaneously at Baghdād and ʿAmmān. It comprised 80 articles in 8 chapters. "Membership of the Union is open to any Arab State desirous of joining", but each State would retain its independent identity and its own system of government; any treaties previously concluded would affect only the States which had signed them. Here again there is no provision on the religion or language of the Union. The seat of government was to be at Baghdād and ʿAmmān alternately; a common emblem was envisaged, but each state was to retain its own flag. Legislative power would belong to the president of the Union (the king of

ʿIrāḳ) and to an Assembly of forty members (20 from each State), who were to be elected for four years by the Chambers of Deputies of ʿIrāḳ and Jordan. Chapter II dealt in some detail with the prerogatives of the President and the role of the Assembly; the following chapter with the executive power, which belonged to the President of the Union assisted by a council of ministers. The President would nominate, dismiss and accept the resignation of the Prime Minister and conclude treaties, and would be the Supreme chief of the army. The ministers were to be collectively and individually responsible to the Assembly of the Union; each ministry had, within a month of its formation, to define its policy in a declaration made to the assembly. In case of urgency, during the interval between sessions of the assembly, the president could promulgate federal decrees having the force of law, provided that he submitted them to the next meeting of the Council of the Union. Chapter IV, which deals with the judicial power, is almost exclusively concerned with the institution of a Supreme Court charged with the task of judging the members of the Assembly and the ministers, of settling any disputes which might arise, of giving its advice on legal questions submitted to it by the Prime Minister, of interpreting the constitution, of determining the constitutionality of laws, and of hearing appeals on sentences of the federal courts. Chapter V deals with the powers of the Union as regards foreign affairs, security, customs, economic questions, and education. The finances of the union (chapter 6) were to be furnished by the member states in defined proportions. The Assembly would discuss the budget, and a Court of Audit was to be instituted. Chapter VII envisages the conditions under which the Constitution could be amended. Finally chapter VIII contains various provisions on the state of emergency, the first assembly, the first budget, the necessity of member States revising their own constitutions to bring them into line with that of the Union.

On 26 March the Jordanian and ʿIrāḳī parliaments ratified the Constitution of the Union. At Baghdād the Chamber of Deputies decided to amend the ʿIrāḳī Constitution of 1925, and was then dissolved to allow the vote on the amendment to be taken by a new assembly; on 10 May the latter voted the amendment, and on 12 May approved the text of the Constitution of the Union. On 18 May the first federal government was formed. On 14 July 1958 the ʿIrāḳī Revolution put an end to the Union and in consequence to the federal Constitution.

Bibliography: *Institutions de la République Arabe Unie*, in *Orient*, v (1958), 181-95; *Constitution des "États Arabes Unis"*, *ibid.*, vi (1958), 183-6; *Formation et institution de l'Union Arabe*, *ibid.*, vi (1958), 167-82; *COC*, xxxvii-xxxviii (1958); Documentation française, *Notes et études documentaires*, no. 2420 of 4 June 1958; relevant dates in *MEA*, *MEJ*, *OM*, etc. (Ch. Pellat)

Amīrates of southern Arabia. In the course of the year 1958 discussions were undertaken with a view to drafting a constitution of federation of a certain number of Arab principalities of the Aden Protectorate. On 20 June 1958 the general secretariat of the Arab League sent to all member countries a memoir drawing their attention to the British intention to create a federal union of all the southern protectorates, allegedly in order to bring the amīrates and sultanates under the British governor of Aden. The federation was not, however, constituted before 3 February 1959, receiving the allegiance of the following six small states: the amīrate of Bayḥān [see bayḥān al-ḳaṣab], the sultanates of ʿAwdhalī [*q.v.*], Faḍlī [*q.v.*] and Ḍāliʿ ([*q.v.*] in Supplement), the Shaykhdom of Upper ʿAwlaḳī [*q.v.*] and the sultanate of Lower Yāfaʿ [*q.v.*]; at the beginning of April 1959 the sultanate of Lāḥidj [*q.v.*], the amīrate of Lower ʿAwlaḳī and the republic of Dathīna [*q.v.*] asked in their turn to participate. On 29 September 1959 the foundation stone of the capital of the Federation (*al-Ittiḥād*) was even laid, erected at Biʾr Aḥmad by the sultan of Lāḥidj, who began to take an important part; other states also demanded admission, and on 29 October 1961 the British government even transferred to the Federation its powers over the forces of public order.

From 11 February 1959 this Islamic Arab Federation provided itself with an elaborate Constitution consisting of a preamble and ten chapters divided into 47 articles. Chap. III (arts. 5-11) institutes a Supreme Council of the Federal Government which wields the executive power; it is composed of six ministers at the maximum, elected for five years by a Federal Council endowed with legislative power (Chap. IV, arts. 12-9); this Council is composed of six representatives of each member State and legislates by regulation (Chap. V, 20-2). Legislation may be carried out by provisional orders of the Supreme Council when the Federal Council is not in session (arts. 23-6) or by decrees of the Supreme Council when a state of emergency has been declared (arts. 27-8). The following chapters deal with the finances of the Federation (arts. 29-35), federal officials (arts. 36-7), responsibilities and powers of the Federation and of the member States (arts. 38-42), the procedure for revision of the Constitution (art. 43), and end with interim provisions (arts. 44-7).

Bibliography: See the account of the events in *OM*, *COC*, *MEJ*, *MEA*, on the dates noted, especially *COC*, xxxix (1959), 127-38. (Ed.)

xix. — Conclusion

The authors who have shared in the composition of the article dustūr have made it their chief endeavour to trace the history of the constitutional movement in the countries concerned and to analyse more or less briefly the promulgated texts. This has the advantage of presenting the reader with a fairly complete synthesis, but also the occasional drawback of obscuring to some extent those points which must be of primary interest to students of Islam, namely the place accorded to Islam in the constitutions of the Muslim countries. We shall therefore set ourselves here to group together the common elements and to note the points of divergence, taking into account only those texts at present (beginning of 1963) in force (or suspended without being replaced), and disregarding constitutions that are too archaic (Saʿūdī Arabia), rigorously secular (Turkey), Soviet, or of a special local character (Lebanon, Indonesia). Thus we shall confine our attention to the constitutions of eight Arabic-speaking states (Egypt, ʿIrāḳ, Jordan, Libya, Morocco, Mauretania, Syria and Tunisia) and three non-Arab Muslim countries (Afghānistān, Īrān and Pākistān).

The chronological order in which these eleven constitutions were promulgated is of no more than secondary interest, for all of them (except that of Afghānistān) can be regarded as recent and on the modern pattern, the oldest (Īrān) having been revised and, so to speak, brought up to date. Both in the monarchies: Afghānistān (with qualifications), Īrān, Jordan, Libya and Morocco, and in the republics, the uni- or bi-cameral parliamentary system has been universally adopted, though the sovereign or head of state enjoys powers that are generally very extensive and participates actively in the country's political life (we cannot fail to notice, moreover, that at the present moment (January 1963) three out of seven republics—not counting the Sudan—are headed by officers brought to power by the army in order to put an end to the abuses of a misconstrued liberal régime).

To the parliamentarianism of democratic tendency is added the solemn proclamation of the Rights of Man and the principles of liberty and equality, painstakingly included in the texts; the functioning of the institutions is minutely regulated, with the result that these constitutions, while far from being identical, are absolutely comparable to those of the Western countries which have more or less served as their models. The difference lies, on the one hand in the fact that the Eastern Arab countries declare themselves to be "an integral part of the Arab nation" and that Tunisia and Morocco proclaim that they belong to the "Greater Maghrib", on the other hand, and above all, in the provisions relating to Islam which they all contain.

To begin with, Islam is expressly declared to be the state religion in all the constitutions enumerated below, with the exception of that of Syria. Morocco takes the precaution (art. 108) of excluding from any future revision the provisions relating to the Muslim religion, *i.e.*, the second half of art. 6 (which additionally guarantees to all the freedom of worship). It goes without saying that in these countries the head of state could not belong to any religion but Islam; four constitutions make express provision to this effect: those of Syria (art. 3), of Pākistān (art. 10[a]), of Tunisia (art. 37) and of Mauretania (art. 10). Art. 120 of the Egyptian Constitution of 1956 is silent about the religion of the head of state, but there can be no doubt as to the will of the framers of the constitution; in the monarchies it is evident that the sovereign must be a Muslim; in Īrān (art. 1) the state religion is Twelver Shīʿism to which the sovereign must necessarily belong; in Afghānistān (art. 1) the King must belong to the Ḥanafī school; in Morocco the King is Commander of the Faithful (*amīr al-muʾminīn*); in Libya (art. 51) the representative of the throne, regent or member of the regency council, must be a Muslim.

Syria (but see also the Sudan) is thus the only Muslim country not to have declared that Islam is the state religion, but in this regard art. 3 of the constitution voted on 5 September 1950 (retained in that of 22 September 1953) is instructive; in effect, the original draft, which actually made Islam the state religion, has been modified by the Constituent Assembly in the following manner:

1. the religion of the President of the Republic is Islam;
2. Islamic *fiḳh* is the principal source of legislation;
3. freedom of belief is guaranteed. The State respects all revealed religions and assures them complete freedom of worship on condition that they do not disturb the public order;
4. the personal status of the religious communities is safeguarded and respected.

This notion of respect for revealed religions only is unique in the constitutional system of the Muslim countries and has no parallel except in the clause of the Afghān constitution on the protection of Hindus and Jews alone, happily replacing the obligation of the *dhimmīs* to pay the *djizya* and wear distinguishing emblems (see above v). The Syrian constitution has sought to take account of the peculiar conditions prevailing in a country where Christians of every sect and Jews live side by side with Muslims; it shows itself liberal in reserving to the religious communities their personal status, but in a sense less tolerant than the other constitutions which guarantee (theoretically at least) to all religions the freedom of worship, on condition that they do not disturb public order. In restricting this freedom to the revealed religions only, the framers of the Syrian constitution have evidently sought to make a concession to the tenets of the *sharīʿa* [*q.v.*], without perhaps devoting any great attention to the problem posed by the definition of *ahl al-kitāb*; they have made another such concession in manifesting the desire, expressed in the text, of deriving all legislation from Islamic *fiḳh*, without however specifying the *madhhab* followed, and perhaps with the ulterior motive of neglecting this provision, for they must certainly have realized how difficult it is to reconcile the rules of the *sharīʿa* with the exigencies of a modern state.

This harmonization of Islamic law and modern legislation was, in fact, one of the major concerns of the first constitution-makers. The constitution of Afghānistān lays down that the laws must be in accordance with the *sharīʿa*, and the Iranian Fundamental Law goes even further, since art. 2 lays down that a committee of *mudjtahids* shall be named to watch over the "Islamicity" of the laws; in practice this provision does not seem to have been punctiliously applied (see above, ĪRĀN). Indeed, in nearly all the countries which had not been subject to foreign domination and which had been able fairly early to enjoy a constitutional life of their own, the elaboration and promulgation of a constitution represented a victory for the partisans of progress over the conservatives entrenched behind the *sharīʿa*; in the other countries, which have gained their independent status more or less recently, the constitution-makers tried to fight against the *ʿulamāʾ*, who were too much attached to legal rules felt to be out-of-date and incompatible with the harmonious development of a modern State, and have elaborated texts that show a progress in the direction of de-Islamization, despite some concessions of principle to the conservatives. The sole, and logically necessary, exception to this rule is Pākistān, whose very *raison d'être* is precisely to allow Muslims to lead a life in total conformity with the teachings of Islam in a State built on a purely Islamic basis. The experiment was interesting, but we know that it has run up against countless difficulties. The preparation of the first constitution bristled with difficulties, although each successive draft of the project marked a set-back for the claims of the *ʿulamāʾ* and a victory for the modernists (see K. J. Newman, *Essays on the Constitution of Pakistan*, Dacca 1956; A. Chapy, *L'Islam dans la Constitution du Pakistan*, in *Orient*, iii (1957), 120-7). The committee for the scrutiny of laws, on which the *ʿulamāʾ* were to be represented, was finally replaced by a kind of manual which the members of the Assembly were supposed to follow, so as to promulgate only such laws as are in conformity with the prescriptions of Islam. The constitution of 1962 has returned to a consultative council on Islamic ideology; but the members of this council, named by the President, must not only know Islam, but also be aware of the economic, legal and administrative problems which Pākistān has to solve; in other words, the *ʿulamāʾ* are virtually excluded from it. Moreover, this council is charged with giving its opinion on the "Islamicity" of the laws at the request of the President of the Republic or of a governor; and the Head of State, though he may respect the *ʿulamāʾ*, knows that he can hardly count on them, and does not fail to invite them to become better informed of the requirements of the modern world. Their incapacity has been shown up clearly by the so-called Munīr report, presented by the commission of enquiry into the disturbances in the Pandjāb in 1953 (*Report of the Court of Inquiry constituted under Punjab Act II of 1954 to enquire into Punjab disturbances of 1953*, Lahore 1954, 200-32, especially 218-9), of which W. C. Smith (*Islam in Modern History*, 233) says that it "publicized further the fact that the *ʿulamāʾ*, the traditional leaders of traditional Islam, were not only unfitted to run a modern state, but were deplorably unable under cross-questioning even to give realistic guidance on elementary matters of Islam. The court of inquiry, and subsequently the world, was presented with the sorry spectacle of Muslim divines no two of whom agreed on the definition of a Muslim, and who were yet practically unanimous that all who disagreed should be put to death".

The application of Islamic law may be studied in the article SHARĪʿA (see meanwhile G.-H. Bousquet, *Du droit musulman et de son application effective dans le monde*, Algiers 1949; J. N. D. Anderson, *Islamic law in the modern world*, London 1959), but we must notice here that the general tendency of the constitutions, even in Pākistān, is to institute civil courts charged with giving judgement, in matters of personal status and succession, on the basis of codes established according to the requirements of Islamic law. It is worth emphasizing, then, that of all the modern constitutions that of Jordan is unique, in the judicial sphere, in providing expressly for the maintenance of religious jurisdictions (art. 104) consisting in *sharʿī* courts and in councils for the other religious communities. The competence of these latter councils in matters of personal status and mortmain property is fixed by the law (art. 109), while the *sharʿī* courts are constitutionally declared competent (art. 105) in the following matters: personal status of Muslims; claims for payment of *diya* [*q.v.*] between Muslims or parties consenting to this mode of settlement; questions concerning *waḳf* [*q.v.*] property. In other countries the *ḳāḍī*s have been retained, but their existence is more or less precarious.

Bibliography: General: A. Giannini, *Le costituzioni degli Stati del Vicino Oriente*, Rome 1931; Helen M. Davis, *Constitutions, electoral laws, treaties of the States in the Near and Middle East*², Durham, N.C., 1953; J. C. Hurewitz, *Diplomacy in the Near and Middle East*, Princeton 1956, 2 vols.; Muhammad Khalil, *The Arab States and the Arab League*, Beirut 1962; G. Lenczowski, *Political institutions*, apud R. N. Anshen (ed.), *Mid-East: World-Center*, New York 1956, 118-72; M. Khadduri, *Governments of the Arab East*, in *Journal of International Affairs*, vi (1952), 37-50; J. E. Godchot, *Les constitutions du Proche et du Moyen-Orient*, Paris 1957; M. Harari, *Government and politics of the Middle East*, Englewood Cliffs, N.J. 1962; H. B. Sharabi, *Governments and politics of the Middle East in the twentieth century*, Princeton N.J. 1962.

DUYŪN-I ʿUMŪMIYYE, the Ottoman public debt, more particularly the debt administration set up in 1881. The Ottoman government had made its first attempts to raise money by internal loans in the late 18th and early 19th centuries (see ASHĀM and ḲĀʾIME). The needs and opportunities of the Crimean War brought a new type of loan, floated on the money markets of Europe. The first such foreign loan was raised in London in 1854, the second in the following year. They were for £ 3,000,000 at 6% and £ 5,000,000 at 4% respectively. Between 1854 and 1874 foreign loans were raised almost every year, reaching a nominal total of about £ 200 million. Usually, since Turkey was regarded as a poor risk, the loans were granted on very disadvantageous terms; the money received was for the most part used to cover regular budgetary expenditure, or else spent on projects unconnected with economic development. The end came on 6 October 1875, when the Ottoman government defaulted on its payments of interest and amortization. A period of negotiations followed, and agreement was finally reached between the government and representatives of the European bondholders. This agreement was given legal effect in the so-called Muḥarram Decree, issued on 28 Muḥarram 1299/20 December 1881, setting up an "Administration of the Public Debt" (*Duyūn-i ʿumūmiyye*—in French *Administration de la dette publique ottomane*), directly controlled by and answerable to the foreign creditors. Its primary duty was to ensure the service of the Ottoman public debt, which was consolidated at a total of £ 106,409,920, or £T. 117,050,912, at the prevailing rate of 110 piastres to the pound sterling. For this purpose, the Ottoman government ceded certain revenues to the Council "absolutely and irrevocably ... until the complete liquidation of the debt". These consisted of the revenues from the salt and tobacco monopolies, stamp-duties, and the taxes on spirits, silk, and fisheries, together known as the *rusūm-i sitte*, six taxes. In addition to these taxes, which it collected directly through its own agents, the Council was to receive tribute from the Balkan principalities, and, if necessary, a share of customs receipts. The executive committee, or Council, consisted of six delegates, representing British and Dutch, French, German, Italian, Austro-Hungarian and Ottoman bondholders, together with a seventh representing a group of priority bonds, most of which were held by the Imperial Ottoman Bank. Already in 1881 the Council had over 3000 revenue collectors at its disposal. By 1911 its total staff stood at 8,931—more than that of the Ottoman Ministry of Finance. The Council of the Debt had become a very powerful body, with far-reaching influence on the financial and economic life of the Ottoman Empire, and even, to an extent that has been variously assessed, on its politics.

The Debt Administration continued to function during the First World War and under the Allied occupation, in spite of the withdrawal of the British, French and Italian delegates during the war and of the German and Austrian delegates after the armistice. The work was carried on under the authority of the remaining delegates, and amounts due to enemy creditors deposited for future payment. It came to an end with the victory of the nationalists under Muṣṭafā Kemāl, and the creation of the republic. The treaty of Lausanne determined the share of the new Turkey in the debt of the defunct Empire. Negotiations followed, and agreements regarding liability and payment were signed in 1928 and 1933. The debt was finally liquidated in 1944.

Bibliography: F. A. Belin, *Essai sur l'histoire économique de la Turquie*, in *JA*, 1885; C. Morawitz, *Les finances de Turquie*, Paris 1902; A. du Velay,

Essai sur l'histoire financière de la Turquie, Paris 1903; A. Roumani, *Essai historique et technique sur la dette publique ottomane*, Paris 1927 (not seen); D. G. Blaisdell, *European financial control in the Ottoman Empire*, New York 1929; Z. Y. Hershlag, *Turkey, an economy in transition*, The Hague, n.d. [? 1960]; B. Lewis, *The emergence of modern Turkey*², London 1962; Aḥmed Rāsim, *ʿOth̲mānli taʾrīk̲h̲i*, iv, Istanbul 1326-30, 2028-47 (*fāʾide*); Refii Şükrü Suvla, *Tanzimat devrinde istikrazlar*, in *Tanzimat*, i, Istanbul 1940, 263-88; Pakalın, i, 487-91; Ziya Karamursal, *Osmanlı malî tarihi hakkında tetkikler*, Istanbul 1940. (B. Lewis)

DŪZAK̲H̲ [see DJAHANNAM].

DÜZME MUṢṬAFĀ [see MUṢṬAFĀ DÜZME].

DWĀRKĀ, a town in the Okhāmanḍal district in the north-west of the Kāthiāwāḍ peninsula of Gud̲j̲arāt, India, associated in Hindū legend with the god Kris̲h̲na and hence considered to be of special sanctity by Hindūs. It is known also by the names of Dwārawatī and D̲j̲agat, and was notorious for its pirates until the 19th century. Under the name Bāruwī (< *dwārawatī*) it is referred to by al-Bīrūnī (*K. Taʾrīk̲h̲ al-Hind*, tr. E. Sachau, London 1888, ii, 105 ff.).

It was sacked by the Gud̲j̲arāt sultan Maḥmūd I "Begḍā" in 877/1473 as a reprisal for an attack by pirates on the scholar-merchant Mawlānā Maḥmūd Samarḳandī: the city was plundered, its temples destroyed, and its idols broken (*Firis̲h̲ta*, tr. Briggs, iv, 59-60, and note). It figures again in the Muslim history of Gud̲j̲arāt at the time of the pursuit of the deposed sultan, Muẓaffar III, by Mug̲h̲al imperial troops in 1000-1/1592-3, although the various accounts differ considerably among themselves.

Bibliography: J. Burton-Page, *"Azīz" and the sack of Dvārkā: a seventeenth century Hindī version*, in *BSOAS*, xx (1957), 145-57, with full bibliography and discussion of the second incident. (J. Burton-Page)

DWIN (pronounced Dvin) was formerly an important town in Armenia and was the capital at the time of the Arab domination. The name of the town, to which Asog̲h̲ik, ii, ch. I, trans. Gelzer and Burckhardt, 47, gives the meaning "hill", is probably, as was shown by Minorsky, *Le nom de Dvin*, in *Rev. des ét. arm.*, x (1930), 119 ff. and *Transcaucasica*, in *JA*, ccxvii/1 (1930), 41 ff., of pre-Iranian origin and said to have been imported by the Armenian Arsacids from their original dwelling-place, the present Turkoman steppe. In the Arab authors it occurs in the forms Dawīn or Duwīn (Yāḳūt, ii, 632; Ibn K̲h̲allikān, Būlāḳ ed., i, 105) and Dabīl (Yāḳūt, ii, 548) which is the most usual form. Neither Yāḳūt nor Abu 'l-Fidāʾ (ii, 2, 150-1), nor the author of the *Muk̲h̲taṣar* of Ibn Ḥawḳal (240; 2nd ed., 337), seems to realise that Dabīl and Dawīn denote one and the same town. The Greek name is sometimes Δόυβιος (Procopius), sometimes τὸ Τίβιον, τὸ Τιβή, τὸ Τιβί (Constantine Porphyrogenitus). The forms Dovin or Tovin, Duin, Douin are found in many European authors.

The town was founded by the Armenian Arsacid king K̲h̲usraw II the Young (330-8 A.D.) in a plain, near the river Azat (Garni Čay), a tributary on the left bank of the Araxes, to replace the ancient Artas̲h̲at (Artaxata), which was situated in the same region of Ararat but a little further south. After the partition of Armenia between the Persians and the Romans in about 387 or 390, Dwin was included in the Persian sector (Persarmenia) and was the capital of Persarmenia after the deposition in 426 of the last Armenian Arsacid.

Besides being the capital and administrative centre, and the residence of the Persian *marzpan* (*marzubān*), Dwin was also, from the 5th century, the seat of the Catholicos: several synods were held there, notably the one in 554 which made a final break with the Greek Church and established the Armenian era, beginning on 1 July 552. But its importance also came from the fact that it was a centre of transit trade between Byzantine Anatolia, Persia and the countries of the Caucasus. Together with Nisibis and Callinicos (Raḳḳa) it was one of the customs-posts where a tithe was levied on the Romans' and Persians' merchandise (Menander in Constantine Porphyrogenitus, *Excerpta de legationibus*, ed. C. de Boor, i, 180 and Güterbock, *Byzanz und Persien*, 75, in W. Heffening, *Das islamische Fremdenrecht*, 109-10).

Dwin was destroyed, Asog̲h̲ik tells us (ii, ch. III, trans. 84-5), by Heraclius during his famous campaign against Persia. The Arabs, advancing from Mesopotamia which they had already conquered, captured the town on 6 October 640 (the date fixed in Manandean's work); it was pillaged, 12,000 Armenians were massacred and 35,000 were carried off as prisoners. Other invasions followed but did not reach Dwin; on the other hand, the invasion by Ḥabīb b. Maslama, which Arab sources place either in 24-5/645-6 or in 31/651-2, and the historian Sebeos in 652-3, ended in the surrender and capture of Dwin and a treaty, the text of which has been preserved by al-Balād̲h̲urī, and in which Ḥabīb granted "the Christians, Zoroastrians and Jews" of Dwin the *amān* and security for their persons, goods, synagogues and churches, in return for payment of *d̲j̲izya* and *k̲h̲arād̲j̲*. The Armenian authors do not seem to have preserved any recollection of the agreement concluded with Dwin and the other towns (Nak̲h̲čawān, Tiflis, S̲h̲amkūr) and only mention the general treaty concluded between Theodore Res̲h̲tuni and Muʿāwiya. The capture of Dwin did not signify a lasting occupation of the town by the Arabs; for some time it was subjected alternately to Byzantine and Arab domination. The emperor Constans II was able to have a synod held in Dwin in 645 (or 648-9), and even after the agreement between Muʿāwiya and Theodore Res̲h̲tuni, this same Constans II penetrated as far as Dwin where he summoned another synod. After this, the town was reoccupied by the Arabs, and then once again by the Byzantine general Maurianos; in 657-8, it was with the help of a new and temporary Byzantine domination that the Catholicos Nerses, who had left Dwin, returned there. Arab sovereignty was only finally established in Dwin and in Armenia when the authority of the new caliph Muʿāwiya was fully affirmed by the Arabs (41/661). Nevertheless, it is from the time of Ḥabīb b. Maslama's expedition that Arab sources mark the start of the administration of Armenia by Muslim governors. Dwin became the residence of these governors, and when, in addition to Armenia, they also had to rule the D̲j̲azīra and Ād̲h̲arbayd̲j̲ān and were not residing in Dwin, they had a deputy there. Thanks to the establishment of an Arab administration whose main task was the collection of taxes, and of a garrison, an Arab population settled in the town and grew constantly bigger. In fact, according to an observation of Markwart (*Südarmenien*, 115), the Arabs, unlike the Persians, caused whole quarters of the towns to be evacuated for their own use, transforming them little by little into Arab towns. Dwin was given a governmental palace (*dār al-imāra*), a mosque, a State prison and a mint. The operation of the mint at Dwin is attested from the beginning of the 2nd/8th century, and it was one of the first to function in the caliph's territories. The place of origin, given on the coins as Armīniyya, is Dwin (see Minorsky, *Studies on Caucasian History*, 117 and Kh. Mushegian, *Contribution to the history of monetary circulation in Dwin, according to finds of coins*, in *Bull. Ac. Sc. Armenian S.S.R.*, xi (1956), 84 (in Russian)).

Dwin was the scene of various events of greater or lesser importance during the Arab domination; it seems to have been a period of decadence for the town which was abandoned by part of its Christian population, especially the nobility, until the end of the 3rd/9th century and the establishment of the monarchy. In the Umayyad period, under the reign of ʿAbd al-Malik, the governor ʿAbd Allāh b. Ḥātim b. al-Nuʿmān al-Bāhilī caused the martyrdom at Dwin of a holy man named David and exiled several Armenian princes to Damascus (Asoghik, ii, ch. II, tr., 73; see other references in Grousset, *Histoire de l'Arménie*, 309 ff.). His brother ʿAbd al-ʿAzīz who was governor from 86-97/705-15, in the reign of al-Walīd, restored Dwin, fortified it and surrounded it with a ditch, and enlarged the mosque (al-Balādhurī, 204; cf. Asoghik, ii, ch. IV, tr. 92; Ghevond, vi, 34-5; Grousset, 314). During the Umayyad period, the Mamikonians were pre-eminent among the great families of the country; with the ʿAbbāsid period the Bagratunis took the lead. However, the rise of the Bagratunis did not affect the position of Dwin which, with Bardhaʿa, remained one of the two bulwarks of Arab power in Armenia and Arrān, and where the governors and their deputies remained firmly established. In the reign of al-Manṣūr (136-58/754-75) and the rule of Ḥasan b. Ḳaḥṭaba a revolt of Armenian nobles broke out. It began with an attack on a tax-collector by Artavazd Mamikonian who had taken up arms in Dwin under the very eyes of the governor; it was carried further by Mushegh Mamikonian who, after seizing Dwin, was defeated and killed in the battle of Bagrevand in 775 (see Grousset, 324 ff.).

During the civil war between al-Amīn and al-Maʾmūn, the Arab *amīr* in command at Manazgerd, al-Djaḥḥāf, of the family of the Kaisikkʿ (Ḳaysites), and who was married to an Armenian princess, took possession of Dwin for himself, and his son ʿAbd al-Malik remained there until he was killed by the actual inhabitants of Dwin in 823-4 (Grousset, 345 ff.; Laurent, *L'Arménie*, 322). In the time of the caliph al-Wāthiḳ (227-32/842-7), Khālid b. Yazīd b. Mazyad al-Shaybānī, governor of Armenia, died, possibly by assassination, during an expedition against the rebellious governor of Georgia; his body was brought back and buried in Dwin in 230/844-5 (Laurent, 345). After the assassination of the governor of Armenia Yūsuf b. Abī Saʿīd Muḥammad in Mūsh in 237/852, the caliph al-Mutawakkil (232-47/847-61) sent into Armenia Bughā al-Sharābī who wintered at Dwin and there, as elsewhere, indulged in numerous massacres (Grousset, 355 ff.; Laurent, 120, n. 5 345-6).

After the recognition of Bagratuni Ashot (Ashūṭ) as prince of princes (*baṭrīḳ al-baṭāriḳa*) in 862, and then as king in 886 (or 887: Asoghik, iii, ch. II, tr. 115; cf. Laurent, 267, 287 ff.; Grousset, 372, 394), Dwin was in theory included in his possession for which he regarded himself as the caliph's vassal; but in fact it was independent of him, and he did not establish his capital there. At the beginning of the reign of Ashot's son Sembat (Sanbāṭ) the Martyr (890-914), two Muslim amīrs, Mahmat (Muḥammad) and Umay (Umayya), brothers of unknown origin, took up position in Dwin, and Sembat had to struggle for two years to subdue them; he captured them and sent them to the emperor Leo VI. But this situation disturbed the ambitious *amīr* of Ādharbaydjān, Afshīn Muḥammad b. Abi 'l-Sādj, who was in theory still governor of Armenia. In spite of the agreement he had concluded with Sembat, he intervened in Armenia. This was after the terrible earthquake which ravaged Dwin in 280/893 and destroyed the Catholicos's palace (the latter consequently decided to move to Ečmiadzin). Afshīn came and occupied Dwin. War with Sembat followed, in the course of which the wives of both Sembat and his son Mushegh were sent as prisoners to Dwin, only being released in 898-9 (see Grousset, 402 ff., 413 ff.). Afshīn was succeeded by his brother Yūsuf who captured Sembat, tortured him to death and exposed his crucified body in Dwin, where many Armenians were martyred. The Catholicos Ter Yohannes fled to Greek territory (Asoghik, iii, ch. V, tr. 123); for these events, see Grousset, 435 ff.). In opposition to Sembat's lawful successor Ashot II, Yūsuf gave his support to his cousin Ashot son of Shapuh whom he established in Dwin and recognized as king. In addition, in the canton of Goghthn, situated on the left bank of the Araxa below Dwin, he set up an Arab *amīr* whose successors were subsequently to play a part in the history of Dwin.

Yūsuf revolted against the caliph and was taken prisoner in 307/919. During his captivity one of his officers, Sbuk (Subuk), governed Ādharbaydjān and Armenia; he re-established good relations with Ashot II, whose rival was compelled to give up Dwin, though it did not, however, return to Ashot's possession. In 921 the emperor Romanus Lecapenus sent an expedition against Dwin under the command of the Domesticos (Demeslikos). According to Asoghik (iii, ch. VI, 124), Subuk (Spkhi) drove him back with the aid of Ashot whom he had called upon for assistance. When Yūsuf returned to Ādharbaydjān in 310/922, Dwin was at first governed by Naṣr Subukī, *ghulām* to Subuk who had just died, and then, after Naṣr's recall, by Bishr (or Bashīr) who started hostilities with Ashot but was defeated by him. In 314/926 Yūsuf left Ādharbaydjān, the caliph having entrusted him with the conduct of the war against the Ḳarmaṭians, in the course of which he met his death in the following year. It was at this point, in 315/927-8, that a new Byzantine expedition took place, commanded by the Domesticos John Corcuas, against Dwin which was defended by Naṣr Subukī. It fell: the Greeks, with the help of siege-engines, breached the walls and succeeded in making their way into the town, but were driven out as a result of the assistance given to the defenders by the inhabitants. This is what Ibn al-Athīr relates (viii, 129-30). It may be questioned whether, in spite of the differences of names and dates, the two expeditions under discussion were not in fact one and the same.

The dynasty of the Sādjids in Ādharbaydjān came to an end in 317/929, though for a time it was continued by Sādjid officers. We then enter a confused period in the history of Dwin. We do not know which *amīr* was in command of Dwin when king Abas (929-53) secured from him the release of the Christian prisoners, nor who was the Muslim personage who, in about 937, came as far as Dwin and inflicted a defeat on Abas, but was then defeated by king Gagik of Vaspurakan, who compelled the Muslim population of Dwin to pay tribute and give hostages. It is possible that at this time Dwin was more or less subject to the authority of Daysam b. Ibrāhīm al-Kurdī, a temporary ruler of Ādharbaydjān who was thus successor to the Sādjids and heir to their rights over Armenia; we possess a coin of his, struck at Dwin in 330/941-2. But at about that date, Daysam was driven out by Marzubān b. Muḥammad b. Musāfir, of the family of the Kangarids of Ṭarom, who founded the dynasty of the Sallārids or Musāfirids [*q.v.*]. Then, Marzubān having been captured by the Buwayhid Rukn al-Dawla in 337/948-9, Daysam succeeded in reconquering Ādharbaydjān and made himself master of Dwin, expelling two adventurers, Faḍl b. Dja'far al-Ḥamdānī and Ibrāhīm al-Ḍābbī, who had seized the town. But already a new power had appeared at Dwin, that of Muḥammad b. Shaddād, founder of the Kurdish dynasty of the Shaddādids which was to rule over the territory between the Kūr and the Araxes. Muḥammad gained control of Dwin in about 340/951, by what means we do not know. Ibrāhīm b. al-Marzubān, acting in the name of his father who was still held prisoner, tried to drive him out of Dwin; the first attempt failed, and Muḥammad built a fortress at the gates of Dwin. A second attempt by Ibrāhīm compelled Muḥammad to flee, and a Daylamite garrison was installed in Dwin itself. But soon the townspeople recalled Muḥammad who triumphantly resisted an attack by king Ashot III the Charitable of Ani. Marzubān, however, had managed to escape from prison in 341 or 342/952 or 953-4 (for the date, see M. Canard, *Hist. de la dynastie des H'amdanides*, i, 533). He disposed of Daysam in Ādharbaydjān and came to attack Dwin. Muḥammad b. Shaddād, caught between Marzubān's army and the Daylamite garrison still in the town, and deserted by the inhabitants, took refuge in Vaspurakan and then in Byzantine territory where he tried in vain to enlist help to reconquer Dwin. He died in 344/955, leaving three sons, one of whom we shall see again later at Dwin.

From the time of Marzubān's reconquest, Dwin seems to have remained in the hands of the Sallārids, although it does not occur in the list of regions paying tribute to the Sallārid, given by Ibn Ḥawḳal for the year 344, perhaps because it was administered directly by a deputy. Ibrāhīm b. al-Marzubān was deprived of Ādharbaydjān in about 368/979 and died four years later. It is no doubt his son Abu 'l-Haydjā', the Aplhač of Delmastan in Asoghik, iii, ch. xii, whom we find still in possession of Dwin in 982-3, but shortly afterwards the town was taken by the *amīr* of Goghthn, Abū Dulaf al-Shaybānī (Aputluph in Asoghik). In 377/987, Abu 'l-Haydjā' al-Rawwādī al-Kurdī, the Arabo-Kurdish *amīr* of Ādharbaydjān and successor to the Sallārids, took it from him, but Abū Dulaf reconquered the town from Mamlān, successor to Abu 'l-Haydjā'. The Bagratuni king Gagik I (990-1020) overcame the *amīr* of Goghthn, and no doubt took Dwin from him.

However, the sons of Muḥammad b. Shaddād after many adventures had set up an amīrate at Gandja (Djanza), north-west of Bardha'a, in 360/971, the territory having been taken from the Sallārids, and they extended their rule between the Kūr and the Araxes. One of them, Faḍl I (375-422/985-1031), also captured Dwin and took tribute from the Armenians. The date of the capture of Dwin is without doubt 413/1022, for it was then that Faḍl's youngest son Abu 'l-Aswār Shāwur became governor, after which he ruled over the whole block of Shaddādid possessions, with his residence at Gandja, from 440/1049 until 459/1067. For the relations between Abu 'l-Aswār and his Armenian neighbours, see Minorsky, *op. cit.*, 51 ff. It was Abu 'l-Aswār, *amīr* of Dwin, the Ἀπλησφάρης of the Byzantines, whom the emperor Constantine Monomachos (1042-54) engaged to attack Gagik II of Ani in order to compel him to give his kingdom to the empire, promising to allow him to have the territories he conquered from Gagik. When Gagik finally abdicated (1045), the emperor wanted Abu 'l-Aswār to restore to him the regions taken from Gagik. He sent an army against Dwin, but it was defeated. Another expedition followed in 1046-7, commanded by the eunuch Constantine and a general of Armenian origin, Kekaumenos, grandfather of the historian Kekaumenos and, according to that writer, formerly "toparch" of Dwin (for the difficulties raised by this point, see Markwart, *Südarmenien* 562 ff.). A further expedition was dispatched against Abu 'l-Aswār in 1048 or 1049 (rather than in 1055-6, see Minorsky, 55, 59 ff., as opposed to Honigmann, *Ostgrenze*, 182). In both expeditions alike, the Byzantines failed to lay siege to Dwin. However, by this time the Turks were already invading Armenia. When, in 446/1054, Ṭughril Beg arrived in Ādharbaydjān and Arrān, Abu 'l-Aswār submitted to him and, in agreement with the Turks, made a raid on Ani, returning laden with booty. He died in 1067.

Dwin then passed into the hands of a branch of the Shaddādids which settled at Ani, after the capture of that town by Alp Arslān (1064) in 1072. This situation lasted until 552/1105, when a Turkish *amīr* seized the town. It then fell to Tughān Arslān, lord of Bitlis and Arzan and vassal of an Artuḳid. As a result of the struggle between Maḥmūd and Ṭughril, it was recovered by the Shaddādid Faḍlūn III, who died in 1130, but was recaptured at that date by a son of Tughān Arslān. According to Minorsky (*op. cit.*, 131), it was at that moment that Saladin's grandfather Shādī, a Kurd born in a village near Dwin, is said to have left the country and gone to Takrīt. (We know, as Ibn Khallikān relates, i, 105, that Saladin's family were natives of Dwin).

In 557/1162 the Georgians sacked the town and destroyed the mosque. But despite repeated attacks they were not able to gain possession, since the town was taken by the atabeks of Ādharbaydjān who were descended from Eldigüz (Ildegiz, vizier of Sultan Maḥmūd). In 1203 Dwin was captured by the Georgians, from whom it was taken by the Khʷārizm-shāh Djalāl al-Dīn in 1225. Then came the Mongols, who destroyed the town between 1236 and 1239.

It will be seen from this sketch that, from the end of the 9th century, Dwin suffered ceaselessly from all the repercussions to the upheavals that took place in Ādharbaydjān, that all the powers which had been built up in the neighbouring countries tried to get possession of it on account of its position and commercial importance, and that it was only in the hands of the Armenians in exceptional circumstances, despite the large Armenian population which no doubt formed the majority. However, several of the Muslim overlords were related by marriage to Armenian princely families, for example, even Abu 'l-Aswār, as son-in-law of king Ashot.

The Arab geographers have left us certain descriptions of Dwin. It was, Ibn Ḥawḳal tells us, a larger town than Ardabīl, surrounded by walls, inhabited by many Christians, and its cathedral mosque stood beside the church, as was the case at Ḥimṣ. Fabrics of goats-hair, called *mirʿizzā*, and wool were woven there; carpets, hangings, cushions, coverlets, mattresses, etc., of what were known as "Armenian" (*armanī*) textiles, dyed vermilion with *kermes* (*ḳirmiz*), patterned silk materials called *buzyūn* comparable and even superior to those from the Byzantine countries. One speciality much prized in Muslim countries was the trouser-lacings (*tikka*, pl. *tikak*). All these products formed the basis of a flourishing export trade. Ibn Ḥawḳal's *Epitome* boasts of the gardens, fruit, and the cultivation of cereals, rice and cotton in the locality of Dwin, the springs and flowing waters; and his account also mentions the destruction of the town by the Georgians. Al-Muḳaddasī says that Dwin is a very cold region, and speaks of its textile products, its gardens, the citadel built of stone and clay, and the markets "in the shape of a cross"; he gives the names of the gates of the town, specifies that the mosque stands high up on an eminence and that in his day the fortress was falling into ruin. According to him, the number of inhabitants, the majority of whom were Christian, was declining. He mentions the rite which was used by the Muslims, that of Abū Ḥanīfa, and says that there was a convent of Ṣūfīs in Dwin.

Excavations have been carried out on the site of Dwin, now occupied by villages. The results will be found in a work of K. Kafadarian, *La ville de Dwin et ses fouilles*, Erevan 1952, in Armenian with a résumé in Russian (see also *BSE*, xiii (1952), 467). In the upper part of the town remains have been found of the governors' palace, built after the earthquake of 893 and, below the ruins, traces of a palace of the same sort but dating from an earlier period. In the centre of the town have been found the remains of the palace of the Catholicos, built in 461 or 485, and also of a church of basilican design with a single nave, dating from the 6th century A.D. But the most important building discovered at Dwin is the cathedral whose complicated history can be retraced: originally a pagan temple with three aisles, built in the 3rd century, converted into a church at the beginning of the 4th century when an apse was added, and in the middle of the 5th century refashioned as a basilica with three aisles, and also possessing an external gallery; then, in the 7th century, with the building of lateral apses and a central cupola resting on four large pillars, it became a cruciform church with a cupola. This great church was destroyed in the earthquake of 893. Remains have also been found of dwellings, workshops for weaving, jewellery etc., cellars, warehouses, tools (ploughshares, iron shovels, etc.), gold and silver articles, pottery, china, architectural fragments decorated with sculptures of secular subjects (grape-gathering) etc. The discoveries have shown that the economic life of Dwin was active particularly from the end of the 3rd/9th century until the 5th/11th century inclusive, that is to say until the rise of the Armenian kingdom.

Bibliography: The history of Dwin is described in detail in Markwart, *Südarmenien und die Tigrisquellen*, see index and in particular 562 ff. (cf. also, by the same author, *Streifzüge*, 404-5), but the outstanding work is V. Minorsky, *Studies on Caucasian history*, London 1952, in which for the first time a study is made of the important historical source of Münedjdjim Bas̲h̲ī, collated with the Armenian sources: see particularly 116 ff., *Vicissitudes of Dwin*; it is upon Minorsky's work that the present article has been based; it has been used in two studies of Ter Łevondian entitled *Dvin under the Sallarids* and *Chronology of Dwin in the 9th and 10th centuries* published in Armenian in the *Bull. Ac. Sc. Armenian S.S.R.* of 1956 and 1957 and of which H. Berberian is now preparing a French translation. For the capture of Dwin by the Arabs, see H. Manandean, *Les invasions arabes en Arménie*, in Armenian, Fr. tr. H. Berberian in *Byzantion*, xviii (1948); the Arab historians for the dates indicated above, the chapter of Balād̲h̲urī entitled *Futūḥ Armīniyya*, ed. Cairo, 202 ff. For the description of Dwin, see Iṣṭak̲h̲rī, 191 ff.; Ibn Ḥawḳal, ed. Kramers, 337, 342-3; Muḳaddasī, 257, 379; Le Strange, 182-4. In addition to their accounts of the conquest, the Arab historians also mention Dwin in connexion with events in Armenia, revolts, etc.: see e.g. Ṭabarī, iii, 1409, 1410, 1414. Details concerning Dwin will be found in Tournebize, *Hist. pol. et rel. de l'Arménie* (index s.v. Tovin); Ghazarian, *Armenien unter der arab. Herrschaft*, reprinted from *Z. für arm. Philologie*, 21 ff., 71; Thopdschian, *Die inneren Zustände von Armenien unter Aschot I*, in *MSOS*, vii/2 (1904), and *Politische und Kirchengeschichte Armeniens unter Aschot I und Sembat I*, in *MSOS*, viii/2 (1905), *passim*; J. Laurent, *L'Arménie entre Byzance et l'Islam ... jusqu'en 886*, Paris 1919, index; idem, *Byzance et les Turcs Seljoucides*, Paris 1913-4, index; R. Vasmer, *Chronologie der arabischen Statthalter in Armenien* (750-887), Vienna 1931 and *Zur Chronologie der Ğastaniden und Sallariden*, in *Islamica*, iii, 170 ff.; Vasiliev, *Byz. et les Arabes. Dynastie macédonienne*, Russian ed., 219, 230, 231; idem, *Justin the First*, Cambridge, Mass. 1950, 357-8; E. Honigmann, *Die Ostgrenze des byz. Reiches von 363 bis 1071*, 19, 29, 158, 174, 167-7, 182; see also De Morgan, *Hist. du peuple arménien* (1919), 105, 116, 118, 123, 134, 135-6, 138, 244. References to the Armenian historians will be found in Grousset, *Histoire de l'Arménie*, Paris 1947, *passim*, and also in the works of Laurent and Minorsky given above. See also G. H. Sarkisian, *Tigranakert* (*Tigranocerta*), *Hist. of the urban communities of ancient Armenia*, Erevan 1960, in Russian, 19, 106, 135. Further to the articles of Ter Łevondian cited above, see idem, *The emirate of Dvin in Armenia in the 9th-10th centuries*, (dissertation of the University of Leningrad, 1958), and *On the question of the origin of the emirate of Dvin in Armenia*, in the volume in honour of I. A. Orbeli, *Researches on the history of the culture of the peoples of the Orient*, Moscow-Leningrad 1960 (in Russian). (M. Canard)

DYEING [see sabbāg̲h̲].

DŽABIĆ, Ali Fehmi, b. Mostar 1853, d. Istanbul 1918, from 1884 *muftī* in Mostar (Herzegovina). The Austro-Hungarian provincial government of Bosnia and Herzegovina re-organized Muslim religious institutions in order to keep them under its control. As early as 1886 the Muslims of Sarajevo aspired to religious autonomy, and the dissatisfaction of the Muslims in Herzegovina, under Džabić's leadership, steadily increased. Džabić sought religious autonomy at the conference of Bosnia-Herzegovina Muslim leaders in Sarajevo in 1893, but he remained in the minority. From the year 1899 onwards, the movement for the religious autonomy of the Muslims in Herzegovina, under Džabić's leadership, entered an acute phase. The movement had linked up with the struggle of the orthodox Serbs for religious autonomy. The Austro-Hungarian authorities persecuted

Džabić's group so that Džabić was removed from his position of *muftī* (1900). In the meantime the movement had also begun to spread in Bosnia, so that the Austro-Hungarian authorities were compelled to enter into negotiations. No agreement was reached, because the Austro-Hungarian authorities were unwilling to accept certain paragraphs in the draft statute which related to the choice of organs of religious administration and to the attestation of the *re'īs al-ʿulemā'* on behalf of the *shaykh al-Islām* in Istanbul. In 1902, when Džabić with five of his friends went to Istanbul for consultations, he was forbidden to return to his country, and stayed in Istanbul until his death. He lectured on Arabic language and literature at the university, and contributed to many journals. On the occasion of the annexation of Bosnia and Herzegovina (1908) he wrote a pamphlet in Arabic to the parliamentary deputies of the Arab countries, in which he attacked Austro-Hungarian rule in Bosnia and Herzegovina and the Turkish government because of its indulgence. As a result, he was removed from the university. He made an anthology of poems by the Companions of Muḥammad, which he wanted to publish in three volumes with his commentary, but he published only one of them: *Ḥusn al-ṣaḥāba fī sharḥ ashʿār al-ṣaḥāba*; he also wrote a commentary on Abū Ṭālib's poem in defence of Muḥammad (printed in Istanbul 1327 A.H.).

Bibliography: V. Skarić, Osman Nuri Hadžić and N. Stojanović, *Bosna i Hercegovina pod austro-ugarskom upravom, Srpski narod u XIX veku*, Belgrade 1938; M. Handžić, *Književni rad bosansko-hercegovačkih muslimana*, Sarajevo 1934.

(BRANISLAV DJURDJEV)

DŽAMBUL DŽABAEV [see DJAMBUL DJABAEV].

E

EAST AFRICA [see BAḤR AL-HIND, BAḤR AL-ZANDJ, DAR-ES-SALAAM, ERITREA, GEDI, ḤABASH, KILWA, MALINDI, MOGADISHU, MOMBASA, SOMALI, SWAHILI, TANGANYIKA, ZANDJIBĀR, etc.].

EBÜZZİYA TEVFİK (Ebu 'l-Ḍiyā' Tewfīḳ) (1848-1913), a well-known Ottoman journalist. Born in Istanbul, he had only a sketchy education, and was largely self taught. At the age of sixteen or seventeen he met Nāmiḳ Kemāl, and, through him, Shināsī, and became a frequent caller at the offices of the newspaper *Taṣwīr-i Efkār*, where the literary *avant-garde* used to meet; he claimed to have been the sixth to register as a member of the Society of New Ottomans (*Yeñi ʿOthmanlīlar Djemʿiyyeti*), founded in 1865, but this claim is questionable.

Tewfīḳ started his journalistic career in 1868-9 by writing articles in *Teraḳḳī*. When Shināsī died, Tewfīḳ and Kemāl (who soon gave up his rights in the venture) bought the printing presses on behalf of the Egyptian prince Muṣṭafā Fāḍil Pasha [*q.v.*]. The first three products of the newly-acquired press were a collection of the political writings of Reshīd Pasha, Nāmiḳ Kemāl's *Ṣalāḥ al-Dīn-i Eyyūbī*, and Tewfīḳ's own first work, the play *Edjel-i Ḳaḍā*. In his preface to this play, which was well received, Tewfiḳ defends the realist thesis that a writer must describe the morals and customs of his age without projecting his own personality. Tewfīḳ was also a regular contributor to Kemāl's *ʿIbret*, which appeared in 1872. He then took over the editorship of *Ḥadīḳa*, as from its issue dated 9 November 1872. When the latter was suspended for two months following its 56th issue, he issued the *Sirādj*, for which he had earlier taken out a licence as a precaution. 25 issues of *Sirādj* were published, the venture finally collapsing when Tewfīḳ was exiled to Rhodes in April 1873. It was in Rhodes that Tewfīḳ composed his anthology, *Nümūne-i Edebiyāt-ī ʿOthmāniyye*, and a collection of encyclopaedic articles, entitled *Māhiyāt*, of which the historical portions were later printed in the magazine *Muḥarrir* (vii-viii; 1295/1878). After the accession of Murād on 31 May 1876, Tewfīḳ returned to Istanbul and resumed his journalistic activity which continued under the new reign of ʿAbd al-Ḥamīd. When the latter had Kemāl exiled to Midilli and Ḍiyā' Pasha to Adana, Tewfīḳ sought release from official pressure by making a journey to Vienna in 1877 on publishing business. In 1880 he obtained from the Minister of Education Münīf Pasha the licence to publish the magazine *Medjmūʿa-i Ebu 'l-Ḍiyā'*, which soon became an organ of the *Tanẓīmāt* "progressives". His annual calendars, called first *Rebīʿ-i Maʿrifet*, then *Newsāl-i Maʿrifet*, had a brisk sale. In 1882 he regained control of his printing-press and named it *Maṭbaʿa-i Ebu 'l-Ḍiyā'*. A flood of publications followed, the printing-press producing on an average one fascicule every five days. There included a series of short biographies, entitled *Kütübkhāne-i meshāhīr* and modelled on the French *La vie des hommes illustres*, the hundred or so thicker volumes of the *Kütübkhāne-i Ebu 'l-Ḍiyā'*, modelled this time on the German *Universal Bibliothek* and written either by Tewfīḳ himself or by other *Tanẓīmāt* intellectuals, as well as various magazines. Before long, however, the authorities began to interfere: in 1888 the publication of Nāmiḳ Kemāl's *ʿOthmanlī ta'rīkhi* was stopped after the first fascicule had sold 6,000 copies. When the authorities demanded that pamphlets and magazines should be submitted for censorship before publicaton, Tewfīḳ closed down his *Medjmūʿa-i Ebu 'l-Ḍiyā'*. He was arrested twice, in 1891 when he was Director of the School of Arts and Crafts, and in 1893 when he was a member of the Court of First Instance of the Council of State, each time on trumped-up charges. Book censorship was relaxed in 1897 when Zühdī Pasha became Minister of Education, and Tewfīḳ once again brought out his *Medjmūʿa*, which survived until 1900 when Tewfīḳ was arrested and exiled to Ḳonya, where he stayed for almost nine years, returning only after the Young Turk Revolution as parliamentary deputy for Antalya. In 1909 he brought out the new *Taṣwīr-i Efkār* in which he described himself as an "independent and moderate progressive". He spent the remaining four years of his life in political discussions and polemics both in that newspaper and in the *Medjmūʿa-i Ebu 'l-Ḍiyā'*, which he also republished. The *Taṣwīr-i Efkār* was closed down for a time, but allowed to re-appear on 25 January 1913 when Maḥmūd Shewket Pasha succeeded Kāmil Pasha as Grand Vizier. Tewfīḳ died two days later having just delivered to his newspaper office an article entitled "New Arrests" on the Government's latest measures.

The importance of Ebu 'l-Ḍiyā Tewfīḳ lies not so much in the literary quality of his writings (although he was a good stylist and helped in the development of simple and clear Turkish prose) and not so much in his ideas, which were often confused and contradictory, as in his tireless work as a popularizer, journalist and above all publisher and printer. He himself was proud of having produced the first illustrated printed texts in Turkey. He was also the first to use Kūfic type face. His memoirs about his famous contemporaries are also important and there is much of interest in his *Shināsī ile mülāḳāt*, *Zamānīmīz ta'rīkhine ʿā'id khāṭirāt*, *Ridjāl-i mensiye*, *Yeñi ʿOthmanlīlar ta'rīkhi* and *Kemāl Beyiñ terdjüme-i ḥāli*, Istanbul 1326/1908), as well as in his autobiographical articles *Rūznāme-i ḥayātīmdan baʿḍī ṣaḥā'if* and *Maḳāme-i tewḳīfiyye* (in *Medjmūʿa-i Ebu 'l-Ḍiyā'*, Nos. 109-27).

Bibliography: The best biography is that by Ihsan Sungur in *Aylık Ansiklopedi*, ix, 266-9, see also *Merḥūm Ḍiyā' Tewfīḳ Bey*, in *Therwet-i Funūn*, no. 28; articles in Bursalī Ṭāhir, *ʿOthmānlī mü'ellifleri* and I. Alâeddin, *Meşhur Adamlar Ansiklopedisi* and references in Aḥmed Midḥat, *Menfā*, Istanbul 1293/1876, 72 ff.; Bereket-zāde I. Ḥaḳḳī, *Yād-ī Māḍī*, Istanbul 1332/1914, 55, 73 ff., 141; Ali Ekrem, *Nâmık Kemal*, Istanbul 1930, 58, 78; Halid Ziya Uşaklıgil, *Kırk Yıl*, Istanbul 1936, ii, 35, 74, 119; Fu'ād Köprülü, *Ebu 'l-Ḍiyā Tewfīḳ Bey: ölümü münāsebeti ile* in *Therwet-i Funūn* (No. 1140, 28 March 1911); *İA*, s.v.

(Fevziye Abdullah)

ECIJA [see istidja'].

ECONOMY [see tadbīr al-manzil]

ECSTASY [see shaṭḥ, also darwīsh, dhikr].

EDEBIYYĀT-I DJEDĪDE, "new literature", the name given to a Turkish literary movement associated with the review *Therwet-i Funūn* [*q.v.*] during the years 1895-1901—that is, during the editorship of Tewfīḳ Fikret [*q.v.*]. See further turks, literature, and the articles on the individual authors.

(Ed.)

EDESSA [see al-ruhā].

EDHEM, ČERKES [see čerkes, edhem].

EDHEM, KHALĪL [see eldem, khalīl edhem].

EDIRNE, Adrianople—a city lying at the confluence of the Tundja and Arda with the Merič (Maritsa); the capital of the Ottomans after Bursa (Brusa), and now the administrative centre of the *vilâyet* (province) of the same name and, traditionally, the centre of Turkish (now Eastern) Thrace (Trakya or Pasha-eli). Its historical importance derives from the fact that it lies on the main road from Asia Minor to the Balkans, where it is the first important staging point after Istanbul. It guards the eastern entrance to the natural corridor between the Rhodope mountains to the south-west and the Istrandja mountains to the north-east. It also dominates traffic down the valleys of the Tundja and the Merič and used to be the starting point of important river traffic down the Merič to the Aegean. In later times the main weight of traffic was transferred to the railway passing through Edirne on its way to Istanbul. Edirne is particularly rich in Ottoman architectural monuments. Its importance, diminished by the transfer of the Ottoman capital to Istanbul, received a great blow when the city was captured by the Russians in 1829. Since the Balkan Wars it has been a Turkish frontier city, which fell briefly under Bulgarian occupation in 1913 and was occupied by the Greeks between 1920 and 1922. The population of Edirne, which exceeded 100,000 in the middle of the 19th century, fell to 87,000 at the beginning of the present century (of whom 47,000 are Turks, some 20,000 Greeks, some 15,000 Jews, 4,000 Armenians and 2,000 Bulgarians), then again to 34,528 at the census of 1927 and, finally, to 29,400 in 1945, since when it has been rising. The population is now largely Turkish, with a small Jewish community.

The city is built inside a bend of the Tundja, just before its junction with the Merič, on gently rising ground reaching a height of 75 metres on the hillock on which the great Selīmiyye mosque is built, and some 100 metres further to the east. The part of the city built on the lower slopes has often been flooded, sometimes catastrophically. The city consists of two main parts, Ḳalʿe-iči, in the western part of the river curve, the district surrounded by the walls, which have now almost completely disappeared, and rebuilt on a geometric pattern after being devastated by fire at the end of the last century, and Ḳalʿe-dīshī to the east. It is the latter which is the centre of the modern city.

The name of the city is given in old Ottoman sources as Edrinus, Edrune, Edrinaboli, Endriye, as well as Edirne or Edrine, the latter form being used in the *fetḥnāme* sent by Murād I to the Ilkhānid sultan Uways Khān. Historical documents also use honorific names, such as Dār al-Naṣr wa 'l-Maymana (Abode of Divinely-Aided Victory and of Felicity), Dār al-Salṭana (Abode of the Sultanate) etc.

The city is believed to have been first settled by Thracian tribes, from whom it was captured by the Macedonians and named Oresteia (or Orestias). It was rebuilt by the Emperor Hadrian in the 2nd century and named after him Hadrianopolis, Adrianople. Adrianople witnessed the victory of Constantine over Licinius in 323, the defeat of Valens by the Goths in 378; it was besieged by the Avars in 586, captured by the Bulgars in 914, besieged again by the Pečenegs in 1049 and 1078. At the battle of Adrianople in 1205 the Latin Emperor of Byzantium Baldwin was defeated and captured by the Bulgars who joined with the Greeks in resisting Catholic encroachment. The Byzantine Greeks then held the city against the Bulgarians. Turks from Asia Minor appeared on the scene in 1342-3 when Aydīn-oghlu Umūr Bey fought as an ally of Cantacuzenus against John Palaeologus, defended Dimetoka [*q.v.*] against the "prince" (*tekfūr*) of Edirne and is said to have killed the latter (see Mükrimin Halil, *Dustūrnāme-i Enverī*, Istanbul 1929, introduction 43-6). In 754/1353 the Ottoman prince Süleymān Pasha joined the forces of Cantacuzenus in Edirne after defeating an army of Bulgars and Serbians. Three years before the final conquest of Edirne, the Ottoman Orkhān Bey advised Süleymān Pasha to keep a close eye on the castle of Edirne. The conquest was accomplished under Murād I by Lālā Shāhīn Pasha, who defeated the *tekfūr* of Edirne at Sāzlī-Dere, to the south-east of the city. The latter then fled secretly by boat from his palace on the banks of the Tundja and in Ramaḍān 763/July 1362 the inhabitants of the town surrendered on condition of being allowed to live there freely. Although Murād I left the administration of Edirne to Lālā Shāhīn Pasha, preferring for a time to hold his court at Bursa or Dimetoka, the city of Edirne became almost immediately the forward base of

Ottoman expansion in Europe. It was from Edirne, furthermore that Yïldïrïm Bāyezīd set out to besiege Constantinople. After Bāyezīd's later defeat in the battle of Ankara, the elder prince Süleymān transferred the treasury from Bursa to Edirne where he ascended the throne. He later lost the city to Mūsā Čelebi, who also ruled from Edirne and minted money there in his name. After his defeat and death, Sultan Meḥemmed I spent most of his eight-year rule in Edirne and died there, being buried like his predecessors in Bursa. It was in Edirne in 825/1422 that the Pretender Muṣṭafā was executed after his defeat by Murād II. The latter's reign saw an increase in the prosperity of Edirne and its environs and the building of the town of Uzun-Köprü (Djisr-i Ergene).

It was at Edirne that Murād II received foreign ambassadors, it is from there that he directed his conquests, and it was also on the island on the Tundja that the circumcision-feasts of his sons ʿAlāʾ al-Dīn and Meḥemmed were celebrated with magnificent pomp. His reign witnessed also a mutiny of the Janissaries at Edirne on the pretext of the fire in the city, a mutiny which was pacified by an increase in the soldiers' pay. Murād II died in Edirne and was succeeded by Meḥemmed II who, however, did not return to the city until he decided to lay siege to Constantinople. The plans of the siege were worked out in Edirne and the siege guns tested in its environs. After the conquest Meḥemmed II again held court in Edirne where he organized in the spring of 861/1457 magnificent circumcision celebrations, lasting two months, for the princes Bāyezīd and Muṣṭafā. Selīm I also held court in Edirne, the city being left to the care of princes when the Sultan campaigned. The prosperity of Edirne continued to grow in the 10th/16th century: Süleymān the Magnificent often stayed there, while the city's greatest mosque was built under his successor. The tranquillity of the city was, however, disturbed by mutinies in 994/1586 and 1003/1595. From the time of Aḥmed I, Edirne became famous for its royal hunting parties, royal celebrations and entertainments in and around the city, attaining particular brilliance under Meḥemmed IV (*Avdjï* = the Hunter). Later the life of the city began to be affected by the successive defeats suffered by Ottoman arms. In 1115/1703, at the famous "Edirne incident", Muṣṭafā II who held his court in Edirne was deposed in favour of Aḥmed III by malcontents coming from Istanbul. The subsequent decline of the city was hastened by the fire of 1158/1745 in which some 60 quarters were burnt down and by the earthquake of 1164/1751. In 1801 Edirne witnessed a mutiny of Albanian troops against Selīm III's reforms. A second "Edirne incident" occurred in 1806 for the same reasons. On the other hands the abolition of the Janissaries occasioned only minor difficulties in Edirne. In the Russian-Ottoman war of 1828-9 Edirne was occupied by the Russians and this occupation deeply affected the local Muslim population. Muslims started emigrating from Edirne, their place being taken by Christians coming in from the surrounding villages. To raise the Muslims' morale Maḥmūd II visited Edirne for some ten days, ordered a large bridge to be built on the Merič (this, however, was only completed in 1842 in the reign of ʿAbd al-Medjīd) and had commemorative coins struck. More devastations were caused by the Russian occupation of Edirne in 1878-9, and by the hostilities in the Balkan wars and following the First World War.

Monuments: Of the castle of Edirne, four of whose towers and nine of whose gates we know by name, only one tower, the Sāʿat Ḳulesi (Clock Tower), originally Büyük Ḳule (the Great Tower), remains in existence, the clock itself being a late 19th century addition. Greek inscriptions in the names of John V and Michael Palaeologus have disappeared.

Palaces: 1. Eski Sarāy (the Old Palace). After the conquest of Edirne, Murād I found the *Tekfūr*'s palace in the castle inadequate, and built a new palace outside the castle, where he moved in 767/1365-6. Ewliyā Čelebi says that this was near the Sultan Selīm mosque in the quarter of Ḳavaḳ Meydan(ï) and that it was later used as a barracks for *ʿadjemī-oghlan*s. During the Hungarian expeditions of Süleymān the Magnificent the old palace could accommodate 6,000 pages, while accommodation for 40,000 Janissaries was provided near by. Ewliyā Čelebi (iii, 456) says that the palace did not have its own gardens, that it was surrounded by high walls, measuring some 5,000 paces in circumference, that it was rectangular in shape and that it had a gate known as *bāb-ï humāyūn*. Although the importance of the old palace diminished after the building of the Sultan Selīm mosque, it was still used for the education of *ič-oghlan*s, the palace organization remaining unchanged from before the conquest of Istanbul. In 1086/1675 Sultan Meḥemmed IV allocated the old palace to his daughter Khadīdja who married Muṣāḥib Muṣṭafā Pasha, hence the later name of Palace of Khadīdja Sulṭān. In the later 19th century a military lycée was built on the site of the old palace.

2. Sarāy-ï Djedīd-i ʿĀmire (the New Imperial Palace), built on an island on the Tundja and on adjoining meadows by Murād II in 854/1450, partly with marble brought from some ruins near Salonica. Construction of the palace was continued the following year by Meḥemmed II who also had thousands of trees planted on the island, which he joined by a bridge to the main palace buildings to the west. Another bridge, this time between the palace and the main city, was built by Süleymān the Magnificent, under whose direction important additions were made to the palace. More pavilions were added in subsequent reigns until the palace grew to twice its size under Meḥemmed II. At the end of the 11th/17th century it contained 18 pavilions, 8 *mesdjid*s, 17 large gates, 14 baths and 5 courts. Some six to ten thousand people lived within the confines of the palace. Dissolution was gradual: there were many attempts at restoration in the 18th century, but in 1827 an official survey said that most buildings were either completely in ruins or half-ruined. Much damage was caused to the palace by the Russian occupation of 1829, Russian troops camping in the palace gardens. More attempts at restoration followed, but the second Russian occupation sounded the death knell of the palace. The Ottomans themselves set fire to ammunition dumps in the palace before evacuating the city, and after returning they quarried the remaining buildings for stone.

Mosques: The first Friday prayers were said in Edirne in a converted church inside the castle, known afterwards as the Ḥalabiye, after its first *müderris*, Sirādj al-Dīn Muḥammed b. ʿUmar Ḥalabī, a teacher of Meḥemmed the Conqueror, and also as Čelebi Djāmiʿi. Ruined in an earthquake in the 18th century and later repaired, it survived until the end of the 19th century. Another church in the castle was converted into a mosque under the name of Kilise Djāmiʿi, but this was pulled down by Meḥemmed II and replaced by one with six

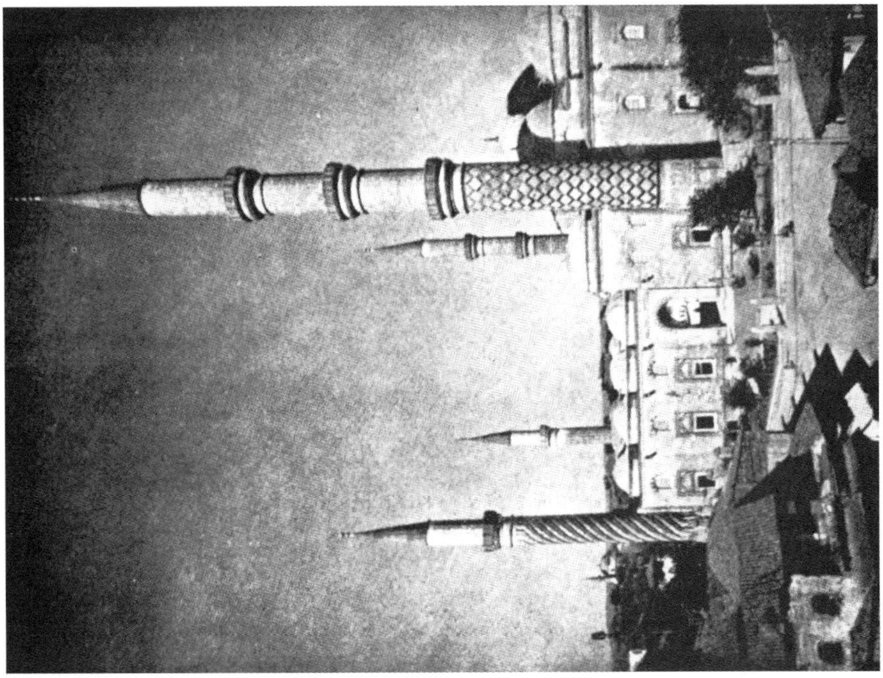

Üč-s̲h̲erefeli D̲j̲āmiʿ, entrée et cour.

(B. Ünsal, *Turkish Islamic Architecture*, Londres 1959.)

Eski D̲j̲āmiʿ.

Mosquée de Bāyezīd II et hôpital.

Selīmiyye D̲j̲āmiʿi.
(B. Ünsal, *Turkish Islamic Architecture*, Londres 1959).

domes which disappeared in the second half of the 18th century. The oldest surviving mosque is that of Yïldïrïm, built in 801/1399, on the foundations of a church ruined in the Fourth Crusade, so that the *miḥrāb* is built into a side wall. During their occupation of 1878 the Russians stripped the inside of the mosque of its tiles and of the two linked marble rings which had given the mosque the name of Küpeli Dj̲āmiʿ (Ear-ring mosque). Another old mosque, the Eski Dj̲āmiʿ (or Old Mosque *par excellence*) was started in 804/1402 by Emīr Süleymān (hence the name of Süleymāniye given it by Meḥemmed I, a name which was later changed into Ulu Dj̲āmiʿ, or Great Mosque, before the present one of Eski Dj̲āmiʿ or Dj̲āmiʿi ʿAtīḳ was finally adopted) and completed in 816/1413 under Meḥemmed I (Pl. X). The interior is square, 9 domes being supported by four columns. An inscription on the western gate, gives the name of the architect as Ḥādj̲dj̲ī ʿAlaʾ al-Dīn of Ḳonya. A stone from a corner of the Kaʿba was placed at the time of building in the window to the right of the *miḥrāb*, and has been venerated ever since. In the 18th century the mosque suffered in a fire and an earthquake and was restored by Maḥmud I. Another mosque, the Murādiye, was built by Murād II first as a house of Mewlewī dervishes, a smaller *mewlewī-k̲h̲āne* being built next to it when the main building was turned into a mosque. This mosque is distinguished by the excellent tiles which cover the *miḥrāb* and part of the walls. In the 10th/16th century this mosque, with its almshouse and other adjuncts, was in receipt of very large revenues. Another formerly rich mosque, the Dār al-Ḥadīt̲h̲ (which had at the beginning of the 11th/17th century a revenue of over half a million aspers), was originally a *medrese*, completed in 839/1435. The minaret of this mosque was destroyed in the siege of 1912. Several princes and princesses are buried in a nearby *türbe*.

Another building going back to Murād II is the Üč-s̲h̲erefeli Dj̲āmiʿ (Three-Balconied Mosque) started in 841/1437-8 and finished in 851/1447-8 (Pl. X). Ewliyā Čelebi says that it was built at the cost of 7,000 purses, being the proceeds of the booty captured at the conquest of Izmir. This mosque has also been known as the Murādiye, Yeni Dj̲āmiʿ (New Mosque) and Dj̲āmiʿ-i Kebīr (Great Mosque). The building is rectangular, a great dome being held up by six columns, there being four medium-sized and four other small domes at the sides of the main one. Four of the columns (at either side of the main gate and the *miḥrāb*) are built into the walls. The *ḥarem* (sacred enclosure, *i.e.*, court-yard), paved with marble, is regarded as the first *ḥarem* of a mosque built by the Ottomans. The cloisters on the four sides of the *ḥarem* are made up of 21 domed vaults, supported by 18 columns. The three-balconied minaret is known as the first Ottoman minaret of this kind. There is also one minaret with two balconies and others with one balcony. Murād II first allocated for the upkeep of this mosque the revenues of the silver mines at Karatova in Serbia. Later Rüstem Pas̲h̲a transferred these mines to the Treasury, allowing the mosque to draw money instead from the *waḳf* of Bāyezīd II. An important event in the history of the mosque was the public condemnation in it by Fak̲h̲r al-Dīn ʿAdj̲emī of the *ḥurūfī* followers of Faḍl Allāh Tabrīzī, who were believed to enjoy the sympathy of Sultan Meḥemmed the Conqueror. Bāyezīd II built on the banks of the Tundj̲a a mosque, baths, a hospital, a *medrese* and an almshouse (Pl. XI). A chronogram on the mosque gate yields the date 893/1488. The building was financed with the booty captured at Aḳ-Kermān.

The mosque is a simple structure, without arches or pillars, the dome being supported by the four walls. Baths (*tāb-k̲h̲āne*), surmounted by nine domes and consisting of four rooms each, adjoin on either side and lead onto the two slender minarets. The marble *minbar* of the mosque is particularly elegant. The mosque contains also the first private gallery (*maḥfil*) built in an Edirne mosque; this is supported by porphyry columns, brought probably from the ruins of some temple. The hospital (*dār al-s̲h̲ifāʾ*) built to the west of the mosque is a hexagonal building, six further rooms for the isolation and treatment of patients standing in the hospital gardens (where, Ewliyā Čelebi tells us, the patients were regularly made to listen to music). The *medrese* stands in front of the hospital, while the almshouse and a bakery lie to the east of the mosque. Bāyezīd II had a quay made on the bank of the Tundj̲a, in front of the *miḥrab* of the mosque, and also widened the course of the river. The most beautiful monuments built in Edirne in the 10th/16th century are the work of the architect Sinān. One of these mosques (the Tas̲h̲lïḳ Dj̲āmiʿi, converted by Sinān from the *zāwiya* of Maḥmūd Pas̲h̲a) is no longer in existence. Three still stand: the Defterdār Dj̲āmiʿi, the mosque of S̲h̲ayk̲h̲ī Čelebi, and finally the mosque of Sultan Selīm (Selīmiye Dj̲āmiʿi), which is the glory of Edirne and the last royal mosque in the city (Pl. XI). Built between 972/1564-5 and 982/1574-5 according to the chronogram on the gate of the *ḥarem*, it cost, Ewliyā Čelebi tells us, 27,760 purses obtained from the booty captured in Cyprus. The great dome of the mosque, which rests on 8 columns, is 6 cubits (*d̲h̲irāʿ*) higher than that of Saint Sophia in Istanbul. The *muʾad̲h̲d̲h̲in*'s gallery under the great dome is supported by 12 marble columns, two metres high; under it there is a small fountain. The mosque library is on the right, and the royal gallery on the left. This *maḥfil*, which rests on four marble pillars, used to be decorated by tiles, which were taken away by the Russians in 1878. The *ḥarem* court-yard is surrounded by cloisters, in which 18 domes are supported by 16 large pillars brought from the Ḳapï-Dag̲h̲ peninsula and from ruins in Syria (according to Ewliyā Čelebi, also from Athens). Four three-balconied minarets stand at the four corners of the mosque, which have often been repaired. As for the mosque itself, it was repaired after the earthquake of 1752 and also in 1808, 1884 and in recent years. The Sultan Selīm mosque forms an architectural whole with the adjacent *medrese*, *dār al-ḳurrāʾ* (*Ḳurʾān* reciters' quarters), school and clock-house. The *müderris* of the Selīmiye *medrese* was considered the chief *müderris* of the city. The *medrese* was subsequently used as a military detention centre and is now a museum of antiquities, while the *dār al-ḳurrāʾ* houses an ethnographic museum. The library was later enriched by many *waḳf* books, but some valuable books were lost during the Bulgarian occupation.

Edirne was an important centre of Islamic learning, which was allowed an independent course, as in Istanbul and Bursa. Apart from those already mentioned, there were important *medrese*s in the court-yard of the Uč-s̲h̲erefeli Dj̲āmiʿ (founded by Murād II) and the Peykler Medresesi, founded in the same place by Meḥemmed II. These *medrese*s, built in the classical Ottoman style, are today ruined, but could still be restored. Many markets were also built in Edirne, largely as a source of revenue for the upkeep of the pious foundations in the city. The first of these is the covered market of Meḥemmed I (14 domes, 4 gates), which was a *waḳf* of the Eski Djāmiʿ. The covered market built by Murād II, known as the Old Market, fell into ruin in the second half of the 11th/17th century. Murād III had a market built by Sinān, and known as Ārasta (73 arches, 124 shops), to provide revenue for the Selīmiye mosque. Sinān also built a market with six gates for Semiz ʿAlī Pasha. The city contained also a large number of *khāns*. Of these Sinān built the Large and the Small *khāns* of Rüstem Pasha and also the Tash-khān built for Sokollu. Another *khān* which is still in existence is that built in the beginning of the 11th/17th century by Ekmekči-zāde Aḥmed Pasha. At the beginning of the 10th/16th century there were in all 16 *khans* and markets in Edirne. Later the number increased, French and English merchants also having their places of work. The trades practised in Edirne included dyeing, tanning, soap-making, distillation of attar of roses, carriage-building etc. Edirne was also famous for its own style of book-binding. The city's water supply was ensured by the Khāṣṣeki Sulṭān aqueduct built in 937/1530. There were also some 300 public fountains, most of which have now disappeared. Apart from the palace bridges, there were in Edirne four bridges over the Tundja and one over the Merič, the oldest being the bridge of Ghāzī Mīkhāl, built in 823/1420.

At first the administration of Edirne was in the hands of a *ḳāḍī* and of a *su-bashi* (who was probably the same person as the *āghā* of Janissaries mentioned by Pococke). After the conquest of Istanbul the *bostāndji-bashi* was made responsible for the administration. The *ḳāḍī* of Edirne, who had a daily allowance of 300 aspers at the beginning of the 10th/16th century, could expect promotion to Istanbul, and had, according to Ewliyā Čelebi, 45 deputies (*nāʾib*). He was appointed and dismissed by the central government. One interesting local official was the Chief Gardener (*ketkhudā-yi bāghbāniyān*), responsible for the care of private gardens and orchards on the banks of the three rivers (Ḥibrī gives their number as 450, suggesting that it had been larger before, *Enīs al-müsāmirīn*, f. 26). The city of Edirne was a crown domain (*khāṣṣ*) of the Sultans, producing a revenue of nearly two million aspers at the beginning of the 10th/16th century. Money was sometimes sent from the Edirne Treasury to help meet the requirements of Istanbul. Edirne used also to be the seat of a Greek Orthodox Metropolitan and of a Chief Rabbi.

With more than 50 *zāwiyas* and *tekkes*, Edirne bred many famous dervish *sheykhs*. Among the most famous were the Mewlewīs Djelāl al-Dīn and Djemāl al-Dīn in the reign of Murād II, and Sezāʾī Ḥasan Dede (d. 1151/1738), considered the second *pīr* of the Gulshenī *ṭarīḳa*. The beauties of Edirne have been described in many poems, including the *Humāyūn-nāme* of ʿAlāʾ al-Dīn ʿAlī and the *Ṭabaḳāt al-mamālik* of Ḳodja Nishāndjī. A local poet, Khayālī, wrote a poem ending in the refrain *Edrine*, and this has often been imitated. Finally, Edirne is graphically described in Nefʿī's *ḳaṣīda* to the Sultan.

Bibliography: A detailed monograph on Edirne, with a history of the years 760-1043/1359-1633, was written by Ḥibrī [*q.v.*] of Edirne in 1046/1636 under the title *Enīs al-müsāmirīn*; it is still unpublished, but is extracted in Ḥādjdjī Khalīfa's *Rumeli und Bosna*, tr. v. Hammer, Vienna 1812, 1-15, and in the so-called *Chronicle* of Djewrī (Istanbul 1291-2), cf. Hammer-Purgstall, *GOR*, x, 691 ff., and Babinger, 213; there is a continuation, called *Riyāḍ-i belde-i Edirne*, by Bādī Aḥmed Efendi (1255-1326/1839-1908). Besides the long section in Ewliyā Čelebi, *Seyāḥatnāme*, iii, there are descriptions by European travellers in the 17th and 18th centuries (John Covel, in Th. Bent, *Early voyages and travels in the Levant*, London 1893; Antoine Galland, *Journal*, ed. Ch. Schefer, Paris 1881; E. Chishull, *Travels in Turkey*, London 1747; *Letters of Lady Wortley Montague*, letters 25-34). The decay of the city in the beginning of the 19th century is described by George Keppel, *Narrative of a journey across the Balcans*, London 1831, i, and by Moltke, *Briefe über Zustände und Begebenheiten in der Türkei*[6], 150 ff.; Nicolas de Nicolay, *Navigations . . .*, gives types of the inhabitants in the 10th/16th century. Views and plans of the mosques and other buildings are given by C. Sayger and A. Desarnod, *Album d'un voyage en Turquie en 1829-1830*, Paris n.d., fol., Thomas Allom and Robert Walsh, *Constantinople*, ii, 73, 77, and notably by C. Gurlitt, *Die Bauten Adrianopels*, in *Orientalisches Archiv*, i, p. i and ii (cf. G. Jacob in *Isl.*, iii (1912), 358-68). Works in Turkish include: the *Sālnāmes* of the vilâyet of Edirne; Rifʿat ʿOthmān, *Edirne Rehnümāsī*, Edirne 1335/1920; Oktay Aslanapa, *Edirnede Osmanlı devri abideleri*, Istanbul 1949; M. Tayyib Gökbilgin, *XV-XVI asırlarda Edirne ve Paşa livâsı*, Istanbul 1952; idem, "Edirne" in *IA*.

(M. Tayyib Gökbilgin)

EDREMIT, town of western Turkey, situated 8 km. from the head of the Gulf of Edremit (on the site of Homer's Thebe) on the lower slopes of Pasha-dagh (a spur of Mt. Ida) overlooking the fertile alluvial plain to the south (39° 35′ N., 27° 02′ E.). The ancient Adramyttion was on the coast at Karatash (4 km. west of Burhaniye [formerly Kemer] and 13 km. south-west of Edremit), where remains of quays, etc., are to be found. The evidence of coins indicates that the city was transferred to its present site not (as Kiepert suggested) under the Comnenes but much earlier, perhaps in the 2nd century A.D. (W. Ruge, in Pauly-Wissowa, art. Thebe, col. 1597). Turkish attacks began at the end of the 11th century: in 1093 Adramyttion was entirely destroyed by Tzachas (Čaka), operating from his base at Smyrna, and re-built by Alexius' general Philokales (*Aléxiade*, ed. B. Leib, iii, 143); and towards 1160 Manuel I strengthened its fortifications against the Turkish danger (Nicetas Choniates, Bonn ed., 194). When in 1261 Michael Palaeologus ceded Smyrna to the Genoese, he granted them also extensive privileges in Adramyttion (W. Heyd, *Hist. du commerce du Levant*, i, 429), and early in the next century a Genoese garrison was defending the city against the Turks (Pachymeres, Bonn ed., ii, 558). Soon afterwards Edremit fell into the hands of the Karasī [*q.v.*] dynasty, to be occupied, along with their other territories, by the Ottomans in the reign of Orkhān (ʿĀshiḳpashazāde, ed. Giese, 41; ʿĀshiḳpashazāde's date, 735/1334-5, is too early, by ten years or more). For five centuries Edremit was administered as a *ḳaḍā* of the *sandjaḳ* of Karasī (for administrative changes 1841-1923 see *IA*, vi, 334). Now the centre of a *kaza* of the *vilâyet* of Balīkesir, it has a thriving olive-oil industry (population [1950] 12,700).

Bibliography: Pauly-Wissowa, s.vv. Adramitteion, Thebe (5); H. Kiepert, *Die alten Ortslagen am Südfusse des Idagebirges*, in *ZGErdk.Berl.*, xxiv (1889), 290-303 (with map); W. Tomaschek, *Zur historischen Topographie von Kleinasien im Mittelalter*, i, 1891 (= *SBAk.Wien*, cxxiv/8), 23-4; V. Cuinet, *La Turquie d'Asie*, 1890-5, iv, 273-6; A. Philippson, *Reisen und Forschungen im Westlichen Kleinasien*, i (= *Pet. Mitt.*, Ergänzungsheft 167), 1910, 30-3; *IA* s.v. (= Mordtmann's article in *EI*[1], with additions by the Turkish editors).

(J. H. MORDTMANN-[V. L. MÉNAGE])

EDUCATION [see TADRĪS, also DJĀMIʿA, MAʿĀRIF, MADRASA and TARBIYA].

EFE (see ZEYBEK).

EFENDI, an Ottoman title of Greek origin, from αὐθέντης, Lord, Master, (cf. authentic), probably via a Byzantine colloquial vocative form, *afendi* (G. Meyer, *Türkische Studien*, i, in *SBAk. Wien* (1893), 37; K. Foy in *MSOS*, i/2 (1898), 44 n. 3; Psichari, 408). The term was already in use in Turkish Anatolia in the 13th and 14th centuries. Eflākī indicates that the daughter of Djalāl al-Dīn Rūmī was known as Efendipoulo—the master's daughter (Cl. Huart, *Les saints des derviches tourneurs*, Paris 1922, ii, 429; on the later Karaite family name Afendopoulo or Efendipoulo see Z. Ankori, *Karaites in Byzantium*, New York-Jerusalem 1959, 199-200). Ibn Baṭṭūṭa found that the brother of the ruler of Kastamonu was called Efendi (*Voyages*, ii, 345; Eng. trans. Sir Hamilton Gibb, *The travels of Ibn Battuta*, ii, Cambridge 1962, 463). This title was also used under the Ottomans (see, for example, ʿĀshîḳpashazāde, chapter 46, where Ḳara Rüstem addresses the Ḳāḍîʿasker Djandarlî Khalīl as Efendi), and in a number of fermāns issued in Greek from the chancery of Meḥemmed the Conqueror the Sultan himself is called ὁ μέγας αὐθέντης—perhaps the original of Grand Signor (Hammer-Purgstall, *Histoire*, ii, 523; F. Babinger-F. Dölger, *Mehmed's II. frühester Staatsvertrag (1446)*, in *Orientalia Christiana Periodica*, xv (1949), 234; A. Bombaci, *Nuovi firmani greci di Maometto II*, in *BZ*, xlvii (1954), 298-319; cf. Deny, *Sommaire*, 561). From the late 15th century onwards the title Efendi was used of various dignitaries, in Turkish as well as in Greek. In the 16th century there still seem to have been doubts of its propriety. A *fatwā* of Abu 'l-Suʿūd [*q.v.*], cited by Pakalın, considers the origin and meaning of the word, and the propriety of applying it to Muslims or to God. The word, he says, is common to Turkish and Greek (*kefere lughatî*), and means the owner of slaves and slave-girls. It is wrong to call God Efendi; whether one may call a Muslim Efendi is an open question. In fact, the word became increasingly common in Ottoman usage, as a designation of members of the scribal and religious, as opposed to the military classes (cf. ČELEBI). It was in particular used of certain important functionaries. Thus, the *Reʾīs al-küttāb* [*q.v.*] was known as the Reis Efendi, the ḳāḍī of Istanbul as Istanbul Efendisi, and the chief secretary of the janissaries as Yeñi Čeri [*q.v.*] Efendisi; the latter's department was called Efendi Kapîsî or Efendi Dāʾiresi. The chief secretaries of the *dīwān* in Istanbul or of provincial governors-general were known as *dīwān efendisi* (in Egypt *dīwān efendi*—Deny, 111-2. For other efendis in Ottoman Egypt see Gibb-Bowen, i/2, 46-7, 65-6; S. J. Shaw, *The financial and administrative organization and development of Ottoman Egypt 1517-1798*, Princeton 1962, index). At the same time, it remained the practice to speak of the Sultan as *Efendimiz*—our master; in the 19th century an Arabicized form of the same expression—*Efendinā*—was used in Egypt of Muḥammad ʿAlī and his successors. It was not uncommon for Muslims to speak of the Prophet as *Efendimiz*—our lord, or for Turkish-speaking Christians to use the same expression of Jesus Christ.

During the 19th century the Ottoman government made attempts to regulate the use of *Efendi*, as of other titles and designations, by law. It was given, for example, to princes of the ruling house; to the wives of the Sultans (*kadîn* [*q.v.*] *efendi*); to the *Shaykh al-Islām*, the *ʿUlemāʾ*, and other, non-Muslim, religious heads; to functionaries up to the rank of *Bālā* [*q.v.*] or, in the armed forces, of *biñbashî* [*q.v.*]. In fact, however, it was used, following the personal name, as a form of address or reference for persons possessing a certain standard of literacy, and not styled Bey (see BEG) or Pasha; it thus came to be an approximate equivalent of the English Mister or French Monsieur. In the records of the first Ottoman parliament of 1877, the deputies are nearly all designated as Efendi or Bey, and the speaker addresses the house as *Efendiler*—gentlemen. The distinction between *efendi* and *bey* in Turkey finally came to be one between religious and secular, the former term being used primarily for men of religion or of religious education, the latter for military and then also for civilian laymen. The title *efendi* was finally abolished in Turkey, together with other Ottoman ranks and titles, in 1934. In the form *efendim* (also *Beyefendim* and *Hanımefendim*)—sir, madam—it remains in common use as a form of address for both men and women.

In the Arab countries formerly under Ottoman rule, where the title Efendi came into general use in the 19th century, it followed a somewhat different line of development, and came to designate the secular, literate townspeople, usually dressed in European style, as against the lower classes on the one hand, and the men of religion on the other. This was in contrast with the Turkish practice, which tended to apply the title more especially to men of religion. After becoming a rough equivalent of Mr. or Esquire, the title Efendi is now disappearing in the Arab lands, being replaced for the most part by Sayyid.

Bibliography: J. Psichari, *Efendi*, in *Philologie et linguistique. Mélanges offerts à Louis Havet*, Paris 1909, 387-427; J. Deny, *Sommaire des archives turques du Caire*, Cairo 1930, 61-2 and index; Köprülüzade Mehmet Fuat (= M. F. Köprülü), *Bizans müesseselerinin Osmanlı müesseselerine te'siri . .*, in *Türk Hukuk ve Iktisat Tarihi Mecmuası*, i (1931), 277-8 (Ital. trans., *Alcune osservazioni intorno all' influenza delle istituzioni bizantine sulle istituzioni ottomane*, Rome 1953, 130-1); S. Kekule, *Über Titel, Ämter, Rangstufen und Anreden in der offiziellen osmanischen Sprache*, Halle 1892, 8; Pakalın, i, 505; *IA* s.v. (Orhan Köprülü); brief entries also in E. Littmann, *Morgenländische Wörter im Deutschen*[2], Tübingen 1924, 107; K. Lokotsch, *Etymologisches Wörterbuch der europäischen . . Wörter orientalischen Ursprungs*, Heidelberg 1927, 44, and the standard dictionaries.

(B. LEWIS)

EFLĀḲ, the Turkish form of the word Wallach, originally applied by Germanic tribes to Latin populations. The Slavs, the Byzantines and, later, the Ottomans used it to denote the Balkan Rumanians and those north of the Danube. It is probable that it lost its ethnic meaning in certain parts of the peninsula, and was applied simply to a pastoral population. Under the Turks, the Wallachians who were incorporated in the organization of the *voynūḳ* [*q.v.*] provided light cavalry units.

The first mention of Rumanian political institutions south of the Carpathians occurs in the diploma granted by the king of Hungary to the Knights Hospitallers (1247). In 1330, Basarab reigned over the whole territory lying between the Danube and the Carpathians (Ţara Românească) as an independent sovereign, after the victory over the Hungarian king Charles Robert. The dynasty founded by Basarab bore his name, which is of Kuman origin. Under his son Nicolaë Alexandru, the orthodox Rumanian Church was raised to metropolitan status. The first contact of Wallachia with the Ottomans took place in 1368 in the reign of Vladislav (1364-74 or 5). The reign of Mircea the Old (1388-1418) is memorable for a long series of struggles against Bāyezīd I. In 1391 Fīrūz Beg attacked Vidin and crossed the Danube into Wallachia. Enough booty was taken to provide endowments for charitable institutions in Bursa. In 1393 Mircea the Old lost Silistria. In the years that followed, war was waged between Wallachia and the Ottomans, and the monarch was temporarily replaced by a certain Vlad who recognized Ottoman suzerainty and, in 1394, paid tribute for the first time. After the battle of Ankara, Mircea intervened in the struggle between the sons of Bāyezīd I over the succession to the throne. The entry of Wallachia into the Turkish orbit gave rise to two political currents. In the struggle against Islam, some of the Boyars sought aid from the Magyar kingdom, and later from the royal houses of Austria or Russia; but rather than endure the wars which this policy provoked, the others preferred to recognize Ottoman suzerainty. The whole course of Rumanian history was profoundly influenced by this conflict. In the 15th century Vlad the Devil (1436-46) struggled against the Turks, but in the end accepted their authority, thereby provoking a Hungarian campaign in the course of which he met his death. His son Vlad the Impaler (1456-62, 1476) fought against Meḥemmed II without success. In the 16th century Radu dela Afumaţi (1522-9) resisted the Turks but was compelled to recognize their suzerainty and in the end was assassinated by the Boyars. It was only in the closing years of the 16th century that Rumanian resistance became at all effective. Michael the Brave (1593-1601), in alliance with the Christian League, started a campaign against the Ottoman Empire and defied its armies. By making forays south of the Danube he harassed the Turks who were at that time fighting against Austria. Attacked by Sinān Pas̲h̲a (1595), he saved his country with the help of Transylvania and Moldavia. The necessities of war and the hesitant policies of the two countries finally led Michael the Brave to conquer them (1599, 1600). His reign over the three principalities was of short duration. He came into conflict with the interests of the throne of Austria, and also those of Poland and the Ottomans. Michael finally lost his conquests and his life as well, being assassinated on the order of general Basta, Commander in Chief of the Imperial forces. In the 17th century the princes Matei Basarab (1633-54) and Şerban Cantacuzino (1678-88) succeeded in limiting Turkish interventions in the country's affairs. Constantin Brâncoveanu (1688-1714) continued Şerban's policy of keeping a balance between Austria and the Ottomans, but the appearance of Russia did not make his task easier. His relations with Peter the Great made him an object of suspicion to the Turks. Lured to Constantinople, he was there executed. The new prince Stefan Cantacuzino (1714-15) perished in similar circumstances. The Ottomans, no longer having confidence in the Rumanian princes who were so ready to take up arms against them, preferred to choose their rulers from the Greek families of the Phanar who had distinguished themselves in the sultan's service. During this period, the wars waged by the House of Austria, and even more by Russia, against Turkey brought constant bloodshed. Wallachia was occupied by the Austrians and Russians in turn. By the treaty of Küčük Ḳaynard̲j̲a, Russia confirmed her right to intervene with the Porte on behalf of Wallachia and Moldavia. The Phanariot regime came to an end in 1821 as a result of the revolt of Tudor Vladimirescu. Acting at first in agreement with the *Hetaira*, he later turned against the Greeks, the instruments of Ottoman domination. In 1829 the Treaty of Andrianople marked a new stage in the Russian penetration into the Balkans, but it also brought Wallachia complete freedom of trade, the beginning of a period of vigorous economic growth. The country received its first constitution in 1834; and this was replaced by a more liberal fundamental law in the anti-Russian revolutionary outburst of 1848. The Porte, urged on by St. Petersburg, quenched the revolution in blood. The Treaty of Paris (1856) was the origin of the union of Wallachia and Moldavia in a single state under prince Alexandru Ion Cuza (1859). As a result of the Peace of Berlin (1878), Rumania was recognized as an independent state.

The entry of Wallachia into the Ottoman system brought profound changes in its social and economic structure. The country lost the right to maintain commercial relations with other countries, and was compelled to provide Constantinople with a part of its supplies of cereals and live-stock. It must be emphasized that, despite the bonds of suzerainty, the Turks never had the right to establish themselves in Wallachia. This country played an important part in upholding eastern Christianity by large donations to the Orthodox monasteries in the Ottoman empire, as well as by printing religious books. It was at Bucharest that one of the oldest books in the Turkish language was printed in 1701.

Bibliography: F. Babinger, *Beiträge zur Frühgeschichte der Türkenherrschaft in Rumelien*, Brünn-Munich-Vienna 1944, 1-21; Ö. L. Barkan, *Kanunlar*, Istanbul 1943, 289, 321, 324-5, 394; N. Beldiceanu, *La région de Timok-Morava dans les documents de Meḥmed II et de Selīm I*, in *Revue des Etudes Roumaines*, iii-iv, Paris 1957, 111-29; M. Berza, *Haraciul Moldovei şi Ţării Româneşti in sec. XV-XIX*, in *Studii şi Materiale de Istorie Medie*, ii, Bucharest 1957, 27; G. I. Brătianu, *Études byzantines d'histoire économique et sociale*, Paris 1938, 127-81, 241-64; idem, *Origines et formation de l'unité roumaine*, Bucharest 1943; V. Costăchel, P. P. Panaitescu, A. Cazacu, *Viaţa feudală în Ţara Românească şi Moldova*, Bucharest 1957, 413-44; N. Drăganu, *Românii în veacurile IX-XIV*, Bucharest 1933; S. Dragomir, *Vlahii din nordul peninsulei balcanice în evul mediu*, Bucharest 1959; F. Giese, *Die altosmanische Chronik des ʿĀšyḳpašazāde*, Leipzig 1929; C. C. Giurescu, *Istoria Românilor*, Bucharest 1944-6, 5 vols.; C. C. Giurescu, *Livres turcs imprimés à Bucarest*, in *Revista istorică română*, xv/3, Bucharest 1945, 275-86; Ibn Kemal, *Tevârih-i âl-i Osman*, Ankara

1954-7, 2 vols.; Ionnescu Gion, *Istoria Bucureştiului*, Bucharest 1899; I. Minea, "*Reforma*" *lui Constantin Mavrocordat*, Iassy 1927; A. Oţetea, *T. Vladimirescu şi mişcarea eteristă în Ţările Româneşti*, Bucharest 1945; P. P. Panaitescu, *Interpretări româneşti*, Bucharest 1947; P. P. Panaitescu, *Mihai Viteazul*, Bucharest 1936; P. P. Panaitescu, *Mircea cel Bătrân*, Bucharest 1944; G. Paris, *Romani*, in *Romania*, i, Paris 1872, 1-22; P. Pelliot, *Notes sur l'histoire de la Horde d'Or*, Paris 1950, 145; L. Rasonyi, *Contributions à l'histoire des premières cristallisations d'Etat des Roumains*, in *Archivum Europae centro-orientalis*, i, Budapest 1935, 251; *Taʾrīkh-i Pečewī*, ii, Istanbul 1283, 152 ff.; *Taʾrīkh-i Selānikī*, Bibl. Nat. Paris, ms. fonds turc suppl. 1060, fol. 215r° ff.; Urudj, *Tewārīkh-i āl-i ʿOthmān*, Hanover 1925; Şt. Zeletin, *Burghezia română. Origina şi rolul ei istoric*, Bucharest 1925; G. Weigand, *Die Aromunen*, Leipzig 1895. (N. Beldiceanu)

EGER [see eğri].

EGERDIR [see eğridir].

EĞIN, now known as Kemāliye, a town in E. Anatolia on the right (west) bank of the Euphrates (Ḳara-Su), 40 kms. from ʿArapkīr [*q.v.*], 130 kms. from El-ʿAzīz and Malaṭya via ʿArapkīr, and 150 kms. from Erzindjān [*q.v.*] (under which it comes administratively as the centre of a *ḳaḍā*) via the station of Ilič on the Sivas [*q.v.*]—Erzurum [*q.v.*] railway. It is near Eğin that the valley of the Euphrates narrows, pressed in by the outposts of the Monzur mountains of Dersim to the east and the Sarî-Čiček mountains to the west. The valley which is situated here, at an altitude of 825 m. above sea level, is overlooked on the eastern side by a precipitous slope rising above it like a wall. The western slope is more gradual, rising like an amphitheatre round a small valley. It is here that Eğin is built at an altitude of from 900 to 1000 metres. A spring higher up, known as Ḳāḍī Gölü, waters the town's gardens, feeds its fountains and turns its mills. It is said that the name Eğin is derived from the Armenian word *agn* (*akn*), meaning "spring", and that the town was founded in the 11th century by a group of Vaspurakan Armenians (see J. Saint Martin, *Mémoire sur l'Arménie*, Paris 1818, i, 189). In ancient times this district was ruled by local lords or changed hands in the wars between Rome and Persia (remains of Roman roads can still be seen). In Islamic times it was for short periods of time autonomous, before the foundation of the Saldjūḳid State and also after that State had become weaker. After the invasion of Tīmūr [*q.v.*], Eğin was annexed to the Ottoman Empire in the reign of Sulṭān Meḥemmed I [*q.v.*]. It was for a long time attached to the *liwā* of ʿArapkīr in the *eyālet* of Sivas [*q.v.*]. In the 19th century it passed into the vilayet of Kharpūt [*q.v.*] and then into that of Maʿmūret ül-ʿAzīz. After the foundation of the Turkish Republic the name of Eğin was changed into Kemāliye after Muṣṭafā Kemāl Pasha (Atatürk). The *ḳaḍā* of Kemāliye formed part successively of the vilayets of El-ʿAzīz, Malaṭya and Erzindjān.

The *Djihān-nümā*, the *Seyāḥatnāme* of Ewliyā Čelebi [*q.v.*] and other 17th century sources mention Eğin as a place of gardens and orchards producing an abundance of fruit. Ewliyā Čelebi says that although Eğin formed a *ḳaḍā* of the *eyālat* of Sivas, its taxes were collected by the *muḥaṣṣil* of Malaṭya. He adds that the castle of Eğin had been surrendered to Sulṭān Meḥemmed I under a treaty and that the 300 Christians living there were immune from taxation. According to him, there were in Eğin some 10,000 well-built houses with earth roofs. Sources in the first half of the 19th century praise the beauty of the town, whose houses were surrounded by greenery. Moltke, who visited Eğin in April 1839, describes it as one of the most beautiful towns in Asia which he had seen, comparable to Amasya [*q.v.*]. Although he found Amasya a more pleasant and original place, he thought Eğin more impressive and beautiful and its river more important. Although Moltke mentions Eğin as a largely Armenian centre, Texier, as well as sources belonging to the second half of the 19th century, state that the Armenians were never in the majority there. According to Texier there were 2,000 Muslim households and only some 700 Armenian households in the town. Towards the end of the 19th century Yorke estimated the population of Eğin at 15,000 and Cuinet at 19,000, of whom some 12,000 were Turks and 7,000 Armenians.

The Muslims of Eğin were engaged in agriculture and particularly in cattle-breeding, as is the case today, while the Armenians were engaged in commerce and crafts. According to Ewliyā Čelebi, the town was famous for its bows, bow-makers occupying most of the bazaar. In more recent times the town produced fine cotton goods, embroidered silks, embroidered head-cloths, handkerchiefs and towels. Moltke mentions that many citizens of Eğin settled in Istanbul, where they found employment as butchers, porters, grocers, builders, merchants and money-changers, returning to their birth-place in their old age and building fine houses there. Some citizens of Eğin reached high rank in the service of the State, including that of Minister. This custom of seeking employment outside their birth-place was also shared by the citizens of ʿArapkīr, as well as by people from neighbouring villages. Some Armenians from Eğin emigrated to America, returning occasionally to their town in their old age. Cuinet writing in 1890 says that while some such Armenians returned rich and made fine houses for themselves their descendants wasted the money they inherited. Local industry declined as a result of European competition and the town lost its prosperity. Eğin was badly affected by the First World War. According to the first results of the 1945 census the population of Eğin amounted to 3,300 while the whole *ḳaḍā*, which covered an area of 1333 sq. kms. and included 34 villages, numbered 16,900 people.

Bibliography: Kātib Čelebī, *Djihan-nümā*, 624; Ewliyā Čelebi, *Seyāḥatnāme* (Istanbul A.H. 1314), iii, 214 ff.; H. von Moltke, *Briefe über Zustände und Begebenheiten in der Türkei* (*1835-1839*), 378 ff.; Charles Texier, *Asie Mineure*, 591; J. Taylor, *Journal of a Tour in Armenia . . . in 1898* (*JRGS*, xxxviii), London 1898; E. Reclus, *Nouvelle géographie universelle* (1884) ix, 363; Ritter, *Erdkunde*, x, 790 ff.; Hommaire de Hell, *Voyage en Turquie et en Perse*, Paris 1855; V. W. Yorke, *A Journey in the Valley of the Upper Euphrates* (*Geographical Journal*, 1896, II), viii, 333 ff.; Lehmann-Haupt, *Armenien einst und jetzt* (Berlin, 1910), i, 496. (Besim Darkot)

EĞRI (Turk., Eğri; Hung., Eger; Ger., Erlau; Lat. and Ital., Agria), an old Hungarian town, 110 km. to the north-east of Buda, situated close to the massif of Bükk, *i.e.*, to the eastern foot-hills of the Matrá mountains, and on the river Eger, which flows into the Tisza (Theiss). Eğri was subject to Ottoman rule from 1005/1596 to 1099/1687.

The Ottomans, in 959/1552, captured Temesvár and Szolnok (important in the future as a base for the concentration of the men and supplies needed for the conquest and thereafter for the retention of Eğri) and then laid siege to Eğri itself, but in vain, all their assaults failing before the desperate resistance of the Christian garrison under Stephen Dobó (Ramaḍān-Shawwāl 959/September-October 1552).

Eğri was not in fact to come into Muslim hands until the long war of 1001-15/1593-1606 between the Austrian Habsburgs and the Ottomans. The first years of this war brought such disaster to the Ottoman cause that Sultan Meḥemmed III (1003-12/1595-1603) was induced to take the field in person for the campaign of 1004-5/1596. Near Szalánkemen the Sultan held a council of war, at which the decision was reached to make the capture of Eğri the main objective of the campaign (one of the Christian sources—Decsi, *Commentarii*, 252—notes that the "Begus Szolnokiensis", *i.e.*, the Sandjaḳ Beg of Szolnok, in the spring of 1004/1596 ("sub idem ferme veris initium"), had reconnoitred and raided in force the lands around Eğri—a foretoken of the fate soon to befall the town). The decision of the Sultan and of the council of war rested on two considerations: that possession of Eğri would enable the Ottomans to threaten the narrow corridor of land through which ran the lines of communication between Austria and Transylvania, then in alliance with the Emperor against the Sultan, and that control of Eğri might bring under Ottoman domination the mines located in the mountainous region to the north of the town (cf. Pečewī, ii, 191; Naʿīmā, i, 146; Ḥādjdjī Khalīfa, i, 71; Decsi, *Commentarii*, 267; Hurmuzaki, iii/2, 216. Marsigli, *Danubius Pannonico-Mysicus*, iii/2, Amsterdam 1726, 19 ff. contains a "Mappa Mineralogica", which shows the mines existing in his own time to the north of Eğri). Eğri fell to the Ottomans after a siege of three weeks (28 Muḥarram-19 Ṣafar 1005/21 September-12 October 1596). Once the fortress was in their hands, the Ottomans began to repair forthwith the damage that it had suffered in the course of the siege, but their continued possession of Eğri was in fact ensured to them only by their defeat of the Imperialists in the great battle of Ḥāč Ovasï (Mezö-Keresztes) fought not far from Eğri in Rabīʿ I 1005/October 1596. Eğri, at first a sandjaḳ in the eyālet of Budin (Buda), was later raised to the status of a beglerbeglik comprising (with Eğri itself) six sandjaḳs, amongst them Szegedin and Szolnok (cf. Tischendorf, 69 and also Gökbilgin in *IA*).

The Christians recaptured Eğri in 1099/1687 during the course of the war waged between Austria and the Ottoman Empire from 1094/1683 to 1110/1699. As a result of the campaigns of 1096/1685 and 1097/1686 the Imperialists won Budin and a number of additional fortresses, including Szolnok and Szegedin on the Tisza. Eğri was now more or less isolated. The Ottomans, in order to retain it, would have had to undertake a major—and highly successful— counter-offensive. All prospect of such an offensive ended with the defeat of the Ottoman forces under the command of Süleymān Pasha at the second battle of Mohács in Shawwāl 1098/August 1687. The fall of Eğri had been foreshadowed in the summer of 1097/1686, when the Imperialists, eager to deprive the fortress even of local sources of men and food, compelled the inhabitants of the villages in the region to leave their homes and to settle elsewhere. Eğri withstood the ensuing blockade until Ṣafar 1099/December 1687, the garrison capitulating in that month to the Imperialist general Antonio Caraffa.

Bibliography: Pečewī, *Taʾrīkh*, Istanbul 1281-3, i, 295 ff. and ii, 190 ff.; Ḥādjdjī Khalīfa, *Fedhleke*, Istanbul 1286-7, i, 69 ff.; Naʿīmā, *Taʾrīkh*, Istanbul 1281-3, i, 144 ff. (cf. C. Fraser, *Annals of the Turkish empire*, London 1832, i, 73 ff.); Silïḥdār Fïndïklïlï Meḥemmed Agha, *Taʾrīkh*, Istanbul 1928, ii, 315 ff.; Rāshid, *Taʾrīkh*, Istanbul 1153, i, 141v ff. (= Istanbul 1282, ii, 32 ff.); Ṣolaḳzāde, *Taʾrīkh*, Istanbul 1298, 517 ff. and 630 ff.; Münedjdjīm Bāshï, *Ṣaḥāʾif al-akhbār*, Istanbul 1285, 501, 588; Ewliyā Čelebi, *Seyāḥatnāme*, vii, Istanbul 1928, 160 ff.; *Tinódi Sebesteyén Összes Müvei 1540-1555* (= XVI. Századbeli Magyar Költök Müvei, Köt. 2, ed. Á. Szilády), Budapest 1881, 105 ff., 435 ff.; *Gr. Illésházy István Nádor Följegyzései 1592-1603* (= Magyar Történelmi Emlékek, Oszt. 2: Írók, Köt. 7, ed. G. Kazinczy), Pest 1863, 30 ff.; *Rerum Memorabilium in Pannonia Exegeses Recensente Nicolao Reusnero ....*, Frankfurt am Main 1603, 82 ff. ("Rerum ad Agriam M.D.LII. gestarum Narratio, Auctore Ioanne Sambuco"— also to be found in earlier publications, *e.g.*, S. Schardius, *Historicum Opus*, Basle 1574; N. Honigerus, *Solymanni XII. et Selymi XIII. .... res gestae ....*, Basle 1577; and A. Bonfinius, *Rerum Ungaricarum Decades ....*, Frankfurt am Main 1581) and 273 ff. ("De Expugnatione Agriae, et Praelio ibidem ad Kerestam .... Narratio Historica, auctore M. Iansonio"); *Nicolai Isthvanfi Pannoni Historiarum De Rebus Ungaricis Libri xxxiv*, Cologne 1622, 337 ff. and 693 ff.; *Joh: Baptistae Vici De Rebus Gestis Antonij Caraphaei Libri iv*, Naples 1716, ii, 178 ff., 218 ff., 244 ff. (cf. also Giambattista Vico, *Scritti storici*, ed. F. Nicolini, Bari 1939, index: 454); *Francisci Forgachii de Ghymes Pannonii .... Rerum Hungaricarum Sui Temporis Commentarii*, Possoni et Cassoviae 1788, 69 ff.; S. Katona, *Historia Critica Regum Hungariae, Stirpis Austriacae*, xxii, Buda 1798, 311 ff. and xxvii, Buda 1794, 307 ff.; *Baronyai Decsi János Magyar Historiája* 1592-1598 (= Magyar Történelmi Emlékek, Oszt. 2: Írók, Köt. 17, ed. F. Toldy), Pest 1866, 252, 267 ff.; Ascanio Centorio degli Hortensii, *Commentarii della Guerra di Transilvania*, Venice 1566, 221 ff. (= *Commentarii*, ed. L. Gáldi, Budapest 1940, 221 ff.); G. Fantuzzi, *Memorie della Vita del Generale Co: Luigi Ferdinando Marsigli*, Bologna 1770, 64 ff.; *Autobiografia di Luigi Ferdinando Marsili*, ed. E. Lovarini, Bologna 1930, 84 ff.; H. Marczali, *A Parisi Nemzeti Könyvtárböl*, in *Magyar Történelmi Tár* (A Magyar Tudományos Akadémia Történelmi Bizottsága), Folyam 2, Köt. 11, Budapest 1877, 83 ff. (*op. cit.*, 113-22 = Narrazione de capitano Claudio Cogonara de Parma della perdita d'Agria .... alli 13. ottobre 1596); Hieronymus Ortelius, *Chronologia oder Historische beschreibung aller Kriegs emporungen ... in Ober und Under Ungern auch Sibenbürgen ....*, Nürnberg 1602, 22v ff. and 101v ff.; *Shakespeare's Europe. Unpublished chapters of Fynes Moryson's Itinerary*, ed. C. Hughes, London 1903, 44 ff.; *Purchas His Pilgrimes*, viii, Glasgow 1905, 304 ff., *passim*; Ferīdūn Beg, *Munshaʾāt al-Salāṭīn*, Istanbul 1264-5, ii, 2 ff. (a *fetḥnāme* on the Ottoman conquest of Eğri in 1005/1596. British Museum Cotton Ms. Nero B.XI, 225r ff. contains an Ital. trans. of the *fetḥnāme*. English translation (from the Italian) in Sir Henry Ellis, *Original letters illustrative of English history*, 3rd Series, iii, London 1846, 140 ff.);

L. Fekete, *Die Siyāqat-Schrift in der türkischen Finanzverwaltung*, Budapest 1955, i, 868 (index); E. de Hurmuzaki, *Documente privitóre la Istoria Românilor*, iii/2 (1576-1600), Bucharest 1888, 214 ff. (nos. 237-40, *passim*); L. Fekete, *A Verlini és Drezdai Gyüjtemények Török Levéltári anyaga*, in *Levéltári Közlemények*, vi, Budapest 1929, 259 ff., *passim* and vii, Budapest 1930, 55 ff., *passim*; idem (ed.), *Türkische Schriften aus dem Archive des Palatins Nikolaus Esterházy 1606-1645*, Budapest 1932, 478 (index); idem, *Gyöngyös Város Levéltárának Török Iratai*, in *Levéltári Közlemények*, x, Budapest 1932, 287 ff., *passim* and xi, Budapest 1933, 93 ff., *passim*; F. Balássy, *Az Egri Vár 1687-diki Feladásának Alkupontjai és A Törökök Maradekai Egerben*, Budapest 1875; I. Gyárfás, *Dobó István Egerben*, Budapest 1879; N. Szederkényi, *Heves Vármegye Története*, ii (1526-96) and iii (1596-1687), Eger 1890, 1891; G. Gömöry, *Eger Ostroma 1552-ben*, in *Hadtörténelmi Közlemények*, iii, Budapest 1890, 613 ff.; V. Pataki, *A XVI. Századi Várépités Magyarországon*, in *Jahrbuch des Wiener Ung. Hist. Inst.*, Erster Jahrgang, Budapest 1931, 98 ff., *passim*; P. A. von Tischendorf, *Das Lehnswesen in den moslemischen Staaten insbesondere im osmanischen Reiche*, Leipzig 1872, 69; A. S. Levend, *Ġazavāt-nāmeler ve Mihaloğlu Ali Bey'in Ġazavāt-nāmesi*, Ankara 1956, 94 ff.; F. E. Karatay, *Topkapı Sarayı Müzesi Kütüphanesi Türkçe Yazmalar Kataloğu*, i, Istanbul 1961, 236 (no. 713), 244 (no. 741); G. Bascapè, *Le Relazioni fra l'Italia e la Transilvania nel secolo XVI.*, Rome 1931, 197-8, *passim*; K. A. Kertbeny, *Ungarn betreffende deutsche Erstlings-Drucke 1454-1600*, Budapest 1880, 296 (no. 1221 ff.); J. Pohler, *Bibliotheca Historico-Militaris*, i, Cassel 1887, 169 ff., *passim*, 303 ff., *passim*, 517 ff., *passim*; Hammer-Purgstall, *Histoire*, vi, 43 ff., vii, 322 ff., xii, 252; A. Huber and O. Redlich, *Geschichte Österreichs*, iv, Gotha 1892, 176, 396-7 and vi, Gotha 1921, 361, 387-8, 396-7, 523; *IA*, s.v. Eğri (M. Tayyib Gökbilgin). (V. J. PARRY)

EĞRIBOZ (also IGHRIBOS/Z, ĀGHRIBOS/Z, EGRIBOS), Turkish name for the island of Euboea and its chief town, the classical Chalkis. Originally the name of the narrow strait separating Chalkis from the mainland, Εὔριπος (vulg. Ἔγριπος) was already by the 12th century currently used for the town; a supposed connexion with the bridge over the strait produced from the acc. [εἰς τὸ]ν Ἔγριπον 'Negroponte', the regular Western name for both town and island. In Byzantine times Euboea formed part of the theme of Hellas. At the partition of the Empire in 1204 it fell to a triarchy of Veronese, but the Venetians, reserving trading rights and appointing a bailo to supervise their settlements, gradually made themselves the effective masters of the island; the town of Negroponte, strongly fortified in 1304, became their principal naval base in the Aegean.

The Turkish danger first appeared with the raids of Umur Pasha of Aydin (see P. Lemerle, *L'émirat d'Aydin*, 1957), and by the beginning of the Ottoman-Venetian war of 867-83/1463-79 practically all mainland Greece was in Ottoman hands. In Dhu 'l-Ḥidjdja 874/June 1470 the fleet under Maḥmūd Pasha [*q.v.*], then Ḳapudan, cast anchor in Vurko Bay, south of the town, while Meḥemmed II with the army advanced overland via Thebes to the mainland shore; the army crossed by a bridge of boats made south of the heavily defended Euripos bridge, and ships were dragged overland to prevent relief approaching from the north. The walls, defended on three sides by the sea and on the fourth by a deep fosse, were finally carried on Thursday 13 Muḥarram 875/12 July 1470, the garrison was massacred and 15,000 prisoners (so Kemālpashazāde) were taken (Western sources on the siege are listed by Miller [see Bibl.], 478; the fullest Turkish account is that of Kemālpashazāde, ed. Ş. Turan, facs. 301-11 = transcription 284-92, with refs. to the other sources; a *fetḥnāme* was published by A. S. Erzi in *Fatih ve Istanbul*, i/3-6 (1954), 300 ff.).

Thereafter until its cession to Greece in 1833 Euboea, with parts of the mainland, was a sandjaḳ belonging to the jurisdiction of the Ḳapudan Pasha, who frequently resided in the town. Ewliyā Čelebi, visiting Euboea in 1081/1670 (*Seyāḥatnāme*, viii, 236-48) describes the strongly-fortified town—it was to resist a siege of over three months during Morosini's campaign of 1688—with 11 Muslim, 1 Jewish and 5 Christian wards, the drawbridge linking it to the Venetian fortress (destroyed when the present swing-bridge was built in 1896) in mid-strait and the second bridge to the mainland, with watermills worked by the freakish currents.

Bibliography: Pauly-Wissowa, s.v. Chalkis (Oberhummer); W. Heyd, *Histoire du commerce du Levant*, 1885-6; W. Miller, *The Latins in the Levant*, 1908; Pīrī Re'īs, *Kitabı Bahriye*, Istanbul 1935, 119-29; İ. H. Uzunçarşılı, *Osmanlı devletinin merkez ve bahriye teşkilâtı*, Ankara 1948; Ḥādjdji Khalfa, *Djihān-numā* = J. von Hammer, *Rumeli und Bosna*, Vienna 1812, 105-11; J. C. Hobhouse, *A journey through Albania* ..., 1813, 445-59; M. F. Thielen, *Die europäische Türkey*, Vienna 1828, 72-5; W. M. Leake, *Travels in Northern Greece*, 1835, ii, 253-66; D. Kalogeropulo, *Contribution à la bibliographie de l'île d'Euboea* ... (*1471-1937*), Athens 1937 (not seen); Hachette's *Greece*, Paris 1955, 314 ff. (V. L. MÉNAGE)

EĞRI DAGH [see AGHRÎ DAGH].

EĞRIDIR, earlier spellings Egirdir or Egerdir in Ibn Baṭṭūṭa, ii, 267, and Ibn Faḍl Allāh al-ʿUmarī, *Masālik al-Abṣār*, report on Anatolia, ed. Taeschner, Leipzig 1929, 39 l. 5, (middle of the 14th century), Akridūr, Greek Akrotiri, possibly—though there is no proof for this—from the name 'Ακρωτήριον; a small town in south-western Anatolia on a penin sula at the southern end of the Eğridir lake, which has no visible outlet but which may have a subterranean outlet to the Mediterranean, thus keeping its water fresh. This is the Limnai of antiquity (924 m. (= 3034 ft.) above sea-level, concerning which cf. F. Loewe, *Beobachtungen während einer Durchquerung Zentralanatoliens im Jahre 1927*, in *Geografiska Annaler* 1935); its geographical position is 37° 50′ north, 30° 53′ east, and it is the capital of a *kaza* of the *vilâyet* of Isparta. It has 5,766 inhabitants, the *kaza* has 26,820 (1950), and it is the terminus of the branch line from Dinar (opened 1912). There are two islands, Çan-adası and Yeşil-ada, facing the peninsula on which Eğridir is built. On the second of these (formerly called Nîs [Νησί] Adasî), there was a monastery with some 1000 Turkish-speaking Greeks up to the end of the First World War.

According to W. M. Ramsay, *The historical geography of Asia Minor*, London 1890, 407 and 417, the episcopal see of Prostanna was located in or near Eğridir. It is assumed that the town, together with the region of Isparta, which was conquered by Ḳilîdj-Arslan III (600-1/1204, see Houtsma, *Recueil* etc., iii, 62; iv, 24; H. W. Duda, *Die Seltschukengeschichte des Ibn Bībī*, Copenhagen 1959, 30), fell into the hands of the Saldjūḳs. After the dissolution of the Rūm Saldjūḳ Empire, Eğridir became the capital of the Turkish principality of the Ḥamīd-oghlu. One of the first rulers of this dynasty, Falak al-Dīn Dündār (at the end of the 13th century), gave the town the name Felekbār or Felekābād (Abu 'l-Fidā', *Taḳwīm*, 379; translation ii, 2, 134). In 783 or 784/towards 1381 A.D., the last Ḥamīd-oghlu, Ḥüseyn Beg, sold his rights to the Ottoman Murād I. Tīmūr conquered both the town and the fortified island Nīs-Adasî on his march through Anatolia (according to Saʿd al-Dīn on 17 Shaʿbān 805/11 March 1403, according to Sharaf al-Dīn on 17 Radjab/10 February). He left them to the Ḳaramānids, whom he had restored, but they, in turn, had to cede them, together with the region of Ḥamīd-eli, to the Ottomans in 1425. It now became a *liwā'* in the *eyālet* of Anadolu. Later on, in the 19th century, Ḥamīd-eli, or Isbarta, as it was temporarily known, became a *sandjaḳ* of the *wilāyet* of Konya.

The most notable building is the citadel, probably built by Keyḳubād I, at the tip of the peninsula of Eğridir. It is separated from the town itself by a wall, and there is an inner wall protecting the innermost part of the citadel, which lies on the tip of the peninsula (where there are further fortifications, including two towers which lean against the rocks). These fortifications, which are now destroyed, were still intact in the 18th century (see *Voyage du Sieur Paul Lucas fait en* 1714 ...., Amsterdam 1720).

There is a mosque, the Ulu Djāmiʿ, with wooden buttresses, near the gate of the citadel in the outer town; its minaret stands on the actual gate of the citadel. Opposite the mosque, there is the Tash Madrasa, a court *madrasa* with an *aywān* and a beautiful Saldjūḳ doorway dated Shawwāl 635/May-June 1238 (*RCEA*, xi, 96, no. 4148); the *aywān* is dated 701/1301-2 (*ibid.*, xiii, 227, no. 5138).

Bibliography: Kâtib Čelebi, *Djihānnümā*, 640; I. H. Uzunçarşılı, *Anadolu beylikleri*, 15; F. Sarre, *Reise in Kleinasien*, 1895, 142 ff.; *IA*, iv, 199-201 (Besim Darkot).

(J. H. Mordtmann-[Fr. Taeschner])

EGYPT [see miṣr].

EKREM BEY, Redjā'īzāde Maḥmūd (1847-1914), Turkish writer, poet and critic, one of the leading personalities in the victory of the modern school of poetry over traditional *dīwān*-poetry. Born in Vaniköy, a suburb of Istanbul on the Bosphorus, he was the son of Redjā'ī Efendi, director of the Government Press, a poet and scholar of some distinction. He attended various schools until the age of fifteen and, like most of his contemporaries, continued his education as an apprentice clerk in the chancellery of the Foreign Ministry (where he met Nāmîḳ Kemāl) and various other government offices. Subsequently he became a senior official of the Council of State (*Shūrā-yi Dewlet*) and taught literature at the Galatasaray Lycée and the Imperial School of Political Science (*Mülkiye*), two of the few leading institutions where the Turkish intelligentsia and ruling classes were educated, and exercised immense influence on the formation of the literary taste of the young generation. After the restoration of the Constitution in 1908 he became, for a short time, Minister of *Waḳf*s and later Minister of Education in the Kāmil Pasha cabinet, but soon resigned as he disagreed with the policy of massive purges in the civil service. He was made a senator in December 1908 and remained so until his death.

Ekrem Bey began by writing poems in the *dīwān* tradition until he came under the influence of the modernist Tanẓīmāt school, particularly of Nāmîḳ Kemāl and ʿAbd al-Ḥaḳḳ Ḥāmid. Then gradually he developed a personality of his own and influenced even Ḥāmid's later work. His poetry is romantic, often over-sentimental and melancholy bordering sometimes on the *funèbre*, constantly elaborating one of the three themes: nature, love and particularly death, helped in this by tragic circumstances in his life (he lost three children at a young age).

Although himself a poet of limited inspiration and not a very skilful versifier, he sincerely believed in a thorough revolution in the form and content of the Turkish *ars poetica*, and became the pioneer fighter of modern Turkish poetry against the traditionalists headed by Muʿallim Nādjī. He was thus a link between the early modernists (Shināsī, Ziya (Ḍiyā') Pasha, Nāmîḳ Kemāl, ʿAbd al-Ḥaḳḳ Ḥāmid) and radical reformists of the Fikret school. The long and often bitter struggle, continued by the generation of Tewfīḳ Fikret (in the literary magazine *Therwet-i Fünūn* where many young talents gathered first round Ekrem Bey), ended with the triumph of modernism during his lifetime, and Ekrem Bey's rôle in this, perhaps more as a critic and movement-leader than as a poet, is decisive. Hence the name Ustād-ı Ekrem given to him by his students and admirers. The individualism and Art for Art's sake tendency of the *Therwet-i Fünūn* school are also partly to be traced to Ekrem who was not as social- or history-conscious as his predecessors.

Apart from articles and poems published in various reviews of the period and some booklets of minor importance, he is the author of: Verse: (I) *Naghme-i seḥer* (1871) and (II) *Yadghār-î shebāb* (1873); (III) *Zemzeme* in three parts (1885), the third of which contains his celebrated poem *Yaḳadjîḳda bir mezārlîḳ ʿālemi*, considered his masterpiece; (IV) *Nāčīz* (1886) a collection of verse translations from the French romantics and La Fontaine; (V) *Pejmürde* (1894). Prose: (I) *Müntekhabāt medjmūʿasî* (1873) a collection of his early writings, articles and translations, in the tradition of the old flowery style; (II) *Mes Prisons Terdjümesi* (1874), translation from the French of Silvio Pellico's *Le mie prigioni*, equally in the old fashioned ornate prose which was severely criticized by Nāmîḳ Kemāl; (III) *Nidjād Ekrem* (1900), in two volumes, interspersed with verse, some in syllabic metre. Into this book dedicated to his beloved son Nidjād, who died very young, the unhappy father put, in all detail, everything he remembered about him. It is on the whole written in a spontaneous and unadorned style and contains some of his best prose; (IV) *Tefekkür* (1888) contains his later, simpler and more personal prose; (V) *Atala* (1872), a translation, in bombastic and old fashioned style, of Chateaubriand's novel; (VI) *Muḥsin Bey* (1889), a rather mediocre sentimental novel; (VII) *ʿAraba sevdāsî* (1889, published 1896 and 1940), a much appreciated novel of social satire, in the manner of Turkish novels which attack and ridicule the aping of Western customs by snobs (cf. Aḥmed Midḥat's *Felāṭūn Bey ile Rāḳîm Efendi* (1875), Ḥüseyn Raḥmī's *Shîḳ* (1897) and *Shîpsevdi* (1900)); (VIII) *Shemsā* (1896), a short narrative about the life and sudden death of a four year old peasant girl, adopted by the poet's family; (IX) *Taʿlīm-i Edebiyyāt* (1882), a book of *ars poetica* with examples, composed of his lectures at the Mülkiye and first mimeographed in 1879, is his most important work, which revolutionized taste and literary theories and standards of the time. Contrary to tradition he gave in this book many examples from contemporary writers and poets and made the new school popular among the majority of the educated youth; (X) *Taḳdīr-i elḥān* (1886), literary criticism. Drama: (I) *ʿAfīfe Anjelik* (1870), (II) *Atala* (1872), a theatrical adaptation of the Chateaubriand novel he had already translated; (III) *Wuṣlat* (1874) inspired by Nāmiḳ Kemāl's *Zavālli Čodjuk*, (IV) *Čok bilen čok yañilir*, a comedy adapted from a tale of the *Alf nahār wa-nahār*, published posthumously (1914 and 1941).

Bibliography: Rushen Eshref, *Diyorlar ki*, Istanbul 1918 *passim*; Ismāʿīl Ḥabīb, *Türk tedjeddüd edebiyyātī taʾrīkhi*, Istanbul 1924; ʿAlī Ekrem, *Redjāʾīzāde Ekrem*, Istanbul 1924; Ismail Hikmet, *Recaizade Ekrem*, Istanbul 1932; Ercüment Ekrem Talu (Ekrem Bey's son), *Recaizade Mahmud Ekrem*, in *Aylık Ansiklopedi*, Istanbul 1945, i, 269; Ibnülemin Mahmud Kemal Inal, *Son asır Türk şairleri*, 274-85; Ahmet Hamdi Tanpınar in *IA*, s.v.; Kenan Akyüz, *Batı tesirinde Türk şiiri antolojisi*, Ankara 1953, 69-105. (Fahir İz)

ELAZIĞ [see maʿmūrat al-ʿazīz].

ELBASAN (T. *él-basan* '[fortress] which subdues the land'), town of central Albania (41° 06′ N., 20° 06′ E.) on the site of the ancient Scampis on the Via Egnatia, a strategic position controlling the fertile valley of the Shkumbî (anc. Genysos), which here emerges from the mountains. The fortress, round which the town grew up, was built with great speed at the command of Meḥemmed II while Krujë (Kroya [*q.v.*]) was being unsuccessfully besieged in the summer of 1466, as a base for future operations against Iskandar Beg [*q.v.*]; it resisted a siege in the following spring. At first administered as part of the sandjaḳ of Okhri (Tursun, *TOEM ʿilāwe*, 135), within a few years Elbasan was made the chef-lieu of a separate sandjaḳ of Rumili, having (ca. 926/1520) four ḳaḍās: Elbasan, Čermenika, Ishbat and Drač (Durazzo). In the later years of the Empire it formed part of the *wilāyet* of Yanya, and finally of Ishkodra.

With the consolidation of the Ottoman hold on N. Albania and the Adriatic coast, the fortress rapidly lost its military importance (it was dismantled in 1832 by Reshīd Pasha and further damaged by earthquake in 1920, so that now only the south side survives); but the town, always and still predominantly Muslim, remained a flourishing trade-centre: Ewliyā describes a prosperous and attractive town (the fortress ungarrisoned), with 18 Muslim and 10 Christian *maḥalles*, 46 mosques, 11 *tekkes*, 11 *khāns*, and a very frequented market. Now linked by rail with Durazzo and Tirana, it is, after Tirana, the chief town of central Albania, with some 15,000 inhabitants.

Bibliography: F. Babinger, *Die Gründung von Elbasan*, in *MSOS*, xxxiv (1931), 94-103 (plan, photograph, inscriptions); H. Inalcık, *Hicrî 835 tarihli Sûret-i defter-i sancak-i Arvanid*, Ankara 1954, introd.; Ö. L. Barkan, *Kanunlar*, Istanbul 1943, 293; Ḥādjdji Khalfa, *Djihān-numā* = J. von Hammer, *Rumeli und Bosna*, Vienna 1812, 134-6; Ewliyā Čelebi, *Seyāḥatnāme*, viii, 716-30 = F. Babinger's abridged trans. and comm., in *MSOS*, xxxiii (1930), 169-76; M. F. Thielen, *Die europäische Türkey*, Vienna 1828, 114 f.; Baedeker's *Dalmatien und die Adria*, 1929, 245 (F. Babinger); *Guide d'Albanie* ('Albturist'), Tirana 1958, 255-9; art. arnawutluk, above. (V. L. Ménage)

ELBISTAN, Abulustayn or Ablistayn in the ancient Arabic writers, Āblistān in the Persian, Ablasta in the Armenian, Plasta in the Byzantine, and Albistān or Elbistān in more recent times: a town in south-eastern Anatolia, 38° 15′ N., 37° 11′ E., at an altitude of 1150 m., on the Sögütlü Dere, one of the sources of the Ceyhan, the Pyramos of antiquity. It is situated in a wide plain which is rich in water and enclosed by high mountains of the eastern Taurus, at the foot of the Shar Daghî (1300 m. = 4265 ft.). It is the capital of a *kaza* in the *vilâyet* of Marash. In 1950, it had 7,477 inhabitants, and the *kaza* had 55,668.

In antiquity, Arabissos (whence the Arabic ʿArabsūs, Afsūs, the early Turkish Yarpuz—later Efsus—and, as capital of the *ḳaḍāʾ*, Afshin) was the capital of the Elbistan plain, which belonged to the Syrian Marches (Thughūr al-Shām), much fought over by the Muslims and Byzantines. Around 333/944 or 340/951, Arabissos was destroyed by the Ḥamdānid Sayf al-Dawla, but as the supposed place of rest of the Seven Sleepers (*aṣḥāb al-kahf*) it was also revered as a place of pilgrimage by the Muslims (see F. Babinger, *Die Örtlichkeit der Siebenschläferlegende in muslimischer Schau*, in *Anzeiger der phil.-hist. Kl. der Österr. Akademie der Wissenschaften*, Year 1957, no. 6, 1-9). Elbistan, however, developed as the political centre.

In the years between 1097 and 1105, Elbistan (Plastantia) was in the hand of the Crusaders. Subsequently it changed hands several times, belonging in turn to the Crusaders of Antioch, the Dānishmandids of Sīwās and the Saldjūḳids of Konya, finally remaining in the hands of these last in 1201. During the Anatolian (Kayseri) campaign in 675/1277, the Mamlūk Sulṭān al-Ẓāhir Baybars gained a great victory near Elbistan over the Mongol army of the Ilkhān Abāḳā on 10 or 13 Dhu 'l-Ḳaʿda/15 or 18 April. From 740/1339 onwards, Elbistan became the capital of the Turcoman principality of Dhulḳadîr, but in 1400 it was destroyed by Tīmūr, and in 1507 by the Ṣafawid Shāh Ismāʿīl; in 921/1515 Selīm I brought it under Ottoman suzerainty, but it was not incorporated into the Ottoman Empire as an independent (*müsellem*) *ḳaḍāʾ* in the *liwāʾ* and *eyālet* of Dhu 'l-ḳadriyye (capital Marʿash) until the time of Sulṭān Süleymān. In 1264/1847, it was assigned to the *sandjaḳ* of Marʿash in the *wilāyet* of Aleppo as an ordinary *ḳaḍāʾ*.

The most notable monument in Elbistan is the Ulu Djāmiʿ, which, according to an inscription over the gateway, was built in 639/1241 (*RCEA*, xi, 132, no. 4199) by the *amīr* Mubāriz al-Dīn Čawlī, but was later restored in the Ottoman style. On the way to Hurman, the same *amīr* built a khān, later destroyed, on whose site now stands the village of Çawlı-Han. On the way to Behisni, there is the ruin of a large khān of the Saldjūḳ *amīr* Ḳamar al-Dīn; there is also a mosque, known as the Himmet-Baba-Djāmiʿ, a small building with one cupola, dating from Ottoman times. It is of special interest because one enters the octagonal *türbe* on the *ḳibla* wall through a door in the *miḥrāb* (reported by K. Erdmann).

Bibliography: V. Cuinet, *La Turquie d'Asie*, ii, 240; Kātib Čelebi, *Djihānnümā*, 599; Yāḳūt, i, 93; d'Ohsson, *Hist. des Mongols*, iii, 480, 488; Hammer-Purgstall, *Geschichte der Ilchane*, 293-311; E. Reclus, *Nouv. géogr. univ.*, ix, 657; Ritter, *Erdkunde*, xix, 15 f.; Ziya Güner, *Elbistan*, Istanbul 1936; *IA*, article *Elbistan* (Mükrimin Halil Yınanç), where further bibliography can be found.

(Fr. Taeschner)

ELBURZ [see alburz].

ELCHE [see alsh].

ELČI, a Turkish word meaning envoy, from *el* or *il*, country, people, or state, with the occupational suffix *či* (= *dji*). In some eastern Turkish texts the word appears to denote the ruler of a land or people; its normal meaning, however, since early times, has been that of envoy or messenger, usually in a diplomatic, sometimes, in mystical literature, in a figurative religious sense. In Ottoman Turkish it became the normal word for an ambassador, together with the more formal Arabic term *sefīr*. From an early date the Ottoman sultans exchanged occasional diplomatic missions, for courtesy or negotiation, with other Muslim rulers (in Anatolia, Egypt, Morocco, Persia, India, Central Asia, etc.) and also sent a number of missions to various European capitals. From the 16th century, in accordance with the growing European practice of continuous diplomacy through resident embassies, European states established permanent missions in Istanbul. The Ottoman government, however, made no attempt to respond to this practice until the end of the 18th century, preferring to rely, for contact with the European powers, on the foreign missions in Istanbul, and on occasional special embassies despatched to one or another European capital for some immediate and limited purpose. It was the custom for such envoys, in addition to their official reports, to write a general account, known as *sefāretnāme*, of their travels and experiences. A number of these accounts have survived in part or in full, and some of them have been published. In 1792 Selīm III decided to establish permanent resident embassies in Europe. The first was opened in London in 1793 (on the reasons for this choice see Djewdet, *Ta'rīkh*², vi, 257-60), and was followed by others in Vienna, Berlin, and Paris. This first experiment gradually petered out, the embassies, left in charge of Greek officials, being finally closed on the outbreak of the Greek War of Independence in 1821. A new start was made in the eighteen-thirties with the opening of permanent embassies in London, Paris and Vienna and a legation in Berlin, and the despatch of envoys extraordinary (*fawḳ al-ʿāda*) to Tehran and St. Petersburg. These were followed by further resident missions in Europe, Asia (Tehran embassy 1849) and America (Washington legation 1867), and the organization of a foreign ministry. In earlier times envoys were usually chosen from the palace corps of pursuivants (see ČAUSH); later from among the bureaucratic and *ʿulemā'* classes. At first there was some uncertainty about grades and ranks; in the 19th century the European terminology of ambassador, minister plenipotentiary, and *chargé d'affaires* for heads of missions, was adopted. The first was rendered *büyük elči* or *sefīr-i kebīr*, the second *orta elči* or simply *sefīr*, the third *maṣlaḥatgüzār*.

Bibliography: Djewdet, *Ta'rīkh*², vi, 85-9, 128-30, 231-2; *IA*, article Elçi (Mecdud Mansuroğlu); J. C. Hurewitz, *Ottoman diplomacy and the European state system*, in *MEJ*, (1961), 141-52 (reprinted in *Belleten*, xxv (1961), 455-66). On European diplomats in Istanbul see B. Spuler, *Die europäische Diplomatie in Konstantinopel bis zum Frieden von Beograd* (*1739*), in *Jahrb. f. Kultur u. Gesch. d. Slaven*, n.s. xi (1935) and *Jahrbücher für Geschichte Osteuropas*, i (1936), and Zarif Orgun, *Osmanlı İmparatorluğunda nâme ve hediye getiren elçilere yapılan merasim*, in *Tarih vesikaları*, i/6 (1942), 407-13. For lists of envoys sent to and from Istanbul until 1774, see Hammer-Purgstall, *GOR*, ix, 303-34 (*Histoire*, xvii, 134-68); Ottoman ambassadors from 1250/1834 onwards are listed in the Ottoman Foreign Office yearbooks (*Sālnāme-i neẓāret-i khāridjiyye*, 1302 A.H., 178-95, and later editions). On the *sefāretnāmes* see Bursalî Meḥmed Ṭāhir, *ʿOthmānlî müʾellifleri*, iii, 189-90; F. Taeschner in *ZDMG*, lxxvii (1923), 75-8; Babinger, *GOW*, 323-32; B. Lewis, *The Muslim discovery of Europe*, in preparation. See further ḲĀṢID, TERDJÜMĀN, VALAVAČ, and, for a general survey of Muslim diplomacy and diplomatic practice, SAFĪR.

(B. LEWIS)

ELDEM, KHALĪL EDHEM, Turkish archeologist and historian, was born on 24 (?) June 1861 in Istanbul. He was the youngest son of the grand vizier Ibrāhīm Edhem Pasha [*q.v.*]. After completing his primary school course in Istanbul, he continued, from 1876, his secondary education in Berlin, and later studied chemistry and natural sciences in the University of Zurich and at the Polytechnic School of Vienna. In 1885 he received the Ph. D. degree from the University of Berne. Back in Istanbul he was appointed to an office in the Ministry of War and transferred later to the General Staff Administration of the Ottoman Empire. He found his vocation when he was nominated in 1892 as deputy administrator of the Imperial Museum, where his eldest brother ʿOthmān Ḥamdī Bey [*q.v.*] occupied the post of administrator-general. Upon the death of his brother, he was charged on 28 February 1910 with the administration of the Imperial Museum, an important post which he held until his retirement, on 28 February 1931. His ability as administrator and scholar is shown in the organization of the Imperial Museum. He enlarged and classified the collections of the main Archeological Museum and founded in 1918, in a separate building, the Ancient Near Eastern Section of the Museum. He also organized the Topkapı Sarayı [*q.v.*] upon the opening of this palace as a museum under his administration. His publications cover the fields of archaeology, numismatics, sigillography, epigraphy and history (for his bibliography see *Halil Edhem Hâtıra Kitabı*, i, 299-302). His works on sigillography and epigraphy are the first studies in these ancillary disciplines of history published in Turkey. The book entitled *Düwel-i Islāmiyye*, Istanbul 1927, a revised and enlarged translation of S. Lane-Poole's *Mohammedan dynasties*, attests his wide knowledge of Islamic history. His scholarship won him a world-wide reputation: he was a member of national and foreign academies, honorary doctor of the Universities of Basle and Leipzig, and honorary professor of the University of Istanbul. He died 16 November 1938 in Istanbul, being a member of the Turkish Parliament.

Bibliography: *Halil Edhem Hâtıra Kitabı*, ii, Ankara 1948; Arif Müfit Mansel, *Halil Edhem Eldem*, in *Ülkü*, xii, 383-6; Aziz Ogan, *Bay Halil Ethem*, in *Yeni Türk*, no. 73, 4-8; Ibrahim Alâettin Gövsa, *Türk meşhurları ansiklopedisi*, Istanbul 1946, 163-4. (E. KURAN)

ELEGY [see MARTHIYA].

ELEPHANT [see FĪL].

ELIČPUR [see GĀWILGAŔH].

ELIJAH [see ILYĀS],

ELISHA [see ALĪSAʿ].

ELITE [see AL-KHĀṢṢA WA'L-ʿĀMMA].

ELIXIR [see AL-IKSĪR].

ELKASS MIRZA [see ALKĀṢ MĪRZĀ].

ELMA DAGHÎ, name of several ranges of mountains in Anatolia: 1) south-east of Ankara, 2) north-west of Elmalî (2505 m. [= 8,218 ft.]).

(FR. TAESCHNER)

ELMALİ, earlier spelling Elmalu (Turkish = "Appletown"), a small town in south-western Anatolia, 36° 45′ N., 29° 55′ E., altitude 1150 m. (= 3,772 ft.), on a small plain, surrounded by high mountains (Elma Daghî 2505 m. (= 8,218 ft.) in the north, Bey Daghlarî 3086 m. (= 10,124 ft.) in the south-east), in the vicinity of the small lake Kara-Göl. This lake flows into a cave, Elmalî Düdeni. Elmalî is capital of a *kaza* in the *vilâyet* of Antalya, and has 4,967 inhabitants (1950); the *kaza* has 23,993 inhabitants.

Elmalî, in the ancient region of Lycia, is a pretty and neat town with a healthy climate. It has a fairly new bazaar, and a classical Ottoman mosque (the ʿÖmer-Pasha Djāmiʿi) of the year 1016/1607. The mosque itself has one cupola and the entrance-hall has five. Outside, there is a minaret on the right face, and at the back, to the left, a *türbe*. There are fourteen tympana of tiles of quite good quality within the mosque itself, and five more in the entrance hall (reported by K. Erdmann).

Elmalî was the capital of the Turcoman principality of Tekke [*q.v.*], which was acquired in 830/1426-7 by Murād II, and henceforth became a *liwāʾ* of the *eyālet* of Anadolu. The main centre of the *liwāʾ* of Tekke shifted to Anṭālya, and Elmalî became a *ḳaḍāʾ*. In the 19th century, it was a *ḳaḍāʾ* of the *sandjaḳ* of Anṭālya (Adalia) in the *wilāyet* of Konya.

The so-called *Takhtadjî*, woodcutters suspected of being Shīʿīs, have settled in the wooded surroundings of Elmalî and they sell their wood in the town. Some 60 km. (37 m.) south of Elmalî is the harbour of Finike (earlier spelling Fineka, 1,382 inhabitants) which once formed part of the *ḳaḍāʾ* of Elmalî, but today forms a *kaza* of its own. Nearby there are the Lycian graves and one Phoenician inscription.

There are three other villages in Anatolia called Elmalî: one is in the *kaza* of Ordu, in the *vilâyet* of the same name; the second is on the shores of lake Van; and the third in the *kaza* Besni (Behesni) in the *vilâyet* of Malatya.

Bibliography: Ewliyā Čelebi, *Seyāḥatnāme*, ix, 277 ff.; E. Reclus, *Nouvelle géographie universelle*, ix, 649, 660; E. Banse, *Die Türkei*, 156; Sāmī Bey Fraschery, *Ḳāmūs al-Aʿlām*, ii, 1025; V. Cuinet, *La Turquie d'Asie*, i, 864; ii, 377; Cemal Arif Alagöz, *Türkiye Karst olayları*, 47; *IA*, s.v. (Besim Darkot).

(Fr. Taeschner)

ELOQUENCE [see BALĀGHA, BAYĀN and FAṢĀḤA].

ELURĀ. The Elurā (Ellora) caves, near Dawlatābād [*q.v.*], appear in the history of Muslim India only as the scene of the capture of the Gudjarāt princess Deval Devī, the future bride of Khiḍr Khān [*q.v.*], for ʿAlāʾ al-Dīn Khaldjī by Alp Khān, who had given his forces leave to visit the cave temples (Firishta, Lucknow lith., i, 117). These caves were justly famous and were described by some early travellers, *e.g.*, Masʿūdī, iv, 95, copied with much distortion of names by Ḳazwīnī, cf. Gildemeister, *Scriptorum Arabum de rebus Indicis*, text 79, trans. 221; Muslim descriptions of more recent times in Rafīʿ al-Dīn Shīrāzī, *Tadhkirat al-mulūk*, ms. Bombay 196a-198b, and in Muḥammad Sāḳī Mustaʿidd Khān, *Maʾāthir-i ʿĀlamgīrī*, 238; tr. Sarkar, Calcutta 1947, 145. The technique of scarping the solid rock here is strikingly similar to that of the great scarp on which the citadel of Dawlatābād stands. (J. Burton-Page)

ELVIRA [see ILBĪRA].

ELWEND [see ALWAND].

EMĀNET [see EMĪN].

EMĀNET-I MUḲADDESE, a Turkicized Arabic expression meaning sacred trust or deposit, the name given to a collection of relics preserved in the treasury of the Topkapı palace in Istanbul. The most important are a group of objects said to have belonged to the Prophet; they included his cloak (*khirḳa-i sherīf* [*q.v.*]), a prayer-rug, a flag, a bow, a staff, a pair of horseshoes, as well as a tooth, some hairs (see LIḤYA), and a stone bearing the Prophet's footprint. In addition there are weapons, utensils and garments said to have belonged to the ancient prophets, to the early Caliphs, and to various Companions, a key of the Kaʿba, and Ḳurʾāns said to have been written by the Caliphs ʿUthmān and ʿAlī. Under the Sultans these relics were honoured in the annual ceremony of the *Khirḳa-i saʿādet*, held on 15 Ramaḍān.

Bibliography: For a detailed description, with illustrations, see Tahsin Öz, *Hırka-i Saadet dairesi ve Emanet-i Mukaddese*, Istanbul 1953; on the Muslim attitude to relics in general, see I. Goldziher, *Muh. St.*, ii, 356-68, and the article ATHAR. (Ed.)

EMBALMING [see ḤINĀṬA].

EMBLEM [see SHIʿĀR].

EMESA [see ḤIMS].

EMIGRATION [see DJĀLIYA, HIDJRA and MUHĀDJIRŪN].

EMĪN, from Arabic *amīn* [*q.v.*], faithful, trustworthy, an Ottoman administrative title usually translated intendant or commissioner. His function or office was called *emānet*. The primary meaning of *emīn*, in Ottoman official usage, was a salaried officer appointed by or in the name of the Sultan, usually by *berāt*, to administer, supervise or control a department, function or source of revenue. There were thus *emīns* of various kinds of stores and supplies, of mints, of mines, of customs, customs-houses and other revenues, and of the *taḥrīr* [*q.v.*], the preparation of the registers of land, tenure, population and revenue of the provinces and the distribution of fiefs (see DAFTAR-I KHĀḲĀNĪ and TĪMĀR). In the words of Prof. Inalcık, "the *emānet* of *taḥrīr* required great experience and knowledge, carried great responsibility, and at the same time was susceptible to corruption and abuse; usually influential beys and *ḳāḍīs* were appointed to it". In principle, the *emīn* was a salaried government commissioner, and not a tax-farmer, grantee, or lessee of any kind. His duty might be to represent the government in dealings with such persons, or himself to arrange for the collection of the revenues in question. When concerned with revenues, he was to have no financial interest in the proceeds, which he was required to remit in full to the treasury. The term *emīn* is also used of agents and commissioners appointed by authorities other than the Sultan—by the *ḳāḍīs*, for example, and even by the tax-farmers themselves, who appointed their own agents to look after their interests. At times, by abuse, the *emīns* themselves appear as tax-farmers.

In the capital, the title *emīn* was borne by a number of high-ranking officers, in charge of certain departments and services. Such for example were the commissioners of the powder magazines (*bārūt-khāne emīni*), of the arsenal (*tersāne* [*q.v.*] *emīni*), and of the *daftar-i khāḳānī* (*defter emīni* or *defter-i khāḳānī emīni*). The highest ranking holders of this title were the four *emīns* attached to the external services (*bīrūn* [*q.v.*]) of the palace: the city commissioner (*Shehr emīni* [*q.v.*]), concerned with palace finances and supplies and with the maintenance of palaces and other royal and governmental buildings in the city; the kitchen commissioner (*Maṭbakh emīni*) and barley commissioner (*Arpa emīni*), concerned respectively with food and fodder for the imperial kitchens (see MAṬBAKH) and stables (see IṢṬABL; the commissioner of the mint (*Ḍarbkhāne emīni*), in charge of the mint in the palace grounds (see DĀR AL-ḌARB, ii).

Bibliography: Halil Inalcık, *Hicri 835 tarihli sûret-i defter-i sancak-i Arvanid*, Ankara 1954, XIX; R. Anhegger, *Beitraege zur Geschichte des Bergbaus im osmanischen Reich*, i/I, Istanbul 1943, 22-3, 32-5, 104-7; R. Anhegger and Halil Inalcık, *Ḳānūnnāme-i sulṭānī ber mūceb-i ʿörf-i ʿOsmānī*, Ankara 1956, index; N. Beldiceanu, *Les actes des premiers Sultans*, Paris-The Hague 1960, index; Barkan, *Kanunlar*, index; L. Fekete, *Die Siyāqat-Schrift in der türkischen Finanzverwaltung*, i, Budapest 1955, 86, and index; U. Heyd, *Ottoman documents on Palestine 1552-1615*, Oxford 1960, 59-60, 93, and index; S. J. Shaw, *The financial and administrative organization and development of Ottoman Egypt 1517-1798*, Princeton 1962, 26-7, 31, and index; ʿAbd al-Raḥmān Wefīḳ, *Tekālīf ḳawāʿidi*, i, Istanbul 1328, 176-84; I. H. Uzunçarşılı, *Osmanlı devletinin Saray teşkilâtı*, Ankara 1945, 375-87; idem, *Osmanlı devletinin merkez ve bahriye teşkilâtı*, Ankara 1948, index; Gibb-Bowen, i/1 84-5, 132-3, 150, i/2 21; Pakalın, i, 525-6.

(B. LEWIS)

EMIN, MEHMED, [see YURDAKUL, MEHMED EMIN].

EMĪN PASHA (Eduard Carl Oscar Theodor Schnitzer) was born on 28 March 1840 at Oppeln in Prussian Silesia. He graduated in medicine at Berlin in 1864. He entered the Ottoman service as a medical officer in Albania in 1865, and assumed the name of Khayr Allāh; later, in the Sudan, he became known as Meḥmed Emīn (Muḥammad Amīn, not al-A.). He went to Egypt in October 1875, whence he proceeded to Khartoum, and (in May 1876) to Lado, the capital of the Equatorial Provinces, where he was appointed medical officer by C. G. Gordon Pasha, the then governor. He was entrusted with political missions to Uganda and Unyoro. In June 1878, Gordon, now governor-general of the Egyptian Sudan, appointed him governor of the Equatorial Provinces, henceforward amalgamated as the Equatorial Province (*Mudīriyyat Khaṭṭ al-Istiwāʾ*). During the first years of his governorship, Emīn continued Gordon's task of extending and pacifying the Egyptian territories in the southern Sudan, and of exploiting their natural resources, the chief of which was ivory. The administrative problems confronting him were enormous, arising from the vast extent and poor communications of his province, the disaffection of the tribes, and his enforced dependence on unreliable and incompetent troops and officials. Many of these were northern Sudanese (Danāḳla) who had originally entered the region in the retinues of predatory traders in ivory and slaves, others were exiles from Egypt. Emīn was indefatigable in touring the province, and made important studies in its natural history. By 1881 he had attained a fair measure of success in establishing administrative order. Reviving prosperity was reflected in increasing revenue; at the start of his governorship, the province had a deficit of £ 30,000; three years later it showed a surplus of £ 1,200. After the outbreak of the Mahdist revolt in 1881, Emīn's position deteriorated. His communications with Khartoum were cut after April 1883. The defeat of an Egyptian expeditionary force at Shaykān (5 November 1883) was followed by the Mahdist conquest of the Baḥr al-Ghazāl [*q.v.*], the neighbouring province to Emīn's. In May 1884, Emīn received a letter from Karam Allāh Kurḳusāwī, the Mahdist military governor of the Baḥr al-Ghazāl, demanding the surrender of his province. Emīn's officers advised capitulation, and to gain time he sent a delegation to Karam Allāh, and moved his headquarters to Wadelai (Walad Lāy) in April 1885. However, the Mahdist forces withdrew from the Equatorial Province. For over two years, Emīn remained undisturbed, although with diminished and precarious authority. In March 1886, he received a despatch from Nūbār Pasha, the Egyptian prime minister, dated 13 Shaʿbān 1302/27 May 1885, informing him of the abandonment of the Sudan, and authorizing him to withdraw with his men to Zanzibar. Meanwhile projects for relieving Emīn were being mooted in Europe. An expedition was organized and partly financed by a British committee including persons interested in East African commerce. The Egyptian government also subsidized the project. The expedition was headed by H. M. Stanley, who was an agent of Leopold II of the Belgians. Taking the Congo route, Stanley met Emīn by Lake Albert on 29 April 1888. Emīn was most unwilling to leave his post, and Stanley put before him alternative proposals: that he should continue to administer the Equatorial Province on behalf of the Congo Free State, or that he should establish a station by Lake Victoria for the British East Africa Company. Emīn rejected these proposals, and Stanley left to bring up the rest of his expedition. During his absence, mutiny broke out among some of Emīn's troops, who were suspicious of recent developments, and unwilling to go to Egypt. Emīn was held by the mutineers at Dufile. Meanwhile, on 11 June 1888, a Mahdist expeditionary force under ʿUmar Ṣāliḥ had left Omdurman in steamers. This reached Lado on 11 October, and summoned Emīn to surrender. The mutineers resisted the Mahdist forces, and on 16 November Emīn was released. He withdrew to Lake Albert, where he was rejoined in January 1889 by Stanley. In April, Stanley began his march to the coast, unwillingly accompanied by Emīn. Emīn then entered the German service in East Africa. He led an expedition in what is now Tanganyika. Thence he entered the fringes of his old province, to try to attract some of his former followers. With his expedition reduced to desperate straits by smallpox, he endeavoured to reach the Congo, but was murdered by a tribal chief on or shortly after 23 October 1892.

Bibliography: Georg Schweitzer, *Emin Pasha: his life and work*, London 1898, 2 vols.; G. Schweinfurth and others (edd.), *Emin Pasha in Central Africa*, London 1888; A. J. Mounteney-Jephson, *Emin Pasha and the rebellion at the Equator*, London 1890. For the rôle of the relief expedition in Leopold II's policy, see P. Ceulemans, *La question arabe et le Congo (1883-1892)*, Brussels 1959, 86-117. For further bibliographical material, see R. L. Hill, *A bibliography of the Anglo-Egyptian Sudan*, London 1939, 126, 145-6 and Index; also *Biography Catalogue of the library of the Royal Commonwealth Society*, London 1961, 114b-115b; Abdel Rahman el-Nasri, *A bibliography of the Sudan, 1938-1958*, London 1962, index. A copy of Emīn's despatch of 1 September 1885 to the Egyptian minister of the Interior is in the Sudan

Government archives (Cairint 3/14, 236); photostat in the School of Oriental and African Studies, London. (P. M. Holt)

EMIR [see AMĪR].

EMĪR SULṬĀN, SAYYID SHAMS AL-DĪN MEHEMMED B. ʿALĪ AL-ḤÜSEYNĪ AL-BUKHĀRĪ, popularly known as Emīr Seyyid, or Emīr Sulṭān, the patron saint of Bursa (Brusa). He is supposed to have been a descendant of the 12th Imam, Muḥammad al-Mahdī, and hence a Sayyid. His father, Sayyid ʿAlī, known under the name of Emīr Külāl, was a Ṣūfī in Bukhārā. He himself, born in Bukhārā (in 770/1368), joined the Nūrbakhshiyya branch of the Kubrawiyya in his early youth. Some *menāḳibnāmes* assert that he was a follower of the Imāmiyya.

After his *ḥadjdj*, Emīr Sulṭān spent some time in Medina, and then went to Anatolia via Ḳaramān, Ḥamīd-eli, Kütāhya and Ine-Göl. Finally he reached Bursa, where he dwelt in a cell (*ṣawmaʿa*) and led a life of good works. Within a short time, he gained great fame, gathered disciples around him, and entered into contact with the *ʿulemāʾ* and *shaykhs* of Bursa. He was highly esteemed by Sulṭān Bayazīd I Yïldïrïm, and married his daughter, Khundī Sulṭān, by whom he had three children (a son and two daughters). He was asked to invest the sultan with his sword when the latter went into battle, and his admonitions decided the sultan to refrain from excessive drinking (cf. the anecdote in Ewliyā Čelebi, *Narrative of Travels*, ii, 25 = *Taʾrīkh-i Ṣāf*, i, 32 f.; missing in the edition of *Seyāḥatnāme*, ii, 48); it is also said that Emīr Sulṭān successfully restrained Bāyezīd from the illegal execution of Tīmūr's ambassadors (ʿĀlī, *Künh*, v, 83 f.). Emīr Sulṭān was captured when Bursa was taken by one of Tīmūr's scouting parties in 805/1402, and brought before Tīmūr, who gave him the choice of accompanying him to Samarkand, but Emīr Sulṭān preferred to return to Bursa (Saʿd al-Dīn, i, 188 f.). Legend does not mention this incident; it does, on the other hand, report that the departure of Tīmūr's troops from Bursa was a miracle worked by the saint (Saʿd al-Dīn, ii, 427). When Murād II began his reign in 824/1421, he asked Emīr Sulṭān to invest him with his sword, and the saint is also said to have accelerated the defeat of the 'False Muṣṭafā' (Muṣṭafā Düzme [*q.v.*]), who contested Murād II's right to the throne, by the force of his prayers (ʿĀlī, 195 f.; Leunclavius, *Hist. Mus.*, 493 f.). In the next year, he, and a following of 500 dervishes, took part in the siege of Constantinople. The fall of the city, which he prophesied, did not, however, occur. Kananos, a Byzantine who took part in the siege, gives a detailed and vivid description of the appearance of the Mīr-Sayyid (Μηρσαίτης Βεχαρ), the 'Patriarch of the Turks', as he calls Emīr Sulṭān (ed. Bonn, 466 ff., 477 f.); the Ottoman historians, on the other hand, do not mention this lack of success. Emīr Sulṭān died in 833/1429 in Bursa, as a result of the plague. Soon afterwards legends told of miracles (*menāḳib*) wrought by the saint.

A splendid mausoleum (which became one of the most visited places of pilgrimage in Turkey) was erected over the grave of Emīr Sulṭān at the eastern end of the town. The mosque attached to it was built in its present form by Selīm III (inscription of 1219/1804).

Bibliography: Tashköprüzāde, i, 76 f. (transl. O. Rescher, 30 f.); Saʿd al-Dīn, ii, 425-7; ʿĀlī, *Künh*, v, 112; *Güldeste-i riyāḍ-i ʿirfān*, 69-79; Ewliyā Čelebi, *Seyāḥatnāme*, ii, 47 ff.; Le Beau, *Histoire du Bas-Empire*, Paris 1836, xxi, 104 ff.; Hammer-Purgstall, i, 234 f., 431, 643 (references of the last two chiefly concern the role played by Emīr Sulṭān in the siege of Constantinople); further bibliography, especially hagiographic, from the *Menāḳibnāmes*, see *IA*, iv, 261-3 (M. Cavid Baysun).

(J. H. Mordtmann-[Fr. Taeschner])

EMPEDOCLES [see ANBĀDUḲLĪS].

EMRELI (ʿEMRĀLĪ, ÏMRʿĀLĪ or ÏMRĀLĪ), a semi-sedentary Turkmen tribe which since the 10th/16th century has dwelt in Khurāsān, in the region of Gürgen. Driven back at the end of the 12th/18th century by the Tekkes (Tekins), the tribe emigrated northwards and, in two successive waves, settled down in Khwārizm (region of Hudjaylī on the Amān Ḳūlī canal), the first in 1803-4 and the second in 1827 when they submitted to the Khāns of Khiva. In 1873 (I. Ibragimov, *Nekotorïe zametki o Khivinskikh Turkmenakh i Kirgizakh*, in *Voennïy Sbornik*, xcviii (1874), no. 9, 133-63), they owned nearly 10,000 tents. At the present time the Emrelis inhabit the Ilyalï region, west of Tashawz, between the Yomuds in the south and the Goklens and Čowdors in the north. An isolated settlement exists in the Ashkābād region (district of Kaakhka).

Since the Russian conquest the Emrelis have been sedentary, and are engaged in agriculture and sheep-rearing.

Detailed information on the history of the tribe in the 19th century is contained in the recent work by Yu. E. Bregel, *Khorezmskie Turkmeni v XIX veke*, Moscow (Acad. of Sc., Institute of Asian Peoples) 1961. (A. Bennigsen)

ENAMEL [see MĪNĀ].

ENDERŪN (pers. Andarūn, "inside"; turk. Enderūn). The term Enderūn (or Enderūn-i Humāyūn) was used to designate the "Inside" Service (as opposed to Bīrūn [*q.v.*], the "Outside" Service) of the Imperial Household of the Ottoman Sulṭān: *i.e.*, to denote the complex of officials engaged in the personal and private service of the Sulṭān—included therein was the system of Palace Schools—and placed under the control of the Chief of the White Eunuchs, the Bāb al-Saʿādet Aghasï (the Agha of the Gate of Felicity—*i.e.*, the gate leading from the second into the third court, proceeding inward, of the Imperial Palace—the Topkapı Sarayı) or, more simply, the Kapï Aghasï (the Agha of the Gate). Further information will be found in the article SARĀY.

Bibliography: Khidr Ilyās Efendi, *Laṭāʾif-i Enderūn*, Istanbul A.H. 1276; Ṭayyārzāde Aḥmed ʿAṭā, *Taʾrīkh*, Istanbul A.H. 1291-3; *Quanto di più curioso .... hà potuto raccorre Cornelio Magni .... in viaggi, e dimore per la Turchia*, Parma 1679, Parte Prima, 502 ff. (= the "Serrai Enderum" of ʿAlī Beg, *i.e.*, of Alberto Bobovi (Bobowski), "Polacco da Leopoli"); N. Barozzi and G. Berchet, *Le Relazioni degli Stati Europei lette al Senato dagli Ambasciatori Veneziani nel secolo decimosettimo*, Serie V: Turchia, fasc. I, Venice 1866, 59 ff. (= *Descrizione del Serraglio del Gransignore fatta dal Bailo Ottaviano Bon*. Cf. also the English version of Robert Withers: *A Description of the Grand Signor's Seraglio, or Turkish Emperours Court*, ed. J. Greaves, London 1650 and 1653); M. Baudier, *Histoire Generalle du Serrail, et de la Cour du Grand Seigneur Empereur des Turcs*, Paris 1624, 1631 (English translation: E. Grimeston, *The History of the Imperiall Estate of the Grand Seigneurs*, London 1635); I. H. Uzunçarşılı, *Osmanlı Devletinin Saray Teşkilâtı* (*Türk Tarih Kurumu Yayın-*

larindan, viii Seri, no. 15), Ankara 1945, 297 ff., *passim*; I. H. Baykal, *Enderun Mektebi Tarihi* (Istanbul Fethi Derneği Neşriyatı: no. 20), Istanbul 1953; B. Miller, *Beyond the Sublime Porte*, New York 1931, 47 ff., *passim* and 205 ff., *passim*; idem, *The Curriculum of the Palace School of the Turkish Sultans*, in *The Macdonald Presentation Volume*, Princeton, New Jersey 1933, 303 ff.; idem, *The Palace School of Muhammad the Conqueror* (Harvard Historical Monographs, no. 17), Cambridge, Mass., 1941; N. M. Penzer, *The Harem*, London 1936, 27 ff. (listing various European accounts of the Seraglio); Gibb-Bowen, i/I, 72, 77 ff., 331 ff.; B. Lewis, *Istanbul and the civilization of the Ottoman Empire*, Norman 1963, 65 ff.

(V. J. Parry)

ENDJÜMEN [see ANDJUMAN, DJAMʿIYYA].

ENGÜRÜ [see ANKARA].

ENGÜRÜS [see MADJĀRISTĀN and UNGURUS].

ENIF [see NUDJŪM].

ENNAYER [see INNĀYĒR].

ENOCH [see IDRĪS].

ENOS (also Inos/z), Ottoman name for the classical Ainos, now Enez, town on the Aegean coast of Thrace (40° 43′ N., 26° 03′ E.) on the east bank of the estuary of the Merič ([*q.v.*], anc. Hebros). From classical times until the last century it was a prosperous harbour, on an important trade route from the upper Merič valley and across the isthmus from the Black Sea, with valuable and much-coveted saltpans. With Lesbos (T. Midilli, [*q.v.*]) it passed in 1355 to Francesco Gattilusio, as the dowry of Maria, the sister of John V Palaeologus. On the death of Palamede Gattilusio in 1455, family quarrels and the complaints of neighbouring Muslims that the citizens sheltered runaway slaves (ʿĀshıḳpashazāde, ed. Giese, § 125; Tursun, *TOEM ʿilāwe*, 68) provided Meḥemmed II with the pretext to intervene: at his approach in Ṣafar 860/January 1456 the citizens submitted, and the region was thenceforth a ḳaḍā of the sandjaḳ of Gallipoli. The silting of the river (now barely navigable), the construction of the railway to Dede-aghač [*q.v.*] and the re-drawing of the frontier in 1913 have reduced Enos to a small fishing-village, now 4 km. from the sea among marshy lagoons.

Bibliography: Pauly-Wissowa, s.v. Ainos (G. Hirschfeld); F. W. Hasluck, *Monuments of the Gattelusi*, in *Annual of the British School at Athens*, xv (1908-9), 248 ff. (sketch-map and references to travellers' descriptions, etc.); S. Casson, *Macedonia, Thrace and Illyria*, 1926, 255 ff.; F. Babinger, *Mehmed der Eroberer und seine Zeit*, Munich 1953, 141 ff.; Ö. L. Barkan, *Kanunlar*, Istanbul 1943, 255-6; Pīrī Reʾīs, *Kitabı Bahriye*, Istanbul 1935, 98-9; Ḥādjdji Khalīfa, *Djihān-numā* = J. von Hammer, *Rumeli und Bosna*, Vienna 1812, 68; M. F. Thielen, *Die europäische Türkey*, Vienna 1828, 76; *Turkey* (Naval Intelligence geog. handbook), 1943, ii, 79.

(V. L. Ménage)

ENWER PASHA, Young Turk soldier and statesman (1881-1922). Enwer was born in the Dīwānyolu quarter of Istanbul, on 22 November 1881, the eldest of six children of Aḥmed bey, then a minor civil servant, and his wife ʿĀʾishe. The family was from Manastir (Bitolj) in Macedonia, and moved there again when Enwer was a boy. After completing his secondary schooling there, Enwer entered the military academy (Mekteb-i Ḥarbiyye) in Istanbul, completing both the regular officers' training course and the advanced general staff course. He graduated second in his class on 5 December 1902 (the first was his close friend and life-long associate Ḥāfiẓ Ismāʿīl Ḥaḳḳī Pasha, 1879-1915; see Muharrem Mazlum [Iskora], *Erkânıharbiye mektebi . . . tarihi*, Istanbul 1930, 246) as a general staff captain and was posted to the Third Army in Macedonia. He spent the next three years in military operations against Macedonian guerrillas. In September 1906, he was assigned with the rank of major to Third Army headquarters in Manastır. There he joined, as member no. 12, the ʿOthmānlī Ittiḥād we Teraḳḳī Djemʿiyyeti, the conspiratorial nucleus of the Young Turk movement, and in the following years helped to spread its organization. When the Istanbul authorities launched an investigation into these secret activities, Enwer, who with a group of soldiers had ambushed one of the investigating officers, deemed it wise to refuse a call for promotion and reassignment to Istanbul; instead, in late June, 1908, he escaped with a group of followers into the Macedonian hills, an example soon followed by *kolaghasi* (senior captain) Aḥmed Niyāzī of Resne and Eyyūb Ṣabrī [Akgöl] of Ohri. Their action proved to be the prelude to the Young Turk revolution of 24 July, 1908. At only 26 years of age, Enwer was widely acclaimed as the foremost hero of revolution and liberty.

While on liaison service with Austrian officers in Macedonia Enwer had studied German and military tactics. In 1909 he was posted as military attaché to Berlin where he deepened his lifelong admiration for German military power and efficiency. In 1909 he briefly returned to Turkey to participate in the action of the Ḥareket Ordusu in suppressing the Istanbul mutiny of 13 April 1909 (the so-called *Otuzbir Mart waḳʿasi*). In the autumn of 1911, he resigned his post in Berlin to volunteer for service in the Libyan war, where he fought with distinction. On 5 June 1912 he earned a double promotion to lieutenant-colonel. In September he also was appointed *mutaṣarrif* of the sandjaḳ of Benghāzī. Back in Istanbul, he participated actively in the politics of the Society for Union and Progress (Ittiḥād we Teraḳḳī Djemʿiyyeti [*q.v.*]) and at its 1912 congress helped secure the post of secretary general for his friend Ṭalʿat [*q.v.*]. On 23 January 1913 he led a raid on the Sublime Porte by a group of Unionist officers and soldiers who forced at gun point the resignation of the aging Grand Wezīr Kāmil Pasha (through the excessive zeal of one of the group, Muṣṭafā Nedjīb, the war minister Nāẓim Pasha and two other persons were killed). The major aim of the participants in this «Sublime Porte Incident» (*Bāb-i ʿĀlī waḳʿasī*) was the energetic resumption of the First Balkan War after the truce at Čataldja (3 December 1912 to 30 January 1913), but instead the campaign of the late winter of 1913 resulted in the complete evacuation of Macedonia and most of Thrace. The *coup* brought to power a Unionist party cabinet under Maḥmūd Shewket Pasha and its long-range effect was the conversion of the constitutional monarchy of 1908 into a partisan and military dictatorship, with only a semblance of parliamentary institutions, which was to last until the defeat of 1918. In the Second Balkan War Enwer was the chief of staff of the left wing, and as such was in the vanguard of the troops re-entering Edirne on 22 July 1913.

On 4 January 1914 Enwer was promoted two more ranks to brigadier-general and appointed minister of war in the Unionist cabinet of Saʿīd Ḥalīm Pasha, and with the impending outbreak of war on 21 October 1914, deputy commander-in-chief (under the Sultan's nominal authority). He became a lieutenant-general in 1915 and a general (*birindji ferik*) in 1917. After the accession of Meḥmed VI Waḥīd al-Dīn his title was changed, on 8 August 1918, from deputy commander-in-chief to chief of the General Staff (*erkān-i ḥarbiyye re'īsi*). His nearly five years in the War Office and at General Headquarters were characterized by intensive efforts to increase the efficiency of the armed forces. In his first few months in office, he presided over a purge in which the aging generals of the ʿAbd al-Ḥamīd period, who were held responsible for the disastrous Balkan War defeat, were put on the inactive list and replaced by energetic younger officers. Enwer is credited with introducing the practice of appointing officers to temporary higher rank so as to test their ability. He also personally designed a new military cap (known as the *Enweriyye*) and invented a simplified Arabic script, based on disconnected letters, which, however, found no wide acceptance. On 5 March 1914, Enwer married Emīne Nādjiye Sulṭān, a niece of the reigning monarch.

In the Ottoman diplomatic moves of the spring and summer of 1914, Enwer was the most consistent advocate of a close alliance with Germany and the Central Powers. After fruitless negotiations by Djemāl Pasha in Paris and Ṭalʿat in Bucharest, Enwer on 22 July approached the German Ambassador, Baron von Wangenheim, with the proposal of a secret offensive and defensive alliance. On the Ottoman side the ensuing negotiations were conducted mainly by Enwer himself and the Grand Vizier Saʿīd Ḥalīm Pasha with the knowledge of only a few of their colleagues; they were kept secret from the other ministers and also from the francophile Ottoman Ambassador to Berlin, Maḥmūd Mukhtār Pasha. The result was a defensive alliance against Russia dated 2 August 1914. In the following weeks, Enwer assiduously worked for early Ottoman entry into the World War, although others in the cabinet and General Staff urged caution in view of the German setback on the Marne. The German admiral Souchon, who in mid-August had entered Ottoman waters and service with his ships Goeben and Breslau, received Enwer's authorization on 14 September to sail into the Black Sea with freedom of action against Russia; but Enwer was promptly forced by his cabinet colleagues to countermand these instructions. A compromise solution on 20 September authorized Souchon's sailing but disclaimed Ottoman responsibility for any belligerent acts. By October several cabinet members had been won over to the war faction and on 22 October Enwer once more instructed Souchon: "The Turkish fleet must win maritime supremacy in the Black Sea. Seek out the Russian fleet and attack it without declaration of war" (Mühlmann, *Deutschland und die Türkei*, 102). On 29 October Souchon's Ottoman fleet attacked Russian ports and ships and the Empire was at war with the Allied powers.

Enwer's conduct of the Ottoman War effort was characterized by close co-operation with German strategy and German officers, by a readiness to attack so as to produce, if possible, early and decisive results, and by extensive use of ideological propaganda and of secret guerrilla operations to reinforce the efforts of the field armies. As many as two or three of the six to nine Ottoman armies and army groups were commanded by German generals; most of the rest had Ottoman commanders with German chiefs of staff—this binational command structure being carried through consistently from General Headquarters down to division and even regiment level. Enwer's own chief of staff throughout most of the war was General Walter Bronsart von Schellendorf, replaced in 1918 by General Hans von Seeckt. By late 1916, as many as seven Turkish divisions were assigned to reinforce the fronts in Galicia, in Rumania, and in Macedonia.

Shortly before the Empire's entry into the World War, on 5 August 1914, Enwer ordered the creation of a Special Organization (*Teshkīlāt-i Makhṣūṣa*) under Süleymān ʿAskerī, "a combination ... of secret service and guerrilla organization" (Rustow in *World Politics*, xi, 518), which engaged in irredentist struggles in Macedonia, Libya, the Caucasus, and Iran. Prominent members of the Ittiḥād we Terakkī inner circle, such as Dr. Bahā' al-Dīn Shākir and Midḥat Shükrü [Bleda], formed part of the Organization's political bureau. The proclamations from Enwer's headquarters relied at first mainly on Islamic or Pan-Islamic themes, later increasingly on Pan-Turkish ones. The 1915 offensive against the Suez Canal was known as the "Islamic" strategy. Even when the Arab Revolt in 1916 cut off the Hidjāz railroad, Enwer refused to withdraw the army corps stationed in the Holy City of Medīna. (The commander ʿÖmer Fakhr al-Dīn [Türkkan] Pasha was so thoroughly isolated by the end of the war that he did not learn of the armistice until two and a half months later; he surrendered with 12 battalions on 10 January 1919.) The offensives in Transcaucasia in the wake of the crumbling Czarist armies in 1918 were known as the "Turanic" strategy, although a guerrilla force created there by the Special Organization was called the "Army of Islam".

In December 1914 Enwer took personal command of the Third Army on the Russian front in the Armenian mountains since the previous commander, Ḥasan ʿIzzet Pasha, had proved reluctant to carry out an encirclement manœuvre against the advancing Russians in the Sarïkamïsh region, which had been planned in advance. As a result of local reconnaissance under Ḥāfiẓ Ḥakkī it was decided to enlarge the pincer movement further—a plan that did not take into account terrain and weather conditions in the steep, icy, and windswept mountains. Hunger and cold destroyed most of the Third Army before it could reach, let alone encircle, the Russian forces; of a total strength of 90,000, casualties have been estimated at 80,000. In mid-January Enwer turned the command of the remaining Third Army units over to Ḥāfiẓ Ḥakkī Pasha and returned to G.H.Q. in Istanbul. Enwer did not again take personal command of battlefield units.

The following years brought some striking Ottoman military successes, notably the defeat of the Allied landing expedition at Gallipoli (April 1915-January 1916) which prevented the loss of the capital, Istanbul, and the opening of communications between the Western Allies and the retreating Russian fronts; the victory at Kūt (see below); and the advance against the Russians in 1917-18. Beginning in the spring of 1917, however, vastly outnumbered Ottoman armies retreated steadily before the British offensives in Palestine, Iraq, and Syria. By the autumn of 1918, the military situation had become untenable, and on 14 October, the Grand Vizier Ṭalʿat Pasha resigned with his Unionist cabinet so as to facilitate the impending armistice negotiations. On 2 November 1918, Enwer, Ṭalʿat, Djemāl [*qq.v.*], Dr. Nāẓīm and other prominent Unionists assembled at night in the house of Enwer's aide-de-camp Kāẓīm [Orbay] in Arnavutköy on the

Bosphorus, and boarded a German naval vessel that brought them to Odessa. Although Enwer had plans to go to the Caucasus (Ziya Şakir, 156 f.), he later joined the others in Berlin, where they arrived in December. In Istanbul, court martial proceedings against the fugitive Unionists began 26 November 1918, and on 5 July 1919 resulted in death sentences in absentia for Enwer, Ṭalʿat, Djemāl, and Dr. Nāẓîm.

Enwer spent the winter of 1918-9 in Berlin. Since the Entente powers were demanding the extradition of the Young Turks, they lived semi-legally; Enwer himself adopted the name "(Professor) ʿAlī Bey", which he later also used in Russia. Whereas Ṭalʿat and other civilian leaders centered their political activities on Berlin and Munich, Enwer and Djemāl proceeded at different times to Russia and then Central Asia, where they were joined by Enwer's uncle Khalīl (see below) and other former associates in a complex web of political manœuvres. In April 1919, Enwer secured the services of a pilot and airplane and with false Russian identity papers set out for Moscow. When mechanical trouble forced the plane to land in Lithuania, Enwer was detained for several weeks until his friends in Berlin established his identity and secured his release. After several months in Berlin, where he visited the Bolshevik leader Karl Radek in his jail in August 1919, Enwer on second try did make his way to Moscow where he arrived early in 1920. He took up contact with the Soviet Foreign Office, with Lenin, with a Turkish nationalist delegation under Bekir Sāmī which was then in Moscow, and, by correspondence, with Muṣṭafā Kemāl. With the encouragement of the Soviet authorities, he proclaimed the formation of a "Union of Islamic Revolutionary Societies" (Islām Ikhtilāl Djemʿiyyetleri Ittiḥādî) and of an affiliated People's Councils Party (Khalḳ Shūrālar Fîrḳasî), the former intended as a Muslim revolutionary international, the latter as its Turkish affiliate. On 1-9 September 1920 he attended the Soviet-sponsored Congress of the Peoples of the East at Baku with the title of Delegate of the Revolutionaries of Libya, Tunis, Algeria, and Morocco (chosen perhaps because of his war record in Cyrenaica in 1911-2); a Kemālist Turkish delegation under Ibrāhīm Ṭāliʿ [Öngören] also was present.

In October 1920, Enwer was back in Berlin where he lived in a villa in the fashionable Grunewald section. He was confident that the Soviets would support nationalist movements in Turkey and other border states. To this end he asked Khalīl to secure approval from the Soviet Foreign Office for a plan whereby two cavalry divisions, to be formed among Ottoman war prisoners and Muslim residents of the Caucasian region, would, under Enwer's command, join the Anatolian resistance movement. Enwer himself, meanwhile, was trying to purchase arms in Berlin. That he had hopes of taking over the supreme command in Anatolia is indicated by Khalīl's statement to Karakhan, Soviet Deputy Commissar for Foreign Affairs, that "Muṣṭafā Kemāl Pasha would not be in favour of creating divisiveness and is accustomed to obeying you [*i.e.*, Enwer]"—an interpretation rather strikingly at variance with Kemāl's record of near-insubordination to Enwer during the World War. (From Khalīl's letter to Enwer, 4 November 1920, quoted by Cebesoy, 165). Enwer's plans, however, were rejected by Karakhan.

After Ṭalʿat Pasha's assassination (15 March 1921), Enwer was the most prominent surviving Union and Progress leader in exile. At its 1921 annual meetings held in Berlin and Rome, the Union of Islamic Revolutionary Societies adopted a set of resolutions according to which the affiliated People's Councils Party was to be the legatee of the Union and Progress Society in Turkey; the Revolutionary Union itself was to work in close conjunction with the Third International and to secure further Soviet aid for the Nationalist struggle in Anatolia. (See Cebesoy, 224 f., who does not, however, give any exact date for the meetings). In Moscow, Enwer had several conversations with ʿAli Fuʾād [Cebesoy], the newly appointed Kemālist ambassador (their first meeting occurred on 26 February 1921) and with Čičerin, both of whom tried to dissuade him from interfering with the Anatolian movement; a protocol to this effect was drawn up by ʿAlī Fuʾād, Enwer, and Dr. Nāẓîm at one of these meetings. On 16 July 1921 Enwer sent a lengthy letter to Muṣṭafā Kemāl complaining of groundless suspicions and assuring Kemāl that he (Enwer) was content to support the Anatolian movement from outside. But the moves of Major Naʿīm Djewād, whom Enwer sent from Russia to Anatolia with quantities of propaganda material for the People's Councils Party and who was arrested by the Kemalists at the Black Sea town of Amasra, indicated that he was pursuing his former plans.

On 30 July, at a time when the Greek offensive toward Ankara was in full progress, Enwer proceeded from Moscow to Batumi where he gathered with other Unionists awaiting an opportunity to enter Anatolia. Close by, the Trabzon Defence of Rights Society was openly supporting Enwer, and in the Ankara Assembly a group of about forty ex-Unionists are said to have been working secretly to replace Kemāl with Enwer. On 5 September, a congress of the "Union and Progress (People's Councils) Party" was held at Batumi which issued an appeal to the Ankara Assembly to abandon its hostility toward the Union and Progress exiles. Meanwhile, however, Kemāl's victory at the Sakarya (2-13 September) consolidated his political position and by November his authority was restored in Trabzon.

Abandoning his Anatolian plans, Enwer left Batumi by way of Tbilisi, Baku, ʿAshḳābād, and Merv, and arrived in Bukhāra in October 1921 accompanied by Kushdjubashîzāde Ḥādjdjī Sāmī of the former Special Organization and others. He seems to have given the impression to Soviet authorities that he would rally Muslims of various parts of Central Asia in a struggle against the British; yet he soon was engaged in efforts to mobilize various Özbek factions into common resistance against Soviet rule and penetration of Türkistān. The major political groupings that he encountered in Özbekistān were (1) the Young Bukhara party under ʿOthmān Khodja, which in a revolution with Soviet support in September 1920 had deposed the Emīr of Bukhārā, ʿAbd al-Saʿīd Mīr ʿĀlim forcing him into exile in Kābul and (2) the tribesmen of the area who were generally loyal to the Emīr, formed armed bands known as Basmadjîs, (*i.e.*, Raiders), and fought both the Republicans and the Soviets. Enwer was welcomed in Bukhārā by ʿOthmān Khodja's representatives, and took up close contact with Aḥmed Zekī Welīdī [Togan], the exiled Bashkir leader, who was then trying to rally various Özbek factions against the Soviets. On 8 November Enwer left Bukhārā with thirty armed followers on the pretext of a hunting trip but actually so as to join the Basmadjîs. He proceeded to Shīrābād and thence eastward along the Afg͟hān frontier, being joined by local armed groups along the way. In the vicinity of Korgantepe, south-west of Düs͟henbe (later Stalinābād) he made contact with Ibrāhīm Lakay, known as the Basmad͟jī leader most staunchly loyal to the Emīr. Lakay, who disapproved of Young Turk revolutionaries as much as he did of Young Buk͟hārans, interned Enwer and his men for six weeks (1 December 1921 to 15 January 1922). Released through the intervention of another Basmad͟jī group under Is͟han Sulṭān, Enwer assembled more than 200 armed Tad͟jik tribesmen and invested the Russian garrison at Düs͟henbe, which evacuated the town on 14 February. On 19 February Enwer was wounded in his arm in an engagement fought in pursuit. Enwer's proclamations of this period were signed "Deputy of the Emīr of Buk͟hārā, Son-in-Law of the Caliph of the Muslims, *Seyyid* Enwer" (Togan, 449) and his initial success rallied other armed men to his headquarters, while some of his associates went to Afg͟hānistān in quest of further reinforcements. On 15 May he sent an ultimatum to the Russians which he signed as "Commander-in-Chief of the National Armies of Türkistān, K͟hīwa and Buk͟hārā" and in which he demanded prompt Russian evacuation of those areas (Togan, 451). But Enwer's forces lost a major engagement at Kāfirān on 28 June. As his troops melted away, he was obliged to join forces with the Basmad͟jī leader, Dewletmand Bek, at Beld͟juwān south-east of Düs͟henbe.

Enwer was killed on 4 August 1922 (Togan, 452 f.; Baysun, 109-11, gives the date as Friday, 5 August, but that day was a Saturday), by a machine-gun bullet while leading a cavalry counter-charge against a superior Russian force at the near-by village of Čeken. Dewletmand also was killed while coming to his rescue, and both were buried at Čeken by their men on the following day.

Enwer was short of stature and slender of waist, with wide-set fiery eyes and an up-pointed, well-groomed moustache. He had great personal courage, boundless energy, and a keen sense of drama—at times melodrama (cf. C. R. Buxton, *Turkey in Revolution*, London 1909, 16 ff.). Soldiers of an older generation such as Liman or ʿIzzet Pas͟ha [*q.v.*] were likely to see in him a brusque, restless upstart. But among his friends and close associates he instilled profound and lasting loyalty, and the masses idolized him. His financial integrity and sincere patriotism are attested even by his rivals and enemies. Despite the Sarīḳamīs͟h disaster, his popularity remained unimpaired throughout the World War. In judging his total performance as supreme commander, it should be recalled that only in 1912 the Ottoman Empire had been roundly beaten by four small Balkan states. The transformation of its armies into a fighting instrument that through four fateful years withstood the combined onslaught of Russia, Britain, and their Allies must be regarded above all as the achievement of Enwer and of the German officers with whom he so closely and consistently co-operated.

Enwer's flight in November 1918 was a turning point that did severe and lasting damage to his reputation. His subsequent efforts to redeem himself by resuming a military role in Anatolia—or failing that, in Central Asia—remain the most obscure and controversial part of his career. A full and balanced account of this period must await more complete publication of his correspondance of those years with K͟halīl, D͟jemāl, Ṭalʿat, Muṣṭafā Kemāl, and others.

Several of Enwer's close relatives also attained prominence in Ottoman-Turkish military and political affairs. His father, Aḥmed Bey (1864-1947), rose in the civil service to the position of *sürre emīni* (*i.e.*, official in charge of delivering the Sultān's annual gift to Mecca) with the (civilian) rank of pas͟ha.

K͟halīl Pas͟ha (Halil Kut) (1881-1957), the son by another marriage of Enwer's paternal grandmother, was a career officer who graduated from the military academy as "distinguished captain" (mümtāz yüzbas͟hī) in 1904. He fought in the Libyan, Balkan and World Wars becoming a Lieutenant-Colonel of the general staff in 1913. In April 1916, with the rank of Brigadier General (mīrliwā) and later Lieutenant General he assumed command of the Sixth Army in ʿIrāq, and in one of the more spectacular Ottoman victories, at Ctesiphon (or Ḳūt al-ʿAmāra), captured General Townshend with an entire British army of 13,000 men. But he had to retreat before a renewed British offensive, abandoning Bag͟hdād in March 1917. In June 1918 he became commander of the Eastern Army Group which undertook the Turkish advance into the Caucasus area and occupied Baku in September.

Following the armistice, he was interned at Batumi but escaped early in 1919 (see *Taṣwīr-i Efkār*, Istanbul, 4 February 1919). After only a few weeks in Istanbul he was again arrested and jailed in the Bekirag͟ha prison on charges of matreatment of Armenians and others during the war. Once again he escaped (8 August 1919) making his way to Anatolia. Tentative plans to have him take a part in military operation in Anatolia (*e.g.*, command of the Izmir front) were abandoned because of the political strain they would have placed on relations between Anatolia and Istanbul. He saw Muṣṭafā Kemāl in Sivas in mid-September 1919 and accepted from him the assignment to try to secure military and financial aid for Anatolia from the Bolsheviki. He made his way to Russia by slow stages, arriving in Baku in December and in Moscow before 24 May 1920. On 1 June he delivered a letter from Kemāl to Čičerin, Soviet Commissar for Foreign Affairs. In negotiations with Čičerin and Karakhan he obtained arms, ammunition, and the equivalent of 100,000 Turkish pounds in gold bullion. (The latter he later delivered in person to Colonel D͟jāwīd [Erdelhun], division commander in Karaköse). In the winter of 1920-1 he was back in Moscow, where he participated intensively in the political negotiations between Enwer and the Bolsheviks. In February 1921 he was in Trabzon to try to build up the Peoples' Councils Party, Enwer's political organization in Anatolia. In 1922 he was expelled from Trabzon by the Kemalists and went to Berlin. After the nationalist victory he returned to Istanbul. His expulsion from the army, decreed by the Istanbul authorities on 18 February 1920, was set aside; instead he was retired in 1923 and took no further part in political and military affairs. Under the law of 1934 he took the family name of Kut after his victory at Ctesiphon.

Enwer's surviving brothers and sisters after 1934 took the family name Killigil. Nuri Killigil (1890-1949), the second son of Aḥmed Pas͟ha and ʿĀʾis͟he, also was a career officer. In 1914, with the rank of major, he was assigned to the Special Organization. From 1915 to 1918, with the honorary rank of major general, he served in Libya "where he was organizing a rather successful resistance to Italian penetration of the hinterland" (Allen and Muratoff, 468, who state erroneously, however, that he was Enwer's half-brother). Toward the end of the World War he was in charge of guerrilla operations of the "Army of Islam" in the Caucasus. He hesitated to heed the Istanbul authorities' call for his return and instead stopped in Erzurūm early in 1919. By January 1920 he was organizing guerrilla forces in Daghestān. Like Khalīl, he returned eventually to private life in Istanbul. He was killed in an explosion of his munitions factory in Sütlüdje on 2 March 1949.

Enwer's younger sister Mediha Killigil (b. 1899) was married (1919-1963) to Colonel (later General) Kâzim [Orbay], Enwer's aide-de-camp in 1914-18, who in 1961 was the presiding officer of the Turkish Constituent Assembly and subsequently became an appointed senator under the Second Republic. His younger brother Kâmil Killigil (-1962) married Enwer's widow, Nādjiye Sultan, (1898-1957) on 30 October 1923. Enwer was survived by two daughters, of whom the younger, Türkân, was married to Hüveyda Mayatepek, a Turkish career diplomat and currently (May 1963) Ambassador to Copenhagen; and one son, Ali Enver.

Bibliography: Ziya Şakir [Soku], *Yakın tarihin üç büyük adamı*: *Talât, Enver, Cemal*², Istanbul 1944, is a popular and not always accurate account. Kurt Okay, *Enver Pascha, der grosse Freund Deutschlands*, Berlin 1935, combines fact and fiction. The memoirs of Enwer's widow appeared in the Istanbul newspaper *Vatan*, 15 December 1952-21 January 1953.

On his political-military career to 1914: A. D. Alderson, *Structure of the Ottoman Dynasty*, Oxford 1956, table xlvii; Tevfik Bıyıklıoğlu, *Trakya'da Millî Mücadele*, Ankara 1955-6, esp. i, 88 ff.; [Resneli Aḥmed Niyāzī], *Khaṭirāt-i Niyāzī*, Istanbul 1326 A.H.; E. E. Ramsaur, *The Young Turks*, Princeton 1957; Ali Fuad Türkgeldi, *Görüp Işittiklerim*², Ankara 1951.

On the German alliance and entry into World War One: İbnülemin Mahmud Kemal İnal, *Osmanlı devrinde son sadrıazamlar*, Istanbul 1940-53, esp. 1896 ff.; *Harp kabinelerinin isticvabı*, Istanbul 1933 (testimony by war cabinet members before parliamentary inquiry of 1919); Carl Mühlmann, *Deutschland und die Türkei, 1913-1914*, Berlin 1929.

On his military leadership in 1914-8: W. E. D. Allen and Paul Muratoff, *Caucasian Battlefields*, Cambridge 1953; [Ahmed Cemal], *Memories of a Turkish Statesman*, by Djemal Pasha, London 1922; M. Larcher, *La guerre turque dans la guerre mondiale*, Paris 1926; Carl Mühlmann, *Das deutsch-türkische Waffenbündnis im Weltkrieg*, Leipzig 1940; Joseph Pomiankowski, *Der Zusammenbruch des ottomanischen Reiches*, Leipzig 1928.

On the activities in exile of Enwer, Khalīl, and Nūrī: Samet Ağaoğlu, *Babamın arkadaşları*, Istanbul 1959, 30-34 (sketch of Nūrī); Abdullah Receb Baysun, *Türkistan Millî hareketleri*, Istanbul 1945; Tevfik Bıyıklıoğlu, *Atatürk Anadoluda*, Ankara 1959, 35, 68 ff.; Wipert von Blücher, *Deutschlands Weg nach Rapallo*, Wiesbaden 1951, 132-5; Olaf Caroe, *Soviet Empire*, London 1953, 114-30; Joseph Castagné, *Les Basmatchis (1917-1924)*, Paris 1928; Ali Fuat Cebesoy, *Moskova hatiralari*, Istanbul 1955, esp. 128-37, 157-88, 220-39, 313-27; Baymirza Hayit, *Turkestan im XX. Jahrhundert*, Darmstadt 1956; Gotthard Jäschke in *WI*, x (1929), 146, n.s. v (1957), 44-52, vi (1961), 185-222, viii (1962), 35-43; Sami Sabit Karaman, *Trabzon ve Kars hatıraları*: *Millî mücadele ve Enver Paşa*, Izmit 1949; Friedrich von Rabenau, *Seeckt*: *Aus seinem Leben 1918-1936*, Leipzig 1940, 95, 356 f.; D. A. Rustow in *World Politics*, xi (1959), 513-52; Otto-Ernst Schüddekopf, *Karl Radek in Berlin*, in *Archiv für Sozialgeschichte*, ii (1962), 87-166 (including German translation of Radek's Berlin memoirs entitled *November*, first published in *Krasnaya nov'*, October 1926), esp. 97 (where there is some confusion between Enwer's first and second attempts to get from Berlin to Moscow) and 152 f.; Ahmed Zeki Velîdî Togan, *Bugünkü Türkili* (*Türkistan*) *ve yakın mazisi*, Istanbul 1947, 434-53. A copy of Enwer's letter to Mustafa Kemal of 16 July 1920 is in the Türk Inkilâp Tarihi Enstitüsü, Ankara.

I have supplemented the above sources with information obtained in personal interviews kindly granted by General Kâzım Orbay (Ankara, 30 and 31 January 1963) and Bay Ali Enver (Istanbul, 4 February 1963); additional data have been generously supplied by Bay Faik Reşit Unat, Ankara.

(D. A. Rustow)

ENWERÎ, Ḥādjdjī Saʿd Allāh Efendi (1733?-1794), minor Ottoman historian. He was born at Trebizond (Trabzon), going to Istanbul as a young man. After completing his studies he found employment with the Sublime Porte.

Enwerī was appointed official historian in 1182/1769 and retained that function, except for four short intervals, under three Sultans, Muṣṭafā III, ʿAbd al-Ḥamīd I and Selīm III. He also undertook additional duties.

From 1184/1771 onwards he was *Teshrīfātdjī*, *Djebedjiler Kātibi*, *Mewḳūfātdjī*, *Büyük Tedhkiredji* and, four times, *Anadolu Muḥāsebedjisi*. Four times he either replaced or was replaced by Wāṣif as official historian.

His history, known as *Taʾrīkh-i Enwerī*, has never been published. It consists of three volumes, of which the first deals with the military and political events concerning the war against Russia which started in 1182/1769. In his introduction the author explains that "he has avoided an elaborate style, endeavouring not to omit any important events and trying to relate them in a clear and precise language" (MS Istanbul University Library, no. T.Y. 2437, fol. 2ᵃ). Wāṣif altered this volume in some important particulars and then called it the first of his history. Djewdet Pasha made considerable use of Enwerī's second volume, which deals with the period 1167-97/1754-83.

Enwerī also wrote poetry, although his work in this field does not deserve much attention. He could write Arabic and Persian, made the pilgrimage to Mecca and was known as a man of excellent character (v. Djemāl al-Dīn, *Āʾīna-i Ẓurafā*, Istanbul 1314, 57—the author's manuscript is at the Istanbul University Library, no. T.Y. 372, Faṭīn, *Tedhkira*, 20).

Bibliography: For the main MSS. of Enwerī, apart from those in the libraries of Istanbul University, Inḳilāb and Topkapîsarayî, see *Istanbul Kütüphaneleri Tarih-Coğrafya Yazmaları Katalogları*, Istanbul 1944, ii, 143-46; Babinger, 320; Meḥmed Thüreyyā, *Sidjill-i ʿOthmānī*, Istanbul, 1308, i, 440; Meḥmed Ṭāhir, *ʿOthmānlî Müʾellifleri*, Istanbul 1342, iii, 22; Sadeddin Nüzhet Ergun, *Türk Şairleri*, iii, 1303; Nail Tuman, *Katalog*, author's MS in Ist. Univ. Lib., 271.

(Abdülkadir Karahan)

ENZELÎ [see bandar ʿabbās].

EPHESUS [see aya solūḳ].

EPIC [see ḤAMĀSA].

EPIGONI [see AL-SALAF WA 'L-KHALAF].

EPIGRAM [see HIDJĀʾ].

EPIGRAPHY [see KITĀBĀT, also KHAṬṬ, NAḲSH].

EQUATOR [see AL-ISTIWĀʾ, KHAṬṬ].

EQUITY [see INṢĀF].

ERBĪL [see IRBĪL].

ERDEL, ERDĪL or ERDELISTĀN, from the Hungarian Erdély (*erdö elve* = beyond the forest); Ardeal in Rumanian; Siebenbürgen in German; the Latin name Terra Ultrasilvas and later Transsilvania being a translation of the Hungarian—the province of Transylvania which now constitutes the western portion of Rumania. In Ottoman sources the name of Erdel occurs first in the *Rūznāme-i Süleymānī* in the course of a description of the reception into the Ottoman army of King Yanosh of the *wilāyet* of Engurūs (*i.e.*, of the Hungarians), who is described as having been formerly the Bey of Erdel (cf. Ferīdūn Bey, *Munshaʾāt*, 2nd ed., Istanbul 1275, ii, 275). The variant Erdelistān occurs also in later sources (Naʿīmā, i, loc. var.; Ewliyā Čelebi, *Seyāḥat-nāme*, i, 181; Muṣṭafā Nūrī Pasha, *Natāʾidj al-wuḳūʿāt*, ii, 72). Geographically speaking, Erdel borders on Boghdān (Moldavia) in the east, Eflāḳ (Wallachia) in the south, the Banat (from which it is separated by the Iron Gates—Demir [Temir, etc.]-Ḳapī) in the south-west, and the province of Marmarosh (Maramureș) in the north. Thus delimited, Erdel is a basin surrounded by the Carpathians and the Transylvanian Alps on three sides, and separated from the Hungarian plain by the Érchegység (Rom. Muntii Apuseni) mountains. Ottoman Erdel often exceeded, however, these geographical limits at the expense of neighbouring countries. Erdel can be subdivided into three main areas: the Erdel plain, higher and more broken than the Hungarian plain and crossed by the river Muresh and its tributaries; the country of the Sekels in the east, and, finally, the area of the southern Carpathians.

The first contact of the Ottomans with Erdel occurred in the middle of the 8th/14th century. In 769/1367, Dénes (Dennis), who had become *voyvoda* (prince) of Erdel after being *ban* (lord) of Vidin, fought the Bulgarians supported by Murād I. The first Ottoman campaign against Hungary and, therefore, Erdel is put by ʿĀshīḳpasha-zāde (ed. Giese, 60) in 793/1391. The large raid which occurred in 823/1420 under Meḥemmed I must have been the work of the frontier guards from Vidin. The following year the frontier *bey* of the Danube, encouraged by the *voyvoda* of Eflāḳ, captured and burnt down the city of Brashov. There were other raids in 829/1426 and 836/1432, the latter being led by Evrenos-zāde ʿAlī Bey, acting in conjunction with the *Bey* of Eflāḳ. Turkish historians speak of another raid by ʿAlī Bey (sent by Murād II) in 841/1437 (ʿĀshīḳpasha-zāde, *op. cit.*, 110; Neshrī, *Tewārīkh-i āl-i ʿOthmān*, Welī al-Dīn Efendī MS, no. 2351, f. 177). The following year, the Sultan himself entered the territory of Erdel for the first time, accompanied by Vlad Dracul, the *Bey* of Eflāḳ, and advanced as far as Sibin (Saʿd al-Dīn, i, 321). An interesting account of Ottoman customs and organization has been left by one of the Saxon prisoners taken during this campaign (*Cronica Abconterfayung der Türkei* . . ., Augsburg 1531). Resistance against the Ottomans stiffened with the appearance on the scene of Yanku Hunyades (in Hung. Hunyadi János), "the White Knight of Wallachia", who after engaging the Ottomans at Semendere in 841/1437 and near Belgrade in 845/1441, defeated and killed the Ottoman commander Mezīd Bey in 846/1442. The same year Hunyadi, supported this time by Vlad Dracul, defeated in Wallachia Khādim Shihāb al-Dīn Pasha, the *Beylerbeyi* of Rūm-īli (Rumeli) and thus seized the initiative in the Balkans, preserving it until the fateful battle of Varna. Ottoman raids were resumed under Meḥemmed II: there was a raid in 879/1474 against Hunyadi's son, Matthias; a force of 30,000 troops entered Erdel in 884/1479, but was defeated; and there was yet another raid in 898/1493. During the temporary cessation of Ottoman raids which then followed, the Hungarian and Wallachian peasants of Erdel revolted (in 920/1514), but were suppressed by the feudal lords, an important part being played by the *voyvoda* of Erdel, John Zápolyai ("Sapolyayi Yanosh" in Pečewī, i, 108), who, after the battle of Mohácz, proclaimed himself King of Hungary at Istolni Belgrad [*q.v.*] (Hung. Székesfehérvár, Ger. Stuhlweissenburg) in 1526. Challenged, however, by the Archduke Ferdinand of Austria, Zápolyai fled to Poland, sending an ambassador to Istanbul to obtain the Sultan's support. This was granted in change for a recognition of Ottoman suzerainty, Zápolyai swearing allegiance to the Sultan in person during the Vienna campaign (Ferīdūn Bey, ii, 570; ʿĀlī, *Kunh al-akhbār*, Ist. Univ. Lib., no. 5959/32, f. 293). In 936/1530, Meḥmed Pasha, the *sandjaḳ-beyi* of Silistre (Silistria), supported by Vlad, *voyvoda* of Eflāḳ, captured Brashov and handed it over to Zápolyai, who appointed Stephen Báthory *voyvoda* of Erdel.

Ottoman supremacy in Erdel (948/1541-1110/1699): a few days before his death in 1540, Zápolyai secured the Sultan's agreement to the succession of his son John Sigismund (Pečewī, "Simon Yanosh" and "Yanosh Jigmon", i, 228 and 434 *passim*; but in other Ottoman sources he is generally called Istefan), this time against payment of a tribute (*kharādj*). During the Budin campaign, the boy was shown to Süleymān the Magnificent who granted him a *sandjaḳ* in the *wilāyet* of Erdel, with the promise of a kingdom later (cf. ʿĀlī, *Kunh al-akhbār*, f. 277). Ottoman supremacy was confirmed in the treaty of 948/1541, which provides for Ottoman protection against payment of a tribute, which was first fixed at 10,000 ducats, was raised to 15,000 between 983/1575 and 1010/1601, was then remitted for ten years and later still fixed again at 10,000. In the second half of the 11th/17th century it was again raised first to 15,000 and then to 40,000 gold coins (*altīn, altun*). It was also customary to give an annual present (*pīshkesh*) of 10,000 to 60,000 coins. The prince of Erdel was nominated by the local Diet, the Sultan confirming the choice by sending him a caparisoned horse, a standard, a sword and a robe of honour (for the order of precedence as between the prince of Erdel and the *voyvodas* of Eflāḳ and Boghdān, see *Natāʾidj al-wuḳūʿāt*, i, 137). There were also cases of the Porte rejecting a nomination or dismissing a prince, as in 1022/1613 with Gábor Báthory and in 1067/1657 with George Rákóczi II. The princes' foreign policy had to conform to the Porte's wishes, but they were free in their internal affairs. They were represented at the Porte first by special envoys, the first permanent agent (*ḳapu kakhyasī* = *kedkhudāsī* (in Erdel documents *kapitiha*), being appointed in 967/1560. This agent represented both the *Bey* of Erdel and the three local *millets* (Hungarians, Germans and Sekels, the Wallachians being denied legal existence). His residence was in the Balat quarter of Istanbul, in a street known today as Macarlar Yokuşu ("Hungatians' Rise") near the residences of the agents of Boghdān and Eflāķ.

During John Sigismund's minority, the Diet appointed as regent the Croatian Catholic friar George Martinuzzi-Utyeszenicz (Uteśenić) (in ʿĀlī, f. 287 "brata", *i.e.*, "brother"), who, however, handed over Erdel to the Habsburgs in 1551. The *beylerbeyi* of Rūm-ili Meḥmed Pasha Sokollu thereupon led an army into Erdel (ʿĀlī, f. 287). Martinuzzi made his peace with the Ottomans, but was then attacked by the Austrian General Castaldo and killed in 1552. A second army was sent to the Banat under Ķara Aḥmed Pasha who captured Temesvár (Timișoara). Castaldo withdrew from Erdel in 1553, the country being for a time ruled by *voyvoda*s on behalf of the Habsburgs, until in 1556 the Diet invited back the Queen Mother Isabella and John Sigismund, who, coming from Poland, established their seat of government in the Belgrade of Erdel (Erdel Belgradî, Rum. Alba Julia, Hung. Gyulafehérvár, Ger. Karlsburg). John Sigismund ruled alone from 1559 to 1571 both over Erdel and over the northern districts of Hungary in constant competition with the Habsburgs. Although by the agreement of Satmar in 1564 he recognized Emperor Ferdinand as King of Hungary, peace was not long preserved, John appealing to the Sultan for help (cf. Pečewī, i, 412), and the latter responding by undertaking the Szigetvár expedition in 1566. John's reign witnessed also the revolt of the Sekels and the suppression of their traditional privileges in 1562 and the proclamation of religious toleration in Erdel by the Diet's decisions of 1564 and 1571. His successor Stephen Báthory (1571-6) managed to preserve a precarious balance between the Habsburgs and the Ottomans, by recognizing the Emperor Maximilian as King of Hungary and thus becoming his vassal by the treaty of Speyer in 1571, while continuing payment of tribute to the Porte. In 1576 he was elected King of Poland by the efforts of the Porte and of the Grand Vizier Sokollu Meḥmed Pasha (see Aḥmed Refīķ, *Sokollu Meḥmed Pasha ve Lehistān intikhābātî*, in *TOEM*, 6th year, 664 ff.), Erdel being governed until 1581 by his brother Christopher Báthory and then until 1602 (although with intervals) by his son Sigismund Báthory. The latter wavered in his loyalty to the Porte, entering the Holy League in 1593 and executing the leaders of the pro-Turkish party in 1594 at a time when he pretended to be getting ready to join the Ottoman army under Ķodja Sinān Pasha. He incited the *voyvoda*s of Boghdān and Eflāķ against the Ottomans and defeated in 1003/1595 the Ottoman army sent to suppress their rebellion. After the severe defeat suffered by the Imperialist forces at the battle of Mezö-Keresztes in the following year, he withdrew from Erdel, relinquishing the rule to his cousin Cardinal Andreas Báthory, who had been brought up at the Polish court and was, therefore, pro-Ottoman. The latter was, however, defeated by the rebellious *voyvoda* of Eflāķ, Mikhal (Michael), who was in turn killed by the Austrians. The latter then occupied the country, foiling an attempt by Sigismund Báthory to re-establish his rule. In 1603 a Sekel nobleman, Székely Mózes, made an unsuccessful attempt to oust the Austrians with Ottoman support. An Erdel nobleman, Stephen Bocskay, who had fled to the Ottomans (see Naʿīmā, i, 386) was more successful, and by the treaty of Vienna in 1606, the Emperor Rudolf recognized him as prince of Erdel. His death was followed by a period of instability which included the tyrannical rule of Gábor Báthory (1608-13), known in Ottoman sources as "the mad king". The *beylerbeyi* of Kanije, Iskender Pasha, succeeded in deposing him and in getting the diet at Kolojvár to elect in his place Gábor Bethlen, whose rule marks the golden age of the principality of Erdel. His death in 1629 was followed by a short interregnum, his policy of safeguarding local autonomy through co-operation with the Ottomans being re-established by George Rákoczi I (1630-48). In 1046/1636 the Ottomans made an unsuccessful attempt to unseat him in favour of Gábor Bethlen's brother, Stephen Bethlen. George Rákoczi I was succeeded by his son George II (1648-57, 1658, 1659-60), whose unsuccessful attempt to gain the crown of Poland against the wishes of the Porte led eventually to his death, Erdel being occupied by Ottoman troops. One of the prisoners taken by the Ottomans in Kolojvar was the young Hungarian who later embraced Islam and became known as Ibrāhīm Müteferriķa [*q.v.*]. Ottoman supremacy in Erdel was re-established in the Köprülü period, the principality being governed from 1072-3/1662 to 1101/1690 by the Ottoman nominee Michael Apafiy. The fate of Erdel autonomy was, however, sealed when Austria gained the upper hand in her wars with the Ottomans, Michael Apafiy himself allowing Habsburg troops to enter his country. In 1102/1691 the famous *Diploma Leopoldinum* fixed the status of Erdel as a Habsburg crown land, the local Diet being, however, kept in existence. Austrian sovereignty was legally recognized by the treaty of Karlowitz (Karlofča) in 1110/1699. Francis Rákoczi II tried in 1703 to put the clock back: after a local revolution he was chosen prince in 1704, but was defeated in 1710 and fled to France the following year. An attempt was made by the Ottomans to make use of him in their war with Austria in 1127/1715, but, after the treaty of Passarowitz he and his Hungarian companions had to withdraw and were settled at Tekirdagh (Rodosto in Thrace) (cf. Rāshid, iv, v, *passim*; Aḥmed Refīķ, *Memālik-i ʿOthmāniyyede Rakoczi ve tewābiʿi*, Istanbul 1338; M. Tayyib Gökbilgin, *Rakoczi Ferenc II ve tevâbiine dair yeni vesikalar*, in *Belleten*, v/20, 1941). A similarly unsuccessful attempt was made by the Ottomans to make use of the latter's son Jozsef, all Ottoman designs on Erdel being finally abandoned with the peace of Belgrade in 1152/1739.

The main events in the post-Ottoman history of Erdel are the submission of a large number of local Rumanian Orthodox to the Pope (the Union of 1700), the Rumanian peasant rising of 1784, the decision of the Diet in 1848 to merge with Hungary and finally the accession of Erdel to Rumania under the treaty of Trianon in 1920.

Bibliography: A. Centorio degli Hortensi, *Commentarii della guerra di Transilvania*, Venice 1566; C. Spontone, *Historia della Transilvania*, Venice 1638; *Regni Hungarici Historia ... a Nicolao Isthuanffio*, Coloniae Agrippinae 1724; G. Kraus, *Siebenbürgische Chronik* (Österr. Akad. d. Wiss., Fontes Rerum Austriacorum, Abh. I, Bde iii-iv), Vienna 1862-4; ed. S. Szilágyi, *Monumenta comitalia regni Transylvaniae. Erdélyi országgülési emlékek*, i-xxi, Budapest 1876-98 (MCRT); idem, *Transylvania et bellum boreo-orientale*, Budapest 1890-1; Hurmuzaki, *Documente privitoare la istoria Românilor*, i-xxxii, Bucharest, from 1887 with supplements; A. Szilády and Al. Szilágyi, *Törökmagyarkori államokmánytár*, Budapest 1868-72, i-vii; *Monumenta Hungariae historica*, Sect. ii, "Scriptores"; ed. A. Veress, *Basta György hadvezér Sevelezése és Iratai (1597-1607)* [Monumenta Hungariae historica. Diplomataria, vols. xxxiv and xxxvii], Budapest 1909-14; ed. idem, *Fontes rerum Transylvanicarum*, i-iii, Budapest 1913; idem, *Documente privitoare la istoria Ardealului, Moldovei şi Tării Romănesti*, Bucharest 1929-38, i-xii; R. Goos, *Österreichische Staatsverträge. Fürstentum Siebenbürgen (1526-1690)*, Vienna 1911; G. E. Müller, *Die Türkenherrschaft in Siebenbürgen* [Südosteuropäisches Forschungs-Institut, Sekt. Hermannstadt, Deutsche Abteilung ii], Hermannstadt 1923; G. Bascapè, *Le relazioni fra l'Italia e la Transilvania nel secolo XVI*, Rome 1931. Other sources have been cited in the course of the article. For further studies see bibliography in *İA*, s.v.

(A. Decei and M. Tayyib Gökbilgin)

EPDJĪSH [see ARDJĪSH].

ERDJIYAS (or Erdjiyes) **DAGHĪ** (modern spelling Erciyas), the Argaeus Mons of antiquity, referred to by Ḥamd Allāh Mustawfī (*Nuzha*, 98, 181) as Ardjāst-kūh, the highest mountain in Central Anatolia. It is an extinct volcano, with a height of 3,916 m. (= 12,847 ft.), which rises rather suddenly from the surrounding plain of an average height of 1000 m. (= 3,280 ft.). It is some 20 km. (12¹/₂ m.) to the south of the town of Kayseri, almost precisely 38° 30′ N., 35° 30′ E., and covers an area of roughly 45 km. (28 m.) from east to west and 35 km. (21¹/₂ m.) from north to south. Certain early sources say it was still active in antiquity. Today, the Erciyas-Dağ is completely bare and permanently covered with snow. In it there rises the Deli-Su, which flows into the Kara-Su, a tributary of the Kızıl-Irmak.

A route, in use since antiquity, leads from Kayseri to Everek and Develi in the south, over the pastures of Tekir Yaylası (at a height of 2000 m. (6,561 ft.)) between the eastern slope of the Erciyas Dağ and its eastern neighbour Koç-Dağı (2500 m. (= 8,202 ft.)). The main route to the south, however (also since antiquity), skirts round Erciyas towards the west, leading via Incesu to Niğde and Bor, the ancient Tyana.

Erciyas Dağ was first climbed by W. J. Hamilton (1837), and then again by Tchihatcheff (1848), Tozer (1879), and Cooper (1879). After these, the most important ascent was that of Penther and his group in 1902. There were several ascents after 1905 (those up to 1928 are listed by E. J. Ritter, *Erdjias Dag*, Innsbruck 1931, 135 ff.). The area has recently been used for ski-ing.

Bibliography: Pauly-Wissowa, ii, 684 (Hirschfeld); Le Strange, 146; Ewliyā Čelebi, *Seyāḥatnāme*, iii, Istanbul 1314, 176 ff.; Kātib Čelebi, *Djihānnümā*, 620; H. v. Moltke, *Briefe über Zustände und Begebenheiten in der Türkei*, Berlin 1911, especially 330; more recent bibliography of works concerning Erciyas Dağ (since Hamilton), compiled by Besim Darkot in his article *Erciyas-Dağı* in *IA*, iv, 286-8, to which must be added a most important contribution, Gerhart Bartsch, *Das Gebiet des Erciyes Daği und die Stadt Kayseri in Mittel-Anatolien*, in *Jahrbuch der Geographischen Gesellschaft zu Hannover für 1934 und 1935*, Hanover 1935, 87-202. (Fr. Taeschner)

EREĞLI, Turkish adaptation of the place-name Heraclea, given to a number of places in Turkey, of which the most important are:

1) Karadeniz Ereğlisi (Ereğli on the Black Sea), Heraclea Pontica, hence formerly (as in *Djihānnümā*, 653) known as Bendereğli: a small town on the coast of the Black Sea, 41° 17′ N., 31° 25′ E., in the region of the coalfields formerly named after it, but now called after Zonguldak.

The *kaza*, now in the *vilâyet* of Zonguldak, was once in the *sandjaḳ* (or *liwā'*) of Bolu. This used to belong to the *eyālet* of Anadolu, and in the 19th century to the *wilāyet* of Kastamonu. The place has 8,815 inhabitants (1960) and the district 67,661.

Bibliography: Pauly-Wissowa, 8, 433; V. Cuinet, *La Turquie d'Asie*, iv, 512.

2) Konya (formerly Ḳaramān) Ereğlisi, τὸ Ἡρακλέως Κάστρον in Theophanes, i, 482 (ed. de Boor), ἡ τοῦ Ἡρακλέος Κωμόπολις of Michael Attaliata, 136 (ed. Bonn), the Hiraḳla of the Arabs, Erāklīya of Ibn Bībī (transl. Duda, 19, 238 f.), in Turkish occasionally in the more archaic form Hirāḳla or Hiraḳlīya, Reclei or Reachia to the Crusaders (Tomaschek, *Zur historischen Topographie von Kleinasien*, 84, 88, 92), Araclie in Bertrandon de la Broquière (ed. Ch. Schefer, 104 f.): a town in south-western Anatolia, near the central chain of the Taurus, from which rivers flow in a northerly direction into the Ereğli plain. These rivers make the town an oasis of vegetation, but disappear further on into marshy ground. The position of the town is 37° 30′ N., 34° 5′ E. It is the capital of a *kaza* in the *vilâyet* of Konya and has 32,057 inhabitants; the district has 46,324 (1960).

South of Ereğli, where the river emerges from a ravine in the Taurus, near Ivriz, there is a famous late Hittite rock carving, depicting the river-god dispensing corn and grapes, and being worshipped by the king of Tyana (Assyr. Urballa, Hitt. Varpallawa, ca. 730 B. C.), the modern Bor.

In Byzantine times, Ereğli was a frontier fortification on the way from Iconium to Cilicia. It was conquered several times by the Arabs, most notably by Hārūn al-Rashīd in Dhu 'l-Ḳaʿda 190/Sept.-Oct. 806 (Ṭabarī, iii, 709 ff. = Theophanes, *loc. cit.*), but remained Byzantine until the Saldjūḳ Turks conquered it (supposedly in 484/1091, see Ewliyā Čelebi, iii, 28). After the collapse of the Rūm-Saldjūḳ empire, the town came under the rule of the Ḳaramānids, and finally, together with the other Ḳaramān regions, it came under Ottoman rule in 871/1466.

The Ulu Djāmiʿ is a rather remarkable mosque with a flat roof. The *Djihānnümā* claims that it was founded by the Ḳaramān-oghlu Ibrāhīm (but the *Menāsik al-ḥadjdj* attributes its foundation to the Saldjūḳ Ḳilīdj-Arslan). The Türbe Djāmiʿi (a small mosque with an estrade built onto it, containing the grave of Shihāb al-Dīn Suhrawardī Maḳtūl which is also mentioned in the *Djihānnümā*) is also worthy of note. There is also a large *khān* in the town, supposed to have been built by Sinān for Rüstem Pasha in the 15th century.

Ereğli was a halt on the pilgrim route, and since 1908 it has become an important station on the Baghdād Railway from Konya.

Bibliography: Kātib Čelebi, *Djihānnümā*, 616 f.; Ewliyā Čelebi, *Seyāḥatnāme*, iii, 28 f.; Meḥmed Edīb, *Menāsik al-ḥadjdj*, 37 f.; Ritter, *Kleinasien*, ii, 268; Cuinet, *La Turquie d'Asie*, i, 818; *IA*, iv, 307-9 (Besim Darkot). Concerning Ivriz, cf. H. Th. Bossert, *Altanatolien*, Berlin 1942, plate 796; Gelb, *Hittite Hiergl. Monum.*, 1939, 15; Maurice Vieyra, *Hittite Art*, London 1955, plate 70, 76. (J. H. Mordtmann-[Fr. Taeschner])

ERETNA (Ärätnä, Ärdäni ?), name of a chief of Uyghur origin, who made his fortune in Asia Minor as an heir of the Ilkhānid régime. The name is perhaps to be explained by Sanskrit *ratna* 'jewel', common among the Oyghur after the spread of Buddhism (communication from L. Bazin); this was of course no bar to the family becoming Muslim, like all the Mongols and Turks in the Ilkhānid state. Eretna, who was probably an officer in the service of Čūbān/Čoban [see ČŪBĀNIDS], settled in Asia Minor as a follower of the latter's son, Tīmūrtāsh, was appointed governor by the Ilkhān Abū Saʿīd, and went into hiding during his master's revolt; after Tīmūrtāsh had been compelled to flee to Egypt, where he was to meet his death (727/1326), Eretna was invested with the succession to the rebel, under the general suzerainty of Ḥasan the Elder, the master of Ādharbāydjān. When, after the disorders which followed the death of Abū Saʿīd, this Ḥasan was defeated by Ḥasan the Younger, son of Tīmūrtāsh, Eretna sought and obtained the protection of the Mamlūk sultan al-Nāṣir Muḥammad (738/1337), and in 744/1343 defeated Ḥasan the Younger who had become master of Ādharbāydjān, which certainly helped his prestige. After this he appears as an independent sovereign over all those territories of central Asia Minor which the Turkoman principalities that arose after the breakdown of the Saldjūḳid-Mongol régime had not divided among themselves; that is, in a more or less stable form, the provinces of Nigde, Aḳsarāy, Ankara, Develi Ḳaraḥiṣār, Derende, Amāsya, Toḳāt, Merzifūn, Samsūn, Erzindjān, Sharḳī Ḳaraḥiṣār, with first Sīwās and later Ḳayseri as capital. He called himself sultan, with the *laḳab* ʿAlāʾ al-Dīn, and struck coins in his own name. He knew Arabic, scholars call him a scholar, and his people, appreciative of an administration which maintained some order in a troubled world, called him, it is said, *Köse Peyghamber*, "the Prophet with the Scanty Beard". He died in 753/1352, leaving his principality to his son Ghiyāth al-Dīn Muḥammad (Meḥmed) who, maintaining the Mamlūk alliance, successfully withstood the revolt of his brother Djaʿfar.

The *begs*, however, were here as everywhere undisciplined, and in 766/1365 Meḥmed fell victim to an attack fomented by them; under his son ʿAlāʾ al-Dīn ʿAlī Beg, who is said to have cared only for pleasure, the *begs* of Amāsya, Toḳāt, Sharḳī Ḳaraḥiṣār, even Sīwās, and especially Tahartan the *beg* of Erzindjān, acted like autonomous or rebel lords, while the Ḳaramānids and the Ottomans stripped the Eretnid principality of its western possessions, and the Aḳ-ḳoyunlu of some of its eastern dependencies. In effect, government was now exercised by the *ḳāḍī* Burhān al-Dīn [*q.v.*], son and grandson of the *ḳāḍī*s of Ḳayseri, who had already been influential under the previous princes. ʿAlī was killed in 782/1380 in a campaign against the rebel *begs*; Burhān al-Dīn, during a struggle by rival claimants, eliminated the young heir Muḥammad (Meḥmed) II, and proclaimed himself sultan directly, thus putting an end to the dynasty.

It is unfortunate that the state of the documentation allows us to form no precise idea of the Eretnid régime. At the most some inferences can be drawn from comparisons between descriptions (Ibn Baṭṭūṭa, al-ʿUmarī) dating from the dawn of the dynasty, and a chronicle (the *Bezm u Rezm*) and travellers' accounts (Schiltberger, Clavijo) of ten or twenty years after its end. The originality of the system of government, the effective reality of which requires examination, lies in the fact that here, from the Mongol régime to the Ottoman conquest, there was no interlude of government by Turkoman dynasties as in all the surrounding territories. The Turkoman element in the central provinces was apparently less strong than the surviving Mongol tribes, and the towns seem to have enjoyed a certain prosperity. The culture of the aristocracy, and commerce also, were perhaps directed more than in the previous period towards the Arabic-speaking Syro-Egyptian domain, without however destroying the interest in Persian culture. The contrasts must not, however, be made too much of; in the Eretnid domain, as in the neighbouring small states, there developed the institution and power of the urban *akhī*s, the influence of the aristocratic (Mewlewī) and popular religious orders, literature in Turkish in the form of translations from Persian (Yūsuf Meddāḥ of Sīwās), learned poetry (that of Burhān al-Dīn, with which in part the Eretnid period must be credited), and popular heroic romances (the second *Dānishmendnāma*, at Toḳāt, an adaptation of a Saldjūḳid original); the few extant specimens of art in the Eretnid regions call for no particular remark. It does not appear that the reign of Burhān al-Dīn, who was himself of Turkish birth, broke with the Eretnid traditions.

Bibliography: The only mediaeval author to give a general résumé of the history of the Eretnid dynasty is Ibn Khaldūn, v, 558 ff., whose information on their relations with the Mamlūks is confirmed by the Mamlūk historians down to al-ʿAynī. On the beginnings of the régime, valuable details are given by Ibn Baṭṭūṭa, ii, 286 ff. (Gibb, ii, 433 ff.), and by Shihāb al-Dīn al-ʿUmarī, ed. Taeschner, 28 *et passim*, and Eflākī, ed. T. Yazıcı, Ankara 1959-61, ii, 978, = tr. Huart, ii, 415 (last chapter), and by the Shāfiʿī *Ṭabaḳāt* of al-Subkī. For the end of the régime, from the point of view of Burhān al-Dīn, see the history of the latter, under the title *Bezm u rezm*, by ʿAzīz b. Ardashīr Astarābādī, [ed. Kilisli Rifat], Istanbul 1928 (analysis and commentary by H. H. Giesecke, *Das Werk des* . . ., 1940), and, for the eastern frontier, the history of the Aḳ-Ḳoyunlu expansion composed under the title of *Kitāb-i Diyārbakriyya* by Abū Bakr Tihrānī (2nd half of the 9th/15th century) and recently published by Faruk Sümer (i, Ankara 1962); see also the Persian (Ḥāfiẓ Abrū, etc.) and Ottoman (Münedjdjim Bashī, in the Arabic manuscript text) general histories; there are many mentions of the Eretnids in the historical romance of Shikārī (ed. M. Mes'ud Koman, 1946), devoted to the Ḳaramānids; the Trebizond, Genoese and Armenian sources should also be examined.—A good inventory of the coins appears in the catalogue of the numismatic collections of the Istanbul Museum by Aḥmed Tewḥīd, iv, 346 ff.; the epigraphic material of the Eretnid regions is collected in vol. xv of *RCEA*, based especially on the researches of Ismāʿīl Ḥaḳḳī [Uzunçarşılı] (*Sīwās Shehri*, *Ḳayserī Shehri*, etc.), and Max van Berchem and Khalīl Edhem, *CIA*, iii, 40 ff. For the archaeology see also A. Gabriel, *Monuments turcs d'Anatolie*, 2 vols.—Here as elsewhere there is the possibility of extracting further information from later Ottoman texts, where traces of earlier institutions may be preserved; there are also *waḳfiyye*s which might be published and exploited. Besides the tables of Khalīl Edhem, *Düwel-i Islāmiyye*, and Zambaur, 155, the only modern general exposé is that of I. H. Uzunçarşılı, *Anadolu beylikleri*, chap. xv, based largely on Aḥmed Tewḥīd, *Benī Eretna*, in *TOEM*, v (1330), 13-22, and reappearing in the same author's résumés in *İA* and in *Osmanlı* *tarihi*, i; see also Mustafa Akdağ, *Türkiye'nin iktisadî ve içtimaî tarihi*, i, 1959, index; Z. Velidi Togan, *Umumi Türk tarihine giriş*, i, 232-6, 448; Spuler, *Mongolen*, esp. 355, and the works cited above of van Berchem, Khalīl Edhem, Giesecke and Gabriel, and also the histories of literature, to be completed by the recent book of I. Mélikoff, *La geste de Melik Dānişmend*, 2 vols. 1960, Preface.

(Cl. Cahen)

ERGANI (Arghanî, sometimes Argani, in European sources Arghana until recent times), centre of a *kaza* in the *vilâyet* of Diyār-Bakr [*q.v.*], called for a time ʿOthmāniyya (Osmaniye), situated on the highroad from Diyār-Bakr to Harput. 18 kms. to the north-west, on the river Tigris, lies the mining town of Erghani-Maʿden(i), which is the centre of a *kaza* of the *vilâyet* of Elazîgh (El-ʿAzīz) called after Erghani. Although the two towns lie apart, they are confused in some sources.

The name ʿOthmāniyya given to Erghani had to be abandoned because it gave rise to confusion with the town of ʿOthmāniyya (Osmaniye) in Djebel Bereket to the east of Adana [*q.v.*]. The town of Erghani is situated at an altitude of 1000 metres on the steep south-east slope, overlooking a deep gully (Hushut Deresi), in a limestone mountain rising to a height of 1526 metres, 10 kilometres from the right bank of the Tigris. Below the town lie fields and gardens, while above on the slope overlooking Erghani lies the old town. A near-by hill is called after Nabī Dhu 'l-Kifl [*q.v.*], who is reported to be buried there. The station of Erghani on the Diyār-Bakr—Malaṭya railway line lies in a valley, 6.5 kms. south of the present town of Erghani.

The town of Erghani, called Argani in Armenian sources, may have inherited the site of Arkania mentioned in cuneiform writings. It is also not impossible that this was also the site of one of the cities of Arsinia mentioned in the Peutinger Table. In Islamic times the fate of Erghani was linked with that of Diyār-Bakr (for history, see diyār-bakr). After the victory of Čaldîran [*q.v.*] won by Selīm I in 920/1514, and through the services of Idrīs Bidlīsī, Erghani became a *sandjak* attached to the *eyālet* of Diyār-Bakr, the district of Diyār-Bakr having been conquered for the Ottomans by Bîyîklî Meḥmed Pasha. Cuinet, writing towards the end of the 19th century, gives the population of the town of Erghani as more than 6,000. It was at that time that the centre of the *sandjak* of Erghani was transferred to the township of Maʿden, in view of the importance of the copper mines there. After the foundation of the Turkish Republic, the *ḳaḍā* of Maʿden was attached to the *wilāyet* of El-ʿAzīz, and that of Erghani (Osmaniye) was left in the *wilāyet* of Diyār-Bakr. The *kaza* of Erghani covers an area of 1595 sq. kms. and includes 68 villages. According to the results of the 1960 census, the population of the district amounted to 28,095 and that of the town of Erghani to 8,542.

The township of Erghani-Maʿden (known now usually simply as Maʿden) is situated on the lower slopes of Miḥrab Daghî overlooking the right bank of the Tigris (Didjla, known here as Erghani-Suyu). Its fortunes have always depended on that of the rich copper vein situated in the vicinity. The existence of the mine was known in ancient times, but it cannot be stated with certainty when it was first exploited. It seems to have been worked in the beginning of the 12th century, since when it was exploited at irregular intervals. Considering that there is no mention of the mine either in Ewliyā Čelebi's *Seyāḥat-nāme* or in the *Djihān-nümā*, exploitation seems to have been interrupted in the middle of the 17th century. At the beginning of the 19th century, the traveller Olivier mentions that part of the ore mined in a place called Hapur was sent to Baghdād. In 1837 Brant states that the local population, which was engaged largely in mining, amounted to 3,500 people. According to Cuinet, at the end of the century the mine was worked by the State, the ore being smelted locally with firewood and refined into black copper and then sent by camel or mule to Tokat where it was further refined into red copper, or exported via Iskenderūn. At the beginning of the 20th century, the fall in the world price of copper, the absence of roads between the mining area and ports of export and the destruction of local forests led to the abandonment of the mine. A resumption of exploitation became possible only after the foundation of the Turkish Republic, when after the completion of the Diyār-Bakr railway in 1935 it became practicable to send coal to the mining area and to export the copper easily. 8,103 tons of copper were produced in 1941. Exploitation has also started of the rich chromium deposits at Ghulemān, north-east of the Erghani copper mine. The *kaza* of (Erghani) Maʿden covers an area of 1,040 sq. kms. and includes 54 villages. According to the results of the 1960 census, there were 19,399 inhabitants of the district and 8,011 of the township.

Bibliography: W. Ainsworth, *Researches in Assyria, Babylonia and Chaldea*, London 1838, 270 ff.; On the mines: Year-book (*Sālnāme*) of the *vilāyet* of Diyār-Bakr for A.H. 1319, 19; Ewliyā Čelebi, *Seyāḥatnāme*, Istanbul A.H. 1314, iv, 22; K. Ritter, *Erdkunde*, x, 701, 801, 913; xi, 14 ff.; E. Reclus, *Nouvelle géographie universelle*, ix, 418; Olivier, *Voyage en Perse fait dans les années 1807, 1808 et 1809*; H. von Moltke, *Briefe über Zustände und Begebenheiten in der Türkei*, index; J. Brant in *JRGS*, London 1836; C. Sandreczki, *Reise nach Musul und durch Kurdistan und Urmia*, Stuttgart 1857, i, 181 ff.; H. F. B. Lynch, *Armenia. Travels and studies*, London 1901, ii, 388, 396; G. L. Bell, *Amurath to Amurath*, London 1911, 328 ff.; Vital Cuinet, *La Turquie d'Asie*, Paris 1891, ii, 475 ff.; Vivien de Saint Martin, *Nouv. Dict. de Géogr. Universelle*, suppl. I; E. Banse, *Die Türkei*, Brunswick 1915, 226; H. Hübschmann, *Indogermanische Forschungen*, xvi, 193 ff.; Streck, *ZA*, xii, 97; W. W. Smyth, *Geological features of the country round the mines of the Taurus*, in *Quarterly Journal* (1844), 330-40; E. Coulant, *Notes sur les mines de cuivre d'Arghana*, in *Annales des Mines*, 11th series, ii, 1912, 281-93; R. Pilz, *Beitrag zur Kenntnis der Kupfererzlagerstätten in der Gegend von Argana Maden*, in *Zeitschr. für prakt. Geologie*, xi-xii (1917); F. Behrend, *Die Kupfererzlagerstätte Argana Maden in Kurdistan*, *ibid.*, xxxiii (1925), 1-12; E. Chaput, *Voyages d'études géologiques et géomorphogéniques en Turquie*, Paris 1936, 142 ff.; V. Kovenko, *Guleman-Ergani madeni metallojenik bölgesi*, in *Maden Tetkik ve Arama Enstitüsü Mecmuasî*, 1944, 1-31, 29 ff.; Sh. Sāmī, *Ḳāmūs al-aʿlām*, s.v.

(Besim Darkot)

ERGENEKON, the name of a plain surrounded by mountains, mentioned in the legend of the origin of the Mongols.

An associated legend in the Chinese Chronicle of Pei-shih (ed. in about 629) explains the origins of the T'u-chüeh as follows. This people lived on the shores of the Western Sea, Hsi-hai. They were massacred by a neighbouring people. Only a young boy survived, although wounded. A she-wolf who protected and fed him became pregnant by him. She led him through a grotto to a plain surrounded by mountains. There she gave birth to ten boys who were the ancestors of the ten clans. The founder of the A-shih-na clan, who was the most intelligent, became the sovereign of the Tʾu-chüeh After some generations, under A-hsien-shih, the T'u-chüeh left the interior of the mountains and submitted to the Juan-juan.

Ras͟hīd al-Dīn, and after him Abu 'l-G͟hāzī Bahādur K͟hān, relate the same legend, with certain variations, and attribute it to the Mongols; the Tatars conquered and wiped out the Mongols. Two princes and their wives were the only survivors of the massacre and, following a narrow track, they took refuge in a plain surrounded by mountains, called Ergenekon. There they multiplied and when, four hundred years later, Ergenekon became too small for them, they contrived to make their way out by causing part of a mountain-side to crumble away by means of a huge fire, on the advice of a blacksmith.

The day consequently became a festival and its anniversary was celebrated by the Mongol sovereigns.

Bibliography: *Pei-shih*, chap. 99; Abu 'l-G͟hāzī Bahādur K͟hān, *S͟hedjere-i Türk*, ed. Riḍā Nūr, Istanbul 1925, 34-8; Fuad Köprülü, *Türk edebiyâtî taʾrīk͟hi*, Istanbul 1926, 65-7. (P. N. Boratav)

ERGİN, OSMAN (ʿOt͟hmān Nūrī) Turkish scholar and publicist, was born in 1883 in Imrin, a village (now a district centre) in the *wilāyet* of Malatya. His father Ḥādjdjī ʿAlī, of a family of humble farmers, tried his fortune in trade and after many journeys, including one in Rumania, settled in Istanbul, where he opened a coffee-house. The little Osman, who had memorized the Ḳurʾān in the village, was brought to Istanbul in 1892 where, after attending various modern schools, he entered the Dār ül-S͟hafaḳa, a leading private school of high standard, and graduated second of his class in 1901. The same year he was appointed an official in the Municipality of Istanbul. Spurred by a love of learning, for three years he attended, in his spare time, the courses of traditional sciences of a *k͟hodja* at the S͟hehzāde mosque. This type of training, which he was later bitterly to criticize, did not satisfy him, and he registered at the Faculty of Letters of Istanbul University whence he graduated in 1907 with a first class degree. Osman Ergin continued as a municipal official until his retirement in 1947, rising in his career from a simple clerk to be a *mektūbdju*, the office he held for twenty-two years. He was also a successful teacher and taught until 1956 in various secondary and professional schools of Istanbul, including his own Dār ül-S͟hafaḳa and the American College for Girls. He died in 1961 in Istanbul.

Osman Ergin had a lively and inquisitive mind and was very erudite. His life-long research in the archives and libraries of Istanbul soon made him a leading authority on the history of municipal and educational institutions of Istanbul. Unbending in his principles, loyal in his friendships, "the *Mektūbdju* Osman Bey" was one of the most remarkable characters among scholars of his generation, liked and respected by everyone.

Apart from his very numerous books on various subjects and his biographical and bibliographical monographs, some still unpublished, he was the author of the following major works:

1) *Medjelle-i Umūr-i Belediyye*, 5 volumes, Istanbul 1330-8, the first of which is a richly documented historical introduction to municipal institutions in Islam and in Turkey, particularly the city of Istanbul, a standard reference book on the subject; the other volumes contain a collection of laws, bye-laws, regulations, Council of State decisions, etc. concerning municipal administration.

2) *Türkiye maarif tarihi*, 5 volumes, Istanbul 1939-43 (a promised sixth volume did not appear). Originally planned as a "History of schools and other educational and scholarly institutions of Istanbul", it was developed later into a history of education in Turkey. This pioneer work, which is a mine of information, remains, in spite of some technical shortcomings, the only comprehensive work of reference on the subject. The history and development of all types of schools in Turkey are elaborately discussed: *medrese*s, the palace school, military schools, old and new style technical and professional schools, semi-educational institutions and their auxiliaries in the Ottoman Empire, European types of schools of all grades, private, foreign and minority schools, universities and various institutions of higher education, etc., are amply treated. Special emphasis is given to the detailed and comparative analysis of the evolution of syllabuses in the many types of school. Many of the controversial educational problems arising from social change in Turkey are discussed at length and the book abounds in anecdotes and personal notes which make it extremely interesting reading.

3) *Istanbul şehri rehberi*, Istanbul 1934, is the outcome of his long research preparatory to the first modern census of the city of Istanbul in 1927 (as part of the first general census in Turkey). This is the best detailed topographical study of Istanbul with street names and thirty-eight maps.

4) *Türkiye'de şehirciliğin tarihî inkişafı*, Istanbul 1936, a survey of most of the problems discussed in the *Medjelle-i Umūr-i Belediyye.*

Bibliography: A. Süheyl Ünver, *Osman Ergin, çalışma hayatı ve eserleri*, in *Belleten*, xxvi/101 (1962), 163-79, with a bibliography including his unpublished works and a list of his articles in the journal of the municipality of Istanbul (*Istanbul Şehremaneti* (*Belediye*) *Mecmuası*) from 1924 to 1936; Orhan Durusoy, *Osman Ergin bibliyografyası*, in *Tıp ve ilimler tarihimizde portreler, I, Osman Ergin* (Istanbul Üniversitesi Tıp Tarihi Enstitüsü neşriyatından, sayı 52), Istanbul 1958; Bedi N. Şehsuvaroğlu, *Osman Ergin'in biyografyası*, in the same publication. (Fahir İz)

ERGIRI (Argiri, Ergeri), Ottoman name of Argyrokastro, Alb. Gjinokastër, principal town of Albanian Epirus (40° 13′ N., 20° 13′ E.) near the foot of the eastern slopes of the Mali Gjerë; overlooking the wide and fertile valley of the Drin, a tributary of the Voyutsa (Vijosë), it controls the route from Valona into Northern Greece. The town, near the site of the ancient Hadrianopolis, probably takes its name from that of an Illyrian tribe. The district came under Ottoman control in the reign of Bāyezīd I. In the *defter* of 835/1431 'Argiri-ḳaṣrī' (its district being called *wilāyet-i Zenebis͟h*, *i.e.*, of the Zenebissi family) appears as the chef-lieu of the sandjaḳ of 'Arvānya'; later (certainly by 912/1506) it formed part of the sandjaḳ of Avlonya; in the last years of the Empire it was again a sandjak, belonging to the *wilāyet* of Yanya. Ewliyā (1670) describes a thriving, solidly-built town, with a predominantly Muslim population. Gjinokastër, now extending into the valley (present pop. ca. 12,000), is dominated by the mediaeval (Venetian?) castle, reconstructed by ʿAlī Pas͟ha of Tepedelen [*q.v.*]; many of its old houses survive, built in the characteristic fortress-like style which impressed Ewliyā.

Bibliography: H. Inalcık, *Arnavutluk'ta Osmanlı hâkimiyetinin yerleşmesi* ..., in *Fatih ve Istanbul*, i/2 (1953), 153-75; idem, *Hicrî 835 tarihli Suret-i defter-i Sancak-i Arvanid*, Ankara 1954, introd.; idem, art. ARNAWUTLUK above; Ewliyā Čelebi, *Seyāḥatnāme*, viii, 674-81 = F. Babinger's abridged trans. and comm., in *MSOS*, xxxiii (1930), 148-50; J. C. Hobhouse, *A journey through Albania* ..., 1813, 92-7; Baedeker's *Dalmatien und die Adria*, 1929, 250 (F. Babinger); *Enc. It.*, s.v. Argirocastro; S. Skendi (ed.), *Albania*, 1957; *Guide d'Albanie* ('Albturist'), Tirana 1958, 310-5.

(V. L. MÉNAGE)

ERITREA, a territory with a sizeable Muslim population in North-East Africa, bordering on the Red Sea, since 1952 federated with Ethiopia, since 1962 fully integrated in the Ethiopian Empire.

(*i*) Geographically, historically, and ethnically Eritrea has generally formed part of a larger unit which will be treated under AL-ḤABASH. In the following, special emphasis will be placed on such features and Islamic manifestations as are peculiar to Eritrea in the narrow sense. 'Eritrea' (from *Mare Erythraeum*) was so named by the Italians in 1890 to describe their growing possessions (initiated in 1869 by the purchase of the port of Assab [*q.v.*]) on the Red Sea coast, the *Baḥrmeder* ('sea country') or *Mareb Mellash* ('beyond the river Mareb') of the Abyssinians.

In the north and west Eritrea's triangular shape (enclosing nearly 50,000 square miles of extremely variegated country) borders upon the Sudan, in the east on the Red Sea, in the south-east corner upon French Somaliland whence the old frontier with Ethiopia proceeds in a north-westerly direction along the Danḳali [*q.v.*] depression and then following the Mareb-Belesa line. The physical configuration of the country is marked by the vast central mountain massif (6500-8000 feet above sea-level) extending southwards into Ethiopia and surrounded by the torrid plains in the east, west, and north.

(ii) Population: With the exception of the Djabart [*q.v.*], the vast majority of Muslim Eritreans live in those hot regions of the east, west, and north. Their number reaches about half a million in a total population of approx. 1,100,000, among whom the monophysite Christian element wields most of the political power. While the Christians and Djabart, concentrated in the densely populated central highlands, speak Tigrinya (see below), the vast majority of the Muslims, sedentary or nomadic in the sparsely inhabited lowlands, use Tigre (see below) and, to a very limited extent, Arabic. They are the descendants of Bedja [*q.v.*] or other Cushitic tribes and early South-Arabian immigrants. The Banū ʿĀmir [*q.v.*] or Beni Amer are the largest tribal federation, numbering about 60,000 (with an additional 30,000 in the Sudan) and occupying a considerable portion of Western Eritrea. They owe allegiance to a paramount chief, the Diglāl [*q.v.*], and acknowledge the religious leadership of the Mirghani family. In the northern hills the Habab, Ad Tekles, and Ad Temariam form the tribal federation of Bet Asgede. The Ad Shaykh have their encampments between the Habab and the Ad Tekles; they claim descent from a Meccan family, but most of these tribal memories are incapable of proof. The Bilen (or Bogos) in the Keren area consist of two large tribes (Bet Tarke and Bet Takwe). The Saho live along the eastern escarpment and the foothills leading to the tribal confederacy of the Danāḳil who inhabit the vast arid depression behind the Red Sea coast, one of the hottest and most barren regions in the world. The population of the port of Massawa (and to a much lesser extent of Arkiko and Assab) is cosmopolitan and includes tribesmen from the hills, Danāḳil, Sudanese, Arabs, Indians and groups of Turkish descent. The unifying factor is Islam. The people of the barren Dahlak [*q.v.*] islands off the Massawa coast were among the first in East Africa to be converted to Islam, and many tombstones in Kūfic characters bear witness to this early Muslim connexion.

(iii) Eritrea's history is so entwined with that of Ethiopia and South Arabia, on the one hand, and the Sudan, on the other, that it is difficult to disentangle the few independent facets of its past. South Arabian immigrants settled along that part of the western Red Sea coast which is now Eritrea. From here they subsequently penetrated into the interior and established the Aksumite Kingdom which has left so many traces within the soil of Eritrea. Later, Eritrea became the base from which the Aksumite hegemony over a large strip of the coast of south-west Arabia was launched. Here also was the avenue through which contacts, hostile as well as cultural, with Meroe and its civilization flowed. As Ethiopia's traditional maritime province and only outlet to the sea, Eritrea became the spring-board of both Muslim assault, leading to centuries of struggle, and Portuguese rescue from that domination. In the 10th/16th century Massawa and Arkiko were the base from which the Turks attempted their invasion of the Christian plateau (an event perpetuated in the title of the *nāʾib* of Arkiko, the representative of the Ottoman power), and in the nineteenth the Egyptians repeatedly fought to gain a permanent foothold in Eritrea until they were decisively defeated by the Emperor John near Gura (1876). Sir Robert Napier launched his successful campaign against Theodore (1867-8) from the Bay of Zula, and the Italians carved out their Eritrean colony from those parts of the maritime province for which the Shoan Emperor Menelik II (in contrast to his Tigrean predecessor John) was either unable or unwilling to fight. Twice within 40 years the Italians despatched their armies from Eritrea into Ethiopia until they were finally dislodged during the Second World War. From 1941 to 1952 a British Military Administration had charge of Eritrea, a period during which both Muslim and Christian political ambitions first asserted themselves. A plan to do away with Eritrea as an artificial political entity (by incorporating the Muslim West with the Sudan and the Christian centre with Ethiopia) finally came to grief when the United Nations decided (1950) to constitute Eritrea as an autonomous federal unit under the sovereignty of the Ethiopian crown. This uneasy arrangement gradually led to Eritrea's full absorption, for no constitutional safeguards could make the territory economically or politically viable. The large Muslim minority enjoys reasonable religious and political expression in the Christian Empire.

(iv) Languages: Tigrinya and Tigre are both successor languages of Semitic Ethiopic (Geʿez); the former is spoken by the Djabart of the highlands, while the latter is the principal tongue of the Muslims in the western and eastern lowlands and the northern hills. In the Kassala province of the Sudan Tigre is called *al-Khaṣṣiya*. Dialectal distinctions within Tigre have not yet been fully worked out. Tigre cannot boast any written literature and it is losing some ground in favour of Arabic, which among Muslims and traders enjoys a cachet which Tigre does not possess. The decision of the Eritrean government, in 1952, declaring Tigrinya and Arabic the official languages of Eritrea (although most Tigre-speakers know little or no Arabic) was a political and prestige resolution—not a linguistic judgement. The two main non-Semitic languages spoken by the Muslims of Eritrea are Bedawiye and Bilin.

(v) Religion: Islam has been a force in Eritrea-Abyssinia ever since Muḥammad sent some of his earliest followers to seek refuge with the Negus. Throughout the Middle Ages Muslim pressure from the Red Sea compelled Abyssinians to fight for their own form of Christianity. But in Eritrea as well as Ethiopia, though nearly half the population are Muslims, Islam has not succeeded in piercing the defensive armour of monophysitism and in transforming its essential fabric. On the contrary, the Djabart have been so completely assimilated to the cultural, linguistic, and national pattern of traditional Abyssinia that their religion seems strangely disembodied. Islam is, however, still making progress among the Cushitic and Nilotic peoples in the lowland areas, but none among the highland population. The universal call of Islam has a special attraction in all those regions where the particularistic and national message of monophysite Christianity has no genuine application.

The Ḳādiriyya became firmly entrenched in the coastal areas of Eritrea, especially at Massawa and its hinterland. But the most influential order in Eritrea is undoubtedly the Mīrghaniyya or Khatmiyya, based on Kassala, which is predominant in the western regions, especially among the Beni Amer, Habab, and other Muslim tribes. According to the last Italian census (1931) the relative strength of the *madhāhib* in Eritrea is as follows: Mālikites: 65%; Ḥanafites: 26%; Shāfiʿites: 9%. While the *sharīʿa* is generally subordinate to customary law among many of the tribes, it still prevails in urban areas. The secular government, both European and Ethiopian, has encouraged the development of Muslim civil law and the establishment of *Ḳāḍī*'s courts.

Bibliography: *Africa Orientale* (Reale Società Geogr. Ital.), Bologna 1936; Brit. Mil. Admin., *Races and tribes of Eritrea*, Asmara 1943; Chamber of Commerce, *Guide book of Ethiopia*, Addis Ababa 1954; *Chi è? dell'Eritrea*, Asmara 1952; C. Conti Rossini, *Principi di diritto consuetudinario dell' Eritrea*, Rome 1916; *Eritrea*, in *Enciclopedia Italiana*; *Guida dell'Africa Orientale*, Milan 1938; S. H. Longrigg, *A short history of Eritrea*, Oxford 1945; N. Marein, *The Ethiopian Empire-federation and laws*, Rotterdam 1954; L. M. Nesbitt, *Desert and forest* (Exploration of the Danakil), Penguin Books 1955; A. Pollera, *Le popolazioni indigene dell'Eritrea*, Bologna 1935; Rennell of Rodd, *British military administration of occupied territories in Africa, 1941-7*, London 1948; *Tensaʾe Eritrea Ityopyawit* (Restoration of Eritrea), Addis Ababa 1952; G. K. N. Trevaskis, *Eritrea, 1941-52*, London 1960; J. S. Trimingham, *Islam in Ethiopia*, Oxford 1952; E. Ullendorff, *The Ethiopians*, London 1960. (E. Ullendorff)

ERIWAN [see REWĀN].

ERMENAK or **ERMENEK**, the ancient Germanikopolis in Isauria (see Pauly-Wissowa, vii, 1258), a small town in southern Anatolia, 36° 35′ N., 32° 50′ E., in the western Taurus mountains, at an altitude of ca. 1200 m. (3937 ft.), above the confluence of two of the source-rivers of the Göksu, the Kalykadnos of antiquity. It is the capital of a *kaza* in the *vilâyet* of Konya, formerly in the *sandjaḳ* of Ičel in the *wilāyet* of Adana. In 1960, it had 7,536 inhabitants and the district 36,380. Mediaeval Oriental writers put Ermenāk two days' journey south of Lārende (the modern Karaman), and three days' journey east of ʿAlāʾiyya (the modern Alanya). Its grotto with a spring was particularly famous.

Ermenāk originally belonged to the kingdom of Lesser Armenia. It was conquered by the Rūm-Saldjūḳ Sulṭān ʿAlāʾ al-Dīn Keyḳubād I in 625/1228. Later it became the seat of the Turcoman dynasty of Ḳaramān. After the collapse of the Rūm-Saldjūḳ empire, the Ḳaramānids set out from there to take possession of the southern part, with Lārende (subsequently Ḳaramān) and Konya. Under Meḥemmed II, Ermenāk and the principality of Ḳaramān came under Ottoman rule.

There are some remarkable buildings in Ermenāk, dating from Ḳaramānid times. Of these, the most important is the Ulu Djāmiʿ, which was built by Maḥmūd Beg b. Ḳaramān in 702/1302-3 (cf. *RCEA*, xiii, Cairo 1944, 239, no. 5154). It is a simple building with three parallel naves, thus built on the plan of the Umayyad mosque in Damascus.

Bibliography: Kātib Čelebi, *Djihānnümā*, Istanbul 1145, 611 f.; Ewliyā Čelebi, *Seyāḥatnāme* ix, 304 f.; Shihāb al-Dīn al-ʿUmarī, *Masālik al-abṣār fī mamālik al-amṣār*, ed. Taeschner, i, Leipzig 1929, 23 and 48; Le Strange, 148; Tomaschek, i, 60, 89, 105; Ritter, *Erdkunde*, xix, 307; Ramsay, *The historical geography of Asia Minor*, London 1890, 363 f.; V. Cuinet, *La Turquie d'Asie*, ii, 77; Ch. Samy-Bey Fraschery, *Ḳāmūs al-aʿlām*, ii, Istanbul 1306, 839 f.; E. Diez, Oktay Aslanapa, and Mahmut Mesut Koman, *Karaman devri sanati*, Istanbul 1950, 5-30; *İA*, s.v. (M. C. Şihâbeddin Tekindağ). (Fr. Taeschner)

ERSOY [see MEHMET AKIF ERSOY].

ERTOGHRUL (T. *er* 'male', *toghrïl* 'kite').— 1. According to tradition, the name of the father of ʿOthmān I [*q.v.*], the founder of the Ottoman dynasty; but it appears in no source, Byzantine or Islamic, before the end of the 14th century, when it is mentioned in a letter (authentic?) of Bāyazīd I to Timur (Ferīdūn, *Munshaʾāt*[2], i, 127) and in the *Dhāt al-shifāʾ* (sub anno 699) of al-Djazarī [*q.v.*]. The traditions presented in the 9th/15th century Ottoman works, largely legendary in tone, fall into two main groups: (a) Ertoghrul, together with Gündüz Alp and Gök Alp, accompanied Sultan ʿAlāʾ al-Dīn of Konya to Sulṭān Öyüğü (near Eskishehir), performed great feats of arms thereabouts and, after ʿAlāʾ al-Dīn had returned to deal with a Tatar attack, conquered the district around Söğüd [*q.v.*] (Aḥmedī, *Iskender-nāme*, ed. N. S. Banarlı, in *Türkiyat Mecmuası*, vi (1936-9), 113 f. and cf. 75-7): echoes of this tradition are given by Yazīdjī-oghlu ʿAlī (M. T. Houtsma, *Recueil*, iii, 217-8), with the addition of the claim that Ertoghrul and his associates belonged to the clan of the Ḳayï [*q.v.*]. The related fuller version in Shükrüllāh's *Bahdjat al-tawārīkh* (ed. Th. Seif, in *MOG*, ii (1923-6), 76-8) adds that Ertoghrul had come into Rūm from the east with 340 followers after the Mongol invasions and settled first at Ḳaradja-dagh (south of Ankara), that he captured Ḳaradja-ḥiṣār (10 km. south-west of Eskishehir), and died at the age of 93; Ḳaramānī Meḥemmed Pasha gives a similar account (tr. M. Khalīl [Yınanç], *TOEM*, no. 79, 87 f.). In one version of this tradition Gündüz is said to be not the associate but the father of Ertoghrul (Ḳ. Meḥemmed Pasha, and cf. Neshrī, ed. Taeschner, i, 21-2, and Enwerī, ed. M. Khalīl, 81). (b) Ertoghrul, Sonkurtegin and Gün-doghdï, the three sons of Süleymānshāh, came to Pasin-ovasï (east of Erzurum) after their father was drowned in the Euphrates near Ḳalʿat Djaʿbar; his brothers returned to the east, but Ertoghrul, remaining with 400 households, was granted by Sultan ʿAlāʾ al-Dīn the region around Söğüd as winter pastures and the hills of Domanïč and Ermeni-beli (to the west) as summer pastures. He died in 687/1288, after ruling his folk for 52 years (Anonymous chronicles, ed. Giese, 5 f. [recension of MS W_3 etc.] = Leunclavius, *Annales*; cf. Urudj, ed. Babinger, 6-7, ʿĀshïḳpashazāde, ed. Giese, § 2). Neshrī succeeds in harmonizing these traditions, adding, on the authority of Mewlānā Ayās (for whom see Tashköprüzāde, *Shaḳāʾiḳ*, tr. Medjdī, 189 f.), the story that Ertoghrul and his followers had rescued ʿAlāʾ al-Dīn in a skirmish with a Mongol force. A *türbe* just outside Söğüd on the Biledjik road (much restored, no early inscription) is revered as that of Ertoghrul (R. Hartmann, *Im neuen Anatolien*, Leipzig 1928, 50, and Tafel 14).

In the later years of the Ottoman Empire, Ertoghrul was the name given to a sandjaḳ of the *wilāyet* of Bursa (V. Cuinet, *La Turquie d'Asie*, iv, 160 ff.).

Bibliography: P. Wittek, *The rise of the Ottoman Empire*, London 1938, 6-13; M. F. Köprülü, *Osmanlı imparatorluğu'nun etnik menşei mes'eleleri*, in *Belleten*, vii (1943), 219-313; *IA*, s.v. Ertuğrul Gâzî, by M. Halil Yınanç (summaries of all the early Ottoman, and of other, accounts); for references to Byzantine sources see G. Moravcsik, *Byzantinoturcica*², ii, 125.

2. The eldest son of Bāyazīd I, born, according to Ismāʿīl Belīgh (*Güldeste*, 40), in 778/1376-7. Appointed governor of a district of Western Anatolia (Sarukhan and Karasï, according to ʿĀshïḳpashazāde, § 59, and hence Neshrī; Aydïn, according to Idrīs, and hence Saʿd al-Dīn, i, 128) after his father's campaign of 792/1389-90, he was killed in 794/1392 in the battle of Kïrk-Dilim near Čorum (for which see ʿAzīz b. Ardashīr, *Bezm ü rezm*, Istanbul 1928, 403-5) and buried by the mosque which he had founded at Bursa (Kâzım Baykal, *Bursa ve anıtları*, Bursa 1950, 107). (V. L. Ménage)

ERTOGHRUL, ii [see BILEDJIK].

ERZEN [see ARZAN].

ERZERUM [see ERZURUM].

ERZINDJAN, modern spelling Erzincan, older forms Arzingan, Arzandjān, a town in eastern Anatolia, 39° 45′ N., 39° 30′ E., on the northern bank of the Karasu (the northern tributary of the Euphrates). It is situated in a fertile plain which is surrounded by high mountain ranges (the Keşiş Dağı, 3,537 m. (11,604 ft.), in the north-east, the Sipikör Dağı, 3,010 m. (9,875 ft.), in the north, and the Mercan Dağı, 3,449 m. (11,315 ft.), which is part of the Monzur range, in the south). It has an altitude of 1200 m. (3,937 ft.), and was once the capital of a *sandjaḳ* in the *wilāyet* of Erzurum. Today it is the capital of the *vilâyet* itself, with the *kaza*s Erzincan, Ilice, Kemah, Kemaliye (Eğin), Refahiye, and Tercan. In 1960, the town had 36,465 inhabitants, the district had 51,721, and the *vilâyet* 243,837. According to Cuinet, Erzincan had 23,000 inhabitants towards the end of the last century. Of these, 15,000 were Muslims. Erzincan has always been an important meeting point for the caravan routes between Sivas and Erzurum. Since 1938, it has been the main station on the railway line between these two towns; it is 337 km. (248 m.) from Sivas, and 245 km. (133 m.) from Erzurum.

According to Armenian sources, Erzincan dates back to before the Christian era, though detailed information does not appear before Saldjūḳ times. The town was in the region over which Muslims and Byzantines fought, and had changed hands several times prior to the battle of Malazkirt (1071). After this, it came under the rule of the Saldjūḳ amīr Mengüdjek, and remained in the hands of his successors until 625/1228, when the Rūm-Saldjūḳ Sulṭan ʿAlāʾ al-Dīn Keyḳubād I forced the last of the Mengüdjekids ʿAlāʾ al-Dīn Dāwūdshāh, to hand it over. Keyḳubād rebuilt the town and its walls (Ḥamdallāh Mustawfī, *Nuzha*, 95, top). On 28 Ramaḍān 627/10 August 1230 the Khwārizmshāh Djalāl al-Dīn suffered a defeat at the hands of the Rūm-Saldjūḳ ʿAlāʾ al-Dīn Keyḳubād I, an ally of the Ayyūbid al-Ashraf, near Yası-Čimen in the vicinity of Erzincan (*Die Seltschukengeschichte des Ibn Bībī*, transl. H. W. Duda, Copenhagen 1959, 166 ff., in particular 171). In 640/1243, Erzincan was taken by the Mongols, who broke into Anatolia from the direction of Erzurum. Thenceforth it belonged to that part of Anatolia which was administered by the Ilkhānid governors. According to Ibn Baṭṭūṭa (ii, 293 f.; Eng. tr. H.A.R. Gibb, ii, 436 f.), the town was largely populated by Armenians in his day, though there were also some Turkish-speaking Muslims. He also mentions the industriousness of the inhabitants of the town (engaged in textiles and copperwork). There was also a branch of the Akhī [*q.v.*] order.

After the collapse of the Mongol Empire of the Ilkhans, Erzincan first belonged to the *amīr* Eretnā [*q.v.*], then to the ḳāḍī Burhān al-Dīn; subsequently, Bāyazīd I incorporated it into the Ottoman Empire for a short time. After his defeat by Tīmūr near Ankara in 804/1402, the town passed to the Ḳaraḳoyunlu and the Aḳ-ḳoyunlu. There are two funerary monuments in the shape of rams (as they are frequently found in cemeteries of eastern Anatolia) which bear witness to their rule. These have been erected in an attractive way near the main road (concerning this, cf. Strzygowski's work on Armenia, and also Hamit Koşay, *Les statues de béliers et de moutons dans les cimetières historiques de l'Anatolie orientale*, Ier Congrès international des arts turcs, Ankara 1959, 58-60). After the victory of Meḥemmed II over Uzun Ḥasan near Tercan (Otluk Beli), the town belonged to local rulers for a time. During Selīm I's campaign against Shāh Ismāʿīl in 920/1514, Erzincan and its district were finally incorporated in the Ottoman Empire as a *liwāʾ* (*sandjaḳ*) of the *eyālet* (later *wilāyet*) of Erzurum. In the 17th century, Erzincan played a part in the Djalālī [*q.v.* in Supplement] rising. During the 19th century it was the seat of a lodge of the reformed Naḳshbandī order, headed by Fehmī Efendi [*q.v.*]. In the First World War, Erzincan was occupied by Russian forces on 24 July 1916, but evacuated again after 18 months, on 26 February 1918.

Erzincan has frequently suffered destruction by earthquakes; the last of these was in 1939. Consequently, nothing remains of its historical buildings. The Ulu Djāmiʿ, which dated from Saldjūḳ times, and the Ḳurshunlu Djāmiʿ and the Tash Khān, which dated from the time of Sultan Süleymān, used to be noteworthy. Thanks to the fertility of the surrounding country, the town has always been able to recover. Today its main exports are horticultural. From a military point of view, it is a main centre of the defence of Turkey's eastern frontier.

Bibliography: in addition to references in the text: Yāḳūt, *Muʿdjam*, i, 205; Abu 'l-Fidā', *Taḳwīm*, 392 f.; Dimashḳī, 228; Ewliyā Čelebi, *Seyāḥatnāme*, ii, 379 (*Travels*, ii, 202); Kātib Čelebi, *Djihānnümā*, 423 f.; Le Strange, 118; K. Ritter, *Erdkunde*, x, 770-4; V. Cuinet, *La Turquie d'Asie*, i, 210 f.; Samy Bey Fraschery, *Ḳāmūs al-aʿlām*, ii, 827; Ali Kemâlî, *Erzincan*, Istanbul 1932; *IA*, s.v. (Besim Darkot).

(R. Hartmann-[Fr. Taeschner])

ERZURUM. one of the principal cities in eastern Turkey, today the chief town of the province of Erzurum with a population of 91,196 (1960 census).

Situated between the Karasu and Aras valleys which formed the main thoroughfare between Turkey and Īrān for caravans and armies, Erzurum has been an important commercial and military centre in the area since antiquity. It was the ancient Ḳarin, also called Ḳarnoi Ḳal(gh)aḳ in Armenian, from which Ḳālīḳalā or Ḳālī in the Arabic sources (cf. Ibn Ḥawḳal, i, 343; Ibn al-Faḳīh, *Akhbār al-buldān*, Leiden 1885, 295) must have been derived. Under the Romans it was fortified and called Theodosiopolis in 415 A.D. The name of Erzurum comes from *Arzan al-Rūm*, *Arzan-i Rūm* or *Arz-i Rūm* (see the Saldjūḳid coins in I. Ghālib, *Taḳwīm-i meskūkāt-i Seldjūḳiyye*, Istanbul 1309H., nos. 10, 147, 152). Arzan (Erzen) was a nearby commercial centre, the population of which took refuge in Ḳālīḳalā upon its destruction by the Saldjūḳids in 440/1048 or 441/1049 (see arzan).

First taken by the Arabs under Caliph ʿUthmān after 33/653, its possession fluctuated between Byzantines and Arabs (Byzantine in 66/686, Arab in 81/700, Byzantine again in 137/754 for a short time and then Arab again until 338/949 when the Byzantines took it, to hold it until the Saldjūḳid conquest). The native Armenian princes in the area played an important part in all these changes. With its strong walls, Ḳālī made a base for the Arabs from which to control the area and organize *ghazā* raids into Byzantine Anatolia. In 153-5/770-2 the local Armenian dynasts organized a large-scale insurrection against the Arabs and came to lay siege to Ḳālī (Ghévond, *Hist. des guerres et des conquêtes des Arabes en Arménie*, trans. Chahnazaryan, Paris 1856, 136-43; Yaʿḳūbī, ii, 447).

Under the Byzantines the chief city of the 'theme' of Theodosiopolis, it withstood the Saldjūḳid onslaught until 473/1080 when Amīr Aḥmad took it, and it was then made the capital of the Turkish principality of the Saltuḳids (see saltuḳ-oghlu). In 597/1201 it came under the Saldjūḳids of Anatolia and was made the seat of a *malik*, prince, possessing the province as his appanage. The city under its new name of Arzan-i Rūm became one of the most prosperous commercial centres in Anatolia (cf. Yaḳūt, *Muʿdjam al-buldān*, s.v. Arzan) and its important monuments belong to this period: the Ulu-djāmiʿ built in 575/1179, the Medrese of Khūndī Khātūn (Čifte-mināre) built in 651/1253, and the mausoleums of the Saltuḳids.

In 639/1242 the Mongols under Baydju took it. Remaining a part of Seldjūḳid territory under Mongol suzerainty, the province of Arzan-i Rūm paid a large annual tribute to the Mongol treasury, 222,000 dīnār in 736/1335 (Z. V. Togan, *Mogollar devrinde Anadolu'nun iktisadî vaziyeti*, in *THITM*, i (1931), 22). After the dissolution of the Ilkhānid empire in Īrān, Erzurum was occupied by the rival Mongol amīrs successively, the Čobanid Shaykh Ḥasan in 741/1340, Muḥammad b. Eretna about 761/1360. Then the city became part of the rising Türkmen states in eastern Anatolia, first of the Ḳara-ḳoyunlu [*q.v.*] from 787/1385, and then of the Aḳ-ḳoyunlu [*q.v.*] from 869/1465. Taken by Shāh Ismāʿīl from the latter in 908/1502, it was conquered by the Ottoman Sultan Selīm I following his victory at Čāldīrān in 920/1514. It was made in 941/1534 the chief city of a new *Beglerbegilik* comprising the sandjaḳs of Erzurum, Shebīn Ḳara-ḥiṣār, Kīghi, Khînîs, Yuḳarî-Pasin, Malazgird, Tekman, Kîzučan, Ispir, Tortum, Nāmervān and Medjinkerd.

The tax regulations of the time of Uzun Ḥasan [*q.v.*], preserved after the Ottoman conquest, were later in 926/1520 and in 947/1540 modified and replaced by the typical Ottoman *ḳānūn* (cf. Ö. L. Barkan, *Kanunlar*, 63; W. Hinz, *Das Steuerwesen Ostanatoliens im 15. und 16. Jahrhundert*, in *ZDMG*, c (1950), 177-201).

Under the Ottomans the city benefited from the active caravan trade between Īrān and Bursa (for a description of it in 1050/1640 see Ewliyā Čelebi, *Seyāḥatnāme*, ii, Istanbul 1314/1896, 203-19). Erzurum became also the chief Ottoman military base during the wars against Īrān and Georgia in the 10th/16th and 11th/17th centuries. In 1031/1622, upon the murder of ʿOthmān II, Abaza Meḥmed Pasha, *beglerbegi* of Erzurum, supported by the population and the Djalālī [*q.v.* in Supplement] groups, rose up against the central government then under Janissary control. Entrenched in Erzurum, Meḥmed defied imperial armies sent against him until Muḥarram 1038/September 1628.

During the Ottoman-Russian wars the Russians occupied Erzurum temporarily in September 1829, in 1878 and in February 1916. On 23 July 1919 the first national congress under Muṣṭafā Kemāl (Atatürk) was held in Erzurum. Today it is the most important city in eastern Turkey with the headquarters of the Third Army and the Atatürk University which was opened on 17 November 1958. The city was linked with the country's railway system in 1939.

Bibliography: Le Strange, 117-8; E. Honigmann, *Die Ostgrenze des byzantinischen Reiches von 363 bis 1071*, (Corpus Bruxellense Hist. Byz. iii), Brussels 1935; A. A. Vasiliev, *Byzance et les Arabes*, French ed. H. Grégoire and M. Canard, 2 vols. (Corpus Bruxellense Hist. Byz. i, ii/2), Brussels 1935-50; St. Martin, *Mémoires sur l'Arménie*, Paris 1818; Şerif Beygu, *Erzurum tarihi, anıtları ve kitâbeleri*, Istanbul 1936; M. Nuṣret, *Ta'rīkhče-i Erzurum*, Istanbul 1338 A. H.; Vehbi Kocagüney, *Erzurum kalesi ve savaşları*, Istanbul 1942; C. Dursunoğlu, *Millî Mücadelede Erzurum*, Ankara 1946; E. Z. Karal, *Zarif Paşanın Hatıratı*, in *Belleten*, iv/16 (1940), 473-94; *Sālnāmes* of the *wilāyet* of Erzurum; *Erzurum Halkevi Mecmuası*; *IA*, Erzurum (by Besim Darkot, M. Halil Yinanç, H. Inalcık). (Halil İnalcık)

ESʿAD EFENDI, AḤMED (1153/1740-1230/1814), Ottoman *Shaykh al-Islām*, son of the *Shaykh al-Islām* Meḥemmed Ṣāliḥ Efendi [*q.v.*]. After being *ḳāḍī* successively of Izmir (from 1184/1770), Bursa (from 1192/1778) and Istanbul (1201/1787), he held office for a short time (1204/1790-1206/1791) as *ḳāḍīʿasker* of Anadolu. One of the prominent personalities consulted by Selīm III (*q.v.*] on the reforms necessary in state affairs, he made proposals particularly for the improvement of military efficiency. As a known advocate of reform, he twice held office as *ḳāḍī*ᶜ*asker* of Rūmeli (from Radjab 1208/February 1794 and Radjab 1213/December 1798), and on 29 Muḥarram 1218/21 May 1803 was made *Shaykh al-Islām*. When in 1221/1806 the attempt was made to apply the *Niẓām-i djedīd* [*q.v.*] in Rūmeli, Esᶜad Efendi issued a *fatwā* condemning those who resisted it, but upon the Sultan's abandoning the attempt to enforce reform he was relieved of office at his own request (1 Radjab 1221/14 September 1806). The influence of the *Shaykh al-Islām* ᶜAṭāʾullāh Efendi and the ᶜ*ulemā*ʾ saved his life during the rebellion of Kabakčï Muṣṭafā [*q.v.*]. When Muṣṭafā Pasha Bayraḳdār [*q.v.*] came to power, Esᶜad Efendi was again appointed *Shaykh al-Islām* (22 Djumādā II 1223/15 August 1808) and took part in the discussions which bore fruit in the *Sened-i ittifāḳ* (see art. DUSTŪR, ii). When Muṣṭafā Pasha fell, Esᶜad Efendi was again saved by the ᶜ*ulemā*ʾ; dismissed on 3 Shawwāl 1223/22 November 1808, he was sent for his own protection to his *arpalïḳ* at Maᶜnīsā. He was later permitted to return to Istanbul and died, on 10 Muḥarram 1230/23 December 1814, in his *yalï* at Kanlïdja.

Bibliography: Wāṣif, *Taʾrīkh*, Istanbul 1219, ii, 151; ᶜĀṣim, *Taʾrīkh*, Istanbul n.d., i, 119, ii, 257; Shānī-zāde, *Taʾrīkh*, Istanbul 1290, i, 45, 72, 139-46; Djewdet, *Taʾrīkh*, Istanbul 1309, iv-ix (index); Meḥemmed Münīb, *Dawḥa-i mashāʾikh-i kibār dhayli* (MS); Süleymān Fāʾiḳ, *Dawḥa-i mashāʾikh-i kibār dhayli* (MS); Aḥmed Rifᶜat, *Dawḥat al-mashāʾikh*, Istanbul (lith., n.d.), 100, 119; Ḥüseyn Aywānsarāyī, *Ḥadīḳat al-djawāmi*ᶜ, Istanbul 1281, i, 123; ᶜ*Ilmiyye sālnāmesi*, Istanbul 1334, 570; *IA*, s.v. (of which the above is an abridgement).

(M. MÜNİR AKTEPE)

ESᶜAD EFENDI, MEḤMED (978/1570-1034/1625), Ottoman *Shaykh al-Islām*, was the second son of the celebrated Saᶜd al-Dīn [*q.v.*]. Thanks to the influence of his father, he advanced rapidly in the theological career, to become in Muḥarram 1007/August 1598 *ḳāḍī* of Istanbul. During his elder brother Meḥemmed's first period in office as *Shaykh al-Islām* (1010/1601-1011/1603) he was for a time *ḳāḍī*ᶜ*asker* of Anadolu; and after two short periods as *ḳāḍī*ᶜ*asker* of Rūmeli he was himself appointed *Shaykh al-Islām* on 5 Djumādā II 1024/2 July 1615 in succession to his brother. During his seven years in office he played a prominent part in the turbulent events of the time, but incurred the enmity of ᶜOthmān II ([*q.v.*], ruled 1027/1618-1031/1622) for having procured the accession of Muṣṭafā I upon the death of Aḥmed I in 1026/1617. This enmity, increased by Esᶜad Efendi's refusal to issue a *fatwā* sanctioning the execution of ᶜOthmān's brother Meḥemmed, was not allayed by the Sultan's marrying Esᶜad Efendi's daughter; ᶜOthmān took the disposition of theological appointments from the *Shaykh al-Islām* and gave it to his *khodja* ᶜÖmer Efendi. When in 1031/1622 ᶜOthmān proposed to make the Pilgrimage, Esᶜad Efendi declared that it was not obligatory on the Sultan to do so; and on the outbreak of the Janissary mutiny that culminated in the Sultan's murder issued a *fatwā* condemning the Palace-favourites against whom the mutineers had risen. He protested, however, against the recognition of Muṣṭafā I as sultan while ᶜOthmān was still alive, and by abstaining from attending ᶜOthmān's funeral was deemed to have resigned office. He was re-appointed *Shaykh al-Islām* in Dhu'l-Ḥidjdja 1032/October 1623, but soon fell out with his supporter Kemānkesh ᶜAlī Pasha, the Grand Vizier. He died in office, on 14 Shaᶜbān 1034/22 May 1625, and was buried at Eyyūb beside his father.

Esᶜad Efendi is the author of a translation of the *Gulistān* of Saᶜdī, entitled *Gül-i khandān* (printed Istanbul, n.d.), a Persian *dīwān* (Bağdatlı Ismail Paşa, *Keşf-el-zunun zeyli*, Istanbul 1945, i, 489, and other works (for details see *IA*).

Bibliography: ᶜAṭāʾī, *Dhayl al-Shaḳāʾiḳ*, Istanbul 1268, 690-2; Solaḳ-zāde, *Taʾrīkh*, Istanbul 1297, 705 ff., 719, 737 ff.; Pečewī, *Taʾrīkh*, Istanbul 1283, ii, 346, 356 ff., 370; Naᶜīmā, *Taʾrīkh*, Istanbul 1280, ii, 214, 232, 294; Kātib Čelebi, *Fedhleke*, Istanbul 1287, ii, 12 ff.; Ḳara Čelebizāde ᶜAbd al-ᶜAzīz, *Rawḍat al-abrār*, Bulak 1248, 481, 529, 541; the *tedhkires* of Ḳïnalï-zāde Ḥasan Čelebi and Riyāḍī (in MS) and of Riḍā, Istanbul 1316, 10; Ḥüseyn Aywānsarāyī, *Ḥadīḳat al-djawāmi*ᶜ, Istanbul 1281, 271 ff.; Müstaḳīm-zāde, *Tuḥfe-i khaṭṭāṭīn*, Istanbul 1928, 445; ᶜ*Ilmiyye sālnāmesi*, Istanbul 1334, 437; *IA*, s.v. (of which the above is an abridgement). (M. MÜNİR AKTEPE)

ESᶜAD EFENDI, MEḤMED (1096/1685-1166/1753), Ottoman *Shaykh al-Islām*, son of the *Shaykh al-Islām* Abū Isḥāḳ Ismāᶜīl Efendi and brother of the *Shaykh al-Islām* Isḥāḳ Efendi, after holding various posts as *müderris* was appointed *ḳāḍī* of Selānik and later (Muḥarram 1147/June 1734) of Mecca. As *ḳāḍī* of the army from 1150/1737 he distinguished himself in the operations against Austria and was one of the Ottoman negotiators of the Treaty of Belgrade. Appointed *ḳāḍī*ᶜ*asker* of Rūmeli for two short periods from Muḥarram 1157/March 1744 and Shawwāl 1159/October 1746, on 24 Radjab 1161/20 July 1748 he became *Shaykh al-Islām*, but was dismissed little more than a year later and banished, first to Sinop and then to Gelibolu. Pardoned in Rabīᶜ II 1165/March 1752, he returned to Istanbul but died the next year (10 Shawwāl 1166/9 August 1753).

Esᶜad Efendi's son Sherīf Efendi twice held office as *Shaykh al-Islām*, and the poetess Fiṭnat [*q.v.*] was his daughter. He himself was a minor poet and a distinguished musician. His best-known works are (1) *Lahdjat al-lughāt*, a dictionary of Turkish (printed Istanbul 1216), and (2) *Aṭrab al-āthār fī tadhkirat* ᶜ*urafā*ʾ *al-adwār* (also called *Tedhkire-i khᵂānendegān*), containing the biographies of 100 musicians (poor edition in *Mekteb*, 3rd year, Istanbul 1311, nos. 1-7 and 10). For details of his other works (poems, *tafsīr*) see *IA*.

Bibliography: Sālim, *Tedhkire*, Istanbul 1315, 72-6; Wāṣif, *Taʾrīkh*, Istanbul 1219, i, 17; Sāmī-Shākir-Ṣubḥī, *Taʾrīkh*, Istanbul 1198, 53b, 121b, 160b, 187a, 201b; ᶜIzzī, *Taʾrīkh*, Istanbul 1199, 3b, 154b, 175b, 206a, 262a; Aḥmed Rifᶜat, *Dawḥat al-mashāʾikh*, Istanbul (lith., n.d.), 86; Sadeddin Nüzhet Ergun, *Türk şairleri*, iii, 1329 ff.; Bursalï Meḥmed Ṭāhir, ᶜ*Othmānlï müʾellifleri*, i, 238-9; *IA*, s.v. (of which the above is an abridgement).

(M. CAVİD BAYSUN)

ESᶜAD EFENDI, MEḤMED (1119/1707-1192/1778), Ottoman *Shaykh al-Islām*, was the son of the *Shaykh al-Islām* Waṣṣāf ᶜAbd Allāh Efendi (in office 1168/1755). After rising to be *ḳāḍī* of Galata (1163/1749-50), he was long out of office because of the influence of his father's opponents. He became *ḳāḍī*ᶜ*asker* of Anadolu in 1182/1768 and of Rūmeli in 1186/1773. Appointed *Shaykh al-Islām* in Shawwāl 1190/December 1776, ill-health brought about his dismissal in Djumādā II 1192/July 1778, and he died a few days later.

Bibliography: Wāṣif, *Ḥaḳā'iḳ al-akhbār*, Istanbul 1219, i, 199; Djewdet, *Ta'rīkh*, Istanbul 1309, ii, 48, 100; Müstaḳīm-zāde, *Dawḥa-i mashā'ikh-i kibār* (MS); idem, *Tuḥfe-i khaṭṭāṭīn*, Istanbul 1928, 711; Aḥmed Rif'at, *Dawḥat al-mashā'ikh*, Istanbul (lith., n.d.), 98, 106; *'Ilmiyye sālnāmesi*, Istanbul 1334, 545-7; *IA*, s.v. (of which the above is an abridgement). (M. MÜNİR AKTEPE)

ES'AD EFENDI, ṢAḤḤĀFLAR-SHEYKHI-ZĀDE SEYYID **MEḤMED** (1204/1789-1264/1848), Ottoman official historiographer (*waḳ'a-nüwis*) and scholar, was left in straitened circumstances by his father's accidental death (December 1804) while on his way to take up the duties of *ḳāḍī* of Medina. After holding various clerical posts, in Ṣafar 1241/October 1825 he succeeded Shānī-zāde 'Atā'ullāh Efendi [*q.v.*] as *waḳ'a-nüwīs*, a post he held until his death. His work *Üss-i ẓafer* attracted the favour of Maḥmūd II: he was *ḳāḍī* of the army in 1828, then *ḳāḍī* of Üsküdar, and was appointed editor of the official gazette *Taḳwīm al-waḳā'i'* (see art. DJARĪDA, col. 465b) when it first appeared in 1247/1831. In September 1834 he was appointed *ḳāḍī* of Istanbul, and in 1835-6 went as special envoy to Persia, to congratulate Muḥammad Shāh on his accession. A long illness interrupted his career, but after the *Tanẓīmāt* [*q.v.*] he was for two years a member of the *Medjlis-i aḥkām-i 'adliyye* (Council for Judicial Ordinances), on 6 August 1841 he was appointed *Naḳīb al-ashrāf*, and from 30 May 1843 to 13 October 1844 he was *ḳāḍī'asker* of Rūmeli. In 1845 he was a member of the commission set up to reform primary education, and in 1846 became a member of the Council for Education (*Medjlis-i ma'ārif-i 'umūmiyye*); appointed its president on 1st January 1848, he died almost immediately afterwards (3 Ṣafar 1264/10 January 1848) and was buried in the garden of the library he had founded in the Yerebatan quarter of Istanbul.

His collection of books, over 4000 in number (3719 of them manuscripts), he deposited in a library which he endowed in 1262/1846: now housed in the Süleymaniye Public Library, they remain one of the most important collections in Turkey. His principal works are: (1) his official history (unpublished) in two volumes, covering the events of the years 1237-41/1821-6: it begins as a continuation of the work of his predecessor as *waḳ'a-nüwīs*, and his drafts for later years were used by his successor, Luṭfī Efendi [*q.v.*] (for the MSS see Babinger, 355; *Istanbul kütüpaneleri tarih-coğrafya yazmaları katalogları*, i/2, Istanbul 1944, 174-6; *IA*, iv, 364b); (2) *Üss-i ẓafer* (chronogram for 1241), an account of the suppression of the Janissaries (the so-called *Waḳ'a-i khayriyye*, see art. YENI ČERI) in 1241/1826; MS Esad Ef. 2071 is said to be the autograph; twice printed in Turkish (Istanbul 1243, 1293), it was translated into French (A. P. Caussin de Perceval, *Précis historique de la destruction . . .*, Paris 1833), Greek, and in part into Russian; (3) *Teshrīfāt-i ḳadīme*, on the court-ceremonial and protocol of the Empire (edition: Istanbul [1287]); (4) *Zībā-i tawārīkh*, an uncompleted translation of the *Mir'āt al-adwār*, in Persian, of Lārī [*q.v.*] (autograph draft: MS Esad Ef. 2410); (5) *Sefer-nāme-i khayr* (chronogram for 1247), an account of Maḥmūd II's tour of Eastern Thrace (autograph: Istanbul, Eski Eserler Müzesi library, MS Recaizade Ekrem 157); (6) *Āyāt al-khayr*, on Maḥmūd II's tour of the Danube province in 1253; (7) *Bahče-i ṣafā-endūz* (chronogram for 1351), a *tedhkire* of poets living between 1135/1723 and 1251/1836 (autograph draft: MS Esad Ef./Esad Arif Bey 4040); (8) *Munsha'āt*: two autograph notebooks (MSS Esad Ef. 3847, 3851) contain letters etc. written on various occasions; (9) *Shāhid al-mu'arrikhīn* (chronogram for 1247), a *tedhkire* of writers of chronograms (autograph: Fatih-Millet library, MSS Ali Emiri, tarih, 362-3). Es'ad Efendi left also a large number of poems and various *risāle*s (for details see *IA*, and Bursalî Meḥmed Ṭāhir, *'Othmānlî mü'ellifleri*, iii, 24-6).

Bibliography: Shānī-zāde 'Aṭā'ullāh, *Ta'rīkh*, Istanbul 1292, iv; Djewdet, *Ta'rīkh*, Istanbul 1309, i and xii; Aḥmed Luṭfī, *Ta'rīkh*, Istanbul 1290-1306, i-vii; *Ta'rīkh-i Luṭfī*, viii, ed. 'Abd al-Raḥmān Sheref, Istanbul 1328, Rif'at, *Dawḥat al-nuḳabā'*, Istanbul 1283, 57 ff.; Faṭīn, *Tedhkire*, Istanbul 1271, 13; Djemāl al-Dīn, *Āyīne-i ẓurefā*, Istanbul 1314, 79 ff.; Ibnülemīn Maḥmūd Kemāl, *Son 'aṣîr türk shā'irleri*, Istanbul 1314, ii, 321 ff.; Sadeddin Nüzhet Ergun, *Türk şairleri*, Istanbul 1944, iii, 1335; *Taḳwīm-i waḳā'i'*, years 1247-64; Babinger, 354-5; U. Heyd, *The Ottoman 'ulemā and westernization in the time of Selīm III and Maḥmūd II*, in *Scripta Hierosolymitana*, ix, *Studies in Islamic history and civilization*, Jerusalem 1961, 63 ff.; *IA*, s.v. (of which the above is an abridgement).
(M. MÜNİR AKTEPE)

ESĀME [see YENI ČERI].

ESCHATOLOGY [see ḲIYĀMA].

ESHĀM [see ASHĀM].

ESHKINDJI, also *eshkündji*, means in Turkish 'one who rushes, goes on an expedition' (*eshkin* is defined by Maḥmūd Kāshgharī [*Dīwān lughāt al-Türk*, i, 100; = Besim Atalay's T. tr., i, 109] as 'long journey', and *eshkindji* as 'galloping courier'; cf. also *Tanıklariyle tarama sözlüğü*, ed. Türk Dil Kurumu, i-iv, s.v.; the verb *eshmek*, to go on an expedition, was later replaced in Ottoman Turkish by *mülāzemet*, Ar. *mulāzama*).

As a term in the Ottoman army *eshkindji* meant in general a soldier who joined the army on an expedition. Thus *eshkindji* timariots (see TĪMĀR) who joined the army were distinguished from *ḳal'a-eri* or *mustaḥfiẓ*, those who stayed in the fortresses as garrison (cf. *Sûret-i Defter-i Sancak-i Arvanid*, ed. H. Inalcık, Ankara 1954, 108, 109).

As a special term *eshkindji* designated auxiliary soldiers whose expenses were provided by the people of *re'āyā* [*q.v.*] status as against *djebelü* equipped by the *'askarī* [*q.v.*]. The obligation was in return for the tax exemptions made on agricultural lands which were considered in principle as under state proprietorship (cf. H. Inalcık, *Stefan Duşan'dan Osmanlı imparatorluğuna*, in *Fuat Köprülü Armağanı*, Istanbul 1953, 134, note 121). In the organizations of *yürük*, *djānbāz*, *yaya*, *müsellem*, *Tatar* and the like, each group of 10, 24, 25, or 30 persons was to furnish the expenses of an *eshkindji* each year. Three or five among them were appointed *eshkindji*s, and the rest *yamaḳ*s, assistants. Each year an *eshkindji* collected in turn, *be-newbet*, a certain sum called *khardjlîḳ* (usually 50 akče per person)from the *yamaḳ*s and joined the Sultan's army on an expedition (under Bāyezīd II *khardjlîḳ* was collected only when an expedition occurred). In return the *eshkindji*s and the *yamaḳ*s were exempted from taxes and dues on their *čiftlik*s [*q.v.*] entirely or partly (cf. *Ḳānūnnāme Sultan Meḥmeds des Eroberers*, ed. Fr. Kraelitz, in *MOG*, i (1921-2), 25, 28; T. Gökbilgin, *Rumeli'de Yürükler, Tatarlar ve Evlâd-ı Fâtihân*, Istanbul 1957, 244-6). The *voynuḳ*s and *Eflaḳ*s can be considered also as *eshkindji* organizations (cf. H. Inalcık, *ibid.* 241). Even the *doghandjîs* [*q.v.*] in some areas, who were organized in the same manner, were to furnish *eshkindji*s.

Another category of *eshkindjis* was provided by the possessors of *wakfs* and *mulks*. Increasingly in need of new troops, Meḥemmed the Conqueror ordered in Ramaḍān 881/December 1476 that the *wakfs* and *mulks* of certain types were to furnish *eshkindjis* for the army (cf. *Fatih devrinde Karaman Eyâleti vakıfları fihristi*, ed. F. N. Uzluk, Ankara 1958, facsimile 3). The measure was applied extensively in the empire, especially in central and northern Anatolia, and resulted in the widespread discontent in the last years of his reign (cf. *IA*, s.v. Mehmed II; Ö. L. Barkan, *Malikâne-Divanî sistemi*, in *THITM*, ii (1932-9), 119-84). It was assumed that such *wakfs* and *mulks*, mostly of pre-Ottoman times, were valid only by the approval of the Ottoman Sultan. In most cases he did not confirm them, on the grounds that they did not meet the conditions required; he then made most of them state-owned lands granted as *tīmār* [*q.v.*] or else required their possessors, in return for the taxes and dues, to equip *eshkindjis* for the army. Such *wakfs* and *mulks* were known as *eshkindjilü*. Under Bāyezīd II, who followed a more tolerant policy, *tīmārs* of this kind too were made *eshkindjilü mulk*. But later records in the defters [see DAFTAR-I KHĀKĀNĪ] show that these were again made *tīmārs*.

An *eshkindji* of the Yürük organization was equipped with a lance, bow and arrows, a sword and a shield, and every ten *eshkindjis* had one horse for joint use and a tent (cf. *Ḳānūnnāme Sultan Mehmeds des Eroberers*, 28).

Eshkindjis from the different groups made up a large part of the Ottoman army in the 9th/15th century, especially under Meḥemmed II. But from the mid 10th/16th century, when the Ottoman army had to consist mainly of infantry with fire-arms, the *eshkindjis* and the various organizations to which they belonged lost their importance and gradually disappeared. (HALİL İNALCIK)

ESHREFOGHLU RŪMĪ [see SUPPLEMENT].

ESKI BABA [see BABA ESKI].

ESKI SARĀY [see SARĀY].

ESKISHEHIR (modern spelling Eskişehir), a town in the western part of Central Anatolia, 39° 47′ N., 30° 33′ E., altitude 792 m. (= 2,597ft.) (railway station) to 810 m. (= 2,657 ft.), on the river Porsuk, a tributary of the Sakarya; it is the capital of a *vilâyet* of 389,129 inhabitants, the district has 56,077, and the town itself 153,190 (all figures for 1960). Eskişehir is famous for its hot springs, and for the meerschaum found nearby (see Reinhardt, in *Pet. Mitt.* 1911, ii, 251 ff.); it is also important as a junction of the Istanbul—Ankara and Istanbul—Konya railways.

Eskişehir has replaced the ancient Dorylaion (Darūliyya of the Arabs), which was situated near the modern Shar-Üyük, 3 km. to the north. In Byzantine times, the wide plain of Dorylaion was the place where the emperor's armies assembled for their eastern campaigns against the Arabs and the Saldjūḳ Turks cf. Ibn Khurradādhbih, 109). In the year 89/708, al-ʿAbbās b. al-Walīd conquered Dorylaion (Ṭabarī, ii, 1197; cf. Theophanes, i, 376, ed. de Boer), and Ḥasan b. Ḳaḥṭaba advanced as far as this point in 162/778 (Ṭabarī, iii, 493; Theophanes, i, 452). Near Dorylaion, on 1 July 1097, the Crusaders won the battle enabling them to pass through the Rūm Saldjūḳ Empire (Konya), but the crusaders under Conrad III suffered such a defeat on 26 October 1147 that further passage through this territory was barred. In 1175 the emperor Manuel Comnenos fortified the town again, after it had been laid waste by the Saldjūḳids, and he drove away the nomadic Yürüks (Kinnamos, 294, 297; Niketas, 236 ff., 246); but only one year later (after the unsuccessful war against Ḳïlïdj Arslan II) he had to undertake to pull down the fortifications, and it was probably shortly after this that the town finally passed into Saldjūḳ possession.

In the 13th century, Ertoghrul settled in the area of Söğüt near Eskişehir, in the region of Sulṭān Üyügi (Sulṭān Önü) (Neshrī, ed. Unat and Köymen, i, 72). In the apocryphal document (*menshūr*) of ʿAlāʾ al-Dīn b. Farāmarz, of early Shawwāl 688/October 1289, in favour of his son ʿOthmān (Ferīdūn², i, 56), the region of Eskişehir was given to ʿOthmān as a *sandjaḳ* (cf. Leunclavius, *Hist. Mus.*, 125, 126 f.). The fortress of Ḳaradja-Ḥiṣār [*q.v.*] south-west of Eskişehir is considered the first Ottoman conquest (cf. Neshrī, 64).

Later on, Eskişehir became the chef-lieu of the *sandjaḳ* (*liwāʾ*) of Inönü in the *eyālet* of Anadolu, and a halt on the pilgrim route. In the 19th century, it became the capital of a *ḳaḍāʾ* in the *sandjaḳ* of Kütahya, *wilāyet* of Bursa, and according to Cuinet it had 19,023 inhabitants at the turn of this century. During the Greco-Turkish war of 1922, the town was almost completely destroyed, but it was rebuilt as an industrial centre after the war. It has the most important railway repair workshops in Turkey.

The Kurshunlu Djāmiʿ (921/1515) was erected by a certain Muṣṭafā Pasha, and is the most notable building of the town. Beside it there is an extensive *khān*, laid out in two parts (*khān* and *bedestan*). The ʿAlāʾ al-Dīn mosque, which dates from Saldjūḳ times, has been completely renovated; but on the base of its minaret there is an inscription by Djadja Beg of the year 666(?)/1268 (*RCEA*, xii, Cairo 1943, 131, no. 4596) which refers to its erection. In 1927 there was still a small bridge, which apparently dated from Saldjūḳ times, over the Sarı Su, which flows into the Porsuk. This bridge could, however, no longer be found in 1955. It is probable that it was removed when the industrial buildings were extended.

Bibliography: Pauly-Wissowa, v, 1577 f. (concerning Dorylaion); Ewliyā Čelebi, *Seyāḥat-nāme*, iii, 12; Kātib Čelebi, *Djihānnümā*, 641 f.; Meḥemmed Edīb, *Menāsik al-ḥadjdj*, 28 f.; Ch. Texier, *Asie Mineure*, 408 ff.; Sāmī Bey Fraschery, *Ḳāmūs al-aʿlām*, ii, 938; *IA*, s.v. (Besim Darkot), where further bibliography can be found.

J. H. MORDTMANN-[FR. TAESCHNER])

ESNE [see ISNĀ].

ESOTERICS [see ẒĀHIR].

ESPIONAGE [see DJĀSŪS].

ESSENCE [see DHĀT and DJAWHAR].

ESZÉK (ESSEG), until 1919 a town in Hungary (Slavonia) on the right bank of the Drave, not far from its junction with the Danube, and since 1919 in Yugoslavia. The name of the town is in Serbo-Croat Osijek, in Hungarian Eszék and in German Esseg; in Turkish it was written as اوسك (Ösek).

During the first decisive phase of the Turkish-Hungarian wars the town is mentioned for the first time in connexion with events relating to Turkish history. After the Turks had overrun Sirmium (Hung. Szerémség), the then commander of the Hungarian army, Paul Tomori, wanted to bring the Turks to a halt on the Drave. The forces of Sultan Süleymān, however, gained possession of Eszék easily, built a bridge over the Drave, crossed the river and advanced on Mohács (932/1526).

The passage over the Drave near Eszék was, for

a century and a half, an important halting-place for Turkish armies on the march into Hungary.

In the course of his later campaigns (1529, 1532, 1541, 1543) Sultan Süleymān, time and again, caused a bridge of boats to be built nearby (cf. J. Thúry, *Török Törtenetirók* [Turkish historians], i, 329, 331, 351 and ii, 103, 107). He had a permanent bridge erected over the Drave only on the occasion of his last campaign against Sigeth (Szigetvár) in 974/1566.

As we know from later accounts in particular, the permanent bridge over the Drave itself rested on boats, while its prolongation on the left bank of the Drave spanned a marshland some 8000 paces broad and was laid on piles (Ewliyā Čelebi, vi, 187). On both sides of the bridge there were parapets (*ḳorḳuluḳ*); in the middle, 'lay-bys', *i.e.* towers (*ḳaṣr*), had been constructed, so that here the pedestrian might rest without impeding the flow of traffic. There was room for two waggons side by side on the main road of the bridge. A horseman needed one and a half hours to cross the bridge. In western sources, too, the bridge at Eszék is mentioned as a remarkable piece of construction work. H. Ottendorff (Vienna, Heeres-archiv, Kartenabteilung K. VII, K. I) offers a description similar to the one given above. A portion of his travel narrative *From Buda to Belgrade in the year 1663* has been published in Hungarian translation (*Budáról Belgrádba 1663*, Pécs 1943). There is available a comprehensive study of the bridge: P. Z. Szabó, *Az eszéki hid* [The bridge of Eszék], Majorossy Imre-Múzeum értesítöje, Pécs 1941.

Bridgeheads were built on both banks of the river to protect the bridge, on the northern bank beyond the marshland near Dárda and on the southern bank not far from the Drave near Eszék. The defences at Dárda consisted only of palisades; the defences near Eszék were constructed of brick, but were, however, only weakly fortified. The Turks feared no attack on these defences, for they lay 200-300 km. inside the Ottoman frontiers. All the greater, therefore, was their surprise at the onslaught of Nicholas Zrínyi, the poet, who in the winter of 1664, avoiding the Turkish frontier fortresses, pushed forward as far as Eszék and on 1 February set the bridge in flames. It was, however, rebuilt by the Turks. The bridge at Eszék was once more burnt down in 1685 by General Lesley and in 1687 was seized definitively from the Turks by the Imperialists.

From the diffuse information of Ewliyā Čelebi (vi, 178 ff.) the following data can be gathered: Ösek, a voyvodalïḳ in the sandjaḳ of Požega, a *ḳaḍā* with a stipend of 150 aḳče. The defences consist of an inner and an outer fortress (*ič ḳalʿa* and *orta ḥiṣār*); outside the outer fortifications lies the town (*varosh*). Ewliyā Čelebi does not mention the fortress as being an especially strong one; on the other hand he writes appreciatively of the religious buildings (above all the *djāmiʿ*s of Ḳāsim Pasha and Muṣṭafā Pasha) and of the *tekke* and the other *khayrāt* (*medrese, sebīl,* and *ḥamām*). He draws particular attention to the much frequented trade fair (*panayir*) held once a year and to the covered market built by Ibrāhīm Pasha of Kanizsa. The speech of the inhabitants, according to Ewliyā Čelebi, was Hungarian, but according to Ottendorff it was Turkish. (L. Fekete)

ESZTERGOM (Gran), a fortress town in Hungary situated on the right bank of the Danube about 80 km. to the north-east of Budapest, in the Turkish period the name and chief town of a sandjaḳ.

The place-name Esztergom is said to be of Frankish origin (osterringun = eastern fortress). The site, named Gran in German, is called Strigonium in Latin, Ostrihom in Slovenian and Esztergom or Esztergon in Hungarian, while in Turkish such forms as استرغون , اوسترغون , اوسترغوم etc. are known.

Gran, in the time of the Arpad dynasty, was on a number of occasions the royal residence—here the founder of the Hungarian Kingdom, Stephen I (St. Stephen), was born—and it was at the same time the seat of the Archbishop of Hungary (the head of the ten bishoprics established by Stephen I) and from about 1200 A.D. his own exclusive possession.

After the conquest of Buda (948/1541) Gran entered the pages of Turkish history. In order to safeguard Buda, now a frontier fortress, Sultan Süleymān ordered his forces to conquer Gran, which fell into Turkish hands after a siege lasting barely two weeks (950/1543). Detailed Turkish sources on this siege are Djalālzāde Muṣṭafā (translated, from the Vienna Ms., by J. Thúry in *Török Történetirók* [Turkish Historians], Budapest 1896, ii, 244 ff.) and Sinān Čawush (*ibid.*, ii, 325 ff.).

A fruitless attempt was made in 1002/1594 to wrest Gran from the Turks (in this fighting there fell, on the Hungarian side, the distinguished Hungarian lyric poet B. Balassi). The assault on Gran in 1003/1595 was, however, successful; after the food and water of the defenders of the fortress had become exhausted, the Turkish garrison mutinied and the commander of the besieging troops, Nicholas Pálffy (called Miḳlōsh [Hung. Miklós] in Ewliyā Čelebi, vi, 258) was able to gain possession of the fortress by capitulation. The Turks tried on several occasions to win back the fortress; eventually the Grand Vizier Lālā Meḥemmed Pasha, who ten years before "had given over the fortress into the keeping of Miḳlōsh" (Ewliyā Čelebi, vi, 259), recovered it in 1605, likewise by capitulation. The history of these sieges is recorded, on the Turkish side, in Pečewī (ii, 175 ff. and 301 ff.), who was present on both occasions at the negotiations over the two-fold surrender of the fortress, and—leaving out of account some statements of little value—in Ewliyā Čelebi (vi, 257 ff.); and on the Hungarian side, in M. Istvánffy (*Historiarum de Rebus Ungaricis libri xxxiv*, Cologne 1622). More modern studies by J. Thúry and G. Gömöry are in *Hadtörténelmi Közlemények* [Communications on Military History], 1891 and 1892.

Thereafter the Turks remained until 1094/1683 undisturbed in their possession of the fortress. Gran, in the autumn of 1683, passed without serious fighting and by agreement into the hands of the Imperialists; Turkish attempts to reconquer it were unsuccessful. Gran, *i.e.* Esztergom, has in Turkish a proverbial fame (the newspaper *Yeni Sabah*, on 19 April 1956, carried on the front page a picture of a fortress with the superscription "Estergon kalesi" and near it, in a caption, the words referring to the still firmly established Menderes régime: Menderes Estergon kalesidir—"Menderes is [strong as] the fortress of Estergon"), but it is difficult to state on what events connected with Gran this fame is based.

The *muḳāṭaʿa* defters of Gran for some ten years between the dates 973/1565 and 991/1582 are extant (Vienna, Flügel Catalogue, no. 1359); in them are recorded the following topographical names relating to the town of Gran: Ḳalʿa-i Bālā, Ḳalʿa-i Zīr, Iskele-i Bālā, Iskele-i Zīr, Īlīdja, Varosh-i Kebīr and Varosh-i Ṣaghīr (or Varosh-i Buzurg and Varosh-i Kūček); these defters, moreover, record the personnel of three Muslim mosques in the upper fortress, in the main town and in the suburb Djigerdelen as receiving salaries from the state. Ewliyā Čelebi (vi, 271-2), in connexion with his visit to Gran in 1074/1663, offers information about several Muslim places of worship and also tells us in some cases who founded them.

To the fortress of Gran belonged, on the left bank of the Danube, the bridge-head of Djigerdelen, Djigerdelen Parkani ("Liver-piercer", "Liver-piercing Fort"—whence the later Hungarian name of the place: Párkány), the point of departure for the subsequent geographical extension of this sandjaḳ.

According to Ewliyā Čelebi (vi, 273) it was Lālā Meḥemmed Pasha who ordered the building of the outer defence work of Gran on the right bank of the Danube, *i.e.*, of the mountain fort of Szenttamás; he is also said to have given to it the name of Tepedelen, "Head-piercer" (a locality of this name existed in Albania: cf. Tepedelenli ʿAlī Pasha).

There is extant also a Turkish survey of the houses in Gran, dating from about 1570 (Vienna, Krafft Catalogue, ccxc). In this survey Muslims and, in lesser number, Orthodox (Pravoslav) are shown as house-holders; there are no Hungarians amongst them. It seems that Hungarians, at that time, cannot have been living in Gran.

The sandjaḳ of Estergom was established after the conquest of the fortress in 950/1543. At first it consisted essentially of some 30 villages on the right bank of the Danube, but, growing outward from the bridge-head of Djigerdelen on the left bank of the river, it became extended later, thanks to the unwearying expansionist activities of the Sandjaḳ Begs, far to the west and north, so that the chief town of the sandjaḳ, Gran, came to be situated on the inner border of the actual administrative area (other examples exist in Hungary of such an expansion, as, for example, the sandjaḳs of Szolnok (Ṣolnoḳ), Istulni Belghrad and Szigetvár (Sigeth), in each of which the chief place, after which the sandjaḳ was named, found itself eventually on the inner border of the actual area administered from it). The "financial frontier" and territorial administration thus brought into being did not receive recognition from the Austrians, now growing stronger, or from the Hungarian kingdom, with the result that numerous villages paid taxes to two masters—a situation which, from the end of the 16th century, gave occasion for countless disputes.

Several tax registers (*taḥrīr*) of the sandjaḳ are preserved at Istanbul and one also, dating from 1570, at Berlin (Berlin, Prussian State Library, Pet. II, Nachtr. I). The tax register preserved at Berlin is available in Hungarian (L. Fekete, *Az Esztergomi szandzsák 1570. évi adóösszeírása* [The tax register of the sandjaḳ of Gran for 1570], Budapest 1943). According to this register there belonged to the sandjaḳ 12 "varosh", *i.e.*, towns, 365 villages (*ḳarye*) and 93 abandoned farms, *i.e.*, puszta (*mezraʿa*) with a total of 4206 households (*khāne*). A number of the villages paid taxes to two masters and so it came about that Nikolaus Oláh, the Archbishop of Gran, caused to be built, around 1580 and near the locality known as Nyárhid, with a view to the hindering of the further advance of the Turks, a fortress (Újvár, later Érsekújvár, Germ. Neuhäusel), the site of which lay more or less in the centre of the Turkish sandjaḳ. After the capture of Neuhäusel by the Turks in 1074/1663 most of the villages of the sandjaḳ of Gran were incorporated in the then established Beglerbeglik of Neuhäusel/Újvár. With the definitive reconquest of Gran by the Imperialists in 1093/1683 the sandjaḳ of Gran fell into dissolution.

(L. Fekete)

ETAWAH [see ITĀWA].

ETERNITY [see ABAD].

ETERNITY OF THE WORLD [see ABAD, ḲIDAM].

ETHICS [see AKHLĀḲ].

ETHIOPIA [see AL-ḤABASH].

ET-MEYDANI [see ISTANBUL].

EUCLID [see UḲLĪDISH].

EULOGY [see MADĪḤ].

EUNUCH [see KHĀDIM, KHAṢĪ, ḲIZLAR AGHASİ].

EUPHRATES [see AL-FURĀT].

EUTYCHIUS [see SAʿĪD B. BIṬRĪḲ].

EVE [see ḤAWWĀʾ].

EVIDENCE [see BAYYINA].

EVORA [see YĀBURA].

EWLIYĀ ČELEBI B. DERWĪSH MEḤMED ẒILLĪ, b. 10 Muḥarram 1020/25 March 1611 in the Unkapan quarter of Istanbul, seems to have died not before the last third of 1095/1684 (cf. *WZKM*, li (1948-52), 226, Anm. 137, and *TM*, xii (1955), 261). For a period of almost forty years (from 1050/1640, perhaps even earlier, to 1087/1676), after he had already started his wanderings in Istanbul in the year 1040/1630-1, he described a series of long journeys within the Ottoman Empire and in the neighbouring lands, undertaken (or allegedly undertaken) sometimes as a private individual, sometimes in an official capacity, either when taken along in the retinue of the Ottoman dignitaries or on his own responsibility, in his work of ten parts generally known as the *Seyāḥatnāme* ("Travels") or according to the Vienna Ms (Flügel, no. 1281) as the *Taʾrīkh-i Seyyāḥ* ("Traveller's chronicle"). For his life and experiences we are dependent solely on his own accounts in the *Seyāḥatnāme*, which are not always trustworthy (see below). His personal name is unknown; Ewliyā is his pen-name, which he adopted in veneration of his teacher the court-*imām* Ewliyā Meḥmed Efendi. His father was the chief jeweller to the court (*Sarāy-i ʿāmire bashḳuyumdjusu, sar-zargarān*), Derwīsh Meḥmed Ẓillī (cf. i, 218 [here and below the Istanbul edition is referred to; see below]), who died Djumādā II 1058/June-July 1648 (cf. ii, 458), according to Ewliyā's assertion aged 117 (lunar) years; he is said to have taken part in the (last) campaigns of the sultan Süleymān Ḳānūnī and to have served and undertaken works of craftsmanship for the later sultans also (cf. i, 218; iv, 102; vi, 267; x, 298). Ewliyā's father must have been a merry and also a poetically talented man, since on this account he was allowed to enjoy the favour of the court. The family tree which Ewliyā claims on his father's side is contradictory and improbable (cf. i, 424-5; iii, 444; vi, 226; x, 915). His paternal ancestors probably came from Kütahya; the family seems to have removed to Istanbul after the conquest of Constantinople in 857/1453, but to have retained the house in Kütahya and to have had also a house in Bursa, in the Ine Bey quarter, and at Manisa, an estate in Sandıklı, four shops in the Unkapan quarter of Istanbul as well as two houses there, and a vineyard in Kadıköy near Istanbul (cf. i, 471; vi, 146; ix, 81). This gives some idea of Ewliyā's economic circumstances, which—in addition to his shrewdness in making himself useful to the dignitaries—made it possible for him to follow his Wanderlust. Ewliyā's mother was from the Caucasus; she came to the *sarāy* in the time of Sultan Aḥmed I (1012-26/1603-17), and was there married to the court jeweller, Ewliyā's father. Ewliyā says that his mother was related to Melek Aḥmed Pasha (cf. Meḥmed Thüreyyā, *Sidjill-i ʿOthmānī*, iv, 509), who was indeed himself of Caucasian origin. Ewliyā's accounts of the degree of this relationship are, however, contradictory; either Ewliyā's and Melek Aḥmed Pasha's mothers were sisters, or Ewliyā's mother was the daughter of Melek Aḥmed Pasha's mother's sister. Ewliyā was also related on his mother's side, according to his story, to Defterdārzāde Meḥmed Pasha (cf. *Sidjill-i ʿOthmānī*, iv, 168) and to Ibshīr Muṣṭafā Pasha (cf. ibid., i, 166; İ. H. Uzunçarşılı, *Osmanlı tarihi*, Ankara 1947 ff., iii/2, 408; cf. *Seyāḥatnāme*, ii, 370, 453; v, 168). Ewliyā declares that he had also one brother and one sister (cf. ix, 81).—After the end of his elementary schooling Ewliyā was for seven years a pupil at the *medrese* of the *Shaykh al-Islām* Ḥāmid Efendi in Istanbul, and attended a Ḳurʾān school for eleven years where he was trained as a Ḳurʾān reciter (cf. i, 360); he also learnt many manual skills from his father (cf. i, 243, 404; ii, 467; vi, 381). In the *laylat al-ḳadr* of the year 1045/1636 Ewliyā distinguished himself by an especially good recitation of the Ḳurʾān, and through this fortunate circumstance he was presented by the then *silīḥdār* Melek Aḥmed Agha to Sultan Murād IV, on whose command he was admitted to the palace, where he received a more extensive training in calligraphy, music, Arabic grammar, and *tadjwīd*. He was often summoned to the Sultan's presence on account of his lively disposition, his common-sense, and his skill as a narrator. Shortly before Murād IV's expedition to Baghdād (1048/1638) Ewliyā was appointed a *sipāhī* of the Porte (cf. i, 258).

In his ten-volume *Seyāḥatnāme* Ewliyā describes in vol. i: the capital city of Istanbul and its environs; in ii: Bursa, İzmid, Batum, Trabzon, Abkhāzia, Crete, Erzurum, Ādharbāydjān, Georgia, etc.; in iii: Damascus, Syria, Palestine, Urūmiyya, Sivas, Kurdistān, Armenia, Rumelia (Bulgaria, Dobrudja), etc.; in iv: Van, Tabriz, Baghdad, Baṣra, etc.; in v: Van, Baṣra, Oczakov, Hungary, Russia, Anatolia, Bursa, the Dardanelles, Adrianople, Moldavia, Transylvania, Bosnia, Dalmatia, Sofia; in vi: Transylvania, Albania, Hungary, Ujvár (Neuhäusel. Here is interpolated the expedition, which is unquestionably only fantasy on Ewliyā's part, of 10,000 Tatars through Austria, Germany and Holland, to the North Sea), Belgrade, Herzegovina, Ragusa (Dubrovnik), Montenegro, Kanizsa, Croatia; in vii: Hungary, Buda, Erlau (here is also described the journey to Vienna, which he undertook in the retinue of the embassy of Ḳara Meḥmed Pasha in 1075/1665, and his alleged residence in Vienna; here also a fictitious journey of Ewliyā's in the regions of the "country of the seven kings"—perhaps the seven electorates are meant here—which, however, is not described in greater detail: blank passage in text), Temesvár (Banat, Rum. Timişoara), Transylvania, Wallachia, Moldavia, the Crimea, Ḳazaḳ, South Russia, the Caucasus, Dāghestān, Azaḳ; in viii: Azaḳ, Kafa, Bāghčesarāy (Crimea), Istanbul, Crete, Macedonia, Greece, Athens, the Dodecanese, Peloponnesus, Albania, Valona, Elbaşan, Ochrida, Adrianople, Istanbul; in ix: (Pilgrimage to Mecca) south-west Anatolia, Smyrna, Ephesus, Rhodes, south Anatolia, Syria, Aleppo, Damascus, Medina, Mecca, Suez; in x: Egypt (with historical excursus), Cairo, Upper Egypt, Sudan, Abyssinia.

Ewliyā seems to have stayed for eight or nine years in Egypt, where he perhaps also completed the last, tenth, part of the *Seyāḥatnāme*. The last date he mentions is 1 Djumādā I 1087/12 July 1676, although he knows of events which took place in 1093/1682 (cf. x, 1048) and later (cf. biographical details discussed above). He seems to have spent the last year of his life in Istanbul editing his book, which had probably been written down piecemeal at various times and required a final redaction which Ewliyā, as the mss show, never fully accomplished.

Ewliyā Čelebi is an imaginative writer with a marked penchant for the wonderful and the adventurous. He prefers legend to bare historical fact, indulges freely in exaggeration, and at times does not eschew bragging or anecdotes designed for comic effect. His *Seyāḥatnāme* thus appears in the first place as a work of 17th century light literature, which satisfied the need of the Turkish intellectuals of his time for entertainment and instruction, and which, thanks to the use at times of a traditional Turkish narrative technique and of the colloquial Turkish of the 17th century, with occasional borrowings of phrases and turns of expression from the ornate style, was intelligible to a wide circle; this obvious purpose of the work explains Ewliyā's lack of concern for historical truth. He also occasionally describes journeys which he himself manifestly cannot have undertaken. His literary ambition often drives him to record things and occurrences as though he had seen or experienced them himself, whereas a close examination reveals that he knows of them only from hearsay or that he is indebted to literary sources which he does not cite.

In spite of these reservations, the *Seyāḥatnāme* offers a wealth of information on cultural history, folklore and geography, which will be especially valuable once the philological groundwork is done and the necessary criticism of content applied. The charm of the work lies not least in the fact that it reflects the mental approach of the 17th century Ottoman Turkish intellectuals in their attitudes to the non-Muslim Occident, and throws some light on the administration and internal organization of the Ottoman empire of that time.

Cavid Baysun, to whom we owe the most comprehensive study to date of Ewliyā Čelebi's life and work (see below), has declared that one of the most pressing needs is the preparation of a new critical edition of the *Seyāḥatnāme*, and that only this would make possible the effective use of the information that it contains. Baysun's suggestions have been in part taken up in the admirable detailed researches of Meşkûre Eren (see below), limited to the first book of the *Seyāḥatnāme*. On the basis of her findings from the mss, Dr. Eren demonstrates Ewliyā's method of working, and points to the many blank and unfinished passages in the *Seyāḥatnāme*, which suggest that the author intended to expand the work further and to give it a final redaction which he did not however complete; she also proves that Ewliyā made abundant use of literary sources for his descriptions and even for the chronograms which he quotes. Dr. Eren classifies these literary sources (all with reference to book i of the *Seyāḥatnāme*) as: (1) those named and used by Ewliyā; (2) those which Ewliyā has used but not cited. In this group fall: ʿĀlī, *Kunh al-akhbār* (cf. Babinger, *GOW*, 126 ff.); Ibrāhīm Pečewī, *Taʾrīkh* (cf. Babinger, 192 ff.); Newʿīzāde ʿAṭāʾī, *Ḥadāʾiḳ al-ḥaḳāʾiḳ fī takmilat al-Shaḳāʾiḳ* (cf. Babinger, 171 ff.); Sāʿī, *Tadhkirat al-bunyān* (cf. Babinger, 137 ff.); ʿAwfī, *Djawāmiʿ al-ḥikāyāt*, in the Turkish translation of Djelālzāde Ṣāliḥ (cf. Ms Istanbul

Topkapısaray, Revan Köşkü no. 1085, 693a); Başīrī, *Laṭā'if* (quoted in the *Tedhkire* of Ḳînalîzāde Ḥasan Čelebi, Ms Istanbul, Üniversite Kütüphanesi, T.Y. 2525, 74a); and chronogram verses from various poets cited by Eren (100-14); (3) those which Ewliyā has cited, but not used.

Mss of the *Seyāḥatnāme.*

Istanbul: Pertev Paşa collection nos. 458-62; Topkapısaray, Bağdat Köşkü nos. 300-4; Beşir Ağa nos. 448-52 (copy of 1158 [= 1745]). These mss include all ten books of the work. Also Topkapısaray, Bağdat Köşkü nos. 304 (i, ii), 305 (iii, iv), 306 (ix), 307 (v), 308 (vii, viii); Topkapısaray, Revan Köşkü nos. 366/1457-369/1460 (vi, vii, viii, ix); Hamidiye no. 963 (x); Halis Efendi no. 2750 (i), ibid. 2750 mükerrer (iii, iv); Üniversite Kütüphanesi no. 2371 (i, copy of 1170 [= 1756-7]), 5939 (i, ii, copy of 1155 [= 1742-3]); Yıldız, Tarih Kısmı, no. 48 (x). Vienna: Nationalbibliothek H.O. 193 (iv), cf. G. Flügel, *Die arabischen, persischen und türkischen Handschriften der kaiserlich-königlichen Hofbibliothek zu Wien*, Vienna 1865-7, ii, 433, no. 1281; Cod. mixt 1382 (i). London: Royal Asiatic Society nos. 22-3 (i, ii, iii, iv). Manchester: Univ. Libr., Lindsay collection no. 142 (iii, iv). Basle: R. Tschudi collection (i, ii, iii). Munich: Bayr. Staatsbibliothek (?), Th. Menzel collection (i, ii, iii, iv, v).

Printed versions of the *Seyāḥatnāme.*

Poor edition of extracts from Bk. i, with foreword, under the title of *Müntekhabāt-i Ewliyā Čelebi*, Istanbul 1258 (150 pp.), 1262 (143 pp.); Būlāḳ 1264 (140 pp.); Istanbul, ca. 1890 (104 pp., quarto). Integral edition: i-vi, Istanbul 1314-8 (Iḳdām Press); i-vi under the editorship of Aḥmed Djewdet and Nedjīb ʿĀṣim, vi with Karácson also. The value of this edition is much diminished by misprints, omissions and censored passages. Books vii and viii appeared as a publication of the Türk Ta'rīkh Endjümeni, utilizing several mss, ed. Kilisli Rifʿat Bilge, Istanbul 1928 (Dewlet and Orkhāniyye Presses). Books ix, Istanbul 1935 (Devlet Matbaası), and x, Istanbul 1938 (Devlet Matbaası) were published by the Turkish Ministry of Education, but unfortunately are in the new official Turkish orthography and are hence of limited use. A critical scholarly edition of the complete *Seyāḥatnāme*, in the original Arabic script, of course, is an urgent necessity.

Bibliography (arranged chronologically): Hammer-Purgstall, *Staatsverfassung*, i, 455-70 (detailed table of contents of books i-iv); idem, *Narrative of travels in Europe, Asia and Africa by Ewliya Efendi*, London 1834-50 (trans. of books i and ii; M. Bittner, *Der Kurdengau Uschnûje und die Stadt Urûmîje*, Vienna 1895; A. Šopov, *Evlija Čelebi*, in *Periodičesko spisanie na Bŭlgarskoto Knižovno Družestvo v Sofija*, lxii (1902); I. Karácson, *Evlia Cselebi török világutazó Magyarországi utazásai 1660-1664*, Budapest 1904 (trans. of the greater part of v and vi); D. S. Čohadžić, *Putopis Evlije Čelebije v srpskim zemljama v XVII v.*, in *Spomenik Srpske Kraljevske Akademije*, xlii (1905); G. Germánus, *Evlija Cselebi a XVII századbeli Törökországi czéhekröl*, in *Keleti Szemle*, viii (1907); I. Karácson, *Evlija Cselebi török világutazó Magyarországi utazásai 1664-66*, Budapest 1908 (trans. of vii to p. 446 of the Istanbul edition); D. G. Gadžanov, *Pŭtuvane na Evlija Čelebi iz bŭlgarskitě zemi prez srědata na XVII v.*, in *Periodičesko Spisanie na Bŭlgarskoto Knižovno Družestvo v Sofija*, lxx (1909); A. H. Lybyer, *The travels of Evliya Effendi*, in *JAOS*, xxxvii (1917), 224-39; G. I. Cialicoff, *Din călatoriă lui Evliya Celebi*, in *Arhiva Dobrogei*, ii (1919); R. Hartmann, *Zu Ewlija Tschelebi's Reisen im oberen Euphrat- und Tigrisgebiet*, in *Isl.*, ix (1919), 184-244; W. Björkman, *Ofen zur Türkenzeit*, Hamburg 1920; Carra de Vaux, *Les penseurs de l'Islam*, Paris 1921, i; F. Taeschner, *Die geographische Literatur der Osmanen*, in *ZDMG*, lxx (1923), 31-80, 144; *ʿOthmānlî mü'ellifleri*, iii; F. Taeschner, *Das anatolische Wegenetz*, Leipzig 1924-6; Babinger, *GOW*; P. Pelliot, *Le prétendu vocabulaire mongol des Kaitak du Daghestan*, in *JA*, ccx (1927); W. Köhler, *Die Kurdenstadt Bitlis nach dem türkischen Reisewerk des Ewlija Tschelebi*, Munich 1928; F. Taeschner, *Die neue Stambuler Ausgabe von Evlijā Tschelebis Reisewerk*, in *Isl.*, xviii (1929), 299-310; F. Babinger, *Ewlija Tschelebi's Reisewege in Albanien*, in *MSOS As.*, xxxiii (1930), 138-78; S. Khudaverdóglou, Ὁ Ἐβλιᾶ Τσελεμπῆ ἀνὰ τὰς ἑλληνικὰς χώρας, in Ἑλληνικά, iv (1931); D. Tzortzóglou, Τὰ περὶ Ἀθηνῶν κεφάλαια τοῦ Ἐβλιᾶ Τσελεμπῆ, in Ἑλληνικά, iv (1931); P. Pelliot, *Les formes turques et mongoles dans la nomenclature zoologique du Nuzhatu-'l-Ḳulūb*, in *BSOS*, vi (1930-2), 555-80; İ. H. Uzunçarşılı, *Kütahya Şehri*, Istanbul 1932; A. Antalffy, *Călătoria lui Evlia Celebi prin Moldava în anul 1659*, in *Buletinul Comisiei Istorice a României*, xii (1933); J. Deny, *Les pérégrinations du muezzin Evliyâ Tchelebi en Roumanie (XVIIe siècle)*, in *Mélanges offerts à M. Nicolas Iorga*, Paris 1933; Mehmed Halid, *Evliya Çelebi'ye göre Azerbaycan şehirleri*, in *Azerbaycan Yurt Bilgisi* (Istanbul), ii (1933); I. Spatháres, Ἡ Δυτικὴ Θράκη κατὰ τὸν Ἐβλιγιὰ Τσελεπήν, περιηγητὴν τοῦ *XVII* αἰῶνος, in Θρακικά, iv (1933); R. Bleichsteiner, *Die kaukasischen Sprachproben in Evliya Çelebi's Seyahetname*, in *Caucasica*, xi (1934), 84-126; P. Wittek, *Das Fürstentum Mentesche*, Istanbul 1934; H. G. Farmer, *Turkish instruments of music in the seventeenth century*, in *JRAS* 1936, 1-43; H. Wilhelmy, *Hochbulgarien*, Kiel 1935-6; A. Sakisian, *Abdal Khan, Seigneur kurde de Bitlis au XVIIe s. et ses trésors*, in *JA*, ccxxix (1937), 253-70; I. Spatháres, (Μετάφρασις) Ἡ Ἀνατολικὴ Θράκη κατὰ τὸν Τοῦρκον περιηγητὴν τοῦ *XVII* αἰῶνος Ἐβλιγιὰ Τσελεμπήν, in Θρακικά, vii (1937); F. Babinger, *Rumelische Streifen (Albania)*, Berlin 1938; H. J. Kissling, *Einige deutsche Sprachproben bei Evliyā Čelebi*, in *Leipziger Vierteljahrsschrift für Südosteuropa*, ii (1938); V. Garbouzova, *Evliya Tchelebi sur les joaillers turcs au XVIIe s.*, in *Travaux du Département Oriental, Musée de l'Ermitage, Leningrad*, iii (1940); F. Bajraktarević, *Türk-Yugoslav kültür münasebetleri*, in *İkinci Türk Tarih Kongresi 1937*, Istanbul 1943; A. Bombaci, *Il viaggio in Abissinia di Evliyā Čelebi (1673)*, in *AIUON*, n.s. ii (1943), 259-75; P. Darvingov, *Un grand voyageur turc*, in *La Bulgarie* of 16 May 1943; F. Babinger, *Beiträge zur Frühgeschichte der Türkenherrschaft in Rumelien*, Brünn 1944; *IA*, art. Evliyā Çelebi (M. Cavid Baysun); H. W. Duda, *Balkantürkische Studien (Üsküb)*, Vienna 1949; R. F. Kreutel, *Ewlijā Čelebis Bericht über die türkische Grossbotschaft des Jahres 1665 in Wien*, in *WZKM*, li (1948-52), 188-242; M. Cavid Baysun, *Evliya Çelebi'ye dâir notlar*, in *TM*, xii (1955); A. Bombaci, *Storia della letteratura turca*, Milan 1956; H. J. Kissling, *Beiträge zur Kenntnis*

Thrakiens im 17. Jahrhundert, Wiesbaden 1956; R. F. Kreutel, *Im Reiche des goldenen Apfels* (Vienna), Graz 1957; M. Eren, *Evliya Çelebi Seyahatnamesi birinci cildinin kaynakları üzerinde bir araştırma*, Istanbul 1960; C. B. Ashurbeyli, *Seyāḥatnāme Evliya Čelebi kak istočnik po izučeniyu sotsial'no-ekonomičeskoi i političeskoi istorii gorodov Azerbaydjana v pervoy polovine XVII veka* (*The Seyāḥatnāme of Evliyā Čelebi as a source for the study of the social-economic and political history of the towns of Azerbaydjān in the first half of the 17th century*), Papers of the Soviet delegation to the XXV International Congress of Orientalists, Moscow 1960; Ewliya Čelebi, *Kniga puteshestviya: perevod i kommentarii*, i, *Zemli Moldavii i Ukrainî*, Moscow 1961. Other references in Pearson, p. 277, and Supp., p. 84. (J. H. Mordtmann-[H. W. Duda])

EWRENOS, (Ghāzī Evrenos) makes his appearance in history after the emirate of Ḳarasî had been occupied by the Ottomans (after 735/1334-5), and given by sultan Orkhān as *tîmār* to his eldest son Süleymān Pasha, into whose service came the begs of the *amîr*s of Ḳarasî, Ḥādjdjī İl-Begi, Edje Beg, Ghāzī Fāḍil and Evrenos. According to the genealogical tree of the family, confirmed by a deed of *waḳf* (published by Ö. L. Barkan, in *Vakıflar Dergisi*, ii, Ankara 1942, 342-3), the father of Evrenos is said to have been ʿĪsā Beg, later called *Prangi* because he died in the village of that name; his son had a mausoleum built there and established a *waḳf*. The name of Evrenos can be found listed among the reinforcements sent by Orkhān under the command of his son to Cantacuzenus, to support him in his struggle against John V Palaeologus. But it is particularly from the moment when Süleymān Pasha (d. 759/1359) crossed the Dardanelles that one can follow continuously the history of Ghāzī Evrenos in the accounts of the Ottoman historians. Installed in the fortress of Ḳoñur Ḥiṣārî, near Gallipoli, beside Ḥādjdjī İl-Begi, Evrenos took part with the latter in raids on the region of Dimetoka [*q.v.*] and distinguished himself personally by occupying Keshān and laying waste Ipsala. Henceforward his name was to be associated with the history of the conquest of Rūmeli, where he made himself famous by his raids. After Orkhān's death Evrenos took part, with Ḥādjdjī Il-Begi, in the capture of Edirne by Murād I (763/1362), who next sent him to occupy the towns of Ipsala and Gümüldjina (Komotini) in Thrace, and appointed him *udj-begi* of the conquered territories. He was present at the battle of Sîrp-Ṣîndîghî, and later, in 772/1371, at that of Tchernomen (Čirmen) or of the Maritza, which brought disaster to the Serbs and their allies and opened the gates of Macedonia to the Turks. As a result, Evrenos was sent to conquer Feredjik (Pherrai) in 1372, and then, while the Turks took Kavala, Drama, Zichna, Serres and Karaferya (Yenidje-i Vardar), he himself occupied the regions of Porî (Peritheorion), Iskedje (Xanthi), Maronea (ʿAwret Ḥiṣārî) from which he levied *kharādj* (1373). As a reward, the sultan gave him the region of Serres which he had subjected and of which he became *udj-begi* (in 784/1382 or 787/1385). He then took part in the occupation of Greater Macedonia, capturing Yenidje-i Vardar and Monastir and, under the command of the vizier Čandarlî Khayr al-Dīn Pasha, assisted in the campaign against king Balsha II of Albania, which came to an end with the death of that prince (1385). Evrenos next went on the Pilgrimage, and on his return was granted an important fief by the sultan; the *fermān* bestowed on him by Murād I on this occasion was for a long time erroneously considered to be apocryphal; it has been the subject of various publications (Diez, *Denkwürdigkeiten von Asien*, ii, Berlin 1815, 101-32; cf. Ferīdūn, *Munshaʾāt al-salāṭīn*², i, 87-8). During the last campaign of Murād I, Evrenos was the sultan's adviser. He distinguished himself by occupying Üsküb (Skoplje), and then, before the Kossovo campaign, by crushing the enemy in a pass, thereby allowing the Turkish army to cross the Morava. On his accession Bāyezīd I (1389-1402), by a *berāt* dated Muḥarram 793/December 1390, confirmed Evrenos in the possession of the fief previously granted him by his father. On behalf of the new sultan, Evrenos occupied Vodena and Kitros and led several incursions into Albania. In 1391 he took part in the Morea campaign. In 1396 he was present at the battle of Nicopolis (Niğbolu), where he was head of the *aḳîndjî*s. Afterwards, as a result of the victory of Nicopolis, he made further raids into Albania and took part in the invasions of Hungary and Wallachia, where Bāyezīd sent him to parley with the enemy; next, with Yaʿḳūb Beg, he made his way into the Morea and captured Corinth and the fortress of Argos (1397). He was present at the battle of Ankara and then, during the interregnum, went into the service of Süleymān Čelebi, assisting him in his campaign against the Ḳaramān-oghlu, whom he besieged in Aḳsaray. On Süleymān's death, fearing reprisals from Mūsā Čelebi, he retired to Yenidje-i Vardar and feigned blindness. In the fratricidal struggle between Mūsā and Meḥemmed, Evrenos and the begs of Rūmeli who were discontented with the former took sides with Meḥemmed and helped him to overcome his brother. Evrenos died in 820/1417 at a very great age at Yenidje-i Vardar, which had become his family's residence (Yenidje-i Vardar was called *"Evrenos Beg yöresi"*: cf. Ewliyā Čelebī, ix, 47). In the time of Murād I, Evrenos had already become one of the greatest feudatories of the Ottoman empire. The extent of the lands belonging to him had become legendary (ʿĀlī, *Künh*, v, 75; Beauséjour, *Tableau du commerce de la Grèce*, i, 111 ff.). The Ottoman historians also refer to his great generosity; he devoted a large part of his wealth to charitable foundations. Together with the Mīkhāl-oghullarî, the Malḳodj-oghullarî and the Tūrākhān-oghullarî, [*qq.v.*], the descendants of Evrenos constitute the four ancient families of the Ottoman warrior nobility.

Bibliography (in addition to works quoted above): ʿĀshîḳpashazāde, ed. ʿĀlī, 51, 53, 54, 57, 58, 60, 61, 63 (= *Osmanlı Tarihleri*, i, Istanbul 1946, 125-8, 130-2, 135); Neshrī, edd. Unat and Köymen, i and ii, *passim*; *Die altosmanischen anonymen Chroniken*, tr. F. Giese, 25, 30, 31, 34, 35, 68, 70; Chalcocondyles, Bonn ed., 79-80, 97-9, 175, 181; Ducas, Bonn ed., 50; Phrantzes, Bonn ed., 62-3, 83; *Epirotica*, Bonn ed., 234, 236; Ḥamīd Wehbī, *Ghāzī Evrenos Beg*, *Meshāhīr-i Islām*, Istanbul 1301-2, 801-40; ʿOthmān Ferīd, *Evrenos Beg Khānedānîna ʿāʾid temlīknāme-i humāyūn*, in *TOEM*, vi (1915), 432-8; N. Jorga, *GOR*, i, Gotha 1908; I. H. Danişmend, *Izahlı Osmanlı tarihi kronolojisi*, i, Istanbul 1947, 12, 27, 39-40, 47, 56, 64, 77, 95, 108, 112, 156, 160, 163, 165; *IA*, s.v. Evrenos (by I. H. Uzunçarşılı); T. Gökbilgin, *XV-XVI asırlarda Edirne ve Paşa livâsı*, Istanbul 1952, 23, 69, 155, 220, 269, 271, 364.
(I. Mélikoff)

EWRENOS OGHULLARÎ. Ghāzī Evrenos had seven sons, whose names are given by the chronicles and the *waḳf* deeds, and several daughters, one of whom married the Grand Vizier Čandarlî Khalīl Pasha and became the mother of Bāyezīd II's Grand Vizier, Čandarlî Ibrāhīm Pasha. Two of his sons became famous in history, ʿAlī and ʿĪsā. ʿAlī was at first head of the *akîndjîs* under the command of his father, then *sandjak begi*. During the interregnum he adopted the cause of Mūsā Čelebī, and was sent by him to join his father who was living in retirement at Yenidje-i Vardar; but on the advice of Evrenos he went into the service of Meḥemmed Čelebī. When Meḥemmed died, the sons of Evrenos, like the other begs of Rūmeli, joined the cause of the pretender known as Muṣṭafā Düzme [*q.v.*]; but at Ulubād they forsook him and went over to Murād II. They were pardoned, and the sultan confirmed their possession of the fief granted to Evrenos by Murād I. In 833/1430, when Murād II was storming Salonika, ʿAlī Beg won distinction by inciting the assailants with promises of booty. In 838/1434-5 he headed a raid into Albania and returned laden with booty. In 1437 he was sent with the *akîndjîs* to make a reconnaissance raid in Hungary; he came back after a month, loaded with spoils, and advised the sultan to invade the country. In 845/1441 he laid siege to Belgrade, but the *akîndjîs* were defeated by the Hungarians and the Turks had to withdraw. During the revolt of the Albanians under the leadership of George Castriotes Iskender Beg (1443-68) [*q.v.*], he several times commanded the Turkish forces sent against the rebel. In 866/1462 he took part with his two sons Aḥmed and Evrenos in the campaign in Wallachia, in which he was leader of the *akîndjîs*. He died after this date; his tomb is at Yenidje-i Vardar.

His brother ʿĪsā Beg was, like him, leader of the *akîndjîs*. In 826/1423 he was sent on a reconnaissance raid into Albania by Murād II, who was just about to undertake his campaign in Albania and the Morea; he headed several other raids into Albania, one in 841/1438 and another in 846/1442. In 847/1443 he was at the battle of Jalovats which saw the defeat of the Turks by John Hunyadi. During the reign of Meḥemmed II, he took part in the Serbian campaign in 858/1454 and occupied the small fort of Tirebdje. In the following year he was sent into Albania and won a victory over Iskender Beg at Berat. In 867/1463 he was involved in the incidents in the Morea which led to the Turco-Venetian war. In 884/1479, together with ʿAlī and Iskender Mīkhāl-oghlu and Bali Malkodj-oghlu, he led the raid into Transylvania which ended in the massacre of the Turks who, too avid for loot, allowed themselves to be taken unawares and were crushed by the voïvode Stephen Bathori. He died after this date; his tomb is at Yenidje-i Vardar, and also a mosque and an *ʿimāret* founded by him.

The two sons of ʿAlī Evrenos-oghlu, Shems al-Dīn Aḥmed and Evrenos, were present with their father on the campaign in Wallachia in 866/1462; Evrenos was sent on a raid to the frontier of Moldavia; the former, whose name occurs in numerous archive-documents, was in 870/1466 beg of the *sandjak* of Trikkala, and then of Semendria; in 883/1478 he took part in the siege of Shkodra in Albania and was afterwards appointed head of the garrison left in the fort. A year before his death (903/1498), he established a *wakf* of which his son Mūsā was put in trust; his other two sons, ʿĪsā and Süleymān, had died in 893/1488 at the battle of Agha-Čayîrî, against the Mamlūks.

Other descendants of Evrenos are recorded at the beginning of the 9th/16th century, notably Meḥemmed, son of ʿĪsā b. Evrenos, *sandjak-begi* of Elbasan, who captured Durazzo in 907/1502; and Yūsuf, grandson of Khîḍr-Shāh b. Evrenos, who was present on Selīm I's Egyptian campaign. The Evrenos family, who won their fame by their raids in Rūmeli, lost their importance as military leaders after the middle of the 10th/16th century. This family, which played a great part in the rise of the Ottoman empire, remained, throughout the course of history, one of the most prominent by reason both of its territorial possessions and also of the statesmen to which it gave birth.

Bibliography: ʿĀshîkpashazāde, ed. ʿĀlī, 84, 106, 118, 123-4, 162, 224 (= *Osmanlı Tarihleri*, i, Istanbul 1946, 148, 157-8, 160, 164, 173, 176-7, 196); Neshrī, edd. Unat and Köymen, ii, 557, 561, 563, 567, 579, 611, 621-3; *Die altosmanischen anonymen Chroniken*, trans. F. Giese, 75, 79, 88-9; Ibn Kemāl, *Tewārīkh-i Āl-i ʿOthmān, VII. defter*, ed. Ş. Turan, Ankara 1954, 215, 219, 608-9; Dursun Beg, *Taʾrīkh-i Abu 'l-Fatḥ, TOEM* supp., Istanbul 1330, 105; Chalcocondyles, Bonn, 181, 217-9, 247, 250-1, 257, 308, 432, 448-50; Ducas, Bonn, 197; Ḥamīd Wehbī, *Evrenoszāde ʿAlī Beg, Meshāhīr-i Islām*, Istanbul 1301-2, 945-6; N. Jorga, *GOR*, i and ii, Gotha 1908-9; A. Gegaj, *L'Albanie et l'invasion turque au XVe siècle*, Paris 1937; I. H. Danişmend, *Izahlı Osmanlı Tarihi Kronolojisi*, i, Istanbul 1947, 189, 190, 203, 204, 206, 209, 220, 275, 279, 281, 302, 341, 343, 410; *Evrenos oğulları*, in *IA* (by I. H. Uzunçarşılı).

(I. Mélikoff)

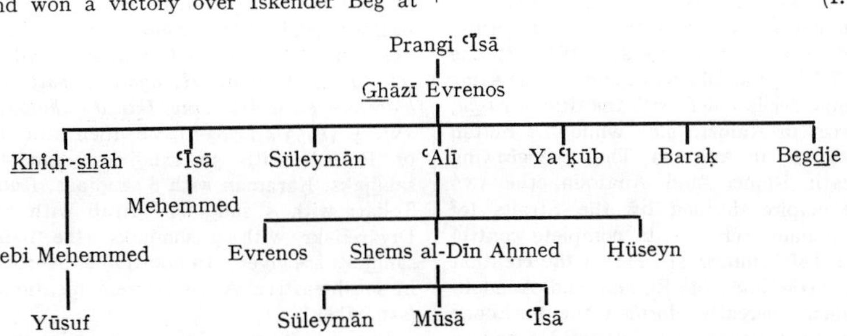

EXEGESIS [see TAFSĪR].

EXISTENCE [see WUDJŪD].

EXORCISM [see RUKYA].

EXPENDITURE [see NAFAKA].

EXPIATION [see KAFFĀRA].

EXTRA-TERRITORIALITY [see IMTIYĀZĀT].

EYĀLET, from the Arabic *iyāla*, "management, administration, exercise of power" (cf. Turkish translation of Fīrūzābādī's *Kāmūs* by ʿĀṣim, Istanbul 1250/1834, iii, 135); in the Ottoman empire the largest administrative division under a *beglerbegi* [*q.v.*], governor-general. In this sense it was officially used after

1000/1591. The assumption that under Murād III the empire was divided up into *eyālet*s (M. d'Ohsson, *Tableau général de l'empire ottoman*, vii, 277) must be an error since the term does not occur in the documents of the period. Instead we always find *beglerbegilik* and *wilāyet* (*wilāya*). *Beglerbegilik* was then the proper term for this administrative division, while *wilāyet* designated any governorship, large or small (cf. *Sûret-i Defter-i Sancâk-i Arvanid*, ed. H. Inalcık, Ankara 1954, index; U. Heyd, *Ottoman documents on Palestine*, Oxford 1960, 50). As a term designating the territory of a *beglerbegilik*, *eyālet* must have been adopted by 1000/1591, while *beglerbegilik* continued to be used rather for the office of a *beglerbegi*.

In early Ottoman history the *beglerbegi* was the commander-in-chief of the provincial forces, in particular timariots, and as such the institution was directly connected with that of the *beglerbegi*, commander-in-chief, found with the Seldjūḳids and Ilkhānids (cf. F. Köprülü, *Bizans müesseselerinin Osmanlı müesseselerine tesiri*, in *THITM*, i (1931), 190-5 [Ital. tr. *Alcune osservazioni...*, Rome 1944]; I. H. Uzunçarşılı, *Osmanlı devleti teşkilâtına medhal*, Istanbul 1941, 59-60, 108). Orkhan during his father's reign, ʿAlāʾ al-Dīn Pasha his brother and Süleymān Pasha his son during Orkhan's reign, were considered as *beglerbegi* (cf. Saʿd al-Dīn, *Tādj al-tawārīkh*, i, Istanbul 1279/1862, 69). But Murād I [*q.v.*] made Shāhīn, his *lālā* [*q.v.*], *beglerbegi* (under the Seldjūḳids some *beglerbegis* bore the title of *lālā*, or the synonymous *atabeg*. In a passage in Rūḥī's chronicle *lālā etmek* means to appoint *beglerbegi*), and set out for his historic conquests in Thrace. The conquered lands there were put under Lālā Shāhīn's military responsibility while Ewrenos [*q.v.*] was made *udj* [*q.v.*] *begi* over the irregular *ghāzī* forces on the marches (Neshrī, *Ğihānnümā*, i, ed. Fr. Taeschner, Leipzig 1951, 54; Orūdj, *Tewārīkh-i Āl-i ʿOthmān*, ed. Fr. Babinger, Hanover 1925, 20, 92). Thus the Ottoman *beglerbegi* became *beglerbegi* of Rumeli, and the rivalry between him and the *udj-begi*s became an important factor of Ottoman history down to Meḥemmed II's time (cf. H. Inalcık, *Fatih Devri*, i, Ankara 1954, 57-8). But the *beglerbegi* of Rumeli was still the only *beglerbegi*, the actual commander-in-chief of the Ottoman army. In the period between 787/1385 and 789/1387 the vizier Čandarlî Khayr al-Dīn was made at the same time the commander-in-chief, with the title of *pasha*, of all the forces in Rumeli [*q.v.*] while the Sultan himself had to stay in Anatolia. Thus the growing responsibilities in Rumeli and Anatolia, the two parts of the empire divided by the Straits (of which the Ottomans were not in complete control until the time of Meḥemmed II), led to the creation of the two *beglerbegilik*s of Rumeli and Anadolu (Anatolia), which thereafter formed the backbone of the empire. In 795/1393 when Bāyazīd I had to leave Anatolia for Rumeli he appointed Ḳara Timurtash *beglerbegi* of Anadolu in Ankara (Neshrī, 86). In his father's time Bāyazīd himself had been a governor on this *udj* area in Kütahya. But the *beglerbegi* of Rumeli preserved his position of primacy in the state by being always considered as the first among the *beglerbegi*s, having the exclusive right to sit with the viziers at Dīwān [*q.v.*] meetings etc. (cf. *Ḳānūnnāme-i Āl-i ʿOthmān*, Meḥemmed the Conqueror's code of laws, ed. M. ʿĀrif, suppl. of *TOEM*, 1330/1912, 13; Süleymān I confirmed these prerogatives in Muḥarram 942/July 1535, see Ferīdūn, *Munshaʾāt al-Salāṭīn*, Istanbul 1274, 595; cf. also *Ḳānūn-i Mīr-i Mīrān*, in *MTM*, i (1331), 527). Maḥmūd Pasha under Meḥemmed II and Ibrahīm Pasha under Süleymān I both held the offices of Grand Vizier and *beglerbegi* of Rumeli at the same time.

It appears that further *beglerbegiliks* in Anatolia were founded subsequently according to the traditional pattern.

The farthest *udj wilāyet*s in Anatolia, which became the nuclei of the new *beglerbegilik*s, continued to be assigned to the Ottoman royal princes. The third *beglerbegilik*, that of Rūm in the Amasya-Tokat region, developed from an *udj* under the royal princes whose *lālā*s, responsible for the actual administration, bore the title of *pasha* and *beglerbegi* from Bāyazīd I's time (cf. Ḥ. Ḥüsām el-Dīn, *Amasya taʾrīkhi*, iii, Istanbul 1927, 157-91). Timur's invasion and later on Shāhrukh's threats (cf. article Murad II, in *IA*) made this region vitally important for the Ottomans, and the new conquests in Djanik and Trebizond were incorporated into it. Also put under a royal prince with his *lālā*s after its conquest in 873/1468 (cf. article Mehmed II in *IA*) the '*wilāyet* of Ḳaraman' (cf. *Fatih devrinde Karaman eyâleti vakıfları fihristi*, ed. F. N. Uzluk, Ankara 1958, fac. 2) developed into a *beglerbegilik* later on (in 922/1516 Khüsrew Pasha was the *beglerbegi*). The development of the *udj wilāyet* of Bosna into a *beglerbegilik* in Rumeli took more than a century from 867/1463 to 988/1580 (the process is examined in detail in the monograph by H. Šabanović, *Bosanski Pašaluk*, Sarajevo 1959). With some variation dependent on the particular conditions of the *udj* sandjaḳs and further conquests (cf. L. Fekete, *Osmanlı Türkleri ve Macarlar*, in *Belleten*, xiii/52 (1949), 679-85), the Ottomans maintained the pre-conquest boundaries, especially in the first '*wilāyet*' stage (cf. H. Šabanović, *op. cit.*, 1-95; H. Inalcık, *Sûret-i Defter* . . ., 33, 55, 75). Later on in reorganizing them as *sandjaḳ*s [*q.v.*] and *beglerbegiliks* they acted more freely and fixed the boundaries according to the situation.

The conquests under Selīm I were organized first as the *wilāyet* of ʿAlāʾ al-Dawla (conquered in 921/1515), the *wilāyet* of ʿArab which included Syria, Palestine, Egypt and the Ḥidjāz, and the *wilāyet* of Diyār-Bakr (conquered in 923/1517, first survey in 924/1518, cf. Barkan, *Kanunlar*, 145 and article Diyarbekir in *IA*). In an Ottoman record of 926/1520 (cf. Ö. L. Barkan, *H. 933-934 malî yılına ait bir bütçe örneği*, in *Ist. Üniv. Iktisat Fakültesi Mecmuası*, xv/1-4 (1953-4), 303-7) we then find the *wilāyet*s of Rumeli with 30 sandjaḳs, Anadolu with 20 sandjaḳs, Ḳaraman with 8 sandjaḳs, Rūm (Amasya-Tokat) with 5 sandjaḳs, ʿArab with 15 sandjaḳs, Diyār-Bakr with 9 sandjaḳs (the names of the sandjaḳs are given). In addition 28 Kurdish *djemāʿat*s in south-eastern Anatolia were mentioned as *liwā*s (sandjaḳs).

In the first years of the reign of Süleymān I events forced him to reorganize the *wilāyet* of ʿArab into the *beglerbegilik*s of Ḥaleb (Aleppo), Shām (Damascus) and Egypt (cf. Gibb-Bowen, i/1, 200-34; B. Lewis, *Notes and documents from the Turkish Archives*, Jerusalem 1952; S. J. Shaw, *The financial and administrative organization and development of Ottoman Egypt*, Princeton 1962, 1-19). The *wilāyet* of ʿAlāʾ al-Dawla too was put under an Ottoman beglerbegi in 928/1522 (cf. article Dulkadırlılar, in *IA*). In 940/1533 Süleymān I also created the *beglerbegilik* of Djezāʾir (Algeria) with the appointment of Khayr al-Dīn Ḳapudān Pasha [*q.v.*]. The development of the sea *udj* into a *beglerbegilik* was precipitated by Andrea Doria's capture of Koron and the crusading activities of Charles V in the Mediterranean. In the western reports of about 941/1534 (Ramberti, A. Gritti in A. H. Lybyer, *The government of the Ottoman Empire in the time of Suleiman the Magnificent*, Cambridge, Mass., 1913, 255-61, 270-4) the *beglerbegilik*s in the Ottoman empire are listed as follows: Djezā'ir under the name of the *beglerbegilik* of the sea, Rumeli, Anadolu, Ḳaraman, Amasya-Tokat, ʿAlā' al-Dawla, Diyār Bakr, Shām and Egypt.

Further conquests under Süleymān I gave rise to the new *beglerbegilik*s: Ādharbāydjān and Baghdād in 941/1534, Van in Radjab 955/August 1548, Erzurum in 941/1534, Aḳča-ḳalʿa in Georgia in Shaʿbān 956/September 1549 (cf. Ferīdūn, *op. cit.*, i, 586, 604, 606) in Asia; Budīn in Djumādā II 948/August 1541, Temeshvar in 959/1552 in Europe (cf. Fekete, *op. cit.*). Thus in appointing *beglerbegis* on the spot immediately after the conquest Süleymān I made an innovation.

In 976/1568 when a large scale expedition was planned in the Volga basin the sandjaḳ of Kefe (Caffa) in the *beglerbegilik* of Rumeli was raised to a *beglerbegilik* (cf. H. Inalcık, *Osmanlı-Rus rekabetinin menşei*, in *Belleten*, xii/46 (1948), 375 = *The origin of the Ottoman-Russian rivalry*..., in *Ann. de l'Un. d'Ankara*, i (1946-7), 75). As, after its conquest, Cyprus had to be protected by large forces, Lefḳosha (Nicosia) was made the centre of a *beglerbegilik* in 979/1571, and, the sandjaḳs of ʿAlā'iyye, Ṭarsūs, Ičel, Sis and Ṭarābulus-Shām (Syrian Ṭripoli) were attached to it.

Of many *beglerbegilik*s created during the occupation of the Caucasian lands between 986/1578 and 999/1590 (cf. B. Kütükoğlu, *Osmanlı-Iran siyâsî münâsebetleri*, Istanbul 1962) only those of Čildir and Ḳarṣ (created in 988/1580) remained after the Persian reaction under ʿAbbās I [*q.v.*].

In the list of ʿAyn-i ʿAlī of 1018/1609 (*Ḳawānīn-i Āl-i ʿOthmān*, Istanbul 1280) are mentioned thirty-two *eyālet*s in the empire. Twenty-three of them were regular Ottoman *eyālet*s subjected to the tīmār system. These were: Rumeli, Anadolu, Ḳaraman, Budīn, Temeshvar, Bosna, Djezā'ir-i Baḥr-i Sefīd [*q.v.*], Ḳibris, Dhülḳadriyye (formerly ʿAlā' al-Dawla or Marʿash), Diyārbakr, Rūm (Amasya-Tokat or Sivas), Erzurum, Shām, Ṭarābulus-Shām, Ḥaleb, Raḳḳa, Ḳarṣ, Čildir, Ṭrabzon, Kefe, Mosul, Van, Shehrizūr. Nine *eyālet*s were with *sālyāne* [*q.v.*], that is to say the tax revenues were not distributed as tīmārs but collected directly for the Sultan's treasury; the *beglerbegi*, soldiers and all the other functionaries were assigned salaries from the annual tax collection of the *eyālet*. The *eyālet*s with *sālyāne* were: Miṣr (Egypt), Baghdād, Yemen, Ḥabesh (Eritrea), Baṣra, Laḥsā, Djezā'ir-i Gharb (Algeria), Ṭarābulus-Gharb (Tripolitania), Tūnus (Tunis). (See further MÜSTETHNĀ EYĀLETLER).

In the list given by Koči Beg about 1640 (*Risāle*, ed. A. K. Aksüt, Istanbul 1939, 99-103) the only difference is the addition of the *eyālet* of Özü which had been created by then primarily with the purpose of stopping the continuing Cossack attacks on the Black Sea coasts. It included the sandjaḳs on the western coasts of the Black Sea and the Danube. In both lists the *eyālet*s of Ḳanizha (Kanizsa) and Egri (Eger) are missing though these were created after their conquest in 1004/1596 (cf. Fekete, *op. cit.*, 681). In Kātib Čelebi's *Djihānnümā* (ed. Ibrāhīm Müteferriḳa, Istanbul 1145/1732, and trans. J. von Hammer, *Rumeli und Bosna*, Vienna 1812) we find the same *eyālet*s with the differences that Marʿash for Dhulḳadriyye, Sivas for Rūm, Ḳonya for Ḳaraman are mentioned, and the *eyālet* of Adana is added.

The term of *eyālet* for *beglerbegilik* appeared by the end of the 10th/16th century. We find it in the previous documents in its general meaning (cf. Ferīdūn, i, 614). Also in the new period the important *eyālet*s were assigned to *beglerbegi*s of the rank of vizier, with three *tugh*s (cf. Gibb-Bowen, i/1, 139-41), who had some authority over the neighbouring *beglerbegi*s of two *tugh*s. Also now the general tendency was to create smaller *beglerbegilik*s which were required to cope with certain military situations. Such was the case with the small *beglerbegilik*s set up in Georgia and Ādharbāydjān after 986/1578. In Syria a fourth *eyālet*, that of Ṣaydā', was created in 1023/1614 for the better control of the area (cf. U. Heyd, *op. cit.*, 45-8).

An *eyālet* was composed of sandjaḳs (*liwās*) under sandjaḳ-begis and, as a sandjaḳ was always the basic administrative unit, the *beglerbegi* himself was at the head of a sandjaḳ called *pasha sandjaghi*. It included certain centrally located towns and districts in each sandjaḳ as his *khāṣṣ* (see TĪMĀR).

The main responsibilities of a *beglerbegi* were summarized in *berāt*s (diplomas) of assignment (see for example the *berāt* of ʿĪsā Beg in Ferīdūn, i, 269; for its date cf. H. Inalcık, *Fatih devri*, Ankara 1954, 77; also see *Ḳānūn-i mīr-i mīrān*, in *MTM*, i, 527-8). Representing the executive power of the sultan on all matters (*umūr-i siyāset*) in the *eyālet* and called in this capacity *wālī* of it, he enforced the *ḳāḍī*'s decisions and the Sultan's orders. He was also entitled to give decisions in the dīwān under him (*beglerbegilik dīwānî*) on matters concerning the persons of *ʿaskerī* [see ʿASKARĪ] status. But the *beglerbegi*s with the rank of vizier had larger and more absolute powers (cf. *MTM*, i, 528). The *beglerbegi*'s main administrative responsibility was to maintain public security, and pursue those who broke the law and opposed the Sultan's orders (for their ceremonial privileges see *MTM*, i, 527-8). It should be emphasized that the *ḳāḍī* and *māl defterdārî* [see DAFTARDĀR] in an *eyālet* were independent of the *beglerbegi*s in their decisions, and, could apply directly to the central government. Also the *agha*s of the Janissary garrisons in the main cities were independent of the *beglerbegi*s, who could never enter the fortresses under the Janissaries' guardianship. These restrictions and frequent changes of their posts were obviously designed to prevent *beglerbegi*s from becoming too independent.

The *Beglerbegilik-eyālet* was essentially based on the *tīmār* system and a *beglerbegi* was responsible primarily for the army of timariot *sipāhī*s in his *eyālet*. Under his command it was the largest military unit in the imperial army. It was the *beglerbegi*'s responsibility to bring it to the Sultan's army in perfect condition. The appointment and promotions of the *sipāhī*s depended on him. He was entitled to grant *tīmār*s up to a certain amount (cf. ʿAyn-i ʿAlī, *op. cit.*, 61-81). Two high officials, the *defter-ketkhüdāsî* and *tīmār-defterdārı* under him, were responsible for these affairs. The copies of the *idjmāl* and *mufaṣṣal defter*s, basic record-books of *tīmār*s drawn up for each sandjaḳ, were sent by the Sultan to the *eyālet*s (H. Inalcık, *Sûret-i Defter*, xxi; Heyd, *op. cit.*, 48).

But in the period of decline when the central authority weakened the whole system deteriorated. In some distant *eyālet*s the Janissaries obtained effective control and constituted ruling castes, as was the case in the North African provinces and Baghdād. In Egypt, however, it was the Mamlūk begs who finally seized the actual control (cf. Shaw, *op. cit.*, 184-5, 316). In the *eyālet*s of Eastern Anatolia the Janissaries' attempt to seize power failed before the violent reaction of the provincial forces and the D̲j̲alālīs (see Supplement, *s.v.*) under Abaza Meḥmed Pas̲h̲a [*q.v.*]. But it was the disorganization of the *tīmār* system that brought about fundamental changes in the *eyālet*s. Now an important part of the tax revenues was not distributed as *tīmār*s, but reserved directly for the Sultan's treasury, and farmed out to the tax-farmers; it then became a widespread practice to assign governorships with the governor himself farming the taxes, a practice applied previously in some distant *eyālet*s like Egypt. Thus on his appointment the governor guaranteed to deliver to the treasury a certain amount of money as the province's tax revenue. Also governors in general were encouraged by the Sultan to maintain forces at their own expense. It was principally these developments that prepared the way for the emergence of autonomous *eyālet*s in the 12th/18th century. In the same period local magnates called *aʿyān* [*q.v.*] acquired power in the *eyālet*s, since the governors were actually powerless without their cooperation. Despite the Sultan's efforts to reserve the rank of pas̲h̲a for his own men, some of these *aʿyān* managed to obtain governorships and even to found real provincial dynasties not only in the remoter provinces but also in Anatolia and Rumeli [see DEREBEY].

In 1227/1812 Maḥmūd II [*q.v.*] opened war against the pas̲h̲as and *aʿyān* of this type to re-establish the authority of the central government in the provinces, and after 1241/1826 reorganized them as *müs̲h̲īriyyet* (*mus̲h̲īriyya*) giving the *müs̲h̲īr*s large powers in military as well as financial affairs with a view to organizing the new army (cf. Luṭfī, *Taʾrīk̲h̲*, v, 107, 172). With the proclamation of the *Tanẓīmāt* [*q.v.*] in 1255/1839 financial affairs in the *eyālet*s were made the exclusive responsibility of the *muḥaṣṣil*s, and later on important changes under Western influence were introduced in the provincial administration: administrative councils were set up in the provinces sharing the governors' responsibilities, and most of the *eyālet*s were reduced in size (see especially the *sālnāme*s (state year books) published since 1263/1847). The *eyālet* system was finally replaced by that of *wilāyet* [*q.v.*] in 1281/1864.

(HALİL İNALCIK)

EYLŪL [see TAʾRĪK̲H̲].

EYMIR (EYMÜR), name of an Og̲h̲uz tribe (*boy*). They are mentioned in a legendary account of the pagan Og̲h̲uz as being the only tribe of the Üč-ok group from whom sprang rulers, but the historical references to them so far known go back only to the 10th/16th century, when they formed part of Türkmen confederations in the Ottoman Empire, in Persia, and south-east of the Caspian Sea.

(1) The Eymir of the Ottoman domains were in two main branches, the one living among the Türkmen of Aleppo, the other with the Dulkadîrlî confederation (*ulus*). The former consisted, in the reign of Süleymān I, of four clans (*oymak*); later in the 10th/16th century their numbers increased, to form 11 clans. At this period another clan of this branch was found among the Yeni-il tribesfolk south of Sivas. After the second siege of Vienna (1683), the Eymir, like other Türkmen groups, were required to serve in the war with Austria. A little later an unsuccessful attempt was made to settle a large group of the Türkmen of Aleppo, the Eymir among them, in the Ḥamā-Ḥims region; their population is recorded in the 12th/18th century as 500 tents.

The Eymir living among the Dulkadîrlî were much more numerous, those of the Marʿas̲h̲ region alone comprising, in the third decade of the 10th/16th century, 49 clans. Like the other groups constituting the Dulkadîrlî confederation, these Eymir were half-settled, engaging in agriculture in their winter camping-grounds and growing rice. During the 11th/17th century they became completely settled in the Marʿas̲h̲-ʿAyntāb region. Some scattered clans of this group were then living in other areas occupied by the Dulkadîrlî confederation—in the sand̲j̲aḳs of Kars (Kadirli) and Bozok, among the Boz-ulus, and in Persia.

Small communities named Eymürlü and Eymürler were found in the regions of Söğüt, Aydîn and Adana, but they took their name probably not from the tribe but from individuals (Eymir/Imir was a common personal name in the 9th/15th and 10th/16th centuries). 'Eymir' or 'Eymür' is a common village-name in central and western Turkey, particularly around Sivas, whence it appears that this tribe formed an important element among the Turkish immigrants into Anatolia.

(2) The Eymir of Persia belonged to the D̲h̲u 'l-Ḳadr confederation, dwelling in Fars, which was one of the seven great Ḳîzîl-bas̲h̲ tribes upon which depended the power of the Ṣafawid dynasty. The D̲h̲u 'l-Ḳadr tribe was a branch of the D̲h̲u 'l-Ḳadr/Dulkadîrlî confederation of Anatolia, from whence it had migrated to Persia.

(3) Eymir were found in the 10th/16th century also among the Sayîn K̲h̲ānlu Türkmen dwelling along the rivers Atrak and D̲j̲urd̲j̲ān north of Astarābād. Upon their submission to S̲h̲āh ʿAbbās, their chief ʿAlī Yār was appointed governor of Astarābād, with the title of K̲h̲ān; after his death in about 1005/1596, his son Muḥammad Yār succeeded him. A remnant of these Eymir, numbering some 200 households, is still living in this region.

Bibliography: V. V. Barthold (tr. V. and T. Minorsky), *Four studies on the history of Central Asia*, iii, Leiden 1962, index (s.v. Eymür); F. Sümer, *Anadolu'da yaşayan bazı Üçoklu Oğuz boylarına mensup teşekküller*, in *Istanbul Ün. Iktisat Fak. Mecm.*, xi (1949-50), 459-66.

(FARUK SÜMER)

EYYŪB [see ISTANBUL].

EZEKIEL [see ḤIZḲĪL].

EZELI [see AZALĪ].

EZRA [see IDRĪS, ʿUZAYR].

F

FĀʾ, 20th letter of the Arabic alphabet, transcribed *f*; numerical value 80, as in the Syriac (and Canaanite) alphabet [see ABDJAD].

Definition: fricative, labio-dental, unvoiced; according to the Arabic grammatical tradition: *rikhwa*, *shafawiyya* (or *shafahiyya*), *mahmūsa*; *f* is a continuation of a *p* in ancient Semitic and common Semitic. For the phonological oppositions of the phoneme *f*, see J. Cantineau, *Esquisse*, in *BSL* (no. 126), 94, 1°; for the incompatibilities, *ibid.*, 134.

Modifications: some examples exist of the passage of *f* to *th*, as in the doublet: *nukāf* and *nukāth* "tumour on a camel's jaw" (a less frequent passage than the reverse: *th* > *f*); see al-Ḳālī, *Amālī*², ii, 34-5, Ibn Djinnī's critique, *Sirr ṣināʿa*, i, 250-1. This passage probably explains the existence of *thumm* "mouth" (nomad) > *təmm* (sedentary), in modern Syro-Lebanese dialects, side by side with *fumm* (the expected form) in central Syria (see A. Barthélemy, *Dict. Ar.-Fr.*, 93 and 622).

(H. FLEISCH)

FABLE [see ḤIKĀYA, ḲIṢṢA, MATHAL].

FAḌĀʾIL [see FAḌĪLA]

FADAK, an ancient small town in the northern Ḥidjāz, near Khaybar and, according to Yāḳūt, two or three days' journey from Medina. This place-name having disappeared, Ḥāfiẓ Wahba in his *Djazīrat al-ʿArab* (Cairo 1956, 15) identified the ancient Fadak with the modern village of al-Ḥuwayyiṭ (pron. Ḥowēyaṭ), situated on the edge of the *ḥarra* of Khaybar. Inhabited, like Khaybar, by a colony of Jewish agriculturists, Fadak produced dates and cereals; handicrafts also flourished, with the weaving of blankets with palm-leaf borders.

Fadak owes its fame in the history of Islam to the fact that it was the object of an agreement and a particular decision by the Prophet, and that it gave rise to a disagreement between Fāṭima [*q.v.*] and the caliph Abū Bakr, the consequences of which were to last more than two centuries. When, in 5/627, Muḥammad took his well-known measures against the Banū Ḳurayẓa [*q.v.*], the Jews of Khaybar and the neighbourhood became alarmed and secretly attempted to form a league in the expectation of an attack; a *ḥayy* of the Banū Saʿd living in the vicinity then offered them help, but Muḥammad sent about a hundred men commanded by ʿAlī against this *ḥayy* in Shaʿbān 6/December 627-January 628; the expedition was reduced to a raid. In the following year, Muḥammad marched against Khaybar, and the Jews of Fadak, frightened by the news of his victories, agreed to hold discussions with a view to concluding an agreement with the Prophet's envoy, Muḥayyiṣa b. Masʿūd al-Anṣārī, even going so far as to propose giving up all their possessions provided that Muḥammad allowed them to depart. An initial agreement was followed by a second pact granted by Muḥammad, sometimes overlooked by the sources (*e.g.* the *K. al-Kharādj*): they were to remain in Fadak while giving up half their lands and half the produce of the oasis; on this point al-Balādhurī (*Futūḥ*, 29) is explicit: *ʿalā niṣf al-arḍ bi-turbatihā* (the emendation suggested in the Glossary, *bi-thamaratihā*, should be rejected). On the subject of the agreement with the Jews of Khaybar, the same author (*Futūḥ*, 23) uses a quite different expression: "*ʿāmalahum* [*Muḥammad*] *ʿalā 'l-shaṭr min al-thamar wa 'l-ḥabb*", that is to say that he concluded an agreement with them for share-cropping, and subsequently confirms this condition in other *khabar*s (*ibid.*, 24, 25, 27; cf. 29; on the difference between the two agreements see also al-Bukhārī, ed. Krehl, iii, 74; Ibn Ḥanbal, *Musnad*, Cairo 1959, i, 58; al-Ṭabarī, i, 1825; Ibn Abi 'l-Ḥadīd, *Sharḥ*, Cairo 1959, vi, 46; al-Ḥalabī, *al-Sīra al-ḥalabiyya*, Alexandria 1280, iii, 172). Unlike the decision reached for Khaybar, where the produce, assigned to the Muslims, was shared annually, Fadak was allocated to Muḥammad (*khāliṣa lahu*), who devoted the revenues from it to needy travellers (*abnāʾ al-sabīl*) and also for the maintenance of the least rich (*ṣaghīr*) of the Banū Hāshim; the reason invoked to justify this measure was that Fadak had been acquired by treaty (*ṣulḥ*^{an}). Two other expeditions of limited importance, in Shaʿbān 7/end of 628-beginning of 629, took place against the tribe of the Banū Murra who in summer lived near Fadak.

It was after the Prophet's death that the disagreement between Fāṭima and Abū Bakr started. Fāṭima maintained that Fadak, like Muḥammad's share of the produce from Khaybar, should come to her as her father's heiress; Abū Bakr, on the other hand, maintained that their attribution should remain exactly as Muhammad had settled it, since it was a question of *ṣadaḳa*s (that is to say public property used for benevolent purposes, like the *zakāt*). The Prophet, he said, had stated that he would have no heirs (*lā nūrathu*); what he left would be *ṣadaḳa* (*mā taraknā, ṣadaḳat*^{un}). ʿAlī supported his wife, and this question of inheritance aggravated his opposition to Abū Bakr. The caliph used a fatherly tone in his conversation with Fāṭima, but remained firm; he invited her to produce witnesses to testify to the donation which she claimed to have been made by her father; but, as she could only produce her husband and a woman named Umm Ayman, he considered their evidence inadequate [see SHAHĀDA], nevertheless admitting that an appropriate income must be guaranteed for the Prophet's family. The rejection of Fāṭima's claim appeared to be an injustice in the eyes of the Shīʿa (see *al-Sīra al-ḥalabiyya*, iii, 607-9 for their grounds for this belief and for a criticism of their arguments). After the failure of her claim, Fāṭima was unwilling to meet Abū Bakr again, and it was only after her death, some months after that of the Prophet, that ʿAlī consented to recognise the election of Abū Bakr and renounced the claims to Fadak.

In the time of ʿUmar, the Jews living in the northern Ḥidjāz suffered a very severe blow: the caliph decided to expel them, since by this time the great number of slaves at the disposal of the Muslims allowed them to exploit all the fertile land in Arabia. While the Jews of Khaybar had to leave the oasis and emigrate to Syria without receiving any indemnity, those from Fadak were granted one, based on the valuation of their property. This fact confirms that the former were regarded simply as usufructuaries, so that the share-cropping agreement with them could thus be broken without compensation, whereas the rights of ownership of the latter to one half of the oasis were recognised. Even after the expulsion of the Jews, ʿUmar used different methods for K̲h̲aybar and for Fadak: to the Muslims who had received from Muḥammad a share in the produce from K̲h̲aybar (or to their heirs), he gave ownership of the land (*raḳabat al-arḍ*, says al-Balād̲h̲urī, *ibid.*, 26) in proportion; as regards Fadak, he did not change the system, and his immediate successors followed his example. However, this assertion by the majority of the sources is explained by a note which Yāḳūt has preserved for us and Ibn Kat̲h̲īr has clarified with some details: when the Muslims, thanks to their conquests, had attained widespread prosperity, ʿUmar, guided by his *id̲j̲tihād*, assigned Fadak to al-ʿAbbās and ʿAlī; these two men quarrelled bitterly, each maintaining his own right of possession, and ʿUmar left them to sort out the matter themselves; it seems that they partitioned the oasis—subsequently, however, there is no further mention of the rights of al-ʿAbbās and his descendants to Fadak—and that one condition had been imposed by ʿUmar, namely that Fadak had to remain a *ṣadaḳa*; consequently, in the caliph's view, ʿAlī and al-ʿAbbās had merely been the administrators of a charitable foundation. It is to be assumed, however, that since the Prophet had used the revenues of Fadak also to meet the needs of his family, ʿAlī, and the ʿAlids after him, put the same interpretation upon the way in which the *ṣadaḳa* should be administered; thus is to be explained their persistence in claiming possession of the oasis, and the promptness with which the caliphs dispossessed them of it as soon as they went into opposition (see below). In later times it was not clearly understood what had happened; the uncertainty of the information is well explained by Yāḳūt, according to whom the disagreement over the question of Fadak sprang from political passions; and further evidence of this is to be found in the *Kitāb al-ʿAbbāsiyya* of al-D̲j̲āḥiẓ (see Ibn Abi 'l-Ḥadīd, *S̲h̲arḥ Nahd̲j̲ al-balāg̲h̲a*, iv, 98; *Rasāʾil*, ed. Sandūbī, 300). Ibn Kat̲h̲īr (*Bidāya*, iv, 203) confirms and explains the above account. According to some *ḥadīt̲h̲s* (e.g. al-Buk̲h̲ārī, ed. Krehl, ii, 271 f.), ʿUmar assigned to ʿAlī and to al-ʿAbbās the *ṣadaḳa* which the Prophet possessed at Medina, but retained Fadak and K̲h̲aybar. In any case, the change in the situation at Fadak took place after the expulsion of the Jews, for the government then had to look for the most convenient means of exploiting the land thus vacated. It was Muʿāwiya who brought the oasis under private ownership by giving it as an *iḳṭāʿ* to Marwān b. al-Ḥakam; however, he took it away from him during the years when he was in disgrace (from about 48/668 to 54/674), and then others vainly coveted it, since it produced an annual revenue of approximately 10,000 dinars (Ibn Saʿd, v, 286). Marwān, in his turn, gave it to his sons ʿAbd al-ʿAzīz and ʿAbd al-Malik. When ʿUmar II came to the throne, the whole property of Fadak was in his possession, since a share of it had been given him by his father ʿAbd al-ʿAzīz, and he had gained possession of the shares belonging to al-Walīd and Sulaymān, ʿAbd al-Malik's heirs. He was thus able to proclaim in a speech in the mosque that he had restored Fadak to its original purpose, and he also told his hearers that the Prophet had refused to make a gift of Fadak to Fāṭima when she had asked him for it (this shows that he was acquainted with a *ḥadīt̲h̲* which described this incident). But he entrusted Fadak to Fāṭima's descendants, and it was they who administered it (Ibn al-At̲h̲īr, ii, 173, states this positively: *fa-waliyahā awlād Fāṭima*; Ibn Saʿd (v, 287) leaves matters vague; the other writers, perhaps being afraid to venture onto dangerous ground, say nothing about it). It is probable that ʿUmar II had re-imposed the solution adopted by ʿUmar I for the Fadak question. It might be supposed that information on this point had been confused and that, instead of two decisions taken by the two ʿUmars, there was in fact only one single decision, taken by one or other of them; but the sources are too specific with regard to the first decision, while the second fits well into the general picture of the measures adopted by ʿUmar II for the purpose of ending the injustices inflicted on the ʿAlids.

This decision did not put an end to the vicissitudes of Fadak. Yazīd b. ʿAbd al-Malik took possession of the oasis, and it was the first of the ʿAbbāsids, al-Saffāḥ, who restored Fadak to Fāṭima's descendants. The change was short-lived, for al-Manṣūr confiscated Fadak after the rebellion of Muḥammad al-Nafs al-Zakiyya [*q.v.*] and Ibrāhīm [*q.v.*]; the oasis reverted to the ʿAlids in the caliphate of al-Mahdī, only to be once again seized by al-Hādī after the revolt of the ʿAlids with its tragic conclusion at al-Fak̲h̲k̲h̲ [*q.v.*]. Finally, in 210/826, al-Maʾmūn consented that it should be granted to Fāṭima's descendants who had come to make this request in the name of the family; he even caused his decree to be recorded in his *dīwān*s. The long letter which he sent to his *ʿāmil* in Medina, preserved by al-Balād̲h̲urī, shows us that the caliph imposed his decision while at the same time he attempted to support it by arguments for which, we can see clearly, he brought pressure to bear on the *faḳīh*s (al-Yaʿḳūbī, ii, 573); however, he was so fully cognisant of the weakness of these arguments that, at the beginning of the letter, he boasted of his position in regard to the religion of Allāh, his responsibility as the Prophet's representative, his relationship with him, his fitness for applying the *sunna*, etc. But al-Maʾmūn's third successor, al-Mutawakkil, did not respect his decree and once again devoted Fadak to its original purpose which Abū Bakr had sanctioned; we must conclude that, under the influence of the *ʿulamāʾ*, he renounced the arguments put forward by al-Maʾmūn. Finally, al-Masʿūdī (viii, 303) and Ibn al-At̲h̲īr (vii, 75) add a further point about the fate of Fadak: they tell us that the caliph al-Muntaṣir, son of al-Mutawakkil, once again restored Fadak to the ʿAlids.

To conclude, the question of Fadak is interesting from the legal point of view (it proves that, from the earliest times of Islam, there was a very precise conception regarding the difference between private and collective property and an awareness of the duties and rights relating to each); it is moreover an example of the difficulties encountered by the rulers who respected the *s̲h̲arīʿa* when, for political motives, they proposed to modify a situation established by the Prophet and his immediate successors.

Bibliography: Ibn Saʿd, I/i, 18, 65, I/ii, 183, II/i, 65, 80, 82, 86, 91, II/ii, 85-7, III/i, 14, III/ii, 83 f., V, 286 f., VIII, 18; Ibn Ḥanbal, *Musnad*, Cairo 1373/1954, i, 9, 14, 25, 55, 58, 60, 78, etc. Balād̲h̲urī, *Futūḥ*, 20, 29-33; idem, *Ansāb*, ed. M. Ḥamīd Allāh, Cairo 1959, i, 519; Abū Yūsuf, *K. al-K̲h̲arād̲j̲*, trans. Fagnan, 78 f.;

Yaḥyā b. Ādam, *K. al-Kharādj*, ed. Juynboll, 21, 22, 27; Ibn Hishām, ed. Wüstenfeld, 764, 776, 779 (English trans. A. Guillaume, 515-6, 523-5); Wāḳidī, *Maghāzī* (Wellhausen), 237, 291, 292, 296, 297; Ṭabarī, i, 1556, 1583, 1589-92, 1825, 2594 f., ii, 85; Yaʿḳūbī, *Historiae*, ed. Houtsma, i, 296, ii, 78, 142, 265, 366, 573; Masʿūdī, *Murūdj*, iv, 158, v, 66, vi, 55 f., vii, 303; idem, *Tanbīh*, *BGA*, viii, 247, 253, 258, 262, 264, 287 ff.; Ibn al-Athīr, ii, 160, 169, 171-3, iii, 381, 413, v, 46, vii, 75; al-Ḳāḍī al-Nuʿmān. *Daʿāʾim al-islām*, ed. Fyzee, Cairo 1370/1951, 449 f.; Ibn Abi 'l-Ḥadīd. *Sharḥ Nahdj al-balāgha*, iv, 88-106 (ed. Abu 'l-Faḍl Ibrāhīm, Cairo 1959, vi, 46-52 ff.), whose source on Fadak is the *K. al-Sakīfa* of al-Djawharī; Ibn Kathīr, *Bidāya*, Cairo 1348-55, iv, 203; Ḥalabī, *al-Sīra al-ḥalabiyya*, Alexandria 1280, iii, 607 f.; Bakrī, *Muʿdjam*, ed. Wüstenfeld, 333, 706; Yāḳūt, *Muʿdjam*, iii, 855-8; Bukhārī, ed. Krehl, ii, 271 f., iii, 131, iv, 282; A. Sprenger, *Das Leben und die Lehre des Muḥammad*, 2nd. ed., Berlin 1869, iii, 232 n. 2, 277 n. 1; L. Caetani, *Annali*, 1 A.H., § 65, 5 A.H., § 55, 6 A.H., § 17, 7 A.H., §§ 33, 46 n. 1, 47 and nn. 2 and 3, 48, 63, 64 and n. 1, 8 A.H., § 32, 9 A.H., § 51, 10 A.H., § 103, 11 A.H., §§ 202 and n. 1 (where the dates are incorrect) 203, 208, 20 A.H., §§ 234, 235, 236, 237 n. 2, 239 and n. 1; I. Hrbek, *Muḥammads Nachlass und die Aliden*, in *ArO* (1950), 43-9. On the way the question was developed in legend and hence in the *taʿziyas*, see E. Rossi and A. Bombaci, *Elenco dei drammi religiosi persiani (fondo mss vaticani Cerulli)*, Citta del Vaticano 1961, 45, 268, 316, 356, 678, 802, 803, 996. (L. Veccia Vaglieri)

FAḌĀLA, town and port on the Atlantic coast of Morocco, 25 km. to the north-east of Casablanca, in the lands of the Zanāta tribe. The origin of the name is unknown; the etymology given by Graberg de Hemsö and by Godard (*fayḍ Allāh* = "bounty of God") is obviously fanciful. The name is perhaps to be compared with that of a section of the neighbouring Ziyāyda tribe, the Faḍḍāla. The toponym appears as early as al-Idrīsī and the Genoese and Venetian portulans. It appears that Christian merchants visited the anchorage in the 14th and 15th centuries. —Sīdī Muḥammad b. ʿAbd Allāh in 1186-7/1773, wishing to make Faḍāla a grain depot for the province of Tamasna, granted export privileges to the European merchants, but withdrew them the following year. He then accorded them to the Spanish company of "los cinco gremios mayores", who also held the monopoly of the trade of al-Dār al-Bayḍāʾ. The port was again abandoned in the 19th century. It had only one *ḳaṣaba* which, like the neighbouring *ḳaṣaba* of al-Manṣūriyya, was used as a staging-post on the route from Rabat to Casablanca.

The concession to build a small port was granted in 1914 to the French company Hersent frères. Today the port of Faḍāla, as an auxiliary to that of Casablanca, is principally a petrol port. The tonnage loaded was 90,000 tons in 1955, 36,000 in 1958; the tonnage unloaded was 331,000 tons in 1955, 233,000 in 1958.

The proximity of Casablanca has encouraged the introduction of a fair number of industries, and the population, mostly composed of workers who have migrated from the neighbouring countryside, has increased rapidly: in 1952 it was 25,189, of which 20,880 were Muslim Moroccans, 449 Jewish Moroccans, and 3,860 were foreigners. In 1960 (provisional census reports) it was 35,000, with 31,750 Muslims, 150 Jews and 3,100 foreigners. The town has the status of a municipality. In 1379/1959 its name was changed by decree to al-Muḥammadiyya, in honour of the reigning sovereign, Muḥammad V.

Bibliography: Idrīsī, *al-Maghrib*, 81; E. de la Primaudaie, *Les villes maritimes du Maroc*, in *R.Afr.*, xvii (1873), 285-6; Budgett Meakin, *The land of the Moors*, London 1901, 230; *Villes et tribus du Maroc, Casablanca et les Chaouïa*, Paris 1915, ii, 34 ff.; M. Lamidey, *Fedala*, in *Bull. Ec. et Soc. du Maroc*, xiv (1950), 27-36. (A. Adam)

al-**FAḌĀLĪ,** Muḥammad b. Muḥammad al-Shāfiʿī, a writer on Islamic dogmatics and teacher of al-Bādjūrī [*q.v.*], d. 1236/1821. Both of his works, *Kifāyat al-ʿAwāmm fīmā yadjib ʿalayhim min ʿilm al-kalām*, and a commentary on the profession of monotheism, *Risāla ʿalā lā ilāha illa 'llāh*, have been commented upon by al-Bādjūrī and have been often printed together with the commentaries.

Bibliography: Brockelmann, II, 641; S II, 744; D. B. Macdonald, in *EI*¹, s.v.; translations of his *Kifāya* by Macdonald, *Development of Muslim theology*, etc., 1903, 315 ff., and by M. Horten, *Muhammedanische Glaubenslehre*, Bonn 1916, 5-45. (J. Schacht)

FADDĀN [see misāḥa].

FADHLAKA, sum, total, from the Arabic *fa dhālika*, "and that [is]", placed at the bottom of an addition to introduce the result. Besides its arithmetical use, the term was also employed for the summing up of a petition, report, or other document, as for example for the summarized statements of complaints presented at the *Dīwān-i humāyūn* [*q.v.*]. By extension it acquired the meaning of compendium and is used, in this sense, in the titles of two well-known works on Ottoman history, written in the 17th century by Kātib Čelebi and in the 19th by Aḥmad Wefīḳ Pasha [*qq.v.*]. (Ed.)

FĀḌIL BEY, Ḥüseyn (ca. 1170/1757-1225/1810) also known as Fāḍil-i Enderūnī, Ottoman poet celebrated for his erotic works, was a grandson of Ẓāhir Āl ʿUmar [*q.v.*] of ʿAkkā, who rebelled against the Porte in the seventies of the 18th century. Taken to Istanbul in 1190/1776 by the *ḳapudān pasha* Ghāzī Ḥasan after his grandfather and father had been slain in battle, he was brought up in the Palace. An amatory intrigue led to his expulsion in 1198/1783-4, and for twelve years he led a vagabond life in poverty in Istanbul. *Ḳaṣīde*s addressed to Selīm III and the statesmen of the day imploring their patronage eventually won him employment, but in 1214/1799 he was banished to Rhodes. There he lost his sight, and was permitted to return to Istanbul, where he died in Dhu'l-Ḥidjdja 1225/ December 1810. His works are (1) a *dīwān*, printed at Būlāḳ 1258/1842 together with (2) *Defter-i ʿashḳ* ('Journal of love'), a long *methnewī* mainly recounting his love-affairs but with some interesting descriptions of life in the Palace School (see saray); (3) *Khūbān-nāme* ('Book of beautiful youths'), a *methnewī* describing the attractions of young men of various nationalities (both from within the Empire and from Europe and the 'New World'!) and (4) *Zenān-nāme* ('Book of women'), a similar work on girls (these two were lithographed at Istanbul in 1838, but the Minister of the Exterior Muṣṭafā Rashīd had the edition confiscated for its indecent subject-matter; new edition 1286/1870; Fazil Bey, *Le livre des femmes* (*Zenan-nameh*), trad. du turc par J. Decourdemanche, Paris 1879); (5) *Čengī-nāme*, a series of stanzas in the tradition of the *Shehr-engīz* [*q.v.*], on the dancing-boys of Istanbul.

Bibliography: Sha̲nī-zāde, *Ta'rīk̲h̲*, Istanbul 1292, i, 407; D̲j̲ewdet, *Ta'rīk̲h̲*, i, 105, ix, 219; Ṭayyār-zāde ʿAṭāʾ, *Ta'rīk̲h̲* (*'Enderūn ta'rīk̲h̲i'*), Istanbul 1292-3, iv, 242-61; Faṭīn, *Te̲d̲h̲kere*, 321 ff.; Hammer-Purgstall, *GOD*, iv, 428-53; Gibb, *Ottoman Poetry*, iv, 220-42; F. Edhem and I. Stchoukine, *Les manuscrits orientaux illustrés de la Bibliothèque de l'Université de Stamboul*, Paris 1933, no. 17; *IA*, iv, 529-31, by Ali Cânib Yöntem.   (J. H. MORDTMANN*)

MUṢṬAFĀ **FĀḌIL PAS̲H̲A**, MIṢIRLI, Ottoman statesman, was born 2 February 1830 in Cairo, the youngest son of Ibrāhīm Pas̲h̲a and grandson of Muḥammad ʿAlī Pas̲h̲a, wālī of Egypt. After his education in Cairo, he went in 1262/1846 to Istanbul, where he was attached to the office of the Grand Vizier. He advanced in government service and was nominated vizier in S̲h̲aʿbān 1274/March-April 1858. On 19 November 1862 he became Minister of Education and was transferred on 12 January 1863 to the ministry of Finance, a post he held until March 1864, when he resigned. On 5 November 1865 he was appointed president of the *Med̲j̲lis-i k̲h̲azāʾin*, from which he was dismissed on 16 February 1866. Being exiled from the Ottoman Empire, he left Istanbul, 4 April 1866, and went to Paris. His exile was probably due to his criticism of the policy of Fuʾād Pas̲h̲a [*q.v.*], who favoured Ismāʿīl Pas̲h̲a, the wālī of Egypt. Ismāʿīl Pas̲h̲a sought to restrict the succession to the hereditary governorship to his own descendants, thus depriving his brother Muṣṭafā Fāḍil Pas̲h̲a of his right to succeed. Muṣṭafā Fāḍil Pas̲h̲a took the leadership of Ottoman liberalism by publishing on 24 March 1867 in the French newspaper *Liberté* a letter addressed to the Sultan ʿAbd al-ʿAzīz, in which he advised the Sultan to accept a Constitution for the Empire (for the text of this letter see *Orient*, no. 5 [1er Trimestre 1958], 29-38). He invited the Young Ottomans [see YEÑI ʿOT̲H̲MĀNLÍLAR] to join him in Europe and helped them in their press campaign against the autocratic government in Turkey. But he profited from the official visit of the Sultan to Western capitals to regain favour and returned on 20 September 1867 to Istanbul. He was nominated, on 25 July 1869, a member of the *Med̲j̲lis-i Wālā* and became for the second time, in Muḥarram 1287/April 1870, Minister of Finance. He was dismissed from this post on 18 December. He occupied from October 1871 to January 1872 the ministry of Justice. He died on 2 December 1875 in Istanbul and was buried at Eyyūb, the holy quarter of the city. His remains were moved to Egypt on 25 June 1929. He was an intelligent and able statesman and succeeded in negotiating the sixth foreign loan of the Ottoman Empire in 1863 during his first term as Minister of Finance. The conditions of this loan were reasonable. His ambition caused him to behave in an opportunist way: he used the Young Ottomans as a tool in his intrigues to become wālī of Egypt. He spent unsuccessfully extraordinary sums in this aim. Nevertheless he patronized such writers as Shināsī [*q.v.*] and artists as Zekāʾī Dede [*q.v.*]. He founded in 1870 the first club in Istanbul: this *End̲j̲ümen-i Ülfet* lasted just over a year.

Bibliography: Mehmed Zeki Pâkalın, *Tanzimat maliye nazırları*, Istanbul 1939-40, ii, 3-65; Marcel Colombe, *Une lettre d'un prince égyptien du XIXe siècle au sultan ottoman Abd al-Aziz*, in *Orient*, no. 5 (1er Trimestre 1958), 23-38; Şerif Mardin, *The Genesis of Young Ottoman thought*, Princeton, N.J. 1962, *passim*; *Sid̲j̲ill-i ʿOt̲h̲mānī*,

iv, 481; Ibrahim Alâettin Gövsa, *Türk meşhurları ansiklopedisi*, Istanbul 1946, 132.   (E. KURAN)

FAḌĪLA (Arab., pl. *faḍāʾil*) an excellence or excellent quality, a high degree in (or of) excellence. The plural *faḍāʾil* indicates a definite category of literature, related to but distinct from the so-called "disputes for precedence". *Faḍāʾil* literature exposes the excellences of things, individuals, groups, places, regions and such for the purpose of a *laudatio*. The polemical comparison or dialogue, characteristic of the "disputes for precedence", is lacking.

Faḍāʾil literature, the opposite to which is *mat̲h̲ālib* literature, may be divided into various branches:

Ḳurʾān. *Faḍāʾil* literature takes its point of departure from the Ḳurʾān. The praise of the Ḳurʾān preserves, modified for the conditions of Islam, the custom of the pre-islamic Arabs to boast (*mufāk̲h̲ara*) of the nobility and exalted rank of their tribes (see Goldziher, *Muh. St.* i, 51, 54 ff.). A comparison of its *faḍāʾil* with others, despite the Arab fondness for comparison, was impossible, for the Ḳurʾān, as the direct and unadulterated word of God, was immeasurable, even in polemic against the *Ahl al-Kitāb* (see Goldziher, *ZDMG*, xxxii (1878), 344 ff.; M. Schreiner, *ZDMG*, xlii (1888), 593 f.). An enumeration of its excellences was furthermore to win back to the study of the incomparable holy book those Muslims who had occupied themselves all too exclusively with profane science, such as that of the *mag̲h̲āzī* and the *amt̲h̲āl* (see Goldziher, *Muh. St.*, ii, 155; Abū ʿUbayd, *K. al-Amt̲h̲āl*, beginning). The nucleus of the *faḍāʾil al-Ḳurʾān* consists of sayings derived from the Prophet, his Companions and their descendents (*ṣaḥāba*, *tābiʿūn* etc.) concerning the excellences of the individual suras and verses and the reward for those who occupy themselves with them. There are also accounts providing information as to when separate revelations were granted to Muḥammad. Questions of Ḳurʾānic readings are treated in special chapters. The oldest preserved *K. Faḍāʾil al-Ḳurʾān* is very likely that of Abū ʿUbayd (died 224/837; see Brockelmann, I, 106, and S I, 166 ff.), see Ahlwardt no. 451; A. Spitaler, in *Documenta Islamica Inedita* (*Festschrift R. Hartmann*), Berlin 1952, 1-24. The list in Ḥād̲j̲d̲j̲ī K̲h̲alīfa (under *ʿIlm Faḍāʾil al-Ḳurʾān*) is incomplete (see Yāḳūt, *Irs̲h̲ād*, indexes; Ibn K̲h̲ayr, *Fihrist*, index; Brockelmann, index). The large collections of traditions, such as Buk̲h̲ārī's (died 256/870) *Ṣaḥīḥ* (book 66), have a separate chapter on the *Faḍāʾil al-Ḳurʾān*.

Companions of the Prophet. Among others Wahb b. Wahb (d. 200/815) had already written a *K. Faḍāʾil al-Anṣār* (*Irs̲h̲ād*, vii, 233, 7), al-S̲h̲āfiʿī (d. 204/820) a *K. Faḍāʾil Ḳurays̲h̲ wa 'l-Anṣār* (*Irs̲h̲ād*, vi, 397, 17), and Aḥmad b. Ḥanbal's (d. 241/855) *K. Faḍāʾil al-Ṣaḥāba* has been preserved (Brockelmann, S I, 310, 312). The 62nd chapter of Buk̲h̲ārī's *Ṣaḥīḥ* contains *faḍāʾil aṣḥāb al-nabī*. The "excellences" of the Companions of the Prophet are for the most part concerned with the experiences which they shared with the Prophet. Historically confirmed traditions, such as that concerning Muḥammad's *hid̲j̲ra* in the company of Abū Bakr, stand beside fantastic prophecies by Muḥammad about the destiny and future of his Companions, and so forth.

Individuals. Al-Madāʾinī (d. 225/840) wrote a book about the *faḍāʾil* of Muḥammad b. al-Ḥanafiyya, D̲j̲aʿfar b. Abī Ṭālib and al-Ḥārit̲h̲ b. ʿAbd al-Muṭṭalib (*Irs̲h̲ād*, v, 313, 9 ff.), and al-Ṭabarī (d. 310/923) one about those of Abū Bakr, ʿUmar, al-ʿAbbās and ʿAlī (*Irshād*, vi, 452, 18f,, 16). Ibn al-ʿUshārī's (d. 441/1029) *K. Faḍāʾil Abī Bakr al-Ṣiddīḳ* has been preserved (Brockelmann, S I, 601); Ibn ʿAsākir (d. 571/1176) dreamed of the *faḍāʾil* of Abū Bakr (for this and others of his various *faḍāʾil* books, see *Irshād*, v, 143 ff.), etc. A work such as that of Ibn al-Djawzī (d. 597/1200) about the *faḍāʾil* of Ḥasan al-Baṣrī (Brockelmann, S I, 917) belongs properly to *manāḳib* [*q.v.*] literature (see also al-Ḳifṭī, *Inbāh*, i, 219; Brockelmann, S III, 1228; Storey, index).

Cities and provinces. Among *faḍāʾil* works those concerning the *faḍāʾil* of particular cities and provinces occupy a special place. H. Ritter (*Über die Bildersprache Niẓāmīs*, Berlin 1927, 20) has already pointed out certain similarities to the *genos epideiktikon*. But the yield of a genuine panegyric of the city, such as G. E. von Grunebaum has sketched (*Zum Lob der Stadt in der arabischen Prosa*, in *Kritik und Dichtkunst*, Wiesbaden 1955, 80-6), is comparatively small, apart from the Islamic West (see below). For these *faḍāʾil* books too consist largely of sayings put into the mouths of Muḥammad and his Companions in which political and regional aims are primarily pursued (see Goldziher, *Muh. St.*, ii, 128 ff.; *al-Aghānī*[1], v, 157, [3]vi, 54 ff.; al-Marzubānī, *al-Muḳtabas*, Ms. Nur. Osm. 3391, fol. 22b ff., 90b). These *ḥadīth*s may be divided into three groups: 1) *Isrāʾīliyyāt*, traditions about the pre-islamic period, in particular about the holy places of prophets, etc., 2) invented *ḥadīth*s which originated in the rivalries between Umayyads, Shīʿīs, ʿAbbāsids etc., or between the Ḥidjāz, Syria and ʿIrāḳ, etc., 3) a few genuine *ḥadīth*s able to withstand even an internal criticism (see Ṣalāḥ al-Dīn al-Munadjdjid's preface to his edition of al-Rabaʿī's (d. 444/1052) *K. Faḍāʾil al-Shām wa-Dimashḳ*, Damascus 1950). The *faḍāʾil* of Baṣra were collected by ʿUmar b. Shabba (d. 264/878) (Ḥādjdjī Khalīfa), those of Kūfa by Ibrāhīm b. Muḥammad (d. 283/896; *Irshād*, i, 295, 13), those of Baghdād by al-Saraḳhsī (d. 286/899; Ḥādjdjī Khalīfa). Probably the oldest surviving work of this nature is the *K. Faḍāʾil Miṣr* of ʿUmar b. Muḥammad al-Kindī (d. after 350/961; Brockelmann I, 155; S I, 230; ed. and tr. by J. Østrup, Copenhagen 1896). For a manuscript of an early book about the *Faḍāʾil al-Kūfa* in the Ẓāhiriyya Library, see H. Ritter in *Oriens*, iii (1950), 82 (for the *Faḍāʾil-i Balkh*, see Storey, i, 1296 ff.; also *Irshād*, ii, 143, 9). Quite different is al-Shaḳundī's (d. 629/1231; Brockelmann, S I, 483) *R. fī Faḍl al-Andalus* (tr. E. G. Gómez according to al-Maḳḳarī, *Analectes*, ii, 126-50: *Elogio del Islam Español*, Madrid-Granada 1934, 123). This small *Risāla* represents indeed an *encomium* of Andalusia, freed of the fetters of eastern *ḥadīth* science: the praise of the power of the state (Umayyad caliphs), of knowledge (famous Andalusian scholars), of poetry, of cities such as Seville, Cordova, etc.

Peoples and Tribes. Abū ʿUbayda's (d. ca. 210/825) *K. Faḍāʾil al-Furs* (*Fihrist*, 54, 10; *Irshād*, vii, 170, 5; *Ṣubḥ al-Aʿshā*, iv, 92, 8: read Abū ʿUbayda instead of Abū ʿUbayd; Brockelmann, S I, 167 also to be corrected thus) might owe its origin to the author's inclinations towards the Shuʿūbiyya. For Djāḥiẓ's *K. Faḍāʾil al-Atrāk*, see Ch. Pellat (*Arabica*, iii (1956), 177), and F. Gabrieli (*RSO*, xxxii (1957), 477-483), for his *K. Faḍl al-Furs*, see *Irshād* (vi, 77, 19). Djāḥiẓ's *K. Faḍīlat al-kalām* and *Faḍīlat al-Muʿtazila* (see Pellat in *Arabica*, iii (1956), 163 and 168) do not actually belong to the *faḍāʾil* literature, but rather are similar to the apologetic nature of the *K. Faḍāʾil al-Imām al-Shāfiʿī* by Fakhr al-Dīn al-Rāzī (d. 606/1209; see Brockelmann, S I, 921). Ibn ʿAbd Rabbih (d. 328/940) devoted a special chapter of his *ʿIḳd al-Farīd* (vol. iii, Cairo 1372/1952, 312-418) to the *faḍāʾil al-ʿArab*. Ibn al-Kalbī (d. 204/819) collected the *faḍāʾil* of Ḳays ʿAylān (*Irshād*, vii, 251, 1), and al-Shuʿūbī (ca. 200/815) those of Kināna and Rabīʿa (*Fihrist* 105, 15 ff.; *Irshād*, v, 66, 16 ff.), etc. To what extent anti-Shuʿūbī tendencies play a part in these works, as seems to have been the case with Aḥmad b. Abī Ṭāhir Ṭayfur's (d. 280/893) *K. Faḍl al-ʿArab ʿala ʾl-ʿAdjam* (*Irshād*, i, 155, 6), has not been clarified.

Various. The *faḍāʾil* of the holy months (Ibn Abī Dunyā, d. 281/894, Brockelmann, I, 160, S I, 247, and others) have been the subject of treatises, as have been those of prayers (Aḥmad b. al-Ḥusayn al-Bayhaḳī, d. 458/1066, Brockelmann I, 446 f., S I, 619, and others), of the *basmala* (al-Būnī, d. 622/1225, Brockelmann I, 655, and others), of the *djihād* (Ibn Shaddād, d. 632/1234, Brockelmann, S I, 550, and others), as well as the "excellences" of quite profane things which have been particularly collected: for example, shaving of the head (al-Ṣaymarī, d. 275/888: *Irshād*, vi, 402 and 403), the days of the week (al-Sīrāfī, d. 368/979; poem, *Irshād*, iii, 89, 5-11), the herb basil (Muḥammad b. Aḥmad al-Nūḳātī, d. 382/992; *Irshād*, vi, 324, 16), archery (al-Ḳarrāb, d. 429/1037; Brockelmann, S I, 619; *IC*, xxxiv (1960), 195-218) and coffee (al-Udjhūrī, d. 967/1559; Brockelmann II, 414 no. 9).

Bibliography: in the article. For "disputes for precedence" see M. Steinschneider, *Rangstreit-Literatur, Ein Beitrag zur vergleichenden Literatur- und Kulturgeschichte*, *SBAW* Vienna, clv/4 (1908), 87 pp.; also O. Rescher, *Zu Moritz Steinschneiders "Rangstreitliteratur"*, in *Isl.*, xiv (1925), 397-401; W. Bacher, *Zur Rangstreit-Literatur, Aus der arabischen Poesie der Juden Jemens*, in *Mélanges H. Derenbourg*, Paris 1909, 131-47; C. Brockelmann, *Fabel und Tiermärchen in der älteren arabischen Literatur*, in *Islamica*, ii (1926), 96-128, esp. 118, 120, 128; E. Littmann, *Neuarabische Streitgedichte*, transcr., ed. and tr., in *Festschrift zur Feier des 200-jährigen Bestehens der Akad. d. Wissensch. Göttingen*, ii, 1951, 36-66; H. Ethé, *Über persische Tenzonen*, in *Abhandlungen und Vorträge des Fünften Internationalen Orientalisten-Congresses*, Erste Hälfte, Berlin 1882, 48-135; E. Littmann, *Ein türkisches Streitgedicht über die Ehe*, in *A Volume of Oriental Studies presented to Edward G. Browne*, Cambridge 1922, 269-84; H. Walther, *Das Streitgedicht in der lateinischen Literatur des Mittelalters*, München 1920, 254 pp. (*Quellen und Untersuchungen zur latein. Philologie des Mittelalters*, v, 2); F. Focke, *Synkrisis*, in *Hermes*, lviii (1923), 327-68; O. Hense, *Die Synkrisis in der antiken Literatur*, Prorectoratsrede, Freiburg i. Br. 1893, 41 pp.; L. Rademacher, *Aristophanes' 'Frösche'*, *SBAW* Vienna cxcviii/4 (1922), esp. 26 ff.; F. de la Granja, *Dos epistolas de Aḥmad ibn Burd al-Aṣgar*, in *Al-Andalus*, xxv (1960), 383-418. (R. Sellheim)

FADJĪDJ [see FIGUIG].

FADJR [see ṢALĀT].

FADJR-I ĀTĪ [see FEDJR-I ĀTĪ].

FAḌL, BĀ, a family of *mashāyikh* of Tarīm in Ḥaḍramawt claiming descent from the Saʿd al-ʿashira clan of Madhḥidj. The name Bā Faḍl seems to derive from an ancestor called *al-faḳīh* Faḍl b. Muḥammad b. ʿAbd al-Karīm b. Muḥammad, whose genealogy cannot be traced beyond that. They seem to have had supreme authority in religious matters in

Tarīm until superseded by the Bā ʿAlawī *sayyids* around the 9th/15th century. They have long been prominent as *ṣūfīs* and *faḳīhs*, jurists. In the 10-11th/16th-17th centuries one branch existed in Aden. The most famous of this branch, and probably the founder, was Djamāl al-Dīn Muḥammad b. Aḥmad b. ʿAbd Allāh, born in Tarīm, who attained prominence in Aden as teacher and *muftī* and was favoured by Sulṭān ʿĀmir b. ʿAbd al-Wahhāb, the Ṭāhirid ruler of al-Yaman. He died in Aden in 903/1498.

Another branch, known as Bal Ḥādjdj, existed in al-Shiḥr, of which the probable founder was ʿAbd Allāh b. ʿAbd al-Raḥmān b. Abī Bakr (d. 918/1513), the author of a number of manuals on *fiḳh* and ṣūfism some of which gained circulation beyond his land and were commented upon by other authors (cf. Brockelmann II 389 and S II 528). He also acted as arbitrator between the rulers of the region and excercised some public authority. He was succeded by his son Aḥmad, known as *al-shahīd*, the martyr, because he was killed in al-Shiḥr in a battle with the Portuguese in 929/1523. The family might then have moved back to Tarīm, for a brother of Aḥmad *al-shahīd*, Ḥusayn (d. 979/1572), was a prominent *ṣūfī* in Tarīm and had inclinations towards the Shādhilī *ṭarīḳa*. A son of this Ḥusayn, called Zayn al-Dīn (d. 1026/1617), was also a *ṣūfī* and jurist in Tarīm. Another Ḥusayn, a descendent of Aḥmad *al-shahīd*, was born in al-Shiḥr in 1019/1610, travelled as a student to Aden, Zabīd, Mecca and Medina and back to al-Shiḥr and then to India and then back to Mecca, where he settled and traded in coffee and cloth between al-Mukhā and Mecca. He became a prominent and rather controversial *ṣūfī* and wrote some *ṣūfī* poetry. He died in Mecca in 1087/1677.

Of the Tarīm branch Muḥammad b. Ismāʿīl (d. 1006/1597) was a prominent teacher, and Aḥmad b. ʿAbd Allāh b. Sālim, called al-Sūdī (d. 1044/1634) was a linguist and grammarian of some merit.

Shaykh Muḥammad ʿAwaḍ Bā Faḍl (d. ca. 1953) is the author of a book of biographies called *Ṣilat al-ahl fī tarādjim Āl Bā Faḍl*, still in manuscript.

Bibliography: Ibn al-ʿAydarūs, *al-Nūr al-sāfir min akhbār al-ḳarn al-ʿāshir*, Baghdād 1934, 23-6, 44, 98-100, 135-7, 207 f., 344-8; al-Muḥibbī, *Khulāṣat al-athar fī aʿyān al-ḳarn al-ḥādī ʿashar*, Cairo 1869, 4 vols.; F. Wüstenfeld, *Die Çufiten in Süd-Arabien im XI (XVII) Jahrhundert*, Göttingen 1883, 86-90; R. B. Serjeant, *The Saiyids of Ḥaḍramawt*, London 1957, 12, 14; idem, *Historians and historiography of Ḥaḍramawt*, in *BSOAS*, xxv (1962), 256; idem, *The Portuguese off the South Arabian Coast*, Oxford 1963, 52-4. (M. A. Ghūl)

AL-FAḌL B. AḤMAD AL-ISFARĀʾINĪ Abu'l-ʿAbbās, the first *wazīr* of Sulṭan Maḥmūd of Ghazna, was formerly the *ṣāḥib-i barīd* (see barīd) of Marw under the Sāmānids. At the request of Subuktigīn, Amīr Nuḥ b. Manṣūr the Sāmānid sent Faḍl to Nīshāpūr in 385/995 as the *wazīr* of Maḥmūd, who had been appointed to the command of the troops in Khurāsān the previous year. Faḍl managed the affairs of the expanding empire of Sulṭān Maḥmūd with great tact and ability until 404/1013, when he was accused of extorting money from the subjects of the Sultan. Instead of answering the charge when he was called upon to do so, he voluntarily placed himself in the custody of the commander of the fort of Ghazna. The Sultan was annoyed at his conduct and allowed him to remain there. Faḍl died in 404/1013-4, during the absence of Sultan Maḥmūd on one of his Indian expeditions.

Bibliography: ʿUtbī, *Kitāb al-Yamīnī* (Lahore ed.), 265-71; *Āthār al-wuzarāʾ* (India Office Ms. no. 1569), fol. 88a-89a; Muḥammad Nāẓim, *The life and times of Sultan Maḥmūd of Ghazna*, Cambridge 1931, 48, 135, 146; C. E. Bosworth, *The Ghaznavids: their empire in Afghanistan and Eastern Iran, 994-1040*, Edinburgh 1963. (M. Nazim)

AL-FAḌL B. MARWĀN, vizier to the ʿAbbāsid al-Muʿtaṣim, and an ʿIrāḳi of Christian origin. He began his career modestly as a retainer of Harthama, the commander of Hārūn al-Rashīd's guard. Later, as a result of his particular talents, he became a secretary in the Land Tax office under the same caliph and subsequently he retired to ʿIrāḳ to the estates he had acquired during the civil war. It was there, in the region of al-Baradān, that he had an opportunity, during the reign of al-Maʾmūn, to gain the attention of the future al-Muʿtaṣim, who admitted him into his service, took him to Egypt in 212-3/827-8, and then had him put in charge of the Land Tax office. It was he who, acting as the caliph's deputy in Baghdād, had the oath of loyalty to al-Muʿtaṣim administered. Appointed vizier in Ramaḍān 218/September 833, he enjoyed wide powers, maintained a firm control over the treasury and attempted to restrict the sovereign's expenditure. This policy was the main cause of his disgrace, which occurred in Ṣafar 211/February 836, at the moment when the caliph decided to move his residence to Sāmarrā.

Al-Faḍl b. Marwān was the first example of the ʿIrāḳi secretaries of Christian origin who, during the 3rd/9th century, were to become numerous. He was held to have little education in religious knowledge, but to be highly competent in the exploitation of landed property. As an expert in land taxes, he also played a part under the succeeding caliphs, particularly al-Wāthiḳ and al-Mustaʿīn. He died in 250/864, about 90 years old.

Bibliography: Ṭabarī, index; D. Sourdel, *Le vizirat ʿabbāside*, Damascus 1959-60, i, 246-53 and index. (D. Sourdel)

AL-FAḌL B. AL-RABĪʿ, vizier to the ʿAbbāsid caliphs al-Rashīd and al-Amīn, was the son of al-Manṣūr's chamberlain al-Rabīʿ b. Yūnus [*q.v.*]. Born in 138/757-8, he very soon won the esteem of Hārūn al-Rashīd, who in 173/789-90 placed him in charge of the Expenditure Office and then in 179/795-6 made him chamberlain. After the disgrace of the Barāmika [*q.v.*] in 187/803, he succeeded Yaḥyā as vizier, though without being granted such wide powers; his part was confined to keeping check on public expenditure and in presenting letters and petitions (*ʿarḍ*), while another secretary directed the financial administration. On the death of al-Rashīd, which took place at Ṭūs in 193/809, it was al-Faḍl who caused the oath of loyalty to al-Amīn to be taken and who led back to Baghdād the whole of the expeditionary force which had been gathered together by the caliph to fight against the rebel Rāfiʿ b. al-Layth. The second heir al-Maʾmūn, who, under the terms of al-Rashīd's testament, was to govern the province of Khurāsān, held al-Faḍl responsible for this withdrawal of the army and tried in vain to make him reverse his decision. Shortly afterwards, it was the advice given by al-Faḍl which encouraged al-Amīn to deprive his brother of his rights to the succession and to confer them on his own son. This tense situation gave rise to a civil war and ended in the siege of Baghdād and the final triumph of al-Maʾmūn.

During the short reign of al-Amīn (193-8/809-14), al-Faḍl remained as before the caliph's most intimate adviser, playing a particularly important part in the episodes of the struggle with al-Maʾmūn. But he did not exercise any general control over the administration, nor was he responsible for the jurisdiction of the *maẓālim.*

On the arrival of al-Maʾmūn's troops he went into hiding, reappearing when the inhabitants of Baghdād, in revolt against the rule of the caliph in Marw who had chosen an ʿAlid as his heir, brought Ibrāhīm b. al-Mahdī (201/816-7) to power. He subsequently gained al-Maʾmūn's pardon when the latter returned to Baghdād, and died in 207/822-3 or 208/823-4.

Al-Faḍl b. al-Rabīʿ thus seems to have been an intriguer of mediocre personality and limited ability. As chamberlain he succeeded by means of adroit manoeuvres in replacing the Barāmika and in exalting himself to the highest government office, the vizierate. He then adopted the cause of al-Amīn, a weak character over whom he planned to exert great influence, but he was unsuccessful in meeting the situation created by the forceful opposition of al-Maʾmūn.

Bibliography: Ṭabarī, index; Djahshiyārī, *K. al-Wuzarāʾ*, index; D. Sourdel, *Le vizirat ʿabbāside*, Damascus 1959-60, i, 183-94 and index.

(D. Sourdel)

AL-FAḌL B. SAHL B. ZADHĀNFARŪKH, vizier to the ʿAbbāsid caliph al-Maʾmūn, had originally been in the service of the Barāmika [*q.v.*]. His father, of Iranian origin and Zoroastrian by religion, had been converted to Islam and had entrusted the Barāmika with his two sons, al-Faḍl and al-Ḥasan [*q.v.*]. Al-Faḍl, who immediately attracted attention on account of his intelligence, was taken into the service of Djaʿfar al-Barmakī, then tutor to prince al-Maʾmūn, and took over this position from him after the fall of the Barāmika; it was in the presence of al-Maʾmūn that he is said to have been converted, in 190/806, at a time when the prince was holding power, deputising for his father who had gone to Anatolia.

From the end of the reign of al-Rashīd, al-Faḍl was to demonstrate the influence that he held over al-Maʾmūn's mind and to give his pupil certain advice of great political significance, namely that he should accompany the caliph on the expedition which he had launched in 192/808 in the eastern provinces. On the death of al-Rashīd, which took place at Ṭūs in 193/809, al-Maʾmūn thus found himself in the centre of the province of which, under the terms of his father's will, he became autonomous governor. While his brother on being proclaimed caliph in Baghdād had the whole of the expeditionary force brought back, he himself stayed on in Khurāsān, though not without being exasperated by al-Amīn's decision, which he held to be contrary to the last wishes of the dead sovereign. His adviser al-Faḍl, urging patience, restored his equanimity.

Relations between the two brothers thus being strained and the situation having deteriorated to the point of civil war, al-Faḍl, who had at his command a well-organized intelligence service in ʿIrāḳ, continued to give al-Maʾmūn helpful advice, promising to secure him the caliphate in the near future. In fact al-Maʾmūn was soon to overcome his brother after the siege of Baghdād and to succeed him, without being the first to infringe the will of al-Rashīd, which al-Amīn had violated by putting forward his own son as heir. As soon as the first victory had been gained by al-Maʾmūn's forces over those of al-Amīn, al-Maʾmūn was proclaimed caliph in the eastern provinces (196/812) and al-Faḍl was made officially responsible for civil and military administration in the occupied territories from Hamadhān to Tibet, while at the same time the honorific title of *Dhu ʾl-riʾāsatayn* "the man with two commands" was conferred on him, a title which appeared on the coinage either together with or in place of the name al-Faḍl, which was already linked with the sovereign's name. Being both *wazīr* and *amīr*, al-Faḍl directed military expeditions in the countries lying beyond the Oxus and secured the conversion of the king of Kābul whose throne and crown were sent to the caliph and then put on view at the Kaʿba, where al-Rashīd's will and the declarations of the two heirs apparent had been affixed.

Al-Faḍl did not let matters rest with this manoeuvre, which was intended to enhance the prestige of the new caliph. In addition, he defined the main outlines of the new policy of fidelity to the Book and the Sunna, an attitude of pietist reformism such as would rally not only the former adherents of the fallen caliph, who was accused in particular of having violated the most sacred pacts, but also the men of religion who had at that time been won over by Shīʿite propaganda based on the same themes. Al-Faḍl probably came to terms with Muʿtazilite circles, who were influential in al-Maʾmūn's entourage, to encourage the new caliph to act as *imām*, a title which appeared on the coinage. On the other hand, there is nothing to prove that he took part in elaborating the plan conceived by al-Maʾmūn to bequeath the caliphate to an ʿAlid, ʿAlī al-Riḍā, but he was nevertheless associated with this reckless attempt which eventually was to compromise him.

Meanwhile al-Faḍl exercised a dictatorial control which, especially in ʿIrāḳ where the nomination of ʿAlī al-Riḍā provoked an actual revolt, aroused violent opposition, even among elements favourable to the caliph. In certain cases he did not hesitate to dispose of his enemies by violence.

Learning by chance of the situation in ʿIrāḳ, al-Maʾmūn decided to return to Baghdād, and it was in the course of this long journey that his vizier was assassinated, at Sarakhs, in Shaʿbān 202/February 818, by members of the caliphal guard. The caliph had the murderers put to death at once, but persistent rumours, which are echoed by the chroniclers, alleged that al-Maʾmūn himself had been the instigator of the murder.

After the death of al-Faḍl, al-Maʾmūn apparently entrusted the vizierate to his brother al-Ḥasan, who was already governor of ʿIrāḳ. While continuing to be a prominent member of the court, since al-Maʾmūn had married his daughter Burān [*q.v.*], al-Ḥasan did not in fact exercise his position, and withdrew from political life. Incidentally, it was at this time that the caliph gave up granting too extensive powers to his officials.

In the course of his brief career, al-Faḍl appears to have been a person of unusual energy, highly dictatorial, often violent, but devoid of ambition and as severe to others as he was to himself. He exercised a dominating influence over the mind of al-Maʾmūn, who nevertheless succeeded in releasing himself from his control. It was certainly unjustly that he was accused of wishing to restore the former Iranian rule and of having had ʿAlī al-Riḍā nominated as heir with this intention, but it is unquestionable that he was the most Iranian of the viziers of the ʿAbbāsid caliphs: imbued with very ancient traditions which he set out to promote in the cultural field, he was particularly in favour of an orientation of policy by the caliph which would have pleased many of the Iranian *mawālī*, and it was no doubt for that reason that he was soon stopped by the Arab and ʿIrāḳī aristocracy.

Bibliography: D̲j̲ahs̲h̲iyārī, *K. al-Wuzarāʾ*, index; Ṭabarī, index; D. Sourdel, *Le vizirat ʿabbāside*, Damascus 1959-60, i, 195-217 and index; idem, *La politique religieuse du calife ʿabbāside al-Maʾmūn*, in *REI*, 1962, 27-48. (D. Sourdel)

AL-FAḌL B. YAḤYĀ AL-BARMAKĪ, the eldest son of Yaḥyā al-Barmakī, played an important part during the reign of Hārūn al-Ras̲h̲īd, in the first years of the domination of the Barāmika [*q.v.*]. As tutor to the crown prince al-Amīn, on whose behalf he caused the customary oath of loyalty to be sworn by the notables, he was particularly distinguished by the benevolence he showed towards the inhabitants of the eastern provinces and by his policy of conciliation with regard to the ʿAlids, perhaps going so far as to support the establishment of an independent Zaydī State in Daylam. His ambiguous attitude won him public execration by the caliph in 183/799 and partly explains the disgrace of the family. Imprisoned at the same time as his father in 187/803, he died at al-Raḳḳa in 193/808, at the age of 45.

Bibliography: Ṭabarī, index; D̲j̲ahs̲h̲iyārī, *K. al-Wuzarāʾ*, index; D. Sourdel, *Le vizirat ʿabbāside*, Damascus 1959-60, i, 134-81 and index; idem, *Le politique religieuse du calife ʿabbāside al-Maʾmūn*, in *REI*, 1962, 27-48. (D. Sourdel)

FAḌL ALLĀH, a family of Mamlūk state officials who traced their descent from the Caliph ʿUmar I, hence their *nisba* al-ʿUmarī, al-ʿAdawī al-Ḳuras̲h̲ī. The family received its name from its founder Faḍl Allāh b. Mud̲j̲allī b. Daʿd̲j̲ān, who was living in al-Karak (Transjordan) in 645/1247. S̲h̲araf al-Dīn ʿAbd al-Wahhāb, a son of Faḍl Allāh, held office as *kātib al-sirr* (head of the chancery) in Damascus, and was transferred to the same office in Cairo by the Sultan al-As̲h̲raf K̲h̲alīl in 692/1293. ʿAbd al-Wahhāb continued to head the central chancery of the Mamlūk his brother ʿAbd al-Wahhāb, served for a time in Ḥimṣ, then returned to Damascus. Summoned to Cairo in 697/1298 to act for his brother who had fallen ill, he returned to Damascus as *kātib al-sirr*, and remained in that office until he was replaced by his brother in 711/1311. After staying out of office for some years, he re-entered the public service in Damascus as a court clerk (*muwaḳḳiʿ fi 'l-dast*) and rose again to be *kātib al-sirr* in 727/1327 or 728/1328. In 729/1329 he was appointed to head the central chancery in Cairo, and he died in this office.

Nothing is known about the progeny of Badr al-Dīn Muḥammad I, if he had any. ʿAbd al-Wahhāb's son Ṣalāḥ al-Dīn ʿAbd Allāh (d. 719/1319) served as a Mamlūk *d̲j̲undī* (soldier), and his grandson Nāṣir al-Dīn Muḥammad b. ʿAbd Allāh (704-64/1304-63) also entered the Mamlūk military service in Damascus and rose to be an *amīr* of 40 (*amīr ṭablak̲h̲ānā*). Nāṣir al-Dīn Muḥammad sired the undistinguished Abū Bakr. It was the progeny of Muḥyī al-Dīn Yaḥyā which maintained a position of distinction for the family for two more generations.

Of Yaḥyā's three known sons, the most distinguished by far was S̲h̲ihāb al-Dīn Aḥmad I (700-49/1301-49) [*q.v.*], author of *Masālik al-abṣār fī mamālik al-amṣār* and *al-Taʿrīf bi 'l-muṣṭalaḥ al-s̲h̲arīf*, and perhaps the most outstanding of all the Faḍl Allāh. Aḥmad assisted his father in the Cairo chancery, and was later *kātib al-sirr* in Damascus. His brother ʿAlāʾ al-Dīn ʿAlī (712-69/1312-68), who also assisted his father in the Cairo chancery, succeeded his father as *kātib al-sirr* of Cairo (738-42, 743-69/1337-42, 1342-68) and died in that office, to be succeeded in turn by his son Badr al-Dīn Muḥammad III (d. 796/1394). Badr al-Dīn Muḥammad II (710-46/1310-45), a third son of Yaḥyā and brother of S̲h̲ihāb al-Dīn Aḥmad, also served as *kātib al-sirr* in Cairo (where he replaced his brother ʿAlī for a few months in 1342) and in Damascus (743-6/1342-5).

Apart from Badr al-Dīn Muḥammad III, ʿAlaʾ al-Dīn ʿAlī had three sons. S̲h̲ihāb al-Dīn Aḥmad II

Banū Faḍl-Allāh al-ʿUmarī

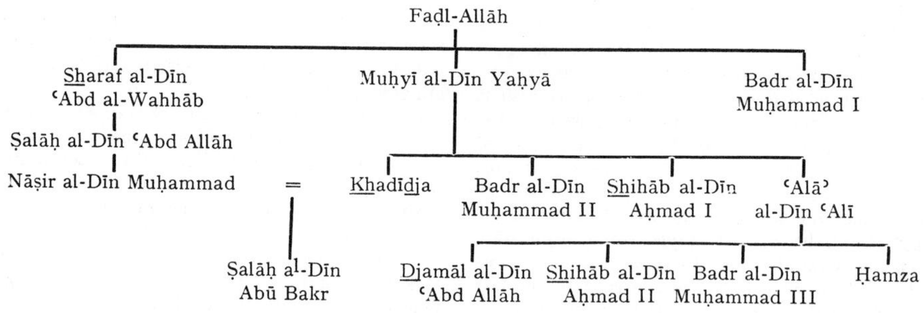

state until 711/1311, when he was transferred back to Damascus. There he died in office in 717/1317.

ʿAbd al-Wahhāb b. Faḍl Allāh was the first member of his family to hold a high position in the Mamlūk civil service. During his lifetime, and for nearly a century after his death, other members of his family distinguished themselves as Mamlūk state officials. Badr al-Dīn Muḥammad I, a younger brother of ʿAbd al-Wahhāb, who died in 706/1306, was a chancery official in Damascus. A still younger brother, Muḥyī al-Dīn Yaḥyā (645-738/1247-1337), began his career in the Damascus chancery under (d. 777/1375) acted as deputy *kātib al-sirr* for his father in Cairo, and died a young man. His brother D̲j̲amāl al-Dīn ʿAbd Allāh (d. 821/1418) was an impoverished *d̲j̲undī*. Equally undistinguished was his brother Ḥamza (d. 796/1394), of whose career nothing is known.

The family of Faḍl Allāh had a family home in Cairo; but they regarded Damascus as their home town, and there had a family cemetery in which most of them were buried.

Bibliography: Brockelmann, S II, 141; al-D̲h̲ahabī, *Duwal al-Islām*, Ḥaydarābād Deccan,

1364; Ibn Ḥadjar, *al-Durar al-kāmina fi aʿyān al-miʾa al-thāmina*, Ḥaydarābād Deccan, 1348-50; Ibn al-ʿImād al-Ḥanbalī, *Shadharāt*; Ibn Iyās, *Taʾrīkh Miṣr* ..., Būlāḳ 1311; Ibn Kathīr, *al-Bidāya wa 'l-nihāya fi 'l-taʾrīkh*, Cairo 1348-58; al-Kutubī, *Fawāt*; Ibn Ḳāḍī Shuhba, *Ṭabaḳāt al-Shāfiʿiyya*, A.U.B. MS 920.02: 1131; Ibn Taghrībirdī; al-Laknawī, *al-Fawāʾid al-bahiyya fī tarādjim al-Ḥanafiyya*, Cairo 1324; al-Maḳrīzī, *Khiṭaṭ*, Cairo 1324-6; al-Maḳrīzī, *al-Sulūk li maʿrifat duwal al-mulūk*, Cairo 1934-58; Ḳalḳashandī, *Ṣubḥ al-aʿshā*, Cairo 1913-9; al-Suyūṭī, *Ḥusn al-muḥāḍara fī akhbār Miṣr wa 'l-Ḳāhira*, Cairo 1321; Gaston Wiet, *Les biographies du Manhal Safi*, Cairo 1932; D. S. Rice, *A miniature in an autograph of Shihāb al-Dīn Ibn Fadlallāh al-ʿUmarī*, in *BSOAS*, xiii (1951), 856-67; R. Hartmann, *Die politische Geographie des Mamlukenreiches*, in *ZDMG*, lxx (1916), 1 ff.

(K. S. Salibi)

FAḌL ALLĀH [see rashīd al-dīn].

FAḌL ALLĀH DJAMĀLĪ [see djamālī].

FAḌL ALLĀH ḤURŪFĪ, the founder of the sect, or more properly, the religion of the Ḥurūfiyya [*q.v.*]. The information given about Faḍl Allāh in the histories closest to his period in no way conforms to the information about him given by those who belonged to his sect and were contemporary with him and those who were inspired by his teachings. While the sources are agreed that he lived in the 8th/14th century, the reports that his name was Djalāl al-Dīn, that he was put to death in 804/1401-2, and especially the statement of later sources like the *Riyāḍ al-ʿārifīn* of Riḍā Kulikhān Hidāyat (d. 1288/1872) that he was a native of Meshhed are totally erroneous. A study of the life of Faḍl Allāh should thus be based on the books of those personally connected with him.

One of the most important of these is the *Istiwā-nāma* of Amīr Ghiyāth al-Dīn Muḥammad b. Ḥusayn b. Muḥammad al-Astarābādī, one of the disciples (*khalīfe* [*q.v.*]) of Faḍl Allāh, according to which Faḍl Allāh was born in 740/1339-40, began to spread his doctrines in 788/1386, and was put to death in 796/1394 (Istanbul, Millet Library, MS Ali Emiri farsça 269, f. 1a). These dates are confirmed in one of the Ḥurūfī books. Both these sources, in addition, call Mīrān Shāh, the man who ordered Faḍl Allāh's execution, "Dadjdjāl", record his name as "Mārān Shāh", and give the date of his death as 803/1400 (same library, MS 1052, f. 7a). Abu 'l-Ḥasan, the foremost disciple of Faḍl Allāh and the one who turned his *Djāwidān* into verse in 802/1400, states that Faḍl Allāh was put to death in 796/1393-4 and that Mīrān Shāh was slain seven years later, that is, in 803/1400-1 (Ṣādiḳ Kiyā, *Wāzha-nāme-i Gurgānī*, Tehran 1330, 26. In this source the date of the death of Mīrān Shāh is given as 810/1407-8; cf. the genealogy in Khalīl Edhem, *Düwel-i Islāmiyye*, Istanbul 1345/1927, 429). The *Khāb-nāma* of Sayyid Isḥāḳ (frequently mentioned in the *Istiwā-nāma* as one of the intimates of Faḍl Allāh) states that in 772/1370-1 Faḍl Allāh entered into a period of retirement (*čile*) in Iṣfahān, being then thirty-two years of age (MS Ali Emiri, Farsça 1042, 25a-b). According to this reckoning the date of his birth is 740/1339-40. Sayyid Sharīf, a contemporary of Faḍl Allāh (as one understands from the eulogies in his *Dīwān*, cf. Istanbul University Library, MS Farsça 152, 16a-18b) mentions in his *Risāla-i maʿādiyya* that Faḍl Allāh was a Sayyid and also records his genealogy, according to which there is a line of twenty persons between Faḍl Allāh and ʿAlī (Ist. Univ. Lib., MS Farsça 1043, 51a). The fact that the ninth ancestor in one list, the eight in the other, is Muḥammad al-Yamānī deserves attention in view of the fact that the Yemen is known to have been one of the most important centres of the Bāṭinīs from the latter part of the 3rd/9th century onwards (Muḥammad b. al-Ḥasan al-Daylamī, *Ḳawāʿid ʿaḳāʾid āl Muḥammad*, ed. R. Strothmann: *Die Geheimlehre der Batiniten: Dogmatik des Hauses Muhammad*, Bibliotheca Islamica II, Istanbul 1938, Introduction vi-ix, 24-5, 95, 96).

One also finds scattered throughout both the *Istiwā-nāma* and the *Khāb-nāma* information relating to the life of Faḍl Allāh and the places which he visited. According to the *Istiwā-nāma* (82b), being at one point—the date is not known—in Iṣfahān, he rejected the notion that the human soul becomes non-existent after death and the assertions of the Ḥurūfīs who denied the existence of the afterlife. In the *Khāb-nāma* also (10b) he is said to have rejected such a claim in Iṣfahān. Again according to this latter book Faḍl Allāh embraced Ṣūfism at the age of eighteen. He was inspired with the ability to interpret dreams in 756/1355 (19a), in which year he was in a place named Tokdji in Iṣfahān; later he went to Tabrīz, where the Djalāʾirid Sultan Uways b. Ḥasan (d. 776/1374-5), Wazīr Zakariyyā, and Ṣāḥib Ṣadr Shaykh Khwādja accepted his teachings (19a-b). In Tabrīz he married a girl from Astarābād on the recommendation of his disciple Kamāl al-Dīn Hāshimī. He wrote a book on *fiḳh* for ʿIzz al-Dīn Shāh Shudjāʿ (d. 786/1384) (24a). He was again in Iṣfahān in 772/1370-1, at the age of thirty-two, and there went into retreat (35a-b). He also spent some time in Dāmghān (38b) and Bākūye (47a). While in Shamāḳhī interpreting a dream of Ḳāḍī Bāyazīd, he foretold his own martyrdom (49b). When he left the house of this *ḳāḍī* and was returning to his cell (*hüdjre*), he was arrested on the strength of a decree from Astarābād and taken to the fortress of Alīndjak (50a). He was imprisoned on the order of Mīrān Shāh (55a). Among those believing in him were important men; he even sent a dervish cap (*dervīsh külāhī*), conveying his blessing, to Sultan Uways (55b-56a). His followers are known as *Darwīshān-i ḥalāl-khor ve rāst-gūy* (48a). A *bayt* in the *Tawḥīd-nāma* of ʿAlī al-Aʿlā, called by the Ḥurūfīs "Khalīfat Allāh" and "Waṣī Allāh", states that Faḍl Allāh was born in Astarābād (Ist. Univ. Lib., MS Farsça 1158, 5b.

There exist three chronograms giving the date of the death of Faḍl Allāh-i Ḥurūfī. In one of these his name is recorded as Shihāb al-Dīn Faḍl Allāh and his death as having occurred on a Friday in Dhu 'l-Ḳaʿda 796/October-November 1394, when he was fifty-six years of age (Millet Library, MS Ali Emiri, Farsça 1043, at the beginning). The second chronogram is in a 16th cent. *madjmūʿa* belonging to the book-dealer Raif Yelkenci. Though the chronogrammatic *miṣrāʿ* is known to all Ḥurūfīs and to all those connected in any way with the Ḥurūfīs (see, for example, Aḥmad Rifʿat, *Mirʾāt al-maḳāṣid fī dafʿ al-mafāsid*, Istanbul 1293, lithograph, 133, where there is also the genealogy of Faḍl Allāh, taken from a *risāla*), I have seen the whole of the chronogram only in this *madjmūʿa*. The author of this chronogram is unknown, as is that of the first chronogram. In the first *bayt* Timur is mocked, in the fourth *bayt* the name of Mīrān Shāh is mentioned, and in the fifth *bayt* it is stated that Faḍl Allāh was put to death on "Thursday, the eve of Friday" the sixth of Dhu 'l-Ḳaʿda. In the first poem, which contains seven *bayts*, it is also stated that he died in Dhu 'l-Ḳaʿda, but on a Friday. It is clear, however, form the specific method of recording the date in the second chronogram, that he was put to death after the afternoon prayer on Thursday, since, according to the custom of the holy law, Friday begins after that time. The year is stated in the sixth and last *bayt* in the form *dhāl u ṣād u wāw*, that is, 796 (according to the conversion-tables, the first day of Dhu 'l-Ḳaʿda 796 corresponds to Friday, 28 August 1394. But the new moon of the month must have been confirmed the day before by observation, in which case the sixth day of Dhu 'l-Ḳaʿda would coincide with Thursday, 3 September 1394). The third chronogram is in a *madjmūʿa* containing the poems of Faḍl Allāh, along with those of Sharīf and ʿAlī al-Aʿlā. In the fourth of the seven *bayts* in this chronogram it is stated that Faḍl Allāh was fifty-six (*Bīst u čār u sī u du*) when he was put to death. The place of his martyrdom is specified in the last *bayt* as "Alīndja" while the date is conveyed by the phrase *Shahīd-i ʿishk-i ū* (Millet Library, MS Kenan Bey, Farsça 186, f. 194b). In a *risāla* of Mīr Fāḍilī is found the note: "The honoured resting-place of that most excellent Prophet (*Ṣāḥib bayān*) is at a town called Alīndja, by Astarābād on the far side of Tabrīz. ʿAlī al-Aʿlā is also buried there, and there is yet another grave. The covering of (Faḍl Allāh's) tomb is black, that of ʿAlī al-Aʿlā's green, and of the other's red" (MS Ali Emiri, Farsça 1039, f. 92b). In his *risāla* entitled *Ṣalāt-nāma* Shaykh Muḥammad, who is known by the name Ishkurt Dede and who is known to have met some of the disciples of Faḍl Allāh, writes while discussing the rules governing the *ḥadjdj* that during the days of the *Tashrīḳ* sixty-three stones are thrown, twenty-one each day, at the Tower of Mīrān Shāh, opposite the Alīndjak fortress, which is also called Sandjariyye, and that the *Ṭawāf* procession occurs in a place called "*Maḳtal-gāh*"; during the course of this discussion he states that Faḍl Allāh was put to death in Alīndjak and that his grave is there (Millet Library, MS Kenan Bey, Farsça 1043, 35b-36a).

To regard certain numbers as sacred and to assign various meanings to certain letters are ancient, magical practices; examples occur in both the Old and the New Testaments. Similarly various meanings have been assigned from time to time to the letters occurring at the beginning of twenty-nine *sūras* of the Ḳurʾān. In both the *Dīwān* of Ḥusayn b. Manṣūr al-Ḥallādj (d. 309/922) (see L. Massignon, *Le Dīwān d'al-Hallaj*, *JA* (1931), 63, 83, 94) and his *Kitāb al-Ṭawāsīn* (ed. L. Massignon, Paris 1913, 13-4, 29, 31, 56-60, 63, 65-67) there are frequent references to letters and numbers and to the correspondence of letters to numbers. His statements relative to points, lines, and letters are transmitted in the *Akhbār al-Ḥallādj* (ed. L. Massignon, Paris 1936, 16, 25-6, 59-60, 71, 95-6); and one finds that he even discusses the equator (*khaṭṭ-i istiwāʾ*) (*ibid.*, 53), which is one of the basic elements in the system of Faḍl Allāh. The Bāṭinī belief in these matters is well-known (see for example Nāṣir-i Khusraw, *Khān al-Ikhwān*, ed. Yaḥyā al-Khashshāb, Cairo 1359/1940, 66-7; and also his *Wadjh-i Dīn*, Berlin 1343, 76-7). Even in the *Futūḥāt al-Makkiyya* of Ibn ʿArabī (d. 635/1240) great importance is given to letters, and particular emphasis is laid upon this idea (Būlāḳ 1272, i, 56-92; section 2, 92-101; ch. 5, 112-30; ii, ch. 79, 135-7. For the sections which explain the Bāṭinī ideas in connection with the *Khatm al-awliyāʾ* together with the complete Bāṭinī system, see iv, ch. 557, 215).

Faḍl Allāh was certainly acquainted with the Bāṭinī methods. The *ṭarīḳa* which he joined while young was one which had adopted the Bāṭinī beliefs. He occupied himself with the meanings given to letters and with numerical relationships. Perhaps he also studied Ibn ʿArabī. Conclusions drawn from the Old and New-Testaments in appropriate places in the *Djāwidān* make it clear that he had read these books (Ali Emiri, MS Kenan Bey 920, 144b). From his *Dīwān* it is evident that he knew Arabic, Persian, and his native language, the Gurgān dialect, that he was well-versed in Persian literaure, and that he was capable of composing poetry in the classical style.

That an *ʿIlm al-ḥurūf* was among those branches of knowledge known as *ʿUlūm gharība* or *ʿUlūm khāfiya* and that it was used for the most part for divination of the occult is well-known (see, for example, *Manāḳib al-ʿarifīn*, begun in 718/1318; ed. Tahsin Yazici, Ankara 1959, 421). Faḍl Allāh thus took over, among other features of Bāṭinī *taʾwīl*, in particular the importance given to letters, and, wherever necessary, the relationships of letters and numbers. He adopted the method of referring all religious commands to the twenty-eight letters of the Arabic alphabet and the thirty-two of the Persian. To the *ʿIlm al-ḥurūf*, which was old and not completely systematized, he gave a form truly original for his period; and, by proclaiming himself Messiah, *Mahdī*, and Manifestation (*maẓhar*) of God, he founded the Ḥurūfī religion. His disciples and those who came later adapted the obligations of ablution, prayer, and the pilgrimage completely to this religion. Although it is reported that Faḍl Allāh rejected the claims of those who denied the existence of the after-life and the continued existence of the soul, it is known that Ḥurūfīs in a number of places like Iṣfahān, Tabrīz, and Geylān considered life to be merely material and denied the continued existence of the soul. In view of this, it seems likely that the rejection of such claims by him and some of his disciples was no more than an instance of *taḳiyya* [*q.v.*], a concealment of their true views, so as not to put off new converts to the religion.

His disciples (*khalīfa*). Sayyid Sharīf, in his *Risāla-i maʿādiyya* (properly entitled *Bayān al-wāḳiʿ*) lists the disciples of Faḍl Allāh, with the note "whom I remember", as follows: Amīr Sayyid ʿAlī, Ḥusayn Kiyā b. Thāḳib. Madjd al-Dīn, Maḥmūd, Kamāl al-Dīn Hāshimī, Khʷādja Ḥāfiẓ Ḥasan, Shaykh ʿAlī Maghzāyish, Bāyazīd, Tawakkul b. Dārā, Abu 'l-Ḥasan, Sayyid Isḥāḳ, Sayyid Nasīmī, Ḥasan b. Ḥaydar, Ḥusayn Ghāzī, Sulaymān.

Later he records that all of them, four hundred in number, were Sayyids, that they were in Faḍl Allāh's company day and night, and that they went with him wherever he went (51b-52a). 'Sayyid ʿAlī' is the ʿAlī al-Aʿlā who, in the *Istiwā-nāma*, is called *Khalīfat Allāh* and *Waṣī Allāh*, and who is known to have been Faḍl Allāh's favourite disciple (2a, 11a, 29b, 37a). The names of Madjd al-Dīn, Isḥāḳ, and Nasīmī occur in the same book (29a, 37a). One meets in the same *risāla* such names as Darwīsh Bahāʾ al-Dīn, Darwīsh ʿAlī, Muḥammad Nāyinī, ʿĪsā Bitlīsī, Muḥammad Tīr-ger, Tādj al-Dīn, Sayyid Muẓaffar, and Ḥusām al-Dīn Yazddjurdī (12a-b, 37a, 40a-b, 43a-b, 80a). Of these, the names of ʿAlī al-Aʿlā, Nasīmī, and Isḥāḳ are found in the *Ṣalāt-nāma* of Ishkurt Dede, as are those of the author of the *Maʿādiyya*, Sayyid Sharīf, and Djāwidī. Besides these, the name of Mīr Fāḍilī is mentioned, and he is reported to have been the disciple (*khalīfa*) of ʿAlī al-Aʿlā. It is also reported that Amīr Ghiyāth al-Dīn was the son of ʿAlī al-Aʿlā's sister, and that, in addition to the *Istiwā-nāma*, he was the author of a *risāla* named *Turāb-nāma* (5a). Djāwidī, in a *risāla* which he wrote in Shawwāl 1000/July-August 1592, reveals that his personal name was ʿAlī (Millet Library, MS Farisi 437). In view of the date in which he wrote his *risāla*, this person must have been connected with one of the disciples of Faḍl Allāh. In the *Muḥarram-nāma* of Sayyid Isḥāḳ one finds the following names: Sayyid Tādj al-Dīn Kehnā-yi Bayhaḳī, one of the intimates of Faḍl Allāh and known to the Ḥurūfīs as *Ṣāḥib Taʾwīl* (see C. Huart, *Textes persans relatifs a la secte des Houroufîs*, Leiden and London 1909, Gibb Memorial Series, 42); Mawlānā Kamāl al-Dīn Hāshimī; ʿAlī Dāmghānī, who, it is reported, had formerly been one of the intimates of Sultan Uways and had been Wālī of Khurāsān; and Pīr Ḥasan Dāmghānī (*ibid.*, 43). Both in this book and in the *Nawm-nāma*, which is attributed to Faḍl Allāh, other names are mentioned in a section devoted to statesmen; but it is impossible to determine definitely the degree of their relationships with Faḍl Allāh (*Wāzha-nāma-i Gurgānī*, 36; examples from the text and translations into Persian, 236-46). Mīr Fāḍilī writes in a *risāla* the names of the disciples ʿAlī al-Aʿlā, Sayyid Abu 'l-Ḥasan, Kamāl al-Dīn Hāshimī Rūmī (*i.e.*, from Anatolia) and Kamāl al-Dīn Hāshimī Iṣfahānī, and says that they are "the four friends of the felicitous one" ("*Ṣāḥib Devletün čār yārīdur*"), thus testifying to a belief that Faḍl Allāh had "four friends" corresponding to the "four friends" of the Prophet Muḥammad (Millet Library, MS Farsça 990, last folio).

The names of the sons, daughters, and grandchildren of Faḍl Allāh are written in a different hand on the last folio of the *Risāla-i maʿādiyya* (61b). Among these is the name of Amīr Nūr Allāh, who was arrested and put to the question along with the author of the *Istiwā-nāma*, Ghiyāth al-Dīn Muḥammad, after the attempt on the life of Shāh Rukh. Among his sons there is one Salām Allāh, who is not to be confused with his elder sister who was appointed by Faḍl Allāh in the last will and testament which he wrote before his arrest as the trustee and guardian for all his children. (Abdülbâki Gölpinarlı, *Fazl-Allāh-ı Hurūfī'nin Waṣiyya-Nāma'sı veya Waṣāyā'sı*, in *Şarkiyat mecmuası*, ii (1958), 54-62. There is a copy of this will also in Millet Library, MS Farsça 1009, 1b-9a, as well as an incomplete copy in the same section of the library, MS 933, 104a-b).

Works. Faḍl Allāh's most famous work is the *Djāwidān-nāma*. From the *Khāb-nāma* one learns that this work became famous after Faḍl Allāh's death (43a). The *Istiwā-nāma* reveals that the *Djāwidān-nāma* begins with the word "*ibtidāʾ*" repeated six times (29b). There is a copy beginning with this word and written in the Gurgān dialect in Millet Library, Farsça, MS Kenan Bey 920. The *Djāwidān-nāma* written in normal Persian and common in both public and private libraries must be a new redaction, separated into sections, and arranged by Faḍl Allāh personally or by one of his disciples, made on the basis of this text. For a copy belonging to the period of Faḍl Allāh but without a colophon see MS Fatih (Süleymaniye) 3728; another copy, written by Darwīsh ʿAlī Sarkhanī in Dhu 'l-Ḥidjdja 845/1442, Millet Library, MS Kenan Bey 1000. MS Ist. Univ. Lib., Farsça 869 (written n 1049/1639) is in the hand of Darwīsh Murtaḍā Baktāshī who translated the second version of the *Djāwidān-Nāma* under the title *Durr-i yatīm*. Among the manuscripts which I gave to the Mevlānā Museum Library in Konya is one written by this same man in the previous year (a rather free and expanded translation). In the *Khāb-nāma* two other works by Faḍl Allāh are mentioned: the *Maḥabbat-nāma* and the *ʿArsh-nāma*. ʿAlī al-Aʿlā also mentions these two works in his *Tawḥīd-nāma* (34b).

Faḍl Allāh also composed poetry, mostly in Persian but some in Arabic, under the *makhlaṣ* Naʿīmī. His poems form a small *dīwān*. In the *medjmūʿa* which contains the chronogram relative to the death of Faḍl Allāh there are thirty-three *ghazals*, seven *ḳitʿas*, nine *rubāʿīs*, four *bayts*, and two *tardjīʿs*. In the *dīwān* in Millet Library, MS Kenan Bey 989, there are seventy-two poems: thirty-six *ghazals*, two *ḳitʿas*, twenty-four *rubāʿīs*, eight *bayts*, and the two *tardjīʿs* in the *madjmūʿa* previously mentioned.

Bibliography: in the article.

(Abdülbâki Gölpinarli)

FAḌL-i ḤAḲḲ al-ʿUmarī, al-Ḥanafī, al-Māturīdī, al-Čishtī (not al-Ḥabashī as misread by Brockelmann, S II, 458), al-Khayrābādī b. Faḍl-i Imām [*q.v.*] was born at Khayrābād [*q.v.*] in 1211/1796-7. Having studied first at home with his father, he later studied *ḥadīth* with Shāh ʿAbd al-Ḳādir al-Dihlawī [*q.v.*] and at the age of thirteen completed his studies. He entered service as a *pīshkār* to the Commissioner of Delhi under the East India Company and later served with the Chiefs of Djhadjdjar, Alwar, Tonk and Rāmpur. He was a leading scholar of his day, well-versed in logic, philosophy, belles-lettres, *kalām*, *uṣūl al-fiḳh* and poetics, and a great teacher and logician who attracted students from far and near. He was often seen teaching *al-Ufḳ al-mubīn* of al-Dāmād [*q.v.*], a rather involved text on logic, while engaged in playing chess. On the doctrine of *imtināʿ al-naẓīr* he entered into a lengthy controversy with Muḥammad Ismāʿīl Shahīd [*q.v.*] in refutation of whose teachings he composed a number of treatises. This controversy greatly agitated the people of Dihlī, and even the reigning monarch Bahādur Shāh Ẓafar and the egalitarian poet Ghālib were involved in it. The controversy later took an ugly turn, and he misused his official position by persuading the *kōtwāl* of Delhi, Mīrzā Khānī, a bigoted Shīʿī, to take preventive measures against Ismāʿīl Shahīd, who was prohibited from delivering public sermons in the congregational mosque. He took a leading part in the military uprising of 1857, was charged with high treason, arrested, tried and sentenced to transportation for life. He died in exile in the Andamans (*Kālā Pānī*), where he was interred, in 1862.

Among his works are: (i) *al-Djins al-ghālī fī sharḥ al-Djawhar al-ʿālī* (a treatise on theology); (ii) *al-Hadiyya al-saʿīdiyya fi 'l-ḥikma al-ṭabīʿiyya*, a treatise on physics begun by Faḍl-i Ḥaḳḳ but completed by his son ʿAbd al-Ḥaḳḳ, Kānpur 1283/1866; (iii) *al-Rawḍ al-mudjūd fī taḥḳīḳ ḥaḳīḳat al-wudjūd*; (iv) *al-Ḥāshiya ʿalā Talkhīṣ al-Shifāʾ*; (v) *al-Ḥāshiya ʿalā al-Ufḳ al-mubīn*; (vi) *al-Ḥāshiya ʿalā Sharḥ Sullam al-ʿulūm* by Ḳāḍī Mubārak Gōpāmawī (Delhi 1899); (vii) *Risāla fi 'l-tashkīk wa fi 'l-māhiyyāt*; (viii) *al-Risāla al-ghadriyya* (or *al-Thawra al-Hindiyya*), a doleful and moving account of the untold sufferings that he underwent in the Andamans as a dangerous political prisoner; published with Urdu transl. and notes as *Bāghī Hindustān* (see Bibliography); (ix) *al-Risāla fī taḥkīk al-ʿilm wa 'l-maʿlūm*; and (x) *al-Risāla fī taḥkīk al-adjsām*.

Bibliography: Faḳīr Muḥammad Djhelamī, *Ḥadāʾiḳ al-Ḥanafiyya*, Lucknow 1906, 480; Raḥmān ʿAlī, *Tadhkira-i ʿulamāʾ-i Hind*, Lucknow 1914, 164-5; Alṭāf Ḥusayn Ḥālī, *Yādgār-i Ghālib*, Lahore 1932, 71; Amīr Aḥmad Mīnāʾī, *Intikhāb-i Yādgār*, Lucknow 1279/1862, 281-95; ʿAbd al-Ḳādir Rāmpūrī, *Rūz-nāma* (*Waḳāʾiʿ-i ʿAbd al-Ḳādir Khānī*), Urdu transl. *ʿIlm-o ʿAmal*, Karachi 1960, i, 258; Ṣiddīḳ Ḥasan Khān, *ʿAbdjad al-ʿulūm*, Bhopal 1296/1878, 915; Muḥammad Muḥsin al-Tirhutī, *al-Yāniʿ al-djanī fī asānīd al-Shaykh ʿAbd al-Ghanī* (on the margin of *Kashf al-astār ʿan ridjāl maʿānī 'l-āthār*), Delhi 1349/1930, 75; Sayyid Aḥmad Khān, *Āthār al-ṣanādīd* (ch. IV, reprinted separately as *Tadhkira-i Ahl-i Dihlī*), Karachi 1955, 86-96; ʿAbd al-Shāhid Khān Shirwānī, *Bāghī Hindustān*, Bijnor 1947, 11-176; Nadjm al-Ghanī Rāmpūrī, *Taʾrīkh-i Awadh*, Lucknow 1919, v, 232; Gul Ḥasan Shāh Pānīpatī, *Ghawthiyya*, Lahore n.d., 124-5; M. G. Zubaid Ahmad, *Contribution of India to Arabic literature*, Allahabad 1946, index; ʿAbd al-Ḥayy Lakhnawī, *Nuzhat al-khawāṭir*, Ḥaydarābād 1377/1958-9, vii, 374-7; Brockelmann, S II, 458-9; Muḥammad Bahāʾ Allāh Gōpāmawī, *Siyar al-ʿulamāʾ*, Kānpur 1346, 22-3; ʿAbd al-Ḥayy, *Dihlī awr uskē aṭrāf*, Dihlī 1958, 30-1, 39-40, 54-5, 61-2, 113; monthly *Taḥrīk*, Dihlī, Aug. 1957-June 1960; Intiẓām Allāh Shihābī, *Mawlānā Faḍl-i Ḥakk wa ʿAbd al-Ḥakk*, Badāʾūn, n.d. (A. S. Bazmee Ansari)

FAḌL-i IMĀM b. Muḥammad Arshad al-ʿUmarī al-Hargāmī, b. Muḥ. Ṣāliḥ b. ʿAbd al-Wādjid b. ʿAbd al-Mādjid b. Ḳāḍī Ṣadr al-Dīn al-Ḥanafī, was a contemporary of Shāh ʿAbd al-ʿAzīz al-Dihlawī, and the first Indian Muslim scholar to have accepted the post of *muftī* and *ṣadr al-ṣudūr* of Delhi under the East India Company, the highest office, equivalent to the modern sub-judge in the Indo-Pakistan sub-continent, which the Company could confer on its native employees. His duties, as *ṣadr al-ṣudūr*, included examining candidates for the posts of *ḳāḍīs*, scrutiny of requests for financial aid or the grant of *amlāk* (fiefs), *aʾimma* lands or *madad maʿāsh* from scholars, divines and needy and learned persons. Born at Khayrābād [*q.v.*], a flourishing centre of learning in the *Purb* (Eastern districts) which Shāhdjahān described as "the Shīrāz of India", in the last quarter of the 12th/18th century he completed his studies with ʿAbd al-Wādjid Kirmānī, a learned scholar of Khayrābād (cf. Raḥmān ʿAlī, *Tadhkira-i ʿulamā-i Hind*, Lucknow 1914, 136). One of his maternal uncles Mullā Abu 'l-Wāʿiẓ Hargāmī was one of the compilers of *al-Fatāwā al-ʿĀlamgīriyya* [*q.v.*]. Specially interested in rational sciences, he devoted his leisure hours to the teaching of logic and philosophy. He was so fond of his pupils that once he strongly upbraided his son Faḍl-i Ḥakk for misbehaving towards a dull student. He seems to have been relieved of his post at Delhi in ca. 1827 when he was succeeded by Ṣadr al-Dīn Āzurda [*q.v.*], one of his pupils. He then entered the service of the chief of Paṭiālā as a minister but soon retired to his hometown where he died in 1244/1829. He left behind three sons of whom Faḍl-i Ḥakk [*q.v.*] gained great distinction.

His works are: (i) *al-Mirḳāt al-mīzāniyya* (ed. Dihlī 1886, 1888), a text-book on logic based mainly on *al-Shamsiyya* by Nadjm al-Dīn ʿUmar b. ʿAlī al-Ḳazwīnī (d. 613/1216) and *Tahdhīb al-manṭiḳ* of al-Taftāzānī (d. 729/1389). It was commented upon by his grandson ʿAbd al-Ḥakk b. Faḍl-i Hakk and has since been translated into Urdu; (ii) *Tashḥīdh al-adhhān fī Sharḥ al-Mīzān* (MSS I.O.; Delhi-Arabic no. 1529; Āṣafiyya, ii, 1566); (iii) *Ḥāshiya ʿalā al-Ḥāshiya al-zāhidiyya al-ḳuṭbiyya* (MS Bankipore no. 2273); (iv) *Ḥāshiya ʿalā al-Ḥāshiya al-zāhidiyya al-djalāliyya* (MS I.O. Delhi-Arabic no. 1513); (v) *Talkhīs al-Shifāʾ* (MSS Aligarh Subḥān-Allāh Collection, no. 80, Rampur, no. 381); (vi) *Āmad-nāma*, a very useful booklet on Persian infinitives for beginners of which chapter v, comprising short biographical notices of some of the leading *ʿulamāʾ* and scholars of Awadh, has been published at Karachi under the title *Tarādjim al-fuḍalāʾ* (1956), with English translation and notes by me; (vii) *Tardjama-i Taʾrīkh-i Yamīnī* (MS Aumer 241).

Bibliography: Sayyid Aḥmad Khān, *Āthār al-ṣanādīd*, Ch. iv (reprinted as *Tadhkira-i Ahl-i Dihlī*), Karachi 1955, 97-8; Rahmān ʿAlī, *Tadhkira-i ʿulamāʾ-i Hind*, Lucknow 1914, 162 (Urdū transl. with additions, Karachi 1961, 376-8); M. G. Zubaid Ahmad, *Contribution of India to Arabic literature*, Allahabad 1946, s.v.; ʿAbd al-Ḥayy Lakhnawī, *Nuzhat al-khawāṭir*, Ḥaydarābād 1378/1958, vii, 374; ʿAbd al-Shāhid Khān Shirwānī, *Bāghī Hindustān*, Bijnor 1947, 16-35; Bashīr al-Dīn Aḥmad, *Wāḳiʿāt-i Dār al-Ḥukūmat-i Dihlī*, Āgra 1919, 414-5; Faḍl-i Imām Khayrābādī, *Tarādjim al-fuḍalāʾ*, Persian text with Eng. transl. and notes, A. S. Bazmee Ansari, Karachi 1956, i-iii, 35-6; ʿAbd al-Ḳādir Rāmpūrī, *Rūz-nāma* (*Waḳāʾiʿ-i ʿAbd al-Ḳādir Khānī*), Urdū transl. under the title *ʿIlm-o ʿAmal*, Karachi 1960, i, 257; Muḥammad Bahāʾ Allāh Gopāmawī, *Siyar al-ʿulamāʾ*, Kānpur 1346 A.H., 21-2; Gul Ḥasan Shāh Pānīpatī, *Tadhkira-i Ghawthiyya*, Lahore n.d., 125; Waḥīd Allāh Badāʾūnī, *Mukhtaṣar sayr-i Hindustān*, Murādābād 1273/1857, 60; Ghālib, *Kulliyāt-i nathr-i Ghālib*, Lucknow 1871, 42-3; Storey, i/I, 252; Ellis, ii, 329-30. (A. S. Bazmee Ansari)

FAḌLAWAYH, Banū, a Kurdish dynasty which ruled in Shabānkāra [*q.v.*] from 448/1056 to 718/1318-9. Very little is known about them except for the founder of the dynasty Faḍlawayh (in Ibn al-Athīr, x, 48: Faḍlūn) and for members of the family during the Ilkhān period [*q.v.*].

Faḍlawayh, son of the chief ʿAlī b. al-Ḥasan b. Ayyūb of the Kurdish tribe Rāmānī in Shabānkāra, was originally a general (Sipāh-Sālār) under the Buwayhids [*q.v.*] and closely connected with their vizier Ṣāḥib ʿĀdil. When the latter was executed after a change of government, Faḍlawayh eliminated the last Buwayhid in 447/1055 and placed himself under the authority of the Saldjūḳs [*q.v.*]. Later, however, he fell out with Alp Arslan [*q.v.*], was defeated by Niẓām al-Mulk [*q.v.*] and finally taken prisoner and executed in 464/1071.

Reports of the Banū Faḍlawayh until the beginning of the 7th/13th century are vague. After 626/1227-8 Muẓaffar al-Dīn Muḥammad b. al-Mubāriz expanded his rule in the direction of Fārs and the coast opposite Hormuz. He asserted himself against the *atabeg* of Fārs, but fell during a siege of his own capital Īdj by Hulagu [*q.v.*] in 658/1260. Until 664/1266 three rulers followed one another in rapid succession: Ḳuṭb al-Dīn, the brother (according to Zambaur the son) of Muẓaffar al-Dīn (murdered 10 Dhu 'l-Ḥidjdja 659/5 November 1261); Niẓām al-Dīn II Ḥasanwayh who fell in Rabīʿ II 662/February 1264; Nuṣrat al-Dīn Ibrāhīm, the brother of the latter, deposed Rabīʿ II 664/Jan.-Feb. 1266, after which more peaceful conditions obtained. The brother of the last named, Djalāl al-Dīn Ṭayyibshāh, ruled for sixteen years under Mongol suzerainty until his execution on 10 Djumādā I 681/16 August 1282. His brother Bahā᾽ al-Dīn Ismā῾īl died a natural death in 688/1289-90. The cousins who succeeded, Ghiyāth al-Dīn b. Djalāl al-Dīn and Niẓām al-Dīn III b. Bahā᾽ al-Dīn, were quite powerless. In the year following the suppression of a revolt in 712/1312-3 a certain Ardashīr, whose lineage is uncertain, succeeded to power. As early as Dhu 'l-Ḳa῾da/February-March 1314 he was eliminated by the founder of the Muẓaffarid dynasty, Mubāriz al-Dīn Muḥammad, and thus the dynasty of the Banū Faḍlawayh came to an end.

Bibliography: On Faḍlawayh: (Ibn al-) Balkhī, *Fārs-nāma*, ed. G. Le Strange and R. A. Nicholson, London 1921, 164 ff. (*GMS*, N.S. i). On the 13th century: Waṣṣāf, lith. Bombay, 1269/1852-3, 423-5; Mustawfī Ḳazwīnī, *Ta᾽rīkh-i guzīda*, i, 613 ff. (*GMS*, xiv); B. Spuler, *Die Mongolen in Iran*², Berlin 1955, 146 ff.; E. de Zambaur, *Manuel*², Pyrmont 1955, 233 (genealogical table with considerable differences from Waṣṣāf, whose version is the basis for the above article). See also SHABĀNKĀRA and its bibliography.

(B. SPULER)

FAḌLĪ (commonly written FADHLĪ), a tribal territory now one of the states of the Federation of South Arabia, area about 1600 square miles with an estimated population of 55,000. Its western bounds touch on the Aden Colony and then run northwest bordering on Laḥdj (῾Abdalī), Ḥawshabī and Lower Yāfi῾ territories; in the northeast it is bounded by ῾Awdhalī and Dathīna, in the east by the Lower ῾Awlaḳī, and on the south by the Arabian Sea. The country consists of two main parts: the lowlands of Abyan in the west, partly desert but containing the only fertile soil, with a mainly settled population; and the steppes and hilly parts in the east, with a mainly tribal population.

The territory was originally a confederation of tribes whose chieftain, a *sulṭān* by title, of the Faḍlī tribe, lived in Shuḳra, the capital and a seaport. After the British occupied Aden the Faḍlī remained hostile to them until in 1865, after the Faḍlīs had attacked a caravan near Aden, the British attacked them by land and sea. In 1888 the Faḍlī *sulṭān* Aḥmad b. Ḥusayn signed a treaty accepting British protection; and in 1944 the Faḍlī *sulṭān* ῾Abd Allāh b. ῾Uthmān signed a treaty with the British whereby he accepted advice on the administration of his country and the expenditure of his revenue. An executive acted for him in all matters in close cooperation with the British Political Officer in Abyan, and Zandjibār (also written Zandjubār) in Abyan became the administrative seat. In December 1962 Sulṭān ῾Abd Allāh b. ῾Uthmān was replaced as ruler by his *nā᾽ib* in Abyan the *de facto* ruler, Sulṭān Aḥmad b. ῾Abd Allāh. The *sulṭān* is aided by a State Council, recently constituted, made up of thirteen members representing the tribes, the fishermen, the farmers and the traders. In June 1963 the State Council passed an ordinance providing for the election of 12 members, four from the settled areas in the west and eight from the tribal areas in the east, who, with five *ex officio* members and the members of the existing State Council will make a legislative body. In 1959 the Faḍlī sultanate or state was among the first territories of the Western Aden Protectorate to join in forming the Federation of Arab Amirates of the South, later called the Federation of South Arabia when Aden Colony joined it in 1962. The present Faḍlī Sulṭān is a member of the Federal Supreme Council and holds a Federal ministerial post.

The economy depends chiefly on agriculture, which is centred in the Abyan delta formed by Wādī Banā and Wādī Ḥasan whose irrigation waters are shared by Faḍlī and Lower Yāfi῾ growers under the control of the joint Abyan Board. The formation of the Board marked the settlement of the long standing dispute between the two territories over the leading channel, *nāzi῾a*, which the Faḍlīs had constructed in the last century to divert water to their land from Wādī Banā in Lower Yāfi῾ territory. Cotton is the main cash crop, with the Faḍlī production in 1963 nearing 5,000 tons. Other products are fruit and vegetables, to supply nearby Aden Colony, crops other than cotton, especially sorghum, and animal husbandry. There is also a fishing industry with good potential. The revenue of the state has reached £ 250,000 a year.

The state has two systems of courts, *sharī῾a* and Customary Law (*῾urf*); a Justice of the Peace system has also been introduced. There is also a State High Court with powers of appeal and with jurisdiction over some constitutional matters.

Education has progressed recently and there are 20 primary schools including two for girls, the first in the Federation outside Aden Colony.

Bibliography: F. M. Hunter and C. W. H. Sealy, *An account of the Arab tribes in the vicinity of Aden*, Bombay 1909, 32-43; G. Wyman Bury, *The Land of Uz*, London 1911, 4-8; W. H. Ingrams, *Arabia and the Isles*, London 1942, 113-34; D. van der Meulen, *Aden to the Hadhramaut*, London 1947, 20-31; Belhaven (A. Hamilton), *The Kingdom of Melchior*, London 1949, 73-84; idem, *The uneven road*, London 1955, 146-57; D. Ingrams, *A survey of social and economic conditions in the Aden Protectorate*, Eritrea 1949, *passim*; T. Hickinbotham, *Aden*, London 1958, 147-53; *Aden 1957 and 1958*, administrative report issued by H.M.S.O., London 1961.

(M. A. GHŪL)

FAḌLI, MEḤMED, better known as ḲARA FAḌLĪ (? -971/1563-4), Turkish poet, born in Istanbul, son of a saddler. Little is known of his early life. He does not seem to have had a regular education, but acquired knowledge in the company of learned people, particularly the poet Dhātī [*q.v.*], whose shop of geomancy had become a sort of a literary club for men of letters, where the old poet helped and encouraged young talents. On Dhātī's suggestion he composed a *ḳaṣīda* on the occasion of the circumcision festivities of prince Meḥmed. When Dhātī had finished reading his poem on the same subject, he introduced to the Sultan, Süleymān the Magnificent, his young disciple who then recited his, which won him the favour of the court. Faḍlī was made *dīwān* secretary to prince Meḥmed and, upon his death, to prince Muṣṭafā. On the latter's tragic end (960/1552) he wrote a long remembered elegy. He then entered the service of the crown prince Selīm who, upon succeeding to the throne, made him his chief secretary with a high fief. The poet died in Kütahya the following year.

Faḍlī was a master of classical formal prose (*inshā᾽*), but he is better known as a poet. Unlike most poets of the classical age, he does not seem to have collected his poems into a *dīwān* and his known poems are scattered in various *medjmū῾a*s. Some of his works, mentioned and praised in *tedhkire*s (the *mathnawī*s *Humā we Humāyūn* and *Lehdjet ul-*

esrār, and a collection of stories in prose, *Nakhlistān*) have not come down to us. Apart from his *ḳaṣīdas*, *ghazal*s, *muṣammaṭ*s and *rubāʿī*s, Faḍlī owes his fame, among minor poets of the 10th/16th century, to his *mathnawī Gül we Bülbül* written in 960/1552-3 and dedicated to prince Muṣṭafā. This is an allegorical romance of the love of the Nightingale for the Rose which, unlike most of its contemporaries, does not follow any particular Persian model. In spite of the fluent and simple style of some passages, the work is on the whole written in an over-elaborated style laden with the conventional *ṣūfī* vocabulary which was in vogue during the period. Hammer's edition and translation of this work (see Bibl.) revived, for a time, the fading interest in this romance.

Bibliography: The *tedhkire*s of Laṭīfī, ʿAhdī, ʿĀshiḳ Čelebi, Ḳïnalï-zāde Ḥasan Čelebi, Riyāḍī and the biographical section in ʿĀlī's *Kunh al-akhbār*, s.v.; Hammer-Purgstall, *Gül u Bülbül, das ist: Rose und Nachtigall, von Fasli*, Pest and Leipzig 1834; Gibb, iii, 108; M. Fuad Köprülü in *IA*, s.v. Fazli. (FAHİR İZ)

FAGHFŪR or BAGHBŪR, title of the Emperor of China in the Muslim sources. The Sanskrit **bhagaputra* and the Old Iranian **baghaputhra*, with which attempts have been made to connect this compound, are not attested, but a form *bghpwhr* (= **baghpuhr*), signifying etymologically "son of God", is attested in Parthian Pahlavī to designate Jesus, whence Sogdian *baghpūr*, Arabicized as *baghbūr* and *faghfūr*; these forms were felt by the Arab authors as the translation of the Chinese *T'ien tzŭ* "son of heaven" (cf. *Relation de la Chine et de l'Inde*, ed. and tr. J. Sauvaget, Paris 1948, 20; al-Masʿūdī, *Murūdj*, i, 306 (tr. Pellat, § 334); *Fihrist*, 350 (Cairo ed., 491): *baghbūr* = son of heaven, that is to say descended from the heavens; Ibn al-Athīr, vii, 221). The form *faghfūr* (*facfur* in Marco Polo, ed. Yule-Cordier, ii, 145, ed. L. Hambis, Paris 1955, 194, to refer to the last emperor of the Sung dynasty), which has been borrowed by Persian (cf. Ferrand, in *JA*, 1924/1, 243; idem, in *BSOS*, vi (1931), 329-39; S. Lévi, in *JA*, 1934/1, 19), seems to be a more eastern form, although it is attested in al-Masʿūdī (*Murūdj*, ii, 200, = tr. Pellat § 622); it appears notably in the *Ḥudūd al-ʿālam*, 84, and in an Arabic inscription in the cemetery of Zaytūn (Ts'iuan-cheou) dated 723/1323 (cf. G. Arnáiz and M. van Berchem, *Mémoire sur les antiquités musulmanes de Ts'iuan-cheou*, in *T'oung-Pao*, xii, 724). In the Arabic texts it appears less frequently than *baghbūr* (the Arabic dictionaries give the vocalization *bughbūr*), the earliest attestations of which go back at least to the 3rd/9th century (Ibn Khurradādhbih, 16; al-Djāḥiẓ, *Ḥayawān*, vii, 180); later authors use it frequently (al-Masʿūdī, *Fihrist*, Ibn al-Athīr, see above; al-Khʷārizmī, *Mafātīḥ*, Cairo 1342, 71, 73; al-Bīrūnī, *Chronology*, 109; *Abrégé des merveilles*, 118; etc.). According to the author of the *Relation de la Chine et de l'Inde* (20), a form *maghbūr* was used, perhaps punningly, by navigators. Al-Masʿūdī, *loc. cit.*, also indicates the title which one gave to the emperor of China when addressing him, and it seems that the reading *Ṭamghāč khān*, "Khān of the Ṭamghāč", must be adopted; this refers to the Chinese (cf. Abu 'l-Fidāʾ, ii/2, 123), *Ṭamghāč* (*Tabghač*) designating the Chinese and China (see P. Pelliot, *Notes on Marco Polo*, i, 274).

The derived forms *faghfūrī* (Persian) and *faghfur* (Turkish) have become synonyms of *čīnī* "Chinese [porcelain]", but later authors who try to explain this word make *faghfūr* a region of China (cf. P. Pelliot, in *T'oung-Pao*, 1931, 458). This term has entered Modern Greek (φάρφουρι) in the sense of "porcelain", and also Slav languages, through the Russian *farfor* (see Berneker, *Slav. etymol. Wörterbuch*, i, 279; Laufer, *Beginnings of porcelain*, 126).

Bibliography: in addition to the references in the text: E. Blochet, *Introduction à l'histoire des Mongols*, GMS XII, 76 n. 1; H. Cordier, in *Mélanges H. Derembourg*, 434; H. Yule and A. C. Burnell, *Hobson-Jobson*², London 1903, s.v. *Faghfur*; G. Ferrand, *Relations de voyages et textes géographiques*, Paris 1913-4, 2; Maspero, *La Chine antique*, Paris 1927, 144; P. Pelliot, *Notes on Marco Polo*, ii, Paris 1963, s.v. *facfur*, devotes a well-developed and documented study to this term. (ED.)

FAGHFŪR, in the sense of 'porcelain' [see ṢĪNĪ].

FAHD (Ar.), (fem. *fahda*, pl. *fuhūd, afhād, afhud, fuhūda*), is the name of the Cheetah (Urdū *čītā* < Sanskrit *čitraka*, "spotted"), *Acinonyx jubatus*, also called "Hunting-leopard and Hunting-cat", (French: "*guépard*", Persian: "*yūz*"), the subspecies *Acin. jub. venaticus* being found from Balūčistān to ʿIrāḳ and Jordan and the subspecies *Acin. jub. hecki* or *guttatus* in northern Africa, from the borders of the Sahara. The noun *fahd*, the form to be preferred to *fahid* which was recommended by al-Ḳalḳashandī (*Ṣubḥ al-aʿshā*, ii, 39 ff.), is connected with the root *FHD* which contains the idea of being "soporific by nature and with a tendency to negligence" in speaking of a man who could thus be compared with the cheetah; it is, however, difficult to know if the animal has taken its name from the earlier root bearing this sense, the cheetah being well-known for its natural sleepiness, or if, on the contrary, the root is derived from the word *fahd* which can equally well be supposed to be an Arabic corruption of the Greco-Latin term πάρδος/*pardus*, "panther".

From remotest antiquity travellers in regions inhabited by cheetahs have not failed to observe this slender wild beast, asleep all day in the shade of a bush, hunting only at dawn or dusk, and, though with the tabby coat of a feline, claiming relationship with the canine family. Modern mammalogists in fact recognize it as a greyhound with the fur of a big cat from the form of the cranium, teeth like those of the canidae, non-retractile claws, its habit of running in strides, each step being a leap of five to six yards, and its peaceful nature; the cheetah does not experience the blind atavistic ferocity shown by the big felines at the sight of blood. It is not therefore surprising that the Mongols, Persians and Hindūs who hunted because they needed food and consequently were close observers of wild animals should at a very early time have had the idea of taming the yards, and making use of its predatory instinct for catching hares and various ungulates with edible flesh; by so doing they gained the services of the swiftest of all quadrupeds, the cheetah having a speed of about eighty miles an hour for a distance of five or six hundred yards. It is probable that the Lakhmid princes, vassals of the Sāsānids, tamed the cheetah in east Syria and ʿIrāḳ, the animal being fairly widespread in those countries; the strain from the Samāwa had the reputation, according to al-Manglī, of being superior to any other in the 14th century.

Although Arab tradition attributes to Kulayb Wāʾil of the Nadjd (second half of the 5th century A.D.) the distinction of first hunting with the cheetah, the animal does not appear to have been commonly employed in hunting by the Arabs before the Islamic conquests. Pre-Islamic poets, to judge by such of their writings as survive, make no mention of them; instead, it must have been regarded, like the panther, as a dangerous wild animal best avoided. Although extant in the Ḥidjāz and the Yemen, the cheetah was never very numerous in Arabia, its elective biotope hardly going beyond the tropic of Cancer and being pre-eminently the dry Mediterranean steppe of grass- and bush-land found between the 25th and 35th parallels. The absence in ancient Arabic of any "collective noun" in *mafʿala* among derivatives from the root *FHD* may to some measure corroborate, if not the ignorance of the Bedouins of pre-Islamic Arabia in respect of the cheetah, at least their confusion of this animal with the panther Leopard, *Panthera pardus*, (*namir*, *nimr*, *arḳaṭ*). This confusion, incidentally, has been perpetuated unfailingly even up to our own time in the works of many western writers since the introduction by the Crusaders in the 14th century of the cheetah to the courts of Sicily and Italy, and subsequently from there to the courts of France, Germany and England. The French name "guépard", after the names "gapard" and "chat-pard" derived from the Italian "gatto-pardo", has only lately, and correctly, been substituted for the incorrect mediaeval old-French appellations "lyépard", "leupart", "léopard", "léopard-chasseur", just as the anglicized term "cheetah" has taken the place of the archaic Middle-English forms of "leopart", "leparde", "lebarde", "libbard", and "hunting-leopard". Many also continue to make a serious error in confusing the cheetah with the Ounce or "Mountain Panther", also called "Snow-leopard", *Felis uncia*, a species of panther confined to the high mountains of central Asia, which only certain Mongolo-Altaic clans ventured to tame for hunting cervidae, and without any great success. The word Ounce, used for "Lonce" (from the Low Latin *lyncea*, lynx), applied to the "Snow-Leopard" revealed the confusion existing between the panther and the lynx which is called in French "Loup-cervier", *i.e.*, Stag-eating wolf, and was in fact trained. Moreover it is an actual fact that the orthodox Muslim has never included a panther of any species, any more than the tiger (*babr* pl. *bubūr*) or lion, in the list of "beasts of prey" (*al-djawāriḥ*) recognised as "lawful instruments" of hunting (*ālāt al-ṣayd*); justifying this position of the Islamic law, Usāma b. Munḳidh, the illustrious Syrian hunter-knight of the 6th/12th century, was certainly the first to expound with precision the well-known anatomical distinctions between the cheetah and the panther, especially in the structure of the cranium, and to insist upon the ineradicable brutality of the second (see *K. al-Iʿtibār*, 111-2). In this connexion, it is to be regretted that L. Mercier (74-5), misled by erroneous sources of later date, failed to realize that the *yūz* of the Persians was actually the cheetah, and not an "unidentified" panther.

However that may be, it was not until the Muslim expansion towards the north-east took place in the 1st/7th century that the Arabs could be seen to have familiarized themselves with this new auxiliary in their hunting expeditions, afterwards taking to it with passionate enthusiasm. Their interest in the cheetah was to be revealed by their concise aphorisms in which the animal served as an example for some of its characteristic features; they said, among other things, "sleepier than a cheetah" (*anwamᵘ min fahd*), "heavier-headed than the cheetah" (*athḳalᵘ raʾsᵃⁿ min al-fahd*), "a better purveyor than a cheetah" (*aksabᵘ min fahd*), "quicker off the mark than a cheetah" (*athwabᵘ min fahd*), "angrier than a cheetah" (*aghḍabᵘ min fahd*); all these axioms are to be found in collections devoted to this literary genre, such as that of al-Maydānī (d. 518/1124).

To be of service in hare and gazelle hunting, the cheetah has to receive a certain training and, for this reason, the Muslims ranked it, like the greyhound and the sporting-bird [see BAYZARA] as one of the "credited carnivora" (*al-ḍawārī*) the use of which in hunting was recognized as lawful on the strength of the Ḳurʾānic ruling (V, 6/4): ". . Reply [to them]: lawful for you are foodstuffs good to eat and any [game] that, at your wish, is captured by beasts of prey which you have trained as you do dogs, according to the method which Allāh has taught you, after you have spoken the name of Allāh over it . . .". It is in imposing this necessary condition of training, (*idjāba*, *ḍarāwa/ḍarāʾa*, *taʿlīm*, *taʾdīb*), and in considering the "bleeding bite" (*ʿaḳr*) made by the beast of prey at the take as a ritual slaughter (*dhabḥ*, *tadhkiya*) of the victim, that the doctors of the Law also admit certain other carnivora (*kāsib*, pl. *kawāsib*) whose training for hunting is identical with that of the cheetah.

First comes the Lynx Caracal (*ʿanāḳ al-arḍ*, *ʿunfuṭ*, *ghundjul*, *ʿundjul*, *ḳundjul*, *fundjul*, *ḥundjul*, *ḥandjal*, *furānik al-asad*, *shīb*, *bawwāḳ*; Ḥidjāz: *tumayla*; Sudan: *umm rīshāt*; Maghrib: (*a*)*bū sbūla*, *ūdān/awdān* for *ādhān*; Persian *siyāh-gūsh*; Turkish *ḳaraḳulaḳ* whence "caracal"); the number of its names is proof that the Caracal was well-known in the countries of Islam, all the more since this large russet-coloured cat, with "ears tufted with black", less heavy to carry than the cheetah and less exacting in its requirements, in addition to its aptitude for "fur hunting" (*ṣayd li 'l-wabar*) was equally adept with feathered creatures (*ṣayd li 'l-rīsh*), partridges, wild geese, bustards and cranes. After the cheetah and the caracal, they trained, with equal success, the Jungle Cat (Fr. *Lynx des marais*, *i.e.*, Marsh lynx), *Felis chaus* (*tuffa*, *tufah*, *tifā*, *tifāwa*) as well as the Serval or Tiger-Cat, *Leptailurus serval* (*washak*, *wishk*, *wishk*, *kiṭṭ-namir*); as for the Ferret, *Mustela putorius furo* (*ibn ʿirs*, *nims*), it was used on rare occasions to flush game from dense coverts and for digging out fox, badger (*zabzab*) and porcupine (*ḍirbān*) (Kushādjim, 227-8; Ibn Munḳidh, 213).

Under the Umayyad dynasty, the cheetah became an indispensable element in the caliphs' diversions; in Yazīd b. Muʿāwiya (680-3) the passion for "hunting with cheetahs" was quite as fervent as his love of hawking, so much so that he was traditionally the first (of the Muslims) to carry on his crupper the noble animal which the ordinary people, with their grey-hounds, looked upon as impossible to tame (*dhū shakīma*). To name all the caliphs and distinguished personages in Islam who kept packs of cheetahs would be lengthy and of little value, since very few of them failed to respond to the powerful fascination exerted by the swift and inexorable hunt to the death as seen in the cheetah's headlong attack. The ʿAbbāsids, following the example of their illustrious general Abū Muslim al-Khurāsānī (718-55), and later the Fāṭimids and the Mamlūks, took such a great interest in this proud beast, forcibly tamed by man, that they delighted in making it take part in their official processions; it may even be thought that they looked upon it as an external mark of their prestige and opulence. The vast expense entailed by the upkeep of a hunt with cheetahs, for which a paid staff of experts was essential, precluded all but the rich from the privilege of this luxurious diversion; the less affluent contented themselves with flying and coursing sports. It is however surprising to note that the Maghrib and Muslim Spain took no interest in the cheetah and never trained it; no reference to it occurs in any of the great number of documents, both Arabic and European, from which we draw our knowledge of Western Islam. The cheetah is known throughout the pre-Saharan zone of the Maghrib, from Tunisia to the Moroccan borders, although it is becoming rare there, and the nomads of the region have always regarded it simply as a permanent danger to their flocks (see L. Lavauden, *Les vertébrés du Sahara*, Tunis 1926, 39-40; idem, *Les grands animaux de chasse de l'Afrique française*, in *Faune des Colonies françaises*, Paris 1934, no. 30, 366-7; idem, *La chasse et la faune cynégétique en Tunisie*, Tunis 1920, 9-10). The Touaregs for their part are pleased, when they capture the beast, either to sell it to Europeans or else to make beautiful saddle-cloths and food-bags (*mizwad*, pl. *mazāwid*) from its skin, but they have never thought of training it; they are, however, aware of its elegance and power, often giving its name (in Tamashaḳ *amayas*) to their children as a first-name (H. Lhote, *La chasse chez les Touaregs*, Paris 1951, 129-30).

In contrast to the indifference shown by the Muslim West towards hunting with cheetahs, the East for its part has until our own time kept this ancient practice very much alive in ʿIrāḳ, Īrān and India; Persian tradition ascribes it to Chosroes Anūshirwān (531-79 A.D.), but in fact it goes back to remotest antiquity. The renowned poet Firdawsī is somewhat nearer the truth when, in his *Shāh Nāma* he names Tahmūras, prince of the legendary dynasty of the Pishdādians, as the inventor of the training of beasts of prey, in these lines: *Siyāh-gūsh o yūz dar miyān bargozīd / Bā čāra biāwūrdash az dasht o kūh* ("He [Tahmūras] chooses from them [the wild beasts] the Caracal and the Cheetah. By artifice he took them from the desert and the mountains").

Muslim writers in the Middle Ages, naturalists like al-Ḳazwīnī (599-682/1203-83) in his *K. ʿAdjāʾib al-makhlūḳāt* and al-Damīrī (742-807/1341-1405) in his *K. Ḥayāt al-ḥayawān*, encyclopaedists like al-Djāḥiẓ (d. 255/868) in his *K. al-Ḥayawān* and al-Ḳalḳashandī (d. 821/1418, *op. cit. supra*), philologists like the Andalusian Ibn Sīda in his *K. al-Mukhaṣṣaṣ*, all spoke of the cheetah, not as connoisseurs but as recorders of the sayings of the Ancients; in this way they perpetuated certain naive and fabulous beliefs which originated in part in the imagination of the Greeks. From the beginning of the Umayyad dynasty a team of anonymous translators, possibly bilingual Ghassānids, had put into Arabic some of Aristotle's writings, in particular his "History of the animals". Al-Djāḥiẓ made use of this work, and tried to complete it; on occasion he in his turn repeated the old fallacies which had been accepted without verification; people will never cease to believe, for example, that the cheetah is a hybrid from the union of a female panther and a lion. Still more typical is the case of the variety of Aconite (*Doronicum pardalianches*) which Greek hunters ground to a paste and used as a poison for wild animals (see Aristotle, *History of Animals*, new Fr. trans. J. Tricot, Paris 1957, ii, 600 [Eng. tr. of *Works*, edd. J. A. Smith and W. D. Ross, iv, 612a]; Xenophon, *Cynegeticus*, Fr. trans. E. Talbot, Paris 1873, i, chap. VI, 338 [Loeb ed. of *Scripta minora*, 1956, 440-1]) and which, from a literal translation of its Greek name "pardalianches" *i.e.*, "that chokes the panther" (which is the actual "Wolf's-bane", with the same meaning; cf. Old-French: "étrangle-loup", "tue-loup"), is called in Arabic *khāniḳ al-fuhūd* or *khāniḳ al-namir*; then, by metonymy, this name has been extended, in al-Djāḥiẓ and those who repeated what he wrote (see *K. al-Ḥayawān*, iv, 228), to mean the effects of poisoning induced by this plant and considered as a malady peculiar to wild carnivores.

In the last resort we have to turn to writers on hunting to find more realistic information about the cheetah's nature, capture and training. Of the numerous Arabic treatises on venery and falconry recorded by lexicographers, very few have survived [see BAYZARA]; the oldest which has come down to us seems, at present, to be the *K. al-Maṣāyid wa 'l-maṭārid*, attributed to the poet Kushādjim (d. 961 or 971): in reality, this is no more than a work at second-hand which, thanks to the compiler, contains long fragments from a much earlier, possibly Umayyad, work; and the treatises in Old-French of "Moamin and Ghatrif" (see the excellent critical edition by H. Tjerneld, Stockholm-Paris 1945) are a complete translation. However that may be, the *K. al-Maṣāyid wa 'l-maṭārid* (very careless edition by A. Ṭalas, Baghdād 1954) contains in the *Bāb al-fahd* (183-201) a useful documentation on the animal's treatment. This chapter is reproduced word for word in the *K. al-Bayzara* (ed. Kurd ʿAlī, Damascus 1953), the work of the hawker (al-Ḥasan b. al-Ḥusayn?) of the Fāṭimid caliph al-ʿAzīz bi'llāh (975-96); however, the anonymous author, in the *Bāb ṣayd al-fahd* (118 ff.), puts forward his own personal remarks which are not lacking in interest. As for Usāma b. Munḳidh (d. 1188), he recalls his childhood days when at his father's house there was a she-cheetah of unusual docility, living in freedom (*musayyaba*) and on perfectly good terms with the fowls and the numerous tame gazelles belonging to the house, although when hunting she displayed a relentless ferocity towards her quarry. From his "Hunting memories" it emerges that he himself took almost no interest in this method of hunting. It was a very different matter with al-Manglī, a famous Mamlūk hunter, who in his treatise dated 773/1371 gives us the fruit of his great experience in the matter of cheetahs; it is certainly the most thorough study on this subject in Arabic that we possess. The works of al-Ashʿari (848/1444) and al-Fākihī (d. 948/1541) of which L. Mercier made use (mss. Paris, B.N., no. 2831 and 2834) are merely repetitions of the earlier writings.

In the light of these texts it is easy to formulate an exact idea of the difficulties which mediaeval Islamic huntsmen had to overcome before being able to experience to the full the excitement engendered by the cheetah's "career" (*ṭalḳ*, pl. *aṭlāḳ*). First it was necessary to find an animal in the prime of life (*musinn*), for the cheetah does not breed in captivity and the cheetah's whelp (*ʿawbar, hawbar*), if deprived of the tutelage of its wild parents, never acquires by itself the instinct of rapine. In fact, the master of a hunt with cheetahs was no more than a spectator on the spot, watching the exploits of the beasts in his menagerie, all the work and the results being the responsibility of the "cheetah-keeper" (*fahhād*, Fr. *guépardier*), a difficult and very restricted occupation for which the rewards had to be lavish. The cheetah-keeper had, in fact, to be "trailer" (*dhānib*), tamer (*rāʾiḍ*, pl. *ruwwāḍ*) and trainer (*muḍarr^in^*, *muḍr^in^*).

Certain tribes had specialized in this activity, like the Banū Ḳurra and the Banū Sulaym in Egypt, and made a profit from selling the animals they captured. The tactics most usually employed in catching the animal that was required, a female for preference, were "to recognize it by its footprints" (*ḥifẓ al-āthār*), to "stalk its lair" (*taḳrīb al-ʿarīn*) with two or three men on horseback, in the heat of the day, to "start it" and to "trail its slot" (*nadjāsha*) slowly, without pressing it too hard; soon the indolent creature lies down to resume its interrupted nap, but is started once again. This manoeuvre is repeated three or four times until the animal is forced by fatigue to "wait steady" (*muḳāwama*) and to "face" (*muʿāraḍa*) its pursuers, if it is not falling asleep from exhaustion. One of the trackers (*nadjdjāshūn*) then dismounts, throws his burnous over it with a rapid and deft movement to blind it by covering it, and immobilizes the animal by holding down its flank with the whole weight of his body. It is at this moment that the cheetah-keeper has to employ all his skill to slip a halter (*maras*) under the garment round the animal's neck and to bind its jaws with a solid "muzzle" (*kimāma, sayr*) while an assistant securely ties together its forelegs and hindlegs two by two, above the pasterns in order not to bruise the muscles, wrapping its feet in pieces of cloth to avoid any injury from the claws; for greater safety its forequarters and hindquarters are made fast to two posts. The animal is left for some time in this painful position; and so fatigue, grief, terror and hunger soon get the better of its savagery. In addition to these natural aids to taming the cheetah-keeper also makes use of the human eye's mastery over the beast's, staring at it at frequent intervals and for longer and longer periods; when the animal closes its eyes or turns away its head, it is humbled and no further reaction of ferocity is to be feared from it. The hobbles from the posts are gradually loosened until the cheetah can raise itself on its fore quarters and can accept from the tamer's hand some pieces of cheese and then meat. With each morsel that is offered the cheetah-keeper utters a cry, as it were inviting his pupil to respond; this is the real start of the "reclaiming" (*idjāba, istidjāba*). In this connexion, Muslim authors have not failed to stress the similarity of the procedures for reclaiming the goshawk and training the cheetah, as well as the technical terminology relating to both; incidentally al-Manglī states: "... *idjābat al-fahd ka-idjābat al-bāzī* ...", "the cheetah's reclamation is like that of the goshawk ...". After about ten days the prisoner's fetters (*withāḳ*, pl. *wuthuḳ*) are replaced by hobbles (*ʿiḳāl*, pl. *ʿuḳul*) binding together the four feet in pairs, following the method used for camels and beasts of burden. Henceforward the cheetah can stand upright and stretch itself; everyone speaks to it, its keeper watches over it ceaselessly and feeds it, but only sparingly so that it still remains hungry (*tadjwīʿ*); at this point it is possible to think about transporting it to its future domicile.

The Indians use a different technique for catching cheetahs; they spread nets round the edges of trees on whose trunks can be seen marks of scratching, where the animal has abraded its claws; sooner or later it is caught in the nets. On the other hand it is difficult to believe the statement, taken from the Greeks, that the cheetah allows itself to be approached without difficulty when it is made to hear a "beautiful voice" (*ṣawt ḥasan*); but it is possible, in spite of everything, that like many wild animals it is responsive to music and singing.

To convey the cheetah to the room set aside for it by its owner is a delicate operation to which the cheetah-keeper devotes particular care: he has to avoid any accident which might impair the animal's fine condition. To do this, he puts it into a "strait-jacket" (*wiʿāʾ, ghirāra, kays*), a large bag, allowing it to pass its head through the opening and, to prevent it being frightened by anything nearby, he accustoms it to wear on its head a hood (*kumma*), a leather visor shaped like a baby's bonnet and tying under the chin; two porters then suffice to carry it safely to its destination when thus "hooded" (*mughaṭṭā 'l-wadjh*).

On reaching its new home the cheetah, like sporting-birds, has to receive some "manning" (*uns, ilf*), training that will make it lose its savageness (*tadjrīd*) completely. For this purpose the cheetah-keeper, leaving the hobbles on its feet, tethers it outside a house facing on to a busy street; the din, the constant movement and the teasing by the children soon result in making it absolutely harmless. They even go so far as to make it walk through the markets, held firmly on a lead and carefully surrounded. In the evening it is taken to its room, a dark stable where it is fastened to a long chain (*midjarr*) which leaves its movements entirely free. For the first nights an ostler (*sāʾis*) watches it by the light of a lamp and prevents it from sleeping in order not to interrupt the process of training; it is only later that it is given a thick carpet (*ṭinfisa*) to sleep on.

All this time and for the rest of its life it receives food only from the hand of its keeper, for it is by means of the daily feed (*ṭuʿm*) that he begins the education (*tahdīʾ*) of his pupil. The art is not in teaching it to hunt, for it already has the instinct to do so, but instead in accustoming it to jump and ride pillion (*irtidāf*) on its trainer's horse at any speed. The Indians avoid this difficult initiation by conveying their cheetahs to the hunting-grounds in small, individual vehicles, shaped like cages and drawn by horses or oxen.

To train it to ride pillion the cheetah-master installs in his pupil's room a wooden vaulting-horse (*mithāl al-dābba*) or a small platform (*dakka, markab*) on trestles of adjustable height, and then having fastened a solid leather collar (*ḳilāda*), fitted with a ring with swivel-pin (*midwar*), round the cheetah's neck, he releases it from the chain and holds it by the leash with one hand; with the other he shakes the bowl with rings (*ḳasʿa*) from which the animal feeds and places it on the raised platform, to start with a cubit and a half above the ground. Repeating this manœuvre several times, he ends by ostentatiously throwing a piece of raw meat into the bowl standing on the platform, at the same time inviting the animal to jump up by pulling lightly at the leash. Egged on by hunger, the cheetah quickly understands that the rattle of rings on the bowl is the announcement of something good for it to eat and that it has to go up onto the platform to get it. In this way the copper or bronze bowl, with rings attached, now continually plays the part of the cheetah's "reclaim", like the sporting-bird's lure. For this same purpose the Indians use a large iron ladle which is easier to handle on horseback than a bowl. By repeating this routine several times a day, each time increasing the height by several centimetres, the keeper accustoms the animal, in less than ten days, to come and look for its food at a height of more than three cubits above the ground, the average height of the crupper on a saddled horse; he does not fail, each time, to give it confidence by patting its flanks. Finally he replaces the platform by a table suspended from the ceiling, like the old breadshelf of former times, and puts on it not only the bowl but also the cheetah's carpet, thereby compelling it to balance itself on an unsteady seat where it is rocked about in exactly the same way as on its trainer's crupper.

Again, it is by using the bowl that the keeper starts teaching the cheetah to mount. He selects a calm, good-natured horse and gets an ostler to hold the bridle; he then goes to fetch the cheetah and brings it on a leash close to the horse; to begin with, he is careful to hood the cheetah before taking it outside, to prevent it being at all alarmed by the sight of the horse. As soon as he is in the saddle he pulls the leash with one hand and with the other makes a clinking sound with the bowl which is placed behind him on the pillion (*rifāda*) or "crupper-seat", fixed to the cantle of the saddle. The animal is attracted and nimbly jumps up to eat the meat in the bowl; intent on its food, it pays no attention to the movement of the seat, the rider having meanwhile made his mount start to move. Patient and frequent repetitions of this manoeuvre quite soon allow the cheetah-keeper to ride at a trot, and then at a gallop, without disturbing his passenger which, being "well-credited" (*rabīb*), sits firmly on its pillion, untied except for its slip which is knotted to the saddle-bow.

The "slipping on live" (*irsāl ʿalā 'l-ṣayd*) of the cheetah is fairly rapid: some train-deer (*kasīra*, pl. *kasāʾir*), hares or gazelle fawns (*k͟his͟hf*, pl. *k͟hus͟hūf*) which are easy to catch and are slaughtered under the cheetah's feet so that it may lap the blood, quickly bring out its hunting instincts. The skilful cheetah-keeper can even ensure that his beast only "sets upon" the gazelle bucks (*faḥl*, pl. *fuḥūl*), the does (*ʿanz*, pl. *ʿunūz*) in venery in East and West alike being always left free for breeding; whenever a doe is seized, the cheetah is deprived of its "right" by being immediately removed from its take, whilst it is allowed to "take its pleasure" (*is͟hbāʿ*) on the bucks it has caught.

When a cheetah is judged to be "well-tried" (*muḥkam*), three ways of hunting are possible. The first, a princely prerogative, is "hunting at force" (*al-mukābara, al-muwād͟jaha*): the huntsmen, having reconnoitred the herd (*sirb*) from a distance, dislodge a buck and run it down until the "finish"; at the same time the cheetah is cast on the exhausted quarry and lays it low without difficulty or fatigue. These tactics entail long rides at random and require great endurance from riders and mounts alike. The second way is greatly relished for the thrilling spectacle that it offers, for it depends on the action of the cheetah alone: it is "stalking" (*al-dasīs*); the cheetah which has been unhooded (*maks͟hūf al-wad͟jh*) "reconnoitres" (*tas͟hawwuf*) from a distance the gazelle as it is browsing and, at a sign from its keeper who has put it down on the ground, it sets off to try to take its quarry by surprise without being betrayed by its scent. The huntsmen take cover in order to see without being seen, and tremble with delight at the cheetah's manoeuvres as, having made its way upwind (*mustaḳbil al-rīḥ*), it steals on and creeps up (*daʾalān, tasallul*) to the quarry, crouches down, remaining stock-still at the first alarm, and starts off again, one foot after another, taking advantage of every undulation of the ground, and so comes up quite close to the gazelle without having put it on its guard; the final charge is a matter of only a few seconds. As for the third way, it is by far the most commonly used by cheetah-keepers and gentlemen farmers (*dihḳān*, pl. *dahāḳīn*) for the small amount of difficulty and fatigue that it entails: it is "trailing" (*al-mud͟hānaba, al-id͟hnāb*); the huntsmen recognize a herd by its footprints and trail it upwind as far as its cover without alerting it. The cheetah, unhooded and "cast on the fur" unawares, is able to lay low several beasts before they have time to escape.

Whichever method of attack is adopted in the course of hunting, the cheetah-keeper cannot call for more than five or six "careers" (*ṭalḳ*, pl. *aṭlāḳ*) from his cheetah since it makes the maximum effort in each career and thus rapidly becomes exhausted; for the same reason, it is only allowed to hunt on alternate days. Furthermore the cheetah-keeper must always cut the quarry's throat while the cheetah is still lying on it (*tamahhud*), biting it hard in the nape of the neck or the throat, and must let it lap the blood caught in the bowl in order to remove it from its quarry and to take away the body. Nor will he neglect to hood the cheetah again as soon as it has remounted the pillion, so that it is not tempted to dash off after some game not intended for it, since it is only lawful to eat the flesh of a wild beast caught in this manner if the cheetah-keeper has pronounced the formula invoking the name of Allāh (*tasmiya*) at the moment when the beast of prey is deliberately let slip (*irsāl bi 'l-niyya*). The cheetah, being subject to laws of nature, becomes vexed and angry when it misses its quarry and turns a deaf ear when its master calls it in; only the clinking of its bowl makes it decide to go back. Although sensitive to reprimands, it is doubtful if this animal goes so far as to learn a lesson, as the legend has it, from a rebuke addressed in its presence but vicariously, to a dog that is in fact blameless.

The excitement of watching coursing with the cheetah has not escaped the inspiration of those Muslim poets who were responsive to subjects provided by the chase (*ṭaradiyyāt*). Some accomplished masters of the *urd͟jūza* have left superb descriptions of the animal and its lightning charges, stressing the beauty of its tabby coat (*mudannar*), the terrifying aspect given by its "tear-streaks" (*al-madmaʿānⁱ*) or "moustaches" (*al-sufʿatānⁱ*, *al-s͟hāhidānⁱ*), the two dark stripes like two *alif*s, stretching from the eyes to the corners of the mouth, its suppleness when creeping, its unparalleled speed and irresistible assault. Of the writings devoted to the cheetah, which are rarer than those describing hounds and sporting-birds, only those by poets of the ʿAbbāsid period have survived; we need note only such famous names as Abū Nuwās, al-Faḍl al-Raḳās͟hī the rival of Abū Nuwās, Ibn al-Muʿtazz, al-Nās͟hiʾ, Ibn Abī Karīma the contemporary of al-D͟jāḥiẓ, Ibn al-Muʿad͟hd͟hal and Ibn al-Ḥusayn al-Ḥāfiẓ. The sport of hunting with cheetahs having remained a diversion for the rich in Islam, it is not surprising to find that only the court poets of caliphs and wealthy patrons have celebrated it in verse; popular poetry and Bedouin songs have scarcely touched on the subject.

Sāsānid Persia gave the cheetah a certain place in its works of art; miniaturists represented it either realistically or else symbolically, by pair affronted or addorsed, on either side of the "tree of life" (*hōm*). The West eagerly borrowed this last motif in the illuminations of the main Middle Ages, as we see in a frontispiece of the IXth century Evangeliary of Lothair (Latin ms. Paris, B.N., no. 226, f° 75v°, according to A. Michel, *Histoire de l'Art*, Paris 1905, I, 1st part, 400-4). The cheetah is also to be seen as an element of animal decoration in ceramics, tapestries, drawings, carving and jewellery; in the Bucharest Museum there are two openwork cloisonné vessels which were discovered in ancient Petrossa and are therefore known as the "Petrossa treasure"; each handle on these vases is made in the form of a cheetah supporting the vessel, the body made of gold and studded with garnets and turquoises (see A. Michel, *op. cit.*, 413-4). Throughout Islam, the dominating influence of Sāsānid inspiration in the minor arts swept through all the Muslim territories and remained effective for several centuries; thus one frequently finds the "cheetah motif" in the works of art in metal or stone left by the artists of Fāṭimid Egypt and Muslim Spain. In this connexion one may wonder if the historians of Muslim art have occasionally been mistaken in regard to some of these decorations with animal figures, and have identified as lions what the artist intended as cheetahs. Finally, we may note that despite the renown it enjoyed among the great in the East, the cheetah never attained the heraldic eminence in Mamlūk heraldry that it reached in the Christian West during the Middle Ages.

Bibliography: In addition to the references given in the article: Usāma Ibn Munḳidh, *K. al-Iʿtibār*, ed. Ph. Hitti, Princeton 1930, chap. i, 111; iii, 206-9; Muḥammad al-Manglī, *K. Uns al-malāʾ bi-waḥsh al-falāʾ*, Arabic ms. Paris, B.N., no. 2832, fol. 18v° ff. and ed. F. Pharaon, Paris 1880, 60 f. with mediocre trans., 61 f.; ʿUmarī, *K. al-Taʿrīf bi 'l-muṣṭalaḥ al-sharīf*, Cairo 1312; Ibn Rushd-Averroès, *Le livre de la chasse*, extr. from the *Bidāyat al-mudjtahid*, text and trans. annotated by F. Viré, in *Revue Tunisienne de Droit*, iii-iv, Tunis 1954; Marco Polo, *Le Devisement du Monde*, ed. A. t'Serstevens, Paris 1960, 168, 201; L. Mercier, *La chasse et les sports chez les Arabes*, Paris 1927, ch. iv; A. Boyer and M. Planiol, *Traité de fauconnerie et autourserie*, Paris 1948, 170-81; L. Blancou, *Géographie cynégétique du monde*, Paris 1959; G. Migeon, *Manuel d'art musulman*², Paris 1927, ii, 403 ff. and *passim*; A. V. Pope, *A survey of Persian art*, Oxford 1939; Mayer, *Saracenic heraldry*, Oxford 1932. For an account of cheetah-hunting in Mughal India and the emperor Akbar's personal interest therein, see Abu 'l-Faḍl ʿAllāmī, *Āʾīn-i Akbarī*, ii, Āʾīn 27; food allowed to cheetahs, the wages of their keepers, and methods of hunting with cheetahs, *ibid.*, Āʾīn 28. On the caracal, *ibid.*, Āʾīn 28. See also Muʿtamid Khān, *Iḳbāl-nāma*, ed. Bibl. Ind., 70. (F. Viré)

FAḤL or Fiḥl, an ancient town in Transjordania situated 12 km. south-east of Baysān [*q.v.*], was known in earliest antiquity, at the time of el-Amarna, under the name *Bikhil*, corresponding to a semitic *p ḥ l*. Macedonian colonists settled there in about 310 B.C., giving it the name of the Macedonian town of Pella, which resembled the native name. After the Roman conquest, Pella was one of the towns of the Decapolis, and the Christians took refuge there during the disturbances which followed the destruction of Jerusalem. Later it belonged to the Second Palestine and was the seat of a bishopric. About six months after the battle of Adjnādayn [*q.v.*], in Dhu 'l-Ḳaʿda 13/January 635, it was near Faḥl that the Muslim armies attacked the Byzantines who had mustered to the east of the Jordan and cut the dikes at Baysān in order to turn the district into a marsh; during the battle, known as the "battle of Faḥl" or "battle of the marsh (*yawm al-radagha*)", the Arab invaders succeeded in crossing the Jordan and taking the town.

In the 3rd/9th century the population of Faḥl, according to al-Yaʿḳūbī, was still half Greek and the town, which formed part of the province of al-Urdunn, seems then to have declined rapidly, for the writers of the 4th/10th century do not mention it. Today the name Faḥl merely denotes a collection of ruins, mostly Roman and Byzantine.

Bibliography: Pauly-Wissowa, s.v. *Pella* (4); F.-M. Abel, *Géographie de la Palestine*, ii, Paris 1938, especially 405-6; Caetani, *Annali*, iii, 187-219; G. Le Strange, *Palestine under the Moslems*, London 1890, especially 439; A.-S. Marmardji, *Textes géographiques arabes sur la Palestine*, Paris 1951, 159; Balādhurī, *Futūḥ*, 115; Ṭabarī, i, 2146, 2155; Ibn al-Faḳīh, 116; Ibn Khurradādhbih, 78; Yaʿḳūbī, *Buldān*, 327 (trans. Wiet, 175); Yāḳūt, *Buldān*, iii, 853. (Fr. Buhl-[D. Sourdel])

FAHRASA, the name given in Muslim Spain to kinds of catalogues in which scholars enumerated, in one form or another, their masters and the subjects or works studied under their direction. The word *fahrasa* is an Arabicization of the Persian *fihrist* by means of a double vocalization *-a-* and the closing of the final *tāʾ*, a fairly frequent modification. In al-Andalus, it is completely synonymous with *barnāmadj*, which is also Persian, while in the east it corresponds with *thabat*, *mashīkha* (*mashyakha*) or *muʿdjam* (this last word is also used in the west). In the east, the best known of these works is *al-Muʿdjam al-mufahras* of Ibn Ḥadjar al-ʿAsḳalānī (d. 852/1449), still in manuscript (see Brockelmann, S II, 73), who adopts the same classification as Ibn Khayr (see *infra*). In the west, the *fahrasas* appear to be more numerous (Ibn Khayr and al-Ruʿaynī [see below] give quite a long list) and some still survive; three of them have already been published: a. Ibn Khayr al-Ishbīlī (502-70/1108-76 [*q.v.*]), *Fahrasat mā rawāh ʿan shuyūkhih min al-dawāwīn al-muṣannaf fī ḍurūb al-ʿilm wa-anwāʿ al-maʿārif*: *Index librorum de diversis scientiarum ordinibus quos a magistris didicit*, ed. J. Ribera Tarragó, *BAH*, ix-x, Saragossa 1894-5. — b. Ibn Abi 'l-Rabīʿ (599-688/1203-89; see Brockelmann, S I, 547), *Barnāmadj*, ed. ʿAbd al-ʿAzīz al-Ahwānī, in *RIMA*, i/2 (1955), 252-71. — c. al-Ruʿaynī al-Ishbīlī (592-666/1195-1268), *Barnāmadj* or *K. al-Īrād li-nubdhat al-mustafād min al-riwāya wa'l-isnād bi-liḳāʾ ḥamalat al-ʿilm fi 'l-bilād ʿalā ṭarīḳ al-iḳtiṣār wa'l-iḳtiṣād*, ed. Ibrāhīm Shabbūḥ, Damascus 1361/1962.

ʿAbd al-ʿAzīz al-Ahwānī has examined the mss. still extant and incorporated the results of his research in an extremely well documented article, *Kutub barāmidj al-ʿulamāʾ fi 'l-Andalus*, in *RIMA*, i/I (1955), 91-120. According to this writer, it is possible to distinguish four categories of *fahrasa* or *barnāmadj*: — I. Catalogue of writings, classified according to the branch of study to which they belong. Ibn Khayr observes the following order: Ḳurʾānic studies, *ḥadīth*, *siyar* and genealogy, *fiḳh*, grammar, lexicography, *adab*, poetry; he does no more than give the names of his masters, without any further observations. To this category belongs the *Barnāmadj* of Ibn Masʿūd al-Khushanī (d. 544/1149) of which only a few pages survive (al-Ahwānī, 99). — 2. A list of masters, with a note of the works studied under their direction. The *Ghunya* of *ḳāḍī* ʿIyāḍ (476-544/1083-1149 [*q.v.*]) who adopts an alphabetical classification, belongs to this category, as does the *Fahrasa* of Ibn ʿAṭiyya al-Muḥāribī (d. 541/1146; see Pons Boigues, *Ensayo bio-bibliográfico sobre los historiadores y geógrafos arábigo-españoles*, Madrid 1898, 207; Brockelmann, S I, 732; ms. Escorial 1733; he recounts the biography of his father and his other masters; al-Ahwānī, 101-2), and the *Barnāmadj* of al-Ruʿaynī who classifies his masters according to the subjects in which they specialized: Ḳurʾān, *ḥadīth*, grammar, *adab*, poetry. — 3. A combination of the two classifications, as in the *Barnāmadj* of Ibn Abi 'l-Rabīʿ (see *supra*) and that of Muḥammad b. Djābir al-Wādiyāshī (d. 749/1348; see Brockelmann, S II, 371, and correct the date and place [Tunis instead of Granada] of his death; ms. Escorial 1726), who first gives the names and biographies of his masters, then the list of subjects and works studied under their direction. — 4. The addition of personal observations, narratives etc. by the author to the above lists.

This genre, which appears to be a particular speciality of the Andalusians, should be associated with the transmission of *ḥadīth*, and indeed it was the traditionists and *fuḳahāʾ* who considered it helpful to leave for posterity a list of their masters (or to entrust it to one of their disciples, as in the case of Ibn Abi 'l-Rabīʿ), sometimes not without indicating the *isnād* of the *ḥadīth* learnt under their direction. But a well composed *fahrasa* such as that of Ibn Khayr possesses an interest of quite a different sort by revealing what studies could be undertaken by a young scholar at some given period, and by providing an inventory of the works favoured by cultivated circles (cf. H. Pérès, *Poésie andalouse*, 28 ff.).

Bibliography: in the article.

(Ch. Pellat)

FAḤṢ al-BALLŪṬ, "Plain of the oaktrees" or, more accurately, "of the acorns" (*ballūṭ*) whose present name Los Pedroches is applied to the wide valley situated to the south-west of Oreto, three days' journey north of Cordova. It stretches as far as the mountains of Almadén and has always been characterized by the great mass of evergreen oaks covering the mountains and the high plateau. *Pedroche* is synonymous with *pedregal*, the designation of the whole region, and the Latin name *petra*, transcribed into Arabic as *biṭra*, has, with the suffix *che*, given Biṭrawsh. In common with al-Idrīsī, the Muslim geographers praised the quality of the acorns which, according to al-Rāzī, were sweeter than *quantas ha en Espanya*, and added that the local inhabitants cultivated these trees with great care and that in years of poor harvest and famine they lived on the crop, for with this species the acorns can be eaten by human beings, not merely by animals. It was a high, mountainous region, inhabited mostly by Berbers, and the principal town Ghāfiḳ was so called from the name of the Maghribī tribe which had settled there. The castle, strongly fortified and well situated on the road leading from Dār al-baḳār to Toledo via Pedroche, was remarkable for the vigour with which its occupants repulsed the Castilians during the raids they made in the time of Alfonso VII and Alfonso VIII. The old fortress of Ghāfiḳ, towering above a little peninsula like an island, was put to new use in the 15th century and transformed into a barbican, on which was built the castle of Belalcázar; its identification with Ghāfiḳ has been finally established and there are no longer any grounds for uncertainty.

The Kūra of al-Balāliṭa, the plural of ballūṭ, included among its castles, in addition to Ghāfiḳ, Pedroche —Biṭrawsh [*q.v.*]—Sadfura on the Djabal ʿAfūr, Ḥiṣn Ḥārūn, identified with the castle of Aznaron and the castle of Cuzna, alongside the river which bears its name and the port, later called Puerto Calatraveño. Al-Ghāfiḳī and al-Ballūṭī are the ethnic names of important personages of the district, among them the great *ḳāḍī* of Cordova, Abu 'l-Ḥakam Mundhir b. Saʿīd, famous for his rectitude and learning in the time of ʿAbd al-Raḥmān III. Abū Ḥafṣ ʿUmar al-Ballūṭī, leader of the émigrés from the outskirts of Cordova who had occupied Alexandria, seized Crete and founded a dynasty which remained there until 309/921.

During the Almoravid period, in 528/1134, the Castilians crossed through the region of the Pedroches and reached the castle of al-Baḳār, where they were routed by Tāshfīn b. ʿAlī and compelled to retreat along the valley of the Guadiato. In the summer of 549/1155 Alfonso VII took Pedroche and Santa Euphemia, but Pedroche was immediately recaptured by the new Almohad governor of Cordova, ʿIbn Īgīt who defeated the count left in command of Pedroche by Alfonso VII, took him prisoner when capturing the castle by storm, and sent him to Marrākush. For a considerable time Ghāfiḳ-Belalcázar remained in the hands of the Almohads for, although we do not know the date when the Faḥṣ al-ballūṭ passed completely into the power of Castile, it is certain that in 580/1184 the caliph Yūsuf b. ʿAbd al-Muʾmin, on his arrival at Seville to start the Santarem campaign, sent his general Muḥammad b. Wānūdīn into exile at Ghāfiḳ, his conduct in action against the Castilians and Portuguese having been somewhat discreditable.

The counts of Sotomayor, when building their castle on the site of the abandoned fortress of Ghāfiḳ, erected a grand tower of extremely picturesque appearance which, standing out prominently in the restricted setting that it commanded, merited the name of Belalcázar; the old name of Ghāfiḳ fell into oblivion, although later it was felt desirable to give it a more Arabic etymology with the tortuous invention of Belalcázar.

Bibliography: Idrīsī, *Descript.*, text 214, trans. 263-4; Himyarī, *al-Rawḍ al-miʿṭār*, ed. Lévi-Provençal, text 139-43, trans. 167-71; *Crónica del moro Rasis*, ed. Gayangos in *Mem. de la R. Academia de Historia*, viii (1850); Khushanī, *Los cadies de Córdoba*, ed. Ribera, 256-7 in the trans.; Hernandez Jiménez, *Estudios de Geog. hist. esp. Gāfiq, Gahet, Gahete = Belalcázar*, in *al-Andalus*, ix/1 (1944), 71-105; Lévi-Provençal, *Hist. Esp. mus.*, i, 172 and 384-5; Ibn ʿIdhārī, *al-Bayān al-mughrib*, trans. Huici, in *Crón. árabes de la Reconquista*, ii, 68; A. Huici, *Un nuevo manuscrito de al-Bayān al-muġrib*, in *al-Andalus*, xxiv/1 (1959), 63-84.

(A. Huici Miranda)

FĀʿIL [see ʿilla].

FĀʿIL [see naḥw].

FAIR [see panāyir, sūḳ].

FAITH [see īmān].

FAKHDH, FAKHIDH [see ʿashīra, ḳabīla].

FAKHKH, a locality near Mecca which is now called al-Shuhadaʾ "the Martyrs". A very ancient tradition relates that certain Companions of the Prophet, in particular ʿAbd Allāh the son of the caliph ʿUmar, were buried there. It is in honour of this famous person, regarded as the local saint, that on 14 Ṣafar a ceremony is held there every year, and not because about a hundred ʿAlids and their partisans met their deaths at Fakhkh in a battle (*yawm Fakhkh*) on 8 Dhu 'l-Ḥidjdja 169/11 June 786.

The latter were, however, the "Martyrs". The battle, which in the time of Snouck Hurgronje was known only to cultivated Meccans but of which the Shīʿa have preserved vivid recollections, was the dramatic conclusion of an ʿAlid revolt which began in Medina and which, though lasting less than forty days, was regarded, because of the final massacre, as the most serious of the revolts after that which culminated in Karbalāʾ. This revolt sprang from more or less long-standing causes in addition to its immediate cause. Al-Yaʿḳūbī tells us that, after the elevation of al-Hādī to the caliphate, there was a renewal of hostilities against the Shīʿa, some of whom went to Medina to complain to the ʿAlids in the town of the persecutions which had been suffered. But so short a time elapsed between that event and the revolt that, even if the information given by this author can be accepted, it is necessary to go further back to find the real causes of the occurrence. The revolt had connexions with that of Muḥammad b. ʿAbd Allāh al-Nafs al-Zakiyya [*q.v.*] and his brother Ibrāhīm [*q.v.*] in 145/762-3, for the ʿAlids who revolted in 169 were closely related to the victims of 145; on the other hand, if we examine word by word the speech which the leader made to his followers, we see that it must have been the culmination of one of those movements of a social character to which the Ṭālibids so often gave their support. For the leader of the movement, the cause and the course of the insurrection, see AL-ḤUSAYN B. ʿALĪ ṢĀḤIB FAKHKH; here we mention only that after resisting for eleven days at Medina Ḥusayn set out with his followers for Mecca, and the clash with the ʿAbbāsid forces took place on the day of the *tarwiya* (8 Dhu 'l-Ḥidjdja 169/11 June 786) at the foot of the mountain of al-Burūd at Fakhkh. Al-Ḥusayn, the *Ṣāḥib Fakhkh* as he is often called, having refused to accept a safe-conduct, fell in battle along with other ʿAlids. For three days their bodies were left unburied, an incident which provided the poets with a moving theme for their elegies. The ʿAlid Idrīs b. ʿAbd Allāh b. al-Ḥasan succeeded in escaping; he took refuge in Egypt, and from there went to the far Maghrib where he founded the state and dynasty of the Idrīsids [*q.v.*].

Bibliography: Yāḳūt, iii, 854 ff.; Chr. Snouck Hurgronje, *Mekka*, The Hague 1888, i, 41, ii, 55 ff.; Abu 'l-Faradj al-Iṣfāhānī, *Maḳātil al-Ṭālibiyyīn*, ed. Aḥmad Saḳr, Cairo 1365/1946, 431-58; Ṭabarī, iii, 551-68; Masʿūdī, *Murūdj*, vi, 266-8; Yaʿḳūbī, *Historiae*, ed. Houtsma, ii, 488; F. Wüstenfeld, *Die Chroniken der Stadt Mekka*, Leipzig 1857-9, i, 435, 501 f., ii, 185 and index; M. J. De Goeje, *Fragmenta historicorum arabicorum*, i, 284 f.; Ibn al-Athīr, vi, 60-4.; Ibn al-Ṭiḳṭaḳā, *Fakhrī*, ed. Derenbourg, Paris 1895, 260 f. (= Eng. tr., C. E. J. Whitting, London 1947, 187 ff.) (inaccurate); Ibn Kathīr, *Bidāya*, x, 157; Muḥsin Amīn, *Aʿyān al-Shīʿa*, s.v. al-Ḥusayn b. ʿAlī b. al-Ḥasan; G. Weil, *Gesch. der Chalifen*, ii, 123-5; S. Moscati, *Le califat d'al-Hādī*, in *Studia Or. ed. Soc. orient. Fennica*, xiii/4 (1946), 9-15. (L. VECCIA VAGLIERI)

FAKHKHĀR, earthenware vase, pottery, ceramics. Pottery is one of the glories of Islamic art and is produced by practically every country in the Islamic world. Ceramic wares have a place in architecture as inlays or as faïence tiles, and they hold an important place in the field of the applied arts. In order to make a necessarily brief study of this vast subject clear, it would seem appropriate to give some idea of the different techniques employed, before proceeding to the naming of the principal centres of manufacture and the periods of their activity.

The basic material for ceramic wares is baked clay, which is termed silicious or plastic according to the element predominant in its composition. The clay may be left bare, thus retaining a brick-like appearance, or be covered with slip (a much paler and thinner clay), which conceals the true colour. Various kinds of decoration may be applied to a vessel while the clay is still soft. A vase thrown on the wheel may be incised with grooves while still being turned on the wheel, ornamented with reliefs luted on with slip (a thin watery clay), impressed with motives laid side by side in a mould, or stamped with independent dies. A pot dried and fired in the kiln may be glazed by covering it with a glaze fluxed with lead, which gives it a glossy appearance and renders it impermeable; this glaze may be coloured or uncoloured. There are various means available to the potter for enriching his work with polychrome effects. A great number of different coloured glazes may be obtained by combining metallic oxides with a colourless fusible material. Apart from tin oxide which gives white, the palette includes cobalt oxide for blue, copper oxide for green and turquoise blue, and manganese oxide for brown and aubergine purple. The decoration may be painted with a brush on a slip-dressed body and appear under the glaze; this is the method used with silicious wares; or the decoration may be painted on a glaze made opaque with tin oxide; this is the method used with tin-glazed wares (*i.e.*, Majolica and Delft).

Western Asia was the birth place of Islamic pottery. Its ultimate ancestors were undoubtedly the glazed bricks of the Achaemenid palaces, and its more recent forerunners the Parthian and Sāsānid wares. Islamic pottery, however, is not known to us until the beginning of the ʿAbbāsid period (3rd/9th century). It is to the excavations at Sāmarrā, the residence of the caliphs from 223 to 269/838-83, that we owe our earliest and in any way precise knowledge of the wares. They seem already very varied and skilfully executed, so that we are led to believe that there had been earlier developments of which we know nothing. In addition to pottery with or without glaze, incised or stamped, there are three main types of wares represented at Sāmarrā; there is a white earthenware decorated with spots or pseudo-calligraphic motives in cobalt blue, an earthenware decorated in polychrome, obviously inspired by Chinese stonewares of the T'ang period (7th-8th centuries); and finally there is an earthenware known as lustre, characterized by its metallic lights. The decoration of this last type is achieved by means of an ochre mixed with powdered silver, or copper, which separates out in the firing and is deposited as a thin film on the surface of the tin glaze; the colour varies from pale gold to ruby red and the iridescence of these tones varies according to the fall of light. Other analogous and doubtless contemporary pieces have been found at Susa. At Baghdād, or at other centres in the ʿAbbāsid empire, this ware, which in appearance rivalled the vessels in precious metals but was never hit by the same interdiction on the part of strict Muslims, seems to have been an item in the lively export trade across the Islamic world. Thus is it that a number of fragments have been dug up at Madīnat al-Zahrāʾ, the royal city of the caliph of Cordova, thus also that the finest collection to come down to us (nearly 150 tiles sent from

Ba<u>gh</u>dād or manufactured there) appear in the surround of the *miḥrāb* in the Great Mosque at Ḳayrawān. In Egypt the workshops of Fusṭāṭ were initiated into the technique of lustre decoration, where we shall meet this ware again.

Persia played a remarkable part in the development of ceramic wares at a very early date. She seems to have profited from foreign as well as from pre-Islamic traditions, as is evidenced by the ware called *gabrī*, after the name of "Guebres", adherents of Zoroastrianism, which Islam had not completely stamped out. The ornamentation of this ware, produced by means of larger or smaller scratches in the slip that covers the body under the transparent partly coloured glaze, consists of schematic representations, recalling the ancient culture of Persia, notably of fire altars, as well as figures of men and beasts, birds, lions and dragons depicted in a curiously stylized manner.

Of all the centres of ceramic production in Īrān, the now ruined city of Rayy, in the vicinity of Tehran, seems the most ancient. It was extremely active until the 7th/13th century and, under the name of Rhages, is the best known to collectors. The wares show great diversity of both form and technique. Lustre wares, often of a greenish gold tone, are frequently represented. Apart from tiles, for facing wall surfaces, cut in eight-pointed stars and in crosses with arms of equal length, Rayy also produced bottles and vases in the form of animals, or ornamented with wild beasts modelled in relief. The predilection displayed by the potters for the representation of living beings, and even their interpretation in the round, is a pronounced characteristic of Persian taste. Inside and on the rims of plates, on the swelling walls of bottles, as well as on wall tiles, mounted soldiers and hunters ride along, rulers and stumpy, doll-faced musicians sit, all bringing to mind the figures depicted in the miniatures of the period. These little figures, standing out against a white or pale blue ground, are dressed in delicately coloured cloths heightened with gold. Inscriptions in golden letters tell of the Iranian legends illustrated in this type of decoration.

Rayy was sacked by Čingiz <u>Kh</u>ān's Mongols in 624/1227; yet although appallingly impoverished, her potters continued production, using the techniques with which they were familiar. Attributed to them, and regarded as of this period, are a number of pieces decorated in black silhouette against a green ground.

The arrival of the Mongols appears to have some connexion with the establishment of stores that were found in the ruins of Gurgān. The pieces, which were found intact, had been packed in large jars, or had been buried at the time of the invasion. The wares are dateable to the end of the 5th-6th/11th-12th century; some of them might be earlier. They include copper lustre wares with a cream or turquoise ground; there are some, too, that may have been imported from Sava.

Under Mongol domination, the ceramic industry remained vigorous, especially in the Persian area, at Āmul and even more so at Sava and Ka<u>sh</u>ān, as well as in the north-east at Samarḳand. Wares with geometric, floral and highly stylized animal decoration, cut through a slip dressing and tinged with green and manganese purple are believed to have been made at Āmul in the 5th-7th/11th-13th centuries.

In the Mongol period we find new centres of production, such as that at Sulṭānābād, springing up. Chinese influence asserts itself and is favoured by the new rulers of Īrān, who brought in Chinese potters, just as they had introduced miniature painters into the occupied territory. Chinese fashions were to persist into the Ṣafawid period, which followed that of the Mongols. The fabulous beasts of the Far East enliven the wares attributed to Kirmān in the time of <u>Sh</u>āh ʿAbbās 995-1037/1587-1628.

The excavations carried out by the Americans before and during the second World War have brought to light the existence of ceramic activity in Nī<u>sh</u>āpūr in Transoxiana, which must have achieved its apogee in the 2nd-5th/8th-11th centuries under the Sāmānids. The wares produced seem to be the earliest ones covered with a very thin dull glaze stained lemon yellow, green or brick red; they display a disorderly grouping of geometric motives, pseudo-calligraphic elements, florets, animals and figures, perhaps derived from ancient Persia, enclosed by black lines.

In the wares of Dā<u>gh</u>istān to the south-west of the Caspian, and in the dishes, somewhat arbitrarily attributed to the small town of Ḳubāča, we find not only late survivals of Chinese influence, but also characteristics that foreshadow the Turkish pottery of Asia Minor. The painted decoration under the glaze, which is colourless or stained green or blue and is often crackled, consists of stylized flowers, animals, usually in silhouette, or turbaned personages against a floral ground.

Apart from pieces of such forms as vases and dishes, Persia produced an abundance of ceramics for architectural purposes, which make a glittering and colourful addition of great charm to the elegantly proportioned buildings. Combinations of brick and glazed tile, and ceramic insets, formed by setting mosaics in monochrome surfaces, make up geometric, calligraphic and floral decorations that have a place both on the inside and on the outside of architectural structures. On the outside these ceramics encase domes, tall minarets and porches, the colours most frequently occurring being dark and light blue; on the inside one is struck by the faïence *miḥrāb*s, especially those made at Kā<u>sh</u>ān, with their flat central panels flanked by pilasters and crowned with a Persian arch with straight members.

The settlement of the Sal<u>dj</u>ūḳ Turks in Asia Minor at first resulted in a considerable spread of Persian art. Ḳonya, which became the capital of the Turkish kingdom of Rūm, and where the sultans established many foundations, had an influx of craftsmen, particularly of potters, from <u>Kh</u>urāsān as the consequence of the Mongol invasion of their country. Dating from the 6th/12th and 7th/13th centuries are some fine wall facings for interiors made from bricks glazed on one side, or of tile mosaics, besides polychrome tiles.

The collapse of the sultanate of Ḳonya at the beginning of the 8th/14th century brought the ceramic production of Anatolia to a standstill. But it was to have brilliant revival, thanks to the Ottoman Turks, who in 726/1326 made Bursa their capital. They endowed the city with fine buildings of which ceramic ornament is the most prominent feature, and of which the mosque and the *turba* are the most justly celebrated. Nevertheless Bursa was not the real centre of the industry; this was at Iznik, a town not far from the capital. It was to remain a flourishing centre for two centuries (from the end of the 8th/14th to the end of the 10th/16th century), in the course of which different stages in style and technique are distinguishable. At the beginning of the 10th/16th century Persian influence was still very marked, but at the end of this century, which saw the polychrome wares of Iznik reach their apogee, the potters freed themselves from Iranian tradition and the wares began to acquire specifically Turkish characteristics. The decoration is painted on slip, and to the colours already in use (cobalt blue, turquoise and green from copper), are added a black to outline the coloured areas, and a splendid tomato red in low relief. The composition of the panels, made up from rectangular tiles, is almost entirely based on floral motives. Four flowers traditionally appearing on them are the rose, jasmine, poppy and tulip.

During the 11th/17th century Iznik ceased production and was replaced by Kütahya, which copied the techniques and styles of Iznik but without equalling them in mastery. The posthumous glory of Iznik reached even Istanbul, where the kilns known as Tekfūr came into operation at the beginning of the 12th/18th century.

Attributed to Damascus are some very fine dishes, related to the Anatolian wares, but distinguished from them as much by the colours (lacking tomato red and using manganese purple and a green from chromium oxide), as by the drawing of the designs, which are less naturalistic, less sensitive and which give greater weight to the background.

The skills of the kiln and the crucible are very ancient in Egypt and it is known that making of glass was first practised there. In the lands of the Pharaohs the people also made pottery and understood the use of glaze. If lustre ware was not first invented there, as some people believe, at least it was made there at a very early date in imitation of that of ʿIrāḳ. There are some pieces of lustre very similar to those from Sāmarrā, dated to the 3rd/9th century, that is the period of the Ṭūlūnids, or even earlier. The decoration, drawn very boldly, introduces somewhat uncouth human figures and pseudo-calligraphic elements. These wares underwent a remarkable development in the course of the 5th-6th/11th-12th centuries under the Fāṭimids. The diversity of the pieces, dishes, lamps and figurines, attests, alongside a very free attitude to the orthodox prescriptions concerning images, a striving after that elegance which imbues all the arts of the Fāṭimid era. The surfaces, covered with a fine gold lustre, are enriched by the details within the field of the lustre itself being delicately traced out with a fine point. The repertory of ornament includes four-footed beasts, birds or fish, and also the human figure, the men wearing turbans and the women with their hair hanging down. The crucifix and representations of Christ with a halo lead one to believe in the existence of Coptic craftsmen.

The same period saw the flowering of a ware with carved decoration under a monochrome glaze, especially a greyish green Chinese celadon colour. The quantity of sherds thrown on the refuse heaps by the potters reveals the extent of activity at the kilns at Fusṭāṭ. In the 7th/13th century a new technique appears of painting decoration on the body under the glaze. The glaze, often crackled, is thick and glossy; the decoration, neatly painted with a brush, frequently consists of animals in silhouette in a good tone of black.

In order to complete this short survey of the ceramic art of Egypt, it is fitting to say something of the pottery with *sgraffiato* decoration under a yellowish or green lead glaze. This was primarily a ware for domestic use, bearing inscriptions and blazons of dignitaries at the Mamlūk court for whom it was made. Syria and Palestine produced the same type of ware during the same period.

North Africa, and particularly eastern Barbary, at least until the 6th/12th century, appears to have been an artistic off-shoot of the Near East and Egypt. We have seen that Ḳayrawān got lustre tiles in the 3rd/9th century from Baghdād; ceramic craftsmen recruited locally may have completed the collection. In the 5th/11th century palace in the Ḳalʿa of the Banū Ḥammād (see HAMMĀDIDS), a pavement has been found made from lustre tiles, in the forms of stars and crosses, which conform to Persian type, but were very probably of local manufacture. Yet the very large amount of pottery of the Ḥammādids of the Ḳalʿa and that of the Zīrids of Ḳayrawān present characteristics that are highly individual. Apart from architectural elements such as inlays for wall surfaces, *claustra*, and stalactite pendentive elements, and in addition to green glazed wares with incised or stamped decoration, excavations have revealed lead glazed polychromes of wares with painting on slip. The decorations are very diverse and summary in treatment with silhouettes and fillers; there are such motives as triangles, ellipses, strap-work, trellis patterns used as fillers, and figures of men and beasts, which are clearly distinguishable from the more easterly examples. The palette comprises only manganese brown, copper green and, more rarely, a yellow from chromium oxide. Cobalt blue appears rather later, in the 6th/12th century, when it occurs in the polychromes produced at Bougie (Bidjāya), to which city the craftsmen of Ḳayrawān and the Ḳalʿa had to retire as the result of the nomadic Arab invasions. Bougie, a maritime city, benefited in other respects from imports from Andalusia.

Moorish Spain was, indeed, a producer of fine ceramic wares. The excavations at Madīnat al-Zahrāʾ, the caliphate city near Cordova, have yielded a great quantity of pottery with decoration consisting of manganese brown painted lines and copper green for the coloured surfaces. These wares, dating like the city from the 4th/10th century, have parallels among the eastern Barbary examples of an appreciably later date. The Islamic ceramics of Sicily (6th/12th century) suggest further parallels of a similar kind. This appearance of family grouping and the relative homogeneity of the wares of Western Islam raises a problem that warrants some attention.

The excavations of Madīnat al-Zahrāʾ show that Spain was aware in the 4th/10th century of the lustre wares imported from the east; yet the Iberian peninsula had its own centres of production also. Malaga from the 7th/13th to 9th/15th century was just such a centre, at which were produced gold lustre dishes and large jars of the type of which the one known as the "Alhambra Jar" is the most famous.

The noble grace of form of these great pottery jars is echoed in the large vases, with impressed decoration, that seem to have the same origin and may perhaps be attributed to the same period. The paste is left unglazed, or is covered with a green enamel-glaze; the decoration, arranged in registers one above another, comprises blind arcading, calligraphic forms, interlacing elements and sometimes animal forms. The same technique and a similar décor is found in the linings for wells and tanks such as those preserved in Andalusia and also in the Maghrib. A fine collection of these stoutly-made ceramic shafts, by which to draw water, has been found at Sīdī Bū ʿUthmān to the north of Marrākush and perhaps dating from the 6th/12th century.

At the beginning of the 6th/12th century Moorish Spain and the Maghrib gave ceramics an important rôle in architectural ornament. Glazed earthenware tiles, which we first encountered in Persia and then in eastern Barbary, are associated with the adornment of minarets and make up panels in rooms. The facility of the craftsmen, specialists in *zallīdj* [*q.v.*], in cutting out shapes in monochrome tiles and assembling them to make geometric, calligraphic and floral decorations, is astonishing. They are equally skilled in a kind of ceramic *champlevé*, which consists of chiselling out the glaze with a graving tool, thus leaving the elements of decoration in reserve. Finally there is recourse to a *cloisonné* treatment, called in Spanish *cuerda seca*, which, using similar interlacing geometrical motives, gives from a distance an impression as of inlay work. It is a very ancient technique, not without analogy with the glazed bricks of the Achaemenid palace at Susa. Each surface is enclosed by a black line, which has an important place in the composition and which serves to prevent contiguous colours spilling over into each other. Neither the potters of Sāmarrā nor those of Madīnat al-Zahrāʾ passed over this technique; and it was practised in North Africa in the 5th-6th/11th-12th centuries. The *cuerda seca* and the technique termed *cuenca*, in which the black line is replaced by a thin line incised in the paste to separate the colours, was to become a special skill of the Spanish centres of production, notably of Seville. At the beginning of the 11th/17th century (1019/1610) the Spanish Moors took the technique with them when they were expelled to Tunisia.

Just as the *azulejos* method of wall revetment prolonged the tradition of ceramic inlay, so the *mudejar* period saw the manufactories of Manises take over the making of lustre ware from Malaga. In the same way the green and brown decorated wares of Paterna, in the region of Valencia, seem, in the 8th/14th and 9th/15th centuries, a late legacy of the Andalusian Caliphate.

Ceramic art was still to survive, not without renown, in North Africa. Morocco still has her cutters and assemblers of tile mosaics (*zallīdj*), and the potters of Fez knew, until quite recent times, how to produce vessels with blue or polychrome decoration as well as dishes of an original kind.

Turkish Algeria used to have a remarkable quantity of earthernware tiles, but they were almost entirely imports from Europe.

Tunisia, and especially Tunis, has not wholly forgotten the mediaeval ceramic arts. It is indeed likely that tin-glazed wares have never ceased to be made while there has been a use for them. The last few centuries have seen the production of vases which preserve quite well the older colours, and panels decorated with blind arcading, vases and covers, in which local traditions merge with contributions from the Levant.

Bibliography: M. Migeon, *Manuel d'art musulman, Arts plastiques et industrielles*, 1927, ii, 158-78; A. Lane, *Early Islamic pottery*; idem, *Later Islamic pottery*; F. Sarre, *Die Keramik von Samarra* (*Die Ausgrabungen von Samarra II*), Berlin 1925; M. Pezard, *La céramique archaïque de l'Islam*, 2 vols., 1920; H. Wallis, *Persian lustre vases*, London 1899; A. U. Pope, *The ceramic art in Islamic times* (*A survey of Persian art*, ii, v), Oxford 1938-9; R. Koechelin, *Les céramiques de Suze au Musée du Louvre*, in *MMAP*, 1928; idem, *La céramique* (*L'Art de l'Islam, Musée des arts décoratifs*), n.d.; Dimand, *Handbook of Muhammedan art*², 1958, 158-229; Walter Hauser, J. H. Upton and C. K. Wilkinson, *The Iranian expedition*, in *Bulletin of the Metropolitan Museum of Art*, xxxii (1937), xxxiii (1938), xxxviii (1943); J. Lacam, *Cahiers de la céramique et des arts du feu*, xx (1960), 244-93; Mehdi Bahrami, *Gurzan faïences*, Cairo; Ch. Kiefer, *Les céramiques musulmanes d'Anatolie*, in *Cahiers de la céramique*, iv (1956); H. Rivière, *La céramique dans l'art musulman*, 1914; D. Fouquet, *Contribution à l'étude de la céramique orientale*, Cairo 1900; Butler, *Islamic pottery*, London 1926; Aly bey Bahgat and F. Massoul, *La céramique musulmane de l'Égypte*, Cairo 1930; A. Abel, *Gaibi et les grands faïenciers égyptiens d'époque mamlouke*, Cairo 1930; E. Kühnel, *Islamitische Kleinkunst*, Berlin 1925; G. Marçais, *Les faïences à reflets métalliques de la grande mosquée de Kairouan*, 1927; idem, *Les poteries et faïences de la Qalʿa des Beni Hammād*, Constantine 1913; idem, *Les poteries et faïences de Bougie*, Constantine 1916; M. Gomez Moreno, *El arte español hasta los Almohades*, in *Ars Hispaniae*, iii, 310; L. Torres Balbas, *Arte almohade, arte nazari, arte mudejar*, in *Ars Hispaniae*, iv; Gonzalez Marti, *Ceramica del Levante español*, 3 vols; A. Wilson Frothingham, *Lustre ware of Spain*, New York 1951; J. Giacomotti, *Carreaux espagnols de revêtement*, in *Cahiers de la céramique*, xi, 113; Folch i Torres, *Notice sobre la ceramica de Paterna*, Barcelona 1919; A. Bel, *Les industries de la céramique à Fès*, Alger-Paris 1918. (G. Marçais)

FAKHR [see MUFĀKHARA]

FAKHR AL-DAWLA, Abu 'l-Ḥasan ʿAlī b. al-Ḥasan, born in about 341/952, third son of the Buwayhid Rukn al-Dawla [*q.v.*] and of a daughter of the Daylamī chief al-Ḥasan b. Fayzurān, a cousin of Mākān b. Kākī [*q.v.*], received his *laḳab* in 364/975 and was summoned in 365/976, with his brothers ʿAḍud al-Dawla [*q.v.*], the eldest, and Muʾayyid al-Dawla, to his father's sick-bed, in order to agree what share each would receive of their father's possessions, under the suzerainty of ʿAḍud al-Dawla; as his portion, Fakhr al-Dawla received the provinces of Hamadhān and Dīnawar, that is to say the Kurdish Djabal, partly under the autonomous domination of the Kurd Ḥasanwayh, situated around the Iran-Baghdād route. When Rukn al-Dawla died (366/977), Fakhr al-Dawla was not content with these territories and, with the object of depriving Muʾayyid al-Dawla, who remained faithful to ʿAḍud al-Dawla, of his share, consisting of the provinces of Rayy and Iṣfahān, he negotiated with ʿIzz al-Dawla Bakhtiyār [*q.v.*], the opponent of ʿAḍud al-Dawla, with Ḥasanwayh, and finally and most important with Ḳābūs b. Washmagīr [*q.v.*], of the Ziyārid dynasty of Djurdjān, the original rivals of the Buwayhids. After first defeating Bakhtiyār in 366, and then the Ḥamdānids of Moṣul, and after Ḥasanwayh's death, ʿAḍud al-Dawla in 369/979 drove out Fakhr al-Dawla, who finally took refuge with Ḳābūs in Khurāsān, under the protection of the Sāmānid governor Ḥusām al-Dawla Tāsh, while Muʾayyid was invested with his territories. From then onwards, Fakhr al-Dawla's attempts to regain his principality are merely one aspect of the long struggle between the Sāmānids and the Buwayhids; in 371/981 the allied army was defeated by Muʾayyid al-Dawla, and the following campaigns, although more successful, achieved no better results [see ʿAḌUD AL-DAWLA].

On the death of ʿAḍud al-Dawla (372/982), Muʾayyid al-Dawla tried unsuccessfully to initiate a reconciliation with his brother, and died in his turn in 373. His vizier Ibn ʿAbbād [*q.v.*] seems to have calculated that no adequate opposition would be put up against Fak͟hr al-Dawla, now the eldest member of the family, or that the sons of ʿAḍud al-Dawla, the masters of ʿIrāḳ and Fārs, already had viziers of their own and would not retain him (Ibn ʿAbbād) in his present position; he appealed boldly to Fak͟hr al-Dawla, the very man whom hitherto he had always opposed and who, travelling to Rayy with all haste, assumed power without difficulty, while the son of Muʾayyid al-Dawla, the governor of Iṣfahān, submitted to him; naturally enough he retained the all-powerful Ibn ʿAbbād as vizier. Despite the difference in temperament of these princes, this fact ensured a certain continuity in policy, and in particular Fak͟hr al-Dawla, despite the debt he owed to Ḳābūs, retained D̲j̲urd̲j̲ān which Muʾayyid al-Dawla had annexed; in K͟hurāsān, the struggles between Tās͟h, whom he supported and welcomed, and Ibn Simd̲j̲ūr, his successor, allowed him on the other hand to combine gratitude with the continuation of an anti-Sāmānid course of action. However, Muʾayyid al-Dawla had become a vassal, and Fak͟hr al-Dawla, the head of the family, was an independent prince. Within his dominions and on the frontiers he seems to have had a more aggressive policy than his brother, to the cost of the local lords, annexing Kurdish or Daylamī fortresses such as S͟hamīrān (Yāḳūt, iii, 150, according to a letter of Ibn ʿAbbād), but also provoking revolts (Ḥasanwayhid Kurds from the district of Ḳumm in 373/983, Ṭabaristān and Ḳazwīn in 377/987, the prince's maternal cousin Naṣr b. al-Ḥasan b. Fayzurān at Dāmg͟hān in 378). Whether from greed or as a matter of policy, with the object of confiscating his possessions he arrested the commander of Muʾayyid al-Dawla's army, ʿAlī b. Kāma, who died as a result. With Ṣamṣām al-Dawla, his nephew in Bag͟hdād, he maintained good relations but, when this prince had been driven out by another son of ʿAḍud al-Dawla, Bahāʾ al-Dawla, with the help of Badr b. Ḥasanwayh Fak͟hr al-Dawla tried to attack the victor through K͟hūzistān; the inadequacy of the rewards he offered to the troops and unexpected floods disorganized his army, whereupon he withdrew (379/989); and in 384/994 he allied himself with Bahāʾ al-Dawla against Ṣamṣām al-Dawla, the latter in the meanwhile having become master of Fārs and now appearing to him to be the more dangerous. Towards the vizier Ibn ʿAbbād, who had shown some irresolution during the K͟hūzistān campaign, Fak͟hr al-Dawla had become somewhat cold, although there was no positive action against him; but when death finally removed him (385) he confiscated his possessions and, as ʿAḍud al-Dawla had done, divided the vizierate between two candidates, selling it to the highest bidder.

From our sources, the personality of Fak͟hr al-Dawla appears less clearly than that of other members of his family. Naturally he maintained his poets, certain of whose works are named in the *Yatīma* of al-T͟haʿālibī, but intellectually he did not have the reputation of certain other Buwayhids or of his own vizier. In his administration he was considered avaricious, and at his death left behind a considerable fortune, augmented by his confiscations; his refusal to increase the pay and *iḳṭāʿ*s of his forces may have been based on sound reasons, but in fact this decision was not consistent with his over-ruling ambition. In general, his internal administration must have resembled his predecessor's, since it was directed by the same man, Ibn ʿAbbād; but we do not possess any documents from his period comparable with those which we have for the preceding reign. We know that the methods of adjudication of fiscal districts, in use at Rayy, helped to make Ibn ʿAbbād unpopular when he tried to introduce them in K͟huzistān; there can be no doubt as to the general vigilance and regularity of the administration under this vizier, and certain minor innovations made by him are recorded in the *Taʾrīkh-i Ḳumm*, written in the days of Fak͟hr al-Dawla, and later the *Siyāsat-nāma* of Niẓām al-Mulk, chap. 41. The geographer al-Muḳaddasī, who also wrote during this reign (see especially 399-400), gives an impression of the prosperity of the country; apart from a mosque, Rayy is also indebted to him for a new citadel (perhaps Tabarak) (Yāḳūt, iii, 855).

Fak͟hr al-Dawla died in S͟haʿbān 387/August 997 and, it is said, the Treasury key being in the possession of his son who was absent, there were no funds available to provide for a decent burial. Some weeks after his death Ḳābūs returned to D̲j̲urd̲j̲ān.

Bibliography: for the sources, see BUWAYHIDS, ḲĀBŪS, SĀMĀNIDS; and in particular for the whole subject Miskawayh-Rud͟hrawārī, completed by Ibn al-At͟hīr viii-ix and (especially the years 376, 385, 387) Sibṭ Ibn al-D̲j̲awzī (MS.); and then, for the period of ʿAḍud al-Dawla, the three collections of correspondence referred to in BUWAYHIDS, and, for relations with the Sāmānids, the sources for their history, Gardīzī, ʿUtbī, and also Ibn Isfandiyār for Ḳābūs; and the sources given in the article *supra*.—Modern works, see BUWAYHIDS, in particular B. Spuler and G. Wiet. (CL. CAHEN)

FAK͟HR AL-DĪN, name of two Lebanese amīrs of the Druze house of Maʿn [*q.v.*]. Fak͟hr al-Dīn I, amīr of the S͟hūf (north-east of Sidon) at the time of the Ottoman conquest of Syria, was among the chieftains who offered submission to the conquering Sultan Selīm I in Damascus in 922/1516. The Sultan, impressed by his eloquence, is said to have sent him back with the title *amīr al-barr* (lord of the land), recognizing him as overlord of the chieftains of the Druze Mountain (the G͟harb, the D̲j̲urd, and the S͟hūf). Fak͟hr al-Dīn I was assassinated in c. 951/1544 under obscure circumstances on the orders of the Pas͟ha of Damascus, and was succeeded by his son Ḳorḳmaz.

Fak͟hr al-Dīn II, son and successor of Ḳorḳmaz, was born in c. 980/1572, and was only a boy when his father died in 993/1585. In the previous year a convoy bearing the annual tribute from Egypt was ambushed and robbed at the bay of ʿAkkār, to the north of Tripoli; and the enemies of the Maʿns in Lebanon, jealous of their rising power, accused Ḳorḳmaz of responsibility for the misdeed before the Ottomans. Consequently, Ottoman troops attacked and ravaged the S͟hūf, and Ḳorḳmaz died in flight. His fall was followed by civil war in the Druze Mountain between the Ḳaysī faction who supported the Maʿns, and the opposing Yamanīs led by the house of ʿAlam al-Dīn. By 1000/1591 the Ḳaysīs had clearly gained the upper hand, and Fak͟hr al-Dīn II could effectively take over his father's position.

The first aim of the young amīr was vengeance against Yūsuf Sayfā, the powerful Kurdish chieftain of the Tripoli region in northern Lebanon who had been the chief instigator of the Ottoman attack on the S͟hūf in 1585. Shortly after Fak͟hr al-Dīn's accession, in 1593, Yūsuf Sayfā had considerably expanded his domain by absorbing the Maronite districts of Bs͟harrī, Batrūn, D̲j̲ubayl and Kisrawān, and extending his hold southwards to include Beirut. Master of the whole of northern Lebanon and of ʿAkkār, Yūsuf Sayfā became the most powerful figure of the time in Syria, and his territory extended northwards to Lattakia and Ḥamā. However, in his struggle against the Sayfā, Fak͟hr al-Dīn had for allies the Maronites who, smarting under Sayfā oppression, looked towards the young Druze amīr as a possible deliverer. Fak͟hr al-Dīn encouraged the Maronites in this attitude, surrounded himself with Maronite advisers, and was soon dreaming of uniting the Druzes and the Maronites of Lebanon under his own dynasty.

Fak͟hr al-Dīn's first step was to make friends with Murād Pas͟ha of Damascus, paying him a formal visit and obtaining from him possession of the port of Sidon, which he made his capital. While in Damascus Fak͟hr al-Dīn also started an intrigue against his enemies ʿAlī Ḥarfūs͟h of Baalbek and D̲j̲abal ʿĀmil and Manṣūr Furayk͟h of the Biḳāʿ, both potential allies of Yūsuf Sayfā. As a result both chieftains were seized and executed by Murād in the following year. Fak͟hr al-Dīn thereupon invaded and seized the Biḳāʿ, making peace with Mūsā Ḥarfūs͟h, ʿAlī's successor, who became the Druze amīr's virtual vassal in Baalbek and D̲j̲abal ʿĀmil.

Beirut and the coastal plain as far north as Nahr al-Kalb had traditionally been under the control of the Druze Amīrs, and in 1007/1598 Fak͟hr al-Dīn secured from Damascus the permission to occupy them. He then proceeded to expel Yūsuf Ṣayfā from the territory and to chase him beyond the Nahr al-Kalb. Next he turned his attention to the south, and with the additional wealth accruing from the trade of Sidon and Beirut he purchased the tenure of the Sand̲j̲aḳ of Ṣafad which bordered on the S͟hūf. The fortresses of Arnūn (Beaufort) and Ṣubayba, which belonged to the sand̲j̲aḳ, were occupied and restored, securing the Druze Mountain against Beduin attack from the south. Fak͟hr al-Dīn then crossed Nahr al-Kalb again in 1014/1605, defeated Yūsuf Ṣayfā at D̲j̲ūniya, and permanently occupied Kisrawān.

Meanwhile, in northern Syria, a Kurdish adventurer called ʿAlī D̲j̲ānbūlād had made himself master of the Sand̲j̲aks of Aleppo, Aʿzāz, and Killīs. His southern boundaries touched the northern boundaries of Yūsuf Ṣayfā; and in 1015/1606 D̲j̲ānbūlād marched into Sayfā's territory, defeated him near Ḥamā, and advanced towards Tripoli. Anxious to stake a claim to Sayfā's southern territories, Fak͟hr al-Dīn quickly allied himself with D̲j̲ānbūlād, and hurried forces to Baalbek to prevent reinforcements sent by Kurd Ḥamza, the commander of the Janissaries in Damascus, from reaching Tripoli. Unable to resist D̲j̲ānbūlād, Yūsuf Sayfā fled by sea to Palestine, then joined Kurd Ḥamza in Damascus. D̲j̲ānbūlād meanwhile entered and sacked Tripoli, then advanced with Fak͟hr al-Dīn against Damascus.

Fak͟hr al-Dīn's earlier friendship with Murād Pas͟ha, now Grand Vizier, saved him from the fate of D̲j̲ānbūlād. Defeated in battle by the resolute Naṣūḥ Pās͟ha of Aleppo, D̲j̲ānbūlād was executed in 1016/1607. But in that same year Murād Pas͟ha arrived in Aleppo to settle the affairs of Syria in person, and Fak͟hr al-Dīn managed to effect a quick return to Ottoman grace by sending a delegation to greet the Grand Vizier with a large present of gold. Murād Pas͟ha, accordingly, confirmed Fak͟hr al-Dīn in the possession of Beirut, Sidon, and Kisrawān, and as a further mark of favour exempted the S͟hūf from the *ḳis͟hlaḳ*—the forced quartering of Ottoman troops.

Fak͟hr al-Dīn, however, realized that Murād Pas͟ha would not remain Grand Vizier for ever, and that some other form of support was needed in case of another clash with the Porte. The Tuscans, who had dreams of establishing a Medici kingdom in the Levant, had as early as 1012/1603 approached Fak͟hr al-Dīn and tried to arouse his interest in the plan. A second approach after 1016/1607 found Fak͟hr al-Dīn willing to listen; and in 1017/1608 a treaty was concluded whereby, in return for his help in an eventual Tuscan attempt to conquer Damascus and Jerusalem, Fak͟hr al-Dīn was to receive Tuscan military aid, and the Medici were to use their influence with the Pope so that the Maronite patriarch would support Fak͟hr al-Dīn against the Sayfā. Indeed, Pope Paul V in 1610 wrote to the Maronite patriarch commending him and his flock to the protection of Fak͟hr al-Dīn; and in the following year a Maronite bishop was sent to Italy to represent the Druze amīr at the court of Tuscany and at the Holy See.

Murād Pas͟ha died in 1020/1611 and was succeeded by Fak͟hr al-Dīn's bitter enemy Naṣūḥ Pas͟ha. Meanwhile, the growing relations between Fak͟hr al-Dīn and Tuscany had greatly increased the suspicions of the Porte. Naṣūḥ Pas͟ha's suspicions were particularly aroused when Fak͟hr al-Dīn began to employ a standing army of mercenaries (the *sukman*—see SEGBĀN) instead of depending on the usual peasant levies, and when he began to show a keen interest in the sand̲j̲aḳs of Nāblus and ʿAd̲j̲lūn, in Palestine and Transjordan, which controlled the road to Jerusalem. Attempts to appease the Grand Vizier with gifts proved useless. When Fak͟hr al-Dīn clashed with Aḥmad Ḥāfiẓ Pas͟ha of Damascus over the two sand̲j̲aḳs, Naṣūḥ Pas͟ha mobilized a powerful army for the command of Ḥāfiẓ. Expecting defeat, Fak͟hr al-Dīn handed over affairs to his brother Yūnus with instructions to move the capital to Dayr al-Ḳamar in the S͟hūf, and himself took ship from Sidon and fled to Tuscany.

The self-imposed exile of Fak͟hr al-Dīn was a temporary retreat after a temporary reverse. In 1023/1614 Naṣūḥ Pas͟ha died. Ḥāfiẓ Pas͟ha was shortly after recalled from Damascus, and Yūnus Maʿn made peace with his successor on the payment on a large sum of money and a promise to dismantle the fortresses of Arnūn and Ṣubayba. Fak͟hr al-Dīn could now return to Lebanon, arriving back at Acre in 1027/1618.

In 1024/1615, during Fak͟hr al-Dīn's absence, Yūsuf Sayfā had sacked Dayr al-Ḳamar. This gave Fak͟hr al-Dīn an excuse, upon his return, to ally himself with ʿUmar Pas͟ha of Tripoli, who wanted Sayfā to pay arrears of tribute. Fak͟hr al-Dīn successfully intervened against Sayfā on behalf of the Pas͟ha, and in return received the districts of D̲j̲ubayl and Batrūn. A formal peace between the two chieftains was arranged in 1028/1619, Fak͟hr al-Dīn taking Sayfā's daughter in marriage. In the same year Fak͟hr al-Dīn procured the tenure of the sand̲j̲aḳs of D̲j̲abala and Lattakia, which had previously belonged to Sayfā. During the next five years fighting between the amīr and his father-in-law continued, Fak͟hr al-Dīn meanwhile seizing the districts of Bs͟harrī and ʿAkkār, until Yūsuf Sayfā died in 1033/1624. Three years later Fak͟hr al-Dīn completed his triumph by obtaining the governorship of Tripoli for his infant son Ḥusayn, a Sayfā on his mother's side.

In the meantime, Fakhr al-Dīn had also obtained the titles to the sandjaḳs of Nāblus and ʿAdjlūn, and it was left to him to evict the occupants of these sandjaḳs. As he campaigned in Palestine for the purpose, Muṣṭafā Pasha of Damascus, incited by Kurd Ḥamza, formed a coalition against the amīr and advanced into the Biḳāʿ in 1032/1623. Fakhr al-Dīn rushed back and met him at ʿAndjar, where Muṣṭafā Pasha was defeated in battle and taken prisoner, then honourably released. During the years that followed this victory Fakhr al-Dīn reached the height of his power; and by 1040/1631 his territory had come to extend westwards to Palmyra, and northwards almost to the borders of Anatolia.

Following 1040/1631, however, troubles began to come upon Fakhr al-Dīn thick and fast. While he campaigned in northern Syria Beduin chieftains revolted against him in Palestine and Transjordan; while in the Shūf the Yamanī ʿAlam al-Gīns, in alliance with the sons of Yūsuf Sayfā, were creating unrest. By 1042/1633 civil war broke out in the Druze Mountain, and Fakhr al-Dīn's firm allies the Ḳaysī Tanūkhs [*q.v.*] were massacred to a man by the ʿAlam al-Dīns. Meanwhile the Ottoman Government, under the vigorous Sultan Murād IV, was becoming concerned about Fakhr al-Dīn's activities in northern Syria and the fortresses that were going up near the Anatolian border. Accordingly, the Grand Vizier Khalīl Pasha instructed Küčük Aḥmad Pasha of Damascus in 1042/1633 to proceed against Fakhr al-Dīn with full support from Istanbul. The amīr's troops, commanded by his son ʿAlī, were defeated at Ṣubayba, and ʿAlī himself was killed. Before the resolute Ottoman attack Fakhr al-Dīn's precariously balanced power collapsed within a few weeks. The amīr himself fled to a cave in the cliffs of Djazzīn, where he was discovered and captured by Küčük Aḥmad, then sent in chains to Istanbul. There Fakhr al-Dīn was executed by strangling in 1045/1635, along with his sons. Only his youngest son, Ḥusayn, was spared, to become a prominent Ottoman courtier and an ambassador of the sultan to India. He was a friend of the historian Shāriḥ al-Manārzāde [*q.v.*], and is cited frequently as a source in those parts of Naʿīmā's history that are based on Shāriḥ al-Manārzāde's lost work. In Lebanon Fakhr al-Dīn was succeeded by his nephew Mulḥim, son of Yūnus.

Fakhr al-Dīn was a rapacious tyrant who weighed his subjects down with taxes, but he was enlightened enough to realize that the better the condition of a people the more they can pay. His policy revolved around the collection of enough revenue to satisfy the rapacity of the Ottoman government and buy the friendship of influential Pashas. Accordingly, to raise the revenue of Lebanon, he introduced a number of innovations to the country, particularly improved agricultural methods, and encouraged commerce. His religious tolerance made him highly popular with his Christian subjects, and was an important factor in promoting the political union between the Maronites and Druzes which was to be of great importance in the subsequent history of Lebanon. Fakhr al-Dīn II, indeed, is regarded by the Lebanese today as the father of modern Lebanon, for it was under his rule that the Druze and Maronite districts of the Mountain became united for the first time, with the adjacent coastlands and the Biḳāʿ, under a single authority.

Bibliography: J. M. Collard, *Fakhr-ed-Din al-Maʿni, a biography* (typescript in my possession); Adel Ismail, *Histoire du Liban du XVIIe siècle à nos jours*; tome V: *Le Liban au temps de Fakhr-ed-Din II, 1590-1633*, Paris 1955; F. Wüstenfeld, *Fakhr ed-din der Drusenfürst und seine Zeitgenossen: die Aufstände in Syrien und Anatolien gegen die Türken in der ersten Hälfte XI. Jahrhunderts*, Göttingen 1886; Paolo Carali, *Fakhr ad-Din II e la corte di Toscana*, Rome 1936; Būlus Ḳaraʾlī, *Fakhr al-Din al-Maʿnī al-thānī amīr Lubnān, idāratuhu wa siyāsatuhu 1590-1635*, Ḥarīsā 1937-8; Hammer-Purgstall, index; Aḥmad b. Muḥammad al-Khālidī, *Taʾrīkh al-amīr Fakhr al-Dīn*, edd. Rustum and Bustānī, Beirut 1936; Muḥammad b. Faḍl-Allāh al-Muḥibbī, *Khulāṣat al-athar fī aʿyān al-ḳarn al-ḥādī ʿashar*, Cairo 1284 A.H., iii, 266 ff.; Naʿīmā⁴, ii, 119-23 (s.a. 1023), iii, 242 (s.a. 1044). (KAMAL SALIBI)

FAKHR AL-DĪN MUBĀRAKSHĀH, originally known by the short name of Fakhrā and posted at Sonārgāwn in East Bengal as a *Silāḥdār* of Bahrām Khān, the local governor in the time of the Dihlī Sultan Muḥammad b. Tughluḳ. After the governor's death Fakhrā revolted, assumed sovereignty at Sonārgāwn and maintained his position by defeating the imperial forces led by the eastern governors of the Tughluḳ Sulṭān. He established the first independent dynasty in Bengal in 739/1338, conquered up to Čāṭgāwn in the south and made a bid for Lakhnawtī in the north-west, but failed in the latter venture. From 739/1338 to 750/1349 he ruled undisputedly at Sonārgāwn, issued silver currency and assumed the titles of *Yamīn-i Khalīfat-Allāh* and *Nāṣir-i Amīr al-Muʾminīn*. In 751/1350 he was succeeded at Sonārgāwn by his son Ikhtiyār al-Dīn Ghāzī Shāh, who in 753/1352 lost his kingdom to Shams al-Dīn Ilyās Shāh, the ruler of Lakhnawtī; the latter united the whole of Bengal under his authority. Ibn Baṭṭūṭa visited Sonārgāwn when Fakhr al-Dīn was the ruler. He pays tribute to the king's generosity towards *pīrs*, and speaks of the cheapness of commodities within the kingdom.

Bibliography: Yaḥyā Sirhindī, *Taʾrīkh-i Mubārakshāhī*, Eng. tr. K. K. Basu, Baroda 1932, 106-7; Ibn Baṭṭūṭa, iv, 212-6 (= H. von Mžik, *Die Reise...*, Hamburg 1911, 384-5); N. K. Bhattasali, *Coins and chronology of the early independent sultans of Bengal*, Dacca 1922; J. N. Sarkar, *History of Bengal*, ii, ed. Dacca, 1948.

(A. H. DANI)

FAKHR AL-DĪN AL-RĀZĪ, Abū ʿAbd Allāh Muḥammad b. ʿUmar b. al-Ḥusayn, one of the most celebrated theologians and exegetists of Islam, born in 543/1149 (or perhaps 544) at Rayy. His father, Ḍiyāʾ al-Dīn Abu 'l-Ḳāsim, was a preacher (*khaṭīb*) in his native town, from whose name comes his son's appellation, Ibn al-Khaṭīb. He was also conversant with *kalām* and, among other works, wrote the *Ghāyat al-marām*, in which he showed himself a warm partisan of al-Ashʿarī. Al-Subkī who gives him a brief review (*Ṭabaḳāt al-Shāfiʿiyya*, iv, 285-6) names among the list of his masters, Abu 'l-Ḳāsim al-Anṣārī, pupil of the Imām al-Ḥaramayn, as well as the author of the *Tahdhīb*. In addition to his father, the young Fakhr al-Dīn had al-Madjd al-Djīlī (al-Djabalī?), whom he followed to Marāgha, as his master in philosophy, and al-Kamāl al-Sumnānī for *fiḳh*.

After finishing studies both literary and religious in Rayy, and, according to al-Ḳifṭī, after having failed in some researches into alchemy, Fakhr al-Dīn went to Khʷārizm where he was engaged in relentless controversies with the Muʿtazilīs who forced him to leave the country. In Transoxania (*Mā warāʾ al-Nahr*), he encountered the same opposition. Returning to Rayy, he entered into relations with Shihāb al-Dīn al-Ghūrī, Sultan of Ghazna, who heaped money and honours upon him. The same thing occurred later with ʿAlāʾ al-Dīn Khʷārizmshāh Muḥammad b. Takash, with whom he lived for some time in Khurāsān. This prince showed him the greatest consideration and caused a *madrasa* to be built for him.

In 580/1184, while on his way to Transoxania in order to reach Bukhārā, he stopped for some time at Sarakhs where he was received with honour by the doctor ʿAbd al-Raḥman b. ʿAbd al-Karīm al-Sarakhsī. As a mark of his gratitude he dedicated to him his commentary on the *Kulliyyāt* of Avicenna's *Canon*. As he did not find the protection on which he had counted in Bukhārā, he went on to Herāt, where the Ghūrid Sultan of Ghazna, Ghiyāth al-Dīn, allowed him to open a school for the general public within the royal palace.

After a certain number of journeys which took him to Samarḳand and as far as India (where perhaps he was sent on a mission), he settled down finally in Herāt where he passed the greater part of his life. He was known there by the title of *shaykh al-Islām*. It is said that at this period, at the height of his glory, more than three hundred of his disciples or followers accompanied him when he moved from one place to another.

He was so poor at the outset of his career that his compatriots in Bukhārā were obliged to make a collection in order to help him when he fell ill there; but later on he came into a vast fortune. He married his two sons to the two daughters of an immensely rich doctor from Rayy and, on this man's death, inherited part of his money.

His lively and penetrating intelligence, his prodigious memory (he is said to have learned the *Shāmil* of al-Djuwaynī by heart in his youth), his methodical and clear mind, caused him to become a teacher celebrated throughout the whole region of Central Asia, from all parts of which people came to consult him on the most diverse questions. He was, moreover, an excellent preacher. Of medium height, well-built, heavy-bearded, endowed with a voice both powerful and warm, he inspired and enflamed his listeners to the point of tears and was himself deeply moved by emotion when he was preaching. His preaching converted many Karrāmīs to Sunnism. Despite his strong grounding in philosophy and numerous controversies he was extremely pious (*kāna min ahl al-dīn wa 'l-taṣawwuf*). In many of his treatises, he ended on a religious note, emphasizing the practical applications that could be made of the subject with which he had dealt. Towards the end of his life, he often meditated upon death and, according to Ibn al-Ṣalāḥ, he reproached himself for having devoted himself so much to the abstract sciences (philosophy and *kalām*) which, as he thought, were not capable of leading to certain truth. He was to write in his "Testament": "I have had experience of all the methods of *kalām* and of all the paths of philosophy, but I have not found in them either satisfaction or comfort to equal that which I have found in reading the Ḳurʾān" (Ibn Abī Uṣaybiʿa, ii, 27).

Al-Rāzī's zeal in the defence of Sunnism was always ardent and caused him to make many bitter enemies. Apart from the Muʿtazilīs, he had to strive with the Karrāmīs, adherents of an anthropomorphic type of exegesis [see KARRĀMIYYA], who did not hesitate to use any calumny to discredit their adversary. In 599/1202, while he was staying at Ferūkūh, an actual riot was set off against him by these last, who accused him of corrupting Islam by preferring to its teaching that of Aristotle, Fārābī and Avicenna. He was also reproached for reporting so much of the arguments of the adversaries of Islam, without being capable of refuting them convincingly.

In 606/1209, seriously ill and feeling the approach of death, he dictated his "Testament" to his disciple, Ibrāhīm b. Abī Bakr al-Iṣfahānī, on Sunday, 21 Muḥarram/26 July. The text of this has been preserved by, among others, al-Subkī and Ibn Abī Uṣaybiʿa. It is a true profession of Sunnī faith and a beautiful example of total resignation to the will of God. He commends his children to the Sultan and asks him, as well as his disciples, to bury him according to all the ordinances of Muslim law on the mountain of Mazdakhan near Herāt. Certain biographers of al-Rāzī have held that he was poisoned by the Karrāmīs. In addition, Ibn al-ʿIbrī (Barhebraeus) and Ibn Abī Uṣaybiʿa pass on a rumour according to which he was buried secretly within his house to prevent the crowd from ill-treating his remains. It is unlikely that either of these reports is true: al-Rāzī's tomb is still venerated at Herāt.

Although he was a convinced follower of al-Ashʿarī, al-Rāzī showed himself, at least in his youthful works, to be an opponent of atomism (cf. *K. al-Mabāḥith al-mashriḳiyya*, ii, 11). It is true that later on (cf. *Mafātīḥ al-ghayb*, z, i, 5 and *K. Lawāmiʿ al-bayyināt*, 229; *K. al-Arbaʿīn fī uṣūl al-dīn*) he seems to have changed his views or at any rate to have shown less severity in his criticism of atomism. He dedicated his *K. al-Djawhar al-fard* (Ibn Abī Uṣaybiʿa, ii, 30) to this subject and al-Ṭūsī gives a short analysis of it in his *Sharḥ al-Ishārāt* (ed. of Istanbul, 4). According to Khʷānsārī (*Rawḍāt al-djannāt*, 730), he also criticized Ashʿarī's doctrine of the divine attributes.

His profound knowledge of *falsafa* (he had studied al-Fārābī and composed a commentary on the *Ishārāt* and the *ʿUyūn al-akhbār* of Ibn Sīnā), allowed him to make use of considerable portions of it in his dogmatic synthesis (cf., for example, the greater part of the *Mabāḥith*). But in doing this, he preserved his freedom of mind, criticizing Avicenna strongly, where he did not wish to follow his opinions. Kraus, who was clearly much impressed by the originality of al-Rāzī, thinks that "the reconciliation of philosophy with theology is achieved, in his view, at the level of a Platonistic system which in the last resort derives from the interpretation of the Timaeus" (*Les "Controverses" de Fakhr al-Dīn Rāzī*, in *BIÉ*, xix (1937), 190). He points out Rāzī's frequent references to the *K. al-Muʿtabar* of Abu 'l-Barakāt b. Malka al-Baghdādī (cf., for example, *al-Mabāḥith*, ii, 286, 392, 398, 475, etc.; *Lawāmiʿ al-bayyināt*, 71-3, where a long fragment of al-Baghdādī on *al-ism al-aʿẓam* is quoted; cf. also Khʷānsārī, 730).

Finally, Goldziher has shown that while al-Rāzī was an opponent of the Muʿtazilīs, he was nevertheless influenced by them in certain respects, for example concerning the problem of the *ʿiṣma* of the Prophet, and the validity of *āḥād* traditions in theological argument (cf. *Aus der Theologie des Fachr al-Din al-Rāzī*, in *Isl.*, iii (1912), 213-47).

For the influence of al-Rāzī's ideas on a mind as uncompromising as that of Ibn Taymiyya, see the remarkable thesis of H. Laoust, *Essai sur les doctrines sociales et politiques de Taḳi-d-din Aḥmad b. Taimīya*, Cairo 1939 (cf. index s.v. Rāzī). Ibn Taymiyya made use of al-Rāzī's principal works, the *Muḥaṣṣal*, the *Maʿālim uṣūl al-dīn*, and the *K. al-Arbaʿīn*, and "on many points he was led to make some concessions to his doctrine of the Prophets. Furthermore, his political sociology remains incomprehensible enough unless we see in it, to some degree, a reaction against the conception of sovereignty and the theory of the Caliphate defended by al-Rāzī. In short, it cannot be denied that Fakhr al-Dīn al-Rāzī led Ibn Taymiyya on towards a deeper personal understanding of philosophy and heresiography" (85). Ibn Taymiyya himself passed a severe enough judgment on al-Rāzī (cf. *Bughyat al-murtād*, Cairo 1329, 107-8).

Works. — The works of Fakhr al-Dīn al-Rāzī are huge in number; they are encyclopaedic but the great majority of them are concerned with *kalām*, philosophy or exegesis. A list of those works whose manuscripts have come down to us is to be found in Brockelmann (S I, 920-4; I², 666-9) who has subdivided them under thirteen headings: I. History; II. *Fiḳh*; III. Ḳur'ān; IV. Dogmatics; V. Philosophy; VI. Astrology; VII. Cheiromancy; VIII. Rhetoric; IX. Encyclopaedia; X. Medicine; XI. Physiognomy; XII. Alchemy; XIII. Mineralogy. ʿAlī Sāmī al-Nashshār has endeavoured to collect all the information provided by his biographers with regard to his literary output and has classed his works in the following manner: Ḳur'ān (exegesis) (5 works), *Kalām* (40), *Ḥikma* and Philosophy (26), Arabic language and literature (7), *Fiḳh* and *uṣūl al-fiḳh* (5), Medicine (7), Talismans and Geometry (5), History (2) (see the introduction to his edition of al-Rāzī's little treatise, *Iʿtiḳādāt firaḳ al-Muslimīn wa 'l-mushrikīn*, Cairo 1356/1938, 26-34). But this list is by no means a critical one. A profound study of al-Rāzī's work still remains to be achieved.

There follows here a list of the main Arabic works of al-Rāzī which exist in print, with a brief glimpse of the contents of each book:

1. — *Asās al-taḳdīs fī ʿilm al-kalām* (Cairo 1354/1935, 197 pp.). This work, dedicated to the Sultan Abū Bakr b. Ayyūb, sets out to study the *via remotionis* applied to the knowledge of God. It consists of four parts: the first studies the proofs that God is incorporeal and does not exist in space; the second shows how to apply the *ta'wīl* (interpretation) of ambiguous terms (*mutashābih*) mentioned in the Ḳur'ān; the third part establishes the doctrine of the Ancients (*madhhab al-salaf*), especially in matters concerning both the clear verses of the Ḳur'ān and the obscure ones; finally the fourth part follows up this account, dealing chiefly with those verses which are ambiguous.

2. — *Lawāmiʿ al-bayyināt fi 'l-asmā' wa 'l-ṣifāt* (ed. Amīn al-Khāndjī, Cairo 1323/1905, 270 pp.), a treatise on the Divine Names, one of the most substantial in Muslim theology. It consists of three parts: the prolegomena (3-73), under the title *mabādi' wa-muḳaddimāt*. In ten chapters, al-Rāzī studies the problems posed by the subject of the name in general, and in the cases where it is applied to God, the nature of name and appellation, the distinction between the name and the attribute, the origin of the Divine Names, their subdivision, etc. Here are to be found excellent developments on the *dhikr* (ch. 6) and on prayers of request (ch. 9). The second and longest part (73-259) studies systematically the ninety-nine Divine Names. Al-Rāzī mentions and discusses the various applications of each of them. The chapter dealing with the name of Allāh consists of more than thirty pages. Generally al-Rāzī finishes his exposition with practical spiritual advice. Finally, the third part, entitled *al-lawāḥiḳ wa 'l-mutammimāt* (256-67), gives some precise details on a number of names other than those previously studied.

3. — *Sharḥ al-Ishārāt* (Constantinople 1290/1873, with commentary by al-Ṭūsī). It is a commentary on the physics and metaphysics in the *Kitāb al-Ishārāt wa 'l-tanbīhāt* of Ibn Sīnā, that is to say from the beginning of the first *namaṭ* (ed. Froget, 90). Firstly, al-Rāzī reproduces in full a paragraph of Avicenna's text, then comments on it, pointing out carefully the plan which the author follows as well as its several component parts.

4. — *Lubāb al-Ishārāt* (Cairo 1326/1908; 2nd ed. Cairo 1355/1936, 136 pp.). A summary of Avicenna's celebrated work, written after the commentary referred to last. It is concerned not with extracts from the work, but with a true digest of Avicenna's thought. Al-Rāzī follows thus each *nahdj* of the logic and each *namaṭ* of the physics and metaphysics.

5. — *Muḥaṣṣal afkār al-mutaḳaddimīn wa 'l-muta'akhkhirīn min al-ʿulamā' wa 'l-ḥukamā' wa 'l-mutakallimīn* (a précis of ideas, scholars, philosophers and *mutakallimūn*, ancient and modern). Although at the beginning al-Rāzī indicates the plan which he intends to follow, in the course of the book's development this design is almost lost. *Kalām*, he says, is divided into four parts which he calls "cornerstones" (*arkān*). He begins immediately with the first, the preliminaries, without mentioning the others which are as follows: 2) being and its several modes; 3) rational theology (*ilāhiyyāt*); 4) the traditional questions (*al-samʿiyyāt*). The preliminaries (1-32) go far beyond those of al-Djuwaynī (in the *Irshād*) and of al-Ghazālī (in the *Iḳtiṣād*). Three important questions are: a) the first ideas, where al-Rāzī speaks of perception, of judgment, and where he examines the divers theories concerning the innate or acquired character of the judgments; b) the characters of reasoning (*aḥkām al-naẓar*), including the setting out and proving of a dozen "theses"; c) apodeictic proof (*al-dalīl*). It is in the second part that the sections are distinguished with less clarity. Al-Rāzī begins by speaking of the *maʿlūmāt* (things known) where we can distinguish with some difficulty three divisions: 1) characters of existing beings; 2) the non-being (*fi 'l-maʿdūm*); 3) the negation of modes (*aḥwāl*) which are intermediary between being and non-being. Al-Rāzī next divides created beings into necessary and possible and goes on to examine the various arguments concerning these two categories, expounding and discussing in turn the theory of the *mutakallimūn* and that of the *falāsifa*. There follow thirty or so paragraphs whose contents are oddly enough assorted (on cold, softness, weight, movement, death, science, the senses, etc.), badly arranged paragraphs which are meant to link up probably with what immediately follows concerning the kinds and properties of accidents. Next the author studies bodies (*adjsām*), their constitution, properties and kinds. Finally, the last section of this part is dedicated to the general characteristics of being, the One and the Many, cause and effect, etc. The two last *rukn*s deal directly with *kalām*. The third study, the *Ilāhiyyāt*, is a demonstration of the existence of the Necessary Being, of its attributes both positive and negative, of its acts, and of the relationship between divine and created acts. Then come some brief lines on the Divine Names. The fourth part, which is exclusively based on "Scripture", comprises four sections: doctrine of the Prophets, eschatology, the "Statutes and Names" (the problem of faith), and finally, the imāmate.

The Cairo edition (the only one in existence; printed at al-Ḥusayniyya, n.d.) has at the bottom of the pages the *Talkhīṣ al-Muḥaṣṣal* of Naṣīr al-Dīn al-Ṭūsī, in which criticism of al-Rāzī is not spared. This commentator remarks that in his time it was the only famous work on dogmatics, but according to him without justification (3). The Cairo edition also contains on the margins the *Maʿālim uṣūl al-dīn* of al-Rāzī. The *Muḥaṣṣal* has been commentated often (see Brockelmann). Horten has made an abridged edition in two volumes (*Die Philosophischen Ansichten von Rāzī und Ṭūsī*, Bonn 1910, and *Die spekulative und positive Theologie des Islams nach Razi und ihre Kritik nach Tusi*, Leipzig 1912), but "their value is diminished, if not indeed made doubtful, by the great number of errors in translation and arbitrary interpretations" (P. Kraus).

6. — *al-Maʿālim fī uṣūl al-dīn*. In his introduction to this work, al-Rāzī writes: "This is a compendium which deals with five kinds of sciences: dogmatics (*ʿilm uṣūl al-dīn*), the methodology of law (*uṣūl al-fiḳh*), *fiḳh*, the principles on which differences of opinion are based (*al-uṣūl al-muʿtabara fi 'l-khilāfiyyāt*), the rules of controversy and of dialectics".

Only the first of these five parts has been printed (on the margin of the *Muḥaṣṣal*, see above, no. 5).

7. — *Mafātīḥ al-ghayb* or *K. al-Tafsīr al-kabīr* (ed. Būlāḳ 1279-89, 6 vols.; Cairo 1310, 8 vols. (reprinted in 1924-27); 1327, 8 vols., with the *Irshād al-ʿaḳl* of Abu 'l-Suʿūd al-ʿImādī on the margin. The most recent and careful edition is that of Muḥammad Muḥyi 'l-Dīn, Cairo 1352/1933, in 32 *djuzʾ*, each comprising on the average 225 pp.). This is certainly al-Rāzī's most important work. It belongs to the class of commentaries at the same time philosophical and *bi 'l-raʾy*, and al-Rāzī put into this all his knowledge both of philosophy and of religion. Whenever the opportunity presents itself, he takes the opportunity of expounding what he wishes to say in the form of a "question" (*masʾala*). He often tries to link the verses logically one to anotner, and, according to his habit, sets forth in answer to each question asked the various opinions with their arguments. The work consists of no less than eight volumes in-quarto, each containing about 600 pages of closely printed text. The commentary opens with a great dissertation (forming the whole of the first volume in the new edition) on the *istiʿādha* and then on the *basmala*. Appreciation of this commentary has varied from author to author. Certain detractors of philosophy and of *kalām*, such as Ibn Taymiyya for example, speak with disdain of this commentary on the Ḳurʾān where everything is to be found except a commentary. To this, admirers of al-Rāzī reply that in addition to the commentary on the Ḳurʾān everything else is to be found there (cf. al-Ṣafadī, *Wāfi 'l-wafayāt*, iv, 254). The influence of al-Rāzī's commentary has made itself felt amongst those who would like to modernize certain aspects of traditional exegesis. Thus a modern author, who helped to introduce the concept of "literary style" into the study of the Ḳurʾān, has remarked: "As far as the ideas contained in the Ḳurʾān are concerned, Rāzī is unique ... attitudes which are considered new and daring in the commentary of the *Manār* or in modern works have already been mentioned by Rāzī" (cf. J. Jomiei, *Quelques positions actuelles de l'exégèse coranique en Égypte révélées par une polémique récente*, in *MIDEO*, i (1954), 51).

8. — *al-Munāẓarāt* (the controversies) (ed. Ḥaydarābād 1354/1935). This is a kind of autobiography in which the author reports in detail sixteen controversies which occurred at different places during his travels. Al-Rāzī disputes with Shāfiʿī and Ḥanafī, Ashʿarī and Māturīdī scholars who cannot always be identified by name. The contents of the *Munāẓarāt* are varied. Almost half of the chapters are given up to subtle questions of canon law. Al-Rāzī makes fun here of the juridical work of al-Ghazālī. The rest deals with matters of philosophy and theology, such as the problem of the Divine Attributes, the origin of our perceptions, a refutation of astrology (ninth controversy), etc. In the tenth controversy, he gives interesting details on the sources of the *Milal wa 'l-niḥal* of al-Shahrastānī. This short work has been analysed by Kraus (who seems to have believed that it had never been published): *Les controverses de Fakhr al-Dīn Rāzī*, in *BIÉ*, xix (1937), 187-214. The full title, added by a later hand, is: "The controversies of Fakhr al-Dīn al-Rāzī which took place during his journey to Samarḳand and then to India".

9. — *Iʿtiḳād firaḳ al-Muslimīn wa 'l-Mushrikīn*. In this little treatise, edited in 1938 by ʿAlī Sāmī al-Nashshār, al-Rāzī refers, in a manner very concise but at the same time precise and objective, to the majority of Muslim sects and to a number of the "sects" of the Zoroastrians, Jews and Christians. A special chapter is reserved to the philosophers. Al-Rāzī points out that he is the only one to regard the Ṣūfīs as a sect.

10. — *al-Mabāḥith al-mashriḳiyya* (Ḥaydarābād 1342, 2 vols. of 726 and 550 pp. respectively). This is a work on "metaphysics and physics" (*fī ʿilm al-ilāhiyyāt wa 'l-ṭabīʿiyyāt*) which, however, does not refer at all to the *samʿiyyāt*. The author does not fail to point out that he is the first to have conceived a work of this sort. At the beginning, he explains clearly the plan which he intends to follow in this work which consists of three "books". Knowledge being the more perfect as its object is more geneial, the author will dedicate the first book to the study of being and its properties, then to its correlative, non-being, then to essence, unity, and multiplicity. Having defined these general principles (*al-umūr al-ʿāmma*), the author studies a certain number of problems connected with them, such as division of being into necessary and possible (12 chapters), eternity and beginning in being (5 chapters). The second book is dedicated to the great divisions of the possible, substance and accident. An introduction studies them in a general manner (15 chapteis), then a first *djumla* consisting of five *funūn* is concerned with accident as follows: 1) quantity; 2) quality; 3) relative categories (*al-maḳūlāt al-nisbiyya*); 4) causes and effects; 5) movement and time (72 chapters). The second *djumla* is concerned with substance as follows: 1) bodies; 2) soul (*ʿilm al-nafs*); 3) intelligence. Finally, the third book (ii, 448-524) deals with "pure metaphysics" (*fi 'l-ilāhiyyāt al-maḥḍa*) and comprises four sections: 1) proof of the existence of the Necessary Being and of its transcendence; 2) its attributes; 3) its acts; 4) prophecy. This work is divided carefully into *funūn*, *abwāb* and *fuṣūl*, which call to mind Avicenna's *Shifāʾ*. From him, whom he calls simply *al-raʾīs*, and to whom he refers very frequently and sometimes quotes verbally, he borrows much important material, above all drawn from the *Shifāʾ* (physics, metaphysics, *de Coelo et Mundo*), the *Nadjāt*, and occasionally the *Ishārāt* (cf. ii, 342). He often accepts his data, but he does not hesitate to dispute freely certain of his principles, pointing out, sometimes with astonishment, what he calls contradictions in him. On the

subject of necessary emanation ("from one can come forth only one") and the theory of the active intellect (cf. ii), he disagrees completely with Avicenna. He reports many opinions, usually unfortunately not naming their authors, and discusses them; nevertheless he does refer by name to Aristotle, Plato, al-Fārābī, Empedocles, Galen, and Thābit b. Ḳurra.

11. — *Kitāb al-Firāsa.* This book on physiognomy has been edited (from the three manuscripts of Cambridge, the British Museum, and the Aya Sofya) by Youssouf Mourad (*La physiognomonie arabe et le* Kitāb al-firāsa *de Fakhr al-Dīn al-Rāzī*, Paris 1939), with a long introduction and a French translation, notes and commentary. The work consists of three dissertations (*maḳālāt*). The first deals with the general principles of this science, the second is made up of four sections as follows: 1) the signs of the temperaments; 2) the conditions special to the four ages; 3) the conditions special to the several states; 4) differences of character arising from the differences of countries, hot and cold climates, etc. Finally, the third dissertation is given up to the significance of numbers.

12. — *Kitāb al-Arbaʿīn fī uṣūl al-dīn* (Ḥaydarābād 1353/1934, 500 pp.). This treatise on theology was written by al-Rāzī for his eldest son Muḥammad. The plan of the questions with which it deals is not indicated by the author. It is nevertheless possible to classify the forty questions as follows: A. Beginning of the world in time (q. 1); the non-being is not a thing (q. 2). B. Existence of God (q. 3). C. Attributes of God (q. 4-40): God is eternal (q. 4), unlike everything which exists (q. 5), His essence is identical with His existence (q. 6), He does not exist in space (q. 7 and 8), it is impossible for His essence to enter anything (q. 9), it is impossible that He should be subject to accident (q. 10); He is all-powerful (q. 11), all-knowing (q. 12), possessed of will (q. 13), living (q. 14), He has knowledge and will (q. 15), He is hearing and seeing (q. 16), speaking (q. 17), everlasting (q. 18), visible (q. 19); His essence can be known by man (q. 20); He is one (q. 21), creator of the acts of man (q. 22), and of all which exists (q. 23), He wills all things (q. 24); good and evil are determined by religious Law (q. 25); the actions of God are not caused (q. 26); the existence of atoms (q. 27), reality of the soul (q. 28), existence of the void (q. 29), resurrection (q. 30), prophecy of Muḥammad (q. 31), impeccability of the Prophets (q. 32), comparison of angels and messengers (q. 33), the miracles of the saints (q. 34); reward and punishment (q. 35), non-eternal nature of the punishment of Muslim sinners (q. 36), the intercession of the Prophet (q. 37); whether proofs based on tradition produce certainty (q. 38), the imāmate (q. 39), methodology concerning rational proofs (q. 40). What is so striking in this treatise is the attitude of al-Rāzī towards atomism which here he seems to approve, whereas in the *Mabāḥith al-mashriḳiyya* he refutes it.

Bibliography: in addition to the works mentioned in the text: Ibn Abī Uṣaybiʿa, *ʿUyūn al-anbāʾ*, ii, 23-30; Ibn al-Ḳifṭī, *Taʾrīkh al-ḥukamāʾ*, Cairo 1326/1908, 190-2; Ibn Khallikān, Cairo 1299/1881, i, 600-2; Ṣafadī, *Wāfī*, ed. Dedering, iv, 248-58; Dhahabī, *Taʾrīkh al-Islām*, ms. Paris 1582, ff. 153b-6a; Subkī, *Ṭabaḳāt al-Shāfiʿiyya*, Cairo 1324/1906, iv, 285, v, 33-40; Ibn al-Sāʿī, *al-Djāmiʿ al-mukhtaṣar*, ix, ed. Muṣṭafa Djawād, Baghdād 1353/1934, 4-6, 171-2, 306-8; Ibn al-ʿIbrī, *Mukhtaṣar al-duwal*, 419; Ibn Ḥadjar, *Lisān al-mīzān*, iv, 426-9; Tāshköprü-zāde, *Miftāḥ al-saʿāda*, Ḥaydarābād 1328/1910, i, 445-51; Khʷānṣārī, *Rawḍāt al-djannāt*, lith. Tehrān, 729-31; Ibn Dāʿī, *Tabṣirat al-ʿawāmm*, ed. ʿAbbās Iḳbāl, Tehrān 1333/1914, 120; Abu 'l-Falāḥ ʿAbd al-Ḥayy al-Ḥanbalī, *Shadharāt al-dhahab*, Cairo 1350/1931, v, 21-2; I. Goldziher, *Aus der Theologie des Fachr al-Dīn al-Rāzī*, in *Isl.*, iii (1912), 213-47; M. Horten, *Die philosophischen Ansichten von Razi und Tusi*, Bonn 1912; idem, *Die spekulative und positive Theologie des Islams nach Razi und ihre Kritik durch Tusi*, Leipzig 1912; G. Gabrieli, *Fachr-al-Dīn al-Rāzī*, in *Isis*, 1925, 9-13; McNeile, *An index to the Commentary of Fakhr al-Rāzī*, London 1933; P. Kraus, *Les controverses de Fakhr al-Dīn al-Rāzī*, in *BIÉ*, xix (1937), 187-214 (= *The controversies of Fakhr al-Dīn Rāzī*, in *Islamic Culture*, xii (1938), 131-53); *Shorter Encyclopedia of Islam*, article on Rāzī by Kramers; R. Arnaldez, *L'œuvre de Fakhr al-Dīn al-Rāzī commentateur du Coran et philosophe*, in *Cahiers de Civilisation médiévale*, iii (1960), 307-23; idem, *Apories sur la prédestination et le libre-arbitre dans le Commentaire de Rāzī*, in *MIDEO*, vi (1959-60), 123-36; G. C. Anawati, *Fakhr al-Dīn al-Rāzī: tamhīd li-dirāsat ḥayātih wa-muʾallafātih*, in *Mélanges Taha Hussein*, Cairo 1962, 193-234; idem, *Fakhr al-Dīn al-Rāzī: éléments de biographie*, in *Mélanges Massé*, Tehrān (forthcoming). (G. C. ANAWATI)

FAKHR AL-**MULK** [see ʿAMMĀR, BANŪ].

FAKHR AL-**MULK** B. NIẒĀM AL-MULK [see NIẒĀMIDS].

FAKHRĪ (d. *ca.* 1027/1618), a native of Bursa, the most celebrated silhouette-cutter in Turkey. This art (*ṣanʿat-i ḳaṭʿ*) was brought from Persia to Turkey in the 10th/16th century, and to the west in the 11th/17th century, where at first, as in the east, light paper on a dark ground was always used. There are specimens of Fakhrī's work—he cut principally examples of calligraphy, flowers and gardens—in the album prepared for Murād III, now in the Vienna Hofbibliothek; for Aḥmed I he cut out a Gulistān, which did not, however, survive his criticism; Murād IV on the other hand thought very highly of the artist. He is buried in Istanbul near the Edirne gate.

Bibliography: Ismāʿīl Belīgh, *Güldeste*, Bursa 1302, 532-4; Ḥabīb, *Khaṭṭ u khaṭṭāṭān*, Istanbul 1305, 261; J. von Karabacek, *Zur orientalischen Altertumskunde*, iv, 46 f., in *SBAk. Wien*, clxxii; G. Jacob, *Die Herkunft der Silhouettenkunst aus Persien*, Berlin 1913. (G. JACOB)

FAKHRĪ, SHAMS AL-DĪN Muḥammad b. Fakhr al-Dīn Saʿīd Iṣfāhānī, an Iranian philologist, author of the *Miʿyār-i Djamālī va-miftāḥ-i Bū Isḥāḳī* ("The bird-trap offered to Djamāl and the key entrusted to Abū Isḥāḳ"), written in Iṣfāhān, after residing in Shīrāz, and dedicated in 745/1344 to Djamāl al-Dīn Abū Isḥāḳ Muḥammad, the last prince of the Indjū dynasty [*q.v.*]. The work consists of four sections: prosody (*ʿarūḍ*), knowledge of rhyme (*ḳawāfī*), rhetorical devices (*badāʾiʿ al-sanāʾiʿ*), a lexicon intermingled with verses in praise of the prince (Persian words arranged according to their final letter: they will be found in recent western dictionaries). Salemann, the editor of this lexicon, also adds a poem of 150 lines of verse, *Marghūb al-ḳulūb* ("Hearts' desire"), moral and mystical in content, its attribution to Fakhrī being questionable (the manuscript of the B.N., Paris, Cat. Blochet no. 158, 3°, used by Salemann, puts it only under the name Shams). In the preface to the *Miʿyār*, writing in a very careful and elaborate style, the author states that in 713/1313, while still a youth, he lived in Lūristān in the company of writers and scholars and there composed a manual on versification which he dedicated to Nuṣrat al-Dīn Aḥmad, the seventh and last *atabek* of the Lūr-i Buzurg (cf. Gantin, 581); he adds that he was intending to revise this manual and to transform it into a basic work—which he intended to achieve by writing the *Miʿyār* (additional details in Blochet, *Catalogue*, nos. 971 and 2423; Pajūh, *Fihrist*, 432-3).

Bibliography: *Shams i Fachrii Ispahanensis lexicon Persicum id est libri Miʿjar Gamāli pars quarta quam ... edidit Carolus Salemann, Fasc. prior textum et indices continens*, Casani 1887; E. Blochet, *Catalogue des mss. persans de la Bibliothèque Nationale de Paris*; Pajūh (Muḥammad Taḳī Dānish), *Fihrist-i nuskhahā-yi khaṭṭī-i kitābkhāna-yi dānishkada-yi adabiyyāt* (catalogue of mss. of the Faculty of Letters), *Review of the Faculty of Letters, University of Tehran*, viii/I (1339 p. /1960); Ḥamd Allāh Mustawfī, *Taʾrīkh-i Guzīda*, the Persian dynasties, ed. and Fr. tr. Jules Gantin, Paris 1903. (H. Massé)

FAĶĪH (A.), plur. *fuḳahāʾ*, in its non-technical meaning denotes anyone possessing knowledge (*fiḳh*) of a thing (syn. *ʿālim*, plur. *ʿulamāʾ* [*q.v.*]). Then, as *fiḳh* passed from denoting any branch of knowledge and became a technical term for the science of religious law (*sharīʿa* [*q.v.*]) and in particular for the science of its derivative details (*furūʿ*), *faḳīh* became the technical term for a specialist in religious law and in particular its *furūʿ*. This development is parallel to that of the term (*iuris*) *prudens* in Roman law. In older terminology, however, *faḳīh* as opposed to *ʿālim* denotes the speculative, systematic lawyer as opposed to the specialist in the traditional elements of religious law. (See on all this the art. FIḲH). A more modest synonym of *faḳīh* is *mutafaḳḳih* "a student of *fiḳh*", whereas a person possessing the highest degree of competence in *fiḳh* is called *mudjtahid* [see IDJTIHĀD]. In several Arabic dialects the word, in forms like *fiḳī* etc., has come to mean a schoolmaster in a *kuttāb* [*q.v.*] or a professional reciter of the Ḳurʾān.

Bibliography: Lane, s.v.; *LA*, s.v.; Tahānawī, *Dictionary of Technical Terms*, 30-3, 198 ff., 1157; E. W. Lane, *Modern Egyptians*, chap. 2; W. Marçais, *Textes arabes de Tanger*, 415 (with further references). (D. B. Macdonald*)

FAĶĪH, BĀ, a family of Bā ʿAlawī *sayyids* of Tarīm in Ḥaḍramawt descended from Muḥammad b. ʿAlī (d. 862/1458), called *mawlā ʿAydīd* or *ṣāḥib ʿAydīd*, after ʿAydīd, now a suburb of Tarīm, to which he moved from Tarīm. His father, ʿAlī b. Muḥammad (d. 838/1434) was called *ṣāḥib al-ḥawṭa*, after an estate he had near Tarīm which he developed as a plantation and which became a sacrosanct enclosure (*ḥawṭa*). The name Bā Faḳīh apparently refers to *ṣāḥib al-ḥawṭa*'s great-grandfather, al-Faḳīh Aḥmad b. ʿAbd al-Raḥmān b. ʿAlī b. Muḥammad (d. 726/1326), whose great-grandfather was Muḥammad *ṣāḥib Mirbāṭ* (d. 556/1162), after the town of Mirbāṭ, then a prosperous town on the coast of Ẓufār, where he moved from Tarīm and where he later died and was buried. From *ṣāḥib Mirbāṭ* are descended all the Bā ʿAlawī *sayyids* of Ḥaḍramawt.

Muḥammad b. ʿAlī, *mawlā ʿAydīd*, the ancestor of the Bā Faḳīh, is described in *sayyid* literature as a great saint, a description, however, which is lavishly used by *sayyid* writers about their ancestors. His descendants known to us were mainly *ṣūfīs*, teachers and jurists. They are descended through his sons (a) ʿAbd al-Raḥmān, (b) ʿAbd Allāh, (c) ʿAlī, (d) ʿAlawī and (e) Zayn.

Through (a) ʿAbd al-Raḥmān were descended his son Zayn (died in al-Shiḥr) and the latter's son ʿAbd al-Raḥmān (d. 950/1543). Through (b) ʿAbd Allāh were descended, from his great-grandson Muḥammad, Abū Bakr b. Muḥammad (d. 1005/1596), a prominent teacher and jurist, called *ṣāḥib Ḳaydūn*, after the town near Dawʿan to which he moved and where he died, and his brother Ḥusayn b. Muḥammad (d. 1040/1630) who was *ḳāḍī* in Tarīm and got involved in disputes between members of the influential ʿAydarūs [*q.v.*] family. Ḥusayn had two sons: Aḥmad (d. 1052/1642 in Mecca) and ʿAbd Allāh, who travelled to India in his youth and settled in Kunūr, where he married the daughter of its governor ʿAbd al-Wahhāb and gained public importance, although he mainly occupied himself with teaching. He seems to have studied mathematics while there and to have applied himself to the pursuit of alchemy. He died in Kunūr. A nephew of Abū Bakr and Ḥusayn, called Muḥammad b. ʿUmar b. Muḥammad, settled in Kunūr where he married the daughter of its governor ʿAbd al-Madjīd and acquired some prominence, which he retained in the days of ʿAbd al-Madjīd's brother and successor ʿAbd al-Wahhāb; but he fell upon bad days after the latter's death and moved to Ḥaydarābād, where he died.

From (c) ʿAlī was descended his great-grandson Aḥmad b. ʿUmar b. ʿAbd al-Raḥmān b. ʿAlī (d. 11th/17th century), whose studies took him to Mecca, Medina and Cairo; then he went back to Tarīm where towards the end of his life he was twice *ḳāḍī*. From (d) ʿAlawī were descended his son Muḥammad b. ʿAlawī (d. 924/1519 in Aden) and his great-grandson ʿAbd al-Raḥmān b. ʿAlawī b. Aḥmad b. ʿAlawī (d. 1047/1637), a prominent *ṣūfī*, jurist and teacher. From (e) Zayn was descended ʿAbd Allāh b. Zayn b. Muḥammad b. ʿAbd al-Raḥmān b. Zayn, a teacher of al-Shillī, author of *al-Mashraʿ al-rawī*, who later moved to India, studying and teaching, until he settled in Bīdjāpūr, where he died.

A chronicler called Muḥammad b. ʿUmar al-Ṭayyib Bā Faḳīh Bā ʿAlawī al-Shiḥrī, about whom no biographical details can be traced, was the author of a chronicle commonly referred to as *Tārīkh Bā Faḳīh al-Shiḥrī* (covering the 10th/16th century); cf. R. B. Serjeant in *BSOAS*, xiii (1950), 292-5; xxv (1962), 245 f.

Bibliography: Ibn al-ʿAydarūs, *al-Nūr al-sāfir min akhbār al-ḳarn al-ʿāshir*, Baghdād 1934; Muḥammad b. Abū Bakr al-Shillī, *al-Mashraʿ al-rawī fī manāḳib al-sāda al-kirām āl Abī ʿAlawī*, Cairo 1319/1901; al-Muḥibbī, *Khulāṣat al-athar fī aʿyān al-ḳarn al-ḥādī ʿashar*, Cairo 1869, 4 vols.; F. Wüstenfeld, *Die Çufiten in Süd-Arabien im XI (XVII) Jahrhundert*, Göttingen 1883, 57-64; R. B. Serjeant, *Materials for South Arabian history*, in *BSOAS*, xiii (1950), 292-5, and xxv (1962), 245 f.; idem, *The Portuguese off the South Arabian Coast*, Oxford 1963, *passim*. (M. A. Ghūl)

FAĶĪH, BAL, a family of Bā ʿAlawī *sayyids* of Tarīm in Ḥaḍramawt descended from al-Faḳīh Muḥammad b. ʿAbd al-Raḥmān, called *al-asḳaʿ*, a prominent scholar who, after studying in his native Tarīm, Aden, Zabīd, Mecca and Medina, settled in Tarīm, where he died in 917/1512. A kind of historical work by him was used as a source of the *Taʾrīkh* of Bā Faḳīh al-Shiḥrī, where it is referred to as *Khaṭṭ*; cf. R. B. Serjeant in *BSOAS*, xxv (1962), 246. His great ancestor was Muḥammad b. ʿAlī b. Muḥammad *ṣāḥib Mirbāṭ*, commonly called *al-ustādh al-aʿẓam wa 'l-faḳīh al-muḳaddam* (d. 653/1255).

The Bal Faḳīh *sayyids* of whom we know were mainly *ṣūfī*s, and in some cases teachers and jurists as well. They were descended from al-Faḳīh Muḥammad b. ʿAbd al-Raḥmān *al-asḳaʿ* through his three sons (a) ʿAbd Allāh, (b) ʿAbd al-Raḥmān and (c) Aḥmad.

The first son ʿAbd Allāh is also called al-ʿAydarūs and is known as *ṣāḥib al-Shubayka*, after the cemetery in Mecca where he was buried. He was born in Tarīm, which he left for Shiḥr, Aden, Mecca, Medina and Zabīd in search of learning, and then went back to it where he became a prominent teacher. He left it later for Mecca, where he lived the last 14 years of his life and where he died in 974/1567. His son ʿAlī, a *ṣūfī*, died in Mecca in 1021/1612. The latter had two sons, Muḥammad, who attained wealth and public importance in Mecca, where he died in 1066/1656, and ʿAbd Allāh, a *ṣūfī*, who died in Mecca in 1050/1640.

From (b) ʿAbd al-Raḥmān were descended his son Muḥammad (d. 1007/1598) and his two grandsons by his son Ḥusayn, Aḥmad b. Ḥusayn b. ʿAbd al-Raḥmān (d. 1048/1638), who was twice *ḳāḍī* of Tarīm and got involved together with Ḥusayn b. Muḥammad Bā Faḳīh in disputes between members of the influential ʿAydarūs [*q.v.*] family; and Abū Bakr b. Ḥusayn b. ʿAbd al-Raḥmān, who travelled to India where he finally settled in Bādjāpūr enjoying the patronage of its ruler Maḥmūd ʿĀdil Shāh until his death there in 1074/1663.

Of (c) Aḥmad's descendants we know of a grandson called Aḥmad b. ʿAbd al-Raḥmān b. Aḥmad who was born in Tarīm, where he studied and then became a teacher and jurist. He was a contemporary and friend of al-Shillī, author of *al-Mashraʿ al-Rawī*.

Bibliography: as for FAḲĪH, BĀ; add R. B. Serjeant, *The Saiyids of Ḥadramawt*, London 1957, 14, 19 and 25. (M. A. GHŪL)

AL-**FĀKIHĪ**, ABŪ ʿABD ALLĀH MUḤAMMAD B. ISḤĀḲ B. AL-ʿABBĀS, 3rd/9th-century historian of Mecca. No information on him was available to later Muslim scholars, or is to us, except what can be learned from his *History of Mecca*, of which the second half is preserved in a single manuscript in Leiden (cod. or. 463). A small portion of the work has been edited by F. Wüstenfeld, *Die Chroniken der Stadt Mekka*, Leipzig 1857-61, ii, 3-51. Al-Fākihī was alive and, it seems, quite young during the judgeship of ʿAbd al-Raḥmān b. Yazīd b. Muḥammad b. Ḥanẓala b. Muḥammad which came to an end in or shortly before 238/852-3 (Wüstenfeld, ii, 43 f.; Wakīʿ, *Akhbār al-Ḳuḍāt*, i, 268 f.); his birth may thus be placed around 225/839, and this agrees with the fact that some of his authorities died in the early 240 s. He was in contact with the leading scholars of Mecca. He completed his work between 272/885-86, a date he himself mentions, and the end of 275/April-May 889 when ʿAbd al-ʿAzīz b. ʿAbd Allāh al-Hāshimī, who is referred to as being still alive, died (Wüstenfeld, ii, 12; *Taʾrīkh Baghdād*, x, 451 f.; or, if the passages cited refer to different men, at the latest 279/892). He left a son, Abū Muḥammad ʿAbd Allāh, who is briefly noticed in al-Fāsī, *ʿIḳd*.

His work is referred to as *Akhbār Makka* or (in the Leiden ms.) *Taʾrīkh Makka*, but *Fihrist* 159 calls it *Kitāb Makka wa-akhbārihā fi 'l-Djāhiliyya wa 'l-Islām*. Its size was more than twice that of the earlier *History of Mecca* by al-Azraḳī [*q.v.*]. It shares with the latter the arrangement and, to a large degree, the material but must be considered an independent scholarly achievement. The *isnād*s prove that al-Fākihī collected his material on his own; certain historical statements and descriptions of architectural features and the like not introduced by *isnād*s agree literally with al-Azraḳī and, therefore, may have been taken over from his work without acknowledgement. The fact that al-Fākihī makes no mention of al-Azraḳī and even appears to suppress references to his family may have its reason in some personal enmity between him and the Azraḳīs and their circle, or the latter may have refused him permission to make use of the material in their possession; at any rate, it does not mean that al-Fākihī was out to conceal an alleged improper use of al-Azraḳī's work, which would, anyhow, have been impossible.

Bibliography: Wüstenfeld, *op. cit.*, i, xxiv-xxix; Brockelmann, I, 143. (F. ROSENTHAL)

FAḲĪR. The word *faḳīr* has four different connotations—etymological, Ḳurʾānic, mystical and popular. Etymologically it means (*a*) one whose backbone is broken (see Ḳurʾān, lxxvii, 25); (*b*) poor or destitute; (*c*) canal, aqueduct or mouth of a canal; (*d*) hollow dug for planting or watering palm-trees. When used in the sense of a pauper its plural form is *fuḳarāʾ*, but when used in the sense of an aqueduct, *fuḳur* is its plural form.

The word *faḳīr* (or *fuḳarāʾ*) occurs 12 times in the Ḳurʾān. It is sometimes used as opposed to *ghanī* (one who is self-sufficient and independent, see xxxv, 16) and is sometimes conjoined with the term *miskīn* to indicate two distinct types of needy persons (ix, 60). According to Imām al-Shāfiʿī, a *faḳīr* is one who neither owns anything nor engages himself in any avocation; a *miskīn*, on the contrary, is one who owns something though it is barely sufficient for his immediate needs. He cites in support of his view the parable of Khiḍr and Moses in which the sailor of a boat is called a *miskīn* (xviii, 79). Imām Abū Ḥanīfa held the other view. According to him a *faḳīr* is one who owns something while a *miskīn* is one who owns nothing. The supporters of this view say that the sailor in the parable was not the owner of the boat but had it on hire. Reconciling all these differences Ibn al-ʿArabī says that these terms are interchangeable and synonymous. According to some commentators the word *fuḳarāʾ* in ii, 273 refers to the *ahl al-ṣuffa* [*q.v.*] who lived in the mosque of the Prophet and devoted all their time to prayers and meditation.

In mystic terminology *faḳīr* means a person who 'lives for the Lord alone'. As Shiblī says: *Al-faḳīr man lā yastaghnī bi-shayʾin dūn Allāh* (a *faḳīr* does not rest content with anything except God.) Total rejection of private property (*ʿadam tamalluk*) and resignation to the will of God (*tawakkul*) were considered essential for a *faḳīr* who aspired for gnosis (*maʿrifa*).

In popular parlance the term *faḳīr* is used for a poor man, a pauper or a beggar. Its use in the English language dates from 1608; see *Oxford English Dictionary*, s.v. Fakir, and H. Yule and A. C. Burnell, *Hobson-Jobson*², London 1903, s.v. Fakeer.

Bibliography: Zamakhsharī, *Kitāb al-Fāʾiḳ*, Ḥaydarābād, ii, 143-4; *LA*, vi, 366: *TA*, iii, 473-5; Shams al-Dīn Aḥmad, *Iṣṭilāḥāt-i Ṣūfiyya*, Lucknow 1904, 32-3; ʿAbd al-Bāḳī, *Al-Minaḥ al-Madaniyya fī mukhtārāt al-Ṣūfiyya*, Madīna 1330, 37-8; ʿIzz al-Dīn Maḥmūd, *Miṣbāḥ al-hidāya wa miftāḥ al-kifāya*, ed. Djalāl al-Dīn Humāʾī, 1365, 375-9; Shihāb al-Dīn Suhrawardī, *ʿAwārif al-maʿārif*,

1292, 105-6; Ḳus̲h̲ayrī, *Risāla*, ʿUt̲h̲māniya Press 1304, 159-64; al-Hudjwīrī, *Kas̲h̲f al-Maḥdjūb*, tr. Nicholson, 19-29, 60; Turāb ʿAlī Ḳalandar, *Maṭālib-i Ras̲h̲īdī*, Nawal Kishore edn., 302.

(K. A. Nizami)

FAḲĪR MUḤAMMAD K̲H̲ĀN, an Urdu writer (Faḳīr is a *tak̲h̲alluṣ*, nom de plume). He is chiefly known as the author of a translation of the *Anwār-i Suhaylī* of Ḥusayn Wāʿiẓ Kās̲h̲ifī [*q.v.*], an adaptation in elaborate Persian prose of the stories from *Kalīla wa-Dimna* [*q.v.*]. The title of the Urdu translation by Faḳīr Muḥammad K̲h̲ān, for which he appears to have been helped by the celebrated Urdu poet Mīr Ḥasan (d. 1200/1786), is *Bustān-i ḥikmat* (Garden of wisdom). The first edition is a lithograph, Lucknow 1845. As a lyric poet, Faḳīr belongs to the Lucknow school and to the *silsila* (poetic school) of the famous Nāsik̲h̲ (d. 1254/1838).

Bibliography: Garcin de Tassy, *Hist. de la litt. Hindoue et Hindoustanie*[2], Paris 1870, i, 443.

(A. Bausani)

FAḲĪRĪ, Kalkandelenli, Turkish poet of the mid-10th/16th century. Very little is known about his life. From the scanty information provided by *tedhkire*-writers, we learn only that he was from Ḳalḳandelen (Tatova) near Üsküb (Skopje); of a modest family, cheerful and easy-going, he was unambitious and died young, while still a student.

Faḳīrī is the author of a *s̲h̲ehrengīz*, a *sāḳī-nāme* and a number of *g̲h̲azel*s scattered in *medjmūʿa*s and *naẓīre* collections, all of which are of rather mediocre quality. He owes his reputation to his original *Risāle-i taʿrīfāt* (Book of Definitions) written in 941/1534 in the tradition and style of *s̲h̲ehrengīz*. This is a collection of short descriptions (in 159 *faṣl*s) of various officials, artisans and types of the Ottoman Empire, and one of the rare examples of social satire in Turkish literature. In every "definition" of three couplets, the characteristics of the type are given in a concise, often colourful description, a vivid and informative parade of the famous and infamous.

After the customary introduction in praise of God, the Prophet and the first four Caliphs and homage to the reigning Sultan, Süleymān the Magnificent, Faḳīrī begins his definitions with the highest ranking official, the vizier, and proceeds to other ranks and classes. The vizier is "the aid of religion and the State, he is the orderer of the country". The *ḳāḍīʿasker*s are not liked by the *ḳāḍī*s as "they give life to some by distributing largesse and take the life of others", the *defterdār*s turn some people's business into gold, and dismiss and deceive others, the *bey*s and *ag̲h̲a*s "lead always a pleasant life, they stage stately *dīwān*s where notables foregather; some, by their justice, make the country prosperous, some, by their tyranny, destroy the world".

Further he describes in short but accurate terms the functions of the *solaḳ*, *silīḥdār*, *čāwūs̲h̲*, *ulaḳ*, *yeñičeri*, *mewālī*, etc., and passes critical judgment on members of various professions: *müderris* "the heirs to the science of the Prophet", the "insatiable" *muʿīd*, the "corrupt" *nāʾib*, etc. The joy of the *manṣūb* (the newly-appointed official) and the sorrow of the *maʿzūl* (the dismissed one), the pangs of expectation of the *mülāzim* (the probationary), the difference between the true devout *s̲h̲ayk̲h̲* and the hypocritical false one, the insincere preacher, *wāʿiẓ*, with an eye to profit are concisely portrayed. The parade continues with the *imām*, *müʾedhdhin*, *ḥāfiẓ*, *kātib*, the poet, the lover, the gentleman, the beauty, the lady's man, the rival, etc. The arts, crafts and professions are represented by the porter, physician, barber, acrobat, musician, dancer, merchant, tailor, town-crier, cobbler, saddler, butcher, blacksmith, etc. Then come characters: the hypocrite, intriguer, liar, idiot, etc. Further come definitions of some national types: Persian, Arab, Fellāḥ. Faḳīrī's uncomplimentary definition of "Turk" (faṣl 80) "with a fur on his shoulder and a *börk* on his head, ignorant of religion and sect" confirms the fact that in the period of the Empire this term meant "uneducated peasant, country boor" as opposed to the town-dwelling Ottomans (Rūmī), who are "refined and educated, but some think of themselves as writers, some as poets, yet when they gather to talk they do nothing but backbite one another".

Faḳīrī is strongly critical in his definition of *sipāhī*, *ʿazab*, *subas̲h̲i*, *ʿases*, *muḥtesib*, *ketk̲h̲udā*, *ʿummāl*, *mütewelli*, etc., and popular complaints about bribery, abuses, tyranny, cruelty, injustices of the times are reflected in these definitions. An edition of the *Risāle-i taʿrīfāt* is in preparation.

Bibliography: The *tedhkire*s of Laṭīfī, Ḳinalīzāde Ḥasan Čelebi, ʿĀs̲h̲iḳ Čelebi, Beyānī and the biographical section in ʿĀlī's *Künh al-Ak̲h̲bār*, s.v.; Köprülü-zāde Meḥmed Fuʾād, *Millī edebiyyāt djereyānînîn ilk mübes̲h̲s̲h̲irleri*, Istanbul 1928, 62-3; idem, *Onundju ʿaṣîr ḥayātîna ʿāʾid wet̲h̲īḳalar*, in *Ḥayāt*, i, 22-3; I. Ulçugür, *Fakiri ve Risale-i Tarifat'ı*, (unpublished thesis in Türkiyat Library no. 220): M. Izzet, *Şehrengizler* (unpublished thesis in Türkiyat Library no. 76). (Fahir İz)

FAʾL, *ṭīra* and *zadjr* are terms which merge into one another and together correspond to and express adequately the concept of "omen" and of οἰωνός. *Faʾl*, a term peculiar to Arabic and equivalent to the Hebrew *neḥas̲h̲īm* and the Syriac *neḥshē*, originally meant natural omen, cledonism. It appears in very varied forms, ranging from simple sneezing (al-Ibs̲h̲īhī, *Mustaṭraf*, trans. Rat, ii 182), certain peculiarities of persons and things that one encounters (al-Nuwayrī, *Nihāya*, 133 ff., trans. in *Arabica*, viii/1 (1961), 34-7), to the interpretation of the names of persons and things which present themselves spontaneously to the sight, hearing and mind of man. On this last point, the *sīra*, tradition (*ḥadīt̲h̲*) and Muslim chronicles give ample evidence depicting this tendency of the Arab mind to draw omens from all kinds of physical movement, all kinds of chance happenings, from all kinds of words heard and all attitudes observed. "After all, the whole of good manners has grown out of *faʾl*" (Doutté, *Magie et religion*, 364). To this must be added the predominant rôle among all Semites, and the Arabs in particular, of euphemism and antiphrasis (see *infra*).

This tendency of the Arab mind reveals itself clearly in the conduct, practice and recommendations of the Prophet. The *sīra* is full of incidents where the Prophet "drew omens from the names of the regions and tribes through which he travelled on his raids" (Ibn His̲h̲ām, 434). Furthermore, he made a considerable number of changes in proper names, with the double design of effacing all traces of Arab paganism from Muslim terminology (cf. Wellhausen, *Reste*[2], 8 f.), and even more of removing from any shocking or unsuitable names of followers which he must hear around him, all baleful influences which might emanate from their meanings. It was for this reason that he changed Ḳalīl into Kat̲h̲īr, ʿĀṣī into Muṭīʿ (Ibn al-At̲h̲īr, *Usd*, iv, 232); and thus also that he gave the future Medina the name of Ṭayyiba in place of Yat̲h̲rib, whose root contained the idea of "calumny" (*Marāṣid al-iṭṭilāʿ*, ed. Juynboll, i, 2). He changed the name of Zayd al-Khayl into Zayd al-Khayr (*Aghānī*[1], xvii, 49). "In the Djāhiliyya, Sulaymān b. Ṣurad was called Yasār (as a euphemism for 'left'); the Prophet called him Sulaymān" (Ibn al-Athīr, *Usd*, ii, 351); "Sahl used to be called Ḥazn but the Prophet renamed him Sahl" (*ibid.* 380; cf. Ibn ʿAbd Rabbih, *ʿIḳd*, i, 226), and so on (cf. *ibid.* ii, 301; al-Bakrī, *Muʿdjam*, ed. Wüstenfeld, 313, 559; Goldziher, in *ZDMG*, li (1897), 256 ff.). "Für Muḥammad wurde ja jedes Nomen, besonders aber jedes Nomen proprium, zum omen" (Fischer in *ZDMG*, lxi (1907), 753, cf. 427). The Prophet was imitated in this respect by his Companions, especially ʿUmar b. al-Khaṭṭāb (cf. Ibn Ḳutayba, *ʿUyūn*, ed. Brockelmann, ii, 148 f.; Ibn ʿAbd Rabbih, *ʿIḳd*, i, 225; al-Ṭabarī, xv, 2609, etc.). On the other hand, omens were not only drawn from the individual's name but also from his appearance. The Prophet wrote to his officials: "When you send me a courier, see that he has a beautiful name and a handsome face" (Ibn Ḳutayba, *l.c.*; Ibn ʿAbd Rabbih, *l.c.*; cf. *Aghānī*[1], ii, 20; xviii, 35). In North Africa, even a man's social position could become a factor from which omens could be drawn; thus to encounter a *sharīf* was a matter of happy omen, while to meet a Jew or a blacksmith was unlucky (Doutté, *op. cit.*, 361). A whole family might be considered as having a baleful influence (cf. the family of Baṣbaṣ, who gave bad advice to the Taghlib, *Ḥamāsa*, 254, l. 5, in Freytag, *Einleitung*, 162). Certain individuals are referred to as *mashʾūm* (cf. al-Djāḥiẓ, *Ḥayawān*, vii, 150 f.); their company augured ill.

Because of this, choice of names was important to parents for their children and to masters for their slaves. With regard to this, the Arabs followed a definite ruling. "Someone asked a Bedouin: 'Why do you give your children the worst of names such as Kalb and Dhiʾb, and to your slaves the best such as Marzūḳ and Rabāḥ?' He replied: 'It is because the names of our children are destined for our enemies, and those of our slaves for ourselves'. He meant to say that the children are a shield against the enemy and arrows in their bosoms; it is for this reason that they give them this kind of name" (al-Diyārbakrī, *Khamīs*, ii, 153; cf. Ibn Durayd, *Ishtiḳāḳ*, ed. Wüstenfeld, 4 f.; Ibn al-Athīr, v, 247; cf. al-Djāḥiẓ, *Ḥayawān*, vi, 65 and i, 158 f., where the author sets out the various motives underlying the choice of names among Arabs).

This process of interpretation was expanded from personal names to the names of precious stones, of fruits and flowers, and even to the words of songs. Thus gold (*dhahab*) means 'departure', onyx (*djazʿ*) sadness and melancholy (al-Tīfāshī, in Reinaud, *Monumens*, i, 14); a lemon (*utrudj*) presages hypocrisy because of the fact that the exterior of the fruit does not resemble the interior (al-Djāḥiẓ, *Ḥayawān*, iii, 142; Ibn ʿAbd Rabbih, *ʿIḳd*, i, 226); the quince (*safardjal*) signifies a journey because its name contains the word *safar* (Ibn ʿAbd Rabbih, *loc. cit.*; cf. *ZDMG*, lxvii (1913), 273 ff., and lxviii (1914), 275 ff.). Lilac (*sūsan*) brings misfortune because its name contains the word *sūʾ* (Ibn ʿAbd Rabbih, *loc. cit.*), and misfortune which will last for a year because its name is made up of *sūʾ* and *sana* (cf. Flügel, *Loosbücher*, 27); basil (*rīḥān*) is at the same time of good and evil omen because on the one hand its name includes the word *rūḥ*, and on the other hand it has a bitter taste, even though it pleases the eye and the nose (al-Djāḥiẓ, *Ḥayawān*, iii, 142). As for the evil presentiments aroused by the contents of a phrase or a song, there are many examples of these in the Arab chronicles (cf. al-Djāḥiẓ, *loc. cit.*, 139; al-Masʿūdī, *Murūdj*, iv, 426 ff.; vii, 269 ff.; al-Ibshīhī, ii, 154). These facts are generally classified under the name of *ṭīra*.

According to Ḥādjdjī Khalīfa, *Kashf*, ed. Flügel, iv, 646 f., *faʾl* is an approval of a man's intentions and thence an encouragement to his carrying them out, while *ṭīra* (or *ṭayara* or *ṭūra*, cf. *Ḳāmūs*, i, 93) is a disapproval and in consequence an obstruction, a postponement until later. This opposition which in the end established itself between two concepts which were originally complementary, seems to have developed from the attitude which Tradition ascribed to the Prophet concerning this predominant variety of *faʾl*. *Ṭīra* (ὄρνις) is in effect a technique whose origin is pastoral and nomadic; Arabia was therefore a very propitious region for its development, as Cicero had already commented: "Arabes (et Phryges et Cilices), quod pastu pecudum maxime utuntur, campos et montes hieme et aestate peragrantes, propterea facilius cantus avium et volatus notaverunt" (*De divinatione*, i, 41; cf. i, 1 and ii, 93-5). Its technical character made it the prerogative of a privileged class of men, which in an organized and developed society enjoyed the status of priesthood. In the short-lived and nomadic civilizations of Bedouin Arabia, the existence of a priestly class which specialized in the interpretation of the flight and cries of birds was as yet hardly perceptible (see KIHĀNA: *ʿāʾif, ḥāzī, zādjir*). It is only by means of comparison between the brief and obscure data of Islamic literature and those of Semitic antiquity, that it is possible to affirm the religious character of *ṭīra* as it was practised in the Djāhiliyya.

It is from this, it would seem, that the hostility displayed by the Prophet towards *ṭīra* arose, even while he was practising and recommending *faʾl*. This also explains the baleful character which was assigned to it later. In fact, certain examples demonstrate that *ṭīra* could be a good omen. "ʿUbayd Allāh b. Ziyād painted a dog, a ram and a lion in the entrance-hall of his house. He said of them: 'a barking dog, a fighting ram and an angry lion'. He drew a good omen (*fataṭayyara*) from these and this was repeated after him" (*Ḥayawān*, i, 158). And from the same author (*ibid.* 159): "When 'ass', 'dog', 'bull' were names borne by honourable men, the Arabs did not hesitate after this to use them, seeing a good omen in them (*taṭayyur*[an])". One *ḥadīth* even seems to give *ṭīra* a wider meaning, including *faʾl* itself which is regarded as that part of it which comes true: "*asdaḳ*[u] *'l-ṭīrat*[i] *al-faʾl*[u]" (Ibn Ḳutayba, *ʿUyūn*, ii, 146). Another *ḥadīth* includes the subject-matter of *ṭīra* in *faʾl*: "There is nothing in the *hām* (the owl regarded as the spirit of a dead man), but the evil eye is true and birds give true omens (*wa-aṣdaḳa 'l-ṭayr*[u] *al-faʾl*[a])" (Ibn al-Athīr, *Usd*, i, 314 and ii, 78). In the same way, there are examples which give *faʾl* the meaning of evil omen (cf. al-Nuwayrī, *Nihāya*, iii, 138; Ibn Durayd, *Ishtiḳāḳ*, 4).

This confusion reveals the existence of a primitive foundation which was not entirely submerged by the powerful wave of puritanism which swept over Arabia in the first two centuries of the Hidjra.

It appears from all this that *ṭīra*, which was originally no more than the observation and interpretation of the flight, cries and perching activities of certain birds used in divination, became the equivalent of the *male ominari* of the Latins and the βλασφημεῖν and δυσφημεῖν of the Greeks.

From this was derived a whole literature, essentially of poetry and proverbs, created to dissuade man from following the ideas inspired in him by *ṭīra*, and to which all men are subject. The Prophet is reported to have said: "There are three dangers which no-one escapes: *ṭīra*, suspicion and jealousy". When asked what remedy there is for this, he replied: "If (on your way) you think you have seen an evil omen (*taṭayyarta*), do not turn back; if you suspect, do not execute; if you are envious, do not commit an injustice" (Ibn Ḳutayba, *ʿUyūn*, ii, 8; Ibn ʿAbd Rabbih, *ʿIḳd*, i, 226). Quotations from poetry on this subject are very numerous (cf. especially al-Buhturī, *Ḥamāsa*, ed. Cheikho, nos. 599, 860-7, 1132; al-Bayhaḳī, *Maḥāsin*, 368 and Ps.-Djāḥiẓ, *Maḥāsin*, 68 f.; al-Djāḥiẓ, *Ḥayawān*, iii, 138, 139, 160; Ibn Ḳutayba, *ʿUyūn*, ed. Cairo, ii, 145 f.).

It is worth remarking that when it means presaging evil, *ṭīra* does not strictly apply only to *signa ex avibus* but also to all other kinds of evil omen (cf. Ibn Ḳutayba, *ʿUyūn*, ii, 147; al-Djāḥiẓ, *Ḥayawān*, iii, 140; al-Masʿūdī, *Murūdj*, vi, 426 ff., 433 f., vii, 269 ff.; *Aghānī*, i, 184; al-Ṭabarī, i/3, 1089; etc.).

But the primitive meaning of *ṭīra* seems to be better preserved in *zadjr*, which is often used as its equivalent, although originally this term designated a technique belonging to *ṭīra*. Indeed, if *ṭīra* is the observation and interpretation of the spontaneous flight and cries of birds, *zadjr* consists on the contrary of the deliberate instigation of these flights and cries; it belongs to the category of *auspicia impetrita*, in contrast to *auspicia oblativa*. Apart from the meaning of *zadjara* (to arouse, chase someone with cries, make fly, draw omens, practise divination), Arab tradition still preserves some accounts of the existence of this practice (cf. *Arabica*, viii/1 (1961), 50 f.).

But in the same way as *faʾl* and *ṭīra*, *zadjr* soon began to lose its primitive meaning and specific character and came to stand for evil omen or divination in general. Indeed sometimes there is a kind of *zadjr* which is confused with *kihāna* (cf. al-Nuwayrī, *Nihāya*, iii, 135-9). This leads us to believe that *zadjr* was, as in Assyria and Babylonia, the prerogative of the soothsayer who, especially in Arabia, combined various functions and acted as a guardian of institutions in a nomadic society which lacked the focal points necessary to fix and safeguard them.

Thus in a passage from Ps.-Djāḥiẓ, Arab *zadjr* includes the interpretation of the cooing of doves, the cries of birds, the sudden appearance of an animal crossing from right to left or from left to right, the rustling of leaves, the sigh of the wind and other similar portents (*ʿIrāfa*, ed. Inostrantseff, 23).

Zadjr is also referred to a *ʿiyāfa* [*q.v.*] which applies to various procedures of divination. As for the birds whose flight and cries form the object of *faʾl*, *ṭīra* and *zadjr*, they are of many kinds, but the bird of divination most regarded by the Arabs is the crow (Corvus capensis Lichtenst., Corvus umbrinus Rüppell, and perhaps also Corvus agricola Tristram which exists in Palestine). Nevertheless, these three procedures do not limit themselves to birds, for any animal is capable of furnishing an omen (on the crow and other birds, animals and insects of divination, cf. *Arabica*, viii/1 (1961), 30-58).

The direction of a bird's flight, or an animal's steps, plays a very important part in the application of the three procedures. Technical terms designate the various directions: *sāniḥ* (that which travels from right to left), *bāriḥ* (that which travels from left to right), *djābih* (that which comes from in front), *ḳaʿīd* or *khafīf* (that which comes from behind). As a general rule, the left is of evil omen (al-Tibrīzī, in Abū Tammām, *Ḥamāsa*, ed. Freytag, i, 165), therefore "*al-sāniḥ* is desired by the Arabs and *al-bāriḥ* is dreaded" (al-Masʿūdī, *Murūdj*, iii, 340). Thus it is by way of euphemism that Arabs call the left side *al-yasār* and the left hand *al-yusrā* (comp. the Greek εὐώνυμος), whereas in fact they signify "difficulty" to them, whence comes the name of *al-ʿusrā*, also used for the left hand (cf. al-Djaḥiẓ, *Ḥayawān*, v, 150).

In other respects too, euphemism and antiphrasis play an important part in *faʾl*. "The desire to hear from the mouth of others a word of happy omen, the fear of hearing some unlucky expression, is moreover found in Islam in all ages and all countries" (W. Marçais, *Euphémisme*, 431). A whole vocabulary has been created in order to avoid certain expressions whose meanings suggest evil omens. Hence the blind is called "seeing", *baṣīr* (cf. other euphemisms for blind and ref. in Fischer, in *ZDMG*, lxi (1907), 425 sqq.), smallpox is described as "blessed", *mubārak*, as also are syphilis, plague and insanity (cf. Greek ἱέρα, the Italian *il benedetto*). It is because of *ṭīra*, al-Djāḥiẓ tells us (*Ḥayawān*, iii, 136), that the Arabs call someone who has been bitten by a snake "safe and sound" (*salīm*), call the desert the "refuge" (*mafāza*); it is for the same reason that they name the blind, for *kunya*, Abū Baṣīr and the negro Abu 'l-Bayḍāʾ (white). Such examples are innumerable (cf. W. Marçais and Fischer, *op. cit.*, Wellhausen, *Reste*², 200 ff.).

For astrological *faʾl*, see NUDJŪM, and for the *faʾl* by drawing lots, see ḲURʿA. For books of divination, see FĀL-NĀMA.

Bibliography: Ibn Ḳutayba, *ʿUyūn al-akhbār*, Cairo, ii, 144-151; Djāḥiẓ, *Ḥayawān*, *passim*; Masʿūdī, *Murūdj*, iii, 334 f.; Nuwayrī, *Nihāyat al-arab*, Cairo, iii, 134 ff.; Ibshīhī, *Mustaṭraf*, tr. Rat, 177 ff.; Ḥādjdjī Khalīfa, iv, 646 f., 174; G. Flügel, *Die Loosbücher der Muhammadaner*, in *B(K)SGW*, phil.-hist. Kl. XII-XIII, 1860-1, 24-74; E. Doutté, *Magie et religion*, 363 ff.; W. Marçais, *L'euphémisme et l'antiphrase dans les dialectes arabes d'Algérie*, in *Or. St. Th. Nöldeke*, i, 425-38; A. Fischer, *Arab. baṣīr 'scharfsichtig' per antiphrasim = 'blind'*, in *ZDMG*, lxi (1907), 425-34; cf. *ibid.*, 751-3 and 849; cf. also lxii (1908), 151-4, 568, 789; J. Wellhausen, *Reste*², 200 ff.; T. Fahd, *Les présages par le corbeau*, in *Arabica*, viii/1 (1961), 30-58. (T. FAHD)

FĀL-NĀMA, book of divination. In the Muslim East (especially in Iranian and Turkish countries), in order to know if not the future, at least the signs or circumstances that are auspicious for some decision, recourse is still sometimes made to certain procedures (cf. Massé, *Croyances*, ch. XI: divination), among others to two kinds of books: 1. collections of poems (*dīwān* of Ḥāfiẓ); 2. special works (*fāl-nāma*). Consulting the *dīwān*, an act within the reach of everyone, consists in opening the book at random and interpreting the text which first strikes the eye (for details, see Massé, *op. cit.*, 244-5; and in particular E. G. Browne, iii, 315-9; also Binning, i, 220). As for the *fāl-nāma*, some are tables of divination, used in the manner of the above-named *dīwān* (cf. the *sortes Virgilianae*; and for the *dīwān* of Ḥāfiẓ, the description of this table in Browne, iii, 312-5); others are booklets containing quadrangular or circular tables (*dāʾira*), preceded by an explanatory text, in which the divisions of the page (*burdj*) contain letters and words arranged in eastern *abdjad* [*q.v.*] order. The *fāl-nāma* which has always been the most authoritative (taking precedence even over the one attributed to ʿAlī) is that of Djaʿfar which is attributed to the imām Djaʿfar al-Ṣādiḳ ([*q.v.*], see also DJAFR) (cf. D. M. Donaldson, *The Shiʾite religion*, ch. XII). The essence of this booklet is as follows (according to the manuscript in the B.N., Paris, Suppl. persan, no. 77): "*Fāl-nāma* of his holiness the imām Djaʿfar Ṣādiḳ. If anyone wishes to consult the omens, he must make his ablutions, recite the *fātiḥa* once, the sūra of the *Ikhlāṣ* three times, the Ḳuʾrānic Throne verse once, and then place his finger inside the table ..." (fol. 40), while keeping his eyes closed, on one of the page divisions containing the letters (for example, the letter *nūn*); each division of the second table contains one of these letters accompanied by a word (*e.g.*, *nūn* — *al-kayl*); then follows a list of these words, each incorporated in a phrase linking it to a sign of the zodiac (*e.g.*, "*Al-kayl*: your *fāl* is fortunate; but refer to the Ram (*ḥamal*) which will elucidate it", etc.); next comes a list of these signs with reference to the planets (*e.g.*, "Sun: good tidings, O ye who seek *fāl*! God has opened the gates of his clemency for you; He will give you your daily bread, multiply your powers, watch over your concerns; your children shall repay you; it will be propitious for you to build, to buy horses and arms, to marry and to travel; in the event of a parent or friend being absent, imprisoned or ill, you must be patient and perform your almsgiving; then God will certainly provide"; these replies, which are all of the same order, justify the Persian proverb "It is the *fāl* of the imām Djaʿfar which cannot do harm" (Dehkhodā, *Amthāl u-ḥikam*, s.v. *Fāl*, and the following proverbs). Sometimes the first table of the *fāl-nāma* is composed not of letters of the alphabet but of figures; in this case the procedure is as follows (beginning of the *Fāl-nāma* manuscript in the B.N., Paris, Suppl. persan 1872, fol. 62 v°): "Hear ye, this is the *fāl-nāma* which his holiness Djaʿfar Ṣādiḳ has learnt from the august divine Word. Whoever has a transaction, dispute or a certain desire and wishes to know what is good, what is evil and what the outcome, must stand face to face with a partner who must act exactly as he does, and place his hand under his arm; then, bringing out their hands, both must show what number of fingers each has chosen; the man concerned must add up the total, and then consult whichever page division contains this number; he must read the sacred verse of the Ḳuʾrān inscribed in the circular table of the *fāl-nāma*; having thus recognized the good and evil features of his plan, let him not deviate from it" (after which he will proceed as above). Another *fāl-nāma*, less well-known and more literary, the versified answers of which are often of a disturbing precision, is that of Shaykh Bahāʾī (d. 1030/1621; see AL-ʿĀMILĪ); it is composed of 48 tables (12 lines each containing 18 letters selected for their numerical values); at the head of the table is the question set (*e.g.*, "Is this news true or false?"; "what will happen to our invalid?"; etc.), paraphrased in two lines of verse; a letter is selected at random; the letters are counted in sixes from the chosen letter; on reaching the foot of the table the six is made up by adding letters from the first line of the table, then continuing in sixes to the chosen letter; two lists of letters are drawn up (one of even letters, the other of odd) starting with those of the first line of the table; thus one obtains the two hemistichs of a verse whose sense then has to be interpreted (example of a precise answer: "Will this association be favourable for me?—This bond will bring you troubles; flee it as one flees an arrow" (table 27).

In addition to these methods, Chardin and other travellers (cf. Massé, *op. cit.*, 247) noted three others based on dice (this practice has not entirely disappeared): in these cases, recourse is made to a specialist known as *fāl-bīn* or *fāl-gīr* (augur) who shakes and then throws the dice (in Persian, *raml*, divination by dice, practised by the *rammāl*; Arabic words distorted from their original meaning); this *raml* is related to the *sortes* of classical antiquity (cf. Fontenelle, *Histoire des oracles*, ch. XVIII).

The *fāl-nāma* of Djaʿfar was translated into Turkish; also there exists in this language (and in Persian) a series of minor works dealing with divination by the lines of the hand, coffee-grounds, beans and chick-peas, stars, molten lead, omoplatoscopy, omens drawn from the quivering of parts of the body, bruises and wounds.

Bibliography: H. Massé, *Croyances et coutumes persanes*, Paris 1938; D. M. Donaldson, *The wild rue*, 196; Binning, *A journal of two years of travel in Persia*, London 1857; E. Blochet, *Catalogue des manuscrits persans de la Bibliothèque Nationale de Paris* (index: *fa'l-nāma*, in particular no. 909 in verse); idem, *Catalogue des manuscrits turcs de la Bibliothèque Nationale de Paris* (index: *fa'l-nāmè*, in particular no. 809 "*fāl li Muhiy al-dīn al-ʿArabi*"); *Fal-namah, a table of the alphabet for divination, professedly from works of Nasir ul-Din Tusi*, in *Khvab namah, a tract on dream interpretation*, lith. Lahore 1870 and 1882; Dehkhodā, *Kitāb-i amthāl u-ḥikam*, Tehran 1310/1932, s.v. *fāl*; *Fāl-nāma-yi Djaʿfarī* (Turkish tr., lith. Istanbul 1270/1854); Ismail Hikmet Ertaylan, *Falname*, Istanbul 1951 (University Publications, 3rd series, no. 4); Tashköprüzāde, *Mawḍūʿāt al-ʿulūm*, Istanbul 1211, 378; Kātib Čelebi, *Kashf al-ẓunūn*, Istanbul 1311, i, 133; A. von Gabain, *Alttürkische Grammatik*, Leipzig 1950, 262-6; Abdülkadir Inan, *Tarihte ve bugün şamanizm*, Ankara 1954, 151-9.

(H. MASSÉ)

FALAK, Sphere, in particular the Celestial Sphere.

a. Etymology and semantic evolution. The word *falak* (pl. *aflāk*) occurs already in the *Ḳurʾān* with the specific significance "celestial sphere" (xxi, 34 "it is He who has created night and day, the Sun and the Moon, each of which moves in its own sphere"; similarly xxxvi, 40). Etymologically and semantically it has a long history: it can be traced back to Sumerian origins, where the stem *bala* ($\gtrless$ **pilak*) already has the meaning "to be round" or also "to turn around". In Akk. it appears as *pilakku*, which denotes the whorl of the spindle as well as the double-edged axe (to be distinguished from the single-edged axe, Akk. *pāšu*, *paštu* > Syr. *pustā*, Aram. *passā* > probably Ar. *faʾs*; cf. H. Zimmern, *Akkadische Fremdwörter als Beweis für babylonischen Kultureinfluss*, Leipzig 1914, 12). The double significance is readily explained by the resemblance of the whorl with the head of the double-axe, both being round and pierced so as to be mounted on the spindle, or else on the handle. The Akk. word is found again in Syr. *pelkā*, "(double-) axe" and, with its other meaning, in Heb. פֶּלֶךְ, "spindle". The original Sumero-Akk. form is best preserved in the Talmudic פילכה, "whorl" (also "spindle") used apparently indiscriminately with פלך and פלכה = Ar. *falaka*, of which the abstract technical term *falak*, "(celestial) sphere" is of course a later derivative. The question may be left open whether also Ar. *falaḳa* and *faladja*, which have both the meaning "to cleave", are derived from the same stem.

On the other hand, the occurrence of the stem **pl-ek* (≷ **pl-et*, cf. E. Boisacq, *Dictionnaire étymologique de la langue grecque*[2], Heidelberg and Paris, 1923, 793, s.v. πλέκω) in a great many (Eastern and Western) Indo-European languages, in all cases with the meaning "to plait", "to pleat", "to coil", "to twist", "to fold", etc., strongly supports the assumption of a common origin of the Sumero-Akk. and the Indo-Europ. words, but seems to exclude (with the exception of Gr. πέλεκυς and Skr. *paraçú-ḥ*, see below) the possibility of a direct loan. Thus we have the various genuine Greek words for (hair-) curl, coil and similar round objects: πλεκτή, πλεκτάνη, πλόκος, πλόκαμος, πλέγμα etc., while the representative of the second significance: πέλεκυς, "double-axe", alone clearly betrays its Akk. origin. (Against this, cf. Walther Wüst, *Idg. *pᶜéʾleḳu—"Axt, Beil". Eine paläographische Studie*, in *Suomalaisen Tiedeakatemian Toimituksia*, Helsinki 1956).

In Greek texts dealing with astronomical subjects, derivatives of πλέκω are not too common, though they do occur occasionally, *e.g.*, *Timaeus* 36 D: ἡ δὲ [ψυχὴ] ἐκ μέσου πρὸς τὸν ἔσχατον οὐρανὸν πάντῃ διαπλακεῖσα κύκλῳ τε αὐτὸν ἔξωθεν περικαλύψουσα, αὐτὴ ἐν αὑτῇ στρεφομένη, though here the idea of roundness inheres in the word στρεφομένη rather than in διαπλακεῖσα ("twisted" or "plaited through"). In the *Myth of Er*, however, (*Republic* X, 616 B-617 D), which adumbrates the later elaborate theory of material spheres revolving inside one another, the word used for the (hollow) whorls, σφόνδυλος (= σπόνδυλος, "vertebra") is of course not derived from the stem **pl-ek*, but clearly betrays its kinship with mod. Engl. "spindle", "to spin", etc. Its original meaning, though, is the same: the whorl as the "spinning object" giving momentum to the turning axis (now called "spindle") is evidently primary, and the application of the term to human and animal anatomy, secondary. A glance at the two first cervical vertebrae (σπόνδυλοι) of larger mammals suffices to show that they are the ideal prototype of the pierced whorl. Lat. *vertebra*, Engl. *whorl* (or *whirl*), Ger. *Wirtel* and *Wirbel*, all stress the idea of turning or whirling round (*vertere*, *wirbeln*, etc.); conversely, the Arabic word for the vertebra, *fiḳra*, emphasizes the other characteristic of the object, viz., its being pierced (*mafḳūr* or *mufaḳḳar*).

The Gr. word σφαῖρα, finally, which later (Eudoxus, Aristotle, Ptolemy, etc.) became the generally accepted technical term, equally reflects the idea of "turning round", since it is obviously akin to σπεῖρα (*σπερ-ḭα), "coiling", "spiral". It is this word which we find generally rendered by the Ar. *falak*.

b. Definitions. *falak* thus corresponds with Gr. σφαῖρα and Lat. *sphaera* or *orbis*, while *dāʾira* can be equated with Gr. κύκλος and Lat. *circulus*. Authors writing in any one of the three languages, however, seldom aim at a perfect consistency in the use of these terms. According to al-Bīrūnī (*Al-Ḳānūn al-Masᶜūdī*, i, Hyderabad-Dn. 1954, 54-5), "*dāʾira* and *falak* are two terms that denote the same thing and are interchangeable; but sometimes *falak* refers to the globe (*kura*), in particular when it is moveable (*mutaḥarrik*); *falak*, thus, does not apply to the motionless [globe]; and it is called "*falak*" only on account of its similarity with the whorl of the rotating spindle (*ᶜalā wadjh al-tashbīh bi-falakat al-mighzal al-dāʾir*)". According to Ibn al-Haytham's *Fī hayʾat al-ᶜālam* (Ms. Kastamonu no. 2298, fol. 6r 11 ff.), the term *falak* "applies to any round quantity of a globular body or surface or of the surface (area) or the circumference of a circle; the body surrounding the world, which turns about the centre (viz., of the Earth), is called in particular *falak*, and this *falak* is divided into many parts, but first and foremost into seven parts, which are spherical bodies (*i.e.*, shells) contiguous with one another in such a way that each one of them surrounds the next one, the concave surface of the surrounding [spherical shell] touching the convex surface of the one surrounded by it. The centre of all of these spheres is the centre of the world, and each one of them individually is also called *falak*".

Of the manifold applications of the term *falak* in Arabic astronomical literature, the following may be mentioned with their Greek and Latin equivalents (cf. C. A. Nallino in *Al-Battānī Op. Astr.*, ii, Milan 1907, 348): *f. al-burūdj* = *minṭaḳat al-b.*, ὁ λοξὸς κύκλος, ὁ διὰ μέσων τῶν ζωδίων κύκλος, *ecliptica*; *f. al-tadwīr* (pl. *aflāk al-tadāwīr*) = ἐπίκυκλος, *epicyclus*; *al-f. al-ḥāmil* (pl. *al-ḥawāmil*) = ὁ φέρων τὸν ἐπίκυκλον ἔκκεντρος, *deferens* (= "*levador*" = mod. Span. *llevador* in the Alphonsine *Libros del Saber*); *al-f. al-khāridj al-markaz* = *f. al-awdj* = ἔκκεντρος, *excentricus*; *al-f. al-māʾil* = ὁ λοξὸς κύκλος (τῆς σελήνης), ὁ ἐγκεκλιμένος (τῶν πλανωμένων), *circulus obliquus* (or *deflectens*); *al-f. al-mumaththal li-f. al-burūdj* = ὁ ὁμόκεντρος τῷ ζωδιακῷ κύκλος, *circulus pareclipticus*; moreover, in spherical astronomy: *f. muᶜaddil al-nahār* = ὁ ἰσημερινός, *circulus aequinoctialis* (the *celestial* equator, not the *terrestrial*, which is called *khaṭṭ al-istiwāʾ*); *al-aflāk al-māʾila ᶜan f. muᶜaddil al-nahār* = οἱ παράλληλοι (the circles parallel to the equator); *al-f. al-mustaḳīm* = ἡ ὀρθὴ σφαῖρα, *sphaera recta* (the celestial sphere as appearing to the inhabitants of the equatorial region, where the celestial equator passes through the zenith).

c. History. There can hardly be a doubt that the conception of a universe consisting of concentric spheres, in which the celestial bodies are carried around at various distances from the Earth, is very old. The earliest document susceptible of such an interpretation is a tablet in the Hilprecht Collection at Jena dating from the Cassite period, but copied probably from a much older original (1st Babylonian Dynasty), see F. Thureau-Dangin, *La tablette astronomique de Nippur*, in *Revue d'Ass.*, xxviii, 85-8. According to O. Neugebauer, *The exact sciences in antiquity*[2], Copenhagen 1957, 100, "This text and a few similar fragments seem to indicate something like a universe of 8 different spheres, beginning with the sphere of the moon. This model obviously belongs to a rather early stage of development of which no traces have been found preserved in the later mathematical astronomy, which seems to operate without any underlying physical model. It must be emphasized, however, that the interpretation of this Nippur text and its parallels is far from secure".

While later Babylonian (Seleucid) astronomy thus no longer shows any trace of such a conception, it reappears, in Greece, in the astronomical and cosmological speculations of Plato (*Myth of Er*, see above, and *Tim.* 36 C-D) and of the late Pythagoreans (Philolaos). The former of these two "models" (the Platonic "whorls") leaves out of account the planets' standstills and retrogradations; the latter, which places the hypothetical "central fire" in the centre of circular motion, is capable of explaining them at least in part, owing to the fact that the Earth, too, is regarded as a planet revolving about the central fire. The first elaborate geometrical model, operating, for each one of the planets, with a set of homocentric (geocentric) spheres revolving about different poles inside one another, was devised by Eudoxus. His model, improved by Callippus, was wrought into a comprehensive (physical) system by Aristotle (*Methaph.* 8, 1073 b 38-1074 a 17), whose aim was to represent and to explain the celestial motions as a whole, from the fixed stars down to the Moon, by the combination of acting and reacting ("unrolling") spheres. This physical model, because of its incapability to account for the varying brilliancy of the planets (above all Venus and Mars, see Simplicius, *Comm. on De caelo*, ed. Heiberg (Berlin, 1894), 504) was later replaced by a new purely geometrical model, based mainly on two theorems of Apollonius (ca. 200 B.C.), in which an eccentric deferent carries around the centre of an epicycle in the circumference of which the planet revolves. This device, which is the governing principle of planetary motion in Ptolemy's *Almagest*, takes into account only the planes (inclined to one another as well as to the ecliptic) of the deferent and of the epicycle, expressly renouncing any attempt at a physical interpretation. In the *Hypotheses*, however, composed after the completion of the *Almagest*, Ptolemy interprets the circles mentioned as sections through solid globes or spherical shells contiguous with one another in such a way that the outer limit of one planetary sphere coincides, without leaving any void, with the inner limit of the next one, counting from the Earth outwards (see *Hypotheses*, Book II, 6, in *Cl. Ptolemaei Opera* II, *Opera astron. minora*, ed. Heiberg, Leipzig 1907; the text of Book II, preserved only in Arabic, is not complete and contains errors). In II, 4, Ptolemy states that it is not necessary to assume *complete* spheres since it suffices (in accordance with the Creator's principle of economy) to postulate, for each one of the planets, the existence of "sawn pieces" or "disks" (Ar. *manshūrāt*, prob. = Gr. πρίσματα) comprised between two circles parallel to and equidistant from the equator of a sphere, in which the whole complicated mechanism of planetary motion is contained. For this reason, Ptolemy's *Hypotheses*, otherwise called *K. al-Iḳtiṣāṣ*, are often quoted by Islamic authors under the title *K. al-Manshūrāt* (see W. Hartner, *Mediaeval views on cosmic dimensions and Ptolemy's Kitāb al-Manshūrāt*, in *Mélanges Alexandre Koyré*, Paris, to appear in 1963 or 1964).

It is, however, the complete, contiguous, spheres, not the spherical prisms (*manshūrāt*) that prevail in Islamic astronomy, starting at the latest by the time of, and with, al-Farghānī (fl. ca. 830 A.D.), whose *Elements of Astrology* were among the first works translated into Latin and served to transmit the late Greek and Islamic views on the structure and the dimensions of the universe to the Latin Middle Ages (Dante, Regiomontanus, etc.). It was not before the end of the 16th century that Tycho Brahe, on the basis of new observations, demonstrated the untenability of the system of contiguous solid spheres (see W. Hartner, *Tycho Brahe et Albumasar*, in *La science au seizième siècle*, Paris 1960, 135-67).

Bibliography (apart from the references given above): K. Kohl, *Über den Aufbau der Welt nach Ibn al Haitam*, in *Sitzungsberichte d. Physik. Med. Sozietät in Erlangen*, liv-lv (1922-3), Erlangen 1925, 140-79; W. Hartner, *The Mercury Horoscope of Marcantonio Michiel of Venice*, in *Vistas in Astronomy* (ed. A. Beer), i, 86-138, see in particular

Part II, 105 ff.; Abū Yaḥyā Zakariyyā al-Ḳazwīnī, *ʿAd̲j̲āʾib al-mak̲h̲lūḳāt wa-g̲h̲arāʾib al-mawd̲j̲ūdāt*, Ar. text ed. F. Wüstenfeld (2 vols., Göttingen, 1848/9, see in particular Vol. I), Vol I, transl. into German by H. Ethé: *Die Wunder der Schöpfung*, Leipzig 1868; G. Rudloff and A. Hochheim, *Die Astronomie des G̲agmînî*, in *ZDMG*, xlvii (1893), 213-75. (W. HARTNER)

FALAḲA (Ar.), Turkish: *falaka, falāka, falaḳ*; Persian: *falaka, falaḳ*; Byzantine Greek: φάλαγγας; Moroccan: *ḳarma, arma.*

One of the favourite punishments of the masters in the Ḳurʾānic schools (see KUTTĀB) was to give the pupil a bastinado on the soles of the feet, more or less severe according to the offence. (There exist detailed scales; see Ibn Saḥnūn, *op. cit. infra*). One or more assistants (*ʿarīf*) immobilized the victim's feet with the help of an apparatus sometimes called *miḳṭara*, but more often *falaḳa*. It existed in three different forms: 1) a plank with two holes in it, of the pillory type; 2) two poles joined at one end; it was possible to confine the ankles by holding the other end tightly; 3) a single, fairly stout pole with a cord fixed at the two ends; the feet were inserted between the pole and the cord and the pole thenturned.

Evidence of the existence of the *falaḳa* in the Arab world dates back to the 4th/10th century, but it is quite possible that it was already in use in the eastern half of the Mediterranean area, perhaps under other names, in times of remote antiquity. While in the East, especially among the Turks, it appears that the *falaḳa* was used as an instrument of torture by all kinds of different authorities, in North Africa its use was confined to the schoolmaster. This usage is still very much alive in the Mag̲h̲rib, not only among Muslims but also in the Talmudic schools.

It is interesting to record that the Byzantines possessed an identical apparatus known by the name of φάλαγγας, the use of which was only forbidden in 1829. It seems to have been in common use in Greek elementary schools, whose methods, curricula and customs in other respects also curiously resemble those of the *kuttāb*.

The etymology of the word clearly poses a problem. An Arabic derivation from the root FLḲ, which means to cleave or split, suggests itself at first. The classical Arabic dictionaries (*LA*, *TA*, etc,) all give *falaḳ/falaḳa* as meaning *k̲h̲as̲h̲aba*, a piece of squared wood (*i.e.*, not unworked wood).

Certain Greek scholars have also considered a Greek etymology (Μεγάλη Ἑλληνικὴ Ἐγκυκλοπαιδεία, Athens 1933, s.v.). This etymology seems to be ruled out by the fact that there is no evidence either of the object or the word before the time of the Turkish conquest.

On the other hand, the form φάλαγγας, despite its close resemblance to φάλαγξ, as much in form as in meaning, is not the only one in existence. The dialect forms φάλακας, φιάλακας, φάλακα, φέλεκας (gender and number uncertain), which are difficult to connect with φάλαγξ, are also to be found.

It seems then more probable to regard it as a Greek borrowing of a Turco-Arabic word which remained almost unaltered in certain Greek dialects, but which, in the written language, was contaminated by φάλαγξ to give φάλαγγας.

If the word appears, pending further information, well and truly of Arabic origin, it still remains possible to regard it as part of a stock common to divers linguistic communities of the Near East. This possibility should be examined not only from the Semitic, but also from the Turkish and Iranian angles.

Bibliography: Ibn Saḥnūn, *Kitāb Ādāb al-muʿallimīn*, Tunis 1931; tr. G. Lecomte, *Le livre des règles de conduite des maîtres d'école*, in *REI*, xxi (1953), 77-105; R. Guilland, *La vie scolaire à Byzance*, in *Bulletin de l'Association Guillaume Budé*, March 1953, 63-83; Ἐλευθερουδάκη Ἐγκυκλοπαιδικὸν Λεξικόν (*Encyclopaedic Dictionary*), Athens 1931; D. Dimitriacos, Μέγα Λεξικὸν τῆς Ἑλληνικῆς Γλώσσης (*Great Dictionary of the Greek Language*), Athens 1951; see further H. and R. Kahane and A. Tietze, *Lingua franca in the Levant*, 866.

See especially in *Arabica*, 1954, 324-36, *Sur la vie scolaire à Byzance et dans l'Islam*: I.—G. Lecomte, *L'enseignement primaire à Byzance et le Kuttāb*; II.—M. Canard, *Falaqa* = φάλαγγας, where the notes give the complete bibliography of this question. (G. Lecomte)

al-**FALAKĪ**, Maḥmūd Pasha, was born in 1230/1815 at al-Ḥiṣṣa (province of al-Gharbiyya), and received his early schooling in Alexandria. He subsequently attended, firstly as a pupil, and then as an officer-instructor, the polytechnic school at Būlāḳ (Muhandiskhāne) founded by Muḥammad ʿAlī. In 1850-1 he was sent to Paris, to specialize in astronomy under Arago. He returned to Cairo in 1859. Afterwards he directed the team which, on the orders of the Khedive Saʿīd, mapped Egypt. He lived long enough to see the whole work almost completed, and the section on Lower Egypt in print. He left many writings in Arabic and French, which are enumerated by his biographers. He represented the Egyptian government at the Geographical Congresses in Paris (1875) and Venice (1881). A high dignitary of Freemasonry, and a member of the Egyptian Institute, he was also a member, and later president, of the Geographical Society in Cairo. For two months Minister of Public Works, but removed from this post as a result of the events of 1882, he was subsequently *Wakīl*, and then Minister of Education (*al-Maʿārif al-ʿumūmiyya*). He died in 1303/November 1885.

Bibliography: Ismāʿīl Bey Muṣṭafā, *Notice nécrologique de S. E. Mahmoud Pacha, l'astronome*, Cairo 1886 (in French with Arabic trans.); Brockelmann, II, 642-3 (490-1); G. Zaydān, *Mashāhīr al-Sharḳ*, ii, 132 ff.; Ziriklī, *al-Aʿlām*², viii, Cairo 1956, 39-40; Gamal el-Din El-Shayyal, *A history of Egyptian historiography in the nineteenth century*, Alexandria 1962, 54-7. (J. Jomier)

FALAKĪ SHIRWĀNĪ. Muḥammad Falakī, poet-astronomer of Shirwān and pupil of Khāḳānī, is the author of a lost *dīwān* of Persian poetry, of which 1512 verses have been recovered and published. Falakī lived 49 years, ca. 501/1108 - ca. 550/1155 and like Abu 'l-ʿAlāʾ and Khāḳānī was a court-poet of the Shirwānshāh Abu 'l-Haydjā Fakhr al-Dīn Minūčihr II, who succeeded his father Farīdūn I on the throne of Shirwān in 514/1120 and ruled for 37 years until *c.* 551/1156. The statement of his contemporary Khāḳānī, that Falakī's life was short-lived and that Manūčihr II ruled for 30 years is not precise, for one of Falakī's odes can be dated 521/1127, and in another Falakī offers condolences to Manūčihr II when his brother-in-law, ex-king Dimitri of Georgia, died between 549 and 551/ 1154-1156. Nowhere does Falakī mention the death of Manūčihr II; he would have done so, if he had survived Manūčihr II; but he describes how Manūčihr II defeated the Alāns and 'Khazars' (in fact Ḳipčāḳs); how with the help of Mīr Ṭughān Arslān (ruler of Arzan and Bidlīs, d. 532/1138) Manūčihr II took (some part of) Arrān from (Nuṣrat al-Dīn) Arslān Abihī (ruler of Marāgha 530-570/1136-1175); how Manūčihr II built the cities of Kardmān and Saʿdūn; and how Manūčihr II rebuilt (in 532/1138) the flood-destroyed Bāḳilānī dam (Band-i-Bāḳilānī) by removing *lān*, leaving *band bāḳī* = "the dam remained". And as for the flood it "went into what remained" (*dar bāḳī shud*), *i.e.*, went into the chains which remained, for *band* also means chains. Such being Falakī's poetry, "how can I reply to his ode?" confesses the well-known poet ʿIṣmat of Bukhārā. Falakī once suffered imprisonment; otherwise he spent a quiet life with astronomy as his hobby; "because of his proficiency in ten sciences, he knew the mystery of the nine heavens", says Khāḳānī.

Bibliography: Hādī Ḥasan, *Falakī: His life, times and works*, pub. *RAS*, 1929; idem, *Dīwān-i-Falakī*, pub. *RAS*, 1930; idem, *Researches in Persian literature*, 12-94, Ḥaydarābād/Dn. 1958; M. Brosset, *Histoire de la Géorgie*, pt. i, 364, St. Petersburg 1849; W. E. D. Allen, *A History of the Georgian people*, 101, London 1932. (Hadi Hasan)

FALĀSIFA, pl. of *faylasūf*, formed from the Greek φιλόσοφος. By its origin this word primarily denotes the Greek thinkers. Al-Shahrastānī gives a list of them: the seven Sages who are "the fount of philosophy (*falsafa*) and the beginning of wisdom (*ḥikma*)", then Thales, Anaxagoras, Anaximenes, Empedocles, Pythagoras, Socrates, Plato, Plutarch, Xenophanes, Zeno the elder, Democritus, the philosophers of the Academy, Heraclitus, Epicurus, Homer (the poet whose wisdom inspired Greece for, with the Greeks, poetry preceded philosophy), Hippocrates, Euclid, Ptolemy, Chrysippus and Zeno, Aristotle (whose philosophy is described according to Themistius), Porphyry, Plotinus (*al-shaykh al-yūnānī*), Theophrastus, Proclus and Alexander of Aphrodisias. The doctrines attributed to these thinkers are often incorrect or anachronistic, perhaps under the influence of the systemization of Aristotle and the Eclectics. Then the *falāsifat al-Islām* are named. The list is somewhat long; we may mention al-Kindī, Ḥunayn b. Isḥāḳ, Abu 'l-Faradj al-Mufassir, Thābit b. Ḳurra, al-Nisābūrī, Ibn Miskawayh, al-Fārābī, etc. But, he writes, the true representative of the *falāsifa* (*ʿalāmat al-ḳawm*) is Ibn Sīnā, and it is his philosophy alone that he expounds. From this point of view the Muslim *falāsifa* appeared merely as the successors of the Greeks: "They followed Aristotle in all he thought . . . except for unimportant expressions on which they adopted the views of Plato and the earlier philosophers". This judgment needs to be radically revised.

a). The word *falāsifa* has retained in Arabic the general sense of the Greek equivalent. It is thus synonymous with *ḥukamāʾ* or *ʿulamāʾ*. This is the meaning it has in al-Djāḥiẓ (*K. al-Ḥayawān*, introd.) where *falāsifat ʿulamāʾ al-bashar* is compared with *ḥudhdhāḳ ridjāl al-raʾy*, in a passage in which human reason and skill, which in the signs of nature discern the wisdom of God, are compared with animals' instinct, the immediate expression of this wisdom.

b). If the general idea of wisdom (which occurs both in the Ḳurʾān and in the Greek philosophical tradition) remains attached to the term *falsafa*, there is justification for describing as *falāsifa* those Muslim theologians who gave a place to human reason and *raʾy*. Indeed, from the very start of Muʿtazilī thinking there can be discerned, in the exposition of problems and in methods of reasoning, a Greek influence, transmitted indirectly by the Christian philosophers of Syria (John of Damascus, Theodore Abū Ḳurra). Later, when the logic of Aristotle (the pre-eminent Master and organizer of this branch of learning in the Arabs' eyes) was known directly, it was utilized by the *mutakallimūn*, but less as an instrument of constructive analysis than as a means of exposition and refutation. In this form it quite soon became general throughout Islam, despite the opposition of the strictly orthodox. An instance of this purely dialectical use of logic can be found in the Ẓāhirī Ibn Ḥazm (5th/11th century) at the beginning of his *Fiṣal*, to refute certain philosophically inspired ideas about the eternity of the world. In the thinking of such Ash^carīs as al-Bāḳillānī and al-Djuwaynī, and especially in al-Ghazālī, despite his opposition to the *falāsifa*, the influence of Greece is even more positive. Al-Bāḳillānī's theory of simple substances (atoms) and accidents, the Mu^ctazilī doctrines concerning essence and existence or the knowledge that God has of created things before and after their creation, derive among other things from pure philosophy. Moreover the *falāsifa* properly speaking are acquainted with these theological schools and sometimes refer to them in order to determine their own situation. An absolute distinction between them cannot be made.

c). As for the *falāsifa* in the restricted sense of the word, it is not possible to give a clear-cut, exclusive definition. In general, they are the successors of Neo-Platonism, which is itself an eclecticism in which are combined Platonic, Aristotelian, Stoic, Pythagorean and many other kinds of ideas. This Neo-Platonism had been sufficiently flexible to integrate Alexandrian learning, as P. Duhem has shown. In this multiplicity of influences, that of Aristotle is distinguished by the part played by his logic. Seen from this point of view, *falsafa* was a consequence of the translation of Greek writings, and certain translators were themselves the first *falāsifa*. Orientalists, following Renan, have regarded *falsafa* as a sect, and this is the opinion of Muslims in general. But if there is a common body of doctrine and strong resemblances, the originality of each thinker and the existence of different tendencies must not be denied.

The sources of the *falāsifa* are no doubt essentially Greek—Plato, Aristotle and the commentators, especially Alexander and Themistius. But we must also observe the influence of scientific thought, particularly of Galen, the scholar and philosopher, and also that of an intellectualist mysticism deriving from Plotinus, and combining theological and cosmological ideas of gnostic type, the theology and angelology of Proclus, the *Theology* of the pseudo-Aristotle, doctrines of Hermetic origin. All the gnoses of the Alexandrian period, which even then were tinged with Iranism, find an echo in Arabo-Muslim thought. The Sabaeans, with their astrology that was at once scientific and religious, and with their conception of an intermediate world of spirits (cf. the exposé of al-Shahrastānī), played a large part. In this situation, Persian-inspired dualism was able to infiltrate without difficulty, either directly or through the Shī^cī sects, especially Ismā^cīlism. From the theoretical aspect, it is difficult entirely to isolate from *falsafa* esoteric mystics such as Suhrawardī whose speculative thinking is Peripatetic and who speaks of light as Aristotle speaks of substance. The thinking of the *falāsifa* is thus very complex; Ibn Sīnā, a scholar and the disciple of Galen, a logician and follower of Aristotle, a Neo-Platonist, exponent of a mysticism that gave rise to that of Suhrawardī, illustrates in a single harmonious entity the complexity of *falsafa*.

But this description is only entirely true of the first *falāsifa*, al-Kindī and, in particular, al-Fārābī and Ibn Sīnā. What characterizes them is their belief, deriving from Greek electicism, in the harmony between the "two sages", Plato and Aristotle (cf. the treatise of al-Fārābī on this subject). Reason, the instrument of truth, can produce only a single system. Insofar as the *falāsifa* concentrated on defining and developing this single system which came to them from Greece, they do indeed form a single school or sect. But al-Ghazālī, under the inspiration of al-Djuwaynī, denounces this mistake: reason is not the supreme arbiter (*ḥakam*); there are as many divergencies (*ikhtilāf*) between philosophers as between theologians. He thus marks the beginning of a second period which is characterized by a better knowledge of Aristotle's works and exemplified in the West by Ibn Bādjdja and, more particularly, by Ibn Rushd upon whom al-Ghazālī was not without influence in spite of their obvious differences, and who reacted against Arab Neo-Platonism. In the East, Fakhr al-Dīn and Naṣīr al-Dīn al-Ṭūsī returned to Ibn Sīnā's doctrine on various important points, while also integrating elements of Ash^carī theology with it, in the case of the former, or of mystical esoterism in the case of the latter.

Finally, side by side with this main stream (Ibn Sīnā, al-Ghazālī, and then Ibn Rushd in the West, al-Rāzī in the East), a further, and Neo-Pythagorean, stream must be pointed out, represented by the Ikhwān al-Ṣafā᾿ whose esoteric and mystical character is more clearly marked. They accuse other philosophers or theologians of having only partially observed the rhythms of the universe. It is not consonant with Wisdom that beings should go only in multiples of two (matter and form, substance and accident, etc.), or of three (the three dimensions, the three modes of existence—necessary, possible and impossible, etc.), or of four, five, six, seven (doctrine of the septimanians), etc. The Pythagoreans (*al-ḥukamā᾿ al-fīthāghūriyyūn*) "accept the right of everything which has a right"; since the number includes everything, measures and balances everything, so their thought takes everthing exactly into account. In their eyes, Pythagoras was a sage adoring the single God; they connected him with the philosophers of Ḥarrān.

How are the *falāsifa* as a whole to be characterized?

a). By their vocabulary. It is composed of *iṣṭilāḥāt*, words that are Arabic or calques from the Greek which have assumed a technical meaning. For the expression of the truth, strictly orthodox theology only allows words of divine origin (texts from the Ḳur᾿ān and from Tradition). However, a large proportion of this vocabulary has been accepted by the *mutakillimūn*. The distinguishing feature of the *falāsifa* is therefore merely the more systematic and independent use which they make of this conventional vocabulary.

b). By logic. As with Aristotle, logic became a true organon (*āla*). It shows from what known starting-point one can reach a certain unknown point, and by what course. It is based on the study of concepts and categories, judgment, syllogism and induction. This analytical and constructive use of logic to discover the structure of truth is not accepted by strict theologians. Al-Ghazālī, however, recognizes that it has a certain value, although not absolute. On the other hand the *falāsifa*, indirectly following Aristotle, have taken account, in their studies of concept and judgment, of principles enunciated by the Arab grammarians. With logic can be connected the division of the sciences, inspired by the Greeks but varying according to the authors (Ikhwān al-Ṣafāʾ; al-Fārābī: *Iḥṣāʾ al-ʿulūm*; Ibn Sīnā: *Aḳsām al-ʿulūm al-ʿaḳliyya*). Its basis is the tripartite division into sciences theoretical, practical and creative.

c). By their study of natural science. The *falāsifa* were all scholars, sometimes of originality. They integrated astronomy, physics, chemistry and medicine with their general metaphysics which was the source of their fundamental concepts. Nevertheless a spirit of experiment, not unrelated to the Muslim tendency to attach value to the experience of the senses, is clearly revealed.

d). By metaphysics. Here the divergences between authors are more marked. But for all of them, metaphysics is a theory of being, built up on the distinction between the necessary and the possible (being necessary in itself, being necessary through another or possible) or the eternal and the contingent. The pure being of all matter is at once the intellect, the agent which intellectualizes, and intelligible. The interplay of these ideas explains the constitution of the world. For the Neo-Platonists and Arab Pythagoreans, from the One only one can emerge, that is to say the first intellect. Ibn Rushd does not accept this postulate. The first intellect on the one hand intellectualizes the being necessary in itself, thus producing a second intellect; on the other hand, it intellectualizes its own essence, either as being necessary through another and thereby producing the form or soul of the sphere, or else as being possible in itself and so producing the body of the sphere (*djirm al-falak*). Upon this general principle of emanation, many variations are to be found in the expositions by the different authors. This process continues up to the last intellect, that is to say the active intellect. Beneath it are placed the sentient beings of the sublunary world. The active intellect plays an important part in human knowledge, but upon this point the *falāsifa* differ considerably. Emanation is of a different character for the Ikhwān al-Ṣafāʾ. From the Creator (*al-Bāriʾ*) is emanated Intellect, which is the immediate expression of his powers and virtues (cf. Philo of Alexandria). From the intellect is emanated the universal Soul which at once receives the forms of all beings. From this emanates universal matter, a simple intelligible substance like the foregoing, which eventually receives the forms. The first form received is the corporeal form in the three dimensions which constitute a sort of intelligible scale, and in this way the absolute body (*al-djism al-muṭlaḳ*) is attained, where emanation is halted. After this comes the diversity of sentient objects, the universal bodies of the spheres and the elements, the individual and composite bodies of our world.

e). By theology. The *falāsifa* here are in agreement with the *mutakallimūn* and the problem of the attributes of God. They are close to the Muʿtazila in that they seek not to multiply the divine essence. But they differ in that, for them, God is at once the source of existences and essences. Their central problem is that of divine knowledge. God, knowing Himself sufficiently, knows Himself as the cause of everything that is; of all kinds, of all species, of all possibilities that enter into existence, that is to say possibilities which are necessary by their cause, and finally of all individual beings, not by a knowledge which would vary with them, but through a universal species (*bi-nawʿ kullī*). Providence leads to the necessary universal order. The *falāsifa* have a theory as to the Prophet: in general, he is a man so gifted that the active intellect acts on his imagination (while it acts on the intelligence of the wise man).

f). By psychology and morality. Morality is a practical science: moral natures, virtues and characters exist, whose value one can learn by reason in order to gain from it a system of life that conforms with the good. These values are in relation to the human soul. In regard to the metaphysical nature of the soul, theories are diverse and reflect the uncertainties of Plato and Aristotle. But gnostic beliefs are intermixed with them: in the cosmos, the soul has an itinerary to follow, stages of purification to traverse, to regain its place of origin (cf. *Theology* of Pseudo-Aristotle). The Aristotelians such as Ibn Rushd do not accept these ideas. Moreover, in all the *falāsifa* we find a morality based on the Greek psychology of the three souls or powers (rational, irascible and concupiscible) and on the doctrine of virtue as the golden mean. Thus, in *falsafa* we meet two moralities, juxtaposed and co-existent for some (Ibn Sīnā), the one a humanist morality (Ibn Rushd), the other mystical (Suhrawardī). Both are at variance with strict orthodoxy which regards the revelation of the Law as the single source of knowledge of both ethical and religious values. But, in their classification of the virtues within the Greek philosophical systems, the *falāsifa* introduced a considerable number of Islamized Arab virtues, for example *ḥilm* (cf. Ibn Sīnā, *Risālat al-akhlāḳ*).

Thus the *falāsifa* often break away from orthodox Islam, but thanks to *taʾwīl* they could still believe that they were in harmony with the Ḳurʾān, from which they quoted unfailingly. But they quoted it purely as evidence, without incorporating it in the body of their argumentation. Thus the theologians, so far as they depart from the revealed texts, are opposed to them. This is how Abū Ḥayyān al-Tawḥīdī speaks of the Ikhwān al-Ṣafāʾ (*K. al-Imtāʿ*, 17th Night). According to them, the Law has been profaned by foolish ignorance and confounded by error. It must be purified by philosophy. By harmonizing Greek philosophy and Arab law, perfection is reached. But their *Epistles* are no more than "ramblings" consisting of "scraps strung together in a kind of patch-work". They have "woven a philosophy in secret" out of the science of the stars and spheres, the *Almagest*, the knowledge of the greatness and works of nature, music, logic. Now there is no question of these sciences in the Revelation. The Muslim community is divided into sects, but none of them has had recourse to the *falāsifa*. "What is the relation between religion and philosophy? (*ayna 'l-dīn min al-falsafa?*)", between what is derived from a heavenborn revelation and what is derived from fallible personal opinion? The prophet is superior to the philosopher. As for reason, it does not pertain in its entirety to any one man, but to mankind as a whole. And al-Tawḥīdī proclaims the ambition of philosophers: their wish is, not to cure men of their maladies, the task to which the prophets confine themselves, but rather to preserve the health of those who possess it. They aspire to the most exalted happiness and to a dignity, thanks to which man becomes worthy of the divine life. But in that case what purpose would the Revelation serve?

For al-Ghazālī (*Munḳidh*; *Maḳāṣid*), certain parts

of philosophy are without danger to the faith, provided that good is made of them: these are mathematics and logic. Physics is also admissible, on condition that it is never forgotten that the only causality is that of God. The useful sciences such as medicine are the *ʿulūm al-dunyā*, and ought to be studied, at least by some (*farḍ kifāya*) for the general good, since life in this world contains the germ of the future life and it must not be neglected (cf. *Iḥyāʾ ʿulūm al-dīn*, ch. on Science). Certain sciences are harmful, like magic and the science of talismans (which still come into Ibn Sīnā's classification); they must be rejected. As for the theology of the *falāsifa*, this is frankly bad, since it teaches that bodies are not resurrected, that it is disembodied spirits that are rewarded or punished, and that penalties are spiritual, not bodily. Moreover, the theories of the eternity of the world and of the knowledge of God who knows only the universals are complete heresies (*kufr*). On the other hand, the doctrine which reduces the divine attributes to essence is not *kufr* in the eyes of al-G͟hazālī since the Muʿtazila, who cannot be charged with infidelity, adhered to it. Finally, the political theory of the *falāsifa* is taken from the ancient prophets (*salaf al-anbiyāʾ*), a very ancient idea which Philo of Alexandria had already rejected; and their moral philosophy is inspired by the mystics. From the end of the period of antiquity the opinion was widespread that Plato was an initiate and inspired.

For al-S͟hahrastānī (6th/12th century), philosophers are men of passions (*ahl al-ahwāʾ*), that is to say men who follow their own judgment and who must be distinguished from those who follow a revelation (*arbāb al-diyāna*), to whom they are diametrically opposed (*taḳābul al-taḍādd*). Later, Ibn Taymiyya (7th-8th/13th-14th centuries), in the *K. al-Radd ʿalā 'l-manṭiḳiyyīn*, denounces the uselessness and inconsequence of the logic of the *falāsifa*. Finally we may mention Ibn K͟haldūn (8th/14th century) who attacked philosophy in his *Muḳaddima* (*Ibṭāl al-falsafa*). Philosophers think that it is reason, not tradition, which confirms the truth of the foundations of the faith. They proceed by successive abstractions, reach the first intelligibles and then integrate them to establish sciences in the manner of second intelligibles. The soul which, in purifying itself, comes to the sciences, experiences joy and has no need of the illumination of the Law. The soul that is ignorant is in affliction. Such is the meaning of the rewards and punishments of the other world. But this opinion is false: when they relate all beings to the first intellect and find this a satisfactory means of reaching the necessary, they reveal a lack of vision in regard to the actual organization of the divine Creation, which surpasses any representations of it that they give. Existence is too vast for man to be able to embrace it in its entirety.

These criticisms make it possible to place the *falāsifa* in relation to orthodox Muslim ideals. But they give too sharp a definition of outline to *falsafa*. In reality, the philosophers of Islam remain truly Muslim, in touch with the theologians and with the mystical elements which have not tried to break away from the teaching of the Ḳurʾān. As for the legacy of Greece, this was first acquired by the Muslim world as a whole, in spite of the opposition raised by strict orthodoxy. If it appears to be systematized in their doctrines, its influence is far from being limited to the *falāsifa* alone. It is therefore impossible to regard *falsafa* as a sect sharply differentiated from the general cultural and spiritual movement which is the pride of Muslim civilization.

(R. ARNALDEZ)

FALCONRY [see BAYZARA, ČAKÎRD͟JÎ-BAS͟HÎ, DOG͟HAND͟JÎ]

FALLĀḤ [see FILĀḤA]

FALLĀḤIYA [see DAWRAḲ]

FALLĀḲ, an Arabic word used particularly in the Beduin dialect form *fəllāg*, pl. *fəllāga* (in the western press principally in the pl., with the spelling: *fellaga, fellagah, fellagha*), and denoting in the first place the brigands and subsequently the rebels who appeared in Tunisia and Algeria.

A connexion with *falaḳa* [*q.v.*] "instrument of torture", of which the etymology is, in any case, obscure (see *Arabica*, 1954/3, 325-36), is certainly to be ruled out. On the other hand, the Arabic root FLḲ (comp. FLD͟J, FLḤ, etc.) seems worthy of retention; Tunisian rural and nomadic dialects make use of *fləg* "deflower, violate", *fəlləg* "split, cleave (wood), split in two (skull)", etc. (M. Beaussier, who gives *felleg* "split" as well as the 5th and 7th forms and other derivatives of the root, is acquainted with a *fellāg* in the Algerian South meaning "of which the stone is easily detached (peach)", while G. Boris, *Lexique du parler arabe des Marazig*, Paris 1958, has only recorded the 7th form, and it is to this root that the Tunisians (who have coined a 10th form *stəfləg* "to take to the hills") generally relate the intensifying adjective *fəllāg*). Originally the term was applied to individuals who wished to escape punishment, to deserters, and to fugitive offenders, who eventually formed bands supporting themselves by brigandage. The first lexicographer to have noted *fallāḳ* is E. Bocthor, who may well have created it himself in order to translate the French word *pourfendeur*; H. Wehr, *Wörterbuch*, on the other hand, lists it with the sense of "bandit, highwayman", but this is obviously a recent usage of the Arabic press, which, moreover, finds the term too pejorative to use it as freely as does the European press.

The real popularity of the word, however, dates from the beginning of the first world war, and the uprising brought about by K͟halīfa b. ʿAskar [*q.v.*] in southern Tunisia; these rebels were in fact designated by the name of *fellāga*, less perhaps by the Tunisians themselves, than by the French troops. Somewhat forgotten between the wars, the term was resurrected on the occasion of the incidents which occurred in Tunisia between 1952 and 1954: the whole of the western press used it to describe the rebels who, for political reasons, formed armed groups fighting against the French army. When the Algerian rebellion broke out in 1954, the term was quite naturally applied to the outlaws, and then to the combatants of the rebel army. It is thus that a Tunisian colloquialism was borrowed by the French army and then by the French press, subsequently spread into western newspapers and the Algerian dialect of Arabic, and made its appearance in the Arabic press in the classicizing form *fallāḳ*.

(CH. PELLAT)

FALLĀTA, although strictly signifying the Fulānī [*q.v.*], is used in the Nilotic Sudan generally for Muslim immigrants from the western *Bilād al-Sūdān*, and in particular for those from northern Nigeria. The term has largely superseded the older *Takārīr* or *Takārna* (which had a similarly loose application), presumably after the Fulānī conquests under ʿUt͟hmān dan Fodio. The Takārīr/Fallāta immigrants are primarily pilgrims *en route* to Mecca: their first appearance in the Nilotic Sudan can hardly have been before the establishment of

Muslim sultanates in Dār Fūr [*q.v.*] and Waddāī during the 11th/17th century. Many have become domiciled in the territories which now compose the Republic of the Sudan. Takārīr founded a border state in the Ḳallābāt (Sudanese-Abyssinian marches) in the 18th century; its ruler, S͟hayk͟h Mīrī, submitted to the Turco-Egyptian governor of Sinnār in 1245/1829-30. A Fallāta settlement exists at the southern end of D̲j̲abal Marra in Dār Fūr. Some Fallāta/Takārīr settlers in Dār Fūr and Kurdufān have intermarried with local Baḳḳāra, become arabized, and now constitute tribal sections. More recent immigrants form an important element in the labour-force of the Republic of the Sudan, as domestic servants, and as labourers employed by the tenants of the Gezira (cotton-growing) Scheme; see Saad Ed Din Fawzi, *The Labour Movement in the Sudan*, London 1957, 5-8.

Bibliography: An important account of the Takārīr pilgrims in the early 19th century is given by J. L. Burckhardt, *Travels in Nubia*, London 1819, 406-14; more generally, see under Felláta (and also Takárír) in the Indexes of H. A. MacMichael, *The Tribes of northern and central Kordofan*, Cambridge 1912; and idem, *A History of the Arabs in the Sudan*, Cambridge 1922. (P. M. Holt)

FALLŪD̲J̲A, name of two districts (*ṭassūd̲j̲*) of ʿIrāḳ, Upper and Lower Fallūd̲j̲a, which occupied the angle formed by the two arms of the lower Euphrates which flow finally into the Baṭīḥa [*q.v.*], the Euphrates proper to the west (this arm is given various names by the geographers and is now called S͟haṭṭ al-Hindiyya) and the nahr Sūrā (now S͟haṭṭ al-Ḥilla) to the east.

Bibliography: Suhrāb, *K. ʿAd̲j̲āʾib al-aḳālīm al-sabʿa*, ed. H. von Mžik, Leipzig 1930, 124-5; Ṭabarī, index; Balād̲h̲urī, *Futūḥ*, 245, 254, 265, 457; Bakrī, index; Yāḳūt, s.v.; Yaʿḳūbī-Wiet, 140; Masʿūdī, *Murūd̲j̲*, v, 337; A. Musil, *The middle Euphrates*, 125; Le Strange, 74; Caetani, *Annali*, ii, 942-3, iii, 259-60; M. Canard, *H'amdânides*, 148. (Ed.)

al-**FALLŪD̲J̲A,** name of an ancient locality, still existing, of ʿIrāḳ; it is situated on the Euphrates down-stream from al-Anbār [*q.v.*] and near Dimmimā, from where the nahr ʿĪsā branched off towards Bag͟hdād. At al-Fallūd̲j̲a nowadays the main road from Bag͟hdād crosses the Euphrates.

Bibliography: Muḳaddasī, 115; Suhrāb, 123; Iṣṭak͟hrī, 84; Ibn Ḥawḳal, 165; Musil, *The middle Euphrates*, 269-71; Le Strange, 66, 68 (distinguishing two villages of the same name, the second at the point where the nahr al-Malik branches off; but there seems to be some confusion here); M. Canard, *H'amdânides*, 147. (Ed.)

FALS (pl. *fulūs*), the designation of the copper or bronze coin current in the early centuries of the Islamic era. The term *fals* for copper coinage, like those of *dīnār* and *dirham* for gold and silver, is of Greek origin, deriving from φόλλις, the name of the Byzantine copper coin. *Fals* denotes any and all copper or bronze coins, regardless of size or weight. The system of varying denominations in which Byzantine copper coinage was originally issued seems already to have disintegrated prior to the Arab conquests. By the time the Arabs arrived in Syria, there was little, if anything, left of the graduated monetary system of copper coinage (cf. Ph. Grierson, *Coinage and Money in the Byzantine Empire*, in *Settimane di studio de centro italiano di studi sull'alto medioevo*, viii, *Moneta e Scambi nell'alto Medioevo*, Spoleto 1961, 437). This point deserves special emphasis, because it explains why the Arabs issued only one standard copper coin without any denominational differentiations. They imitated the system they found prevalent in the former Byzantine territories, and the pattern established in the early years of their rule continued throughout the Umayyad and ʿAbbāsid Caliphates. The glass *fals* weights issued in Egypt during most of the eighth century in denominations of from nine to thirty-six *k͟harrūba*s may indicate a possible exception. However, the exact use of these glass coin weights is a problem that remains yet to be solved (cf. G. C. Miles, *On the varieties and accuracy of eighth century coin weights*, in the forthcoming memorial volume for Leo A. Mayer).

The copper coins previous to the monetary reform of ʿAbd al-Malik (ca. 77/696) fall into three broad categories.

Arab-Byzantine: Immediately following the conquests the Arabs continued to strike copper coins almost exactly as they found them—religious formulae, obsolete dates and all. These imitations, frequently barbarized, are probably the earliest extant Islamic coins. While the basic Byzantine types were maintained until ʿAbd al-Malik's reform, various modifications of an Arabicizing nature were introduced before that date. Among the most important of these are the addition in the margin of short religious formulae, indication of the mint in Arabic characters, the addition of words such as *baraka*, *ṭayyib*, etc., as well as the occasional mention of the governor or local *ʿāmil* under whose authority the coin was issued. The most interesting departure from the Byzantine style is to be found in the "Standing Caliph" type, on the obverse of which the sword-girt figure of the Caliph dressed in typical Bedouin garb displaces the likeness of the Emperor with his cross, crown and orb, while maintaining a modified form of the reverse Byzantine type. The stance of the Caliph appears to be an attempt to portray him in the posture of leading the prayer service. The fact that all five extant *dīnār*s of this type, as well as most of the *fulūs*, date from the early part of ʿAbd al-Malik's reign, and immediately precede his monetary reforms, is an indication that these coins are to be considered as a transitional type through which the emerging Islamic state was attempting to find an appropriate iconographic form for its coinage (cf. John Walker, *A Catalogue of Muhammadan coins in the British Museum*, ii, London 1956, pp. xxviii-xxxii, 22-43).

Arab-Sāsānian: These copper coins are very rare. They have the regular Sāsānian bust on the obverse, and some modification of the fire altar and attendants on the reverse. (For examples cf. Walker, *Catalogue*, i, 73, 125, 161, 170-2, and G. C. Miles, *Excavation coins from the Persepolis region*, New York 1959).

Byzantine-Pahlavi: This type exists only in copper. These coins represent a unique combination of Byzantine and Sāsānian elements, with the obverse usually following the Byzantine model, and the reverse the Sāsānian one (cf. Walker, *Catalogue*, ii, pp. li-liii, 81-3).

The purely epigraphic, non-pictorial coin which resulted from ʿAbd al-Malik's reforms appeared in copper somewhat later than in gold and silver. The earliest preserved dated epigraphic *fals* is of the year 87/705-6 struck at Damascus. The effect of the reform on the copper coinage was purely epigraphic with no metrological aspects as in the case of gold and silver (cf. Ph. Grierson, *The monetary reforms of*

ʿ*Abd al-Malik*, in *JESHO*, iii, 246-7). Neither the size, weight or epigraphic content of the copper coins was uniform. They all contained some religious formula, and sometimes the mint, date and names of the issuing official or officials.

Unlike the centralized system of copper minting in Byzantium, its emission in Islam was highly proliferated and decentralized. In the period immediately preceding the conquests there were twelve known copper mints in the entire Byzantine Empire, only three of which were in Syria, Egypt and Africa. Under the Umayyads there were fifty-three known copper mints, thirty-three of them in the former Byzantine provinces. The number of mints increases to eighty-three under the ʿAbbāsids, with most of the new mints in the eastern part of the Empire.

Copper coinage was a token currency issued to fill the need for petty commercial transactions, and passed by tale and not by weight. Its emission was left to the discretion of governors and local authorities, without any centralized control. As a result, the *fals* varied greatly in weight, size, and probably value from one district to another. The weight variation was sometimes as much as five grams between contemporary *fulūs* from different mints (*e.g.*, a *fals* from al-Mawṣil dated 157 weighs 10.63 grams, while one of Bag̲h̲dād from the same year weighs 5.42 grams). It is for these reasons that the circulation of the *fals*, unlike that of the *dīnār* or *dirham*, was limited to the near vicinity of its emission.

This may help to explain why small sums of money are so infrequently expressed in the written sources in terms of *fulūs*, but rather in terms of minute weights of gold and silver. Such small sums as 1/144th or 1/288th of a *dīnār* mentioned in the Arabic papyri, or the fractional division of the *dirham* into *ḳīrāṭ*, *dāniḳ* and *ḥabba* have no counterpart in actual gold or silver coins. These are rather monies of account pegged to the fluctuating and diversified value of the *fals*, and were the only standard way to express small sums of money.

The simultaneous circulation of coins in gold, silver and copper implies a fixed and known rate of exchange between them. We possess occasional references to the established ratio between *dīnārs* and *dirhams* and its periodic modifications, but our knowledge of the ratio between these denominations and *fulūs* is poorly documented. That such a ratio existed in Umayyad and ʿAbbāsid times is known from various anecdotes (*e.g.*, Ibn Abī Uṣaybiʿa, ʿ*Uyūn*, i, 185; Ibn K̲h̲allikān, *Wafayāt*, tr. de Slane, ii, 125), from legal discussions related to the problems of converting *dirhams* into *fulūs* and *vice versa* (cf. material collected by H. Sauvaire, in *JA*, vii/15, 262-6), and from al-Ṭabarī's rendering of the amount in *dirhams* spent on the construction of Bag̲h̲dād into its equivalent in *fulūs* (*Taʾrīk̲h̲*, ed. de Goeje, iii, 326). For Mamlūk Egypt al-Maḳrīzī (*Traité des Famines*, in *JESHO*, v, 68-9), and others (cf. references in Grohmann, *Einführung*, 218) provide us with some information on the *dirham*: *fals* ratio. All these sources indicate a ratio fluctuating between twenty-four and forty-eight *fulūs* to the *dirham*.

During the first half of the 3rd/9th century there was a sudden cessation of copper minting throughout the Islamic world. This scarcity of copper coinage lasted for several centuries. That the absence in our collections of *fulūs* for this period is not a mere coincidence is confirmed by the results of excavations at such important Islamic sites as Rayy, Persepolis (Iṣṭak̲h̲r) and Antioch. From among the large number of copper coins found at these sites only one dates after 207/822. The only exception to this general pattern are the mints of Transoxania. The mints of Buk̲h̲ārā and Samarḳand have a continuous series of copper coins throughout the late ninth and tenth centuries. The absence of copper coinage in western Europe during most of the Middle Ages is ascribed to the self-sufficient nature of the feudal system and to the negligible volume of petty trade, an explanation which is eminently unsuitable for the Islamic world of the 3rd/9th to 6th/12th centuries. An explanation of this phenomenon may be connected with the inflationary trend created by the greatly increased production of silver and gold which occurred at this period, and which would have made the production of copper coins more expensive and less necessary.

The plural form *fulūs* persisted in use as the designation of the autonomous copper coins of Persian localities in the eighteenth and nineteenth centuries (*e.g.*, R. S. Poole, *The coins of the Shāhs of Persia*, London 1887, 212-61). To the present day *fils* designates the petty coin of ʿIrāḳ and Jordan, and the plural *fulūs* (*flūs*) is a general term for money in colloquial Arabic in Egypt, Morocco and elsewhere.

Bibliography: For the coins see the standard catalogues of various collections, especially: Berlin (H. Nützel), British Museum (S. Lane-Poole, J. Walker), Istanbul (Ismāʿīl G̲h̲ālib), Paris (H. Lavoix) and St. Petersburg (W. Tiesenhausen). See also A. Grohmann, *Einführung und Chrestomathie zur arabischen Papyruskunde*, Prague 1955, 214-9; al-Maḳrīzī, *Traité des monnaies musulmanes*, tr. de Sacy, Paris 1797, 44-8; G. C. Miles, *The early Islamic bronze coinage of Egypt*, in *Centennial Volume of the American Numismatic Society*, New York 1958, 471-502; H. Sauvaire, in *JA*, vii/15 (1880), 257-70. See also SIKKA.

(A. L. UDOVITCH)

FALSAFA, 1. — Origins. — The origins of *falsafa* are purely Greek; the activity of the *falāsifa* [*q.v.*] begins with Arabic translations of the Greek philosophical texts (whether direct or through a Syriac intermediary). Thus *falsafa* appears first as the continuation of φιλοσοφία in Muslim surroundings. But this definition leads at once to a more precise formulation: since strictly orthodox Sunnī Islam has never welcomed philosophic thought, *falsafa* developed from the first especially among thinkers influenced by the sects, and particularly by the S̲h̲īʿa; and this arose from a certain prior sympathy, such sects having absorbed gnostic ideas, some related to Hellenistic types of gnosis, others to Iranian types—for Persia is known in any case to have been an influence on religious and philosophical speculation throughout the Eastern Mediterranean since the Alexandrian epoch.

But it is more difficult to give precise significance to the concept of a Greek legacy; Greek thought is far from unified. Though *falsafa* may be called a continuation of Greek thought there is no perfect continuity, since the Arabic-speaking Muslims were not part of the movement in which φιλοσοφία was developing. They were forced to integrate themselves into it as if foreign bodies: they could not simply follow on; they had to learn everything, from the pre-Socratic teachings to the writings and commentaries of Proclus and John Philoponus. They started therefore from an acquired knowledge of a conspectus of Greek thought, comprehensive and abstract, which they envisaged as a separate culture lacking any historical dimension. They were not unaware that thought had a history but this knowledge came almost exclusively from their reading of Aristotle, and in practice, for them, he seems the culmination of this movement; after him, they only see commentators or works written under his direct inspiration. Even Neoplatonism itself is not viewed as an original system but in the light of a generalized Aristotelian influence.

It would be an easy solution of this difficulty to describe *falsafa* as having assumed one particular form of post-classical Greek thought: eclecticism, which had already appeared in the middle period of Stoicism and exercised considerable influence in the development of Neoplatonism. Certainly this school, in spite of its internal diversity, favoured the development of *falsafa* and contributed to the spread of the belief that Greek philosophy was unified. A text such as the *Theology* of the pseudo-Aristotle would confirm this belief. Nevertheless it is difficult to suppose that the *falāsifa* failed to notice the differences, not only between Aristotle and Plato, but also between the commentators, or that they passively took over eclecticism, which is itself a synthesis and in any case necessarily varies from one writer to another. Primitive *falsafa* could not establish itself as a "sect" (to use the term employed by Renan) except insofar as it borrowed from Hellenistic and post-Hellenistic philosophy a common form, a general concept of the world, a comprehensive theory of the spirit, the soul, man and human knowledge, with a technical vocabulary to become the familiar jargon of the schools. In detail, beyond the structural uniformity, each *faylasūf* made his own choice, and the first *falsafa* is much more original than one would suppose if it were described as nothing but Arab Neoplatonism.

2. — Utilization of Greek sources. — Ibn al-Ḳifṭī (568-646/1172-1248), though remote from the beginnings and later than al-Ghazālī, provides some interesting information. He enumerates seven sects of Greek philosophy, adding that the two principal ones are that of Pythagoras and that of Plato and Aristotle. He considers in fact two great sections of Greek philosophy: natural philosophy, which is that of the ancients, exemplified by Pythagoras, Thales of Miletus, the Sabaeans and the Egyptians; and "political" philosophy, which characterizes the moderns, with Socrates, Plato and Aristotle. He explains that this division comes from Aristotle. But he does not separate them absolutely, since he goes so far as to say that Plato achieved the level of Pythagoras in the study of intelligible realities (*fi 'l-umūr al-ʿaḳliyya*) and the level of Socrates in the questions of the constitution of the perfect city (*fī siyāsat al-madīna al-fāḍila*). Thus in the eyes of the Muslims philosophy, culminating in Aristotle, the disciple of Plato, is a synthesis which studies the universe in relation to human life, which views man in the whole and which conceives of the whole as the medium in which man by knowledge and virtue realises his ultimate goal in re-discovering the principle of his being. The philosophy of nature opens out into a mystical cosmology in which the central concept is the Stoic *cosmopolis*. It is comprehensible that in this light Neoplatonism, which embodies all these viewpoints in one system, should have appeared to them as the final formulation of a philosophic ideal in harmony with the religious ideal put forward by a more or less heterodox form of Islam. It is clear that the primary motive for the choice of *falsafa* is religious by nature, since the *falāsifa* always rejected with horror that type of thought also offered by ancient Greece, known as that of the *dahriyya* [*q.v.*], of whom Ibn al-Ḳifṭī also says: "This is a sect of ancient philosophers who deny the Creator, the director of the Universe. They assert that the world has not ceased to be what it is in itself, that it has no creator who made it and freely chose to do so; that the circling motion has no beginning, that man comes from a drop of sperm, and the sperm from man, the plant from the seed and the seed from the plant. The most famous philosopher of this sect is Thales of Miletus; those who follow him are called *zanādiḳa*".

Since Thales was classed among the "physicists" (*ṭabīʿiyyūn*), it is clear that there are in fact two kinds of physicists: those who are purely materialist and rejected, and those who may be taken over by the "metaphysicists" (*ilāhiyyūn*) as Pythagoras is by Plato. It may be argued that Aristotle, in spite of his metaphysics, does not lend himself to use by religious thought: God, νόησις νοήσεως, is not the efficient cause of the world; He is the end, but not the principle. In reply it could be said that the *Uthūlūghiyā* intervened here most aptly, "since it seemed to present the theodicy absent from the *Metaphysics*, though itself brief on the divine attributes and silent on the creation" (A. M. Goichon, *La Philosophie d'Avicenne et son influence en Europe médiévale*, Paris 1951, 12). But it should not be forgotten that Porphyry, the disciple of Plotinus, had steeped himself in Aristotelian thought and saw no opposition in it to that of Plato. Equally, the Neoplatonic commentator Simplicius (6th century), educated both in Alexandria and Athens, had already attempted to harmonize the systems of Plato and Aristotle (as al-Fārābī was to do). Now Simplicius, who had emigrated to Persia upon the closure of the School of Athens by Justinian in 529, was well known to the Muslims (cf. Ibn al-Ḳifṭī: art. *Samlis*). Syrianus also (*ibid.*, art. *Sūryānūs*) was as frequently quoted by the specialists; and he, though he did not believe that the two sages of antiquity were in agreement, at least saw the study of Aristotle as a preliminary to the understanding of Plato. The Muslims therefore did not lack precedents authorizing them not to make too great a gulf between the two great masters of Greek thought.

Nevertheless it would appear that the 'Plotinus source', as F. Rosenthal calls it (*Aš-Šayḫ al-Yūnānī and the Arabic Plotinus source*, in *Orientalia*, xxi (1952), xxii (1953), xxiv (1955), played very much a major rôle, together with the *Uthūlūghiyā* which is related to it. On this point P. Kraus, *Plotin chez les Arabes, Remarques sur un nouveau fragment de la paraphrase des Ennéades*, in *BIÉ*, xxiii (1940), 41, may also be consulted.

Thus everything combined to give a Neoplatonic form to the meeting of Plato and Aristotle in Muslim thought. P. Duhem (*Le système du monde*, iv, 322) observes that Neoplatonism permitted the conservation in a single harmonious whole of what could be saved of the Aristotelian theory of the universe together with what theology claimed.

At the same time certain elements of the Greek inheritance could not be absorbed with comfort in this synthesis. On the one hand, the whole Gnostic, or, rather, theurgic tradition as it developed from Iamblichus to Proclus, becoming burdened with Egyptian and Hermetic ideas, preoccupied with every religion and every god, developing a fantastic angelology, was ready to fuse with the mystic concepts of Persia and India and revivify that esoteric cult which is still alive. These tendencies, subjugated to the discipline of *falsafa* by Avicenna, were to flourish freely in the philosophy of *Ishrāḳ*. On the other hand, an Aristotelianism which had remained more faithful to Aristotle, confining itself to the correction of those points where he displayed weaknesses, difficulties, obscurities or incoherence, had never ceased to be represented in the post-Hellenistic period up to the 6th century. Alexander of Aphrodisias (2nd century) tries to explain Aristotle and defend him against the doctrines of other schools. In doing so, he insists on the naturalist aspect of his teaching and professes a nominalism. The universal exists only in human thought; "separated from the intellect which thinks it, it is destroyed." Thus it neither preexists particular things nor is drawn from them; it appears only as a consequence of the experience which thought has of these things: thus the soul is a form of the body and cannot subsist without it. As for the doctrine of the intellect, a distinction must be drawn between the νοῦς φυσικός or ὑλικός (natural or material, which is potential), the νοῦς ἐπίκτητος or καθ' ἕξιν (acquired and possessing the habitus of intelligible thought), and the νοῦς ποιητικός which makes the transition from the potentiality of the former to the habitus of the latter but which does not belong to the human soul, coming to it from outside (θύραθεν). This theory of the intellect was to be the constant subject of consideration in the *falsafa* of every age. But the Aristotelianism of Alexander was especially to characterize the Western philosophers: Ibn Bādjdja (Avempace) and particularly Ibn Rushd (Averroes) and to exercise some influence in the East on the thought of Fakhr al-Dīn al-Rāzī. It is thus associated with a transformation of primitive *falsafa* which takes place in consequence of al-Ghazālī's criticism of the *falāsifa*. We should also refer to Themistius (4th century), a late Peripatetic: he uses Plato, believing him in agreement with Aristotle, but "prefers to the novelties of Neoplatonism that more ancient Platonic-Aristotelian philosophy" (W. Stegemann, *Real Encyclopädie*, art. *Themistios*). He was above all interested in ethics, to which he regarded logic and physics as merely ancillary. This idea passed into *falsafa*. His aim was practical; he wished to render Aristotle more easily accessible, in "paraphrases" in which he gathered together the ideas of the master clearly and concisely. This is why the Muslims turned frequently to him; some indeed adopted his method of exposition by means of paraphrase.

Falsafa, as an encyclopaedic system of knowledge, also owes much to the physician Galen (2nd century). He again is the author of an original and very wide electicism. He made explicit the idea that medicine is founded on a philosophical basis, an idea which was to dominate the activity of the *falāsifa*, who were nearly all savants and physicians. In logic, physics, and metaphysics Galen bases himself on Aristotle, but his eclecticism is touched with Stoic ideas and it is in part through him that Islam made the acquaintance of the Stoa. In psychology, he follows the Platonic teaching of the tripartite division of the soul. Though concentrating on the study of positive reality as accessible to experience, he believes in the existence of God and in Providence, which is manifested in the harmony of the parts of the universe and the bodily organs. Fakhr al-Dīn al-Rāzī depends on him, at the beginning of his commentary on the Ḳur'ān, in order to demonstrate the sympathy of all beings in the universe, from which it follows that the slightest search is linked with every other. Nevertheless, though Galen integrated philosophy with science and thus laid the foundations for a system to be found in every Muslim philosopher, he did not distract *falsafa* from its Neoplatonic preference, for he nourished a philosophical literature "which, starting from the Timaeus of Plato and passing through the commentary of Posidonius on the Timaeus, ended in Neoplatonism" (Ueberweg, *Grundriss der Geschichte der Philosophie des Altertums*, Berlin 1920, 576). At the same time Galen represents above all to the Muslims, if we may believe Ibn al-Ḳifṭī, a physical philosopher (*favlasūf ṭabīʿī*) who understood the method of demonstrative proof (*ʿālim bi-ṭarīḳ al-burhān*) and applied it to all sciences. He concerned himself with the problem of distinguishing causes (the question of the *asbāb al-māsika* to which Ibn al-Ḳifṭī draws attention), an important problem which is equally central in Proclus and over which *falsafa* and *kalām* were to divide.

Another commentator of Aristotle familiar to the Muslims is John Philoponus (Yaḥyā al-Naḥwī). He was a Christian, who contested with Proclus the doctrine of the eternity of the world, basing himself primarily on considerations of physics. In this manner he demonstrated that the scientific spirit, freed from the extremist metaphysics of the Athenian Neoplatonists, could have room for the fundamental dogma of revealed monotheism.

The Greek heritage is therefore a very varied body of doctrines and trends of whose multiplicity the Muslims were not unaware. Thus *falsafa* had to make a choice, and this explains the varied forms it assumed from time to time, reflecting no doubt different philosophical temperaments but also religious attitudes to dogma and theology and to the history of the sects and of *kalām*.

3. — The establishment of *falsafa*. — The influence of translations is of prime importance. But that *falsafa* was born at all is due to the fact that most of the translators were also original thinkers. Original work was often linked to the translation by the intermediary of commentary. Thus Ḳustā b. Lūḳā made use of technical language gleaned from translations to produce individual work, as shown in the *Book of characters* (ed. P. Sbath, in *BIÉ*, xxiii (1940-1)). Ibn al-Nadīm (d. 386/996) appreciated his value as a philosopher. Ḳustā reveals great subtlety in analysis, and a spirit of synthesis which enables him to borrow from the different sciences whatever material he needs to deal with his subject. It is important to note that a thinker like al-Kindī, who is revered by posterity as a philosopher and savant, is also a translator. Moreover, all the great *falāsifa* applied themselves to commentaries on Greek texts. Thus, *falsafa* does not follow from works of translation and commentary; it is born amongst them and continues them; its lexicon (*iṣṭilāḥāt*) was not written as a purely philological exercise unrelated to it; *falsafa* gained definition by an undertaking which combined translations, commentaries, personal reflections and practical examples.

4. — The first period of *falsafa*. — This could be called Avicennan. It takes shape in the East between the 3rd/9th and the 5th/11th centuries, with al-Kindī, al-Fārābī, and Ibn Sīnā (Avicenna). It is a synthesis of Neoplatonic metaphysics, natural science and mysticism: Plotinus enriched by Galen and Proclus.

This first *falsafa* is quite distinct from the *kalām* which preceded it (Muʿtazilī *kalām*); although it takes pleasure in the rediscovery of Ḳurʾānic texts or ideas, it does not make them a starting point, but is presented as a method of research independent of dogma, without, however, rejecting the dogma or ignoring it in its sources. Nevertheless, its problems are not unrelated to those of theology. The Muʿtazila, in order to preserve the absolute transcendence of the divine unity, had distinguished essence from existence in created beings. For them, there was in God no paradigm (*mat̲h̲al*) for the essence of the creature, and creation consisted simply in bestowing existence on essences which were in "a state of nothingness". The creative act was conceived in a positive sense as what causes essences to pass from non-existence to existence (*lam yakun fayakūnu*). God, Whom nothing resembles, was therefore beyond the essence and the existence of creatures here below. The first *falsafa* is based on an ontology which also makes a distinction between essence and existence. But it did not find the idea of creation *ex nihilo* in the Greeks. It preserved the absolute transcendence and unity of God by introducing precisely this distinction between essence and existence in all beings other than the Godhead. For God alone, existence is identical with essence. But for this reason He is the unifying and unique mainspring of the two orders of being. Thus this *falsafa* unites seemingly contradictory concepts of the universe; on the one hand there is a First Principle in whose unity are rooted both the essences and the existences of all beings, and in consequence a continuity is postulated between the Being and beings, which is not interrupted by any creative act; on the other hand, there is an absolute discontinuity between the modes of being of the Principle and of that which proceeds from the Principle. Thus it is possible to speak of a cosmological continuity between the universe and its source (theory of emanation), tending to a form of monism, and of an ontological discontinuity between the necessary and the possible, tending to re-establish the absolute transcendence of God. Furthermore, the possible beings, in whom essence is distinct from existence, are only possible if considered in themselves. But they are necessary if considered in relation to the Principle: granted a Being necessary *on its own account*, everything else is necessary *because of it*. As was to be the case with Spinoza and Hegel, the possible is always real. Hence we return to monism. Is that a reason for considering that this *falsafa* is incoherent? Up to now we have considered only the cosmology and the ontology of the first *falsafa*, which means that this *falsafa* needed to be completed by a third attitude to Being: the mystical. *Falsafa* of the Avicennan type may be analysed as regards its system in the following manner: a first upward movement going from beings to the Being, which seeks an ontological foundation for given reality; this is human intelligence in search of a principle of intelligibility in the universe; then a second, downward movement, an attempt to explain the universe on the basis of a declared principle, which should provide a total explanation of it; these two movements involve only human thought; but in the first, the principle is attained so to speak in perspective, as the limit where conditions of intelligibility converge; thus there may well be some lack of continuity of thought, since it is logically impossible for thought to reach this limit; whilst in the second movement, thought starts from the idea which corresponds in it to this Principle, and tries to produce from it the world from which it came itself; this is a difficult task, since it is beyond the scope of logical deduction, and recourse must be made to images (metaphors of light) through which the continuity which is postulated but not demonstrated can be re-established. Then comes the third movement, which is a second ascent, but this time no longer a simple discursive procedure, since it is by intelligible intuitions of the spiritual realities themselves, already identified, that progress is made. Man first sees himself in his contingency, separated from his Principle, endowed with a precarious existence. But ontology has taught him that his whole being is rooted in God, and cosmology supplies him with a spiritual itinerary, whose postulated continuity will be verified by mystical experience. The last word therefore is with this experience.

A second theme which Greek philosophy had touched on, and which Muʿtazilī *kalām* had studied very closely, is that of the knowledge God has of particular things. The first *falsafa*, in its theory of the possible, considerably simplified the problem posed by the theologians who believed that contingent things could be or not be. However, there still remained the difficulty of the knowledge of the particular as such: God could not make contact with this in itself in its materiality, but only in His universal knowledge of that which is. *Falsafa* was thus obliged to interpret the verses of the Ḳurʾān where God declares that nothing, not even a grain of mustard seed (Ḳurʾān, xxi, 47), escapes Him. This question is, moreover, closely linked with the concept of creation held by the first *falsafa*. There is no doubt that it rejects the dogmatic idea of creation *ex nihilo*, but it aggravates its case by adopting the principle that from the One only the one can proceed, which led it into complicated theories on the successive procession of the Intellects and of their spheres, from the first Intellect onward; this procession plays a part not only in cosmology, but in the theory of knowledge, of prophetic revelation and of mystical experience. In this context must be placed the doctrine of the intellect as agent and its rôle in man's intellection. On this point explanations vary slightly from one philosopher to another. In conclusion we may note that the problem of the immortality of the soul is closely related to this doctrine.

Such are the fundamental themes of the first *falsafa*. Each philosopher of this school, and above all Avicenna, has been the object of varying interpretations, according to whether emphasis was laid on his scientific works, on the relationship of his metaphysics with Western scholasticism, on his fidelity to Greek thought, or on his mystical ideas. In fact, all these points of view must be considered together, not forgetting moreover that *falsafa* penetrates into the Muslim environment and that even if it was rejected by strict orthodoxy it was none the less steeped in Islamic thought considered as a whole; we have seen that it was not ignorant of *kalām*; even in its logic, where the Aristotelian inspiration is clearest (for example in the *S̲h̲ifāʾ* of Avicenna), allusions to the concepts of the Arab grammarians are easily discernible. Finally, *falsafa* interested itself in political problems, not only by preserving Greek works on *politeia*, but in relation to the political, and therefore religious, problems of the Muslim world of that time. The temporal organization of a city has the double purpose of achieving the well-being of men and of preparing them for the future life. The union of members of the earthly community foreshadows the union of souls with souls, and of souls with God, in the after life. Political theory thus itself embraces mysticism; these ideas are so strong that they will be respected by al-G͟hazālī and will reappear in another context as late as Ibn K͟haldūn. It may be said that *falsafa* wished to support *s͟harīʿa, fiḳh*, and *aḥkām sulṭāniyya*, and that it is thus opposed to the spirit of the Ḳurʾān. This is true as far as rigorously orthodox Islam is concerned. But *falsafa* developed in more liberal surroundings, where there was a desire for a less legalistic view of religion and for an Islam which would be cultural and universal in character.

5. — The reaction of al-G͟hazālī. — If Avicenna is a much discussed figure, al-G͟hazālī is discussed much more. Some see him as a reactionary who brought to an end the blossoming of the rational thought of the philosophers, and made supreme a theology which was itself the slave of dogma. For others he clipped the wings of mystical thought by fighting the Bāṭiniyya, whose teachings were in harmony with the great spiritual constructions of *falsafa*. Whatever value one may place on the thought of al-G͟hazālī, the historical significance of his work demands recognition. Even if he conceived his religious system only for political ends associated with the passing circumstances of the disturbed period in which he was living, yet he introduced Greek philosophy into the realm of Sunnī thought, through the way he developed As͟hʿarism and criticized the *falāsifa*. In *falsafa*, as in esoteric mysticism, he denounced Gnostic trends opposed to the Ḳurʾānic spirit. No doubt he remained a *mutakallim*; it would be an abuse of language to say that he created a Sunnī *falsafa*. He simply allowed *falsafa*, and mysticism too, to detach itself from S͟hīʿī heterodoxy and to become acclimatized in an orthodox environment.

The principal points of his criticism (which were to be taken up again by Ibn al-Ḳifṭī) may be brought together under three headings: against *falsafa* he maintains (a) the resurrection of the body and the materiality of the rewards and punishments of the after life; (b) the creation of the world in the proper sense and its real contingency; (c) God's knowledge of particular things. As for the other philosophical sciences—mathematics, logic, physics—they are harmless provided that their methods are not generalized rashly and that they are not allowed to exceed their proper limits. The metaphysics of the Greeks and their imitators is on the other hand a privileged place for innovations and impieties since in this field logical reasoning is not infallibly applied. Al-G͟hazālī, like his master al-D͟juwaynī, was struck by the differences which rule between metaphysicians in spite of their common appeal to reason. There is a level of reality where human reason cannot grasp truth by its own efforts; it needs the help of revelation which alone provides certitude in these questions. These ideas, put forward by G͟hazālī in a dogmatic and theological context, reappear in a philosophical context in his successors.

6. — The second period of *falsafa*. — This may be called post-G͟hazālī. It is distinguished geographically by having one centre in the East with Fak͟hr al-Dīn al-Rāzī and another in the West with Avempace (Ibn Bād͟jd͟ja), Ibn Ṭufayl and Averroes (Ibn Rus͟hd). The period is characterized in part by its diversity, the teachings no longer displaying that unity of approach which the preceding period showed; and in part by the fact that this *falsafa* is much more integrated in the whole intellectual and spiritual culture acquired by Islam over the formative centuries: theology, law, *tafsīr*, mysticism, constitute disciplines which from now on are established and rich in content and influence, whereas the first *falsafa* found itself taking shape at a time when all mental activities were seeking an appropriate way for themselves, and only Muʿtazilism so far had taken up fixed positions.

Of the three who most adorned Western *falsafa*, Avempace displayed the least religious spirit. His *Rule of the solitary* (*Tadbīr al-mutawaḥḥid*) has as its ideal isolation from the mass of mankind in a purely intellectual contemplation of the intelligible. In his *Risālat al-Ittiṣāl* he shows how it is possible to unite with the agent Intellect, by studying the development of the human individual from his embryonic life to the speculative life. This is a philosophical psychology of knowledge.

This "evolutive" aspect of Avempace's thought recurs in Ibn Ṭufayl, where some influence of the Ik͟hwān al-Ṣafāʾ may also be discerned. The mysticism of Ibn Ṭufayl tries to go further than the purely speculative mysticism of Avempace, being inspired both by Avicenna and al-G͟hazālī.

Averroes, in his refutation of the *Tahāfut al-falāsifa*, was led to take up again the problems with which Avicenna's philosophy had faced Sunnī orthodoxy. He replies to al-G͟hazālī, not in order to defend Ibn Sīnā but in order to set out his own teaching, more directly inspired by Aristotle and the Peripatetic commentators than the first *falsafa* had been. The meaning of Averroism has been much discussed. Some, with Renan, view him as a pure rationalist. According to L. Gauthier, Ibn Rus͟hd only rejects the kind of theology which encloses itself in the revealed texts and desires to comprehend them dialectically; but he allows literal belief to the uneducated, who react to the rhetoric of images, while philosophers should submit everything to apodictic proof. It appears that this explanation by means of the theory of the three classes of spirit (apodictic, dialectic, rhetorical) does not entirely cover the thought of Averroes. In fact, he was responsive to the warning of al-G͟hazālī: rigorous proof is only superior where the object is accessible to human intelligence. When this is not so and obscurities remain, as in the questions of creation, the attributes of God, and the nature of the after life, philosophy has no real privilege, and risks indeed encouraging doubt, while revealed knowledge, though in itself inferior, gains the advantage since it brings assurance. To the fundamental problems of the first *falsafa* as criticised by al-G͟hazālī, Averroes replies like a *mutakallim*: he gives up the postulate that from the One nothing but the one can emerge; God moves the world by His *amr* which permits Him to act while remaining unmoved (cf. the unmoved prime mover of Aristotle); God has no will resembling the human will, since He has nothing to desire, having all; but the idea of a voluntary act better represents what creation is than the idea of an involuntary emanation (a viewpoint to be found in al-Rāzī in his commentaries on the divine attribute of life, *ḥayāt*); God does not know particular things in a sentient manner; but the knowledge He has of them resembles the sentient knowledge by which man grasps them rather than our abstract and general knowledge. These few observations suffice to show that Averroes took note of the theological criticisms of al-G͟hazālī.

In the East, Fak͟hr al-Dīn al-Rāzī is an As͟hʿarī

like al-Ghazālī, whom he takes for guide, while remaining attached to the thought of Avicenna. He criticizes the Muʿtazila but he borrows from them what he can use. He attacks the extremist sects but without breaking down the bridges to them. Irenic in outlook, in spite of his polemical vigour, he is endowed with great powers of synthesis and it is perhaps in him that the richest, widest and most open system is to be found. He explains Avicenna while correcting him. He achieves a profound union of *kalām* and *falsafa*. Thus, like his adversary al-Ṭūsī, he studies the Muʿtazilī notion of mode (*ḥāl*) in relation to the problem of the divine attributes. For him, philosophical reason may well collect ideas into coherent systems, but it is for revelation to pronounce upon their truth. Finally, the sacred text is a stimulus for philosophical thought. Al-Rāzī therefore clearly differs from Averroes in his approach; he does not limit recourse to dogma and *kalām* to certain difficult cases: with him philosophy and theology are co-extensive and interpenetrating.

7. — The tradition of Avicenna in the philosophy of *ishrāḳ*. — The work of al-Ghazālī was not accepted by the whole of Islam; in particular those circles, of Shīʿī tendencies, who resisted his criticism developed the most mystical aspects of Avicenna's thought in order to produce a union of Avicennian type *falsafa* with a mystical *kalām* of Gnostic inspiration.

Here we must mention the philosophical *corpus* of Abu 'l-Barakāt al-Baghdādī (d. 550/1155), which develops into an angelology. But the great representative of *Ishrāḳ* is al-Suhrawardī (d. 578/1191), who was influenced philosophically by Avicenna but gives an important position to Aristotelian concepts in the exposition of his mystical ideas. On the philosophical plane, it was Naṣīr al-Dīn al-Ṭūsī (d. 672/1273) who was to undertake the Shīʿī defence of Avicenna's thought against al-Rāzī, a defence which is not, however, accompanied by absolute fidelity: the *real* distinction between essence and existence is denied, and one finds in the end an explicit monism in al-Suhrawardī, al-Ṭūsī and Ṣadr al-Dīn al-Shīrāzī (d. 1050/1640). This monist philosophy developed above all in the Iranian areas and is often expressed in Persian. It remained alive and flourishing for a long period.

8. — *Falsafa* as scholasticism. — In spite of the great names which adorn even the last period of *falsafa*, it must be recognized that from now on thinkers are in possession of received ideas and that they develop them in variations which offer interest but without real invention. The union of *falsafa* and *kalām* was completed: the stages of this process are marked by Tustarī, Ḳuṭb al-Dīn al-Rāzī (d. 765/1364) and al-Īdjī (d. 756/1355), for whom *kalām* includes metaphysical questions and logical procedures while offering the greater security of reason founded on tradition. Al-Īdjī appears in this period as the leader of a school whose disciples were to diverge in different directions, some attaching themselves to Ashʿarī orthodoxy, such as al-Djurdjānī (d. 816/1413), others remaining more faithful to Avicenna, like Sayf al-Dīn al-Abharī (8th/14th century), al-Fanārī (d. 886/1481), al-Siyālakūtī (d. 1069/1659). Thus the earlier discussions over the opposition of Avicenna and Ghazālī are taken up again: in these the partisans and continuers of Avicenna are Djamāl al-Dīn al-Ḥillī (d. 726/1326), a leading theologian of the imāmiyya, and Ḳushdjī (d. 749/1348); while those who attacked Avicenna's school in the spirit of Ashʿarī *kalām* and in the tradition of al-Ghazālī included al-Iṣfahānī (d. 749/1348) and al-Taftazānī (d. 791/1389). The "scholastic" character of this *falsafa* is basically what unites it in spite of the diversity of trends. It is clearly indicated by the flourishing of commentaries, no longer on Greek, but on Arabic and Persian works. Thus, al-Djurdjānī writes a commentary on the *Mawāḳif* of al-Īdjī; al-Dawwānī on Suhrawardī and on the *ʿAḳāʾid*, also of al-Īdjī; while al-Fanārī comments on al-Fārābī.

This *falsafa* is also scholastic in its method of exposition, which multiplies divisions and subdivisions. This method was not, of course, new, but it becomes more and more formal.

9. — Supplementary and conclusion. — To enumerate here all the theological philosophers of the last period would be tedious. We ought rather to mention those works of previous centuries which, though philosophical, do not exactly fit into the categories we have outlined. We should first recall that theologians like the Ashʿarīs al-Bāḳillānī and al-Djuwaynī or the Ẓāhirī Ibn Ḥazm, wrote of purely philosophical questions from a point of view which was properly that of *kalām* (*e.g.*, al-Bāḳillānī's theory of causality and atomism). On the other hand, the *Rasāʾil* of the Ikhwān al-Ṣafāʾ deserve mention; these develop Pythagorean ideas, frequently with remarkable originality, on the fringes of the school of Avicenna but in an analogous spirit, in spite of the popularizing character of these writings. Ibn Masarra, who has been studied by Asín Palacios, was influenced by the philosophy of Empedocles and Bāṭinī mysticism (cf. Ibn al-Ḳifṭī, art. *Abīdhaḳlīs*).

Further, it should be noted that in order to study not *falsafa* as such but the philosophical ideas current in Islam one should also consider the use of Greek concepts by sages such as ʿAlī b. Rabban al-Ṭabarī and above all Abū Bakr Muḥammad b. Zakariyya al-Rāzī and many others. The corpus of Djābir also, in the analysis of it by P. Kraus, should not be neglected by those seeking to establish the function of Pythagoreanism in the alchemical concepts of Islamic scholars. In another field, the examination of the theories of the grammarians, particularly Ibn Djinnī, would supply very interesting information on the influence of Greek ideas in Arabic grammar. In special philosophical disciplines such as ethics, Ibn Miskawayh should be mentioned, whose thought extensively overlaps pure questions of morals and reflects the life of his age. The literary circle of Baghdād made known to us by Abū Ḥayyān al-Tawḥīdī, is very representative of philosophical culture in the Muslim East of the 4th/10th century.

To sum up, *falsafa* was a focus of reflection on the legacy of Greek thought. It was not at the beginning a matter of Muslim apologetics utilizing Hellenic philosophy to explain and justify the faith. *Falsafa* began as a search by Muslims with Shīʿī leanings for a coherence in their intellectual and spiritual life, that is, the quest for a religious humanism, with all that humanism implies in freedom of spirit. Later it evolved, grew closer to orthodox *kalām* and ended by fusing with it. Only then did *falsafa* begin to burden itself with apologetic elements: *fides quaerens intellectum* or, conversely, faith illuminating and fortifying knowledge. Only the mysticism of *ishrāḳ* retained the primitive humanism of Avicenna (cf. *al-Insān al-kāmil*). In the course of its development, *falsafa* spread Greek ideas in every realm of thought. But it concluded by becoming a school activity. It is perhaps this decline which inspired the disillusioned observations of Ibn Khaldūn on the pernicious effects of education in the Muslim world.

This great thinker of the 8th/14th century, who spared nothing and no-one in his scientific criticism of societies, appears at least in his *Muḳaddima* as the most profoundly rationalist of all Muslim philosophers. The interest in political philosophy which animates the first *falāsifa* reappears in him, but purged of all Neoplatonic metaphysics. Ibn Khaldūn indeed saw in these great systems concepts inspired by the characteristics of social life. In this sense one can say that he destroyed *falsafa* in accomplishing his ideal. For the universality which it assumed for itself, because it claimed to achieve a self-sufficing intelligible, he substituted the actual universality of a positive all-embracing science, the science of human societies.

Bibliography: ʿA. Badawī, *Arisṭū ʿind al-ʿArab*, Cairo 1947; idem, *Neoplatonici apud Arabes*, Cairo 1955; idem, *Manṭiḳ Arisṭū*, Cairo 1947-52, 3 vols.; idem, *Al-Uṣūl al-Yūnāniyya li 'l-naẓariyyāt al-siyāsiyya fi 'l-Islām*, 1954; T. J. de Boer, *Geschichte der Philosophie im Islam*, Stuttgart 1901; Carra de Vaux, *Les penseurs de l'Islam*, iv, Paris 1923; P. Duhem, *Le système du monde*, iv, Paris 1916; Gardet and Anawati, *Introduction à la théologie musulmane*, Paris 1948; Ḥannā al-Fākhūrī and Khalīl Djurr (Georr), *Taʾrīkh al-falsafa al-ʿarabiyya*, Beirut; S. Horowitz, *Über den Einfluss d. griech. Philosophie auf die Entwicklung d. Kalam* (*Jahresber. d. jüd.-theol. Seminars*, Breslau 1909); M. Horten, *Die Philosophie des Islams*, Munich 1924; M. Klamroth, *Über die Auszüge aus griechischen Schriftstellern bei al-Yaʿḳūbī*, iii: *Philosophen*, in *ZDMG*, xli (1887); I. Madkour, *L'Organon d'Aristote dans le monde arabe*, Paris 1934; idem, *La place d'al-Fārābī dans l'école philosophique musulmane*, Paris 1934; S. Munk, *Mélanges de philosophie juive et arabe*, Paris 1859, republ. 1927; W. Kutsch and S. Marrow, *Alfarabi's commentary on Aristotle's De Interpretatione*, Beirut 1962; M. Mahdi, *Al-Farabi's Philosophy of Aristotle*, Beirut 1961; idem, *Al-Farabi's Philosophy of Plato and Aristotle*, New York 1962; A. Schmölders, *Essai sur les écoles philosophiques chez les Arabes*, Paris 1842; M. Steinschneider, *Die arab. Übersetzungen aus dem Griechischen*, (*Beih. z. Centralbl. für Bibliothekw.*, xii), Leipzig 1893; R. Walzer, *Greek into Arabic, Essays on Islamic philosophy*, Oxford 1962; W. M. Watt, *Islamic philosophy and theology*, London 1962.—For a bibliography of each philosopher, see the appropriate article. In the context of this article we would nevertheless refer to the works of A. M. Goichon, Henri Corbin, and Louis Gardet on Avicenna. Cf. also Averroes' *Tahāfut al-Tahāfut*, English trans. with notes (very important) by S. van den Berg, *GMS*, N.S. xix, London 1954. On Rāzī, Ṭūsī and questions concerning *kalām*, see M. Horten, *Die Modus Theorie des Abū Haschim, Ein Beitrag zur Geschichte der Philosophie im Islam*, in *ZDMG*, lxiii (1909). For a general bibliography, see J. de Menasce, *Arabische Philosophie*, Berne 1948. (R. Arnaldez)

FAMAGUSTA [see maghosha].

FAMILY [see ʿāʾila].

FAN [see mirwāḥa].

FANĀʾ [see baḳāʾ].

FANAK (pl. *afnāk*; from Pers. *fanak/fanadj*) may refer, at different times and with different authors, to various animals of different orders or families. In the Muslim west *fanak* is commonly applied to the fennec-fox, *Fennecus zerda*, a small wild member of the genus *Vulpes* of the Canidae with very large ears, a pale dun coat, and a spreading bushy tail. The nocturnal habits of this puny carnivore, and its essentially desert distribution from the Sahara to Arabia, have caused it to be practically ignored by Arabic writers, naturalists, encyclopaedists and poets; al-Djāḥiẓ, for example, frankly confesses his ignorance of the real *fanak* (*Ḥayawān*, vi, 32). For a better knowledge of the fennec it is necessary to turn to the desert tribes; one finds, for example, six terms at least in the various dialects of Tamaḥaḳ which refer to this animal (see Ch. de Foucauld, *Dictionnaire Touareg-Français*, Paris 1952, ii, 962, s.v. *akhōrhi*; H. Lhote, *La chasse chez les Touaregs*, Paris 1951, 133). In the eastern countries which do not know the fennec proper of the Sahara fauna, *fanak* is used for the Corsac or Karagan Fox, *Vulpes corsac* (from Turk. *ḳūrsāḳ*), found from Turkestan to Mongolia; this little animal when domesticated enjoyed a great vogue as a lady's pet in Europe in the 16th century, when it was known as "adive".

However, neither of these two foxes is meant by the term *fanak* in the imagination of all the authors who have used the word; all mean a member of the Mustelidae whose pelt was greatly esteemed in the luxury fur-trade and which ranked with such fur-bearing animals (*dhawāt al-wabr wa 'l-firāʾ*) as the ermine (*ḳāḳum*), sable (*sammūr*), Siberian squirrel (*sindjāb*) and otter (*kalb al-māʾ*). The skins of the *fanak* were imported, at great expense, from central Europe and Asia (*min arḍ Khwārizm, min bilād al-Ṣaḳāliba*). Although the identification of this animal has troubled many translators, there is no doubt that it must be the mink, *Mustela lutreola*; sufficient proof of this is given by Ibn al-Bayṭār (tr. L. Leclerc, *Traité des simples*, Paris 1877-83, iii, no. 1708), who says of the *fanak* "... this is a species of marten, and its fur is brought from the land of the Slavonians, or from the lands of the Turks and Russians". It is difficult to understand how the *fanak*, worn in cloaks (*farwa*) by the young Andalusian dandies and poets of the 4th-5th/10th-11th centuries, could have been identified with the weasel (see H. Pérès, *La poésie andalouse ... au XIème siècle*², Paris 1953, 320 and notes) which, common in Spain, has never been used by furriers, its pelt being too small and of mediocre quality; moreover the weasel, *Mustela nivalis*, has never been known in Arabic by any name other than *ibn ʿirs*. Finally, it is of interest to note that the flesh of the *fanak* is recognized, according to al-Damīrī (*Ḥayāt al-ḥayawān*, ii, 225), as legitimate for human consumption among Muslims, which indicates that in the eyes of the legists the *fanak* cannot belong to the Canidae, the canine species, domestic or wild, being absolutely impure, on the authority of many traditions of the Prophet.

Bibliography: in addition to references in the text: Ps.-Djāḥiẓ, *K. al-Tabaṣṣur bi 'l-tidjāra*, ed. H. H. Abdul Wahab, Cairo 1935, 28, and Fr. tr. Ch. Pellat in *Arabica*, 1954, 159; Djāḥiẓ, *Ḥayawān*, v, 484; vi, 27, 32, 305; Ḳalḳashandī, *Ṣubḥ*, ii, 49; L. Blancou, *Géographie cynégétique du monde*, Paris 1959, *passim*; L. Lavauden, *Les vertébrés du Sahara*, Tunis 1926, 34; P. Bourgoin, *Animaux de chasse d'Afrique*, Paris 1955, 179; V. Monteil, *Faune du Sahara occidental*, Paris 1951, 57. (F. Viré)

FANĀR [see fener and manār].

al-**FANĀRĪ** [see fenārī-zāde].

FANN, the (modern) Arabic name for art. Individual treatment of aspects of the art of Islam will be found in articles under the following headings;

the examples are given as a guide and are not intended to be exhaustive.

1. Techniques, *e.g.*, ARCHITECTURE, BINĀʾ (building), FAKHKHĀR (the potter's craft), FUSAYFISĀʾ (mosaic), ḲĀLĪ (carpets), KHAṬṬ (calligraphy), ḲUMĀSH (textiles), METALWORK, TAṢWĪR (painting), etc.

2. Materials, *e.g.*, ʿĀDJ (ivory), BILLAWR (crystal), DJIṢṢ (plaster), KHAZAF (pottery and ceramics), ʿIRḲ AL-LUʾLUʾ (mother-of-pearl), LIBĀS (costume), etc., as well as description of materials in the articles on techniques.

3. Objects, types of buildings, artistic features, *e.g.*, ḲALAMDĀN (pencases); BĀB (gates), BĀʾOLĪ (step-wells), BURDJ (towers), BUSTĀN (gardens), ḤAMMĀM (baths), ḤIṢN (fortification), ḲANṬARA (bridges), MAḲBARA (tombs), MANĀRA (minarets), MASDJID (mosques), SABĪL (fountains), etc.; ʿAMŪD (capitals), ARABESQUE, ĪWĀN (arcades), MUḲARNAS (stalactites), etc.

4. Artists, *e.g.*, BIHZĀD, MANṢŪR, SINĀN, etc.

5. Music, theatre, etc., *e.g.*, MŪSĪḲĪ; articles on individual musical instruments, *e.g.*, DUFF, ṬANBŪR; CINEMA; MAṢRAḤIYYA (drama); LAʿB (games).

6. Countries and cities, *passim*.

7. Dynasties, and in some cases individual rulers *passim*. (ED.)

The idea of a specifically Islamic art can hardly be conceived without preliminary reference to the idea of an Islamic civilization which allows the bringing together, across the apparent contradictions of form, style and material, of monuments widely separated in time and space and objects produced according to widely different techniques. If it be indeed commonly admitted that a new faith and a new spirit may invoke a similar renaissance in the domain of aesthetics, it must as readily be conceded that the perpetuation of certain modes of life and thought, in a society dominated by a rigid legalism of a religious character and faithful until the dawn of the modern era to the principles established in the Middle Ages, has produced a similar fixedness of artistic traditions, as seen in the most diverse natural surroundings from the moment when they were first incorporated in the world of Islam; thus we may group under a common heading, in spite of all the exterior reasons for differentiation, works which derive, over more than thirteen centuries of history, from the most diverse countries and peoples.

In this sense one can speak of the unity of Islamic art, the principal factor of which was without doubt the constitution, in the first centuries of Islam, of that immense empire of the Caliphate, Umayyad and later ʿAbbāsid, which brought together under a single authority many regions formerly independent of one another; it thus provided an environment favouring the elaboration of a primitive "classicism" which was to serve as a point of reference for the later developments, and to bring into being, according to clearly discernible lines of affiliation, local or national flowerings which could not fail to develop individually in the years that followed.

Sprung therefore from the conjunction of several inheritances, in the first rank of which were a Hellenistic heritage from the southern provinces of the Byzantine empire and an Iranian heritage which shortly before had been crystallized under the aegis of the powerful Sāsānid dynasty, this first Islamic art deserves primarily to be described as profoundly eclectic, through its having gathered and mingled without restraint, while the conquerors were willingly susceptible to the atmosphere of the arts around them, structural or decorative elements borrowed from the practices of the conquered countries, with the one proviso that these elements be adapted, in conformity with the observance of certain rules, to the needs of the new Muslim society.

This practice was to be perpetuated in the ensuing periods, and although the first phenomena of absorption and transformation, particularly noticeable in the Near Eastern regions which might be called the heart of the empire, marked Islamic art as such with Syro-Mesopotamian features, it must not be forgotten that other influences, sometimes transmitted throughout the Muslim world, more often integrated in lands on the periphery whence they could have but a weak diffusion—this is exemplified in North Africa or Spain just as in Khurāsān or in India—, continually influenced here and there the traditional modes which had gradually spread from the active capitals of Damascus or Baghdād. The receptivity, demonstrated very early, to trends coming from the East, which brought into ʿIrāḳī sculpture the characteristic rhythms and scrolls of that Asian art known as "Steppic", was thus soon to be surpassed by the facility with which, from the Saldjūḳ era onwards, modifications of taste and feeling directly attributable to the Turkish invaders were to be imposed. Similarly the reception by Persia of a decorative repertoire of Chinese origin, which had been carried across the Mongol empire and was to stimulate the imagination of its miniaturists, was to have as a counterpart that extraordinary perfection of architectural techniques accomplished in 10th/16th century Ottoman Turkey by artists who applied themselves to the school of the Byzantine masters and who were to succeed in equalling, if not surpassing, Byzantine chefs-d'œuvre by erecting the great series of imperial mosques in Istanbul.

One may also understand in this perspective the multiplication of regional styles [see articles on the relevant countries or dynasties] within an art whose faculty of assimilation remains its dominant characteristic and whose various stages develop within varying ethnic groups and as a result of borrowings which are undisguised; these borrowings have, however, in the course of their transmission undergone a subtle transformation which makes it impossible—even in a creative milieu as clearly individualized as that of Īrān, for example—to confuse works anterior to Islam and those which belong, after the lasting triumph of the new religion, to a differently orientated cycle of aesthetic experience.

Indeed, whatever be the type of monuments or objects under consideration, it would appear that the artistic production of Muslim countries has always conformed to a double set of requirements; the one imposed by the material organization of a society in which artistic patronage was bestowed principally by princes and sovereigns, impressing on the art an aulic, sumptuary and dynastic character whereby the taste for richness and brilliant ornament was necessarily developed; the other, and more important, inspired by the particular form of intellectual and religious outlook which came into being in the 7th century with the preaching of Muḥammad and which, far from becoming more tractable, became more and more rigid in its claims to model the life of the Muslim community according to the dictates of the holy law and the opinions of its practitioners, providing the dominant themes of architecture and encouraging the increasingly systematic employment of decoration in accordance with stereotyped formulas, remote from all realism and spontaneity.

Indeed, it is this deliberate impoverishment of plastic imagination, with its aniconic tendency, which most frequently comes to mind when one attempts to define the basic originality of Islamic art, whether the emphasis is put only on the abstract character of the surface ornamentation which it uses in such profusion, or whether this characteristic is more precisely related with the religious prohibitions peculiar to Islamic doctrine or with a system of theologico-philosophic opinions which dwells on the illusory and precarious character of the visible world as contrasted with God Who alone endures. This may be a somewhat simplified view of a very complex problem, all the more since the exclusion of images was not observed with the same rigour in every region or period; to deny this would be to ignore some of the most beautiful Muslim achievements, starting with those of the schools of illuminators who were well able to portray or transpose with delicate touch the scenes which surrounded them. Yet one should not disregard the large share of truth which such an axiom contains.

As a general rule, indeed, artists working in the Muslim milieu have remained unaffected by a concern to reproduce faithfully the forms of the living world, forms which certainly served them as sources of inspiration, but which became relegated to second place through the treatment to which they were subjected: either they were reduced to filling an accessory rôle in larger compositions — an effort is necessary to discover, for example, the medallions with human or animal representations which are on so many objects enmeshed by networks of arabesques, and the miniatures themselves were conceived solely as an appendage to the manuscript page which they were to enrich — or else recourse was had to them merely for the guiding lines of stylizations which were to be repeated, divorced from all direct contact with nature. This is not unrelated to the lack of favour with which work in high relief was regarded, a technique which more than any other was likely to disturb the rigorists by producing from its medium an inanimate copy too close to its original; it is connected also with the growing disregard, which visibly asserts itself, for the feeling for the third dimension: it disappears in the interplay of flat colours with which the surfaces of monuments were covered, as in the productions of the artistic workshops or in the *grisaille* of moulded interlacing work which filled the previously compartmented borders and panels.

Thus it is justifiable to define Islamic art as a whole as an art of decorators and ornamenters, concerned to decorate every surface with a multiplicity of figures springing from their own imagination in accordance with a repertoire of motifs which had long passed to the stage of studio prescriptions, motifs often executed in relief or in shallow patterns which were vibrant with light and shade effects, but to which was frequently added the refinement of notes of colour, obtained from very different media according to the period or the region. This art of the ornamenters thus corresponded to a peculiar regard for agreements and harmonies, founded, not without some aridity, on the observation of rules such as the horror of the void and the continuation of the line, in a climate which produced also the melodic line of Arab music and the cadences of its poetry.

It is also true to say, however, that this precious art was first and foremost a scholarly and intellectual art, which grew from a continual recourse to geometrical design and to complicated calculations, permitting decorative forms which were sometimes of a rudimentary nature to be used effectively. This is admirably illustrated by the use of stalactite corbelling, with straightlined or curvilinear cells [see MUḲARNAS], which were ultimately used in the adornment of domes or semi-domes (for example in the coping of portals) according to extremely complex constructional schemes, and which demanded a very specialized technique from the artisans who carried them out, empirical though this may have been. This is revealed also by the study of the basic lines of so many opulent arabesques [*q.v.*], whose value lies in the convolutions of their stylized vegetal stems which are in other respects rather poor; or by analysis of the innumerable combinations of star-shaped polygons on which are based systems of interlacing which often serve as the starting-point for further stylizations. This is also expressed by the variations developed from the angular or cursive letters of the Arabic script, letters which had the double advantage of offering continually fresh themes to the invention of artists, and of being in themselves shapes with an inherent meaning and embodying the results of a long development [see KH̲AṬṬ]. The growing development of ornamental compositions of this genre, apparently without regard for calligraphic exactitude or legibility, is certainly to be included among the most typical aspects of art in Islamic countries.

It goes without saying, however, that such considerations alone do not suffice to characterize the creative vigour of an art which was not content merely to impress its sign manual on certain modes of aesthetic expression, notably in the field of ornament, but was also able to demonstrate, in the field of architecture, its ability to respond, with new programmes, to the situation resulting from the development of Islam and its establishment in regions where there was an older civilization—regions already so enriched with past monumental glory as to prevent the conquerors from being content with the primitive constructions of Mecca or Medina. In this connexion it is necessary to emphasize once more the importance as a model of what was always the Muslim building *par excellence*—the great mosque or *d̲j̲āmiʿ* [see MASD̲J̲ID], created as a whole to meet the needs of the *kh̲uṭba* ceremonial in the Umayyad period, and later reflecting, in a progressive conversion of its various parts to more purely religious purposes, the transformations which the corresponding institutions had similarly undergone. To these transformations of a functional order are to be added also the effects of different architectural fashions, inducing new steps in an evolution which one often underrates by taking account, in archaeological definitions, only of monuments which can truly be called Mediterranean, but which in fact reveals, for anyone who attempts to view Muslim art as a whole, successive adaptations of a structure which was, above all, living.

This is only one example among many, for the origin and the conditions of evolution of other Muslim buildings of a more or less religious character can be viewed in the same light, *e.g.*, the *madrasa* [*q.v.*] with its variants in the *dār al-ḥadīth̲* and the *zāwiya*; the convent illustrated by the forms of the *ribāṭ*, the *kh̲ānḳāh* and the *tekke* [*qq.v.*]; and finally the *mash̲had* [*q.v.*] and the *ḳubba* [*q.v.*] or *turba* [*q.v.*], whose particular characteristics, linked with the development of certain hardly orthodox ways of worship, were also influenced by regional funerary customs and by the growing extravagance of governors or other rich persons in building tombs designed to glorify their memory.

It is no less significant to notice, on a different level, the various interpretations taken, from the beginning of Islam to the present day, by royal palaces [see ḲAṢR], for which there has been a continuous need since the early conquests, and the building of which has been the principal care of each Muslim dynast. Nor are the less grandiose aspects of civil and military architecture to be overlooked, as illustrated by, for example, works of public utility such as waterworks, fountains [see SABĪL], baths [see ḤAMMĀM], warehouses [see ḲAYṢARIYYA] and covered markets [see SŪḲ], simple private houses, or the various types of fortification [see BURDJ, ḤIṢN] represented as much by town walls as by the defence systems of isolated strongholds. Here also one may see the preservation of constant traditions, which it is difficult to separate from the strictly mediaeval historical conditions within which they have been perpetuated, but which nevertheless deserve to be described as Islamic inasmuch as the limits of the geographical region in which they appear correspond exactly with those of the territories characterized by adhesion to Islam.

Bibliography: A complete bibliography is provided by K. A. C. Creswell, *A bibliography of the architecture, arts and crafts of Islam, to 1 Jan. 1960*, London 1962. To general works which have appeared recently on Islamic art (among which must be mentioned G. Marçais, *L'art de l'Islam*, Paris 1946, republished as *L'art musulman*, Paris 1962; G. Wiet, *L'Islam et l'art musulman*, apud R. Huyghe, *L'art et l'homme*, ii, Paris 1958, 133-48, and iii, Paris 1961, 206-9; J. Sourdel-Thomine, *L'art de l'Islam*, in *Encyclopédie de la Pléiade, Histoire de l'art*, i, Paris 1961, 932-1087; E. Kühnel, *Die Kunst des Islam*, Stuttgart 1962) should be added various studies: L. Massignon, *Les méthodes de réalisation artistique des peuples de l'Islam*, in *Syria*, ii (1921); E. Kühnel, *Die Arabeske*, Wiesbaden 1949; idem, *Kunst und Volkstum im Islam*, in *Die Welt des Islams*, N.S., i (1951), 247-82; B. Farès, *Essai sur l'esprit de la décoration islamique*, Cairo 1952; R. Ettinghausen, *Interaction and integration in Islamic art*, in *Unity and variety in Muslim civilization*, Chicago 1955, 107-31; F. Gabrieli, *Corrélations entre la littérature et l'art dans la civilisation musulmane*, in *Classicisme et déclin culturel dans l'histoire de l'Islam*, Paris 1957, 53-70; H. Terrasse, *Classicisme et décadence dans les arts musulmans*, *ibid.*, 71-80; J. Sourdel-Thomine, *Art et société dans le monde de l'Islam*, in *XXIIIe Semaine de Synthèse* (Paris), in the press.

(J. SOURDEL-THOMINE)

FĀO [see AL-FĀʾŪ].

FĀRĀB, a small district on both sides of the middle Jaxartes at the mouth of its tributary, the Aris, which flows from Isfīdjāb. It is also the name of the principal settlement in this district. The older Persian form Pārāb occurs in *Ḥudūd al-ʿālam*, (72, 118 ff., 122), the form Bārāb in Iṣṭakhrī (346) and Muḳaddasī (273; but also Fārāb) as well as in the later Persian sources. The extent of the district in both length and breadth was less than a day's journey (Ibn Ḥawḳal, 390 ff.). According to Masʿūdī (*Tanbīh*, 366) the region was flooded annually at the end of January, and traffic between the settlements was possible only by boat. (In fact the Jaxartes is usually frozen at that season.)

The principal settlement of the district was originally apparently Kadar (Kadir?), with a Friday mosque and lying about half a parasang east of the Jaxartes (Iṣṭakhrī, 346). Near there but of later origin (according to Barthold) was a new centre, called after the district Fārāb, and first mentioned by Muḳaddasī (262, 273). According to the latter it was an extensive fortified city of 70,000 (?) inhabitants (mostly Shāfiʿīs, according to Samʿānī, *GMS*, xx, fol. 415b), with a Friday mosque, a citadel and a marketplace. Kadar and Fārāb fought for pre-eminence in the area. Also worthy of mention in the district of Fārāb is Wasīdj, a small village on the left bank of the river somewhat below the mouth of the Aris and, according to Ibn Ḥawḳal, the birthplace of the philosopher al-Fārābī [*q.v.*], who got his name from the district where he was born.

Fārāb is rarely mentioned in historical sources. In 121/738 for example the prince of Čāč (Tashkent), owing to the pressure of the Arabic provincial government, had to banish to Fārāb an Arab who had taken refuge with him (Ṭabarī, ii, 1694: the only mention of Fārāb by this historian). Islam did not penetrate Fārāb apparently until the Sāmānid period [*q.v.*], after the conquest of Isfīdjāb [*q.v.*] in 225/839-40 (see Balādhurī, *Futūḥ*, 422; Samʿānī, fol. 286b, lines 11-13, s.v. Sāmānī). Wasīdj was mentioned as late as the 12th century as a fortress. For a long time Fārāb lay on the north-east border of Islamic territory, until 349/960 when the neighbouring Turks were also converted to Islam. One of the overland routes which led to the land of the Kimäk Turks had its point of departure in Fārāb (Gardīzī, 83).

According to the common view of the Islamic sources the city of Fārāb corresponds to the later Otrār (for evidence see that article) which, according to Sharaf al-Dīn ʿAlī Yazdī (*Ẓafarnāma*, Calcutta edition, ii, 668), lay two parasangs from the right bank of the Jaxartes. For the further development of the town see OTRĀR. (The ruins of Otrār are in fact about 10 km. from the river).

Bibliography: Le Strange, 484 ff.; Barthold, *Turkestan*, 176-9; *Ḥudūd al-ʿālam*, index, and 358. See also the bibliography to OTRĀR.

(W. BARTHOLD-[B. SPULER])

AL **FĀRĀBĪ**, ABŪ NAṢR MUḤAMMAD B. MUḤAMMAD B. TARKHĀN B. AWZALAGH (UZLUGH?), referred to as Alfarabius or Avennasar in medieval Latin texts. One of the most outstanding and renowned Muslim philosophers, he became known as the "second teacher", the first being Aristotle.

i. — LIFE

Very little is known of al-Fārābī's life. There neither exists an autobiography nor do we have any report by contemporaries. Al-Fārābī was of Turkish origin. He was born in Turkestan at Wasīdj in the district of the city of Fārāb [*q.v.*] and is said to have died at the age of eighty or more in 339/950 in Damascus. His father, described as an officer (*ḳāʾid djaysh*), may have belonged to the Turkish body-guard of the Caliph, and al-Fārābī may have come to Baghdād with him early in life. He settled down there for many years as a private individual; he did not belong to the society of the court nor was he a member of the secretarial class. For reasons unknown he accepted in 330/942 an invitation of the Shīʿī Ḥamdānid ruler Sayf al-Dawla [*q.v.*] and lived in his entourage, mainly in Aleppo, together with other men of letters, until his death.

His teacher in philosophy was a Christian, the Nestorian Yuḥannā b. Haylān. Al-Fārābī himself

(Ibn Abī Uṣaybiʿa, ii, 135, 8 ff.) and al-Masʿūdī (*Tanbīh*, 122 ff.) connect him ultimately with a branch of the Greek philosophical school of Alexandria, which somehow continued to exist after the Arab conquest; some of its representatives are supposed to have come to Antioch, and the school subsequently spread to Marw and Ḥarrān and from there to Baghdād. Yuḥannā is reported to have come from Marw to Baghdād after 295/908. The possibility that he had taught al-Fārābī in Marw cannot be ruled out. Apart from this, we learn that al-Fārābī was somehow in touch with the great translator and commentator Abū Bishr Mattā b. Yūnus (d. 329/940), a prominent figure in the Baghdād school of Christian Aristotelians, and that he had a great influence on Yaḥyā b. ʿAdī (d. 362/972), its main representative in the next generation. Al-Fārābī's extant philosophical works bear out his dependence on the 10th century syllabus of Christian Aristotelian teaching in Baghdād and the impact of the late Alexandrian interpretation of Greek philosophy on his thought (cf. M. Meyerhof, *Von Alexandrien nach Baghdad*, in *Sitzungsber. d. Preuss. Akd.*, Phil. hist. Klasse, 1930, xxiii).

ii. — Thought

Al-Fārābī was convinced that philosophy had come to an end everywhere else and that it had found a new home and a new life within the world of Islam. He believed that human reason is superior to religious faith, and hence assigned only a secondary place to the different revealed religions which provide, in his view, an approach to truth for non-philosophers through symbols. Philosophical truth is universally valid whereas these symbols vary from nation to nation; they are the work of philosopher-prophets, of whom Muḥammad was one. Al-Fārābī thus went beyond al-Kindī [*q.v.*], who naturalized philosophy as a kind of appropriate handmaiden of revealed truth; on the other hand, he differs from al-Rāzī [*q.v.*] by not condemning the prophets as impostors but allotting, like his master Plato, an important and indispensable function to organized religion. There is some evidence to suggest that al-Fārābī reached this view gradually.

Al-Fārābī set out to explain how Greek philosophy—which had reached him as an almost closed system of truth and an established method of reaching felicity—could provide valid explanations of all the important issues raised in contemporary Islamic discussion. Greek natural theology shows the truth about God as the first cause of emanation, about divine inspiration (*waḥy*) as the outcome of the supreme perfection of the human mind, about the true nature of creation and divine providence as it manifests itself in the hierarchic order of the universe and about immortality, which is by no means granted to every human being. As *magistra vitae*, philosophy gives the right views about the freedom of moral choice and of the good life altogether. The perfect man, the philosopher, ought also to be the sovereign ruler; philosophy alone shows the right path to the urgent reform of the caliphate. Al-Fārābī envisages a perfect city state as well as a perfect nation (*umma*) and a perfect world state.

Apart from building up a philosophical syllabus for different levels of study, al-Fārābī had to rethink the existing Islamic sciences and to give them a new meaning and a new function in his novel theistic philosophy: a grammar adaptable to every language (cf. P. Kraus, *Jābir et la science grecque*, Cairo 1942, 251, n. 2); a dialectical theology (*kalām*) and a jurisprudence (*fiḳh*) restricted to the service of a particular religion, its "legal theology", and using the forms explained in Aristotle's *Topics* and *Sophistici Elenchi* (cf. Gardet-Anawati, *Introduction à la théologie musulmane*, Paris 1948, 102 ff.); the metaphysician is also the true lawgiver, as Plato has shown in his *Laws*, which were translated into Arabic a second time by al-Fārābī's contemporary Yaḥyā b. ʿAdī [see AFLĀṬŪN]. Rhetoric and Poetic provide the best method for bringing home the truth to non-philosophers, *i.e.*, the majority of men, by working on their imagination; no Greek philosopher would ever have envisaged that Rhetoric and Poetic could be applied to Muslim scripture, and to the Muslim creed (cf. R. Walzer, *Greek into Arabic*, Oxford 1962, 129 ff.).

Only a few characteristic tenets of al-Fārābī can be mentioned here. Like many later Greek thinkers, he believed in the ultimate identity of Plato's and Aristotle's views. He based himself on Aristotle, as understood by the Greek commentators of late antiquity, in logic, natural science, psychology, metaphysics (these metaphysics however understood and developed on moderate Neoplatonic lines). In political science he preferred to follow Plato's *Republic* and *Laws*, as understood by middle Platonic thinkers, convinced that Plato's theoretical philosophy had been superseded by Aristotle and the Neoplatonists, but that his analysis of the imperfect states and his solution of the problems of politics remained valid and compatible with the changed political conditions. The Greek antecedents of this particular branch of later Platonism—which also appealed strongly to Ibn Rushd [*q.v.*]—are lost and can be reconstructed only from al-Fārābī and other Arabic writers (cf. R. Walzer, *Aspects of Islamic political thought*, in *Oriens*, 1963).

According to al-Fārābī, the first cause is at the same time the Plotinian one, the eternal creator of an eternal world, and the Aristotelian Divine Mind, a conception which is probably of middle-Platonic origin. Aristotle's νοῦς ποιητικός is for al-Fārābī neither identical with the first cause nor situated within the human soul but has become a transcendental entity mediating between the higher and the sublunar world and the human mind—probably another later Greek interpretation of the difficult Aristotelian chapter *De an.*, III 5. Very remarkable is the theory of imagination and prophecy adopted by al-Fārābī; it may also derive from some otherwise lost Greek original (cf. R. Walzer, *Greek into Arabic*, 206 ff.). Prophecy, though being an indispensable ingredient in man's perfection, is auxiliary to his rational faculty, being confined to the inferior faculty of representation. It is neither described as a state of possession by supernatural powers nor understood as a mystic 'state'. Divine inspiration may be granted to the perfect man who has reached the highest philosophical level together with the highest form of prophecy.

The Christian-Arabic Aristotelian teaching in 4th/10th century Baghdād is the immediate background of al-Fārābī's thought. His proximate ancient sources are within the orbit of the Greek philosophical schools in 6th century Alexandria. To a large extent, he appears to continue a tradition which became extinct during the later centuries of Byzantine civilization and whose original form may now be reconstructed from Arabic versions and imitations only. His particular variation of Neoplatonic metaphysics and his full acknowledgment of the political aspects of Plato's thought distinguish him from Proclus and his followers. Much more of Porphyry's thought may be preserved in al-Fārābī's work than is apparent to us today. His ultimate roots seem to lie in a pre-Plotinian platonizing tradition.

Al Fārābī's importance for subsequent Islamic philosophers is considerable, and would well deserve to be described in detail. His impact on the writings of 4th/10th century authors such as the Ikhwān al-Ṣafā', al-Mas'ūdī, Miskawayh, and Abu 'l-Ḥasan Muḥammad al-Āmirī is undeniable. Ibn Sīnā seems to have known his works intimately and Ibn Rushd follows him in the essentials of his thought. Maimonides appreciated him highly. His political ideas had a belated and lasting success from the 13th century onwards (cf. T. W. Arnold, *The Caliphate*, Oxford 1924, 125 ff.). A few of his treatises became known to the Latin Schoolmen; more were translated into mediaeval Hebrew.

iii. — Works

More than one hundred works of varying size are attributed by the Arab bibliographers to al-Fārābī, not all of them genuine. One, the *Risālā* known as *al-Fuṣūṣ fi 'l-ḥikma*, is most probably by Ibn Sīnā (cf. S. Pines, in *REI*, 1951, 121 ff.), and its wrong attribution to al-Fārābī has made it unnecessarily difficult to realise how fundamental the differences between these two most influential Islamic philosophers are, in spite of many obvious similarities.

a. First to be mentioned among the genuine works are the great scholarly commentaries on a number of Aristotle's lecture courses; they continue the tradition of the late Greek schools without a gap (cf. the twenty-two volumes of the *Commentaria in Aristotelem graeca* published by the Berlin Academy); they seem to have been used by Ibn Bādjdja [*q.v.*] and especially by Ibn Rushd [*q.v.*] and have to a large extent been superseded by their commentaries. One of them, on the Περὶ ἑρμηνείας, has just been edited for the first time, with valuable and copious indexes, by W. Kutsch and S. Marrow (Beirut 1960); it is based on a Greek original different both from the 6th century A.D. commentary by Ammonius (*Comm. in Arist. graeca*, iv, 5) and the Greek work used by his Latin contemporary Boethius; all three seem somehow to depend on a lost commentary by Porphyry. We learn about similar commentaries on all the remaining parts of the *Organon*, including the *Rhetorics* (widely, I think, used by Ibn Rushd), on the *Physics* (which al-Fārābī read more than forty times), the *De caelo*, the *Meteorology* and parts of the *Nicomachean Ethics* (depending probably on a lost commentary by Porphyry). There may well have been more. A commentary on Alexander of Aphrodisias' *De anima* is mentioned. A commentary on Porphyry's *Isagoge* attributed to al-Fārābī is in fact by Abu 'l Faradj b. al-Ṭayyib (cf. S. M. Stern, in *BSOAS*, xix (1957), 119 ff.). I assume that Ibn Rushd's *Commentary on Plato's Republic* (ed. E. I. J. Rosenthal, Cambridge 1956) depends on a similar work by al-Fārābī.

b. A number of relatively small introductory monographs 'τοῖς εἰσαγομένοις'.

A. Logic. *Al-tawṭi'a fi 'l manṭiḳ*, ed. M. Türker, with Turkish translation, Ankara 1958; *Introductory sections on logic*, ed. D. M. Dunlop, with English translation, in *I Q*, 1955; ed. M. Türker, with Turkish translation, Ankara 1958; *Paraphrase of Porphyry's Isagoge*, ed. D. M. Dunlop, with English translation, in *I Q*, 1956; *Paraphrase of Aristotle's Categories*, ed. D. M. Dunlop, with English translation, in *I Q*, 1958; *Paraphrase of Aristotle's Prior Analytics*, ed. M. Türker, with Turkish translation, Ankara 1958, with a very interesting opening chapter; English translation prepared by N. Rescher; *Treatise on the canons of the art of poetry*, ed. A. J. Arberry, with English translation, in *RSO*, 1938 (Arabic text reprinted by A. Badawi, Cairo 1953).

B. Physics. *On vacuum*, ed. Necati Lugal and Aydın Sayılı with Turkish and English trans., Ankara 1951 (see further A. Sayılı in *Belleten*, xv/57 (1951), 151-74); *Against Astrology*, ed. F. Dieterici, *Alfarabi's Philosophische Abhandlungen*, Leiden 1890, with German translation, 1892; cf. C. A. Nallino, *Raccolta di scritti*, vi, 1944, 23 ff.; *De Intellectu (fi 'l 'aḳl)*, critical edition by M. Bouyges, Beirut 1938; medieval Latin translation ed. E. Gilson (with translation by himself), in *Archives d'histoire doctrinale et littéraire du moyen âge*, iv (1929), 113 ff.

C. Metaphysics. *About the scope of Aristotle's Metaphysics*, ed. F. Dieterici, *op. cit.*, with German translation; *On the One (fi 'l-Wāḥid wa 'l-waḥda)*, critical edition and English translation by H. Mushtaq (in preparation).

D. Ethics and Politics. *Reminder of the Way of Happiness (al-tanbīh 'alā sabīl al-sa'āda)*, ed. Hyderabad 1326/1908; mediaeval Latin translation ed. H. Salman, in *Recherches de théologie ancienne et médiévale*, xii (1940), 33 ff.; *Aphorisms of the statesman (Fuṣūl al-madanī)*, ed. D. M. Dunlop, with English translation and notes, Cambridge 1961; *Compendium Legum Platonis*, ed. F. Gabrieli, with Latin translation and notes, *Plato Arabus III*, London 1952; *On the best religion (fi 'l-milla al-fāḍila)*, an important but still unedited treatise.

E. Miscellanea. *Harmony between the views of Plato and Aristotle (al-djam' bayna ra'yay al-Ḥakīm Aflāṭūn al-ilāhī wa-Arisṭuṭalis)*, ed. F. Dieterici, *op. cit.*, with German translation; ed. Nader, Beyrouth 1960. *Answers to questions (Djawāb masā'il su'ila 'anhā)*, ed. F. Dieterici, *op. cit.*, with German translation; ed. Hyderabad 1344/1925. *Main questions ('Uyūn al-masā'il)*, ed. F. Dieterici, *op. cit.*, with German translation.

The very titles of three not yet traced refutations of philosophical adversaries help to circumscribe Al-Fārābī's position among the philosophers of his time. One is against Galen (Djālīnūs)—known to the Arabs not only as a physician but as a philosopher as well—and rejects Galen's attacks against Aristotle's first cause, most probably in the wake of Alexander of Aphrodisias' refutation of Galen [see DJĀLĪNŪS]. Another is against John Philoponus (again in defence of Aristotle) and, by implication, al-Kindī [*q.v.*], who both adhere to the creation of the world from nothing (cf. R. Walzer, *Greek into Arabic*, 193 ff.). In a third treatise al-Fārābī set out to refute Muḥammad b. Zakariyyā al-Rāzī [*q.v.*], presumably because of his belief in atoms and the creation of the world in time. A treatise against Ibn al-Rawandī may have been concerned with his radical rejection of prophecy altogether (cf. P. Kraus, *Beiträge zur islamischen Ketzergeschichte*, in *RSO*, 1932).

d. There is finally a group of important major works which sum up the results of philosophical research and al-Fārābī's further reaching intentions. They all are concerned with the sovereign position to be given to philosophy within the realm of thinking and with the organization of the perfect society and the philosopher-king. Their right understanding provides, in my view, the key to al-Fārābī's thought; this, however, is made particularly difficult for us, since he is, from the very outset, determined to let the reader find out the application for himself (cf. the first page of *Plato Arabus III*).

I. *Survey of the Sciences* (*K. Iḥṣā' al-ʿulūm*). Best edition by ʿUthmān Amīn, Cairo 1931-48. Mediaeval Latin translation by Gerard of Cremona, printed by A. Gonzáles Palencia, Madrid 1932 (together with an edition of the Arabic text and a Spanish translation).

II. A work in three books, in contents very similar to III and IV, but perhaps earlier. (1) *On attaining felicity* (*fī taḥṣīl al-saʿāda*), ed. Hyderabad 1345/1926. Critical edition and English translation prepared by M. Mahdi. (2) *On the philosophy of Plato*, ed. with Latin translation and notes by F. Rosenthal and R. Walzer, *Plato Arabus II*, London 1943. New ed. and Eng. trans. prepared by M. Mahdi. (3) *On the philosophy of Aristotle*, ed. M. Mahdi, Beirut 1961. English translation prepared by the same author.

III. *On the principles of the views of the inhabitants of the excellent state* (*fī mabādi' arāʿ ahl al-madīna al-fāḍila*). Editions by F. Dieterici, Leiden 1895, and A. Nader, Beirut 1959. Ger. trans. (*Der Musterstaat*) F. Dieterici, Leiden 1900; Fr. trans. R. P. Jaussen and others, Cairo 1949; Span. trans. M. Alonso Alonso, in *al-And.*, xxvi-xxvii (1961-62). A critical edition, with English translation and commentary, is being prepared by R. Walzer.

IV. *On political government* (*al-siyāsa al-madaniyya*), a similar survey of the whole of philosophy, written with the same definite political purpose in mind. Edited Hyderabad 1346/1927. Ger. trans. (*Die Staatsleitung*), by F. Dieterici, Leiden 1904. A critical edition and an English translation are being prepared in Chicago.

Bibliography: C. Brockelmann, I², 232 ff.; S I, 375 ff., 957 ff.; Pearson, nos. 4713-50 and Supplement, 1342-58; A. Ateş, *Farabinin eserlerinin bibliyografyası*, in *Belleten*, xv/57 (1951), 175-92; N. Rescher, *Al-Farabi. An annotated bibliography*, Pittsburg 1962; M. Steinschneider, *Die Hebräischen Übersetzungen des Mittelalters und die Juden als Dolmetscher*, reprint, Graz 1956, 158 ff.; idem, *Al-Farabi*, in *Mémoires de l'Académie Impériale des Sciences de Saint-Petersbourg*, 1869; Ibrahim Madkour, *La place d'Al-Fārābī dans l'école philosophique musulmane*, Paris 1934; P. Kraus, *Plotin chez les Arabes*, in *BIÉ*, xxiii (1940), 263 ff.; idem, *Jābir et la science grecque*, Cairo 1942, *passim*; Leo Strauss, *Farabi's Plato*, in *Ginsberg Jubilee Volume*, New York 1945; idem, *How Farabi read Plato's Laws*, in *Mélanges Massignon*, iii, Damascus 1957; E. I. J. Rosenthal, *Political thought in medieval Islam²*, Cambridge 1962, 122 ff.; Saʿīd Zāyid, *al-Fārābī* (Nawābigh al-fikr al-ʿarabī, 31), Cairo 1962; *İA* (art. Fârâbî by Abdülhak Adnan [Adıvar]). (R. WALZER)

FARADJ, AL-MALIK AL-NĀṢIR ZAYN AL-DĪN ABU 'L-SAʿĀDĀT, 26th Mamlūk Sultan of Egypt and second of the Circassians [see ČERKES ii and BURDJIYYA]. The son of Sultan Barḳūḳ [*q.v.*] and a Greek mother, Shīrīn, Faradj was born in Cairo in 791/1389 and succeeded to the Sultanate upon the death of his father on 15 Shawwāl 801/20 June 1399. Owing to his youth Faradj began his reign under the guardianship of two of his father's *amīrs*: Taghrī Birdī al-Bashbughāwī (father of the historian) and Aytimish al-Badjasī, but disagreements among the *amīrs* and their factions soon led to an early proclamation of his majority, in Rabīʿ I 802/November 1399. The first reign of Faradj lasted six years, until he was deposed at Cairo in favour of his younger brother ʿAbd al-ʿAzīz, who took the regnal name al-Malik al-Manṣūr, on 25 Rabīʿ I 808/20 September 1405. Seventy days later, on 5 Djumādā II 808/28 November 1405, Faradj was restored to power for a second reign, which lasted until his deposition at Damascus on 25 Muḥarram 815/7 May 1412. A few weeks later, on 16 Ṣafar 815/28 May 1412, after having been succeeded unwillingly by the ʿAbbāsid Caliph al-Mustaʿīn bi'llāh [*q.v.*], Faradj was publicly humiliated and killed in Damascus.

Neither of the reigns of Faradj represents a particularly constructive period in Mamlūk history, a result of the continual strife of high-ranking *amīrs*, aggravated by the consequences of Barḳūḳ's policy of introducing large numbers of Circassians into Egypt and Syria and of favouring them over the hitherto predominant Turkish mamlūks. Both factions found leaders among the anyway quarrelsome *amīrs*, and the resulting clashes, usually based on rival headquarters in Egypt and Syria, account for most of Faradj's movements in both his reigns, during which he made no less than seven expeditions to Syria. The major protagonists in these internal Mamlūk struggles included the *amīrs* Yashbak al-Shaʿbānī, favoured at first by Faradj and supported by Circassians, and Aytimish al-Badjasī, who led the Turkish faction and was supported by Tanam, viceroy (*nā'ib*) of Damascus. After the defeat and execution of Aytimish by Faradj at Gaza and Damascus (3 Shaʿbān 802/30 March 1400), a fresh conflict broke out between Yashbak and Nawrūz al-Ḥāfiẓī at Cairo, in which the former fell from power and favour. The struggle was further confused by the complicity of the *amīrs* Djakam, Shaykh al-Maḥmūdī, now viceroy of Damascus, Baybars (later atabeg [see ATĀBAK AL-ʿASĀKIR]), and Taghrī Birdī al-Bashbughāwī. On 25 Rabīʿ I 808/20 September 1405, upon report that Faradj had fled in the company of Taghrī Birdī to Syria, it was Yashbak and Baybars who arranged the accession of ʿAbd al-ʿAzīz. After the restoration of Faradj, Djakam and Nawrūz revolted in Syria, the former proclaiming himself Sultan, with the regnal name al-Malik al-ʿĀdil (11 Shawwāl 809/21 March 1407), but was killed soon after in his siege of Āmid. Syria, however, remained in the hands of Nawrūz, who succeeded in winning over Shaykh al-Maḥmūdī, the *amīr* sent by Faradj to replace him. Despite three expeditions against them Faradj was unable to break the power of these two *amīrs*, who defeated him finally at Ladjdjun (Dhu 'l-Ḥidjdja 814/March-April 1412), and forced his deposition at Damascus whither he had fled. After a brief reign of six months by his puppet, the Caliph al-Mustaʿīn, Shaykh himself became Sultan, taking the regnal name al-Mu'ayyad [*q.v.*].

The only exception to the bleak rule of *amīrs*' rivalries in this period is provided by the appearance in Syria of Tīmūr [*q.v.*]. Although Faradj, after some hesitation and refusals of aid to the Djalā'irid and Ottoman rulers against the threat from the East, did make a stand at Damascus against Tīmūr, it would not be true to assert either that the external challenge provoked any real degree of internal consolidation within the Mamlūk Sultanate, or that fear of defeat at the hands of Faradj made Tīmūr turn north to Anatolia and Bāyazīd I rather than south to Egypt, after plundering Damascus (Radjab 803/March 1401). The chronicler Abu 'l-Maḥāsin b. Taghrī Birdī [*q.v*] does, however, report Tīmūr's respect for the Egyptian army, whose effectiveness he considered reduced only owing to the youth of the Sultan and the lack of unity among its commanders (*Nudjūm*, vi, 46). The brief encounter between the two rulers at Damascus also provided the occasion for an interesting if inconclusive meeting between Tīmūr and Ibn Khaldūn who, though out of office, had been prevailed upon to accompany Faradj to Syria.

With regard to the rôle of Faradj in Mamlūk history the two Egyptian chroniclers al-Maḳrīzī and Ibn Taghrī Birdī represent diametrically opposed opinions. Whereas the former ascribes to him the ruin of Egypt and Syria because of poor administration, debased coinage, corrupt officials, and oppressive taxation (*Khiṭaṭ*, cited *Nudjūm*, vi, 271-3), the latter gives Faradj a most favourable obituary despite his observation that the Sultan had brought about the financial ruin of his family and indirectly the death of his father (*Nudjūm*, vi, 270-4). In fact the remarks of Ibn Taghrī Birdī must be considered with the greatest care, owing to the involvement of his family's affairs with those of Faradj, who had married a sister of his and, during an acute crisis, appointed his father atabeg (810/1407-8). His son's portrait of Taghrī Birdī as a loyal and self-sacrificing subject of the Sultan may not be inaccurate, but it is bound to have affected the chronicler's view of the recipient of such loyalty and sacrifice. Such observations as are found among the commercial records of Western powers then active in Egypt and Syria would suggest that al-Maḳrīzī's evaluation of Faradj as one addicted to arbitrary fiscal policies and indifferent to the importance of a sound and consistent administration, is not unfounded.

Bibliography: Ibn Taghrī Birdī, *Nudjūm*, vi, 1-300; idem, *Manhal ṣāfī*, fol. 507 (no. 1789; see Wiet, in *Mém. Inst. Égypte*, xix, 265, for further bibliography, including inscriptions); Ibn Iyās, *Badāʾiʿ al-zuhūr*, i, index; al-Ḳalḳashandī, *Ṣubḥ al-aʿshā*, iii, 439; vii, 305-25, 407-11; Weil, *Geschichte der Chalifen*, v, 72-105, 108-25; W. Heyd, *Histoire du commerce du Levant*, ii, 471-2; Gaudefroy-Demombynes, *La Syrie à l'époque des Mamelouks*, xxiv-xxvii, cvii; W. J. Fischel, *Ibn Khaldun and Tamerlane*, *passim*; Mayer, *Mamluk costume*, index.

(J. Wansbrough)

AL-**FARADJ BAʿD** AL-**SHIDDA** [see NĀDIRA].

AL-**FARĀFRA**, an oasis in the eastern Libyan desert, in Egypt, situated approximately on lat. 27° N. and long. 28° E., equidistant from the Nile and the Libyan frontier. It is a halting stage between the oases of al-Dākhla 170 km. to the south-west and those of al-Baḥriyya 160 km. to the north-north-east; the routes are motorable only with difficulty. Al-Farāfra is a single village of about 1,000 inhabitants. Its mud huts surround a slightly raised fortification. Village and oasis are situated in a vast plain 70 to 90 m. high, partially covered with sand and surrounded by an immense barren plateau of Lower Eocene limestone extending all round, some 300 m. in height; the depression includes a score of wells and springs, the most abundant of which are ʿAyn al-Bellad and ʿAyn Ebsay. They provide the irrigation for a plantation of palms with a few olive-trees, pomegranates, and some barley, wheat, sorghum and onions. Groups of wild palms mark other areas with water. The inhabitants sell dates and a few olives, and buy in particular grain.

Al-Farāfra is said to be the *T3-iḥw* (land of oxen) of Pharaonic times and the *Trinytheos* of Graeco-Roman antiquity. Al-Bakrī (37) describes the alum and vitriol mines (the latter including iron or copper sulphate) in the vicinity; he extols its importance, and attributes to it a Coptic population. It is now Muslim. It appears to have suffered much in the course of time from the razzias of the nomads of Egypt and Cyrenaica (Barka), and more recently, since 1860, from the seizure of its estates by the Sanūsiyya.

Bibliography: al-Bakrī, *L'Afrique septentrionale*, tr. de Slane, 2nd ed. Algiers 1913; G. Rohlfs, *Drei Monate in der libischen Wüste*, Cassel 1871, and map in *Pet. Mitt.*, 1875; H. J. L. Beadnel, *Farafra, its topology and geology*, Geological Survey of Egypt, 1889.

(J. Despois)

FARĀH, town in south-western Afghānistān, capital of the district (*ʿalā-ḥukūmat*) of the same name. The town is located on the Farāh river 62° 5′ E. 32° 23′ N., alt. 1738 m.

Farāh is located where trade routes from Harāt, Ḳandahār and Seistān join and the site has been occupied from ancient times. The name of the river is probably found in Avestan Fradaθā (*Yasht*, xix, 67). The town is mentioned by many classical authors under various names; Prophthasia, Propasta, and Phrada (see Bibliography).

Farāh is not mentioned in Arabic works dealing with the conquests, but it is mentioned (as Farah) by the geographers Iṣṭakhrī (247), Ibn Ḥawḳal (420), and al-Muḳaddasī (306). The bridge over the river, and Khāridjīs in the town are both noted. Although the town is mentioned by later geographies (*Ḥudūd al-ʿālam*, Yāḳūt, etc.) it never had any historical importance. It was abandoned in the time of the Mongols, rebuilt, and sacked by Nādir Shāh, and today has ca. 15,000 inhabitants.

Bibliography: Classical sources are discussed in Pauly-Wissowa, xx, 738; xxiii, 817. Arabic sources are summarized in Le Strange, 341. On the present town see E. Caspani and E. Cagnacci, *Afghanistan crocevia dell Asia*, Milan 1951, 256.

(R. N. Frye)

FARAḤ ANṬŪN, (Anṭūn being the family name; 1874-1922), Arab author and journalist. Trained in a Greek-Orthodox school near Tripoli (now in Lebanon), he migrated to Egypt, and published a journal in Alexandria. He then migrated to the U.S.A. but, following the Turkish revolution of 1908, went back to Egypt and became active in the national movement.

Well versed in French literature (and translations) he was attracted mostly by social-political-ethical and philosophical-religious themes, but he lacked method, system, and consistency. His adherence to Westernism in the spirit of the French Revolution, as well as his lucid exposition, felicity of expression and a ceaseless search for new ideas and the 'latest word' marked him as a representative of enlightenment. He was essentially a gifted eclectic, translator and excerpter, exponent of Western ideas and of their conflicts in his mind. Thus he brought to the Arab reader Renan's ideas on the origins of Christianity and on Ibn Rushd; discussions of Nietzsche and Tolstoy, of socialist theories. A proclivity for polemics caused him to clash with literary and public figures (notably with Muḥ. ʿAbduh, on Ibn Rushd).

His *New Jerusalem* (1904) is a novel set in the time of the Arab conquest, and, though it suffers from lengthy ideological monologues, has a place in the history of the novel in Arabic. He was also a playwright.

His influence was considerable and he used to be studied in schools as a classical author, mainly on account of scope and style.

Bibliography: Brockelmann S III, 192-4;

Y. Dāgher, *Maṣādir al-dirāsa al-adabiyya*, ii, Beirut 1956, 147-52; I. Yu. Kračkovskiy, *Izbr. Soč.*, iii, 40-2. (M. Perlmann)

FARAḤĀBĀD, the name of a place in Māzandarān, situated 36° 50′ N., 53° 2′ 38″ E., 17 m. north of Sārī and 26 m. north-west of As͟hraf [*q.v.*], near the mouth of the Tid͟jin (or Tīd͟jān, or Tid͟jīna) river. Formerly known as Ṭāhān, the site was renamed Faraḥābād by S͟hāh ʿAbbās I, who in 1020/1611-2 or 1021/1612-3 ordered the construction of a royal palace there. Around the palace were built residences, gardens, baths, bazaars, mosques and caravanserais. The new town, according to Pietro della Valle, was peopled by S͟hāh ʿAbbās with colonies of different nationalities—including many Christians from Georgia—transplanted from territories overrun by Ṣafawid forces. Faraḥābād was linked to Sārī by S͟hāh ʿAbbās's famous causeway (completed in 1031/1621), and until his death in 1038/1629 S͟hāh ʿAbbās regularly spent the winter either at Faraḥābād or As͟hraf, usually not returning to his capital Iṣfahān until after Naw-rūz. The *Taʾrīk͟h-i ʿĀlam-ārā-yi ʿAbbāsī* uses the terms *dār al-salṭana* and *dār al-mulk* with reference to Faraḥābād; this suggests that it had become virtually a second capital (cf. also *A Chronicle of the Carmelites in Persia*, London 1939, i, 282).

Pietro della Valle, who visited Faraḥābād in 1618, declared that the circuit of the walls was equal to, if not greater than, that of Rome or Constantinople, and that the town contained streets of more than a league in length, and Chardin, who saw it forty years later, stated that the palace housed a vast treasure of dishes and basins of porcelain or china, cornaline, agate, coral, amber, cups of rock-crystal, and other varieties without number. In 1668, however, Faraḥābād was sacked by the Cossacks under Stenka Razin, and it suffered further destruction during the period of anarchy which followed the collapse of the Ṣafawid dynasty in the 18th century. Hanway, who passed through Faraḥābād in 1744, stated that the place had been abandoned, only a few Persian and Armenian inhabitants remaining there, and Fraser, who was there in 1822, described the ruins as "vastly inferior to those of Ashraf".

At the present day Faraḥābād is only a small village; it gives its name to a district (*bulūk*) of Māzandarān (see Rabino, 119-20).

Bibliography: Iskandar Beg, *Taʾrīk͟h-i ʿĀlam-ārā-yi ʿAbbāsī*, ii, Tehrān 1335 s./1956, index; Pietro della Valle, *Viaggi*, quoted in J. de Morgan, *Mission scientifique en Perse*, ii, Paris 1894, 223, 228; J. Hanway, *An historical account of the British trade over the Caspian Sea etc.*, London 1753, i, 209; Sir John Chardin, *Voyages ... en Perse* (ed. Langlès), Paris 1811, iii, 454-9; J. B. Fraser, *Travels and adventures etc. on the southern banks of the Caspian Sea*, London 1826, 70-4; G. N. Curzon, *Persia and the Persian question*, London 1892, i, 378; H. L. Rabino, *Māzandarān and Astarābād*, London 1928, 49, 63. (R. M. Savory)

FARĀʾIḌ (a.), plural of *farīḍa* [see farḍ], literally "appointed or obligatory portions", is the technical term for the fixed shares in an estate (1/2, 1/4, 1/3, 1/8, 2/3 and 1/16) which are given to certain heirs, who are called *d͟hawu 'l-farāʾiḍ* or *aṣḥāb al-farāʾiḍ*, on the basis of Ḳurʾān, IV, 11-2 and 176. These Ḳurʾānic enactments aim at modifying a system of purely agnatic succession, under which only men can inherit, in favour of the nearest female relatives (including half-brothers on the mother's side), the spouse, and also the father (who is protected against being excluded by existing male descendants). It is rare that the concurrence of several shares leads to the exclusion of near male relatives; this can never happen to the descendants and ascendants. Islamic law, by some consequential extensions and distinctions, has systematically completed the rules given in the Ḳurʾān; it has also provided solutions for those exceptional cases in which the aggregate of the shares amounts to more than one unit, or the mechanical application of the rules would lead to a solution which is considered unjust. For the details of all this see mīrāt͟h, ʿawl and akdariyya.

The rules concerning *farāʾiḍ* are the most typical feature of the Islamic law of inheritance, and are rather complicated in detail; because of their importance the whole of the Islamic law of inheritance is called *ʿilm al-farāʾiḍ*, and it has often been treated in separate works. A person skilled in the science of *farāʾiḍ* is called *fāriḍ* or *faraḍī*.

Bibliography: F. Peltier and G.-H. Bousquet, *Les successions agnatiques mitigées*, Paris 1935; Juynboll, *Handbuch*, 247-55; idem, *Handleiding*, 253-60; Santillana, *Istituzioni*, ii, 505-14; L. Milliot, *Introduction*, 461-71; A. A. A. Fyzee, *Outlines*, 2nd ed., 336-8, 341-56; J. Schacht, *Introduction to Islamic Law* (forthcoming), chap. 23 (with bibliography); L. Hirsch, *Der überfliessende Strom in der Wissenschaft des Erbrechts*, Leipzig 1891 (Arabic text and translation); idem, *The overflowing river*, etc., 2nd ed., Aden 1899. (Th. W. Juynboll*)

FARĀʾIḌIYYA, a Muslim sect in Bengal established at the beginning of the 19th century by Ḥād͟jd͟jī S͟harīʿat Allāh. The setting in which the sect was born and developed was eastern Bengal in the period immediately following the British conquest. Peasant life in that State, perhaps more than in other parts of India, was influenced by Hindu customs and practices. At that time the virtual loss of political supremacy by a section of the governing Muslim class, the support which the British sometimes gave to the Hindu elements, the unbridled power of the *zamīndārs* [*q.v.*], rich landed proprietors both Hindu and Muslim, over the peasant masses the majority of whom were Muslim, British "liberalism" which in the end actually increased this power, all these factors helped to form a religio-social reaction which found particular expression in the *farāʾiḍiyya* (local Indo-Persian pronunciation *farāʾiẓiyya*). Ḥād͟jd͟jī S͟harīʿat Allāh was born at an uncertain date in a humble family in the *pargana* of Bandarkhola, a district of Farīdpūr (eastern Bengal); when hardly 18 years old he went to Mecca, where he remained for a long time (about twenty years apparently) and is said to have been the pupil of S͟hayk͟h Ṭāhir al-Sunbul al-Makkī, a S͟hāfiʿī scholar. The date of his return to Bengal varies in the different sources, which give it as 1807, 1822 or 1828, while certain writers affirm that he made two journeys to Mecca, returning home to his country in the interval. If we accept the latest date, it is unquestionable that S͟harīʿat Allāh was in touch with the Wahhābī reformers in Mecca. A specific Wahhābī influence is in no sense indispensable for an understanding of the orientation of S͟harīʿat Allāh's activities in Bengal, which are to be explained above all by the contrast he so vehemently resented between a certain type of Islam in his own country and the "Arab" Islam of the Prophet's native land; *mutatis mutandis*, other Muslim reformers in India (beginning with S͟hāh Walī Allāh of Delhi himself) had had the same experience. On returning to his native country,

S̲h̲arīʿat Allāh launched a reform movement which mainly attracted the lower classes of Muslims in Bengal, and in substance of a legal rather than mystical nature, aiming at the widespread application of the *s̲h̲arīʿa* so often spoken of in Islam, but so laxly applied. The very name of the movement (from *farāʾiḍ* "religious duties") underlines this aspect. To Western observers today, some of the reforms envisaged by S̲h̲arīʿat Allāh might seem to be of little interest; thus, besides various para-Hindu customs, he rejected the celebration, with funerary lamentations and special ceremonies, of the martyrdom of Ḥusayn at Karbalāʾ, the pomp and ceremonial that had been introduced into the very simple, austere rites of Muslim marriage and burial, the offering of fruit and flowers at tombs, etc.; moreover, he prohibited the use of the mystical terms *pīr* and *murīd* ("master" and "disciple"), which at that time conveyed an almost Brahmin-like implication of total devotion of the disciple to his spiritual master, out of keeping with the sturdy Islamic tradition, and instead proposing the two terms *ustād̲h̲* and *s̲h̲āgird* (also Persian, but more "secular"); the initiation ceremony common to the various Muslim confraternities, the *bayʿa*, was also prohibited and replaced by a simple statement of repentance (*tawba*) and a changed life made by the *murīd* (or *s̲h̲āgird*). Another significant precept of S̲h̲arīʿat Allāh was the prohibition of communal prayers on Fridays or feastdays, based on the exclusion of British India from the *dār al-Islām*. But S̲h̲arīʿat Allāh does not seem to have gone so far as to preach the *d̲j̲ihād*, the holy war. His preoccupations, more concretely, were with the wretched condition of the oppressed Bengal peasants (especially as their lack of financial means prevented them from turning to the courts, which in certain cases could have given them justice). He tried to alleviate their miserable state by living among poor peasants as one of them and by making efforts to organize them to escape from the unjust demands of the land-owners, whom he revealed as transgressors of the pure holy law of Islam.

S̲h̲arīʿat Allāh's son Muḥammad Muḥsin, known as Dūdhū Miyān (1819-60), had a more vigorous temperament, a talent for organizing and a natural authority; under his direction the Farāʾiḍiyya became a homogeneous and disciplined organization with Dūdhū Miyān himself at its head; by a curious violation of the founder's precept he was called *pīr*. The territory of eastern Bengal (especially the region of Bāḳargand̲j̲, Dacca, Farīdpūr and Pabna where the sect was most active) was divided into districts entrusted to special agents whose duty it was to make converts and to organize resistance to the rich proprietors. An especially effective and important measure was the prohibition made by Dūdhū Miyān of recourse to the ordinary courts; disputes between the Farāʾiḍiyya themselves had to be settled by him personally. Since in many cases the impossibility of the poor peasants securing justice sprang from their individual lack of resources, as has been said, "collections" were organized in order to indict the *zamīndārs* in the courts in cases of injustice to peasants unable to defend themselves without help. In other words, the Farāʾiḍiyya did not restrict themselves to upholding the beauty of the theoretical principles of "ancient" Islam, like "The earth is God's" (as Dūdhū Miyān in fact used to proclaim), but they had found quite effective ways of putting them into practice. Since the taxes and forced labour imposed by landlords on peasants were illegal from the point of view of the *s̲h̲arīʿa*, Dūdhū Miyān advised landless peasants to leave the privately-owned estates and settle on the *k̲h̲āṣṣ maḥall*, that is, State property, thus avoiding all taxes other than those owed to the government. It is certain that, faced by a movement so efficiently organized, the rich *zamīndārs* and indigo planters united and tried to destroy it. As in similar cases, two methods were used; firstly, they tried violence, both privately and officially (Dūdhū Miyān was even prosecuted on charges, which were more or less proved, of rapine, etc. Numerous disturbances broke out in the areas controlled by the Farāʾiḍiyya and the landowners resorted to barbarous tortures); secondly, on the strength of certain religious juridical statements by the Farāʾiḍiyya, they tried to demonstrate their "heterodoxy" and at the same time, placing the discussions on a theoretical-religious basis, they tried to turn the Farāʾiḍiyya aside from practical action. To a certain extent this second method became effective, while the Farāʾiḍiyya lost the sympathy of some neutral Muslims of the neighbourhood (easily persuaded by the Muslim landowners) on account of the mistakes made by them and by Dūdhū Miyān who, from Bahādurpūr where he generally lived, "excommunicated" by declaring "non-Muslim" those who were not willing to accept all the doctrines of the sect. Disturbances became more and more serious and frequent and, in 1836, the enemies of the Farāʾiḍiyya succeeded in having Dūdhū Miyān sent to prison in ʿAlīpūr. The movement continued to vegetate under the direction of Dūdhū Miyān's sons, who were lacking in energy and whose qualities of organization were very inferior to those of their father. Dūdhū Miyān died in 1860 and was buried in Bahādurpūr, but a subsequent flood has left no trace of his tomb. The sect dwindled, to become one of the very many purely religious communities in India, while its social effectiveness was lost.

Bibliography: Abdul Bari, *The reform movement in Bengal*, in *A history of the freedom movement (being the story of Muslim struggle for the freedom of Hindo-Pakistan, 1707-1947)*, i, Karachi 1957, 542 ff. (with copious bibliography).

(A. Bausani)

FARAS (A.) (pl. *afrās, furūs, fursān*) denotes the Horse (*Equus caballus*), in the sense of saddle-horse; philologists further restrict the meaning of the word to "saddle-horse of the Arabian breed". This original name is applied to both sexes without distinction, and serves as a noun of unity for the collective of the species *k̲h̲ayl* (*Equidae*); hence this term is found in agreement with either gender, the feminine, however, seeming the more usual, in ancient Arabic (see Ch. Pellat, *Sur quelques noms d'animaux en arabe classique*, in *GLECS*, viii, 95-9). The word *faras*, pronounced *fras*, pl. *frāsāt*, with the meaning "thoroughbred horse", has survived in the Bedouin dialects on the borders of the Sahara, whereas the Mag̲h̲rib dialects only really recognise *ḥiṣān* (Tunisia) and *ʿawd* (Algeria, Morocco) to denote the horse (for the etymology of *ʿawd*, see Ph. Marçais, *Document de dialectologie maghrébine*, in *AIEO-Alger*, vi (1947), 206-7). The immense interest taken by the Arabs in their breed of horses, both before and after Islam, and the considerable part which this animal played in Muslim expansion have endowed the language with a great number of terms, many of them qualifying words, to complete all that *faras* left unspecified as to sex, age, origin, external peculiarities and temperament; from it sprang the philology of the horse which, in amplitude, is in no way inferior to that of the camel. For example, to distinguish the sex, the pure-bred stallion (*faḥl*) will be called *ḥiṣān*, that is to say "one who reserves his seed jealously", and the pedigree brood-mare (*farasa*) will be *ḥidjr*, that is "forbidden to all comers", while the mare of mixed breed will be merely *ramaka*, that is "the offspring of misalliance". The age of an animal is determined by the stage of development of the teeth, as is the present practice; at birth the foal is called *muhr*, then, up to one year of age *filw* (= weaned), up to two years *ḥawlī*, to three *thanī*, to four *rabāʿin*, to five *ḳāriḥ*, after which it becomes *mudhakkin* for the rest of its life.

The origin of the so-called "Arabian" breed of horses has been the subject, in the written documentation of the Arabs, of a multitude of traditions, from which we must exclude those of a purely religious character as well as works of natural history strongly influenced by Greek thought. Pre-islamic poetry alone can provide some information on this subject, for it represents the least distorting medium for the oldest Arab traditions. Without hoping to find in these archaic poems any precise expositions on the subject, we can nevertheless glean from them the names of celebrated horses and great horsemen which can be tolerably well placed in history, and so reconstruct a chronology in the genealogy of ancient families of Arabian horses. The first of these is said to have sprung up among the Azd in the Yemen and the Taghlib in Baḥrayn, descended from Zād al-Rākib (= "the horseman's viaticum"), a famous stallion given by king Solomon to the Azdī delegation on the occasion of their visit to that illustrious monarch and his celebrated stud (*ḥimā*). Of the same descent was the sire al-Aʿwadj, owned by Ḥudjr, king of Kinda who had emigrated from the Ḥaḍramawt in the 5th century B.C. to the borders of the Syrian desert. The son of this Ḥudjr is none other than the great poet Imruʾ al-Ḳays whose lines giving a description of his steed "with its fine-haired coat" (*mundjarid*) in his classic *Muʿallaḳa* (lines 51 ff.) have remained unequalled, though very often subsequently imitated. Of the seven other families of horses known to tradition, four are also connected with Zād al-Rākib. To one of these strains was attributed the stallion Dāḥis, the fruit of an accidental mating of the noble pure-bred Dhu 'l-ʿuḳḳāl. This degrading origin caused Dāḥis, as the outcome of a race, to become the cause of the famous war of Ghaṭafān which lasted for forty years; consequently his strain soon became extinct since it was thought to bring bad luck. Of the three remaining strains, one is purely Persian and the other two of forgotten origin. The story of Dāḥis demonstrates the importance which the Arabs originally used to attach in the pedigree to the stallion, whilst after Islam the genealogy was traced through the mares; there is here a curious contradiction.

With Islam, a new version of the facts comes to light; we now go back to Ismāʿīl, to whom is attributed the domestication of the horse, the special gift of Allāh, though without omitting the episode of Solomon's stallion. Then we leap over the centuries of the *Djāhiliyya* and start again with an authentic historical event, the breaching of the dam of Maʾrib, in the Yemen, which occurred in the middle of the 6th century A.D., to explain the origin of the Arabian breed. The flooding of the country is said to have driven the horse population into the desert where they became wild; five mares from these wandering herds were seen by the people of Nadjd and captured in a curious manner. Five lines of descent sprang from these five mares and one of their descendants, taken to Syria, in her turn began five thoroughbred strains. From one of these the celebrated mare Kuḥaylat al-ʿAdjūz became the eponym for every pure-blooded creature; the term *kuḥaylān*, with its variations *kaḥlānī*, *kaḥayl*, and *kaḥīl*, even now still denotes the thoroughbred Arab.

In reality, the greatest confusion reigns among the horse-breeders of Arabia and Syria on the matter of these "five strains" (*al-kaḥāʾil al-khams*), in which they take such pride and to which they claim that their own stock is related. Inquiries undertaken in the interests of historical and scientific truth by trustworthy travellers like Niebuhr (1779), Burkhardt (1836), Blunt (1882), von Oppenheim (1900) and in particular Major Upton (1881) (see *Bibl.*) have not succeeded in establishing logical connexions between the statements of the various parties consulted; nor could it be otherwise, as the Bedouins have never kept any written pedigrees and entrust the recollection of their prized lines of descent to memory alone.

After the Ḳurʾānic revelation, the victorious Muslims created a corpus of mythical traditions making the horse the chosen mount of Allāh, of supernatural origin; this was justified by the fact that they owed their victorious expansion to that animal. Together with the angels' winged horses and those of king Solomon, and al-Burāḳ, the Prophet's celestial steed, the charger (*djawād*) of the warrior for the Faith (*al-mudjāhid*) became, on earth, a powerful agent for ensuring the final reward in the hereafter; that explains what solicitude and care the Muslim rider had to devote to his beast, which in times of shortage was often given precedence over his wife and family. Among certain tribes in Morocco, popular superstition even went so far as to make the horse a mascot and bringer of luck. On the other hand, the time has now long passed when the horse received so much attention from its master in Arabia; the indignant testimony of all the investigators (see above) bears this out.

In the countries of the Near East we can still today find pedigrees (*ḥudjdja*) drawn up when there is a sale of horses, in the form of official deeds and attesting the animal's highly aristocratic origins: these are merely the inventions of horse-copers. But, like the mediaeval treatises on hippology, they betray a preoccupation with the classification of horses, according to the purity of their breeding, in four degrees; thus we have—(a) *al-ʿarabī* or *al-ʿatīḳ*, the "thoroughbred", well-proportioned, of moderate size, and with a flat forehead; its parents are noble, and the belief is that the devil will not approach its owner; (b) *al-hadjīn* or *al-shihrī*, the "mixed breed", whose sire is better bred than the dam; (c) *al-muḳrif*, the "approacher", whose dam is of better breeding than the sire; (d) *al-birdhawn*, of common parentage: this is the draught-horse or pack-horse. According to the etymologists, it is from this term that the French have derived the words "*bardot*" or "*bardeau*" to describe the offspring of the union of the she-ass and the horse. The horse, other than the saddle-horse, is still called *kadīsh* (in Persian *ikdīsh*), or *khardjī*, "bastard". A gelding (*khaṣī*) can be a thoroughbred, but its sterility deprives it of all estimation in the eyes of the Muslims, the Prophet having disapproved of castration.

Leaving aside those Arab traditions which do not stand up to historical criticism, the origin of the

Arabian breed of horses has been the subject of extensive research by such discerning historians and mammalogists as Piétrement, Ridgeway, von Oppenheim and S. Reinach (see *Bibl.*), whose conclusions prove irrefutably the very recent character of this breed. Assyria and the Caspian region, long before Arabia, possessed horses very closely resembling the Egyptian and the Barb, and very clearly distinguished from the type of the steppes of central Asia and the Przewalski. Syria first of all became acquainted with this source, which must have been crossed with certain Libyan horses imported during the reigns of David and Solomon, while northern and central Arabia for many centuries remained unaware of the existence of this noble beast. Strabo, writing at the start of the Christian era, testified (*Geography*, XVI, 768, 784) to the absence of the horse from Arabia in his day. It was only later, in the 4th century, that the large migrations of tribes from southern Arabia towards Syria and ʿIrāḳ brought a new reinforcement to the horse population of those countries with the Dongola breed; the Yemen had for some centuries had the benefit of Ethiopian exports from this Egypto-Libyan source. From the contact of the two existing stocks, that of Syria-Palestine in the north and that of Nad̲j̲d-Yemen in the south, both of them of Libyan origin, the Arabian type began to become fixed; the nomadic element, and in particular the tribe of ʿAnaza, by their seasonal migrations for pasturage in effect created a permanent link between the two centres. The great Islamic conquests in the 1st and 2nd/7th-8th centuries further increased the infusion of new blood, first Assyrian, later Caspian, into Arab breeding, horses being one of the forms of booty most highly prized by the Muslim warriors. Furthermore, their rapid advance in the west, with the occupation of the Mag̲h̲rib, made them appreciate the excellence of the Barb horse and Berber cavalry, the inheritors of the reputation of the ancient Numidian cavalry; in them they found an inexhaustible source of supply for remounting their squadrons; in fact, in the view of Ibn K̲h̲allikān (*Wafāyāt*, trans. M. G. de Slane, Paris-London 1843-71, iii, 476), we know that, in the twelve thousand Berber cavalry who disembarked in Spain under the command of Ṭāriḳ, there were only twelve Arab horses. The theory of the introduction of the Arab horse into the West by Islam is therefore no longer tenable since, on the contrary, it was on the Barb stock, of Libyan breed and perfectly unified, that the Muslims drew so constantly; they hastened to introduce a number of fine stallions to Arabian studs, and these newcomers succeeded in giving the Arabian type its perfect form. From the 7th/13th century Arabia ceased to be at the head of the Islamic world and became isolated; consequently she no longer received any regenerating assistance from abroad in the matter of breeding, which, for good or ill, took place in enclosed conditions, among the Bedouins of the Nufūd. The important nomadic ʿAnazī breeders, for their part, left the Nad̲j̲d for Syria, so condemning the stocks of horses in Arabia to a decline which has inevitably become more and more marked until the present time. Today, only the very largest fortunes derived from oil can bid for the extremely rare pure-bred Arab stallions, and it has to be admitted that this noble race is on the way to extinction.

Having been one of the principal factors in securing the victories of Islam, the horse was the inspiration of many literary works in Arabic in both verse and prose, especially during the first five Muslim centuries. In poetry, there were scarcely any poets who did not try to describe the horse, but always in an occasional way, the *waṣf al-faras* never having constituted a true theme. It is among the great masters of verse that we must seek the most beautiful expressions of this kind, although none of them, not even Abū Tammām, al-Buḥturī, al-Mutanabbī, Ibn al-Muʿtazz and others, abstained from using ready-made metaphors collected together in the pre-islamic *ḳaṣīdas* or from resorting pedantically to rare archaic terms (*g̲h̲arīb*); in Muslim Spain, the Andalusian poets revealed no greater originality and, like their masters in the East, merely applied themselves to an external description of the animal with all the conventionalism imposed by their concern with philological erudition (see H. Pérès, *La poésie andalouse, en arabe classique, au XIe siècle*,² Paris 1953, 235-6). In prose, the number of works dealing with the horse would be well over a hundred had they all survived; there are frequent mentions of titles such as *K. al-Faras*, *K. al-K̲h̲ayl*, *K. K̲h̲alḳ al-faras*, and *K. Ṣifāt al-k̲h̲ayl* in the lexicographers and encyclopaedists devoted to *adab*; Ibn al-Nadīm, in his *Fihrist*, gives quite a long list of them. Of the various manuscripts of this sort preserved in the libraries, very few have been published, in view of their striking similarity in form and substance. In all periods, the chief preoccupation of the writers of these treatises was to reproduce the terminology relating to the horse, very often at the cost of scientific reality. Moreover, the large place given in these works to superstitious interpretations of the physiognomy of the *faras* deprives them of what technical value one might wish to find in them; every anatomical detail, when considered from this angle, implies consequences either good or ill for the animal's owner; in this attitude we can see the mark of the nomad, with his excessive credulity, and similarly in the curious nomenclature of the horse borrowed from the names of desert birds. It is sufficient to consult the classic *K. Ḥilyat al-fursān wa-s̲h̲iʿār al-s̲h̲ud̲j̲ʿān* of the Andalusian Ibn Hud̲h̲ayl, of the 8th/14th century (see Brockelmann, S II, 379 and the excellent translation, with full comments, by L. Mercier under the title *La parure des cavaliers et l'insigne des preux*, Paris 1924) to establish that the Arabs have always relied solely on the external features of the horse to determine its qualities of temperament. Thus their criterion of appreciation was founded on the interpretation of the particular features of the colour of the coat (*lawn*) and the "signs" (*s̲h̲iyāt*) constituted by the "blaze" (*g̲h̲urar*), light patches on the head, the "stockings" (*taḥd̲j̲īl*), white markings at the foot of the legs, and the *dawāʾir*, tufts of hairs growing in different directions; other points to be considered are the shape of the "upper parts" (*al-aʿālī, al-samāʾ*), and the "under side" (*al-asāfil, al-arḍ*), and of the "forehand" (*al-maḳādim*) and "hindquarters" (*al-maʾāk̲h̲ir*), the animal's attitude in repose, its walk and trot, its bad habits both natural and acquired, its speed and staying-power. In their writings, these authors have never made a distinction between equitation, hippology and the veterinary art, and these three ideas are fused, in their works, in the synonyms *farāsa, furūsa* and *furūsiyya* [*q.v.*]. It is interesting to note that *firāsa*, from the same root, means "physiognomy".

The principles of rearing, teaching and training (*taḍmīr, iḍmār*) specified in these writings and in general use among the Muslims are very often completely contrary to the nature of the horse and differ sharply from modern scientific methods; the same is true of veterinary treatment, when not taken directly from ancient Greek practice. For equitation, see FURŪSIYYA.

There is another category of works which are fairly numerous, mostly written by non-Arab Muslims, on subjects concerning the horse regarded from the viewpoint of military usefulness; they served as "manuals of instruction" for the use of the warriors of the Caliph's cavalry squadrons [see FURŪSIYYA]. Arabia gradually lost the passion for the race-course, in proportion as the number of horses declined. The other Muslim countries have remained quite interested in racing, but the sport is at present governed by rules imported from the west, and the Anglo-Arab thoroughbred is everywhere supplanting its illustrious ancestor.

To sum up, we may say that the horse reached its apogee, in the Near East, between the 5th and 15th centuries A.D., and that Arab horsemanship was in no respect inferior to that of European chivalry. But the lack of rational methods in breeding, on the one hand, and the replacement of steel by fire-arms on the other, condemned the Arab cavalry to an inevitable decline. Those Bedouins who still ride horses today use only violent and cruel methods to break in an animal that by nature is good-tempered and gifted with rare qualities of intelligence; it must be realised that these horsemen are not and never will be as close to the *faras* as were their mediaeval ancestors. We may add that, but for the judicious and praiseworthy intervention of English horse-lovers and breeders, the breed of the pure-bred Arabian would long since have been extinct.

Bibliography: In addition to the works referred to in the text: Sources in Arabic (in addition to the exhaustive bibliographies of Hammer-Purgstall, *Das Pferd bei den Arabern*, in *Denkschr. d. K. Akad. d. Wiss. zu Wien*, vi, 1855-6 and of L. Mercier, *op. cit.*): Ibn Sīduh, *Mukhaṣṣaṣ*, Alexandria 1904, vi, 135-98; Ibn al-ʿAwwām, *K. al-Filāḥa*, trans. Clément-Mullet, *Le livre de l'agriculture*, Paris 1864-7; Khūrī Nadjīb, *al-Khayl wa-fursānuhā*, Baabda (Lebanon) 1916; Damīrī, Cairo 1356, i, 309 ff., ii, 209 ff.; Ṣaʿīdī, *al-Ifṣāḥ fī fiḳh al-lugha*, Cairo 1929, 322-44; Saʿdī Rashīd, *K. Ghāyat al-murād fi 'l-khayl al-djiyād*, Bayān Press, 1896; Ḳazwīnī, *ʿAdjāʾib*, Cairo 1356, ii, 190 ff.; Ḥāṣibānī, *K. Sirādj al-layl fī surūdj al-khayl*, Beirut 1881; Ibn al-Kalbī and Ibn al-Aʿrābī, *K. Asmāʾ khayl al-ʿArab wa fursānihim*, ed. G. Levi Della Vida, *Les "Livres de chevaux"*, Leiden 1928; Masʿūdī, *Murūdj*, iii 59, iv 23, viii 359 (on racing); *Rasāʾil Ikhwān al-Ṣafāʾ*, ed. Bombay, ii 145; Djāḥiẓ, *Ḥayawān* (see index s.vv. *khayl* and *faras*). References to numerous manuscript works on *faras* and *furūsiyya* preserved in the great European libraries are to be found in Hammer-Purgstall and L. Mercier, *op. cit.*—European sources (in alphabetical order):—H. d'Allemagne, *Du Khorassan au pays des Backhtiaris*, Paris 1911, 4 vol. (*passim*); E. Aureggio, *Les chevaux du Nord de l'Afrique*, Algiers 1893; L. Azpeitia de Moros, *En busca del caballo árabe*, Madrid 1915; Lady Anne Blunt, *Bedouin tribes of the Euphra'es*, London 1879; eadem, *A pilgrimage to Nejd*, London 1881; Boucault, *The Arab horse, the thoroughbred and the turf*, London 1912; J. L. Burkhardt, *Travels in Arabia*, 1829; Chevalier Chatelain, *Mémoire sur les chevaux arabes*, Paris 1816; A. Le Clercq, *De l'origine commune des chevaux arabes et des chevaux barbes*, 1854; Gen. Daumas, *Les Chevaux du Sahara et les mœurs du désert avec les observations de l'Emir Abdelkader*, Paris 1864; idem, *Principes généraux du cavalier arabe*, Paris 1854; Gen. Descoins, *L'équitation arabe: ses principes, sa pratique*, Paris 1924; H. R. P. Dickson, *The Arab of the desert*, London 1949, ch. xxx; C. Doughty, *Travels in Arabia Deserta*, 1888; Cdt. Duhousset, *Notices et documents sur les chevaux orientaux*, in *Journal de médecine vétérinaire militaire*, vii (Dec. 1862); R. Dussaud, *Les Arabes en Syrie avant l'Islam*, Paris 1907; idem, *Les régions désertiques de la Syrie et le cheval arabe*, in *Bull. Soc. Anthropologie*, series V, vol. iv; A. Haffner, *Das Kitāb Al Chail von Al Asmaʿi*, Vienna 1895; Hammer-Purgstall, *Sur la Chevalerie des Arabes antérieure à celle de l'Europe*, in *JA*, 1849; Hamont, *Des races chevalines orientales*, in *Revue de l'Orient*, 1843; Hommel, *Die Namen der Saeugethiere bei den Südsemitischen Voelkern*, Leipzig 1879; A. Jaeger, *Das orientalische Pferd und das Privat-Gestüte des Koenigs von Würtemberg*, 1846; H. Lammens, *Le Berceau de l'Islam*, Rome 1914; Gen. Margueritte, *Chasses de l'Algérie et notes sur les Arabes du Sud*, Paris 1869; J. Mazoiller, *Les chevaux arabes de la Syrie*, Paris 1854; Ch. de Meffray, *Des chevaux Nedjdis Keuheylans et de la possibilité de fonder en Algérie un haras de Keuheylans*, Grenoble 1866; Gen. Mennessier de la Lance, *Essai de bibliographie hippique*, Paris 1915; L. Mercier, *La chasse et les sports chez les Arabes*, Paris 1927; Prince Mohammed Ali, *Notes prises dans l'ouvrage du Cheikh El Hafez Siradj ed Din Ibn Baslan ... sur le sport arabe* (*XIIe siècle*), Paris n.d.; C. Niebuhr, *Description de l'Arabie*, Paris 1779; Von Oppenheim, *Von Mittelmeer zum Persischen Golf*, Berlin 1900; W. G. Palgrave, *Personal narrative of a year's journey through central and eastern Arabia*, London 1865; Dr. Perron, *Le Nāceri ou la Perfection des deux arts, trad. du K. Kāmil al-ṣināʿatayn d'Abū Bakr b. Badr al-Nāṣirī, Traité complet d'hippologie et d'hippiatrique arabes*, Paris 1852-60, 3 vols.; idem, *Nobiliaire des chevaux arabes*, Paris n.d.; D. C. Phillot, *Faras Nama e Rangin, or the Book of the Horse by Rangin* (translated from Hindustani), London 1911; Piétrement, *Les chevaux dans les temps préhistoriques et historiques*, Paris n.d.; Prisse d'Avennes, *Des divers races chevalines de l'Orient*, in *Revue contemporaine*, Paris 1854; S. Reinach, *Analyse d'un ouvrage de Ridgeway sur l'origine et l'influence du pur-sang*, in *L'Anthropologie*, Paris xiv (1903), 200-3, 270; Reinaud, *De l'art militaire chez les Arabes au moyen-âge*, in *JA*, 1848; Ridgeway, *Origin and influence of the Thoroughbred Horse*, Biological Series, University Press, Cambridge, n.d.; W. Rzewuski, *Sur l'introduction du sang oriental des chevaux en Europe*, Paris n.d.; idem, *Notice sur les chevaux arabes*, Paris n.d. (reproduced in *Mines d'Orient* of Hammer-Purgstall, v); W. O. Sproull, *An Extract of Ibn Kutaïba's Adab Al Kātib*, Leipzig 1877; E. Süe, *Histoire de Arabian Godolphin*, in *Revue du Cheval de Selle*, Paris 1921; Col. Tweedie, *The Arabian Horse*, n.p., n.d.; Major R. D. Upton, *Gleanings from the Desert of Arabia*, London 1881; Vallée de Loncey, *Le cheval algérien*, Paris 1889; F. Vatin, *Le cheval arabe dans le Nord de l'Afrique*, 1911. (F. VIRÉ)

FARASĀN (FARSĀN), a group of islands in the Red Sea opposite Abū ʿArīsh. They are not mentioned in the *Periplus*. In the *Martyrdom of St Arethas* the Φαρσὰν islands are said to have contributed seven hips to the Christian expedition against the Yaman. The name is tribal. According to Hamdānī, the Banū Farasān, though claimed as Ḥimyarī by the Ḥimyarī genealogists, belonged to Taghlib and had once been Christian; there were ruined churches on the islands. They were at war with the Banū Madjīd and traded with Abyssinia. They were also found in the Tihāma. The islands had some strategic value in the naval wars of the 16th century. The Egyptians landed there in 912/1506. Albuquerque considered occupying them. The Sharīf Abū Numayy II seized them but was ejected by the Turks. According to Ovington 'Fersham' exported corn to Arabia and the inhabitants were employed by Banians in pearling. Despite Yamanī claims the islands became part of Idrīsī, and later, Saʿūdī territory. Philby found a few troops there. They were visited by Ehrenberg and Hemprich (1825), by Bové (1830-1), and later by oil geologists.

Bibliography: J. Boissonade, *Anecdota graeca*, v, 44; Hamdānī, *Djazīra*, 53, 119; Yāḳūt, iii, 873-4; Albuquerque, *Cartas*, i, 280; W. Foster, *The Red Sea and adjacent countries*, 178; Philby, *Arabian Highlands*, index. (C. F. Beckingham)

AL-**FARAZDAḲ**, "the lump of dough", properly Tammām b. Ghālib (Abū Firās), famous Arab satirist and panegyrist, died at Baṣra about 110/728 or 112/730.

Born in Yamāma (Eastern Arabia) on a date which is uncertain (probably after 20/640), this poet was descended from the sub-tribe of Mudjāshiʿ, of the Dārim group of the Tamīm. His father, Ghālib [*q.v.*], is said to have played some part, in the Baṣra area, in the conflict between ʿAlī and Muʿāwiya; to this fact must be attributed the later idea that al-Farazdaḳ entertained pro-ʿAlid sympathies which, however, are not very apparent in his works. The talent for verse does not seem to have been widespread in his family; however al-Farazdaḳ, endowed with a prodigious memory and precocious talent, seems very soon to have made himself known in his tribe by laudatory and epigrammatic compositions in the Bedouin style. The accession of the Umayyad dynasty must have been a decisive factor in the career of the young poet, because of the choices to which it limited him. By the bonds of affinity as much as by obligation, al-Farazdaḳ was first led to choose himself protectors in Yamāma, then at Baṣra, amongst people more or less bound to the fortunes of the family ruling in Syria. This attitude is particularly noticeable in the relations he maintained, for example, with the Banū Bakra, who were secretly flirting with the ʿAlids, though supporting the Umayyads.

The satire attributed to al-Farazdaḳ against the caliph Muʿāwiya, contrary to what Nallino maintains, is far from being definitely authentic.

Nevertheless circumstances, fortuitous or contrived, must have affected his behaviour occasionally: it is known, for example, that al-Farazdaḳ, as a result of some rather obscure proceedings, had to flee from ʿIrāḳ and seek refuge in Medina to escape the threat that Ziyād, the governor of Baṣra, laid upon his life (in 49/669). At Medina the poet was welcomed most warmly by the local authorities, and he remained in this town till 56/675-6; he then returned to ʿIrāḳ immediately after the death of Ziyād to attach himself to the latter's son, ʿUbayd Allāh. In 67/686, the panegyrist confirmed his attachment to the Umayyad branch of the Marwānids which was in power, by celebrating prince Bishr, who had come to ʿIrāḳ, and his brother ʿAbd al-ʿAzīz, whose praises he sang in a threnody in 85/704 (*Dīwān*, ed. Ṣāwī, 225 ff.). There is no doubt that under the governorship of al-Ḥadjdjādj [*q.v.*], probably because of the intrigues of his enemy Djarīr, who was in the good graces of this powerful personage, al-Farazdaḳ was more or less in disgrace. Nevertheless he dedicated a number of laudatory poems to al-Ḥadjdjādj and to some members of his family. Perhaps his delicate position in relation to the governor of ʿIrāḳ prevented al-Farazdaḳ from obtaining the protection of the caliph ʿAbd al-Malik and it is to be noted that no ode was addressed by him to this ruler. On the other hand, under Walīd I, al-Farazdaḳ became the official poet of the caliph, as witness numerous panegyrics dedicated to him and to his two sons. Under Sulaymān he enjoyed the same favour. It was otherwise on the accession of ʿUmar II in 99/717, when al-Farazdaḳ was rather in the shade. However, the insurrection of Yazīd b. al-Muhallab gave the poet the chance to recover favour and, under the caliph Yazīd II, he violently attacked the rebel whom he had celebrated several years before, at the time of his power (see the panegyrics to Yazīd II and to Maslama, dated 101/720 and 102/720-1 in *Dīwān*, 262-7 and 201). At this time, al-Farazdaḳ, who was eighty years old, hardly ever left Baṣra. Caught up in the whirlwind of conflicts between the "Yemenī" and Ḳaysī factions, he experienced many difficulties with governors of ʿIrāḳ belonging to one or other of them. Twice he was thrown into prison because of this, but succeeded in getting out thanks to local support.

In his career, struggles against rivals occupied a prominent place. Political attitudes, notably attachment to the "Yemenī" or the Ḳaysī faction, provoked or aggravated these enmities. In the background one can also sense some tribal partisanship. This is the reason for the implacable hostility nursed by al-Farazdaḳ for Djarīr, also a Tamīmī, but of another branch. There is no doubt that the contentions between these two rivals have been a fruitful source for anecdotal literature (as one can ascertain from *Kitāb al-Aghānī*[3], viii, 32-7). Moreover, it is certain that this opposition inspired al-Farazdaḳ—and his enemy likewise—with the poems which most clearly characterize their work. These diatribes should not however, allow us to forget those other relationships, of a different kind, maintained with al-Aḥwaṣ [*q.v.*] at Medina, with the "reader"-grammarian Abū ʿAmr ibn al-ʿAlāʾ [*q.v.*], or with al-Ḥasan al-Baṣrī (cf. *Aghānī*[1], xix, 14).

Al-Farazdaḳ seems to have been too unusual a figure not to have stimulated the imagination of the "logographers" who interested themselves in him. In the biographical facts we have, there often comes to light a tendency to exaggerate the eccentricities of his personality, to accentuate his cowardice, bawdiness, drunkenness, and venality. This harsh approach is in fact of little concern because it does not touch on the essentials. What is important in reality is to discover in al-Farazdaḳ the traits which are of relevance for the panegyrist, the satirist, and the representative of a generation torn between bedouin culture and the new ethics. On these lines might be explained certain traits of his character, his recantations and his final impenitence, all to be found echoed in his poetry.

The greater part of his poetry has survived, because of Tamīmī particularism on the one hand, and also because of the favour al-Farazdaḳ still retained in learned circles in Baṣra. After an oral transmission about which we have few facts, his poetry was equally well received at Kūfa (see *Aghānī*[1], xix, 2, 11 f.) There is no doubt that it is from this time that al-

Farazdaḳ, along with Djarīr and al-Akhṭal [*q.v.*], becomes one of a trio who for several centuries furnished a theme for discussion among the cultivated. In his own lifetime, al-Farazdaḳ did not hesitate to appropriate the verses of his contemporaries (cf. Ibn Sallām, 126 and *Aghānī*[3], ii, 266-7, viii, 96); there is also reason to doubt the authenticity of many of the poems which appear in al-Sukkarī's recension in the 3th/9th century. The *Dīwān*, in Ṣāwī's edition, numbers about 7,630 verses, which is the largest total that is known in the whole of Arabic poetry. His work is presented in the form of fragments or of complete poems of 20 to 30 verses, rarely more. Many poems are in *ḳasīda* form. With al-Farazdaḳ this form had a tripartite structure with a short *nasīb* (*e.g.*, *Dīwān*, ed. Ṣāwī, 7, 8, 74-6, etc.), but usually—and this is remarkable—this elegiac prelude is omitted (so *ibid.*, 84-7, 99 f., 228-33 etc.), and very frequently the *ḳaṣīda* is reduced to the laudatory elements alone (so *ibid.*, 57-9, 63-7, 70-1, 99-101, 309-14, etc.). The thematic sequence in the *ḳaṣīda* with *nasīb* often anticipates the sequence which imposed itself on the "classical" theoreticians (so *ibid.*, 219-24, 302-8 etc.). Too often the threnodic form is difficult to find in this poet, but we have a good specimen in the threnody composed on Bishr (*ibid.*, 268-70). The various types of poem are unequally represented in al-Farazdaḳ. First and foremost come the laudatory themes made up of the traditional sterotypes, among which should be pointed out the traditional theme of the greatness as caliph and the religious value of the Caliph-Imām (so *ibid.*, 63-7, 89-92 lines 12 ff., 219-24 lines 18 ff. etc.). Naturally enough, tribal and personal *fakhr* is frequent in this poet. Like his contemporaries, al-Farazdaḳ treated the epigram in short impromptus or developed it as a thematic element in a *ḳaṣīda*. In this latter case he obtains an effect of contrast with the laudatory elements (so *ibid.*, 115-23 where the glories of the Dārim are contrasted with the "shames" of the Kulayb, Djarīr's tribe). In al-Farazdaḳ, more than in his contemporaries, the satirical genre has a rare vigour and obscenity (*e.g.*, the piece directed against al-Tirimmāḥ, in *Dīwān*, 135-7). The traditional wisdom, poorly represented in the work of this panegyrist and satirist, is of a distressing banality, and the Islamic ethic has in no way enriched in depth a spirit completely impregnated with Bedouin culture. Sometimes, however, the poet seems to have been able to strike a moving tone, in lamenting, for example, the death of a child (so *Dīwān*, 764 and *Aghānī*[1], xix, 12-3). It is worth noting that, dissolute as al-Farazdaḳ is supposed to have been, he did not to all intents and purposes write in the Bacchic genre (cf. Ibn Ḳutayba, 294). Likewise this epicurean hardly felt the need to celebrate his loves, and the ode composed on a gallant adventure confirms this deficiency in his sensibility (*ibid.*, 255-62). Similarly in the fragments, in any case suspect, on his separation from his wife Nawār, the poet is without deep emotion and reduced to repeating banal formulas (see *Aghhānī*[1], xix, 9).

The language and style of the works ascribed to al-Farazdaḳ are of a remarkable homogeneity: very rarely does one find a laboured effect due to the use of rare terms or *hapax legomena*. In this poet as in his contemporaries of the ʿIrāḳī circle, only the five current metres are employed; *radjaz* is employed only sporadically. From this point of view, his work is well worth attention, in the sense that it enables us to assess the prosodic resources available in this epoch to a poet dependent on the Tamīmī tradition. Put beside the poetry of Djarīr, it is thoroughly representative of the poetry of the great nomads of Eastern Arabia at its height, at the very moment when, in contact with the big ʿIrāḳī cities, it was to yield before new influences.

Bibliography: Ibn Sallām, *Ṭabaḳāt*, index; Ibn Ḳutayba, *Shiʿr*, index; *Aghānī*[3], i, 116, 148-9, viii, index and especially 33-8, 44-5, xv, 441-7, and *Aghānī*[1], xix, 1-61; Āmidī, 166 and index; Marzubānī, *Muʿdjam*, ed. Krenkow, 272, 477, 486-7; idem, *Muwashshaḥ*, index; Ibn Khallikān, *Wafayāt*, Cairo 1310, ii, 196-202; Baghdādī, *Khizāna*, Cairo 1347, i, 202-7 (summarizes or quotes Ibn Ḳutayba and *Aghānī*). The ʿIrāḳī anthologists and others have frequently quoted or mentioned al-Farazdaḳ, see esp.: Djāḥiẓ, *Bayān*, index; Ibn Ḳutayba, *ʿUyūn*, index; Ibn ʿAbd Rabbih, *ʿIḳd*, Cairo 1359/1940, index (72 mentions and quotations); Ḳurashi, *Djamhara*, 336-44. Edition of the *Dīwān* by Sukkarī (see *Fihrist*, 158, l. 27-8); for the manuscripts of the *Dīwān*, see Brockelmann, I, 56, S I, 85; Muḥ. b. Ḥabīb, *Naḳāʾiḍ Djarīr wa'l-Farazdaḳ*, ed. Bevan, *passim*; editions of the *Dīwān* by R. Boucher, *Divan de Ferazdaq, récit de Muḥ. b. Ḥabīb*, Paris 1870 (1st part, 270 nos.) and by J. Hell, photolithographic ed., Munich-Leipzig 1900-1 (2nd part); note also other editions, Beirut (n.d. and 1937), Cairo (1293, very defective); another edition by Ṣāwī, *Sharḥ Dīwān al-Farazdaḳ*, Cairo 1354/1936 (782 poems and fragments, amounting to about 7630 verses; besides the fragments and short pieces, it includes about 80 long satires, 94 panegyrics, 24 threnodies, often brief; it is an uncritical and mediocre edition, with glosses often of slight importance; there is no indication how the known mss. were utilised; it seems to reproduce Boucher and Hell, but it has the advantage that it adds the text of the *Naḳāʾiḍ*); a partial French translation by Boucher (Paris 1870-5); and by Hell (Leipzig 1902: trans. of the panegyric to Walīd II), also idem, in *ZDMG*, lix (1905), 595-600 and lx, 1-35; on the Muhallabids, cf. Rosen in *Zapiski*, xvii (1906), 931-48; Schwarz in *ZDMG*, lxxiii (1919), 80-5 and Krenkow in *Islamica*, ii, 344-54. Notes and studies: Caussin de Perceval, *Notice sur ... al-Farazdaq*, in *JA*, xiii (1834), 507-52; Hell, *Einleitung über das Leben des Farazdaḳ*, Leipzig 1902; Lammens, *Etudes sur le règne du Calife omaiyade Mo'awia I*[er], in *MFOB*, iii (1908), 145 ff. (= 281-448 of the offprint); Nallino, *Littérature arabe*, index; Blachère, *Litt.*, III, 3rd part, chap. I, section C.

(R. Blachère)

FARD (adj., can be taken as a subst.), pl. *afrād*, used of the individual, and so with the meanings of *only, solitary, unique, incomparable*; the *half*, that is to say *one* of a pair or couple (pl. *firād*, *Ḳāmūs* root *f.r.d*); and other derivative meanings. The word has been used to denote Allāh, as the single Being who has no parallel: *al-fard fī ṣifāt Allāh* (al-Layth, *Lisān*, iv, 327/iii, 331a), but it does not occur in the Ḳurʾān or in *ḥadīths* as an epithet of Allāh. It is for that reason that al-Azharī (*ibid.*) found fault with this usage. There is every reason for believing that *al-fard* was at that time simply used as an equivalent of *aḥad*, in accordance with the verse *huwa'llāhu aḥad* (Ḳurʾān, CXII, 1) "où se résume le dogme de l'unicité divine", as R. Blachère said (*Le Coran*, Paris 1949, ii, 123). In addition, *al-fard* serves as a technical term in different sciences: (a) in poetry it denotes a line of verse taken in *isolation* (intact or reduced to a single hemistich); (b) in lexicography, the *afrād* are the words handed down by *one single* lexicographer (see al-Suyūṭī, *Muzhir*³, i, ch. 5), distinct from *āḥād* (*ibid.*, i, 114, lines 8-12) and *mafārīd* (*ibid.*, ch. 15); (c) in grammar, *al-fard* has been said to signify "the singular" by de Sacy (*Gr. Ar.*², i, 149), Fleischer (*Kleinere Schriften*, i, 97), Wright (*Ar. Gr.*³, i, 52B). This can only be a recent or exceptional meaning of the word, which should be dropped and replaced by the traditional terms *al-wāḥid* or (more often used today) *al-mufrad*; (d) in the science of *ḥadīth,fard* is synonymous with *gharīb muṭlaḳ*: a tradition in which the second link of the chain of those who have transmitted it is only represented by a *single tābiʿī*; (e) in astronomy, *al-fard* denotes the star *alpha* in Hydra (*al-shudjāʿ*), and hence the most brilliant (idea of isolation); (f) in arithmetic, *al-ʿadad al-fard* is "the odd number" (from 3 upwards, inclusive), as opposed to *al-ʿadad al-zawdj* "even number" (al-Khʷārizmī, *Mafātīḥ al-ʿulūm*, ed. van Vloten, 184), other uses of *fard* in the divisibility of numbers, *ibid.*, 184-5; (g) for theologians and philosophers, *al-fard* denotes the species, as restricted by the bond of individuation.

Bibliography: in the text; see also Tahānawī, *Dictionary of technical terms*, ii, 1087, 1107, 1178 foot and 1179; Lane, *Lexicon*, s.v.

(H. FLEISCH)

AL-**FARD** [see NUDJŪM]

FARḌ (A.), also *farīḍa*, literally "something which has been apportioned, or made obligatory", and as a technical term, a religious duty or obligation, the omission of which will be punished and the performance of which will be rewarded. It is one of the so-called *al-aḥkām al-khamsa*, the "five qualifications" by which every act of man is qualified in religious law [see AḤKĀM]. A synonym is *wādjib*. The Ḥanafī school makes a distinction between *farḍ* and *wādjib*, applying the first term to those religious duties which are explicitly mentioned in the proof texts (Ḳurʾān and *sunna*) as such, or based on *idjmāʿ*, and the second to those the obligatory character of which has been deduced by reasoning. This distinction is not made by the other schools, and as a norm for action *farḍ* and *wādjib* are equally binding. Islamic law distinguishes the individual duty (*farḍ ʿayn*), such as ritual prayer, fasting, etc., and the collective duty (*farḍ kifāya*), the fulfilment of which by a sufficient number of individuals excuses the other individuals from fulfilling it, such as funeral prayer, holy war, etc.

Bibliography: Tahānawī, *Dictionary of technical terms*, 1124-6, 1444-8; N. P. Aghnides, *Mohammedan theories of finance*, New York 1916, 112 ff.; Santillana, *Istituzioni*, i, 57 ff. See also FURḌA.

(TH. W. JUYNBOLL*)

FARGHĀNĀ, Ferghānā, a valley on the middle Jaxartes (Sîr-Daryā), approximately 300 km. long and 70 km. wide, surrounded by parts of the Tianshan mountains: the Čatkal range (Ar. Djadghal, up to 3,000 m. high) on the north, the Ferghānā mountains (up to 4,000 m.) on the east, and the Alai mountains (up to 6,000 m.) on the south. The only approach (7 km. wide) accessible in all seasons is in the west, at the point where the Jaxartes leaves the valley and where the trade-route (and since 1899 the railway from Samarḳand to Ōsh) enters it. The Farghānā valley covers approximately 23,000 km.²; the irrigated land (9,000 km.²) has increased during the last decades, owing to the constant extension of irrigation. The interior of the area consists of a desert.

The Farghānā valley has always been fairly densely populated since the earliest irruption of Islam, and even in pre-Islamic times, according to Chinese sources. As a consequence, the indigenous population has been able to withstand the Turks, who have pressed in repeatedly ever since early Islamic times; thus the Turks have only settled in one part of the district (cf. the present political distribution below). Since the end of the nineteenth century the Russians have also settled almost exclusively in the towns, leaving the agricultural areas in the hands of the indigenous population.

Evidently Farghānā became known to the Chinese in 128 B.C., from the description of an envoy who had travelled through it. But the connexion of the Chinese accounts with individual areas or persons cannot be established with any certainty. After the spread of the second (western) Kök-Turkish kingdom Farghānā was exposed to Turkish attacks and, after continued fighting between 627 and 649 A.D., came under Turkish dominion. A Turkish prince took up residence in Kāsān (Chinese Kʿo-sai), the capital of that time. After the overthrow of the first west-Turkish kingdom by the Chinese, in 657, the whole district was governed from Kāsān by a Chinese governor. The indigenous Iranian dynasty, whose influence had for some time been weakened by a succession of local princes (as reported by the Chinese envoy Hüan-tsang in 630), was evidently supplanted by a Turkish ruling family, after the elimination of Chinese rule in about 680. In 739 Arslan Khān is mentioned as ruler of Farghānā.

An Arab-Muslim advance into Farghānā, alleged to have taken place in the time of the Caliph ʿUthmān under the leadership of Muḥammad b. Djarīr, who is said to have fallen at Safīd Bulān at the head of 2700 warriors (according to Djamāl Ḳarshī apud Barthold, *Turkestan*, 160), certainly belongs to the realm of legend. The legend formed the basis for a Persian folk-tale (said to have been translated from Arabic) which later spread throughout Central Asia, and was finally translated into Turkish (cf. *Protokolî Turkest. Kružka Lyubiteley Arkheologii*, iv, 149 f.).

In fact the Muslim invasion of Farghānā is connected with the occupation of Transoxania by Ḳutayba b. Muslim [*q.v.*]. He first advanced into the country in 94/712-3 and attempted a revolt from there against the Caliph in 96/715, but was killed by his own soldiers (Ṭabarī, ii, 1256 f., 1275-81; S. G. Klyashtorniy, *Iz istorii borʾbî narodov Sredney Azii protiv arabov* [*Remarks on the history of the struggle of the peoples of Central Asia against the Arabs*], in *Épigrafika Vostoka*, ix (1954), 55-64: this treats mainly of the events of 712). Ḳutayba's grave is still pointed out today close to the village of Djalāl Ḳuduḳ, near Andīdjān (*Protokolî*, iii, 4). This revolt and the battles which followed in Persia in the next decades, finally leading to the downfall of the Umayyads in 749-50, prevented for some time the consolidation of Arab-Islamic rule over Farghānā. The Muslims apparently had to leave the country again and in 103/721-2 the indigenous Sogdian prince was able to recall and resettle in part of his country those Sogdians who had migrated further eastwards to avoid the summons to adopt Islam (Spuler, *Iran*, 37, 254 f.). At that time the local nobility (gentry: *Dihḳāns* [*q.v.*]) played the leading rôle in Farghānā, as in the rest of Transoxania. The local prince also bore this title beside that of Ikhshēdh (cf. IKHSHĪDIDS, and Olʾga I. Smirnova, *Sogdiyskie monetî kak novîy istočnik dlya istorii Sredney Azii* [*Sogdian coins as a new source for the history of Central Asia*], in *Sovetskoe Vostokovedenie*, vi (1949), 356-67; further, A. Yu Yakubovskiy [ed.]: *Trudi sogdiysko-tadžikskoy ékspeditsii . . . [Works of the Sogdian-Tādjīk expedition . . .*], i, Moscow-Leningrad 1950, 224-31; further as sources: al-Balādhurī, *Futūḥ*, 420; al-Ṭabarī, ii, 1442, 2142; *Ḥudūd al-ʿālam*, ed. Minorsky, 115-17, 355; idem in *BSOAS*, xvii/2 (1955), 265).—In the year 121/739 the Arabs were once more able to send a governor to Farghānā (al-Ṭabarī, ii, 1694), but there was still continued opposition to Islam, especially as the permanence of Arab rule had again been put in doubt by the advance of Chinese armies into Western Central Asia as far as Transoxania, between 745 and 751 (cf. Spuler, *Iran*, 302 and the sources and studies given there). An envoy sent to the Caliph al-Manṣūr by the local prince, who had evidently fled to Kāshghar, was held prisoner for a long time owing to his refusal to adopt Islam (Yaʿḳūbī, ii, 645). The Caliphs al-Mahdī, Hārūn al-Rashīd (175-6/791-3) and al-Maʾmūn were also forced to send troops to Farghānā to overcome the opposition to Islam and Arab rule (Yaʿḳūbī, ii, 465 f., 478; Gardēzī, 19; further Spuler, *Iran*, 51 f.). Only the inclusion of Farghānā in the dominions of the Sāmānids [*q.v.*] in approximately 205/820-1, under the administration of the governor Nūḥ b. Asad (d. 227/841-2), opened the last doors to Islam, both in Kāsān (al-Yaʿḳūbī, *Geogr.*, 294, al-Yaʿḳūbī, ii, 478; al-Ṭabarī, ii, 1257), the centre of administration, and Ūrast. The indigenous dynasty had in the meantime disappeared. From then on, the inhabitants of Farghānā supplied soldiers for the guards of the Caliph al-Muʿtaṣim (218-27/833-42: al-Balādhurī, 431; Spuler, *Iran*, 137, 185, fn. 8). They thereby strengthened the influence of the Iranian element in Mesopotamia, which moreover increased continually under the Sāmānids.

Farghānā in the time of the Sāmānids has been amply described by Arab geographers. At that time a change in the economic importance of the several parts of the country appears to have taken place. According to Ibn Khurradādhbih, 30, the road leading into the country from the west crossed the Jaxartes at Khodjand ([*q.v.*]; now Leninābād), and continued to Akhsīkath [*q.v.*], along the right bank, then to Ḳubā, Ōsh and Özkänd (Ūzgand) along the left bank. Al-Iṣṭakhrī, 335, on the other hand considers the road running south of the river to be the main one and lists several populated places along it; only a secondary road led to Akhsīkath at that time. The Farghānā valley then formed the frontier district against the (still unconverted) Turks, who had recently been driven back north-eastwards in several places. There were strong garrisons in Ōsh and some neighbouring forts, used as observation posts against them. Akhsīkath (al-Iṣṭakhrī, 333) was the capital at that time, a position it held as early as the middle of the seventh century, according to Chinese reports and al-Balādhurī (*Futūḥ*, ed. de Goeje, 420). On the other hand Ḳubā is designated as larger, and as the actual capital of the country by al-Muḳaddasī, 272, though its period of prosperity was certainly short.—In the tenth century Farghānā was divided into three provinces and many administrative districts, which are listed by the geographers. They stress the fact that the villages of the country were bigger than elsewhere in Transoxania and occasionally extended as much as a day's journey. Islam (of the Ḥanafī school of law) had asserted itself successfully in the meantime, and convents (*Khānḳāh*) of the Karrāmiyya [*q.v.*] are also mentioned by al-Muḳaddasī, 323. Nothing else is reported about adherents of other religions, such as Christians, Manichaeans and Zoroastrians. Nevertheless an Arabic inscription dating from 433/1041-2 was discovered in the gorge at Wārūkh (in the south), showing a Sassanian and Christian (*rūmī*) date beside the Muslim one (*Protokolī*, viii, 46 f.). A further Arabic inscription (without this peculiarity in the dating) from the year 329/940-1 was found in Ōsh in 1885 (*Otčët Imp. Arkheol. Kommissii za 1882-1888 godī*, p. LXXIII). Buildings from Sāmānid times, on the other hand, have evidently not been preserved.

The mountain ranges surrounding the valley supplied gold, silver and coal (already then used for heating, al-Iṣṭakhrī, 334), and furthermore petroleum, iron, copper, lead, turquoises, sal ammoniac and a medicament called Kū/īlkān (cf. *BGA*, iv, 344; particulars in Spuler, *Iran*, 387, 389, 399, with sources, especially al-Muḳaddasī, 326; Ibn Ḥawḳal^2, 384). Turkish slaves, iron and copper, swords and armour as well as textiles were exported from Farghānā and Isfīdjāb (*Ḥudūd al-ʿālam*, 116; Spuler, *Iran*, 407 f.). Judging by the growth in revenue the country's prosperity increased greatly in Sāmānid times. According to Ibn Khurradādhbih, 38, it amounted to 280,000 dirhems; Ibn Ḥawḳal^2, 470, writing about 130 years later, in 977, puts it already at one million (Spuler, *Iran*, 476).

After the collapse of the Sāmānid state in 389/999, Farghānā came under the dominion of the Ḳarluḳs [*q.v.*] and thus of the ruling dynasty of the Ilig-Khāns or Ḳarakhānids [*q.v.*]. Özkänd [*q.v.*], where twelfth-century buildings and tomb-stones are still preserved, now became the centre of administration. It was there that most coins were minted (often bearing the province name Farghānā as the place of coinage), but other minting-places also occur. The whole of Transoxania was originally administered from Özkänd. After the divisions which soon took place within the Ḳarakhānid dynasty (cf. O. Pritsak, in *Isl.*, xxxi/1 (1953), 17-68), the princes of Farghānā settled in Özkänd, where they withstood a Saldjūḳ advance in the years 482-3/1089-90. In 536/1141 Farghānā came under the dominion of the Gürkhāns [*q.v.*] of the Ḳarakhitāy [*q.v.*], but the indigenous dynasty was still tolerated, as elsewhere within this state. Until 560-74/1165-79, this dynasty seems also to have ruled over Samarḳand, which later again came under the rule of a separate branch of the Ḳarakhānids. From 1212 to 1218 Farghānā was disputed between the Khʷārizmshāh Muḥammad II [*q.v.*] and first the Nayman prince Küčlüg, who had fled westwards, then the Mongols; with the subjection of the prince of Akhsīkath and Kāsān, the province subsequently fell to the Mongols (Ulus of Čaghatāy; cf. the article ČINGIZIDS, above) for whom it was long administered by Maḥmūd and his son Masʿūd Yalavač in the thirteenth century. Local princes in Farghānā were tolerated for a long time; the sheltered position of the valley induced Baraḳ Khān, the Mongol governor, and the Ḳarakhitāy before him, to keep the treasury there (Waṣṣāf, Bombay ed., 67 bottom; Djuwaynī, i, 48). The newly founded town of Andīdjān [*q.v.*] (known to the Arab geographers only as the village Anduḳān) was the capital of the Farghānā valley at the end of the thirteenth century. Marghīnān now also gained in importance.

After the Ulus of Čaghatāy split into two opposing sections in the fourteenth century, both the western kingdom (Transoxania) and the eastern kingdom (then called Mogholistān) contended for Farghānā at different times, up to the time of Tīmūr. As Farghānā belonged to Mogholistān during the greater part of this struggle, its administration shared certain aspects of the administration of the Tarim valley: the tax districts in both countries were called Určin, not Tūmān (Mongolian *tümen*: unit of ten thousand) as in the rest of Transoxania.

Under the Tīmūrids [*q.v.*] Farghānā mostly belonged to Khurāsān (*i.e.*, to the dominion of Shāhrukh [*q.v.*] and his son Ulugh Beg [*q.v.*]) and from 873-99/1469-94 had its own ruler in ʿUmar Shaykh [*q.v.*], a great-great-grandson of Tīmūr. He was succeeded by his son Bābur, who from Farghānā moved against the intruding Shaybānids [*q.v.*] and advanced as far as Samarḳand; but in 909/1504, after eventful battles he saw himself forced to surrender Farghānā, and finally fled altogether to India (for details see BĀBUR). It is to him that we owe a more exact description of Farghānā at a time when power-relationships in Central Asia were undergoing a decisive change, through the fall of the Tīmūrids, the advance of the Shaybānids at the head of the Özbegs [*q.v.*], as well as the establishment of the Shīʿī Ṣafavids [*q.v.*] in Persia. At that time there were nine larger towns in Farghānā, to which Bābur also adds Khodjand. Khoḳand, the later capital, was only a village at the time. The capital was Andīdjān, which was already completely turkicized. (According to Bābur, it was here that Čaghatay, raised to a literary language by ʿAlī Shīr Nawāʾī, was spoken). Marghinān was then still Iranian.—At the time of Bābur there were numerous orchards and gardens in Farghānā and various kinds of wood used for making quivers, bird-cages and similar articles; also a reddish-white stone, discovered in about 1492 and used for making knife-handles and articles of that kind. Iron and turquoise were obtained from the mines; but Bābur makes no mention of coal-mining or the manufacture of weapons, two formerly important branches of the economy. According to his estimate the country was only sufficiently rich to support an army of 3-4000 men.

After the final expulsion of the Tīmūrids, Farghānā belonged to the Özbeg state of the Shaybānids; Andīdjān was then the seat of a local dynasty and gave its name to the whole valley (cf. Maḥmūd ibn Walī, *Baḥr al-asrār*, MS India Office 575, fol. 102b). After the collapse of the Shaybānid state in 1598-9, several Khodja families divided the country up among themselves. They lived under the nominal dependency of Bukhārā, in Čadak, north of the Jaxartes, and had to submit to a number of arrangements with the Ḳazakhs and Kirgiz, who repeatedly pressed into the valleys of the mountains surrounding Farghānā. In 1121/1709-10 the Farghānā valley became a separate Özbeg Khānate under Shāhrukh Bī (Mullā Niyāz Muḥammad, *Taʾrīkh-i Shāhrukhī*, ed. N. N. Pantusov, Kazan 1885, 21; cf. Ivanov, 178-214). From then until 1876 the Farghānā valley was the centre of the Khānate of Khoḳand (*q.v.* for details about the name and history of the town).

In 1876 the Khānate was annexed by the Russians and became the centre of the "Farghānā district" (Ferganskaya Oblastʾ), an area of 160,141 km.^{2} (according to Brockhaus-Efron) with 1,560,411 inhabitants (in 1897). The seat of the military government was the town New Margelan, founded by the Russians, called Skobelev from 1907-24, and subsequently Farghānā (pop., 1951, approx. 50,000) and still today the centre of administration of the "Farghānā district" in Uzbekistan (8029 km.^{2} with approximately 720,000 inhabitants [in 1951]). The towns of Khoḳand and Namangān were, however, considerably larger and of greater economic importance (Khoḳand had approximately 113,000 inhabitants in 1912, and Namangān 70,000; in 1951, in contrast, approximately 93,000 and 115,000 respectively).

The Russians forthwith raised Farghānā's cotton-production considerably, introduced new American kinds of cotton and made Farghānā (as Central Asia generally) one of their main providers of cotton and silk. The most important source of uranium of the Soviet Union is also situated in the Farghānā valley (especially near Tuya-Muyun); petroleum and coal are also extracted.—The ancient system of irrigation has been expanded and improved and, as the "Farghānā system", it has gained significance for the entire irrigation economy of the USSR: construction of the great Farghānā canal in 1939; Farhat dam on the Jaxartes.—The sudden economic advance caused an inflation which led to a revolt in 1898. From 1916 to 1922 Farghānā was involved in the fighting between the indigenous Turkish Basmači associations and the Russians, and later the Bolsheviks. After the October revolution the Farghānā valley was no longer a single administrative unit. Instead the central and eastern areas—essentially according to the nature of the majority of the population—were handed over to the Uzbekistan republic, and the west to Tādjīkistān. The mountains surrounding the Farghānā valley belong for the most part, however, to Kirgizistān: this division demonstrates the result of the gradual advance of Turkish tribes into this area and, since the sixteenth and seventeenth centuries, into the mountains, as well as the retreat of the Iranians. This political organization has had no significance for the development of the valley's economy or system of communication. The knowledge of Russian has increased greatly in the last decades among the indigenous population, but without supplanting the indigenous languages.

Bibliography: Chinese and Köktürks: Edouard Chavannes, *Documents sur les Tou-kiue (Turcs) occidentaux*, St. Petersburg 1903, especially 148 ff.; Hsüan-Tschuang (Hiouen-Tshang), *Mémoires sur les contrées occidentales*, ed. Stanislas Julien, 2 vols., Paris 1857-8; Yu. A. Zadneprovskiy, *Drevnezemledelʾčeskaya kulʾtura Ferganī* (*The ancient agrarian culture of Farghānā*), Moscow and Leningrad 1962 (Materialī i issledovaniya po arkheologii SSSR, cxviii).

Islamic period: Barthold, *Turkestan*, 155-65, 186-202 and index; idem, *Zwölf Vorlesungen über die Geschichte der Türken Mittelasiens*, Berlin 1935; idem, *Four Studies*, ed. V. Minorsky, i, Leiden 1956; Bertold Spuler, *Iran in früh-islamischer Zeit*, Wiesbaden 1952, index; P. P. Ivanov, *Očerki po istorii Sredney Azii* [*Sketches in the history of Central Asia*], Moscow 1958, *passim*, especially 178-213.

Geography: Le Strange, 476-80; A. von Middendorff, *Einblicke in das Farghānā-Tal*, St. Petersburg 1881 (Mém. de l'Acad., vol. xxix); W. Busse, *Bewässerungswirtschaft in Turan*, 1915; W. Leimbach, *Die Sowjetunion*, Stuttgart 1950, 42 ff., 147, 526; Th. Shabad, *Geography of the USSR*, New York 1951, 388-99 and index; V. Masalʾskiy in Brockhaus-Efron, *Éntsiklopedičeskiy Slovarʾ* xxxv A (70), St. Petersburg 1902, 560-4; *Bolʾshaya Sovetskaya Éntsiklopediya*^{2}, xliv (1956), 617-20 (both articles are geographical-statistical).

Maps: 7th cent.: A. Herrmann, *Atlas of China*, Cambridge Mass. 1935, 37; 10th cent.: Spuler, *op. cit.*, end; modern: *Bolʾshaya Sovetskaya Éntsi-*

*klopediya*², xliv, facing p. 618 (with illus.); Diercke, *Weltatlas*, 91st ed., 1957, p. 93; Leimbach, 340; Shabad, 395. (W. Barthold-[B. Spuler])

AL-FARGHĀNĪ, the mediaeval astronomer *Alfraganus*. His full name is Abu 'l-ʿAbbās Aḥmad b. Muḥammad b. Kathīr al-Farghānī, that is to say, a native of Farghāna in Transoxania; not everyone, however, is agreed upon his name: the *Fihrist* only speaks of Muḥammad b. Kathīr, and Abu 'l-Faradj of Aḥmad b. Kathīr, while Ibn al-Ḳifṭī distinguishes between two persons, Muḥammad and Aḥmad b. Muḥammad, in other words father and son; however it is very probable that all the references are to the same personage, an astronomer who lived in the time of the Caliph al-Maʾmūn (d. 833) and until the death of al-Mutawakkil (861), for Abu 'l-Maḥāsin and Ibn Abī Uṣaybiʿa refer to a certain Aḥmad b. Kathīr al-Farghānī who, in 247/861, is said to have been sent by al-Mutawakkil to Fusṭāṭ to supervise the construction of a Nilometer.

His principal work, which still survives in Arabic at Oxford, Paris, Cairo and the library of Princeton University, bears different titles: *Djawāmiʿ ʿilm al-nudjūm wa 'l-ḥarakāt al-samāwiyya*, *Uṣūl ʿilm al-nudjūm*, *al-Madkhal ila ʿilm hayʾat al-aflāk*, and *Kitāb al-fuṣūl al-thalāthīn*. It was translated into Latin by John of Seville and Gerard of Cremona. According to Steinschneider, a translation into Hebrew by Jacob Anatoli also exists at Berlin, Munich, Vienna, Oxford, etc. The Latin translation by John of Seville was printed at Farrara in 1493, Nuremberg in 1537, Paris in 1546, Berkeley (F. J. Carmody) in 1943; the translation by Gerard of Cremona was published by R. Campani (Città di Castello, 1910). From Jacob Anatoli's translation into Hebrew Jacob Christmann made a Latin translation which appeared in 1590 at Frankfurt-am-Main. In 1669, at Amsterdam, Jacob Golius edited the Arabic text with a translation and a copious commentary, under the title: *Muhammedis fil. Ketiri Ferganensis, qui vulgo Alfraganus dicitur, Elementa astronomica, Arabice et Latine.* Apart from this work which, before Regiomontanus, was more widely circulated in the west than that of any other Arabic astronomer, since it was fairly short and easily understood, al-Farghānī also wrote two books on the astrolabe, *al-Kāmil fi 'l-asṭurlāb* and *Fī ṣanʿat al-asṭurlāb* (the Arabic text of which is extant in Berlin and Paris) and certain other works, references to which are given in Brockelmann and Carmody.

Bibliography: *Fihrist*, i, 279; Ibn al-Ḳifṭī, ed. Lippert, 78 and 286; Abu 'l-Faradj (ed. Ṣālḥānī), 236; Ibn Abī Uṣaybiʿa, i, 207; Ibn Taghrībirdī, i, 742; M. Steinschneider, *Die europäischen Übersetzungen aus dem Arabischen bis Mitte des XVII Jahr., SBAk. Wien, phil.-hist. Klasse*, cxlix, 22 and 44; Brockelmann, I, 221 S I, 392-3; Suter, *Abhandlungen zur Gesch. der mathem. Wissensch.*, x, 18 and xiv, 160; Sarton, *Introduction*, i, 567; P. Duhem, *Système du monde*, ii, 204-14; F. J. Carmody, *Arabic astronomical and astrological sciences in Latin translation*, Berkeley 1956, 113-6. (H. Suter-[J. Vernet])

AL-FARGHĀNĪ, the name of two tenth-century historians, Abū Muḥammad ʿAbd Allāh b. Aḥmad b. Djaʿfar (b. 282/895-6, d. 362/972-3) and his son, Abū Manṣūr Aḥmad b. ʿAbd Allāh (327/939-398/1007). ʿAbd Allāh's great-grandfather had been brought to the ʿIrāḳ from Farghāna and had become a Muslim under al-Muʿtaṣim. ʿAbd Allāh himself was a student of the great Ṭabarī, whose works he transmitted, and he achieved high rank in the army. He went to Egypt where his son, it seems, was born, and he and his family remained there. He wrote a continuation of al-Ṭabarī's historical work, entitled *al-Ṣila* or *al-Mudhayyal*, and his son wrote a further continuation, entitled *Ṣilat al-Ṣila*. Both works are known only from quotations in the works of other historians, though it has been suggested that a papyrus leaf containing the account of a battle from the reign of al-Muḳtadir may derive from the *Ṣila*; they were probably much more widely used than citations under their names indicate. The younger Farghānī also wrote biographies of Kāfūr al-Ikhshīdī and the Fāṭimid al-ʿAzīz, both of which, unfortunately, have been lost along with most of the historical literature written under the Fāṭimids.

Bibliography: *Taʾrīkh Baghdād*, ix, 389; *Taʾrīkh Dimashḳ*, vii, 277; Yāḳūt, *Udabāʾ*, i, 161 f.; Ṣafadī, *Wāfī*, under Aḥmad (who follows Yāḳūt); intro. to Ṭabarī, xx; R. Guest, in *A volume of Oriental studies presented to E. G. Browne*, Cambridge 1922, 173; F. Rosenthal, *A history of Muslim historiography*, Leiden 1952, 73; N. Abbott, *Studies in Arabic literary papyri*, i, Chicago 1957, 109 ff. (F. Rosenthal)

FARHĀD PASHA [see FERHĀD PASHA].

FARHĀD WA-SHĪRĪN. A. Christensen (*Sassanides*, 469 and index) has collected together the information relating to Shīrīn (Pehlavi *Shīrēn* "the sweet"; cf. Γλυκέρα, Glycera), a Christian favourite of the Sāsānid king of Īrān, Khusraw II Parvīz (Pehlavi *Abharvēz* "the victorious", 590-628). According to Sebeos, she was a native of Khuzistān; Khusraw married her at the beginning of his reign and she maintained her influence over him although inferior in status to Maria the Byzantine whom he had married mainly for reasons of policy; she protected the Christian clergy, probably lived for a time in the palace, the ruins of which still survive at Ḳaṣr-i Shīrīn [*q.v.*], and she did not forsake the king in the last hours immediately before his assassination; their son, Mardānshāh, was put to death when Shēroē, Maria's son, overthrew him and ascended the throne. Legends concerning the love of the king and Shīrīn soon came into being, and some of the details were collected by al-Thaʿālibī (691) and Firdawsī (*Shāh-nāma*, trans. Mohl, vii), in particular Shīrīn's suicide over the body of Khusraw; this romantic episode, together with that of Shīrīn and Farhād (Pehlavi *Frahādh*), became the subject of a series of romances in verse, in Persian, Turkish (see below) and Kurdish (Duda, 3, n. 7 and 8). Moreover Christensen (*Gestes*, 116-9) has noted certain features in the *Persica* of Ctesias in which he sees elements which helped to form the legend of Farhād and Shīrīn—Semiramis creating a garden near Mount Bagistanon (Bīsutūn), having a way cut through the Zagros mountains to allow for the passage of a canal, and having a royal castle built for her own use.

After the occupation of Īrān by the Arabs, the first text in their language to mention Shīrīn and her lovers is the Chronicle of al-Ṭabarī; in its Persian adaptation by Balʿamī, we read: "Shīrīn was loved by Farhād whom Parvīz punished by sending him to the quarries of Bīsutūn" (trans. Zotenberg, ii, 304 and index, s.v. Ferhād, Schīrīn). The Arab geographers mention them; thus Yāḳūt claims to see Shīrīn's image among the sculptures of Ṭāḳ-i Būstān, according to poems which he quotes (*Buldān*, iii, 252-3) and records a narrative (iv, 112; and Barbier de Meynard, *Dictionnaire de la Perse*, 347-8 and 448-9) explaining how the king had a castle built for her, named Ḳaṣr-i Shīrīn [*q.v.*]. In the Persian language Firdawsī, when writing the history in verse of the reign of Khusraw, tells briefly at the appropriate place of his relations with Shīrīn, though without giving them in his epic the importance which they were later to assume in the eyes of other poets: Parvīz had parted from this childhood friend; meeting her again while hunting, he took her to the palace and decided to marry her, in spite of powerful opposition; then Shīrīn poisoned her rival Maryam whose son Shīrūya was cast into prison; some time afterwards, the troops mutinied, released him and proclaimed him king, while Parvīz was held prisoner in his palace, only accepting food prepared by Shīrīn; the leaders had him stabbed to death. Later, Firdawsī gave reign to his imagination: Shīrīn, on Shīrūya's orders, consented to appear before an assembly of the nobility; she justified herself in respect of all the accusations brought against her, returned to her palace, made her final dispositions, asked Shīrūya for permission to see Khusraw once more, in his tomb, and there she took a violent poison and died at his side.

It was Nīẓāmī who, in his *Khusraw wa-Shīrīn* (completed in 576/1180), created the romance of Farhād and Shīrīn, a notable part of this vast poem, from which it can be detached to form a complete work in itself. It would be superfluous to analyse the contents of this and the following poems, which have been studied by H. W. Duda; but a brief analysis of this romance, from which all the others are derived, is indispensable (leaving aside the first part): Shīrīn wishes to construct a canal; Farhād is assigned to her for this purpose and begins work; Shīrīn comes to inspect the project, and they fall in love with each other; Khusraw, being apprised of this, has Farhād brought before him and, finding his passion unshaken, gives him orders to cut a way through Mount Bīsutūn and to renounce his association with Shīrīn; but she comes back to see him; the king has false news of Shīrīn's death given to Farhād who hurls himself from the mountain top and kills himself; the king has been left a widower by the death of Maryam and is on the point of marrying again; Shīrīn lives alone, in despair; but one day, visiting Ḳaṣr-i Shīrīn on the pretext of hunting, the king meets Shīrīn again; after a long discussion, reminiscent of that between Wīs and Rāmīn [see GURGĀNĪ], they are reconciled and marry; the end of the reign and Khusraw's assassination correspond, in essentials, with the records of the historians; after his death Shīrīn, scorning Shīrūya's attentions, kills herself in Khusraw's tomb.

The poet Amīr Khusraw Dihlawī is the author of a *Shīrīn and Khusraw* in which the narration is more lively and the style simpler than in Niẓāmī's romance; his account of the reign and the amorous exploits of Khusraw (apart from the romance with Shīrīn) is different from Niẓāmī's; Farhād is no longer a simple engineer but is a son of the emperor of China, an exile who has become an artist; after his tragic death, Shīrīn takes revenge by having her rival, a favourite of the king, poisoned (just as she poisoned Maryam in the *Shāh-nāma*). ʿĀrifī (who lived in Ādharbāydjān in about 770/1368-9: not to be confused with the author of *Gūy u-čūgān*, d. 853/1449), desiring to use the same theme once again, succeeded merely in producing an involved work with a complicated and protracted plot, even to analyse which would be tedious; in brief, prince Farhād became a sculptor and architect in order to win the hand of a girl named Gulistān; later, when a widower, he met Shīrīn and fell in love with her; then ʿĀrifī follows his predecessors quite closely, until Farhād dies, poisoned by the mother of a young man whom Gulistān had spurned. Hātifī (about 1520) for the most part kept to the traditional account, but he added various episodes: for example, Khusraw had Farhād imprisoned in a pit in the mountains to keep him away from Shīrīn; but when digging a tunnel, Farhād came across a vein of precious stones; he managed to escape and was then recaptured. The inspiration of Waḥshī, in his *Farhād and Shīrīn* (966/1558-9, completed by Wiṣāl, 1265/1848-9), some details of which were taken from Amīr Khusraw Dihlawī, is lyrical rather than narrative: the sentimental incidents are in some respects reminiscent of the inspirations of Western poets of love and chivalry. In the short *Farhād and Shīrīn* (about 400 lines of verse) of ʿUrfī (d. about 1590), which is even more lyrical than the work of Waḥshī, the hymn to the beauty of nature and the meditation on the diverse emotions of love form the essential parts of this poem in which sentiment is personified by Shīrīn, the author refraining from repeating the legend itself which he assumes will already be familiar to the reader. Finally, in 1920 Dhabīh Behrūz published the script of a film "The king of Iran and the Armenian princess".

Bibliography: Faruk K. Timurtaş, *Iran edebiyatında Husrev ü Şirin ve Ferhad ü Şirin yazan şairler*, in *Şarkiyat Mecmuası*, iv (1961), 73-86; A. Christensen, *L'Iran sous les Sassanides*, 1936; H. W. Duda, *Ferhād und Schīrīn*, Prague 1933 (essential); Schwarz, *Īrān*, index, s.v. Farhād, Širīn; Thaʿālibī, *Histoire des rois des Perses*, ed.-trans. Zotenberg, 1900; Firdawsī, *Shāh-nāma*, ed.-trans. Mohl in-fol., or trans. in-12, vii and index; A. Christensen, *Les gestes des rois dans les traditions de l'Iran antique*, Paris 1936; Niẓāmī, *Khusraw wa-Shīrīn*, ed. Waḥīd Dastgardī, vol. ii of the complete works, Tehrān 1333-55; on the *poetae minores* who have treated this subject in Persian from the 17th to the 20th centuries, Timurtaş, *loc. cit.*, Duda, *op. cit.*, 116 ff., and *Gr. I. Ph.*, ii, 246 and 247. *Schirin, ein persisches romantisches Gedicht nach Morgenländischen Quellen*, by Hammer-Purgstall, Leipzig 1809, is based on an amalgam of extracts from Niẓāmī, Amīr Khusraw Dihlawī, Hātifī and the Turkish writers Āhī and Shaykhī , freely translated (cf. Duda, *op. cit.*, 12; *Gr. I. Ph.*, ii 242-3 and Rieu, *CPM*, 566b).

(H. MASSÉ)

This theme penetrates very early into Turkish literatures. There exist two very old versions of the poem *Khusraw and Shīrīn*, dating back to the first half of the 8th/14th century : one adapted by Ḳuṭb (ca. 741/1341) in the territories of the Golden Horde (ed. A. Zajączkowski, *Najstarsza wersja Turecka Ḫusräv u Širīn Quṭba*, Warsaw 1958), another written by Fakhr al-Dīn Yaʿḳūb in Western Anatolia, in the principality of the Aydîn Oghullarî (ca. 767/1366; Ms: Marburg, Westdeutsche Bibl., Or. Qu. 1069). There is also a fairly close Turkish translation of Niẓāmī's poem by Sheykhī [*q.v.*], made early in the 9th/15th century.

In Eastern Turkish literature the theme was first treated by Nawāʾī, who gave first place to the person of Farhād; Farhād, possessed with love for Shīrīn, pierces a mountain and dies on hearing the false news of Shīrīn's death. Many subsequent Turkish poets elaborated this topic, for example: *Khusraw and Shīrīn*: Aḥmed Riḍwān, Ṣadrī, Ḥayātī, Āhī, Djelīlī; *Farhād and Shīrīn* or *Farhād-nāme*: Ḥarīmī (Prince

Ḳorḳud), Lāmiʿī, S̲h̲ānī, Nākām, etc. (see Faruk K. Timurtaş, *Türk edebiyatında Husrev ü Şirin ve Ferhad ü Şirin hikâyesi*, in *Ist. Ün. Türk Dili ve Edebiyatı Dergisi*, ix (1959), 65-88).

There exist alsc some versions presenting the story in the form of a dramatic play, *e.g.*, the *Farhād wa S̲h̲īrīn* by the Azerbaydjan poet Samed Vurgun (d. 1956) and that by the modern Turkish poet Nazim Hikmet Ran (d. 1963), translated into Russian as "A Legend of Love".

Bibliography: (further to that given above) Gibb, *Ottoman Poetry*, i, 321 ff. and index ii, s.vv. *Ferhád-Náme, K̲h̲usrev u S̲h̲irin*; G. Aliyev, *Iz istorii voznikoveniya obraza Farhada v literaturak̲h̲ narodov Vostoka*, in *Kratkiya soobs̲h̲ḟeniya Inst. vostok.*, xxvii (1958), 50-7; idem, *Legenda o Khosrove i S̲h̲irin v literaturak̲h̲ narodov Vostoka*, Moscow 1960; A. Zajączkowski, *La traduction turque-osmanlie du Ḥusräv u S̲h̲irin de S̲h̲eyk̲h̲ī*, Warsaw 1963; Fevziye Abdullah, in *İA*, s.v. Ferhad ile Şirin; Muharrem Ergin, in *Türkoloji bölümü çalışmaları*, Istanbul 1962, 113-39.

(A. ZAJĄCZKOWSKI)

FARHANG [see ḲĀMŪS and MAʿĀRIF].

FARHANGISTĀN [see MAD̲J̲MAʿ].

FARḤĀT, D̲J̲ARMĀNŪS, Arabic philologist and poet, forerunner of the nineteenth century literary renaissance in the Arab countries, born at Aleppo 20 November 1670, and died there 10 June 1732. He was Maronite archbishop of his native town from 1725 to 1732, but we are not concerned here with his activity as an organizer, which was of the greatest importance to the Maronite church, nor with the majority of his dogmatic and polemic writings and his works of edification and history; he must however be mentioned in the history of Arabic literature as a lexicographer, grammarian and poet.

Aleppo was one of the few Arab towns which after the Ottoman conquest had retained and to a certain extent developed a literary tradition. This tradition had been fortified by certain European influences, particularly among the Arabic-speaking Christians. The establishment of the Maronite college at Rome in 1584 and the presence at Aleppo of a large colony of European merchants played an important part in this; it must not be forgotten that J. Golius (1625-6) and E. Pococke (1630-6) both spent some time there. Some literary activity flourished in all the Christian communities, and the Orthodox patriarch Makāriūs b. al-Zaʿīm al-Ḥalabī (d. 1672) is only one example out of many.

Born of a prosperous Maronite family, the Maṭar, Farḥāt received an excellent education from the Christian and Muslim scholars of Aleppo: Buṭrus al-Tūlawī, a pupil of the Maronite college of Rome (d. 1745; cf Manas̲h̲ in *Machriq*, vi (1903), 769-77; idem, *Mustaṭrafāt*, 7; Cheikho, *Catalogue*, 76-8, no. 270; Masʿad, *D̲h̲ikrā*, 9-11), Yaʿḳūb al-Dibsī, a great authority on rhetoric (cf. Cheikho, *op. cit.*, 97, no. 344), and the famous Muslim scholar S̲h̲ayk̲h̲ Sulaymān al-Naḥwī al-Ḥalabī. Besides his native languages, Syriac and Arabic, he learnt in his youth Latin and Italian. After having taken monastic vows in 1693, with the name of D̲j̲ibrāʾīl, he undertook a journey to Jerusalem (cf. *Dīwān*, 131) and then settled in Lebanon where he sat at the feet of the famous Maronite patriarch Isṭifān al-Duwayhī (1630-1704). Ordained priest in 1697, he became in 1698 abbot of the monastery of Mart Mūra at Ihdin; in 1711-2, as a result of certain complications (see *Dīwān*, 403, 469), he went on a journey to Rome, which made a deep impression on him (see *Dīwān*, 87,

131, 146, 294, 434, 438, 448), to Spain, Sicily (*op. cit.*, 220, 404) and Malta (*op. cit.*, 229). As archbishop of Aleppo (from 1725) he formed an important collection of manuscripts which still exists (cf. Zaydān, *Taʾrīk̲h̲ ādāb al-lug̲h̲a al-ʿarabiyya*, iv, Cairo 1914, 135) and he gathered round him a circle of poets and scholars. Among the friends whom he names in his *Dīwān* the following especially deserve mention: Niḳūlā al-Ṣāʾig̲h̲ (1692-1756), of Greek descent, who shares with him the glory of being the most popular poet (*Dīwān*, 150; Cheikho in *Machriq*, vi (1903), 97-111, with portrait; idem, *Catalogue*, 131, no. 484; idem, *S̲h̲uʿarāʾ*, 503-11); Mikirdīd̲j̲ al-Kasīḥ, an Armenian by birth (*Dīwān*, 239, 466; Cheikho, *Catalogue*, 195-6, no. 751; idem, *S̲h̲uʿarāʾ*, 498-501); the poet Niʿmat Allāh al-Ḥalabī (d. c. 1700; see *Dīwān*, 64; Manas̲h̲ in *Machriq*, v (1902), 396-405; Cheikho, *Catalogue*, 205-6, no. 796; idem, *S̲h̲uʿarāʾ*, 396-405); ʿAbd Allāh Zāk̲h̲ir (1680-1748), who applied himself with enthusiasm and success to printing (*Dīwān*, 158; Cheikho, *Catalogue*, 108-9, no. 386; idem, *S̲h̲uʿarāʾ*, 501-3; Zaydān, *Taʾrīk̲h̲*, iv, 45); the theologian Ilyās b. al-Fak̲h̲r (d. c. 1740; see *Dīwān*, 214; Cheikho, *Catalogue*, 39-40, no. 122), etc.

As a philologist, Farḥāt understood above all the need to make available to his fellow countrymen textbooks which would facilitate for them the study of Arabic. In almost all fields—lexicography, grammar, rhetoric—he wrote such textbooks, some of which have remained until recently in common use among Syrian Christians. Although they are based mainly on Arabic tradition, here and there, particularly in grammar, can be detected traces of European influence, especially of the Roman Maronites and of the school of Erpenius. Among his works of lexicography we have *al-Mut̲h̲allat̲h̲āt al-durriya* (Ṭāmīs̲h̲ (Lebanon) 1867, and *Dīwān*, 92-106), an imitation in verse, composed in 1705, of the famous *Mut̲h̲allat̲h̲āt* of Ḳuṭrub [*q.v.*], and provided later with a commentary (manuscripts of it are not uncommon: one, of 1712, is in the Asiatic Museum in Leningrad; see v. Rosen, *Les manuscrits ar. de l'Inst. des Langues Or.*, St. Petersburg 1877, 71, no. 156). His dictionary, *Iḥkām bāb al-iʿrāb min lug̲h̲at al-Aʿrāb*, completed in 1718, is of greater importance; it is based for the most part on the *Ḳāmūs* of al-Fīrūzābādī [*q.v.*], but contains many modern words and terms used by Christian Arabs; the Maronite patron of learning, the emigré Rus̲h̲ayd al-Daḥdāḥ (1813-89), collated five manuscripts of it with the *Ḳāmūs* and published the resulting dictionary under the title *Dictionnaire arabe par Germanos Farhat, maronite, éveque d'Alep. Revu, corrigé et considérablement augmenté sur le manuscrit de l'auteur par Rochaid de Dahdah, scheick maronite*, Marseilles 1849, with portrait of the author (Arabic title: *Iḥkām bāb al-iʿrāb*); as an appendix to the dictionary is printed the treatise *al-Faṣl al-maʿḳūd fī ʿawāmil al-iʿrāb*. Among Farḥāt's grammatical works, the *Baḥt̲h̲ al-maṭālib* (cf. Manas̲h̲ in *Machriq*, iii (1900), 1077-83; Masʿad, *D̲h̲ikrā*, 111-2) was particularly successful; written on a very large scale, in 1705, and provided the following year with notes, it was abridged in 1707 by the author himself, and it is this abridged form which has been published in many editions with commentaries by Fāris al-S̲h̲idyāḳ [*q.v.*], Malta 1836; by Buṭrus al-Bustānī, Beirut 1854; by Saʿīd al-S̲h̲artūnī, Beirut, 1865, 1883, 1891, 1896, 1899, 1913 etc.). As the zealous pupil of Yaʿḳūb al-Dibsī, Farḥāt compiled also a manual of rhetoric and poetics under the title: *Bulūg̲h̲ al-arab fī ʿilm al-adab* (only in manuscript; see P. Sbath, "*L'arrivée au but dans l'art de la littérature*": *Ouvrage sur la rhétorique par Germanos Farhat*, in *BIÉ*, xiv (1932) 275-9 with portrait; cf. *Dīwān*, 89; Cheikho, *Catalogue*, 151, no. 6). In the field of prosody two small treatises of his are known: *al-Tadhkira fi 'l-ḳawāfī* (printed with the *Dīwān*, 13-22) and a *Risālat al-fawāʾid fi 'l-ʿarūḍ* (cf. Cheikho, *Catalogue*, 161, no. 7).

Farḥāt is famous not only as a scholar but also as a poet. He himself collected the poems of his *Dīwān* under the title of *al-Tadhkira*, and it is in this form that the *Dīwān* has been published three times (Beirut 1850—lithogr. 1866, 1894—with the commentary of Saʿīd al-Shartūnī, based on three manuscripts; on the last edition cf. C. F. S[eybold], in *Litterarisches Zentralblatt*, 1895, col. 1447). This collection does not contain all his poetic works, many of which were later printed separately (cf. for example Cheikho, *Shuʿarāʾ*, 463-8, and also in *Machriq*, vii (1904), 288, xxiv (1926), 397 and *passim*). His work is interesting from the point of view of literary history as representing a systematic effort to apply the forms of Arabic poetry to specifically Christian themes: the form of the *ghazal* to hymns to the Virgin, the *khamriyyāt* to the Eucharist, etc. Farḥāt was of course not the first to do this: as early as the 8th/14th century we have the *Dīwān* of a certain Sulaymān al-Ghazzī (cf. Cheikho, *Shuʿarāʾ*, 404-24) devoted to the same religious themes, but his name and his works are almost forgotten, and he did not found a school. The Christian element is largely predominant in the *Dīwān* of Farḥāt, although it cannot be denied that he possessed a fairly deep knowledge of Arabic poetry in general; we find in it vigorous polemics directed against Abu 'l-ʿAlāʾ al-Maʿarrī (248, 420, 439), many traces of the influence of Ibn al-Rūmī (257), Ibn al-Fāriḍ (295), al-Suhrawardī (310), an imitation of Avicenna's famous *ḳaṣīda* on the soul (274-7) etc. The form of his poems is in general classical, but he used also different types of *muwashshaḥ*, *takhmīs* and *tasmīṭ*. His language is not always faultless and he has been rightly accused of too free recourse to poetic licence.

The bicentenary of Djarmānūs Farḥāt was celebrated at Aleppo in 1932, and in 1934 a monument was erected to him in the palace of the Maronite archbishop (*Machriq*, xxix (1931), 949; xxxii (1934), 300; cf. also the article by F. A. al-Bustānī in *Machriq*, xxx (1932), 49-53; on the volume published in his honour, cf. *ibid.*, xxxi (1933), 789-90).

Bibliography: G. Manache (Manash), *Historical note on the bishop Djarmānūs Farḥāt* (in Arabic), in *Machriq*, vii (1904), 49-56, 105-11, 210-9 (with portrait); idem, *The works of the bishop Djarmānūs Farḥāt, ibid.*, 354-61 (a list of 104 works, of which 37 are original, the rest being the works of other authors annotated, translated and edited by Farḥāt); idem, *al-Mustaṭrafāt fī ḥayāt al-Sayyid Djarmānūs Farḥāt*, 1904; B. Masʿad. *al-Dhikrā fī ḥayāt al-Maṭrān Djarmānūs Farḥāt*, Djūniya 1934; Mārūn ʿAbbūd, *Ruwwād al-nahḍa al-ḥadītha*, Beirut 1952; F. Taoutel, *Mgr. Djarmānūs Farhat, spiritual director*, in *Machriq*, xxxii (1934), 261-72 (with portrait and autograph); Buṭrus al-Bustānī, *Dāʾirat al-maʿārif*, Beirut 1882, vi, 437-8; A. Baumgartner, *Geschichte der Weltliteratur*, i/2, Freiburg 1897, 413-4; Cl. Huart, *Littérature arabe*², Paris 1912, 41-2; K. T. Khaïrallah, *La Syrie*, Paris 1912, 41-2; Djirdjī Zaydān, *Taʾrīkh ādāb al-lugha al-ʿarabiyya*, Cairo 1914, iv, 13-4 (with portrait); L. Cheikho, *Catalogue of the Christian Arabic authors since Islam* (in Arabic), Beirut 1924, 160-2, no. 609 and p. 240 (additions from the libraries of Leningrad by I. Yu Kračkovskiy, in *Machriq*, xxiii (1925), 681); idem, *Kitāb Shuʿarāʾ al-naṣrāniyya baʿd al-Islām*, Beirut 1927, 459-68; J. E. Sarkis, col. 1441-2.

(I. Kratschkowsky-[A. G. Karam])

FARĪD PASHA [see DĀMĀD FERĪD PASHA].

FARĪD AL-DĪN [see ʿAṬṬĀR].

FARĪD AL-DĪN MASʿŪD "GANDJ-I-SHAKAR", one of the most distinguished of Indian Muslim mystics, was born some time in 571/1175 at Kahtwāl, a town near Multān, in a family which traced its descent from the caliph ʿUmar. His grandfather, Ḳāḍī Shuʿayb, who belonged to a ruling house of Kābul, migrated to India under the stress of the Ghuzz invasions. Shaykh Farīd's first teacher, who exerted a lasting influence on him, was his mother, who kindled that spark of Divine Love in him which later dominated his entire being, and moulded his thought and action. Shaykh Farīd received his education in a *madrasa* attached to the mosque of one Mawlānā Minhādj al-Dīn Tirmidhī at Multān where, later, he met Shaykh Ḳuṭb al-Dīn Bakhtiyār Kākī [*q.v.*], *khalīfa* of Shaykh Muʿīn al-Dīn Čishtī [*q.v.*], and got himself admitted into the Čishtī order. According to Ghawthī Shaṭṭārī, Shaykh Farīd excelled all other saints in his devotions and penitences. At Učč h he performed the *ṣalāt-i maʿkūs* by hanging head downwards in a well, suspended from the boughs of a tree. He observed fasts of all types, the most difficult of them being *Ṣawm-i Dāʾūdī* and *Ṭayy*. He had committed to memory the entire text of the Ḳurʾān and used to recite it once in twenty-four hours. Accounts of his visits to foreign lands by later writers are hardly reliable because no early authority refers to them. Besides Shaykh Ḳuṭb al-Dīn Bakhtiyār Kākī, he received spiritual benedictions from Shaykh Muʿīn al-Dīn Čishtī also. For nearly 20 years he lived and worked at Ḥānsī, in the Ḥiṣār district. Later on he moved to Adjodhan (now called Pāk Pattan on his account) from where his fame spread far and wide. He died at Adjodhan on 5 Muḥarram 664/17 October 1265. During the last 700 years his tomb has been one of the most venerated centres of pilgrimage for the people of the sub-continent. Hindūs, Muslims and Sikhs alike hold him in high esteem. Numerous rulers, including Tīmūr and Akbar, have visited his grave for spiritual blessings. The town of Farīdkōṭ was named after him. He left a big family which spread in the country and many of his descendants (e.g. Shaykh Bahāʾ al-Dīn of Radjabpur, near Amroha, and Shaykh Salīm Čishti of Fateḥpur Sikri) set up important mystic centres.

To Shaykh Farīd belongs the credit of giving an all-India status to the Čishtī *silsila* and training a number of eminent disciples—like Shaykh Djamāl al-Dīn of Hānsī, Shaykh Niẓām al-Dīn Awliyāʾ of Dihlī and Shaykh ʿAlāʾ al-Dīn Ṣābir of Kalyar—who disseminated its teachings far and wide. By establishing close personal contact with people, he transformed the Čishtī order—which was, till then, limited in its sphere of influence—into a powerful movement for the spiritual culture of the masses. He attracted towards Islam many of the Hindū tribes of the Pandjāb. The impact of his teachings is discernible in the sacred book of the Sikhs, the *Guru Granth*, where his sayings are respectfully quoted. His knowledge of *tafsīr*, *ḳirāʾāt* and *fiḳh*, besides his mastery of Arabic grammar, impressed even the specialists. He introduced the *ʿAwārif al-maʿārif* into the mystic syllabus of those days, taught it to his disciples and himself prepared a summary of it.

Since all sorts of people—*djogīs* and *kāfirān-i siyāh posh*, Hindūs and Muslims, villagers and townsfolk—came to him, his *djamāʿat khāna* grew into a veritable centre for cultural intercourse between different social groups. Some of the earliest sentences of *Hinduwī* (the earliest form of Urdū) were uttered in his dwelling. He also helped in the development of some local dialects of the Pandjāb by recommending religious exercises in the Pandjābī language (Shāh Kalīm Allāh, *Kashkōl-i Kalīmī*, Dihlī 1308, 25).

Bibliography: The following three works are the earliest and the most reliable sources for his life: Amīr Ḥasan Sidjzī, *Fawāʾid al-fuʾād*, Lucknow 1302; Ḥamīd Ḳalandar, *Khayr al-madjālis*, ed. Niẓāmī, ʿAlīgarh; Amīr Khurd, *Siyar al-awliyāʾ*, Dihlī 1302. The following collections of *malfūẓāt*—*Fawāʾid al-sālikīn*, *Asrār al-awliyāʾ*, *Rahat al-ḳulūb*—are apocryphal (see Nizami, *The life and times of Shaikh Faridu'd-Din Ganj-i Shakar*, ʿAlīgarh 1955, 118-20). Among later sources, the following Persian *tadhkiras* may be mentioned: Sayyid Muḥ. Akbar Ḥusaynī, *Djawāmiʿ al-kalim*, Kānpur 1356, 230-1, 151, etc.; Djamālī, *Siyar al-ʿārifīn*, Dihlī 1311, 31-59; ʿAbd al-Ḥaḳḳ, *Akhbār al-akhhyār*, Dihlī 1309, 51-9; Muḥ. Ghawthī Shaṭṭārī, *Gulzār-i abrār*, As. Soc. Bengal Ms. 259, f. 13-13v; ʿAbd al-Ṣamad, *Akhbār al-aṣfiyāʾ*, Ms. Ethe 64; ʿAbd al-Raḥmān Čishtī, *Mirʾāt al-asrār*, Ms. personal collection; Mīr ʿAlī Akbar Ardistanī, *Madjmaʿ al-awliyāʾ*, Ms. Ethe 645; Allāh Diya Čishtī, *Siyar al-aḳṭāb*, Nawal Kishore 1881, 161-77; ʿAlī Aṣghar Čishtī, *Djawāhir-i Farīdī*, Lahore 1301; Darā Shukoh, *Safīnat al-awliyāʾ*, Nawal Kishore 1900, 96-7; Ghulām Muʿīn al-Dīn ʿAbd Allāh, *Maʿāridj al-wilāyāt*, Ms. personal collection; Muḥ. Bulāḳ Čishtī, *Maṭlūb al-ṭālibīn*, Ms., personal collection; *Rawḍa-i aḳṭāb*, Dihlī, Muḥibb-i-Hind Press, 58-61; Muḥ. Akram Barāswī, *Iḳtibās al-anwār*, Lahore 1895, 160-75; Raḥīm Bakhsh Fakhrī, *Shadjarat al-anwār*, Ms., personal collection; Muḥ. Ḥusayn Murādābādī, *Anwār al-ʿārifīn*, Lucknow 1876; Nadjm al-Dīn, *Manāḳib al-maḥbūbīn*, Lucknow 1873; Ḳāḍī Sher Muḥ., *Risāla Farīdiyya bihishtiyya*, Lahore 1300; Ghulām Sarwar, *Khazinat al-aṣfiyāʾ*, Lucknow 1872, i, 287-305. References are found in the following historical works: ʿAfīf, *Taʾrīkh-i Fīrūz Shāhī*, Bibl. Indica, 198; Ibn Baṭṭūṭa, iii, 135-6 = H. von Mžik, *Die Reise*..., 52-4; Muḥ. Biḥāmid Khānī, *Taʾrīkh-i Muḥammadī*, Brit. Museum MS Or. 137, ff. 144-6; Abu 'l-Faḍl, *Āʾīn-i Akbarī*, Sir Sayyid edition, ii, 208; Abu 'l-Ḳāsim Hindū Shāh, *Taʾrīkh-i Ferishta*, Nawal Kishore 1865, ii, 383-91; Sujjan Rai Bhandārī, *Khulāṣat al-tawārīkh*, Dihlī 1918, 33, 35, 61-3. See also, ʿAbd al-Wāḥid, *Sabaʿ sanābil*, Kanpur 1299, 58; Fayḍī, *Dīwān-i Fayḍī*, Dihlī 1268, 183. Urdū and English accounts: Pīr Muḥ. Ḥusayn, *Waḳāʾiʿ Ḥaḍrat Bābā Farīd Gandj Shakar* (Urdū), Lahore 1312; Ghulām Sarwar, *Ḥadīḳāt al-awliyāʾ* (Urdū), Lahore 1293, 36-8; Mirẓā Muḥ. Akhtar, *Tadhkira awliyāʾ-i Hind* (Urdū), Dihlī 1928, i, 43-6; Muḥ. Naẓīr Aḥmad Deobandī, *Tadhkirat al-ʿābidīn*, ʿAlīgarh 1901, 22-8; Mushtāḳ Aḥmad, *Anwār al-ʿāshiḳīn*, Haydarabad-Deccan 1332, 34-6; Rashīd Aḥmad Riḍwī, *Iʿlān-i siyādat-i Farīdī*, Amroha 1332; ʿAbd al-Ḥaḳḳ, *The Sufis' work in the early development of the Urdu Language* (Urdu), Dihlī 1939, 5-7; *Imperial Gazetteer of India*, x, 532; *Punjab Gazetteer*, ii; *Report on a tour in the Punjab (1878-9)*, in *ASI*, xiv; Ibbetson, *Panjab castes*, Lahore 1916; M. Irving, in *Jour. Punj. Hist. Soc.*, i (1911-2), 70-6; F. Mackeson, *Journal of Captain C. M. Wade's voyage from Lodiana to Mithankot*..., in *JASB*, vi (1837), 190-3; *Oriental College Magazine*, Lahore, xiv, xv, xvii; Munshi Mahan Lal, *A brief account of Masud, known by the name of Farid Shakarganj or Shakarbar*, in *JASB*, v (1836), 635-8; K. A. Nizami, *The life and times of Shaikh Farid-u'd-Din Ganj-i Shakar*, ʿAlīgarh 1955.

(K. A. Nizami)

FARĪḌA [see farāʾiḍ, farḍ].

FARĪDKŌṬ, formerly a small feudatory princely state in the Pandjāb, now merged with the Fīrūzpur Division of the Indian Pandjāb, and lying between 30° 13′ and 30° 50′ N. and 74° 31′ and 75° 5′ E. with an area of 642 sq. miles. Both the State and the principal town of the same name are unimportant. The town, lying in 30° 40′ N. and 74° 49′ E., 20 miles south of Fīrūzpur [*q.v.*], has a fort built by Rādja Mokulsī, a native Rādjpūt chief, in the time of Farīd al-Dīn Gandj-Shakar [*q.v.*], popularly known as Bāwā (Bābā) Farīd, after whom the fort was named Farīdkōṭ (*kōṭ* = fort). The founder was apparently an admirer and devotee of the saint, who was equally popular with the Muslims and the non-Muslims. The former ruling family belonging to the Siddhū-Brār clan of the Djāṭs [*q.v.*], who later embraced Sikhism, occupied the town and the neighbouring territory during the time of Akbar [*q.v.*]. They were, however, involved in several petty quarrels with the surrounding Sikh states belonging to their kinsmen. Offended at the hostility of their neighbours, the ruling family sided with the British during the Sikh Wars, being rewarded with the restoration of certain lost territory. Again during the military uprising of 1857 the ruler, Wazīr Singh, remained loyal and actively assisted the British, receiving a further handsome reward. Farīdkōṭ, along with the other Phulkian States ruled by the Sikh Rādjas of the same common family, was badly disturbed during the communal riots of 1947 which followed in the wake of Partition, and is now without any Muslims, who have all migrated to Pakistan.

Bibliography: Aitchison, *Engagements and Sanads* ..., s.v.; *Imperial Gazetteer of India*, Oxford 1908, xii, 51-2. (A. S. Bazmee Ansari)

FARĪDPUR, head-quarters of a district bearing the same name in East Pakistan. The district was created in 1807 out of the older division of Dacca-Djalālpur. It embraces an area of 2,371 square miles and has a population of 2,709,711 (1951 census). The city (pop. 25,287), which is named after that of the local *pīr* Shaykh Farīd, is situated on an old channel of the Padmā, called the *Marā* (dead) *Padmā*. It is generally identified with the Fatḥābād of the Muslim period. The *Āʾīn-i Akbarī* mentions Sarkār Fatḥābād, and this name is believed to originate from that of Djalāl al-Dīn Fatḥ Shāh, the Bengal Sultan (886-92/1481-6). But Fatḥābād as a mint town is known to have been first started by Djalāl al-Dīn Muḥammad (818-31/1415-35) after his conquest of the Hindū Rādjā of south Bengal. Since then Fatḥābād maintained its integrity, rising to an almost independent status in the time of the Dihlī emperor Akbar under the local *zamīndār* Madjlis Ḳuṭub, who was finally subjugated in about 1013/1609 by Islām Khān, the Mughal *ṣubadār* of Bengal. It is in this district that the Farāʾiḍiyya [*q.v.*] movement was started by Ḥādjdjī Sharīʿat Allāh in the early 19th century, which was of a rural character and hence spread far and wide in the riparian districts of lower Bengal.

Bibliography: Mīrzā Nāthān, *Bahāristān-i Ghaybī*, Eng. tr. M. I. Borah, Gawhatī 1936,

45-60; L. S. S. O'Malley, *Bengal district gazetteers: Faridpur*, Calcutta 1925; A. H. Dani, *House of Rādjā Gaṇeśa of Bengal*, in *JASB*, 1952; Muʿīn al-Dīn Aḥmad Khān, *History of the Farāʾiḍī movement in Bengal*, to be published by the Asiatic Society of Pakistan, Dacca. (A. H. Dani)

FARĪDŪN (Pahlavi, Frēdun; ancient Iranian, Thraētaona), the son of Abtiyān or Abtīn, one of the early kings of Īrān. The most complete text on the subject is the account of his reign by Firdawsī, in verse; some of the sources for it will be found in pre-Islamic texts. §§ 130-8 of the *Yasht*s of the Avesta reveal the names of the first kings of Īrān in their original order (the first being Yima [see djamshīd]), whose conqueror and murderer, Azhī-Dahāka, was overthrown in his turn and put to death by Thraētaona; the latter was rewarded by a share of the aureole of glory (*hvareno*) which, from the throne of Ahura-Mazda, descends upon the heads of saints and heroes, and which as the result of a grave transgression had forsaken Yima (*Yasht* 19); Thraētona the son of Athwya, the priest responsible for preparing the sacred potion known as *haoma*, saved the world from the domination of the monstrous demon Azhī-Dahāka, liberated Arnavāk and Sahavāk (Firdawsī: Arnawāz and Shahrnāz), the daughters of the dead Yima, became king of Īrān and then, in old age, divided his empire between his three sons, one of whom, Iradj, was assassinated by the other two, leaving a daughter; Thraētona married her, with the object of procreating an avenger for his son (J. Darmesteter, *Zend-Avesta*, i, 131, n. 15, sees in this consanguineous union, subsequently transformed by national tradition, an early instance of *khetuk-das*; cf. the same author, *Études iraniennes*, ii, 217 ff., and al-Masʿūdī, *Murūdj*, ii, 145). According to religious tradition, Thraētaona fought against the demons of Māzandarān (national tradition describes him as an expert in magic). In the national tradition, handed down by the *Shāh-nāma* of Firdawsī, Azhī-Dahāka (Persian: Zahhāk) retains only one feature of his monstrous appearance —two serpents which sprang from his shoulders at the kiss of the devil, and which he has to feed by demanding the daily sacrifice of a group of his subjects; one night, in a dream, he sees the young warrior who overthrows him; he consults his soothsayers and learns that Farīdūn will be born and will overthrow him; he orders the execution of the father of Farīdūn, for whom he has a vigorous search made from the time of his birth, though in vain; aided by partisans led by the blacksmith Kāvah, Farīdūn defeats Zahhāk's troops and imprisons him, in a cave on Mount Damāwand [*q.v.*]; being proclaimed king of Īrān, he established justice and peace in the land; three sons were born to him and, in due time, he divided his empire between them; the two eldest, jealous of their younger brother, put him to death—a murder which gave rise to interminable wars; from the union of Iradj and a slave-girl married to a nephew of Farīdūn was born Manučihr who succeeded his father on the throne of Īrān, overthrew and put to death his two uncles whose heads he sent to Farīdūn; the latter ended his life in solitude, mourning his sons, his eyes fixed on their three skulls.—To this narrative, Arab and Iranian authors add little. According to Ibn Isfandyār, (*History of Tabaristan*, trans. E. G. Browne, 15; ed. Iḳbāl, Tehrān, index), Farīdūn was born in the village of Warka, a dependency of Lāridjān; Ibn al-Balkhī (*Fārs-nāma*, ed. Le Strange, index) credits him with a fantastic genealogy (12), the stature and corpulence of a giant, a very wide field of knowledge, the inauguration of the autumn feast of *mihrgān* [*q.v.*], the re-establishment of justice, the use of simples and magic practices to cure illnesses of both humans and animals, the creation of the mule(36); Balʿamī (*Chronique*, trans. Zotenberg, index s.v. Afrīdūn) speaks of Farīdūn's knowledge of astronomy and fancifully attributes the Khʷārizmian Tables to him; al-Thaʿālibī (*Histoire des rois des Perses*, ed.-trans. Zotenberg) relates, according to the Pahlavi *Āyīn-nāmagh* (Book of institutions) that, in his reign, men were classed according to merit and to services performed (15); furthermore, he records sentences and proverbs ascribed to Farīdūn (40); al-Shahrastānī (*Milal*, trans. Haarbrucker, i, 298) credits him with the construction of a pyraeus; al-Bīrūnī (*Chronology*, trans. Sachau, 213 and index s.v. Frēdūn) indirectly attributes to him the introduction of the Sada, a periodic bonfire, whilst Firdawsī connects him with the invention of fire by king Hūshang (*Shāh-nāma*, trans. Mohl, i, 26) and attributes the custom of the *mihrgān* fire to Farīdūn (i, 85).

Bibliography: in addition to the sources quoted above, see also: Justi, *Iranisches Namenbuch* (Thraētaona); Ṭabarī, index, s.v. Afrīdūn; Schwarz, *Irān* (index, s.v. Afrīdūn); Masʿūdī, *Murūdj*, index; idem, *Avertissement*, trans. Carra de Vaux, index (in particular 126, n. 1, quotation from Abū Tammām); Ḥamza Isfāhānī (ed. Gottwald, i, 13, brief mention); Yāḳūt, index, s.v. Afrīdūn (his enthronement, his sons) and Barbier de Meynard, *Dictionnaire de la Perse*, 5, n. 2; Maḳdisī, *Création et histoire*, ed.-trans. Cl. Huart, iii, 8, 149; *Mudjmil al-tawārīkh*, in *JA*, xi (1841), 157 (short résumé of the reign, following Firdawsī); *ʿUlamā-i Islām*, trans. Blochet, in *RHR*, xxxvii (1898), 45 (mention only); A. Christensen, *Heltedigtning og Fortaellingslitteratur hos Iranerne i Oldtiden*, Copenhagen 1935; M. Molé, *Le partage du monde dans la tradition iranienne*, in *JA*, ccxl (1952), 455 ff. (H. Massé)

FARĪDŪN [see ferīdūn beg].

FARĪGHŪNIDS (Āl-i Farīghūn, Banū Farīghūn), ruling dynasty of Gūzgān (Gūzgānān, Gūzgānyān, Arabic al-Djūzdjān [*q.v.*]) in east Khurāsān, now in north-west Afghānistān. In the 4th/10th century they appear among the principai vassals of the Sāmānids [*q.v.*]. The name is perhaps to be connected with that of the legendary Afrīdhūn (Farīdūn), cf. *Ḥudūd al-ʿālam*, § 23, 46, or somewhat more probably with that of Afrīgh (Farīgh), who is said to have ruled in Khʷārizm in pre-Islamic times (see al-Bīrūnī, *Chronology*, 35, transl. 41). There is no evidence, though this remains a possibility, that tbe Farīghūnids were descended from the pre-Islamic rulers of Gūzgān, the Gūzgān Khudāhs, on whom Ṭabarī has some details (ii, 1206, 1569, 1609-11, 1694, cf. Ibn Khurradādhbih, 40, trans. 29).

The names and number of the Farīghūnid rulers have never been determined with certainty, owing principally to contradictory statements in the text of the *Taʾrīkh-i Yamīnī* of ʿUtbī [*q.v.*], a contemporary authority, who has been followed by the later historians (Ibn al-Athīr, Rashīd al-Dīn, Ibn Khaldūn, etc.). The list as usually given includes:

(a) Aḥmad b. Farīghūn, *amīr* of Gūzgān about 287/900. He was a prince of importance, who according to Narshakhī refused the friendship of the *amīr* of Marw, whereupon the latter turned to Ismāʿīl, the Sāmānid ruler of Transoxiana. Aḥmad b. Farīghūn subsequently did homage to ʿAmr b. Layth, the

Ṣaffārid (Narshakhī, ed. Schefer, 85, transl. R. N. Frye, *History of Bukhara*, Cambridge, Mass., 1954, 87).

(b) Abu 'l-Ḥārith Muḥammad b. Aḥmad b. Farīghūn. He is first mentioned apparently as Abu 'l-Ḥārith b. Farīghūn (in connexion with his secretary Dja'far b. Sahl b. al-Marzubān, who was famous for his hospitality and the most popular man in Khurāsān) by al-Iṣṭakhrī (148), and later by Ibn Ḥawḳal (ed. De Goeje, 208, ed. Kramers, 292). Al-Iṣṭakhrī wrote according to De Goeje not later than 933 (Barthold, Preface to *Ḥudūd al-ʿālam*, 6, 19), but the date 951 is often given (cf. Minorsky, *Ḥudūd al-ʿālam*, 176). Abu 'l-Ḥārith Muḥammad b. Aḥmad b. Farīghūn evidently gave his daughter in marriage to the young Sāmānid sovereign Nūḥ b. Manṣūr, some time after the latter's accession in 365/976 (Gardīzī, ed. M. Nāẓim, 48), and in 372/982 he received the dedication of the geographical work *Ḥudūd al-ʿālam*, possibly written by another Ibn Farīghūn (see Minorsky in *A Locust's Leg*, 189-96).

After 380/990 Abu 'l-Ḥārith as Sāmānid *amīr* of Gūzgān was ordered to oppose Fā'iḳ, the *amīr* of Harāt, who was then in rebellion. He assembled a large force and advanced from Gūzgān against Fā'iḳ, last heard of at al-Tirmidh across the Oxus. Fā'iḳ sent a cavalry force of 500 men, Turks and Arabs, who routed the army of the Farīghūnid and returned thereafter to Balkh (ʿUtbī-Manīnī, i, 166, cf. Ibn al-Athīr, *sub anno* 383). In 383/993 Nūḥ b. Manṣūr, on the way to chastise rebellious subjects in Khurāsān, crossed the Oxus into Gūzgān and met its governor, the *amīr* Abu 'l-Ḥārith al-Farīghūnī, remaining there till all his forces arrived (ʿUtbī-Manīnī, i, 184). Sabuktakīn [*q.v.*] was at this time in command of the Sāmānid forces, and in 385/995 he and his son Maḥmūd requested Abu 'l-Ḥārith al-Farīghūnī to join them in Harāt, which he did (ʿUtbī-Manīnī, i, 209; Gardīzī, 56). At some time a double marriage alliance united the two families, Maḥmūd marrying a daughter of Abu 'l-Ḥārith and Maḥmūd's sister being given to the son of Abu 'l-Ḥārith, Abū Naṣr (ʿUtbī-Manīnī, ii, 101, cf. Ibn al-Athīr, *sub anno* 401, Ibn Khaldūn, ed. Lebanon 1958, iv, 790). Later, when Sabuktakīn died (387/997) Abu 'l-Ḥārith al-Farīghūnī attempted to mediate between his sons Maḥmūd and Ismāʿīl (ʿUtbī Manīnī, i, 275), and Maḥmūd, when about to march on Ghazna, wrote a letter to inform him (*ibid.*, i, 277). Eventually, towards 389/999, Maḥmūd committed Ismāʿīl to the safe keeping of the governor of Gūzgān, Abu 'l-Ḥārith (*ibid.*, i, 316).

It is somewhat striking that Abu 'l-Ḥārith Muḥammad b. Aḥmad b. Farīghūn is apparently never named by ʿUtbī. In his formal account of the Farīghūnids (ʿUtbī-Manīnī, ii, 101-5) he states that Abu 'l-Ḥārith Aḥmad b. Muḥammad was the father of Abū Naṣr, who in the sequel appears as the head of the family (below, (*c*)). It seems feasible that some time after 372/982 Abu 'l-Ḥārith Muḥammad, who had already enjoyed a career of perhaps as long as 50 years, was succeeded by a son with the same *kunya*, Abu 'l-Ḥārith Aḥmad, who would then be the Farīghūnid who engaged in the various campaigns mentioned by ʿUtbī between 990 and 995. But the texts of the passage vary: Minorsky has already pointed out that in ʿUtbī-Manīnī (ii, 101) Abu 'l-Ḥārith Aḥmad b. Muḥammad is succeeded by his son Abū Naṣr Aḥmad *b. Muḥammad*, which is impossible, from which he concludes that Abu 'l-Ḥārith Aḥmad b. Muḥammad never existed (*Ḥudūd al-ʿālam*, 176), and although in the same passage the Delhi (1847, p. 283) and Lahore (1300/1882, p. 227) editions of ʿUtbī give, as the son of Abu 'l-Ḥārith Aḥmad b. Muḥammad, Abū Naṣr Muḥammad b. Aḥmad b. Muḥammad, no positive conclusion is afforded. Elsewhere ʿUtbī names Abū Naṣr Aḥmad b. Muḥammad al-Farīghūnī (ʿUtbī-Manīnī, ii, 84, also Delhi, 271, Lahore, 218). The successor of b. Abu 'l-Ḥārith Muḥammad b. Aḥmad is usually said to be

(c) Abū Naṣr Aḥmad b. Muḥammad b. Farīghūn. In 389/999, when Maḥmūd destroyed the Sāmānid power in Khurāsān and established himself at Balkh, the local rulers who had previously acknowledged the Sāmānids, submitted to him, including Āl-i Farīghūn, rulers of Gūzgān (ʿUtbī-Manīnī, i, 316, cf. Ibn al-Athīr, *sub anno* 389). Thus when the Īlek Khān crossed the Oxus to attack Maḥmūd, Abū Naṣr al-Farīghūnī the governor of Gūzgān fought in the centre with the Sultan's brother Naṣr against the Ḳara-Khānids at the battle of Čarkhiyān in 398/January 1008 (ʿUtbī-Manīnī, ii, 84, cf. Ibn Khaldūn, iv, 788). Later in the same year, or in the following year, Maḥmūd invaded India. His brother-in-law Abū Naṣr al-Farīghūnī accompanied him, and played a prominent part (ʿUtbī-Manīnī, ii, 98, cf. Ibn Khaldūn, iv, 789). Abū Naṣr had been confirmed in the possession of Gūzgān at his father's death, and continued to enjoy all his rights there till his own death in 401/1010-1 (ʿUtbī-Manīnī, ii, 102, cf. Ibn al-Athīr, *sub anno*, Ibn Khaldūn, iv, 790).

(*d*) Ḥasan b. Farīghūn, once mentioned by Bayhaḳī (*Ta'rīkh*, ed. Morley, 125, cited Minorsky, *Ḥudūd*, 177), apparently did not succeed to, or did not retain, the governorship of Gūzgān, which was ruled from 408/1017-8 as a Ghaznawid fief by Abū Aḥmad Muḥammad b. Maḥmūd (married to a daughter of Abū Naṣr al-Farīghūnī) (ʿUtbī-Manīnī, ii, 236).

Nothing can be gleaned concerning the Farīghūnids from the portion of the *Ṭabaḳāt-i Nāṣirī* of al-Djūzdjānī translated by H. G. Raverty, who in his notes mentions a Ma'mūn b. Muḥammad Farīghūnī, *i.e.*, Ma'mūn b. Muḥammad [*q.v.*] of Khʷārizm. This man is called Farīghūnī also by the late (16th century) writer Ghaffārī (Giffārī) (cf. *Ḥudūd al-ʿālam*, 174; *Čahār maḳāla*, ed. Mīrzā Muḥammad Ḳazwīnī, GMS, 1910, 243), and this is usually reckoned a mistake. It is possible, however, that Ma'mūn b. Muḥammad (whose genealogy is still unknown) belonged to a collateral branch of the family of the Khʷārizm Shāhs whom he dispossessed in 386/996, in which case he might claim descent from the Afrīgh or Farīgh of Khʷārizm mentioned earlier in this article.

In the 10th century under the Farīghūnids Gūzgān appears to have possessed greater importance than at other times in its history. Apart from their political activity, the Farīghūnids were also patrons of learned men and poets, including Badīʿ al-Zamān al-Hamadhānī and Abu 'l-Fatḥ al-Bustī (ʿUtbī-Manīnī, ii, 102-5, cf. Ibn al-Athīr, *sub anno* 401; Ibn Khaldūn, iv, 790) and of course the author of *Ḥudūd al-ʿālam*.

Bibliography: V. V. Barthold, Preface to *Ḥudūd al-ʿālam*, 4-7; V. Minorsky, *ibid.*, 173-8 (the best and most complete account); idem, *Ibn Farīghūn and the Ḥudūd al-ʿĀlam*, in *A Locust's Leg, Studies in honour of S. H. Taqizadeh*, London 1962, 189-96; E. Sachau, *Ein Verzeichnis muhammedanischer Dynastien*, in *Abhandlungen der preussischen Akademie der Wissenschaften*, Phil.-hist. Klasse, 1923, i/5, p. 5 (based on the 17th century author Münedjdjim-Bashī); D. M. Dunlop, *The Jawāmiʿ al-ʿUlūm of Ibn Farīghūn*, in *Z. V. Togan'a armağan*, Istanbul 1955, 348-53; Muhammad Nāẓim, *Life and times of Sultan Mahmud of Ghazna*, Cambridge 1931, Appendix C, The Farighunids, 179-80; C. E. Bosworth, *The Ghaznavids* ..., Edinburgh 1963, index; Zambaur, 205.

(D. M. Dunlop)

FĀRIS (A., pl. *fursān* and also *fawāris*, probably for the sake of expressiveness) denotes the rider on horseback, and in principle cannot be applied to the man riding a donkey or mule. The horse was considered in the article FARAS, equitation will be discussed in FURŪSIYYA, and in the present article we shall not dwell on subjects relating to the horse, but rather concentrate on the rider. It will be noticed immediately that, in Arabic, to 'ride a horse' is rendered by *rakiba*, with the result that the active participle *rākib* has the general sense "horseman", while *fāris* has the form of an active participle of *farusa* "to be an expert on horses" and, with the root *f. r. s.* implying an idea of capacity for judging at a single glance and guessing hidden qualities by external inspection [see FIRĀSA], there is a curious semantic convergence which has not received any satisfactory explanation. D. J. Wiseman, consulted on Semitic parallels, writes as follows: "The Hebrew פרש (probably *parraš*) is used of a '(warrior) rider' in 44 passages. I do not agree with S. Mowinckel, *Vetus Testamentum* XII/3 (July 1962), p. 290, that the meaning 'horse' (which is considered probable in 7 passages) should apply in all these passages. The word does not occur in Akkadian (the verb *parāšu* means 'to fly along') where *rākib* (as also in Hebrew) is used of the horseman".

However that may be, during the Djāhiliyya and the first centuries of Islam *fāris* appears in texts with the sense of simple horseman, which in itself indicated membership of a well-to-do class, but also, though the nuance is not always apparent, to denote, in conjunction with the more explicit *baṭal* and *faḥl*, the valiant, the champion, the intrepid warrior, to such an extent that one is sometimes tempted to translate this term by "cavalier", "knight", though not without the risk of leading the reader into error, for during the period in question no social institution existed among the Arabs comparable with the chivalry of mediaeval Europe.

Nevertheless the fact remains that the translation of *fāris* by "knight" is not in itself an error, for chivalry was nascent even in the pre-Islamic period and the first centuries of Islam, and the practices, customs and sentiments of "chivalry" were widely disseminated in at least one section of Arab society; by force of arms, the *fāris* defended first his "country" in the shape of the tribal patrimony, and then his religion; he protected the weak, the widows and orphans either in an entirely disinterested way or to increase his prestige; he addressed verses somewhat in the "courtly" tradition [see NASĪB] to his Lady, eschewed force in dealing with a conquered enemy, was to the highest possible degree conscious of his dignity [see ḤILM], despised riches and was content with provision merely for subsistence, occasionally making use of practices which morality would condemn. In the more or less idealized portrait of the *fursān* we can thus discern the noble features of chivalry, but in this case it is a personal chivalry, so to speak, without any precise code, initiation ceremonies, investiture or accolade.

To be a *fāris*, all that was in fact needed was to own a horse, an attribute which secured for the mounted warrior a rate of pay and share of the booty twice as large as those of the plain foot-soldier [see ʿAṬĀʾ, GHANĪMA], but to rank among the true *fursān* it was necessary to have performed deeds of prowess on the battle-field and, in single combat, to have shown courage above the ordinary. When warring armies came face to face, the *fāris* stepped forward from the ranks and, after certain preliminaries, issued a challenge to the foe: "Is there a champion (*mubāriz*) [ready to prove himself against me]?". In the wars waged by the Arabs, single combats often formed the first phase of the battle; historians give the names of the *fursān* and describe with satisfaction the deeds that they accomplished, a notable feature being that they did not always belong to the military aristocracy and often held only a very subordinate rank; their feats of arms nevertheless won them generous rewards. In battle, the *fāris* remained composed, encouraged his comrades in arms, hastened to the rescue of those who were hard pressed, was ready to give up his mount for an unhorsed officer and to continue the combat on foot, etc. When the army was put to flight, he stayed on until the end to fight a delaying action, once again brought solace to his companions, gave aid to the footsore, and finally sacrificed himself to minimize the results of the defeat. The *fāris* wore a light coat of mail and carried a sabre, a javelin and also a lasso (*wahaḳ*) which, in single combat, was used to unhorse his adversary and make him bite the dust (for later developments, see DJAYSH and ḤARB).

Works of *adab* and history enumerate the *fursān* of the various tribes, some of whom have become proverbial; in particular, there is the saying *afras min Summ al-fursān* "a better *fāris* than Summ al-fursān" [= ʿUtayba b. al-Ḥārith of the Tamīm], *afras min Mulāʿib al-asinna* [= ʿĀmir b. Mālik of the Ḳays], *afras min ʿĀmir* [*b. al-Ṭufayl*], *afras min Bisṭām* [*b. Ḳays al-Shaybānī*], etc. Ḥamza b. ʿAbd al-Muṭṭalib is regarded as the *fāris* par excellence of Ḳuraysh, ʿUmayr b. al-Ḥubāb al-Sulamī as the *fāris* of Islam; ʿAntara is called ʿAntarat *al-fawāris*, etc. Some of these *fursān* have become the heroes of "romances of chivalry" which in Arabic bear the name *Sīra* [see ʿANTAR, BAṬṬĀL, DHU 'L-HIMMA, SĪRA].

Bibliography: Maydānī, *Amthāl*, Cairo 1352, ii, 32 ff.; Ibn ʿAbd Rabbih, *ʿIḳd*, Cairo 1346/1928, i, 60 ff.; Ibshīhī, *Mustaṭraf*, bābs 40-1; Wacyf Boutros Ghali, *La tradition chevaleresque des Arabes*, Paris 1919, *passim*; Bichr Farès, *L'honneur chez les Arabes avant l'Islam*, Paris 1932, 22 ff.; see also FUTUWWA, SIPĀHĪ, SUVĀR. (Ed.)

FĀRIS B. MUḤAMMAD, alias ḤUSĀM AL-DĪN ABU 'L-SHAWḲ [see ʿANNAZIDS].

FĀRIS AL-SHIDYĀḲ, Lebanese writer, lexicographer, journalist and poet, born at ʿAshḳūt in 1804 (B. al-Bustānī, *Dāʾira*, x, 428; Ṭ. al-Shidyāḳ, *Akhbār al-aʿyān*, 194; Zaydān, *Mashāhīr*, ii, 74; al-Dibs, *al-Djāmiʿ al-mufaṣṣal*, 534; Ṭarrāzī, *Taʾrīkh al-ṣiḥāfa*, i, 96), and not at Beirut (as Brockelmann, II, 505), nor in 1805 (as Masʿad, *Fāris al-Shidyāḳ*, 16; Y. Yazbik, in *al-Makshūf*, no. 172, 8). In 1809 his parents moved to Hadath (15 km. from Beirut, Ḥārat al-Buṭm), where Fāris received his early education, later going on to the seminary of ʿAyn Waraḳa (Kisrwān, Lebanon: see *al-Sāḳ*, 14-7; *Dāʾira*, x, 428; Masʿad, *op. cit.*, 17). As the result of a political clash and the death of his father (in 1820: Masʿad, 17; *al-Sāḳ*, 31-2), he embarked on the profession of his brother Ṭannūs (1791-1861), the copying of manuscripts (*Akhbār*, 193, 197; *al-Sāḳ*, 31-2, 45-8, 68), finding the necessary materials in his father's library. It is in 1830 that there occurred the dramatic event which profoundly affected his life, his character and the direction of his talents—the passion and martyrdom of his brother Asʿad (1798-1830), who, because of his conversion to Protestantism, was arbitrarily imprisoned and tortured to death by the Maronite Patriarch Yūsuf Ḥubaysh (d. 1845, see *Khabariyyat Asʿad al-Shidyāḳ*, in B. al-Bustānī, *Ḳiṣṣat Asʿad al-Shidyāḳ*, 31-59, 93-104, 106, 109, 120-1). Fāris's conversion to Protestantism is to be dated towards the end of 1825 (Cheikho, *Ādāb*, ii, 79, Ṭarrāzī, *Ṣiḥāfa*, i, 96, and Masʿad, 18, who allege that he was converted in Malta, *i.e.*, between 1834 and 1848, are to be rejected: see *al-Sāḳ*[1], 377-8 and the dispute between Khardjī and Sūḳī; pages 130-2 confirm that he attached himself to the Protestant Evangelical Mission before his departure for Egypt).

His stay in Egypt (1825-34) was marked by his first marriage (his wife, a Maronite born at al-Ṣūlī, was the mother of his two sons Salīm, 1826-1906, and Fāyiz, 1828-56), and by his coming under the influence of men of learning and of letters such as Naṣr Allāh al-Ṭarābulusī (1770-1840) and Shihāb al-Dīn Muḥammad b. Ismāʿīl al-Mālikī (1803-57). He found there an environment conducive to the study of Arabic, of logic, of theology, of *kalām* and of prosody. Winning the favour of Muḥammad ʿAlī, he was appointed Arabic editor of the official gazette, *al-Waḳāʾiʿ al-Miṣriyya*, in place of Rifāʿa al-Ṭahṭāwī [*q.v.*] (see *al-Aʿyān*, 198; *Dāʾira*, x, 428; Masʿad, 18; *Makshūf*, no. 170, 1938, 12; ʿAbbūd, *Ṣaḳr*, 135-6; Dāghir, *Maṣādir*, ii, 472-3).

At the request of the head of the Protestant Evangelical Mission, he moved to Malta, where he spent several years (1834-48: see *Wāsiṭa*, 3) teaching Arabic, writing text-books and correcting manuscripts; he interrupted this austere existence only twice (*al-Sāḳ*, 436, 474-7, 478-82; *Wāsiṭa*, 14; ʿAbbūd, 171), to return secretly to Lebanon in 1837 and to visit England in 1845 (see Najm, *Thesis*, 61).

In 1848 he was invited to London (*Kashf al-mukhabbā*, 67) to assist in the translation of the Bible (*Kanz al-raghāʾib*, i, 168-70); there, divorcing his first wife, he married an Englishwoman, obtained British protection (*Kashf*, 280, on the oath) and lost his third child (*al-Sāḳ*, 613-7). When the translation of the Bible was completed (in less than 20 months), he took up residence in Paris (*ibid.*, 633-41). Two panegyrics, the one addressed to Aḥmad Pasha, Bey of Tunis (*zārat Suʿād*, 1851: see *ZDMG*, v, 249 ff.; H. Pérès, in *al-Makshūf*, no. 314, 2), the other to Sultan ʿAbd al-Madjīd in 1854 (see *al-Sāḳ*, 665-72), were to change the course of his life. He received a warm welcome at Tunis (1857), where he embraced Islam, adopting the personal name Aḥmad and abandoning the patronymic al-Shidyāḳ (see Cheikho, *Ādāb*, ii, 80; *Dāʾira*, x, 429, § 1); his wife and son did likewise (*Dāʾira*, *loc. cit.*). According to Ṭarrāzī he had no part, as has been claimed, in the establishment of *al-Rāʾid al-Tūnisī* (*Ṣiḥāfa*, i, 66).

But it was in Istanbul (end of 1857) that Fāris was to reach the summit of his fame. In favour with the Sultan, who had summoned him officially, and loaded with honours, he established (yet only after many reverses: see *Dīwān*, 24-6, 28-9) the weekly paper *al-Djawāʾib* (2 July 1861 until 1884: the statement of Cheikho, *Ādāb*, ii, 80, Ṭarrāzī, *Ṣiḥāfa*, i, 61, *Dāʾira*, x, 429, § 2, that publication began in 1860 is to be rejected: see *Kanz al-raghāʾib*, vii, 110-1, Masʿad, 21, Najm, *Thesis*, 247-75), thus inaugurating a new era in Arab journalism (ʿAbbūd, *Ṣaḳr*, 157-62 and DJARĪDA).

After a cordial welcome and a brief stay in Cairo (1886), Fāris al-Shidyāḳ returned to Istanbul (26 May 1887: *al-Ahrām*, issue of that day), where he died a few months later, on 20 September 1887, in his summer residence at Kadıköy. The assertion that he finally returned to Catholicism is completely baseless (the hypothesis of Cheikho, *Catal.*, 123, no. 447 and of Yazbik, in *al-Djumhūr*, no. 99 (1938), 8, 104, is to be rejected: see ʿAbbūd, *ibid.*, no. 102, 15, Najm, *Thesis*, 69-73). On Wednesday 5 October 1887 his body was received at Beirut (see Masʿad, 25-42; *Lisān al-ḥāl*, no. 997 (6 October 1887); Āṣaf, *Huwa 'l-Bāḳī*, Cairo 1888) and buried at Ḥāzmiyya (a suburb of Beirut).

Of his numerous works (*Dāʾira*, x, 430, §§ 1-2; Sarkis, §§ 1104-8; Dāghir, *Maṣādir*, ii, 474-6), only the most characteristic will be mentioned here. *K. al-Sāḳ ʿala 'l-Sāḳ fīmā huwa 'l-Fāryāḳ ʿan ayyām wa shuhūr wa aʿwām fī ʿudjm al-ʿArab wa 'l-ʿAdjam* (1st edition Paris 1855, for details see *Kashf al-mukhabbā*, 285, 289; 2nd and 3rd editions Cairo 1919 and 1920) is certainly the most basic, and one of the most distinguished Arabic works of the 19th century. The noun Fāryāḳ is made up from the first syllable of his personal name (Fāris) and the second syllable of his family name (al-Shidyāḳ). In this autobiographical miscellany, packed with memories of childhood and youth, are combined narrative skill, observation, and social, moral and religious criticism.

Al-Wāsiṭa fī maʿrifat aḥwāl Mālṭa (1st ed. Malta 1836, 2nd ed., together with *al-Kashf*, in *al-Djawāʾib*, 1299/1881) is written in the style of the mediaeval Arab travellers; the author recounts the observations made during his stay in Malta, dealing with its physical geography (6-11), demography and climate (11-8, 27), ethnology and sociology (21, 29, 30, 31-44, 55), politics (44-50), philology (23-5, 56-66), art, and notably music, singing (50-4) and architecture (25, churches), illustrated sometimes by statistics and sometimes by comparative analyses.

According to the author, the *Kashf al-mukhabbā ʿan funūn Urubbā* (1st ed. Tunis 1866, 2nd ed. Istanbul 1881) forms the second part of *al-Wāsiṭa*, consisting of his travel-notes in Europe. In it are found recorded historical facts (Napoleon, 260; Joan of Arc, 262; other famous figures, 258), thoughts on civilizations (London: 290-306, 313-36; Paris: 238, 247, specially 271, 276-7) and different systems of government (279 ff.), reflections on religion (189, 256), and some tales in the manner of the *Gulistān* (285, 289). The digressions and the tales are recounted in a precise and direct style. Apart from a few extravagances, the two works are not without order and clarity.

As a linguist, al-Shidyāḳ is to be remembered for his debates with his chief followers; Y. al-Asīr (1815-90) and I. al-Aḥdab (1826-91) on the one hand, and then N. al-Yāzidjī, his son Ibrāhīm (1847-1906), Buṭrus al-Bustānī (1819-83), Adīb Isḥāḳ (1856-86) on the other (see *al-Djinān*, 1871; *al-Ḍiyāʾ*, iv, 190; Shiblī, *passim* and texts, 62-349; ʿAbbūd, *Ṣaḳr*, 74-84, 162-7). In *al-Djāsūs ʿala 'l-Ḳāmūs* (Istanbul 1299/1881) he points out, in the course of a long introduction (2-90), the shortcomings of the Arabic dictionaries, establishes the reason for this (3-5), and demonstrates the principal errors committed by their various authors (10-45, with biographical notes 22-4, 71-2, 77-9). He then draws up an extended and passionate criticism of al-Fīrūzābādī, and probably al-Bustānī, his imitator, analysing the 24 weaknesses which he finds in al-Fīrūzābādī's *Ḳāmūs* (90-519). In spite of its importance, this work occupies only a secondary position in comparison with *Sirr al-layāl fi 'l-ḳalb wa 'l-ibdāl* (i, Istanbul

1884; vol. ii appears to exist in MS in private hands, see Najm, *Thesis*, 196), in which the author undertakes the study of the verbs and nouns in current use, which he arranges according to their pronunciation in order to demonstrate the links connecting them, their origin and the nuances distinguishing them, as well as of permutation, inversion and synonyms; he also supplies some of the omissions of al-Fīrūzābādī (*Sirr*, 6).

The author of a text-book of grammar (*Ghunyat al-ṭālib*, 1288/1871), he laughed at the extravagant exponents of the subject (*Fāryāḳ*, 68-9, 238) and wrote two text-books of Arabic grammar, in French (with G. Dugat, Paris 1854) and in English (*Practical Arabic grammar*, 2nd ed. London 1866). Drawing on the old lexicons, he undertook the translation of a work on the nature of animals (Malta 1841), assisted in the translation of the Bible, borrowed extensively from Western journals, and composed a trilingual (Persian-Turkish-Arabic) dictionary (Beirut 1876).

Extensive though it is, al-Shidyāḳ's poetical production (*Dīwān* of 22,000 lines: *Mashāhīr*, ii, 82; *Dā'ira*, x, 430; selections published Istanbul 1291/1874; various poems in *al-Sāḳ*, *al-Wāsiṭa*, *Kashf*; see especially *Kanz al-raghā'ib*, iii and introduction to the *Dīwān*) remains on the whole linked with the classical tradition. Besides the quatrains in which he expresses his misfortunes, there are some satirical effusions and some lyrical outbursts (*Kanz*, iii, e.g. 8, 11, 56-7, 80, 85, 87 and *passim*; *Dīwān*, 11, 12, 15, 16, 22, 30, 33, 43, 80, 84, 88, 89). The rest is a more or less servile imitation of the older writers, most of it occasional verse.

The *Kanz al-raghā'ib* (7 vols.), selections from *al-Djawā'ib*, reflects the results of his reading, his travels, his translations and his personal contacts. It is a mixture of ethics, sociology, politics (i and ii), history (v-vii), literature and linguistic discussions, composed of numerous diverse elements and assorted pieces of information which have aroused interest in both Oriental and European circles (*al-Muḳtabas*, vi).

In the religious sphere no faith satisfied him, and he remained a sceptic, a cynic, a realist, a materialist in search of honours and pleasures. Yet he rebelled, and, though joining the pan-Islamic movement, extolled the principles of the French Revolution. In revolt against feudalism and all forms of slavery, a supporter of the equality of man and the emancipation of women, a political and a social critic (*Kanz*, i, 101-3, 226-8; *Kashf*, 128 ff.), yet he lived and wrote in accordance with the behests of the Sultan or the Khedive.

Despite this ambivalence of culture and outlook we can discern in his works some of the features which characterize the writings of his contemporaries, and the seeds of a literature of innovation which blossomed after him. Concerned with the everyday problems of the century, he is the creator of the genre of the Maḳāla, the newspaper article [see MAḲĀLA], and the forerunner, if not actually the first, of the progressive reformers. Conservative and radical, traveller, linguist, man of learning and journalist, this humanist is undoubtedly one of the chief representatives of 19th century Arabic literature.

Bibliography: M. ʿAbbūd, *Ṣaḳr Lubnān*, Beirut 1950; B. al-Bustānī, *Dā'irat al-maʿārif*, x, 1898; idem, *Ḳiṣṣat Asʿad al-Shidyāḳ*², Beirut 1878; Brockelmann, II, 505-6, S II, 867-8; Cheikho, *al-Ādāb al-ʿarabiyya fi 'l-ḳarn al-tāsiʿ ʿashar*, Beirut 1908-26; idem, *Catalogue*, Beirut 1924, no. 447, 123; Dāghir, *Maṣādir al-dirāsa al-adabiyya*, ii, Beirut 1956; Kurd ʿAlī, *Nahḍat al-ʿarabiyya al-akhīra*, in *al-Muḳtabas*, vi, 1908; *al-Makshūf*, nos. 170 (17 October 1938), 314, 315, 316 (1941); B. Masʿad, *Fāris al-Shidyāḳ*, Beirut 1934; M. Najm, *Aḥmad Fāris al-Shidyāḳ*, M.A. thesis of the American University of Beirut, 1948; H. Pérès, in *al-Makshūf*, 314-6 (1941); Sarkīs, vi, 1104-7; M. Ṣawāyā, *Aḥmad Fāris al-Shidyāḳ*, Beirut 1962; A. Shiblī, *al-Shidyāḳ wa 'l-Yāzidjī*, Djunyeh 1950; Ṭ. al-Shidyāḳ, *Akhbār al-aʿyān fī Djabal Lubnān*, Beirut 1859 (see other editions; *al-Makshūf*, no. 170, 12); F. Ṭarrāzī, *Ta'rīkh al-ṣiḥāfa al-ʿarabiyya*, i, Beirut 1913; I. al-Yāzidjī, in *al-Djinān*, 1871, *al-Ḍiyā'*, iv, 1902; Dj. Zaydān, *Mashāhīr al-Sharḳ*, ii, Cairo 1922; idem, *Ta'rīkh al-ādāb*, iv, Cairo 1957; Sāmī Frasheri, *Ḳāmūs al-aʿlām*, v, 3326-7; H. Ewald and H. L. Fleischer, *Eine neuarabische Qaṣîde*, in *ZDMG*, v, 249-57; Brockelmann, G II 505, S II 867; Albert Hourani, *Arabic thought in the liberal age 1798-1939*, London 1962, 97-9 and index; H. Pérès, *Les premières manifestations de la renaissance littéraire arabe en Orient au XIX*ᵉ *siècle. Nāṣīf al-Yāziǧi et Fāris aš-Šidyāḳ*, in *AIEO Alger*, i (1934-5), 240 ff.; A. J. Arberry, *Fresh light on Ahmed Faris al-Shidyaq*, in *IC* (1952), 155-68

(A. G. KARAM)

AL-FĀRISĪ, ABŪ ʿALĪ AL-ḤASAN B. ʿALĪ, one of the outstanding grammarians of the 4th/10th century. Born 288/900 at Fasā [*q.v.*], he studied at Baghdād under Ibn al-Sarrādj, al-Zadjdjādj, and others. In 341/952 he joined the court of Sayf al-Dawla at Aleppo, where he consorted with Mutanabbī. He transferred himself to the service of the Būyid Aḍud al-Dawla sometime before the latter's conquest of Baghdād in 319/979 (cf. the story in Yāḳūt, *Irshād*, iii, 11). He died at Baghdād in 377/987. Amongst his numerous pupils were Ibn Djinnī (who attended him for 40 years and became his successor) and his nephew Abu 'l-Ḥusayn al-Fārisī, who became the teacher of ʿAbd al-Ḳāhir al-Djurdjānī. Fārisī was suspected of Muʿtazilism, and indeed commented upon the exegesis of the Muʿtazilī Muḥammad al-Djubbā'ī in a (lost) work called *al-Tatabbuʿ*. Among his other works the chief one s *al-Īḍāḥ fi 'l-naḥw*, an advanced grammar, with a more difficult appendix, *al-Takmila*. The popularity of this work in his time is proved by the numerous MSS preserved and by the five extant commentaries and two *shawāhid* commentaries. A large part is printed in Girgas-Rosen, *Arabskaya Khrestom.*, 378-434. Further works (extant items marked *): *al-Īḍāḥ al-shiʿrī*, perhaps identical with **K. al-shiʿr* or *al-ʿAḍudī*, MS. Berl. 6465 (a part printed in Io. Roediger, *De nominibus verborum arabicis commentatio*, Halle 1870), and with *Sharḥ abyāt al-Īḍāḥ* mentioned *Fihrist* 646; a commentary on al-Zadjdjādj's *Maʿānī al-Ḳur'ān* called **al-Ighfāl* (confused in *Fihrist*); perhaps on the same work (or identical) *Abyāt al-Maʿānī*; a commentary on Ibn Mudjāhid's *al-Ḳirā'āt al-sabʿa* called **al-Ḥudjdja* (*wa 'l-ighfāl*?); *al-Tadhkira*, on difficult verses; **Djawāhir al-naḥw*; *Mukhtaṣar ʿawāmil al-iʿrāb* (called by Ibn Khallikān *al-ʿAwāmil al-mi'a*); *al-Maḳṣūr wa 'l-mamdūd*; *Abyāt al-iʿrāb*; a comm. on Ḳur'ān, V, 8; and a number of collections of **Masā'il*, named after various localities (where Fārisī taught?); it is not clear what was the nature of his *Naḳḍ al-hādhūr* ("The Babbler Confounded").

Bibliography: Brockelmann, I, 116; S. I, 175; Flügel, 110; *Fihrist*, 64; Ibn Khallikān, no. 155; Yāḳūt, *Udabā'*, iii, 9-22; al-Anbārī, *Nuzha*, 387-9; *Ta'rīkh Baghdād*, vii, 275; Ibn al-

Athīr, ix, 36; Ibn Taghrībirdī, 533-4; Ibn al-ʿImād, *Shadharāt*, iv, 88-9; Suyūṭī, *Bughya*, 216.

(C. Rabin)

FĀRISIYYA [see īrān].

al-**FĀRISIYYA**, Djazīrat, island in the Persian Gulf in Lat. 27° 59′ N., Long. 50° 10′ E., about midway between the shores of Saudi Arabia and Iran. Like Djazīrat al-ʿArabiyya, 14 statute miles to the south, al-Fārisiyya is low and less than one square mile in area. The island is administered by Iran which maintains a meteorological station there (although Kuwayt and Saudi Arabia have also advanced claims on it), and the Persian Gulf Lighting Service maintains a navigation light.

(W. E. Mulligan)

FARK [see faṣl].

al-**FARKADĀNi** [see nudjūm].

FARMĀN, basic meanings: 1. Command, 2. (preparation in writing of a command) Edict, Document.

Ancient Persian *framānā* (*fra* = "fore", Greek πρό), modern Persian *farmān* through dropping the ending ā and insertion of a vowel owing to the initial double consonant (still *fra-* in Pahlavi). In the derived verb *farmūdan* the ā of the stem became ū (after the third century: *far-mūdan*, analogous to *āz-mūdan* "to try", *pay-mūdan* "to measure", *nu-mūdan* "to show", etc.).

In Firdawsī *farmān* is found with the following meanings: command, authority, will, wish, permission; and *farmūdan* accordingly: to command, to regulate, to have something done, to say, to announce, as well as "to permit"; in those meanings mentioned first it is construed with (1) the content of the command as direct object, (2) a following infinitive, (3) with *tā* "that", or (4) *ki* "that", and (5) with *ki* introducing direct address. In addition the forms *farmān dādan* (or *kardan*) "to command" and *farmān burdan* "to obey" are also found in Firdawsī. Among composite forms Firdawsī has *farmāndih* "commander", "master", *farmānrawā* "one whose commands are accepted", "commanding", "powerful", and *farmānbar* "servant", "slave", as well as *farmānpadhīr* "submissive", "yielding". In the *Farhang-i Nafīsī* on the other hand nine composite forms occur, which are to a degree identical with those mentioned above and which may be divided into the same two groups according to meaning: *f.-dih*, *f.-rawā*, *f.-farmā*, *f.-godhār* (to command), and *f.-bar*, *f.-bardār*, *f.-padhīr*, *f.-shenū*, *f.-niyūsh* (to obey). There are in Firdawsī isolated examples of the Arabic equivalents of *farmān*: *ḥukm* (sentence, decision, command) and *amr* (command), although the "Command of God" is called *farmān-i yazdān*.

Farmān in the sense of "document" does not, however, occur in Firdawsī, who uses only the three Arabic (!) expressions *raḳam* (sign, script, writing, decree), *manshūr* (diploma, decree, investiture) and *barāt* (diploma, assignment). Firdawsī also uses the word *nishān* only in the sense of "sign", "emblem", "trace", "target", etc., though in the *ʿAtabat al-kataba* (mid 12th century) *nishān* is already a common term for edicts and diplomas in the broadest sense of the word. But *farmān* as a designation for the writing itself came only very slowly into usage and became part of the official language of administration at a very late date. Thus we find in the earlier period *farmān* in the sense of "document" in examples of language which is not quite official, such as the *Siyāsat-nāma* of Niẓām al-Mulk, where *farmān* is employed occasionally as a parallel to *mithāl* (ed. Hubert Darke, Tehrān 1962, 90), clearly designating two different kinds of document, one of which (*farmān*) was issued by the ruler himself, and the other (*mithāl*) by authorities of lower rank (cf. *Isl.*, xxxviii (1962), 195-8). A diploma, which would later be called officially *farmān* or *nishān*, is designated by Niẓām al-Mulk (ed. Darke, 191), still dependent upon Arabic usage, *ʿahd-nāma*, a term which more accurately applies to treaties in a narrower sense. In religious matters of course a treaty is (now) called *ʿaḳd-nāma*. *Farmān* in the strict sense of "document" cannot be unquestionably established before the 15th century, when it occurs as "... *dar farāmīn* (here in the Arabic broken plural) *masṭūr ast*", "... (as is) written in the documents" (Busse, *Untersuchungen*, Document No. 3). Until well into modern times expressions such as *ḥukm*, *manshūr*, *nishān*, etc. are used beside *farmān* with very little difference, occasionally in the combination *ḥukm-i farmān* or *ḥukm-i mithāl*, and it is not always possible to establish without reservation whether by *farmān* the actual command or the writing of it is meant. In this double application of the term *farmān* an echo of an older juridical concept is perceptible, according to which the document was only the writing down of an originally oral (which alone was authoritative) decree. During the Ṣafawid period the edicts of subordinate authorities were called *mithāl* or *raḳam* (pl. *arḳām*), and in the Ḳādjār period the terminology had become consolidated to the extent that *farmān* was reserved for the ruler's edicts, while those of governors were called according to their rank either *raḳam* or *ḥukm* (cf. diplomatic, iii, Persian, 309).

Like rulers' titles the various designations for edict and document are distinguished by epithets: *nishān* (*farmān*, *ḥukm*)*-i humāyūn* "royal edict" (Firdawsī: *dirafsh-i humāyūn* "felicitous, glorious, royal banner"); *aḥkām-i muṭāʿ-i humāyūn* "royal edicts, which are obeyed"; *arḳām wa-aḥkām-i muṭāʿāt*; *farāmīn-i muṭāʿāt lāzim al-iṭāʿat-i humāyūn* "royal edicts which are and must be obeyed"; *ḥukm djahānmuṭāʿ wa-āftāb-shuʿā* "edict, obeyed by the world and shining (like) the sun's rays"; *farmān-i aʿlā khudāʾiganī-yi aʿẓamī-yi shāhinshāhī* "most high, lordly, most noble, imperial edict"; *raḳam-i mubārak-i ashraf* "blessed and most honoured edict". In comparison to the elatives are the basic forms *ʿālī* and *sharīf*, which were employed for edicts not originating from the ruler himself in the highly developed nomenclature of the Ḳādjār period, and to some extent even earlier. A formula of benediction likewise follows mention of the edict or command: *aʿlāhu'llāh taʿālā wa-khallada nifādhahu* "May God elevate it and make abiding its effect"; *lā zāla munfadhᵃⁿ fi 'l-aḳṭāʿ wa 'l-arbāʿ* "may it be always effective in the regions and quarters of the earth", and other formulae of the kind.

In the *Dispositio*, that part of the document containing the resolution of the ruler, firmly established formulae are employed: (1) Substantive plus *farmūdan*: *ḥukm f.*, *mithāl f.*, *manshūr f.*, *ḥawālat f.* (to make an assignment), *maḥmadat f.* (to proclaim praise); (2) Arabic verbal noun II plus *farmūdan*: *taḳrīr f.*, *tafwīḍ f.*, etc.; (3) Arabic passive participle II plus *farmūdan*: *muḳarrar f.*, etc. In the first group of formulae *farmūdan* can be replaced by *dādan*, in those of the second and third groups by *kardan* or *dāshtan* and *gardānīdan*. Very frequently two formulae are combined: *maḥramat farmūdīm wa-arzānī dāshtīm* "we have shown and conceded favour" (in Firdawsī *arzānī* means "worthy" or "poor"; in Vullers *arzānī dāshtan* is 'dignum putare, tanquam digno largiri, concedere, conferre'; thus also in Steingass). In the *Dispositio* impersonal formulae are also favoured: *ḥukm* ... *ba-nafādh andjāmīd* "a ... command has been issued"; *ḥukm* ... *samt-i iṣdār yaft* "a ... command has found the path of issue"; *ḥukm* ... *ʿizz-i iṣdār wa-sharaf-i nafādh yaft* "a ... command has found the honour of issue and the esteem of promulgation". Out of these and the equally current formulae with *shud* (*ḥukm shud, muḳarrar shud*) the introductory formulae (*tughra*) developed, which predominated in the early Ṣafawid period for particular kinds of documents: *farmān-i humāyūn shud, farmān-i humāyūn sharaf-i nafādh yaft*, and *ḥukm-i djahānmuṭāʿ shud*, with the later distinction also here between *aʿlā* and *ʿālī* as adjectives for *farmān* and *ḥukm*. The issuing authorities and the rank of the originator can be determined by the various introductory formulae, which to some extent, however, depend upon the content of the document or the addressee. Directly related to the introductory formulae are the seals affixed and parts of the protocol (invocation) sometimes used.

The designations for edict and command can in addition be made more precise for various purposes by a following substantive or adjective, thus: according to content (*nishān-i ṣadārat*, diploma for a *ṣadr*, *manshūr-i taḳlīd* (or *tafwīḍ*), diploma of investiture; *ḥukm-i mudjammalī*, a general edict addressed to everyone); according to the promulgating authority (*mithāl-i dīwān al-ṣadāra*); for an original document or a confirmation (*raḳam-i muthannā, mudjaddad, ḥukm-i imḍā* or *tadjdīd-i nishān*); and for further processing of the document by the authorities (*raḳam-i daftarī* and *bayāḍī*, that is, documents which were registered and those which were not). For seals, script, registration, etc., cf. DIPLOMATIC, iii, Persia.

We also find *Farmān* as the pen-name (*takhalluṣ*) of a poet (cf. Justi, *Iranisches Namenbuch*, s.v.), and in the form *Farmān-farmā* as the nick-name of the Ḳādjār prince Ḥusayn ʿĀlī, the son of Fatḥ ʿĀlī Shāh (d. 1834).

Bibliography: in addition to that given in the article DIPLOMATIC, iii, Persia: Fritz Wolff, *Glossar zu Firdosis Schahname*, Berlin 1935. To be added to the bibliography in Diplomatic iii. — Persia: M. R. Arunova, *Firman Nadir-Shakha*, in *SO*, ii (1958), 116-20; P. I. Petrov, *Ferman Shakha Sultan Huseyna Vakhtangu VI*, in *SO*, iv (1957), 127-8 (both with facsimile reproductions). A. D. Papazyan, *Dva novootkrytykh il'khanskikh yarlyka*, in *Banber Matenadarani*, vi (1962), 379-401; idem, *K voprosu o tekhničeskom značenii nalogovogo termina "malodžakhat"*, in *Izvestiy Akademii nauk Armyanskoy SSR*, 1961, No. 2, 61-82 (both with facsimile reproductions).

(H. BUSSE)

ii.—Ottoman Empire

Fermān, in Turkish, denotes any order or edict of the Ottoman sultan. In a more limited sense it means a decree of the sultan headed by his cypher (*tughra*) and composed in a certain form which generally differs from that of the *berāt* (*nishān*, *yasaḳnāme*) and *nāme* [*qq.v.*]. Synonymous terms are, particularly in the early Ottoman Empire, *biti*, *yarlïgh*, *mithāl*, *ḥüdjdjet* (for a certain type), *menshūr*, *tewḳīʿ* and, in most periods, *emr*, *ḥükm* (and, in Arabic, *marsūm*). All these terms are usually followed by epithets, such as *sherīf*, *humāyūn*, *refīʿ*, *ʿālī*[-*shān*], *djihān-muṭāʿ*, etc. Imperial princes serving as provincial governors sometimes issued *fermān*s under their own *tughra*s (so far one has been published: *Belleten*, v (1941), 108-9, 126-7). In late Ottoman Egypt an edict of the wālī also used to be called *faramān*.

Preparation. Most *fermān*s were not issued by order of the sultan himself. According to the *ḳānūnnāme* of Meḥemmed II (*TOEM*, 1330, suppl., 16), three high officials were authorized to give orders (*buyuruldï*) to issue a *fermān* in the sultan's name and under his *tughra* : the Grand Vizier on general subjects, the *defterdār*s on fiscal matters and the *ḳāḍī-ʿasker*s on questions of *sharīʿa* law. In many cases they did so after the affair had been discussed and decided upon in the imperial council (*dīwān-i humāyūn* [*q.v.*]) or the Grand Vizier's council (*ikindi dīwānï*), with or without the sultan's subsequent express approval. Later *ḳānūnnāme*s (*e.g.*, *MTM*, i (1331), 500, 523) extended this authority to the Deputy Grand Vizier (*ḳāʾim-maḳām*) during the Grand Vizier's absence from the capital and to viziers appointed commanders-in-chief (*serdār*).

Most *fermān*s were prepared in the imperial chancery (*dīwān-i humāyūn ḳalemi*). A draft made by a junior clerk (see Ferīdūn, *Munshaʾāt al-salāṭīn*[1], i, 20) was corrected and approved by the *mümeyyiz*, the *beylikdji*, the *reʾīs al-küttāb* [*q.v.*] (for his *resīd* see *MTM*, i, 516-7) and, exceptionally, the sultan himself. *Fermān*s on fiscal matters, which were prepared in the Finance Department (*māliyye*), passed through other stages (see L. Fekete, *Die Siyāqat-Schrift*, Budapest 1955, i, 68, n. 2). On the fair copy the *tughra* [*q.v.*] was drawn by the *nishāndjï* [*q.v.*] (or the *tughra-kesh*), or by one of the viziers in the dīwān or, in certain cases, the Grand Vizier himself (see *MTM*, i, 499, 509, 515). The right of governors of vizier rank in frontier provinces to affix the sultan's *tughra* to *fermān*s drawn up by them was abolished by the Grand Vizier Kemānkesh Muṣṭafā Pasha (1638-44) (*Taʾrīkh-i Naʿīmā*, 1147, ii, 11). The Grand Vizier and certain other viziers when away from the capital and the Deputy Grand Vizier in Istanbul were often provided with blank papers on which the *tughra* had been drawn beforehand to enable them to issue *fermān*s on the spot.

The completed *fermān* was put in a small bag (*kīse, kese*) and used to be conveyed to its destination either by government couriers (*ulaḳ* [*q.v.*]) or by the permanent representative of the addressee (provincial governors, etc.) in Istanbul (*ḳapï ketkhudāsï*) or the person who had submitted a petition and asked for the decree. The latter is frequently referred to in the document as its 'bearer' (*dārende, ḥāmil, rāfiʿ*, etc.). The persons in whose favour a *fermān* was issued were often explicitly allowed to keep it after it had been shown to its addressee (and copied into the local *ḳāḍī*'s register), so that they could present it in case of a violation of their rights in future.

Internal structure. In its composition, which changed surprisingly little over the centuries, the *fermān* bears much similarity to certain occidental documents. It opens with an *invocatio* (*daʿwet, taḥmīd*) of God, the shortest form of which is *huwa*. Beneath a considerable blank space, a sign of respect, there follows the *tughra*, which, particularly in later periods, is sometimes richly decorated. The text begins with the address (*inscriptio*) which mentions the office, and often also the name and rank, of the addressee preceded by his honorific titles (*elḳāb*) and followed by a short benediction (*duʿā*) (see *TOEM*, 1330, suppl., 30-2; Ferīdūn, *Munshaʾāt*[1], i, 2-13). The addressee is not a private citizen but mostly a government official in the capital or the provinces, a dependent Christian ruler, and the like. Many *fermān*s are addressed jointly to two or more such persons, others to a class of officials in a certain province, along a given road or in the whole Empire.

Following an introductory formula, such as *tewkīʿ-i refīʿ-i humāyūn wāṣîl olîdjaḳ maʿlūm ola ki* ('when the exalted imperial cipher arrives, be it known that . . .'), most *fermān*s then relate the facts that caused the order to be issued (*narratio, iblāgh*). Usually this section is a summary, partly verbatim, of an incoming report or petition.

Thereupon follows the main part of the *fermān*, the *dispositio* (*ḥükm, emr*), which may open with the words *öyle olsa, imdi* (*gerekdir ki*), etc. In many *fermān*s it consists of two parts. The first, ending in *emr ėdüb, fermānîm* (*ṣādîr*) *olmushdîr*, and the like, states the sultan's decision in the form of a short, impersonal order. This clause seems to be the 'documentary commission' which, as mentioned above, was generally written by a high official or the sultan himself in the upper margin of the incoming communication or on a separate piece of paper and was sometimes reproduced verbatim in the *fermān*. The second (or only) part of the *dispositio*, which sets forth the sultan's command to the addressee in greater detail, mostly begins *buyurdum ki*. The space left empty after these words in many *fermān*s was originally reserved for the name of the official who was to convey the document to its destination. In some *fermān*s this space is filled with the much elongated words *ḥükm-i sherīfimle* (*vardîḳda*).

Numerous *fermān*s add a *sanctio* or *comminatio* (*teʾkīd*), which emphasizes the importance of the order, exhorts the addressee to carry it out without delay and threatens him with punishment for any disobedience. The subsequent *corroboratio* refers to the *tughra* (*ʿalāmet-i sherīf*) as attestation to the authenticity of the document. Neither a signature nor, with few exceptions (*e.g.*, in certain fiscal *fermān*s), a seal is affixed. At the end, the (*Hidjra*) date and, mostly in the lower left corner, the place of issue are given. In *fermān*s issued by the Finance Department these were generally added by a special bureau in smaller letters and a different handwriting.

On the back, various annotations may be found, such as *ṣaḥḥ* denoting that the document has been examined and approved, the peculiar signature (*ḳuyruḳlî imḍā*) of the *defterdār*, registration comments, the address, a short reference to the contents, etc.

To give a *fermān* greater weight or confer distinction upon its recipient, the sultan often added a few words in his own hand near the *tughra*. The later standard formula is *mūdjebindje ʿamel oluna*, but sometimes the note is more elaborate (cf. Babinger, *Archiv*, 50; *TM*, vi (1936-9), 228, 234). Such documents are called *khaṭṭ-i humāyūn* or *khaṭṭ-i sherīf* [*q.v.*], a term also used in other meanings (see *IA*, s.v. *Hatt-i Hümâyûn*).

Contents and external form. *Fermān*s deal with a wide range of subjects—administration, military affairs, finance, judicial decisions, etc. Some are communiqués on Ottoman victories, travel permits, safe-conducts, permits for foreign ships to pass through the Straits, courier orders, etc. Many *fermān*s which contained rules of general applicability became 'regulations' (*ḳānūn*) and were incorporated in *ḳānūnnāme*s [*q.v.*], the codes of Ottoman secular law.

Generally, *fermān*s are written in Ottoman Turkish. Exceptions are some early Ottoman *yarlîgh*s written, in a different form, in Central Asian Turkish and Uyghūr characters (with interlinear text in Arabic letters) (see R. Rahmeti Arat in *TM*, vi, 285-322 and *Ann. del R. Ist. Sup. Orient. di Napoli*, N.S., i (1940), 25-68). Until the 16th century *fermān*s were also issued in other languages (Greek, Slavonic, Arabic, etc.).

The script used in *fermān*s is some kind of *tewḳīʿ* or *dīwānī*. Frequently gold dust (*altîn rīg*) was sprinkled on the writing before it had dried. Like other Ottoman documents, *fermān*s are usually written on long and relatively narrow sheets of paper with the lines slightly rising towards the left. While a margin is left on the right, the last word in a line is often lengthened to prevent interpolations. Forgers of *fermān*s incurred capital punishment (see Hammer, *GOR*[1], vii, 375; Stephan Gerlach, *Tage-Buch*, Frankfurt a.M. 1674, 376).

The composition and form of the Ottoman *fermān* were certainly influenced by oriental (Saldjūḳ, Mamlūk, etc.) and, possibly, occidental models, but this question has not yet been adequately studied.

Originals and copies. Original *fermān*s are preserved in the archives and libraries of Turkey, other parts of the former Ottoman Empire and many European countries. A number of them have been published (see *Bibl.*). Other *fermān*s have survived in the form of individual copies, often legalized by a *ḳāḍī* (see *MOG*, ii, 138 ff.). Innumerable *fermān* texts, generally without the 'protocol' at the beginning and the end, are found in various registers, such as the *Mühimme Defteri* [*q.v.*], *Shikāyet Defteri, Aḥkām Defteri* and a few others, most of which are kept today in the *Başvekâlet Arşivi* [*q.v.*] in Istanbul. Collections of such copies have been published by Aḥmed Refīḳ (especially for Istanbul), H. T. Dağlıoğlu (for Bursa), D. Šopova (for Macedonia), U. Heyd (for Palestine), İ. H. Uzunçarşılı (for Ottoman history and institutions in general), and others. The registers (*sidjill* [*q.v.*]) of the *sharīʿa* courts also contain a large number of *fermān* copies (see publications by J. Grzegorzewski, H. İnalcık, M. Ç. Uluçay, H. Ongan, J. Kabrda, H. W. Duda-G. D. Galabov, etc.). Finally, many copies of *fermān*s, including early ones, are found in *inshā* works by Ferīdūn and others, collectanea (*medjmūʿa*) and chronicles.

Bibliography: D'Ohsson, *Tableau général de l'empire othoman*, iii, Paris 1820, 339-40; Fr. Kraelitz, *Osmanische Urkunden in türkischer Sprache*, Wien 1921; L. Fekete, *Einführung in die osmanisch-türkische Diplomatik*, Budapest 1926; J. Deny, *Sommaire des archives turques du Caire*, Cairo 1930, esp. 145-9; İ. H. Uzunçarşılı, *Osmanlı devletinin saray teşkilâtı*, Ankara 1945, 279-87; A. Zajączkowski-J. Reychman, *Zarys dyplomatyki Osmańsko-Tureckiej*, Warsaw 1955 (English translation in the press); M. Guboglu, *Paleografia şi diplomatica turco-osmană*, Bucarest 1958 (with extensive bibliogr.); U. Heyd, *Ottoman documents on Palestine 1552-1615, a study of the firman according to the Mühimme Defteri*, Oxford 1960. For texts and photostats of *fermān* originals see: Kraelitz, *op. cit.*; Guboglu, *op. cit.*; Fr. Babinger, *Das Archiv des Bosniaken Osman Pascha*, Berlin 1931; İ. H. Uzunçarşılı, in *Belleten*, v/17-8 (1941), 101-31; P. Lemerle-P. Wittek, in *Arch. d'hist. du droit oriental*, iii (1947), 420 ff.; Gl. Elezović, *Turski spomenici*, i-ii, Belgrade 1940, 1952; Ć. Truhelka, in *Glasnik zem. Muzeja*, xxiii (1911); see also BERĀT; BUYURULDU; DIPLOMATIC iv—Ottoman Empire; IRĀDE.

(U. HEYD)

iii.—India.

The authentic texts of many formal written royal orders have survived from the Mughal period, in originals located in the archives of former princely states, of the descendents of great merchants or of religious communities. From the references collected in I. H. Qureshi, *The administration of the sultanate of Dehli*, Lahore 1942, 86, it would seem that the procedures of Mughal times designed to ensure that *farmāns* were intentional, authentic and effective were founded on long-established Indo-Muslim precedent, though in the absence of extant texts from the sultanate period, many details are lacking.

The formalizing of the discourse of the Mughal *pādshāh* into a state document could, the *Āʾīn-i Akbarī* suggests, be stately and elaborate. First, the speech and actions of the *pādshāh* were recorded daily by two *wāḳiʿ-nawīs*, the record being confirmed by the *pādshāh* before a *yād-dāsht* or memorandum of actual orders was prepared therefrom and countersigned by the *mīr ʿarḍ*, the *parwānčī* and the officer who had placed it before the *pādshāh* for a second approval. *Farmāns*, which were distinguished from *parwānčas* in point of force and generality of application by the attachment of a royal seal, were often, but not always, prepared from a *taʿlīḳa* or abridgment of the *yād-dāsht*, particularly in the granting of money or of an office entailing the grant of money. Although the *pādshāh* was bound by no invariable rule, *farmāns* were usually issued for appointments as *wakīl*, *wazīr*, *ṣadr*, *mīr bakhshī* or *nāẓim* or for the grant of a *manṣab*, *djāgīr* or *sayūrghāl*. They were also sent to tributary princes, to foreign rulers and used to grant privileges to religious communities and trading organisations.

The procedure for a *farmān* appointing to a *djāgīr* or *manṣab* involved many checks against inaccuracy, fraud and caprice. The *farmān* was drafted both on the basis of a *sarkhaṭ* or certificate specifying the salary being granted (the details of which were copied in the *bakhshī*'s department from the *taʿlīḳa*), and on the basis of a *taʿlīḳa-yi tan* or certificate of salary which went to the *dīwān* or finance minister. These preliminary documents went before the *pādshāh* for continuing approval at various stages and were signed and sealed by such officials as the *mīr bakhshī*, the *mustawfī-i dīwān* and the *ṣāḥib-i tawdjīh* (accountant in the *bakhshī*'s department). The *farmān* of grant or appointment called *farmān-i thabtī* received the seals of the *bakhshīs*, the *dīwān* and the *wakīl* before receiving a royal seal. Confidential and important *farmāns*, not involving sums of money, received only a royal seal and were folded and dispatched in such a way that their contents remained private to the recipient. They were called *farmān-i bayāḍī*.

The two most important royal seals were the *uzuk* seal (a 'privy' seal), kept often either by one of the royal ladies or by a trusted official, and a large linear seal (a 'great' seal), the *muhr-i muḳaddas-i kalān*, on which was engraved the name of the *pādshāh* and of his ruling ancestors from Tīmūr. This was particularly but not exclusively used for *farmāns* to foreign rulers and to tributary princes. Besides the seal, a *tughra* or 'sign manual', giving the full name and titles of the *pādshāh* himself, written in *naskh*, was superscribed.

The *pādshāh* might favour the addressee of a *farmān* by adding his own signature to the seal, or by writing a few lines in his own hand, or by impressing the mark of the royal hand (*pandja-yi mubārak*) upon the *farmān*. Shāh Djahān sometimes wrote out the entire *farmān* himself.

Bibliography: Abu 'l-Faḍl, *Āʾīn-i Akbarī*, i, Calcutta 1872, 192-6; Muḥammad Kāẓim, *ʿĀlamgīr-nāma*, Calcutta 1868, 1101; Fr. Felix, *Mughal farmāns, parwānahs and sanads issued in favour of the Jesuit missionaries*, in *JPHS*, v/1 (1916), 1-53; idem, *The Mughal Seals*, in *JPHS*, v/2 (1916), 100-25; M. S. Commissariat, *Imperial Mughal farmans in Gujarat*, in *Journal of the University of Bombay*, ix/1 (July 1940), 1-56; S. M. Jaffar, *Mughal farmans in Peshawar*, in *Proceedings of the Indian Historical Records Commission*, xviii (1942), 236-45; idem, *An important farman of Aurangzeb*, in *Proc. IHRC*, xxii (1945); A. Halim, *A farman of Emperor Shah Jahan*, in *Proc. IHRC*, xix (1943), 56-60; idem, *A farman of Emperor Akbar*, in *Proc. IHRC*, xxii (1945), 33-5; B. N. Reu, *Some imperial farmans addressed to Ratho and Durgadas*, in *Proc. IHRC*, xxv/2 (1945), 186-9; idem, *Some Imperial Farmans addressed to the rulers of Jodhpur*, in *Proc. Ind. Hist. Congress*, 1947, 350-7; M. L. Roy Chaudhuri, *Jahangir's farman of 1613 A.D.*, in *Proc. IHRC*, xix (1943), 56-60; P. Saran, *A farman of Farrukhsiyar*, in *Proc. IHRC*, xix (1943), 74-9; Jadunath Sarkar, *Studies in Mughal Administration*, Calcutta 1924, 230-5; Ibn Hasan, *The central structure of the Mughal empire*, London 1936, 93-106. (P. Hardy)

FĀRMĀSŪN [see MĀSŪNIYYA].

FARMING [see FILĀḤA].

FARMING OF TAXES [see BAYT AL-MAL, ḌARĪBA, ILTIZĀM, MUḲĀṬAʿA].

FARMŪL (also FARMUL). A town east of Ghazna in Afghanistan near Gardēz. It is mentioned by al-Muḳaddasī (296), and the *Ḥudūd al-ʿālam* (251). The exact location of the town is unknown and it no longer exists. (R. N. Frye)

AL-**FARRĀʾ**, the sobriquet of the grammarian of al-Kūfa, Abū Zakariyyāʾ Yaḥyā b. Ziyād, who died in 207/822; according to al-Samʿānī, *Ansāb*, f° 420a (quoted by Ibn Khallikān, ii, 229, l. 34), al-Farrāʾ appears to signify, not "the Furrier" but "one who skins, *i.e.*, scrutinises language". He was born at al-Kūfa in about 144/761, of a family that were natives of Daylam (see Yāḳūt, *Udabāʾ*, xx, 9), and he remained as a dependent of an Arab clan, either the Asad or the Minḳār (see *Fihrist*, 66 and *Taʾrīkh Baghdād*, xiv, 149); he received an education in *ḥadīth* that went back to the well-known traditionists (*Taʾrīkh Baghdād*, al-Samʿānī, *loc. cit.*); naturally, it is on the subject of his grammatical education that we possess the fullest particulars, but these must, however, be used with discretion; on the authority of the "Kūfan" Thaʿlab (d. 291/904) [*q.v.*], it has been customary to regard al-Farrāʾ as one of the masters and indeed one of the founders of the "grammatical school of al-Kūfa"; the fact is that al-Farrāʾ holds a place in the list of Kūfans who were influenced by al-Ruʾāsī [*q.v.*] and al-Kisāʾī [*q.v.*] (see anecdotal material in *Fihrist*, 64, l. 16, repeated by al-Anbāri, 65, in which *amyazu* must be read, not *asannu*); in any event, al-Farrāʾ would only have met al-Kisāʾī in Baghdād when in his years of maturity, and what is more, it is not admissable to accept that at that time the division between the "School of al-Kūfa" and that of al-Baṣra had already assumed the intensity which it later attained during the grammarians' polemics at the end of the 3rd/9th century and in the following century (cf. Fleisch, 14 and al-Makhzūmī, who refer to Weil, *Inṣāf*, Introduction); like his contemporaries, al-Farrāʾ seems in fact to have made wide use of direct inquiry among Bedouin informants; to some degree he was influenced by Baṣran scholars such as Yūnus al-Thaḳafī, perhaps also al-Aṣmaʿī, Abū Zayd al-Anṣārī and Abū ʿUbayda (cf. Abu 'l-Ṭayyib al-Lughawi (?) *apud* al-Suyūṭī, *Muzhir*, ii, 403); like most if not all the Kūfans, al-Farrāʾ had an intimate knowledge of the *Book* of Sībawayh (cf. the information going back to al-Djāḥiẓ, in Ibn Khallikān, i, 385, l. 21, where the polygraph says a gift was made to the vizier Ibn al-Zayyāt of a copy of this work, originating from the library of al-Farrāʾ and executed by the latter himself); in fact the problem of the Baṣran influences on al-Farrāʾ remains partly obscure since the evidence is contradictory (cf. Yāḳūt, *Udabāʾ*, xx, 10 and al-Suyūṭī, *Bughya*, 411 and also the summary by al-Makhzūmī, 146 ff.); in any case, he does not seem to have undergone direct influences of master on disciple. By his personality, the austerity of his habits, his disinterestedness, and also as a result of his position in relation to the caliph al-Rashīd (see Zubaydī, 143; Ibn Khallikān, ii, 228, l. 12) and especially al-Maʾmūn who appointed him tutor to his two sons (see *Taʾrīkh Baghdād*, xiv, 150, repeated by al-Anbārī, 130-1), al-Farrāʾ appears to have largely deserved the renown which his erudition had won. His knowledge was encyclopaedic and derived simulnaneously from *ḥadīth*, *fiḳh*, astrology, medicine, the "Days of the Arabs", and, naturally, from grammar (see *Taʾrīkh Baghdād*, xiv, 151, condensed in Yāḳūt, *Udabāʾ*, xx, 11 and al-Anbārī, 132-3); his Muʿtazilī leanings are certain but, according to al-Djāḥiẓ, al-Farrāʾ had no real gift for *kalām* (see Ibn Khallikān, ii, 229, l. 13; cf. Yāḳūt, *loc. cit.*). It is above all as a grammarian of the "School of al-Kūfa" that the reputation of al-Farrāʾ has been perpetuated; his immediate disciples like Salama b. ʿĀṣim, Abū ʿUbayd Ibn Sallām, Muḥammad b. Djahm al-Simmarī were of importance in that respect (cf. *Fihrist*, 67, 71; *Taʾrīkh Baghdād*, xiv, 149; Yāḳūt, xx, 10; Zubaydī, 150); but it is mainly due to Thaʿlab that he came to be recognised as the leader of the "School of al-Kūfa" (cf. *Fihrist*, 74 and *Taʾrīkh Baghdād*, *loc. cit.*); it is worth noting that his authority extended as far as Spain (see Zubaydī, 163 and the statement by his uncle; see also *ibid.*, 278 and al-Suyūṭī, *Bughya*, 213 ff. on what Djūdī of Toledo owes to al-Farrāʾ and the Kūfans).

The writings of al-Farrāʾ are known to us from the list of works given in the *Fihrist*, 67, enumerating 13 titles (cf. *Maʿānī al-Ḳurʾān*, Introd. by the editors, 10-1, who include 17 titles; this initial list serves as the basis for those given by Yāḳūt, Ibn Khallikān, and al-Suyūṭī, *Bughya*, which includes only 11 titles); a number of these works appear to be lost; note also that certain titles appear to apply to chapters of the *Ḥudūd*. His work consists of: (*a*) writings on grammar such as — 1. *K. Mulāzim* (?) (see Yāḳūt, xx, 14; Ibn Khallikān, ii, 229, l. 30; the *Fihrist*, 67, gives a *Ḥadd mulāzamat radjul* (sic) among the chapters of the *Ḥudūd*); — 2. *K. al-Ḥudūd*, "Definitiones grammaticae", thought by some to have been dictated at the instance of al-Maʾmūn, after 204/819 (cf. *Taʾrīkh Baghdād*, xiv, 149) or, more probably, before that date (see Cairo ed., i; cf. al-Makhzūmī, 151); according to the *Fihrist*, 67, we possess the list of 45 chap., but al-Suyūṭī, *Bughya*, gave it as 46 and al-Zubaydī, 150, speaks of 60; the work was imitated by the Kūfan Ibn Saʿdān (d. 231/845; cf. *Fihrist*, 70, l. 5); — 3. *K. Faʿala* (?) *wa-afʿala* (see *Fihrist*, 67); the *K. al-Ḥudūd* contains a chapter with the same title; a small work possibly quoted by al-Suyūṭī, *Muzhir*, ii, 95; — 4. *K. al-Maḳṣūr wa 'l-mamdūd* (*Fihrist*, 67); quoted by al-Suyūṭī, *Muzhir*, ii, 255 ff. and by Ibn al-Sikkīt, *ibid.*, ii, 106; for the MSS, see Brockelmann, S I, 179; — 5. *K. al-Mudhakkar wa 'l-muʾannath* (*Fihrist*, 67); the *K. al-Ḥudūd* contains a chapter with the same title; ed. Muṣṭafā Zaraʿī, Beirut/Aleppo 1345 in *Madjmūʿa lughawiyya*; — 6. *K. al-Wāw* (see Yāḳūt, *Udabāʾ*, xx, 14 and Ibn Khallikān, ii, 229). — (*b*) writings on lexicography such as 7. *K. al-Ayyām wa 'l-layālī* [*wa 'l-shuhūr*] (al-Suyūṭī, *Muzhir*, i, 219 and ii, 76-7, 158 l. 3, 248: 3 quotations); ed. Ibr. al-Ibyāri, Cairo 1956, 1 vol. in 8°, 64 pp.; perhaps composed on the basis of "current dictations" going back to al-Farrāʾ and certain other Kūfans; — 8. *K. al-Fākhir* (*Fihrist*, 67 and Yāḳūt, xx, 14; not *al-mafākhir* as in Ibn Khallikān, ii, 229, l. 29); for the MSS, see Brockelmann, S I, 179; deals with proverbs; it should be noted that Mufaḍḍal b. Salama, son of al-Farrāʾ's disciple, in his turn also later wrote a work on proverbial sayings with the same title; — 9. *K. al-Nawādir* (*Fihrist*, 67), handed down by Salama and two other disciples of the author (*ibid.*, 88, l. 8; cf. Yāḳūt, xx, 14); note that the Kūfan al-Kisāʾī had himself composed a work on this subject in three versions (*Fihrist*, *loc. cit.*); — 10. *K. Ālāt al-kuttāb* (*Fihrist*, 67); — 11. *K. Mushkil al-lugha* (*Taʾrīkh Baghdād*, xiv, 150; Yāḳūt, xx, 14 and Ibn Khallikān, ii, 229, l. 24, in two editions, the one *major*, the other *minor*); — 12. *K. Yāfiʿ wa-yafaʿa* (?) (Yāḳūt, xx, 14, giving the variant *wa-yāfiʿa*; Ibn Khallikān, ii, 229, l. 31), which comprised 50 f^os^ with the *K. Mulāzim*); — 13. *K. al-Bahāʾ* (so given in Ibn Khallikān, ii, 229; not *al-bahī*, as in *Fihrist*, 67 and in Yāḳūt, xx, 13; the full title in al-Suyūṭī, *Bughya*, 411, is *K. al-Bahāʾ fī mā talḥanu fī-hi 'l-ʿāmma*); written for ʿAbd Allāh b. Ṭāhir (*Fihrist*, *loc. cit.*); repeated with certain additions by Thaʿlab in his *K. al-Faṣīḥ* (Ibn Khallikān, *loc. cit.*). — (*c*) works on the *Ḳurʾān* such as — 14. *K. al-Maṣādir fi 'l-Ḳurʾān* (*Fihrist*, 67); — 15. *K. al-Djamʿ wa'l-tathniya fi 'l-Ḳurʾān* (*ibid.*); — 16. *K. Lughāt al-Ḳurʾān* (*ibid.*, 35, l. 10 and 67); — 17. *K. al-Waḳf wa 'l-ibtidāʾ fi 'l-Ḳurʾān* (*ibid.*, 36, l. 2 and 67); — 18. *K. Ikhtilāf ahl al-Kūfa wa 'l-Baṣra wa 'l-Shaʾm fi 'l-maṣāḥif* (Yāḳūt, xx, 13); — 19. *K. Maʿānī al-Ḳurʾān*, written in about 204/819, whether before or after the *K. al-Ḥudūd* (see above), at the request of ʿUmar b. Bukayr the "logograph" and genealogist in the entourage of the vizier al-Ḥasan b. Sahl (*Fihrist*, 67, l. 5 and 107); the well-known copy belonging to Ibn al-Nadīm consisted of four volumes; the work is in process of being edited (i, Cairo 1374/1955) by Aḥmad Nadjatī and Muḥ. Nadjdjār (for the MSS see Introd., 3-6 and Brockelmann, S I, 173); other Kūfans had written works bearing the same title, among them al-Ruʾāsī, al-Kisāʾī and Ḳuṭrub (see *Fihrist*, 34); in the same way, the Baṣran al-Ḥasan al-Akhfash had written a *K. Maʿānī al-Ḳurʾān* which had served as a model for al-Kisāʾī and al-Farrāʾ (see Zubaydī, 71); a refutation by Ibn Durustawayh mentioned in *Fihrist*, 63, l. 16; an abridgement of it was made by al-Dīnawāri (see Zubaydī, 234). The Cairo ed. reproduces the version of Muḥ. b. al-Djahm al-Simmarī, probably following the "current dictations" of al-Farrāʾ (cf. i/1); in places, however, al-Farrāʾ seems to be quoted textually (i, 21, l. 10 and 351, l. 11).

At present we can really only judge al-Farrāʾ by the published part of the *K. Maʿānī al-Ḳurʾān*. The work is highly disappointing and without any general theme, being confined for the most part to argumentation on casual syntax; if here and there certain interpretations of a Muʿtazilī character are to be observed (as in i, 353: *nūr-īmān*) or lexicographical remarks which are not devoid of subtlety (i, 385 on *fataḥa* "to judge"), on the other hand the comments on the "lectures" are curious rather than convincing (i, 455). Bearing in mind that this work has not come down to us in the form which the master gave to it, we reach the conclusion that al-Farrā' mainly owes his importance to the influence which he exerted over his pupils, either through writings received from him or through his personal authority. In general his followers have, without exception, been distinguished by the same grammatical anomalism, of which so many instances are to be found in the *K. Maʿānī al-Ḳur'ān*, based upon respect for usage particularly when aberrant (see the discussions on certain "readings", *op. cit.*, i, 353, 355, 357-8, 363, 375, 460).

Bibliography: *Fihrist*, 30, 34 ff., 36, 41, 63, 66-7, 70, 71, 74, 75, 88, 107; *Ta'rīkh Baghdād*, xiv, 149-55; al-Anbārī, *Nuzha*, 65 ff., 126-37, ed. Samarra'ī (Baghdād 1959), 34, 65-8 (repeating the previous work without acknowledgement); Yāḳūt, *Udabā'*, ii, 276-8 = ed. Rifāʿī, Cairo 1936 onwards, xx, 9-14; Ibn al-ʿImād al-Iṣfahānī, *Shadharāt al-dhahab*, ii, 19 ff. and Ibn Khallikān, *Wafayāt*, Cairo 1310, ii, 228-30 (all three going back to or summarizing the *Ta'rīkh Baghdād*); Suyūṭī, *Bughya*, 411 (probably summarizes Yāḳūt or Ibn Khallikān); Abu 'l-Ṭayyib al-Lughawī, *Marātib al-naḥwiyyīn*, ed. Muḥ. Ibrāhīm, Cairo 1375/1955, 88 and *passim*; Zubaydī, *Tabaḳāt al-naḥwiyyīn*, 69 ff., 143-6, *passim*; Samʿānī, *Ansāb*, f° 420*a*; Suyūṭī, *Muzhir*, Cairo 1942, i, 19 quotations or mentions, ii, 33 quotations or mentions, particularly p. 410. Articles or studies by Aḥmad Amīn, *Duḥā 'l-Islām*, ii, 307-8 (biographical synthesis); Makhzūmī, *Madrasat al-Kūfa*, Baghdād 1374/1955, 99 ff., 144-71 (important); H. Ritter, in *Isl.*, xvii (1928), 249-57; Pretzl, in *Islamica*, vi (1933), 16; H. Fleisch, *Traité de philologie arabe*, Beirut 1961, 13-5, 30, 48 and index; Brockelmann, I, 46 and S I, 178.

(R. BLACHÈRE)

FARRUKHĀBĀD, name of a town and district in the Uttar Pradesh state of India; situated between the Ganges and the Yamuna (Djamnā) between 26° 46′ and 27° 43′ N. and 78° 8′ and 80° 1′ E., with an area of 1,685 sq. miles. Before the establishment of Pakistan the Muslims were in a majority but many of them later migrated to Pakistan.

While the district can boast of an ancient past, the town itself is of comparatively recent growth, having been founded in 1126/1714 by Muḥammad Khān Bangash (b. *c.* 1076/1665), an Afghan military adventurer belonging to Ma'ū-Rashīdābād (now a mere name), a village near Ḳā'imgandj, where his father ʿAyn Khān was employed as a trooper by one ʿAyn Khān Sarwānī. A dashing soldier, Muḥammad Khān had collected about him a band of Afghan mercenaries. When Farrukh-Siyar [*q.v.*] contested the title to the throne of Dihlī, he joined him and helped him to win the throne by providing a force of 12,000 men on the battle-field of Samūgaṛh (1124/1713), nine miles east of Āgra [*q.v.*]. Soon afterwards Ḳāsim Khān Bangash, father-in-law of Muḥammad Khān, was killed in a clash with the local Rādjpūts, and the king, as a token of gratitude, granted his daughter (Muḥammad Khān's wife) five *maḥālls* by way of blood-money. He also ordered the building of a town, named after him, in memory of the slain Bangash chieftain. Thus was founded the town of Farrukhābād, which soon grew in prosperity: and an Imperial mint was established there at which coins (mostly silver rupees) continued to be minted even for the later Mughal emperors. The coins of ʿĀlamgīr II, Shāh Djahān III and Shāh ʿĀlam II also carry the second name of the town—Aḥmadnagar—derived from Nawwāb Aḥmad Khān, younger son of Muḥammad Khān, who had defeated the forces of Ṣafdar-Djang, the Nawwāb-Wazīr of Awadh, in 1163/1750 and recovered from him his lost patrimony, Farrukhābād, which had been captured by the Awadh forces in 1161/1748. This second name appears for the first time on coins minted at Farrukhābād in 1170/1756. Even after the British occupation of the town in 1191/1777 the Farrukhābād mint continued to function for the East India Company, who used it up to 1835, minting silver rupees in the name of Shāh ʿĀlam II, although he had died years earlier in 1221/1806. These rupees bore the legend (*sikka*) of Shāh ʿĀlam II in Persian and were known as the *Farrukhabadi Sicca* rupee.

The earliest account of the district is that of the Chinese traveller Hiuen Tsiang, who mentions some of its ancient sites including that of Sankīsā. The historic Kanawdj, capital of the empire of Harsha Vardhana in the 7th century A.D., which was plundered and sacked by Maḥmūd of Ghazna in 409/1018, captured by the Ghūrī Sulṭān Shihāb al-Dīn Muḥammad b. Sām in 580/1193, and gave shelter to the fugitive Delhi monarch Maḥmūd Tughluḳ in 805/1402, is also situated in this district. However, the real history of Farrukhābād begins with its foundation early in the 12th/18th century by the first of the Bangash Nawwābs, Muḥammad Khān Karlānī. In addition to being the chief (*ra'īs*) of Farrukhābād and several other *parganas* granted to him by Farrukh-Siyar, Muḥammad Khān was also the governor of the province of Allāhābād for a time and later of that of Mālwa. On his death in 1156/1743 he was succeeded by his eldest son Ḳā'im Khān, who as a result of the machinations of Ṣafdar-Djang of Awadh, the old enemy of his house, got embroiled with the Rohillas and consequently lost his life in a clash with them in 1161/1748-9 near Badā'ūn. After his death Farrukhābād was annexed to the kingdom of Awadh and ceased to exist as an independent territory. However, the very next year Aḥmad Khān, younger brother of Ḳā'im Khān, defeated and slew the Awadh governor and recovered his lost patrimony. Ṣafdar-Djang appealed for help to the Marāṭhas, who besieged Aḥmad Khān in the fort of Fatḥgaṛh near Farrukhābād, and successfully beat off his confederates, the Rohillas. Aḥmad Khān suffered a virtual defeat, escaped to the Himalayan jungles and was allowed to return only on ceding a large portion of his territory. He bided his time, however, and by rendering good service to the invaders when Aḥmad Shāh Durrānī fought the Marāṭhas in 1175/1761 on the battle-field of Pānīpat, was able to regain, through Imperial favour, much of his lost possessions. The fortunes of Farrukhābād, however, still hung in the balance and in 1185/1771 the Marāṭhas again made good their loss. Before the dispossessed ailing Nawwāb (Aḥmad Khān) could do anything he died. At this time the state virtually became a vassal of the Awadh *durbār*. In 1191/1777, in response to an appeal by the ruler of Awadh, with whom the Marāṭhas had fallen out, British troops were stationed at Fatḥgaṛh (3 miles from Farrukhābād) to guard against Marāṭha inroads, and in 1194/1780 a British Resident was posted there. In 1802, Imdād Ḥusayn Khān Nāṣir Djang (1796-1813), the fifth Nawwāb of Farrukhhābād, virtually ceded the territory to the British, although he continued to be recognised as a "native prince". His grandson Tadjammul Ḥusayn Khān Ẓafar Djang was addicted to a life of luxury and ease; the Persian-Urdu poet Mīrzā Ghālib makes a very delightful reference to it in one of his Urdu *ghazals*. The last of the line, Tafaḍḍul Ḥusayn Khān, who had succeeded to the title in December 1846, considering the Mutiny an opportune moment to proclaim independence, sided with the mutinous Bengal Army with his 30,000 troops and recovered Farrukhābād, which he held till January 1858. During these seven months the Nawwāb enjoyed the active support of the great rebel leader Bakht Khān [*q.v.*] of the Bareilly Brigade and the Mughal fugitive prince Fīrūz Shāh. After the disturbances had been quelled, the Nawwāb was secured, his territory confiscated and for his complicity in the Mutiny he was exiled to Mecca in 1859.

There are numerous sites of historical importance in the district, but they all belong to the pre-Muslim era. The tombs of the Nawwābs to the west of the town are the only buildings of note of the later Muslim period. These are, however, in a sad state of disrepair and neglect. The tomb of Muḥammad Khān was used as late as 1940 as a godown for storing tobacco (cf. *al-ʿIlm* (Urdū quarterly), Karachi, xii/2 (Jan.-March 1963), 12-3). For a description of the city see *JASB*, xlvii (1878), 276-80.

Bibliography: (Muftī) S. Muḥ. Walī Allāh Farrukhhābādī, *Taʾrīkh-i Farrukhābād* (MS), Subḥān Allāh Collection, Muslim University Aligarh; Mīr Ḥusām al-Dīn Gawāliyārī, *Muḥammad Khānī*, (MS in Persian), I.O. 3896; Elliot and Dowson, *History of India* . . ., viii, 44; *Imperial Gazetteer of India*, Oxford 1908, xii, 62-73; W. Irvine, *Later Mughals*, Calcutta 1922, index s.v. Muḥammad Khān Bangash; idem, *The Bangash Nawábs of Farrukhábád*, *JASB*, xlvii (1878), 259-383, xlviii (1879), 49-170; H. N. Wright, *Catalogue, coins of the Indian Museum*, Oxford 1908, iii/xlvi; W. Crooke, *N.W. Provinces of India*, London 1897, 116, 722; S. Lane-Poole, *Catalogue of Moghul coins in the British Museum*; Storey, i, 693-4; Muḥammad ʿAlī Khān Anṣārī, *Taʾrīkh-i Muẓaffarī, sub anno* 1156 A.H. (biography of Muḥammad Khān); Ghulām Ḥusayn Khān Ṭabāṭabāʾī, *Siyar al-mutaʾakhkhirīn*, Lucknow 1314/1897, 422, 433, 437-9, 443, 451, 456.

(A. S. Bazmee Ansari)

FARRUKHĀN Gīlān-shāh, *ispahbad* of Ṭabaristān, known as the Great (*buzurg*) and the Virtuous (*dhu 'l-manāḳib*), son of Dābūya, conquered Māzandarān and restored peace to the frontiers. When defeated by the Daylamīs in their revolt, he fled to Āmul and entrenched himself in the castle of Fīrūzābād; he saved himself by the ruse of making his besiegers believe that he had enormous stocks of bread. He gave asylum to the Khāridjīs when they were being pursued by al-Ḥadjdjādj, but fought against them and put their chiefs to death on the approach of an army commanded by Ṣufyān b. Abi 'l-Abrad al-Kalbī. Yazīd b. al-Muhallab, governor of Khurāsān under Sulaymān b. ʿAbd al-Malik, tried in vain to conquer the country and could count himself fortunate to be able to withdraw in return for a sum of money, as compensation for the depredations that had been committed. Farrukhān died a year or two later, after reigning for seventy years. He was the maternal grandfather of al-Manṣūr, the son of the caliph al-Mahdī. His capital was Sārī, which he had rebuilt and embellished. His son Dādh-Mihr succeeded him.

Bibliography: Ibn Isfandiyār, *History of Ṭabaristān* (tr. Browne), 99 ff.; Ẓahīr al-Dīn, *Taʾrīkh Ṭabaristān*, ed. Dorn, 45 ff.; J. L. Rabino di Borgomale, *Māzanderān and Astarābād*, 1928, index. See also ispahbad and māzandarān.

(Cl. Huart)

FARRUKHĪ Sīstānī, Abu 'l-Ḥasan ʿAlī b. Djūlūgh, the celebrated Iranian poet, a native of the town of Sīstān (cf. Yāḳūt, s.v.; Ḳazwīnī, *Nuzhat*, s.v.), as he says in a hemistich: "I place (other towns) after Sīstān, because it is my (native) town". The *takhalluṣ* Farrukhī unites the ideas of happiness and physical beauty. His father, Djūlūgh (according to ʿAwfī and Dawlatshāh) or Kūlūgh (according to Adhar and Hidāyat) was in the service of the governor of the province of Sīstān. According to Niẓāmī-i ʿArūḍī, who gives the most reliable information, Farrukhī very soon revealed his talents for poetry and music; being in the service of a *dihḳān* [*q.v.*] and wishing to marry, he asked for an increase in salary which was refused; Niẓāmī relates in detail how two of his most beautiful poems (*Dīwān*, 177 and 331) which he recited in the presence of the *amīr* governor of Ṣāghāniyān (Barthold, *Turkestan*, index s.v.) won him the favour of that prince, Fakhr al-Dawla Abu 'l-Muẓaffar, the last of his line (cf. Niẓāmī-i ʿArūḍi, *Čahār maḳāla*, trans. E. G. Browne, 122-3; ed. Muʿīn, Tehrān, 178-88), and then after 377/987-8, the date of his predecessor's tragic death, he took the place of the poet Daḳīḳī, as he states at the end of the poem (181). In 389/999 Maḥmūd, Abu 'l-Muẓaffar's suzerain, ascended the throne of Ghazna; some time later, Farrukhī became one of the poets attached to his court; singing his poems to his own accompaniment on the lute (*rūd*), he lived in Ghazna for the rest of his life, loaded with honours by sultan Maḥmūd, his brothers and the sultan's first two successors, whose praises he celebrated without fulsomeness, mentioning their bounty in several of his *ḳaṣīdas*; he also wrote poems in honour of leading court dignitaries. On several occasions he accompanied the sultan on his expeditions against India (witness these lines: "Three times was I with you on the immense sea . . .", "the trials and fatigues of the journey from Kanawdj have broken me"). The collected edition of his poems (*dīwān*) contains more than 9,500 lines of verse; while the treatise on rhetoric *Tardjumān al-balāgha*, often attributed to him, is in reality the work of Muḥammad b. ʿUmar al-Radūyānī (end of 5th/11th and beginning of 6th/12th centuries; ed. Ahmed Ateş, Istanbul 1949—important introduction). He died probably in 429/1037-8, while still young, according to the lines of his contemporary Labībī (quoted by Radūyānī): "If Farrukhī died, why did not ʿUnṣurī die? The old man lingered on; the young man went so soon" (*Tardjumān*, 32). His *ḳaṣīdas*, which are panegyrics, are characterized by the ease and vigour of their style; uncomplicated ideas and sentiments are expressed in sober, clear and fluent language which gives his poetry a particular charm. According to Rashīd-i Waṭwāṭ (*Ḥadāʾiḳ al-siḥr*), his talent is reminiscent of that of the Arab poet Abū Firās. His shorter poems (a small number only: *ḳiṭʿa*, *ghazal*, *rubāʿī*) are remarkable for their freshness and spontaneity of feeling, and for the occasionally ironical and pungent subtlety of thought which sometimes transforms a *ḳiṭʿa* into an excellent epigram; in short, the delicacy he shows in the *ghazal* is just as great as the rhetorical force in the *ḳaṣīda*. His mastery was universally acclaimed, and numerous poets imitated his manner.

Bibliography: *Dīwān*, ed. ʿAli ʿAbd al-

Rasūlī, Tehrān 1331/1953; Niẓāmī-i ʿArūḍī, *Čahār maḳāla*, tr. E. G. Browne and ed. Muʿīn (index); Muḥammad ʿAwfī, *Tadhkirat al-shuʿarāʾ*, ed. Browne, ii, 47; Djāmī, *Bahāristān*, trans. H. Massé, 168 (short notice and *ḳiṭʿa*, the text of which is in *Dīwān*, 435); Dawlat-Shāh, *Tadhkirat al-shuʿarāʾ*, ed. Browne,55;. Riḍā Ḳulī Khān, *Madjmaʿ al-fuṣaḥāʾ*, i, 439 ff.; Ṣafā (Dhabīh Allāh), *Taʾrīkh-i adabiyāt dar Īrān*, i, 534 ff.; H. Massé, *Anthologie persane*, 38 ff.; *IA* (art. Ferruhi, by H. Ritter).

(Cl. Huart-[H. Massé])

FARRUKH-SIYAR, Abu 'l-Muẓaffar Muḥammad Muʿīn al-Dīn, the second son of Muḥammad ʿAẓīm (ʿAẓīm al-Shān), the third son of Bahādur Shāh [*q.v.*], reigned as Mughal Emperor from 13 Dhu 'l-Ḥidjdja 1124/10 January 1713 to 7 Rabīʿ II 1131/27 February 1719. Born at Awrangābād in the Deccan, apparently in 1094/1683, in his tenth year he accompanied his father to Āgra, and in 1108/1697 to Bengal, when that province was added to his charge. In 1119/1707, when ʿAẓīm al-Shān was summoned to the court from Bengal by Awrangzīb, Farrukh-Siyar was nominated his father's deputy there, which post he held till his recall by ʿAẓīm al-Shān in 1123/1711. However, during this period he exercised no real power, the affairs of the province being dominated by the *dīwān*, Murshid Ḳulī Khān [*q.v.*].

When Bahādur Shāh died at Lahore on 19 Muḥarram 1124/27 February 1712, Farrukh-Siyar was at Paṭna, having tarried there since the previous rainy season. Following the defeat and death of his father in the contest at Lahore, Farrukh-Siyar proclaimed himself king at Paṭna on 29 Ṣafar 1124/6 March 1712 (the official beginning of the reign), having won over to his side the deputy-governor, Sayyid Ḥusayn ʿAlī Khān Bārha [*q.v.*], with whom he had had many differences earlier. Farrukh-Siyar now marched on Delhi, being joined on the way by the elder Sayyid brother, ʿAbd Allāh Khān, who was the deputy-governor of *ṣūba* Ilāhābād, and by many nobles from the eastern parts. He defeated Djahāndār Shāh [*q.v.*] on 13 Dhu 'l-Ḥidjdja 1124/10 January 1713 after a hard-fought battle at Sāmūgaṛh near Āgra. Farrukh-Siyar's part in the victory was, however, slight, the chief credit undoubtedly belonging to the two Sayyid brothers, who were aided by division and demoralisation in Djahāndār Shāh's camp. ʿAbd Allāh Khān was now appointed the *wazīr*, and Ḥusayn ʿAlī the chief *bakhshī*. Djahāndār Shāh and his *wazīr*, Dhu 'l-Fiḳār Khān were executed by Farrukh-Siyar's order, and many others suffered confiscation of property and imprisonment.

The internal history of Farrukh-Siyar's reign consists of a series of contests between Farrukh-Siyar and his two leading ministers, the Sayyid brothers. The Sayyid brothers were clearly determined not to relinquish voluntarily their offices, which they considered theirs by right, and to dominate the affairs of the state as far as possible. Their claims were resented by the youthful monarch, and even more by his personal favourites who had been accorded important posts at the court. The Sayyids were also accused, not without some justification, of being negligent in matters of administration and of leaving it in the hands of corrupt underlings. Farrukh-Siyar and his favourites gave little proof of capacity to rule, and, moreover, they lacked the courage and resources to challenge the Sayyids openly, and dared not apply to any of the old nobles for fear of exchanging one set of masters for a worse. Farrukh-Siyar, therefore, had recourse to hatching plots against his ministers, and inciting the nobles and elements outside the court against them. As a result, the court became divided into two opposing factions, the administration suffered, and the prestige of the central government was undermined. However, it does not seem correct to identify the court factions as "Mughals" and "Hindustānīs", with the Sayyids acting as the leaders of the latter. A close study shows that the factions were not based on any religious or ethnic groups in the Mughal nobility, personal and family attachments and considerations being the main factor. Taking advantage of dissatisfaction at Farrukh-Siyar's patronage of unworthy favourites, the Sayyids gradually succeeded in winning over to their side or in neutralizing most of the important nobles—Radja Djay Singh Kaččwāha of Āmber remaining a notable exception. Matters rapidly came to a head. In February 1719, Ḥusayn ʿAlī, who had assumed personal charge of the Deccan in May 1715, re-entered Delhi at the head of a large army, which included a force of 15,000 Marāthā horsemen under the command of the Peshwa, Bālādjī Wishwanāth. After a proffered compromise had been rejected by Farrukh-Siyar, he was deposed and blinded on 9 Rabīʿ II 1131/28 February 1719, and a new prince, Rafīʿ al-Dardjāt, was proclaimed. Soon afterwards, in the night of 9 Djumādā II 1131/27-28 April 1719, Farrukh-Siyar was strangled.

The chief importance of Farrukh-Siyar's reign lies in a clear breach with Awrangzīb's policies in a number of spheres. The *djizya* was abolished even while Farrukh-Siyar was in Bihār. After his victory, an effort was made to conciliate the leading Rādjpūt Rādjahs by granting them high *manṣab*s and appointing them to important posts. The marriage of Farrukh-Siyar to the daughter of Mahārādja Adjīt Singh of Djodhpur, which was celebrated with great pomp and ceremony in December 1715, was intended as a symbol of the reconciliation. Under the stress of the factional struggle at the court, the Sayyids also befriended the Djaṭ Rādja, Čūrāman, acquiescing in his usurpation of many areas in the neighbourhood of Āgra, and made far-reaching concessions to the Marāthās, recognising Rādja Shāhū's right to levy *cauth* and *sardeshmukhī*—contributions amounting to 35% of the revenue, in the six *ṣūba*s of the Deccan. Farrukh-Siyar actively opposed the concessions to the Djāṭs and the Marāthās. He also sought, belatedly, to rally the othodox elements to his side by reviving *djizya* in 1129/1717. The impost was again abolished by the Sayyids after his deposition.

Another development, which marked an important phase in the growth of the English East India Company, was the grant to it in 1129/1717 of *farmān*s securing the right to carry on trade free of duties in Bengal, Bihār and Orissa, and at Sūrat and Madras, besides sundry other privileges. There is, however, little justification for the view that these grants were made by Farrukh-Siyar out of gratitude to the English surgeon, Dr. William Hamilton, who had successfully treated him. Dr. Hamilton's services were rewarded by the grant of a robe, a horse, five thousand rupees and other costly gifts. But it was not within the power of Farrukh-Siyar to make grants of the nature desired by the English without the agreement of ʿAbd Allāh Khān, the *wazīr*, whose domination over the affairs of the state was almost complete at this time. The English realized this only when two successive applications made by them through the King's favourite, Khān-i-Dawrān, proved fruitless. Finally, they approached ʿAbd Allāh Khān, and he sanctioned their petition, over-ruling the objections advanced by the officials of the revenue ministry (*Early annals of the English in Bengal*, ed. C. R. Wilson, ii/1, 235, ii/2, p. xxiv-xxvii, 48-173). ʿAbd Allāh K͟hān accepted no personal gratification, and his motives in approving the grants can only be guessed at.

Though Farruk͟h-Siyar possessed none of the qualities of greatness, his deposition and death made him a martyr in popular eyes, and contributed to the subsequent downfall of the Sayyid brothers. He was apparently survived by only one daughter who married the emperor Muḥammad S͟hāh [*q.v.*] in 1131/1720-1.

Bibliography: Documents as well as contemporary and secondary works for the reign of Farruk͟h-Siyar are very numerous. For details, see *Later Mughals*, by W. Irvine, ed. J. Sarkar, Calcutta and London 1921; Satish Chandra, *Parties and politics at the Mughal court, 1707-1740*, Aligarh 1959; from detailed personal enquiries I have learnt that no ms. of the type described in the *Oriental College Magazine*, ii/4 (Aug. 1926), p. 58, no. 70, and referred to by Storey (sec. II, no. 767) exists in the Punjab Univ. Lib. See also M. Muʾmin b. Muḥammad Ḳāsim al-D̲jazāʾirī al-S͟hīrāzī, *K͟hizānat al-k͟hayāl*, J.R. Lib., ff. 182a-197a (summarized by A. Mingana, in *Bull. J.R.Lib.*, viii (1924), 150-65); *Miḥakk al-sulūk wa miṣkat al-nafūṣ*, I.O. no. 1012, ff. 520a-542b, 647-8; Iʿtimād K͟hān, *Mirʾāt al-ḥaḳāʾiḳ*, Bod. Lib., Fraser no. 124, ff. 129a-148b (contents summarized by R. Sinh, in *Procs. IHRC*, xvii (1941) 356-62); *Early annals of the English in Bengal*, ed. C. R. Wilson, 3 vols., London 1895-1917; *Home Misc. Series*, lxix; Satish Chandra, *Jizyah in the post-Aurangzib period*, in *Proc. Ind. Hist. Cong.*, 1946, 320-6; idem, *Early relations of Farrukh Siyar and the Saiyid brothers*, in *Med. Ind. Quart.*, Aligarh 1957, 135-46; B. N. Reu, *Letter of Maharaja Ajit Singh relating to the death of Farrukh Siyar*, in *Proc. 9th A.I. Or. Conf.*, 1937, 839-42; A. G. Pawar, *Some documents bearing on imperial Mughal grants to Raja Shahu*, in *Procs. IHRC*, xvii (1941), 204-15; S. H. Askari, *Bihar in the first quarter of the 18th century*, in *Proc. Ind. Hist. Cong.*, 1941, 394-405; Balkrishna, *The Magna Carta and after*, in *Procs. IHRC*, vii (1925), 79-87. For works dealing with the revenue and administrative history of the period, see N. A. Siddiqi, *Mughal land revenue system in Northern India in the first half of the eighteenth century*, (unpublished thesis, Aligarh University).

(SATISH CHANDRA)

FĀRS, the arabicized form of Pārs, which itself was derived from Parsa, the Persis of the Greeks. The province of Fārs, which has now become the seventh *Ustān*, extends from long. 50° to 55° E. (Greenwich) and from lat. 27° to 31° 45′ N. Its greatest length, from Linga in the south to Yazdik͟hʷāst in the north, is 680 km. while its maximum breadth, from Bandar Dilam in the west to Abādeh in the east is 520 km. The total area of the province, including the islands off the coast, is approximately 200,000 sq. km. In 1951 the estimated population was 1,290,000 (Razmārā and Nawtās͟h, *Farhang-i D̲jughrāfiyā-yi Īrān*, vii, 120). Fārs is bounded on the north-west by the sixth *Ustān* (K͟hūzistān), on the north-east by the tenth *Ustān* (Iṣfahān, formerly known successively as al-D̲jibāl [*q.v.*] and ʿIrāḳ ʿAd̲jamī), on the east by the eighth *Ustān* (Kirmān) and on the west and south-west by the Persian Gulf. The province is divided into 8 *s͟hahristāns* (districts), namely, S͟hīrāz [*q.v.*], Būs͟hahr [*q.v.*], Lār, Fasā [*q.v.*], Kāzarūn, D̲jahram, Fīrūzābād [*q.v.*] and Abādah. Much of the province is mountainous, and there are some difficult passes, particularly on the route connecting S͟hīrāz with Būs͟hahr. Fārs is watered by a number of rivers most of which flow into the Persian Gulf; some, such as the Kurr, flow into lakes on the further side of the watershed.

In the 7th century B. C., Teispes, the son of Achaemenes and king of Anshan, threw off the yoke of the Medes and added Parsa to his realm. In the oldest Achaemenian tablet known, in cuneiform Old Persian, Ariaramnes states: 'This land of the Persians which I possess, provided with good horses and good men, it is the great god Ahuramazda who has given it to me. I am lord of this land' (R. Ghirshman, *Iran*, 1954, 120). It was from Pārs, Herodotus's 'scant and rugged land', that Cyrus the Great (559-530 B.C.) started on his phenomenal career of conquest which culminated in the establishment of the greatest empire of the ancient world. Two centuries later, Pārs, together with the rest of Persia, was overrun by Alexander the Great. Little is known of the province in Seleucid and Parthian times save that it was ruled by a series of *frataraka*s or *fratadara*s (governors). Ardas͟hīr, the son of Pāpak and grandson of Sāsān, was, like Cyrus the Great, a native of Pārs of which he became king in 228 A.D. His grandfather and father had both been tenders of the sacred fire in the temple of Anāhit (Venus) at Iṣtak͟hr (A. Christensen, *L'Iran sous les Sassanides*², Copenhagen 1944, 86). In 224 A.D. Ardas͟hīr revolted, killed Artavan, the last Arsacid, in battle, and thus threw off the Parthian yoke. In this way the Sasanian dynasty and empire were founded. Not without reason did E. C. Browne (ii, 92) describe Pārs as the 'cradle of Persian greatness'.

In Sāsānian times Pārs was divided into 5 districts, namely, Ardas͟hīr-K͟hurra, S͟hāpūr-K͟hurra, Arrad̲jān, Iṣtak͟hr and Dārābgird.

It was during the caliphate of ʿUmar that the Muslim Arabs made their first attempt to conquer Pārs (or Fārs, as they called it), when al-ʿAlāʾ b. al-Ḥaḍramī, the governor of Baḥrayn, sent ʿArfad̲ja b. Hart͟hama al-Bārikī to attack it from the sea, but the enterprise proved unsuccessful. When ʿUt͟hmān b. Abi 'l-ʿĀṣ succeeded ʿAlāʾ b. al-Ḥaḍramī as governor of Baḥrayn, he sent his brother al-Ḥakam to effect the conquest of the province. Al-Ḥakam, after seizing some islands off the coast, landed on the mainland, but was unable to penetrate far into the interior. During the caliphate of ʿUt͟hmān [*q.v.*] the Arabs made a further attempt to overrun Fārs. At Tawwad̲j (or Tawwaz), near Rīs͟hahr, ʿUt͟hmān b. Abi 'l-Aṣ and his men fought a desperate battle with the Sāsānian forces under the command of the *marzbān* S͟hahrak; victory at length went to the Arabs after S͟hahrak and many of his men had fallen (Balād͟hurī, 386). Simultaneously, another Arab army, under the command of Abū Mūsā al-As͟hʿari, set out from Baṣra and invaded Fārs from the west. The two generals, having joined forces, penetrated deeply into Fārs, capturing S͟hīrāz; in the north the town of Sīnīz (the ruins of which are near Ganāfa (D̲jannāba)) also fell into their hands. ʿUt͟hmān then detached his forces and captured Dārābgird (which then became arabicized as Dārābd̲jird), Pasā (Fasā [*q.v.*]) and S͟hāpūr (Sābūr). In 28/648-9 the army under ʿAbd Allāh b. ʿĀmir besieged and captured the city of Iṣtak͟hr; he then marched southwards and took Fīrūzābād [*q.v.*], thus completing the subjugation of Fārs. The land-tax (*k͟harād̲j*) was fixed first at 33 million *dirhams*; later, in the reign of al-Mutawakkil, it was raised to 35 million. The poll-tax (*dj̲izya*) brought in a revenue of 18 million *dirhams*.

Under the Caliphate Fārs was appreciably larger than it had been before, as the district of Iṣṭak̲h̲r was extended north-eastwards to include Yazd and other towns in proximity to the great desert; moreover, in the north the boundary lay between Ḳumīsha and Iṣfahān. After the Mongol conquest, however, these additional territories were detached (Le Strange, 248, 249, 275).

With the decline in the temporal authority of the Caliphate in the 3rd/9th century, Fārs came under the sway of Yaʿḳūb b. Layt̲h̲, the founder of the Ṣaffārid dynasty. He made S̲h̲īrāz his capital city, where his brother ʿAmr b. Layt̲h̲ built the great cathedral mosque on the site of which the present Masdj̲id-i Dj̲āmiʿ stands. The Buwayhids later obtained possession of Fārs, one of whom, ʿAḍud al-Dawla, extended his power over most of Persia and part of Mesopotamia; one of his notable achievements was the construction of the great barrage over the river Kurr which was called the Band-i Amīr or the Band-i ʿAḍudī after him. The Buwayhids were succeeded as rulers of Fārs by the Saldj̲ūḳs [*q.v.*]; when the power of the latter was on the wane, Sunḳur, the first of the Salg̲h̲urid Atabegs, gained possession of the province in 543/1148-9 and refused to acknowledge the suzerainty of the Saldj̲ūḳs. The Salg̲h̲urid Atabegs maintained themselves as rulers of Fārs until that remarkable woman Ābis̲h̲ K̲h̲ātūn, after ruling for a year, married Mangū Tīmūr, a son of the Il-K̲h̲ān Hūlāgū K̲h̲ān, in 667/1268 (Ḥamd Allāh Mustawfī, *Taʾrīk̲h̲-i Guzīda*, 509); thenceforward her authority was only nominal.

Mubāriz al-Dīn Muḥammad, the founder of the Muẓaffarid dynasty, added Fārs to his dominions in 754/1353. The Muẓaffarids ruled over Fārs until Mubāriz al-Dīn's grandson S̲h̲āh Manṣūr was defeated and killed outside S̲h̲īrāz in a fierce encounter with the forces of Tīmūr in 795/1393.

Shah Ismāʿīl I, the first of the Ṣafawid line of rulers, who was enthroned at Tabrīz in Muḥarram 907/July 1501, established his authority in Fārs two years later. Under him and his successors both Fārs and its capital S̲h̲īrāz prospered. During the reign of S̲h̲āh ʿAbbās I [*q.v.*] Imām Ḳulī K̲h̲ān, the great Governor-General of Fārs, maintained almost regal state in S̲h̲īrāz where, in March 1628, he sumptuously entertained the English envoy, Sir Dodmore Cotton, and his suite (see Sir Thomas Herbert, *Travels in Persia, 1627-1629*, edited by E. Denison Ross, London 1928, 74-83).

S̲h̲īrāz, in common with many other places in Fārs, suffered severely in the fighting between the Persian forces under Nadr Ḳulī Beg (Ṭahmāsp Ḳulī K̲h̲ān, the future Nādir S̲h̲āh) and the G̲h̲alzay Afg̲h̲āns under As̲h̲raf. This fighting ended with the complete defeat and virtual annihilation of the Afg̲h̲āns in 1730 (see L. Lockhart, *The fall of the Ṣafavi Dynasty and the Afghan occupation of Persia*, Cambridge 1958, 336-9). Fārs suffered again in the disturbances which occurred after the assassination of Nādir S̲h̲āh in 1160/1747, but the accession to power of the beneficent Karīm K̲h̲ān Zand [*q.v.*] who made S̲h̲īrāz his capital, soon resulted in a return of peace and prosperity. After Karīm K̲h̲ān's death in 1193/1779 Fārs suffered once more during the struggle for supremacy between various members of the Zand family and, subsequently, between the gallant Luṭf ʿAlī K̲h̲ān Zand and his relentless foe Ag̲h̲a Muḥammad Khān Ḳādj̲ār.

In more recent times the history of Fārs has been comparatively uneventful except on the following occasions: In 1250/1834, following upon the death of Fatḥ ʿAlī S̲h̲āh, his brother Ḥusayn ʿAlī Mīrzā, the Governor-General of Fārs, had himself enthroned in S̲h̲īrāz, but was soon after defeated and forced to relinquish his claims by his nephew Muḥammad S̲h̲āh (for details of the battle, which was fought near Ḳumīs̲h̲a, see Baron de Bode, *Travels in Luristan and Arabistan*, London 1845, i, 61-2; see also Ḥādj̲dj̲ī Mīrzā Ḥasan 'Fasāʾī', *Fars-Nāma-yi Nāṣirī*, Tehrān 1313/1895-6, 288). Four years later, in consequence of Muḥammad S̲h̲āh's insistence on maintaining the siege of Herāt despite protests by Great Britain, that power occupied the island of K̲h̲arg, 35 miles north-west of Būs̲h̲ahr, and threatened to declare war on Persia. The S̲h̲āh thereupon gave way, and the troops were subsequently withdrawn from K̲h̲arg. On 5 Dj̲umādā I 1260/23 May 1844 Sayyid ʿAlī Muḥammad announced in S̲h̲īrāz that he was the *Bāb* or 'Gateway' (to the divine Truth), a development which led to very serious disturbances not only in Fārs but throughout the country (see BĀB, BĀBĪS). In 1273-4/1856, when the seizure by Persia of Herāt involved her in war with Great Britain, the latter power again occupied K̲h̲arg and then landed a force on the coast of Fārs. This force, after taking Būs̲h̲ahr, advanced some distance inland; the conclusion of peace prevented any further military operations. An interesting event at the present time (1960) is the inauguration of the crude oil loading terminal on K̲h̲arg island, where oil-tankers of even the largest size can berth. The crude oil is brought by a pipe-line 99 miles (160 km.) long from the Gač Sarān oilfield on the mainland; for 23 miles (37 km.) of its length this pipe-line is beneath the waters of the Persian Gulf.

Bibliography: In addition to references in the text: *Ḥudūd al-ʿālam*, 6, 19, 25, 34, 36, 40, 52-55, 65, 66, 74, 80, 83, 123, 125-31, 163, 212; Ibn al-Balk̲h̲ī, *Fārs-nāma*, edited by G. Le Strange and R. A. Nicholson, London 1921, *passim*; Ḥamd Allāh Mustawfī, *Nuzha*, Eng. tr. by Le Strange, London 1919, 111-36; Ḥādj̲dj̲ī Mīrzā Ḥasan 'Fasāʾi', *Fārs-nāma-yi Nāṣirī*, *passim*; F. Spiegel, *Eranische Alterthumskunde*, i, 214; Le Strange, 248-98; Barbier de Meynard, *Dictionnaire géographique de la Perse*, 410-3; G. N. Curzon, *Persia and the Persian Question*, London 1892, ii, 64-236; Sir Arnold Wilson, *The Persian Gulf*, Oxford 1928, 60, 61, 71-5, 85, 86, 94, 96, 172, 175. (L. LOCKHART)

FARSAK̲H̲, Persian measure of distance on a time basis, from the Parthian word **frasak̲h̲*, which came into Armenian as *hrasak̲h̲*, into Syrian as *parsᵉḥā*, to continue in both Arabic and modern Persian as *farsak̲h̲*. Beside this, there is also the modern Persian *farsang*, derived from the Middle Persian *frasang*, the Old Persian **parāt̲h̲anga*, to be found in Herodotus and Xenophon as παρασάγγης. Originally the distance which could be covered on foot in an hour, or 'marching mile', this developed (presumably as early as Sāsānid times) into a standard measure of distance. Herodotus takes the *parasang* to be 30 stadia, though it must be borne in mind that he refers not to the Attic, but to the Babylonian-Persian stadium of 198 m. Thus the Old Persian *parasang* would be a distance of 5.94 km.; this, however, only for the cavalry. The foot-soldiers' *parasang* (or hour's march) was—as Xenophon's data prove—only about 4 km. In Islam, the *farsak̲h̲-i s̲h̲arʿī* was officially fixed at 3 Arab *mīl* ('miles'), each of 1000 *bā*ʿ ('fathoms'), each of 4 canonical ells (cf. *al-dhirā*ʿ *al-sharʿiyya*), each of 49.875 cm., = 5.985 km. Both terms, *farsakh* and *farsang*, continue to be used in Iran today, but *farsakh* is the more usual. It has now been fixed at precisely 6 km.

Bibliography: W. Hinz, *Islamische Masse und Gewichte*, Leiden 1955, 62-3; P. Horn, in *Grund. Iran. Phil.*, i/2, 127; H. S. Nyberg, *Hilfsbuch des Pehlevi*, ii, 73; F. Segl, *Vom Kentrites bis Trapezus*, Erlangen 1925, 12; F. Lehmann-Haupt, in *Gnomon*, 1928, 339-40; H. Roemer, *Shams al-Ḥusn*, Wiesbaden 1956, 126.

(W. Hinz)

FARSH [see ĶĀLĪ].

FĀRSĪ [see ĪRĀN].

AL-**FĀRŪĶ** [see ʿUMAR B. AL-KHAṬṬĀB].

AL-**FĀRŪĶĪ**, ʿABD AL-BĀĶĪ, an ʿIrāķī poet and official, born in Mosul in 1204/1790, who traced back his ancestry to ʿUmar b. al-Khaṭṭāb, whence his *nisba* of al-Fārūķī or al-ʿUmarī. While still very young, he became an assistant of the *wālī* of Mosul and was later appointed governor of the town by Dāwūd Pasha [*q.v.*]; when the Porte decided to restrict the independence which Dāwūd had until then enjoyed in Baghdād, ʿAbd al-Bāķī at first accompanied his uncle Ķāsim Pasha, who failed in his mission, and then ʿAlī Riḍā Pasha who made him his deputy; he remained in office in Baghdād until his death, which took place in 1278/1862.

ʿAbd al-Bāķī composed an *adab* work, *Ahillat al-afkār fī maghānī al-ibtikār* which appears to be lost; a biographical collection, *Nuzhat al-dahr fī tarādjim fuḍalāʾ al-ʿaṣr* (unpublished); a short *dīwān*, religious in character, *al-Bāķiyyāt al-Ṣāliḥāt* which he published in 1270; another *dīwān*, which also includes pieces not written by himself, published in Cairo in 1316 under the title *al-Tiryāķ al-fārūķī min munshaʾāt al-Fārūķī*.

His secular poetry returns to the classical themes of wine, music, etc., but it also contains certain descriptions of nature or curiosities (*e.g.*, the telegraph) and a number of allusions to contemporary political events. ʿAbd al-Bāķī's religious poetry is copious but devoid of originality; in particular it includes panegyrics and elegies of the great figures of Islam (the Prophet, ʿAlī, the Ahl al-Bayt, Ibn ʿArabī, etc.).

Bibliography: Dj. Zaydān, *Tarādjim mashāhīr al-Sharķ*, ii, 193 ff.; L. Cheikho, *La Littérature arabe au XIX siècle*², 1924-6, index; ʿAbbās al-ʿAzzawī, *Taʾrīkh al-ʿIrāķ bayn iḥtilālayn*, v, Baghdād 1955, 139-40 and index (s.v. ʿAbd al-Bāķī al-ʿUmarī); M. M. al-Baṣīr, *Nahḍat al-ʿIrāķ al-adabiyya*, Baghdād 1365/1946, 89-113.

(CH. PELLAT)

AL-**FĀRŪĶĪ**, MULLĀ MAḤMŪD B. MUḤAMMAD B. SHĀH MUḤAMMAD AL-DJAWNPŪRĪ, one of the greatest scholars and logicians of India, was born at Djawnpūr [*q.v.*] in 993/1585. This date is, however, doubtful as the Mullā died in 1062/1652 when he was, according to his family tradition, less than forty years of age (cf. *Mullah* [sic] *Mahmood's Determinism and Freewill* (ed. Ali Mahdi Khan), Allahabad 1934, 19-22). He received his early education from his grandfather and later from Ustādh al-Mulk Muḥammad Afḍal b. Ḥamza al-ʿUthmānī al-Djawnpūrī. A brilliant student, he completed his education at the comparatively early age of 17, specializing in logic and philosophy, and then became a teacher in his home-town. His fame soon spread and even reached the Emperor Shāhdjahān, who summoned him to Āgra and ordered his chief minister Saʿd Allāh Khān ʿAllāmī to receive him with full honours on arrival in the city. His name was subsequently included in the list of the Court *ʿulamāʾ* and he was given the *manṣab* of *sih ṣadī* (commander of three-hundred). He invariably accompanied the emperor on his journeys as a member of his *entourage*. On one Imperial visit to Lahore he was severely reprimanded by Mullā Shāh Mīr Badakhshī, the spiritual guide of Shāhdjahān, for having become too much engrossed in worldly affairs, and advised to give up the service of the emperor. Deeply affected, the Mullā resigned and went back to teach in his home-town. His project for an observatory at Āgra with financial help from the state failed to win the support of the chief minister Āṣaf Khān [*q.v.*] and was consequently turned down by the emperor on the ground that money was urgently required for the Balkh campaigns (1055-8/1645-8), which ultimately proved disastrous. Disappointed, he returned to Djawnpūr and engaged himself in academic activities. In the meantime he was invited to Dacca by Shāh Shudjāʿ, second son of Shāhdjahān and the then governor of Bengal, who read with him books on philosophy and logic. This must have happened before 1052/1642, when Mullā Maḥmūd contracted his *bayʿa* with Niʿmat Allāh b. ʿAṭāʾ Allāh al-Fīrūzpūrī and compiled a tract containing the *obiter dicta* and the esoteric prayers of his *shaykh* (cf. Muḥammad Yaḥyā b. Muḥammad Amīn al-ʿAbbāsī al-Allāhābādī, *Wafayāt al-aʿlām*). A great authority on philosophy and rhetoric, he is rated very high as a scholar. He is said to have never uttered a word which he had to withdraw later or contradicted a statement once solemnly made. Contrary to the views of the majority of Sunnī scholars and writers, Shāh ʿAbd al-ʿAzīz al-Dihlawī [*q.v.*], counts him among the veteran Shīʿī theologians (cf. *Tuḥfa Ithnāʿasharī*, Lucknow 1295/1878, ch. iii, 166). His death in 1062/1652 was deeply mourned by his teacher Ustādh al-Mulk Muḥammad Afḍal, who followed his pupil to the grave within forty days. His tomb outside the town still exists and is well known to the inhabitants.

He is the author of: (i) *Al-Shams al-bāzigha*, his *magnum opus*, a commentary on his own philosophical text entitled *al-Ḥikma al-bāligha* (litho. Delhi 1278/1861, Ludhiana 1280/1863, Lucknow 1288/1871). Unlike other works on philosophy, it follows the pattern '*ķult*ᵘ *aķūl*ᵘ', *i.e.*, 'I said and now I say'. Equally famous glosses on this work are by (a) Mullā Niẓām al-Dīn Sihālī, (b) Ḥamd Allāh Sandīlī, (c) Mullā Ḥasan Lakhnawī, and (d) ʿAbd al-Ḥalīm Anṣārī Farangī = Maḥallī, all being prescribed as final courses of study in religious institutions in India and Pakistan; (ii) *al-Farāʾid fī sharḥ al-Fawāʾid* (ed. Cawnpore 1331/1913), a commentary on ʿAḍud al-Dīn al-Īdjī's *al-Fawāʾid al-Ghiyāthiyya*, a work on rhetoric; (iii) *al-Farāʾid al-Maḥmūdiyya*, his glosses on (ii) above (most probably prepared for Nawwāb Shāʾistah Khān, governor of Bengal, who read them with the author during his stay at Āgra); (iv) *Ḥāshiya ʿala 'l-Ādāb al-Bāķiyya*, a super-commentary on ʿAbd al-Bāķī b. Ghawth al-Islām al-Ṣiddīķī's commentary on Sayyid Sharīf al-Djurdjānī's *al-Risāla al-Sharīfiyya fī ʿilm al-munāẓara* (MS Farangī Maḥall Lib.); (v) *Risāla fī Ithbāt al-hayūlā*, as the name indicates a treatise on *hayūla* (matter), a popular subject with Muslim logicians in India; same as no. (vii) below; (vi) *Risālat Ḥirz al-īmān* (or *Ḥirz al-amānī*) in refutation of *al-Taswiya* by Muḥibb Allāh Allāhābādī; (vii) *Al-Dawḥa al-mayyāda fī taḥķīķ al-ṣūra wa 'l-mādda* (litho. 1308/1890); and (viii) *Risāla Djabr u ikhtiyār* (Determinism and Free-will), ed. with Eng. transl. and notes by ʿAlī Mahdī Khān, Allahabad 1934. A treatise on the kinds of women and a *dīwān* of Persian poems is also attributed to him.

Bibliography: Āzād Bilgrāmī, *Subḥat al-mardjān fī āthār Hindustān*, Bombay 1303 A.H., 53-66; idem, *Maʾāthir al-kirām*, Agra 1910, 202-3; Ṣiddīḳ Ḥasan Ḳannawdjī, *Abdjad al-ʿulūm*, Bhopal 1296/1878, 901-2; Nūr al-Dīn Zaydī Ẓafarābādī, *Tadjallī-yi nūr* (or *Shigraf Bayān*), Djawnpūr 1900, 48; Raḥmān ʿAlī, *Tadhkira-i ʿulamāʾ-i Hind*, Lucknow 1332/1914, 221; M. G. Zubaid Ahmad, *Contribution of India to Arabic literature*, Allahabad 1946, 125 ff.; Faḳīr Muḥammad Lāhorī, *Ḥadāʾiḳ al-Ḥanafiyya*, Lucknow 1308/1891, 412-3; al-Ziriklī, *al-Aʿlām*, viii, 62; ʿAbd al-Ḥayy Lakhnawī, *Nuzhat al-khawāṭir*, Ḥaydarābād (Ind.), 1375/1955, vi, 397-9; Brockelmann, II, 420, S II, 621; Ṣādiḳ Iṣfahānī, *Ṣubḥ-i Ṣādiḳ* (MS), *mudjallad siwum*, *maṭlaʿ* 12; Muḥammad Yaḥyā b. Muḥammad Amīn al-ʿAbbāsī al-Allāhābādī, *Wafayāt al-aʿlām* (MS Dār al-Muṣannifīn, Aʿẓamgaṛh); Muḥ. Ṣāliḥ Kambōh, *ʿAmal-i Ṣāliḥ*, Calcutta 1939, iii, 391. 441; Khayr al-Dīn Muḥ. Djawnpūrī, *Tadhkirat al-ʿulamāʾ*, ed. with Engl. transl. and notes by Muhammad Sana Ullah, Calcutta 1934, 45-8 (Persian text), 51-5 (Eng. transl.).

A. S. BAZMEE ANSARI)

FĀRŪḲIDS, the Fārūḳī dynasty (so-called because of claimed descent from the *khalīfa* ʿUmar al-Fārūḳ) established and ruled the semi-independent Muslim principality of Khāndēsh between the rivers Tāptī and Narbadā for two centuries, until, in 1009/1600-1, Akbar captured most of the surviving members of the Fārūḳid family, forced them to become Mughal pensioners, and converted Khāndēsh into the Mughal *ṣūba* of Dāndēsh. The founder of the dynasty, Malik Rādjā (or Rādjā Aḥmad) was probably a younger son of Khwādja Djahān, *wazīr* to ʿAlāʾ al-Dīn Bahman Shāh the first Bahmanī sultan and his successor Muḥammad I. Becoming *wazīr* in succession to his father, Rādjā Aḥmad was involved (c. 767/1365-6) in a rebellion against Muḥammad I led by the latter's nephew Bahrām Khān Māzandarānī, and fled to Dawlatābād. Thence he made his way to the court of Fīrūz Shāh Tughluḳ of Dihlī, possibly as a member of the embassy from Bahrām Khān which waited on Fīrūz, in an effort to persuade him to intervene, when the latter was engaged in the expedition against Thaṭṭha in the period 767-8/1366-7 (ʿAfīf, *Taʾrīkh-i Fīrūz Shāhī*, Calcutta 1890, 224). (Haig, *The Fārūqī dynasty of Khāndesh* (see *Bibl.*), 114-5, has wrongly placed the Thaṭṭha expedition in 765/1363 and spoken of two embassies from Bahrām Khān to Fīrūz Shāh; the alleged second embassy was in fact from Maʿbar, see ʿAfīf, 261). For services on the hunting field Rādjā Aḥmad was rewarded at his own request with the village of Karwand near Thālnēr by Fīrūz Shāh Tughluḳ. He proceeded there in 772/1370, enlarging his hold locally and increasing the surrounding area under cultivation. (Tradition recorded in the *Āʾīn-i Akbarī* and *Gulzār-i abrār* speaks of an earlier association of the Fārūḳids with the district). Forcing the neighbouring Rāthor Rādjā of Baglāna to submit and raiding Gondwāna, Rādjā Aḥmad acquired resources sufficient to act independently of Dihlī after c. 784/1382. He died in Shaʿbān 801/April 1399. (The above account of the origins of the Fārūḳids has been deduced from Firishta, *Ẓafar al-Wālih* and the *Āʾīn*, sources which are considered to offer different but not wholly contradictory or wholly independent accounts of the same events). The maintenance of the independence of the Fārūḳids depended until Akbar's time upon adroit management of relations with the rulers of the more powerful neighbouring Muslim successor kingdoms to the Dihlī sultanate, namely Mālwa, Gudjarāt, the Bahmanī sultanate and its contiguous heir, Aḥmadnagar. These rulers did not recognize the Fārūḳids as equals; the Gudjarāt, Bahmanī and Aḥmadnagar sources usually refer to the ruler of Asīr and Burhānpur [*q.v.*] as *ḥākim* or *wālī*. Rādjā Aḥmad married a daughter to Hūshang, son of the founder of the Mālwa sultanate, Dilāwar Khān, but Rādjā Aḥmad's successor in eastern Khāndēsh, Naṣīr Khān, was forced to abandon this alliance for the overlordship of Gudjarāt after Hūshang Shāh of Mālwa had proved (820/1417) incapable of protecting him from the Gudjarāt sultan Aḥmad I who had intervened in Khāndēsh to support Naṣīr's brother Ḥasan against the former's attempts to prevent Ḥasan from exercising any authority at Thālnēr. Unreconciled, however, to the supremacy of Gudjarāt, in 833/1429 Naṣīr concluded a marriage alliance between his daughter and ʿAlāʾ al-Dīn Aḥmad, son of Aḥmad Shāh Bahmanī, but this move did not save Khāndesh from being overrun in the following year by Gudjarāt troops, replying to an attack by the Bahmanī and Khāndēsh forces on the Gudjarāt border district of Nandurbār. In 839/1435, disillusioned with the connexion with the Bahmanīs, Naṣīr Khān attacked Berār with the approval of Aḥmad Shāh of Gudjarāt but was twice severely defeated by the Bahmanī general Malik al-Tudjdjār, suffering the plunder of his capital Burhānpur before the threatened intervention of Aḥmad Shāh's forces persuaded Malik al-Tudjdjār to withdraw. Naṣīr Khān died in Rabīʿ I 841/August-September 1437. Naṣīr Khān's immediate successors, ʿĀdil Khān (died Dhu 'l-Ḥidjdja 844/April 1441) and Mubārak Khān (died Djumādā II or Radjab 861/May or June 1457) accepted Gudjarāt's overlordship without apparent stir, but ʿĀdil Khān II (died Rabīʿ I 907/September 1501), successful in forays against the *rādjās* of Gondwāna and Djhārkand and against the predatory Kolīs and Bhīls, delayed paying the customary tribute until, in 904/1498, Maḥmūd Bāyḳarā, advancing to the Tāptī, obliged him to make amends. The story, unlikely as it stands, in the *Burhān-i maʾāthir* (220-5) of the intervention at this time of Aḥmadnagar in Khāndēsh in support of a mythical Maḥmūd Shāh Fārūḳī against Maḥmūd Bāyḳarā, is probably a garbled version of efforts by ʿĀdil Khān II to loosen the ties with Gudjarāt, garbled, as Haig (*op. cit.*, 120) suggests, to disguise the discomfiture of Aḥmad Niẓām Shāh.

Following the death of ʿĀdil Khān II, the political life of Khāndēsh was torn by dynastic rivalries which invited the intervention of the stronger neighbouring powers. First, a struggle occurred between Dāwūd Khān, brother of ʿĀdil Khān, who had succeeded to the throne (though not without first having to overcome opposition by some of the *amīrs*), and an unspecified relation, ʿĀlam Khān Fārūḳī, a *protégé* of the ruler of Aḥmadnagar, Aḥmad Niẓām Shāh. Dāwūd successfully sought aid from Mālwa rather than provide Maḥmud Bāyḳarā with further oppurtunity for intervention in Khāndēsh, and the Aḥmadnagar forces were forced to withdraw (910/1504). Then, the death of Dāwūd Khān (Djumādā I 914/August 1508) precipitated a further open clash between Gudjarāt and Aḥmadnagar over Khāndēsh, with Maḥmūd Bāyḳarā supporting another ʿĀlam

Kh̲ān, a descendant of Ḥasan Kh̲ān the brother of Naṣīr Kh̲ān (see above), against the Niẓām Sh̲āh's Fārūḳī client, the previously-named ʿĀlam Kh̲ān. Invading Kh̲āndēsh̲ in Sh̲aʿbān 914/November-December 1508, Maḥmūd captured Thālnēr and Burhānpur from the forces of the Niẓām Sh̲āh and his supporters and in Dh̲u 'l-Ḥid̲j̲d̲j̲a 914/April 1509 installed the Gud̲j̲arāt candidate as ʿĀdil Kh̲ān III of Kh̲āndēsh̲. The latter married the daughter of the later Muẓaffar II of Gud̲j̲arāt. ʿĀdil Kh̲ān III's son Muḥammad I (*regnabat* Ramaḍān 926/August 1520 to Dh̲u 'l-Ḳaʿda 943/April 1537 [following the *Mirʾāt-i Sikandarī*]) remained faithful to Gud̲j̲arāt, acting in concert with his uncle Bahādur Sh̲āh Gud̲j̲arātī [*q.v.*] against Aḥmadnagar in 935-6/1528-9 and 939/1533, and against Māndū and Čitor in 938-9/1532-3. Bahādur Sh̲āh rewarded him by granting him the title of *sh̲āh* and by designating him heir-presumptive to the sultanate of Gud̲j̲arāt. Muḥammad I died, however, before he could consolidate the Fārūḳid claim to succeed Bahādur Sh̲āh in Gud̲j̲arāt.

The reign of Muḥammad I's successor in Kh̲āndēsh̲, Mubārak Sh̲āh II (died D̲j̲umādā II 974/December 1566) witnessed the first encounter of the Fārūḳids with the Mug̲h̲als. In 962/1562, Akbar's general Pīr Muḥammad followed Bāz Bahādur [*q.v.*] into Kh̲āndēsh̲ burning and killing before being defeated by a combination of the forces of Mubārak, Bāz Bahādur and Tufāl Kh̲ān of Berār and drowned in the Narbadā. In 972/1564, Akbar himself marched to Mālwa and compelled Mubārak to accept Mug̲h̲al overlordship and a marriage alliance. At first Mug̲h̲al overlordship did not prove any more restrictive than that of Gud̲j̲arāt and the Fārūḳids remained free to pursue their rivalries with their neighbours, subject to the obligation to give military and other support to the Mug̲h̲als in their enterprises. In 975-6/1568-9 Mīrān Muḥammad II (died 984/1576) invaded Gud̲j̲arāt to take advantage of the dissensions of its *amīrs* under the puppet Muẓaffar III, but after some initial success was obliged to retire rebuffed. In 982/1574 Muḥammad II in collusion with the sultans of Bīd̲j̲āpur and Golkonda attempted to win Berār, newly annexed by Murtaḍā Niẓām Sh̲āh I, but the forces of the Niẓām Sh̲āh overmatched those of the Fārūḳid ruler and the latter was obliged to buy off a siege of Asīr for 900,000 or 1,000,000 *muẓaffarīs*.

From c. 993/1585, however, with Akbar rounding out his empire in the north, Mug̲h̲al pressure to the south began seriously to be felt and in 994/early 1586, Rād̲j̲ā ʿAlī Kh̲ān (or ʿĀdil Sh̲āh IV, killed D̲j̲umādā II 1005/February 1597), the last Fārūḳid with any ability for successful diplomatic manœuvre, was desired to give passage and aid to a Mug̲h̲al army appointed to intervene in Aḥmadnagar. Overtly complaisant, Rād̲j̲ā ʿAlī Kh̲ān covertly engaged the support of the Berār forces against which the Mug̲h̲als wished to move, and Mīrzā ʿAzīz Kōka, Kh̲ān-i Aʿẓam, Mug̲h̲al governor of Mālwa, retired from the Deccan discomfited. In 999/1591, however, Rād̲j̲ā ʿAlī Kh̲ān actively furthered Akbar's policy of aiding Burhān Niẓām Sh̲āh (II) to become ruler of Aḥmadnagar, being mainly responsible for the victory of Rohankhed, D̲j̲umādā II or Rad̲j̲ab 999/April or May, 1591. Rād̲j̲ā ʿAlī Kh̲ān now probably assisted indirect Mug̲h̲al intervention in the Deccan in hope of staving off direct Mug̲h̲al intervention, but the death (Sh̲aʿbān 1003/April 1595) of Burhān Niẓām Sh̲āh II, followed by appeals from one of the Aḥmadnagar factions for Mug̲h̲al aid, precipitated the direct Mug̲h̲al military interference which Rād̲j̲ā ʿAlī had tried to head off. Rād̲j̲ā ʿAlī, bending with good grace before the wind, joined Akbar's forces in the siege of Aḥmadnagar (Rabīʿ II to Rad̲j̲ab 1004/December 1595 to March 1596) which ended in the negotiation of the cession of Berār to Akbar. An uneasy peace was soon broken by disputes over the limits of the ceded area and in D̲j̲umādā II 1005/February 1597 Rād̲j̲ā ʿAlī Kh̲ān, supporting the Mug̲h̲als against the forces of Aḥmadnagar, Bīd̲j̲āpur and Golkonda, was killed at the battle of Āsh̲tī. Unfortunately for friendship between his son and successor Bahādur Sh̲āh and Akbar, Mug̲h̲al troops, in ignorance of his death but from his absence suspecting Rād̲j̲ā ʿAlī Kh̲ān's loyalty, plundered his camp, an action which appears to have embittered Bahādur Sh̲āh's attitude towards the Mug̲h̲als and to have led him into a maladroitly-managed opposition to them which Akbar, inbued by contemporary ideas of the duties of locally autonomous princes towards their overlord, was so strongly to resent that he encompassed the fall of the Fārūḳid dynasty by actions which for Vincent Smith, *Akbar the Great Mogul 1542-1605*[1], Oxford 1917, constituted 'perfidy' (281) and 'base personal treachery' (285).

At the beginning of his reign, Bahādur accepted the proposal of Sultan Murād, who was commanding the Mug̲h̲al forces in Berār, for a marriage alliance. But in D̲j̲umādā II-Rad̲j̲ab 1008/January 1600, Bahādur slighted Sultan Dāniyāl, Akbar's youngest son, while on his way to replace Sultan Murād in Berār. Akbar sent Abu 'l-Faḍl to persuade Bahādur to make amends by presenting himself at Akbar's court, but to no avail, and in Ramaḍān 1008/April 1600 Akbar himself arrived at Burhānpur and ordered the siege of Asīr where Bahādur had taken refuge. The fact that Akbar did not have a siege train ready suggests that he had expected Bahādur to submit on terms tantamount to a restoration of the previous Mug̲h̲al-Fārūḳid relationship; Bahādur too, once the Mug̲h̲als began the siege in earnest, thought he could and should still obtain similar terms, while being prepared to use the threat of continued resistance by the fortress if Akbar appeared unwilling. That Akbar cut the diplomatic knot by inveigling Bahādur out of Asīr by a promise to maintain him in his possession of Kh̲āndēsh̲, provided that Asīr was surrendered, and then detaining him by force, may, it is argued, be explained by Akbar's knowledge that Bahādur intended to prolong the siege as a diplomatic bargaining counter and had instructed the garrison commander accordingly (knowledge gained from the defecting Kh̲āndēsh̲ *amīr*, Sādāt Kh̲ān). Moreover, Akbar desired to deal a further blow at the already waning morale of the garrison by forcing Bahādur Sh̲āh to order it to capitulate, whereupon refusal to obey, despite his secret instructions to ignore such an order, could be interpreted as rebellion against Bahādur Sh̲āh and treated as such. It is possible that Akbar decided not to restore Kh̲āndēsh̲ to Bahādur after the fall of Asīr (22 Rad̲j̲ab 1009/27 January 1601 N.S.) because he may have thought the continued resistance of the garrison after Bahādur's detention (in D̲j̲umādā II/December 1600) was further evidence that Bahādur was both false and irreconcilable and because he needed the warlike stores of Asīr (and Asīr itself) under immediate Mug̲h̲al control for further unhampered operations in the Dekkan. Furthermore the Fārūḳid practice of imprisoning the other male members of the ruler's family under Ḥabsh̲ī guard enabled Akbar, following their capture in Asīr, easily to send the entire dynasty into exile, without fear of subsequent local opposition finding a focus in a Fārūḳid claimant. (According to *Firishta*, ii, 568, Bahādur died at Āgra in 1033/1623-4).

The extant evidence for the history of the Fārūḳids mainly displays them in their dealings with outside powers and not with their own servants and subjects. From the references given in hagiological literature (*e.g.*, *Gulzār-i abrār*, available to me only in the Urdū translation *Adhkār-i abrār*) it appears that Burhānpur [*q.v.*], the Fārūḳid capital, was a favourite burial place for *ṣūfīs*, and that the Fārūḳids provided *madad-i maʿāsh* lands for the disciples of Shaykh Burhān al-Dīn Gharīb, said to have foretold the foundation of the later Burhānpur and the rule of the Fārūḳids there. The details and the significance of this apparent association between the Fārūḳids and the *mashā'ikh* have yet to be critically established. C. F. Beckingham, *Amba Gešen and Asirgarh*, in *JSS*, ii (1957), 182-8, has noted the parallels between Ethiopian and Khāndēsh custom in keeping imprisoned the male members of the ruling dynasty in an attempt to avoid dynastic quarrels. Ḥabshīs became prominent in Gudjarāt under Bahādur Shāh and his successors and it may be suggested that Ḥabshī prominence in Khāndēsh as *amīrs* and as guardians of imprisoned relatives of the ruler also dates from this period of close association between Bahādur Shāh Gudjarātī and Muḥammad I and of the involvement of Mubārak Shāh II of Khāndēsh in the domestic politics of Gudjarāt under Sultan Aḥmad Shāh III (961-8/1554-61).

The survival of the Fārūḳids as autonomous rulers of a principality weak, compared with its neighbours, in men and resources, may be attributed in part to the geographical situation of Khāndēsh as a marchland occupying the area between the Tāptī and the Narbadā and protected by the difficult terrain of Gondwāna to the east. So long as a balance of power was maintained between Mālwa, Gudjarāt and the Bahmanī sultanate and later Aḥmadnagar, Khāndēsh was free of all but a loose tie with Gudjarāt; but chaos in Gudjarāt after the death of Bahādur Shāh Gudjarātī, the Mughal take-over in Mālwa in the time of Bāz Bahādur, and the growing involvement of Aḥmadnagar in hostilities with Bīdjāpur and Golkonda destroyed the power equilibrium on which Fārūḳid autonomy depended, while a bungling diplomacy made it impossible for the dynasty to lay claim to that honourable mediatized status within the Mughal system which Akbar had been prepared to concede to the Rādjpūt chiefs.

Bibliography: Firishta, ii, 541-68; ʿAbd Allāh Muḥammad b. ʿUmar al-Makkī, *Ẓafar al-wālih bi muẓaffar wa ālih*, three vols., ed. E. Denison Ross as *An Arabic history of Gujarat*, 1910-28, i, 51-87; other references given under individual Fārūḳids in *index*, iii; Shaykh Sikandar b. Muḥammad Mandjhū, *Mir'āt-i Sikandarī*, ed. S. C. Misra and M. L. Rahman, Baroda 1961, 17, 46-8, 59, 147-9 *passim*, 268, 272-3, 281, 286, 289, 294, 319, 323, 326-8, 332, 390-97, 414-7 *passim*, 439-40; Abū Turāb Walī, *Ta'rīkh-i Gudjarāt*, ed. E. Denison Ross, Calcutta 1909, 15, 38-9; Anon. (see Storey, 725-6), *Ta'rīkh-i Muẓaffar Shāhī*, India Office Persian MS 3842, fols. 39b-40a, 55; Anon., *Ḍamīna-yi ma'āthir-i Maḥmūd Shāhī*, (*Ta'rīkh-i Maḥmūd Shāhī*?) I.O. MS 3841, fols. 37a-59a; ʿAlī b. Maḥmūd al-Kirmānī, *Ma'āthir-i Maḥmūd Shāhī*, King's College, Cambridge, Persian MS no. 67, fols. 275a-276b; ʿAlī b. ʿAzīz Allāh Ṭabaṭabā, *Burhān-i ma'āthir*, Ḥaydarābād (Delhi printed) 1355/1936, 55, 77-8, 124, 220-5, 276, 357, 457, 466-7 *passim*, 475-82, 488, 490, 547-8, 550, 583, 585, 587-9 *passim*, 595, 608, 610, 612-3, 627; Niẓām al-Dīn Aḥmad, *Ṭabaḳāt-i Akbarī*, ii, Calcutta 1931, 156-7, 330, 333, 336, 340, 384, 393-4, 412; iii, Calcutta 1935, 21, 26-7, 66, 75-7 *passim*, 102-3, 104, 115-7, 222, 223, 226, 235-7 *passim*, 252, 290, 336-7; Abu 'l-Faḍl, *Akbar-nāma*, Calcutta 1873-87, ii, index s.v. Rādja ʿAlī Khān, Bahādur Khān *marzubān-i Khāndēsh*, Khāndēsh, Asīr and Burhānpūr; idem, *Ā'īn-i Akbarī*, Calcutta 1867-77, index s.v. Khāndēsh and Dāndēsh; idem, *Mukātabāt*, Lucknow 1863, 68-75; Ilāh-dād Fayḍī Sirhindī, *Akbar-nāma*, British Museum Or. 169, fols. 252a-275a; *Adhkār-i abrār*, (Urdū translation of Muḥammad Ghawthī Shaṭṭārī, *Gulzār-i abrār*), Āgra 1326/1908, 90; see also under those saints and scholars listed in the index as having their *madfan* at Burhānpur or Asīr; T. W. Haig, *The Fārūqī dynasty of Khāndesh*, in *Indian Antiquary*, xlvii (1918), 113-24, 141-9, 178-86; *Cambridge History of India*, 1928; the account of Khāndēsh in (ed.) R. C. Majumdar, *The Delhi Sultanate*, Bombay 1960, 169-73, 238, has been written in apparent ignorance of much contemporary or near-contemporary evidence and of important modern studies; C. P. Singhal, *Coins of Nāsir Shāh Faruqi of Khandesh*, in *Journal of the Numismatic Society of India*, vi (1944), 46-7; idem, *A copper coin of Bahadur Shāh Fāruqi of Khāndesh*, in *JNSI*, xii (1950), 154-6; M. K. Thakore, *Coins doubtfully assigned to Qādir Shāh of Malwā*, in *JNSI*, ix (1947), 36-44; M. Ḥamid Kuraishī, *Some Persian, Arabic and Sanskrit inscriptions from Asīrgarh in Numār District, Central Provinces*, in *EIM*, 1925-6, 1-6. For the controversy over Akbar's detention of Bahādur Khan Fārūḳī and the fall of Asīrgarh (inadequately referenced in the article Asīrgarh) see also Vincent A. Smith, *Akbar, the Great Mogul 1542-1605*, Oxford 1917, 272-86, 297-300; Fernão Guerreiro, *Relaçam annual das cousas que fizeram os Padres da Companhia de Jesus na India & Japao*, i, Evora 1603, fols. 7b-9a, trans. H. Heras, *The siege and conquest of the fort of Asirgarh by the Emperor Akbar*, in *Indian Antiquary*, liii (1924), 33-41; C. H. Payne, *Akbar and the Jesuits*, London 1926, 102-9, 251-8; *Cambridge History of India*, iv, 1937, 147-8; E. Maclagan, *The Jesuits and the Great Mogul*, London 1932, 58, 372; John Correia-Afonso, *Jesuit letters and Indian history*, Bombay 1955, 86-7; Shāhpūrshāh Hormasji Hodīvālā, *Studies in Indo-Muslim history*, i, Bombay 1939, 589-90, *Supplement* = vol. ii, Bombay 1957, 289-91. For valuable remarks on the historical geography of Khāndēsh see O. H. K. Spate, *India and Pakistan: a general and regional geography*², London 1957, index s.v. Khandesh.

(P. HARDY)

FARW (A.) or FARWA (pl. *firā'*), 'a fur; a garment made of, or trimmed with, fur.' Although *farwa* can mean also a cloak of camel-hair, it is likely that when this term is encountered in ancient poetry it refers to sheepskins with the wool left on (what in Morocco are called *haydūra*), used as carpets, to cover seats, or for protection against the cold; the *farwa* which Abū Bakr had with him and which he spread on the ground in the cave for the Prophet to rest on (al-Bukhārī, v, 82) was presumably a sheepskin. The wearing of costly furs was introduced only after the Arabs had reached a fairly advanced stage of civilization, at which time the name *farrā'* ('furrier'), borne by certain individuals well-known in other connexions, was applied no longer only to the maker of sheepskin cloaks but also to the dealer in costly furs.

The furs most often mentioned are grey squirrel (*sindjāb*), sable (*sammūr*), ermine (*ḵāḵum*), fox (*thaʿlab*), beaver (*ḵunduz* or *ḵundus*, *ḵhazz*), mink [? see FANAK], lynx (*washaḵ*) and weasel (*ibn ʿirs*). The geographers and travellers provide information on the origins of these furs: they came chiefly from the lands of the Bulg̲h̲ar [*q.v.*] of the Volga (Ibn Faḍlān; al-Muḵaddasī, *BGA*, iii, 324-5; Ibn Rusta-Wiet, 159), and of the Burtās [*q.v.*] (al-Masʿūdī, *Murūd̲j̲*, ii, 14-5), but also from other regions, including the Slav lands, the Turkish lands in Central and Eastern Asia, and Tibet (*Ḥudūd al-ʿālam*, 92, 94 ff.). Ḵabāla in Ad̲h̲arbāyd̲j̲ān supplied many beaver skins (*Ḥudūd*, 144); Tudela in Spain was famous for its sables (al-Muḵaddasī, *BGA*, iii, 239-40 = *Desc. de l'Occ. Mus.*, Algiers 1950, 51; *Ḥudūd*, 155, cf. ibid., 417). The Bulg̲h̲ars and their neighbours obtained furs from remoter peoples by tribute, trade, and dumb barter (Ibn Faḍlān, ed. Dahān, 129, 135, 145, tr. Canard in *AIÉO Alger*, 1958, 101, 106-7, 115; Marwazī, ed. Minorsky, 20, tr. 32-4; Abū Ḥāmid-Dubler 14, tr. 56-7, comm. 300-3; Abu 'l-Fidā, *Taḵwīm*, ed. Reinaud, i, 284; Ibn Baṭṭūṭa, ii, 400-2 = Gibb, ii, 491-2 etc.). Furs were sent from Bulg̲h̲ar to Kh̲ʷārizm (al-Muḵaddasī, *BGA*, iii, 324-5), where there were establishments for their manufacture (Yaʿḵūbī-Wiet, 83). Ibn Kh̲urradād̲h̲bih (*BGA*, vi, 92, tr. 67, and 151-3, tr. 114 = *Descr. du Maghreb et de l'Europe*, Algiers 1949, 21-3) gives some information on the routes followed by the European Jewish merchants called Rād̲h̲āniyya [*q.v.*] and the Russian merchants, who carried their wares, including furs, to Egypt and the lands of the eastern Caliphate. Furs were sent to Spain across Europe, both by sea from the Baltic ports (Ibn Ḥawḵal, ii, 392 on the export of beaver-skins from the Baltic; cf. T. Lewicki in *Isl.*, xxxv, 33) and across the lands of the Slavs and Franks (al-Masʿūdī, *Tanbīh*, 63; French tr., 94). The travellers occasionally mention fur garments which they wore in cold countries: Ibn Faḍlān (tr. M. Canard, in *AIÉO Alger*, 1958, 63-4) wrapped himself in a sheepskin cloak and other furs; Ibn Baṭṭūṭa (ii, 445; tr. Gibb, ii, 514) had with him three fur coats when he left Constantinople; etc.

Al-Masʿūdī (*loc. cit.*) esteemed highly the pelts of black and red foxes which the Burtās exported to all countries, and particularly to the 'Arab kings', who preferred them to sable, *fanak* and other furs. The Ps.-D̲j̲āḥiẓ (in *Arabica*, 1954/2, 157), expressing the view of the dealers, places highest the back of the ermine, together with the squirrel of the Caspian and of Kh̲ʷārizm; he notes that the black fox of the Caspian is more highly prized than the red and the grey, and considers the sable of China superior to that of the Caspian. This passage indicates that trade in furs must have been fairly brisk, and that the wealthy could acquire them without difficulty; it shows also that rabbit-fur was already being used by dishonest furriers to hide defects in a pelt and that dye was used to increase the value of light-coloured furs. Andalusian authors of works of *ḥisba* battled against the frauds and malpractices engaged in by dealers in furs and pelts who used the skins of sheep and rabbits (see E. Lévi-Provençal, *Séville musulmane*, Paris 1947, 131; R. Arié, in *Hespéris-Tamuda*, 1960/3, 352-3).

In the legal field, furs seem to have occasioned hardly any special regulations; and they posed no legal problem except in connexion with the validity of prayer: indeed both Sunnīs (see, *e.g.*, al-Ḵayrawānī, *Risāla*, ed. and tr. Bercher, 297) and S̲h̲īʿīs (see, *e.g.*, the Ismāʿīlī ḵāḍī al-Nuʿmān, *K. al-Iḵtiṣār*, ed. Muḥ. Waḥīd Mīrzā, Damascus 1376/1957, 100) permit the wearing of garments made from the skin of prohibited animals or animals not ritually slaughtered, except during the prayer.

On the use of fur in robes of honour and other garments see KHILʿA, LIBĀS. On furs in the Ottoman Empire see SAMMŪR.

Bibliography: in addition to that given in the article: B. Schier, *Wege und Formen des ältesten Pelzhandels in Europa*, Frankfurt 1951, 21-45; Th. Lewicki, *Il commercio arabo con la Russia e con i paesi slavi d'Occidente nei secoli IX-XI*, in *AIUON*, n.s. viii (1958), 57-8; cf. *ibid.* 47-8, where other writings on Arab trade with Eastern Europe are cited; C. E. Dubler, *Abū Ḥāmid el Granadino . . .*, Madrid 1953, index and glossary, s.vv. *sammūr, sindjāb, ḵāḵum*, etc.; L. A. Mayer, *Mamluk costume*, Geneva 1952, 23, 25, and index, under the names of the individual furs; Maḵrīzī, *Khiṭaṭ*, ii, 103 (on the furriers' market: cf. Dozy, *Dictionnaire . . . des noms des vêtements chez les Arabes*, Amsterdam 1845, 357).

(ED.)

FARWĀN (also PARWĀN), ancient town in the Hindū-Ḵush mountains and a modern administrative district of Afg̲h̲ānistān, the capital of which is Charikar.

The modern town of D̲j̲abal al-Sirād̲j̲ (alt. 3751 m.) is located near the site of the ancient Farwān, *ca.* 69° 15′ E., 35° 7′ N. by the Pand̲j̲s̲h̲īr river near its junction with the G̲h̲ūrband river.

Farwān may have occupied the ancient site of Alexander's Alexandria of the Caucasus or Alexandria-Kapisa. It was conquered by the Arabs ca. 176/792 (Ibn Rusta, 289) and included in the province of Bamiyān. Coins were struck in Farwān by the G̲h̲aznawid rulers, and it was the centre for silver mining of the Pand̲j̲s̲h̲īr valley. Many geographers mention the town, but it achieved prominence only under D̲j̲alāl al-Dīn Kh̲ʷārizms̲h̲āh when he defeated the Mongols there in 618/1221. The site of the battle, however, may be another Farwān (*Ḥudūd al-ʿālam*, 348). The site was the scene of a battle in the first British-Afg̲h̲ān war in 1840, but there is no indication of a settlement. In 1937, with the construction of a textile factory in the new town of D̲j̲abal al-Sirād̲j̲, the area began a new history.

Bibliography: Lane Poole, *Cat.*, ii 128; H. Raverty (trans.), *Ṭabaḵāt-i Nāṣirī*, Calcutta 1881, 288; W. Erskine, *Memoirs of Bābur*, London 1826, 139; D̲j̲uwaynī, ii, 138; Ḵ. Ris̲h̲tiya, *Afg̲h̲ānistān dar ḵarn-i nuzdahum*, Kabul 1951 (Russian trans., Moscow 1958, 174).

(R. N. FRYE)

FARWARDĪN [see TAʾRĪKH].

FARYĀB (also FĀRIYĀB and PARYĀB), name of several towns in Iran:

1. A town in northern Afg̲h̲ānistān, now called Dawlatābād, formerly in the province of D̲j̲ūzd̲j̲ān. It was conquered by al-Aḥnaf b. Ḵays in 65/685 (al-Balād̲h̲urī, 407). Many geographers mention the town as large and flourishing until the Mongol conquest when it was destroyed. It never regained its former importance.

2. A small town in southern Fārs province (Le Strange, 257, 296).

3. A village in Kirmān (Le Strange, 317).

4. A village in Sug͟hd (Barthold, 138; Frye, *The History of Bukhara*, 1954, 152).

Bibliography: Barthold, *Turkestan*, 79; *Ḥudūd al-ʿālam*, 335; Le Strange, 425.

(R. N. Frye)

FĀS (Fès, Fez), a town of Northern Morocco situated at 4° 54′ W., 34° 6′ N. It stands at the north-east extremity of the plain of the Sāʾis, at the exact place where the waters of the eastern side of this plain go down into the valley of Sebou via the valley of the Wādī Fās. It is therefore on the easiest route between the Atlantic coast of Morocco and the central Mag͟hrib. Furthermore, one of the least difficult roads across the Middle Atlas to the south passes by way of Sefrou, 30 kms. south of Fās, and the communications between this last town whether with the Mediterranean coast (Bādis or Vélez) or with the Straits of Gibraltar (Tangier) are relatively easy, too. It might be said that Fās is clearly situated at the point of intersection of two great axes of communication, indicated by the general contours of the country: one axis north-south between the Mediterranean or the Straits of Gibraltar and the Tāfīlālt and so beyond to the negro countries; the other west-east between the Atlantic coast and central Mag͟hrib.

Moreover, the site of Fās is rich in water; apart from the river itself and its tributaries, which it has been easy to canalize and turn to urban use, numerous springs rise from the steep banks of the water-courses, especially from the left bank, which is actually inside the town. In the immediate vicinity there are quarries which provide building stone, sand and lime, while the cedar and oak forests of the Middle Atlas are not far away and offer wood of very good quality. Finally, for considerable distances around, the neighbouring country is favourable to all types of farming. Cereals, vines, olives and various kinds or fruit-trees grow here, while not only sheep and goats but cows also can be raised here.

Nevertheless it seems that no urban centre existed on this privileged site before the Muslim town came into being. Archaeology has not confirmed the vague legendary tradition of the *Rawḍ al-Ḳirṭās*, according to which a very ancient town existed long ago on the site of Fās. It can therefore be regarded as likely that Fās came into being at the end of the 2nd/8th century at the desire of the Idrīsids [*q.v.*]. It has even long been believed, on the strength of the *Rawḍ al-Ḳirṭās*, supported by numerous other authors, that Fās was founded by Idrīs b. Idrīs on I Rabīʿ I, 192/4 January 808. The young king was thought to have then founded his town on the right bank of the Wādī Fās, and a lunar year later to the day, that is to say on 22 December 808, to have founded a second town on the left bank. Intrigued by this double foundation for which no explanation has been given, E. Lévi-Provençal studied the question very thoroughly and showed (*La Fondation de Fès*, in *AIEO Algers*, iv (1938), 23-52), that there existed another tradition less well-known but older on the founding of Fās; this took it back to Idrīs b. ʿAbd Allāh, father of Idrīs b. Idrīs. He is said to have founded the town on the right bank in 172/789 under the name of Madīnat Fās. Death intervened before he had time to develop it and twenty years later his son is believed to have founded a town for himself on the left bank, which was given the name of al-ʿĀliya. This tradition seems much more likely.

In any case, it is certain that for several centuries two cities, barely separated by the trickle of water in the Wādī Fās but frequently ranged against each other in bitter rivalry, co-existed and developed with difficulty, each hindering the other. During the whole time of the Idrīsids, that is to say until the beginning of the 4th/10th century, dynastic quarrels disturbed the life of the double city; then, during the first third of that century, it became one of the stakes in the struggle between the Umayyads of Spain and the Fāṭimids of Ifrīḳiya, which was frequently staged in the north of Morocco. During the thirty years between 980 and 1012, it lived under the protection of the Umayyads and seems then to have enjoyed a certain prosperity. When the Caliphate of Cordova began to be in jeopardy, it came under the authority of the Zenāta Berbers who, far from always agreeing among themselves, revived the ancient rivalries between the twin towns up to the time of the coming of the Almoravids [see al-murābiṭūn].

The traditional date of the conquest of Fās by the Almoravid, Yūsuf b. Tās͟hufīn, is 461/1069, but in a posthumous article (*La fondation de Marrakech*, in *Mél. d'Hist. et d'Archéol. de l'Occ. Mus.*, Algiers 1957, ii, 117-120) E. Lévi-Provençal, following al-Bakrī, showed that the traditional chronology should be treated with caution and that the foundation of Marrākus͟h and consequently the conquest of Fās, which occurred after this, ought probably to be dated a few years later. Whatever the case, the Almoravid conquest marks a very important date in the history of Fās, since Yūsuf b. Tās͟hufīn combined the two towns into one and made it his essential military base in northern Morocco. There is therefore good right to consider the Almoravid conqueror as the second founder of Fās: it was he who did away with the duality which had for so long prejudiced the city's development; it was he also who marked out for it the direction in which it was to develop in the future by building to the west of the two original towns and on the very edge of the plain of the Sāʾis, an important fortress, now disappeared, which stimulated the growth of more new quarters between it and the original ones. The Almoravids were also responsible for the growth in importance of the principal sanctuary of the left bank area, the Ḳarawiyyīn mosque (D̲j̲āmiʿ al-Ḳarawiyyīn [*q.v.*]). This sanctuary had been built of modest size, it seems, in the 4th/10th century. The Almoravid, ʿAlī b. Yūsuf, had it destroyed with the exception of the minaret which still stands (Pl. XV) and in its place built a mosque of vast dimensions, sumptuously ornamented by Andalusian artisans. It is also probable that the principal works in the Wādī Fās, thanks to which the city has possessed a system of running water from a very early date, go back to the Almoravid epoch. Fās lived thus under the Almoravids for almost three-quarters of a century (467?-540/1075?-1145), one of the most prosperous periods of its existence, but a period about which unfortunately we have all too little detailed information.

The Almohad conquest [see al-muwaḥḥidūn] marks a brief pause in the history of Fās. When ʿAbd al-Muʾmin [*q.v.*] attacked it in 540/1145, the city, which had every good reason for remaining faithful to the Almoravids, put up a violent resistance. The Almohad only conquered it after a hard siege, and punished the town by razing the Almoravid *ḳaṣaba* and the city ramparts. But like the Almoravids, the Almohads had need of Fās and the town grew afresh in proportions of which al-Idrīsī's account gives a fair idea. It is a city in full development and at the height of economic progress that he describes in his work, The fourth Almohad Caliph, al-Nāṣir, even ordered on the very day after the defeat of Las Navas de Tolosa (1212), that the ramparts of Fās should be reconstructed. The general outline of these and a good part of their masonry date from this period (Pl. XIII). Thus the old city of Fās attained the proportions that we now know. Its surrounding wall is pierced by eight huge gates, four on each bank, and it seems certain that empty spaces, gardens and orchards, once existed within this enclosure.

A century later, Fās changed masters anew and came under the authority of the Marīnids [*q.v.*]. Though badly received at first, the new masters succeeded in raising the city's prosperity to a height as yet unknown. Unlike the Almoravids and the Almohads, they did not come from the south but from the east, and Fās was the first large town which they had succeeded in conquering; hence they made it their capital and relegated Marrāku<u>sh</u> to second place. Because of this the fortunes of Fās were assured for several centuries. The new court lived at first in the *ḳaṣaba* which the Almohads had reconstructed on the site of the ancient Almoravid *ḳaṣaba*, in the district now called Bū <u>Dj</u>ulūd (probably a popular corruption of Abu 'l-<u>Dj</u>unūd). They soon found themselves cramped for space here; hence the Marīnid sovereign Abū Yūsuf (1258-1286) decided to found a royal and administrative town to the west of the ancient one, on the extreme borders of the plain of the Sā'is, and the foundations were laid out on 3 Shawwāl 674/21 March 1276. This new urban centre was at first named *al-Madīnat al-Bayḍā'* (the white city), but has been known for a very long time and still is known as Fās al-<u>Dj</u>adīd (New Fās). It consisted essentially of the palace, various administrative buildings, a great mosque to which were added little by little various other sanctuaries, barracks, the homes of various important Marīnid dignitaries, and later, in the 9th/15th century, a special quarter in which the Jews were compelled to live. From the beginning, this town was surrounded by a double city wall, broken by only a few gates. In the 10th/16th century, these were reinforced by a number of bastions capable of supporting cannon.

Thus Fās became again a double urban centre, with a middle-class and commercial town, Fās al-Bālī (Ancient Fās), known locally as 'al-Madīna' (i.e. the 'town' proper) and an administrative and military centre which complemented rather than entered into competition with the first. The description which Leo Africanus gives of Fās at the beginning of the 16th century gives the impression of an active and heavily populated city, so heavily populated indeed that several areas of lightly constructed buildings had been established outside the ramparts, especially to the north-west of the ancient city. It was a commercial and industrial city (notable for its textiles and leather-goods), but also a city of religion and learning, where around the Ḳarawiyyīn Mosque flourished what J. Berque has called 'the School of Fās' (*Ville et Université. Aperçu sur l'histoire de l'École de Fās*, in *Rev. hist. de Droit fr. et étr.*, 1949), and finally a centre of art, thanks to the country palaces built by the Marīnids on the hills which dominate Fās to the north, thanks above all to the colleges (*madrasas*) built mainly in the 8th/14th century by various Marīnid princes around the Ḳarawiyyīn Mosque, the Mosque of the Andalusians in the upper part of the old town, and in Fās al-<u>Dj</u>adīd. These colleges are almost all ornamented with good taste and variety and form one of the greatest adornments of Fās. This favourable situation lasted for three centuries during which Fās enjoyed political, economic and intellectual priority throughout Morocco as well as in the western regions of what is now Algeria, and was in economic and cultural relations with the western Sahara as far as the loop of the Niger. In 870-1/1465, the city was the scene of an attempt to restore the Idrīsids, which hung fire; the Waṭṭāsids, successors of the Marīnids, do not seem to have been very hard in their treatment of those concerned, as is shown by the description of Leo Africanus who describes an active and flourishing city.

Nevertheless the Saʿdī [*q.v.*] <u>sh</u>arīfs, masters of Marrāku<u>sh</u> since 931/1524 (R. Le Tourneau, *Les débuts de la dynastie saʿdienne*, Algiers 1954) gradually extended their influence over the rest of Morocco, threatened Fās from 954/1547 on, and thanks to inside intrigues, managed to get hold of it on 28 <u>Dh</u>u 'l-Hi<u>dj</u>dja 955/28 January 1549. This change of dynasty was not a good thing for the city, for the Saʿdīs, a southern people, had already made Marrāku<u>sh</u> their capital. Fās became once again the second city of the <u>Sh</u>arīfian empire. At first it accepted this situation very unwillingly and welcomed the Waṭṭāsid pretender, Abū Ḥassūn, when he put the Saʿdīs to flight on 2 Ṣafar 961/7th January 1554 with the help of a small Turkish force which had accompanied him from Algiers. But this venture was not to be successful for long; the Saʿdīs returned in force in <u>Sh</u>awwāl 968/September 1554. Abū Ḥassūn, who had been forced to discharge his over-enterprising Turkish allies, was killed in battle beneath the walls of Fās, and the city came back into the possession of the conquerors. These did not long continue to treat the opposition harshly, reinforced its defences, perhaps in order to hold it more strongly, and put in hand works of improvement and embellishment at the Ḳarawiyyīn Mosque. A diminished but still prosperous situation was the lot of Fās in the second half of the 10th/16th century.

When the Sultan Aḥmad al-Manṣūr [*q.v.*] died at Fās on 16 Rabīʿ I 1012/25 August 1603, his sons fought savagely over the succession and brought about a state of anarchy in Morocco which lasted more than sixty years (R. Le Tourneau, *La décadence saʿdienne et l'anarchie marocaine au XVIIe siècle*, in *Ann. de la Fac. des Lettres d'Aix*, xxxii (1958), 187-225). Fās was caught up in this whirlwind of violence, conquered by naked force, and despoiled in various reconquests; very grave internal disputes added to its misfortunes and for more than fifty years it suffered the darkest period of its history. It was an exhausted city of which the ʿAlawid pretender, Mawlāy al-Rā<u>sh</u>id, took possession in 1076/1666.

Under the power of this energetic prince, the wounds of Fās began to heal and it began to come to life again with the help of a sovereign who was putting in hand great works of public utility (construction of a bridge over the neighbouring Sebou, of two fortresses to the west of the ancient town, restoration of a bridge over the Wādī Fās, creation of a new *madrasa* in addition to those built by the Marīnids) when he was killed accidentally in 1082/1672. His brother, Mawlāy Ismāʿīl [*q.v.*], who replaced him, was also a remarkable man but he detested Fās; he had a new capital constructed at Meknès and continued to insult and offend the people of Fās throughout his long reign of fifty-five years, to such a degree that the city was becoming depopulated. On the death of Mawlāy Ismāʿīl (1139/1727) matters became even worse; several of his sons fought over the succession and, just as in the preceding century, Morocco fell back into a grave state of anarchy. Once again, for a period of thirty years, Fās was delivered up to the caprices of ephemeral rulers, among them Mawlāy ʿAbd Allāh who detested its people, and to the pillaging of the soldiery, especially that of the military tribe of Ūdāya. At last, when Sayyidī Muḥammad (1171-1204/1757-1790) succeeded his father, ʿAbd Allāh, Fās was granted a long period of respite, which was disturbed only briefly by the disorders which darkened the end of Mawlāy Sulaymān's reign (1207-1230/1792-1824). Its position as capital was restored and it shared this with Marrākus̲h̲ up to the beginning of the 20th century. Then Mawlāy ʿAbd al-ʿAzīz [*q.v.*], freed from the tutelage of his Vizier, Bā Aḥmad, adopted a policy of modernization which raised a large part of the Moroccan population against him.

In the course of the second half of the 19th century, many Fās merchants had entered into contact with various European or African countries (England, Spain, France, Italy, Germany, French West Africa) and the city was gradually being drawn into international trade. Moreover a number of Europeans and Americans (soldiers, diplomats, clergy, doctors, businessmen) came and settled in the city of Idrīs. The destiny of Fās, like that of the rest of Morocco, was beginning to take a new turn. Furthermore the Sultan Mawlāy al-Ḥasan (1290-1311/1873-1894) [*q.v.*] had undertaken important public works in this city where he normally lived when he was not travelling around the country at the head of his army: he set up a small-arms factory near his palace, the Makīna; he connected by long walls the two urban areas of Fās al-D̲j̲adīd and the Madīna, which had remained separated so far, and had a new palace built at Bū D̲j̲ulūd, on the edge of the Madīna.

From 1901 on, Fās once again faced disturbed conditions; it was threatened in 1903 by the pretender, Bū Ḥmāra [*q.v.*]; then when Mawlāy ʿAbd al-ʿAzīz was forced to abdicate in 1908, Fās put into power a descendant of its founder Idrīs, the S̲h̲arīf Muḥammad al-Kattānī; but he did not succeed in raising an army and could not prevent the Sultan proclaimed in Marrākus̲h̲, Mawlāy ʿAbd al-Ḥafīẓ, from installing himself in the city. Unrest continued, however, and the new sovereign, threatened in his capital by Berber tribes from the Middle Atlas, finally appealed to the French army for help in 1911. A column commanded by General Moinier came and encamped under the walls of Fās, the first time that a European army had been in contact with the city; the troops established themselves south of Fās al-D̲j̲adīd, at Dār al-Dubaybag̲h̲ (colloquial pronunciation: Dār ad-Dbībag̲h̲), a country house built by Mawlāy ʿAbd Allāh in the 18th century. On 30 March 1912, in the following year, the Protectorate treaty between France and Morocco was signed in a room of the palace of Bū D̲j̲ulūd. A few days later (16 and 17 April 1912), Moroccan troops revolted and massacred a number of Europeans, while at the same time others were rescued by the people of Fās. A little later, General Lyautey, the first French Resident-General of Morocco, was besieged in Fās by revolting Berber tribes; the town was set free by a column under General Gouraud (end of May - beginning of June, 1912). From that time on Fās was able to live in peace and organize itself for a new type of life.

A European town soon began to rise on a vast flat area in the region of Dār ad-Dbībag̲h̲; it was called Dār ad-Dbībag̲h̲ in Arabic and the 'Ville Nouvelle' in French. The palace of Bū D̲j̲ulūd became the seat of the Resident-General, and the Bū D̲j̲ulūd district began to fill up with many Europeans. Behind the city walls of Mawlāy al-Ḥasan, there arose administrative buildings adapted to their mediaeval style. The merchants of Fās quickly accommodated themselves to the new economic conditions of the country. Very early on, some of them went and established themselves at Casablanca, without however breaking off all contact with their ancestral city. A system of modern education was organized alongside the traditional religious teaching.

Perhaps startled by so many novelties, the city of Fās retired into its shell for a few years, but soon began to take an attitude of discreet opposition to the new régime. The Rif war and the first successes of ʿAbd al-Karīm (1925) raised fear of pillage and hopes of liberation. Little by little, a young people's party turned towards political action hostile to the Protectorate, and led the opposition against the *ẓahīr* on the organization of justice in Berber regions (16 May 1930). In 1937 and 1944, at the time of political crises which ended finally in the demand for independence of 11 January 1944, Fās was the scene of important demonstrations. Nevertheless the political centre of gravity of Morocco was shifting towards Rabat and Casablanca, and Fās played no more than a secondary part in the events which, between 1953 and 1956, led to the proclamation of Morocco's independence. At present, Fās is the capital of a province and ranks as the third city of Morocco after Casablanca and Marrākus̲h̲.

The city, whose population is 179,400 (census of 1952) of whom 15,800 are Europeans, is made up of four main centres: (1) the Madīna, in which empty spaces have almost disappeared, but where certain areas on the outskirts have been opened to motor traffic; (2) Fās al-D̲j̲adīd, itself composed of three elements: a little Muslim town of rather humble people which is called Fās al-D̲j̲adīd; the palace and its dependencies; the Jewish quarter or Mellāḥ; (3) the New City (Ville Nouvelle), where many Jews and some Muslim families live; (4) a new Muslim town situated to the north-west of the palace and created since 1950 according to modern standards. Around these urban areas, general areas of lightly constructed buildings have sprung up, inhabited by poor people recently come from the country, and these are generally nicknamed 'bidonvilles'.

Fās is connected with the outer world by excellent roads and by a railway which connects the Atlantic coast and Tangier with Oujda on the Algerian frontier. It has also an aerodrome of moderate importance.

Its economic life is founded above all, just as in the past, on its relations with the neighbouring countryside. Its industry has to a great extent remained traditional (textiles, leather-goods, industries connected with food) and has been only partly modernized; the adaptation of its artisans to modern economic conditions is one of its principal problems. By contrast, its agricultural hinterland has grown considerably into a wide belt around the city. The main business city of Morocco at the beginning of the century, it has been dethroned by Casablanca where, however, a good number of its inhabitants have settled.

Not less than as the economic metropolis, Fās has

Fās Bālī — *Madrasa* of Abū ʿInān: court, and façade of the prayer-hall.
(*Service des Monuments Historiques du Maroc*, photograph by Jean Latour)

Fās Bālī — General view from the north, with the Almohad walls in the foreground.
(*Service des Monuments Historiques du Maroc*, photograph by Jean Latour)

Fās Djadīd — The Great Mosque: *ṣaḥn* and minaret.
(*Service des Monuments Historiques du Maroc*, photograph by Jean Latour)

Fās Bālī — *Ṣaḥn* of the Ḳarawiyyīn mosque: Zenāta minaret and Saʿdid pavilion.
(*Service des Monuments Historiques du Maroc*, photograph by Jean Latour)

Fās Bālī — *Madrasa* of Abū ʿInān: *miḥrāb* of the prayer-hall.
(*Service des Monuments Historiques du Maroc*, photograph by Jean Latour)

Fās Djadīd — The Great Mosque: *mihrāb*.
(*Service des Monuments Historiques du Maroc*, photograph by Jean Latour)

Fās Bālī — The Ṣahrīdj *madrasa*: north-west façade of the courtyard.
(*Service des Monuments Historiques du Maroc*, photograph by Jean Latour)

Fās Bālī — *Madrasa* of the Sharrāṭīn: courtyard.
(*Service des Monuments Historiques du Maroc*, photograph by Jean Latour)

long been the intellectual metropolis of Morocco, thanks to its great centre of traditional learning, the Djāmiʿ al-Ḳarawiyyīn. In modern Morocco it seems to be having some difficulty in keeping this priority, since the modern Moroccan University created after independence is situated in Rabat. Fās continues nevertheless to be an important centre both of traditional and modern learning and of intellectual life.

All in all, it seems questionable whether Fās, despite remaining one of the principal cities of Morocco, has succeeded in taking up again the rôle of outstanding importance which it has played so many times in its long history. At the moment, the population seems stationary or has perhaps even slightly diminished since independence, following the departure of many French and Jews. In the political arena it seems to have been overtaken by Rabat, the capital, as well as Casablanca. In brief, events in Morocco since the beginning of the 20th century do not appear to have been favourable to Fās.

Bibliography: Ibn Ḥawḳal (10th cent.), *Descr. de l'Afr. Sept.*, ed. Kramers, 90; trans. de Slane, in *JA*, 1842, 236 ff.; Bakrī (11th cent.), *Descr. de l'Afr. Sept.*, ed. and trans. de Slane, text 115-8, trans. 262-8; Idrīsī (12th cent.), *Descript.*, text 75-6, trans. 86-7; Abu 'l-Ḥasan ʿAlī al-Djaznāʾī (14th cent.), *Zahrat al-Ās*, ed. and trans. A. Bel, Algiers 1923; Ibn Faḍl Allāh al-ʿUmarī 14th cent.), *Masālik al-abṣār*, i, *L'Afrique moins l'Égypte*, trans. M. Gaudefroy-Demombynes, Paris 1927; Ibn Abī Zarʿ al-Fāsī (14th cent.), *Rawḍ al-Ḳirṭās*, ed. and Latin trans. Tornberg, 2 vols., Upsala 1843 and 1846, French trans. Beaumier, Paris 1860; Leo Africanus (16th cent.), *Description de l'Afrique*, trans. A. Épaulard, Paris 1956, i, 179-241; Marmol (16th cent.), *De l'Afrique*, trans. Perrot d'Ablancourt, Paris 1667, ii, 157-95; Ibn al-Ḳāḍī (17th cent.), *Djadhwat al-iḳtibās*, lith., Fās 1309; Muḥammad b. Djaʿfar al-Kattāni (19th cent.), *Salwat al-anfās*, 3 vols. lith., Fās 1316; H. Gaillard, *Une ville d'Islam: Fez*, Paris 1905; A. Mouliéras, *Fez*, Paris 1902; G. Lucas, *Fès dans le Maroc moderne*, Paris 1937; R. Le Tourneau, *Fès avant le Protectorat*, Casablanca 1949 (with bibliography); idem, *Fez in the age of the Marinids*, Oklahoma University Press, Norman Okla., 1961; F. Charles-Roux and J. Caillé, *Missions diplomatiques françaises à Fès*, Paris 1955. (R. Le Tourneau)

Monuments

Under the Idrīsids. — We know of the two places of prayer which formed the origins of the two great sanctuaries of the city only from brief accounts. The mosque of Fāṭima in the quarter of the Ḳarawiyyīn (242/857) and the mosque of the Andalusians in the quarter of the same name (245/859-60) were buildings of medium size, with naves parallel to the *ḳibla* wall, with *ṣaḥn*s planted with trees, and minarets of very modest height.

Some rubble remains of the surrounding wall exist in the quarter of the Karawiyyīn but, in the absence of all traces of doors or towers, these are not sufficient to allow us to plot the main lines of this first rampart.

The settlements founded by the two Idrīs attained urban status only very gradually, and there can have been few monuments built during this period.

Under the Zenāta Emirs. — After a troubled period, the city began to develop a certain amount of artistic activity under the Zenāta Emirs, who were allies and vassals of the Umayyads of Cordova. After a Fāṭimid incursion, the mosque of Fāṭima, from that time on called the Ḳarawiyyīn, and that of the Andalusians became the cathedral-mosques of the two quarters (321/933). The two structures were rebuilt and enlarged under the Maghrāwa Emirs: their naves, still parallel to the wall of the *ḳibla*, were made of rows of horseshoe brick arches; the axial naves were bordered with bastions of stone with a four-leaved plan. The two minarets, built in 349/956, still exist. That of the Ḳarawiyyīn (Pl. XV) was built on the orders and at the expense of Sultan ʿAbd al-Raḥmān III of Cordova. In their proportions and their square plan with staircases surrounding a central newel, the two stone towers resemble the Andalusian type of minaret, but their copings of projecting string-courses and cupolas belong to the Ifrīḳiya type. Andalusian influences were only beginning to be added to the African and oriental elements which had come from Aghlabid Tunisia.

The actions of the Umayyads in the Maghrib were hardly ever concerned with the spread of artistic influence: the ancient *minbar* of the mosque of the Andalusians, detached from a more recent one in the course of a restoration of the sanctuary, bears witness to the persistence of oriental influences. Made in 369/980 at the time of the occupation of Fās by the Zīrid, Buluḳḳīn, this pulpit of turned and carved wood is of a completely Fāṭimid style. When in 375/986 an Umayyad expedition retook the town, they began by destroying this Shīʿī pulpit; but once this pious fury had passed, they saw that the ancient *minbar*, repaired and provided with a new seat-back to the greater glory of orthodoxy, could very well continue to be used, and an artist was found to make the repairs and additions in the original style. This pulpit, after that of Ḳayrawān the oldest of all the *minbar*s which have come down to us, is the only monument which remains as a witness of the struggles between the Fāṭimids and the Umayyads in Morocco.

Thus Fās awakened little by little to artistic life under the prevailing influence of Ḳayrawān, and in the middle of the 4th/10th century had also received some influences from Andalusian sources.

Under the Almoravids. — The period of the Almoravids was a decisive one in the architectural history of Fās. Although the Ṣanhādjī Emirs took Marrākush, the city which they had founded, as their capital, they nevertheless did not forget the great city of the north. Yūsuf b. Tāshufīn united the two quarters of the Ḳarawiyyīn and the Andalusians and at their highest point built the Ḳaṣba (*ḳaṣaba*) of Bū Jlūd (Abu 'l-Djulūd). He was soon to become master of Muslim Spain, the whole of whose artistic resources were put at the service of the African emirs. Hispano-Moorish art, which became the dominant factor in Fās as in Marrākush, eliminated the Ifrīḳiyan influences under which the city had lived up to this time. In becoming attached to the artistic tradition under which it was to continue up to our own times, Fās became an artistic metropolis.

The second Almoravid sultan, ʿAlī b. Yūsuf, gave the Ḳarawiyyīn mosque its present dimensions and form by enlarging it on the *ḳibla* side and on the side of the *ṣaḥn*, and by working over all the earlier parts. The work was executed between 529/1135 and 536/1142. The arrangement of naves parallel to the wall of the chevet was retained, but a higher axial nave leading to the *miḥrāb* was inserted between the ancient and new naves of the hall of prayer. A row of rich cupolas—above all domes with stalactites—covered it.

The Almoravid enlargements were made of glazed or bonded brick, which on the outer wall of the *miḥrāb* formed a very beautiful interlacing design. Inside the building, in the great axial nave, rich sculptured decorations, heightened with colour, had been covered with plaster by the Almohads in the period of their rigorous puritanism. These magnificent ornaments, mainly epigraphic and floral, were uncovered in the course of a restoration of the whole of the building directed by the author of this article. The whole art of Muslim Spain, as it had been elaborated in the 5th/11th century, with its profuse richness, its erudite composition and its nervous elegance, is revealed in this Moroccan mosque.

The al-Ḳarawiyyīn mosque preserves the *minbar* of carved wood and marquetry which was given to it by ʿAlī b. Yūsuf. Second in Morocco only to the one at present in the Kutubiyya at Marrāku<u>sh</u>, the work of the same ruler, it is one of the most beautiful in all Islam. The great mosque of Fās, long unknown in detail, has become once again the greatest witness to Hispano-Moorish art in the time of the Almoravids.

Under the Almohads. — The Almohads, who kept Marrāku<u>sh</u> as their capital, were slower to interest themselves in Fās. They gave a cathedral-mosque to the Ḳaṣba of Bū Jlūd. Under Muḥammad al-Nāṣir, the mosque of the Andalusians was reconstructed, with the exception of its minaret. The ancient Zīrid and Amīrid *minbar* was covered, except for its seat-back, with a new sculptured decoration. At the Ḳarawiyyīn, which was given a great ornamental chandelier and a room for ritual ablutions, some works of detail were carried out. But the greatest work of the Almohads was the reconstruction of the great city wall (Pl. XIII) which still to-day surrounds Fās al-Bālī. Bāb Gīsa (<u>Dj</u>īsa) and Bāb Maḥrūk, more or less repaired or altered, date for the main part from this period.

During the whole time of the Almohads, Fās was very prosperous, and Andalusian influences continued to prevail there without rival.

Under the Marīnids. — Under the Marīnids, Fās became the capital of Morocco. In 674/1276, a little while after his victory over the last of the Almohads, Abū Yūsuf Yaʿḳūb founded, at a short distance to the west of the old town, a new administrative city, Fās al-<u>Dj</u>adīd. Here he built his palaces, which he endowed with a great mosque (Pls. XIV, XVII) and here he installed his guard and the administrative services of the state. Fās al-<u>Dj</u>adīd was surrounded by a mighty rampart with inner and outer walls and furnished with monumental gates. Three of these gates, Bāb al-Sammārīn, Bāb al-Bākākīn, and Bāb al-Ma<u>kh</u>zan still exist to-day, very little altered. The palaces of the Marīnids have been replaced by more modern buildings, but some of their vaulted store-houses are still to be seen there.

Other sanctuaries were built later on at Fās al-<u>Dj</u>adīd: the al-Ḥamrāʾ mosque, doubtless in the reign of Abū Saʿīd (710-31/1310-31), the little sanctuary of Lāllā Zhar (Zahr, 759/1357) built by Abū ʿInān, and finally the mosque of Lāllā <u>Gh</u>arība (810/1408), whose minaret alone has been preserved. The great mosque of al-Ḥamrāʾ and Lāllā Zhar are beautiful buildings of harmonious proportions and quiet luxury. In 720/1320, Abū Saʿīd had a *madrasa* constructed, which to-day is in a very damaged condition.

The Marīnids did not forget Fās al-Bālī. There they built several small mosques such as the <u>Sh</u>arābliyyīn and Abu 'l-Ḥasan, whose sanctuaries have been rebuilt but which still preserve some carved wood from this period and, even more important, their graceful minarets. All the Marīnid minarets of Fās al-<u>Dj</u>adīd and Fās al-Bālī consist of square towers with turrets. Their façades are decorated with interlaced designs in brick enclosing backgrounds of mosaic faïence. Other *azulejos* in the form of polygonal stars cover the wide string-course at the top of the tower. They are perfect examples of the classic type of Hispano-Moorish minaret.

But the old town was indebted above all to the Marīnids for the glorious beauty of the *madrasa*s of this period. These are students' colleges arranged around luxurious court-yards at the back of which are situated halls of prayer. As early as 670/1271, the founder of the dynasty, Abū Yūsuf Yaʿḳūb, built the *madrasa* of the Ṣaffārīn. The Ṣahrī<u>dj</u> (720/1321), (Pl. XVIII), Ṣbaʿiyyīn (723/1323) and ʿAṭṭārīn (743/1346) *madrasa*s were built in the time of Abū Saʿīd. Abu 'l-Ḥasan founded the Miṣbāḥiyya (743/1346), and Abū ʿInān the one which bears his name, the Bū-ʿInāniyya (Pls. XII, XVI). Outwardly each of different appearance, all the *madrasa*s built in this last great epoch of Hispano-Moorish art are extremely beautiful. The decorations which cover them are admirably arranged and the detail of the ornament is worthy of the harmony of the whole. The latest in date and the largest, the Bū ʿInāniyya, which is the only one to possess a *minbar* and a minaret, is the last great masterpiece of the classic period of Hispano-Moorish art to be found in Morocco.

The Almoravid and Almohad monuments were planned and decorated by artists who came from Spain, but towards the end of the 7th/13th century Fās had its own workshops, closely linked with those of Granada. From the beginning of the 8th/14th century on, beautiful houses were erected both in Fās al-<u>Dj</u>adīd and Fās al-Bālī, which, like the *madrasa*s, were adorned with floors and facings of faïence mosaic, plaster and carved wood. The same decorative style prevailed in sanctuaries, palaces and rich homes.

The masonry, also very homogeneous in style, is less beautiful but almost as delicate as the ornament. In the walls, stone gives place to bonded or glazed brick, and often also to cobwork. Cedar wood plays a large part in all the architecture of Fās. Whether in beams, lintels, corbelling, ceilings or *artesonados* domes, it provides both roof beams and cover for all types of buildings. In the framework of doors and openings and in joinery, it is moulded, decorated with pieces of applied ornament, or carved. At the tops of walls and court-yards, it is worked into friezes and projecting porches resting upon carved and painted corbels. This wide use of wood, the frequency of pillars and the rarety of columns, are the only characteristics which distinguish the Marīnid monuments from contemporary Naṣrid buildings.

Vaulted architecture is to be found only in the great store-houses of Fās al-<u>Dj</u>adīd and in the *ḥammām*s which follow the very simple plans of the Andalusian baths.

Thus under the Marīnids Fās received not only its shape as two distinct agglomerations, but also its architectural appearance. From then on it was, second only to Granada, the most active centre of Hispano-Moorish art. Once Muslim Spain had disappeared, all the processes of masonry, techniques and ornamental forms inherited from the 14th century continued to be used in Fās up to our own times, in a slow decline and with a touching fidelity.

Under the Saʿdīs. — The end of the Marīnid dynasty and the reign of the Banū Waṭṭās produced no great monuments in Fās. Nevertheless, its buildings maintained the same architectural and decorative traditions as those of the art which preceded this period. Relations with Granada had become more rare, and from the end of the 8th/14th century onwards, the latest innovations in ornament of the Alhambra of Muḥammad V had not been passed on to Fās. And in 896/1492, Granada was reconquered. In the victorious thrust of Renaissance art in Spain, Hispano-Moorish art became confined by the 10th/16th century to its African domain. Under the Saʿdīs, who struggled for a long time against the Banū Waṭṭās for the possession of Fās, the city went through difficult times. Marrākus̲h̲ once again became the capital of Morocco and the sultans distrusted the metropolis of the North. They reinforced the ramparts of Fās al-D̲j̲adīd, which remained the headquarters of government, with bastions for the use of cannon. Two works of the same kind but even more powerful, the northern *burd̲j̲* and the southern *burd̲j̲*, dominated and overlooked Fās al-Bālī. The Ḳarawiyyīn was enriched with two fountain kiosks, jutting out of the shorter sides of the *ṣaḥn* (Pl. XV). In the anarchy in which the Saʿdī dynasty went down, Fās passed through terrible times and in such a troubled period no monuments could be constructed

Under the ʿAlawīs. — The founder of the dynasty, Mawlāy al-Ras̲h̲īd, hastened to give Fās al-Bālī a new *madrasa*, that of the S̲h̲arrāṭīn (1081/1670). His successor, Mawlāy Ismāʿīl, transferred his capital to Miknās. Nevertheless, he had the mausoleum and sanctuary of Mawlāy Idrīs rebuilt.

At the beginning of the 18th century, Fās once again became the customary residence of the sultan and the central government. Almost all the sovereigns, from Sīdī Muḥammad b. ʿAbd al-Allāh on, had work done on the palaces of Fās al-D̲j̲adīd. The most important groups of buildings which still exist to-day date mainly from Mawlāy ʿAbd al-Raḥmān (1237-75/1822-59) and Mawlāy al-Ḥasan (1289-1311/1873-94). The ramparts were repaired many times and one of the great gates, Bāb al-Futūḥ, was entirely rebuilt by Mawlāy Sulaymān.

Numerous sanctuaries, whether cathedral-mosques or simple places of prayer, were built in Fās under the ʿAlawī sovereigns and very often through their initiative. The most important of these were the mosques of Bāb Gīsa (D̲j̲īsa), of al-Raṣīf and of al-Siyād̲j̲ at Fās al-Bālī, and the mosque of Mawlāy ʿAbd Allāh at Fās al-D̲j̲adīd. Local mosques, places of prayer dedicated to saints, headquarters of brotherhoods, were built in great numbers. Sanctuaries of reasonably large dimensions consisted according to local tradition of naves parallel to the wall of the *ḳibla*. The minarets were square towers surmounted by turrets but the decoration of a network of interlacing and faïence was almost always omitted and the walls of brick, glazed or not, were ornamented with simple blind arcades. Some little sanctuaries still keep their 'platform' minarets of a very archaic type. An occasional *madrasa* was built: those of Bāb Gīsa and al-Wād preserve very nearly the traditional arrangement.

Most of the houses of Fās date from the ʿAlawī period but continue the Marīnid tradition. The walls are made either of cobwork or more commonly of brick, and sometimes of coated rubble. In the old town, the houses rise vertically, mostly on two floors around narrow court-yards. These houses, though poor in light and ventilation, are nevertheless sometimes sumptuous; the pillars of the court-yard and the bases of the walls are panelled in faïence mosaics; carved plaster often ornaments the door and window frames and the tympanums of the openings, and sometimes even the walls themselves. A cornice of moulded or even carved cedar-wood crowns the whole. The ceilings and the joinery—also of cedar-wood—are worked with care. In the less dense outlying districts, there are lower houses around vast court-yards and even gardens.

The *funduḳ*s, with several storeys and galleries, follow the same arrangement as that of the Marīnid hostelries, and are, in this city of commerce, very often beautiful buildings.

Thus in the work of these last centuries there is nothing new, but a remarkable fidelity to a great architectural and decorative tradition. Despite the baldness of the ornamental detail, both the civil and the religious architecture of Fās preserves, sometimes not without grandeur, a sense of balance which does not exclude the picturesque. Above all, a perfect unity of style, maintained by guilds of artisans, knowing and loving their work, has given Fās al-Bālī and even more, Fās al-D̲j̲adīd, an astonishing harmony. Regulations concerning matters of art have succeeded in preserving in Fās, as in other ancient cities in Morocco, their originality and beauty. In Fās, more than elsewhere, there has been preserved the architectural and decorative climate of Muslim Andalusia.

Bibliography: H. Gaillard, *Une ville de l'Islam: Fès*, Paris 1905; G. Marçais, *L'architecture musulmane d'Occident*, Paris 1950; H. Terrasse, *L'art hispano-mauresque des origines au XIIIe siècle*, Paris 1932; idem, *Les villes impériales du Maroc*, Grenoble 1937; idem, *La mosquée des Andalous à Fès*, Paris 1949; R. le Tourneau, *Fès avant le Protectorat*, Casablanca 1949; D. Maslow, *Les mosquées de Fès et du Nord du Maroc*, Paris 1937. (H. Terrasse)

FASĀ (formerly Pasā), is situated in 28° 56′ N. Lat. and 53° 39′ E. Long. (Greenwich); it is 1,561 metres above sea level. Fasā is 164 km. from S̲h̲īrāz, 55 from Dārābd̲j̲ird and 70 from D̲j̲ahrum. The district (*s̲h̲ahristān*) of which Fasā is the capital forms part of the seventh *Ustān* (Fārs). The Muslim Arabs under ʿUt̲h̲mān b. Abi 'l-ʿĀṣ captured Fasā in 23/644. According to Ḥa md Allah Mustawfī (*Nuzha*, 124), it was originally called Sāsān and was triangular in shape. Ibn al-Balk̲h̲ī (*Fārs-nāma*, 130) stated that Fasā was as large as Iṣfahān; it had been destroyed by the S̲h̲abānkāra tribes, but was rebuilt by the Atabeg Čawlī. The climate was temperate and the surrounding district produced the fruits of both the cold and hot regions. The abundant water supply was entirely from *ḳanāt*s, there being no wells. The cathedral mosque was of burnt brick and rivalled that of Madīna for splendour (Muḳaddasī, 431). Fasā was famous for its carpets and brocades and also (according to the *Ḥudūd al-ʿālam*, 127) for its rose-water. In 1951 the population was 8,300. 4 km. to the south of the town is the ancient mound known as the Tell-i Ḍaḥāk.

Bibliography: in the text, and: Yāḳūt, iii, 891; J. Karabacek, *Die persische Nadelmalerei Susandschird*, Leipzig 1881, 107; Ḥād̲j̲d̲j̲ī Mīrzā Ḥasan Fasāʾī, *Fārs-nāma-yi Nāṣirī*, ii, 228 ff.; Flandin and Coste, *Voyage en Perse*, vol. i (text), 28-30, vols. i and ii (plates), 30; Oliver St. John, *Narrative of a journey through Baluchistan and*

Southern Persia, in *Eastern Persia*, i, 109; Le Strange, 290, 293, 294; *Rāhnamā-yi Īrān*, 176 (with plan on 177). (L. LOCKHART)

FASĀD [see FĀSID, KAWN].

FAṢĀḤA, an Arabic word, properly "clarity, purity", abstract noun from *faṣīḥ*, "clear, pure". To summarize the definitive analysis of the concept as it was achieved in the work of Djalāl al-Dīn al-Ḳazwīnī, the Khaṭīb Dimashḳ (666-739/1267-1338), and his commentator, Saʿd al-Dīn al-Taftazānī (722-91/1322-89), in Arabic rhetoric *faṣīḥ* is applied to: (1) a single word when it is not difficult to pronounce, is not a foreign or rare word and its form is not an exception to the usual; (2) a whole sentence, when it does not contain an objectionable construction, a discord, an obscurity (through a confusion in the arrangement of the words) or a metaphor too far-fetched and therefore incomprehensible. The first kind of *faṣāḥa* is called *faṣāḥat al-mufrad*, the latter *faṣāḥat al-kalām*. There is also (3) a *faṣāḥat al-mutakallim*. This is peculiar to a person whose style conforms to the above conditions (Ḳazwīnī, *Talkhīṣ al-Miftāḥ*, Cairo 1342/1923, i, 70-6, with Taftazānī's *Mukhtaṣar*). The adjective *faṣīḥ* denotes a word or a sentence only when free from objection in itself; it is distinguished from *balīgh*, which also implies that the expression is relevant in its context.

From its inception Arabic theory gravitated towards a strict separation between the stylistic areas where the ideal accomplishment is represented by *faṣāḥa* and *balāgha* respectively; in practice, the dividing line between the two concepts was not always clearly drawn. A number of critics tended to enlarge the scope of *faṣāḥa* at the expense, as it were, of *balāgha*, and the general public, as Nuwayrī (d. 732/1332), *Nihāya*, vii, 7, observes, was inclined to use the two terms indiscriminately. (Similarly, Ḳazwīnī, *Īḍāḥ*, i, 136-7. Cf. Ibn Ḳayyim al-Djawziyya (d. 751/1350), *Fawāʾid*, Cairo 1327/1909, 9, where the opinion of some authorities is noted that *faṣāḥa* and *balāgha* are alternative terms for the same concept).

Without attempting to develop an integrated concept, al-Djāḥiẓ (d. 255/869) collects a great deal of the materials and states a number of the value judgments that later theorists were to work into a system. Every language has certain sounds that are characteristic for it, such as the 's' in Greek. Among its sounds there will be some that do not agreeably fit together; in Arabic, *e.g.*, the *ḥarf* 'dj' cannot stand side by side with ẓ, ḳ, ṭ, gh; and the 'z' with ẓ, s, ḍ and dh (*Bayān*, Cairo 1932, i, 69-72). The best *kalām* in all the world is the mode of speech, or narrative, of the *faṣīḥ* among the *ʿArab*; but the common people, too, sometimes achieve pertinence in their speech (i, 133). Solecism, *laḥn*, endangers *faṣāḥa* but does not necessarily destroy it. For in the view of Abū ʿAmr b. al-ʿAlāʾ (d. c. 153/770), al-Ḥasan al-Baṣrī (d. 110/728) and al-Ḥadjdjādj (d. 95/714) were *afṣaḥ* of all, yet not entirely free from *laḥn* (i, 146; a list of the most disturbing *alḥān* is given, i, 134; the worst is the manner of speaking of Bedouins whose speech has been affected by that of the town mob; cf. also i, 146 on the deteriorating influence of the language of the city on that of the Bedouin. In the 5th/11th century Khafādjī, *Sirr*, 53, was to note that the Bedouin had become dependent on the townsman for linguistic perfection). Altogether *kalām* must be graded in various *ṭabaḳāt* (*djazl, sakhīf, malīḥ, ḥasan, ḳabīḥ, khafīf* and *thaḳīf*) precisely as the people themselves. Since the speaker, *khaṭīb*, should adapt his speech to both his ideas and his audience he must ordinarily refrain from using the vocabulary of the *mutakallimīn* (here: scholars in the technical sense) even if he should himself be one of them. In scientific discussion, on the other hand, the employment of the terminology of the *mutakallimīn* is indicated. It is they who developed (*takhayyarū, ishtaḳḳū, iṣṭalaḥū*) a scientific language in regard to which they are *salafᵃⁿ li-kull khalaf*, (authoritative) ancestors to all posterity. While the *khaṭīb* must use their terms only when common expressions fail to convey his thoughts, their insertion into poems is allowable as a piece of witticism, *ʿalā djihat al-taẓarruf wa 'l-tamalluḥ* (i, 128-31).

The clever though disjointed remarks of Djāḥiẓ are interesting in themselves but significant mainly as a foil to the rapid consolidation of the theorists' ideas on *faṣāḥa*, spurred as it was by the need to document the uniqueness, *iʿdjāz*, of the Ḳurʾān from the formal point of view. Abū Hilāl al-ʿAskarī (d. after 395/1005) makes the (often repeated) statement that after theology the science most worthy to engage our study is *ʿilm al-balāgha wa-maʿrifat al-faṣāḥa*, by means of which the *iʿdjāz* is recognised (*Kitāb al-ṣināʿatayn*, Constantinople 1320, 2). To ʿAskarī *faṣāḥa* is the perfect tool, *āla*, of clear exposition, *bayān*; the scope is confined to the wording because the idea of tool bears only on the wording and not on the idea, *maʿnā*. Hence a parrot could be called *faṣīḥ*, but never *balīgh*. An isolated *kalām*, however, may be described as *faṣīḥ balīgh* provided it is clear in concept and smoothly fluent, *sahl*, in style (*ibid.*, 7; some authorities require in addition a certain stateliness, *fakhāma*, without which a discourse may qualify as *balīgh* but not *faṣīḥ*; this reversal of the usual terminology deserves to be noted).

ʿAbd al-Ḳāhir al-Djurdjānī (d. 1078 or 1081; cf. Ritter, *Asrār*, German translation, Wiesbaden 1959, 5*) clearly felt dissatisfied with the treatment accorded *faṣāḥa*. The more he studied what scholars had to say about it the more did he realise that their statements failed because of their all too general character. After all, nothing much is gained from explanations where *faṣāḥa* is merely described as a peculiar trait in the putting together of words, *khuṣūṣiyya fī naẓm al-kalim* (*Dalāʾil al-iʿdjāz*, Cairo 1331/1913, 30). Specifically, he is critical of those who maintain that *faṣāḥa* has no meaning beyond the "harmony within the words and the adjustment of the sequence of the letters so the meeting in pronunciation of letters that are difficult for the tongue will be avoided", *al-talāʾum al-lafẓī wa-taʿdīl mizādj al-ḥurūf ḥattā lā yatalāḳā fī 'l-nutḳ ḥurūf tathḳulu ʿala 'l-lisān*. This view would lead to separating *faṣāḥa* from *balāgha* (as a separate science or approach) and would constitute euphony the only criterion of rhetorical perfection and the *iʿdjāz al-Ḳurʾān*, or at least lend it too much importance against such virtues as *ḥusn al-tartīb*, good organization. The reason why the ancients, *al-ḳudamāʾ*, maintained the strict division between *lafẓ* and *maʿnā* and stressed the function and merits of the *lafẓ* is that the *maʿānī* are manifested by words only. Hence the custom of attributing to the word what in fact belongs to the *maʿnā* and to speak, *e.g.*, of *lafẓ mutamakkin*, solid wording, when actually the ideas expressed are intended by this characterization (*ibid.*, 45-51).

From these remarks one is led to conclude that Djurdjānī did not know al-Khafādjī's (d. 465/1073) *Sirr al-faṣāḥa* (completed 2 Shaʿbān 454/11 August

1062; cf. *Sirr*, Cairo 1932, 276), perhaps the most thorough examination of the concept. Khafādjī, too, was, ostensibly at least, motivated by a desire to investigate the *iʿdjāz al-Ḳurʾān* whose *faṣāḥa* "broke the custom", in other words, was miraculous, *ibid.*, 4. The special excellence which Khafādjī claims for his work consists in its comprehensiveness—the *mutakallimūn* neglect the study of phonetics; the grammarians that of the principles, *al-aṣl wa 'l-uss*; the critics, *ahl naḳd al-kalām*, do not rise above the *aperçu*, *ibid.*, 5. Khafādjī is deeply concerned with the phonetic aspect. He observes that Arabic disposes of 29 (or according to al-Mubarrad, who does not count the *hamza*, 28) *ḥurūf*; actually, the language has 14 more for which there does not exist any graphic representation. Of these, six add to the *faṣīḥ* (*e.g.*, the *imāla*, the *z* for *ṣ* in the pronunciation '*mazdar*' in lieu of *maṣdar*), whereas eight detract from it (*e.g.*, the *sh* for *dj* in the pronunciation '*kharashat*' for *kharadjat*; 19, 21-2). Other languages have in part different *ḥurūf*; thus Armenian has 36 against the Arabs' 29 (53). The putting together of *ḥurūf* into words is guided by aesthetic principles; three consonants of the same phonetic category are avoided in the formation of any given word. The best procedure is to combine sounds with distant bases of articulation (53-4).

Faṣāḥa then, as a property confined to individual words (55), can be attributed to the *alfāẓ* if certain requirements, *shurūṭ*, are met. (A) Some of these are manifest in the isolated word, (B) others when the words are connected one with the other (60). The *shurūṭ* of the first type (A) are the following: (1) the words must be composed of sounds whose bases of articulation are varied; (2) over and above this condition their sequence must be acoustically pleasing; (3) the words must be neither 'raw' nor barbarous, *mutawaʿʿir* and *waḥshī* (Suyūṭī, *Muzhir*, Cairo 1282, i, 114-15, offers a definition of the *waḥshī* and a listing of [near-]synonyms of this term); (4) nor must they be low and vulgar, *sāḳiṭ* and *ʿāmmī* (both these requirements are to be found in Djāḥiẓ, Khafādjī observes); (5) the words must conform to correct Arabic usage, *ʿurf*; here objections may arise from fourteen causes, such as (a) the un-Arabic origin of a word; (b) the wrong use of an Arabic word; (c) the unwarranted shortening or (d) lengthening of a word; (e) the extreme rarity of a word or the particular form of a common word as, *e.g.*, an unusual plural; etc. Trespasses of this kind do not impair *faṣāḥa* very badly yet had better be avoided. (6) The word must not have a second meaning which brings to mind something one does not wish the hearer to think of; (7) the word should be "well-balanced" and not composed of (too) many *ḥurūf*; (8) if the word is a diminutive it should be used only where a diminutive is directly appropriate: Khafādjī dislikes the *taṣghīr bi-maʿnā al-taʿẓīm*.

Of these *shurūṭ*, nos. 1 to 6 apply also to (B) *al-alfāẓ al-muʾallafa*, *i.e.*, they constitute requirements for a sequence of words exactly as for a sequence of *ḥurūf* within the individual word; in fact, nos. 2 to 4 depend in *taʾlīf* entirely on their occurrence in the *lafẓa mufrada*. A7 and A8 do not bear on B. To be *faṣīḥ*, *taʾlīf* must instead fulfil these additional *shurūṭ*: (1) the words must be placed exactly where they belong; no unjustified changes of the customary word order are allowable (thus *taḳdīm* and *taʾkhīr* as well as the *ḳalb al-kalām* are to be avoided); (2) they must exhibit *ḥusn al-istiʿāra*, appropriate metaphors; (3) be free from *ḥashw*, padding; in opposition, however, to both the Muʿtazilī al-Djubbāʾī (d. 303/915) and his orthodox critic al-Rummānī (d. 387/994), Khafādjī admits (140-1) that some *ḥashw* enriches the meaning and adds lustre to the discourse; (4) there must not be any unnecessary repetitions; (5) the words must be properly selected according to the purpose; this includes the use of *kināya*, metonymy, where *taṣrīḥ*, plain speech, would be out of place; (6) technical terms are inadmissible (60-161).

There is another set of properties of *faṣāḥa* which Khafādjī treats separately (162 ff.) even though they could be subsumed under the requirements of (B). These are: (1) *munāsaba* or *tanāsub*, correspondence between words in regard either (i) to their pattern or (ii) to their meaning. It is under (i) that Khafādjī deals with *sadjʿ* and *izdiwādj*, *ḳawāfī*, *luzūm mā lam yalzam* and *taṣrīʿ* (internal rhyme), *tarṣīʿ*, *ḥaml al-lafẓ ʿala 'l-lafẓ fi'l-tartīb* (an unusual name for *al-laff wa 'l-nashr*; *plokē*), *al-tanāsub fi 'l-miḳdār* (requirements concerning the relative length of the various *cola* in a *sadjʿ* passage), *al-mudjānas* (covering both *figura etymologica* and paronomasia) and, as the lowest form of *tanāsub*, *al-taṣḥīf* (paronomasia based on modifications of the graphic representations of two words and not on sound).

By introducing category (ii) of *tanāsub*, which is concerned with closeness and contrast of the meaning of two *lafẓa*, Khafādjī leaves definitely the area which Arabic theory is generally willing to assign to *faṣāḥa*. Considering that *ṭibāḳ*, antithesis, for instance, clearly derives from meaning and not from the word pattern or its *ḥurūf*, it can hardly be viewed as a component of *faṣāḥa* which, after all, Khafādjī himself had explicitly tied to the word while leaving the meaning to *balāgha*. Khafādjī goes on to consider *īdjāz*, concision, as a *sharṭ* of both *faṣāḥa* and *balāgha*. The same applies to clarity, *an yakūna maʿnā al-kalām wāḍiḥ*^{an} *ẓāhir*^{an} *djaliyy*^{an}. Khafādjī justifies its connexion with *faṣāḥa* by pointing to six reasons for obscurity of discourse (210), two each inherent in (a) the isolated word: the unusual expression; the use of homonyms; (b) the composition of words, *taʾlīf al-alfāẓ baʿḍa-hā maʿa baʿḍ*: excessive concision; confusion; and (c) the *maʿnā* as such: over-subtlety; too much advance knowledge required for understanding. In this context Khafādjī (212-5) takes sides in a controversial issue by asserting that some parts of the Ḳurʾān are more *afṣaḥ* than others. Since everybody agrees that Torah, Gospels and Psalms although *kalām Allāh* are less *faṣīḥ* than the Ḳurʾān there is no reason why all of the Book should be on the same level of *faṣāḥa*. Additional characteristics, *nuʿūt*, of *balāgha* and *faṣāḥa* (not integrated in any classification by Khafādjī) are (1) the designation of an idea not by its usual name but by an expression implying it, and (2) the rendering of an idea through a simile, *tamthīl*. Only at this point does Khafādjī definitely turn to the examination of the *maʿānī* and their properties such as (224 ff.) soundness, *ṣiḥḥa* (eight sub-categories), completeness, or emphatic presentation.

Fakhr al-Dīn al-Rāzī's (d. 606/1209) motivation in discussing *faṣāḥa* is the same as Khafādjī's: its *faṣāḥa* makes the Ḳurʾān *muʿdjiz* (*Nihāyat al-īdjāz*, Cairo 1317, 5). This fact makes its investigation research into the noblest of all religious subjects, *viz.* the manner in which the Holy Book indicates the veracity of Muḥammad (7). But although Rāzī follows his predecessor in overextending the content of *faṣāḥa* his presentation is much more orderly and shows the progress of scholastic disciplining of scientific thinking in the intervening century.

Faṣāḥa is defined (9) as *khulūṣ al-kalām min al-taʿḳīd*, the freedom of the discourse from obscurity, or confusion, from anything that "ties" tongue and mind. (This definition recurs, *e.g.*, in Ibn Ḳayyim, *Fawāʾid*, 9; the concept of *taʿḳīd* is discussed by Ḳazwīnī and Taftazānī, *Talkhīṣ*, i, 102-108). The purpose of *kalām*, the conveying of meaning, is achieved on the verbal and the intellectual level. Neither *faṣāḥa* nor *balāgha* can be predicated of the connexion, established θέσει, between word and meaning, the signifier and the signified. Were it otherwise, *faṣāḥa* would have to inhere in the individual *ḥurūf* or in their agglomeration which, however, could not possess any *ṣifa* lacking in the individual *ḥarf*. Also in this case, a person ignorant of the Arabic tongue would have to be able to recognize *al-kalām al-ʿarabī al-faṣīḥ*. Besides, *faṣāḥa* is a "plus" achieved by the free choice of the speaker; the qualities of the individual words, on the other hands, are due to the *waḍʿ al-wāḍiʿ*, not to the speaker. Furthermore, a word will be *faṣīḥ* in one, *rakīk*, "weak", in another context. The Prophet challenged the Arabs to match the *faṣāḥa* of the Book; had this *faṣāḥa* rested on the individual words the challenge could easily have been met. Metaphor, metonymy and simile are for Rāzī as for Khafādjī *abwāb al-faṣāḥa*; since these figures of speech have reference to the *maʿnā*, not to the *lafẓ*, *faṣāḥa* cannot, in its entirety, be word-bound (12-4). The objection (15-6) that everybody speaks of *lafẓ faṣīḥ* and nobody of *maʿnā faṣīḥ* is countered by the observation that the attribution of *faṣāḥa* to the *lafẓ* refers to its *dalāla maʿnawiyya* (not its *dalāla lafẓiyya*). In disposing of the criticism that since the same *maʿnā* may often be expressed by two *lafẓ*, one *faṣīḥ*, the other *rakīk*, *faṣāḥa* cannot refer to the *maʿnā*—nor would if it did the *tafsīr al-mufassir* be inferior in beauty to the poetic passage which it explains—, Rāzī gropes for the concept of the emotive etc. associations surrounding the different words and phrases without quite piercing through to an adequate terminology. Rāzī insists correctly that the *faṣāḥa* of a *kināya* (against *ifṣāḥ*, Rāzī's term for *taṣrīḥ*; 18) has to do with the intellectual rather than the phonetic and lexicographical structure of the phrase, an insight which, incidentally, al-Djurdjānī had acquired before him without tying it so closely to the concept of *faṣāḥa*.

Ḍiyāʾ al-Dīn Ibn al-Athīr (d. 631/1234), who veers away sharply from the blurring between the areas of *faṣāḥa* and *balāgha* which is characteristic of Khafādjī's and Rāzī's position, is concerned with reducing the subjective element in ascribing *faṣāḥa* to a given expression. The frequently proposed definition of the *faṣīḥ* as *al-ẓāhir al-bayyin* is inadequate. For it is open to three objections: (1) a *lafẓ* would be judged *faṣīḥ* when clearly understood and non-*faṣīḥ* when not clearly understood by the hearer; thereby a subjective element would become decisive; (2) consequently an expression would become *faṣīḥ* to Zayd and *ghayr faṣīḥ* to ʿAmr, whereas the *faṣīḥ* is uncontrovertibly so for everybody; (3) an ugly word would be *faṣīḥ* as long as it was *ẓāhir* and *bayyin*, evident and clear; yet *faṣāḥa* is *waṣf ḥusn al-lafẓ lā waṣf ḳubḥ*, *i.e.*, it indicates the properties which make a word beautiful, not those that make it ugly. Unfortunately, Ibn al-Athīr's amendment to the definition fails of its objective when it explains understandability by familiarity in prose and poetry and accounts for this familiarity by the beauty of the particular expressions which induces the writers to seek them out. The criterion is phonetic attraction, which proves that *faṣāḥa* is not connected with the *maʿnā* but merely with the acoustics of the expression (26)—a position which Ibn al-Ḥadīd (d. 655/1257), *al-Falak al-dāʾir ʿala 'l-mathal al-sāʾir*, Bombay 1308, 39-40, was seriously to question. If it is argued that to equate the *faṣīḥ* with the *mafhūm* would raise the problem that many Ḳurʾānic verses even though necessarily *faṣīḥ* require a commentary, the answer (which applies to many a poem and other literary document as well) is that the individual words are all clear and *faṣīḥ*; a *tafsīr* is needed because of the profundity of the *maʿnā* (*al-Mathal al-sāʾir*, Cairo 1312, 27). Ibn al-Athīr notes that every language has its own *faṣāḥa* (and *balāgha*) but Arabic is superior to all other tongues because of its amplitude, *tawassuʿāt* (28). (On 73 Ibn al-Athīr reports the opinion of an unidentified Jew that Arabic is the most beautiful language because it was the last to be created and the *Wāḍiʿ* improved on the defects of those created earlier. Nuwayrī, vii, 6, was to reserve *faṣāḥa*, defined as freedom from *al-lukna al-aʿdjamiyya*, exclusively for the Arabs; by contrast, Ibn Ḳayyim, *Fawāʾid*, 9, states expressly that neither *faṣāḥa* nor *balāgha* are peculiar to *al-alfāẓ al-ʿarabiyya*; the concepts apply to any phrase whose wording is unusual and which is yet easily understood, *lafẓu-hu gharīb wa-fahmu-hu ḳarīb*). It is foolish to maintain as some do that every word is *ḥasan* because the *Wāḍiʿ* has not coined any ugly word. In (unstated) agreement with the principles of legal *idjmāʿ*, Ibn al-Athīr considers *ḥasan* and *ḳabīḥ* what has always been so considered by the Arabs. In doing so personal preferences are eliminated (59-60). It must be realised that the class of beautiful words comprises such words as have always been in use and others that were in use formerly but are no longer (*e.g.*, many expressions occurring in Ḳurʾān and *ḥadīth*)—this fact restricts the use of *ʿurf* as a criterion of beauty (62, 61). On the whole, Ibn al-Athīr makes his own the criteria for the beauty of a *lafẓa* which Khafādjī had developed. (Ibn al-Athīr's eight requirements correspond to Khafādjī's A 1, 5, 8, 4, 3, 6, 7, 2; in 2 the agreement is slightest; in regard to 7 he differs, 72-3, with Khafādjī on detail and is, in turn, attacked by Ibn al-Ḥadīd, 85-6, who (83-4) also finds fault with his position on 1. Ibn al-Athīr's description of the effect of phonetic *tanāfur*, 60-1, is deservedly referred to by Taftazānī, *Mukhtaṣar*, i, 80).

Ibn al-Athīr's treatment of "composition", *ṣināʿat taʾlīf al-alfāẓ*, is superior to Khafādjī's in clarity. He lists eight "parts" (74), the first five of which are traceable in Khafādjī: *musadjdjaʿ* (= *sadjʿ* and *izdiwādj*), *taṣrīʿ*, *tadjnīs* (= *mudjānas*), *tarṣīʿ* and *luzūm mā lam yalzam*; a sixth, *muwāzana*, corresponds to Khafādjī's *tanāsub fi 'l-miḳdār*; for the seventh, *ikhtilāf ṣiyagh al-alfāẓ*, the variation of the aesthetic effect when the same root appears in different moulds, Ibn al-Athīr claims originality (110); the eighth, *takrīr al-ḥurūf*, is in the actual discussion replaced by two: *al-muʿāẓala al-lafẓiyya*, the "crowding of one part of *kalām* upon another" (cf. Lane, 2086a), and, again presented as an original contribution, *al-munāfara bayn al-alfāẓ fi 'l-sabk* (118-9), the juxtaposition of words that do not fit together in the particular context.

To carry the presentation to the conventional limits of the Middle Ages reference may be made to al-Suyūṭī (d. 911/1505) who, *Muzhir*, i, 91-2, adopts Ḳazwīnī's concept except for the tacit omission of the *faṣāḥa* pertaining to a whole sentence. Usage would appear to be for Suyūṭī the decisive factor constituting an expression *faṣīḥ*. *Faṣāḥa* allows of gradation. Some words are more *afṣaḥ* than others; thus *burr* in relation to *ḳamḥ* and *ḥinṭa* (i, 105; cf. Ibn al-Athīr, 26-7 and 59-60 with Ibn al-Ḥadīd, 40, on *muzna* and *dīma* as *afṣaḥ* than *buʿāḳ*); so of course are some speakers, and the Prophet is *afṣaḥ* of all (103).

To be fully understood, the distinction between *faṣāḥa* and *balāgha* must be seen, on the one hand, in the context of the dualism of form and content that dominates the critical thought of the Arab-Muslim theorist and, on the other, in the context of the dualism which the Muslim philosophy of language predicates of its subject. When the activity which results in language is analysed into its two components, *faṣāḥa* emerges as the "virtue" co-ordinated with man's physiological, phonetic effort and *balāgha* as the "virtue" registering the realization of his mental endeavour (for the Ikhwān al-Safāʾ as representatives of this "dualism of language" cf. J. Lecerf, *Stud. Isl.*, xii (1960), 22-3).

Bibliography: In the article; in addition: F. A. Mehren, *Die Rhetorik der Araber*, Copenhagen and Vienna, 1853, 15-8.

(G. E. VON GRUNEBAUM)

FASANDJUS (BANŪ), the name of one of the families which hereditarily shared among themselves the high administrative offices under the Buwayhid régime. The founder of this family's fortune was Abu 'l-Faḍl al-ʿAbbās b. Fasandjus, a rich notable of Shīrāz who, after being fined 600,000 dirhams by ʿAlī b. Buwayh (ʿImād al-Dawla), had taken a part in the farming of taxes for that prince (322/934), and then, in 338/949, had entered the service of Muʿizz al-Dawla, for whom he administered the finances of Baṣra. It was there that he died in 342/953, at the age of 77, leaving his son Abu 'l-Faradj Muḥammad to inherit his position; the latter, on the death of the vizier al-Muhallabī, succeeded him, though without the title, at the head of the administration of ʿIrāḳ (352/963). In 355/966 Muʿizz al-Dawla sent him to conquer ʿUmān (a letter from al-Ṣābī has been preserved, replying to his report of the victory, Paris MS arabe 6195, 167 v°); he returned on the death of that ruler in the following year. Under ʿIzz al-Dawla Bakhtiyār he shared the vizierate and then came into conflict with Abu 'l-Faḍl al-ʿAbbās al-Shīrāzī, and finally lived in retirement from 360 until 370 (971-81) when he died. However, his death did not bring about the ruin of his family, which apparently remained strongly established in Fars. Abū Muḥammad ʿAlī, brother of Abu 'l-Faradj, was vizier to Sharaf al-Dawla in 373-4/984-5, and Abu 'l-Faradj's son Abu 'l-Ḳāsim Djaʿfar (355-419/966-1029) also vizier to Sulṭān al-Dawla, in Fārs and then for a time in Baghdād (408-9/1017-8). The son of Abu 'l-Ḳāsim, named like his grandfather Abu 'l-Faradj Muḥammad, with the additional name Dhu 'l-Saʿādāt, was vizier to Djalāl al-Dawla in ʿIrāḳ from 421/1030 at the latest until that ruler's death in 435/1044; he was retained in the same office by Abū Kālīdjār, who however had him arrested in 439/1047 and put to death in the following year, at the age of 51 (Ibn al-Athīr gives the name of Djalāl al-Dawla's vizier in 428/1037 as Abu 'l-Faḍl al-ʿAbbās b. al-Ḥasan b. Djaʿfar, another member of this family, who in any case cannot have held this office for any length of time). Abu 'l-Faradj's son, ʿAlāʾ al-Dīn Abu 'l-Ghanāʾim Saʿd, seems to have been vizier to the last Buwayhid in Baghdād, al-Malik al-Raḥīm, at the time of Tughrīl-Beg's entry into the city; the Saldjūḳid vizier al-Kundurī had him made governor of Wāsiṭ, perhaps because in his father's lifetime he had successfully fought against the lord of Baṭīḥa there; but, feeling his position to be insecure, he had the town fortified, an action which resulted in making him suspect. Attacked by a Saldjūḳ force, he openly allied himself with al-Basāsīrī [*q.v.*] and proclaimed the Fāṭimid *khuṭba* in Wāsiṭ (the Fāṭimid envoy al-Muʾayyad al-Shīrāzī who alludes to this event in his *Sīra*, 136-7, gives the governor's name as Ibn Ḳāʾid b. Raḥma). Defeated and taken prisoner at the beginning of 449/March-April 1057 with his brother, he was crucified and dismembered, and from that time nothing further is heard of the family.

Bibliography: The chronicles of Miskawayh, Abū Shudjāʿ Rudhrawārī, al-Hamadhānī, and then of Ibn al-Djawzī, Ibn al-Athīr and Sibṭ Ibn al-Djawzī referred to in BUWAYHIDS, and also the two texts mentioned in the article. The genealogical table of Zambaur is entirely invalidated as a result of the division of Abu 'l-Ḳāsim into two homonyms, and the untenable identification of Abu 'l-Faradj II with al-Maḥalbān of Takrīt (because each had a son named Abu 'l-Ghanāʾim).

(CL. CAHEN)

AL-**FĀSHIR** (EL FASHER), the capital of Dār Fūr [*q.v.*], formerly a sultanate, now a province of the Republic of the Sudan. The term *fāshir*, meaning a royal residence, more precisely signified an open space, serving for public audience by a sultan, or as a market-place, and was also used in Sinnār under the Fundj [*q.v.*], and in Waddāī, where *wara* appears as a synonym (see J. L. Burckhardt, *Travels in Nubia*, London 1819, 486). The *fāshir* of the Fūrāwī sultan was established in 1206/1791-2 at Wādī Tandaltī, on a sandy ridge, overlooking a seasonal lake. Around this royal residence, the town developed. It was visited between 1793-6 by W. G. Browne, who has left a plan and description of the palace area, but says nothing of the town. Fuller information, and an elaborate but schematized plan of the palace area, were given by al-Tūnusī, who spent eight years in Dār Fūr from 1218/1803. Outside the palace area, which was surrounded by a triple thorn-fence (*zarība*), were the houses of royal officials, holy men (*fuḳarāʾ*) and others. The inhabitants were divided into two groups, the people of *Warradayā* (the Men's Gate of the palace), and those of *Warrabayā* (the *Ḥarīm* Gate). The houses of the poor were built of millet straw, those of the ruler and notables of mud. Al-Fāshir remained the capital of the sultanate until the annexation of Dār Fūr to the Egyptian Sudan in 1291/1874. Sporadic Fūrāwī resistance continued, and on one occasion al-Fāshir nearly fell to the troops of the shadow-sultan Hārūn. In January 1884, the khedivial garrison surrendered to Muḥammad Khālid Zuḳal, the first Mahdist governor of Dār Fūr. When the Mahdist state was overthrown in 1898, al-Fāshir became the capital of the revived Fūrāwī sultanate of ʿAlī Dīnār. In 1916 Dār Fūr was annexed to the Anglo-Egyptian Sudan, and al-Fāshir became again a provincial capital. Although al-Fāshir has long superseded Kubbayh (Cobbé), which in Browne's time was the trade-centre of Dār Fūr, its difficulty of access from the east has led in recent years to a shift of road-traffic southwards to Nyala, to which town a railway-line was opened in 1959. The population of al-Fāshir, of varied origins, was estimated at c. 2,650 in 1875, and c. 10,000 in 1905. In 1959 it was 26,161.

Bibliography: for the following principal sources, see under DĀR FŪR: Browne, al-Tūnusī, Nachtigal, Slatin, Shuḳayr. Also K. M. Barbour, *The republic of the Sudan*, London [1961], 155-6.

(R. CAPOT-REY and P. M. HOLT)

FĀSHŌDA proper, the royal village of the Shilluk, lies near the west bank of the White Nile at 9° 50′ N., 31° 58′ E. It is the principal site of the elaborate ceremonies by which a *Reth* of the Shilluk is invested with his 'divine' attributes.

An Egyptian expedition under the *Ḥukmdār* ʿAlī Khūrshīd reached Fāshōda in 1830. In 1855 a government post was founded on the river some 18 kms. downstream, at 9° 53′ N., 32° 07′ E., and was named after Fāshōda as the nearest place of importance. In 1863 this post became the headquarters of the newly-created *mudīriyya* of the White Nile. Its garrison contributed to the suppression of the riverain slave-trade, but Fāshōda acquired an evil reputation as an unhealthy 'punishment station' for criminal and political exiles. Heavy taxation and forced recruiting led to conflict with the Shilluk. Although the Egyptians were sometimes able to procure the election of friendly *Reth*s, in 1866 and again in 1875 the post was almost overwhelmed by Shilluk risings.

On 9 December 1881, near Djabal Ḳadīr in south-eastern Kordofān, Muḥammad Aḥmad al-Mahdī [*q.v.*] annihilated a force from Fāshōda under the *mudīr* Rāshid Aymān. The rout of this strong, but ill-planned and unauthorized, expedition greatly increased the Mahdī's prestige and influence. Further Mahdist successes in Kordofān, culminating in the total defeat of Hicks at Shaykān (5 November 1883), threatened communications with Fāshōda and enforced its evacuation early in 1884.

In 1891, the Shilluk having refused to pay *zakāt*, Fāshōda was occupied and the Shilluk country harried by a Mahdist force under al-Zākī Ṭamal. Late in 1892 the Mahdists withdrew, leaving the *Reth*ship in the hands of their nominee, Kūr Galdwan *alias* ʿAbd al-Fāḍil. *Reth* Kūr maintained Fāshōda as a staging-post in the Mahdist communications with Equatoria and paid occasional tribute in grain; the Mahdists supported him against rival claimants and disaffected Shilluk sections.

On 10 July 1898 J.-B. Marchand, with about 100 men, occupied the former Egyptian fort at Fāshōda. On 25 August he repelled an attack by a Mahdist flotilla under Saʿīd al-Ṣughayyar. On 3 September, by treaty with *Reth* Kūr, he placed the Shilluk country under French protection. On 19 September Kitchener arrived from Omdurmān with five steamers and a mainly Egyptian force of over 1,000 men. Marchand's presence and status were referred to Europe for diplomatic solution; but Kitchener hoisted the Egyptian flag and installed H. W. Jackson as Egyptian *mudīr* of Fāshōda. The ensuing Anglo-French crisis was resolved on 3 November, when the French Cabinet, under an implicit British threat of war, agreed to withdraw Marchand from Fāshōda unconditionally. This news, unnecessarily delayed by Cromer, did not however reach Fāshōda until 4 December; meanwhile, relations between the rival commanders had deteriorated almost to the point of armed conflict. Marchand evacuated Fāshōda on 11 December 1898.

From 1898 until 1902, when Baḥr al-Ghazāl was constituted as a separate province, the entire southern Sudan was administered from Fāshōda. In 1903 the 'administrative' Fāshōda was re-named Kodok (after the nearest Shilluk hamlet), and the Fāshōda Province was henceforth termed Upper Nile Province. Its equatorial regions became a separate province (Mongalla) in 1906. In 1914 the headquarters of the truncated Upper Nile Province were transferred to Malakāl: Kodok has since been merely the headquarters of Shilluk District.

Bibliography: W. Hofmayr, *Die Schilluk*, Venna 1925; P. P. Howell and W. P. G. Thomson, *The death of a Reth of the Shilluk and the installation of his successor*, in *S[udan] N[otes and] R[ecords]*, xxvii (1946), 5-85; P. P. Howell, *The election and installation of Reth Kur wad Fafiti of the Shilluk*, *ibid.*, xxxiv/2 (1953), 189-204; R. L. Hill, *Egypt in the Sudan*, London 1959; J. R. Gray, *A history of the Southern Sudan*, London 1961; P. M. Holt, *The Mahdist State in the Sudan*, Oxford 1958; H. W. Jackson, *Fashoda 1898*, in *SNR*, iii/1 (1920), 1-9; J. Emily, *Mission Marchand*, Paris 1913; [A.-E.-A.] Baratier, *Souvenirs de la Mission Marchand: Fachoda*, Paris 1941; W. L. Langer, *The diplomacy of Imperialism*², New York 1951; P. Renouvin, *Les origines de l'expédition de Fachoda*, in *Revue Historique*, cc/408 (1948), 180-97; G. N. Sanderson, *The European Powers and the Sudan in the later nineteenth century*, in *SNR*, xl (1959), 79-100; R. Robinson and J. Gallagher, *Africa and the Victorians*, London 1961.

(G. N. SANDERSON)

AL-**FĀSĪ**, TAḲĪ AL-DĪN MUḤAMMAD B. AḤMAD B. ʿALĪ AL-MAKKĪ AL-ḤASANĪ AL-MĀLIKĪ (775-832/1373-1429), historian of Mecca, was, through family connexions and upbringing, eminently qualified for his lifework as the outstanding historian of his native city. His father Aḥmad (754-819/1353-1416) had received an excellent scholarly education and was married to a daughter of the Meccan chief judge Abu 'l-Faḍl Muḥammad b. Aḥmad b. ʿAbd-al-ʿAzīz al-Nuwayrī; a daughter of his, and half-sister of the historian, was, in her first marriage, married briefly to the amīr of Mecca, Ḥasan b. ʿAdjlān. Among al-Fāsī's teachers we find the author of Mālikī biographies, Ibn Farḥūn, with whom he studied al-Maṭarī's *History of Medina* in Medina (where he had already lived for a few years as a young boy) in 796/1393-4. In Damascus, he studied with Abū Hurayra, the son of al-Dhahabī, and of Ibn Khaldūn, whom he may have met in Egypt, he speaks as "our shaykh". Thus, the interest in historical studies, which was characteristic of his times, came to him naturally.

His professional life followed the usual pattern. He travelled much as a student and in later life. His first visit to Egypt took place in 797/1394-5, followed by a trip to Damascus and the scholarly centres of Palestine in the next year and, in 805/1402-3, by a first trip to South Arabia, where he spent much time later on; his remarks on the history of the composition of his works, which he conscientiously appended to them, permit us to follow his travels in some detail. He was appointed Mālikī judge of Mecca in 807/1405 and remained in this position, with brief interruptions in 817/December 1414-January 1415 and 819-20/January-May 1417, until he became blind four years before his death. He managed to obtain a *fatwā* from Mālikī authorities in Cairo permitting him to remain in office for a while, but soon he had to retire permanently; during his blindness, he continued his scholarly work. His learning, character, and social bearing were highly praised, but there must have been some latent discontent stored up in him since the *waḳf* deed for his works contained the stipulation that they be not lent to a Meccan.

His numerous works included an abridgment of the *Ḥayāt al-ḥayawān* of his teacher, al-Damīrī, and a number of writings on *ḥadīth* and other religious subjects, of which two are preserved, *Djawāhir al-uṣūl fi 'l-ḥadīth* and *al-Arbaʿūn al-ḥadīth al-mutabāyināt al-isnād*. Biographical works on religious scholars included his Supplement to Ibn Nuḳta's *Taḳyīd* (which also contained an autobiography of his) and a negative appreciation of Ibn ʿArabī. Of general historical titles, we may mention the *Muntakhab al-Mukhtār*, an abridgment of Ibn Rāfiʿ's supplement to Ibn al-Nadjdjār's supplement to the *Taʾrīkh Baghdād* (Baghdād 1357/1938; another old ms. in Mecca, cf. *Shifāʾ*, ii, 432, n. 2); a partly preserved supplement to al-Dhahabī's *Nubalāʾ* (Berlin 9873); a supplement to the same author's *Ishāra* and a History of the Rasūlids (not preserved).

Al-Fāsī's fame, however, rests upon his works on the history of Mecca, a subject which had been strangely neglected practically since the times of al-Azraḳī and al-Fākihī [*q.v.*]. His basic works are *Shifāʾ al-gharām bi-akhbār al-balad al-ḥarām* (Mecca-Cairo 1956; some chapters in Wüstenfeld, *Die Chroniken der Stadt Mekka*, Leipzig 1857-61, ii, 55 ff.) and *al-ʿIḳd al-thamīn fī taʾrīkh al-balad al-amīn* (Cairo 1289-90; Mecca 1314; additional mss. Cairo Taymūr, *taʾrīkh* 849; Yale L-305 [Cat. Nemoy 1179]; Kattānī, cf. *Revue Inst. Mss. ar.*, v [1959], 184; Istanbul Feyzullah [*not* Fatih] 1482; al-Azhar, cf. *Fihris al-makhṭūṭāt al-muṣawwara*, ii/1, 181 f., ii/2, 106, etc.). The *Shifāʾ* contains (1) the description and history of the physical features, both natural and man-made, of Mecca and environs, including a discussion of the holy places and the rituals connected with them; (2) the ancient pre-Islamic history of the city; (3) a chronological list of its governors and rulers; and (4) a selection of historical events connected with it. The *ʿIḳd*, on the other hand, although it starts out with the holy topography of the city (abridged from the *Shifāʾ* and entitled *al-Zuhūr al-muḳtaṭafa min taʾrīkh Makka al-musharrafa*), is a collection of biographies of persons connected in some way with the city, beginning with a biography of the Prophet (entitled *al-Djawāhir al-saniyya fi 'l-sīra al-nabawiyya*) and biographies of the other Muḥammads and Aḥmads, including a lengthy autobiography of the author in the third person, and then using an alphabetic arrangement. Of the *Shifāʾ*, al-Fāsī produced five or six successive abridgments, among them *Tuḥfat al-kirām bi-akhbār al-balad al-ḥarām* and, as an abridgment of the *Tuḥfa*, *Taḥṣīl al-marām min taʾrīkh al-balad al-ḥarām* (additional mss. in Princeton 594 [393B]; Bursa, Hüseyin Çelebi 794). An abridged edition of the *ʿIḳd* is preserved in *ʿUdjālat al-ḳirā li 'l-ghārib fī taʾrīkh Umm al-Ḳurā*. A work entitled *al-Muḳniʿ fī akhbār al-mulūk wa 'l-khulafāʾ wa-wulāt Makka al-musharrafa* was published by F. Erdmann (Kazan 1822), and a work on Medina, *al-Riḍā wa 'l-ḳabūl fī faḍāʾil al-Madīna wa-ziyārat al-Rasūl*, appears in the margin of the Meccan edition of the *ʿIḳd* (neither of them seen by this writer).

Biography: Wüstenfeld, *op. cit.*, ii, vi-xvi; Brockelmann, II, 221 f., S II, 221 f. In addition to the autobiography in the *ʿIḳd*, cf., for instance, Muḥammad Ibn Fahd, *Laḥẓ al-alḥāẓ*, Damascus 1347, 291-7; Sakhāwī, *Ḍawʾ*, vii, 18-20; idem, *Iʿlān*, in F. Rosenthal, *A history of Muslim historiography*, Leiden 1952, 404, 408, 414 f. (and *ibid.*, 524, for al-Sakhāwī, *al-Djawāhir wa 'l-durar*); Ibn al-ʿImād, *Shadharāt*, vii, 199. According to *Ḍawʾ*, al-Fāsī also has biographies in works of younger contemporaries such as Ibn Ḥadjar, *Inbāʾ* and *Muʿdjam*; al-Maḳrīzī, *ʿUḳūd*; ʿUmar b. Muḥammad Ibn Fahd (who also wrote monographs on the Meccan families of the Fāsīs and Nuwayrīs [*Ḍawʾ*, vi, 128 f.] as well as a continuation of the *ʿIḳd*), *Muʿdjam* of his father.

(F. ROSENTHAL)

FĀSID WA BĀṬIL, In the terminology of the Ḥanafī jurists, *bāṭil* denotes the act which lacks one of the elements essential for the existence of any legal activity. *Buṭlān* embodies the notion of non-existence, and the act which lacks one of these elements which are considered fundamental is, in effect, deemed non-existent.

If, while fulfilling the necessary conditions for its formation, a legal act does not observe the conditions of validity *stricto sensu* required for its perfection (*awṣāf*, sing. *waṣf*, quality), it is then said to be *fāsid*, or vitiated and therefore null. But this nullity (*fasād*) is of a fundamental nature, and therefore has nothing in common with the relative nullity familiar to the Western jurist, who sees only in this latter concept a means of protecting those of defective legal capacity and all those whose agreement has been tainted by duress, error or deceit. Although it sometimes happens—by negligence or inadvertence—that *fāsid* and *bāṭil* are used interchangeably, even by Ḥanafī authors who have a reputation for the scientific rigidity of their definitions, it is none the less true that the distinction between *bāṭil* and *fāsid* is the principal characteristic of the Ḥanafī theory of nullity.

The three other orthodox schools, as well as the former Ẓāhiri school, reject this distinction. According to their writers, there cannot be two degrees of invalidity based upon the nature of the rules whose non-observance is the subject of legal sanction. Thus they use the terms *fāsid* or *bāṭil* indifferently to describe the legal act which is not valid in the eyes of the law. In the doctrine of these schools, the two terms are synonymous, the synonymity reflecting their notion of a single sanction. However, we must state at the outset that for the Shāfiʿīs and the Ḥanbalīs this uniform nullity corresponds to the *bāṭil* form of nullity in Ḥanafī law, while for the Mālikīs its incidents coincide almost exactly with those of the *fāsid* type of nullity as expounded by Ḥanafī law.

If the practical application of the principles we have just expounded does not present serious difficulties, even in Ḥanafī law, when it is only a question of dealings with property (sale, hire, pledge, etc.), it appears, on the contrary, singularly complicated in relation to the contract of marriage. In this sphere, the fluctuations of the classical doctrine, as it grappled with a contract arbitrarily classified in the same category as sale or hire (*tamlīkāt*), but which, in fact, is radically distinct from them, have reverberated down the course of the centuries in the works of authors and have reappeared at the present time—always on the same point—in the codes and laws of personal status recently promulgated in numerous Arab countries. It is therefore necessary to study the theory of nullity in the sphere of marriage separately in a third section.

I. Ḥanafī doctrine. (A). Non-existence, *al-buṭlān*. This, as has just been explained, is the sanction for the lack of any of the essential elements of a legal act, *e.g.*, free will of the two parties (in contracts), which, furthermore, must be expressed by the use of a verb in the past tense and which must be declared in those conditions of time and place which together constitute what is called the session of the contract or the *madjlis*. Free will is presumed impossible (thence occasioning the non-existence of the act) in the case of a mentally defective person, a minor of tender years, and even in the case of a minor who has reached the age of discretion, when this latter performs an act, such as gift, which must necessarily cause him a material loss. Further elements considered fundamental are the actual existence of the object, its quality of legal property and the possibility of its delivery (the sale of fish in the sea and birds in the air is *bāṭil*).

The *bāṭil* act, since it is considered non-existent, cannot have any legal effect, whether there has been delivery or not. Reasoning on the classical hypothesis of sale—the same rules applying *mutatis mutandis* to all legal acts—it follows that the purchaser, who has not become the owner, cannot constrain the vendor to deliver to him the sale object, no more than the vendor can require the purchaser to pay him the agreed price. If, in fact, there has been a performance of the agreement reached between them (which is no more than the semblance of a sale) the *status quo* must be restored, *i.e.*, the vendor must return the price received and the purchaser the object delivered, without any need of recourse to law, at least to establish the non-existence of the act. Suppose, now, that after a *bāṭil* sale followed by delivery the transferee in turn alienates the object, either for a consideration or gratuitously, or that he subjects it to some kind of lien, or that he hires it out or constitutes it as a *wakf*. In either event, the original vendor will not be deprived of the right to regain his property from the hands of a third party, whether this latter be a purchaser for value, a lessee, or the beneficiary of a *wakf*. The property, in fact, has never left his ownership because the sale concluded by him was legally non-existent—so much so, the Ḥanafī authors state, that his heirs will succeed to his right and will be able, after his death, to reclaim from the third party the object of which they are now the owners.

There is one case where the application of the principles outlined above may possibly result in injustice. This is where the object sold has perished when in the possession of the transferee.

Strict logic would require that the risks should lie with the vendor: he has remained the owner, since, by reason of the *bāṭil* character of the sale, transfer of ownership has not been effected. The transferee, after having taken possession of the object, can only be considered, at most, as a trustee; and risks, in the case of a trust, lie with the owner. There exists on this point some uncertainty in the doctrine. In general, authors confine themselves—without taking one side or the other—to expounding two applicable arguments: (a) the transferee is simply a trustee (*amīn*), and the loss of the object releases him; (b) the transferee is a guarantor of the object, for this has been delivered to him not in the interests of the owner, but in his own interests. His taking of possession more closely resembles *ghaṣb* (usurpation) than a trust (*amāna*).

It would seem that this latter argument prevailed. In the *bāṭil* sale, therefore, the risks will lie with the purchaser, when this latter has taken possession of the sale object which has then perished in his possession. He becomes liable for its value if it is a specific object, and where it is a fungible commodity, he will be bound to restore its equivalent (*mithl*).

(B). Fundamental nullity, *fasād*, is the sanction for the infringement of conditions of validity which do not have the character of constituent elements of a legal act. Such are held to be the precise determination of the object, as regards both its nature and its value, the absence of any illicit gain (*ribā*) and of the majority of accompanying conditions, and the exclusion of any prejudice which would be occasioned by the delivery of possession. As for the act obtained by duress, this also is regarded as *fāsid* in Ḥanafī law; but this kind of *fāsid* nullity is regulated in a particular fashion which distinguishes it from the *fāsid* nullity of common law.

As a general proposition, we may say that the great majority of *fāsid* acts derive their character, in Ḥanafī law, from the fact that they contain accompanying conditions: an uncertain term or a suspensive condition (in the majority of the *tamlīkāt*), immoral or illegal stipulations, or simply conditions which are not in harmony with the nature of the act to which they are attached. This extends considerably the sphere of *fāsid* nullity, which can thus be regarded as parallel with the nullity of common law, as opposed to the *bāṭil* nullity whose rôle is most often confined to those theoretical arguments of a school which have no real practical interest.

The effects of *fāsid* nullity are less extreme than those attached to *bāṭil* nullity. This is easily explained inasmuch as the *fāsid* act, although void, is nevertheless constituted; juridically speaking, it exists, although it is vitiated and therefore needs to be negated. The difference between the two kinds of nullity is especially apparent after the delivery of possession or voluntary performance. (a) *Before* delivery of possession (or, for certain contracts, voluntary performance) the *fāsid* act is not greatly distinct from the *bāṭil* act. As is the case with the latter it does not give any of the parties the power to compel performance from the other. Each of them has the right, and the duty, to avail himself of the nullity. A judicial decree is not at all necessary, and the nullity will be established by the declaration of one of the parties or even by the simple act, of the vendor, for example, in alienating the object for the benefit of a third party. The judge who has knowledge of such an act, must, by virtue of his office, pronounce its nullity. It is self-evident that *fāsid* nullity cannot be removed by confirmation. The act must be performed again in its entirety. However, if the nullity does not stem from a defect in the sale object, but results from the presence of a prohibited condition, the elimination of the offending condition will validate the act, which, thenceforth, will produce its normal effects. A usurious sale, from which the parties, by common agreement, have eliminated the clauses which gave it this character, will transfer ownership from the moment that the forbidden clause disappeared. (b) *After* the taking of possession authorized by the vendor (reasoning always on the basis of a sale), the *fāsid* act will produce certain effects which the *bāṭil* act can never have. It is not that the taking of possession transforms it into a valid act (*ṣaḥīḥ*): this is certainly not so. It continues to be tainted with an absolute nullity, although the vendor has authorized the purchaser to take possession; and this latter is bound to restore the object received and to take back the price he has paid. Delivery of possession, then, following upon a *fāsid* sale, does not transfer ownership in Ḥanafī law, although such an assertion is often made without the necessary reservations.

According to the opinion which prevails in the school, delivery of possession does not in reality transfer ownership, or at least ownership in the normal sense, since the vendor can always reclaim his property as long as it is in the possession of the transferee. Furthermore, this transferee cannot enjoy or use the thing which he has received (with the agreement of the vendor). "He cannot eat it, nor wear it (if it is a garment), nor ride it (if it is a beast of burden), nor live in the house (which he has bought), nor avail himself of the services of the slave girl that he has acquired" (al-Kāsānī). What does result from delivery of possession following a *fāsid* sale is solely the transferee's power validly to dispose of the object delivered to him, either gratuitously or for a consideration—*e.g.*, he may sell it, give it away, constitute it as a *waḳf*, or, if it is a slave, set him free. This fiction of ownership, albeit an odd ownership (*khabīth*a, bad, defective) in that it confers upon the one in whom it vests the *abusus*, but not the *usus* or the *fructus*, is quite obviously designed to protect subsequent transferees against a claim for restitution by the original vendor, in so far as their title cannot be impugned on the ground that they acquired the property from one who was not the owner. It is this Ḥanafī system, perhaps, which appears the least complicated.

Apart from this result, vital for the protection of future transferees, delivery of possession or performance following a *fāsid* contract operates to produce two other effects, less important but not altogether devoid of interest. In the first place, where *fāsid* nullity is solely the result of the incorporation of a prohibited term within the transaction (an uncertain period, for example), the party in whose interests the term was stipulated has the option of relying upon the nullity or, on the other hand, validating the transaction by renouncing the benefit of the term; whereas, prior to delivery of possession, confirmation of the transaction by repudiation of the offending term could only have been effected by the mutual agreement of the two parties. The second result of the *fāsid* character of a legal transaction comes into play where the transferee has in fact utilised the property delivered to him, or, in case of a contract for services, these services have been performed, or, of course, where the first transferee has alienated the property sold. In this case, in order that nullity may not result in unjust enrichment, the price, rent or wages which become due will not be the agreed price, rent or wages (since the contract is null), but will be the market value of the property, or the rent customarily payable, or the usual wages.

II. The doctrine of the other schools. The three other schools refuse to admit degrees of invalidity. To fail to observe the conditions required by the Sharīʿa for the validity of an act is equally serious whether it is a question of a fundamental condition or of an attribute (*waṣf*), which, although it does not have an essential character, is nevertheless imposed by the law. In both cases there is "disobedience" to the rules of the Sharīʿa which must be sanctioned by the same nullity.

For the Shāfiʿīs and the Ḥanbalīs, this single nullity corresponds with the *bāṭil* nullity of Ḥanafī law, at least as far as concerns the invalidity of acts of disposition effected by the transferee in a void sale: subsequent transferees are not protected against the claim of the original vendor. On this point the texts are explicit. However, outside contracts which operate to transfer ownership, the Shāfiʿīs and the Ḥanbalīs sometimes accept the distinction between *bāṭil* and *fāsid* in order to avoid, as far as possible, the injustice which would be entailed by the voluntary performance of a void contract if the *status quo ante* was purely and simply restored as the principle of *buṭlān* would require. Finally, the possibility, admitted by both these schools, of the partial annulment of a composite contract concluded by a single legal transaction (*ṣafḳa*), which contains both valid and invalid components (the sale, at the same time, of a free man and a slave), fortunately serves to relax, to some degree, the rigidity of their principles.

The Mālikīs, on their part, regulate the single nullity which sanctions invalid acts (termed *fāsid* or *bāṭil*) in a different way, with the result that their system is closely parallel to the system of *fāsid* nullity in Ḥanafī law, at least as far as concerns sale, the prototype contract of Islamic law. Recovery by the original vendor in a void sale is impossible, state the Mālikī authors, when the purchaser has disposed of the property to the profit of a third party, whether by way of sale for a consideration or by gift, or when he has set free a slave, or even when he has merely made the property a pledge or has transferred it to a bailee. In these last two cases the original vendor is bound by the pledge or the bailment for their full duration. Equally, recovery by the original vendor is inadmissible when the form (*ṣūra*) of the sale-object has been changed, by "increase or decrease", while in the possession of the first transferee. In this case the vendor will have to be satisfied with monetary compensation.

III. Nullity of marriage. Certain Ḥanafī authors of authority assert that the distinction between *bāṭil* and *fāsid* which, for reasons readily understandable, does not apply to ritual obligations (*ʿibādāt*), is equally alien to the contract of marriage, where all defects, whether they attach to the essence of the contract or to its external conditions of validity, are sanctioned by the same single nullity which is neither exactly a *fāsid* nullity nor exactly a *bāṭil* nullity. In point of fact, the thought of the classical authors is difficult to follow on this matter, and the question of nullity in marriage presents one of the most difficult problems of Ḥanafī law. For the other schools the problem is hardly more simple, and the solutions which appear to have prevailed with them seem, paradoxically enough, to establish the distinction between *bāṭil* and *fāsid* which they rejected in other spheres of the law.

Difficulties and uncertainties stem from the fact that the question is bound up with a problem peculiar to Islamic penal law—that of *shubha*, or semblance, which is one of the grounds for avoidance of the fixed penalties. The doctrine of each school —and, in the Ḥanafī school, the two doctrines there adopted concerning nullity in marriage—are directly influenced by the position taken by the jurists in regard to this theory of *shubha*. Indeed, it must not be forgotten that the annulment of a marriage, with its retrospective effect, results in the assumption that the spouses have never in fact been married; if, therefore, there has been consummation, this will, in principle, be held to be fornication, punishable by the severe fixed penalty (*ḥadd*) prescribed in cases of *zinā*. This penalty, like all the other fixed penalties (*ḥudūd*), is avoided whenever there exists a *shubha*, or semblance, between the deed with which the accused is charged and another deed of the same nature which is indisputably not criminal. According to Abū Ḥanīfa, such a semblance is found in three sets of circumstances: firstly, when the action with which the accused is charged resembles an action which is normally permissible (*shubha fi 'l-fiʿl*), although here the accused must have acted in good faith and in ignorance of the criminal character of the act—a husband, for example, has had sexual relations with his wife, believing them to be permissible, during the period of retirement which follows an irrevocable repudiation; secondly, when the illegality founded upon a proof text may appear dubious because of the existence of another, ambiguous text (*shubha fi 'l-maḥall*) which precludes any unanimity of juristic opinion on the point concerned,—a Ḥanafī, for example, could believe that the presence of witnesses at the moment of the conclusion of a marriage is not indispensible since they are not required, at that moment, by the Mālikīs; finally, when the act has been done as the result of a contract which observed merely the conditions of formation (*shubhat al-ʿaḳd*). This third category of *shubha* is admitted by Abū Ḥanīfa alone, and is rejected by his two pupils (Abū Yūsuf and al-Shaybānī) and by the three other Imāms: its result is the avoidance of the *ḥadd* for fornication in every case where the dissolution of a marriage has taken place for any reason whatsoever, even where it is a case of a contract vitiated in its essence. Accordingly, in the opinion of Abu Ḥanīfa—and in his opinion alone—if the contract of marriage is ostensibly valid because it fulfills all the necessary conditions of formation, but its nullity is nevertheless manifest because there exists an impediment to marriage between these two spouses (too close a blood-relationship, foster relationship, the husband already having four wives, the wife already being married to another man who has not repudiated her, etc.) then, in these cases, the penalty for fornication will not be applied after the separation of the couple; and this will be so whether or not the spouses acted in good faith, *i.e.*, whether they knew, or did not know, of the prohibition they were infringing. The two pupils of Abū Ḥanīfa, and all the jurists of the three other schools, did not admit the *shubhat al-ʿaḳd*, and accordingly decided that in such a case the penalty for fornication would lapse only if one, at least, of the two spouses believed that the law was not being broken by their contract of marriage—this, by applying the *shubha fi 'l-fiʿl*. In other words, the dissolution of a marriage on the ground that there existed a legal impediment between the spouses will entail the application of the *ḥadd* only where the two spouses acted in bad faith, knowing that they were being married in contravention of a legal prohibition.

In seeking to reconcile the preceding solutions, which are of a penal nature and are strictly concerned only with the offence of fornication, with the rules relating to the conditions of formation and validity of a marriage, the authors arrived at two systems of nullity. The Ḥanafī school always hesitated between the two, while the three other schools adopted the second. It is necessary, at the beginning, to stress that if the ground for nullity is established before consummation, the marriage is deemed, purely and simply, never to have existed: there is no dower, no maintenance and no rights of succession should one of the spouses die before the declaration of nullity. Any Muslim has the right to invoke such a declaration by the court, if the spouses themselves have not made it: this, in fact, they are obliged to do and, moreover, no formalities are required. On this point there is a consensus of opinion. When nullity is established after consummation, Abū Ḥanīfa distinguishes between the fact that it results from the absence of a condition of the existence of marriage (legal capacity of the spouses, mutual agreement in the course of the same contractual session) and the fact that it results from any other cause external to the formation of the contract. In the first case the marriage does not exist. It is *bāṭil* and it produces no effect, neither entitlement to succession, nor legitimacy of children, nor the obligation of the wife to observe the 'waiting period' (*ʿidda*). However, because of the *shubhat al-ʿaḳd* which results from the semblance of a contract the spouses are not liable for the *ḥadd* penalty, and, because there is no *ḥadd*, the wife is entitled to the dower, by virtue of the maxim: 'Sexual relations with a woman entail either a payment (*ʿuḳr*) or a penalty (*ʿaḳr*). In the second case, there exists a marriage which, as a matter of form, is ostensibly valid although the violation of a legal prohibition renders it null (*fāsid*): Abū Ḥanīfa accordingly ascribes to the union certain of the effects which flow from a valid marriage, even though the two spouses should be aware of the illicit nature of their union: (a) firstly, there is no longer any question of the *ḥadd*, the spouses being relieved therefrom by *shubhat al-ʿaḳd*: (b) because the penalty is avoided, the woman has the right to a dower—the proper (customary) or stipulated dower, whichever is less; (c) the woman will be bound to observe the period of retirement, which will last until the completion of three menstrual periods (*ḳurūʾ*); (d) the issue born of this sexual relationship will be the legitimate children of their father; (e) finally, the *fāsid* marriage will raise a bar to marriage between the relatives of the spouses whose union has been terminated.

According to the two pupils of Abū Ḥanīfa and the three other Imāms (al-Shāfiʿī, Mālik and Ibn Ḥanbal), when nullity is incurred on the ground that the marriage has been concluded in defiance of some prohibition concerning blood relationship, affinity, fosterage, religion, or the fact that the woman was already married or in her period of retirement, or that the husband already had four wives etc., in all cases enquiry must first be made as to whether the ground of nullity is or is not disputed. Where there is no unanimity of the jurists that an impediment in fact exists, the spouses will benefit from the *shubha* which arises from such disagreement. And even when it is admitted that the *idjmāʿ* condemns the union, still enquiry must be made as to whether the spouses were acting, at the moment of the conclusion of the marriage, in good or in bad faith. Where they acted in good faith, the marriage, although naturally null or *fāsid*, will nevertheless give rise to the limited effects which, in Abū Ḥanīfa's view, follow the dissolution of a *fāsid* marriage—although certain schools hold that the wife is necessarily entitled to the proper dower, even if this exceeds the agreed dower.

Where the two spouses acted in bad faith, they are liable to the *ḥadd* for fornication, and none of the normal effects of marriage follows the dissolution of their union (except the *istibrāʾ* of one menstrual period in Mālikī law).

One cannot help drawing a parallel between this system and the institution of putative marriage in Christian canon law. In any event, those who adopt it are returning, without acknowledging it and, indeed, without mentioning it, to the distinction between *fāsid* and *bāṭil*.

The contemporary Codes of Personal Status or laws on the status of the family, which have been recently promulgated (Ottoman Law of 1917, arts. 52-8 and 75-6; Jordanian Law of 1951, arts. 28-9, 37-8; Syrian Code of 1953, arts. 47-51; Tunisian Code of 1956, arts. 21-2; Moroccan Code of 1958, art. 37), although freed from the concern of having to avoid the *ḥadd* for fornication, which is no longer anywhere applied, have adopted the thesis of Abū Ḥanīfa in its broad outlines. However, the Ottoman Law and the Syrian Code consider as *bāṭil* the marriage of a Muslim woman with a non-Muslim, and the Jordanian Law attributes the same character to a marriage between persons within the prohibited degrees, neither of which rules agrees with the principles of Abū Ḥanīfa. The criterion of good faith appears only in a single Code—the Moroccan Code, where art. 37, sec. 5, provides that "where good faith is established, a void marriage will result in a legal connexion between the children born of such a union and their parents".

Bibliography: I. Kāsānī, *Badāʾiʿ al-ṣanāʾiʿ*, Cairo 1327, v, 299 ff.; Ibn al-Ḥumām, *Fatḥ al-Ḳadīr*, and other commentaries of the *Hidāya*, v, 227 ff.; Ibn Nudjaym, *al-Baḥr al-rāʾiḳ*, vi, 90 ff.; Modern authors: Chafik T. Chehata, *Théorie général de l'obligation en droit musulman*, Cairo 1936, 127 ff.; Sanhūrī, *Maṣādir al-ḥaḳḳ*, Cairo 1957, iv, 142 ff.; O. Spies, *Das System der Nichtigkeit im islamischen Recht*, in *Deutsche Landesreferate zum VI. Internationalen Kongress für Rechtsvergleichung 1962*, Berlin and Tübingen 1962, 87-99.

II. Shāfiʿī law: Zakariyyāʾ al-Anṣārī, *Sharḥ al-bahdja ʿala 'l-minhādj*, ii, 435; Suyūṭī, *al-Ashbāh wa 'l-naẓāʾir*, ed. Muṣṭafā Muḥammad, Cairo 1359, 233. Mālikī law: Dasūḳī-Dardīr, *al-Sharḥ al-kabīr*, iii, 70 ff.; Ibn Rushd, *Bidāyat al-mudjtahid*, ed. *al-Istiḳāma*, ii, 191 ff. Ḥanbalī law: Ibn Ḳudāma, *Mughnī*³, iv, 231, 232.

III. Ibn Nudjaym, *op. cit.*, iii, 184, v, 16 ff.; Ibn ʿĀbidīn, *Radd al-Muḥtār*³, Būlāḳ, ii, 835; Ibn al-Ḥumām, *op. cit.*, ii, 382, 468 ff.; Ibn Ḳudāma, *op. cit.*, vi, 455 ff. Among contemporary writers: Abū Zahra, *al-Zawādj*², Cairo 1950, 142 ff.; ʿUmar ʿAbd Allāh, *al-Aḥwāl al-shakhṣiyya*², Cairo 1958, 103 ff.; J. N. D. Anderson, *Invalid and void marriages in Hanafi Law*, in *BSOAS*, xiii/2 (1950), 357 ff. (Y. LINANT DE BELLEFONDS)

FAṢĪḤ [see FAṢĀḤA].

FAṢĪḤ DEDE, AḤMED (d. 1111/1699), Turkish poet of the Mewlewī order, born in Istanbul. He was the son of Meḥmed, of the Dūḳakīnzāde family. After a thorough grounding in oriental literatures he entered the service of the grand vizier Köprülüzāde Aḥmed Pasha, but soon abandoned this easy life to enter the order of the Mewlewīs, and became a disciple of Ghawthī Dede, the sheykh of the famous Galata convent.

Apart from a *dīwān* he is the author of many poems in Persian and Arabic and several *mathnawīs*, strongly mystic in nature and terminology.

Bibliography: The *tedhkires* of Sālim, Ṣafāʾī, Belīgh, Esrār Dede, s.v.; Abdülbâki Gölpınarlı, *Mevlânâ'dan sonra Mevlevilik*, Istanbul 1953, index; *Sidjill-i ʿOthmānī*, iv, 21; Bursalī Ṭāhir, *ʿOthmanlī müʾellifleri*, ii, 366; *Istanbul kütüphaneleri türkçe yazma divanlar kataloğu*, ii, 494.

(FAHIR İZ)

FĀSIḲ, unjust man, guilty of *fisḳ*,—that is to say, one who has committed one or several "great sins" (*kabāʾir*). Most of the authors of *ʿilm al-kalām* avoid extending the term *fāsiḳ* to the believer who is guilty only of "lesser sins" (*ṣaghāʾir*).

The "name and status" (*al-ism wa 'l-ḥukm*) of the *fāsiḳ* is one of the cardinal points discussed by the *kalām*. Its origin goes back to the battle of Ṣiffīn and to the question which believers then raised, as to the destiny on earth and the future destiny of the Muslim leader, and hence of all Muslims who sinned.

Two initial trains of thought: a) the Khāridjīs purely and simply condemned the unrepentant *fāsiḳ* to eternal hell and, on earth, denied his right to stand at the head of the Community. To commit an act of *fisḳ* rendered the *imām* unable to hold his office. (N.B.: for the Shīʿa, the lawful *imām* is inherently sinless). b) The Murdjiʾīs made the unjust man subject, on earth, to the fixed legal penalties (*ḥudūd*); but once this debt to the Community was paid, he remained in full exercise of his status as a believer, and, for the life to come, every believer is saved in hope.

These extreme solutions were to undergo certain modifications in the course of scholastic controversies, but were also to be a source of inspiration for them. It was on this theme that the Muʿtazila elaborated the thesis of the so-called "intermediary status", one of their particular characteristics which is attributed to Wāṣil ibn ʿAṭāʾ. The *fāsiḳ* is not entirely a believer (*muʾmin*) nor entirely an infidel (*kāfir*), but "in a position between the two", *fī manzilatⁱⁿ bayna 'l-manzilatayn*. On earth, he is answerable to the laws of the Muslim Community; but if he does not repent, he will be punished with eternal hell (e.g. *Ḳurʾān*, XXXII, 20)—though his punishment, it is true, will be less severe than that of the *kāfir*. This reply is entirely dependent on the conception of faith (*īmān*) which is involved. In the eyes of the Muʿtazila indeed, to be a believer signifies at once adhering in one's heart, professing with the tongue, and witnessing "with the limbs" by performing the actions prescribed by the Law. Whoever does not fulfil the third condition cannot truly be a believer, and so cannot be saved.

In the *Ibāna* (Cairo 1348, ii) and the *Maḳālāt* (ed. Ritter, i, 293) Abu 'l-Ḥasan al-Ashʿarī defines the faith as "words and deeds", *ḳawl* and *aʿmāl*, thereby appearing to integrate the "witness of the limbs" with it, like the Muʿtazila. But his *Kitāb al-Lumaʿ* (ed. McCarthy, Beirut 1953, 75/104) states: "faith in God is *taṣdīḳ* (adherence) to God". And he taught clearly that it was impossible for a *fāsiḳ* to be neither a believer nor an unbeliever; if he was a believer before becoming a sinner, he said, the "great sin" committed will not invalidate his standing as a believer (*Lumaʿ*, 75-6/104-6). And al-Ashʿarī upholds this opinion with the tradition of the *ahl al-istiḳāma* ("people of Rectitude", in R. J. McCarthy's translation). The later Ashʿarites were to maintain the same principle even more forcibly since, for them, faith came to be identified solely with *taṣdīḳ*, adherence, inner judgement.—The same solution appears in the Ḥanafī-Māturīdī line of thought which defines faith as *taṣdīḳ* and its avowal in the spoken word (thus *Fiḳh Akbar I*, 1; *Waṣiyyat Abī Ḥanīfa*, 4; *Fiḳh Akbar II*, 14). The *fāsiḳ* is a sinner, but a believer.

In its apparent sense, verse XXXII, 18 of the Ḳurʾān certainly seemed to open the way to the Muʿtazila solution: "Is then the man who is a believer like him who is *fāsiḳ*? (No), they are in no way the same". But from the 4th/10th century, the dominant tendencies of *ʿilm al-kalām* taught that the *fāsiḳ* would be saved in the Hereafter. He *can* be punished by a certain time in the (eternal) hell:

As͟hʿarīs; or he will *certainly* be punished in that way: Māturīdīs (*Fiḳh Akbar II*, 14). But finally God will make him enter Paradise. "Those whose heart contains only an atom of faith", says the *ḥadīt͟h*, "will leave hell" (al-Buk͟hārī, *Īmān*, 33). According to the opinion which became generally accepted, good deeds enhance faith, but cease to form an integral part of its expression; to fail in a prescribed duty does not therefore render faith invalid.—Abū Ḥāmid al-G͟hazzālī, who accepted as equally legitimate both the definition which identifies faith with internal adherence alone, and also that which adds verbal profession and bodily actions (cf. *Iḥyāʾ*, Cairo 1352/1933, i, 104-5), defended the same thesis. He defines the *fāsiḳ* as the Muslim who adhered to the faith in his heart, professed it in his words, performed *certain* prescribed actions, but who committed "great sins".

The As͟hʿarī solution is, in short, that of the *ahl al-sunna* taken as a whole, including the Ḥanbalīs, the opponents of *kalām*. It will be found for example in Ibn Taymiyya, and subsequently it became one of the articles of the Wahhābī profession of faith (cf. H. Laoust, *Doctrines sociales et politiques de Taḳī-d-Dīn Aḥmad b. Taimīya*, Cairo 1939, 621).

Two problems. — 1) Can a prophet be said to be *fāsiḳ*? Literalists (called *has͟hwiyya* by their adversaries) have admitted this; but it is a question of purely material or unintentional sins, some will point out. The majority of Sunnīs will consider it blasphemous to attribute the name of *fāsiḳ* to a prophet. In his case they will admit, at most, only "minor sins", and that only insofar as neither the transmission of the message received from God (cf. al-Bād͟jūrī, *Ḥās͟hiya* ... *ʿalā D͟jawharat al-tawḥīd*, Cairo 1352/1934, 71-3), nor even the personal observance of the Law by the prophet is concerned. Moreover, certain acts which appear to be sins have been performed by prophets merely "by way of teaching". The S͟hīʿa (*e.g.*, Naṣīr al-Dīn al-Ṭūsī, Ḥillī) were to teach the absolute sinlessness (*ʿiṣma*) of the prophet, and their doctrine was to influence their adversaries themselves. Thus the "modern" Fak͟hr al-Dīn Rāzī [*q.v.*], who nevertheless maintains the possibility of trifling errors arising from involuntary forgetfulness or from obscurities in the regulations; but still more the Ḥanbalī Ibn Taymiyya who adopts the S͟hīʿa thesis in its entirety, though making the *ʿisma* a gratuitous (and no longer "obligatory") favour of God (cf. Laoust, *op. cit.*, 191).

2) Is it lawful to rise against an *imām* who is *fāsiḳ*? Yes, answered the K͟hārid͟jīs and Muʿtazila, who even regarded insurrection as a duty in that event. The same attitude is found with the Zaydīs (moderate S͟hīʿa) and various S͟hīʿa trends, but the dogma of the *imām*'s sinlessness widely prevailed among the S͟hīʿa.—Certain jurists make a distinction: no revolt against the *imām* who is *fāsiḳ*, but refusal to obey the agents who are enforcing the injustice. Common Sunnī doctrine calls for obedience to the *imām* (and his agents), even if he be *fāsiḳ* in his private life, so long as he orders nothing contrary to Ḳurʾānic law. But if a command of his runs counter to a precise Ḳurʾānic or traditional precept, disobedience is permitted and even obligatory; if there is a guarantee of success, he must be deposed, if necessary by force.

In legal terminology, *fāsiḳ* is the opposite of *ʿadl* [*q.v.*].

Bibliography: in the article; and all the treatises on *ʿilm al-kalām* under the heading *al-aḥkām wa 'l-asmāʾ* (e.g. Baḳillānī, D͟juwaynī, D͟jurd͟jānī, Bād͟jūrī, etc.); A. J. Wensinck, *The Muslim Creed*, Cambridge 1932, index s.v.; L. Gardet, *Les noms et les statuts*, in *Stud. Isl.*, iii, Paris 1956. (L. Gardet)

FĀṢILA in its original usage indicates a separative: "a pearl (*k͟haraza*) which effects a separation between two other pearls in the stringing of the latter" when a necklace or piece of jewellery is being made (see Lane s.v.); *fāṣila*, with this sense of separative, has received two technical usages, one in Arabic prosody, the other in Ḳurʾānic terminology.

In Arabic prosody (*ʿarūḍ* [*q.v.*]), *fāṣila* denotes a division in the primitive feet, meaning three *ḥurūf mutaḥarrika* followed by one *ḥarf sākin*, *e.g.*: *ḳatalat* (*al-fāsila al-ṣug͟hrā*), or else four *ḥurūf mutaḥarrika* followed by one *ḥarf sākin*, *e.g.*: *ḳatala-hum* (*al-fāṣila al-kubrā*). Al-K͟halīl (according to *LA*, xiv, 38, l. 21-2/xi, 523b, l. 27 ff.) used *fāṣila* for the first group and *fāḍila* for the second. The first denotes the series two short syllables + one long syllable, the *anapaest* of Graeco-Latin prosody; the second denotes the series three short syllables + one long syllable, the *fourth paeon* in the said prosody. But there is an important difference: the anapaest and the fourth paeon denote rhythmic units, whilst *fāṣila ṣug͟hrā* or *kubrā* relate to divisions, groups, within primary rhythmic units (the *tafāʿīl*), in order to explain the composition of the latter.

The Ḳurʾānic text carries rhymes. The question was raised in the Muslim world, by what technical term are these rhymes to be designated? There was no hesitation in rejecting the *ḳāfiya* of *s͟hiʿr*, for the Ḳurʾān is not a work of *s͟hiʿr* (poetry). Was the Ḳurʾān *sad͟jʿ* [*q.v.*]? Many of those who did not profess As͟hʿarism (this must refer to the Muʿtazila) adopted and defended this point of view. But after al-As͟hʿarī and al-Bāḳillānī it was abandoned: in fact, on the one hand the verses of the Ḳurʾān, in general, are not balanced according to the rules of *sad͟jʿ* and the rhymes are given a freedom not permitted by the latter (see Th. Nöldeke, *Geschichte des Qorans*², i, 37-41); on the other hand, Muslim religious sentiment was reluctant to apply to the Ḳurʾān, *kalām Allāh*, a designation not derived from Him, and which was moreover taken from a human source, namely the *sad͟jʿ* of the soothsayers, whom Muḥammad disliked. The solution was to consider the Ḳurʾānic text as prose of a particular kind and to designate its rhymes by a special term, *fāṣila*, pl. *fawāṣil*, which could be compared with the Ḳurʾānic expression *faṣṣalnā 'l-āyāt* (VI, 97, 98, 126). Ibn K͟haldūn repeats the opinion which for long had been common, when he writes on the subject of the Ḳurʾān: *wa-in kāna min al-mant͟hūr illā annahū . . . laysa yusammā mursalᵃⁿ iṭlāḳᵃⁿ wa-lā musad͟jd͟jaʿᵃⁿ*, "although it is prose, it is however not free prose, nor rhymed prose (*sad͟jʿ*)" and he expounds its particular character (*Muḳaddima*, iii, 322; Eng. tr., Rosenthal, iii, 368).

The technical designation of rhyme is thus established according to a triple division: *ḳāfiya* for *s͟hiʿr* (poetry), *fāṣila* for Ḳurʾānic prose, and *ḳarīna* for *sad͟jʿ*, and the Ḳurʾānic *fāṣila* was explained by comparison with its partners: *al-fāṣila kalimat āk͟hir al-āya ka-ḳāfiyat al-s͟hiʿr wa-ḳarīnat al-sad͟jʿ*, "*al-fāṣila* is the word at the end of the verse, like the *ḳāfiya* in poetry and the *ḳarīna* in *sad͟jʿ*" (al-Suyūṭī, *Itḳān*, beginning of Ch. 59); see also *Ḳāmūs*, root *f ṣ l*.

Bibliography: in addition to the references in the text, for *fāṣila* of *ʿarūḍ*, *LA*, xiv, 38/xi, 523b; writers on Arabic prosody, D. Vernier,

Gr. Ar., ii, 515; S. de Sacy, *Gr. Ar.*², ii, 619, etc. For the Ḳurʾānic *fāṣila*, see particularly ch. 59 of the *Itḳān* of Suyūṭī; for both, the *Dict. of techn. terms*, ed. A. Sprenger, ii, 1140-1 (cf. i, 672-3). (H. FLEISCH)

FAṢĪLA, verbal adjective of the *faʿīl* type in the passive sense, as the Arab lexicographers record, denoting an object which is "separated", like the young animal when weaned (young camel or calf), in the feminine *faṣīla*; and the same feminine form is used for a palmtree sucker when transplanted. It is no doubt the same semantic derivation which explains the meaning of the smallest "section" of a tribe, the closest relatives: thus ʿAbbās, according to the *LA*, is called *faṣīlat al-Nabī* "close kinship with the Prophet". However, Arabic philological doctrine advances one meaning of *faṣīla* "fragment of the flesh of the thigh" by virtue of the principle which makes every term of this tribal nomenclature correspond with the name of one part of the body. Robertson Smith has, not without probability, claimed to discern in the origin of this series various allusions to the female organs such as *baṭn* "belly" (starting with *ḥayy* which seems to be connected), upon which the denominations of male organs would be superimposed when the patriarchal organization was substituted for the matriarchy. (J. LECERF)

AL-**FĀSIYYŪN** or AHL FĀS, a name given to the inhabitants of Fās. In the local dialect this name does not apply to all those who live in Fās, but to those who were born there and have right of citizenship through having adopted the ways and customs of the city and its code of good manners.

The population of Fās was formed little by little of many diverse elements. The original basis was certainly made up of Berbers and some Arab companions of the Idrīsids. From the beginning of the 3rd/9th century on, the population grew through the coming of political refugees from Cordova and Ḳayrawān, who brought the traditions and techniques of long-rooted urban peoples to the new town. Even though the people of Ḳayrawān did not continue to swarm into Fās, the Muslims of Andalusia came time after time to establish themselves there, at any rate up to the conquest of Granada by the Catholic Kings (1492).

In addition, various groups were added to the original kernel of the population through the circumstances of Morocco's dynastic history: Berbers from South Morocco under the Almoravids and the Almohads; Berbers from East Morocco and members of Arab tribes under the Marīnids; Berbers from the oases of the Sahara and negroes under the Saʿdīs; Filālīs and negroes under the ʿAlawids. At different periods, the Muslim population of the town was augmented by a number of families of Jewish converts to Islam of whom several, the Cohens for example, have preserved their original names. It must also not be forgotten that, at any rate in the 19th century, groups of Muslims came to Fās from outside for the purpose of practising various specialized trades, Berbers of the High Guir, for instance, who are porters, the people of Tuwāt who handle fatty substances, those from the Draʿ who are gardeners, those of Sūs who are dealers in fatty substances, and those of the Rīf who take part in the pressing of the olives. It is interesting that the Middle Atlas, although so near, has provided Fās with very few immigrants.

Since the French conquest of Algeria, Fās has formed a refuge for a number of families from the Oran area, notably Tlemcen, who preferred emigration to foreign domination. This was the case especially first in 1835 and then in 1911.

Before the 20th century the population scarcely ever seems to have passed the 100,000 mark, if it was as high, but no reliable document exists on this subject. Since the Protectorate, the number of Muslim inhabitants has grown, but in modest proportions compared with many other Moroccan towns: 163,000 in the 1952 census. This relative stagnation means that the traditional citizens have not been swamped in an enormous mass of new arrivals but preserve their personality and pre-eminence. This personality is characterized by a happy balance between economic activity, intellectual activity, and the religious life of the city, and by the existence of an etiquette (*ḳāʿida*) which rules most stringently the relationships of the people of Fās amongst themselves. Only those whose roots are truly in the city follow this etiquette, and they alone have a right to the name of Fāsiyyūn. They can be divided into several social strata which complement rather than compete with each other: at the top of the social ladder are the big merchants, the high functionaries and the religious leaders who form the middle-classes; then come the small tradesmen and the artisans; finally there are the workmen settled in the city or about to become a part of it. The mass of labourers originally from the country who live miserably in their 'bidonvilles', form a quite separate society entirely different from the people of Fās. The strong personality of these people has caused them to preserve almost up to the present time a great number of legal and social customs inherited from their ancestors; the rules and ceremonies of marriage are an example. This state of things is in the course of being modified owing to European influence, which was most marked during the Protectorate. The behaviour of the Europeans living in Fās, and even more the ideas which they spread, the contact which they helped to establish between the society of Fās and the outside world, introduced the seeds of transformation into the city, not only in matters to do with the habits of daily life but also in matters concerning family and social structure and behaviour. It is still too early to judge how far this evolution will go.

There is every right to consider the Jews as Fāsiyyūn because they were to be found in Fās from the time of its foundation and for centuries lived in the Madīna side by side with the Muslims. It was only in the 9th/15th century that they were compelled to live in a special quarter, the Mellāḥ. Apart from those Jews installed there since the city's beginnings, whose exact origin it is impossible to discover, it is well known that the Jewish community has been enriched on a number of occasions by families or individuals emigrating from Spain; in the 19th century Spanish was still the daily language of more than a few families. In general, the relationship between the Jews and the Muslim middle classes has been correct and sometimes cordial. On the other hand, it has happened that the people of Fās al-Dj̲adīd have broken out against the Mellāḥ, as was the case in April 1912, at the time of the revolt of the Moroccan troops. More rarely, the government has persecuted the Jewish community, notably during the short reign of Mawlāy al-Yazīd (1790-1792). Even more than the Muslims, the Jews of Fās have been affected by European influences since the beginning of the 20th century; many have left the Mellāḥ for the New Town (Ville Nouvelle).

Bibliography: Leo Africanus, *Descr. de*

l'Afrique, trans. A. Épaulard, i, 179-232; J. and J. Tharaud, *Fez ou les bourgeois de l'Islam*, Paris 1930; F. Bonjean, *Les confidences d'une fi'le de la nuit*, Paris 1939; R. Le Tourneau. *Fès avant le protectorat*, Casablanca 1949, Books iii and viii. See also the bibliography to the art. FĀS.

(R. LE TOURNEAU)

FASKH—The term *faskh*, in the language of the Islamic jurists, has a very wide meaning. It serves in a general way to designate the dissolution of any contractual bond whatever (Ibn Nudjaym, *al-Ashbāh*, ii, 114). Whether or not the contract was validly formed, the intervention of *faskh* will reduce it to nought. But *faskh* presupposes a contract which at least fulfils all the conditions necessary to its formation, *i.e.*, a *munʿaḳid* contract. A non-existent contract cannot be the object of *faskh*. On the other hand, a formed contract which happens to be vitiated by some irregularity (*fāsid*) can be dissolved only by means of *faskh*, even though in the meantime it does not produce any of its legal effects. *Faskh*, in this case, is equivalent to annulment. In cases of error or injurious misrepresentation Islamic doctrine does not regard the contract as *fāsid*. It is nevertheless subject to *faskh*, under certain conditions. *Faskh* in this case constitutes the sanction of an express or implied condition included in the contract. Generally speaking, *faskh* is admitted whenever one of the contracting parties fails to fulfil one of the express or implied conditions stipulated in the contract. It is by the application of this principle that a sale is annulled in cases of redhibitory defect or eviction. In this sense *faskh* can be identified with rescission. But the domain of rescission is singularly restricted in Islamic law. In effect, in the absence of an express or implied rescissory clause, it is impossible in Islamic law to obtain the rescission of a contract by reason of the failure of the other party to discharge his obligation. The only remedy available is compulsory performance (Chafik Chehata, *Théorie de l'obligation en droit musulman*, 147, 204).

Faskh is not only annulment or rescission. The revocation of a gift, or of any other contract revocable by its nature, takes place equally by way of *faskh*. Likewise, a contract by nature irrevocable becomes susceptible of *faskh*, or revocable, whenever it includes a right of option (*khiyār*).

Finally, an irrevocable contract can be dissolved by *mutuus dissensus* (*iḳāla*). This dissolution effected by a mutual agreement is equally termed *faskh* by the jurists—at least with regard to relations *inter partes*.

Thus the term *faskh* comes to embrace also the cases of revocation and cancellation.

In every case *faskh* is effected, as a rule, by means of a declaration of intention pronounced in the presence of the other contracting party. This is why *faskh* is regarded by the jurists as a juridical act in its own right. However, in certain cases *faskh* must be obtained by judicial process. This is so in the case of redhibitory defects discovered after the delivery of the object sold. Likewise, the revocation of a gift must, as a rule, be pronounced by the judge. It should be mentioned here that the judge can pronounce officially the *faskh* of a vitiated contract when one or other of the parties has not requested it.

Moreover, *faskh* is clearly distinguished in the texts from *infisākh*, which comes about without the need of any declaration or judicial decree. An example is provided by the case of impossibility of performance. If the object sold perishes before delivery to the buyer, the contract is dissolved by the normal operation of the law. Here the authors are fond of the term nullity or *buṭlān* (Sarakhsī, xii, *Mabsūṭ*, xii, 174). Likewise in the case where proof of the contract is held impossible by reason of the conflicting oaths sworn by either side, the contract is dissolved by the normal operation of the law: *infisākh* (Kāsānī, *Badāʾiʿ*, v, 238).

Once *faskh* is effected the contract stands dissolved, and things must be restored to their former condition: the *status quo ante*. This is why *faskh* becomes impossible if the thing representing the object of a contract has happened to perish in the meantime. As a rule, *faskh* has a retro-active effect (Kāsānī, v, 239): the contract is held never to have existed. The effects of the contract disappear as from the day it was formed. However, with a view to protecting the rights of third parties, the *mutuus dissensus* (*iḳāla*) is considered a new alienation with respect to third parties. As far as they are concerned it does not have a retroactive effect. Likewise the alienation of a thing to the profit of a third party prevents the operation of *faskh*. Thus the right to dissolve the contract is destroyed, and the thing is established in the ownership of the third party who has acquired it.

We must notice, finally, that in family law *faskh* is distinguished from *ṭalāḳ*. *Ṭalāḳ*, which is the exclusive right of the man, brings about the dissolution of the marriage by a simple unilateral declaration. It always presupposes a validly formed contract. Dissolution of marriage by way of *faskh* takes place at the instance of the wife or her relatives. It generally comes about by judicial process. Like any other *faskh*, this dissolution embraces cases of failure to fulfil an express or implied condition, as well as those cases where the contract is vitiated by some irregularity. The grounds for dissolution of marriage by way of *faskh* are defined by the law, and *faskh* constitutes the legal means open to the wife of dissolving the conjugal tie in case of serious cruelty (Egyptian laws, no. 25 of 1920, no. 25 of 1929).

Bibliography: Chafik Chehata, *Théorie générale de l'obligation en droit musulman*, Cairo 1936; Ḥasan ʿAlī al-Ẓanūn, *al-Naẓariyya al-ʿāmma li 'l-faskh fi 'l-fiḳh al-islāmī wa 'l-ḳānūn al-muḳāran*, Cairo 1946; ʿAlī al-Khafīf, *Furaḳ al-zawādj fi 'l-madhāhib al-islāmiyya*, Cairo 1958; M. Morand, *Quelques particularités du droit musulman des obligations*, in *Bulletin de Législation Comparée*, 1929, 305-69; al-Sanhūrī, *Maṣādir al-ḥaḳḳ fi 'l-fiḳh al-islāmī*, vi, Cairo 1959.

(CHAFIK CHEHATA)

FAṢL etymologically, like *farḳ*, expresses the general meaning of separation or disjunction (for the various meanings, see *LA*, xiv, 35-9 for *faṣl*; xii, 174-82 for *farḳ*; Abu 'l-Baḳāʾ, *K. al-Kulliyyāt*, 275). In logic, *faṣl* signifies "difference" and especially "specific difference", the διαφορά of the five predicables of Porphyry (1. γενός, *djins*, genus; 2. εἶδος, *nawʿ*, species; 3. διαφορά, *faṣl*, difference; 4. ἴδιον, *khāṣṣa*, property; 5. συμβεβηκός, *ʿaraḍ*, accident. The Ikhwān al-Ṣafāʾ add, in the tenth *risāla*, *shakhṣ*, person). For the logicians, *faṣl* has two meanings: the first covers every attribute by which one thing is distinguished from another, whether it be individual or universal, the second, in transposition (*ʿalā naḳl*), covering that by which a thing is essentially distinguished. In transposition in this way, *faṣl* is used, *per prius et posterius* (*bi-ḥasab al-taḳdīm wa 'l-taʾkhīr*) to designate three ideas; common dif erence (*al-faṣl al-ʿāmm*), particular difference (*al-*

faṣl al-khāṣṣ), and the particular of the particular (*khāṣṣ al-khāṣṣ*). Common difference (*al-faṣl al-ʿāmm*) is what allows a thing to differ from another and that other to differ from the former; equally it is what allows a thing to differ from itself at another time. This is the case of separable accidents. Particular difference (*al-faṣl al-khāṣṣ*) is the predicate which is necessarily associated (*lāzim, comitans*) with accidents, *e.g.*, the difference between a horse and a man constituted by the whiteness of the latter's skin Finally, specific difference or the particular of the particular (*khāṣṣ al-khāṣṣ*) is what constitutes the species. It is the simple universal attributed to the species in reply to the question: what is it (*in quale quid*) in its essence in relation to its genus (*fī djawāb ayyu shayʾ huwa fī dhātihi min djinsihi*), *e.g.*, rationality for man.

The Platonic method of analysis or division (διαιρεσίς) is distinguished by the name of *ṭarīḳ al-ḳisma* from the Aristotelian *ṭarīḳ al-ḳiyās* (συλλογισμός) (al-Fārābī, *Abhandlungen*, ed. Dieterici, 2).

For the metaphysical difference between the incorporeal and the body, *farḳ* (χωρισμός) is used. God is *mufāraḳ*, that is, separated, free of all that is material or corporeal. In the essence of God, there is neither *farḳ* nor *faṣl* (*Theology of Aristotle*, ed. Dieterici, 40). Purely spiritual beings (*ʿuḳūl*), the intelligences of the spheres and the heavenly bodies are *mufāraḳāt* (syn. *mudjarradāt*).

Bibliography: I. Pollak, *Die Hermeneutik des Aristoteles*, Leipzig 1913, glossary; the major text for *faṣl* is that of Ibn Sīnā, *Shifāʾ*, *al-Madkhal*, pub. Cairo 1952, ch. XIII, 72-82; the Latin translation of this text was used by Prantl, *Geschichte der Logik*, ii, 345-8; cf. also A. M. Goichon, *Lexique de la langue philosophique d'Ibn Sīnā*, no. 504, and Madkour, *L'Organon d'Aristote dans le monde arabe*, Paris 1934, 70-133; see also DJINS and ḤADD.

(TJ. DE BOER-[G. C. ANAWATI])

FAṢL [see FILĀḤA, MAFṢŪL].

FASTS [see ṢAWM].

FATĀ, pl. *fityān*, strictly "young man", has assumed a certain number of meanings in Arabic [see FUTUWWA]: here we confine ourselves to one exclusively Andalusian usage. In Muslim Spain the slaves, whether eunuchs or not, employed in the service of the prince and his household, and then of the *ḥādjib* [*q.v.*] at the time when the latter was in practice taking over the reins of power, were in fact called *ghilmān* (sing. *ghulām* [*q.v.*]), whilst those who held an elevated rank in the palace hierarchy bore the title *fatā*, the entire management of the household being placed under the control of two majordomos or "high officers", *al-fatayānⁱ al-kabīrānⁱ*. In the course of the history of al-Andalus a certain number of these slaves, generally of European origin [see ṢAḲĀLIBA], after obtaining the status of free men, were promoted to the highest positions in the social hierarchy and played an outstanding political part, even succeeding in creating independent principalities for themselves, like the ʿĀmirid *fatā* Mudjāhid [*q.v.*] of Denia. Their elevation inevitably gave rise to disputes with the aristocratic Arab families, with whom they came to blows, not without sometimes resorting to arguments of a Shuʿūbī character (see I. Goldziher, in *ZDMG*, 1898).

Bibliography: E. Lévi-Provençal, *Xᵉ siècle*, index; idem, *Hist. Esp. Mus.*, index. (ED.)

FATALISM [see AL-ḲAḌĀʾ WAʾL-ḲADAR].

AL-FATĀWĀ AL-ʿĀLAMGĪRIYYA, a compendium of Ḥanafī law, in India ranking second only to al-Marghīnānī's *Hidāya*, compiled by order of Awrangzīb during the years 1075/1664-1083/1672. The intention was to arrange in systematic order the most authoritative decisions by earlier legists which were scattered in a number of *fiḳh* books, and thus provide a convenient work of reference. The board in charge of the compilation was presided over by Shaykh Niẓām of Burhānpur (d. 1090/1679), who had four superintendents under him: Shaykh Wadjīh al-Dīn of Gopāmaw, Shaykh Djalāl al-Dīn Muḥammad of Mačhlīshahr; Ḳāḍī Muḥammad Ḥusayn and Mullā Ḥāmid, both of Djawnpur; each of them was assisted by a team of ten or more *ʿulamāʾ*. The book has repeatedly been printed (see Brockelmann).

Bibliography: Muḥammad Kāẓim, *ʿĀlamgīr-nāma* (Bibl. Ind.), 1072; Muḥammad Sāḳī Mustaʿidd Khān, *Maʾāthir-i ʿĀlamgīrī* (Bibl. Ind.), 529; *Mirʾāt al-ʿālam*, in *Oriental College Magazine* (*Supplement*), Lahore Aug.-Nov. 1953; Khʷāfī Khān, *Muntakhab al-Lubāb* (Bibl. Ind.), ii, 251; Nūr al-Dīn Zaydī Ẓafarābādī, *Tadjallī-i nūr*, Djawnpur 1900, ii, 77-89, 93, 119-20; Shāh Walī Allāh, *Anfās al-ʿārifīn*, 24; ʿAbd al-Ḥayy Lakhnawī, *Nuzhat al-khawāṭir*, Ḥaydarābād 1375, v, 18, 34, 149, 281, 364, 420, 430; *Maʿārif* (Urdū monthly), Aʿẓamgaṙh, Dec. 1946, Jan., Feb., Oct. 1947, Jan. 1948; Faḍl-i Imām Khayrābādī, *Tarādjim al-fuḍalāʾ* (trans. Bazmee Ansari), Karachi 1956, 12-3, 27-8; Khūb Allāh Allāhābādī, *Wafayāt al-aʿlām* (Ms.); *Āthār-i sharaf* (Ms.), fol. 94; Muḥammad ʿAlī Ḥaydar, *Tadhkira mashāhīr-i kākawrī*, Lucknow 1927, 354-6; A. S. Bazmee Ansari in *al-Islām*, Karachi July-Dec. 1953, Jan. 1954; Ṣabāḥ al-Dīn ʿAbd al-Raḥmān, *Bazm-i Tīmūriyya*, Aʿẓamgaṙh 1948, 236-43; Brockelmann, II, 549, S II, 604.

(A. S. BAZMEE ANSARI)

FATḤ [see ḤARAKA].

AL-FATḤ B. KHĀḲĀN was the son of Khāḳān b. ʿUrṭūdj (or Ghurṭūdj) of the Turkish ruling family at Farghānā and chief of the Turkish soldiers from Central Asia who formed part of the troops of the guard of the caliph al-Muʿtaṣim. Biographical information concerning him is scarce: he must have been born ca. 200/817-8, because he was probably the same age as al-Mutawakkil, son of al-Muʿtaṣim, with whom he was educated since infancy at the court of the caliph, who had adopted him at the age of seven. Hardly had al-Mutawakkil been elected caliph in 232/846-7 when he made him his secretary (*kātib*, and not *wazīr* as incorrectly stated in some sources), and later, in 235/848-9 or 236/849-50, appointed him superintendent of works at Sāmarrā; in 242/855-6 governor of Egypt for a short time in place of his son al-Muntaṣir; and in 244/857-8 as his lieutenant at Damascus. He was a member of the caliph's literary circle, and was a great patron of young and little-known authors, a friend of many writers and poets such as al-Djāḥiẓ and al-Buḥturī, of historians like al-Thaʿlabī, etc. He was himself a writer and poet, but of his works (*K. Akhlāḳ al-mulūk*, *K. al-Ṣayd wa 'l-djawāriḥ*, *K. al-Rawḍa wa 'l-zuhr*) none has come down to us, and only 13 verses of his poetry are known (cf. Yāḳūt, *Udabāʾ*, vi, 118). In his palace at Sāmarrā he had collected a very valuable library (consisting in particular of philosophical works), which was much visited by many students of Baṣra and Kūfa. On the night of 4 Shawwāl 247/11 December 861, at the caliph's palace in the new capital al-Mutawakkiliyya (or al-Djaʿfariyya) he was murdered with his caliph and friend defending him with his own bodv against the hired assassins sent by al-Muntaṣir, son of al-Mutawakkil.

Bibliography: O. Pinto, *al-Fatḥ b. Ḫāqān, favorito di al-Mutawakkil*, in *RSO*, xiii (1932), 133-49; D. Sourdel, *Le vizirat ʿabbāside de 749 à 936* . . ., Damascus 1959, i, 282-3; *Fihrist*, 116-7; Yāḳūt, *Udabāʾ*, vi, 116-24. (O. PINTO)

AL-FATḤ B. MUḤAMMAD B. ʿUBAYD ALLĀH B. **KHĀḲĀN**, ABŪ NAṢR AL-ḲAYSĪ AL-ISHBĪLĪ, an Andalusian anthologist whose history is somewhat obscure. We do, however, know that he studied seriously under well-known teachers and that he led an adventurous life, travelling through much of Muslim Spain and enjoying to the full pleasures strictly forbidden by the laws of Islam. Despite this, he obtained a position as secretary to the governor of Granada, Abū Yūsuf Tāshfīn b. ʿAlī, but did not keep it and went to Marrākush where, at the instigation of an Almoravid prince or even perhaps of Sultan ʿAlī b. Yūsuf b. Tāshfīn, he was assassinated in a *funduḳ* at a date which, in various sources, varies between 528/1134 and 555/1160, the year 529/1134 being the most probable.

When he decided to compile the first of his anthologies, dedicated to the brother of the above-mentioned sultan, Abū Isḥāḳ Ibrāhīm b. Yūsuf b. Tāshfīn, he wrote to a certain number of prominent personalities who were reputed to be also men of letters, informing them of his project and asking them to send him some of their own documents; those who accepted and included gifts as well as documents were made the subject of panegyrics, while the others were passed over in silence or criticised adversely. This was the treatment accorded to Ibn Bādjdja [*q.v.*] in particular, except that it was his privilege to have two notices, one of blame, the other of praise (text in Yāḳūt). For the earlier writers, Ibn Khāḳān had no hesitation in ransacking the anthologies and, it is said, even involved himself in a lawsuit with his contemporary Ibn Bassām [*q.v.*].

He is the author of two anthologies. The first, entitled *Ḳalāʾid al-ʿiḳyān fī* (var. *wa-*) *maḥāsin al-aʿyān*, was published in Marseilles-Paris in 1277/1860 in the journal *al-Bardjīs* and as an independent volume, later at Būlāḳ in 1283-1284; R. Dozy included some chapters from it in his history of the ʿAbbādids, and H. Pérès published extracts from it in Algiers in 1946; it is divided into four parts: princes, viziers, *ḳāḍīs* and jurists, poets and men of letters. A commentary, *Farāʾid al-tibyān alā Ḳalāʾid al-ʿiḳyān*, was written by Muḥ. b. Ḳāsim Ibn Zākūr al-Fāsī (d. 1120/1708); H. Pérès (see *Poésie andalouse*², xxxii) has a manuscript of it in his possession; but the French translation announced by E. Bourgade has still to appear.—The second anthology, *Maṭmaḥ al-anfus wa-masraḥ al-taʾannus fī mulaḥ ahl al-Andalus*, seems to have been made in three versions, large, medium and small, but only the last of the three has survived (published in Istanbul in 1302 at the *al-Djawāʾib* press [see DJARĪDA] and in Cairo in 1325; cf. also Dozy, *Abbadides*); it is in some way complementary to the preceding work, in three parts: viziers, *ḳāḍīs* and jurists, men of letters.—To these anthologies we should add a biography of one of the author's teachers, al-Baṭalyawsī [*q.v.*], followed by a short anthology (see Derenbourg, *Mss. ar. de l'Escurial*, 448), and a *maḳāma* on his teacher (Derenbourg, *op. cit.*, 538), as well as a *Bidāyat al-maḥāsin wa-ghāyat al-muḥāsin* and a collection of his letters which is lost.

In the two published anthologies, the articles contain biographical and historical information (cf. A. Cour, *De l'opinion d'Ibn al-Ḫaṭīb sur les ouvrages d'Ibn Ḫâqân considérés comme source historique*, in *Mél. R. Basset*, ii, Paris 1925, 17-32), but it requires the application and long experience of H. Pérès (see *Bibl.*) to understand and interpret them, for the rhyming prose, which is made up of short clauses and used exclusively, holds the reader spell-bound and prevents him from paying attention to the meaning, in the opinion even of a modern critic, Aḥmad Ḍayf. This prose, which can be regarded as *vers libres*, eventually becomes wearisome, but it is acknowledged to possess a rare elegance, and anthologists show unconcealed pleasure in reproducing long extracts from it (see especially al-Maḳḳarī, *Analectes*, index). The principal interest of the *Ḳalāʾid* and the *Maṭmaḥ* rests, however, in the poetical works which Ibn Khāḳān has saved from oblivion and which form fundamental sources for the study of Arabic literature in Spain, principally in the 5th/11th century.

Bibliography: Ibn al-Abbār, *Muʿdjam*, ed. Codera, Madrid 1898, no. 285; Ibn Khallikān, ed. Cairo 1310, ii, 407; Yāḳūt, *Muʿdjam al-udabāʾ*, xvi, 186-92; Maḳḳarī, *Analectes*, index; Weyers, *Specimen criticum exhibens locos Ibn Khacanis de Ibn Zeiduno*, Leiden 1831; R. Dozy, *Scriptorum arabum loci de Abbadidis*, Leyden 1846, i, 1-10; idem, *Recherches*³, *passim*; Wüstenfeld, *Geschichtschreiber*, 238; Pons Boigues, *Ensayo*, no. 162; Nāṣirī Salāwī, *Zahr al-afnān min ḥadīḳat Abi 'l-Wannān*, Fās 1314, ii, 356; M. Ben Cheneb, *Étude sur les personnages de l'idjāza de Sīdī ʿAbd al-Qādir al-Fāsy*, Paris 1907, no. 241; A. Ḍayf, *Balāghat al-ʿArab fi 'l-Andalus*, Cairo 1342/1924, 211-5; A. González Palencia, *Literatura*², Barcelona 1945, 204, 206-8; H. Pérès, *Poésie andalouse*², Paris 1953, index; idem, *Glanes historiques . . . dans les Qalâʾid al-ʿIqyân*, in *Mél. d'hist. et d'archéol. de l'Occ. mus.*, ii, Algiers 1957, 147-52.

(M. BEN CHENEB-[CH. PELLAT])

FATḤ ʿALĪ ĀKHUND-ZĀDA [see ĀKHUND ZĀDA, MĪRZĀ FATḤ ʿALĪ].

FATḤ-ʿALĪ SHĀH, the second ruler of the Ḳādjār [*q.v.*] dynasty, was born in 1185/1771 and bore the name Bābā Khān. He was made governor of Fārs, Kirmān, and Yazd by his uncle, Āḳā Muḥammad Khān, and heir apparent in 1211/1796-7. He succeeded to the throne in 1212/1797. He died in 1250/1834 and was buried at Ḳumm. Much of his reign of 38 years and 5 months was spent in military expeditions against internal rebels and external foes. On the assassination of Aḳā Muḥammad Khān in 1212/1797 Bābā Khān hastened from Shīrāz to Tehrān, where Mīrzā Muḥammad Khān Ḳādjār had closed the gates pending his arrival. On reaching Tehrān he ascended the throne as Fatḥ ʿAlī on 4 Ṣafar 1212/30 July 1797, but was not crowned until 1 Shawwāl 1212/21 March 1798. Ṣādiḳ Khān Shakākī, who opposed his succession, was defeated near Ḳazwīn. Various attempts at rebellion by Fatḥ ʿAlī's brother, Ḥusayn Ḳulī Mīrzā, Ṣādiḳ Khān Shakākī, and Muḥammad Khān b. Zakī Khān were defeated; and in a series of expeditions to Khurāsān Fatḥ ʿAlī succeeded in establishing his nominal authority over most of that province. Relations with Europe were actively joined. In 1798 Lord Wellesley, the Governor General of India, sent Mihdī ʿAlī Khān, the East India Company's resident at Bushire, to the Persian Court to induce it to take measures to keep the Afghān ruler, Zamān Khān Durrānī, in check. A subsequent mission sent under Captain (later Sir) John Malcolm resulted in a political and commercial treaty concluded in 1801. In 1802 France made unsuccessful overtures to

Persia for a Franco-Persian alliance against Russia. In 1804 the Perso-Russian war was resumed. Fatḥ ʿAlī sent an envoy to India to seek aid under the British alliance but his request was coldly received. In 1805 a French envoy, Romieux, reached Tehrān and urged Persia to repudiate the British alliance. Disappointed of British help, Fatḥ ʿAlī sent Mīrzā Muḥammad Riḍā to treat with Napoleon. A treaty was signed at Finkenstein (1807), but was nullified almost immediately by the Franco-Russian treaty of Tilsit. Renewed French activities and the possibility of Franco-Russian activities in Persia induced the British Government to send a mission under Sir Harford Jones to the court of Fatḥ ʿAlī. In March 1809 a Preliminary Treaty was concluded. This was followed by a Definitive Treaty in March 1812, which was superseded in 1814 by the Treaty of Tehrān. Under this treaty Persia undertook not to allow any European army to advance on India through Persia and Britain undertook in the case of a European nation invading Persia to send a military force or in lieu thereof to pay an annual subsidy. The subsidy articles were abrogated in 1828. The long war with Russia was concluded by the peace of Gulistān [*q.v.*] (1813), by which Georgia and a number of other districts were acknowledged as belonging to Russia, Russian vessels of war were given the exclusive right of navigation of the Caspian Sea, and a 5% *ad valorem* duty on Russian imports into Persia was fixed. A rebellion in Khurāsān fomented by Maḥmūd Shāh of Afghānistān gave Fatḥ ʿAlī an opportunity to seize Herāt (1813), but he failed to keep it. A war with the Porte (1821-3) was concluded by the Treaty of Erzurum (1813). In 1826 war broke out again with Russia and ended disastrously for Persia. In addition to the territory going to Russia under the Treaty of Gulistān, Persia lost Erīvān and Nakhdjivān; and the exclusive right of Russian vessels of war to navigate the Caspian was reaffirmed. A commercial treaty signed on the same day gave Russian subjects extra-territorial privileges and established the pattern of the capitulations enjoyed by Europeans in Persia under the Ḳādjār dynasty. Fatḥ ʿAlī died in 1834. He was survived by fifty-seven sons and forty-six daughters. His favourite son ʿAbbās Mīrzā [*q.v.*], who had been declared *walī ʿahd*, died in 1833. ʿAbbās Mīrzā's son, Muḥammad Mīrzā, was proclaimed *walī ʿahd* and succeeded to the throne on Fatḥ ʿAlī's death.

The rule of Fatḥ ʿAlī was arbitrary and autocratic. Pomp and ceremony distinguished his public audiences, but much of his time was spent in camp on military expeditions. Military reform was begun during his reign, first under French officers accompanying General Gardane, who came to Persia as envoy in 1806, and later under British officers, when an attempt was made to introduce European methods and discipline into the army in Ādharbāydjān commanded by ʿAbbās Mīrzā. Fatḥ ʿAlī is described by some European travellers as being intelligent and having a lively and curious mind, by others as being ignorant and vain. Like many of the Ḳādjār princes he had a great love of hunting. His besetting sin was avarice. He made, or repaired, a number of buildings in Tehrān, Ḳumm, Kāẓimayn, Karbalāʾ and elsewhere.

Bibliography: ʿAbd al-Razzāḳ b. Nadjafḳulī, *Maʾāthir-i sulṭāniyya*, Tabrīz 1241/1826 (translated by H. T. Brydges, *The Dynasty of the Kajars*, London 1833); Mīrzā Taḳī Sipihr, *Taʾrīkh-i Ḳādjāriyya* (being the ninth volume of the *Nāsikh al-tawārīkh*), Tabrīz 1319/1901-2; Ḥādjdjī Mīrzā Ḥasan Fasāʾī, *Fārs-nāma-i Nāṣirī*; Saʿīd Nafīsī, *Taʾrīkh-i idjtimāʿī wa siyāsī-i Īrān*, Tehrān 1335 (solar); R. G. Watson, *A history of Persia*, London 1866; Amédée Jaubert, *Voyage en Arménie et en Perse*, Paris 1821; J. B. Fraser, *Narrative of a journey into Khorasan*, London 1825; Fonton, *La Russie dans l'Asie Mineure*, 231 f.; L. Dubeux, *Perse*, 376 f. (portrait, pl. 58 and pl. 84); *Grundr. d Iran. Phil.*, ii, 596 f.; M. E. Yapp, *The control of the Persian Mission, 1822-1836*, in *University of Birmingham Historical Journal*, vii (1960), 162-79.

(A. K. S. LAMBTON)

FATḤNĀME, an official announcement of a victory. This definition excludes large numbers of '*fatḥnāmes*' written by private persons as literary exercises, such as the *Maḥrūse-i Istanbul Fatḥnāmesi* of Tādjīzāde Djaʿfar Čelebi [*q.v.*], which was composed at least a generation after the conquest (*TOEM*, nos. 20-1) and works such as Murādī's *Fatḥnāme-i Khayr al-Dīn Pasha* (A. S. Levend, *Ġazavāt-nāmeler*, Ankara 1956, 70-3), a versified narrative of the exploits of Barbarossa and his brother Oruč. According to Uzunçarşılı (*Osmanlı devletinin saray teşkilâtı*, Ankara 1945, 288), a *fatḥnāme* consists of 15 elements: (1) praise to God, (2) encomia on the Prophet, (3) the sovereign's duty to relieve oppression, (4) reasons for ending the wrong-doing of the tyrant in question, (5) the Sulṭān's departure, (6) the multitude of his troops, (7) the position of the enemy, (8) the boldness of the enemy, (9) description of the battle, (10) the Sulṭān's victory, (11) thanks to God, (12) occupation of the enemy's territory, (13) this success to be proclaimed by land and sea (only in *fatḥnāmes* addressed to the Sulṭān's own dominions), (14) the names of the place to which the *fatḥnāme* is sent and of the bearer, (15) the Sulṭān's joy at the victory, his communication of the good tidings to the recipient and his request for prayers. Although this scheme may well have served as a model to literary men, there is some reason to suppose that it was not closely followed by the official (usually the *nishāndjī*?) entrusted with composing the *fatḥnāme* after a battle. It is difficult to be precise on this subject because of the dearth of original *fatḥnāmes* available for study. Of the dozens of examples in Ferīdūn there is none of whose genuineness we can be sure, nor do they seem to bear out Pakalın's statement (s.v. *Fetihname*) that *fatḥnāmes* are of great historical importance as being short histories of battles. What Ferīdūn describes as the *fatḥnāme* on the conquest of Eger in 1005/1596, for instance (*Madjmūʿa-i munshaʾāt al-salāṭīn*, Istanbul 1265, ii, 2-3), contains no mention of the massacre of the garrison (see G. L. Lewis, *The Utility of Ottoman Fetḥnames*, in Bernard Lewis and P. M. Holt, *Historians of the Middle East*, Oxford 1962, and cf. Naʿīmā, *Taʾrīkh*, Istanbul 1281, i, 151). Nor does Ferīdūn's text bear any relation to Naʿīmā's statement (*ibid.*, 173) that the Nishāndjī Lām ʿAlī Čelebi was dismissed for exaggerating, in this same *fatḥnāme*, the part played in the conquest by Djighalazāde Sinān Pasha. On the other hand, we do have one published *fatḥnāme* which appears to be the genuine article and not a literary exercise: the Uygur account of Meḥemmed II's victory in 878/1473 over Uzun Ḥasan (R. Rahmeti Arat, *Fatih Sultan Mehmed'in yarlıġı*, in *TM*, vi (1939), 285-322; cf. idem, *Un yarlık de Mehmed II, le Conquérant*, in *Annali del R. Ist. Sup. Orientale di Napoli*, n.s. i (1940), 25-68). It is laconic in style and full of information, including a complete order of battle with the names of the principal commanders on both sides. There is none of the verbosity and sanctimonious self-justification which we see in the literary *fatḥnāmes*; the occasion for the campaign is refreshingly stated thus: 'Uzun Ḥasan having burned the city of Tokat, we came to fight him'. The most suggestive feature of the document is its conclusion: the Sulṭān is coming to winter in Istanbul and adjures various officials there to be steadfast in their work and not to neglect the business of the *dīwān*; the chief men of all towns are to keep the mosques in a flourishing state, to perform the five daily prayers in congregation and to fulfil the ordinances of the *sharīʿa* and the commandments of God. Yet the fact that the document is in Uygur shows that it was intended only for the eastern territories. The inference is that for this victory, at any rate, there was only one *fatḥnāme*, of which copies and, in this special case, a translation were sent to all parts of the Sulṭān's dominions. Ferīdūn (*op. cit.*, i, 283-6) gives the texts of three accounts of the victory: a *ḥukm-i sherīf* to Prince Djem, a letter (*nāme-i humāyūn*) to Ḥusayn Bayḳarā and a *fatḥnāme* 'to the Guarded Dominions'. None contains any useful details of the campaign; compared with the Uygur *yarlīḳ* their historical value is negligible. For the victory of Čaldirān, 41 years later, Ferīdūn gives no fewer than ten different *fatḥnāmes*, none of them giving a full account of the battle (for a partial analysis see Lewis's article cited above). A working hypothesis is that there was only one true *fatḥnāme* for each victory, which would add greatly to our knowledge of Ottoman military history if only we could lay hands on it. Other so-called *fatḥnāmes* are merely elegant variations on a theme, their value being mainly literary, though they may be of some interest as early specimens of war-propaganda. The last word cannot be said on this subject until more work has been done in the Ottoman archives, particularly perhaps on the *ordu mühimmesi* registers (see Uriel Heyd, *Ottoman documents on Palestine*, Oxford 1960, 5).

Bibliography: Works cited in text. Pakalın's article consists mainly in a lengthy quotation from M. F. Köprülü, *Bizans müesseselerinin ... tesiri*, in *Türk Hukuk ve Iktisat Tarihi Mecmuası*, i (1931) [Italian translation, *Alcune osservazioni ....*, Pubblicazioni dell'Inst. per l'Oriente di Roma, 1944], rejecting the theory of a connexion between the *fatḥnāme* and the Roman *litterae laureatae*. For some examples see G. Vajda, *Un bulletin de victoire de Bajazet II*, in *JA*, 236 (1948), 87-102; L. Fekete, *A fetḥnāméról*, in *A Magyar Tudományos Akadémia Nyelv — és Irodalomtudományi Osztályának Közleményei*, xix/1-4 (1963), 65-101 (a *fatḥnāme* of Uzun Ḥasan); Adnan Sadık Erzi, *Türkiye Kütüphanelerinden notlar ve vesikalar*, ii, in *Belleten*, xiv/56 (1950), 612 ff.

(G. L. Lewis)

FATḤPŪR-SĪKRĪ, a deserted city, 23 miles from Agra, situated in 27° 5′ N. and 77° 40′ E., on a ridge of sandstone rocks near the ancient village of Sīkrī. In 1569 when Akbar visited Shaykh Salīm Čishtī, who was living in a cave on the Sīkrī ridge, the saint foretold the birth of a son to the childless monarch, and in 1570 Sulṭan Salīm, afterwards known as the Emperor Djahāngīr [*q.v.*] was born there. Akbar then commenced building a city, covering an area of about 1¾ sq. m. and enclosed by a wall (still standing) 3¾ m. long. On his return from his campaign in Gudjarāt in 1574, he found his new capital ready for occupation and named it Fatḥpūr (the City of Victory); he resided here until 1586, when he abandoned it as a capital, probably on account of the brackish nature of the water obtainable there, and shortly after his death it began to fall into ruin. Many of the buildings, however, still remain in an excellent state of preservation; among these may be mentioned the official buildings, such as the mint, the treasury, the record office, and the hall of public audience, and the royal palace, including the private apartments of the Emperor and the residences of several of his wives. The house of the Turkī Sulṭāna is remarkable for the elaborate carving with which it is covered, both within and without; the interior is decorated with a dado, 4 ft. high, divided into eight oblong panels, richly decorated with carvings representing forest and garden scenes. The two-storeyed building, known as Bīrbal's house (though it was undoubtedly the palace of one of Akbar's queens), is similarly covered with carving exhibiting a profuse variety of patterns executed in minute detail. In close proximity to the royal apartments are some curious buildings, of a unique design, *e.g.*, the Pānč Maḥall, a five-storeyed pavilion, each storey of which is smaller than the one on which it rests, and the so-called Dīwān-i-Khāṣṣ (or private audience hall), a building consisting of one room only, in the centre of which rises an octagonal column surmounted by an enormous circular capital, from the top of which radiate four narrow causeways, each about 10 ft. long, to the corners of the building; the top of this capital is thus connected with a gallery, running round the upper part of the room and communicating by staircases (made in the thickness of the wall) both with the roof and the courtyard below. It is not possible to enumerate here the many other buildings connected with the emperor and his court, but special mention must be made of the great mosque, which is one of the finest monuments of Mughal architecture. It covers an area of 438 ft. by 542 ft., having a central court (360 ft. by 439 ft.) enclosed by cloisters, except at the three gateways, of which the Buland Darwāza (facing the south), erected by Akbar in 1602 to commemorate his victories in the Dakkan, ranks as one of the noblest gateways in India. In the court of the mosque stands the tomb of Shaykh Salīm Čishtī, a single-storeyed building, encased in white marble and surmounted by a dome; the marble lattice screens which enclose the veranda of this building are of extraordinary delicacy and intricacy of geometrical pattern; over the cenotaph is a wooden canopy inlaid with mother-of-pearl arranged in beautiful geometrical designs.

Among the noteworthy features of the buildings at Fatḥpūr-Sīkrī are the evidences of the influence of Hindu architecture, in construction and decoration, and the frescoes painted on the walls of the Khʷābgāh and the Sōnahrā Makān, and the colour decoration of the Ḥammām and other buildings.

Bibliography: *Tūzuk-i-Djahāngīrī*, Aligarh 1864, 2; E. W. Smith, *The Moghul Architecture of Fathpur-Sikri*, in *Archaeological Survey of India*, Allahabad 1894-8; *Keene's Handbook for visitors to Agra and its neighbourhood*, re-written by E. A. Duncan, 7th ed. Calcutta 1909, 222-57; E. W. Smith, *Wall paintings recently found in the khwabgah, Fathpur Sikri, near Agra*, in *Journal of Indian Art*, vi (1894); Muhammad Ashraf Husain, *A guide to Fatehpur Sikri*, Delhi 1937; P. Brown, *Indian architecture (the Islamic period)*, Bombay 1942; Pearson, nos. 6734-5, 6737-8, 6788, and *Supplement (1956-60)*, nos. 1779, 1796. See further HIND—Architecture.

FĀTIḤA, "the opening (Sūra)", or, more exactly, *Fātiḥat al-Kitāb* "(the Sūra) which opens the scripture (of revelation)", designation of the first Sūra of the Ḳurʾān. Occasionally the terms *umm al-kitāb* (according to Sūra III, 7; XIII, 39; XLIII, 4) and *al-sabʿ al-mat̲h̲ānī* (according to Sūra XV, 87) are also found. With reference to the last-named term one must count the Basmala which comes before the Sūra as a verse on its own, to make up the total of seven verses (= *mat̲h̲ānī*).

While the other Sūras are arranged fairly accurately according to length (that is to say, the longer they are the nearer the beginning they are to be found, the shorter they are, the nearer the end) the Fātiḥa, despite its shortness, is prefaced to the Ḳurʾān as a sort of introductory prayer. Like the last two Sūrās (*al-muʿawwid̲h̲atān*), it is said not to have been preserved originally in the Codex of Ibn Masʿūd. It is markedly liturgical in character, as is also shown by the use of the first person plural (verses 5 and 6). Its chronological position (within the Mecca period) cannot be established more precisely.

The Fātiḥa is an indispensible component of the prayer-ritual. It must be recited at the beginning of every *rakʿa*, that is to say at least seventeen times a day (twice at the morning *ṣalāt*, three times at the sunset *ṣalāt*, and four times at each of the other three hours of prayer). It is often said at other times too. "With this recitation a seal is put on almost all important resolutions, almost all prayer formulae at the holy places are closed, and all joyful news is welcomed: while tradesmen who cannot come to terms over the price of goods seek in the united recitation of the fâtihah new strength for a decision" (Snouck Hurgronje, *Mekka*, 1931, 29). On many tombs there is an inscription asking the traveller visiting the spot to pray a *fātiḥa* for the soul of the dead man (H. Ritter, *Meer der Seele*, 1955, 317). In some respects, therefore, the *fātiḥa* may be compared with the Lord's Prayer in Christian practice. However, H. Winkler's attempt to show that the one is derived from the other must be said to have failed (*ZS*, vi, 1928, 238-46). M. Gaster's guess that the Fātiḥa is an imitation of the Samaritan Enṣira (*EI*[1], iv, art. Samaritans) is equally unconvincing.

Buk̲h̲ārī and Muslim tell of a sick man who was cured by exorcism with the *umm al-kitāb*. There are numerous examples of the *fātiḥa* being used as a powerful prayer in the making of amulets. The *sawāḳiṭ al-fātiḥa*, that is, the seven letters which are significant by their absence from the *fātiḥa*, play an important part in this. Al-Būnī gives the requisite instructions in his book of magic *S̲h̲ams al-maʿārif*.

In certain Arab countries, particularly in North Africa, the term *fātiḥa* (or *fatḥa*) is used to mean a prayer ceremony in which the arms are stretched out with the palms upwards, but without any recitation of the first Sūra (Snouck Hurgronje, *Mekka*, 1931, 29, note; E. Westermarck, *Ritual and belief in Morocco*, 1926, i, 186, note). Philipp Vassel gives as a translation "prayer with open hands" (*MSOS*, v, 1902, ii, 188). But it seems probable that even this prayer-ceremony is called after the first Sūra, and that originally it involved a recitation of the *fātiḥa* which only subsequently and as a result of much repetition disappeared to be replaced by a silent prayer.

Bibliography: Buk̲h̲ārī, *Id̲j̲āra*, 16; *Tafsīr al-Ḳurʾān*, 1; *Faḍāʾil al-Ḳurʾān*, 9; *Ṭibb*, 33 f.; Muslim, *Ṣalāt*, 34-44; *Salām*, 65 f.; Ṭabarī, *Tafsīr*, 1321, i, 35-66; Zamak̲h̲s̲h̲arī, *Kas̲h̲s̲h̲āf*, Cairo 1373/1953, i, 1-15; Suyūṭī, *Itḳān*, Cairo 1317, i, 54 f.; ii, 152; *Gesch. des Qor.*, i², 1909, 110-7; Blachère, *Le Coran*, i, 1949, 125-7; A. Jeffery, *A variant text of the Fātiḥa*, in *MW*, xxix (1939), 158-62; al-Būnī, *S̲h̲ams al-maʿārif*, Cairo 1319, 68 f., 71, 95-9; E. Doutté, *Magie et religion dans l'Afrique du Nord*, Algiers 1909, 159, 211 ff.; Snouck Hurgronje, *Mekka in the latter part of the 19th century*, 1931, *passim*; E. Westermarck, *Ritual and belief in Morocco*, i and ii, 1926, *passim*; J. Jomier, *La place du Coran dans la vie quotidienne en Égypte*, in *IBLA*, xv (1952), 131-65, 149; H. Winkler, *Fātiḥa und Vaterunser*, in *ZS*, vi (1928), 238-46.

(R. Paret)

al-**FĀTIK** [see nad̲j̲āḥ, banū].

FĀṬIMA, daughter of Muḥammad and K̲h̲adīd̲j̲a, wife of ʿAlī b. Abī Ṭālib, mother of al-Ḥasan and al-Ḥusayn, was the only one of the Prophet's daughters to enjoy great renown. She became the object of great veneration by all Muslims. This may be because she lived closest to her father, lived longest, and gave him numerous descendants, who spread throughout the Muslim world (the other sons and daughters of Muḥammad either died young or, if they had descendants, these soon died out); or it may be because there was reflected upon her, besides the greatness of her father, the historical importance of her husband and her sons; or because, as time went on, the Muslims attributed to her extraordinary qualities. Throughout the Muslim world, as is well known, it is customary to add to her name the honorific title al-Zahrāʾ, "the Shining One", and she is always spoken of with the greatest respect; but it was above all the S̲h̲īʿīs who surrounded her with a halo of beliefs and glorified her some centuries after her death. That Fāṭima—a woman who, unlike other women associated with the Prophet, remained on the fringe of the great events of the early years of Islam and hence receives little attention in the historical sources—should be exalted to the level of legend, presents no problem to the believer: Western scholars, on the other hand, have set themselves to recover the real Fāṭima from the haze which envelops her. Did she really possess merits so special as to explain her posthumous fame, or is this fame to be attributed to a complex of circumstances which includes the human tendency to render extreme veneration to Woman? Two eminent European orientalists, Father Henri Lammens and Louis Massignon, have presented diametrically opposed judgements of Fāṭima.

The former, in *Fāṭima et les filles de Mahomet*, has sketched, in sparkling and lively style, ingeniously but not without malice, a thoroughly gloomy portrait of the daughter of the Prophet: as he describes her, Fāṭima becomes a woman devoid of attraction, of mediocre intelligence, completely insignificant, little esteemed by her father, ill-treated by her husband, "caractère chagrin et perpétuellement voilé de deuil", "ombre gémissante de femme", anaemic, often ill, prone to tears, who died perhaps of consumption. It is profitable to read the criticism of this thesis by G. Levi Della Vida, in *RSO*, vi (1913), 536-47 and C. H. Becker, *Grundsätzliches zur Leben-Muhammed-Forschung*, in *Islamstudien*, i, 520-7 = *Prinzipielles zu Lammens' Sīrastudien*, in *Isl.*, iv (1913), 263-9.

Massignon, on the other hand, has made Fāṭima sublime, elevating her to a position often reminiscent of that which the Virgin Mary holds among Christians. He accuses Lammens of having contented himself with putting together isolated fragments of anecdotes without attempting to arrange them in plausible patterns so as to bring them to life. "Yet it is only this method", he says, "which allows us to understand how Fāṭima's intuitive actions (hardly consciously performed) have, throughout the collective history of Islam, penetrated the tangle of deceptions, accommodations and theories". Fāṭima, as he conceives her, is the Woman whose soul was unappreciated during her lifetime, who enjoyed privileges (*k͟haṣāʾiṣ*) accorded her by her father; she is Mistress of the Tent of hospitality, the Hostess of the Prophet's freedmen and of the non-Arab converts, and, as such, she represents the beginnings of universal Islam (*La notion*, 118 f.). To avoid any misrepresentation of Massignon's conception, we reproduce verbatim some of the concluding sentences of his *Mubāhala*. According to him, Fāṭima had a "vie secrète ... voilée bien au delà de la jalousie de ʿAyisha, par une autre Jalousie, celle de Dieu. Vie de compassion intérieure, de larmes, prières pour les morts (à Uḥud) et dans les cimetières, voeux de jeûne, choses de peu de poids pour des théologiens philosophes ou canonistes. Vie qui les survole et les surplombe en Islam, comme une menace, de plus en plus imminente, de la Grâce de Dieu: du Voeu secret de la Femme, Vierge ou Mère qui transcende tous les axiomes et serments des hommes. L'hyperdulie des âmes en douleur, en Islam, pour Fāṭima, n'est selon le Coran lui-même qu'une figure de l'hyperdulie mariale ...". This interpretation of the figure of Fāṭima will doubtless satisfy the mystic who lives in a world of extraordinary religious experiences and, perhaps, the scholar concerned with religious problems, because it gives a psychologico-religious explanation for the origin and development of the legend of the daughter of the Prophet and bridges the gap between legend and reality, as Lammens's book fails to do; but it cannot escape the objections of the historian, who will consider that the author subordinates the facts to beliefs about Fāṭima which appeared only later.

In the following survey will be found, placed in chronological order, arranged schematically, and accompanied sometimes by a commentary, the references to Fāṭima which can be collected from the sources belonging to the 2nd/8th and 3rd/9th centuries and the first half of the 4th/10th century (particularly al-Balād͟hurī, *Ansāb*, Ibn Saʿd and collections of *ḥadīt͟h*s regarded as canonical by the Sunnīs, for Ibn His͟hām and the historians had little occasion to concern themselves with Fāṭima, so obscure was the life that she led; later sources such as Ibn ʿAbd al-Barr's *Istīʿāb*, Ibn al-At͟hīr's *Usd al-g͟hāba*, Ibn Ḥad͟jar's *Iṣāba*, the *Sīra al-Ḥalabiyya* and the *Taʾrīk͟h al-k͟hamīs*, have purposely been ignored, the aim being to get as near as possible, if not to the reality, at least to the time when Fāṭima lived). In the survey some apparently trivial facts have been mentioned: this is because they had, particularly among the S͟hīʿīs, unforeseen developments; Fāṭima's trousseau, for example, became the subject of Persian religious dramas, the famous *taʿziya*s.

The Historical Fāṭima

Birth and childhood. The date of Fāṭima's birth is uncertain; however that indicated as most probable is the year of the re-building of the Kaʿba, *i.e.*, five years before the beginning of the Prophet's mission. This implies, as will appear, that the girl was married when she was over 18, a rather unusual age for an Arab bride. But if we take her birth as being a few years later (see al-Yaʿḳūbī, ii, 19) we encounter another difficulty—that when she was born her mother K͟hadīd͟ja would have been over fifty. The question of Fāṭima's age is treated at some length in Lammens's book (8-14). There is also some uncertainty as to Fāṭima's place in the sequence of Muḥammad's daughters, who are generally listed in the order: Zaynab, Ruḳayya, Umm Kult͟hūm, Fāṭima. Of her childhood and her life at Mecca two episodes only are related: (1) she was overcome by grief at her mother's death, and the Prophet consoled her by saying that D͟jibrīl had come down to tell him that God had built for K͟hadīd͟ja in Paradise a pavilion of brilliant pearls (*ḳaṣab*; see Lane, s.v., 2529 f.), free of weariness and noise (al-Yaʿḳūbī, ii, 35); (2) she removed the refuse which ʿUḳba b. Abī Muʿayṭ, one of the Ḳurays͟h most hostile to Islam, had flung over the Prophet while he was at prayer, and her indignation led her to curse the offender (al-Buk͟hārī, ed. Krehl, ii, 300).

Journey from Mecca to Medina and betrothal. After the Hid͟jra, Muḥammad moved his daughters Fāṭima and Umm Kult͟hūm and his wife Sawda bint Zamaʿa from Mecca to Medina, charging his adopted son Zayd b. Ḥārit͟ha [*q.v.*] and Abū Rāfiʿ to go and fetch them, giving them two camels and a sum of money. There is however a completely different version of this: al-ʿAbbās escorted these women to Medina and the departure was not a peaceful one, for al-Ḥuwayrit͟h b. Nuḳayẓ b. Wahb prodded their camels, causing them to be thrown to the ground, for which act, it is said, he was killed after the occupation of Mecca. On the betrothal of Fāṭima and ʿAlī the sources give much information, but, as usual, they do not completely agree. Both Abū Bakr and ʿUmar had asked for Fāṭima's hand, but Muḥammad had refused, saying that he was waiting for the moment fixed by destiny (*ḳaḍāʾ*: Ibn Saʿd, viii, 11). ʿAlī did not dare to put forward his proposal because of his poverty, and it was Muḥammad who made his task easier; he reminded him that he owned a breast-plate which, if sold, would provide him with enough money for the bridal gift (*mahr*). ʿAlī, adding to the breast-plate some other objects and a camel or a ewe, raised the very modest sum of 480 dirhams or thereabouts. Of this money he spent, on Muḥammad's advice, one-third or two-thirds on perfumes, and the rest on objects necessary for the household. When Muḥammad informed his daughter of the promise which he had made to ʿAlī, Fāṭima (according to Ibn Saʿd) said nothing, and her silence was interpreted by the Prophet as consent (according to other sources, she protested and her father had to console her by saying that he had married her to that member of the family who was the most learned and wise, and who had been the first to embrace Islam).

Marriage. The accounts are at variance concerning the year and the month of the marriage and its consummation: the first or second year of the Hid͟jra, more likely the latter. According to some sources the consummation was postponed for a few days or for a few months, and some say that it did not take place until ʿAlī's return from the expedition of Badr. To celebrate their marriage, the bridegroom prepared a feast, Muḥammad having told him that this was necessary; the Anṣār gave their contributions in *d͟hura*, and ʿAlī killed a sheep. Two wives of the Prophet, ʿĀʾis͟ha and Umm Salama, arranged the house and prepared the wedding-feast. It is said that at this time ʿAlī was 25 and Fāṭima between 15 and 21. The sources give a rather long account of a rite inaugurated by the Prophet: having warned the bridal pair to expect him, Muḥammad went to their house on the wedding-night, asked for water in a jar, washed his hands in it (or spat in it, or spat back into it the water he had used to rinse his mouth) and sprinkled with it the breast (the shoulders and the forearms) of ʿAlī and of Fāṭima; finally he invoked God's blessing on them.

Poverty of the household. At night the newly-married pair lay on the fleece of an untanned sheepskin, which contained camel fodder during the day; for a covering they used an old piece of striped Yemenī cloth, which was not large enough to cover both feet and head. The pillow was of leather stuffed with *līf* (palm fibres); the trousseau was indeed meagre: a goatskin bottle, a sieve, a duster, a cup. Muḥammad had made some wedding-gifts: a velvet garment (*khamla* or *khamīl*), two pitchers, a leather bottle, a pillow and some bunches of fragrant herbs. Fāṭima, having no maid-servants, ground the corn herself, which gave her blisters; ʿAlī, to earn a little money, drew water from the wells and watered other people's land; because of this hard work he complained of pains in the chest. One day, the Prophet having received some slaves, ʿAlī sent Fāṭima to ask for one, and, as his wife lacked the courage to make this request, he went with her himself but met with a refusal. "I cannot allow the *ahl al-ṣuffa* [*q.v.*] to be tormented with hunger", exclaimed the Prophet, "I shall sell the slaves and spend the money to help them". To console his daughter and son-in-law, Muḥammad went later to their house and taught them some litanies (so many repetitions of *Allāh akbar*, so many of *al-ḥamdu li'llāh*, so many of *subḥān Allāh*), and ʿAlī did not fail to repeat them every night before going to sleep.

There seems no reason to reject the *ḥadīth*s which speak of the poverty of the household of ʿAlī and Fāṭima; only its duration must be limited to the first years of their marriage; many members of the community were just as poor and it was only after the occupation of Khaybar that the situation improved for ʿAlī and Fāṭima, as for a good number of Muslims, for they then received shares in the produce of the rich oasis and ʿĀʾisha could exclaim: "Now we shall eat our fill of dates".

Fāṭima's house after the marriage. ʿAlī built a dwelling not far from that of the Prophet but, as Fāṭima wanted to live nearer to her father, the Medinan al-Ḥāritha b. al-Nuʿmān gave up his own house to them.

Sons of ʿAlī and Fāṭima. Al-Ḥasan was born in 2/624 (but in this case the consummation of the marriage cannot have taken place after Badr!) or in 3/625, in Ramaḍān; al-Ḥusayn was conceived 50 days after the birth of al-Ḥasan and born in 4/626, in the first days of Shaʿbān. Besides these two sons and a third, Muḥassin (or Muḥsin), still-born, Fāṭima had two daughters, who were called by the names of two of their aunts: Umm Kulthūm and Zaynab [see further ʿALIDS].

Disputes between ʿAlī and Fāṭima, and Muḥammad's intervention. ʿAlī and Fāṭima did not always live in harmony. ʿAlī treated his wife with too much harshness (*shidda, ghilāẓ*), and Fāṭima went to complain to her father. There are some *ḥadīth*s which are real vignettes of family life, describing in a vivid and fresh manner how the Prophet intervened and how his face shone with satisfaction after the reconciliation of those dear to him. The most serious disputes between the pair arose when the Banū Hishām b. al-Mughīra of the Ḳuraysh suggested to ʿAlī that he should marry one of their women. ʿAlī did not reject the proposal, but Muḥammad, when some of the tribe came to sound him on the matter, came to the defence of his daughter. "Fāṭima", he said, "is a part of me (*baḍʿa minnī*) and whoever offends her offends me" (al-Balādhurī, *Ansāb*, i, 403; al-Tirmidhī, ii, 319, etc.) or "what angers her angers me also" (this *ḥadīth* has many variants which, however, do not much change the meaning). It seems that at the same time ʿAlī was asking in marriage a daughter of Abū Djahl nicknamed al-ʿAwrāʾ (the One-eyed). Muḥammad protested from the *minbar* against ʿAlī, who proposed to shelter under one roof the daughter of the Apostle of God and the daughter of the enemy of God (*i.e.*, Abū Djahl). On this occasion also the Prophet pronounced the phrase: *Innahā baḍʿa minnī* ("she is indeed a part of me"), and added that if ʿAlī wanted to accomplish his project he must first divorce Fāṭima (Aḥmad b. Ḥanbal, *Musnad*, Cairo 1313, iv, 326; al-Bukhārī, ed. Krehl, ii, 440, etc.). Some authors have deduced from this that monogamy was one of the *khaṣāʾiṣ* of the daughter of the Prophet.

The name Abū Turāb, "the man of dust", given to ʿAlī has, among other explanations, one connecting it with the disputes between ʿAlī and Fāṭima: instead of answering his wife in anger, ʿAlī would go out of the house and put dust on his head; Muḥammad, seeing him do this, gave him the famous nickname.

Historical events in which Fāṭima was involved during the life of Muḥammad. The following is all that can be collected: (1) After the battle of Uḥud Fāṭima tended Muḥammad's wounds and was charged by him and by ʿAlī to clean their bloodstained swords; after this it became her custom to go to pray on the graves of those killed in this battle; (2) Abū Sufyān, foreseeing the occupation of Mecca, sought her and ʿAlī's intercession with Muḥammad (al-Ṭabarī, i, 1623); (3) she received a share of the products of Khaybar and ʿAlī another, separate, share; (4) she went to Mecca while the town was being occupied, and on this occasion Abū Sufyān begged her to give him her protection, but she refused and refused also to allow her child to do so, the Prophet having prohibited this (al-Wāḳidī, 324); in 10/632 she performed the *ʿumra*; (5) with her husband and her sons, Fāṭima played an important part in the *mubāhala*, an episode which had strong repercussions among the Shīʿa [see MUBĀHALA].

Fāṭima as one of the five members of the *Ahl al-bayt*. A verse of the Ḳurʾān (XXXIII, 33) says: "God wishes only to remove from you the uncleanness, O People of the House" (*Ahl al-bayt* [*q.v.*]). The preceding verses contain instructions to the wives of the Prophet, and there the verbs and pronouns are in the feminine plural; but in this verse, addressed to the People of the House, the pronouns are in the masculine plural. Thus, it has been said, it is no longer a question of the Prophet's wives, or of them alone. To whom then does it refer? The expression *Ahl al-bayt* can only mean "Family of the Prophet". The privilege accorded by God to the latter (originally entirely spiritual, but later not merely so) naturally led all the relatives of Muḥammad—those nearest to him, those belonging to the collateral branches of the family, and beyond this such groups of the community as the Anṣār, or indeed the whole of the community—to claim a place in the *Ahl al-bayt*. But there is a story given in many traditions according to which Muḥammad sheltered under his cloak (or under a covering or under a sort of tent), in varying circumstances (including the occasion when he was preparing for the *mubāhala*), his grandchildren al-Ḥasan and al-Ḥusayn, his daughter Fāṭima and his son-in-law ʿAlī; and so it is these five who are given the title *Ahl al-kisāʾ* [*q.v.*] or "People of the Mantle". Efforts have been made to include among the latter Muḥammad's wives; in general however the number of the privileged is limited to these five. Now according to the Shīʿa, without exception, but also according to the pro-ʿAlid Sunnīs, the *Ahl al-bayt* are identical with the *Ahl al-kisāʾ*. The verse quoted above (XXXIII, 33) is associated with Fāṭima and ʿAlī on one other occasion: it is related that Muḥammad, rising early in the morning to perform the *ṣubḥ*, was in the habit of knocking on their door and using this verse to remind them of the duty of prayer.

During the Prophet's illness. Fāṭima, who loved her father greatly, was much grieved by his illness and wept and lamented. During this period she received a confidence from Muḥammad. It is ʿĀʾisha who relates the episode in many *ḥadīth*s: she saw Fāṭima weep when her father spoke to her in secret and then smile. After the Prophet's death, she asked her what her father had said to her on that occasion; Fāṭima replied that Muḥammad had told her that Djibrīl came down once a year to bring him the Ḳurʾān, but that, as he had recently come down twice, he deduced that the end of his life was near, then he had added that she, Fāṭima, would be the first member of the family to join him in the next world. Then Fāṭima had wept. But Muḥammad had said to her: "Are you not pleased to be the *sayyida* of the women of this people?" (or "of the women of the Believers", or "of the women of the world", or "of the women of Paradise"—all these variants are found in the *ḥadīth*s). Then Fāṭima had smiled. As will be seen, this story is interesting because of the developments it underwent among the Shīʿa.

After the death of the Prophet. Fāṭima, a timid woman who had never taken part in political matters, found herself indirectly involved in some of the events which followed the death of the Prophet. After his election, Abū Bakr made his way with some companions towards Fāṭima's house, where a number of Anṣār and of ʿAlī's supporters had assembled. The newly-elected Khalīfa wanted to obtain the homage of these dissidents also, but ʿAlī went forward to meet him with sword drawn, and Fāṭima, when her husband had been disarmed by ʿUmar and the party was preparing to enter the house, raised such cries and threatened so boldly to uncover her hair that Abū Bakr preferred to withdraw (al-Yaʿḳūbī, ii, 141). There are other accounts of the same episode: Fāṭima saw in ʿUmar's hand a brand, and asked him if he intended to set fire to her door because of his hostility to her (al-Balādhurī, *Ansāb*, i, 586). In one book, *al-Imāma wa 'l-siyāsa* (which is certainly very early, even though the attribution to Ibn Ḳutayba is wrong), the episode is related with more serious details: ʿUmar really had evil intentions; he had wood brought and threatened to burn the house with everything in it. When he was asked, "Even if Fāṭima is there?", he replied in the affirmative. Then those who were in the house came out and rendered the homage demanded—except for ʿAlī. Fāṭima, appearing at the door, reproached them: "You have left the body of the Apostle of God with us and you have decided among yourselves without consulting us, without respecting our rights!" When Abū Bakr and ʿUmar repeated their attempts to make ʿAlī comply, she is said to have cried out, "O father! O Apostle of God! What evils we have suffered at the hands of ʿUmar and Abū Bakr after your death!" When they came back to her house and asked permission to enter, she again refused, and it was ʿAlī who let them in. Fāṭima turned her face to the wall. If one is to believe another account preserved in the same book (12), Fāṭima played an active part at the time when the decision was being made on the choice of a successor to the Prophet in the capacity of head of the community: she went on horseback with ʿAlī to the meeting-places of the Anṣār to ask them to support her husband; but the Anṣār replied that ʿAlī had come to them too late, when they were already committed to Abū Bakr. We have spent some time on these episodes because (1) even if they have been expanded by invented details, they are based on fact; (2) they represent Fāṭima's only political action; (3) to the motives for the hatred felt by the Shīʿa for ʿUmar they add one more, true or false: his treatment of the daughter of the Prophet.

Fāṭima's claim to Muḥammad's estate. After the death of her father, Fāṭima asked Abū Bakr to hand over the possessions of Muḥammad which he was holding. It is not clear whether these possessions included the property which Mukhayriḳ, the Jew converted to Islam, had given to the Prophet at Medina on the land of the Banu 'l-Naḍīr; probably there was no dispute about this. It was over the land of Fadak [*q.v.*] and over the share of Khaybar [*q.v.*] that Abū Bakr met Fāṭima's claims with a flat refusal, asserting that he had heard the Prophet say that he had no heirs and that everything that he left would be *ṣadaḳa* [*q.v.*]. Nor is it known whether the claim to the inheritance was put forward by Fāṭima alone or together with al-ʿAbbās; the examination of many *ḥadīth*s leads us to believe that the attempt to gain possession of this property was made twice and with different arguments, on the first occasion probably by both of them, on the second by Fāṭima alone. This dispute between such a prominent person as Abū Bakr and the daughter of the Prophet has always been disagreeable to Muslims; consequently they have tried to minimize its gravity by maintaining, for example, that Fāṭima claimed Fadak intending to give the rents of it to the poor (Shīʿī sources add: to the *mawālī*); they like to depict Abū Bakr as grieved by the duty of refusing a request of the daughter of the Prophet, but forced to act thus by the conduct of Muḥammad himself. The Shīʿa naturally do not forgive the Caliph for having disbelieved Fāṭima, who maintained that she had received Fadak as a gift from her father, and have continued for centuries to argue about this question.

Illness and death of Fāṭima. Fāṭima fell ill soon after her father's death. According to some sources she was reconciled during her illness with Abū Bakr, who had asked to visit her, but, according to the majority she remained angry to the end. There is an oft-repeated story about the last moments of her life: she prepared for death by washing herself, putting on coarse garments and rubbing herself with balm, and she charged her sister-in-law, Asmāʾ b. ʿUmays, the widow of Djaʿfar b. Abī Ṭālib, who was helping her with these tasks, that no-one should uncover her after her death; then she lay down on a clean bed in the middle of the room and awaited the end. As she had complained about the custom of covering the dead with a material which revealed their forms, Asmāʾ prepared for her a bier made, in the manner of the Abyssinians, of wood and fresh palm-leaves.

Fāṭima was content with this. Unfortunately these accounts which would allow us to assume that Fāṭima was gentle, modest, and calm in the face of death are contradicted by others: according to al-Yaʿḳūbī (ii, 128-30), she rebuked severely the Prophet's wives and the women of the Ḳuraysh who came to visit her during her illness; through Asmāʾ she prevented ʿĀʾisha from entering; her anxiety to hide her form from people's gaze was prompted by shame at her extreme thinness (al-Ṭabarī, iii, 2436); it was ʿAlī who washed the body, or it was she herself who begged her husband to perform this task. It is difficult, if not impossible, to choose among these different accounts.

There is the same uncertainty over the date of her death as surrounds other events of her private life: it was certainly the year 11, but the month is doubtful; the commonest report is that she died six months after the Prophet. Her death was kept secret and her burial took place by night. According to most versions, neither Abū Bakr nor ʿUmar was informed; but there are accounts which relate that Abū Bakr recited the ritual prayers over Fāṭima's grave. Nearly all the sources agree that Fāṭima was buried in the Baḳīʿ, and some specify the place of her grave: near the mosque called, from the name of the woman who built it, Masdjid Ruḳayya, at the corner of the *dār* of ʿAḳīl (ʿAlī's brother), seven cubits from the road etc., but according to other sources, either immediately after the burial or some time later, the exact position of the grave was no longer known. Al-Masʿūdī (*Murūdj*, vi, 165) asserts that there was a tomb which bore an inscription giving as the names of those buried there Fāṭima and three ʿAlids (he is however the only one to give this detail), but al-Muḳaddasī (*BGA*, iii, 46) includes the tomb of the daughter of the Prophet in the list of places on which there is disagreement, for it was also possible that Fāṭima had been buried "in the room" (*fi 'l-ḥudjra*). Nowadays Shīʿī pilgrims, to pay homage to the *sayyidat al-nisāʾ*, visit three places: her house, the Baḳīʿ and the space in the Great Mosque between the *rawḍa* and the tomb of the Prophet. For a small *maḳṣūra* which may mark her place of burial and "Fāṭima's Garden", also in the Great Mosque, see *EI*[1], art. al-Madīna, 90 f.

Physical and moral attributes. Fāṭima had a very strange *kunya*: Umm Abīhā, "mother of her father". The explanations given for this name make us suspect that it originated among the Shīʿa, all the more so that it is apparently mentioned only in the more recent sources, *e.g.*, the *Usd al-ghāba*. An Imāmī source says that she was called "mother of her father" because she learned through a revelation that the name of her very last descendant would be Muḥammad, like that of her father. There are other explanations, for which see below, sections on The celestial apple and Fāṭima's names. Given the connexions between the cult of Mary among Christians and that of Fāṭima among Muslims (to which Massignon has drawn attention), it is possible that the title arose as a counterpart to that of "Mother of God".

Fāṭima was certainly not a beautiful woman, for the sources are silent about her appearance, whereas they mention the beauty of her sister Ruḳayya; they confine themselves to reporting that she resembled the Prophet in her gait. In any case she cannot have appeared the weak and sickly woman which Lammens took her to be on the strength of two *ḥadīth*s, which may refer to purely temporary situations, for there are other facts (her bearing five children; her discharge of arduous household tasks, her two journeys to Mecca) which prove that Faṭima enjoyed fairly good health.

In attempting to form a judgement on the moral qualities of Fāṭima we encounter many obstacles. When some accounts permit us to attribute to her a certain characteristic, there are others which contradict it. It seems certain that she was hardworking, content to perform her domestic work diligently and patiently. She appears to have taken pleasure in helping others, and the Prophet's wives used her as a spokesman to express their resentment over the preference which he showed for ʿĀʾisha; we can easily imagine, however, that she performed this service willingly, for she herself had no great fondness for ʿĀʾisha. On this occasion she proved incapable of defending the case for which she had approached her father, for when he asked her: "Do you not love what I love?" (meaning ʿĀʾisha), she quickly agreed that she too loved her; so the Prophet's wives had to choose a less timorous advocate from among their number to maintain their rights. Are we then to conclude from this and other accounts that Fāṭima was timid? On the day of her marriage she stumbled on the hem of her garment, but we see her support her husband so boldly against Abū Bakr that there is no question of timidity, and she appears as a woman of quite different calibre. There is no doubt that she was meek and submissive towards the Prophet, but what was her attitude to her husband? It was really she who prevented ʿAlī from taking a second wife, and in the affair of the inheritance, when it was a question of defending the interests of the family, although she was obliged to yield to the wishes of the head of the State, she did it unwillingly, refusing to acknowledge the validity of Abū Bakr's decision.

The Fāṭima of Legend

As no systematic study of this subject exists, we have limited ourselves to selecting the main themes of the Fāṭima legend from three early Shīʿī works (see *Bibl.*) in which some chapters are devoted to the daughter of the Prophet. The authors are: (1) Ibn Rustam al-Ṭabarī who, according to the editor of his *Dalāʾil al-imāma*, lived in the 4th/10th century (siglum: IRṬ); (2) Ḥusayn b. ʿAbd al-Wahhāb, who began to write in 448/1056-7 the work which we have used and which was one of the sources of al-Madjlisī's *Biḥār al-anwār* and of al-Baḥrānī's *Madīnat al-maʿādjiz*; he presents some stories about Fāṭima which differ strikingly from those of the other sources (siglum: ḤʿAW); (3) Ibn Shahrāshūb, who died in 588/1192. Of the three works, his *Manāḳib Āl Abī Ṭālib* yields the most information and quotes form the largest number of sources (siglum: ISh).

Khadīdja's pregnancy and accouchement. Khadīdja was despised by the Ḳuraysh because of her marriage with a poor man from a social class lower than her own (IRṬ, 8). On going in to her, Muḥammad told her that Djibrīl had informed him that she would bear a daughter, a pure and blessed soul, and that from this daughter would spring his posterity and the *imām*s destined to be the rulers on earth when his own inspiration ended (IRṬ, 8). Fāṭima, while still in her mother's womb, conversed with her (IRṬ, 8; ḤʿAW, 48, 51; ISh, 119). Because of their contempt for Khadīdja, the women of the Ḳuraysh refused to help her during her confinement. So four women came down from Paradise to assist her: Sāra, Āsiya, Mary and Ṣafūrāʾ, daughter of Shuʿayb and wife of Mūsā. Ten houris came with a bowl and a jug filled with water from the Kawthar, and the first of them washed the new-born child, wrapped her in perfumed fine linen, and handed her, pure, purified, fortunate, blessed also in her posterity, to Khadīdja, who suckled her (IRṬ, 9; ḤʿAW, 48; ISh, 119). Fāṭima grew as much in a month as other children in a year (IRṬ, 9; ISh, 119). The women who had come to assist her mother departed as soon as they had completed their task, but before they went the new-born child greeted them by their names (ḤʿAW, 48). At the moment of Fāṭima's birth, light spread over the sky and the earth, to the West and to the East (hence her title al-Zahrāʾ) (IRṬ, 9; ISh, 119). Immediately after her birth Fāṭima uttered the profession of faith, praised God, recognized the imamate of ʿAlī, recited the Ḳurʾān and predicted future events (IRṬ, 9; ḤʿAW, 48, 51; ISh, 119).

Betrothal. ʿAbd al-Raḥmān b. ʿAwf wished to marry Fāṭima and offered an enormous *mahr* (100 camels loaded with Coptic cloth, and 10,000 *dīnārs*). ʿUthmān then offered the same *mahr*, and advanced the argument that he had embraced Islam earlier than ʿAbd al-Raḥmān. This flaunting of wealth angered Muḥammad, who threw at ʿAbd al-Raḥmān (or placed on the hem of his garment) pebbles which turned into pearls (a single one of them worth all the riches of ʿAbd al-Raḥmān). Djibrīl descended from heaven to announce that ʿAlī was to be the husband of Fāṭima, for God had already commanded the angel Riḍwān to adorn the four Paradises and another angel to built a *minbar* of light (IRṬ, 12; ISh, 123).

Marriage of Fāṭima and ʿAlī. The Ḳuraysh women criticized Fāṭima's marrying ʿAlī, a poor man, but Muḥammad had destined her for him because he had learned through Djibrīl (or through an angel named Maḥmūd) not only that this was the will of God but that the marriage had already taken place in heaven, with God as *walī*, Djibrīl as *khaṭīb* and the angels as witnesses. The *mahr* had been half of the earth (or a fifth, or a quarter) and, in addition, Paradise and Hell (hence Fāṭima enables her supporters to enter the one and consigns her enemies to the other). The *mahr* on earth was only about 500 *dirhams* because it was to serve as *sunna* for the community. Perhaps in order to leave the *mahr* at this low figure, there are some references to a *niḥla* from ʿAlī, consisting of a fifth of the earth, two-thirds of Paradise, and four rivers: the Euphrates, the Tigris, the Nile and the Oxus. The tree *Ṭūbā* or the *Sidrat al-muntahā*, at God's command, covered itself with robes, pearls and precious stones, and scattered them in vast quantities; the houris gathered these jewels and will keep them until the Day of Resurrection, for they are Fāṭima's *nithār*. The same tree, according to some accounts, let fall also missives written in light, which the angels gathered up because they are the safe-conducts of the supporters of the ʿAlids (IRṬ, 12 f., cf. also 14, 18, 19 f., 23 f.; ḤʿAW, 48 f.; ISh, 109, 123, 128, 134 f.). When Muḥammad learned this, he called to him ʿAmmār b. Yāsir, Salmān, and al-ʿAbbās and in their presence told ʿAlī what God's will was; on his advice, ʿAlī sold his breast-plate to Diḥya [*q.v.*], who then made him a present of it (Diḥya = Djibrīl: IRṬ, 14). The marriage in heaven, according to two of our sources, took place forty days before the marriage on earth (or on the night of the *isrāʾ*). The angel Maḥmūd revealed also the reason for the union: light must be joined to light (*ibid.*).

Trousseau. Muḥammad charged Asmāʾ bint ʿUmays, Umm Salama and a freedwoman, ʿAmmār, Abū Bakr and Bilāl to make the purchases necessary for the household of Fāṭima and ʿAlī. The list of their purchases is recorded, in some cases with the prices (ISh, 123). Umm Salama bought the mattress-cover of Egyptian cloth which was to be filled with *līf*; Bilāl or ʿAmmār saw to the perfumes (IRṬ, 14 f., 26).

The marriage ceremony. During the marriage ceremony on earth, Djibrīl cried from heaven "*Allāhu akbar*"; Muḥammad heard him, and he too, with his Companions, cried "*Allāhu akbar*". This was the first *takbīr* to be called during a wedding procession (*zifāf*) and from that day onwards it became *sunna* (ḤʿAW, 51). But there is another and stranger story concerning this *takbīr*: Muḥammad mounted Fāṭima on his mule and pushed the animal, while Salmān led it; suddenly there was great confusion in the street: Djibrīl and Mīkhāʾīl, each at the head of 70,000 angels, had come down for the ceremony and raised with Muḥammad the cry "*Allāhu akbar!*" (IRṬ, 23, 25).

Gifts from heaven. Djibrīl brought to Muḥammad a clove and an ear of corn from Paradise, announcing that God had commanded him to adorn Paradise for the marriage of Fāṭima and ʿAlī (IRṬ, 14, 20). ʿAlī, told by Muḥammad to look up into the sky, saw richly-clad maidens bringing presents: these were his own and Fāṭima's future servants in Paradise (IRṬ, 26). When ʿAmmār brought to Fāṭima the perfume which Muḥammad had sent him to buy for her, Fāṭima announced that the angel Riḍwān had sent her some from heaven, brought by houris each of whom had in her right hand a fruit and in her left some basil; these gifts were intended for the people of her House and for her supporters (IRṬ, 26). Like Mary who, according to the Ḳurʾān (III, 32/37), received a necessary provision (*rizḳ*), Fāṭima received pomegranates, grapes, apples, quinces, etc., and ate besides things which other creatures had never tasted since the fall of Adam and Eve (ISh, 135). One day Muḥammad entered Fāṭima's house while she was at prayer, and saw behind her a steaming cauldron; he asked what this was and she replied: "Divine Providence" (ISh, 135). Another day ʿAlī invited Salmān to the house because Fāṭima had received a gift from heaven and wished to share it with him. Three houris had brought it to her, with a message of sympathy from God while she was weeping for the death of her father. These three houris were called Dharra, Miḳdāda and Salmā, because they had been created for Abū Dharr [*q.v.*], Miḳdād [*q.v.*] and Salmān [*q.v.*] respectively. The gift was a dish of white dates, cooled and so fragrant that Salmān was asked, as he was taking five of them home, whether he had perfumed himself with musk. The dates had no stones; God had created them for Fāṭima beneath His throne from the prayers which Muḥammad had taught her (IRṬ, 29). Fāṭima wished for a ring, and asked it of God during the night-prayer, Muḥammad having taught her that she should make her requests at those times. A mysterious voice informed her that the ring was under the prayer-rug. In a dream Fāṭima saw castles destined for her in Paradise and noticed that the ring had been made from the foot of a bed which was in one of these castles and which had only three feet; but next day Muḥammad told her that the family of ʿAbd al-Muṭṭalib should set their attention on the next world and not on earthly things, and ordered her to put the ring back under the rug. In a dream Fāṭima saw the bed, which now again had four feet (ISh, 118). After the death of her father, Fāṭima received from heaven a book with covers of red chrysolite and pages of white pearl, which contained nothing from the Ḳurʾān, but instruction on all that had been and would be until the Day of Resurrection (in IRṬ, 27, the source which speaks of this book, there is a summary of the information contained in it: it ranged from the numbers of the angels, the Prophets, etc. to the names of places on the earth, statistics of the believers, the events which would take place during 50,000 years, etc.). This book was brought to Fāṭima while she was at prayer, and the angels waited until she had completed her devotions before giving it to her and returning to heaven. Fāṭima read the book, and all—men, *djinn*s, birds, beasts, prophets and angels—are bound to obey her. Later the book was handed on to ʿAlī, and after that to the *imām*s (IRṬ, 227 f.).

Physical privileges. Having been born pure and purified (she was a houri from heaven: ḤʿAW, 50), Fāṭima was exempt from the physiological troubles of women: she did not menstruate, and lost no blood during her confinements. She gave birth through the left thigh, while Mary gave birth through the right thigh (ḤʿAW, 48, 51). Her pregnancies lasted only nine hours.

Miracles. Several miracles were worked by Fāṭima: the stone for grinding corn turned without anyone moving it, an angel (Ḳūḳabīl or Djibrīl) rocked her baby's cradle. One of her garments, given as a pledge to a Jew by the wife of Zayd b. Ḥāritha, gave forth light, and the Jew and eighty other people, astonished at this miracle, embraced Islam (ISh, 16 f.). When, after the election of Abū Bakr, those who wanted to compel ʿAlī to offer the *bayʿa* made him leave the house, Fāṭima went to the mosque and, standing near her father's tomb, threatened to uncover her head; at that moment Salmān saw the walls of the mosque rise up: "My mistress and my patroness", he cried, "God sent your father in His mercy: you should not bring us misfortune!" The walls then returned to their place (ISh, 118). When Fāṭima was weeping for her father's death, it was Djibrīl himself who consoled her. The miracles continued even after Fāṭima's death, benefiting one of her servants and the descendant of one of her servants (ISh, 16 f.).

Fāṭima in Paradise. Fāṭima will be the first person to enter Paradise after the Resurrection (ISh, 110). All will have to lower their gaze when she crosses the Bridge (*ṣirāṭ*) which leads across Hell to Paradise. She will be escorted by seventy houris. In Paradise she will proceed, mounted on a wondrous camel with legs of emerald, eyes of ruby, etc., under a dome of light. It will be Djibrīl who leads the camel up to the throne of God. There she will descend and ask God to mete out justice to those who were guilty of the deaths of al-Ḥasan and al-Ḥusayn. Then God will say to her, "My beloved, daughter of my beloved, ask of me what you will and I will grant it to you". Fāṭima will procure entry into Paradise for all her own people and all her supporters (ISh, 107-9). She is called al-Zahrāʾ because of the dome of rubies which hangs over her in Paradise—a wonderful dome of immense height (a whole year's journey), upheld in the sky neither suspended from above nor supported from below, with 10,000 doors and 100 angels at each one (ISh, 111). In Paradise Fāṭima will have a privilege: she will be the sole wife of ʿAlī, while other men will have as many houris as they please (ISh, 106); it was the houris who told her this (IRṬ, 26; ISh, 106), and it is out of respect for Fāṭima that there is no mention of houris in Sūra LXXVI, where Paradise is described (ISh, 106).

The celestial apple. An early story, which goes back at least as far as al-Ghullābī (d. 298/910) runs as follows: Muḥammad, on being reproached for embracing Fāṭima but not his other daughters, told how Djibrīl had presented him with an apple of Paradise, which he had eaten and which had become water in his loins; he then placed it within Khadīdja, who conceived Fāṭima. He finished by saying that he smelled in Fāṭima the fragrance of Paradise. Other similar accounts are given in the same source (ḤʿAW, 49 f.), with slight variants: Muḥammad ate the apple and a date in Paradise during the *miʿrādj* [*q.v.*]; both were transformed into water in his loins, etc. In ISh (135) Djibrīl gives Muḥammad a celestial date instead of an apple; the story then continues as above. A notable difference appears when there is introduced into the story the Light which forms the central point of other accounts; the themes then become interwoven: God created the light of Fāṭima and Fāṭima uttered His praises; then He placed the light of Fāṭima in a tree of Paradise, which shone with the splendour of it; Muḥammad, ascending to Paradise, was advised by God to pick the fruit of this tree. God caused its juice to pass into the throat of ʿAlī, and then placed Fāṭima in the loins of Muḥammad, who deposited her in Khadīdja; the latter bore Fāṭima, who was of that light: she knew what was, what would be and what was not (ḤʿAW, 47). This last account (the Light of Fāṭima lodged in the loins of Muḥammad) would explain her *kunya* Umm Abīhā.

The Light and Fāṭima. Muḥammad explained thus the reason for the preference accorded to the People of the House: God, he said, created me and ʿAlī as light, and separated off from our light that of my descendants; then He separated from our light the light of the Throne, and from that of my descendants the light of the sun and of the moon. We teach the angels the *tasbīḥ*, the *tahlīl* and the *taḥmīd* (*i.e.*, the formulas for the praise of God). God then said to the angels: "By My power, My majesty, My generosity, My eminence, I will act", and He created the light of Fāṭima like a lamp, and it is through her that the heavens were illuminated. Fāṭima was called al-Zahrāʾ because the horizon took its light from her (ḤʿAW, 46). This story is of particular interest because, with its description of successive divine emanations, it contains some features characteristic of Ismāʿīlī beliefs. Another story collected by ISh (106) also speaks of light, but in a different way: God created Paradise from the light of His countenance; He took this light, and threw it; with a third of it He struck Muḥammad, with another third Fāṭima, and with the remaining third ʿAlī and the People of the House. Whoever is thus struck recognizes the *walāya* [*q.v.*] of the family of Muḥammad.

Fāṭima's names. Attempts have been made to see a significance in the name Fāṭima. As the root has the meaning of "weaning a child", "breaking someone of a habit", she has been said to be so called because she, and her descendants and supporters, will be spared from Hell, or because she was exempt from evil (ISh, 110, cf. 107), or because she was removed from polytheism (IRṬ, 10). The list of her names in IRṬ (10 f.) consists of nine: Fāṭima, al-Ṣiddīḳa, al-Mubāraka, al-Ṭāhira, al-Zakiyya, al-Raḍiyya, al-Rāḍiya, al-Muḥaddatha, al-Zahrāʾ. She was called al-Muḥaddatha because the angels spoke to her as to Mary, and she to them; they told her "God has chosen you and purified you; He has chosen you from among the women of the world". According to ḤʿAW (46), her names on earth are: Fāṭim (*sic*, in the masculine), Fāṭir, al-Zahrāʾ, al-Batūl, al-Ḥaṣān, al-Ḥawrāʾ, al-Sayyida, al-Ṣiddīḳa, and Maryam al-Kubrā. Ibn Bābūya (d. 381/991) knew of 16 names for Fāṭima on earth and three in heaven, and Ibn Shahrāshūb (133) who records them appends a list of 69 names and attributes which must have served as a litany, for they are linked by the rhymes in groups, usually of three. Among the names listed by ḤʿAW should be noted Fāṭir, *i.e.*, Creator, for not only is it masculine, but it carried with it a glorification of Fāṭima which seems to be characteristic of the extreme Ismāʿīlīs and of aberrant sects such as the Nuṣayrīs (Bausani, 189) rather than of the Imāmīs. Have we here a borrowing by the latter from the former? The belief that Fāṭima is Fāṭir, Creator, would also explain her *kunya* Umm Abīhā.

References to Fāṭima in the Ḳurʾān; her other merits. The Ḳurʾān too is made to contribute to the glorification of Fāṭima, thanks to the exegesis of Shīʿī writers, who maintain that many verses allude to ʿAlī and his wife. When the Book speaks of women in general, a hidden reference to Fāṭima is intended: thus in III, 193/195, "I shall not permit to be lost the work of one who works [well] among you, male or female", the "male" is ʿAlī and the "female" Fāṭima at the time of the *hidjra*. Similarly they identify with ʿAlī and Fāṭima the reference to the creation of man and woman in XCII, 3.

Twelve women are alluded to in the Ḳurʾān without their names being mentioned (*e.g.*, Eve, Sarah, Pharaoh's wife, etc.). There is such an allusion to Fāṭima in LV, 19, which speaks of two seas which God has caused to flow together: this confluence is the reconciliation of ʿAlī and Fāṭima after a dispute, for he is the sea of knowledge and Fāṭima the sea of prophecy; the barrier between them, mentioned in the following verse, is the Apostle of God, who prevents ʿAlī from distressing himself over the life of this world and Fāṭima from quarrelling with her husband over earthly things; the pearls and the coral of verse 22 are, since they come from these seas, allusions to al-Ḥasan and al-Ḥusayn (ISh, 101, 102 f.). Each of the women of the Ḳurʾān has a particular quality which is apparent from a phrase in the Book, *e.g.*, Eve has repentance (cf. Ḳurʾān, VII, 22/23), Pharaoh's wife desire (LXVI, 11), Fāṭima *ʿiṣma* (because of the *mubāhala*, III, 54/61). Ten of these women received a gift from God, Fāṭima's being knowledge. Support for all these, and other, assertions is found in verses of the Ḳurʾān (ISh, 102-4). The best women of Paradise are Fāṭima, Khadīdja, Āsiya bint Muzāḥim, Pharaoh's wife, and Maryam bint ʿImrān (= Mary), but Fāṭima is the *sayyida* par excellence (an angel had announced this to Muḥammad: ḤʿAW, 51; ISh, 104 f.). Fāṭima is often compared with Mary. On one occasion she asked the angels, "Is not Mary the chosen one?", to which the reply was "Mary is the *sayyida* of her world; God has made you the *sayyida* of the women of this world and the next" (IRṬ, 10); further, Fāṭima had the privilege of being married to a great man in this life and the next (ISh, 105), and thus is superior. And although Mary preserved her virginity, so did Fāṭima, whence her title al-Batūl (also explained, however, as meaning that no woman comparable with her ever existed) (ISh, 134 f.). Fāṭima is numbered among the four best known "returners to God" (*tawwāb* [*q.v.*]): Ādam, Yūnus, Dāwūd and Fāṭima, and it is to her that the Ḳurʾān refers in III, 188/191; the best known "weepers" (*bakkāʾ* [*q.v.*]) number seven: Ādam, Nūḥ, Yaʿḳūb, Yūsuf, Shuʿayb, Dāwūd, Zayn al-ʿĀbidīn, and she is the eighth; she had become so accustomed to weep at all times for the death of her father that the people of Medina urged her to devote herself to weeping either by night or by day (ISh, 104).

Fāṭima in the *taʿziyas*. The rich collection of *taʿziyas* presented by Enrico Cerulli to the Vatican Library (of which E. Rossi and A. Bombaci have published the Index, and the latter proposes to publish resumés) presents several texts based on episodes of the Fāṭima legend, *e.g.*, her trousseau (Salmān and Abū Dharr are commissioned to make the purchases); her invitation to the wedding of a woman of the Ḳuraysh, which led to the conversion of those present; her hard work to support herself; the misappropriation of Fadak and the violence shown by ʿUmar to her and ʿAlī; the visit of Abū Bakr and ʿUmar during her last illness; her will; her death (a pomegranate is brought to her from heaven); her arrival at the camp of al-Ḥusayn on the 10th Muḥarram to visit the People of the Tent, and on the day following the massacre to see her son's body; various of her miracles, etc. In the introduction to the work mentioned above will be found references to other collections of these Persian sacred dramas, where too, very probably, Fāṭima plays the principal or a leading role.

The cult of Fāṭima today. Popular sympathy for Fāṭima among the Shīʿa has caused several feasts to be dedicated to her: that of the *mubāhala* (21, 24 or 25 Dhu 'l-Ḥidjdja) is the only canonical one; others, held in private, celebrate her birth (20 Ramaḍān) or her death (3 Djumādā II and 2 Ramaḍān) or an episode of her life: the marriage to which she was invited and for which, she having no suitable garments, Djibrīl clad her in a sumptuous robe and put on her two ear-rings, the one green, foreshowing the poisoning of al-Ḥasan, the other red, a symbol of the martyrdom of al-Ḥusayn; on seeing her so beautiful the bride died of jealousy, but was at once restored to life by Fāṭima (on these feasts see Massignon, *La notion*, 107-11; on prayers to her, *ibid.*, 102-6). In his book *The wild rue*, Donaldson has introduced some popular tales which do not differ substantially from the accounts preserved in the Arabic and Persian texts. Only that on page 77 seems to offer some new details: after the Resurrection the earth will become a desert; Muḥammad, Fāṭima and the *Imāms* will appear, and Fāṭima will tell the women that all those who have wept for al-Ḥusayn and preserved their tears, thus acquiring great merit, will go to Paradise. Fāṭima will be clad in a garment with a magnificent fringe, the women will cling to it and pass over the Bridge with her in the twinkling of an eye. One further belief may be noted: the Shīʿa believe that the "Five" are present at difficult moments of their lives and hear their prayers.

Fāṭima in the beliefs of the Ismāʿīlīs. The study of the development of the Fāṭima legend among the Ismāʿīlīs and the deviant sects of Islam is more difficult than among the Imāmīs because of their esotericism and because they are split up into numerous groups, each holding varying beliefs; and what is known of these beliefs has not yet been systematically assembled in any one study embracing all the material. Some information on Fāṭima can be drawn from the works of Massignon, and some more from the writings of Ivanow and of Corbin. Here some general observations may be made: Among the Imāmīs the Fāṭima of legend preserves almost always links with the Fāṭima of history, even in the more fantastic accounts (whose texts, furthermore, contain an admixture of *ḥadīth*s having nothing of the fantastic about them, whether they are from Sunnī or from other collections). In the more extravagant exaltation accorded to Fāṭima by the Ismāʿīlīs these links are often preserved; but in their systems of cosmogony she becomes a secondary element among a host of other gnostic or semi-gnostic elements, and she is then to some extent overshadowed by these and all links with her historical self are generally lost. Among the Ismāʿīlīs and the deviant sects there appear other beliefs, of which we have found no trace in the Imāmī sources, *e.g.*, the identification of Fāṭima with al-Masḏjid al-Aḳṣā in Jerusalem, with the Cave of the Seven Sleepers, with the rock of Moses which gushed forth miraculous water (the ancestral motif of Water), and the idea that she conceived through the ear and gave birth through the navel, etc. Among the Ismāʿīlīs and the deviant sects there has been a more extensive assimilation of the themes of the Christian devotion to Mary, the Mother of God. There is also, according to Massignon (*La notion* . . ., 113 f.), a tendency to identify the figures of Mary and Fāṭima in the style of depicting them in icons (Fāṭima enthroned in heaven, with a diadem, a sword, and ear-pendants).

Although the *Umm al-kitāb*, the curious holy book of groups of Ismāʿīlīs of Central Asia (published and analysed by Ivanow, *REI*, 1932, 419-82; *Isl.*, xxiii (1936), 1-132), is of limited importance—it is almost unknown to the other Ismāʿīlīs—we may summarize here its account of the Creation, noting that it bears a certain resemblance to that of Ḥusayn b. ʿAbd al-Wahhāb summarized above. God, a being of light (*shakhṣ nūrānī*) before the Creation, with five limbs: hearing, sight, the senses of smell and taste, and speech (which on earth were to become Muḥammad, ʿAlī, Fāṭima, al-Ḥasan and al-Ḥusayn), manifested Himself when the world began in ʿAlī, and then in successive theophanies; that of Fāṭima took place in Paradise after the creation of primordial men as a figure adorned with thousands of colours and seated on a throne with a crown on her head (Muḥammad), two ear-rings in her ears (al-Ḥasan and al-Ḥusayn), and a sword carried in a shoulder-belt (ʿAlī); all the garden of Paradise shone upon the appearance of this radiant figure.

Conclusion. In preparing this article we have taken note of the gaps left unfilled, and therefore indicate here the course that should be followed by future students of the legend of Fāṭima. It would be advisable to collect all the references to the daughter of the Prophet in the Shīʿī *ḥadīth*-collections (*e.g.*, that of al-Kulaynī) and in the *akhbār Fāṭima*, which Āghā Buzurg has listed in his *Ḏharīʿa* (i, 243 f., 331) and, if they no longer survive, to reconstruct them, at least in part, from the numerous quotations from them in later texts; it will be necessary to establish, from al-Maḏjlisī, the beliefs accepted by the Ṣafawids, to collect together the ideas of the Ismāʿīlīs, and finally, with the help of al-Ḳāḍī al-Nuʿmān or other authors, to establish the esoteric beliefs of the Fāṭimids. Use should be made of the Persian lithographs (excluded from this study as being confused and difficult to consult) as a source for other legendary themes, for it is very probable that the themes developed as time went on. Parallels in Ṣūfī anecdotes should also be studied. Finally, the

investigator will have also to interpret the themes, and to trace what connexion they have either with beliefs which existed long before Islam, of which they could be a recrudescence, or with ideas which, although incompatible with Islam, survived in the countries conquered by the Muslims, or with details preserved in *ḥadīth*s and with genuinely Islamic ideas. In our view the last is likely in most cases to prove to be the real connexion, even when the themes have expanded into stories which are completely fantastic.

Bibliography: Ibn Hishām, *Sīra*, 121, 776 (Cairo ed. 1937, i, 206; iii, 407); Wāḳidī, ed. Wellhausen, 118 f., 143, 287, 324, 421, and index; Ibn Saʿd, viii, 11-20; Balāḏhurī, *Ansāb*, i, ed. Muḥammad Ḥamīdullāh, Cairo 1959, 125, 269, 324, 390, 400, 402, 403, 404, 405, 414, 415, 559, 583, 586; idem, *Futūḥ*, 30-2; Ibn Ḥabīb, *K. al-Muḥabbar*, Ḥaydarābād 1361/1942, 18 (Fāṭima's female ancestors) and index; Ṭabarī, i, 1128, 1140 1272, 1273, 1367, 1426, 1431, 1623, 1624, 1751, 1825, 1869, 3470, iii, 2302 f., 2423, 2434-6, 2440, 2463; Yaʿḳūbī, ii, 19, 35, 42, 91, 128 f., 141, 142; Ibn Ḳutayba (attrib.), *al-Imāma wa 'l-siyāsa*, ed. Rāfiʿī, Cairo 1322/1904, 20-4 (2nd ed., Cairo 1377/ 1957, 12, 13 f.); idem, *ʿUyūn al-akhbār*, Cairo 1343-9/1925-30, iv, 70; Ibn ʿAbd Rabbihi, *ʿIḳd*, Cairo 1293, ii, 3 f. For *ḥadīth*s, numerous citations in A. J. Wensinck, *A handbook of early Muhammadan tradition*, Leiden 1927, s.v. Fāṭima and also s.v. ʿAlī (the collections with the richest notices on Fāṭima are those of al-Tirmidhī and of Aḥmad b. Ḥanbal; the former devotes a chapter to *Faḍl Fāṭima bint al-nabī*: *Ḏjāmiʿ*, [Cairo] 1292, ii, 319-21; in Bukhārī the following references are to be consulted: 56, 85, 163, 57, 1, 62, 12, 16, 29, 64, 24, 38, 83, 67, 123, 69, 6, 7, 76, 27, 79, 43, 80, 11, 85, 3); Masʿūdī, *Murūḏj*, iv, 146, 156, 157, 161, vi, 55, 56, 165; Ibn ʿAbd al-Barr, *Kitāb al-Istīʿāb*, Ḥaydarābād 1318-9, 770-3 = no. 3406; Ibn al-Athīr, *Usd*, s.v. *Fāṭima bint Rasūl Allāh* = v, 519-25, for al-ʿAwrāʾ v, 419; Ibn Ḥaḏjar, *Iṣāba*, iv, 724-31 = no. 823, for al-ʿAwrāʾ iv, 715 = no. 791; Diyārbakrī, *Taʾrīkh al-khamīs*, [Cairo] 1302, i, 313-5, 407 f., 462-4; Ḥalabī, *al-Sīra al-Ḥalabiyya*, Alexandria 1280, iii, 529, 607-9.

For the *mubāhala*: Ṭabarī, *Tafsīr*, Cairo 1958- , vi, 478-82; Zamakhsharī, *Kashshāf*, Cairo 1308, i, 308 f., and the other *tafsīr*s; a short modern work: ʿUmar Abu 'l-Naṣr, *Fāṭima bint Muḥammad umm al-shuhadāʾ wa Sayyidat al-nisāʾ*, Cairo 1366/1947 (*al-shīʿa al-ūlā fī 'l-Islām*), 22-70; other citations in Ziriklī, *Aʿlām*, v, 329. Shīʿī imāmī works: Kulaynī (Muḥammad b. Yaʿḳūb), *al-Kāfī fī ʿilm al-dīn*, Tehrān 1313/1895-6, 185-7; Ibn Rustam al-Ṭabarī, *Dalāʾil al-imāma*, Nadjaf 1369/1949, 1-58; Ḥusayn b. ʿAbd al-Wahhāb, *ʿUyūn al-muʿḏjizāt*, Nadjaf 1369/1950, 46-51; Ibn Shahrāshūb, *Manāḳib Āl Abī Ṭālib*, Nadjaf 1956, iii, 101-40; Muḥammad Bāḳir Maḏjlisī, *Biḥār al-anwār*, x-xiii, lith. Tehrān 1305 (the notices on Fāṭima collected officially by the Ṣafawids are in vol. x, *bāb*s 1-6, pp. 2-65: (1) birth, (2) virtues and miracles, (3) habits, including domestic habits, (4) marriage, and relations with ʿAlī, (5) end of her life, (6) revenge and eschatological events. The popular version in Persian of these notices, regarded as canonical, is in: idem, *Ḏjilāʾ al-ʿuyūn*, Tehrān 1332/1953, *bāb* 2, 82-166—birth, virtues, life and miracles, habits, marriage, relations with ʿAlī, death, revenge); Muḥsin Fayḍ al-Ḳāshānī, (= al-Kāshī), *al-Wāfī*, Tehrān 1376/1957, 172 f. For the canonical prayers of the Imāmīs in honour of Fāṭima: Shaykh ʿAbbās Ḳummī, *Kulliyyāt-i mafātīḥ al-djinān*, Tehrān 1316(s.)/1937-8, 41 f., 57, 301, 318, 322-4 (commentary: 244, 428, 429, 488). An Ismāʿīlī work: al-Ḳāḍī al-Nuʿmān, *Daʿāʾim al-Islām*, ed. A. A. A. Fyzee, i, Cairo 1370/1951, 203 (*tasbīḥ* of Fāṭima), 285, and index). Modern authors: Abu 'l-Ḥasan Marandī, *Madjmaʿ al-nūrayn wa multaḳā al-baḥrayn fī aḥwāl badʿat Sayyid al-thaḳalayn wa umm al-sibṭayn al-ṣiddīḳa al-kubrā al-batūl al-ʿadhrāʾ al-Sayyida Fāṭima al-Zahrāʾ*, Tehrān 1328/1907, chaps. 1-23, 26-30, 35-7, 43-59 (cited by Massignon); ʿImād al-Dīn Ḥusayn al-Iṣfahānī, *Madjmūʿa-i zindigānī-i čahārdah maʿṣūm*, Tehrān 1330 (solar), i, 221-358; Muḥsin al-Amīn, *Aʿyān al-shīʿa*, ii, 535-639; *Nāma-i Fāṭimī*, MS (Rieu, ii, 708: 'a Shīʿite poem on the life of Fāṭimah'); A. Sprenger, *Das Leben und die Lehre des Moḥammad*, i, 199, 203, ii, 462; L. Caetani, *Annali*, Intr. 160, 1 A.H., § 53, 2 A.H., §§ 17, 102, 3 A.H., § 11, 7 A.H., §§ 42, 47 no. 3, 8 A.H., §§ 80, 203, 11 A.H., §§ 19 n. 1, 37 n. 3, 59, 202-3, 203 n. 1, 205-8, 238; H. Lammens, *Fāṭima et les filles de Mahomet. Notes critiques pour l'étude de la Sīra*, Rome 1912 (Scripta Pontificii Instituti Biblici); L. Massignon, *Der gnostische Kultus der Fatima im schiitischen Islam*, in *Eranos Jahrbücher*, 1938, 167 ff.; idem, *La Mubâhala de Médine et l'hyperdulie de Fatima*, Paris 1955; idem, *La notion du voeu et la dévotion musulmane à Fāṭima*, in *Studi orientalistici in onore di Giorgio Levi Della Vida*, Rome 1956, ii, 102-26; B. A. Donaldson, *The wild rue: a study of Muhammadan magic and folklore in Iran*, London 1938, 39, 55, 69, 109, 119; A. Bausani, *Persia religiosa*, Milan 1959, 188, 384-6, 390. For the *taʿziyas*: E. Rossi and A. Bombaci, *Elenco di drammi religiosi persiani (fondo Mss. Vaticani Cerulli)*, Vatican 1961 (Studi e testi 209), index s.v. Fāṭima.

(L. Veccia Vaglieri)

FĀṬIMIDS, dynasty which reigned in North Africa, and later in Egypt, from 297/909 until 567/1171.

ʿUbayd Allāh (al-Mahdī), 297-322/909-34.
Al-Ḳāʾim, 322-34/934-46.
Al-Manṣūr, 334-41/946-53.
Al-Muʿizz, 341-65/953-75.
Al-ʿAzīz, 365-86/975-96.
Al-Ḥākim, 386-411/996-1021.
Al-Ẓāhir, 411-27/1021-36.
Al-Mustanṣir, 427-87/1036-94.
Al-Mustaʿlī, 487-95/1094-1101.
Al-Āmir, 495-525/1101-30.
Al-Ḥāfiẓ, 525-44/1130-49.
Al-Ẓāfir, 544-9/1149-54.
Al-Fāʾiz, 549-55/1154-60.
Al-ʿĀḍid, 555-67/1160-71.

The dynasty takes its name from Fāṭima, for the Fāṭimid caliphs traced their origin to ʿAlī and Fāṭima. It is also possible that another Fāṭima, the daughter of Ḥusayn, who transmitted some *ḥadīths* of her grandmother and had foreknowledge of the Mahdī, played a part in the attribution of this name (see L. Massignon, *Fāṭima bint al-Ḥusayn et l'origine du nom dynastique "Fāṭimites"*, in *Akten des XXIV. intern. Orientalisten-Kongresses*, Munich 1957, 368). It should also be mentioned that the mother of ʿAlī was a Hāshimite called Fāṭima bint Asad (Ibn Ḥadjar, *Iṣāba*, Cairo 1328, iv, 380) and that among the Ahl-i Ḥaḳḳ she is connected with the legend of Salmān (see al-Mokri, *Le "secret indicible..."*, in *JA*, ccl (1962), 375), who plays an important part in Fāṭimid tradition.

According to W. Ivanow (*Ismaili traditions concerning the rise of the Fatimids*, Bombay 1942, Isl. Res. Ass. Series, no. 10, 80), the name Fāṭimiyyūn, which, according to al-Ṭabarī (iii, 2219, *sub anno* 289), had been adopted by the Bedouin Banu 'l-Aṣbagh of the Syrian desert whose leader was the Ḳarmaṭo-Ismāʿīlī Yaḥyā b. Zikrawayh, was the first name of the Ismāʿīlīs. But Massignon (*op. cit.*) reminds us that the name is already found in Bashshār b. Burd, used in a pejorative sense. The origin of the Fāṭimid movement, which in North Africa brought the Fāṭimids to power in the person of ʿUbayd Allāh al-Mahdī, must be sought in Ismāʿīlism [see ISMĀʿĪLIYYA], a Shīʿī doctrine which was at the same time political and religious, philosophical and social, and whose adherents expected the appearance of a Mahdī descended from the Prophet through ʿAlī and Fāṭima, in the line of Ismāʿīl, son of Djaʿfar al-Ṣādiḳ.

Genealogy of the Fāṭimids

The Fāṭimids trace their origin to Ismāʿīl, but as they did not announce their genealogy publicly and officially for some time, and as, during the period of the Hidden Imāms, the *satr* [*q.v.*], the names of the imāms between Muḥammad b. Ismāʿīl and ʿUbayd Allāh al-Mahdī were intentionally left in the dark, several different genealogies became current; with the result that, even today, the origin of the Fāṭimids is still wrapped in obscurity. The enemies of the Fāṭimids denied their descent from ʿAlī and declared that they were impostors. Following the ancient Arab habit of giving a Jewish origin to people they hate (Goldziher, *Muh. St.*, i, 204), ʿUbayd Allāh has even been presented as the son of a Jew.

According to the traditional Fāṭimid genealogy, ʿUbayd Allāh was the son of Ḥusayn b. Aḥmad b. ʿAbd Allāh b. Muḥammad b. Ismāʿīl b. Djaʿfar al-Ṣādiḳ. The general anti-Fāṭimid tradition has it that he was the son of Ḥusayn b. Aḥmad b. Muḥammad b. ʿAbd Allāh b. Maymūn al-Ḳaddāḥ, that he was really called Saʿīd, and that it was only in North Africa that he took the name of ʿUbayd Allāh (or ʿAbd Allāh) and claimed to be of ʿAlid descent and to be the Mahdī (on Maymūn al-Ḳaddāḥ and his son ʿAbd Allāh and their relations with Djaʿfar al-Ṣādiḳ and his grandson Muḥammad b. Ismāʿīl, see ʿABD ALLĀH B. MAYMŪN).

On the genealogy of the Fāṭimids, the different forms, both anti-Fāṭimid and Ismāʿīlī, in which it has been presented, and the complex problems which it raises and which seem to defy a satisfactory solution, information is to be found in various works: S. de Sacy, *Exposé de la religion des Druzes*, Paris 1838; Wüstenfeld, *Gesch. der Fatimiden-Chalifen*, Göttingen 1881; C. H. Becker, *Beiträge zur Geschichte Ägyptens*, Strasbourg 1902-3; De Goeje, *Mémoire sur les Carmathes*, Leiden 1886; P. H. Mamour, *Polemics on the origin of the Fatimi Caliphs*, London 1924. The question has been studied afresh in more recent works: W. Ivanow, *Ismaili traditions concerning the rise of the Fatimids*, 1942, 154 f., 223 f.; idem, *Ismailis and Qarmatians*, in *JBRAS*, 1940, 70 f.; idem, *The alleged founder of Ismailism*, Bombay 1946, 169 f. (Ism. Soc. Series, no. 1); B. Lewis, *The origins of Ismāʿīlism*, Cambridge 1940 (Arabic translation, Baghdad 1947). Still more recently have appeared: Husayn F. al-Hamdani, *On the genealogy of Fatimid Caliphs*, Cairo 1958, and W. Madelung,

Das Imamat in der frühen ismailitischen Lehre, in *Isl.*, xxxvii (1961), an article which is a continuation of *Fatimiden und Bahrainqarmaten*, in *Isl.*, xxxiv (1959).

We can do no more here than glance at the questions which are discussed in these works and the difficulties which are encountered in studying the origin of the Fāṭimids, considering the many divergences which are found in the sources and the very different standpoints taken by the authors who concern themselves with these questions—even by the Ismāʿīlī writers, in considering whose works we must take into account the very different treatment they give to a question according to whether the work is exoteric or esoteric.

Here are a few of the difficulties which arise: In the Ismāʿīlī sources the series of imāms preceding ʿUbayd Allāh is not everywhere the same and the names do not always agree (see Ivanow, *Rise*, 46 f.). Even the name of the father of ʿUbayd Allāh varies; there is one tradition which presents him as the son not of Ḥusayn but of one Aḥmad. ʿUbayd Allāh appears sometimes as ʿAlī b. al-Ḥusayn, but on the other hand an ʿAli b. al-Ḥusayn is considered as a fourth Hidden Imām, not found in the list given above. Was Ḥusayn, the father of ʿUbayd Allāh, the regular imām or was the imām not rather Muḥammad b. Aḥmad, uncle of ʿUbayd Allāh? In that case the uncle would not have been able to hand down the imāmate to ʿUbayd Allāh, since the doctrine decrees that, apart from the case of Ḥasan and Ḥusayn, it is transmitted only from father to son. This Muḥammad b. Aḥmad bears also the name of Abū ʿAlī al-Ḥākim with the *kunya* Abu 'l-Shalaʿlaʿ (or Shalaghlagh) and the surname Saʿīd al-Khayr. He is also presented as the father of ʿUbayd Allāh. As ʿUbayd Allāh is also Saʿīd, it can be seen what a source of confusion these different names must have been (see *Rise*, 31, Madelung, *Imamat*, 56, 71, 75, and similarly S. de Sacy and De Goeje).

ʿUbayd Allāh himself gave other versions of his origin than that of the Fāṭimid tradition mentioned above. In a letter to the Ismāʿīlī community of the Yemen (see Madelung, 70), he claims to be descended not from Ismāʿīl b. Djaʿfar, but from another son of Djaʿfar, ʿAbd Allāh. In the interview which he had with ʿAbdān, the emissary of Ḥamdān Ḳarmaṭ, as it is reported by Akhū Muḥsin (admittedly a strongly anti-Fāṭimid sharīf), ʿUbayd Allāh claimed a Ḳaddāḥī descent (Madelung, 60).

A further uncertainty lies in the relationship between ʿUbayd Allāh and the second Fāṭimid caliph, Muḥammad Abu 'l-Ḳāsim al-Ḳāʾim bi-amr Allāh. The latter bears the name attributed by tradition to the expected Mahdī who must have the same name as the Prophet; the Ḳāʾim is strictly the Mahdī (the two names are used interchangeably). ʿUbayd Allāh took the title of al-Mahdī, but did he really in his heart consider himself as the expected Mahdī, given that he did not have the necessary characteristics? Al-Ḳāʾim may not have been the son of ʿUbayd Allāh, although the latter always considered him officially as his son. According to the *Ghāyat al-mawālīd* of al-Khaṭṭāb b. al-Ḥasan (6th/12th century), he was the son of that fourth Hidden Imām ʿAlī mentioned above (see Ivanow, *Rise*, texts, 37, and Madelung, 77). ʿUbayd Allāh's attitude to Abu 'l-Ḳāsim al-Ḳāʾim in conferring on him when he entered Raḳḳāda a rank apparently superior to his own (see the facts in Madelung, 66, and see also 72) seems to imply that he considered Abu 'l-Ḳāsim as the awaited Mahdī. Similar doubts are raised by various other details concerning al-Ḳāʾim (see Ivanow, *Rise*, 50, 204 and the *Sīrat Djaʿfar al-Ḥādjib*, 304, tr. in *Hespéris*, 1952, 120). However it is difficult to be definite on this subject.

Another difficulty is that arising from the contradiction between the official genealogy and that which links the Fāṭimids with Maymūn al-Ḳaddāḥ. Even in the reign of al-Muʿizz, the fourth Fāṭimid caliph, an attempt was made in certain heterodox Ismāʿīlī circles to reconcile the two genealogies by identifying ʿAbd Allāh b. Maymūn al-Ḳaddāḥ with the ʿAbd Allāh b. Muḥammad b. Ismāʿīl b. Djaʿfar of the Fāṭimid genealogy and thus introducing a non-ʿAlid into the family (see Ivanow, *Rise*, 140; S. M. Stern, *Heterodox Ismāʿīlism at the time of al-Muʿizz*, in *BSOAS*, xvii/i (1955), 12 f.). B. Lewis resolves the contradiction by showing, on the evidence of Ismāʿīlī and Druze works, how it was possible to consider the Ḳaddāḥīs as Fāṭimid imāms, as the result of a spiritual adoption. Among the Ismāʿīlīs spiritual paternity holds an important place beside physical paternity. (It may be recalled that in his letter to the community of the Yemen, ʿUbayd Allāh, who included in the list of the imāms his uncle Muḥammad b. Aḥmad, stated that he himself was called ʿAbd Allāh b. Muḥammad because he was *fi'l-bāṭin* the son of this Muḥammad b. Aḥmad, who transmitted the imāmate to him: see Husayn F. Hamdani, in Madelung, 71-2).

Apart from the real, true imāms, descended from ʿAlī and Fāṭima, and called *mustaḳarr* (literally 'permanent'), there were, says B. Lewis, imāms called *mustawdaʿ*, trustees or guardians of the imāmate (on these two terms see Stern, *op. cit.*, 16), whose function was to "veil" the true imām in order to protect him, and who acted by right of an assignment (*tafwīḍ*) which so to speak allowed them to enter the family of the true imāms. Maymūn al-Ḳaddāḥ, who had received from Djaʿfar al-Ṣādiḳ the charge of his grandson Muḥammad b. Ismāʿīl, said that his own son ʿAbd Allāh was the spiritual son of Muḥammad b. Ismāʿīl and his heir, and it is by virtue of this that he proclaimed him imām. Thus a series of Ḳaddāḥī imāms is found side by side with a series of ʿAlid imāms. The last Ḳaddāḥī of the series was ʿUbayd Allāh Saʿīd, the *mustawdaʿ* imām of al-Ḳāʾim, the ʿAlid and *mustaḳarr* imām. Thus, in the person of al-Ḳāʾim, the imāmate returned to the ʿAlid family.

For all the questions which arise and which cannot be dealt with here, reference should be made to the very detailed and fully documented article of Madelung on the imāmate in early Ismāʿīlī doctrine, to which we shall return when discussing the religious policy of the Fāṭimids.

From the historical point of view, that which concerns us directly in this question of the genealogy is the attitude of the ʿAbbāsids, who naturally contested the ʿAlid origin of their rivals the Fāṭimids, to whom it gave great prestige. ʿArīb (*sub anno* 302, 51 f.), following al-Ṣūlī, reveals that at Baghdād at this time it was said that the master of the Maghrib was descended from a freedman of Ziyād b. Abīhi's [*q.v.*] chief of police. All the same, it was not until later that official documents appeared, signed by jurists and ʿAlids, one of 402/1011 and the other of 444/1052, which denied that they were of ʿAlid origin (see Ibn al-Djawzi, *Muntaẓam*, vii, 255; Ibn al-Athīr, *sub annis* 402, 444; Ibn Khaldūn, *Proleg.*, tr. de Slane, i, 39, tr. Rosenthal, i, 45, and *Hist. des Berbères*, tr. ii, 55; al-Maḳrīzī, *Ittiʿāẓ*, Cairo ed., 58 f.; Abu 'l-Maḥāsin, Cairo ed., iv, 229, v, 53; cf. Goldziher,

Die Streitschrift des Ġazâlî gegen die Bâṭinijja-Sekte, Leiden 1915, 15).

The Sunnī historians are in general not well disposed towards the Fāṭimids. Hardly any of them except al-Maḳrīzī and Ibn Khaldūn pronounce their ʿAlid descent to be authentic. Moreover, the argument advanced by these two writers that ʿUbayd Allāh would not have been persecuted by the ʿAbbāsids if they had not been convinced of the ʿAlid descent of the Fāṭimids is not very convincing, for, ʿAlid or not, he represented ideas which were dangerous to those in power and it was natural that the authorities should harry him. While the supporters of the Fāṭimids refer to their dynasty as ʿAlid (*al-dawla al-ʿalawiyya*: see e.g. al-Muʾayyad fi 'l-Dīn, *Sīra*, passim), several Sunnī historians speak of them only as ʿUbaydids and as the ʿUbaydid dynasty. Ibn Ḥamādo (Ḥammād [*q.v.*]) calls them *mulūk Banī ʿUbayd*. Similarly Abu 'l-Maḥāsin speaks of al-Muʿizz al-ʿUbaydī, al-ʿAzīz al-ʿUbaydī.

Foundation of the Dynasty

Whoever ʿUbayd Allāh-Saʿīd may have been, he laid the foundations of the dynasty in North Africa. He lived at Salamiyya in Syria, a centre of Ismāʿīlī propaganda. The way had been prepared for him by the *dāʿīs* [*q.v.*], the Ismāʿīlī missionaries. Ibn Ḥawshab Manṣūr al-Yaman, the *dāʿī* of the Yemen, where he was firmly established, had sent missionaries into North Africa, the last and most important of whom was Abū ʿAbd Allāh al-Shīʿī [*q.v.*]. When ʿUbayd Allāh decided to leave Salamiyya, either to escape ʿAbbāsid investigations, or as the result of the obscure affair of a conspiracy against him within the Ismāʿīlī movement (that of the "three Ḳarmaṭī brothers" as Ivanow puts it in *Rise*, 75 f.), he could have gone either to the Yemen, or to North Africa, where the missionary Abū ʿAbd Allāh al-Shīʿī had been working successfully among the Kutāma Berbers since 280/893. He went first to Ramla in Palestine, thence to Egypt, probably in 291/903; then when he was harassed by the ʿAbbāsid governor, and when his followers expected him to set off for the Yemen, he decided to go to North Africa where Abū ʿAbd Allāh al-Shīʿī was occupied in undermining the Aghlabī domination. Being unable to join the missionary at once, he went to Sidjilmāsa where he was put under house arrest, if not actually imprisoned, by the *amīr* of the country. It was there that Abū ʿAbd Allāh, after having made himself master of the Aghlabī capital Raḳḳāda and expelling Ziyādat Allāh in Radjab 296/March 909, came to seek him to lead him in triumph, on 29 Rabīʿ II 297/15 January 910, to Raḳḳāda where he publicly took the titles of Mahdī and of Amīr al-Muʾminīn (on all this, see, besides the historians, the *Sīrat Djaʿfar al-Ḥādjib*, one of the faithful companions of ʿUbayd Allāh, mentioned above).

The African period of the Fāṭimid Caliphate

The first four Fāṭimid caliphs, ʿUbayd Allāh al-Mahdī, al-Ḳāʾim, al-Manṣūr and al-Muʿizz, lived in North Africa, the last until, in 362/973, he left for Egypt, which had been conquered by his general Djawhar [*q.v.*].

During the African period, the Fāṭimid caliphs encountered many difficulties. In North Africa, split between Sunnism, mainly in its Mālikī form, and Kharidjism, in its Ibāḍī and Ṣufrī forms, the new doctrine could not fail to bring trouble. The existence in the Maghrib of two rival Berber groups, the Zenāta in the west and the Ṣanhādja (who included the Kutāma) in the east, was a further disrupting factor. Settled in the centre and the west of the country were two dynasties of eastern origin, the Khāridjī Rustamids of Tāhert and the (ʿAlid) Idrīsids of Fez, which the new dynasty could not allow to remain independent. The Umayyads of Spain were in possession of a part of the Maghribī territory lying nearest to the Iberian peninsula. Finally, if we consider that, from the very beginning, the new masters of Ifrīḳiya had considered it only as a base from which to move on, that they intended one day to move to the East, to supplant the ʿAbbāsids there, that in order to do this they had to keep up a powerful and expensive army and a navy of some consequence, and that apart from this they were to come into a troubled inheritance in Sicily, the full scope of the difficulties with which they were faced becomes clear. To solve all the problems which the situation presented to them, Fāṭimid caliphs could rely only on a fairly restricted number of supporters, apart from the Kutāma, who were not always tractable, and on their own political skill and their energy. It is a wonder that they succeeded.

Within his own party, ʿUbayd Allāh was not long in coming into conflict with the *dāʿī* Abū ʿAbd Allāh, either because the latter had doubts of his really being the Mahdī, or because his master had limited his power. ʿUbayd Allāh had Abū ʿAbd Allāh and his brother assassinated, and this provoked a revolt of the Kutāma, who proclaimed a new Mahdī, a child. The revolt was suppressed with much bloodshed. Later, in the reigns of al-Manṣūr and al-Muʿizz, there were discords within the Fāṭimid family itself, hints of which are revealed in the *Sīrat al-ustādh Djawhar* (see the translation of this work by M. Canard, 19, 91 f., 147, 150, 174, 181); the revocation of the investiture of Tamīm, the son of al-Muʿizz, as *walī al-ʿahd* is compatible with this (*op. cit.*, 213 and n., 339 and 467). In addition, it was necessary to combat extremist opinions within the sect (see below).

In the religious and politico-religious field, the Fāṭimids had to struggle in North Africa against both Sunnī and Khāridjī opposition. The Mālikī Sunnī opposition has been well explained by G. Marçais in his work *La Berbérie musulmane et l'Orient au Moyen Age*, Paris 1946, in the chapter *Les causes du divorce*, 136 f., which, although based on prejudiced Sunnī sources, gives a striking picture of the manifestations of this opposition, which was sometimes sternly quelled and at other times extinguished by bribery. In M. Bencheneb, *Classes des savants de l'Ifrikiya*, 288-304, is to be found the curious story of a doctrinal controversy between some jurists and the brother of the Dāʿī. This opposition, however, seriously troubled those in power only when Ḳayrawān, although very orthodox, made a temporary alliance with the Khāridjī Abū Yazīd [*q.v.*]. Indeed, on the Khāridjī side, the opposition took a very dangerous form with the revolt of this curious personality, who took possession of several important towns, laid siege for a year to Mahdiyya, and was not defeated until 336/947. The revolt, which began in 332/943-4, exhausted al-Ḳāʾim, who succumbed to the fatigues of war at Sūs, and it did not end until the reign of al-Manṣūr. Abū Yazīd, supported by the Umayyad ruler of Cordova, brought the Fāṭimid dynasty to the brink of ruin.

The Zenāta of the west were another source of difficulty. The Khāridjī Rustamids of Tāhert had been expelled in 296/909 by Abū ʿAbd Allāh al-Shīʿī, but a revolt broke out and the place had to be retaken in 299/911 by Maṭāla b. Ḥabūs who next, subjugating the Idrīsid, took possession of Fez in 308/920, then of Sidjilmāsa in 309/921. After the death of Maṣāla, his lieutenant and successor, Mūsā b. Abi 'l ʿĀfiya, effectively subdued the Maghrib, taking Fez from the Idrīsids, but he ended by defecting to the Umayyad ruler in 320/932. Also al-Ḳāʾim, who had already conducted campaigns in the Maghrib during his father's lifetime and founded the fortress town of Masīla (Muḥammadiyya) in the Zāb, was obliged, after his accession, to send an expedition to reconquer Fez and all the western Maghrib from Ibn al-ʿĀfiya, as well as Tāhert. He re-established the Idrīsids in their domains, but under Fāṭimid authority. It was only al-Muʿizz who, through his wise and prudent behaviour and the military skill of his general Djawhar, subdued all the west and re-established peace there, as the result of a great campaign by Djawhar, extending as far as the Atlantic. The same caliph had also pacified the Aurès and defeated the maritime offensive of the Umayyad ʿAbd al-Raḥmān III in 344/955.

In order to have a window open onto the East, ʿUbayd Allāh founded on the eastern coast of Ifrīḳiya the town of al-Mahdiyya, which he made his capital in 308/920. A few years after his accession he tried to establish himself in Egypt. But the two expeditions which his son al-Ḳāʾim made in 301-2/913-5 and 307-9/919-21 were unsuccessful and, after initial successes which led him at one time as far as the gates of al-Fusṭāṭ and at another time to Fayyūm, they ended in heavy defeats. In the second expedition, the Fāṭimid fleet was destroyed. Barḳa, however, remained in Fāṭimid hands. After his accession, al-Ḳāʾim tried a third time in 323/925 to conquer Egypt, but again without success.

In none of these operations does the Fāṭimid ruler seem to have been helped by any campaign undertaken on their side by the Ḳarmaṭīs of Bahrain; this is contrary to the opinion advanced by De Goeje (on this subject see W. Madelung, *Fatimiden und Bahrainqarmaten*, in *Isl.*, xxxiv (1959), 46 f., who denies that there was a collaboration between Fāṭimids and Ḳarmaṭīs and maintains that the letter of ʿUbayd Allāh to Abū Ṭāhir after the taking of the Black Stone—for which see the historians *sub anno* 317—is no proof of an alliance between Fāṭimids and Ḳarmaṭīs).

The new power, as successor of the Aghlabids, could not be indifferent to Sicily. But two successive governors sent to Sicily had to withdraw, and the inhabitants elected a governor of their own, Ibn Ḳurhub. He declared for the ʿAbbāsid caliph and twice sent a fleet against Ifrīḳiya, but the second time the fleet suffered a serious defeat; finally the Sicilians rid themselves of Ibn Ḳurhub by giving him up to ʿUbayd Allāh, who had him put to death in 304/916. It was only after this that a new Fāṭimid governor was able to take possession of the island. But Sicily was later to suffer disturbances. In 336/948 al-Manṣūr sent as governor al-Ḥasan b. ʿAlī b. al-Kalbī, and from then on it was from this family that the governors of Sicily were taken, tending more and more towards autonomy.

The Fāṭimid caliphs of North Africa were naturally driven to fight against the Byzantines who were settled in Sicily and to exchange embassies with them. Several times armies and fleets were sent from Ifrīḳiya against the Byzantines in Italy and in Sicily. During the time of ʿUbayd Allāh, at a date which is uncertain (between 914 and 918) the Byzantine emperor concluded a treaty with the governor of Sicily, by which he undertook to pay annually a tribute of 22,000 gold pieces; some years later the caliph reduced this to 11,000, to thank the emperor Romanus Lecapenus for having freed the African ambassadors whose ship had been captured when they were travelling to the court of the king of the Bulgars, in the company of Bulgar emissaries who had come to Africa to propose to the Fāṭimid ruler an alliance against Byzantium. Because of this the projected alliance between Fāṭimids and Bulgars fell through. At about the same time an expedition was sent from Africa against Genoa, Corsica and Sardinia. In the time of al-Ḳāʾim, during the revolt of Girgenti (see DJIRDJENT and Amari, *Storia*, ii, 218 f.; Vasiliev, *Byz. et les Arabes*, ii, 261), the Emperor tried to support the rebels. Al-Manṣūr, at the height of his struggle against Abū Yazīd, received in 335/946 a Byzantine embassy, which had come to apprise itself of the situation. In the time of al-Muʿizz, during the hostilities with the Umayyads, the Umayyad caliph having in 344/955-6 asked and obtained from the Emperor help against the Fāṭimid caliph, the Emperor proposed to al-Muʿizz that he would withdraw his troops if he was willing to grant him a long-term truce. Al-Muʿizz refused, and sent in 345/956-7 a fleet under the command of ʿAmmār (of the Kalbī family) and Djawhar, which gained a great success over the Byzantines and disembarked troops in Italy, but was scattered by a storm on the return voyage. It was after this that in 346/957-8 a Byzantine ambassador came to bring tribute and obtained a truce of five years. This truce was broken by al-Muʿizz when the Cretans appealed to him for help against Byzantium. Al-Muʿizz's help to the Cretans, if it was sent, was of no use (see M. Canard, *Les sources arabes de l'histoire byzantine*, in *Revue des Études Byzantines*, xix (1961), 284 f., and on the embassy of 346 and related events, S. M. Stern, *An embassy of the Byzantine Emperor to the Fatimid Caliph al-Muʿizz*, in *Byzantion*, xx (1950), 239-58; on other Byzantine embassies, see Amari, *Storia*, ii, 314-22).

Some years later, in the time of Nicephorus Phocas, who had refused to continue to pay the tribute and had resumed hostilities in Sicily, the Fāṭimid army and fleet inflicted two defeats on the Byzantines (Battle of Rametta and Battle of the Straits) at the beginning of 965. The resulting negotiations ended in a peace treaty in 356/967, and this treaty was concluded all the more easily as al-Muʿizz was engaged at the time in preparing his Egyptian expedition.

The Conquest of Egypt

The success of al-Muʿizz in North Africa had allowed him to devote himself to the pursuit of an eastern policy, and to undertake the conquest of Egypt in which ʿUbayd Allāh and al-Ḳāʾim had failed. The conquest, carefully planned in its practical aspects, and psychologically by skilful political propaganda (see G. Wiet, *L'Égypte arabe*, vol. iv of *Hist. de la Nat. Égypt.*, 147 f., and M. Canard, *L'impérialisme des Fāṭimides et leur propagande*, in *AIEO-Alger*, vi, 167 f.) in a country which was in a state of internal chaos and ravaged by famine, was achieved without much difficulty by Djawhar, who entered al-Fusṭāṭ on 12 Shaʿbān 358/1st July 969. Egypt then became for two centuries a Shīʿī country, at least superficially. Djawhar had the name of the ʿAbbāsid caliph suppressed in the *khuṭba*, but introduced Shīʿī formulae only very gradually. He concentrated at first on taking measures against the famine and on restoring order, and acted with considerable generosity. To house his troops he built a new town—Cairo—and laid the first stone of the al-Azhar mosque on 24 Ḏjumādā I 359/4 April 970.

THE FĀṬIMIDS IN EGYPT

1. Territorial expansion: its vicissitudes. Ḏjawhar made great efforts to extend Fāṭimid domination beyond the frontiers of Egypt over the countries which were dependencies of the Iḵẖsẖīdid emirate. The two holy cities of Mecca and Medina, where the gold liberally distributed by al-Muʿizz had achieved its propagandist purpose, surrendered readily in 359/970-1, and remained under Fāṭimid suzerainty, apart from a few interruptions over questions of money, until the reign of al-Mustanṣir. It was more difficult to establish a foothold in Syria, for there the Iḵẖsẖīdid governor had made a pact with the Ḳarmaṭīs of Baḥrayn, who in turn had the support of the Buwayhid ruler of Baghdād. Ḏjawhar's lieutenant, Ḏjaʿfar al-Falāḥ, was able to seize Damascus, but he was killed in a battle against the leader of the Ḳarmaṭīs, al-Ḥasan al-Aʿṣam, at the end of 360/August 971 (on the attitude of the Ḳarmaṭīs to the Fāṭimids see al-Maḳrīzī, *Ittiʿāẓ*, 248 f.; De Goeje, *op. cit.*, 183 f.; Ḥasan Ibrāhīm Ḥasan and Ṭaha Sẖaraf, *al-Muʿizz*, 115 f.; Madelung, *Fat. und Bahrainqarm.*, 62 f. and AL-ḤASAN AL-AʿṢAM). The Ḳarmaṭī intended to proceed without delay as far as Egypt, but he encountered a successful defence by Ḏjawhar (end of 361/December 971) and fled. All the same Ḏjawhar was able to re-occupy only a part of Palestine. Al-Ḥasan al-Aʿṣam returned to attack Cairo in 363/ beginning of 974, while al-Muʿizz, who had left Ifrīḳiya on 21 Sẖawwāl 361/ 5 August 972, entrusting the government of the Maghrib to the Ṣanhāḏjī Berber chief Bulukkīn, was already in Cairo, which he had entered on 7 Ramaḍān 362/11 June 973. But the Bedouin auxiliaries of al-Ḥasan al-Aʿṣam, won over by Fāṭimid gold, abandoned him and he was routed. Following this the Fāṭimid army was able to reoccupy Damascus, but shortly afterwards Damascus fell into the hands of a Turkish adventurer, Alptekīn, against whom al-Muʿizz, on the eve of his death in 365/975, was proposing to march.

The new caliph al-ʿAzīz succeeded in re-taking Damascus in 368/978, but in order to procure the withdrawal of the Ḳarmaṭīs, who supported Alptekīn, he was obliged to pay them tribute. Possession of Palestine and Syria was necessary to al-ʿAzīz, whose ultimate plans also required the seizure of Aleppo, but there was continued trouble in Palestine and Syria, fomented either by rebels like the powerful Ṭayyī family of Palestine, the Ḏjarrāḥids [*q.v.*], or by dissident governors or generals. The attempts of al-ʿAzīz failed in 373/983, 382/992-3 and 384/994-5, and his power barely extended as far as Tripoli. Nevertheless it was then that Fāṭimid sovereignty was recognized from the Atlantic to the Red Sea, in the Ḥidjāz, in the Yemen (by the Yaʿfurid ʿAbd Allāh b. Ḳaḥṭān in 377/987 [see ṢANʿĀ']), in Syria and even for a time as far as Mosul, in the time of the ʿUḳaylid Abu 'l-Dawādh b. al-Musayyib. But they were unable to reach any understanding with the Buwayhid of Baghdād, although he was a Sẖīʿī.

The troubles in Syria continued, and it is possible to say that this country was never a solidly Fāṭimid possession. In the time of al-Ḥākim the amirate of Aleppo fell under Fāṭimid rule in 406/1015, and in 408/1017 received a Fāṭimid governor; but he was sometimes in revolt. In Palestine the Ḏjarrāḥid

Mufarriḏj b. Daghfal was able to have an anti-caliph proclaimed in the person of a *sẖarīf* of Mecca, and it was only by buying Mufarriḏj off that al-Ḥākim could rid himself of the danger which he had stirred up. Under al-Ẓāhir, Fāṭimid domination in Syria was endangered by the alliance between the Ḏjarrāḥids, the Kalbīs of central Syria and the Kilābīs of northern Syria. Aleppo fell into the hands of the Kilābī Ṣāliḥ b. Mirdās [*q.v.*] in 415/1025. The fact that the Kalbīs changed sides allowed the Fāṭimid general Anusẖtekīn al-Duzbarī to win the battle of al-Uḵẖuwāna in Palestine, to re-occupy Damascus and to re-take Aleppo from the Mirdāsids in 429/1038 (in the reign of al-Mustanṣir). Thanks to Anusẖtekīn, Fāṭimid domination extended as far as Ḥarrān, Sarūḏj and Raḳḳa, but he fell a victim to the intrigues of the vizier al-Ḏjardjarāʾī; his successor was a descendant of the Ḥamdānids, Nāṣir al-Dawla [*q.v.*], and Aleppo fell again to a Mirdāsid in 433/1041. In spite of two attempts to re-take it in 440/1048 and 441/1049 and its surrender to the Fāṭimids in 449/1057-450/1058, it returned into Mirdāsid hands in 452 and was then irrevocably lost to the Fāṭimids, for it surrendered to the caliph of Baghdād and to the Salḏjūḳ sultan Alp Arslān in 462/1069-70, and had a Salḏjūḳ governor from 479/1086-7.

Nor did Syria and Palestine remain for long under Fāṭimid domination in the 5th/11th century. There was continual unrest there. The Fāṭimid general Badr al-Ḏjamālī [*q.v.*] tried vainly in 455/1063-456/1064 and again in 458/1066-460/1068 to maintain Fāṭimid sovereignty in Damascus. In 461/1069, in the course of fighting between Maghribī and Eastern elements of the army, the Umayyad mosque was burned. In 468/1076 Damascus was occupied by a former Fāṭimid officer, the Turcoman Atsïz, who threatened even Cairo in 469/1077, and Damascus had a Salḏjūḳ *amīr* from 471/1079. In 463/1071 Atsïz had taken Jerusalem, which later passed into the hands of Suḳmān b. Artuḳ. In Palestine there remained in Fāṭimid hands only ʿAsḳalān, which was to be occupied by the Crusaders in 548/1153, and a few coastal towns—Beirut, Tyre, Sidon and Acre. None of the attempts of Badr al-Ḏjamālī to recover Syria and Damascus was successful.

2. Relations with North Africa and Sicily. Already in the reign of al-ʿAzīz North Africa began to loosen its links with the Fāṭimid caliphate under the governorship of Manṣūr b. Bulukkīn (373/984-386/996). In the time of al-Ḥākim difficulties arose over Barḳa and Tripoli. With Muʿizz b. Bādīs (406/1016-454/1062), after he had taken several measures which were hostile to the Fāṭimid caliphate, there came about a complete rupture in 443/1051; the Ṣanhādjī *amīr* threw off Fāṭimid suzerainty and obtained investiture from the caliph of Baghdād. The invasion of Ifrīḳiya by the Banū Hilāl is attributed to the desire of the Fāṭimid vizier al-Yāzūrī for reprisals. Tamīm b. al-Muʿizz (454/1062-501/1108) returned temporarily to Fāṭimid allegiance in the first years of his reign. Similarly in 517/1123 we find the *amīr* Ḥasan b. ʿAlī (515/1121-543/1148) paying homage to the Fāṭimid caliph al-Āmir and asking him to intervene with Roger II of Sicily to stop him from attacking Ifrīḳiya. But it can be said that in fact the rupture lasted for more than half a century.

Sicily also became virtually independent of the Fāṭimid caliphate. The Kalbid governors limited themselves to accepting retrospective investiture from Cairo. They had far more contacts with the Zīrids of Ifrīḳiya, whose suzerainty the Sicilians recognized in about 427/1036 (see Amari, *Storia*, ii, 435), than with Cairo. All the same, until the time of al-Ẓāhir and even under his successor, their coins still bore the name of the caliph (Amari, ii, 276-7). It is not impossible that the attacks which the Sicilians launched on the Byzantine coasts were supported by Cairo, for, in his negotiations with the Fāṭimid al-Ẓāhir in 1032, the emperor Romanus Argyrus expressly demanded that the Fāṭimid government should not aid *Ṣāḥib Sikilliyya* in his campaigns against the Byzantines, and promised for his part to observe the same neutrality. In practice, Cairo had no longer any power over Sicily and seems to have lost interest in it. The Norman conquest was tacitly accepted, and contacts with Roger II were frequent and friendly (see above for the caliph al-Āmir). Al-Ḥāfiẓ also maintained excellent relations with him: there was correspondence in 531/1137 (see M. Canard, *Une lettre du caliphe fāṭimite al-Ḥāfiz .... à Roger II*, in *Atti del Convegno Intern. di Studi Ruggeriani*, Palermo 1955, 125-46); in 537/1142 he sent an embassy to Roger, and in about 537/1143 he concluded a commercial treaty with him. But later, in 1153, 1155, 1169 and 1174, there were Norman attacks by sea against Tinnīs, Damietta and Alexandria (see Amari, index).

3. Relations with the Byzantine Empire. In their propaganda already in their African period the Fāṭimids proclaimed aloud that universal sovereignty was given to them by divine decree and that they were called to displace the Umayyads of Spain as well as the ʿAbbāsids of Baghdād and the Byzantine emperors (see M. Canard, *L'impérialisme ....*, *passim*). We have seen above what their relations with Byzantium had been during the African period. Al-Muʿizz received several Byzantine embassies. In Egypt, in the very year of his death in 365/975, he received an embassy from John Tzimisces. Al-ʿAzīz, in this attempt to take Aleppo, clashed with the Greeks as protectors of the Ḥamdānid amīrate of Aleppo, who each time prevented him from achieving his object. Although al-ʿAzīz did not succeed in his attempts, he nevertheless obtained in 377/987-8 from the emperor Basil II, who was threatened by the renewal of the revolt of Bardas Skleros, an advantageous treaty stipulating that the Byzantine commercial prohibitions should be lifted and that the prayer should be said in his name in the mosque of Constantinople (Abu 'l-Maḥāsin, Cairo ed., iv, 151-2). Immediately before his death, this caliph was preparing a great expedition against Byzantine territory, and he died while setting off on this campaign.

Hostilities continued in northern Syria during the reign of al-Ḥākim, for his aim, like his predecessor's, was to seize Aleppo, and rebels in Syria against Fāṭimid authority often appealed to the Emperor. The Byzantines helped al-ʿAllāḳa at Tyre, whereas in 387/997 they had refused to help the Fāṭimid general Mangūtekīn. They were defeated at sea off Tyre and again in the same year when they were besieging Apamea, a Fāṭimid enclave in northern Syria (388/998), and the emperor Basil then made proposals for peace. But it was not until 391/1001 that a ten-year truce was signed, and in the interval Basil had conducted a victorious campaign in northern Syria, though he had failed to take Tripoli. The destruction of the Church of the Holy Sepulchre on the orders of al-Ḥākim was probably one of the causes of the breaking off of commercial relations ordered by Basil in 406/1015-6. Attempts at reconciliation were made in 412/1021, just before the death of al-Ḥākim.

At the beginning of the reign of al-Ẓāhir, in 414/1023, the regent Sitt al-Mulk ([*q.v.*], d. 415/1024-5) had re-opened negotiations but without success. They were not resumed until 423/1032, and were soon broken off because of the caliph's refusal to accept the return of Ḥassān b. al-Mufarridj [see DJARRĀḤIDS], when agreement had been reached on the rebuilding of the Church of the Holy Sepulchre. It was not until 429/1038 that a peace of thirty years could be signed, at the beginning of the reign of al-Mustanṣir: the Byzantines obtained permission to rebuild the church, and sent architects and money for this purpose.

From this time on begins a period of friendly relations between Fāṭimids and Byzantines. Although Byzantium had agreed to support a rebel Sicilian *amīr* and had given him the title of *magister* in 1035-6 (Amari, ii, 434), yet when in 443/1051-2 the Zīrid Muʿizz b. Bādīs had recognized ʿAbbāsid suzerainty, his ambassador returning from Baghdād was arrested in Byzantine territory and sent to al-Mustanṣir. In 439/1048 the treaty of 1038 had been renewed.

Constantine Monomachus (1042-54) maintained excellent relations with al-Mustanṣir, who asked him to supply Egypt with wheat after the famine of 446/1054. But the death of the Emperor and the demands of his successor, the empress Zoë, who wanted in return a treaty of military aid (against the Saldjūḳs), led to a cooling of relations and even a resumption of hostilities. The rupture was aggravated when a Fāṭimid ambassador, al-Ḳuḍāʿī, noticed at Constantinople that the prayer was said in the mosque no longer in the name of the Fāṭimid, but for the Saldjūḳ sultan Toghrīl Beg, for the Emperor had entered into relations with the latter in 441/1049 in gratitude for his having freed the king of the Abkhāz, and it seems, to judge from the *Sīra* of the Fāṭimid missionary al-Muʾayyad fi 'l-Dīn (p. 95), that there had been a project for an alliance between the two against the Fāṭimid ruler. Relations were resumed however and the Byzantine writer Psellus states that they were excellent in the reign of Constantine Monomachus (ed. Renault, ii, 64) and were still so between 1057 and 1059, during the reign of Isaac Comnenus (*op. cit.*, ii, 122).

The exchange of embassies continued, the more so because the same danger, the Saldjūḳs, was threatening both Egypt and Byzantium. There was for example a Fāṭimid embassy during the reign of Romanus Diogenes in 461/1069, a letter from Alexis Comnenus to the vizier al-Afḍal in about 1098, after Antioch had been taken by the Crusaders, and an embassy from the same emperor to al-Afḍal in 1105 to negotiate the ransom of Frankish prisoners. Manuel Comnenus also maintained good relations with Egypt and in 553/1158 requested the help of a Fāṭimid fleet against Sicily. In the same year, the vizier Ṭalāʾiʿ b. Ruzzīk sent to Manuel the brother of the Count of Cyprus whom he had taken prisoner. Some years later however, in 1168, Manuel concluded a pact with king Amalric of Jerusalem for an attack against Egypt, which took place the following year, but failed.

4. Relations with the ʿAbbāsid East. Ibn Hāniʾ al-Andalusī, the eulogist of al-Muʿizz, tempts his master with the prospect of a Fāṭimid entry into Baghdād, and shows him, wide open, the old imperial Persian highway, the road to Khurāsān. One tradition has it that al-Muʿizz declared to a Byzantine ambassador in Cairo that on his next visit he would find him in Baghdād. Al-ʿAzīz set himself to achieve this goal, but by means of negotiations, trying to

get himself recognized by the Buwayhid ʿAḍud al-Dawla. An exchange of embassies took place in 369/979-80, but without result. Like the ʿAbbāsid caliph later, the Buwayhid contested the authenticity of the ʿAlid genealogy of the Fāṭimids. Al-Ḥākim was no more successful with the Ghaznawid ruler in 403/1012-3, nor was al-Ẓāhir in 415/1024. The *khilaʿ* sent were despatched to Baghdād and burnt. Al-Ẓahir did not give up, and in 425/1034 sent missionaries to the ʿAbbāsid capital to take advantage of the disturbances caused by the Turkish soldiery during the reign of the Buwayhid Djalāl al-Dawla [*q.v.*], and they made vigorous propaganda there. Al-Mustanṣir [*q.v.*] cemented relations with several governments in the East. The activities of his missionaries spread as far as Sind (see S. M. Stern, *Ismāʿīlī propaganda and Fāṭimid rule in Sind*, in *IC*, xxiii (1949), 298-307; B. Lewis, *The Fatimids and the route to India*, in *Rev. de la Fac. des Sc. économ. de l'Univ. d'Istanbul*, 1953). For a time al-Mustanṣir could believe that the Fāṭimid dream was about to become reality. In ʿIrāḳ the Turkish *amīr* al-Basāsīrī [*q.v.*] caused the sovereignty of the Fāṭimid ruler to be recognized in various places, at Mosul in 448/1057, then in Baghdād for a year in 451/1059. This extension of Fāṭimid sovereignty had been prepared in particular by the propaganda of the missionary al-Muʾayyad fi 'l-Dīn [*q.v.*], who had even converted the Buwayhid Abū Kālīdjār [*q.v.*] at Shīrāz to Ismāʿīlism. The Saldjūḳs, as Sunnīs, naturally had no sympathy for the Fāṭimids. In 447/1055, Toghrīl Beg had announced his intention of marching on Syria and Egypt and of putting an end to the reign of al-Mustanṣir. The affair of al-Basāsīrī strengthened the determination of the Saldjūḳs to direct their policy towards Syria and the Mediterranean, especially as the vizier al-Yāzūrī [*q.v.*], who decided to abandon his support of al-Basāsīrī, had entered into correspondence with Toghrīl Beg (so at least certain sources allege). The fact remains that from then on the Saldjūḳs did nothing but gain territory from the Fāṭimids: at Mecca the name of the Fāṭimid ruler was omitted from the *khuṭba*, temporarily in 462/1069-70 and finally in 473/1088. In his rebellion against al-Mustanṣir, the *amīr* Nāṣir al-Dawla appealed for help, in 462/1069-70, to the Saldjūḳ sultan Alp Arslān, asking him to send an army to help him to re-establish the ʿAbbāsid *khuṭba*. The Saldjūḳ sultan got as far as Aleppo the following year, and the Mirdāsid ruler abandoned the Fāṭimid *khuṭba*. Alp Arslān was unable to proceed further, because of the invasion of Armenia by the Byzantine emperor. Apart from this, we have already noticed the Saldjūḳ penetration into Syria and Palestine.

In the Yemen, the Fāṭimids found fervent supporters in the dynasty of the Ṣulayḥids of Ṣanʿāʾ, which ruled from 429/1038 to 534/1139. The founder was a *dāʿī* who established Fāṭimid domination in the Yemen. This dynasty included a remarkable ruler in the person of Sayyida Ḥurra, and maintained uninterrupted relations with Cairo: the letters from the chancery of al-Mustanṣir to the Ṣulayḥids have survived (*Al-Sidjillāt al-Mustanṣiriyya*, ed. A. M. Magued, Cairo 1954).

5. The Fāṭimids and the Crusades. At the time when the Crusaders arrived in northern Syria the Fāṭimids no longer held any territory in Syria, and in Palestine they retained only ʿAsḳalān and a few coastal towns. They were less interested in the struggle against the Franks than were the Turkish *amīrs* of Syria. Ibn al-Athīr, *sub anno* 491/1097-8, relates a tradition according to which the Fāṭimids, being uneasy over the plans of the Saldjūḳs and their intentions against Egypt (for the *amīr* Atsïz had already, in 469/1077, launched an unsuccessful attack against Cairo), requested the intervention of the Franks in the East. This does not seem very likely. Be that as it may, the Franks received a Fāṭimid embassy outside Antioch at the beginning of 1098 and sent delegates to Cairo, who set off with the Egyptian ambassadors. But the project for an alliance against the Turks, giving Syria to the Franks and Palestine to the Fāṭimids, did not come to anything, although the Fāṭimids were better disposed towards the Franks than towards the Turks, and in spite of the good intentions of the Franks, who were able to learn through Alexis Comnenus what was the Fāṭimid attitude to the Turks. In these circumstances the vizier al-Afḍal decided to take Jerusalem from Suḳmān, succeeded in 491/August 1098 after a siege of forty days, and continued his advance to beyond Beirut. It is difficult in these circumstances to see why—for presumably he re-took Jerusalem in order to hold it—he did nothing to prevent the Crusaders from seizing it on 15 July 1099, and allowed himself to be surprised and beaten in August outside ʿAsḳalān in a battle which had been preceded by the capture of several places, including Yāfā (Jaffa).

Following this, in 494/1100-1, the Crusaders took in Palestine Ḥayfa, Arsūf and Caesarea, and then Acre (ʿAkkā) in 497/1104. The Egyptians took part in the struggle against the Crusaders but were unable to prevent the fall of Tripoli, which had called on them for help at the end of 503/1109, nor the fall of Beirut and Sidon (Ṣaydā) in 504/1110, nor the fall of Tyre in 518/1124: it is true that the Fāṭimid governor of Tyre had signed an agreement with the *amīr* of Damascus. The Franks were even able, at the end of 517/1118, to advance as far as Faramā. Yet it was not until much later that they turned their attention to Egypt and actively prepared to attack ʿAskalān [*q.v.*]. The Egyptian vizier, Ibn al-Sallār, entered into negotiations with Nūr al-Dīn [*q.v.*], master of Aleppo, in 545/1150, and the Egyptian fleet launched a great offensive against the Frankish ports. In 548/1153, the Franks seized ʿAskalān after bloody fighting.

Next the vizier Ṭalāʾiʿ b. Ruzzīk carried out some operations against the Crusaders and gained a victory near Ghazza, then at Hebron (al-Khalīl) in 553/1158; but this had little result because Nūr al-Dīn, master of Damascus since 549/1154, when he was approached again, was still not willing to become involved because of the internal unrest in Cairo.

Ṭalāʾiʿ was assassinated at the instigation of the caliph al-ʿĀḍid in 556/1161; his son succeeded him and met the same fate in 558/1163. From then on, the relations of Fāṭimid Egypt with the Crusaders on the one hand and with Nūr al-Dīn on the other were influenced by the rivalry between Shāwar, who succeeded Ṭalāʾiʿ's son, Ruzzīk, and Ḍirghām [*qq.v.*], and by the versatile and personal policy of Shāwar. The latter, when expelled by Ḍirghām, had taken refuge with Nūr al-Dīn and persuaded him to intervene in Egypt, particularly as the king of Jerusalem, Amalric I, had made a first incursion into Egypt in 1161 and exacted a payment of tribute from Ṭalāʾiʿ, had returned in 1162, but had had to retreat before the deliberate flooding of the Nile Delta. Nūr al-Dīn sent an army with Shīrkūh [*q.v.*] and his nephew, Saladin (Ṣalāḥ al-Dīn). Ḍirghām was killed in Ramaḍān 559/August 1164, and

Shāwar resumed the vizierate. There is no room here to trace in detail the events which ensued, and the confused tangle of the successive interventions by Shīrkūh and Amalric. The main details will be found in the articles SHĀWAR and SHĪRKŪH. The result was that Shīrkūh, finally answering a joint appeal by the caliph and Shāwar, procured the evacuation of the country by the Franks in 564/1169, rid himself of Shāwar by assassination, and was granted the post of vizier to the Fāṭimid caliph. He died soon after; Saladin succeeded, and put an end to the Fāṭimid caliphate in 567/1171, re-establishing Sunnism and ʿAbbāsid sovereignty in Egypt.

Internal Policy of the Fāṭimids

1. Caliphs and viziers. In the Sunnī system, the appointment of the caliph is the result of an election or of a nomination by the predecessor ratified by a pseudo-election. In the Ismāʿīlī system, the caliph is the successor of him who, by virtue of a Divine decree and nomination, has been chosen to be the heir (*waṣī*) of the Prophet, namely ʿAlī, and the imāmate is transmitted from father to son (with the exception of the case of Ḥasan and Ḥusayn) within the family of ʿAlī. In these circumstances there could be no question of an election, nor of the conditions demanded by Sunnism for holding the office of imām. The imām is chosen by the personal nomination of his predecessor, by the *naṣṣ* [*q.v.*], a manifestation of the Divine will (on this subject see al-Nuʿmān, *Daʿāʾim al-Islam*, i, 48 f.; the *Tādj al-ʿaḳāʾid* of ʿAlī b. Muḥammad b. al-Walīd, d. 612/1215, in Ivanow, *A creed of the Fatimids*, Bombay 1936, paras. 30-32).

The succession of the imāms was thus governed by the *naṣṣ*. This nomination could be hidden from the people and known only to certain trusted persons and revealed only when desired (see examples in the *Sīrat al-ustādh Djawdhar*). It was possible for the elder son not to be chosen. Already Djaʿfar al-Ṣādiḳ had nominated Ismāʿīl, who was not the eldest of his sons. Similarly ʿAbd Allāh was preferred to Tamīm, the eldest son of al-Muʿizz, mainly for moral reasons (see the same *Sīra*). When ʿAbd Allāh died in 364/974-5, the successor nominated was his brother Nizār (al-ʿAzīz). So far everything had been quite regular. But, after the disappearance of al-Ḥākim, the nominated heir, the caliph's nephew ʿAbd al-Raḥmān b. Ilyās, was arrested and imprisoned on the orders of Sitt al-Mulk, who had the young son of al-Ḥākim, ʿAlī, proclaimed imām under the name of al-Ẓāhir. He was only 16, but there was no stipulation regarding age: al-Ḥākim himself had mounted the throne at 11 years of age. The throne often fell to a child, as in the cases of al-Mustanṣir, aged 7, of al-Mustaʿlī, who was only 8, al-Āmir, who was 5, al-Ẓāfir, who was 17, al-Fāʾiz, who was 5, and al-ʿĀḍid, who was 9 years of age. The result was that power was often in the hands of a regent (or a female regent like Sitt al-Mulk, or of a queen-mother, like the mother of al-Mustanṣir), and that on various occasions it was generals or viziers who held the real authority, even after the new caliph had reached maturity, and that the caliphs were often powerless against their viziers and their generals.

The succession proceeded regularly without any serious objections until al-Mustaʿlī, the first caliph whose nomination was violently contested and gave rise to disturbances. The vizier al-Afḍal had caused the elder son of al-Mustanṣir, Nizār, who had been nominated in the regular manner, to be passed over in favour of the younger son, al-Mustaʿlī. As a result Nizār led a revolt, which ended in his death and produced a schism which still exists today in the Ismāʿīlī community [see NIZĀR]. After the death of al-Āmir, the victim of a Nizārī plot in 524/1130, the succession was assured by completely irregular means. No nomination had been made, and al-Ḥāfiẓ [*q.v.*], the cousin of al-Āmir, was at first only regent before he proclaimed himself caliph, following the precedent of ʿAlī, who was the cousin of the Prophet. With his reign began a tremendous crisis, with bloody periods of revolution and treachery, and with struggles of rival factions in the midst of military and civil disturbances in the capital and in the provinces.

The weakness of the caliphs showed itself as early as the reign of al-Mustanṣir, who was reduced to penury and forced to sell his treasures to satisfy the demands of Nāṣir al-Dawla and of the Turkish guard which he commanded, and who only once showed a spark of energy. From the time of al-Mustaʿlī, the real masters were the "Viziers of the Sword". It could happen that the caliph was thrust aside by the vizier, and avenged himself by having the vizier assassinated when opportunity arose: it was thus that al-Āmir had al-Afḍal assassinated.

After a certain period, even the idea of the legitimacy of the Fāṭimids was less generally accepted. Already during the reign of al-Mustanṣir there had been an attempt to restore ʿAbbāsid suzerainty. In 462/1070, Nāṣir al-Dawla, at Alexandria, had the *khuṭba* said in the name of the ʿAbbāsid caliph, and in 464/1072, when he was temporarily master of Cairo, he entered into relations with him. Al-Ḥāfiẓ had a vizier, Kutayfāt, who was openly Imāmī; then followed a Sunnī vizier, Ibn al-Sallār. We cannot give in detail here all the vicissitudes through which the Fāṭimid caliphate passed, but refer the reader to the articles on the individual caliphs. The Fāṭimid caliphate, beset by troubles, declined rapidly to its end, which was finally hastened by its inability to resist the Crusaders, and not only by internal disorder.

The evolution of the vizierate. In the history of the Fāṭimid dynasty, the viziers occupied a place of gradually increasing importance. During the North African period there had been no ministers bearing the title of vizier. In Egypt, the first to receive this title, from the caliph al-ʿAzīz, was Yaʿḳūb b. Killis [*q.v.*], the organizer of the administration and the finances for the first two Egyptian caliphs. Thereafter the caliphs sometimes governed without the help of a vizier; sometimes they had a minister to whom they gave neither the title nor the office of vizier, but only the duty of acting as intermediary between them and their officials and subjects (*safāra*, *wasāṭa*, the one who fulfilled this function bearing the title of *wāsiṭa*); sometimes they had a minister who did in fact bear the title of vizier. Up to a certain time these viziers, whatever their power and their influence over the caliphs may have been, were considered as agents for the execution of the sovereign's will (called by al-Māwardī *wazīr al-tanfīdh*), but from the second period of the reign of al-Mustanṣir, when, in order to restore order and remedy a catastrophic situation, he appealed for help to the commander of the troops of Syria, Badr al-Djamālī, the latter obtained from him full powers: that is to say he was the equivalent of what al-Māwardī calls *wazīr al-tafwīḍ*, vizier with delegated powers; and as he was of military status he was called "Vizier of the Pen and of the Sword", or simply "Vizier of the Sword". From this time on all the viziers who followed, whether they were nominated by the caliph or whether they had seized the position for themselves by force, had full powers and were Viziers of the Sword. The Vizier of the Sword was not only head of the armies, with the title of *amīr al-djuyūsh*, but the head of all the civil, the judicial and even the religious administration, for among his titles were those of chief *ḳāḍī* and of chief missionary. We have seen that the vizier often left no power to the caliph and even thrust him aside; from the time of Riḍwān, the vizier of al-Ḥāfiẓ in 531/1171, it was made still clearer that the vizier had full powers by his taking the title of al-Malik, accompanied by a varying epithet, analogous to that which the last Buwayhid *amīr* of Baghdād had adopted in 440/1048. The importance of this event is that the title passed via Shīrkūh, who assumed the vizierate in 564/1169, to his nephew Saladin and hence to all the members of the Ayyūbid dynasty.

One remarkable fact concerning the Fāṭimid vizierate is that several viziers, whether they possessed the title or not, were Christians. An example is ʿĪsā b. Nasṭūrus, vizier of al-ʿAzīz, and similarly Zurʿa b. ʿĪsā b. Nasṭūrus, who succeeded yet another Christian, Manṣūr b. ʿAbdūn. We do not know whether the Armenian Yānis, who was for some months in 562/1132 the vizier of al-Ḥāfiẓ and who was a freedman of al-Afḍal, had remained Christian. But there is the very curious case of another vizier of al-Ḥāfiẓ, an Armenian who remained Christian, and nevertheless was Vizier of the Sword with full powers and surnamed Sayf al-Islām [see BAHRĀM]. On the other hand, it does not seem that Jews, although they often held important posts, ever became viziers without embracing Islam. Ibn Killis, the vizier of al-ʿAzīz, was a convert, as was Ḥasan b. Ibrāhīm b. Sahl al-Tustarī, vizier for a short time of al-Mustanṣir, and also Ibn al-Fallāḥī.

The career of a vizier in the Fāṭimid period was a dangerous one, as in fact was that of officials of every rank. Disgrace, confiscation of goods, imprisonment and the punishment of the bastinado were events of frequent occurrence. The execution or the assassination of a vizier on the orders of the caliph or by a rival became more and more common. As early as 390/1000 the *wāsiṭa* Bardjawān [*q.v.*] was assassinated by order of al-Ḥākim, and six of his successors suffered the same fate; al-Yāzūrī was executed in 450/1058 during the reign of al-Mustanṣir; then al-Afḍal was assassinated in 515/1121 by order of the caliph al-Āmir. The same caliph, in 519/1125, imprisoned al-Maʾmūn al-Baṭāʾiḥī, who was hanged three years later. Al-Ḥāfiẓ in 526/1131 had Kutayfāt put to death, and then in the next year Yānis. Ṭalāʾiʿ b. Ruzzīk was assassinated in 556/1161 on the orders of one of the aunts of the young caliph al-ʿĀḍid.

Broadly speaking, the main characteristic of the vizierate of the Fāṭimids is the insecurity of the viziers. While al-ʿAzīz had eight viziers in a reign of twenty years, and al-Ḥākim eight in nineteen years, under al-Mustanṣir there were five viziers between 452/1060 and 454/1062, and between 454/1062 and 466/1074 there was a continual coming and going of viziers. Ibn Muyassar reckons that this caliph had twenty-four viziers, some of whom held office three times.

2. Disturbances, rebellions and revolutions. Given the progressive decline of the caliphs from power to impotence, the insecurity of the viziers, and the prevailing anarchy, it is not surprising that the Fāṭimid caliphate went through periods of serious disturbances, resulting from various causes —political, military, religious, economic and social.

Under al-Ḥākim there was the revolt of Abū Rakwa, who claimed to be related to the Umayyads of Spain and whose aim was to re-establish the Umayyad dynasty. At the beginning of the reign of al-Mustanṣir, an impostor, al-Sikkīn, claiming to be al-Ḥākim, gathered supporters and marched with them as far as the gates of the palace: they were all captured, brought to the gallows and riddled with arrows (434/1043). The revolt of Nizār, the heir nominated by al-Mustanṣir and ousted from the succession by the all-powerful vizier al-Afḍal in favour of al-Mustaʿlī, had tremendous consequences, for the famous Ḥasan-i Ṣabbāḥ [*q.v.*] had taken his side and started a movement which led to the foundation of the sect of the Assassins [see HASHĪSHIYYA, NIZĀRĪS]. In 524/1130, the caliph al-Āmir, assassinated by a follower of Nizār, died without male issue. But some declared that he had a son, al-Ṭayyib, and a new schism occurred (see Ivanow, *Rise*, 20, and S. M. Stern, *The succession of the Fāṭimid imām al-Āmir, the claims of the later Fāṭimids to the imāmate and the rise of Ṭayyibī Ismāʿīlism*, in *Oriens*, 1951, 193 ff.). In 543/1148 yet another rebellion was stirred up, by one who claimed to be the son of Nizār.

There were numerous military disturbances, especially when the dynasty was declining, when factions of the army made and unmade ministers and fought continually among themselves. But long before this the very composition of the army provoked disturbances which sometimes took the form of racial rivalry. Berbers (*Maghāriba*), Turks (who had been enrolled since the reign of al-ʿAzīz), Daylamīs (*Mashāriḳa*), and also black Sudanese slaves bought for the army (*ʿabīd al-shirāʾ*) and numerous since the regency of the mother of al-Mustanṣir, herself a former black slave—all were jealous of and hated one another. These corps were generally undisciplined and they or their leaders either stirred up rebellions themselves or readily allowed themselves to become involved in them. Thus in the struggle between the Kutāmī Ibn ʿAmmār and Bardjawān at the beginning of the reign of al-Ḥākim, there were the Berbers on one side and on the other the Turks, the Daylamīs and the black slaves. The hatred between the Turks and the black slaves, stirred up by al-Mustanṣir's mother, provoked murderous battles in 454/1062 and 459/1067, in which the Berbers sided with the Turks. Nāṣir al-Dawla, the commander of the Turks and victor over the black slaves, wrested all power from the caliph al-Mustanṣir, who had to sell his treasures in order to pay the Turks with their ever-increasing demands. The disturbances provoked by the tyranny of Nāṣir al-Dawla and aggravated by the famine (see below) lasted until the dictatorship of Badr al-Djamālī. From the reign of al-Ḥāfiẓ onwards, the various corps of the army distributed their loyalties among the various claimants to the vizierate, some of whom, to forward their cause, raised special corps (e.g. the Barḳiyya of Ṭalāʾiʿ b. Ruzzīk) or recruited Bedouins (as did Ibn Maṣāl and Shāwar [*qq.v.*]).

Disturbances of religious origin arose when a certain group of missionaries wanted to have the divinity of al-Ḥākim recognized: in 411/1020 the mob massacred the missionaries, and this resulted in uproar and the burning of al-Fusṭāṭ on the caliph's orders. In 531/1137, Riḍwān had no difficulty in rousing the Muslim mob against the vizier Bahrām, an Armenian Christian.

But it was the economic crises and famines (which Egypt has always suffered periodically when the Nile rises insufficiently) which in the Fāṭimid period caused most disorders: shortage of food, looting, crimes, acts of cannibalism, and horrors of every description. In 414/1024-415/1025, under al-Ẓāhir, there was a famine which obliged the populace to eat all the domestic animals, so that the caliph had to forbid the slaughter of plough-oxen. This famine was accompanied by looting by the black troops, who carried off the dishes set out for the banquet of the Feast of Sacrifices in 415 (12 February 1025). But the worst crisis of all was the great famine in the reign of al-Mustanṣir. In 446/1054-5 the caliph was obliged to ask Constantine Monomachus to supply food for Egypt (see above). The dearth, followed by disease, was worse in the following year. For seven years from 457/1065 to 464/1072 there persisted a famine so terrible that people were reduced to eating dogs and cats, and even human flesh (see al-Maḳrīzī, *Khiṭaṭ*, i, 337). Looting, and the kidnapping of men and women in order to kill and eat them, led to a general breakdown of order which was aggravated by the struggles between the Turkish and the Negro regiments of the army. The economic situation improved in the vizierate of Badr al-Djamālī and his son al-Afḍal.

3. Religious policy. The religious policy of the Fāṭimids, so far as it is concerned with Ismāʿīlī doctrine and its evolution, cannot be treated here in detail. For this subject the reader is referred to the article ISMĀʿĪLIYYA and to W. Madelung's work (cited above), in which are studied the 'reforms' introduced into the doctrine by ʿUbayd Allāh, and then al-Muʿizz, the theories of the Persian Ismāʿīlīs, the schism under al-Ḥākim, and the doctrine in the time of al-Mustanṣir. The first Fāṭimid caliphs had to justify themselves to the different Ismāʿīlī communities with their different emphases, and to combat heterodox or extremist opinions which might constitute a danger to them. They were confronted with the fact that the hopes which the Ismāʿīlī community has placed in the appearance of the Mahdī had not been realized: the law of Muḥammad had not been abrogated, the hidden meaning of the religious duties and of the Ḳurʾān had not been revealed, a more perfect law, in which there was no longer any distinction between the *bāṭin* and the *ẓāhir*, had not been promulgated, Fāṭimid rule had not spread throughout the world, but had, on the contrary, encountered unsurmountable obstacles. Policy and reason of state had obliged them to retain the fundamental duties of Islam, and the *ẓāhir* continued to exist beside the *bāṭin*. It had to be admitted that the complete reversal of positions and the victory over the Infidels which the Mahdī was expected to bring about had been postponed to the end of time, that the Mahdī had done no more than to restore fully the rights of the family of the Prophet, and that the mission would be continued by his successors until God should fulfil this promise through the Ḳāʾim. The system elaborated by the great Fāṭimī jurist al-Nuʿmān in his *Daʿāʾim al-islām* did not differ fundamentally, on numerous points, from Sunnism, and in his esoteric treatises he too postponed the awaited changes to the end of time. In general, the Fāṭimid caliphate showed itself opportunist and moderate, and it could not be otherwise in seeking to establish a state religion.

But this religion was not universally accepted, and it was necessary to embark on a struggle with the Sunnism to which a large part of the population of Egypt and Syria remained loyal. The observance of the Sunna continued, as is testified by ʿAbd al-Ḳāhir al-Baghdādī, *al-Farḳ bayn al-firaḳ* (275; cf. Goldziher, *Streitschrift des Ġazālī ...*, 7), and there were numerous reactions against Shīʿī practices (*Khiṭaṭ*, ii, 340; Kindī-Guest, 594). Propaganda [see DĀʿĪ and DAʿWA] and the teaching of Fāṭimī *fiḳh* were organized. The *ḳāḍī* al-Nuʿmān, later his sons, and also the vizier Ibn Killis exerted all their efforts to implant the new doctrine (see *Khiṭaṭ*, ii, 341, 363; Yaḥyā b. Saʿīd, *P.O.*, xxiii/3, 434). The *Dār al-ḥikma* [*q.v.*] of al-Ḥākim was also a centre of religious and legal teaching. At first Sunnī *shaykh*s were admitted, but al-Ḥākim soon had them executed (Abu 'l-Maḥāsin, iv, 178, 222-3). The establishment was closed in the time of al-Afḍal because it was attended by people holding heretical opinions and it was feared that it would become a centre of Nizārī propaganda. After al-Afḍal's death, it was re-opened by the vizier al-Maʾmūn al-Baṭāʾiḥī, but at some distance from the palace and under the supervision of the *Dāʿī*.

Policy towards the Sunnīs fluctuated. Sunnī practices were in general forbidden, but there were some periods of tolerance and some of strictness. In 307/919-20, a *muʾadhdhin* of Ḳayrawān was executed for not having pronounced in the call to prayer "Come to the best of works" (on the differences between the Ismāʿīlī system and Sunnism, see the *Tādj al-ʿaḳāʾid* of ʿAlī b. Muḥammad b. al-Walīd in Ivanow, *A creed of the Fatimids*, Bombay 1936; al-Nuʿmān, *Daʿāʾim al-islām*; al-Muḳaddasī, 237-8; cf. R. Brunschvig, *Fiqh fatimide et histoire de l'Ifriqiya*, in *Mélanges d'hist. et d'arch. de l'Occident musulman*, Algiers 1957, ii, 13-20). The *tarāwīḥ* [*q.v.*] prayer in Ramaḍān had been forbidden in North Africa, as it was in Egypt in 372/982-3 by al-ʿAzīz, but it was allowed again in 399/1009 by al-Ḥākim (see al-Maḳrīzī's chapter, *Khiṭaṭ*, ii, 341 f., on the *Madhāhib ahl Miṣr*). Al-ʿAzīz was very strict towards the Mālikīs; al-Ḥākim sometimes tolerated them, sometimes persecuted them. Al-Ẓāhir expelled the Mālikī *faḳīh*s from Egypt in 416/1025-6. In 525/1131, on the other hand, the vizier Kutayfāt, an Imāmī, showed great tolerance: there were, besides an Ismāʿīlī and an Imāmī ḳāḍī, also a Mālikī ḳāḍī and a Shāfiʿī. Al-Ḳalḳashandī could say (*Ṣubḥ*, iii, 524) that the Fāṭimids were tolerant to the Sunnīs, with the exception of Ḥanafīs.

As for the Christians and the Jews, they held a relatively favourable position throughout the Fāṭimid period. We have noticed that several caliphs had Christian viziers: al-ʿAzīz, al-Ḥākim, who had three (Fahd b. Ibrāhīm, Manṣūr b. ʿAbdūn and Zurʿa b. Nasṭūrus), al-Ḥāfiẓ, with Bahrām. In spite of the discontent, sometimes openly expressed, of the Muslim population, Christians could always hold the highest offices. Throughout the period of the dynasty, non-Muslims continued to occupy numerous posts in the administration, especially in the finance departments. In the time of al-ʿAzīz the Jews rose to hold important offices and were sometimes very powerful, as they were at the court of al-Mustanṣir during the regency of his mother. Tolerance to Christians and Jews is one of the characteristics of the dynasty. The Armenian Abū Ṣāliḥ testifies to the tolerance of the Fāṭimid caliphs in the matter of the building of churches and their benevolence towards Christian establishments (see *The Churches and monasteries of Egypt*, ed. and tr. Evetts, Oxford 1895). For the Jews, see J. Mann, *The Jews under the Fatimid Caliphs*, Oxford 1920-2; R. J. H. Gottheil, *A decree in favour of the Karaites of Cairo dated 1024*, in *Festschrift A. Harkavy*, St. Petersburg 1908, 115 ff.; S. D. Goitein, *A Caliph's decree in favour of the*

Rabbinite Jews of Palestine, in *Journ. of Jew. stud.*, 1954; id., *The Muslim government, as seen by its non-Muslim subjects*, in *J. Pak. Hist. Soc.*, 1964; id., *Evidence on the Muslim poll tax from non-Muslim sources*, in *JESHO*, 1964; see further Cl. Cahen, *Histoires coptes d'un cadi médieval*, in *BIFAO*, lix (1960), 133 ff.

4. Organization of the State. The Fāṭimid state in North Africa, although it already surrounded itself by some ceremonial, was not yet a complex organization. But from the very beginning of the Egyptian period the caliphs al-Muʿizz and al-ʿAzīz laid the solid foundations of the power of the dynasty. The strict organization which they introduced in the administration and the finances, and which Djawhar had prepared together with Ibn Killis and Uslūdj, was the basis for a complex system of institutions which progressively developed, became modified, or were transformed, and whose functions have been studied in various works: Ibn al-Ṣayrafī, *Ḳānūn dīwān al-rasāʾil*, ed. Ali Bahgat, Cairo 1905, tr. Massé, in *BIFAO*, xi (1914); al-Maḳrīzī, *Khiṭaṭ*, i; al-Ḳalḳashandī, *Ṣubḥ*, iii (reproduced in *Les Institutions des Fatimides en Egypte*, Bibl. de l'Inst. d'Ét. Supér. Isl. d'Alger, xii (1957)); trans. by Wüstenfeld, *Calcaschandi's Geographie und Verwaltung von Aegypten*, *AKGWG*, xxv, Göttingen 1879. Some modern works also have been devoted to these questions: Dr. ʿAbd al-Munʿim Mādjid (Magued), *Institutions et cérémonial des Fatimides en Egypte*, 2 vols., Cairo 1953-5; Dr. ʿAtiya Muṣṭafā Musharrafa, *Nuẓum al-ḥukm bi-Miṣr fī ʿaṣr al-Fāṭimiyyīn*, Cairo, 2nd ed., no date. Again, one special chapter (ix) deals with the organs of the administration and another (xii) with ceremonial in Ḥasan Ibrāhīm Ḥasan's *Taʾrīkh al-dawla al-fāṭimiyya*, Cairo 1958 (revised version of *Al-Fāṭimiyyūn fī Miṣr*, 1932), 264-325, 628-73.

Fāṭimid administration was a strongly centralized system, having at its head the caliph and the vizier, either with executive or with delegated powers (from Badr al-Djamālī onwards, the vizier is a Vizier of the Sword). Everything was under the control of the central administration, the provincial organs of government having no real autonomy although some governors, such as the govenor of Ḳūṣ for example, were able at time to attain great power. Administration was carried on through the *dīwāns* (offices or ministries), which were assembled sometimes at the palace of the vizier (as for example under Ibn Killis and al-Afḍal), sometimes at the palace of the caliph [see DIWĀN ii].

Officials, both civil and military (*arbāb al-aḳlām* and *arbāb al-suyūf*), both in the personal service of the caliph (*khawāṣṣ al-khalīfa*) and in the public service (military, administrative, financial, judicial, religious), were strictly organized in a hierarchy, the degrees of which were marked not only by differences of pay but also by the insignia peculiar to each rank and the places occupied in receptions held at the palace and in public processions. Some of the military officers belonged to the public service, like the Vizier of the Sword, the Grand Chamberlain, the *Isfahsalār*, the Bearer of the Umbrella, the Sword-bearer, the Grooms, etc., others belonged to the private service: these were eunuchs, those most exalted in dignity being the *muḥannak* eunuchs, distinguished by a special style of turban, among whom were the Master of the Audience-chamber, the Message-Bearer, the Major-Domo, the eunuch responsible for arranging the caliph's headgear (*shādd al-tādj*) etc. The officers of the pen included the Vizier of the Pen (when there was no Vizier of the Sword), the heads of the chancellery and the various *dīwāns*, the Administrator of the Public Treasury, some religious officials like the Chief *Ḳāḍī*, the Chief Missionnary, the *Muḥtasib*, the Ḳurʾān-reciters and other court-officials, like the palace physicians and poets. All these officials resided in the capital, this list not including those of the provinces. See the article MIṢR, and for more details the descriptions of al-Maḳrīzī, al-Ḳalḳashandī, and the works cited above; also M. Canard, *Le cérémonial fâtimite et le cérémonial byzantin: essai de comparaison*, in *Byzantion*, xxi (1951) fasc. 2, 355-420. For Fāṭimid ceremonial, see TASHRĪFĀT; for the processions, see MAWĀKIB; for the insignia and emblems of sovereignty, see MARĀSIM.

5. Economic activity during the Fāṭimid period. ʿUbayd Allāh al-Mahdī had found North Africa in a flourishing condition, thanks to the development of town life. This prosperity permitted the first Fāṭimids to dispose of valuable resources and to set about the establishment of a powerful fleet and army.

In spite of disturbances, rebellions and disorders, Fāṭimid Egypt in general enjoyed great prosperity, thanks to the stability of its administrative and financial apparatus, its rich revenues arising from taxes and dues, the income from state-owned shops, trade and custom-dues, and the influx of gold from he mines of Nubia. The annual rise of the Nile enriched its soil and sustained its agriculture, so that numerous different crops were produced, and, except when the river failed to rise high enough or when the dams and canals were neglected, agricultural productivity was sufficient. The crops are listed in Ḥasan Ibrāhīm Ḥasan, *op. cit.*, 576 f.: wheat, barley, various vegetables, sugar-cane, dye-plants, animal-fodder; yet wheat had to be imported. The chief industrial crops were flax, sugar-cane, and, to a lesser degree, cotton. Production of wood—and that only soft-wood (sycamore, acacia)—was inadequate. For this subject see the geographers, ʿAbd al-Laṭīf al-Baghdādī, *Al-Ifāda wa 'l-iʿtibār bi-mā fī Miṣr min al-āthār*, tr. S. de Sacy, *Relation de l'Egypte par Abd al-Latîf*; D. Müller-Wodarg, *Die Landwirtschaft Aegyptens in der frühen Abbasidenzeit*, in *Isl.*, xxxii (1955); Ali Bahgat, *Les forêts en Egypte et leur administration au Moyen Age*, in *Bull. de l'Inst. d'Egypte*, 4e série, i (1901), 141-58.

Industry flourished. The first place was occupied by weaving, encouraged by the cultivation of flax and carried on in the region of Tinnis, Damietta, Dabīḳ [*q.v.*]. At Cairo also were manufactured silk-stuffs, with various names: it was into a '*ḳurḳubī tustarī*' silk, blue in colour, that al-Muʿizz had had the map of the various regions woven (*Khiṭaṭ*, i, 417). For the textile industry in Egypt see Serjeant, *Islamic Textiles*, in *Ars Islamica*, xiii-xiv (1948), 110 ff.; Ali Bahgat, *Les manufactures d'étoffes en Egypte au Moyen Age*, in *Mém. de l'Inst. Egyptien*, 1903; Ḥ. Zayyāt, *Thiyāb al-sharb*, in *Machriq*, xli/1, 137-41. Among the other industries, should be noted the wood-industry (for ship-building: on the arsenals see *Khiṭaṭ*, i, 193 f.), glass and crystal at al-Fusṭāṭ and Alexandria, pottery, ceramics, mosaic; metalwork (iron and copper: making of knives and scissors at Tinnīs), work in ivory and leather, paper-making, sugar, oil. For further details see Ḥ. Ibrāhīm Ḥasan's chapter *al-Ṣināʿa*.

In general, industry benefited from the luxury and pomp of the court, the liberal distribution of gifts and garments by the caliphs, and by the extravagance of viziers like al-Yāzūrī and al-Afḍal.

Trade, both internal and external, thrived, and Egypt carried on commercial relations with many countries. An important role in trade was played by the Jews, for the Fāṭimids do not seem to have imposed discriminatory customs tariffs, varying according to whether the traders were Jewish, Christian or Muslim. Trade with India was carried on through Ḳūṣ and Ayd͟hāb on the Red Sea, from whence the merchant-ships embarked. Cairo was in commercial relations with Abyssinia, Nubia, Constantinople (reached in twenty days' sailing), Italy—Amalfi, trade with which was particularly brisk (see Yaḥyā b. Saʿīd, *PO*, xxiii, 447; Rosen, *The Emperor Basil Bulgaroctonus* (in Russian), 293-6; Gay, *L'Italie méridionale . . .*, 585-6; Heyd, *Commerce du Levant*, i, 99, 104-6), Pisa, Genoa, Venice (which sent wood for ship-building, to the profound displeasure of the Byzantine Emperor)—, Sicily (twenty days' sailing), North Africa, Spain, and Europe, particularly via Sicily. These countries bought spices, clothes, etc., and sent in return the commodities which Egypt lacked or could not produce in sufficient quantities: wheat, iron, wood, silk (Fayyūm produced only a little), wool, and cheese (which the Jews consumed in large quantities).

Details on trade will be found in al-Idrīsī, in Nāṣir-i K͟husraw, in the articles by B. Lewis and S. M. Stern noted above for India, and in S. M. Stern, *An original document from the Fatimid Chancery concerning Italian merchants*, in *Mél. Levi Della Vida*, ii, Rome 1956, 529-38. The studies of S. D. Goitein are particularly important in this connexion: *Records from the Cairo Geniza*, in *Exhibition Amer. Or. Society*, April 1961; *From the Mediterranean to India: Documents on the trade to India, South Arabia and East Africa from the eleventh and twelfth centuries*, in *Speculum*, xxix; *The Jewish India merchants of the Middle Ages*, in *India and Israel*, 1953; *New light on the beginnings of the Karimi merchants*, in *JESHO*, i (1958); *The main industries of the Mediterranean area as reflected in the records of the Cairo Geniza*, *ibid.*, iv/2 (1961); *The Cairo Geniza as a source for the history of Moslem civilisation*, in *Studia Islamica*, iii (1955), 75-91; *The Documents of the Cairo Geniza as a source for Mediterranean social history*, in *JAOS*, lxxx/2 (1960), 91-100; *Petitions to Fatimid Caliphs from the Cairo Geniza*, in *Jew. Quart. Rev.*, xi (1954), 30 ff.; *L'état actuel de la recherche sur les documents de la Geniza du Caire*, in *REJ*, 3e série, 1959-60, i; *La Tunisie du XIe siècle à la lumière des documents de la Geniza du Caire*, in *Études d'Orientalisme dédiées à la mémoire de Lévi-Provençal*, ii, 1962, 559 ff. This author has promised a comprehensive work on the whole question. See also his *Jews and Arabs, their contact through the ages*, New York 1955 (French edition, *Juifs et Arabes*, Paris 1957). For Fāṭimid trade see also Ḥ. Ibr. Ḥasan, *op. cit.*, 595 ff.; Rashīd Muḥ. al-Barrāwī, *Ḥālat Miṣr al-iḳtiṣādiyya fī ʿahd al-Fāṭimiyyīn*, Cairo 1948; G. Wiet, *Hist. de la Nat. égypt.*, *L'Égypte arabe*, 303-8; idem, *Les communications en Égypte au Moyen Age*, in *Rev. de la Soc. Royale d'Economie politique, de statistique et de législation*, xxiv, Cairo 1933; R. Idris, *Commerce maritime et ḳirāḍ en Berbérie orientale*, in *JESHO*, 1961, 226-39.

Contemporary sources of the Fāṭimid period give a picture of the economic activity of Cairo and al-Fusṭāṭ, for example the Persian traveller, Nāṣir-i K͟husraw in his *Safar-nāma* (on whom see, besides Schefer, who edited and translated the work, Yahya el-Khachab, *Nâṣir e Ḫosraw*, Cairo 1940). Similarly it is after contemporary sources that al-Maḳrīzī described the extraordinary wealth of the treasuries (*k͟hazāʾin*) of the caliphs, and thus indicates how flourishing were luxury industries (*K͟hiṭaṭ*, i, 408 f.; cf. al-Ḳalḳas͟handī, *Ṣubḥ*, iii, 475 f.); following the *K. al-D͟hak͟hāʾir wa 'l-tuḥaf* of the Ḳāḍī al-Ras͟hīd b. al-Zubayr, he lists all the contents of al-Mustanṣir's treasury of garments and his treasury of jewels, perfumes and valuables (see the edition by M. Ḥamīdullāh, Kuwait 1959, 249 f. These treasuries, described also in Magued, *op. cit.*, ii, had earlier been studied by Quatremère, *Mém. géogr. et hist. sur l'Egypte*, ii, 366 ff., by Inostrant͟sev, *Toržestvenniy vežd fatimidskik͟h K͟halifov*, St. Petersburg 1905, 92 ff. and by Kahle, *Die Schätze der Fāṭimiden*, in *ZDMG*, xiv (1935), 329 ff. with trans. of *K͟hiṭaṭ*, i, 414-6. The inventory of the treasures of the palace of al-Afḍal (Ibn Muyassar, 57 f.), which it took al-Āmir and his secretaries forty days to make, also testifies to the same luxury and economic prosperity.

6. Cultural activity in the Fāṭimid period. In the Fāṭimid period an intense intellectual, literary and artistic activity developed.

In North Africa court-poets flourished, one of whom, Ibn Hāniʾ [*q.v.*], was a fervent Ismāʿīlī. On al-Iyādī and other poets, see H. H. ʿAbdal-Wahhāb, *Al-muntak͟hab al-madrasī min al-adab al-tūnisī*, Tunis 1944. The caliphs themselves composed verses (see the *Sīrat D͟jawd͟har*). The *dīwān* of Tamīm, the son of al-Muʿizz, has been published. Verses by him, and by various Fāṭimid caliphs, will be found in Muḥammad Ḥasan al-Aʿẓamī, *ʿAbḳariyyat al-Fāṭimiyyīn*, Cairo 1960, 133 f., 235 f. In North Africa too the *ḳāḍī* Abū Ḥanīfa al-Nuʿmān [*q.v.*] composed his historical, juridical and esoteric works, as did D͟jaʿfar b. Manṣūr al-Yaman [*q.v.*], who left the Yemen for North Africa after the death of his father. The caliphs al-Manṣūr and al-Muʿizz took part in these activities: some works of al-Nuʿmān, it is known, owe much to the collaboration of al-Muʿizz.

ʿUbayd Allāh was responsible for the foundation of the town of al-Mahdiyya, with its mosque, palace, and various public buildings; al-Manṣūr founded Ṣabra (al-Manṣūriyya) with its sumptuous palaces. On this subject see G. Marçais, *L'architecture musulmane d'Occident*, Paris 1954, 65-6, 69-70, 78-81, 89-92, 93-118; S. M. Zbiss, *Mahdia et Sabra-Mansoûriya, nouveaux documents d'art fâtimite d'Occident*, in *JA*, ccxliv (1956), 79-93; Ḥ. Ibr. Ḥasan, *op. cit.*, 524-6. On these two towns see also the *Sīrat D͟jawd͟har* (index).

In Egypt, cultural activity was still more vigorous. Poetry was cultivated by the caliphs themselves, and their court welcomed even non-Ismāʿīlī poets, such as ʿUmāra al-Yamanī [*q.v.*]. There was vigorous encouragement of works on religion, on the exposition of Ismāʿīlī doctrines, on the allegorical commentary of the Ḳurʾān, on philosophy, and on the popularization of scientific learning. The Fāṭimid period is characterized by a burst of intellectual curiosity analogous to that of the 18th century in Europe. See Ḥ. Ibr. Ḥasan, ch. xi; Muḥammad Kāmil Ḥusayn, *Fī adab Miṣr al-fāṭimiyya*, Cairo 1950; Brockelmann, S I, 323 f., 714 f.; Ivanow, *Rise*; and the articles on the philosophers Abū Ḥātim al-Rāzī, Ḥamīd al-Dīn al-Kirmānī, Aḥmad b. Ibrāhīm al-Nīsābūrī, al-Muʾayyad fi 'l-Dīn al-S͟hīrāzī, Ḥātim b. Ibrāhīm al-Ḥāmidī, etc., and on the Encyclopaedia of the Ik͟hwān al-Ṣafāʾ.

The Fāṭimid period was also distinguished by men of learning: the mathematician Ibn Hayt͟ham al-Baṣrī, invited to Egypt by al-Ḥākim; the astronomer

ʿAlī b. Yūnus al-Ṣadafī, author of *al-Zīdj al-Ḥākimī*; the physicians Ibn Saʿīd al-Tamīmī, in the entourage of Ibn Killis, Mūsā b. Alʿazār al-Isrāʾīlī and his sons Isḥāḳ and Ismāʿīl, in the reigns of al-Muʿizz and al-ʿAzīz, the famous Ibn Riḍwān, whose dispute with Ibn Buṭlān has been studied by J. Schacht and M. Meyerhof, *The medical controversy between Ibn Buṭlān of Baghdad and Ibn Riḍwān of Cairo* (publication no. 13 of the Faculty of Arts of the Egyptian University), Cairo 1937 (cf. J. Schacht, *Ueber den Hellenismus in Baghdad und Cairo*, in *ZDMG*, xc/xv (1936), 526 ff.), Manṣūr b. Sahlān b. Muḳashshir, al-Ḥākim's Christian physician (cf. Yaḥyā b. Saʿīd, *PO*, xxiii, 464).

The Fāṭimid period was also rich in authors on various subjects; the historians Ibn Zūlāḳ, al-Musabbiḥī, al-Kuḍāʾī, the author of *K. al-Diyārāt*, al-Shābushtī, the librarian of al-ʿAzīz, al-Muhallabī, the author of a geographical work composed for al-ʿAzīz, Ibn al-Maʾmūn al-Baṭāʾihī, son of the vizier, an important source of al-Maḳrīzī, the *ḳāḍī* al-Rashīd b. al-Zubayr, author of the *K. al-Dhakhāʾir wa 'l-tuḥaf*, Ibn al-Ṣayrafī, al-Ḳurṭī, who composed his history in the reign of the last Fāṭimid caliph, etc. [*qq.v.*].

The Fāṭimid period, as G. Wiet has also said, is "une des plus passionantes de l'histoire de l'Egypte musulmane". The dynasty, born of an original ideological movement within Shīʿism which developed to a degree hitherto unknown and aroused extraordinary devotion for the triumph of the cause, established itself by force of arms in North Africa and formed a powerful empire in Egypt. To them were turned the eyes and aspirations of the Ismāʿīlīs throughout the Muslim world and their sympathizers. The history of this dynasty dominates the history of the Mediterranean Near East for two centuries. Having suffered from the prejudices and hostility of the Sunnīs, it has not always been described by Sunnī writers with understanding; but for some years now it had enjoyed a renewal of interest.

The Fāṭimid dynasty had periods of greatness, thanks to its administrative and financial organization, its economic development, the flourishing intellectual and artistic activity, the pomp of court and palace, which was, as William of Tyre testifies, maintained up to the end, the ceremonial and ostentatious feasts, which immediately provoke comparison with Constantinople and far surpass what had previously been known at Baghdād. But it suffered also periods of misery and famine, bloody struggles between military factions, and a disastrous end, among the intrigues of rival viziers appealing for the intervention of foreign powers. Its history is full of contrasts. Both its greatness and its decadence offer attractive material to the historian and confer upon the dynasty a niche of its own in history.

Bibliography: To the Arab historians who are listed by M. ʿAbd Allāh ʿInān in his *Miṣr al-islāmiyya*, Cairo 1931, 34 ff. and by Ḥasan Ibrāhīm Ḥasan add: Ibn Ẓāfir, Ms. Br. Mus. Or. 3685, ff. 41 f.; Ibn al-Dawādārī, *Die Chronik des Ibn ad-Dawādārī, Sechster Teil: Der Bericht über die Fatimiden*, ed. Ṣalāḥ ad-Dīn al-Munaǧǧid, Cairo 1961 (Deutsches Arch. Inst. Kairo, Quellen zur Gesch. des isl. Aegyptens 1 f.), reviewed by B. Lewis in *BSOAS*, xxvi (1963), 429-31. For Sibṭ Ibn al-Djawzī, add MS Paris 5866, year 358/969 onwards. Several sources are discussed in the preface to Wüstenfeld, *Gesch. der Fatimiden-Chalifen* and in C. H. Becker, *Beiträge zur Gesch. Aegyptens unter dem Islam*, with, in particular, a study on a fragment of al-Musabbiḥī. Cl. Cahen, *Quelques chroniques anciennes relatives aux derniers Fatimides*, in *Bull. de l'IFAO*, xxxvii (1937), has examined a certain number of sources used by Ibn al-Furāt and drawn attention to the value as a source of the Shīʿī Ibn Abī Ṭayyiʾ. For North Africa, the chronicle of Abū Zakariyyāʾ is now accessible in a new French translation by R. Le Tourneau and R. Idris, in *Revue Africaine*, 1960-2. On Fāṭimid coins, besides the standard coin catalogues and numismatic handbooks, see: H. Sauvaire, *Matériaux pour servir à l'hist. de la numismatique* ..., in *JA*, xv (1880), xix (1882); J. Farrugia de Candia, *Monnaies fatimites du Musée du Bardo*, in *RT*, xxvii-xxviii (1936) and xxix (1937); M. Troussel, *Les monnaies d'or musulmanes du Cabinet des Médailles du Musée de Constantine*, in *Rec. des Not. et Mém. de la Soc. Arch. de Constantine*, lxv (1942); G. C. Miles, *Fatimid coins in the collection of the Univ. Museum Philadelphia and the American Numismatic Society*, New York, Amer. Num. Soc., lii (1951); A. S. Ehrenkreutz, *Studies in the Monetary history of the Near East in the Middle Ages*, in *JESHO*, 1959, 1963, 1964; id., *Contribution to the monetary history of Egypt in the Middle Ages*, in *BSOAS*, xvi (1954).—To works mentioned in the course of the article add Hodgson, *The Order of Assassins*, The Hague 1955; S. M. Stern, *Three petitions of the Fatimid period*, in *Oriens*, 1962, 172-209 and *A Fatimid decree of the year 524/1130*, in *BSOAS*, 1960, 439 ff.; A. Grohmann and P. Labīb, *Ein Fatimidenerlass vom Jahre 415 AH (1024 AD)*, in *RSO*, 1957, 641 ff.; G. Levi Della Vida, *A marriage contract on parchment from Fatimite Egypt*, in *Eretz-Israel*, xii (1963).—For a general survey of the history of the Fāṭimids, besides the works of S. Lane-Poole, *A history of Egypt in the Middle Ages*², London 1914, and *The Mohammedan dynasties*, London 1894, of Wüstenfeld, and of De Lacy O'Leary, *A short history of the Fatimid Khalifate*, London 1923, see G. Wiet, *Précis de l'histoire de l'Egypte* and *Histoire de la Nation égyptienne, L'Egypte arabe*, cited above.

(M. Canard)

FĀṬIMID ART. The political history of the Fāṭimids forms an indispensable background to an understanding of the development of their art. It allows us to distinguish two successive periods in it: one Ifrīḳiyan period, which extends from 308/908, the date of the installation of the Mahdī in Ḳayrawān and of the foundation of al-Mahdiyya, until 362/973, which saw the departure of al-Muʿizz and the establishment of Cairo as the city of the Caliphs; then an Egyptian period, which lasts from 362/973 up to the collapse of the Caliphate in 567/1171. To this division in time a geographical division must be added. The art which the Fāṭimids transplanted into Egypt continued to flourish in eastern 'Barbary', thanks to the Zīrids and the Ḥammādids, vassals of Cairo, and it extended its influence over both Muslim and Norman Sicily.

Al-Mahdiyya, the city of the Mahdī on the Tunisian coast, preserves, apart from the ruins of its Fāṭimid fortifications, a mosque and traces of the palace of al-Ḳaʾim. The mosque, very much altered, has a porch projecting in front whose central bay is framed on either side by two storeys of niches. This motif, which reminds us of Roman triumphal arches, was to pass into the Fāṭimid style of Egypt. The palace of al-Ḳāʾim (322-34/934-46) which stood opposite the palace of the Mahdī, his father, still keeps its beautifully constructed walls, with an entrance jutting out from the façade, and a hall of state whose floor is covered with a stone mosaic, the last North African use of this kind of pavement. A palace of Ṣabra Manṣūriyya at the gates of Ḳayrawān seems to date from the time of the Fāṭimid Caliph al-Manṣūr (334-41/946-53). Here we see a large hall, a kind of ante-room from which, side by side, open three deep rooms, the central one of which, having no front wall, appears in the shape of an *īwān*. A similar arrangement relates this palace of Ṣabra, which is presumed Fāṭimid, to the Ṭūlūnid houses of Fusṭāṭ. It reveals connexions between Egypt and Ifrīḳiya prior to the departure of the Caliph al-Muʿizz.

Even before this departure took place, the Fāṭimid general, al-Djawhar, had undertaken the construction in Cairo of the mosque of al-Azhar, which was to be considerably enlarged later on and to become the Muslim university which we know to-day. The original sanctuary shows by its plan and decorations the survival of the Ṭūlūnid tradition; but the influence of Ifrīḳiya, whence the new masters of the country came, is also to be found. The five transversal aisles which make up the hall of prayer, as in the mosque of Ibn Ṭūlūn, are interrupted in the middle by a perpendicular aisle which is wider, bordered with columns joined in pairs and having a cupola at each end, probably influenced by the Great Mosque of Ḳayrawān.

The mosque of al-Ḥākim (384-94/990-1003) combines in the same way elements imported from Ifrīḳiya and elements preserved from Ṭūlūnid architecture. The porch, projecting from the front of the building and covered by a vault giving entrance to the vast court-yard, seems Ifrīḳiyan, inspired by the mosque of Mahdiyya. The influence of the mosque of Ibn Ṭūlūn shows itself in the hall of prayer with its five transversal aisles, whose *arcs brisés* rest on brick pillars cantoned with small false columns. The two minarets which rise at the front angles of the mosque have a cylindrical core enveloped in a solid mass of square design. Like that of the porch, the ornamentation of these towers in very low relief employing geometrical and vegetal designs marks a decisive step in the elaboration of Muslim decorative art. One hundred and twenty-two years later than the mosque of al-Ḥākim, the little al-Aḳmar mosque (519/1125) is worth notice also for the ornamentation on its façade. The entrance in the projecting forepart of the building is ornamented with a great high-relief flanked by two storeys of niches.

The mosque of al-Ṣāliḥ Ṭalāʾiʿ is the latest in date of the Fāṭimid mosques (555/1160). Built above shops, its façade is made up of two projecting foreparts joined by a portico. The sanctuary has three transversal aisles, the central passage which leads up to the *miḥrāb* being distinguished only by a wider separation of the pillars.

Apart from these mosques, the Fāṭimid period saw the construction of a great number of mausoleums such as those of al-Djaʿfarī, Sayyida ʿĀtika, al-Ḥaṣawātī and Shaykh Yūnus. They consist traditionally of a square chamber with a cupola. This cupola is supported by squinches at the four corners. In the 6th/12th century these squinches multiplied and were superimposed upon each other, producing corbels of *muḳarnas* (= stalactites), whose original model seems likely to have come from Persia.

A tomb constitutes at any rate the essential element of the *mashhad* of al-Djuyūshī, built in 478/1085 on the Muḳaṭṭam Hill by the *wazīr* Badr al-Djamālī to hold his sepulchre. This building consists of four parts: a front portion, surmounted by the minaret, where the door is situated; a middle portion with a court flanked by two chambers with wagons-vaulted roofs; at the back there is a sanctuary of three aisles covered with herring-bone vaulting and a great cupola in front of the *miḥrāb*; finally there is the chamber of the tomb itself which is joined laterally to the sanctuary. Certain peculiarities may be observed in this monument which were to perpetuate themselves in Egyptian art: the minaret formed of three towers one on top of the other, two square in design and one octagonal which surmounts a cornice of *muḳarnas* and is capped by a dome, a possible prototype of the future minarets of Cairo. Equally worth noticing is the importance given to the cupola in the sanctuary, the sharp-angled profile of this cupola, and the outline analogous with the so-called "Persian" arches whose two vertical sides are bent to form a right-angle at the summit.

Between 480/1087 and 484/1091, the same all-powerful *wazīr*, Badr al-Djamālī, gave Cairo a new city wall. Armenian by birth and surrounding himself with Armenian troops, he brought from his country architects to whom the Fāṭimid capital owes three of its most beautiful buildings, the three gates called Bāb Zuwayla, Bāb al-Naṣr and Bāb al-Futūḥ. Construction and ornamentation, the magnificence of the walls, the outline of the vaults and semi-circular arches, everything in these majestic entrances to the city springs from Hellenistic tradition.

Whereas the palaces known from manuscripts to have been built by Fāṭimid Caliphs in the centre of Cairo have disappeared, those of the Ḳalʿa of the Banū Ḥammād preserve, perhaps, the record of their civil foundations. This Berber capital was built among the mountains of eastern Algeria at the beginning of the 5th/11th century, but it profited greatly by the ruin of Ḳayrawān, victim of the invasion of the Banū Hilāl, and at the end of this same century knew a brief period of splendour. A mosque whose minaret dominates the vast field of ruins, traces of palaces of which two, the keep of Ḳaṣr al-Manār (the Castle of the Lighthouse) and the Dār al-Baḥr (the Palace of the Lake), were excavated in 1908 and a third is now being excavated, give us knowledge of this North African architecture nourished by oriental influences, inspired not only by Egypt but also by ʿIrāḳ and Persia. It suffices to remember the long niches which decorate the front of the minaret and those of the palaces, a theme deeply imprinted in the architecture of the Sāsānids, the mirror of water in the court-yard of Dār al-Baḥr, the inlaid ceramic work paving and lining the great halls where faïence with metallic reflections is used, and finally the *muḳarnas* (stalactites), proved to be an Iranian invention, whose first use in the Islamic west is to be found at the Ḳalʿa.

The excavations of the Ḳalʿa have filled an important gap in our knowledge. Bougie, to which the Banū Ḥammād moved at the beginning of the 6th/12th century, does not provide a similar store of riches. Only some parts of the city wall and the great stone arch, which formed the entry to the harbour and its boats, have survived out of the buildings of the second Ḥammādid capital.

Nevertheless we are inclined to regard Bougie as an important step on the road taken by Fāṭimid art in its penetration of Sicily; many indications authorize this belief. It was from Bougie undoubtedly as well as from al-Mahdiyya, refuge of the last

Zīrids, or from the Tunis of the Banū Khurāsān, rather than from Cairo, that Palermo received the ground-plan of the pavilions on its outskirts. The Ḥammādid palaces help us to understand better the Ziza and Cuba of the Norman kings.

Within the Maghrib and as far as Andalusia, there is no place that has not to some extent been influenced by Fāṭimid art. To this distant influence can be attributed the adoption by the Islamic west of *muḳarnas* (stalactites) and inlays of enamelled clay in the Almohad period.

The propagation of these art forms can be explained by the journeys of artisans (the ruin of the cities of eastern 'Barbary' following on the invasion of the nomad Arabs must have provoked numerous departures among them) and also by the export of *objets d'art* from one place to another.

Fāṭimid Egypt produced indeed a remarkable amount of activity in the decorative arts and an amazing development of luxury. The opulence of the Caliphs and the high functionaries is vouched for by Arab authors such as al-Maḳrīzī who describes the treasure of the Caliph al-Mustanṣir, or Ibn Muyassar enumerating the riches of the *wazīr* al-Afḍal, son of Badr al-Djamālī. The artistic creations of the Fāṭimid epoch above all in Egypt but sometimes also in Spain (the kinship between the works of the two countries leaves us sometimes in doubt of their origin) are the glory of European museums and church treasures.

In the 11th and 12th centuries techniques concerned with bronze, faïence, glass and cut crystal, jewels and textiles were the most flourishing and show an extremely refined artistic taste. The same decorative elements were used as in monumental sculpture: lettering, interlacing, either star-shaped and geometrical or based on plant and occasionally animal motifs. Indeed, notwithstanding strict orthodoxy, there were many representations of living creatures both human and animal. Such in the Cairo Museum are the friezes in carved wood from a Fāṭimid palace displaying musicians, dancers and hunters, or the ewers and fountain motifs in bronze of which the most celebrated is the griffin in the Campo Santo at Pisa, or the gilded faïences with representations of persons, or the brocades decorated with animals confronting each other. The freedom of the Shīʿī masters with regard to the *sunna* undoubtedly explains the attitude of the artisans in the matter of iconography, but certainly another factor was the personality of these artisans and the traditions which they continued. Fāṭimid art is a cross-roads of influences, as will have been made clear by what has been said so far. To architectural elements from Ifrīḳiya, to the Ṭūlūnid and Mesopotamian heritage, to the Syrian contribution which shows itself in military construction, is added, above all in ornamentation and the decorative arts, the legacy of Persia which the common faith united with the masters of Egypt, and, no less important, the Hellenistic legacy handed down by the Copts. It is impossible to exaggerate the part played by the Christians of Egypt in the formation of the Fāṭimid style and of that which we designate by the rather vague but traditional name of arabesque.

Bibliography: G. Wiet and L. Hautecœur, *Les Mosquées du Caire*, 2 vols., Cairo 1932; G. Wiet, *L'exposition d'art persan à Londres*, in *Syria*, 1932; Arnold, *Painting in Islam*, Oxford 1928, 22; *The mosques of Egypt*, Publ. of Ministry of Wakfs, chap. 3; K. A. C. Creswell, *The Muslim architecture of Egypt*, Oxford 1952; idem, *The great salients of the mosque of al-Ḥākim*, in *JRAS*, 1923; idem, *A bibliography of painting in Islam*, Publ. of IFAO, Cairo, Art Islamique, I, Cairo 1953; idem, *A bibliography of glass and rock crystal*, in *Bull. of the Fac. of Arts*, xiv, Cairo 1952; M. S. Briggs, *Muhammedan architecture in Egypt and Palestine*, Oxford 1924; M. van Berchem, *Matériaux pour un Corpus inscriptionum arabicarum, Égypte*, I; idem, *Notes d'archéologie arabe*, in *JA*, xvii (1891), 429 ff.; idem, *Une mosquée du temps des Fāṭimides*, in *MIE*, ii (1889); S. Flury, *Die Ornamente der Hakkim und Azhar Moschee*, Heidelberg 1912; idem, *Islamische Schriftbänder*, Bâle-Paris 1920; V. Monneret de Villard, *La necropoli musulmana di Aswan*, Cairo 1930; idem *Le pitture musulmane al sofitto della Capella Palatina in Palermo*, Rome 1950; L. de Beylié, *La Kalaa des Beni Hammad*, Paris 1909; G. Marçais, *L'architecture musulmane d'Occident*, Paris 1954; idem, *Les figures d'hommes et de bêtes d'époque fatimite*, in *Mélanges Maspéro*, ii; idem, *Les Poteries et faiences de la Qalʿa des Beni Hammad*, Constantine 1913; G. Migeon, *Manuel d'art musulman*, 2 vols., Paris 1927; Pauty and Wiet, *Les bois sculptés jusqu'à l'époque ayyoubide*, Cairo 1931; Panty, *Bois sculptés d'églises coptes*, Cairo 1930; J. David-Weill, *Les bois à épigraphes jusqu'à l'époque mamlouke*, Cairo 1931; A. Bahgat Bey and F. Massoul, *La céramique musulmane d'Égypte*, Cairo 1930; E. Kühnel, *Islamische Stoffe aus Agyptischen Gräbern*, Berlin 1927; idem, *The textile Museum. Catal. of dated Ṭirāz Fabrics*, Washington 1953, 59 sq.; R. Ettinghausen, *Painting in the Fatimid period; A reconstruction*, in *Ars Islamica*, ix (1942), 112-24; Lane-Poole, *The art of the Saracens in Egypt*, London 1886; R. Pfister, *Toiles à inscriptions abbasides et fatimides*, in *Bull. d'Ét. Or.*, Damascus xi (1948), 47-90; Zakī Muḥammad Ḥasan, *al-Fann al-islāmī fī Miṣr*, 1935; idem, *Zakhārīf al-mansūdjāt al-ḳibṭiyya*, in *Rev. de la Fac. des Let. de l'Univ. du Caire*, xii/1 (1950); D. S. Rice, *A drawing of the Faṭimid period*, in *BSOAS*, xxi/1 (1958). See also the bibl. given by Ḥ. Ibr. Ḥasan, and for a comprehensive survey, G. Wiet, *Précis de l'Hist. de l'Égypte*, Cairo 1932, 199-216. For the Faṭimid inscriptions, see the *Corpus inscriptionum arabicarum* and G. Wiet, *Nouvelles inscriptions fâṭimides*, in *Bull. de l'Inst. Egypt.*, xxiv (1941-2), 145-58 and *Une nouvelle inscription fâṭimide au Caire*, in *JA*, 1961, 13-20. For G. Wiet's other works relating to the Fāṭimid period, see the *Bibliographie de l'œuvre scientifique de G. Wiet*, by A. Raymond, in *Bull. de l'IFAO*, Cairo, xlix (1960), ix-xxiv. The reader should consult also *Ars Islamica*. (G. Marçais)

FAṬĪN, pseudonym of **DĀWŪD**, (1229-83/1814-67), Turkish biographer and poet, the last of the Ottoman *tedhkire*-writers. He was born in Drama, in Western Thrace, the son of the local notable Ḥādjdjī Khālid Bey. After spending several years in Egypt, wheιe his uncle lived, he returned to Istanbul and occupied various minor posts in government offices.

His *dīwān*, published posthumously by his son, shows him as a mediocre poet. His main work, the *Khātimat al-ashʿār*, is the continuation of the *tedhkire* of Ṣafāʾī (completed in 1132/1720) and that of Sālim (completed 1134/1721) and contains the biographies of poets from 1135/1722 to his own day.

Completed in 1269/1852 and printed lithographically in Istanbul in 1271/1855, Faṭīn's *Tedhkire* is of particular use for the biographies of his own contemporaries.

Bibliography: Faṭīn, *Dīwān*, Istanbul 1288 (with an introduction on Faṭīn's life); Babinger, 359; Ibnülemin Mahmud Kemal Inal, *Son asır türk şairleri*, Istanbul 1930, i, 8; ii, 367; Orhan F. Köprülü, in *IA*, s.v. An incomplete revised edition of the *Khātimat al-ashʿār*, made by Shināsī, has now been found by Ö. F. Akün: see *Türk Dili ve Edebiyatı Dergisi*, xi (1961), 66-98.

(Fahir İz)

FATRA (Ar.), which in general means a relaxing, and then an interval of time (*e.g.*, the modern *fatrat al-intiḳāl* "period of transition"), is applied more particularly to the period separating two prophets or two successive messengers (*rasūl*); al-Djāḥiẓ (*Rasāʾil*, ed. Sandūbī, Cairo 1352/1933, 133-4), in his exposition of prophetic history, uses the term *fatra* for the end of the period separating two prophets, making it clear that the "slackening" (of observance of the earlier prophet's teachings) is not a "break" (*ḳaṭʿa*). Al-Masʿūdī (*Murūdj*, iii, 85) for example uses this term to denote the lapse of time that intervened between Hūd [*q.v.*] and Ṣāliḥ [*q.v.*], but in its more current usage (see *LA*, s.v.) it is applied to the period without prophets from the time of Jesus Christ to Muḥammad. It seems that the Muslims who had heard of a considerable number of pre-Christian prophets did not take long to remark the gap of six centuries which was revealed between Jesus and Muḥammad; and so they attempted, if not to fill this gap, at least to discover personages who had rejected the worship of idols without necessarily adopting Judaism or Christianity, lived a more or less ascetic life and, in some instances, had announced the coming of the Prophet. Ibn Ḳutayba, probably on the basis of sources of the 2nd/8th century, is the first, it seems, to enumerate (*Maʿārif*, ed. ʿUkāsha, Cairo 1960, 58) "the men who had a religion before the mission of the Prophet"; in this way he names Riʾāb al-Shannī, Waraḳa b. Nawfal, Zayd b. ʿAmr b. Nufayl, Umayya b. Abi 'l-Ṣalt, Asʿad Abū Karib, Ḳuss b. Sāʿida, Ṣirma b. Abī Anas, Khālid b. Sinān. But he does not use the word *fatra*, whilst in the following century al-Masʿūdī, who clearly relies on the *Maʿārif*, describes as *ahl al-fatra* (*Murūdj*, i, 124-48) the personages named by Ibn Ḳutayba, to whom he adds some others who, he states, "have believed in a single God and in the resurrection". He even asserts that two of them, Ḥanẓala b. Ṣafwān [*q.v.*] and Khālid b. Sinān, are regarded as prophets by part of the Muslim community.

In later times the term *fatra* was also applied, by analogy, to periods of political interregnum, as for example in Spain after the collapse of the Caliphate and in the Ottoman Empire after the capture and death of Bāyazīd I. (Ch. Pellat)

FATTĀḤĪ, Persian poet of the Tīmūrid period, born at Nīshāpūr at an unspecified date, died in 852 or 853/1448-9. His name was in fact Muḥammad Yaḥyā b. Sībak, and the *takhalluṣ* "Fattāḥī" is simply derived from the anagram of the Arabic translation of his Persian name Sībak ("little apple", Ar. *tuffāḥ* "apple"). His most famous work is the *mathnawī* of about 5,000 distichs in *hazadj* metre (⏑– – –/⏑– – –/⏑– – –), entitled *Dastūr-i ʿushshāḳ* (The rule of lovers) and known also by the title *Ḥusn u-Dil* (Beauty and Heart), from the names of its two allegorical protagonists. It was completed in 840/1436-7; as, towards the end, the author mentions the plague of 838/1434-5, its composition must have been spread over several years. It is impossible in a few lines to summarize the contents of this poem in which all the "concepts" of the unique but varied "drama of love" of the classical Persian *ghazal* appear in the form of persons: Heart (*dil*), son of King Intellect (*ʿaḳl*), Beauty (*ḥusn*), daughter of King Love (*ʿishḳ*), Glance (*naẓar*), Mouth (*dahān*), Eyelash (*muzha*), Body (*badan*), Tresses (*zulf*), Rival (*raḳīb*), etc., so much so that the poem has justly been called an "Index der Bildersprache der orientalischen Erotik". The style is overloaded with rhetorical embellishments (particularly in the letters exchanged between the two lovers), and, despite its undoubted interest from the point of view of knowledge of the metaphorical language of Persian lyrics, the general effect of the poem finally becomes somewhat tedious as a result of the perpetual use of allegory. However, it is not accurate to speak of "decadence", as certain contemporary Persian critics have done. It was a question of searching for new ways to excape from the "perfect" world of Ḥāfiẓian symbolism. The living symbol is here replaced by allegory by means of the personification of abstract concepts, a device also used by other poets of the period (*e.g.*, Kātibī), which became one of the basic elements of what is called the "Indian style". Another element of this style which was already in existence at that period and even occurs in Fattāḥī is the marked tendency to use hyperbole (in the description of a perfectly smooth castle wall, he writes "the stones of its wall were so limpid that they reflected a hair several *farsangs* away"); moreover, the sophistication of the psychological study of the characters (a matter in which Niẓāmī excelled, but here carried to extremes), the use of bookish terms in metaphors (the letters of the alphabet, for example) or of words denoting objects in current use, are all elements which appeared in the "Indian style", though functioning in a new way. More readable (and an excellent example of Persian prose intermingled with verse), but perhaps less interesting from the point of view of style, is the summary in prose of the same poem which Fattāḥī made under the title *Ḥusn u-dil*. In addition, the poet also wrote a *Shabistān-i khayāl* (Bedroom of Fantasy), again in verse and prose (completed in 843/1439-40), a short poem entitled *Taʿbīr-nāma* (Book of interpretation of dreams), a *Kitāb-i Asrārī wa-khumārī* (unpublished, and of which only very few mss. exist; perhaps a discussion between a wine drinker and a hashish smoker, with *taḍmīn* (insertion of lines from famous poets). The titles alone suffice to show the new orientations for widening the content of poetry in this period which, far from being decadent, lays the foundations for possible new stylistic developments. But these developments continued along these lines perhaps more in "outer Iran" (meaning India, Central Asia and Ottoman Turkey) than in Iran proper. In fact, if it is true that Fattāḥī's secluded life as a dervish left him comparatively little known in Iran, the success of his narrative, in which personified concepts took a dramatic part (this seems to be an invention and he himself was aware of its originality, as he was to state in his own poem) was very great: he was imitated in verse and prose in various Islamic literatures. For India, besides the *Sab-ras* of Wadjhī (1044/1635), in Deccan Urdu prose, we should mention Khwādja Muḥammad Bīdil who, in 1094/1683, attempted an adaptation of it into elaborate Persian prose, while an unpublished *mathnawī*, also in Persian, is the work of a certain Dāwūd Elči (1054/1644) and is preserved in the Bombay University Library. In addition, Dhawḳī (1108/1697),

Mud̲j̲rimī (1086/1675), Sayyid Muḥammad Walī Allāh Ḳādirī (about 1180/1766) imitated him in Deccan Urdu, and Kh̲ʷād̲j̲a (1264/1848) wrote on the same subject in northern Urdu. In Ottoman Turkish he was imitated by Lāmiʿī (d. 937/1531), Āhī (d. 923/1517) and Walī Ṣidḳī.

Bibliography: Dawlat S̲h̲āh, *Tad̲h̲kirat al-s̲h̲uʿarāʾ*, 417-8; ʿAlī S̲h̲īr Nawāʾī, *Mad̲j̲ālis al-nafāʾis*, 13, 135; Kh̲ʷāndamīr, *Ḥabīb al-siyar*, iii/3, 108, 133; Yār-i S̲h̲āṭir, *S̲h̲iʿr-i fārsī dar ʿahd-i S̲h̲āhrūk̲h̲*, Tehran 1334 ff., 180-4 and *passim*; J. Rypka, *Iranische Literaturgeschichte*, Leipzig 1959, 275; A. Bausani, *Storia delle letterature del Pakistan*, Milan 1958, 111-7 (with a detailed résumé of the poem). The *Ḥusn u-dil* in prose has been translated into English (A. Browne, Dublin 1801; W. Price, 1828) and German (Dvořák, Vienna 1889, with the Persian text, an introduction and important notes). The *Dastūr-i ʿus̲h̲s̲h̲āḳ* has been published by Greenshields (Berlin 1926). Part of the *S̲h̲abistān-i k̲h̲ayāl* (ch. I) has been translated by Ethé (Leipzig 1865, 1868).

(A. Bausani)

FATWĀ, opinion on a point of law, the term "law" applying, in Islam, to all civil or religious matters. The act of giving a *fatwā* is a *futyā* or *iftāʾ*; —the same term is used to denote the profession of the adviser;—the person who gives a *fatwā*, or is engaged in that profession, is a *muftī*;—the person who asks for a *fatwā* is a *mustaftī*.

The institution of the *futyā* corresponds with the Roman institution of *jus respondendi* and is comparable with it in many respects.

The need for legal advice was soon felt in Islam. The ever-increasing number of the adherents of the new religion, which governed, through its totalitarian character, the temporal as well as the spiritual aspects of daily life, and the survival of the laws and customs of the conquered territories, which had to be harmonized, in some way or another, with novel precepts and integrated within the nascent Muslim *corpus juris*, necessitated a continual recourse to the opinions of competent persons.

Furthermore, the *muftīs*, like the *prudentes* of Roman law, played a considerable part in building up the structure of Islamic law. Compilations of "responsa" by *muftīs* of repute count among the most important legal manuals.

The conditions required by the classical doctrine for the exercise of the profession, or even for the delivery of a *fatwā*, are: Islam, integrity or *ʿadāla* [see ʿAdl], legal knowledge (*id̲j̲tihād*), or the ability to reach, by personal reasoning, the solution of a problem. Accordingly, authors observe that, in those times when there exist no jurists having this ability but only those who report the opinion of their predecessors, their opinions do not constitute *fatwās* properly so-called but simple 'reports of opinion'.

As opposed to a judge, a *muftī* can be a woman, a slave, a blind or dumb person (except in the case of a *muftī* who is a public official).

The afore-mentioned conditions are equally required whether it is a case of an individual and isolated *fatwā* being given or of *futyā* being exercised in a professional capacity.

Fatwās may be given to private individuals, to magistrates in the exercise of their profession, and to any other authorities. The law, indeed, particularly urges magistrates to seek opinions; and in those countries, like Muslim Spain, where the institution of the *s̲h̲ūrā* [*q.v.*] developed, permanent *muftīs* were attached to the courts of magistrates as advisers (*mus̲h̲āwir*).

In principle *futyā* was an independent profession, but became associated with public authority in a variety of ways. The State controlled the exercise of the profession, such control normally being one of the functions of the magistrate, who could, in necessary cases, subject a *muftī* to "interdiction". From the 1st/7th century, the State itself undertook the designation of jurists qualified to act as *muftīs* in order to influence the choice made by private individuals. Later, official posts of *futyā* were created, and it thus became a public office, ranking, like the judicial magistracy, in the category of religious functions. Holders of these posts, however, remained at the service of private individuals; but they were more directly attached to the public service. Thus in the Mamlūk State, these *muftīs* formed part of the Council of Justice (*mad̲j̲lis al-maẓālim*) of the Sultan and the provincial governors.

At certain periods and in certain areas, as in the Ottoman Empire, the function of *muftī* could be combined with that of magistrate; the holder of the office was merely forbidden to give *fatwās* in relation to a legal action which was brought in his court.

The public function of *futyā* is without prejudice to the private exercise of the profession. However, with the introduction of codes and their provisions borrowed from European systems in almost all the branches of law, the profession has fallen into disuse; even in those matters which, like personal status and *waḳfs*, are still generally governed by the principles of Islamic law, the practice of *fatwās* seems to be becoming obsolescent.

It remains only as a public office, rather in the manner of a historical survival, stamped with the Islamic character of the State. Furthermore, Islamic states with a modern political structure no longer have recourse to the holders of this office in order to establish the legitimacy of their legislative activities. In States where the Islamic community forms only a part of the total population—Lebanon, for example—the function of *futyā* has undergone a remarkable transformation: the "Mufti of the Republic" has become "the religious leader of the community and its representative, in this respect, with the authorities"; he is the head of all the officials of the Muslim cult and the service of *waḳfs*; he is elected for life by a college composed of qualified members of the community (Legislative Decree 18, of 13 January 1955). There remain, however, *muftīs* in the traditional sense, under the authority of the "Mufti of the Republic".

Bibliography: Ibn K̲h̲aldūn, *Muḳaddima*, ed. Imprimerie Belles-Lettres, Beyrouth, 220 (Eng. tr., Rosenthal, i, 451 ff.); Tyan, *Histoire de l'organisation judiciaire en pays d'Islam*, in *Ann. Univer. de Lyon*, i, 1938, first ed., 323 ff. and the references there indicated; Juynboll, *Handbuch des islāmischen Gesetzes*, Leiden 1910, 55 ff.; Ibn Nud̲j̲aym, *al-Baḥr al-rāʾiḳ*, Cairo n.d., 265 ff.; Damas Efendi, *Mad̲j̲maʿ al-anhur*, Istanbul 1328/1910, 154 ff. (E. Tyan)

ii.—Ottoman Empire

Among the early Ottomans the function of *iftāʾ* appears to have been of the same casual nature it had hitherto exhibited in all other regions of Islamic domination: anyone prominent for his learning and piety could be asked to act as a mutually acceptable arbiter in a dispute involving a point of law and his opinion was allowed to be decisive. However, as the orderly administration of the rapidly expanding empire was seen to demand a more unified system of legal practice, such authority was gradually confined to a few individuals of public position (the *ḳāḍi 'l-ʿasker*s, the preceptors of the Sultans, the *ḳāḍī*s of great cities like Bursa and Edirne, etc.) to whom appeal could be made against the decisions of lesser *müftī*s. But this, too, was unsatisfactory as it seemed to secularize the divine law and make it an instrument of the ruler's will; sometime, therefore, in the reign of Murād II (824-55/1421-51) the right to issue *fetwā*s was vested exclusively in an individual known as the *shaykh al-islām* [*q.v.*], who, although appointed by the Sultan, had no part in the councils of the state, received no fees for the decisions he delivered, and was held to be above worldly considerations. He had no contact with the litigants or their advocates; every matter to be put before him was drafted in hypothetical terms by a clerk of the *fetwā odasī* known as the *müsweddedji* and examined as to correctness of presentation by another clerk of the same office, the *mümeyyiz*, so that ultimately it was only a pure question of law on which he had to decide. These decisions were recorded and preserved by the *fetwā emīni* in a special records office (*fetwākhāne*) where they could be referred to did the occasion arise. It was these three individuals who shared the fee charged for a *fetwā*, which in the middle of the 17th century was eight *aḳče* (Paul Rycaut, *The Present State of the Ottoman Empire*, London 1670, 109). Although in the course of time the office of the *shaykh al-islām* expanded greatly to include numerous other departments and officials (cf. its organization under Muṣṭafā Khayrī Ef. in 1914-6 as given in the *ʿIlmiyye sālnāmesi*, Istanbul 1334, 140 ff.), the section concerned with the *fetwā* remained substantially as described. Selections from the *fetwā*s of certain distinguished *shaykh*s were occasionally collected into book form, but neither these nor any of the decisions preserved in the *fetwākhāne* were of value as legal precedents; case-law as such is unknown.

Individuals with the title of *müftī* are to be found acting along with the *ḳāḍī*s throughout all the provinces but they have no connexion with *fetwā* other than in etymology. While in theory the *müftī* should be a man deeply versed in the canonical works of his *madhhab* and of an unimpeachable character, in practice it was only the latter quality that was demanded in these provincials. For as the *ḳāḍī* was usually a transient and a stranger to the district to which he was appointed, and was felt, moreover, to be the agent and the voice of the secular power, his judgments only achieved the authority of religion when they had the implicit sanction of some elderly person locally respected for his piety and somewhat above the very low average level of education. Occasionally a *ḳāḍī* who had retired from office might serve in this capacity in his place of residence, as might a member of one of the local learned families in the larger cities, but otherwise the *müftī*s were not of the *ʿulemā* class and their presence in the provinces was only necessary to satisfy the legalistic distinction between *ḳaḍāʾ*, "case judgment", and *iftāʾ*, "interpretative judgment" (cf. Ö. N. Bilmen, *Hukukı Islâmiyye ve ıstılahatı fıkhiyye kamusu*, Istanbul 1948-52, i, 258; vi, 487) and to avoid the expense and delay of constantly having to refer to Istanbul for rulings from the *shaykh al-islām*. Though these *müftī*s would hold a document of appointment from the latter, they were in no sense part of a centralized organization and their only income from the office was a share in the *ḳāḍī*'s fee for cases in which they participated. Such was the position in the "homelands" of the Ottoman Empire (Rūmili and Anatolia) where the Ḥanafī *madhhab* was followed exclusively. However, in the Arab provinces (Egypt, Syria, North Africa) where *ḳāḍī*s were appointed from Istanbul only to a few prominent cities (Cairo, Damascus, Aleppo, Jerusalem, Mecca, Medina)—and these merely as sinecures on the road to higher office—earlier traditions and practices were allowed to remain in force; here the *müftī*s of the various other *madhhab*s were frequently the chief religious and judicial dignitaries and were recognized as such by the *shaykh al-islām* who (for a price) issued their patents of office and by the civil authority who enforced their judgments.

The *fetwā* document was of a conventional form and varied little over the centuries. It was headed by a pious invocation in Arabic, often written in a very involved and stylized manner and varying from period to period according to the preferences of the drafting clerk; after the middle of the 12th/18th century, however, the formula *al-tawfīḳ minhu*, "guidance is from Him", became invariable. The remainder of the document was in Turkish and was introduced by the words: *bu mesʾele* (or *khuṣūṣ*) *beyānında eʾimme-i ḥanefiyyeden djewāb ne wedjhledir ki . . .*, "in what way is this problem answered by the Ḥanafī imāms . . .", and there followed an exposition of the matter in dispute couched in hypothetical terms with the identity of the parties involved concealed behind aliases (Zayd, ʿAmr; Hind, Zaynab). The exposition concluded, the single point at issue was presented as a direct interrogative, and this was followed by some variation of the formula of petition: *beyān buyurulup methāb ve meʾdjūr oluna*, "may this be explained, and may it (the explanation) be rewarded in the Hereafter", which later was always abbreviated to *beyān buyurula*. The decision was written on the same page in the *shaykh*'s own hand; introduced by the word *al-djawāb*, "answer", the characters of which were extended so as to mark a division between what preceded and what followed, the fallibility of all human judgement is immediately acknowledged by the phrase *Allāhu aʿlam*, "God knows best", written on the same line. The answer is always very brief, frequently a mere "yes" or "no" (*olur, olmaz*), never supported by reasons or citations from authority, and the document concludes with the signature of the *shaykh* (the use of a seal was prohibited unless his physical condition made writing impossible).

The office of Shaykh al-Islam was abolished in 1924, at the same time as the Ottoman Caliphate. It was replaced by a department for religious affairs, attached to the office of the Prime Minister, with a head appointed by him.

Bibliography: see SHAYKH AL-ISLĀM.

(J. R. WALSH)

FĀʾW (ḲARYAT AL-, WĀDĪ AL-)—At approximately 45° 10′ E and 19° 15′ N, some 70 km. south of the Wādī al-Dawāsir gap, the bed of Wādī al-Fāʾw cuts across the prominent Central Arabian escarpment of Djabal Ṭuwayḳ. At the widest point the banks of the gap are about 18 km. apart. The wādī is generally dry, and in the rare floods drains north-eastward to join Wādī al-Dawāsir. Near the southern edge of the Wādī al-Fāʾw gap, approximately two km. from the scarp itself, are three wells and the extensive remains of the ancient settlement of Ḳaryat al-Fāʾw. The wells are still being used, but permanent habitation ceased a number of centuries ago. The ruins of the large settlement consist of remains of a number of houses, tombs, and a few mounds of undetermined nature. Construction is of brick and stone masonry with lavish use of the locally available gypsum. Present indications, based on pottery, are that this settlement was in existence during the 2nd century B.C., and from other surface remains as well as from inscriptions in the vicinity it seems likely that it was once a Sabaean outpost. Surface finds also indicate that the settlement was, at least during a part of its existence, contemporaneous with that of al-Ukhdūd in Wādī Nadjrān.

Bibliography: H. St. J. B. Philby, *Two notes from Central Arabia*, in *GJ*, cxiii, Jan.-June 1949, map; P. Lippens, *Expédition en Arabie Centrale*, Paris 1956. (F. S. VIDAL)

FAWDJ [see ḤARB, vii—India].

FAWDJDĀR, as described by Abu' l-Faḍl (cf. *Ā'īn-i Akbarī*, Eng. transl. by Jarrett, Calcutta 1949, 41-2) was both an executive and military officer, the administrative head of a *sarkār* (district) under the Mughals. However, during the Sultanate period the *kōtwāls* [*q.v.*], who were stationed in newly-built fortresses at strategic points to police the roads, came later to be called *fawdjdārs*; but the *kōtwāls* also continued to exist and perform the duties of modern prefects of city police. While the responsibility for the general administration and civil affairs rested with the *shiḳḳdārs*, the *fawdjdārs* were charged with the maintenance of law and order within their respective jurisdictions. Baranī [*q.v.*] speaks of both *shiḳḳdārs* and *fawdjdārs* during the reign of Fīrūz Shāh Tughluḳ (752-90/1351-88). He speaks of their being jointly detailed to quell agrarian disturbances in the Doāb (cf. *Ta'rīkh-i Fīrūzshāhī*, Calcutta 1862, 479). The *fawdjdārs* in the pre-Mughal period were akin to the modern zone-commanders under Martial Law, collaborating with the civil authorities but having different areas under their control. The *fawdjdārs* under Shēr Shāh Sūr (945-52/1538-45) performed two kinds of functions: they acted both as reguiar heads of the *sarkārs* and in cases of emergency or for military purposes acted as *ḳalʿadārs* (commandants) of frontier forts or outposts. The back-bone of the central administration, they could be deputed to perform any kinds of duties throughout the empire. Normally one *fawdjdār* was appointed in every *sarkār* but two could also be appointed when necessary.

The *shiḳḳdārs* of the Sultanate were replaced by *fawdjdārs* under the Mughals. They combined in themselves the dual functions of both the executive and the military head of the district administration corresponding to the District Magistrate-*cum*-Superintendent of Police (but not the Collector) of British India. In importance and status the *fawdjdārs* ranked next to the *ṣūbadārs* (provincial governors). Their main function, apart from police duties, was to assist the *ʿamalguzār* (revenue-collector) or the *amīn* (revenue assessor) in the collection of land-revenue. It was the primary duty of a *fawdjdār* to ensure that the local *zamīndārs* paid the revenue regularly. The *fawdjdār* was required to guard the roads and should any merchant or traveller be robbed in daylight he was obliged to pay compensation to the victim. It was also his duty to protect the ryots, and to assist and provide armed escort to the *gumāshtas* (agents) of the *djāgīrdārs* and the assignees of Crown-lands in the collection of land-revenue. His other duties included the prevention of unauthorized arms manufacture, cutting of jungles, suppression of agrarian unrest and minor uprisings, forcible dispersal of robber-gangs and bandits, and taking cognizance of major crimes committed within his jurisdiction.

Although subordinate to the provincial governor, the *fawdjdār* was a very important official. In all probability he was appointed directly by the emperor through a *farmān-i thabatī*; the border (*nāḥiya*) *fawdjdār* or the commandant of a frontier outpost, consisting of several *thānās*, had direct dealings with the central government, and could call for help on the provincial government in cases of emergency. The duties of a border-*fawdjdār* were to keep watch over the frontiers falling within his jurisdiction, suppress turbulent and rebellious chiefs, punish aggressors, collect tribute from the local *rādjās* and when possible to conquer or subjugate enemy territory. A class of border *fawdjdārs* was known as *ghāṭwāls*; but their posts were semi-military in character. They existed as late as the later part of the 12th/18th century when they were replaced by the new police force organized by Lord Cornwallis, the Governor-General of Fort William, Calcutta (1786-93). Although the district *fawdjdār* was a central official, yet the provincial governor had powers to appoint the *fawdjdār-i gird* (*i.e.*, the *fawdjdār* of the environs) for the protection of the suburbs of the city. This officer in his turn appointed the *fawdjdārs* of the *nākās* and the *thānā-dārs*. An echo of their official designation is heard in the former province of Sind in Pakistan where the city police-station is still known as the *fawdjdārī*.

Apart from his police and administrative duties the *fawdjdār* also exercized judicial powers under the Sultans. He could try petty offences and take "security" proceedings, *i.e.*, the binding over of potential or suspected criminals. In the early Mughal period he was frequently transferred from one place to another and was, like the modern Martial Law Administrators, sometimes deputed to conduct purely military operations (cf. Khāfī Khān, *Muntakhab al-Lubāb*, i, 505). His judicial powers in criminal cases were enhanced by the later Mughals, who empowered him to try non-capital offences (cf. M. B. Ahmad, *The Administration of justice in medieval India*, Aligarh 1941, 165). The criminal courts in Pakistan and India are still known as *ʿAdālathā-yi Fawdjdārī* and criminal cases as *fawdjdārī muḳaddimāt*. Sometimes *fawdjdārs* were also appointed in certain *parganas*, as a purely temporary measure, and they enjoyed the same powers as the *fawdjdār-i sarkār*. In a few districts (*sarkārs*) there were no separate *fawdjdārs*; the same person performed the duties of the *amīn* (controller of expenses and revenue assessor) as well as of the *fawdjdār* in addition to his own duties (cf. Shāhnawāz Khān, *Ma'āthir al-umarā'* (Bibl. Ind.), ii, 37, which mentions Diyānat Khān being appointed both as the *amīn* and the *fawdjdār* of Sirhind on the reversion of Ray Kāshī Dās); while in certain cases the duties of the *fawdjdār* were performed either by the local *shiḳḳdār* or the *kōtwāl*.

Bibliography: Abu 'l-Faḍl, *Ā'īn-i Akbarī*,[2] Eng. transl. by Jarret, Calcutta 1949, 41-2; Baranī, *Ta'rīkh-i Fīrūzshāhī* (Bibl. Indica), 479-80; Jadu Nath Sarkar, *Mughal administration*[3], Calcutta 1935, 63-6; P. Saran, *Provincial government of the Mughals*, Allahabad 1941, 189 ff. (contains the best discussion on the subject); Ishtiaq Husain Qureshi, *The Administration of the Sultanate of Delhi*,[4] Karachi 1958, 201, 214; M. B. Ahmad, *The Administration of justice in medieval India*, Aligarh 1941, 121, 123, 164-5, 167, 171, 174, 179, 183, 194, 200, 209, 214, 245; ʿAlī Muḥammad Khān, *Mir'āt-i Aḥmadī* (Supplement), Baroda 1930, 174; S. A. Q. Husaini, *Administration under the Mughals*, Dacca 1952, 203, 214-5, 224; Ibne Hasan, *The central structure of the Mughal Empire*, Oxford 1936, index; S. M. Jafar, *Some cultural aspects of the Muslim rule in India*, Peshawar 1950, 28; N. Manucci, *Storia do Mogor*, transl. W. Irvine, London 1907, ii, 450-1; W. H. Moreland, in *Journal of Indian History*, vi/2 (1927); R. P. Tripathi, *Some aspects of Muslim administration*, Allahabad 1936, index; Anon., *Dastūr al-ʿAmal* (*Manual of officers' duties* drawn up in Awrangzīb's reign), Ethé (I.O.L.) MS. no. 307, s.v. *fawdjdār*; S. R. Sharma, *Mughal government and administration*, Bombay 1951, 105, 217; *Bahār-i ʿAdjam* (Persian dictionary), s.v. *fawdjdār*; W. W. Hunter, *Annals of rural Bengal*², New York 1868, i, 123 f.

(A. S. Bazmee Ansari)

FAWRĪ (Fevrī), Aḥmad b. ʿAbd Allāh, a 16th century Ottoman poet and scholar, was born a Christian. After his conversion to Islam he was called, in accordance with contemporary custom, ʿAbd Allāh-oghlu in the *tadhkira*s (v. Lāṭifī, Istanbul 1314, 269; Ḥasan Čelebī, Istanbul University Library, T.Y. 304, 253b).

Fawrī was deeply influenced by Naḳḳāsh ʿAlī Bey, the father of his master Lāmiʿī, and also by the *müderris* Dursun Efendi. Fawrī's profound knowledge of theology and of Arabic, a language in which he wrote poetry (*Mashāʿir al-shuʿarāʾ*, Ist. Univ. Lib., T.Y. 2406, 253 et seq.; *Ḥadāʾiḳ al-ḥaḳāʾiḳ*, Istanbul 1268, 142 et seq.), are mentioned by his friends ʿĀshiḳ Čelebī and Newʿī-zāde ʿAṭāʾī.

A *müderris* himself, Fawrī Aḥmad Efendi was both a notable scholar and a teacher. He visited Mecca and later, in 960/1553, he took part in the expedition against Nakhčiwān under Sultan Süleymān, whose patronage he secured by means of numerous panegyrics. Fawrī died in Damascus where he had filled the post of Muftī, in Dhu 'l-Ḳaʿda 978/April 1571.

He is the author of the following works: *Dīwān*, which is preceded by the *Terdjeme-i Ḥadīth-i Arbaʿīn* (v. Abdülkadir Karahan, *Islâm-Türk edebiyatında Kırk Hadis*, Istanbul 1954, 320-1; MSS. Ist. Univ. Lib., T.Y. 2873; Topkapı-Revan 763, Murad Molla Lala Ismail, 473); a marginal commentary on the *Durar wa Ghurar*, a *risāla* on calligraphy, a Persian dictionary in Turkish and, finally, the *Akhlāḳ-i Süleymānī*.

Fawrī is the editor of the poems of Sultan Süleymān (1520-1566). According to Riyāḍī, Fawrī was the first Ottoman poet to compose *takhmīs* and *tasdīs* (*Riyāḍ al-shuʿarāʾ*, Ist. Univ. Lib , T.Y. 761, 108).

Bibliography: ʿĀlī, *Kunh al-akhbār*, unpublished part, Ist. Univ. Lib., T.Y. 5959, 492; Beyānī, *Tadhkira*, same lib., T.Y. 2568, 68ᵇ-69ᵃ; Fāʾizī, *Zubdat al-ashʿār*, same lib., T.Y. 2472, 87ᵇ; Mustaḳīm-zāde Saʿd al-Dīn, *Tuḥfat al-khaṭṭāṭīn*, Istanbul 1928, 98; Esrār Dede, *Tadhkira*, Ist. Univ. Lib., T.Y. 3894, 161; Sabri Kalkandelen, Catalogue of Istanbul University Library MSS.

(Abdülkadir Karahan)

FAWZĪ al-MAʿLŪF [see maʿlūf].

FAYʾ, in pre-Islamic times used for chattels taken as booty, like *ghanīma* [*q.v.*], to be divided between victors, either in fifths (*e.g.*, *Mufaḍḍaliyyāt*, ed. Lyall, 599, 1) or in fourths (*Ḥamāsa*, ed. Freytag, 458, 18, Cairo 1335, i, 428; G. Jacob, *Altarabisches Beduinenleben*, Berlin 1897, 215), the leader being entitled to one of the parts. This custom was upheld by the Prophet after the battle of Badr, and Sūra VIII, 42 mentions five employments for the Prophet's one fifth (*khums*), to figure in future budgets. The old use of the word *fayʾ* never became completely obliterated. But when territorial conquests began and political responsibility grew on the Prophet's mind, procedure had to be changed. So the conquests of the Banu 'l-Naḍīr, Khaybar, and Fadak led to a new precedent. The Banu 'l-Naḍīr surrendered after a siege, and Sūra LIX, 7-10 maintains that this result was not due to the assailants' having prevailed, but to God's interposition in favour of His Apostle, so that it was *fayʾ* to him exclusively to the ultimate benefit of Muslim society. In fact the same incumbents are mentioned as for the *khums*, but those actually held in view were the destitute *muhādjirūn* (Ibn Hishām, Cairo ed. 1937, iii, 193 ult.). Traditions about Khaybar and Fadak are at variance, but it is certain that Muḥammad also on these occasions followed his own equity (al-Balādhurī, *Futūḥ*, 23-33).

The theocratic explanation based on the meaning of *afāʾa*, "to bring back", as by right belonging to God and consequently to Muslim society (al-Bayḍāwī *ad* Sūra LIX, 7) cannot be supported by another Ḳurʾānic passage, Sūra XXXIII, 49. Ḳudāma derives the word in the same way, but understands it to connote annual return, namely of revenue. Otherwise, too, theorists found it difficult to define the content of *fayʾ*. The longevity of bedouin custom left the possibility that the four-fifths could be divided among the conquering troops instead of being kept as state land. Another opinion was that the revenue (*fayʾ*) of such lands should be subjected to the *khums* for the canonical purposes, while the rest went to state expenses for the army and to public services of different kinds (*maṣāliḥ*). It seems, however, that already ʿUmar I had made it one budget, and that *fayʾ* early began to be classed with *waḳf* or *ḥubs* (mortmain) for the benefit of all Muslims. Support for this is the identical employment of both categories mentioned in the Ḳurʾān. This cancelling of the freer disposal of the *khums* of the leader in fact made for centralized power.

According to theory *fayʾ* lands arise from unconditional surrender (conquests made *ʿanwatan*, *ḳasran*, or *ḳahran*), even if this does not wholly square with the Prophet's precedent, as negotiations had taken place then. The theoretical alternatives are division among Muslims, in which case it would become *ʿushr* land [*q.v.*], while its inhabitants became serfs, or that it should be left *in statu quo* for the exploitation of the Muslim community, the inhabitants remaining free, but liable to *kharādj* on the land, in which case the *kharādj* is regarded as a sort of tenure to the state. Thus it would seem that the *fayʾ* notion is intended to support the right of the state to heavy taxation, the inhabitants holding the usufruct, *manfaʿa*, while their ownership is held precarious. This, however, does not exclude the right of inheritance. On the other hand *ṣulḥ* lands, originally paying a stipulated tribute, *shayʾ musammā*, or other more favourable dues, increasingly came to pay *kharādj*, so, apart from the actual ownership, it became difficult in theory to uphold a strict division between the two, as the economic result tended to become identical. On the problems of *kharādj* lands, see kharādj.

From of old the leader of a foray had a right to reserve for himself—apart from the fifth—any special object of the booty which attracted him, the *ṣafiyya* (pl. *ṣafāyā*). Likely enough this right was very limited, or it could have been used by the Prophet in the Banu 'l-Naḍīr case. The term, however, stuck to state domains as *ṣawāfī* [*q.v.*].

Bibliography: Abū Yūsuf, *Kitāb al-Kharādj*, Būlāḳ 1885, 10 ff.; al-Māwardī, *Kitāb al-Aḥkām al-sulṭāniyya*, ed. Enger, 1853, 217 ff., 237 ff., 293 ff.; Ḳudāma, *Kitāb* [*al-Kharādj wa-*]*ṣanʿat al-kitāba*, Bibliothèque Nationale, Paris, ms. no. 5907, fols. 91 ff. (the section specially handled by Ibn al-Djawzī ?); al-Shīrāzī, *Kitāb al-Tanbīh*, ed. Juynboll, 1879, 292 ff.; M. Hartmann, in *OLZ*, 1904, 413-25, 462-68; D. C. Dennett, *Conversion and the poll tax in early Islam*, 1950, 20 ff.; H. A. R. Gibb, in *Arabica*, 1955, 1-16; Cl. Cahen, in *Arabica*, 1954, 136 ff.; and the references to authorities in F. Løkkegaard, *Islamic taxation in the classic period*, 1950, 38-72.

(F. Løkkegaard)

FAYḌ [see Supplement].

al-**FAYḌ** b. **ABĪ ṢĀLIḤ** Shīrawayh, Abū Djaʿfar, vizier (?) of the ʿAbbāsid caliph al-Mahdī. Born at Nīshāpūr of a Christian father, al-Fayḍ seems to have been one of the *ghilmān* of Ibn al-Muḳaffaʿ [*q.v.*]; he attracted attention by his talent and culture and, according to al-Djahshiyārī (*Wuzarā'*, 164-6), followed by Ibn Khallikān (vi, 25; tr. de Slane, iv, 358) and *al-Fakhrī* (ed. Derenbourg, 255-7; tr. Fagnan, 314-8; tr. C. E. J. Whitting, 183), he was appointed *wazīr* by al-Mahdī after the dismissal of Yaʿḳūb b. Dāwūd [*q.v.*] in 166/782; he remained in office until the caliphate of al-Hādī (169/785), but was then removed from the administration. However, al-Ṭabarī mentions him (ii, 841) only in the list of secretaries of al-Mahdī, and al-Yaʿḳūbī (ii, 483) makes Muḥammad b. al-Layth the successor of Yaʿḳūb. Al-Fayḍ appears again under al-Rashīd, where he acted as agent (*wakīl*) in a matter concerning some land and where the poet Abu 'l-Asad Nubāta praises his exceptional generosity. He was also famous for his pride and his arrogance. He died in 173/789-90.

Bibliography: Besides the sources quoted, see: Ibn ʿAbd Rabbih, *ʿIḳd*, v, 116; Wakīʿ, *Akhbār al-ḳuḍāt*, ii, 145; Tanūkhī, *Faradj*, i, 103; al-Makīn, Leiden 1625, 109; De Goeje and De Jong, *Fragmenta historicorum arabicorum*, Leiden 1869, i, 281 (al-Fayḍ b. Sahl); *Aghānī*, xii, 176 (in the biog. of Abu 'l-Asad); Ibn al-Djawzī, in *JRAS*, 1907, 26; S. D. Goitein, *The vizierate*, 383; S. Moscati, *Nuovi studi storici sul califfato di al-Mahdī*, in *Orientalia*, xv/1-2 (1946), 167; D. Sourdel, *Vizirat*, 111 and index.

(L. Veccia Vaglieri)

FAYḌĀBĀD, (Fyzabad), a town in the district of the same name in India, situated in 26° 47′ N. and 82° 10′ E., 4 miles from the ancient town of Ayōdhyā, which gave its name to the province of Awadh (Oudh) and the Shīʿī kingdom founded by Saʿādat Khān Burhān al-Mulk [*q.v.*]. The town grew up around a wooden lodge (*bangla*), surrounded by a large and expansive compound, which Burhān al-Mulk had built for himself on his appointment in 1132/1719-20 as the *Nā'ib Nāẓim* of Awadh. Other buildings, mostly of mud, for the *ḥarem* and barracks for the troops sprang up all around converting the humble habitation into a respectable settlement. Even after his assumption of power as the Nawwāb-Wazīr, Burhān al-Mulk continued to stay in the same wooden lodge. On the accession of his nephew Abu 'l-Manṣūr Ṣafdar Djang [*q.v.*] to the *masnad* in 1152/1739 more buildings were added to the growing township which was given the name of Fayḍābād. (To the people of Awadh Fayḍābād is still known by its earlier name *Bangla*). Gardens were laid out and *bāzār*s sprang up all around, resulting in the decline of Ayōdhyā which suffered both in population and prosperity. Shudjāʿ al-Dawla, the third Nawwāb (1170-88/1756-75), stayed chiefly at Lucknow but after his defeat by the British at Buxar in 1764 he moved to Fayḍābād and made it his head-quarters. He added many new buildings, and in order to strengthen the defences of the town dug a moat around the citadel and also built two mud-forts. Before the end of 1189/1775 Āṣaf al-Dawla, the fourth Nawwāb, abandoned Fayḍābād and moved permanently to Lucknow, which thenceforward became the seat of government of the Nawwābs of Awadh. However, both the mother and the widow (Bahū Bēgum) of Shudjāʿ al-Dawla continued to live at Fayḍābād which soon declined in importance. It was his alleged maltreatment of these two Bēgums which led to the impeachment of Warren Hastings. After the death of Bahū Bēgum in 1232/1816 Fayḍābād lost further in importance and glory. It continued to decay till the British annexation of Awadh in 1847 when an era of development opened and the general deterioration was arrested. The Urdū poet Mīr Ḥasan in his *mathnawī*, *Gulzār-i Iram* praises Fayḍābād for its well-kept streets and wide roads.

Shudjāʿ al-Dawla was responsible for constructing many of the historic brick buildings and monuments of the city. He lies buried in a beautiful tall mausoleum, which he himself erected during his life-time in the centre of a charming rosegarden, the *Gulāb-bārī*, laid out by Ṣafdar Djang. The tomb of Bahū Bēgum, mother of Āṣaf al-Dawla, on the south of the town is a fine domed building which cost Rs. 300,000 to build. The entire amount was paid out of the queen mother's personal property. The fortress constructed by Shudjāʿ al-Dawla is now in ruins, and so are the palaces built by the Nawwābs and the nobles. The town was badly disturbed during the military uprising (Mutiny) of 1857 when Mawlawī Aḥmad Allāh gained prominence for the deeds of valour performed by him. He came to be known and dreaded as the 'Mawlawī of Fayḍābād'.

Bibliography: Muḥammad Fayḍ Bakhsh, *Faraḥ-bakhsh*, (Eng. transl., *Memoirs of Delhi and Faizábád, being a translation of the "Tárikh Farahbaksh"*..., by W. Hoey, 2 vols., Allahabad 1888-9); Ghulām Ḥusayn Naḳawī, *ʿImād al-Saʿādat*[2], Lucknow 1897; Nadjm al-Ghanī Rāmpurī, *Ta'rīkh-i Awadh*, Lucknow 1919, i, 36-8; B. Carnegie, *A History of Fyzabad*, (not seen); *Imperial Gazetteer of India*, Oxford 1908, xii, 110-1, 117-8; Mīr Ḥasan, *Gulzār-i Iram* (Urdu *mathnawī* still in MS.); Munshī Lāl-djī, *Sulṭān al-Ḥikāyāt* (MS. in Persian); Storey, i/II, 706-8; S.N. Sen, *Eighteen Fifty-seven*, Calcutta 1958, 154, 186-7, 355, 402.

(A. S. Bazmee Ansari)

FAYḌĪ (later Fayyāḍī), Abu 'l-Fayḍ b. Shaykh Mubārak al-Mahdawī, Persian poet, commentator of the Ḳur'ān, one of the nine jewels (*naw ratan*) of the court of Akbar, younger brother of the historian Abu 'l-Faḍl ʿAllāmī [*q.v.*], was of Yamanī extraction; one of his ancestors Shaykh Mūsā had migrated to Sind and settled at Rēl, a small place near Sīwastān (modern Sehwān). His grandfather Shaykh Khiḍr came down to Nāgor [*q.v.*], where Fayḍī's father Mubārak was born. In 950/1543-4 Shaykh Mubārak migrated to Āgra, where he married and his first child Fayḍī was born in 954/1547. He soon aroused the hostility of the ʿ*ulamā'* on account of his unorthodox ideas and heretical beliefs as a Mahdawī (see A. S. Bazmee Ansari, *Sayyid Muḥammad Jawnpūrī and his movement*, in *Islamic Studies*, ii/1 (1963), 68,

73, and AL-DJAWNPŪRĪ). The Shaykh along with his grown-up sons, Fayḍī and Abu 'l-Faḍl, had a very hard time for several years. Unable to bear any longer the rigours of an outlaw's life Fayḍī persuaded his father to surrender himself to the emperor. In 974/1566 Shaykh Mubārak was granted an audience at Āgra and Fayḍī, welcoming the opportunity, greatly impressed the emperor with his extraordinary ability and achievements (cf. Fayḍī's *Ḳaṣīda* in *Āʾīn-i Akbarī*, Eng. transl. by Blochmann, 620 ff.). This marked the beginning of a long and brilliant career as a court-poet, statesman and a *manṣabdār*, which brought him several honours and distinctions. In 984/1576 he was created *Malik al-Shuʿarāʾ* by Akbar. In order to vindicate his claim to this high-sounding title he planned to compose a *khamsa* in 987/1579, after the famous *khamsa* of Niẓāmī [*q.v.*]. The five poems to be included were: (i) *Markaz-i Adwār*, mostly composed in Fatḥpūr Sīkrī; (ii) *Sulaymān u Bilḳīs*, commenced in Lahore but never completed; (iii) *Nal-Daman*, his best known poem (ed. Calcutta 1831); (iv) *Haft kishwar* and (v) *Akbar-nāma* on the lines of the *Sikandar-nāma*. Of these only (i) and (iii) were completed several years later at the persistent urging of Akbar while the remaining three, in spite of Abu 'l-Faḍl's assertion to the contrary (cf. *Akbar-nāma, sub anno* 39 regnal) remained incomplete.

An accomplished scholar, physician, and poet, he was appointed in 987/1579 tutor to prince Dāniyāl; he also claims to have instructed Djahāngīr, and Murād (cf. *Akbar-nāma*, Bibl. Ind., ii, 311). Of these Dāniyāl was also a poet in Bradj-bhākā, suggesting that his tutor was a master of that dialect as well as of classical Arabic and Persian. In 993/1585 he was sent on an expedition against the Yūsufzaʾīs of Pēshāwar. Treated as a close companion, he was included in the royal *entourage* during Akbar's visit to Kashmīr in 997/1588. In 999/1590-1 he was sent as an envoy to the courts of Rādjā ʿAlī Khān, ruler of Khāndesh, and Burhān Niẓām Shāh, the king of Aḥmadnagar. After the completion of his mission he returned to Fatḥpūr Sīkrī, the capital, in 1001/1592.

Generous and hospitable by nature, he even helped his enemies. When his worst critic al-Badāʾūnī [*q.v.*] fell from imperial favour in 1000/1591, Fayḍī, who was then on a mission to Gudjarāt, wrote a letter to Akbar strongly pleading the case of the disgraced historian (see al-Badāʾūnī, iii, 303-5). Yet he received very harsh treatment at the hands of Badāʾūnī, who attributes to him every possible vice and depravity and even accuses him of open enmity towards the Muslims and making fun of Islam; he also holds him responsible for Akbar's anti-Islamic activities and practices. But most of these charges are ill-founded and seem to be the result of some personal grudge, as there are in Fayḍī's *dīwān* poems in praise of the Prophet and his Companions. He died of asthma at Āgra on 10 Ṣafar 1044/5 October 1595. He was buried at Āgra alongside his father, who had died in Lahore in 1001/1592. Al-Badāʾūnī quotes several uncomplimentary chronograms of his death composed by orthodox poets. On his own showing he had accepted the "Divine Faith", instituted by Akbar (cf. *Akbar-nāma*, Bibl. Ind., ii, 311), which was denounced by the *ʿulamāʾ* as an unwarranted innovation.

A great lover of books, he had in his library more than 4,600 volumes on such varied subjects as medicine, astrology, music, philosophy, *taṣawwuf*, trigonometry, arithmetic, exegesis, *ḥadīth*, *fiḳh* etc. On his death many of these books, mostly autographs or copied during the lifetimes of their authors, were transferred to the imperial library by order of Akbar, in all probability under the law of escheat.

He is said to be the author of 101 books (apparently an exaggeration), of which very few are now extant. In addition to the incomplete *khamsa*, he compiled a *dīwān* of poems in Persian (ed. Dihlī, 1261/1845). There are, however, conflicting opinions about his poetical achievements, on which his fame chiefly rests. Shiblī Nuʿmānī [*q.v.*] regards him as one of those non-Iranian poets "whose verse would pass as the work of a genuine Persian". E. J. W. Gibb believes that after Djāmī [*q.v.*], ʿUrfī and Fayḍī were the chief Persian poets to influence Turkish poetry (*Ottoman Poetry*, i, 5, 127, 129). Al-Badāʾūnī, on the other hand, says that he was not so popular in his day as were his contemporaries ʿUrfī and Thanāʾī [*q.v.*]. A master of the Arabic language, he composed two books in the *ṣanʿat ihmāl, i.e.*, employing no dotted letter, simply to display his lexicographical abilities. One of these, the *Mawārid al-kilam* on ethics (ed. Calcutta 1241/1825), which contains pithy and laconic sentences defining terms like *Islām, ʿilm al-Kalām, Ādam, Kalām Allāh, ahl Allāh* was intended to be a preliminary to the writing of the *Sawāṭiʿ al-ilhām*, a voluminous commentary on the Ḳurʾān without any dotted letter, characterised by critics to be almost a "useless piece of Arabic writing", finished in 1002/1593 (ed. Lucknow 1306/1889). Al-Badāʾūnī bitingly remarks that he composed this book in a state of drunkenness and ritual impurity (*al-djanāba*). In view of this the claim of the Mudjaddidīs that Aḥmad Sirhindī [*q.v.*] collaborated in the composition of a part of this work seems wholly untenable (see Bibliography).

He also translated Līlāvatī, a Sanskrit work on arithmetic (ed. Calcutta 1826), and some portions of the epic poem *Mahābhārata* into Persian at the express command of Akbar, in collaboration with al-Badāʾūnī and Mullā Shīrī. *Laṭīfa-i Fayḍī*, a posthumous collection of his letters, was compiled by his nephew Nūr al-Dīn Muḥammad ʿAbd Allāh b. ʿAyn al-Mulk (MSS, Rieu 792, 984). According to Shiblī these are couched in a simple unornate language, in contradistinction to the high-flown bombastic style then in vogue in Persian letter-writing (*inshāʾ*), of which his younger brother, the celebrated Abu 'l-Faḍl was a great master (cf. his letters to Fayḍī in the second *daftar* of his *Inshāʾ*).

Bibliography: Abu 'l-Faḍl ʿAllāmī, *Akbar-nāma*, Bibl. Ind., Calcutta 1873-87, iii, index; idem, *Har sih daftar Abu 'l-Faḍl*, Lucknow 1292/1875, 138 ff., 202-14; idem, *Āʾīn-i Akbarī*², Eng. trans. by Blochmann, Calcutta 1939, 490-1, 548-50, 618 ff., 112-3 (where several *rubāʿīs* of Fayḍī which were stamped on the royal coinage are quoted); Ṣamṣām al-Dawla Shāh-Nawāz Khān, *Maʾāthir al-umarāʾ*, Eng. transl. by H. Beveridge, Calcutta 1941, 513 ff.; al-Badāʾūnī, *Muntakhab al-tawārīkh*, Bibl. Ind., ii, 393-4, 405-6; iii, 299-310; Āzād Bilgrāmī, *Subḥat al-mardjān*, Bombay 1303/1885, 45-6; idem, *Maʾāthir al-kirām*, Agra 1910, 198-200; idem, *Khizāna-i ʿāmira*, Cawnpore 1871, 318; Niẓām al-Dīn Aḥmad, *Ṭabaḳāt-i Akbarī*, Bibl. Ind., ii, 486-8; Browne, iv, 242-5; Sh. Farīd Bhakkarī, *Dhakhīrat al-Khawānīn*, Karachi 1961, i, 64-7; Ṣiddīḳ Ḥasan Khān Ḳannawdjī, *Abdjad al-ʿulūm*, Bhopal 1295/1878, 897-8; ʿAbd al-Ḥayy Lakhnawī, *Nuzhat al-khawāṭir*, Hyderabad 1375/1955, v, 26-31; Shiblī Nuʿmānī, *Shiʿr al-ʿAdjam*, Lahore 1924, iii, 28-72; Shīr Khān Lōdhī, *Mirʾāt* *al-khayāl*, Bombay 1324/1906, 79-81 (where his *kunya* is given as Abu 'l-Fayḍ and his title as Fayyāḍī, which are both erroneous); M. Ḳudrat Allāh Gopāmawī, *Tadhkira natā'idj al-afkār*, Bombay 1334 solar, 533-7; Muḥ. Ḥusayn Āzād, *Darbār-i Akbarī*[4] (in Urdu), Lahore 1927, 359-418; Storey, i/II, 540; Brockelmann, II, 417, S II 610; Sarkīs, col. 1472 (where his name is given as Fayḍ Allāh and his *kunya* as Abu 'l-Faḍl, obviously wrong); *JASB* (1869), 137, 142; Āghā Aḥmad ʿAlī, *Haft Āsmān*, Calcutta 1873; Taḳī Kāshī, *Khulāṣat al-ashʿār wa zubdat al-afkār* (MS); Khān-i Ārzū, *Madjmaʿ al-nafā'is* (MS Bankipur, viii, 695-16); Wālih Dāghistānī, *Riyāḍ al-shuʿarā'* (MS Bankipur, viii, 693); Rieu, 450; M. G. Zubaid Ahmad, *Contribution of India to Arabic literature*, Allahabad/Jullunder 1946, index; A. Sprenger, *Oudh Catalogue*, 401-2; Ibrāhīm Khān Khalīl, *Khulāṣat al-kalām* (MS Bankipur); Bindrāban Dās Khʷushgū, *Safīna-i Khʷushgū* (MS Bankipur); Kamāl al-Dīn Muḥ. Iḥsān, *Rawḍat al-Ḳayyūmiyya* (MS in Persian), Urdu transl., Lahore n.d., i, 60, 62-3; Badr al-Dīn Sirhindī, *Ḥaḍarāt al-Ḳuds* (MS in Persian), Urdu transl., Lahore 1341/1922, ii, 9-10; S. Muḥ. Ikrām, *Rūd-i Kawthar*, Karachi n.d., 87-98 (to be used with care); Z. A. Desai, *Life and works of Faidi*, in *Indo-Iranica*, Calcutta, xvi/3 1963). (A. S. Bazmee Ansari)

FAYDJ [see fuyūdj].

FAYLASŪF, philosopher: he who studies falsafa [*q.v.*], thence frequently used as an epithet for deep thinkers. The Arab philologists know the literal meaning of this word as *muḥibb al-ḥikma* (lover of wisdom). Al-Ḳindī [*q.v.*] was known for preference as the *faylasūf al-ʿArab* (philosopher of the Arabs), presumably because he was a philosopher of genuine Arab origin in contrast to most Muslim philosophers who belonged to non-Arab nations (cf. the correct explanation of this name given to al-Kindī by T. J. de Boer in the *Archiv für Gesch. der Philos.*, 1899, xiii, 154 ff.).

In popular language *faylasūf* is applied in an uncomplimentary sense to freethinkers or unbelievers. Even the Jewish king Jeroboam is called *faylasūf* in this sense (*Revue des Études Juives*, xxx, 23 ult.). An idea of contempt is associated with the forms *faylafūs*, *fulfūs* (also *falafsūn*, Syr.), plur. *falāfis*, current in the popular language; this is applied to frivolous, imprudent people, good-for-nothings and charlatans (examples in *ZDMG*, xxxviii, 681); Vollers, (*ibid.* li, 300, 4) gives *fulfūs*. The verbal form *yufalfis* (*Bāsim le forgeron*, ed. Landberg, 38, 5) is also connected with this: "he could not wriggle out". See falāsifa and falsafa. (I. Goldziher)

FAYṢAL [see saʿūd, āl].

FAYṢAL I, of ʿIrāḳ, was born at Ṭā'if in 1301/1883, third son of the Sharīf (later king) Ḥusayn b. ʿAlī. After a boyhood of desert and oasis life, he accompanied his father to Istanbul in 1309/1891, there to pass 18 years. He married his cousin, Ḥazīma, in 1323/1905. Returning to Mecca with Sharīf Ḥusayn in 1327/1909, he took part in expeditions against the Idrīsī of ʿAsīr in 1331-2/1912-3, and was elected to the Turkish parliament. Resentful of Turkish severity against Arab dissidents in Syria in 1915, and admitted to knowledge of the Arab political secret societies, Fayṣal in 1916 joined, and was for two years to command with distinction, the armies of the Mecca-based Sharīfian "Arab Revolt". His two-year effort thereafter to consolidate an Arab monarchy in Syria (1337-9/1918-20) failed in the face of French opposition; he was expelled from Damascus in July 1339/1920. But British favour and ʿIrāḳī election secured him a throne in Baghdād (August 1340/1921), and he could for the twelve years following play a conspicuous, indeed indispensable, part in the foundation, consolidation and ultimate liberation from the British Mandate of the young and aspiring kingdom. Fayṣal, holding a balance between British requirements and local patriotism, showed admirable qualities of patient leadership. ʿIrāḳ was admitted to the League of Nations in 1351/1932. Fayṣal died suddenly in Switzerland in September 1352/1933, succeeded by his son, Ghāzī.

Bibliography: The Arabic and European literature of the 1914-8 war, the Mandates, and Arab and ʿIrāḳī affairs between 1914 and 1933 is very extensive. For British and Arab views of Fayṣal see T. E. Lawrence, *The seven pillars of wisdom*, London 1935; Amīn Rīḥānī, *Fayṣal al-Awwal*, Beirut 1353/1934; Sāṭiʿ al-Ḥuṣrī, *Yawm Maysalūn*, Beirut 1945. For German and Turkish views of his war-time role see Liman von Sanders, *Fünf Jahre Türkei*, Berlin 1920 (Eng. tr. *Five years in Turkey*, Annapolis 1927; Fr. tr. *Cinq ans de Turquie*, Paris 1923) and Ali Fuad Erden, *Birinci Dünya Harbinde Suriye Hatıraları*, i, Istanbul 1954. For French views, see L. Jovelet, *L'évolution sociale et politique des «pays arabes»*, in *REI*, vii (1933), 473-81; R. de Gontaut-Biron, *Comment la France s'est installée en Syrie*, Paris 1922, 232 sqq.; M. Pernot, *L'inquiétude de l'Orient: II, En Asie musulmane*, Paris 1927, 147. In general, see S. H. Longrigg, *Syria and Lebanon under French Mandate*, Oxford 1958; idem, *ʿIraq 1900 to 1950*, Oxford 1953. (S. H. Longrigg)

FAYṢAL II, of ʿIrāḳ, son of King Ghāzī and grandson of Fayṣal I [*q.v.*], was born in Baghdād May 1354/1935, and, aged four, became King under the Regency of his uncle the Amīr ʿAbd al-Ilāh on the accidental death of his father in 1358/1939. Educated by an English governess and at Harrow, he passed an uneventful childhood, suffering intermittently from asthma. He assumed his royal functions in May 1953, and during his five-year effective reign showed excellent intentions, accepting guidance from his veteran statesman Nūrī al-Saʿīd [*q.v.*] and from his uncle. He appeared generally popular and travelled widely. Recently engaged to be married to a Turkish-Egyptian princess, Fayṣal was, with his uncle and most of his immediate family, shot by insurgent troops during the revolutionary *coup* of 14 July 1958. (S. H. Longrigg)

al-FAYYŪM, a geographical region of Egypt, which today, as usually in the past, forms an administrative province. The Fayyūm, which derives its name from the Coptic, *Phiom* ("the Sea"), is a roughly triangular depression, about 35 miles from north to south, and about 49 miles from east to west. It is in Middle Egypt, lying in the Libyan Desert, east of the Nile valley. The cliffs separating it from the river valley are breached at one point, thereby admitting a stream which branches off from the Nile near Asyūṭ. Now known as Baḥr Yūsuf, this stream was called by medieval writers Khalīdj al-Manhā. Its entry into the depression of the Fayyūm has been controlled since Pharaonic times by sluices at Illahūn. On entering the Fayyūm, the waters are canalized for irrigation, the surplus escaping to form a permanent lake, now known as Birkat Ḳārūn. The principal town and provincial capital is Madīnat al-Fayyūm. The Fayyūm plays an important part in the Judaeo-Islamic legend of Joseph, who is said to have constructed the canal of al-Manhā (hence the modern name), the sluices of Illahūn, and the canals which drained the great marsh (*al-d̲j̲awba*) formerly covering the region. Two variants of this legend are given by Ibn ʿAbd al-Ḥakam, and it also appears in al-Maḳrīzī's *K̲h̲iṭaṭ* and other sources. With it is connected a folk-etymology of the name, al-Fayyūm: the Egyptian king, on seeing Joseph's achievements, said, "This is the work of a thousand days [*alf yawm*]". Abū Ṣāliḥ derives the name also from an eponym. The intimate association of the Fayyūm with the Joseph legend is perhaps due to the presence there of an ancient Jewish settlement, of which documentary evidence exists as early as the 3rd century B.C. Jewish influence may perhaps also be traced in the assertion, recorded by ʿAlī Mubārak, that S̲h̲ayk̲h̲ al-Rūbī, the *walī* of Madīnat al-Fayyūm, was a descendant of Reuben; a possible indication of an islamized Jewish shrine. During the Arab invasion of Egypt, the Fayyūm was occupied without difficulty, although it lay off the main routes of the conquerors: Ibn ʿAbd al-Ḥakam gives three variant traditions of its discovery and capture. It continued for some centuries to be an important centre of Coptic Christianity: Abū Ṣāliḥ, writing in the opening years of the 7th/13th century, says that there were (by implication, before his time) 35 monasteries, and he devotes some space to those still surviving. At the opening of the Muslim period, the Fayyūm seems to have been a fertile and prosperous region, as is indicated by the legend of its 360 villages, each of which could provision the whole of Egypt for one day. Rice and flax were among its chief products. It suffered a gradual decline in the succeeding centuries. Its remoteness, and the difficulty of access to it during the Nile flood, laid it open to the raids of Arab and Berber tribes. The associated phenomenon of the sedentarization of nomads in the Fayyūm has been recurrent down to modern times. Like other parts of Egypt, the Fayyūm was affected by the administrative reorganization and economic development which took place under Muḥammad ʿAlī Pas̲h̲a and his successors of the Albanian dynasty. The establishment of a railway link with the Nile valley (1874) ended the isolation of the province, while the area under cultivation was extended, cotton being developed as a cash-crop.

Bibliography: For a general bibliography, see Maspéro-Wiet, *Matériaux*, 142-3. Al-Maḳrīzī, *K̲h̲iṭaṭ* (Būlāḳ edn.), i, 241-50; ʿAlī Mubārak, *al-K̲h̲iṭaṭ al-d̲j̲adīda*, xvi, 84-94; Ibn ʿAbd al-Ḥakam, *Futūḥ Miṣr* (ed. Torrey), 14-6; B. T. A. Evetts and A. J. Butler, *The churches and monasteries of Egypt*, Oxford 1895, 49-56, 202-10; H. Lorin, *L'Egypte d'aujourd'hui*, Cairo 1926, 53-60.

(P. M. Holt)

FAZĀRA, a North Arabian tribe, reckoned part of D̲h̲ubyān, which was itself included in G̲h̲aṭafān [*q.v.*]. Its main pasture-grounds were in Wādi 'l-Rumma in Nad̲j̲d, and the names of many localities associated with it have been preserved (cf. Yāḳūt, index, s.v. Fazāra). In the D̲j̲āhiliyya the famous war of Dāḥis between Abs and D̲h̲ubyān arose out of a wager between Ḳays b. Zuhayr, chief of Abs, and Ḥud̲h̲ayfa b. Badr of Fazāra about their respective horses Dāḥis and G̲h̲abrā. The latter won because of underhand acts by some men of Fazāra, and this led to the killing of a brother of Ḥud̲h̲ayfa. In the long war which followed D̲h̲ubyān was led by Ḥud̲h̲ayfa, and then by his son Ḥiṣn (A. P. Caussin de Perceval, *Essai sur l'histoire des Arabes avant l'Islamisme*, Paris 1847, ii, 424-43, etc.). After peace was made with Abs, Fazāra became involved in fighting with ʿĀmir b. Ṣaʿṣaʿa, D̲j̲us̲h̲am and other tribes, the command being latterly in the hands of ʿUyayna b. Ḥiṣn b. Ḥud̲h̲ayfa. In Muḥammad's period at Medina ʿUyayna was the leader of Fazāra and joined in the siege of Medina (affair of the K̲h̲andaḳ) in 5/627 with 1000 men. Some months later part of Fazāra ambushed a Muslim trading expedition led by Zayd b. Ḥārit̲h̲a, and in 6/628 Zayd made severe reprisals on Fazāra. At the siege of Medina, Muḥammad had tried to bribe ʿUyayna to abandon his allies, and made similar offers during the expedition to K̲h̲aybar in 7/628, where ʿUyayna with a large force of G̲h̲aṭafān was supporting the Jews. Though furious at the eventual failure of these intrigues ʿUyayna came to terms with Muḥammad, joined the expeditions to Mecca and Ḥunayn (in 8/630), and received a hundred camels at al-D̲j̲iʿrāna along with "those whose hearts are to be reconciled"; this seems to have been the share of the leader of a non-Muslim contingent, though ʿUyayna is not said to have had any following. Shortly afterwards he led a Muslim expedition against Tamīm, but he was not a member of the deputation (*wafd*) from Fazāra. After Muḥammad's death most of Fazāra joined the *ridda* under Ṭulayḥa, but eventually had to submit (cf. W. Hoenerbach, in *Abhandlungen der Akademie der Wissenschaften und der Literatur*, Geistes- und sozialwissenschaftliche Klasse, no. 4, 1951, 242-6. They are later heard of in North Africa (al-Ḳalḳashandī, *Nihāyat al-arab*, Cairo 1959, 392 f.).

Bibliography: in addition to the references in the article: *Mufaḍḍaliyyāt*, ed. Lyall, i, 38, n. 2; ii, 288-90; etc.; al-Hamdānī, see *Index historicus;* al-Bakrī, *Muʿd̲j̲am*, Cairo, index; *Ag̲h̲ānī*, Tables; al-Ṭabarī, ii, 1381-90 (Fazārī in revolt of 101); iii, 1342 f., 2008 (in Arabia in 231, 267); Montgomery Watt, *Muḥammad at Medina*, Oxford 1956, 91-5, etc.

(W. Montgomery Watt)

FĀZĀZ, name borne in mediaeval times by the north-western extremity of the Moroccan Middle Atlas. This territory lay to the south of Fez and Meknès. It was bounded to the east by the upper course of the Wādī Subū (=Wādī Gīgū); westwards, it extended as far as the upper course of the Wādī Umm-Rabīʿ (=Wādī Wānsīfan); its southern boundary was the so-called Tīg̲h̲ānīmīn pass, where the Malwiyya rises. It coincided with the territory now occupied by the Berber-speaking tribes called in Arabic: Bnī Mṭīr, Bnī Mgīld, Gerwān, Zemmūr and Ẓāyān. It is a high plateau, with an average altitude of 1500 m./5000 ft., from which some mountains rise. Geologically, it is of the 'causse' type (karst, limestone plateau), here and there volcanic, and cut by numerous canyons; it is covered by forests of oaks, thujas (arbor vitae) and cedars, where are found monkeys and panthers (and, as late as the end of the 19th century, lions).

Northwards and westwards this high plateau shades off into lower foothills (peneplains). The abundant rain and snow give rise to many copious springs: here rise the three most important rivers of Morocco, the Malwiyya, the Subū and the Umm Rabīʿ, and many left tributaries of the last two.

As in the rest of central Morocco, the oldest known population consisted of Ṣanhād̲j̲a [*q.v.*], or, more strictly, Ẓanāga, the Arabic adaptation of the Berber plural *Iẓnāgen*, sing. *Āẓnāg*. Some Arabic authors call them also 'Banū Fāzāz', as though the second element were the name of an eponymous ancestor; but this name must arise from a careless translation of the Berber 'Ayt Fāzāz' = A. *ahl Fāzāz*, 'the people of the Fāzāz'.

The geographers describe them as pastoral mountain-folk, raising cattle, sheep, and also very sturdy horses. They practised transhumance: they spent the summers on the high plateaus, but the snows of winter obliged them to move to the valleys of the Lower Atlas: to the north, those of Tāgrāgrā (the *Guraigura* of Leo Africanus, modern Tīgrīgra) and Āsāis (between Fez and Meknès), to the west, that of Ādek͟hsān, on the upper Umm Rabīʿ.

In 173/789, Idrīs I took possession of the Fāzāz and applied himself to converting the population to Islam, for they had, for the most part, remained loyal to Judaism or Christianity. From the reign of his successor Idrīs II (188-213/804-28) there survive numerous *dirhams*, struck at Wazaḳḳūr. This mint must have been located on the present Bū-Uzeḳḳūr, a small tributary of the Umm Rabīʿ, some 3 km/2 miles south of K͟hnīfra. When in 213/828 the domains of Idrīs II were shared out between his sons, the Fāzāz was divided: the northern part was annexed to the principality of Fez whose *amīr*, the eldest son Muḥammad, struck *dirhams* at Tāgrāgrā; the southern part fell to ʿĪsā, whose principality included also the northern Tāmasnā with the city of S͟hālla. Shortly afterwards ʿĪsā rose in revolt against his elder brother Muḥammad, who entrusted to another brother, ʿUmar, the task of subduing the rebel. ʿĪsā was defeated and left the Fāzāz; he died in the Tādlā, where his tomb is still venerated among the Ayt ʿItāb as that of Mūlāy ʿĪsā ben Drīs.

During the second half of the 4th/10th century, the Zenāta of the central Mag͟hrib were pushed westwards by the Ṣanhād͟ja of Buluggīn, who was governing Ifrīḳiya in the name of the Fāṭimids of Cairo; it is at this period that the Mag͟hrāwa and the Banū Yafran settled in Morocco. The latter carved out for themselves a principality whose boundaries corresponded to those of the principality of ʿĪsā b. Idrīs, with its capital at S͟hālla. One clan, the Banū Yad͟jfas͟h, occupied the Fāzāz; their chief, Tawālā, built there a *ḳalʿa*—the famous Ḳalʿat Mahdī b. Tawālā—which was inherited by his son Mahdī.

In 452/1060 the Almoravid *amīr* Abū Bakr b. ʿUmar conquered the mountain district of the Fāzāz, except for the Ḳalʿa, which his successor Yūsuf b. Tās͟hufīn was able to occupy, on terms, only after a nine-year investment (456-65/1063-72). For some months the luckless al-Muʿtamid [*q.v.*] was held prisoner in the Ḳalʿa before being finally interned at Ag͟hmāt.

Thereafter the Fāzāz was conquered in turn by the Almohads and the Marīnids. This district controlled the most direct route from Fez to Marrākus͟h, that passing through the Tādlā; it had also two silver-mines, at ʿAwwām and Wārknās.

From the 9th/15th century onwards the name Fāzāz seems to have fallen out of use. Leo Africanus, who crossed the district in 1515, does not mention it. Indeed in the course of the 10th/16th century the land was overrun by new waves of Berbers (also belonging to the Ṣanhād͟ja group) who had come from the upper valley of the Malwiyya, following in the wake of the Arab tribes, the Banū Ḥasan (= Bnī Ḥsen) and the Zuʿayr (= Zʿēr) as they migrated towards the north-west of Morocco.

Thenceforward the history of the Fāzāz is the history of the marabouts of the *zāwiya* of al-Dilāʾ and their Berber fellow-tribesmen the Ayt Īdrāsen (to the north) and the Ayt Ūmālū (to the west), and their struggles against the ʿAlawī sultans (especially al-Ras͟hīd, Ismāʿīl and Sulaymān) and later against the troops of the French Protectorate.

Two Idrīsid mints in the Fāzāz, Wazaḳḳūr and Tāgrāgrā, are (as has been noted) easily identified, but this is not true of the two other famous place-names of the district. As regards the silver-mine called Maʿdin ʿAwwām, there exists nowadays a D͟jabal ʿAwwām, some 10 km/6 miles west of Mrīrt, and thus 120 km/75 miles south-west of Fez, where there is a mine of silver-bearing lead; but Leo Africanus, who passed that way, speaks of an iron-mine on the Bū Ragrāg. Still more difficult is the case of the famous Ḳalʿa. Al-Bakrī does not mention it: indeed his route from Ag͟hmāt to Fez via the Tādlā passed some way to the west of the Fāzāz; while al-Idrīsī locates it, on the same route, between Ṣufrūy [*q.v.*] and the town of Tādlā, two stages (some 100 km/60 miles) from each, on a very high mountain. The anonymous author of the *Kitāb al-Istibṣār* notes that when Al-Muʿtamid was a prisoner there it was built of wood and the majority of its population consisted of Jewish merchants. But Leo Africanus, who saw it when it was ruined and calls it *Mahdiyya*, says that it was built almost on the plain. He might be referring to a township built below a mountain-fortress, but he locates it 'ten miles' (15 km) from ʿAyn al-Aṣnām (the present Anoceur), i.e. 35 km/22 miles (barely one stage) from Ṣufrūy. It seems that the site of the Ḳalʿa of Mahdī b. Tawālā is to be sought for in the area between Timahdit and Mrīrt, perhaps at Timahdit itself.

The Fāzāz has produced few famous men apart from the founder of the Ḳalʿa, but the following may be mentioned: (1) the secretary of state and religious poet ʿAbd al-Raḥmān b. Yak͟hlaftan al-Fāzāzī, who died in 627/1230 (see Brockelmann, I, 273, where he is called in error *al-Fazārī*; S I, 482); (2) the great historian al-Ẓayānī, who died in 1230/1815 (see Lévi-Provençal, *Les historiens des Chorfa*, 142).

Bibliography: See the indexes of al-Idrīsī, the *Kitāb al-Istibṣār*, the *Extraits inédits relatifs au Maghreb* (tr. Fagnan), Ibn K͟haldūn (*Histoire des Berbères*, tr. de Slane), and Leo Africanus (tr. Epaulard), under the toponyms mentioned in the article.

(G. S. Colin)

FĀZIL ḤUSAYN BEY [see FĀḌIL BEY].

FAZL [see FAḌL].

FAZLĪ [see FAḌLĪ].

FAZLULLĀH [see FAḌL ALLĀH].

FĀZŪG͟HLĪ, a region of the upper Blue Nile, within the modern Republic of the Sudan, and near to the Ethiopian border. Its historical importance is solely due to the presence of alluvial gold. The ruler (*makk*) of Fāzūg͟hlī was a vassal of the Fund͟j [*q.v.*] sultan of Sinnār, and wore the horned cap (*taḳiyya umm ḳarnayn*) as his insignia of office. This usage long survived the downfall of the Fund͟j sultanate (see A. W. M. Disney, *The coronation of the Fung king of Fazoghli*, in *Sudan Notes and Records*, xxvi/1, Khartoum 1945, 37-42, describing the investiture of a *makk* in 1944). In 1237/1821-22 Fāzūg͟hlī was conquered by Ismāʿīl Kāmil Pas͟ha, *serʿasker* of Muḥammad ʿAlī Pas͟ha's invading forces, and a levy of gold was laid on its merchants. Muḥammad ʿAlī endeavoured, with the aid of European technicians, to exploit the gold of Fāzūg͟hlī, but had little success. Under ʿAbbās I Fāzūg͟hlī became a place of banishment. Thereafter it lost all importance.

Bibliography: Count Gleichen, *The Anglo-Egyptian Sudan*, London 1905, i, 123-6; O. G. S. Crawford, *The Fung Kingdom of Sennar*, Gloucester 1951, 82-3; Richard Hill, *Egypt in the Sudan 1820-1881*, London 1959, Index.

(P. M. Holt)

FAZZĀN (Fezzān), one of the three provinces, with Tripolitania and Cyrenaica, of the United Kingdom of Libya which dates from 1951. An entirely desert region of 551,000 sq. km., it extends as far as 600 km. to the south of the Mediterranean, between latitudes 24° and 28°, at the longitude of Tripolitania and Chad. The most direct routes from the Sudan to the Mediterranean lie across Fezzan. The climate is very arid, and localities there have an average rainfall of only 5 to 12 mm.; frost is rare; the summers are very hot, but not among the most torrid.

Fezzan consists of a number of depressions enclosed by plateaux of an altitude of from 400 to 600 m., the surface of which is rocky (*ḥamāda*) or covered with gravel (*serīr*): calcareous and sandstone plateaux, cretaceous and tertiary, in the north and east (*Ḥamāda al-Ḥamrā*ʾ, Gargāf and Ḥarūdj), sometimes covered with black basalt deposits (Djabal al-Sōda, Ḥarūdj al-Aswad); tertiary sandstone plateaux in the south, rising to the Djabal Ben Guenēma and the vast primary and volcanic massif of Tibesti. West of the primary sandstones lie the slopes of the Messak and Tadrart (1,000 to 1,200 m.), on the edge of the Tassili.

The two Fezzanese depressions, separated by the Ḥamāda of Murzuḳ and the Serīr al-Gaṭṭūsa, are made up of two *ramla*s (erg or edeien) encircled by depressions of 300 to 450 m. in depth, where underground water is present near the surface and which are inhabited: the *ramla* of Ubāri with the oases of Shāṭi, al-Bwānis and Wādi ʾl-Adjal, the *ramla* of Murzuḳ, al-Ḥofra, al-Shergiyya and, in the south-east, Gatrun (Ghaṭrūm). The sparse rainwater which soaks through into the sandstone, limestone and sand supplies the underground water-table in the depressions, and sometimes the deeper artesian water-channels.

The word Fezzān which goes back to antiquity (*Phasania*) is applied to the oases as a whole, excluding those in the Ghāt and Ghadāmes regions. The Fezzanese (*Fazāzna*, sing. *Fazzānī*) are the cultivators of these oases. They have often been menaced and robbed by the nomadic shepherds of the neighbourhood, "Arabs" from the Gibla (plateaux in south Tripolitania), connected with Shāṭi, the Touareg Ajjer whose home is in Ghāt and south of Ghadāmes but who also live as nomads in west Fezzan, and the Tebou, who are few in number, in the south-east. The Fezzanese, who are strongly interbred with negroes, are, like the nomads in the north who have remained much whiter, all Arabic speakers: their dialects "are related to the general type of Maghribī Arabic. But with them the Maghribī type is already assuming an oriental tinge" (W. Marçais), as regards both the sedentary inhabitants and also the nomads whose dialects "differ phonetically, and often grammatically as well". The Touareg Ajjer, who are tall but often of mixed breeding, are Berber-speaking (but many are bilingual); the Tebou, who are few in number and also partly of mixed breeding, are somewhat tall and slender, black but of a non-negroid type, and speak a Sudanic dialect. All the inhabitants of Fezzan, both the settled population and the herdsmen, are Sunnī Muslims of the Mālikī rite; there are no Jews.

Fezzan has been inhabited, even in what are now the most desert regions such as the *ḥamāda*s, since the old palaeolithic age. Worked stones from the mid-palaeolithic age, which are much more numerous, are already concentrated in the depressions; this is even more the case with the plentiful and fine stone relics of the age of polished stone. Fezzan shared in the great Saharan civilization of the neolithic age, to which we must certainly attribute a notable part of the rock paintings, those of the "pre-camel" period which represent, in a naturalistic style, elephants, giraffes, rhinoceroses, bovines, and men armed with bows. The most recent and diagrammatic of the rock paintings, which depict camels (dromedaries), horses, various domestic animals and men armed with shields and lances, are thought to date from the end of the neolithic period and prehistory, perhaps even from the beginning of our own era. The Garamantes who are mentioned by Herodotus and with whom the Romans were in contact, were already a mixed race composed of white Berbers like the Touareg today, half-castes and negroes, as is shown in the great number of tombs that have been excavated, particularly by Italian scholars, and whose funerary furnishings include Roman ceramics and glassware from the 2nd to the 6th centuries A.D.

The Garamantes, living over 500 km. south of the Tripolitanian *limes* but often allied with the turbulent Getuli, had to endure several "punitive" expeditions by the Romans under Cornelius Balbus in 20-19 B.C. and Valerius Festus in 69-70. However, they collaborated with Roman troops in two expeditions against the "Ethiopians", their southern neighbours, and carried produce from their country and from Sudan to the Tripolitanian ports (Leptis Magna, Oea and Sabratha). Draught oxen, donkeys, horses, and carts drawn by two horses were the forerunners of camels, the use of which spread only slowly, over the desert tracks. But only dromedaries had the ability to carry to the coast sufficient quantities of dates, precious stones, ostrich feathers, ivory and, no doubt, some black slaves from the Sahara and Sudan. From the end of the 3rd century the Garamantes came on several occasions to plunder Tripolitania. The only Roman monument in Fezzan is a mausoleum at Djerma (Garama), surrounded by cremation tombs (probably of Roman or Romanized merchants). It is likely that the technique of *foggāra*s (underground conduits for collecting water), possibly of Iranian origin, spread towards the end of the Roman period.

Being independent and ignored by the Vandal and Byzantine Maghrib, Fezzan long remained outside the sphere of Arab expansion, though conquered by ʿUḳba b. Nāfiʿ in 46/666-7. We know only that the town of Zawīla was founded in 306/918 in the Shergiyya by a Berber, Ibn Khaṭṭāb al-Hawwārī; it was a flourishing caravan centre, particularly for the slave trade, a small open city with a mosque and baths, and from it the Banū Khaṭṭāb ruled Fezzan. The country was then prosperous, irrigated by wells and numerous *foggāras*; Djerma (Garama), Sebha, Tsāwa, and Tmessa were the principal centres. But as early as the 12th century "the Arabs spread through the countryside, doing as much damage as possible" (al-Idrīsī, trans. 158); Zawīla was surrounded by walls which are now falling into ruin. In 1190 the dynasty of the Banū Khaṭṭāb fell before the attacks of Ḳarāḳush al-Ghuzzī, a Turcoman adventurer from Armenia who had the support of the Arab tribes of Sulaym and was already master of Tripolitania.

Fezzan then passed under the domination of the

negro kings of Kanem (13th-15th centuries); they were represented by a governor (*mai*) who lived in the new capital, Trāghen (70 km. east of Zawīla); as a result there followed a widespread immigration of negroes (not slaves) and, no doubt, closer connexions with the Sudan; but the abandonment of the *foggāras* appears to date from this period.

The negro domination finally declined at the beginning of the 16th century as a result of the wars of Kanem against the Bornu and the long struggles with the Awlād Muḥammad dynasty, the founders of Murzuḳ and of Moroccan and Sharīfian origin. The Awlād Muḥammad, when finally they became masters of Fezzan, certainly contributed to its Islamization and Arabization; Murzuḳ was made the capital of the country, remaining so until the 20th century, while it was also a busy caravan centre and a stopping-place for pilgrims from the west on their way to Mecca.

The Turks, who occupied Tripoli in 1551, attempted to establish their authority in Fezzan only in 1577-8. At times they had governors there, several of whom were assassinated; they sent punitive expeditions such as that of 1679 during which Murzuḳ was completely sacked. But for the most part they were compelled to recognize Fezzan's *de facto* independence, in return for payment of tribute in gold and negro slaves by the Awlād Muḥammad.

The Ḳaramanlī dynasty which ruled over Tripoli from 1710 until 1835 was unable to keep control over Fezzan, in spite of armed intervention in 1716, 1718, 1731-2 and 1811. In the second half of the 18th century the country was, however, reasonably peaceful, under what was in practice a ruling family that paid tribute. But in 1831 Fezzan fell into the hands of the dreaded nomads, the Awlād Slēmān, under their chief ʿAbd al-Djalīl Sīf al-Naṣr.

The Turks, returning to Tripoli in 1835, made themselves masters of Fezzan in 1842, after killing Sīf al-Naṣr and driving back the Awlād Slēmān into Kanem. They remained there until 1911. The country became a *sandjaḳ* subordinate to the *wilāyet* of Tripoli and was divided into districts (*ḳaḍā*) and sub-districts (*nāḥiya*) with Ghāt in Touareg country. The Ottoman Government found Fezzan a convenient place of exile for the Young Turks, both civilians and military, whom it was anxious to keep at a distance; the tombs of several of them can be seen at Murzuḳ.

The principal halting place for trans-Saharan trade was Zawīla, Trāghen and then Murzuḳ. But the story was only known in detail long after, from the correspondence of the French Consuls in Tripoli and explorations at the end of the 18th and in the 19th centuries. On their way from Sudan to Tripoli came caravans, their chief merchandise being black slaves numbering from 500 to 2,000 a year, and also gold (either dust or in ingots); less important were ivory, ostrich feathers, copper (from Bornu) and hides. Fezzan exported only dates and natron (carbonate of soda). In the opposite direction the caravans carried various manufactured articles from Europe or the East; Venetian glassware, brocades and brass, coarse cloth from Naples and Marseilles, cottons from England and silks from Lyons (19th century), arms, ironmongery and pharmaceuticals from Italy and France, oriental fabrics, carpets and spices. The Fezzanese had some share in this traffic, which was mainly financed by the merchants from the oases in the north, in Tripoli and Ghadāmes, the Tebou of Bilma and the Bornu negroes; and the government of Murzuḳ levied duties on camel-loads and slaves. The suppression of slavery, progressively observed, and the occupation of the Guinea Coast by the European Powers brought about first the decline and then the almost total disappearance of trans-Saharan trade. In addition, the Fezzan suffered greatly from the banditry of nomads during the ten years of the Awlād Slēmān's domination and, much more recently, between the two Italian conquests.

The Italians actually disembarked in Tripoli on 5 October 1911—taking over from the Turks in Libya as a result of the Treaty of Ouchy (19 October 1912)—but were able to occupy Fezzan only between January and August 1914. The Miani force, coming from Syrte through Sokna, and outflanking Gibla which was occupied by hostile nomads, took Brak, Sebḥa, Murzuḳ, Ubāri and Ghāt in succession. But owing to the opposition of the nomads who were spurred on by the propaganda of the Sanūsiyya fraternity, and also to the outbreak of the first world war, into which Italy was to make her entry, the Italian troops were withdrawn, though not without difficulty, in December 1914 and January 1915, leaving the country unprotected against the brigandage of the nomads for fifteen years. In fact, the Italians only returned in December 1929; in a combined advance of three columns, under the command of General Graziani, they passed through Derdj, al-Gueriat and Hūn (Djofra) and had no great difficulty in reoccupying Fezzan, including Ghāt and the Gatrūn region (February 1930).

It was a ruined country which had to be organized and equipped. Fezzan became a military command dependent on the Governor General of Libya; later (1936) it was transferred to the South Libya Command, set up at Hūn. The Italians started to link up the different parts of the Fezzan and Ghāt with Tripoli and Miṣrāta by motor roads; they set up a number of schools and hospitals, and regularized and controlled the traditional administration of the *mudīrs*. Fezzan enjoyed a period of peace that was sorely needed.

The peaceful atmosphere was scarcely disturbed by the arrival of the Free French troops under the command of General Leclerc who, coming from the south in December 1942, easily occupied Murzuḳ on 7 January 1943, and then Sebḥa and the rest of the country before linking up with the British 8th Army in the advance on Tunisia. As a result of the Franco-British Agreement of January 1943, Fezzan and Ghadāmes formed a territory placed under the direct authority of the Direction des Territoires du Sud de l'Algérie, while Ghāt was annexed to the territory of Djanet (Fort-Charley). The French divided Fezzan into 3 subdivisions (Shāṭi, Sebḥa-Ubāri, Murzuḳ), maintained the administration by *mudīrs* and continued the educational, medical and economic work undertaken by the Italians; in addition, they dug several artesian wells.

Since 24 December 1951, the date of the creation of the United Kingdom of Libya under the sovereignty of Muḥammad Idrīsi al-Sanūsī, Fezzan has been one of the three autonomous provinces of this now independent country. The French forces provisionally maintained in Fezzan evacuated it, together with Ghāt and Ghadāmes, by the terms of the Franco-Libyan Treaty of 10 August 1955; Ghadāmes has subsequently been added to Tripolitania. The *wālī*, the governor who represents the king at Sebḥa, the chief town of Fezzan, is assisted by an executive council composed of minor ministers (*nāẓir*) and a legislative council, three-quarters of whose members are elected and whose chairman shares authority with the *wālī*.

The census of 1954 recorded 54,400 inhabitants in Fezzan province, three-quarters of whom are sedentary. Agriculture is in fact the main source of livelihood, in particular the cultivation of date-palms of which there are between eight and nine hundred thousand. To be accurate, the date-palms are, for the most part, neither cultivated nor even irrigated, but merely fertilized. The underground water-table is sufficiently close to the surface for the palmtrees' roots to reach the level of moisture; but the annual production of dates is hardly more than 4 to 6 kg. per tree, whilst with irrigation it reaches from 30 to 50 kg., particularly in Sh̲āṭi. Another characteristic: outside the palm-groves cultivation is for the most part practised by means of a balance-well (*k̲h̲eṭṭāra*), especially in the south, and in particular by means of a well operated by an animal [see BIʾR] in which the goatskin water-container (*dalw*) is drawn up by a donkey helped by a man. Cereals—wheat and barley in winter, millet (*gṣob*) and sorghum (*gāfūli*) in summer—are almost the only form of cultivation: they are grown in succession on the same piece of land which is then left fallow; the rotation of crops near the wells is thus carried out in from 2 to 5 successive crops. The cultivated strips are protected by temporary hedges of palm leaves. Trees (pomegranates, vines) are very rare and are always planted at the side of the wells (or springs). Fertilization of the date-palms, drawing of water and irrigation are undertaken by the proprietors themselves or by hired labourers, serfs by origin, former negro slaves or tribes of very mixed antecedents, the *Sh̲wāsh̲na* (sing. *Sh̲ūsh̲ānī*): these are the *Ḥarātīn* of other parts of the Sahara. The sedentary inhabitants possess only a few sheep and goats; donkeys and dromedaries are used for wells and for transport. The workers are very poor. Emigration, both temporary and permanent, is by tradition made mainly to Tripolitania, but also to Tunisia.

The villages are generally of wretched appearance. The huddled buildings, partly or wholly in ruins, testify to a state of insecurity either formerly or recently. The houses, built of dry stone or baked bricks, with flat roofs and opening onto a court which is also sometimes covered (*kawdi*), are built close together in barely two-thirds of the villages. It is only in the chief centres like Brāk (Sh̲āṭi), Murzuḳ or the oases of Sebḥa and al-Bwānis that they assume a somewhat more comfortable and urban aspect. There are numerous hamlets. In the poorest regions habitations are merely huts of palm leaves (*zarība*), and are widely spaced for fear of fire. The placing of houses, either adjoining one another or at a distance, is the result of the degree of social cohesion of the villagers and of the types of dwellings, not of economic differences. Stockbreeding is almost the sole activity of the more or less nomadic shepherds in the outlying regions of the Fezzan. The Tebou in the south-east wander in small scattered groups, from the Tibesti to the D̲jabal Ben Guenēma and the neighbourhood of Gatrūn; they have temporary oblong huts made of the ribs of palmleaves and matting (*būsh̲i*). The Touareg Ajjer (Imangh̲assaten and Urāg̲h̲en), from the neighbourhood of G̲h̲adāmes and the Messāk, drive their flocks as far as the approaches to Sh̲āṭi, on the edge of the Wādi 'l-Ad̲jal, and the Murzuḳ region. They live in tents of hides or in little round temporary huts made of matting. The shepherds from the north, the "Arabs", are far more numerous. The Gdādfa, the Urfella, the Awlād Busīf and the Zintān from Gibla, and also part of the Megārha, come to Sh̲āṭi at the end of the summer at the time of the date harvest. But most of the Megārha and the Ḥasāwna own date-palms and land which they have cultivated by the Sh̲wāsh̲na: they are semi-nomadic, living alternately in houses and tents: the Ḥotmān, Zwayd and Gwāyda, formerly semi-nomadic, are today almost completely settled in western Sh̲āṭi. All the Arabs' tents are of the "black tent" type which is to be found from Afghanistan to the Atlantic.

Fezzan sells part of its dates to all the neighbouring shepherds, and part of its cereals to the Tebou and Touareg. The nomads in the north, who grow cereals in the Gibla depressions, are the largest purchasers of dates, consuming a good part of them themselves, while by tradition they take the rest to markets in Tripolitania, to be exchanged for manufactured goods landed at Tripoli; some caravans go to south Tunisia.

But the dates and cereals, and also the natron taken by the Dawāda from the small lakes south of the *ramla* of Ubāri, are now almost always carried by lorry along the roads linking Misrata and Tripoli. It is also by lorry that the manufactured goods that are increasingly needed are brought from Tripoli. New roads lead to the oil-drilling centres recently opened in west and north-west Fezzan; but they are on the fringe of the country. Sebḥa, the capital of Fezzan, which includes a certain number of administrative and modern business buildings, has on the other hand become an important aerodrome.

Bibliography: Bakrī, *Description de l'Afrique septentrionale*, tr. de Slane, 2nd ed. Algiers 1911; Idrīsī, *Description de l'Afr. et de l'Esp.*, trans. Dozy and De Goeje, Leiden 1866; Ibn K̲h̲aldūn, *Histoire des Berbères*, tr. de Slane, 2nd ed. Paris 1925-56; P. Masson, *Histoire des établissements et du commerce français dans l'Afrique barbaresque*, Paris 1903; H. Barth, *Reisen und Entdeckungen in Nord und Central Afrika*, i, Gotha 1858; H. Duveyrier, *Les Touareg du Nord*, Paris 1854; G. Nachtigal, *Sahara und Sudan*, i, Berlin 1879; E. Scarin, *Le oasi del Fezzan*, Bologna 1924; Soc. Geogr. Italiana, *Il Sahara italiano*, i, *Fezzan e oasi del Gat*, Rome 1937; J. Despois, *Mission scientifique du Fezzan*, iii, *Géogr. Humaine*, Paris 1946; J. Lethielleux, *Le Fezzan, ses jardins, ses palmiers*, in *IBLA*, 1948; P. Bellair, etc., *Mission au Fezzan* (1949), Publ. Inst. des Hautes Et. de Tunis, i, Tunis 1953; Ct Cauneille, *Le nomadisme des Mgarha*, in *Travaux de l'Institut de recherches sahariennes*, Paris 1954; idem, *Le nomadisme des Zentan*, *ibid.*, 1957; idem, *Les Hassaouna*, in *Bull. de liaison saharienne*, Algiers 1955, xix; idem, *Le nomadisme des Guedadfa*, *ibid.*, xxxii (1958); idem, *Les Gouneyda d'Ouenzerik*, *ibid.*, xxxviii (1960); W. Meckelein, *Der Fezzan heute*, Stuttgarter Geogr. Studien 1957; L. Richter, *Inseln der Sahara. Durch die Oasien Libyens*, Leipzig 1957; B. Vernier, *Histoire d'un pays saharien. Le Fezzan*, in *Orient*, xiv (1960). See further LIBYA.

(J. DESPOIS)

FEDALA [see FAḌĀLA].

FED̲JR-I ĀTĪ, the coming dawn, a Turkish literary group active in the period following the Young Turk Revolution of 1908, and associated with the review *T̲h̲erwet-i Fünūn* [*q.v.*], where its initial manifesto was published. See further TURKS, literature, and the articles on the individual authors. (Ed.)

FEHĪM, SÜLEYMĀN (1203-62/1789-1846), a minor Ottoman poet who wrote in the first half of the 19th century, during the declining decades of the classical school. A government official in Istanbul and in the Balkans, he soon retired and devoted his life to study and writing, teaching Persian occasionally.

His little *dīwān* (Istanbul 1262) contains poems inspired by the "Indian style" of Persian poetry. He is also the author of *Sefīnet al-shuʿarāʾ* (Istanbul 1259), an expanded translation of Dawlatshāh's *Tadhkirat al-shuʿarāʾ*.

Bibliography: Djewdet, *Taʾrīkh*², xii, 184; Faṭīn, *Tedhkire*, 336; İbnülemin Mahmud Kemal, *Son asır Türk şairleri*, 379-81; A. C. Yöntem, in *IA*, s.v. (Fahir İz)

FEHĪM, UNDJUZĀDE MUṢṬAFĀ known as Fehīm-i Ḳadīm (? -1058/1648), Turkish poet, one of the most appreciated of the minor poets of the 17th century. According to scattered information found in various *tedhkire*s and in Ewliyā Čelebi, he was born in Istanbul, the son of an Egyptian pastrycook. Without a regular education or settled position, stricken by poverty he left Istanbul, joining the suite of Eyyūb Pasha, governor of Egypt. Because of a colleague's intrigue, he lost the favour of the Pasha and decided to leave Egypt, where he does not seem to have been very happy or prosperous. Thanks to the mediation of Newālī Bey, the commander of the Janissaries in Egypt, he was allowed to join the caravan conveying the yearly tribute from Egypt to the Capital, but he died on the way at Ilghīn in 1058/1648, apparently in his early twenties.

His *dīwān*, his only work, which according to *tedhkire*s he completed at the age of eighteen, shows that he was an unconventional poet of great promise and although fascinated by the work of the Persian poet ʿUrfī, in his lyrics he did not always follow the latter's precious and bombastic style, but succeeded in developing, at that early age, a personality of his own. Especially in his *ghazal*s, in the middle of hackneyed clichés, characteristic of the school, it is not rare to come across sincere personal notes and glimpses of his *ambiance*. During the attempt at a classical revival in the second half of the 19th century, many latter-day *dīwān* poets, headed by Leskofdjalī Ghālib, started a vogue of Fehīm and wrote many *naẓīra*s to his poems. Even the modernist Nāmiḳ Kemāl joined this admiration of Fehīm and rebuked Ziya (Ḍiyā) Pasha (*Takhrīb-i kharābāt*, Istanbul 1291, 76) for not having included him in the *Kharābāt*, his classical anthology of *dīwān* verse.

Bibliography: The *tedhkire*s of Ṣafāʾī, Riḍā and Sheykhī's *Waḳāʾiʿ al-fuḍalā*, s.v.; Ewliyā Čelebi, *Seyāḥatnāme*, iii, 17; Gibb, iii, 290; Sadettin Nüzhet Ergun, *Fehim Divanı*, Istanbul 1934 (not a critical edition as he uses only a few of nearly 30 MSS); Ali Canib Yöntem in *İA*, s.v. (Fahir İz)

FEHĪM PASHA, chief of the secret police under the Ottoman sultan ʿAbd al-Ḥamīd II. He was born in Istanbul in 1873 (?). Being the eldest son of the *ethwābdjībashī* ʿIṣmet Bey, foster-brother of the sultan, he was educated in the special class of the *Mekteb-i Ḥarbiyye* from where he was gazetted captain in 1894. Two years later he became *yāver-i shehriyārī* and received the title of *pasha* in 1898. Fehīm Pasha was appointed director of the secret police of the sultan, a post he held for many years. He maintained the trust of ʿAbd al-Ḥamīd II by enlarging the network of *khafiye* (secret agents) throughout the capital. He was feared by the people, especially by the native and foreign merchants whom he taxed unlawfully. He was dismissed from his position and sent to Bursa on 17 February 1907; his banishment was due to the intervention of the German ambassador von Bieberstein, supporting the claims of a German merchant against Fehīm. He was lynched at Yenishehir, near Bursa, after the revolution of 1908.

Bibliography: Mahmud Kemal Inal, *Osmanlı devrinde son sadrıazamlar*, Istanbul 1940-53, 1608-11, 1613-5; P. Fesch, *Constantinople aux derniers jours d'Abdul-Hamid*, Paris 1907, 116-22; ʿOthmān Nūrī, *ʿAbd al-Ḥamīd-i thānī we dewr-i salṭanatī*, Istanbul 1327, ii, 554-61; de la Jonquière, *Histoire de l'Empire ottoman*², Paris 1914, ii, 679-80; Ibrahim Alâettin Gövsa, *Türk meşhurları ansiklopedisi*, Istanbul 1946, 133. (E. Kuran)

FEHMĪ, Sheykh, Naḳshbandī-Khālidī Sheykh of Erzindjān. Muṣṭafā Fehmī succeeded Pīr Meḥmed Wehbī Khayyāṭ after the latter's death in 1264/1848 (see Ismāʿīl Pasha, *Hadiyyat al-ʿārifīn*, i, 643) as Sheykh of the Khālidī order in Erzindjān; Pīr Wehbī had introduced the order in Erzindjān after making there the acquaintance of ʿAbd Allah Efendī, the pupil of Mewlānā Khālid in Damascus. Fehmī died on his third pilgrimage on 21 Muḥarram 1299/14 December 1881, in Mecca, and was buried at the foot of Khadīdja's grave.

His position as head of the order does not seem to have been always unopposed; close beside him was ʿAbd al-Ḥamīd Efendi, the son-in-law of Pīr Wehbī, whom in the early days he often consulted when taking decisions, and who after a quarrel made it impossible for him to remain in his own convent for a considerable time. In spite of this, Fehmī was greatly esteemed. When he made his first two pilgrimages (winter 1276/1859-60 to 1277/1861, and Shawwāl 1282/February 1866 to Dhu 'l-Ḥidjdja 1283/ April 1867) the population of Erzindjān took a lively interest, saw him off, and gave him a musical welcome on his return with the band of the local garrison. Not only did he have connexions with the merchants and officials of the area, but he was on terms of particular trust with members of the military aristocracy, such as Čerkes Ismāʿīl Pasha (1805-61), the Turkish general in the wars with Croatia and Russia (see Ibrahim Alâettin Gövsa, *Türk meşhurları ansiklopedisi*, 1945, 193) and Derwīsh Pasha (1812-96, see *IA*, s.v.). The latter looked after him in his illness, and received "spiritual support" from him for the war against Russia (1877-8); in Djumādā II 1282/October-November 1865, he took him with him to Istanbul, where Fehmī made a speech before the General Assembly (*medjlis-i ʿumūmī*) of the Sublime Porte. The building of the Dergāh in Erzindjān (opened 12 Rabīʿ I 1284/14 July 1867, having taken two years to build) was financed by contributions from numerous important persons.

In his demeanour, Fehmī combined outward modesty with extreme self-confidence. He avoided ostentatious piety and asceticism; though never wearing European dress, he did not criticize its use by others; in his house the daily *dhikr* was combined with the forbidden playing of the flute. At the same time, he kept jealous watch over the loyalty of his followers and interfered in their private lives, and was not averse to being considered the *Sulṭān-i ʿulamāʾ bi'llāh*, that "spiritual *Khalīfa*" who manifests himself once in every generation, now in one *ṭarīḳa*, now in another, and who was then believed to be appearing in the Naḳshbandiyya. His piety contains national elements, especially the belief in the *erenler*, the "men of God" (*mardān-i Khudā*; for meaning and etymology see Schaeder in *OLZ*, xxxi (1928), 734, n.); the "superstructure" of his thought is strongly influenced by Ibn ʿArabī.

Bibliography: The most important source for his life and thought is the three volume autobiography of Ashčī Dede Ibrāhīm Khalīl b. Meḥmed ʿAlī (preserved in the Istanbul manuscripts, Üniversite Kütüphanesi T 3222 and T 78-80) who was his pupil from 1273/1856 onwards; see also M. L. Bremer, *Die Memoiren des türkischen Derwischs Aşçı Dede Ibrāhīm*, Waldorf-Hessen 1959 (*Beiträge z. Sprach- u. Kulturgesch. des Or.*, Heft 12). (M. L. van Ess-Bremer)

FELLAGHA [see fallāk].

FELLATA [see fallāta].

FELT [see keče, libād].

FEMALE CIRCUMCISION [see khifāḍ].

FENĀRĪ-ZĀDE, prominent family of Ottoman scholars and jurists, the founder of which, Shems al-Dīn Meḥemmed Fenārī, is regarded in native tradition as the first supreme *muftī* (*shaykh al-islām*) of the Empire. He was born in Bursa in 751/1350-1, the son of a certain Shaykh Ḥamza who, despite the impossibility of the dating, is said to have been a pupil of the famous *ṣūfī* scholar Ṣadr al-Dīn Ḳōnewī (d. 672/1273-4; Brockelmann, I, 449). Having studied under some of the most distinguished scholars of his age in Anatolia and Egypt, in 770/1368-9 he was appointed teacher at the Manāstir *medrese* in Bursa and the following year made *ḳāḍī* of this capital city. What the political influence was which could manoeuvre a youth of twenty into such an important position remains unknown, but that there was a special connexion with the dynasty is to be inferred from the great wealth he was able to amass, the distinction he was accorded among the statesmen and the special privileges granted to his children and his grandchildren by Murād II and Meḥemmed II. The sources give no specific date for his appointment as *muftī*, but it would seem that he retained this office even after relinquishing the *ḳāḍī*-ship of Bursa to Mollā Yegān in 822/1419-20 in order to go on the pilgrimage, for we hear of no other individual with this title until after his death in Radjab 834/15 March-13 April 1431), when Fakhr al-Dīn ʿAdjemī was appointed. He was buried in the courtyard of the mosque which he built in Bursa. The most famous of his numerous works is the *Fuṣūl al-badāʾiʿ*, a compilation on the *uṣūl al-fiḳh* (Brockelmann, II, 233, to whose biographical sources should be added Ismāʿīl Belīgh, *Güldeste-i riyāḍ-i ʿirfān*, Bursa 1302, 239-44; Muṣṭafā ʿĀlī, *Künh al-akhbār*, 4th *rükn*, Istanbul 1285, 108-10; Ṭashköprüzāde, *Shaḳāʾiḳ al-nuʿmāniyya* (trans. Medjdī), Istanbul 1269, 47-53; *ʿOthmānlī müʾellifleri*, i, 390; İ. H. Uzunçarşılı, *Osmanlı tarihi*, ii, Ankara 1949, 644; *ʿIlmiyye sālnāmesi*, Istanbul 1334, 322-6; Müstaḳīm-zāde Süleymān Efendi, *Dawḥat al-mashāʾikh*, litho., Istanbul n.d., 3).

Although Nishāndjī Meḥemmed Pasha (*Taʾrīkh-i Nishāndjī*, Istanbul 1290, 123) is probably in error in saying that he was also a *wazīr*, one of his sons, Aḥmed Čelebi (later Pasha), did follow a secular career, and after having been *defterdār* for a period and served in the campaign of 878/1473 against Uzun Ḥasan Aḳḳoyunlu (in which he was taken captive), in 884/1479 he was appointed *lālā* (mentor) to Prince Bāyezīd (later Bāyezīd II) in his governorship of Amasya; afterwards, he held the appointment of *nishāndjī* on two occasions (885/1480-81 and 887/1482-83; for a discussion of these dates, cf. İsmail Hami Danişmend, *İzahlı Osmanlı tarihi kronolojisi*, i, Istanbul 1947, 462-3). On being dismissed from office in 890/1485-6, he retired to Bursa where he died in 893/1487-8 (cf. Nishāndjī Meḥemmed Pasha, 163).

The next member of the family to achieve high office was Shems al-Dīn's grandson, ʿAlāʾ al-Dīn ʿAlī b. Yūsuf Bālī, who, after having been *ḳāḍī* of Bursa from 872/1467-8 to 877/1472-3, was appointed *ḳāḍī 'l-ʿasker* the following year, in which post he remained until 881/1476-7. Towards the end of the reign of Meḥemmed II this office was divided into two, and in 894/1488-9 he was appointed *ḳāḍī 'l-ʿasker* of Rūmili, holding this charge until 900/1494-5, when he was made chief *ḳāḍī* of Anatolia. He died in 903/1497-8 and was buried in his grandfather's mosque in Bursa (Ṭashköprüzāde, 199; Belīgh, 245). His son, [Muḥyi 'l-Dīn] Shāh Meḥemmed, also had a distinguished career. From the time of his birth (ca. 883/1478-9) he was the recipient of a stipend from the Sultan, and after having been *ḳāḍī* of Bursa (919/1513-4), Istanbul and Edirne (the dates in the sources are confused), in 925/1519 he was appointed *ḳāḍī 'l-ʿasker* of Anatolia and in 926/1519-20 of Rūmili. He died in 929/1522-3 at the age of forty-six while in this latter office, and was buried in the family graveyard in Bursa (Ṭashköprüzāde, 386; Belīgh, 248; Sehī, *Hesht Bihisht*, Istanbul 1325, 28).

His younger brother (and not his son, as stated in Ṭashköprüzāde, 387, and the sources which derive therefrom), Muḥyi 'l-Dīn Meḥemmed, attained even greater dignity. Having been *ḳāḍī* of Edirne (925/1519) and Istanbul, in 929/1522-3 he was made *ḳāḍī 'l-ʿasker* of Anatolia and, in the following year, of Rūmili. Having held this post for fourteen or fifteen years, he was retired on pension in 944/1537-8, but in 949/1542-3 was recalled to office by appointment as *shaykh al-islām* in succession to ʿAbd al-Ḳādir Efendi. Retiring at his own request in 952/1545, he died on 24 Dhu 'l-Ḳaʿda 954/5 January 1548 and was buried in Eyyūb. He is mentioned (as Muḥyī) among the poets of his age, and is said to have built a mosque in the Topkhāne quarter of Galata. (The sources often confuse him with his brother and should be used with caution: Müstaḳīm-zāde, 22; *ʿIlm. sāl.*, 361; Danişmend, ii, 432; Sehī, 29; Laṭīfī, *Tedhkere-i shuʿarā*, Istanbul 1314, 307; Ḥuseyn Ayvānsarāyī, *Ḥadīḳat al-djewāmiʿ*, Istanbul 1281, ii, 66, 131). Although descendants of this line appear as teachers and *ḳāḍī*s down to the 12th/18th century, none achieved outstanding prominence. (Cf. for example, Ṭashköprüzāde, 400 (Zeyn al-Dīn Meḥemmed), 486 (Pīr Meḥmed); ʿAṭāʾī, *Dheyl-i Shaḳāʾiḳ*, Istanbul 1268, 13 (Ḥasan b. Zeyn al-Dīn), 35 (ʿAbd al-Bāḳī Efendi and Yūsuf Efendi), 418 (Maḥmūd Efendi)). (J. R. Walsh)

FENER, the name of a quarter of Istanbul which, according to tradition, was allotted to the Greeks by Meḥemmed II after the conquest in 857/1453; for the topography, monuments, etc. see istanbul. After the conquest the seat of the Greek Patriarch was transferred from St. Sophia to the Church of the Holy Apostles, and three years later to the nearby Church of the Pammakaristos. In 994/1586, when this church was converted into a mosque (Fetḥiye Djāmiʿi), the Patriarch moved down into the Fener quarter, to establish himself finally in 1011/1603 at the Church of St. George (re-built in 1720), still the seat of the Orthodox Patriarchate. At quite an early period there settled in the neighbourhood, in addition to the ecclesiastical and secular officials of the Patriarchate, the few old Byzantine families that had remained in Istanbul and other distinguished and wealthy members of the community; in the school of the Patriarchate, conducted by the clergy, the ancient classical studies were cultivated. The prominent Greek families resident around the Patriarchate were known collectively as the 'Phanariots' (T. *Fenerliler*). Thanks to their links with and knowledge of the Christian world (many of them were educated in Italy), the Porte, particularly in the 12th/18th and early 13th/19th centuries, drew on them to fill various influential employments. Members of these families acted as dragomans of the Porte and of the Arsenal [see TARDJUMĀN], and as contractors for the supply of furs and meat to the Saray, etc.. Since they were regarded as more reliable than the native princes, for some of whom they had earlier acted as 'agents at the Porte' (*kapî ketkhüdâsî*), it was from the Phanariots that were appointed, for over a century, the *voyvoda*s (hospodars) of Moldavia (from 1123/1711, see BOGHDĀN) and Wallachia (from 1128/1716, see EFLĀĶ). The best-known names were Kantakouzenos, Skarlatos, Maurokordatos, Gkikas, Karatzas, Soutsos, Khantzeres (Handjeri), Maurogenes, Hypsilantes, Mourouzes, Kallimakhes, Mousouros, Aristarkhes, etc. In the second half of the 12th/18th century the Phanariot families began to move from Fener to the more salubrious villages along the Bosphorus—Ķuručeshme, Arnawutköy, Tarabya; after the Greek War of Independence many of them migrated to Greece. Descendants of Phanariot families are still found in modern Rumania.

Bibliography: M. Crusius, *Turcograecia*, Basle 1578, 91, 497; de la Croix, *État présent de la Nation et de l'Église grecque*, 3 ff.; W. Eton, *A survey . . .*, London 1798, 331 ff.; J. Dallaway, *Constantinople ancient and modern*, London 1797, 98 ff.; *Le livre d'or de la noblesse phanariote . . . , par un Phanariote* [= Eugène Rizo-Rhavgabê], Athens 1892; Epaminondas I. Stamatiadis, Βιογραφίαι τῶν Ἑλλήνων Μεγάλων Διερμηνέων τοῦ Ὀθωμανικοῦ Κράτους, Athens 1865; *IA*, s.v. Fenerliler (by A. Decei), with numerous further references.

(J. H. MORDTMANN*)

FERDĪ, *makhlaṣ* (nom-de-plume) of some minor Ottoman poets, one of whom died young early in the reign of Süleymān I (Laṭīfī, 263; the *tedhkire*s [in MS] of ʿĀshiķ Čelebi and Ḥasan Čelebi; ʿĀlī, *Kunh al-akhbār*, Ankara Un. DTCF Lib. MS, f. 210a); another, Arayîdjîzāde Ḥüseyn, died in 1121/1709 (Sālim, 525; for MSS of his works see F. E. Karatay, *Topkapı Sarayı ... türkçe yazmalar kataloğu*, Istanbul 1961, nos. 2449, 2697); a third, 'Derwīsh' Ferdī, died in 1125/1713 (Sālim, 527); a 'Kātib' Ferdī is also known (Babinger, 83, n.).

A detailed history in Turkish of the reign of Süleymān I from his accession in 926/1520 to 949/1542 was long attributed to a 'Ferdī' (Hammer-Purgstall, iii, intr. v, 710; Flügel, *Die ... Handschriften der Kais.-kön. Hofbibl. zu Wien*, ii, 222 f.; J. Thury, *Török történetirók*, ii, Budapest 1896, 39; cf. Babinger, 83), while von Karabacek, taking the name of the copyist of the Vienna MS, 'Muṣṭafā āl-i ʿOthmān' as that also of the author, attributed the work to Süleymān's son Prince Muṣṭafā (see J. von Karabacek, *Geschichte Suleimans des Grossen, verfasst und eigenhändig geschrieben von seinem Sohne Mustafa, Zur orientalischen Altertumskunde*, vii, Vienna 1917). These attributions are without foundation. The word *'ferdī'*, appearing in a Persian poem in the work, is not a proper name but bears its ordinary lexicographical meaning, 'one person'; the author's *makhlaṣ* in fact appears, in a poem at the end of the work, as 'Būstān', and hence reveals him to be Muṣṭafā Būstān b. Meḥemmed, 'Būstān Efendi', a *ķāḍīʿasker* under Süleymān I, b. 904/1498, d. 977/1570 [see BOSTĀNZĀDE].

Bibliography: Hüseyin G. Yurdaydın, *Ferdî'nin Süleymannâmesinin yeni bir nüshası*, in *Ank. Ün. DTCFD*, viii (1950), 201-23; idem, *Bostan'ın Süleymannâmesi (Ferdi'ye atfedilen eser)*, in *Belleten*, xix (1955), 137-202.

(HÜSEYIN G. YURDAYDIN)

FERHĀD PASHA (? — 1004/1595), Ottoman Grand Vizier. One Venetian *relazione* of 1585 gives his then age as about 50 years, while other Venetian *relazioni* of 1590-4 describe him as a man of about 65 or 70 years. Ferhād Pasha was of Albanian origin (some of the Venetian accounts refer to him as "di nazion schiavone", "di nazione schiava") and, according to Lazaro Soránzo, a native of "Andronici Castello dell'Albania". After he had gone out from the *enderūn-i humāyūn* towards the end of the reign of Sultan Süleymān Ķānūnī (d. 974/1566), his career embraced the offices of Mīr Akhor-i Kebīr, *i.e.* Grand Master of the Imperial Horse (while holding this appointment he was sent in 986/1578 to Budin (Buda) with orders to execute the Beglerbeg of Budin, Muṣṭafā Pasha, the nephew of the then Grand Vizier Meḥemmed Ṣoķollu) and also of Yeñičeri Aghasî, *i.e.*, Agha of the Janissaries (an office that he lost in 990/1582). Ferhād Pasha became Beglerbeg of Rūmili late in 990/1582 and not long thereafter was raised, with the rank of vizier, to the eminence of *serdār*, *i.e.*, commander-in-chief, of the Ottoman forces engaged in the war which had broken out against Persia in 986/1578. During the campaigns of 991/1583-992/1584 he relieved with new supplies and reinforcements the Ottoman garrison at Tiflis in Georgia and in addition fortified Eriwān, together with a number of strong positions on the routes leading into Georgia. The supreme command on the eastern front was assigned, for the year 1585, to the famous ʿOthmān Pasha, then at the height of his renown as a soldier in view of the brilliant campaigns that he had waged in the Caucasus during the earlier phases of the war. After the death of ʿOthmān Pasha in Dhu 'l-Ķaʿda 993/October 1585 the appointment as *serdār* was given once more to Ferhād Pasha, who now retained it until the end of the long conflict with Persia in 998/1590. His solid achievement as a soldier was crowned in 996/1588, when he conquered Gandja and the region of Ķarabāgh in Persian Adharbaydjān. Ferhād Pasha became Grand Vizier in Shawwāl 999/August 1591, but a revolt amongst the Janissaries brought about his dismissal from office in Djumādā II 1000/March-April 1592. As second vizier, and during the first years of the long war of 1001/1593-1015/1606 between the Ottoman Empire and Austria, he was *ķāʾim-maķām* at Istanbul in the absence of the Grand Vizier Ķodja Sinān Pasha on the Hungarian front. Soon after the accession to the throne of Sultan Meḥemmed III in 1003/1595 Ferhād Pasha became Grand Vizier for the second time (Djumādā II 1003/February 1595). His renewed tenure of the office was destined, however, to be brief—as he was preparing for a campaign against Wallachia (at that time aligned on the side of Austria), the intrigues of his bitter rival Ķodja Sinān led to his dismissal in Shawwāl

1003/July 1595 and not long afterwards to his execution, on the order of the Sultan, in Ṣafer 1004/ October 1595. Some of the sources describe Ferhād Pas̲h̲a ("detto Charailam, cioe, nero serpente" (= Ḳara Yilan), in the words of Lazaro Soranzo) as a rough and ignorant man, overbearing and avaricious in his conduct. None the less, on the evidence of a career not devoid of notable achievements, above all in the war against Persia, he has some claim to be regarded as one of the most able viziers of his time.

Bibliography: Selānīkī, *Taʾrīk̲h̲*, Istanbul A.H. 1281, 67, 169, 172, 202, 204, 212 ff., *passim*, 220 ff., *passim*, 232 ff., *passim*, 243 ff., *passim*, 259-60, 268, 285-6, 295, 302, 308, 310-2, 320; Pečewī, *Taʾrīk̲h̲*, Istanbul A.H. 1281-1283, i, 423 and ii, 19, 73, 86 ff., *passim*, 107 ff., *passim*, 122 ff., *passim*, 164 ff., *passim*; Ḥād̲j̲d̲j̲ī K̲h̲alīfa, *Fed̲h̲leke*, Istanbul A.H. 1286-1287, i, 3, 46 ff., *passim*, 76; Naʿīmā, *Taʾrīk̲h̲*, Istanbul A.H. 1281-1283, i, 66 ff., *passim*, 110, 117 ff., *passim*; Ṣolāḳ-zāde, *Taʾrīk̲h̲*, Istanbul A.H. 1298, 605 ff., *passim*; I. H. Uzunçarşılı, *Osmanlı Tarihi*, Ankara 1954, iii, Pt. 2, 347-9 and 608 (index); A. S. Levend, *Ġazavāt-nāmeler*, Ankara 1956, 89 ff. (information on the Persian campaigns of Ferhād Pas̲h̲a can also be found in Iskandar Beg Muns̲h̲ī, *Taʾrīk̲h̲-i ʿālam-ārā-yi ʿAbbāsī*, Tehrān 1955, *passim*); G. T. Minadoi, *Historia della Guerra fra Turchi et Persiani*, Venice 1594, 216 ff., *passim*, 345 ff., *passim*; L. Soranzo, *L'Ottomanno*, Ferrara 1599, 82; E. Alberi, *Relazioni degli ambasciatori Veneti al Senato*, ser. iii, Florence 1840-1855, ii, 283 ff., 353 ff. and iii, 290 ff., 371, 416 ff.; *Calendar of State Papers, Venetian*, (*1581-1591*), 591 (index) and (*1592-1603*), 597 (index); Hammer-Purgstall, *Histoire*, vii, 62, 107 ff., 123, 148, 209, 214 ff., 241, 296 ff. (V. J. Parry)

FERHĀD u-S̲H̲ĪRĪN [see farhād wa-s̲h̲īrīn].

FERĪDŪN BEG (d. 991/1583), private secretary of Meḥemmed Pas̲h̲a Sokollu [*q.v.*], head of the Ottoman chancery and compiler of the *Muns̲h̲aʾāt al-salāṭīn*. Nothing is known of his origins; his personal name was Aḥmed, and his *waḳfiye* (see Bibl.) refers to him as 'ibn ʿAbd al-Ḳadīr'. Educated in the household of the *defterdār* Čiwi-zāde ʿAbdī Čelebi, in the year of the latter's death (960/1553) he entered the service of Meḥemmed Pas̲h̲a Sokollu, then *beglerbegi* of Rūmeli, as secretary. As Sokollu rose to supreme power, so Ferīdūn played an increasingly important part in state affairs, notably in the negotiations for the extradition of the fugitive prince Bāyezīd from Persia and in the crisis of Süleymān's death at Szigetvar (974/1566); his personal bravery during this siege was rewarded with a *ziʿāmet* and promotion to *mutafarriḳa*. On 8 Muḥarram 978/12 June 1570 he was appointed *Reʾīs al-küttāb* (for his *berāt* see *Muns̲h̲aʾāt*[2], ii, 572) and on 3 Ramaḍān 981/27 December 1573 promoted to *nis̲h̲änd̲j̲ï*. When, on the death of Selīm II, Murād III was hastening from Maʿnīsa to Istanbul, he had a stormy crossing from Mudanya in a small boat belonging to Ferīdūn which happened to be available (*Muns̲h̲aʾāt*[2], i, 17, cf. Pečewī, i, 26-7). A month later, on 9 S̲h̲awwāl 982/ 22 January 1575, Ferīdūn presented his *Muns̲h̲aʾāt al-salāṭīn* to the new Sultan, but received scant thanks for it (Selānikī, 137): as the protégé of Sokollu he was regarded coldly by Murād III, and his dismissal from the post of *nis̲h̲änd̲j̲ï* and banishment from the capital on 11 Muḥarram 984/10 April 1576 (S. Gerlach, *Tagebuch*, 175-6) was the first of several measures aimed at weakening Sokollu's position (Pečewī, i, 26; ii, 7). In D̲j̲umādā II 985/ August 1577 he was appointed *sand̲j̲aḳ-begi* of Semendre (Smederevo), arriving at Belgrade, the chef-lieu of the *sand̲j̲aḳ*, four months later (Gerlach, 375; S. Schweigger, *Reyssbeschreibung*, 39); before long (by 988/1580, see Hammer-Purgstall, iv, 82, note *e*) he was transferred to Köstendil. In Muḥarram 989/February 1581 (a year after Sokollu's assassination) he was recalled to Istanbul and re-appointed *nis̲h̲änd̲j̲ï*; and on 12 Rabīʿ I 990/6 April 1582 he was given in marriage ʿĀys̲h̲e Sulṭān, the daughter of Rüstem Pas̲h̲a [*q.v.*] and Süleymān's daughter Mihrimāh (Selānikī, 162-3; the tradition that he was married to Sokollu's widow is baseless, see Hammer-Purgstall, iv, 104, note *b*). He died in office, of a haemorrhage, on Wednesday 21 Ṣafar 991/16 March 1583 (Selānikī, 172), and is buried in a *türbe* at Eyyūb (Ewliyā, i, 405; cf. ʿ*OM*, ii, 363-4).

Ferīdūn's *Muns̲h̲aʾāt al-salāṭīn* (chronogram for 982, the year of its completion) is a collection of state-papers—imperial letters, *fermāns*, *fetḥnāmes*, *berāts*, treaties, with some campaign-diaries. According to Selānikī (137), the presentation volume, of over 250 gatherings (*d̲j̲uzʾ*) and divided into eleven sections for the eleven Ottoman sultans to Selīm II, contained 1880 documents, but no known MS approaches this length. The work has been printed twice (1) Istanbul 1264-5/1848-9, containing 735 documents, of which 41 relate to the early period of Islam; and (2) Istanbul 1274-5/1858 (the standard edition), containing 840 documents, many of which, however, are later than the date of presentation. From the examination of MSS in European libraries (the Istanbul MSS remain to be investigated) K. Holter concludes that *Muns̲h̲aʾāt*[2] i and ii, 1-100 (528 documents) and perhaps also ii, 536-74 (30 docs.) belong to Ferīdūn's original collection, while ii, 100-536 (282 docs. of the late 16th and the 17th centuries) reproduce a single separate collection, similar in scope to that represented in MS Göttingen Univ.-bibl. turc. 29. Mükrimīn K̲h̲alīl's demonstration that several of the documents purporting to belong to the reigns of ʿOt̲h̲mān G̲h̲āzī and Ork̲h̲ān are spurious, being modelled on documents in a collection of correspondence of the K̲h̲ʷārizm-s̲h̲āhs entitled *al-Tawassul ila 'l-tarassul* (Ḥād̲j̲d̲j̲ī K̲h̲alīfa, ed. Flügel, no. 3730), prompted grave doubts on the authenticity of the whole collection (see J. H. Mordtmann in *Isl.*, xiv (1925), 362n.); but recent studies suggest that these were exaggerated: it is for the most part a highly reliable source.

The *Muns̲h̲aʾāt* is introduced (i, 24-8) by a short treatise on ethics, *Miftāḥ al-D̲j̲annat* (chronogram for 982/1574) and followed (ii, 574-600) by an essay, written early in the reign of Murād III, on the measures needed to restore order in Egypt. Ferīdūn composed also *Nuzhat al-ak̲h̲bār dar safar-i Sigetwār*, a history of the Szigetvar campaign (974/1566) and the events of the two years following; MSS: Leiden, Univ.-bibl. Warn. 277; Istanbul, Millet-Ali Emiri 330; Istanbul, Hazine 1339 (this, dated 976 and containing 20 miniatures [Karatay, no. 692], is presumably the presentation-copy). In 980/1572, as *reʾīs al-küttāb*, he caused to be translated, from French, a history of France down to the year 1563; MS: Dresden (H. O. Fleischer, *Catalogus*, no. 120).

Bibliography: Ferīdūn's introduction to his work, *Muns̲h̲aʾāt*[2], i, 14-23; ʿAṭāʾī, *Ḥadāʾiḳ al-ḥaḳāʾiḳ*, 336-7; J. H. Mordtmann, s.v., in *EI*[1] (= *IA*, s.v.), followed by Babinger, 106-8 (with further references); Mükrimīn K̲h̲alīl [Yınanç],

Ferīdūn Beg Münshe'āti, in *TOEM*, no. 77, pp. 161-8, no. 78, pp. 37-46, no. 79, pp. 95-104, no. 81, pp. 216-26; J. Rypka, *Briefwechsel der Hohen Pforte mit den Krimchanen* ..., in *Festschrift Georg Jacob*, Leipzig 1932, 241-69; K. Holter, *Studien zu Aḥmed Ferīdûn's Münše'ât es-selâṭîn*, in *Mitt. d. Österreichischen Inst. f. Geschichtsforschung*, Erg.-Bd. xiv, Innsbruck 1939, 429-51 (with further references). Two copies of his *waḳfiye* (providing for the support of a mosque in Istanbul, etc.) are recorded in *Ist. küt. tarih-coğrafya yazmaları katalogları*, i/11, Istanbul 1962, 846 f. (J. H. Mordtmann-[V. L. Ménage])

FERMAN [see farmān].

FĒRŌZ [see fīrūz].

FĒRŌZKŌH [see fīrūzkūh].

FESTIVAL [see bayram, ʿīd].

FETWA [see fatwā].

FEUDALISM [see iḳṭāʿ].

FEZ [see fās, and (for the head-gear) libās].

FEZZĀN [see fazzān].

FIDĀʾ [(1) see hadjdj; (2) see harb—i].

FIDĀʾĪ (or, more often, *fidāwī*), one who offers up his life for another, a name used of special devotees in several religious and political groups. Among the Nizārī Ismāʿīlīs it was used of those members who risked their lives to assassinate the enemies of the sect. They acted also on behalf of political allies of the Nizārīs, sometimes at a price. At Alamūt they may have become, in later years, a special corps; but normally tasks of assassination seem to have been assigned to anyone who was fit. The mediaeval Western tradition developed an elaborate account of them as highly trained specialists, evidently based partly on Muslim tales, partly on imaginative deduction. Mediaeval Muslim legends gave rise later to the idea that *ḥashīsh* was used in motivating the *fidāʾīs*, but there is no evidence for this (see M. G. S. Hodgson, *The Order of Assassins*, The Hague 1955).

In Algeria, *fidāwī* means a narrator of heroic deeds, and *fidāwiyya* a tale or song of heroic deeds. During the Persian revolution *fidāwī* was applied in the first place to the adherents of the republican party, later to the defenders of liberal ideas and the constitution.

Fidāʾī was also the pen-name of Shaykhzāda Lāhidjī, who was sent by the Ṣafawī Shāh Ismāʿīl as ambassador to Muḥammad Khān Shaybānī and afterwards retired to Shīrāz where he died (Riḍā Ḳūlī Khān, *Madjmaʿ al-fuṣaḥāʾ*, ii, 27). It was also the pen-name of Sayyid Mīrzā Saʿīd of Ardistān, who lived at Iṣfahān and was the favourite poet of Muḥammad Shāh Ḳādjār (Riḍā Ḳūlī Khān, ii, 383).

Bibliography: Ibn Khaldūn-de Slane, i, 122, 5; Lane, *Modern Egyptians*, ii, 147; H. d'Allemagne, *Du Khorassan au pays des Backtiaris*, Paris 1911, iv, 304 (photographs, 294, 299); Browne, ii, 206 ff.; idem, *Persian Revolution*, 127, 151; *RMM*, i, 49; iv, 176; v, 361; xii, 217.

(Cl. Huart-[M. G. S. Hodgson])

FIDĀʾIYYĀN-I ISLĀM, a small politico-religious terrorist group based in Tehrān which during its twelve years of activity (1943-55) became notorious for its responsibility for numerous political murders. The Fidāʾiyyān were organized secretly, but held open rallies and announced their aims publicly. Their goals included strict enforcement of the *sharīʿa* and the ending of irreligiousness. They combined fundamentalism with violent xenophobia, and considered attacks on foreigners and politicians with foreign connexions a defence of the *Dār al-Islām*. The Fidāʾiyyān proclaimed the government of "xenophiles" illegitimate, and called such men enemy spies whose blood must be shed. They demanded the revocation of all laws which they considered inconsistent with Shīʿī law, and tried to re-establish the veiling of women and other traditional Islamic practices.

The notoriety of the Fidāʾiyyān began with the abortive attempt by their young founder, Sayyid Mudjtabā Mīrlawḥī, later called Nawāb-i Ṣafawī, on the life of the famous scholar and religious reformer, Aḥmad Kasrawī [see kasrawī], in March 1945. In February 1946 the Fidāʾiyyān assassinated Kasrawī during open court proceedings in the Palace of Justice in Tehrān. Ṣafawī and a few associates were arrested, but none of those who had been present would testify against them and they were acquitted. Āyat Allāh Kāshānī's protection of the Fidāʾiyyān and their influence in the Tehrān *bāzār* played a part in the acquittal, as did the fear of reprisals, which now grew. In October 1949 the Fidāʾiyyān assassinated the Minister of Court, ʿAbd al-Ḥusayn Hazhīr, whom they accused of having foreign connexions and of interfering in elections to the Madjlis. This murder was a factor in the annulment of the Tehrān elections to the 16th session of the Madjlis, and in the new elections the National Front led by Dr. Muḥammad Muṣaddiḳ made gains. The hostility of the Prime Minister, Gen. Ḥādjdjī ʿAlī Razmārā, to the National Front's proposal to nationalize oil brought about his assassination in March 1951 by a fanatical Fidāʾī, Khalīl Ṭahmāsbī. Threats from the Fidāʾiyyān soon led to the resignation of the next prime minister, Ḥusayn ʿAlā, after which Muṣaddiḳ became prime minister. Nawāb-i Ṣafawī was arrested in June 1951 and Muṣaddiḳ and his government faced threats to their lives from the Fidāʾiyyān unless Ṭahmāsbī and Ṣafawī were released. Ḥusayn Fāṭimī, a member of the government, was shot and wounded by a Fidāʾī in February 1952. Influenced by fear and by the claim of Kāshānī and his followers that Razmārā's assassin was a hero, the Madjlis voted to pardon Ṭahmāsbī in August 1952. As threats from the Fidāʾiyyān continued, however, the Muṣaddiḳ government moved against them and banished some of their members to Bandar ʿAbbās, an insalubrious port on the Persian Gulf.

After the overthrow of Muṣaddiḳ the activity of the Fidāʾiyyān decreased, and for a time they restricted themselves to issuing occasional harsh statements against the new government. Then an abortive attempt on the life of the prime minister Ḥusayn ʿAlā in October 1955 gave the government a basis for prosecuting them. The arrested Fidāʾiyyān, among whom were Nawāb-i Ṣafawī, Wāḥidī and Ṭahmāsbī, were executed and no more was heard from the group.

The Fidāʾiyyān had ties with the Ikhwān al-Muslimīn [*q.v.*] in ʿIrāḳ and Egypt, and like the Ikhwān as well as many politico-religious groups of the past they called each other "brethren". In the Arab-Israeli dispute they gave vocal support to the Arab cause. Their members appear to have been primarily very young men with a limited and traditional education. They drew on traditional ideas of the sacredness of self-sacrifice and of using force in combating irreligion. Their programme was chimerical, but in appealing to real resentments and frustrations they had an influence beyond their small numbers, while the fear they instilled influenced the acts even of their opponents, particularly in the years 1951-3. Although defended and protected by

Kā**sh**ānī, they were not directly led by him and at least once differed with him publicly.

Bibliography: The Fidā'iyyān issued their programme in a booklet, *al-Islām yaʿlū wa lā yuʿlā ʿalayh*, Tehran, 1951. There is as yet (1963) no published study of the group in either Persian or a Western language. Their activities are covered in newspapers like the *New York Times*, which carried an interview with Nawāb-i Ṣafawī on May 6, 1951. See also the remarks in Leonard Binder, *Iran*, California 1962, and D. N. Wilber, *Contemporary Iran*, New York 1963. More can be found in Persian newspapers and periodicals, including *Taraḳḳī, Dunyā, Waẓīfa,* and *Parčam-i Islām*, in the years 1949-55. Particularly interesting is a series of articles which appeared in *Kh^w^ āndanīhā*, vols. 16-7, which was discontinued because of the arrest and execution of their author. See also *OM, COC*, etc.

(N. R. Keddie and A. H. Zarrinkub)

FIḌḌA, silver, because of the variety of its application was in great demand in Muslim society. Its abusive accumulation, however, was to be avoided, since, according to the Ḳur'ān, "those who treasure up gold and silver and do not expend them in the way of Allāh" would meet with a painful punishment (*Sūra* ix, 34). Functionally the significance of silver resembled that of gold (see DHAHAB). Its economic importance arose from the fact that silver, along with gold, constituted the basis for the official Muslim coinage (see DIRHAM). Under normal economic circumstances the value of silver, as against gold, was established at 10 : 1, which ratio underlay the legal principle of the exchange rate between the silver and gold coinage (cf. C. Cahen, *Problèmes économiques de l'Iraq Buyide*, in *AIEO*, x (1952), 338). During the mediaeval period the needs of Near Eastern markets were adequately met by silver supplies of local provenance. Although mediaeval sources refer to many mining areas, the argentiferous districts of Khurāsān and Transoxania were particularly famous for an intensive exploitation of silver ore (cf. D. M. Dunlop, *Sources of gold and silver in Islam according to al-Hamdani, 10th Century A.D.*, in *Stud. Isl.*, viii (1957), 29-49; S. Bolin, *Mohammed, Charlemagne and Ruric*, in *Scandinavian Economic History Review*, i/1 (1953), 19-23). Near Eastern silver resources seem to have been rich enough to afford an export of this metal to Europe. This was particularly true in the course of the 4th/10th century, when large quantities of Near Eastern silver in the shape of Muslim dirhams were absorbed by trading regions of Eastern and Northern Europe. (For different viewpoints on the significance of the circulation of Near Eastern silver in the Middle Ages, see S. Bolin, *op. cit.*; R. P. Blake, *The circulation of silver in the Moslem East down to the Mongol epoch*, in *Harvard Journal of Asiatic Studies*, ii (1937), 291-328; F. J. Himly, *Y a-t-il emprise musulmane sur l'économie des états européens du VIIIe au Xe siècle?*, in *Schweizerische Zeitschrift für Geschichte*, v/3 (1955), 31-81).

As in the pre-Islamic period, silver was used in jewellery, metalwork and decorative incrustation (R. Harari, *Metalwork after the early Islamic period*, in *Survey of Persian Art*, iii, 2476-529). Luxurious silver vessels were also in demand, particularly during the Buwayhid régime (cf. E. Kühnel, *Die Kunst Persiens unter den Buyiden*, *ZDMG*, cvi, 1 (N. F. xxxi) (1956), 83 ff.), although their use for eating purposes was condemned by Muslim tradition.

Silver attracted the attention of Muslim alchemists who referred to it by a number of different names, *e.g.*, the moon, mother, servant (cf. E. Wiedemann, *Beiträge zur Geschichte der Naturwissenschaften*, xxiv, 82; A. Siggel, *Decknamen in der arabischen alchemistischen Literatur*, Berlin 1951). Albeit accepting the theory of transmutation of metals (cf. G. Sarton, *Introduction to the history of science*, ii, 2, 1045) Muslim alchemists were well acquainted with various chemical processes aiming at the extraction and refining of silver (E. J. Holmyard, *The makers of chemistry*, Oxford 1931, 77; D. M. Dunlop, *op. cit.*, 46-8; A. S. Ehrenkreutz, *Extracts from the technical manual on the Ayyubid mint in Cairo*, in *BSOAS*, xv (1953), 429).

Finally, silver was used in Muslim medicine. It was applied in the form of filings which, when mixed with drugs, were effective against melancholy, palpitation of the heart, and similar afflictions (cf. Ibn al-Bayṭār, ed. Leclerc, *Notices et extraits*, iii, 36). See also DĀR AL-ḌARB; METALWORK; SIKKA.

(A. S. Ehrenkreutz)

FIDJĀR "sacrilege"; *ḥarb al-fidjār* "the sacrilegious war" is the name of a war waged towards the end of the 6th century A.D. during the holy months between the Ḳuraysh and Kināna on the one side and the Ḳays-ʿAylān (without the Ghatafān) on the other. Our sources mention eight days on which fighting took place. The first three of them—usually put together as the first war but sometimes counted as the first three wars—were mere brawls. Of real importance was only the second (or, according to the second reckoning, fourth) war which lasted four years. It started when during the holy season ʿUrwa al-Raḥḥāl of the Banū ʿĀmir b. Ṣaʿṣaʿa, whilst escorting a caravan of al-Nuʿmān III (reigned 580-602 A.D.) from al-Ḥīra to the fair of ʿUkāẓ, was treacherously murdered by al-Barrāḍ b. Ḳays al-Ḍamrī al-Kinānī. The patron of al-Barrāḍ, Ḥarb b. Umayya, was at that time together with other chieftains of the Ḳuraysh at ʿUkāẓ. As soon as they heard of this misdeed, the Ḳuraysh and Kināna started for Mecca; they were overtaken by the pursuing Hawāzin and attacked at Nakhla, but the night enabled them to reach the sacred territory. This *yawm Nakhla* is generally counted as the first battle-day of the second Fidjār war, but sometimes added as the fourth day to the first war. A year later both parties—but without the Banū Kaʿb and Kilāb of the ʿĀmir b. Ṣaʿṣaʿa—met again at Shamṭa (v.l. Shamẓa) near ʿUkāẓ and the Hawāzin were victorious (*yawm Shamṭa*). The same happened next year at ʿUkāẓ (*yawm al-ʿAblā'*). It was only in the following year that the Ḳuraysh and Kināna carried the day (*yawm ʿUkāẓ* or *yawm Sharab*). A fifth engagement on the Ḥarra near ʿUkāẓ (*yawm al-Ḥurayra*) resulted again in the victory of the Hawāzin. After this there were only some skirmishes and then peace was restored. Of the many poems which according to Wāḳidī (*apud* Ibn Saʿd i/1, 82, 1) were composed about this war only a few verses have come down to us.

Whilst it is admitted that the Prophet was present at the Fidjār war, there is much controversy about the particulars. Some say that he took part in the fighting, and that at Shamṭa, where the Ḳuraysh were defeated, he was praised for his courage (*Aghānī*, xix, 78, 2). Others maintained that he only supplied his uncles with arrows (*e.g.*, Ibn Hishām, 117 pu; 119,1); but experts on the *ayyām al-ʿArab* knew that none of his uncles except al-Zubayr took part (*Aghānī*, xix, 81 f.). In support of these conflicting views alleged sayings of the Prophet are adduced. Also the years given for his age range from 14 to 28 (*Aghānī*, xix, 75, 1-3).

The Fidjār war was waged for four years in the holy season, when in normal times trade was flourishing unhampered by tribal feuds; it involved two great confederations including townsfolk of Mecca and al-Ṭāʾif, and it even gave its name to an era. The real aim of it was the control of the trade routes in the Nadjd and consequently the benefit of the great gains which this trade offered. In this great contest the Ḳuraysh were leading; they procured the weapons for their confederates and defrayed all expenses. Amongst their opponents the Thaḳīf together with the Banū Naṣr b. Muʿāwiya offered the hardest resistance but had finally to give in and, worn out by years of war, left the victory to the Ḳuraysh.

Bibliography: Ibn Hishām, 117-9; Ibn Saʿd, i/1, 80-2; Ibn ʿAbd Rabbih, *ʿIḳd* (1316 H.), iii, 77-80; *Aghānī*[1], xix, 73-82; Yaʿḳūbī, i, 14-6; Masʿūdī, *Murūdj*, iv, 120-2, 125, 150 ff.; idem, *Tanbīh*, 208 f.; Bakrī, *Muʿdjam* s.v. ʿUḳāẓ; Suhaylī, *al-Rawḍ al-unuf*, i, 120; Yāḳūt, iii, 579 s.v. Ẓallāl; Ibn al-Athīr, i, 439-45; Diyārbakrī, *Taʾrīkh al-Khamīs* (1302 H.), i, 288 f., 293; Ḥalabī, *Insān al-ʿuyūn* (1308 H.), i, 137 ff. (with Zaynī Daḥlān's *Sīra* on the margin p. 105); Bīrūnī, *Chronologie*, 34, 12; Sachau; Ch. Lyall, *The Mufaḍḍalīyāt*, ii, 302-5; H. Lammens, *La cité arabe de Ṭāʾif à la veille de l'Hégire* (= *MUB* viii, 4) 240/98; idem, *La Mecque à la veille de l'Hégire* (= *MUB* ix, 3) 326/230; A. M. Watt, *Muhammad at Mecca*, 14 f.

(J. W. Fück)

FIDYA, (which becomes, according to the area concerned, *fedu, fadu, fadwa* and even *fdīya*) is a general designation among Syro-Palestinians for a blood sacrifice made for purposes of atonement. From this point of view, its meaning is close to that of *ḍaḥiyya*. Indeed, in the Negeb and other parts of former Palestine, these two terms are sometimes used to designate one and the same thing. In fact, however, while the *ḍaḥiyya* is essentially an offering to the dead made on the occasion of *ʿīd al-aḍḥā*, the *fidya*, on the other hand, is practised in the interests of the living, without any limitation of time. It is offered up before Allāh for the delivery of a man, his family, his cattle and his goods, from some imminent misfortune, such as an epidemic. See also ḤADJDJ.

Bibliography: S. Curtiss, *Primitive Semitic religion to-day*, ch. XVI, London 1902; Jaussen, *Coutumes des Arabes au pays de Moab*, 361-2, 372; T. Canaan, *Mohammedan saints and sanctuaries in Palestine*, 164-6; H. Granqvist, *Child problems among the Arabs*, Helsingfors 1950, 131-2.

((J. Chelhod)

FIEF [see DJĀGĪR, IḲṬĀʿ, TĪMĀR].

FIGHĀNĪ (Bābā), pseudonym of a celebrated Persian poet whose patronymic, like his first name, is unknown. He was a native of Shīrāz where he started by helping his brother, a cutler by trade, and it was on that account that he first took the pseudonym Sakkākī when he began to write poetry. In his youth, which was spent at Shīrāz, he lived a life of debauchery, and then made a journey to Herāt where he became acquainted with the great poet Djāmī, but his poetry was not appreciated by the poets of Khurāsān. From there he went to Ādharbaydjān, to the court of sultan Yaʿḳūb (884-96/1479-91), of the Aḳ-Ḳoyunlu dynasty, one of the greatest patrons of the age. At this prince's court in Tabrīz he received every favour, and his protector called him *Bābā-yi shuʿarā* (father of poets). There he continued with his life of debauchery, recklessly spending everything that he earned. While he was accompanying his patron on one of his campaigns, the manuscript of his *dīwān* together with his baggage was looted. He wrote to his brother and asked him for a copy of the poems which he had left in his native town, and made a new selection. On sultan Yaʿḳūb's death he left Tabrīz, after spending more than seventeen years there; he went to Shīrāz and then to Khurāsān, living in the towns of Nasā and Abīward and following the same life. At the end of his life he repented and went to live in Mashhad, where he took to a life of devotion and died in 925/1519. Fighānī is one of the best lyric poets of his time and his *ghazals* were highly esteemed by poets, who continued to imitate him until the 17th century. His *dīwān* includes in particular some *ghazals* and certain *ḳaṣīdas* specially dedicated to the Shīʿī *imāms*. Ten of his *ghazals* have been published by Bland in his "Century" (34-37). The Iranian scholar Ḥusayn Āzād published a French translation of some of his poems under the title *Les perles de la couronne, choix de poésies de Baba Féghani, traduites pour la première fois du persan avec une introduction et des notes par Hocéyne-Azad*, Paris 1903. There are two editions of the Persian text of his *ghazals*: (1) *Dīwān-i Fighānī* with an introduction in Urdū by Manmōhan Lāl Māthur of Dihlī, Lahore n.d.; (2) *Dīwān-i Bābā Fighānī-yi Shīrāzī* with emendations by Suhaylī Khunsārī, Tehran 1316 s.

Bibliography: Rieu, *Cat. Pers. man.*, 651; Ethé in *Gr.I.Ph.*, ii, 307-10; Browne, iv, 164, 229-30, 342; *The Tuhfa i Sami of Sam Mirza Safawi*, edited . . . by Mawlawi Iqbal Husain, Patna 1934, 36-8, 53, 95, 171; idem, Tehran edition 1314 s., 102-3, 130; Luṭf ʿAlī Ādhar, *Ātashkadeh*, Bombay edition 1299, 306; Said Naficy, *Taʾrīkhče-yi Adabiyyāt-i Īrān*, in *Sāl-Nāma-yi Pārs*, Tehran 1326 s., 18.

(Said Naficy)

FIGHĀNĪ, pseudonym of **RAMAḌĀN** (?-938/1532), Ottoman poet. Very little is known of his early life, except that he was a native of Trabzon and that after a summary education he became a minor clerk in government offices in Istanbul, where together with his fellow-poets and boon-companions he frequented taverns and places of amusement, leading an irregular and dissolute life. He seems to have lived in near poverty and without proper patronage, in spite of the poems which he dedicated to the great. We are told of his extraordinary memory where he stored enormous amounts of Arabic and Persian verse and all his own compositions. At the start of a very promising poetic career he met a sudden and tragic end: a Persian epigram which he wrote (or which was attributed to him) subtly attacked the Grand Vizier Ibrāhīm Pasha for the statues which he had brought from Budin and had erected in front of his palace in the Hippodrome: "Two Ibrāhīms came to this world: one destroyed idols (meaning the patriarch Abraham), and the other erected them", and the unfortunate poet was hanged after an ignominious parade.

His *ghazels* and *ḳaṣīdes* are scattered in various *medjmūʿas* and unmistakably show a great talent that was liberating itself from the influence of Persian models and his Ottoman predecessors. Most *tedhkire*-writers agree that his *ḳaṣīdes* in particular are outstanding.

Bibliography: The *tedhkires* of Sehī, Laṭīfī, ʿĀshiḳ Čelebi, Riyāḍī, Ḳïnalïzāde Ḥasan Čelebi, Ḳāf-zāde, s.v.; Gibb, *Ottoman Poetry*, iii, 34 ff.;

M. Fuad Köprülü, in *İA*, s.v.; A. Karahan, *Figani ve şiirleri*, in *Türk Dili ve Edebiyatı Dergisi*, iii/3-4 (1949), 389-410; *Istanbul Kitaplıkları Türkçe yazma divanlar kataloğu*, i, 100-1; *Topkapı Sarayı Müzesi Kütüphanesi Türkçe yazmalar kataloğu*, Istanbul 1962, Index. (FAHİR İZ)

FIGUIG (Ar. FADJĪDJ), a group of seven *ḳṣūr* isolated in the south-east of Morocco and surrounded on three sides by the Algerian frontier. It is situated to the east of the *djabal* Grūz at the meeting point of the Sahara Atlas and the Sahara plateau, in a broad hollow 850-900 metres in altitude (long. 1° 15′ W., lat. 32° 5′). The seven *ḳṣūr* fall into three groups: al-Ūdāghīr, al-ʿAbīd, Awlād Slīmān and al-Maïzz to the north-west, the two Ḥammām (Fūḳānī and Taḥtānī) to the north-east, and Zenāga, the most important, two kilometres to the south. Zenāga, which has 7,000 inhabitants out of a total population of 15,000, is situated at the foot of the high sinter plateau of al-Djorf, on which the other *ḳṣūr* stand; the new administrative centre is situated on the plateau half-way between these and Zenāga. The houses of the *ḳṣūr*, made of unfired brick (*ṭūb*) on a sub-foundation of dry stone, are almost always two or three storeys high and give a distinctly urban impression; at al-Maïzz, the rooms which give on to the terraces are open on the south side. The streets, partly covered, are relatively broad at al-Ūdāghīr and Zenāga. Each *ḳṣar* is surrounded by walls. Al-Ūdāghīr and Zenāga have a small *mellāḥ* inhabited by a few Jewish families, and Zenāga has many *ḥarāṭīn* among its population. The whole of the population, which is of very varied origin, is Berber-speaking, but the men know Arabic as well; the few families of Shorfa and the Marabouts, Awlād Sīdī Shaykh, are Arabic-speaking.

The *ḳṣūr* to the north and their gardens are supplied with water from thermal springs (31.5° C.) situated along a fault in the Jurassic limestone, and Zenāga gets its water from *foggāras*. The 200,000 palm-trees cultivated here suffer from the altitude and attacks of *bayūḍ* (a cryptogamic disease); other crops (apricots, peaches, pears, turnips, onions, red peppers or pimentos) are of secondary importance. The amount of time allowed for irrigation is measured by means of a floating copper container pierced with a small hole, which sinks when it is full. Some of the palm trees belong to the nomads who camp around them and deposit their stores there: Beni Guil, ʿAmūr of the west and Awlād Sīdī Shaykh Ghrāba. The artisan class (burnous, carpets, painted and embroidered leather goods, jewellery made by the Jews) is declining in number. A great many men emigrate to Algeria and other parts of Morocco as labourers or masons; smuggling is rife.

Although the region has certainly been inhabited for a long time, as is proved by the rock engravings, the name Fadjīdj appears only in the 8th/14th century. Ibn Khaldūn (*Hist.*, i, 240) speaks of its being active and ruled by the Banū Sīd al-Mulūk, a family of the Maṭghāra of the group of Banū Fāten: these used to form the greater part of the population of Sidjilmāsa, a caravaneers' market and capital of Tafilālet, then already waning in importance, and to whose position as a meeting-point of caravan tracks Figuig perhaps succeeded. In the 16th century, Leo Africanus (435) praises the fineness of the woollen stuffs woven by its women, the intelligence, commercial vigour and culture of its men; in the seventeenth century, al-ʿAyyāshī draws attention to the flourishing condition and richness of its libraries (*Voyage*, tr. Berbrugger, 159). Figuig seems always to have been an independent territory, thanks to its isolated position. The expedition which Mawlāy Sulaymān undertook in 1807, like that of the powerful Mawlāy Ismāʿīl at the end of the seventeenth century, was never followed up. Nevertheless, when the French began the conquest of Algeria, the Convention of Lālla-Maghnya (18 March 1845) left Figuig to Morocco. It was the refuge of the Awlād Sīdī Shaykh who rose against France from 1864 on, of the adventurer, Bū ʿAmāna, and the pillaging Zegdu. In 1883, the Sultan, Mawlāy Ḥasan, installed a representative there, who had, however, no authority. Even after the Franco-Moroccan agreement of 1902 the Sultan was unable to command obedience in this region, and a column of French soldiers accompanying Jonnart, the governor-general of Algeria, to Beni-Ounif was attacked on 30 May 1903; a military counter-action forced the *djemāʿa* of Zenāga to surrender the criminals and hostages. There were no more outbreaks and Figuig came with Morocco under the French Protectorate and was incorporated into the administration of the Makhzen.

The disappearance of the slave-trade aud of commerce across the Sahara and the arrival of the railway between Oran and Colomb-Béchar, which had reached Beni-Ounif by 1903, contributed to the economic decline of Figuig. Moreover the region was often weakened by internal quarrels, especially those which set the two principal *ḳṣūr*, al-Ūdāghīr and Zenāga, against each other over the possession of ʿAyn Thaddert, and also those which divided the two Ḥāmmām. The walls of the *ḳṣūr* were for protection against neighbours as much as nomads, and watch-towers still overlook the gardens. The Marabout families have continually done their utmost to keep or restore the peace.

Although so isolated and cut up into *ḳṣūr*, Figuig does not ever appear to have enjoyed political unity. Each *ḳṣar* has traditionally its *djemāʿas* of administrative subdivisions which bring together the heads of families, and also its own *djemāʿa* made up of elected notables which judges according to its *ḳānūns* (not very differently from one *ḳṣar* to another). In matters of civil law, the *ḳāḍī* judged according to the *sharʿ* and also the *ʿurf*. Since Figuig has been re-united with Morocco, the meetings of the *djemāʿa* of the *ḳṣar* are presided over by the representative of the king of Morocco and the *ḳāḍī* is nominated by the Makhzen. The people are at the same time pious and superstitious and are fervent adepts of brotherhoods (Ṭayyibiyya, Kerzāziyya, Zayyāniyya, Nāṣiriyya, etc.). Habous (*waḳf*) properties are numerous but their purpose is above all to deprive women of the right of succession. Sīdī ʿAbd al-Ḳādir Muḥammad, patron saint of Figuig, has his *ḳubba* to the north-east of al-Ḥammām.

Bibliography: Ibn Khaldūn, *Hist. des Berbères*, tr. de Slane, 2nd ed., Paris 1925-56; Leo Africanus, *Description de l'Afrique*, tr. Épaulard, Paris 1956; de Castries, *Notes sur Figuig*, in *Bull. de la Société de géogr.*, Paris 1882; de La Martinière and Lacroix, *Documents pour servir à l'étude du N.-O. africain*, ii, Algiers 1896; E. Doutté, *Figuig*, in *La Géogr.*, Paris 1903; E. F. Gautier, *La source de Thaddert à Figuig*, in *Annales de géogr.*, Paris 1917; M. Bonnefous, *La palmeraie de Figuig*, Rabat 1952.

(J. DESPOIS)

FIḤL [see FAḤL].

AL-FIHRĪ, ABŪ ISḤĀḲ IBRĀHĪM B. ABI 'L-ḤASAN ʿALĪ B. AḤMAD, composed in 632/1234 an anthology of the works of Spanish stylists and poets of the 5th/11th and 6th/12th centuries entitled *Kanz al-*

kuttāb wa-muntak͟hab al-ādāb (see H. Krafft, *Die ar., pers. und türk. Hdss. der k. k. orient. Akademie zu Wien*, Vienna 1824, no. 147). (C. BROCKELMANN)

FIHRIST [see BIBLIOGRAPHY, FAHRASA, IBN AL-NADĪM, ṬŪSĪ].

FIḲH (A.), originally "understanding, knowledge, intelligence", and applied to any branch of knowledge (as in *fiḳh al-lug͟ha*, the science of lexicography), has become the technical term for jurisprudence, the science of religious law in Islam. It is, like the *iurisprudentia* of the Romans, *rerum divinarum atque humanarum notitia* and in its widest sense covers all aspects of religious, political and civil life. In addition to the laws regulating ritual and religious observances (*ʿibādāt*), containing orders and prohibitions, it includes the whole field of family law, the law of inheritance, of property and of contracts and obligations, in a word provisions for all the legal questions that arise in social life (*muʿāmalāt*); it also includes criminal law and procedure, and finally constitutional law and laws regulating the administration of the state and the conduct of war.

All aspects of public and private life and business should be regulated by laws based on religion; the science of these laws is *fiḳh*.

In older theological language the word did not have this comprehensive meaning; it was rather used in opposition to *ʿilm*. While the latter denotes, beside the Ḳurʾān and its interpretation, the accurate knowledge of the legal decisions handed down from the Prophet and his Companions (Ibn Saʿd, ii/2, 127, [16]: *al-riwāyāt wa 'l-ʿilm*, as synonyms), the term *fiḳh* is applied to the independent exercise of the intelligence, the decision of legal points by one's own judgment in the absence or ignorance of a traditional ruling bearing on the case in question. The result of such independent consideration is *raʾy* (opinion, *opinio prudentium*), with which it is also sometimes used synonymously. In this sense *ʿilm* and *fiḳh* are regarded as distinct qualities of the theologian (Nawawī, *Tahd͟hīb*, ed. Wüstenfeld, 703, [2]); also *fiḳh wa-riwāya* (Ibn Saʿd, v, 327, [10]). The sum total of all wisdom is defined by Mud͟jāhid (in explanation of Sūra ii, 269: *man yuʾta 'l-ḥikma*) as composed of the following elements: *al-Ḳurʾān wa 'l-ʿilm wa 'l-fiḳh* (Ṭabarī, *Tafsīr*, iii, 56, [2]), and, similarly, the Jewish Karaitic expositor of the Bible, Jepheth b. ʿAlī (910-80 A.D.), translates *tiftāyē* in Daniel, iii, 2 (ed. D. S. Margoliouth, *Anecdota Oxoniensa*, 1889, 33, [7]) by *ahl al-ʿilm wa 'l-fiḳh*. Hārūn al-Ras͟hīd instructs his governor Hart͟hama to consult the *uli 'l-fiḳh fī dīn Allāh* and the *uli 'l-ʿilm bi-kitāb Allāh* in doubtful cases (Ṭabarī, iii, 717, [10]). Further passages are quoted in Goldziher, *Muh. Stud.*, ii, 176, n. 6.

In this sense, *ʿālim* (plur. *ʿulamāʾ*) is distinguished from *faḳīh* (plur. *fuḳahāʾ*), or the combination of both sciences in one individual is expressed by the combination of these two ephitets or their synonyms. Ibn ʿUmar was *d͟jayyid al-ḥadīt͟h* but not *d͟jayyid al-fiḳh* (Ibn Saʿd, ii/2, 125, [5]); on the other hand Ibn ʿAbbās was *aʿlam* with reference to decisions handed down by Tradition and at the same time *afḳah* (or *at͟hḳafu raʾy^{in}*) in new cases that arose, for which no precedent could be found in Tradition and in which it was necessary to use one's own judgment (*ibid.*, 122, 124); the same is true of Zayd b. T͟hābit (*ibid.*, 116); cf. *faḳīh fi 'l-dīn ʿālim fi 'l-sunna* (*ibid.*, iii/1, 110). Saʿīd b. al-Muṣayyib is *faḳīh al-fuḳahāʾ* on the one hand and *ʿālim al-ʿulamāʾ* (*ibid.*, ii/2, 129, 130; v, 90) on the other. Among the *tābiʿūn* there were *fuḳahāʾ wa-ʿulamāʾ*, *i.e.*, those who were authorities on the transmission of *ḥadīt͟h* and *āt͟hār* as well as those who were authorities on *fiḳh* and competent to give (independent) decisions, *fatwā* (*ibid.*, ii/2, 128). Abū T͟hawr was *aḥad aʾimmat al-dunyā fiḳh^{an} wa-ʿilm^{an}* (D͟hahabī, *Ṭabaḳāt al-ḥuffāẓ*, viii, 106).

In the earliest period of the development of Islam the authorities entrusted with the administration of justice and the control of religious life had in most cases to fall back on the exercise of their own *raʾy* owing to the scarcity of legislative material in the Ḳurʾān and the dearth of ancient precedents. This was regarded as a matter of course by everyone, although they were naturally very pleased if the verdict could as far as possible be based on *ʿilm*. When ʿAṭāʾ b. Abī Rabāḥ (d. 114/732) was giving a judgment, he was asked: "Is this *ʿilm* or *raʾy*?" If it was founded on a precedent (*at͟har*), he said it was *ʿilm* (Ibn Saʿd, v, 345). The *raʾy* was not, however, thereby discredited. It was considered an equally legitimate factor in the decision of a point of law and its results were destined in the near future to be regarded as the decisions of old authorities and in later times to be actually considered an element of *ʿilm*. From the very beginning one could have recourse to it as soon as *ʿilm* failed. According to an old story which certainly reflects the conditions of the Umayyad period, although it does not actually date from the time in which its scene is laid, Muʿāwiya finally applied to Zayd b. T͟hābit on a legal question, on which neither he nor other Companions to whom he propounded it could quote any ancient evidence (*falam yūd͟jad ʿindahū*—or *ʿindahum*—*fīhā ʿilm*); the latter gave a verdict based on this own independent *raʾy* (Ṭabarī, *Tafsīr*, ii, 250 *ult.*, on Sūra II, 228). The *ḳāḍī* of Egypt asked the advice of the Caliph ʿUmar II on a point not provided for in Tradition; the latter wrote to him: Nothing has reached me on this matter, therefore I leave the verdict to you to be given according to your opinion (*bi-raʾyik*) (Kindī, *Governors and Judges of Egypt*, ed. Guest, 334; ed. Gottheil, 29) [cf. ID͟JTIHĀD].

This recognition of *raʾy* [*q.v.*] as an approved source of law found expression in the instructions attributed to the Prophet and the early Caliphs, which they gave to the officials sent to administer justice in the conquered provinces, and in their alleged approval of the principles of their decisions which the judges whom they had sent out submitted to them (Goldziher, *Ẓâhiriten*, 8 ff.; cf. Ibn al-At͟hīr, *Usd al-g͟hāba*, i, 314; Mubarrad, *Kāmil*, 9 ff.; Ibn Ḳutayba, *ʿUyūn al-ak͟hbār*, 87). In the more elaborate versions of these reports which were developed from their original, rudimentary forms we find already mentioned explicitly the principle of deduction from decisions of similar cases (*as͟hbāh, naẓāʾir*; cf. *ʿUyūn al-ak͟hbār*, 72), *i.e.*, the use of analogy (*ḳiyās*, [*q.v.*]) as a methodological regulator of *raʾy*. In the investigation of the *ʿillat al-s͟harʿ*, the motive of law (*ratio legis*), and the resulting reduction of doubtful cases to a rational point of view, we find this principle given systematic validity. At the same time—there is evidence of it at a very early period—a kind of popular element entered the number of constitutive sources for the deduction of laws: the conception of the general usage of the community (*sunna*, [*q.v.*]) which had been established by general agreement or consensus (*id͟jmāʿ*, [*q.v.*]) in wider circles of believers, independent of written (*i.e.*, Ḳurʾānic), traditional, or inferred law.

This usage contained an appreciable amount of foreign elements. It was only natural that the legal, commercial, and administrative practices which prevailed in the conquered provinces should have survived under Islam, just as ancient Arab legal and commercial practices had survived, and should have been adopted by the Muslims as far as they were compatible with the demands of the new religious ideas. That the retention of pre-Islamic legal institutions was the normal procedure is shown by a passage in Balā*dh*urī: "Abū Yūsuf held that if there exists in a country an ancient, non-Arab *sunna* which Islam has neither changed nor abolished, and people complain to the Caliph that it causes them hardship, he is not entitled to change it; but Mālik and *Sh*āfiʿī held that he may change it even if it be ancient, because he ought to prohibit (in similar circumstances) any valid *sunna* which has been introduced by a Muslim, let alone those introduced by unbelievers" (*Futūḥ*, 448). In this way, elements from Roman Byzantine (including Roman provincial) law, Talmudic law, the canon law of the Eastern churches, and Persian Sāsānian law entered Islamic law during its formative period. The influence of Talmudic law manifested itself above all in matters of ritual and worship. Influences of Persian Sāsānian law (and of the canon law of the Eastern churches) have been established in a few individual cases, but their full extent remains to be investigated. In the case of Roman and of Talmudic law, these influences extended not only to rules and institutions of positive law, but to legal concepts and maxims, to methods of reasoning (*ḳiyās*, and conclusions *a maiore ad minus* and *a minore ad maius*), and even to fundamental ideas of legal science; for instance, the highly organized concept of the consensus of the scholars as formulated by the ancient schools of Islamic law (see below), seems to have been modelled on the concept of the *opinio prudentium* of Roman law (cf. *Digest*, i, 3, 38: *In ambiguitatibus quae ex legibus proficiscunter, consuetudinem aut rerum perpetuo similiter iudicatarum auctoritatem vim legis obtinere debere*; *Institutes*, i, 2, 9: *Nam diuturni mores consensu utentium comprobati legem imitantur*). Goldziher has repeatedly drawn attention to this and to the fact that parallels between Roman and Islamic law in the field of legal science are usually doubled by parallels in Talmudic law. (Goldziher has even suggested that the terms *fiḳh* and *fuḳahāʾ*, in their special technical reference to the sacred law and its practitioners, as well as the corresponding Jewish terms *ḥokhmā* and *ḥᵃkhāmīm*, may have been influenced by the Latin terms *(iuris)prudentia* and *(iuris)prudentes*; in *Die Kultur der Gegenwart*[2, 3], I/iii/1, 103). Some of the borrowings from Roman law may, in fact, have been made through the medium of the Jews, as was first suggested by von Kremer (*Culturgeschichte des Orients*, i, 535). This adoption of Roman (and other) legal concepts and maxims occurred not through direct influence of one legal system on another at the technical level, but through the medium of the cultured non-Arab converts to Islam, whose education in Hellenistic rhetoric had made them acquainted with the rudiments of law and who brought their familiar ideas with them into their new religion. When Islamic legal science came into being towards the end of the first century of Islam (early 8th century A.D.), the door of Islamic civilization had been opened wide to these potential transmitters. That the early jurists of Islam should consciously have adopted any principle of foreign law is out of the question. The subject remains, in the words of Goldziher, "one of the most attractive problems of this branch of Islamic studies".

With the gradual recognition of Ḳurʾān, *sunna*, *idjmāʿ* and *ḳiyās* as the four official "roots" or sources of legal knowledge, methodological principles from which legal rules might be legitimately derived [see UṢŪL], the terms *fiḳh* and *fuḳahāʾ* gradually lost their original limitation to deductions not based on tradition. *Fiḳh* came to mean the science which co-ordinated and included all the branches of knowledge derived from the four roots; similarly those who were masters of this science were called *fuḳahāʾ*, *i.e.*, jurists. Or *fiḳh* was used for the result of deduction from the sources of positive law, the sum total of the deductions derived from them, *e.g.*, *wa-fī hā*dh*a 'l-ḥadī*th* ḍurūb min al-fiḳh* (Mubarrad, *Kāmil*, 529, cf. *WZKM*, iii, 84). The Arabic sources contain numerous reports about scholars who arranged the *ʿilm* or *sunan* in chapters and thence deduced the *fiḳh* inferences (*Muh. Stud.*, ii, 211). Of ʿAbd Allāh b. al-Mubārak it is said: *dawwan al-ʿilm fi 'l-abwāb wa 'l-fiḳh* (*Dh*ahabī, *Ta*dh*kirat al-ḥuffāẓ*, i, 250); of Abū *Th*awr: *ṣannaf al-kutub wa-farraʿ ʿala 'l-sunan* (*ibid.*, ii, 95). Little value can be attached to the statement ascribed to Hi*sh*ām b. ʿUrwa that many *kutub fiḳh* of his father's perished in the flames on the day of the battle of the Ḥarra (*Biographien*, ed. Fischer, 41). At that ancient period (ʿUrwa died in 94/712, the so-called "year of the *fuḳahāʾ*", when many *fuḳahāʾ* died; Ibn Saʿd, vi, 135) there could be no real *kutub* in existence; the report can therefore refer, at the utmost, to rough notes only. We might also mention the statement that Zuhrī's *fatwā*s were collected in three, Ḥasan al-Baṣrī's in seven books (*asfār*) arranged in the order of the *abwāb al-fiḳh* (Ibn Ḳayyim al-Djawziyya, *Iʿlām*, i, 26).

In a still wider meaning, *fiḳh* was used for religious science in general (*al-Ḳurʾān wa 'l-fiḳh* in opposition to the study of poetry: *A*gh*ānī*, vii, 55, [22]; *laysa bihim ra*gh*ba fi 'l-dīn wa-lā ra*gh*ba fi 'l-fiḳh*: *Musnad* of Aḥmad b. Ḥanbal, i, 155; cf. also the titles *al-Fiḳh al-Akbar* and *al-Fiḳh al-Absaṭ* and the text of these treatises, on which see ABŪ ḤANĪFA). *Fuḳahāʾ* was correspondingly applied to students of religion, theologians (not only students of law) *e.g.*, Ṭabarī, *Tafsīr*, xii, 73, [13]; *fuḳahāʾunā wa-ma*sh*āʾi*kh*unā*; *ibid.*, 112, [8], where Abū ʿUbayd al-Ḳāsim b. Sallām says with reference to an explanation by Abū ʿUbayda Maʿmar of a word in the Ḳurʾān contrary to the traditional explanation: *al-fuḳahāʾ aʿlam bi 'l-taʾwīl minhu*, "the *fuḳahāʾ* are more conversant with exegesis than he" (who is not a theologian but only a philologist); cf. also *Ẓâhiriten*, 19. (I. GOLDZIHER-[J. SCHACHT])

The traditional opinion of the Muslim scholars projects the origins of Islamic jurisprudence back into the generation of the Companions of the Prophet. According to it, the Caliphs of Medina and a few specialists in religious law among the Companions started to draw conclusions from the Ḳurʾān and the words and acts of the Prophet as they remembered them or as they had been reported to them, by independent reasoning; their conclusions were approved, explicitly or silently, by the other Companions and became thereby binding on the community; their Successors continued this activity and the generation following the Successors saw the foundation of the schools of religious law.

Recent historical research, however, has shown that Islamic jurisprudence came into being towards the end of the first century of the hi*dj*ra (early 8th century A.D.). During the greater part of the 1st/7th century, Islamic law, in the technical meaning of the term, and therefore Islamic jurisprudence, did not as yet exist. As had been the case in the time of the Prophet, law as such fell outside the sphere of religion, and so far as there were no religious or moral objections to specific transactions or modes of behaviour, the technical aspects of law were a matter of indifference to the Muslims. Not only did Arab customary law, as modified and completed by the Ḳurʾān, survive to a considerable extent, but the Muslims did not hesitate to adopt the legal, commercial and administrative institutions and practices of the conquered territories, and even legal concepts and maxims, as far as they were compatible with the demands of the new religious ideas (see above). As supreme rulers and administrators, the Caliphs of Medina acted to a great extent as the lawgivers of the community, and they were followed in this by the Umayyad Caliphs and their governors; during the whole of the first century of Islam, the administrative and legislative activities of the Islamic government cannot be separated. The Umayyad governors also appointed the first ḳāḍīs who by their decisions laid the foundations of what was to become Islamic law. They gave judgment according to their own discretion or "sound opinion" (raʾy), basing themselves on customary practice and on administrative regulations, and taking the letter and the spirit of the Ḳurʾān and other recognized Islamic religious norms into account. Subsequent developments brought it about that the part played by the earliest ḳāḍīs in laying the foundations of Islamic law was not recognized by Islamic jurisprudence.

Towards the end of the first century of the hidjra (early 8th century A.D.) only we encounter the first specialists in religious law whose activity can be regarded as historical, such as Ibrāhīm al-Naḵẖaʿī in Kūfa, and Saʿīd b. al-Musayyib and his contemporaries in Medina. They were pious persons whose interest in religion caused them to survey, either individually or in discussion with like-minded friends, all fields of contemporary activities, including the field of law, from an Islamic angle, to impregnate the sphere of law with religious and ethical ideas, and to elaborate, by individual reasoning (raʾy, istiḥsān, idjtihād [qq.v.]), an Islamic way of life. Their reasoning represents the beginnings of an Islamic jurisprudence. Islamic jurisprudence did not grow out of an existing Islamic law; it created Islamic law by endorsing, modifying or rejecting the popular and administrative practice of the Umayyad period. Members of this group, such as Radjāʾ and Abū Ḳilāba, were among the familiars of the Umayyad Caliphs from the last decades of the 1st/7th century onwards, and the ḳāḍīs came increasingly to be recruited from them.

As the groups of pious specialists grew in numbers and in cohesion, they developed, in the first few decades of the 2nd/8th century, into the "ancient schools of law" of which those of Kūfa, of Medina and of Syria are known to us in some detail. The differences between them were caused in the first place by geographical factors, such as local variations in social conditions, customary law and practice, but they were not based on any noticeable disagreement on principles or methods. The great centre of nascent Islamic jurisprudence at the end of the 1st/7th and during the 2nd/8th century was ʿIrāḳ; influences of the doctrine of one school on that of another almost invariably proceeded from ʿIrāḳ to Ḥidjāz, and the doctrinal development of the school of Madīna often lagged behind that of the school of Kūfa. The ancient schools shared not only

a considerable body of common doctrine but the essentials of a legal theory the central idea of which was that of the "living tradition of the school". This idea dominated the development of Islamic jurisprudence during the whole of the 2nd/8th century. Retrospectively, it appears as sunna or "practice" (ʿamal), i.e., the ideal practice, the practice as it ought to be, or "well-established precedent" (sunna māḍiya) or "ancient practice" (amr ḳadīm). Synchronously, it is represented by the consensus (idjmāʿ, al-amr al-mudjtamaʿ ʿalayh), the common doctrine of the majority of the representative religious scholars of each centre (cf. above). Originally, the living tradition of the ancient schools was anonymous; it was the average opinion of their representatives that counted, and not the individual doctrines of the most prominent scholars. From the first decades of the 2nd/8th century onwards, however, it began to be projected backwards and to be ascribed to some of the great figures of the past. The earliest specialists, such as Ibrāhīm al-Naḵẖaʿī, had not done more than give opinions on questions of ritual and perhaps on kindred problems of directly religious concern, cases of conscience concerning alms-tax, marriage, divorce, and the like, and technical points of law appeared only at the stage of doctrine represented by the teaching of Ḥammād b. Abī Sulaymān (d. 120/738). By a literary convention which found particular favour in ʿIrāḳ, scholars used to put their own doctrines under the aegis of their masters. In this way, the main contents of the Kitāb al-Āthār of Abū Yūsuf and of the Kitāb al-Āthār of S̲h̲aybānī represent themselves as having been derived from Abū Ḥanīfa, "from" (ʿan) Ḥammād, "from" Ibrāhīm. The Medinese followed suit and projected their own teaching back to a number of ancient authorities who had died in the last years of the first or in the very first years of the second century, seven of whom were later singled out to form the group of the so-called "seven lawyers of Medina" (fuḳahāʾ al-Madīna al-sabʿa: Saʿīd b. al-Musayyib, ʿUrwa b. al-Zubayr, Abū Bakr b. ʿAbd al-Raḥmān, ʿUbayd Allāh b. ʿAbd Allāh b. ʿUtba, Khāridja b. Zayd b. Thābit, Sulaymān b. Yasār, and al-Ḳāsim b. Muḥammad b. Abī Bakr). The transmission of legal doctrine in Ḥidjāz becomes ascertainable at about the same time as in ʿIrāḳ, with Zuhrī ([q.v.]; d. 124/742) and his younger contemporary Rabīʿa b. Abī ʿAbd al-Raḥmān for Medina, and with ʿAṭāʾ b. Abī Rabāḥ for Mecca. At the same time at which the doctrine of the school of Kūfa was retrospectively attributed to Ibrāhīm al-Naḵẖaʿī, a similar body of doctrine was directly connected with the very beginnings of Islam in Kūfa by being attributed to Ibn Masʿūd [q.v.], a Companion of the Prophet who had come to live in that city, and Ibrāhīm al-Naḵẖaʿī became the main transmitter of that body of doctrine, too. In the same way, another Companion of the Prophet, Ibn ʿAbbās [q.v.], became the eponym of the school of Mecca, and the school of Medina claimed as its main authorities among the Companions of the Prophet the caliph ʿUmar [q.v.] and his son, ʿAbd Allāh b. ʿUmar. One further step in the search for a solid theoretical foundation of the doctrine of the ancient schools was taken in ʿIrāḳ, very early in the second century of Islam, by transferring the term "sunna of the Prophet" from its political and theological into a legal context and identifying it with the sunna, the ideal practice of the local community and the corresponding doctrine of its scholars. This term, which was taken over by the school of Syria, expressed the axiom that the practice of the Muslims continued the practice of the Prophet, but did not yet imply the existence of positive information in the form of "traditions" (*ḥadīth*) that the Prophet by his words or acts had in fact originated or approved that practice.

It was not long before there arose movements of opposition to the opinions held by the majorities in the ancient schools. In Kūfa, where Ibn Masʿūd had become the eponym of the school, the doctrines which were put forward in opposition to it and which do not embody the coherent teaching of any one group were regularly attributed to the caliph ʿAlī [*q.v.*], who had made Kūfa his headquarters, not indeed on account of any Shīʿī bias, which is absent from them, but because the name of ʿAlī represented an authority equal to and possibly even higher than that of Ibn Masʿūd. These opinions generally did not prevail in the school of Kūfa, but in Medina the corresponding doctrines succeeded in gaining recognition to a considerable extent. In contrast with the opposition in Kūfa, the opposition in Medina already reflected the activity of the Traditionists. The movement of the Traditionists (*ahl al-ḥadīth*, [*q.v.*]) is the most important single event in the history of Islamic jurisprudence in the second century of the hidjra; it opposed to the "living tradition" of the ancient schools, which was to a great extent based on *raʾy*, the authority of individual traditions (*ḥadīth*, [*q.v.*]) from the Prophet which its adherents put into circulation in ever increasing numbers. According to the traditionists, *fiḳh* had to be based exclusively on traditions from the Prophet, whom they reported as having said: "Luck to the man who hears my words, remembers them, guards them and hands them on; many a transmitter of *fiḳh* is no *faḳīh* himself, and many a one transmits *fiḳh* to a person who is a better *faḳīh* than he is" (Shāfiʿī, *Risāla*, 55, 65). Traditionists existed in all great centres of Islam, where they formed groups in opposition to, but nevertheless in contact with, the local schools of law, and the polemics between them and the ancient schools occupied most of the second century. But the ancient schools had no real defence against the rising tide of traditions; they had to express their own doctrines in traditions which allegedly went back to the Prophet and to take increasing notice of the traditions produced by their opponents, and finally the outlines and many details of Islamic jurisprudence were cast into the form of traditions from the Prophet. Later Muslim scholars, who in the nature of things were unable to acknowledge such a fundamental change in the bases of Islamic legal thought, represented this struggle as a struggle between the *ahl al-ḥadīth* and the imaginary group of the *aṣḥāb al-raʾy* [*q.v.*]. The Traditionists of the 3rd/9th century attacked the ʿIrāḳians and the school of Abū Ḥanīfa with particular venom, and castigated their use of the formula *araʾayta* "what do you think of . . ., supposing . . ." as typical of the casuistry of the *aṣḥāb al-raʾy*.

The literary productions of Islamic jurisprudence begin soon after the middle of the 2nd/8th century (the *Madjmūʿ al-fiḳh* attributed to the Shīʿī pretender Zayd b. ʿAlī [*q.v.*], who died in 122/740, though of an early date, is not authentic; cf. Bergsträsser, in *OLZ*, 1922, 114-24; Strothmann, in *Isl.*, xiii (1923), 27-40, 49), and from then onwards its development can be followed step by step from scholar to scholar. For ʿIrāḳ, and Kūfa in particular, successive stages are represented, after Ḥammād (d. 120/738; see above), by the doctrines of Ibn Abī Laylā ([*q.v.*] d. 148/765), of Abū Ḥanīfa ([*q.v.*]; d. 150/767), of Abū Yūsuf ([*q.v.*]; d. 182/798), and of Shaybānī ([*q.v.*]; d. 189/805) respectively. Outside the line of doctrine represented by the *isnād* Abū Ḥanīfa—Ḥammād—Ibrāhīm stands another scholar of Kūfa, Sufyān al-Thawrī ([*q.v.*]; d. 161/778); his doctrines are known to us through the *Kitāb Ikhtilāf al-fuḳahāʾ* of Ṭabarī ([*q.v.*]; d. 310/923), which also contains information on other early lawyers. The Syrian Awzāʿī ([*q.v.*]; d. 157/774) represents an archaic type of doctrine, which takes us very near to the beginnings of Islamic jurisprudence. Mālik b. Anas ([*q.v.*]; d. 179/795) in his *Muwaṭṭaʾ* aimed at expounding the average doctrine of the school of Medina in his time. Much information on the opinions of Mālik himself, of his disciple Ibn al-Ḳāsim ([*q.v.*]; d. 191/806), and of the older authorities of Medina is contained in the *Mudawwana* of Saḥnūn ([*q.v.*]; d. 240/854).

Shāfiʿī ([*q.v.*]; d. 204/820) belonged originally to the school of Medina, but he accepted the thesis of the Traditionists on the overriding authority of the traditions from the Prophet, identifying their contents with the *sunna*, defended it in vigorous polemics with the followers of the ancient schools, elaborated on its basis a new body of doctrine by which he cut himself off from the continuity of doctrine in the ancient schools, and composed in his *Risāla* the first treatise on the method of legal reasoning, becoming thereby the founder of the science of *uṣūl al-fiḳh* [see UṢŪL]. (In contrast with the *uṣūl*, the "roots" or sources of legal knowledge, the body of positive rules derived from them is called *furūʿ*, plural of *farʿ*, "branches"; the earliest existing work of pure *furūʿ*, presented in a didactic manner, is Shaybānī's *Kitāb al-Aṣl.*) Shāfiʿī's writings, which to a great extent are cast in the form of dialogues with unnamed opponents and most of which were brought together by his disciples in a collection which received the name of *Kitāb al-Umm*, are an important source for the history of Islamic jurisprudence in the second century. Shāfiʿī was not a mere Traditionist; on the contrary, he deplored their faulty reasoning, and himself accompanied his reliance on traditions from the Prophet by systematic legal thought (*ʿaḳl, maʿḳūl*) of exceptionally high quality, excluding *raʾy* and *istiḥsān* and insisting on strict *ḳiyās*. It happened, however, that some of his disciples, and in particular Aḥmad b. Ḥanbal ([*q.v.*]; d. 241/855), emphasized the traditionist element in his doctrine and derived their legal teaching exclusively from traditions, avoiding human reasoning as far as possible. This avoidance of drawing conclusions was erected into a principle by Dāwūd b. Khalaf ([*q.v.*]; d. 270/884), called al-Ẓāhirī because he relied exclusively on the literal meaning (*ẓāhir*) of Ḳurʾān and *ḥadīth* and rejected not only *raʾy* and *istiḥsān* but reasoning by *ḳiyās* as well.

About the middle of the 2nd/8th century, groups or circles within the ancient schools of law began to form themselves round individual masters, such as the "followers of Abū Ḥanīfa" within the school of Kūfa, and the "followers of Mālik" within the school of Medina. Several factors favoured this process, and by the middle of the 3rd/9th century the ancient schools of law had transformed themselves into "personal" schools, which perpetuated not the living tradition of a city but the doctrine of a master and of his disciples. In this way, the bulk of the ancient school of Kūfa transformed itself into the school of the Ḥanafīs, another group of scholars into the school of Sufyān al-Thawrī, the ancient school of Medina into the school of the Mālikīs, and the ancient school of Syria into that of Awzāʿī. Although Shāfiʿī had disclaimed any intention of founding a school, his disciples, being neither mere Traditionists nor members of another school, became his personal followers, and the doctrinal movement started by him has always been known as the Shāfiʿī school. The school of legal thought originated by Aḥmad b. Ḥanbal, too, became known as the school of the Ḥanbalīs; this school never absorbed its parent movement, that of the Traditionists, as completely as the Ḥanafī and Mālikī schools absorbed theirs. The followers of Dāwūd b. Khalaf al-Ẓāhirī formed the only school of law whose name, Ẓāhiriyya [*q.v.*], is derived from a principle of legal theory. These and some other later schools of law (such as a short-lived one founded by Ṭabarī) are called *madhāhib* (pl. of *madhhab*, "way of thinking, persuasion"). Since about 700/1300 four of them only have survived in orthodox Islam, the Ḥanafī, Mālikī, Shāfiʿī and Ḥanbali schools (cf. ḤANĀBILA, ḤANAFIYYA, MĀLIKIYYA, SHĀFIʿIYYA); they are regarded, and regard one another, as alternative and equally valid interpretations of the religious law of Islam. Notwithstanding their divergent doctrinal roots, the orthodox schools of law share a common legal theory (cf. UṢŪL) which asserted itself in the 3rd/9th century, and which accepted Shāfiʿī's (and the Traditionists') principle of the overriding authority of the traditions from the Prophet as the only evidence of *sunna* but subordinated its practical application to the consensus of the scholars. The theory of the *uṣūl al-fiḳh* is therefore of little direct importance for the positive doctrines of the schools of law. From the middle of the 3rd/9th century, too, the idea began to gain ground that only the great scholars of the past had the right to independent reasoning in law (*idjtihād* [*q.v.*]), and in the 4th/10th century a consensus gradually established itself in orthodox Islam to the effect that all future activity would have to be confined to the explanation, application, and, at the most, interpretation of the doctrine as it had been laid down once and for all (*taḳlīd* [*q.v.*]). This implied the obligation to join one of the existing schools. Even under the rule of *taḳlīd*, Islamic jurisprudence did not lack manifestations of original thought in which the several schools competed with and influenced one another. But this original thought could express itself freely in nothing more than abstract systematic constructions which affected neither the established doctrine of positive law nor the theory of the *uṣūl al-fiḳh*. New sets of facts, too, constantly arose in life, and they had to be decided by the specialists with the traditional tools of legal science; such a decision is called *fatwā* [*q.v.*], and the scholar who gives a *fatwā* is called *muftī*. Once recognized as correct by the common opinion of the scholars, the decisions of the *muftī*s became part of the doctrine of each school. The activity of the *muftī*s is essentially of the same kind, though carried out against a different background, as that of the first specialists in religious law.

The legal doctrines of the Khāridjīs [*q.v.*] and of the Shīʿa [*q.v.*], which split from the orthodox or Sunnī majority on political grounds about the middle of the first century of Islam (ca. 660 A.D.), differ from those of the Sunnīs on the question of the leadership of the community [see IMĀM] and consequential questions of *uṣūl*, but on other questions they do not differ from those of the orthodox schools of law more widely than these last differ from one another. From this, it must not be concluded that the features common to Khāridjī, Shīʿa, and Sunnī law are older than the schisms which split the Islamic community within its first century. For a considerable period, and during the 2nd/8th and 3rd/9th centuries in particular, these ancient sects remained in a sufficiently close contact with the Sunnīs for them to adopt the doctrines which were being developed in the orthodox schools of law, introducing only such superficial modifications as were required by their particular political and dogmatic tenets. Certain doctrines which in themselves were not necessarily either Shīʿī or Sunnī became adventitiously distinctive for Shīʿa as against Sunnī law.

When the Umayyads were overthrown by the ʿAbbāsids in 132/750, Islamic jurisprudence, though still in its formative period, had acquired its essential features. For reasons of dynastic policy, and in order to differentiate themselves from their predecessors, the ʿAbbāsids posed as the protagonists of Islam, recognized Islamic law as it was being taught by the pious specialists as the only legitimate norm in Islam, and set out to translate their doctrines into practice. They regularly attracted specialists in religious law to their court and made a point of consulting them on problems that might come within their competence. At the request of the Caliph Hārūn al-Rashīd, Abū Yūsuf wrote his *Kitāb al-Kharādj*, a long treatise on public finance, taxation, criminal justice, and connected subjects. The *ḳāḍī*s, who under the Umayyads had been appointed by the governors, were now appointed by the caliph, they had to be specialists in religious law, and they had to apply nothing but the sacred Law, without interference from the government [see ḲĀḌĪ]. But this effort to translate into practice the ideal doctrine which was being elaborated by the specialists, was short-lived. The early specialists who had formulated their doctrine not on the basis of but in a certain opposition to Umayyad popular and administrative practice had been ahead of realities, and now the early ʿAbbāsids and their religious advisers were unable to carry the whole of society with them. The *ḳāḍī*s, theoretically independent though they were, had to rely on the political authorities for the execution of their judgments, and, being bound by the formal rules of the Islamic law of evidence, their inability to deal with criminal cases became apparent, so that the administration of the greater part of criminal justice was taken over by the police (*shurṭa* [*q.v.*]). The administrative "investigation of complaints" [see MAẒĀLIM] very soon led to formal Courts of Complaints being set up, which by their very existence show the breakdown of a considerable part of the administration of civil justice by the *ḳāḍī*s as well. [See also SIYĀSA]. In this way, a double administration of justice came into being, and it has prevailed in most Islamic countries, the competence of the *ḳāḍī*s' tribunals being restricted to matters of family law, inheritance, and *waḳf*. [See MAḤKAMA].

This is one aspect of the tension between theory and practice (*ʿāda*, *ʿurf* [*qq.v.*]), between jurisprudence and customary law, which existed in Islamic law from its very beginnings. The most remarkable and, for a time, the most successful effort on the part of a state of high material civilization to bridge this gulf, was made in the Ottoman Empire [see ABU 'L-SUʿŪD, ḲĀNŪN-NĀME, SHAYKH AL-ISLĀM]. Islamic jurisprudence, too, took notice of the practice which it could not overcome, and tried at least to control and regulate it in the works on *ʿamal*, on *ḥiyal*, and on *sh͟hurūṭ* [*qq.v.*], which form an important branch of its literary productions.

Until the early ʿAbbāsid period, Islamic jurisprudence had been adaptable and growing, but from then onwards it became increasingly rigid and set in its final mould. This essential rigidity helped it to maintain its stability over the centuries which saw the decay of the political institutions of Islam. Taken as a whole, it reflects and fits the social and economic conditions of the early ʿAbbāsid period. If it grew more and more out of touch with later developments of state and society, in the long run it gained more in power over the minds than it lost in control over the bodies of the Muslims. The *fiḳh* is, in the words of Snouck Hurgronje, a "doctrine of duties", the interpretation of a religious ideal not by legislators but by scholars, and the recognized handbooks of the several schools are not "codes" in the Western meaning of the term. Islamic law is a "jurists' law" par excellence: Islamic jurisprudence did not grow out of an existing law, it itself created it. [See also SH͟HARĪʿA].

In British India and in French Algeria, Islamic jurisprudence, being fused with Western legal thought and affected by Western legislation, gave birth, respectively, to Anglo-Muhammadan law [see HIND] and to the *droit musulman algérien* [see AL-DJAZĀʾIR] both of which became independent legal systems. Only in the 20th century, Islamic Modernism, whilst accepting the postulate that Islam as a religion ought to regulate the sphere of law as well, has denied the validity of traditional Islamic jurisprudence. Under the influence of modern constitutional and social ideas, many institutions of Islamic law have been reshaped, and sometimes changed out of recognition, by secular legislation in a number of Islamic countries. Once again, jurists prepared, provoked, and guided a new legislation. On the other hand, the programme was formulated of deriving a new, modern law from the general formal principles which were elaborated by the early Islamic jurists. Both tendencies are inspired by the desire to put a new Islamic jurisprudence in the place of the old one. [See ḲĀNŪN].

Bibliography: Lane, s.v.; *LA*, s.v.; Tahānawī, *Dictionary of technical terms*, 30-3.—Traditional accounts: Muḥammad b. al-Ḥasan al-Ḥadjwī, *al-Fikr al-sāmī fī taʾrīkh al-fiḳh al-islāmī*, 4 vols., Rabat-Fes-Tunis 1345-9/1926-31; Muḥammad Yūsuf Mūsā, *Muḥāḍarāt fī taʾrīkh al-fiḳh al-islāmī*, 3 vols., Cairo 1954-6.—Modern historical studies: I. Goldziher, *Die Ẓâhiriten*, Leipzig 1884; idem, *Muh. St.*, ii, 66-87 (Fr. transl. L. Bercher, *Études sur la tradition islamique*, Paris 1952, 79-105); idem, *Vorlesungen*, 35-79 (² 30-70, 309-21); *Selected works of C. Snouck Hurgronje*, ed. G.-H. Bousquet and J. Schacht, Leiden 1957; D. S. Margoliouth, *The early development of Mohammedanism*, London 1914, 65-98; Juynboll, *Handbuch*, 22-38 (*Handleiding* ³ ᵃⁿᵈ ⁴, 16-32); F. Köprülü, art. *Fıkıh*, in *IA* (1947); R. Brunschvig, *Polémiques médiévales autour du rite de Mālik*, in *Al-Andalus*, 1950, 377-435; J. Schacht, *The origins of Muhammadan jurisprudence*³, Oxford 1959; idem, *Introduction to Islamic law*, Oxford 1964, with detailed bibliography.—On foreign elements: J. Schacht, in *Mémoires de l'Académie Internationale de Droit Comparé*, iii/4, Rome 1955, 127-41, and in *XII Convegno "Volta"*, Rome 1957, 197-218; on influences of Jewish law and ritual in particular: I. Goldziher, in *REJ*, xxviii, 78, xliii, 4; A. J. Wensinck, in *Isl.*, i (1910), 101 f.; E. Mittwoch, *Zur Entstehungsgeschichte des islamischen Gebets und Kultus* (*Abh. Pr. Ak. W.*), Berlin 1913.—On the literature of fiḳh: Juynboll, *Handbuch*, 360-3 (*Handleiding*, 373-8); N. P. Aghnides, *Mohammedan theories of finance*, New York 1916, 177-94; J. Schacht, *Introduction*, chap. 16 and bibliography.

(J. SCHACHT)

FIKR, pl. *afkār*, thought, reflection. The Ḳurʾān employs the 2nd and 5th forms of the root *fkr*, to urge men "to reflect". In the vocabulary of *falsafa* and *ʿilm al-kalām*, the *maṣdar fikr* denotes the intellectual faculty in the act of thought, reflecting upon an object of intellection. It is distinguished from *idrāk*, the intellectual faculty of grasping, of perception. The result of the operation of *fikr* is expressed by the noun of unity *fikra*.

In *taṣawwuf*, *fikr* is used habitually in contrast to *d͟hikr* [*q.v.*], recollection. *Fikr* can thus be translated by reflection or meditation. In the performance of *fikr* the Ṣūfī, concentrating upon a religious subject, meditates according to a certain progression of ideas or a series of evocations which he assimilates and experiences; in *d͟hikr*, concentrating on the object recollected—generally a Divine Name—, he allows his field of consciousness to lose itself in this object: hence the importance granted to the technique of repetition, at first verbal, later unspoken. The "meditations" of al-Ḥallād͟j on the "night-journey" and "ascension" (*miʿrād͟j*) of the Prophet, or on the meeting of Moses and Iblīs, can be taken as examples of *fikr*. Another instance of it will be found in the "scrutiny of conscience" (*ḥisāb*) advocated by al-Muḥāsibī.

The problem of the respective merits of *fikr* and *d͟hikr* confronted the Ṣūfīs of the first centuries. Al-Ḥasan al-Baṣrī insisted upon *fikr*. It is, he said, "the mirror which makes you see what good there is in you, and what evil". The Muʿtazila, the Karrāmiyya and the Imāmiyya taught that reflection must precede recourse to *samʿ*, scriptural or traditional authority; hence, in their view, the superiority of *fikr* to *d͟hikr*. Al-Ḥallād͟j, notes L. Massignon, "does not make a decision": he considers both methods to be legitimate, since both must lead to the Goal, but only on the condition that the "initiate" (*ʿārif*) should not cling to his approach as an end in itself. In a celebrated passage of his meditation on the *miʿrād͟j*, he speaks of the "garden of *d͟hikr*" which Muḥammad visited "without deviating", and of the "process of *fikr*" which he followed without "passing beyond".

However, al-Ḥallād͟j also seems to have given his preference to *fikr* rather than *d͟hikr*. Some of his texts follow this trend. But it is evident that in these texts *fikr* must not be rendered solely by "discursive meditation", the effort of the spirit following the human method of procedure, as distinct from the "passive" state of recollection in prayer. *Fikr* is clearly distinguished from *ḥads*, just as reflection is distinguished from an intellectual flash of illumination or intuition. But in the reply of Iblīs to Moses, the *Kitāb al-Ṭawāsīn* contrasts *al-fikra* ("pure thought", following Massignon's translation) with *d͟hikr*: "O Moses, pure thought (*fikra*) has no need of recollection (*d͟hikr*)". The fact is, al-Kalābād͟hī explains in commenting on a phrase of Ḥallād͟j, the fruits of *d͟hikr* are refreshment for the soul, while meditations (*afkār*) guide the initiate towards the single divine majesty, the reverential fear of God, His favours and His gifts. *Dhikr* appeals to the organs of the senses (the tongue, the physical heart), *fikr* purely to intellectual concentration. By means of *dhikr* and its rhythmical use of oral prayers the Ṣūfī is almost certain to succeed in attaining subjective spiritual "states" (*aḥwāl*); *fikr* tends to put him within the possibility of experiencing transcendant truths.

But in the event, it was the superiority of *dhikr* to *fikr* which was to be most generally affirmed. There was distrust of the illusions which the practice of *fikr* could engender: as early as the 3rd/9th century, Khashīsh Nisaʾī said that, "some, by force of "meditation", claim to enjoy in this world the spiritual life of God, the angels and the prophets, and to feast with the ḥūris" (quoted and trans. Massignon); whilst *dhikr*, though appealing as it does to the organs of the senses, at least has the merit of depriving the spirit of everything other than the object recollected. Monographs were written on *dhikr*, its techniques and achievements, but not on *fikr* and its methods.

There remains the fact that the gnostic soarings of those who profess *waḥdat al-wudjūd* ("Unity of Being") can be regarded as deriving from a *fikr* in which the use of typified symbols replaced the "process" of discursive reasoning.

Bibliography: Ḥallādj, *Kitāb al-Ṭawāsīn*, ed. Massignon, Paris 1913, 33, 46-7; Kalābādhī, *Kitāb al-Taʿarruf*, ed. Arberry, Cairo 1352/1934, 74-5; L. Massignon, *Lexique technique de la mystique musulman*, Paris 1954, 114, 192; idem, *Passion d'al-Ḥallâj*, Paris 1922, index s.v.

(L. Gardet)

FIKRET, TEVFIK [see tewfīk fikret].

FIKRĪ, ʿAbd Allāh Pasha, an Egyptian statesman, poet and prose-writer, regarded as one of the authors who have helped to give a simpler, more modern character to Arabic literary style. Born in 1250/1834 in Mecca where his father, an Egyptian officer, was serving, and later brought up in Cairo, he studied at al-Azhar and consorted with the Ṣūfīs. From 1267/1851 he was an administrative official and attracted the attention of Khedive Ismāʿīl who, in 1284/1866, chose him to teach Arabic, Turkish and Persian to his sons Tawfīḳ, Ḥasan and Ḥusayn. His biographers reveal him as a man of integrity, with sincere religious beliefs, and distinguished by his family's piety (his paternal grandfather ʿAbd Allāh taught at al-Azhar). He often visited Istanbul on official missions. In 1870 he took part in founding the Khedivial library, as the subordinate of ʿAli Pasha Mubārak [*q.v.*] with whom subsequently he often worked. In 1878 he was *wakīl* of the Minister of Public Instruction, at that time ʿAli Pasha Mubārak. In 1882, for four months, he was himself Minister of Public Instruction in the ministry of al-Bārūdī, a follower of the movement of ʿUrābī Pasha [*q.v.*]. Imprisoned for that reason and then released, he remained thenceforth in obscurity. He made the pilgrimage to Mecca in 1302/1885, and attended the Stockholm Congress of Orientalists in 1889 as an official Egyptian delegate. He died on 11 Dhu 'l-Ḥidjdja 1307/27 July 1890.

After his death, his son Amīn Pasha Fikrī published a collection of his father's poems, letters, etc. under the title *al-Āthār al-Fikriyya*, Cairo 1315, and a description of his father's travels under the title *Irshād al-alibbāʾ ilā maḥāsin Urubbā*, Cairo 1892. The list of his other writings is given in Brockelmann, II, 474 ff. and *Suppl.*, and also in his biographies.

Bibliography: ʿAlī Pasha Mubārak, *Khiṭaṭ djadīda*, ii, 46 ff.; Muḥammad ʿAbd al-Ghanī Ḥasan, *ʿAbd Allāh Fikrī, ʿaṣruhu, ḥayātuhu, adabuhu*, Cairo 1946; Sayyid ʿInānī, *ʿAbd Allāh Bāshā Fikrī, ḥayātuhu wa-āthāruhu wa-makānatuhu 'l-adabiyya*, Cairo 1946; Ziriklī, *al-Aʿlām, ḳāmūs tarādjim* ..., iv, 252-3, giving additional bibliographical information.

(J. Jomier)

FĪL (Ar.; from Persian *pīl*), elephant. The word appears in the title and first verse of *Sūra* CV, which alludes to the expedition of Abraha [*q.v.*], but the Arabs were barely acquainted with this animal which is a native of India and Africa; consequently when, towards the end of the 2nd/beginning of the 8th century, a troop of elephants arrived in Baṣra, it was a matter of curiosity for the population (see al-Nawawī, *Tahdhīb*, 738). The subject had already come up in the *Kalīla wa-Dimna* (trans. A. Miquel, Paris 1957, 53), but the first Arab author truly to concern himself and to undertake a personal investigation was al-Djāḥiẓ (*Ḥayawān*, in particular vii, *passim*) who, on the basis also of the poems of a certain Hārūn b. Mūsā who had lived in Mūltān, collected together most of the known facts and beliefs relating to this huge and curious creature, for which the name *zandabīl* was also used, although it was not really known whether that term denoted the male or the female.

The outcome of a metamorphosis, it is the father of the pig which has a vague resemblance to it. The points that attract most attention, apart from its size, are its trunk, which serves as both nose and hand and is used for work and as a weapon, and its tusks which, some say, are hollow at the base and attain a weight of from 2 to 300 *manns*. Equally striking are its ugliness and its over-short neck, its huge ears and small eyes. The tongue is reversed, that is to say the tip points inwards, and were it not for this fault it would be able to learn to speak. In spite of its massive body it has a feeble cry; it runs swiftly and can move with agility and dexterity. As its only joints are in the shoulder and thigh, it is unable to lie down and has to sleep standing up, against a tree or wall; if it falls down on its side, its companions haul it up again by means of their trunks. It can swim, keeping its trunk above water in order to breathe. The thick secretion from its forehead is sweeter then musk, and is collected with the utmost care; the dung is a remedy to prevent conception, and various parts of the body are used in medicine.

Elephants do not breed in ʿIrāḳ, and the birth of an elephant calf at the court of a king of Persia is referred to as a curiosity. In its fifth year the animal, whose testicles are inside the body, near the kidneys, is capable of reproduction. In the rutting season the male is endowed with extraordinary strength and reverts to a state of savagery, while the female becomes intractable and bad-tempered; once she is pregnant she is no longer touched by the males; she calves every seven years, and to find the calf it is necessary to search in the jungle, near to a river, where the mother deposits it to save it from a dangerous fall. The elephant calf, which is born with teeth, is entrusted to the care of a *fayyāl* responsible for its training. In captivity, the elephant lives from 80 to 100 years, but in the wild state its longevity is much greater, and certain individuals live to the age of 400.

The elephant is very intelligent, patient and docile; it is able to recognize its master and understands orders given by its *fayyāl* who, seated on its back, touches its forehead with a curved stick and talks to it in an Indian language. It possesses a curious gift for imitation and becomes very friendly; normally of a playful disposition, and in fact addicted to jokes, it is terribly vindictive and has the ability to choose the best moment to wreak its vengeance. It takes to flight at the approach of the rhinoceros, which is thought to be able to lift it up with its horn; similarly, the lion utterly terrifies it, and the cat profits from its resemblance to the king of beasts, so much so that one way of effectively dealing with a force containing war-elephants is, on their approach, to release a quantity of cats which have been kept in readiness in sacks. Its worst enemy is, however, a small creature called the *zabraḳ*, which kills it by spraying it with its urine.

The Arab authors are aware that the elephant lives in Africa also, but in the wild state, and al-Masʿūdī (*Murūdj*, iii, 5-7) relates how the Zandj set about killing it and taking its tusks. Al-Dimashḳī, for his part, gives details of the way in which a wild elephant is captured by trapping it in a pit; men wearing brightly coloured clothes maltreat it and strike it, but a trainer, dressed in white, drives them away and starts to tame the animal by giving it food; after a certain time the hunters return, and the same manoeuvre is repeated until the elephant has enough trust in the *fayyāl* to allow itself to be ridden away.

To judge by the tales of travellers, geographers and historians, the various Indian sovereigns used by tradition to keep a varying but very large number of elephants for ceremonial use and for war. With the body shielded by bands of iron and cork, and the trunk protected by a curved sabre (*ḳarṭal*), each war-elephant was accompanied by 500 men who in turn preceded 5,000 horsemen. Ibn Baṭṭūṭa says that he had seen some trained for executions.

The existence of certain elephants in ʿIrāḳ is attested by the texts; thus, it was on a grey elephant offered by an Indian king to al-Maʾmūn that al-Muʿtaṣim in 223/838 had his prisoner Bābak [*q.v.*] carried to Sāmarrā, before handing him over to the executioner; similarly, at about the same period, al-Djāḥiẓ was able to see some for himself and to take part in conversations in which the respective merits of the camel and the elephant were debated. In general, however, this animal remained purely an object of curiosity throughout the Muslim world west of India, with the possible exception of East and West Africa. On the other hand, ivory was well known and was used in the making of various articles [see ʿĀDJ].

When seen in a dream, the elephant generally presages some important business, but it is capable of more varied and subtle interpretations.

Bibliography: Djāḥiẓ, *Ḥawayān*, index; Masʿūdī, *Murūdj*, index; Damīrī, *Ḥayāt al-ḥayawān*, s.v.; Ḳazwīnī, ed. Wüstenfeld, i, 400; Dimashḳī, ed. Mehren, 156; Ibn Baṭṭūṭa, ed. Defrémery and Sanguinetti, iii, 330, 354, iv, 45; Ibn al-Bayṭār, *Traité des simples*, ed. Leclerc, iii, 51; M. Perron, *Nâcérî*, ii, 404-17, 465-74; R. Mauny, *Tableau géographique de l'Ouest africain au moyen âge*, Dakar 1961, 264-5.

(J. RUSKA-[CH. PELLAT])

As beasts of war. The use in western Asia of elephants for war stems from India. They were used in the warfare described in the *Mahābhārata* and their tactical use is discussed in Kauṭilya's *Arthaśāstra*. From this treatise we learn certain facts which remain valid in the Indo-Persian world of the Islamic period: that elephants were regarded as a royal monopoly and private possession of them was forbidden, and that they might be provided with armour plating and have mounted on their backs archers, swordsmen and mace-bearers (cf. B. P. Sinha, *The art of war in ancient India 600 B.C.-300 A.D.*, in *Cahiers d'Histoire Mondiale*, iv, 1957, 132-6, and S. H. Hodivala, *Studies in Indo-Muslim history*, Bombay 1939, 139-40). From India, their use passed to Achaemenid Persia. Alexander the Great first met Persian elephants when he defeated Darius III at Arbela in 331 B.C.; the Greek rulers in Bactria used them; Seleucus I introduced them to Syria, and the later Seleucids used them against Rome.

The Sāsānids regularly used war elephants (Masʿūdī, *Murūdj*, ii, 230; Christensen, *L'Iran sous les Sassanides*[2], 208). At Ḳādisiyya in 14/635, the Persian general Rustum deployed thirty of them in his centre and on his wings, and their appearance spread terror amongst the Bedouins; the Arabs finally stopped them by cutting their girths and dislodging the troop-laden howdahs, and also by attacking vulnerable parts like the eyes and trunks (Sir W. Muir, *The Caliphate, its rise, decline and fall*[4], Edinburgh 1915, 102 ff.). Despite new contacts with the Persian world, the military use of elephants did not spread during the Umayyad and early ʿAbbāsid periods. They were imported into the Caliphal lands from the fringes of the Indian world, *scil.* Kābul, Makrān and Sind (cf. Ṭabarī, i, 2708, and Ibn al-Athīr, vii, 89), but they were mainly used as stately mounts on ceremonial occasions; the Caliph al-Manṣūr is said to have favoured them for this (*Murūdj*, iii, 18-20). The Buwayhid ʿAḍud al-Dawla had a number of war elephants, *fuyūl muḳātila*, which he used in battle, but it is not recorded that they played any significant part in the fighting (Miskawayh, *Eclipse of the ʿAbbasid Caliphate*, ii, 368, tr. v, 402).

It was the Ghaznavids, the first Islamic dynasty whose empire spanned both the Persian and northern Indian worlds, who first used elephants in large numbers for military purposes and who first assigned them a definite place in their tactical theory. The next two centuries, the 5th/11th and the 6th/12th, were the heyday of the elephant as a military weapon in the Islamic world. Sebüktigīn and Maḥmūd of Ghazna captured elephants in hundreds from the Indian princes. These beasts fell within the Sultan's fifth of plunder. Their use was jealously guarded by the Sultans and by their successors in northern India, the Ghūrids and the Slave Kings of Delhi, and only as an exceptional mark of favour were they bestowed on great men of state. Armour plating was often placed over their heads and faces. In battle, they were usually placed in the front line; their metal accoutrements and ornaments were jangled to make a terrifying din, and they were then stampeded towards the enemy. This tactic was used with demoralizing effect on the Ḳarakhānids in 398/1008 and 416/1025 (cf. C. E. Bosworth, *Ghaznevid military organisation*, in *Der Islam*, xxxvi (1960), 61-4, and M. Nāẓim, *The life and times of Sulṭān Maḥmūd of Ghazna*, Cambridge 1931, 139).

Influenced by Ghaznavid practice, the sporadic use of elephants is recorded in the empire of the Great Saldjūḳs from the time of Berk-yāruḳ onwards, especially in Khurāsān and the east. At the battle outside Ghazna in 510/1116-17, Sandjar's Saldjūḳ troops were initially thrown into confusion at the sight of the fifty elephants of the Ghaznavid Arslān Shāh, but they dealt with the beasts by ripping open the soft under-belly of the leading elephant and stampeding it back into its own camp (Bosworth, *op. cit.*, 64). When Sandjar defeated his nephew Maḥmūd b. Muḥammad at Sāwa in 513/1119, he had in his forces forty elephants with troops mounted on them (Ibn al-Djawzī, *al-Muntaẓam*, ix, 205; Ibn al-Athīr, x, 387). The Ghūrids used elephants in their warfare with the Khwārizm Shāhs, and beasts captured from the Ghūrids were used by ʿAlāʾ al-Dīn Muḥammad for the defence of Samarḳand against the Mongols in 617/1220 (Djuwaynī, tr. Boyle, i, 117, 322-3). Although the Ḳara Khiṭāy used elephants captured from the Khwārizm Shāh for their assault on Balāṣāghūn, the use in war of these slow-moving and cumbersome beasts did not commend itself to the swift-moving Mongol cavalrymen. After he had taken Samarḳand, Čingiz Khān refused to allot fodder for the elephants captured there, and they were turned out in the steppe to die of hunger (Djuwaynī, tr. Boyle, i, 120, 360).

Outside Muslim India, elephants never thereafter regained their popularity as tactical weapons of war, although they were still used in the Persian world for ceremonial occasions.

Bibliography (in addition to the references given above): B. Spuler, *Iran in früh-islamischer Zeit*, 492-3; C. E. Bosworth, *The Ghaznavids: their empire in Afghanistan and eastern Iran 994-1040*, Edinburgh 1963, 115-18. (C. E. Bosworth)

Iconography. The earliest known representation of an elephant in Islamic art is the so-called Elephant Silk, perhaps from Khurāsān, which was originally in the church at St. Josse-sur-Mer, Pas-de-Calais, and is now in the Louvre. In company with other decorative motifs, it shows elephants in yellow confronting each other which have been reproduced in terms of inlay. The colours are a deep purple for the ground, with clear blue and tan which may have once been red. Each elephant bears elaborate trappings and a saddle-cloth. Although the colours are sumptuous enough, the design of this piece of silk is rather crude. The Kufic inscription in yellow below the two elephants mentions the name of Abu 'l-Manṣūr Bakht-tegīn, an Amīr of Khurāsān whose death took place in 349/960. Part of a similar elephant pattern is found on a fragment of silk at Siegburg which is of uncertain date. The treatment is again very stylised, the elephant having an excessively thin trunk and jointed legs. Mez (*Renaissance*, 437; English trans., 465) mentions that elephant designs were used in the decoration of carpets made at Ḥīra. In this connexion some fragments of a carpet bearing an elephant's head are now in the Musée des Arts Décoratifs at Paris.

Elephants appear only very rarely in Islamic metal work. Some bronze incense-burners, supported by small figures of elephants, are known. In the Pennsylvania Museum of Art is a panel from Rayy showing a king seated on a throne which rests on the backs of elephants. This may possibly represent Ṭoghrīl II (d. 590/1193-4).

Several early examples are known of the elephant in its role as one of the pieces in the game of chess. These ivory chessmen can be paralleled by a small black Sāsānid elephant which may have formed part of a set. According to Kühnel, one of these, in the Bargello Museum at Florence, is Mesopotamian work of the 3rd/9th century. Another, in which the elephant is shown picking up a smaller animal with its trunk, was in the possession of Dr. F. R. Martin, who states that it is Tīmūrid. Two ivory caskets from Cordova are in the Victoria and Albert Museum. A panel on one of these represents a person of rank travelling in state upon an elephant. This bears the date 359/969-70. Another, which is probably early 5th/11th century, has a number of circular panels each bearing a pair of different animals facing each other. One panel contains elephants with bushy tails upon the backs of which peacocks are resting.

In contrast to most of the elephants mentioned above, those depicted on Islamic pottery are more faithfully drawn. Examples are fairly numerous, the majority showing a king with two or more attendants riding in an elaborate howdah. This may represent Bahrām Gūr's return from Sind. One plate in the Possession Moussa is dated 616/1219-20. Others, with the same scene, are in the Freer Gallery at Washington, the Possession Rabenou and the Collection Allan Balch. These are mostly *mīnāʾī* ware from Rayy, belonging to the first half of the 7th/13th century. A spotted elephant with rich caparison appears on a star-shaped basin in a Kāshān lustre ware. Other ceramic objects of artistic merit with elephants are a basin from Āmul with some Chinese characteristics now in the Art Institute of Chicago, a bowl and a pitcher in the Louvre, and a plate in the Kelekian Collection which was formerly on exhibition at the Victoria and Albert Museum.

Copies of the *Manāfiʿ al-ḥayawān* of Ibn Bukhtīshūʿ with their wealth of animal paintings provide us with several pictures of elephants in which an attempt has been made to show every detail. The older copies were made and illustrated in the 7th/13th century. A bluish elephant with gilded saddle and a trunk composed of a series of loops (Pl. xx) appears in a British Museum manuscript of this work (OR. 2784, f. 136r°). Another, better known, is the famous Elefantenpaar in a manuscript illustrated towards the end of the 7th/13th century for Ghāzān Khān at Marāgha which is now in the Morgan Library at New York. The two elephants, each adorned with gold circlets bearing bells around foreheads and ankles, are embracing each other with their trunks against a background of foliage. The smaller elephant is blue with darker stripes; the larger is grey-brown with lighter stripes. Elephants' heads in gold occasionally appear among the very varied marginal decorations of some 9th/15th century manuscripts, notably the pocket encyclopaedia in the British Museum (ADD. 27261) which is dated 814/1410-11, an anthology of approximately the same date, and a *Shāh-nāma* in the Gulbenkian Foundation at Lisbon (Nos. 117 and 121 in *Arte do Oriente Islâmico*, Lisbon, 1963). These are very finely drawn and, for the first time, an accurate representation of an elephant is encountered.

The best sources of elephant miniatures are illustrated copies of the *Shāh-nāma* of Firdawsī. Scenes like Rustam killing the White Elephant or lassoing the Khāḳān of Čīn, the death of Ṭalḥand (Pl. xxii), and Iskandar's battle with Fūr have all provided much scope for the portrayal of elephants, ranging from exact drawings to figures of somewhat bizarre appearance, like those in mediaeval bestiaries (*e.g.* B.M. MS. Harl. 3244 f. 39r°). In some *Shāh-nāma* illustrations the heroes bear the device of an elephant on their banners. Other literary themes in which elephants appear—but rather less frequently—are the story in the *Mathnawī* of Rūmī of the elephant who trampled to death the travellers who had eaten her calf (Pl. xxi), the *ʿAdjāʾib al-makhlūḳāt* of Ḳazwīnī, and the Court of Solomon (Sulaymān) where an elephant sometimes appears among the animals grouped around the throne with angels and *djinn*.

Elephant, 7th/13th century. British Museum, OR. 2784, fol. 136r°.

The elephant killing the travellers who had eaten her calf. Miniature in the *Mathnawī* of Djalāl al-Dīn Rūmī, written c. 937/1530.

British Museum, ADD. 27262, fol. 134r°.

Gav being shown the body of Ṭalḥand. Miniature in a manuscript of Firdawsī's *Shāh-nāma*, dated 994/1586.
British Museum, ADD. 27302, fol. 519v°.

Bābur hunting rhinoceros. Miniature from the Persian translation of the *Bābur-nāma* by ʿAbd Al-Raḥīm Kh̲ān, written about the close of the 10th/16th century. British Museum, OR. 3714, fol. 352.

The earliest appearance of an elephant in the Islamic art of India is probably an ivory chessman bearing an Arabic inscription on its base in the Cabinet des Médailles of the Bibliothèque Nationale. This piece was reputed to have been sent by Hārūn al-Rash̲īd to Charlemagne, and certainly formed part of the Treasure of St. Denis as early as 1505. The elephant is shown in battle, unhorsing an enemy rider. On its back a king sits in a howdah, the exterior of which is fashioned in the form of a wall, guarded by soldiers with swords and round bucklers. Although some authorities have dated it much earlier, the latest study suggests that it was made in Gud̲j̲arāt in the 8th/14th or 9th/15th century. Two stone elephants which were discovered in the Red Fort of Dihlī now flank one of the doorways. It is thought that they were made in the reign of Akbar.

With the flowering of Mug̲h̲al painting which began during this period, elephants appear with increasing frequency. Several of the finest examples from the artistic point of view are in the *Akbar-nāma* at the Victoria and Albert Museum. One shows Akbar crossing a river mounted on an elephant. A painting of the reign of D̲j̲ahāngīr depicts elephants fighting and is in the Metropolitan Museum, New York.

Even though elephant heads are found in one of the Fātiḥ Albums at Istanbul, these have been proved by Ettinghausen to be Tīmūrid work of the 9th/15th century. One example is known of a very life-like elephant's head as a gold marginal ornament in a British Museum manuscript (OR. 2708) which was apparently painted during the third quarter of the 10th/16th century. Otherwise most of the relatively few Ottoman drawings of elephants resemble more or less that upon which Sitt K̲h̲ātūn, the wife of Meḥemmed (Muḥammad) II, is seated in a Byzantine miniature now in the Bibliotheca Marciana at Venice. This elephant is closely akin to those depicted in mediaeval Western manuscripts. A very similar elephant is to be seen in the *Hümāyūn-nāme* of ʿAlī Čelebi (B.M. ADD. 15153, f. 388r°, dated 997/1589) illustrating the story of King Hīlār of India.

In the field of sculpture, there is a stone slab at Ḳonya showing an elephant being pursued by a griffin. This was built into the wall of the Sald̲j̲ūḳid citadel, dating from the early part of the 7th/13th century.

Bibliography: *Survey of Persian Art*, iii, 2002-3; pl. 186, 604a, 663, 671, 692a-b, 758b; G. Wiet, *L'exposition d'art persan*, Cairo 1935, pl. 28; E. Kühnel, *Islamische Kleinkunst*, Berlin 1925, 194; J. Beckwith, *Caskets from Cordoba*, London, H.M.S.O., 1960, 29, pl. 19. See the article ʿĀD̲J̲, pl. 2, fig. 2; B. Gray and D. Barrett, *The painting of India*, Lausanne 1963, pl. 91; Ajit Ghosh, *Some old Indian ivories*, in *Rupam*, No. 32 (Oct. 1927); *Oriental Art* (New Series) i/2 (1955), 51; T. Arnold and A. Guillaume (edd.), *The legacy of Islam*, Oxford 1931, 134 and fig. 43.

(G. M. Meredith-Owens)

al-**FĪL,** is the title of the early Meccan Sūra cv which deals with God's judgment on the "men of the Elephant". This is an allusion to a story which must have been very familiar to the Meccan contemporaries of the Prophet; the background of the allusion is explained by the commentators and historians as follows. The Yemenite king Abraha [*q.v.*], bent on a policy of destroying the power of the Meccan sanctuary, led an expedition against Mecca, hoping to destroy the Kaʿba, and the expeditionary troops were supported by an elephant (some versions say, more than one). But on arriving at the frontier of Meccan territory, the elephant kneeled down and refused to advance further towards Mecca, although when his head was turned in any other direction he moved. Flights of birds then came and dropped stones on the invading troops, who all died. The authority of ʿIkrima [*q.v.*] is given for the rationalizing explanation that they were in fact smitten by an epidemic of smallpox. Abraha himself is said to have been afflicted with a loathsome disease and carried back to Yemen to die. For the student of Islam, the main relevance of the episode is that the birth of the Prophet is said to have taken place at this time, in the "year of the Elephant". And according to the commonly accepted chronology of the Prophet's life, this event would have to be dated in or around 570 A.D.

Not unnaturally, the South Arabian inscriptions contain no direct reference to this disaster. The possibilities involved are, however, illustrated by an earlier occasion described in the Murayg̲h̲ān inscription, Ryckmans 506. This records that while Abraha was campaigning in central Arabia against Maʿadd, who were subject to the suzerainty of the kingdom of Ḥīra, another part of the South Arabian army was operating in the Ḥid̲j̲āz and inflicted a defeat on a tribal confederation of the ʿĀmir b. Ṣaʿṣaʿa [*q.v.*] at the oasis of Turaba (approximately 100 km. due east of Ṭāʾif). This is dated in 662 of the Sabaean era, *i.e.*, the late forties or early fifties of the sixth century A.D.; in any case it cannot be later than 554 A.D., since it mentions al-Mund̲h̲ir (who was assassinated in that year) as king of Ḥīra. How much later than this we can reasonably date the "year of the Elephant" is problematical. But the fairly substantial cluster of texts from the decade or so preceding the Murayghān inscription, coupled with the complete cessation of South Arabian records from shortly thereafter (our latest being a private text of 665 of the Sabaean era), tend to suggest that it is somewhat unlikely that Abraha and his kingdom continued so to flourish as to be able to stage a full scale attack on Mecca, until so late as 570 A.D.

A striking proposal advanced by C. Conti Rossini (*JA*, xi sér., xviii, 30-2) deserves a passing mention, although it has not been endorsed by general approval. This is that the story as we know it is a contamination of two records of South Arabian attacks on Mecca: that by Abraha, and a much earlier one led by the Aksumite king Afilas, whom numismatic evidence assigns to around 300 A.D. It was at or shortly after this time that the kingdom of Aksūm did in fact exercise a short-lived hegemony over South Arabia, and a military enterprise further north is not impossible. Conti Rossini appeals to this event in order to suggest that a conflated story of this nature was the one known to the Prophet's contemporaries, and that *al-fīl* in this context is a later corruption of the name Afilas.

Bibliography: See the bibliography cited under abraha. (A. F. L. Beeston)

FIʿL, "action", is regarded as a noun derived from the verb *faʿala yafʿal* inf. *faʿl*, "to do" (Lane, vi, 2420a, b). This noun is the technical term in Arabic grammar for denoting the verb. Where traditional English grammar distinguishes between eight "parts of speech", the grammar of the Arabs established only three principal divisions: *ism, fiʿl, ḥarf*. This tripartite division into *noun, verb* and *particle* came to the Arabs from Aristotelian *logic* and not from the *grammar* of the Greeks; this fact seems sufficiently established (see *Arabica*, iv, 14-5 and *Traité*, 23-4). Acquaintance with the latter would have given Arabic grammar a different organization, something like the parts of speech referred to above, which in essence derive precisely from this Greek grammar through the intermediary of the Latin grammarians. Besides, a division which establishes the *noun* and the *verb* as the principal categories finds its justification in general linguistics (see *Traité*, § 53).

The *Kitāb* of Sībawayh (i, ch. I) starts with the enunciation of this main division: *ism, fiᶜl, ḥarf*. Its definition of the verb (*a*) on the one hand stresses the origin of the personal forms of the verb: *amma 'l-fiᶜl fa-amthilat ukhidhat min lafẓ aḥdāth al-asmā'*: these are the 'forms taken from the word expressing the "happenings" of nouns' [the infinitives]; this is already the Baṣrī theory of the *infinitive-maṣdar*, that is, the 'origin' of the verb; *ḥadath*, pl. *aḥdāth* (inf. of *ḥadatha* (*u*) "to happen, take place") can be well translated by "happening", a meaning very close to the idea of "process", used in modern general linguistics to define the verb; (*b*) on the other hand expresses the temporal value of the verb: *buniyat* (they have been constructed) *li-mā maḍā* (past), *wa-li-mā yakūn wa-lam yaḳaᶜ* (future), *wa-mā huwa kā'in lam yanḳaṭiᶜ* (present).

Thus, from the very start, so far as can be traced, a temporal value is attributed to the verb as something self-evident, requiring no justification. We have here the indication that this was an accepted doctrine, accepted as something established, and not the fruit of the personal investigations of the Arab grammarian; for the latter, always so ready to explain or legitimize everything, would have advanced reasons or reasonings in support of any basic definition which he had drawn up. The same holds good for the tripartite division, simply stated. Like the latter, in fact, the temporal values of the verb came to the Arabs from Aristotelian logic (as has been said above), but this fact does in no way impair the originality of their construction of grammar (see *Arabica*, iv, 16 and *Traité*, 25).

The theory of the *infinitive-maṣdar* has been challenged by grammarians of the Kūfa tradition (Ibn al-Anbārī, *K. al-Inṣāf*, disputed question no. 28, ed. Weil). But the whole grammatical tradition teaches the temporal value of the verb, regarding this as the feature that distinguishes it from the noun (*ism*) (likewise Ibn Yaᶜīsh, according to 26, l. 10-1, in spite of what is said later).

The definition given by the *Mufaṣṣal* of al-Zamakhsharī is clear: *al-fiᶜl mā dalla ᶜala 'ḳtirān ḥadath bi-zamān* [*muḥaṣṣal*] (§ 402) "the verb is that which indicates the connexion of an event with a [determined] time": for the noun (*ism*), the contrary (§ 2).

Ibn Yaᶜīsh blames the vagueness of *mā*: for a strict definition by closest genus and specific difference, he requires a more precise word, *kalima* or *lafẓa* (912, l. 2). As for *muḥaṣṣal*, put by us in brackets as a reminder of the insistence of certain writers (according to 911, l. 6), on the need to distinguish the infinitive from the personal forms of the verb, Ibn Yaᶜīsh states that this is needless: the *maṣdar* is clearly enough distinguished in itself; it too is verb but it expresses time in another way (*min khāridj, min lawāzimih*); see 911, l. 8-13.

He also finds fault, in the definition, with the predominance allowed to the connexion with time in regard to *ḥadath*. The verb in itself indicates both things, the *ḥadath* and the time of its existence (911, l. 9), but the verb was not established to indicate this very connexion: it indicates a *ḥadath* in connexion, the latter comes secondarily, *wa 'l-iḳtirān wudjida tabaᶜan* (912, l. 5-6). However, Ibn al-Ḥādjib (*Kāfiya*, in the *Sharḥ al-Kāfiya*, ii, 207, l. 23) had said: *al-fiᶜl mā dalla ᶜalā maᶜnā fī nafsih muḳtarin bi-aḥad al-azmina al-thalātha*, without mentioning *ḥadath*; and al-Astarābādhī repeats: *kull ism fa-huwa ghayr muḳtarin, kull fiᶜl fa-huwa muḳtarin* (*ibid.*, l. 26 and 30), "a noun of any kind has no connexion [with time]"; "a verb of any kind connotes the connexion [with time]". *Remark*: al-Sīrāfī, in his *Sharḥ* of the *Kitāb* (ms. Cairo², II, 134) professes, for the definition of the verb, the doctrine of the *ḥadath muḳtarin bi-zamān muḥaṣṣal* (Part 1, p. 8).

As to the definition of the *Kitāb*, related in the beginning of this article, al-Sīrāfī explains *amthila* and *aḥdāth al-asmā'* as follows: *amthila*: *arāda abniya* because the *abniyat al-afᶜāl* are various (*mukhtalifa*), *i.e.* *faᶜala, faᶜila faᶜula*, etc. (p. 8 at the end). The *aḥdāth* are *al-maṣādir allatī tuḥdithuha 'l-asmā'* and the *asmā'* are the *aṣḥāb al-asmā' wa-hum al-fāᶜilūn* (p. 9, lines 3-4). Afterwards he expresses the Baṣrī theory of the *maṣdar* origin of the verb, contained in *amthila ukhidhat min lafẓ aḥdāth al-asmā'*.

This shows clearly enough how essential the Arabs considered the temporal value to be, in the definition of the verb. They ignored the *aspect*. In ancient Greek, an important part devolved upon aspect in verbal value; at the same time the Greeks did not recognize it as such (it is an acquisition of modern linguistics). The Arabs' notions of grammatical tenses being derived from Aristotelian logic, they were led along a false trail, under conditions most unfavourable for considering their aspect-governed verb from the point of view of time: immediately came the difficulty of differentiating three tenses, past, present and future, under a system which only contrasts two forms. They called the one *māḍī*. Ibn al-Ḳūṭiyya (d. 367) said *mustaḳbal* "future" for the other (*K. al-Afᶜāl*, 1 l. 18, 2 l. 18, 3 l. 3, etc., ed. Ign. Guidi). He was logically contrasting two terms of the same order, but the present was left aside. Grammatical tradition habitually uses *muḍāriᶜ* "resembling (the agent noun)", but formally the term is no longer opposed to *māḍī*; it enters into the grammatical speculations on the system of *ḳiyās* (*Traité*, 6).

For better or worse, the Arab grammarians were only able to systematize the value of the verb in respect of time by incorporating with the verb certain external elements: *sa-, sawfa, ḳad*, which they call its *khaṣā'iṣ* "its properties" (*Muf.*, § 402). Now it is important to understand the true position: aspect characterizes the verb in classical Arabic; the latter makes a contrast between an *accomplished* (conjugated by suffixes), and an unaccomplished form (conjugated by prefixes and suffixes), which are thus designated by an important but not exclusive nuance of aspect. *The tense emerges from the phrase*, without any established system (for the past, see below).

With an unaccomplished form, the future requires a mark : the verbal indicators *sa-, sawfa*, for example: *kallā sa-yaᶜlamūna thumma kallā sa-yaᶜlamūna* (Ḳur'ān, LXXVIII, 4-5), "No! they will know [it]. No! No! they will know [it]!", or else a temporal adverb, a temporal adverbial complement, etc., or simply the situation. The present results spontaneously from the absence of this mark, *e.g.*: *li-ma tabkī* "Why are you weeping?"

For the past, a distinction must be made: the accomplished gives the tense of the narrative for historical accounts; the verb then expresses the past tense, corresponding to the French *passé simple.* But this *māḍī* is also the accomplished form, and the language possesses only this *one single form* for historic narrative and conversation, according to the distinction formulated by E. Benveniste (*Les relations de temps dans le verbe français*, in *BSL*, liv/1 (1959), 69-82). It often indicates something resulting, it may be merely a resultative or a simple accomplished form without any temporal value. It therefore cannot be called purely and simply a tense, a *māḍī* (see *Esquisse*, 85-8; *Études*, 3: *Temps et aspect*, 170-7). The examples quoted can be examined in the light of the above distinction (published only in 1959), and the part played by the phrase and the verbal indicators will be noted.

As to the division of the verb, Arab grammarians teach: *maᶜlūm/madjhūl = known/unknown*; this referring to the agent. In fact, the Arabic verb falls into two divisions: the verb with agent (the subject being considered as the agent) and the verb of quality (the subject being simply the thing qualified). The verb with agent is subdivided:

a) agent pure and simple: *faᶜala yafᶜi/ulu*, like *ḍaraba* (*i*) "to strike", *ṭalaba* (*u*) "to ask".

b) agent with an interest: *faᶜila yafᶜalu*, like *rabiḥa* (*a*) "to gain", *sakira* (*a*) "to get drunk". This category includes part of *faᶜila.*

c) agent unknown: *fuᶜila yufᶜalu*, like *ḍuriba, rubiḥa.*

Agentive is a good term for the first two as opposed to the third: the *madjhūl*, to turn to the Arabic designation for lack of an appropriate English term. When wishing to denote the second specifically, one can use the term "verb with interested agent".

The verb of quality (or qualitative verb) includes the whole form of *faᶜula yafᶜulu* (with two exceptions), *e.g.*: *karuma* (*u*) "to become generous" and the other part of *faᶜila yafᶜalu*, which is thus divided into two: the verb with interested agent, described above, and the verb of quality, *e.g.*: *kabira* (*a*) "to become old".

The verb of quality is not static. It signifies: "to acquire a quality", or "to become such and such" (according to the quality in question), *karuma* "to become *karīm* (generous)"; or else as a consequence of the acquisition: "to have a quality", or "to be such and such", it is a resultative, *karuma* "to be *karīm* (generous)".

The *madjhūl* is the verb whose agent is not known or, if known, remains unexpressed and *cannot be expressed*: it is the *fiᶜl mā lam yusamma fāᶜiluh*, according to the expression of *Muf.* (116, l. 5). If it is used with a person as the subject, *e.g.*, *ḍuriba Zayd*, from the fact that Zayd is the subject of the verb, attention is concentrated on him, the idea of enduring takes shape to some extent, it may predominate and in that case we are led to translate by a passive: "Zayd was beaten", instead of "One has beaten Zayd", which would have revealed that the agent was unknown. This is to be judged according to the context. But none the less the Arabic verb remains the *madjhūl.* It cannot be coupled with "a complement of a passive verb", contrarily to its morphological character. One sees how deceptive it is to call *fuᶜila* "passive".

The impersonal verb exists in classical Arabic, although the Arab grammarians have not spoken of it; it exists, it can be constructed on any transitive indirect verb with agent (this being very widely interpreted, see the examples, *Esquisse*, 160), giving it the form of *madjhūl* which remains invariable in the 3rd person singular. This is the impersonal *madjhūl*, which provides the perfect example of the "verb whose agent is unknown". With the personal verb we can say: *kharadjtu min al-dār* "I left the house", *nazaltu ᶜalā ᶜAmr* "I went down to ᶜAmr's"; in the impersonal, *khuridja min al-dār* , *nuzila ᶜalā ᶜAmr*: "they went out of the house", "they went down to ᶜAmr". These verbs are often difficult to translate exactly, because for each of them we need to find the corresponding impersonal expression; in its absence "they" is used, as in the preceding examples.

Some verbs have come to the point of acquiring an impersonal usage without taking the form of the *madjhūl*: *kafā, badā, rāᶜa, ḥabba* (see Brockelmann, *Grundriss*, ii, 124-5; A. Spitaler, mā rāᶜa-hū illā bi- *und verwandtes*, in *Serta Monacensia*, Leiden 1952, 171-83); an example: *wa-kafā bi 'llāhi shahīdan* (Ḳurʾān, IV, 81/79), "it suffices with Allāh as witness".

Arab grammarians have recognized a *djāmid* or *ghayr mutaṣarrif* verb, like *ᶜasā, niᶜma, laysa*, as opposed to the *mutaṣarrif* verb which possesses all its verbal forms: *māḍī*, etc. or nomino-verbal forms: n. ag., etc. (*Dict. of T. T.*, 1143, l. 7-9). But they have not recognized the impersonal verb. They judged the impersonal *madjhūl* (*e.g.*: *nuzila ᶜalā ᶜAmr*), as if it were the *madjhūl* of a direct transitive, acting on the meaning of *mafᶜūl bih* (see *Études*, 167-8; on their kind of conception of *al-fiᶜl al-mutaᶜaddī*, the transitive verb, *Muf.* §§ 432-3, Ibn Yaᶜīsh 966-71, especially 970 l. 11-8). This lacuna is the logical consequence of their ignorance of the idea of subject and its rôle in grammar, for the impersonal verb is based throughout on this notion of the subject. The impersonal verb must, however, find a place in any accurate account of the morphology of the classical Arabic verb.

The Arabic verb presents contrasts: on the one side, great simplicity, on the other side complexity. Simplicity: in personal moods only two verbal forms, one acomplished, one unaccomplished, which are sufficient to give an opposition of aspect, and one imperative (2nd person); one conjugation, "the common conjugation" (*Esquisse*, 80-5), which employs *the same* prefixes or suffixes for verbs of all kinds, triliteral and derived forms, quadriliteral and derived forms, variations resulting from phonetic accidents arising from the combination of these prefixes or suffixes with the verbal root. The simplicity of the internal flexion of vowels which, by an interplay of contrasts between the three vowels *a, i, u*, characterizes the verb in its divisions *agentive/madjhūl*, not only in the simple triliteral or quadriliteral verb but in all derived forms for every agent verb; moreover, the simplicity of the *external* flexion of vowels which determines the moods: *yafᶜul-u* (indicative), *yafᶜul-a* (subjunctive), *yafᶜul* (jussive). Complexity: the multitude of derived forms: 14 for the triliteral verb, 3 for the quadriliteral verb; the multitude of forms of the infinitive or noun of action for the simple triliteral verb: Wright (*Ar. Gr.*[3], 110-2) lists 44 of them, either rare or common.

But these numerous derived forms have one advantage: they allow one to express synthetically notions which, in French, must be enunciated separately in accordance with its analytical character, *e.g.*: *farasa* (*i*) "to devour" (a prey, wild beast), *farrasa "to cause* to be devoured" (a prey), *afrasa "to allow* his flock to be devoured" (shepherd), *taḍārabū* "they fought *each other*", etc. They contribute considerably to the synthetic character of the Arabic language.

Affective language expresses itself through the Arabic verb. Briefly, we may mention the 2nd *faʿʿala* intensive form and the 5th *tafaʿʿala* which is correlative to it; the so-called "rare" forms, with gemination (14th form) or repetition (12th and 13th forms), a procedure that was abandoned; quadriliteral formations, especially by repetition of a biliteral element (type 1212) (*Esquisse*, 102-3). In addition, the *energetic*.

The energetic forms a part of the "common conjugation". It is formed by the suffix *-anna* or *-nna*, most often used, added to the unaccomplished in its jussive (or apocopated) form and to the imperative. It gives a vigorous expression to a personal feeling: *conviction* in an affirmation or negation, *astonishment* or *impatience* in interrogation. It is used especially to emphasize an expression of an act of will: an order, prohibition, threat, promise, wish. After an oath the energetic always occurs (if one uses the unaccomplished form), and in addition the corroborative *lam* (examples, Wright, ii, 42A).

Bibliography: Muḥ. Aʿlā, *Dictionary of Technical Terms*, (ed. A. Sprenger), i, 707 foot and 708, 711 l. 13-712 l. 3; ii, 1142-3; Zamakhsharī, *al-Mufaṣṣal*, 2nd ed. J. P. Broch, §§ 1, 2, 402, 403; Ibn Yaʿīsh, *Sharḥ K. al-Mufaṣṣal*, ed. G. Jahn, 20-9, 911-5; Raḍī al-Dīn al-Astarābādhī, *Sharḥ al-Kāfiya*, Istanbul ed. 1275, i, 8 l. 14 ff., 5 l. 21 ff.; ii, 207 l. 23 ff.; M. S. Howell, *Grammar of the Classical Arabic Language*, ii, Allāhābād 1880, 1-3 (§ 402); i, Allāhābād 1883, 1-3 (§ 2); H. Fleisch, *L'arabe classique, Esquisse d'une structure linguistique*, Beirut 1956 (*Recherches*, vol. v), 80-104 (quoted as *Esquisse*); idem, *Études sur le verbe arabe*, in *Mélanges Louis Massignon*, 1957, ii, 153-81 (quoted as *Études*): 1. *La Iʳᵉ forme du verbe et ses divisions*, 153-9; 2. *La question du madjhūl*, 160-1701; 3. *Temps et aspect*, 170-7; idem, *Traité de philologie arabe*, i, Beirut 1961 (quoted as *Traité*). Other references in the text.

(H. Fleisch)

FIʿL, pl. *afʿāl*, actuation, act, and sometimes the result of an act, that is to say effectuation, effect. From its current usage in Arabic, this word very quickly became a technical term (*iṣṭilāḥ*), not only in grammar but also in *falsafa* and in *ʿilm al-kalām*. If *ʿamal* [*q.v.*] designates the realms of 'doing' and 'acting' (whence 'work', human acts, and moral action), and thus has at least in its last meaning an ethical connotation, *fiʿl* refers above all to noetic and ontological values: the fact of actuating, of passing (or causing to pass) to the performance of an act. Hence the translation by R. Blachère of *Ḳurʾān*, xxi, 73: 'et Nous leur révélâmes la réalisation des bonnes œuvres' (*fiʿl al-khayrāt*). It should be noted that the distinction between *ʿamal* and *fiʿl* often becomes less marked: *akhlāḳ wa-afʿāl*, '(human) mores and actions', says Ibn Sīnā, for instance, (*Aḳsām*, 107), in order to define ethics.

Falsafa.

Fiʿl belongs to the language of logic and noetics. (a) In logic it is one of the ten categories, *actio* opposed to *passio*, *infiʿāl*. It is worth mentioning here that the suppleness of its verbal forms allows Arabic to emphasize the connexion, at the same time opposed and complementary, of the *muḳābal* pair, *actio* and *passio*, by using the same root, *fʿl*, in the first form active and in the seventh passive. In consequence, the active element is *al-fāʿil* and the passive element, *al-munfaʿil*. This use of *fʿl* and its derivations may be found over and over again in all treatises on logic, both in the philosophical introductions of the *ʿilm al-kalām* and also in *falsafa*.

(b). In noetics and metaphysics, the complementary opposition is no longer *fiʿl-infiʿāl*, but *fiʿl-ḳuwwa*, act-potentiality (faculty, *in posse*). Potentiality, in so far as it is the principle of change and becoming, may be in its turn either 'active' (*fiʿliyya*) if it resides in the agent (*fāʿil*), or passive (*infiʿāliyya*) if it resides in the passive element (*munfaʿil*). The expression *bi 'l-fiʿl*, 'actually', which is used for every faculty of the human spirit, is of especially wide and well-known usage in noetics, where it is used to designate one of the states of the intellect, *al-ʿaḳl bi 'l-fiʿl*, the intellect in action or the active intellect, as distinguished from *al-ʿaḳl bi 'l-ḳuwwa*, the intellect *in posse*, or potential intellect. Moreover, *al-ʿaḳl bi 'l-fiʿl* must be distinguished from *al-ʿaḳl al-faʿʿāl*, the acting intelligence, *i.e.*, continually in action, which is the last of the separate Intelligences and the same for all men. The *ʿaḳl bi 'l-fiʿl*, in becoming more and more actual, receives the illumination of the *ʿaḳl faʿʿāl* and becomes similar to it. The hierarchy of the intellects according to al-Kindī, al-Fārābī, Ibn Sīnā and Ibn Rushd, and the differences of meanings applied to these terms by the several authors, are well-known. For the *ʿaḳl bi 'l-fiʿl* according to al-Fārābī and Ibn Sīnā, see ʿAḳl; contrary to what is suggested by the Latin translations referred to by F. Rahman in this last article, it does not seem necessary to translate differently the meaning of *al-ʿaḳl bi'l-fiʿl* according to al-Fārābī (*in effectu*) and Ibn Sīnā (*in actu*). The real differences of thought between the two philosophers can perhaps best be expressed, whether in translation or in Arabic, by the use of an identical terminology. The ancient Latin translations, in fact, often prefer *effectus* for *fiʿl*, while the modern ones (such as that of Mgr. N. Carame) are more in favour of *actus*. The difference which can be noted between act (or action) and effect diminishes when we go back to the more specifically appropriate technical terms 'actuation' and 'effectuation'.

ʿIlm al-kalām

The *mutakallimūn* use *fiʿl* and *bi 'l-fiʿl* in the same sense as the *falāsifa* when they in their turn speak of the subjects of logic, noetics and metaphysics. But the term, above all in its plural form, *afʿāl*, comes up frequently when they discuss 'questions concerning God' (*ilāhiyyāt*). *Fiʿl* then designates the action of God *ad extra*, 'what it is possible (not necessary) for God to do'. Thus al-Ashʿarī writes in his *Kitāb al-Lumaʿ*: 'the fact that God wills a thing, signifies that He does it' *faʿalahu*; ed. McCarthy, Beirut 1953, 15-6; cf. English translation, 21).

Later on, the subject of the treatise concerning the effects of Divine Omnipotence *ad extra* is thus called *afʿāluhu taʿālā*, 'the Acts of God, the Most High'. It is essentially the problem of secondary causes (*asbāb*), the relations of God with mankind, the divine pre-determining decree (*ḳadar* and *ḳaḍāʾ*), and human free-will (*ikhtiyār*). For the details of the problems dealt with, and the solutions of the various schools, see Allāh, 412 ff.

The treatise on *afʿāluhu taʿālā* is preceded by a treatise on the divine attributes, *ṣifāt Allāh*. One of the subdivisions of this last is concerned with the *ṣifāt al-afʿāl*, which may be translated as the 'attributes of action' and which refer to what God may or may not do: visibility, creation, commandment, decree (*loc. cit.*, 411).

These discussions of the 'actions of God' do not supersede the normal usage of *fiʿl* and *afʿāl* to designate the act or acts of man, sometimes almost as synonyms of *ʿamal* and *aʿmāl*, more often with the psychological and legal background meaning 'an act which must be performed', leaving to *ʿamal* the wider background meaning of 'human behaviour in general'. Thus *fiʿl* is distinguished from *tark*, lack of action, action to be avoided. It is thus also that at the beginning of the *Iḥyāʾ ʿulūm al-dīn* (Cairo 1352/1933, i, 13-5), al-Ghazzālī teaches that man under Law is, in order to guide his conduct (*ʿamal*), under the obligation of knowing: the creed of the faith (*iʿtiḳād*), the act (*al-fiʿl*) which must be performed at a given moment (*e.g.*, the times of prayer), and what it is obligatory not to perform (*tark*). These terms, moreover, are reminiscent of the vocabulary of *ḥadīth*, since the text of a *ḥadīth* relates a saying or an action or the absence of an action on the part of the Prophet.

Bibliography: apart from the references given in this article, reference should be made to the well-known treatises and chapters of the great philosophers (a) on the categories, (b) on *ʿaḳl*; also the various treatises of *ʿilm al-kalām* (*e.g.*, Fakhr al-Dīn al-Rāzī, *Muḥaṣṣal*, Djurdjānī, *Sharḥ al-Mawāḳif*, etc.), in the chapters *Ṣifāt Allāh* and *Afʿāluhu taʿālā*. (L. Gardet)

FILĀḤA, agriculture.

Falḥ, the act of cleaving and cutting, when applied to the soil has the meaning of "to break up in order to cultivate", or "to plough". *Fallāḥ* "ploughman", *filāḥa* "ploughing". But from pre-Islamic times the word *filāḥa* has assumed a wider meaning to denote the occupation of husbandry, agriculture. In this sense it is synonymous with *zirāʿa*, to which the ancients preferred *filāḥa* (all the earlier writers called their works on agriculture *Kitāb al-Filāḥa*). At the present time this latter word is very widely used in North Africa, both in official language and in everyday speech. Thus, in Morocco, the Ministry of Agriculture is called *wizārat al-filāḥa*, whilst in Egypt, Syria, Lebanon, Jordan and ʿIrāḳ it is called *wizārat al-zirāʿa*. It is only since the last century that the word *zirāʿa* has taken precedence in official and literary circles in the Arab East; but the word *filāḥa* is still very widely used in the language of agricultural workers. The following articles will deal primarily with agricultural methods and techniques. [See further, for settlement and sedentarization, ISKĀN; for irrigation, ḲANĀT, MĀʾ; for land-tenure, IḲṬĀʿ, TENURE OF LAND, and the articles listed under ARḌ].

i. — Middle East

1. — Technical and historical survey. — Agriculture in the Arab countries is under the influence of two different types of climate: in the south of the Arabian peninsula (Yemen, Ḥaḍramawt and ʿUmān), and also in the Sudan, the Indian monsoon brings abundant rainfall in summer which enables various tropical plants to be cultivated (coffee, datepalms, custard-apples, mangoes, pawpaws, bananas, *catha edulis*, tamarinds etc.). Throughout the rest of the Arab world the mediterranean climate prevails. This climate is characterized by a cold wet winter season, followed by a long summer period which is hot and without rain. The further one goes from the Mediterranean coast the more the rainfall diminishes, until it ceases entirely in certain hot deserts in Arabia and the African Sahara. This basic climatic system divides the zones of Arab countries into two distinct categories; in the first, the extent and distribution of the rainfall favour the economic cultivation of various crops. In the second category the winter rains, though not sufficient to allow of economic cultivation, nevertheless permit the natural growth of certain grasses and various succulent, bulbous and halophytic plants which constitute the pasturages of the desert steppes. In order to make use both of their agricultural land and of the steppes, the Arabs have at all times led two sorts of lives—as a rural or urban sedentary population, and as pastoral nomads.

Nomadism is a necessity in the desert steppes where the winter rainfall varies in extent between 50 and 150 mm., but the Bedouin tribes are not opposed to a sedentary existence. It is in this way that the Yemeni tribes, long before Islam, founded their civilization on irrigation and intensive cultivation of the land. After the Islamic conquests, the Arab tribes soon intermingled with Aramaeans from Syria and ʿIrāḳ, Copts from Egypt and Berbers from north Africa, and with the Ibero-Latins of the Spanish peninsula, in order to exploit together the vast territories of the present Arab countries and of former Muslim Andalusia.

The mediterranean climatic system being everywhere the same, we find throughout these territories three agricultural climates. Firstly, in most of the coastal plains (the coasts of Syria, Lebanon, Palestine, Tunisia, Algeria and Morocco), thanks to a mild winter temperature and an annual rainfall of from 500 to 1,000 mm., it is possible without irrigation to cultivate cereals, annual leguminous plants, various vegetables, tobacco, olives in particular, and even cotton. With the help of irrigation, a vast number of annual or perennial agricultural crops can be successfully grown—citrus fruits, bananas, pomegranates, loquats, early vegetables, aromatic or ornamental plants, etc.

Secondly, in the plains, hills and inland plateaus of Syria, Upper Mesopotamia and North Africa, where the density of rainfall varies between 250 and 500 mm., dry-farming is the dominant system of cultivation for vast areas of non-irrigated land. Of the chief annual plants cultivated in these regions we may mention wheat, barley, sorghum, lentils, chick-peas, vetch, gherkins, melons, watermelons and sesame, while the principal fruiting trees and shrubs are olives, vines, figs, hazelnuts and pistachios.

In these regions, irrigation is indispensable for the cultivation of most fruit trees, ornamental trees, vegetables, leguminous and industrial plants—apples, pears, apricots, peaches, eggplant, tomatoes, gumbo, artichokes, potatoes, lucerne, clover, cotton, hemp, groundnuts, poppies, roses, jasmine, etc.

Thirdly, in regions with a desert climate (Lower Mesopotamia, central Arabia, Egypt, inland regions of Libya and North Africa) where rain is rare and the average annual temperature reaches or exceeds 21° C. it is only by means of irrigation that such plants as date-palms, mangoes, orange trees, cotton, rice, sugar-cane and others can be successfully cultivated.

During the Middle Ages, the Arabs were familiar with and cultivated most of the agricultural plants now known to the Arab world. It was they who introduced Seville oranges and lemons from India to ʿUmān, and thence to Baṣra, Egypt and the coast of Syria and Palestine (cf. al-Masʿūdī, *Murūdj*, ii, 438, viii, 336). From Andalusia and Sicily they disseminated throughout the Mediterranean basin the cultivation of cotton, sugar-cane, apricots, peaches, rice, carobs, water melons, eggplant, etc. (cf. De Candolle, *L'Origine des plantes cultivées*[5], Paris 1912). Moreover, the European names of many cultivated plants are of Arabic origin, that is to say borrowed directly or indirectly from words either purely Arabic or long Arabicized.

2. — Works on agriculture. — The oldest Arabic work on agriculture which we know is *al-Filāḥa al-nabaṭiyya* (Nabataean agriculture) of Ibn Waḥshiyya [*q.v.*], written (or translated from the Nabataean!) in 291/904. A little later there appeared a work entitled *al-Filāḥa al-rūmiyya* (Greek or Byzantine agriculture). This book, published in Cairo in 1293/1876, bears the names of Ḳusṭūs al-Rūmī as author and of Sardjīs b. Hilyā al-Rūmī as translator from Greek into Arabic. According to Ḥādjdjī Khalīfa (*Kashf al-ẓunūn*, ii, 1447), the author's full name was Ḳusṭūs b. Askūrāskīna, and we think that this is the name of Cassianus Bassus to whom agronomic works collected from Greek and Latin authors are attributed. Ḥādjdjī Khalīfa names three other translators of this book, one of them being said to be Ḳusṭā b. Lūḳā [*q.v.*]. From another source we know that the agronomic work of Anatolius of Berytos (4th century A.D.) had been translated into Syriac by Sardjīs Rāsaʿnī (d. 536 A.D.), and there is reason to believe that this text was also translated subsequently into Arabic and that no manuscripts of it have survived (cf. *BIE*, xiii, 47). In any case, in the two Arabic works that we know (*al-Filāḥa al-nabaṭiyya* and *al-Filāḥa al-rūmiyya*), we find a reasonable knowledge of agricultural practice, side by side with superstitious advice.

In Egypt, the best presentation of agricultural questions at the time of the Ayyūbids is to be found in a work of Ibn Mammātī (d. 606/1209), entitled *Ḳawānīn al-dawāwīn*, published in Cairo in 1943 by the Royal Agricultural Society (cf. *MMIA*, xxxiii, 556). In the following century Djamāl al-Dīn al-Waṭwāṭ (d. 718/1318) wrote in Cairo the (unpublished) book entitled *Mabāhidj al-fikar wa-manāhidj al-ʿibar*, the fourth volume of which is devoted to plants and agriculture. In the 10th/16th century, a Damascene author named Riyaḍ al-Dīn al-Ghazzī al-ʿĀmirī (935/1529) wrote a large book on agriculture which has not survived; but later ʿAbd al-Ghanī al-Nābulusī (d. 1143/1731) gave a summary of it in a work entitled *ʿAlam al-milāḥa fī ʿilm al-filāḥa* published in Damascus in 1299/1882.

In general, the writers of ancient Arabic works on agriculture dealt with the following subjects: types of agricultural land and choice of land; manure and other fertilizers; tools and work of cultivation; wells, springs, and irrigation channels; plants and nurseries; planting, prunung and grafting of fruit trees; cultivation of cereals, legumes, vegetables, flowers, bulbs and tubers, and plants for perfume; noxious plants and animals; preserving of fruit; and sometimes zootechny.

It may be noted that the writers of these works used several non-classical agricultural terms (*muwallad*; cf. *MMIA*, ii, 193 and xxxiii, 560), and made a distinction between plants which fertilize (legumes) and those which exhaust the soil (cereals and others).

The chief principles of dry-farming were not unknown to them, and similarly the principles of variation and rotation of crops. Certain Arab agronomists in Andalusia had at their disposal botanical gardens and trial grounds where they experimented with native and exotic plants, practised methods of grafting and tried to create new varieties of fruit and flowers. We should also note that several ancient Arabic dictionaries, encyclopaedic works and Arabic treatises on agriculture and botany contain the names of numerous varieties of fruit, cereals, flowers and other cultivated plants. Thus al-Badrī (9th/15th century) in his *Nuzhat al-anām fī maḥāsin al-Shām* gives the names, in Syria, of 21 varieties of apricots, 50 varieties of grapes, 6 varieties of roses, etc.

All the early Arabic (or other) works on agriculture, being based on observation alone, are only of historical and terminological value. It was only in the 19th century that, in Egypt, there appeared the first Arabic agricultural work based on modern science; it was produced by Aḥmad Nadā who, after being sent to France on an educational mission, wrote the two-volume *Ḥusn al-ṣināʿa fī ʿilm al-zirāʿa*, published in Cairo in 1291/1874. At the present time, text books in the Arabic language exist in all branches of agriculture, written by the teachers of the faculties and practical schools of agriculture.

3. — Terminology and literature. — For the Arabic terminology of agronomic science there exists a dictionary compiled by the writer of this article (*Dictionnaire français-arabe des termes agricoles*, Damascus 1943, Cairo 1957), containing about ten thousand terms concisely defined in Arabic.

The Arabic language is rich in agricultural terms, particularly in relation to date-palms, vines, cereals and desert plants (cf. the *Mukhaṣṣaṣ* of Ibn Sīda), and the imagination of the poets of antiquity has endowed it with a vast and original literature on the nature of plants and their connexions with human beings. Not only flowers (roses, narcissi, jasmine, violets, pinks, irises, anemones, etc.) and fruit (dates, apricots, apples, pears, pomegranates, jububes, Neapolitan medlars, quinces, Seville oranges, lemons, etc.) but also a great quantity of cereals, legumes, vegetables and wild plants of the fields , pasturages and prairies are mentioned or described in verse.

4. — Legislation relating to land. — The code on landed property (*Ḳānūn al-arāḍī*) and the civil code (*al-Madjalla*), which were in force in the Arab countries that were separated from the Ottoman Empire after the 1914-8 war, are based on Muslim law (*sharīʿa*) and Muslim jurisprudence (*fiḳh*). The *Madjalla* divides land into five categories: *arḍ mamlūka*, land to which there is a right of ownership; *arḍ amīriyya*, land to which the original title (*raḳaba*) belongs to the State, while its exploitation (*taṣarruf*) can be conceded to individuals (this is the case with most agricultural land); *arḍ mawḳūfa*, land set aside for the benefit of a religious endowment; *arḍ matrūka*, land placed at the disposal of corporate bodies; and lastly *arḍ mawāt*, waste land, defined as free land, situated away from inhabited areas and out of ear-shot of houses. For details see TENURE OF LAND.

The *Madjalla* also defines and codifies questions relating to metayage (*muzāraʿa*), leases for orchard-planting (*musāḳāt*), the repair and clearing of communal watercourses used for irrigation, reclamation of waste land (*iḥyāʾ al-mawāt*), the enclosure (*ḥarīm*) of wells and subterranean watercourses (*ḳanawāt*), etc.

At the present time, the land laws of most of the Arab States, while incorporating substantial improvements, still uphold the principles respecting either the distinction between categories (and sub-categories) of land, or else their legal status and the rights based on them.

According to Muslim jurisprudence, it is the duty

of the State to construct and maintain dams, and also to excavate and clear the main irrigation channels. In former times, this work was carried out either directly by the governors of provinces or by holders of fiefs. The history of the Umayyads and the first ʿAbbāsid caliphs provides examples of the execution of several large-scale irrigation schemes, and also of the repairing of several ancient dams on the Tigris, Euphrates, Kh̲ābūr, Orontes and Baradā.

Bibliography: In addition to the sources quoted above: J.-J. Clément-Mullet, *Le Livre de l'Agriculture d'Ibn al-ʿAwwām*, Fr. trans., Paris 1864-7, 2 vols. in 3; Don J. A. Banqueri, *Libro de Agricultura, su autor el doctor excellente A.Z.J.B.M.B. el-ʿAwām*, Ar. text and Span. trans. Madrid 1802, 2 vols.; B. Lewin, *The Book of plants of Abū Ḥanīfa al-Dīnawarī*, Part of the alphabetical section (ز — ا), Leiden 1953; A. Risso and A. Poiteau, *Histoire naturelle des orangers*, Paris 1819, 7-10; G. Schweinfurth, *Arabische Pflanzennamen aus Aegypten, Algerien und Iemen*, Berlin 1912; E. Sauvaigo, *Les cultures sur le littoral de la Méditerranée*, Paris 1913; Ch. Rivière and H. Lecq, *Culture du Midi, de l'Algérie et de la Tunisie*, Paris 1915.

(Mustafa al-Shihabi)

ii. — Muslim West

So far as we know at present, it was exclusively in the Iberian peninsula, the home of the celebrated Latin agronomist Junius Columella of Gades/Cádiz, that an agricultural literature in the Arabic language was created and developed, particularly during the 5th/11th and 6th/12th centuries , in the brilliant period of the satraps (*mulūk al-ṭawāʾif*) and the Almoravid governors who followed.

The principal centres of this literature were Cordova, Toledo, Seville, Granada and, to a lesser extent, Almeria. In Cordova the great doctor Abu 'l-Ḳāsim al-Zahrāwī, who died in 404/1010, known as Albucasis in the Middle Ages, is reputed to be the author of a Compendium on agronomy (*Mukh̲taṣar kitāb al-filāḥa*) which Professor H. Pérès has recently discovered and intends to publish.

In Toledo, at the court of the renowned al-Maʾmūn [*q.v.*], the great "garden lover", lived the celebrated doctor Ibn Wāfid (d. 467/1075) known as Abenguefith in the Middle Ages. He was appointed by al-Maʾmūn to create his royal botanical garden (*D̲j̲annat al-sulṭān*). Among other works, he wrote a treatise (*mad̲j̲mūʿ*) on agronomy which was translated into Castilian in the Middle Ages. Another inhabitant of Toledo, Muḥammad b. Ibrāhīm Ibn Baṣṣāl, devoted himself exclusively to agronomy. He performed the regular pilgrimage, travelling via Sicily and Egypt, and brought back many botanical and agronomic notes from the East. He also was in the service of al-Maʾmūn, for whom he wrote a lengthy treatise on agronomy (*dīwān al-filāḥa*); this work was subsequently abridged into one volume with sixteen chapters (*bāb*), with the title *Kitāb al-Ḳaṣd wa 'l-bayān* "Concision and clarity". This work, which was translated into Castilian in the Middle Ages, was published in 1955 with a modern Castilian introduction. The treatise by Ibn Baṣṣāl is singular in that it contains no reference to earlier agronomists; it appears to be based exclusively on the personal experiences of the author, who is revealed as the most original and objective of all the Hispano-Arabic specialists.

The name of this writer's father has not been established conclusively. Writers who quote from him give the name with or without the definite article; the initial *bāʾ* is sometimes replaced by *fāʾ* (subpunctuated in Magh̲ribī orthography), or the *ṣād* by *ṭāʾ*. Nevertheless the form Baṣāl/Baṣṣāl seems to be the most probable, but it is not certain that it is a name with any etymological connection with *baṣal* "onions". It might be a Romance diminutive in *-él* of the adjective *bāṣo/bāṣṣo* (Castilian *bazo*), "brown", a name borne by several Muslims in Spain; and *Baṣ(ṣ)él* would then be synonymous with the well-attested name of *Maurél*.

After the capture of Toledo by Alfonso VI of Castile (478/1085), Ibn Baṣṣāl withdrew to Seville, to the court of al-Muʿtamid [*q.v.*] for whom he created a new royal garden.

In Seville Ibn Baṣṣāl again met ʿAlī Ibn al-Lūnḳuh of Toledo, a doctor and disciple of Ibn Wāfid, and like him interested in botany and agronomy. He had left his native town shortly before its capture and settled in Seville in 487/1094. He died at Cordova in 499/1105.

He also encountered Abū ʿUmar Aḥmad b. Muḥammad b. Ḥad̲j̲d̲j̲ād̲j̲ al-Ish̲bīlī, the author of several works on agronomy, among them *al-Muḳniʿ*, written in 466/1073. This writer is distinguished from others by his scorn for "the inadmissible tales of stupid yokels" (*ahl al-gh̲abāwa min ahl al-barārī wa-aḳwāluhum al-sāḳiṭa*) and his almost exclusive use of ancient agronomists, especially Yūniyūs. However, he also recounts his personal experiences in al-Sh̲araf. There he became acquainted with the agronomist Abu 'l-Kh̲ayr al-Ish̲bīlī [*q.v.*] whose work, with title unknown, is often quoted by Ibn al-ʿAwwām. All that we know about him is that in 494/1100 he was studying with the Seville doctor Abu 'l-Ḥasan Sh̲ihāb al-Muʿayṭī.

In Seville, Ibn Baṣṣāl and Ibn al-Lūnḳuh were the masters of the mysterious "anonymous botanist of Seville", the author of the *ʿUmdat al-ṭabīb fī maʿrifat al-nabāt li-kull labīb*, a botanical dictionary of considerable merit and far superior to that by Ibn al-Bayṭār. He seems to have been a certain Ibn ʿAbdūn, to be distinguished from the doctor (Al-D̲j̲abalī) and the literary writer (al-Yāburī). The only fact about him in our possession is that he was a member of the diplomatic mission which went to the Almohad court of Marrākush̲ in 542/1147 and that he wrote his *ʿUmda* after that date.

In Granada, the principal agricultural writer was Muḥammad b. Mālik al-Ṭigh̲narī (from the name of a village now known as Tignar, a few kilometres north of Granada). He worked in succession in the service of the Ṣanhād̲j̲ī princeling ʿAbd Allāh b. Buluggīn (466/83/1073-90) and then of the Almoravid prince Tamīm, son of Yūsuf b. Tāsh̲fīn, at the time when that prince was governor of the province of Granada (501-12/1107-18). It was for the latter that he wrote a treatise on agronomy in twelve books (*maḳāla*) entitled *Zuhrat al-bustān wa-nuzhat al-adh̲hān*. Al-Ṭigh̲narī also went on pilgrimage to the East. Probably while staying in Seville he came into contact with Ibn Baṣṣāl and was able to profit from his experiences. It is probably with al-Ṭigh̲narī that we should identify the anonymous agronomist whom Ibn al-ʿAwwām frequently quotes under the name al-Ḥād̲j̲d̲j̲ al-Gh̲arnāṭī. It should be noted that several manuscripts of the *Zuhrat al-bustān* are attributed to a certain Ḥamdūn al-Ish̲bīlī, who is otherwise unknown.

Towards the end of the 6th/12th century or in the first half of the 7th/13th century (the capture of Seville by the Christians took place in 646/1248),

Abū Zakariyyā Yaḥyā b. Muḥammad Ibn al-ʿAwwām of Seville wrote a lengthy *Kitab al-Filāḥa* in 35 books (*bāb*). We know nothing of his life. To orientalists, however, he is celebrated since he was the first to be published and also translated, into Spanish by J. A. Banqueri, Madrid 1802, then into French by Clément-Mullet, Paris 1864-7, and finally into Urdū. He is also the only agronomist whom Ibn Khaldūn (second half of the 8th/14th century) thought worthy of quoting in his *Muḳaddima* (tr. de Slane, iii, 166; he regards the *K. al-Filāḥa* as an abridged version of *al-Filāḥa al-nabaṭiyya* [see IBN WAḤSHIYYA]. He is, however, far from being the most important of the Arabo-Hispanic agronomists. His work is essentially an extensive and useful compilation of quotations from ancient writers and from his Hispanic predecessors, Ibn Baṣṣāl, Ibn Ḥadjdjādj, Abu 'l-Khayr and al-Ḥādjdj al-Gharnāṭī. It is only occasionally at the end of a chapter that he records his own personal observations (introduced by the word *Lī* "this is my own"), made in the neighbourhood of Seville, especially in the district of al-Sharaf. For Ibn al-ʿAwwām, see C.C. Moncada in *Actes du 8e Congrès des Orient.*, Stockholm 1889, ii, 215-57; E. Meyer, *Gesch. der Botanik*, iii, 260-6; Brockelmann, S I, 903).

Finally, towards the middle of the 8th/14th century, a scholar of Almeria, Abū ʿUthmān Saʿd b. Abū Djaʿfar Aḥmad Ibn Luyūn al-Tudjībī (d. 750/1349) wrote his *Kitāb Ibdāʾ al-malāḥa wa-inhāʾ al-radjāḥa fī uṣūl ṣināʿat al-filāḥa*. The work of an amateur, it is an abridgement in verse (*urdjūza*), based essentially on Ibn Baṣṣāl and al-Ṭighnarī; but it also contains certain valuable information which the author recorded in the words of local practitioners (*mimmā shāfahahu bih ahl al-tadjriba wa 'l-imtiḥān*).

These treatises on *filāḥa* contain far more than their titles would indicate; in fact, they are true encyclopaedias of rural economy, based on a plan closely in line with that followed by Columella in his *De re rustica*. Naturally, the essential feature is of course agronomy (*filāḥat al-araḍīn*): the study of types of soil, water, manure; field cultivation of cereals and legumes; but arboriculture is also dealt with at length (particularly vines, olives and figs), with additional matter on pruning, layering and grafting; and also horticulture and floriculture. Zootechny (*filāḥat al-ḥayawānāt*) also takes a leading place: the rearing of livestock, beasts of burden, fowls and bees; veterinary practice (*bayṭara*). All these fundamental questions are completed by chapters on domestic economy: farm management, the choice of agricultural workers, storage of produce after harvest, etc. Some writers also provide information on measurement of land (*taksīr*) and the seasonal agricultural calendar.

We may imagine that specialists of many sorts were led to contribute to such encyclopaedic works. To start with, there were practitioners and professional workers: farmers (*fallāḥūn*), fruit-growers (*shadjdjārūn*), horticulturists (*djannānūn*); but there were also "scientific workers"—herbalists (*ʿashshābūn*), botanists (*nabātiyyūn*), doctors interested in medicinal plants (*mufradāt*) and dietetics; and there were also pure theoreticians (*ḥukamāʾ*, *mutakallimūn*).

On the other hand, Hispano-Arab treatises on *filāḥa* were often the work of many-sided writers (*mushārikūn, mutafanninūn*). Beside Ibn Baṣṣāl who was essentially an agronomist, Ibn Wāfid was primarily a doctor. Ibn Ḥadjdjādj was described by Ibn al-ʿAwwām as *imām* and *khaṭīb*. Al-Ṭighnarī and Ibn Luyūn are well-known poets. Finally, the enigmatical Seville botanist Ibn ʿAbdūn could well be the same as his contemporary Ibn ʿAbdūn of Seville, the author of a treatise on *ḥisba* [*q.v.*], published and later translated by E. Lévi-Provençal.

In this connexion one is reminded of Aristotle, both philosopher and naturalist and creator of a botanical garden, and Virgil, author of the *Georgics*.

The Hispano-Arab agronomists were familiar with and made wide use of ancient writers. A list of them (in which the names are often inaccurate) will be found at the beginning of the translation edition of Ibn al-ʿAwwām by Banqueri. Among the Arab sources, they made use of *Kitāb al-Nabāt* of the polygraph al-Dīnawarī [*q.v.*] and, in particular, the *Filāḥa nabaṭiyya* of Ibn Waḥshīyya [*q.v.*], though for the most part leaving out his farrago of magic recipes. However, in this branch of instruction they have not confined themselves to repeating their precursors' writings. They made their own personal observations and experiments, in order to adapt their works to the realities of the Spanish soil and climate. They also introduced original chapters on the cultivation of new plants—rice, sugar-cane, date palms, citrus fruits, cotton, flax, madder, apricots, peaches, pears, watermelons, eggplant, pistachios, saffron, etc.

As we have seen, two Arabo-Hispanic treatises on agronomy were translated into Castilian. In this way, Ibn Wāfid's work was widely used by the Spanish agronomist Alonso de Herrera in his famous *Agricultura General* (1513).

Finally we should note that it was in Muslim Spain, during the 5th/11th century, in Toledo and later in Seville, that the first "royal botanical gardens" of Europe made their appearance, both pleasure gardens and also trial grounds for the acclimatization of plants brought back from the Near and Middle East. In the Christian world we have to wait until the middle of the 16th century to see the establishment of gardens of this sort, in the university towns of Italy.

Bibliography: The essentials will be found in the introduction to *Kitāb al-Filāḥa* of Ibn Baṣṣāl, edited with Spanish translation by Millás Vallicrosa and ʿAzīmān (Tetuán 1955). See also: García Gómez, *Sobre agricultura arabigoandaluza*, in *Andalus*, x (1945), 127; Millás Vallicrosa, *ʿIlm al-filāḥa ʿind al-muʾallifīn al-ʿArab bi'l-Andalus*, Ar. trans. ʿAbd al-Laṭīf al-Khaṭīb, Tetuán 1957; Ibn al-Ḳāḍī, *Durrat al-Ḥidjāl*, ed. Allouche, Rabat 1936 (no. 1352 = biography of Ibn Luyūn); Ibn Khaldūn, *Muḳaddima, faṣl* vi, no. 20 = trans. de Slane, iii, 165 = tr. Rosenthal, iii, 151; S. M. Imamuddin, Al-Filāḥah (*Farming*) *in Muslim Spain*, in *Islamic Studies*, i/4 (1962), 51-89.

(G. S. COLIN)

iii.—PERSIA

Agriculture in Persia was from earliest times regarded as the fundamental basis of the prosperity of the country. From early times also there has been a dichotomy between the agricultural and the pastoral elements of the population. The Avesta was unequivocal in its approval of the settled life of the peasant and of the practice of agriculture. Agricultural prosperity, which was also in Islamic times traditionally regarded as the basis upon which stable government rested, was closely connected with irrigation [see MĀʾ], security, and taxation.

Rulers were urged by mediaeval Islamic theorists to foster agriculture in order to ensure a full treasury and thus prevent the decay of the kingdom. To this end irrigation works were to be carried out, security established, and extortion against the peasantry prevented. The philosophers and encyclopaedists similarly regarded agriculture as the basic industry, upon which the good order of the world and the perpetuation of the human race depended (cf. Maḥmūd Āmulī, *Nafāʾis al-funūn*, Tehrān, ii, 159).

Invasion and dynastic struggles have been the cause of frequent interruption in, not to say decay of, agriculture. For example in Kh̲ūzistān, where there had been considerable development under the Sāsānians, the agricultural economy failed to return quickly to its previous level after the Arab invasion in the first half of the seventh century A.D. and there was until modern times a cumulative, though not uninterrupted, decline (R. A. Adams, *Agriculture and urban life in early south-western Iran*, in *Science*, vol. 136, no. 3511, 13 April 1962). The quartering of soldiers on the population in Būyid times appears to have materially contributed to agricultural decline (cf. Ibn Miskawayh, *Eclipse*, ii, 96, and Ibn al-Ath̲īr *Taʾrīkh̲*, viii, 342). It has always been the practice of government officials, civil and military, to live upon the country, a custom highly detrimental to agriculture. At no time, perhaps, did the evils of the system reach greater heights than under the Īlkh̲āns (cf. Rash̲īd al-Dīn, *Gesch. Ġāzān Ḫān's*, ed. K. Jahn, *passim*). In the Ḳād̲j̲ār period the evil was also widespread. In times of war, continuous or intermittent, it was sometimes the practice deliberately to lay waste frontier areas. Thus the Turco-Persian frontier area in Ṣafawid times was reduced to a desert (*A chronicle of the Carmelites in Persia*, London 1939, i, 140). Many examples at different periods of Persian history could be cited of local officials imposing such severe contributions on the cultivators of the soil as to cause their dispersal and thus lead to the ruin of their land.

Tribal warfare and raiding was another major cause of agricultural decay. Such raiding was common whenever the central government weakened; further, when the tribal population and its flocks rose above the level which could be maintained by the limited pasture available, either because of a period of drought or because of natural increase, there would be a movement, violent or otherwise, into the settled areas. The balance between the settled and semi-settled elements of the population was extremely precarious, and inevitably adversely affected agriculture on the borders of the tribal regions. Various tribal groups, notably in Fārs, during the course of the late nineteenth and early twentieth centuries became settled and practised agriculture. Riḍā Sh̲āh made an abortive attempt to settle the nomadic population of the country, notably in Fārs, the Bakh̲tiyārī, and parts of Kurdistān. Since about 1956 there has been a movement by Turkomans and others to reclaim the Gurgān steppe.

Another factor militating against agricultural development has been insecurity of tenure both as regards the peasant and the landowner [see TENURE OF LAND].

Agriculture is also subject to interruption by the capricious nature of the climate. Drought, due to insufficient spring or winter rain, causing partial or complete crop failures, and floods, with the accompanying destruction of irrigation channels and *ḳanāt*s, are of common occurrence. Earthquakes have also been a contributory factor causing local and temporary dislocation. Ravages by pests, notably the *sunn* pest and locusts, not infrequently cause heavy losses. High winds in many areas and violent hailstorms are other detrimental factors. Deterioration of the soil because of a change in the water table due to over-lavish irrigation or inadequate drainage, or both, is a major problem in some parts of the country, especially Kh̲ūzistān and Sīstān; and in some places on the central plateau the soil is salty and the water too saline to be used for irrigation. On the south and south-east borders of the central desert there is a marked tendency for the desert to encroach upon the surrounding area (cf. Ḥamd Allāh Mustawfī, *Nuzhat*, 142, *Taʾrīkh̲-i Sīstān*, ed. Bahār, Tehrān 1936-8, 21). Soil erosion is widespread, notably in Ād̲h̲arbāyd̲j̲ān. Its primary causes are climatic and geological, but uncontrolled grazing by goats and the destruction of forests for fuel have steadily increased the tendency towards erosion. Little attention has been given to its control or reduction by modifying existing practices of arable and animal husbandry, or by contour ploughing, which is made difficult by the relatively small size of the holdings. Terracing in mountain valleys, however, is often carried out with considerable skill.

Irrigated and dry farming are both practised, the latter in large areas of Ād̲h̲arbāyd̲j̲ān and Kurdistān, and to a lesser extent in Kh̲urāsān and Fārs, and on the Caspian littoral for crops other than rice. Everywhere with the exception of the Caspian littoral rainfall is the main limiting factor on agriculture. Gīlān and Māzandarān have a relatively heavy rainfall, well distributed throughout the year with a maximum in early autumn, varying from 50-60 inches in the west to 20 inches in the east and rising to over 100 inches on the northern slopes of the Elburz. The natural vegetation is thick deciduous forest, found up to a height of 7,000-8,000 ft.; where this is cleared fruit, rice, cotton, and other crops thrive. The eastern end of the Persian Gulf littoral comes under the influence of the south-west monsoon. The average rainfall in the coastal district of Persian Balūčistān is 3-4 inches; Bushire has an average rainfall of about 10 inches; and Kh̲ūzistān 12-15 inches, with a maximum in December. The plateau, the average elevation of which varies between 3,000-5,000 ft., is ringed by mountain ranges, the general trend of which is from north-west to south-east. The seasons on the plateau are regular but considerable variations of climate are found. Within the mountains the plateau lies in the rain shadow. In general the 10 inch rainfall line follows the inner foothills of the Zagros-Elburz-Kopet Dagh ring of mountains and marks the boundary between areas where cereals can be cultivated extensively without irrigation and areas dependent upon irrigation. The summer grazing of the nomadic tribes also lies in or near the 10 inch line. Rain begins in November and continues intermittently to the end of March and, in the south and north-east, to the end of April. Heavy snowfalls are common in winter. Vegetation is limited but some forest is found in Kurdistān and Luristān; and a narrow belt of oak forest in Fārs. Considerable areas, notably in Ād̲h̲arbāyd̲j̲ān, Kurdistān, and northern Fārs consist of mountain pasture. South-east of Tehrān are two great salt deserts, the Dash̲t-i Kavīr and the Dash̲t-i Lūṭ, which together with Sīstān have a relatively low elevation. The climate of Sīstān is one of extremes and the average annual rainfall only 2½ inches. It is estimated that only 10-14 per cent of the total area of the whole country is under cultivation. Some 30 to 35 per cent is desert and waste. The remainder is grazing-land and forest.

Grain crops. Wheat and barley are the staple crops and are grown as irrigated (*ābī*) and unirrigated (*daymī*) crops up to an elevation of about 10,000 ft. Maize and millet have also been widely grown throughout the country since early times (cf. B. Spuler, *Iran in früh-islamischer Zeit*, Wiesbaden 1952, 387). Wheat is mainly grown as a winter crop; but in the high valleys of the Zagros and Elburz it is also grown as a spring crop. The regions with the greatest production of wheat are the neighbourhood of Mas͟hhad in K͟hurāsān, western Ād͟harbāyd͟jān, Hamadān, Kirmāns͟hāh, and Iṣfahān. In south Persia wheat and barley are sown between the first week in November and the first week in January, and in central Persia between the end of October and the end of November; and spring wheat between the end of February and the end of April. Wheat is harvested in the south about the end of April or the beginning of May; in the upland areas of Fārs about a month later, and on the plateau some two to two and a half months later. Barley is harvested about three to four weeks earlier than wheat (cf. Mīrzā Ḥusayn K͟hān, *D͟jug͟hrāfiyā-yi Iṣfahān*, ed. M. Sutūdeh, Tehrān 1953-4,55 ff.). The yield on wheat varies greatly in different parts of the country. In general it is low. The peasant normally saves part of his crop for the following year's seed.

Rice. The main rice-growing area is in the Caspian provinces. Some rice is also grown in the Lind͟jān and Alind͟jān districts of Iṣfahān (*D͟jug͟hrāfiyā-yi Iṣfahān*, 55 ff.) and, on a small scale, in Fārs, K͟hūzistān, Kurdistān and other districts (Spuler, *op. cit.*, 387, Ḥamd Allāh Mustawfī, *Nuzhat*, 162, 163, Sanīʿ al-Dawla, *Maʾāt͟hir al-āt͟hār*, Tehrān, lith. 1888-9, 115). According to tradition rice was originally imported from India (*Kitāb-i ʿIlm-i filāḥat wa zirāʿat dar ʿahd-i G͟hāzān K͟hān*, ed. ʿAbd al-G͟haffār Nad͟jm al-Dawla, Tehrān 1905-6, 86). In some areas rice is sown broadcast, but in the main rice-growing areas such as Māzandarān and Iṣfahān it is sown in nurseries (*k͟hazāna*) and transplantation (*nis͟hāʾ*) takes place after a month. In Māzandarān the land is ploughed in April, flooded and then ploughed twice more. A fortnight after transplanting weeding (*vid͟jīn*) begins, the weeds being trampled into the mud. The rice fields are kept permanently under water for two to three months. Rice is reaped in September. The main varieties are known as *ṣadrī*, *girda*, *dum-i siyāh* and *ʿambarbū* (see also J. B. Fraser, *Travels and adventures in the Persian provinces*, London 1826, 119-20).

Sugar cane. This was mainly grown in K͟hūzistān in early Islamic times and in the middle ages (cf. Spuler, *op. cit.*, 388, *Kitāb-i ʿIlm-i filāḥat wa zirāʿat*, 102); and to a minor extent in Māzandarān. In the later middle ages its cultivation in K͟hūzistān died out. An attempt was made in Ḳād͟jār times to revive it (*Waḳāyiʿ-i ittifāḳiyya*, Tehrān,no. 55), and also to cultivate sugar cane in Gīlān (*Maʾāt͟hir al-āt͟hār*, 118) and Iṣfahān (*D͟jug͟hrāfiyā-yi Iṣfahān*, 58). In recent years the cultivation of sugar cane in K͟hūzistān has begun on a more extensive scale as a result of new irrigation developments. Planting takes place in March or April and the cane is cut in November.

Sugar beet. An abortive attempt was made to introduce sugar beet by a Belgian company at Kahrīzak near Tehrān in 1886-7. Under Riḍā S͟hāh the cultivation of sugar beet was encouraged and it is widely cultivated at the present day especially in the Tehrān, Tabrīz, Kirmāns͟hāh, S͟hīrāz, Kirmān, and Mas͟hhad areas.

Cotton. This appears to have been widely grown on the plateau in early Islamic times (Spuler, *op. cit.*, 389; Ḥamd Allāh Mustawfī, *Nuzhat*, 52, and *passim*). American sea island cotton was first introduced into the Urūmiyya region about the year 1852 from whence its cultivation spread (*Letters from Persia written by Charles and Edward Burgess 1828-1855*, ed. B. Schwarz, New York 1942, 117). During the reign of Riḍā S͟hāh a long stapled variety was introduced and came to be known locally as *filistānī* (from the village where it was first cultivated). This variety is grown in Ād͟harbāyd͟jān, Kirmāns͟hāh, Fārs, and K͟hūzistān. A shorter stapled American variety is grown in the Caspian provinces, including Gurgān, and a native short stapled variety of inferior quality but hardy growth is grown in marginal areas. Cotton is grown as an irrigated crop up to an elevation of about 5,000 ft. It is sown in April or May and reaped in the autumn. The land is normally watered once before sowing and the crop is irrigated several times during the period of vegetation. Cotton is the main cash crop of Persia. It is also grown extensively for its seed, which yields an edible oil (cf. *D͟jug͟hrāfiyā-yi Iṣfahān*, 56).

Tobacco. This is grown in many districts for local use and especially in the north-west and south-east Zagros and in the Caspian provinces. It appears to have been first cultivated in Persia in the 11th/17th century, having been introduced by the Portuguese in the early part of that century. It began to be cultivated in Gīlān in 1875-6 (Taḳī Bahrāmī, *Taʾrīk͟h-i kis͟hāvarzī-i Īrān*, Tehrān 1951-2).

Opium. It is difficult to establish when the opium poppy was first cultivated in Persia. Muḥammad b. Zakariyā (Rhazes) refers to the wild and cultivated poppy. By the end of the 11th/17th century opium cultivation was well established (cf. Kaempfer, *Amoenitas Exoticae*). It spread in the nineteenth century as an alternative to the declining silk industry. It was first introduced into Fārs in 1868-9 (Mīrzā Ḥasan Fasāʾī, *Fārs nāma-i Nāṣirī*, Tehrān 1894-6, ii, 3). The main opium-growing areas, until the prohibition of the cultivation of the opium poppy, which was first made in 1953 and became effective in 1956, were Iṣfahān, Fārs, and K͟hurāsān; it was also grown in Hamadān and Kirmānshāh. The best opium came from Ābāda, Kirmān, Yazd, Burūd͟jird, and Varāmīn. The seed is sown from October to December, or more rarely in spring. The crop is weeded and thinned in spring; and irrigated during May and June. The collection of the sap begins in May, or a month earlier in the hotter districts of the south, and continues until August. A vertical or diagonal incision is made in the seed capsule in the evening; the sap oozes from the incisions during the night, partially dries, and is scraped off with a blunt knife the next morning. This operation is performed twice or, if the crop is exceptionally good, three times at an interval of several days (A. R. Neligan, *The opium question with special reference to Persia*, London 1927).

Tea. An abortive attempt was made by Ṣanīʿ al-Dawla to introduce the cultivation of tea into Māzandarān in the late nineteenth century. Subsequently there was some cultivation on a small scale; in 1928-9 seed was imported from the Far East, since when there has been a great expansion in tea cultivation in western Māzandarān.

Silk. This is a traditional product of Persia. In the 7th/13th century the silk trade was important; the high water mark in the production of silk was reached in the 11th/17th century. In the nineteenth century production declined because of a disease among the silk worms, which began in 1864. New strains were subsequently introduced (Taḳī Bahrāmī, *op. cit.*, 99 ff.). Mulberry trees, on the leaves of which the silk worms feed, are widespread throughout the country, especially in the north. In northern Persia a curious custom exists for the hatching of the eggs of the silk worm. These are attached to a piece of paper and exposed to the warmth of the human body by being worn next to the skin (Hanway, *An historical account of the British trade over the Caspian Sea*, London 1762, i, 189 ff.; Curzon, *Persia*, i, 369; see also ḤARĪR).

Minor crops. Pulses and oil seeds are widely cultivated; and some fodder crops, such as lucerne and clover. A great variety of vegetables is grown especially near urban centres. Potatoes were introduced into Persia by Sir John Malcolm during the reign of Fatḥ ʿAlī S͟hāh (*Maʾāt͟hir al-āt͟hār*, 112; Kaye, *Life and correspondence of Major-General Sir John Malcolm*, ii, 47-8). Dye-plants, mainly in the central Zagros region and Kirmān, and other plants used in industry such as saffron, hemp, flax and, in the Dizful and S͟hustar areas, indigo (which was introduced by the Būyid, ʿAḍud al-Dawla, see Ibn al-At͟hīr, *Taʾrīk͟h*, viii, 513), madder, and, round Yazd and Kirmān, henna, and, in Māzandarān, jute, have been cultivated since early times (cf. Spuler, *op. cit.*, 389). Vegetable gums, including gum tragacanth and asafoetida, are cropped mainly for export. The latter was known in early Islamic times (cf. *Ḥudūd al-ʿālam*, 108-10). Oak-gall is produced mainly in Kurdistān. A variety of flowers and a kind of willow were cultivated for scent (Spuler, *op. cit.*, 389-90); the former also contributed to bee-keeping.

Fruit. Persia has been famous for fruit-growing since early times (cf. Spuler, *op. cit.*, 388). Many varieties of vine are cultivated and found up to an altitude of 4,500 ft. Vine cultivation is mainly by irrigation, except in some areas of Kurdistān. On the plateau the vines are covered with earth in the winter. Apricots, peaches, nectarines, figs, melons, pomegranates, plums, cherries, pears, and apples are widely grown. Citrus fruits are important in the Caspian provinces and south Persia, especially in K͟hūzistān and southern Fārs. Recently citrus cultivation has been extended to Bam. Dates are widely cultivated in south Persia and on the coastal plains bordering the Persian Gulf. The female plant is impregnated by the male in March or April, some two males going to a plantation of fifty (cf. Naṣīr al-Dīn Ṭūsī, who was aware of this peculiarity of the date palm, *Ak͟hlāḳ-i Nāṣirī*, Tehrān n.d., 25-6). Nut trees, especially almonds and pistachios, are of importance. Olives were cultivated in early Islamic times in Nīs͟hāpūr, Gurgān, Daylam, and Fārs (Spuler, *op. cit.*, 387). The main area of cultivation at the present day is Rūdbār in Māzandarān, where cultivation increased after the decline of silk production in the middle of the nineteenth century (T. E. Gordon, *Persia revisited*, London 1896, 163; Curzon, *Persia*, i, 368). The grafting of vines and other fruit trees has long been practised (cf. Fak͟hr al-Dīn Rāzī, *D͟jāmiʿ al-ʿulūm*, B.M., OR. 2972, ff. 132a-133b and *Čahārdah risāla*, ed. Sayyid Muḥammad Bāḳir Sabzawārī, Tehrān 1962, 146-51). At the present day in Kirmān and Fārs almonds and pistachios are grafted on to the wild almond tree (*bāna*).

Although large landownership has been the dominant form of land tenure, large-scale farming was not (and is not) practised, except exceptionally. The agricultural unit was the ploughland (*d͟juft*, *k͟hīs͟h*, *zawd͟j*) and agriculture was carried on mainly as subsistence agriculture; this is still predominantly the case. Broadly the ploughland consists of an area which a pair of oxen can cultivate annually; but it varies in size according to the nature of the soil, the type of agriculture practised (dry or irrigated), practices with regard to fallow, the kind of crops grown, the draught animals used, and the pressure or otherwise on the land. The average ploughland ranges from some 60 to 20 acres; but in some areas holdings are much smaller, as for example in Mārbīn, one of the districts of Iṣfahān, where cultivation is mainly carried on by spade. The relation between the peasant and the landowner was formerly usually regulated, and to some extent still is, by a crop-sharing agreement (*muzāraʿa* [*q.v.*]). The ploughland or peasant-holding is usually run as a family concern by the peasant and his sons or other members of the family; extra labour may be required at harvest time and at certain other seasons of the year. In some areas three or four ploughlands are run together as a unit (*buna*). Periodical redistribution of the ploughlands among the peasants of a village used to take place, usually by lot, in some districts.

The main draught animal used on the plateau is the ox. Donkeys and, especially in K͟hūzistān, mules, and in the Persian Gulf littoral, Miyāndoāb (in Ād͟harbāyd͟jān), and Mahābād (in Kurdistān), buffaloes, and in Persian Balūčistān, the camel, are also used. In some areas, notably Sīstān, oxen are hired for ploughing to the cultivators by graziers. Where the soil is stiff more than one pair of draught animals may be required (cf. Morier, *Second journey through Persia, Armenia and Asia Minor to Constantinople in the year 1810 and 1816*, London 1818, 304). Donkeys and camels are the main pack-animals. Small bullock carts are found in western Ād͟harbāyd͟jān and some of the Armenian villages in Firaydan.

The plough (*k͟hīs͟h*) used is of the hook type having a large or small steel share. The plough beam is linked to the yoke by means of a rope sling. There is no mould board and the soil is ripped open leaving an open, coarse, cloddy tilth. There are slight differences between the plough used in (i) Fārs, Kirmān, and Sīstān, (ii) Iṣfahān, Hamadān, Tehrān, and Ād͟harbāyd͟jān, and (iii) Gīlān and Māzandarān. Seed is sown broadcast.

In addition to the plough, a kind of harrow (*māla*) is used; it differs slightly in shape in south and central Persia on the one hand and north-west Persia on the other. Two kinds of levelling board are in use, a relatively large board drawn by a draught animal, and a smaller board (known in central Persia as *katar*), which is used for the preparation of irrigation check banks, and operated by two men, one pulling and the other pushing. Three types of spade are used, one in Fārs, which has a wooden cross bar, the second in central Persia, which has a turned footrest, and the third in Ād͟harbāyd͟jān, which has a rolled edge.

Grain is cut with a sickle (*dās*) which has a plain cutting edge; scythes are used in northern Ād͟harbāyd͟jān, where they were introduced from Russia at the end of the nineteenth century. A small toothed sickle is used for cutting grass and lucerne, etc. Corn is tied into sheaves and left to dry or carried straight to the threshing floor (*k͟harmangāh*). Pod crops, such as peas, beans, linseed, and carraway seed, are mainly threshed by beating with rods; and in those parts of the country where draught animals are scarce, corn is also threshed in this way. A threshing board, the bottom surface of which is studded with sharp pieces of flint stone held in position by wooden wedges, is used to thresh grain. It is attached by a rope to a yoke and drawn, while a man stands on it, in a circle by an ox or oxen or other animal over the threshing floor. A threshing wheel or wain (*čūn*, ?*čān*) is used, especially in north-eastern, central and south Persia. This is a sledge-like carriage, usually drawn by two oxen with two sets of rollers, which turn round as the sledge beams slide over the sheaves. The rollers carry sharp-edged steel discs, sometimes with fine saw teeth, or have steel knives or prongs with sharp edges, one roller having the edges parallel to the axis, and the other having them at right angles. In some parts of Ā͟dharbāyd͟jān the wain has wooden spokes. The third method of threshing is for the grain to be trodden out by strings of oxen, donkeys, or horses driven round the threshing floor. Winnowing is done by wooden forks, the grain being thrown six or seven feet into the air. The grain drops straight down while the chaff is carried by the wind and settles on a separate heap. A second winnowing done by wooden shovels is sometimes necessary. Finally the grain is sifted to separate it from the stones and earth with which it may have become mixed during threshing and winnowing. Two men can winnow and sift 20-25 cwt. of corn a day. Donkeys and other pack animals take the grain in sacks to the granaries. The chaff is removed in nets and used as fodder for horses, donkeys and oxen (H. E. Wulff, *Agricultural implements in Persia*, in *Power farming and better farming digest*, Sidney, Oct. 1958).

Sheep and goats are commonly grazed on stubble fields, which thus receive a slight benefit from their manure. For the most part, however, animal dung is used as fuel. In some dry farming areas there is insufficient rainfall to rot the manure even if it were used. Household sewage mixed with earth is used as fertilizer in some areas, especially round urban centres. Earth from old walls and ruined buildings is also broken down and spread on the fields (cf. J. B. Fraser, *Winter's journey*, London 1838, ii, 65). Gardens tend to be manured more regularly than fields and to be cultivated annually. Pigeon lime, collected in pigeon towers, is used in the Iṣfahān district for the cultivation of melons and pear trees (cf. Chardin, *Voyages*, Amsterdam 1711, ii, 75). Fak͟hr al-Dīn Rāzī mentions the use of bird lime and weed-killers (*D͟jāmiʿ al-ʿulūm*, f. 132a). Fish manure is used in Kirmān for pistachio trees. Chemical fertilizers have been introduced in recent years but their use is comparatively rare.

Practices in fallow, during which the land may or may not be ploughed, and crop rotation vary very widely. Unirrigated land tends to be left fallow for long periods. Irrigation is usually by inundation. In vineyards, melon land, and market gardens the water is let into the land by irrigation trenches. In land watered by *ḳanāt*s the tendency is to cultivate more intensively the land nearest the mouth of the *ḳanāt* to avoid water loss while that at the end of the *ḳanāt* is less frequently cultivated.

In many parts of Persia the crops have to be guarded, especially at night, to prevent depredations by wild pig and other animals. Scarecrows (*matarsak*) are erected in some districts (cf. C. E. Yate, *Khurasan and Sistan*, London 1900, 168, 283).

In recent years there has been some development in mechanization. An increasing number of tractors and combine harvesters have been in use especially since 1952, but the numbers are still relatively small except in Das͟ht-i Gurgān, where cultivation in the grain-growing areas has been wholly, and in the cotton-growing areas, partially mechanized.

The state did not interest itself in the conduct of agriculture except so far as crown lands (*k͟hāliṣa*) were concerned; though it was interested in the prosperity or otherwise of agriculture from the point of view of taxation. A Ministry of Agriculture, Commerce and Public Welfare, was first founded in 1879; at the same time an Agricultural Council was set up. In 1891-2 the department of agriculture and commerce was transferred to the Ministry of National Economy and Roads. The following year departments general of agriculture, commerce, and industry were set up. In 1893-4 agriculture and industry were once more united in one department, but were subsequently again divided. In 1897-8 the Ministry of Crown Lands (*wizārat-i k͟hāliṣad͟jāt wa raḳabāt-i dār al-k͟hilāfa*) became the Ministry of Crown Lands and Agriculture. Subsequently crown lands (*k͟hāliṣa*) were transferred to the Ministry of Finance. During the constitutional period agriculture suffered various vicissitudes administratively. The first agricultural magazine to be published was a fortnightly journal of agriculture and commerce issued in 1880 by the Ministry of Agriculture and Commerce.

The first agricultural school in Persia was the Madrasa-i Muẓaffarī at Tehrān which was opened in 1901-2. It closed after six years. The next attempt to open an agricultural school was at Karad͟j near Tehrān in 1919. This became a high school in 1933-4 and a college in 1943-4. In 1948-9 it was transferred from the Ministry of Agriculture to Tehran University and in 1952-3 separated into two colleges, the college of agriculture and the college of veterinary science, which were fully incorporated into the university. Experimental work is done in government agricultural stations, notably at Karad͟j.

Bibliography: (In addition to the works mentioned in the text): A. K. S. Lambton, *Landlord and Peasant in Persia*, Oxford 1953; Taḳī Bahrāmī, *D͟jughrāfiyā-yi Kis͟hāvarzī-i Īrān*, Tehrān 1954-5; *Farhang-i Rustāʾī*, 3 vols., Tehrān 1927-38; W. B. Fisher, *The Middle East*, London 1950; *The Middle East, A political and economic survey*, 3rd edition, Oxford 1958; ʿAbd al-Raḥīm Ẓarrābī, *Taʾrīk͟h-i Kās͟hān*, ed. Irad͟j Afs͟hār, Tehrān 1956-7, 144 ff.; Macdonald Kinneir, *A geographical memoir of the Persian Empire*, London 1813; P. H. T. Beckett, *The soils of Kerman, South Persia*, in *The Journal of Soil Science*, ix (1 March 1958); idem, *Agriculture in Central Persia*, in *Tropical Agriculture*, xxxiv (1 January 1957); H. L. Rabino, *Report on the production of rice in the provinces of Gilan, Mazandaran and Astarabad*, in *Board of Trade Journal*, 25 April 1907; idem, *Silk culture in Persia*, in *ibid.*, 6 June 1907; H. L. Rabino and D. F. Lafont, *La culture du riz en Gilan*, in *Annales de l'Ecole Nationale d'Agriculture de Montpelier*, 1911, *Culture du tabac en Guilan*, in *Progrès viticole*, Montpelier 1911, *Culture de la gourde a Ghalian en Gilan et en Mazandaran*, in *RMM*, xxviii (1914), *Culture de la canne à sucre en Mazandaran*, in *ibid*; Mohamed Hossein Danechi, *Vocabulaires agricoles en langue persane*, thesis, Paris 1963 (not published).— Scattered references to agriculture are also to be found in the works of the Arab and Persian geographers and in local histories. (A. K. S. Lambton)

iv. — Ottoman Empire

During the period between the 8th/14th and 11th/17th centuries, when the *tīmār* [*q.v.*] system prevailed in the Ottoman Empire, the *raḳabe*, *i.e.*, the freehold ownership of agricultural lands was regarded as vested in the State. The tenure of lands held as *waḳf* and *mülk* in the pre-Ottoman Muslim states of Anatolia was in part confirmed, but Meḥemmed II converted some of them to *mīrī*-land (see *IA*, s.v. Mehmed II, 533), as he did the land belonging to Christian monasteries in the territories of Trebizond (Başvekâlet Arşivi, Maliye defter no. 828): generally speaking the central authority, when it was powerful, attempted to increase the extent of *mīrī*-land.

According to the typical *ʿörfī ḳānūn*s promulgated in these centuries [see ḲĀNŪN], land was granted on lease to farmers in parcels usually termed *čift* or *čiftlik* [*q.v.*]. The peasant could not transfer these *raʿiyyetlik* lands as *mülk* or as *waḳf* or as a gift. If he wished to sell them or give them up he was obliged to obtain the permission of the *sipāhī* and pay a fixed charge, the *ḥaḳḳ-i ḳarār* (in the 11th/17th century, 3% of the selling price). Thus the peasant possessed merely the right of usufruct (*istig̲h̲lāl*); and this right could pass directly only to his sons (for the later recognized rights of daughters and other relatives, see Ö. L. Barkan, *Türk toprak hukuku* . . ., in *Tanzimat*, i, Istanbul 1940, 358-421). The *čift* unit of land could not be divided: if more than one son inherited they enjoyed the usufruct jointly. In principle, the peasant could not leave this land: if he did, he was obliged to pay the *čift bozan resmi* (50 *aḳče* [*q.v.*] in the 9th/15th, 75 *aḳče* in the 10th/16th century; as the number of peasants leaving the land increased so the *čift bozan resmi* was increased, with the fall in the value of the *aḳče*, to 300 *aḳče*s). If the peasant left the land unworked for more than three years, the timariot could grant it to another. The use to which the land was put could not be changed: agricultural land, for example, could not be converted to pasture, vegetable-growing or fruit-growing. Agricultural land turned over to vine- or vegetable-growing without the *sipāhī*'s permission could, if less than ten years had passed, be restored to its former use. The State expected the peasant to sow a definite quantity of seed on land of a given area. Vineyards and vegetable-gardens near towns or around houses were exempt from these regulations, being subject to the *s̲h̲arʿī* rules of ownership. The status of the land and the farmer was confirmed by the *taḥrīr* [*q.v.*] carried out at fixed intervals.

The problem in the Ottoman Empire was not shortage of land but shortage of labour; and it is probably for this reason that the peasant was bound to the soil. On the *tīmār*s there were several areas of untenanted land, known as *mezraʿa* and *ekinlik*. The State was concerned above all to prevent the peasants abandoning the land and moving away: the *sipāhī* who provoked this was severely punished, while those who could persuade farmers to settle on vacant land were rewarded. The *taḥrīr* registers of the time of Süleymān I, however, show that new land, referred to as *ifrāzāt*, had then been brought under cultivation, for at this period the population had increased considerably and the State encouraged the cultivation of *mawāt* lands, heretofore left unused; such lands were exempt from *tapu resmi* until the next *taḥrīr* was carried out.

A further degree in State control of the land and of agriculture is found in the active participation by the State, exemplified particularly in rice-growing. Under this system, applied with the object of ensuring supplies for the army, rice-growing was carried out under the supervision of *emīn*s, responsible for the administrative and financial organization, and of *čeltik reʾīsleri*, responsible for the actual cultivation. Every *čeltikd̲j̲i* was obliged to sow a definite amount of seed on a definite area, both prescribed by the State. The irrigation-canals were kept in repair under the supervision of the *reʾīs*. From the harvested rice, after seed had been set aside, the State took one-half (in some areas two-thirds). As compensation for this, the *čeltikd̲j̲iler* so organized were exempt from certain taxes (mainly the *resm-i čift, resm-i g̲h̲anem, ʿawāriḍ*; for the *čeltikd̲j̲iler* see Barkan, *Kanunlar*, 54, 202-3, 205; for a *čeltik ḳānūnu* see Ankara Un., DTCF library, Ismail Saip collection MS 5120, 130-9). The cultivation of rice was introduced into Rūmeli by the Ottomans, and extensive rice-fields under State control appeared in the valleys of the Merič (Maritsa), Karasu, Vardar and Salambria (see M. T. Gökbilgin, *Edirne ve Paşa Livâsı*, Istanbul 1952, 125-50). A similar system of State participation prevailed in the villages which, in order to ensure the food-supply of Istanbul, were created in the vicinity of the city by the settlement of prisoners of war, '*ortaḳd̲j̲ī ḳullar*' (see Barkan, *Kanunlar*, 86-109, and idem, *XV ve XVI. asırlarda Osmanlı imperatorluğunda toprak işçiliğinin organizasyonu şekilleri*, in *Iktisat Fak. Mecm.*, i (1939), 29-74, 198-245, 397-447. On the food supply of the capital see further W. Hahn, *Die verpflegung Konstantinopels durch staatliche Zwangswirtschaft*, Stuttgart 1926; R. Mantran, *Istanbul dans la seconde moitié du XVIIe siècle*, Paris 1962, 179-213).

Thus the principal characteristic of the classical Ottoman land-system was direct State control of the peasant and the soil, a system which had grown up to meet the military and financial needs of an absolutist administration, and in which the state's main concern was to ensure the revenues of the *tīmār*s. This *tīmār* organization and the Ottoman land-system broke up in the period of anarchy which began at the end of the 10th/16th century (see Ḳočī Beg, *Risāle*, ed. A. K. Aksüt, Istanbul 1939, 24-56). Lack of settled conditions and heavy taxes caused the peasantry to abandon the soil in droves: in the first half of the 11th/17th century this movement from the land reached disastrous proportions and was called 'the great flight', '*büyük ḳačḳun*' (see M. Akdağ, *Türkiyenin iktisadî vaziyeti*, in *Belleten*, xiii/51 (1949), 537-64, xiv/55 (1950), 319-405). In many districts local dignitaries and Janissaries turned the abandoned agricultural land into pastures for their flocks of sheep (M. Akdağ, *Belleten*, xiv, 374, 394). The new *ḳānūn*s concerning the use of land and the *raʿāyā* which were promulgated in the early 11th/17th century (they are found together in *MTM*, i (1331), 49-112, 305-48) are the result of efforts to solve this problem.

In the 11th/17th and 12th/18th centuries the most important change in agricultural conditions was brought about by the spread of the systems of *muḳāṭaʿa* and *iltizām* [*qq.v.*]. There arose a new class of *ag̲h̲a*s, *aʿyān* and derebeys [*qq.v.*] in Rūmeli and Anatolia who, holding possession of the land for life, became in practice great land-owners (for Western Anatolia see Ç. Uluçay, *18.ve 19. yüzyıllarda Saruhan'da eşkiyalık ve halk hareketleri*, Istanbul 1955; see further A. F. Miller, *Mustafa Pasha Bayraktar*, Moscow 1947). Although Maḥmūd II succeeded, after 1227/1812, in putting down the great *aʿyān*s and derebeys, the village *ag̲h̲a*s and the lesser *aʿyān* maintained themselves as the ruling class in the social sphere. In many areas the peasant had now sunk to the position of tenant or share-cropper on the lands held as *muḳāṭaʿa* by the *ag̲h̲a*s: in this state of affairs is to be found the basic reason for the peasant risings in the Balkans in the 19th century (see H. İnalcık, *Tanzimat nedir?*, in *Tarih araştırmaları*, Ankara 1941, 237-63).

Difficulties of communication meant that agricultural products were in general disposed of in local markets. Cereals were distributed further afield only in areas near the coasts or in the vicinity of cities or along the great military routes. In the 8th/14th and 9th/15th centuries Venice bought large quantities of cereals from Western Anatolia, Thrace and Thessaly (see F. Thiriet, *Régestes des délibérations du Senat de Venise concernant la Romanie*, i-iii, Paris 1958-60). In the same period cotton and dried fruits were exported from Western Anatolia to countries in the north (this appears particularly from the customs-registers of Akkerman and Kili, Başvekâlet Arşivi, Maliye no. 6). From the 9th/16th century onwards increased trade with Western Europe led to an increase in the export of the cotton and cotton goods of Western Anatolia (P. Masson, *Hist. du commerce français dans le Levant*, Paris 1896-1911, appendix VIII; E. Arup, *Studier i Engelsk og Tysk Handelshistorie*, Copenhagen 1907, 109 ff., 191 ff.). In the the 19th century, as was observed by P. de Tchichatchef (*Asie Mineure*, 3 vols., Paris 1867), G. Perrot (*Souvenirs d'un voyage en Asie Mineure*, Paris 1867) and A. Ubicini (*Lettres sur la Turquie*, Paris 1851, 244-65), the agricultural methods of the peasantry were dictated entirely by tradition. In this field ethnographical observations (e.g. Hâmit Z. Koşay, *Türkiye halkının maddî kültürüne dair araştırmalar*, in *Türk Etnografya Dergisi*, i (1956), 7-55; *Contribution à l'étude de la culture matérielle des Bulgares*, in *Bulletin du Musée Nat. d'Ethnographie à Sofia*, viii, 55-109, x-xi, 130-65, xii, 62-85) can be supplemented from the *ḳānūn*s for sandjaḳs and notes in the registers concerning agriculture and irrigation (see, *e.g.*, Barkan, *Kanunlar*, and *Monumenta Turcica*, i, Sarajevo 1957). The *mufaṣṣal defterler* [see DAFTAR-I KHĀḲĀNĪ] contain much material—as yet unstudied—on the crops grown in various areas and their productivity; the various agricultural implements are to be found listed in the *ḳāḍīs*' registers of effects (*metrūkāt*). The Anatolian peasant divided his land into three or two sections, and followed the principle of leaving each fallow for two years or one year (*nadas*, see Barkan, *Kanunlar*, s.v.). Important details on the irrigation methods employed in the Ilkhānid period in Anatolia are found in the letters of Rashīd al-Dīn (see Z. V. Togan, *Reşideddin'in mektûplarında Andadolu'nun iktisadî ve medenî hayatına ait kayıtlar*, in *Ist. Ün. Iktisat Fak. Mecm.*, xv (1953-4), 33-50; Khwādja Rashīd al-Dīn Faḍl Allāh, *Kitāb-i Mukātabāt-i Rashīdī*, ed. M. Shafi, Lahore 1363/1935, 220-30, 234-6). In the Ottoman period, in arid districts like Central Anatolia and Diyārbakr there was a special régime for irrigation (for this *mīrāblīḳ* see Barkan, *Kanunlar*, 42, 46; *Ḳānūnnāme* of Süleymān, *TOEM* Supplement, 65-6).

The Ottomans were naturally acquainted with Muslim works on *ʿilm al-filāḥa*. The *K. al-Filāḥa* of Shaykh Abū Zakariyyāʾ Yaḥyā b. al-ʿAwwām was translated into Turkish in 998/1599 by Muṣṭafā b. Luṭf Allāh (MSS: Bayezid Lib., Veliyeddin 2534, Bursa müzesi E 32; Ist. Univ. Lib.). Two works by Ottoman authors were well-known: *Rawnaḳ-i bustān* by al-Ḥādjdj Ibrāhīm b. Meḥemmed (MS: Süleymaniye, Esad Ef. 1019; editions: Istanbul 1260; Konya 1285; and ed. Hadiye Tunçer [in modern script, unsatisfactory], Ankara 1961), and *Gharsnāme* by Kemānī, composed in 1047/1637 (see *Türk ziraat tarihine bir bakış* [I. Köy ve Ziraat Kalkınma Kongresi yayını], Istanbul 1938, 43). Both these works are concerned with the growing of fruit trees, and contain chapters on the soil, planting, pruning, grafting, the diseases of trees and their treatment. The author of the *Rawnaḳ-i bustān* discussed in a final section the gathering and keeping of fruit; he had himself, he says, made an orchard near Edirne and added to the data of books on *filāḥa* what he had learned from experience.

In the history of horticulture, the Ottomans hold an especial position as cultivators of flowers, particularly tulips, in the 12th/18th century (see Djewād Rüshdī, in *Edebiyyāt-i ʿUmūmiyye Medjmūʿasī*, nos. 29, 35, 36). At the Palace, there was a separate corps of flower-gardeners controlled by the *shükūfe-bashī* (*čičekči-bashī*) (see Ferīdūn, *Munshaʾāt al-salāṭīn*², ii, 224-5). There was overt competition among great men to raise new varieties, a successful grower receiving the title *ṣāḥib-i tukhm*. In that century the Ottomans are said to have produced 839 types of tulip (A. Refīḳ, *Lāle devri*, 46-7). Ottoman authors wrote many works on flower-growing (the best-known being Meḥemmed Remzī's *Lālezār-i bāgh-i ḳadīm*, ʿAlī Čelebi's *Shükūfe-nāme*, Fetḥī Čelebi's *Tuḥfat al-ikhwān*, Lālezārī Meḥemmed's *Mīzān al-azhār*, ʿOthmān Efendi's *K. al-Nabāt*, ʿAbd Allāh Efendi's *Shükūfe-nāme*, Ḥādjdjī Aḥmed's *Natāʾidj al-azhār*, etc., see Djewād Rüshdī, *op. cit.*). The biographies of prominent growers were also collected in such works as ʿAbd Allāh Efendi's and Rüshdī-zāde Remzī's *Tedhkire-i shükūfedjiyān* (MSS: Halis Ef. and Ali Emiri collections).

In the period of the Tanẓīmāt [*q.v.*] attempts were made, under European influence, to improve agricultural methods. The issue of the *Taḳwīm al-waḳāʾiʿ* of 14 Rabīʿ II 1254/7 July 1838 reports the setting-up of a *Zirāʿat ve Ṣanāʾiʿ Medjlisi*; and in 1259/1843 a *Medjlis-i Zirāʿat* was founded, attached to the Ministry of Finance. Directors of Agriculture were sent to the provinces (13 Radjab 1260/29 July 1844) and on 23 Rabīʿ II 1261/1 May 1845 an Agricultural Congress of delegates from the provinces was held in Istanbul. The chief matters raised by the participants were the need to reduce the taxes on agriculture, to provide agricultural credits, to control rivers and to build roads (A. Ubicini, *Letters sur la Turquie*, 244-65, dwells on the same points). Finally in Ṣafar 1262/February 1846 there was constituted a Ministry of Agriculture, which was later united with the Ministry of Commerce, and in 1310/1892 reconstituted as the Ministry of Forests, Mines and Agriculture (*Orman, Maʿādin ve Zirāʿat Neẓāreti*). The first School of Agriculture and model farm was founded on the Aya-Mama estate near Istanbul, but did not last long. The promotion of scientific agriculture in Turkey is the work of the Halkalı College of Agriculture and Veterinary Science, founded in 1308/1890.

Various attempts were made in the Tanẓīmāt period to improve the lot of the peasant. In some regions proposals were made—but not put into effect—to transfer *muḳāṭaʿa*-land from the *agha*s to the peasants (see H. İnalcık, *Tanzimat ve Bulgar meselesi*, Ankara 1943). Measures taken to promote the ownership of land with the right of inheritance were inadequate (see Ö. L. Barkan, *Türk toprak hukuku*, in *Tanzimat*, i, 399-341), and favoured rather the holders of large estates. The land law of 1274/1858 contains some new European ideas, but is basically merely a codification of the old Ottoman land-regulations. To protect the peasant from moneylenders, the maximum interest was fixed by law at 15% (Başvekâlet Arşivi, Mühimme def. no. 253, 8-10), and the sum of 20 million ḳurus̲h̲ per annum was set aside to provide credits to peasants. The measures taken to improve agriculture in the Dobrud̲j̲a [*q.v.*] deserve particular mention. A French expert was called in to survey the agricultural situation and make recommendations (see A. Gaudry, *Recherches scientifiques en Orient*, Paris 1860). The distribution of good varieties of seed to the peasants, tax-exemption granted to promote the culture of olives and mulberries, encouragement to use modern implements—all these sprang from the adoption of the new outlook, whose effects are best exemplified in the activities of Midḥat Pas̲h̲a [*q.v.*] in the Danube province (northern Bulgaria): he was the first to import from Europe reaping- and threshing-machines, he founded a model farm, and set up '*Menāfiʿ sandīḳlarī*' to supply credit on easy terms to farmers (see ʿAlī Ḥaydar Midḥat, *Midḥat Pas̲h̲a, ḥayāt-i siyāsiyyesi*. . ., Istanbul 1325/1909, 29). In this period the export of agricultural products to Europe, especially to Great Britain, increased greatly (see F. E. Bailey, *British policy and the Turkish reform movement*, Cambridge, Mass. 1942, 76, and tables 8-14). Cotton-growing expanded considerably, with British encouragement, during the American Civil War (see *Türk ziraat tarihine bir bakış*, 127-36).

Bibliography: in the article. (H. İnalcık)

v. — India

This section offers a survey of agriculture in India during the mediaeval period, *i.e.*, from the time of the arrival of the Muslims to the British conquest.

1. Agriculture. The natural setting of agriculture in India, despite various important variations, displays a surprising degree of uniformity. The larger part of the country consists of plains: the great Indus and Gangetic Plains of the north and the broad river valleys of the south. Except for the extreme tip of the southern peninsula, where there is a significant winter monsoon as well, the rainfall received is mainly from the summer monsoons. These are so bountiful that nearly half of the area of the Union of India has an average annual rainfall of over 100 cm. Some mediaeval writers could, therefore, be excused for their exaggeration when they said, as Abu 'l-Faḍl (*Āʾīn-i Akbarī*, Bibl. Ind., ii, 5-6), that the whole of the land of India was cultivable or, as Bābur (*Bāburnāma*, tr. A. S. Beveridge, ii, 488), that its crops needed no artificial irrigation. Nature has also made possible another phenomenon, regarded in mediaeval times as the special characteristic of Indian agriculture, *viz.*, the sowing and reaping of two harvests in the year—one (*k̲h̲arīf*) collected after the end of the rains, and the other (*rabīʿ*) at the end of the winter.

A comparison of 11th/17th century area statistics (preserved in the *Āʾīn-i Akbarī*, c. 1595, and in certain documents from Awrangzeb's reign) with modern returns suggests that the cultivated area during the 11th/17th century was about half of the area cultivated at the beginning of this century in such large regions as Bihār, eastern and central Uttar Pradesh, Berār and Western Pākistān. In western Uttar Pradesh, eastern Pand̲j̲āb and Gud̲j̲arāt, the area cultivated was smaller by one-third to one-fifth. (See Irfan Habib, *Agrarian system of Mughal India*, 1-22; Moreland, *India at the death of Akbar*, 20-2, offers a still lower estimate of the extent of cultivation under Akbar). The great extent of forest in mediaeval times is also indicated by the information we possess about particular localities. We know, for example, from the chroniclers' accounts of campaigns in Kaṭehr (now Rohilkhand) that extensive forests existed in this region in the 13th and 14th centuries. While these were largely cleared during the following three or four centuries, the Tarāʾī forest still covered, further to the east, most of north-eastern Uttar Pradesh (now a densely populated area), down to the end of the 18th century (cf. Rennell's *Atlas of Bengal*, 1781, Map X).

All descriptions of mediaeval agricultural practice apply equally well to the traditional practice in Indian villages today. There existed the same combination of simple and crude tools with certain ingenious methods and devices. While the fitting of the "iron point" to the wooden plough is referred to in a work as old as the *Manusmriti* (x, 84), Fryer (1672-81) found that in fact the "coulters" of Indian ploughs were "unarmed mostly, Iron being scarce", and that hard wood was being used instead. Yet on the other hand, Amān Allāh Ḥusaynī (early 17th century) notices the use of dibbling in sowing cotton, and Thévenot in Gud̲j̲arāt observed the use of fish manure in planting sugar-cane.

Rainfall was generally supplemented by artificial irrigation, from wells, tanks and canals. Bābur has described for us the two most common methods of lifting water out of wells. One involves lifting water in a leathern bucket (*čaras*) pulled out of the well by yoked oxen drawing a rope passed over a wooden wheel, "a laborious and filthy method". The other (the *rahaṭ* or *arhaṭ*), which deeply interested Bābur, is called in English the Persian wheel (*Bāburnāma*, tr. Beveridge, i, 388; ii, 486). The *ḍhenklī*, based on the use of weights, has been described by Fryer. Large tanks for irrigation purposes were usually constructed by damming streams and rivulets. Fīrūz S̲h̲āh (752-90/1351-88) is said to have built several tanks by means of such dams (*bands*) (ʿAfīf, *Taʾrīk̲h̲-i Fīrūz-s̲h̲āhī*, Bibl. Ind., 330). The Udaypūr lake, created by a massive dam in the 16th century, was originally about 40 miles in circumference (*Āʾīn*, i, 509). Abandoned channels of rivers, which became active during the inundations, served as natural canals and were important sources of irrigation in the Indus basin. Human effort was often needed to keep them in use by clearing silted sections. In addition there were some big man-made canals. The best known of these was Fīrūz S̲h̲āh's West Jamunā Canal, re-excavated and re-aligned by S̲h̲āhd̲j̲ahān. Among other important mediaeval works were the East Jamunā Canal (early 18th century), a long canal drawn from the Sutled̲j̲ by Fīrūz S̲h̲āh, a network of Mug̲h̲al canals drawn from the Rāvī near its entry into the plains, the Sidhnai (which the Rāvī took as its main bed in or before the 16th century), the Begārīwah in upper Sind (17th or 18th century) and the K̲h̲ānwah in the Indus delta (early 16th century).

Most of the major crops raised today were also raised in mediaeval times. A few new crops were introduced during the mediaeval period itself. Tobacco cultivation became well established throughout the country during the earlier part of the 17th century. Coffee cultivation had its beginnings late in the same century, while the cultivation of capsicum spread rapidly in the earlier part of the next. Among the purely modern crops may be counted maize, potatoes, tea and groundnuts.

The geographical distribution of the crops in the 17th century (and so presumably earlier) was different in some important respects from that prevailing today. There was the same broad division into rice and wheat zones marked by the 40- or 50-inch isohyets. But the cultivation of cash crops, notably cotton and sugar-cane, was far more widespread in mediaeval times, the conditions of transport prohibiting concentration. Indigo claimed a large area, in mediaeval times as well as till late in the 19th century; but its cultivation has now practically disappeared. Similarly, opium and hemp were more widely cultivated than now. On the other hand, jute, though known to have been cultivated in certain localities in Bengal, was far from being an important cash crop during mediaeval times. Sericulture, which has undergone a great decline since, flourished mainly in Bengāl and Ka<u>sh</u>mīr.

Among fruits the most prominent were the mango and the coco-nut. The pine-apple was introduced during the 16th century through the agency of the Portuguese, and was rapidly acclimatized. The practice of grafting seems to have been widely applied in Mug<u>h</u>al times. <u>Dj</u>ahāngīr describes its application to cherries and apricots in Ka<u>sh</u>mīr (*Tuzuk*, ed. Sayyid Aḥmad, 299). Amān Allāh notices its use in planting mangoes, and a history of Shāh<u>dj</u>ahān's reign declares that great improvement in citrus fruits resulted from grafting (British Museum MS, Or. 174, f. 102a). The Emperors and their nobles were generally fond of laying out orchards. Fīrūz <u>Sh</u>āh is said to have planted 1200 orchards around Delhi (ʿAfīf, 295). The Mug<u>h</u>als have given their name to a particular type of garden, laid out in squares and criss-crossed by channels of flowing water obtained by various devices (see BUSTĀN II).

2. Mediaeval Works on Agriculture. Very few works seem to have been written on agriculture in mediaeval India, to judge from their extreme paucity in modern collections. There exists in some MSS, *e.g.*, India Office Library I.O. 4702, Aligarh Lytton Fārsiya ʿUlūm 51, and Brit. Mus. Or. 1741, ff. 25a-48a, a tract on agriculture which is really Chapter XI of an encyclopaedic work, the *Gan<u>dj</u>-i Bād-āward*, of Amān Allāh Ḥusaynī, <u>Kh</u>ān Zamān, d. 1046/1637. This tract embodies, with acknowledgment, the whole of the *Kitāb <u>Shadj</u>arat al-nihāl*, a work mainly concerned with horticulture and written in Persia or Central Asia in the 15th century (Brit. Mus. Add. 1771, ff. 157b-269b, etc.). But Amān Allāh has introduced considerable additions, including detailed descriptions of the cultivation of Indian fruits and notices of various crops grown in India. Yet, despite certain interesting statements, Amān Allah's work is much too superficial, and he follows the *Kitāb <u>Shadj</u>arat al-nihāl* in recommending a number of quack-practices. Abu'l-Faḍl in his famous work on Akbar's administration, the *Āʾīn-i Akbarī* (ed. Blochmann, Bibl. Ind., Calcutta, 1867-77), gives much information relating to agriculture. In its detailed accounts of the provinces of Akbar's Empire, the book contains lists of prices of agricultural products, tables of revenue-rates on the various crops, and area statistics and sundry information on cultivation and irrigation.

Bibliography: Modern works only. Moreland's *India at the death of Akbar*, London 1920, also contains a description of the system of agriculture. On Mug<u>h</u>al gardens there is a charming book by C. M. Villiers Stuart, *Gardens of the Great Mughals*, London 1913. Irfan Habib's *Agrarian system of Mughal India*, Bombay 1963, may be consulted for a fuller treatment of several points touched upon in this article.

Watt's *Dictionary of economic products of India*, 6 vols., is a monumental work of reference, giving detailed historical, technical and other information on almost everything produced in India. For an examination of Indian agricultural practice see J. A. Voelcker, *Report on the improvement of Indian agriculture*, London 1893; see also the Royal Commission on Indian Agriculture, *Report*, London 1928. Modern agricultural statistics, given by districts, are available in the volumes of *The agricultural statistics of India*, issued by the Department of Revenue, etc., Government of India, at irregular intervals since 1884-5.

(IRFAN HABIB)

FILĀLĪ [see TAFILALT].

FILASṬĪN, colloquially also Falasṭīn, an Arabic adaptation of the classical Palestine (Greek Παλαιστίνη, Latin Palaestina), the land of the Philistines. The name was used by Herodotus (i, 105; ii, 106; iii, 91; iv, 39) and other Greek and Latin authors to designate the Philistine coastlands and sometimes also the territory east of it as far as the Arabian desert. After the suppression of the Jewish revolts in 70 and 132-5 A.D. and the consequent reduction in the Jewish population the name Syria Palaestina, later Palaestina, was adopted by the Romans in place of Judaea. The Roman province of Palestine was later extended by the annexation to it of other, adjoining territories. By the 5th century there were three provinces of Palestine, Palaestina Prima, with its capital at Caesarea, including Judaea, Idumaea, Samaria, and part of Peraea, Palaestina Secunda, with its capital at Scythopolis (Baysān), including the valley of Esdraelon, Galilee, and parts of the Decapolis and of Gaulanitis, and Palaestina Tertia or Salutaris, with its capital at Petra, including the Negev, Nabataea and part of the Sinai peninsula.

(ED.)

1.—PALESTINE UNDER ISLAMIC RULE.

The name of Filasṭīn was applied first to the administrative and military district (*<u>dj</u>und* [*q.v.*]) established by the Arab conquerors on the territory of the ancient Byzantine province known as *Palaestina prima*. The latter comprised roughly Samaria and Judaea with the coastal area stretching from Mt. Carmel in the north to <u>Gh</u>azza in the south. This corresponded with a fairly varied region from the geographical point of view, the largest part of which was made up of a mountainous chain of medium height, with summits rarely exceeding 1,000 metres (mountains of Samaria in the north, with Mt. Gerizim, the mountains of Judaea in the centre, and the mountain of Hebron in the south), extending to the west in a series of hills bordering the coastal plain and to the east in expanses of steppe, of which the most important was the desert of Judah.

It is difficult to reconstruct with accuracy the story of the conquest of Palestine by the Arabs. The expedition sent out by Abū Bakr and commanded by ʿAmr b. al-ʿĀṣ invaded the region of <u>Gh</u>azza in <u>Dh</u>u'l-Ḥi<u>dj</u>dja 12 or Muḥarram 13/February or March 634. After the fall of <u>Gh</u>azza, ʿAmr marched on Ḳaysariyya (Caesarea by the sea) and began to besiege it in <u>Dj</u>umādā I 13/July 634, but he was forced to retreat on the approach of a new Byzantine army, which he was ready to confront only after uniting his troops with those brought by <u>Kh</u>ālid from Syria. After the victory over the Byzantines of A<u>dj</u>nādayn [*q.v.*] in <u>Dj</u>umādā I or II/July-August 634, ʿAmr occupied most of the towns of Palestine: Sabasṭiya (Samaria), Nābulus, Ludd (Lydda), Yubnā,

ʿAmwās (Emmaus), Bayt Djibrīn and Yāfā (Jaffa). It was only after the battle of the Yarmūk [*q.v.*] that he was able to pursue the siege of Īliyā (Jerusalem, see AL-ḲUDS), whose inhabitants are said to have refused to submit to anyone but the Khalīfa himself. ʿUmar b. al-Khaṭṭāb then visited Syria for this purpose (16/637). As for the town of Ḳaysariyya, ʿAmr took up the siege again, but left it shortly afterwards to go to Egypt, leaving as his successor Yazīd b. Abī Sufyān, who, soon dying, was succeeded by his brother Muʿāwiya. It was Muʿāwiya who obtained possession of the town by betrayal in 19 or 20/640 or 641 and completed the conquest of Palestine by occupying ʿAsḳalān (Ashkelon).

The Arab conquerors permitted the previous administrative organization to continue, transforming the former *Palaestina prima* into *djund Filasṭīn*; they set up the capital first at Ludd, and then at al-Ramla, a new town which was founded by Sulayman b. ʿAbd al-Malik when he was governor of Palestine and in which he continued to reside after he had become caliph in 96/715. The *djund Filasṭīn*, still mentioned as such by Ibn Shaddād, survived until the Mongol invasion as an administrative district, but its territory appears to have been extended from the 4th/10th century onwards, both towards the east, and to the south and south-east. The geographer al-Muḳaddasī in fact counts Arīḥa (Jericho) and ʿAmmān (the ancient Philadelphia) among the towns of this district, and is followed in this by Yāḳūt. Al-Iṣṭakhrī and Ibn Ḥawḳal, for their part, join to Palestine the south of the Ghawr [*q.v.*], al-Djibāl [*q.v.*] and al-Sharāt [*q.v.*], that is to say, on the one hand the lands situated to the north of the Dead Sea, and on the other those to the south of it on the other side of the rift-valley which extends as far as the gulf of al-ʿAḳaba. Further, the vast area called al-Tīh, covering the present day Negev and Mt. Sinai, was also in practice attached to Palestine. Under the Mamlūk sultans, Palestine received a new administrative organization. It was attached more or less directly to the *niyāba* of Damascus, and comprised six districts, those of Ghazza, Ludd and Ḳāḳūn on the one hand (these three districts being sometimes considered as forming a separate *mamlaka*) and those of al-Ḳuds (Jerusalem), al-Khalīl (Hebron) and Nābulus on the other.

Palestine was particularly honoured in the Umayyad period. Muʿāwiya is reported to have had himself proclaimed caliph at Jerusalem and it was under one of his successors that the ancient court of the Temple, called the *ḥaram*, received its two principal monuments, *Ḳubbat al-Ṣakhra* and *al-Masdjid al-Aḳṣā*, both built by ʿAbd al-Malik (65-86/684-705). This caliph had the interior of the Dome of the Rock decorated with mosaics evoking the superiority of Islam over Christianity and the domination of the world by the Muslim rulers. In the ʿAbbāsid period Palestine reverted, with Syria, to the rank of a mere province; its official capital continued to be al-Ramla, but the monuments of Jerusalem maintained sufficient renown for the caliph al-Maʾmūn, inspired by hostility for the Umayyads' memory, to feel the need to substitute his own name for that of ʿAbd al-Malik in all the inscriptions commemorating the latter's foundations.

Palestine was occupied by the Fāṭimids immediately after Egypt (359/969) and thus broke free for some time from the authority of the caliphs of Baghdād, which had already become nominal under the Ṭūlūnids [*q.v.*] and then under the Ikhshīdids [*q.v.*]. But Fāṭimid rule was never firmly established there, and brief revolts ensued, of which the most spectacular was the one which led to the installation of a new ʿAlid caliph at al-Ramla by a Bedouin *amīr* of the Banu 'l-Djarrāḥ [see DJARRĀḤIDS]. Jerusalem, on the other hand, was the victim of the violent measures adopted against the Christians by al-Ḥākim, and at his command the Holy Sepulchre was destroyed. In the late 5th/11th century, Palestine was briefly occupied by the Turcoman chief Atsiz b. Uvak [*q.v.*]; shortly afterwards a minor Turkish dynasty, founded by Artuḳ [see ARTUḲIDS], occupied Jerusalem, but it was soon expelled by a Fāṭimid counter-attack (479-90/1086-98). This Fāṭimid success was nullified by the arrival of the First Crusade, which achieved the foundation of the Latin Kingdom of Jerusalem and led to the Crusaders' occupation of the Holy Places for nearly a century (492-587/1099-1187).

The Arab geographers provide some scattered information on conditions in Palestine during the period between the Arab conquest and the arrival of the Crusaders. In the 3rd/9th century Palestine was occupied by a numerous population of Arab origin (belonging to various tribes). There was, however, also a certain proportion of non-Muslims, Christians, Jews and Samaritans, the size of which we naturally cannot estimate; al-Yaʿḳūbi refers to the presence of "non-Arabs" in the town of al-Ramla. At this period the region was crossed by the pilgrimage route from Damascus; at Ayla, near the gulf of al-ʿAḳaba, this met the route followed by pilgrims from Egypt and the Maghrib; it was also a trade-route used long since for traffic with Egypt or Arabia. There was also a route connecting Jerusalem with ʿAmmān via Jericho. In the 4th/10th century Palestine was one of the most fertile regions of the province of al-Shām, since it was well watered with rain and, in the Nābulus region, boasted abundant streams. Al-Muḳaddasī informs us of its principal products, among which agricultural produce was particularly copious and prized: fruit of every kind (olives, figs, grapes, quinces, plums, apples, dates, walnuts, almonds, jujubes and bananas), some of which were exported, and crops for processing (sugar-cane, indigo and sumac). But the mineral resources were equally important: chalk earth (*al-ḥawwāra*), marble from Bayt Djibrīn, and sulphur mined in the Ghawr, not to mention the salt and bitumen of the Dead Sea. Stone, which was common in the country, was the most generally used building-material for towns of any importance. Al-Muḳaddasī also gives us brief indications of the main Muslim religious trends; there were some Shīʿīs at Nābulus, no Muʿtazilīs openly confessing their beliefs, and some well organized Karrāmīs at Jerusalem; at the end of the 4th/10th century the juridical schools followed were the Shāfiʿī and the Fāṭimī. The mediaeval geographers also notice briefly the places of pilgrimage, which were especially numerous in Jerusalem and Hebron (the town of Abraham *al-Khalīl*).

During the period of the Crusades, Palestine was the scene of battles and ambushes, periodically interrupted by the truces which were from time to time established by treaties; such a treaty is that of 626/1229 by which the Ayyūbid al-Kāmil restored the demilitarized city of Jerusalem to the Franks of Acre for ten years. This situation, which in any case became more settled after the recapture of Jerusalem by Ṣalāḥ al-Dīn, did not, however, prevent the continuation of economic interchange between Egypt and Syria; the caravans were merely subject to "transit tolls" imposed by the Franks or, in certain circumstances, were the victims of hostile raids. Nor did it prevent the establishment of fruitful commerce, particularly under the successors of Ṣalaḥ al-Dīn, between the European merchants (Italian, French or English), living mainly at Acre, and the Muslim towns of the interior. It was also at this time that Palestine was celebrated by certain Muslim writers as the especial land of Prophets, and the places of pilgrimage experienced their greatest popularity; whether at Jerusalem or at Nābulus or Hebron relics of the Biblical prophets venerated by the Muslims were not scarce, and to these were added the monument at ʿAsḳalān, reputed to contain the head of al-Ḥusayn b. ʿAlī [*q.v.*], and the tomb at G͟hazza of Hās͟him, grandfather of the Prophet.

At the end of the 7th/13th century (690/1291), the Franks, from whom the Mamlūk sultan Baybars had already taken the stronghold of ʿAsḳalān in 668/1270, were expelled by al-As͟hraf K͟halīl from their last possessions, Caesarea and Acre; thus all Palestine and the neighbouring provinces were again under Muslim rule. The territories west of the Jordan continued thus during the Mamlūk period to play an important part as a trunk route, followed as much by the merchants as by the official couriers who linked Cairo with Damascus and Aleppo along a post-road adopted and improved to permit greater despatch.

In 922/1516, after the battle of Dābiḳ, the region fell under Ottoman rule, which was to last almost without interruption until 1917-18. During the 16th century Palestine consisted of the sand͟jaḳs of G͟hazza, Jerusalem, Nābulus, Lad͟jd͟jūn and Ṣafad, all forming part of the *eyālet* of Damascus. The sand͟jaḳ of Lad͟jd͟jūn was not under an Ottoman governor but was held by the local Bedouin clan of Ṭurābāy, who revolted on more than one occasion. From the late 16th century there is a noticeable decline, due to falling standards in the administration, frequent changes of governors, attempts by local chieftains to gain independence, and the campaigns carried out on the soil of Palestine originating in neighbouring regions. As early as the end of the 10th/16th century, indeed, the little Druze state of Fak͟hr al-Dīn [*q.v.*], which controlled the districts stretching from Beirut to Mt. Carmel, attempted, between 1595 and 1634, to make itself independent of the Sublime Porte; following this episode, in about 1660 a new province distinct from that of S͟hām was created, named Ṣaydā and including the *liwā*s of Ṣafad and al-Lad͟jd͟jūn. This measure did not prevent the continued activities of local chieftains the most notable of whom, Ẓāhir Āl ʿUmar [*q.v.*], a chief of bedouin origin, established himself round ʿAkkā between 1750 and 1775. Shortly thereafter it was the turn of Aḥmad al-D͟jazzār to attempt to emancipate himself from Ottoman tutelage in the same region, though not without vigorously resisting the attacks of Napoleon Bonaparte who, although he had captured Yāfā in 1213/1799, was unable to make himself master of ʿAkkā. In the 19th century, the son of Muḥammad ʿAlī, Ibrāhīm Pās͟hā [*q.v.*], was another who desired to take Palestine and Syria from the Ottomans and thus assure his mastery over the lands of the Arabs. He captured ʿAkkā and Damascus in 1832, but in 1840 Palestine was returned to the sultan ʿAbd al-Mad͟jīd in consequence of the intervention of Britain and Austria.

During the later Ottoman period Palestine became a subject of increasing interest to the Great Powers of Europe, on economic as much as religious grounds. The custody of the Holy Places there had been acknowledged as in the hands of the Orthodox Patriarchate of Jerusalem in the 16th century and was reaffirmed at the request of Russia by firmans of 1853; the Latin clergy there also had, since the 16th century, been under the protection of France. This situation was the occasion for frequent intervention by the European States in the affairs of the Ottoman Empire. But Palestine also had European commercial factories, mainly French, such as those of Acre and Ramla, and here, as well as at Jerusalem, there resided Consuls charged with protecting their nationals by virtue of the agreements known as Capitulations [see IMTIYĀZĀT].

From the 18th century onwards, European economic penetration increased in Palestine as elsewhere in the Arab East. European products were sold there either by European merchants themselves or by Christians or Jews native to the area who sometimes, by taking a European nationality, succeeded in enjoying the advantages conferred by the Capitulations, avoiding part of the '*avania*s' to which those merchants who were Ottoman subjects were exposed and thus obtaining practically a monopoly of important trade [see BERATLĪ]. In the 19th century, Christian missions, both Catholic and Protestant, contributed in Palestine as in the Lebanon to the raising of the general level of education, while with European help modern technology began to spread; thus a French company completed the building of the first railway line, that connecting Jaffa with Jerusalem, in 1892.

Palestine had some Jewish inhabitants throughout the period of Islamic rule, though their numbers were much reduced during the Crusades. They were from time to time reinforced by immigration from other countries, notably in the 16th century. A new type of immigration began in the late 19th century, with the establishment of the first Zionist agricultural settlements in the eighteen eighties. Despite attempts by the Ottoman government to restrain it, this movement gained force. It found its ideology in Zionism, whose official beginnings may be dated 1897, when the congress inspired by Th. Herzl was held at Basle; at the beginning of the 20th century it became ever more marked, so much so that the number of Jews resident in Palestine rose from 25,000 in 1880 to 80,000 in 1914.

Bibliography: F.-M. Abel, *Géographie de la Palestine*, Paris 1933-38, especially ii, 171-4; Le Strange, *Palestine*; A.-S. Marmardji, *Textes géographiques arabes sur la Palestine*, Paris 1951, especially 95-111; N. A. Mednikov, *Palestina*, St. Petersburg 1897-1902; De Goeje, *Mémoire sur la conquête de la Syrie*, Leiden 1864; Ibn K͟hurradād͟hbih, 56-9; Ibn al-Faḳīh, 92-103; Yaʿḳūbī, *Buldān*, 328-30; Ibn Hawḳal, 111-3; Muḳaddasī, 154-5, 175, 180, 184; Balād͟hurī, *Futūḥ*, 138-44; Ṭabarī, indices; Ibn S͟haddād, *al-Aʿlāḳ al-k͟haṭīra, Liban, Jordanie, Palestine*, ed. Dahan, Damascus 1963; Ibn D͟jubayr, *Riḥla*, ed. De Goeje, 300-3; J. Richard, *Le royaume latin de Jérusalem*, Paris 1953; M. Gaudefroy-Demombynes, *La Syrie à l'époque des Mamelouks*, Paris 1923; W. Popper, *Egypt and Syria under the Circassian Sultans*, Berkeley-Los Angeles, 1955; J. Sauvaget, *La poste aux chevaux dans l'empire des Mamelouks*, Paris 1941; U. Heyd, *Ottoman documents on Palestine (1552-1615)*, Oxford 1960; R. Mantran and J. Sauvaget, *Règlements fiscaux ottomans*, Paris 1951; B. Lewis, *Studies in the Ottoman archives - I*, in *BSOAS*, xvi/3 (1954), 469-501; idem, *The Ottoman archives as a source for the history of the Arab lands*, in *JRAS*, (1951), 139-55; I. Ben-Zvi, *Ereṣ-Yisrael ve-yishūvah biyemē ha-s͟hilṭōn ha-ʿOt͟hmānī*, Jerusalem 1955; Gibb-Bowen, i/1, particularly 221-4; G. Young, *Corps de droit ottoman*, Oxford 1905; Guérin, *Description géographique, historique et archéologique de la Palestine*, Paris 1868-81; *The survey of Western Palestine*, London 1884; *The survey of Eastern Palestine*, London 1889; Parkes, *The emergence of the Jewish Problem (1898-1939)*, London 1946; L. A. Mayer, *Some principal religious buildings in Israel*, Jerusalem 1950; A. L. Tibawi, *British interests in Palestine, 1800-1901*, London 1961.

(D. Sourdel)

2. — The British Mandate

Turkish rule in Palestine ended with the First World War, which led to the dismemberment of the Ottoman Empire, ratified in 1920 by the abortive Treaty of Sèvres, and again in the Treaty of Lausanne of 1923. Great Britain, who had occupied Palestine during the war (General Allenby entered Jerusalem on 9 December 1917), had asked the League of Nations as early as 1919 to entrust her with the administration of the territory under the form of an international Mandate. The British proposal, which was amended in 1920, was approved by the Council of the League in July 1922, and the Mandate entered into force in September 1923, after the conclusion (July 1923) but before the entry into force (August 1924) of the Treaty of Lausanne, which regulated the future of the territories split off from the Ottoman Empire. Although the Mandate covered the areas on both sides of the Jordan, direct British administration was established only in the region to the west of the river. That to the east formed the Amirate of Transjordan, with an autonomous government, whose powers were limited by a treaty with Britain.

The policy of the British mandatory government in Palestine was from the beginning influenced by the promises made by Britain to the Jews to establish a Jewish National Home in Palestine. In August 1897 the Basle Congress had defined Zionism in the following formula: "the object of Zionism is the establishment for the Jewish people of a home in Palestine secured by public law". The execution of this programme was undertaken by a "Zionist Organization", which committed itself to political action, with especial encouragement from Great Britain, and which achieved a great success in 1917, when the latter declared officially that "His Majesty's Government view with favour the establishment in Palestine of a National Home for the Jewish people, and will use their best endeavours to facilitate the achievement of this object, it being clearly understood that nothing shall be done which may prejudice the civil and religious rights of existing non-Jewish communities in Palestine" (Balfour Declaration, 2 November 1917); France, Italy and the U.S.A. subsequently accepted the policy set out in the British declaration.

Parallel with the obligations Great Britain had assumed towards the Zionist Organization, she was bound by the promises of independence she had made to the Sherif Ḥusayn to encourage him to revolt against the Turks (Ḥusayn-McMahon correspondence, 1915). The British Government subsequently declared that Palestine was excluded from the territories promised to the Arabs for their independent State; in the Churchill Memorandum of June 1922, accepted by the Zionist Organization, it further stated that "the terms of the Declaration referred to do not contemplate that Palestine as a whole should be converted into a Jewish National Home, but that such a Home should be founded *in Palestine*", and gave the Arabs various assurances that an autonomous government would be established in Palestine. But the Arabs, disappointed in their hopes and disturbed by the massive immigration of Jews, who in 1939 already numbered 400,000, refused to cooperate with the Palestine administration and, under the inspiration of the Arab Higher Committee for Palestine, directed by al-Ḥād͟jd͟j Amīn al-Ḥusaynī, *muftī* of Jerusalem, reacted with violence: in 1928, 1929, 1933, 1936 and 1939 bloody disturbances broke out in Jerusalem, Jaffa and Haifa.

In spite of the Arab reaction, the Zionists pursued their efforts with success; they consolidated their international position by the creation (Zurich Congress 1929) of the "Jewish Agency", which included also representatives of non-Zionist Jews. The situation in Palestine disturbed the League of Nations Permanent Mandates Commission, which in 1930 severely condemned the British administration for failing to meet and reconcile Arab and Jewish needs. The British Government gave assurances that no more land would be put at the disposal of Jewish immigrants; this measure was, however, mitigated by an assurance given to the Zionists that there was no question of an absolute prohibition but rather of the imposition of controls on land purchase. Nevertheless, faced with unshakeable opposition from the Arabs, and obliged continually to reinforce the garrison in order to put down the disturbances, Britain was forced to give an ever more restricted interpretation to the Balfour Declaration. After a fruitless attempt to bring Arab and Jewish delegates together to settle their differences (the Round Table Conference, London, February-March 1939), the British Government published a White Paper (May 1939) which restricted Jewish land purchases and immigration and envisaged the establishment after ten years of a Palestinian State in which Arabs and Jews would share the government. The solution proposed by the British Government excluded the establishment of the Jewish National Home, and the publication of the White Paper was followed by an outburst of Jewish violence. The situation grew steadily worse during the Second World War. The Jews surviving the holocausts gazed with hope towards Palestine; the British authorities began to force the immigrants back; and the Jewish secret organizations entered on a campaign of terror against the British, who in 1946 proclaimed martial law.

Great Britain's efforts at conciliation had failed and she therefore referred the question to the United Nations Organisation. The U.N. General Assembly appointed a ten-member Special Committee in 1947. Its report was then considered by the Palestine Committee of the whole Assembly, which produced a partition plan, adopted by the Assembly on 29 November 1947, and envisaging the creation of two independent States, Arab and Jewish, and of an international zone covering the Jerusalem area under U.N. control.

The plan was accepted by the Jews but rejected by the Arabs. Arab volunteers attacked the Jewish forces, who were making efforts to occupy the areas assigned to them by the partition plan. Fighting broke out in the Jerusalem area, in which the Jewish forces gained some success; Arab opinion was moved by this to call for the intervention of the Arab regular armies; but divergencies of opinion arose in the Arab League and between the Arab governments.

On giving up the Mandate on 15 May 1948, Britain withdrew her troops from Palestine. The day before, David Ben Gurion had proclaimed the birth of the State of Israel. The Arab armies advanced, but the Jews confronted them everywhere. The Security Council imposed a truce, accepted by both Arabs and Jews, but the United Nations' efforts at conciliation ended in failure. In December 1948, the battle recommenced, but Egypt was the only Arab State fighting, for ʿIrāḳ, Syria and Transjordan withheld their troops from the operations. Despite their numerical superiority the Egyptian forces withdrew before the Jews, whom the ceasefire imposed by the Security Council halted 20 km. beyond their borders. The armistice between Israel and Egypt, signed at Rhodes on 24 February 1949, and those signed successively thereafter between Israel and Lebanon, Jordan, and Syria, put an end to the fighting between the Arabs and the Jews and established the partition of Palestine.   (P. MINGANTI)

FILIBE, Ottoman name for the town of Plovdiv in Bulgaria, situated on and around six syenite hills in the Thracian plain along the Maritsa. Called Pulpudeva by the Thracians, Philippopolis by the Greeks, Trimontium by the Romans, and Pludin by the Slavs, it was an important fortress throughout antiquity and the Middle Ages, being held successively by Byzantines, Bulgarians and Latins between the 6th and 14th centuries A.D. At the time of the Ottoman invasion of the Balkans it was in the hands of the Bulgarians. The Ottoman chroniclers record the conquest of Filibe immediately after the fall of Edirne, i.e., in about 765/1363-4. According to Saʿd al-Dīn the governor of the town attempted to resist but, not risking an open battle, was obliged to retreat to the fortress; the besiegers made a fierce onslaught and the governor was compelled to cede the town to Lālā S̲h̲āhīn. According to Ewliyā Čelebi, Filibe was besieged at seven points, bridges having been built across the Maritsa, and was taken by assault after heavy fighting. There is no doubt that the town offered stubborn resistance, but it was probably taken on terms (cf. Chalcocondyles, Bonn ed., 32). It was made the chef-lieu of the *eyālet* of Rūm-ili, with Lālā S̲h̲āhīn as the first *beglerbegi*. In registers dating from the end of the 9th/15th century, Filibe is referred to as the chef-lieu of a *wilāyet* and a *nāḥiye*, while during the first half of the 10th/16th century it figures among the nine *ḳāḍīlīḳs* (*nāḥiyes*) of the *pas̲h̲a liwāsī*. In the early 10th/16th century the town belonged partly to the *k̲h̲āṣṣ* of the Sultan and partly to the *k̲h̲āṣṣ* of Ayās Pas̲h̲a. The large revenues arising from the rice-fields (*čeltik*) in the surrounding region were farmed out as *muḳāṭaʿas*.

The colonization of Filibe and its district by Turks and Tatars was begun by Murād I. Bāyazīd I transported here nomads from Saruk̲h̲ān, and Meḥemmed I Tatars from Anatolia; one of the sons of Isfendiyār was settled here by Meḥemmed II. According to de la Broquière, the population was predominantly Bulgarian in 1433. Turkish sources show that in the early 10th/16th century Filibe had 29 Muslim and 4 Christian *maḥalle*s, and a Jewish and a Gypsy community, while in the 11th/17th century it had 23 Muslim *maḥalle*s and 7 *maḥalle*s inhabited by Bulgarians, Serbians, Jews, Greeks, etc. The surrounding region was mainly inhabited by Bulgarians. The town was the seat of a Greek metropolitan.

Situated on a large river on the main road between Belgrade and Istanbul, Filibe became, during the 10th/16th and 11th/17th centuries, an important centre of trade and industry. Rice growing flourished in the district, and the town was famous for the fine wool of the neighbourhood and for the manufacture of fine woollen cloth (*aba*). The guild of clothmakers was active and influential: its code of regulations, of the 11th/17th century, has been preserved. Merchants from all over the Ottoman Empire came to the Filibe fair; hides were bought by the merchants of Ragusa (Dubrovnik), the cloth was sold as far away as Syria and Germany, and the raw wool was taken by Venice.

The appearance of Filibe changed greatly during the period of Ottoman domination. The old fortress on the Trimontium was used by the Turks until the beginning of the 9th/15th century, but thereafter fell into ruin. The centre of the town shifted towards the north-west. New mosques, public buildings and palaces were built, notably the Ulu Djāmiʿ, the ʿImāret Djāmiʿ (of 848/1444-5, founded by S̲h̲ihāb al-Dīn Pas̲h̲a), the Kurs̲h̲un K̲h̲ān, and an extensive bazaar (9th/15th century), and the K̲h̲unkār Ḥammāmī; a clock-tower was erected on one of the hills of the town (early 11th/17th century); a new wooden bridge spanned the Maritsa, and near the town extensive stabling was built for the Imperial camels. Besides Muslim buildings, Filibe possessed a number of old churches (St. Marina, St. Constantine, St. Demetrius) and a mansion for the Metropolitan. During the 18th and 19th centuries the town flourished and acquired its predominantly Bulgarian appearance.

Bibliography: Fr. Giese, *Die altosmanische Chronik des ʿĀsiḳpas̲h̲azāde*, Leipzig 1929, 50, 66 f., 80 f., 154; Nes̲h̲rī, *Djihān-nümā* (ed. Taeschner, i, index); F. Babinger, *Die frühosmanischen Jahrbücher des Urudsch*, Hanover 1925, 21, 110; Saʿd al-Dīn, *Tādj al-tawārīk̲h̲*, i, 76 f.; Leunclavius, *Hist. Mus.*, Frankfurt 1591, cols. 337 f.; Chalcocondyles, Bonn ed., 32, 101; Ewliyā Čelebi, *Seyāḥat-nāme*, iii, 381-7; J. von Hammer, *Rumeli und Bosna*, Vienna 1812; M. T. Gökbilgin, *XV-XVI asırlarda Edirne ve Paşa Livâsı*, Istanbul 1952, index; idem, *Kanunî Sultan Süleyman devri başlarında Rumeli eyaleti* ..., in *Belleten* xx (1956), 247-94; F. Babinger, *Beiträge zur Frühgeschichte der Türkenherrschaft in Rumelien*, Vienna-Munich 1944, 49; St. Šiškov, *Plovdiv v svoeto minalo i nastojašte*, i, Plovdiv 1926; V. Peev, *Grad Plovdiv, minalo i nastojašte*, i, Plovdiv 1941; G. Rudolf-Hile and O. Rudolf, *Grad Plovdiv i negovite zgradi*, in *Izvestia na Bálgarskija archeologičeski Inst.*, viii; C. Jireček, *Die Heerstrasse von Belgrad nach Constantinopel* ..., Prague 1877, 94 f.; B. Cvetkova, *Matériel documentaire relatif aux agglomérations et aux constructions en Bulgarie aux XVe et XVIe siècles*, in *Bull. de l'Inst. d'urbanisme et d'architecture*, Sofia, vii-viii (1955), 459-518; H. J. Kissling, *Beiträge zur Kenntnis Thrakiens im 17. Jh.*, Wiesbaden 1956, 29-33. Among the descriptions of travellers (15th-19th centuries) may be mentioned: B. de la Broquière, ed. Schefer, Paris 1892, 200; K. Zen-Starine, *Jugoslavenska Akademija znanosti i unijetnosti*, x, Zagreb 1878, 213; H. Dernschwam, *Tagebuch* ..., ed. Fr. Babinger, Munich-Leipzig 1923, 20 f., 249 f.; Pigafetta-Starine, *Jug. Ak. znanosti i unijetnosti*, xxii, Zagreb 1890, 175; S. Gerlach, *Türkisches Tag-Buch*, Frankfurt 1674, 515-7. Many documents concerning the history of Filibe in Ottoman times are preserved in the Oriental Section of the National Library, Sofia.   (B. CVETKOVA)

FILORI, Ottoman name for the standard gold coins of Europe (see H. Sahillioğlu, *Bir mültezim zimem defterine göre XV. yüzyıl sonunda Osmanlı* *darphane mukataaları*, in *Ist. Ün. Iktisat Fak. Mecm.*, xxiii (1962-3), 145-218); also a tax amounting to one *filori*, in which sense it is usually referred to as *resm-i filori*. The tax, paid especially by the Eflāḳ (i.e. the semi-nomadic Vlachs of the Balkans, and especially of Serbia), was, together with other supplementary imposts, also called *Eflāḳiyye ʿādeti*.

According to the oldest surviving Ottoman *Ḳānūn* for the Eflāḳ (see H. Inalcık, *Stefan Duşan'dan Osmanlı Imperatorluğuna*, in *Fuat Köprülü armağanı*, Istanbul 1953, 222), the Eflāḳ subject to the *resm-i filori* paid one *filori* per household or family per year. Each household also paid two sheep (one ram and one ewe). According to the same *Ḳānūn*, twenty households formed one *ḳatun* or *ḳatuna*, and each *ḳatuna* was obliged to supply annually one tent (*čerge*), one cheese, three ropes (*urg̲h̲an*), six halters (*yular*), one skin-bag of butter and one sheep; but according to the *taḥrīr*-register of 873/1468 for Bosna (Istanbul Belediye Library, Cevdet collection, O 76), one *ḳatun* consisted of 50 households, and each *ḳatun* paid one tent, or 100 *aḳče* as its equivalent, and two rams, or 60 *aḳče* (for other later changes see *Kanun i Kanun-name* (Mon. Turc. Hist. Slav. Merid. Illust., i), Sarajevo 1957, 12-7; *Sulṭān Süleymān Ḳānūn-nāmesi*, *TOEM*, *ʿilāve*, 64; Ö.L. Barkan, *Kanunlar*, i, Istanbul 1943, 324-5).

The *resm-i filori* was a local tax older than the Ottoman occupation. According to the code of Stefan Dushan, each household paid to the ruler one *hyperpyron* (*careva perpera*) (at Zeta one Venetian ducat; see G. Ostrogorskij, *Pour l'histoire de la féodalité byzantine*, trans. H. Gregoire and P. Lemerle, Brussels 1954, 200, 240, 255). The Ottomans continued this taxation-system for the Eflāḳ, who had from of old been subject to a special ordinance (*jus valachicum*); but as rulers of a Muslim state they interpreted the *resm-i filori* as being equivalent to the *d̲j̲izya* [*q.v.*] prescribed by the *s̲h̲arīʿa* and to the *ʿurfī raʿiyyet rüsūmu*, from both of which the Eflāḳ were consequently exempt.

Similarly the tax of one *filori* per household which the Ottomans exacted in Hungary was nothing but the continuance of a tax formerly paid to the kings of Hungary (see the *Ḳānūn* for Lipve, of 961/1554, in Barkan, 322); this tax too was regarded as the equivalent of the *d̲j̲izya* (ibid., 304, 316).

The *resm-i filori* was usually paid in *aḳčes*, so that the number of *aḳčes* which it represented increased with the increase in the relative value of gold (45 *aḳčes* in 873/1468, 50 under Süleymān I, 70 in 974/1566, 80 in 976/1568).

In view of the lightness of this tax the Ottomans imposed military service on the Eflāḳ (cf. in this connexion the Yürük [*q.v.*]), every five households supplying one *voynuḳ* (from Slavonic *voynik*, 'soldier').

The Ottomans imposed the *filori* tax, sometimes under the name of *Eflāḳ ʿādeti*, on other groups who rendered services to the state. Thus the *raʿāya* miners in the Rudnik district paid one *filori* per household instead of *k̲h̲arād̲j̲* (*i.e.*, *d̲j̲izya*) and *ispend̲j̲e* [*q.v.*] (*Kanun i Kanun-name*, 15-6; for the Eflāḳ employed as guardians of passes (*derbendd̲j̲i*), *ibid.*, 62); towards 936/1530 the Čingene in the sand̲j̲aḳ of Semendire (Smederevo) also paid 80 *aḳče* per household under the name of *resm-i filori* (Barkan, 250); but these groups may have some connexion with the Eflāḳ.

In general the *resm-i filori* was collected by an official called *filorid̲j̲i* (*Kanun i Kanun-name*, 78, 130, 147), to be paid direct into the treasury of the Sultan, although sometimes it was allocated to the *sand̲j̲aḳ-begi*. In the 11th/17th century those subject to the *filori* tax were called *filorid̲j̲i ṭāʾifesi*, or *filorid̲j̲iyān*; in *Ḳānūns* of this period (*Ḳānūn-nāme*, Ankara Ün. DTC Fakültesi Library, I. Saip collection, MS 5120, 141) the *filorid̲j̲i* is defined as a person who is exempt from the *ʿös̲h̲ür* [see ʿUS̲H̲R] and the *raʿiyyet rüsūmu* [*q.v.*] and pays only a fixed sum annually. The *resm-i filori* was paid (in *aḳčes*) in two instalments, on the day of K̲h̲iḍr-Ilyās [*q.v.*] (23 April, O.S.) and on *Ḳāsim günü* [*q.v.*] (26 October, O.S.).

Bibliography: in the article.

(H. İNALCIK)

FILS [see FALS].

FINANCE [see BAYT AL-MĀL, DAFTARDĀR, MĀL, MĀLIYYA].

FINDIḲLI [see ISTANBUL, and SIKKA].

FINDIḲLILI MEḤMED [see SILĀḤDĀR].

FINE [see D̲J̲URM].

FINE ARTS [see FANN].

FINYĀNA, Sp. FIÑANA, a small town of some 5,000 inhabitants engaged in agriculture. It is situated in the province of Almería, about 30 km. from Guadix, in the *partido judicial* of Gérgal. It lies on the southern slope of the Sierra de Baza, which joins the Sierra Nevada on the west. It is overlooked by an ancient fortress of which only ruins remain. Within the town there was a mosque, now converted into a church where services are held. The Muslim inhabitants were *muladíes* of Hispano-Roman origin and had nobody of Arab descent among them. They lived peacefully occupied in agriculture, preferably the cultivation of mulberry trees and the rearing of silkworms. An industry grew up of which the products were highly esteemed: the manufacture of *ṭuruz*—handkerchiefs and shawls of silk and brocade. These were exported even to Christian territory and were much sought after in León, where they were known as *alfiniane* from their mark of origin. But already in the 14th century this industry and the culture on which it was based had disappeared and today no trace of it remains. During the rebellion of Ibn Ḥafṣūn the inhabitants of Finyāna showed a disposition to join him but ʿAbd al-Raḥmān III, when he occupied the *kūra* of Baza during his campaign of 300/913 against eastern Andalusia, made a diversion against Finyāna and there, on 4 S̲h̲awwāl 300/14 May 913, captured the emissaries whom Ibn Ḥafṣūn had sent to them. No more details of its mediaeval history until it was taken by the Catholic Monarchs when they won Baza are known.

Bibliography: Idrīsī, *Descr.*, text 201, tr. 246; Ḥimyarī, *al-Rawḍ al-miʿṭār*, ed. Lévi-Provençal, text 143-4, tr. 172; Lévi-Provençal, *Histoire de l'Espagne musulmane*, ii, 10; iii, 311; Sánchez Albornoz, *Estampas de la vida en León durante el siglo X*, 11-4.

(A. HUICI MIRANDA)

FIRABR, early (*e.g.*, *Ḥudūd al-ʿālam*, 113) named also Firab (Farab), in Ḳudāma (BGA vi, 203) as well as Yāḳūt (iii, 867) also called Ḳaryat ʿAlī or Ribāṭ Ṭāhir ibn ʿAlī, is a town opposite Āmul [*q.v.*, 2]. It lay a parasang north of the Oxus (Āmū Daryā, [*q.v.*]) on the road to Buk̲h̲ārā and was the centre of a fertile region with many villages as well as the seat of an inspector for water-control (*Mīr-i rūd̲h̲*: *Ḥudūd*, see above). The city was protected by a fortress and possessed a Friday-mosque and an open space for public worship (*muṣallā*) with a hostel for travellers who were also boarded there (Muḳaddasi, 291; Ibn Faḍlān, ed. Z. V. Togan, 1939, 4, § 4: written *Āf.rb.r*; cf. trans. Canard, in *AEIO Alger*, xvi (1958), 54). According to a presumably legendary account by

Abu 'l-Ḥasan ʿAbd al-Raḥman ibn Muḥammad al-Naysābūrī (Nī̲sh̲āpūrī) in his *K̲h̲azāʾin al-ʿulūm* (continuator and editor of Nars̲h̲ak̲h̲ī's description of Buk̲h̲ārā, ed. Ch. Schefer, 6, also in his *Chrestomathie persane*, 13; tr. R. N. Frye, 1954, 8 and 119, note 97) the founding of Firabr followed the conquest of Paykand by the Kök Turks towards the end of the 6th century (conjectures regarding this report in J. Markwart, *Wehrot und Arang*, Leiden 1938, 145-8; and Franz Altheim-Ruth Stiehl, *Finanzgeschichte der Spätantike*, Frankfurt 1957, 257-62, who object to an interpretation of Naysābūrī, unconfirmed by sources, in S. P. Tolstow, *Auf den Spuren der altchoresmischen Kultur*, Berlin 1953, 235 f., and other works of Tolstow mentioned there).

Bibliography: Iṣṭak̲h̲rī, 314; Ibn Ḥawḳal, 2nd ed., 489; Ibn K̲h̲urradād̲h̲bih, 25, 173; Yāḳūt, Beirut 1957, iv, 245 ff. (with the index of the scholars of this town); Le Strange, 403 ff., 443.

(B. Spuler)

FIRĀSA, a technique of inductive divination which permits the foretelling of moral conditions and psychological behaviour from external indications and physical states: *al-istidlāl bi'l-k̲h̲alḳ al-ẓāhir ʿala'l-k̲h̲ulḳ al-bāṭin* (cf. al-Rāzī, *Firāsa*, ed. Mourad, 4; Ḥād̲j̲d̲j̲ī K̲h̲alīfa, ii, p. VIII; iv, 388 ff.; al-Ḳazwīnī, i, 318; cf. Ps.-D̲j̲āḥiẓ, *ʿIrāfa*, ed. Inostrants̲e̲v, 17 ff.). These indications are provided by colours, forms and limbs; they reveal to experts the secrets of characters and minds. "Peculiarities of character cannot be concealed even if a man does his utmost to keep silence about them and to hide them; for nature unveils them and lets them show through. Sooner or later, God reveals them through the actions, movements and gestures of the man. Indeed the Ḳurʾān (XLVII, 30) says: 'And if We wish it, We shall make thee see them (= the false Muslims); thou shalt recognize them by their physiognomy (*sīmā-hum*); thou shalt recognize them by their *lapsus linguae* (*laḥn al-ḳawl*)" (Ps.-D̲j̲āḥiẓ, *op. cit.* 17). ʿAlī is related to have said: "No-one considers something within his conscience without its being revealed by the slips of his tongue or the expression of his face" (al-Ibs̲h̲īhī, *Mustaṭraf*, tr. Rat, ii, 187). It has even been said that "the eyes of servants unveil the conscience of their masters" (al-D̲j̲ināʿī, *al-Darad̲j̲a al-ʿulyā fī tafsīr al-ruʾyā*, ms. ar. Strasbourg 4212, f° 97).

Firāsa is an Islamic science whose Arab ancestor is *ḳiyāfa* (sometimes confused with *ʿiyāfa* which is essentially concerned with portents drawn from the behaviour of birds).

The classification of the sciences which are included under the name of *firāsa* bears witness to the breadth of territory which this technique of divination covers. In fact, it includes (Ḥad̲j̲d̲j̲ī K̲h̲alīfa, i, 34; cf. al-Rāzī, *op. cit.* 10 ff.; al-D̲j̲āḥiẓ, *Ḥayawān*, v, 93; Ps.-D̲j̲āḥiẓ, *ʿIrāfa*, 16): birth-marks and beauty spots (*al-s̲h̲āmāt* and *al-k̲h̲ayalān*), palmistry (*ʿilm al-asārīr* or *ʿilm al-kaff*), character as revealed from shoulder-blades (*ʿilm al-aktāf*), examination of foot-prints (*ʿilm ʿiyāfat al-at̲h̲ar*), examination of morphoscopic or genealogical lines (*ʿilm ḳiyāfat al-bas̲h̲ar*), finding one's bearings in deserts (*ʿilm al-ihtidāʾ fi 'l-barārī wa'l-ḳifār*), dowsing (*riyāfa*), detection of precious metals (*ʿilm istinbāṭ al-maʿādin*), signs foretelling rain (*ʿilm nuzūl al-g̲h̲ayt̲h̲*), the unravelling of secret analogies between present and future events (*ʿilm al-ʿirāfa*), divination by means of palm-trees (palmomancy) (*ʿilm al-ik̲h̲tilād̲j̲*).

To this divinatory meaning of *firāsa* regarded as a technique of observation of external signs betraying intentions, qualities, defects, courage, intelligence and thoughts (cf. Ps.-D̲j̲āḥiẓ, *loc. cit.*, 12-14; al-Nuwayrī, *Nihāya*, iii, 149 ff.; al-Ibs̲h̲īhī, *op. cit.*, 188 ff.), must be added a psychological meaning which gives it an intuitive and almost prophetic character. This meaning is peculiar to religious and mystical literature. It is derived from verses of the Ḳurʾān (XV, 75; XLVII, 30; XLVIII, 29) in which the term *sīmāʾ* is equivalent to *firāsa*. There appears already in these texts the idea of a divine influx which assists certain privileged persons to an intuitive understanding of the secrets of men's consciences. Tradition only enriches and develops this idea while applying it to *firāsa*. This last is then defined as "a light which God causes to penetrate the heart" or "a thing which God causes to penetrate their hearts and their tongues"; and the Prophet is made to say: "Fear the intuitive eye of the true believer, for he sees with the light of God." These definitions of *firāsa* derived from the collections of *ḥadīt̲h̲s*, are widely commented on and developed in mystical writings (cf. al-Ḳus̲h̲ayrī, *al-Risāla al-Ḳus̲h̲ayriyya*, ed. Būlāḳ 1284/1867, *Bāb al-firāsa*, 137-43). "If you converse with truthful persons," recommends Aḥmad b. ʿĀṣim al-Anṭākī, "speak the truth to them, for such persons are spies (*d̲j̲awāsīs*) of hearts; they penetrate into your heart and out again before you have realized it" (*ibid.*, 139). *Firāsa* becomes one of the distinguishing qualities (*k̲h̲awāṣṣ*) of faith, to which a close bond unites it: "He who has the deepest faith has also the most penetrating *firāsa*" (*ibid.*, 137).

Ḥadīt̲h̲ has another term even more expressive which regards *firāsa* as the fruit of inspiration (*ilhām*). The Prophet is made to say: "The nations which came before you had their inspired ones (*muḥaddat̲h̲ūn*); if there is one to be found in my nation it can only be ʿUmar (b. al-K̲h̲aṭṭāb)" (Tas̲h̲köprüzāde, *Miftāḥ al-saʿāda wa-miṣbāḥ al-siyāda*, i, 272; see also Ibn al-At̲h̲īr, *Nihāya*, i, 240; Ibn K̲h̲aldūn, *Muḳaddima*, i, 200, tr. de Slane, i, 228, tr. Rosenthal, i, 223; Ḥarīrī, *Maḳāmāt*, ed. de Sacy, 601).

Finally, *firāsa* preserves the main meaning of Arab *ḳiyāfa*, the recognition of signs of paternity. The *Ḳāʾif* was called in to settle genealogical disputes (al-Rāzī, *Firāsa*, 12 ff.; Ibn Ḳayyim al-D̲j̲awziyya, *al-Ṭuruḳ al-ḥukmiyya*, Cairo 1323, 195-213, 208; Goldziher, *Muh. St.*, i, 185). Speaking of physiognomy for the use of princes, Ibn Ḳayyim al-D̲j̲awziyya proves that the law is not based only on objective criteria but also on subjective impressions such as the deductions drawn from *firāsa* (on the controversy concerning the legal value of *firāsa*, cf. Mourad, *La physiognomie arabe*, 135 ff.).

The far-reaching development which separates *firāsa* from *ḳiyāfa* is due on the one hand to the psychological and religious elements introduced by Ḳurʾān and Tradition, and on the other hand to the translation of Greek treatises on physiognomy whose characteristics strongly influenced *firāsa*. The most important of these were the treatise of Pseudo-Aristotle called *Sirr al-asrār*, used by al-Rāzī and al-Dimas̲h̲ḳī (cf. M. Steinschneider, *Die arabischen Übersetzungen aus dem Griechischen*, Leipzig 1897, 79 ff.), that of Polemon (al-D̲j̲āḥiẓ, *Ḥayawān*, iii, 46, 83, 87 ff.; likewise Ḥād̲j̲d̲j̲ī K̲h̲alīfa, iv, 388 ff.; cf. Steinschneider, *op. cit.*, 107 ff.; a *Kitāb al-Firāsa* under the name of Filīmūn was edited at Aleppo in 1929; on this person and his work, see the excellent article by Willy Stegemann in Pauly-Wissowa, xxi, 2 (1952), col. 1320-57 (cf. col. 1345 ff.)) and that of Menas (Mīnas—Μήνας) al-Rūmī (?), *Kitāb al*

Khayalān and *Kitāb al-Shāmāt* (*Fihrist*, 314). In another connexion, Ps.-Djāḥiẓ (*ʿIrāfa*, 120) quotes Djawbar al-Hindī as the author of a treatise on *firāsa*.

Bibliography: A great number of treatises on physiognomy (in Arabic, Turkish and Persian) are to be found in the different catalogues of MSS. Among the best-known should be mentioned: *K. al-Firāsa* of Shams al-Dīn Abū ʿAbd Allāh Muḥammad b. Ibr. b. Abī Ṭālib al-Anṣārī al-Ṣūfī al-Dimashḳī (d. 727/1327) sometimes called *al-Siyāsa fī ʿilm al-firāsa* or *al-Firāsa li-adjl al-siyāsa* or again *Aḥkām al-firāsa* (cf. *ZDMG*, xxi, 384). Several copies of it are known, especially Bursa, Ḥusayn Čelebi 33, I (the second part of the manuscript contains the *Risāla fi'l-firāsa* of Yaʿḳūb b. Isḥāḳ al-Kindī; cf. O. Rescher, in *ZDMG*, lxviii (1914), 53), Aya Sofya 3782, Paris 2759, 5928, etc. The work was edited in Cairo in 1300/1882. No less famous is the treatise of Fakhr al-Dīn al-Rāzī (d. 606/1209), *Risāla fī ʿilm al-firāsa* or *Djumal aḥkām al-firāsa* (cf. MS. Aya Sofya 2457, 2, containing also the *K. al-Firāsa* of Filīmūn). The work was edited at Aleppo in 1929 by Muḥ. Rāghib al-Ṭabbākh, then re-edited, translated and annotated, with an introduction and a bibliography, by Yousef Mourad in his complementary thesis, *La Physiognomonie arabe et le 'Kitāb al-firāsa' de Fakhr al-Dīn al-Rāzī*, Paris 1939. Cf. also the treatise attributed to Djāḥiẓ called *Bāb al-ʿIrāfa wa'l-zadjr wa'l-firāsa ʿalā madhhab al-Furs*, edited, translated into Russian and annotated by K. Inostrantsev, *Materyalî iz arabskikh istočnikov dlya kulʾturnoy istorii Sasanidskoy Persii*, in *Zapiski Vostočnago Otʾdeleniya Imperatorskago Russkago Arkheologičeskago Obshčestva*, xviii (1907-8), 113-232.

(T. Fahd)

FIRʿAWN (pl. Farāʿina), Pharaoh. The Arabic form of the name may derive from the Syriac or the Ethiopic. Commentators on the Ḳurʾān (II, 46-49) explain the word as the permanent title (*laḳab*) of the Amalekite kings [see ʿamālīḳ], on the analogy of Kisrā, title of the sovereigns of Persia, and Ḳayṣar of the emperors of Byzantium. As the designation of the typical haughty and insolent tyrant, the name Firʿawn gave rise to a verb *tafarʿana* "to behave like a hardened tyrant".—If one disregards certain verses of Umayya which are probably not authentic, it was in fact the Ḳurʾān which, at the time of the first Meccan period, introduced the figure of Pharaoh (only that of Exodus) into Arabic literature. Broadly speaking, the narrative in the Ḳurʾān, so far as one can synthesize it artificially by the help of texts extending almost from the beginning of the revelation to the third year of the Medina period, covers the first fourteen chapters of the book of Exodus: the oppression of the children of Israel, the birth of Moses [see mūsā], the mission of Moses and Aaron [see hārūn], the hardening of Pharaoh's heart, Moses' miracles, the plagues, the Exodus, the crossing of the Red Sea and the drowning of Pharaoh; like all narrative elements of this sort in the Ḳurʾān, the history of Pharaoh is seen in relation to Muḥammad's own mission—the determined rejection of the divine message by the unbelievers who in the end are severely punished, while the believers among them are saved. In the fragmentary accounts given in the Ḳurʾān, certain non-biblical elements may be detected, the chief ones being the following. Firʿawn is given the name (LXXXIX, 9/10 and XXXVIII, 11/12) *dhu 'l-awtād* "master of the stakes (posts)" perhaps on account of his buildings (cf. XXVIII, 38), but this interpretation (J. Horovitz) is scarcely less uncertain than those which have been put forward by Muslim commentators. The place of Pharaoh's daughter is taken by his wife, to whom commentators give the name of Āsiya [*q.v.*]. As Pharaoh's counsellor there appears a certain Hāmān who is responsible in particular for building a tower which will enable Pharaoh to reach the God of Moses (XXVIII, 38 and XL, 38/36): the narrative in Exodus is thus modified in two respects, by misplaced recollections of both the book of Esther and the story of the tower of Babel (Genesis, xi) to which no other reference occurs in the Ḳurʾān. The unnamed believer in Pharaoh's entourage who pleaded for Mūsā (XL, 29/28 ff.) cannot be connected with any known Jewish or Christian legend, unless it be related to a vague recollection of the Aggada which makes Jethro one of Pharaoh's advisers.—The conversion of the magicians who were in consequence threatened with cruel punishments by their master is an innovation of the Ḳurʾān (cf. however Exodus, viii, 15 and x, 7), whilst Firʿawn's aspiration to divinity (XXVIII, 38) is Aggadic, as is also his conversion *in extremis*, which God rejects (X, 90-2).

Muslim tradition (both exegesis and historiography) does not confine itself to commenting on and amplifying the Ḳurʾānic version, particularly with the aid of Aggada elements. Its field of interest extends beyond that of the inspired book, and it deals with the kings of Egypt both before and after the *Firʿawn* of Mūsā, connecting them with the "Amalekites" and also, later, drawing on the stock of local legends. Thus the Firʿawn of Ibrāhīm [*q.v.*] and Yūsuf [*q.v.*] is discussed; he is given the name al-Rayyān b. al-Walīd (or al-Walīd or even Dārim b. al-Rayyān) and his successor Ḳābūs b. Muṣʿab (al-Masʿūdī, *Murūdj*, i, 92, but written al-Walīd b. Muṣʿab). Isolated traditions, regarded with utter disdain by the author of *al-Badʾ wa 'l-taʾrīkh*, attribute an Iranian origin to Firʿawn and Hāmān (al-Ṭabarī, *Tafsīr*, xx, 28: Firʿawn was a native of Iṣṭakhr; *Badʾ*, iii, 81 ff./84: Firʿawn a native of Balkh and Hāmān of Sarakhs).

The New Testament theme of the massacre of the innocents is introduced into the account of the birth of Moses, and the Midrashic legend of the proving of Moses by the crown and burning coals came into the account of the education of the future liberator of Israel who was brought up at Pharaoh's court.

Similarly, it was with the Jewish Aggada (*Abōth of Rabbi Nathan*, recension A, ch. XXVII and *Pirkey Rabbi Eliʿezer*, ch. XLII) and through it possibly to an ancient Egyptian related form that is connected the legend of the mare ridden by Gabriel which led Firʿawn's army into the abyss, the vanguard of the army being commanded by Hāmān. After the drowning of Firʿawn, whom Gabriel prevented from making his profession of faith until the very end by cramming his mouth with sea slime, Mūsā sent to Egypt a military expedition commanded by Joshua and Caleb. The *Badʾ wa 'l-taʾrīkh* (iv, 37/36) is aware that the Jews celebrate the feast of unleavened bread in memory of their delivery from the hands of Firʿawn (cf. also al-Bīrūnī, *Āthār*, ed. Sachau, 281, *Chronology*, 275), but certain traditions also exist which give the same motive for the celebration of the fast of *ʿAshūrā* by the Jews (texts quoted from G. Vajda, *Hebrew Union College Annual*, xii-xiii (1937-8), 374, but whose authenticity is rejected by al-Bīrūnī, *ibid.*, 330 ff./327 ff.).

A later Firʿawn bears the name Aʿradj "the lame"; this, no doubt, is Necho (Nekō, II Chron. xxxv and xxxvi), whose name is thus interpreted by the Jewish Aggada (Targum, also Peshiṭṭa, *Leviticus-Rabba* xx/1, ed. M. Margulies, 442); al-Masʿūdī, *Murūdj*, ii, 410, however, calls him Bilūnah. —The theological problem of the "hardening of heart" of Firʿawn did not fail to occupy the attention of the Muʿtazila (see *Badʾ*, i, 106/97 ff.). The Mystics and in particular al-Ḥallādj meditated in their fashion on the revolt and the conversion *in extremis* of Firʿawn (see L. Massignon, *La Passion d'al-Hallāj*, 357, 416, n. 1, 615, 935-9 and H. Ritter, *Das Meer der Seele*, 74 and 272), but with them also he remains one of the prototypes of pride, concupiscence and refusal to renounce self (see, *e.g.*, al-Muḥāsibī, *Riʿāya*, 236 ff. and H. Ritter, *ibid.*, 51, 98 ff., 114, 577; a more favourable view, 320).

Bibliography: Ḳurʾān, index to R. Blachère's translation, s.vv. *Pharaon, Plaies d'Egypte, Haman*; Ṭabarī, *Tafsīr* on these passages; idem, *Annales*, i, 378-9, 442-89; Yaʿḳūbī, *Historiae*, ed. Houtsma, i, 30 ff. (G. Smit, *Bijbel en Legende*, 39-44); Masʿūdī, *Murūdj*, i, 92-3; ii, 368-9, 397-8, 410-4; iii, 273; *al-Badʾ wa 'l-taʾrīkh*, ed. C. Huart, passages quoted in the article and i, 106/97-8; ii, 209/180; iii, 27-29, 93-6/95-8; iv, 72/68; Kisāʾī, ed. Eisenberg, 195-218; Thaʿlabī, *ʿArāʾis al-madjālis*, Cairo 1370/1951, 102-20; Ibn Kathīr, *Bidāya*, i, 202, 237-74.—Harawī, *Guide des lieux de pèlerinage*, ed. J. Sourdel-Thomine, index, s.v. *Firʿawn*; J. Horowitz, *Koranische Untersuchungen*, 130 ff.; A. Jeffery, *The foreign vocabulary of the Qurʾan*, 225; D. Sidersky, *Les origines des légendes musulmanes*, 73-87; H. Speyer, *Die biblischen Erzählungen im Qoran*, 1931, 224-92; Ch. G. Torrey, *The Jewish foundation of Islam*, New York 1933, 109 ff., 117 ff.; M. Gaudefroy-Demombynes, *Mahomet*, Paris 1957, 393-7; Grünbaum, *Neue Beiträge z. sem. Sagenkunde*, 152 ff.; B. Heller, *Egyptian elements in the Aggada* (in Hungarian), in *Magyar Zsido Szemle*, liv (1937), 280; G. Wiet, *L'Egypte de Murtadi*, Paris 1953, especially the Introduction, 16-47.

(A. J. Wensinck-[G. Vajda])

FIRDA [see furḍa].

FIRDAWS [see djanna].

FIRDAWSĪ (Ferdosi), Persian poet, one of the greatest writers of epic, author of the *Shāhnāma* (*Shāhnāmè*, the Book of Kings). His personal name and that of his father are variously reported (Manṣūr b. Ḥasan, according to al-Bundārī [*q.v.*]); it is agreed that his *kunya* [*q.v.*] and his pen-name were Abu 'l-Ḳāsim Firdawsī. According to Niẓāmī ʿArūḍī, the oldest source (*Čahār maḳāla*, tr. E. G. Browne, 54), he was born at Bāzh, a village in the Tabaran quarter of Ṭūs [*q.v.*]. The date of his birth (ca. 329-30/940-1) is reliably deduced from his statement that in the year of the accession of Sultan Maḥmūd (387/997) he was 58 years old (*Shāhnāma*, ed. Mohl, iv, 8). Sprung from a family of *dihḳāns* [*q.v.*], he was, according to Niẓāmī ʿArūḍī, a man of influence in his village, of independent means thanks to the revenues from his lands. Numerous passages of his work reveal his love for Iran. He was certainly acquainted with Arabic; and early in life had acquired a deep knowledge of the history and the legends concerning Iran, to which his family environment had predisposed him. Until he had exhausted his resources by devoting them to his work, he made no approach to the rulers of his day. The writing of the *Shāhnāma* was undertaken no doubt after the assassination of Daḳīḳī (ca. 370/980); before this he had tried out his talents in composing some epic passages and some lyric poems, of which a few have survived. At the beginning of his epic he speaks of how Daḳīḳī had begun to put into verse an ancient book, of how this work was prematurely interrupted by Daḳīḳī's death, and how a friend had procured the book for him (ed. Mohl, i, 16-20). For several episodes he had other sources, for the story of Bijen and Manīja, for example (for which he followed a manuscript which a woman-friend read to him, ed. Mohl, iii, 293-4), and for the death of the hero Rustam (following a redaction by Āzād Sarw, ed. Mohl, iv, 701). In spite of great political upheavals, recounted by the historians, his *Shāhnāma* was undertaken by 370-1/980-1 at the latest.

In the course of the 4th/10th century, the Iranians, reviving a pre-Islamic custom, had applied themselves to gathering the historical facts and the legends concerning their national history. Collections were made in imitation of the Pahlavi *Khwatāy-nāmak* (Book of Rulers) composed towards the end of the Sāsānid period (Christensen, *L'Iran sous les Sassanides*, 54), which is lost, as are Arabic translations of it. Ancient tales were assembled in other collections. The oldest and most famous of the prose works of the 4th/10th century is the *Shāhnāma* of Abu 'l-Muʾayyad Balkhī, a collection of heroic traditions which is echoed here and there in Firdawsī's epic and in some historical works (notably a fragment in the *Taʾrīkh-i Sīstān*, Tehrān ed., 35). Another *Shāhnāma* is that of Abū ʿAlī Muḥammad b. Aḥmad al-Balkhī, praised by al-Bīrūnī (*al-Āthār al-bāḳiya*, Leipzig ed., 99), which derives particularly from written sources, translated from Pahlavi into Arabic, but lost. The third important *Shāhnāma* known to us is that to which Firdawsī refers in his introduction (ed. Mohl, i, 17-8): the *pahlavān* of whom he there speaks was probably Abū Manṣūr Muḥammad b. ʿAbd al-Razzāḳ, governor of Ṭūs in about 335/946; he gathered together men who knew the history and the ancient legends and ordered them to compose a *Shāhnāma* under the supervision of his vizier, Abū Manṣūr Muḥammad al-Maʿmarī (preface to Abū Manṣūr's *Shāhnāma*, dated 346/957, published by Muḥammad Ḳazwīnī in *Bīst maḳāla*, ii, Tehrān 1313/1935, 24-25); their work was used by Daḳīḳī (about a thousand of whose verses were incorporated by Firdawsī in his *Shāhnāma*), then by Firdawsī, then by al-Thaʿālibī (d. 429/1038). Besides these, there existed other documents and traditions which were treated by epic poets who came after Firdawsī (notably on the heroes Garshāsp, Bārzū, Sām [see ḥamāsa]).

At Ṭūs, various persons whom Firdawsī names had supported him in his work, but he was looking for a more powerful protector to whom to dedicate his work. Finally he chose the greatest monarch of the age, Sultan Maḥmūd of Ghazna; this was probably when he was about 65 years old (ed. Mohl, iv, 8), in 394/1004, when he found himself in straitened circumstances (ed. Mohl, *loc. cit.*, and vii, 500).

The Arabic translation of the *Shāhnāma* by al-Bundārī and the *Ghurar akhbār mulūk al-Furs* of al-Thaʿālibī (which uses sources identical with, or at least very close to, those of Firdawsī) omit several episodes found in Firdawsī's work; it may therefore be agreed that the final redaction of the *Shāhnāma* was preceded by a less complete redaction; furthermore, al-Bundārī's translation and some manuscripts give on the last leaf the date 384/994, and not that of the final completion (400/1010).

Maḥmūd was a man of little erudition, but gathered at his court, even by force, men of learning and letters and particularly panegyrists. His attention was perhaps first drawn to Firdawsī by Abu 'l-ʿAbbās Faḍl b. Aḥmad al-Isfarāyinī, who was his first vizier (from 384/994 until 401/1010) and whose kindness is praised in the *Shāhnāma* (ed. Mohl, iv, 7-8). No doubt Firdawsī had composed various sections of his work, not in a systematic order but as inspiration came to him and inclination prompted; afterwards he linked them together by passages of transition; he then, as his fame spread, set about revising and polishing his epic. At the end of his poem (ed. Mohl, vii, 500) he states: "When I had passed the age of 65 years, the care of my sufferings increased; I was occupied always with the history of the kings"; great men were having copies of his epic made, "but I received in return only praise". (He adds that three noble inhabitants of Ṭūs provided him with material help and encouragement). In the course of this revision, followed by the making of a fair-copy by a copyist, he probably inserted or amplified the passages in which Maḥmūd is praised (one of these eulogies, for example, was inserted after the composition of the account of the death of Rustam, for the poet speaks in it of his old age and his infirmities: ed. Mohl, iv, 702). At this point his protector, the vizier Faḍl b. Aḥmad al-Isfarāyinī, was dismissed; the poet was left without a supporter and his work was ill-received when he presented it to the sultan. Various stories have been handed down concerning his journey to Ghazna and the presentation of the poem, but they are not reliable: all that is to be accepted is that the journey took place, and that it resulted in a disappointment, expressed by Firdawsī in the words: "Such a monarch, so generous, shining among the sovereigns, did not cast a glance at my poem: the fault lies with slanderers and with ill-fortune" (ed. Mohl, vii, 294). According to a tradition frequently repeated (it is given by Niẓāmī ʿArūḍī), Maḥmūd had promised one *dīnār* for each verse, but gave only a *dirham*. Firdawsī, offended at the contrast between this reward and those heaped on the panegyrists living at the court, divided the sum he received among three persons before abruptly leaving Ghazna. One of his biographers claims that he worked on his epic for some months at the court of Maḥmūd, who loaded him with honours; this report, like other similar ones, is not to be accepted: Firdawsī travelled to Ghazna simply to present his work. On reading the biographers, one is led to presume that the chief cause of Firdawsī's dissatisfaction was the inadequacy of his reward. But the causes of misunderstanding between the sultan and the poet were more serious. In the first place, Firdawsī was a Shīʿī and Maḥmūd a Sunnī—each enthusiastically; according to Niẓāmī ʿArūḍī, the poet was accused of being a *Muʿtazilī* and a *Rāfiḍī* (a 'rejecter' of Sunnism), and he quotes in support some verses of Firdawsī (*op. cit.*, 56); as for his Shīʿism, Firdawsī does not announce it directly but allows it to be inferred in the introduction of his poem (ed. Mohl, i, 14-6). Futhermore, he had in his poem praised a vizier who had fallen out of favour, thus laying himself open to misrepresentation by his detractors. Finally, and most important, the poet could not tolerate the sultan's lack of interest ("Such a monarch ... did not cast a glance at my poem"): Maḥmūd appreciated only lyric poems, and particularly those devoted to his praise—slight and frivolous works in comparison with a vast and powerful epic.

According to Niẓāmī ʿArūḍī (p. 57), Firdawsī, on leaving Ghazna, spent six months at Herāt, returned to Ṭūs, and then went to Ṭabaristān to the court of the prince Shahriyār. It is impossible to confirm the truth of this. Moreover a legend gradually grew up on the relations between Maḥmūd and Firdawsī, but it is impossible to give credence to its account of how the poet, loaded with honours, stayed for a long time at the court of Maḥmūd, and of the sultan's belated change of heart. This very romantic legend, given authority by the preface to the *Shāhnāma* written by the Tīmūrid prince Baysunghur (829/1426), was used by Macan and Mohl in the prefaces to their editions. Firdawsī is said to have written a satire against Maḥmūd (published in the editions and translated by Mohl, i, introd.); it is said that Shahriyār pacified him and advised him to leave intact the passages of the *Shāhnāma* composed in praise of Maḥmūd, and that of his satire there remain only six authentic verses, quoted by Niẓāmī ʿArūḍī; but the text of it as given in the manuscripts varies in length up to as many as a hundred verses, including some borrowed here and there from the *Shāhnāma*. These satirical verses, examined as a whole, show the same qualities of style and composition as the *Shāhnāma*, so that it would be rash to affirm that they are not authentic (cf. Nöldeke, *Gr. I. Ph.*, ii, 155 ff.).

The date when he finally completed his epic is recorded on its last page: "When I was 71 years of age the heavens paid homage to my poem; for 35 years, in this transient world, I composed my work in the hope of a reward; as my efforts were spent for nothing, these 35 years were without result; now I am nearly 80 and all my hope has gone with the wind. The last episode of my epic was completed on the day of *ard* of the month of *isfendarmadh*, five times 80 years of the Hidjra having elapsed" (therefore in 400/25 February 1010). In other words, he had completed his poem at the age of 71 (in 400 A.H.), and when he was nearly 80 he added to it a note of the date of completion. He spent his last years at Ṭūs. According to Dawlatshāh, he died in 411/1020. Perhaps, as Nöldeke assumes (*loc. cit.*), the satire against Maḥmūd was found among his papers and communicated to various people who spread copies of it around. According to Niẓāmī ʿArūḍī, he was refused burial in a Muslim cemetary because he was a *Rāfiḍī*; he was buried in a garden which belonged to him (on his grave and on his present mausoleum, see ṬŪS).

In a manuscript in the British Museum (text and tr. in Nāṣir-i Khusraw, *Safar-nāma*, ed. and tr. Ch. Schefer; text reproduced with emendations in Firdawsī, *Shāhnāma*, Tehrān 1935, vii, 3019), it is related that Firdawsī made in 384/994 a journey to Iṣfahān and Baghdād, and that he offered to the *amīr* of ʿIrāḳ his poem *Yūsuf u-Zalīkhā* [*q.v.*]: Nöldeke (*Gr. I. Ph.*, ii, 229 ff.) and S. H. Taḳīzāda (in the review *Kāveh*, 1921, no. 10) have praised this poem, whose attribution to Firdawsī is now questioned (Z. Safa, *Taʾrīkh*, ii, 477) for several reasons, notably the presence of many more Arabic words than are found in the *Shāhnāma*, apart from peculiarities of style. In any case this journey to ʿIrāḳ seems doubtful. The death of a son at the age of 37 (the poet being then 65) inspired some sublime verses (ed. Mohl, vii, 190). Niẓāmī ʿArūḍī says that he had a devoted daughter, of whom however he makes no mention. Such are the generally accepted facts and dates of the life of Firdawsī.

It is impossible to give more than a brief outline of the vast S̲h̲āhnāma (amounting in several manuscripts to some 60,000 verses). It begins with the creation of the universe; some time later the first kings of Iran were reigning, benefactors of humanity for which they established the various elements of social life, at the same time struggling against the demons which infest the world. For more than a thousand years these good and evil powers confronted each other in an unremitting duel full of dramatic episodes. At last one of these mythical kings established a general peace for half a century; but after his death his three sons, among whom he had shared out the civilized world, could not agree, and one of them, who ruled over Iran, was treacherously assassinated by his brothers. This murder begins an endless cycle of revenge: a merciless war is waged for several centuries between the settled Iranians and the nomadic Turanians of Central Asia. Whether he is describing pitched battles, skirmishes or single combats, the poet exhibits an unequalled skill in varying the situations, and in maintaining a note of the most ardent patriotism, which does not however lead him to belittle the bravery of the enemy: throughout the poem the adversaries are worthy of each other. This cycle of wars is divided into several "gestes", corresponding to the exploits of the heroes who dominate the action—heroes of superhuman proportions and strength, among whom the famous Rustam stands out. This epic, while dealing mainly with war, contains some splendid love-stories, by which Firdawsī, the incomparable creator of the national epic, became at the same time the founder of the romantic narrative poem which was to have such a brilliant future in Persia. His sensibility, as lively as it is deep, shows itself in a series of sentimental episodes where paroxysms of passion alternate with those of despair. While two-thirds of the poem are essentially heroic and legendary, the last part is more historical and recounts poetically the reigns of the Sāsānid kings; this part is the product of the poet's old age, whence the numerous moral reflexions and the digressions on politics and metaphysics. Firdawsī's ideas would demand a lengthy study. His view of the universe is entirely pessimistic; an implacable fate, the sister of that which dominates Greek tragedy, hangs over the principal actors of the epic until the final catastrophe in which ancient Iran perishes. Yet man must ceaselessly struggle against fate: Firdawsī's moral philosophy (which corresponds, though not deliberately, with that of the Avesta) vehemently preaches action and the love of good, which uphold in man reason—his unique privilege and his true claim to superiority over all other beings. Reason must always guide us: it teaches us to accept the (sometimes only apparent) injustice of fate and enables man to retain that feeling of tender sympathy which Firdawsī himself so often shows for luckless heroes and for suffering animals; for the character of this poet as a man is in harmony with his exceptional gifts as an artist—nobility and purity of heart, family affection, complete self-sacrifice for the sake of his work, love of glory, kindness to the weak and the defeated, ardent patriotism, religious tolerance and a profound sense of the Divine. In short, he combines harmoniously what he drew from his sources with what he owed to personal inspiration and he made magnificent use of the gifts which he possessed. As for his style, whether in the fantastic elements demanded by the epic of the supernatural or in the gracefulness of descriptions of the countryside or in heroic episodes,

he excels at describing and explaining the facts and at expressing sentiments and ideas in a clear and simple language, firm but eloquent, and remarkable for the aptness of the terms used and the nobility of the thoughts. The level of expression is always equal to that of the ideas, which does not preclude the generous use of images; he varies his expressions according to the type and rank of the characters; he sometimes uses the different rhetorical figures common in the East, but not to excess, and his style remains sober even among the exaggerations proper to the epic genre. There are very few Arabic words in the poem: he wanted to revive the ancient Iran, but to do it in the Iranian tongue, remaining faithful to his sources; it is in the story of Alexander the Great that most Arabic words are to be found (for he was using a non-Iranian source, translated into Pahlavi [see ISKANDAR NĀMA]). His influence on Persian literature and indeed on the spirit of the people of Iran has been as profound as it has been lasting, and in itself would merit a serious study; in particular it led to the writing of numerous epics which, though not the equal of his own, are of real (and still insufficiently recognized) interest from the points of view both of literature and of folklore [see ḤAMĀSA].

Bibliography: A full bibliography would itself constitute a detailed study. Complete editions of the S̲h̲āhnāma: Turner Macan, The Shah-Nama ..., Calcutta 1829, 4 vols.; J. Mohl, Le Livre des Rois ..., text and French translation, Paris 1838-78, 7 vols., and translation alone, Paris 1876-8, 7 vols.; J. A. Vullers and Landauer, Liber Regum ..., Leyden 1877-84, 3 vols. (incomplete). These three editions were used for the Firdawsī Millenary edition (with notes and variants, Tehrān, Beroukhim, 1934-5, 9 vols.), which is now the most easily accessible (it gives the pagination of the Calcutta and Paris editions at the head of each page). Parts i and ii of a critical text prepared under the editorship of E. E. Bertels appeared in Moscow in 1960 and 1961. Besides Mohl's translation, it has been translated into Italian verse by Pizzi (Turin 1886-8), into German by F. Rückert (Berlin 1890-5), into Gudjarātī by J. J. Modi (Bombay 1897-1904), into English by A. G. and E. Warner (London 1905-12), into Danish (selections) by Arthur Christensen (Copenhagen 1931); many sections have been translated into various languages. An Arabic prose version was made by AL-BUNDĀRĪ [q.v.]. The essential study on the poet and his work (still of value although out of date on certain points) is Nöldeke, Das Iranische Nationalepos, in Gr. I. Ph., ii, Persian translation, Ḥamāsa-i millī-i Īrān, Tehrān 1327), to which is to be added Éthé, Firdausi als Lyriker, in München. Sitzungsberichte, 1872, 275-304, and 1873, 623-53. In Persian there are the notable works of Z. A. Safa, Ḥamāsa-sarāyī dar Īrān and Taʾrīkh̲-i adabiyyāt dar Īrān, ii. Finally, numerous articles and studies assembled in volumes or dispersed in periodicals, published in Iran and other countries. See further IA (Firdevsi, by H. Ritter), and Pearson 774-5.   (CL. HUART-[H. MASSÉ])

There are three principal translations of the S̲h̲āhnāma in Ottoman Turkish: (1) a prose version, completed by an unidentified writer in 854/1450-1 (Flügel, Die ... Handschriften des Kais.-kön. Hofbibl. zu Wien, i, 495; F. E. Karatay, Topkapı Sarayı ... türkçe yazmalar kataloğu, Istanbul 1961, no. 2154; cf. Blochet, Cat. des manuscrits turcs, ii, 220); (2) a verse translation (in hazad̲j̲ metre) made in Egypt by a certain Sherīf or Sherīfī, a member of the entourage of Prince Djem, who spent ten years on the task before presenting his work to Sultan Ḳānṣūh Ghūrī (see Rieu, *CTM*, 152; W. D. Smirnow, *Manuscrits turcs* ..., St. Petersburg 1897, 78-82; the presentation-copy, completed in 916/1510, is in the Topkapı Sarayı at Istanbul, MS Hazine 1519, see Karatay, no. 2155); (3) another prose version made early in the 11th/17th century for ʿOthmān II by Derwīsh Ḥasan, Medḥī [*q.v.*] (see Blochet, i, 314; Smirnow, 82-7). There is a translation into modern Turkish (in the series '*Dünya edebiyatından tercümeler*') by N. Lûgal and K. Akyüz, 3 vols., Istanbul 1945. There are at least two translations into Özbek Turkish (see Blochet, ii, 129; *Firdausī Celebration* ..., ed. D. E. Smith, New York 1936, 93 f.). For the influence of the *Shāhnāma* upon Turkish popular literature see Irène Mélikoff, *Abū Muslim* ..., Paris 1962, ch. 1.

To compose '*Shāhnāmes*' in praise of the Ottoman sultan became the vogue under Meḥemmed II, and in the second half of the 10th/16th century the official historiographer-panegyrists of the court were known as '*shehnāme-khwān*' [see LOḲMĀN, SAYYID]. (V. L. MÉNAGE)

FIRDEWSĪ, called RŪMĪ also UZUN or ṬAWĪL (857/1453- ?). Turkish poet and polymath, author of the voluminous *Süleymānnāme* (the Book of Solomon). He was probably born in Aydïndjïk, where he spent his childhood, and educated at Bursa, where he had as master the poet Melīḥī, and lived for a while at Balïkesir. According to information in the introduction of a *Süleymānnāme* copy, seen by M. Fuad Köprülü (see Bibl.) but now unavailable, his ancestors were all illustrious men of arms who served the Empire from ʿOthmān I onwards, and his father Ḥādjdjī Genek Bey was given the fief of Aydïndjïk for his services at the conquest of Istanbul. He is the author and translator of many books of very diverse subjects of which only some have come down to us. But he is particularly known for his *Süleymānnāme*, an encyclopaedic work in verse and prose which includes all contemporary knowledge on history, genealogy, philosophy, geometry, medicine, etc., and all the tales and anecdotes, found in religious literature, concerning Solomon. In its 81st volume he himself tells how he came to write the book: in the year 876/1472 he translated a portion of Firdawsī's *Shāhnāma* into Turkish verse and presented it to Meḥemmed II through Maḥmūd Pasha, the Grand-Vizier. The Sultan, remarking that the *Shāhnāma* was widely known and that it was unnecessary to repeat it, encouraged the poet to write a book on Solomon. Firdewsī searched for sources in the Imperial Library and toured Anatolia. He based his first three volumes on the biblical David legend and the next three on a Persian book of Solomon which he had bought from an Arab at Niksar. He presented the first six volumes of his work to Meḥemmed II, who promised a reward when the work was completed. The Sultan however died while Firdewsī was writing the seventh volume. Eventually Bāyezīd II came to hear of this and asked for a copy. The first 82 volumes were submitted to the Imperial Library except for this 81st volume which somehow, owing to the copyist's error, was not. It was eventually submitted to Selīm I (*Süleymānnāme*, 81st volume, Millet Kütüphanesi, Tarih-Coğrafa Yazmaları no. 317, 3b-4a and 123a).

Firdewsī had planned his enormous work originally in 366 volumes divided into 1830 *medjlis*, as he states at the end of certain early volumes (see for instance Topkapı Sarayı, Hazine K. no. 1525, 287b), and asked God for health and long life to be able to complete the work. Upon completion each volume was duly presented to the Imperial Library. Uzun Firdewsī continued to write at Bāyezīd II's order (whom incidentally he refers to as *Ildirim*) and speaks of himself as an aged man (*pīr*). He says that he has devoted 40-50 years of his life to the compilation of the book, writing most of it at Balïkesir (Topkapı Sarayı, Koğuşlar K. 892, 83a). From these circumstances no doubt arises Laṭīfī's tradition, later repeated by most sources, that Bāyezīd II chose only 80 parts and had the rest destroyed.

At the end of the 79th volume Firdewsī reduces his plan to 99 volumes from the original 366 (Topkapı Sarayı, Hazine K., no. 1537, 387a). This revised plan is repeated at the end of volumes 80 and 81. There is also reference to intrigues and rivals. We have no indication whether he was able to write the remaining 17 volumes. No library possesses a complete set. The best set is at the Topkapı Sarayı Library. The style of the *Süleymānnāme* is very much like that of popular story books of the period though more repetitive and less vivid.

Bibliography: Laṭīfī, *Tedhkire* s.v.; Bursalï Ṭāhir, *ʿOthmanlï Müʾellifleri*, ii/2, 357; Babinger, *GOW*, 32; *Istanbul Kütüphaneleri Tarih-Coğrafya yazmaları Kataloğu*, Istanbul 1944, II, 147; M. Fuad Köprülü in *IA*, s.v. (with critical bibliography and list of works); Fehmi Edhem Karatay, *Topkapı Sarayı Müzesi Kütüphanesi Türkçe yazmalar kataloğu*, Istanbul 1961, ii, 290-2.

(FAHİR İZ)

FIRE [see NĀR], GREEK FIRE [see BĀRŪD and NAFṬ].

FIREWORKS [see SHENLIK].

FIRISHTA [see MALʾAK].

FIRISHTA, by-name of MUḤAMMAD ḲĀSIM HINDŪ SHĀH ASTARĀBĀDĪ, Indo-Muslim historian, writer on Indian medicine and servant of the Aḥmadnagar and Bīdjāpūrī sultanates. As Storey (whose account of Firishta's biography is followed here) states, the date and place of his birth remain conjectural but the context of *Gulshan-i Ibrāhīmī*, Bombay ed., ii, 288, suggests that Firishta was probably born a few years before 980/1572. His father was one Ghulām ʿAlī Hindū-Shāh. That Firishta was to be found among the *gharībān* and *gharīb-zādahā* the 'foreigners' and their descendants who migrated for safety to Bīdjāpūr in 997/1589 (*Gulshan-i Ibrāhīmī*, ii, 295) suggests that his family was of recent domicile in Aḥmadnagar. He was a Shīʿī (*Gulshan*, i, 27). Entering the service of Murtaḍā Niẓām Shāh (972-96/1565-88) [*q.v.*] Firishta was employed as a member of the royal guard. Commissioned by Murtaḍā Niẓām Shāh to discover why an army, gathered by the *waḳīl* and *peshwa* Mīrzā Khān ostensibly to resist invasion by Bīdjāpūr, had remained immobile, Firishta discovered a plot between Mīrzā Khān and the Bīdjāpūrī 'regent' Dilāwar Khān to depose Murtaḍā Niẓām Shāh in favour of his son Mīrān Ḥusayn. Firishta warned Murtaḍā but was unable to save him from assassination. Firishta himself only escaped death through Mīrān Ḥusayn recognizing his claims as a former school-fellow. A forced migration of *gharībān* from Aḥmadnagar to Bīdjāpūr in 997/1589 followed the murder of Mīrān Ḥusayn and on 19 Ṣafar 998/28 December 1589 Firishta was presented at the Bīdjāpūrī court and on 1 Rabīʿ I 998/8 January 1590 took service under Ibrāhīm ʿĀdil Shāh. Later that year Firishta acted as a go-between for Burhān

Niẓām Shāh who was seeking Bīdjāpūrī support for the deposition of his son Ismāʿīl. In the subsequent struggle between the forces of Bīdjāpūr and Aḥmadnagar, Firishta was wounded and captured, but escaped. In Radjab 998/May-June 1590 he accompanied Ibrāhīm ʿĀdil Shāh on his night excursion to remove the 'regent' Dilāwar Khān. In Ṣafar 1013/July 1604 Firishta accompanied Bēgam Sulṭān, daughter of Ibrāhīm ʿĀdil Shāh, upon her journey to marry Akbar's son Dāniyāl. At the beginning of Djahāngīr's reign, Firishta was sent upon some unspecified mission to Lahore. Unless the reference to the death of Bahādur Khān Fārūḳī at Āgra in 1033/1623-4 was inserted by a later hand, Firishta was still alive in that year.

Firishta's reputation rests upon his well-known history the *Gulshan-i Ibrāhīmī*, extant in two recensions, the first dated 1015/1606-7 and the second, with a new title, *Ta'rīkh-i Nawras-nāma*, dated 1018/1609-10. The *Gulshan-i Ibrāhīmī* sets out (i, 4) to narrate the annals of the *pādshāhān-i Islām* and the biographies of the *mashā'ikh* who have been connected with the ordering (*niẓām*) of the countries of Hindustān (*mamālik-i Hindūstān*) from Sebüktigīn of Ghazna onward. The annals (*wāḳiʿāt*) are prefaced by a *muḳaddima* giving an abstract of Hindū history and are followed with a *khāṭima* on the geography of Hindustān, on Hindū chronometry and on the great Hindū *rādjās* of Firishta's time who keep their territories, Firishta says (ii, 788), on payment of tribute.

The typical *genres* of Indo-Muslim historiography in Firishta's day were the general history of Muslim rulers from the time of the Prophet and the regional history of the significant behaviour of Muslim rulers and saints in Hindustān since the Ghaznavid invasions. 9th/15th century Persian models appear to have been important in the universal histories that were written under the Mughals and under the sultanate of Gudjarāt, with lines of influence running from the *Rawḍat al-ṣafā* through Khʷānd Amīr's *Khulāṣat al-akhbār* (905/1500) and *Ḥabīb al-siyar* (c. 930/1524) to the *Ta'rīkh-i alfī*, commissioned by Akbar in 993/1585, and from the *Rawḍat al-ṣafā* through ʿAbd al-Karīm b. Muḥammad al-Namīdīhī's (?) *al-Ṭabaḳāt al-Maḥmūd Shāhiyya* (c. 905/1490-1500) and Fayḍ Allāh Banbānī's *Ta'rīkh-i Ṣadr-i Djahān* (c. 907/1501-2) (both authors being in the service of Maḥmūd Shāh Bēgṛā). Akbar had stimulated the production of regional histories both by sponsoring the writing of those which might serve to link his rule psychologically with that of pre-Mughal Muslim sultans in India, *e.g.*, ʿAbbās Khān Sarwānī's *Tuḥfa-yi Akbar-Shāhī* (c. 987/1579) and Abu 'l-Faḍl's *Akbar-nāma*, and by re-creating a great regional empire which needed to be matched by a great regional history—*e.g.*, Niẓām al-Dīn Aḥmad's *Ṭabaḳāt-i Akbarī* (1001/1592-3). Firishta himself, acquainted with both al-Namīdīhī's and Banbānī's work, states (ii, 153-4) that Ibrāhīm ʿĀdil Shāh gave him a copy of *Rawḍat al-ṣafā* and encouraged him to write the annals of the countries of Hind and to include more data on the sultans of the Deccan than Niẓām al-Dīn Aḥmad had done in his *Ṭabaḳāt*.

The *Gulshan-i Ibrāhīmī* is an annalistic compilation from earlier histories, oral tradition and Firishta's own eyewitness, intended for the edification of Muslims. It is an adaptation and extension of the *Ṭabaḳāt-i Akbarī*, an imitation rather than a copy. Thus Firishta's abstract of pre-Muslim Hindū history and his account of early Arab movements towards Hindustān, of the origin of the Afghāns and of their deeds between Arab penetration of the Kābul valley and the reign of Sebüktigīn of Ghazna, supplement Niẓām al-Dīn. In his use of data, Firishta follows no consistent principle. Thus (i, 104) he corrupts the late tradition in *Ta'rīkh-i Alfī* and in *Ṭabaḳāt-i Akbarī* by calling the assassins of Muḥammad b. Sām of Ghor at Damyak in 602/1206 (Hindū) 'Ghakkars' and does not assess the statements in the near-contemporary *Tādj al-ma'āthir* and the rather later *Ṭabaḳāt-i Nāṣirī* (listed by Firishta as among his sources) that they were *mulāḥida*. (See H. G. Raverty, trans. *Ṭabaḳāt-i Nāṣirī*, i, London 1881, 485 n. 3). Firishta sometimes behaves as a mere copyist of the *Ṭabaḳāt-i Akbarī*; thus he copies (i, 122) Niẓām al-Dīn's misstatement, *Ṭabaḳāt-i Akbarī*, i, Calcutta 1927, 72, (probably derived from a faulty MS of the *Ṭabaḳāt-i Nāṣirī*) that in 642/4 Čingīz Khān invaded Lakhnawtī. (See Raverty, *op. cit.* 665 n. 8). In going behind Niẓām al-Dīn to their common sources Firishta is often arbitrary. He follows Yaḥyā b. Aḥmad Sirhindī's *Ta'rīkh-i Mubārak Shāhī*, Calcutta 1931, 92, in dating the accession of Ghiyāth al-Dīn Tughluḳ in 721/1321, in preference to Baranī's 720/1320 (*Ta'rīkh-i Fīrūz Shāhī*, Calcutta 1862, 425), the date followed by the *Ṭabaḳāt-i Akbarī* (92) and which is supported by the numismatic evidence. Firishta appears to have seen the sources of the *Ṭabaḳāt-i Akbarī* independently. His account (i, 183) of the dialogue between the *kotwāl* of Dihlī and Sultan ʿAlā' al-Dīn Khaldjī (i, 183) is textually closer to that of Baranī (264-5) than to that of the *Ṭabaḳāt* (145). Firishta glosses his sources without explanation. Thus he speaks (i, 240) of Muḥammad b. Tughluḳ's intention to conquer the *wilāyat-i Čīn* when Baranī (477), and following him Niẓām al-Dīn (102), refer to an expedition to conquer the mountain of Ḳarāčil between India and China. Occasionally, in handling his data, Firishta shows independence of mind. He imputes (i, 238) Baranī's silence about a reported invasion of Muḥammad b. Tughluḳ's territories by Tarmashīrīn of Transoxania to his position in the reign of Muḥammad's successor, Fīrūz Shāh (an imputation which, in the light of Baranī's strong criticism of Muḥammad, seems invalid). He attempts (i, 235) to assess the truth behind the conflicting accounts of the death of Ghiyāth al-Dīn Tughluḳ in 725/1325, before concluding that the real truth is with God. To supplement his written data, Firishta draws upon oral tradition personally ascertained. His account (i, 230-1) of the origin of Ghiyāth al-Dīn Tughluḳ is based on personal inquiries at Lahore during his visit there at the beginning of Djahāngīr's reign.

Firishta evinces the same characteristics as an annalist of the Muslim sultanates of the Deccan. The story of the Ottoman origin of Yūsuf ʿĀdil Shāh of Bīdjāpūr is given as 'the best of tales' (ii, 1) but without a personal affirmation of its authenticity. [See BĪDJĀPUR]. His report (ii, 6) that Yūsuf ʿĀdil Shāh assumed the title of ʿĀdil Shāh and had the *khuṭba* read in his name in 895/1489 is not consistent with the evidence of Rafīʿ al-Dīn Shīrāzī, *Tadhkirat al-mulūk*, B.M. Add. 23,883, fols. 32a-33b, a work contemporary with *Gulshan-i Ibrāhīmī* or with such inscriptional evidence as is now extant (see *EIM*, 1939-40, 14-6). Firishta's evidence for the assumption of royal titles by Sulṭān Ḳulī Ḳuṭb al-Mulk of Golkonda has similarly been shown to be doubtful testimony (see *Journal of the Hyderabad Archaeological Society*, 1918, 89-94). As a historian of the Bahmanī sultanate, Firishta is no less suspect.

He states (i, 575) that the fifth Bahmanī sultan was Maḥmūd and not Muḥammad as the coinage (O. Codrington, *Coins of the Bahmani dynasty*, in *Numismatic Chronicle*, 3rd series, xviii (1898), 259-73), and ʿAlī b. ʿAzīz Allāh Ṭabāṭabā, *Burhān-i maʾāthir* (1003/1594), Ḥaydarābād 1355/1936, 36-8, and Shīrāzī's *Tadhkirat al-mulūk*, fol. 16a-b, suggest. On the discrepancies between the *Gulshan-i Ibrāhīmī* and the *Burhān-i maʾāthir* in other respects see Sir Wolseley Haig, *The history of the Nizām Shāhī kings of Aḥmadnagar*, in *Indian Antiquary*, xlix-lii, 1920-3. The differences between the accounts of Deccan and Gudjarāt history by Niẓām al-Dīn Aḥmad and Firishta have been exhaustively noticed in the translation of the *Ṭabaḳāt-i Akbarī* by Brajendranath De, iii/1, *Bibl. Ind.*, Calcutta 1939.

Criticism of Firishta as a historian, often by anachronistic criteria (*e.g.*, S. H. Hodivala, *Studies in Indo-Muslim history*, i, Bombay 1939, 594-5), has perhaps been the more severe by reason of the reputation and status of an 'authority' which he enjoyed among European writers on Indo-Muslim history from the middle of the 18th century. Alexander Dow, *The history of Hindostan*, 2 vols., London 1768, introduced the *Gulshan-i Ibrāhīmī*, (*maḳāla*s i and ii only), to a European public in the form of an interpretation in which there is little to distinguish a very free translation from Dow's own glosses. As a general annalist of Muslim rule in Hindustān Firishta provided a basis for that general history of India before the attainment of political authority by the East India Company for which Dow hoped his countrymen were, by reason of their growing involvement in India, ready. A translation of the eleventh *maḳāla* on Malībār in the *Asiatick miscellany*, ii, Calcutta 1786, and of the third *maḳāla* by Jonathan Scott, *Ferishta's history of Dekkan*, 2 vols., Shrewsbury 1794, further established Firishta as an 'authority' and Thomas Maurice, *History of Hindostan*, 2 vols. and 2 parts, London 1802-10, David Price, *Chronological retrospect*, 3 vols., London 1811-21, and James Mill, *History of British India*, 3 vols., London 1817, drew more or less heavily upon him. In 1829, Lt. Col. John Briggs published a translation of all the *Gulshan-i Ibrāhīmī* except the part containing the biographies of the *mashāʾikh* and, in 1831-2, the Bombay two-volume edition of the entire Persian text. Both translation and text are based upon a collation of unspecified MSS but without an indication of variant readings or other critical apparatus. Later editions of the *Gulshan-i Ibrāhīmī* (see Storey, 448) cannot be said to have established a definitive text. Mountstuart Elphinstone in his *History of India*, 2 vols., London 1841, gave a powerful impetus to the process of change from treating the *Gulshan-i Ibrāhīmī* as an historical 'authority' to treating it as historical data, when he went behind Firishta to many of Firishta's own sources. Sir Henry Elliot and John Dowson took the process further with (Elliot's) *Bibliographical index to the historians of Muhammedan India*, Calcutta 1849, and *The history of India as told by its own historians*, 10 vols., London 1867-77. Now that subsequent publication of literary, numismatic, inscriptional and other material on Indo-Muslim history and subsequent development of a more critical technique have destroyed dependence on Firishta (and the concept of dependence upon 'authorities'), the time is ripe for a new assessment of his character and achievement as a historical writer.

Bibliography: In addition to references in the text; Storey, 442-50; Baini Prashad, Preface to vol. iii of Brajendranath De's translation of the *Tabaḳāt-i Akbarī*, Calcutta 1939, xxxii-xxxiii; S. H. Hodivala, *Studies in Indo-Muslim History*, 2 vols., Bombay 1939, 1957, in the course of his commentary on Elliot and Dowson's *History of India*, gives incidentally an indispensable critique of Firishta's work; Jagtar Singh Grewal, *British historical writing (from Alexander Dow to Mountstuart Elphinstone) on Muslim India*, unpublished doctoral thesis, University of London, 1963.

(P. Hardy)

FIRISHTE-OGHLU (Firishte-zāde, Ibn Firishte, also Ibn Malak), patronymic of two Turkish writers, brothers, who flourished in Anatolia in the 9th/15th century.

1. ʿAbd al-Laṭīf b. Firishte ʿIzz al-Dīn b. Amīn al-Dīn, known particularly as Ibn Malak, lived at Tire first in the period of the Aydïn-oghullarï and later under Ottoman rule (so that he is listed in biographical works among the *ʿulamāʾ* of the reign of Bāyezīd I), and won enduring fame as the author of works in the fields of *fiḳh* and *ḥadīth*. The chronologically impossible statement in the *Shaḳāʾiḳ* that he was active in the reign of Meḥemmed b. Aydïn (d. 733/1333) arises from a confusion of him with his father, the *ḳāḍī* of Birgi whom Ibn Baṭṭūṭa met in that year (Ibn Baṭṭūṭa, ii, 296, 300=Eng. tr. H. A. R. Gibb, ii, 438, 440). According to Ewliyā Čelebi (*Seyāḥatnāme*, ix, 74) he was educated at Maghnīsā. He taught for many years in Tire at the *medrese* founded by Meḥemmed Beg (to which later his own name was attached), and lies buried beside it. The date of his death is differently reported: the gravestone dated 797/1394-5, which Bursalï Meḥmed Ṭāhir [see Bibl.] thought to be his, in fact commemorates someone else; the year 801/1398-9 is reported by Ismāʿīl Pasha, 820/1417 by Meḥmed Thüreyyā, and 821/1418 by Faik Tokluoğlu (*Tire*, n.p., 1957, 12); all these dates seem to be too early, since one of his works was composed in 824/1421.

Of his works (reported by Ewliyā to be 700 in number) the chief are (in Arabic): (1) *Mabāriḳ al-azhār fī sharḥ Mashāriḳ al-anwār*; (2) *Sharḥ Manār al-anwār* (autograph, dated 824, in Necip Paşa Kütüphanesi, Tire)—these two works, long regarded as classics, were printed in several editions in the 19th century ; (3) *Sharḥ Madjmaʿ al-baḥrayn*; (4) *Sharḥ al-Wiḳāya*; (5) *Manāfiʿ al-Ḳurʾān*; (6) *al-Ashbāh wa 'l-naẓāʾir*; (7) *Munyat al-ṣayyādīn fī taʿlīm al-iṣṭiyād wa-aḥkāmih* (on hunting); (in Persian): (8) *K. al-Maẓāhir*. His best-known work is his rhyming Arabic-Turkish dictionary of certain words found in the Ḳurʾān known as *Firishte-oghlu lughatï*: this was the model for the later rhyming dictionaries of Ottoman literature. The *Badr al-wāʿiẓīn wa-zuhr al-ʿābidīn* and the *Sharḥ Tuḥfat al-mulūk*, sometimes attributed to him, are in fact by his son Meḥemmed, and the *Lughat-i Ḳānūn-i ilāhī* by another son ʿAbd al-Madjīd.

Bibliography: Tashköprüzāde, *Shaḳāʾiḳ*, tr. Medjdī, 66-7; ʿĀlī, *Kunh al-akhbār*, Ist. Un. Lib., MS T 5459, f. 36r.; Taḳī al-Dīn b. al-Tamīmī, *al-Ṭabaḳāt al-saniyya fī tarādjim al-ḥanafiyya*, Süleymaniye Lib., MS 829, f. 260v.; Ḥādjdjī Khalīfa, ed. Flügel, ii, 29, 240=ed. Yaltkaya and Bilge, i, 231, 275; Ewliyā Čelebi, *Seyāḥatnāme*, ix, 74, 166; Mustaḳīm-zāde, *Madjallat al-nisab*, Süleymaniye Lib., MS Halet Ef. 628, f. 53r.; Aḥmed Ḥasīb, *Silk al-laʾāliʾ*, Ist. Un. Lib., MS T 104, f. 80; Meḥmed Thüreyyā, *Sidjill-i ʿOthmānī*, iii, 454; Bursalï Meḥmed Ṭāhir, *Aydïn wilāyetine mensūb meshāʾikh, ʿulemāʾ, shuʿarāʾ, müwerrikhīn ve eṭibbānīñ terādjim-i aḥwāli*, Izmir 1324, 36-8; idem, *ʿOthmānlî müʾellifleri*, i, 219-20; Sarkis, *Muʿdjam*, Cairo 1346, i, 252-3; al-Shawkānī, *al-Badr al-tāliʿ*, Cairo 1348, i, 374; Brockelmann, S II, 315-6; Ismail Paşa, *Asmāʾ al-muʾallifīn*, Istanbul 1951, i, 617; Faik Şişik, *Abdüllatîf Ibn-i Melek*, in *Küçük Menderes Mecmuası*, nos. 10 and 11 (Izmir 1942); idem, *Ibn-i Melek-zâde Mehmet Efendi, ibid.*, no. 12 (1942).

2. ʿAbd al-Madjīd b. Firishte ʿIzz al-Dīn b. Amīn al-Dīn, known usually simply as Firishte-oghlu, was one of the chief disciples of Faḍl Allāh [*q.v.*], founder of the Ḥurūfī sect [see ḤURŪFIYYA] in the line: Faḍl Allāh—Sayyid Shams al-Dīn—Mewlānā Bāyazīd—ʿAbd al-Madjīd. (Medjdī in his translation of the *Shaḳāʾiḳ* denies his connexion with the Ḥurūfiyya, from the desire to avoid compromising his honoured and orthodox brother). Little is known of his life; he is reported to have died in 864/1469. His *ʿIshḳ-nāme* remained for centuries, with Faḍl Allāh's *Djāwidān-nāme*, one of the principal books of the sect. Works (all in Turkish): (1) *ʿIshḳ-nāme* (lith., Istanbul 1288/1871 and n.d.), begun in 833/1430, is partly an abridged translation of Faḍl Allāh's *Djāwidān-i kabīr*, partly original; it formed the basis for Isḥāḳ Efendi's refutation of the Ḥurūfiyya (*Kāshif al-asrār*, 31 ff.); (2) *Hidāyet-nāme*, composed 833/1434; (3) *Khʷāb-nāme*, translation from Shaykh Abu 'l-Ḥasan Iṣfahānī; (4) *Ākhiret-nāme* (the last three are preserved in Ist. Un. Lib., MS T 9685). The dictionary to the Ḳurʾān sometimes attributed to him is the work of his nephew ʿAbd al-Madjīd,see above.

Bibliography: Tashköprüzāde, *Shaḳāʾiḳ*, tr. Medjdī, 67; Isḥāḳ Efendi, *Kāshif al-asrār*, Istanbul 1291, 157; J. K. Birge, *The Bektashi order of dervishes*, London 1937, 152-4.

(Ömer Faruk Akün)

FIRḲA [see ḤIZB (on political parties), AL-MILAL WA'L-NIḤAL, ṬARĪḲA].

FIRMAN [see FARMĀN].

FIRRĪSH (Sp. Castillo del Hierro), in the province of Seville, north of the Guadalquivir valley between Cazalla de la Sierra and Hornachuelos, in the neighbourhood of Constantina. The *kūra* (or region) of Firrīsh, adjacent to that of Faḥṣ al-Ballūṭ [*q.v.*], lay two stages distant to the north-west of Cordova. There were and still are chestnuts and cork-oaks in its region, but its forests were composed then as now chiefly of evergreen oaks as in Faḥṣ al-Ballūṭ. Its principal wealth lay in the exploitation of its iron, which gave it its names of Castillo del Hierro and Constantina del Hierro, and which was used throughout al-Andalus on account of its excellent quality. The deposits, however, must soon have been exhausted for no trace of this industry now remains. According to the *Rawḍ al-miʿṭār* Constantina was a great Roman town, and indeed ruins of Roman origin have been found there in the Cerro del Almendro, as also ruins of a Muslim fortress. Remains of another fortification, which might be Almoravid, have been encountered in the Cerro del Castillo. There are also prehistoric remains as yet unexplored.

In the listing of the regions of al-Andalus all the geographers place Firrīsh adjacent to Faḥṣ al-Ballūṭ and in the levy of troops which Muḥammad I made in 249/863 for the expedition against Galicia Firrīsh appears with 342 horsemen alongside Faḥṣ al-Ballūṭ which provides 400. Both Firrīsh and Constantina lie to the west of Cordova, not the north-west as stated in the *Rawḍ al-miʿṭār*. Between them and the district of Los Pedroches lies the wide band of uninhabited and uncultivated land constituted by the Sierra Morena which must be crossed before the descent of the deep valley of the Guadiato with its castle of al-Baḳār. In 230/844 the Normans, temporarily masters of Seville, launched raids in all directions and thus reached not only Morón and Cordova but also Firrīsh, which at that time was working, besides its iron mine, a quarry of highly esteemed pure white marble.

Bibliography: Ḥimyarī, *al-Rawḍ al-miʿṭār*, ed. Lévi-Provençal, text 143, tr. 171-2; Idrīsī, *Descr.*, text 207, tr. 256; Dozy, *Recherches*³, ii, 294; Lévi-Provençal, *Histoire de l'Espagne musulmane*, i, 218; idem, *L'Espagne musulmane au Xᵉ siècle*, 117; Yāḳūt, *Muʿdjam*, iii, 889-90.

(A. Huici Miranda)

FĪRŪZ SHĀH KHALDJĪ [see DIHLĪ, SULTANATE OF].

FĪRŪZ SHĀH TUGHLUḲ (b. 707/1307-8) was the son of *Sipahsālār* Radjab, younger brother of Ghiyāth al-Dīn Tughluḳ Shāh, and Bībī Nāʾila, daughter of a Hindū *zamīndār* of the Bhattī tribe of southern Pandjāb. (No contemporary or later Persian source uses 'Tughluḳ' with Fīrūz Shāh's name. The addition of 'Tughluḳ' after his name is a modern innovation, convenient but inaccurate.) During the reign of Muḥammad b. Tughluḳ, Fīrūz occupied the high position of Nāʾib Amīr Ḥādjib and played an important part in the affairs of state. On the death of Muḥammad b. Tughluḳ near Ṭhaṭṭha in Sind in Muḥarram 752/March 1351, Fīrūz was elected to the throne by the nobles and notables (including several influential religious leaders) present in the imperial camp. He had no difficulty in overcoming the opposition of Khwādja Djahān Aḥmad Ayāz, the *wazīr* of the late Sultan, at Dehlī.

Despite his pacific temperament, Fīrūz Shāh was not without imperial ambitions. He had a keen desire to regain the provinces lost during the previous reign. The two successive campaigns he led to Bengāl (754-5/1353-4 and 760-2/1359-61) gained practically nothing. His prolonged and costly expedition against the Samma chiefs of Ṭhaṭṭha (767-8/1366-7) resulted only in the extension of his suzerainty to the distant province, as did his invasion of Kāngṛa (764/1363). As a general Fīrūz Shāh was thoroughly incompetent: his conduct of war suffered from his professed desire to avoid all bloodshed and his vacillating judgment. It was therefore fortunate that he did not go ahead with a projected invasion of the Deccan (prob. 764/1363) and that sometime later, on the advice of his *wazīr*, Khān Djahān, he resolved not to undertake any further expeditions.

Fīrūz Shāh ordered a new revenue survey of the empire. He followed a liberal agrarian policy, levying only one-fifth of the produce as revenue. He issued orders to his revenue staff to deal leniently with the peasants. He dug several canals and numerous irrigation wells. The resulting extension of cultivation, apart from benefiting the peasantry, contributed to a cheaper and more plentiful supply of food-grains in the urban areas. Fīrūz Shāh abolished twenty-nine taxes, most of which were urban cesses: the measure benefited the small shop-keeper, the artisan and the craftsman.

Fīrūz Shāh humanized the government and softened the code of punishment. But his benevolence often bordered upon weakness. He granted big *iḳṭāʿ*s to his nobles, leaving them practically free to manage these estates as they chose. The measure enriched the nobles and impoverished the state. Fīrūz Shāh failed to check corruption in the administration. Indeed, some of his own measures contributed to corruption and inefficiency. The Sultan's weakness was to some extent balanced by the wisdom and firmness of his *wazīr*, Khān Djahān Maḳbūl (a convert, from Telingānā in South India), whom he trusted implicitly and who served him with rare loyalty. Another buttress which Fīrūz Shāh built up to offset his weakness was the large body of personal slaves he acquired and maintained. These slaves, known as the *bandagān-i Fīrūz Shāhī*, though loyal to their master, created much trouble towards the end of the Sultan's reign and after his death.

In religious matters Fīrūz Shāh was strongly orthodox. He suppressed extremist sectarian manifestations and outbreaks of what he considered heretical movements in his kingdom. On the advice of the *ʿulamāʾ* (whom he frequently consulted), he extended *djizya* to the Brahmans, who had so far been exempt from the tax, though he allowed them to pay it at the lowest rate. Fīrūz Shāh was the last Sultan of Dehlī to receive investiture from the ʿAbbāsid caliph, himself by now a powerless pensionary in Cairo.

Fīrūz Shāh was a prolific builder. He founded several towns, including a new city of Dehlī named Fīrūzābād, and Djawnpūr, named after his late imperial cousin Djawnā Khān alias Muḥammad b. Tughluḳ. He built many mosques, *madrasas* and other royal and public edifices. Architecturally his buildings, though possessing a conspicuous style, were not of a high order. He also showed interest in preserving old monuments and repaired many of these, including the Ḳuṭb Mīnār. His transplanting of two Asokan pillars from their original sites to the city of Dehlī was a creditable feat of mediaeval engineering. The operation in all its phases—the uprooting of the pillars, transporting them across the river Djamunā and refixing them in the sites where they stand to this day—is described in elaborate detail in the *Sīrat-i Fīrūz Shāhī* (see *ASI Memoirs*, no. 52, cited in Bibl. below). The many gardens Fīrūz Shāh laid out around Dehlī substantially increased the supply of flowers and fruits to the city.

Fīrūz Shāh died in Ramaḍān 790/September 1388 and lies buried in a simple and dignified mausoleum at the Ḥawḍ Khāṣṣ outside Delhi. The ease and plenty of his reign, the widespread distribution of charity, the corruption in the civil as well as the military administration, and the very peace and tranquillity which made the people "forget the profession of arms" (ʿAfīf), sapped the vigour of the ruling community and thereby contributed to the rapid decline of the Sultanate after nim. The invasion of Tīmūr a decade after the Sultan's death only hastened the process of decay which had already begun.

Bibliography: Among the Persian sources, ʿAfīf's *Taʾrīkh-i Fīrūz Shāhī* gives the fullest account of the reign. Though professedly favourable to Fīrūz Shāh, ʿAfīf seldom slurs over his faults. Fīrūz Shāh's own brochure, the *Futūḥāt-i Fīrūz Shāhī* (inscribed in a dome, no longer extant, in the Masdjid-i Fīrūz Shāhī in Fīrūzābād) is a revealing document. See Elliot and Dowson, iii, 265-388, for translations of excerpts from Persian accounts. For modern writings, see articles by Riazul Islam, B. N. Roy, K. K. Basu and others listed in Pearson, *Index Islamicus*, pp. 631-2, *Supplement*, p. 203. The more important articles are given below.

Original sources: Ḍiyāʾ al-Dīn Baranī, *Ta'rīkh-i Fīrūz Shāhī* (Bibl. Indica), Calcutta 1862; ʿAyn al-Mulk Māhrū Multānī, *Munshaʾāt-i Māhrū*, Asiatic Society of Bengal MS, Cat. No. 338, Ivanow, pp. 145-48; Anon., *Sīrat-i Fīrūz Shāhī*, Oriental Public Library, Bankipore, Catalogue, vii, 28-33, MS No. 547; Fīrūz Shāh, *Futūḥāt-i Fīrūz Shāhī*, (i) B.M. MS Or. 2039, see Rieu, *Cat. Pers. Mss.*, iii, 920 (ii) text with translation and introduction by Sh. Abdur Rashid, Aligarh 1943; Shams Sirādj ʿAfīf, *Taʾrīkh-i Fīrūz Shāhī* (Bibl. Indica), Calcutta 1890; Muḥammad Bīhāmid Khānī, *Taʾrīkh-i Muḥammadī*, B.M. MS Or. 137.

Modern authorities: Riazul Islam, *The rise of the Sammas in Sind*, in *IC*, xxii (1948), 359-82; idem, *A review of the reign of Fīrūz Shah*, in *IC*, xxiii (1949), 281-97; idem, *The age of Firoz Shah*, in *Med. India Qly.*, Aligarh, i/1 (1950), 25-41; idem, *Fīrūz Shah Tughluq's relations with the Deccan*, in *IC*, xxvi/3 (1952), 8-12; idem, *Fīrūz Shah's invasion of Bengal*, in *JPak. H.S.*, iii (1955), 35-9; Sh. A. Rashid, *Fīrūz Shah's investiture by the Caliph*, in *Med. India Qly.*, Aligarh, i/1 (1950), 66-71; N. B. Roy, *Futūḥāt-i Fīrūz Shāhī*, in *JASB*, ser. iii, viii (1941), 61-89; Syed Hasan ʿAskari, *Side-lights on Firuz Shah and his times*, in *Ind. Hist. Cong. Proc.*, xxi (1958), 33-37; K. K. Basu, *Firuz Shah Tughluq as a Ruler*, in *IHQ*, xvii, 386-93; *Memoirs of the Archaeological survey of India*, no. 52: *A Memoir on Kotla Firoz Shah, Delhi*, by J. A. Page, Delhi 1937. (RIAZUL ISLAM)

FĪRŪZĀBĀD (formerly Pīrūzābād, 'the town of victory', and originally known as Gūr or Čūr) is situated in 28° 50′ N. Lat. and 52° 34′ E. Long. (Greenwich); it is 1356 m. above sea level. The present town, which had 4,340 inhabitants in 1951, is 3 km. to the south-east of the ancient site. Fīrūzābād, besides being one of the chief centres of the Ḳash-ḳaʾī tribe [*q.v.*], is the chief administrative centre of the district (*shahristān*) of the same name in the seventh *Ustān* (Fārs). The surrounding country is very fertile and well-watered and the climate is temperate.

The ancient town is said to have been built by Ardashīr on the site of his great victory over Artabanus V. It was circular in shape and had four gates, one at each cardinal point; these gates were called Mithra (the Sun), Bahrām (Mars), Hormuz (Jupiter) and Ardashīr. In the centre of the town was a lofty tower (now in ruins) on the top of which was a fire-altar; near-by was a large fire-temple. North of the town are the remains of the palace which Ardashīr built shortly before his successful revolt; it is thus the oldest Sāsānid building in existence (see F. Sarre and E. Herzfeld, *Iranische Felsreliefs*, Berlin 1910, 128). Gūr became the capital of the province of Ardashīr-khurra ("Glory of Ardashīr"). According to al-Balādhurī (315 and 389), Gūr and Iṣṭakhr were the last two towns in Fārs to surrender to the Muslim Arabs. In the 3rd/9th century Gūr was as large as Iṣṭakhr, but was smaller than Shīrāz (Iṣṭakhrī, 97). The district produced excellent rose-water which was exported far and wide; it was also celebrated for its fruit. The Buwayhid ruler ʿAḍud al-Dawla [*q.v.*] used to frequent Gūr; his courtiers, disliking the name (which means 'grave' in Persian), persuaded him to change it to Pīrūzābād 'the town of victory'. Ḥamd Allāh Mustawfī (*Nuzha*, 137) stated that the inhabitants were noted for their piety and honesty.

Bibliography: in addition to the references in the text, see Muḳaddasī, 432; Ibn al-Balkhī, *Fārs-nāma* (ed. Le Strange and Nicholson), 137-139; Yāḳūt, iii, 146; Barbier de Meynard, *Dictionnaire de la Perse*, 174-176; T. Nöldeke, *Araber und Perser*, 11, note 3; Flandin and Coste, *Voyage en Perse*, vol. i, 36-45 and plates xxxv to xliv; Oscar Reuther, *Sasanian Architecture*, in *A Survey of Persian Art*, vol. i, 493; A. Christensen, *L'Iran sous les Sassanides*, 87, 93, 94, 114 and 168; R. Ghirshman, *Iran from the earliest times to the Islamic Conquest*, 320-21, 323-24, 328; *Rāhnamā-yi Īrān*, 180 (with town plan on 181); Razmārā and Nawtāsh, *Farhang-i Djughrāfiyā-yi Īrān*, vol. vii, 168. (L. Lockhart)

al-**FĪRŪZĀBĀDĪ**, Abu 'l-Ṭāhir Muḥammad b. Yaʿḳūb b. Muḥammad b. Ibrāhīm Madjd al-Dīn al-Shāfiʿī al-Shīrāzī, from his father's town Fīrūzābād, was born at Kāzarūn, a town near Shīrāz (Īrān) in Rabīʿ II or Djumādā II 729/February or April 1329. From the age of eight he was educated in Shīrāz, then in Wāsiṭ and, in 745/1344, in Baghdād. In 750/1349 he was attending the classes of Taḳī al-Dīn al-Subkī in Damascus (Brockelmann, II, 106).

His long life can be divided into three main periods, spent in Jerusalem, Mecca and in the Yemen.

In the same year 750 he accompanied al-Subkī to Jerusalem where he stayed for ten years as a teacher and then, while still a young man, became a master. Subsequent travels took him to Cairo and Asia Minor.

The information to be found in his biographers in regard to his journeys varies very greatly (see Brockelmann, II, 232 n.). We have here followed, like Brockelmann, *ibid.*, the account given in the *K. al-Rawḍ al-ʿāṭir* of al-Nuʿmānī, which seems to be the most trustworthy. According to al-Sakhāwī's account (*Ḍaw*, x, 85 foot), a long biography of al-Fīrūzābādī is given in the *ʿUḳūd* of al-Maḳrīzī; this must be the *Durar al-ʿuḳūd al-farīda fī tarādjim al-aʿyān al-mufīda*; the MS Gotha 1771 cannot include it, but perhaps it is contained in MS Mawṣil 1264, no. 5 (Brockelmann, S II, 37), which should correctly be 264, no. 5. From al-Maḳrīzī interesting details might be expected. The ms. is at the present time in Baghdād, in the possession of the al-Djalīlī family who do not allow it to be consulted.

In 770/1368 he went to live in Mecca, breaking his stay there to travel to India and spending five years in Dihlī; after that came more travelling.

In 794/1392 he went to Baghdād at the invitation of Sultan Aḥmad b. Uways, and afterwards to Persia. Tīmūr Lang, after taking Shīrāz (795/1393), greeted him with the greatest respect. But his native land, ravaged by the Mongol invasion, could no longer keep him: from Hormuz he set sail for southern Arabia.

In Rabīʿ I 796/January 1394 he reached the Yemen and lived in Taʿizz for 14 months in the house of Sultan al-Malik al-Ashraf Ismāʿīl b. ʿAbbās, who appointed him chief ḳāḍī of the Yemen on 6 Dhu 'l-Ḥidjdja 797/22 September 1395 (with residence in Zabīd) and gave him his daughter in marriage. In 802/1400 he once again made the pilgrimage and in his house in Mecca set up a modest Mālikī *madrasa* with three teachers. He was in Medina in 803/1401 when he heard of the death of his father-in-law al-Malik al-Ashraf. In Ramaḍān 805/April 1403 he made another journey to Mecca, but returned to Zabīd without delay. He died there on 20 Shawwāl 817/3 January 1415.

An active man with a thirst for knowledge, he is said when travelling to have taken with him quantities of books which he used to read at the halts. He bought many books, the necessary equipment for the work of compilation, as practised in his time. A spendthrift (but see *Ḍaw*, x, 81 l. 23), he used to sell during a famine and buy back when times of plenty returned. His works were concerned with *tafsīr*, *ḥadīth* and history, but lexicography remained the branch in which he excelled.

He had certain pretensions: born near Shīrāz, he claimed to be a descendant of the celebrated Shāfiʿī Abū Isḥāḳ al-Shīrāzī (Brockelmann, I, 484) who had, however, died without issue. After achieving his brilliant position in the Yemen, he called himself and wrote by the name of Muḥammad al-Ṣiddīḳī, as though a descendant of the caliph Abū Bakr al-Ṣiddīḳ (*Ḍaw*, x, 85 l. 12-3; al-Nuʿmānī, *Rawḍ*, 218r.), no doubt the eccentricity of a man who enjoyed great renown. He had more serious ambitions: he wished to compile a dictionary in 60 (*Ḳāmūs*, Preface, 3 l. 13) or, it is even said, in 100 volumes: *al-Lāmiʿ al-muʿallam al-ʿudjāb al-djāmiʿ bayn al-Muḥkam wa 'l-ʿUbāb*, which only reached the 5th volume (Ibn al-ʿImād, *Shadharāt*, vii, 128; *TA*, *Preface*, 14, l. 10). He made a summary of it, his *Ḳāmūs*, its full title being *al-Ḳāmūs al-muḥīṭ wa 'l-ḳābūs al-wasīṭ al-djāmiʿ li-mā dhahaba min al-ʿarab shamaṭīṭ*. But then he set himself up as the rival, to use no stronger a term, of al-Djawharī in his *Ṣiḥāḥ*. The often unjustified criticism that he made of the latter (*e.g.*, *Ḳāmūs*, *Preface*, 3 l. 20-1, 4 l. 18-20) will come as no surprise.

Of his numerous works the following are printed: 1. the *Taḥbīr al-muwashshīn fī-mā yuḳāl bi 'l-sīn wa 'l-shīn*, vocabulary of Arabic words written indiscriminately with either *s* or *sh*, Algiers 1909 (also published Beirut 1330/1912); 2. narratives derived from the life of the Prophet, *Sufar al-saʿāda* or else *al-Ṣirāṭ al-mustaḳīm*, written in Persian, translated into Arabic by Abu 'l-Djūd Muḥ. b. Maḥmūd al-Makhzūmī in the margin of *al-Fawz al-kabīr maʿa fatḥ al-ḥabīr fī uṣūl al-tafsīr* of Walī Allāh b. ʿAbd al-Raḥīm (Cairo or Jerusalem 1307, 1346), and in the margin of *Kashf al-ghumma* (Cairo 1317, 1332) of al-Shaʿrānī; see Brockelmann, S II, 235, no. 10; 3. the *Tanwīr al-miḳbās min* (*Tanwīr al-miḳyās fī*, Ḥādjdjī Khalīfa, *Kashf al-ẓunūn*, no. 3706) *tafsīr Ibn ʿAbbās*, Cairo 1290, 1316 (in the margin of *al-Nāsikh wa 'l-mansūkh* of Ibn Ḥazm), 1345/1926. 18 works are extant in manuscript, see Brockelmann, II, 233-4 and S II, 235-6; of these, we may single out *al-Bulgha fī ta'rīkh a'immat al-lugha* (*Suppl. ibid.*, no. 7), perhaps the most important; and, a unique manuscript, *al-Mirḳāt al-wafiyya fī ṭabaḳāt al-Ḥanafiyya*, Medina, Library of Shaykh al-Islām ʿĀrif Ḥikmet Bey, register *Sulayman Nadwī*, no. 128, see O. Spies, in *ZDMG*, xc (1936), 99 and 117; cf. Ḥādjdjī Khalīfa, *op. cit.*, no. 7895, 11830; the work derives from the *Ṭabaḳāt* of ʿAbd al-Ḳādir al-Ḥanafī (*Ḍaw*, x, 82).

The *Preface* to the *TA* (i, 13-4) provides a biography of al-Fīrūzābādī and a list (incomplete) of 45 works; Brockelmann (S II, 236) must have referred to it, for the *Preface* to the *Ḳāmūs* does not include a comparable list. 49 works, according to *Ḍaw* (x, 81-3): *tafsīr* 6, *ḥadīth* and history 27, lexicography *et alia* 16, but 61 in the *ʿUḳūd al-djawhar* of Djamīl Bey al-ʿAẓm (i, 302-6), lists, however, that are open to criticism.

Al-Fīrūzābādī is "the author of the *Ḳāmūs*", his name remains connected with this famous book. The work is preeminently a compilation of the *Muḥkam* of Ibn Sīda and of the *ʿUbāb* of al-Ṣaghānī.

He venerated al-Saghānī as a model (*Ḍaw*, x, 83). But from whom did he take the *ziyādāt*? It would be helpful to discover if he is indebted for certain elements to the *Shams al-ʿulūm* of Nashwān al-Ḥimyarī (a first vol. published by K. V. Zetterstein, Leiden 1951). The *Ḳāmūs* was completed in Mecca in his house *ʿala 'l-ṣafā* (end of *Ḳ.*, iv, 415) during the second main period described above (cf. *Ḍaw*, x, 83 and 85), before his stay in the Yemen. But it is hardly likely that such an expert lexicographer as he was would have been unacquainted with this dictionary which incidentally devotes so much space to matters concerning the Yemen.

Very brief definitions or explanations allowed him to present an extremely rich vocabulary in a volume of modest size. This brevity has given rise to innumerable misapprehensions (see Lane, *Lexicon, Preface*, XVII l. 14-6 and *ZDMG*, iii (1849), 95 ff.). It was the subject of numerous glosses and criticisms, and commentaries of every sort, both by admirers, in particular the *Tādj al-ʿarūs* of al-Sayyid Murtaḍā al-Zabīdī (d. 1205/1791), 10 vols., Būlāḳ 1306-7, who in this commentary incorporates the work of his master Abū ʿAbd Allāh al-Fāsī, the *Iḍā'at al-rāmūs*, and by detractors, defending the *Ṣiḥāḥ* of al-Djawharī; see I. Goldziher, *Beiträge zur Geschichte der Sprachgelehrsamkeit bei den Arabern*, Vienna 1872, ii, 602 ff. and the judgement of al-Suyūṭī, *Muzhir*³, i, 101 and 103. In the last century we may also quote the criticisms of Aḥmad Fāris al-Shidyāḳ (d. 1305/1887), *al-Djāsūs ʿala 'l-Ḳāmūs*, Istanbul 1299 and, more recently, the *Taṣḥīḥ al-Ḳāmūs* (Cairo 1343/1925) of Aḥmad Taymur Pasha.

The *Ḳāmūs* was published for the first time in Calcutta (1230-2) and Üsküdār (1230), and on very many occasions subsequently. The 4th edition (Cairo 1357/1938) in 4 vols., of the Maṭbaʿat Dār al-Ma'mūn (cited in this article), is well presented typographically.

The *Ḳāmūs* has been translated into Persian (see Brockelmann, S II, 234), and also into Turkish by ʿĀṣim Efendi (d. 1235/1819 or 1248/1832): *al-Ūḳiyānūs al-basīṭ fī tardjamat al-Ḳāmūs al-muḥīṭ*, published in Būlāḳ 1250, Istanbul 1305, etc. This Turkish edition was favoured by nineteenth century orientalists and is often quoted, *e.g.*, by Fleischer and Goldziher.

In the West the *Thesaurus linguae Arabicae* of A. Giggeius (Milan 1632, 4 vols.) was based on the *Ḳāmūs*. For his *Lexicon* (Leiden 1653), J. Golius added to it the *Ṣiḥāḥ*. Freytag (Kazimirski) and Belot did the same. The two rivals were associated together to provide a dictionary for European orientalism; and Lane took as the basis of his great *Lexicon* the *Tādj al-ʿarūs*, the commentary on the *Ḳāmūs* referred to above.

Bibliography: Brockelmann, II, 181-3; II² (*angepasst*) 231-4; S II, 234-6; J. Kraemer, in *Studien zur altarabischen Lexikographie*, in *Oriens*, vi (1953), 232-4, particularly on the subject of the *Ḳāmūs*, and also Ḥusayn Naṣṣār, *al-Muʿdjam al-ʿarabī*, ii (Cairo 1956), 540-603. F. Wüstenfeld, *Die Geschichtsschreiber der Araber und ihre Werke* (Göttingen 1882), no. 464, made use of the *Ṭabaḳāt al-Shāfiʿiyya* of Taḳī al-Dīn Ibn Ḳāḍī Shuhba, MS Gotha 1763; Sharaf al-Dīn b. Ayyūb al-Nuʿmānī, *al-Rawḍ al-ʿāṭir*, MS Wetzstein II 289 (Ahlwardt 9886), fols. 217v-219v (cited as *Rawḍ*). Shams al-Dīn Muḥ. al-Sakhāwī, *al-Ḍaw al-lāmiʿ li-ahl al-ḳarn al-tāsiʿ*, x, 79-86 (Cairo 1355), detailed information but with confused chronology (cited as *Ḍaw*); Suyūṭī, *Bughyat al-wuʿāt*, 117-8 (Cairo 1326); ʿAlī b. al-Ḥasan al-Khazradjī, *al-ʿUḳūd al-lu'lu'iyya*, trans. Redhouse, GMS, III/2, 248-9 and note 1557 (III/3, 212); ʿAbd al-Ḥayy Ibn al-ʿImād, *Shadharāt al-dhahab*, vii, 126-31 (Cairo 1351); Ibn Taghribirdi, *al-Nudjūm al-zāhira* (ed. Popper), vi, 446-8; Ṭāshköprüzāde, *al-Shaḳā'iḳ al-nuʿmāniyya*, in the margin of *Wafayāt al-aʿyān* of Ibn Khallikān (Būlāḳ 1299), i, 92-3. Other references, Brockelmann, S II, 234.

(H. Fleisch)

FĪRŪZADJ, the turquoise, a well-known precious stone of a bright green or "mountain green" to sky-blue colour with a gloss like wax; in composition it is a hydrated clay phosphate with a small but essential proportion of copper and iron. The colour is not permanent in all stones, and is said to be particularly affected by perspiration. It is almost always cut as an ornament *en cabochon*, *i.e.*, with a convex upper surface; only stones with an inscription are given a flat upper surface. The provenance of serviceable stones is limited to a few places whose history may be traced back for thousands of years. Turquoise mines were worked by the kings of Egypt in the peninsula of Sinai. Major Macdonald discovered them again in 1845 in the Wādī Maghāra and its neighbourhood and worked them again for a number of years. No mention of the stone or the mines has survived from the Hellenistic period; on the other hand in addition to marvellous details of the method of procuring the pale green *callais* in Carmania (east of Persis), Pliny knows a good deal about its properties, and his description can only refer to our turquoise; for the statement that the *callais* loses its colour when affected by oil or ointment is found in al-Kindī on the *fīrūzadj* and in all later mineralogical works. It can hardly be doubted that the turquoise was obtained in the Sāsānid period and even earlier in the mines around Nīshāpūr. Al-Tīfāshī (d. 651/1253) says of the kings of Persia that they adorned their hands and necks with turquoises, because they averted danger of death by land or water; but we often meet with the assertion that the turquoise detracts from the majesty of kings. It was considered to contain copper and to be formed in the vicinity of copper mines. Different kinds are distinguished according to the different colours (sky-blue, milk-blue, green, spotted); the best kind is considered to be the *būsḥāḳī* (*i.e.*, *Abū Isḥāḳī*) and the finest variety of this is the sky-blue *azharī*. Large pieces are very rare and are correspondingly costly, small pieces on the other hand are very common. The best specimens retain their colour, apart from the influences detailed below; after 10-12 years many lose their colour entirely and the stone is then said to be dead. All stones, however, show a certain variation in colour. They are brilliant in a clear sky and dim when the sky is clouded; they alter their colour with the state of health of the wearer, and when affected by sweat, oil or musk; fat is believed to restore the colour again.

Taken internally it is a poison, but in collyrium it is useful for clearing the sight, also if it is stared at for some time. Gold takes away its beauty (unlike lapis lazuli), *i.e.*, probably, the greenish blue colour does not harmonize as well with the yellow of the gold as the dark blue of the lapis lazuli.

Ibn al-Akfānī (d. 749/1348) explains the name *fīrūzadj* as "stone of victory"; whence it is also called *ḥadjar al-ghalaba*. The word *fīrūzadj* is found in many corrupt forms in the Latin translations of the middle ages (*farasquin*, *febrognug*, *peruzegi* etc.), but none of these can be considered the original of the word turquoise; for as early as the 13th century we find the form *turcoys*, *turquesa* and *turquesia*, and it may safely be assumed that this was a new name given to the stone from the land of its origin, the ancient home of the Turks.

The edition of al-Bīrūnī's *al-Djamāhir fī maʿrifat al-djawāhir* (1355/1937) has revealed that almost all particulars mentioned above are already to be found there and that the essential contents of his short article (169-71) were practically quoted in full.

The use of the turquoise for magical purposes is remarkably limited. Ibn al-Akfānī quotes on the authority of Hermes a talisman made of it. In the great magical work *Ghāyat al-ḥakīm* the turquoise appears in the list of stones among those belonging to Saturn; but only one single talisman engraved on turquoise is mentioned.

General Sir A. Houtum-Schindler who was governor of the mining area and director of operations at the mines in the "eighties" of last century has given a detailed account of the Persian turquoise mines at Mashhad in Khurāsān, which is quoted in Bauer's *Edelsteinkunde* (2nd ed., 490 *et seq.*).

Bibliography: *Das Steinbuch des Aristoteles* (ed. Ruska), 151; al-Kindī, in E. Wiedemann, *Zur Mineralogie bei den Arabern*, in *Arch. f. d. Gesch. d. Naturw.*, i (1909), 210; al-Tīfāshī, *Azhār al-afkār*, trans. Reineri Biscia, 2nd ed., 70 f.; Ibn al-Akfānī, *Nukhab al-dhakhā'ir*, ed. P. Anastase-Marie, 1939, 55-62 (Wiedemann's trans. in *Beiträge*, xxx (1912), 225 f. is to be corrected accordingly); Ḳazwīnī (ed. Wüstenfeld), i, 232; Dimishḳī (ed. Mehren), 68; Ibn al-Bayṭār, trans. by Leclerc in *Notices et extr.*, xxvi, 50; Clément-Mullet, *Essai sur la min. arabe*, in *JA*, ser. vi, vol. xi, 150 f.; *Ghāyat al-ḥakīm*, ed. H. Ritter, 1933, 106, 120 = trans. H. Ritter and M. Plessner, 1962, 113, 127; H. Brugsch, *Wanderung nach den Türkis-Minen und der Sinai-Halbinsel*, 1866, 66 f.; W. Flinders Petrie, *Researches in Sinai*, 1906, 41, etc.; Bauer, *Edelsteinkunde*², 386-495; H. Fühner, *Lithotherapie*, 1902, 138-40.

(J. Ruska-[M. Plessner])

FĪRŪZĀNIDS, Banū Fīrūzān (Pērōzān), a Persian tribe which in the 4th/10th century had considerable influence in the district of Shukūr (Ṭabaristān). The only member of the tribe of real significance was Mākān b. Kālī (Kākī ?) who started as an officer in the service of the ʿAlids of Ṭabaristān, and later held various official positions; in 329/940 he died in battle (for details see mākān). After his death one of his relatives (his cousin, according to Ibn Miskawayh, ii, 3-7; his uncle, according to Zambaur), al-Ḥasan b. Fīrūzān, succeeded in gaining control of the neighbourhood of Ḳūmis for a short time. One of his daughters (name unknown) married the Būyid Rukn al-Dawla [*q.v.*]. The last member of the family to be mentioned was Ḥasan's grandson, Kanār b. Fīrūzān, in 388/998.

Bibliography: B. Spuler, *Iran*, 91-4 (with references to sources); Zambaur, 216 (with genealogical table). See also bibl. to mākān.

(B. Spuler)

FĪRŪZKŪH (Fērōzkōh). The name of several localities.

1. The capital of the Ghūrid [*q.v.*] kings, in the mountains east of Herat on the upper Harī-rūd *ca.* 64° 22′ E. Long. (Green.) and *ca.* 34° 23′ N. Lat. The site has been identified with the present Djām [*q.v.*] where a large minaret still exists.

The town of Fīrūzkūh was built by Ḳuṭb al-Dīn Muḥammad as the capital of the district of Warshāda in Ghūr which he ruled. When Ḳuṭb al-Dīn was poisoned in Ghazna, his brother Bahā al-Dīn moved from his appanage, Mandesh in the east, to Fīrūzkūh. Bahā al-Dīn became ruler of Ghūr in 544/1149 and thus founded the Ghūrid kingdom. For more than sixty years Fīrūzkūh was the capital of the Ghūrid state and to it were brought the spoils of the conquests of the Ghūrids. It was a cultural centre where writers and poets flourished. After the death of Ghiyāth al-Dīn in 599/1202 the empire fell to pieces and Fīrūzkūh lost its importance. Ghiyāth al-Dīn built the minaret which still stands.

The town was conquered by ʿAlā al-Dīn Khʷārizm Shāh in 607/1210, and it was finally destroyed by Ögödei son of Čingiz Khān in 619/1222. The Fīrūzkūh nomads probably derived their name from this site.

2. The name of a castle in Ṭabaristān near Mt. Damāwand in a district called Wīmah. We do not know when the castle or town of Fīrūzkūh was built and Casanova's attempt to identify it with Firīm, capital of a dynasty of Ispāhbads in the 4th/10th century, was refuted by Ḳazwīnī (Djuwaynī, iii, 381). Fīrūzkūh is mentioned as an important stronghold under the Khʷārizmshāhs and especially under the Mongols. It was taken by the Mongols in 624/1227 (Djuwaynī, ii, 210). Afterwards the Ismāʿīlīs of Alamut obtained possession of it. It fell again to the Mongols under Hülegü in 654/1256. The area was a summer resort for the Il-Khāns, and the name appears in accounts of Tīmūr's conquests. The town is now linked to Tehrān by rail (202 km.); it has over 5,000 inhabitants and is the centre of a district of the same name.

Bibliography: 1. A. Maricq and G. Wiet, *Le Minaret de Djam*, Paris 1959, with references to all Islamic sources; ʿAwfī, *Lubāb*, *passim*, for literary references; on the Fīrūzkūhī tribe see H. F. Schurmann, *The Mongols of Afghanistan*, The Hague 1962, 54-6.

2. Le Strange, 371-2; P. Casanova, *Les Ispehbeds de Firīm*, in *A Volume of Oriental Studies presented to E. G. Browne*, ed. T. W. Arnold, Cambridge 1922, 117-9; *Farhang-i Djughrāfiyā-yi Īrān*, i, Teheran 1950, 153; *IA*, *s.v.*, by M. Fuad Köprülü.

(R. N. Frye)

FĪRŪZPŪR (Fērōzpūr). A district in the Pandjāb which takes its name from the principal town. It forms part of the Djalandhar division, lying between 29° 55″ and 31° 9′ N. and 73° 52′ and 75° 26′ E. Area 3202 sq. m. Until 1947, the principal Muslim tribes of the district were Rādjpūts, Arains, Dogars and Wattus, and also an ascetic tribe known as Bodla, believed to possess powers of incantation. The ancient site of Djanēr, supposed to be the Hadjnīr of Bayhaḳī, was the capital of the Punwar Rādjpūts. Soon after the Muslim invasion the Bhaṭṭi Rādjpūts adopted Islām and invaded the district from the south. The Gil, Dhālīwāl and other Djaṭ tribes entered it later. The Dogars, a wild and predatory tribe, were more recent immigrants. The town of Fīrūzpūr was reputedly founded in the time of Sultan Fīrūz Shāh III of Dihlī and named after him. In Akbar's time it was part of the Sūba of Multān and not of Sirhind, and probably lay on the right bank of the river Satladj, and not on the left as at present. The Sidhū Djaṭs appear towards the end of Akbar's reign and soon adopted the Sikh religion. It was in this tract that Guru Govind was defeated after a three days fight by Awrangzīb's army; the site was held sacred and the tank (Mukat-sar = Tank of Salvation) became a place of pilgrimage, where a 3 days' festival was held in January. Round it the important town of Mukatsar has grown up. The Sikhs got possession of the country after the retirement of Aḥmad S̲h̲āh Durrānī: the Bhangī Misl under Gūd̲j̲ar Singh took the principal part in the conquest. Rand̲j̲īt Singh threatened this country with the minor Sikh states, and this move (1808) led to British intervention. Fīrūzpūr was occupied, and annexed in 1835, thus interposing between Rand̲j̲īt Singh's kingdom and the minor states. The Muslim Nawwābs of Ḳaṣūr also found a refuge at their estate of Mamdot near Fīrūzpūr in 1807, and were recognized as ruling chiefs. Their territory was annexed in 1855, but was afterwards restored to the Nawwābs, who held it until 1947. It was a large and wealthy estate.

The first Sikh war between the British and the K̲h̲ālsa army was fought in this tract. The Sikh army crossed the Satlad̲j̲ in December 1845. The battles of Mudkī and Phērū-s̲h̲ahr (often wrongly called Fīrūz-s̲h̲ahr or Fīrūz-s̲h̲āh) were fought soon after. The Sikh army was repulsed but not crushed, and recrossed the Satlad̲j̲, only to invade British territory again higher up the river near Ludhiāna. The decisive battle of Alīwāl was fought outside the district of Fīrūzpūr, but the desperate struggle of Subrāwāṅ (Sobraon) which ended the war, was fought within its limits.

In more recent times the district was enlarged by the addition of the Taḥsīl of Fazilka in the south from the former district of Sirsa (1884). The sandy tracts to the east and south of the district have been rendered fertile by irrigation from the Sirhind canal, and the inundation-canals constructed by Col. Grey in the riverain tract also added greatly to its productiveness. The Sikh D̲j̲aṫs are excellent farmers and take full advantage of these conditions. There is a large export of wheat from the Fīrūzpūr district. The Muslim population of the city, and of the district, emigrated to Pākistān during the Partition Riots of 1947.

Bibliography: Various provincial and district Gazetteers and settlement reports issued by Pand̲j̲ab Govt. Press Lahore; Cunningham, *History of the Sikhs*, London 1849; Ibbetson, *Outlines of Punjab Ethnography*, Calcutta 1883.

(M. Longworth Dames)

FISCAL SYSTEMS [see bayt al-māl, ḍarība, etc.].

FISH [see samak].

FIS̲H̲EK [see s̲h̲enlik].

FISḲ [see fāsiḳ].

FĪT̲H̲ĀG̲H̲ŪRAS, or Fūt̲h̲āg̲h̲ūras (rarely Būt̲h̲āg̲h̲ūras or other individual transliterations), Pythagoras, the Greek philosopher of the sixth century B.C., as celebrated and as elusive a figure in Islam as in the West. The distinction between the man and the school, or schools, bearing his name was occasionally sensed but, of course, not really understood, and no true distinction was made between the two.

The partly historical and mostly legendary circumstances of his life were known in considerable detail through a lengthy summary of his biography from Porphyry's *Philosophos Historia*, preserved in al-Mubas̲h̲s̲h̲ir 52 ff. and Ibn Abī Uṣaybiʿa, i, 38 ff. (cf. F. Rosenthal, in *Orientalia*, *N.S.* vi (1937), 43 ff.). His lifetime was assumed, on the basis of various synchronisms, to have spanned the reigns of Cyrus and Cambyses (Mubas̲h̲s̲h̲ir, Ibn Abī Uṣaybiʿa), to have been fixed by his position as the second in a chain of five philosophers (between Empedocles [who, in fact, lived later than Pythagoras] and Socrates) (see anbaduḳlīs), or to have fallen in the reign of an Artaxerxes (Saʿīd [Eutychios], *Annals*, i, 77). The customary dating "in the time of Sulaymān" used for men and events of great antiquity is occasionally mentioned (S̲h̲ahrastānī), as he was also supposed to have been in touch in Egypt with followers (*aṣḥāb*) of Sulaymān. His claim to being the founder of philosophy was recognized as disputed by other theories concerning the history of philosophy (*Fihrist*, 245; Sid̲j̲istānī, *Ṣiwān*, according to Ms. Murad Molla 1408, 2a), but, following *Flwṭrk̲h̲s* (Plutarch ?), it was constantly repeated that he had coined the word "philosophy", and, following the introductions to the Aristotelian Logic, that he had given his name to the philosophical school of the Pythagoreans. He was sometimes believed to have elaborated on the doctrines of Empedocles (Ṣāʿid al-Andalusī, trans. Blachère, 60; Ḳifṭī, 258 f.), or to have been a forerunner of the Platonic theory of ideas (*Picatrix*, trans. Ritter and Plessner, 154). In addition to his role in the history of philosophy, his main achievements were the invention of the science of music and the propagation among the Greeks of arithmetic and geometry (Yaʿḳūbī, i, 134; or the introduction of geometry, physics, and metaphysics from the East: Abu 'l-Ḥasan al-ʿĀmirī, *Amad*, Ms. Servili 179, 80b; Ṣāʿid; Ḳifṭī; Ibn Abī Uṣaybiʿa). The Ḥarrānian Ṣābians are said to have adopted him as one of their prophets (Bīrūnī, *Chronology*, 205; Ik̲h̲wān al-Ṣafāʾ, cf. P. Kraus, *Jābir*, Cairo 1942-3, ii, 223 n. 1), and his mystico-religious character was noted (Masʿūdī, *Murūd̲j̲*, iii, 348; Ibn Abī Uṣaybiʿa). In addition to his own contacts with the East, we hear about students of his who went east and influenced Zoroastrianism and Indian religious philosophy (from the doxographical work of Ammonios, Ms. Aya Sofya 2450, cited by Bīrūnī, *Chronology* [cf. H. S. Taqizadeh, in *BSOS*, viii (1935-7), 947 ff.], and S̲h̲ahrastānī, 277 f. and 455 ff.).

Of the works ascribed to him, the *Golden Words* (*Chrysâ epê*) enjoyed extraordinary fame and a wide circulation in their Arabic translation, which, in the course of transmission, underwent slight but at times meaningful variations. They are usually referred to as *al-Risāla* (*al-Rasāʾil*) *al-d̲h̲ahabiyya* or *Waṣāyā* (*Waṣiyya*); once they are also referred to as the "Golden Epistle and Exhortation for Diogenes" (*Ras. Ik̲h̲wān al-Ṣafāʾ*, Cairo 1347/1928, iv, 100 to be connected with i, 92 f.). The appellation "golden" is said to go back to Galen who read the poem daily and copied it with gold letters, a statement for which the Greek authority remains to be found. Separate editions by J. Elichmann, *Tabula Cebetis* (1640, from Miskawayh); L. Cheikho, *Traités inédits*, 2nd ed. (1911); M. Ullmann (Diss. Munich 1959, not yet published); cf. also F. Rosenthal, in *Orientalia*, *N.S.*, x (1941), 104 ff., and M. Plessner, in *Es̲h̲kōlōt*, iv (1962), 68. The Muslims knew of various commentaries on the work. One is ascribed to Proclus (*Fihrist*, 252; Ḳifṭī, 89) and listed as extant in a summary made by ʿAbd Allāh b. al-Ṭayyib (d. 435/1043) in Ms. Escurial 888 (8); its relationship, if any, to the commentary of Hierocles has not yet been investigated. A recension of Sid̲j̲istānī, *Ṣiwān* (Murad Molla 1408, 13a) introduces its (uncommented) quotation of the work as being "a summary of the book of Iamblichus in explanation of the 'Golden' Exhortations". A manuscript of this commentary appears to be preserved in Princeton (J. Kritzek, in *MIDEO*, iii (1956), 380). The existence of a commentary by Aḥmad b. al-Ṭayyib al-Sarak̲h̲sī (p. 55, Rosenthal) is poorly attested (a confusion with the afore-mentioned ʿAbd Allāh b. al-Ṭayyib ?). ʿAlī b. Riḍwān's *Commentary on Pythagoras on Virtue* (Ibn Abī Uṣaybiʿa, ii, 104) may have dealt with the *Golden Words*.

The famous Pythagorean *symbola* were known and often cited (cf. B. R. Sanguinetti, in *JA*, v/8 (1856), 188; G. Levi Della Vida, in *RSO*, iii (1910), 595 ff.; *Picatrix*, trans. Ritter and Plessner, 422). A good deal of doxographical material was available in the translations of philosophical texts, *e.g.*, that of Ps.-Plutarch's *Placita Philosophorum*. Excerpts on the intellect and emanation ascribed to Pythagoras appear in al-Ṭabarī, *Firdaws*, 70 f., 72 f. Siddiqi, a passage on the connexion between the soul and physical perfection in al-Tawḥīdī, *Ris. al-Ḥayāt*, 68 f. (*Trois Épîtres*, ed. Keilani). A valuable exposition of Pythagorean cosmology has been preserved by al-Shahrastānī, 265 ff. (cf. D. Kövendi, in F. Altheim, *Gesch. der Hunnen*, v,32-71). A large number of wise sayings was ascribed to Pythagoras; Ḥunayn's chapter on Pythagoras in the *Nawādir* is restricted to the *Golden Words*, but extensive collections are found in the *Ṣiwān*, Ibn Hindū, Mubashshir, Ibn Abī Uṣaybiʿa, aud Anon. Ms. Aya Sofya 2469. Although of Greek origin, they can rarely be traced to sayings connected with the name of Pythagoras in Greek tradition (cf., *e.g.*, F. Rosenthal, in *Orientalia, N.S.* xxvii (1958), 29 ff.). We cannot, however, be certain in all cases as to whether their attribution to Pythagoras was effected in the Greek or, rather, the Oriental tradition.

Many other Pythagorean writings are mentioned by the sources. It was known that Plato had asked Dion to buy three books by Pythagoras (Ḳifṭī, 20, as in Iamblichus). According to another statement of Greek origin quoted in the name of Porphyry but not contained in Porphyry's Greek text (Ibn Abī Uṣaybiʿa, i, 42), Archytas collected eighty works by himself and 200 more from other members of the Pythagorean school; thus, there once existed 280 genuine works (Mubashshir, Ibn Abī Uṣaybiʿa), and, in addition, a number of works on a great variety of subjects, mentioned by title, that were not genuine. The Muslims knew three treatises with a commentary by Iamblichus (*On Spiritual Polity*, *To the Tyrant of Sicily*, and *To Sīfan.s on the Discovery of Ideas*) (*Fihrist*). The general references to "works on arithmetic and music" do not seem to aim at any specific work, but Ibn Abī Uṣaybiʿa attributes to Pythagoras a *Book on Arithmetic* and five further titles. *A Treatise on the Natural Numbers* (*al-aʿdād al-ṭabīʿiyya*) is cited by a writer on alchemy (Kraus, *Jābir*, ii, 45 n. 5; *ibid.* ii, 289 n. 9, on the *Miftāḥ al-ḥikma known as Nuzhat al-nufūs*). Some surviving works may be described as Neo-Pythagorean products, such as the *Oikonomikos* of Bryson (ed. M. Plessner, Heidelberg 1928), the excerpts on domestic life by a certain female philosopher named Pythagoras (?) (Abu 'l-Ḥasan [al-ʿĀmirī], *al-Saʿāda wa 'l-isʿād*, 389 ff. Minovi), or a brief treatise on the *Education of the Young* ascribed to Plato (F. Rosenthal, in *Orientalia, N.S.* x (1941), 383 ff.).

Like other great names of Antiquity, that of Pythagoras served to give greater prestige to alchemical teachings, and the Djābir-Corpus contained a *Muṣaḥḥaḥāt F.* (Kraus, *Jābir*, i, 94; ii, 45 n. 5). There also existed a *Kitāb al-Ḳurʿa* on divination in his name (*Fihrist*, 314) (= P. Tannery, in *Notices et Extraits*, xxxi/2 (1886), 231 ff. ?).

An authority on *materia medica* named Badīghūras is cited numerous times in al-Rāzī's *Ḥāwī* and other authors on the subject. The form of the name is not easily reconciled with Pythagoras, and such an identification went probably unnoticed by al-Rāzī; it is not impossible, but other Greek names may be involved (such as Diagoras). The pre-Hippocratic physician Pythagoras (Būthāghūras), in the sketch of the ancient history of medicine going back to Yaḥyā al-Naḥwī, appears to be a figment of the imagination inspired by the figure of Pythagoras (*Ṣiwān*, 8b, where he is distinguished from the contemporary philosopher Fūthāghūras; Ibn Abī Uṣaybiʿa, i, 23).

The influence of Pythagoras and Pythagoreanism on Muslim civilization must be rated rather high. Greco-Arabic theories of music and numbers go back ultimately to them (Nicomachus of Gerasa, the author of the *Arithmêtikê Eisagôgê*, was even thought to have been identical with the father of Aristotle). The Ikhwān al-Ṣafāʾ may not have been entirely unaware of the organizational precedent of Pythagoreanism, and al-Rāzī, among others, is stated to have been inspired by the Pythagoreans and to have written in their defence (Masʿūdī, *Tanbīh*, 162; Ṣāʿid, trans. Blachère, 75). However, the name of Pythagoras must often be considered a mere label, as in his alleged appearance, together with Plato and Aristotle, in Ismāʿīlism (Maḳrīzī, *Khiṭaṭ*, Būlāḳ 1270, i, 394).

Bibliography: In the article, supplementary to M. Steinschneider, *Die arabischen Übersetzungen* (1889), repr. Graz 1960, 4-8. (F. ROSENTHAL)

FITNA, the primary meaning is "putting to the proof, discriminatory test", as gold, al-Djurdjānī says in his *Taʿrīfāt* (ed. Flügel, Leipzig 1845, 171), is tested by fire. Hence the idea of a temptation permitted or sent by God to test the believer's faith, which, for the man wedded to his desires, would have the appearance of an invitation to abandon the faith. "Your goods and children are *fitna*" (Ḳurʾān, VIII, 28; LXIV, 15). The term *fitna* occurs many times in the Ḳurʾān with the sense of temptation or trial of faith ("tentation d'abjurer", according to R. Blachère's translation); and most frequently as a test which is in itself a punishment inflicted by God upon the sinful, the unrighteous. "Taste your *fitna*" (LI, 14); this saying is addressed to those who are "tried by the Fire" (of Gehenna)". It is not a matter of an inner, secret temptation, but of external circumstances in which faith succumbs or may succumb. "O Lord, do not place us in *fitna* before those who are unfaithful!" (Ḳurʾān, LX, 5). The idea of scandal is associated with it (VII, 3), to such an extent that to take a part in this putting to the test is for man a very grave fault: "the *fitna* of believers is worse than murder" (*ibid.*, II, 191; cf. II, 217).

On the one hand, *fitna* will thus be employed in the sense of the "trial of the grave", or even the torments of hell; but on the other hand *fitna* will be essentially a state of rebellion against the divine Law in which the weak always run the risk of being trapped. The idea which is to become dominant is that of "revolt", "disturbances", "civil war", but a civil war that breeds schism and in which the believers' purity of faith is in grave danger. There are numerous *ḥadīth*s which proclaim the troubles to come, which will destroy the Community and from which the believer must flee. For example: "after me there shall break forth such troubles (*fitna*) that the believer of one morning shall, by evening, be an infidel, while the believer of the evening shall, next day, be an infidel—save only for those whom God will strengthen through knowledge" (quoted in the "Profession of Faith" of Ibn Baṭṭa, in H. Laoust's translation).—In view of the fusion of spiritual and temporal characteristic of Islam, the great struggles of the early period of Muslim history are *fitna* (pl. *fitan*), inasmuch as the questions contested regarding the legitimacy of the *Imāms* or caliphs and the armed conflicts that they aroused have a direct bearing on the values of faith.

The series of events which includes the murder of ʿUthmān, the designation of ʿAlī as *Imām*, the battle of Ṣiffīn and the development of both the *shīʿat ʿAlī* [*q.v.*] and the *khawāridj* [*q.v.*] schisms, and the seizing of power by Muʿāwiya, is often called "the first *fitna*", and also "the *fitna*" *par excellence* or "the great *fitna*". On account of the struggles that marked Muʿāwiya's advent, the term *fitna* was later applied to any period of disturbances inspired by schools or sects that broke away from the majority of believers (*al-djumla*). We read of the *fitna* of the Murdjiʾa, which Ibn al-Nakhaʿī apparently described as "graver" than that of the Azāriḳa Khāridjīs. And every "innovator", every man guilty of *bidʿa*, is potentially an instigator of *fitna*. Reversing the terms, al-Ḥasan al-Baṣrī gives this definition: "all those who foment disturbances (*fitna*) are innovators (*muḥdith*)". The "men of Tradition and the Community", *ahl al-sunna wa 'l-djamāʿa* have the strict duty to obey the legitimate sovereign so long as his orders do not run counter to the Ḳurʾān, and to shun all *fitna*. It is in this spirit that the first Sunnī professions of faith (*e.g.*, *Fiḳh Akbar*, i, 5) "rely upon God" in the dispute between ʿUthmān and ʿAlī, and regard the successive proclamation to the *Imāma* of both of them as equally valid.

Although the struggle between ʿAlī and Muʿawiya and its consequences institutes the era of *fitna* par excellence, during which schisms came into being which were never to be resolved, the term *fitna* was none the less applied, in the course of history, to other and more localized disturbances. It is in this way, for example, that some chronicles, denouncing the struggles and seditions which more than once pitted Ashʿarīs and Ḥanbalīs against each other, are apt to speak of *fitna*, as is the case at Baghdād, shortly after the death of al-Ashʿarī, when his gravestone was overturned, or at Damascus in 835/1432, when the majority of the *ʿulama*ʾ anathematized Ibn Taymiyya.—On the other hand, to denote the persecution of the followers of the "righteous Ancients", which also affected Ibn Ḥanbal under al-Maʾmūn, at the time of the triumph of the Muʿtazila, the annalists are more inclined to speak of *miḥna* [*q.v.*]. The chroniclers concerned are those who came after al-Mutawakkil's reaction and were opposed to *muʿtazilī* tendencies; according to this point of view, there was no element of "rebellion" under al-Maʾmūn, since it was the central power which protected the *bidʿa*. The *ahl al-djamāʿa* thus underwent a "testing" (*miḥna*) for the sake of their faith, there was no *fitna* (that is to say armed revolt led by "innovators" and "agitators") whatsoever.

It is in the chapter on the *imāma* that the treatises of *ʿilm al-kalām* raise the question of *fitna*. It is taught that the nomination of an *imām* is "obligatory" (*wādjib*) for the Community, an obligation justified 'rationally" (*ʿaḳlan*) according to the Muʿtazilīs, "'legally" (*sharʿan*) or "traditionally" (*samʿan*) according to the Ashʿarīs. And one of the arguments most readily put forward is that only an *imām* can prevent the disturbances of *fitna*, or restore peace if they have already broken out. Indeed, certain schools with Khāridjī tendencies teach that it is obligatory to nominate an *imām* in the event of *fitna*, but not if peace is prevailing; others, on the contrary, hold that he should only be nominated in a period of peace, never in a time of unrest, for fear that the nomination should give rise to fresh revolts. The Ashʿarīs, for their part, require the *imām* to lead the Community during *fitna* and in times of peace alike, and consider as the authority in favour of their opinion the history of the early years of Islam.

All these discussions relate implicitly to a notion of *fitna* defined as disturbances, or even civil war, involving the adoption of doctrinal attitudes which endanger the purity of the Muslim faith; and every mention of *fitna* evokes "the great *fitna* of Islam" which culminated at Ṣiffīn. We may say in fact that somewhat later summaries of the question—or more accurately, the nomenclatures of the schools in which they result—are closer or more distant echoes of the attitudes and opinions which the "great *fitna*" had caused to be adopted. At that time (early 2nd/7th cent.), certain traditionists of Baṣra and the first Muʿtazilīs declared that "the era of the *fitna*" having opened, every *mudjtahid*, every man capable of "making an effort", was entitled to seek for the solution; the Karrāmiyya, for their part, upheld the concomitant legitimacy of the two *imāms* in dispute; the Shīʿa maintained the sole legitimacy of ʿAlī; while the majority of the Sunnīs maintained that it was better to obey the established power and refrain from taking sides, in order to have no part in civil war, and thereby to hasten the return to peace. It is on this last attitude that the Ashʿarīs and Māturīdīs were later to base their views. For the *fitna* in Muslim Spain, see AL-ANDALUS, vi, 5.

Bibliography: the various treatises of *ʿilm al-kalām*, *e.g.*, Djurdjānī, *Sharḥ al-Mawāḳif*, ed. Cairo 1325/1907, viii, 344 ff.; A. J. Wensinck, *The Muslim Creed*, Cambridge 1932, 104, 109-10; H. Laoust, *Essai sur les doctrines sociales et politiques de Taḳī-d-Dīn Aḥmad b. Taimīya*, Cairo 1939, index, s.v.; idem, *La Profession de Foi d'Ibn Baṭṭa*, Damascus 1958, index, *s.v.*

((L. GARDET)

FIṬNAT, pseudonym of ZÜBEYDE (?-1194/1780), a Turkish poetess. Little is known of her early life. She was the daughter of the Shaykh al-Islām Meḥmed Esʿad Efendi (d. 1166/1753) the well known scholar of the reign of Meḥemmed IV, whose father Abū Isḥāḳ Ismāʿīl had also been a Shaykh al-Islām. She was married to Derwīsh Meḥmed Efendi who became ḳāḍīʿasker of Rumeli under Selīm III.

Her short *dīwān* contains all the usual conventional poems written for various occasions and *ghazal*s which do not vary in style or content from those of her contemporary male poets. She tends on the whole to follow the Nābī—Ḳodja Rāghib Pasha school of "wisdom-poetry", full of aphorisms and fatalistic statements. But occasionally she is inspired by the carefree and joyful style of Nedīm (see her *musaddas* in Gibb, vi, 395). She writes with great ease in a polished and fluent style.

Bibliography: Faṭīn, *Tedhkire*, s.v.; Gibb, *Ottoman Poetry*, iv, 150 ff.; A. C. Yöntem, in *İA*, s.v.

(FAHİR İz)

FIṬR [see ʿĪD AL-FIṬR].

FIṬRA is a "noun of kind" (Wright, *Grammar*,[3] i, 123[d]) to the infinitive *faṭr* and means (an Ethiopic loan-meaning, see Schwally, in *ZDMG*, liii, 199 f.; Nöldeke, *Neue Beiträge*, 49), "a kind or way of creating or of being created". It occurs in Ḳurʾān, XXX, 29 (*khilḳa*, Bayḍāwī) and other forms of its verb in the same meaning occur 14 times. But though

Muḥammad uses derived forms freely, it was obscure to his hearers. Ibn ʿAbbās did not understand it until he heard a Bedouin use it of digging a well, and then the Bedouin probably meant the genuinely Arab sense of shakk (*Lisān*, vi, 362, l. 20). Its theologically important usage is in the saying of Muḥammad, "Every infant is born according to the *fiṭra* (*ʿala 'l-fiṭra*; *i.e.*, Allāh's kind or way of creating; "on God's plan", cf. Macdonald, *Religious attitude in Islam*, 243); then his parents make him a Jew or a Christian or a Magian". This is one of several contradictory traditions on the salvability of the infants of unbelievers. On the whole question the theologians were uncertain and in disagreement. This text evidently means that every child is born naturally a Muslim; but is perverted after birth by his environment. But in this interpretation—that of the Muʿtazilīs (cf. *Kashshāf*, ed. Lees, ii, 1094)—there were found serious theological and legal difficulties. (i.) It interferes with the sovereign will (*mashīʾa*) and guidance (*hidāya*) of Allāh. Orthodox Islam, therefore, holds that the parents could be only a secondary cause (*sabab*) and that the guiding aright and leading astray must come from Allāh himself. (ii.) This view, and indeed almost any view of the tradition, would involve that such an infant, if his parents died before he reached years of discretion, could not inherit from them, and that if he died before years of discretion, his parents could not inherit from him. For this presupposes that he is a Muslim up to years of discretion, and canon law lays down that a Muslim cannot inherit from a non-Muslim or vice versa (*Ḥāshiya* of al-Bādjūrī on the *sharḥ* of Ibn Ḳāsim on the *matn* of Abū Shudjāʿ, ed. Cairo 1307, ii, 74 f. and Sachau, *Muhammedanisches Recht*, 186, 204, 206—a favourite subject for hair-splitting). Two attempts have been made to escape this. (i.) This statement of Muḥammad is to be regarded as a decision (*ḥukm*) and was abrogated by the later decision as to inheritance. But it is pointed out that it is not really a decision, but a narrative (*khabar*) and that narratives are not abrogated. (ii). The being made a Jew, Christian or Magian is to be regarded as not actual, but figurative, and takes place in this figurative sense from the point of birth; the legal religion of the infant is automatically that of his parents, although he comes actually to embrace that religion only with maturity of mind. Another view was that being created according to the *fiṭra* meant only being created in a healthy condition, like a sound animal, with a capacity of either belief or unbelief when the time should come. Another was that *fiṭra* meant only "beginning" (*badʾa*). Still another was that it referred to Allāh's creating man with a capacity of either belief or unbelief and then laying on them the covenant of the "Day of *Alastu*" (Ḳurʾān, VII, 171). Finally that it was that to which Allāh turns round the hearts of men.

Bibliography: Mālik b. Anas, *Muwaṭṭa* (ed. Cairo 1279-80 with Zurḳānī), ii, 35; *Dict. of tech. terms*, 1117 f.; *Lisān*, vi, 362 f.; *Risāla* on *Īmān* by Abū Manṣūr Muḥammad al-Samarḳandī prefixed to the Ḥaydarābād ed. of the *Fiḳh al-akbar* of Abū Ḥanīfa, 25 f.; *Miṣbāḥ* of al-Fayyūmī s.v.; Krehl, *Beiträge z. muh. Dogm.*, 235; Hughes, *Dict. of Islam* under *Infants*; Rāzī, *Mafātīḥ al-ghayb*, iv, 16; vi, 480 of ed. of Cairo 1308; Ṭabarī, *Tafsīr*, xxi, 24.

(D. B. Macdonald)

FIṬRAT (Fiṭra), ʿAbd al-Raʾūf, inspirer and theorist of the reform movement in Turkestan. Very little is known of his life: born at the end of the 19th century into a family of small traders in Bukhārā, he was at first a teacher, and then devoted all his time to his activities as a writer, poet and journalist. Fiṭrat was active from 1908-9 in the reform movement of Bukhārā (the *Djadīds*, who were originally concerned with educational reform, but from 1917 were to form themselves into a political party, the 'Young Bukhārians'), of which he soon became the ideological leader. From 1910 to 1914 he took part in the creation of a reformed system of teaching in Bukhārā and in Turkestan, and actively promoted the sending of students to Turkey. In 1920, after the inauguration of the People's Republic, he held office in the government at first as Minister of Education, then as Minister of Foreign Affairs. After the suppression of the republic in 1924, he took no part in the government of the Uzbekistan Republic (unlike some of his comrades in arms, such as Fayḍ Allāh Hožaev [see KHODJAEV]), and taught at the University of Samarḳand until his arrest in 1937. His fate after that is unknown.

Like Djamāl al-Dīn al-Afghānī, with whom he has much in common (though he himself does not claim it), ʿAbd al-Raʾūf Fiṭrat studies in all his works the causes of the spiritual and temporal decay of the Muslim world, examines the external signs of it, and seeks a means of salvation from it. Fiṭrat studied this crisis as seen in the example of Bukhārā, which, perhaps more than any other Muslim country, showed the full extent of it: one of the chief centres of Islam delivered over to the Russian conqueror, the *madrasas* deserted, the formerly powerful state sunk into anarchy, the Muslim faith reduced on the one hand to a fossilized religion, fettered by all the weight of an obsolete legalism, on the other, to the superstition and the fetishism of the masses (*Munāẓara*).

Fiṭrat saw for it only one possible salvation: the return to a dynamic religion freed from a rigorism which was completely foreign to the fundamental rules of Islam, and freed first of all from servile respect for *taḳlīd*.

But although criticism forms a considerable part of Fiṭrat's work, it is not merely critical and destructive. He gave much thought to the means by which his country and all the Islamic community could overcome this crisis. In this search for its salvation, Fiṭrat seems to represent the two fundamental aspects of Muslim renewal. He was a reformer, an educator and a politician whose thought was mainly revolutionary. He considered that all reform must start with assiduous work among the people. True to his first vocation as an educator, he held that no regeneration of the Muslim community was possible without the preparation and education of individuals, and a consequent rebirth in each of an understanding and grasp of the meaning of Islam. Fiṭrat stressed continually the importance of the individual and the part which he must play, maintaining that personal reform was an absolute condition of the whole of Islam. He gives a considerable place in his works to the problem of reformed methods of teaching (*Munāẓara*, 26, 35-6, 43, 48, 52; *Bayānāt*, 29). Traditional education having proved incapable of developing, even of recognizing the necessity for change, he regarded the reformation of the *maktabs* as the only road to salvation. An important feature of Fiṭrat's thought is his pragmatic conception of knowledge. He considers that the only learning which is worthy of human effort is learning which is of value not only to man's ultimate salvation but also to his earthly existence; it is also a learning which can be acquired within a reasonable period, leaving man time to put it to use for the good of humanity. Thus he opposed the preservation of scholasticism, which 'is of no help to man in the modern world' (*Munāẓara*, 28), and insisted that all knowledge should be submitted to the criticism of the intellect and not accepted blindly.

In this field Fiṭrat, while recognizing that 'one must seek knowledge where it is to be found', denied that Islam needed to borrow anything from the West or to seek inspiration from it or to imitate it, for, he maintained, everything that has contributed to the temporal greatness of the West derives from Islam (*Bayānāt*, 32-3). But Fiṭrat did not consider that the salvation of the Muslim community would come only from below, through a regeneration of all Muslims; he held that there was another task to be accomplished, the transformation of Muslim society from above, and it is here that we see in him the political thinker. No institution is spared in Fiṭrat's political programme; he insists throughout his works on the importance of the individual and of individual initiative, and on man's ability to dominate everything around him, from Nature to his own destiny. Analysing the economic and social bases of power, he clearly distinguishes spiritual demands from physical, considering that men's conduct is ruled primarily by natural conditions. Without arriving at any definite separation of the spiritual and the temporal, Fiṭrat indicated that the solutions to the problems of the adaption of Islam to the modern world were to be sought along these lines. Similarly, he considered that a complete revision of social relations, leading to a more equitable distribution of wealth, was indispensable and in no way contrary to the teaching of Islam. In his view, one of the causes of the decadence of Islam was that it had become the ideology of the wealthy classes, and thus its salvation lay in the destruction of this ideology. Another equally important course to be followed was the introduction of a new kind of relationship within society. *ʿĀʾile* ('The Family') is devoted to a study of the reform necessary in family relationships. And the reform enunciated by Fiṭrat was not a compromise between the structure of Islamic society and that of Western society, but a radical choice, a break with the past, the complete re-making of family relationships, in which Fiṭrat gave a very important place to the raising of the status of women. For Fiṭrat, the internal renewal of the Muslim community could be brought about only by a double process: a spiritual renewal, involving the education of each individual, and a political and social revolution which would leave remaining nothing of the ideas, the institutions and the human relations of the period of stagnation, and which would give birth to a modern society and a modern state. This internal regeneration was indispensable in order to achieve external liberation. The salvation of Islam would imply the end of foreign domination, which was a consequence of the degradation of Islam: and the struggle for liberty does not come after the work of internal regeneration, but is one of the aspects of it. Fiṭrat constantly reminds his readers that 'the *djihād* is an obligation for every Muslim'. For Fiṭrat, this internal regeneration and the resultant progress would contribute to the Holy War, and in a very direct fashion: 'Learn at the same time the traditional learning and the new learning, and thus you will be able to prepare the material means which are indispensable for the defence of Islam, the *djihād*, which is obligatory for all' (*Munāẓara*, 48). Thus Fiṭrat's thought develops into the ideas of the unity of Islam and of Pan-Islamism.

Like Djamāl al-Dīn al-Afghānī, Fiṭrat thought that the renaissance of Islam had to come from the Muslims themselves. The incitement to action, the rejection of passivity, of quietism and of reluctance to accept responsibility, which are such noticeable features of the works of Djamāl al-Dīn, are similarly prominent in those of Fiṭrat. Fiṭrat followed Djamāl al-Dīn along the path which he had opened up by stressing the temporal history of Islam, and it is probably for this reason that his works are more concerned with defining the means of achieving a new vitality than with re-defining the content, or more simply the methods, of the Faith. The originality of Fiṭrat's work lies in the fact that to reformism and Pan-Islamism there is added a call to social justice and to a revolt against the rich and those in power.

His principal works are (1) *Munāẓara*, first published in Istanbul in 1908, and re-published in Persian at Tashkent in 1913; Russian trans. by Col. Yagello, Tashkent 1911, under the title *Spor Bukharskogo mudarrisa s evropeytsem v Indii o novometodnikh shkolakh*. (*Istinnîy resultat obmena mîsley*) pervoye izdanie sočineniy Bukhara, Fiṭrat; (2) *Bayānāt-i sayyāḥ-i hindī*, first publ. at Istanbul (n.d.), then by Behbūdī in a Russian trans. at Tashkent in 1913 as: Abd ur Rauf, *Rasskazî indiyskogo puteshestvennika* (*Bukhara kak ona 'est'*); (3) *Sāʾiḥa*, Istanbul 1910; (4) *Rahbar-i nadjāt*, n.p. 1915; (5) *ʿĀʾile*, n.p., n.d.

He published also various novels (notably *Ḳiyāmat*, Tashkent 1961) and poems in *Millî Edebiyat*, Berlin, i (1943).

Bibliography: Veli Kajum Khan, introductory article to the review *Millî Edebiyat*, i (1943), 4-5; A. Zavqi and I. Tolqun, *Şair Colpan*, in *Millî Turkestan*, lxxvi (1952), 17-23; Erturk, *Abdur Rauf Fitrat*, in *Millî Turkestan*, lxxx-lxxxi (1952), 9-16; F. Khodjaev, *O mlado Buhartsah*, in *Istorik Marksist*, i (1926), 123-41; idem, *K istorii revolyutsii v Bukhare*, Tashkent 1926; S. Aini, *Buhoro inqilobi ta'rihi učun materiallar*, Moscow 1926. (H. Carrère d'Encausse)

FLAG [see liwāʾ].

FLOOD [see ṭūfān].

FLORI [see filori].

FLOWER [see nawriyya].

FOGGARA [see ḳanāt].

FOLKLORE [see ḥikāya, taḳālīd].

FOOD [see ghidhāʾ].

FOREIGN AFFAIRS [see khāridjiyya].

FORESTS [see ghāba].

FORNICATION [see zināʾ].

FORTIFICATION [see burdj, ḥiṣār, ḥiṣn, ḳalʿa, sūr].

FOUNTAIN [see sabīl].

FRAGA [see ifragha].

FRANKS [see al-ifrandj].

FRAXINETUM was in the middle ages the name of the village now called La-Garde-Freinet, lying in a gap in the Mt. des Maures (département of Var, France). This locality only finds a place in this Encyclopaedia because it was occupied for 80 years by Muslim pirates who had come from Spain between 278-81/891-4. Having gained a footing in the gulf of Saint-Tropez, they occupied a natural fortress (Fraxinet, Freinet) near the modern village of La-Garde-Freinet; "soon reinforced by new groups from the Iberian peninsula, the invaders visited the county of Fréjus with fire and the sword, and sacked the chief town". They then infiltrated westwards, ascended the Rhône, and extended their influence as far as the Alps and Piedmont. About 321/933 "light columns, very mobile, held—at least during the summer—all the country under a reign of terror, while the bulk of the Muslim forces was entrenched in the mountainous canton of Fraxinetum, in the immediate vicinity of the sea". The States concerned reacted slowly, and only in 361 or 362/972 or 973, after several unsuccessful attempts, did the vassals of Otto the Great "arrive to free Provence and the transalpine regions from the Muslim peril and to drive away for ever these pirates from their lair in the gulf of Saint-Tropez". Thus ended this "strange Islamic State encapsulated within a wholly Christian land" (J. Calmette, *L'effondrement d'un empire et la naissance d'une Europe*, 117).

Bibliography: No Arabic chronicle refers to these events, for which the *Antapodosis* of Liutprand, ed. Becker, Hanover-Leipzig 1915, is the principal source; J. T. Reinaud, *Invasions des Sarrazins en France*, Paris 1836 (Eng. tr., Lahore 1956), gives the history of these corsairs in detail, for which see also: R. Poupardin, *Le royaume de Provence sous les Carolingiens*, Paris 1901, 243-73; idem, *Le royaume de Bourgogne*, Paris 1907, 87-107; G. Pinet deManteyer, *La Provence du Ier au XIIe siècle*, Paris 1908, 238 ff.; E. Lévi-Provençal, *Hist. Esp. Mus.*, ii, 154-60 (which has been taken as the basis of this entry) supplies a more detailed bibliography.

(Ed.)

FREE WILL [see IKHTIYĀR, ḲADAR].

FREEMASONRY [see MĀSŪNIYYA].

FRONTIER [see ʿAWĀṢIM, GHĀZĪ, MURĀBIṬ, RIBĀṬ, THUGHŪR].

FRUNZE [see PIČPEK].

FU'ĀD AL-AWWAL, king of Egypt. Aḥmad Fu'ād was born in the Gizeh palace on 26 March 1868, of a Circassian mother. In 1879 his father, the Khedive Ismāʿīl, who had been deposed by the Sublime Porte, took him with him into exile. He studied in Geneva and Turin, and in 1885 entered the Italian military academy. At Rome in 1887, as a second-lieutenant in the artillery, he frequently visited the Italian royal family. Having been Ottoman military attaché at Vienna, he finally returned (1892) to Egypt after a stay at Istanbul. As prince he accepted the first Rectorship of the Free University of Cairo (1908-13). On the death of his brother Ḥusayn (9 October 1917) he succeeded him as sultan of Egypt. The British considered him as not at all Anglophobe, though regretting that he enjoyed neither great popularity nor much influence among the Egyptians (Lord Lloyd). He assumed the title of king of Egypt from 15 March 1922, and d. 28 April 1936. He had a respect for decorum and tradition, and during his lifetime the queen and the princesses, excepting his own daughters, remained veiled.

The age in which he reigned is significant in the history of the Egyptian awakening. The nationalist movement, then embodied in the person of Saʿd Zaghlūl and the *Wafd*, launched the open struggle against the British occupation immediately after the armistice of 11 November 1918. A campaign of signed petitions, demonstrations in Cairo, and strikes (1919, again in 1921) forced Great Britain to recognize Egypt as a "sovereign and independent state" (1922). While profiting by the action of the *Wafd*, which helped him to counteract British influence, king Fu'ād dreamed of an authority too absolute for him not to fear the nationalist leaders. A constitution envisaging two chambers was promulgated on 19 April 1923. The 1924 elections were a triumph for the *Wafd*. But the assassination of the *Sirdār* (November 1924), the difficulties in the negotiations, several times broken off and then resumed, with the British with a view to drawing up a treaty, the intervention of the British in Egypt and their Sudanese policy, all added to the crises. Parliament was dissolved four times, and the elections always returned a Wafdist majority (1925, 1926, 1929), except that of 1931 which the *Wafd* boycotted. In spite of this, there were only three rather brief periods of Wafdist ministry (Saʿd Zaghlūl in 1924, Muṣṭafā al-Naḥḥās in 1928 and 1930). That is to say, the king did as he pleased with the constitution, which was abrogated in 1930, immediately superseded, then re-established in 1935. He relied on minority parties or on unattached politicians; he appealed to, among others, Aḥmad Ziwar (1924-6), Muḥammad Maḥmūd (1928-9), and Ismāʿīl Ṣidḳī (1930-3). At the end of his reign the Italian menace (Abyssinian war) demonstrated the urgency of an agreement with Britain. The treaty was signed in London on 26 August 1936, four months after his death.

From the economic point of view, the foundation of the Miṣr bank marked the first step in his reign towards economic independence. He had no share in it, nor did he deposit his private fortune there, which, however, he did not neglect. On the other hand, he took a lively interest in the intellectual development of the country. He founded schools, encouraged the new university at Gizeh (Fu'ād al-Awwal University, 1925) and the reform of al-Azhar [*q.v.*], an establishment on which his internal policies greatly relied. He promoted the creation and rejuvenation of numerous cultural institutions (Royal Society of Political Economy, of Geography, etc.). He insisted that Cairo should be the venue of great international congresses. He was however accused of mistrusting Egyptians and confiding in foreigners. He always patronized, without any fanaticism, all those who, outside politics, could contribute to the development of modern Egypt, especially in the cultural sphere. He was a true Maecenas, visiting schools and institutions. The personal prestige which he enjoyed abroad and the historical studies which he patronized enlarged the world reputation of Egypt.

Bibliography: G. Hanotaux, *Histoire de la nation égyptienne*, vii, specially pp. iii-xxxii (by Henri Dehérain); M. Colombe, *L'évolution de l'Égypte (1924-1950)*, Paris 1951, with detailed bibliography; Karīm Thābit, *al-Malik Fu'ād, malik al-Nahḍa*, Cairo 1944.

(J. Jomier)

FU'ĀD PASHA, Kečedji-zāde Meḥmed, five times Ottoman Foreign Minister and twice Grand Vizier, was born in Istanbul in 1815, the son of the poet ʿIzzet Molla [*q.v.*]. Upon his father's exile to Sivas in 1829 Fu'ād switched from the usual theological curriculum to the new medical school, where he learned French, the key to his future career. From 1834-5 he spent three years as an army doctor in Tripoli in Africa; but since the Porte's diplomatic business was rapidly increasing, his French gained Fu'ād appointment to the Translation Bureau in November 1837. Like his life-long colleague Meḥmed Emīn ʿĀlī [see ʿĀLĪ PASHA MUḤAMMAD AMĪN] he became a protégé of Muṣṭafā Reshīd Pasha [*q.v.*].

During the next decade Fu'ād advanced rapidly as interpreter and diplomat through the ranks of the Ottoman bureaucracy and gained firsthand experience of Europe. In 1839 he became dragoman of the Porte; in 1840 he was dragoman, and from 1841 to 1844 first secretary, of the Ottoman embassy in London; in 1844 he went on special mission to Spain when Isabella II was declared of age to rule. In March 1845 Fuʾād was appointed member of an ad hoc commission on education whose report of August 1846 recommended a new state school system. He became dragoman of the imperial Dīwān in June-July 1845, and on 18 February 1847 *āmeddji* [*q.v.*]. Late in 1848 Fuʾād was sent to Bucharest to ensure smooth relations with the Russian forces which had entered the Principalities to suppress the revolution. When in 1849 Magyar and Polish refugees sought asylum in Ottoman territory Fuʾād was dispatched to St. Petersburg to uphold Reshīd's policy of no extraditions. Nicholas I received Fuʾād on 16 October. Fuʾād's mission was successful. In reward he was advanced to *ṣadāret müsteshārī*, in effect Minister of the Interior. After returning via Jassy and Bucharest to Istanbul on 11 April 1850 he sat on a special commission of the *medjlis-i wālā* to deal with Christian complaints from Vidin.

Fuʾād went to Bursa in mid-September 1850 to take baths for his rheumatism. There he wrote with Aḥmad Djewdet [*q.v.*] the first modern Ottoman grammar published in the empire, *Ḳawāʿid-i ʿOthmāniyye*, 1851. In that year, on the founding of the Endjümen-i Dānish [see ANDJUMAN], Fuʾād was appointed a member. In Bursa Fuʾād and Djewdet also drafted a proposal for the Bosporus ferry-boat company, which became the first joint-stock company in the empire. From April to July 1852 Fuʾād was in Egypt on a special mission to see to the application of Tanẓīmāt [*q.v.*] decrees and solve questions of railway building, inheritance, and the Egyptian tribute. That year Fuʾād advocated a European loan to help the finances of the empire, but Sultan ʿAbd al-Medjīd refused.

On 9 August 1852 Fuʾād was appointed Foreign Minister, three days after ʿĀlī succeeded Reshīd as Grand Vizier. This marks the first time Reshīd's two disciples had worked together in the highest offices, and the beginning of their involuntary estrangement from their master. This turbulent period brought the Leiningen mission with Austria's ultimatum on Montenegro. Fuʾād was also involved in the pro-Latin decision on the Holy Places. Prince Menshikov, Russia's special envoy, consequently deliberately snubbed Fuʾād, causing his resignation in early March 1853. For a year from March 1854 Fuʾād was special commissioner with military authority in Epirus and Thessaly, successfully repressing Greek insurgents who sought to profit from the Crimean War situation. Thereafter he was appointed to the new Tanẓīmāt Council, and in early May 1855, when ʿĀlī again succeeded Reshīd as Grand Vizier, again became Foreign Minister, with the rank of *vezīr* and *müshīr*. Fuʾād had a major share in elaborating the *Khaṭṭ-i Hümāyūn* [*q.v.*] of 18 February 1856. He did not, however, attend the Paris peace congress; ʿĀlī was the Ottoman plenipotentiary. Owing to Stratford's pressure concerning the Principalities Fuʾād resigned in early November 1856. In early August 1857 he was again President of the Tanẓīmāt Council.

Fuʾād again became Foreign Minister, and ʿĀlī Grand Vizier, on 11 January 1858, four days after Reshīd's death. As Foreign Minister he represented the empire at the Paris conference on the Principalities, 22 May to 19 August 1858; Couza's double election the next year, however, sabotaged the plan adopted for separate administrations. When Druze attacks on Maronites provoked intervention by the great powers, Fuʾād was sent on 12 July 1860 to Beirut with full civil and military powers. News of massacres in Syria took him to Damascus, where he had over 700 persons tried and 167 executed, including the *wālī* Aḥmed Pasha. This severity, earning Fuʾād the local nickname "father of the cord", successfully forestalled further penetration by French troops. Back in the Lebanon, Fuʾād punished some guilty Druze, though the French claimed he let most escape. He was chairman of the international commission that sat there from 5 October 1860 to 4 May 1861, although missing the first five sessions. The new Lebanese administrative statute of 9 June 1861 resulted.

On 6 August 1861, while still in Syria, Fuʾād was appointed Foreign Minister for the fourth time, and on 22 November Grand Vizier, which post he took up on arriving in Istanbul on 21 December. His first job was to deal vigorously with a financial crisis of panic proportions; he withdrew the *ḳāʾime* [*q.v.*], drew up a budget, and negotiated the successful loan of 1862. A Montenegrin campaign was successfully concluded, but the Belgrade incident of 1862 forced Turkish evacuation of two Serbian fortresses. Fuʾād helped secure new *millet* constitutions for the Greeks, Armenians, and Jews. He resigned on 2 January 1863. His famous letter of resignation to ʿAbd al-ʿAzīz pointed out financial difficulties and the danger of Balkan nationalisms; it was evidently also an effort, though vain, to present a united ministerial front. On 13 January Fuʾād was president of the *medjlis-i wālā*, and on 14 February *serʿasker*. In this capacity he accompanied ʿAbd al-ʿAzīz to Egypt in April, and regained the imperial favour. On 1 June 1863 he was again appointed Grand Vizier, keeping the war ministry also.

Fuʾād's three-year term was marked by the *wilāyet* law, prepared by Fuʾād and Midḥat [*q.v.*] in 1864 for the new provincial administration experiment in Bulgaria; by the final authorization of the construction of the Suez Canal; by the necessity of recognizing Karl of Hohenzollern as the new prince of Roumania; by the firman of 27 May 1866 granting Khedive Ismāʿīl's heirs direct succession from father to eldest son; and by Fuʾād's growing feud with Muṣṭafā Fāḍil Pasha [*q.v.*] over finances. Fuʾād was dismissed on 5 June 1866 because he opposed ʿAbd al-ʿAzīz's taking a daughter of Ismāʿīl as wife.

When ʿĀlī once more became Grand Vizier, on 11 February 1867, Fuʾād became Foreign Minister again. His masterly memorandum of 15 May for the Powers delineated Ottoman progress under the Tanẓīmāt, but, with ʿĀlī, Fuʾād was subject to increasing attacks from New Ottoman writers, especially over the Cretan rebellion and the final Turkish military evacuation of Serbia. From 21 June to 7 August 1867 Fuʾād accompanied ʿAbd al-ʿAzīz on his trip to Paris, London, and Vienna; Fuʾād kept the sultan from blunders, and the trip succeeded in diminishing the likelihood of serious foreign intervention in Crete, as well as interesting the sultan in western material progress. Fuʾād returned exhausted. Nevertheless he also was acting Grand Vizier in the autumn of 1867 when ʿĀlī went to Crete. He helped develop plans for the Council of State (*Shūrā-yi Dewlet* [*q.v.*]) and the Galatasaray lycée, both inaugurated in 1868. On medical advice, for his heart condition, Fuʾād travelled via Italy to Nice for a rest in the winter of 1868-69. There he died on 12 February 1869. His body was brought to Istanbul by the French dispatch-boat Renard.

Fuʾād was a convinced westernizer. He worked on many of the reforms of the later Tanẓīmāt period. He may have favoured representative government, though he was in no hurry to achieve it. His main objective was preservation of the Ottoman Empire through diplomacy and reform. He loved high office, but was not so jealous and grudging as ʿĀlī, and rather bolder in innovation. His honesty has been impugned, especially as regards gifts from Ismāʿil, but his objectives remained constant. Fuʾād was a brilliant conversationalist. He was completely at home in French. His witticisms are famous; some imputed to him are apocryphal. He also wrote well, although sometimes carelessly, and helped to clarify Ottoman Turkish by having vowel marks put in the 1858/59 *sālnāme* and in his grammar. His so-called political testament is not proven genuine; it does, however, reflect his known views.

Bibliography: Contemporary accounts and documents include Djewdet, *Tezâkir*, i (1-12), ii (13-20), iii (21-39), ed. C. Baysun, Ankara 1953, 1960, 1963; Challemel-Lacour, *Les hommes d'état de la Turquie*, in *Revue des deux mondes*, 73 (15 Feb. 1868), 917-23; Fāṭima ʿAliyye, *Aḥmed Djewdet Pasha wezamānī*, Istanbul 1332, 85-90, 109; Meḥmed Memdūḥ, *Mirʾāt-i Shuʾūnāt*, Izmir 1328, 127-33; Melek-Hanum, *Six years in Europe*, London 1873, 199-203; ʿAlī Ḥaydar Midḥat, *Tabṣire-i ʿibret*, Istanbul 1325, 23-4; Frederick Millingen, *La Turquie sous le règne d'Abdul Aziz*, Paris 1868, 272-84, 324-6; Charles Mismer, *Souvenirs du monde musulman*, Paris 1892, 13-6, 110; [A. D. Mordtmann], *Stambul und das moderne Türkenthum*, Leipzig 1877-8, i, 25-6, and ii, 143-50, 175-6; J. F. Scheltema, ed., *The Lebanon in turmoil*, New Haven 1920, 38, 143-58; I. de Testa, *Recueil des traités de la Porte ottomane*, Paris 1884-1911, vi, 90-285, and vii, *passim*; J. H. Abdolonyme Ubicini, *La Turquie actuelle*, Paris 1855, 177-84; Franz von Werner (Murad Efendi), *Türkische Skizzen*, Leipzig 1877, 166-71.

Of later studies, Orhan Köprülü's in *IA*, iv, 672-81, is the best, with many references, often to unpublished materials. See also ʿAbd al-Raḥmān Sheref, *Taʾrīkh muṣāḥabeleri*, Istanbul 1339, 98-104, 108; ʿAlī Fuʾād, *Ridjāl-i mühimme-i siyāsiye*, Istanbul 1928, 59, 141-74; I. H. Danişmend, *Izahlı osmanlı tarihi kronolojisi*, iv, Istanbul 1955, index; R. H. Davison, *The question of Fuad Paşa's 'Political Testament'*, in *Belleten*, xxiii/89 (1959), 119-36; R. H. Davison, *Reform in the Ottoman Empire, 1856-1876*, Princeton 1963, chap. 3 and index; A. Du Velay, *Essai sur l'histoire financière de la Turquie*, Paris 1903, 174-96, 260-75; Ibnülemin Mahmud Kemal Inal, *Osmanlı devrinde son sadrıazamlar*, Istanbul 1940-53, 149-95; M. Jouplain, *La question du Liban*, Paris 1908, 414-82; Adel Ismail, *Histoire du Liban du XVIIe siècle à nos jours*, iv, *Redressement et déclin du féodalisme libanais*, Beirut 1958, 352-75; E. Z. Karal, *Osmanlı tarihi*, vi and vii, Ankara 1954-6, index; B. Lewis, *The emergence of modern Turkey*[2], London 1962, 115-21, index; T. W. Riker, *The making of Roumania*, London 1931, 55-9, 75, 155-80, index; Harold Temperley, *England and the Near East*, London 1936, 262, 267-8, 306-10; idem, *The Last Phase of Stratford de Redcliffe, 1855-1858*, in *English Historical Review*, xlvii (1932), 237-55. See also the biographical dictionaries: Sāmī, *Ḳāmūs al-aʿlām*, v, 3440; *Sidjill-i ʿOthmānī*, iv, 26.

(R. H. Davison)

AL-FUḌAYL B. ʿIYĀḌ, Abū ʿAlī al-Tālaḳānī, of the tribe of Tamīmī, an early Ṣūfī, disciple of Sufyān al-Thawrī, was born in Samarḳand, grew up in Abiward, and in his youth was a highway robber. After his conversion, he betook himself to the study of *Ḥadīth* at Kūfa. He was summoned to give ascetic addresses to Hārūn al-Rashīd, who called him "The chief of the Muslims". He settled in Mecca and died there 187/803.

Mentioned frequently as a transmitter of Traditions, he was also a noted ascetic and advocate of other-worldliness, known as one who lived with God. "The servant's fear of God", he said, "is in proportion to his knowledge of Him and his renunciation of this world is in proportion to his desire for the next", and again, "Satisfaction (*riḍā*) with God is the stage of those who are close to Him, who find in Him joy and happiness". Asked what he thought of the condition of mankind, Fuḍayl replied, "Forgiven, but for my presence among them". It was said that when Fuḍayl left the world, sadness disappeared.

Bibliography: Ibn Saʿd, v, 366; al-Sulamī, *Ṭabaḳāt al-Ṣūfiyya*, Cairo 1953, 6-14; Abū Nuʿaym, *Ḥilyat al-awliyāʾ*, viii, 84-139; al-Hudjwīrī, *Kashf al-maḥdjūb*, (tr. Nicholson), 97 ff.; ʿAṭṭār, *Tadhkirāt al-awliyāʾ*, (ed. Nicholson), i, 74 ff.; Ibn Khallikān, No. 542; Shaʿrānī, *Ṭabaḳāt*, i, 58, 59.

(M. Smith)

AL-FUDJAYRA, (officially, al-Fujairah), one of the seven Trucial Shaykhdoms in Arabia and the only one lying in its entirety on the eastern side of the peninsula separating the Gulf of ʿUmān from the Persian Gulf. The tiny state is wedged between the Sultan of Muscat's territory of Rūs al-Djibāl, to the north, and the once independent territory of Kalbā (Kalba in Yāḳūt, *TA*, and the *Ḳāmūs* of al-Fīrūzābādī), to the south. Kalbā, since 1371/1952 a part of the Trucial Shaykhdom of al-Shāriḳa (Sharjah), lies between al-Fudjayra and the central part of the Sultan of Muscat's domains. From Kalbā north to Rūs al-Djibāl, the narrow littoral and steep eastern watershed of the mountains of al-Ḥadjar behind the coast constitute the region known as al-Shamāliyya.

The little town of al-Fudjayra is at the mouth of Wādī Ḥām and about two miles from the sea. Most of the inhabitants of the town and wādī are members of the tribe of al-Sharḳiyyūn. Strung along the coast to the north are other villages of the state: Sakamkam, al-Ḳurayya, Murbiḥ, Ḍadna and a part of Dabā. Between Murbiḥ and Ḍadna is the enclave of Khawr Fakkān (Fukkān in Yāḳūt, *TA*, and the *Ḳāmūs* of al-Fīrūzābādī) belonging to al-Shāriḳa.

Al-Fudjayra has long been under the influence of al-Ḳawāsim of Raʾs al-Khayma and al-Shāriḳa, who were occupying Khawr Fakkān as early as 1188/1775. Al-Fudjayra, however, became virtually independent in 1321/1902 and was recognized as such by Great Britain in 1371/1952, when the Ruler, Shaykh Muḥammad b. Ḥamad al-Sharḳī, subscribed to the agreements in force between Britain and the Trucial Shaykhdoms.

Bibliography: Admiralty, *A Handbook of Arabia*, London 1916-7; C. Aitchison, ed., *A Collection of Treaties*[5], xi, Calcutta 1933; *al-ʿArabī*, Nov. 1960 (Kuwait periodical); Aḥmad al-Būrīnī, *al-Imārāt al-Sabʿ*, Beirut 1957; *Selections from the records of the Bombay Government*, n.s., xxiv, Bombay 1856; R. Hay, *The Persian Gulf states*, Washington 1959; J. Lorimer, *Gazetteer of the Persian Gulf, ʾOmān, and Central Arabia*, Calcutta

1908-15; Reference Division, Central Office of Information, *The Arab states of the Persian Gulf and South-East Arabia*, London 1959.

(ʿAbd al-Hafez Kamal)

FUḌŪLĪ, Muḥammad b. Sulaymān (885?-963/1480?-1556), (in Turkish Fuzūlī) one of the most illustrious authors of Classical Turkish literature. He was born in ʿIrāḳ at the time of the Aḳ-Ḳoyunlu (White Sheep Dynasty) domination, probably at Karbalā, although Baghdād, Ḥilla, Nadjaf, Kirkūk, Manzil and Hīt are also mentioned as his birthplace. It is reported on uncertain authority that his father was *muftī* of Ḥilla, that he was taught by one Raḥmat Allāh, that he first took to poetry when he fell in love with this teacher's daughter and that his literary taste was formed by the Ādharī poet Ḥabībī. It can, however, be said with certainty that Fuḍūlī came from an educated family and was himself fully trained in all the learning of the age. His learning is also attested by the titles of *Mollā* and, later, *Mawlānā* which are given to him. It appears that his education commenced at Karbalā and was continued at Ḥilla and Baghdād.

Meḥmed b. Sulaymān (v. Ḥādjdjī Khalīfa, 255, 645, 805, 914, 1075, 1571, 1719) invariably used the *makhlaṣ* (pen-name) Fuḍūlī in all his verse and prose works and is, therefore, mentioned among poets known by their *takhalluṣ* (Sām Mīrzā, *Tuḥfa*, Tehran 1314, 136). He explained the choice of this original pseudonym, meaning both "inappropriate" and even "improper" and also, if taken as the plural of *faḍl*, "of great value", in the preface to his Persian *Dīwān* (Br. Mus. Or. 4911; Fāʾiḳ Reshād, *Fuḍūlī'nin ghayr-i maṭbūʿ eshʿārî*, Istanbul 1314, 43; Suleymān Naẓīf, *Fuḍūlī* (1925), 13-14). In the preface to his Turkish *Dīwān* he speaks of his innate artistic temperament and mentions that he started writing poetry at a very early age (*Türkçe Divan*, Ankara 1958, 4 ff.). His first known poem is a *ḳaṣīda* in praise of Elvend Bey (904-8/1498-1502), a grandson of the Aḳ-Ḳoyunlu Uzun Ḥasan (*Madjmūʿa-i nafīsa*, in the author's possession, 178a-b). When the Ṣafawī Shāh Ismāʿīl captured Baghdād in 914/1508, Fuḍūlī was already quite well known as a young man of literary and religious learning. He dedicated to this Shīʿī Shāh (Fuḍūlī being himself a Shīʿī) his first *mathnawī*, *Beng-ü-Bāde*. He enjoyed the patronage of the Ṣafawid Wālī of Baghdād, Ibrāhīm Khān Mawṣillü, and dedicated *ḳaṣīdas* to him (*Türkçe Divan*, 87, 89; *Beng-ü-Bâde*, Istanbul 1956, 3-4; Ṣādiḳī, *Madjmaʿ al-khawāṣṣ*, İst. Üniv. Kütüph. T.Y. 408, 533b, 34b —for a Persian translation of this see Khayyāmpūr, Tabrīz 1327).

When Sultan Suleymān the Magnificent conquered ʿIrāḳ in 941/1534, Fuḍūlī addressed *ḳaṣīdas* to him too, feeling no embarrassment at the change of administration and hastening to sing the praises in *madḥiyyas* of members of the entourage of the new conqueror. These included the Grand Vizier Ibrāhīm Pasha, the *Ḳāḍīʿasker* Ḳādir Čelebi, the *Nishāndjî* Djalāl-zāde Muṣṭafā Čelebi (cf. *Turkçe Divan*, 85, 98, 101; see also ʿĀlī, *Kunh al-akhbār*, unpublished part, İst. Üniv. T.Y. 5959, 385a-b; ʿĀshiḳ Čelebi, *Mashāʿir al-shuʿarāʾ*, Istanbul Ali Emirî Lib. No. 772, 528; Ḥasan Čelebī, *Tadhkira*, same lib. No. 761, 221a-222a). Fuḍūlī met also two poets who participated in the campaign, Khayālī (d. 964/1557) and Tashlîdjalî Yaḥyā (d. 990/1582). While the Sultan was in Baghdād, Fuḍūlī was promised a pension payable from *waḳf* funds. Difficulties arose, however, when a later *berāt* stipulated the payment of nine aspers a day from *zewāʾid* funds. These difficulties are the subject of the letter known as the *Shikāyet-nāme* (Abdülkadir Karahan, *Fuzûlî'nin mektupları*, Istanbul 1948, 31-8). Fuḍūlī entered also into correspondence with Aḥmed Bey, the *Mīr-i liwā* of Mawṣil, Āyās Pasha, the *Ḳāḍī* ʿAlā al-Dīn (cf. Karahan, op. cit., 38-41, 42-4, 44-6) and the *Shehzāde* Bāyezīd (Hasibe Çatbaş, *Fuzûlî'nin bir mektubu*, in *AÜDTCFD*, iv (1948), 139-46.

Fuḍūlī composed *ḳaṣīdas* praising the Pashas Uways, Djaʿfar, Āyās and Meḥmed, when they were *Wālīs* of Baghdād, and also the *Ḳāḍī* of Baghdād Fuḍayl Efendi. He also wrote some of his most important works, including *Ḥadīḳat al-suʿadāʾ* and *Laylī wa Madjnūn*, under the Ottomans. Although he spoke with longing of travel in his poems, and although in his youth he hoped to visit Tabrīz and in his mature age to go to India and Asia Minor, Fuḍūlī never left the confines of ʿIrāḳ. He seems to have spent a large portion of his long life in employment at the *ʿAtabāt-i ʿĀliya* in Nadjaf (cf. the Persian *ḳaṣīdas* in praise of the *Imām* ʿAlī in the *Madjmūʿa*, in the author's possession, fols. 166 ff.). He died and was buried at Karbalā in 963/1556 during a plague (*ṭāʿūn*) epidemic (ʿAhdī, *Gulshen-i shuʿarāʾ*; Ali Emirî Lib. No. 774, 155a; Riyāḍī, *Riyāḍ al-shuʿarāʾ*, İst. Üniv. T.Y. 3250, 46 etc.). The year 970/1562 is sometimes given in error as the date of his death (Ḥasan Čelebi, loc. cit.; Ḥādjdjī Khalīfa, loc. cit., gives both dates).

The only known member of Fuḍūlī's family is the poet's son Faḍlī Čelebi. In his religion the poet can be described as a moderate *Ithnā ʿasharī* Shīʿī. In spite of traditions to the contrary, it was unlikely that he was a Bektāshī (ʿAlī Suʿād, *Seyāḥatlerim*, Istanbul 1330, 100-7), a Ḥurūfī (ʿAbbās al-ʿAzzawī, *Taʾrīkh al-ʿIrāḳ*, Baghdād 1939, iii, 246) or a Bāṭinī (A. Gölpınarlı, *Fuzûlî'nin Bâtınîliğe temayül* . . ., in *Azerbaycan Yurt Bilgisi Mecmuası*, no. 8-9, 265 ff.; for objections cf. Sadeddin Nüzhet Ergun, *Türk musikisi antolojisi*, ii, 640). Nevertheless it is right to consider Fuḍūlī as standing above sects and schools in his *ṣūfī* approach (cf. Karahan, *Fuzûlî-Muhiti, hayatı ve şahsiyeti*, Istanbul 1949, 144 ff.).

Fuḍūlī wrote some fifteen works in Arabic, Persian and Turkish, as follows: (*a*) Arabic: (1) *Dīwān*; (2) *Maṭlaʿ al-iʿtiḳād*; (*b*) Persian; (3) *Dīwān*; (4) *Haft-djām* (or *Sāḳī-nāma*); (5) *Anīs al-ḳalb*; (6) *Risāla-yi muʿammayāt* (he also wrote riddles in Turkish); (7) *Rind wa zāhid*; (8) *Ḥusn wa ʿishḳ* (or *Ṣiḥḥat wa maraḍ*); (*c*) Turkish: (9) *Dīwān*; (10) *Beng-ü-bāde*; (11) *Leylī vü Medjnūn*; (12) *Ḳirḳ ḥadīth terdjemesi*; (13) *Shāh-ü-gedā*; (14) *Ḥadīḳat al-suʿadāʾ*; (15) Letters.

Four other works are attributed to him on doubtful grounds. These are: *Suḥbat al-athmār*, *Djumdjume-nāme*, a Turkish-Persian rhyming dictionary and the *Konya Risālesi* (Müze Ktph. 2617).

The known manuscript of Fuḍūlī's Arabic poems and of the tract entitled *Maṭlaʿ al-iʿtiḳād* is to be found in a *Ḳulliyāt-i Fuḍūlī*, preserved in the Asian Museum in Leningrad (see E. Bertels, *Arabskie stikhi Fuzulī*, in *Zapiski Kollegii Vostokovedov*, v, Leningrad 1930; idem, *Novaya rukopis 'Kulliyata Fuzuli'*, in *Izvestya Ak. Nauk*, iv, 1935). *Maṭlaʿ al-iʿtiḳād*, together with the Arabic *ḳaṣīdas*, was published in Baku in 1958. Another edition is being printed in Turkey. There are many manuscripts in existence of the poet's works in Persian, many of which have also been printed (for details see Abdülkadir Karahan, *Fuzûlî*; Müjgân Cunbur, *Fuzûlî hakkında bir bibliografya denemesi*, Istanbul 1956)

There is a Turkish translation of the Persian *Dīwān* (which is also about to be published), with the exception of the *ḳaṣīdas* (Ali Nihad Tarlan, *Fuzûlî'nin Farsça divanı*, Istanbul 1950). *Haft-d̲j̲ām* has been printed several times under the title of *Sāḳī-nāma* as part of Fuḍūlī's collected works (a Turkish translation was added at the end of the translation of the Persian *Dīwān*). Other published works are as follows; *Anīs al-ḳalb*, ed. Süleyman Cafer Erkılıç, Istanbul 1944; *Risāle-i muʿammayāt*, ed. Kemal Edib Kürkçüoğlu, Ankara 1949; *Rind wa zāhid*, same ed., Ankara 1956; *Ḥusn wa ʿis̲h̲ḳ* as *Safar-nāma-i Rūḥ*, ed. Muḥ. ʿAlī Nāṣiḥ, in *Armag̲h̲ān* (Tehrān), xi, 418-24, 505-17);the same work as *Ṣiḥḥat wa maraḍ*, ed. Necati Hüsnü Lugal and O. Reşer, Istanbul 1943—for the latest Turkish translation and a summary in French, see Fuzuli, *Sihhat ve maraz*, Istanbul 1940.

Critical editions of most of Fuḍūlī's Turkish works have appeared recently. Of the *Dīwān* 26 printed editions and more than a hundred MSS are known to exist (cf. op. cit., by Karahan and Cunbur, also *Istanbul kitaplıkları Türkçe yazmalar kataloğu*, Istanbul 1947, 124-37; a MS copied during the poet's lifetime is in the author's possession). The latest edition of the *Beng ü bāde* is that by K. E. Kürkçüoğlu, Istanbul 1956. An interleaved edition of *Leylī vü Med̲j̲nūn* by Necmettin Halil Onan has been published by the Turkish Ministry of Education (Istanbul 1950) (for a German translation of this famous work see N. Lugal and O. Reşer, *Des Türkischen Dichters Fuzûlîs Poëm "Laylâ-Meğnûn" und die Gereimte Erzählung "Benk u Bâde" (Haşiş und Wein)*, Istanbul 1943; Engl. tr. by Sofi Huri, *Leyla and Mejnun*, in *Fuzûlî ve Leylâ ve Mecnun*, published by the Turkish National UNESCO Committee, Istanbul 1959). The author has edited the first published version of the *Ḳirḳ ḥadīth terd̲j̲emesi* (A. Karahan, *Fuzûlî'nin tetkik edilmemiş bir eseri: Kırk hadîs tercemesi*, in *Selâmet Mecmuası*, Istanbul 1948, nos. 57, 59, 61, 63, 64, 66). It was later published by Kürkçüoğlu, Istanbul 1951. *S̲h̲āh ü gedā* is known only through a reference in Ṣādiḳī, op. cit. A critical edition of the *Ḥadīḳat al-suʿadāʾ* is in preparation; MSS of this work are numerous (in addition to the works cited above, cf. catalogues by Rieu, Flügel, Pertsch, Blochet and Rossi). Five letters by Fuḍūlī are known: the author of this article has published four (*Fuzûlî'nin mektupları*, Istanbul 1948), while the fifth was published by Hasibe Çatbaş (*Fuzûlî'nin bir mektubu*, Ankara 1948).

Both Fuḍūlī's artistry and his wide learning are reflected in almost every one of his works. The penetrating quality of his thought and his scholarship in many fields are made clear in many passages, chief amongst them being the *tawḥīd* (praise of Divine unity) in the form of a *ḳaṣīda* at the beginning of his Turkish *Dīwān*. Fuḍūlī's notions on medicine, material and spiritual welfare, love and beauty can be gathered from his tract *Ḥusn wa ʿis̲h̲ḳ*; his *ṣūfī* philosophy and the advice which he had to give are made clear in *Rind wa zāhid*; *Haft-d̲j̲ām* is full of the *ṣūfī* symbolism in which mystic love and wine are equated; mystic love and ṣūfism inspire also *Leylī vü Med̲j̲nūn* and the *g̲h̲azal*s; stories about the prophets and the poet's feelings about the tragedy at Karbalā can be found in the *Ḥadīḳat al-suʿadāʾ*; the *Dīwān*s (especially in the brief *ḳiṭʿa*s) and *Anīs al-ḳalb* reflect the poet's philosophy of life in general.

Fuḍūlī was a brilliant linguist. No fault can be found with the language and technique of his Arabic poetry. Nevertheless in feeling they are overshadowed by his work in Persian and Turkish. It is true that in spite of their technical brilliance and richness of content his poems in Persian cannot compete with the great masters of Persian literature, in which Fuḍūlī is ranked as a better than average second class writer. In Turkish literature, however, he ranks with the greatest. Fuḍūlī does not owe this reputation to the originality of his subject-matter, which he drew from earlier Persian writers. Thus, the subject of the *Ḥadīḳat al-suʿadāʾ*, which can be classed as a *maḳtal* (a description of the tragedy at Karbalā) is drawn from the *Rawḍat al-s̲h̲uhadāʾ* of Ḥusayn Wāʿiẓ Kās̲h̲ifī; the desert story narrated in *Leylī vü Med̲j̲nūn* had been told many times before, particularly in the poems of the same name by Niẓāmī and Hātifī; the forty traditions of the Prophet in *Ḳirḳ ḥadīth terd̲j̲emesi* are drawn from D̲j̲āmī's *Tard̲j̲ama-i arbaʿīn ḥadīth* (cf. A. Karahan, *Islâm-Türk edebiyatında kırk hadîs*, Istanbul 1954, 100-6, 167-72). Fuḍūlī succeeded, however, in impressing the particular stamp of his personality on his treatment of this common subject-matter. His treatment of the themes of love, suffering, the impermanence of this world, the emptiness of worldly favours and riches and of the theme of death attain to a lyricism and directness which no other Turkish poet has reached. He is the Turkish poet who has expressed with the greatest effect a feeling of pity for the unfortunate, of patience in the face of adversity and of separation.

Fuḍūlī's Turkish has the characteristics of literary Ād̲h̲arī. This is true both of his grammar and of his vocabulary. The works of his age of maturity reflect, however, some Ottoman influences which followed naturally the Ottoman conquest of ʿIrāḳ in 941/1534. Fuḍūlī's fame and influence, marked already in his lifetime, have not ceased to grow in the Muslim Turkish world. He has always been the most popular poet in all the countries inhabited by Turks. He has influenced many classical Turkish writers, such as Rūḥī, Newʿī-zāde ʿAṭāʾī, Nāʾilī, Nābī, S̲h̲eyk̲h̲ G̲h̲ālib and Nigārī. Such writers wrote imitations (*naẓīras*) of his poems, or *tak̲h̲mīs* and *tasdīs* to his *g̲h̲azals*.

Traces of Fūdulī's influence occur also in post-*Tanẓīmāt* modern Turkish literature, as well as in poems written specially for musical settings (*sāz*). Many of his own poems have also been set to music, starting from the 17th century. Even today, some of his *g̲h̲azal*s are sung by *k̲h̲ʷānende*s and are occasionally recorded.

Bibliography: In addition to the works cited in the article see: Laṭīfī, *Tad̲h̲kira*, Istanbul 1314, 265-6; Sām Mīrzā, *Tuḥfa*, Tehrān 1314, 136; Beyānī, *Tad̲h̲kira* (Ali Emirî Lib. no. 757), 148; Amīn Aḥmad Rāzī, *Haft iḳlīm*, Calcutta 1358, 122-3; Fāʾiḍī, *Zubdat al-as̲h̲ʿār* (Ist. Univ. Lib. no. 1646), 84a-86a; Mīrzā Muḥ. Ṭāhir, *Tad̲h̲kira-i Naṣr-ābādī*, Tehrān 1317, 519; K̲h̲os̲h̲gū, *Safīna (Daftar-i t̲h̲ānī)* (Bodleian, Elliot 395), 316b-17a; Gibb, *Ottoman poetry*, iii, 70-107; Ibrāhīm ʿAs̲h̲ḳī, *Fuḍūlī*, Istanbul 1338; Muḥ. ʿAlī Tarbiyat, *Danis̲h̲mandān-i Ād̲h̲arbayd̲j̲ān*, Tehrān 1314, 300; Kevork Terzibas̲h̲yan, *Nimus̲h̲ Arewelyan mistik panasdeg̲h̲dzutyan gam Fuzulî megnapanvadz*, i-ii, Istanbul 1928-9; Tâhir Olgun, *Fuzûlîye dâir*, Istanbul 1936; Mehmed Mihrī, *Fuzûlî'nin şerh ve tefsirli divanı*, Istanbul 1937; Muḥ. ʿAlī Tabrīzī, *Rayḥānat al-adab*, Tehrān 1328, iii, 222-3; Celil Özulus, *Fuzulî*, Niğde 1948; Ahmed Ateş, *Fuzulî'nin el yazısı*, in *Türk Dili*, v (1956), 545-63; Hasibe Mazioğlu, *Fuzûlî-Hâfız*, Ankara 1956;

Zeynep Korkmaz and Selâhettin Olcay, *Fuzûlî'nin dili hakkında notlar*, Ankara 1956; Ali Hüseynzade, *Doktor Abdülkadir Karahan Fuzûlî hakkında*, in *Ilmî-Tedkikî Meseleler Medjmuası*, Baku 1958, 315-33; Hamid Araslı, *Böyük Azerbaydjan shairi Füzuli*, Baku 1958; Ḥusayn ʿAlī Maḥfūẓ, *Fuḍūlī al-Baghdādī*, Baghdād 1378. For detailed bibliography see A. Karahan's monograph on Fuḍūlī.

(ABDÜLKADİR KARAHAN)

FULANI [see FULBE].

FULBE, pl. of *Pullo* (called Fula(s) in Gambia and Sierra Leone; usual French name: Peuls; usual English name: Fulani; their language is variously called Fula, Fulani, Peul (French usage), Ful (German usage), their own name for it being variously *Pular*, in Senegal, Gambia and Sierra Leone, and *Fulfulde*, in Mali and territories further east), a pastoral people—the only people of white (or red) stock in negro Africa—the 'cattle-men' who for more than a thousand years have been moving in groups across Africa at its greatest width. Wearing their would-be white rags with unfailing pride, they look at you with a glance of aristocratic nonchalance. They are one of the few nomadic societies of negro Africa, and G. Vieillard, who professed a brotherly affection for them, spoke of the Fulani as "parasites on the bovine species". Living amongst groups of stalwart negro farmers, the Fulani seem relatively frail, their frailty offset, according to Gautier (*Afrique noire occidentale*, 167) by a certain intellectual superiority.

According to Barth, Peul means "light-brown, red", in contrast to *Olof* (black), while according to Gaden the term *Fulbe* means "the scattered ones". Peul being the Wolof name which was adopted by the French, coming from the coast of Senegal, it is more correct to speak of *Pul* or *Ful*, or in the plural *Fulbe*, the name by which the Fulani call themselves.

Al-Maḳrīzī (765-845/1364-1442) was probably the first to speak of the Fūlāniyya, a term which was used again by al-Saʿdī in the *Taʾrīkh al-Sūdān* (1667). João de Barros speaks of them at length in his *Asia*, as do the various explorers who travelled through Africa from the 18th century onwards (Moore, René Caillé, d'Avezac (1829), Clapperton (1825), the Lander brothers (1830), d'Eichtal (1842), Barth (1850-55). Substantial studies have been devoted to them by De Crozals (1883), Gaden, Delafosse (1912), Mischlich (1931), and finally Tauxier (1937) who during his official career was for more than ten years in charge of districts containing many Fulani groups, and who produced an excellent comprehensive study. Vieillard (1938), Lhote (1951) and de Lavergne de Tressan must also be mentioned, as must Colonel Figaret, who settled at Bamako on his retirement, and died there in 1943.

Reference must also be made to the monographs by the British writers, East (on Adamawa), Stenning and Hopen, by the Germans Passarge and Strümpell, and by the Frenchmen Lacroix, Richet and Froelich, and also the works of Wolf and Ahmadou Hampaté Ba on Macina and Senegambia.

Origin of the Fulani. The problem of the origin of the Fulani is one that is the subject of hot dispute among Africanists. In fact it seems vital to know whence came these pastoralists, often turned warriors, who have played such an important part in the establishment of various African kingdoms, from Senegal to central Cameroon. Racial resemblances, or reminders of some passage in the Bible or the Ḳurʾān, have often led well-meaning authors along innumerable false trails which it is pointless to follow, now that considerable light has been shed on the existence in neolithic times of a humid Sahara, which for several millennia sheltered cattle-owning pastoralists who came from the east of Africa and are most probably the ancestors of the Fulani. Until quite recently, ignorance of the Sahara's climatic changes obliged authors to search, far or near, for peoples bearing a physical resemblance to the Fulani, and to conjure out of nothing a migration route which would have led them to Futa Toro in Senegal, the place where they are first mentioned in history. The various theories, many of which read like pure fiction, can be grouped under two headings; non-African origins, and African origins.

It has been maintained in all seriousness that the Fulani were descended from the Tziganes, from the Pelasgians, primitive inhabitants of Greece and Italy, or from Gauls or Romans who vanished in the sands of the desert. In support of the Judaeo-Syrian theory, supported as early as the end of the 18th century by Winterbottom and Matthews, the explorers of Sierra Leone, M. Delafosse in his *Haut-Sénégal-Niger* put forward plausible arguments which for long were generally accepted. On this view the Fulani would have been the descendants of Jews from Tripolitania and Cyrenaica, a party of whom are known to have fled into the desert after the great Roman persecution of 115 A.D. Travelling by way of Fezzan, Aïr and Macina they would have reached the region between upper Senegal and the Niger, occupied by the ancient kingdom of Ghāna. Tauxier, writing with merciless accuracy, has disproved this theory.

The supposed Indian origin of the Fulani has been upheld by many writers, including Faidherbe and Binger. It has been reinforced by the linguistic theories of which Mlle. Homburger has made herself the ardent propagandist, arguing as she does a relationship between the Dravidian languages and certain African languages such as "Serer-Peul", a relationship rejected by most writers. Finally Etienne Richet, in a lengthy study entitled *Peuls de l'Adamaoua*, has adduced evidence of anthropological and sociological similarities between the Fulani and the ancient Iranians.

Two original African stocks have been invoked as representing the ancestors of the Fulani. The closest, geographically speaking, is the most difficult to defend. It seems clear that the Fulani are not Arabo-Berbers, as Cortambert, F. Dubois and C. Monteil have maintained—Monteil claiming that the Fulani are the descendants of the Honainen, mentioned by al-Bakrī as the grandchildren of the soldiers sent in 734 by the Umayyads against the kingdom of Ghāna. The Nubian-Ethiopian origin seems much more worthy of consideration. It has moreover been supported by the greatest number of authors. Mollien, the first of these, in his *Voyage dans l'intérieur de l'Afrique aux sources du Sénégal et de la Gambie*, 1818, sees a resemblance between the features, character and customs of the Fulani and those of the Barabra of Nubia; he makes them a race of red Ethiopians. Barth (1855) is inclined to admit that the Fulani occupied western Africa prior to the expansion of the Berber people; he likens the Fulani to the *Pyrrhi Aethiopes* of Ptolemy, Ethiopians burnt to a copper-red colour. Coming from the east of Africa, the Fulani would have passed by southern Morocco (approximately 150 B.C.) and then, under pressure from the Arabs (from about 132/750), would have reached Senegal, occupying the region of Futa Toro. This theory was supported (1868) by F. Müller, who connects Fulfulde, the language of the Fulani, with Nuba in Kordofan, relates the Fulani to the Nuba or Nuba-Fula people, and supposes that the Fulani occupied North Africa, displacing the Berbers. Two years later Schweinfurth associated the Mangbutu (Mombutu) with the *Pyrrhi Aethiopes*, and found in them a resemblance to the Fulani, whose origin he too placed in eastern Africa. This theory was to be revived some years later (1881) by O. Lenz in his book on Timbuctoo; he makes the Fula and Nuba halfway between negroes and Mediterranean Hamites. About the same time E. H. Haeckel (1868-75), in his *Natürliche Schöpfungsgeschichte*, takes the hair as a fundamental criterion, and this leads him to group together the Nubians and Fulani who are euplocomes (soft curly hair) like the Dravidians and Mediterranean peoples. He states: "the Nubians, properly so-called, inhabit the regions of the Upper Nile (Dongola, Changalla, Barabra, Kordofan), from there the Fula or Fellata migrated towards the west and at present occupy a large zone in the western Sahara between the Sudan in the north and the negro peoples in the south". Haeckel, then, makes the Nubians and Fulani a race half-way between whites and negroes. He includes in these groups some lower Hamites or Cushites (Beja, Galla, Somali, Danakil), some elements of which have more negro features than the Fulani, who resemble rather the upper Hamites (Egyptians and Berbers) and Semites (Jews, Arabs, Indo-Europeans). Topinard (1879) says that the Fulani are a red people; he connects them with the Barabra and with the Aḥmar described by Caillaud in the course of his explorations in Upper Egypt (1823).

Hartmann (1876) makes the Fulani some kind of sub-Ethiopians, a kind of cross between Berbers and Nigritians. Quatrefages and Hamy, in their *Crania Ethnica*, indicate a close connexion between Fulani and Egyptians, at the same time suggesting that there are fairly clear signs of admixture with negro peoples. Machat, in 1906, revives the theory of Dr. Tautain (1895) and of Dr. Verneau showing the relationship of the Fulani to the peoples of Upper Egypt and Nubia, which was supported by the Fulani traditions collected by Olivier de Sanderval and Hecquard. Verneau's view was confirmed by Dr. Lasnet, who however connects the Fulani with the 240,000 soldiers of Psammetichus who in the 6th century B.C. left Egypt for Nubia; reaching the south of Morocco they would have become the leuco-Ethiopians and would then have moved down towards the Senegal. Deniker, in *Les races et les peuples de la terre*, after studying the Ethiopians or Cushito-Hamites, points to a Fula-Sande group derived from a mixture of Ethiopian and Nigritian stock. He makes the Fulani essentially Ethiopians with Berber or negro admixture. Montandon, in his *Ologonèse humaine*, places the Fulani among the pan-Ethiopian races (which include also Barabra-Danakil-Somali, Abyssinians-Galla-Masai, Badima), while Chantre, in his contribution to the study of the human races in western Sudan, connects the Fulani with the Beja in view of the following common features: colour of skin, which is not black but reddish; texture of hair, which is not woolly; the principal indices, which often differ only by a few millimetres; numerous common ethnographic features. Seligman, in his book *The races of Africa* (1936), attempts to show that the Fulani are really Hamites and not Semites or Judaeo-Syrians, that the Fula language is an ancient Hamitic language, sister of the language whose impact on the previously Sudanic-like negro languages produced the Bantu languages.

On the other hand it can now be said that the Fulani are not the very tall men which the statistics of Verneau (1.74 m./5 ft. 8½ ins.) and Deniker (1.75 m.) seem to suggest. Although they are taller than the average of negro peoples, they are shorter than the Wolofs. The height of the Fulani varies according to the region, and the samples taken give from 1.67 to 1.71 m. (5 ft. 5¾-7¼ ins.) for men and 1.54 to 1.62 m. (5 ft. 0½-3¾ ins.) for women.

The Fulani are distinctly dolichocephalic (average horizontal cephalic index 74) and platyrrhine (average nasal index 96). These anthropological data enabled Dr. Verneau (1897-99), Deniker (1926) and Seligman to confirm the theory according to which the Fulani would be lower Hamites, Ethiopians. Tauxier, to whom we are indebted for the most complete study of the Fulani which has so far appeared, notes in this connection that they have always given the name *Phouta* or *Fouta* (*Futa*) to the countries where they have settled—Futa Toro, Futa D̲j̲allon, Futa Damga (west of Nioro Circle)—and he underlines the similarity of these names to the country of Phout (Fut) in Nubia. A. Berthelot accepts that the Fulani are Ethiopians, and 'red'-skinned, and relates them to the Barabra and the Baḳḳāra, and makes their language a negro language. Recently S̲h̲eyk̲h̲ Anta Diop has supported this Nilotic origin by identifying the only two typical totemic proper names of the Fulani with two equally typical concepts in Egyptian metaphysical beliefs, *Ka* and *Ba*. On the other hand he supports the close connexion existing between the Fula language, Wolof and Serer.

The Fulani have no firm national tradition about their origin. They regard themselves sometimes as Arabs, sometimes as a cross between Jews and Arabs, sometimes as a cross between Arabs and negroes, or between Moors and negroes. In actual fact the legends most often date from the time of islamization, and on that account lack any kind of validity.

Saharan route of the Fulani. Although a number of authors have found little difficulty in demonstrating the relationship of the Fulani to the Nubians and the Masai, the difficulty of crossing the Sahara seems to have caused a diversion of the Fulanis' supposed migration routes, so that almost all are made to pass by the northern fringe of the desert, in fact all over the Mag̲h̲rib. It is only quite recently that the explorer H. Lhote has thrown light on a probable travel route across the present desert, a route possible in the climatological conditions of the 3rd millenium B.C. when the terrain of the Sahara resembled the present-day Sudan zone. More than a thousand rock engravings and paintings are found at intervals across the desert from Egypt to the Atlantic, depicting cattle and their herdsmen. The cattle portrayed belong to two types—longhorns, and the short-horned cattle, long ago domesticated in Egypt, which are indigenous to Africa. The style recalls that of Egypt—in the way the animal is depicted in profile and full face, and in the presence of a spherical object or appendage between the horns, suggestive of a cult identical with or related to the cults of Egypt; the human figures, with the hair fashioned into a crest, are identical with those of present-day Fulani women.

The tools (polished axes, grinding stones) which

have been recovered near these engravings, particularly at Mertutek (Hoggar) date from the neolithic period (perhaps the 3rd millennium B.C.). It was probably around this period that these pastoralists left the Upper Nile and moved into a pastoral zone covering the presentday Sahara. They reached the Djebel Wenat, where some very beautiful paintings of cattle have been found, then reached the Fezzan, travelled along the high plateaus of Tassili, passed by way of the deep canyons to the Hoggar uplands, and then followed the valleys of the Hoggar and of Wādī Tamanrasset. They passed to the north of Adrar of the Ifoghas, and were unknown in Mauretania until quite recently (their art, probably learnt in Egypt, had been lost). These movements are explained by the search for new pastures and the need for continual change of habitat that is typical of nomadic peoples, and also no doubt by the gradual encroachment of desert conditions through changes of climate; a contributory factor may also have been the importance which the Fulani attach to their cattle.

The vexed question of the origin of the Fulani is as hotly disputed by Africanists today as it has been in the past. Various branches of science—anthropology, ethnology, linguistics and prehistory—have made their contribution towards the solution of the problem. The type of the hair (Haeckel, Chantre), cranial indices (Tautain, Verneau, Deniker, Chantre), linguistic relationships (Mlle. Homburger, F. Müller, Seligman), and the ethnographic context (Lhote, Tauxier) constitute a body of important presumptions concerning the common origin of these light-skinned peoples who set out from the vicinity of Ethiopia with their cattle, one group going west, the other south, peacefully driving their cattle before them. Often superior to the tribes they encountered, they became their advisers and their suppliers of meat—a luxury commodity—and then, when circumstances were favourable, they seized power, assisted by the fact that they were also skilled horsemen, and that in the open country of the savannah regions cavalry is always at an advantage, especially when the opposing infantry is equipped only with bows and featherless arrows, which make it impossible to shoot any distance.

Spread of the Fulani. Futa Toro plays an important role as the centre of the dispersal of the Fulani élite. It is nevertheless probable that where these élite have succeeded in establishing their authority, it is to a large extent due to the presence on the spot of other Fulani elements. It was probably in the 11th century that the Fulani established themselves at Futa Toro, and from there, at the time of the fall of the empire of Ghāna, they spread towards the east by way of Dhombogo and Kaarta, where several clans remained. Others mingled with the settled Mandinka population to produce the *Fulanke*. A fairly large group remained up to the end of the 14th century at Kaniagan (south of Bagana), whence Maga Djallo and his companions were to set out at the beginning of the 15th century in the direction of Macina. Another section was to settle at Bakunu. Another contingent from Futa Toro was to reach the northern shore of Lake Debo and then, after crossing the Niger at Say, was to settle first in the Sokoto area and then in Adamawa. From Macina were to come the Fulani of the Dogon country and of Liptako, as well as those of Futa Djallon. By intermarriage with the local negro population the Fulani were to produce six groups which were to be of considerable importance in the evolution of the African continent. The alliance of Fulani with Serer was to produce the *Tukulors*, the *Futanke* and the *Toronke*, important groups in the valley of the Senegal. Crossed with the Mandinkas they formed the groups of Fulanke who number more than 100,000 in the vicinity of Bafoulabe, Kita, Bougouni and Sikasso. The *Khassonke* and *Wassulonke*, who evolved during the 18th century at Wassulu, were to distinguish themselves during the struggle against the Fulani of Futa Djallon (1760).

The supremacy of the Fulani. The Fulani are normally regarded as fierce Muslims. Although this is true in general, nevertheless numerous pagan customs still persist, and their influence made itself felt at first in a pagan reaction against Islam.

The details of the spread of the Fulani have often been described. At first, as guardians of the cattle which farmers entrusted to them, they played an important economic role, and were fully conscious of their intellectual superiority. As a second step, the owner was reduced to slavery and his land and cattle appropriated. The extraordinary spate of Fulani conquests of the 18th and 19th centuries is then readily understandable. The extent of the Fulani dispersion from Chad to Senegal made it possible for them to rely on the support of one or other of the various Fulani communities. Moreover their herds constituted a reserve of food which gave them great mobility. Richard Mollard has rightly observed that the two most important Fulani empires, Adamawa and Futa Djallon [*qq.v.*], were also two mountain massifs—"two well-watered castles, the two Fulani bastions; it was certainly the mountains which provided this race with the ideal base for establishing a solid empire, thanks to the nature of the terrain, the climate, the suitability of its soil for pasture as well as for agriculture, and the miserable standard of living of the pagans, who were powerless to resist, having nothing to offer in opposition, and who were often quite ready to admire, to submit and to serve". From Futa Toro the Fulani, or at least their ruling classes, set out towards the east, establishing kingdoms as they went, first Macina, then Futa Djallon, and the Fulani empires of Nigeria and of Adamawa.

The Fulani empire of Macina was created by one Maga Djallo at the end of the 14th century. The Ardos resisted the assaults of the Songhai of the Sonni Ali Ber, and then came under the control of the Moroccans of Gao before finding themselves, at the end of the 18th century, caught between the Bambara invasions and the Tuareg expansion. It was left to Sēku (Sheku) Hamadu (1810-44) to carry the Fulani empire of Macina to the peak of its power, thanks to the rise of Usman (ʿUthmān) dan Fodio. He established his capital at Hamdallahi ("Praise to God") in 1815, and organized his states into provinces, with governors, judges, and fiscal and military systems. Sēku Hamadu succeeded in converting to Islam almost all the Fulani and a considerable number of Bambara. After Hamadu Sēku (1844-52), who established his suzerainty over Timbuctoo, his son Hamadu Hamadu (1852-62) saw his army of 50,000 warriors defeated at Sayewal at the hands of Al-Ḥādjdj ʿUmar's 30,000 Tukulors. Hamdallahi was conquered and Hamadu Hamadu put to death. Two years later his brother Ba Lobbo was to succeed in defeating the Tukulor army while Al-Ḥādjdj ʿUmar was to escape into the cave at Degembere with his reserves of ammunition. But Tīdjānī, nephew of Al-Ḥādjdj ʿUmar, soon took his revenge. From that time on, the Tukulors were to be in control of Macina.

The Fulani (Fulas) of Futa Djallon came from Macina around 1694, led by a certain Saʿīdī. As soon as the Fulani felt themselves strong enough, they were to seize power and wage a succession of holy wars against the pagans. The position of Almamy was to be held alternately by the Sorya and Alfaya families; the most famous of the Almamys was Ibrahim Sori Maudo (1751-84).

The Fulani of Nigeria are among the best known of the Fulani groups, owing to the many written documents which have survived. Here, as elsewhere, a distinction is made between the *Fulanin Gida*, who took up a sedentary life and often intermarried with the local inhabitants, and the *Bororo*, who still faithfully tend their herds of cattle. In contrast to many of the Filanin Gida, the Bororo are tall and slim, with a proud carriage, light skin, aquiline nose and thin lips. According to the Kano Chronicle, it was in the 18th century that the Fulani came from Futa Toro to establish themselves in the kingdom of Gobir, one of the Seven Hausa States.

Usman dan Fodio (born 1754) set himself up in opposition to the Emir of Gobir, declared a holy war, defeated the Emir's troops (21 June 1804), and had himself proclaimed Sarkin Musulmi ("Commander of the Faithful"). Thereafter he extended his authority over Kano, where he established his base while his armies overthrew the Hausa states of Katsina, Kebbi, Nupe, Zaria and Liptako. Usman attacked Bornu (1808), although its people too were Muslims, but was repulsed by El-Kanemi (1810) and died some time afterwards in a fit of religious frenzy. Abdullahi, brother of Usman, received the western provinces (with their capital at Gwandu) while Muhammadu Bello, son of Usman, was given the recently-conquered eastern provinces and established himself at Sokoto. Under Muhammadu Bello the Fulani empire of Nigeria reached its zenith, and included the emirates of Katsina, Kano, Zaria, Hadejia, Adamawa, Gombe, Katagum, Nupe, Ilorin, Daura, and Bauchi. In spite of his many campaigns, Muhammadu Bello found time to write works of history, geography and theology. Unfortunately, he had the papers and documents of the Hausa kingdoms destroyed. In 1824 and 1826 he received the British explorer, Lieutenant Clapperton, and sent a friendly letter to the King of England.

Usman dan Fodio and Muhammadu Bello established an administration based on the Ḳurʾānic law. The nature and value of a person's property determined the tax (*zakāt*) he was to pay. The ruler was assisted by a *Waziri* (chief minister), a *Ma'aji* or *Ajiya* (treasurer) and a *Sarkin Dogarai* (chief of police). The corruption in this administration at the end of the 19th century was to be a factor favourable to the establishment of British rule.

The Fulani empire of Usman dan Fodio was to give rise to two important chiefdoms, those of Liptako and of Adamawa.

The Fulani influence at Liptako had started with the Ferobe ("those who have abandoned their land"), who came from Macina under the leadership of Birmali Sala Pate. The latter established himself at a place called Bayel near Wendu, and began to win over to Islam the Fulani who had been in the country for a long time. The success of Usman dan Fodio enabled the Fulani to rise against the Gurma chiefs. The battle of Dori (April 1810), which resulted in seven deaths among the Gurmas, established the authority of Brahima bi Saidu, grandson of Birmali. Salifu bi Hama, who succeeded him in 1817, founded Dori. He overcame the Gurmas in the south, but had to abandon the north (Udalam) under pressure from the Tuaregs. The reign of Sori (1832-61) was to be a glorious one, but was marred in 1840 by the bloody battle of Kassirga (1900 dead). After Lieutenant Monteil had passed through Liptako (1891), and the Tukulor troops of Ali Bori had been wiped out by Capt. Blachère at Duentza (1894), Bubakar Sori signed a protectorate treaty with Capt. Destenave (4 October 1895).

The Fulani of Adamawa entered the plateau areas during the 18th century in search of pasture. They settled peacefully among the Bata, Fali, Mundang, and Masa tribes in the neighbourhood of the Mandara mountains and the Benue, Mayo Kebbi and Logone rivers.

At the call of Usman dan Fodio the Fulani seized power. Summoning the influential *malam*s (those learned in the Ḳurʾān) to Kano, Usman dan Fodio appointed Adama of the Ba clan to carry his standard. Adama installed himself at Yola and conducted a campaign against the pagans of the north "for the faith, not to capture slaves and fill his harem". Meanwhile he attacked the chief of Mandara before carrying the war against the hill tribes of the Fali, Mufu and Daba. He overcame the Mundang of Mayo Kebbi, and to the south he fought the Vere, Chamba, Namchi and Doni. After the wars of liberation were to come the wars of domination. The captives made a plentiful labour force for tilling the soil. The Fulani themselves settled in the best-situated villages abandoned by the pagans.

On the death of Adama (1847) the conquest was practically complete. The country which had up to then been called Fombina ("the South") in the Fula language became Adamawa ("country of Adama"), subdivided into several chiefdoms (such as Banyo, Garua, Ngaundere, Rai and Tibati), whose incumbents received their appointments from Yola. After the death of Adama the chiefdoms of Ngaundere, Tibati and Bindere became independent, while the southern areas remained vassals of Yola.

The half-century between the death of Adama and the arrival of the Germans saw the gradual attrition of Yola's authority. The emirs were much more preoccupied with possible profitable raids and the sale of slaves to the Kanuri, the Arabs and the Hausas, than with converting the infidels.

Society and language. Fulani society is marked by a caste system consisting of nobles (*rimbe*, plural of *dimo*), serfs (*rimaibe*), traders and herdsmen (*jawambe*), singers and weavers (*mābube*), leatherworkers (*sakēbe* or *gargassābe*), woodworkers (*laōbe* or *sakaēbe*) and smiths (*wailbe*).

The language of the Fulani (Fula, Fulani, Pular, or Fulfulde) has been the subject of a great many studies. Once considered a Hamitic language related to the Berber dialects, Fula is generally grouped with the languages of Senegal and Guinea. It is a language with characteristic noun classes, marked by sets of suffixes and a pronominal system of an alliterative type. The roots are mainly monosyllabic roots consisting of closed syllables (consonant + vowel + consonant) like those of the other languages in the area. The verbal system is very rich, and includes three voices—active, middle and passive—and various moods and aspects.

Bibliography: Crozals, *Les Peuhls*, Paris 1883; Lhote, *Les Peuls*, in *Enc. col. et mar.*, mars 1951, 66-9; Mischlich Adam, *Über die Herkunft der Fulbe*, in *MSOS*, 1931; Tauxier, *Mœurs et histoire des Peuls*, Paris 1937; Vieillard, *Les Peuls dans notre Afrique*, in *Monde colonial illustré*, no. 174

(1937), 288-9.—Futa Toro: Kane Issa, *Histoire et origine des familles du Fouta Toro*, in *Ann. et mémoires du GEHSAOF*, 1916, 325-44; K. Wolff, *Die Entstehung der frühen Ful Staeten in Senegambien, Beiträge zur Gesellungs und Völkerwissenschaft*, in *Festschrift Thurnwald*, Berlin 1950, 435-45.— Macina: Amadou Hampate Ba and Jacques Daget, *L'empire peul du Macina*, 1955.—O. Durand, *Mœurs et institutions d'une famille Peule du cercle de Pita*, in *BSCHSAOF*, 1929, 1-85; G. Vieillard, *Notes sur les Peuls du Fouta Djalon*, in *Bull. IFAN*, Janv.-av. 1940, 85-210.—Futa Djallon: Demougeot, *Notes sur l'organisation politique et administrative du Labé*, Paris 1944; Bouché and Mauny, *Sources écrites relatives à l'histoire des Peuls et des Toucouleurs*, in *Notes africaines*, July 1946, 7-9; Monteil, *Réflexions sur le problème des Peuls*, in *Journal de la Soc. des africanistes*, 20-2-1950, 153-92.—Niger: M. Dupire, *La place du commerce et des marchés dans l'économie des Bororo nomades du Niger*, *IFAN* 1962.—Nigeria: Palmer, *An early conception of Islam (tambiku'l Ikhwan)*, in *JAS*, xiii (1913), 407, xiv, 53, *Western Sudan history, The Raudhatu'l Afkari*, xv (1915), 251; Brass, *Eine neue Quelle zur Geschichte des Fubreiches Sokôto*, in *Isl.*, x; Meek, *The Northern Tribes of Nigeria*, i (esp. 23, 28, 94) and ii, Oxford 1925; E. Arnett, *The rise of the Sokoto Gulani*, Kano 1930; C. N. Reed, *Notes on some Fulani Tribes and Customs*, in *Africa*, v (1932), 422 ff.; D. J. Stenning, *Savannah nomads*, London and Oxford 1959.—Adamawa: S. Passarge, *Adamawa*, Berlin 1895; A. H. M. Kirk Greene, *Adamawa past and present*, London 1958; K. Strumpell, *Die Geschichte Adamauas*, in *Mitt. der geog. Gesellschaft*, Hamburg 1912; E. Richet, *Les Peuls de l'Adamaoua*, Paris 1922; R. M. East, *Stories of old Adamawa*, Lagos and London 1934; Pfeffer, *Die Djafun Bororo* (thesis), Berlin 1936; P. F. Lacroix, *Matériaux pour servir à l'histoire des Peuls de l'Adamawa*, in *Études camerounaises*, sept.-déc. 1952, 361, mars-juillet 1953, 340; J. C. Froelich, *Le commandement et l'organisation sociale chez les Foulbé de l'Adamaoua*, in *Études camerounaises*, sept.-déc. 1954, 91.—Language: Faidherbe, *Essai sur la langue poul*, Paris 1875; Reichardt, *Grammar of the fulbe language*, London 1876; Grimal de Guiraudon, *Manuel de la langue Foule*, Paris-Leipzig 1894; Westermann, *Handbuch der Fulsprache*, London 1909; Meinhof, *Das Ful in seiner Bedeutung für die Sprachen der Hamiten, Semiten und Bantu*, in *ZDMG*, 1911; Gaden, *Le Poular, dialecte peul du Fouta sénégalais*, Paris 1912; idem, *Proverbes et maximes peuls et toucouleurs*, Paris 1932; Klingenheben, *Die Präfixklassen der Ful*, in *Zeits. für eingeborenen Sprachen*, xiv (1923-4), 189-222, 290-315; idem, *Die Permutation des Biafada und des Ful*, ibid., xv (1924-5), 180-213, 266-72; F. W. Taylor, *Fulani-Hausa readings*, Oxford 1929; idem, *Fulani-English dictionary*, Oxford 1932; L. Homburger, *Éléments dravidiens en peul*, in *JA*, 1948, 135-43; idem, *Les représentants de quelques hiéroglyphes égyptiens en peul*, in *MSLP*, xxiii/5, 277-312; Lavergne de Tressan, *Du langage descriptif en peul*, in *Bull. IFAN*, xiv/2 (1952), 636-59; H. Labouret, *La langue des Peuls ou Foulbé*, Dakar 1952; F. W. Taylor, *A grammar of the Adamawa dialect of the Fulani language*, Oxford 1953; Engeström Tor, *Apport à la théorie du peuple et de la langue peule*, Stockholm (Statens Etnografiska Museum) 1954; Labouret, *La langue des Peuls ou Fulbé, Lexique francais-peul, Mém.*

IFAN, Dakar 1955; D. W. Arnott, *The middle voice in Fula*, in *BSOAS*, xviii (1956), 130-44; idem, *Some features of the nominal class system of Fula ...*, in *Afrika und Ubersee*, xliii (1960); A. Klingenheben, *Die Sprache der Ful*, Hamburg 1963; M. Dupine, *Peuls nomades. Etude descriptive des Woôaabe du Sahel Nigérien*, Mâcon 1963.

(R. CORNEVIN)

FŪMAN (FŪMIN), the centre of a region (*kaṣaba*) in Gīlān [q.v.], with (in 1914) about 27,000 inhabitants (mostly S̲h̲īʿī Persians: Gīlak) whose main crops are rice and some cereals, and who also produce silk. The town of Fūman is 21 km. W.S.W. of Ras̲h̲t [q.v.] on the right bank of the Gāzrūdbār and it contains some four hundred houses. Before the advent of Islam in the 7th-8th century it was the seat of the Dābūya dynasty [q.v.] and for part of the middle ages it was considered the most important town in Gīlān. After the country's surrender to the Mongols in 1307, the prince of Fūman, said to be a descendant of the Sāsānids and the only S̲h̲āfiʿī of the country, was, after the ruler of Lāhīdjān [q.v.], the Ilk̲h̲ān's confidant in Gīlān. Fūman was then the centre of a fertile agricultural area and an important market for trading, and was considered the focal point of the Daylam [q.v.] district. (The assertions of al-ʿUmarī, in *Notices et extraits des mss. de la Bibliothèque du Roi*, ed. M. E. Quatremère, xiii, Paris 1838, 298, and Ḥamd Allāh Mustawfī, *Nuzha*, i (text), 162 = ii (trans.), 159, contradict each other in many respects). Thereafter, until 980/1572-3, Fūman remained the capital of the Bīya-pas ("beyond the river") region (see GĪLĀN) which was then transferred to Ras̲h̲t. After that Fūman was the centre for two important clans, one of which migrated to Ras̲h̲t in the nineteenth century. Today Fūman is a small country town of little significance.

Bibliography: H. Louis Rabino di Borgomale, *Les provinces caspiennes de la Perse: le Guîlân*, Paris 1917, 160-81 (history, geography, statistics, list of place-names); idem, *Rulers of Lâhîjân and Fûman in Gîlân*, in *JRAS*, 1918, 85-100 (for the period from 1349 to 1628); Le Strange, 174; B. Spuler, *Mongolen²*, 109, 166, 545.

(B. SPULER)

FŪMANĪ [see ʿABD AL-FATTĀḤ FŪMANĪ].

FUNDJ Origins: The Fund̲j̲ appear in the early 10th/16th century as a nomadic cattle-herding people, gradually extending their range down the Blue Nile from Lūl (or Lūlū), an unidentified district, to Sinnār. The foundation of Sinnār, subsequently the dynastic capital, is ascribed to ʿAmāra Dūnḳas in 910/1504-5. Hypotheses of remoter Fund̲j̲ origins among the Shilluk, in Abyssinia, or among the Bulala, are unsubstantiated, while the Sudanese tradition of their Umayyad descent is a typical device for the legitimation of a parvenu Muslim dynasty.

Fund̲j̲ kings to the establishment of the Regency. (Dates from the list obtained by James Bruce at Sinnār in 1772: Bodleian Library, Oxford, MS Bruce 18(2), ff. 54b-57a).

1. ʿAmāra I (Dūnḳas) b. ʿAdlān, d. 940/1533-4.
2. Nāyil b. ʿAmāra, d. 957/1550-1.
3. ʿAbd al-Ḳādir I b. ʿAmāra, d. 965/1557-8.
4. ʿAmāra II (Abū Sikaykīn) b. Nāyil, deposed 976/1568-9.
5. Dakīn b. Nāyil, d. 994/1585-6.
6. Dūra b. Dakīn, deposed 996/1587-8.
7. Ṭayyib b. ʿAbd al-Ḳādir, d. 1000/1591-2.
8. Ūnsa I b. ?, deposed 1012/1603-4.

9. ʿAbd al-Ḳādir II b. Ūnsa, deposed Radjab 1015/ November 1606.
10. ʿAdlān b. Ūnsa, deposed 1020/1611-2.
11. Bādī I (Sīd al-Ḳawm) b. ʿAbd al-Ḳādir, d. 1025/ 1616-7.
12. Rubāṭ b. Bādī, d. 1054/1644-5.
13. Bādī II (Abū Diḳan) b. Rubāṭ, d. 6 Dhu ʾl-Ḥidjdja 1091/28 December 1680.
14. Ūnsa II b. Nāṣir b. Rubāṭ, d. 21 Ramaḍān 1103/ 6 June 1692*.
15. Bādī III (al-Aḥmar) b. Ūnsa, d. 20 Rabīʿ II 1128/ 13 April 1716*.
16. Ūnsa III b. Bādī, deposed 1 Shaʿbān 1132/8 June 1720*.
17. Nūl, d. 16 Shawwāl 1136/8 July 1724*.
18. Bādī IV (Abū Shulūkh) b. Nūl, deposed 2 Ramaḍān 1175/27 March 1762.

* Date of accession of the next king.

The early monarchy: The northward expansion of the Fundj coincided with a southward Arab expansion under the hegemony of the ʿAbdallāb dynasty, connected with the overthrow of the Christian Nubian metropolis of Sūba. The two migrations clashed near Arbadjī, the southernmost ʿAbdallābī town, on the Blue Nile, in the Gezira (Djazīrat Sinnār, Dj. al-Hōī, Dj. al-Fundj). The victorious Fundj chief became the high-king in a partnership with the ʿAbdallābī *shaykh*, whose own authority extended over the nomads and sedentaries northwards as far as the Third Cataract. The tradition that ʿAmāra Dūnḳas and the ʿAbdallābī eponym, ʿAbd Allāh Djammāʿ, combined to overthrow Sūba is probably a face-saving legend. The Fundj rulers were early converted to Islam. ʿAmāra had Muslims in his retinue, and his second successor, ʿAbd al-Ḳādir I, bore a Muslim name, and one which furthermore indicates the predominant role of the Ḳādiriyya *ṭarīḳa* in the Fundj territories. Our principal source of information on the islamization of the region, the *Ṭabaḳāt* of Wad Ḍayf Allāh, says little about the true Fundj lands, but is almost wholly concerned with the ʿAbdallābī districts further north. The dual hegemony was subjected to severe strain, when the ʿAbdallābī chief, ʿAdjīb al-Māndjilak (*i.e.*, "the Viceroy"), revolted against ʿAdblān b. Ūnsa, and was killed in the battle of Karkūdj (1016/1607-8). Peace was restored, and the ʿAbdallābī dynasty re-established, through the mediation of an influential Ḳādirī shaykh, Idrīs b. Muḥammad al-Arbāb (d. 1060/1650).

The heyday of the monarchy: Fundj power expanded across the southern Gezira into Kordofān, west of the White Nile. The first stages were the conquest of the isolated hills of Saḳadī and Mūya, ascribed to ʿAbd al-Ḳādir I, c. 1554, and the securing of the crossing of the White Nile, at this time dominated by the Shilluk, a pagan tribe, celebrated for their canoe raids. Bādī II defeated the Shilluk, and raided the Muslim hill-state of Taḳalī, south of Kordofān, which he laid under tribute. The command of al-Ays, the Fundj bridge-head on the White Nile, was always held by a member of the royal clan. The plains of Kordofān proper, ruled by the Musabbaʿāt, kinsmen of the Kayra dynasty of Dār Fūr [*q.v.*], were not conquered until the reign of Bādī IV. Fundj expansion eastwards was barred by Abyssinia. Two Fundj-Abyssinian wars are recorded: the first (known only from Abyssinian sources) in 1618-9, and the second in the reign of Bādī IV, culminating in a Fundj victory (Ṣafar 1157/March-April 1744). The auriferous district of Fāzūghlī [*q.v.*] on the upper Blue Nile, under a tributary chief, formed the southern limit of the Fundj dominions.

The monarchy in decline: On several occasions the dynasty showed signs of internal weakness, as indicated by the deposition of monarchs. Bruce's statement that there was a custom of regicide (*Travels*, vi, 372) seems, however, to be a gratuitous generalization. A development of great importance was the creation of a slave-army by Bādī II, as a consequence of his successful raid in the west. These slaves, augmented by natural increase, purchase and further raiding, were settled in villages around Sinnār. Their existence created tensions between the dynasty and the Fundj warrior aristocrary. Bādī III overcame a revolt of the Fundj of Sinnār and al-Ays, who were supported by the ʿAbdallāb, but his son, Ūnsa III, was deposed after the "troops of Lūlū" had marched northwards on the capital. This marked the end of the direct male line. The next king, Nūl, was connected through his mother with the former royal clan, the Ūnsāb; there are other traces of matrilineal customs. Under Nūl and his son, Bādī IV, the monarchy temporarily regained strength. Bādī was, however, overthrown by his victorious commander and viceroy in Kordofān, Muḥammad Abū Likaylik, who profited from the renewal of dissensions between the king and the Fundj aristocracy to march on Sinnār and depose Bādī. Although the succession of Fundj monarchs continued, power now passed to Abū Likaylik and his clan as hereditary regents. This indicated the revival of a submerged element in the population, which had been overwhelmed by the Arab and Fundj migrations: Abū Likaylik is described as belonging to the Hamadj (*i.e.*, autochthons), or as a Djaʿalī (*i.e.*, an arabized Nubian; see DJAʿALIYYŪN). After his death, the Hamadj wasted their power in struggles over the regency. Simultaneously with the Fundj, the ʿAbdallāb were in decline. Their old capital, Ḳarrī, was abandoned for Ḥalfāyat al-Mulūk in the eighteenth century, while Arbadjī was devastated in 1198/1783-4. The arabized Nubians along the main Nile revived, notably the Saʿadāb Djaʿaliyyūn, whose capital, Shandī, was the commercial metropolis of the Nilotic Sudan in the early nineteenth century. A dynasty of religious teachers, the Madjādhīb, made al-Dāmir into a centre of learning and devotion. The Shāyḳiyya, who had revolted against the ʿAbdallāb in the reign of Bādī I, formed an independent and predatory confederacy. At the time of the Turco-Egyptian invasion of 1821, neither the ʿAbdallābī chief, Shaykh Nāṣir, nor the last Fundj king, Bādī VI, offered any resistance to the forces of Muḥammad ʿAlī.

Bibliography: R. L. Hill, *Bibliography of the Anglo-Egyptian Sudan . . . to 1937*, London 1939; Abdel Rahman el Nasri, *Bibliography of the Sudan 1938-1958*, London 1962; Makkī Shibayka (ed.), *Taʾrīkh mulūk al-Sūdān*, Khartoum 1947; al-Shāṭir Buṣaylī ʿAbd al-Djalīl, *Makhṭūṭat kātib al-shūna fī taʾrīkh al-salṭana al-sinnāriyya wa ʾl-idāra al-miṣriyya*, n.p., n.d. [? Cairo 1961]; Muḥammad [wad] Ḍayf Allāh b. Muḥammad al-Djaʿalī al-Faḍlī, *K. al-Ṭabaḳāt*, (a) ed. Ibrāhīm Ṣiddīḳ Aḥmad, Cairo 1348/1930, (b) ed. Sulaymān Dāʾūd Mandīl, Cairo 1349/1930; H. A. MacMichael, *History of the Arabs in the Sudan*, Cambridge 1922, especially ii, 217-323, 354-438; S. Hillelson, *Sudan Arabic texts*, Cambridge 1935, 172-203; idem, *Tabaqât Wad Ḍayf Allah*, in *Sudan Notes and Records*, vi/2 (1923), 191-230; idem, *David Reubeni, an early visitor to Sennar, ibid.*, xvi/1

(1933), 55-66; Ewliyā Čelebi, *Seyāḥatnāme*, x, Istanbul 1938; James Bruce, *Travels to discover the source of the Nile*[2], Edinburgh 1805, vi; J. L. Burckhardt, *Travels in Nubia*, London 1819; Naʿūm S͟hukayr, *Taʾrīk͟h al-Sūdān*, Cairo [1903], ii, 71-107; J. S. Trimingham, *Islam in the Sudan*, London 1949; O. G. S. Crawford, *The Fung kingdom of Sennar*, Gloucester 1951; al-S͟hāṭir Buṣaylī ʿAbd al-Dj̲alīl, *Maʿālim taʾrīk͟h Sūdān wādī al-Nīl*, Cairo 1955; Sadik Nur, *Land tenure during the time of the Fung*, in *Kush*, iv (1956), 48-53; P. M. Holt, *A Sudanese historical legend*: *the Funj conquest of Sūba*, in *BSOAS*, xxiii/1 (1960), 1-12; idem, *Funj origins*: *a critique and new evidence*, in *Journal of African History*, iv/1 (1963), 39-55.

(P. M. HOLT)

FUNDUḲ, a term of Greek origin (πανδοχεῖον) used, particularly in North Africa, to denote hostelries at which animals and humans can lodge, on the lines of the caravanserais or *k͟hān*s of the Muslim East. These hostelries consist of a court-yard surrounded by buildings on all four sides. The ground floors are generally used to house animals from caravans or owned by passing country-dwellers and also, when necessary, any merchandise stored there until such time as the consignee takes delivery of it. On the upper floor (usually there is only one), small rooms give onto a gallery which encircles the entire building; it is here that people are housed. The gate to the street is large enough to allow fully laden animals to pass through. In the Middle Ages it often happened that in towns open to international trade *funduḳ*s were placed at the disposal of European traders on a "national" basis. Thus in Tunis there was a *funduḳ* for the French, in Cairo a *funduḳ* for the Venetians, etc. These hostelries were patronized almost exclusively by the poor; others went out of their way to avoid the discomfort, the contiguity with the animals, and in many cases the presence of prostitutes who often occupied several rooms where they entertained travellers.

In Morocco the same type of building is often used by a group of merchants to store their goods. The court-yard is shared, and each participant hires one or more rooms; in this type of *funduḳ* there is no stabling for animals. It also happens that groups of artisans, often of the same trade, hire the various rooms in a *funduḳ* and use them as a collective workshop, each member remaining fully independent.

In general, *funduḳ*s belong to the administration of religious estates (*ḥubūs* or *awḳāf*) which let them out to the various occupants, in the case of traders or artisans, or to a concessionaire in the case of a hostelry.

Some of these buildings are of artistic merit, such as the *funduḳ al-nadjdjārīn* and the *funduḳ al-Tiṭṭawniyyīn* in Fez. *Funduḳ*s for storage or workshops are found in the industrial or trading quarters, while *funduḳ*s in the sense of hostelries are usually situated near the main gates of the town.

Bibliography: No work exists dealing specifically with *funduḳ*s. Information relating to Fez will be found in R. Le Tourneau, *Fès avant le Protectorat*, Casablanca-Paris 1949, in particular 190-1 and 317-8. See also K͟HĀN.

(R. LE TOURNEAU)

FÜNFKIRCHEN [see PÉCS].

FUNG [see FUNDJ].

FUR [see FARW].

AL-**FURĀT** is the Arabic name of the Euphrates, called in Sumerian BU-RA-NU-NU, Assyr. *Purātu*, Hebrew פְּרָת, Syriac ܦܪܬ; in Old Persian it was called *Ufrātu*, whence Middle Persian *Frat*, modern Turkish *Fırat*. On the name and the notices by authors in antiquity see Pauly-Wissowa, art. *Euphrates* (by Weissbach). The main stream of the Euphrates is formed by the junction of two principal arms, now called the Karasu (length 450 km./280 miles) and the Murad-suyu (650 km./400 miles). The former, though the shorter, long bore (and in its lower course still bears) the name Furāt/Fırat, and is regarded by all the sources as the true Euphrates. Its headwaters are the numerous streams flowing down from the high mountains (Gavur-dağı [see GAWUR DAG͟HLARI], Dumlu-dağı, Karga-Pazarı-dağı) north of the plain of Erzurum. According to the Arab geographers, it rises in the district of Ḳālīḳalā [see ERZURUM] in a mountain called ʾFRDK͟HS or some such name, in which we may probably recognise the Παρυάδρης ὄρος of Ptolemy, and the *Mons Paruerdes* of the Tabula Peutingeriana. For the upper course of the river we have the very important description by Ibn Serapion, whose text has been published with translation by G. Le Strange in *JRAS*, 1895; his statements were discussed by Tomaschek in a valuable paper in the *Festschrift für H. Kiepert*, 1898, 137-49.

After leaving the marshy plain of Erzurum, the river flows westward through narrow gorges, accompanied by the line of the Erzurum-Erzincan-Sıvas railway; the Erzurum-Trabzon road turns off north-west at Aşkale. Twisting south, between the ranges of the Cemal and Keşiş dağları, it is joined by the Tuzla çayı flowing from Tercan [see TERDJĀN], and then turns west again to emerge into the plain of Erzincan [see ERZINDJĀN] (altitude 1200 m./4000 ft.). From there it proceeds through very steep and narrow gorges along the foot of the northern slopes of the Monzor range. Turning sharply south-east, it receives the Çaltısuyu (the Nahr Abrīḳ of Ibn Serapion), which flows from Divriği [see DIWRĪĞĪ] to meet it, passes by Eğin [*q.v.*] /Kemaliye, receives the Arabkir-suyu (the Nahr Andjā of Ibn Serapion), and some 12 km./8 miles north of Keban, at an altitude of 680 m./2230 ft., is joined by the other main arm, the Murad-suyu.

The Murad-suyu rises in the volcanic Aladağ and Tendürük mountains north of Lake Van, and flows westwards to traverse the Kara-köse plain. Alternately passing through steep gorges and across broad plains [see MALĀZGERD, TUTAK], it enters from the north the extensive plain of Muş [see MŪS͟H], where it is joined by the Kara-su, flowing westward across the plain from the Nemrut-dağı. Now accompanied by the recently constructed railway to Elâzığ, it again flows westward, receiving from the left the Harinket-deresi, which drains the plain of Elâzığ, and from the right the Peri-suyu, before uniting with the Kara-su.

The name of the Murad-su in antiquity was Arsanias, whence the Nahr Arsanās of the Arab geographers, who describe it as rising in Ṭarūn (Taraunitis) and being joined near S͟himS͟hāṭ (Arsamosata) by the Nahr al-D͟hiʾb and the Nahr Salḳiṭ (identified by Tomaschek with the Peri-suyu and the Sungut-suyu respectively). The origin of the name Murad is not clear; the hypotheses of Belck (*Beiträge zu alten Geographie*, i, 45), that it may be a popular etymology for Purāt, and of Tomaschek (*Sasūn*, 17), that it rises in a mountain region once called Murad, should be mentioned. Although some European maps and text-books refer to the Murad-su as the 'Eastern' and the Kara-su as the 'Western' Euphrates, such a distinction is not known in the region itself (and indeed the 'Western' Euphrates is in fact the northern arm).

The united stream flows, first south-west and then south, past Ḥiṣn al-Minshār (the modern Muṣar; Khalīl al-Ẓāhirī, *Zubda*, 52: Mūshār), receives on the west bank the Kuru-çay or Hekimhan suyu (probably the Nahr Djardjāriyya of the mediaeval geographers, reported as flowing from the neighbourhood of Kharshana) and the Tohma-çayı. The latter (the mediaeval Nahr Ḳubāḳib), into which flow the Nahr Ḳurāḳis = Sultan-su and the Nahr al-Zarnūḳ, which irrigates by a branch Malaṭya, is crossed by the celebrated Ḳanṭarat Ḳubāḳib, the modern Kırkgözköprü (see Yorke in the *Geogr. Journ.*, viii (1896), 328 f.; Lehmann-Haupt, *Armenien*, i, 486). On the east bank the Euphrates receives the Nahr Henzīṭ (Büyük çay) which still preserves the name of the capital of the old district of Anzitene and then, breaking through the south-east Taurus, enters the cataract district, which it does not leave till it reaches Gerger (see von Moltke, *Briefe über Zustände ..... in der Türkei*[6], 305-10; E. Huntington in *Zeitschr. für Ethnol.*, 1901, 183-204; idem, in *Geog. Journ.*, xx (1902), 175-200).

Leaving the mountainous country the Euphrates divides the flat tableland into two, and forms the boundary between Syria and al-Djazīra below Samsat (Ṣumayṣāṭ [*q.v.*]). At first the river continues as before to receive important tributaries from the west only. Of these the most important is the Nahr Sandja or Nahr al-Azraḳ crossed by the famous Ḳanṭarat Sandja, which, like the Singas of the ancients (cf. R. Kiepert, *Formae Orbis Antiqui*, text to sheet 5, p. 1[b]), is certainly to be identified with the Göksu. Below the rocky citadel of Ḳalʿat al-Rūm and the crossing of al-Bīra, of particular importance since the Crusading period [see BĪREDJIK], there is still the Nahr Sādjūr (modern Turkish Sacur) to be mentioned. Immediately after being crossed by the bridge of the Aleppo-Baghdād railway, the river crosses the frontier into Syria.

In the early middle ages Djisr Manbidj (the later Ḳalʿat al-Nadjm) and al-Raḳḳa [*q.v.*] were the main places where the Euphrates could be crossed. After Meskene [see BĀLIS], where it swings eastwards, the river is navigable. It passes the battlefield of Ṣiffīn [*q.v.*], near which is the ruined citadel of Djaʿbar [*q.v.*] with the reputed tomb of Süleymān-shāh [*q.v.*]. Below al-Raḳḳa the al-Balīkh, rising in the neighbourhood of Ḥarrān, joins the mainstream at al-Raḳḳa al-Ṣawdāʾ, the modern ruins of al-Samrāʾ (see Sarre and Herzfeld, *Archäol. Reise im Euphrat- und Tigris-Gebiet*, i, 160). The now very important crossing at Dayr al-Zōr has only become of any considerable importance in modern times. The place held by Dayr al-Zōr at the present day was held in ancient times by Circesium, the Ḳarḳīsiyā of the Arabs, at the mouth of the Khābūr; this river flowing from Raʾs al-ʿAyn formed, according to the repeated statements of the Arab authors, with its tributary the Hirmās from Ṭūr ʿAbdīn, a navigable connection between the Euphrates and the Tigris in the Nahr al-Tharthār, but, according to the investigations of Sarre and Herzfeld, *op. cit.*, i, 193, this must be regarded as more than doubtful. The rôle of the ancient Circesium and of the modern Dayr al-Zōr was filled, particularly in the later middle ages, by the double village of Raḥba, or the Dāliya of Mālik b. Ṭawḳ, a little south of the former, the lands of which were watered by the Nahr Saʿīd canal, which began before Ḳarḳīsiyā, and was called after Saʿīd b. ʿAbd al-Malik b. Marwān (see Peters, *Nippur*, i, 127, 129-30; A. Musil, *In Nordwestarabien und Südmesopotamien*, p. 10 of the reprint from the *Anzeiger der phil.-hist. Kl. der Wiener Akad.*, 1913, I).

While modern geographers make Southern Mesopotamia begin at ʿĀna [*q.v.*], already celebrated in the Middle Ages for its palms, where the cultivation of the datepalm in the Euphrates valley begins, the writers of the Middle Ages as a rule place the boundary between al-Djazīra and al-ʿIrāḳ much farther south on the Euphrates. The Čerī Saʿde, which was led out of the Euphrates downwards from Hīt, the course of which can be traced almost as far as Nadjaf (see Peters, *Nippur*, i, 166 and 313; ii, 327; Meissner, *Von Babylon nach den Ruinen von Ḥīra und Ḫuarnaq*, 15), has unfortunately not been sufficiently explored to establish its real importance and relation to Khandaḳ Sābūr (see Nöldeke, *Sasaniden*, 57; Le Strange, 65) and to the Wādī ʿAyn al-Tamr (see Musil, *op. cit.*, 11), which, according to Ibn Serapion, flowed into the Euphrates at Hīt. According to Ibn Serapion a canal, called Nahr Dudjayl, flowed from the Euphrates at al-Rabb (7 *farsakh* from al-Anbār, 12 from Hīt; possibly the Umm al-Ruʾūs in Peters, *Nippur*, ii, 45) to the Tigris near ʿUkbarā (see Streck, *Die alte Landschaft Babylonien*, 24), but it seems soon to have been silted up, as the later geographers give this name only to a Tigris-canal perhaps originally connected with the ancient Dudjayl (see Streck, *op. cit.*, 33 and 220 f.).

Only a little farther down, at al-Anbār [*q.v.*] begins the great network of the Babylonian canal system, which dates back into remote antiquity, although only the remains survive today. The usual identification of the four main canals, Nahr ʿĪsā, Nahr Ṣarṣar, Nahr al-Malik and Nahr Kūthā, led from the Euphrates, is given in the article DIDJLA (for details see Streck, *op. cit.*, 25 f.), but in the present state of our knowledge of the country it can only be regarded as highly hypothetical. Shortly after they branch off, the Euphrates divides into two arms. The western arm, according to the Arabs the river proper, which flows past Kūfa and is finally lost in the Baṭīḥa [*q.v.*] west of Wāsiṭ, is also called al-ʿAlḳamī, which Musil (*op. cit.*, 13) has found east-north-east of Karbalāʾ as the name of an ancient canal, perhaps forming the northern continuation of the modern Hindiyya arm. The eastern arm of the Euphrates, which even in Ibn Serapion's time held a greater stream of water, for the first part of it corresponded to the bed of the modern Euphrates proper until, since about 1889, the river began to pour the greater part of its waters into the Hindiyya arm (see Peters, *Nippur*, ii, 335; Sachau, *Am Euphrat und Tigris*, 38 and 57), again divides near Bābil. Its eastern arm, which flows to the Tigris under the names Nahr Sūrā al-Aʿlā, Sarāt al-Kabīra, Nahr al-Nīl, or Nahr Sābūs via the town of al-Nīl (the modern Nīliyya), has been thoroughly explored by Sarre and Herzfeld (*Arch. Reise*, i, 234-47) except for its eastern extremity. How far the western branch, the Nahr Sūrā al-Asfal, corresponds to the modern course of the Euphrates or the canals Shaṭṭ al-Nīl, Shaṭṭ al-Kār, which flow to the southeast, cannot yet be exactly determined. This arm likewise ends in the great swampy area of the Baṭīḥa, the outflow from which, Nahr Abi 'l-Asad, which runs into the Didjlat al-ʿAwrāʾ, may in a way be described as the lower course of the Euphrates.

This is in its main outlines the picture drawn by the Arab geographers, particularly Ibn Serapion.

That the details which they give us are not always intelligible is not remarkable, considering the deficiencies in our knowledge of the country; that contradictions seem to be found in them need not cause surprise, when we consider how much the river has changed its course, of which the shifting to the south in quite recent times of its confluence with the Tigris is a striking example (see *Geogr. Journ.*, xxxv, 11 with map). The Arabs themselves knew of considerable changes in the course of the Euphrates; for example, Masʿūdī (*Murūdj*, i, 216) says that in the period of Ḥīra's prosperity sea-going ships came up as far as Nadjaf in the old riverbed (*al-ʿatīḳ*). A detailed account has been given above (s.v.) of the Arabs' knowledge of the history of the Baṭīḥa, which is at the same time the history of the Lower Euphrates. It is perhaps evidence of the gradual alteration in this area of swamps that, according to certain authors (see *BGA*, iii, 20, note 1; cf. also Yāḳūt, iii, 860 f.), an arm of the Euphrates—it can only be the Nahr Sūrā al-Asfal—entered the Tigris at Wāsiṭ. Not only is the history of the Euphrates in antiquity and the middle ages still very obscure, but we have only very meagre information regarding the changes in its course in recent times.

Bibliography: The Arab geographers and the more important western works are given under DIDJLA; we may here mention as a cartographical aid R. Kiepert's excellent *Karte von Kleinasien* (1: 400,000). For further details see the separate articles. For the course, tributaries, etc. of the Euphrates in the modern Turkish Republic, see *IA*, s.v. Fırat (by Besim Darkot) and Naval Intelligence Handbook, *Turkey*, 2 vols., 1942-3, index.

(R. HARTMANN*)

The Euphrates measures 2333 km./1480 miles from the confluence of the Karasu and the Murad-suyu to Baṣra. It drains an enormous basin, which is made up as follows: Karasu, 21,500 sq. km./8400 sq. miles; Murad-suyu, 39,700 sq. km./15,500 sq. miles; the Euphrates as far as Djarablus (where it enters Syria), 96,000 sq. km./37,500 sq. miles; as far as ʿĀna (where it enters ʿIrāḳ), 229,000 sq. km./89,300 sq. miles; to the point where it enters the Gulf, 444,000 sq. km./173,000 sq. miles. It must however be realized that the greater part of this area is complete desert and contributes no water at all to the river.

The area from which the Euphrates is fed is virtually confined to the mountainous area to the North, which consists of 82,330 sq. km./32,110 sq. miles, only some 20% of the total area of the basin, 80% of which is made up of steppe and desert. After it has left the mountains the Euphrates is nothing more than an artery for carrying away the rains and snows which have fallen in Eastern Turkey. Consequently, very soon—from Djarablus, on the Turco-Syrian frontier, 1980 km./1230 miles from the Persian Gulf—the river begins to dwindle. At Hīt, its average annual flow is 838 cubic metres/29,595 cubic feet per second; at Hindiyya, 629 cu. m./ 22,213 cu. ft.; at Shināfiyya, 573 cu. m./20,236 cu. ft.; at Nāṣiriyya, 458 cu. m./16,174 cu. ft. (for comparison, the figure for the Rhine is 2200 cu. m./ 77,696 cu. ft. per sec.; for the Loire, 935 cu. m./ 33,020 cu. ft.; for the Oder, 510 cu. m./18,011 cu. ft.; for the Seine, 485 cu. m./17,127 cu. ft.). Between Hīt and Nāṣiriyya (680 km./420 miles) the Euphrates loses 46% of its water.

Similarly wide variations are found between different years. Although the average annual flow at Hīt is 838 cu m./29,595 cu. ft. per sec., in 1941, a very high year, it rose there to 1140 cu. m./40,260 cu. ft., while in 1930, a very low year, it fell to 382 cu. m./ 13,489 cu. ft.

There are also fairly wide variations between the different months of the year. During the hot season the flow decreases: (at Hīt), August, 354 cu. m./ 12,501 cu. ft.; September, 293 cu. m./10,347 cu. ft. In the autumn it begins to rise again with the first rains: November, 433 cu. m./15,291 cu. ft.; December, 547 cu. m./19,317 cu. ft.; January, 587 cu. m./ 20,730 cu. ft., and rises still further during the winter: February, 668 cu. m./23,590 cu. ft.; March, 962 cu. m./33,973 cu. ft.; April, 1880 cu. m./66,394 cu. ft.; May, 2230 cu. m./78,755 cu. ft.; June, 1210 cu. m./ 42,732 cu. ft. Thus 63% of the water carried by the Euphrates flows during March, April, May and June only, and in May there flows $7^1/_2$ times as much water (2230 cu. m./78,755 cu. ft.) as in September (293 cu. m./10,347 cu. ft.).

Especially striking is the rapidity with which the average flow declines in the space of two months—June and July—and also how late the annual maximum flow is reached (in May), whereas in the Tigris it appears a month earlier (in April). This is explained by the fact that the Euphrates is supplied to a large extent by snow which, on the high plateaus, does not melt until very late spring.

In addition to its extreme seasonal variations in rate of flow, the floods of the Euphrates are also extreme, though much less so that those of the Tigris. At Hīt on 6 September 1938 a flow of 5200 cu. m./183,645 cu. ft. per sec. was recorded. On such occasions the Euphrates would burst its banks and spread eastwards as far as the eye could see, reaching as far as the suburbs of Baghdād.

The countries through which the Euphrates flows are very varied: the mountains of Turkey, where the river is more or less torrential; the Syrian steppes of al-Djazīra, where it is slightly sunk below the level of the surrounding plateau and where the slope averages 30 cm. per km. between Djarablus and Hīt; Mesopotamia proper, where the slope falls to 10 cm. per km. between Hīt and Shināfiyya. After Shināfiyya and Nāṣiriyya the slope practically disappears: 3 cm. per km.

A very important feature of the geography of Mesopotamia is the fact that the Euphrates between Hīt and Shināfiyya flows at a slightly higher level than the section of the Tigris between Baghdād and Kūt. The northern part of Mesopotamia is thus irrigated by canals which lead off from the Euphrates to the east and the south-east, and this has been so since remotest antiquity (no canal can lead off to the west because of the edge of the Syrian plateau), while the southern part on the other hand is irrigated by canals leading off from the Tigris, the main one—practically the only one—being the Gharrāf, in whose bed the Tigris itself at one time flowed.

From Samāwa to the Shaṭṭ al-ʿArab, the Euphrates clings to the desert plateau, the slope is very slight, and the area was formerly filled by the great marsh which, according to some sources, appeared in the 5th century A.D., while others say that it appeared at the time of the great flood of 629 A.D. The last traces of it are now represented by the 110 km./ 70 miles of lake Hammar.

At all periods embankments have been built to combat the floods. Since the building of the Ramādī barrage in 1955-6, it has been possible when the water level is very high to divert 2800 cu. m./ 98,900 cu. ft. per sec. in the direction of Lake Habbāniyya along a canal 8.5 km./5 miles long and 210 metres/230 yards wide. In the same year there was completed on the Tigris at Sāmarrā a similar barrage, which is capable of diverting 9000 cu. m./318,000 cu. ft. per sec. towards the depression of the Wādī Thar̲th̲ār along a canal 65 km./40 miles long. Now, and for the first time in history, Mesopotamia is protected from the catastrophe of floods.

Bibliography: E. de Vaumas, *Études irakiennes*, in *Bulletin de la Société de Géographie d'Égypte*, xxviii (1955), 125-94; idem, *Études irakiennes* (2e série), *Le contrôle et l'utilisation des eaux du Tigre et de l'Euphrate*, in *Revue de géographie alpine*, xlvi (1958), 235-331; idem, *Structure et morphologie du Proche-Orient*, *ibid.*, xlix (1961), 226-74, 433-509, 645-739. In these works will be found a complete description of the climatology, hydrology, structure and relief of the Middle East, as well as the relevant bibliographies.

(E. DE VAUMAS)

AL-**FURĀT, BANŪ** [see IBN AL-FURĀT].

FURḌA, a term used interchangeably in Ottoman documents and Arabic texts with *firda*, in reference to personal taxes. Attested in Ottoman Egypt after about 1775 as one of the many illegal charges imposed on peasants by soldiers of the provincial governors, in 1792 this tax was legalized under the name *Firdat al-taḥrīr*, as a comprehensive levy to replace all the previous illegal charges. It was not a regular imposition, nor was it applied everywhere at the same time, but only where and when local authorities needed money for special purposes. The total amount levied on each village and individual varied according to ability to pay and the amount of money needed. It was one of the *mukh̲ridj̲āt* revenues of the Treasury, *i.e.*, those collected and spent locally, without being sent to Cairo, although they were included in the accounts of revenues and expenditures of the central treasury. It was also considered to be one of the *Kush̲ūfiyye-i dj̲edīd* taxes. In 1798, 7,096,194 *paras* were collected in this way, approximately five per cent of the total Treasury revenues. In March 1801 it was abolished by the French, along with most of the other taxes inherited from Ottoman times.

After the departure of the French, Muḥammad ʿAlī restored the *firda* and changed it into a general personal tax, theoretically an income tax (called *Firdat al-ruʾūs*). This was levied annually on Muslim and non-Muslim males alike, with only European subjects and natives in the employ of foreign consulates being exempted. In the large cities, it was levied on individuals at a rate of about eight per cent of their incomes or salaries, but no one had to pay more than five hundred piastres. The tax was deducted directly from the salaries of government employees and was a major cause of their discontent. In the villages and smaller towns, it was levied on households, which were divided into three classes according to ability to pay. It provided about one-sixth of the Treasury's revenues, and was used principally to pay for the expenses of the rapidly expanding armed forces. The *firda* was also collected in Syria during the period of Egyptian occupation.

Bibliography: S. J. Shaw, *The financial and administrative organization and development of Ottoman Egypt, 1517-1798*, Princeton N.J. 1962, 92-93; idem, *Ottoman Egypt in the age of the French Revolution*, Cambridge Mass. 1964, 124, 146; Helen A. B. Rivlin, *The agricultural policy of Muḥammad ʿAlī in Egypt*, Cambridge Mass. 1961, 133; ʿAbd al-Raḥmān b. Ḥasan al-Dj̲abartī, *ʿAdj̲āʾib al-āth̲ār*, 4 vols., Cairo 1888-94, ii, 82, 104; M. R. X. Estève, *Mémoires sur les finances de l'Égypte depuis la conquête de ce pays par le Sultan Selim Ier jusqu'à celle du général en chef Bonaparte*, in *Description de l'Égypte*[2], Paris 1821-9, xii, 59, 61-62, 92, 98; Michel-Ange Lancret, *Mémoires sur le système d'imposition territoriale et sur l'administration des provinces de l'Égypte dans les dernières années du gouvernement des Mamlouks*, *op. cit.*, xi, 491; E. W. Lane, *Manners and customs of the modern Egyptians*, London 1954 (Everyman ed.), 134, 388, 547-8; A. B. Clot-Bey, *Aperçu général sur l'Égypte*, 2 vols., Bruxelles 1840, ii, 191-2; ʿAbd al-Raḥmān al-Rāfiʿī, *ʿAṣr Muḥammad ʿAlī*[3], Cairo 1951, 629; W. R. Polk, *The opening of South Lebanon 1788-1840*, Cambridge Mass. 1963, 38, 154-7.

(S. J. SHAW)

FURFŪRIYŪS, *i.e.*, Πορφύριος, Porphyry (A.D 234-about 305) of Tyre, amanuensis, biographer and editor of Plotinus, and outstanding as the founder of Neoplatonism as a scholastic tradition. The philosophical syllabus common in Arabic philosophy is ultimately due to him: since his days it became customary to use the lecture courses of Aristotle as set-books in the Neoplatonic schools of late antiquity and to start with the *Categories*. He himself wrote commentaries on Aristotle and Plotinus, which seem to have reached the Arabs either in their original or in some diluted form. It is not impossible that his conviction that Plato's and Aristotle's views were basically identical—he wrote a lost work, in seven parts, Περὶ τοῦ μίαν εἶναι τὴν Πλάτωνος καὶ Ἀριστοτέλους αἵρεσιν (Suda, s.v. Πορφύριος) —became of some importance for Muslim philosophers like Al-Fārābī [*q.v.*] or Ibn Sīnā [*q.v.*]. Most of his very numerous Greek works are not preserved. A long and careful survey of his life and his huge literary output, by R. Beutler, is to be found in Pauly-Wissowa, Kroll, xliii, 1953, cols. 275-313; it is, however, still indispensable to consult in addition J. Bidez, *Vie de Porphyre le philosophe néoplatonicien*, Gand-Leipzig 1914, reprinted Hildesheim 1964, and E. Zeller, *Philosophie der Griechen*, iii/2[4], 693 ff. For a brilliant sketch of the man cf. R. Harder, *Kleine Schriften*, Munich 1960, 260 ff.

A very sketchy Arabic account of Porphyry's works is to be found in Ibn al-Nadīm, *Fihrist*, 253 (= Cairo ed., 354), cf. Ibn al-Kifṭī, *Taʾrīkh̲ al-ḥukamāʾ*, 256 (ed. Lippert); cf. Bidez, *op. cit.*, 54 ff.; also F. Rosenthal, *Isḥāḳ b. Ḥunayn's Taʾrīkh̲ al-aṭibbāʾ*, in *Oriens*, vii (1954), 69-79, and F. Gabrieli, *Plotino e Porfirio in un eresiografo musulmano*, in *La parola del Passato*, i, 1946, 338 ff.

(1) Only one of Porphyry's surviving Greek works is preserved in a complete Arabic version as well, the *Isagoge* (cf. *Commentaria in Aristotelem Graeca*, IV, 1), a rather elementary treatise on logic, which had become the first philosophical book to be studied in the schools. It became as popular in the Islamic world as it had been in Greek and Latin (cf. W. and M. Kneale, *The Development of Logic*, Oxford 1962, 187 ff.). The translator is Abū ʿUth̲mān al-Dimash̲ḳī (flor. A.D. 900); it can be read in two Egyptian editions, both published 1952, by Aḥmad Fuʾād al-Aḥwānī, and by ʿAbd al-Raḥmān Badawī (*Manṭiḳ Arisṭū*, 1021-68), together with the corrections given in S. M. Stern's article on Ibn al-Ṭayyib's commentary on the *Isagoge*, *BSOAS*, xix (1957) 419 ff. The *Isagoge* was well known to all the Arabic philosophers. from the days of Al-Kindī's [*q.v.*] *First Philosophy*. Ibn Sīnā's [*q.v.*] treatment of its subject matter is now available in a critical edition by Dr. Ibrahim Madkour and others: *Al-Sh̲ifāʾ, La Logique. I. L'Isagoge*, Cairo 1952. The commentary of Porphyry's work by Ibn Sīnā's contemporary Ibn al-

Ṭayyib (434/1043) is preserved in the Bodleian MS Marsh 28. The 7th/13th century commentary by Al-Abharī (cf. Brockelmann, I², 609, S I, 841) became most popular in later centuries, was in its turn frequently commented upon and eventually completely replaced the original work.

(2) Commentaries on Aristotle. (a) The *Fihrist*, 252, 2 (= Cairo ed. 351, 21), refers to a lost commentary on the *Nicomachean Ethics*, in twelve books (translated by Isḥāķ b. Ḥunayn), which is not mentioned in the Greek tradition but was obviously used by Arabic writers. Al-Fārābī [*q.v.*], for example, mentions it in the essay on the identity of Plato's and Aristotle's views, *al-Djamʿ bayna raʾyay al-ḥakīmayn Aflāṭūn wa-Ariṣṭū* (ed. Dieterici, 17; ed. Nader, 95, 17): "As Porphyry and many commentators after him say". We are not in a position to decide whether he made much use of it in his other writings but it is obviously likely. Abu 'l-Ḥasan Muḥammad al-ʿĀmirī (d. 382/992) refers to Porphyry four times by name in his very interesting ethical work *Fi'l-saʿāda wa'l-isʿād* (ed. M. Minovi, Wiesbaden 1957-8); once, p. 53, he mentions the commentary expressly while discussing Aristotle's treatment of pleasure. The definition of felicity (p. 5) is given according to Porphyry; the other references occur on pp. 192 and 353, but much more in that book may ultimately be derived from this commentary or from other ethical works by Porphyry. Porphyry as an interpreter of Aristotle's ethical doctrines is again referred to in the beginning of the third chapter of Miskawayh's *Tahdhīb al-akhlāķ*; moreover, chapters 3-5 of the treatise reproduce selections from a Neoplatonic commentary on the *Nicomachean Ethics*, and it is an obvious guess to think of Porphyry as its author (cf. R. Walzer, *Greek into Arabic*, Oxford 1962, 224 ff.). The possibility that the late Greek ethical treatise tentatively attributed to Nicolaus of Laodicea and discussed in *Oriens*, xiii-xiv (1960-1), 34 ff. by M. C. Lyons may be connected with Porphyry's commentary deserves certainly to be considered. (b) A reference to the second book of Porphyry's *Commentary on Aristotle's Physics* I-IV (translated by Basīl) occurs in Muḥammad b. Zakariyyā al-Rāzī [*q.v.*], *Opera philosophica*, i, 121 (ed. P. Kraus, Cairo 1939). (c) It is very likely that Al-Fārābī used Porphyry's commentary on the Περὶ ἑρμηνείας; a comparison of his commentary (ed. W. Kutsch-Stanley Marrow, Beyrouth 1960) with the commentaries by Boethius and Ammonius and Stephanus may yield interesting results.

(3) Porphyry's *History of Philosophy* in four books (Greek remnants of it were edited by A. Nauck, *Porphyrii Opuscula*, Leipzig 1886, 3-52) was known in Syriac (*Fihrist*, 245, 12 = Cairo ed., 355) and in Arabic (the *Fihrist* (i, 245) mentions a translation of two books by Abu 'l-Khayr al-Ḥasan ibn Suwār). The Arabic text of the *Life of Pythagoras* (Nauck, 11-52) is accessible in Ibn Abī Uṣaybiʿa, *ʿUyūn al-anbāʾ*, ed. A. Mueller, 38, 18-41, 4, and is discussed by F. Rosenthal, *Arabische Nachrichten ueber Zeno den Eleaten*, in *Orientalia*, vi (1937), 43 ff.; F. Rosenthal edited from al-Mubashshir a section of Porphyry's life of Solon (*ibid.*, 40 f.), and an unknown biography of Zeno of Elea (*ibid.*, 30 ff.), which is most likely derived from Porphyry's work. Al-Bīrūnī, *Hind* (Sachau, 21-43), seems to refer to this book. R. Beutler (*op. cit.*, 287) does not mention the Arabic tradition at all.

(4) The so-called *Theology of Aristotle* [see ARISṬŪṬĀLĪS and AL-SHAYKH AL-YŪNĀNĪ], a running paraphrase of Plotinus, IV 3, IV 4, IV 7, IV 8, V 1, V 2, V 8, VI 7, arranged in a systematic order, is introduced in its Arabic text as 'the interpretation (*tafsīr*) of Porphyry of Tyre'. There is, in my view, every likelihood that it must ultimately somehow be connected with Porphyry's explanations of the *Enneads* (ὑπομνήματα and κεφάλαια) which he mentions in § 26 (l. 29 ff.) of his biography of Plotinus. An English translation of the work by G. Lewis, arranged in the order of Plotinus' *Enneads*, is to be found in the second volume of P. Henry and H.-R. Schwyzer's monumental critical edition of Plotinus, Paris-Bruxelles 1959, cf. particularly p. XXVI ff. Whether the *Epistula de Scientia Divina* (cf. P. Kraus, *Plotin chez les Arabes*, in *BIE*, xxiii (1941), 263 ff.) which contains similar extracts from *Enneads* V 3, V 4, V 5, V 9 (also translated by G. Lewis in the same volume) goes back to the same source, is uncertain but it is quite probable.

(5) A fragment from a treatise *On soul* was published and translated into German by W. Kutsch S.J.; *Ein arabisches Bruchstueck aus Porphyrios (?)* Περὶ ψυχῆς *und die Frage des Verfassers der Theologie des Aristoteles*, in *Mélanges de l'Université St. Joseph*, xxxi (1954), 265 ff.; cf. S. M. Stern, *Ibn Ḥasday's Neoplatonist*, in *Oriens*, xiii-xiv (1960-1), 92 and n. 1; P. Merlan, *Monopsychism, mysticism, metaconsciousness*, The Hague 1963, 25 f. It looks as if Ibn Sīnā, *Shifāʾ* v, 6 (ed. Raḥmān, 240, 3 ff.; ed. Bakoš, 236) and *Ishārāt* (ed. Forget, 180) has either this treatise in mind or the Ἀφορμαὶ πρὸς τὰ νοητά (which he seems to quote as the treatise *Fi 'l-ʿaķl wa'l-maʿķūl* in the *Ishārāt*) while voicing his dissatisfaction with Porphyry's view of the *unio mystica* (cf. F. Rahman, *Prophecy in Islam*, London 1958, 15 ff.). As one 'who is not among the most subtle of philosophers' Porphyry is blamed by Ibn Rushd, *Tahāfut al-Tahāfut*, ed. Bouyges 250, 10 ff. (cf. van den Bergh, *Incoherence* . . ., i, 154, ii, 100) for his explanation of the cause of plurality. Porphyry's view on matter is rejected in the *Epitome of Aristotle's Metaphysics* (Amīn, 73), cf. S. van den Bergh, *Die Epitome der Metaphysik des Averroes*, Leiden 1924, 63 and 201.

(6) The *Letter to Anebo* (recent edition of the Greek and Latin fragments by A. R. Sodano, Naples 1958) is referred to by al-Masʿūdī, *Kitāb al-Tanbīh wa 'l-ishrāf*, 162, 6 (p. 222 of Carra de Vaux's French translation). A rather long fragment of it is quoted by al-Shahrastānī *K. al-Milal wa 'l-niḥal*, ed. Cureton, 345, 8-347; German translation by Th. Haarbruecker, *Religionspartheien*, Halle 1850-1, ii, 208 ff.; Italian translation by F.Gabrieli, *La parola del passato*, i, 1946, 344 ff. Muḥ. b. Zak. al-Rāzī wrote a refutation of the book. Cf. P. Kraus, *Jābir ibn Ḥayyān II*, in *MIE*, xlv (1942), 128, n. 5. These passages are not mentioned by Sodano.

(7) The great corpus of Alchemy attributed to Djābir ibn Ḥayyān refers to a most probably spurious work of Porphyry entitled 'The book of Generation', a book in which the creation of artificial human beings was discussed at some length. It is mentioned neither in Greek nor in Arabic lists of Porphyry's works. It is described by P. Kraus, *op. cit.*, 114 ff., 122 n. 3; cf. E. R. Dodds, *The Greeks and the irrational*, Los Angeles 1951,295. (R. WALZER)

FURGAČ [see ʿIZZET PASHA, AḤMED].

FURĶĀN, soteriological expression used in the Ķurʾān. The word occurs in various connexions in the Ķurʾān and is usually translated as "discrimination", "criterion", "separation", "deliverance", or "salvation", where it is translated at all. The Aramaic word *purķān* on which it is modelled, means "deliverance", "redemption", and (in the Christian sense) "salvation". The Arabic root *faraḳa*, which must be considered as another element in the *furḳān* of the Ḳurʾān, means "to separate", "to divide", "to distinguish".

Sūra VIII, 29 runs: "O believers, if you fear God, He will assign you a *furḳān* and acquit you of your evil deeds, and forgive you". In *Sūra* VIII, 41 "the day on which the two hosts met" (which must refer to the battle at Badr) is described as "the day of the *furḳān*". At the same time it is said that on that day something which must be believed in was "sent down" to the Prophet. On the five other occasions where the word is used it is always in connexion with the giving of divine revelation; twice Moses, or Moses and Aaron, are named as those who receive the revelation (II, 53; XXI, 48); on three occasions it is mentioned in connexion with Muḥammad and the Ḳurʾān (II, 185; III, 4; XXV, 1).

The difficulty of interpreting these passages springs chiefly from the fact that the relationship between revelation-writings and *furḳān* is not always defined in the same way. In *Sūra* XXV, 1 the *furḳān* seems to be identified with the Ḳurʾān (*tabāraka 'lladhī nazzala 'l-furḳāna alā ʿabdihī li-yakūna li'l-ʿālamīna nadhīr^an*). Again, *furḳān* may perhaps be identified with the Ḳurʾān in III, 4. The phrase *wa-anzala 'l-furḳāna* must then be a repetition, since the "sending-down" of the Ḳurʾān (and the Torah and the Indjīl) have already been mentioned in the previous verse (*nazzala ʿalayka 'l-kitāba bi 'l-ḥaḳḳi muṣaddiḳ^an li-mā bayna yadayhi wa-anzala 'l-tawrāta wa 'l-indjīla min ḳablu hudan li'l-nāsi*). In XXI, 48 *furḳān* could mean the Torah (*wa-la-ḳad ātaynā Mūsā wa-Hārūna 'l-furḳāna wa-ḍiyāʾ^an wa-dhikr^an li'l-muttaḳīna*). But in II, 53 this is hardly possible, for here "the scriptures" are named first and then afterwards, in the same connexion, the *furḳān* (*wa-idh ātaynā Mūsā 'l-kitāba wa 'l-furḳāna laʿallakum tahtadūna*). The terms used in *Sūra* II, 185 are noteworthy (*shahru Ramaḍāna 'lladhī unzila fīhi 'l-ḳurʾānu hudan li'l-nāsi wa-bayyināt^in mina 'l-hudā wa 'l-furḳāni*). This means that the giving of the Ḳurʾān (especially in Ramaḍān) should serve man as moral guidance and as "proof of moral guidance and the *furḳān*".

Even the early commentators made some effort to interpret the term satisfactorily. Since the time of Abraham Geiger western orientalists have made renewed attempts at interpretation but without ever reaching any certain conclusions. See the review of the whole question in A. Jeffery, *The foreign vocabulary of the Qurʾān*, Baroda 1938, 225-9. W. Montgomery Watt, *Muhammad at Medina*, 1956, 16, is in general agreement with the conclusion first reached by Richard Bell in *The origin of Islam in its Christian environment*, 1926, 118-25, and adds: "In VIII, 41 'the day of the *furqān*, the day the two parties met' must be the day of Badr; and *furqān*, in virtue of its connexion with the Syriac word *purqānā*, 'salvation', must mean something like 'deliverance from the judgement'. This being so the *furqān* which was given to Moses (II, 53; XXI, 48) is doubtless his deliverance when he led his people out of Egypt, and Pharaoh and his hosts were overwhelmed. Similarly, Muḥammad's *furqān* will be the deliverance given at Badr when the Calamity came upon the Meccans. That was the 'sign' which confirmed his prophethood. Perhaps there is also a reference to the experience, analogous to the receiving of revelation, which Muḥammad apparently had during the heat of the battle, and as a result of which he became assured that the Muslims had invincible Divine assistance".

In his *Introduction to the Qurʾān*, 1953, published posthumously, Richard Bell again tackled the question (136 ff., *Note on al-Furqān*), and put forward an interpretation of the whole subject which is both well-considered and complete in itself. According to Bell, "it was from Christian sources that the word was derived, but Muhammad must have associated it with the Arabic root *faraqa* to separate, and taken it to imply the separation of an accepted religious community from the unbelievers". To explain the places where the *furḳān* is said to have been given to Moses (and Aaron) he adduces *Sūra* V, 25, in which Moses, referring to his people's hesitation to enter the Holy Land, prays to God: "I control no one but myself and my brother: make a separation (*fa-'fruḳ*) between us and the reprobate people". And he accounts for the passages referring to Muḥammad's own period by reference to the situation at (and before) the battle of Badr. "The victory at Badr was not only a "deliverance" of the small band of Moslems who had gone out with Muḥammad expecting to intercept a caravan and had found themselves face to face with an army. It was a final separation between Muḥammad's followers and the unbelieving Meccans". "Here [in the Ḳurʾān passages referred to] then, we have the appearance of the Qurʾān as the distinctive Scripture of an independent Moslem religious community, linked with the *furqān*, the separation of believers from unbelievers, and the assurance of forgiveness and acceptance with God; and both linked with the day of Badr".

Bibliography: A. Geiger, *Was hat Mohammed aus dem Judentum aufgenommen*, 1902, 55 f.; H. Hirschfeld, *New researches into the composition and exegesis of the Qoran*, 1902, 68; Nöldeke, *Neue Beiträge zur semitischen Sprachwissenschaft*, 1910, 23 f.; *Gesch. des Qor.*, i, 34, note; A. J. Wensinck, *Furḳān* in *EI*¹; M. Lidzbarski, in *ZS*, i (1922), 90-2; J. Horovitz, *Koranische Untersuchungen*, 1926, 76 f.; idem, *Jewish proper names and derivatives in the Koran*, in *Hebrew Union College Annual*, ii (1925), 145-227, 216-8; R. Bell, *The origin of Islam in its Christian environment*, 1926, 118-25; A. Jeffery, *The foreign vocabulary of the Qurʾan*, Baroda 1938, 225-9; W. Montgomery Watt, *Muhammad at Medina*, 1956, 16; R. Bell, *Introduction to the Qurʾān*, 1953, 136-8. (R. PARET)

AL-FURS, one of the two terms used by the Arabs to denote the Persians, the other being al-ʿAdjam [*q.v.*]. In the following lines we shall attempt to show in precisely what way the Arabs were acquainted with the Persians and their civilization; for other aspects, see ĪRĀN.

From remotest antiquity, the Arabian peninsula had maintained relations with Persia; shortly before Islam, these connexions were established, in the north-east, through the Lakhmids [*q.v.*] of al-Ḥīra, and, in the south, through the medium of the Yemen, a vassal of Persia, and the *Abnāʾ* [*q.v.*] who were settled in the country. The word *Furs* does not appear in the Ḳurʾān, which, however, contains a certain number of words of Persian origin, but among the Prophet's entourage there was in particular one Salmān al-Fārisī [*q.v.*], whom legend has made a figure of outstanding importance. Already in the 1st/7th century, relations between Arabs and Persians were strengthened as a result of the Islamic conquests, and some elements of Iranian civilization penetrated to Mecca and Medina through prizoners who became *mawālī* [*q.v.*] and played an essential part in the history of the first centuries of Islam. However, it was only in the 2nd/8th century, and especially through the efforts of Ibn al-Muḳaffaᶜ [*q.v.*], that there first began to circulate Arabic translations of Pahlavi works such as the *K͟hᵂatāy-nāmak* (*K. Siyar mulūk al-ᶜAd͟jam* or *al-Furs*), the *Āʾīn-nāmak*, the *Tād͟j-nāma*, etc., which helped to nourish the growing *adab* [*q.v.*] and Arabic historiography, and later served as a source for Firdawsī (see F. Gabrieli, *L'opera di Ibn al-Muqaffaᶜ*, in *RSO*, xiii/3 (1932), 197-247).

The dissemination of these translations and of the works they inspired coincided with the accession and rise of the ᶜAbbāsid dynasty, which drew closer to Persia and, through its officials, increased Iranian influence to the point when it sometimes gives the impression of being heir to the Sāsānids (cf. D. Sourdel, *Vizirat, passim*). It is unnecessary to dwell here on the considerable importance of the *kuttāb* who, while attempting to acquire Arab culture, perceptibly followed the Iranian tradition, nor upon the rôle played by the *S͟huᶜūbiyya* [*q.v.*] in the shaping of Islamic civilization.

What must be noted is the introduction into Arabic historiography, from the end of the 2nd/8th century or beginning of the 3rd/9th, of the history of Persia in the form of monographs (al-Hayt͟ham b. ᶜAdī, Abū ᶜUbayda, etc.) which, together with the translated sources, were to serve as the basis for "universal" history. From then onwards historians writing in Arabic, among whom Iranians are not uncommon, were able to plan and write universal history, to include first the Biblical data and the legends transmitted by non-Muslims, representing a kind of scriptural history from Adam to Jesus Christ and then to Muḥammad; then a summary of the actual or legendary events that had occurred since the earliest times in non-Arab countries now under Muslim rule; and finally the history of Islam up to the writer's own period. Muslim Spain and the Mag͟hrib are somewhat neglected by the eastern historians, who on the other hand are better informed on the subject of Egypt, and in particular Persia. Basing themselves in this way on translations from Pahlavi, on previously published monographs and occasionally on traditional accounts transmitted orally, authors such as al-Ṭabarī, al-Dīnawarī, al-Yaᶜḳūbī, Ibn Ḳutayba, al-Masᶜūdī, al-T͟haᶜālibī and Ḥamza al-Iṣfahānī devoted one or several chapters of their works to the ancient history of Persia, from Kayūmart͟h to the last Sāsānid sovereigns who were conquered by the Arabs, though not without falling into various errors which derive from the state of the sources used, or from accepting legends and myths handed down by tradition as authentic historical facts. Thus al-Masᶜūdī, for example (*Murūd͟j*, trans. Pellat, i, 197 ff.), enumerates the mythical Kayānids, and then passes immediately to Alexander and Darius (Dārā [*q.v.*]), ignoring the Achaemenids who preceded him or, rather, confusing them with the "kings of Babylon", deals cursorily with the Arsacids (*Mulūk al-ṭawāʾif* [*q.v.*]), but is happier to dwell on the Sāsānids, with whom he is obviously more at his ease.

It is very natural that the Sāsānids should be the most familiar to the Arabs, and Arab sources have provided the historian of the dynasty, A. Christensen, with a large part of his documentation (see *L'Iran sous les Sassanides*², Copenhagen 1944, 59-74); this work deals partly with the historical facts properly speaking, and partly with Persian society, especially with the religions of Persia, which seem to have been fairly well known. While the glories of the Sāsānids provided the *S͟huᶜūbiyya* with something to boast about without fear of contradiction, those who upheld the supremacy of the Arab element found in Mazdaism and Manicheism arguments against this same *S͟huᶜūbiyya*. In fact, the Persian religions were known only rather superficially, but we do know that the system of the *kis͟hwārs* which inspired the division of the world made by the Arab geographers [see DJUG͟HRĀFIYĀ] was familiar to al-D͟jāḥiẓ (see *Tarbīᶜ*, ed. Pellat, index) who, what is more, was acquainted with certain other details of Mazdaism and Manicheism. Incidentally, for him there were only four civilized nations on earth—the Arabs, the Indians, the Byzantines and the Furs (*al-Ak͟hbār*, in *Lug͟hat al-ᶜArab*, ix, 174 ff.) and it is a matter of surprise to him that these last, so brilliant in other respects, should have accepted certain religious practices, allowed incestuous unions, worshipped fire, etc. We may feel sure that, in private conversations, these questions must have given rise to passionate discussions. A little later Ṣāᶜid al-Andalusī, who acknowledged that eight nations "were distinguished for their taste for things of the mind", the Indians, Persians, Chaldeans, Greeks, *Rūm*, Egyptians, Arabs and Israelites, attributed to the Persians "a marked taste for the art of medicine and a profound knowledge of astrology and the influence of the stars on the sublunary world" (*K. Ṭabaḳāt al-umam*, tr. R. Blachère, Paris 1935, 49-52). Ibn al-Nadīm, in the *Fihrist*, gives some particulars concerning the religions of Persia, but the Arabic author best acquainted with these questions certainly seems to be al-S͟hahrastānī, who drew upon the early sources and gave a comparatively objective account.

It must not be forgotten that the Arabic translation of *Kalīla wa-Dimna* [*q.v.*] can be regarded as one of the first monuments—if not the first—of simple prose, and that *adab*, which is the core of secular prose literature, is a product of Iranian influence. The early authors who sought to achieve a balance between the component elements of Arabic culture took pains to restrict borrowings from Iranian civilization, but they were unable to prevent the Arabs from adopting and handing down with marked pleasure those traditions that had most impressed them. The names of emperors like Ardas͟hīr or Anūs͟hirwān, even though obscured in the mists of legend, were well known to the authors who delighted in reproducing passages from the testaments (*ᶜahd*) of Persian sovereigns, and, thanks to the *adab* which popularized the figure of Buzurgmihr [*q.v.*], gave the whole nation a reputation for wisdom and political adroitness, at least at a time when the S͟huᶜūbī threat had been removed.

Bibliography: it is hardly feasible to give a restricted bibliography of the subject dealt with in the above article, since it would mean listing all ancient works which mentioned the Persians. We confine ourselves therefore to referring to the articles ᶜADJAM, ĪRĀN and S͟HUᶜŪBIYYA, and also to the works of M. Inostranzev, *Iranian influence on Moslem Literature*, i, trans. G. K. Nariman, Bombay 1918 and R. N. Frye, *The heritage of Persia*, London 1962, 234 ff. (CH. PELLAT)

FÜRSTENSPIEGEL [see SIYĀSA].

FURŪᶜ [see FIḲH, UṢŪL].

FURŪG͟H, the pseudonym of two Persian poets: (1) Abu 'l-Ḳāsim K͟hān, younger son of Fatḥ ᶜAlī K͟hān Ṣabā, poet laureate at the court of Fatḥ ᶜAlī S͟hāh Ḳād͟jār, was regarded as one of the scholars of his time and had been well educated. He spent some time in Mas̲h̲had in the civil service and, after the crown prince ʿAbbās Mīrzā had visited the region, he entered his service, principally as a poet. Later he returned to Tehrān where he retired from public life and lived until the end of the 19th century. (2) Muḥammad Mahdī ibn Muḥammad Bāg̲h̲ir Iṣfahānī lived until the time of Muḥammad S̲h̲āh Ḳād̲j̲ār (1250-64/1834-48) and wrote a most interesting work on the *Siyāḳ* numerals, mathematics, calligraphy, weights and measures, contemporary currencies and accountancy, entitled *Furūg̲h̲istān*, dedicated to the Grand Vizier Ḥād̲j̲d̲j̲ī Mīrzā Āḳāsī. The author of the *Mad̲j̲maʿ al-fuṣaḥāʾ* (ii, 396-9), who included some of his poems, referred to him incorrectly as Furūg̲h̲ al-Dīn, and said that he was born in Tabrīz in 1223/1808, had a good education from the age of seven, entered the service of the crown prince ʿAbbās Mīrzā and his eldest son Farīdūn Mīrzā, travelled in Ād̲h̲arbayd̲j̲ān and Fārs, finally settled in Tehrān where he entered the finance department, and wrote various works including the *Ṣaḥāʾif al-ʿālam* and the *Tad̲h̲kirat al-s̲h̲abāb* ("Recollections of youth"), a kind of autobiography in which he included poems in Arabic and Persian. He also must have lived until the end of the 19th century.

Bibliography: Riḍā-Ḳulī K̲h̲ān, *Mad̲j̲maʿ al-fuṣaḥāʾ*, ii, 370-82 and 396-9; *Furūg̲h̲istān*, contemporary manuscript dating from the month of Rabiʿ II 1259/May 1843, in the author's possession. (Said Naficy)

FURŪG̲H̲ AL-DĪN [see furūgh 2].

FURŪG̲H̲Ī, the pseudonym of three Persian poets: 1) Mīrzā Muḥammad Iṣfahānī, a scholar and native of that town. During his travels in the middle of his life he attached himself to Tīmūr S̲h̲āh, amīr of Afghanistan (1187-1207/1773-93) and became his court poet. 2) Mīrzā ʿAbbās, son of Āḳā Mūsā Bistāmī, born in 1213/1798 in ʿIrāḳ, where his father was travelling. As a youth he travelled in Māzanderān and Karmān where he started his career as a poet, at first using the pseudonym "Miskīn". After taking the name "Furūg̲h̲ī" he came and settled in Tehrān, living under the protection of his paternal uncle Dūst ʿAlī K̲h̲ān, the court treasurer. After joining the circle of the Čis̲h̲tī Ṣūfīs, he led a retiring life of devotion and died in 1274/1858. Furūg̲h̲ī ranks among the best modern lyric poets and his *g̲h̲azals* are very popular, seven editions of them having been published in Tehrān. He is regarded as one of the best followers of the school of Saʿdī. 3) Mīrzā Muḥammad Ḥusayn, son of Āḳā Muḥammad Mahdī Arbāb-i Iṣfahānī, born in 1255/1839 in Iṣfahān where he was educated. As a youth he went with his father to India where he was engaged in trade. Later he lived in ʿIrāḳ, and finally went to Tehrān where he later served in the Ministry of the Press, under the direction of the celebrated publicist Muḥammad Ḥasan K̲h̲ān Ṣanīʿ al-Dawla, later Iʿtimād al-Salṭana. He collaborated in the publication of both official and unofficial newspapers of the time, as well as in some of his director's publications. At the end of his life he received the honorary title of D̲h̲akāʾ al-Mulk, a title which was granted to his eldest son Mīrzā Muḥammad ʿAlī K̲h̲ān who chose the family name Furūg̲h̲ī. The father was later appointed head of the translation department at court and director of the School of Political Science. He died in Tehrān in 1908. He was very active as poet, writer, translator, publicist and journalist. On 11 Rad̲j̲ab 1314/16 December 1896 he started publication in Tehrān of the weekly *Tarbiyat* which was influential in introducing modern ideas into Īrān and which appeared until his death. His chief activity was the editing of works which his eldest son translated from European languages, including *La Chaumière Indienne* by Bernardin de Saint-Pierre, *Le Tour du Monde en 80 Jours* by Jules Verne, *The Seventh Great Oriental Monarchy* by George Rawlinson, etc. His eldest son started his career by teaching in secondary schools in Tehrān, was then elected Deputy and Leader of the Chamber of Deputies during the second legislature. He was nominated several times as ambassador, president of the Court of Cassation, Minister and Prime Minister. He died in Tehrān on 5 Ad̲h̲ar 1321 s/27 November 1943. From the time of the founding of the Iranian Academy (*Farhangistān-i Īrān*) he was elected a member, and ranked among the best writers and translators of his day. He translated other works into Persian without his father's collaboration, in particular Plato's Dialogues, the *Discours sur la Méthode* of Descartes and the *Kitāb al-S̲h̲ifāʾ* of Ibn Sīnā.

Bibliography: Riḍā-Ḳulī K̲h̲ān, *Mad̲j̲maʿ al-fuṣaḥāʾ*, ii, 383, 394-6; *Dīwān-i D̲h̲akāʾ al-Mulk Mīrzā Muḥammad Ḥusayn K̲h̲ān mutak̲h̲alliṣ bi-Furūg̲h̲ī*, Tehrān 1325. (Said Naficy)

FURŪSIYYA, (A.), the whole field of equestrian knowledge, both theoretical and practical, including the principles of hippology (*k̲h̲alḳ al-k̲h̲ayl*), the care of horses and farriery (*bayṭara*), and *siyāsat al-k̲h̲ayl*, a more exact rendering of the concept of "equitation" in European languages, which can be defined as the art of training and using correctly a saddle-horse. The words *farāsa* and *furūsa*, more rarely used, embrace the same group of ideas. If we consult the indexes of the classical catalogues, such as the *Fihrist* of Ibn al-Nadīm or the exhaustive bibliographies on this subject compiled in the 19th century by Hammer-Purgstall, we gain the quite erroneous impression that a great number of works still exist from which a detailed study of riding could be made. However, this excess of material must not deceive us, and a critical study of these works reveals little material of any use. The Arabic sources can be divided according to the following principle of classification: works of lexicography and *adab*, and treatises on *furūsiyya*.

The lexicographical works do not present any great interest for those who wish to study riding under the Arabs, since they are the work of philologists, not horsemen. The earliest, the *Kitāb al-K̲h̲ayl* of al-Aṣmaʿī (ed. Haffner, Vienna 1875), has been widely used and drawn upon by later authors; we may also mention His̲h̲ām al-Kalbī and Ibn al-Aʿrābī, whose works have been partly edited by G. Levi Della Vida (Leiden 1928) and Abū ʿUbayda, said to be the author of three works entitled *Kitāb al-Sard̲j̲*, *K. al-K̲h̲ayl* and *K. al-Lid̲j̲ām*, mentioned in the *Fihrist*, the only parts of which to have survived are certain fragments incorporated by al-Dimyāṭī in his *K. Faḍl al-k̲h̲ayl*. The *Kitāb al-Ḥayawān* of al-D̲j̲āḥiẓ quotes from works no longer extant. It is mainly in texts not dealing specifically with horses, like the *Risāla fī manāḳib al-Atrāk* of al-D̲j̲āḥiẓ, that valuable information about riding is to be found.

Treatises on *furūsiyya* appeared at a late stage in Arabic literature. The writers of these treatises were horsemen, veterinary surgeons or riders who in their writings rehashed or quoted passages wholly or in part from works of lexicography, as proof of their erudition. Very fortunately, they also added some pages on riding, in which they describe various methods of schooling or the principles to be inculcated in the young rider.

It is essential to make a fundamental distinction between two types of riding which co-existed in the Muslim world, that practised by the Arabs in the desert, and, at a later stage, high school riding. With regard to the former, we possess few documents which allow us to build up a detailed picture of it. It occurred in two basic forms, for war and for racing. The tribal warriors, basing their riding on the tactics of *al-karr wa 'l-farr* (attack and flight), practised it in small bands of combatants (*katība*) using the sabre and lance in preference to the bow, their handling of the latter being decidedly clumsy in the eyes of al-Djāḥiẓ, according to whom "the Khāridjī when fighting at close quarters relies solely on his lance. Neither the Khāridjīs nor the Bedouins are renowned for their skill as archers when mounted". The problem of harness is also difficult to solve for this period. The poems do not help us to decide what sort of saddle was used by the tribal horsemen.

The question of the bit also arises. From the accounts of 19th century travellers we know that the curb bit was very seldom used by Arab horsemen in the East, their preference being for the bozal (*rasan*). We may question whether the word *lidjām*, in passages of ancient poetry, in fact represents the curb bit. Perhaps bits were used for horses only at the time of an action, to make it possible to perform sudden halts and swift half-turns. We possess fuller documentation on the subject of horse-racing (*sabḳ*, *sibāḳ*). Though with certain discrepancies in points of detail, writers have described the conditions of training (*taḍmīr*, *iḍmār*). This lasted from 40 to 60 days and had the effect of bringing the horses into good condition by a suitable system of feeding, while excessive weight was sweated off under blankets. Horses thinned down in this way were called *ḥinād*, and the sweat they lost *sirāḥ*. In pre-Islamic Arabia, races covering very great distances and over varied terrain were organized between the horses of the different tribes; they were often the source of long and bloody wars [see FARAS], although even at that time they were governed by rules. The field (*ḥalba*) consisted of 10 horses; seven tokens were placed on lances, in an enclosure into which the first eight horses of the field made their way; seven received a prize proportionate with their placing, and only the eighth received no prize, its admission being purely a matter of honour. Each horse was given a name, according to the order of finishing, but the list of these names varies in the different authors. According to al-Masʿūdī, they were: 1st - *sābiḳ*, 2nd - *mutabarriz*, 3rd - *mudjallī*, 4th - *muṣallī*, 5th - *musallī*, 6th - *tālī*, 7th - *murtāḥ*; al-Thaʿālibī, following al-Djāḥiẓ, gives a slightly different list, in which the 3rd is called *muḳaffī* and the 5th *ʿāṭif*; the 9th and 10th have the same names in the two traditions, *laṭīm* (knocked out of the enclosure by a blow) and *sukkayt* (silenced by shame at finishing last).

The Prophet did not forbid racing, which fostered rivalry between breeders and encouraged the preservation and increase of the stock of horses so much reduced by the wars. During his lifetime he made regulations for them, and by his advice tried to establish what were for the most part open competitions by making the size of the field uniform and fixing the distance to be covered according to the age of the horses taking part. The traditionists relate that he organized races at Medina, from Ḥafya to Thaniyyat al-Wadāʿ (60 *ghalwa*) for mature horses and from Thaniyyat al-Wadāʿ to Banū Zurayḳ (10 *ghalwa*) for young horses. He himself presented substantial prizes for these competitions and entered his own horses. A ruling on the subject of betting (*rihān*) had been made earlier by the *ḥukamāʾ* of the large tribes. As Islam forbade the *maysir*, the ancient custom was slightly modified to include the entry, among the other runners, of a horse called *muḥallil* or *dākhil*, whose owner made no wager and gained the whole amount staked by all the other entrants if his horse won.

The wars of conquest waged by the Arabs under the first caliphs brought them into contact with foreign equestrian traditions and led them to organize new tactics for warfare on horseback. Three foreign traditions contributed, Iranian, Turkish and Greek. The arabized names of the Iranian or Turkish riders referred to by the writers of treatises on riding are an indication of the part placed by foreigners in the elaboration of the new equestrian art. This influence made itself felt at a very early period; even in the 1st/7th century the *fatā* Ḳanbar, a freedman of ʿAlī, had, according to the traditionists, tamed an unridable horse belonging to that caliph (see *TA*, iii, 507). To make a chronological study would be of little interest; indeed, in riding, two series of factors alone can determine any radical evolution—the type of horse used, and the use of new arms. The first of these factors cannot enter into it, even though the Arab stock was very largely interbred with the stock owned by the conquered peoples [see FARAS]; the resulting progeny was still of the eastern type. The second of these factors, which is closely concerned with the art of war, had a decisive influence on the Islamic equestrian art which sprang up in the 2nd/8th century, and whose apogee can be placed in the 6th/12th and 7th/13th centuries in Spain and Egypt.

Principles of schooling.—Treatises on the first steps of dressage for the young colt, started at about the age of three, might bear the signature of modern riders, but the principles of the more elaborate schooling are somewhat obscure. The terminology is often Turkish or Iranian: the term *maydān* must represent the "track" and the *nāward ḳazan* the circular show-ring where the horse is made supple (*istikhradj al-khayl fi 'l-nāward*). The expression *tartīb al-maydān* can no doubt be interpreted in the sense of organized movements of groups of horsemen; they doubtless served the same purpose as our show-ring movements. The riders also alluded to the balance between front-quarters and hind-quarters (*taʿdīl*) and to the flexibility of the jaw (*ʿalk al-lidjām, lawk al-lidjām*). The advice given to aspiring riders is very simple: the secret of riding rests in the firmness of the seat (*thabāt*) and the evenness of the reins (*taswiyat al-ʿinān*). This firmness is acquired by riding bare-back (*ʿala 'l-ʿārī*), the rider being held in position by the grip of his thighs. As soon as he has some measure of experience, the young rider uses a saddle and fork seat. It will be seen how different such methods of riding are from that practised today in North Africa and Andalusia under the name *a la jinete*. This style is difficult to date and no doubt corresponds to the appearance of the cross-bow and gun. Writers have drawn up long lists of vices both natural and acquired, from which we can give a typical list: *ḥarūn*, a horse that refuses to walk forward; *rawwāgh*, a horse that shies; *djamūḥ*, that checks its head to escape from control by the hands; *munāziʿ*, that takes the bit in its teeth and jerks the hands; *ramūḥ*, a horse that kicks; *khabūṭ*, that stamps its fore-feet; *shabūb*, that rears; *shamūs*, difficult to mount; *ḳalūḳ*, a horse of uncertain temper; *nafūr*, that swerves and shies; finally, the *ṭamūḥ* is regarded as impossible to ride. In this list the writers have classed faults in carriage of the head and withers; the horse with bad head carriage is called *munakkis*. The remedies suggested for dealing with these defects are often brutal and sometimes fantastic.

Harness.—The treatises define with considerable precision the nomenclature of the harness (*lidjām*) which includes the reins (*ʿinān*), the cheek straps (*idhār*) and the browband (*ʿiṣāb*). Three types of bits were used—the *īwān*, a light bit, the *fakk* a snaffle bit (?) and the *nāzikī*, which must be the equivalent of the modern bit used by the Spahis. The bit is composed of branches (*shākima*), mouthpiece and port (*faʾs*) and curb-chain (*ḥakma*); in other cases, this term also denotes the bozal or martingale. The saddle used, the so-called saddle of Khʷārizm, was flat and wide, the pommel (*ḳarbūs*) and cantle (*muʾakhkhara*) being only slightly raised. It rested on a pad (*mirshaḥa*), held in position by one or two girths (*ḥizām*) and a breast-strap (*labab*). The horse was provided with collars (*ḳilāda*) and cloths (*kabūsh* and *shalīl*, the terms *tashāhir* and *djulla* being confined to stable-cloths). The war-horse wore *barāsim* (carapaces) and *barāḳiʿ* (helmets).

Throughout the whole of this period (6th-7th/12th-13th centuries) equestrian sports were regularly practised. Horsemen took part in *djerīd* [*q.v.*] or *burdjās*, a chivalrous duel with lances, in polo [see ČAWGĀN], venery (*ṭard*) and hunting by means of a closed drive (*ḥalḳa*), a favourite sport of the Mamlūks. All these sports provided men and horses alike with excellent training for the *djihād*. Various works, with abundant illustrations, deal with the technique of fighting with the sabre and lance, giving detailed descriptions of lunges and parries (*al-bunūd wa 'l-tabṭīl*); they also describe training in archery with a small target (*kabaḳ*) or with the long bow (*niḍāl*). All these activities were abandoned in turn, and in the modern Muslim world where racing is governed by western rules, only the "fantasia" (*laʿb al-bārūd*, *laʿb al-khayl*) remains as a last vestige of the equestrian displays of bygone ages.

Bibliography: see FARAS. (G. DOUILLET)

IN THE MAMLŪK STATE

Mamlūk historical sources contain exceptionally ample data on *furūsiyya* exercises. By far the most important of these sources is Abu 'l-Maḥāsin Yūsuf b. Taghrībirdī [*q.v.*], who was the son of a high-ranking Mamlūk *amīr* and had close links with some of the great *furūsiyya* masters of his time. It should, however, be stressed that full use of the data furnished by the historical sources will only be possible after a very much more extensive study of Muslim military technical literature.

According to Ibn Taghrībirdī, "*Furūsiyya* is something different from bravery and intrepidity (*al-shadjāʿa wa 'l-iḳdām*), for the brave man overthrows his adversary by sheer courage, while the horseman (*fāris al-khayl*) is one who handles his horse well in the charge (*karr*) and the retreat (*farr*), and who knows all that he needs to know about his horse and his weapons and about how to handle them in accordance with the rules known and established among the masters of this art" (*Nudjūm*, ed. Popper, vi, 445). This is undoubtedly an excellent definition of the strict technical meaning of the term *furūsiyya*. In everyday use, however, the distinction between *furūsiyya* and *shadjāʿa* (or *iḳdām*) had become blurred, and Mamlūk historians confuse them frequently. Sometimes, though very rarely, *furūsiyya* was even used in the meaning of 'high moral character' or 'chivalry'.

In most cases the term *furūsiyya* does not appear independently, but in conjunction with another word. The most common combinations are *funūn al-furūsiyya* and *anwāʿ al-furūsiyya*, *i.e.*, the 'branches' or 'kinds' or 'arts' of the military exercises. Sometimes the word *funūn* appears alone in the sense of *funūn al-furūsiyya*. The expression *funūn al-Atrāk* in the same sense is rather rare. The expression *fann al-furūsiyya* (in the singular) is not very common. The term *ʿilm* ('science') *al-furūsiyya* is rare in Mamlūk historical sources, but frequently found in some of the technical military treatises. The combination *anwāʿ al-malāʿib* or *anwāʿ al-malāʿib* (the 'branches of games') in the meaning of *anwāʿ al-furūsiyya* is quite common. Mastery of the *furūsiyya* exercises constituted a prerequisite for the Mamlūk horseman. These exercises (or high proficiency in them) were sometimes called *kamālāt* ('perfections', 'accomplishments') or *faḍāʾil* ('excellent qualities' or 'virtues').

In any study of the *furūsiyya* training, special attention must be paid to the condition of the 'hippodromes' (*mayādīn*, sing. *maydān*). No intensive cavalry training is possible for any length of time in dilapidated hippodromes. Their number and state of repair are, therefore, useful indications of the level of training reached. During the Baḥrī period (648/1250-784/1382) there was a considerable number of hippodromes in Cairo and its immediate vicinity, where *furūsiyya* exercises were carried out systematically and intensively, especially under Sultan Baybars (658/1260-676/1277) and to a lesser degree under Sultans Ḳalāūn (678/1279-689/1290) and al-Nāṣir Muḥammad (693/1293-741/1340, with interruptions). After al-Nāṣir Muḥammad's death the disintegration of the Ḳalāūnid dynasty set in; and it seems that the accompanying disturbances also had an adverse effect on Mamlūk training. Sultan al-Ashraf Shaʿbān (764/1363-778/1376) attempted to arrest the deterioration of *furūsiyya* training, but in vain. The decline continued at an accelerated pace during the Circassian period (784/1382-923/1517), with a short interruption during the reign of Sultan Ḳanṣūh al-Ghawrī (905/1500-922/1516).

The standard of the *furūsiyya* training is clearly reflected in the state of the hippodromes. In the Baḥrī period there were the following hippodromes, most of which did not remain in use throughout that period: a) al-Maydān al-Ṣāliḥī, built in 641/1243 by Sultan al-Ṣāliḥ Nadjm al-Dīn Ayyūb, the founder of the Baḥriyya regiment; b) al-Maydān al-Ẓāhirī, built by Sultan Baybars; c) Maydān al-Ḳabaḳ, built by the same sultan in 665/1267; d) Maydān Birkat al-Fīl built by Sultan al-ʿĀdil Kitbughā (694/1294-696/1296); e) al-Maydān al-Nāṣirī or al-Maydān al-Kabīr al-Nāṣirī, built by Sultan al-Nāṣir Muḥammad in 712/1312-3; f) Maydān Siryāḳus, built by the same sultan in 724-5/1323-5; g) Maydān al-Mahāri, built by the same sultan in 720/1320.

From the end of the reign of al-Nāṣir Muḥammad and up to that of Ḳanṣūh al-Ghawrī no sultan is reported to have built a hippodrome. The remaining Baḥrī hippodromes were abandoned in the first years of Circassian rule. Towards the middle of the 9th/15th century, exercises were performed on a limited scale in the Royal Courtyard (al-Ḥawsh al-Sulṭānī) in the Citadel. The performance of such exercises near Birkat al-Ḥabash is also mentioned in the sources from time to time, but no source refers to the existence of a hippodrome there.

Ḳanṣūh al-Ghawrī was the only Circassian sultan who constructed (in 909/1503) a hippodrome in Egypt. But his attempt to revive *furūsiyya* training came too late, for the decline of traditional military training in the Mamlūk Sultanate coincided with the slow but steady rise of fire-arms, which revolutionized the whole art of war and, necessarily, of training for it (for a discussion of this aspect of *furūsiyya* see my *Gunpowder and firearms in the Mamluk Kingdom*, London 1956, 46-140, and art. BĀRŪD above).

Furūsiyya included the following 'branches': a) the lance game (*laʿb al-rumḥ*, *thaḳafat al-rumḥ*, *thaḳāfa* or *thiḳāf*); b) the polo game (*laʿb al-kura*, *al-ḍarb bi 'l-kura*, *laʿb al-ṣawladjān*); c) the *ḳabaḳ* (or 'gourd' game); d) archery (*ramy al-nushshāb*, *al-ramy bi 'l-nushshāb*); e) fencing (*al-ḍarb bi 'l-sayf* or *ḍarb al-sayf*); f) the *birdjās* game (*sawḳ al-birdjās*); g) the mace game (*fann al-dabbūs*); h) wrestling (*ṣirāʿ*); i) the games accompanying the *maḥmil* procession (*sawḳ al-maḥmil*); j) hunting (*ṣayd*); k) shooting with the crossbow (*al-ramy bi 'l-bunduḳ*); l) horse racing (*sibāḳ al-khayl*).

The information furnished by the sources on the first three 'branches', as well as on the games accompanying the *maḥmil* procession, is considerably richer than that supplied on the other 'branches'. The mace game is mentioned rarely in the sources. Fencing is mentioned quite frequently in the enumeration of *funūn al-furūsiyya*, but is rarely referred to independently. The *birdjās* game is often mentioned; but without any details. Though the sources frequently speak of the games of archery, they furnish no details regarding them. This is particularly disappointing, seeing that the bow was the main weapon of the Mamlūks and was far more important in battle than the lance. The game of chess (*shitrandj*) was very popular among the Mamlūks. Though it cannot be included among the *furūsiyya* games in the strict sense of the word, the mastery of chess was considered an accomplishment deserving of mention side by side with the Mamlūk's accomplishments in the field of *furūsiyya*.

The *furūsiyya* master (or expert or instructor) was called *muʿallim*. If he was an expert in the handling of the lance, he was called *muʿallim al-rumḥ* (or *rammāḥ*). If he was an expert in the handling of the bow and arrows he was called *muʿallim al-nushshāb*, and so on. The name *ustādh* in the same sense is also mentioned from time to time in the Mamlūk sources, but it is much more frequent in technical military literature. We know the names of a considerable number of such masters, especially from the Circassian period.

Bibliography: D. Ayalon, *Notes on the Furūsiyya exercises and games in the Mamluk Sultanate*, in *Scripta Hierosolymitana*, ix (*Studies in Islamic History and Civilization*), Jerusalem 1961, 31-62 (see the literature cited there).

(D. AYALON)

FUSAYFISĀʾ mosaic. The fact that the Arabic word for the mosaic itself is ultimately derived from the Greek ψῆφος, perhaps through Aramaic **פסיפס**, and the word *faṣṣ*, used for the little coloured cubes which are arranged according to a pre-designed cartoon, derives from the Greek πεσσός, leads us to consider this form of architectural decoration as a borrowing by Muslim art from Byzantine art. This borrowing is undeniable and we shall examine it later. All the same, apart from this importation from abroad, Muslim art of the early centuries seems to have included a form of mosaic which was rather different from any whose technique could have been learned from Constantinople and which the Islamic peoples must have found still flourishing in the countries which they conquered. The Byzantine mosaic is characterized by the use made in it of cubes of glass, called *smalts*, and by its use to cover walls, arches and domes. The pavement mosaic which derives from the Roman tradition is quite different, being composed almost exclusively of cubes of stone of various colours, mostly cut from pieces of marble. Being limited to these mineral components, the colouring of these pavements is usually confined to a few warm tones: creamy white, black, red, bistre and grey-green; the cartoons are often composed of large areas of geometrical motifs, chequered designs and polygonal figures, interlaced plant forms, and plaits, which, in state rooms, frame a central picture (*emblema*).

This type of decoration, appearing first in the Greek lands of the Near East, spread across the Mediterranean world with the Roman conquest. Not only in Italy, but in Syria and in North Africa and southern Gaul it enjoyed great popularity. The triumph of Christianity extended its domain and increased the uses to which it was put. The mosaics which had covered the floors of villas and baths now, in a rougher style and with a less elaborate technique, adorned the apses and naves of churches. Pagan forms now represented Christian symbols. Nevertheless, these survivals from antiquity became suspect to the strict: fear of profanation caused these pictures to be banished from the chancels, while long inscriptions and geometrical patterns, often of improverished invention, covered vast areas. Paving mosaic underwent a great decadence, yet it did not disappear completely from Christian buildings: in the form of ornamented pavements it is still found in basilicas of the 8th and 9th centuries A.D.

Fairly recent discoveries allow us to state that at about the same period, and even later, Islam preserved the taste for mosaics and the technique for making them.

North of Jericho, excavation has revealed the ruins of an Umayyad palace, called *Khirbat al-Mafdjar* [*q.v.*]. To this princely residence is attached a magnificent bath. A vast columned hall, 30 metres long, with a central dome and with walls containing scooped-out apses, has a pavement consisting of thirty-eight mosaic panels, all different. The geometrical decoration consists of rectilinear and curvilinear interlacing patterns, chevrons and imbrications, splendidly executed and with a harmonious colouring produced solely by cubes of stone. In one corner of this monumental *frigidarium* is a small apsidal hall whose floor is adorned with a particularly elaborate decoration. A leafy tree rears itself along the axis, separating two groups of animals very realistically drawn: on one side two gazelles, on the other a third gazelle attacked by a lion. The very recent excavations of Khirbat al-Miniya [*q.v.*], another Umayyad building, have revealed halls and courtyards paved with mosaic. The exclusively geometrical ornament consists of strapwork, lattice work, Greek key patterns and other related themes.

Although less well represented in the West, the tradition inherited from pagan and Christian mosaic-artists is attested by remains found in eastern Barbary. Five miles from al-Ḳayrawān there has been identified the site of al-Raḳḳāda which was, at the end of the 3rd/9th and the beginning of the 4th/10th centuries, the seat of the Aghlabid *amīrs*, vassals of the Baghdād caliph. Cubes of mosaic are found there, either at ground level or buried in the masonry. Beside an enormous pool there had been erected palaces, of which very little remains. All the same, some rooms paved with mosaic are still to be found. The very simple decoration, of black on a white background, consisted of scatterings of geometrical figures, square, lozenge-shaped and hexagonal, and of compartments adorned with knots and of spirals arranged in crosses. These pavements of Ifrīḳiya, executed in about 290/900 and so similar to Christian mosaics, betray themselves as being the work of local craftsmen who put at the disposal of Arab *amīrs* a technique and a style of decoration which had been entirely inherited from their Romanized Berber ancestors.

Some forty years later was executed a mosaic revealed by the excavations of Mr. Sliman Zbiss at Mahdiyya (in Tunisia), among the ruins of the palace of the Fāṭimid caliph al-Ḳā'im (322/934-334/946). This fine pavement covered the floor of a room of state 13 yards long and 4 yards wide. It consisted of a central panel adorned with quatrefoils interlaced like the rings of a coat of mail and a wide border containing pelta-ornaments, quatrefoil squares and circles. The colours represented are black and white, with ochre and bistre. Neither the colours nor the polygonal shapes are foreign to what is attested in Roman work. Yet the theme of interlacing patterns gives the decorative scheme an oriental character (for interlacing polygonals are hardly ever found in Roman pavements); the compact plant themes enclosed by these polygons belong still more obviously to the flora of ʿAbbāsid ʿIrāḳ or Ṭūlūnid Egypt. The craftsmen working at Mahdiyya would seem to have been using cartoons imported from the East; just as the contemporary architecture of Ifrīḳiya bears the stamp of the same foreign influences.

This pavement mosaic, whose survival in the first centuries of Islam is attested only by excavation, is to be distinguished from mural mosaic, of which East and West alike have preserved magnificent examples. In the East, they are to be found at the Ḳubbat al-Ṣakhra [*q.v.*] in Jerusalem, built in 72/691 by ʿAbd al-Malik, and at the Great Mosque of Damascus, built in 86/705 by al-Walīd; in the West, at the Great Mosque of Cordova, in the superb *ḳibla* of the caliph al-Ḥakam I [*q.v.*], of 350/961. As is evident, these are the three most important religious buildings of the Umayyads owing their adornment to mosaics. The interior of the Ḳubbat al-Ṣakhra is largely covered with mosaic, which adorns the peripheral arcades, the drum surmounting them, and the dome. As for the Great Mosque of Damascus, only fragments survive of the pictures representing a great gilded vine and whole towns, the most striking of them adorning some surfaces of the arcade surrounding the courtyard. As for the Great Mosque of Cordova, in it are preserved, more or less worked over, the frame of the *miḥrāb* and of the doors flanking it, and also the dome in front of the *miḥrāb*. These three examples, from East and West, have many features in common, but are distinguished one from another by more than one characteristic. The materials used show clearly their interrelation. White and black cubes of marble and red or pink stones are to be found, as in the mosaic pavements; but much more numerous (85% at Damascus) are the cubes of glass paste coloured throughout, and particularly such cubes consisting of a brown base of glass paste upon which is applied gold leaf, which in turn is covered with a protecting layer of glass. It is the use of gold which creates the richness and the harmony of the Byzantine mosaic. The varied positions of the cubes, stuck in either vertically or slightly inclined towards the spectator, diversify the tones and, in particular, relieve the monotony of the areas of gold and bring life to these shining surfaces.

The subjects of the decorations vary from one monument to another. That of the Ḳubbat al-Ṣakhra is the richest, and in it floral designs predominate. The most frequent theme is that of acanthus leaves or vine leaves with grapes, the main stem emerging from a cluster of leaves, a bowl or a cornucopia. Narrow panels are provided with vertical supports reminiscent of the antique candelabras on which are placed trays, foliage or fruit. The plant themes, arranged in bands placed side by side, alternate with motifs of jewellery, ribbons, bandeaus, and pendants inspired by necklaces and diadems; plaques cut from mother-of-pearl add their lustre to these themes of adornment. This ornamentation derives almost entirely from Hellenistic tradition; the jewellery motifs seem to be inspired by the imperial decoration of Byzantium; some palm-branches in the form of wings and some flowers derived from the lotus are probable borrowings from the Sāsānid flora and were familiar also to Syrian sculpture of the same period.

Quite different are the very beautiful mosaics of the Great Mosque of Damascus, at any rate those which the removal of the layer of plaster has revealed in the courtyard. They contain large green trees rising up among groups of buildings: fortresses whose walls border on the terraces alternate with balconied houses with pitched roofs and wide cornices, pavilions with colonnades and conical roofs, and exedras; lower down, more modest houses overlook the shore lapped by lively waves. The Pompeian character of the architecture has been remarked. The waters which form the foreground of the decoration have been thought to be the Barada, the river which flows through the oasis of Damascus. This realistic interpretation, which associates a familiar and not very highly esteemed landscape with the adornment of a great mosque, does not seem compatible with Muslim aesthetic. Perhaps we should rather consider this decoration of the courtyard as the complement of the geographical pictures which spread across the walls of the prayer hall, and identify the tumultuous waters on the shore with those of the surrounding Ocean (*al-baḥr al-muḥīṭ*) which, according to the Arab geographers, encircles all the inhabited lands of the world.

According to the traditions which Ibn Idhārī has transmitted and which we shall examine, the Umayyad caliph al-Ḥakam II, following the example set by his ancestor al-Walīd, the builder of the mosque of Damascus, obtained from the emperor of Constantinople the despatch of a mosaicist and the necessary materials to decorate the Great Mosque of Cordova, which he was providing with a new *ḳibla*. In fact the mosaics of the *miḥrāb* of Cordova and the parts which frame it or lead to it scarcely recall the picturesque decoration of Damascus. This is not surprising, for two and a half centuries separate the Syrian from the Andalusian work. The latter presents a simplified and schematic flora with its central stems rigid or slightly curving, regularly bent into foliated scroll-patterns or doubled and forming wide symmetrical interlacings. These stems bear palm leaves with two or three incurved fronds, flowers, or bunches of grapes, each separate. The inscriptions play an important part here and their Kūfic script is sober and elegant. One seeks in vain Christian mosaics of the same period analagous to these Muslim mosaics; on the contrary, analysis reveals the relation between this flat and coloured decoration and the sculptured decoration which surrounds it. We find the same floral themes portrayed by the two techniques, sculpture and mosaic, but both belong to the same Islamic art.

Nevertheless the historical conditions make it probable that mosaics were sent from Byzantium to Cordova. Relations between the two powers, interrupted for over a century, had been resumed since 346/958, and at the end of the reign of ʿAbd al-Raḥmān III they were active and cordial. The sending of gifts—notably of Byzantine mosaics—served for the embellishment of the Madīnat al-Zahrāʾ. The continuation of these relations between al-Ḥakam II and Nicephorus Phocas is therefore not surprising and we have no difficulty in accepting the tradition, albeit three hundred years old, related by Ibn ʿIdhārī (*Bayān*, ii, 253, tr. ii, 392). At the request of al-Ḥakam, a mosaicist came from Constantinople with 320 quintals of mosaic cubes. The caliph assigned to him a certain number of slaves (some of whom had already begun to learn the craft at Madīnat al-Zahrāʾ). They worked under the direction of the Greek and were not long in surpassing their master in skill. When the latter left Cordova, where he had been lodged magnificently, he received from the caliph gifts and robes of honour; his pupils continued the work alone and completed it. The story seems to be historically possible.

However, we have seen that (according to Ibn ʿIdhārī) al-Ḥakam, in requesting the Byzantine emperor to send a mosaicist, was following the example of al-Walīd, the founder of the Damascus mosque. Now it seems that this is a legend which was unknown to the earliest sources and which does not appear until the 6th/12th century. According to Ibn ʿAsākir (d. 571/1176) al-Walīd accompanied his request with the threat to overrun the territory of Byzantium and destroy the churches on his own lands if the Basileus refused; and the Basileus complied. The attribution of such an attitude to the two rulers is doubtful. But although the story cannot be applied to the Damascus mosque it may be possible to associate it with the mosque of Medina. According to al-Yaʿḳūbī, al-Wāḳidī and al-Ṭabarī, for the re-building of this mosque, a request for a mosaicist was made to the emperor of Byzantium and was granted. This is nevertheless rather surprising. Al-Balādhurī (d. 279/892), speaking of the work on the mosque of Medina, gives a more likely report. Al-Walīd, he says, wishing to embellish the Mosque of the Prophet, obtained the collaboration of mosaicists and other craftsmen of Rūm recruited in Syria and in Egypt. This supposes the existence in these countries of ateliers or individual artists, presumably of Greek origin, continuing in the 2nd/8th century the technique of Byzantine mosaic. The tradition of this fine craft, which had formed the glory of Antioch, could have survived in Syria from Christian times, which saw the building of the Church of the Ascension in Jerusalem, the Basilica of the Nativity in Bethlehem and the churches of Edessa and of Lydda. It seems very possible that for the first religious foundations of Islam local mosaicists as well as builders were recruited, and probably they were still available during the following centuries to complete and restore the decorations of the sanctuaries of Syria. In Jerusalem there are the mosaics of the Fāṭimid al-Ẓāhir (411-27/1021-36), of the Ayyūbid Ṣalāḥ al-Dīn (570-89/1174-93), and of the Mamlūk Tanḳiz (729/1329), and at Damascus those of Baybars. The date of the mosaics of the Kaʿba of Mecca described by Ibn Djubayr is not known.

In Egypt, which, as we have seen, had possessed, like Syria, artists from 'Rūm', who practised the art of Byzantine mosaic, only a few and late examples of this work remain. In Cairo, the tomb of Shadjar al-Durr (648/1250) retains a *miḥrāb* the lower part of which is decorated with cubes of blue, green, red and gilded glass with the addition of mother-of pearl. Of the same type are the decoration of the *miḥrāb* which the sultan Lādjīn gave to the mosque of Ibn Ṭūlūn in 696/1296, and the *miḥrāb*s of the *madrasa*s of Ṭaybars (709/1309) and of Aḳbughā (740/1339), dependencies of the Al-Azhar mosque.

Bibliography: P. Gauckler, *Musivum opus*, in *Dictionnaire des Antiquités*; Max van Berchem, *Matériaux pour un corpus inscriptionum arabicarum, Jerusalem-Haram*, 274 ff.; Marguerite van Berchem, in K. A. C. Cresswell, *Early Muslim architecture*, i, 277 ff.; eadem, in *Monuments Piot*, 1930; E. de Lorey, *Les mosaïques de la mosquée des Omeyades de Damas*, in *Syria*, xii (1931), 326 ff.; H. Zayat, *Les mosaïques de la mosquée des Omayades de Damas furent-elles l'oeuvre des Grecs de Byzance ou des Grecs melkites de Damas?*, in *al-Khizāna al-Sharḳiyya*, ii, Beirut 1937; R. W. Hamilton, *Khirbat al-mafjar, an Arabian mansion in the Jordan Valley*, Oxford 1959, 327-42; idem, *A mosaic carpet of Umayyad date at Khirbat al-Mafjar*, in *Quarterly of the Department of Antiquities of Palestine*, xiv (1950), 120; J. Sauvaget, *Monuments historiques de Damas*, 1932, 67-8; Selim Abdul-Hak, in *Annales archéologiques de Syrie*, 1958-9, 5; G. Wiet and Hautecoeur, *Mosquées du Caire*, 116 and *passim*; G. Marçais, *Architecture musulmane d'Occident*, 28, 45, 98; J. M. Solignac, *Recherches sur les installations hydrauliques en Ifriqiya*, in *AIEO-Alger*, x (1952).

(G. Marçais)

AL-FUSṬĀṬ, the first city to be founded in Egypt by the Muslim conquerors and the first place of residence of the Arab governors. It was built on the east bank of the Nile, alongside the Greco-Coptic township of Babylon or Bābalyūn [*q.v.*], traces of which are still preserved in the ramparts of the Ḳaṣr al-Shamʿ. A bridge of boats, interrupted by the island of al-Rawḍa [*q.v.*], linked the Ḳaṣr with the city of Giza (al-Djīza) on the other bank of the Nile. Al-Fusṭāṭ was partly built beside the river, which at that time followed a more easterly course, and partly on high desert ground, shaped in the form of a saddle and extending for more than four km. from north to south. The hills to the south of Sharaf were called al-Raṣad after 513/1119; those to the north were called Djabal Yashkur. It was not far from Djabal Yashkur that the Khalīdj started, the Pharaohs' canal connecting the Nile with the Red Sea, which was restored on the orders of ʿAmr b. al-ʿĀṣ.

In former times the name al-Fusṭāṭ was written in various ways, enumerated by the Arab authors, which betray uncertainty as to the true origin of the word. One of the meanings suggested is that of "tent"; for the town was founded on the spot where ʿAmr b. al-ʿĀṣ had pitched his tent (*fusṭāṭ*) during the siege of Babylon. It seems likely that this name was merely the arabization of the word

Φοσσάτον, camp, encampment, used by the bilingual papyri to denote the town. The chroniclers also use the expression Fusṭāṭ-Miṣr or even simply Miṣr, colloquially pronounced Maṣr. The quarter of modern Cairo, which contains the remains of al-Fusṭāṭ and Babylon, is called Maṣr al-ʿAtīḳa, Old Cairo.

When ʿAmr b. al-ʿĀṣ returned from the first siege of Alexandria, probably early in 22/643, he established the foundations of a permanent encampment at al-Fusṭāṭ which was gradually transformed into a town. The proximity of Babylon made it easy for the Arabs to employ and control Coptic officials. Later came the distribution of the land and the building of the mosque (D̲j̲āmiʿ ʿAmr or al-D̲j̲āmiʿ al-ʿAtīḳ). This mosque, the first to be built in Egypt, originally measured 50 by 30 cubits. It is possible that it had a *minbar* from the start; but the *miḥrāb*, in the form of a niche, seems to have been built only in 92/711. Reconstructed and enlarged several times, it attained its present dimensions in 212/827. It served simultaneously as a place of prayer, council chamber, court room, post (office) and as lodgings for travellers. It was there that the main grants of leases of land were made. Not far away was ʿAmr's house and the army stores. There was also a *muṣallā*, an immense place of prayer in the open air, where, on the *ʿid al-Fiṭr* 43/January 664, prayers were offered over the body of ʿAmr b. al-ʿĀṣ, who had died the previous night. Each tribe was allotted a certain fixed zone (*k̲h̲iṭṭa* which, in Fusṭāṭ, is the equivalent of the *ḥāra* in Cairo, that is to say quarter or ward). Certain *k̲h̲iṭaṭ* included inhabitants belonging to different tribes, for example, the *k̲h̲iṭṭat ahl al-rāya* surrounding ʿAmr's mosque, the *k̲h̲iṭaṭ al-Lafīf* just to the north of it, and the *k̲h̲iṭaṭ ahl al-Ẓāhir*, the last-named being reserved for new arrivals who had been unable to settle with their own respective tribes (cf. Guest, in *JRAS*, 1907, 63 f.). Each *k̲h̲iṭṭa* had its own mosque. In 53/673, for the first time, minarets were built for ʿAmr's mosque and for those in the *k̲h̲iṭaṭ*, with two exceptions. The Arab army of conquest included a very large proportion of Yamanīs. Christians and Jews from Syria with political affiliations with the Muslims had accompanied the invading armies; they were settled in three different quarters near the river, named respectively, going north from ʿAmr's mosque, *al-Ḥamrāʾ al-dunyā*, *al-Ḥamrāʾ al-wusṭā*, and *al-Ḥamrāʾ al-ḳuṣwā*. Other *d̲h̲immīs* settled with them.

The original encampment was gradually transformed. The different quarters were separated by open spaces. Whole zones, particularly to the north in the desert, were then abandoned, only to be reoccupied later. Permanent structures multiplied. The treasury, *bayt al-māl*, was built (Becker, *Beiträge zur Geschichte Ägypten*, ii, 162). Al-Fusṭāṭ was not fortified and, in 64-5/684, the K̲h̲āridjīs of Egypt who had seized power had a ditch built on the east side to defend the town against the caliph Marwān and his forces. The governor ʿAbd al-ʿAzīz b. Marwān, who founded or developed Ḥulwān, where he had taken refuge from the plague (70/689-90), also built houses, covered markets and baths in Fusṭāṭ. The Copts imperceptibly became intermingled with the conquerors. Coptic was spoken in Fusṭāṭ in the 2nd/8th century. Some churches also were built, and are occasionally mentioned by the chroniclers. Warehouses were set up along the Nile for waterborne merchandise. When the last Umayyad caliph Marwān II, in flight before the ʿAbbāsids, went through Fusṭāṭ (132/750) he caused the stores of grain, cotton, chopped straw and barley, and indeed the whole town, to be set on fire, according to Severus of As̲h̲munayn (*Patr. Orient.*, v, 168). Further east, between Fusṭāṭ and the cliffs of Muḳaṭṭam was the cemetery of al-Ḳarāfa [*q.v.*]. The ʿAbbāsid governors did not reside in the centre of Fusṭāṭ; they chose instead the old *al-Ḥamrāʾ al-ḳuṣwā*, in the open spaces of the original encampment, to found the suburb of al-ʿAskar. Al-Maḳrīzī explains in this connexion that the actual town of Fusṭāṭ was divided into two districts—the *ʿamal fūḳ* or upper district with its western section (the high ground in the south as far as the Nile) and eastern section (the rest of the desert as far as al-ʿAskar), and the *ʿamal asfal* or lower district, including the remainder. The ʿAbbāsids tried a new and short-lived settlement on the D̲j̲abal Yas̲h̲kur, as a refuge from an epidemic, in 133/751. Later they settled at al-ʿAskar where a "Palace of the Amirate" (*dār al-Imāra*) was built and then in 169/785-6, just beside it, a large mosque (*d̲j̲āmiʿ al-ʿAskar*, also called *d̲j̲āmiʿ Sāḥil al-G̲h̲alla*). All around there grew up a real town, with shops, markets and fine houses. Nothing now remains of it.

In the 3rd/9th century Aḥmad b. Ṭūlūn also created his own capital called al-Ḳaṭāʾiʿ, between the north-east tip of the D̲j̲abal Yas̲h̲kur (where he had a large and striking mosque built) and the *mas̲h̲had* of Sayyida Nafīsa and the future Rumayla square. The mosque (*d̲j̲āmiʿ Ibn Ṭūlūn*), the oldest in Greater Cairo still existing in its original form, was completed in 265/879. The architect, a Christian and probably of Mesopotamian origin, took his inspiration from the buildings of Sāmarrā. He had previously built an aqueduct, the ruins of which still stand to the north-west of Basātīn, leading towards ʿAyn al-Ṣīra. Besides the mosque and a number of houses, al-Ḳaṭāʾiʿ also included a palace, a *dār al-Imāra* and some magnificent gardens. It was all to vanish very swiftly. On the fall of the Ṭūlūnids (292/905), the ʿAbbāsids demolished the palace. They did not touch the mosque, which was later restored by sultan Lād̲j̲īn (696/1297) (cf. Salmon, *Études sur la topographie du Caire*, in *MIFAO*, 1902, where also all necessary details on the later history of the district are given).

The founding of al-Ḳāhira (358/969) did not put an end to the prosperity of Fusṭāṭ which, in the Fāṭimid period, was one of the wealthiest towns of the Muslim world, with its lofty houses of from five to seven stories (Nāṣir-i K̲h̲usraw, in the *Safar Nāma*, trans. Schefer, 146, even speaks of fourteen stories), the crowded souks round ʿAmr's mosque and the network of narrow streets recently excavated on the desert plateau. Al-Ḳāhira, where the houses were lower and furnished with gardens, was then the city of the caliphs and the military aristocracy; Fusṭāṭ, more populous, remained the home of commerce and industry, as is testified by very fine ceramics and pieces of glassware discovered during excavations, as will as texts on papyrus and paper. In the 7th/13th century the town still manufactured steel, copper, soap, glass and paper (Ibn Duḳmāḳ, iv, 108), not to mention its production of sugar and textiles. In 513/1119 the town was able to produce a massive ring of polished copper, graduated, and measuring more than ten cubits in diameter, weighing several tons and intended to act as a support for an apparatus for astronomic observations. However, during the anarchic reign of the caliph al-Mustanṣir, over a period of eighteen years (from 446/1054 to 464/1072) the town suffered sixteen years of severe famine, accompanied by epidemics. Al-ʿAskar, al-Ḳaṭāʾiʿ and whole zones of the desert quarters of Fusṭāṭ were consequently abandoned. The vizier Badr al-Djamālī then caused the materials of the ruined buildings to be removed for re-use in Cairo. A second operation of this kind took place between 495/1101 and 524/1130; it was concerned with those buildings which the owners, despite a general warning, had failed to put into a state of repair. The year 564/1168-9 was catastrophic. The Frankish armies of Amalric were encamped just to the south of al-Raṣad, at Birkat al-Ḥabash; Shāwar, their former ally, had summoned them four years earlier, and he himself was now attacked by them. Fearing that they would occupy Fusṭāṭ, which had no ramparts to defend it and which might be used by them as a base against Cairo, he had the town evacuated and his men systematically set it on fire. The conflagration lasted for fifty-four days. After all these cataclysms life began once again; the place was rebuilt. All the same, to prevent the recurrence of such incidents Ṣalāḥ al-Dīn built a city wall enclosing Cairo, the citadel and Fusṭāṭ. The remains of this wall can be seen to the south of the citadel, and also 900 metres to the east as well as to the south-east of ʿAmr's mosque. New quarters were built on the abandoned land by the Nile, while the notables erected pleasure pavilions alongside the water. The eastern districts were increasingly neglected, while ʿAmr's mosque remained a flourishing centre of religious instruction until the great plague of 749/1348. Under the Mamlūk sultans, however, Cairo attracted great commerce; it was the souks of Cairo, not of Miṣr, that the astonished European travellers described. Fusṭāṭ (which name disappears, being replaced by Miṣr) fell into obscurity. It remained merely the administrative capital of Upper Egypt whose produce was constantly brought by ship to its river banks. At the time of Napoleon's expedition, Old Cairo contained 10,000 inhabitants, 600 of whom were Copts.

Bibliography: Maḳrīzī, *Khiṭaṭ*; Ibn Duḳmāḳ, *Kitāb al-Intiṣār*; ʿAlī Mubārak, *al-Khiṭaṭ al-djadīda*. Besides the works mentioned earlier, A. F. Mehren, *Câhira og Kerâfat*, Copenhagen 1870; S. Lane Poole, *The story of Cairo*, London 1906; idem, *A history of Egypt in the Middle Ages*², London 1914; Casanova, *Essai de reconstitution topographique de la ville d'al-Foustât ou Miṣr*, in *MIFAO*, xxxv (1919); U. Monneret de Villard, *Ricerche sulla topografia di Qasr eš-Šamʿ*, in *Bull. Soc. Géog. Egypte*, xii (1923-4), 205-32, xiii (1924-5), 73-94; M. Clerget, *Le Caire, Étude de géographie urbaine et d'histoire économique*, 2 vols., Cairo 1934, with very abundant references; ʿAlī Bahgat Bey and A. Gabriel, *Fouilles d'al-Foustât*, Paris 1921; eidem, *Kitāb Ḥafriyyāt al-Fusṭāṭ*, 1 vol., with an album of photographs, Cairo 1928; Maspero and Wiet, *Matériaux pour servir à la géographie de l'Égypte*, in *MIFAO*, xxxvi (1919); K. A. C. Creswell, *The Muslim architecture of Egypt*, i, Oxford 1952; Van Berchem, *CIA*; Gabriel Hanotaux, *Histoire de la Nation Égyptienne*, vol. iv, *L'Égypte arabe (642-1517)* by G. Wiet; Guest, *Miṣr in the Fifteenth Century*, in *JRAS*, 1903, 791-816 [see further AL-ḲĀHIRA]. (J. JOMIER)

FŪTA DJALLON (accepted French spelling Fouta), principal massif of tropical West Africa, situated at the north-east of the Republic of Guinea. This group of mountains has been thoroughly studied by J. Richard Molard (1913-51). It is twice the size of Switzerland and of very varied character. Its eastern section has a crystalline base which rises to about 700 m./3000 ft., with some peaks of over 1000 m./3,300 ft. The Tinkisso, a tributary of the Niger, rises there. The central Fouta is an internal "Tassili" divided into three masses: in the north the massif of Mali (with its highest point at Mount Tennsira, 1515 m./4,970 ft), in the centre the plateau of Timbi, Labé and Popodara, with an average height of 1000 m./3,300 ft., which is divided by numerous canyons with impressive waterfalls (Ditinu, Kinkon, Kambadaga, the Sala, etc.), and finally in the south the massif of Dalaba (1425 m./4,675 ft. at Mount Tinka). From these massifs with their sheer cliffs (those of Massi reach 800 m./2,600 ft.) rise the Bafing, the principal feature of Senegal, the Upper Gambia, the Rio Grande of Portuguese Guinea and many mountain rivers, which together form the water tower of the western region of Africa. Because of its altitude the Fouta enjoys a favourable climate. It has a high rainfall in summer and its winter is a healthy dry season, the effect of which is further increased from December to February by the 'harmattan'; the rainy season is from July to September. The scorching heat of the Sahara attracts the Atlantic clouds and each year Dalaba has a rainfall of 2035 mm./80 ins., Pita 1882 mm./73 ins., Labé 1764 mm./70 ins. and Mali 1893 mm./76 ins. Three types of vegetation are found in the Fouta: (a) bush, either brushwood (*bururhe*) or trees (*fitare*); (b) sparse grassland, sometimes on the shores of a small lake (*dunkere*) on the clay covering a plateau (*hollande*), sometimes on sand which fills a depression (*dantari*); (c) the *bowal*, which covers three quarters of the surface of the Fouta and which is "in the dry season a vast and torrid surface of desert, marked at intervals by mushroom-shaped white-ant-heaps" (Richard Molard).

Population. The Fouta is a mountain district suitable for the rearing of livestock. As Vieillard says: "half-way between the Sahelian steppe and the dense forest: the former stretches over the endless barren plains of the high plateaus, the latter clothes the sides of the mountains in the form of tall riverside forests. This hybrid environment has favoured the formation of a composite society, a mixture of settled forest-dwellers and of shepherds and cowherds". The Baga and Landuman, probably autochthonous, were driven out in the 13th century by the Susu-Dialonke expelled by the Mandinkas of Sundjata. In 1534, the Fulakunda of Koli Tenguela came from the Fouta Toro to settle to the west of this group of mountains. Finally, in 1694, Fulani who had come from Macina formed an empire which was to last for two centuries. Apart from these great movements, there were small migrations from the plains of the north. The Fulani replaced the hump-backed cattle by the *ndama* which was more or less immunized against trypanosomiasis. They enslaved or drove out the former negro inhabitants of the forests, borrowing features of their material civilization. According to Vieillard they "brought with them their language, their faith which permitted the foundation of a Muslim fraternity, and a harsh exploitation mitigated by intermarriage.

Of the 750,000 inhabitants of the Fouta, two-thirds are Fulani and the others are former slaves who have adopted the Fulani language and belonged to the feudal system of the Fouta. These vassals, *rimaibe* (singular *dimadio*), cultivate the ground for their Fulani masters. They live in *runde*s near the country house of the master (*marga*).

The administrative organization consists of the *missidi* (village mosque) at the bottom, then the *teku*, a group of *missidis* with the *lamdo-teku* at the head. When the system of alternative government came into operation the chief of a *diwal* (province) was changed every second year, at the same time as the *almamy*.

The fiscal laws were very carefully worked out. The tax on inheritance consisted of the *homidia* (assigning to the marabout a quarter of the possessions of the deceased) and the *kombabete*, collected by the chief of the *diwal* or the *lamdo-teku* five months after the death. The *assaka* (or *saka* or *fariba*) was due to the chief of the *missidi* for the poor. The *ussuru* was a tithe on manufactured goods. In addition the ruler of the Fouta received a fifth of the booty of war and the tributes (*sakkale*) paid by the vassal peoples of the coast.

History. A large contingent of the Fulani of the Fouta came from Macina at the end of the 17th century, led by Seri or Sidi. After Muhammadu Saïdi, elected chief in 1700, they chose the pious Kikala, then his son Sambigu, whose two sons disputed the succession (1720-26). So the Fulani called on Ibrahima Mussu, called also Karamoko Alfa, a man of immense piety, who was invited to wage war against the pagans. Karamoko Alfa inaugurated that permanent state of Holy War which was to become one of the characteristic political features of the Fouta. In the Fouta D̲jallon Islam served as a justification for the seizure of power. A committee of insurrection consisting of Karamoko Alfa and six other members was formed and the movement was supported by young Islamized Dialonkes and Malinkes. The fetishist Dialonke were conquered and Timbo and Fukumba occupied. But some years later, Puli Garme, chief of the pagan Dialonke, re-took Timbo. Karamoko Alfa died insane in 1751, Ibrahima Sori (= early-rising) took his place; he was given the by-name of Mawdo (= the great) and his reign was marked by military campaigns against the Wassulonke and the Sulima. Tradition has it that he exterminated 174 kings (who were probably nothing more than village chiefs), he subdued the Fulani chief of Labe, seized the Mandingo province of Niokolo (Upper Gambia) and forced Maka, the king of the Bundu, to become a Muslim. But these military successes disturbed the council of the elders, and particularly its president Modi Maka, who caused Abdulay Ba Demba, son of Karamoko Alfa, to be appointed in place of Ibrahima Sori Mawdo. But the latter was soon recalled because of dangers which threatened from outside. Ibrahima Sori then transferred his capital from Fukumba to Timbo. On the death of Ibrahima Sori Mawdo (1784) the principle was adopted of rule alternating every two years between the Alfaya and Sorya families; but it was put into practice only with difficulty. The 19th century was dominated by the reign of the Almani Omar (1837-72) who had to suppress the rising of the fanatical Hubbus. These, won over by the Modi Mamadu D̲joue, took the name of *Hubbu rasul Allai* (one who loves the Messenger of God). These Hubbu, fighting in the name of an intransigeant Islam, took Timbo (1859) before being beaten at Kuni and Kusogogya. Mamadu D̲joue died after taking refuge in the mountains between Bafing and Tinkisso. His son, Mamadu Abal (= the wild), was to be defeated. Umaw died during the campaign undertaken in the Rio Grande. In 1887-8, an extraordinary nobleman, Aimé Olivier, Count (?) of Sanderval, got himself recognized by the Almami as a citizen of the Fouta D̲jallon, and obtained the grant of the uplands of Kahel and the right to mint coins. He played an important part in helping the chief of Labe to fight Bokar Biro. The latter, put on to the throne by French authority, signed the treaty of the protectorate with *Bissimilahi* (*bi-'smi 'llāh*) instead of his own name. Then Captain Müller marched on Timbo and Bokar Biro and his 1500 warriors were defeated at Poredaka. This was the end of the independence of the Fouta, which was divided by the French administration into districts.

The Fulani chiefdoms, which had been retained throughout the colonial period, were suppressed by the Council of Government set up during the summer of 1957. But by then they were already of very little significance. The Fouta D̲jallon had ceased to be an independent fortress and had become fully integrated into the political and economic life of Guinea.

Bibliography: General works, travellers' accounts: Mollien, *Voyage dans l'intérieur de l'Afrique, aux sources du Sénégal et de la Gambie*, Paris 1820; Hecquard, *Voyage sur la côte et dans l'intérieur de l'Afrique occidentale*, Paris 1853; Lambert, *Voyage dans le Fouta Djallon, Tour du Monde*, 1862; Olivier (de Sanderval), *De l'Atlantique au Niger par le Fouta Djallon*, Paris 1883; Dölter, *Über die Cap Verden nach dem Rio Grande und Futah Djallon*, Leipzig 1884; Dr. Bayol, *Voyage en Sénégambie*, Paris 1888; Noirot, *A travers le Fouta Djallon et le Bambouc*, Paris 1889; Madrolle, *Notes d'un voyage en Afrique occidentale*, Paris 1893; Dr. Maclaud, *A travers la Guinée et le Fouta Djallon*, in *Bull. Com. Afr. Franç.*, 1899; Manchat, *Les rivières du Sud et le Fouta Djallon*, Paris 1909;—Physical structure: Fras, *Les résultats scientifiques de la mission du Fouta Djallon*, in *Bull. Soc. Géog. commerciale*, Bordeaux 1891; J. Chautard, *Étude géographique et géophysique sur le Fouta Djallon*, Paris 1905; Chevalier, *Les hauts plateaux du Fouta Djallon*, in *Annales de géographie*, 1909; J. Richard Molard, *Les traits d'ensemble du Fouta Djallon*, in *Revue de géographie alpine*, xxxi/2 (1943); G. Sautter, *Le Fouta Djallon*, in *Bull. de la Soc. languedocienne de géog.*, Montpellier, 2e série, xv/1 (1944), 3-76; J. Tricart, *Dégradation du milieu naturel et problèmes d'aménagement au Fouta Djalon* (*Guinée*), in *Revue de géographie alpine*, 1956/1, 7-36; J. Pouquet, *Aspects morphologiques du Fouta Djallon*, in *Revue de géographie alpine*, 1956/2, 215-46; idem, *Le plateau de Labé* (*Guinée Française, AOF*), in *Bulletin de l'IFAN*, xviii-B/1 (1956), 1-24.—Peoples: Bérenger Féraud, *Les peuples de la Sénégambie*, Paris 1878; L. Guebhard, *La religion, la famille, la propriété et le régime foncier au Fouta Djallon*, in *Revue coloniale nouvelle, série IX*, 1909; idem, *Les Peuls du Fouta Djallon*, in *Revue des études ethnographiques*, ii (1909); G. Vieillard, *Notes sur les Peuls du Fouta Djalon*, in *Bull. de l'IFAN*, Jan.-April 1940, 85-210; J. Richard Molard, *Les densités des populations au Fouta Djalon et dans les régions environnantes*, in *XVIe Congrès Intern. de géog.*, Lisbon 1949; idem, *Essai sur la vie paysanne au Fouta Djalon. Le cadre physique, l'économie rurale, l'habitat*, in *Revue de géographie alpine*, xxxii/2 (1944), 135-240; idem, *Notes démographiques sur la région de Labé. Hommage à Jacques Richard Molard*, in *Présence africaine*, xv, 83-94; idem, *Islam ou colonisation au Fouta Djalon*, in *Bulletin des missions évangéliques*, xvi (Oct. 1953); Saïkhou Balde, *Les associations d'âge chez les Foulbé du Fouta Djalon*, in *Bull. de l'IFAN*, 1959/1, 89-109; —History: Hecquard, *Coup d'œil sur l'organisation politique, l'histoire, les mœurs des Peuls du*

Fouta Djallon, Paris n.d.; Olivier (de Sanderval), *La conquête du Fouta Djallon*, Paris 1890; J. Guebhard, *Histoire du Fouta Djallon et des Almamys*, in *Bull. du Com. de l'Afr. Fr.*, 1909; A. Arcin, *Histoire de la Guinée Française*, Paris 1911; P. Marty, *L'Islam en Guinée*, Paris 1921; Ch. Le Cœur, *Le culte de la génération et l'évolution religieuse et sociale en Guinée*, Paris 1932; L. Tauxier, *Histoire des Peuls du Fouta Djallon*, in *Mœurs et histoire des Peuls*, Paris 1937, 218-382; Demougeot, *Notes sur l'organisation politique et administrative du Labé*, Paris 1944; F. Rouget, *La Guinée française*; A. Teixeira da Mota, *Nota sobre a historia dos Fulas. Coli Tengvela e a chega da dos primeiros Fulas a Futa Jalom*, 2e CIAO, Bissao 1947, Lisbon 1950, v, 53-70; Schnell, *Vestiges archéologiques et agriculture ancienne dans le nord du Fouta Djalon*, in *Bull. de l'IFAN*, B-xix/1-2 (1957), 295-301.

(R. Cornevin)

FŪTHĀGHŪRAS [see fīthāghūras].

FUTŪḤĀT [see ṭarābulus (al-sha'm)].

FUTUWWA, a term invented in about the 2nd/8th century as the counterpart of *muruwwa* [*q.v.*], the qualities of the mature man, to signify that which is regarded as characteristic of the *fatā*, pl. *fityān*, literally "young man"; by this term it has become customary to denote various movements and organizations which until the beginning of the modern era were wide-spread throughout all the urban communities of the Muslim East. The study of these movements is made difficult by the fact that, in the course of history, they have assumed very diverse forms, corresponding with which are two fundamental categories of documentation, the information from which often appears for that reason to be irreconcilable. Thus, from the time when, over a century ago, Hammer-Purgstall drew attention to them, many representations of them have been given and, despite the advance that has been made in our knowledge of them, it cannot be said that even now we really know exactly what they were. Hammer-Purgstall for his part regarded the *futuwwa* as a form of chivalry, and one finds this interpretation repeated up to our own time; but, for the past fifty years, particular attention has been given to the connexions maintained by the *futuwwa* at a late period on the one hand with Ṣūfism, and on the other with the professional groupings; however, even in the latter case the nature of the treatises specifically devoted to it has resulted in its being approached from the doctrinal or psychological angle rather than being integrated within the social structure, of which nevertheless it constitutes an important element. It is to this last aspect that I wish to give especial emphasis.

In the pre-Islamic and early Islamic periods, the Arabic language does not use the term *futuwwa*, but only *fatā*, itself used in the singular rather than in the plural, in that the word denoted individuals, not groups. At that time the *fatā* was a man still young and vigorous, valiant in warfare, noble and chivalrous: an essentially personal attitude and, though obviously linked with tribal society and its combats, one not dependent on any collective activity or explicit religious belief; and indeed it so happens that a modern work will still extol this type of character under the name *futuwwa*. The semi-legendary model for it in ancient Arabian society was prince Ḥātim al-Ṭā'ī [*q.v.*]; but, in Islam, the gradual growth of the figure of ʿAlī has resulted in his being regarded as the *fatā* par excellence, as is expressed in the old saying *lā fatā illā ʿAlī*.

Quite soon, however, in the complex society of the Arabo-Islamic Empire new *fityān* (now in the plural) made their appearance; it is however impossible to trace their origin back exclusively to the ancient Arab tradition. Indeed, these new *fityān* themselves are presented to us in two categories of portraits which are at first sight incompatible.

A first group of texts, consisting for the most part of relatively late accounts of mystics, but also of earlier narrations of the lives of poets, presents the *fityān* as young adults living in small communities, coming from varied social, ethnic (and, to start with, religious?) circles and, free from any sort of attachment to family (they were frequently bachelors), profession (even if they had one) or tribe, associating together to lead in common the most comfortable possible life in an atmosphere of solidarity, mutual devotion and comradeship (with joint ownership of goods), without which such an aim could obviously not be achieved. The setting was more extensive than that of a single town, in the sense that a fraternity existed between the *fityān* of each town and others elsewhere by whom they were received when travelling, like the old "companions" in Europe. It seems that they wore a special costume. It was still largely under this aspect that Ibn Baṭṭūṭa, the famous traveller of the 8th/14th century, was to see them when he encountered them among the common people in Turkish Asia Minor; but among the Persian aristocracy also, where *futuwwa* was translated by *djavānmardī*, the life of the *fityān* appeared to a prince such as the author of the *Ḳābūsnāma* (5th/11th century) to be a desirable vocation, indeed an ideal.

In contrast, however, to these peaceful impressions the ancient chroniclers record many others which are far less so. In this connexion the name *fityān* is not in fact the one that occurs most frequently; since they were discussing elements of disorder, the writers, who belonged to the official classes, gave them names suggestive of the mob or rabble; the most general term, which the recipients adopted with just as much pride as did other men of the people in revolutionary France the term *sans-culotte*, is *ʿayyār(ūn)* "vagrant, outlaw"; other quite common terms were *awbāsh* "riff-raff", *shāṭir*, pl. *shuṭṭār* "artful [ones]" and, from the time of the Saldjūḳids, *rind* [*q.v.*], pl. *runūd* "scamp". It is with their condition in Baghdād that we are through the documentation most familiar, but it must not be forgotten that the special character of that town may mean that they did not occur there in their widely-spread form, and it is important to study them also in any other place where it is possible to do so.

In Baghdād, we see the *ʿayyārūn* emerging from obscurity in the periods when authority was relaxed. Well-known pages of al-Ṭabarī and al-Masʿūdī evoke them for us, armed with stones and staves and with no protection other than helmets made of palm-leaves, standing together in defence of the caliph al-Amīn against the attacks of the Khurāsānīs who supported his brother al-Ma'mūn, or, half a century later, in the cause of al-Mustaʿīn against the troops of al-Muʿtazz. The three centuries from the 4th/10th to the 6th/12th are full of tales of disturbances fomented by them or in which they took part, their exploits only ceasing at exceptional times under strong rulers (the Būyid ʿAḍud al-Dawla, the three great Saldjūḳids). During the civil wars of the last years of the independent caliphate, numerous leaders sought their help and enrolled them in their police forces. In 361-2/972, when arms had been distributed to those who had declared themselves ready to set off for the Holy War against the Byzantine invaders, disorders ensued which were ended only by burning down a quarter of the town. In about 420-5/1028-33 two of their leaders, Ibn al-Mawṣilī and al-Burd̲j̲amī, were the real masters of the capital and forced the appointment as head of police of Muḥammad al-Nasawī who was regarded as one of their friends and who in any case treated them with consideration and relied on them. If we are to believe later traditions, it is possible that the Būyid Abū Kālīd̲j̲ār was in league with them. In the following century the head of the *fityān* in Bag̲h̲dād in about 530/1135 and the succeeding years included the governor and members of the vizier's and the sultan's families among his followers. These are only a few instances out of a multitude of other less striking ones. When they were strong, they succeeded in plundering, but the chief complaint of the merchants in the *sūḳ*s was in general less of their "thefts" than of the "protection" k̲h̲ifāra, ḥimāya [*qq.v.*] which, following the example of certain great men, they extended over the *sūḳ*s for the sake of the spoils that fell to them. They were particularly powerful in the outlying districts, but also in certain quarters of Kark̲h̲, inhabited by artisans, on the left bank of the Tigris and, later, at Bāb al-Azad̲j̲ on the right bank, at the gates of the capital which provided their livelihood.

Who were they, what were their aims? In the first place they were clearly humble people, often without any established or definite profession; but more exalted persons readily mingled with them, either being attracted by them or, from ambition, desiring to have followers. They certainly had no 'programme' in the sense that a modern popular party would have, and often an inclination towards plunder and the rewards derived from it seem to have been their sole motivation; however, at the same time they had a more specific ambition, which may cause some surprise: they wanted to be enrolled in the police (s̲h̲urṭa), partly of course for the sake of the regular pay, but also and primarily because to join the police is the surest way of avoiding trouble with them. This is also the reason why one sometimes comes across reformed ʿayyārūn who, acting as volunteers (muṭṭawiʿūn), helped the government against their former companions. Among the masses, the true ʿayyārūn enjoyed the popularity of thieves who attack the rich, an elementary form of class repossession to which no moral stigma was attached. Their leaders claimed official recognition for the title of ḳāʾid which they assumed and which, besides gratifying their self-esteem, gave them a secure place in the social hierarchy. Finally, as regards religion, they included S̲h̲īʿīs and Sunnīs; the Ismāʿīlīs may have attempted to penetrate their groupings in order to organize political activities there (as in the case of the "plot" which a pious organization denounced in 473/1080 to the government of the Caliph under the Sald̲j̲ūḳid protectorate); and the Ḥanbalīs certainly had their social "base" among some of them: but these diverse movements co-existed, and the *futuwwa*, in its general character common to all, owes nothing to them and is not more specifically affected by any one of them than by any other.

What we have just said applies, we repeat, more particularly to Bag̲h̲dād, where the importance of the forces of the government and the aristocracy in general thrust back ʿiyāra (*i.e.*, the quality and posture of the ʿayyārūn) into a role of extra-legal op-

position. But the picture suggested by the documentation relating to other towns is, despite its deficiencies, somewhat different. There was not a single town in the Iranian and peri-Iranian world, from Central Asia to Mesopotamia, which did not have its ʿayyārūn, and although they appear to be somewhat similar to what we have just seen in the capital of the Caliphate they nevertheless seem to be more closely linked with the local bourgeoisie, even in the functioning of official political institutions. Sometimes they joined forces with the bourgeoisie in support of a native prince, as in the Sāmānid territory; sometimes the bourgeoisie relied on them in resisting the authorities whom it resented as foreigners, particularly during the Turkish period. Their greatest success, in Sīstān, was the elevation to princely authority of a dynasty that had sprung up from themselves, that of the Ṣaffārids, which had started out by superseding the inadequate forces of the Caliph during the struggle against the bedouin K̲h̲ārid̲j̲īs; and without going as far as that, there were many occasions when they made and unmade princes. More usually, in the majority of towns which had no s̲h̲urṭa, they formed an indispensable local militia, whose quality was enhanced by their active traditions of sporting and military training and upon whom the *raʾīs* of the city relied, whether or not he was their actual leader (see the case of Buk̲h̲ārā, where the *K. al-D̲h̲ak̲h̲āʾir* clearly shows the official standing of their battalions alongside the army and the *g̲h̲āzīs*).

It will naturally be asked what connexion there is between the *fityān* whom we described at the beginning of this article and the ʿayyārūn of whom we are now speaking. The texts, however, make it clear beyond question that many of the *fityān* of the first sort called themselves or were called ʿayyārūn or some equivalent name, while many of the ʿayyārūn on the other hand called themselves *fityān* or followers of the *futuwwa*. An at least partial equivalence is therefore indisputable, and the only question is to know if this is or is not absolute and, insofar as it is confirmed, to understand its significance. To find the answer, we have to remember the existence of the urban ʿaṣabiyyāt. In eastern towns certain kinds of factions existed almost everywhere under this name, feuding in the name of some particular doctrine or eponym; but they are more profoundly characteristic of a certain type of urban society. Now the texts also leave no doubt that the concepts of ʿaṣabiyya and *futuwwa* were, at least in part, inter-related. In the moral sense, ʿaṣabiyya is the principle of solidarity of a group, *futuwwa* the individual qualities by which it can be achieved. This being said, it is evidently as impossible to attribute any great numerical strength to the sodalities of *fityān* of the mystico-literary texts as it is to deny it to the ʿayyārūn belonging to the ʿaṣabiyyāt who inspired the accounts in the historical and related works; but we see very clearly that, in a sense that is materially elastic but morally no less strong, the members of the ʿaṣabiyyāt could have regarded themselves as true adherents of the *futuwwa* and that, among the *fityān* in the apparent idyllic sense, many individuals or groups may in fact have been steeped in the ʿaṣabiyyāt and the disturbances that they engendered. Consequently the *futuwwa* must apparently be considered neither as an interesting but marginal socio-ideological institution, as most of the ancient descriptions imply, nor even solely or precisely as a form of reaction by the destitute classes, but as a general and fundamental structural element of urban society in the mediaeval East.

Within which frontiers, in the East? Though attested throughout the whole Irano-Mesopotamian territory, the *ʿiyāra-futuwwa* is not recorded, at least under those names, in Syria or Egypt. There were militias there, it is true, the *aḥdāth* [*q.v.*], a name which, like *fityān*, evokes "youth"; they are found first in the 4th/10th century, ranged against the authorities while simultaneously entrusted with the functions of the *shurṭa*; later, towards the end of the following century, they became an officially accepted institution, their *raʾīs* then being *raʾīs* for the town, sometimes almost by inheritance; however, they progressively declined in face of the organization of new powers relying on military garrisons. The resemblance to the *fityān*, both in the facts and the meaning of the name, is evident; and yet the analogy is not absolute. The status of the *aḥdāth* became more systematically official than that of the *fityān*, their recruitment was perhaps more bourgeois, and above all there is no indication that their organization was in any way concerned with the communal life, the rites of initiation and the ideological elaboration which, as we shall see, characterize the *futuwwa*; if we add to this that the latter's domain was that of Sāsānid tradition, while the *aḥdāth* only existed in the former Syro-Byzantine territories, we shall concede that, in spite of a certain parallelism in conditioning and evolution, there may be differences in their historical origins. But in Damascus the ordinary *aḥdāth* were sometimes opposed by more popular *aḥdāth* who were accused of *ʿiyāra*; in Egypt, at Tinnīs, there was in the 4th/10th century a large organization of *shabāb shudjʿān* "young heroes", who combined communal life with violent anti-aristocratic activities; though Muslims, they were denounced by the Christian notables to the Fāṭimid caliph al-Muʿizz who had them exterminated, like others in Damascus (*Histoire des Patriarches d'Alexandrie*, ed. Soc. d'Arch. Copte, ii/2, 88-9); and later, in Cairo, there were popular groups then called *ḥarāfīsh* who reveal an undeniable relationship with the *ʿayyārūn*, if not explicitly with the *futuwwa* in the strict sense of the term, with whom they do not appear to have claimed kinship (see W. Brinner, *The significance of the ḥarāfīsh and their Sultan*, in *JESHO*, vi/2 (1963)). Nothing comparable seems to have been recorded in western Islam.

The *futuwwa* is often represented as being linked with the guild organizations, and it has even been suggested that, through the initiation rites to which we shall return later, both of these were influenced by the Ismāʿīlīs, who were credited with particular interest in the world of labour. We have already said what we think about this last point. More generally, it is important to make a careful chronological distinction. In the later Middle Ages (*v. infra*) a certain kind of interpenetration between the trade guilds in the Irano-Turkish territories and the *futuwwa* is undeniable; but until the 7th/13th century, when guild life remained very much under State control, the most that could be said is that the *futuwwa* clientèle was evidently recruited for the most part at a popular level. On the one hand, it was apparently not the well-established masters of regular trades who constituted the chief recruits; on the other hand there is in any case nothing to indicate that the corporate groups of *futuwwa* were set up and marked off from one other on an occupational basis. No doubt relationships in respect of their work can be traced; but if a European parallel may be cited, it is that of the inter-professional Companies and not the trade guilds, and the term 'corporation' must not be taken implicitly as the equivalent of 'profession'.

The point remains that the *futuwwa*, as we have noted, is strictly speaking an urban phenomenon. Naturally it happened that, in the course of their activities, the *fityān* went beyond urban boundaries and mingled with other social categories, and the diversity of the groups and the uncertainties of terminology in the various writers perhaps permit us to admit the existence of some intermediate cases between the true *futuwwa* and other corporate organizations. But it seems necessary to make a distinction in principle between the urban *fatā* and the *ṣuʿlūk* [*q.v.*], the knight-errant of the desert (even if he derives from the proto-Arab *fatā* or the *djavānmard* of Persian tradition); and although, in the frontier zone, the *fatā* may be replaced by the *ghāzī*, for the rest he is a phenomenon of wider occurrence, and even there generally coexisted with the other without confusion.

These remarks on the *ʿayyārūn* apply particularly to the period up to the 5th/11th century; at that time there occurred an evolution, both among them and in the surrounding society, which in itself is of great historical importance, but which furthermore, as we shall see, is at the origin of the appearance of that form of literature on *futuwwa* which, when compared with the reality, is at first sight so misleading. The growing importance of the *fityān-ʿayyārūn*, attracting persons of high social rank and an increasing number of men of erudition, provoked a tendency among them to clarify and scrutinize the values that the *futuwwa* in fact implied; in the second place, and simultaneously with this process, another movement came into being within Ṣūfism which, for long restricted to individual forms of asceticism and mysticism, became organized into communities where, very naturally, the problems of collective life brought them into touch with the experience of *futuwwa*; it was perhaps the extra-legal aspect of the *futuwwa* which formed the attraction for some Ṣūfīs like the Malāmatiyya. It was in these circles, from the 5th/11th century, that a specific literature on *futuwwa* made its appearance, the characteristic feature of which is that it provides us with a spiritual elaboration of the subject, with the addition of certain pseudo-historical traditions and a selective and idealized portrayal of the ancient *fityān* (such as we described earlier, partly from this source), without any other allusion being made to the real organizations of *fityān* and the use of violence, of which nevertheless the chroniclers continue to provide such irrefutable evidence—to such an extent that we might well wonder if we really are dealing with the same people, were it not that we know that at least from the 7th/13th century some of the writers of the treatises of this type were well-known as leaders of authentic groups of real *fityān*.

The attitude of the governments and aristocracy towards the *futuwwa* was consequently modified. It is true that they continued their struggle against those who fomented disturbances or who were suspected of heterodoxy, but, far from being opposed to the concept of the *futuwwa*, they were hostile only to what they called distortions, or deviations from what it should in fact be. Niẓām al-Mulk, the great Saldjūḳid vizier, in whose lifetime a vizier of the Caliph persecuted the group of *fityān* suspected of Ismāʿīlism to whom we have already referred, was at the same time the man to whom one of the first treatises of *muruwwa* and *futuwwa* was dedicated.

Again, during the following century, in the well-known pages where the Ḥanbalī Ibn al-Djawzī attacked the *fityān* of his day and their conception of sexual honour, their acts of violence, etc., what he preaches is not so much their destruction as the taking over of the *futuwwa*, in its anarchic condition, by a superior authority capable of guiding it towards its true aims.

It was this reform that the caliph al-Nāṣir (577/1181-620/1223) was to accomplish. The dominating preoccupation of this remarkable man was his attempt to regroup under the aegis of the Caliphate all spiritual families and all organizations claiming kinship with Islam. At a very early date (578/1182 according to Ibn Abi 'l-Damm and al-Sakhāwī quoted in Muṣṭ. Djawād, see *Bibl.*) he had himself initiated into the Baghdād *futuwwa* by its grand master, *shaykh* ʿAbd al-Djabbār. As we have seen, the *futuwwa* was to a greater or lesser degree diversified, and in the time of al-Nāṣir in Baghdād there were five branches of it, one of which, the *Nabawiyya*, whose existence is attested as early as the 4th/10th century and which was also known elsewhere in the 6th/12th century by Ibn Djubayr, devoted itself to fighting against the heretic and the infidel, while another was the *Raḥḥāṣiyya*, ʿAbd al-Djabbār's branch. Al-Nāṣir cannot have been a simple, ordinary devotee of the *futuwwa*. Legislating in this domain as in others, he tried to unify, discipline and co-ordinate the *futuwwa* of Baghdād while at the same time encouraging the ruling circles of religious, military and administrative society to belong to it, with the aim of converting into an instrument of social education and general solidarity what had previously been a source of disturbance and discord, and also to reconcile the Ṣūfī-influenced *sharīʿa* of his conception with a corpus of regulations and customs that had grown up independently of it. Afterwards he exhorted the princes of the whole Muslim East to adhere to this new *futuwwa*, to develop its organization in their respective States, to associate themselves generally with him in the establishment, under his aegis, of a pan-Islamic *futuwwa*. For the aristocratic clientèle, privileges had to be found; hence the emphasis placed on the monopoly of performance of certain sports to which the *fityān* had long devoted themselves with enthusiasm. Indeed in Syria and Egypt the *futuwwa*, in this form, remained aristocratic. But it so happens that it was with this form that Hammer-Purgstall was acquainted, with the result that he looked upon it as an order of chivalry; we can see to what extent this view is, if not misdirected, at least restricted in fact to a single tardy excrescence, destined not to last and in no way representative of the real *futuwwa*. In Baghdād society the caliph's efforts were nullified, after his death, by the Mongol conquest. Strangely enough, it was in Anatolian-Turkish society, during its first phase of organization, that the great caliph's initiative was to rouse the strongest echoes; the *futuwwa* that developed there in the original form of the *akhī*s [*q.v.*] never ceased to be ascribed to the patronage of al-Nāṣir (see below).

It is through the writings on *futuwwa* that resulted from al-Nāṣir's policy that we are best acquainted with the organization of the *fityān*, without of course being able always to specify exactly which elements of the description given would also have been valid in the preceding centuries, and which were al-Nāṣir's innovations. The treatises of Ibn al-Miʿmār, who is the most factual, al-Khartaburtī who is more imbued with the spirit of Ṣūfism, and al-Suhrawardī, the first of a series of writers in Persian, inaugurated a literary category which, in Irano-Turkish territories (and also in Egypt during the Ottoman period), was to continue until the beginning of modern times. The rôle of communal initiatory groups which they ascribed to the *futuwwa* organizations is certainly applicable, though not uniformly, in the "classical" periods of Islam. Membership, preceded by a period of probation, was accompanied by a ceremonial which entailed in particular the drinking of a cup of salt water during a communal meeting at which a belt was buckled round the new devotee; he also adopted the distinctive clothing of the *futuwwa*, the trousers being especially significant. He was introduced by a sponsor to whom he was bound as by the inflexible duty of the son (*ibn*) or junior, inferior man (*ṣaghīr*) to the father (*abū*) or senior (*kabīr*). In al-Nāṣir's *futuwwa*, an interval of time separated the first ceremony of adoption of the novice (*murīd*) from the presentation of the trousers, the action which alone conferred the rank of full member, comrade (*rafīḳ*). The *Futuwwatnāma* of Suhrawardī adds a hierarchy between the simple adepts by the spoken word only (*ḳawlī*) and those who had girded on the sword (*sayfī*), but we do not know how far this corresponded to reality; at the end of the century an intermediate stage was still spoken of, that of those who had drunk the cup (*shurbī*). Solidarity between comrades had to be absolute. The general organization, in which the Grand Master was the caliph assisted by a *naḳīb*, was divided into a certain number of sub-groups (*aḥzāb*, pl. of *ḥizb*), each of which consisted of several *buyūt*; and a kind of autonomous internal jurisdiction settled their disputes by a procedure in which the oath of honour of the *futuwwa* played a great part. The books on *futuwwa* do not mention any sporting privileges; but we know that these did apply to the rearing and flying of homing pigeons, an ancient occupation of the *fityān* but despised by the aristocracy, and the sport of the *bunduḳ* [see KAWS] (accompanied by the shooting of birds), the rules for which were then officially promulgated, and which seems to have been a favourite diversion of the Turkish military caste; we may suppose that this aspect of the *futuwwa* did not interest the writers who were considering the *futuwwa* in its moral and religious aspects.

There is no doubt, however, that from then onwards there was a certain convergence between the popular *futuwwa* and the *futuwwa* of the Ṣūfīs. One of the most ardent disseminators of the reformed institution was the same Suhrawardī, general theological adviser to al-Nāṣir and founder of an order of Ṣūfīs, and one who commanded extraordinary respect, especially in Asia Minor. A certain reciprocal penetration took place between the combative spirit of the *fityān* and the spiritual ideal of the Ṣūfīs. One manifestation of this was the adoption for the *futuwwa* of *isnād*s inspired by Ṣūfī models, by means of which each group claimed attachment to ancestors, whether true or suppositious, whose patronage was morally significant: generally, in the end, to ʿAlī, on account of the ambivalence of the word *fatā*, and very often after him to Salmān, the patron of the Irano-Mesopotamian artisans. In more general terms, we thus see the *futuwwa* demonstrating in its own particular way the method of absorption of popular movements by Ṣūfī organizations which from the end of the Middle Ages to our own time has characterized such large sectors of social evolution in Muslim countries. It is merely necessary to repeat that the literature that resulted from this evolution cannot be taken as a guarantee of what the classical *futuwwa* had been in earlier times.

Bibliography: It is impossible to enumerate here all the historical, literary, religious etc. works which provide occasional and sometimes valuable documentation on *futuwwa*; references will be found in the articles listed below, particularly those of Fr. Taeschner and Cl. Cahen; we shall confine ourselves to adding two works which have more recently become known, the *K. al-Dhakhā'ir wa 'l-tuḥaf* of al-Rashīd b. al-Zubayr, ed. Ḥamīdullah, Kuwait 1959 (on Bukhārā, 153), and the *Ta'rīkh* of Ibn Abi 'l-Damm, unpublished, passage quoted by Muṣṭafā Djawād in the work listed *infra*, 52. In the section following we shall consider only those treatises which, either wholly or in part, are devoted specifically and explicitly to the *futuwwa*, with the reservations noted in the article. The earliest is that of Sulamī (about 400/1010), ed. Fr. Taeschner, *As-Sulami's Kitab al-Futuwwa*, in *Studia Orientalia Joanni Pedersen ... dicata*, Copenhagen 1953, which is followed by some special sections on the *futuwwa* in the larger works of mysticism or *muruwwa* of Thaʿālibī (Brockelmann, I, 286), of ʿAbd Allāh al-Anṣārī (Abdülbaki Gölpınarlı, *op. cit.*, *infra*, 10), of Ibn Djadawayh (ed. Taeschner in *Documenta Islamica Inedita* [*Festschrift R. Hartmann*], 1952) and of Ḳushayrī (*Risāla*, see R. Hartmann, *al-Kuschairis Darstellung des Sufitums*, Türk. Bibl. XVIII, Berlin 1914). In the following century appeared the critical chapter of Ibn al-Djawzī in his *Talbīs Iblīs*, ed. Cairo 1340, 421-2. But it was naturally around the caliph al-Nāṣir that works on *futuwwa* especially developed. The most notable of these is the *Basṭ madad al-tawfīḳ* of the Ḥanbalī Ibn al-Miʿmār (and not ʿAmmār, as has been read until recently), which was studied by Thorning (see *infra*) as early as 1913, though its attribution to al-Nāṣir's circle was only established by P. Kahle in his article *Die Futuwwa-Bündnisse des Kalifen al-Nasir*, in *Festschrift Georg Jacob*, 1932; the last-named writer has now, under the same title, produced a German translation of the work in his *Opera Minora*, 1956; the same text has been published with a scholarly introduction, under the title *K. al-Futuwwa*, by Muṣṭafā Djawād and Muḥammad al-Hilālī (with two other collaborators), Baghdād 1958, who have established the true name of the author. To the writings of al-Nāṣir's circle belong also the *Tuḥfat al-Waṣāyā* of Ilyās al-Khartaburtī analysed by Taeschner in *Islamica*, v (1932), and published in facsimile with Turkish translation by Abdülbaki Gölpınarlı in his *Islam ve Türk illerinde fütüvvet teşkilatı ve kaynakları*, in *Istanbul Üniversitesi Iktisat Fakültesi Mecmuası*, xi (1952) (the French edition of the same review, *Revue d'Histoire Economique*, reproduces the introduction), and a treatise, the precursor of a series in Persian, by al-Nāṣir's spiritual adviser, Shihāb al-Dīn ʿUmar Suhrawardī, analysed by Fr. Taeschner in *Oriens*, xv (1962), in which he refers to another treatise by the same author. Moreover, P. Kahle has extracted from the Chronicle of Ibn al-Sāʿī, ed. Muṣṭ. Djawād, 227 ff., and translated and studied the text of the caliph's decree of 604/1207 on the reorganization of the *futuwwa*, *Der Futuwwa-Erlass des Kalifen al-Nasir*, in *Festschrift Oppenheim* (= Beiheft I zum Archiv f. Orientforschung, 1932). For subsequent works after al-Nāṣir's time, see the second part of this article.

As has been said, the first European writer to have noted—in however fortuitous and digressive a manner—the existence of the *futuwwa* was J. v. Hammer-Purgstall, in his article *Sur la chevalerie des Arabes*, in *JA*, 1849 (mainly following Ibn al-Furāt). After him, however, it was in fact H. Thorning who, from an entirely different approach, inaugurated the study of the *futuwwa*, to which P. Kahle in the articles enumerated above made decisive contributions; but the principal specialist, to whom we are indebted for a mass of information and ideas, has for over thirty years been Franz Taeschner. This scholar has from time to time undertaken various restatements of the problem, the last general one being his *Futuwwa, eine gemeinschaftbildende Idee im mittelalterlichen Orient und ihre verschiedene Erscheinungsformen*, in *Schweizerisches Archiv für Volkskunde*, lii (1956), 122-58; nevertheless, although in this article the author has on certain points completed and modified his earlier expositions, the latter should still be consulted for detailed information, particularly his principal works: *Die islamischen Futuwwabünde, das Problem ihrer Entstehung und die Grundlinien ihrer Geschichte*, in *ZDMG*, lxxxvii (1933); *Futuwwa-studien*, in *Islamica*, v (1932); *Der Anteil des Sufismus an der Formung des Futuwwaideals*, in *Isl.*, xxiv (1937); *Islamisches Ordensrittertum zur Zeit der Kreuzzüge*, in *Die Welt als Geschichte*, iv (1938); *Das Futuwwarittertum des islamischen Mittelalters*, in *Beiträge zur Arabistik, Semitistik und Islamwissenschaft*, Leipzig 1944 (not to mention his contributions on the later Turkish *futuwwa* and the *akhīs*, for which see below). More recently, critical views of varying validity have been expressed by G. Salinger, *Was the Futuwwa an oriental form of Chivalry?*, in *Proceedings of the American Philosophical Society*, xciv (1950). A valuable and illuminating study of social psychology has been made by L. Massignon, *La futuwwa ou pacte d'honneur entre les travailleurs musulmans au Moyen Age*, in *La Nouvelle Clio*, 1952. After bringing to light certain details concerning *Les Débuts de la futuwwa d'al-Nasir*, in *Oriens*, 1953, Cl. Cahen has attempted, by a more complete use of historical information, to further our knowledge of the *futuwwa* organizations as an organic part of oriental urban society, in his *Mouvements populaires et autonomisme urbain dans l'Asie Musulmane du Moyen Age*, in *Arabica*, 1958-9 (also printed separately, 1959; abridged German version: *Zur Geschichte der städtischen Gesellschaft im islamischen Orient des Mittelalters*, in *Saeculum*, ix (1958), 59-76), and quite recently the *fityān* of Khurāsān have attracted the attention of C. E. Bosworth in *The Ghaznevids*, Edinburgh 1963, chap. VI. Of the Arab scholars, besides the contributions of Muṣṭafā Djawād reproduced in the introduction to his edition of Ibn al-Miʿmār, we should add S. ʿAfīfī, *al-Malāmatiyya wa 'l-Ṣūfiyya wa ahl al-futuwwa*, Cairo 1364/1945. For the Turkish scholars, who for the most part have concerned themselves with the Turkish period of the *futuwwa*, see below.

The *fatā*, in its ancient Arab form, has been the subject of expositions, for example in Bishr Farès, *L'honneur chez les Arabes avant l'Islam*, Paris 1932, ʿUmar al-Dasūḳī, *al-Futuwwa ʿind al-ʿArab*, Cairo 1953, and M. Bravmann, *On the spiritual background of Early Islam*, in *Muséon*, lxiv (1951).

(CL. CAHEN)

Post-Mongol Period

(i) Survival of the courtly *futuwwa* after the Mongol Invasion.

When Hülegü, the grandson of Čingiz Khān, conquered Baghdād in 1258, putting a bloody end to the ʿAbbāsid Caliphate, he also dealt a blow to the *futuwwa* organization, which the Caliph al-Nāṣir li-Dīn Allāh had reformed and brought to new greatness by introducing it into courtly life. *Futuwwa* writings, which had come into being under al-Nāṣir, survived for a time to the extent of entries in the great encyclopaedias (here I would mention the Persian encyclopaedia *Nafāʾis al-funūn fī masāʾil al-ʿuyūn* of Āmulī, and the *Tuḥfat al-ikhwān* of ʿAbd al-Razzāḳ Kāshānī), which have a chapter on *futuwwa*, giving extracts from the *Kitāb al-Futuwwa* of the Ḥanbalī *faḳīh* Abū ʿAbd Allāh Muḥammad al-Shārim (?), known as Ibn al-Miʿmār, which was written for the *futuwwa* circles of the caliph al-Nāṣir. But it is doubtful whether this literary survival was matched by any actual survival of the organizational *futuwwa* in its courtly form.

For some time, however, the courtly *futuwwa* did in fact persist in Egypt. This was connected with the move of the ʿAbbāsid Caliphate to that country under the Mamlūk sultan al-Ẓāhir Baybars (658-676/1260-1277). Before he left for Damascus on 19 Ramaḍān 659/18 August 1261, the ʿAbbāsid prince who had fled to him, and whom he recognized as Caliph al-Mustanṣir II, clothed him with the "garment of the *futuwwa*" (*libās al-futuwwa*). After Mustanṣir II had been killed on his unsuccessful campaign against the Mongols, a second supposed ʿAbbāsid descendant arrived in Cairo, and was in turn recognized by Baybars as the Caliph al-Ḥākim bi-amr Allāh, and Baybars in his turn now bestowed on him the "garment of the *futuwwa*". Baybars's successors maintained the investiture with the "garment of the *futuwwa*" for some time. They invested Mamlūk *amīr*s and foreign princes with it, issuing the relevant documents, *e.g.*, that made out for the Mamlūk sultan al-Ashraf Khalīl in 691/1292 in respect of the Kurdish prince ʿAlāʾ al-Dīn al-Hakkārī. Mamlūk *amīr*s who had received the *futuwwa* showed this in their coat of arms. As time went on, however, interest in the *futuwwa* seems to have waned. During the 8th/14th century, or at the latest during the 9th/15th, courtly *futuwwa* appears to have become extinct even in Egypt—at least, no more is heard of it. Only Ḳalḳashandī, in his work *Ṣubḥ al-aʿshā*, makes brief mention of the ceremony of admission, the girding (*shadd*). There are also a few documents opposing the *futuwwa*, written by members of the *ʿulamāʾ*, such as the one by the famous Ḥanbalī reformer Ibn Taymiyya (died 728/1328), but otherwise no further evidence has come to light.

Bibliography: Concerning the Egyptian *futuwwa*: E. Blochet, *Moufazzal ibn Abilfazaïl, Histoire des Sultans Mamlouks* (*Patrologia Orientalis*, xii, treatise iii), Paris 1919, 426 [84]; *Chronicle of Aḥmed ibn ʿAlī al-Maḳrīzī, entitled Kitāb al-Sulūk fī maʿrifat duwal al-mulūk*, ed. by M. Muṣṭafā Ziada, vol. I, Part 2, Cairo 1936, 459, note 5 (reproduction of Mufaḍḍal's report); Fr. Taeschner, *Eine Futuwwa-Urkunde des Mamlukensultans al-Aschraf Chalīl von 1292*, in *Aus der Geschichte des islamischen Orients* (*Philosophie und Geschichte* 69), Tübingen 1949, 1-15; al-Ḳalḳashandī, *Ṣubḥ al-aʿshā*, Cairo 1336/1918, 274-9 (reproduction of the above-mentioned *futuwwa* document, and a further one with an introduction); I. Goldziher, *Eine Fetwā gegen die Futuwwa*, in *ZDMG*, lxxiii (1919), 127 f.; J. Schacht, *Zwei neue Quellen zur Kenntnis der Futuwwa*, in *Festschrift Georg Jacob*, Leipzig 1932, 276-87.

(ii) Popular *futuwwa*. The Turkish *Akhīlīk*.

Wherever *futuwwa* once existed, it continued in a different form, by becoming linked with the crafts, and thus, in time, it became the rule of the guilds. This process, occurring in all the countries of the Islamic Orient, is by no means clear, but we know more about its history in Turkey than in most other places. This is due to the fact that here (*i.e.*, in Saldjūḳ Anatolia), it took on a rather interesting form among the urban craftsmen, noticeable because the bearer of the *futuwwa* (Turkish *fütüwwet*), the *fütüwwetdār*, was referred to as *Akhī*; hence the Turkish name *Akhīlīk* (see AKHĪ) for this particular Anatolian form of *futuwwa*.

We know from the historian Ibn Bībī that courtly *futuwwa* did exist in Anatolia. He reports that the Rūm-Saldjūḳ Sultan ʿIzz al-Dīn Kaykāwūs I had requested and received the "garment of the *futuwwa*" from the Caliph al-Nāṣir (c. 611/1214). In the time of his successor ʿAlāʾ al-Dīn Kayḳubād I (616-634/1219-1236), the great Shaykh Abū Ḥafṣ ʿUmar al-Suhrawardī—al-Nāṣir's theological adviser—came to Konya as ambassador and, amongst other duties, performed the *futuwwa* rituals. One might be justified in assuming that this contributed to the spread of *futuwwa* in Anatolia, yet this impetus from courtly *futuwwa* does not seem to be solely resonsible for the development of *Akhīlīk*.

The existence of this form of *futuwwa* in Iran can be proved even before that in Anatolia, and everything points to the fact that it must have reached Anatolia from there. This theory is also supported by the cult of Abū Muslim [*q.v.*]—the propagator of the ʿAbbāsid revolt against the Umayyads—who (rather like Sayyid Baṭṭāl [*q.v.*]) became a sort of national hero, first for the Persians and later also for the Turks. However, whilst Sayyid Baṭṭāl was regarded as the model of fighters for the faith—the Ghāzīs—Abū Muslim was the model for the artisans and the lesser people, who formed a corporate body under the name of *Akhī*. According to a widespread tale which was responsible for shaping the picture of Abū Muslim in the imagination of the people, the *Akhī*s led by him—especially those of Marw and Khurāsān—were the ones chiefly concerned with the ʿAbbāsid rising. Even if one regards this as a mythical elaboration of the figure of Abū Muslim, one may still assume that the institution as a popular element in the social structure of Iran dates quite a long way back.

Although there is clearly a connexion between the *futuwwa* and the *Akhīlīk*, there is some question about the earlier Islamic and Iranian antecedents of the *futuwwa* (see above). *Akhī* Faradj Zindjānī (died 457/1065), one of the most famous saints in Iran, is the earliest personality on Iranian soil who is mentioned as an *Akhī*, and he is also revered by the Anatolian *Akhī*s (whose adherence to the *futuwwa* is beyond doubt) as one of their own shaykhs, appearing in their rolls of honour (*silsila*). *Akhī* Faradj Zindjānī is held to be the master of the great Persian poet Niẓāmī, but as the latter was born only in 535/1141 (that is to say 80 years after Zindjānī's death), one can only regard Niẓāmī as a spiritual disciple of the great master.

In the 7th/13th and 8th/14th centuries, when *Akhīlīk* flourished in Anatolia (as is borne out by numerous documents) it also flourished in Iran. There were a number of *A*k*h*ī*s in the time of Shaykh Ṣafī al-Dīn Ardabīlī (1252-1334), the ancestor of the Ṣafawid Shāhs, and some of them must be numbered among his own companions and followers. Notable amongst these is *Akhī* Sulaymān of Gilkhʷārān, the father-in-law of the Shaykh. In connexion with these, one should probably also mention a certain *Akhī* Aḥmad al-Muḥibb ..... al-Ardabīlī, by whom we have a *Kitāb al-Futuwwa* in Arabic (which contains, however, only quotations from the Ḳurʾān and *ḥadīth*, and sayings concerning generosity). The Ṣafawid *Akhī* tradition may also be the basis of the fact that we find the word *Akhī* (with reduced significance) several times in the *Dīwān* of Khaṭāʾī (*i.e.*, Shāh Ismāʿīl), as a name for followers of the Ṣafawiyya.

Further evidence for the existence of the Iranian institution is to be found in the work of the great Persian Ṣūfī Shaykh and saint Amīr Sayyid ʿAlī b. Shihāb al-Dīn Hamadānī, called ʿAlī II (714-786/1313-1384), entitled *Risāla-i Futuwwatiyya*, in which he not only equates *futuwwa* and *taṣawwuf* (and where the 'possessor of the *futuwwa*', the *futuwwatdār*, is referred to by the name of *Akhī*), but where there is also clear reference to the institution as such.

Like the Anatolian *Akhīs*, the Iranian ones occasionally intervened in politics. This can be seen from the example of Akhīdjūḳ [*q.v.*] who gained power in Tabrīz and Ādharbāydjān for three years (758-760/1357-59), until the Djalāʾirid Shaykh Uways conquered Tabrīz.

Bibliography: Concerning *Akhī* writing see [besides the works mentioned in the article AKHĪ (Nāṣirī, Gülshehrī)] the following: *Gülşehrī, Manṭiḳu't-ṭayr*, a facsimile edition with an introduction by Agâh Sırrı Levend, Ankara 1957 (the relevant *fütüwwet* chapter at 180 ff.); Abdülbâki Gölpınarlı, *Burgâzî ve "Fütüvvet-Nâme" si*, in *Iktisat Fakültesi Mecmuası*, xv (1953), 76-153, transliterated edition with an introduction. Concerning Abū Muslim: I. Mélikoff-Sayar, *Abu Muslim, patron des Akhis* (in *Akten des xxiv. intern. Orientalisten-Kongresses, München*, Munich 1957, 419-21). Concerning the institution in Iran: Fr. Taeschner, *Spuren für das Vorkommen des Achitums ausserhalb von Anatolien*, in *Proceedings of the Twenty-second Congress of Orientalists, held in Istanbul Sept. 15th to 22nd 1951*, vol. II, Leiden 1957, 273-77; H. W. Duda, *ʿImāduddīn Faqīh und die Futuwwa*, in *ArO*, vi (1933), 112-24; B. Nikitine, *Essai d'Analyse du Ṣafvat-uṣ-Ṣafā* [of Ibn Bazzāz, died 773/1371-72], in *JA*, 1957, 385-94 (particularly 393, *Akhīs* in the entourage of Shaykh Ṣafī); concerning *Akhī* Aḥmad al-Muḥibb al-Ardabīlī cf. *Islamica*, v (1932), 314, under no. 5; A. K. Borovkov, *K istorii bratstva "Achi" v Sredney Azii* (Concerning the history of the *Akhī* constitution in Central Asia), in *Akademiku V. A. Gordlevskomu ... sbornik statey*, Moscow 1953, 87 ff.; Fr. Taeschner, *Der Achidschuk von Tebriz und seine Erwähnung im Iskendername des Aḥmedī*, in *Charisteria Orientalia* (Festschrift Jan Rypka), Prague 1956, 338-44.

(iii) *Futuwwa* as a system of guilds.

There have probably always been guilds (*ṣinf*, [*q.v.*], pl. *aṣnāf*, Turkish *esnaf*) in the towns of the Islamic Orient. This is also indicated by the fact that whereas individual trades are scattered all over the town in the Occident, those in the Orient are grouped around the market area in streets bearing their name. In the absence of clear evidence, one cannot state with any certainty what the organization of the guilds was like in the Middle Ages, and whether there has always been a link with the *futuwwa*. The few guild documents which we do possess are of a relatively more recent date (at the earliest of the 9th/15th century): that is to say, dating from the era of the great Ottoman expansion which grew until its rule extended over three continents. In the documents of the guild records, there is a corresponding prominence of Turkish writings with evidence of their having influenced the Arabic.

These guild documents, now generally referred to as *Fütüwwet-nāmes*, primarily—not to say exclusively—deal with the organization of the guilds. The numerous catechisms which survive, collections of questions put to the apprentice who was being examined and their answers, are exclusively concerned with matters of organization and ritual and not with questions of training in the trades. From these, it appears that it is not only the *Akhīliḳ*, as we know it from its writings, which is responsible for the organization of guilds as a *futuwwa* union; the documents differ in several respects, so that it appears probable that other *futuwwa* groups also exerted their influence over the guilds.

The so-called "Great *fütüwwetnāma*" (*fütüwwetnāme-i kebīr*) of Sayyid Meḥmed b. Sayyid ʿAlāʾ al-Dīn al-Ḥüseynī al-Raḍawī, dated 931/1524, the full title of which is *Miftāḥ al-daḳāʾiḳ*, is the most important of these documents. It describes the *fütüwwet* customs of the guilds in full detail, and from this it appears that the *fütüwwet* of the guilds had nine grades (whereas that of the *Akhīliḳ* had three). The first three of these, *nāzil*, *nīm-ṭarīḳ*, and *meyān-beste*, may be taken to correspond to the three grades of a trade: apprentice (*terbiye*, or *čirak*), journeyman (*ḳalfa*), and master (*usta*), which do not, however, appear under these names in the *fütüwwetnāme*. The next three grades (that is to say, 4 to 6), are those of the master of ceremonies, the *naḳīb*: *bīshrewīsh* (*i.e.*, the assistant of the *naḳīb*), *naḳīb*, and head *naḳīb* (*naḳīb al-nuḳabāʾ*); the three top grades (7 to 9), are those of the Shaykh: the representative (*khalīfe*) of the shaykh, also known as *Akhī*, the *Shaykh*, and the Supreme Shaykh (*shaykh al-shuyūkh*). The *Akhī*, therefore, is the seventh grade in the hierarchy of this particular guild *fütüwwet*.

There is a further difference: whereas the *Akhīliḳ* shows a division into two classes, the *fütüwwetnāmes* of the guilds give evidence of a division into three: *Ḳawlī*, *Shürbī* and *Seyfī*. Thus there is an intermediate class between the lowest members—those who are committed by their word only—and the full members—those who have received the accolade; this is the class of those who have partaken of the ritual cup.

A further interesting custom of the guild-*fütüwwet* is the one by which the novice, or apprentice—the *nāzil*—chooses not only a master as "Patron of the Journey" (*yol atasî*), but at the same time he has to chose two "Brothers of the Journey" (*yol kardeshleri*)—apparently from among the older apprentices—who are to assist him along the path of the *fütüwwet*.

A further thing which emerges clearly from almost every page of the "Great *fütüwwetnāme*" of Sayyid Meḥmed b. Sayyid ʿAlāʾ al-Dīn, is its decidedly Shīʿī (and more specifically "Twelver" Shīʿī, Imāmī) character. Doubtless this is because at the time when it was written, at the beginning of the 10th/16th century, the "Twelver" Shīʿa enjoyed a time of expansion because of the Ṣafawiyya, and this led to the foundation of the new Persian Empire. It threatened to spread also to Ottoman territory, until Sultan Selīm I put an end to the threat of the new Shīʿī Persians by his campaign against Shāh Ismāʿīl, over whom he won the victory of Čāldirān [*q.v.*] in 1514. This was also the time when the Shīʿī order of the Bektāshiyya [*q.v.*] was organized by Bālim Sulṭān. There are, in fact, some points of contact between the "Great *fütüwwetnāme*" of Sayyid Meḥmed, and the Bektāshiyya: a number of the *terdjümān*—the short verses mentioned there which were recited or sung at the celebrations of the guilds—can also be found in the book *Mirʾāt al-maḳāṣid fī dafʿ al-mafāsid* of Sayyid Aḥmad Rifʿat, which describes the Bektāshī ceremonies.

There appear to be only a few complete manuscripts of the "Great *fütüwwetnāme*" of Sayyid Meḥmed. There are, however, shorter guild extracts in all libraries, and these are usually also called "*fütüwwetnāme*". They are generally excerpts from the "Great *fütüwwetnāme*". One may therefore assume that every guild compiled its own little *fütüwwetnāme* from that source. It is worth noting that the Shīʿī character of the original no longer emerges in these. This fact reflects a trend in the history of religion of the Ottoman Empire where—after earlier indecision between Sunnī and Shīʿī—the Sunnī creed progressively gained ground from the days of Selīm I onwards. Arabic *futuwwa* writings (discussed by Thorning in a study which has become an indispensable basis for all work on *futuwwa*) also seem to be based on the Turkish "Great *fütüwwetnāme*" of Sayyid Meḥmed, and to represent Arabic translations of excerpts from this work.

Whilst there were other *futuwwa* traditions besides *Akhīlīk* in most of the guilds whose rule was Sayyid Meḥmed's "Great *fütüwwetnāme*", there was also a group of guilds which must be regarded as the direct continuation of *Akhīlīk*, namely the tanners and all trades concerned with the treatment of leather, such as saddlers and cobblers. All these paid homage to their *pīr* Akhī Ewrān [*q.v.*], properly Evren, an *Akhī* saint of Kîrshehir in Central Anatolia (south-east of Ankara), who is himself said to have been a tanner. They did not use Sayyid Meḥmed's "Great *fütüwwetnāme*" as their rule, but the original *fütüwwetnāme* of the *Akhī*s, which is that of Yaḥyā b. Khalīl al-Burghāzī. There is, however, in most of these manuscripts which come from tanner circles, an appendix informing the reader of the more modern terms, and these are the terms familiar to us from Sayyid Meḥmed's "Great *fütüwwetnāme*". Thus there is evidence that influence was exerted by the *fütüwwet* tradition represented by the latter over the *Akhī* tradition kept up by the tanners.

For their part, the tanners, thanks to their *Akhī* tradition, could exert their own influence over the other guilds, particularly as they had a firm and centralized organisation which had its centre at the grave of their patron saint Akhī Evren in Ḳîrshehir. At this place there was a *tekye* whose guardian, called Akhī Baba [*q.v.*], was taken to be a descendant of Akhī Evren, and regarded (admittedly only in the Turkish provinces of the Ottoman Empire, Anatolia, Rumelia, Bosnia and even the Crimea, but not in the Arab provinces) as the head of all the tanners in the Ottoman Empire. This Akhī Baba, or his representative, travelled through the provinces every year, receiving the apprentices into the guild. The main part of this ceremony was their girding with the belt (*ḳushaḳ ḳushatmasî*). Naturally, such ceremonies brought a certain income, and this formed the financial basis of the organization. The Akhī Babas succeeded in gaining the privilege of girding the apprentices of other guilds as well, and thus they gained a position of considerable power among the craftsmen of the ancient Ottoman Empire. Akhī Evren thus became *pīr* not only of the tanners but of the whole of the Turkish guilds. This position of the Akhī Babas of Ḳîrshehir was repeatedly confirmed by edict and, on the whole, the Ottoman sultans protected the guilds and their organizations. These were useful to them on several counts: firstly, they supplied not only the general populace, but in particular the armies on their campaigns, and secondly they were a reserve of men—some of the guilds were bound to do military service; in the earliest days, the guilds were also the only means of reaching the whole population of the Empire. This was the purpose of the occasional processions of the guilds. Ewliyā Čelebi describes one which took place under Murād IV in 1048/1638. Such gatherings gave the ruler a picture of the military and economic strength of his country.

There were, however, some protests from *ʿulemāʾ* circles, both against the Shīʿī leanings of the "Great *fütüwwetnāme*" by Sayyid Meḥmed, and against the Akhī Evren cult of the tanners. A learned man by name of Münīrī (Ibrāhīm b. Iskandar) Belghrādī wrote a book entitled *Niṣāb al-intisāb wa-ādāb al-iktisāb*, attacking these things and presenting the crafts from the strictly Sunnī point of view. The book was of no avail; probably it never even reached the hands of those for whom it was intended.

There is a great amount of important documentation concerning the guilds (including their rules and regulations) in Turkish archives, the major part of which has not been studied.

The European provinces, including those inhabited by other races, like Bosnia, took part in the general development of the Turkish guilds; they also relied on the same writings.

As has already been mentioned, the "Great *fütüwwetnāme*" of Sayyid Meḥmed b. Sayyid ʿAlāʾ al-Dīn was also the accepted authority in the Arabic provinces of the Ottoman Empire. There, the guilds used extracts, written in Arabic, and adapted them to their special needs. This is the material on which H. Thorning based his epoch-making work. There is a description of the guilds in Damascus in 1883 by Elia Qoudsî, from which it becomes clear that the organization at that time was still essentially the same as that which we know to have existed among the Turkish guilds.

A valuable document concerning the *fütüwwet* as an organization of the guilds comes from Persia. This is the *Fütüwwetnāme-i sulṭānī* of the well known writer Kamāl al-Dīn Ḥusayn Wāʿiẓ Kāshifī (died 910/1505), a nephew of the famous poet Djāmī. Unfortunately only one manuscript has so far come to light; it is in the British Museum, but is incomplete and still awaits an editor. One may hope, though, that further manuscripts of this important work, and of others concerning the *futuwwa* and the guild organizations, will emerge from the still largely unexplored libraries of Iran.

In Turkestan also it can be shown that *futuwwa* is at the basis of the guild organizations. The eastern Turkish guild treatises (of which there was quite a number in the collection of the Berlin orientalist Martin Hartmann), are generally called *risāla*. It has recently been shown that there is even a reference to the Anatolian saint of the guild,

Akhī Evren. Thus the effects of his cult stretched as far as Turkestan.

In the course of the 19th century, with the influx of European goods and the expansion of the European type of commerce, the guild-organizations fell into decay in all states of the Islamic Orient. For this reason it has been gradually abolished in all countries of the Islamic world. In Turkey, it was discontinued in Young Turk times, and replaced by chambers of commerce (by a law of 13 February 1325 *mālī*/26 Feb. 1910; chambers of commerce were instituted in 1943). A few surviving features were abolished in the time of the Turkish Republic. With this, therefore, the organization of the *futuwwa* also came to an end.

In the Arabic dialect of Egypt, *futuwwa* means "ruffian"; cf. the *Mudhakkirāt futuwwa*, 2nd ed., Cairo 1927, written in colloquial Arabic.

Bibliography: On Turkish guilds in general: ʿOthmān Nūrī [Ergun], *Medjelle-i umūr-i belediye*, Istanbul 1338/1922, ch. VI: *Eṣnāf teshkīlātī ve tidjāret uṣūllarī*; Fr. Taeschner, *Das Zunftwesen in der Türkei*, in *Leipziger Vierteljahresschrift für Südosteuropa*, v (1941), 172-188. Concerning the "Great *fütüwwetnāme*" of Seyyid Meḥmed b. Seyyid ʿAlāʾ al-Dīn al-Hüseynī al-Raḍavī of the year 931/1524: A complete copy of this was in the possession of Prof. Tschudi, Basle, excerpts from it in Ewliyā Čelebi, *Seyāḥatnāme*, i, 487 ff., as an introduction to his description of the great procession of the guilds in 1638 (translated by J. v. Hammer, *Narrative of Travels ... by Evliyâ Efendi*, i, 2, London 1834, 90 ff.). Concerning Akhī Evren: Fr. Taeschner, *Gülschehrīs Mesnevi auf Achi Evran, den Heiligen von Kïrschehir und Patron der türkischen Zünfte*, Wiesbaden 1955. Guild documents: Fr. Taeschner, *Ein Icāzetnāme aus dem Kreise der Achis* (dated Muḥ. 876/July 1471), in *Jean Deny Armağanı*, Ankara 1958, 249-254; idem, *Eine Urkunde für den Stiftungsinhaber der Zaviye des Ahı Evran in Kırşehir von 1238/1822-23*, in *Vakıflar Dergisi*, iii, Ankara 1957, 309-313; idem, *Ein Zunft-Fermān Sultan Muṣṭafās III von 1773*, in *Westöstliche Abhandlungen* (Festschrift Rudolf Tschudi), Wiesbaden 1954, 331-337 (a similar document of 1197/1783 is reproduced in Âfet Inan, *Aperçu général sur l'Histoire économique de l'Empire Turc-Ottoman*, Istanbul 1941, pl. XVIII; table of contents pl. XIX); further guild documents in M. Djewdet, *L'Éducation aux foyers des gens des métiers* (Arabic), Istanbul 1350/1932; there is a reproduction of a 17th century miniature depicting the ceremony of accepting an apprentice into the guild in Taeschner, *Alt-Stambuler Hof- und Volksleben*, Hanover 1925, plate 24; also *Isl.*, vi (1916), 169-172. The procession of the guilds in 1048/1638, described by Ewliyā Čelebi, *Seyāḥatnāme*, i, Istanbul 1314/1896-97, 506 ff. (partially and not faithfully translated from a defective manuscript by J. v. Hammer, *Narrative of Travels* ....., vol. i, part 2, London 1834, 104 ff.). Concerning Ibrāhīm b. Iskender Belghrādī, cf. Bursalī Meḥmed Ṭāhir, *ʿOthmānlī müʾellifleri*, ii, 25 f. Concerning the guilds in Bosnia cf. studies by Hamdija Kresevljakōvić, *Esnafi i Obrti u Bosni i Hercegovini (1463-1878)* ("Guilds and Companies in Bosnia and Herzegovina"), i *Sarajevo*, Zagreb 1935 (expanded new edition, Sarajevo 1958), ii *Mostar*, Zagreb 1951; Fr. Taeschner, *Das bosnische Zunftwesen zur Türkenzeit*, in *BZ*, xliv (1951), 531-559. The guilds in the Crimea: Vl. Gordlevskiy, *Organizatsiya tsekhov u krimskikh tatar* ("The organization of guilds among the Tatars of the Crimea") in *Trudi Etnografo-Archeologičeskogo Muzea*, Moscow 1928, 56-65. Concerning the guilds in the Arab provinces of the Ottoman Empire: H. Thorning, *Beiträge zur Kenntnis des islamischen Vereinswesens auf Grund von Basṭ Madad et-Taufīq* (*Turk. Bibl.* 16), Berlin 1913; Carlo Landberg, *Notice sur les corporations de Damas par Elia Qoudsî, fils de ʿAbdo Qoudsî*, Leiden 1884 (German translation by O. Rescher as appendix II, *Über die Zünfte in Damaskus*, in *Die "Nawâdir" von el-Qaljûbî*, Stuttgart 1920, 280-309). The *fütüwwetnāme-i sulṭānī* is part of a manuscript in the British Museum, Ms. Add. 22,705 (Rieu, 44). Concerning the guilds in Turkestan: M. Hartmann, *Die osttürkischen Handschriften der Sammlung Hartmann*, in *MSOS*, vii/2 (1904), 16, no. 9 (artisan *Risāle*s); M. Gavrilov, *Les corps de métiers en Asie Centrale et leur status* (*Rissala*), tr. from the Russian by J. Castagné in *REI*, 1928, 202-230; A. K. Borovkov, *K istorii bratstva "Achi" v Sredney Azii* ("Concerning the history of the Akhī union in Central Asia"), in *Akademiku Vl. A. Gordlevskomu ...*, Moscow 1953, 83 ff.; Pearson, 281-2. (Fr. Taeschner)

al-FUWAṬĪ [see ibn al-fuwaṭī].

FUYŪDJ, pl. of faydj, (from Persian *payk*), is the name not only of the couriers of the government *Barīd* [*q.v.*], but also of the commercial mail serving the population at large. This term was common all over North Africa and Egypt during the 5th/11th and 6th/12th centuries, while on the Egypt-Syria route the word *kutubī*, letter-bearer, was used. Occasionally, *rasūl* appears in the same sense, although the latter is more regularly applied to special messengers (see below).

Since only a few letters written in Arabic script on paper have been published, for the time being our information about the *fuyūdj* is derived exclusively from the letters of the Geniza [*q.v.*], which are written in the Arabic language but in Hebrew script.

In addition to carrying letters between the cities of a country, the *fuyūdj* provided the international mail services during the winter, when the sea was closed, and in midsummer, since the ships used to sail in convoys in spring time and in the autumn. As with the *Barīd*, one and the same man would carry the dispatches entrusted to him from the starting point to the final destination, *e.g.*, from al-Ḳayrawān to Cairo, or even from Almeria, Spain, to Alexandria. For the task of the *fuyūdj* was of a confidential nature. The names of the *fuyūdj* (mostly Muslim, some Jewish) are often referred to in a way which indicates that they must have been personally known to the addressee, albeit coming from a distant country.

No traces of any guild organization of the *fuyūdj* have been found thus far, but the times for their departures and arrivals must have been more or less fixed. The Geniza letters suppose that there was a weekly service between Cairo and Tyre (and presumably also other Syro-Lebanese-Palestinian cities, see below), while that between Cairo and al-Ḳayrawān also was regular, but dependent on the caravans, which, in normal years, seem to have made the double journey three times during one winter.

As to the speed of this service, the way between Cairo and Alexandria required four days approximately. A letter from the Egyptian capital to Ascalon, Palestine, took twelve days, while those carried between Tunisia and Egypt required from one to two and a half months, depending on the length of the stay of the caravans in each of the localities visited by them (which stay was used by the *fuyūdj* for collecting additional mail).

The cost of the forwarding of a letter from Jerusalem to Ramle was half a *dirham*, that from Alexandria to Cairo one *dirham* exactly, that from Almeria to Alexandria, referred to above, one and a half *dirham*s, four letters being sent to the same address. These prices are indicated in the letters preserved because payment was to be made after delivery. The prices were certainly not fixed, but probably customary.

The payments to special messengers, called *rasūl*, of which three cases have been traced thus far, were up to fifty times as high as those made to *fuyūdj*. A service midway between the latter, who moved too slowly, and the special messengers, who were too expensive, was provided by the *faydj ṭayyār*, or express courier. The request *tuṭayyir lī kitābak*, "fly your letter to me", most probably refers not to carrier pigeons, but to this express service. Carrier pigeons might have been intended in another letter, in which the addressee is asked to send a *barā*ʾ, or release, *ma*ʿ*a'l-ṭayr*, "with the birds", possibly a technical term, parallel to the usual request to send a letter either *bi 'l-marākib*, "by boat" or *ma*ʿ*a 'l-fuyūdj*, "with the mail couriers".

Bibliography: S. D. Goitein, *The commercial mail service in medieval Islam*, in *JAOS*, lxxxiv (1964); idem, *A Mediterranean society*, chapter IV, section 3 (in the press). (S. D. Goitein)

FUẒŪLĪ [see FUḌŪLĪ].

FYZABAD [see FAYḌĀBĀD].

G

GABAN, properly Gabnopert (cf. Abu 'l-Faradj, *Chron. Syr.*, ed. Bruns, 329 and Καπνίσκερτι φρουρίον, Cinnamus, i, 8), an Armenian mountain stronghold on the Tekir-Su, a tributary of the Djayhān, now called Geben and belonging to the *ilçe* of Enderin in the *il* of Maraş. Here the kings of Armenia kept their treasures and retired in case of need; the last king Leon VI de Lusignan entrenched himself here in 776/1374, for example, but had to surrender after a siege of nine months to the Mamlūk Sultan al-Malik al-Ashraf Shaʿbān.

Bibliography: Ritter, *Erdkunde*, ix/2, 36, 157; Defrémery, in *Documents arméniens*, *Recueil des historiens des crois.*, s. Index; Cuinet, *La Turquie d'Asie*, ii, 243.

GABÈS [see ḲĀBIS].

GABON, one of the few African countries into which Islam was introduced in the colonizer's baggage-train. It was in 1843 that the first Senegalese soldiers (Wolofs or Tukulors) were stationed with the garrison of Fort d'Aumale and then in the camp on the plateau at Libreville; some of these soldiers, on the completion of their service, chose to settle in Gabon where for the most part they went into trade along the Ogoué, the Ngounié or the Fernan Vaz lagoon. They married Gabon women who remained Christian, and their children generally attended the Catholic school of the St. Mary mission.

A garrison of colonial infantry mainly composed of riflemen who were natives of Senegal and French Sudan meant the constant introduction of new Muslim contingents, but they stayed two or three years and then returned to their country. Hausa and Dyula pedlars and shopkeepers had to replace these soldiers. Some of these Muslims acted as professional fortune-tellers or witch-doctors, taking advantage of the credulity of the peasants in the bush.

It is not possible to speak of autochthonous Islam; the total number of converts in Gabon does not exceed a few dozen.

The statistics for 1959, given in the year-book of missions in the apostolic prefecture of Dakar, arrived at a total (probably an under-estimate) of 2,000 Muslims (1090 in the prefecture of the estuary, 266 in the Woleu Ntem, 175 in maritime Ogoué, 80 in Ogoué Ivindo, 31 in the Ngounié, 21 in the Ogoué-Lolo, 10 in the Nyanga and 4 in Upper Ogoué).

The paucity of Muslims is matched by the small number of mosques, one at Port Gentil, one at Lambaréné, two at Libreville, the biggest of which was built at the expense of the French Government.

The Muslims in Gabon, representing 0.4% of the population, were of importance only during the colonial period in the capacity of subordinates in the administration. They still play a certain part as a commercial bourgeoisie.

Bibliography: Some lines in the various works relating to Gabon. The Abbé Raponda-Walker has very kindly furnished the essential features of the information contained in the above article. (R. Cornevin)

GABR, term generally used in Persian literature—with rather depreciative implications—to indicate Zoroastrians. Philologists have not yet reached agreement on its etymology. Several suggestions have been made, *e.g.*, (a) from Hebrew *ḥabher* ("companion") in the sense of *Ḳiddūshīn* 72a; (b) from Aramaeo-Pahlavi *gabrā* (read *mart*), especially in the compounds *mōġ-martān* ("the Magi") (written *mōġ-gabrā-ān*); (c) from a Persian corruption of Arabic *kāfir* ("unbeliever"). The first two etymologies are very improbable, so that the derivation from A. *kāfir* seems the most acceptable. In Persian literature the word takes often the depreciative suffix *-ak* (*gabrak*, pl. *gabrakān*). Persian knows also the form *gawr*/*gaur*, Kurdish the forms *gebīr* (applied to Armenians), *gawr* (Zoroastrians), *gāvir* (applied to Europeans, especially Russians), Turkish the well-known word *gâvur* (unbeliever). In Persian literature the word is applied only secondarily to "unbelievers" in general, the oldest texts using it especially and technically for Zoroastrians. This, together with the iranization of the Arabic word which probably lies behind it, points to a very old origin—purely "oral"—of the loan, certainly at a period preceding that when Arabic words were introduced in abundance into new-Persian, at the birth of new-Persian *written* literature.

Bibliography: *Gr. I. Ph.*, ii, 697; *Burhān-i ḳāṭi*ʿ, ed. M. Muʿīn[2], Tehrān 1342s., iii, 1773-4, 1850; M. Muʿīn, *Mazdayasnā wa ta*ʾ*thīr-i ān dar adabiyyāt-i Pārsī*, Tehrān 1326, 395-6 (and new ed. in 2 vols., Tehrān 1338); A. Akbar Dihkhudā, *Lughat-nāma*, fasc. 30, Tehrān 1335s./1956, 94-100.

(A. Bausani)

GABRIEL [see djabrā'īl].

GAFSA [see ķafṣa].

GAFURI [see ghafūrī, madjīd].

GAGAUZ, a small Turkic tribe speaking a Turkic language but Orthodox Christian in religion. At the present time they are settled in the south of the Moldavian S.S.R. (Bessarabia) in the district of Komrat, Čadîr-Lunga, Kangaz, Tarakliya, Vulkanešti; in the south of the Ukrainian S.S.R. in the district of Zaporože and Odessa (Izmail) and in the district of Rostov in the Russian S.S.R. There are also small Gagauz settlements in Central Asia—in the districts of Kokpektī, Žarma, Čarskiy, Aksuat and Urdžar in the region of Semipalatinsk and in the eastern Kazakh and Pavlodar region of the Kazakh S.S.R. The Gagauz also live in the region of Frunze in the Kirghiz S.S.R. and in the district of Tashkent in the Uzbek S.S.R. The total number of Gagauz in the U.S.S.R. is 124,000 (1959). In Bulgaria the Gagauz occupy the villages in the district of Varna, near Provadya, in the Dobrudja near Kavarna and in the south of Bulgaria in the district of Yambol and Topolovgrad. In Rumania there are only a few Gagauz villages left—and those in the Dobrudja.

The ancestry and origin of the Gagauz are not clear. According to one hypothesis the Gagauz originate from the Kumans or Polovtsians who played an active role in the history of the south Russian steppes until 1237. According to another theory the Gagauz are possibly the descendants of the Torks or Uzes who were related to the Kumans and who are well known to the old Russian chronicles under the name of Black Caps (*čornīye klobuki*) (11th century). These Karakalpaks seem to have been a very mixed tribe; with Russian rule they also adopted the Russian religion (Greek Orthodoxy). Since the Gagauz too are Christian and Orthodox, it is possible to equate them with the Karakalpaks.

Bulgarian scholars, however, consider the Gagauz to be descendants of the Bulgars who were turkicized in the 15th-19th centuries but who retained Orthodox belief.

The most probable hypothesis seems to be the one which regards the Gagauz as descendants of the Turkish-Oghuz tribes (and of the Seldjūķs). The area which was later named the Dobrudja was inhabited in the first half of the 13th century by Turkish tribes and bore the name of Karvuna-land after its capital Karvuna (later Balčîķ). The Byzantines obtained their troops from among the population of that area, especially from among the Uzes. The Oghuz tribes often threatened the security of the Byzantine empire as they joined forces with other tribes during their raids. Byzantium, therefore, had always to beware of them and strove to subject them in order to utilize their forces for itself. In 1261 there appeared at the court of Michael VIII Palaeologus the Seldjūķ Sultan ʿIzz al-Dīn Kay Kā'ūs, who had fled before the Mongols from Anatolia. The Byzantine Emperor enfeoffed him with the possession of land in the Dobrudja, where he established an independent Oghuz state with the capital Karvuna (Balčîķ). The ethnic appelation Gagauz seems to stem from the name Kay Kā'ūs. Greek Orthodoxy was recognized as the dominant religion. Ecclesiastical authority was exercised by the Patriarch of Constantinople through the agency of the exarch in Karvuna. The newly founded state was strengthened by the incorporation of Seldjūķ Turks and created its own army and fleet. As a result of the struggles between the tribes, Balîķ came to the fore and, at the head of the Oghuz tribes, was chosen to be ruler of the state. In 1346 Balîķ took part in the disorders in Constantinople where he sent 1,000 horsemen to the aid of the Regent Anne of Savoy. After the death of Balîķ, Dobrotič came to the throne (1357). In his reign the state was strengthened considerably. Dobrotič increased his fleet. The name Karvuna-land was changed to Dobrotič-land. The form 'Dobrudja' became current at a later date. Dobrotič was followed by Yanko (1386)—according to other sources Ivanko—the last Oghuz ruler. In 1398 he was obliged to acknowledge the suzerainty of the Ottoman Turks. After the fall of the Oghuz state some of the population accepted Islam but the rest remained true to Christianity. With the conquest of Constantinople the Ottoman Sultan recognized the Greek Patriarch of Constantinople as head of all the Christians without reference to their nationality. Although the sources are silent for many years concerning the Gagauz, it must be assumed that they too came under the authority of the Patriarch. There is evidence relevant to this from the year 1652 concerning the decision of the Patriarch to give authority over all towns and villages to the local bishop instead of to the exarch in Karvyna.

From 1750 until 1846 there occurred a migration of the Gagauz of the Balkan peninsula—in connexion with a similar movement by the Bulgars—over the Danube to Russia (until 1769 into the province of New Russia; between 1787 and 1791 and most strongly between 1801 and 1812 to Bessarabia). Initially this went on without any apparent interference from the Russian government, which only later introduced order into the management of the land and the administration. This migration was apparently caused by the oppression of the robber bands (the Daghlî and Ķîrdjalî) of Pasvand-oghlu ʿOthmān [*q.v.*], the notorious Pasha of Vidin, and of Ķara Feydī).

Since 1940 the territory of the Bessarabian Gagauz has belonged to the U.S.S.R. In 1949 all the Gagauz villages in the Moldavian and Ukranian S.S.R. were collectivized together with those in Bulgaria and Rumania. The Gagauz work mainly in agriculture, cattle-raising, wine growing and, on the coast, fishing. As a result of being the long-standing neighbours of the Bulgarians, the Gagauz have borrowed much from their way of life, their customs and their domestic activity. The most salient characteristics of the Gagauz are diligence, hospitality, cheerfulness and contentment.

The language of the Gagauz belongs to the southern group of Turkic languages, *i.e.*, it is closest to the Turkish of Turkey, of Ādharbaydjān and of Turkmenistān. Several phonetic features, almost the whole syntax and phraseology as well as most of the morphology and vocabulary of the Gagauz are not Turkish. The following points may be enumerated here:

(1) the softening of consonants before front vowels;
(2) the appearance of the gender suffixes *-ka*, *-yka*;
(4) syntactically the Gagauz language is completely Slavicized and un-Turkish;
(4) the strong foreign element in the vocabulary (Greek, Rumanian and Slavonic).

For a long time the Gagauz possessed no literature of their own. For ecclesiastical purposes the Greek Church used 'Ķaramanlî' books written in the Turkish language and in the Greek alphabet. These books contain lives of the saints and prayers. By contrast a rich folk poetry has developed, together with riddles (*bilmeydžă*), proverbs (*söleiš*), folk-songs (*türkü*, *mani*), stories (*masal*), anecdotes (*fĭḳra*) etc. The Gagauz alphabet, based on the Russian with additional letters, was created in the Moldavian S.S.R. in 1957. Since 1958 elementary education in the Gagauz language has been introduced. For this purpose text books are being compiled. Work is gradually going on towards the development of a Gagauz literary language. In Kishinev a Gagauz newspaper is published twice a month as a supplement to the *Moldova Socialistă*.

Bibliography: C. Jireček, *Das Fürstentum Bulgarien*, Vienna 1891; V. Moškov, *Gagauzĭ Benderskogo uyezda*, in *Etnografičeskoye Obozrenye*, 1900-2, xliv, xlviii, xlix, li, liv, lv; idem, *Mundarten der bessarabischen Gagauzen*, i-ii, in *Proben der Volksliteratur der türkischen Stämme*, x, St. Petersburg 1904; T. Kowalski, *Les Turcs et la langue turque de la Bulgarie du Nord-Est*, Kraków 1933; E. M. Hoppe, *I Gagauzi, popolazione turco-cristiana della Bulgaria*, in *OM*, xiv (1934); M. Čakïr, *Besarabieală Gagauzlarân istorieasâ*, Chişinâu 1934; A. I. Manov, *Potekloto na gagauzite i tekhnite običai i nravi*, Varna 1938 (Turkish translation by Türker Acaroğlu, *Gagauzlar*, Ankara 1940); P. Wittek, *Yazïjïoghlu ʿAlī on the Christian Turks of the Dobruja*, in *BSOAS*, xiv (1952); idem, *Les Gagaouzes—les gens de Kaykāūs*, in *RO*, xvii (1953); V. Marinov, *Prinos k'm izučavaneto na bita i kulturata na turcite i gagauzite v Severoiztočna Bulgariya*, Sofia 1956; I. I. Meščeruk, *Antikrepostničeskaya bor'ba gagauzov i bolgar Bessarabiyi v 1812-1820 gg.*, Chişinâu 1957; N. K. Dmitriyev, *Gagausische Lautlehre*, in *Ar O*, iv (1932) and v (1933); idem, *Stroy tyurkskikh yazĭkov*, Moscow 1962; G. Doerfer, *Das Gagausische*, in *Philologiae Turcicae Fundamenta*, i, 1959; L. A. Pokrovskaya, *Osnovnĭye čertĭ fonetiki sovremennogo gagauzskogo yazĭka*, in *Voprosĭ dialektologii tyurkskikh yazĭkov*, ii, Baku 1960; *Budžaktan seslär*, Chişinâu 1959; R. I. Bigayev, P. A. Danilov, M. U. Umarev, *O gagauzakh Sredney Azii*, in *RO*, xxv (1961); V. Drimba, *Remarques sur les parlers gagaouzes de la Bulgarie du Nord Est*, in *RO*, xxvi (1963); W. Zajączkowski, *Przyczynki do etnografii Gagauzów*, in *RO*, xx (1956); idem, *Gagauskie teksty forklorystyczne*, in *Yezikovedsko-etnografski izsledvaniya v pamet na akad. St. Romanski*, Sofia 1960; idem, *Sostoyaniye i bliżayšiye zadači izučeniya gagauzov*, in *Folia Orientalia*, ii (1960).

(WŁODZIMIERZ ZAJĄCZKOWSKI.)

GAKKHAŔ, a war-like Muslim tribe, inhabiting mostly the Hazāra district and parts of the districts of Rāwalpindī, Attock and Djehlam (Jhelum) of West Pakistan and that part of the Indian-held territory of Djammū which lies to the west of the Čināb; it is of indigenous origin. Agriculturists by profession, the Gakkhars are considered socially high and stand apart from the local tribes of Rādjpūt descent who resent their arrogance and racial pride. Many of the religious and social ceremonies observed by them reflect Hindu influences. They do not permit remarriage of widows and observe very strict *pardah*. According to their own legends they are descended from Anūshirwān and Yezdigerd and claim the title of Kayānī; their eponym is said to have been one Sultan Kaygawhar (later corrupted into Gakkhaŕ), a native of Kayān in Işfahān. Cunningham's opinion that they are Kushāns seems nearer the truth, as the territory inhabited by them up to this day (described by Djahāngīr, *Tūzuk*, tr. Rogers, i, 99, ending at

the Mārghala pass between Rāwalpindī and Ḥasan Abdāl) was once the stronghold of Buddhism. Buddhism flourished in northern India during the rule of the Kushān dynasty, who were mostly Buddhists. The claim of the Gakkhaŕs that they entered India in the train of Maḥmūd of Ghazna (*reg.* 388-421/998-1030) and that they once ruled Tibet as vassals of the Chinese, is evidently fictitious. According to Firishta (Lucknow ed., 26), it was the Gakkhaŕs (and not the orthographically similar Khokhars) who joined the confederacy of the local Hindū *rādjā*s against Maḥmūd of Ghazna in 399/1008. No less than 30,000 Gakkhaŕs "with their heads and feet bare, and armed with various weapons" stormed the camp of the Sultan at Peshāwar but had to suffer badly for their audacity as did the Mēḍs and the Djāṭs [*q.v.*] of Sind who had harrassed and attacked Maḥmūd's rear on his return from Somnāth in 417/1026.

In 601/1204-5 they rose in revolt against the rule of the Ghūrid Sultan Muʿizz al-Dīn Muḥammad b. Sām, who took strong measures against them and quelled the rebellion with an iron hand. After this crushing defeat they were so thoroughly demoralized that their chief, simply because a Muslim captive had initiated him into the tenets of Islam, willingly became a convert, followed *en masse* by the whole of the tribe soon afterwards. However, this mass conversion was a mere act of expediency as these very Gakkhaŕs, only the next year (602/1205), treacherously fell upon the retreating Sultan *en route* to Ghazna, while he was encamped at Damyak, a small place on the bank of the Djehlam, three-quarters of a mile from modern Sohāwa, and murdered him. The place where he was murdered is still known to the local population as "*Ghūrăň dă phaŕ*", *i.e.*, passage of the Ghūrids. Raverty's lengthy discussion (*Ṭabaḳāt-i Nāṣirī*, tr. i, 485 *n*) on the identification of the tribe to which the Sultan's assassins belonged leaves the question open as Ibn al-Athīr (*sub anno* 602 A.H.) and the *Tādj al-maʾāthir* of Ḥasan Niẓāmī, a contemporary source, describe them as *malāḥida* and *fidāʾīs* (*i.e.*, agents of the Alamūt Ismāʿīlīs), which is somewhat curious in view of the recent conversion of the Gakkhaŕs to Islam. There is, therefore, reason to suppose that the assassins of Muḥammad Ghūrī were most probably Khokhars, who might have turned Ismāʿīlī under the influence of the Carmathians of Multān, their close neighbours. On the other hand since the murder took place in the territory of the Gakkhaŕs there is equally strong reason to suspect them of the crime or of complicity in it, for no strangers to the place could be bold enough to break into the royal camp and murder a powerful Sultan who had not only ravaged their territory and inflicted a crushing defeat on them but was also instrumental in their conversion to Islam. It is also possible that some disgruntled members of the tribe, who had unwillingly abandoned the faith of their forefathers, might have nurtured a grudge against the Sultan and, finding a suitable opportunity, wreaked their vengeance. Here again we are confronted with a difficulty in that history does not record any large-scale defections on the part of the Gakkhaŕs. The *Ṭabaḳāt-i Nāṣirī* (Raverty, i, 485) also says that the Sultan "attained martyrdom at the hand of a disciple of the Mulahidah (*sic*)", who was apparently a Muslim, and not a Hindū as stated by Ḥamd Allāh Mustawfī (*Taʾrīkh-i Guzīda*, i, 412), and al-Djuwaynī (tr. Boyle, i, 326; where 'Hindu' has been wrongly translated as 'Indian'), as he was found on capture to have been circumcised. He could not, therefore, have been a Khokhar as there is no evidence to prove that the Khokhars had embraced Islam long before the assassination of Muʿizz al-Dīn Muḥammad G̲h̲ūrī. Piecing all the recorded evidence together one is led to believe that the assassin was a Gakkhaŕ, smarting under the insult and humility suffered by his tribe. It was the result of a personal vendetta and had no political or religious implications as has been suggested by Ras̲h̲īd al-Dīn (D̲j̲āmiʿ al-tawārīk̲h̲, ed. Smirnova, i, 58) and Ibn al-At̲h̲īr (sub anno 602 A.H.) involving even Fak̲h̲r al-Dīn al-Rāzī [q.v.] in the conspiracy.

The Gakkhaŕs continued to harry the Delhi Sultans and in 645/1247 even a peace-loving prince like Nāṣir al-Dīn Maḥmūd had to take measures against them. He appointed Balban, who reduced their country, took revenge on them for their continued incursions, chastised them for having allowed passage to the Mongols through their territory and made thousands of them captives. Malik Altūniya, who had forcibly married Raḍiyya Sultāna, most probably had pressed these very Gakkhaŕs, along with the D̲j̲āts and other tribes, into an army with which he opposed the forces of the slave king Muʿizz al-Dīn Bahrām S̲h̲āh but was defeated. Almost a century later they invaded the Pand̲j̲āb in 743/1342, during the reign of Muḥammad b. Tug̲h̲luḳ, killed Tatār K̲h̲ān, the viceroy of Lahore and "completed the ruin of the province". Taking advantage of the disturbed conditions in the wake of Tīmūr's invasion of India (802/1399), they tried to harrass the great conqueror but had to pay dearly for their audacity. They again gave trouble to Bābur [q.v.] during his victorious march (932/1525) against the Delhi Sultan Ibrāhīm Lodī. Bābur seized their fort Paŕhālah (now called Phaŕwāla, but mostly in ruins, about 12 miles east of Rāwalpindī), ruled by Hātī K̲h̲ān, their chief, who had to flee before the onslaught of the Mug̲h̲als. At the end of 933/1526 Hātī K̲h̲ān waited on the emperor during his return to the Pand̲j̲āb and assisted greatly in procuring supplies for the Mug̲h̲al army. Bābur fully recognized his services, made him a handsome present and conferred on him the title of Sultān (proudly retained by the Gakkhaŕs till the middle of the 18th century when they were subjugated and reduced by the Sikh generals Gud̲j̲d̲j̲ar Singh Bhangī and Ṣāḥib Singh). During the reign of Humāyūn, the Gakkhaŕ chief Sultān Sārang gained much prominence. He became so powerful that he struck his own money, included his name in the k̲h̲uṭba and refused to recognise S̲h̲ēr S̲h̲āh Sūr, on the defeat of Humāyūn, as the new sovereign of India. He even obstructed by all the means at his disposal the construction in 948/1541 of the historic Rohtās fort by S̲h̲ēr S̲h̲āh. This act of open hostility coupled with his contumacious behaviour enraged S̲h̲ēr S̲h̲āh who personally led an expedition against him resulting in the rout of the Gakkhaŕs, the capture of Sultān Sārang and his subsequent execution. His tomb still exists at Rawāt, near Rāwalpindī. He was succeeded by his brother Sultān Ādam, who had several skirmishes with the troops of Islām S̲h̲āh Sūr. Ādam was so powerful that in 959/1552 prince Kamrān, the rebel brother of Humāyūn, who had been refused shelter by Islām S̲h̲āh, sought refuge with him. He was, however, betrayed and given up to Humāyūn who had him blinded, Ādam receiving robes of honour, kettle-drums and other insignia of nobility as a reward for his treachery (cf. D̲j̲awhar Āftābaċī, Tad̲h̲kirat al-wāḳiʿāt, Urdu transl., Karachi 1955,

151-7). Following a family scandal, Sultān Ādam had to suffer disgrace at the hands of his own nephew Kamāl K̲h̲ān, a son of Sultān Sārang, who confined him in the fort of Phaŕwāla, where he subsequently died, and hanged his son Las̲h̲kar K̲h̲ān, who had been guilty of an illicit love-affair with the wife of Kamāl K̲h̲ān's brother. Abu 'l-Faḍl gives a different version omitting all reference to the love-affair and asserting that on a petition from Kamāl K̲h̲ān, Akbar ordered the division of the Gakkhaŕ territory between him and his uncle Ādam; this resulted in a dispute which culminated in a pitched battle in which Ādam was utterly defeated and captured. This was clearly a stratagem which Akbar employed in order to punish the refractory chief by pitting his own kinsmen against him and to implant his suzerainty firmly in the territory of the Gakkhaŕs (cf. Akbarnāma, Bibl. Indica, iii, 560 ff.). In order further to cement his relations with the Gakkhaŕs and to use them as an ally against the turbulent Afghans, Akbar, in accordance with his well-known policy, contracted matrimonial alliances with them. Prince Salīm (sc. D̲j̲ahāngīr) was married to a daughter of Sayd (Sayyid ?) K̲h̲ān, a brother of Kamāl K̲h̲ān. Sayd K̲h̲ān had fought under the Mug̲h̲al general Zayn K̲h̲ān Kōkah against the Afghans in Swāt and Bād̲j̲awŕ [qq.v.]. Later Awrangzīb also honoured the Gakkhaŕ chief, Allāh Ḳulī K̲h̲ān (1093-1117/1681-1705), by marrying one of his daughters to his son, Prince Muḥammad Akbar. Thus two Gakkhaŕ ladies, apart from several Rād̲j̲pūt princesses, found their way into the Imperial ḥarem. Akbar's policy of pacification and reconciliation had its desired effects and we find the Gakkhaŕs leading a peaceful, uneventful life during the major part of the Mug̲h̲al rule. They seem, however, to have reluctantly accepted the Tīmūrids as their overlords, inasmuch as a celebrated Gakkhaŕ warrior-chief, Muḳarrab K̲h̲ān, sided with Nādir S̲h̲āh Afs̲h̲ār [q.v.] and took part in the battle of Karnāl (1152/1739), which showed up the cracks in the crumbling fabric of the Mug̲h̲al empire. As a reward for his services he was confirmed in his possession of the fort of Phaŕwāla and on return to Kābul, Nādir S̲h̲āh conferred upon him, as a mark of further favour, the title of Nawwāb. (This seems to have been a personal title as no later Gakkhaŕ chief ever used it). He was defeated by the Sikhs at Gud̲j̲rāt [q.v.] in 1179/1765 and had to surrender the whole of his possessions up to the D̲j̲ehlam to the victors. Four years later he was treacherously captured and put to death by a rival chief, Himmat K̲h̲ān. The Sikhs, finding it a suitable opportunity, annexed the entire Gakkhaŕ territory to the Sikh kingdom of the Pand̲j̲āb. Muḳarrab K̲h̲ān's two elder sons were, however, allowed to retain the Phaŕwāla fort as a d̲j̲āgīr; this too was confiscated in 1234/1818 by the Sikh governor of the area. Chafing under successive insults and acts of expropriation, the Gakkhaŕs revolted in 1835 but were crushed by the Sikhs who put their chieftains—S̲h̲ādmān K̲h̲ān and Muddū K̲h̲ān—along with their families in confinement, where both of them died. On the annexation of the Pand̲j̲āb in 1849, the British conferred a pension of Rs. 1200 per annum on Ḥayāt Allāh K̲h̲ān, a son of S̲h̲ādmān K̲h̲ān, he and the other members of his family having been released from captivity by the British two years earlier. In 1853 Nādir K̲h̲ān, the Gakkhaŕ chief of Māndla, joined a Sikh conspiracy against the British. The rising, which might have been serious, was promptly quelled and Nādir K̲h̲ān was captured and hanged. Apart from this incident the Gakkhaŕs remained loyal and peaceful; they joined the army and served the British well, who honoured one of their chiefs, Rād̲j̲a D̲j̲ahāndād K̲h̲ān (d. 1906) of Hazāra (K̲h̲ānpur), by conferring upon him the order of C.I.E. The present chief of the tribe is Sulṭān Īrad̲j̲ Zamān K̲h̲ān, an 18-year old youth, who succeeded to the title in October 1963 after the accidental death of his father, a grandson of D̲j̲ahāndād K̲h̲ān.

The Gakkhaŕs are divided into several clans, the leading being: the Būgīyāl, Iskandarāl, Fīrūzāl, Sārangāl and Ādamāl. Of these the last two are more influential and powerful; they are the descendants of Sārang and Ādam respectively, the two chiefs who gained prominence during the reigns of Humāyūn and Akbar. While the Sārangāls are found in Hazāra and Attock, the Ādamāls inhabit the districts of Rāwalpindī and D̲j̲ehlam. As compared with the Gakkhaŕs of Hazāra and D̲j̲ehlam those of the Rāwalpindī district are generally considered the senior and most important branch of the tribe (for details see *Rawalpindi District Gazetteer*, 63 ff.).

Bibliography: In addition to the authorities cited in the text: J. G. Delmerick, *A History of the Gak'khars*, in *JASB*, 1871, Pt. I, 67-101; *Gazetteer of the Rawalpindi District*, Lahore 1909, 35, 38-44, 62-6; *Gazetteer of the Hazara District (1883-84)*, Lahore n.d., 20-22, 29, 32; al-D̲j̲ūzd̲j̲ānī, *Ṭabaḳāt-i Nāṣirī*, tr. Raverty, i, 481 ff.; Lepel Griffin, *Panjab Chiefs*, Lahore 1872, 574 ff.; Ibbetson, *Outlines of Panjab ethnography*, Calcutta 1883, 255; H. A. Rose, *A glossary of the tribes and castes of the Punjab* ..., Lahore 1911-14, s.v. Gakhars; *The Tūzuk-i Jahāngīrī*, tr. Rogers and Beveridge, London 1909, i, 96-9; Cunningham, *Later Indo-Scythians*, in *Numis. Chron.*, 1893, 94; *Baber's Memoirs*, tr. Erskine, London 1826, 259; Storey, ii, 675-6: *Cambridge History of India*, iii, under "*Khokhars*" (makes no mention of the *Gakkhaŕs* and confuses them with the *Khokhars*); Elliot and Dowson, *History of India* ..., ii, appendix, 444; Massy, *Chiefs and families of the Panjab*, Allahabad 1890, 424; Firis̲h̲ta, Lucknow 1284 A.H., 26-58 (= Brigg's tr., i, 146-82); *Archaeological Survey of India* (Report for 1863-64), see "Rohtas—the fortress of—"; Abu 'l-Faḍl, *Āʾīn-i Akbarī*, tr. Blochmann, Calcutta 1873, i, 486. On the confusion between Gakkhaŕs and Khokars, see Rose, *Khokars and Gakkhars in Panjab history*, in *Ind. Antiquary*, 1907. (A. S. Bazmee Ansari)

GALATA [see istanbul].

GALATA-SARAY [see g̲h̲alaṭa-sarāyī].

GALEN [see d̲j̲ālīnūs].

GALICIA [see d̲j̲illīḳiya].

GALLA (own name *Oromo*, 'the people'). A people widespread in the modern state of Ethiopia, speaking a language belonging to the Eastern (or Low) Kushitic group which includes ʿAfar-Saho and Somali). They irrupted from the region south of the Webi during the first half of the 16th century, almost contemporaneously with the campaigns of Aḥmad Grāñ [*q.v.*] and spread fanwise, penetrating deeply into the Abyssinian highlands. For long they were a menace to the existence of the Ethiopian state but were finally subjected by Menelik II between 1872 and 1888.

When their expansion began they were all nomadic herdsmen with an elaborate political system based on a cycle of generation-sets (*gada*), but in consequence of their tribal movements and settlement in different environments many groups underwent profound changes. When they first expanded they came into contact first with Islam and then with Ethiopian Christianity. Their gradual and qualified adoption of the one or the other religion was slow, piecemeal, and tribal or regional. Although all the other Hamitic nomads of north-east Africa (Bed̲j̲a, Saho, ʿAfar and Somali) had long been Muslim, and although the important Muslim city of Harar [*q.v.*] and the southern Muslim states of Bali and Dawaro lay in their path, the Galla remained impervious to religious change so long as they remained nomads and their *gada* system intact. But when they settled in contact with Amhara and Sidama they became either Christian or Muslim.

The vast number of tribes forbids any formal classification here, whilst the syncretistic character of their religion, whatever they call themselves, also prevents any clear-cut religious classification. The southernmost Galla, small groups of Warday or Orma of Tanaland in Kenya, detached from the rest by Somali expansion, have adopted Islam in this century. So have many Bōran of northern Kenya. But the nomadic Bōran of southern Ethiopia, occupying a vast territory between the Lake Stephanie region and the River D̲j̲uba, and those Arsi (Arūsi in Amharic), living to the north of the Bōran between the Somali of Ogaden and the Sidama, who continue to maintain a pastoral nomadic life, remain pagan. Some Arsi are Muslim and in their territory lies the famous Muslim-pagan pilgrimage sanctuary of S̲h̲ayk̲h̲ Ḥusayn. Muslims are the northernmost Galla of the highlands (Yed̲j̲u and Raya or Azebo), who inhabit a region once occupied by a Muslim population known as Dobʿa, and the Wallo, covering a wide area of the eastern highlands north of the Tulama, who played an important part in the history of the empire in the 18th and 19th centuries, during which many embraced Christianity. Among the Shoan Galla (collectively known as Tulama) Christianity prevails. The Galla who penetrated the Gibē region of south-west Ethiopia, where they mingled with Sidama, were transformed in form of government, forming a group of five monarchical-type states (D̲j̲imma, Limmu, Gera, Gomma and Guma), and became Muslim between 1820 and 1870. Many of the Macha tribes (*e.g.*, Nonno) to the north of these states have Muslim minorities. In the west the Leqa Galla of the Waleqa region are pagan, very few being influenced by Islam, whilst the chiefs are generally Christian. In the south-east the sections who live in the Harar region became Muslim during the last century: Nolē and D̲j̲aso north of Harar, Ala around the city, Itu to the west, and Ania (Ennia) to the south.

Bibliography: C. F. Beckingham and G. W. B. Huntingford, *Some records of Ethiopia: 1593-1646*, Hakluyt, 1954; E. Cerulli, *The Folk-Literature of the Galla of Southern Abyssinia*, in *Harvard African Studies*, iii (1922), 9-228; idem, *Etiopia Occidentale*, 1929-33; E. Haberland, *Galla Süd-Äthiopiens*, Stuttgart 1963; G. W. B. Huntingford, *The Galla of Ethiopia*, 1955; P. Paulitschke, *Ethnographie Nordost-Afrikas*, Berlin 1896; J. S. Trimingham, *Islam in Ethiopia*, 1952. (J. S. Trimingham)

GALLIPOLI [see gelibolu].

GAMBIA, British Colony and Protectorate, West Africa, 13° 25′ N., 16° W.; 4,000 square miles in extent with a population of about 260,000. It forms a narrow enclave in the surrounding territory of Senegal, occupying both banks of the Gambia river to a distance of 200 miles from the coast and being nowhere more than 39 miles broad. The principal tribal groups are Mandingo, Fula and Wollof.

The country is entirely agricultural, millet and rice providing the staple food of the people. The main economic crop is groundnuts, which accounts for nine-tenths of the revenue in an average year. There is no mining and apparently no mineral wealth. The only town is the capital Bathurst (population, 20,000). Under the constitution introduced in May 1962, the country has attained full internal self-government, the prime minister being Mr. D. Jawara the leader of the People's Progressive Party. A measure of union with Senegal is under active consideration (1964).

The British trading interest in the Gambia dates from early in the seventeenth century, and from 1662, when the fort on James Island was seized from the Duke of Courland, the succession of British African Companies maintained permanent occupation of one or more trading posts. The eighteenth century was a period of intense commercial rivalry with the French, who had established a factory at Albreda on the north bank and were not finally excluded from the river until 1857. Bathurst was founded in 1816 to provide an additional base for the campaign against the slave trade.

At least four-fifths of the indigenous population are Muslim. Islam was first introduced in the period from the 5th/11th to the 8th/14th century but conversion remained very superficial until towards the close of the eighteenth century, and the present strength of orthodoxy dates only from the period of the "marabout" wars, about a hundred years ago. All Gambia Muslims follow the Mālikī school of law and most of them are attached to one of two Ṣūfī orders, the Ḳādiriyya or the Tidjāniyya, the latter being dominant, at least on the lower river. In some areas literacy in Arabic is not uncommon. Protestant and Catholic missions have been at work for more than a century, but there are very few Christians outside Bathurst.

Bibliography: J. M. Gray, *History of the Gambia*, London 1940; J. N. D. Anderson, *Islamic Law in Africa*, London 1945; D. P. Gamble, *The Wollof of Senegambia*, London 1957; *Gambia Annual Reports*; A. Gouilly, *L'Islam dans l'Afrique Occidentale Française*, Paris 1952.

(D. H. Jones)

GAMES [see LAʿB].

GANĀFA [see DJANNĀBA].

GANDĀPUR, the name of a Pathan tribe which lives in the Dāmān area of the Dēra Ismāʿīl Khān district of Pakistan. The tribe is now, for the most part, absorbed in the population of the area.

The tribe descended from the Afghan highlands to the plains of Dāmān during the 17th century. The centre of their winter quarters developed into a town in the 19th century, probably because of the trading activities of the tribesmen between Khurāsān and India. This town is at present called Kulāčī.

The Gandapūr tribe took part in Pathan tribal wars during the 18th century but under British rule the tribe became settled and peaceful, mixing with other Pashto-speaking settlers. The origin of the name is unknown, as is the history of the people.

Bibliography: *Gazeteer of the Dera Ismail Khan District*, Lahore 1884, 53, 109, 202; M. Elphinstone, *An account of the Kingdom of Caubul*, London 1839, ii, 67; I. M. Reisner, *Razvitie feodalizma i obrazovanie gosudarstva u Afgantsev*, Moscow 1954, *passim*. (R. N. Frye)

GANDJA, Arab. DJANZA, the former ELIZAVETPOL, now KIROVABAD, the second largest town in the Azerbaijan S.S.R.

The town was first founded under Arab rule, in 245/859 according to the *Taʾrīkh Bāb al-abwāb* (V. Minorsky, *A History of Sharvān and Darband*, Cambridge 1958, 25 and 57). It is not mentioned by the oldest Arabic geographers like Ibn Khurradādhbih and Yaʿḳūbī; it seems to have taken its name from the pre-Muslim capital of Ādharbaydjān (now the ruins of Takht-i-Sulaymān). Iṣṭakhrī, 187 and 193, mentions Gandja only as a small town on the road from Bardhaʿa [*q.v.*] to Tiflīs; according to him the distance between Bardhaʿa and Gandja was 9 *farsakh*, according to Yāḳūt (ii, 132) 16 *farsakh*. After the decline of Bardhaʿa Gandja became the capital of Arrān; the Shaddādid dynasty ruled here from *ca.* 340/951-2; after it had been overthrown by Sultan Malik Shāh, the latter's son Muḥammad was granted Gandja in fief. In 533/1138-9 the town was destroyed by an earthquake in which, according to ʿImād al-Dīn al-Iṣfahānī, there perished some 300,000 persons (130,000 according to Ibn al-Athīr), including the wife and children of Ḳara-Sonḳur, *amīr* of Ādharbaydjān and Arrān, who was absent at the time; Demetrius, king of Georgia, sacked the ruined town and carried off one of its gates. ʿImād al-Dīn says that the Georgians built a new town in their country, gave it the name Djanza and set up the gate they had carried off there; soon afterwards Ḳara-Sonḳur destroyed the new town and brought the gate back to Gandja. The latter statement does not agree with the facts; the gate that was carried off still exists in the Gelathi monastery in Kutais; a Georgian inscription gives an account of its removal; and there has also survived on the gate itself an Arabic inscription of the year 455/1063 (the year of its erection) which has been deciphered by Frähn (Mém. de l'Acad., 6th Ser., *Sciences politiques*, iii, 531 ff.).

Ḳara-Sonḳur died in 535/1140-1, his successor Čavlī in Djumādā I 541/9 October-7 November 1146; Rawādī is next mentioned as ruler of Arrān; but a few years later we find Arrān reunited with Ādharbaydjān under the rule of the Ildegizids. The town of Gandja is said to have been rebuilt by Ḳara-Sonḳur "in all its splendour"; in the 7th/13th century it was considered one of the most beautiful cities of Western Asia (cf. the verses in the *Nuzhat al-ḳulūb*, *GMS*, 91); the poet Niẓāmī Gandjawī [*q.v.*] belongs to this period; Ibn al-Athīr (xii, 251) calls Gandja "mother of the cities of Arrān". When the Mongols appeared before Gandja in 618/1221, they did not dare to attack the strongly fortified town, the inhabitants of which had proved their courage in frequent battles with the Georgians; but the retreat of the enemy had to be purchased with money and clothstuffs. In 622/1225 Gandja, whither the last Ildegizid, Öz-Beg [*q.v.*], had fled from Tabrīz, was taken by Sultan Djalāl al-Dīn Khʷārizmshāh [*q.v.*]; a few years later all the Khʷārizmīs were massacred in a rebellion of the inhabitants; nevertheless, after suppressing this rising Djalāl al-Dīn refused to allow his troops to sack the town and only had the ringleaders, 30 in all, executed (618/1231). Four years later (1235) the town was captured and burned by the Mongols. On this occasion also it was soon rebuilt but does not seem to have attained great importance again. Under the Il-Khāns Arrān with Gandja as its capital was one of their provinces; the land afterwards usually shared the lot of Ādharbaydjān and from the reign of Ismāʿīl Shāh Ṣafawī [*q.v.*] onwards formed part of the Persian kingdom; under Persian rule the governor of Gandja bore the title of Khān. In 991/1583 Khān Imām Ḳulī was defeated by the Turks, who in 996/1588 captured the town itself; invested in Shawwāl 1014/February-March 1606 by Shāh ʿAbbās I it was recovered for the Persians after a six months' siege. Shāh ʿAbbās transferred the town to another site about 1 *farsakh* "higher", *i.e.*, to the south-west. The new Gandja was captured by the Turks in 1135/1723; regained by Nādir Shāh in 1148/1735 it remained after his death under the rule of Khāns who were practically independent, passed at the end of the 18th century into the power of the Ḳādjārs and was stormed on the 3rd (15th) January 1804 by the Russians under Prince Tsitsianov to be definitely ceded to Russia by the treaty of Gulistān [*q.v.*]. On the 13th (25th) September 1826 Paskevič defeated a Persian army under ʿAbbās Mīrzā in the immediate neighbourhood of the town. Called Elizavetpol by the Russians, Gandja resumed its old name in 1924, to change it again in 1935 to Kirovabad in honour of the Soviet statesman S. M. Kirov.

The modern town with a population (1959) of 116,000 inhabitants, lies on both banks of the Gandja Čay, a tributary of the Kura. In the older western half of the town, fortifications and the so-called "Tatar" mosque have survived from the time of Shāh ʿAbbās; the "Persian" mosque belongs to a later period. The climate is unhealthy and malarial but favourable to the growth of vegetation. Vines, fruit trees, vegetables and tobacco are cultivated in the surrounding countryside; it is also a centre of sericulture.

Bibliography: In addition to the works mentioned above: *The history of the Caucasian Albanians* by Movsēs Dasxuranç̣i, transl. C. J. F. Dowsett, London 1961; V. Minorsky, *A history of Sharvān and Darband in the 10th-11th centuries*, Cambridge 1958; idem, *Studies in Caucasian history*, London 1953; A. A. Ali-zade, *Sotsial'no-ekonomičeskaya i političeskaya istoriya Azerbaidzhana XIII-XIV vv.*, Baku 1956; B. Lewis, *Registers on Iran and Âdharbâyjân in the Ottoman* Defter-i Khâqânî, in *Mélanges Massé*, Tehran 1963, 259 ff. (on registers dating from the first and second Ottoman occupations); *IA*, s.v. Gence, by Mirza Bala, with further bibliography.

(W. Barthold-[J. A. Boyle])

GANDO [see fulbe].

GANGĀ, the Ganges (also Gang گنگ, کنک in the Muslim historians of India), the principal river of Upper India [see hind] which rises in the snows of the Himālaya in the district of Gaŕhwāl at an altitude of some 3100 m., flows through the present provinces of Uttar Pradesh, Bihār and Bengal, and falls in the Bay of Bengal after a course of about 2500 km., the last 500 km. through the Bengal delta. Above the delta it receives successively the waters of the Rāmgangā, Yamunā (Djamnā, [*q.v.*]), Gōmatī, Gōgrā, Sōn, Gandak and Kōsī; above the Djamnā confluence at Prayāg (Allāhābād, [*q.v.*]) it is fordable. The delta commences south of the ruins of Gawŕ [see lakhnawtī], the westernmost channel which passes close to Murshīdābād [*q.v.*] being known in its upper reaches as the Bhāgīrathī and in its lower as the Hūglī [*q.v.*]. The main (eastern) channel, known also as the Padmā, runs south-east to Goālanda where it joins the (Bengal) Djamnā, *i.e.*, the lower reaches of the Brahmaputra. The confluence forms a broad estuary, now called the Meghnā, which enters the Bay of Bengal near Noākhālī as the most easterly of a number of channels. The delta is fertile in the north, and the swampy Sundarbans (salt, timber for boat-building) form its southern base; the Hūglī is its main commercial channel. Until the construction of the railways the Ganges formed, with its tributaries, a most important traffic artery (J. Rennell, *Memoir of a map of Hindoostan ...*[3], London 1793, 335 ff.), its major towns (*e.g.*, Kanawdj, Allāhābād, Fayḍābād, Banāras, Paṫnā, Munger, Rādjmaḥall [*qq.v.*]) having in many cases stone or brick landing stages. Its irrigation waters are extended by the Upper and Lower Ganges canals, with headworks at Hardwār.

In its lower reaches the fall is no more than from 1 to 3 cm. per kilometre, and hence its course is very liable to change under the weight of monsoon rainfall; for example, before the Muslim conquest of Bengal the main stream instead of turning south at its present point ran eastwards to Mālda and then turned south along the present course of the Mahānadā, running east of Gawŕ (cf. E. V. Westmacott in *JASB*, 1875, 7 ff.); the transfer of the Bengal capital from Gawŕ to Pānḋuā in 739/1338-9 was evidently occasioned by such a change, as was a subsequent removal of the court from Gawŕ to Tānḋā about 850/1446. The differences between the present courses of the Ganges and its deltaic tributaries and those shown on Rennell's map (*op. cit.*, facing p. 364; cf. *ibid.*, 345 ff.) are striking. For further details of change of course see hūglī.

To the Hindūs the Ganges is a sacred river, having its source in paradise whence it is precipitated on to the earth as the centre of seven streams; this legend, represented in Sanskrit sources in the *Matsyapurāṇa*, *Vāyupurāṇa*, *Rāmāyaṇa*, etc., is recounted in al-Bīrūnī's *K. al-Hind*, Eng. tr. E. Sachau, London 1888, i, 261. Its water has a special ritual purity, either for bathing at the confluences, especially at Allāhābād when the sun is in Aquarius, or for drinking (for the express courier which took Ganges water to Muḥammad b. Tughluḳ's court in Dawlatābād see Ibn Baṭṭūṭa, iii, 96, tr. Gibb, 184; for Akbar's use of Ganges water see Abu 'l-Faḍl, *Āʾīn-i Akbarī*, i, 55; and cf. Tavernier's observation (*Voyages*, Eng. tr. ed. W. Crooke, London 1925, i, 95) that the emperor (Shāhdjahān) and his court drink no other). For the Hindū practice of self-immolation in its waters, and casting the ashes of the dead therein, see Ibn Baṭṭūṭa, i, 79, iii, 141 f., tr. v. Mžik, 57; tr. Gibb, 193; V. Minorsky, *Gardīzī on India*, in *BSOAS*, xii (1947-8), 639 f.

Bibliography: in addition to the references in the text, see *Imperial Gazetteer of India*, ed. 1908, s.v. Ganges.

(J. Burton-Page)

GANZA [see gandja].

GAO, a town in the republic of Mali, situated on the left bank of the Niger (10,000 inhabitants), is one of the oldest commercial centres in West Africa, standing at the point where the caravan route from Tilemsi reaches the Niger. In older writers, Gao is referred to under the names Kaukau, Kawkaw, Kookou, Kankou and Kounkou. Two etymologies are suggested: according to al-Bakrī (*Description de l'Afrique*, 399), the name Kaukau derives from the sound of tom-toms; Houdas (*Taʾrīkh al-Sūdān*, 6, n. 3) suggests that it is an abbreviation of ***kokoy Korya*** (the king's town).

Probably founded in about 690 A.D. by the Sorko Faran fishermen expelled from Kukia by the Songhai Gao became an important commercial centre. It is probably the town referred to by al-Khwārizmī (before 218/833) and, in about 258/872, by al-Yaʿḳūbī as "Kawkaw, the greatest and most powerful of the kingdoms of the Sudan", which would anticipate by some twenty years the date 890 given by Barth as marking the extension of the authority of the Songhai rulers of Kukia over Gao.

Gao was then very much frequented by traders from the Maghrib. Hence it happened that, according to Ibn Khaldūn (*Berbères*, trans. de Slane, iii, 201), it was at Gao, during one of his father's business journeys, in about 271/885, that Abū Yazīd [*q.v.*], "the man on the donkey", was born.

Al-Muhallabī tells us: "The king of this people sets his subjects the example of the faith of Islam, and the majority of them follow his example. It has a town on the east bank of the Nile (Niger) named Sarna; this town contains markets and merchandise and is regularly frequented by people from all countries. The king also has a town on the west of the Nile where he lives with his nobles and intimates. He has a mosque where he prays, while the people have their own *muṣallā* between the two *madrasas*. In his town the king has a palace which no-one lives in except himself and which now harbours only a single eunuch. They are all Muslims. The king and his principal companions wear tunics and turbans and ride horses bareback". These lines, quoted by Y. Kamal (*Monumenta Cartographica Africae et Aegypti*, iii/2, 683), were written in about 385/996, that is to say 15 years before the date given for the conversion to Islam and the settling at Gao of Dia Kossoï (1009-10).

Al-Bakrī (459/1067) describes the division of the town into two quarters: "(Kawkaw) consists of two towns, one is the residence of the king and the other is inhabited by the Muslims. Their king bears the title of *Kanda*. Like other negroes, they wear a loin-cloth and a jacket of skins or other material, the quality of which varies according to the wealth of the individual. Like the negroes, they worship idols... When a new king mounts the throne, he is given a seal, a sword and a Ḳur'ān ... Their king professes the faith of Islam, they never entrust the supreme authority to anyone other than a Muslim" (*Descr. de l'Afr. sept.*, trans. de Slane 1859, Algiers 1913, 342-3).

In 1939, royal steles of the 12th century were discovered at Sane (9 km. east of Gao). Al-Zuhrī (before 545/1150) noted a greater volume of trade came from Egypt and Wargla than through the Tafilelt.

Gao was captured by Sagamandia, one of the generals of Kango Mūsā (Mansa Musa), at the time of the return from pilgrimage of the emperor of Mali (724/1324) who had a mosque with *miḥrāb* built, perhaps on the plans of the poet al-Sāḥilī. Dia Assibaï, a vassal of Mali, had to surrender his two sons as hostages. One of them, ʿAlī Kolen (the cricket), managed to escape and restored the Songhai empire by deposing the *dia* Bada who was governing Gao on behalf of the Mali. He was called *Sonni* (the liberator) and founded the second dynasty which ruled from 739/1339 until 898/1493.

Gao, however, remained a highly prosperous capital and, after his visit in 753/1352, Ibn Baṭṭūṭa stated that it was one of the most beautiful and extensive cities in the Negroes' country, and most abundantly supplied with foodstuffs. But during the 8th/14th century the Songhai were driven back to the former capital of Kukia. It was only in 802/1400 that the Sonni Ma Daou (or Ma Dogo, that is, the Giant) passed to the attack and sacked the town of Mali. The last ruler Sonni ʿAlī (868/1464-898/1493) or ʿAlī Ber (the Great) brought the Songhai empire to its apogee when he captured Timbuctoo (872/1468) and Djenne (877/1473). But it was a period of pagan resurgence and of persecution of the Muslims.

When nominated chief of the Songhai on 21 January 1493, the Sonni Barou refused to adopt Islam; he was compelled to fight against ʿAlī Ber's best commander, the Sarakole (Soninke) Muḥammad Toure who won a victory (12 April 1493) and took the name *Askia* (signifying *usurper* or *it is not he*). Muḥammad Askia (898/1493-934/1528) made the pilgrimage to Mecca (1497-8), and then extended and organized his conquests. He received a visit (907/1502-909/1504) from the reformer al-Maghīlī who had just had the Jewish colonies at Touat (Tuat) massacred.

The 16th century represents the great period of the empire of Gao. The *Ta'rīkh al-Fattāsh* enumerates 7626 houses, which represents a large town. Leo Africanus, who probably visited Gao at the beginning of the 16th century, related: "Gao is a very large city without walls ..., the greater part of the houses are ugly in appearance; however, there are some quite handsome and commodious buildings in which the king lives with his court". In 999/1591, the army of the pasha Djawdhar captured Gao. But, accustomed to the splendours of Morocco, Djawdhar was disappointed: "the head donkey-driver's house in Marrākush is better than the Askia's palace" (*Ta'rīkh al-Sūdān*, 221).

But dependence on Morocco was soon no more than nominal. In any case, it merely took the form of plundering the educated and bourgeois classes, which explains the utter collapse of Islamic culture. After 1021/1612, the pashas commanding the Moroccan army no longer came from Morocco, but were appointed on the spot by the soldiers. The *Arma*, half-breed descendants of Moroccans, had difficulty in fighting against the Tuareg who occupied Gao for the first time in 1091/1680, but were driven from it in 1099/1688 by the pasha Manṣūr Seneber, who however left no further garrisons there.

Thereafter, decline set in, and in 1184/1770 Gao, following Timbuctoo, was under Tuareg control.

At the time of Barth's visit in 1854, Gao was no more than a wretched village with from three to four hundred huts, where only a single partly ruined monument was to be seen, the tomb of the great Askia Muḥammad. Although they reached Timbuctoo in 1893, the French military authorities established a base there only in 1899 (Lt.-Col. Klobb). On their arrival, the French found merely a small group of *sharīfs* called *Sherifikalo* in the neighbourhood of the Askia tomb.

The peace brought by French rule permitted the intermingling of the various races which nevertheless retained some degree of specialization, with Songhai farmers, Arma artisans, Moorish shopkeepers, Hausa traders and Bambara fishermen and tailors.

Bibliography: R. Basset, *Essai sur l'histoire et la langue de Tombouctou et des royaumes de Songhay et Melli*, Louvain 1889; Béraud-Villars, *L'Empire de Gao*, Paris 1943; Boulnois and Boubou Hama, *L'Empire de Gao*, Paris 1954; Delafosse, *Haut-Sénégal-Niger*, Paris 1912; Dubois, *Tombouctou la mystérieuse*, Paris 1897; idem, *La Région de Gao, berceau de l'Empire Songhay*, in *BCAF*, 1909, 47 ff.; Dutel, *Comparaison entre une généalogie Sonraï de tradition arabe et la généalogie des Askia de Gao donnée par les sources historiques*, in *Notes africaines*, xxv (January 1945), 22-3; R. Mauny, *Notes d'archéologie au sujet de Gao*, in *BIFAN*, 1951, 837-52; idem, *La tour et la Mosquée de l'Askia Mohammed à Gao*, in *Notes Africaines*, xlvii (July 1950); Capt. Péfontan, *Les Armes*, in

BCHSAOF, 1926, 153-79; J. Rouch, *Les Songhay*, Mémoire IFAN, Dakar 1952; J. Sauvaget, *Notes préliminaires sur les épitaphes royales de Gao*, in *REI*, 1948, 5-12; idem, *Les épitaphes royales de Gao*, in *Andalus*, xiv/1 (1949); J. Spencer Trimingham, *A History of Islam in West Africa*, Oxford 1962. (R. Cornevin)

GARDEN [see bustān].

GARDĪZ, town of modern Afghanistan, headquarters of Paktiya Province (originally called 'The Southern Province'), situated 65 km. east of Ghaznī in the direct line, though further by road, in 69° 6′ E. 33° 36′ N. Gardīz stands on the route from Ghaznī towards the Kurram Valley, which there joins the route passing south-eastwards from Kābul through the Logar Valley. The town stands at an altitude of 2289 metres amid extensive orchards in the Zurmatt plain, surrounded except to the south-west by substantial mountains. It is dominated by an artificial fortress-mound, the Bālā Ḥiṣār, which is crowned by an elegant fortress apparently dating from the 19th century. Within these fortifications are contained a barracks, and a *ziyārat* which occupies the remains of an ancient mud-brick bastion. Local tradition attributes the foundation of the city to a certain Zamar, who is apparently not otherwise documented. None the less, the discovery in 1947 at Mir Zakah, 53 km. east-north-east of the town, of a sacred spring containing an important treasure of Indo-Bactrian and Indo-Scythian coins, suggests that Gardīz was a place of consequence already in the second century B.C. Preserved at Kābul is an image of the elephant-headed god Gaṇeśa, bearing a Sanskrit inscription of the eighth year of the Hūna king Khingāla (Khingila). The image is reputed to have been brought to Kābul from Gardīz, and this if true would attest the importance of the place in the 6th century A.D. According to the *Taʾrīkh-i Sīstān* (p. 24) Gardīz was founded (or re-founded) by the Khāridjī leader Ḥamza b. ʿAbd Allāh in about 181/797. The connexion of the Kharidjīs with this town is confirmed in the *Ḥudūd al-ʿālam*, but the later history of its Khāridjī *amīrs* is little known. A bilingual Arabic-Sanskrit inscription from the Tochi Valley now in the Peshawar Museum dated 243/857 contains the words *fī barrⁱ ʿUmān* 'in the land of ʿUmān', which appears to refer to the well-known Khāridjī connexions beyond the Persian Gulf. The ruler's name has not been read, but the early date suggests that he must have been one of the princes of Gardīz. The historian Gardīzī [*q.v.*] (*Zayn al-akhbār*, ed. Nazim, 11) reports an attack by the Ṣaffārid Yaʿḳūb b. al-Layth on the *amīr* of Gardīz, Abū Manṣūr Aflaḥ b. Muḥammad b. Khāḳān in 256/869. In 364/974 Bilgetegin, one of the predecessors of Maḥmūd of Ghaznī, died whilst he was undertaking a siege of Gardīz. However, the town soon fell into the hands of the Ghaznawids, for during the reign of Sebüktigīn, in 385/995 according to Barthold, the former was housing political prisoners in the fortress of Gardīz. With the loss of its independence, the historical importance of the town began to diminish. During the Mongol invasion it was the scene of a counter-attack by the Sultan Djalāl al-Dīn upon the Mongol vanguard. The Emperor Bābur, in his Memoirs, mentions it as a strong fortress, and the scene of a skirmish with the "ʿAbd al-Raḥmān Afghans'. Modern research has devoted little attention to Gardīz, and it is remarkable that its earlier rulers are apparently unknown to numismatics.

Bibliography: R. Curiel and D. Schlumberger, *Le trésor de Mir Zakah près de Gardēz*, in *Trésors monétaires d'Afghanistan* (Mémoires de la Délégation archéologique Française en Afghanistan, Tome XIV), Paris 1953, 67-99; D. C. Sarcar, *Three early medieval inscriptions*, in *Epigraphia Indica*, xxxv (1963), 45-7; Malik al-Shuʿarā Bahār (ed.), *Taʾrīkh-i Sīstān*, 24; *Ḥudūd al-ʿālam*, 91, 251; Muhammad Hamid Qureshi, *A Kufic Sarada inscription from the Peshawar Museum*, in *Epigraphia Indo-Moslemica*, 1925-6, 27; Barthold, *Turkestan*², 264, 445; Sir Lucas King (ed.), *Memoirs of Zahīr-ed-dīn Muhammed Bābur*, London 1921, i, 241; ii, 122 ff.; Muḥammad Nāẓim, *The life and times of Sulṭān Maḥmūd of Ghazna*, Cambridge 1931, 27. (A. D. H. Bivar)

GARDĪZĪ, Abū Saʿīd ʿAbd al-Ḥayy b. al-Ḍaḥḥāk b. Maḥmūd, Persian historian who flourished in the middle of the 5th/11th century. Nothing is known of his life. His *nisba* shows that he came from Gardīz [*q.v.*]; since he says that he received information about Indian festivals from al-Bīrūnī [*q.v.*], he may have been his pupil. His work, entitled *Zayn al-akhbār*, was written in the reign of the Ghaznawid Sultan ʿAbd al-Rashīd (440/1049-443/1052). It contains a history of the pre-Islamic kings of Persia, of Muḥammad and the Caliphs to the year 423/1032, and a detailed history of Khurāsān from the Arab conquest to 432/1041: no sources are named, but for the history of Khurāsān Gardīzī must have been mainly following al-Sallāmī [*q.v.*]; the work includes also a valuable chapter on the Turks, based on the works of Ibn Khurradādhbih, al-Djayhānī and Ibn al-Muḳaffaʿ [*qq.v.*] (ed. with Russian tr. by W. Barthold, in *Otčet o poezdke v Srednuyu Aziyu* (Zap. Imp. Akad. Nauk po Ist.-Phil. Otd., i, no. 4), St Petersburg 1897, 78 ff., and with Hungarian tr. by G. Kuun in *Keleti Kútfök*, 1898, 5 ff. and *KS*, 1903, 17 ff.), a chapter on India (see E. Sachau, *Alberuni's India*, London 1888, ii, 360, 397 and V. Minorsky, *Gardīzī on India*, in *BSOAS*, xii (1948), 625-40), and essays on Greek sciences, chronology, the religious festivals of various peoples, and genealogy. Only two incomplete manuscripts are known: Bodleian, Ouseley 240, dated 1196/1782, which is a transcript of Cambridge, King's College 213, dated (?)930/1524. The contents, so far as they survive, are listed by E. Sachau and H. Ethé (*Catalogue .... Bodleian Library*, i, 9 ff.). Historical sections on the Ṭāhirids, Ṣaffārids, Sāmānids and Ghaznawids have been edited by Muhammad Nazim, *Kitab Zainu 'l-akhbar*, Berlin-London 1928 (E. G. Browne Memorial Series, i).

Bibliography: Introduction to M. Nazim's edition and Barthold, *Turkestan*², 20-1, and references there given; *Ḥudūd al-ʿālam*, index. (W. Barthold*)

GARĔBĔG [see ʿīd and indonesia—v].

GARMSĪR [see ḳishlaḳ].

GARSĪF (in the Marīnid period *Agarsīf* occurs quite as frequently; the occlusive Berber *g* is some times transcribed in Arabic characters as *djīm*, sometimes as *kāf*, each distinguished by three diacritical points), the Guercif of French maps, a small place in eastern Morocco 60 km. east of Taza, in the middle of the immense Tāfrāṭa steppe. It is situated on the spit of land between the Mulullū and Moulouya rivers at their confluence; hence its name (Berber *ger-* "between" and *āsīf* "river").

Marmol wished to identify Guercif with Ptolemy's *Galapha*; but this is scarcely likely, since the Greek geographer clearly put the latter place east of Molochat (= Moulouya): Tāwrīrt seems a more probable identification.

Guercif was founded towards the middle of the 3rd/9th century by the Banū Abi 'l-ʿĀfiya, one of the tribes of the Miknāsa, a Berber people who led a nomadic life in the Moulouya valley. It became the centre of the lands of Mūsā b. Abi 'l-ʿĀfiya (d. 327/938) and then of his sons who were renowned for their wars with the Idrīsids and Fāṭimids.

Its commercial and strategic importance was due to its situation at the intersection of two important routes, one from Fez to Tlemcen, the other from Sidjilmāsa to Melilla. In the middle of the 5th/11th century al-Bakrī described it as an important village with a considerable population (*ḳarya ʿāmira*). But after being captured and destroyed by the Almoravid Yūsuf b. Tāshfīn in 473/1080 it lost its former importance; and al-Idrīsī (middle of the 5th/11th century) did not know it.

At the beginning of the 7th/13th century, the site of Guercif was frequented by the Banū Marīn, nomadic Berber tribes belonging to the Zanāta group. In summer they came down from the high plateaus of the pre-Saharan zone and spent the summer in the lower Moulouya valley. It was at Guercif that they stored their stocks of grain; it was also there that, at the approach of autumn, their tribes met before returning to their grazing-lands in the Sahara. In 610/1213, taking advantage of the enfeebled state into which the Almohad empire had fallen as a result of the disaster at al-ʿUḳāb, the Banū Marīn settled down along the lower Moulouya and occupied Guercif. It was there that, in 646/1248, they lay in wait for the Almohad army in its retreat from Tlemcen to Fez, and then defeated and routed it. In about 1275 the Marīnids became masters of the whole of Morocco. However, on the eastern borders of their empire the Zayyānid kings of Tlemcen constituted a dangerous enemy. Along with the neighbouring localities of Tāwrīrt and Dubdū [*q.v.*] Guercif formed a march (*thaghr*), barring access to the interior of Morocco. In 721/1321 the Marīnid Abū Saʿīd had the walls rebuilt. Later, after a revolt by the inhabitants, Guercif was sacked and part of the fortifications were destroyed by Abū ʿInān.

After his death (759/1358) Guercif, together with the fortified castle of Murāda (15 km. to the north-west, on the Moulouya) became a fief of the celebrated Wanzammār b. ʿArīf, chief of the Suwayd Arabs, who was in command of all the Bedouin tribes supporting the Marīnids, and the mentor of the kings of that dynasty. Numerous attacks were made against it by Abū Ḥammū, king of Tlemcen, and the two fortified places were on several occasions captured and sacked.

Later, Guercif lost its military importance when the boundary between Morocco and Turkish Algeria was moved east of Oujda; the Saʿdids and ʿAlawids preferred Tāwrīrt.

From 1912 Guercif was occupied by France and acquired a measure of importance through being at the head of the railway from Oujda. After the line had been extended, first to Taza, then to Fez, the village declined rapidly. With Msoun, it is one of the two centres of the Hawwāra, an important tribe who move with their flocks to summer pasturages and who devote themselves to sheep-rearing.

Bibliography: Bakrī, index; Ibn Khaldūn, *Histoire des Berbères*, index; Leo Africanus, ed. Schefer, ii, 329, tr. Epaulard, 299. (G. S. Colin)

GASPRALI (GASPRINSKI), ISMĀʿĪL, prominent ideological writer of the Turks, more particularly of the Russian Turks, was born in 1851 in the village of Avčī, near Baghčesarāy. His father, Muṣṭafā Agha, was one of the notables of the village of Gaspra, between Yalta and Alupka (whence their family name Gasprali, later Gasprinski), and a graduate of the Military Lycée in Odessa. At the time of the Battle of Sevastopol in 1854 Muṣṭafā Agha settled in Baghčesarāy and sent his son Ismāʿīl first to the Zindjirli Medrese in Baghčesarāy and later, at the age of ten, to the Simferopol Gymnasium. Two years later Ismāʿīl went to the Voronezh Military Lycée and was then transferred to the Moscow Military Lycée. Together with Muṣṭafā Mīrzā Davidovič, a Lithuanian Tatar in origin, he attracted the attention of their principal teacher, Ivan Katkov, the famous Pan-Slavist and editor of the newspaper *Moskovskiya Vedomosti*, who invited them every week to his house. At the time of the rebellion in Crete in 1867 the hostility which Katkov showed toward Turkey produced a reaction in these two youths, and they went to Odessa with the intention of serving in Crete as volunteers on the Turkish side. As they had no passports, however, they were arrested and sent back to their homes in the Crimea. Ismāʿīl Bey was appointed a teacher in Russian, the study of which was compulsory, in the Zindjirli Medrese in Baghčesarāy. He constantly thought of going to Turkey and becoming an officer; and when he discovered that it was necessary to learn French to do this, he learned French during his four-year appointment at Baghčesarāy. He had, in fact, acquired some knowledge of this language while at the Military Lycée in Moscow. In 1871 he resolved to go to Istanbul; but, seeking to perfect his French, went by way of Vienna to Paris. The results of his observations in Paris were reflected in works which he later published in Russia—especially in his work named *Rūsyā Islāmlighī* ('*The Muslim Community in Russia*')—and also in a work named *Avrūpā medeniyetine bir naẓar-ī müvāzene* ('*A balanced view of European civilization*') which he wrote while still in Paris.

While in Paris he earned his living by working as at ranslator in an advertizing agency. Since his aim was to go to Turkey, he did not mix much with the Young Ottoman circles in Paris. Finally in 1874 he went to Istanbul and stayed with his paternal uncle, Süleymān Efendi, who had settled there earlier. He made great efforts to enter the Turkish War College, but when the Russian Ambassador Ignatiev learned of this he brought influence to bear on the Grand Vizier Maḥmūd Nedīm Pasha and prevented it. After vainly waiting a year, Ismāʿīl returned to the Crimea. While in Istanbul he published non-political articles describing Eastern life for some Russian newspapers appearing in St. Petersburg and Moscow.

Between the years 1874 and 1878 he became familiar with the village life of the Crimean Turks, and described this period of his life in his story *Gün Doghdu*, published in 1906. In this he refers to himself under the name "Dāniyāl Bey". While becoming familiar with the needs of his nation, with education and village life, this Dāniyāl Bey sees the vital need of bringing out a newspaper and making his nation aware of the world. In 1878 Ismāʿīl Bey was elected mayor of Baghčesarāy, and in 1879 he applied to the Czar's government for permission to bring out a newspaper, but was refused. He thereupon wrote in the Russian-language newspaper *Tavrida*, published in Simferopol, serious political articles pertaining to the Muslims of the Russia Empire. He also published occasional collections of articles: *Tunguč* (lithograph, Simferopol); *Shefeḳ* and *Laṭāʾif* (Ünsizādeler Press, Tiflis); and, later, *Ay*, *Yïldïz* and *Günesh*. These writings were mostly in the Crimean dialect. In the next year (1882) Ismāʿīl Bey expanded a little the articles he had published in Russian in the newspaper *Tavrida* and published them in the form of a fifty-four page work with the title *Russkoye Musulmanstvo* (*'Russian Islam'*). This work was a pioneer work relative to the political and cultural problems of the Muslim subject-peoples of the Russian Empire. Although Ismāʿīl Bey presented himself in this work as a loyal Russian subject, even speaking approvingly of the salvation of the Russians from Tatar domination, Russian circles believed this to be a device and regarded this work with suspicion. In it he considered the "Turco-Tatars" under Russian rule as a single Russian Muslim community and showed the road by which they might join Western civilization. In the pamphlets which he published in Turkish he pointed out that if the Turco-Tatar group were to remain dispersed the result would be calamitous: he tried to explain that the sole road of salvation for them was to work together to join the new Western civilization by means of their own languages. In the year 1883 he received permission to publish a newspaper named *Terdjümān*. The Russian title of the newspaper was *Perevodčik*; and in the first issues the Russian-language section was more important. It explained that it was to perform the role of translator in the matter of spreading Western civilization among the Russian Muslim community. The Turkish-language section gradually expanded and became more serious and later, in 1890, *Terdjümān* became "the national newspaper concerning politics, education, and literature". After 1905, it took the name *Terdjümān-i Aḥwāl-i Zamān*, and at the head of the newspaper was the slogan: "Unity in language, work, and thought". Finally the part in Russian was abandoned altogether, and the newspaper became the interpreter of the thoughts and aims of the Muslim community in the Russian Empire. All the Turks living in the regions of Kazan, the Caucasus, Turkistan, and Siberia recognized this newspaper as being the disseminator of their national ideas. The deep influence of this newspaper on Turkish intellectuals may be judged from the first novel in the Tatar language, entitled *Molla Ḥusām al-Dīn* by Mūsā Aḳyegitzāde, published in 1886, from the speeches and gifts of the delegates who came from every part of the Russian Empire on the occasion of the twenty-fifth anniversary of the appearance of *Terdjümān* in 1908, and from the increased numbers of newspapers that year.

Ismāʿīl Bey married Zehrā Khanïm, a member of the Aḳčura (Akčurin) manufacturing family, one of the noble Kazan families. Through this marriage his ties with the Kazan Tatars became close. He was in constant touch with Azerbaijan Turkish writers, Ḥasan bek Melikov, Ünsizāde, Topčïbashï and others. Muṣṭafā Davidovič, the Lithuanian Muslim who had studied with him at the Moscow Military Lycée, settled in Baghčesarāy, where he was mayor for twenty years, helping Ismāʿīl Bey in all his enterprises. The work with which Ismāʿīl Bey was most occupied was to create modern primary schools for Russian Muslims and to publish textbooks for these. He also wanted to ensure modern methods of instruction by opening teachers' courses in Baghčesarāy and other places, and to assure the opening of this type of school throughout the Muslim community of Russia. He himself visited every part of that community, including Tashkent, Bukhārā, and Siberia. He set up and printed personally on his own press *Khʷādje-i ṣibyān*, *Maʿlūmāt-i nāfiʿa* and other works which he brought out for the primary schools. Together with his wife, Zehrā Khanïm, and the mayor, Muṣṭafā Davidovič, he opened a handicrafts institute for girls on the twenty-fifth anniversary of the appearance of *Terdjümān*, an idea which spread to other provinces as well. He brought out the first magazine for women, entitled *ʿĀlem-i niswān*, and placed his daughter Shefīḳa at the head of it. He also published a work concerning women's rights, entitled *Ḳadïnlar ülkesi*. Inspired by Shams al-Dīn Sāmī's *Ḳāmūs al-aʿlām*, he began to publish an encyclopaedia for Russian Muslims, but was unable to complete it. He became occupied with problems of language and literature. After the 1905 Revolution he planned a programme especially designed to deal with the problems of instruction and "literary language". It envisaged that in the first three years of primary school instruction would be carried out in the local Turkish dialects; afterwards, the "common literary language" would become the general language of instruction. His original idea of the "common literary language" was some addition of Ottoman to a language which was mainly Tatar; but the Ottoman influence increased under the influence of those who were working with him, and the result was a simple Ottoman which could be understood by the Muslims of Russia. National Turkish literature, according to Ismāʿīl Bey, would consist of novels which would reflect the life of the regions in which the Turks lived and which would inculcate in them new thoughts and ideals. The supplements named *Ḍamīme-i Terdjümān*, which he published as additions to *Terdjümān* in the years 1892-4, and his novel *Dār al-Rāḥat Müslümānlarï* are important in this respect. In language, Ismāʿīl Bey earnestly opposed the domination of Arabic and Persian in Ottoman and also the tendency among the Kazan Tatars to take words from Russian, and he put forward the idea of drawing on popular literature for the literary language. His stories *Arslan Ḳïz* and *Güldjemāl Bikeč* telling of the 18th century Chinese occupation of Kāshghar, and his writings entitled *Baghčesarāydan Tashkende*, which included the memoirs of his travels, were serialized in many issues of the *Ḍamīme*. In 1893 he published stories about Baghdād Khātūn [*q.v.*], who played an important role in the history of the Ilkhānids. He also published an expanded version of the treatise *Türklerde ʿilim ve funūn* of Bursalï Ṭāhir, publishing some of it—the discussions of Saʿd al-Dīn Taftāzānī, for example—in the *Ḍamīme*.

At first Ismāʿīl Bey valued Islam as being useful in preserving for the Turks their national identities but, aside from the "pocket Ḳurʾān", he did not devote much space to religious publications. After the 1905 Revolution he saw the adverse results of Socialism and Communism, which were beginning to appear in those years in Kazan and Baku, and became frightened of those movements, especially in the face of publications which, opposing the separate political institutions of the Russian Muslims, claimed allegiance solely to the Russian socialist parties, and which made haphazard efforts to impose Russian as the literary language. In the series of articles which he published in *Terdjümān* under the title "*Ishtirākiyyūn*", he moved noticeably to the right and began to think of bringing about a cultural unity among Islamic nations. With this aim in mind he wanted to convene a general Muslim congress in Egypt in 1907, and, having gone there himself, even began to publish an Arabic newspaper named *Al-Nahḍa* with ʿAbd Allāh Taymas. He also made a journey to India to further this endeavour; but when these efforts did not give the results he had hoped for, he resumed his old activities in Bag̲h̲česarāy.

Among the other publications of Ismāʿīl Bey are the *Mebādiʾ-i temeddün-i Islāmiyyān-i Rūs*, published in 1901, and the twenty-page work *Rūs ve S̲h̲arḳ anlas̲h̲masî*, published in Russian (*Russko-vostočnoye soglas̲h̲enye*) in 1896. Ismāʿīl Bey, having seen the positive results of his efforts, fought in the last years of his life against the excessive bias which viewed Westernization as a form of spiritual suicide for Turks and other Muslims in Russia. Ismāʿīl Bey, carried away with new hopes at the time of the beginning of the First World War, died on 11 September 1914, in his house in Bag̲h̲česarāy and was buried there. His son and daughters carried on for a period after his death the publication of the newspaper *Terd̲j̲ümān* which had continued for thirty-one years.

Bibliography: The biography of Ismāʿīl Bey has been written by Yusuf Akçura in *Türk Yılı*, 1928, 338-46. Cafer Seydahmet also published a fairly large work entitled *Gaspralı Ismail Bey* in 1934. A complete set of *Terd̲j̲ümān* is preserved in the Leningrad Public Library; outside Russia, some copies of this newspaper may be found in the Helsinki University Library, the Inkilap Library in Istanbul, the British Museum, the Ankara National Library, and in various private libraries. The Centre Russe de l'École Pratique des Hautes Études in the Sorbonne is now collecting microfilms of all the years of publication of this newspaper. (Z. V. Togan)

GATE, GATEWAY [see bāb].

GAUR [see lakhnāwtī].

GÂVUR [see kāfir].

GĀWĀN, MAḤMŪD [see maḥmūd gāwān].

GĀWILGAŔH, in the histories also Gāwīl, Gāwīlgaŕh, a fortress "of almost matchless strength" (Abu 'l-Faḍl, *Āʾīn-i Akbarī*, Eng. tr. Jarrett, ii, 237) in Berār, Central India, lat. 21° 20′ N., long. 77° 18′ E., seven *kos* (about 25 km.) north-west of Eličpur (Iličpur [*q.v.*]). According to Firis̲h̲ta the fortress was built by Aḥmad S̲h̲āh Walī [see bahmanīs] in 829/1425-6; but from its name it appears to have been a former stronghold of the Gāwalī chiefs, and it is more likely that Aḥmad S̲h̲āh merely strengthened the fortifications during the year he spent at Eličpur in the consolidation of his northern frontiers before proceeding to his attacks on the Vid̲j̲ayanagar kingdom on his south. A Brāhman captured in an earlier Vid̲j̲ayanagar campaign who was received into Islam under the name Fatḥ Allāh was sent for service under the governor of Berār; later, under the Bahmanī minister Maḥmūd Gāwān, this Fatḥ Allāh, with the title ʿImād al-Mulk, was himself made governor in 876/1471. The increasing loss of power by the Bahmanī sultans to their Barīdī ministers in the capital, Bīdar, had led Fatḥ Allāh to prepare against possible opposition by strengthening the defences of Gāwilgaŕh in 893/1488 (inscription on Fatḥ Darwāza), from which time also dates the rebuilding of the D̲j̲āmiʿ Masd̲j̲id "with the old stones" and Fatḥ Allāh's use of the Vid̲j̲ayanagar emblems on the gates (see below, Monuments). Two years later Fatḥ Allāh assumed independence [see ʿimād s̲h̲āhī] with headquarters at Eličpur and the fortresses of Gāwilgaŕh and Narnālā as his strongholds, and these remained ʿImād S̲h̲āhī possessions until the extinction of the dynasty in 982/1574 when Berār became a province of the Niẓām S̲h̲āhī [*q.v.*] dynasty of Aḥmadnagar. After the cession of Berār to the Mug̲h̲als in 1004/1596 Gāwilgaŕh was still held by *amīr*s of Aḥmadnagar, and Akbar's son Prince Murād, reluctant to besiege it, made Bālāpur his principal stronghold; two years later, however, it fell to Abu 'l-Faḍl. The description of the *sūba* of Berār was added to the *Āʾīn-i Akbarī* immediately after the cession of Berār, obviously before the Mug̲h̲als had had time to reorganize the province, and thus the place given to Gāwīl as the largest and richest of the thirteen *sarkār*s must reflect the pre-Mug̲h̲al administrative division. This division was substantially unchanged in the great scheme of reorganization of the Deccan provinces under Awrangzīb as viceroy in 1046/1636. In the Marāṫhā troubles in the Deccan in the early 12th/18th century the province was held together by Āṣaf D̲j̲āh Niẓām al-Mulk, but on his absence in Dihlī in 1151/1738 Berār with its great fortresses of Gāwilgaŕh and Narnālā was taken by the Bhonsla Marāṫhās. In 1803 Gāwilgaŕh fell to Wellesley, but was retained by the Bhonsla in the treaty which followed; in 1822, however, it was restored to the Niẓām. In 1853 it was assigned to the East India Company, and the fortifications were dismantled five years later.

Monuments. Much of the walling of the fort still remains, with gates and bastions. One fine tall bastion on the west wall, the Burd̲j̲-i Bahrām, gives its date of repair (985/1577 by chronogram) by Bahrām K̲h̲ān, governor of Gāwilgaŕh under the Niẓām S̲h̲āhīs at a time when it was expected that Akbar's forces would advance. The Dihlī Darwāza is most interesting for its sculptured symbols: the lions with elephants beneath their paws, level with the top of the arch, are devices of the Gond kings, but the two-headed eagles holding elephants in each beak, which lie over the lions, are the *gaṇḍa-bherunda* symbols of the Vid̲j̲ayanagar empire; this is the northern gate, which leads to the outer fort built in the 12th/18th century by the Marāṫhā Bhonslas of Nāgpur. The D̲j̲āmiʿ Masd̲j̲id stands on the highest point within the fort, and in its present form doubtless represents the rebuilding by Fatḥ Allāh recorded in the inscription on the Fatḥ (south-west) Darwāza; the western *līwān* was three bays deep behind the seven-arched façade, on which was some blue tile decoration in addition to fine stonework, and bore a rich *čhad̲j̲d̲j̲ā* on carved brackets; the *miḥrāb* wall has fallen. The most interesting feature, characteristic of the local style, is the pylon standing at each end of the *līwān* façade, which bears not a *minār* as in the other Deccan styles but a square *čhatrī* with projecting eaves, rich brackets, and *d̲j̲ālī* screens in each side. A large walled *ṣaḥn* stands in front of the *līwān*, with a great eastern gateway. To the north-east of the great mosque stands a smaller unnamed mosque, similar but supported on octagonal columns. Few other buildings remain.

Bibliography: Almost the sole source for the history of Berār is Muḥammad Ḳāsim b. Hindū S̲h̲āh Firis̲h̲ta, *Guls̲h̲an-i Ibrāhīmī*, *passim*. See also T. W. Haig, *Inscriptions of Berar*, in *EIM*, 1907-8, 10-21; *Archaeological Survey of India, Annual Report 1920-1*, Plate VIIIa; *ibid.*, *Report 1922-3*, 56-8 and Plate XXIc; *ibid.*, *Report 1926-7*, 36-8; *Dispatches of ... the Duke of Wellington ...*, London 1838, ii, 560 ff. (J. Burton-Page)

GAWR [see lakhnāwtī].

GAWUR [see kāfir].

GĀWUR DAGHLARĪ, literally "the mountains of the unbelievers", the name given by the Turks to several mountainous massifs, notably to (1) that where the Euphrates has its source to the north of Erzurum, and especially to (2) the Amanos, an arc of mountains which forms the south-western extremity of the eastern Taurus. It consists of a vast anticline rising to 7,411 ft./2,262 metres, orientated north-north-east/south-south-west, changing to north-east/south-west in its southern section after the col of Belen, with a structure of palaeozoic strata, accompanied by chalk and greenstone, which forms a fragment of the north-western edge of the Syrian plateau, rising, then descending below the level of it along the great fracture of the lower Orontes. The Amanos is very well watered and on it at a high level is found an isolated region of humid forest, where *Fagus orientalis* mingles with evergreen oaks and *Pinus nigra*, with peaty soils. The population consists of Turks and ʿAlawīs. Apart from the permanent villages (which are found up to a height of about 3,000 ft./900 metres) there are *yaylas* (Belen, Sorkun) which in summer are occupied especially by the inhabitants of the coastal towns and villages. The official Turkish name is now Amanos. For the other names, which are very varied, see Streck, art. ALMA DAGH, in *EI*¹. The most important is the Arabic: Djabal al-Ukkām = Turkish Kara dağ, "the black mountain", very probably the origin of the name Akma daghī used by several European travellers, owing to a confusion with Alma (or Elma) daghī.

Bibliography: see in general *İA*, s.v. Gâvur dağları (B. Darkot); on (2) for structure: E. de Vaumas, *Structure et morphologie du Proche-Orient*, in *Revue de Géographie Alpine*, 1961, 469-72; idem, *L'Amanus et le Dj. Ansarieh, étude morphométrique*, in *Revue de Géographie Alpine*, 1954, 633-64; for vegetation: H. Louis, *Das natürliche Pflanzenkleid Anatoliens*, Stuttgart 1939, 98; among the travel accounts see also Th. Kotschy, *Reise in den Amanus*, in *Petermanns Mitteilungen*, 1863, 340 ff. (X. DE PLANHOL)

GAYKHĀTŪ, Īlkhān [*q.v.*] from 1291 until 1295, the younger son of Abaḳa, was raised to power by the leaders of his country after the death of his brother Arghūn [*q.v.*]. He ascended the throne on 23 Radjab 690/22 July 1291, when he also adopted the Buddhist (Tibetan) names Rin-čhen rDo-rje "precious jewel"; he was, however, in no way hostile to the Muslims, and he was the only Īlkhān who did not carry out any executions. Earlier, as an official in Asia Minor, he had been renowned for his unbounded liberality; now he squandered the State Treasury within a short space of time, devoted himself to drunkenness and pederasty and—apart from an attack against Asia Minor in 1292—paid no attention to State affairs. In order to prevent financial disaster, Ṣadr al-Dīn Aḥmad b. ʿAbd al-Razzāḳ Khālidī (also called Zandjānī), his Finance Minister (*Ṣāḥib dīwān*) since 1292, advised him to introduce paper money on the Chinese pattern; the name *čāw* (from Chinese *ṭṣʿau*) was retained in Persia [see ČAO]. Since the population was not familiar with this type of currency and since it was not covered by treasury resources, the State finances collapsed in the autumn of 1294 (under circumstances described most dramatically by Rashīd al-Dīn). Gaykhātū was consequently deserted by his *amīrs* and troops when Prince Bāydū of Baghdād advanced against him. Three days after his defeat at Hamadān (3 Djumādā I 694/21 March 1295) he was taken prisoner and executed. The paper money was again withdrawn.—After six months of civil war, his nephew Ghāzān [*q.v.*] succeeded him.

Bibliography: Rashīd al-Dīn, *Geschichte der Īlḫāne Abāġā bis Gaiḫātū*, ed. K. Jahn, Prague 1941 (²The Hague 1957), 81-90; Waṣṣāf, lith. Bombay 1852, iii, 259-84; K. Jahn, *Das iranische Papiergeld*, in *ArO*, x (1938), 308-40; B. Spuler, *Mongolen*², 86-9, 541 (with further data on sources and bibliography). (B. SPULER)

GAYOS [see ATJEH].

GAZA [see GHAZZA].

GAZELLE [see GHAZĀL].

GAZI ANTEP [see ʿAYNṬĀB].

GAZŪLA [see DJAZŪLA].

GAZŪLĪ [see DJAZŪLĪ].

GEBER [see GABR and MADJŪS].

GEBER [see DJĀBIR].

GEBZE (formerly *Geğbize, Geğibüze*), the ancient Dakibyza, a small town in north-west Anatolia, 40° 48′ N., 29° 26′ E., situated in undulating country not far from the mouth of the Gulf of Izmit in the Sea of Marmara; at one time a *ḳaḍā* in the *liwā* (*sandjaḳ*) of Ḳodja Eli (chief town Iznikmid/Izmit, *Eyālet* of Djezāʾir [islands]), later (in the 19th century) in the *vilâyet* of Istanbul, today in the *vilâyet* of Kocaeli; population, in 1960, of the town 8,018, and of the *ḳaḍā* 30,442.

At the time of Orkhan Geğibüze seems to have been already occupied by the Ottomans; in any case, the town was from the time of Meḥemmed I certainly Ottoman. The *ḳāḍī* of the town, by name Faḍl Allāh, who played a certain part under Meḥemmed I, was a descendant of Aḳča Ḳodja, the conqueror of this region under Orkhan.

Buildings in the town that are worthy of note are the Orkhan-Djāmiʿ, a simple construction with a single cupola and an entrance hall, and, in particular, the mosque of Čoban Muṣṭafā Pasha with *türbe*, *ʿimāret* and *medrese*. The builder was an official from Egypt who had the decoration of his mosque carried out in the Egyptian Mamlūk style (925/1519, but according to Ewliyā Čelebi 930/1525-6). The *türbe* is in the high Ottoman style.

The plain near Gebze bears the name Tekfūr Čayrī or Khunkar Čayrī in ancient sources. It was a halting-place on the route followed by the imperial armies on their campaigns in the east and south-east. It was here that sultan Meḥemmed II died on 4 Rabīʿ I 886/3 May 1481. Not far from Gebze can be seen the grave of Hannibal who met his death nearby, at Libyssa, when his protector king Prusias of Bithynia was planning to hand him over to the Romans.—Beyond Gebze, on the shores of the Gulf of Izmit, stand the picturesque ruins of a castle, Eskiḥiṣār.

Gebze is situated on the great military and caravan routes that lead across Anatolia from Istanbul to the east and south-east. The imperial armies followed these along the north shore of the gulf as far as Izmit, where they curve southwards towards Iznik; the pilgrim caravans, on the other hand, continued south-eastwards from Gebze for about 10 km. to Dil Iskelesi, a port situated at the narrowest point of the gulf, where they crossed to Hersek in order to go on to Iznik. Since 1873 Gebze has been connected with Ḥaydarpasha by a railway.

Bibliography: Kātib Čelebi, *Djihānnumā*, Istanbul 1145, 662; Ewliyā Čelebi, *Seyāḥatnāme*, ii, Istanbul 1314, 168-70; Ch. Samy Bey Fraschery, *Ḳāmūs al-aʿlām*, Istanbul 1314, v, 3870; V. Cuinet,

La Turquie d'Asie, iv, 687; C. Frh. v. d. Goltz, *Anatolische Ausflüge*, Berlin 1896, 74 ff.

(Fr. Taeschner)

GEDI or **GEDE,** a late mediaeval Arab-African town, built on a coral ridge four miles from the sea and ten miles south of Malindi on the Kenya Coast of East Africa. It is shown on sixteenth century Portuguese maps as Quelman, a rendering for the Swahili Kilimani, meaning "on the hill". Gedi is a Galla word meaning "precious", the name which the site acquired in the seventeenth century.

The ruins, excavated during the years 1948-58 and maintained as a National Park, cover an area of forty-five acres, and are surrounded by a town wall. They include a *d͟jāmiʿ*, seven other mosques, a palace, a number of private houses and three pillar tombs. The excavations have produced large quantities of Chinese porcelain and Islamic faïence, and also glass beads.

The single dated monument is a tomb with date 802/1399-1400. The original settlement may go back to the 7th/13th century, but the majority of the structures remaining are unlikely to be older than the 9th/15th century. It may have been destroyed in the early 10th/16th century, but was re-occupied at the end of the century. In the early 17th century it was abandoned as a result of the southern advance of the Galla from Somalia.

Bibliography: J. S. Kirkman, *Gedi the Great Mosque: Architecture and Finds*, Oxford 1954; idem, *Historical Archaeology in Kenya 1948-1956*, in *Ant. J.*, xxxvii (1957); idem, *The Tomb of the Dated Inscription at Gedi*, Roy. Anthropological Inst. Occ. Paper 14, 1959; idem, *Gedi, the Palace*, The Hague 1963. (J. S. Kirkman)

GEDIK [see ṢINF].

GEDIZ ČAYÎ, a river in west Anatolia, the former Hermos; it takes its modern name from Gediz, a place (39° 3′ N., 29° 29′ E.) near its source. It rises on Murat Dağı (2312 m.) and in its upper reaches flows through the Lydian mountains.

In its central section the Gediz Čay traverses the broad plain which is bounded on the south by Mount Sipylos (Manisa Daği), at the foot of which ties the town of Manisa [*q.v.*] (formerly Mag͟hnisa, the ancient Magnesia). Further along on the southern extremity of this plain lie the towns of Turgutlu (Kasaba) and Salıhlı which have been connected with Izmir by a railway since 1863. In this plain are also to be found the remains of the ancient Sardes, near Sartköy.

After forcing its way through a ridge of mountains the Gediz Čay flows past Menemen in the plain near to its mouth in the Gulf of Smyrna (Izmir). And indeed in ancient times and in the Middle Ages the river-mouth was dangerously near to the old port of Smyrna. Since the land round the river-mouth was continually being enlarged by deposits from the river and Izmir was in danger of being cut off from the sea, in 1886 the mouth was removed above Menemen, so that it now flows into the more open part of the Gulf. (Fr. Taeschner)

GEG [see ARNAWUTLUḲ].

GELIBOLU, in English Gallipoli, town on the European coast and at the Marmara end of the Dardanelles (Turkish: Čanaḳ-ḳalʿe Bog͟hazî [*q.v.*]), in the Ottoman period a naval base and the seat of the ḳapudan-pas͟ha [*q.v.*], now an *ilçe* belonging to the *il* of Çanakkale; the name derives from the Greek Kalliopolis, Kallioupolis, also Kallipolis (for the various forms see E. Oberhummer, in Pauly-Wissowa, x, 1659-60).

When, towards 700/1300, the Turks of Anatolia first concerned themselves with the town, it was one of the greatest and strongest Byzantine fortresses in Thrace (P. Lemerle, *L'émirat d'Aydin, Byzance et l'Occident*, Paris 1957, 69-70), the base, towards 720/1320, for all the crews of the Byzantine fleet. In the winter of 704/1304-5, the Catalans in the service of Byzantium were stationed there, and when their leader Roger de Flor was killed in the following year they seized and fortified this strategic position (L. Nicolau d'Olwer, *L'expansió de Catalunya en la Mediterrània oriental*, Barcelona 1926, *passim*). Some 500 Turks, led by Ed͟je K͟halīl, came from Ḳarasî [*q.v.*] to join them. When these Turks, returning from the raids they had made with the Catalans in Thrace, wished to cross back from the Gallipoli peninsula into Anatolia, they were attacked by the Byzantines (709/1309) and obliged to stay there two years longer (P. Wittek, *Yazîjîog͟hlu ʿAlī on the Christian Turks of the Dobruja*, in *BSOAS*, xiv (1952), 639-68, at 662-7). In 731/1331 or 732/1332 Umur Beg [*q.v.*] of Aydîn made an unsuccessful attack on Gelibolu with his fleet, but was able to seize and sack the fortress of 'Lazgöl' (Lazu ?) (Lemerle, *op. cit.*, 70). Enwerī (*Düstūrnāme*, ed. M. K͟halīl [Yınanç], Istanbul 1928, 25-6; ed. and tr. I. Mélikoff-Sayar, *Le Destan d'Umur Pacha*, Paris 1954, 62) states explicitly that this fortress was on the harbour, but Lemerle thinks it might be a small fort in the neighbourhood.

The Ottomans, under the command of Süleymān Pas͟ha [*q.v.*] and as allies of John Cantacuzenus, in 753/1352 occupied the fortress of Tzympe (in the Ottoman registers and in the *waḳfiye* of Süleymān Pas͟ha, 'D͟jinbi'), north of Gelibolu, and, occupying the whole of the hinterland, cut Gelibolu off from Thrace. In order to maintain pressure on the strong fortress, the Ottomans made an *ud͟j* here, under the command of Yaʿḳūb Ed͟je and G͟hāzī Fāḍil (ʿAs͟hiḳpas͟hazāde, ed. Giese, 45; tr. R. Kreutel, 77). While the Byzantines were trying to buy them off (Cantacuzenus, Bonn ed., iii, 278-81; Fr. tr. Cousin, *Hist. de Constantinople*, viii, Paris 1774, 230-1), a violent earthquake, on 7 Ṣafar 755/2 March 1354, destroyed the walls of Gelibolu (*Düstūrnāme*, 82; P. Wittek, in *Byzantion*, xii (1937), 320; P. Charanis, in *Byzantion*, xiii (1938), 347-9; idem in *Byzantinoslavica*, xvi (1955), 113-7). The Ottomans immediately occupied Gelibolu, and other neighbouring fortresses whose walls had been thrown down. Süleymān Pas͟ha crossed from Anatolia, repaired the citadel, and settled there Turks brought over from Anatolia (Cantacuzenus, *loc. cit.*). This occupation of Gelibolu made it possible for the Ottomans to install themselves in Europe: Süleymān Pas͟ha made Gelibolu the base for the conquests in Thrace (ʿAs͟hiḳpas͟hazāde, ed. Giese, 47; tr. Kreutel, 80), and Gelibolu became the first centre of the *Pas͟ha sand͟jag͟hî* in Rumeli. After Süleymān's death (758/1357), he was succeeded at Gelibolu by Prince Murād (later Murād I): the *taḥrīr*-registers mention his palace at Gelibolu (Tapu def. no. 67 [see *Bibl.*], 428). On 15 D͟hu 'l-Ḥid͟jd͟ja 767/23 August 1366, the Duke of Savoy, Amadeo VI, attacked Gelibolu with a Crusader fleet and captured it. The Crusaders handed it over to the Byzantines on 15 S͟hawwāl 768/14 June 1367 (N. Jorga, *GOR*, i, 226; idem, *Philippe de Mézières*, Paris 1896, 334-5). In a speech made in the summer of 773/1371, N. Cydones was urging that Gelibolu must not be returned to the Turks (*Oratio de reddenda Gallipoli*, in Migne, *PG*, cliv, 1009; R. J. Loenertz, *Les recueils de lettres de Demetrius Cydones*, Vatican 1947, 112), but finally

Andronicus IV yielded to the Sultan's insistence and returned the fortress to the Ottomans on 14 Rabīʿ II 778/3 September 1376 (G. Ostrogorsky, *History of the Byzantine State*, tr. J. Hussey, Oxford 1956, 483).

During the reign of Murād I Gelibolu was the regular crossing-point for Ottoman armies, and became also the principal base for the Ottoman fleet. In 791/1389 Murād I transported the army to Rumeli under the protection of the fleet stationed here, and left Yanīdj̲ Beg at Gelibolu to protect his line of communications with Anatolia (Nes̲h̲rī, ed. Taeschner, i, 68). In 790/1388 Venice had sent her fleet to make a threatening demonstration off Gelibolu (N. Iorga, *La politique vénitienne dans les eaux de la Mer Noire*, in *Bull. de la sec. d'histoire de l'Acad. Roumaine*, no. 2-4 (1914), 14-5). Indeed, during the 8th/14th and 9th/15th centuries, to blockade the Strait and destroy the Ottoman fleet at Gelibolu were always two main objectives in the plans of the Crusaders (such a plan had been mooted even before 767/1366: O. Halecki, *Un empereur de Byzance à Rome*, Warsaw 1930, 63-144; for the plan of 798/1396 see M. Silberschmidt, *Das orientalische Problem zur Zeit der Entstehung des türkischen Reiches*, Berlin 1923, 145; for the plan of 848/1444 see H. Inalcık, *Fatih devri* . . ., i, Ankara 1954, 12, 30); G. de Lannoy wrote in 825/1422: "Et qui auroit dit chastel et port les Turcs n'auroient nul sçeur passage plus de l'un à l'autre et seroit leur pays qu'ilz ont en Grèce comme perdu et deffect" (*Voyages et ambassades de Messire G. de Lannoy 1399-1450*, Mons 1840, 117-8).

Bāyezīd I well understood the vital importance of Gelibolu for his imperial policy. He rebuilt completely the ruined citadel and fortified with a strong tower the harbour, which was capable of accommodating large galleys. His aim was to control the Strait (Ducas, ed. Grecu, 41 = Turkish tr. by V. Mirmiroğlu, Istanbul 1956, 9; Silberschmidt, 115). In 806/1403, Clavijo saw a great arsenal and docks at Gelibolu and reported that the fortress was full of troops and that there were about 40 ships in the harbour; between the inner and the outer basins there was a bridge with a three-storey tower (presumably that which Ducas mentions) at one end of it to protect the inner harbour. G. de Lannoy, who visited Gelibolu in 825/1422, speaks of a "ville très grande" outside the wall; there was a citadel with eight towers, and a fine large square tower to protect the harbour. The harbour was protected on the seaward side by a wall (for a 16th century engraving see F. Kurtoğlu, *Gelibolu ve yöresi tarihi*, Istanbul 1938, 17), with a small gateway in it by which galleys entered the harbour; there was no chain. In the Gelibolu *defter* of 879/1475 (Cevdet O. 79 [see *Bibl.*], 154-62) this tower, 'Birg̲h̲oz-i Gelibolu' (Greek πύργος, reproduced with various spellings in Turkish), is mentioned separately from 'Ḳalʿe-i Gelibolu': it had a garrison of 42, 9 of them *tīmār*-holders and 33 on stipend (*ʿulūfeli*). The upper part of this tower was destroyed in 1920 (Kurtoğlu, *op. cit.*, pl. 32). In 1069/1659 Ewliyā Čelebi described Gelibolu as a strong fortress, hexagonal in shape, with 70 (?) towers of hewn stone (*Seyāḥatnāme*, v, 315).

By thus making Gelibolu into a powerful fortress and naval base and by strengthening the fleet (Silberschmidt, 159), Bāyezīd I hoped to establish complete control over the Strait, and compel foreign ships to halt off Gelibolu, undergo inspection and pay a due for the right of passage. But Venice decided to fight for the right of free passage through the Strait. In alliance with Hungary she planned to destroy both the naval base and the Ottoman fleet (Silberschmidt, *op. cit.*, 111-2, 145; F. Thiriet, *Régestes des délibérations du Sénat de Venise concernant la Romanie*, i, Paris 1958, docs. 881, 896). The Ottoman fleet was not in fact very powerful (Bāyezīd had 17 galleys); it would emerge from the shelter of the strong base at Gelibolu and attack Venetian territory and merchant ships in the Aegean, but only when the Venetian fleet was not at sea; and it could not prevent Marshal Boucicaut from sailing past Gelibolu in 1399, although it seriously hindered Venetian attempts to bring relief to Constantinople, then under investment by Bāyezīd (see Thiriet, *op. cit.*, ii, Paris 1959, doc. 1023). After the Ottoman defeat at Ankara (804/1402), the Venetian fleet was ordered to seize Gelibolu (Thiriet, *op. cit.*, ii, docs. 1070, 1078), but the plan was not carried out, and the Ottoman threat continued in the reign of Emīr Süleymān, so that Venice was obliged to send warships to protect her merchant ships in their passage through the Strait (Thiriet, *op. cit.*, ii, docs. 1283, 1431). In 812/1409 Emīr Süleymān built another fortress (the so-called 'Emīr Süleymān Burḳozī') at Lapseki on the Anatolian coast, primarily as a protection against his rivals in Anatolia. While the struggle among the Ottoman princes continued, Venice encouraged the Byzantines in their hopes of recovering Gelibolu (Thiriet, *op. cit.*, ii, doc. 1415) and came to an agreement with Mūsā Čelebi by which he granted her free passage through the Strait. In 817/1414 she was unable to renew this agreement with Meḥemmed I (Thiriet, *op. cit.*, ii, doc. 1538), so that Gelibolu became the main object of dispute in Venetian-Ottoman relations. When, in 818/1415, an Ottoman fleet based on Gelibolu attacked Venetian territory in the Aegean, the Venetian fleet, under Pietro Loredano, appeared off Gelibolu and, when the Ottoman fleet rashly emerged from the well-protected harbour, destroyed it (1 Rabīʿ II 819/29 May 1416; see Jorga, *GOR*, i, 372). Maḳrīzī (*al-Sulūk li-maʿrifat duwal al-mulūk*, MS. Istanbul, Fatih 4380, fol. 66a) mentions that the Venetians captured 12 ships (Venetian sources say 14, Ducas says 27) and killed 4000 Muslims. In spite of this victory, Venice was unable to achieve complete control of the Strait and remained obliged to convoy her merchant ships (see Thiriet, *op. cit.*, ii, docs. 1667, 1708, 1749, 1783, 1896). During the peace negotiations of 822/1419 Venice endeavoured above all to obtain freedom of passage past Gelibolu and exemption from tolls (Thiriet, ii, doc. 1750). In the Venetian-Ottoman war of 826/1423-834/1430 (for possession of Salonica/Selānik [*q.v.*]), Venetian attacks were mainly aimed at Gelibolu (see Thiriet, ii, docs. 1931, 1949; Jorga, *GOR*, i, 401; idem, *Notes et extraits* . . ., 2nd series, i, Paris 1899, 374). When her merchant ships were seized, the Venetian fleet under Silvestro Mocenigo launched an attack on the inner harbour: Mocenigo broke through the 'palissade' of the bridge and penetrated the inner harbour, but was obliged to retire (Iorga, *Notes et extraits* . . ., i, 505-6; *Tarihî takvimler*, ed. O. Turan, Ankara 1954, 26); the aim of the Venetians was to destroy once more the Ottoman fleet (Thiriet, ii, docs. 2189, 2212; Jorga, *GOR*, i, 409). At about this time the Emīr Süleymān Burḳozī at Lapseki was destroyed on the orders of Murād II, for fear that it should be occupied by the enemy (*Tarihî takvimler*, 26; according to Ducas, 149 = Turkish tr., 67, this occurred in 1417).

In 824/1421 the authorities at Constantinople hoped that the struggle for the throne between Murād II and his uncle Muṣṭafā would enable them to recover Gelibolu by negotiation, but neither of the rivals was willing to relinquish control of this important base (see *IA*, art. Murad II, 599-601). In the reign of Meḥemmed II, when the long war with Venice broke out (winter of 868/1463-4), two strong fortresses, named Kilīd al-baḥr and Ḳalʿe-i sulṭāniyye, were built on opposite sides of the Strait towards the Aegean end, and an arsenal and harbour were constructed in Istanbul at Ḳadirgha Limanî (see *IA*, art. Mehmed II, 523); nevertheless Gelibolu remained the principal harbour and naval base of the Empire (Iorga, *Notes et extraits*, iv, Bucharest 1915, 339) until superseded by the great arsenal and base constructed on the Golden Horn in 921/1515 (F. Kurtoğlu, *op. cit.*, 57-8). When the Venetian fleet attempted to gain control of the Strait during the war for Crete, two more fortresses were built at the Aegean entrance to the Strait, Seddü 'l-baḥr (Sadd al-baḥr) and Ḳum-ḳalʿesi, also called Khāḳāniyye and Sulṭāniyye (Naʿīmā, iv, 420; Silāḥdār, i, 168). By this time, according to Ewliyā (v, 317), Gelibolu had lost its former military importance and counted as '*ič-el*'.

When the Ottomans first occupied Gelibolu, the upper class of the Greek population fled by ship to Constantinople (*Düstūrnāme*, 83). Those that remained settled in the area known as Eski Gelibolu and the nearby village of Ḳozlu-Dere. The *taḥrīr*-register of 879/1474 (Cevdet O 79, see *Bibl.*) shows the Greeks of Gelibolu organized into two principal *djemāʿat*, the *kürekčiyān* (rowers) and the *zenberekčiyān* (arbalesters); of the latter, a group of 35 served in the citadel and a group of 22 in the 'tower'. A further 95 Greeks were organized into various *djemāʿat*s for ship-building and repair, and for the maintenance of the base. Some of these were paid a daily wage, others were recompensed by exemption from *kharādj*, *ispendje* and *ʿawāriḍ-i dīwāniyye*. The register of 925/1519, however, shows that all the members of these *djemāʿat*s were by then Muslims. It shows the Greeks living in six *maḥalle*s, and records also 80 Greeks as '*khaymāne*', organized in five *djemāʿat*s: these are presumably migrants who had come to settle at Gelibolu.

After the occupation, Gelibolu developed as a typical Ottoman city. The population at various dates, as revealed by the *taḥrīr*-registers, was:

879/1474	39 *maḥalle*s comprising 1095 households (*khāne*)
924/1518	55 *maḥalle*s comprising 1305 households
1009/1600	58 *maḥalle*s (four of them Christian and one Jewish).

Each *maḥalle* was usually named after the founder of the mosque which served it: most of these founders belonged to the military or to the theological class (*e.g.*, Ḥasan Pasha, Ṣarudja Pasha, Aḥmed Beg, Ḳapudan, Ḥādjdjī Dizdār, Shaykh Meḥmed, ʿAlī Faḳīh, Mütewellī Khoshḳadem, etc.); some were merchants (Kečedji Ḥādjdjī, Weled-i Ḳilabdandjī, Khwādja Ḥamza); the founder of the Ḥādjdjī Khiḍr mosque (Tapu def. 67, 509) was presumably the Ḥādjdjī Khiḍr who had accompanied Süleymān Pasha into Rumeli. According to Ewliyā Čelebi there were in his day some 300 two-storeyed houses in the fortress; outside the walls the city, with most of the principal buildings to the west, contained seven or eight hundred fine two-storeyed houses. The population in the middle years of the 19th century was 12-17,000 (N. V. Michoff, *La population de la Turquie et de la Bulgarie*, iv, Sofia 1935, 58, 94, 112, 128).

According to a register (Tapu def. 12), at the end of the reign of Meḥemmed II the principal buildings were: (1) the mosque of Ghāzī Khudāwendgār (Murād I), also known as Eski Djāmiʿ, with a bath (*ḥammām*) and a shop (*dükkān*) among its *waḳf*-properties; (2) the *zāwiye* and mosque of Ḳaradja Beg, built by the close associate of Emīr Süleymān, who was killed with him (Hammer-Purgstall, i, 349; on his grave-stone at Gelibolu he is called Ghāzī Ḳaradja b. ʿAbd Allāh and the date of his death is given as first decade of Shawwāl 813/end of February 1411); (3) the *ʿimāret* (with inscription dated 840/1436) and *medrese* of Ṣarudja Pasha, who was *beglerbegi* of Rumeli until 840/1436, when he was dismissed and banished to Gelibolu (see H. Inalcık, *Fatih devri* . . ., i, 86; Saʿd al-Dīn, i, 374): he appears as *sandjaḳ-begi* of Gelibolu until the winter of 847/1443; the *waḳf*-properties of his foundations were, at Gelibolu, a *bezzāzistān*, a *kārbānsarāy*, 96 shops, a bath and two abattoirs (see M. T. Gökbilgin, *Edirne ve Paşa Livâsı*, Istanbul 1952, 248); (4) the *zāwiye* and mosque of Khāṣṣ Aḥmed Beg (b. ʿAbd Allāh), an officer of Murād II; his *waḳfiye* (reproduced in M. T. Gölkbilgin, *op. cit.*, 257-61) is dated Shawwāl 863/August 1459; among the endowments he made are several shops and fields and a *kārbānsarāy* beside the quay at Gelibolu; for the property-grants (*temlīk*) made by Murād II there are deeds of confirmation (*muḳarrer-nāme*) issued by Meḥemmed II in 856/1452 and by Bāyezīd II in 886/1481; (5) the *medrese* of Balaban Pasha; the *waḳfiye* (Gökbilgin, *op. cit.*, 223), dated 846/1442, endows the *medrese* with a bath and some shops; (6) the *zāwiye* and *türbe* of Güyegü (Güvey = Dāmād) Sinān Pasha, the husband of Bāyezīd II's daughter ʿAyshe (ʿĀʾisha) Khatun; as *beglerbegi* of Anatolia he played a part in bringing Bāyezīd II to the throne; in 907/1501 he was *beglerbegi* of Rumeli, and from then until his death in 909/1503 was governor of Gelibolu and *Ḳapudan* (Saʿd al-Dīn, ii, 220-1); the *zāwiye*, of which the ruins survive, was built in 896/1491; the *türbe* was, in Ewliyā's day, a place of pilgrimage.

These and several other similar religious foundations, and the khans, markets, baths and shops, whose revenues supported them, promoted the development of Gelibolu as one of the chief cities of the Ottoman Empire. This development was most pronounced during the reign of Murād II, but important buildings were added in later years, such as the mosques of Mesīḥ Pasha [*q.v.*] and of Aḥmed Pasha (941/1534). Ewliyā Čelebi credits Gelibolu with 164 mosques, *zāwiye*s and *tekke*s, 14 *ʿimāret*s, 900 shops and 8 baths. The *tekke*s of Yazîdjîzāde Meḥmed [*q.v.*] and of the Mewlewī order (detailed description in Ewliyā, v, 318) were especially famous.

Gelibolu, known as 'Dar al-mudjāhidīn', remained the principal naval base and arsenal of the Empire until the 10th/16th century, so that a high proportion of its population consisted of fighting men. The register of 879/1474 shows the sailors organized in 4 *djemāʿat*s: captains (*reʾīs*) and *ʿazeb*s of (1) the galleys (*ḳadirgha*), (2) the galleots (*galyata*), (3) the '*ḳayiḳ*s' (at this period a *ḳayiḳ* was a transport big enough to take 14 horses), and (4) the horse-transports (*at gemileri*). Each *djemāʿat* was divided (like the *djemāʿat*s of the Janissaries [see YENI ČERI]) into a number of *bölük*s [*q.v.*]. The *djemāʿat* of the galleys comprised 92 *bölük*s: the first, that of the *Ḳapudan*, contained also, in two separate *djemāʿat*, 7 *mehter* [see MIHTER] and 5 non-Muslim '*kümi*' (from Latin *comes*, Greek κόμης, officer in charge of the galley-slaves, see Tietze and Kahane, *The Lingua Franca in the*

Levant, Urbana 1958, no. 789; these were mostly non-Muslims, Greeks or Genoese); it was headed by the *ḳapudan* and a *ser-oda*, the rest being *ʿazeb*s, *i.e.*, seamen. Each of the other *bölük*s was similarly composed of a *reʾīs* (captain), a *ser-oda*, a *kümi*, and a number of *ʿazeb*s. The captains and *ʿazeb*s were all Muslims (a captain named 'Frenk Ilyās' is presumably a convert). The *dj̲emāʿat* of the galleys comprised 1112 men, and the division into 92 *bölük*s shows that the strength of the fleet at that time was 92 galleys. There were 5 *bölük*s in the *dj̲emāʿat* of the galleots (hence 5 in number) and 11 in that of the *ḳayïḳ*s. In the register of 925/1519 we find 93 *bölük*s in the *dj̲emāʿat* of the galleys, and very little change in the organization. At the time of the Malta campaign of 973/1565, the construction of a new arsenal was begun (*Mühimme* register no. 5, p. 183; I. H. Uzunçarşılı, *Osmanlı devletinin merkez ve bahriye teşkilâti*, Ankara 1948, 395, n. 3).

Of the 59 captains making up the *dj̲emāʿat* of horse-transports, nine were holders of *čiftlik*s [*q.v.*] in the neighbourhood, the rest drew stipends (*ʿulūfe*); they served only on campaigns. In 925/1519 they were all stipendiary, *i.e.*, more closely bound to the service of the state. 181 *k̲h̲āne* (households) of *ʿazeb*s were registered as living in various *maḥalle*s of the town, liable to be called to serve when necessary. In the town and in the nearby Greek villages of Maydos and Kirte there were living Christian *kürekči*s (rowers) who served in the fleet in return for exemption from taxes.

Besides these naval crews, there were the garrisons of the citadel (*ḳalʿe*), consisting in 879/1474 of 56 men (27 with *tīmār*s, 29 with *ʿulūfe*), and of the 'tower', consisting of 42 men (9 with *tīmār*s, 33 with *ʿulūfe*). The *dj̲emāʿat*s of Christians who rendered service as arbalesters or in the upkeep of these fortresses numbered 60-65 men.

The first *odj̲aḳ* of *ʿadj̲amī og̲h̲lan*s [*q.v.*] was established at Gelibolu. In the 10th/16th century they numbered between four and five hundred, and served on the transports plying between Gelibolu and Čardaḳ.

Particularly in the 9th/15th century, Gelibolu was the most important point on the great trade-route between Bursa (via Mik̲h̲ālič—Big̲h̲ā—Lapseki or Čardaḳ) and Rumeli (see H. Inalcık, in *Belleten*, xxiv/93 (1960), 55). From Gelibolu the Florentines carried the silk which they had bought in Bursa overland, via Edirne, Foča and Ragusa; at Gelibolu, Italian ships took on cotton and nut-gall (W. Heyd, *Hist. du commerce du Levant*, ii, Leipzig 1936, 300, 337, 665). The register of 879/1474 records five families of 'Franks' at Gelibolu, that of 925/1519, eight. At about this time 15 Jewish families had come from Istanbul to settle here as merchants. In the reign of Meḥemmed II there were also Venetian trading-houses (Heyd, *op. cit.*, ii, 328).

Before the capture of Constantinople, Gelibolu was one of the principal customs-houses of the Ottoman Empire. Under Meḥemmed II the *muḳāṭaʿa* ([*q.v.*] tax-farm) of the Gelibolu customs was included in that of the customs of Istanbul. The customs levied at all harbours from Edj̲e-ovasî to Tekfur-dag̲h̲î (Rodosto) were farmed out as a separate *muḳāṭaʿa*; in about 880/1475 the 'Gelibolu customs' brought in some 9000 gold ducats (about 400,000 *aḳča*s) a year (F. Babinger, *Die Aufzeichnungen des Genuesen Iacopo de Promontorio-de Campis* ..., Munich 1957 (*SBBayr.Ak.*, 1956/8), 63); in 1009/1600 it brought in 766,663 *aḳča*s (*Mufaṣṣal* register 141 [see *Bibl.*]); Ewliyā Čelebi (v, 316) gives a similar figure—700,000 *aḳča*s—for 1069/1658-9. But by this time the port was declining, and the French consulate there was closed in 1100/1689. Customs dues (for the rates see MAKS) were levied at Istanbul or Gelibolu on all cargoes, and it was also the practice that a 'gift' (*armag̲h̲an*) should be given to the *sandj̲aḳ-begi* and the *emīn* ([*q.v.*], 'intendant') (R. Anhegger and H. Inalcık, *Ḳānūnnāme-i sulṭānī ber mūceb-i ʿörf-i ʿOsmānī*, Ankara 1956, 48, 63, 79; cf. N. Beldiceanu, *Les actes des premiers sultans* ..., Paris-The Hague 1960, 112 ff, 133 ff., 151-2). Every foreign ship, after being inspected at Istanbul, was inspected again at Gelibolu before passing out into the Mediterranean and issued with an *idj̲āzet ted̲h̲kiresi* ('clearance'); in about 1091/1680 the charge for this '*id̲h̲n-i sefīne*' was about 100 *ḳurus̲h̲*; the revenue from these charges amounted in 1009/1600 to 610,000 *aḳča*s. By article 27 of the French capitulation of 1153/1740, ships inspected at Istanbul were relieved from the obligation to be inspected again at Gelibolu.

Gelibolu served also as the principal control-point for traffic between Rumeli and Anatolia. A traveller going in either direction was obliged to obtain from the *ḳāḍī* of his starting-point a 'chit' (*ted̲h̲kire*) attesting the purpose of his journey and produce it to the authorities at Gelibolu. The '*pendj̲ik resmi*' [see PENDJ̲IK], levied on enslaved prisoners-of-war being transported from Rumeli to Anatolia, was collected at Gelibolu by the '*pendj̲ik emīni*'. Gelibolu was also a centre for the slave-trade. Here too a tax of four *aḳča*s a head was levied on sheep and goats being taken from Rumeli to Anatolia; this tax brought in 66,499 *aḳča*s in 1009/1600. There was an additional levy of 80 *aḳča*s per thousand sheep, which was assigned to the *k̲h̲āṣṣ* of the *sandj̲aḳ begi*.

The chief exports from Gelibolu were wheat (see A. Refik, *Onaltıncı asırda Istanbul hayatı*, Istanbul 1935, 82), cotton, fish, wine and arrack (idem, *Hicri onikinci asırda Istanbul hayatı*, Istanbul 1930, 119), bows and arrows, and naval stores such as cables and sails. In 1009/1600 the 'municipal' taxes, which were assigned to the *k̲h̲āṣṣ* of the *sandj̲aḳ-begi*, amounted to 15,000 *aḳča*s from *iḥtisāb* [see ḤISBA] dues, 12,000 *aḳčas* from *niyābet* [*q.v.*] dues, and 3,500 *aḳčas* from the *s̲h̲emʿk̲h̲āne* [see S̲H̲AMʿ].

Until 940/1533 Gelibolu was the chef-lieu of a *sandj̲aḳ* belonging to the *beglerbegilik* of Rumeli (see M. T. Gökbilgin, in *Belleten*, xx/78 (1956), 252). As commander of the fleet, the *sandj̲aḳ-begi* of Gelibolu held a position of especial eminence among the other *sandj̲aḳ-begis*: his *k̲h̲āṣṣ* approached in value the *k̲h̲āṣṣ* of a *beglerbegi* (500,000 *aḳča*s early in the reign of Süleymān I, 605,000 later in that reign). The post of *sandj̲aḳ-begi* was often given to prominent statesmen—dismissed viziers or *beglerbegis*, or pas̲h̲as with the rank of *beglerbegi*. When in 940/1533 K̲h̲ayr al-Dīn Pas̲h̲a [*q.v.*] ('Barbarossa') was appointed both *beglerbegi* of Algiers and Ḳapudan Pas̲h̲a [*q.v.*], Gelibolu was incorporated in this *beglerbegilik*; later it became the chef-lieu of the *eyālet* of *Dj̲azāʾir-i Baḥr-i Safīd* [*q.v.*], *i.e.*, the '*Pas̲h̲a-sandj̲ag̲h̲î*' of the Ḳapudan Pas̲h̲a [see EYĀLET, SANDJ̲AḲ]. According to the register of 1009/1600, the *nāḥiye*s of the *sandj̲aḳ* were: Gelibolu and Evres̲h̲e (together), Lemnos, Tas̲h̲oz (Thasos), Mig̲h̲alḳara (Malkara) and Harala (together), Abri, Kes̲h̲an, Ipsala, Gümüldj̲ine. In the time of ʿAyn-i ʿAlī (*Ḳawānīn*, Istanbul 1280, 20 = German tr. by P. A. von Tischendorf, *Das Lehnwesen* ..., Leipzig 1872, 70 f.) it contained 14 *zeʿāmet*s and 85 *tīmār*s, in the time of Ewliyā Čelebi (v, 316), 6 *zeʿāmet*s and 122 *tīmār*s.

During the confinement there of the pseudo-Messiah Shabbetay Ṣebi [*q.v.*] in 1666, Gelibolu briefly became a place of pilgrimage for his Jewish disciples.

By the new provincial law of 1281/1864, Gelibolu became a *sandjak* (*liwāʾ*) of the *wilāyet* of Edirne, containing in 1287/1870 six *ḳaḍās*: Gelibolu, Sharköy, Firedjik, Keshan, Malḳara and Enoz (*Edirne sālnāmesi*, 1271). The *sandjak* was later reduced in size, to comprise only the three *ḳaḍās* of Keshan, Mürefte and Sharköy (*Edirne sālnāmesi*, 1309). The town is now the centre of an *ilçe*, population (1960) 12,945.

Bibliography: I. Archive material: (1) *Defter-i esāmī-i sandjak-i Gelibolu* (awāʾil Shawwāl 879/February 1475), Istanbul, Belediye Library, Cevdet collection no. 79 (a *mufaṣṣal* register, lacking at the end the section on Malḳara); (2) *Gelibolu sandjaghî müsellemān ve piyādegān defteri* (the *taḥrīr* of 879/1475), Istanbul, Başvekâlet Arşivi, Tapu defteri no. 12; (3) *Gelibolu sandjaghî müsellemān ve piyādegān defteri* (Dhu 'l-Ḳaʿda 925/November 1519), Istanbul, Başvekâlet Arşivi, Tapu defteri no. 67 (the *ḳānūn-nāme* at the beginning of this register has been published by Ö. L. Barkan, *Kanunlar*, Istanbul 1943, 240-2); (4) *Gelibolu sandjaghî mufaṣṣal taḥrīr defteri* (Dhu 'l-Ḳaʿda 925/November 1519), Istanbul, Başvekâlet Arşivi, Tapu defteri no. 75 (its *ḳānūn-nāme* published by Barkan, *op. cit.*, 235-6); (5) *Gelibolu sandjaghî mufaṣṣal taḥrīr defteri*, Ankara, Tapu ve Kadastro Umum Müdürlüğü, Eski Kayıtlar dairesi, mufassal def. no. 141 (with a *ḳānūn-nāme* at the beginning); (6) *Defter-i idjmāl-i Gelibolu*, as (5), no. 293 (defective at the end).

II. Travellers: Ewliyā Čelebi, *Seyāḥat-nāme*, v, 320-9 (description used by A. D. Mordtmann, *Ein Ausflug nach Gallipoli*, in *Das Ausland*, xxxii (1859), 166, and J. H. Kissling, *Beiträge zur Kenntnis Thrakiens im 17. Jh.*, Wiesbaden 1956, 49-53); Kātib Čelebi (Ḥādjdjī Khalīfa), *Djihān-nümā*, tr. Hammer, *Rumeli und Bosna*, 59 ff. (the *Djihānnümā-i Avrūpā* attributed to Sheykh Meḥmed [Istanbul, Süleymaniye Lib., MS Hamidiye 932, fols. 11-12] is more detailed); Samuel Yemshel, in B. Lewis, *A Karaite itinerary through Turkey in 1641-2*, in *Vakıflar Dergisi*, iii (1957), 317-8; G. de Lannoy, *Voyages et ambassades de Messire Guillebert de Lannoy, 1399-1450*, Mons 1840, 117-8; Pierre Belon, *Les observations de plusieurs singularitéz . . .*, Paris 1553, 76 v.; F. de la Boullaye-le-Gouz, *Les voyages et observations*, Paris 1653, 24-5; V. Stochove, *Voyage du Levant*, Rouen 1687, 25.

III. Studies: Fevzi Kurtoğlu, *Gelibolu ve yöresi tarihi*, Istanbul 1938; idem, *XVI ıncı asrın ilk yarımında Gelibolu*, in *Türkiyat Mecmuası*, v (1935), 291-306; H. Högg, *Türkenburgen an Bosporus und Hellespont*, Dresden 1932; ʿAlī Riḍā Seyfī, *Čannaḳḳalʿe Boghazî ve djiwārî*, Istanbul 1327. (Halil Inalcik)

GEMLIK, the ancient Kios, a small port in north-west Anatolia, 40° 25′ N., 29° 9′ E., on the Gulf of Gemlik, an inlet on the Sea of Marmara, at the end of a depression through which flows a stream (Gardak Su, formerly the Askanios) and which after 15 km. leads to the Iznik Gölü, the Lake of Iznik/Nikaia (formerly Askaniē limnē, 80 m. above sea-level), between the mountains of the Samanlî Daghî in the north and the Ḳaṭîrlî Daghî in the south, and situated on the road leading from Bursa to the port of Yalova; a *ḳaḍā* in the *vilāyet* of Bursa, at one time in the *liwā* of Khudāwendkār (Bursa) of the *eyālet* of Anadolu. Population in 1960: the town, 12,640, the *ilçe* 30,673, before the first world war mostly Greeks (the modern Greek name of the town is Kio).

By the time of ʿOthmān, probably towards the end of his life, Gemlik had apparently already come under his sway, being the last of his conquests.

Bibliography: Kātib Čelebi, *Djihānnümā*, Istanbul 1145, 658; V. Cuinet, *La Turquie d'Asie*, iv, 141; Ch. Samy Fraschery, *Ḳāmūs al-aʿlām*, v, Istanbul 1314, 3888 f. (Fr. Taeschner)

GENEALOGY [see NASAB].

GENEROSITY [see KARAM].

GENIE [see DJINN].

GENIL [see SHANĪL].

GENIZA, a Hebrew word of the same Persian origin as Arabic *djanāza*, designates a place where Hebrew writings were deposited in order to prevent the desecration of the name of God which might be found in them. As a term of scholarship, Geniza, or Cairo Geniza, refers to writings coming from the store-room of the "Synagogue of the Palestinians" in Fusṭāṭ [*q.v.*] and, to a small extent, from the cemetery al-Basātīn near that ancient city. When the synagogue was pulled down and rebuilt in 1889-90, a good deal of the manuscripts preserved in its Geniza were dispersed and acquired by various libraries in Europe and the United States, until, in 1897, Solomon Schechter brought the bulk of what remained to the University Library, Cambridge, England, where it forms the famous Taylor-Schechter Collection.

Naturally, it was mostly Hebrew literature which gained from these treasures. Paul E. Kahle's book with the somewhat misleading title *The Cairo Geniza* (second edition, New York 1960) deals exclusively with this aspect. For Islamic studies, it is mainly the documentary material, such as letters, accounts, court records, contracts etc., which is of immediate interest. Most of these documents come from Fāṭimid and Ayyūbid times; there is little from the Mamlūk period; but from the 10th/16th century onwards, the Geniza was again used somewhat more frequently, albeit in a sporadic way. This article is concerned with "the classical Geniza", the three hundred years between 354/965 and 663/1265 approximately.

The major part of the documentary material of the Cairo Geniza is written in Arabic language, though in Hebrew characters. Business letters were invariably and family letters generally written in Arabic, and the same applies to court records and other legal documents with the exception of writs of divorce, deeds of manumission and the formal—but not the substantial—parts of marriage contracts. Only subjects related to religion or the life of the Jewish community were largely, but by no means exclusively, transacted in Hebrew. As to the number of the Geniza documents preserved, if we disregard mere scraps and confine ourselves to complete pieces and fragments which are self-contained, meaningful units, we arrive at a total of about ten thousand items.

In addition to Egypt itself, Tunisia and Sicily are conspicuously represented in the Geniza. This has its reason in their prominence in Mediterranean trade during the first half of the 5th/11th century and the migration of many Maghribīs to Egypt in the second half (see S. D. Goitein, *La Tunisie du XIe siècle à la lumière des documents de la Geniza du Caire*, in *Études d'Orientalisme . . . Lévi Provençal*, 1962, 559-79). Most of the Geniza letters dealing with the India trade come from the 6th/12th century, but here again we find that the majority of the Mediterranean merchants active in South Arabia and India were Maghribīs (see idem, *Letters and documents on the India trade in medieval times*, in *IC*, xxvii (1963), 188-205). Spain is only sparsely represented during the 5th/11th century (see E. Ashtor, *Documentos españoles de la Genizah*, in *Sefarad*, xxiv (1964), 41-80), and somewhat more generously during the 6th/12th, but Spanish products loom large in the Geniza papers and so do persons called 'Andalusī', although many of these seem to have originated in countries other than Spain. There is much correspondence from Palestine and the cities on the coast of Lebanon and Syria, but very little from Damascus and other Syrian and Mesopotamian cities and next to nothing from Baghdād. On the other hand, thousands of responsa (*fatwās*) and a number of letters of the heads of the two Jewish academies of Baghdād have been found in the Geniza. Most of them were addressed to places in Tunisia and Morocco, but were preserved in Fusṭaṭ, partly because they were copied there before being sent on to the West and partly because they were brought back by immigrants from the Maghrib. Still, the discrepancy between the abundance of official correspondence with Baghdād and the almost complete absence of business and private letters is not easily explained. A few Persian items (see D. S. Margoliouth, *A Jewish Persian law-report*, in *JQR* xi (1898-9), 671-5 (there are more)), and one or two beautifully written Arabic letters from Iran have also been found.

Material in Arabic characters also made its way into the Geniza, either because blank reverse sides of Arabic documents were used for Hebrew writings, or because the persons concerned were Jewish, or for no apparent reason. Much of this material is dispersed all over the various Geniza collections. In the Cambridge University Library some of it was put aside in boxes labelled 'Mohammedan', which is, however, somewhat inaccurate, since most of the documents contained in them concerned Jews. There are a number of pieces from the Fāṭimid chanceries (see *Bibl.*) as well as a variety of material on widely different topics: thus, two Christians lease from a Muslim two-thirds of his vegetable garden (the vegetables to be grown are specified) on the outskirts of Alexandria; an archer (*aḥad al-rumāt*) in prison requests his commander to work for his release; a *fundukānī*, or proprietor of a caravanserai, undertakes to transport to the *ṣināʿa*, the customs station on the Nile at Fusṭāṭ, all consignments for which no customs had been paid, whether brought to his own *funduk* or to any other in the city; a tax-farmer makes a contract with a representative of the caliph al-Mustanṣir; the *al-sāda al-fukahāʾ* are requested to give a *fatwā* in a disputed case of inheritance, etc. Jews also corresponded sometimes with each other in Arabic characters. When a schoolmaster writes a complaint to a father about his son in this way, he certainly did so because he did not want the boy, who thus far had learned only the Hebrew letters, to read it. When a scholar boasting of his Jewish learning asks a notable for financial help in a letter written in Arabic characters, he followed that course because he knew that the addressee was more fluent in Arabic than in Hebrew (there is an express statement to this effect). However, even a letter addressed to the Gaon, or head of the Jewish academy of Jerusalem, and dealing exclusively with communal affairs, is written in Arabic characters.

Research on the Geniza documents began immediately after their discovery in the eighteen-nineties. A survey of the widely scattered publications is contained in S. Shaked (see *Bibl.*). Jacob Mann's work, although intended to serve Jewish history, is important for Islamic studies as well, and so are the publications of S. Assaf and D. H. Baneth, which are, however, all in Hebrew. The importance of the Geniza documents for the economic, social and cultural history of mediaeval Islam, as well as for the history of the Arabic language, is being more and more recognized. Joshua Blau, *A Grammar of mediaeval Judaeo-Arabic*, Jerusalem 1961, is a mine of linguistic information, and, albeit in Hebrew, can be used with profit also by scholars not familiar with that language, since each paragraph has also a name in English and consists mainly of examples culled from the Geniza and similar sources. E. Ashtor is completing a book on prices in mediaeval Islam, based largely on the Geniza. N. Golb has prepared an edition of the magnificent series 18 J of the Taylor-Schechter Collection with an English translation and commentary. S. D. Goitein has written two volumes containing a general survey of the Geniza material under the title *A Mediterranean society: The Jewish communities of the Arab world as portrayed in the Cairo Geniza*, accompanied by a volume of selected translations in English, called *Readings in Mediterranean social history*. His collection of Geniza papers dealing with the India trade amounts now to 315 items. M. Michael is preparing an edition of letters emanating from or addressed to Nahray ben Nissim, a prominent Ḳayrawānī merchant scholar and public figure who was active in Egypt in the second half of the 5th/11th century. Muhammad El-Garh of Cairo University is preparing a selection in Arabic characters of Geniza documents written in Hebrew script.

The Geniza contains also a considerable number of fragments of Judaeo-Arabic literature (see, *e.g.*, the series of articles *The Arabic portion of the Cairo Genizah at Cambridge*, in *JQR*, xv-xvi (1902-4), by H. Hirschfeld), and some items from Islamic Arabic literature, which might not have been preserved otherwise, *e.g.*, a manual of correspondence prepared for Muhadhdhab al-Dawla ʿAlī b. Naṣr (cf. D. S. Margoliouth, *Eclipse*, Index 93), publ. by Richard Gottheil in *BIFAO*, xxxiv (1933), 103-28, under the title *Fragments from an Arabic Commonplace book*, or *A Muhammedan book of augury in Hebrew characters*, publ. I. Friedlaender, in *JQR*, xix (1907-8), 84-102. Cf. also H. Hirschfeld, *A Hebraeo-Sufic poem*, in *JAOS*, xlix (1929), 168-73, and the literature on the subject noted by S. M. Stern, in *JQR*, l (1960), 356, n. 21.

Bibliography: S. Shaked, *A tentative bibliography of Geniza documents*, Paris-The Hague 1964; S. D. Goitein, *The Documents of the Cairo Geniza as a source for Mediterranean social history*, in *JAOS*, lxxx (1960), 91-100; idem, *Studies in Islamic history and institutions*, Leiden 1965, chapters XII-XVIII; Jacob Mann, *Texts and studies*, Philadelphia 1935; R. Gottheil and W. H. Worrell, *Fragments from the Cairo Genizah in the Freer Collection*, New York 1927; A. Merx, *Documents de paléographie hebraique et arabe*, Leiden 1894; David Kaufmann, *Beiträge zur Geschichte Aegyptens aus jüdischen Quellen*, in *ZDMG*, li (1897), 436-52; idem, *Letter sent to Constantinople by Alafdhal's ex-minister of finance*, in *JQR*, x (1897-8), 430-44; J. H. Greenstone, *The Turkoman defeat at Cairo, by Solomon ben Joseph ha-Kohen*, in *AJSLL*, xxii (1905-6), 144-75; E. J. Worman, *Forms of address in*

Genizah letters, in *JQR*, xix (1907-8); I. Goldziher, *Formules dans les lettres de "Gueniza"*, in *REJ*, lv (1908), 54-7; E. Ashtor, *Le coût de la vie dans l'Égypte médiévale*, in *JESHO*, iii (1960), 56-77; idem, *Matériaux pour l'histoire des prix dans l'Égypte médiévale*, in *JESHO*, vi (1963), 158-89; idem, *Le coût de la vie en Palestine au moyen âge*, in *Eretz Israel*, vii (1964), 154-64; S. D. Goitein, *The main industries of the Mediterranean area as reflected in the records of the Cairo Geniza*, in *JESHO*, iv (1961), 168-97; idem, *Slaves and slavegirls in the Cairo Geniza records*, in *Arabica*, ix (1962), 1-20; idem, *Evidence on the Muslim poll tax from non-Muslim sources: a Geniza study*, in *JESHO*, vi (1963), 278-95; idem, *The commercial mail service in medieval Islam*, in *JAOS*, lxxxiv (1964); N. Golb, *Legal documents from the Cairo Geniza*, in *Jewish Social Studies*, xx (1958), 17-46; S. M. Stern, *An original document from the Fatimid chancery concerning Italian merchants*, in *Studi ... Levi Della Vida*, ii, Rome 1956, 529-38; idem, *Three petitions of the Fatimid period*, in *Oriens*, xv (1962), 172-209; idem, *Studies in Ibn Quzman IV*, in *Andalus*, xvi (1951), 411-21; Sophie Walzer, *An illustrated leaf from a lost Mamlūk Kalīlah wa-Dimnah*, in *Ars Orientalis*, ii (1957), 503-5; Abdul-Jalil Badria Abdul-Kader, *Arabic Epistolary Art in the twelfth century* (M. A. thesis, Univ. of Pennsylvania, 1962). (S. D. Goitein)

GEOGRAPHY [see <u>DJUGH</u>RĀFIYĀ].

GEOMANCY [see RAML].

GEOMETRY [see HANDASA].

GEORGIA [see KURDJ].

GERDEK RESMI [see ʿARŪS RESMI].

GERMIYĀN-OGHULLARÎ. Germiyān, at first the name of a Turkoman tribe, was afterwards applied to a family, then to an amīrate. Mentioned from the 6th/12th century in the history of the Anatolian Turks, the Germiyān appeared for the first time in 636-7/1239 in the reign of the Saldjūḳid Ghiyāth al-Dīn Kaykhusraw II; at this time the Germiyān Muẓaffar al-Dīn b. ʿAlī Shīr, installed in the region of Malaṭya, was sent at the head of a troop of Kurds and Germiyān against the Turkoman rebel Baba Isḥāḳ (cf. Ibn Bībī, ed. Houtsma, 229, 232). It was, however, in western Anatolia, in the region of Kütāhya, that the Germiyān were in 675-6/1277 when, under the leadership of Ḥusām al-Dīn b. ʿAlī Shīr, they took part in the punitive expedition against Djimrī and his ally Meḥmed the Ḳaramānid (cf. Ibn Bībī, 326-7, 332). After the execution of Ghiyāth al-Dīn Kaykhusraw III by the Mongols in 682/1283, and the accession of Masʿūd II, it seems that the Germiyān sought to break their bonds of vassalage towards the Saldjūḳids and to proclaim their independence. The downfall of Masʿūd, however, put an end to the hostilities between the Germiyān and the Saldjūḳids, as is revealed by an inscription in the mosque of Ḳîzîl Beg at Ankara, dated 699/1299, according to which Yaʿḳūb b. ʿAlī Shīr, whose possessions at that time extended up to this town, declared himself a vassal of ʿAlāʾ al-Dīn Kayḳobād III. This Yaʿḳūb b. ʿAlī Shīr was the founder of the amīrate of Germiyān, under the nominal suzerainty of the Saldjūḳ sultan and the Mongol Ilkhān; the breakdown of the central power was progressively to give him complete independence. According to al-ʿUmarī he was the most powerful of the Turkish amīrs; he led a princely life and exercised a suzerain's authority over the neighbouring amīrs, many of whom, such as his former *ṣubashî* Meḥmed Beg Aydîn-oghlu, had at first waged war in his name before becoming independent; the Byzantine emperor paid him an annual tribute of 100,000 pieces of gold. The amīr of Germiyān, whose capital was Kütāhya, occupied the greater part of the ancient Phrygia, according to Gregoras (i, 214); his sovereignty extended to the region of Ṭoñuzlu-Lādīḳ, which was governed by a member of his family, and to that of Ḳaraḥiṣār, where his son-in-law was amīr; Pachymeres (ii, 426, 433, 435) attributes to him possession of Tripoli on the Menderes, and al-ʿUmarī that of Gümüsh-Shār (not to be confused with the town of the same name in northern Cappadocia) where there were important silver and alum mines, and of Sivri-Köy, a rice-producing region; the conquest of the regions of Sīmav and Kula, regained by the Catalans and then reconquered by his son Meḥmed, is attested by the inscription of the *madrasa* of Yaʿḳūb II at Kütāhya; Yaʿḳūb b. ʿAlī Shīr also coveted Philadelphia (Alashehir), to which he laid siege but which was liberated by the Catalans in the spring of 703/1304 (cf. Pachymeres, ii, 421, 427-8); we learn, however, from an inscription in the Wādjidiyya *madrasa* in Kütāhya that in 714/1314 the town of Alashehir, the only Byzantine possession in Turkish territory, had been forced by him to pay the *djizya*. In the reign of Yaʿḳūb I the amīrate of Germiyān was prosperous; it was famous for its breeding of horses, the best in all Anatolia, and for its cloths and brocades; thanks to the Menderes it maintained an active commerce, transporting goods by this waterway as far as the Aegean Sea ports. The date of the death of Yaʿḳūb I is not known; it took place after 720/1320. His successor was his son Meḥmed Beg, on whom there is little information; a court romance composed for his elder son, Süleymān Shāh, relates that Meḥmed Beg was surnamed Čakhshadān (cf. *Khurshīdnāme*, B.M. ms. Or. 11408, fol. 14 v°). We also know, from the inscription of his grandson mentioned above, that he reconquered the regions of Sīmav and Kula which the Catalans had retaken from his father. The date of his death is not known; but, from the inscriptions of his son Süleymān Shāh, it is known that the latter was reigning by 764/1363. In Süleymān's time the Germiyān amīrate was no longer the prosperous state described by al-ʿUmarī: separated from the sea by the coastal principalities founded by his former vassals, Aydîn-oghlu, Ṣarukhan, Ḳaresi, the Germiyān amīrate was reduced to the situation of an inland state confined by the states of two rival powers, the Ḳaramān-oghlu and the ʿOthmānlî. Before the increasing threats towards him by the amīr of Ḳaramān, Süleymān Shāh decided, forgetting the hostilities which had opposed his family to that of the ʿOthmānlî, to align himself with the latter and to consolidate their friendly relations by matrimonial ties: in 783/1381 he gave his daughter Dewlet Khātūn in marriage to the prince Yîldîrîm Bāyazīd, with the towns of Kütāhya, Sīmav, Egrigöz (Emed) and Ṭawshanlî as dowry, and himself withdrew to Kula (cf. ʿĀshîḳpashazāde in *Osmanlı tarihleri*, i, 129-31; Neshrī, Türk Tarih Kurumu ed., i, 203-9). Süleymān Shāh was a generous and benevolent prince and a patron of men of letters; many works were written for him: at his request Baba ʿAlī b. Ṣāliḥ b. Ḳuṭb al-Dīn translated the *Ḳābūs-nāme* and the *Marzbān-nāme* from Persian; Shaykh-oghlu Muṣṭafā, who filled the offices of *nishāndjî*, *defterdār* and treasurer at his court, composed for him a work in prose entitled *Kanz al-kubarāʾ* and, in particular, the *Khurshīdnāme*, a verse romance manuscripts of which exist in Istanbul, London and Paris, and which is a valuable source of information; from this work we learn that Süleymān died in 789/1387. His son Yaʿḳūb II, called Yaʿḳūb Čelebi in his inscriptions, succeeded him. In 791/1389, on the death of Murād I, Yaʿḳūb Čelebi, in connivance with the Anatolian amīrs, turned against the sultan Bāyazīd I, and tried to regain the towns given to his sister as dowry; but Bāyazīd I, free from the affairs of Rumeli, chastised the Anatolian begs in 792/1390, imprisoned Yaʿḳūb in the fortress of Ipsala, and annexed the whole of the Germiyān amīrate (cf. ʿĀshîḳpashazāde, 139-40; Neshrī, i, 315). After nine years in captivity Yaʿḳūb succeeded in making his escape and, in disguise, reached Syria by sea, where he joined Tīmūrleng. During the battle of Ankara he contributed to the capture of Bāyazīd I by pointing him out to Tīmūrleng on the battlefield (cf. ʿĀshîḳpashazāde, 142-4; Neshrī, i, 343, 353). After his victory Tīmūr restored the Germiyān amīrate to Yaʿḳūb, together with the towns which had been given to his sister as dowry (804/1402). In the dynastic struggle which involved the sons of Bāyazīd I, Yaʿḳūb aligned himself with his sister's son Meḥmed Čelebi. Robbed once more of his principality in 814/1411 by the amīr of Ḳaramān, who took the opportunity in this troubled period to enlarge his territories, he had his amīrate restored to him, after two and a half years of exile, by Meḥemmed I, who had triumphed first over his brothers and then over the amīr of Ḳaramān. Yaʿḳūb II was thereafter able to reign under the protection of the ʿOthmānlîs. In 824/1421, however, on the death of Meḥemmed I, he upheld, with the amīr of Ḳaramān, the claim to the throne of the young brother of Murād II, Küčük Muṣṭafā (cf. ʿĀshîḳpashazāde, 160-1; Neshrī, ii, 567-71). After the tragic end of this unfortunate prince relations between Yaʿḳūb II and Murād II became more and more friendly. In 831/1428 the amīr of Germiyān, at the end of his life and without male heirs, decided to bequeath by will his principality to Murād II; on this occasion the sultan offered him a sumptuous reception at Edirne. Yaʿḳūb II was to die a year after this event, at Kütāhya, and, in accordance with his last wishes, Murād II annexed the principality of Germiyān (cf. ʿĀshîḳpashazāde, 171-2; Neshrī, ii, 605-7). Like his father, Yaʿḳūb II had been a learned prince, renowned for his generosity, and a great patron of men of letters; his court was adorned with scholars like Isḥāḳ Faḳīh, and with poets like Aḥmedī, his brother Ḥamzawī, Aḥmed-i Dāʿī, and above all Shaykhī, known as *Shaykh al-shuʿarāʾ*, who in his *ḳaṣīdas* celebrated the virtues of his patron. All these poets and scholars were to move on to the court of the ʿOthmānlî sultans and there contribute to the development of classical poetry.

Bibliography: in addition to the references in the text: ʿUmarī, ed. Taeschner, 22, 30, 32-40, 42, 47, 50; I. H. Uzunçarşılı, *Kütahya şehri*, Istanbul 1932; idem, *Anadolu beylikleri*, Ankara 1937; idem, *Osmanlı tarihi*, i, Ankara 1947, 14-5; idem, in *IA*, art. Germiyân-Oğulları; Cl. Cahen, *L'origine des Germyan*, in *JA*, ccxxxix (1951), 349-54.

(I. MÉLIKOFF)

GERONA [see DJARUNDA].

GEVHERÎ, MEḤMED, Turkish folk poet, a contemporary of ʿĀshîḳ ʿÖmer with whom he shared a wide-spread and lasting popularity among both the educated classes and the ordinary people. He flourished during the second half of the 11th/17th and the first half of the 12th/18th century. Very little is known about his life. From scanty and scattered information in available sources and in his own works, we learn that he probably came from the Crimea or had some connection with that area, he travelled in Syria, Arabia and the Balkans, was at one time secretary to Meḥmed Baḥrī Pasha (d. 1112/1700), wrote at Eger an elegy on the death of Aḥmed Agha, an officer of the Fort and grandfather of Ibrāhīm Naʿīm al-Dīn of Temeshvar, author of the *Ḥadīḳat al-shühedā*, who gives us this information, and wrote a poem in honour of Selīm Giray I, Khān of the Crimea, on the occasion of his visit to Istanbul in 1100/1689.

Apart from his *koshmas*, *türküs*, *türkmanis*, etc., in the popular tradition, Gevherī also wrote, like most folk poets, many poems in the classical style. He was better educated than most folk-poets. This made him a better imitator of the classical form and style, but at the same time adversely influenced the language of his more spontaneous folk-poems, where the use of the vocabulary and mannerisms of "upper class literature" is sometimes overdone. In his poems in the *dīwān* tradition he is repetitive and achieves nothing but an awkward and uninspired imitation of classical poets, particularly of Fuḍūlī. In his poems in the folk tradition, which revolve on themes of love, separation, nostalgia and epic exploits, he proves to be a most original and spontaneous poet, one of the strongest representatives of the ʿĀshîḳ [*q.v.*] literature. Some of his poems have been set to music and are still sung.

Gevherī seems to have died after 1150/1737 (see H. Dizdaroğlu in *Fikirler*, no. 262 and 263, Izmir 1944).

Bibliography: Köprülüzade M. Fuad, *Türk sazşairlerine ait metinler ve tetkikler*, i, *Gevheri*, Istanbul 1929; idem, *Türk sazşairleri*², ii, Istanbul 1962, 191-249; M. Halit Bayrı, *Aşık Gevheri*, Istanbul 1958 (with detailed bibliography).

(FAHİR İZ)

AL-GHĀB, name of the foundered trough, about 200 m./650 ft. above sea-level, crossed by the Orontes half-way along its course, between the plain of Ḥamāt and the narrow valley of Djisr al-Shughr [*q.v.*], characterized by unhealthy swampland. The faulted rock ledges of the Djabal Anṣāriyya in the west and the Djabal Zāwiya in the east stand out in sharp relief against the absolute flatness of the sedimentary levels where the river stretches out and receives yet more waters rising from many springs. Thus is presented the strange landscape which continues into northern Syria the series of tectonic rift-valleys marking the western edge of the Arabian plateau and which is situated exactly on the axis of the plains of al-Buḳayʿa [*q.v.*] and al-Biḳāʿ [*q.v.*].

This region, today semi-desert, was remarkably prosperous in antiquity, when the Seleucids raised here their horses and elephants near the city of Apamea which they had founded, an important town and the centre of their military power. There is no doubt that at that time a drainage system was in existence, about which we have little information but which continued to function well into the Middle Ages. Arabic geographers of the time of the Crusades did in fact know about the two lakes of Afāmiya [*q.v.*], which must have collected the overflow of stagnant water, and a certain amount of activity seems to have continued in this valley, which the Franks occupied until its reconquest by Nūr al-Dīn in 544/1149, at the time of the victory of Inab. It is known also that up to the Ottoman period a north-south traffic was carried on, as is borne out by the ruins of Ottoman caravanserais, one of them that of Ḳalʿat al-Muḍīḳ, near the site of the ancient Apamea/Afāmiya. The gradual spread of reed-covered lagoons and the ravages of malaria explain the increasing abandonment of this area, where there soon remained no more than some few poor villages, almost surrounded by lakes, living by buffalo-breeding and chiefly by fishing for catfish, carried on every winter on a very big scale. However, important modern land improvement works have already been started; besides the control of the course of the Orontes by damming, they provide for the drainage of the swamps and the installation of a new system of irrigation.

Bibliography: R. Dussaud, *Topographie historique de la Syrie*, Paris 1927, 196-8; Le Strange, *Palestine*, 70, 384-5, 473; M. Canard, *Histoire de la dynastie des Hʾamdanides de Jazīra et de Syrie*, Paris 1951, especially 209-10; Cl. Cahen, *La Syrie du Nord à l'époque des Croisades*, Paris 1940, esp. 163-4, 383, 474; Gaudefroy-Demombynes, *La Syrie à l'époque des Mamlouks*, Paris 1923, 21-2; J. Weulersse, *L'Oronte, étude du fleuve*, Tours 1940, 71-7 and *passim*; idem, *Le pays des Alaouites*, Tours 1940, especially 347-54 and 372-5.

(J. Sourdel-Thomine)

GHĀBA, forest. The territory of Islam, lying for the most part within the arid and semi-arid districts of the Old World, includes comparatively few areas of dense and continuous forest. The monsoonal forests of parts of East Pakistan, Malaysia and Indonesia are of course exceptional. The hazel woods of the coastal mountains of north-east Turkey and the adjacent parts of the Caucasus, the forests of plane and alder which overlook the Caspian shores of Iran, and the stands of deodar and pine in the district of Chitral in north-west Pakistan all occupy those limited areas of the Middle East where the rainfall is copious and virtually perennial. But there is abundant evidence that forests were much more extensive in south-west Asia during the Ice Ages, when conditions were both cooler and wetter than at present, and these regions formed a refuge for the flora of the glaciated parts of Central and Northern Europe. After the retreat of the ice, this flora recolonized Europe and within the Middle East, which was becoming progressively drier, withdrew to those mountains and seaward slopes where the drought of summer was less extreme. The rich variety of species which can still be found even in small and isolated areas of woodland, such as those on the slopes of Mount Erciyas [see ERDJIYAS DAGHĪ], bears witness to the more extensive nature of the forests of earlier Quaternary times, of which these are the few remaining outliers.

In view of the anxiety of many modern Islamic states to replant their forests, it is of practical as well as academic interest to know when and why the natural vegetation deteriorated, and in particular to understand how far this degeneration has been due to natural causes and how far to human intervention. The Chicago expedition to Kurdistan, for example, has made abundantly clear the degree to which the vegetation has declined since neolithic times. But from the accounts of classical authors, notably Strabo, it would seem that the forests of the Eastern Mediterranean lands and the Middle East were as recently as 2000 years ago much more abundant and widespread than at present. There is evidence from the study of mountain moraines that there has been no significant decline in rainfall in this region since that time, and the main cause of the devastation of the forests would appear to have been their reckless exploitation during Hellenistic times for ships' timbers, resin, and fuel for smelting metals. The rapid rate of silting of many harbours of the Levant between the third century B.C. and the third century A.D. was a direct result of the widespread destruction of forests and loosening of topsoil at this time. By comparison with the devastation wrought during this period, the injury done to the natural vegetation by the nomadic incursions of the Middle Ages was much less serious. Yürük, Kurdish and Arab tribes have been guilty of tapping pines for turpentine, cutting wood for charcoal, lopping branches for fodder, digging up roots for tannin, and allowing their animals to crop the seedlings. The general effect of their economy, however, has been not so much to destroy trees as to prevent their regeneration. But there are signs of serious encroachment on the few remaining forests of the Middle East during the twentieth century. Timber has often been cut for railway fuel, and the woods about Shaubak in Jordan, for example, were felled to feed the engines of the Hejaz line. The soil scientist, John Nowland, has remarked the recession of the forests of Pamphylia since Tchihatcheff described them in the last century, and Professor Orhan Yamanlar has lately studied in detail the encroachment of farmers and herdsmen on woodland in various parts of Turkey, a consequence, doubtless, of growing numbers and pressure on the means of subsistence. Replanting has as yet been only local and experimental, and may in turn give rise to new problems, as when the afforestation of high valleys in Cyprus led to the desiccation of wells downstream.

Bibliography: R. J. Braidwood and B. Howe, *Prehistoric investigations in Iraqi Kurdistan*, Chicago (Oriental Inst.) 1960; W. C. Brice, *The history of forestry in Turkey*, in *İstanbul Üniv. Orman Fak. Dergisi*, v (1955), 19-38; Government of Cyprus, *Land use in a Mediterranean environment*, Nicosia 1947; P. de Tchihatcheff, *Asie Mineure*, 4 vols., Paris 1853; idem, *Une page sur l'Orient*, Paris 1877; Ali Bahgat, *Les forêts en Egypte ...*, in *BIE*, 1901, 141-58; W. B. Turrill, *The plant-life of the Balkan Peninsula*, Oxford 1929; O. Yamanlar, *Marmara havzası ve bilhassa Yalova mıntakası için arazi tasnifinin erozyon kontrolu üzerine yapacağı tesirler*, Istanbul (İ. Ü. Orman Fakültesi) 1956. (W. C. Brice)

GHADAMÈS (Ghdāms), a little oasis in the Lybian Sahara, situated approximately on the 30th parallel and the 10th meridian east of Greenwich (at almost the same longitude as Ghāt, Gabès and Tunis). It lies at an altitude of 350 m. between the great oriental erg and the arid plateaus of al-Ḥamāda al-Ḥamrāʾ, almost at the meeting-place of the Libyan, Algerian and Tunisian frontiers. It owes its very ancient existence and its continuance to the artesian spring called ʿAyn al-Fres (*faras*) (temperature 30° C., 2-3 grammes per litre of sodium and magnesium chloride), and also to its situation, almost equidistant from Gabès, Tripoli, Ouargla, the heart of the Fezzān and Ghāt. Far more than its very limited agriculture, it was trans-Sahara trade which made its fortune over the course of the centuries and it is the disappearance of this trade which explains its decline.

Paleolithic and Neolithic implements have been discovered in the neighbourhood. In 19 B.C. Cornelius Balbus camped in this Libyan centre, which was to become Cydamus, and, under Septimus Severus, an advance post with a garrison of the 3rd Augusta legion, 200 km. to the south-west of the *limes*. In Byzantine times, it had a church and a bishop; the "idols" (*al-aṣnām*) which stand nearby are ancient ruins, Byzantine mausolea or perhaps even more ancient remains. The Arab conqueror, ʿUḳba b. Nāfiʿ, occupied it with a detachment of cavalry between his conquest of Fezzān and his march on Gafsa in 47/667. It was Ibāḍī between the 2nd/8th and the 4th/10th centuries. Ibn Khaldūn (*Berbères*, iii, 303), far more than al-Bakrī (340), dwells on the prosperity and importance of this "port" of the desert, both for traders and pilgrims. In the 10th/16th century again, Ghadamès seems to have consisted of several *ḳṣūr*. Then it seems to have become concentrated into a single village which has preserved its appearance and its sharply graded society. Ghadamès, on the boundaries of Ifrīḳiya, was able to safeguard, both for its trade and for itself, an independence which was, however, always limited by its obligatory association with the Touareg Ajjer, and the no less compulsory good relations with Tunis and Tripoli. It suffered several attacks by Ḥafṣid and Turkish troops but always managed to free itself rapidly from the taxes imposed by Tunis. It was nevertheless obliged to recognize the authority of the Turks of Tripoli in 1860. It then became a seat of a *ḳāʾimmaḳām* and after 1874 was given a little garrison; it continued none the less to administer itself with a *shaykh* and a *djamāʿa* formed from the heads of noble families.

The Italians, who disembarked at Tripoli in 1911, did not at first occupy Ghadamès, but did so later from April 1913 to November 1914, then from February to July 1915, and finally and more permanently from 15 February 1924 on. They left it before the arrival of General Leclerc's troops on 27 January 1943. First of all attached to the Territory of Fezzān [*q.v.*], it was provisionally administered by the Tunisian Protectorate from January 1948 until 1 July 1951; but following the proclamation of independence of the United Kingdom of Libya on 24 December 1951, and then of the Franco-Libyan treaty of 10 August 1955, Ghadamès was evacuated by the French authorities. It was attached to the province of Tripoli in the spring of 1957.

All the texts are in agreement to show that trans-Sahara trade was the essential activity of Ghadamès. They dwell on the comings and goings of the caravans, on the remarkable aptitude of its traders who were to be encountered in the Sudan as far away as Timbuktu, as well as at Tunis and Tripoli, and who made large profits under the protection, for which they paid tribute, assured to their caravans by the Touareg Ajjer, at the extreme limit of whose territory Ghadamès was situated. Caravans coming from the south brought above all slaves, as well as gold, leather and hides, ostrich feathers, ivory and incense. On the return journey, they carried cotton goods and cloth, sugar, and various products manufactured in Europe. The extreme points of their journeys were Tunis and Tripoli in the north, Agadès, Kano and, more rarely, Timbuktu (for which Ghāt was the first halt) in the south.

Trade profited above all the nobles (*aḥrār*), who also possessed gardens and sometimes herds; they had many black slaves (*agnaw*) whom they sometimes allowed to become free men (*atāra*); the *ḥumrān* formed a small and not very numerous middle class of artisans and shopkeepers; mostly, no doubt, of foreign origin, they formed the retainers of the principal noble families.

In the middle of the 19th century, Duveyrier notes the beginning of the decline in trade, following the abolition of the slave trade, for the most part still little enough respected. In 1910, Pervinquière, the geologist, described the stagnation of a much diminished cross-Sahara trade which had turned away from Ghadamès. To-day it is practically dead, the towns of the Mediterranean coast no longer needing the produce of the Sudan region, which in its turn is provisioned by sea. At the same time, the artisans, once extremely prosperous, many-sided, and since the 5th/11th century famous for their hides, have almost ceased to exist, lacking raw materials.

The people of modern Ghadamès are almost all reduced to cultivating their little oasis, and the Touareg to the raising of camels, sheep and goats. The palm-grove has barely 20,000 palms and the whole area of the gardens is only 75 hectares. It seems that the flow of ʿAyn al-Fres has become less since 1872-7. The Italians opened an artesian well in 1932 and another was sunk by the French but their flow also tends to diminish. The departure of a great number of *atāra* and former slaves, now become free men, provoked a man-power crisis which brought about the ruin of most of the nobles, only a few of whom were willing to apply themselves to agriculture.

The population of Ghadamès, estimated at 7,000 by Duveyrier round about 1850, had fallen to 1,900 by 1952. Most of the people have emigrated to Tripolitania or Tunisia; nearly 2,000 live in Tunis, the town to which the young people used to go in former times to get their initiation into the business world, which led to a local proverb saying: 'Ghadamès gives birth and Tunis brings up'.

Ghadamès is a pretty little oasis which attracted some tourists in Italian times. The palm-grove and gardens are surrounded by crumbling mud walls, and the village, all of unfired brick, is in the interior, a little to the south-east, beside the attractive pool of ʿAyn al-Fres. Most of the houses are very unusual with their urban appearance, rooms placed in uneven storeys or spanning the streets, often transforming them into dark tunnels. The inhabitants, Berbers of the Beni Wazit and Beni Ulīd, and the Awlād Bellīl who consider themselves of Arab origin, used to live as enemies, one group against another, shut up in seven districts isolated from one another by walls whose gates were shut at night. Despite these divisions, hard to understand for people travelling between the Mediterranean and the Sudan, the little urban centre of Ghadamès has been able to maintain across the centuries its personality as a city of caravaneers, its own Berber dialect (a little different from that of the Touareg), its social castes, its original houses and, for a long time, its independence.

Three kms. west of Ghadamès, Tounin is no more than a hamlet with a few palm-trees. The poor oases of Derdj and Sināwan are situated on the trail which goes via Nalout to Tripoli. Oil research has been going on in this area since 1956.

Bibliography: *Descr. de l'Afr. sept.*, trans. de Slane, 2nd ed., Algiers 1911; Ibn Khaldūn, *Histoire des Berbères*, trans. de Slane, 2nd ed., Paris 1925-56; Leo Africanus, *Description de l'Afrique*, trans. Épaulard, Paris 1956; P. Masson, *Histoire des établissements et du commerce français dans l'Afrique barbaresque*, Paris 1903; Mircher, Polignac, Vatonne, Hoffmann, *Mission à Ghadamès*, Algiers 1863; H. Duveyrier, *Les Touareg du Nord*, Paris 1864; V. Largeau, *Le Sahara*, Paris 1877; A. de Motylinski, *Le dialecte berbère de R'edamès*, Paris 1904;

L. Pervinquière, *La Tripolitaine interdite, Ghadamès*, Paris 1912; A. Piccioli, *La porta magica del Sahara*, Tripoli 1931; J. Aymo, *Notes de sociologie et de linguistique sur Ghadamès*, in *Bull. de liaison saharienne*, Algiers 1959, n° 34; idem, *La maison Ghadamsie*, in *Trav. de l'Inst. de Rech. sahariennes*, Algiers 1958. (J. Despois)

al-GHAḌANFAR [see ḤAMDĀNIDS].

GHAḌANFER AGHA [see ḲAPÎ AGHASÎ].

GHADĀR [see KHAZAF].

GHADĪR KHUMM, name of a pool (or a marsh) situated in an area called Khumm, between Mecca and Medina, about 3 miles from al-Djuḥfa. The waters from which it was formed came from a spring which rises in a *wādī*, and from it they flowed to the sea about six miles away, along a valley which was also called Khumm; the name is no longer in use. As the place was frequently watered by rain, there were there bushes and thorn trees which provided large shady areas around the pool and the mosque built in honour of the Prophet between the pond and the spring. The climate there was very hot and unhealthy, and the inhabitants, belonging to the Khuzāʿa and Kināna tribes, who in any case were not numerous, finally abandoned the region because of the fevers which afflicted them and the lack of pasturage.

Ghadīr Khumm is famous in the history of Islam because of a sentence (or some sentences) in favour of ʿAlī which the Prophet uttered there during a discourse, the circumstances of which, according to the most detailed accounts which are preserved in some *ḥadīth*s, were as follows. On his return from the Farewell Pilgrimage, Muḥammad stopped at Ghadīr Khumm on 18 Dhu 'l-Ḥidjdja 10/16 March 632. As he wanted to make an announcement to the pilgrims who accompanied him before they dispersed, and as it was very hot, they constructed for him a dais shaded with branches. Taking ʿAlī by the hand, he asked of his faithful followers whether he, Muḥammad, was not closer (*awlā*) to the Believers than they were to themselves; the crowd cried out: "It is so, O Apostle of God!"; he then declared: "He of whom I am the *mawlā* (the patron?), of him ʿAlī is also the *mawlā* (*man kuntu mawlāhu fa-ʿAlī mawlāhu*)". Nothing which can explain the inner meaning of the main sentence is added either by the additions supplied by several *ḥadīth*s, *e.g.*, "O God, be the friend of him who is his friend, and be the enemy of him who is his enemy (*Allāhumma wāli man wālāhu wa-ʿādi man ʿādāhu*)", or by the variants (the most interesting of which is the substitution of the word *walī* for *mawlā*, which proves that the meaning of the latter word, at least in its metaphorical sense, was not very precise). Most of those sources which form the basis of our knowledge of the life of the Prophet (Ibn Hishām, al-Ṭabarī, Ibn Saʿd, etc.) pass in silence over Muḥammad's stop at Ghadīr Khumm, or, if they mention it, say nothing of his discourse (the writers evidently feared to attract the hostility of the Sunnīs, who were in power, by providing material for the polemic of the Shīʿīs who used these words to support their thesis of ʿAlī's right to the caliphate). Consequently, the western biographers of Muḥammad, whose work is based on these sources, equally make no reference to what happened at Ghadīr Khumm. It is, however, certain that Muḥammad did speak in this place and utter the famous sentence, for the account of this event has been preserved, either in a concise form or in detail, not only by al-Yaʿḳūbī, whose sympathy for the ʿAlid cause is well known, but also in the collections of traditions which are considered as canonical, especially in the *Musnad* of Ibn Ḥanbal; and the *ḥadīth*s are so numerous and so well attested by the different *isnād*s that it does not seem possible to reject them. Several of these *ḥadīth*s are cited in the bibliography, but it does not include the *ḥadīth*s which, although reporting the sentence, omit to name Ghadīr Khumm, or those which state that the sentence was pronounced at al-Ḥudaybiya. The complete documentation will be facilitated when the *Concordances* of Wensinck have been completely published. In order to have an idea of how numerous these *ḥadīth*s are, it is enough to glance at the pages in which Ibn Kathīr has collected a great number of them with their *isnād*s. This author informs us that al-Ṭabarī, in a two-volume work (probably the unfinished work mentioned by Yāḳūt, *Irshād*, vi, 452, the title of which was *K. al-Faḍāʾil*) in which he reported the Prophet's discourse at Ghadīr Khumm, had collected, he says, "the fat and the thin, the strong and the weak". Abu 'l-Ḳāsim Ibn ʿAsākir (d. 571/1176) also reproduces many *ḥadīth*s on the same subject and it is from his collection that Ibn Kathīr has chosen the principal traditions, which however, he adds, supply no basis for the Shīʿī claims.

The beliefs of the latter concerning the affair of Ghadīr Khumm are as follows: Muḥammad had already known through divine inspiration (or by revelation on the night of the *Miʿrādj*) that ʿAlī was to become his successor as leader of the Muslim community, but he had kept this divine decision secret, waiting for the moment when there should be no more opposition to ʿAlī among the Muslims. At Ghadīr Khumm he received the revelation: "O Apostle, communicate that which was revealed to you by your Lord" (Ḳurʾān, V, 71/67). Then, in the presence of the Companions, taking ʿAlī's hand in his own, he pronounced the sentence *man kuntu mawlāhu* etc., which is thus a *naṣṣ* [*q.v.*] nominating ʿAlī as *imām* of the Muslims after the death of their Prophet. On the same occasion, Muḥammad announced his impending death and charged the Believers to remain attached to the Book of God and to his family. After the communal prayer he went into his tent and, on his orders, ʿAlī received, in his tent, the congratulations of the Muslim men and women, who greeted him with the title of *amīr al-muʾminīn*. Among them was ʿUmar b. al-Khaṭṭāb. Ḥassān b. Thābit recited, with Muḥammad's approbation, some verses in honour of ʿAlī (some verses by him, affirming that ʿAlī was named as the successor of the Prophet on the day of Ghadīr Khumm, are quoted by Ibn Shahrāshūb (ii, 230) and, if they are authentic, they are, apart from the *ḥadīth*s, the earliest attestation of the event at Ghadīr Khumm, and not, as Goldziher has suggested, the verse of al-Kumayt). It is said that the same day Muḥammad received at Ghadīr Khumm the revelation of Ḳurʾān, V, 5/3 ("Today I have perfected your religion for you, and I have completed my blessing upon you, and I have approved Islam for your religion"), which is generally accepted to have been revealed at ʿArafāt a few days earlier.

The Sunnīs do not deny that Muḥammad may have expressed himself in the above manner concerning ʿAlī, but they consider that in the sentence in question he was simply exhorting his hearers to hold his cousin and son-in-law in high esteem and affection. On this point, Ibn Kathīr shows himself yet again to be a percipient historian: he connects the affair of Ghadīr Khumm with episodes which took place during the expedition to the Yemen, which was led by ʿAlī in 10/631-2, and which had returned to Mecca just in time to meet the Prophet there during his Farewell Pilgrimage. ʿAlī had been very strict in the sharing out of the booty and his behaviour had aroused protests; doubt was cast on his rectitude, he was reproached with avarice and accused of misuse of authority. Thus it is quite possible that, in order to put an end to all these accusations, Muḥammad wished to demonstrate publicly his esteem and love for ʿAlī. Ibn Kat͟hīr must have arrived at the same conclusion, for he does not forget to add that the Prophet's words put an end to the murmurings against ʿAlī.

Because of the importance in their eyes of Muḥammad's discourse at G͟hadīr K͟humm, the S͟hīʿīs have considered 18 D͟hu 'l-Ḥid͟jd͟ja as an anniversary to be celebrated with solemnity. In ʿIrāḳ, the *id G͟hadīr K͟humm* was introduced by Muʿizz al-Dawla Aḥmad b. Būya in 352/964 and in Egypt by al-Muʿizz in 362/973; under the Fāṭimids, with the exception of some years of the reign of al-Ḥākim, it was one of the most important religious feasts. In Persia today it is celebrated by making for the occasion three pastry figures filled with honey, which represent the caliphs Abū Bakr, ʿUmar and ʿUt͟hmān, and by stabbing them with knives: the honey which comes out symbolizes the blood of the three hated usurpers. This feast also holds an important place among the Nuṣayrīs.

Bibliography: Description of the place: Yaʿḳūbī, *Buldān*, *BGA*, vii, 314; Bakrī, 232, 311, 318; Yāḳūt, *Muʿd͟jam*, ii, 35f., 471; L. Caetani, *Annali dell'Islām*, 1 a.H., §§ 76 n. 4, 78 n. 3; Mosque erected in the place: F. Wüstenfeld, *Die von Medina auslaufenden Hauptstrassen*, 37 f. *Ḥadīt͟h*s where Muḥammad's sentence concerning ʿAlī is linked with G͟hadīr K͟humm: Ibn Ḥanbal, *Musnad*, i, 84, 118, 119, 152, iv, 281, 370, 372, v, 419 (cited by Wensinck, *Handbook*, 15), Cairo ed. in progress, ii, 641, 670, 950, 951, 952, 961, 964, 1310, etc.; al-Muttaḳī al-Hindī, *Kanz al-ʿummāl fī sunan al-aḳwāl wa 'l-afʿāl*, Ḥaydarābād 1312-14, vi, 152 nos. 2522-3, 153 no. 2534, 154 nos. 2563, 2567-9, 390 nos. 5967, 5969-70, 397 nos. 6054, 6057, 398 no. 6067, 399 no. 6074, 403-4 nos. 6121-3, 406 no. 4146, 407 no. 6149 (cf. C. van Arendonk, *De Opkomst van het Zaidietische Imamaat in Yemen*, Leiden 1919, 19 n. 2; Fr. tr., Leiden 1960, 19 n. 2). According to Ibn Kat͟hīr, Muḥammad's discourse is reported also by al-Nasāʾī in his *Sunan* and in his book on the *k͟haṣāʾiṣ ʿAlī*, by Ibn Mād͟ja, Abū Dāwūd and al-Tirmid͟hī. On the Prophet's discourse, see also Ibn al-Kalbī, *D͟jamhara*, MS British Museum, fol. 256 v.; Yaʿḳūbī, *Historiae*, ed. Houtsma, ii, 125; Masʿūdī, *Tanbīh*, *BGA*, viii, 234; Ibn ʿAbd al-Barr, *al-Istīʿāb*, 473; Ibn al-At͟hīr, *Usd*, iv, 28; Ibn K͟hallikān, *Wafayāt*, no. 699, Cairo 1950 iv, 318 f., tr. de Slane, iii, 383 (Ibn K͟hallikān mentions the discourse in favour of ʿAlī, but without reporting the famous sentence. A partial variant is found in some *ḥadīt͟h*s: Ibn Ḥanbal, *Musnad*, Cairo ed., i, nos. 950, 964 and 1310); Muḥibb al-Dīn al-Ṭabarī, *al-Riyāḍ al-nāḍira*, Cairo 1327, ii, 169; D͟hahabī, *Taʾrīk͟h*, MS Paris, fols. 188-9; Ibn Kat͟hīr, *al-Bidāya wa 'l-nihāya*, 1348-55, v, 208-14.—A discussion by a Muʿtazilī: al-D͟jāḥiẓ, *ʿUt͟hmāniyya*, Cairo 1374/1955, index.—On the beliefs of the S͟hīʿīs: Ibn S͟hahrās͟hūb, *Manāḳib Āl Abī Ṭālib*, Nad͟jaf 1376/1956, ii, 224-56 (unsystematic in treatment, but interesting because it mentions the authors who have dealt with the subject and many verses by early poets, including some attributed to Ḥassān b. T͟hābit); Mad͟jlisī, *Ḥayāt al-ḳulūb*, Tehrān 1374, iii, 39-46; Muḥsin al-Amīn al-ʿĀmilī, *Aʿyān al-s͟hīʿa*, iii/1, 524-32 (a lucid modern treatment); I. Goldziher, *Beiträge zur Literaturgeschichte der Šīʿâ und der sunnitischen Polemik*, in *Sitzungsb. der phil.-hist. Classe der K. Ak. der Wissenschaften*, lxxviii (1874), 496 f.; idem, *Muh. Studien*, ii, 115 f.; idem, *Vorlesungen über den Islam*[1], Heidelberg 1910, 239, cf. 274 (Fr. tr., *Dogme*, Paris 1920, 192, cf. 292). On the work of Ṭabarī, idem, *Die liter. Thätigkeit des Ṭabarī nach Ibn ʿAsākir*, in *WZKM*, ix, 366; L. Caetani, *Annali dell'Islām*, 40 A.H., § 293; D. M. Donaldson, *The Shīʿite Religion*, London 1933, 1-3. On ʿAlī's behaviour during the expedition to the Yemen: Ibn His͟hām, 947 f.; Wāḳidī-Wellhausen, 418; Ṭabarī, i, 1752 f.; Ibn al-At͟hīr, *Usd*, 27 f.; Caetani, *Annali*, 10 A.H., § 17 (p. 322). On the festival: Maḳrīzī, *K͟hiṭaṭ*, Būlāḳ 1270, i, 388 f.; R. Dussaud, *Histoire et religion des Noṣairîs*, Paris 1900, 137-41; Hughes, *Dict. of Islam*, 138. Certain practices of the ʿAlawīs of Syria inspired Jehan Cendrieux with a novel entitled *Al-Ghâder* (sic) *ou le sexe-Dieu*, Paris 1926.

(L. Veccia Vaglieri)

al-G͟HĀḌIRĪ, hero of a series of anecdotes collected, probably in the 3rd/9th century, under the title *Kitāb al-G͟hāḍirī* (*Fihrist*, 435). He is said to have been a foundling, who became a humourist of Medina and rival of As͟hʿab [*q.v.*]; the name of al-Ḥasan b. Zayd [*q.v.*], governor of Medina from 150 to 155/767-72, which appears in one anecdote, would seem to give some grounds for thinking him a historical personality. However, as the Banū G͟hāḍira have a reputation as wits, it is possible that the anonymous collection referred to by Ibn al-Nadīm is made up of anecdotes attributed to various members of this group, among whom they had existed as a common heritage.

Bibliography: D͟jāḥiẓ, *Ḥayawān*, v, 241-3; idem, *Buk͟halāʾ*, ed. Ḥad͟jirī, 192, 365; Ibn Ḳutayba, *ʿUyūn*, ii, 52; Ḳālī, *Amālī*, ii, 242; *Ag͟hānī*, v, 132, xvii, 101; Ḥuṣrī, *Zahr*, 160-1; idem, *D͟jamʿ*, 69, 152; Ābī, *Nat͟hr al-durar*, MS Dār al-Kutub, ii, 208; Āmidī, *Muʾtalif*, 161; F. Rosenthal, *Humour*, 7, n. 4.

(Ch. Pellat)

G͟HAFFĀRĪ, Aḥmad b. Muḥammad, Persian historian, descendant of a family originating from Sāwa, later established at Ḳazwīn, and descended from the S͟hāfiʿī *imām* Nad͟jm al-Dīn ʿAbd al-G͟haffār (d. 665/1266), author of the work *Ḥāwī al-ṣag͟hīr*, whence the patronymic "G͟haffārī". Five of his ancestors had held the office of *ḳāḍī*. His father (d. 932/1526), who composed poetry under the pseudonym of Wiṣālī, as well as his brother, had held the same office at Rayy. Since he lived at Ḳazwīn and bore the title of *ḳāḍī*, it would seem that he had held the same post in his native town. It is said that at the end of his life he had resigned the official functions he performed for the princes. He made a journey from Ḳazwīn to Kās͟hān in the company of the *amīr* Taḳī al-Dīn Muḥammad, the grandson of the *amīr* D͟jamāl al-Dīn Muḥammad Ṣadr, and of the poet Nit͟hārī of Tabrīz. During this journey he met the great poet Muḥtas͟ham of Kās͟hān. At the end of his life he made the pilgrimage to Mecca and on his return he died at Daybūl (Sind) in 957/1567. Although a poet, he composed two considerable works of history: *Negārestān*, a collection of historical anecdotes collected from the best known works and arranged in chronological order, completed in 959/

1552 and dedicated to the Ṣafawid Shāh Tahmāsb; *Nusakh-i djahān-ārā*, a history of the dynasties from the beginning up to 972/1564, dedicated to the same sovereign.

Bibliography: Sām Mirzā Ṣafawī, *Tuḥfa-yi sāmī*, Tehrān 1314/1936, 72-4 (six members of the family, with printing errors in the names); *The Muntakhab al-tawārikh of Abd al-qādir bini-Malūk shāh al-Badaoni*, iii, Calcutta 1860, 185-6; Amīn Aḥmad Rāzī, *Haft iḳlīm*, Tehrān, iii, 178; Luṭf ʿAlī Beyk Āzar, *Āteshkadeh*, Bombay 1299, 228; Raḥmān ʿAlī, *Tadhkira-yi ʿulamā-yi Hind*, Lucknow 1914, 18; Sayyid Muḥammad Ṣiddīḳ Khān, *Shamʾi andjuman*, Delhi 1293, 57; ʿAlī Shīr Ḳāniʿ Tatawī, *Maḳālāt al-shuʿarāʾ*, Karachi 1957, 17-18; Storey, section II, 114-6; Saïd Naficy, *Taʾrīkh-i naẓm o nathr dar Īrān wa dar zabān-i Fārsī*, Tehrān 1342/1963, 354, 508. (S. Naficy)

al-**GHĀFIḲĪ**, Muḥammad b. Ḳassūm b. Aslam, Spanish-Arab scholar and oculist, probably of the 6th/12th century. The Arabic chroniclers are silent with regard to his biography and we know almost nothing of his life. It has been no more than supposed that he was born in Cordova and that he practised for a long time in this city. According to Wüstenfeld, he was the father of Abū Djaʿfar Aḥmad b. Muḥammad al-Ghāfiḳī [*q.v.* in Supplement], the famous doctor and pharmacologist, author of the *Kitāb al-Adwiya al-mufrada.*

Of Muḥammad al-Ghāfiḳī, there remains only the *Kitāb al-Murshid fi 'l-kuḥl*, "The Oculist's Guide", of which a single copy exists in the Escorial (N. 835). This book is regarded as a summary of all the knowledge of ophthalmology possessed by the Arabs of both the Islamic east and west, in its author's time. It is divided into six sections of which, in fact, only the fifth (partially) and the sixth (entirely) treat of the medicine and the hygiene of the eyes.

Although the *K. al-Murshid* is considered to be the most remarkable ophthalmological text of the Islamic west, it has been said of it that it is no more than a vast compilation without original contributions, that the part which concerns the oculist in reality only occupies a limited space in relation to that dedicated to general medicine, and that it lacks a sense of proportion (Hirschberg). But in judging it from the point of view of present-day knowledge, it is precisely in the plan of the work and the arrangement of its material that it is possible to catch a glimpse of a kind of anticipation of the modern conception of the pathology of the eye, necessarily linked to and following as a corollary on that of the entire organism.

Bibliography: L. Leclerc, *Histoire de la médecine arabe*, Paris 1876, ii; F. Wüstenfeld, *Geschichte der arabischen Ärzte und Naturforscher*, Göttingen 1840; J. Hirschberg, *Die arabischen Lehrbücher der Augenheilkunde*, Berlin 1905; M. Meyerhof, *L'ophtalmologie de Mohammad al-Ghāfiqī*, Barcelona 1923; P. Pansier, *Breve conspecto de la oftalmologia árabe* (tr., ed. and notes by J. M. Millás Vallicrosa), Barcelona 1956. (T. Sarnelli)

GHAFŪRĪ, MEDJĪD, one of the best-known national poets of the Bashḳurts and Tatars. He was born in 1881 in the village of Djilim Ḳaran, a village inhabited by both Tatars and Bashḳurts belonging to the Isterlitamak administrative district of Bashḳurdistan. He died in 1934, a Soviet poet. His father, Nurgani, was the village teacher, and Medjīd (ʿAbd al-Madjīd) received his primary education from him. For his intermediate schooling he went to the *medrese* in the neighbouring village of Ötesh, and from 1898 to 1904 he studied in the *Resūliye Medresesi* in the city of Troysk. Through teaching among the Ḳazaḳs he became attracted to their style of literature. He published his first poetry in *Terdjümān* in 1902, and later, in 1904, in the form of a collection with the title *Sibir Temiryolu yaki Aḥwāl-i millet.* He subsequently published small collections of poems with titles like *Yash ʿömrüm* (1906), *Millet Maḥabbeti* (1907), *Zamāne shiʿirleri* and *Medjīd Ghafūrī shiʿirleri* (1909), *Teʾeththürātīm* (1910), *Muñ-Zar* (1911), *Millī shiʿirler we emthāl* (1913), and *Yangan Yürek* (1915). As he knew little Russian, he did not derive much inspiration from Russian literature, being influenced only by Krylov's *Fables* and some of the works of Gorky. His first poems, written under the influence of Ḳazaḳ literature and especially of the Ḳazaḳ poet Aḳmolla, were beautiful, and bring a fresh style to Bashḳurt and Tatar literature. After 1907 he wrote his poems wholly in Tatar, in the classical metres (*ʿarūḍ*). Because of lack of variety in his thoughts and carelessness in metre and style, however, he was considered to be in the second rank of poets, compared with men like Shams al-Dīn Izek and Sheykhzāde Babič among the Bashḳurts, and ʿAbd Allāh Toḳay among the Tatars. In *Zamāne shiʿirleri*, in which he imitated Ṣūfī Allāhyārī, he made it clear that he had read Čaghatāy literature first by way of poetry. In his collected works, which appeared in 1904, he complained of the backwardness of the Bashḳurts and Tatars, of the ignorance of the Mollas and so on. He manifested his belief that the Siberian railway, which was completed in 1902, "the longest railway in the world", would bring about some changes in the life of the eastern Turks. In his works generally, he reflected the early twentieth-century life of the Tatars and Bashḳurts and also their complaints and desires. Before the 1917 Revolution, the works which he had written under the influence of the popular literature of the Ḳazaḳs and the Bashḳurts, not attempting to rival the Tatar poets, had made him very popular in his own land. One of his finest works is the *ḳaṣīde Aḳ-Edil*, published at Ufa in 1911. After 1923 he was drawn into propaganda work by the Soviets, and he was much used for this purpose. In the Soviet period his collected works were published in five volumes, which included the greater part of his early writings, as well as later works of an entirely different character and outlook.

(Z. V. Togan)

GHĀʾIB, absent, usually means in law the person who at a given moment is not present at the place where he should be. But, in certain special cases (see below), the term is applied also to the person who is at a distance from the court before which he was to bring an action or who does not appear at the court after being summoned.

If to this first notion is added that of uncertainty concerning the person's existence, the term used is not *ghāʾib* but *mafḳūd*, although sometimes the state of the *mafḳūd* is called also *ghayba*, to which is added the epithet *munḳaṭiʿa* (absence not interrupted by information on the person's existence). This state of affairs may give rise to juridical consequences of greater or less importance according to circumstances. If such an absence extends to a period when persons of the same generation as the missing person are dead, the judge declares him dead: his estate goes to his heirs, and his marriage or marriages are dissolved. Up to this time, the estate of the *mafḳūd* continues to be administered by his agent, if he had appointed one, or, failing such an appointment, by a trustee nominated by the judge; inheritances which are due to him remain in suspense; his marriage or marriages continue to subsist.

Ghayba, in its normal and general sense, gives rise to various juridical consequences, particularly the following:

As regards marriage, the absence of a husband which extends beyond a certain term—four years, four months and ten days, according to the majority opinion—permits the wife to apply for judicial divorce if she is not regularly receiving alimony.

Ghayba is also a reason for suspending the prescription of an action at law. In this connexion, it lies in the plaintiff's being three days' journey (on foot) away from the place where he should have brought his action. But this absence must be continuous (in this case too called *ghayba munḳaṭiʿa*), so that if during the period when prescription is suspended the plaintiff once more comes to the place where he could bring his action, the period of his absence is no longer of any affect.

The non-appearance of a litigant at a hearing does not permit the judge to decide the case by default, a procedure which, in principle, is not recognized, although various means may be employed to compel the litigant to appear, provided that he is not too far away. Nevertheless in the most recent stage of Muslim law, as it is represented by the Ottoman codification of the second half of the 19th century, judgement by default is admitted.

In public law, in certain states (for example the Mamlūk Empire) the Sultan, when himself absent from the capital, often appointed a *locum tenens*, who was called *nā'ib al-ghayba* (literally, 'substitute of absence').

In public worship, *ṣalāt al-ghā'ib* ('prayer of the absent') is the name given to the prayer said for a dead person whose body cannot be produced.

Bibliography: *Madjalla* (Ottoman Civil Code), arts. 1663 ff., 1833 ff.; E. Tyan, *Histoire de l'organisation judiciaire en pays d'Islam*, Paris, i, 41 ff.; idem, *Institutions du droit public musulman*, Paris, ii, 177; [2]Leiden, 369 ff.; idem, *La procédure du "défaut" en droit musulman*, in *St. Isl.*, 1957, 115 ff.; Dozy, *Supplément*, 60; Ottoman Family Law of 1917; all the works of *fiḳh*, under the heading "*mafḳūd*". (E. Tyan)

GHALĀFIḲA (or Ghulāfiḳ(a), Ghulayfiḳa; pl. of *ghalfaḳ*=*ṭuḥlub* "sea-moss"), a coast town in the Tihāma of Yaman, situated half-way between Ḥudayda and Zabīd, at the southern end of a bay (Khor Ghalāfika). Here was in earlier times the main port of Zabīd, whose west gate is called "Bāb Ghulāfiḳa". The geographer Muḳaddasī, who visited this place, mentions its famous mosque, its date- and cocoapalms, and several wells—Ghalāfiḳa is said to be the only place in this part of the coast with a supply of fresh water—but says that the climate is pestilential and mortal to strangers. According to Ibn al-Mudjāwir (7th/13th century) Persians from Sīrāf, *viz.* fugitives from Djidda, restored the town after a period of decay. Towards the end of the Middle Ages the place lost its importance in favour of the "lower" port of Zabīd, al-Ahwāb, and Mokhā, the great harbour for the export of coffee. In 1763, Niebuhr found Ghalāfiḳa a miserable village, difficult to reach even with small boats, owing to the coral reefs. In our days, according to the *Red Sea and Gulf of Aden pilot*, the harbour can still afford anchorage for small craft, its depth being 3-4 fathoms, but it is gradually silting up.

Bibliography: *BGA*, ii, 19; iii, 53, 69, 86, 95, 101, 105; vi, 141, 148; vii, 319; viii, 260; Hamdānī, *Ṣifa*, ed. Müller, 52, 119, tr. Forrer, 37, 50; Yāḳūt, iii, 808; ʿUmāra, *Ta'rīkh al-Yaman* (Kay, *Yaman*), 8, 11, 194, 197, 221; Ibn al-Mudjāwir, *Ta'rīkh al-mustabṣir*, ed. Löfgren, 46, 74, 147, 184, 238-43; Idrīsī, *Géographie*, tr. Jaubert, i, 49, 146 (text corrupt); Abu 'l-Fidā', *Géographie*, tr. Reinaud, ii/1, 121; A. Sprenger, *Post- u. Reiserouten des Orients*, 157; idem, *Die alte Geographie Arabiens*, p. 64 (§ 62); C. Niebuhr, *Beschreibung von Arabien*, 227; A. Grohmann, *Südarabien als Wirtschaftsgebiet*, i, 181, 230; ii, 77, 85 f., 124, 127 f., 130, 134; *Red Sea and Gulf of Aden pilot*, 8th ed., 1932, 323 f.; L. O. Schuman, *Political history of the Yemen at the beginning of the 16th century*, 1960, 75. (O. Löfgren)

GHALAṬA [see ISTANBUL].

GHALAṬA-SARĀYÎ, Palace School and later modern lycée at Pera (Beyoğlu) across the Golden Horn from Istanbul. It was founded during the first years of the Ottoman Sultan Bāyezīd II (886-918/1481-1512), as one of the palace schools in Istanbul and Edirne for the education of the *ʿadjami oghlāns* [*q.v.*]. It covered a large area on which numerous buildings, dormitories, a hospital, a kitchen, baths, mosques and a *ḳaṣr* (small palace) for the sultan, were built. The administration of the school was entrusted to an *agha* (or *bashagha*) who had under him the teaching staff and a large body of servants. The students were divided into three *odas* (rooms) called *küčük*, *orta* and *büyük*, each comprising at the beginning 200 boys. Their number varied with time. They were recruited at first mainly through the *devshirme* [*q.v.*], but from Süleymān the Magnificent's reign on, Muslim boys too were accepted. The students were educated in Islamic sciences and liberal arts, instructed in the palace ceremonial and trained in military exercises. After completing their education, which lasted from seven to fourteen years, the most able were chosen for the imperial palace, the Topḳapî sarāyî [*q.v.*] where they continued their studies at the *Enderūn*. Other joined the permanent cavalry regiments (*sipāhīs*).

Ghalaṭa-sarāyî was changed many times into a *medrese* but from its restoration in 1127/1715 under Aḥmed III it remained a palace school, up to its closing in 1251/1835-6. During this period Maḥmūd I had added a library to the school in 1167/1753. Burnt in the first years of Maḥmūd II's reign, the school was rebuilt in 1235/1819-20. Ghalaṭa-sarāyî became a medical school under the name of Ṭîbbiyye-i ʿadliyye-i shāhāne [*q.v.*] in 1254/1838. European and Turkish doctors taught there modern medicine for ten years: a fire in August 1848 obliged the Ṭîbbiyye to move into Khalîdjîoghlu on the Golden Horn.

Ghalaṭa-sarāyî was later reconstructed in stone and was opened as a preparatory school to the military academies in 1862. But this did not last for long. On 1 September 1868 the Imperial lycée or Mekteb-i sulṭānī was opened there. Thanks to the initiative of the Grand Vizier ʿĀlī Pasha and the Minister of Foreign Affairs Fu'ād Pasha, the new institution was supported by the French government. It was modelled after the French lycées, had to be administered by a French director and the teaching was to be mainly in French. The school aimed at producing Western-educated officials for the Ottoman administration. 341 boys from all nationalities of the empire were accepted at the opening. When the French director, M. de Salve, left in 1872, a Christian Ottoman was appointed to this post. Later only Turkish directors were nominated to the administration of the school. Except for two short intervals, the Impérial lycée remained on the same site. In September 1873 it moved into Gülkhāne, to provide accommodation for the Faculty of Medicine. But three years later, in 1876, it returned to its old premises. On 6 March 1907 a fire burnt the school, and courses continued in a pavilion in the courtyard. The construction of the new building ended the next year, offering more space to the school.

The programmes were revised after the proclamation of the Turkish republic in 1923. Meanwhile the main courses continued to be given in French, mostly by French teachers. Able directors and distinguished professors, many of them famous Turkish poets, scholars and scientists, served in the lycée of Ghalaṭa-sarāyî (now Galatasaray). Graduates of the school contributed much in all fields of activities in Turkey, the Balkans and the Arab countries. The share of the lycée of Ghalaṭa-sarāyî in the modernization of Turkey is important. It still continues to educate Western-minded young men.

Bibliography: D'Ohsson, *Tableau général de l'Empire othoman*, Paris 1788-1824, vii, 47-9; ʿAṭā, *Taʾrīkh*, Istanbul 1293, 5 vol., *passim*; Osman Ergin, *Türkiye maarif tarihi*, Istanbul 1939-43, i, 23-9, ii, 401-5; B. Miller, *The Palace School of Muhammad the Conqueror*, Cambridge Mass. 1941, *passim*; I. Hakki Uzunçarşılı, *Osmanlı devletinin saray teşkilâti*, Ankara 1945, 1939-43, i, 23-9, ii, 401-5; I. Hakkı Uzunçarsılı, *Osmanlı devletinin saray teşkilâtı*, Ankara 1945, 302-6; Fethi Isfendiyaroğlu, *Galatasaray tarihi*, Istanbul 1952, i; Ed. Engelhardt, *La Turquie et le Tanzimat*, Paris 1884, ii, 12-6, 108-10; De La Jonquière, *Histoire de l'Empire ottoman*[2], Paris 1914, ii, 563-7; Hasan-Ali Yücel, *Türkiyede orta öğretim*, Istanbul 1938, 522-4; Ihsan Sungu, *Galatasaray lisesinin kuruluşu*, in *Belleten*, vii (1943), 315-47; idem, *Galatasaray lisesi*, in *Aylık Ansiklopedi*, Istanbul 1945, i, 138-40; Bernard Lewis, *The emergence of modern Turkey*[3], London 1965, index, s.vv. Galatasaray and Imperial Ottoman Lycée; R. Davison, *Reform in the Ottoman Empire, 1856-1876*, Princeton 1963, index, s.v. Galatasaray lycée. (E. KURAN)

GHALAṬĀT-I MESHHŪRE, Ottoman term meaning literally 'well-known errors' and hence 'solecisms sanctioned by usage'. Arabic and Persian loan-words in Ottoman Turkish generally retained the spelling current in the parent languages and were modified in pronunciation only so far as was essential to accommodate them to the Turkish repertory of consonants and vowels. Occasionally, however, phonetic changes characteristic of Turkish produced more drastic modifications in the loan-words; when the modified forms supplanted the original forms in the literary language they were branded by the purists as '*ghalaṭāt-i meshhūre*'. Some of these 'solecisms' consist only of the change of a single vowel: *djenāze* for *djināze*, *terdjüme* for *terdjeme*, *ḳandīl* for *ḳindīl*, *ḳumāsh* for *ḳimāsh*, etc. But sometimes the modification was more drastic: *merdiven* < *nerdubān*, *mushamba* < *mushammaʿ*, *sehpā* < *sepā*, *pabuč* < *pāpūsh*, *čamashīr* < *djāma-shūy*, *čarshaf* < *čādir-i sheb*, *bedāwā* < *bād-i hawā*, etc.; many Arabic broken plurals are used in Turkish as singulars: *ṭalebe*, *elbise*, *khademe*, *ʿamele*, *eshkiyā*, *eshyā*, *aʿḍā* (*aza*); some abstract nouns, unknown to Arabic and Persian, were invented by analogy with Arabic 'measures': *nezāket* ('refinement' < P. *nāzik*), *felāket* ('disaster'), *ṭabābet* ('medicine'), *ṣalāḥiyet* ('authority'), etc.; new words were formed by the addition of an Arabic or a Persian suffix to a Turkish word: *variyet* ('wealth' < T. *var*), *gidishāt* ('goings-on', pseudo-A. pl. of *gidish*), *oyunbāz* ('trickster'), *emekdār* ('veteran'), *sandjaḳdār* ('standard-bearer'), *ishgüzār* ('officious'), etc.

From the 10th/16th century onwards Ottoman scholars and pedants compiled treatises of *ghalaṭat-i meshhūre*, among them Kemāl Pashazāde (*al-Tanbīh ʿalā ghalaṭ al-djāhil wa 'l-nabīh*, see Brockelmann, II 452, S II 671 (no. 106); tr. and printed, Istanbul 1289, as *Terdjüme-i Ghalaṭāt al-ʿawāmm*), Abu 'l-Suʿūd and Khusrew-zāde Meḥmed; many such treatises were written in the period of the Tanẓīmāt [*q.v.*] and after, when there was increased controversy over the rules of correct usage. A number of these Ottoman 'well-known errors' have been accepted in modern Arabic usage.

Bibliography: ʿAlī Seydī, *Defter-i ghalaṭāt*, Istanbul 1324; Muṣṭafā ʿIzzet, *Taṣḥīḥ al-ghalaṭāt wa 'l-muḥarrafāt fi 'l-lughāt*, Istanbul 1303; ʿAlī Himmet, *Fāḍiliñ ghalaṭāt defteri*, Samsun 1338; Sîrrî, *Ghalaṭāt*, Istanbul 1301. For a discussion of the phonetic phenomena involved (dissimilation, assimilation, labialization, etc.) see J. Deny, *Principes de grammaire turque*, Paris 1955; T. Banguoğlu, *Türk grameri, i: sesbilgisi*, Ankara 1959. (G. ALPAY)

GHALČA, an imprecise designation of those mountain peoples of the Pamirs who speak Iranian lamguages. The term has been used in English scholarly literature for the Iranian Pamir languages. In New Persian the word means 'peasant' or 'ruffian', while in Tādjikī it means 'squat, stupid'. In old Yaghnābi *ghalča* meant 'slave'. The origin of the word is uncertain, for one might compare Sogdian γδ 'to steal', (Pashto γəl 'thief') or Sogdian γr 'mountain', hence 'mountaineer'. Usually the term Ghalča has been used in modern literature to cover the speakers of the following languages and dialects (from north to south): Wandjī, Yazgulāmī, Orošorī, Bartangī, Sarikolī, Rošānī, Shughnī, Wakhī, Ishkāshmī, Mundjī, Sanglēčī, Yidgha. A wider use of the term would include such tongues as Yaghnābī in the north and Parāčī near Kābul.

The earliest attested use of the word by an European is found in the travel account of Benedict de Goès *circa* 1603 (Lentz 12). The term Ghalča was brought into prominence by Shaw, who early investigated some of the languages.

Little is known of the history of the Pamir region. Although much of the area paid tribute to Muslim rulers in Balkh in the first three centuries A. H., it is probable that the majority of the population of Islam remained non-Muslim until the Ismāʿīlī missionary activity of the 5th/11th century. The most famous missionary in neighbouring Badkhshān was the author Nāṣir-i Khusraw. Various forms of the Shīʿa creed remained among the populace down to the present. Today the area is divided between Afghanistan, the USSR and China.

Bibliography: W. Lentz, *Pamir-Dialekte*, Göttingen 1933, 9-15; R. Shaw, *On the Ghalchah Languages*, in *JASB*, 1876-7; W. Geiger, *Die Pamir-Dialekte*, in *Gr. I Ph.*, I[2], 288; A. M. Mandelštam, *Materialī k istoriko-geografičeskomu obzoru Pamira*, Trudī Akad. Nauk Tadjikskoy SSR, 53, Stalinabad 1957. (R. N. FRYE)

GHĀLIB [see WAHHĀBIYYA].

GHĀLIB B. ʿABD AL-RAḤMĀN, AL-ṢIḲLABĪ, freedman (*mawlā*) of ʿAbd al-Raḥmān III, in whose time and those of his son al-Ḥakam and grandson

Hishām he was one of the great generals. He led expeditions against the Christians of the Peninsula and also against the Idrīsids and Fāṭimids in Morocco and Ifrīḳiya. In 335/946 he was appointed chief of the Upper Frontier and rebuilt Medinaceli, which he made the base for operations against the Christian positions of the middle and upper Duero valley. His expeditions against Castile in 342/953 were very successful as concerns prisoners and booty but achieved no territorial gains. In 344/955 his fleet attacked the coast of Ifrīḳiya in order to avenge the sack of Almería by the Sicilian fleet of al-Muʿizz the Fāṭimid. This first attack failed but in the following year, 345/956, he returned with another squadron of 70 ships, took and set fire to Marsā al-Kharaz (La Calle) and laid waste the districts of Susa and Ṭabarḳa. In 357/968 he attacked Calahorra and was sent in 361/972 to Morocco to subdue the Idrīsids. After a long and victorious campaign he brought them back in subjection to Cordova. In 364/974 he undertook a carefully prepared expedition against the Castile-Navarre-Leon coalition in which he beat firstly the Christian allies under the walls of Gormaz, then count García Fernández at Langa, south of the Duero, on 25 Shawwāl 364/8 July 975. At this time he took the title of Dhu 'l-Sayfayn and established himself at Medinaceli where he had Ibn Abī ʿĀmir, the famous Almanzor, as his intendant general. When Hishām succeeded to the throne Ibn Abī ʿĀmir joined with Ghālib in his campaigns as commander of the forces of the capital and married his daughter in 367/978. But discord soon broke out between father-in-law and son-in-law when the old general, devoted to the Umayyads, saw the affront suffered by the dynasty at the hands of the parvenu Ibn Abī ʿĀmir, who restricted the activities of the young caliph to pious exercises. The conflict now open, Ibn Abī ʿĀmir seized Medinaceli, Ghālib's fief, at the head of big Berber contingents. Ghālib, to spite him, allied himself with his old enemies the count of Castile and the king of Navarre. The first encounters went in his favour, but Almanzor decided to wager all and provoked a decisive engagement on 4 Muḥarram 371/10 July 981. The battle took place near the castle of San Vicente, probably the modern Torre Vicente about half way between Atienza and Gormaz. In spite of his 80 years Ghālib gave, as always, proof of his courage and boldness, but in a furious attack his horse stumbled and, pierced in the breast by his saddle-bow, he fell dead. The field was thus left free to the unbridled ambition of his lucky rival.

Bibliography: Lévi-Provençal, *Histoire de l'Espagne musulmane*, ii, 64, 68, 108, 116-234; iii, 58, 80, 122, 318, 500; on Medinaceli, Maḳḳarī, *Analectes*, i, 252-6; on Calahorra, Ibn Khaldūn, *ʿIbar*, iv, 145; Maḳḳarī, i, 248; on Gormaz, Codera, in *Bol. Acad. Hist.*, xiv (1889); Ibn Ḥayyān, *Muḳtabis*, iii, 49, 233, 239, 240, 242; idem, 91, 116-8; on Asmāʾ daughter of Ghālib, Ibn Bassām, *Dhakhīra*, iv, 47; Maḳḳarī, ii, 62; Ibn ʿIdhārī, *al-Bayān al-mughrib*, ii, text 285, tr. 443; Ibn al-Khaṭīb, *Aʿmāl al-aʿlām*, 71-4; Ibn Ḥazm, *Naḳt al-ʿarūs*, 21 (ed. Seybold, 239); Ibn ʿAbd al-Malik al-Marrākushī, *al-Dhayl wa 'l-takmila*, Rabat MS. f. 246. (A. Huici Miranda)

GHĀLIB b. Ṣaʿṣaʿa b. Nādjiya b. ʿIḳāl b. Muḥammad b. Sufyān b. Mudjāshiʿ b. Dārim, an eminent Tamīmī, famous for his generosity, the father of the poet al-Farazdaḳ.

The tradition that Ghālib was a contemporary of the Prophet (*lahū idrāk*) seems to be valid; the tradition that he visited the Prophet and asked him about the reward of the deeds of his father in the time of the Djāhiliyya (*Aghānī*, xix, 4) seems however to be spurious. Ghālib belonged to the generation after the Prophet; his name is connected with the names of Ṭalba b. Ḳays b. ʿĀṣim and ʿUmayr b. al-Sulayl al-Shaybānī, tribal leaders in the time of Muʿāwiya, in the story of the men of Kalb who tried to find the most generous man (*Aghānī*, xix, 5; in Ibn Abi 'l'Ḥadīd's *Sharḥ*, iii, 426, ed. 1329 A.H., Ghālib is mentioned with Aktham b. Ṣayfī and ʿUtayba b. al-Ḥārith, which is an obvious anachronism). The most generous man among the three sayyids was indeed Ghālib. (Ghālib was a neighbour of Ṭalba in al-Sīdān, in the vicinity of Kāẓima). He is said to have visited ʿAlī b. Abī Ṭālib and introduced to him his son al-Farazdaḳ; ʿAlī recommended him to teach his son the Ḳurʾān. (According to the tradition of *Aghānī*, xix, 6 he visited him in Baṣra after the battle of the Camel. According to the story quoted in Baghdādī's *Khizāna*, i, 108, Ghālib was then an old man; al-Farazdaḳ was in his early youth).

Ghālib earned his fame by his generosity. Muḥ. b. Ḥabīb counts him in his list of the generous men of the Djāhiliyya (*al-Muḥabbar*, 142); al-Djāḥiẓ stresses that he was one of the generous men of the Islamic period, not inferior to the generous men of the Djāhiliyya, although public opinion prefers the latter (*al-Ḥayawān*, ii, 108, ed. ʿAbd al-Salām Hārūn). Ghālib is said to have granted bounteous gifts to people, not asking them even about their names. The story of his contest with Suḥaym b. Wathīl al-Riyāḥī in slaughtering camels in the time of ʿUthmān is quoted in many versions. Al-Farazdaḳ mentions this deed of his father boastfully in his poems; Djarīr refers to it disdainfully; the competition was censured in Islam as a custom of the Djāhiliyya (Goldziher, *Muh.St.*, i, 60). A peculiar story in *Naḳāʾiḍ* 417 tells how he threw to the populace in Mecca (*anhaba*) 40,000 dirhams.

Ghālib was assaulted by Dhakwān b. ʿAmr al-Fuḳaymī in consequence of a quarrel between Fuḳaymī men and a servant of Ghālib, who tried to prevent them from drinking water from a reservoir belonging to Ghālib in al-Ḳubaybāt. Mudjāshiʿī tradition denies the Fuḳaymī claim that Ghālib died in consequence of this assault. He died in the early years of the reign of Muʿāwiya and was buried at Kāẓima.

Al-Farazdaḳ mourned his father in a number of elegies (cf. *Dīwān al-Farazdaḳ*, 163, 210, 611, 676, ed. al-Ṣāwī). His tomb became a refuge for the needy and the oppressed who asked help, which had indeed always been granted to them by al-Farazdaḳ (cf. *Dīwān al-Farazdaḳ*, 94, 191, 757, 893 and *Naḳāʾiḍ* 380). Al-Farazdaḳ often mentions him in his poems as "Dhu 'l-Ḳabr" or "Ṣāḥib al-Djadath" (Goldziher, *Muh. St.*, i, 237).

Bibliography: In addition to the sources quoted in the article: Balādhurī, *Ansāb*, Ms. 971a-b, 972a, 974a, 978b, 992a, 1043b; al-Marzubānī, *Muʿdjam*, 486; al-Mubarrad, *al-Kāmil*, 129, 280; Ibn Ḳutayba, *K. al-ʿArab* (*Rasāʾil al-Bulaghāʾ*, 350; idem, *Shiʿr*, ed. de Goeje, index; Ibn Durayd, *Ishtiḳāḳ*, ed. Hārūn, 239-40; Al-Djāḥiẓ, *al-Bayān*, ed. al-Sandūbī, ii, 187, 225, iii, 139, 195; *Aghānī*[2], index; *Naḳāʾiḍ*, ed. Bevan, index; al-Djumaḥī, *Ṭabaḳāt*, ed. Shākir, 261; al-Ḳālī, *Amālī*, ii, 120; idem, *Dhayl al-Amālī*, 52, 77; Yāḳūt s.v. Ṣawʾar, Miḳarr; Ibn Ḥadjar, *al-Iṣāba*, s.v. Ghālib (N. 6925), Suḥaym (N. 3660), al-Farazdaḳ (N. 7029), Hunayda (N. 1115-women);

al-Baghdādī, *Khizāna*, i, 462; al-ʿAynī, *al-Maḳāṣid*, i, 112 [on margin of *Khizāna*]; al-Farazdaḳ, *Dīwān*, ed. al-Ṣāwī; Ṭabarī, ed. Cairo 1939, iv, 179.

(M. J. Kister)

GHĀLIB dede, Meḥmed Esʿad, also Shaykh Ghālib (1171/1757-1213/1799), Turkish poet, the last of the five great representatives of the *dīwān* literature (the others being Bāḳī, Fuḍūlī, Nefʿī and Nedīm [*qq.v.*]). He was born in Istanbul at the Yenikapı Mewlewīkhāne, in 1171/1757, as is recorded in two famous chronograms: *ether-i ʿishḳ* and *djezbet-ullāh*. His father Muṣṭafa Reshīd, poet and scholar, belonged to a Mewlewī family, and exercised a decisive influence on Ghālib's life and his choice of career. Of his mother we only know, from a chronogram by Ghālib himself, that her name was Emīne and that she died in 1209/1794. Ghālib does not seem to have had a regular *madrasa* training, but to have been thoroughly educated in Islamic classics in the family circle and in the Mewlewī convent. After his father, his main teacher and guide seems to have been Ashdjî-bashî Ḥüsayn Dede who became the Shaykh of the Ghalaṭa convent in 1194/1790. Ghālib began to write poetry at a very early age and was able to arrange a *dīwān* at the age of twenty-four, while at the same time serving as an official at the Beylikdji Odasî of the Dīwān-ı Hümāyūn. At the suggestion of the poet Neshʾet he adopted as pen-name (*makhlaṣ*) Esʿad, which he later changed to Ghālib. Ghālib became increasingly interested in the works of Djelāl al-Din Rūmī and the Mewlewīs. He suddenly decided in 1198/1783 to join the order and went to Ḳonya accompanied by his young friend Ibrāhīm Khān-zāde Yūnus Bey to perform the necessary rites in the headquarters of the order, under the guidance of the head of the Mewlewīs, Seyyid Ebū Bekir Čelebi. On his return he completed his *čille* at the famous Ghalaṭa convent of the order and then retired to his house in Sütlüdje on the Golden Horn where he wrote a commentary to Yūsuf Sīnečāk's *Djezīre-i Methnewī*.

His appointment by the Čelebi of Ḳonya as the *shaykh* of the Ghalaṭa convent is a turning point in Ghālib's life. He soon attracted the attention of the Sultan Selīm III, himself a poet and musician, an admirer of Djelāl al-Dīn Rūmī and a member of the Mewlewī order. The Sultan became a great personal friend of Ghālib and used to pay him frequent visits in the convent, and the poet was always welcome in the Imperial Palace. With the Sultan's help Ghālib succeeded in restoring the convent and its annexes completely and then in making it the most important literary centre of the capital; he himself moved to the living quarters of the convent. Princess Beyhan, the sister of Selīm III, a cultured and intelligent woman, had great sympathy for the poet, which seems later to have developed into an attachment. She helped and protected him in many ways until his death. Ghālib reveals his great respect and admiration for her in many of his poems. It is not impossible that he was in love with her, judging from the many passages where feeling and affection are couched in expressions of reverence.

In the circle of the Mewlewīs Ghālib's best friend was Esrār Dede, poet and biographer, on whose death he wrote his famous elegy. Ghālib himself died in 1209/1799, at the age of forty-two. The sources are not in agreement as to the causes of his early death. It seems likely that he fell victim to tuberculosis. He is buried at the Ghalaṭa convent cemetery by the side of Ismāʿīl Rüsūkhī Dede, the famous 11th/17th century *Mathnawī* commentator.

Ghālib owes his great fame mainly to his *mathnawī Ḥüsn u ʿAshḳ*. His *dīwān*, which contains the richest variety of forms and metrical patterns of the classical school and contains many poems of high standard, has often been qualified by most critics as second rate, for his brilliant and unusual *mathnawī* eclipsed for them everything else he wrote. *Ḥüsn u ʿAshḳ* is an allegorical romance of mystic love. One night a boy Ḥüsn (Beauty) and a girl ʿAshḳ (Love) are born in the Benī Maḥabbat (Sons of Love) tribe. They are at once betrothed by the elders of the tribe. They go to the same school where their teacher is Mollā-yi Djünūn (The Master of Folly). The two are devoted to each other. In the garden Nüzhet-geh-i Maʿnā (The Promenade of Meaning) where they go, they meet an old man Sukhan (Word), the owner of the garden who becomes their go-between. Ḥayret (Astonishment), the local judge, tries to prevent their meeting. But ʿIṣmet (Chastity), the guardian of Ḥüsn, and Ghayret (Zeal), the nurse of ʿAshḳ, try to console and help them in their difficulties. ʿAshḳ asks for Ḥüsn from the tribe, but they make fun of her. She must first go to the Kingdom of the Ḳalb (Heart) and on the way overcome many trials. But ʿAshḳ is prepared to face all things and sets out with Ghayret. At the first step they fall into the bottomless well of a giant who wishes to fatten and eat them. Sukhan rescues them by a rope he lets down. Then freezing Winter detains them on their way and they fall into the power of a wizard. Again Sukhan comes with a horse (Ashḳar) and a sword (*Tīgh-i āh* 'Sword of Sighs') from Ḥüsn, and they set out on their journey reaching the Deryā-yi Ātesh (the Sea of Fire) where there are ships of wax. They have no choice but to fly over, which Ghayret does by opening his wings. ʿAshḳ mounts on Ashḳar who goes without hesitation into the fire. Thus they reach the borders of China. The Emperor's daughter Hūsh-Rübā (Reason-captivating) assumes the shape of Ḥüsn and deceives ʿAshḳ, shutting her up in the Dhāt al-Ṣuwer (painted) fortress. Again Sukhan comes in the shape of a nightingale and tells ʿAshḳ that there is a treasure in the castle and it is necessary to burn the castle to get the treasure. So the castle and all its paintings are burnt. ʿAshḳ becomes thin and ill and can no longer stand even the weight of her clothes made of cloth of moon silk. But a more auspicious day dawns. Sukhan comes as a healing doctor and orders ʿAshḳ to go the castle of the *Ḳalb* (Heart) where Ḥüsn is King. ʿAshḳ sees that the castle of the *Ḳalb* (Heart) is like the fortress Dhāt al-Ṣuwer, but it is truly real. There she sees all her old teachers and nurses. Sukhan tells her that there are no perils or dangers, that it had been he who slew the monsters, and had been the nightingale and the doctor, and now he invites her to come to union with her beloved. Love is Beauty and Beauty is Love and no evil tongue can separate them.

Ghālib, as the last great exponent of *dīwān* poetry, occupies a unique place in the history of Ottoman Turkish literature. From the late 7th/13th until the 11th/17th century, Ottoman Turkish *dīwān* poets were mainly inspired by the great Persian classics the last of whom was Djāmī [*q.v.*]. But in the Indian courts of Babur's descendants there developed a new style of Persian poetry (*sabḳ-i Hindī* [*q.v.*]) in the 10th/16th and 11th/17th centuries, which, abandoning the tradition of the great classics, made fashionable the exaggerated use of conceits, allegory and ornate expressions, and laid emphasis on symbolic and obscure style and unusual words with over-elaborate and far-fetched colour-imagery. This 'Indian School' of poetry began to influence 11th/17th century Ottoman poets like Nefʿī and more particularly Nāʾilī and a host of other minor writers.

The appearance of a poet of genius like Nedīm in the early 12th/18th century seemed to announce a radical change in the Persian-inspired tradition of Ottoman poetry. Nedīm, although not daring to do away with traditional themes, forms and clichés, made great efforts to "depersianize" Ottoman poetry, introducing many themes and motives from his time and surroundings and using unconventional and often colloquial language. Ghālib, with his poetical genius, unusual power of imagination and mastery of form, might have achieved what Nedīm had started: to create a thoroughly Turkish *dīwān* poetry in the classical tradition, had he chosen to follow his example. Instead, although he admired Nedīm and owes much to him in some of his poems, he decided to turn the clock back and picked up again the "Indian School" tradition where Nāʾilī had left off. But as he was a greater poet with more vision and imagination, and imbued with mysticism, he created, at the close of the classical period, his original blend of both sources.

Bibliography: Esrār Dede, *Tedhkire-i shuʿarā-yi Mewlewīyye*, Istanbul University Library MS, T.Y. 3894, s.v.; Thākib Dede, *Sefīne-i nefīse-i Mewlewiyye*, Cairo 1283, s.v.; Faṭīn, *Tedhkire*, Istanbul 1271, s.v.; Gibb, *Ottoman Poetry*, iv, 175 ff.; M. F. Köprülü, *Eski şairlerimiz, Divan edebiyatı antolojisi*, Istanbul 1931, s.v.; Sadettin Nüzhet Ergun, *Şeyh Galip*, Istanbul 1932; Vasfi Mahir Kocatürk, *Hüsn ile Aşk*, Istanbul 1944 (paraphrased in modern Turkish); Ibrahim Kutluk, *Şeyh Galip ve as-Sohbet-üs-Safiyye*, in *Türk Dili ve Edebiyati Dergisi*, iii (1948), 21 ff.; Abdülbaki Gölpınarlı, *Şeyh Galip, Hayatı, Sanatı, Şiirleri*, Istanbul 1953; A. Bombaci, *Storia della letteratura turca*, Milan 1956, 388 ff.; Sedit Yüksel, *Şeyh Galip, eserlerinin dil ve sanat değeri*, Ankara 1963 (with detailed bibliography and information on MSS and editions of Ghālib's works).

(Fahir İz)

GHĀLIB, Ismāʿīl [see ismāʿīl ghālib].

GHĀLIB, Mīrzā Asad Allāh Khān, one of the greatest Muslim poets of the Indo-Pakistani subcontinent. He was born in 1797 at Āgra in an aristocratic Muslim family; his childhood and early boyhood were passed at Āgra where he received the classical Mughal education (Persian being one of its chief subjects). He moved to Delhi when he was about 15 years of age and lived in the Mughal capital till his death on 15 February 1869, except for a brief sojourn in Lucknow and Benares on his way to Calcutta where he remained two years (1830-32) in connexion with an unsuccessful attempt to have his pension increased. Returning to Delhi, he lived on pensions granted him in recognition of his talents first by the nawab of Oudh, then by the court of Delhi. Thus Ghālib lived a major part of his life near the degenerate Mughal court of his times and witnessed the hard days of the famous "Mutiny" of 1857. Only with great difficulty and after painful humiliations did he succeed in freeing himself of suspicion of having taken part in the Mutiny and get his pension restored to him by the British Government. Apart from domestic unhappiness (he lost his father at the age of five years, all his seven sons died in infancy, etc.) Ghālib's life was rather quiet and colourless. Hardly any hints at the grave political events of his time can be found in his poetry. He was not even passionately concerned with the Muslim religion, and his broad and tolerant attitude in this respect is shown in a letter to Munshī Hargopāl Tāfta, to whom he writes: "I hold all human beings, Muslim, Hindu or Christian, dear to me, and regard them as my brothers"; the mystical imagery present in his lyrics is due rather to his following the traditional style than to genuine Ṣūfī feeling. The real protagonist of all his poetry is his own mind, which creates extremely refined intellectual images; his poetry, chiefly of a very melancholic trend, is therefore extremely fragmentary, but those "fragments" (he himself defines his *Dīwān* as a "selection") are amongst the most perfect specimens of Urdu literature.

Ghālib's more important works are: (1) His Urdu *Dīwān* first published in 1841 and then, with additions, four times again during his life (last edition in Ghālib's life in 1863 with 1795 *bayt*s), and numerous times after his death (*Dīwān-i Ghālib*, ed. Dhākir Ḥusayn, Berlin 1925 is an attractive pocket edition without notes; the last good edition is: *Dīwān-i Urdū*, ed. and annotated by Imtiyāz ʿAlī ʿArshī, ʿAlīgaṛh 1958); (2) His Persian *Kulliyyāt*, consisting of *ḳaṣīda*s, *ghazal*s, short *mathnawī*s, *ḳiṭʿa*s etc., first published in 1845 and then repeatedly, especially by Nawalkishore in Lucknow (1862, 1924 etc.); (3) Various works in Persian prose included in his *Kulliyyāt-i nathr* first published together by Nawalkishore in Lucknow in 1868. They are: *Pandj gandj-i āhang* (a treatise on Persian grammar and stylistics), *Mihr-i nīm-rōz* (first part of a *Partavistān*, which was a history of the Mughals and the Mughal Empire, the second part of which never came out), and *Dastānbū* (an account of the Indian Mutiny as seen by Ghālib); (4) *Ḳāṭiʿ-i Burhān*, a critical work on the famous Persian Dictionary *Burhān-i ḳāṭiʿ*, first published in Lucknow in 1861-62, and then, with additions, in 1865-66 as *Dirafsh-i Kāviyānī*; (5) The two famous collections of letters in Urdu, the *ʿŪd-i Hindī* first published in 1868 (162 letters) in Meerut, and *Urdū-e Muʿallā* (472 letters) published only 19 days after his death, in March 1869 in Delhi; further letters, fragments in Persian and Urdu etc. were repeatedly published afterwards.

Ghālib expressly stated that he entrusted his fame and renown not to his Urdu, but to his Persian works, and his letters reveal his keen interest in Persian grammar, lexicography and stylistics. He declares that at first he was fascinated by Bīdil [*q.v.*] and his difficult style, but afterwards he preferred a sounder and simpler, more classical Persian. Actually the most mature part of his Persian work is far superior to that of many Indo-Persian writers, but historically speaking its value is rather reduced by the fact that Persian had, already in Ghālib's time, been superseded in the Indian administration by Urdu and had practically no future in India. Therefore a more durable trace was left by Ghālib's Urdu productions. In spite of the difficulty, the wealth of conceits and the extreme over-persianization of its style, his small Urdu *Dīwān* shows what has been called by some of his commentators a "passionate intensity of thought", partly at least derived from his former master Bīdil. In some of his fragments he tries even the supremely refined experiment of simplicity. Simplicity—in contrast to his rather complicated Persian prose—is the chief and revolutionary aspect of his Urdu letters, an unsurpassed model of direct, unaffected expression. Ghālib can therefore be considered the father of modern Urdu prose; for what concerns poetry, he is the father of only one aspect of modern Urdu poetry, the intellectual and psychological deepening of the old imagery; his complete aloofness from outward reality (no more than 15-20 lines out of the nearly 1800 verses of his Urdu *Dīwān* have Nature as the main theme!) renders him a not very suitable source of inspiration for modern realistic writers of poetry, who may rather look to Urdu poets of the *gīt* type (*e.g.*, Naẓīr Akbarābādī). Attempts at translations of Ghālib into European languages are therefore very scanty, though some of his poems well deserve a modern European re-interpretation.

Bibliography: Books and articles on Ghālib are numerous, especially in India and Pakistan. We mention only: A. H. Ḥālī, *Yādgār-i Ghālib*, 1897; ʿAbd al-Raḥmān Bijnaurī, *Maḥāsin-i kalām-i Ghālib*, Agra 1928; S. M. Ikrām, *Ḥakīm-i farzāna*, Lahore 1957; Khalīfa ʿAbd al-Ḥakīm, *Afkār-i Ghālib*, Lahore 1954; a useful commentary on the Urdu *Dīwān* is: Āghā Muḥammad Bāḳir, *Bayān-i Ghālib*, Lahore 1946 (includes also opinions of earlier commentators); an attempt at a free English translation of fragments of Ghālib's Urdu poetry is: J. L. Kaul, *Interpretations of Ghalib*, Delhi 1957. See also A. Bausani, *The position of Ghālib (1796-1869) in the history of Urdu and Indo-Persian poetry*, in *Isl.*, xxxiv (1959), 99-127. (A. Bausani)

GHĀLIB, Sharīf [see hāshimids and makka].

GHĀLIB PASHA [see mehmed saʿīd ghālib pasha].

GHALZAY (Ghaldjī, Ghilzay), a large western Afghān (Pashto speaking) tribe with many subdivisions, mainly located between Ḳandahār and Ghazna.

Much has been written about the origins of the Ghalzay and one may assume they are a mixture, including Hephthalite and Turkish elements. The name in Pashto would mean 'the son of Ghal,' which in turn means 'thief'. This is the popular explanation of the name Ghalzay. According to legends in the *Makhzan-i Afghānī*, the Ghalzays are descended from Mato, a daughter of Bitan (or Batnī) who was a son of Ḳays, the eponymous ancestor of all Pathans. Mato had an affair with Shāh Ḥusayn, a refugee prince of Ghūr, and Ghalzay was born of this union, the progenitor of the tribe.

It is probable that the name Ghalzay is derived from Khaladj, a Turkic (or Hephthalite?) tribe, which lived in the Ghazna area in the 4th/10th century (cf. Minorsky). The Khaldji (Khildji) dynasty of India was founded by leaders of this tribe, and a mixture of 'Turks and Afghāns' is indicated by the *Djahān-nāma*, a geographical text of the early 7th/13th century. Bābur campaigned against the Ghaldjī near Ghazna, and we may assume this is the earliest mention of the name of the Ghalzays. The Ghalzays came into prominence in the 11th/17th century when they moved into the region of Ḳandahār, occupying territory vacated by Abdālī tribesmen who had been moved to Harāt by Shāh ʿAbbās I. In 1707 Mīr Ways, leader of the Ghalzays of Ḳandahār, revolted against the Persians, slew the governor and declared his independence. Mīr Ways died in 1715 and was succeeded, after some conflict, by his son Maḥmūd. The latter captured Kirmān in 1720 and the Ṣafawī capital Iṣfahān in 1722. The Ghalzays ruled Persia under Maḥmūd and Ashraf until 1730. With the victories of Nādir Shāh the power of the Ghalzays melted away. In place of the Ghalzays, the Abdalīs or Durrānīs became the principal tribe of Afghānistān, led by Aḥmad Shāh.

The Ghalzays aided Shāh Shudjāʿ to take Kābul in 1218/1803, and ties of marriage joined the Ghalzay chiefs to the ruling Durrānī tribe. In more recent times a Ghalzay force was defeated at Aḥmad Khēl in 1880 by a British detachment under Stewart marching from Ḳandahār to Kābul. The Ghalzays revolted against the ruler of Afghānistān, ʿAbd al-Raḥmān in 1886, and have participated in many local uprisings and raids since that time.

At present the Ghalzays are mainly found east and south-east of Ghazna, although groups of them are settled in northern Afghānistān near Maymāna and in Badakhshān. They are divided into two main groups, the Turān (Tōkhī and Hōtakī sub-tribes) and the Burhān (Sulayman-khēl, ʿAlī-khēl, Tarakkī and Isḥākzay). There may be almost two million Ghalzays, of whom three-quarters live in Afghānistān, and the rest in Pakistān.

Bibliography: V. Minorsky, *The Turkish Dialect of the Khalaj*, in *BSOS*, x (1940), 417; O. Caroe, *The Pathans*, London 1958, *passim*; D. Wilber, *Afghānistān*, New York 1963; *Makhzan* trans. B. Dorn, *History of the Afghans*, London 1836; *Djahān-nāma*, ed. Yu. E. Borshčevskiy, Moscow 1960, 17b; *Sovremenniy Afganistan*, ed. N. A. Dvoryankov, Moscow 1960. (R. N. Frye)

GHĀMID, tribe and district in western Saudi Arabia. The tribe is said to descend from Ghāmid b. ʿAbd Allāh of al-Azd of Ḳaḥtān, who moved northward from the Yaman and settled in the area now called Bilād Ghāmid in the highlands of southern al-Ḥidjāz, centred around approximately 20° N. and 41° 45′ E.

The tribe is now subdivided into a large number of sections, most of which are sedentary. The few nomadic sections, called Āl Ṣayyāḥ, roam along the northern and eastern edges of the settled district and own a few gardens in al-ʿAḳīḳ and along Wādī Ranyā.

The district of Ghāmid is relatively thickly settled, fertile, and prosperous. Rainfall allows dry farming, and fruits, wheat, barley, beans, and tobacco are grown. The villages consist for the most part of stone houses, made from locally quarried granite blocks. The fertility of the area, the extreme fragmentation of tribal splinter groups, and the raids by the Bedouin, formerly always at odds with the farming population, led to the construction of innumerable defensive towers, also made of granite blocks, which are characteristic of the area. Many of these towers have been allowed to decay.

Before the First World War Ghāmid owed allegiance to either the Turks or the Sharīf of Mecca, and its administrative centre was in the village of al-Ẓafīr (from Āl al-Ẓafīr section of Ghāmid). Since the establishment of the Saudi government, the district of Ghāmid and that of Zahrān [*q.v.*] to the north have been administered as a unit. The seat of local government is now some 15 miles south of al-Ẓafīr at Baldjurshī (or Baldjurashī), a name designating twenty-four small settlements scattered over a wide plain (altitude 1,960 meters). Four of these settlements: al-ʿAwadha, al-Ṣilmiyya, al-Rukba, and al-Ghāzī, collectively referred to as Dār al-Sūḳ, are close together and form the administrative and marketing centre.

Bibliography: Fuʾād Ḥamza, *Ḳalb Djazīrat al-ʿArab*, Mecca 1933; ʿUmar Riḍā Kaḥḥāla, *Muʿdjam Ḳabāʾil al-ʿArab*, Damascus 1949; M. F. von Oppenheim, *Die Beduinen*, ii, Leipzig 1943; Admiralty, *A Handbook of Arabia*, London 1916-7. (F. S. Vidal)

GHĀNA, a town in the Nigerian Sudan in the

Middle Ages, now vanished, the site of which should apparently be identified with Kumbi Ṣāliḥ (15° 40′ N., 8° W.), some 330 km./200 miles north of Bamako, 95 km./60 miles west-north-west of Nara and 70 km./44 miles south-south-east of Timbedra. Kumbi Ṣāliḥ belongs to the administrative district of Aïoun el Atrous (*ʿUyun al-ʿatrūs*) (subdivision of Timbedra) in the Islamic republic of Mauritania.

The term *g͟hāna* signified sovereign in the Awkār. By extension, it denoted the capital city of the first negro kingdom of Nigerian Sudan. Al-Fazārī (before 184/800) is the first to speak of "G͟hāna, the land of gold", which is mentioned also by al-Yaʿḳūbī (256/870) and, in particular, by Ibn al-Faḳīh al-Hamad͟hānī who died probably in 290/903 and who, in his *Kitāb al-Buldān* (*BGA*, vi, 87), provides some amusing details (ed. and trans. M. Hadj-Sadok, Algiers 1949, 51): "from Ṭarḳala to G͟hāna it is three months journey on foot through the desert; in the country of G͟hāna, gold grows in the sand like carrots (*d͟jazar*); it is dug up at sunrise; the natives live on millet (*d͟hura*) and beans (*lūbiyā*); their name for millet is *duk͟hn*; they clothe themselves in panther skins since these animals are abundant in their country".

The first eyewitness account by a traveller is that of Ibn Ḥawḳal, who in 366/977 wrote the *K. al-Masālik wa 'l-mamālik* in which he says "The king of G͟hāna is the richest in the land on account of the gold mines he governs", but gives almost no other information about his visit to the Sudan.

Al-Saʿdī (d. *ca.* 1065/1655), inthe *Taʾrīk͟h al-Sūdān* (ed.-tr. O. Houdas, Paris 1900, 2nd ed. Paris 1964) mentions 44 princes of white stock of unknown origin, 22 of whom are said to have ruled before the *hid͟jra* and 22 afterwards, but Delafosse thinks (*Haut Sénégal-Niger*, iii, 1912, 23) that the tradition mentioned 44 sovereigns, a number of whom were before the *hid͟jra*, and that the writer of the *Taʾrīk͟h* translated *a number* by *half*. In fact nothing is known about this period, except that the Soninke, a negro race, co-existed with these princes of white stock; R. Mauny, however, disputes that there was in this period a race of white princes, whom al-Idrīsī (549/1154) is the first writer to mention. In about 174/790, Kaya Maghan Cissé, the first negro *tounka* (king) of G͟hāna, drove back the Whites towards Tagant, Gorgol and Fūta. This kingdom included Awkār, Bagana, Diaga, Kaniaga, northern Beledugu, Kaarta, Kuigui, Diafunu and Wagadu. Almost nothing is known about this kingdom until the first Berber attacks in the 3rd/9th century which have been described for us by Ibn Abī Zarʿ (*Rawḍ al-ḳirṭās*) and Ibn K͟haldūn. This Berber invasion led to the kingdom of Awdag͟host [*q.v.*] which became a vassal of G͟hāna. In 380/990 the town of Awdag͟host was taken by the king of G͟hāna, who appointed a negro governor to ensure that the dues on their caravans were paid by his Berber vassals. For half a century G͟hāna was the most powerful kingdom of the Sudan; thanks to al-Bakrī (460/1067-8) we have a good deal of information about it. The capital consisted of two towns, one of which was inhabited by Muslims among whom were several jurists and other scholars; it had twelve mosques to which *imāms*, *muʾad͟hd͟hins* and readers (*rātibūn*) are attached; the Friday prayer is observed in one of them. The other, situated six miles away, was the royal town. Here the sovereign had a palace comprising a castle and a number of huts with round roofs, the whole being surrounded by a wall. Not far from the king's court stood a mosque for the use of Muslims visiting the Prince on special missions. The houses were made of stone, a unique feature in the Sudan, or of wood of the gum-tree. Nearby were extensive woods, from which the royal town took its name of *g͟hāba* (forest). In huts in this forest lived the sorcerers and priests who guarded the idols; it was there also that the kings' tombs and the prisons were located. The people were fetish-worshippers, as was their sovereign, though in fact he treated the Muslims with great respect, and thus chose his interpreters, his treasurer and most of his ministers from among them; according to al-Bakrī, they had also special privileges of dress. Since Delafosse, many descriptions have been given of the royal audiences. They began with the beating of drums (*daba*). The king's subjects prostrated themselves and threw earth over their heads, but the Muslims showed respect by clapping their hands.

The commercial rôle of G͟hāna was very important. The Mag͟hribī traders arrived from Tafilalet with stocks of merchandise, in particular salt bought at Teg͟hāza and aromatic wood which was used to sweeten the water-skins and to make the water kept in them for a long time fit to drink. The wares brought from the north included copper earrings and rings. From the Sahara came caravans laden with salt. But the principal commodity was gold from the mines of Wangara (Upper Senegal and Faleme basin) which the traders fetched from Gadiaro, 18 days' journey from G͟hāna and probably near Kayes, and which they exchanged by silent barter. The figures given by al-Bakrī relating to the strength of the G͟hāna army (200,000 warriors, 40,000 of them archers) are obviously an exaggeration.

Awdag͟host was captured by the Almoravids of Yaḥyā b. ʿUmar (446/1054). After checking the revolt of the Berber Maṣṣūfa, Abū Bakr b. ʿUmar decided to put their bellicose instincts to good use and sent them to attack Bassi, the king of G͟hāna (1061) who was renowned for his justice and for his friendship towards the Muslims; he was succeeded the next year by his nephew Tounka Menin. After 15 years of warfare, Abū Bakr took possession of G͟hāna (1076). The inhabitants were massacred or compelled to accept conversion. The death of Abū Bakr ibn ʿUmar (480/1087) must have allowed G͟hāna to regain its independence. But the various provinces had broken away, with the result that in the 6th/12th century the authority of the ruler of G͟hāna hardly extended beyond Bassikūnū and Awkār. In 1203 Sumangūrū Kante, the ruler of the Sosso, took G͟hāna and established in it a pagan garrison from which the Muslim Sorinke had to flee to Walata (1224), which replaced G͟hāna as the centre of trading caravans and of Muslim education, and to Dienné (1250). In 1240 Soundjata Keita captured G͟hāna, which was entirely destroyed.

Nevertheless, al-ʿUmarī, writing before 750/1349, stated: "In the length and breadth of the lands of the lord of this kingdom (of Mali), there is no-one who bears the title of king save the lord of G͟hāna, who is, however, his deputy, despite his title of king". Incidentally, Ibn K͟haldūn speaks of his meeting in 796/1393 with S͟hayk͟h ʿUt͟hmān, *muftī* of the inhabitants of G͟hāna. These two passages seem to indicate the persistence, after the expeditions of the 7th/13th century, of an important community perhaps residing at Walata and including a king and *muftī*.

It was the extraordinary renown of this negro kingdom that induced Dr. Nkrumah, the political leader of the Gold Coast, to name his country Ghana when it attained independence in 1957.

Bibliography: Ibn Ḥawḳal, trans. de Slane, in *JA*, 1842, 240; Bakrī, *Desc. de l'Afrique*, trans.

de Slane, 381 ff.; *Tarikh el-Fettach*, trad. O. Houdas and M. Delafosse, Paris 1913, ²Paris 1964; Idrīsī, trans. de Goeje, 9; Ibn Khaldūn, *Berbères*, trans. de Slane, ii, 110; Yāḳūt, iii, 370; *K. al-Istibṣār*, ed. Saʿd Zaghbūl ʿAbd al-Ḥamīd, Alexandria 1958, index (trans. Fagnan, *L'Afrique sept. au 12ᵉ siècle*, 195, 199-204); H. Barth, *Reisen*, iv, app. IX, 600 ff.; Bonnel de Mézières, *Recherches de l'emplacement de Ghana (Fouilles à Koumbi et à Settah)*, in *Acad. des insc. et belles lettres. Mémoires présentés par divers savants*, xii/1, Paris 1920; idem, *La question de Ghana et la mission Bonnel de Mézières*, in *Ann. et Mémoires du Comité Historique et Scientifique de l'AOF*, 1916, 40-61; M. Delafosse, *Le Ghana et le Mali et l'emplacement de leurs capitales*, in *BCHSAOF*, 1924, 479-509; R. Mauny, *État actuel de la question de Ghana*, in *BIFAN*, 1951, 463-75; idem, *The question of Ghana*, in *Africa*, 1954; P. Thomassey and R. Mauny, *Campagne de fouilles à Koumbi Saleh*, in *BIFAN*, 1956, 436-62; J. Vidal, *Le mystère de Ghana*, in *BCHSAOF*, 1923, 512-24; Ch. Monteil, in *Hespéris*, xxxviii, 441 ff.; J. D. Fage, *Ancient Ghana . . .*, in *Trans. of the hist. Soc. of Ghana*, 1957; Yusuf Kamal, *Monumenta cartographica Africae et Aegypti*, Cairo 1926-38, esp. iii; D. F. McCall, *The traditions of the founding of Sijilmasa and Ghana*, in *Trans. of the Hist. Soc. of Ghana*, v/1 (1961); J. SpencerTrimingham, *A Hist. of Islam in West Africa*, Oxford 1962. (R. Cornevin)

GHANA. Islam first spread into the area comprised in the modern Republic of Ghana, the former British colony of the Gold Coast, probably in the late 8th/14th or early 9th/15th century, when the Muslim Dyula—specialized trading groups of Malinke and Soninke affiliations—extended their activities from the metropolitan districts of Mali outwards to various centres of primary economic production far beyond the imperial frontiers. Attracted into the Voltaic region to the south mainly by its abundant resources of gold, the Dyula established themselves in small colonies distributed along the trade-paths leading from the goldfields northwards to the greater markets on the Niger, termini of the trans-Saharan caravan trails. A Dyula centre of early importance, from which many later Muslim communities in both the Ivory Coast and Ghana stemmed, was at Begho, on the western border of Ghana near the modern Nsorkor; before its collapse probably in the early 18th century it had become one of the main focuses of Muslim activity within the Voltaic region. Another early centre was that of Wa, in northern Ghana, where the present *amīr al-muʾminīn*, the Dyula-mansa or Shehu Wangara, claims to be forty-second in office.

A second course of Muslim influence was that from the north-east. Muslim merchants from the Hausa states, active in the kola trade, may, on the evidence of the *Kano Chronicle*, have extended their activities into Ghana as early as the mid-9th/15th century. With the expansion of the trade in the 18th century, Hausa immigration into Ghana was greatly stimulated, and important settlements grew up in such northern market centres as Salaga and Yendi.

On the available evidence, it was not until the later 10th/16th century that Islam began to spread beyond the confines of the Dyula and Hausa trading communities. At that time the Begho *shaykh* Ismāʿīl, and his son Muḥammad al-Abyaḍ, converted to the faith the Malinke-Bambara ruling aristocracy of Gonja, then the rising power in northern Ghana. This was the period when, according to the *Taʾrīkh Kunta*, the disciples of ʿUmar al-Shaykh (d. ca. 949/1552-3) were planting the Ḳādiriyya order throughout the Western Sudan, and it may be that the Begho movement is to be seen against this background.

Not until a century and a half after the Gonja conversions does Islam appear to have made further significant gains in Ghana. In the early years of the 18th century the Dagomba ruler Muḥammad Zanjina became a convert to Islam, as did, at much the same time, Atabia (d. 1154/1741-2), king of the sister state of Mamprusi. Thus by the early 18th century the three major states of northern Ghana, Gonja, Dagomba, and Mamprusi, each had a Muslim ruler. None developed, however, into an Islamic state on the model of the 18th century imāmates of Futa Toro and Futa Jalon: since their political and socio-legal systems had become rigid in earlier times, they preserved, beneath an Islamic super-structure, an essentially pre-Islamic sub-structure.

In the late 18th and early 19th centuries Muslim communities established themselves further to the south. In Kumasi, capital of the Ashanti empire, Muslims served on the king's council, staffed the chancery, and, with the concurrence of the king who was apprehensive of the growth of a revolutionary native Ashanti merchant class, established their control over important sectors of the Ashanti economy.

The early 19th century Muslim reform movement initiated by ʿUthmān dan Fodio, which led to the establishment of the Fulani amīrates of northern Nigeria, made some impact upon north-eastern Ghana Muslim communities such as that of Yendi, the Dagomba capital, but by its doctrinal emphasis upon non-cooperation with pagan rulers perhaps tended in general to retard the spread of Islam further south. In the second half of the same century a wave of Islamization in the north-west, affecting in particular sections of the Sisala, appears to have resulted from the *djihād* of al-Ḥādjdj Maḥmūd Karantao of Wahabu (Republic of Volta), whose forces included Dagari-Dyula contingents from Wa. Later in the century the Wa area, and western Gonja, were for a brief time brought under the dominion of the Mandinka empire of Samori Ture, while in the central districts of northern Ghana the Zabarima and locally-recruited forces of Alfa Kazare, Babatu and Hamaria were creating the nucleus of a Muslim state in the midst of the pagan 'Grunshi'. An alliance between the Muslim forces of Samori, Babatu and Mukhtār ibn al-Ḥādjdj Maḥmūd Karantao, and even the non-Muslim Ashanti, directed against the British and French, failed to consolidate in time and by the beginning of the present century the strength of each had been broken by the colonial powers.

Muslim immigration increased in volume throughout the 19th and into the 20th century, Zabarima, Hausa and Yoruba constituting the bulk of the settlers. Today no town in Ghana is without its Muslim section. The recent spread of Islam has been largely a result of this process, though in the extreme south Islam gained new ground among the Fante as a result of the proselytizing activities from c. 1885 of Abū Bakr, a northern *malam*, and his two Fante disciples Benjamin Sam and Madhi Appah.

No census of the Muslim population of Ghana has been made. Over the country as a whole the proportion of Muslims is unlikely to be less than 10%, and may be significantly higher. The largest concentrations are found in the capital, Accra, which probably has about 75,000 Muslims (total population: 388,000), and in Kumasi with probably about 60,000 (total population: 221,000). Estimates of the extent of Islamization in northern Ghana vary widely from 15% to 50%; much depends upon the view taken of the many marginally Muslim groups there.

No detailed study of Muslim organization in Ghana has yet been made. The Ḳādirī and Tidjānī orders are both established. The history of the former in Ghana, as already suggested, may date back to c. 960/1550, though its main growth took place in the early 19th century, largely through Hausa intermediaries. The Tidjāniyya spread widely, often at the expense of the Ḳādiriyya, in the second half of the 19th century and is still ascendent. The Tidjānī *wird* in Ghana is probably partly of ʿUmarī origin (al-Ḥādjdj ʿUmar of Segu, d. 1864), but has certainly also been received immediately from the Senegambia, and, through pilgrims, from Meccan contacts. There are no reliable estimates of the numerical strength of either order. In addition, since 1921 Aḥmadī missionaries have been active especially in Saltpond in the extreme south, in Kumasi, and in Wa. In 1963 they claimed a following of between thirty and forty thousand. In the political life of Ghana Muslims are represented by the Moslem Council, a wing of the ruling Convention Peoples Party. The Moslem Association, founded in 1932 as an eductional and cultural organization, as the Moslem Association Party joined the opposition to the C.P.P. in 1956, but was disbanded in late 1957.

The development of Islamic learning in Ghana was one result of the spread of the faith. A tradition of local authorship was certainly well established by the early 18th century; it is exemplified in the extant *Kitāb Ghundjā*, an important historical work of Gonja authorship compiled in the middle of that century. The tradition is still a thriving one, and is excellently represented in the works of al-Ḥādjdj ʿUmar b. Abī Bakr of Salaga and Kete Krachi (b. Kano, c. 1850; d. Kete Krachi, 1934), of which over a hundred are known. They are characterized by their lively treatment of topical events,—the coming of the Christians; the Salaga civil war; the influenza epidemic; the claims of a false Mahdī; etc. Al-Ḥādjdj ʿUmar's pupils are now widely dispersed throughout Ghana and the surrounding territories. The Institute of African Studies in the University of Ghana has a growing collection of works in Arabic script from Ghana; these are mainly in the Arabic language but also include items in Hausa, Dagbane, Mamprule and Guan.

The ancient Western Sudanese tradition of mosque architecture, best known from the Niger Bend, is represented in about thirty surviving buildings in northern Ghana, of which the Friday mosques at Larabanga and Bole (Gonja) are particularly worthy of note. In general, however, the old mosques are rapidly being replaced by undistinguished (though more commodious) structures of concrete and corrugated iron. Much of the domestic architecture of north-western Ghana is also heavily Sudano-Islamic in style. (I. Wilks)

GHANAM [see BADW (ii,a), YÜRÜK, ZAKĀT].

GHANĪ, *takhalluṣ* of the Persian poet Mullā Muḥammad Ṭāhir Ashaʾī of Kashmīr, who flourished during the reign of the Mughal emperors, Shāhdjahān and Awrangzīb [*qq.v.*]. Nothing is known with certainty either about the date of his birth or the origins of the clan—the Ashaʾīs—to which he belonged. It is, however, certain that he was the son of an obscure poor *shālbāf* (a weaver of woollen shawls). A pupil of Muḥsin Fānī, assumed by some scholars to be the author of *Dabistān-i madhāhib*, Ghanī began writing poetry at the early age of twenty. The numerical value of his pen-name Ghanī (*i.e.*, 1060/1650) supplies the date. True to the literal meaning of his poetical name, he hated and detested meeting and attending on princes, potentates or men of power and riches. When his fame as a great poet reached the emperor Awrangzīb, he wanted to see him and ordered the governor of Kashmīr, Sayf Khān, to send Ghanī to Delhi. Learning of the governor's intention the poet refused to comply with his wishes and asked Sayf Khān to inform the emperor that Ghanī had gone mad. Finding the governor adamant, the poet all of a sudden tore his collar and rolled in the dust. Three days later he died (1079/1688). Gifted with an extraordinarily fertile imagination and a high-soaring intellect he composed fine poetry rich in *īhām* [*q.v.*].

His *dīwān*, comprising *ghazals*, *rubāʿīs* and *ḳaṣīdas*, was arranged and edited posthumously by Muḥammad ʿAlī Māhir, a Hindu convert to Islam and an adopted son of Mīr Djaʿfar Muʿammāʾī. It contains over 2,000 select verses and was printed in Lucknow in 1261/1845. Given to composing verses which admitted of more than one interpretation, Ghanī has few rivals in this field of *sanʿat-i īhām-gūʾī*. Piqued and offended, he gave up attending on ʿInāyat Khān, son of Ẓafar Khān Aḥsan, the Mughal governor of Kashmīr and a great patron of art and culture, as the former had once remarked that a couplet which could not be properly understood on the first hearing or reading was absurd and meaningless. Ghanī lies buried in the Gurgāṛī Maḥalla (formerly known as Ḳuṭb al-Dīnpūr), Zayna Kadal, Srinagar where his grave is still extant. His cottage in Rādjwer Kadal, a quarter of the same city, is also pointed out to visitors although the simple brick-built structure does not show any signs of age.

Bibliography: Ṭāhir Naṣrābādī, *Tadhkira-i Naṣrābādī*, Teheran 1317 S., 445-6; Muḥammad Afḍal Sarkh^w^ush, *Kalimāt al-shuʿarāʾ*, Madras 1951, 138-41; Muḥammad Ṣāliḥ Kanbōh, *ʿAmal-i Ṣāliḥ* (Bibl. Ind.), Calcutta 1939, iii, 426, 428; Shīr Khān Lodhī, *Mirʾāt al-khayāl*, Bombay 1324/1906, 141-3; Ghulām ʿAlī Āzād Bilgrāmī, *Sarw-i Āzād*, Agra 1913, 103-5; idem, *Yad-i Bayḍāʾ* (MS. Āṣafiyya), fol. 170a; Wālih Dāghistānī, *Riyāḍ al-shuʿarāʾ* (Bankipore MS.), fol. 28; Sirādj al-Dīn ʿAlī Khān Ārzū, *Madjmaʿ al-Nafāʾis* (Bankipore MS.), ii, fol. 344b; Bindrāban Dās Kh^w^ushgū, *Safīna-i Kh^w^ushgū*, ed. Shāh Muḥammad ʿAṭāʾ al-Raḥmān ʿAtāʾ Kākawī), Patna 1378/1959, 38, 348; Muḥammad Ḥusayn Āzād, *Nigāristān-i Fārs*, Lahore 1922, 182-4; G. M. D. Ṣūfī, *Kashīr*, Lahore 1949, ii, 462-9; Rieu, ii, 692; Ethé, 1127; Bankipore, Cat., iii, 136-9; A. Sprenger, *The Oudh Catalogue*, 113, 151, 410; Ṣiddīḳ Ḥasan Khān, *Shamʿ-i Andjuman*, Bhopal 1876, s.v. "Ghanī", (simply reproduces the notice in *Sarw-i Āzād*, without acknowledgement); Ḥādjdjī Mukhtār Shāh Ashaʾī, *Risāla dar Fann-i Shālbāfī*, Lahore 1887, 1; Sir Walter Lawrence, *The Valley of Kashmir*, London 1895, 309. (A. S. Bazmee Ansari)

GHANĪ B. AʿṢUR B. SAʿD B. ḲAYS (B.) ʿAYLĀN, an Arab tribe. They were, according to the genealogists, the brothers of Bāhila [*q.v.*]. Their grazing-grounds lay between Bīsha [*q.v.*] and the later *ḥimā* Dariyya [*q.v.*]. Being small in number they were never prominent. In pre-Islamic times one of them, Riyāḥ b. Ashall, killed towards the middle of the 6th century A.D. Shaʾs, the son of Zuhayr b.

Djadhīma, the powerful chieftain of the ʿAbs (*Aghānī*[1], x, 9 ff., 16). Riyāḥ's daughter Khabiyya was married to Djaʿfar b. Kilāb b. Rabiʿa (*Naḳāʾiḍ Djarīr wa 'l-Farazdaḳ*, 106, 10; *Mufaḍḍaliyyāt*, 353, 1 and 710, 17; Mubarrad, *Kāmil*, 482, 16), the ancestor of the leading "house" of the Banū ʿĀmir b. Ṣaʿṣaʿa. Since then the Ghanī were in subordinate alliance with them, though not considered their equals (*Naḳāʾiḍ*, 533, 17; cf. also *Mufaḍḍaliyyāt*, no. 105, 19). The Ghanī fought about 580 A.D. on the side of the Banū ʿĀmir b. Ṣaʿṣaʿa at Shiʿb Djabala (*Aghānī*[1], x, 37, 20; *Naḳāʾiḍ*, 659, 18). Men of the Ghanī took part in the fight on the Day of al-Raḳam (*Mufaḍḍaliyyāt*, 31, 18) towards the end of the 6th century and on other occasions (*Naḳāʾiḍ*, 227, 1; 1060, 12; 1061, 9; 1063, 6). Some time afterwards they suffered heavily on the Day of Muḥadjdjar, when Zayd al-Khayl al-Ṭāʾī (d. 10/632) fell upon the Banū Kilāb and Banū Kaʿb; but they soon took revenge on him (*Aghānī*[1], xvi, 52 and vii, 147; Ṭufayl b. ʿAwf, nos. I and III).

It seems that the Ghanī were indifferent towards the rising power of Muḥammad; there was, to be sure, amongst his earlier companions Abū Marthad al-Ghanawī, but he was a confederate (*ḥalīf*) of Ḥamza b. ʿAbd al-Muṭṭalib (Ibn Hishām, 322, 3 etc.). After the battle of Ḥunayn (8/630) the Ghanī accepted Islam without resistance, nor did they take part in the revolt (*ridda*) after Muḥammad's death (11/632). During the conquests many of them went to Syria. In the wars that ensued after the battle of Mardj Rāhiṭ (64/684) between the Kays and the Yemenīs and later the Taghlib, the Ghanī with the Banū ʿĀmir, Bāhila and Sulaym fought against the Taghlib (Ibn al-Athīr, iv, 256, 259 ff.).

The best known poet among the Ghanī is Ṭufayl b. ʿAwf, nicknamed Ṭufayl al-Khayl for his skill in describing horses (the Ghanī were renowned horse-breeders, see Ṭufayl no. I, 22). Then there is one Kaʿb b. Saʿd al-Ghanawī of the early Islamic period, whose *Bāʾiyya* is considered to be one of the finest elegies (*Ḳālī, Amālī*[1], ii, 150 ff., etc.). The otherwise unknown Abū Khālid al-Ghanawī (*Fihrist*, 105, 10) wrote a *Kitāb Akhbār Ghanī wa-ansābihim* which is lost.

Bibliography: in the article. Consult also the indexes to Hamdānī and Yāḳūt. For their religious customs in the *djāhiliyya* see Ibn al-Kalbī, *Aṣnām*, 27, 12; 42, 4 and ʿĀmir b. al-Ṭufayl, no. 8. For Ṭufayl al-Ghanawī see F. Krenkow's introduction to his edition *The poems of Ṭufail ibn ʿAwf* etc., *GMS*, xxv. (J. W. Fück)

GHANĪMA, or *ghunm*: booty. The term *maghnam* denotes either the mass of the booty or that part of it which goes to the central government (al-Balādhurī, 145, 11). In Bedouin tribal society, where the basic problem is the provision of the bare necessities of life, plunder has always been a salient feature. Notwithstanding the risk of initiating blood-feuds, the Arabs were proud to have the reputation of being indomitable raiders, even, when hard-pressed, upon related tribes (cf. al-Ḳuṭāmī, ed. Barth, 58 ff.). Far from being considered criminal the *ghazw*s [*q.v.*] were regarded as normal practice, and no doubt served to suppress other criminal activities, appealing as they did to collective responsibility and small-scale co-operation. Customary rules for the sharing of moveable booty existed in pre-Islamic times. The leader was entitled to one fourth or one fifth in addition to the *ṣafī*, or items that especially attracted him. Furthermore he had the right to dispose of, firstly the *nashīṭa*, or casual plunder obtained while journeying to meet the enemy—no doubt because such plunder was taken in less dangerous circumstances and was therefore handed over to the one who controlled the whole group—, and secondly the *fuḍūl*, or surplus items, the strict division of which would be wasteful, such as a horse or a camel (*LA*, s.v. *nashīṭa*; *Ḥamāsa* (Abū Tammām), 458). It is known that the deputy (*ridf*) of the king of al-Ḥīra obtained one fourth of the booty (*Mafātīḥ*, ed. v. Vloten, 128), probably not because he and the king together claimed half of it, but rather in his capacity as a leader in warfare. It would thus seem that the *ghanīma* was not regarded as the concern of the State.

Under Islam it was difficult to maintain the simple Bedouin method of division, for the amount of the booty was vast and complicated strategic situations preceded its acquisition. Moreover there was the need for an enhanced State authority and the responsibility for upholding the existing administrative and economic regime. All this opened the door to foreign influence.

While the neglect of any rules for the division of immovables or landed property did not trouble the Bedouins, who dealt with them under the heading of communal reserves, *ḥimā*, it would have posed a serious problem for the urban societies of the Arabian peninsula. But apart from this the Prophet's deviations from ancient custom as to the division of moveables were, in principle, few and insignificant. Nevertheless he was forced on several occasions as a matter of policy to make considerable adaptations, lest, in view of the vital interest taken in this question by his followers, discontent should become serious.

Most later theorists regard it as a settled rule that the spoils (*salab*), comprising the clothes, weapons and occasionally the mount of an adversary killed in battle, are the property of the victor and are not to be included in the rest of the booty. But after Badr the Prophet, according to one tradition, hesitated to comply with this custom in one case (al-Bayḍāwī, *Tafsīr*, on VIII, 1).

Certain scholars hold that the *anfāl*, or bonus shares given to those warriors who have distinguished themselves, should be provided for out of the leader's portion of the *khums* (see FAYʾ); but Sūra VIII, 1, seems best interpreted as deciding a major problem, and the fact that the Prophet was free to dispose of his personal share of four per cent of the booty (*khums al-khums*) as he wished could scarcely have given rise to discontent. There is some authority for the view that *nafal* should be promised before the battle as a fixed share of the expected booty (*Ikhtilāf*, 118 ff.), but this view was not generally regarded as valid. Criticism was especially severe after Ḥunayn, when the political insight of the Prophet led him to reconcile former opponents with Islam (*taʾalluf al-ḳulūb ʿala 'l-islām*) by bestowing upon them large shares of the booty to the detriment of his old supporters (cf. Sūra IX, 60). There is hardly any reason for posterity to attempt to exculpate the Prophet for this manœuvre on the ground that the booty in fact went to persons who had already embraced Islam. Since the obvious political aim of Muḥammad was to secure a stable centre among the wavering Bedouin tribes it was essential for him to establish his position in Mecca. The *ridda* after Muḥammad's death demonstrated, in its extreme form, a situation which he had successfully kept in check during his lifetime—rival prophetic movements in certain tribes which detested a centralized government and aversion to the poor-tax. Subsequent opponents of the Umayyads, using in their invectives against the dynasty the term *al-mu'allafatu ḳulūbuhum* (al-Dīnawarī, 175, 1), failed to appreciate that the Prophet had won over the ablest politicians of the day, who were destined to provide an effective government at a time of crisis. Once triumphant, however, Islam could afford to abandon this line of approach and was not loth to do so. But, of course, even in later Islam the way to political influence was occasionally paved by economic means, although other names were used. When al-Māwardī (239) calls transferred property (*amwāl manḳūla*, cf. *Mafātīḥ*, 64, 11) by the term *ghanā'im ma'lūfa*, it shows that he was not unaware of the fact that such property was taken from the shares of the militia [see further TA'LĪF AL-ḲULŪB].

A highly interesting example of the vast amount of booty and the unpreparedness of the government for sweeping successes in the field appears in the tradition of Djarīr and his tribe Badjīla. After the latter's exploits in ʿIrāḳ the laxity of the rules for division left them in possession of some of the richest areas known at that time. According to one tradition they had previously been promised a third of the booty as *nafal* over and above the *khums* (al-Balādhurī, 253). The most widespread tradition, however, maintains that they formed one fourth of the conquering force, and that they got one fourth of the Sawād, the conquered territory. In fact the tradition seems to concern the leader's customary one fourth. One cannot doubt that there is a basis of historical fact to these traditions; nor can other traditions be doubted that relate how ʿUmar I realized, on second thoughts, how dangerous this precedent would be. Having appealed to their honour they were faced with the alternative of accepting his proposals or acknowledging that their share of the booty was a payment of the category of *ta'alluf* (al-Balādhurī, 268). Perhaps there were more powerful arguments in reserve, but at any rate such a blot on his honour could not be borne lightly by any good Muslim.

The traditions are undoubtedly right in maintaining that it was ʿUmar I who first settled fixed annual pensions or incomes on the most influential and deserving of the inner circle of conquerors and on the Prophet's widows. The transfer of the militia to a *dīwān* of fixed stipends also took place under his leadership, a process which undoubtedly continued to develop under ʿUthmān. A Muslim could choose the state of *hidjra*, or military service, and so become entitled under the law governing the *dār al-hidjra* to *fay'* contributions (Abū Yūsuf, 85; al-Dīnawarī, 131, 141; al-Balādhurī, 275).

In the systematized rules enunciated by the jurists for the division of the booty it is possible to trace the growth of Islam from its small beginnings and the development of skirmishes into large scale operations. The booty was divided on the basis of military potential. As with regular pay a distinction was drawn between foot soldiers and mounted troopers. The precedent may have been set by the Prophet but the aim behind it was well suited to the armament of the times. Every man was given one share, but the mounted soldier got one or two extra shares for his mount. Some jurists would go even further and give to the horseman one share for each of his mounts. This no doubt marks the trend of development. An illustration is provided by a case in the 4th/10th century of an increase in pay in the ratio 10 : 1 (al-Ṣūlī, *Akhbār al-Rāḍī wa 'l-Muttaḳī*, ed. J. Heyworth Dunne, 1935, 226).

Where large armies were engaged it was naturally not only upon those in the front ranks or those who actually came to grips with the enemy that victory depended. Tradition in fact represents ʿUmar I as faced with the situation of the appearance of certain troops after the battle had been won (al-Balādhurī, 256). He is said to have decided that they were entitled to booty if they had arrived before the dead had been buried. Some jurists claim that even if the army is returning to the *dār al-islām* and is then met by other troops or auxiliaries, these latter can claim part of the booty. Furthermore the next of kin of fallen soldiers may inherit their shares. On the other hand, since only free Muslims are entitled to booty, bondmen, women and *dhimmī*s who may in some way have contributed to victory may take only a bonus share, *raḍkh*, to be given at the discretion of the Imām. Such shares may even be given to those who are temporarily absent. It is not clear whether this also applies to those who are represented by a hired substitute (*badīl*). Such shares are usually small, and ought not in any case to exceed the normal share of one person.

As regards ransom money there was a precedent from Badr, where the captor received it for his own captive. With Ḳur'ānic support this was later regularly added to the booty to be distributed by the Imām. In general the majority of jurists emphasize the free discretion of the latter, and in so doing undoubtedly reflect what was growing practice. Here also precedents from the Prophet might be adduced. Irregular warfare is curbed and the necessary condition that the troops have been officially dispatched is underlined. Of course such rules could never be invariably applied in practice, since situations varied and hired troops occasionally got out of control. Plundering and rioting soldiery mark the decline of the ʿAbbāsid power, although this naturally falls outside normal conditions. See also BARANTA, GHAZW, YAGHMĀ.

Bibliography: s.v. FAY'. In addition, *Das Konstantinopler Fragment des Kitāb Ikhtilāf al-Fuqahā' des ... aṭ-Ṭabarī*, ed. J. Schacht, 1933, 20 ff., 68-196; Yaḥyā ibn Ādam, ed. Juynboll, 1896, 3-51 *passim*; A. J. Wensinck, *Handbook*, references s.v. *booty*; F. F. Schmidt, *Die occupatio im islamischen Recht*, in *Isl.*, i, 303-5; W. Montgomery Watt, *Muhammad at Medina*, 1956, 255 ff., 348 ff.; Ṣāliḥ Aḥmad al-ʿAlī, *al-Tanẓīmāt al-idjtimāʿiyya wa'l-iḳtiṣādiyya fi'l-Baṣra*, Baghdad 1953, 125 ff., and references above.

(F. LØKKEGAARD)

GHANĪMAT, MUḤAMMAD AKRAM, Indian poet who wrote in Persian, a descendant of a family of *muftī*s who originated from the village of Kandjāh five miles from Gudjrāt (Pandjāb). Nothing is known about his life and it is not proved that he was governor of Lahore from 1106 to 1108/1695-7, as is asserted by Éthé (*Gr.Ir.Ph.*, ii, 251). He was in the service of Mukarram Khān at Gudjrāt and we do not even know the exact date of his death, which occurred, it is said, at the end of the 9th century A.H. (about 1690). He is best known for a *mathnawī*, highly esteemed in India, entitled *Neyrang-i ʿIshḳ*, which tells of the love of the young prince ʿAzīz (who seems to have been the son of his patron) for a gipsy dancer named Shāhid; Éthé gives the date 1096/1685 for the composition of this poem. He left also a small collection of *ghazal*s which have recently been published (Lahore, 1337).

Bibliography: Mīr Ḥusayn Dust Sanbhli, *Tadhkira-i Ḥusaynī*, Lucknow 1875, 230-2; Muḥammad Afḍal Sarkhush, *Kalimāt al-shuʿarā'*, Madras 1951, 140-1 (Lahore ed. 1942, 82); Muḥammad Ḳudrat Allāh Gupāmawī Ḳudrat, *Natā'idj al-afkār*, Madras 1259, 317-9 and recent Bombay edition; Sayyid Muḥammad Ṣiddīḳ Khān, *Sham'i andjuman*, Delhi 1293, 356-7; Muḥammad Ẓafar Khān, *Mathnawī-yi Neyrang-i ʿishḳ*, in *Hilāl*, iv/2 (Karachi August 1956), 22-9; *Neyrang-i ʿishḳ*, several Lucknow editions between 1885 and 1925.

(S. Naficy)

GHĀNIYA, Banū, family of Ṣanhādja Berbers who, in the Almohad epoch (6th/12th century), attempted to restore the Almoravids in North Africa.

The feminine name Ghāniya which designates them is that of an Almoravid princess who was given in marriage by the Almoravid sultan Yūsuf b. Tāshfīn to ʿAlī b. Yūsuf, head of the family. He had two sons by her, Yaḥyā and Muḥammad. Yaḥyā fought victoriously against Alfonso the Battler, king of Aragon (528/1133), and was governor of Murcia and Valencia. Thirteen years he successfully defended Cordova against Alfonso, but following fresh attacks by the Christian king was forced to submit.

Meanwhile, the Almohads had just landed in Spain (541/1146). Yaḥyā b. Ghāniya was one of the last defenders of the peninsular part of the Almoravid domains. He died at Granada in 543/1148.

Muḥammad, Yaḥyā's brother, had been nominated governor of the Balearic islands by ʿAlī b. Yūsuf in 520/1126. At the time of the Almoravid collapse many members of the fallen clan came to join him there. The governor was declared an independent sovereign and this was the beginning of a new dynasty. Following a palace revolution authority passed to Isḥāḳ b. Muḥammad (560/1156). Under his rule the small Almoravid kingdom enriched itself by piracy at the expense of the Christians; the islands were peopled by refugees and prisoners. Isḥāḳ himself died in 579/1183 during a piratical expedition. The eldest of his many children, Muḥammad, succeeded him, but he was compelled to submit to the threats of the Almohad Abū Yaʿḳūb, who forced him to recognize his sovereignty. Majorca was given a representative of Almohad authority. The Majorcans, having revolted, gave the power to ʿAlī, Muḥammad's brother. ʿAlī, pressed by the Almoravid refugees who surrounded him, decided to carry on the battle against the Almohads in Barbary. Thirty-two ships disembarked the Majorcan troops near Bougie. This town had once been the capital of the Ṣanhādja Banū Ḥammād, but had become the capital of an outlying province dependent on Marrākush. It cannot easily have tolerated this loss of status and no doubt sheltered partisans of the overseas Ṣanhādja, so it was easily taken while the Almohad garrison was absent and the inhabitants were at the mosque (6 Shaʿbān 580/12 November 1184).

ʿAlī Ibn Ghāniya, having conquered the Almohad troops who returned towards Bougie, gained the support of numerous nomad Arabs of the Hilālī tribes of Riyāḥ, Athbadj, and Djudhām. Leaving the government of Bougie to his brother Yaḥyā, he marched westwards, seized Algiers, Muzāya, and Miliana, then, returning eastwards and recruiting numerous allies on the way, occupied Ḳalʿat Banī Ḥammād and laid siege to Constantine. However, the Almohad caliph Yaʿḳūb al-Manṣūr, informed of the Almoravid success, had sent an army which retook the lost cities and expelled Yaḥyā b. Ghāniya from Bougie. ʿAlī was forced to raise the blockade of Constantine. Fleeing to the desert, he passed to the south of the Aurès and reached the Djarīd (S. Tunisia), which became his base of operations from then on.

Helped by Arabs of the region, he took Tozeur and Gafsa. Setting himself up as sovereign, he paid homage to the ʿAbbāsid caliph, who promised him his support. From Gafsa he went to Tripoli, where he met the Armenian Ḳarāḳūsh, the freedman of a nephew of the Ayyūbid Saladin, who ruled the country with a troop of Turkomans (Ghuzz). An understanding between the two chiefs was effected. The Almoravid troops, reinforced by Ghuzz contingents who had been joined by Arabs from the Banū Hilāl and Banū Sulaym, entered the country, leaving a trail of ruin in Ifrīḳiya. The taking of Mahdiyya and Tunis were the aims of the expedition. Not having been able to seize them, and learning of the arrival of the caliph al-Manṣūr with an Almohad army, ʿAlī Ibn Ghāniya retired to the Djarīd. Six thousand Almohad horsemen followed him there, and he inflicted a bloody defeat on them on the plain of al-ʿUmra (583/1187). Al-Manṣūr then went at the head of his troops and gained a victory at al-Ḥamma near Gabès, and reoccupied Tozeur and Gafsa, whose ramparts were razed. ʿAlī Ibn Ghāniya and Ḳarāḳūsh fled to the desert. Scarcely had al-Manṣūr retaken the road to the Maghrib than the two allies reformed, rallied their followers, and began their campaign afresh. In the midst of all this ʿAlī Ibn Ghāniya died (584/1188). Power passed to his brother Yaḥyā, who for nearly fifty years was to deal the heaviest blows against the Almohad might.

His action began with two fruitless attempts against Constantine. He retired to the desert, the traditional refuge of the vanquished, and rejoined Ḳarāḳūsh there. Not that his relations with the Armenian condottiere were unclouded. They had broken off their alliance many times. The dubious attitude of Ḳarāḳūsh with respect to the Almohads and his severity towards the Arabs caused opposition, and conflict broke out in 591/1195. Yaḥyā Ibn Ghāniya, helped by the Sulaym Arabs, seized Tripoli and Gabès and then proceeded north, where he took Mahdiyya from Ibn ʿAbd al-Karīm al-Ragrāgī, a curious character who had declared himself its independent sovereign. Two years' campaigning had made him master of Béja, Biskra, Tébessa, Kairouan, and Bône; then, on 7 Rabīʿ II 600/14 December 1203, the Almohad governor of Tunis, the Sīd Abū Zayd, surrendered to him. Learning that the Khāridjīs of Djabal Nafūsa were profiting by his absence to stage an uprising, he mounted a rapid expedition against them, defeated them, and extorted a crushing indemnity from them. Yaḥyā Ibn Ghāniya, master of eastern Barbary, was then at the height of his power. He was at Tunis when he learnt that the Almohad caliph al-Nāṣir was on the way to attack him. He did not wait for him but withdrew towards the Djarīd. He was overtaken on the Tādjura plain, where he suffered a heavy defeat. Al-Nāṣir re-took possession of Mahdiyya and Tunis, where he appointed Abū Muḥammad ibn Abī Ḥafṣ governor, with orders to continue the reconquest of the country. Knowing the danger which hung over him in Ifrīḳiya, the Almoravid chief transferred his efforts to the central Maghrib. With his Arab allies he wished to halt al-Nāṣir on his return but was overwhelmingly defeated on the Chélif plain. Passing along the edge of the desert he rallied fresh nomad allies, met Abū Muḥammad ibn Abī Ḥafṣ on the river Shabrū near Tébessa, and suffered a fresh defeat. He returned westwards as far as Tāfilālt and took Sidjilmāsa, which he gave up to pillage. Loaded with booty, he encountered the Almohad governor of Tlemcen and beat him, and passed through Tiaret, which he devastated along with many small towns of the central Maghrib of which Ibn Khaldūn, in the 8th/14th century, was to say "there no more will you find a lighted hearth, nor hear any more the crowing of the cock". On his return from this campaign of destruction a meeting with Abū Muḥammad proved disastrous for him; a second battle fought in the Djabal Nafūsa was still more catastrophic (606/1209).

Thus decisively driven out of Ifrīḳiya, Yaḥyā Ibn Ghāniya sought refuge in Waddān in the south of Tripolitania. Ḳarāḳūsh the Armenian was installed there but capitulated, unable to resist his old rival. Yaḥyā had him executed and took his place.

Abū Muḥammad ibn Ḥafṣ had been replaced in the governorship by the Muʾminid prince Abu ʾl-ʿAlāʾ, who resumed the struggle against the Almoravid. The latter, taking the field again, took possession of Biskra; he even conceived a bold plan of marching anew on Tunis. At Madjdūl, not far from Tunis, a bloody battle decimated the Almoravid force and put Yaḥyā to flight (620/1223).

Having lost all hope of action in Ifrīḳiya the indefatigable rebel, having got himself new allies in the south, again took the road to the central Maghrib and once more sowed ruin there. He went on to Bougie, laid siege to Dellys, Mitīdja, and Algiers, and stirred up a revolt at Tlemcen which came almost to the point of recognizing Almoravid sovereignty. He fled before an army from Tunis which was marching on his heels and took refuge at Sidjilmāsa (624/1226). The eleven years of life left to him saw a hopeless prolongation of his activity. He gave up hope of returning to a too well defended Ifrīḳiya but he pursued to the end of his career the harrying and pillaging along the border of the central Maghrib and perished on the banks of the Chélif, not far from Miliana, in 633/1237. He left three daughters whom he entrusted to the generosity of the Ḥafṣid Abū Zakariyyāʾ who was governor of Tunis. They were treated considerately and housed in a palace called Ḳaṣr al-Banāt (Palace of the Daughters) which a Tunis boulevard (Bāb Banāt) still commemorates.

As a conclusion to this account of a turbulent enterprise which lasted more than 50 years some observations may be made to fix its place in history and underline its importance.

The attempt to restore the Almoravids failed completely and could scarcely have succeeded. But although apparently a mere episode in the past of Barbary it was one of the gravest crises which befell the country and its consequences were long-lasting. Four may be indicated.

1. By stirring up the nomad Arabs and feeding their passion for loot, the exploits of the Banū Ghāniya appears as a prolongation of the invasion begun by the Banū Hilāl and continued by the Banū Sulaym. It was an aggravation—after some 130 years—of the catastrophe from which eastern Barbary was never fully to recover.

2. The Banū Ghāniya extended the Arab scourge to the central Maghrib. In this region, which had remained relatively flourishing, urban centres disappeared which we can hardly locate on the maps. Only Tlemcen, which resisted, profited by the surrounding devastation and began to assume its rôle as capital of a kingdom.

3. If the Almoravid enterprise ended in failure at least it hastened the downfall of the Almohad state. Engaged elsewhere in resisting the Christian reconquest, torn between Spain and eastern Barbary, the empire of ʿAbd al-Muʾmin's successors could not fend off the double danger and began to decine.

4. More evident than the rise of Tlemcen in central Barbary is that of Tunis in Ifrīḳiya, where a strong rule was established which delivered the province from the danger of the Almoravids. The handing over of the government by the Almohads to the Ḥafṣids, who soon assumed autonomy, seems to be one of the only happy consequences of the epic of the Banū Ghāniya.

Bibliography: Ibn Khaldūn-de Slane, ii; Ibn al-Athīr, trad. Fagnan; Ibn Abī Dīnār, *al-Muʾnis fī akhbār Ifrīḳiya wa-Tūnis*², Tunis 1350/1931; tr. Pelissier and Rémusat (*Histoire de l'Afrique*), Paris 1845; Tidjānī, *Riḥla*, partial tr. Rousseau, *JA*, series IV, xx (1852), series V, i (1853); *Kitāb al-Istibṣār*, ed. von Kremer, Vienna 1852; ed. Saʿd Zaghlūl ʿAbd al-Ḥamīd, Alexandria 1958; tr. Fagnan, *Recueil de la Société Archéologique de Constantine*, xxx (1899-1900); Ghubrīnī, *ʿUnwān al-dirāya*, ed. Ben Cheneb, Algiers 1910; A. Bel, *Les Benou Ghânya* (*Publications de l'École des Lettres d'Alger*, XXVII), Paris 1903; G. Marçais, *Les Arabes en Berbérie du XIe au XIVe siècle*, Constantine-Paris 1913; R. Brunschvig, *La Berbérie orientale sous les Ḥafṣides*, 2 vols., Paris 1940-7.

(G. Marçais)

GHARB, part of the Moroccan coast situated approximately between the Wādī Lukkus, the Wādī Subū and the mountains which border the coastal plain to the east. This territory has never been precisely defined, but its limits have varied according to the tribes which occupied it and were or were not considered as tribes of the Gharb. It is an alluvial plain, humid and marshy, along the coast and bordered to the east by rolling hills.

The Gharb, thus roughly defined, was at first inhabited by Berbers and probably formed part of the territory of the Barghawāṭa [*q.v.*]. These were exterminated by the Almoravids and the Almohads, leaving an uninhabited area so that the Almohad Yaʿḳūb al-Manṣūr could establish there at the end of the 6th/12th century levies of the Hilāl Arabs which he intended to use in his battles against the Christians of Spain. The Marīnid rulers Abū Yūsuf and Abū Thābit similarly used the Maʿḳil Arabs in the 7th and 8th/13th and 14th centuries. Hence the population of the Gharb is almost entirely of Arab origin (Banū Mālik, Sufyān, Khluṭ and Ṭlīḳ) and, until the 19th century, the tribes inhabiting this territory were fighting tribes and nomadic rather than settled, pastoral rather than agricultural, which have been of some importance, particularly during the period of Saʿdid anarchy (first half of the 17th century).

With the French colonization, heavy in this region, the Gharb became a prosperous agricultural district, where the growing of rice particularly has flourished.

With the possible exception of al-Ḳaṣr al-Kabīr and the large market of Sūḳ al-Arbaʿ, no thriving urban centre has so far flourished in this area.

Bibliography: Leo Africanus, *Description de l'Afrique*, tr. Epaulard, i, 250 ff. (in his time, the usual place-name was Azghār and not Gharb); L. Massignon, *Le Maroc dans les premières années du XVIe siècle*, 237; E. Michaux-Bellaire, *Le Gharb*, in *Arch. Mar.*, xx (1913); Mission Scientifique du Maroc, *Rabat et sa région*, iv, *Le Gharb (les Djebala)*, Paris 1918; M. Nahon, *Notes d'un colon du Gharb*, Casablanca 1925; J. Berque, *Sur un coin de terre marocaine. Seigneurs terriens et paysans*, in *Ann. d'Hist. éc. et soc.*, no. 45 (1937), 227-35; a geographical thesis on the G͟harb by J. Le Coz will be published shortly. (R. LE TOURNEAU)

G͟HARB AL-ANDALUS, Algarve, the West of Andalusia. This name, now that of the southernmost province of Portugal, was applied by the Muslim historians and geographers to the territory lying to the south-east of Lisbon, reaching as far as both banks of the Guadiana estuary. Mūsā b. Nuṣayr [*q.v.*] took Mérida in 94/713 and his son ʿAbd al-ʿAzīz made himself master of Niebla, Beja, and Ocsónoba, but the G͟harb soon began to show itself a focus of rebellion with the revolt of the Berbers, who were beaten in the Mérida region by the governor T͟haʿlaba in 124/742. The Syrian *d͟jund* of Ḥimṣ settled in Niebla and a part of that of Egypt in Beja and Ocsónoba. Niebla was the scene of a revolt of Yemenites against ʿAbd al-Raḥmān I, whose son Sulaymān also revolted against his nephew al-Ḥakam I. In 213/828, Mérida was the centre of a prolonged Berber rebellion under Muḥammad b. al-D͟jabbār. Hemmed in by the forces of ʿAbd al-Raḥmān II, he withdrew to a fortified position on Monte-Sacro, not far from the present-day town of Faro in the Ocsónoba district, but soon emigrated to Galicia, where he was killed by Alfonso II in 225/840. During the reign of the amīr Muḥammad I one ʿAbd al-Raḥmān b. Marwān b. Yūnus, known as Ibn al-D͟jillīḳī (son of the Galician) as being a member of a *muwallad* family originally from the north of Portugal but long settled in Mérida, proclaimed himself champion of independence in the west of Andalusia and in alliance with Alfonso III kept up a struggle in Badajoz, Esparraguera (between the Guadiana and Almadén), and Antaniya (*Idanha a Velha*, about 140 km. from Mérida and 30 km. north-west of Castelo-Branco). His dynasty, the B. Marwān, survived till 318/930, in which year ʿAbd al-Raḥmān III recovered Badajoz. Soon afterwards he also recovered the little principalities of their vassals in Beja, Santa María del Algarve, and Silves. On the fall of the caliphate of Cordova, during the first period of 'party kings', the petty kingdom of the B. Muzayyin was formed at Silves and lasted from 420/1028 to 445/1053. In 433/1041 Muḥammad b. Saʿīd b. Hārūn made himself independent at Santa María del Algarve but had to submit to al-Muʿtaḍid the emir of Seville. At Huelva and Saltes there reigned ʿAbd al-ʿAzīz al-Bakrī, the father of the famous geographer Abū ʿUbayd al-Bakrī, from 403/1012 to 443/1051 when he surrendered to al-Muʿtaḍid. Niebla suffered the same fate. Tād͟j al-Dawla came to power there in 414/1023 and was recognized by Huelva and Gibraleón. On his death in 433/1041 he was succeeded by his brother Muḥammad al-Yaḥṣubī, who retired to Cordova in 443/1051 leaving the power to his nephew Nāṣir al-Dawla who handed it over to al-Muʿtamid and took refuge in Cordova in 450/1058. When the Almoravid power declined a party kingdom re-formed in Algarve under Ibn Ḳasī at Mértola, who was acknowledged by Sidrāy b. Wazīr at Évora and Beja, Muḥammad al-Mund͟hir at Silves, and Yūsuf al-Biṭrūd͟jī at Niebla. However, finding himself soon betrayed and attacked, he summoned the Almohads, and ʿAbd al-Muʾmin, after taking Marrākus͟h, sent an army to the Peninsula under the command of Barrāz al-Massūfī who subdued all the petty kings of Algarve. They gave in easily but equally easily rose again when they saw the speed and scope of Ibn Hūd al-Māssī's rebellion and his initial victory. Yūsuf al-Biṭrūd͟jī ejected the African garrison from Niebla as did Ibn Ḳasī at Silves and Muḥammad b. al-Ḥad͟jd͟jām at Badajoz. But when ʿAbd al-Muʾmin was as victorious in Andalusia against Ibn G͟hāniya and Alfonso VII as he had been in Morocco against the followers of al-Māssī and the Barag͟hwāṭa they asked for *amān*. They were summoned to Salé and attached to the Caliph's court except for Ibn Ḳasī who did not accede to the summons and allied himself with the king of Portugal. He was killed by his own followers in 546/1151. In 560/1165 the Portuguese under Giraldo Sem Pavor seized Jurumeña, besieged Badajoz, and took Évora, Beja, and Serpa. In 564/1169 the Almohads took Tavira, which still preserved its independence under al-Wuhaybī; and though Sancho I of Portugal besieged and took Silves in 585/1189 Yaʿḳūb al-Manṣūr retook it in 587/1191, along with Alcaçer do Sal. The great Almohad incursions into Portugal end with this campaign. Castile had still to endure the rout of Alarcos, be victorious at Las Navas de Tolosa, and put an end to the danger of the B. Marīn at El Salado. Little by little the Portuguese retrieved their cities and fortresses, which had fallen again into Muslim hands from Alcaçer do Sal to Silves, and met no more than the sporadic resistance put up by each locality as it found itself encircled. The lack of definite information makes the chronology uncertain. Herculano fixes it thus: 1232 Mora and Serpa taken; 1234 Aljustrel; 1238 Mértola; 1239 Tavira and Cacella. But according to the *Cronicas dos sete primeiros reis* Mértola and Aljustrel were not conquered till 1243. The battle in the neighbourhood of Tavira took place in 1244. It may be deduced from the new edition of the *Crónica de Alfonso II* that Maestro Payo Correa took Tavira, Silves, Estombar, and Alvor between 1243 and 1246 and that in 1249-50 Alfonso III took Faro and in 1250, finally, Loulé and Aljazur.

Bibliography: E. Lévi-Provençal, *Hist. Esp. Mus.*, i, 25, 30, 142-9, 297-9; Codera, *Decadencia y desaparición de los Almorávides*, 33-52; Ibn al-Abbār, *al-Ḥulla al-siyarāʾ*, 199, 202, 239, 242; Ibn ʿAbd al-Munʿim, *al-Rawḍ al-miʿṭār*, s.vv. Beja, Silves, Santa María del Algarve, Niebla, Mértola, Badajoz, Saltes, Oscónoba; Ibn al-K͟haṭīb, *Aʿmāl al-aʿlām*, 285 ff.; A. Pietro y Vives, *Los reyes de Taifas*, 72-3; Ibn ʿId͟hārī, *Bayān*, iii, 240 ff.; A. Huici, *Historia politica del imperio almohade*, i, 145, 156, 266-71, 277, 347, 358, 478; Herculano, *Historia de Portugal*, iii, 211-2, iv, 239-87; da Silva Tarouca, *Cronicas dos sete primeiros reis*, i, 171, 254, 262-7. (A. HUICI MIRANDA)

AL-G͟HARBIYYA, a province of Lower Egypt, lying within the Nile Delta, now composed of nine districts. An administrative unit of this name has existed since the early Muslim period (cf. Becker art. EGYPT in *EI*[1]). In the time of Abū Ṣāliḥ (7th/13th century) it comprised 165 villages; it was described by al-Ḳalḳas͟handī (d. 821/1418) as fertile and prosperous. Cotton is now extensively grown, while al-Maḥalla al-Kubrā (until 1836 the provincial capital), which has an old tradition of spinning and weaving, is now the centre of the most modernized textile manufacture in Egypt. Ṭanṭā, now the capital of the province, has the tomb of Sayyid Aḥmad al-Badawī [*q.v.*], where the annual feasts attract thousands of devotees. The population of the province in 1960 was 1,815,000 persons.

Bibliography: Maspéro-Wiet, *Matériaux*, 102, 132, 164; Abū Ṣāliḥ, tr. and ed. B. T. A. Evetts and A. J. Butler, *The churches and monasteries of Egypt*, Oxford 1895, 17; al-Ḳalḳashandi, tr. Wüstenfeld, *Die Geographie und Verwaltung von Aegypten*, 114; J. Lozach, *Le Delta du Nil, étude de géographie humaine*, Cairo 1935; Muḥammad Ramzī, *al-Ḳāmūs al-djughrāfī li 'l-bilād al-miṣriyya*, Cairo 1958, 3-153. (R. Herzog)

GHARDĀYA (current spelling: Ghardaïa), the chief town of the Mzab, situated 635 km. by road south of Algiers on the parallel 32° 30′. Between 500 and 560 metres in altitude, it is built over a rounded hillock on the right bank of the Wādī Mzab, which cuts a hundred metres into the completely desert-like and deeply channeled limestone plateau of the *shebka* ("net") of the Mzab.

Ghardaïa was founded in 445/1053, after al-Ateuf (al-ʿAṭf, 407/1011), Bou Noura (Bū Nūra), Beni Isguen (Isgen) and Melīka, its lower neighbours, by the Ibāḍīs who, little by little, abandoned Sedrata (south of the oasis of Ouargla), their first refuge in the Sahara, after the ruin of their capital, Tiaret (Tāhart), in 296/909 by the Fāṭimids. It was families from Ghardaïa who later founded Guerara (Grāra) in 1631 and Berriān in 1679, 100 km. to the north-east and 50 km. to the north respectively. Ghardaïa, like all the other towns of the Mzab, gives the impression that it has always lived by trading across the Sahara, and, above all since the 10th/16th century, by its dealings with Algiers, far more than by an agriculture seriously limited by shortage of water.

The Mzabis have remained fiercely Ibāḍī and attached to their Berber speech. Ghardaïa has grown over the centuries owing to Ibāḍī immigration. To the Awlād ʿAmmī ʿĪsā and Awlād Bā Slīmān, the groups which founded the city, have later been added Ibāḍī groups from Tafilalet, from the Wādī Rīgh, Djerba and Djabal Nafūsa. It has grown equally through the Mdābīḥ, Mālikī Arabs from the *ḳṣar* of al-Māya, on the foot-hills of the Djabal ʿAmūr, and little by little, through some Benī Merzūg families from the old *ḳṣar* of the Shaʿanba of Metlili; Mdābīḥ and Benī Merzūg are Arabic speaking and belong to the Mālikī school. Ghardaïa also shelters a community of Jews, of whom the earliest are supposed to have come from Djerba from the 14th century on, and others from Morocco, Tripolitania and Algeria.

Ghardaïa surrendered to France with the rest of the Mzab in 1853 and was peacefully occupied in 1882. To-day it has a population of 16,000 (1957), of whom about 1,000 are Arabs and about 1,500 Jews, and there is a small number of Europeans. Both in its appearance and in the way it functions, even more than from the size of its population, Ghardaïa is a true city and not a simple Sahara *ḳṣar*.

Originally, its shape was oval and its plan concentric and radiating. Its single mosque, focal point of the city, place of worship, refuge and storehouse in the troubled times of the past, dominates the whole town with its annexes (schools, *takerbust* for the ablutions of the scholars) and its great truncated cone of a minaret (*ʿassās*), twenty metres high, which overlooks the whole surrounding countryside. The circular streets, with others radiating from them, narrow but rarely covered, and lined with houses side by side, are the main thoroughfares of the district which surrounds the mosque. To the south-west there is a way down to the edge of the town through a place where the ancient ramparts have been demolished to form a rectangular market place, 75 by 44 metres in extent, lined with porticos of irregular arches and shops—the souk. Eight streets coming from three directions of the compass, lead into this and here are to be found the shopkeepers and artisans. This is the economic centre of the town as well as the political and administrative one, where the *ḳāʾid* has his office and the *djamāʿa* meets. To the south-east, the little Jewish quarter leads into the new business district; the Mdābīḥ live together to the north-west. Several vast cemeteries enclosed by walls cover the land immediately surrounding the town.

Ghardaïa is primarily a town of merchants and business men. Little by little, the trade across the Sahara has disappeared, but its population lives mainly on the profits of its approximately 2,000 shopkeepers, grocers and textile merchants in the towns of the Tell. Ghardaïa is also the principal market of the Mzab and a transit post for food supplies for the stations further south. Arabs and Jews share the transport business with the Ibāḍīs. Since 1920, lorry traffic has little by little replaced the traditional caravan. Tourists visiting the Mzab usually stay in Ghardaïa. It is also the chief town of the administrative district (*cercle*) of the Mzab. Some of the traditional artisans (the women make carpets and woollen textiles, the men are coppersmiths) are encouraged by the schools and workshops of the White Sisters and find some exterior outlets. Blacksmiths, carpenters, tailors, shoemakers, work for the local population as do the Jewish jewellers; the building industry has always been active.

Agriculture, on the contrary, shows a debit balance. The 60,000 palm trees and the gardens in the lower part of the valley, watered with difficulty by deep wells, which are worked by animal traction, or flooded by the rare spates of the Wādī Mzab, are used more as pleasure gardens where, for the last threequarters of a century, the people of Ghardaïa have built houses of an urban type in which they live during the summer. The profits of trade pay for the upkeep of these gardens.

In many features of its activities, in its type of housing, in its particular form of administration, and even more in its social and religious life, Ghardaïa is inseparable from the other cities of the Mzab [*q.v.*].

Bibliography: see mzab. (J. Despois)

GHARDJISTĀN, Gharshistān, a territory in the mountains of Afghānistān east of Harāt on the upper valley of the Murghāb River and north of the upper Harī Rūd. Al-Muḳaddasī (309) was probably right in explaining the word as "mountain", hence "country of the mountaineers".

Little is known of this land before the time of the Sāmānids [*q.v.*], but we may assume that it was ruled by petty Hephthalite princes. Ghardjistān was raided by Asad b. ʿAbd Allāh al-Ḳasrī, governor of Khurāsān in 107/725-6. The local ruler Namrūn (?) made peace and accepted Islam (al-Ṭabarī, ii, 1488-9). The title of the ruler of Ghardjistān was *shār*, derived from an Old Iranian word for "king" (Marquart). The Muslim geographers knew that *shār* meant "king" (al-Muḳaddasī, 309; *Ḥudūd al-ʿālam*, 105), but Ibn Khurradādhbih (39) says that the king of Ghardjistān was called Barāz bandah, which is probably a confusion with the ruler of neighbouring Mānshān.

The geographers (al-Muḳaddasī, 50; Ibn Ḥawḳal, 443; Yāḳūt, s.v. *Gharshistān*) speak briefly of two principal towns in the country, Bas͟hīn and S͟hūrmīn, which cannot be located.

Muḥammad b. Karām (d. 255/869) converted many people in G͟hard͟jistān to his heretical doctrines (al-Bag͟hdādī, 202), and centres of this heresy remained in the mountains (al-Muḳaddasī 323). The rulers of G͟hard͟jistān acknowledged the suzerainty of the Sāmānids but Maḥmūd of G͟hazna had to conquer the territory in 403/1012 after it had previously submitted. The S͟hār, Abū Naṣr Muḥammad, a man of learning well versed in Arabic, was taken to G͟hazna where he died in 406/1015 (ʿUtbī, 146). The kingdom of G͟hard͟jistān was placed under the governor of Marw al-Rūd͟h, but apparently local princes resumed control of the country for we hear of several S͟hārs again in the time of the G͟hūrids (D͟jūzd͟jānī, 49). The founder of the dynasty of K͟hʷārizms͟hāhs, Nus͟h Tegīn, was a Turkish slave from G͟hard͟jistān (D͟juwaynī, ii, 1).

The name of G͟hard͟jistān appears in many annals of the G͟hūrīd and Mongol periods, while the "kings" of G͟hard͟jistān are mentioned as late as 715/1315 (*Taʾrīk͟h-nāma-i Harāt*, ed. M. Z. Siddiqi, 626). Thereafter the name does not appear in relevant sources.

Bibliography: Le Strange, 415; *Ḥudūd al-ʿālam*, 327; J. Marquart, *Ērānšahr*, 79; ʿUtbī, *Taʾrīk͟h al-Yamīnī*, ed. A. Manīnī, ii, Cairo 1386/1869, 133-46; M. Nazim, *Sultān Maḥmūd of G͟hazna*, Cambridge 1931, 60-2; D͟jūzd͟jānī, *Ṭabaḳāt-i Nāṣirī*, ed. Raverty, Calcutta 1864, passim; C. E. Bosworth, *The Ghaznavids* . . ., Edinburgh 1963, index. (R. N. Frye)

G͟HARĪB, literally: "strange", "uncommon", a technical term in philology and in the science of tradition. As a term in philology it means: "rare, unfamiliar (and consequently obscure) expressions" (in which sense the terms *waḥs͟hī* and *ḥūs͟hī* are also used), and frequently occurs in the titles of books, mostly such as deal with unfamiliar expressions in the Ḳurʾān and in the Tradition (books carrying the titles *G͟harīb al-Ḳurʿān* and *G͟harīb al-Ḥadīt͟h* seem to have existed as early as the second century). The term also occurs in works on literary theory (where it may also have the non-technical, laudatory sense of "uncommon", "original"). More or less anecdotal reports purport to show that some Umayyad and early ʿAbbāsid critics rejected the use of unfamiliar language by certain contemporary poets such as Ṭirimmāḥ, Kumayt, and Ibn Munād͟hir, because this unfamiliar language was not part of the native vocabulary of these poets, but resulted from an archaizing tendency. Most classical scholars of literary theory follow the same line with regard to the poet's vocabulary, allowing only expressions that are known in the poet's own time, and likewise condemn the use of the *g͟harīb* in prose and oratory. Ibn al-At͟hīr, however, who deals with the subject at great length, holds that unfamiliar expressions may be used in poetry as long as they are not unpleasant to the ear.

For the technical meaning of the term *g͟harīb* in the science of tradition see ḤADĪT͟H.

Bibliography: al-D͟jāḥiẓ, *Bayān*, Cairo 1948, i, 144, 378-80; Ḳudāma b. D͟jaʿfar, *Naḳd al-S͟hiʿr*, Leiden 1956, 100-3; al-Āmidī, *Muwāzana*, Istanbul 1287, 120-1, 190-1; al-Marzubānī, *Muwas͟hs͟hah*, 191-2, 208-9, 295-6, 310-1, 369-70, 376; Abū Hilāl al-ʿAskarī, *Ṣināʿatayn*, Cairo 1952, 3, 61; Ibn Ras͟hīḳ, *ʿUmda*, Cairo 1325, ii, 205-6; al-K͟hafād͟jī, *Sirr al-faṣāḥa*, Cairo 1953, 69-77; Ibn al-At͟hīr, *al-D͟jāmiʿ al-kabīr*, Bag͟hdād 1956, 41-9; idem, *Mat͟hal*, Cairo 1939, i, 155-78; J. Fück, *ʿArabīya*, Berlin 1950 (Fr. tr., Paris 1955), index; von Grunebaum, *Kritik und Dichtkunst*, Wiesbaden 1955, index; Amjad Trabulsi, *La critique poétique des Arabes*, Damascus 1956, 167-70. (S. A. Bonebakker)

AL-**G͟HARĪḌ** ('the fresh [voice]') was the nickname given to Abū Zayd (? Yazīd) or Abū Marwān ʿAbd al-Mālik, a renowned singer of the Umayyad era. He was a half-breed of a Berber slave and a *mawlā* of the famous ʿAbalāt sisters of Mecca who were noted for their elegies. It was one of these—T͟hurayya, of whom ʿUmar b. Abī Rabīʿa sang in praise—who placed al-G͟harīḍ under the tutelage of the famous singer Ibn Surayd͟j [*q.v.*], but the former soon outshone his teacher as an elegiast (*nāʾiḥ*), so much so that the latter abandoned that career for that of an ordinary singer (*mug͟hannī*), although as late as 105/724 he performed as an elegiast at the obsequies of Ḥabāba [*q.v.*] the beloved of Yazīd II. Even as a *mug͟hannī* al-G͟harīḍ challenged Ibn Surayd͟j. Having passed into the household of Sukayna bint al-Ḥasan [*q.v.*] greater fame was to come his way, and he sang at the court of al-Walīd I. On one occasion when these two musicians appeared before Sukayna, both were singing to the verses of the Meccan poet ʿAbd Allāh al-ʿArd͟jī [*q.v.*]. Sukayna confessed that she could not say which of these two musicians was the better, simply likening them to two exquisite necklaces, one of pearls and the other of rubies. When Nāfiʿ b. ʿAlḳama became governor of Mecca he made an edict against wine and music, which compelled Al-G͟harīḍ to seek refuge in the Yaman, where he is said to have died about 98/716-17, although another account shows him at the court of Yazīd II (101/720-105/724). According to the legend, he died at the hands of the *d͟jinn*s at a festive gathering in the bosom of his family. Like others of his profession—Ibrāhīm al-Mawṣilī and Ziryāb—he is said to have been inspired by the *d͟jinn*s. It was the success of Al-G͟harīḍ in the *ramal* and *hazad͟j* rhythms which led Ibn Surayd͟j to follow in that path. Perhaps it was the tenderness (*g͟harīḍ*) in his voice—due to his training as a *nāʾiḥ*—that brought him fame, especially with the womenfolk of Mecca, and pilgrims to the Holy City clamoured for him. He participated in the concerts of D͟jamīla [*q.v.*] so elaborately described in the *Kitāb al-Ag͟hānī*, and also excelled as a performer on the lute (*ʿūd*), tambourine (*duff*) and rhythmic wand (*ḳaḍīb*). Isḥāḳ al-Mawṣilī [*q.v.*] placed al-G͟harīḍ as the fourth in eminence among the great musicians of Islam, and even compiled a *Kitāb Ak͟hbār al-G͟harīḍ*, whilst Abū Ayyūb al-Madīnī also wrote a *Kitāb al-G͟harīḍ*, both of which would seem to prove the high esteem in which this singer was held in the early days of Islam.

Bibliography: D͟jāḥiẓ, *Ḥayawān*, i, 302, vi, 208; Masʿūdī, *Murūd͟j*, iii, 327; *Ag͟hānī*³, ii, 359; Ibn ʿAbd Rabbihi, *Al-ʿIḳd al-Farīd*, Cairo 1887-8, iii, 187; *Fihrist*, 141, 148; *JA*, Nov.-Dec. 1873, 457; Kosegarten, *Liber Cantilenarum*, Griefswald 1840, 44; H. G. Farmer, *History of Arabian music*, London 1929, 80 (translated into Arabic by Ḥusayn Naṣṣār and ʿAbd al-ʿAzīz, Cairo 1956); Muḥammad Kāmil Ḥad͟jd͟jād͟j, *al-Mūsīḳā al-s͟harḳiyya*, Alexandria 1924, 20; Julian Ribera, *Music in ancient Arabia and Spain*, Stanford University, U.S.A., 1929, 34-8, 40, 44; O. Rescher, *Abriss*, i, 231-3. (H. G. Farmer)

G͟HĀRIM (*g͟harīm*, according to the lexicographers, is a synonym): debtor or creditor. By analogy with other legal terms this semantic distinction was favoured by the jurists. In Islam the *gh̲ārim* was entitled to a share of the *zakāt* (Sūra IX, 60) to pay his debt, provided he was destitute and the debt did not arise from any disreputable cause or, if it had so arisen, the debtor had duly repented. Other debtors had this claim although they were not destitute, if the debt had been incurred "for God's sake", *i.e.*, for Islam or for an unselfish purpose. The *zakāt* of relatives might be employed to this end as an exception. This latter case reflects pre-Islamic standards, where it was praiseworthy for a man of standing to take upon himself the burden (*ḥamāla*) of blood money (*diya*) in order to prevent or stop a blood feud (Ḥātim al-Ṭāʾī, ed. Schulthess, 1897, lii, 40 (ar.) ff.; *Ḥamāsa*, Cairo 1335, i, 145; *The* Naḳāʾiḍ *of Dj̲arīr and al-Farazdaḳ*, ed. Bevan, i, 345, 8; 382, 14; ii, 789, 17; 1046). The Prophet also paid *diya* on several occasions (al-Buk̲h̲ārī, 87, 22; 93, 38).

Bibliography: Abū Dāwūd, *Ṣaḥīḥ sunan*, Cairo 1280, i, 165; al-Māwardī, *Kitāb al-Aḥkām al-sulṭāniyya*, ed. Enger 1853, 212; al-S̲h̲īrāzī, *al-Tanbīh*, ed. Juynboll 1897, 62, 113, 288.

(F. Løkkegaard)

G̲H̲ARNĀṬA, Granada, the capital of the province and ancient kingdom of that name, does not come into prominence in Spanish history until the early 5th/11th century when a collateral branch of the Ṣanhād̲j̲a Zīrids (ruling in the Ḳalʿa of the Banū Ḥammād, and later in Bougie) realized that its power was waning and offered its services to the first minister of His̲h̲ām II, ʿAbd al-Malik al-Muẓaffar, son and successor of al-Manṣūr Ibn Abī ʿĀmir. The reply was satisfactory, so they embarked with a considerable band of fellow-tribesmen and retainers, with Zāwī b. Zīrī at its head, soon to become one of the most important and turbulent sections of the Berber army recruited by the ʿĀmirids. On the death of ʿAbd al-Raḥmān Sanchol they espoused the cause of the leader of the Berber party in Spain, Sulaymān al-Mustaʿīn, and contributed largely to his succession to the Caliphate. When Sulaymān rewarded his chief followers by the grant of fiefs, to these he allotted the district of Elvira, *i.e.*, the rich lands of the high valley of the Genil and the surrounding rocky heights, so called because its capital was the ancient city of Illiberis-Elvira; but before long it was to be supplanted by its neighbour Granada, a more recent foundation hitherto inhabited mainly by Jews.

Historians and geographers of Muslim Spain are at one in stressing the beauty of Granada and the fertility of its plains. The admiration inspired in the Zīrids by this fine prospect is best expressed by the last amīr ʿAbd Allāh, who says in his *Memoirs* that "they gazed astonished on that lovely plain, furrowed by streams and clothed in trees. They admired the mountain where the city of Granada now stands, entranced by its situation ... and they were persuaded that if an enemy were to lay siege to it, he would be unable to prevent them from entering or leaving to provision it. So they decided to found a city there, and everyone, Andalusian or Berber, set about building a house, and soon Elvira fell in ruins".

During the Roman period, certainly by the reign of Augustus, there was a township of Elvira, nestling on the slopes of the range of this name, in whose neighbourhood archaeological remains have been found, of Roman, Early Christian and Arab origin. We have no details of the Barbarian invasion of the 5th century, nor of the devastation caused in the Illiberis-Granada country when Leovigildo subsequently broke in by way of Baza with his army to pacify the whole of the south of the Peninsula. With the coming of the Muslims, Mūṣā b. Nuṣayr left to his son ʿAbd al-ʿAzīz the task of subduing eastern Andalusia and Levante. On his way to overcome the princedom of Orihuela-Murcia, he occupied Málaga and Elvira-Granada. Abu 'l-K̲h̲aṭṭār al-Ḥusām b. al-Ḍirār became governor in 125/743 and allotted the district of Elvira-Granada to the men of the Syrian *d̲j̲und* of Damascus, whose pro-Umayyad *s̲h̲ayk̲h̲*s supported the landing of ʿAbd al-Raḥmān I. Under the rule of amīr ʿAbd Allāh the *kūra* of Elvira witnessed many a bloody struggle between the *muwallad*s loyal to the central power, and the Arabs under Sawwār b. Ḥamdūn. While besieged in the palace of the Alhambra, the latter made a bold sortie and put the Andalusians to flight in the Battle of the City (*waḳʿat al-madīna*), as it was to be called. The beaten troops entered the service of Ibn Ḥafṣūn who proceeded to Elvira to continue the struggle in the Genil plain, taking and losing Elvira by turns, until he lost it finally during the rule of ʿAbd al-Raḥmān III.

There is now no disputing the once doubtful identification Illiberis-Granada-Elvira: the administrative and military territory of the *kūra* of Elvira corresponded roughly during the Middle Ages to the present province of Granada. There was indeed a diocese of Illiberis before the time of the Muslims, where a council was held between 309 and 312, and the first Muslim governors lived in Illiberis (which they Arabicized into Ilbira) until the provincial *wālī*s preferred, as they often did, to move to a new foundation near the ancient capital. Thus, not long before the Umayyad restoration, the new capital, Castilia or Castella, was built not far from Illiberis; nevertheless, the district continued to be called the *kūra* of Elvira, and this name prevailed, displacing that of Castella, just as the name Illiberis was later replaced by Granada, which itself in the 3rd/9th century was no more than a large walled village on the right bank of the Darro, near its confluence with the Genil. Few Muslims lived there; there were more Christians, while Jews were so numerous that it was sometimes known as "Granada of the Jews". Opposite on a rocky escarpment dominating the left bank of the Darro arose an old citadel which got its name of "the Red" (*al-Ḥamrāʾ*) from its reddish colour. The Alhambra was to be the seat of the Naṣrid kings, and famous in history.

In the story of the Zīrid dynasty (treated at length in the article zīrī (banū)) the principal events directly affecting the city of Granada are: the siege by the caliph al-Murtaḍā, who incited and betrayed by the ʿĀmirid *fatā*s al-Mund̲h̲ir and K̲h̲ayrān sought to drive out the Zīrids, only to flee and perish in Guadix, after a shameful defeat. After this unexpected victory and the consolidation of the dynasty during the amīrates of Ḥabūs and of Bādis, and with the effective support of the Jewish viziers Samuel and his son Yūsuf b. Nagralla (Negrello), Granada was the scene of a notorious pogrom, whose victims included the vizier Yūsuf as well as a large number of his co-religionists. Just after this the amīr Bādis, old and conscious of the threat to his rule, spent large sums on making the old *alcazaba* of Granada strategically impregnable, judging that if the nearby states, or his enemies, or his own rebellious subjects should drive him to a last resort, he might shut himself up in it with the possibility of embarking at need for Ifrīḳiya, as his grandfather Zāwī had done before him. Of the last

Zīrid amīr, ʿAbd Allāh, Bādis's grandson, who began his reign when little more than a child, we have only to mention that after a chequered career of plots, risings and wars with his Muslim and Christian neigbours, he finally incurred the enmity of the Almoravids, and prepared for armed resistance against them by provisioning and fortifying his castles, and building walls adjoining the *alcazaba*. However, when Yūsuf b. Tās͟hfīn appeared before Granada, his innate cowardice and the advice of his ministers and his mother decided him to go out to welcome the Almoravid amīr, to open the gates of Granada to him, and give him all the treasures of his palace.

After this, Granada was administered by Almoravid governors from 483/1090 to 551/1166, when it passed into the hands of the Almohads. Its first Almoravid governor was Abū Muḥammad ʿAbd al-ʿAzīz, himself followed by the amīr Yaḥyā b. Wasīnū, related to Yūsuf. The latter returned to the Peninsula for the last time in 496/1102 to safeguard the position of his son ʿAlī as heir apparent (he had been proclaimed the year before in Marrākus͟h), proceeded via Granada, whose governor at the time was Abu 'l-Ḥasan b. al-Ḥad͟jd͟j, and went first to Levante. Attacked by Alfonso VI at Medinaceli, he counter-attacked through Toledo and Talavera, but was defeated and died on the field of battle. The next governor was Abu 'l-Ḥasan's brother Muḥammad b. al-Ḥād͟jd͟j; he, with the Granada forces, came to the help of the amīr Sīr, governor of Seville, whose territory was threatened by Alphonso VI, but at al-Muḳāṭiʿ, close to Seville, he was forced to retire with heavy losses. The following year (499/1105) we find as governor Abū Bakr b. Ibrāhīm al-Lamtūnī who, on the death of Yūsuf b. Tās͟hfīn (500/1106), attempted some opposition to the proclamation of ʿAlī b. Yūsuf; the citizens of Granada, however, gave him no support, and he was captured and sent to Marrākus͟h. ʿAlī, accompanied by his faithful but incompetent elder brother Abu 'l-Ṭāhir Ṭamīm, went straight to Andalusia to stifle this attempt at revolt and another which had broken out in Cordova, and appointed Ṭamīm governor of Granada. The latter organized the expedition against Uclés, during which Alphonso VI's son the Infante Sancho met his death. However, he was dismissed in that same year, and after a brief period under the governor of Valencia, ʿAbd Allāh b. Fāṭima, the governorship of Granada was taken over by ʿAli b. Yūsuf's cousin the amīr Mazdalī b. Sulankān. Though his attack at Guadalajara (506/1112-3) had no success, in the year following (507/1113) he took Oreja, and in July 1114 attacked the Sagra of Toledo, pillaged Peginas, Cabañas and Magán, and defeated the alcaide Rodrigo Aznárez. His success was short-lived, for during S͟hawwāl 508/March 1115 this great ally of Yūsuf b. Tās͟hfīn and his successor ʿAlī was defeated and killed. His son ʿAbd Allāh b. Mazdalī, who succeeded him as governor of Granada, went with his forces to the assistance of Abū Bakr b. Yaḥyā b. Tās͟hfīn, amīr of Cordova; he was engaged by the Castilians around Baeza, and was defeated with heavy losses. In 519/1125, while Ṭamīm was once again in Granada, Alphonso I (the Battler) undertook his great expedition across Andalusia, in the course of which he twice camped before Granada but did not manage to lay siege to it; he defeated Ṭamīm at Aranzuel. Dismissed at last for his inefficiency, Ṭamīm was succeeded by Abū ʿUmar Īnālū, grandson of Yūsuf b. Tās͟hfīn and a former governor of Fez, who had engaged Alphonso during the retreat before Guadix. When Ibn Rus͟hd told ʿAlī b. Yūsuf what had been happening in Andalusia and advised him to complete the fortifications of Marrākus͟h, he felt bound to offer the same advice about Andalusia. Orders were therefore sent to the governors of Seville, Granada, Cordova and Almería to mend and reinforce the walls and defences of their cities. In Granada the new governor Īnālū made great efforts to get this done even though while the work was in progress the Genil rose and swept away his building materials around Bāb al-Ramla and Bāb Ilbīra, and many lives were lost. ʿAlī dismissed Īnālū on D͟jumādā 522/May 1128 and ordered him to Marrākus͟h to face serious charges preferred by the Mozarabs of Granada. These were proved at a court of inquiry, and he was imprisoned and sentenced to make good the wrongs he had committed. This unpublished episode from the Almoravid *Bayān* shows clearly that by no means all the Mozarabs were deported to Morocco, no more were they all accomplices and collaborators of Alphonso the Battler, for the majority of them suffered no punishment or reprisals, and even after the great damage caused by him, their rights were respected and justice was done to them. The new governor Abū Ḥafṣ ʿUmar, a son of ʿAlī b. Yūsuf, campaigned in Levante and seized an unnamed castle, only to be deposed after four months (May-September 1128) and replaced by another of ʿAlī's sons, the famous and unfortunate Tās͟hfīn, who for ten years struggled with vigour but without success against the Castilians. In 526/1132 he had to take on as well the governorship of Cordova, and therefore delegated that of Granada to Abū Muḥammad al-Zubayr b. ʿUmar, the Azuel of the Christian chronicles, whose valorous exploits came to a tragic end in 538/1143, when he was beaten and slain by the heroic Toledan *alcaide* Muño Alfonso.

The last of the governors answerable to Marrākus͟h was ʿAlī b. Abī Bakr, son of ʿAlī b. Yūsuf's sister Fannū; he died during the revolt of Ibn Aḍḥā who gave up Granada to Sayf al-Dawla (Zafadola) the last descendant of the Banū Hūd of Saragossa, who had made his submission to Alphonso VII. The Almoravids, shut up in the old *alcazaba*, firmly resisted the assaults of Sayf al-Dawla and forced him to retire after killing his son ʿImād al-Dawla during a sortie. After the Granadan populace had expelled ʿAlī b. Aḍḥā who retired to Almuñecar, they acknowledged the sovereignty of the Almoravids of the *alcazaba*. Commanded by Ibn G͟hāniya's lieutenant Maymūn b. Yiddar, they stood their ground until 551/1156, but the achievements of the Almohad governors of Cordova and Seville, added to their sense of isolation and dwindling numbers, moved them to write to Marrākus͟h and sue for peace. Their offer to surrender the city was accepted, and orders went to ʿAbd Allāh b. Sulaymān, admiral of the Ceuta fleet, and to the new governor of the two coasts of the Straits, the *sayyid* Abū Saʿīd ʿUt͟hmān, to set sail for Algeciras and take the road to Granada. Maymūn b. Yiddar gave up the city, and he and all the Almoravids of Granada were removed to Marrākus͟h, where they were suitably accommodated.

The new governor of Granada made thorough preparations for a land attack on Almería, in the hands of the Castilians, while the Ceuta fleet was blockading it by sea, and he succeeded in reconquering it. Alphonso VII and his ally Ibn Mardanīs͟h hastened to its support, but could not hinder its encirclement. So they tried to surprise Granada, whose garrison was absent in Almería, but the vizier Abū Dja'far Aḥmad b. 'Aṭiyya and the *sayyid* Yūsuf b. 'Abd al-Mu'min, having expedited the surrender of Almería, were able to outpace him, and assured the defence of Granada. Meanwhile Ubeda and Baeza were relieved, and Alphonso VII died at the foot of the Despeñaperros, in Fresneda, on 21 August 1157. Granada now enjoyed five years of peace, broken in 577/1162 by Ibn Hamushk who, enraged at the loss of Carmona, made an assault on Granada with the connivance of the Jewish and Mozarab population. The Almohad garrison entrenched itself in the old *alcazaba*, which Ibn Hamushk attacked with battering-rams from the Alhambra in the Sabīka. He appealed for reinforcements to Ibn Mardanīsh, who arrived with his soldiers and the Christian mercenaries commanded by Alvar Rodríguez the Bald, grandson of Alvar Fáñez. The governor of Granada, the *sayyid* Abū Sa'īd 'Uthmān, was absent in Marrākush, so he set off and crossed the Straits to bring help to the beleaguered city, and from Málaga he reached the plain of Granada, picking up reinforcements from Seville; but at a place called Mardj al-rukad ("sleepy meadow") some four miles from the city he suffered defeat and fled to Málaga. 'Abd al-Mu'min, in Rabat at the time, sent picked forces over the Straits, commanded nominally by his son and heir Yūsuf but in reality by the veteran Yūsuf b. Sulaymān, who scaled by night the rocky cliffs above the Genil, near to the Sabīka and the Alhambra, surprised the enemy encampment at dawn, and achieved total victory. He freed the beleaguered garrison and received the submission of all the dwellers of the plain (who had already submitted to Ibn Hamushk), and provisioned and restored the liberated Alcazaba. In 563/1168, at the very moment when Granada had recognized Yūsuf I as *amīr al-mu'minīn*, its governor defeated between Granada and Guadix a detachment of Christian mercenaries in the service of Ibn Mardanīsh which had got as far as Ronda. Returning from his abortive expedition against Huete (autumn 568/1172) Yūsuf I came by Granada where he left as governor his brother Abū Sa'īd 'Uthmān, who had been with him on this campaign. Nothing of importance occurred in Granada during the reign of the subsequent Almohad caliphs until al-Ma'mūn, who, proclaimed in Seville, before he left for Morocco had to tackle Muḥammad b. Yūsuf b. Hūd al-Djudhāmī, the personification of general insurrection of the Spanish Muslims. During al-Ma'mūn's absence, Ibn Hūd quickly mastered the whole of Andalusia. He had recognized the sovereignty of the 'Abbāsid caliph al-Mustanṣir, and in 630/1232 the caliph's ambassador was received with due solemnity when he came to invest Ibn Hūd with the title of amīr of all Andalusia. But Ibd Hūd was assassinated in Almería in 535/1237, and his enemy Ibn al-Aḥmar rose in Arjona and took possession of Granada in 536/1238 and founded the Naṣrid dynasty.

One of his first tasks was to make a thorough inspection of the Alhambra. He traced the foundations of the Alcázar, appointed the excavators, and before the year was out many defensive works had been built. He brought water from the river, set up an *azūd* and dug a dike to feed it. When this work was just beginning he put to death in the Alhambra itself the tax-gatherer of Almería, Abū Muḥammad b. 'Arūs, and later other collectors of revenue, demanding from them the sums needed for his building programme. When the Almohad caliph al-Rashīd died in 640/1242 he transferred his allegiance to the Ḥafṣid amīr of Tunis, Abū Zakariyā', from whom he received considerable sums intended to be used by the Spanish Muslims in the holy war; but Ibn al-Aḥmar spent them on the works he had undertaken and on the extension of the mosques of the city, and made the *ḳāḍī* Muḥammad b. 'Ayyāsh swear that this money from the Tunisian sovereign was not intended for any definite purpose, but could be spent at will. For the rest of the long and eventful story of the Naṣrid dynasty up to the capture of Granada by the Catholic Kings, see the article NAṢRIDS.

Bibliography: E. Lévi-Provençal, *Hist. Esp. Mus.*, i, 342; ii, 330; R. Dozy, *Hist. des Musulmans d'Espagne*², iii, 70, 143; idem, *Recherches*³, i, 228-31; E. Lévi-Provençal, *Les «Mémoires» de 'Abd Allāh, dernier roi zīride de Grenade*, in *al-Andalus*, iii, 223-344; iv, 29-145; vi, 1-62; L. Torres Balbás, *La Alhambra antes del siglo XII*, in *al-Andalus*, v, 155 ff.; Ibn 'Idhārī, ed. Lévi-Provençal, iii, 113, 125, 129; 'Abd al-Mun'im, *al-Rawḍ al-mi'ṭār*, ed. Lévi-Provençal, 29-30; Ibn al-Khaṭīb, *A'māl al-a'lām*, 139, 260-70; idem, *Iḥāṭa*, Cairo edition, i, 334-7; Codera, *Decadencia y desaparición de los Almorávides*, 136; A. Huici, *Las grandes batallas de la Reconquista*, 19-134; idem, *Historia política del Imperio almohade*, i, 156, 202, 205; ii, 468; idem, *El Bayān almohade*, in *Colección de Crónicas árabes de la Reconquista*, ii, 309, 355; iii, 103, 109-10, 125-6; idem, *La salida de los Almorávides del desierto y el gobierno de Yūsuf b. Tasfin*, in *Hespéris*, 1959, 179; idem, *'Alī b. Yūsuf y sus empreses en el Andalus*, in *Tamuda*, 1959, 17-114. (A. Huici Miranda)

Monuments

A. — The town

The Roman and Visigothic town. — Granada originated in a small Roman town, Illiberis, built on the site where, in the 5th/11th century, the palace of the Zīrids, *al-Ḳasaba al-ḳadīma*, arose, and on the hillside sloping down towards the Darro. Ancient tombs have been discovered on the other side of the river, at the foot of the Alhambra hill. The remains found in the ground at Granada are inadequate for a reconstruction of the topography of the town, or for assessing the value of its monuments. A Visigothic inscription preserved at Granada, but which may have come from somewhere else, mentions the founding of three churches in an unspecified place. Hence the history of the monuments of Granada can only be written from the Muslim period onwards.

Granada in the 4th/10th century. — Up till the 5th/11th century Granada was not the most important town in the region. The chief town in the district was Madina Elvira, at the foot of the ridge of mountains of that name, where excavations have unearthed remains of the period of the caliphs with painted or carved decorations. However, from the 4th/10th century onwards Granada had monuments of a certain importance, built according to the techniques current in Spain under the caliphate. The minaret which served as the base for the bell-tower of the church of San José is similar in its plan and arrangement of stretchers and bondstones to all the minarets of that date. As early as that period the town had a fortified wall, some remains of which are still in existence: the wall was of concrete: the towers and the remains of a gateway are chained with free-stone. Old drawings show that the façades of the gates of Elvira and of Hernán Román had kept their 4th/10th century work up to modern times. The bridge over the Genil, several times altered and replastered, seems to go back to this same century as far as its original construction is concerned. So Hispano-Moorish art, which had its source and principal home in Cordova, was flourishing already in 4th/10th century Granada, which proves that the town had acquired importance and wealth.

Zīrid Granada. — It was in the century of the *Mulūk al-Ṭawā'if* that Granada came into its own. The *amīr*s Ḥabūs (409-29/1019-38) and Bādīs (429-65/1038-73) gave their capital a strong surrounding wall which still exists, inside the present town, from the gate of Elvira to the Puerta Nueva. It is a high concrete rampart with irregular quadrilateral or semicircular towers. There are two gates in this part of the wall : the Puerta Monaita and the Puerta Nueva or Arco de los Pesos. They have arches made of stone or brick, surmounted by brick lintels and relieving arches. They are the oldest known examples in Spain of gateways with crooked entry made of vaulted halls, interrupted, at the Puerta Monaita, by an open bay. The gates of Bibarambla and of the Mauror, now vanished, belonged to this enclosing wall.

This rampart was prolonged on the left bank of the Darro by a stone archway between two towers, allowing the curtain to cross the river without interrupting the route of the patrol. What remains of this beautiful work is commonly known as the Bridge of the Ḳādī. The wall reached right up to the summit of the Alhambra plateau, where it was supported by two small fortresses. It enclosed a fairly extensive suburb in the quarter of the Mauror, where wealthy houses were erected. What is left of this Zīrid enclosure remains one of the finest fortifications of the Andalusian 5th/11th century.

The palace of the Zīrids occupied the upper part of *al-Ḳaṣaba al-ḳadīma*. Nothing of it remains beyond a cistern with four cradle-vaulted bays, and several pieces of wall utilized in later buildings.

Of the buildings of the town itself only a *ḥammām* called the Bañuelo remains. After a room for undressing and resting—with a basin in its centre and which doubtless comprised galleries on the first floor—come three parallel vaulted rooms: the *tepidarium* had columns along three sides; the *frigidarium* and the *caldarium* were prolonged by little loggias reached through twin arches. The columns, with neither base nor astragal, are surmounted by re-used antique capitals. The walls are made of a very hard concrete; the arches and vaults of brick. The Bañuelo with its row of three parallel rooms is the perfect example of a Hispano-Moorish bath, which persisted in Spain during the following centuries and is often found in Morocco.

Few remains of decoration have been found in Granada, apart from a few capitals. A curious piece of sculptured marble, divided into several sections and decorated with a Kufic inscription, preserved at Madrid in the Instituto de Valencia de Don Juan, seems to have been a spice tray.

Granada under the Almoravids and the Almohads. — Under the African dynasties Granada apparently did not undergo great changes. It is possible that the fortification to the west of the Alhambra, now known as Torres Bermejas, goes back in the main to the 6th/11th century.

Some carved woodwork and fragments of moulded plasterwork of the Mauror, all of which have been collected in the Archaeological Museum, seem to be of the Almoravid period. They are of excellent quality. This continuity of the Granada workshops played its part in assuring the rise of Naṣrid art.

Naṣrid Granada. — With the dynasty of the Naṣrids, the founder of which, Muḥammad Ibn al-Aḥmar, settled in Granada in 635/1238, Granada became, and remained till its conquest by the Catholic monarchs in 897/1492, the capital of the last Muslim state in Spain (see NAṢRIDS).

Naṣrid Granada, while maintaining profitable economic relations with Castile and Aragon, was closed to all spiritual and artistic influence from the Christian world. It shut itself up within its Muslim traditions, which it preserved, without renewing them, with pious faithfulness. Naṣrid art was thus the final outcome and the supreme flowering of Muslim art in Spain.

The end of the 7th/13th century and the 8th/14th century were the periods of active construction: architecture and decoration, within formulas now become classical, continued to evolve slowly. But in the 9th/15th century in this increasingly threatened kingdom, often shaken by internal strife, buildings of importance seem to have been very rare, while the decoration of monuments lost its spontaneity and fine quality.

The surrounding wall. — From the moment that it became the capital of Muḥammad ibn Aḥmar, Granada was transformed, especially by the influx of refugees. The wall was extended to the north in order to take in the Albaycín quarter; a concrete rampart with oblong quadrilateral towers, a part of which still exists, enclosed this extension. The rest of the city wall was underpinned and reinforced. In engravings made shortly after the reconquest, the wall appears with *albarranas* towers in many places. But all this fine array of fortifications was demolished when the modern enlargement of the city took place.

Religious buildings. — Granada has kept hardly any of its religious buildings. The church of the Salvador retains some remains of the *ṣaḥn* of the great mosque of the Albaycín, the site of which it occupies. From an old description we know that this Naṣrid sanctuary was a beautiful building with nine naves, the arcade of which rested on eighty-six marble columns. A 7th/13th century minaret serves as the belfry of the church of San Juan de los Reyes. It is a square tower, with a cradle-vaulted staircase rising round a square central newel. The outside walls are decorated with a pattern of interlaced links in brick. The top band of the tower's decoration is in the form of a frieze of star-shaped polygons. This minaret, which belonged to a small 7th/13th century mosque, has neither the size nor the sumptuousness of the great Marīnid minarets of Fez which belong to the same architectural style: it lacks ceramic decoration.

Of the *madrasa* which was built in 750/1349 only the hall of prayer remains, and now much restored. Some remains of the façade have been assembled in the Museum. Finally, outside the old city, the *ermita* of San Sebastián is a small Muslim sanctuary of the 9th/15th century, probably a funerary building, of square form, covered by a sixteen-sided cupola with fine and numerous ribs.

Secular buildings. — Naṣrid Granada had many public baths: only one has been preserved, that of the Calle Real. It is of thoroughly classical type: its three vaulted rooms, on parallel axes, are preceded by a room for undressing and resting, with a gallery on the first floor.

The hospital—the *Māristān*—has been destroyed; but its plan has been preserved. Its central court was bordered by porches with pointed arches on the ground floor, and wooden lintels on the first floor. The rooms opened through twin bays onto galleries. Its façade was symmetrically disposed. Above the entrance archway, richly decorated, and above its lintel, an arcade contained the foundation inscription: on the first floor there were windows, single or geminated.

Of the many *funduḳ*s which Granada boasted, only one has been preserved: the Corral del Carbón. The court, the arrangement of which is similar to that of the *Māristān*, is surrounded by a two-storied colonnade on lintels. Of purer lines and better proportions, it has the same plan that one finds in Marīnid hostelries of the same period in Fez. This utilitarian building, the interior of which remains very sober, had a monumental doorway which was richly decorated. Its approach reveals a short vestibule with a horse-shoe arch, surmounted by a false lintel and a geminated window framed in two arcades. All this arrangement is decorated with moulded plaster. The ceiling of this type of portico is made of stalactites. One enters the court by a door with a lintel surmounted by a geminated arcade. The *funduḳ*s of Fez retained, up till the modern period, the tradition of monumental doors, decorated to a greater or lesser extent.

Although the public buildings of Granada have nearly all disappeared, five beautiful dwelling-houses, more or less restored, still remain in part.

The convent of Santa Isabel la Real retains the remains of the Daralhorra: a court whose shorter sides consist of three arches on the ground floor and first floor, and whose big halls have an alcove at each end.

In the convent of Santa Catalina de Zafra can be seen the remains of a house with a court which had, in its original form, the same arrangement as that of Santa Isabel la Real, and the decoration of which was mainly painted. These two fairly simple houses, the disposition of which is often to be found in the Morisco houses of the 16th century, seem to date back to the middle of the 9th/15th century.

The Casa de los Girones has been much restored. It too had porticoes along the shorter sides of its court. Its beautiful staircase had groined vaulting. Its richly moulded plaster-work on a coloured background dates it as late 7th/13th century.

Outside the city wall the Naṣrid sovereigns and persons of high rank in the kingdom had, *extra muros*, beautiful country houses.

At the Cuarto Real de Santo Domingo a tower which formed part of the city wall contains a beautiful square room, entered by a portico. The walls are decorated with moulded plaster and with very lovely faïence mosaic panels, which, in the older parts, belong to the end of the 7th/13th century.

The buildings of the Alcazar Genil have been even more restored than those of the Cuarto Real de Santo Domingo. There remains a tower with a square room flanked by two alcoves with two interior basins. The moulded plaster-work belongs to the 8th/14th century.

These only too rare remains show us the same intention, the same structure, the same decoration in the houses of Granada as in the palace of the Alhambra, and frequently of an equally good quality. Luxury and refinement in their dwellings was not the prerogative of the sovereigns. These private houses testify to the perfect architectural and decorative unity of the art of Granada.

B. — The Alhambra

The Alhambra before the 7th/13th century. — The name of al-Ḥamrā᾿ appears at the end of the 3rd/9th century: it was applied to a small fortress where the Arabs who were being pursued by the rebel peasants took refuge during the revolts that took place under the Umayyad *amīr* ʿAbd Allāh. This fortress must have been built on the westernmost point of the plateau of the Sabīka. The Naṣrid Alhambra was later to cover the whole of this plateau. This castle, built at the end of the 3rd/9th century, was doubtless abandoned during the latter years of the caliphate and during the first half of the 5th/11th century. It was rebuilt and without doubt enlarged by the Jewish vizier Samuel Ibn Nagrello between 443/1052 and 447/1056. The Zīrid *amīr* ʿAbd Allāh improved it, inspired by the arrangement of the Christian castle of Belillos which he had just captured.

This castle is mentioned several times in the struggle of the Spanish *amīr*s against the Almoravids and the Almohads. It was of small dimensions, for the Christian contingents of Ibn Hamū<u>sh</u>k had to camp outside its walls. Some stretches of wall of very hard rubble and some remains of towers with corners chained with flat stones and bricks, in the neighbourhood of the present Alhambra wall, show that the fortress previous to that of the Naṣrids was very plainly built.

The Alhambra, seat of the Naṣrid government. — When Muḥammad Ibn al-Aḥmar entered Granada in Ramaḍān 635/May 1238 he took up residence in the Zīrid Alcazaba, in the town itself. But he lost no time in ordering the construction of the present Alhambra, work on which began after a few months. The new foundation was something quite different in its intention and size from the original fortress. The Alhambra is more than a fortress and a palace: it is a royal city, a seat of government, as had been Madīnat al-Zahrā᾿, al-Madīna al-Zāhira and the Almohad Ḳaṣaba of Marrāku<u>sh</u>.

Opposite the commercial part of the town there was a *ḳaṣaba* which had been enlarged for the governmental needs of the Naṣrids. It contained, in addition to the royal palaces, the State administration: offices, mints, barracks for the guards, accommodation for the palace servants and some high dignitaries; in short, all the organs necessary to the administrative city's ordinary life: workshops, shops, a great mosque, baths.

Never was the separation of town and palace more happily reflected in the landscape: above the Darro and its confluence with the Genil, the hill of the Sabīka is the last platform of a spur that comes down from the Sierra Nevada. It is a narrow plateau, rising almost sheer above the Darro, easy to defend in all other respects, and separated by a ravine from the slopes which overlook it from the direction of the mountain. This "enormous boat anchored between the mountain and the plain", as L. Torres-Balbás has described it, has a maximum length of 740 metres and width of 220.

Work began with the construction of an aqueduct which brought in the water coming from the mountains: there was water flowing everywhere in the town and in the palaces of the Naṣrids. The enclosure and the first palaces were probably not completed till the time of the second *amīr* Muḥammad II (671-701/1273-1302). The Naṣrids never gave up their residence there.

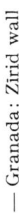

1 — Granada: Zirid wall

Granada: the Alhambra. General view

3 — Granada: the Alhambra. Patio of Comares

4 — Granada: the Alhambra. Hall of the Ambassadors

5 — Granada: the Alhambra. Hall of the Abencerages

6 — Granada: the Alhambra. The Partal

7 — Granada: the Generalife

The Alhambra is first of all a powerful fortress. The high rampart flanked by strong towers which surrounds it is not one of the least of its beauties. The interior of the enclosure, sloping at either end, was divided into three parts: to the west a compact block of fortifications: the Alcazaba; on the highest part, the main body of these palaces; on the gentle slopes which stretch to the east, the town itself.

The fortress. — At the end of the hill, facing the Vega, the Alcazaba formed a sort of fortified keep, completely independent of the rest of the Alhambra. A large parade-ground, then occupied by small houses, is surrounded by a strong triangular wall made up of high curtains, flanked by towers, reinforced by three powerful vaulted bastions, and with an outer wall to the east. This fortress had its own gateway opening into the exterior.

The wall which surrounded the whole of the Alhambra and which the Alcazaba completed to the west consisted of a single rampart made of concrete. This wall is exceptionally high and is strengthened by twenty-three high, wide towers, in the upper storeys of some of which there are halls or small houses belonging to the palaces. The whole of the surrounding wall was built by Muḥammad I and Muḥammad II. In the 8th/14th century, during the reign of Yūsuf I (733-55/1333-54), were built the towers of Comares, of Machuca, of the Candil, and the three great monumental gateways of la Justicia, of Siete Suelas, and of las Armas. The tower of the Peinador was completed under the following sultan, Muḥammad V. So the surrounding wall acquired its present appearance as far back as the middle of the 8th/14th century. The last sultans, in the face of the Christian threat, contented themselves with building platforms for cannon at the foot of the three great gateways.

Three of the Alhambra gates, those of la Justicia, of Siete Suelos and of los Picos, opened onto the exterior. Only the gate of las Armas which flanked the Alcazaba linked the Alhambra to the town.

The Alhambra gates, of huge proportions, form deep masses of masonry enclosing vaulted passages with two or even three bends, often cut across by an open bay. They were made of concrete with façades and arches of brick, sometimes set off by ceramic decorations. Quite apart from their military value, they are beautiful examples of architecture. The gate of la Justicia, which is not flanked by towers, but which forms part of a raised bastion, is pierced by an arch with high piers and has a vigorous elegance all its own. The others do not differ from the great gates of the Almohads or Marīnids in Morocco, especially when they are flanked by two towers.

The curtains, which are very high, had a sentry-walk edged by a parapet crowned by merlons with pyramidions. The lay-out of the ramparts, closely following the contours of the terrain, often makes use of re-entrant angles. The spacing of the towers, which is fairly irregular, reaches and sometimes exceeds fifty metres.

The high bastions of the surrounding wall are often big enough to contain, at the top, one of the halls of the palace, or a small house with a courtyard. The Hall of the Throne, or Hall of the Ambassadors, occupies the top floor of a huge square bastion. All these halls and dwelling-houses overlooked, through numerous windows, the beautiful view of the town and of the Vega.

The magnificent group of fortifications built by the Naṣrid Sultans was never attacked. The numerous Christian incursions to reach Granada stopped before the walls of the town, which never underwent a formal siege, till the last campaign of the Catholic Monarchs, in 896-7/1491-2. The town capitulated and the surrender of the keep took place on 1 Rabīʿ I 897/2 January 1492. Ferdinand and Isabella made their entry into the Alhambra on 6 January. Thus the ramparts of the Alhambra and the palaces they enclosed suffered no damage during the progressive collapse of the kingdom and the fall of the dynasty.

The palaces. — The palaces of the Alhambra, like all Hispano-Moorish palaces, are arranged in groups of buildings round courtyards. The main element is not the body of the building, but the court, more or less spacious, with or without porticoes surrounding it, onto which open the state and living rooms. These groups of buildings often have different axes: they are linked together by corridors or by connecting chambers. The palaces of the 7th/13th century were demolished in the following century to make room for the present palaces. A first group of buildings to the west, long since ruined, and recently uncovered by excavations, comprised a square court onto which opened some small rooms and a small mosque. This fairly simple dwelling-house was followed by a huge court, the patio of Machuca, bordered to the north by a portico which gave access to a hall in the top of one of the towers of the enclosing wall.

The present palaces form two groups built round two courts with perpendicular major axes. The first group, the Cuarto de Comares, preceded by a vestibule, by the Mechouar, and by a small patio, was built by Yūsuf I (733-55/1333-54); the second, the Cuarto de los Leones, by Muḥammad V (755-9/1354-8 and 769-94/1368-92). Some older baths and a mosque link these two 8th/14th century groups.

To the south of the Cuarto de los Leones was the burial-ground of the dynasty, the *Rawḍa*, the plan of which has been rediscovered through excavations. The Partal, a pavilion bordering a pond, the rich houses which complete the towers of the Peinador de la Reina and of the Captive, form separate groups.

The two big patios are surrounded by porticoes or buildings on all four sides. The reception halls are always on the ground floor: the living rooms, of much smaller proportions, occupied the first floor. Thus each of the quarters of this palace forms a small enclosed world round its patio. But, with happy inconsistency, the higher parts are pierced with bays and open galleries surmounted by belvederes.

The architectural composition. — It is in the patio of Comares, known also as the patio of la Alberca or of the Myrtles, the work of Yūsuf I, that we can grasp the methods of composition of the Granada architects. The centre of the court, a very elongated oblong, is occupied by a large pond, emphasized by two borders of myrtles. The buildings which surround this vast patio are disposed in three different styles. The long sides have walls pierced by doors on the ground floor, and by twin windows on the first floor. A mezzanine with single or double windows is inserted along the south front between two colonnades of slender pillars. To the north there is a portico of equally graceful elegance, dominated, above a tile roof, by the huge mass of the bastion that contains the Hall of the Ambassadors, the throne room of the Naṣrid palace. This paradoxical composition which contrasts occupied spaces with empty ones, smooth walls with airy colonnades, which aims at picturesqueness and variety rather than unity, for all its apparent and intentional lack of balance, yet remains a work of the most consummate skill.

Classical traditions govern the arrangement of the state rooms, which open onto the south of the court. The gallery gives access to a very long ante-room, the hall of la Barea. From this sumptuous antechamber one enters the Hall of the Ambassadors: of huge proportions and square in form, it has no middle support: its vast dome rests directly on its walls. It is lit only by nine bays, three to a side, at ground floor level. From these windows one can gaze at the Generalife and the mountain side, the town rising in tiers on its double hill beyond the gully of the Darro, the Vega edged by the distant *sierras*. The bright light in the lower part of the room shades off little by little on the moulded plaster-work. The decoration forms a faint grisaille network: the delicacy of this facing does not detract from the dimensions of the room. The architect who worked for Yūsuf I had, to a rare extent, a taste for architectural contrast and decorative paradoxes.

It is round the famous Court of the Lions that are grouped the majority of the buildings which Sultan Muḥammad V built in the second half of the 8th/14th century. On a plan, the disposition of the four rooms which flank the patio, different in size and in shape, seems to lack severity. But seen from above, the masses of the roofs combine a happy equilibrium with a picturesque variety. The architect has voluntarily deprived himself of the facile resources of symmetry of detail. When one goes through these halls, where perspectives of arches and bays have been skilfully contrived to form axes of light, one cannot help admiring the vital and yet subtle discipline of the architectural arrangement. In spite of the great variety of the decoration the rows of arches re-establish the unity of the composition through the spacing of their lacework of light and shade.

The Court of the Lions itself is of a very classical style: it is divided by two paths which intersect at right angles: their intersection is marked by a fountain whose basin rests on stone lions doubtless belonging originally to a 5th/11th century palace. Four projecting pavilions occupy the middle of the sides. The porticoes and pavilions are made of rich arcades of moulded plaster resting on high and slender marble columns. On the ground floor the portico makes use of one motif only—the ringed column with palm-leaf capitals: here the architecture seems to melt into music. However, the vigorous masses of the tile roofs and pavilions which dominate this ethereal portico save the composition from insipidity. The very placing of the columns shows a rare subtlety: sometimes isolated, sometimes paired, the little columns form symmetrical groupings which link up on successive axes and sometimes overlap. Thus, in the Court of the Lions, the architecture itself becomes a symphony of decoration, through the play of association and repetition of motifs.

At the Partal there is a pool along whose edge runs a long pavilion with a five-arched portico surmounted by tile roofs. This colonnade faces the interior of the palace; but the great hall which opens onto this portico and its central pool have, like the Hall of the Ambassadors, windows at ground level which unite the whole of the landscape with this pleasure pavilion. The left hand side of the patio has a belvedere above it, also pierced by windows which allow one to enjoy the whole panorama of the palace, the mountain, and the town.

Thus the arrangement and classical themes of the Muslim palace have been treated here with true originality. The Naṣrid architects have not been seeking what is grand and massive, but have made use of contrast and nuance with incomparable virtuosity and variety.

The interior decoration. — The Alhambra is famous all over the world for the beauty and opulence of the decorations which overspread its halls. Throughout the palace the tradition of covering everything with decoration dominates. Examples of walls left bare or covered by a fairly large and simply engraved geometrical net-work are rare. The decoration is distributed on three levels. On the floor and on the panels at the base of the walls are to be found ceramic facings. On the floors there are usually geometrical motifs with juxtaposed elements, sometimes star-shaped. But on the panels there are polygonal stars ceaselessly sending out a whole complex of lines, and, through a subtle interweaving, rejoining and forming themselves into frames. In the less important rooms the faïence mosaics are sometimes replaced by glazed paintings, composed of geometrical networks in which are set epigraphic and floral motifs. The middle part of the walls is covered by moulded plasterwork. As a rule it is divided into panels, which, especially in the first half of the 8th/14th century, are arranged with as much skill as variety, thanks to the subtle play of axes and levels. The frames, made up of interlacing bands of inscriptions of varying width and content, allow for both precision and nuance in the grouping of these panels. But in the second half of this century, long high friezes tend to cover, with their uniform distribution, a large proportion of these walls.

In this moulded plasterwork one often finds geometrical networks which make up the general plan. But it is in the epigraphs and floral design that we seek the essentials of the decoration. Kufic script expresses eulogies and spreads out into complex arcatures, but it is the *naskhī* which dominates nearly everywhere: thanks to the balance of its movement it has acquired monumental dignity. Some of the Alhambra inscriptions are perhaps the finest examples of cursive epigraphy. The abundant floral design, usually disposed in foliated scrolls, unites the palm leaf, single or double, ribbed or smooth, to the pine cone and the palmette. Under Muḥammad V an effort was made to renew the forms of the palm and the palmette. But it is not so much a case of innovation as of inspiration rooted in the past, sometimes even in the art of the Cordovan caliphate. But this attempt was short-lived, and apparently limited to the Alhambra.

The quality of the detailed forms is still excellent in the work produced under Yūsuf I. But at the end of the 8th/14th century a certain stiffness appears in the moulding and even in the forms. This incipient decadence became more pronounced in the 9th/15th century, in the moulded plasterwork of the Tower of the Infantes, one of the few buildings of the last Naṣrid rulers in the palace of this dynasty.

This moulded plaster-work composes delicate symphonies in grey, each panel with a shade of its own, because of the distribution of light and shade. The movement of the lines also counts. The double play of light and line prevents any banality or monotony, and gives personality to each panel.

Colour was often used to enhance the moulding, particularly in the background, but sometimes covered the floral or epigraphic forms themselves. The shades—mainly blues and reds—were usually fairly dark, but gold was not lacking. This polychromy, in spite of its sobriety, sometimes impaired the delicate play of light and shade.

All this ornamentation, though no longer renewing either its methods of composition or the forms of its details, yet shows great artistry and real beauty. Its worth lies in its exquisite sense of nuance: but it has lost the vigour of the art of the 6th/12th century.

Above all, it no longer troubles to produce an original composition for each panel. Indefinitely repeated motifs—the background decoration—overrun the whole of the *décor*. This decorative art of the 8th/14th century, in its delicate classicism and its artistry, is already imprisoned in the past: it lacks the boldness of the architecture which it covers. The main motifs—apart from the quadrangular panels—are the arched doorway, its palm-leaf spandrels, its bold rectangular setting, and its arcading, isolated or in tiers.

The ceilings are always most luxurious. Roofs with an interlacing framework, or *artesanados*, are still used. They are nearly always painted. But the biggest and most beautiful halls are covered by domes with stalactites. The *muḳarnas* are small in size, and some of their sides are moulded and painted. These small stalactites are created with great variety, and provide a play of line and shadow both rigorous and hallucinating. The cupolas of the halls of the Kings, of the Two Sisters, and of the Abencerrajes boast a richness and complexity which have never been surpassed.

The human figure is found in some of the famous paintings which cover some of the vaults of the Hall of the Kings: but these have been painted by artists of Christian upbringing. However at the Partal small paintings have been found which in their subjects—scenes of hunting and war and domestic reunions—belong to the Muslim tradition. The costumes and arms are those of the Muslims of Granada.

The Alhambra is the supreme example of monumental decoration in Muslim Spain in its final stage: an art which is still wonderful, but imprisoned in a tradition which it no longer attempts to renew, and already in its decline.

The gardens. — The largest of the patios of the Alhambra must have been laid out as gardens. But the most beautiful were to be found beside the pleasure pavillions, such as the Partal, and above all in the country houses which the sovereigns and wealthy citizens owned in the Vega and on the lower slopes of the mountain. These gardens hardly ever include vast prospects and distant views: they are contained within walls, in a network of alleys intersecting at right angles. More often than not there were just four hollowed-out beds between two raised walks, with a basin at their intersection. Throughout the Alhambra beautiful gardens have been laid out following this tradition, bringing back the gardens of the 8th/14th century, if not in their exact form, at least in their spirit.

It was the Christians who supplied the abundant foliage which today provides so magnificent a screen of greenery to the Alhambra. Although there was running water in the town and palaces of the Naṣrids, the walls and their towers overlooked bare slopes.

The town. — Hardly anything remains, apart from the remains of two houses, of the town enclosed by the walls of the Alhambra, to the south and to the east of the palace. The great Mosque was on the site of the church of Santa Maria de la Alhambra. The *madrasa*, the baths, and the richest houses have disappeared. Excavations have revealed the foundations of houses similar to those still to be found in the business part of the town. To the east was the artisan quarter. The ordinary life of the Muslim city was reproduced at the foot of the palaces, which, in themselves, aimed rather at elegance than at majesty. And this moderation which is expressed by a concern for maintaining the human scale remains one of the great values and charms of the Alhambra.

The Generalife. — On the spur which dominates the Alhambra the Naṣrids had a series of country houses: only the nearest of the palaces, the Generalife, remains. Its water comes from the same aqueduct as supplies the Alhambra.

The gardens are much more extensive than the buildings. After two or three entrance patios one emerges into a long rectangular walled garden. Contrary to the general rule, this *Patio de la Acequia* is not entirely closed in: one of its sides is pierced by arches through which the landscape can be seen; a belvedere marks the centre of this line of arches. The main axis of the garden is formed by a canal with water gushing up along its sides, flanked by two long flower-beds. At both ends of the gardens there are pavilions, the one to the north having three floors. The most sumptuous of the halls, which overlooks both the garden and the vast landscape of Granada, is on the top storey. The halls are richly decorated. The whole of this pleasure pavilion, built for height, dates from the beginning of the 8th/14th century. The style of its plaster mouldings is excellent.

A slightly higher garden stretched out to the east: but it has been greatly altered. Nevertheless, the lay-out of its walks may date back to the Muslim era. With its constantly renewed trees and flowers and the flowing and bubbling of its water, the Generalife evokes, even better than the Alhambra, the private life of the Naṣrid princes. And the architects of Granada have never surpassed this perfect alliance of gardens, water, landscape and architecture, which was their supreme aim, and sets the seal upon their art.

The Alhambra in modern times. — The Alhambra is the only palace of the Muslim Middle Ages to come down to us whole and well preserved. We owe this unique good fortune to the Christian conquerors, who were able to love the Alhambra and defend it against the incurable fragility of its buildings. The Catholic Monarchs, Ferdinand and Isabella, had the palaces they had conquered strengthened and restored. Their successors, the kings and emperors of the house of Habsburg, continued this pious work of preservation. The palace of Charles V was not built after the demolition of part of the Naṣrid residences, but beside them. It was not till the 18th century, under the Bourbon dynasty, that the Alhambra ceased to be looked after: it was partly abandoned to the poor and to the gipsies, who set up their homes within its walls.

In the 19th century the great task of restoration was begun: by clearing the ground, excavating and laying out new gardens, the total of Naṣrid remains has been increased and assured an admirable presentation.

Historic value of the Alhambra. — It is mainly the art of the 8th/14th century that is revealed by the Alhambra. In the following century the sovereigns of Granada were too poor to rebuild the palaces of their predecessors. Otherwise work of less value—such as the few alterations to the Tower of the Infantes then made—would have replaced the masterpieces of Yūsuf I and Muḥammad V. And so

Naṣrid art has left us the *chef d'œuvre* of its classical age, the greatest testimony of its architecture and art of decoration. And the Alhambra has naturally become nothing less than a place of pilgrimage for all who wish to know, and for all who love, the arts of Spanish Islam in their final flowering.

Bibliography: M. Gómez Moreno, *El arte árabe español hasta los Almorávides*, in *Ars Hispaniae*, iii (1951), 173-9, 254-65; L. Torres Balbás, *Arte Almohade, arte nazari, arte mudéjar, ibid.*, iv (1949), 83-195; G. Marçais, *L'architecture musulmane d'Occident*, Paris 1948; H. Terrasse, *Islam d'Espagne*, Paris 1958, 202-32; detailed bibliography on the Muslim monuments of Granada in K. A. C. Creswell, *A bibliography of the architecture, arts and crafts of Islam*, London 1961, 351-63; cf. particularly the many articles by L. Torres Balbás. (H. Terrasse)

GHAṢB, usurpation, *i.e.*, "highhanded appropriation", is neither robbery as it is often translated, nor larceny (*sariḳa*), both of which pertain to the field of criminal law, but the illegal appropriation of something belonging to another or the unlawful use of the rights of another. *Ghaṣb* is thus restricted to civil law, so that it is dealt with by the Islamic jurists in the *Kitāb al-Buyūʿ*. While contractual, legal possession by the non-owner (*e.g.*, tenants, depositaries) is regarded as trusteeship (*amāna*), illegal possession not based on a contract is regarded as *ghaṣb*. The Islamic jurists consider *ghaṣb* from the point of view of an obligation arising from a tort. Hence the question is primarily whether the *ghāṣib* has to return the object obtained by unlawful interference (*maghṣūb*) to the deprived person (*maghṣūb minhu*) or to pay compensation. If the return of the object is no longer possible on account of loss (*halāk*) or as a result of specification, commixtion and confusion, he has to repay the value. As the *ghāṣib* has illegally taken possession of another's property, a high degree of liability is incurred: in all cases of loss, even through *force majeure*, he is liable, *e.g.*, if a usurped child dies from lightning or snake-bite. In the case of *ghaṣb* of *res immobilis* (*ʿaḳār*) jurists disagree over the question of liability.

As far as the consequences, under the law of property, of specification and confusion are concerned, two schools exist in Islam, just as in Roman and Jewish law: the Shāfiʿīs, like the Sabinians or the school of Shammay, direct their attention to the substance of the resulting article, the Ḥanafīs, like the Proculians or the school of Hillel, to the work performed. The Mālikīs represent a *media sententia*, which, however, diverges materially from the Code of Justinian, while the Jewish *media sententia* coincides with the Roman and certainly goes back to it.

Bibliography: The relevant extracts in Islamic law-books, in particular al-Kāsānī, *Badāʾiʿ* and Sarakhsī, *Mabsūṭ*; Bergsträsser-Schacht, *Grundzüge des islam. Rechts*, 80-1; D. Santillana, *Istituzoni*, ii, 455-8; A. d'Emilia, *Il "Kitāb al-Ġaṣb" nella Mudawwanah di Saḥnūn*, in *RSO*, xxviii (1953), 79-98; idem, in *Proceedings of the 22nd Congress of Orientalists, held in Istanbul 1951*, Leiden 1957, 137-46; R. Grasshof, *Über das Ghasb*, in *Mittl. d. Ges. f. vergl. Rechts- und Staatswiss. zu Berlin*, Jhg. I, 1895; O. Spies, *Verarbeitung und Verbindung nach den Lehrmeinungen des islam. Rechts*, in *Zeitschr. f. vergl. Rechtswiss.*, xliv (1928), 41-128. (O. Spies)

GHĀSHIYA, (a.), "the covering", particularly, a "covering for a saddle". Among the Saldjūḳs, Mamlūks etc., the *ghāshiya* was one of the insignia of royal rank and carried before the ruler in public processions (see C. H. Becker, *La Ghâshiya comme emblême de la royauté*, in *Centenario M. Amari*, ii, 148 ff.). *Ghāshiya* is also used metaphorically of a great misfortune that overwhelms someone; in this sense it is found in Sūra LXXXVIII, 1, for the day of the last judgement or for the fires of hell, and from this the Sūra has received the name *al-Ghāshiya*.

GHASĪL al-MALĀʾIKA, nickname by which Ḥanẓala b. Abī ʿĀmir (= ʿAbd ʿAmr) b. Ṣayfī al-Awsī, a Companion of the Prophet, is known. Son of a Christian monk counted among the "People of the Interval" [see fatra], he embraced Islam and took part in the battle of Uḥud; he was about to kill Abū Sufyān [*q.v.*], when he was mortally wounded by one of the enemy (some think that he fell at the hand of Abū Sufyān who, by killing a Ḥanẓala, would thus have avenged his own son Ḥanẓala who had fallen at Badr). On hearing of his death, the Prophet exclaimed: "The angels will prepare his body for burial", and this earned him posthumously the name of Ghasīl al-Malāʾika. He was buried at Uḥud with the many other Muslims killed in this battle.

Bibliography: *Sīra*, ed. Saḳḳā, etc., ii, 75, 123; Ṭabarī, i, 1410, 1412; Ibn Ḳutayba, *Maʿārif*, 343; Muṣʿab al-Zubayrī, *Nasab Ḳuraysh*, 123; Nawawī, *Tahdhīb*, 221-2; Harawī, *Ziyārāt*, 95; Asḳalānī, *Iṣāba*, no. 1863; Ibn al-Athīr, *Usd*, s.v.; Caetani, *Annali*, s.a. 3; M. Hamidullah, *Le Prophète de l'Islam*, i, 121, 152, 510. (Ch. Pellat)

GHASSĀN, a division of the great tribal group al-Azd who migrated from South Arabia, wandered in the Peninsula, and finally settled within the Roman *limes* ca. A.D. 490, having accepted Christianity and agreed to pay tribute.

After a short period of co-existence with Salīḥ [*q.v.*] as tributaries, ὑπόφοροι, they overpowered the latter group and superseded them as the new Arab allies, σύμμαχοι, of Byzantium in A.D. 502-3. Their relations with the Empire were regulated by a treaty, *foedus*, according to which they received annual subsidies, *annonae foederaticae*, and in return they contributed mounted contingents to the Byzantine army. Their leaders in the various provinces were technically called phylarchs, φύλαρχοι, and were generally endowed with the rank *clarissimus*, λαμπρότατος. The chief Ghassānid phylarch whose seat was Djābiya in the province of Arabia was accorded the highest honours and titles; he was *patricius*, *biṭriḳ* [*q.v.*], and *gloriosissimus*, ἐνδοξότατος, and was allowed to wear the crown of a client king. Although Romanized in many respects and passionately attached to Monophysitism, the Ghassānids remained Arabs at heart. Poets from the Peninsula, like Nābigha and Ḥassān b. Thābit [*q.v.*], visited their courts and composed on them panegyrics which give intimate glimpses into their inner life and document their history for three decades.

As allies, σύμμαχοι, politically and militarily, the Ghassānids performed for Byzantium their most important function: (*a*) they supplied the Army of the Orient with an efficient, mobile contingent in the war against the Persians. Their most notable political and military contribution was during the reign of al-Ḥārith b. Djabala [*q.v.*], A.D. 529-69, and before disagreements with the Roman Emperors Justin II, Tiberius, and Maurice limited and frustrated their military efforts. Ḥārith participated regularly in the two Persian Wars of Justinian's reign (A.D. 527-65) and fought with distinction at Callinicum (A.D. 531) and in Belisarius' Assyrian

Campaign (A.D. 541); (*b*) the war against the Lakhmids was successfully prosecuted. Ḥārith triumphed signally over the Lakhmid Mundhir at *Yawm* Ḥalīma [*q.v.*] in A.D. 554 near Ḳinnasrīn, and his son Mundhir triumphed over Ḳābūs, possibly at ʿAyn Ubāgh [*q.v.*], in A.D. 570, captured Ḥīra, and burnt it. Ghassānid military superiority over the Lakhmids solved for Byzantium its most serious Arab problem; (*c*) from their main base in Arabia and Palaestina Tertia, the Ghassānids kept the nomads in check and conducted military operations against the Jews of Ḥidjāz. The Arabian aspect of their function included, also, the protection of Byzantine commercial and political interests along the spice-route, and their importance in this sector is reflected by their participation in the diplomatic mission to Abraha [*q.v.*], the Abyssinian ruler of *Arabia Felix*.

In the history of Syrian Monophysitism the Ghassānids were a determining factor. It was mainly through the efforts of their king Ḥārith b. Djabala that the Monophysite Church in Syria was resuscitated after its disestablishment during the reign of the Chalcedonian Emperor Justin I, A.D. 518-27. Around A.D. 540, and with the help of the Empress Theodora, Ḥārith secured the ordination of two Monophysite bishops, Theodorus and the famous Jacob Baradaeus, after whom the Syrian Monophysite Church was called Jacobite. The indefatigable efforts of these two bishops put the Monophysite Church in Syria on its feet again. The Ghassānid kings, Ḥārith and his son Mundhir, continued to protect the Monophysite Church not only against the hostility of the Chalcedonians but also against divisive movements from within: *e.g.*, the Tritheistic heresy of Eugenius and Conon; the discord which broke out between Jacob Baradaeus and Paul the Black; and the patriarchal strife between the sees of Antioch and Alexandria. But they did not neglect the Arabian Peninsula. Their missionary activities, particularly in Nadjrān, were important contributions towards the propagation of Christianity in those southern parts. Although their staunch support of the Monophysite movement ruffled their relations with the Orthodox Emperors and brought about the downfall of their king Mundhir [*q.v.*], A.D. 569-82, and his son Nuʿmān [*q.v.*], it was through Monophysitism that the history of these war lords underwent that spiritual refinement which made of it the maturest expression of a Christian Arab culture.

The Ghassānids made important contributions to the urbanization of Syria and to its architectural life in the sixth century: (*a*) they were credited with the building of a number of towns, *e.g.*, Djilliḳ, and of public works, *e.g.*, the cisterns, *ṣahāridj*, of Sergiopolis (Ruṣāfa); (*b*) genuinely pious, and living in an age which witnessed a great building activity, they erected churches and monasteries for the resurgent Monophysite Church, *e.g.*, the *Ecclesia extra muros* (possibly a *praetorium*) at Sergiopolis; (*c*) anticipating later Umayyad practice they built, in and near the desert, palatial residences which were sometimes also military establishments, *maṣāniʿ*. [In addition to the dated monument in Sergiopolis there are at least three more, arranged here in chronological order: (i) the tower of the monastery in Ḳaṣr al-Ḥayr al-Gharbī, of 559 A.D., by Ḥārith b. Djabala (D. Schlumberger, *Les fouilles de Qasr el-Heir el-Gharbi*, in *Syria*, xx (1939), 366-72); (ii) a house in al-Hayāt (Ḥawrān) built by Flavios Seos in 578 (H. C. Butler, *Syria, Princeton Expedition, division II*: *Archtecture, section A*: *Southern Syria*, Leiden 1919, 362-3); (iii) the castle in Ḍumayr, built by al-Mundhir (569-82) (described in Brünnow-Domaszeski, *Die Provincia Arabia*, Strassburg 1909, iii, 200; at that time the foundation inscription (Wetzstein, no. 173, Waddington, 2562c) was lost, but in the summer of 1963 I was able to rediscover it on the site, and the Syrian Service of Antiquities is going to exhibit it in the Damascus Museum).— note communicated by K. Brisch]. The prosperity of the province of Arabia in the sixth century, archaeologically attested, can to a great extent be made explicable by the activities of this energetic dynasty whose main base was Arabia, and who, consequently, animated the region and relieved it of its technically insignificant and provincal status.

Relations between Byzantium and the Ghassānids were not uniformly smooth. Their independent spirit, but more, their unflinching support of Monophysitism crossed the will of Orthodox Byzantium. Around A.D. 580, the Emperor Tiberius had Mundhir arrested and brought to Constantinople, and in A.D. 582-3?, Maurice gave the same treatment to his son Nuʿmān. This considerably weakened the Ghassānid Phylarchate. But it was the Persian invasion of A.D. 613-14 that dealt the crushing blow to the Ghassānids who, however, re-emerge, serving in the army of Heraclius and represented by the Djabala b. al-Ayham [*q.v.*] at the decisive battle of Yarmūk, A.D. 536.

The Muslim Conquest of Syria swept away the Ghassānids beyond recall. Some of them went over to Byzantium and settled in Anatolia; others adopted Islam and were assimilated in the new Arab Muslim community; the rest remained Christian and stayed on in Syria. To these, some of the Arab Christian families of the contemporary Near East trace their descent.

Bibliography: Greek Sources: Procopius, *History*, I, xvii, 45-8; xviii, 26, 35-7; II, i, 1-11; xix, 12-8, 26-46; *Anecdota*, ii, 23, 28; Malalas, *Chronographia* (Bonn), 434-5; 441-2; 445-7; 461-5; Menander Protector, in *Excerpta Historica*, ed. C. de Boor, Pars i, 180; Evagrius, *Ecclesiastical history*, ed. Bidez and Parmentier, 216, 223; Syriac Sources: John of Ephesus, *Historica Ecclesiastica*, in *Corpus Scriptorum Christianorum Orientalium*, no. 105 (versio), 90, 129-33; 135-6; 163-70; 212-7; 237, 238; Michael the Syrian, *Chronique*, French trans. by J.-B. Chabot, ii, 245-8, 285, 308-9, 323-5, 344, 345, 349-51, 364-71; Arabic sources: Nābigha, in *The Divans of the Six Ancient Arabic Poets*, ed. W. Ahlwardt, poems 1, 2, 11, 13, 18, 20, 21, 25, 27; Ḥassān b. Thābit, *Dīwān*, ed. H. Hirschfeld, *GMS*, poems 13, 79, 86, 92, 125, 138, 155, 160; Ḥamza al-Iṣfahānī, *Taʾrīkh*, ed. Gottwaldt, 114-22. Cf. also Th. Nöldeke, *Die Ghassānischen Fürsten aus dem Hause Gafna's*, in *Abh. Pr. Ak. W.*, 1887; R. Aigrain, *Arabie*, in *Dictionnaire d'histoire et de géographie ecclésiastiques*, iii, cols. 1200-19; J. Sauvaget, *Les Ghassānides et Sergiopolis*, in *Byzantion*, xiv (1939), 115-30; Irfan Kawar, *Procopius and Arethas*, in *BZ*, 1957; idem, *The Patriciate of Arethas*, in *BZ*, 1959. For Ghassānid residences, those certain and those under discussion, see further K. A. C. Cresswell, *EMA*, i; A. Musil, *Arabia Petraea*, Vienna 1907, i; idem, *Palmyrena*, New York 1928 (index); idem, *Northern Negd*, New York 1928 (index). (IRFAN SHAHĪD)

AL-GHASSĀNĪ, ABŪ ʿABD ALLĀH MUḤAMMAD

(Ḥammū) B. ʿABD AL-WAHHĀB, descendant of an Andalusian family which emigrated to Morocco towards the end of the Middle Ages, was secretary to Mawlāy Ismāʿīl (1082/1672-1139/1727), who entrusted him with various diplomatic missions: one to Spain (1101/1690-1102/1691) for the ransoming of Muslim captives and another to Algiers (1103/1692) as a member of the suite of Muḥammad al-Ṭayyib al-Fāsī. He wrote the story of his journey in Spain under the title *Riḥlat al-wazīr fī iftikāk al-asīr* (ed. and Spanish tr. by A. Bustani, Larache 1940; partial French tr. by H. Sauvaire, Paris 1884). In it he shows himself to be an acute observer and uses the chronicle entitled *Fatḥ al-Andalus* as a source of his historical information. He gives only a few details of the way in which he accomplished the mission with which he was charged, namely to obtain 5,000 books and 500 captives in exchange for the Spanish garrison of Larache imprisoned by Mawlāy Ismāʿīl; if he should not obtain all the books the number of captives was to be increased to 1,000. The Spanish archives complete the information which he gives: he arrived at Madrid on 4 Rabīʿ I 1102/6 Dec. 1690 and after he had presented himself to Charles II the king ordered Cardinal Portocarrero to conduct the negotiations which terminated to the satisfaction of all before 27 Shaʿbān 1102/27 May 1691, the date on which al-Ghassānī set out again for Morocco. The ransomed captives were assembled at Barcelona, Cartagena, and Alicante, whence they were sent to Cadiz and must have crossed to Morocco some time after March 1692.

Bibliography: Brockelmann, S II, 172; Lévi-Provençal, *Historiens des Chorfa*, 284-6; H. Pérès, *L'Espagne vue par les voyageurs musulmans de 1610 à 1930*, Paris 1937, 5-17; E. García Gómez, *Novedades sobre la cronica anonima titulada "Fatḥ al-Andalus"*, in *AIEO Algers*, xii (1954), 31-42; J. Vernet, *La embajada de al-Gassānī (1690-1691)*, in *Al-Andalus*, xviii (1953), 109-31.

(J. VERNET)

GHASSĀNIYYA, name given by later Sunnīs to the Murdjiʾī position associated with Abū Ḥanīfa. In Ashʿarī (*Maḳālāt al-Islāmiyyīn*, ed. Ritter, i, 138 f.), Abū Ḥanīfa appears as head of a section of the Murdjiʾa asserting that *īmān* is the affirmation of God and the Prophet, however poorly these are understood; some of his followers, including Ghassān, differ from him in including reverence within *īmān* and allowing that it may increase. Al-Baghdādī (*Al-farḳ bayn al-firaḳ*, ed. Muḥammad Badr, 191) cites this latter difference as proof that Ghassān did not follow Abū Ḥanīfa at all, and then ascribes the whole position to Ghassān under the name of Ghassāniyya, omitting Abū Ḥanīfa from the Murdjiʾa. Going still further, Shahrastānī (*Kitāb al-Milal wa 'l-niḥal*, ed. Cureton, 263-5) transfers Ashʿarī's quotations of Abū Ḥanīfa to Ghassān al-Kūfī himself. (M. G. S. HODGSON)

GHĀT, a *ḳṣar* of the Sahara among the Touareg Ajjer on the frontier between the Fezzān (Libya) and the Algerian Sahara, in the neighbourhood of the 25th parallel and the 10th meridian. It stands at an altitude of 780 metres, 3 km. to the west of the Wādi Tanezzouft, whose valley lies in a north-south direction between the bank of primary sandstone on the side of the Tadrart in the east and the similar plateaus of the Tassili of the Ajjer in the west. It owes its existence to the richness and shallowness of the phreatic underground water-level and to its situation on the route of the ancient trans-Sahara track which, coming from Kano, Zinder and Agadès, leads towards southern Tunisia by way of Ghadamès, and to Tripoli either via Ghadamès or via the Fezzān, thus avoiding the mountains of the Tassili and the ergs of the Fezzān.

The region was inhabited in ancient times, as is proved by the numerous rock engravings and more than one necropolis such as those of al-Barkat and of Tin Alkoun, but it has never been proved that the *oppidum* of Rapsa mentioned by Pliny was situated there. Ghāt itself does not go back for longer than 700 years and is mentioned for the first time by Ibn Baṭṭūṭa in the 8th/14th century. Its prosperity depended upon the vicissitudes of trade across the Sahara, about which our only exact information comes from some 19th century travellers, in particular Muḥammad al-Otsman al-Hachaïchi (al-Ḥashāʾishī); he remarks, at the end of the century, that if for the Touareg Ajjer "Ghāt is their Paris", most of the traders of Ghāt "which is the Marseilles of the Sahara" are people of Ghadamès and people from Tripoli; the Touareg hired their camels to the traders, but the essential part of the cross-Sahara traffic already went via the Fezzān. This trade disappeared little by little in the early years of the twentieth century.

For a long time Ghāt remained independent, governed by an hereditary *amghar* [*q.v.*] and an elected municipality, but nevertheless under the somewhat heavy protection of the Touaregs. In 1875, the Turks of Tripoli installed a garrison there and a *ḳāʾimmaḳām*, and remained its masters until 1914. Ghāt was occupied for the first time by the Italians, conquerors of Libya, from April to December, 1914, and a second time from February 1930 until January 1943. It was then taken by the French troops of southern Algeria at the same time as the expedition of General Leclerc made itself master of the Fezzān; it was annexed to the region of Djanet (Fort Charley). French forces left Ghāt after the Franco-Libyan treaty of 10th August, 1955, and Ghāt was attached once more to the Fezzān, a province of the United Kingdom of Libya.

Ghāt is a picturesque *ḳṣar*, fortified in an irregular rectangle 700 by 500 metres in area, surrounded by a crenellated wall with five gates; part of it also are the suburbs of Tadramt and Tounin. Al-Fewet, 10 km. away to the west, and the fortified *ḳṣar* of al-Barkat, 8 km. to the south, as well as some hamlets scattered within modest palm groves, are under its control. The whole area has more than 2,000 inhabitants. The Kel Ghāt fall into five groups: the Tel Talaḳ and the Tel Makammazan who are the oldest, the Iadhenan, the Tel Inan Tamalgat and the Tel Khabsa; some Arabicized families, Ghadamesians, Touaregs who have become sedentary (especially at Fewet and al-Barkat) and many negro share-croppers of Sudanese origin, called here *atāra*, complete the population. All speak Tamāhaḳḳ but many understand Arabic and even Hausa which is spoken by the negroes.

Ghāt is the centre for about 1,000 Imanan and Oraghen nomads and for some Imanghassaten families. Some springs and shallow wells (both the type worked by animal traction and those worked by balancing poles) make possible the irrigation of 21,000 palm trees, some fruit trees, winter cereals (corn and barley) and summer cereals (sorghum and Indian millet). The nomads raise dromedaries, goats and a few sheep. The artisan class (skins and woodwork) is declining rapidly. Trade to-day is reduced to modest exchanges between the nomads and the sedentary population and the importation of some manufactured goods from the Fezzān. But if oil research to the north and the east comes to anything, it may perhaps change very rapidly the modest economy of Ghāt.

Bibliography: D. Denham, H. Clapperton and W. Oudrey, *Narratives of travels and discoveries in northern and central Africa*, London 1826; J. Richardson, *Travels in the great desert of Sahara*, London 1848; H. Barth, *Reisen und Entdeckungen in nord- und central Afrika*, Gotha 1858; J. Bouderba, *Voyage à Ghat*, in *Bull. de la Soc. de géogr.*, Paris 1860; H. Duveyrier, *Les Touareg du Nord*, Paris 1864; M. el Otsman el-Hachaïchi, *Voyage au pays des Senoussia à travers la Tripolitaine et les pays Touareg*, Paris, 2nd ed., 1912; E. de Agostini, *La conca di Gat*, in *Boll. geogr. del Gov. della Tripolitania*, Tripoli n° 5-6 (1933-34); Soc. geogr. italiana, *Fezzan e l'oasi di Gat*, Rome 1937; Nehlil, *Étude sur le dialecte de Ghat*, Paris 1909.

(J. Despois)

GHAṬAFĀN, name of a group of Northern Arabian tribes, belonging to the Ḳays ʿAylān [*q.v.*] and represented in the genealogical system as the descendants of Ghaṭafān b. Saʿd b. Ḳays b. ʿAylān. Their lands lay between the Ḥidjāz and the Shammar mountains in that part of the Nadjd which is drained by the Wādī al-Rumma. Here lived from West to East their principal tribes: the Banū Ashdjaʿ, the Dhubyān (with the sub-tribes Fazāra, Murra, and Thaʿlaba), the ʿAbs, and—in the region al-Ḳasīm—the Anmār. Of these tribes the Banū ʿAbs (b. Baghīḍ b. Rayth b. Ghaṭafān) rose to prominence c. 550 A.D., when their chief, Zuhayr b. Djadhīma, gained power not only over all Ghaṭafān, but also over the Hawāzin, the other important group of the Ḳays-ʿAylān. After Zuhayr was slain by Khālid b. Djaʿfar of the Banū ʿĀmir b. Ṣaʿṣaʿa, the power of the ʿAbs declined. A quarrel between Ḳays b. Zuhayr b. Djadhīma und Ḥudhayfa b. Badr, chief of the Banū Fazāra (b. Dhubyān b. Baghīd b. Rayth b. Ghaṭafān), led to the so-called war of Dāḥis between the ʿAbs and Dhubyān; during it nearly all Ghaṭafān took up arms against the ʿAbs and forced them to leave their pasture grounds. After many wanderings they found shelter with the Banū ʿĀmir b. Ṣaʿṣaʿa and c. 580 A.D. both groups defeated in the battle of Shiʿb Djabala [*q.v.*] the coalition of Tamīm, Dhubyān, Asad, and other tribes (see the poem of Khurāsha b. ʿAmr al-ʿAbsī in *Mufaḍḍaliyyāt*, no. 121). Later on peace was restored between the ʿAbs and Dhubyān through the good offices of two chiefs of the Banū Murra (b. ʿAwf b. Saʿd b. Dhubyān) named al-Ḥārith b. ʿAwf and Harim b. Sinān, both of whom were praised by Zuhayr b. Abī Sulmā [*q.v.*] in his *muʿallaḳa*. After this reconciliation the ʿAbs and Dhubyān stood together against the Banū ʿĀmir b. Ṣaʿṣaʿa (see Bakrī, *Muʿdjam* s.v. al-Bathāʾa) and were often joined by the other Ghaṭafān tribes, *e.g.*, in the battle of al-Raḳam (see the poem of Salama b. Khurshub al-Anmārī in *Mufaḍḍaliyyāt*, ed. Lyall, no. 5). About the same time the Ghaṭafān concluded an alliance with their neighbours the Ṭayyiʾ and Asad. There were also fights between the Ghaṭafān and the Hawāzin and Sulaym till the rising power of Islam ended these clashes. The Ghaṭafān were, like almost all Bedouins, hostile towards Muḥammad and his religion. At this time ʿUyayna b. Ḥiṣn al-Fazārī, of the famous "house" of Badr, was the leading chief amongst the Ghaṭafān, and the Meccans tried to win his support, whilst Muḥammad was eager to forestall all hostile movements (*e.g.*, in the expedition of al-Kudr against Sulaym and Ghaṭafān). After the expulsion of the Banu 'l-Naḍīr from Medina to Khaybar, the Jews and Meccans made an alliance and gained the support of the Ghaṭafān and Sulaym. A contingent of the Banū Fazāra and perhaps of the Banū Murra under ʿUyayna took part in 5/627 in the siege of Medina (the so-called War of the Trench), but when this attempt had failed, the Banū Ashdjaʿ, who of all Ghaṭafān lived nearest to Medina, concluded a treaty with Muḥammad (Ibn Saʿd, i/2, 48), and ʿUyayna thought it best to refrain from open opposition. He was in Muḥammad's camp during the conquest of Mecca in 8/630, accompanied him during the subsequent campaign of Ḥunayn, and the Prophet honoured him at Djiʿrāna, when the spoils were distributed, by a special gift of one hundred camels, to the chagrin of al-ʿAbbās b. Mirdās al-Sulamī, who got only four, though the Sulaym had taken an active part in the fighting. It was only in 9/631 that a deputation of the Fazāra and the Murra, led by Khāridja b. Ḥiṣn and al-Ḥārith b. ʿAwf, went to Medina to announce their tribes' conversion. But in the revolt (*ridda*) that broke out immediately after Muḥammad's death, the Ghaṭafān and the Banū Asad took up arms. A band of them, led by Khāridja b. Ḥiṣn, attacked Abū Bakr in his camp near Dhu 'l-Ḳaṣṣa but was driven back. Then Khālid b. al-Walīd defeated the Banū Asad under Ṭulayḥa and a corps of the Fazāra under ʿUyayna b. Ḥiṣn in the battle of Buzākha [*q.v.*] and broke the last resistance of Khāridja b. Ḥiṣn at Ghamr in Fazāra territory. In consequence of this defeat the Fazāra lost part of their grazing-ground. ʿUyayna b. Ḥiṣn was brought as captive to Medina, but pardoned by Abū Bakr. His daughter Umm al-Banīn became wife to ʿUthmān b. ʿAffān (Ṭabarī, i, 3056-7).

In the wars of conquest the warriors of the Ghaṭafān joined the armies; some of them settled in the newly conquered countries. The Syrian army which was sent after Muʿāwiya's death in 60/680 against Medina was led by Muslim b. ʿUḳba of the Banū Murra. In Kūfa we find members belonging to the leading families of the Banū Fazāra, *e.g.*, Manẓūr b. Zabbān, father-in-law to Ḥasan b. ʿAlī, Muḥammad b. Ṭalḥa b. ʿUbayd Allāh, al-Ḥadjdjādj, ʿAbd Allāh b. al-Zubayr, and Mundhir b. al-Zubayr (Ibn Durayd, *Genealogisch-etymologisches Handbuch*, 173 etc.). Hind bint Asmāʾ b. Khāridja b. Ḥiṣn was married to ʿUbayd Allāh b. Ziyād, then to Bishr b. Marwān, and later to al-Ḥadjdjādj.

In the contest between the Northern (*Muḍar*) and the Southern (*Kalb*) Arabs the Ghaṭafān naturally sympathized with the former. They fought at Mardj Rāhiṭ 65/684 under al-Ḍaḥḥāk b. Ḳays al-Fazārī against the Banū Kalb. It seems that later on the Fazāra at Kūfa supported Zufar b. al-Ḥārith of the Banū Kilāb b. ʿĀmir and ʿUmayr b. Ḥubāb al-Sulamī in their fight against Ḥumayd b. Ḥurayth al-Kalbī (see Ibn al-Athīr, iv, 259, 19). When Ḥumayd killed some of the Fazāra in their homeland in Arabia the latter took revenge in the battle of Banāt Ḳayn in the Samāwa c. 74/693 (see Wellhausen, *Das arabische Reich*, 128 f.). It was to the advantage of the Fazāra that Wallāda bint al-ʿAbbās, one of the wives of ʿAbd al-Malik and mother of the caliphs al-Walīd and Sulaymān (Ṭabarī, ii, 1174) was a descendant of Zuhayr b. Rawāḥa al-Fazārī (see the verses in Abū Tammām, *Ḥamāsa*, 672). When ʿUmar b. Hubayra al-Fazārī [*q.v.*] was viceroy of the East in 102/721-105/725 all Ḳays were again in the ascendency. After the downfall of the Umayyad Empire we hear little of the Ghaṭafān. The Fazāra, Ashdjaʿ, and Thaʿlaba are mentioned in connexion with the revolt of the Bedouin tribes in 230/844-5 which was put down by Bughā al-Kabīr (Ṭabarī, iii, 1342 ff.). But the majority of the Ghaṭafān had left Arabia, and their lands were occupied by the Ṭayyiʾ. There were apparently no Ghaṭafān groups among the Northern (Ḳays) Arabs settled by order of Hishām b. ʿAbd al-Malik in 107/725-6 in Egypt (see Haytham b. ʿAdī *apud* Maḳrīzī, *al-Bayān wa 'l-iʿrāb*, 39 f., Wüstenfeld). Later on we find clans and families claiming descent from Ghaṭafān tribes in Egypt, Libya, the Maghrib and in Spain.

Amongst the poets of the *Muʿallaḳāt* there are two belonging to the Ghaṭafān: ʿAntara b. Shaddād al-ʿAbsī [*q.v.*] and al-Nābigha al-Dhubyānī [*q.v.*]. Lesser poets of the Ghaṭafān are ʿUrwa b. al-Ward and al-Ḥuṭayʾa from the ʿAbs; al-Ḥādira and al-Shammākh from the Thaʿlaba b. Saʿd; Ibn Mayyāda (see *Aghānī*[3], iii, 261-340) from the Banū Murra b. ʿAwf; and Ibn Dāra (see *Ḥamāsa*, ed. Freytag, 191 ff.) of the Banū ʿAbd al-ʿUzzū, commonly called Banu 'l-Muḥawwala because the Prophet changed their ancestor's name into ʿAbd Allāh, and ʿUwayf al-Ḳawāfī (see *Aghānī*[1], xii, 105-118) from the Fazāra.

Very little is known of the pagan religion of the Ghaṭafān. They worshipped like other tribes an idol called al-Uḳayṣir [*q.v.*]. They also had a sanctuary of al-ʿUzzā at Buss—misrepresented by Muslim writers as a rival institution to the Kaʿba at Mecca—which was destroyed in the first half of the 6th century by Zuhayr b. Djanāb al-Kalbī (see *Aghānī*[1], xxi, 94; xii, 126). Then there is Khālid b. Sinān al-ʿAbsī, who according to a saying attributed to Muḥammad was "a prophet whom his people let perish" (Ibn Saʿd, xii, 42, 7; Ibn Ḥadjar, *Iṣāba*, Cairo 1328 A.H., i, 466 ff.).

The etymology of the name Ghaṭafān is unknown. Besides the well-known Ghaṭafān of the Ḳays-ʿAylān there are also clans of the same name amongst the Djuhayna, Djudhām, and Iyād (Wüstenfeld, *Gen. Tabellen*, i, 19; 5, 18; A 12; see also Nöldeke, in *ZDMG*, xl, 180). Ghaṭafān b. Unayf al-Kalbī was a poet of the 1st/7th century (Ṭabarī, ii, 456, 799). One of the secretaries of Marwān b. al-Ḥakam had the *kunya* Abū Ghaṭafān (Ṭabarī, ii, 837; see also Ibn Ḥadjar, *Tahdhīb al-Tahdhīb*, xii, 199).

Bibliography: in the article; see also: The indices to Yāḳūt, *Geogr. Wtb.*; Ibn Saʿd; Ṭabarī; the *Naḳāʾiḍ* of Djarīr and al-Farazdaḳ; *Mufaḍḍaliyyāt*; and *Aghānī*. See further v. Oppenheim, *Die Beduinen*, ed. W. Caskel, iii, 7-14; Wellhausen, *Skizzen und Vorarbeiten*, vi, 7 ff. (J. W. Fück)

AL-**GHAWĀR**, a tract of broken limestone hills, now (1963) an important oil field, in Eastern Arabia. Centred 30 kilometres southwest of the oasis town of al-Hufūf, al-Ghawār proper is an elevated area elongated along a north-south axis. Bounded on the north by the depression of Djaww Umm ʿUnayḳ, the tract extends 50 kilometres south to Wādī al-Ḳuṣūr. It averages 20 kilometres in width. Al-Ghawār has only a few poor quality hand-dug wells, and Bedouins consider it a poor pasture area. The machine-drilled wells near the oil field camp of al-ʿUḍayliyya now provide a reliable source of summer water for small groups of Āl Murra and al-Dawāsir tribesmen. Darb Mazālīdj, formerly an important camel track between al-Ḥasāʾ and Central Nadjd, passes through al-Ghawār from northeast to southwest. The hill of al-ʿUthmāniyya and the hill and rock shelter of Ghār al-Shuyūkh, both well-known landmarks of the area, lie near this trail. The derivation of the name al-Ghawār is popularly explained as an alternative plural of *ghār* (common plural *ghīrān*), "rock shelter, shallow cave", or as a plural of *ghawr*, "low ground, depression".

The central portion of Ghawār (Ghawar) Oil Field coincides with al-Ghawār proper. Extending north to Fazrān and south to Wādī al-Sahbāʾ, the oil field has a total length of 256 kilometres. This, with an average width of 20 kilometres, gives it a greater surface area than any other oil field in the world. Discovered by the Arabian American Oil Company in 1948, Ghawār Field yielded an average of 715,200 barrels daily during 1962, nearly one-half of the Company's total production.

Bibliography: J. Lorimer, *Gazetteer of the Persian Gulf, ʾOmān, and Central Arabia*, Calcutta 1908-15, ii, 581-2; Map: U.S. Geological Survey, *Geographic map of the Western Persian Gulf quadrangle, Kingdom of Saudi Arabia*, Miscellaneous geologic investigations, Map I-208 B, 1:500,000, 1958. (J. Mandaville)

GHAWĀZĪ [see ghāziya].

AL-**GHAWR**, "depression", "plain encircled by higher ground", a geographical term denoting various regions in the Muslim countries.

1. The best known is the Ghawr in Palestine, which corresponds with the deep hollow, called *Aulôn* in the Septuagint, through which the Jordan flows, between Lake Tiberias and the Dead Sea, and which is merely a section of the central Syro-Palestinian rift-valley. At first, the Ghawr consists of a plain, overshadowed by the mountains of Samaria on the one side and Mount ʿAdjlūn on the other, 105 km./65 miles long, and sloping down gradually from -208 m. /-680 ft. on the shores of Lake Tiberias to -394 m. /-1300 ft. by the Dead Sea; the width of the plain, though variable, does not exceed 12 km./8 miles in the northern part but reaches 20 km./12$^1/_2$ miles in the Jericho region. It then embraces the basin of the Dead Sea, the deepest point of which goes down to -793 m. /-2600 ft., while the width reaches 12 km./8 miles [see baḥr lūṭ]. Finally, it is continued by the Wādī al-ʿAraba, as far as the approaches to the gulf of ʿAḳaba.

From the earliest times of the Muslim occupation, the Ghawr belonged, for administrative purposes, to two different provinces, the *djund* of al-Urdunn and that of Filasṭīn. The Arab geographers describe it as a very hot, unhealthy district with bad water, but possessing numerous streams and covered with pasturages and sub-tropical plantations (palm-trees, sugar-cane and indigo). Besides the capital Arīḥā (Jericho), they mention Ṭabariyya (Tiberias), Baysān, ʿAmmatā and lastly Zughar to the south of the Dead Sea. As for the region called al-ʿArabāt and belonging to the Ghawr in Palestine where, according to Ibn Isḥāḳ (Ṭabarī, i, 2125; cf. 2107), ʿAmr b. al-ʿĀṣ linked up with the forces from the east of the Jordan before the battle of al-Adjnadayn, this no doubt corresponds with the steppe zone lying to the South of the Dead Sea.

In the Mamlūk period, the Ghawr was divided into several administrative districts, all forming part of the second or southern march of the province of Damascus. It was followed by the trade and post route between Damascus and Ghazza. At the beginning of the Mamlūk period, the couriers made the crossing of the Jordan near Baysān, at a place where the river could be forded in normal times or crossed by ferry-boat in times of flood; in the middle of the 8th/14th century, the route was modified to spare couriers from having to climb too steep gradients; they made use of the bridge of al-Madjāmiʿ, further to the north, at the confluence of the Jordan and the Yarmūk.

Bibliography: F.-M. Abel, Géographie de la Palestine, i, Paris 1933, particularly 10, 80-1, 93-4, 423-9; Le Strange, Palestine, 30-2; A.-S. Marmardji, Textes géographiques arabes sur la Palestine, Paris 1951, 158-9; Yaʿḳūbī, Buldān, 326; Ibn Hawḳal, iii, 114; Yāḳūt, iii, 822; Dimas̲h̲ḳī, ed. Mehren, 201; Gaudefroy-Demombynes, La Syrie à l'époque des Mamelouks, Paris 1923, particularly 64 ff.; J. Sauvaget, La poste aux chevaux dans l'empire des Mamelouks, Paris 1941, 73.

2. Another G̲h̲awr is G̲h̲awr Tihāmat al-Yaman or G̲h̲awr Tihāma (al-Farazdaḳ, ed. Boucher, 20), called also, as a dual, G̲h̲awrā Tihāma (al-Ṭabarī, ii, 219). The statements by the geographers regarding it are very vague, for it is sometimes identified with Tihāma and sometimes described as a separate district adjoining it. For example, according to Ḳudāma b. D̲j̲aʿfar, it stretched from Nad̲j̲d to the extreme borders of Tihāma; on the other hand, according to a passage in al-Bakrī, it lay between Tihāma (the district from D̲h̲āt ʿIrḳ to two days' journey beyond Mecca) and the Sarāt.

Bibliography: Ibn K̲h̲urradād̲h̲bih, 248; Hamdānī, 46, 48, 210, 233; Bakrī, Geographisches Wörterbuch, ed. Wüstenfeld, 7, 11, 36, 818; Yāḳūt, iii, 821.   (F. Buhl-[D. Sourdel])

AL-**G̲H̲AYB** (A.). The two connotations of the root are g̲h̲āba ʿan, to be absent, and g̲h̲āba fī, to be hidden. In current usage, g̲h̲ayb (and especially g̲h̲ayba) may signify "absence" (and g̲h̲ayba, correlated with s̲h̲uhūd, "presence", may be a technical term of Ṣūfism); but more frequently g̲h̲ayb may indicate what is hidden, inaccessible to the senses and to reason—thus, at the same time absent from human knowledge and hidden in divine wisdom. It is to this second meaning that al-g̲h̲ayb refers, as a technical term of the religious vocabulary. It may then be rendered by "the mystery". Such is its meaning, with rare exceptions, in the Ḳurʾān. Its use there is frequent.

"Al-g̲h̲ayb belongs only to God" (Ḳurʾān, X, 20); "He has the keys of al-g̲h̲ayb which are known only to Him" (VI, 59), etc. Reference is here made to the Divine mystery, of itself inaccessible to man. Hence the translation adopted (by R. Blachère) of 'Inconnaissable', "Unknowable". The idea which reappears most often is the inaccessibility of al-g̲h̲ayb, which remains totally hidden. "God knows the Unknowable and enlightens no-one about it" (LXXII, 26), "He does not raise you up to the Unknowable" (III, 174). The g̲h̲ayb nevertheless is an object of faith (II, 3), just as is the Word revealed to the Prophet (II, 4). Man ought therefore to cling to the unknowable mystery "from where God is" (ladunī), and God, if He wishes, will reveal it in part to him. "This is part of the story (anbāʾ) of the Unknowable which We reveal to you" (III, 44; cf. II, 49; XII, 102). It is thus, as Gaudefroy-Demombynes emphasizes, that the g̲h̲ayb of the Ḳurʾān is "sometimes the Revelation, sometimes the Unknowable, sometimes both together" (Les sens du substantif G̲h̲ayb dans le Coran, in Mélanges Louis Massignon, ii, Damascus 1957, 250). In fact, the common denominator is still the notion of (divine) Mystery, sometimes unrevealed, sometimes revealed in fragments—to the extent that this revelation is necessary to lead man along the straight path (hidāya). The Ḳurʾān does not com-

municate all the g̲h̲ayb to man, but the whole Ḳurʾān is a (partial) communication of the g̲h̲ayb. It is in this sense that Fak̲h̲r al-Dīn al-Rāzī was to entitle his great commentary "The keys of the Mystery", Mafātīḥ al-g̲h̲ayb.

This partial revelation of the g̲h̲ayb is explained by L. Massignon (Passion d'al-Ḥallād̲j̲, Paris 1922, 500) as a participation which God vouchsafes to the prophets in His "essential mystery" (al-sirr al-d̲h̲ātī, as al-D̲j̲urd̲j̲ānī says in Taʿrīfāt, Leipzig 1845, 169). In the commentaries on the Ḳurʾān and in religious literature, al-g̲h̲ayb is in fact applied at times to the absolute mystery of God Himself, but more often it is the invisible world taken as a whole. The distinction frequently appears between ʿālam al-g̲h̲ayb and ʿālam al-s̲h̲ahāda, the world of the invisible mystery, created and uncreate, and the perceptible world, also called ʿālam al-mulk. These refinements of meaning are found in the tafsīr commentaries on Ḳurʾān, II, 3. Al-Bayḍāwī there explains the g̲h̲ayb in which belief is required as "that which is not perceived by the senses or which is not immediately understood by the reason". But al-Ṭabarī, on the other hand, there defines the g̲h̲ayb which is an object of faith as being the Will of God—thus an "attribute of the Essence".

However, this resort to the Divine Will seems to relate the idea of g̲h̲ayb to the Decreee of God, rather more than to the notion of "essential Mystery". In his profession of faith, the Ḥanbalī Ibn Baṭṭa lays down: "One must throw oneself (taslīm) upon the Divine Omnipotence (ḳudra) and have faith in the Divine Mystery (g̲h̲ayb), for the individual reason is unable to raise itself to the understanding (maʿrifa) of this mystery" (cf. the translation of H. Laoust, La profession de foi d'Ibn Baṭṭa, Damascus 1958, 105). This "Divine Mystery" is thus simultaneously the "mystery of things" and the destiny of men (and of each man). It is reserved to God, who reveals it to his prophets to the extent that He wills.

Other usages of the expression al-g̲h̲ayb: — (a) in S̲h̲īʿī theology, the imām has, of himself, knowledge of the g̲h̲ayb; a view attacked by the Ḥanbalī al-Barbahārī and others. Mafātīḥ al-g̲h̲ayb is the title of a work of the S̲h̲īʿī S̲h̲īrāzī (Mullā Ṣadrā). — (b) Ibn Baṭṭa compares astrology with "the pretension to know the g̲h̲ayb" and condemns both severely (cf. H. Laoust, op. cit., 155). Under the same title of Mafātīḥ al-g̲h̲ayb (Cairo 1327) the Egyptian Aḥmad al-Zarḳāwī treats of magic and divination. — (c) Ibn ʿArabī uses the same title again, but this time to designate Ṣūfī maʿrifa. In fact taṣawwuf frequently interprets the g̲h̲ayb as the threefold world of d̲j̲abarūt, malakūt and lāhūt [cf. ʿĀLAM], but also as the hidden essence of all that is, whether visible or invisible. It is then the g̲h̲ayb al-huwiyya ("mystery of selfhood") or absolute g̲h̲ayb (muṭlaḳ) (cf. al-D̲j̲urd̲j̲ānī, Taʿrīfāt, 169-70).—The hierarchy of the abdāl, the "saints apotropéens" (Massignon), crowned by the Ḳuṭb ("Pole"), is called "the men of the Mystery" (rid̲j̲āl al-g̲h̲ayb, Lane, Arabian Nights, xxx, n. 17).—And according to C. Wells (Mehemet the Kurd ..., 129), ibn al-g̲h̲ayb describes a child begotten without a father and endowed with mysterious intellectual faculties.

Al-g̲h̲ayb, the Mystery, therefore, may be understood in three possible meanings. — 1) Normal religious sense: the mystery of the Divine Decree, unknowable in itself, partially revealed in the Ḳurʾān. — 2) The invisible world which magic, occultism and astrology try to penetrate (but the man who persists in crossing its boundaries by his own powers is committing a sin). — 3) In Ṣūfism, *al-ghayb* means, according to context, the reality of the world beyond the senses and beyond discursive reason which gnosis (*maʿrifa*) experiences,—the hierarchy of the invisible worlds,—the beings of these worlds,—and even the world of the Divine Essence. (The penetration of the *ghayb* through a pleasurable intellectual experience was to become extremely suspect to the adversaries of *taṣawwuf*).—Finally, we should note that in Shīʿism, the *ghayb* known to the *imām* recalls the latter's actual condition when he has become *ghāʾib* and his state of *ghayba*, absence, or better, "occultation".

Bibliography: Further to references given in the text: *Dict. of tech. terms*, 1033 f. (s.v. *ʿālam*), 1090, 1539 f. (s.v. *huwiyya*): Max Horten, *Theologie des Islam*, 219 f.

(D. B. Macdonald-[L. Gardet])

GHAYBA (*maṣdar* of *ghāba*) means "absence", often "absence of mind". The latter sense was developed by the Ṣūfīs as the obverse of *ḥaḍra* [*q.v.*], absence from the creation and presence with God. The word is also used for the condition of anyone who has been withdrawn by God from the eyes of men and whose life during that period (called his *ghayba*) may have been miraculously prolonged. It is so used of al-Khaḍir [*q.v.*]. A number of Shīʿī groups have recognized the *ghayba*, in the latter sense, of one or another *imām*, with the implication that no further *imām* was to succeed him and he was to return at a foreordained time as Mahdī [*q.v.*]. The first instance of this was that of Muḥammad b. al-Ḥanafiyya.

Among the Ithnāʿasharī Imāmīs, the *Ghayba* became a major historical period, lasting from the disappearance of the twelfth *imām* until his reappearance in eschatological times. It was divided into two parts. In the "lesser *Ghayba*", from 260/874 to about 329/941, the Hidden Imām was represented among his followers by *safīrs* [*q.v.*], held to be in touch with him and exercising his authority. They maintained the organization, in its legal and financial functions, which had grown up around the later *imāms* (cf. Javad Ali, *Die beiden ersten Safīre des zwölften Imāms*, in *Isl.*, xxv (1939), 197-227). The fourth of these did not pass on his authority to a successor; on his death, therefore, began what is called the "greater *Ghayba*" when the Imām is represented only indirectly or through occasional miraculous interventions. Though kept generally invisible, the Imām still lives on earth, has from time to time been seen by some and been in written correspondence with others (for instance, he receives letters placed on holy tombs), and maintains a control over the fortunes of his people. At the time of pilgrimage he is at Mecca, unrecognized, scrutinizing the hearts of the believers. The earlier organization of the sect has been replaced by the presence of independently learned *mudjtahids* in the various Shīʿī centres, recognized by the community as qualified to interpret the Imām's will. The *Ghayba* has legal effects on account of the absence of the *imām*, whose active presence in the community is regarded as necessary for validating certain community actions. Hence some have regarded *djihād* as in abeyance during the *Ghayba*, as well as the full celebration of the *ṣalāt al-djumʿa*. It has not been excluded from the thought of many Imāmīs that another direct representative of the Imām should appear under the title *Bāb*, an equivalent of *safīr*; but none of the claimants to this office has been generally recognized. (On the Imāmī *Ghayba* see I. Goldziher, *Vorlesungen*, 232 ff., 269 f.; idem, *Abhandlungen zur arabischen Philologie*, ii, p. lxii ff.; Ibn Bābūya al-Ḳummī, *Kamāl al-dīn wa-tamām al-niʿma fī ithbāt al-ghayba*, ed. Ernst Möller *Beiträge zur Mahdilehre des Islam*, I, Heidelberg 1901).

The corresponding periods of absence of an *imām* among the Ismāʿīlī groups are differently interpreted, and called *satr* [*q.v.*]. But among the Durūz [*q.v.*], the concept and term were revived to refer to the period of absence of al-Ḥākim and Ḥamza.

(D. B. Macdonald-[M. G. S. Hodgson])

GHAYLĀN b. **MUSLIM**, Abū Marwān al-Dimashḳī al-Ḳibṭī, is chiefly known as one of the first advocates of free will [see ḳadariyya], at the same time as Maʿbad al-Djuhanī [*q.v.*]. The son of a freed slave of ʿUthmān b. ʿAffān, he appears, like Maʿbad, to have been the disciple of a Christian from ʿIrāḳ, but he lived in Damascus where he held the position of secretary in the chancellery. Al-Djāḥiẓ (*Bayān*, iii, 29) mentions him on the same footing as Ibn al-Muḳaffaʿ, Sahl b. Hārūn and ʿAbd al-Ḥamīd, and even one so strictly orthodox as al-ʿAsḳalānī acknowledged his professional ability (*Lisān al-Mīzān*, iv, 424), while Ibn al-Nadīm (*Fihrist*, 171) estimated his *rasāʾil* to amount to about 2,000 leaves; they were probably not all of an administrative and diplomatic character, to judge by al-Khayyāṭ (*Intiṣār*, ed. and trans. Nader, Ar. text 93, trans. 115) who when answering the accusations of Ibn al-Rāwandī [*q.v.*] appealed to their content and stated that they were very widely known; he added that Ghaylān believed in the five Muʿtazilī principles, but the heresiographers rank him solely among the Ḳadarīs. According to al-Shahrastānī (margin of Ibn Ḥazm, i, 194), who names him as one of the Murdjiʾī Ḳadarīs, his principal doctrine concerned the primary, innate knowledge (*maʿrifa*) which allows it to be known that the world has an Artificer created by Himself; the *īmān* is only the secondary, acquired knowledge.

The activities of Ghaylān, who apparently embraced the cause of al-Ḥārith b. Suraydj al-Kadhdhāb [see djahm b. ṣafwān], earned him the imprecations of ʿUmar b. ʿAbd al-ʿAzīz, but it was only Hishām b. ʿAbd al-Malik (105-25/724-43) who gave orders that his hands and feet should be cut off and who had him crucified, after al-Awzāʿī (born about 87/706, d. 157/774 [*q.v.*]) had subjected him to interrogation and given a verdict in favour of his execution.

Bibliography: Djāḥiẓ, *Bayān* and *Ḥayawān*, index; Ibn Ḳutayba, *Maʿārif*, 484, 625; idem, *ʿUyūn*, index; Ibn al-Nadīm, *Fihrist*, 171; Ashʿarī, *Maḳālāt*², ed. Ritter, Wiesbaden 1963, index; Baghdādī, *Farḳ*, ed. Badr, 190, 193, Eng. trans. A. S. Halkin, 1, 6-7; Dhahabī, *Mīzān al-iʿtidāl*; ʿAsḳalānī, *Lisān al-Mīzān*, iv, 424; Ibn Baṭṭa, ed. and trans. H. Laoust, 169; A. N. Nader, *Muʿtazila*, 6; A. S. Tritton, *Muslim theology*, London 1947, index; Montgomery Watt, *Free will and predestination*, London 1948.

(Ch. Pellat)

GHAYLĀN b. **ʿUḲBA** [see dhu 'l-rumma].

GHAYN, 19th letter of the Arabic alphabet, here transcribed *gh*; numerical value: 1000.

Definition: a voiced postvelar fricative; according to the Arab grammatical tradition: *rikhwa madjhūra mustaʿliya*. As regards the *makhradj*: *min adnā 'l-ḥalḳ* (from the part of the throat nearest to the mouth). The Arabs thus made *ghayn* (and *khāʾ*) guttural. They contrasted them with *ʿayn* and *ḥāʾ*, *min awsaṭ al-ḥalḳ*; and with *hāʾ* and *hamza*, *min aḳṣā 'l-ḥalḳ* (al-Zamakhsharī, *Muf.*² § 732). The velaric articulation of *ghayn* is well described by

R. Růžička as "between the soft palate (velum) and the back of the tongue" (*Existence du gh*, 182). The soft palate is divided into two areas: upper (prevelar) and lower (postvelar). The articulation of *ghayn* takes place in the latter area, hence the adjective employed in the definition. To the extent that a channel is formed on the back of the tongue permitting the uvula to vibrate, *ghayn* approximates to uvular *r*.

In a few cases the passage from *gh* to *kh* is quoted (J. Cantineau, *Cours*, 94), see Ibn al-Sikkīt (*al-Ḳalb wa 'l-ibdāl*, 32). But particularly interesting is the passage from *ʿayn* to *ghayn*, which has been illustrated with numerous examples by R. Růžička, notably in *L'alternance de* ع — غ *en arabe* (*JA*, ccxxi (1932), 67-115). Since his article in *ZA*, xxi (1907), 293-340, he has sustained and defended the theory of the secondary origin of *ghayn* in Semitic, by the passage of *ʿayn* into *ghayn* in Arabic and only in Arabic (references to these writings: *Ar. Or.*, xix (1951), 100, n. 4).

One of his last articles summarizes his ideas and his activity in this controversy: *La question de l'existence du gh dans les langues sémitiques en général et dans la langue ougaritienne en particulier*, in *Ar. Or.*, xxii (1954), 176-237 (quoted as *Existence du gh*). K. Petráček, his pupil, who is loyal to his ideas (*Ar. Or.*, xxi (1953), 240-62 and xxiii (1955), 475-8), acknowledges (*ibid.*, xxi, 243, n. 16) that only H. Torczyner has accepted the theory. During the lifetime of its author, and to his great chagrin, it seems to have encountered only indifference or neutrality in the world of orientalists. S. Moscati, in his recent *Lezioni di linguistica semitica* (Rome 1960), includes *ghayn* among the phonemes of common Semitic (41-3), as had W. Leslau in the *Manual of phonetics* (ed. L. Kaiser, Amsterdam 1957), 327. The existence of doublets is not sufficient to prove the secondary character of the Arabic *ghayn* (according to the judgment of J. Cantineau, *Cours*, 94). Further, R. Růžička appears to have underrated the data of South Arabian epigraphy and to have misinterpreted those of Ugaritic (cf. S. Moscati, *loc. cit.* and *Rend. Lin.*, series VIII, xv/3-4 (1960), 87; compare also the account of C. H. Gordon, *Ugaritic manual*, Rome 1955, i, ch. 5, 8). We would ourselves also retain *ghayn* among the articulations of common Semitic. The most recent documents to be discovered (see *GLECS*, *Comptes rendus*, viii, 73; C. Virolleaud, *Palais d'Ugarit*, ii, 201, *Mission Ras Shamra*, vii, 1957), pending a fuller report, do not contradict this view.

But the dispute has at least brought to light a certain instability in the Arabic *ʿayn* (which can pass into *ghayn*), *at least among certain tribes*; (we must also eliminate false doublets arising from simple graphic errors in the manuscript tradition). An analogous case seems to be reproduced in present day dialects, where *ghayn* is seen to have passed into *ḳāf*: dialects of North Arabian nomads: Rögga, the Mawāli; the majority of the dialects of the Algerian Sahara, an immense region which seems to cover also the South Moroccan and Mauritanian Sahara (see J. Cantineau, *Cours*, 95).

In Classical Arabic *ghayn* undergoes few conditioned changes (*ibid.*, 94). For the phonological oppositions of the phoneme *gh* see J. Cantineau, *Esquisse*, in *BSL* (no. 126), 105, 22°; for its incompatibilities see *ibid.*, 135.

For a general discussion of the phonetics of Arabic as seen by the classical grammarians, see ḤURŪF AL-HIDJĀʾ; for modern studies, see LINGUISTICS and PHONETICS.

Bibliography: in the text and under ḤURŪF AL-HIDJĀʾ. (H. FLEISCH)

GHAYR MAHDĪ [see MUḤAMMAD AL-DJAWNPŪRĪ].

GHAYṬA, GHĀʾITA or GHĪTA. A reed-pipe of cylindrical bore or an oboe of conical bore, popular in Muslim Spain and North Africa. The word is not Arabic, but originated in the low Latin *wactare* and the French *guetter*, whence the old English term *wayte*—the modern *wait*—who sounded the hours at night on an instrument thus named. Delphin and Guin say that the *ghayṭa* was introduced by the Turks, but it is mentioned by Ibn Baṭṭūṭa (d. 779/1377) who likens the instrument to the Mesopotamian *surnāy*. It was blown by means of a single or double reed (*ḳaṣba*) placed in the inflation end of the instrument. It is practically identical with the Eastern *zamr* or *mizmār*. Like the mediaeval shawmer of Europe, the player takes the entire inflation reed (*ḳaṣba*) into his mouth as far as a disc called *ʿarrāḍ*, which means that the player's lips have no more control over the tone of the instrument than have those of a bagpiper. The 'bell' of the instrument is widely conical as that term implies, and is perforated with tiny holes. The tube of the *ghayṭa* is perforated with seven finger holes on its breast with one on its back for the thumb. Nowadays these holes on the breast—from the top to the bottom—bear Iranian names, *viz.*, *yaka sāʿida*, *shashka*, *bandjka*, *djahārka*, *sīka*, *dūka*, and *yaka*, the thumb-hole at the back being *haftakā*. Persian musical terminology is current even in conservative Morocco, and the instrument is delineated in Höst, *Nachrichten von Marokos und Fes*, 1787. The *ghayṭa* is chiefly an out-door instrument and is usually accompanied by a drum (*ṭabl*) played with two sticks, and a larger drum termed *ṭanbar*, *i.e.*, the French *tambour*, which is struck with an animal bone. In southern Tunisia it retains the old Arabic name of *zammāra*, which in Egypt is reserved for a double reed-pipe because — perhaps — the term signifies 'shackled'. Strangely enough Ibn Khaldūn calls the instrument *zallāma*, which A. Cour considered to be a metathesis of *zammāra*. On the other hand there was a certain musician named Zunām mentioned in the 18th *maḳāma* of al-Ḥarīrī who is claimed to have been the inventor of a *nāy zunāmī* or *nāy zulāmī*, and he was at the court of Hārūn (d. 193/809) and onwards. Al-Shaḳundī (d. 628/1231) of Seville calls it *zulāmī*. In some places of North Africa, where Turkish influence once prevailed, the instrument is known as the *zurna*; the term *zukra* is also used in Tunisia. In modern Spain the *gaïta Gallega* is still favoured in Galicia, and since that land was held by the Muslims for a mere five years, it is likely that the name of this instrument is not of Arabic origin; nevertheless the initial *ghayn* in the arabicized word has bred the crossed Spanish forms *gaita*, *raita* and *raica*. The Turkish form is *ghaydā* (modern Turkish *gayda*) and this term is used in a part of the Slavonic field for a kind of bagpipe.

Bibliography: G. Höst, *Nachrichten von Marokos und Fes*, Copenhagen 1787; T. Shaw, *Voyages dans la Régence d'Alger* (trans. by MacCarthy, Algiers 1830, 89 ff.); F. Salvador Daniel, *La musique arabe*, Paris 1863, Algiers 1879 (trans. by Farmer as *Arab music and musical instruments*, London 1915, 117, 224, 243-4); Delphin and Guin, *Notes sur la poésie et la musique arabes*, Paris 1886, 47-9; W. Marçais, *Textes arabes de Tanger*, Paris 1911, 152 fn. 3, 407; A. Bel, *La Djâzya*, Paris 1903,

93 ff.; J. E. Budgett Meakin, *The Moors*, London 1901, 202-3; Bū ʿAlī, *K. Kashf al-Ḳināʿ*, Algiers 1904, 98-104; Farmer, *History of Arabian music*, London 1929, 131; idem, *Oriental studies: mainly musical*, London 1953, 6; idem, *EI*[1], s.v. MIZMĀR; M. Snoussi, in *REI*, xxix/1 (1961), 143-57.

(HENRY G. FARMER)

GHAZAL, "song, elegy of love", often also "the erotico-elegiac *genre*". The term is Arabic, but passed into Persian, Turkish and Urdu and acquired a special sense in these languages.

The semantic development of the word from the root *gh z l*, "to spin", "spinning", is not in doubt, but presupposes intermediary meanings for which we have no evidence; the *ghazal* was not in fact a song of women spinning, like that of which Tibullus speaks (ed. Rat, Paris 1931, Book II, no. 1, line 60), but a man's song addressed to a girl; contamination by the noun *ghazāl* "gazelle", from the images and comparisons associated with it, is not perhaps to be excluded (cf. "to make sheep's eyes"). Whatever the reason, the idea evoked by the term *ghazal*, like the English "gallantry" and particularly the noun "gallant", now fallen into disuse, became elaborated in a realm of ideas where there mingle the notions of flirtation, compliments made to a lady, complaints at her coldness or inaccessibility and the description of effeminate languishing attitudes on the part of the lover (cf. the noun-adjective *ghazil*, "affected, mincing, without vigour"; on the ambiguity of the idea, see Ḳudāma, 42, to be compared with the definition in *LA*, xiv, 4, line 20, where the stress is on the idea of "amorous addresses"). The word *ghazal*, as early as in a line of al-Akhṭal (ed. Ṣalḥānī, 142), is associated with *lahw* "pleasure"; in a contemporary poet, Surāḳa (ed. Ḥusayn, in *JRAS*, 1936, no. 20, verse 9), the term appears in the phrase *yalhū ilā ghazal al-shabāb* "he seeks his pleasure in the *ghazal* of youth". The meaning of love-song inspired by youthfulness is clear in a verse attributed to Waḍḍāḥ [*q.v.*], where the composition of *ghazals* and the fear of death are contrasted. By the 3rd/9th century, *ghazal* had finally acquired the general sense given above (see *al-Washshāʾ*, 54 bottom, Ibn Ḳutayba, *Poesis*, 525); the comparative *aghzalu* is as much applied to a verse as to a poet and thus represents the general idea of preeminence in this genre (see *Aghānī*[3], i, 114, line 5, and Ibn Rashīḳ, ii, 115). The noun-adjective *ghazil* means the "elegiac poet" as early as the 3rd/9th century (thus *Aghānī*[3], viii, 352 and *Aghānī*[3], xx, 149 onwards). The 5th form of the verb, *taghazzala*, before it meant "to compose love-songs", would seem to have had the meaning "to express a sorrow of love" (see the passage in Ibn Rashīḳ, ii, 118); for his period, Ḳudāma established a distinction between *ghazal* and *taghazzul* (see Ḳudāma, 42, where the basis of the *ghazal* is further distinguished from that of the *nasīb*).

To the same realm of ideas as *ghazal* there belong the verbal noun and the verb *tashbīb* and *shabbaba*, whose etymology, curiously enough, was not discovered by certain Arab critics (see Ḳudāma, in Ibn Rashīḳ, ii, 121); the term is quite certainly derived from *shabāb*, "youthfulness, youth"; it is frequently used as a simple synonym for *ghazal* and *nasīb* (*LA*, i, 463, line 21). According to Ibn Durayd (in Ibn Rashīḳ, ii, 122 bottom), the term *nasīb* would be more commonly used; the origin of this remains obscure; perhaps it originally described a type of dedicatory verse addressed to a lady; but the possibility must not be excluded of a relationship, by loss of emphasis, with the word *naṣb*, "a kind of camelman's lament similar to the *ḥidāʾ*" (see al-Djāḥiẓ, *Tarbīʿ*, index; *Aghānī*[3], ix, 133 and also vi, 63, where it is a matter of a singer bearing the tribal name of al-Naṣbī). The word *nasīb*, in ancient times, designates the elegiac *genre*, in a list in which there also figure the poem of praise, the satire and the *fakhr* (thus in Ibn Rashīḳ, i, 100 and especially Ibn Sallām in *Aghānī*[3], viii, 6, line 4; cf. *ibid.*, 97, line 12); sometimes this genre appears in a five-fold list (see Ibn Rashīḳ, *loc. cit.*, bottom of page). In certain passages, the verb *nasaba* constructed with *bi-* clearly means "to sing of the beauty of a lady and the agitation she inspires" (thus in *Aghānī*[3], vi, 219, viii, 99, 123). It is well known that in its common meaning *nasīb* designates the amatory elegiac prologue at the beginning of a *ḳaṣīda*. Ḳudāma, 42, attempted very artificially to establish a distinction between the thematic elements of the *ghazal* and those of the *nasīb*.

i. — THE *Ghazal* IN ARABIC POETRY

1. The amatory elegy in Arabic poetry can be made the subject of historical and critical study only from the last quarter of the 6th century A.D. onwards. Of course, we have no text originating in this era, but those which have come down to us under the names of poets belonging to this period, such as Imruʾ al-Ḳays, Ṭarafa and a number of others, are very instructive. At that time the *ghazal* was handled according to a tradition which is clearly ancient and honoured. According to all the evidence, this genre was one of those most current in "spontaneous poetry", that is, in the camelman's chant (or *ḥidāʾ*); at this level it must have been improvised and for this reason no example of it has come down to us. Under what influences, where, and when did there appear and become established the custom of prefacing the *ḳaṣīda* with an amatory elegiac prelude, known from the 1st/7th century onwards as the *nasīb*? We can only guess at the answers to these questions. Since the *ḳaṣīda* was both originally and essentially not a framework but a lyrical movement consisting of a sequence in the key of *fakhr* or a Dionysiac expression of the ego, it is possible that the *nasīb* owed its place to the very importance of the carnal and psychic impulses which it evoked; in fact there also occur in the *ahal* of the Tuaregs the same lyrical flights introducing identical explosions of boasting; the procedure is not therefore peculiar to the Arabs. Though at first episodic in the poetry of the nomads of Central and Eastern Arabia, the elegiac production known as *nasīb* seems to have become incorporated in the *ḳaṣīda* under the influence of a fashion current among or created by poets belonging to groups on the Euphrates steppe; certain data accepted among ʿIrāḳī scholars indeed assume that the *nasīb* is the invention of a certain Ibn Ḥidhām (see Ibn Sallām, ed. Hell, 13, line 9) or of the famous Muhalhil [*q.v.*] (*ibid.* and also al-Djāḥiẓ, *Bayān*, ed. Hārūn, ii, 297) or even in fact of Imruʾ al-Ḳays (Ibn Ḳutayba, 40, 52); as may be seen, these indications demonstrate the existence of a tradition which was still living in the 3rd/9th century and according to which the *nasīb* was associated with an idea peculiar to the Bakrī poets or others in the orbit of al-Ḥīra (see Blachère, *Litt.*, chap. V, § C.). This feature is significant since, in so far as it may be historically acceptable, it permits us to infer that this centre, with its musicians and its circle of poets, probably exercised an influence on the *ghazal* cultivated in the desert. It would seem that this

influence became apparent in the last quarter of the 6th century A.D. at the latest. From certain indications it may be possible to descry a similar phenomenon in other centres closely linked with the *badawī* way of life such as Tayma', Mecca and al-Ṭā'if. Most probably, though of still uncertain date, the verse texts attributed to ancient poets like Ṭarafa, Zuhayr, ʿAlḳama, Imru' al-Ḳays, Ḥassān b. Thābit, al-Aʿshā Maymūn, and al-Ḥuṭay'a, to mention only the most representative, evoke reasonably well the themes which were habitually developed in the amatory elegiac *nasīb* of this period. The apostrophe to the deserted encampment, the description of the migrating group disappearing into the distance, the sorrow aroused by the separation, the memory left in the poet's heart by the promises of the beloved, the recital of the efforts made to rejoin her, all constitute a thematic sequence arising from the environment; even the detail of the development, as much as the stock phrases, derives from the same origin; to a certain extent, the thematic elements belong to the real world but they are transposed into a kind of fiction by the use made of them. Already at this time convention may well have been very powerful; everything leads us to believe that the elegiac poet from now on makes use of a vocabulary, of formulas, of stock phrases, whose use reinforces the tyranny of convention.

2. Among the generation of poets which arose about 50/670, the amatory elegiac *genre* received a particular twist which conditioned its subsequent development. This generation to varied degrees freed itself from the grip of the poetic tradition inherited from Central and Eastern Arabia. The three areas of the Muslim Arab East which were to struggle for leadership during the eighty years or so which followed differed in the extent of their contribution to this change. Syria and Palestine were of secondary importance and followed the lead of the Arabian peninsula and ʿIrāḳ. The latter, while occupying a prominent place in the poetic movement, carried on the previous tradition; the artists and versifiers were led by circumstances to specialize in the laudatory, satirical and descriptive styles; in the works of the representative ʿIrāḳī poets, amatory elegiac themes occur only in the *nasīb*s of the *ḳaṣīda*s; in some, like al-Farazdaḳ, they are in fact noticeably neglected; in all, they are treated in a manner which suggests a mere prolongation of the tradition passed on from the desert and cultivated at al-Ḥīra or under its influence.

In the Ḥidjāz on the other hand, and more particularly in Mecca, al-Ṭā'if and Madīna, the situation was entirely different. The influx of wealth from the conquest, the disruption of the social structure resulting from the enrichment and political advancement of certain families such as the Umayyads, the Zubayrids, and several Makhzūmī clans, the introduction into the population of Mecca and Madīna of foreign elements, particularly captives brought from Palestine and ʿIrāḳ, as well as the choice of Madīna as political capital, had all played their part in turning this province, with its urban centres, into a world very different from that which the generation of the Caliph ʿUmar I had known. The establishment of the Umayyad dynasty in Syria, the gradual political and religious rise of the cities of ʿIrāḳ and the ten years during which the revolt of the Zubayrids cut off the Ḥidjāz from the rest of the Empire, succeeded in giving society in Madīna and Mecca a character of its own. Certain aristocratic elements renounced an active rôle and sought solace for their unsatisfied ambitions in the pursuit of pleasure and the taste for sentimental intrigues. The anecdotal literature collected by Abu 'l-Faradj al-Iṣfahānī from the writings of the ʿIrāḳī "logographers", especially the *ḳāḍī* of Mecca, al-Zubayr b. Bakkār (d. 256/870), subject to the necessary critical adjustments, helps us to form an idea of what life in this circle was like. Women occupied an important place, together with dilettanti, aristocrats with violent passions, intriguers, characters of doubtful morality, singers and singing-girls. The setting was favourable to the development of lyric poetry; by a happy chance, the aristocracy produced several poets like al-ʿArdjī, al-Aḥwaṣ and ʿUmar b. Abī Rabīʿa, who devoted their talent to the celebration of their love affairs; others of more humble origin like Kuthayyir and Nuṣayb imitated them, without entirely being able to avoid becoming court poets. In this poetic movement a significant part is played by singers and singing-girls, as much by reason of the practices they introduced as because they took part in the composition of the works; often in fact they selected fragments of verse or commissioned them from poets, which implies an artistic production entirely governed by musical considerations.

The study of the amatory elegiac verse which developed in the Ḥidjāz between about 50/670 and the end of the first quarter of the 2nd/8th century comes up against the difficulty posed by the state of the texts. On the one hand a considerable volume of verse has disappeared; on the other, what has survived has often been preserved only in anthologies or late or even very recent recensions, as is for example the case with the poems of Kuthayyir (ed. Pérès, Algiers 1928-30) and those of Nuṣayb (ed. Rizzitano in *RSO*, xxii, 1943); frequently, these recensions consist only of fragments which poorly represent the original outpouring; even in the case of the relatively important *Dīwān* attributed to ʿUmar b. Abī Rabīʿa (ed. P. Schwarz, Leipzig 1901-2, 1909; reprinted by ʿAbd al-Ḥamīd, Cairo 1952), many problems arise; it is in fact apparent that this collection includes pieces which give evidence of reconstruction, retouching, and indeed the hand of imitators. The very conditions in which the *ghazal* of the Ḥidjāz was born explain the disappearance of these works and the state of those which survive; many were simply extempore compositions, occasional pieces, ephemeral by nature; some seem to have been commissioned by musicians, singing girls or dilettanti from poets forced to compose in haste and to refurbish earlier works. The uncertainties of attribution are great; it was indeed enough for a piece to contain the name of ʿAzza for it to be attributed to Kuthayyir, who was accustomed to celebrate a lady of this name; often too, single lines or pieces attributed to a poet are nothing more than elaborations in verse drawn from fictional biographies or romances about the poet; thus the small historical and literary value to be accorded to such compositions is easily seen. Taken together, nevertheless, the amatory elegiac texts which have been preserved allow us to evoke satisfactorily the general characteristics of the style in the period under consideration. In order to estimate the extent to which this is possible, however, we must constantly keep in mind the fact that our texts contain passages where the influence of the courtly style of ʿIrāḳ appears, as indicated below.

The poetic instrument used by the poets of the Ḥidjāz was substantially different from that of their contemporaries in Central and Eastern Arabia.

Under local influences the connexion between poetry and music remained very much alive; this is shown especially in the use of metres practically unknown to the poets in the desert tradition; thus, the ***khafīf***, the ***hazadj***, the ***ramal*** are found to be extensively represented among the elegists, and the identity of these with the musical modes of the same names must be emphasized. Among the poets of this school ***enjambement*** is much less rare than among their desert rivals. The vocabulary is equally characteristic; free from rare words and ***hapax legomena***, it aims at simplicity and naturalness; the dialogue form is frequent and corresponds to the description of real scenes; naturally, many expressions are proper to the evocation of feelings connected with the excitements of the heart and the flesh.

The elegists of the Ḥidjāz were primarily poets of the desert school. Their surroundings simply brought about a development which set them aside from the main stream of the *badawī* tradition. This can easily be shown from the texts. Often, for example, the elegist of Madīna and Mecca invokes the deserted encampment, describes the departure of a migrating group, bewails his sorrow at a separation; thus thematic elements proper to the ***nasīb*** of the ***ḳaṣīda*** continue to appear (cf. specimens in Kuthayyir, ed. Pérès, no. 44, and ʿArdjī, no. 2, lines 7 ff. and no. 5, lines 1-4). These remnants of the desert setting lead quickly to stylization, but they still do not preclude a certain realism of description. This derives from the abiding nature of things. The elegist is above all a lyric poet and self-expression cannot do without a minimum of sincerity in its references to life. The various themes which he develops are in effect the highlights of the more or less stylized narration of known circumstances or real events; even the poetical texts inserted in fictional or romantic narratives still represent elements of verisimilitude within the pattern of the whole. It is clear that the elegist of the Ḥidjāz loves to note those details which evoke reality. We can therefore say that this lyric poetry was above all marked by an effort to express sentiments and emotions which were really felt, to represent scenes where the participants retained their attitudes and reactions; this is so unquestionable that in many cases the poet felt obliged to allude to the lady by a name other than her own.

A rapid examination of several themes treated by the elegists of the Ḥidjāz demonstrates the trends just sketched and emphasizes the persisting *badawī* influences. The thematic sequence relating to the obstacles encountered by the poet in seeking to find his lady reproduces the essential features of what is found in the desert tradition. There are few novelties; at the most we may note a certain harping on the obstacles arising from the separation of the sexes and the rigour of the new ethic in the society of Madīna and Mecca; we may also note the realism concealed beneath the fiction of conventional personages such as the ***raḳīb*** or "censor", the ***kāshiḥ*** or "ill-wisher", the ***ʿādhil*** or "blamer"; according to our biographical information, these personages correspond to known real persons. The poetical texts also refer very often to the difficulties which arise from human nature, to the quarrels and misunderstandings between lovers, to the rupture of relations never to be resumed (thus ʿUmar b. Abī Rabīʿa, ed. ʿAbd al-Ḥamīd, 61, and also al-ʿArdjī in *Aghānī*[3], i, 392). One element, however, is original: in these elegists, an important rôle is played by the evocation of the meeting of the poet and a lady on the occasion of the Pilgrimage; clearly the theme in question does not refer to imaginary circumstances; a typical example is to be found in al-ʿArdjī (see *Dīwān*, no. 13 and the account in *Aghānī*[3], i, 408). In these meetings, the lady acts the part of "the silent one" but the lyricism of the poet requires nothing more than her presence for its release. Similarly, the thematic sequence concerned with rediscovery is very suggestive, and appears frequently; here again the poet refers to events he has experienced, to night rides to rejoin his lady, to the surprise caused by his unexpected arrival; hardly have they met when the two lovers enter upon a dialogue whose simple pattern evokes a conversation which has actually taken place; the amorous quest is recorded as an exploit, which re-establishes the connexion between the elegiac theme and ***fakhr*** (thus in ʿUmar b. Abī Rabīʿa, ed. ʿAbd al-Ḥamīd, no. 1, line 25 ff.; no. 6, line 10 and no. 258); among the Ḥidjāz poets rediscoveries are given substance by the description of details designed to emphasize the reality of the experience; thus, the lover, either alone or with companions, surprises the lady amusing herself with her women; sometimes the event is prearranged and organized by the lady; the two lovers meet in a secluded spot (thus in al-ʿArdjī no. 13, line 15, no. 23, line 2); the account very frequently ends with a description of the beloved and the evocation of sensual excitement between the two lovers (thus ʿUmar b. Abī Rabīʿa, no. 1, lines 35-41, no. 5, lines 10 ff., no. 258, lines 9 ff.; al-ʿArdjī, no. 47, lines 6-26).

There emerges from the whole pattern of these amatory elegiac themes a certain literary concept of love, which, for convenience, we shall call the Ḥidjāz manner. This concept is seen primarily in the images formed of the lover and his lady. The latter remains a somewhat unfocussed character, owing to the lack of any poetess able to express herself in verse with the authority of such men as ʿUmar b. Abī Rabīʿa, Nuṣayb or Kuthayyir; her physical appearance is described according to the canon already established in the traditional *nasīb*, evoking a softness and luxury that correspond with an ideal of womanhood having little in common with the generality of real *badawī* women; socially, she belongs to a noble family, which does not at all imply any insistence on the part of the elegist on celebrating her intellectual merits; on the contrary, under the influence of a tradition which may have already been established for centuries, the lady is depicted as a creature formidable in charm, coquetry and beauty, which she wields with a kind of unself-consciousness and at times with manifest cruelty. Nevertheless, on this point, the feminine ideal differs from what seems to have been the ideal of the desert poets; in the texts we are considering, there is a certain contradiction in the fact that the Ḥidjāz elegist takes pleasure in saying that his lady is the embodiment of womanly love, humble in the face of Destiny, eagerly submissive to her seducer (as in ʿUmar b. Abī Rabīʿa, ***passim***, and esp. no. 7, lines 1-4, nos. 181 and 187, lines 13-18, and no. 242); this attitude is what distinguishes the Ḥidjāz lady most completely from her ʿIrāḳī sister, so imbued with courtly spirit. The poet-lover, in contrast to the lady, emerges from our texts with more defined features; two thematic sequences can be distinguished: in the first the lover represents himself according to the psychology and in the attitudes already familiar in the desert tradition; like his *badawī* brother, the elegist of Madīna and Mecca appears to us as a victim of his love for his lady, a prey to the hostility of a world in which he is alone with his agony and despair; his tears flow easily and his complaints are shrill; a fairly large number of clichés strengthen the already apparent links with a completely traditional mentality; at many points, even in his plaintive attitudes, the poet-lover reveals his latent *badawī* traits, and, conspicuously, his *fakhr*; one example of this lies in his boast of *kitmān*, or "discretion", and of *ṣabr* or "constancy and courage in love"—two virtues to display which is to infringe them. A second thematic sequence comprises dominant ideas deriving from a certain realism; of particular importance in this field are those fragments of passages in which the poet portrays himself as a breaker of hearts, a kind of Don Juan whom no beautiful woman can resist (see details in *Aghānī*³, i, 119, 139, 144, 166 f.; ʿUmar b. Abī Rabīʿa, no. 10, lines 10-18, and no. 45); the realities of life are also evident in the developments which might be grouped under the title "love withers with age"; indeed, the poet often stresses the transience of the passions he has aroused or felt; this theme is further linked with the tendency of the desert poets to replace the elegiac *nasīb* with a stereotyped sententious reflection on the flight of youth (thus al-Farazdaḳ, ed. Ṣāwī, 78 and 89). Whatever the reason, the Ḥidjāz manner stands in absolute contradiction here to one of the basic principles of the courtly spirit, which imposes on the lover the obligation of submission to the lady of his choice. There is also another point on which this contradiction is accentuated even more decisively; the Ḥidjāz manner excludes *ʿiffa*, that is, a refusal to yield to desire, both in the lover and the lady. These poets adhere to what is human and do not seek to transcend it; their sensuality is as much part of their love as is their constancy (cf. the strikingly sensual passages in al-ʿArdjī, no. 15, lines 19-21, no. 5, lines 11 f., no. 131, line 7, no. 28, lines 1, 9; and frequent also in ʿUmar b. Abī Rabīʿa, as no. 28, lines 2, 5). In view of this, these poets have been named *ibāḥiyyūn*, "licentious"; it is justifiable, provided one makes it clear that their licence does not descend to indecency or depravity; it is very noteworthy in this connexion that the Ḥidjāz manner never offends against nature and a certain respect for good manners.

3. A new phase in the development of the amatory elegiac genre begins at the point where one can observe the characteristic features of *ʿUdhrī* [*q.v.*] love or the courtly spirit. It is very difficult to fix the *terminus a quo* when this phase makes its appearance; in the texts ascribed to the Ḥidjāz elegists there are in fact widespread courtly traces to be noticed, which arise from the uncertainties of subsequent revision; this very delicate question has not so far been the subject of any very profound research, even though it affects the whole problem. The origins of *ʿUdhrī* love are nevertheless illuminated with a new clarity by a very elaborate examination of the poetic texts attributed to Djamīl [*q.v.*] or Madjnūn [*q.v.*]; this examination must of course be linked with an enquiry into these poets and their ʿUdhrī rivals. Here and now it can be postulated that the amatory elegiac poetry of courtly inspiration acquired its character under influences coming from outside the primitive Arab homeland; certain factors are strictly ʿIrāḳī and to be sought in the preoccupations and tastes of some elements of society in Baṣra, Kūfa or Baghdād; others derive from contacts between centres in ʿIrāḳ and the Ḥidjāz; indeed, when in the first quarter of the 2nd/8th century Madīna was purified of worldly occupations, singer-composers left to settle in ʿIrāḳ, carrying with them the spirit which had favoured the flourishing of the Ḥidjāz manner; without creating it, this current could not but whet the curiosity of a certain ʿIrāḳī public regarding the stories which had spread about the elegists of Madīna or Mecca. From the end of the 2nd/8th century and in the following twenty-five years, there developed in Baṣra and Baghdād a semi-romantic, semi-historical literature, of which Ibn al-Nadīm, *Fihrist*, 306, cites several authors, such as Ibn al-Kalbī, al-Madāʾinī, or al-Haytham b. ʿAdī; these writings, widely utilized by Abu 'l-Faradj al-Iṣfahānī in his *Kitāb al-Aghānī*, demonstrate that the poet-lovers sometimes underwent a genuine transfiguration, which in certain cases turned real persons like Djamīl into veritable heroes of love. From then on the poetical works collected or mis-attributed under the names of these poet-lovers could not but reflect the psychology of the heroes who figured in the romances or romanticized biographies. Can certain tribal groups of Western Arabia have been familiar in their folklore from the 1st/7th century or even earlier with love stories centred on a more or less legendary personality? It is very possible. In particular it seems that the little tribe of the ʿUdhra, which in the 1st/7th century frequented an area extending from the oasis of Taymāʾ to the Wādī 'l-Ḳūra (see *Aghānī*³, viii, 123, 126, lines 4-5) prided itself on having produced one of these heroes, the famous Djamīl. The ʿUdhra were not, however, the only ones to claim such a title to fame; the Nahd of the same area were equally proud of having given birth to the *sayyid* Ibn ʿAdjlān, who later became the hero of a love saga (cf. Ibn Ḳutayba, *Poesis*, 449; *Aghānī*¹, xix, 102-4 and xx, 22; Blachère, *Litt.*, ii, chap. IV, § B). Under the pressure of tribal particularism, other groups seem later to have developed creations of a similar kind in the ʿIrāḳī centres where they had installed themselves; such seems to have been the case with the ʿĀmir b. Ṣaʿṣaʿa and Madjnūn, their "fool of love" who became a famous hero through his passion for Laylā.

Before it was finally established in a closely defined system, the courtly spirit seems to have spread through diffuse influences as a kind of heightening of the Ḥidjāz spirit. There is no doubt that the poet Bashshār b. Burd (b. about 95/714, d. about 167/784) played a considerable part in popularizing certain themes at Baṣra; in his *Dīwān*, which is unfortunately incomplete, it is easy to note, among verses or fragments addressed to ʿAbda and other female personalities of the city, lyric pieces where in fact his love is from the first known to be hopeless and draws its lasting character from this certainty. The setting in which Bashshār was composing his *ghazal*s was in any case favourable to such emotional exaltation; it was the time indeed when at Baṣra mystical experiences were particularly to be observed among women; it was also the time when, in this centre as at Kūfa, a giddy society, free thinking and morally lax, was plunging into easy pleasures which, in occasional flashes, inspired a thirst for purer and serener joys. Bashshār himself seems to have experienced such disillusion, like his contemporary of Kūfa, Muṭīʿ b. Iyās (d. 170/787); here and there in Bashshar's elegiac works he gives evidence of a fruitless desire to detach himself from carnal pursuits. The merit of having achieved such an escape must be ascribed to his younger compatriot, al-ʿAbbās b. al-Aḥnaf (b. about 133/750, d. about 193/808). The work of this poet is unique in the history of Arabic poetry; it is exclusively a song of courtly love. Inspired by real love for a lady designated by various names, this elegist composed occasional pieces and more elaborate works all concerned with one ideal; for the poet, the lady is the unattainable, the distant incarnation of a desired being which one owes it to oneself to love while obeying a self-imposed rule never to try to go beyond dreaming. Renunciation is the law imposed from the moment when the heart ceases to heed the reason; nothing can permit one to dream of being healed from an affliction sent by fate. To express his experience, this courtly poet turns to the instrument developed by the elegists of the Ḥidjāz for their own purposes; he employs the same metres, *khafīf*, *ramal* and *hazadj*; he shares their taste for a flexible vocabulary free of lexical pathos; for him even rhetoric has a certain spontaneity. A number of indications suggest that his poems were composed to be set to music; without doubt, many were composed at the request of certain aristocratic women of Baghdād; it is plausible that the chosen lady of al-ʿAbbās was the princess ʿAlya, as ʿĀtika Khazradjī seems to have established. All this tends to show that the courtly *ghazal* is a genre born among the aristocratic society of the ʿIrāḳī cities; it corresponds to a certain sophistication cultivated by the youth of both sexes who described themselves as *ẓarīf* [*q.v.*], "smart" (pl. *ẓurafāʾ*, fem. pl. *ẓawārif*).

The emergence of Abū Nuwās (b. between 130/747 and 145/762, d. at Baghdād about 200/815) represents a new stage in the development of the amatory elegiac *genre*. The work attributed to this name offers many problems. In the two available recensions it might well in fact not be one individual's works at all, but a collection; whatever the case, if the greater part of it is from the pen of Abū Nuwās alone, this clearly implies a convergence of influences; the poet was actually the child of an Iranian mother and a half-Arab father, and seems to reflect a double trend in which the Arab tradition is no longer the only dominant. In many characteristics the elegiac poems brought together under his name certainly resemble those of other poets of Baṣra. Though they lack much of the courtly spirit of al-ʿAbbās b. al-Aḥnaf, they are nevertheless written in the fluid style typical of that elegist and offer notable similarities to the poems of Bashshār; the setting of Baghdād where Abū Nuwās lived for many years certainly must be taken into account here. There remain nevertheless features which specifically distinguish Abū Nuwās or his school; the courtly spirit occupies a secondary place in these works and must be sought in some pieces addressed to the enigmatic Djanān. These poems prefer to develop, with significant exuberance and insistence, an Epicureanism which embraces every kind of satisfaction; to a certain extent the Bacchic pieces verge, in certain episodes, on the elegy of sentiment; but the poet's eyes are no longer turned towards a chosen lady but towards loose women, or towards young men who, in these works, inflame passions which are hardly Platonic. If, as one may be justified in accepting as a hypothesis, the collection attributed to Abū Nuwās is not the work of one individual, it follows that this lyricism, so definite in character, corresponds to the taste and manners of one sector of Baghdād society. The break with the courtly spirit and romantic love on the part of this sector is clear; in opposition to an idealism lacking relation to the human, there now arises an unashamed naturalism which refuses to blame itself.

4. The 3rd/9th century saw the elaboration of a coherent doctrine of the courtly ideal under the growing influence of neo-Platonism. This ideal is represented by the kind of treatise on sophistication which the *Kitāb al-Muwashshā* of al-Washshāʾ [*q.v.*] constitutes; it is also illustrated by that notable anthology of love which we owe to the Ẓāhirī theologian Muḥammad b. Dāwūd al-Iṣfahānī (d. 297/909), called *Kitāb al-Zahra*. It is unnecessary here to recall the characteristic traits of this spirit [see ʿUDHRA]. But we must indicate the connexions which seem to have existed between this concept of love and its reflexions in the neo-classical poetry whose principal representatives in the East are Abū Tammām, al-Buḥturī and al-Mutanabbī. Among the poets of this period the field of expression of the amatory elegiac genre became more restricted; the only developments to be found are confined in fact to the *nasīb*s prefacing *ḳaṣīda*s. In several respects this is a recollection of the *badawī* tradition, but the tone differs completely and the themes are treated more intellectually and are reduced to the notation of states of mind, and the expression of aphorisms on the vanity and fleeting nature of love, on the sorrow it inspires and the dissatisfaction to which it leads. This lyricism is sinking into conventionality and frigidity. Nevertheless, some urban poets of lesser fame, both in ʿIrāḳ and in the Muslim West, composed poems of a more personal lyricism in the *ghazal* manner. Their tone is given by certain pieces by the ʿAbbāsid prince Ibn al-Muʿtazz (b. 247/861, d. at Baghdād 296/908); the influence of the courtly spirit is perceptible in these works but it does not go so far as to exclude references to a lived experience, in which emotion seeks to express itself with a spontaneity which is frequently suppressed. During the 4th/10th century, similar efforts are visible in other Baghdād poets, particularly those who flourished in great numbers under the Būyids; many names could be cited, but the most typical seem Ibn Sukkara (d. 385/995) and al-Salāmī (d. 393/1003). In this group of poets the influence of Abū Nuwās is undeniable. Like their predecessor these artists sing as much of the joy of loving as of the emotional troubles which passion brings; in all of them we find a stylistic simplicity which in its directness of expression is decidedly a characteristic of the genre. Certain works of the Baghdād poet Ibn al-Ḥadjdjādj (d. 391/1001) raise the question already put regarding Abū Nuwās; should they be cited in connexion with this *genre*? As far as Ibn al-Ḥadjdjādj is concerned, the reply is of even greater delicacy, since the amatory elegiac inspiration of this poet is usually nothing but cynical eroticism. A more elaborate analysis of the *genre* at this stage in its development may lead to the conclusion that two currents are forming: the one idealistic and courtly; the other realistic, either with the moderation of the Ḥidjāz manner or with the extremism of the obscene poems of Ibn al-Ḥadjdjādj. Whatever the case may be, the latter tendency shows itself only sporadically, since the conventionalism and the religious ethic of society do not offer it a favourable soil in which to develop.

In the period we have now reached, poetry in Arabic was cultivated in all the intellectual centres of the Muslim world. The amatory elegiac *genre* naturally therefore had its representative figures in each of these centres. In ʿIrāḳ under the Saldjūḳs, they were numerous, competent in the manipulation of their instrument, but entirely without originality (see al-Ṭāhir, ii, 97-102 and the examples given). In Egypt, the same comment is valid, though under the Ayyūbids al-Bahāʾ Zuhayr (b. 581/1187, d. at Cairo 656/1258) frequently manages to achieve tones which recall Abū Nuwās in their sincerity. In Spain, the Cordovan Ibn Zaydūn (b. 394/1003, d. at Seville 463/1071) contrived also to give the *genre* a somewhat newer air by the employment of a more elaborate vocabulary and the substitution here and there in the traditional thematic material of more acute psychological analyses. Similarly, Ibn Ḥamdīs of Syracuse (b. 447/1055, d. at Bougie (?) 527/1132) achieved the combination of a generalized lyricism with amatory elegiac movements of real charm. It seems also that the cultivated society of the cities of Spain particularly relished this spirit, which induced a sort of "sad delight".

5. Faced with their incapacity to revivify the thematic elements of the *ghazal*, the Arabic Muslim poets from the 5th/11th century onwards turned their efforts at originality in another direction. Both in the East and the West, there were groups who abandoned the exclusive cultivation of this *genre* by means of the resources of the classical vocabulary and prosody only. The signal was given in Spain by the composition of lyrical and elegiac pieces in the *muwashshaḥ* [*q.v.*] or *zadjal* [*q.v.*] forms. From the West, this novelty passed to the East, where Ibn Sanā᾽ al-Mulk (b. about 550/1155, d. 608/1211) in Egypt (see Rikābī, 69 ff.) and Ṣafī al-Dīn al-Ḥillī (b. 677/1278, d. about 750/1359) in ʿIrāḳ compiled treatises with examples of these new poetic forms. These attempts signified an effort to return to the very foundations of all lyric poetry, but they did not aim at what was essential, namely a profound renewal of the themes dealt with in the *ghazal*.

In modern times throughout the Middle East we are witnessing efforts aimed precisely at effecting such a revolution. Poets of this persuasion are subjected to the influence of the Symbolists and indeed of the Surrealists who have gained importance in some literary circles of Western Europe. These efforts deserve our interest, but it is too early as yet to say whether they will be sufficiently widely followed to give new life to elegiac lyricism in Arabic poetry.

Bibliography: For the study of the poets up to the end of the 3rd/9th century, see the accounts in *K. al-Aghānī*[3] (Cairo 1923-, 16 vols. publ.) and in Ibn Ḳutayba, *Shiʿr*. For the subsequent periods see Thaʿālibī, *Yatīmat al-dahr* (Damascus 1303, and ed. ʿAbd al-Ḥamīd, Cairo 1366/1947); al-ʿImād al-Iṣfahānī, *Kharīdat al-Ḳaṣr* (ed. Sh. Fayṣal, Damascus 1375/1955 and 1378/1959; Syrian section). The principal poetical texts to be used are: al-ʿArdjī, *Dīwān* (in the recension of Ibn Djinnī, ed. Khiḍr al-Ṭā᾽ī, Baghdād 1375/1956); Kuthayyir, *Dīwān* (ed. Pérès, 2 vols., Algiers 1928-30); ʿUmar b. Abī Rabīʿa, *Dīwān* (ed. ʿAbd al-Ḥamīd, Cairo 1371/1952); Djamīl, *Dīwān* (ed. Naṣṣār, Cairo no date; on its relation to the ed. of F. Gabrieli see Masnou, in *Arabica*, ix (1962), 88-90); Bashshār b. Burd, *Dīwān* (ed. Ṭ. Ben ʿAshūr, 3 vols., Cairo 1950-57); al-ʿAbbās b. al-Aḥnaf, *Dīwān* (ed. ʿĀ. Khazradjī, Cairo 1373/1954); Muslim b. al-Walīd, *Dīwān* (ed. S. Dahhān, Cairo 1376/1957); Abū Nuwās, *Dīwān* (see *EI*², i, 144b); Ibn al-Ḥadjdjādj, *Dīwān* (part established by Āl Ṭāhir according to the summary of al-Asṭurlābī; unpublished thesis, Sorbonne 1955); Ibn Zaydūn, *Dīwān* (ed. K. Kīlānī and ʿA. Khalīfa, Cairo 1351/1932); Ibn Ḥamdīs, *Dīwān* (ed. Schiaparelli, Rome 1897); also the abundant quotations in Thaʿālibī and al-ʿImād al-Iṣfahānī.

On the courtly spirit in poetry and the related romantic literature see Washshā᾽, *K. al-Muwashshā*, ed. R. Brünnow, Leyden 1886; Muḥammad b. Dāwūd al-Iṣfahānī, *K. al-Zahra*, ed. Nykl and Tukan, Chicago 1351/1932; *Fihrist*, 306; ʿAlī al-Daylamī, *K. ʿAṭf al-alif al-ma᾽lūf ʿala 'l-lām al-maʿṭūf*, ed. J. Vadet, Cairo 1962.

On the aesthetics of the elegiac movement, see Ḳudāma, *Naḳd al-shiʿr*, Istanbul 1302; Ibn Rashīḳ, *al-ʿUmda*, ed. ʿAbd al-Ḥamīd, Cairo 1353/1934, ii, 43, 98, 114, 116, 119.

Studies: Blachère, *Litt.*, ii, iii (printing); idem, *Les principaux thèmes de la poésie érotique au siècle des Umayyades de Damas*, in *AEIO Alger*, v (1939-41), 82-128; idem, *Problème de la transfiguration du poète tribal en héros de roman "courtois" chez les "logographes" arabes du III/IX siècle*, in *Arabica*, viii (1961), 131-6; Ṭ. Ḥusayn, in *Ḥadīth al-arbiʿā᾽*, Cairo 1925, 2nd printing, i, 183-298; F. Gabrieli, *Ǧamīl al-ʿUdrī, studio critico e raccolta dei frammenti*, in *RSO*, xvii (1937), 40-172; I. Yu. Kračkovskiy, *Rannyaya istoriya povesti o Madžnūne i Leyle v arabskoy literature*, reprinted in I. Yu. Kračkovskiy, *Izbrannîe Sočineniya*, ii, Moscow-Leningrad 1956, 588-632, German translation by H. Ritter, *Die Frühgeschichte der Erzählung von M. und L. in der arab. Literatur*, in *Oriens*, viii (1955), 1-50 (cf. J. Vadel in *Arabica*, iv (1957), 81-2); Z. Mubārak, *Ḥubb b. Rabīʿa (sic) wa-shiʿru-hu*, Cairo 1928; Jabbur, *ʿUmar b. A.R., his age, life and works*, 2 vols., Beirut 1935; H. Pérès, *La Poésie andalouse en arabe classique au XI siècle*[2], Paris 1953; Dj. Rikabi, *La poésie profane sous les Ayyubides*, Paris 1949; al-Ṭāhir, *al-Shiʿr al-ʿarabī fi 'l-ʿIrāḳ wa-bilād al-ʿAdjam*, Baghdād 1958 (trans. with publication of a thesis for a State Doctorate, Sorbonne 1955), i, 124-7 and ii, 97-102; F. Ghazi, *La littérature d'imagination en arabe du II/VIII s. au V/XI s.*, in *Arabica*, iv (1957), 164-78; Dj. Aḥ. ʿAllūsh, *Ṣafī al-Dīn al-Ḥillī*, Baghdād 1379/1959 (cf. Blachère in *Arabica*, x (1963), 104-5); A. T. Hatto (ed.), *Eos*, The Hague 1965, 244-73; J. Vadet, *La littérature courtoise dans les cinq premiers siècles de l'Hégire* (in preparation). (R. Blachère)

ii. — In Persian Literature

The *ghazal* is one of the most common instruments of Neo-Persian lyrics. In its present form it consists of a few *bayts* (verses, or distichs), generally not less than five and no more than twelve, with a single rhyme (often accompanied by a *radīf*); in the first *bayt*, called *maṭlaʿ*, both hemistichs too rhyme together; the last *bayt*, called *maḳṭaʿ*, contains the nom-de-plume (*takhalluṣ*) of the author; the contents of the *ghazal* are descriptions of the emotions of the poet in front of love, spring, wine, God, etc., often inextricably connected.

The problem of the origin of the neo-Persian *ghazal* coincides practically with the problem of the origin of neo-Persian poetry. Various hypotheses have been proposed, *e.g.*: (a) the neo-Persian *ghazal* originated from the *tashbīb* or *nasīb* of the Arabic *ḳaṣīda* [*q.v.*], isolated from its context and later developed into an independent form (Shiblī Nuʿmānī, etc.); (b) its origin lies in Persian folk-songs, antedating Arabic influence (Braginskiy and other Soviet authors); (c) a distinction between a "technical *ghazal*" and a more generic *ghazal* should be made: the first can be said to have found its final form only in Saʿdī (7th/13th century), the second owes its origin to folk poetry, later refined at the courts under Arabic influence (Mirzoev). All these hypotheses have their share of truth. Actually it should always be borne in mind that neo-Persian poetry in its specific sense has its origin in the literary experiment of adapting the Persian language to Arabic metres and forms, an experiment first begun at the courts of the first independent Persian dynasties of Khurāsān by people with a perfect knowledge of Arabic. On the other hand "Arabic", in this case, does not imply an ethnic meaning, as many Arabic poets of the time were, ethnically, Persians, and, from the point of view of its content, Arabic poetry of that period was in its turn influenced by Persian ideas. A very useful distinction is that between *ghazal* in its technical sense and *ghazal* in its generic sense, proposed especially by Mirzoev. In its generic sense the *ghazal* may also have been influenced, in its origins, by elements from folk-poetry, though this can in no way be demonstrated by documents, as we know nothing about Persian folk-poetry of the 3rd/9th century, and the very little we know about pre-Islamic Persian poetry shows us something totally different, technically, even from the oldest and least specific and technical forms of the neo-Persian post-Islamic *ghazal*.

The formal history of the neo-Persian *ghazal* can be divided roughly into five periods. The first is the period of the origins, rather obscure, as we have seen, for which we possess actually only fragments of poetical compositions not too different from fragments of *nasīb*s of *ḳaṣīda*s. Many elements of the "technical" *ghazal* still are lacking (*e.g.*, *takhalluṣ*, regular *maṭlaʿ* and *maḳṭaʿ*) and the style is rather decorative/descriptive, with a certain unity and congruity of meanings in the same composition (as compared with the conceptual incongruity of the "technical" *ghazal*) accompanied by a lack, or rarity, of *taghazzul* (the name given to the hardly definable general *Stimmung* of the classical *ghazal*). Rūdagī and Daḳīḳī may be regarded as the greatest poets of this period (3rd/9th and 4th/10th centuries).

The second period could be called the formative one (4th/10th to 7th/13th centuries). In it the proto-*ghazal* acquires a very important element: the mystical experience. At the end of this period the classical *ghazal* is perfectly formed, though the "atmosphere" of the *ghazal* is either mystic in tendency (*e.g.*, ʿAṭṭār), or predominantly profane, as in Anwarī, best known as a *ḳaṣīda* writer but clearly distinguishing the *ghazal* as a special literary genus having as its object the *maʿshūḳ* "the Beloved" whereas the *ḳaṣīda* has as its object the *mamdūḥ*, "the Praised" (Prince or patron).

The third period (7th/13th to 10th/16th centuries) could be called the classical period. The *ghazal* finds its perfectly defined present shape, both from the point of view of form (all the technical elements implied in the definition of *ghazal* given above are present) and from the point of view of content: the decorative style of the origins, after the mystical injection of the formative period, passes into a highly refined and complex symbolic style. Saʿdī and Ḥāfiẓ are the supreme *ghazal* writers of this period. Especially in Ḥāfiẓ the chief object of the *ghazal*, the *maʿshūḳ*, the (earthly) Beloved, becomes inextricably connected not only with the *maʿbūd*, the divine Beloved (God, or better His representative on earth, the mystical Initiator) but even with the *mamdūḥ*, the traditional object of the *ḳaṣīda*: it has been demonstrated, recently especially by Lescot, that the Beloved of the *ghazal*s of Ḥāfiẓ is often his Prince or patron.

The fourth period, that of the so-called Indian style (10th/16th to 12th/18th centuries) [see SABK-I HINDĪ], sees an intellectual reflection on the accepted symbols of the classical *ghazal*, which becomes an arena for a quasi-philosophical exercise of the mind. The *ghazal* finds a renewed congruity of meaning, and its protagonist, instead of the *maʿshūḳ/mamdūḥ/maʿbūd* seems to be the Mind of its Author, creating ever new purely intellectual combinations of the old worn-out symbols. (The greatest poet of this period is probably Ṣāʾib).

The fifth and last period is not easily definable: in Iran a tendency to revive the classical and even pre-classical *ghazal* is followed by attempts to use the *ghazal* for more modern and profane purposes, for which this poetical form, with the refined neo-Platonic symbolism acquired in its classical period, seems rather inadequate.

A description of classical *ghazal* at the time of its "perfection" can be given only by showing the features and symbolic motifs of a single concrete example. We have selected for this purpose the *ghazal* of Ḥāfiẓ whose *maṭlaʿ* is:

rawnaḳ-i ʿahd-i shabāb-ast digar bustān-rā
mīrasad mozhdè-yi gul bulbul-i khush-alḥān-rā

(for full text see edition by M. Ḳazwīnī and Ḳ. Ghanī, Tehrān n.d., 7-8).

1. Once more the age of youth has returned to the garden—and the sweet-singing nightingale receives the good news of the Flower.

2. Oh, gentle breeze! should you once more reach the budding plants in the meadow, give my greetings to the Basil, the Rose, the Cypress tree.

3. The young Son of the Magi, the Vintner, appears before me in such charming motions that I am ready to sweep with my eyebrows the dust of the Tavern.

4. Oh, thou who coverest with purest amber the face of the Moon, do not perturb yet more this man perplexed by love.

5. I greatly fear that those who laugh at wine-bibbers may at last make a tavern of their Faith in God.

6. But mayest thou remain a friend of the Holy Men, for in the Ship of Noah there is still a handful of Mud that knows how to defy the Deluge.

7. Go out from this Dwelling, that has the Heavens for roof, and do not ask it for Food, for that Vile One at the end shamelessly kills her Guest.

8. And say to those whose last resting-place will be a handful of Dust: "Friend, what avails it to raise high palaces to the Skies?"

9. Oh, moon of Canaan! The throne of Egypt has been allotted thee; it is now high time that thou shouldst say farewell to the Prison!

10. Oh Ḥāfiẓ, drink wine, and be a libertine, and live joyfully, but take care not, as others do, to make a snare of the Book of God!

We have here an excellent example—the poem has been chosen almost by chance—of many features characteristic of the style of Persian lyrical poetry of the golden age. Let us list, first of all, the several motifs: of the images indeed none, without exception, is original.

(1) Nightingale-Rose. It may seem strange, but this motif, perhaps the one that occurs most frequently in Persian lyrics, has never been the object of historical research.

It appears in the most ancient Persian lyrics of the 4th/10th century. In the maturer lyrical forms (Ḥāfiẓ) it contains the following meanings:

The rose is Beauty aware of itself, the supreme, inaccessible symbol of the divine *istighnā*; often the rose disdainfully derides the nightingale but as soon as it blossoms it dies. This is the cause of the twofold sadness of the nightingale, which mourns over the rapid death of the rose and its disdainful rejection of union. But between the two there is a kind of mysterious connection: the Bird of Dawn (an epithet very frequently applied to the nightingale) alone understands the secret language of the rose. The nightingale sings in *Arabic*—the sacred language—invitations to partake of the mystic wine. Inebriated with the perfume of the rose it fears to end as did the magician-angel, Mārūt. As the prayer offered at dawn is of special value and has special power (cf. Ḳurʾān, XVII, 78), so the lament of the nightingale is the auroral prayer. But it is a doleful prayer, offered to something inaccessible, for, as Muḳaddasī says in his charming book translated in the middle of the last century by Garcin de Tassy, "my song is a song of grief and not of joy . . . Each time that I flutter over a garden I warble of the affliction that will soon replace the gaiety that reigns there". In an Indian Muslim allegory, the romance of the *Rose of Bakāwalī*, the inaccessible Rose, so difficult to find, is the only remedy that can restore the sight of King Zayn al-Mulūk, etc. The God-Rose identity in the famous preface of the *Gulistān* of Saʿdī can be clearly seen when the Mystic who travels in the transcendental world is unable to bring back any gift from his travels because: "I had in mind that when I reached the Rose-tree I would fill my lap with roses as gifts for my friends, but when I reached it I was so inebriated with the perfume of the Rose that the hem of my robe slipped from my hand".

The enthusiastic pan-Iranist, Pizzi, has endeavoured, but without adequate evidence, to show influence of the Persian Rose motif in the mediaeval *Roman de la Rose*, whose symbolism is reminiscent of this. But in the absence of definite documentary evidence and of preparatory studies we cannot exclude the opposite hypothesis, namely that a Hellenistic motif may have penetrated into both cultures, derived from that civilization which in various ways and forms fertilised them both, *i.e.*, the late Hellenistic symbolism. One should, however, bear in mind that what we refer to is a *motif* and not *an emotional and original perception* by Ḥāfiẓ of the "romantic" and vivid reality of the Spring and the flowers.

(2) And here we have another "personage", the *ṣabā*, "the zephyr", the springtime breeze, generally held to be—and not for the first time by Ḥāfiẓ but by innumerable poets before and after him—the Messenger *par excellence*. The breeze also is personified in a bird, more especially the hoopoe. Why? because with a very slight change in the transcription, the pronunciation of its name is identical to that of the famous region of *Sabāʾ* whose Queen, we read in the Ḳurʾān, sent a hoopoe as her messenger to King Solomon. Thus the "secondary images" aroused in the mind of the listener by the word *ṣabā* are quite other than those awakened in us by the word "zephyr", now ineradicably associated in our minds with Metastasio and Watteau. *Sabā* is a sound that reverberates with a rich symbolism which can be traced back historically and clearly to a "gnostic" world. Basil (*rayḥān*), mentioned soon after, which to us suggests little more than the idea of "perfume", is instead a word used in the Ḳurʾān. The fragrance of basil is one of the chief components of the olfactory joys of the Islamic paradise (cf. Ḳurʾān, LVI, 89), and singularly enough, of the Zoroastrian paradise also (cf. *Mēnōkē Xrat*, ch. VII). On the other hand, the Cypress, familiar to all amateur collectors of Persian carpets and miniatures, in its charming conventionalized shapes, is the sacred tree of Zoroaster. It is identified with the Prophet himself who planted a specially memorable cypress (that of Kās͟hmar) just at the time when the ecstatic-prophetic experience first thrilled him. It is a motif that seems to have come straight from a Central Asian spiritual area: the Shaman, indeed, plants a tree when starting on his "prophetic" career. Thus, even if in the case in point the words are not always intentionally and knowingly symbolical, they are not merely descriptive but are related to verbal-psychological cycles with which they have no connexion in our languages.

(3) In the springtime scenery summoned before us, the nightingale, the rose, the zephyr, the cypress, basil and the "young" (plants) of the meadow are playing a part in a scene which, even from our descriptive standpoint, might acquire a certain unity. But now there enters a character who to our eyes may seem truly extraneous. He is the young Magian (*mog͟hbaččè*), the vintner, and the *Tavern*. The "Zoroastrian" character of the images connected with wine, with the *Superior* of the Magi, and with the Young Magian (the connexion between inebriety and forbidden practices with Zoroastrian belief dates back to Daḳīḳī) are but words used to summon up the idea of that which is forbidden, of sacred impiety. Poets, ancient and modern, to evoke this idea use indiscriminately the words *Magian*, *Christian*, *temple of fire* or *church*. Saʿdī, although the differences were known to him, uses indiscriminately the words "priest", "bishop", "Brahmin" "Magian", "temple of fire", "church", "monastery" in the same poem. The ideas that these lyrical-symbolic images summon up are not something precisely and theologically Zoroastrian (wine indeed is only a secondary element in the Zoroastrian ritual); they serve as signs indicating an esoteric rite. As lyrical poetry was traditionally condemned both by Islam and by Zoroastrianism, the motif of *self-abasement* is added to this intricate image-motif. The poet, the Initiate, is willing even to wipe with his face the door of the tavern-temple where the Young Magian reigns. Here is summed up the material inherited from the frankly libertine poetry of the Arab *mutaʾak͟hk͟hirīn* (wine-Christian Convent, already found in pre-Islamic Arab poetry) with the mystical gnostic motif of a Rite of the Wine which is of ancient syncretic-gnostic origin.

(4) And now, as in a filiform succession of images, the Young Magian takes on the ambiguous appearance of a beautiful boy. The fourth verse should more accurately be translated as: "Oh thou, who drawest across the moon a polo-stick (*čawgān*) of the purest amber, do not make me, whose head whirls (like a polo ball), yet more confused". And we must then add that the game of polo, which is of Persian origin, supplies a wealth of images to this lyric. The polo stick, with its characteristic hooked shape, is the *zulf*, the long wisp of hair, black as the night, and the moon is no other than the face (the roundness of the face is traditionally greatly admired in this lyric). The Child-Magian who is also the Beloved of the Poet (or his *Initiator*, or *God*) has the brilliant and round face of the moon. By mischievously half-veiling it with his black curl, shaped like a polo stick, he only makes the already confused head of the poet whirl like a polo-ball.

(5) In this verse the poet introduces another motif: he upbraids the *doctors of the law*, the *orthodox*. But Ḥāfiẓ must not for this be taken for an "anticlerical", a "progressive". There may be cases in the traditional poetry of Persia of *mullā*s who, when indulging in

this literary style, are obeying its conventions in abusing . . . themselves as a class. This motif can only have arisen from the fact that this kind of poetry gave a gnostic-Neoplatonic interpretation to materials —derived from the Arabian ʿAbbāsid libertine poetry —quite alien to Islamic orthodoxy. The result was a strange combination of libertinism and mysticism, that confers on it a special kind of style of its own.

(6) The verse that follows contains a transparent allusion to the superiority of the Saint (the man of God) over the Doctor of the Law, very skilfully expressed. Noah's ship is the human race, the handful of mud that it contains, possessing, however, the supreme faculty of overcoming any deluge, is the Perfect Man, the Saint, the mystic Master. He is "earth", mud indeed, but one which—as the original puts it—*be-ābī nak͟harad ṭūfānrā*, that is to say "would not buy the deluge for a drop of water", *i.e.*, gives no importance to external "deluges" (and here note the word-play water-deluge-earth). We should therefore be friends of those Masters and not of the doctors of the law.

(7-8) The ethical-mystical warning continues. But, be it always remembered, without undue personal tension. The world is seen as a house, an "old dilapidated convent". But the world—in Arabic a word of feminine gender—is also often compared by the Persian poets to a malicious, faithless *old woman*. Here the word we have translated by "Vile One" is *siyah-kāse*, "of the black pot", also "miserly" "despicable"; hence the play of words "food"-"pot".

(9) The following verse contains a metaphor which may be familiar to the Westerner also: Joseph the Israelite, the symbol of perfect beauty, or of the Soul, for whom the throne of Egypt is prepared, but who yet groans in prison (a typical Neoplatonic metaphor). The last verse reiterates the traditional accusation of hypocrisy addressed to the *mullās*.

In classical *g͟hazal* each verse forms a closed unit, only slightly interconnected with the others. Some modern scholars, to explain this, have invoked the "psychology of depth" to show that there is unity, but an *unconscious* one, in the *g͟hazal*. However this may be, external incongruity would seem to be a real rule in classic Persian poetry. We are in the presence of a bunch of motifs only lightly tied together.

Bibliography: articles *Ghazal* in *Lug͟hat-nāma* by A. A. Dehk͟hodā, Tehrān, i, 207-210 and *Gazel* by A. Ateş in *IA*; A. G. Mirzoev, *Rūdakī va inkis͟hāf-i g͟hazal*, Stalinabad 1957; A. G. Mirzoev, *Rudaki i razvitie gazeli*, Stalinabad 1958; I. S. Braginskiy, *O vozniknovenii gazeli v tadžikskoy i persidskoy literature*, in *SV*, ii (1958), 94-100; A. Pagliaro and A. Bausani, *Storia della letteratura Persiana*, Milan 1960, 239-526; J. Rypka, *Iranische Literaturgeschichte*, Leipzig 1959, 71-112.

Further bibliography will be found in the above mentioned works. (A. Bausani)

iii. — Ottoman Literature

[Circumstances beyond our control have obliged us to refer the reader to the Supplement. Editors' note].

iv. — In Urdu Literature

In spite of its difficulty the *g͟hazal* enjoyed a wide popularity in all literatures belonging to the Islamic cultural cycle. Urdu literature was born under the strong influence of Persian culture, more precisely, of the Persian literature of the period wrongly called of "decadence", the period of Indian style (10th/16th to 12th/18th centuries). This fact accounts for some special features of the Urdu *g͟hazal*. Its history should be divided into some four periods. The first period is that of *dakhnī* Urdu (9th/15th to 11th/17th centuries). In it the *g͟hazal* is only one, and not the most successful, of the instruments of Urdu lyrics, that prefer indigenous poetical forms. Dakhnī *g͟hazal*s are generally descriptive and more congruous than the classical Persian ones. With Walī (1668-1741) the experiment of adapting the contemporary Persian style to Urdu poetry is widened and deepened. Urdu *g͟hazal*s, more or less imitating the contemporary Indian-style Persian *g͟hazal*s, find acceptance also in the literary circles of North India; so begins the classical period of the Urdu *g͟hazal*, culminating perhaps in Mīr Taḳī Mīr (d. 1810). G͟hālib (d. 1869 [*q.v.*]) initiates the modern period of Urdu *g͟hazal*, which finds still newer developments in the contemporary period, the greatest names of which are, besides Iḳbāl (d. 1938 [*q.v.*]), who uses the *g͟hazal* in his peculiar ideological way as a symbolic channel to introduce ideas, Asg͟har of Gondwāna (1884-1936), Ḥasrat Mohānī (1875-1951), Fānī of Badāyūn (1879-1941) and D͟jigar of Murādābād (b. 1890).

The Urdu *g͟hazal*, born under the influence of the Indian-style Persian *g͟hazal* (*e.g.*, Bīdil of Paṭna, d. 1721, who left almost no trace in the development of the Persian *g͟hazal* of Iran, had an enormous influence on Urdu *g͟hazal*), shows a more marked intellectualistic character than Persian *g͟hazal*, together with a comparatively greater congruence in meaning. In later times this led *g͟hazal* writers to use this form too as an ideological instrument, especially under the influence of Ḥālī (d. 1914) and Iḳbāl (d. 1938). Ḥālī advocated, in his stylistical treatise *Muḳaddima-i s͟hiʿr u s͟hāʿirī*, added as a preface to his own *Dīwān*, a reform of the classical *g͟hazal* in a modern sense, based on a widening of the scope of *g͟hazal* so as to include real love, and other human emotions of our times; the rather limited *Wortschatz* of the classical *g͟hazal* should also be widened, according to Ḥālī, while the *malāmatī* and anacreontic aspects of the old *g͟hazal* should be abandoned. The renovation brought about in Urdu *g͟hazal* by the aforementioned personalities led to the result that now, in the Indo-Pakistani subcontinent the *g͟hazal* has become a serious instrument of modern poetry and its old popularity has found an interesting development in a modern sense.

Bibliography: M. Garcin de Tassy, *Histoire de la littérature hindouie et hindoustanie*², Paris 1870 (3 vols.); R. B. Saksena, *A history of Urdu literature*, Allahabad 1927; A. Bausani, *Storia delle letterature del Pakistan*, Milan 1958 (esp. 99-237); Abu 'l-Layt͟h Ṣiddīḳī, *G͟hazal aur mutag͟hazzilīn*, Lahore 1954; A. Bausani, *Alṭāf Ḥusain Ḥālī's ideas on g͟hazal*, in *Charisteria Orientalia*, Prague 1956, 38-55. (A. Bausani)

G͟HAZĀL, (A., fem. *g͟hazāla*, pl. *g͟hizlān*, *g͟hizla*), is the source of our term 'gazelle' denoting, in the Bovidae family, the species, all wild, of the subfamily of the Antilopinae. It is a noun much more restricted in application than *ẓaby*, which covers indiscriminately antelopes and gazelles, that is the Tragelaphini, Alcelaphinae, Oryginae, Reduncini, Antilopinae and Cephalophini. *G͟hazāl*, in common with a number of names of animals, is at once a masculine singular denoting the male, and a collective noun denoting the species (see Ch. Pellat, *Sur quelques noms d'animaux en Arabe classique*, in *GLECS*, viii, 95-9), but its most frequent use is in the wider sense. Herbivores, small of stature, both sexes having tapering horns which are ringed for the lower two thirds and curve forward at the tip, gazelles are creatures of the semi-desert steppe and the savannah; thus they bulk large among the fauna of the Arabic-speaking countries in general, and among those of the Muslim world in particular. The desert-dwellers, nomads and camel-drivers, have from ancient times distinguished different species of gazelle, and the Arabs early gave them different names according to their coats; the modern systematic classification accords perfectly with these denominations, so that we have: — a. the Goitrous Gazelle, *Gazella subgutturosa* (*ghazāl*), in western Persia, Mesopotamia, and north-eastern Arabia; — b. the Rhim or Loder's Gazelle, or Slender-horned Gazelle, *Gazella leptoceros* (*rʾim/rīm*, pl. *ārām*), with the sub-species *G. l. loderi* on the fringe of the Sahara and *G. l. marica* in Arabia, Palestine and Sinai; — c. the Dorcas or Atlas Gazelle, *Gazella dorcas* (*ādam*, pl. *udm*, *ādamī*, *sīn*, *sīnī*), with the sub-species *G. d. saudiya* in northern Arabia, Palestine and Sinai, *G. d. dorcas* in Egypt, *G. d. neglecta* in the Sahara and *G. d. massaesyla* in Morocco; and the three sub-species *G. d. littoralis*, *tilonura* and *Pelzelni* occurring by turns along the Red Sea coast; — d. the Dama Gazelle or "Biche Robert", *Gazella dama* (*aryal*, *adraʿ*), with geographical sub-species the Mhorr or Nanguer Gazelle, *G. d. mhorr*, in southern Morocco, *G. d. dama* (the sub-species bearing the specific name) in the central Sahara, the Red-necked Gazelle or Addra Gazelle, *G. d. ruficollis*, and the Korin or Red-fronted Gazelle, *G. d. rufifrons* (*umm djaʿba*, *ḥamra*), the two last-named being widely scattered throughout the scrub zones of Arabia and Africa; while the distribution of the Soemmering's Gazelle, *G. d. Soemmeringi*, extends from Somalia across into the coastal border of southern Arabia; — e. the Arabian Gazelle, *Gazella gazella* (*aʿfar*, *yaʿfūr*), with the sub-species *G. g. arabica* in the mountainous areas of Arabia, *G. g. gazella* in Syria and Palestine, and *G. g. cuvieri* (Maghribī: *ādam*) throughout the Maghrib.

The excellence of its meat, a food permitted by the Ḳurʾān, and the difficulty of capturing a beast so fleet-footed, made the gazelle, "daughter of the sand" (*bint al-raml*), from earliest times highly prized game alike for the nomad in search of sustenance and the prince whose main pastime was hunting. Methods of capture varied with the hunter's rank. For the well-to-do, there was the noble chase (*ṭarad*, Sahara: *taldjādj*) with gazelle-hounds (*sulūḳiyya*), usually in the heat of the day (*taḥmīṣ*); this hunting down in strength, together with the lightning attack of the trained cheetah [see FAHD], were the forms which venery most often took in the Orient, the Arabs preferring them to the spectacular massacres in a closed battue (*ḥalḳa*) in which the Sāsānids took pride. The gazelle was also hunted by means of falconry, with eagles, gerfalcons, sakers and goshawks trained for this purpose [see BAYZARA]. Partaking less of sport, but more productive, were capture by net (*ḥibāla*, *ḥibāka*, *kaṣīṣa*), snare (*nushka*), or radial trap (*miḳlā*, *ḳula*) set at the approaches to watering-places; advantage was even taken of the animals' being dazzled by fires at night (*nār al-ṣayd*), when driven in towards them for capture (see al-Djāḥiẓ, *Ḥayawān*, iv, 349, 484). Moreover, wealthy Muslims often kept domesticated deer in their parks, Persian-fashion; Usāma Ibn Munḳidh, the famous Syrian gentleman huntsman of the 6th/12th century, notes (*K. al-Iʿtibār*, ed. P. Hitti, Princeton 1930, 207-8) that his father's residence had a score of white gazelles and Atlas or Dorcas gazelles, male and female, grazing at liberty and breeding, each year, undisturbed, and reckoned among the domestic animals (*al-dawādjin*) of the household.

From the first century of Islam, Arab philologists active in linguistic enquiry among the nomad tribes assembled a valuable lexicographic collection of terms differentiating the gazelle as to species, shape, age, coat, posture at rest, leap, gait at speed, quavering call and habits, which forms no negligible aid to the ecological study of the animal. The fawn, for example, was known successively as: *ṭalw/ṭalāⁿ* at birth, *khishf* at a day old, when already on its feet, *shādin* at the appearance of the protuberances later to be horns, *rashaʾ* when weaned, *shaṣar/shafar* at a month, *djaḥsh* or *djady* at six months, *djidhaʿ* at a year, and finally *thanī* at two years and for the rest of its adult life; the gazelle differs from other ungulate ruminants in that the *thanī* is not succeeded by the *ribāʿī*, or *sadasī*, *ṣāliʿ*, or lastly *shabūb*, terms denoting the increasing ages of the young animals as determined by teeth development.

Without the gazelle, Arabic literature would have been without an important source of inspiration. The treatises on falconry and hunting [see BAYZARA and FAHD], in the first place, would virtually have lacked a raison d'être, the antilopinae being in Arab countries the noble game which the cervidae are for the West. Then poetry, classical and popular, would have been without its hunting themes (*ṭaradiyyāt*) in *radjaz*, with their vivid descriptions of the hunt in full cry and triumphant halloo, and erotic writing, in its search to idealize feminine grace and attractions, without countless metaphors drawn from the slender delicacy of the gazelle, its wild starting shyness and maternal tenderness, and the velvety glance owed to the contrast (*ḥawar*) of the ebony pupil set in ivory; such transports of earthly beatitude were induced by these eyes in the heart of the Oriental that the gazelle was to surrender them to the virgins of Paradise, the "houris" (*al-ḥūr al-ʿīn*), promised to the Muslim elect in the after-life (Ḳurʾān, XLIV, 54, LII, 20, LV, 72, LVI, 22).

The aura of lyricism enveloping the gazelle must not obscure the saddening fact that in our day the number of these gracious animals has dwindled considerably in the Islamic countries as a result of firearms and the reckless destruction made possible by modern vehicles; if stringent measures are not taken for the gazelle's protection, the species will be speedily on the way to extinction, and the term *ghazāl* will become an archaism in the Arabic language.

For the *ghazāl al-misk*, see MISK.

Bibliography: In addition to references given in the text: Ḳazwīnī, *ʿAdjāʾib al-makhlūḳāt*, s.v. *ẓaby*; Damīrī, *Ḥayāt al-ḥayawān*, s.v. *ẓaby* and *ghazāl*; Djāḥiẓ, *Ḥayawān*, s.v. *ẓaby* and *ghazāl*; Masʿūdī, *Murūdj*, *passim*; Ibn Sīduh, *Mukhaṣṣaṣ*, viii, 21-42, s.v. *ẓaby*; Ḳalḳashandī, *Ṣubḥ*, ii, 45; Kushādjim, *K. al-Maṣāyid wa 'l-maṭārid*, Baghdad 1954, 201 f. and *passim*, = *al-Bayzara*, Damascus 1953, 133 f.; Manglī, *K. Uns al-malāʾ bi-waḥsh al-falāʾ*, Paris 1880, 37 f.; G. Blaine, *On the relationship of Gazella isabella to Gazella dorcas*, in *Ann. and Mag. of Nat. Hist.*, Ser. 8, xi (1913); L. Blancou, *Géographie cynégétique du monde*, Paris 1959; W. T. Blanford, *Zoology of Eastern Persia*, London 1876; P. Bourgoin, *Animaux de chasse d'Afrique*, Paris 1955; F. Edmond-Blanc, *Le grand livre de la faune africaine et de sa chasse*, Monaco 1954; J. Ellerman and T. C. S. Morrison Scott, *Checklist of Palaearctic and Indian Mammals*, British Museum, London 1951; P. Grassé (ed.), *Traité de zoologie. Mammifères*, Paris 1955; Th. Haltenorth and W. Trense, *Das Grosswild der Erde*, Bonn-Munich-Vienna 1956; L. Joleaud, *Études de Géographie zoologique sur la Berbérie*, ii, *les Bovidés*, in *R.Afr.*, no. 295 (1918); Kobelt, *Die Saügethiere Nordafricas*, in *Der Zool. Gart.*, 1886; L. Lavauden, *La chasse et la faune cynégétique en Tunisie*[2], Tunis 1924; idem, *Les Vertébrés du Sahara*, Tunis 1926; idem, *Les Gazelles du Sahara central*, in *Bull. Soc. d'Hist. Nat. de l'Afrique du Nord*, January 1926; idem, *Les grands animaux de chasse de l'Afrique française*, in *Faune des colonies françaises*, v/7, Paris 1934; Lydekker, *Catalogue of the Ungulate mammals in the British Museum*, London 1913-7; H. Lhote, *La chasse chez les Touaregs*, Paris 1951, 90-102; I. T. Sanderson, *Living mammals of the world*, Fr. trans.: *Les Mammifères vivants du monde*, Paris 1957; *Survey of Iraq fauna*, by members of the Mesopotamia Expeditionary Force, Bombay n.d.; R. Ward, *Record of Big Game*, London 1928.—Mention of gazelles is further to be found in the works of the Arab geographers, and in the many "accounts of journeys" of travellers, Arabic and European, in the regions where the animal is found.

(F. Viré)

al-GHAZĀL, Yaḥyā b. Ḥakam al-Bakrī, a native of Jaén, was called by this name ('the gazelle') in his youth because of his slenderness and good looks. He became prominent, along with ʿAbbās b. Firnās, at the court of al-Ḥakam I, who, on returning from his continual campaigns, liked to take part in the poetical tournaments of the little literary group which he had allowed to spring up round him. Al-Ghazāl was already 50 years old when his star shone even brighter at the court of ʿAbd al-Raḥmān II, who made him one of his favourite poets. In 225/840, after receiving with every honour the embassy of the Byzantine emperor Theophilus and being much flattered by this acknowledgement of his power, ʿAbd al-Raḥmān II caused the Constantinople ambassador, when he returned to his country, to be accompanied by two Muslim emissaries: the poet Yaḥyā al-Ghazāl and another Yaḥyā called *ṣāḥib al-munayḳila* ('the man with the little clock'). These two were charged with bearing the amīr of Cordova's reply to Theophilus's letter, in which he had proposed an alliance against the ʿAbbāsids of the East and their vassals the Aghlabids of Ifrīḳiya because of their naval activities in Sicily. After delivering ʿAbd al-Raḥmān II's reply and presents to Theophilus in Constantinople al-Ghazāl caused a stir at the Byzantine court with his talent and sparks of sly wit which he demonstrated brilliantly before the Emperor himself, his wife Theodora, and the crown prince Michael. By his charming manners and notorious cupidity he obtained jewels for his daughters from the Empress, just as he had contrived, before embarking on his mission, that the Cordovan amīr assign them a pension in case he should not return. His witty and sometimes coarse repartee was as famous as his avarice. He was a poet of mordant wit and greatly dreaded for his merciless satires. They were composed in a clear style devoid of rhetorical figures, which placed them within reach of the common people. Besides the personal gifts made to him by the court he brought back from his stay in Constantinople stocks of a variety of fig tree, of which the figs, called *doñegal*, are still known under the variant name *boñigar* given s.v. *higo* in the Dictionary of the Spanish Academy. During his time the musician Ziryāb [*q.v.*] introduced the game of chess to Cordova, where it had a great success. But it was not approved by al-Ghazāl, for in a poem addressed to a nephew of his who was a keen chess-player he declared it to be sinful and an invention of the devil. Al-Ghazāl's unusual diplomatic mission and the memory of Viking incursions gave rise to the legend invented in the 12th or 13th century by the Valencian Ibn Diḥya (*Muṭrib*, Khartoum 1954, 130 f.) according to which ʿAbd al-Raḥmān II, satisfied with the way in which al-Ghazāl and his companion had carried out their mission, entrusted to them in later years another embassy to the North with the aim of dissuading the king of the Vikings from attempting a fresh landing in Andalusia. According to this story the poet and his companion fulfilled their task in northern Europe and returned to Cordova after a dangerous voyage of nine months in Atlantic waters. The falseness of this is obvious at a glance. The more or less marvellous elements of which it is formed are copied for the most part from episodes attributed in the 10th century to al-Ghazāl's journey to the Greek emperor. No doubt the unusual activity of the Byzantine emperor in Cordova and the daring landing of the Vikings on Spanish territory, enriched with romantic details, finally amalgamated in the popular beliefs of Andalusia and so gave rise to a combined legend which little by little distorted the historical reality.

Bibliography: E. Lévi-Provençal, *Un échange d'ambassades entre Cordoue et Byzance au IX*[e] *siècle*, in *Byzantion*, xii (1937), 1-24 (republished in *Islam d'Occident*, i, 79-107); idem, *Hist. Esp. Mus.*, i, 251-4; on al-Ghazāl's alleged embassy to northern Europe, G. Jacob, *Arabische Berichte von Gesandten an germanischen Fürstenhöfe aus dem 9. und 10. Jahrhundert*, Berlin and Leipzig 1927, 35; E. Dubler, *La crónica arábigo-bizantina del 741*, in *Andalus*, xi (1946), 342; Arne Melvinger, *Les premières incursions des Vikings en Occident ...*, Uppsala 1955, 58 ff. and index; D. M. Dunlop, *The British Isles according to medieval Arabic authors*, in *IQ*, iv (1957), 12-4; W. E. D. Allen, *The poet and the spae-wife*, Dublin 1960. See also Dozy, *Recherches*[2], ii, 267-78; E. García Gómez, *Sobre agricultura arábigo-andaluza*, in *Andalus*, x (1945), 134; F. M. Pareja, *Libro del ajedrez, de sus problemas y sutilezas, de autor árabe desconocido*, Madrid-Granada 1935; Pons Boigues, 281-3, no. 238.

(A. Huici Miranda)

al-GHAZĀLĪ, Abū Ḥāmid Muḥammad b. Muḥammad al-Ṭūsī (450/1058-505/1111), outstanding theologian, jurist, original thinker, mystic and religious reformer. There has been much discussion since ancient times whether his *nisba* should be Ghazālī or Ghazzālī; cf. Brockelmann, S I, 744; the former is to be preferred in accordance with the principle of *difficilior lectio potius*.

1. Life

He was born at Ṭūs in Khurāsān, near the modern Meshhed, in 450/1058. He and his brother Aḥmad were left orphans at an early age. Their education was begun in Ṭūs. Then al-Ghazālī went to Djurdjān and, after a further period in Ṭūs, to Naysābūr, where he was a pupil of al-Djuwaynī Imām al-Ḥaramayn [*q.v.*] until the latter's death in 478/1085. Several other teachers are mentioned, mostly obscure, the best known being Abū ʿAlī al-Fārmadhī. From Naysābūr in 478/1085 al-Ghazālī went to the "camp" of Niẓām al-Mulk [*q.v.*] who had attracted many scholars, and there he was received with honour and respect. At a date which he does not specify but which cannot be much later than his move to Baghdād and which may have been earlier, al-Ghazālī passed through a phase of scepticism, and emerged to begin an energetic search for a more satisfying intellectual position and practical way of life. In 484/1091 he was sent by Niẓām al-Mulk to be professor at the *madrasa* he had founded in Baghdād, the Niẓāmiyyā. Al-Ghazālī was one of the most prominent men in Baghdād, and for four years lectured to an audience of over three hundred students. At the same time he vigorously pursued the study of philosophy by private reading, and wrote several books. In 488/1095, however, he suffered from a nervous illness which made it physically impossible for him to lecture. After some months he left Baghdād on the pretext of making the pilgrimage, but in reality he was abandoning his professorship and his whole career as a jurist and theologian. The motives for this renunciation have been much discussed from the contemporary period until the present day. He himself says he was afraid that he was going to Hell, and he has many criticisms of the corruption of the *ʿulamāʾ* of his time (*e.g.*, *Iḥyāʾ*, i); so it may well be that he felt that the whole organized legal profession in which he was involved was so corrupt that the only way of leading an upright life, as he conceived it, was to leave the profession completely. The recent suggestion (F. Jabre, in *MIDEO*, i (1954), 73-102) that he was chiefly afraid of the Ismāʿīlīs (Assassins) who had murdered Niẓām al-Mulk in 485/1092, and whom he had attacked in his writings, places too much emphasis on what can at most have been one factor. Another suggestion is that of D. B. Macdonald (in *EI*[1]) that contemporary political events may have made al-Ghazālī apprehensive; shortly before he left Baghdād the Saldjūḳid sultan Barkiyārūḳ [*q.v.*] executed his uncle Tutush, who had been supported by the caliph and presumably al-Ghazālī; and it was soon after the death of Barkiyārūḳ in 498/1105 that al-Ghazālī returned to teaching.

From al-Ghazālī's abandonment of his professorship in Baghdād to his return to teaching at Naysābūr in 499/1106 is a period of eleven years, and it is sometimes said, even in early Muslim biographical notices, that al-Ghazālī spent ten years of this in Syria. Careful reading of his own words in the *Munḳidh* (see below), and attention to numerous small details in other sources, makes it certain that he was only "about two years" in Syria. On his departure from Baghdād in Dhu 'l-Ḳaʿda 488/ November 1095 he spent some time in Damascus, then went by Jerusalem and Hebron to Medina and Mecca to take part in the Pilgrimage of 489/ November-December 1096. He then went back for a short time to Damascus, but his own phrase of "nearly two years there" (*Munḳidh*, 130) must be taken loosely. He is reported to have been seen in Baghdād in Djumādā II 490/May-June 1097 (Jabre, *op. cit.*, 87; cf. Bouyges, *Chronologie*, 3), but this can only have been a brief stay in the course of his journey to his home, Ṭūs. It is sometimes said that al-Ghazālī visited Alexandria, but scholars are now inclined to reject this report; if he did go to Egypt it can only have been for a short time.

In this period of retirement at Damascus and Ṭūs al-Ghazālī lived as a poor ṣūfī, often in solitude, spending his time in meditation and other spiritual exercises. It was at this period that he composed his greatest work, *Iḥyāʾ ʿulūm al-dīn* ("The Revival of the Religious Sciences"), and he may have lectured on its contents to select audiences. By the end of the period he had advanced far along the mystic path, and was convinced that it was the highest way of life for man.

In the course of the year 499/1105-6 Fakhr al-Mulk, son of Niẓām al-Mulk and vizier of Sandjar, the Saldjūḳid ruler of Khurāsān, pressed al-Ghazālī to return to academic work. He yielded to the pressure, partly moved by the belief that he was destined to be the reviver of religion (*mudjaddid*) at the beginning of the new century, in accordance with a well-known Tradition. In Dhu 'l-Ḳaʿda 499/ July-August 1106 he began to lecture at the Niẓāmiyya in Naysābūr and not long afterwards wrote the autobiographical work *al-Munḳidh min al-ḍalāl* ("Deliverance from Error"). Before his death, however, in Djumādā II 505/December 1111, he had once again abandoned teaching and retired to Ṭūs. Here he had established, probably before he went to Naysābūr, a *khānḳāh* or hermitage, where he trained young disciples in the theory and practice of the *ṣūfī* life. Several names are known of men who were his pupils at Ṭūs (cf. Bouyges, *Chronologie*, 4 n.).

2. Works and doctrines

(a) *Questions of authenticity and esotericism.* A great difficulty in the study of al-Ghazālī's thought is that, while he undoubtedly wrote many books, some have been attributed to him which he did not write. Bouyges in his *Essai de Chronologie* (composed before 1924 but only published posthumously in 1959 with additional notes on subsequent publications by M. Allard) lists 404 titles. Many of these are taken from lists of his works and no copies are known to exist. In other cases the same book appears under different titles, and a great deal of work has still to be done on manuscripts before scholars know exactly what is extant and what is not. Further, at least from the time of Muḥyi 'l-Dīn b. al-ʿArabī (d. 638/ 1240) allegations have been made that books have been falsely attributed to al-Ghazālī (cf. Montgomery Watt, *A forgery in al-Ghazālī's* Mishkāt?, in *JRAS* 1949, 5-22; idem, *The authenticity of the works attributed to al-Ghazālī*, in *JRAS*, 1952, 24-45). The works whose authenticity has been doubted are mostly works expressing advanced ṣūfistic and philosophical views which are at variance with the teaching of al-Ghazālī in the works generally accepted as authentic. There are difficulties, owing to the richness of his thought, in establishing conclusively the existence of contradictions. Ibn Ṭufayl (d. 581/1185), however, who called attention to contradictions, also suggested that al-Ghazālī wrote differently for ordinary men and for the élite, or, in other words. that he had esoteric views which were not divulged to everyone (*Ḥayy b. Yaḳẓān*, Damascus, 1358/1939, 69-72). This complicates the problem of authenticity: but there is no reason for thinking that, even if al-Ghazālī had different levels of teaching for different audiences, he ever in the "higher" levels directly contradicted what he maintained at the lower levels. An alternative supposition, that he adopted extreme philosophical forms of ṣūfism in his last years, seems to be excluded by the discovery that *Ildjām al-ʿawāmm*, in which he holds a position similar to that of the *Iḥyāʾ*, was completed only a few days before his death (Bouyges, *Chronologie*, 80 f.; G. F. Hourani, *The chronology of Ghazālī's writings*, in *JAOS*, lxxix (1959), 225-33). In the present state of scholarship the soundest methodology is to concentrate on the main works of undoubted authenticity and to accept other works only in so far as the views expressed are not incompatible with those in the former (cf. Montgomery Watt, *The study of al-Ghazālī*, in *Oriens*, xiii-xiv (1961), 121-31.

(b) *Personal.* A year or two before his death al-Ghazālī wrote *al-Munḳidh min al-ḍalāl*, an account of the development of his religious opinions, but not exactly an autobiography, since it is arranged schematically not chronologically; *e.g.*, he knew something of ṣūfism before the stage of development at which he describes it in the book. Most of the details about his life given above are derived from the *Munḳidh*. He is also concerned to defend himself against the accusations and criticism that had been brought against his conduct and the views he had expressed. A small work answering criticisms of the *Iḥyā'* is the *Imlā'*.

(c) *Legal.* Al-Ghazālī's early training was as a jurist, and it was probably only under al-Djuwaynī that he devoted special attention to *kalām* or dogmatic theology. Some of his earliest writings were in the sphere of *fiḳh*, notably the *Basīṭ* and the *Wasīṭ*, but he apparently continued to be interested in the subject and to write about it, for a work called the *Wadjīz* is dated 495/1101, while the *Mustaṣfā* was written during his period of teaching at Naysābūr in 503/1109 (Bouyges, *Chronologie*, 49, 73). The latter deals with the sources of law (*uṣūl al-fiḳh*) in a manner which shows the influence of his earlier philosophical studies but is entirely within the juristic tradition. It is reported in biographical notices that at the time of his death al-Ghazālī was engaged in deepening his knowledge of Tradition.

(d) *Philosophy and logic.* After the period of scepticism described in the *Munḳidh*, al-Ghazālī in his quest for certainty made a thorough study of philosophy, a subject to which he had been introduced by al-Djuwaynī. This occupied all the earlier part of the Baghdād period. What he studied was chiefly the Arabic Neoplatonism of al-Fārābī and Ibn Sīnā. Though his final aim was to show in what respects their doctrines were incompatible with Sunnī Islam, he first wrote an exposition of their philosophy without any criticism, *Maḳāṣid al-falāsifa*, which was much appreciated in Spain and the rest of Europe in the twelfth and thirteenth centuries. This he followed by a criticism of the doctrines entitled *Tahāfut al-falāsifa*, "The incoherence (or inconsistency) of the philosophers"; this was finished at the beginning of 488/1095 (Bouyges, *Chronologie*, 23). In it he noted twenty points on which the philosophers' views were objectionable to Sunnīs or inconsistent with their own claims; in respect of three of these they were to be adjudged unbelievers. In the *Tahāfut* al-Ghazālī concentrates on demonstrating the inconsistencies of the philosophers and does not argue for any positive views of his own. Because of this he has been accused of having remained something of a sceptic. This accusation fails to notice that the *Tahāfut* was written just before the crisis which caused him to leave Baghdād; it is therefore possible that at the time he was somewhat uncertain of his positive beliefs, but a few years later when he was writing the *Iḥyā'* he was in no doubt about what he believed. What impressed al-Ghazālī most of the various branches of philosophical studies was logic, and in particular the Aristotelian syllogism. For the sake of Sunnī jurists and theologians to whom philosophical books were not easily accessible or, because of their technical language, not readily understandable, he wrote two books on Aristotelian logic, *Miʿyār al-ʿilm* and *Miḥakk al-naẓar*. A justification of the use of this logic in religious matters is contained in *al-Ḳisṭās al-mustaḳīm*, apparently written for some comparatively simple-minded believers who were attracted by Bāṭinī (Ismāʿīlī) doctrines. While full of enthusiasm for philosophy al-Ghazālī wrote a work on ethics, *Mīzān al-ʿamal*, though whether the whole of the extant text is authentic has been questioned (*JRAS*, 1952, 38-40, 45). Since al-Ghazālī does not appear to refer to the *Mīzān* in his later works, and since he became very critical of philosophical ethics (*Munḳidh*, 99 ff.), it is possible that, as his enthusiasm waned, he rejected much of what he had written in this work.

(e) *Dogmatic theology.* His chief work of dogmatics is *al-Iḳtiṣād fi 'l-iʿtiḳād*, probably composed shortly before or shortly after his departure from Baghdād (Bouyges, 34). This book deals with roughly the same topics as the *Irshād* of al-Djuwaynī, but it makes full use of Aristotelian logic, including the syllogism. In this respect Ibn Khaldūn (iii, 41) is correct in making al-Ghazālī the founder of a new tendency in theology, although there is no striking novelty in his dogmatic views. In *Kitāb al-Arbaʿīn*, (Cairo 1344, 24), written after the *Iḥyā'*, al-Ghazālī says that the *Iḳtiṣād* is more likely to prepare for the gnosis (*maʿrifa*) of the ṣūfī than the usual works of dogmatics; and this continuing approval strengthens the view that al-Ghazālī never ceased to be an Ashʿarī in dogmatics, even though he came to hold that intellectual discussions in religion should range far beyond the limited field of dogmatics, and that detailed discussions in dogmatics had no practical value. To dogmatic theology might also be assigned *Fayṣal al-tafriḳa bayn al-Islām wa-'l-zandaḳa*. This is partly directed against the Bāṭiniyya, but is mainly a defence of his own views on the extent to which *ta'wīl* is justified, and on the relative places of *tawātur* and *idjmāʿ* as sources of religious knowledge. *Ildjām al-ʿawāmm ʿan ʿilm al-kalām*, which appears to be his last work, warns of the dangers in the study of *kalām* for those with little education.

(f) *Polemics.* The *Mustaẓhirī*, edited in abridged form by Goldziher as *Streitschrift des Gazālī gegen die Bāṭinijja-Sekte* (1916), is a searching theological critique of the Nizārī Ismāʿīlīs or Assassins. A Persian work, edited by O. Pretzl as *Die Streitschrift des Gasālī gegen die Ibāḥīja* (1933), attacks the antinomianism of certain mystics. The authenticity of a work of anti-Christian polemic, *al-Radd al-djamīl ʿalā sarīḥ al-indjīl* (ed. and tr. R. Chidiac, Paris 1939), is doubted by Bouyges (126), but defended by Louis Massignon (in *REI*, 1932, 491-536).

(g) *Ṣūfistic practice.* Al-Ghazālī's greatest work, both in size and in the importance of its contents is *Iḥyā' ʿulūm al-dīn*, "The revival of the religious sciences", in four volumes. This is divided into four "quarters", dealing with *ʿibādāt* (cult practices), *ʿādāt* (social customs), *muhlikāt* (vices, or faults of character leading to perdition), *mundjiyāt* (virtues, or qualities leading to salvation). Each "quarter" has ten books. The *Iḥyā'* is thus a complete guide for the devout Muslim to every aspect of the religious life—worship and devotional practices, conduct in daily life, the purification of the heart, and advance along the mystic way. The first two books deal with the necessary minimum of intellectual knowledge. This whole stupendous undertaking arises from al-Ghazālī's feeling that in the hands of the *ʿulamā'* of his day religious knowledge had become a means of worldly advancement, whereas it was his deep conviction that it was essentially for the attainment of salvation in the world to come. He therefore, while describing the prescriptions of the Sharīʿa in some detail, tries to show how they contribute to a man's final salvation. *Bidāyat al-hidāya* is a brief statement of a rule of daily life for the devout Muslim, together with counsel on the avoidance of sins. *K. al-Arbaʿīn* is a short summary of the *Iḥyā*ʾ, though its forty sections do not altogether correspond to the forty books. *Al-Maḳṣad al-asnā* discusses in what sense men may imitate the names or attributes of God. *Kīmiyāʾ al-saʿāda* is in the main an abridgement in Persian of the *Iḥyā*ʾ (also translated in whole or in part into Urdū, Arabic, etc.), but there are some differences which have not been fully investigated.

(h) *Ṣūfistic theory.* It is in this field that most of the cases of false or dubious authenticity occur. *Mishkāt al-anwār* ("The niche for lights", tr. W. H. T. Gairdner, London 1924; cf. idem, in *Isl.*, v (1914), 121-53) is genuine, except possibly the last section (*JRAS*, 1949, 5-22). *Al-Risāla al-laduniyya* deals with the nature of knowledge of divine things, and its authenticity has been doubted because of its closeness to a work of Ibn al-ʿArabī and because of its Neoplatonism (cf. Bouyges, 124 f.). There are numerous other works in the same category, of which the most important is *Minhādj al-ʿābidīn.* These works are of interest to students of mysticism, and their false attribution to al-Ghazālī, if it can be proved, does not destroy their value as illustrations of some branches of ṣūfistic thought during the lifetime of al-Ghazālī and the subsequent half-century.

3. His influence

A balanced account of the influence of al-Ghazālī will probably not be possible until there has been much more study of various religious movements during the subsequent centuries. The following assessments are therefore to some extent provisional.

(a) His criticism of the Bāṭiniyya may have helped to reduce the intellectual attractiveness of the movement, but its comparative failure, after its success in capturing Alamūt, is due to many other factors.

(b) After his criticism of the philosophers there are no further great names in the philosophical movement in the Islamic east, but it is not clear how far the decline of philosophy is due to al-Ghazālī's criticisms and how far to other causes. Its continuance in the Islamic west, where the *Tahāfut* was also known, suggests that the other causes are also important.

(c) Al-Ghazālī's studies in philosophy led to the incorporation of certain aspects of philosophy, notably logic, into Islamic theology. In course of time theologians came to devote much more time and space to the philosophical preliminaries than to the theology proper. On the other hand, his speculations about the nature of man's knowledge of the divine realm and his conviction that the upright and devout man could attain to an intuition (or direct experience —*dhawḳ*) of divine things comparable to that of the worldliness of the *ʿulamā*ʾ does not seem to have led to any radical changes.

(d) He undoubtedly performed a great service for devout Muslims of every level of education by presenting obedience to the prescriptions of the Sharīʿa as a meaningful way of life. His *khānḳāh* at Ṭūs, where he and his disciples lived together, was not unlike a Christian monastery; and it may be that he gave an impetus to the movement out of which came the dervish orders (but this requires further investigation).

(e) His example may have encouraged those forms of ṣūfism which were close to Sunnism or entirely Sunnī. Before him, however, there had been much more ṣūfism among Sunnī *ʿulamā*ʾ than is commonly realized. His influence on the ṣūfī movement in general, however, requires further careful study.

Bibliography: (a) *Life, General.* P. Bouyges, *Essai de chronologie des œuvres de al-Ghazali*, ed. M. Allard, Beirut 1959 (pp. 1-6 contain very full references to the main biographical sources); D. B. Macdonald, *The life of al-Ghazzālī*, in *JAOS*, xx (1899), 71-132 (still useful but requires to be supplemented and corrected); Margaret Smith, *Al-Ghazālī the mystic*, London 1944 (contains large biographical section, also chapter on his influence); W. Montgomery Watt, *Muslim intellectual*, Edinburgh 1963; W. R. W. Gardner, *An account of al-Ghazālī's life and works*, Madras 1919; S. M. Zwemer, *A Moslem seeker after God*, London 1920.

(b) *Works.* Brockelmann, I, 535-46; S I, 744-56; Bouyges, *Chronologie* (as above). In *ZDMG*, xciii, 395-408, Fr. Meier gives information about the Persian *Naṣīḥat al-mulūk* and its Arabic translation *al-Tibr al-masbūk*; English tr. by F. R. C. Bagley, *Ghazālī's book of counsel for Kings*, London 1964. Translations and studies later than Brockelmann: W. Montgomery Watt, *The faith and practice of al-Ghazālī*, London 1953 (*Munḳidh*, *Bidāyat al-hidāya*); G.-H. Bousquet, *Ih'ya ou Vivification des sciences de la foi, analyse et index*, Paris 1955; *Iḥyā*ʾ, xi, Ger. tr. H. Kindermann, Leiden 1962; xii, Fr. tr. G.-H. Bousquet, Paris 1953; xxxi, Susanna Wilzer, *Untersuchungen*, in *Isl.*, xxxii, 237-309, xxxiii, 51-120, xxxiv, 128-37; xxxiii, Eng. tr. W. McKane, Leiden 1962; *Tahāfut*, Eng. tr. S. A. Kamali, Lahore 1958; Fr. trs. of *Ḳisṭās* by V. Chelhot in *BÉt.Or.*, xv, 7-98; and of *Munḳidh* by F. Jabre, Beirut.

(c) *Doctrines.* M. Asín Palacios, *La espiritualidad de Algazel y su sentido cristiano*, Madrid 1935, etc.; J. Obermann, *Der philosophische und religiöse Subjektivismus Ghazalis*, Vienna and Leipzig 1921; A. J. Wensinck, *La pensée de Ghazâli*, Paris 1940; Farid Jabre, *La notion de certitude selon Ghazali*, Paris 1958; idem, *La notion de la* Maʿrifa *chez Ghazali*, Beirut 1958; M. Smith, *al-Ghazālī the Mystic* (as above); Roger Arnaldez, *Controverses théologiques chez Ibn Hazm de Cordoue et Ghazali*, in *Les Mardis de Dar el-Salam*, Sommaire, 1953, Paris 1956, 207-48. (W. MONTGOMERY WATT)

AL-GHAZĀLĪ, AḤMAD B. MUḤAMMAD, brother of the more renowned Muḥammad Ghazālī, the Ṣūfī and popular preacher, made his way via Hamadān to Baghdād, and took his brother's place when the latter retired from teaching at the Niẓāmiyya. He died in 520/1126 in Ḳazwīn. He wrote an abridged version of the *K. al-Iḥyā*ʾ of his brother, which has not survived; an exposition in sermon form of his confession of faith, *al-Tadjrīd fī kalimat al-tawḥīd* (Turkish translation by M. Fewzī, *el-Tefrīd fī terdjemet el-Tedjrīd*, Istanbul 1285); a discussion of the admissibility of *samāʿ* (Ṣūfī music and dancing), *Bawāriḳ al-ilmāʿ fi 'l-radd ʿalā man yuḥarrimu 'l-samāʿ*, ed. J. Robson in *Tracts on listening to music* (Or. Transl. Fund, NS v), London 1938; a subtle psychology of love, *Sawāniḥ*, ed. H. Ritter (Bibl. Islamica, xv) 1942; (probably) the *Risālat al-Ṭayr*, which was the inspiration for the *Manṭiḳ al-ṭayr* of Farīd al-Dīn ʿAṭṭār (see H. Ritter, *Das Meer der Seele*, 8-10); and other minor writings which have not yet been investigated. His sermons were very popular in Baghdād, and were collected in two volumes by Ṣāʿid b. Fāris al-Labbānī; of these however, only extracts are preserved in Ibn al-Djawzī. In them he undertook the defence of Satan (*al-taʿaṣṣub li-Iblīs*), popular in many Ṣūfī circles since Ḥallādj, which was soon afterwards further developed by ʿAṭṭār (see *Das Meer der Seele*, 536-50), and which presumably gave the so-called Devil worshippers, the Yazīdīs, the justification for their worship of Satan (Aḥmad Taymūr Pāshā, *al-Yazīdiyya*, Cairo 1352, 59-61).

Bibliography: Brockelmann, S I, 756, I², 546; ʿUmar Riḍā Kaḥḥāla, *Muʿdjam al-muʾallifīn*, Damascus 1957, iii, 147; L. Massignon, *Recueil de textes inédits concernant l'histoire de la mystique en pays d'Islam*, Paris 1929, 95-8; H. Ritter, *Das Meer der Seele*, Leiden 1955, index; Ibn al-Djawzī, *al-Muntaẓam*, s. a. 520; idem, *Akhbār al-ḳuṣṣās wa 'l-mudhakkirīn*, ms. Leiden 2156, fol. 77 a-b; Ibn Khallikān, no. 37; Subkī, *Ṭabaḳāt al-ṣūfiyya*, iv, 54.

(H. Ritter)

AL-GHAZĀLĪ, Djānbirdī, governor of Damascus under Selīm I. Originally a *mamlūk* of Ḳāʾit Bāy (873/1468-901/1495), he took his *nisba* from the Egyptian village of Minyat Ghazāl (Sharḳiyya), where he was *shādd* (superintendent). He obtained promotion, ultimately becoming *nāʾib* (governor) of Ḥamā (917/1511). After the battle of Mardj Dābiḳ (24 Radjab 922/23 August 1516), he was nominated governor of Damascus, first by fugitive *amīr*s in that city, then in Cairo, whither he had fled, by Ṭūmān Bāy. He commanded an expedition against the Ottomans in Syria, but was defeated by Sinān Pasha near Baysān (Dhu 'l-Ḳaʿda 922/December 1516). On 18 Muḥarram 923/10 February 1517, after the Ottoman victory at al-Raydāniyya, he submitted to Selīm I, with whom he had secretly been in communication. His atrocities against the Arabs of the Sharḳiyya led to the intervention of the Grand Vizier, Yūnus Pasha. On 5 Ṣafar 924/16 February 1518, Selīm appointed him governor of Damascus with the tax-farm (*taḥadduth*) of southern Syria. He suppressed tribal insubordination, and secured the safe passage of the Pilgrimage caravan. He built up a private army, chiefly of Arabs and Mamlūk refugees from Egypt, which included a corps of musketeers. In Dhu 'l-Ḳaʿda 926/October-November 1520, on the accession of Süleymān, Djānbirdī displaced the Ottoman sub-governors in his province, captured the citadel of Damascus, and endeavoured to involve Khāʾir Bey, the viceroy of Egypt, in the revolt. Khāʾir Bey remained loyal, and Djānbirdī, who had assumed the sultanic title of *al-Malik al-Ashraf Abu 'l-Futūḥāt*, marched on Aleppo. In spite of siege and bombardment, Aleppo held out, and, on 9 Muḥarram 927/21 December 1520, Djānbirdī began to retreat, followed by Ottoman forces. At Damascus, he prepared for resistance, but on 26 Ṣafar 927/5 February 1521, his supporters were routed. He was killed, and his head sent to Istanbul.

Bibliography: Paul Kahle and Muhammad Mustafa (edd.), *Die Chronik des Ibn Ijâs*, vols. iii-v: the most important references are vol. v, 376-8, 418-9, for which cf. Gaston Wiet, *Journal d'un bourgeois du Caire*, ii, [Paris] 1960, 369-71, 405-6; Henri Laoust, *Les gouverneurs de Damas sous les Mamlouks et les premiers Ottomans*, Damascus 1952, 151-9, 171-4.

(P. M. Holt)

GHAZĀLĪ, Meḥmed (?-942/1535), Ottoman poet, also known as "Deli Birader". His father's name was Durmush; his teacher, in his youth, Muḥyī al-Dīn ʿAdjamī. Ghazālī very soon abandoned an early interest in Ṣūfism and took up teaching in the *medreses*. His first official appointment was as *müderris* at the Bāyezīd Pasha *medrese* in Bursa; shortly afterwards, however, he went off to the court of Prince Ḳorḳud, the son of Bāyezīd II, in Manisa. Ḳorḳud grew in a short time to like both Ghazālī's company and his witticisms and made him his inseparable companion, even taking him with him to Egypt. Although Ḳorḳud became angry with him at one point there and ordered that he be executed, Ghazālī was successful in winning over the *kapîdjî-bashî* and thus saving himself (for details, see the *Tedhkere* of ʿĀshiḳ Čelebi).

Ghazālī wrote for Piyāle Bey, who had introduced him to Ḳorḳud, a *risāla* entitled *Dāfiʿ al-ghumūm wa rāfiʿ al-humūm* (Istanbul Un. Lib., Turkish MSS nos. 1400, 9659), in imitation of the *Alfiyya wa-shalfiyya* of Ḥakīm Azraḳī, and presented this *risāla* to Ḳorḳud. According to one account, Ḳorḳud was angered by this indecent *risāla* and sent Ghazālī away; but a more reasonable tradition relates that they were not separated until Ḳorḳud was put to death by Selīm I, and that only after Ḳorḳud's death did Ghazālī become *shaykh* at the *tekke* of Geyikli Baba in Bursa. It was at this point that he adopted the *makhlaṣ* "Ghazālī".

Quickly becoming bored with the life of a *shaykh*, he became *müderris* in Sivriḥiṣār. Later he became successively *müderris* in Akshehir with a daily salary of 50 *akče* and then at the Ḥüseyniyye *medrese* in Amasya. Through the good offices of Ḳadrī Efendi, he went from there to become *müftī* in Aghras.

Not happy in any place to which he had been, he finally went to Istanbul with a pension of 1000 *akče* and built in Beshiktash a garden, a bath, a mosque and a *zāwiye*. He began to operate the bath with Āteshīzāde Memi Shāh, but after a very short time complaints were lodged with the Grand Vizier Ibrāhīm Pasha. Ibrāhīm Pasha sent 100 *ʿadjemī oghlan* and the bath was pulled down, so much to the joy of some that chronograms were written to commemorate the event. Ghazālī wrote a poem of 25 *bayt*, the *Kapludjanāme*, in which he expressed his grief. Following the death of Memi Shah and the execution of Iskender Čelebi, he made his way in 938/1531 to Mecca where he built a garden, a mosque and a *zāwiye* and where he remained until his death. Although there is disagreement about the date of his death, the date 942/1535, which is given in a chronogram, seems acceptable.

His *risāla Dāfiʿ al-ghumūm wa-rāfiʿ al-humūm* shows clearly Ghazālī's outlook on life. Although Ghazālī grew ashamed of this *risāla* in his old age and tried to collect the copies of it in order to destroy them, he was not successful in doing so. The work is divided into seven chapters and is filled from beginning to end with indecent stories. Along with this aspect of Ghazālī's nature, however, it is worth noting the sincerity which he showed to those whom he loved. After the executions of Prince Ḳorḳud and Iskender Čelebi, he wrote for each an elegy in which he manifests the grief he felt.

He also wrote a *risāla* entitled *Miftāḥ al-hidāya* concerning precepts relative to the ritual ablution and the prayer. This *risāla* was extracted from the *Bidāya* and the commentary upon it called the *Hidāya* (Istanbul Un. Lib., Turkish MS no. 3273, fol. 3a). His various anecdotes, short poems (*ḳiṭʿa*) and chronograms are very fine. Both Kātib Čelebi and Bursalī Ṭāhir record that he wrote a history in Persian entitled *Mir'āt-i kā'ināt*, but Bursalī Ṭāhir adds that no copy has yet come to light.

He received the nickname "Deli Birader" because of a *bayt* which he wrote.

Bibliography: Tashköprü-zāde, *al-Shaḳā'iḳ al-nuʿmāniyya*, 527 (Gn. tr., Rescher, 299; Turkish tr., Medjdī, 471); *Tedhkere*s of Sehī and Laṭīfī, s.v.; Ḥasan Čelebi, *Tedhkere*, Istanbul Un. Lib., Turkish MS no. 2579, 232b; Riyāḍī, *Tedhkere*, Istanbul Un. Lib., Turkish MS no. 761, 101b; Beyānī, *Tedhkere*, Istanbul Un. Lib., Turkish MS no. 2568, 72a; ʿĀshiḳ Čelebi, *Tedhkere*, Istanbul Un. Lib., Turkish MS no. 2406, 356b; Ḥāfiẓ Ḥüseyin al-Aywān-Serāyī, *Ḥadīḳat al-djawāmiʿ*, Istanbul 1281, ii, 115; Ismāʿīl Belīgh, *Güldeste*, Bursa 1287, 496; ʿĀlī, *Kunh al-akhbār*, Istanbul Un. Lib., Turkish MS no. 2377, 204b; Fuat Köprülü, in *IA*, s.v.; Bursalī Ṭāhir, *ʿOthmānlī mü'ellifleri*, ii, 348; Gibb, *Ottoman Poetry*, iii, 36; Hammer-Purgstall, *Gesch. d. osm. Dichtkunst*, ii, 198.

(G. Alpay)

GHĀZĀN, Maḥmūd, Ilkhan [*q.v.*] from 694/1295 until 713/1304, was born on 20 Rabīʿ I 670/5 November 1271, being the eldest son of Arghūn [*q.v.*], then only in his thirteenth year. Upon his father's accession Ghāzān was appointed governor of Khurāsān, Māzandarān and Ray, which provinces he continued to administer during the reign of Gaykhātū [*q.v.*]. He had been brought up as a Buddhist and, whilst governor, had ordered the construction of Buddhist temples in Khabūshān (Ḳūčān); but shortly before his accession, during the war with Bāydū [*q.v.*], he had been persuaded by his general Nawrūz to become a Muslim. In his reign Islam was recognized as the state religion, the régime was organized on a basis of Muslim culture, charitable endowments, mosques, theological schools etc., were erected in and around the new capital Tabrīz, descendants of the Prophet were sometimes mentioned in the first place in the state record before princes and princesses of the blood, and lastly the turban was introduced as the court headgear. But Ghāzān was more a Mongol than a Muslim; as ruler and legislator his activities were entirely free from biassed pietism. Particular attention was devoted to the finances of the country, the currency etc.; Ghāzān no longer appears on the coins (the inscriptions on which were in Arabic, Mongol and Tibetan), like his predecessors, as representative of the Great Khān in Pekin, but as ruler "by the grace of God" (in Mongol *tngri-yin küčündür* "in the power of heaven"). He carried out his plans with ruthless vigour; everyone whom he believed to be dangerous to the peace of the realm or to his autocratic rule was disposed of without compunction; among these was the Amīr Nawrūz himself, to whom he owed his throne. On the other hand Ghāzān's measures increased the prosperity of the country and in particular protected the peasantry from oppression and extortion. The revenue of the state is said to have risen during his reign, from 1700 to 2100 *tūmān*s. Like other Mongol rulers Ghāzān particularly esteemed those arts and sciences which might be useful to the State; he himself is said to have been conversant with natural history, medicine, astronomy, chemistry and even several handicrafts; attached to an observatory built by his orders in Tabrīz was a special school for secular sciences (*ḥikmiyyāt*). In addition to his native Mongol Ghāzān is said to have had some knowledge of the Arabic, Persian, Hindī, Kashmīrī, Tibetan, Chinese and Frankish (*i.e.*, French or Latin) languages. Notwithstanding his conversion to Islam, he took a great interest in the history and traditions of his own people, on which indeed he was an authority. It was at his suggestion that his minister the famous historian Rashīd al-Dīn [*q.v.*] compiled his *Djāmiʿ al-tawārīkh*, in which his source for much of the information about the Mongols was none other than Ghāzān himself. Continuing the anti-Mamlūk policy of his predecessors, Ghāzān twice invaded Syria. In the first campaign (1299-1300) he occupied Aleppo, defeated the Egyptian army before Ḥims and entered Damascus; but upon his return to Persia in Djumādā I 699/February 1300 the country was at once re-occupied by the Mamlūks. For the second campaign he sought the alliance of Christian Europe. There has been preserved in the Vatican archives a letter from Ghāzān to Pope Boniface VIII dated 12 April 1302. "We for our part", says the Īlkhān, "are making our preparations. You too should prepare your troops, send word to the rulers of the various nations and not fail to keep the rendezvous. Heaven willing we [*i.e.*, Ghāzān] shall make the great work [*i.e.*, the war against the Mamlūks] our sole aim." The expedition to which Ghāzān refers was undertaken in the spring of 702/1303: the Mongols were decisively defeated at Shahḳab near Damascus (2 Ramaḍān 702/20 April 1303) and never again attempted the conquest of Syria.

Bibliography: Rashīd al-Dīn, *Geschichte Ġāzān-Ḫan's*, ed. K. Jahn, London 1940; idem, *Djāmiʿ al-tawārīkh*, iii, ed. A. A. Ali-zade, Russian transl. A. K. Arends, Baku 1957; B. Spuler, *Mongolen*[2]; A. Mostaert and F. W. Cleaves, *Trois documents mongols des Archives secrètes vaticanes*, in *HJAS*, xv/3-4, 419-506 (467-478).

(W. Barthold-[J. A. Boyle])

GHAZĀT [see ghazw].

GHĀZĪ, Arabic active participle (pl. *ghuzāt*) used to indicate those who took part in a razzia [see ghazw], later in a *ghazwa* [*q.v.*] "raid against the infidels". This name later grew to be a title of honour reserved for those who distinguished themselves in the *ghazwa*, and it became part of the title of certain Muslim princes, such as the *amīr*s of Anatolia and more particularly the first Ottoman sultans. Corporations of *ghāzī*s are attested in Transoxiana and Khurāsān from the Sāmānid period; these were wandering bands who obtained their living chiefly from booty won in the *ghazwa*, and who offered their services wherever war was to be waged against unbelievers or heretics. Their leaders often achieved great fame and even an official status. But these soldiers of fortune, for whom war was an economic necessity and who were easily transformed by lack of occupation into brigands, became, in times of peace, a danger to the government which employed them; al-Ṭabarī records, in 205/821 (iii, 1044), a revolt in Khurāsān, stirred up by one of these mercenaries; Ibn al-Athīr (viii, 155) mentions that these seditious elements took part in the revolt of Bukhārā against the Sāmānid Naṣr, about 318/930. However, these groups, referred to by historians as *ghuzāt*, *fityān*, *ʿayyārūn* [*q.v.*], etc., formed a reserve of troops always available to whoever had need of them: Maḥmūd of Ghazna drew on them extensively, taking with him to India as many as 20,000 *ghāzī*s (ʿUtbī-Manīnī, ii, 262 f.); he was always in need of money to pay his mercenaries, burdening his people with taxes for this before each campaign (*ibid.*, ii, 168). These groups of soldiers of fortune mentioned by the historians in Transoxiana and Khurāsān offered at the same time a refuge for political or religious dissidents and an occupation for adventurers of all races, attracted by the lure of plunder. However, for centuries in these eastern provinces the Turks especially were the reservoir from which Persians and then Arabs recruited their mercenaries; hence, although these groups were originally without any national character, the Turkish element, as constituting the military class *par excellence*, was soon to predominate. Such organizations were not peculiar to the eastern provinces; they existed everywhere where there was fighting to be done, expecially in the regions of the frontier zones. Thus they were also found in the Arab-Byzantine frontier zones where, ever since the Umayyad period, a state of war had existed. In these regions, where, since the reign of the caliph al-Muʿtaṣim (218-27/833-42), the Turkish element formed the majority of the fighting men, the Arab-Byzantine frontier battles were more and more to become Turco-Byzantine wars. In this zone where the *g͟hāzī*s were fighting against the *akritai*, guardians of the Byzantine frontiers who were themselves often recruited from among Turkish mercenaries, there came into existence a population of the marches which to a considerable extent was ethnically the same on both sides of the frontier. We find proof of this state of affairs in the epic literature, both Byzantine and Arabo-Turkish, whether in the Byzantine epic of Digenis Akritas, the Arabic epic story of Delhemma [see D͟HU 'L-HIMMA], or the Turkish story of Sayyid Baṭṭāl [see BAṬṬĀL]. In this area where pilgrimages maintained a continual state of crusade, the defence of both sides of the frontier was organized in the same way: on both sides there was a spontaneous organization, growing up independently of the frontiers and outside the framework of the state, imbued with the same half-military half-religious spirit. In about 595/1200 the caliph al-Nāṣir, seeking to strengthen the caliphate against its enemies, reorganized the corporations which were already linked to the principles of the *futuwwa* [*q.v.*], the code of rules for a virtuous life, according with the tenets of Islamic mysticism and held in common by the artisan, military and religious corporations. In the first place he turned his attention to the military element, which he bound to his own person by new bonds of vassalage. The *g͟hāzī*s, who had at first consisted of a popular movement in which were mingled adventurers and dissidents, were grouped into a corporation which possessed the attributes of a Muslim chivalry and was organized like a religious fraternity, with a ceremony of investiture conferring the title of *g͟hāzī*, the granting of arms and of ritual emblems, and which was joined henceforth by princes and rulers. In the marches of Asia Minor, however, where in the 5th/11th century the *g͟hazī* element was reinforced by the massive immigration of Og͟huz tribes, the movement retained a popular and nomadic character, opposed to the settled and Persianized population of the Sald͟jūḳ towns. It was these turbulent elements of the marches, taking advantage of the slackening of Byzantine defences after the defeat of Mantzikert, impelled by the need to obtain their livelihood from plunder and at the same time inspired by the ideal of the Holy War, who, without the acquiescence of the Sald͟jūḳ government, carried out the conquest of Anatolia. The first Turkish conqueror of Cappadocia was a *g͟hāzī* leader, Emīr Dānis͟hmend; with him *g͟hāzī* makes its appearance among the titles of the emirs of Asia Minor; the term is even given as a personal name to the elder son of the emir; the Greek legend on the coins of Dānis͟hmend's successor reads: Ο ΜΕΓΑϹ ΑΜΗΡΑϹ ΑΜΗΡ ΓΑΖΗ (cf. I. Mélikoff, *Geste de Melik Dāniṣmend*, i, Paris 1960, 106). But this first *g͟hāzī* principality of Asia Minor, lacking the elements necessary for the organization and colonization of the conquered countries, could not survive after it had exhausted such resources as were readily to hand, and was forced to fall back before the attacks of the Sald͟jūḳs. The *g͟hāzī*s were forced back towards the frontiers (*ud͟j*) and brought under the control of the central power, which bridled their turbulence by sending them to fight: to the north of Cappadocia, against the Greek empire of Trebizond, to the south, against the Armenians of Cilicia. These elements are known in Turkish sources under the name "Turks of the *Ud͟j*" and their leaders are called "*Ud͟j begi*". However, in the 7th/13th century, the Mongol invasion brought to Anatolia a new migration of Turkish tribes; large numbers of dervishes, fleeing from the invaded Iranian provinces, came to join the fugitives who had taken refuge in the frontier regions. As a result of the disruption of the Sald͟jūḳ state and the weakness of Byzantine resistance, there arose a new ferment in the frontier regions, where the dervishes brought a new access of enthusiasm for the Holy War. This ferment was to result, at the beginning of the 8th/14th century, in the formation of the Turkish emirates in Anatolia. The 14th century sources and the first Ottoman chroniclers have left in their writings testimony to what the *g͟hāzī* spirit was which animated these warlike principalities. "Put on the white cap for the *g͟hazā*!" exclaims the historian ʿĀs͟hīḳpas͟hazāde (ed. Giese, 40), while Eflākī (ed. T. Yazıcı, Ankara 1959-61, i, 485; tr. Huart, ii, 10) tells us that the use of this white cap, the characteristic head-gear of the *g͟hāzī*s, was introduced in the frontier regions in the 7th/13th century by Meḥmed Beg of the *Ud͟j*. This same Eflākī describes the ceremony of initiation of the "sultan of the *g͟hāzī*s", Meḥmed Aydïnog͟hlï, by the *Mawlawī s͟hayk͟h* of Konya, Amīr ʿĀrif: "Meḥmed Beg, taking the club from the Čelebi, placed it on his head and said: 'I shall beat down my passions with this club, and with it I shall strike dead the enemies of the faith' " (cf. Eflākī, ii, 947-8; tr. Huart, ii, 391-2). The poet Aḥmedī gives the following definition of the *g͟hāzī*: "A *g͟hāzī* is the instrument of the religion of God, a servant of God who cleans the earth from the defilement of polytheism; a *g͟hāzī* is the sword of God, he is the protector and the refuge of the Believers; if he becomes a martyr while following the paths of God, do not think him dead, he lives with God as one of the blessed, he has Eternal Life" (cf. P. Wittek, in *Byzantion*, xi, 304). But these *g͟hāzī* principalities, whose aim was conquest and who supported themselves by plunder, who were made up of warlike elements and lacked the social classes necessary to organize the conquered territories, were doomed to grow progressively weaker and to die out. Only one of these principalities was able to survive and develop: this was the Ottoman state. A *g͟hāzī* principality like the others, it was the only one which was able to acquire the elements necessary for the organization of its conquests, thanks to its geographical position and to the proximity of the Byzantine capital, which obliged it to maintain a continual state of war. The first Ottoman sultans, just like the other Anatolian emirs, had included in their titles that of *g͟hāzī*, which is given them by the historians of their dynasty, such as ʿĀs͟hīḳpas͟hazāde, and which figures in their first inscriptions, as is shown in the inscription of 737/1337, concerning the building of the

Bursa mosque, where Orkhān is called "*sulṭān ibn sulṭān al-ghuzāt, ghāzī ibn al-ghāzī, Shudjā' al-Dawla wa 'l-Dīn, marzbān al-āfāḳ, pehlevān-i djihān,Orkhān ibn ʿUthmān*". ʿĀshiḳpashazāde also reveals that in the first centuries of the Ottoman empire there were four corporations, the first of which he calls the *ghāziyān-i Rūm*, the others being the *akhiyān-i Rūm, abdālān-i Rūm* and *badjiyān-i Rūm*. But when the Ottoman principality grew into an empire and the central power became firmly established, the *ghāzīs*, who had taken an active part in the conquest of Anatolia, were subjected to the authority of the state and the corporations were gradually disbanded. The work of the conquerors was accomplished and they had now to give place to the organizers of the empire.

Bibliography: Aḥmedī, in Atsız, *Osmanlı Tarihleri*, i, Istanbul 1949, 7-8; ʿĀshiḳpashazāde, *ibid.*, 237-8; Eflākī, *Manāḳib al-ʿārifīn*, ed. T. Yazıcı, Ankara 1959-61, i, 485, 506, ii, 947-8 (=Fr. tr. Cl. Huart, *Les saints des derviches tourneurs*, ii, Paris 1922, 10, 36, 391-2); Barthold, *Turkestan*, 214-5, 239, 242, 287, 291, 295, 312, 345; Fuʾād Köprülü, *Türkiye Taʾrīkhi*, Istanbul 1923, 81 f.; idem, *Les origines de l'Empire Ottoman*, Paris 1935, 88-133; Paul Wittek, *Deux chapitres de l'histoire des Turcs de Roum*, in *Byzantion*, xi (1936), 285-319; idem, *The rise of the Ottoman Empire*, London 1938; idem, *De la défaite d'Ankara à la prise de Constantinople*, in *REI*, xiv (1938), 1-34. (I. Mélikoff)

GHĀZĪ, King of ʿIrāḳ, son of King Fayṣal I and his cousin Ḥazīma, was born in the Ḥidjāz in 1912, moved to Baghdād in 1921, and spent his childhood there until he was sent to Harrow School in England. He mounted the throne in the autumn of 1933, equipped with excellent social gifts; but he lacked seriousness or any taste for public affairs. He married ʿAliyya, daughter of ex-King ʿAlī shortly after his accession, becoming the father of the future Fayṣal II in 1935. His short reign was marked by repeated military interventions in the Government, including the short-lived *coup* of General Bakr Ṣidḳī, 1936-7. He died in a motor accident in the spring of 1939.

Bibliography: S. H. Longrigg, *ʿIraq 1900 to 1950*, Oxford 1953: Majid Khadduri, *Independent ʿIraq*, Oxford 1951. (S. H. Longrigg)

GHĀZĪ, Sayf al-Dīn, Zangid prince of al-Mawṣil from 541/1146 to 544/1149. See al-mawṣil, nūr al-dīn, zangids.

GHĀZĪ, Sayf al-Dīn, Zangid prince of al-Mawṣil from 565/1170 to 576/1180. See al-mawṣil, nūr al-dīn, salāḥ al-dīn, zangids.

GHĀZĪ ČELEBI, ruler of Sinope (700/1300?-circa 730/1330 ?) known especially for his piratical exploits against the Genoese, and sometimes alliance with and sometimes against the Greeks of Trebizond (it is known that there were actions in 1313-14, 1319, 1324); there are attributed to him in these raids lack of scruples (*e.g.*, taking guests captive), audacity (typified by an attack on Kaffa in the Crimea), and skill (he is said to have been able, by swimming under water, to pierce the hull of enemy ships), all of which testify to his reputation (see the episodes and the sources, Genoese, Byzantine (Panaretos) and Muslim (Abu 'l-Fidāʾ and Ibn Baṭṭūṭa), in W. Heyd, *Histoire du commerce du Levant*, i, 485 and especially 451, and ii, 98). It is probable that this maritime activity represents the most important feature of his policy—certainly nothing is known of him beyond this; indeed—and this is not without significance—even his identity is in doubt. According to ʿĀlī, *Kunh al-akhbār*, v, 22 (following Rūḥī), he was the son of the Saldjūḳid sultan of Rūm, Masʿūd II, and on the death of the last sultan, ʿAlāʾ al-Din (at the beginning of the 8th/14th century), was granted by the Īlkhān Ghāzān all the northern coastlands of Asia Minor; but this is a late version, perhaps entirely due to the fact that the tombstone of Ghāzī Čelebi (*TOEM*, ii, 422) calls him the son of Masʿūd Čelebi, or to the fact that the career of Masʿūd II and of his father Kay-Kāʾūs in the Black Sea was well remembered; more nearly contemporary authors (Ibn Baṭṭūṭa, ii, 350-2, tr. Gibb, ii, 466-7, and, less clearly, Abu 'l-Fidāʾ *Taḳwīm*, ed. Reinaud-de Slane, 393) make Ghāzī Čelebi a descendant of the famous Muʿīn al-Dīn Sulaymān the Pervāne, whose sons Muḥammad and, more especially, Masʿūd had retained Sinope, their father's fief, until 1300 (cf. Münedjdjim bashī, iii, 31), and this version, although dubious, is not impossible. Ghāzī Čelebi died, if the inscription on the tombstone has been read correctly, in 722/1322, a date which conflicts with reports of his being active in 1324. In any case when Ibn Baṭṭūṭa passed through Sinope (in 1331 or 1333 ?) he was certainly dead—from an excess of *hashīsh* it was said—and the town had been occupied by the Isfandiyārid of Ḳastamūnī, but it is possible that Ghāzī Čelebi had accepted the suzerainty of the latter before his death (it is possible thus to interpret al-ʿUmarī, ed. Taeschner, 23). It is in any case impossible to deduce—as some authors have done—from the confused data on the Isfandiyārids [*q.v.*] that Ghāzī Čelebi lived until 1356.

Bibliography: apart from the sources mentioned in the article, see Aḥmed Tewḥīd, in *TOEM*, i, 199, 257, and 317, and xv (1925), 305; Zambaur, 148 (inaccurate); Ibn Baṭṭūṭa, tr. H. A. R. Gibb, ii, 466, n. 195; *EI*[1], art. Sīnūb. (Cl. Cahen)

GHĀZI 'L-DĪN ḤAYDAR (not Ḥaydar al-Dīn Ghāzī as given in the *Cambridge History of India*, v, 575, 578), the eldest son of Nawwāb Saʿādat ʿAlī Khān, ruler of Awadh (1212-29/1798-1814), was born at Basawlī in Rohīlkhand in 1188/1774. He succeeded his father as the Nawwāb-Wazīr of Awadh in accordance with the rule of primogeniture, in 1229/1814.

Right from the time of his accession he was under the influence of the British Resident, Col. John Bailey, who did not hesitate to interfere in the day-to-day administration of the state. Supported by the Governor-General of British India, Lord Hastings, who wanted to reduce the prestige of the Mughal emperor of Delhi, he declared his independence in 1234/1819 and assumed the royal title of Abu 'l-Muẓaffar Muʿizz al-Dīn Shāh-i Zamān Ghāzi 'l-Dīn Ḥaydar. A huge sum of two crores of rupees (20,000,000) was spent on the manufacture of a throne, made of pure gold and silver and studded with precious stones, and a canopy richly decorated with pearls and gold and silver thread. The same year he struck his own coinage bearing the legend: *sikka zad bar sīm-u zar az faḍl-i rabb-i dhu 'l-minan, Ghāzi al-Dīn Ḥaydar-i ʿālī nasab shāh-i zaman*. The obverse bore a coat of arms with two fishes (the insignia of the House of Burhān al-Mulk [*q.v.*]), supported by two tigers bearing banners. These coins, which replaced the *pahiyyah-dār* rupee of Shāh ʿĀlam II, were in circulation from 1235/1819 until 1242/1827.

A fine silver medal, commemorating the commencement of his rule, was also issued during the first year of his reign. This medal carried his full-faced portrait. An unsuccessful ruler, Ghāzi 'l-Dīn Ḥaydar was a debauchee. He was under the baneful influence of rapacious and unscrupulous ministers like Sayyid Muḥammad Khān, commonly known as Āghā Mīr and entitled Muʿtamad al-Dawla, an upstart who had been one of the pages of Ghāzi 'l-Dīn Ḥaydar before his accession. His maladministration, combined with his extravagance and dishonesty, hastened the decline of the Awadh dynasty.

Ghāzi 'l-Dīn Ḥaydar was benevolent towards the poor and the needy, and provided dowries for innumerable poor girls from the public treasury. Among the notable buildings constructed during his reign are: the Ḳadam Rasūl, where a piece of stone, said to contain the footprint of the Prophet, was enshrined and the Imāmbāŕah Shāh Nadjaf, an imposing building dedicated to mourning for Ḥusayn b. ʿAlī and the martyrs of Karbalāʾ. Ghāzi 'l-Dīn Ḥaydar died in 1243/1827 and was buried in this building.

The Persian dictionary *Haft Ḳulzum*, (publ. Lucknow 1882), a slightly re-arranged version of *Burhān-i ḳāṭiʿ*, which is ascribed to him, is in fact the compilation of Ḳabūl Aḥmad, who fathered it on the king apparently for some monetary consideration (cf. Ethé, in *Gr.I.Ph.*, ii, 265, 348).

Bibliography: Muḥammad Nadjm al-Ghanī Khān, *Taʾrīkh-i Awadh*, Lucknow 1919, iv, 108-211; Sayyid Kamāl al-Dīn Ḥaydar, *Taʾrīkh-i Awadh* (*Ḳayṣar al-tawārīkh*), Lucknow 1296/1877, 205-66; Muḥammad Ṣādiḳ Khān "Akhtar" Huglawī, *Guldasta-i Maḥabbat*, Lucknow 1239/1823 (an account, in prose and verse, of the meeting of Lord Hastings and Ghāzi 'l-Dīn Ḥaydar); anon., *Taʾrīkh-i Shāhiyya-i Nīshāpūriyya*, MS. Riḍā (Raza) Library, Rampur; Muḥ. Muḥtasham Khān, *Taʾrīkh-i Muḥtasham* or *Muḥtasham Khānī*, MS. Bankipore, vii, 605; Durgā Prāśād, *Taʾrīkh-i Ajodhyā* (MS.); Durga Parshād 'Mihr', *Bustān-i Awadh*, Lucknow 1892; Amīr ʿAlī Khān, *Wazīr-nāma*, Cawnpore 1293/1876; Lāl-djī b. Sītal Parshād, *Sulṭān al-ḥikāyāt*, MS. India Office 3902; Pūran Čand, *Iʿdjāz al-Siyar*, MS. India Office 3886; ʿAbd al-Aḥad b. Muḥammad Fāʾiḳ, *Waḳāʾiʿ Dil-padhīr*, MS., Storey 708; J. Mill, *History of India*, London 1857, viii and ix; Irwin, *The Garden of India*, London 1880. (A. S. Bazmee Ansari)

GHĀZI 'L-DĪN KHĀN [see SHIHĀB AL-DĪN, MĪR; MUḤAMMAD PANĀH, MĪR; ʿIMĀD AL-MULK].

GHĀZI EVRENOS BEG [see EWRENOS].

GHĀZĪ GIRĀY I, Khān of the Crimea, reigned for about six months in 930/1523-4. He was proclaimed khān in Muḥarram 930/November 1523 after conspiring with the Crimean *begs* to rebel against his father Meḥmed Girāy I [*q.v.*] and procuring his death. The Ottoman Sultan (Süleymān I) refused to recognize him and, in agreement with Memish Beg of the Shīrīn, the leader of the *begs*, appointed as khān Ghāzī Girāy's uncle Saʿādet Girāy (Djumādā II 930/April 1524). Ghāzī Girāy, unable to resist, accepted Memish Beg's proposal that he should be *ḳalghay* ([*q.v.*] 'heir-apparent') to Saʿādet Girāy, but was killed four months later (Shawwāl 930/August 1524).

Bibliography: Sayyid Muḥammad Riḍā, *Al-Sabʿ al-sayyār fī akhbār al-mulūk al-Tātār*, ed. Kazim Bek, Kazan 1832, 88 ff.; Ḥalīm Girāy, *Gülbün-i khānān*, Istanbul 1287, 13; ʿAbd al-Ghaffār, *ʿUmdat al-tawārīkh*, supplement to *TOEM*, 99; *IA*, s.v. Gâzi Giray I (Halil Inalcık).

(Halil Inalcik)

GHĀZĪ GIRĀY II, known as *Bora* ('tempest'), twice Khān of the Crimea (996/1588-1005/1596 and 1005/1596-1016/1607). Born in 961/1554, he first distinguished himself in 986/1578 as general of Crimean forces operating in support of the Ottomans against Persia, and won the regard of Özdemir-oghlu ʿOthmān Pasha [*q.v.*] (ʿĀlī, *Kunh al-akhbār*, MS; idem, *Nuṣret-nāme*, MS Istanbul, Esad Ef. [Süleymaniye] 2433; Āṣafī, *Shedjāʿat-nāme*, MS Istanbul Un. Lib. 6043; Iskandar Munshī, *Taʾrīkh-i ʿālam-ārā-yi ʿAbbāsī*, Tehrān 1314, 191, 197). Taken prisoner by the Persians in 988/1580 and refusing to co-operate with them against the Ottomans, he was imprisoned in the fortress of Alamūt, but escaped in 993/1585 and managed to rejoin ʿOthmān Pasha's army. Upon the death of ʿOthmān Pasha he went to Istanbul and settled at Yanbolu (Yamboli in Bulgaria). His bravery and loyalty prompted the Sultan (Murād III) to appoint him khān and send him with a fleet to the Crimea (Radjab 996/May 1588). The *begs* of the Crimea accepted him, but the Czar was supporting his own candidate, Murād Girāy. Ghāzī Girāy set on foot negotiations for an alliance with Poland and Sweden, and in 999/1591 made an incursion against Moscow. The next year the Crimean begs raided Russia again. When summoned by the Ottoman Sultan to serve in Hungary in the war with Austria, he made peace with Russia (ratified by Ghāzī Girāy in Radjab 1002/April 1594), the Czar undertaking to pay an annual tribute of 10,000 roubles and to send each year various stipulated gifts (*tiyish* and *bölek*) (two of his *yarlighs* to the King of Poland were published by V. Velyaminov-Zernov and H. Feyizhan, in *Matériaux pour servir à l'histoire du Khanat de Crimée* ...., St. Petersburg 1864, 9-19; cf. I. Novoselskiy, *Borba Moskovskogo gosudarstva s Tatarami v pervoy polovine XVII veka*, Moscow 1948, 118-9).

In Hungary, he took part in the siege of Raab/Yanïḳ (summer of 1002/1594), and in the following year led a brisk campaign to reduce to obedience the rebellious princes of Moldavia and Wallachia. His proposal that Moldavia should be granted to one of the Crimean princes having been rejected by the Porte, he did not appear in person for the campaign of 1005/1596, but sent the *ḳalghay* Fetḥ Girāy. As a consequence he was deposed, but was restored after three months. As the Crimea was now being threatened by the Ḳazaḳs, he began the building of the fortress of Ghāzī-kirman. At the Sultan's insistence, he joined the Ottoman army in Hungary in 1006/1598, and stayed on in winter-quarters at Sonbor/Szombor. His request that the *eyālet* of Silistre be granted him as *arpalïḳ* [*q.v.*] was brusquely rejected, and he refused to stay on in Hungary through the next winter (1008/1599-1600). The Austrians, in the hope of detaching him from the Ottomans, were promising him 10,000 gold pieces a year. Only in 1011/1602, when he saw that his behaviour was endangering his throne again, did he consent to return to Hungary, spending the next winter at Pečüy/Pécs [*q.v.*] and amusing himself with hunting and the writing of poetry. Next spring he returned to the Crimea. His ambassadors met a delegation from the Emperor at Kolozsvár (Klausenburg) to discuss terms of peace, but inconclusively. Throughout the Ottoman-Hapsburg war of 1001/1593-1015/1606 Ghāzī Girāy played a prominent part, both politically and in the military operations.

When peace was signed, he renewed his alliance with Poland against the Czar. The Sultan asked him to send 10,000 men for the operations against the Djelālīs [*q.v.* in Supp.] in Anatolia, but he sent only a small force. Next year (1016/1607) he was ordered to advance through Shirwān to attack Persia (Ferīdūn, *Munsha'āt al-salāṭīn*², ii, 119), but died soon after of plague (Shaʿbān 1016/November 1607). His son and *ḳalghay* Toḳtamīsh Girāy, whom he had nominated to succeed him, was proclaimed khān by the *beg*s of the Crimea, but the Porte refused to recognize him.

Ghāzī Girāy, one of the greatest khāns of the Crimea, managed to steer a course between the Porte, which wished to have the Crimean forces always at its disposal, and the Crimean aristocracy, which was seeking independence of the Porte. During his reign the Khānate co-operated more closely than ever with the Porte, and Ottoman influence, in culture and in administration, greatly increased: the *ḳapu-aghasî* (*eshik-aghasî*, *bash-agha*), appointed from among the Circassian slaves, came to occupy a predominant place in the government comparable with that of the Grand Vizier; and a corps of mounted musketeers (*tüfenkči*), bound to the ruler's person, was formed. Ghāzī Girāy was at the same time a genuine literary artist, occupying a unique place in Crimean literature and in the Ottoman *dīwān* tradition. In a sincere and fluent style, he wrote prose and poetry in Persian, in Arabic, and in Crimean, Čaghatay and Ottoman Turkish (he used as *makhlaṣ* 'Ghazāyī' and 'Khān Ghāzī'), introducing into *dīwān* poetry the new theme—later much imitated—of the valiant sentiments of the soldier. His works include (1) a small *dīwān* (incomplete manuscript published in fascimile by I. H. Ertaylan [see Bibl.]); (2) a *mathnawī* entitled *Gül ü Bülbül*, in Čaghatay Turkish (Ertaylan, 50-3, 62 n. 2, where the suggestion that it is a *naẓīre* to Fuḍūlī's *Nīk u bad* is rejected); (3) a lost 'contention-poem' (*munāẓara*) between Coffee and Wine (see Pečewī, *Ta'rīkh*, ii, 251); and (4) several letters in prose and verse (to be found in various *inshā'* collections, *e.g.*, British Museum MS Or. 6261; see also Abdullah-oğlu Hasan, *Kırım tarihine ait notlar ve vesikalar*, in *Azerbaycan Yurt Bilgisi*, iii (1932), 118-22, iv-v, 159-66, vi-vii, 249-52). He figures prominently in a romantic novel by Nāmīḳ Kemāl [*q.v.*].

Bibliography: Hasan Ortekin, *Bora Gazi Giray, hayatı ve eserleri* (unpublished *mezuniyet* thesis), Türkiyat Enstitüsü, Istanbul; C. M. Kortepeter, *The relations between the Crimean Tatars and the Ottoman Empire, 1578-1608..*, (unpublished University of London Ph. D. thesis, 1962); I. H. Ertaylan, *Gazi Giray Han, hayatı ve eserleri*, Istanbul 1958; *IA*, s.v. Gâzî Giray II (by Halil Inalcık), with further references.

(Halil Inalcik)

GHĀZĪ GIRĀY III, Khān of the Crimea from 1116/1704 until 1118/1707. In Radjab 1110/January 1699 he was appointed *Nuradin* (*Nūr al-Dīn* [*q.v.*]) by his brother Dewlet Girāy II, but rebelled, in collusion wtih the Noghay, and was dismissed. He came to Edirne and was exiled by the Porte to Rhodes. Upon the accession of his father Selīm Girāy [*q.v.*] in 1114/1702, he was recalled and made *ḳalghay* [*q.v.*], and at his death succeeded him as Khān (3 Ramaḍān 1116/30 December 1704). In spite of the Porte's pacific attitude, he himself followed an anti-Russian policy during the Russo-Swedish wars, which provoked Russian protests at Istanbul. For this, and for his resistence to the Porte's efforts to bring the Noghay directly under Ottoman control, he was deposed (Dhu 'l-Ḥidjdja 1118/March 1707) and ordered to reside at Karin-ābād (Karnobat, in Bulgaria), where in Rabīʿ II 1120/June 1708, aged 36, he died of plague.

Bibliography: Rāshid, *Ta'rīkh*, iii, 168, 172, 201, 215; Fîndîḳlîlî Meḥmed Agha (Silāḥdār), *Nuṣret-nāme*, MS; Sayyid Muḥammad Riḍā, *Al-Sabʿ al-sayyār fī akhbār al-mulūk al-Tātār*, Kazan 1832, 270 ff.; *IA*, s.v. Gâzî Giray III (by Halil Inalcık), with further references.

(Halil Inalcik)

GHĀZĪ KHĀN [see Supplement].

GHĀZĪ MIYĀN, popular title of Sipāh Sālār Masʿūd Ghāzī, one of the earliest and most celebrated of Indo-Muslim saints, who lies buried at Bahrāič, in Uttar Pradesh. According to Ḍiyā al-Dīn Baranī, he was a soldier in the army of Sultan Maḥmūd of Ghazna. Abu 'l Faḍl says that he was a kinsman (*khweshāwand*) of the Sultan. ʿAbd al-Ḳādir Badā'ūnī quotes a saint of Khayrabād who once remarked about the Sālār: "He was an Afghān who met his death by martyrdom". No early record of his life exists. Later generations have introduced many mythical and romantic elements in his biography. The *Mir'āt-i Masʿūdī* of ʿAbd al-Raḥmān, written during the reign of Djahāngīr (1014/1605-1037/1627), has consolidated all these later legends, though the author claims to have utilized an early Ghaznawid account of the saint in *Ta'rīkh-i Mullā Muḥammad Ghaznawī*, which is now lost. It is generally held that Sālār Ghāzī passed his youth in the field by the side of his father Sālār Sāhū. At the age of sixteen he started on his invasion of Hindustān. With Satrik (in Bāra Bankī) as his base of operations, he sent out his lieutenants in every direction to conquer and proselytize the country. Sayyid Sayf al-Dīn and Miyān Radjab of his army were sent to Bahrāič but they failed to achieve their objective. Sālār Masʿūd then marched in person to Bahrāič. He was successful in the beginning but was ultimately overthrown and slain with his followers on 18 Radjab 424/30 June 1033. His servants buried him at a spot he had earlier chosen for his resting-place. The fact that his name and his grave survived through the long years between the Ghaznawid invasion and the Ghūrid occupation of northern India shows that there was some Muslim population to look after the grave and to preserve for posterity the tradition of Sālār's martyrdom (Niẓāmī, *Some aspects of religion and politics in India during the 13th century*, ʿAlīgarh 1961, 76-7). Iletmish's son, Nāṣir al-Dīn Maḥmūd, was the first prince of the ruling house of Delhi to live in Bahrāič and during his governorship Muslim colonization began in that region; but there is no reference to Sālār Masʿūd in Minhādj's account of the prince. According to Führer (*Archaeological survey report*, ii, 292), the first building over his grave was constructed by Nāṣir al-Dīn Maḥmūd. Muḥammad b. Tughluḳ (725/1325-752/1351) was the first sultan of Delhi to visit his grave. Fīrūz Shāh Tughluḳ also made a pilgrimage to Bahrāič in 776/1374 and was so overwhelmed by its spiritual atmosphere that he had his head shaved (*maḥluḳ shud*) in the mystic fashion and adopted an other-worldly attitude (ʿAfīf, *Ta'rīkh-i Fīrūz Shāhī*, 372). Some buildings, wells, shades and verandas are said to have been constructed by him.

The tomb of Sālār Masʿūd is one of the most popular centres of pilgrimage in India. Hundreds of thousands of Hindus and Muslims visit it every year. The legend of Ghāzī Miyān—also known as Bālāy Miyān, Bālā Pīr, Hataylā Pīr etc.— occupies a unique place in the cultural life of the people of northern India, particularly in the villages of eastern Uttar Pradesh, Bihar and eastern Bengal. Many tales about him are current amongst the people, and many fairs, festivals and feasts are held in different towns and villages of Uttar Pradesh (*e.g.* Meerut, Sambhal, Badāʾun) to commemorate different events of his life. There are several towns in northern India where certain old graves are considered to be those of his martyr-companions (*e.g.*, the grave of Mīrān Mulhim in Badāʾun, see Raḍī al-Dīn, *Kanz al-tawārīkh*, Badāʾun 1907, 51). The tradition of Ghāzī Miyān has assumed the form of a popular superstition in the villages of eastern Bengal, where large number of symbolic graves of the saint have been put up and thousands of Hindu and Muslim villagers make offerings to them. As it is believed that he was slain while his nuptial ceremonies were being celebrated —which thus became in a double sense his *ʿurs*—marriage processions in his memory are held at many places with *ʿalams* (banners) on the first Sunday of the month of Djayth (May-June). As this festival led to some immoral practices, Sikandar Lōdī (894/1489-923/1517) banned it, but it was revived later. Once the Emperor Akbar (963/1556-1014/1605) witnessed this festival incognito in the vicinity of Agra. The death of the saint is commemorated on the 12th, 13th and 14th of Radjab every year.

Bibliography: The earliest reference to the saint is found in Amīr Khusraw's *Iʿdjāz-i Khusrawī* (Nawal Kishore ed., ii, 155), wherein the author refers to his country-wide popularity. For other sources, see Ḍiyā al-Dīn Baranī, *Taʾrīkh-i Fīrūz Shāhī*, Bibl. Indica, 491; Ibn Baṭṭūṭa, *Riḥla*, Cairo 1346/1928, ii, 69-70; ʿAfīf, *Taʾrīkh-i Fīrūz Shāhī*, Bibl. Indica, 230; ʿAbd Allāh, *Taʾrīkh-i Dāʾūdī*, ʿAlīgarh 1954, 38; Niʿmat Allāh, *Taʾrīkh-i Khān Djahānī*, Dacca 1960, i, 217; Abu'l Faḍl, *Akbar Nāma*, Bibl. Indica, ii, 145; ʿAbd al-Ḳādir, *Muntakhab al-tawārīkh*, Bibl. Indica, iii, 27; Firishta, *Taʾrīkh-i Firishta*, Nawal Kishore ed., i, 139; ʿAbd al-Raḥmān, *Mirʾāt-i Masʿūdī* (for MS see Storey 1006-7); Dārā Shukoh, *Safīnat al-awliyāʾ*, Nawal Kishore, Kānpur 1900, 160-1; Ghulām Muʿīn al-Dīn ʿAbd Allāh, *Maʿāridj al-walāyat*, MS in personal collection, ii, 494-505; Ghulām Sarwar, *Khazīnat al-aṣfiyāʾ*, Nawal Kishore 1873, ii, 217-24; Muḥammad ʿAbbās Khān Sherwānī, *Ḥayāt-i Masʿūdī* (Urdu), ʿAlīgarh 1935; ʿInāyat Ḥusayn, *Ghazā Nāma-i Masʿūd* (Urdu), Nāmī Press, Lucknow 1894; R. Greeven, *The heroes five*, Allahabad 1893; Garcin de Tassy, *Mémoire sur ... la religion musulmane dans l'Inde*, Paris 1869, 72-9; *Asiatic Annual Register*, vi (1801); *JASB*, 1892, Extra number, p. 17; *Statistical and descriptive account of north-west provinces of India*, Allahabad 1874, 118; *District gazetteers of the United Provinces of Agra and Oudh*, xlv, Bahrāič ed. H. R. Nevill, Allahabad 1903; Elliot and Dowson, *History of India*, ii, 513-49; *Voyages de Nikolaes van Graaf aux Indes Orientales*, Amsterdam 1719.

(K. A. NIZAMI)

GHĀZĪ MUḤAMMAD [see ḲĀḌĪ MUḤAMMAD].

GHĀZĪPUR [see Supplement].

GHĀZIYA (A.) plur. *ghawāzī*, the name for Egyptian public dancing-girls. In the 19th century, according to Lane, they came from a single tribe and married only within it. They gave lascivious performances in the streets and courtyards, and performed privately in the *ḥarīms* for certain celebrations or in special places for audiences of men. Lane regarded them as among the most beautiful women in Egypt and as common prostitutes; he distinguished the *ghāziya* from the *ʿālima* [*q.v.*] or female singer.

Today this distinction is less sharp. In Egyptian cities both the dancing-girl and the singer are now called *ʿalma* (colloquial), while in the villages the dancer is still often called *ghāziya*. The dancers do not come from a distinct tribe but from various sorts of low-income families, usually urban. They are taught the art, after showing some natural ability, by female teachers who are sometimes called *ʿawālim* (plur.) too. Both the *ghāziya* and the *ʿālima* must now be distinguished from the better-paid, better-trained "Oriental" dancer (*rāḳiṣa*) who performs in the modern night clubs and films and at private celebrations.

The *ghawāzī*, according to Lane, preferred to call themselves *Barāmika*. *Ghāziya*, the origin of which is uncertain, is still a derogatory term avoided by the dancer herself. In the villages it connotes a woman outside the pale of respectability. *Ibn ghāziya* is thus a serious insult. See further RAḲṢ.

Bibliography: Lane, *Manners and Customs of the Modern Egyptians*, ch. xix; Dozy, *Suppl.*, s.v.; M. Berger, *The Arab Danse du Ventre*, in *Dance Perspectives*, x (1961). (M. BERGER)

GHAZNA, a town in eastern Afghānistān situated 90 miles/145 km. south-west of Kābul in lat. 68° 18′ E. and long. 33° 44′ N. and lying at an altitude of 7,280 feet/2,220 m.

The original form of the name must have been **Ganzak* < *gandja* "treasury", with a later metathesis in eastern Iranian of *-nz-/-ndj-* to *-zn-*, and this etymology indicates that Ghazna was already in pre-Islamic times the metropolis of the surrounding region of Zābulistān. The parallel forms *Ghaznī* (in present-day use) and *Ghaznīn* must go back to forms like *Ghaznīk* and *Ghaznēn*; the geographer Muḳaddasī and the anonymous author of the *Ḥudūd al-ʿālam* (end of 4th/10th century) have *Ghaznīn*, and Yāḳūt says that this is the correct, learned form.

The oldest mention of the town seems to be in the second century A.D., when Ptolemy gives Ga(n)zaka in the region of Paropamisádai, locating it 1,100 *stadia* from Kābul, but to the north of that town. It must have been of some significance under the successive waves of military conquerors in this region, such as the Kushans and Ephthalites. The Chinese Buddhist pilgrim Hiuen-Tsang (7th century A.D.) mentions it as Ho(k)-si(k)-na = Ghaznīk, and describes it as the chief town of the independent kingdom of Tsau-kiu-ch'a = Zābulistān. Buddhism was known in the region, for recent excavations at Ghazna have uncovered a Buddhist site and many clay and terracotta buddhas have been found. (It should be noted that A. Bombaci, in *East and West*, vii (1957), 255-6, doubts the accepted identification of Ghazna with the places mentioned by Ptolemy and Hiuen-Tsang.)

The history of Ghazna in the first three Islamic centuries is most obscure. The armies of the Arab governors of Khurāsān and Sīstān penetrated into Zābulistān in ʿAbd al-Malik's reign and fought the local ruler, the Zunbīl, whose summer quarters were in Zābulistān (Balādhurī, *Futūḥ*, 397; Ṭabarī, ii, 488). The population of this area was doubtless basically Iranian, but with a considerable admixture of Turkish and other Central Asian peoples brought in by earlier waves of conquest; as the homeland of Rustum, Zābulistān plays a part in the Iranian national epic as the homeland of heroes. At the end of the 3rd/9th century, the Ṣaffārids Yaʿḳūb and ʿAmr b. Layth reached Ghazna and Kābul, defeating the Zunbīl of that time, but it is only with the 4th/10th century that the history of G͟hazna, by then a theoretical dependency of the Sāmānids, becomes reasonably clear.

In 351/962 a Sāmānid slave commander, Alptigin, came to G͟hazna with an army and established himself there, defeating the local ruler Abū ʿAlī Lawīk or Anūk, described as a brother-in-law of the Hindūs͟hāhī Kābul-S͟hāh. In 366/977 another slave commander, Sebüktigin, rose to power in G͟hazna, and under the dynasty which he founded, that of the G͟haznavids, the town enters the two most glorious centuries of its existence. It now became the capital of a vast empire, stretching at Sultan Maḥmūd's death in 421/1030 from western Persia to the Ganges valley, and it shared with Kābul a dominating position on the borderland between the Islamic and Indian worlds; according to Ibn Ḥawḳal[2], 450, G͟hazna's Indian trade did not suffer with the coming of Alptigin's army and the temporary severance of political links with India. It was still at this time, and for several decades to come, a frontier fortress town on the edge of the pagan Indian world; in the reign of Masʿūd I of G͟hazna (421-32/1030-41) there was still a Sālār or commander of the *g͟hāzī*s of G͟hazna (Bayhaḳī, *Taʾrīk͟h-i Masʿūdī*, ed. G͟hanī and Fayyāḍ, Tehrān 1324/1945, 254; cf. the anecdote in the first discourse of Niẓāmī ʿArūḍī's *Čahār maḳāla* describing the attacks in Maḥmūd's reign of the infidels on the nearby town of Lāmg͟hān). The geographers of the later 4th/10th century stress that G͟hazna was an entrepôt (*furḍa*) for the trade between G͟hazna and India, that it was a resort of merchants and that its inhabitants enjoyed prosperity and ease of life. They expatiate on its freedom from noxious insects and reptiles and its healthy climate. In winter, snow fell there extensively, and the historian Bayhaḳī describes graphically how in the summer of 422/1031 torrential rain caused the stream flowing through the G͟hazna suburb of Afg͟hān-S͟hāl to swell and burst its banks, carrying away the bridge and destroying many caravanserais, markets and houses. G͟hazna itself was not in a fertile spot and had few or no gardens, but the surrounding country of Zābulistān was fertile and the town accordingly enjoyed an abundance of provisions. T͟haʿālibī lists among the specialities of the G͟hazna region *amīrī* apples and rhubarb, and Fak͟hr-i Mudabbir Mubāraks͟hāh mentions monster pears from there, *pīl-amrūd* "elephant-pears".

Muḳaddasī describes the layout of G͟hazna as it was during Sebüktigin's time. It had a citadel, *ḳalʿa*, in the centre of the town (the modern Bālā-Ḥiṣār), with the ruler's palace; a town proper or *madīna*, in which many of the markets were situated, and which had a wall and four gates; and a suburb, *rabaḍ*, containing the rest of the markets and houses. The citadel and *madīna* had been rebuilt by Yaʿḳūb and ʿAmr b. Layt͟h (Bayhaḳī, 261). Recent work by the Italian Archaeological Mission at G͟hazna has shown that the houses of the great men lay on the hill slopes to the east of the modern town, on the way to the Rawḍa-yi Sulṭān, where lies Maḥmūd's tomb. In this vicinity are the two decorated brick towers built by Masʿūd III and Bahrām S͟hāh, which may be the minarets of mosques, and not necessarily towers of victory as early western visitors to G͟hazna imagined. The site of a fine palace has also been uncovered here. We learn from Bayhaḳī that Maḥmūd had a palace at Afg͟hān-S͟hāl, the Ṣad-Hazāra garden and the Fīrūzī palace and garden where he was eventually buried. His son Masʿūd decided in 427/1035-6 to build a splendid new palace to his own design (Bayhaḳī, 499, 539-41). For the erection and decoration of these and other buildings, the spoils of India were used; it seems that objects of precious metals and captured Hindu statues were directly incorporated into the palace fabrics as trophies of war. With the plunder brought back from the expedition of 409/1018 to Kanawd͟j and Muttra, Maḥmūd decided to build a great new mosque in G͟hazna, to be known as the *ʿArūs al-Falak* "Bride of the Heavens"; to this was attached a *madrasa* containing a library of books filched from K͟hurāsān and the west (ʿUtbī-Manīnī, ii, 290-300). Other constructional works by Maḥmūd included elephant stables (*pīl-k͟hāna*) to house 1,000 beasts, with quarters for their attendants, and various irrigation works in the district; one of his dams, the Band-i Sulṭān, a few miles to the north of the town, has survived to this day. For all these building works, it is probable that the early G͟haznavids imported skilled artisans from Persia and even from India, for Zābulistān had no artistic traditions of its own.

After the G͟haznavids' loss of their western territories, G͟hazna and Lahore became their two main centres, and the minting of coins was concentrated on these two towns. In the first half of the 6th/12th century, G͟hazna was twice occupied by Sald͟jūḳ armies (510/1117 and 529/1135), but a much greater disaster occurred in 545/1150-1 when ʿAlāʾ al-Dīn Ḥusayn of G͟hūr sacked the town in vengeance for two of his brothers killed by the G͟haznavid Bahrām S͟hāh; this orgy of destruction earned for him his title of D͟jihān-sūz "World-incendiary". However, G͟hazna seems to have recovered to some extent. It was finally lost to the G͟haznavids in 558/1163, and after an occupation by a group of G͟huzz from K͟hurāsān, passed into G͟hūrid hands, becoming the capital of the Sultan Muʿizz al-Dīn Muḥammad. After the latter's death in 599/1203, it was held briefly by one of the G͟hūrids' Turkish slave commanders, Tād͟j al-Dīn Yïldïz, but in 612/1215-16 came into the possession of the G͟hūrids' supplanters, the K͟hʷārizm-S͟hāhs. But D͟jalāl al-Dīn Mingburnu's governorship there was short. He was driven into India by Čingiz K͟hān's Mongols in 618/1221 and the town was then sacked by the latter.

This was really the end of G͟hazna's period of glory; coins now cease to be minted there. In Īl-K͟hānid times, it passed to the Kart ruler of Harāt, Muʿizz al-Dīn Ḥusayn. Tīmūr granted it in 804/1401 to his grandson Pīr Muḥammad b. D͟jihāngīr, who used it as a base for raids on India. In 910/1504 Bābur appeared at G͟hazna and forced its then ruler Muḳīm b. D͟hi 'l-Nūn Arg͟hūn to retire to Ḳandahār. Bābur has left a description of the town as it was at this time, a small place where agriculture was difficult, only a few grapes, melons and apples being produced; he marvelled that so insignificant a place should once have been the capital of a mighty empire. Under the Mug͟hals and native Afg͟hān dynasties, G͟hazna played no very great rôle. It was besieged in 1059/1649 by a Persian army, but Awrangzīb succeeded in holding on to it, despite his loss of Ḳandahār. Nādir S͟hāh captured it in 1151/1738 before occupying Kābul and marching on Delhi in the next year, and after his assassination in 1160/1747, Aḥmad S͟hāh Durrānī used G͟hazna and Kābul as springboards for attacks on India. During the First Afghan-British War of 1839-42 G͟hazna was twice taken by British forces, and on the second occasion the British commander sent back to India, at the Governor-General Lord Ellenborough's request, the alleged Gates of Somnāth captured by Maḥmūd of Ghazna eight centuries previously.

Today, Ghazna is a town of some importance; it lies on the Kābul-Ḳandahār road and is the junction for the roads eastward to Gardīz and Mātūn, Urgun and Tōčī. It is the administrative centre of the province (*wilāyat*) of Ghazna. The great majority of the people are Persian-speaking and are Sunnī in religion.

Bibliography: 1. Historical. Primary sources: ʿUtbī and Bayhaḳī (for the early Ghaznavid period), Ibn al-Athīr, Niẓāmī ʿArūḍī, Djuwaynī and Djūzdjānī (for the later Ghaznavid, Ghūrid and Mongol periods). Secondary sources: Pauly-Wissowa, vii, 887 s.v. *Gazak* (Kiessling); E. Benveniste, *Le nom de la ville de Ghazna*, in *JA*, ccxxi (1935), 141-3; Marquart, *Ērānšahr*, 37, 39-40, 293-8; idem, *Das Reich Zābul*, in *Festschrift E. Sachau*, Berlin 1915, 257-8, 261, 272; M. Nāẓim, *The life and times of Sulṭān Maḥmūd of Ghazna*, Cambridge 1931, 166-7; C. E. Bosworth, *The Ghaznavids: their empire in Afghanistan and eastern Iran 994-1040*, Edinburgh 1963, 35 ff., 134-41; I. M. Shafi, *Fresh light on the Ghaznavîds*, in *IC*, xii (1938), 189-234; A. Bombaci, *Ghazni*, in *East and West*, N.S. viii (1957), 247-59; Sir T. Holdich, *The gates of India*, London 1910; Sir P. Sykes, *History of Afghanistan*, London 1940.

2. Geographical, travellers' narratives. Iṣṭakhrī, 280; Ibn Ḥawḳal[2], 450; *Ḥudūd al-ʿālam*, 111, 345-7; Muḳaddasī, 296-7, 303-4; Thaʿālibī, *Laṭāʾif al-maʿārif*, ed. de Jong, 122-3; Yāḳūt, ii, 904-5, iii, 798; Ḳazwīnī, *Āthār al-bilād*, Beirut 1380/1960, 428-9; Ibn Baṭṭūṭa, iii, 88-9; Ḥamd Allāh Mustawfī, *Nuzha*, 146-7; *Bābur-nāma*, tr. Beveridge, 217-9; Le Strange, 348-9; G. T. Vigne, *A personal narrative of a visit to Ghuzni, Kabul and Afghanistan*, London 1840; C. Masson, *Narrative of various journeys in Balochistan, Afghanistan and the Punjab*, London 1842; J. Humlum *et al.*, *La géographie de l'Afghanistan, étude d'un pays aride*, Copenhagen 1959, 117-8, 139-40.

3. Archaeological, architectural, epigraphy, numismatics. E. Thomas, in *JRAS*, 1848, 1860; Lane-Poole, *Cat.*, i; S. Flury, *Das Schriftband an der Türe des Maḥmūd von Ghazna 998-1030*, in *Isl.*, viii (1918), 214-27; idem, *Le décor épigraphique des monuments de Ghazna*, in *Syria*, vi (1925), 61-90; A. Godard, *Ghazni*, in *ibid.*, 58-60; D. Sourdel, *Inventaire des monnaies musulmanes anciennes du Musée de Caboul*, Damascus 1953; J. Sourdel-Thomine, *Deux minarets d'époque seljoukide en Afghanistan*, in *Syria*, xxx (1953), 108-21; A. Bombaci and U. Scerrato, *Summary report on the Italian Archaeological Mission in Afghanistan*, in *East and West*, N.S. x (1959), 3-55; Bombaci, *Ghaznavidi*, in *Enciclopedia Universale dell' Arte*, Venice-Rome, vi, 6-15 (this author is also preparing a study of the ʿArūs al-Falak Mosque at Ghazna); Scerrato, *Islamic glazed tiles with moulded decoration from Ghazni*, in *East and West*, N.S. xiii (1962), 263-87.

(C. E. Bosworth)

GHAZNAWIDS is the name given to the dynasty of Turkish origin which was founded by Sebüktigin, a General and Governor of the Sāmānids [*q.v.*]. With Ghazna [*q.v.*] for long its capital, the dynasty lasted for more than 200 years, from 367/977-8 to 583/1187, in eastern Īrān and what is now Afghānistān, and finally only in parts of the Pandjāb (with Lahāwur/Lahore as centre). For a long time its rulers held the official title of Amīr, although historians call them Sulṭān from the start; on coins, Ibrāhīm (no. XII below) was the first to bear this title.

From the time when Alptigin established himself in the region of Ghazna in 344/955-6 and made himself to a great extent independent of the Sāmānids, the area surrounding this town remained in the hands of Turkish rulers (for details see GHAZNA). In 367/977-8 (I) Sebüktigin gained power, and continued to rule until his death in 387/997. The new ruler, on the evidence of his coinage, acknowledged the overlordship of the Sāmānids, and gave them help against the Sīmdjūrids [*q.v.*] in 992 and 995. He also turned his attention to the Hindū Empires in the Pandjāb [*q.v.*] and in particular the Shāhū dynasty, whose head, Djaypāl, he defeated in 979 and 988, thereby acquiring the fortresses on the Indian frontier. His empire furthermore included northern Balūčistān, Ghūr, Zābulistān and Bactria (Tukhāristān) (on the subject of these and all further geographical references in this article see the entries under individual words). In this way, Sebüktigin, an extraordinarily powerful and ambitious ruler, and a convinced Sunnī, laid the foundations of one of the most lasting empires in the Indo-Afghān border regions.

On this foundation, Sebüktigin's son (III) Maḥmūd, who after quarrelling at one time with his father had become reconciled with him towards the end of the latter's life, was able to embark upon the conquest of the Pandjāb. By so doing, he created for Islam an extensive territory in India, and laid the foundation for the religious division of this area, the latest effect of which has been the creation of the independent state of Pākistān. Maḥmūd swiftly superseded his brother (II) Ismāʿīl, who had been designated by his father as his successor, and by 389/999 had finally made himself secure. There is no doubt that he is the most important ruler of the dynasty. Culturally already strongly inclined towards Īrān and receptive to the developing new Persian literature, he perseveringly encouraged Firdawsī [*q.v.*], although he did not fulfil the exaggerated demands made by the latter since he could not overlook the expenses for his task of spreading Islam in India. Politically Maḥmūd was in a fortunate position, since on his ascending the throne the Sāmānids had lost their influence and he was able to come to an agreement with the victorious Ḳarakhānids [*q.v.*], which in essence laid down that the Oxus should be the frontier between the two kingdoms. A convinced Sunnī like his father, Maḥmūd exchanged the ties which Sebüktigin had had with the Sāmānids for an allegiance to the ʿAbbāsid Caliph al-Ḳādir [*q.v.*], an allegiance which remained purely nominal, since at that time distant Baghdād could not exert any influence so far east, and the Caliphs were in any case dominated by the Shīʿī Būyids [*q.v.*]. The latter had passed the zenith of their power and were several times the target of attacks by Maḥmūd, who thereby also rendered a service to the Caliph. At the same time as his 17 campaigns in the Pandjāb, Maḥmūd was able to push the Būyids back a considerable distance and exert his influence in Khwārizm [*q.v.*]. On his death (23 Rabīʿ II 421/30 April 1030), his empire comprised the Pandjāb and parts of Sind (plus a series of Hindū states in the valley of the Ganges which acknowledged his overlordship), northern Balūčistān (around Ḳuṣdār), Afghānistān including Ghazna, as well as Gharčistān and Ghūr (where native potentates had submitted to his overlordship), Sīstān, Khurāsān, and Persia generally as far as Djibāl (Media); and finally Tukharistān and some border areas on the Oxus (for all details see MAḤMŪD B. SEBÜKTIGIN).

After Maḥmūd's death his son (IV) Muḥammad at first succeeded him, but was immediately opposed by his brother Masʿūd, who, having been his father's victorious general (governor of Iṣfahān and Rayy), was favoured by the army. An army despatched against him by Muḥammad deserted to him, in Herāt; Muḥammad was blinded and taken captive.

(V) Masʿūd I, a bold warrior, addicted, it is true, to drink, and lacking the diplomatic capabilities of his father, continued Maḥmūd's campaigns in India, and attempted to drive the Būyids further back; but he was able to gain possession of Kirmān [*q.v.*] only for a short time (424/1035). From a military standpoint his position was considerably less favourable than that of his father, who had had no opponent of his own calibre in Persia. Now, however, just at the time when Masʿūd came to the throne, the Saldjūḳs [*q.v.*] began to cross the Oxus and little by little to occupy Khurāsān. Masʿūd's resistance had little success; considerable parts of his army were engaged in the Pandjāb, and his forces were made up of very diverse elements: Iranians of various races, and also Indians; his own fellow Turks were only sparsely represented. On 8 Ramaḍān 431/23 May 1040, on the steppes of Dandān(a)ḳān, Masʿūd was decisively defeated by the Saldjūḳs under Toghrïl [*q.v.*], a defeat which cost him his Persian possessions (cf. B. N. Zakhoder, *Dendanekan* (in Turkish), in *Belleten*, xviii/72 (1954), 581-7). On a march to India Masʿūd was overthrown by a conspiracy and murdered forthwith in prison (433/1041). (For details see MASʿUD B. MAḤMUD).

An attempt to restore the blinded (IV) Muḥammad to the throne was foiled by the swift advance of Masʿūd's son (VI) Mawdūd, who pressed forward to Kābul from Balkh (where his father had left him as commander against the Saldjūḳs). He defeated Muḥammad in 434/1042 at the battle of Nagrahār, and killed him. In other ways too Mawdūd took bloody revenge on the murderers of his father. His brother Madjdūd, who also put forward claims, died even before a battle could be joined, probably of poison. Mawdūd's attempts to halt the advances of the Saldjūḳs into Persia continued fruitlessly for years. In 436-7/1044-6 they advanced beyond Bust into the countryside around Zamīndāwar and threatened Ghazna. Here general Bāsī-tigin was able to repulse them and thereby save the home territory of the Ghaznavids; it was also possible to divide the rebellious Ghūr and force them once more into submission to Mawdūd. In a similar way it was possible on the whole to maintain the power of the dynasty in India, even though some areas were temporarily lost and even Lahāwur was threatened for a time. Mawdūd was about to set forth himself on a campaign against the Saldjūḳs to attempt the recovery of Sīstān, when he died in Ghazna on 20 Radjab 440/18 December 1048 after a short illness.

Apart from Persia, now finally lost, Mawdūd had been able to preserve the kernel of his dynasty's territory, but the bloody quarrels which broke out after his death between several claimants to the throne seriously weakened the Ghaznavid position. Through the machinations of generals and viziers who wished to consolidate their own power, the 6-year-old (VII) Masʿūd II (really Muḥammad), Mawdūd's son, succeeded to the throne, followed on 1 Shaʿbān 440/9 Jan. 1049 by Mawdūd's brother (VIII) ʿAlī b. Masʿūd I and on his overthrow, in

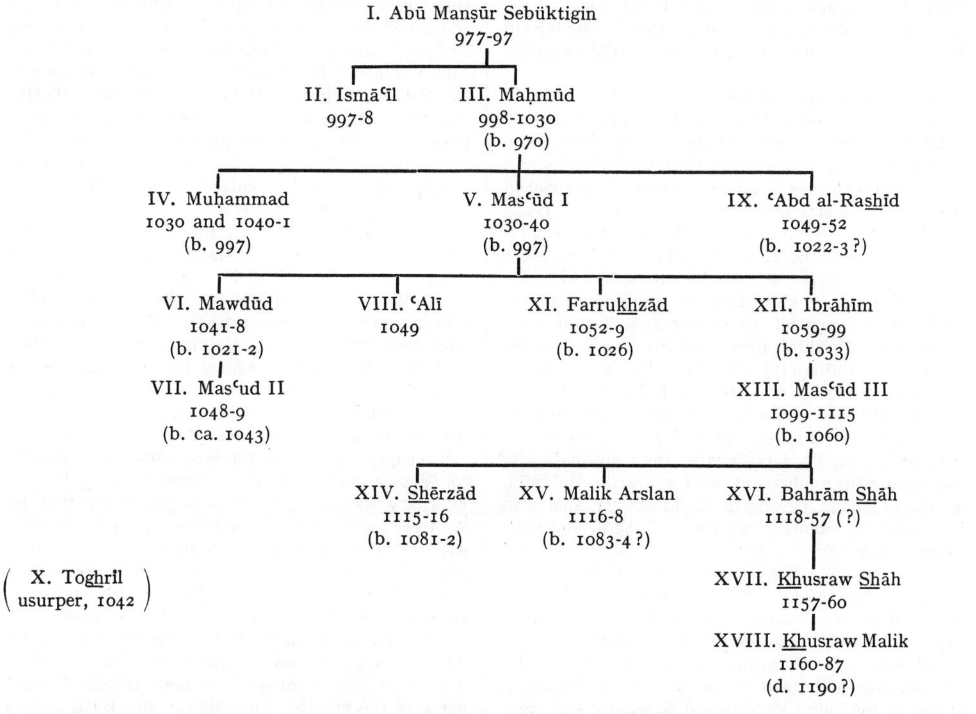

The numbers in this table correspond with those given in the text of the article

May 1049, by (IX) ʿAbd al-Rashīd b. Maḥmūd. Although this ruler lived in peace with his neighbours, he did not succeed in restoring internal stability. The dignitaries took exception to his relations with a certain slave, Tümen, who was forcibly removed as soon as ʿAbd al-Rashīd himself was murdered on 10 Shawwāl 443/14 February 1052. The murderer, a former slave of Masʿūd I and now Commandant of Zarandj, (X) Toghrïl, disposed of other members of the royal house and himself attempted to seize supreme power, but was murdered by followers of the dynasty on 17 Dhu 'l-Kaʿda 443/ 21 March 1052.

With (XI) Farrukhzād b. Masʿūd I the hereditary ruling family returned to the throne. With the help of General Nūsh-tigin, who had already served ʿAbd al-Rashīd loyally, the new ruler was able to repel the Saldjūḳs, who in the meantime were making further advances on Baghdād and Anatolia, when they attacked his central territories; on the other hand, Makrān was lost to them. Farrukhzād died at the early age of 34, in Ṣafar 451/March 1059 apparently of cholera.

His brother and successor (XII) Ibrāhīm b. Masʿūd I, signed a treaty of friendship with the Saldjūḳs, being obliged to cede to them Khuttalān, Čaghāniyān and Ḳubādiyān. Marriage alliances and later rich presents sealed the settlement thus reached with their long-standing main opponents in the West, who for their part promised to abandon their expansionist policy in the East. In other ways too, the new ruler proved himself an able diplomat and a cautious politician, avoiding dangerous undertakings, but essentially capable of preserving and defending his possessions. Ibrāhīm thus had his hands free for exploits in India (465-8/1072-6). He succeeded in capturing a number of fortresses and in re-establishing the influence of the Ghaznavids in the Pandjāb. Thenceforward Ibrāhīm called himself 'Sulṭān' on his coinage. Finally he delegated the continuation of the campaigns to his son Sayf al-Dawla Maḥmūd, whom he made Governor of Lahāwur, and who succeeded immediately in capturing Agra, and later other strongholds. When he attempted to seize power from his father, he was thrown into prison with his friends (481/1088). Ibrāhīm died on 5 Shawwāl 492/25 August 1099, after a reign of 40 years, the longest recorded in this dynasty.

His son and successor, (XIII) Masʿūd III, immediately embarked on an attack on Kanawdj, whose Hindū rulers were forced to submit and were brought to Ghazna in chains; a later attempted revolt in the town was suppressed. Otherwise, Masʿūd III kept up the ties of friendship and marriage with the Saldjūḳs and had a peaceful reign, until his death, at the age of 56, in Shawwāl 508/February-March 1115.

As had happened two generations earlier, the death of Masʿud III meant the outbreak of fratricidal war. Three of his sons took their turn as head of state. (XIV) Shērzād was forced after one year (Shawwāl 509/Feb.-March 1116) to flee to Ṭabaristān before his brother (XV) Malik Arslan, and early in 510/middle of 1116 he fell in an attempt to regain control of Ghazna. But Malik Arslan's days were also numbered. Another brother, who had escaped his sword, (XVI) Bahrām Shāh, won the help of Sandjar [*q.v.*], and was able to march into Ghazna in his train on 12 Shawwāl 511/6 February 1118 after two successful battles; Malik Arslan had fled to India.

Bahrām Shāh had to acknowledge the suzerainty of the Saldjūḳs and pay them high tribute; as a guarantee of this one of their tax controllers remained in Ghazna when Sandjar vacated the town after 40 days, taking with him the State Treasure. Although these conditions were onerous, they also guaranteed Bahrām Shāh Sandjar's solid support. It was only with Saldjūḳ help that he could fend off an attack by Malik Arslan from India; his brother fell into his hands and was executed in Djumādā II 512/September-October 1118. Bahrām Shāh then established his authority in the Pandjāb in three campaigns (Ramaḍān 512/January 1119, Djumādā II-Shawwāl 514/end of 1120, and 523/1129). Otherwise the first decade and a half of his reign appear to have passed peacefully; at any rate no records of battles have survived. In 1135-6 Bahrām Shāh tried in vain to rid himself of Sandjar's overlordship together with the crushing tribute, of 1000 *dīnār*s per day (so at least according to the sources!). Nevertheless, in spite of his defeat by Sandjar, Bahrām Shāh was confirmed in his hereditary territories just as was the Khwārizm Shāh Atsïz [*q.v.*] after his rebellions. Like the latter, Bahrām Shāh now remained loyal to the Saldjūḳ Sultan, although he fell out with the rulers of Ghūr, and had one of them—his son-in-law—poisoned whilst visiting Ghazna. A brother of this man, after losing a battle (2 Muḥarram 544/12 March 1149), was publicly hanged on Bahrām Shāh's orders, with many of his advisers. Both these acts were revenged in the most terrible way by a third brother, ʿAlāʾ al-Dīn Ḥusayn, in an attack on Ghazna towards the end of 1150. The complete destruction of the capital and the utterly ruthless murder, rape and deportation of the inhabitants—who were certainly not responsible for the conduct of their ruler—rightly gained for this monster the name of Djahānsūz (Burner of the World), by which he is known to history. Bahrām Shāh had meanwhile fled to India; thence, when ʿAlāʾ al-Dīn had been taken captive by the Saldjūḳs, he apparently returned to Ghazna and died, it is thought, early in 552/ February-March 1157. There is no doubt that by his treacherous murders and the personal cowardice with which he deserted his subjects in a moment of crisis Bahrām Shāh contributed, in a completely personal way, to the distintegration of his ancestors' empire, which now could no longer be checked.

The rule of Bahrām Shāh's second son (XVII) Khusraw Shāh, was restricted to Ghazna, Zābulistān and Kābul—apart from the Pandjāb. Further parts of the empire, Zamīndāwar and Bust, had in the meantime been taken over by the Ghūrids [*q.v.*]; Tiginābād also fell into their hands after a clash with Khusraw Shāh in the middle of 552/summer of 1157. As Sandjar died just at this time, Khusraw Shāh lost his only helper against his ever more powerful enemies in Ghūr. By Radjab 555/July 1160 he was dead.

His son and heir (XVIII) Khusraw Malik, saw his possessions dwindle bit by bit, until the empire of the Ghaznavids ceased to exist. Already at the beginning of 558/1163 he lost Ghazna and all his Afghān lands to the Oghuz ([*q.v.*] see also GHUZZ) to whom Eastern Persia too was exposed after the death of Sandjar. It was not long before the Ghūrids seized power here also; a member of their ruling house, Shihāb al-Dīn, was put in charge of these territories, and used them, as Maḥmūd had done before him, as a jumping-off ground for an advance on the Pandjāb, where Khusraw Malik still retained Lahāwur (his capital), Pēshāwar, Multān and Sind. On the pretext that he was obliged to take action against the

native Ḳarmaṭīs, S̲h̲ihāb al-Dīn took Multān in 571/
1175-6; in 575/1179-80 Pes̲h̲āwar fell into his hands.
Finally he forced K̲h̲usraw Malik in Lahāwur to pay
him tribute and give up his son, Malik S̲h̲āh, as
hostage. Even so it was no easy task for the G̲h̲ūrid
prince to dispose of G̲h̲aznavid rule completely, for
the Indian tribe of the K̲h̲ok̲h̲ars was collaborating
with K̲h̲usraw Malik. Only after Lahāwur had been
besieged several times was K̲h̲usraw Malik forced by
hunger to yield, in Djumādā I and II 583/July-
August 1187. After some delay he was sent to
G̲h̲ūristān, and imprisoned in a castle in G̲h̲arčistān.
There he was put to death with his sons, probably at
the end of 585/beginning of 1190, when the G̲h̲ūrids
found themselves threatened by the K̲h̲ʷārizm S̲h̲āhs.

"Thus Sebüktigin's house came to an end, and
nothing was left of these mighty rulers but the
historical memory" (Mīrk̲h̲ōnd, Bombay (lithograph) 1849-50, 135), almost at the same time,
incidentally, as the last Saldjūḳs also disappeared
from history before the advance of another new
dynasty, the K̲h̲ʷārizm S̲h̲āhs.

In contrast to the Sāmānids and the Saldjūḳs, the
cultural significance of the G̲h̲aznavids after
Maḥmūd's death was slight. As far as can be seen,
the dynasty assimilated Persian influence in the
realms of language and culture as quickly as did
other Turkish ruling houses. But, leaving Firdawsī
aside, they were not privileged to have a really
important poet at their court. On the other hand,
we are indebted to one of their leading officials,
Bayhaḳī [q.v.], for a uniquely detailed picture of
early Islamic-Iranian history; for the period of
Sultan Masʿūd I, it is also a mine of information on
cultural and diplomatic matters and the technique
of government.

The life of the court, with its receptions and
parties, and the form of government were in accordance with the customs of other Sunnī empires on
Persian territory at this time. It is however worth
noting that the principal ministers rarely changed,
and therefore must on the whole have worked in
harmony with their rulers.

Accession to the throne took place with the
customary ceremonial, especially when the succession
was peacefully established. The rulers counted
among their principal duties a reverent attitude to
the Caliphs, and the protection and dissemination
of the Sunna—in opposition to the Hindus as well
as the S̲h̲īʿīs and the Ḳarmaṭīs in Multān. The
fact that at the same time execution and torture
were allowed in the repression of revolts or the
"punishment" of defeated enemies was in accordance
with the ideas of the time. The financial demands
made on their subjects certainly varied according to
what was required for waging war, paying tribute,
and possibly also supporting an extravagant court,
although it would appear that they did not exceed
the usual average elsewhere, just as the rulers of the
dynasty after Masʿūd I were average personalities.
Of the longer-lived members of the dynasty,
Bahrām S̲h̲āh can be considered the least conscientious and indeed also the least capable.

Bibliography: Sources: Besides Islamic
world-histories (such as Mīrk̲h̲ōnd, Firis̲h̲ta, etc.),
and numismatic catalogues (including Thomas,
in *JRAS*, 1848 and 1859), see especially ʿUtbī,
Bayhaḳī, Djūzdjānī; ʿAwfī, *Djawāmiʿ* and *Lubāb*;
Gardīzī, al-Rāwandī, Ibn al-At̲h̲īr, Ḥamd Allāh
Mustawfī Ḳazwīnī, *Taʾrīk̲h̲-i guzīda* (see these
articles and also Storey, i, index). Studies: M.

Nazim, *The life and times of Sultan Mahmud of
Ghazna*, Cambridge 1931, with map; B. Spuler,
Iran, 111-24; bibliographies to MAḤMŪD and
MASʿŪD; Y. A. Hashmi, *Political, cultural and
administrative History under the later Ghaznavids*,
Hamburg 1956 (thesis), map, bibliography; idem,
Society and religion under the Ghaznavids, in
Journal of the Pakistan Historical Society, vi/4
(Oct. 1958), 254-68 (both comparatively useful
works, the first to give a comprehensive critical
picture of the period after 1040); Gulam Mustafa
Khan, *A history of Bahrām S̲h̲āh of Ghaznin*, in
IC, xxiii (1949), 62-91, 199-235; Muhammad Abdul
Ghafur, *The G̲h̲ūrids* (thesis), Hamburg 1959; C. E.
Bosworth, *The Ghaznavids, their empire in Afgha-
nistān and eastern Iran (994-1040)*, Edinburgh
1963; idem, *The imperial policy of the early
Ghaznavids*, in *Islamic Studies*, i/3 (1962), 49-82;
idem, *Ghaznevid military organization*, in *Isl.*, xxxvi/
1-2 (1960), 37-77; Browne, ii, 90-164, 305 ff.; D.
Sourdel, *Inventaire des monnaies musulmans
anciennes du Musée de Caboul*, Damascus 1963,
xii-xvi, 26-81; C. E. Bosworth, *The titulature of
the early Ghaznavids*, in *Oriens*, xv (1962), 210-33;
idem, *Early sources for the history of the first four
Ghaznavid Sultans (977-1041)*, in *IQ*, vii/1-2 (1963),
3-22.   (B. SPULER)

ART AND MONUMENTS

Corresponding with the pre-eminence of the
G̲h̲aznawid dynasty there was, for about a century,
an efflorescence of architecture and craftsmanship
promoted by the tastes and opulence of those
powerful patrons, and with its geographical centres
in the eastern provinces of Iran, which for so long
were a meeting-point of Islamic and foreign artistic
currents. Quite certainly, this flowering sprang
directly from the earlier experiences of the Sāmānid
centres in K̲h̲urāsān or Transoxania and, in its last
phase, it intermingles with the development of the
art commonly denoted by the name Saldjūḳid, which
was destined to achieve a renown that reached far
beyond the limits of the empire of the Great Saldjūḳs.
But the style developed within the G̲h̲aznawid
territories, from the reign of Maḥmūd b. Sebüktigin
and under his immediate successors, took an equally
significant part in innovation, thus allowing us to
emphasize its importance as well as the exemplary
character, for the later evolution of Islamic art, of
the works of art then executed in the residences,
distant though they were, of G̲h̲azna, Bust, Balk̲h̲,
Harāt or Nīs̲h̲āpūr.

Too often, we have to deplore the ruin and
disappearance in the centuries that followed, of
these monumental works, as well as of their furnishings. The sites of the ancient G̲h̲aznawid capitals are
today deserted, and the chroniclers' accounts can
restore nothing to us save the astonishment of
contemporaries at the ornateness of their edifices,
the brilliance of the official ceremonies that were
performed in them and the collection of objects of
value which the conquest of India had made it
possible to bring together. This is the point that
emerges for example from the unfruitful attempt
made earlier by A. U. Pope to evoke G̲h̲aznawid
art by starting from the imprecise facts contained
in the literary sources (cf. *A survey of Persian
Art*, ii, 975-80).

On the other hand, the various archaeological
remains which have survived to our own time,
our knowledge of which has been considerably
increased within recent years, provide an insight,

stimulating in itself, into the art that flourished under the aegis of the Ghaznawids, and it is to be deplored that they have not yet given rise to any general work, pending the coming of the new discoveries which will perhaps one day complete the instruction they have imparted.

In these remains, traces of imposing edifices can be found, from the minarets at Ghazna to the castles in the "royal town" of Bust [*q.v.*], all situated within modern Afghanistan, to which no doubt should be added the half-ruined remains of the so-called mausoleum of Arslān Djādhib at Sangbast, of which we have only a description made some time ago (cf. E. Diez, *Churasanische Baudenkmäler*, Berlin 1918, 52-5).

The minarets had long been known in the field of ruins at Ghazna, where their prism-shaped brick plinths still stand, entirely covered with decorations and inscriptions; but only recently have both been attributed to Ghaznawid sovereigns of the last period, Masʿūd III (d. 508/1114) and Bahrām Shāh (d. 547/1152), after having formerly been incorrectly described, on the strength of ancient travellers, as "victory towers" of the conqueror of India and his son Masʿūd I. Their archaeological significance has thereby been slightly modified, particularly in regard to the date of the appearance in Ghazna of these brick decorations, obtained by the simple use of variety in the bonding, which adorn the silhouette of the last minaret, so long regarded as being a century older.

The ruins of Lashkari Bāzār, on the other hand, on the site of Maḥmūd's "camp" in the suburbs of Bust, which also became a favourite residence of Masʿūd I, constitute an architectural ensemble, the great extent of which has only just been revealed by excavations conducted by the French Archaeological Mission in Afghanistan—and still incompletely, since as yet only a preliminary report has been published. Three palaces built in a line along the bank of the Hilmand, formerly surrounded with enclosures and gardens, as is shown by their high outer walls, testify to the vigour of an architectural tradition directly related to the customary methods of construction in use in palaces of the Caliphs in ʿAbbāsid ʿIrāḳ. But the details of their plans, in which traces of successive alterations do not fail to raise delicate problems of date and attribution, also deserve attention, starting with the cruciform lay-out of the *īwāns* round the central courtyard of the South castle, where we can see the application of a typically Khurāsānian formula and a clear statement of the welcome subsequently accorded in Iran to this kind of concentric composition. At the same time can be seen traces of a surface decoration worthy of comparison with the embellishment of walls in the buildings of Sāmarrā, yet showing true originality in the details of panels of sculptured stucco, both inscribed and anepigraphic, as also in the frescoes with figures which ornamented the walls of the principal audience chamber and which still depict the rows of guards who once surrounded the sovereign's throne. We should note also the existence of a large mosque, standing outside the South castle though opening onto its fore-court, and characterized by the classically Muslim form of its pillared hall of prayer. Moreover, the two rows of booths stretching for more than half a kilometre along the avenue which led to the royal residence and connected it with the neighbouring town of Bust reveal, in their general treatment, a feeling for town-planning that somewhat transcends the narrow limits of palatine architecture and its exclusive concern with the sumptuous.

A second category of archaeological remains is provided by the abundant series of fragments of architectural decoration and ornamental or funerary inscriptions, mainly on marble slabs, which come from the site of Ghazna; some were discovered forty years ago, others as the result of the excavations at present being carried out by an Italian expedition, concerning which our information is still very incomplete. These fragments are almost all remarkable for their fine decorative quality, combined with richness of materials, which together give the arabesques traced on them a supple elegance of line and modelling for which no exact equivalent in Muslim Iran is known. Probably we should recognize here, to some extent, the results of Indian and Central Asian influences, which can also be seen in the choice of certain motifs containing figures (especially persons, or animals such as elephants). But the basic principles of an ornamentation that is both divided into sections and also characterized by a restricted variety of floral stylizations thus remain faithful to the spirit of ʿAbbāsid art, which can also be discerned in the prominence given here to the epigraphic bands with angular or cursive writing. Among the most significant of the fragments, besides sections from the frieze, are the remains of stone *miḥrābs*, where the niche reveals a lobed profile, and tombs attributed to Sebüktigin and Maḥmūd.

Finally, in the third category are the various products of luxury crafts, of which interesting specimens have been preserved, though without attracting any but the most spasmodic attention, except for ceramics. Here, in fact, the discoveries at Lashkari Bāzār, enriched by the results of digging on the actual site of the town of Bust, have been subjected to a methodical analysis; there is a sufficient range of material for comparison to provide significant fixed points for the hitherto highly confused chronology of certain main categories of Muslim ceramics. The significant features of Ghaznawid pottery, glazed and unglazed, are in any case now precisely defined in its two principal stages, firstly in the 5th/11th century in its relation with Sāmānid pottery, which provided it with its first models, and later at the end of that century and the beginning of the 6th/12th century in relation to Persian Saldjūḳid ceramics, from which it then began to draw inspiration.

One could wish that the Ghaznawid bronze objects, which for the most part are in the museum at Kābul, might be studied in the same way. As for the carved woodwork, of which the doors of Maḥmūd's tomb provide the most famous illustration, it occupied in the art of the period a place which some have already underlined, but which has not yet been defined with the requisite precision or based upon sufficiently detailed analyses.

Bibliography: E. Diez, *Persien. Islamische Baukunst in Churasan*, Gotha 1923; O. von Niedermayer and E. Diez, *Afghanistan*, Leipzig 1924; A. U. Pope, *A Survey of Persian Art*, Oxford 1939, 981 ff. (architecture), 1352-6 (carved stone), 2609-12 (wood); S. Flury, *Das Schriftband an der Türe des Mahmūd von Ghazna*, in *Isl.*, viii (1918), 214-27; idem, *Le décor épigraphique des monuments de Ghazna*, in *Syria*, vi (1925), 61-90; Y. A. Godard, *L'inscription du minaret de Masʿūd III*, in *Āthār-e Īrān*, i, 367-9 and ii, 351; J. Sourdel-Thomine, *Deux minarets d'époque seljoukide en Afghanistan*, in *Syria*, xxx (1953),

108-36; D. Schlumberger, *Le palais ghaznevide de Lashkari Bazar*, in *Syria*, xxix (1952), 251-70; J. Sourdel-Thomine, *Les décors de stuc dans l'est iranien à l'époque salǧuqide*, in *Akten des XXIVen Or. Kongr.*, Wiesbaden 1959, 342-4; D. Schlumberger, etc., *Lashkari Bazar I. Les édifices* (forthcoming); A. Bombaci, *Summary report on the Italian Archaeological Mission in Afghanistan*, i, in *East and West*, x (1959), 3-22; U. Scerrato, *Summary report*, ii, in *East and West*, x (1959), 23-55; J. C. Gardin, *Lashkari Bazar II, Les trouvailles*, Paris 1963. (J. Sourdel-Thomine)

GHAZW (A.), expedition, usually of limited scope, conducted with the aim of gaining plunder. The noun of unity *ghazwa* (pl. *ghazawāt*) is used particularly of the Prophet's expeditions against the infidels [see maghāzī], but has also special meanings (for which see Dozy, *Suppl.*, s.v.).

In its most common sense, *ghazw* (and the dialectical variants) signifies a raid or incursion, a small expedition set on foot by Bedouins (both in the Sahara and in northern Arabia) with booty as its object, and also the force which carries it out. The term has passed into French in the form *rezzou*, which preserves the original meaning of *ghazw*, whilst it is the synonym *ghāziya* (pl. *ghawāzī*) which has given the English word *razzia*, current also in French (where, however, with the verb *razzier*, it tends to have a pejorative implication). In the Berber dialect of the Touareg of the Ahaggar, *tamagh layt* means a *ghazw* of a few men (see Ch. de Foucauld, *Dict. touareg-français*, Paris 1951-2, iv, 1726) and *igən* a group of more than 15-20 men (*op. cit.*, i, 456), the verb *ədəg* (*op. cit.*, i, 263) corresponding exactly to the Arabic *ghazā*.

The *ghazw* (colloquial *ghazu*, pl. *ghizwān*) was one of the oldest institutions of the camel-breeding tribes of Northern Arabia and continued, unmoderated by Islam, well into the present century. Unlike the other warlike activities of the Bedouin, namely war for territory (*manākh*) and punitive raids of retaliation (*tha'r*/coll. *thār*), its primary concern was the acquisition of camels. In practice it operated as a fairly effective means of redistributing economic resources in a region where the balance could easily be upset by natural calamities (Sweet, *Camel raiding*).

The *ghazu*, therefore, minimized the effect of localized drought or disaster on the breeding of properly balanced camel herds, the only form of wealth which could give economic security in this society. Since the acquisition of camels was the aim of a *ghazu*, very little blood was ordinarily shed during the course of it, mercy (*manʿ*) being freely granted. Indeed the whole course of a *ghazu* was governed by elaborate protocol.

A raid on a tribal section was usually initiated by a series of petty thefts of camels, disturbing the existing state of truce. These were often carried out by small parties on foot (*ḥanshal*, sing. *ḥanshūlī*: Hess, *Beduinen*, 96). When these thefts had become of sufficient gravity, and presumably the tolerance with which they were viewed varied according to the condition of the herds of the tribal section concerned, the truce was formally severed and mutual raiding could then be expected to ensue (Musil, *Rwala*, 505-6; Dickson, *The Arab of the Desert*, 343). The person chosen to lead a raid (*ʿaḳīd*, colloquial *ʿadzīd*, *ʿagīd*) was usually the *shaykh* of the section, unless incapacitated by weakness or age, or a member of his family. The *ʿadzīd* gathered his force (*ḳawm*, colloquial *gōm*), for a small raid mounted on perhaps 20-30 camels (*djaysh*/*djēsh*), or on camels and horses if the section to be raided was not far distant. The objective was kept secret from all but a few until the moment of departure, which would be postponed if necessary till the omens were favourable. Scouts (*ʿuyūn*) were then sent out to reconnoitre the ground over which the raiding party would pass. When these reported that the objective was nearby, an advance-party (*sabr*, pl. *subūr*) made a final estimate of the position and brought back a report (*ʿilm*, pl. *ʿulūm*) and if possible a prisoner. The attack itself, provided the raiders were genealogically and socially close to the section to be raided, was made at sunrise (*ṣabāḥ*) or sunset, or at such times in between as the herds were not scattered (cf. Hess, *Beduinen*, 98). A night-attack (*bayāt*), though it would succeed most easily, was considered dishonourable (*ʿayb*, colloquial *ʿēb*).

The captured herds were driven back to the *ʿadzīd*, and the raiders divided into a rear-guard (*kamīn*/*tsamīn*), to ward off the inevitable counter-attack (*fazʿa*), and a party which drove the captured camels to the raiders' last camp, and then as fast as possible to their home-camp.

Although the community attacked was seldom taken by surprise and counter attacks were often effective (Musil, *Arabia Deserta*, 181), most raids would seem to have been successful.

When the raiders came from further afield the raiding party was likely to be larger, and the concern with protocol and the desire to avoid bloodshed would then appear to have been less, since in these circumstances genealogical ties were more likely to be remote (Doughty, *Travels*, ii, 393). In general the more closely related were the parties involved, the more stringent were the rules governing the actual raid.

In its heyday the institution of the raid permeated the whole of Bedouin society, its social and economic life, and its folk literature. It reinforced the fissiparous and predatory nature of tribal society, and for long prevented the emergence of any political organization more complex than short-lived confederations. However, the rise of a strong central power in Arabia under Ibn Saʿūd marked the end of the traditional mode of life based on the *ghazu*. More recently the rise of the oil industry has further hastened the decline of traditional society by accelerating the trend towards the de-tribalization of the Bedouin and their re-grouping along modern industrial lines.

Bibliography: A. Blunt, *Bedouin tribes of the Euphrates*, 2 vols., London 1879; J. L. Burckhardt, *Notes on the Bedouins and Wahabys*, London 1830; H. P. R. Dickson, *The Arab of the Desert*, London 1949; Doughty, *Travels in Arabia Deserta*; J. Euting, *Tagbuch einer Reise in Inner-Arabien*, 2 vols., Leyden 1896 and 1914; C. Guarmani, *Northern Najd*, London 1938; J. J. Hess, *Von den Beduinen des innern Arabiens*, Zürich/Leipzig 1938; R. Montagne, *La civilisation du désert*, Paris 1947; V. Müller, *En Syrie avec les Bédouins*, Paris 1931; A. Musil, *The Northern Ḥeǧâz*, New York 1926; idem, *The manners and customs of the Rwala Bedouins*, New York 1928; idem, *Arabia Deserta*, New York 1927; W. G. Palgrave, *Narrative of a year's journey through Central and Eastern Arabia (1862-63)*, 2 vols., 1865; L. E. Sweet, *Camel Raiding of North Arabian Bedouin* (monograph awaiting publication); J. R. Wellsted, *Travels in Arabia*, 2 vols., London 1838. See also R. Montagne, *Le Ghazou de Šâyè' Alemsâḥ*, in *Mélanges Maspéro*, iii, Cairo 1935-40, 411-416 and

Contes poëtiques bedouins, in *BEO*, v (1935), 33-119. See further GHĀZĪ (as frontier-warriors).

(T. M. JOHNSTONE)

GHAZZA, a town in southern Palestine which from ancient times had been an agricultural and caravan centre, situated 4 km. from the sea, on the route leading from Palestine to Syria and at the junction of the caravan-routes coming from Arabia. A frontier-town which often changed hands through the course of the centuries, the ancient *ʿAzza*, which had been one of the capitals of the Philistines, later became, under the Greek name *Gaza*, a flourishing Hellenistic city, and afterwards a Roman town belonging to Judaea. In the Byzantine period it formed part of Palestina Prima and was christianized in the 5th century; the seat of a bishopric, it was also renowned for its school of rhetoric and, at the beginning of the 7th century, it was described as a rich city where foreigners were welcomed. Merchants from Mecca visited it regularly, and it was in the course of one of these journeys that the Prophet's great-grandfather Hāshim is said to have died there, so conferring a particular dignity upon Ghazza, "the town of Hāshim". According to tradition, it was also there that ʿUmar b. al-Khaṭṭāb acquired his fortune. Finally, it was in the immediate vicinity of Ghazza, in a place sometimes called Dāthin, sometimes Tādūn, that the Patricius of Ghazza was defeated by Arab troops sent by the first caliph Abū Bakr; but according to the most trustworthy accounts, the town itself was conquered by ʿAmr b. al-ʿĀṣ; although the inhabitants were well treated, the soldiers of the garrison were massacred and henceforth regarded in the Christian world as martyrs.

Between the 1st/7th and 3rd/9th centuries, the town of Ghazza is rarely mentioned in the texts. We know only that at the end of the 2nd/8th century the town had to endure the conflicts between the Arab tribes that had settled in Syria and Palestine, and that in 150/767 the great jurisconsult al-Shāfiʿī was born there. In the 4th/10th century, the period when it came beneath the domination of the Fāṭimids, the geographers described it as an important town possessing a beautiful Great Mosque; extending to the edge of the desert and to within a mile of the sea, it was surrounded by vast orchards and vineyards; its port was Mīmās, the ancient Maioumas mentioned as early as the 3rd century B.C., the site of which corresponds with the modern al-Mīna.

The town of Ghazza was afterwards occupied by the Crusaders, who found it in ruins. They started to rebuild it in 544/1149, and the new citadel was given to the Templars by king Baldwin III of Jerusalem, while around it there began to grow up an unprotected lower town inhabited by peasants and merchants. This stronghold helped the Crusaders in their capture of ʿAskalān [*q.v.*], which took place in 548/1153. Some years later the town was assaulted by Ṣalāḥ al-Din who, in 565/1170, sacked the lower town, though he was unable to capture the citadel. It was finally surrendered to this sovereign by the Grand Master of the Templars after the fall of Jerusalem. Recaptured by Richard Cœur de Lion, it became a stake in the negotiations which started between the Crusaders and the Muslims, and was then restored to the latter under the terms of the treaty of 626/1229. Soon afterwards, in 636/1239 and 642/1244, it was the scene of two serious defeats for the Crusaders, and immediately before the Mongol invasion it was a source of rivalry between the Syrian Ayyūbids and the Egyptians, before being itself occupied by the armies of Hūlāgū, marking the furthest limit of their advance.

In the Mamlūk period, Ghazza became the chief town of a district that for the most part belonged to the province of Damascus, though at times it was independent. The town was then very rich and very extensive, if one is to believe the accounts of contemporary geographers and travellers, all of whom stress its economic prosperity, which derived partly from the richness of the surrounding district, abundantly irrigated by subterranean water, and partly from the energy of its merchants. Its most sought-after products were the grape and the fig, but the abundance of its *sūḳ*s was also a source of pride and, according to the Arab authors, it combined three types of social life represented by the merchants, farmers and stock-breeders. The population, belonging to various tribal groups, was very turbulent and always involved in strife. Ghazza eventually possessed numerous public buildings—mosques, *madrasa*s, convents, a hospital and caravanserais, some of which still survive. The chief mosque, built on the foundations of the Crusader church of St. John through the efforts of the governor al-Djāwlī at the beginning of the 8th/14th century, remained standing until the 1914-18 war.

The arrival of the Ottomans in 922/1516 brought suffering to Ghazza. The inhabitants, misled by a false report of a Mamlūk victory into thinking that they could massacre the new Turkish garrison, were the victims of severe reprisals and a certain number of them were executed. They seem, however, to have made a good recovery. The Ottoman *tapu* registers [see DAFTAR-I KHĀḲĀNĪ] show an increase in population in the city from under 1000 households in 932/1525-6 to well over 2000 in 955/1548-9; the survey of 963-4/1555-7 shows a slight decline. The population was predominantly Muslim, with Christian and Jewish minorities and a small group of Samaritans—18 households in 963-4. The registers also show a number of retired members of the former *djund al-ḥalḳa* as living in the city. Kurdish and Turcoman quarters are also shown. At the end of the 11th/17th century, in about 1070/1660, Ghazza enjoyed a period of particular prosperity, under the government of a family of pashas, the most celebrated of whom, Ḥusayn Pasha, succeeded in putting a stop to the periodic raids of the Bedouins, while he maintained good relations with the Christians and Europeans. As the Chevalier d'Arvieux put it, the town at that time acted as the capital of Palestine, and Arabic, Turkish and Greek were all spoken there. Among its principal buildings were six mosques, besides the Great Mosque, numerous baths and markets and two churches, one Armenian and the other Greek.

The 18th century, on the other hand, was characterized in Ghazza by various disturbances and by the turbulence of the Bedouins, whom the Ottoman authorities had some difficulty in subduing; it closed with Napoleon's victory in 1799 immediately outside the town. In the 19th century Ghazza shared the fate of Palestine, being for a time attached to Egypt and then made directly subject to Ottoman governors; at the end of the 1914-18 war, it formed part of Palestine under the British mandate.

The period of peace experienced by Ghazza at the end of the 19th and the beginning of the 20th century brought about a marked increase in its population, which rose from 16,000 inhabitants in 1882 to 40,000 in 1906 (of whom 750 were Christians and 160 Jews). By 1932, however, the population had declined to approximately 17,000, of whom a small minority were Orthodox Greeks, who maintained a church dating from the 12th century with the revered tomb of St. Porphyry, bishop of G̲h̲azza in the 5th century. The Muslims who, since the 1914-18 war, had gathered for prayer in a place near the site of the now destroyed Great Mosque, also venerated a sanctuary dedicated to Nabī Hās̲h̲im, which is found mentioned as early as the 6th/12th century. Despite the progressive disappearance of caravans, the town was for a long time to possess a flourishing market with abundant supplies of various commodities, while the costume and mode of life there were very close to those of Egypt. But its direct attachment to the latter country after the armistice of 1949 was to mark the decline of its commercial activity, though at the same time reaffirming its former strategic importance.

Bibliography: Pauly-Wissowa, s.v.; M. A. Meyer, *History of the city of Gaza*, New York 1907; F.-M. Abel, *Géographie de la Palestine*, ii, Paris 1938, 327-8, 374-5; Le Strange, *Palestine*, 441-3; A.-S. Marmardji, *Textes géographiques arabes sur la Palestine*, Paris 1951, 154-7; Balād̲h̲urī, *Futūḥ*, 108; Ṭabarī, i, 1083, 1091, 1561, 2396-8; Eutychius, *Annales*, ed. Cheikho, 1904, ii, 9; Yaʿḳūbī, *Buldān*, 329-30; Ibn Ḥawḳal, 113; Muḳaddasī, 155, 177; Idrīsī, in *ZDPV*, viii, 112; Harawī, *K. al-Ziyārāt*, Damascus 1952, 60; Ibn Baṭṭūṭa, i, 114 (trans. H. A. R. Gibb, i, Cambridge 1958, 73); E. N. Adler, *Jewish travellers*, London 1930, 179-85 (travels of Meshullam of Volterra, 1481 A.D.); M. Gaudefroy-Demombynes, *La Syrie à l'époque des Mamelouks*, Paris 1923, 50-5; Quatremère, *Sultans Mamlouks*, i/b, 228-35; R. Grousset, *Histoire des Croisades*, Paris 1934-36, index; L. A. Mayer, *Arabic inscriptions of Gaza*, in *Journal of the Palestine Oriental Society*, iii, 69-78, iv, 66-8, v, 64-8, ix, 219-25, x, 59-63, xi, 144-51; idem, in *Quarterly of the Department of the Antiquities of Palestine*, xi, 27-9; *RCEA*, nos. 940, 4659, 4898, 4942, 4979, 5047, 5339, 5400, 5587, 5606, 5636, 5686; for the inscriptions and monuments, see also the Max van Berchem collection (Geneva), carnet VII, 54-136 and envelope 24; B. Lewis, *Studies in the Ottoman archives—I*, in *BSOAS*, xvi (1954), 469 ff.; U. Heyd, *Ottoman documents on Palestine 1552-1615*, Oxford 1960, index; Baedeker, *Palestine et Syrie*, Leipzig 1893, 157; *Guide Bleu, Syrie Palestine*, Paris 1932, 622.   (D. SOURDEL)

AL-G̲H̲AZZĀLĪ [see AL-G̲H̲AZĀLĪ].

G̲H̲ĪBA [see PANDJĀB].

G̲H̲IDHĀʾ, (A., plur. *ag̲h̲d̲h̲iya*) indicates strictly in Arabic "that which ensures the growth and the good health of the body" (*Ḳāmūs*, s.v.), in other words feeding and food. We shall deal here only with the factors which determined the diet of the principal Muslim peoples in the classical period (though sometimes making modern comparisons), in particular with the laws of the Muslim religion concerning food. The descriptive section will be limited to the pre-Islamic period. The more particularly culinary aspects, *i.e.*, those concerning the preparation of special dishes, will be dealt with in the article ṬABK̲H̲. We have omitted for lack of space several aspects of the subject: the variations of food in the contemporary Muslim world, its place in social life (and in particular the question, often dealt with by Muslims, of the *ādāb al-akl*—rules of table manners), the estimated nutritional value in quality and in quantity of the food in the various Islamic countries, etc.

i. — FOOD OF THE PRE-ISLAMIC ARABS

The food of the inhabitants of the Arabian peninsula (apart from the agricultural and civilized states of the south) was—and in large measure still is today—typical of the diet of a pastoral people in a desert region with scattered cultivated oases. We can get an idea of this food from ancient poetry, the classical texts and the Ḳurʾān (the sources have been examined by G. Jacob, *Altarabisches Beduinenleben*, Berlin 1897, 88-109; M. ʿI. Darwaza, *ʿAṣr al-Nabī*, Damascus 1365/1946, 80-6; M. S̲h̲. Alūsī, *Bulūg̲h̲ al-arab fī maʿrifat aḥwāl al-ʿArab²*, i, Cairo 1343/1924, 380-5; M. Kurd ʿAlī, *Maʾākil al-ʿArab*, in *al-Muḳtabas*, iii (1908), 569-79). We have examined in addition the *ḥadīt̲h̲*s, the data of which are acceptable on this matter, since even forgers took great pains to add to the credibility of their work by the archaism of the customs to which they referred.

The essential product from the raising of domestic animals was milk (*laban* rather than *ḥalīb*), one of the two basic foods of the Arabs. The Ḳurʾān (XVI, 68/66) pays an eloquent tribute to this liquid, calling it "sweet to drinkers", and numerous traditions witness how greatly the Bedouin longed for it (*ʿayma*) when they were deprived of it (H. Lammens, *Études sur le siècle des Omayyades*, Beirut 1930, 325 = *MFOB*, iv (1910), 91 ff.). Mainly camel's milk was drunk, also that of goats and sheep. It could be drunk diluted with water, but sour milk (*ḥāzir*) was despised (G. Jacob, *Altarab. Beduinenleben*, Berlin 1897, 95). Milk-products from it were: *samn* "clarified butter" which was used for cooking and which disgusted the Romans of Aelius Gallus when they found it used instead of oil in the Ḥidjāz (Strabo, xvi, 4, 24; it is probably his βούτυρον); *aḳiṭ* "sour-milk cheese" (al-Buk̲h̲ārī, lxx, 8, 16; Abū Dāwūd, xxvi, 27; Imruʾ al-Ḳays, ed. Ahlwardt, *The divans*, London 1870, 162, no. 68, verse 5); *d̲j̲ubn*, cheese of an unknown sort (Abū Dāwūd, xxvi, 38). Camels were slaughtered only in cases of great necessity. In general it was rare for meat to be eaten, but this made it all the more appreciated (Aḥmad b. Ḥanbal, iii, 303, etc.). They seem to have eaten chiefly mutton, sometimes from sheep kept near the house and specially fattened for the table (*dādjin*) (Ibn Ḥanbal, iii, 303, etc.; al-Ṭabarī, i, 1523; cf. Ibn His̲h̲ām, 735), of which the Prophet preferred the shoulder and the fore-leg (al-Buk̲h̲ārī, lxx, 26, 58; Ibn Ḥanbal, vi, 392; cf. Ibn Saʿd, i/2, 108, 109; Abū Dāwūd, xxvi, 20; Ibn His̲h̲ām, 764). The Medinans were extremely fond of the fat from its fat tail (*alya*) and of that from the camel's hump, which they cut from the living animal, a practice which Muḥammad forbade (al-Dārimī, vii, 9; references in poetry *apud* G. Jacob, *Altar. Beduinenleben*, 94; the same practice in the eastern Sahara: W. Besnard, *Que mangent-ils?*, Paris 1947, 47 f.). Specially prized parts of the camel were the udder, the liver, the foetus, etc. but the stomach and the tail were the food of slaves (Jacob, *ibid.*). It seems that it was not only in time of famine that they ate blood drawn from the veins of a living camel and allowed to coagulate or put into pieces of gut and cooked (al-Maydānī, ii, 119; *Ḥamāsa*, 645; *Ag̲h̲ānī*, xvi, 107: 20; W. R. Smith, *Lectures on the religion of the Semites²*, 234). They ate very little beef (*ibid.*; Lammens, *Berceau de l'Islam*, Rome 1914, 132) or goat meat. Pigs and fowls (Jacob, *ibid.*, 84 f.) seem to have been scarcely known, although some *ḥadīt̲h̲*s relate that the Prophet ate the latter (al-Dārimī, viii, 22).

The agriculture of the oases provided mainly dates, another basic food of the Arabs (Lammens, *Berceau de l'Islam*, 82 f.; idem, *Fāṭima*, 44, n. 2). In the oases they were almost the only food. "When the Prophet died, we were nourished only by the two black things: dates and water" (saying attributed to ʿĀʾis̲h̲a: al-Buk̲h̲ārī, lxx, 6, 41; cf. Lammens, *Berceau*, 105, n. 3; for the inhabitants of the Fertile Crescent, on the other hand, the staple foods, even in the desert, were bread and water: *Genesis*, XXI, 14; *I Kings*, XVIII, 14). A scarcity of dates is the equivalent of famine (al-Dārimī, viii, 26; Abū Dāwūd, xxvi, 41; Muslim, xxxvi, 152, 153; cf. *Ag̲h̲ānī*, ii, 161). They liked to stress their therapeutic qualities and they formed the stock provisions when setting off on an expedition (Abū Dāwūd, xxvi, 46). They were eaten also at festivals, such as the *walīma* in honour of the marriage of Muḥammad with Ṣafiyya (al-Bukhārī, lxx, 8, 16; Abū Dāwūd, xxvi, 2). They were eaten dried (*tamr*), fresh (*ruṭab*)—when they were especially relished (Muḥammad was particularly fond of them eaten with cucumber, *ḳut̲h̲t̲h̲āʾ*, cf. Wensinck, *Index*, s.v.)—or when they were beginning to ripen (*busr*). A special variety called *ʿad̲j̲wa* was particularly sought after (especially those grown in the upper region of Medina) and considered as a sovereign remedy against poisons and sorcery (al-Buk̲h̲ārī, lxx, 48; Muslim, xxxvi, 155-6, etc.).

Bread may not have been such an aristocratic food as has been thought, for barley bread at least was not uncommon among the settled populations. All the same, the Prophet and his family never ate bread made from wheat flour three days running during the period between the Hid̲j̲ra and his death (al-Buk̲h̲ārī, lxx, 23, 27; the *ḥadīt̲h̲* of Abū Hurayra according to which the Prophet never ate barley bread is contradicted by several others). The only one of his wedding feasts at which Muḥammad offered his guests bread was that on the occasion of his marriage with Zaynab (Aḥmad b. Ḥanbal, iii, 172, cf. 99). The flour was not sifted—Muḥammad had never seen a sieve—but simply blown to separate it from any coarse residue of husks (Ibn Saʿd, i/2, 109; al-Buk̲h̲ārī, lxx, 22, 23). Among the nomads, however, bread was very rare (Ammianus, xiv, 4, 6; Lammens, *Berceau*, 141; Nöldeke, *Neue Beiträge zur sem. Sprachwiss.*, Strasbourg 1910, 56 f.). Strabo, following Aelius Gallus, speaks of a region of the Ḥid̲j̲āz where the only cereal is ζειά, perhaps a sort of soft wheat (xvi, 4, 24).

Bread was eaten with a "condiment" (*udm, idām*) which was moreover singularly meagre. Those who were able to season their bread with vinegar or oil were not considered as "living on dry bread" (root *ḳfr*) (Zayd b. ʿAlī, *Corpus iuris*, ed. Griffini, Milan 1919, no. 1011: read *yaḳtafiru*) and Muḥammad pronounced vinegar the best of condiments (cf. Wensinck, *Handbook*, s.v. Food; also Abū Dāwūd, xxvi, 39). We also hear of his being content with a date as flavouring for a loaf of barley bread (Abū Dāwūd, xxvi, 41). According to a *ḥadīt̲h̲* attributed to ʿAlī, the best accompaniment was meat, the worst salt and the middle place was given to *samn* or oil (Zayd b. ʿAlī, no. 450; cf. al-Buk̲h̲ārī, lxiv, 29). But it is possible that some at least of these *ḥadīt̲h̲*s were contaminated by later ascetic trends.

The settled agricultural populations were able to enjoy also some vegetables. Among the *buḳūl*, "herbs", the Prophet preferred *hindibāʾ*, "chicory". He was also fond of beets (*silḳ*; al-Buk̲h̲ārī, lxx, 17) and of some vegetables belonging to the gourd family which are difficult to identify exactly (*dubbāʾ* "a kind of marrow?", *ḳut̲h̲t̲h̲āʾ* "a kind of cucumber", *ḳarʿ* "marrow"). Leeks (*kurrāt̲h̲*) were forbidden, though not *ḥarām* (Ibn Ḥanbal, i, 15, iii, 397), and so were raw garlic and onions. But according to other traditions, Muḥammad merely expressed his personal dislike of them and forbade those who had recently eaten them to come to the place of prayer (references in Wensink, *Handbook*, s.vv. *Garlic, Onion*, and *Concordance*, s.v.; also al-Dārimī, viii, 21). Olives also were eaten (Ḳurʾān, VI, 142/141) and the pith of the palm-tree (*d̲j̲ummār*; al-Buk̲h̲ārī, lxx, 42, etc.). Fruits mentioned are the citron (*utrud̲j̲d̲j̲a*; al-Buk̲h̲ārī, lxx, 30), which is thought to be found also (according to the parallel Jewish text and certain Muslim commentaries) in Ḳurʾān, XII, 31 (under the name of *mitk, matk*, to be read in place of *muttakaʾ*, or disguised by a corruption in the text), the pomegranate (Ḳurʾān, VI, 99, 142/141; lv, 68), the grape (cf. Ḳurʾān, VI, 142/141; cf. Lammens, *Berceau*, 90 f.; the dried raisins of Ṭāʾif were famous). The apple and the fig are scarcely mentioned by the poets (Jacob, *Altar. Bed.*, 230) or in *ḥadīt̲h̲*s (Wensinck, *Concordance*, s.vv.).

The pastoral nomads were able to use also, in addition to the meat and the milk-products provided by their flocks, wild vegetables, game and small desert animals. Among the plants may be mentioned *kabāt̲h̲*, the ripe fruit of the thorn tree *arāk* (*Capparis sedata*; cf. Lammens, *Berceau*, 69; al-Buk̲h̲ārī, lxx, 50; Muslim, xxxvi, 163), desert truffles, which, according to a saying attributed to Muḥammad, came from the manna sent to the Israelites (Muslim, xxxvi, 157-62; cf. Dāwūd al-Anṭākī, *Tad̲h̲kira*, Cairo, 1356/1937, i, 252; Lammens, *Berceau*, 49), etc. The game mentioned in the traditions are the hare (Abū Dāwūd, xxvi, 26; al-Dārimī, vii, 7) and the bustard (*ḥubārā*; Abū Dāwūd, xxvi, 28); in addition they ate the flesh of the large desert lizards, food which is said to have disgusted Muḥammad, as a member of a settled community (Ibn Saʿd, i/2, 112); he is said to have regarded these lizards as the metamorphosis of an Israelite tribe (cf. Wensinck, *Concordance*, s.v. *ḍubb*; Robertson Smith, *Kinship...*, new ed., London 1903, 75, n. 2, 230 f.; Cl. Huart, in *JA*, 10th series, xii (1908), 450, n. 1; *Rev. biblique*, xii (1903), 104; a food of Ḥimyar according to a poet of Hud̲h̲ayl: Wellhausen, *Skizzen und Vorarbeiten*, i, Berlin 1884, no. 147[2], tr. 114); the flesh of hedgehogs (Abū Dāwūd, xxvi, 29b), of grasshoppers (Abū Dāwūd, xxvi, 34; al-Dārimī, vii, 5 ff.; cf. Robertson Smith, *Kinship*[2], 75, n. 2, 288; and art. D̲J̲ARĀD), and even that of mice, lice and vermin (Jacob, *Altar. Bed.*, 95, 247 f.).

The inhabitants of coastal regions could also add fish to their diet (Ḳurʾān, V, 97/96).

Besides milk and water (often muddy and seldom plentiful), the Arabs were familiar with a certain number of fermented drinks prepared from dates, honey, wheat, barley, raisins. But wine made from grapes, which (in spite of the fact that there were vineyards at Ṭāʾif for example) was generally imported, was an expensive luxury. It was drunk in the taverns (*ḥānūt*) which were run by the Jews or the Christians of Ḥīra (*ʿIbādī*) and in which women singers (*ḳayna*) performed (Jacob, *op. cit.*, 96-109, 248-54; I. Goldziher, *Muhammedanische Studien*, i, 1889, 21 ff.; I. Guidi, *L'Arabie antéislamique*, Paris 1921, 53 ff.; and art. K̲H̲AMR).

These various resources, which combined foods of agricultural and pastoral origin but which included no, or very few, products from countries outside

Arabia, were prepared in a very elementary fashion. The meats were roasted (roots *sh.w.y*, *ḥ.n.dh*, *ṣ.l.y.*) or baked (*ṭ.b.kh*). The meat was cut in slices or in thin strips which were left to dry in the sun (*ḳadīd*) (*e.g.*, Abū Dāwūd, xxvi, 36a; Abu 'l-Hindī *apud* Alūsī, *Bulūgh*, i, 380; in general on the methods of cooking, see Jacob, *Altar. Beduinenleben*, 90 ff.). A *ḥadīth* is cited according to which the Prophet announced "I am only the son of a woman of the Ḳuraysh who fed on *ḳadīd*" (cited in an epigraph by Bint al-Shāṭiʾ, *Umm al-Nabī*, Cairo 1958, 5). The oven proper seems to have been little known. The only word for oven attested in early Arabic, *tannūr*, is a borrowing from Aramaic (cf. Landberg, *Glossaire datînois*, i, 238 f.) and the purely Arabic word *ṭābūn* seems originally to have meant the cavity in which fire was made to shelter it from the wind (cf. Lane).

The cooking was simple and made use of very few different combinations of food. Two of the dishes mentioned are *tharīd*, associated with the tribal tradition of the Ḳuraysh, consisting of bread crumbled into a broth of meat and vegetables, and *ḥays*, a mixture of dates, butter and milk, both being among the favourite dishes of the Prophet, who said that ʿĀʾisha held among women the place which *tharīd* held among food (Wensinck, *Concordance*, i, 290). They made many kinds of broth (*maraḳ*, *maraḳa*), to which tradition prescribes that plenty of water should be added in order to be able to give some to neighbours (al-Dārimī, viii, 37), especially a broth of marrows (*dubbāʾ*) and of *ḳadīd*. When on expeditions, soldiers took with them *sawīḳ*, a kind of dried barley meal to which was added water, butter or fat from the tails of sheep. Several dishes belong to the broad category of gruels, the usual food of agricultural peoples (*e.g.*, gruels made with milk and with *samn*; al-Bukhārī, lxx, 48; Ibn Ḥanbal, iii, 147, etc.); these include *ḥarīra*, made from flour cooked with milk (al-Bukhāri, lxx, 15), *talbīna*, a similar dish eaten at funeral meals, *khazīr* (or *khazīra*), a gruel generally made from bran and meat cut up into small pieces and cooked in water (al-Bukhārī, lxx, 15, etc.). We notice that the general tendency is a search for fat, for greasy and heavy food, a tendency which still continues in Bedouin cooking and which is probably dictated by physiological needs. There is little tendency mentioned to spiced foods. The Arabs engaged in the transport of spices, but they were too precious a merchandise for them to use themselves at all frequently. We find mentioned, however, camphor and ginger (Ḳurʾān, LXXVI, 5, 17), cloves, pepper, aloes and the sweet wood called lignum aloes (a few references in poetry *apud* Jacob, *op. cit.*, 150, 258).

There seem to have been few prohibitions concerning food, imposed rather by custom (as with us) than by a definite code of laws, and often restricted to one or to several tribes (cf. Wellhausen, *Reste*², 168 ff.). It is, at least in part, against pagan taboos of this sort that the Ḳurʾān seems to inveigh (II, 163/168 ff., VI, 118 ff.); there were often prohibitions concerning specific animals (and not a whole species), not as impure, but as consecrated to the Divinity (Ḳurʾān, V, 102, VI, 139/138, where there is also mentioned a harvest—*ḥarth*—which is taboo; the flesh of newly-born animals was forbidden to women, with the exception of still-born animals: Ḳurʾān, VI, 140/139). Even at Mecca itself, at the time of the *iḥrām*, the *ḥums*, *i.e.*, the holy families serving the local sanctuaries (Lammens, *L'Arabie occidentale avant l'hégire*, Beirut 1928, 130), abstained from meat, from clarified butter, from *aḳiṭ* (and perhaps from all milk-products) as well as from oil [see ḤUMS]. There were various portions of meat which were not eaten: the heart among the Djuʿfī tribe (Ibn Saʿd, i/2, 61 f.), the fat tail of the sheep among the Balī of Ḳuḍāʿa who, not being assimilated with the rest of the Islamic population, still retained this taboo in Andalus (Ibn Ḥazm, *Djamharat ansāb al-ʿArab*, ed. E. Lévi-Provençal, Cairo 1948, 415; cf. H. Pérès, in *Mél. W. Marçais*, Paris 1950, 293 f.), the testicles, at least on feast days (al-Ṭabarī, *Tafsīr*, Cairo 1321/1903, xxx, 166); but there may have been here, as in present-day Arabia (in spite of the religious agitation which appears to have been provoked among the Djuʿfī who were forced by Muḥammad to break the taboo) "rational" motives: in north-western Arabia they do not eat the hearts of birds for fear of becoming as timorous as they are (A. Musil, *The manners and customs of the Rwala Bedouins*, New York 1928, 97; *Arabia Petraea*, iii, Vienna 1908, 150); Hudhalī poets reproach the South-Arabian tribe of Marthad for eating grasshoppers (*Dīwān Hudhayl*, 57, 147), but this was rather a special distaste for this food, or an affectation. A later saying claimed that the Bedouin ate "everything that crawls or walks except the chameleon" (*umm ḥubayn*; Ibn ʿAbd Rabbih, *ʿIḳd*, ed. A. Amīn, etc., iii, Cairo 1942, 485; Ibn al-Ukhuwwa, *Maʿālim al-ḳurbā*, ed. R. Levy, London 1938, 101 f.; cf. Alūsī, *Bulūgh*, i, 380; Kurd ʿAlī, *Maʾākil*, 570). According to Sozomenus (5th century A.D.), the Saracens abstained from pork and observed a number of Jewish ceremonies (*Ecclesiastical history*, vi, 38 = *PG*, lxvii, 1412); it was probably a case of the Arab neighbours of Palestine coming under Jewish-Christian influences. But Pliny had already noted (*Nat Hist.*, viii, 78 = 52, § 212) the absence of pork in Arabia. In case of vital necessity, which often arose in the severe conditions of desert life, all the taboos were relaxed, even the general taboo on human flesh (*Dīwān Hudhayl*, 161 ff.; Procopius, *Bell. Pers.*, I, 19, 4) though it should not therefore be thought that cannibalism was general (J. Henninger, *Kannibalismus in Arabien?*, in *Anthropos*, xxxv-xxxvi (1940-1), 631 ff.), but during battles the heat of passionate hatred, or particular rites, often led men to drink or lick up the blood or the brains, to gnaw the liver of the dead, etc. (Ammianus, xxxi, 16; Ibn Hishām, 581, etc.; cf. Robertson Smith, *Kinship*², 75, n. 2, 295 f.; Nallino, *Raccolta*, iii, 86). Vows were made of temporary abstinence: from *samn*, milk, meat, wine, sometimes even to fast completely [see NADHR]. In some regions wine must have played a religious part. Some rather doubtful texts speak of libations of wine poured on tombs (Jacob, *Altar. Beduinenleben*, 143; Wellhausen, *Reste*², 182 f.; Lammens, *Arabie occid.*, 204). In Liḥyān it is perhaps a case of a large offering of wine to Dhū Ghābat to expiate a murder (W. Caskel, *Lihyan und Lihyanisch*, Cologne-Opladen 1954, no. 82). At Palmyra, wine was ceremonially drunk at the funeral banquets of the *thiasoi* (J. G. Février, *La religion des Palmyréniens*, Paris 1931, 194 f.; R. Dussaud, in *RHR*, xiv (1927), 200 ff.). It is perhaps to this sacred importance that we are to attribute the frequent use in Saphaitic of names such as Shrb (Sharīb? "drinking companion") and Skrn (Sakrān "drunk" "intoxicated"; G. Ryckmans, *Noms propres sud-sémitiques*, Louvain 1934, i, 212, 149, ii, 130, 99). At Mecca, at the moment of deconsecration which concluded the *ḥadjdj*, there was ritually drunk a fermented beverage with a basis of grapes (*sharāb*, *nabīdh*) or of barley and honey (*sawīḳ*) and this rite was continued under Islam until the 2nd/8th century; a similar rite at the beginning of the ceremonies could explain the name of *yawm al-tarwiya* which is given to the first day (Gaudefroy-Demombynes, *Le pèlerinage à la Mekke*, Paris 1923, 89-101). But, in other regions, in other circumstances or in other cults, there was abstinence. Wine was one of the things which people most often vowed to renounce; in particular those swearing vengeance abstained from it until their vengeance was accomplished (Lammens, *L'Arabie occidentale avant l'hégire*, Beirut 1928, 185; art. NADHR; Alūsī, *Bulūgh*, iii, 24). The Nabataeans did not drink wine (Diodorus, xix, 94, 3) and the Arabs in general had the reputation of being water drinkers (Ammianus, xiv, 4, 6; Spartianus, *Pescennius Niger*, 7). A Nabataean set up at Palmyra in 132 A.D. two altars to his god Shayʿ al-ḳawm who, as he emphasizes, probably with polemic intent, "does not drink (or perhaps: does not allow to drink) wine" (*CIS*, ii, 3973[5]). This is very probably the god known in Greek as Λυκοῦργος (inscr. Waddington 2286a), who was regarded as the opposite of Aʿara Dhu 'l-Sharā, in Greek Δουσάρης and identified with Dionysos [see DHU 'L-SHARĀ], hence the mythical story of the fight between the god of wine and his enemy (Nonnos, *Dionys.*, xx, xxi).

Shortly before the time of the Prophet, those who were attracted to monotheism [see ḤANĪF] would seem to have adopted certain prohibitions in order to conform to the Noachic precepts enjoined upon Jewish proselytes and in general adopted by the Christians (*Acts*, xv, 29). An example is Zayd b. ʿAmr from the ʿAdī clan of the Ḳuraysh, who is said to have abstained from animals which had not been ritually slaughtered, from blood and from meat which had been sacrificed to idols (Ibn Hishām, 144). Others, probably from asceticism, under the influence of the earlier practices mentioned above and of the abstinence which was enjoined by Manicheism, by the Christian ascetics and certain Christian sects, and which was practised by other Semitic peoples (if the fact is indeed true), are said to have abstained from drinking wine—*e.g.*, another Ḳurashī, ʿUthmān b. Maẓʿūn, who was later to embrace Islam (Ibn Saʿd, iii/1, 286). Musaylima forbade wine as well as sexual relations to those who were already fathers (Sayf b. ʿUmar, *apud* al-Ṭabarī, i, 1916; as against Ibn Hishām, 946). It has been possible to compile a list of those who abstained from wine in the Djāhiliyya (critical list in Caetani, *Annali*, i, 586).

The epigraphic sources add hardly anything to this picture for central and northern Arabia. They do, however, illustrate the importance attached there to game and hunting. This importance is also reflected in the rock engravings which accompany the graffiti or are contemporary with them (cf., *e.g.*, E. Littmann, *Thamūd und Ṣafā*, Leipzig 1940, 34 f., 100). They hunted gazelle, ostriches, ibex, perhaps also wild asses etc. A "Thamudean" text mentions the capture of a lizard (*wrl*), perhaps for food (*ibid.*, 60, no. 77 = Eut. 44, but A. van den Branden, *Les inscriptions thamoudéennes*, Louvain 1950, 69 reads *wʿl* "chamois"). The domestic animals mentioned: camels, cattle, sheep, horses, donkeys, were used partly for food (cf., *e.g.*, van den Branden, *op. cit.*, 8). The reference to an abundance of milk (*drr*, *Corpus Inscriptionum Semiticarum*, pars v, vol. i, Paris 1950, no. 362) and the reference to bees (van den Branden, inscr. HU 250) are dubious, as are the references to dates (A. van den Branden, *Les textes thamoudéens de Philby*, i, Louvain 1956, 5). Fish caught in the pools of stagnant water on the edges of the desert were preserved by drying (*CIS*, v, 4902, 4384).

ii. — Pre-Islamic Southern Arabia

Southern Arabia was much more agricultural and thus afforded a much greater variety of vegetable food. The dates (*tmr*) supplied by the many palm groves (*nkhl*) which are often the subject of the inscriptions (*e.g.*, *CIS*, pars iv [cited hereafter as *CIH*], 375, 403, 414, 615, 616, etc.; cf. Ammianus Marcellinus, XXIII, 6, 45-7, Eratosthenes *apud* Strabo, XVI, 4, 24) must have been one of the staple foods. The sweet pith from the centre of the trunk of the palm tree (in Arabic *ḳulb*, *ḳalb*, *lubb*, etc., often confused with *djummār*, palm-cabbage; cf. al-Aṣmaʿī, *K. al-Nakhl wa 'l-karm*, ed. A. Haffner, Beirut 1908, 5, and notes; *Tuḥfat al-aḥbāb*, ed. H. P. J. Renaud and G. S. Colin, Paris 1934, no. 107) seems to us to be the *lbb* which was preserved in a temple (*CIH*, 548[13]; Rodinson, *Comptes Rendus du GLECS*, ix (1960-3), 103 f.). Wheat was produced only in moderate quantities and had to be imported (*Periplus of the Erythrean Sea*, §§ 24, 28, 32). Taxes were paid in flour (*ṭḥn* Gl. 1571[3], cf. N. Rhodokanakis, *Altsab. Texte*, i = *SBAK. Wien*, ccvi/2, 1927, 104-7). Flour (*ṭḥn*, flour in general, *dḳḳ*, the flour of cereals, perhaps *khrṣ*?) was made with wheat (*br*), barley (*shʿr*), dates (*tmr*), *gdhdht*, which was perhaps a kind of wheat (it seems difficult to translate it literally as its Arabic equivalent *djadhīdha* "wheat husked and crushed"), and in addition semolina (*sdl*, cf. Ethiopic *sendālē*; *CIH*, 540: 39-40, 83, 86-8; 541: 120). We may have in *CIH*, 408 a reference to a field (*mʿlṣ(t)*; with the emphatic, *ṣ*!) in which would be grown the variety of wheat called in Arabic *ʿalas*; this inscription seems to refer to it in two aspects *yhr* and *frʿ* (cf. *CIH*, 352: 7, 11; cf. also *dhrʾ*, in *RES*, 2774: 4). Vegetable gardens (*tbḳlt*, in *RES*, 4636: 6, 7), orchards (*mḥgrt*, in *CIH*, 204: 3, 546: 11; *ḳshmt*, in *CIH*, 308: 9), vineyards (*ʾʿnb*, in *CIH*, 342: 11-2, 604: 3, *wyn*, in *CIH*, 228: 2, 276: 3, etc.) were numerous. They produced vegetables (*bḳl*, in *SE*, 48[3], translated "broad beans" by Conti-Rossini) and fruit (*thmr*). The country produced sesame oil (Pliny, *Nat. Hist.*, VI, 28 (32), § 161), but not enough for its needs and had to import it via Moscha (*Periplus*, § 32). As a condiment they used capers which they soaked (*kbr wlkh*, in *RES*, 2845; cf. N. Rhodokanakis, *Studien* . . ., i = *SBAK Wien*, 178, 4, 10 f.), and they imported saffron (*Periplus*, § 24) for the same purpose. Cinnamon, also imported in transit, obtained too high prices on the Roman market to be used locally (Pliny, *Nat. Hist.*, XII, 93). The *dbs* which was distributed in large quantities to the workers on the dam of Mārib (*CIH*, 540: 96; cf. also 548: 12 f.) must have been a treacle of grapes or of other fruits, different from the honey which according to Pliny was produced in abundance in the kingdom of Saba (*Nat. Hist.*, VI, 32: 18, § 161). Eratosthenes mentions numerous apiaries (? μελιτουργεῖα) in Southern Arabia (Strabo, XVI, 4: 2, § 768).

The meat (*bshr*, in *CIH*, 563: 3) was in the main that of animals slaughtered (*ṭbkh*, in *CIH*, 541: 122-3, cf. Hebrew *ṭibʰḥâh*) probably according to the usual Semitic rites. For the workers engaged on the repairs to the dam of Mārib they slaughtered thousands of cattle (*bḳr*) and probably also sheep (cf. Dionysios, *Periegesis*, 942 f.), one sort of which had the characteristic name of *dhbyḥ* (Ar. *dhabāʾiḥ* "victims") and the other the enigmatic name of *ḳrṣ*, and, on one occasion, 207,000 *ḳṭnt*, which seems to represent portions rather than head of sheep and goats (cf. Gl. 1142: 9). They were given also 1100 *ʾḏḥ* ("lambs used for sacrifice" to judge from Ar. *aḍāḥī*, pl. of *ḍaḥiyya*) and *ʿḍwd* (perhaps "fat lambs" to judge from Ar. *ʿaḍid*?; *CIH*, 540: 41 ff., 88 ff.; 541: 122 ff.). The sheep were called elsewhere *khrf*, in *RES*, 2959: 2 (Min.), Van Lessen i: 9 (Ḳatab.), and in the Minean colony of the Ḥidjāz *ḏʾn* (in contrast to the goats *mʿzy*, in *JSa*, 19: 11, called in Saba *sfr*, Gl. 1000 A 3). According to Eratosthenes they ate also birds, except for geese and hens (Strabo, XVI, 4, 2 = 768). On the shores of the Indian Ocean, some communities ate mainly fish (*Periplus*, § 27) and the nomads lived on game (Pliny, *Nat. Hist.*, VI, 32: 18 = § 161). These people drank milk (*ibid.*) and the workers of Mārib were supplied with butter (*khmʾt*, Hebrew *ḥèmʾâh*, Akkadian *khimētu*, etc.; *CIH*, 540: 96 f.).

The main drink (*CIH*, 563: 2 ?) seems to have been palm wine (Strabo, XVI, 4, 25, § 783; Pliny, *Nat. Hist.*, VI, 28 (32), § 161), which was called *mzr^m^ dh-tmr^m^* (*CIH*, 540: 50-1; cf. Ar. *mazar*, *mizr*, the word for various fermented drinks) or *sḳy^m^ dh-tmr^m^*, perhaps with a north Arabic gloss *al-ḥalab* (*CIH*, 541: 129-30, but the hypothesis of J. M. Solá Solé, *Las dos grandes inscripciones sudarábigas del dique de Mârib*, Barcelona-Tübingen 1960, 37, raises some difficulties). However, the numerous vineyards (cf. above, and the popularity of the Dionysiac themes making use of the vine in sculpture) provided grape wine (*Periplus*, § 24) and a certain amount was imported (*ibid.*, §§ 24, 28). The workers on the Mārib dam were provided with more of this than of palm wine. A distinction was made between the fermented beverage (*sḳy*) made with the excellent grapes of Ghirbīb (*ghrbb*, cf. the classical dictionaries) and that prepared from dried raisins (*fṣy*, cf. *fuṣa^n^*; *CIH*, 540; 46-8, 91-4; 541: 127-8). The *shnn* kept in a temple (*CIH*, 548[12]) is probably the *shanīn* "whey or milk diluted with water" known in various Arab countries (cf. the classical dictionaries and Dozy). We do not know whether the thermal springs of therapeutic value, which according to Ammianus (XXIII, 6, 46) were numerous, were used for drinking.

Almost nothing is known about the ritual use of foods. Libations (*msty*, in *CIH*, 563: 2 ?) were made on special altars (*mslm*, in *RES*, 3512), but we do not know what was the liquid used. Nor is anything known about the prohibitions concerning food. Nevertheless Eratosthenes mentions the absence of pigs among the domestic animals of the region (Strabo, XVI, 4, 2 = 768).

iii. — Regulations concerning food in early Islam

Muḥammad's reforms were made under the influence of a milieu in which each religious community was distinguished by its own regulations concerning food. We have seen how in the pagan milieu the situation was rather chaotic, and there was the influence of the Noachic code, imposed on proselytes by the Jews and coinciding more or less with the original Christian code. The Revelation (texts conveniently brought together by D. Masson, *Le Coran et la Révélation judéo-chrétienne*, Paris 1958, ii, 577-86) in this respect also was to put an end to ignorance and errors and the Prophet was to declare lawful (*ḥalāl*) "good" foods (*al-ṭayyibāt*) and unlawful (*ḥarām*) unclean foods (*al-khabāʾith*; Ḳurʾān, VII, 156/157). But the Ḳurʾān insists above all on the beneficial nature of food in general. Food is one of the greatest of Divine blessings (often in the Meccan *sūras*: LXXX, 24; XVII, 72/70; XVI, 74; XIV, 37/32, etc.; cf. index of Blachère's tr., s.v. nourriture), which, however, must be used with moderation (VII, 29, Medinan) and which must not be rejected except in specific circumstances. The word "eat (*kulū*) . . ." occurs nearly thirty times. Muḥammad is said to have obliged two newly converted Djuʿfīs to eat heart, taboo in their tribe, without which their conversion would have been incomplete (Ibn Saʿd, i/2, 62, l. 5 f.). The Ḳurʾān inveighs against men who arbitrarily deprive those who listen to them of certain foods (II, 163 f./168 f.; V, 89 f./87 f.; VI, 118 ff.; VII, 30/32; XVI, 117/116, texts which seem to belong to the beginning of the Prophet's stay at Medina). In some cases it is certain that the adversaries aimed at are pagans observing the prohibitions described above (II, 165; VI, 139-51/138-50; X, 60/59); but at Medina it became important to define Islam as against Judaism.

The mass of Jewish prohibitions concerning food led to the emphasizing of the fact that Allāh does not wish to impose too many burdens on His faithful people (II, 286). It seems that the Ḳurʾān is sometimes criticizing Judaizers or *ḥanīf*s who imposed on themselves excessive restrictions (VI, 118 ff.) and who wanted to influence the Prophet to do the same (VI, 116). The Jewish prohibitions (rather inexactly defined in VI, 147/146) are explained as a Divine punishment of the sins of the Israelites (IV, 158; XVI, 119). This is proved by the fact that they were not imposed on them before the revelation of the Torah, except for a prohibition, not of divine origin, which Isrāʾīl (Jacob) had imposed on himself (III, 87/93), a reference to the prohibition of the sciatic nerve after the struggle of Jacob and the angel (*Gen.*, XXXII, 33). They were moreover partially lifted by Jesus (III, 44/50). "Today" (V, 7) these forbidden foods are therefore permitted. We have here ideas taken from the Christian polemic against the Jews, particularly as exemplified by the Syriac writer of Iran, Aphraates (4th century A.D.); cf. his fifteenth homily (ed. Wright, London 1869, 309 ff.; cf. H. Speyer, *Die biblischen Erzählungen im Coran*, Gräfenheinischen 1931, reprinted Hildesheim 1961, 318 ff.). Only a limited number of prohibitions were retained: blood (and consequently "strangled" meats), *mayta*, *i.e.*, the flesh of a dead animal or one not killed specially for meat, pork, animals consecrated to a pagan divinity (II, 168/173; V, 4/3; VI, 146/145; XVI, 116/115; on the date of these passages, see J. Schacht, in *EI*[1], s.v. maita). In addition, during the Pilgrimage it was forbidden to those in a state of ritual purity to kill or (*a fortiori*) to eat game (V, 1, 95/94 ff.), while fish was permitted (V, 97/96; cf. XVI, 14). It was necessary only to invoke (*dhakara*) the name of Allāh on lawful foods (VI, 118 ff., 139/138; XXII, 35/34). Involuntary infringements of these rules, through force majeure or compulsion, are moreover regarded by Allāh with indulgence (II, 168/173; V, 5/3; VI, 119, 146/145; XVI, 116/115). They defined the Muslim community, but only as a particular category within the wide family of the Possessors of the Scripture, since it is permitted to eat the food of the *ahl al-kitāb* and vice-versa (V, 7/5). In fact, these prohibitions go further in conformity to the Jewish regulations than the Noachic regulations, which the Jews theoretically admitted as sufficient for any strangers allowed to live with them (only not to eat unbled meat, according to *Gen.*, IX, 4; cf. E. Schürer, *Geschichte des jüdischen Volkes im Zeitalter Jesu Christi*[4], Leipzig 1901-11, iii, 164 ff., 178, n. 77). There was, in short, a falling into line with the primitive Christian position (which remained very closely observed in the East) as it is defined by the decree of the Apostles (*Acts*, XV, 29; cf. especially K. Böckenhoff, *Speisesatzungen mosaischer Art in mittelalterlichen Kirchenrechtsquellen des Morgen- und Abendlandes*, Münster i. W. 1907). They went further in demanding also abstention from pork. This abstention, one of the first to be practised by Judaizing pagans (Juvenal, XIV, 98 f.), was also the rule among certain Judaeo-Christians (*Didascalia*, 121, 27 ff.; cf. H. J. Schoeps, *Theologie und Geschichte des Judenchristentums*, Tübingen 1949, 341, n. 2) and it was presumably through this route that it became adopted in Arabia (see above, col. 1059 b); it was also adopted by the Christians of Ethiopia in imitation of the Old Testament (*Confessio fidei Claudii regis Aethiopiae*, ed. J. M. Wansleb, London 1661, 3 and n. 11; E. Ullendorff, in *JSS*, i (1956), 240-3; J. Baeteman, *Dictionnaire amarigna-français*, Dire Dawa 1929, col. 574; cf. M. Rodinson, in *Bibliotheca Orientalis*, xxi (1964), 241). The insistence on the lawfulness of fish arose perhaps from opposition to a Judaeo-Christian and Samaritan practice (Schoeps, *op. cit.*, 189 f.). In addition, an entirely new restriction appears in the Divine revelation: at first it praises the virtues of wine (XVI, 69), which is one of the delights promised to the elect in Paradise (XXXVII, 44/45 ff.; XLVII, 16/15), but later has reservations about it (II, 216/219), and then forbids it (V, 92/90). The commentators and the historians disagree on the causes and the date of this prohibition [see KHAMR]. The association with the prohibition of *maysir* suggests a link between wine and pagan usages (W. Montgomery Watt, *Muhammad at Medina*, Oxford 1956, 298 f.; M. Gaudefroy-Demombynes, *Mahomet*, Paris 1957, 570 f.; cf. above, col. 1059 b) and we have seen above that abstention from wine was a religious practice fairly common in Arabia in various milieus and on various occasions. It does not seem easy to agree with W. Montgomery Watt that it was also partly a case of discouraging the import of an expensive commodity which came from enemy countries. The initial indifference about it and the injunction contained in verse IV, 46/43 seem to indicate that this prohibition was essentially a reaction against the deplorable effects of drunkenness within the Medinan community, one of them perhaps being excessive extravagance. This does not exclude the possibility that the practices of abstention mentioned above contributed to the enactment of the prohibition. In addition to these general prohibitions on the eating of specific foods, Islam decreed a general temporary abstention from food at periodic intervals—the fast of Ramaḍān [see ṢAWM].

iv. — Food in the traditional Muslim world

In the Arab empire, which after 132/750 became the Muslim empire, the food in the various occupied countries naturally continued to be the same as it had been before they were conquered. The Arab conquerors adopted it, after a certain period of adaptation, perhaps adding certain dishes or practices of their own. For the food of each country reference should be made therefore to works describing the diet in the pre-Islamic civilizations. For Egypt, see A. Ruffer, *Food in Egypt*, Cairo 1919 (= *Mémoires présentés à l'Institut d'Egypte*, i); A. Erman and H. Ranke, *Ägypten and ägyptisches Leben im Altertum*, Tübingen 1923, 219-29; A. Wiedemann, *Das alte Ägypten*, Heidelberg 1920, 287-309 and also 250 ff., 259 ff., 271 f., 275 ff. On Syria and Palestine see especially R. A. S. Macalister, art. *Food* in J. Hastings, *Dictionary of the Bible*, ii, Edinburgh 1899, 27-43; A. Bertholet, *Kulturgeschichte Israels*, Göttingen 1919, 130-4; P. Thomsen, art. *Nahrung* in M. Ebert, *Reallexikon der Vorgeschichte*, Berlin 1924-32, viii, 429-31. On Mesopotamia, see B. Meissner, *Babylonien und Assyrien*, Heidelberg 1920-5, i, 413-20. The picture had been somewhat modified by the influence of Greek and Roman customs, on which see especially Orth, art. *Kochkunst* in *Pauly's Realencyclopädie d. class. Altertumswissenschaft*, Neue Bearb., xi/1, Stuttgart 1921, 944-82 and J. André, *L'alimentation et la cuisine à Rome*, Paris 1961 (= *Études et commentaires*, 38). For Sāsānid Iran, see A. Christensen, *L'Iran sous les Sassanides*[2], Copenhagen-Paris 1944, 477-9.

However, the Muslim conquest created a relatively coherent cultural area which survived the fragmentation of the political unity which had brought it into being. Yet the differences between countries are important. To give a picture of the food and its variations throughout the whole of this area would be a vast and difficult enterprise for which the necessary detailed monographs do not exist. We shall limit ourselves here to indicating the main factors which influence all these diets. References to precise facts have in most cases only the value of examples taken at random.

1. Products consumed. The formation of new cultural frontiers leads to the spread throughout the territory concerned of products which have formerly been known only in one section of it. In the case of products too heavy to transport, this spread can take place only by their being grown or made locally. The most striking phenomenon in the Muslim world was the spread of the growing of rice and of sugar cane.

Rice, originally from India, was already in pre-Islamic times being cultivated in Iran, in ʿIrāḳ and in Syria, but had hardly been used as food in the Roman world (only as a thickening for sauces); it spread as a crop and as food as far as Spain. It became a common item of food and especially of the poor (particularly in the form of bread made from rice flour) in the areas where it was intensively cultivated, but elsewhere it remained relatively a luxury food, used only in recherché dishes. In any case it did not take the place of wheat and did not acquire the importance which it had in India and in the Far East (cf. M. Canard, *Le riz dans le Proche-Orient aux premiers siècles de l'Islam*, in *Arabica*, vi (1959), 113-31, and art. RUZZ).

Sugar, introduced to Iran from India perhaps shortly before the Muslim conquest, spread after this through the whole of the Mediterranean world (cf. N. Deer, *The history of sugar*, i, London 1949, 68 ff., 74 ff.; and art. SUKKAR). It was used in the food of princes and wealthy people, but among the poor was found chiefly as a medicine (a significant text in the *K. al-Ḥarb al-maʿshūḳ* ..., tr. J. Finkel, in *Zeitschrift für Semitistik*, viii (1932), 5). Honey was generally less expensive, and in particular *dibs*, a treacle of grapes, carob etc., was the sugar of poor people (cf. M. Rodinson, *Recherches sur les documents arabes relatifs à la cuisine*, in *REI*, 1949, 147).

Large-scale transport was particularly necessary to bring to the towns from the surrounding countryside food products such as wheat which were consumed in large quantities. Wheat was everywhere a commodity traded on a large scale (cf. for example R. Le Tourneau, *Fès avant le protectorat*, Casablanca 1949, 377 ff., and art. ḲAMḤ).

Certain heavy products regularly consumed were however transported by caravans or by ships (river or sea transport) considerable distances from the specific region in which they were originally grown. Examples are Syrian olive oil coming down the Euphrates, the dates of Lower ʿIrāḳ or of Arabia, etc., and, later, coffee from Arabia [see ḲAHWA, ZAYTŪN]. A list of Iranian food products exported in this way is found in B. Spuler, *Iran*, 406 f., a picture of the trade in foodstuffs between the various provinces of the Ottoman empire in Gibb-Bowen, i/1, 304. Thus there were great differences in price for the same commodity in the regions in which it was produced and those which were at varying distances from them (*e.g.*, for rice, cf. W. Hinz, in *Die Welt des Orients*, ii (1954-9), 57 ff.), a further factor being the difficulty or otherwise of the transport (the price of rice rose in Istanbul when unfavourable winds delayed the ships from Alexandria, W. Hinz, *op. cit.*, 60).

The products of all the regions of the Muslim world were thus available throughout every part of it to those who could afford the sometimes high prices; but in addition there were available products imported from outside. Thus, in the Middle Ages, the Near East imported from Russia and the Slav countries dried and salted fish, honey and hazel nuts. (G. Jacob, *Welche Handelsartikel bezogen die Araber des Mittelalters aus den nordisch-baltischen Ländern*[2], Berlin 1891, 56 ff., 62 f.). In times of scarcity, Egypt in the 5th/11th century imported wheat from the Byzantine Empire (G. Wiet, *L'Egypte arabe*, Paris 1937, 230). Imports from Europe became numerous from the 6th/12th century onwards. Frederick II sold cereals to Tunisia and Andalusia (A. Schaube, *Handelgeschichte der romanischen Völker des Mittelmeergebiets*, Münich-Berlin 1906, 304, 327), the Pisans exported Tuscan oil to Tunisia (*ibid.*, 298), southern France in the 7th/13th century sent to the Maghrib wine, chestnuts, broad beans, saffron etc. (*ibid.*, 31 f.). Tuscan saffron was on sale in the Maghrib, in Egypt and in Frankish Syria (*ibid.*, 187, 206, 283, 398). Egypt imported cheese from Sicily and from Crete (S. D. Goitein, *Artisans en Méditerranée orientale au haut Moyen-Age*, in *Annales*, xv (1964), 863). In the Middle Ages, Iran imported from India peas, wheat, barley and millet (Spuler, *Iran*, 403). In the 12th/18th century Europe exported to the Levant spices, sugar, coffee etc. (Gibb-Bowen, i/1, 307).

Spices were imported from still more distant places, their lightness for transport and the high prices they commanded justifying the long journeys. From China, the Sunda Isles, India and East Africa came pepper, ginger, cinnamon, cloves, cardamom, mace, betel, musk and nutmeg [see TAWĀBIL].

2. Storage and preservation. The preservation of food is an important problem in all societies. The Muslim civilization had inherited processes from the ancient East and from the classical civilizations. Cereals were stored either in granaries [see AGADIR] or in silos (*maṭmūra* [*q.v.*]) and the agronomists recommended various processes to preserve them from decay, weevils, etc. (Ibn al-ʿAwwām, *K. al-Filāḥa*, ed. J. A. Banqueri, Madrid 1802, i, 678 ff.; tr. J.-J. Clément-Mullet, Paris 1864-7, i, 638 ff.). For fruit, especially grapes, there were handed down various recipes for preserving them from any deterioration and keeping them fresh (*e.g.*, Ibn al-ʿAwwām, i, 660 ff., tr. Clément-Mullet, i, 619 ff., to be compared with processes used by the Romans, J. André, *L'alimentation* ..., 89). Preservation by cold storage was known; melons from Transoxania were transported to Baghdād packed in ice inside lead boxes (al-Thaʿālibī, *Laṭāʾif al-maʿārif*, ed. P. De Jong, Leiden 1867, 129). Drying was a less expensive and more widely used process. We have seen that before Islam the Arabs were already familiar with the drying of meat (*ḳadīd*) and of fish. Desert truffles were also dried (*Wuṣla*, ch. viii, § 44), also figs, pistachio nuts, etc. (Ibn al-ʿAwwām, i, 675 ff., tr. Clément-Mullet, i, 634 ff.). Fruits were often preserved in a sealed air-tight container which was sometimes buried in the ground (Ibn al-ʿAwwām, i, 662 f., 664 f., tr. i, 622, 624, etc.). The curing or smoke-drying of meat seems to have been very little known among the Arabs; it is described in the *Wuṣla* (ch. viii, § 45, mss. A, B, D) as being a Greek process. It was, however, one of the processes applied to *sharāʾiḥ*, slices of meat, in particular to those known as *miṣriyya*, "Egyptian" (*Wuṣla*, ch. v, § 2a), and known in some places as *mudakhkhana* "smoked" (*ibid.*, § 2d). The crystallizing of fruits in honey or sugar, a process known to ancient Rome and a speciality of modern Damascus, was known there at this time according to A. von Kremer, *Culturgeschichte des Orients unter den Chalifen*, Vienna 1875-7, ii, 333, who however quotes no evidence. *Ḳadīd*, or dried meat, must have been coated with fat (cf. the modern Algerian recipe in J. Desparmet, *Enseignement de l'arabe dialectal moderne*[2], Algiers 1913, ii, 184, tr. H. Pérès and G. H. Bousquet, *Coutumes, institutions et croyances des indigènes de l'Algérie*, i, Algiers 1939, 260). But the chief method of preservation was by means of antiseptic agents, particularly salt and vinegar, often used together and with the addition of many condiments; hence the names of these preserves: *mukhallalāt, mulūḥāt*. In addition to vinegar and salt (steeping in salted water, impregnating with salt), a great deal of honey, or its substitutes sugar and treacle (*dibs*), was used in these preparations, also lemon juice, oil, mustard, walnuts or hazel nuts roasted and crushed, all kinds of herbs and spices, etc. In this way were preserved, for long or short periods according to the preparation used, vegetables, fruits and also (using vinegar, oil, etc.) small fishes and birds (*ʿuṣfūr*). Special preserves were made (often to be kept for a shorter period) to be used, spread on bread or otherwise, as a kind of hors d'œuvre: many condiments and salted herbs, or herbs mixed into salted goat's *laban*. In their preparation, *laban* and *ḳanbarīs* (curds; *Wuṣla*, ch. viii, §§ 1-25) were sometimes used. Spices made possible also the preservation of sausages, of which those considered the best contained only mutton without beef, goat-meat etc., and not too much semolina; their name, *laḳāniḳ, naḳāniḳ*, betrays their Roman origin (*lucanicae*, sausages of Lucania; Ibn al-Ukhuwwa, ed. R. Levy, London 1938, 94 f., 107; Ḥ. Zayyāt, *al-Khizāna al-sharḳiyya*, iv, Beirut 1948, 21, l. 3, 23, l. 6). The principal method of preserving milk was in the form of cheese. The eastern Jews sometimes transported kosher (*ḥalāl*) cheese very great distances (S. D. Goitein, *Jews and Arabs*, New York 1955, 112); the transport of food over medium or long distances enabled the inhabitants of the larger cities to enjoy a rich variety (*e.g.*, for Mamlūk Egypt, list in *K. al-Ḥarb al-maʿshūḳ, apud* J. Finkel, *Zeitschrift für Semitistik*, ix (1933-4), 11 f.). Generally speaking, the preservation of food was sometimes done by the producers for home consumption or for sale (*e.g.*, cheeses), sometimes by the wives or the servants in private households or in

palaces (whence the chapters of recipes for preserves in books of cookery like the *Wuṣla*), and sometimes it was the work of specialist craftsmen and prepared to be sold at a later date, sometimes after transport. The manuals of *ḥisba* [*q.v.*] enjoin the *muḥtasib* to make sure for example that any fish left unsold was salted (al-Nabrawī *apud* W. Behrnauer, *Mémoire sur les institutions de police chez les Arabes les Persans et les Turcs*, Paris 1861, 155; Muḥammad b. Abī Muḥammad al-Saḳaṭī, ed. G. S. Colin and E. Lévi-Provençal, *Un manuel hispanique de ḥisba*, i, Paris 1931, 35). But there was very little which resembled the modern food-preserving industry, though one might so classify the sausage-sellers (*naḳāniḳiyyūn*, see above), perhaps those who sold slices of meat (*sh̲arāʾiḥiyyūn*), and the sellers of confectionery (*ḥalwāniyyūn*), traders who themselves preserved food for sale. Among them should also be included the *bawāridiyyūn*, makers and sellers of *bawārid*, cooked green vegetables preserved in vinegar or other acid liquids (cf. M. Rodinson, *Recherches* . . ., 142 and the treatises of *ḥisba*).

3. Preparation. Foods often went through varying degrees of preparation before reaching the consumer, thus reducing the work done domestically (cf. S. D. Goitein, in *JESHO*, iv (1961), 193-7). Flour-grinding, work done by the women in country districts, was often in towns done by mills which provided flour ready prepared (*ṭaḥḥān* "miller"). Kneading of dough was generally done at home, but sometimes by bakers (*kh̲abbāzūn*). The Mālikī and Abāḍī schools sometimes stipulated that a wife could not be obliged to grind corn and that her husband, in this case, was to supply her with flour and not grain (ʿAbd al-ʿAzīz al-Muṣʿabī, *K. al-Nīl*, tr. E. Zeys, *Droit mozabite, Le Nil, Du Mariage*, i, Algiers 1891, 71; Saḥnūn, *apud* M. Ben Cheneb, in *Revue indigène*, xxxiv (1909), 68). But in most cases dough was taken to the owner of a bakehouse (*farrān*) to be cooked (see, *e.g.*, R. Le Tourneau, *Fès avant le protectorat*, Casablanca 1949, 327 f.). Pastries and sweetmeats were also made by craftsmen, as were the various dishes which were sold ready cooked by the *ṭabbākh̲ūn* "keepers of cook-shops", the *harrāsūn* or *harāʾisiyyūn*, sellers of *harīsa* in its popular form (minced meat and wheat cooked with fat), the *bawāridiyyūn* "sellers of *bawārid*" (see above), etc., to be taken away or eaten in the shop (lively description of a *shawwāʾ*, proprietor of a restaurant where all kinds of food could be eaten, in the *Maḳāma bag̲h̲dādiyya* of al-Hamad̲h̲ānī, ed. M. ʿAbduh, Beirut 1889, 57 ff.). European visitors to Cairo in the Middle Ages speak of 10,000 to 12,000 cooks in the streets, the 'Saracens' seldom doing any cooking at home (G. Wiet in *Revue du Caire*, August 1944, 351 f.). Meat was dealt with by specialists who carried out the slaughter (*d̲h̲abbāḥ*), the cutting up or the final marketing (*ḳaṣṣāb*, *d̲j̲azzār* with variations in terminology). More specialized products were prepared by the maker and seller of sausages (*naḳāniḳī*, see above), or of slices of meat (*sh̲arāʾiḥī*, see above), the roaster (*sh̲awwāʾ*), the seller of cooked livers (*kubūdī*), of cooked sheeps' (or other animals') heads (*rawwās*), etc. The manufacture of oil gave rise to a real industry, using presses which were sometimes very costly (P. S. Girard, *apud Description de l'Égypte, État moderne*, ii/1, Paris 1812, 605 ff. = 2nd ed., xvii, Paris 1824, 229 ff.). The industries of wine and other fermented drinks were widespread, for the use of Christians and Jews, although varying numbers of Muslims did not fail to take advantage of them; thus in the Mamlūk period Syria was a wine-growing country while Egypt was not (al-Ḳalḳash̲andī, *Ṣubḥ*, tr. Gaudefroy-Demombynes, *La Syrie à l'époque des Mamelouks*, Paris 1923, 28). The prohibitions applied to this manufacture were only of fairly limited extent; *e.g.*, under the Ottoman empire in the 11th/17th century it was forbidden to make wine or *rāḳī* (*raḳī*) within Istanbul (A. Refik, *Hicrî on birinci asırda Istanbul hayatı*, Istanbul 1931, 32, no. 63; cf. R. Mantran, *Istanbul dans la seconde moitié du XVII*ᵉ *siècle*, Paris 1962, 205 ff., 257, 448 f.). The extraction and refining of cane sugar formed an important industry; Ibn Duḳmāḳ mentions 58 factories at Fusṭāṭ (iv, Būlāḳ 1309, 41-6); it is known that it was an important state monopoly under the Mamlūks (M. Sobernheim, *Das Zuckermonopol unter Sultan Barsbai*, in *ZA*, xxvii (1912), 75-84; A. Darrag, *L'Égypte sous le règne de Barsbay*, Damascus 1961, 146-51); later it was at Cairo that sugar was refined for the use of the palace of the Ottoman Sultan (*Ḳānūnnāme*, in Digeon, *Nouveaux contes turcs et arabes*, Paris 1781, ii, 276 f.). Sugar was also refined in Syria (al-Ḳalḳash̲andī, *ibid.*), in Sicily (M. Amari, *Storia dei Musulmani di Sicilia*, Florence 1854-68, ii, 445, iii, 785 f.), in Iran (Spuler, *Iran*, index), etc. The confectioners used sugar and honey in various ways (see, *e.g.*, a good description of the work of the maker of *kunāfa*, a kind of vermicelli with sugar or honey, etc., in G. Martin, *Les bazars du Caire et les petits métiers arabes*, Cairo-Paris 1910, 60). Fish was dried and salted so that it could be transported long distances (Spuler, *Iran*, 407; Gibb-Bowen, i/1, 299); in Egypt the production of botargo (*baṭrakh̲*, *baṭrīkh̲*) from mullet roes, an industry known from Pharaonic antiquity, still continued (L. Keimer, in *BIÉ*, xxi (1938-9), 215-43). In the Fayyūm, rose-water was distilled (P. S. Girard, *op. cit.*, 609 = 2nd ed., 236 ff.).

4. Distribution. We have given above some details of the distribution of food when it was done by those who had prepared or preserved it. It should be noted that the handbook on trade by Abu 'l-Faḍl D̲j̲aʿfar b. ʿAlī al-Dimish̲ḳī (5th-6th/11th-12th centuries?) classifies grocers as half traders and half craftsmen (see H. Ritter, in *Isl.*, vii (1917), 6). The peasant producers came to sell their produce either in the country, in temporarily set up regional markets (cf. R. Brunschvig, *Coup d'œil sur l'histoire des foires à travers l'Islam*, in *Recueils de la Société Jean Bodin*, v (1953), 43-75; F. Benet, *Weekly suqs and city markets*, in *Research for development in the Mediterranean Basin, a proposal*, ed. C. A. O. van Niewenhuijze, The Hague 1961, 86-97), or in the towns, in markets which were more or less permanent. In the larger towns there were wholesale markets supplying the large markets which served the whole of a large town district and also the small local markets. Private householders bought their provisions from the two latter types (good description by R. Le Tourneau, *Fès avant le protectorat*, Casablanca 1949, 368-97 and R. Mantran, *Istanbul* . . ., 185 ff.). These retail markets consisted of specialized little shops: fruit and vegetable sellers, butchers, dried fruit merchants, sellers of spices (*ʿaṭṭār*), grocers who sold various kinds of fats (*baḳḳāl* in Morocco, elsewhere usually *zayyāt*, *sammān*, etc. with many variants, cf. D̲j̲amāl al-Dīn al-Ḳāsimī, *Ḳāmūs al-ṣināʿāt al-sh̲āmiyya*, Paris-The Hague 1960, 48), etc. There are found in the works on the corporations extensive lists of these retailers (*e.g.*, L. Massignon, *Enquête sur les corporations musulmanes d'artisans et de commerçants au Maroc*, an offprint from *RMM*, Paris 1925). As we have said, many variations are

to be found in the demarcation and naming of specializations in the different regions. In certain countries at certain times the state played an important part at several stages in the distribution of commodities.

5. Food consumption and its variations. In the sociological study of food, special attention must be paid to how consumption varies with different groups and categories of individuals (R. Firth, *The sociological study of native diet*, in *Africa*, vii (1934), 410 f.). These variations are due either to natural, geographical and economic differences in the food resources available to each group, or to cultural traditions of varying origins. Muslim civilization provides many instances of this phenomenon, which is worthy of more detailed study; here we shall give only some examples.

The geographical variations are obviously due to the variety of the resources available, and thus to natural conditions. But, at the sociological level, based on these conditions and extending beyond them, the establishment of cultural traditions regarding the choice and the preparation of dishes has created regional specialization. Thus, in the Middle Ages, Egyptian cuisine had a high reputation (cf. Ḥ. Zayyāt, *al-Khizāna al-sharḳiyya*, iv, Beirut 1948, 14). In Turkey, the cooks of Bolu were and remain very famous (see BOLU, and Nazim Hikmet, *Les romantiques*, Fr. tr., Paris 1964, 8, 156). Cooks from places which were renowned for their food were employed in far distant regions. Al-Ṭāhir brought to Baghdād a Khurāsānī cook (Ṭayfūr, *apud* Spuler, *Iran*, 510), and Egyptian women-cooks were employed everywhere (even in the household of an orientalized Frankish knight of Antioch, cf. Usāma b. Munḳidh, *K. al-Iʿtibār*, ed. P. K. Hitti, Princeton 1930, 140; tr. P. K. Hitti, New York 1929, 169 f.). This specialization gave rise to the numerous adjectives of geographical origin which accompany or represent the names of many dishes: *e.g.*, there are cakes called *akhmīmiyya*, *asyūṭiyya*, a sweet called *ḥalwā makkiyya*, etc. (cf. M. Rodinson, *Recherches* ..., 150). For the regional specialities of Andalus, see A. Huici Miranda, in *Revista del Instituto de Estudios Islámicos en Madrid*, v (1957), 139; a recent ethnographic survey in Turkey traces the local variations of the same dish, see Z. Koşay and A. Ülkücan, *Anadolu yemekleri ve Türk mutfağı*, Ankara 1961; similarly, on local varieties of *palōv* (Ottoman *pilav*, *pilaf*) in Uzbekistan, see Karim Mahmudov, *Uzbekskie blyuda*, Tashkent 1963, 6, 77 ff., and cf. N. K. Alhazov, etc., *Azerbaydžanskaya kulinariya*, Baku 1963, 65 ff. Regional foods or dishes were made far from their place of origin, the recipes being transmitted orally or in writing. Thus as early as the 7th/13th century we find in the East recipes for Maghribī couscous (*ibid.*, 138; for the longing for couscous felt by Maghribī exiles in the East, see Maḳḳarī, Būlāḳ, iii, 137; cf. H. Pérès, in *Bull. des Études Arabes*, iii (1943), 140; R. Brunschvig, *La Berberie orientale sous les Ḥafṣides*, Paris 1940-7, 271). Food is today one of the channels for patriotic fervour. In literature and films, Egypt's national food (*ṭaʿmiyya*, Egyptian beans—*fūl mudammas miṣrī*, Jew's mallow or *mulūkhiyya*) is contrasted with the cosmopolitan dishes affected by snobs (see, *e.g.*, Maḥmūd Taymūr, *La belle aux lèvres charnues*, Fr. tr., Paris 1952, 87). A school textbook relates how an Egyptian student is delighted to find in Oxford an atmosphere of his native country in a restaurant kept by an Egyptian and serving *fūl mudammas* (Saʿīd al-ʿUryān, A. Duwaydār and M. Zahrān, *Mudammas Uksfūrd*, Cairo 1950). Egyptian emigrants returning home dream of a good hot *ṭaʿmiyya* rissole (Yūsuf Idrīs, *Umm al-dunyā*, in his collection *Arkhaṣ al-layālī*, Cairo 1954, series *al-Kitāb al-dhahabī*, 94).

When massive emigrations take place, the emigrants introduce their traditional dishes into their new habitat. Thus, the great emigrations of Muslims from Spain at the time of the Reconquista brought many Andalusian recipes to the Maghrib (see E. Gobert, in *Cahiers de Tunisie*, iii (1955), 529 ff.), for example the famous *bəṣṭēla* (from Span. *pastel*) of Morocco (see L. Brunot, *Textes arabes de Rabat*, ii, Paris 1952, 52; detailed recipe in Z. Guinaudeau, *Fès vu par sa cuisine*, Rabat 1957, 33 ff.).

Variations according to the different religious groups are of more importance ideologically. We shall deal later with the development of the principles laid down in the Ḳurʾān, and it is necessary to mention here only that each group tended to mark itself off distinctly from the others by having its own series of rules concerning food. To eat just like others implied, generally speaking, that a group did not consider itself completely split off from them. In principle one should not eat with the *kāfir* (Goldziher, *Vorlesungen*, 182, Fr. tr. Paris 1920, 152), which gave rise to the vast question of who exactly is to be regarded as *kāfir*. The Ḳurʾān allowed Muslims to eat the food of the *Ahl al-kitāb* and vice versa (V, 7/5, see above). But there is attributed to the Prophet a letter to the Mazdeans of Hadjar according to which Muslims were not to eat meat which they had killed as a sacrifice (Ibn Saʿd, i/2, Leiden 1917, 19, l. 8; al-Balādhurī, *Futūḥ*, 80; cf. Spuler, *Iran*, 184, n. 5). Even in relation to the *Ahl al-kitāb*, the law was more restrictive than the Ḳurʾān, at least concerning animals killed while hunting or by ritual slaughter. It was not forbidden but reprehensible (*makrūh*), according to certain Mālikīs, to eat what a *Kitābī* had slaughtered for himself; according to others, on the contrary, this applied to meat slaughtered by a *Kitābī* for a Muslim. In all cases it was reprehensible to obtain meat from a non-Muslim butcher (Mālikīs). It was advisable to make sure that the name of Allāh had been invoked and not the Cross, or Jesus, etc., though it was permissible to eat, according to all the schools except the Ḥanbalīs, if no name at all had been invoked. However, a *fatwā* of Muḥammad ʿAbduh supporting the same position, issued in about 1903, seems to have provoked heated arguments (M. Rashīd Riḍā, *Taʾrīkh al-ustādh al-imām*, iii, Cairo 1324, 84, 167; see also C. C. Adams, in *Macdonald presentation volume*, Princeton 1933, 13-29). But it was reprehensible to eat anything destined for the synagogues, the churches or the feasts of the *Ahl al-kitāb*. In any case meat obtained from an idolater, a Mazdean, a pagan or an apostate was prohibited. To this list was sometimes added Christian Arabs (prohibited by Shāfiʿīs, and reprehensible according to certain Mālikīs) (ʿAbd al-Raḥmān al-Djazīrī, *K. al-Fiḳh ʿala 'l-madhāhib al-arbaʿa*, ii/3, Cairo n.d., 21-6, etc.). The application of these principles has remained fairly strict until the present day. In China, many of the Muslim carriers take their own bread with them on journeys in order to avoid eating food prepared by infidels (M. Broomhall, *Islam in China*, London 1910, 230 f.). Usāma chose his food carefully in the house of the orientalized Frankish knight mentioned above. However, it is well known that Jewish food conforms to the Muslim rites and thus may be eaten, unlike that of Christians, hence a well-known proverb giving the advice to sleep in Christian beds (which are clean). but to eat Jewish food (Freytag, *Arabum proverbia*, iii, 13, no. 73; W. Marçais and A. Guîga, *Textes arabes de Takroûna*, ii, *Glossaire*, vi, Paris 1959, 2932; E. Westermarck, *Ritual and belief in Morocco*, London 1926, ii, 4). However the eastern Christians often tended to conform with the Muslim regulations (Barhebraeus, *Nomocanon* [in Syriac], ed. P. Bedjan, Paris 1898, 463 ff., tr. J. A. Assemani *apud* A. Mai *Scriptorum veterum nova collectio*, x, Rome 1838, 229 ff.; Ibn al-ʿAssāl, *Nomocanon*, ch. 23, ms. Paris, ar. 245, fol. 94 ff., Ethiopic tr. *Fatḥa Nagašt*, ed. I. Guidi, Rome 1897, 147 ff., tr., Rome 1899, 209 ff.), At the same time Christians and Jews very often avoided Muslim food. The Christians of Ethiopia reproached Europeans with eating meat killed by Muslims, which they considered as amounting practically to apostasy (Abba Tékla-Haïmanot, *Abouna Yacob ou le vénérable De Jacobis*, Paris 1914, 14; Mansfield Parkyns, *Life in Abyssinia*, London 1853, ii, 92 f.). The Christians of Nābulus before the 1914-18 war limited themselves to avoiding the meat of animals sacrificed during the Feast of Sacrifices (J.-A. Jaussen, *Naplouse*, Paris 1927, 311), while the Copts in Egypt in the 11th/17th century bought no food of any sort from Muslims during this feast (J. M. Vansleb, *Nouvelle relation ... d'un voyage fait en Égypte*, Paris 1698, 383). But the Jews of Bu<u>kh</u>ārā in the 12th/18th century had no scruples about eating animals killed by Muslims (J. Wolff, *apud* A. Yaʿarī, *<u>Sh</u>ĕlūḥê ʾĕrĕṣ yiśrâʾél*, Jerusalem 5711/1951, 665). The Afrīdīs of Af<u>gh</u>ānistān, who claim to be of Jewish origin, eat, therefore, meat cooked by Jews, but, being also Sunnīs, refuse meat prepared by <u>Sh</u>īʿīs (Y. Ben-Zvi, *Niddĕḥê Yiśrâʾél*[2], Tel Aviv 5716/1956, 194, Eng. tr. *The exiled and the redeemed*, London 1958, 223). A similar separatism concerning food is to be found therefore among the various sects, but was rather exceptional. In the 4th/10th century a jurist of Ḳayrawān refused to eat sugar which came from Fāṭimid Sicily (*Riyāḍ al-nufūs, apud* M. Amari, *Storia* ..., iii, 785 f.; 2nd ed. iii/3, 808 ff.). The question of eating meat which has been sacrificed arises more often. A saying attributed to Ṭalḥa b. Muṣarrif (d. 112 or 113/730 or 731) and used by the Ḥanbalīs extends to the Rāfiḍa the prohibition decreed by Muḥammad concerning the Mazdeans: it was forbidden to marry their women or to eat the animals which they had slaughtered as sacrifices (Ibn Baṭṭa, *apud* H. Laoust, *La profession de foi d'Ibn Baṭṭa*, Damascus 1958, 38, tr., 64). The Ismāʿīlīs forbade eating the meat of sacrifices offered by *mu<u>sh</u>rikūn* or *ahl al-<u>kh</u>ilāf*, unless one had witnessed that the name of God had been pronounced over it (Ḳāḍī Nuʿmān, *K. al-Iḳtiṣār*, ed. M. W. Mirza, Damascus 1957, 105). They were thus assimilated to the *Ahl al-kitāb*. The Mālikīs discouraged the eating of meat which came from a *bidʿī*, while for the <u>Sh</u>īʿīs that which came from the enemies of the *ahl al-bayt* was unlawful (ʿAbd al-Raḥmān al-<u>D</u>jazīrī, *op. cit.*, 22; Abu 'l-Ḳāṣim <u>D</u>jaʿfar b. Muḥ. al-Ḥillī, *<u>Sh</u>arāʾiʿ al-Islām*, Calcutta 1839, 396 top, tr. A. Querry, *Droit musulman*, Paris 1871-2, ii, 214, § 50).

The variations according to way of life are probably the most considerable. The Bedouins differ from the settled populations in their food as well as in other details (see, *e.g.*, al-<u>D</u>jāḥiẓ, *Bu<u>kh</u>alāʾ*, ed. Ḥā<u>d</u>jirī, Cairo 1948, 164, Fr. tr. Ch. Pellat, Paris 1951, 259). Bedouin women refused to marry town-dwellers because they hated the food of the towns, especially green vegetables (W. R. Smith, *Kinship and marriage in early Arabia*[2], London 1903, 75, n. 2) and the same repugnance is found also among the nomadic Ḳazaḳs in Central Asia (J. D. Littlepage and D. Bess, *In search of Soviet gold*, New York [1937], 110 f.; cf. *Narodī Sredney Azii i Kaza<u>kh</u>stana*, ii, Moscow 1963, 428). Milk products were a typical food of nomads everywhere in the ancient world (B. Laufer, *Some fundamental ideas of Chinese culture*, in *The Journal of Race Development*, v (1914), 167-70; H. G. Creel, *The birth of China*, London 1936, 80 f., Fr. tr. Paris 1937, 77 f.) and they suffered if they were deprived of them when in settled districts (cf. above, col. 1057 b). The difference between peasants and town-dwellers was also often emphasized. It was the subject in Egypt of literary works such as, in the 9th/15th century, the *K. al-Ḥarb al-maʿ<u>sh</u>ūḳ* ..., and in the 11th/17th century the *Hazz al-ḳuḥūf* of al-<u>Sh</u>irbīnī (cf. Rodinson, *Recherches* ..., 113-5).

There was hardly any difference between the food of men and women, except perhaps that the idle lives of rich women inclined them to greediness, the love of sweet things, etc. (see, *e.g.*, E. de Amicis, *Constantinopoli*[3], Milan 1877, 333, Eng. tr. *Constantinople*, London 1878, 234 f.). The excursions of groups of women of leisure for picnics etc. were accompanied also by purchases of cakes, fruit, ices, etc. (*ibid.*, 306 f., Eng. tr., 214 f.; L. M. J. Garnett, *Turkish life in town and country*, London n.d., 67). Hence a regulation of the 10th/16th century forbidding women to go into the shops of the *ḳaymaḳčīs* of Eyyūb and laying down that the Christians should avoid them (A. Refik, *On altıncı asırda Istanbul hayatı*[2], Istanbul 1935, 40, no. 5; cf. R. Mantran, *Istanbul dans la seconde moitié du XVIIème siècle*, Paris 1962, 68). Similarly when in the baths women ate sweetmeats and special dishes (Kulsum Naneh, *Le livre des dames de la Perse*, tr. L. Thonnelier, Paris 1881, 28, 35 f.). In Iran, the offerings to Fāṭima are eaten only by men, at least in one of the first phases of the rite (H. Massé, *Croyances et coutumes persanes*, Paris 1938, ii, 302). Moreover, in some places, customs based on magic forbid certain foods to women (E. Westermarck, *Ritual and belief in Morocco*, London 1916, ii, 363).

Differences in diet according to age depend on theoretical (and even scientific) opinions concerning food. We shall deal with them below. On the other hand a certain number of differences according to social classes can be traced to economic and social factors. Naturally considerations of price alone restricted the food of the poor both in quantity and quality and had the same effect on that of misers, who were voluntarily poor. In some of the literature about misers, particularly in the masterpiece of al-<u>D</u>jāḥiẓ, the *K. al-Bu<u>kh</u>alāʾ*, much is said about their meagre diet. The food of the poor and of misers was apt to include in particular "filling" dishes which were, at least in appearance, rich in nutritional value while consisting of inexpensive ingredients, like Harpagon's haricot of mutton. Several such dishes are mentioned in the time of al-<u>D</u>jāḥiẓ: *ṭif<u>sh</u>īla, harīsa, fu<u>d</u>jliyya, kurunbiyya* (*Bu<u>kh</u>alāʾ*, ed. Ḥā<u>d</u>jirī, 60; tr. Pellat, 99). At the beginning of the 7th/13th century lentils also were mentioned as a dish of poor people (M. Rodinson, *Recherches* ..., 153) and they were again despised as the food of the *fallāḥ* by al-<u>Sh</u>irbīnī. The distinction between the dishes of the poor and those of the rich was clearly understood by the collective consciousness, as expressed in proverbs, popular literature, etc. Examples of this are found in current proverbs about *burghul* (Turkish *bulgur*) "crushed wheat", a dish of the poor and peasants in Syria-Palestine and Turkey in contrast to rice, the dish of the wealthy town-dwellers (M. Feghali, *Proverbes et dictons syro-libanais*, Paris 1938, 248, no. 1097; cf. X. de Planhol, *De la plaine pamphylienne aux lacs pisidiens*, Paris 1958, 177). The *K. al-Ḥarb al-maʿshūḳ* has precisely as its main theme the contest between the food of the poor and that of the rich (J. Finkel, in *Zeitschrift für Semitistik*, viii (1932), 122-48, ix (1933-4), 1-18; cf. M. Rodinson, *Recherches* . . ., 113 ff.). The food of the rich was distinguished by the variety of the dishes, their complexity, their expensiveness, the length of time needed for their preparation, an ostentatious freedom of choice expressed by eating foods of little nutritional value. There was obviously an effort to improve the quantity and quality of the diet, but still there were applied the rules of "conspicuous consumption" in food (Thorstein Veblen, *The theory of the leisure class*, ch. iv, New York 1934, 73 f.) intended to set apart the élite from the masses. The members of the élite were expected to be familiar with the most esoteric dishes, and they either wrote themselves such treatises on cookery as those produced by people of importance in the ʿAbbāsid period (M. Rodinson, *Recherches* . . ., 99 ff.) or had these books written for them (cf. introduction of the book of Ibn Sayyār al-Warrāḳ in Ḥ. Zayyāt, *al-Khizāna al-sharḳiyya*, iv, Beirut 1948, 20). Those who aspired to refinement in 4th/10th century Baghdād, the *ẓurafāʾ*, had strict rules in this matter (Al-Washshāʾ, *K. al-Muwashshā*, ed. R. E. Brünnow, Leiden 1886, 94 f., 130 ff., etc.; cf. M. F. Ghazi, in *Studia Islamica*, xi (1959), 61). The rulers had huge kitchens for themselves and their court, well stocked and equipped, staffed by numerous cooks and their assistants, under the direction of officers such as the *djashnagīr*, the *shādd al-sharāb-khāna* and the *ustādār al-ṣuḥba* at the court of the Mamlūks (Gaudefroy-Demombynes, *La Syrie à l'époque des Mamelouks*, Paris 1923, LX f.), the *kilārdji bashi*, "master of the larder" and his subordinates like the *peshkir bashi*, etc., all supplied with their provisions by the *maṭbakh emīni* and his staff at the Ottoman Palace (Gibb-Bowen, i/1, 78, 85, 332 f., 336 f.).

The quest for the exotic, the partial adoption of the cuisine of foreigners, especially when their civilization enjoys a certain prestige, is another means by which the élite may demonstrate its distinction from ordinary folk. Hence, in the Arab world, the vogue for Iranian dishes, which seems to have begun in pre-Islamic times (cf. ʿAbd Allāh b. Djudʿān's introduction of *fālūdhadj* at Mecca, Alūsī, *Bulūgh*², i, 381) and was very pronounced in the ʿAbbāsid period (Rodinson, *Recherches* . . ., 148 ff.), and later the fashion for things Turkish (*ibid.*, 151). European influence began in the period of the Crusades (*ibid.*, 150; Rodinson, in *Comptes Rendus du GLECS*, ix (1960-3), 106 f.), and has naturally been very powerful since the 19th century, as all modern cookery-books demonstrate (see, *e.g.*, H. Stumme, in *Islamica*, ii (1926), 538-49). Deep though its influence has been (see, for example, on the influence of Russian diet in Central Asia, K. Mahmudov, *Uzbekskie blyuda*, Tashkent 1963, 6, with illustrations of how this trend has been resisted by the Muslim 'clergy', who call potatoes 'food of Satan' and tomatoes 'fruits made of human blood'), in all countries the traditional dishes retain their popularity. Conversely, Muslim diet exercised a pronounced influence on Christian Europe in the Middle Ages (see M. Rodinson, in *Romania*, lxxi (1950), 433-49, in *Scritti orientalistici in onore di G. Levi Della Vida*, Rome 1956, ii, 425-35, and in *Études d'orientalisme . . . . Lévi-Provençal*, Paris 1962, 733-47).

6. Factors of secular ideology in food. We can class as ideological the recommendations or prescriptions which are based either on a rational deduction from various principles and assumptions, or on the Divine will elucidated in greater or less degree by reasoning. Recommendations and prescriptions of this sort play an important part in food habits. We have seen above how certain of them are connected with differences in diet according to social groups and we shall now deal with some others, beginning with the non-religious ones.

Certain general ideas which are prudent deductions from experience are handed on by popular tradition. Thus we have a list of nourishing foods, and of those which cause wind (cf. Ibn ʿAbd Rabbih, *Al-ʿIḳd al-farīd*, ed. A. Amīn etc., vi, Cairo 1949, 320 ff.). But generalizations of a "magic" type are often found: they can grow up from a basis of real attributes which have been observed (birds are timorous, testicles are connected with sexual activity, honey is sweet, etc.), or be deduced from systems of symbolic connexions (yellow is beneficial, black is ill-omened, etc.; cf. the remarkable and unfortunately unique study by J. Jouin, *Valeur symbolique des aliments et rites alimentaires à Rabat*, in *Hesperis*, xliv (1957), 299-327). But these wide and rash generalizations are based on the magic principles of contagion by propinquity, the law of similarity and of opposites, etc. Thus we have seen that in north-western Arabia it is believed that whoever eats birds' hearts becomes himself timorous (see above, col. 1059 b); similarly medical treatises explain that sheep's liver, heart or kidneys strengthen the liver, heart or kidneys of whoever eats them, while to eat sheep's brains causes loss of memory and stupidity because the sheep is senseless and stupid (Dāwūd al-Anṭākī, *Tadhkira*, Cairo 1356/1937, i, 207; cf. the conversation recorded by Naʿīmā (anno 1063, A.H.) and translated by B. Lewis, *Istanbul and the civilization of the Ottoman Empire*, Norman Okla. 1963, 171-2); in present-day Morocco young boys newly-circumcised are made to drink soup made from sheep's testicles to strengthen them, and it is also the recognized diet for people who are exhausted (J. Jouin, *op. cit.*, 309). *Ḥalwāʾ* made with saffron has been recommended because yellow is a source of gaiety (Niẓāmī, *Haft paykar*, Tehrān 1334, 197², tr. C. E. Wilson, London 1924, i, 156). Honey with its sweetness assuages mental suffering (J. Jouin, *op. cit.*, 315) as does *talbīna*, a dish made with honey (see above, col. 1059 a), hence their consumption at funerals. It is possible that the dictum attributed to the *faḳīh* of Medina, Rabīʿa b. Abī ʿAbd al-Raḥmān (d. 136/753-4), according to which the eating of *khabīṣ* (jelly made with starch) fortifies the brain (Ibn ʿAbd Rabbih, *al-ʿIḳd al-farīd*, vi, Cairo 1949, 293), belongs to this class of popular opinions.

But as well as these there was also the corpus of scholarly opinions, transmitted by books and stemming for the most part from the scientific medicine systematized by the Greeks. It consisted of generalizations based sometimes on systematic research on data which were certainly not self-evident (such as the presence in the human body, besides blood, of the pituitary glands, yellow and black bile), from which the Greeks had drawn up a carefully worked out system, avoiding symbolic data and open in principle to revision, consisting as it did of hypotheses which could be verified or invalidated. It was based on the theory of humours, from which had been deduced all kinds of conclusions on the nature of each food and its suitability to one or another human temperament. Thus all the books of medicine contain a long chapter enumerating, usually in alphabetical order, the attributes and faults of each food from the point of view of bodily and spiritual well-being. Special works are also devoted to this branch of medicine, dietetics. Some of them were translated into Latin and had a considerable influence on European dietetics (cf. M. Rodinson, *Recherches* ..., 110 f.). The educated classes paid a great deal of attention to dietetic precepts, so that this science was of no small practical importance. To choose one example among scores, there was the book on dietetics written by Maimonides for al-Malik al-Afḍal. Numerous examples of rulers who could not do without dieticians at their table are given in Ḥ. Zayyāt, *al-Khizāna al-sharḳiyya*, iv, Beirut 1948, 10 ff., cf. H. R. Idris, *La Berbérie orientale sous les Zīrides*, Paris 1962, i, 251. Moreover, these scholarly theories penetrated deeply among the masses, where they became inextricably mixed, sometimes in a debased form, with current ideas coming from other sources. At the same time the learned works came more and more to take account of popular ideas on diet. Thus the famous doctor-philosopher Abū Bakr al-Rāzī (d. 311/923 or 320/932) wrote that fresh dates caused ophthalmia, an idea which re-appears later in Ibn al-Bayṭār in the 7th/13th century. It is probable that this theory, which was unknown to the Greeks and to Ḥunayn b. Isḥāḳ, came from popular ideas in the East (M. Meyerhof, *apud* P. Kraus, in *Orientalia*, iv (1935), 326).

Scholarly ideas on dietetics were influenced by popular ideas, particularly when it came to dealing with diets for special cases. For example the diet of women in child-birth is the subject of only a few general recommendations by the Greek physicians and the first Arab theorists who derived their ideas from them (cf., *e.g.*, Ibn Sīnā, *Ḳānūn*, iii, fann 21, maḳāla 2, faṣl 3). But later the subject was developed under the influence of popular recipes. Thus a 9th/15th century writer recommends, in addition to foods and medicines intended as remedies for stomach pains etc., fresh ripe dates (*ruṭab*) and, if they are not available, ordinary dates also. This is justified by a *ḥadīth* and by the example of the Virgin Mary in Ḳurʾān, XIX, 25 (Ibrāhīm b. ʿAbd al-Raḥmān al-Azraḳ, *K. Tashīl al-manāfiʿ*, Cairo 1356, 140 f.).

7. Post-Ḳurʾānic religious regulations. The pious specialists on religious questions who, in the 2nd/8th century, began to advise on the way of life which best conformed to the Muslim ideal recommended or discouraged the eating of certain foods, in accordance with current practice (see J. Schacht, *Esquisse d'une histoire du droit musulman*, Paris 1953, 22 ff.). Gradually these recommendations became canonized, as they were attributed to earlier and earlier authorities ending with the Prophet himself, at the same time that attempts were made to deduce from them general rules, to systematize them and also to bring them into harmony with the few prescriptions, later more precisely defined and systematized, which are contained in the Ḳurʾān. We cannot here follow the development of this process (on this see, *e.g.*, J. Schacht, *EI*¹, art. MAITA) and we shall deal only with its final results.

The prohibitions concerning food are part of the vast system of Muslim ethics. For this reason there are used for them the usual categories, which include all the degrees, from obligation to prohibition, by way of recommendation, indifferent permission and reprobation. Efforts are made to state the attitude to be taken in every possible case, and even in some very unlikely cases. Procedures are established to settle doubtful cases, all else failing, by ordeal: drawing lots to indicate which animal of a flock has been the object of an act of bestiality and is therefore impure (Abu 'l-Ḳāsim Djaʿfar b. Muḥ. al-Ḥillī, *Sharaʾiʿ al-Islām*, Calcutta 1839, 402, tr. Querry, *Droit musulman*, ii, 231, § 17); in cases of doubt as to the provenance of birds' eggs, which would decide whether they were lawful, to use those whose ends differ in width (*ibid.*, 403 = Querry, ii, 233 f., § 37 [Shīʿīs]).

The categories of the permitted and the forbidden in this field are (apart from some exceptions) identical with those of the clean and the unclean. There follows from this the obligation to apply to these cases the general idea of contagion, of the contaminating power of uncleanliness, which gives rise to a number of delicate problems to determine the limits of this contagion. The milk and the eggs of unclean animals are obviously unclean; but does an animal who has drunk wine or sow's milk, both of them unclean, become by this act unclean itself? (al-Ḥillī, *op. cit.*, 402; tr. Querry, ii, 230 f.). A dog, being unclean, makes unclean any liquid which it has begun to lap or game which it has begun to eat (D. Santillana, *Istituzioni di diritto musulmano malichita*, i, Rome 1926, 321); but there may be another juridical reason for the prohibition in the latter case (cf. al-Ghazālī, *Iḥyāʾ*, Cairo 1352/1933, ii, 91; H. Laoust, *Le précis de droit d'Ibn Qudāma*, Beirut 1950, 230). The question was much discussed as to how far a mouse (or other unclean animal) which had fallen into a food which was clean caused it to be unclean (al-Dārimī, viii, 41; Abū Dāwūd, xxvi, 47; cf. Santillana, *Istituzioni*, i, 321). In general it is admitted that the uncleanliness is transmitted to the whole of any liquid or fluid matter, but only to the parts of any solid matter which are near to the part touched (unless the mouse has remained there for a long time, according to the Mālikī Saḥnūn: Ibn Abī Zayd al-Ḳayrawānī, *Risāla*, ed. and tr. L. Bercher², Algiers 1948, 158). The crossing of a clean with an unclean animal makes their progeny unclean (*e.g.*, the mule; see also, *e.g.*, Ibrāhīm b. ʿAlī al-Shīrāzī, *K. al-Tanbīh*, ed. and tr. Bousquet, i, Algiers 1949, 123 [Shāfiʿī]).

It became necessary also to lay down the course to be followed when there arose a conflict between the system of regulations concerning food and other principles and exigencies of social life, and to make general rules also for borderline cases. Thus, suicide being forbidden, man has a duty to keep himself alive and in good health. From this is deduced the prohibition of injurious substances, notably intoxicants (cf. al-Ghazālī, *Iḥyāʾ*, ii, 83, l. 16 f. concerning *bandj* [*q.v.*] "henbane"; in the Mughal Empire, non-Muslims as well as Muslims were, from social and humanitarian motives, forbidden to use it, see Sri Ram Sharma, *The religious policy of the Mughal Emperors*², London 1962, 25 f., 93, 109 ff.; but nowadays this prohibition is stressed especially with regard to opium, *ḥashīsh*, cocaine, etc., cf. ʿAbd al-Raḥmān al-Djazīrī, *K. al-Fiḳh ʿala 'l-madhāhib al-arbaʿa*, ii², Cairo n.d., 4). But in cases of famine and of extreme necessity, the principle of keeping one's self alive conflicts with the prohibition of what is unclean, and it is acknowledged that the latter must be sacrificed, at least to the minimum degree necessary to maintain life. But limits are set, and also a graduated table of degrees of uncleanliness is established (cf. al-Ḥillī, 406-8, tr. Querry, *Droit musulman*, ii, 242-6, which is especially detailed). The question arose and still arises particularly in relation to medicines prescribed by doctors. In the same way a compromise is established between the duty to keep alive and the rights of property: in certain conditions and within certain limits it is permissible to seize by force from a reluctant owner the means for sustaining one's life. In some cases the duty of acting humanely towards animals can also have an influence on what food is eaten (*e.g.*, the recommendation not to slaughter a sheep which is suckling, Muslim, xxxvi, 140a).

The *fiḳh* naturally upheld the food prohibitions laid down by the Ḳurʾān, endeavouring only to define their scope. The prohibition of blood, linked with that of the meat of animals which are dead without having been ritually slaughtered, led to many developments. It was necessary to define very precisely the method and conditions of slaughter [see DHABĪḤA], etc. Although "carrion" (*mayta*), an animal simply found dead, remains completely forbidden except in case of absolute necessity [see MAYTA], attempts have been made to mitigate a little the more precise prohibition, given in Ḳurʾān, V, 4/3, of the flesh of animals found strangled or gored, victims of a fall or killed by a blunt instrument. If even a breath of life remains in them they may still be ritually slaughtered and thus rendered lawful to eat. This is the "purification" mentioned in the Ḳurʾān. It was necessary to define in the greatest detail the signs by which the presence of this flicker of life could be recognized or presumed to exist (a good summary of the position of the Sunnī schools in al-Djazīrī, *K. al-Fiḳh*, ii³, 4 and n. 3). More serious difficulties are caused by hunting. In general it is necessary to perform the ritual slaughter of the animal before its death, if this is possible. But where this is impossible, it is conceded that the fact of having killed an animal while formulating the intention of slaughtering it ritually and pronouncing the *tasmiya* ("in the name of God") at the moment of sending off the missile may take the place of this ritual slaughter. Naturally the pilgrim who has entered the state of ritual purity (*muḥrim*) may not take advantage of these privileges (in view of the Ḳurʾānic prohibition mentioned above). However some traditions authorize him to eat a wild ass which has been hunted down (al-Bukhārī, lxx, 20) or, in return for compensation, a hyena (Abū Dāwūd, xxvi, 31; cf. Gaudefroy-Demombynes, *Le pèlerinage à la Mekke*, Paris 1923, 10, n. 2, 11 ff.). On the other hand, efforts were made to specify how far the unlawfulness of the *mayta* extends to its skin, its milk, its eggs or to any foetus which it might contain. An exception from the prohibition of blood is generally made for the liver and the spleen, which are considered as a solid form of blood (*ḥadīth*: two kinds of blood have been made lawful for us, Ibn Mādja, xxix, 31; Aḥmad b. Ḥanbal, ii, 97). Ritual slaughter is not necessary for fish (or any marine animals), nor for locusts (cf. art MAYTA and below). For *khamr*, the same processes of interpretation are applied to the Ḳurʾānic prohibition. We shall limit ourselves here to mentioning that, on the one hand, the idea of *khamr* is defined by the intoxicating power of the liquor concerned (taking advantage of the meaning of *khāmara* "to be mixed together"), and that on the other hand the prohibition makes it, in accordance with the logic of the system, a drink impure in itself, even in a quantity too small to produce drunkenness. The result is a logical contradiction, which is illustrated when al-Ghazālī contrasts the Muslim law with the supposed prohibition of wine by Jesus, based solely on its ability to intoxicate. Ghazālī gets over the difficulty by asserting that the drinking of small quantities leads to that of large quantities and drunkenness (*Iḥyaʾ*, iv, 81, l. 3 f.), which is the line taken in the modern interpretation, which emphasizes the moral, hygienic and social justifications for this prohibition (cf. al-Djazīrī, *K. al-Fiḳh*, ii, 6-9).

Food can sometimes be affected by impurities which have nothing to do with the food itself. Thus the impurity of menstruation (Ḳurʾān, II, 222, and much developed later) leads to the conclusion that the meat of menstruating female animals is impure (*e.g.*, the hare: Abū Dāwūd, xxvi, 26b), just as the impurity of women in this state can be transmitted to the food which they prepare (al-Ḥillī, 406, tr. Querry, *Droit musulman*, ii, 242, § 97 f.; a regulation which was applied at Nābulus according to Jaussen, *Naplouse*, 311). The same applies to food prepared by infidels (including the *ahl al-dhimma*, according to certain authors), perhaps even to that eaten in their company (*ibid.*, 404, 405, tr. Querry, ii, 236, 239, and col. 1065 b above) or, in practice, that prepared in utensils which they have used (a pathetic case cited by M. Broomhall, *Islam in China*, 226).

The Mālikī school endeavoured to limit the prohibitions to foods declared impure by Ḳurʾānic prescription, with only those restrictions set out above: that the food eaten should be neither harmful nor the property of others. But in general the idea of uncleanliness was extended, as we have seen, to other foods. It concerns always animal food, except where it relates to edible earth, which was sometimes discouraged or forbidden, and, among the Shīʿīs, to water from hot springs, which was discouraged. Lists are given of the impure parts of animals, generally faecal matter and urine (the urine of the camel is, however, permitted as a medicament); to these are sometimes added the sexal organs and other parts. Similarly, acts of bestiality make unclean the meat of the animal concerned, also the eating of excrement. This leads to the case of the *djallāla*, "scatophagous animal", mentioned in *ḥadīth* (Abū Dāwūd, xxvi, 24, 33, etc.) and developed in great detail by the *fiḳh*, which specifies in particular the length of time which the animal must be kept in supervised isolation and fed with clean food in order to regain its cleanliness and be eaten lawfully.

But, above all, a certain number of animals are added to the pig, which is the only one actually prohibited as such by the Ḳurʾān. For some of these, such as humans and dogs, it is obvious that all that is being done is to make explicit prohibitions which are implicit in the sayings reported from the Prophet. In the case of certain others, a thorough study would be necessary to determine which are of pre-Islamic Arab origin and which arise from the customs already existing among peoples who have become Islamicized. In general, however, Islamic jurisprudence has developed extensively the chapter on the juridical classification of the various animals, with perceptible divergences among the schools: a summary of the attitudes adopted by the principal juridical schools will be found in the article ḤAYAWĀN—iv.

Over and above the categories elaborated by the schools, on the basis of the Ḳurʾān and Tradition, of foods whose consumption is forbidden or reprehensible, the zealous Muslim may wish to carry the imitation of the Prophet so far as to abstain from foods which, according to Tradition, displeased him personally, but which he did not forbid to others (at least according to most of the texts), although he forbade those smelling of them to enter the mosque: garlic, onion and often leeks (*kurrāth*; cf. references *apud* Wensinck, *A handbook of early Muhammedan tradition*, Leiden 1927, s.vv.; recommendations to which attention is still paid today, cf. J. Jomier, *Le commentaire coranique du Manâr*, Paris 1954, 142), which is probably the reason why according to the commentaries (*ad. loc.*) leeks are excluded from the *buḳūl* laid out on the "spread table" sent from Heaven to Jesus and the apostles (Ḳurʾān, V, 111 ff.). Perhaps the lizard should also be added to this list (see above, col. 1058 b).

In the course of the centuries there have come to be added to this list of prohibited goods new edible products; the fact that they were *bidʿa* reinforced their qualities of being harmful, intoxicating etc., to induce—but in vain—their prohibition. This has been the case with coffee [see ḲAHWA], *ḳāt* [*q.v.*], tobacco [see TÜTÜN], etc.

Each Muslim sect, formulating for itself a complete doctrine on all points of dogma and practice, has had to make its decisions on the problem of prohibitions concerning food. In general the Ḳurʾānic prohibitions have been adhered to, but some have considered them to have only an allegorical significance or that an era was beginning in which there was no further justification for them. The extra-Ḳurʾānic prohibitions have been deliberately criticized in some circles. The consumption of dogs, habitual in the Saharan Maghrib, was regarded with indulgence by some jurists (cf. M. Canard, in *Hespéris*, xxxix (1952), 298, n. 1; H. R. Idris, *La Berbérie orientale* ..., 592, 631). The Ḳarmaṭīs of Baḥrayn allowed the meat of cats, dogs, donkeys, etc. to be sold, dogs to be fattened for the table and, at one time at least, seem to have permitted wine (De Goeje, *Mémoire sur les Carmathes du Bahraïn*[2], Leiden 1886, 174 f.; cf., *e.g.*, M. b. Mālik al-Ḥamādī, *Kashf asrār al-bāṭiniyya*, ed. M. Zāhid Kawtharī, Cairo 1939, 13). But Ismāʿīlī dogma follows the classical pattern of regulations concerning food, forbidding the flesh of carnivorous animals and birds of prey, that of the hyena and the fox, the mule and the donkey, discouraging that of the lizard and the hedgehog, authorizing that of the hare and the horse (on condition that the latter should not be ritually slaughtered unless it is exhausted with fatigue) as well as that of locusts and fish with scales, both to be caught alive; condemning the eating of marrow, spleen, kidneys or the genital organs of animals, etc.; forbidding all fermented drinks and discouraging the use of wine-vinegar (Ḳāḍī Nuʿmān, *K. al-Iḳtiṣār*, ed. M. Wahid Mirza, Damascus 1957, 95-7). Al-Ḥākim forbids in addition to this some plants: *mulūkhiyya* ('Jew's-mallow'), *rashād* (cress or rocket), *mutawakkiliyya* (a dish rather than a plant?), and lupins, because of their name or because they were liked by ʿĀʾisha, Abū Bakr, Mutawakkil, etc. (S. de Sacy, *Exposé de la religion des Druzes*, Paris 1838, i, CCCIX f.). As a further example we may mention the prohibition among the Yazīdīs of the chicken and the gazelle, of cauliflower and lettuce, accompanied by a tolerance towards the use of alcohol (R. Lescot, *Enquête sur les Yezidis de Syrie et du Djebel Sindjār*, Beirut 1938, 76 f.). Among the Nuṣayrīs are found in general at least those Muslim prohibitions which are very widespread (camel, eel, cat-fish), the prohibition of the hare, which is strictly Shīʿī, and, among the *Shamsiyya*, equally widespread prohibitions such as those of crabs and shell-fish, that of the porcupine, which is also unlawful for the Shīʿīs, as well as the more surprising prohibition of the gazelle and of vegetables (pumpkins, gumbo, tomatoes). The prohibition laid by this same group upon female animals is reminiscent rather of the practice of the Christian monks of the East. But there were of course local variations (L. Massignon, in *EI*[1], s.v. Nuṣairī; R. Strothmann, *Die Nuṣairī im heutigen Syrien*, Göttingen 1950 = *Nachrichten der Ak.d. Wiss. in Göttingen*, Phil.-hist. Kl., 1950, no. 4, 55).

It would be useful to make a study of the strictness with which these theoretical regulations are applied in practice in the different Muslim countries. The laxity or strictness of observance varies greatly according to regions, social categories, families, etc. The attitude even of the same group or the same individual may vary, according to whether it is a case of one regulation or another. Broadly speaking, for example, it seems that the prohibition of pork has always been more strictly observed than that of alcoholic drinks. Nevertheless in China, where the Muslims live in an area where pork is very much liked, they not infrequently eat it, with or without the precaution of calling it "mutton" (M. Broomhall, *Islam in China*, London 1910, 225 f., 230 f.). The non-Ḳurʾānic prohibitions are often less strictly observed, advantage sometimes being taken of the variations between the *madhāhib*. Thus, at Maʿān and often among the Bedouin of Arabia, there are eaten crows and eagles, which are forbidden by the majority of the schools (A. Jaussen, *Coutumes des Arabes au pays de Moab*, Paris 1908, 67, n. 1; C. Doughty, *Travels in Arabia Deserta*, Cambridge 1888, i, 604). Rich Ottomans had sent to them by Christians (to celebrate *Bayram*!) mussels, concealed under green cloth (Marie Sevadjian, *L'amira*, Fr. tr. F. Macler, Paris 1927, 38 f.), etc.

In the category of religious prohibitions should be included those which the ascetics imposed on themselves, and which are nowhere prescribed by the Law. Among these is abstinence from meat, which is an ancient practice (Goldziher, *Vorlesungen*, 150, 152, Fr. tr. *Le dogme et la loi de l'Islam*, Paris 1920, 122, 124), probably adopted in order to rival the zeal of Christians, Manicheans, etc. (L. Massignon, *Essai sur les origines du lexique technique de la mystique musulmane*[2], Paris 1954, 61), and which may have been reinforced by Hindu and Buddhist influence (for Abu 'l-Alā al-Maʿarrī, see H. Laoust, in *BÉO*, x (1943-4), 152). The dervish-orders too propagated various prohibitions, thus provoking the protests of the reformers (J. Jomier, *Le commentaire coranique de Manâr*, Paris 1954, 209).

It would be interesting to study the way in which the *fuḳahāʾ*, the theologians, the mystics and the philosophers have attempted to justify the prohibitions concerning food. We cannot do it here, but would merely mention that there has always existed a tendency to interpret them in a rational way. Thus al-Marghīnānī points out that the aim of the prohibition is to preserve the nobility of the human body by preventing its being sullied through absorbing the substance of base animals (*Hidāya*, ms. Paris ar. 6763, fol. 247v., tr. C. Hamilton, London 1791, iv, 74). This tendency has developed particularly in modern times, when the apologists lay especial stress on the social advantages and the benefits to health of the prohibition of wine (*e.g.*, J. Jomier, *Le commentaire coranique du Manâr*, Paris 1954, 209 f., and above, col. 1069 b). The mystics favour rather a symbolic exegesis. But the predominant tendency has been to see in these regulations a sign of God's arbitrary will. The expressions of this doctrine often coincide with that of certain contemporary sociologists, who insist on the arbitrary character of the regulations of social life. These regulations are seen as forming a system corresponding to a necessary pattern which is understood only by God: He sets himself against the ignorant anarchy of men, who are not directed by the Revelation but obey only their own psycho-physiological impulses. This is very well expressed in a *ḥadīth* which is said to have been uttered by Ibn ʿAbbās: "The people of the *djāhiliyya* used to eat certain things and abstain from others simply from distaste. But God sent His Prophet and revealed His Book; He allowed that which was lawful and forbade that which was unlawful in His eyes. That which He has permitted is lawful, that which He has forbidden is unlawful and that on which He has kept silent is tolerated (*ʿafw*). Then Ibn Abbās recited the Ḳurʾān, VI, 146/145" (Abū Dāwūd, xxvi, 30; cf. M. Rodinson, in *Trudi dvadtsatʾ pyatogo meždunarodnogo kongressa vostokovedov*, i, Moscow 1962, 362-6).

8. Aesthetic factors. Certain ideas, attitudes and recommendations concerning food are based neither on the categories of useful or harmful (ideas and recommendations of secular ideology) nor on those of good or evil (religious ideas, recommendations and regulations), but on those of what is agreeable or disagreeable. Several of these ideas and attitudes are in a sense "natural", that is to say linked with a conditioning which is specific (pertaining to the human species in general), ethnic (with variations due in part to geographical conditions) or individual, based on the physiological peculiarities of the species, the group or the individual respectively. But the physiological facts influencing the species or the group leave at the same time a certain margin of choice. Within this margin, each society chooses and inculcates in its members from childhood a system of values in taste (in the widest sense, *i.e.*, including not only the sense of taste but the sense of smell and others), comprising distinctions and preferences. It is moreover still often difficult (given the lack of sufficiently detailed studies) to distinguish within this system between the elements which are "natural" (based on physiology) although transmitted by tradition and those which belong to the arbitrary rules of social conduct. Furthermore, some small groups set up and propagate their own systems of values, generally within the margin left by the social system, but sometimes exceeding this. Finally, individuals are subject to their own physiological and psychological conditioning, also within the system inculcated by the society and the group, but sometimes going beyond it.

We can mention here only some of the features which are connected with this aesthetic approach to food. Among the distinctions made are of course the four specifically gustative flavours: sweet, sour, salt, bitter (Arabic *ḥulw*, *ḥāmid*, *malīḥ*, *murr*) with the various degrees and varieties of insipidity (Ar. *malīkh*, *masīkh*, "completely insipid"; *tafih* "without either real sweetness, acidity or bitterness", cf. al-Thaʿālibī, *Fiḳh al-lugha*, ed. Cheikho, Beirut 1885, 272); the qualities, perhaps connected with a chemical sensitivity, such as highly-spiced (in Arabic, as in English, called "hot", *ḥārr*, hence a group of seeds called "hot seeds", *abzār ḥārra*; cf. in French the four "semences chaudes": fennel, carraway, cumin, aniseed), piquant (*ḥāriṣ*, not always interchangeable with sour, *ḥāmiḍ*), astringent (*ḳābiḍ*), pungent (*ʿafiṣ*), etc. or those which correspond more closely to the chemical composition of the foods (fat, Ar. *samīn*, *i.e.*, rich in fats, similarly "oily, greasy, λιπαρὸς", Ar. *dasim*); those connected with smell (cf. Ibn Sīnā, *Psychology*, ed. J. Bakoš, Prague 1956, 76; tr., *ibid.*, 52 f.; cf. Aristotle, *De anima*, II, 10, 422b, and, for the terminology, the Arabic tr. of A. F. El-Ehwany and G. Anawati, 2nd ed., Cairo 1960, 80 with the appended glossaries; Ibn Sīnā addes to the qualities of savour listed by Aristotle, though it is possible to contest this, *bashāʿa*, an unpleasant taste, and *tafah*, insipidity), etc. To these should be added the sensations due to heat and cold, to a brittle or soft consistency, etc. The various preferences are expressed with reference to these distinctions. The taste for fat is readily discernible among both the early and the present-day Bedouin (cf. above, col. 1059 a). Those Muslims of today who are anxious to bring their cooking partly into line with European taste condemn the excessive use of fat meat in their dishes (cf. M. Rodinson, *Recherches* . . ., 107). The taste for highly-spiced foods and for sweet things appeared at a more advanced stage of Muslim civilization; it was simply a continuation of the tastes of classical antiquity (against which Sophon and Damoxenos waged a vain campaign in the 4th century B.C.), as were some more specific tastes which have now become disagreeable to us, such as that of rue (*sadhāb*), or that of products which have a very strong smell (cf. J. André, *L'alimentation et la cuisine à Rome*, 223 ff.).

The art of cooking consists in preparing and combining the basic elements in such a way as to produce a pleasant flavour. The combinations take into account the distinction between the sensory qualities, mentioned above, which are attributed to the foods, and the compatability (with a hierarchy of degrees of compatibility) and incompatibility of ingredients, whether used together or eaten following each other. Europeans have often remarked on the use in Muslim cooking of combinations in one dish of foods not in accordance with their own taste, for example that of highly-spiced with sweet and bland ingredients, without a sauce of intermediate flavour to lessen the contrast; there have even been drawn from this deductions, not beyond dispute, on collective psychology (E. F. Gautier, *apud* L. Massignon, in *RMM*, lvii (1924), 151). In fact these combinations are not confined to Muslim cooking; they are found in European and American cooking, and were used in the past even more than today. Much use is made of sauces for combining ingredients, as was done in the Middle Ages. Present-day Turkish cooking seeks to avoid having in one dish the taste of meat (roasted or grilled) and that of cooked vegetables (I. Orga, *Turkish cooking*, London 1958, 14). Vegetables cooked in oil are often eaten cold in the Middle East. As among the Romans, meat in the mediaeval Muslim world was usually boiled before being baked or roasted, and for some meat this was a necessity, either because of tradition or in order to make it tender (cf. J. André, *L'alimentation et la cuisine à Rome*, 223).

At the more elegant levels of society there has developed, following the tradition of the Ancient World, a custom of serving at one meal a succession of dishes of varying flavours. It was introduced in Cordova in the 3rd/9th century by the Baghdādī Ziryāb (E. Lévi-Provençal, *Hist. Esp. mus.*, i, 271). This arrangement seems to have been less generally adopted in the East than in the West.

It is natural that some preferences and abstentions which have a national or religious origin or are the result of an arbitrary social tradition should sometimes be justified also by aesthetic arguments. The preferring of mutton to beef is perhaps an example of this.

Aesthetic considerations which have nothing to do with taste are also important. Among them is the visual appeal of dishes, to which there are many references in the mediaeval culinary treatises. Great care is always taken over how a dish is served, and saffron, for example, is often used more for its "rich" golden colour than for its flavour. Also with the aim of delighting or surprising the beholder there were evolved an increasing number of the "disguises" (to use a term from ancient cookery) which were so popular also in Europe in the Middle Ages. Hence dishes with such significant names as *muzawwar(a)* "counterfeit", *maṣnūʿ* "artificial", etc., and recipes such as those for "mock brain" or omelette in a bottle (M. Rodinson, *Recherches . . .*, 157 f.), or the dish composed of 5 animals each inside the other which was devised for Abu 'l-ʿUlā, the governor of Ceuta and brother of the Almohad caliph Yūsuf I (A. Huici Miranda, in *Revista del Instituto de Estudios Islámicos en Madrid*, v (1957), 140, 142, n. 3). Nowadays, on the contrary, names of this sort are given rather to economical dishes which are imitations of the more luxurious ones (*e.g.*, Turkish *yalancı dolma*). But attention is always paid to the appearance of a dish, so that even one so common as purée of chick-peas (*ḥummuṣ be-ṭḥīne*), a speciality of Damascus, is always decorated with powdered red pepper, whole chick-peas, etc.

The systematic discrimination of the foods with the pleasantest taste, the drawing up of the rules which govern this according to increasingly subtle criteria, and the search for the most delicious combinations of food, formed the preoccupations not only of head cooks but of a whole distinguished society of gourmets and gastronomes. Gastronomy was especially esteemed in the ʿAbbāsid period, hence the gastronomical gatherings organized by several of the caliphs (cf. Ḥ. Zayyāt, *al-Khizāna al-sharkiyya*, iv, 4 ff.). Gourmets at the highest level of the social hierarchy took pleasure in preparing and in inventing dishes which were often called by their names (cf. M. Rodinson, *Recherches . . .*, *passim* and, for the Muslim West, A. Huici Miranda, *op. cit.*, 138 ff.). The abundance and the popularity of their writings on this subject were already arousing the anger of Ṣāliḥ b. ʿAbd al-Ḳuddūs (d. 167/783; Goldziher, *Transactions of the 9th International Congress of Orientalists*, London 1893, ii, 104 ff.); they wrote especially many treatises on cookery (*Fihrist*, 317, l. 6-10; cf. M. Rodinson, *Recherches . . .*, 100 ff.) which are now unfortunately lost; poems were composed to celebrate certain dishes (*op. cit.*, 112). The interest in food of the ʿAbbāsid upper classes has left its trace in the names of dishes created by its most eminent members, for example the *ibrāhīmiyya*, which is named after the prince (at one time anti-caliph) Ibrāhīm b. al-Mahdī. Within the Muslim world, gastronomy, although later less widespread and certainly less paraded because of the growth of puritanism, nevertheless always had its adherents and its poets (cf. Rodinson, *op. cit.*, *passim*).

Bibliography: In the article. For the manuscript works on cooking mentioned (especially the *Wuṣla ila 'l-ḥabīb*), see M. Rodinson, *Recherches sur les documents arabes relatifs à la cuisine*, in *REI*, 1949, 95-165. (M. Rodinson)

Banū **GHIFĀR** b. Mulayk b. Ḍamra b. Bakr b. ʿAbd Manāt b. Kināna, a small Arab tribe, being a subdivision of the Banū Ḍamra b. Bakr, who in their turn formed a branch of the Kināna. The Ghifār lived in the Ḥidjāz between Mecca and Medina; some of their abodes are mentioned by the geographers. Very little is known of their history in pre-Islamic times: one of their members is mentioned (*Aghānī*[1], xix, 74, 5) in the brawls preceding the Fidjār-war [*q.v.*]. A quarrel between the Ghifār and the Banū Thaʿlaba b. Saʿd b. Dhubyān is referred to in a poem quoted by Yāḳūt, *Muʿdjam*, ii, 202 f. A woman of the Ghifār was wife to the poet ʿUrwa b. al-Ward al-ʿAbsī (Ibn Hishām, 653 f.). A confederacy (*ḥilf*) between them and the Banū Mālik of Kināna is mentioned in *Aghānī*[1], xi, 126 ff. Living as they did in the neighbourhood of Medina it was essential to the Prophet that they should not take sides with the Ḳuraysh; he therefore guaranteed them in one of his earliest letters the protection (*dhimma*) of Allāh and His messenger for their lives and goods (Ibn Saʿd, i, 2, 26 f.). In this treaty Muḥammad did not insist on their conversion; but by 8/630 they had embraced Islam and took part in the conquest of Mecca. Some of them had settled at Medina, *e.g.*, Abū Dharr [*q.v.*] and his nephew ʿAbd Allāh b. al-Ṣāmit; Sibāʿ b. ʿUrfuṭa as well as Abū Ruhm are even said to have been left by the Prophet as his representatives in Medina during some of his expeditions (Ibn Hishām 668, 810, 896, 966).

After the Prophet's death the Banū Ghifār did not join in the revolt (*ridda*), nor were their deeds outstanding in the time of the conquests (*futūḥ*). We hear of the quarter (*khiṭṭa*) they had in Fusṭāṭ, when ʿAmr b. al-ʿĀṣ conquered Egypt in 20/641 (Yāḳūt, *Muʿdjam*, ii, 746).

In 45/665 Ḥakam b. ʿAmr, a younger Companion of the Prophet (see Ibn Ḥadjar, *Iṣāba*, s.v.), was appointed to the governorship of Khurāsān; he died at Marw in 51/671. He was called al-Ghifārī, though his ancestor was not Ghifār, but the latter's brother Nuʿayla, whose descendants being few in number had affiliated themselves to the Banū Ghifār (Ṭabarī, ii, 80 f., 84 f., 109-11).

Bibliography: Indexes to Ibn Hishām; Wāḳidī (transl. by Wellhausen); Ṭabarī; Yāḳūt, *Muʿdjam*; *Aghānī*, Tables; Wüstenfeld, *Genealogische Tabellen*, N 13, index 172; W. M. Watt, *Muhammad at Mecca*; idem, *Muhammad at Medina* (indexes). For Ghifār in the tradition see Wensinck, *Concordance*, iv, 529, 42-6. (J. W. Fück)

GHILZAY [see ghalzay].

GHINĀʾ (a), song, singing. This is the specific meaning of the word, although it stands for music in its generic sense, an interpretation accepted by the Ikhwān al-Ṣafāʾ (4th/10th century) who say (Bombay ed., i, 87): "*mūsīḳī* is *ghināʾ*, and the *mūsīḳār* is the *mughannī*" (see R. Payne-Smith, *Thes. Syr.*, 977, s.v. *hedhrula*). The origin and development of the song must be traced through the folk. From a musical point of view there is no difference between the simple chant of the *faḳīr* and the artless song of the *saḳḳāʾ* (water-carrier), or between the elaborate cantillation of the *muʾadhdhin* (caller to prayer) and the highly festooned vocal work of the professional *mughannī* (singer). In some lands *ghināʾ* is classified according to the structure of the music whether classical or popular, whilst in other lands it is grouped according to the class of verse used. In Morocco the song is divided into folk song or popular song called *ḳarīḥa* (natural talent), and the art song called *āla* (classical) or *ṣanʿa* (art work). In Algeria it is grouped under *kalām al-hazl* (profane song) and *kalām al-djidd* (serious song).

The Djāhiliyya. Just as we see the double meaning of the Latin *carmen* (charm, song), so the Arabic *laḥana* and *shaʿara* (from which we derive *laḥn* (melody) and *shiʿr* (poetry)) have, in their pristine significance, the meaning of 'he understood' in the cryptic sense. Perhaps the *ḥudāʾ* (camel driver's song) was, at first, a 'charm' against the *djinn* (genii) of the desert. The *ḥudāʾ*/*ḥidāʾ* was not confined to the camel driver. The toil or industrial song was to be found on every hand. Indeed we read of the Arabs of old singing at toil for their Assyrian task-masters. That dominating factor of repetition not only relieved the monotony of work but it regulated and disciplined it. Ibn Djinnī (d. 392/1002) has said that the drawer of water will go on working as long as the *radjaz* chant continues. The water carrier, the boatman, the weaver, the gleaner, and even the women of the tent or household sang at work just as they do today. Al-Masʿūdī avers that the *ḥudāʾ* was developed out of the *bikāʾ* (lament) of the women. Out of this came the *nawḥ* (elegy) and the *naṣb* (secular song) which found expression on all occasions of joy, and would include wedding songs, children's songs and lullabies.

We know nothing of the verse or music of these early folk songs, any more than we know the character of those mentioned in *Exodus*, XV, 21 or *Numbers*, XXI, 17, although the names of some singers have been preserved. Al-Djawharī (d. 396/1006) and Ibn Sīda (d. 458/1066) affirm that the *naṣb* was peculiar to the Arabs but was no more than a refined *ḥudāʾ*, and al-Ghazzālī (d. 505/1111) says that its measure (*wazn*) was based on the prosody (*ʿarūḍ*) of the verse. Probably much of pre-Islamic poetry was sung, as Brockelmann suggested. Only by this means could full justice be done to the poetic language. It was not a mere guess which prompted St. Guyard and Landberg to suggest that Arabic prosody was based on musical principles. That verse was originally in the colloquial may be accepted, hence the term *laḥn* came to imply the colloquial. Certainly the folk song is partly responsible for perpetuating corruptions in speech, and both melody and measure are sovereign perpetuators, as we see in the *malḥūn* of Morocco. The melodic framework of folk song is quite simple, a solitary musical phrase being the general rule, and that is repeated with each *bayt* (verse) or even each *miṣrāʿ* (hemistich). The compass is generally tetrachordal or pentachordal, although even two notes might carry the limit of a toil song. Adornments (*taḥsīn*) of the melody by means of grace notes—always the mark of ability in the professional *mughannī* (singer)—is rarely indulged in by the folk. Three types of *ghināʾ* are practised,—the solo, chorus, and antiphon. Both the measured (*mīzān al-shiʿr*) and unmeasured (*ghayr mawzūn*) are in use. The former is called the *nashīd*, *inshād*, *unshūda*, and the latter the *tartīl*.

Needless to say the art song existed with the *ḳaynāt*, *dādjināt*, *mudjināt*, or *ḳarīnāt* (professional singing-girls) of the tribes, wine shops, and private families, the term *musmiʿat*, found in al-Aʿshā Maymūn, being probably post-Islamic. History—or legend—mentions these singing-girls among the old Banū ʿAmālīḳ (see al-Ṭabarī, i, 231; al-Masʿūdī, *Murūdj*, iii, 296), and certainly the *ḳinītu* was known to ancient Assyria. That all played a prominent part in social life is evident from the story of the Prophet Muḥammad himself. Lyall, in his *Mufaḍḍalīyāt* (XXVI, 87), opines that these *ḳaynāt* were 'all foreigners' and that they sang 'probably to foreign airs', but he gives no evidence; whilst the statement of von Kremer that they did not even sing in Arabic is likewise unacceptable. That *some* of them came from Persia, or more likely al-Ḥīra, and even Byzantium, and that *some* of their songs were sung in an alien tongue is quite admissible, but we know that some came from Mecca. Al-Nābigha the poet was corrected by a *ḳayna* for using faulty rhymes (*iḳwāʾ*). That one—at least—was scarcely a foreigner (*Aghānī*, ix, 164; xvi, 15). Most of the great pagan poets were entranced by those singing-girls, and among them Bishr b. ʿAmr, al-Aʿshā Maymūn b. Ḳays, and ʿAbd Yaghūth. Even Ṭarafa, Labīd, and ʿAbd al-Masīḥ were overjoyed to hearken to the *djank* (harp) and *tardjīʿ* (refrain) of the tavern *ḳayna*. Perron says that before Islām, 'music was little else than unpretentious psalming (*tarannum*), varied and embroidered by the singer'. Everyone sang in unison or octave, harmony—in our sense of the term—being unknown. What took its place was what the Arabs called *īḳāʿ* (rhythm) supplied by a *ḳaḍīb* (rhythmic wand), *duff* or *mizhar* (tambourines), or, failing the latter, a *ghirbāl* (a parchment-bottom sieve). Every singer decorated her melody with vocal ornaments (*zawāʾid*). Ṭarafa reveals how the song began on a low note, whilst another describes a singer who 'prolonged the final vowels with a high trill (*tudhrī*)' and clearly enunciated the syllables in the *tartīl* fashion.

Under Islam. At the birth of Islam there was no opposition to singing, since even the Prophet Muḥammad himself had joined in the toil-song at the digging of the trenches at Mecca, yet the four Orthodox Caliphs are reported to have been—more or less—in opposition to any indulgence in listening (*al-samāʿ*) to singing or any music. As a result, the rigid school of religious law in ʿIrāḳ prohibited, and that, more accommodating, of Madina, allowed singing, and a whole library of literature—both for and against—came into existence on *al-samāʿ*. Indeed a legal fiction arose which argued that the cantillation (*taghbīr*) of the Ḳurʾān was not the same as singing, as we read in Ibn Khaldūn. Yet, as Ibn Ḳutayba pointed out, the rule and practice of cantillation and singing were identical, and—as we read in the *ʿIḳd* of Ibn ʿAbd Rabbih—if the artistic song was illegal, so was the chanting of the Ḳurʾān. Human nature, being what it is, could not accept the bigoted ruling of the pious, and so there arose, in addition to the privately owned *ḳayna* or singing-girl, the professional musician (*mughannī*), the first recorded being Ṭuways (10/632-92/711 [*q.v.*]). He, and a *mughanniya* named ʿAzzat al-Maylāʾ [*q.v.*], are said to have introduced a new type of song called the *ghināʾ al-mutḳan* (artistic song) or *ghināʾ al-raḳīḳ* (graceful song). According to Ibn al-Kalbī, 'the *ghināʾ* is of three kinds —(1) the *naṣb*, which was the song of the riders (*ghināʾ al-rukbān*) and the singing-girls (*ḳaynāt*): (2) the *sinād*, which had a slow refrain (*tardjīʿ*), but was full of notes (*naghamāt*): and (3) the *hazadj* which was quick (*khafīf*)'. Yet a new element had arisen called *īḳāʿ* (rhythm), which was distinct from *ʿarūḍ* (metre), and was external because it was supplied by *taṣfīḳ* (handclapping), or a pulsatile instrument such as the *ḳaḍīb* (wand), *duff*, *mizhar*, or *ghirbāl* (tambourine). All the *aṣwāt* (songs) contained in the *Kitāb al-Aghānī* are in the *ḳaṣīda* (ode) or *ḳiṭʿa* (fragment) forms, and many collections of songs were made by Yūnus al-Kātib (d. *c.* 148/765), Ibn Djāmiʿ (d. *c.* 187/803), Yaḥya al-Makkī (d. *c.* 205/820), Isḥāḳ al-Mawṣilī (d. 236/850), Ḥasan b. Mūsā al-Naṣībī (d. *c.* 246/860), Ibn Bāna [*q.v.*] or Bānata (d. 278/891), and al-Wazīr al-Maghribī (d. 417/1026). Later new popular forms of song appeared such as the *muwashshaḥ*, *zadjal*, *mawwāl*, *billīḳ* and *kānkān*. Indeed the first named was lifted into a premier place in Muslim Spain. Alas! not a note has been preserved. All that we know of the songs in the *Kitāb al-Aghānī* of al-Iṣfahānī, is the name of the tonal mode (*aṣbaʿ*) and rhythmic mode (*ḍarb*) in which they were sung. It is not until the time of Ṣafī al-Dīn ʿAbd al-Muʾmin (d. 693/1294) that we get a notation—or rather a tablature—of a song in Arabic books on music, whilst ʿAbd al-Ḳādir b. Ghaybī (d. 838/1435) is the earliest of the Persians to use a notation or tablature for a song. In the 8th/14th-9th/15th centuries three definite types of vocal music were recognized,—the *nashīd*, the *basīṭ*, and what was contained in the *nawba*, the latter being a vocal and instrumental *suite des pièces*. The *nashīd* comprised two parts, the first being an unrhythmical setting of two verses called the *nashr al-naghamāt*, the second being a rhythmic setting called the *naẓm al-naghamāt*. The *basīṭ* was a *ḳiṭʿa* set in one of the *thaḳīl* rhythms.

All singing in the Islamic East is basically homophonic, *i.e.*, purely melodic. Harmony, in our connotation of the term, is unknown. The greater part of the Islamic East conceives music horizontally, whereas Europe views it vertically. All melody is modal. In the days of the *Kitāb al-Aghānī* there were but eight modes, but with the later impingement of Iranian culture there were eighteen or more. These were originally called *asābiʿ* (fingers), but later were named *naghamāt* (notes), *maḳāmāt* (places), or *ṭibāʿ* (natures), the latter term revealing the belief in the innate character of a particular mode. Then there are and were motives or patterns in the melody, some being hoary with antiquity. As every verse of a song is complete in itself, *i.e.*, it contains a compact thought, it originally consisted of the same melodic phrase, but from the time of Ibn Muḥriz (d. *c.* 96/715) the second verse was set to a different melody. These factors do not imply monotony, because the singer varies her or his rendition of the melody differently by means of ornaments (*zawāʾid*, *taḥāsin* or *zuwwāḳ*). For vocalizing these latter, special syllables are introduced such as *ah*, *yā* and *lā*, when the more conventional *yā laylī* or *tirī ṭār* do not suffice. These occur in various places, viz., in the bosom of a word, and the end of a phrase, or the close of a hemistich, verse, or song, and in the last position it is called *shughl* (work). Of course in the folk or toil songs none of the above artistries occur, although some chants of the pearl fishers off the Bahrain coast reveal something of the sort. It is highly probable that the metric melodies (*naghamāt al-buḥūr*), which are still used in North Africa to probe the scansion of verse, may be survivals of many of the old types of songs, even as far back as the days of early Islam.

Bibliography: General. J. Ribera, *La música de las cántigas*, Madrid 1922; translated into English as *Music in ancient Arabia and Spain* by E. Hague and M. Leffingwell, Stanford, California 1929; Aḥmad al-Shubrāwī, *Rawḍat ahl al-fakāha*, Cairo 1317; Aḥmad b. Muḥammad b. ʿAlī al-Ḥidjāzī, *Rawḍ al-adab*, faṣl 6, Cairo MS; ʿAlī b. Muḥammad al-Ḥaddād, *Ḥadīḳat al-munādama*, bāb 29, Cairo MS; Muḥammad b. Muḥammad Saʿd al-Miṣrī, *Tuḥfat ahl al-fakāha*, bāb 9, Cairo 1307; R. Lachman, *Musik des Orients*, Breslau 1929; H. G. Farmer, *History of Arabian music*, London 1929. — Arabia and Mesopotamia. Landberg, *Critica arabica*, in *Arabica*, iii ff., Leiden 1895; Sachau, *Arabische Volkslieder aus Mesopotamien*, Berlin 1889; Meissner, *Neuarabische Gedichte aus dem Iraq*, in *MSOS*, vii/2 (1904); Idelsohn, *Gesänge der jemenischen Juden*, Leipzig 1914; Djurdjī Ibrāhīm al-Dimashḳī, *Nuzhat al-ṭalab*, Cairo 1310; ʿAbd al-Rāziḳ al-Ḥusaynī, *al-Aghānī al-shuʿūbiyya*, Baghdād 1348; ʿAbbās al-ʿAzzāwī, *al-Mūsīḳī al-ʿirāḳiyya*, Baghdād 1370; ʿAbd al-Karīm al-ʿAllāf, *al-Ṭarab ʿind al-ʿarab*, Baghdād 1364.

The Maghrib. G. Höst, *Nachrichten von Marokos und Fes*, Copenhagen 1787; A. Christianowitsch, *Esquisse historique de la musique arabe*, Cologne 1863; F. Salvador Daniel, *La musique arabe, ses rapports avec la musique grecque et le chant grégorien*, Algiers 1879; translated as *The music and musical instruments of the Arab* by H. G. Farmer, London 1915; G. Delphin and L. Guin, *Notes sur la poésie et la musique arabes dans le Maghreb algérien*, Paris 1886; Stumme, *Tripolitanisch-tunisische Beduinenlieder*, Leipzig 1893; idem, *Tunisische Märchen und Gedichte*, Leipzig 1893; Fischer, *Das Liederbuch eines marokkanischen Sängers*, Leipzig 1918; O. Sonneck, *Six chansons en dialecte Maghrebin*, in *JA*, 1899; idem, *Chants arabes du Maghreb*, Paris 1902; E. Yafil and J. Rouanet, *Répertoire de musique arabe et maure*, Algiers 1904 ff.; E. Yāfīl, *Madjmūʿ al-aghānī wa ʾl-alḥān min kalām al-Andalus*, Algiers 1904; Laffage, *La musique arabe, ses instruments, ses chants*, Tunis 1905; R. Mitjana, *L'Orientalisme musical et la musique arabe*, in *MO*, i (1906), 184-221; J. Rouanet, *La musique arabe*, in Lavignac, *Encyclopédie de la musique*, v, Paris 1922; Lens, *Ce que nous savons de la musique et des instruments de musique du Maroc*, in *Bull. Inst. des Hautes Études Marocaines*, i (1920), 137-52; Al-Ḥāʾik [Collection of Songs, in many libraries in the Maghrib]; Chevrillon, *Chants dans la nuit à Marrakech*, in *France-Maroc*, 1918; A. Chottin, *Airs populaires recueillis à Fès*, in *Hespéris*, 1923-24; idem, *La pratique du chant chez les musiciens marocains*, in *Zeitschr. f. vergleichende Musikwissenschaft*, Berlin 1933; idem, *Corpus de musique marocaine*, i, Paris 1931; Derwil and Essafi, *Chansons marocaines*, in *Revue Méditerranéenne*, 1932; R. Lachmann, *Die Musik in den tunisischen Städten*, in *Archiv f. Musikwissenschaft*, 1923; E. von Hornbostel, *Phonographeierte tunesische Melodien*, in *Samml. Intern. Musikgesellschaft*, 1906; Desparmet, *La poésie arabe actuelle à Blida*, in *Actes du XIVème Congrès Intern. des Orient.* — Turkestan. Fitrat, *Uzbīḳ ḳilāsīḳ mūsīḳāsī*, Tashkent 1927; Uspensky-Belayev, *Turkmenskaya muzika*, Moscow 1928; idem, *Shash maḳām*, 1924; Mironov, *Pesni Fergani Bukhari i Khivi*, Tashkent 1931; R. Lach, *Die Musik der türkischen ... und Kaukasusvölker*, in *Mitt. d. Anthrop. Gesellschaft in Wien*, vol. l; P. Aubry, *Au Turkestan. Notes sur quelques habitudes musicales chez les Tadjiks et chez les Sartes*, Paris 1905. — Turkey: E. Littmann, *Türkische Volkslieder aus Kleinasien*, in *ZDMG*, 1899; E. von Hornbostel and Abraham, *Phonographeierte türkische Melodien*, in *Samml. f.*

vergleichende Musikwissenschaft, Munich 1904; E. Borrel, *La musique turque*, in *Revue de Musicologie*, 1923; Raʾūf Yektā Bey, *La musique turque*, in Lavignac, *Encycl. de la musique*, v, Paris 1922; idem, *Sharḳ mūsīḳī taʾrīkhi*, Istanbul 1343; idem, *Esātīd-i Elḥān*, Istanbul 1303; Maḥmūd Rāghib, *Anadolu türküleri*, Istanbul 1928; Sayf al-Dīn and Sezāʾī Bey, *Yurdumuzuñ naghmalarī*, Istanbul 1926; *Dār al-elḥān kulliyyatī*, Istanbul; *Chansons populaires turques*, Istanbul (these two latter published by the Dār al-elḥān). See also the publications of Shāmlī Iskandar and Tewfīḳ, notably the *Aheng* of Sāmī Bey, the *Madjmūʿa-i elḥān* of Djewdet Bey, and the collections of the Dār al-taʿlīm-i mūsīḳī, the publications of Shāmlī Selīm. — Syria, Lebanon, Palestine. E. Littmann, *Neuarabische Volkspoesie*, in *Abh. G. W. Gott*, 1902; H. G. Farmer, *Grove's Dictionary of Music*, viii, 251-8; G. Dalman, *Arabische Gesänge*, in *Palästinajahrbuch*, 1924; idem, *Nachlese arabischer Lieder aus Palästina*, in *Beiträge zur alttestamentlichen Wissenschaft*, 1920; idem, *Palästinischer Diwan*, Leipzig 1906; Outry, *La musique arabe en Palestine*, in *Rev. musicale*, 1905; M. Hartmann, *Arabische Lieder aus Syrien*, in *ZDMG*, 1897; H. M. Huxley, *Syrian songs, proverbs, and stories*, in *JAOS*, 1902; M. Mushāḳa, *al-Risāla al-Shihābiyya fī ṣanʿat al-mūsīḳī*, Beirut 1899 (English tr. in *JAOS*, i; French tr. in *MFOB*, vi); al-Safardjalānī, *al-Safīna al-adabiyya*, Damascus 1308; Ṣāllḥānī, *Ranāt al-mathālith*, Beirut 1888; Buṭrus al-Bustānī, *Dāʾirat al-maʿārif*, Beirut 1304; Nasīm al-Dalw al-Lubnānī, *Izālat al-shudjūn fī aghānī*, Beirut 1910; R. A. Stewart Macalister, in *Palestine Exploration Fund Quarterly Statement*, 1900; J. Parisot, *Rapport sur une mission scientifique en Turquie d'Asie*, Paris 1899; idem, *Rapport sur une mission scientifique en Turquie et Syrie*, Paris 1903; A. Idelsohn, *Die Maqamen der arab. Musik*, in *Sammelbände der intern. Musik-Gesellschaft*, xv, Leipzig 1913; idem, *Gesänge der orient. Sefardim*, Berlin 1922. — Egypt. G. A. Villoteau, in *La Description de l'Égypte*, Paris 1809-26; E. Lane, *Modern Egyptians*[5], London 1860; Bouriant, *Chansons populaires arabes en dialecte du Caire*, Paris 1893; Ibrāhīm al-Dandarāwī, *Mukhtārat al-aghānī*, Cairo; Ibrāhīm Ghanīmat al-Ḳānūndjī, *Ṣayd al-ḥamām*, Cairo; Loret, *Quelques documents relatifs à la littérature et la musique populaires de la Haute-Égypte*, in *Mém. Mission archéol. française*, i, Paris 1889; Aḥmad Rāmī, *Aghānī Rāmī*, Cairo 1927; Ḥabīb Zaydān, *Madjmūʿat al-aghānī*, Cairo 1928; Ḥasan al-Alātī, *Tarwīḥ al-nufūs*, Cairo 1889; Muḥammad b. Ismāʿīl, *Safīnat al-mulk*, Cairo 1309; ʿAbd al-Raḥman Maḥmūd, *al-Mughannī al-miṣrī al-ḥadīth*, Cairo; Kāmil al-Khulaʿī, *Kitāb al-Mūsīḳī al-sharḳī*, Cairo 1332; idem, *Nayl al-amānī*, Cairo; idem, *al-Aghānī al-ʿaṣriyya*, Cairo 1341; Muṣṭafā Ṣādiḳ al-Rāfiʿī, *al-Nashīd al-Miṣrī al-waṭanī*, Cairo 1339; Marsā Shākir al-Ṭanṭāwī, *Aghānī al-shabāb*, Cairo 1341; ʿAlī Imām ʿAṭiyya, *al-Mūsīḳī wa 'l-aghānī*, Cairo 1348; Darwīsh Muḥammad, *Ṣafāʾ al-awḳāt*, Cairo 1328; Muḥammad A. al-Ḥifnī, *Sayyid Darwīsh*, Cairo 1955, Umm Kulthūm, *Ashhar al-aghānī*, Cairo c. 1960. — Berbers: F. Salvador Daniel, *La musique arabe* (with a *Notice sur la musique Kabyle*), Algiers 1879; Hanoteau, *Poésies populaires de la Kabylie*, Paris 1867; Rouger, *Chansons berbères*, in *France-Maroc*, 1920; E. von Hornbostel and R. Lachmann, *Asiatische Parallelen zur Berbermusik*, in *Zeitschr. f. vergleichende Musikwissenschaft*, 1933; Coliac, *Chansons berbères de la Région d'Azilal*, in *France-Maroc*, 1920; Chottin, *Musique et danses berbères du pays chleuh*, in *Corpus de musique marocaine*, ii, Rabat 1933.

(Henry G. Farmer)

GHIRBĪB b. ʿABD ALLĀH, minor poet of Toledan origin who played a political rôle in his native town soon after the succession of the *amīr* al-Ḥakam I (180/796) by supporting the agitation stirred up by one ʿUbayd Allāh b. Khamīr (variant names). Ghirbīb, who exercised great influence at Toledo, had conceived a grudge against al-Ḥakam and, having fled from Cordova, set to work to foster an atmosphere of hostility to the Umayyad *amīr* at Toledo by means of his mordant verses. The latter finally entrusted the task of restoring order to the *muwallad* ʿAmrūs, who put down the revolt savagely and decimated the Toledan bourgeoisie on the "Day of the Ditch" (*waḳʿat al-ḥufra*). E. Lévi-Provençal has established that this event took place in 181/797 (and not in 191/807 as is generally accepted); and as, according to tradition, al-Ḥakam feared Ghirbīb too much to embark on an expedition against Toledo as long as the poet was alive, there is reason to think that he died in 181/797. Nothing remains of his poetical output except a few lines of no great value.

Bibliography: Ḍabbī, *Bughya*, no. 1281; Ibn al-Ḳūṭiyya, in E. Fagnan, *Extraits inédits relatifs au Maghreb*, Algiers 1924, 196; González Palencia, *Literatura*[2], 47, 53; Dozy, *Hist. Mus. Esp.*, ii, 62; E. Lévi-Provençal, *Hist. Esp. Mus.*, i, 159.

(Ed.)

GHIRSH [see sikka].

GHIYĀR (Arabic: distinguishing, distinction, cognizance) is a term denoting the compulsory distinctive mark in the garb of *dhimmī* [*q.v.*] subjects under Muslim rule. It is considered probable that the *ghiyār* became the prototype of the Jewish badge in Christian Europe.

In Islamic lands it was part and parcel of the dispositions concerning the status of the *dhimmīs* which can be traced back to the time of Mutawakkil's enactments (233/849), but had been known even earlier; thus under Hārūn al-Rashīd they were discussed in Abū Yūsuf's *K. al-Kharādj* (72 f.) where they are ascribed to ʿUmar. From time to time when a recrudescence of anti-*dhimmī* restrictions occurred the re-introduction of the *ghiyār* figures in the reports.

It is described as a piece of cloth, a patch of a stipulated colour (red, blue, yellow) placed over the shoulder. The *Tādj* mentions that some considered it the badge of the Jew. On the other hand, in various sources the word denotes any kind of garb distinction imposed upon *dhimmīs*, and indeed the garment which bears the mark. Both the wider connotation and the narrower seem well attested. Thus the *zunnār* (a special belt) of the Christians often comes under this heading. The colours changed in the course of time for each infidel community. The *muḥtasib* [*q.v.*] was supposed to see to it that the statutes concerning the *dhimmīs* in general were enforced, and the wearing of the *ghiyār*, in particular, observed.

In the Maghrib the name *shakla* occurs for the *ghiyār*.

Bibliography: Lane s.v.; R. Dozy, *Dictionnaire ... des vêtements ...*, Amsterdam 1845, 24 ff., esp. 28, 196 ff.; *IA*, iv, 781; A. Fattal, *Le statut légal des non-musulmans ...*, Beirut 1958, 96-110; A. S. Tritton, *The caliphs and their non-Muslim subjects*, London 1930, Ch. viii; D. Santillana, *Istituzioni*, vi, 101; Juynboll, *Handbuch*,

352 f.; Ibn al-Ukhuwwa, *Maʿālim al-Qurba*, ed. R. Levy, London 1938, 41/14 and 46/15; A. Mez, *Renaissance*, 45 f.; R. Brunschvig, *La Berbérie* . . ., i, Paris 1940, 403 ff.; E. Strauss, *The history of the Jews in Egypt and Syria under Mamluk rule*, ii (Hebrew) Jerusalem 1951, 210-8; S. W. Baron, *A Social and religious history of the Jews*, iii, Philadelphia 1957, 139 ff., 298; E. Strauss in *Paul Hirschler Memorial Volume*, Budapest 1950; E. Fagnan in *REJ*, xxviii (1894), 294-8; Ilse Lichtenstaedter, *The distinctive dress of non-Muslims in Islamic countries*, in *Historia Judaica*, xxx, 1943, 35-52; Ḥ. Zayyāt in *Machriq*, 1949, 161 ff., esp. 235 f. (M. PERLMANN)

GHIYĀTH AL-DĪN [see DIHLĪ SULTANATE, KAY-KHUSRAW, MUḤAMMAD].

GHIYĀTH AL-DĪN NAḲḲĀSH, Tīmūrid courtier. If he was an artist, as the name indicates (*naḳḳāsh* = painter, etc.), his speciality is unknown. He was a protégé of Bāysonghor [*q.v.*], the gifted son of Shāh Rukh, and was attached by his patron to the Tīmūrid embassy to China in 823/1420-825/1422, with the special duty of drawing up a day-to-day descriptive account of the embassy. This report of the journey from Harāt to Khānbāligh (Pekin) and back, giving first-hand information about China which is not to be found elsewhere, at one time existed in writing, and has been incorporated into the *Zubdat al-tawārīkh* of Ḥāfiẓ Abrū, the *Maṭlaʿ al-saʿdayn* of ʿAbd al-Razzāḳ al-Samarḳandī, etc. On the 18th century Turkish translation, called *ʿAdjāʾib al-laṭāʾif*, by Küčük Čelebizāde, see Babinger 293-4.

Bibliography: E. Quatremère, *Notices et Extraits*, xiv, 1, 1843, 308 ff., 387 ff. (Persian text and Fr. tr. of the version of ʿAbd al-Razzāḳ al-Samarḳandī); M. Shafīʿ, *Oriental College Magazine*, vii, 1 (Lahore Nov. 1930), 1-66 (Persian text, with notes, of the version of Ḥāfiẓ Abrū); K. M. Maitra, *A Persian Embassy to China; being an extract from Zubdatu't Tawarikh of Hafiz Abru*, Lahore 1934; D. M. Dunlop, *Ḥāfiẓ-i Abrū's Version of the Timurid Embassy to China in A.D. 1420*, in *Glasgow University Oriental Society Transactions*, xi (1946), 15-19. (D. M. DUNLOP)

GHIYĀTH AL-DĪN TUGHLUḲ I (GHĀZĪ MALIK), founder of the Tughluḳ dynasty and ruler of India from 720/1320 to 725/1325, was by origin a Ḳarawna Turk and an immigrant from Khurāsān, who took service under the Khaldjīs. In 705/1305 he was appointed governor of Dīpālpūr in the Pandjāb, and as warden of the marches he held the Mongols at bay for fifteen years, conducting annual raids against them in the Kābul and Ghazna areas.

The prestige thus gained was his main asset when he rose against Khusraw Khān, a Khaldjī general of low-caste Hindu Parwārī origin, who had massacred the last Khaldjī ruler, Ḳutb al-Dīn Mubārak (716/1316-720/1320) and all the Khaldjī princes, seized the throne, apostatized from Islam and begun a reign of terror in Dihlī. Most of the Muslim governors had accepted Khusraw Khān's rule passively, probably owing to the lack of reliable intelligence from Dihlī. Ghāzī Malik addressed his *daʿwa* of *djihād* to only six governors of western India, of whom one joined him, two who refused to join were murdered by their own troops, while another who promised to help was restored to authority by his formerly rebellious troops. The Tughluḳ revolution was therefore the work of the rank and file of the Muslim army, rather than of the Muslim ruling élite. Three decisive victories ending in the capture and execution of Khusraw Khān left Ghāzī Malik the undisputed master of the Sultanate. Despite his refusal, he was raised to the throne by the *idjmāʿ* of the nobles, as the defender and restorer of Islamic power in India against the double challenge of Mongol threat and Hindu subversion. He assumed the title Ghiyāth al-Dīn.

Contemporary Muslim historiography eulogises him as the saviour of Islam in India, and Baranī presents him as the ideal sultan who combined a heroic rôle with personal virtues of continence, chastity and piety. The hagiographical tradition is much less complimentary owing to the Sultan's differences with the Čishtī mystic Niẓām al-Dīn Awliyā on two points: acceptance by the latter of a large gift of money from Khusraw Khān, which he was unable to restore to the treasury when called upon; and the practice of the Čishtiyya [*q.v.*] to listen to music (*samāʿ*). To settle the second point the Sultan convened a great congress of *ʿulamāʾ* and Ṣūfīs, and finally imposed some restriction on the *samāʿ* of the heterodox Ṣūfīs, without interfering with the practices of the Čishtī leader. Anecdotes of subsequent bitterness seem to be later apocryphal legends connected with the death of Ghiyāth al-Dīn which found their way from later hagiographical writings like those of Djamālī into the serious historical works of Firishta and others; they are not traceable either in contemporary chronicles or near-contemporary hagiographies like Ḥamīd Ḳalandar's *Khayr al-madjālis*.

Administratively Ghiyāth al-Dīn's first problem was to restore the economy of the state after its upheaval and thorough fiscal chaos under Khusraw Khān. He had to resort to a policy of confiscation of *djāgīrs* granted by his reckless predecessors, and to the more unpopular measures of appropriating older land-grants and army pensions (ʿIsāmī, 389-91). His taxation policy, which affected mainly the Hindu agricultural and land-owning classes, was to strike a *via media*, denying them opportunities of accumulation of wealth which might lead to rebellion, but granting them security of subsistence to enable them to pursue their husbandry. Between 722/1322 and 723/1323, consolidation and expansion of the Sultanate was effected by this son Djawnā Khān (also known as Ulugh Khān, later Sultan Muḥammad b. Tughluḳ [*q.v.*]), who re-subjugated the rebellious Kakātīya radja Pratāparuraveda II of Warangal after an initial reverse; annexed the Pāṇḍya Hindu kingdom of Madura (Maʿbar); invaded Djādjnagar and made incursions into the independent Hindu principality of Orissa. Ghiyāth al-Dīn personally led an expedition intervening in the civil war in Bengal, which was partly annexed to the sultanate and partly placed under a vassal ruler Nāṣir al-Dīn. During his five years' rule Ghiyāth al-Dīn had thus consolidated the sultanate and extended its borders considerably beyond the Khaldjī frontiers.

On his way back from Bengal in 725/1325 Ghiyāth al-Dīn was crushed to death under the roof of a wooden pavilion constructed hastily upon the orders of his son Djawnā Khān, which collapsed during an elephant parade after a banquet. Djawnā has been accused of parricide by two near-contemporary chroniclers, Ibn Baṭṭūṭa and ʿIṣāmī, both with strong prejudices against him. Other historians of the age, Baranī and Yaḥyā b. Aḥmad Sarhindī, make no such accusation. Sir Wolseley Haig's theory of the involvement of Niẓām al-Dīn Awliyā in this alleged intrigue seems to be far-fetched.

Bibliography: Baranī, *Taʾrīkh-i Fīrūz Shāhī*, Bibl. Ind., Calcutta 1862, 411-43; ʿIṣāmī, *Futūḥ al-salāṭīn*, ed. A. S. Usha, Madras 1948, 375-421; Yaḥyā b. Aḥmad Sarhindī, *Taʾrīkh-i Mubārak Shāhī*, Calcutta 1921, 87 f.; Amīr Khusraw, *Tughluḳ Nāma*, ed. Hashimi Faridabadi, Awrangābād 1933; Firishta, *Gulshan-i Ibrāhīmī*, Lucknow 1905, *passim*; ʿAbd al-Ḳādir Badāʾūnī, *Muntakhab al-tawārīkh*, Bibl. Ind., Calcutta 1868, i, 221-5 (= Eng. tr. by Ranking, Calcutta 1898, 296-301); Abu ʾl-Faḍl ʿAllāmī, *Āʾīn-i Akbarī* (Eng. tr. Jarrett), Calcutta 1949, ii, 311; ʿAbd al-Bāḳī Nihāwandī, *Maʾāthir-i Raḥīmī*, Bibl. Ind., Calcutta 1924, i, 340-5; Niẓām al-Dīn Aḥmad, *Tabaḳāt-i Akbarī* (Eng. tr. B. De), Bibl. Ind., Calcutta, i, 208-15; Ḥāmid b. Faḍl-Allāh Djamālī, *Siyar al-ʿārifīn*, I.O. Pers. Ms. 1313, ff. 164b-166b; Muḥammad b. Tughluḳ (attributed to), Fragment of memoir in B.M. Add. Ms. 2578, ff. 316a-317b; Ibn Baṭṭūṭa, iii, *passim* (H. von Mžik, *Die Reise* ..., Hamburg 1911, index); E. Thomas, *Chronicles of the Pathan Kings of Dehli*, London 1871, 186 f.; Mahdi Husain, *Life and times of Muhammad bin Tughluq*, London 1938, 45 f., 66-74; Ishwari Prasad, *History of the Qaraunah Turks*, Allāhābād 1936, 2-51; N. Venkataramanayya, *Early Muslim expansion in south India*, Madras 1942, 126 f.; Shaykh Muḥammad Ikrām, *Āb-i Kawthar*, Karachi/Lahore 1958, 270-5, 447-57; R. C. Majumdar, in *The Delhi Sultanate*, (Vol. vi of *The history and culture of the Indian people*), Bombay 1960, 52-9, and *passim*; T. Wolseley Haig, *Five questions in the history of the Tughluq dynasty of Dihli*, in *JRAS* (1922), 319-72; Aziz Ahmad, *The Ṣūfī and the sultān in pre-Mughal Muslim India*, in *Isl.*, xxxviii (1962), 142-53; S. K. Banerji, *Ghiyasuddin Tughluq Shah as seen in his monuments and coins*, in *J. of U.P. Hist. Soc.*, xv (1942), 45-54; K. K. Basu, *The House of Tughlaq*, in *JASB*, n.s. xxvi (1930), 247-69; K. A. Nizami, *Some religious and cultural trends in the Tughluq period*, in *J. Pak. Hist. Soc.*, i (1953), 234-43; idem, *Early Indo-Muslim mystics and their attitude towards the state*, in *IC*, xxii (1948), 387-98; xxiii (1949), 13-21, 162-70, 312-21; xxiv (1950), 60-71; S. Moinul Haq, *Baranī's History of the Tughluqs. Ghiyāth al-dīn Tughluq*, in *J. Pak. Hist. Soc.*, vii (1959), 1-23, 127-64.

(Aziz Ahmad)

GHIYĀTH AL-DĪN TUGHLUḲ SHĀH II IBN FATḤ KHĀN IBN SULṬĀN FĪRŪZ SHĀH TUGHLUḲ [*q.v.*] (790/1388-791/1389) succeded to his grandfather's throne according to his will, superseding a number of relatives. This led to the internecine dynastic wars which led to the decline, and finally the overthrow of the Tughluḳ dynasty. The Sultan's inexperience, his love of pleasure and his tactlessness in imprisoning his own brother Sālār Khān led to the revolt of his nephew Abū Bakr son of Ẓafar Khān, who defeated and killed him with the aid of the *wazīr* Rukn al-Din Čanda. The reign of Ghiyāth al-Dīn Tughluḳ II marks the acceleration of chaos and civil strife in which the Delhi Sultanate rapidly disintegrated: a process which also marks the provincialization of Muslim culture in India during the 9th/15th century.

Bibliography: Badāʾūnī, i, 257-8 (= Eng. tr. by Ranking, i, 341-2); Nizām al-Dīn Aḥmad, *Tabaḳāt-i Akbarī*, Bibl. Ind., Calcutta 1927, i, 241-2 (= Eng. tr. by B. De, Bibl. Ind., i, 261-2); Firishta (Briggs), i, 466-86; ʿAbd al-Bāḳī Nihāwandī, *Maʾāthir-i Raḥīmī*, i, 381-2; Sikandar ibn Muḥammad 'Manjhū', *Mirʾat-i Sikandarī*, ed. S. C. Misra and M. L. Raḥmān, Baroda 1961, 12; ʿAlī Muḥammad Khān, *Mirʾat-i Aḥmadī*, Calcutta 1928, i, 40.

(Aziz Ahmad)

GHUBĀR [see ḤISĀB, KHAṬṬ].

GHUBRĪNĪ, *nisba* of the B. Ghubrīn, a branch of the Zawāwa Berbers who formerly inhabited the eastern end of Great Kabylia in Algeria (Ibn Khaldūn, *Berbères*, Index s.v. Ghobrîn) and who are still represented in the same area by the Ait Ghobri (Brunschvig, *Berbérie orientale*, i, 286). Two Ghubrīnīs played a rôle in Ḥafṣid history:

(1) Abu ʾl-ʿAbbās Aḥmad b. ʿAbd Allāh, b. 644/1246 at Bidjāya (Bougie) where he spent all his life and attained the rank of *ḳāḍi ʾl-ḳuḍāt*. In 704/1304 he was sent by the Ḥafṣid ruler of Bougie, Abu ʾl-Baḳāʾ Khālid, as an emissary to establish friendly relations with the rival Ḥafṣid at Tunis, Abū ʿAbd Allāh. On his return he was accused of treason and of having been implicated in the death of Abū Isḥāḳ Ibrāhīm (who had been captured in Ghubrīnī territory 22 years previously) and was put to death.

He wrote a collection of biographies of Bougiotes entitled *ʿUnwān al-dirāya* ... which was edited by Muḥammad b. Abī Shanab (Mohammed Ben Cheneb) and published at Algiers in 1910.

Bibliography: Ibn Farḥūn, *Dībādj*, Cairo 1351/1932, 80 (correct the date to 704); Nubāhī, *Taʾrīkh ḳuḍāt al-Andalus*, 132; Ibn Khaldūn, *Berbères*, ii, 394, 418; Ben Cheneb, *Idjâza*, no. 354.

(2) Abū Mahdī ʿĪsā, who became *ḳāḍi ʾl-djamāʿa* at Tunis in 787/1385 and died there about 813/1410.

Bibliography: Ibn Nādjī, *Maʿālim al-īmān*, Tunis 1320/1902, iii, 103; Ibn al-Ḳāḍī, *Durrat al-ḥidjāl*, ed. Allouche, Rabat 1934, no. 1158; Aḥmad Bābā, *Nayl al-ibtihādj*, Cairo 1351/1932, 193.

(J. F. P. Hopkins)

GHUDJDUWĀN (today Gižduvan), a large village in the northeastern part of the oasis of Bukhārā, on the tributary of the Zarafshān River at present called Pirmast, formerly the Kharḳān Rūd.

The origin of the village and etymology of the name are unknown. It is mentioned as a village of the town of Rāmitīn by al-Muḳaddasī (267c), but no notices are found in other geographies. Al-Samʿānī (406b) says the village was six farsakhs from Bukhārā, and was an important commercial centre. It is mentioned several times in Islamic texts as the home of several learned men. A lieutenant of the heretic al-Muḳannaʿ came from there according to Narshakhī (see below). Bābur in 918/1512 was defeated here by the Özbeks. Thereafter little is heard of the village although the citadel was the scene of fighting several times. At present the village is sixteen kilometres/10 miles from the railroad station of Kyzyl-Tepe and ca. 50 km/30 m. from Bukhārā.

Bibliography: Barthold, *Turkestan*, 119-20; Narshakhī, trans. R. Frye, Cambridge, Mass. 1954, note 249; Faḍl Allāh Khundjī, *Mihmān-nāme-yi Bukhārā*, ed. M. Sutūdah, Tehrān 1962, 62, *et passim*; M. Munshī, *Mukim-khanskaya Istoriya*, trans. A. A. Semienov, Tashkent 1956, 125.

(R. N. Frye)

GHUDJDUWĀNĪ, KHWĀDJA ʿABD AL-KHĀLIḲ B. ʿABD AL-DJAMĪL, famous ṣūfī *shaykh*, born in Ghudjdawān (according to al-Samʿānī) or Ghadjduwān (according to Yāḳūt). His father, whose name has sometimes been corrupted into ʿAbd al-Djalīl, lived at Malātya (Melitene); he migrated from there to the vicinity of Bukhārā, where his son received his education. Certain writers trace his ancestry to a royal dynasty of Rūm (Asia Minor); others consider him to be a descendant of the *imām* Mālik b. Anas and another source traces him back through ten generations to Abu 'l-Ḥasan Kharaḳānī, a famous ṣūfī *shaykh* who died in 424/1033; this seems inadmissible, since only 193 years separate the date of the death of Kharaḳānī from that of the death of Ghudjduwānī (which appears the more exact) and during that time ten generations cannot be admitted; moreover Kharaḳānī lived in Khurāsān and the ancestors of Ghudjduwānī seem always to have been in Asia Minor. The only information we possess on his life tells us that he studied at Bukhārā where, at the age of 22, he met his *shaykh* Abū Yaʿḳūb Yūsuf Hamadānī, who died on Thursday 8 Muḥarram 535/24 August 1140 (in reality a Saturday). Thanks to the latter he entered the sect of Ṣūfīs then called *Tarīḳat-i Khʷādjegān*, later known as the Naḳshbandiyya from the time of Bahāʾ al-Dīn Naḳshband. Most of his biographers place his death in 575/1179, while another version gives the date 617/1220, which seems more correct because he twice mentions the date 600/1204 in his *Risāla-i Ṣāḥibiyya*; what is more, his successor in the *ṭarīḳa*, Khʷādja Aḥmad Ṣiddīḳ, died in 657/1259, so that if Ghudjduwānī had died in 575 his successor would have disappeared 80 or 82 years after him, which is hardly likely. He was buried in Ghudjduwān.

He has left a work in Persian comprising: several quatrains, the *Risāla-i ṭarīḳat*, the *Waṣiyyat-nāma* or *Wāṣāyā* (which was the subject of a commentary composed by Faḍl Allāh b. Rūzbihān Iṣfahānī, known under the title of Khʷādja Mawlānā, died after 921/1515), the *Risāla-i Ṣāḥibiyya*, eulogies of his master Yūsuf Hamadānī, a *Dhikr-i Khʷādja ʿAbd al-Khāliḳ*, mentioned by Storey (mss. of Leyden, of the British Museum and of the India Office). The *Risāla-i Ṣāḥibiyya* has been published with a commentary by the author of this article. We possess another anonymous *risāla* in Persian eulogizing him and his successor Khʷādja ʿĀrif-i Riv-Gari, also published by the author of this article.

Bibliography: *Risāla-i Ṣāḥibiyya*, in *Farhang-i Īrān Zamīn*, i/1 (1332), 70-110; *Maḳāmāt-i ʿAbd al-Khāliḳ-i Ghudjdawānī wa ʿĀrif-i Riv-Gari*, *ibid.*, ii/1 (1333), 1-18; Samʿānī, *Ansāb*, fol. 406b; Khʷādja Muḥammad Pārsā, *Faṣl al-Khiṭāb*, Tashkent 1331, 518-20; *The Nafaḥāt al-Ons min Hadharāt al-qods by Mawlānā Noor al-dīn Abd al-Raḥmān Jāmi*, Calcutta 1859, 431-3; Fakhr al-Dīn ʿAlī al-Ṣāfī, *Rashahāt-i ʿAyn al-ḥayāt*, Tashkent 1329, 18-28, Cawnpore 1912, 18-27; Muḥammad Murād b. ʿAbd Allāh Ḳāzānī, *Tardjamat-i ʿAyn al-ḥayāt*, Mecca 1307, 25-23; Dārā Shukūh, *Ṣafīnat al-awliyā*, Lucknow 1872, 76; Amīn Aḥmad Rāzī, *Haft iḳlīm*, Tehrān, iii, 425-7; Riḍā Ḳūlī Khān, Hidāyat, *Madjmaʿ al-fuṣaḥāʾ*, i, Tehrān 1295, 338; idem, *Riyāḍ al-ʿārifīn*, Tehrān 1305, 105, ²Tehrān 1316, 172; Muḥammad Muẓaffar Ḥusayn Ṣabā, *Rūz-i rawshan*, Bhopal 1295, 433-4; Ghulām Sarwar Lahorī, *Khazīnat al-aṣfiyā*, Cawnpore 1914, i, 532-4; C. A. Storey, i/2, 1055; Said Naficy, *Taʾrīkh-i naẓm wa nathr dar Īrān wa dar zabān-i fārsī*, Tehrān 1342/1963, 110-1, 220, 252. (S. Naficy)

GHUFRĀN, *maṣdar* of *ghafara*, to forgive; refers to the two Ḳurʾānic Divine Names, *al-ghafūr* and *al-ghaffār*, the Forgiver and He who unceasingly forgives. Thus: act of man forgiving an offence, but essentially: act of God forgiving sins. The term *ghufrān* belongs to the vocabulary of *ʿilm al-kalām*, e.g. treatise on the "Last Things" (*al-waʿd wa 'l-waʿīd*) and chapter on *tawba*; and to the vocabulary of *taṣawwuf*, e.g. "dwelling-place" (*maḳām*) of repentance (*tawba*). Frequent synonym: *al-ʿafw*, which places the emphasis on forgiveness conceived as (total) annulment of the sinful act.—The conditions and methods of Divine forgiveness are analysed in the article TAWBA. (L. Gardet)

GHŪL (A., pl. *ghīlān* or *aghwāl*), fabulous being believed by the ancient Arabs to inhabit desert places and, assuming different forms, to lead travellers astray (sometimes, like the Bedouins, lighting fires on the hills the more easily to attract them), to fall upon them unawares and devour them; certain isolated sources (cf. al-Masʿūdī, *Murūdj*, iii, 315) affirm however that it fled as soon as it was challenged; according to al-Djāḥiẓ (*Ḥayawān*, i, 309), it rode on hares, dogs and ostriches; men could kill it, but only by giving it one single blow, for a second restored it to life, and this is why it always asked anyone courageous enough to resist it to strike it again. The root of the word *ghūl* seems to contain two different ideas: on the one hand the ability to assume different forms and on the other the treacherous attack. Indeed the *ghūl* is considered as apt to change its form continually and to appear to travellers under the most attractive guises, its ass's hooves alone remaining unchangeable. The word denotes also any misfortune which happens unexpectedly to a human being (cf. al-Djurdjānī, *Taʿrīfāt*, s.v.; Horten, *Theol. des Islams*, 335); it is also used, notably by Kaʿb b. Zuhayr in verse 8 of his *Burda* (cf. R. Basset, *Bânat Soʿâd*, 102) to indicate fickleness, the ability of the *ghūl* to change its shape and colour having become proverbial; in the same sense it is also sometimes given the name of *khaytaʿūr* (see *LA*, s.v.).

Early sources, while observing that *ghūl* denotes a male as well as a female being, make it clear that the Arabs tended to regard it as a female; later sources however make it into a diabolical *djinn* and certain of them prefer to apply the word *ghūl* to the male, of whom the female is called *siʿlāt* (pl. *saʿālī*), while others consider the *ḳuṭrub* as the male of the latter (see al-Damīrī, s.v. *ḳuṭrub*); indeed these authors are not far from thinking that *ghūl* and *siʿlāt* are the same thing, while al-Djāḥiẓ (*Ḥayawān*, vi, 159), followed by al-Ḳazwīnī (*ʿAdjāʾib*, following the *Ḥayāt al-ḥayawān* of al-Damīrī, Cairo 1956, 214), states that the *siʿlāt* was distinguished from the *ghūl* by the fact that she did not change her form; she was considered among the *djinn*s, as a kind of witch (*sāḥira*). However, although grammatical agreement with the word *ghūl* is in the feminine, those who regard *siʿlāt* as the feminine of *ghūl* can point to the fact that popular usage has formed a feminine *ghūla*, and that, in a certain number of traditions, we find men having fruitful sexual relations with *saʿālī* but rarely with *ghīlān*. Attached to this group is the *ʿudār*, an equally fabulous animal, a male whose habit was to make men submit to assaults, which proved mortal if worms developed in the anus of the victim; there is moreover a proverb: *alwaṭ min ʿudār*; it survives in the Yemen, in the Tihāma and even in Upper Egypt (al-Djāḥiẓ, *Ḥayawān*, vii, 178; al-Masʿūdī, *Murūdj*, iii, 319).

The Ḳurʾān contains none of the above terms, but the Prophet was aware of popular beliefs on the subject of the *ghīlān*; according to one *ḥadīth* he denied their existence, but some commentators consider that he denied only their ability to change shape, all the more because, according to another *ḥadīth*, he advised the repetition of the call to prayer as a way of escaping their evil deeds (cf. *LA*, s.v.; al-Damīrī, s.v.). Hence it is not surprising that this belief survived in Islam to the point that al-Ḳazwīnī, followed by al-Damīrī, does not hesitate to state that these beings are not uncommon in the thickets and reedy marshes and that if they can seize a man they play with him "like a cat with a mouse".

However, the Muʿtazila, in the first place al-Djāḥiẓ, but also for example al-Zamakhsharī (commenting on Ḳurʾān, XXXVII, 46), set out to demonstrate that this fabulous being did not exist. Al-Djāḥiẓ considers that the poets, in their vanity, have bolstered up the legend, for the interpretations, in which the imagination of the *ruwāt* has had a free rein, are based to a great extent on verses such as those of Taʾabbaṭa Sharr^{an} who boasts of his familiarity with the *saʿālī* or the *ghīlān* which he met in the desert (cf. *Aghānī*, xviii, 209 ff.). Al-Masʿūdī (*Murūdj*, iii, 314-22) devotes to the *ghīlān* a whole chapter in which he tries to bring the discussion on to a higher level; unable to deny their existence, for ʿUmar b. al-Khaṭṭāb himself is said to have seen and killed one (and other Companions too, see al-Ḳazwīnī and al-Damīrī, s.v.), he reports a philosophical opinion—taken up later by al-Ḳazwīnī—according to which the *ghūl* is a freak animal, naturally defective, which has strayed from all other animals to take refuge in inaccessible deserts; he suggests also that these beings are the offspring of the constellation Perseus (*Ḥāmil raʾs al-ghūl*) which, on rising, begets shapes and objects which are to be seen in deserts and even in inhabited regions.

In Berber lands, belief in ogres and other fabulous creatures is of great antiquity and manifests itself in a great many stories, where, however, they tend to be islamized (see Westermarck, *Ritual and belief in Morocco*, ii; E. Laoust, *Des noms berbères de l'ogre et de l'ogresse*, in *Hespéris*, xxxiv (1947), 253-65; idem, *Contes berbères du Maroc*, Paris 1949, ii, 125 ff.). For belief in the *ghūl* in Persia, see H. Massé, *Croyances et coutumes persans*, ii, 351 ff.; for Egypt, see especially C. E. Padwick, *Notes on the Jinn and the Ghoul in the peasant mind of Lower Egypt*, in *BSOAS*, iii (1923-5), 421-46.

In popular language *ghūl* (*ghūla*, *ḳuṭrub*, etc.) is frequently used to indicate a cannibal, man or demon, and this ogre is often invoked as a threat to naughty children; it also appears in many stories and has even passed into French and English, where *goule* (fem.) and *ghoul* respectively correspond to the old Arabic original and indicate in addition a kind of vampire which digs up bodies at night to devour them (cf. Lane, *Modern Egyptians*, ch. x).

Bibliography: Apart from the works quoted: Wellhausen, *Reste*, 137 ff.; G. van Vloten, in *WZKM*, vii (1893), 178; R. Basset, *Bânat Soʿâd*, Algiers 1910, 102, n. 2 and bibl. there given; idem, *1001 Contes*, i, 80-4, 153; Ibn Abi 'l-Ḥadīd, *Sharḥ Nahdj al-balāgha*, iv, 444 ff. — Persian stories: J. Malcolm, *Sketches of Persia*, ch. xvi. — Egyptian stories: Spitta Bey, *Contes arabes*, s.v. *ghūl*. — North African stories: J. Desparmet, *Contes populaires sur les ogres recueillis à Blida et traduits* (Coll. de contes et chansons pop., xxxv), Paris 1909-10, 2 vols.; H. Basset, *Essai sur la litt. des Berbères*, Algiers 1920, 129-35. — Turkish stories: Kúnos, *Türkische Volksmärchen*, index s.vv. *dew* and *dschinn*. On the *ghūl* which induces hydrophobia, see R. Burton, *Pilgrimage*, ch. xviii; on *Ṣaydāna*, borrowed from Ethiopic, see Nöldeke, *Neue Beiträge*, 50. See further DIW, DJINN, ʿIFRĪT, etc.

(D. B. MACDONALD-[CH. PELLAT])

GHULĀM (A., pl. *ghilmān*), word meaning in Arabic a young man or boy (the word is used for example of the ʿAbbāsid princes al-Muʿtazz and al-Muʾayyad, sons of al-Mutawakkil, at the time when their brother, the caliph al-Muntaṣir, attempted to make them renounce their rights to the succession (al-Ṭabarī, iii, 1485), while the son of al-Wāthiḳ, whom they hesitated to proclaim caliph because of his youth, is described as *ghulām amrad* "beardless" (al-Ṭabarī, iii, 1368)); then, by extension, either a servant, sometimes elderly (cf. Ch. Pellat, *Milieu*, Paris 1953, 69) and very often, but not necessarily, a slave servant (on this use see ʿABD); or a bodyguard, slave or freedman, bound to his master by personal ties; or finally sometimes an artisan working in the workshop of a master whose name he used along with his own in his signature (cf. D. S. Rice, in *BSOAS*, xv (1963), 67, and Mayer, *Metalworkers*, 14).

Every person of a certain rank in Arab Muslim society of the first centuries had in his service, sometimes in addition to free *ghilmān*, a number of *ghilmān* of servile status whose exact origin is not usually indicated and who are usually distinguished from the eunuchs, *khadam* [see KHĀDIM] (as for example in the description of the household of the vizier al-Ḳāsim under al-Muktafī, preserved in the *Nishwār* of al-Tanūkhī, ii, 159). Rulers owned an often impressive number of slave *ghilmān* who served as attendants or guards and could rise to fairly high office in the hierarchy of the palace service, as well as others who formed a component of varying importance in the armed forces. It is with these latter *ghilmān* and the role which they played in the running of various eastern and western Muslim states that this article is chiefly concerned.

i.—THE CALIPHATE

We find hardly any mention of *ghilmān* at the court or in the palace of the Umayyad caliphs, but Slavs and Berbers who were or had been slaves are already found in the entourages of certain princes or in their armies (T. Lewicki, in *Folia Orientalia*, iv (1962), 319 ff.). Certainly from the time of the foundation of the "Round City" of Baghdād, there is mention of the presence of *ghilmān* in quarters inside the wall of the main fortification. But it is only under al-Muʿtaṣim that the *ghilmān* proper took their place in the history of the Muslim world, after the slave element, notably in the person of the famous eunuch Masrūr, had begun to play a rôle in the processes of government under Ḥārūn al-Rashīd.

At the end of the reign of al-Maʾmūn, his brother, the future al-Muʿtaṣim, had caused to be bought at Samarḳand about three thousand Turkish slaves who were to form the nucleus of the new guard of the caliph and of the new army. The constitution of this guard is said to have been the cause of the transfer of the capital to Sāmarrā in 221/836, although there must also have been other causes, connected with the policy followed by the caliph at that time. To the Turks recruited in Transoxania were added various slaves, also Turkish, who were in the service of certain dignitaries of Baghdād and who, according to al-Yaʿḳūbī, were bought by the caliph. The new militia thus grew rapidly and, at Sāmarrā, the Turkish *ghilmān* were housed in special quarters, away from the Arab or Arabicized population, and obliged to take for wives young slaves of the same origin as themselves from whom they were never allowed to separate. They were divided into several groups under the command of leaders such as Ashnās, Waṣīf and Afshīn who were themselves freedmen, and whose duty it was to lead their troops when on campaign.

What was the reason for the establishment of this force of armed slaves, which was to supplant not only the earlier Arab contingents but also the Khurāsānī troops who had appeared with the ʿAbbāsid dynasty and who, not long before, had effectively supported al-Maʾmūn? It was almost certainly the anxiety of the new caliphs to avoid the repetition of a civil war such as had broken out between al-Maʾmūn and al-Amīn, and to strengthen the central power by enabling it to rely on forces free from all local attachments. In fact, these *ghilmān*, whose numbers grew rapidly to several tens of thousands (20,000 or 70,000 according to the estimates of Arabic writers), did not remain aloof from partisan struggles; their appearance, though it caused profound changes in the functioning of the political régime, did not make the caliphate any more stable.

It was not long before their commanders, usually freedmen, who enjoyed the unconditional loyalty of their troops, began to occupy important positions, either as governors in the provinces, or at the court where they ended by interfering in affairs of government and in the problems of the succession to the caliphate. It was some of these officers who assassinated the caliph al-Mutawakkil in 247/861 and, during the following years, their disputes were the basic cause of the dynastic troubles which constantly recurred until the regent al-Muwaffaḳ and then his son al-Muʿtaḍid succeeded in imposing their authority on the soldiery. Meanwhile there were numerous quarrels between these Turkish officers and the representatives of the secretarial class which they tried to dominate.

Although the situation appears calmer during the reign of al-Muʿtaḍid (279-89/892-902), the military chiefs still belonged to the new aristocracy formed by the descendants of the first *ghilmān*; thus Badr, who was the caliph's supreme general and was often given the title of *ghulām*—in the broadest sense—of the Caliph, was the son of a freedman of al-Mutawakkil. The regiments of *ghilmān*, whose importance had grown during the war against the Zandj, were at this time very numerous. Each regiment bore the name of the leader who commanded it or who had formed it (thus the *Bughāʾiyya* was no doubt called after the name of an officer of al-Mutawakkil, Bughā al-Sharābī [*q.v.*] and the *Nāṣiriyya* after that of the regent al-Muwaffaḳ al-Nāṣir li-dīn Allāh), though this name did not indicate with any certainty in whose service they actually were. Among these *ghilmān* of the army of the caliph, those of which we know most, thanks to the list of the court expenses preserved by Hilāl al-Ṣābiʾ (*K. al-Wuzarāʾ*, 11-18), are the ones who formed the various detachments of the guard. There was first of all a group of former slaves of varying origins, white such as Daylamīs and Berbers, or black such as Nubians and former Zandj prisoners taken by al-Muwaffaḳ during the preceding reign, who were employed to form a line of troops (*maṣāff*) in the reception rooms and who were probably the origin of the corps of the *Maṣāffiyya* mentioned below. There were also others bought especially by al-Muʿtaḍid to be on duty in the "halls" (*ḥudjar*) of the Palace, from which they took their name (*al-Ḥudjariyya*), and placed under the command of eunuchs called *ustādh*s; to these were later added an élite of soldiers chosen from among the various detachments. In addition to these the personal guard of the caliph was made up of freedmen of al-Muwaffaḳ, called *al-ghilmān al-khāṣṣa*.

During the reign of al-Muḳtadir (295-320/908-32), these corps of *ghilmān*, the respective size and importance of which it is difficult to assess (we know only that the *Maṣāffiyya*, who were under the command of the Chamberlain, numbered 10,000 men), commanded by leaders who were often rivals, once again influenced political events and the palace intrigues. Thus in the two abortive coups d'état of 296/908 and 317/929 against the caliph, the guards played a decisive rôle and, in 317/929, it was the *Maṣāffiyya* who forced al-Ḳāhir to flee. In addition, the demands of the *ghilmān*, on whom in large measure the fate of the caliphate depended (in the capital as well as in the provinces where they were often sent as reinforcements), gave rise to financial difficulties and several times they procured the removal from the vizierate of figures such as ʿAlī b. ʿĪsā, who tried to restore financial order by making cuts in this expenditure. The interference of the *ghilmān* in political affairs led to the elimination of one regiment after another. The *Maṣāffiyya* were massacred in 318/930, then the *Sādjiyya* (on the origin of the name, see M. Canard, tr. of al-Ṣūlī, *Akhbâr ar-Râḍî*, i, 49 n. 3) were imprisoned in 324/936 by the *amīr al-umarāʾ* Ibn Rāʾiḳ, who shortly afterwards had the *Ḥudjariyya* exterminated in order to deprive the caliph of all power.

By this time the caliph had lost practically all control over the regiments of *ghilmān*. At Baghdād their commanders no longer respected his authority. Furthermore, persons such as the viziers were in a position to form in due course for themselves personal bodyguards capable eventually of repulsing the troops of the caliph. The provincial governors, who more and more often combined military and fiscal functions, for their part maintained troops who were completely loyal to them. Thus certain governors went so far, with the aid of their own regiments, as to seize effective power for themselves, and a number of them forced the caliph to recognize them as *amīr al-umarāʾ*; after several years they were replaced by the famous Buwayhid *amīr*s, whose Daylamī guards were from then on installed in the palace of the *amīr* side by side with the Turkish *ghilmān* who were still used.

In the western provinces the same development had already given rise to local attempts to attain autonomy from the second half of the 3rd/9th century onwards. Thus Aḥmad b. Ṭūlūn [*q.v.*], who in Egypt achieved a large measure of independence from the central government and managed to establish a short-lived dynasty there, was the son of a slave bought at Bukhārā under al-Maʾmūn. Similarly al-Ikhshīd [*q.v.*], who was later to repeat this success in the same country, was the descendant of a Turk who came to Sāmarrā under al-Muʿtaṣim. The ephemeral dynasties thus founded themselves formed slave armies. The army of Ibn Ṭūlūn is said to have included 24,000 Turkish and 42,000 black slaves in addition to the smaller number of free soldiers; al-Ikhshīd also had a large slave army, and had as minister, as regent for his sons and ultimately as successor, the famous black slave Kāfūr [*q.v.*].

The tradition continued in Fāṭimid Egypt. There were at the Palace, as retainers holding more or less honorific offices and as guards, black or white slaves, some eunuchs and some not, most of the former originating from the Sudan and the latter from the Slav countries. The rôles of Djawhar [*q.v.*], who was a freedman of Slav origin, and of the eunuch freedman Djawdhar [*q.v.*], also a Slav, who was the right hand man of the caliph al-Muʿizz, are well known. Later Turkish and Daylamī units were added. (On the rivalries between the different ethnic groups see FĀṬIMIDS, 858.)

A little later, the Saldjūḳids, who were not of slave origin and who had installed themselves in the eastern provinces of the ʿAbbāsid empire with the aid of the Turcomans, were nevertheless soon forced also to have recourse to a professional army and to recruit Turkish *ghilmān* (see below) as both soldiers and assistants. Thus the *atābak*s [*q.v.*] were in general former slaves. The *atābak*s of Syria themselves employed slaves of various origins for their personal bodyguard (such as those who assassinated Zangī [*q.v.*]), but their army does not seem to have been based on the recruitment of slaves. On the other hand, their successors the Ayyūbids, who were the descendants of a Kurdish officer, recruited Turkish slaves along with the Kurdish contingents, and the last ruler of this dynasty, al-Malik al-Ṣāliḥ, tried to save his threatened throne by installing in Cairo an important troop of Turkish slaves. It was these slaves who were finally to found the first regime in which the power was officially wielded by the slave militia, that of the Mamlūks [*q.v.*].

In Muslim Spain, the slave element of European origin had also played an important rôle both in the army and in the palace service. The freedmen, usually called *fityān* [see FATĀ], but also *ghilmān* as in the East, came to control the main governmental offices and even to found, as the Umayyad state disappeared, small local dynasties [see AL-ANDALUS, 495].

In the Maghrib the name *ghulām* does not seem to have been in current use for the slave mercenaries, and although the rulers of the Maghrib had almost all had, since the Aghlabid period, black bodyguards (the members of which are generally called *ʿabīd*) and employed, in proportions which varied and which are difficult to ascertain, slave mercenaries of diverse origins, often Europeans, the slave militias never had in this region the importance which they had in the East. See further DJAYSH, MAMLŪK.

Bibliography: There is no thorough study of the subject. General information is given in R. Levy, *The social structure of Islam*, London 1958, 416-51 *passim*. On the situation at Sāmarrā and at Baghdād see: E. Herzfeld, *Geschichte der Stadt Samarra*, Hamburg 1948, 88-9; D. Ayalon, *The military reforms of Caliph al-Muʿtaṣim* (a paper read at the Congress of Orientalists at New Delhi, January 1964); Yaʿḳūbī, *Buldān*, 255-6; Ṭabarī, iii, 1017, 2265; Kindī, *Wulāt Miṣr*, ed. Guest, 188; Ibn Khurradādhbih, 37, 39; Masʿūdī, *Murūdj*, vii, 121, 291; Maḳrīzī, *K. al-Nizāʿ wa 'l-takhāṣum*, Leiden 1888, 63 (a passage mentioned by D. Ayalon); D. Sourdel, *Le vizirat ʿabbāside*, Damascus 1959-60, especially i, 325, 330, 370-5; ii, 403, 413, 451-4, 587-8; W. Hoenerbach, *Zur Heeresverwaltung der Abbasiden*, in *Isl.*, xxix (1950), 267; Mez, *Renaissance*, Engl. tr., 141, 165; Miskawayh, in Amedroz and Margoliouth, *Eclipse*, i, 38, 116, 157, 195, 202, 333, 335, 351-2, 357-8; Hilāl al-Ṣābiʾ, *K. al-Wuzarāʾ*, ed. Amedroz, 11-18, 26, 49, 51, 60, 88 (Cairo ed., 15-22, 31, 56, 59, 70, 100); idem, *Rusūm dār al-Khilāfa*, ed. Mīkhāʾīl ʿAwād, Baghdad 1964, 8, 12, 16, 25, 85, 91; Ṣūlī, *Akhbâr ar-Râdî* ..., tr. M. Canard, Algiers 1946-50, i, 71 n. 8, and index (s.v. H'ujarites, Masâffites, Muʾnisites, Sâjites); Ibn al-Zubayr, *K. al-Dhakhāʾir wa'l-tuḥaf*, Kuwayt 1959, index. On Egypt: G. Wiet, *L'Egypte arabe*, Paris 1937, passim; I. Hrbek, *Die Slawen im Dienste der Fatimiden*, in *ArO*, xxi (1953), 543-81; *Vie de l'Ustadh Jaudhar*, tr. M. Canard, Algiers 1958, 15-6; H. A. R. Gibb, *The armies of Saladin*, in *Cahiers d'histoire égyptienne*, iii (1951) (reprinted in idem, *Studies on the civilization of Islam*, London 1962, 74-90). On the west: E. Lévi-Provençal, *L'Espagne musulmane au Xe siècle*, 28-31, 105-7; idem, *Hist. Esp. mus.*, iii, 97; M. Vonderheyden, *La Berbérie orientale sous la dynastie des Benoû' l'-Arlab*, Paris 1927, 197-9; H. R. Idris, *La Berbérie orientale sous les Zirides*, Paris 1962, index; R. Brunschvig, *La Berbérie orientale sous les Hafsides*, ii, 47, 79-81; J. F. P. Hopkins, *Medieval Muslim government in Barbary*, London 1958, 71 ff. (D. SOURDEL)

ii.—PERSIA

The institution of military slavery in the Persian world is post-Islamic. Whilst slavery was known under the Achaemenids, Seleucids, Arsacids and Sāsānids, it was essentially for temple service, for state purposes like building or for domestic duties. At no time in the pre-Islamic period does slavery seem to have been as widespread in the Persian world as in other parts of the Middle East (R. N. Frye, *The heritage of Persia*, London 1963, 152-3). Military organization under all the historic pre-Islamic dynasties of Persia was based on the classes of greater nobility and lesser nobility or gentry (*vuzurgān* and *āzādhān* in Sāsānid terminology), and the free cavalryman was the backbone of the army. Within the army there was usually an élite body surrounding the Emperor, the Achaemenid "corps of immortals" or the Sāsānid *gyān-avspar* "those who sacrifice their lives", but there is no indication that these were anything but freemen and probably they were sons of the nobility (cf. Christensen, *L'Iran sous les Sassanides*², 206 ff., 368). Any slaves in these armies can only have been employed in the little-regarded infantry rump, which was basically a rabble of conscripted peasants.

The carrying of Arab arms beyond the borders of Armenia and Persia opened up vast reservoirs of slave labour from the South Russian, Central Asian and northern Indian worlds. In particular, the Turks early acquired the reputation of being fierce fighters, skilled riders and archers, who because of their nomadic life in the harsh and extreme conditions of the Eurasian steppes were inured to danger and discomfort (cf. Djāḥiẓ, *Risāla fī manāḳib al-Turk*, tr. C. T. Harley-Walker, *JRAS*, 1915, 631-97, analysed by F. Gabrieli, *RSO*, xxxii (1957), 477-83). Turkish prisoners-of-war began to fall into the hands of the Arab governors of Armenia and Khurāsān, and it is with the military use of these captives—a writer of the 5th/11th century, Ibn Ḥassūl, emphasizes that the Turks are too proud a race to make good domestic slaves—that the institution of the *ghulām* in Persia begins. The Ṭāhirid governors of Khurāsān forwarded to the ʿAbbāsids in Baghdād Turkish slaves for use in the Caliphal palace guard. Whilst details of the Ṭāhirids' own use of *ghulām*s are lacking, their example here must have been decisive for succeeding dynasties in Persia.

The spread of military slavery in Persia also reflects the growing economic and commercial prosperity of the land during the 3rd/9th and 4th/10th centuries, for this enabled rulers to pay professional, slave armies rather than to rely on the Arab elements settled in the garrison towns or on local Persian troops. The advantage of slave troops lay in their lack of loyalties to anyone but their master and the fact that they had no material stake in the country of their adoption. Such ties were deliberately avoided by the most strictly professional of slave commanders: the Sāmānid *ghulām* general Ḳaratigin Isfīdjābī (d. 317/929) laid down that "a soldier must be able to take with him everything which he possesses, wherever he may go, and nothing must hold him back" (Ibn al-Athīr, viii, 157).

Juridically, the slave soldier belonged to his master and was heritable property like any other chattel. In practice, personal loyalties and attachments were usually taken into account. When in the middle of the 4th/10th century the Ṣaffārid Amīr of Sīstān, Abū Aḥmad Ḥusayn b. Ṭāhir, died, his *ghulāms* should have passed to his successor Khalaf b. Aḥmad, but the latter gave them the choice of entering his own service or of seeking independent careers; in fact, they elected to stay with Khalaf, and he assigned them houses, estates and concubines (*Taʾrīkh-i Sīstān*, 341). One of Masʿūd I of Ghazna's old and trusted *ghulām* commanders was manumitted before his death and the Sultan respected his last wishes concerning the disposal of his personal *ghulāms* (Bayhaḳī, cited by C. E. Bosworth, *Ghaznevid military organisation*, in *Isl.*, xxxvi/1-2 (1960), 49-50). It was clearly in the interest of the master to treat his slaves well, for the particular concern of the *ghulāms* was normally to act as a dependable élite force within the wider body of the army and as a personal bodyguard. Under such dynasties as the Ghaznavids and Saldjūḳs, *ghulāms* filled such important household and palace offices as Keeper of the Stables, Keeper of the Wardrobe, Keeper of the Sulṭān's Armour and Weapons, Bearer of the Ceremonial Parasol or *čatr* and Keeper of the Washing Vessels (cf. Bosworth, *op. cit.*, 47-8; İ. H. Uzunçarşılı, *Osmanlı devleti teşkilâtına medhal*, Istanbul 1941, 35-41; İ. Kafesoğlu, *Sultan Melikşah devrinde Büyük Selçuklu imparatorluğu*, Istanbul 1953, 143-5). This last office of *ṭasht-dār* was held during the reign of the Saldjūḳ Malik Shāh by the *ghulām* Anūshtigin Gharčaʾī; it was the stepping-stone to his appointment as governor of Khwārizm and the consolidation there in the 6th/12th century of his descendants as Khwārizm-Shāhs. When a ruler or commander lost the loyalty of his *ghulāms*, his position could become very insecure. The Ziyārid Mardāwīdj b. Ziyār was murdered in 323/935 because he had ill-treated his Turkish *ghulāms*, putting reins and saddles on them as if they were horses and leading them into stables (Masʿūdī, *Murūdj*, ix, 29-30; Miskawayh, *Eclipse of the ʿAbbāsid Caliphate*, i, 162-3, 312-15, tr. iv, 182-4, 353-6; Ibn al-Athīr, viii, 222-3). The *ghulāms* of the Sāmānid Amīr Aḥmad b. Ismāʿīl killed him in 301/914 allegedly because he had become alienated from them through his excessive frequenting of the *ʿulamāʾ* (Barthold, *Turkestan*, 240).

In considering the personal relationship between master and slave, the sexual aspect should certainly not be neglected; the ethical climate of Persia in this period condoned homosexual liaisons (cf. Kay Kāʾūs, *Ḳābūs-nāma*, ch. xv, and for more recent times, Olearius, *Voyages and travels . . . to the Great Duke of Muscovy and the King of Persia*, Eng. tr. London 1669, i, 238: "Sodomy not punish'd in Persia"), and the master of youthful slaves was well-placed for indulging unnatural and sadistic tastes. Resentments aroused by practices of this kind seem to have been behind the murder in 541/1146 of Zangī b. Aḳ Sonḳur. Zangī's personal guard was drawn from the sons of the great men of the Turks, Greeks and Armenians, whose fathers he had killed or banished; he had then kept the sons after castrating them to preserve their boyish and beardless appearance. These *ghulāms* had long sought an opportunity for revenge, and eventually assassinated him (Bundārī, 208-9). Eunuch *ghulāms* from the Byzantine, Armenian and Khazar regions may have been castrated within their homelands, but this operation was also done within the borders of Islam, especially in the case of Turks. Emasculation was often accepted voluntarily as a recognized way to preferment (cf. *Murūdj*, viii, 148-9); thus one of the most highly-honoured of the Saldjūḳ *ghulām* generals under Alp Arslan and Malik Shāh, ʿImād al-Dawla Sāwtigin, had castrated himself (Ḥusaynī, *Akhbār al-dawla al-Saldjūḳiyya*, 30-1).

The Ṣaffārids, successors to the Ṭāhirid heritage in Khurāsān, are the first Persian dynasty about whose employment of *ghulāms* we have detailed information. Yaʿḳūb b. Layth's known skill as a military organizer makes it unlikely that he would pass over the adoption of an institution so useful for buttressing a despotic ruler's power. Both Masʿūdī, *Murūdj*, viii, 49-54, and the *Taʾrīkh-i Sīstān*, 222, say that he had a corps of 2000 *ghulāms* who on ceremonial occasions paraded on either side of his throne, richly clothed and armed with golden and silver shields, swords and maces, all captured from the treasury of Muḥammad b. Ṭāhir at Nīshāpūr. Masʿūdī adds that there was within this general body the Amīr's personal bodyguard, the *ghulāms* of the *khawāṣṣ*, who slept round his tent and executed his personal orders. The equipment and functions of these Ṣaffārid *ghulāms* bear a remarkable resemblance to those of the Ghaznavid *ghulāms* of 150 years later as depicted on the walls of Lashkar-i Bāzār (see below).

Contemporaneously with the Ṣaffārids, the Sāmānids in Transoxania and later in Khurāsān were making a slave guard the nucleus of their army. Naṣr b. Aḥmad (d. 331/943) is said to have had as many as 10,000 *ghulāms*. The Amīrs hoped that these Turkish troops, with their personal bond of fealty to the ruler, would counterbalance the military influence of the indigenous Iranian *dihḳān* class, which was hostile to the dynasty's centralizing policy, but the rôle of the *ghulāms* in various palace revolutions and assassinations shows that this hope was not always realised. However, the geographer Iṣṭakhrī praises the Sāmānid slave army for its discipline and boldness in battle. It was, of course, from the slave guard of the Sāmānids that Alptigin, the conqueror of Ghazna, and Sebüktigin, founder of the Ghaznavid dynasty in Afghanistan and northern India, arose.

In the course of the 4th/10th century, the use of military slaves spread throughout the Persian world to such Daylamī dynasties as the Ziyārids and Būyids and to Arab ones like the Ḥamdānids. The Turkish cavalry of the Būyid armies soon grew more numerous than the free Daylamī infantrymen, and under Muʿizz al-Dawla (d. 356/967) were preferred above the Daylamīs in pay and the granting of *iḳṭāʿ*s (Miskawayh, ii, 99-100, 163-4, 166, 173-4, 234, tr. v, 104-5, 175-6, 178, 186-8, 248; Ibn al-Athīr, viii, 343). Amongst the Persian dynasties of Ādharbaydjān and the eastern Caucasus, as amongst the Christian principalities of Georgia and Armenia, slave troops were drawn from the Khazar and Russian lands to the north. The Yazīdī Sharwān-Shāhs had personal guards of *ghulāms*, and the Hāshimī ruler of Darband, Maymūn b. Aḥmad, had Rūs *ghulāms* who were still pagan, although these may have been adventurers of Slav-Scandinavian origin rather than slaves (cf. Minorsky, *A history of Sharvān and Darband in the*

10th-11th centuries, Cambridge 1958, tr. 28-9, 45-6, 51, 113-15, 121, 123, 127).

The G̲h̲aznavids, themselves of servile origin, built their multi-racial army around a slave core, mainly of Turks but also including some Indians. In the reign of Masʿūd b. Maḥmud (d. 432/1041), the *g̲h̲ulām*s numbered between 4,000 and 6,000. Headed by their own general, the *Sālār-i G̲h̲ulāmān*, they were used in battle as a crack force, and on ceremonial occasions they had rich uniforms and bejewelled weapons; the depiction of these *g̲h̲ulām*s in the recently-discovered murals of the palace of Las̲h̲kar-i Bāzār at Bust accords well with the descriptions of them in the written sources. We also see at work at this time, as under the later Sāmānids, the process whereby provincial governors and commanders themselves collected extensive slave guards (cf. Bosworth, *Ghaznevid military organisation*, 40-50).

The Turkish dynasties who in the 5th/11th century irrupted into the Persian world from the Central Asian steppes soon adopted slave troops as a more reliable fighting instrument than the tribal bands who were their original following. As early as 398/1008 the Ḳarāk̲h̲ānid Ilig- K̲h̲ān Naṣr had a body of Turkish *g̲h̲ulām* archers which he used against Maḥmūd of G̲h̲azna (ʿUtbī-Manīnī, *Yamīnī*, ii, 85), and in the next century, the Ḳarāk̲h̲ānid *g̲h̲ulām*s numbered several thousands (Bundārī, 264). In particular, the Great Saldjūḳs found that a paid, professional army was necessary to extend and protect their empire, since their original supporters, the Turkmens, were an anarchic and uncontrollable force. Within this professional army, the Saldjūḳ *g̲h̲ulām*s were prominent; their commanders were active on *g̲h̲azw* in the Caucasus and Armenia and against the Arab dynasties of the west. They usually remained loyal to their masters the Sultans even when the fidelity of other Turkish and Turkmen troops wavered, *e.g.*, in Malik S̲h̲āh's battle of 465/1073 with his uncle Ḳāwurd and in the battle of 526/1132 of Dāʾūd b. Maḥmūd and Aḳ Sonḳur Aḥmadīlī against T̲og̲h̲rïl b. Muḥammad (Bundārī, 48, 160-1). As well as Turks, the *g̲h̲ulām*s of the Saldjūḳs included Greeks, Armenians and even negroes (*al-k̲h̲uddām al-ḥubūs̲h̲*), whose *amīr*s are described as being especially influential under Masʿūd b. Muḥammad (*ibid.*, 193, cf. Rāwandī, 243). The great Vizier Niẓām al-Mulk collected around himself a corps of *g̲h̲ulām*s of regal dimensions, and after his death this body, the *Niẓāmiyya*, still acted as a cohesive body in politics. In the 6th/12th century we see the seizure of power by *g̲h̲ulām* commanders of the increasingly ineffective Saldjūḳ Sultans, nominally as Atabaks or tutors for young Saldjūḳ princes. Hereditary lines of slave Atabaks tended to form in such parts of Persia as Ād̲h̲arbaydjān, Fārs, K̲h̲ūzistān and K̲h̲urāsān, and in this latter province the *g̲h̲ulām*s of Sandjar claimed to carry on the administrative traditions of their old master before they were swept away by the rising tide of the G̲h̲ūrids and K̲h̲wārizm-S̲h̲āhs.

Both the G̲h̲ūrids and the K̲h̲wārizm-S̲h̲āhs relied heavily on slave troops. Djalāl al-Dīn Mingburnu's *g̲h̲ulām*s were armed with the traditional weapon of such troops, the mace (Nasawī, 232, tr. 386: *čumāk̲h̲dāriyya*). The Turkish *g̲h̲ulām*s of the G̲h̲ūrids did not always act harmoniously with the native G̲h̲ūrī troops (cf. Djuwaynī-Boyle, 461), but the troops of Muʿizz al-Dīn or S̲h̲ihāb al-Dīn Muḥammad, the *Muʿizziyya*, continued to revere that Sultan's name and in the 7th/13th century the principalities which they founded in northern India were ostensibly constituted in his name.

The invasions of the Mongols brought into Persia an entirely new set of military traditions. The Mongol commanders used the captured populations of towns as auxiliaries and as pioneers and sappers (cf. Spuler, *Mongolen*[2], 402, 416-19), but *g̲h̲ulām*s in the older sense of professional slave soldiers did not reappear until the Mongols and their successors had been assimilated to Persian ways. The institution may be discernible in the 9th/15th century amongst the Turkmen Aḳ Ḳoyunlu in western Persia and eastern Anatolia. In an ʿArḍ-nāma dating from the time of Uzun Ḥasan (d. 883/1478) are mentioned 3,900 ḳullug̲h̲čīs "servants" in the total of some 10,000 for the Right Wing of the army; it is unclear whether these were mounted or went on foot (W. Hinz, *Irans Aufsteig zum Nationalstaat in fünfzehnten Jahrhundert*, Berlin-Leipzig 1936, 107-8; Minorsky, *A civil and military review in Fārs in 881/1476*, in *BSOS*, x (1939-42), 155, 164).

The military basis of the Ṣafawid state was originally the Ḳïzïl-bās̲h̲ tribal divisions, but S̲h̲āh ʿAbbās I (995-1037/1587-1628) invited men of all tribes and nations to enroll in a new salaried body of troops, the S̲h̲āh-sewans, who would be entirely devoted to the sovereign and free from tribal ties (cf. Minorsky, *EI*[1], s.v.). Also notable in this reign was the increased rôle in the Ṣafawid state of Georgians, Armenians and Circassians, many of whom were captured in the wars in the Caucasus and entered the Ṣafawid service as slave converts to Islam. In 994/1586 a Georgian was *lala* or tutor to the Ṣafawid prince Ṭahmāsp b. ʿAbbās, this office corresponding in many ways to the old one of Atabak (R. M. Savory in *BSOAS*, xxiv (1961), 84-5). With such soldiers and officials as these, the institution of the *g̲h̲ulām* takes on a new lease of life as an important component of the new troops. The Ṣafawid "slaves" (*ḳullar* or *g̲h̲ulāmān-i k̲h̲āṣṣa-yi s̲h̲arīfa*) were mainly slaves or sons of slaves. The military *g̲h̲ulām*s were numbered by Chardin at 10,000 and by Tavernier at 18,000 (a substantial proportion of the whole body of *g̲h̲ulām*s was used for court and administrative service; in the *Tad̲h̲kirat al-mulūk*, tr. Minorsky, 56-7, 127-8, the term *g̲h̲ulām* is also used for the young eunuchs and pages of the S̲h̲āh's private household). The *g̲h̲ulām* body in general was headed by the extremely influential *Ḳullar Āg̲h̲āsï*, and there was for it a special Vizier and *Mustawfī* of the Department of the G̲h̲ulāms (*Tad̲h̲kirat al-mulūk*, tr. 46-7, 73). Tavernier noted that the *g̲h̲ulām*s very rarely rebelled, "For being all Slaves, and of different Nations, there are no ties of Affection or Kindred between them: And if the King has an occasion to punish any of them, the chief of their Body is to execute his orders" (*Travels*, Eng. tr. London 1684, i, 224-5).

In the reign of the Ḳādjār Fatḥ ʿAlī S̲h̲āh (1211-50/1797-1834), the term *g̲h̲ulām* was still applied to the royal bodyguard, and Georgians were still prominent here (Sir Harford Jones Brydges, *An account of the transactions of His Majesty's mission to the court of Persia in the years 1807-11*, London 1834, i, 325, 331, 382); but in the course of the 19th century, as western influences grew in Persia and personal slavery disappeared, *g̲h̲ulām* simply came to denote a runner or messenger employed by a foreign diplomatic or consular agency.

The term is still in current use in Persian Balūčistān, where until recently the *g̲h̲ulām*s were slave retainers of the local Balūč chiefs or *sardār*s; although now legally free, they are still regarded as a socially inferior class (see B. J. Spooner, *Kūch u Balūch and*

Ichthyophagi, in *Iran, J. of the British Inst. of Persian Studies*, ii (1964), 61-2).

Bibliography: given in the article. There are no special studies, but surveys of the institution in the Persian world up to and including the Ghaznavids are given by C. E. Bosworth, *Ghaznevid military organisation*, in *Isl.*, xxxvi/1-2 (1960), 40-50, and idem, *The Ghaznavids: their empire in Afghanistan and eastern Iran 994-1040*, Edinburgh 1963, 98-106. (C. E. Bosworth)

iii. — India.

The Muslim conquest and occupation of Hindūstān at the end of the 7th/13th century, although initiated and directed by the free chiefs of the Ghūrid dynasty, was mainly the achievement of Turkish *ghulāms* (more frequently referred to as *bandagān* in the Indo-Persian histories). In the frequent absences of Muʿizz al-Dīn Muḥammad ibn Sām, his slave Ḳuṭb al-Dīn Aybak, who began in India as military commander (*sipah-sālār*) of Kuhrām, led the Ghūrid forces against Rādjput strongholds. On the death of Muʿizz al-Dīn in 602/1206, Ḳuṭb al-Dīn assumed power in Lahore, at that time probably without having been manumitted. The so-called *Taʾrīkh-i Fakhr al-Dīn Mubārak Shāh*, ed. E. Denison Ross, London, 1927, 35-6, intended for Ḳuṭb al-Dīn, has a remarkable eulogy of Turkish slaves for their fidelity and for their capacity to win advancement to the rank of *amīr* and *sipahsālār*, without regretting their former free life in Turkistān.

Hindūstān was not, however, conquered exclusively by slave agents of the Ghūrids whether as commanders or as troopers. Lakhnawtī was conquered by the free Khaldjī Muḥammad Bakhtiyār; Khaldjīs also formed part of the Ghūrid armies.

Until the reign of Djalāl al-Dīn Khaldjī (689-95/1290-6) the sultans of Dihlī were all either military slaves or their descendants. Iletmish was not manumitted until after appointment as *amīr* of Gwāliyār, *malik* of Badāʾūn and after holding the *iḳṭāʿ* of the *ḳaṣba* of Baran (Minhādj al-Sirādj, *Ṭabaḳāt-i Nāṣirī*, Calcutta 1864, 169-70). Balban had presumably been freed before his marriage to the daughter of Sultan Nāṣir al-Dīn Maḥmūd. Under Iletmish (and there is no reason to conclude that his successors changed the practice) Turkish slaves rose to provincial military command through service in the royal household as Keeper of the Stables, Keeper of the Washing Vessels, Keeper of the Leopards or royal bodyguard (*Ṭabaḳāt-i Nāṣirī*, 229-324, *passim*). Slaves did not, however, enjoy a monopoly of office; Baranī, *Taʾrīkh-i Fīrūz Shāhī*, Calcutta 1862, 26, speaks of the Turkish slaves ousting the free officers (*mulūk-i aḥrār*) in the reigns of Iletmish's children. Some of these officers were fugitives from the Mongols. Antagonism appears to have been evinced by Turkish slaves towards certain non-Turkish slaves, the *ḥabshī* Djamāl al-Dīn Yāḳūt and the Hindu eunuch Imād al-Dīn Rayḥān. Minḥādj (*Ṭabaḳāt*, 300) specifically states that Turkish and Tadjīk slaves resented Rayḥān because he was of the tribes of Hindūstān (*az ḳabāʾil-i Hindūstān*).

Under the Khaldjī and Tughluḳ sultans, slaves continued to become high officers and to form an important component of the sultan's army. The Turkish element among the slaves appears to have been diluted somewhat and the rise to power of Hindū slaves is noteworthy in this period. How far the historian Baranī's hostility to their elevation was shared by his contemporaries is a moot point. The Hindū Khusraw Khān Barwarī, recipient of the homosexually-inspired favours of Sultan Mubārak Shāh Khaldjī, murdered his master (720/1320) and assumed the throne before being deposed by the free *malik*, Ghiyāth al-Dīn Tughluḳ. The Telingana Brahmin, Khān-i Djahān Maḳbūl, became *wazīr* to Fīrūz Shāh Tughluḳ. Slaves were apt to resent a former member of their number usurping the position of the ruling family. Slave commanders of fifty and a hundred, raised by Sultan ʿAlāʾ al-Dīn Khaldjī, successfully plotted the overthrow of the famous eunuch, Malik Kāfūr, conqueror of the Deccan, when he began to kill off the sultan's family after ʿAlā al-Dīn's death (Baranī, *Taʾrīkh-i Fīrūz Shāhī*, 376).

Sources for the Khaldjī and Tughluḳ periods give figures for the number of slaves in service. The army of Muḥammad ibn Tughluḳ was reputed to have 20,000 Turki *ghulāms*, 10,000 eunuchs as well as large numbers of slave bodyguards always accompanying him (al-ʿUmarī, *Masālik al-abṣār fī mamālik al-amṣār*, edited text and Urdū translation by Khūrshīd Aḥmad Fārūḳī, Delhi 1962?, 25). ʿAfīf, *Taʾrīkh-i Fīrūz Shāhī*, Calcutta 1891, 267-73, gives the most elaborate account available of the slave establishment in the sultanate period. Fīrūz Shāh is said to have encouraged the provincial *muḳṭaʿ*s to collect slaves to present them to the sultan, receiving in return an allowance from the revenue to be remitted to headquarters equal to the value of the slaves. Such slaves were stationed in the principal fortress towns (*e.g.*, Multān, Dīpalpur, Sāmānā) and were paid both in cash and by the grant of revenue from villages. ʿAfīf says that Fīrūz Shāh had 180,000 slaves in the capital and in the provinces. A *dīwān* separate from the *dīwān-i wizārat* existed to manage the slaves. They were to be found not only in such familiar household offices as Keeper of the Washing Vessels, Keeper of the sultan's armour and weapons, Bearer of the Ceremonial Parasol, but also employed in the *dīwān-i wizārat* and the *dīwān-i arḍ*, and as *muḳṭaʿ*s, *parganadārs* and *shaḥnagān* (market overseers), becoming *amīrs* and *maliks*. Under the Sayyid sultans too, slaves are found as *muḳṭaʿ*s and *parganadārs*. Under the Lodīs, the sources yield the impression that the majority of officers were free Afghans.

The rôle of military slaves in the provincial Muslim kingdoms did not differ substantially from that in the Dihlī sultanate. Indeed, Ahmad Niẓām Shāh, founder of the independent sultanate of Aḥmadnagar, Yūsuf ʿĀdil Shāh of Bīdjāpūr, Ḳulī Ḳuṭb Shāh of Golkonda and Malik Sarwar of Djawnpur had all been *ghulāms*. *Ḥabshī* [*q.v.*] slaves were prominent in the politics of Gudjarāt, Aḥmadnagar, Bīdjāpūr and Bengal. In Bīdjāpūr, *ḥabshīs* took over the regency (*niyābat*) in the last phase of the sultanate, while in Bengal the former *ḥabshī* slaves Shāhzāda and Sidī Badr seized the throne at the end of the 9th/15th century. The latter had 5,000 *ḥabshīs* in his service. Under the Fārūḳids [*q.v.*] of Khāndesh, *ḥabshī* slaves were employed to guard the junior members of the ruling family in enforced seclusion (cf. C. F. Beckingham, *Amba Gešen and Asirgarh*, in *JSS*, ii/2 (1957), 182-8).

Under the Mughals, slaves played a very minor part in administration and in the army, though not in the household. Mughal rule was established by free Mughal, Turkish and Persian officers and the Mughal army was commanded by *manṣabdārs*, the vast majority of whom were free in origin. A test-sample of 225 of the 730 biographies of Mughal dignitaries in Ṣamṣām al-Dawla Shāh-nawāz Khān, *Maʿāthir al-umarāʾ*, Calcutta 1888-91 (*pānṣadīs* and upwards under Akbar, *sih-hazārīs* and upwards thereafter to the middle of Aurangzīb's reign and then *pandj-hazārīs* or *haft-hazārīs*) shows that only one, Baḳī Khān Čela Ḳalmāḳ, a slave of Shāh Djahān, had been a slave. One, Fīrūz Khān a eunuch, and two, Ātish Khān and Ḥabsh Khān, were *ḥabshīs* who had entered Mughal service from the Deccan sultanates. The *Maʾāthir al-umarāʾ*'s list is, however, not exhaustive; a number of slaves, including three of Bābur's and Humāyūn's, were given *manṣabs* and *djāgīrs* under Akbar and one, Iʿtibār Khān, was appointed governor of Dihlī (see *Āʾīn-i Akbarī*, tr.², Calcutta 1927-39, 442, 444, 483, 485, 488, 491). Such promotions, however, form a very small proportion of Akbar's appointments.

Mughal *manṣabdārs* did on occasion, however, employ slaves as their own subordinate commanders. Mīrzā Nathan, *Bahāristān-i Ghaybī*, a history of Bengal in Djahāngīr's time (trans. M. I. Borah, two vols., Gauhati 1936) shows a slave, Islām Ḳūlī Ghulām thus employed as *Mīr Baḥr* (Commander of the fleet of boats). Examples of slaves holding minor military commands may be met with in the *Bahāristān-i ghaybī* under the names (see index) Ṣaʿadat Khān Khʷādja, Khʷādja Lal Beg, and Shīr Maydān.

Akbar employed a contingent of slave foot soldiers, described as *čelas* in the *Āʾīn-i Akbarī*, Calcutta 1872, 190. An interesting account of the use of *čelas* by a provincial governor in the period of the decline of the Mughal empire under Farrukh-siyar and Muḥammad Shāh is given in W. Irvine, *The Bangash Nawâbs of Farrukhābād — a chronicle (1173-1857)*, in *JASB*, 1878, 340-7. Muḥammad Khān, the Bangash Nawwāb of Farrukhābād, encouraged his local military and revenue officers to obtain Hindū boys, the sons of Brahmins and Radjputs, some by consent, some by payment and some in default of revenue. 500 were trained as matchlockmen and others found employment not only in the Nawwāb's household, but also in his army and revenue service. By the end of Muḥammad Khān's rule, he had 4,000 such slaves. For the recruitment of slaves through the pressure of famine and inability to meet the revenue demands of the Mughal government, see the references given in Irfan Habib, *The agrarian system of Mughal India (1556-1707)*, London 1963, 110, 322-4, *passim*.

The explanation of the continuing existence of military slavery in India and the acquiescence of the slaves themselves in the system must be hypothetical. Deracinated, the Turkish *ghulāms* of the period of the Ghūrid conquest found membership of the conquering élite the only satisfying rôle possible in a compartmented society from which they were divided by religion and the attitudes of caste. The rewards of loyal and efficient service were great and, as the fate of Iletmish's children suggests, it was in the sultan's interest to treat his slaves generously. The Hindū slave, converted to Islām and cut off from his former caste fellows with no hope of reintegration into his old environment had every incentive to make the best of his new, forced, situation. The economic position of a slave was often preferable to that of many free men and those in special favour could hope for manumission. The homosexual aspect of the relationship between master and slave, to which Dr. Bosworth draws attention above (col. 1082 a), was important also in India, as the careers of Malik Kāfūr and Khusraw Khān Barwarī bear witness. The continuing existence of a large free element in the military and bureaucratic service of the Dihlī sultans probably prevented the slaves from acting successfully as a Pretorian guard or as Ottoman janissaries. An attempt by the Hindū *payks* immediately responsible for killing Malik Kāfūr in 716/1316 to assume airs of grandeur was soon suppressed by the new sultan, Ḳuṭb al-Dīn Mubārak Shāh Khaldji (Baranī, *Taʾrīkh-i Fīrūz Shāhī*, 376-7).

Bibliography: given in the article. For slaves and *ḥabshīs* in Gudjarāt see ʿAbd Allāh Muḥammad b. ʿUmar al-Makkī, *Ẓafar al-wālih*, ed. E. Denison Ross as *An Arabic History of Gujarat*, iii, 1928, index s.v. *ḥabshī*; also, Sikandar b. Mandjhū, *Mirʾāt-i Sikandarī*, ed. S. C. Misra and M. L. Rahman, Baroda 1961, 245, 323, 384 f., 427, 433, 444; for Bengal see, *History of Bengal*, ii, ed. Jadunath Sarkar, Dacca 1948; Ibn Baṭṭūṭa, iii, *passim*; on the rôle of slaves in the politics of the Deccan sultanates, see Sayyid ʿAli Ṭabāṭabā, *Burhān-i Maʾāthir*, Delhi 1355/1936, 76, 517, 523, 586, 594-6 *passim*; Niccolao Manucci, *Storia do Mogor*, ii, London 1907, 351, iv, London 1908, index s.v. slaves; K. M. Ashraf, *Life and conditions of the people of Hindustan 1200-1550*, in *JASB*, 1935, 187-191. Some references for this article were kindly supplied by Dr. J. S. Grewal.

(P. Hardy)

iv.—Ottoman Empire

Besides *ghulām*, the terms used in the Ottoman Empire for a young slave subjected to a special training to equip him to serve the Sultan, a member of the military class or an ordinary individual were (A.) *ghilmān* (pl. of *ghulām* used as sing.), (P.) *djuwān*, or (T.) *oghlan* and (rarely) *čeleb*. A Palace page of the *Enderūn* [*q.v.*], of slave origin or recruited through the *devshirme* [*q.v.*], who had not yet been promoted to any post, was known as *oghlan* or *ič-oghlanī* [*q.v.*]; these were known collectively as *ič-khalḳī* or *ghilmānān-i Enderūn*.

The Ottoman administration was based upon the *ghulām* system. This principle of training young slaves for the Palace service and the service of the state had certainly been inherited by the Ottomans from the Seldjūḳ Sultanate of Rūm (see I. H. Uzunçarşılı, *Osmanlı devleti teşkilâtına medhal*, Istanbul 1941, 85-94, 108-22; M. F. Köprülü, *Bizans müesseselerinin Osmanlı müesseselerine tesiri*..., in *THITM*, i (1931), 208-21, 242-6; idem, *Osmanlı Imparatorluğunun etnik menşe'i meseleleri*, in *Belleten*, vii/28 (1943), 275); the names of various prominent commanders of *ghulām* origin in the service of this Seldjūḳ Sultanate are known, *e.g.*, Sharaf al-Dīn Ghulām, Khāṣṣ Balaban and the brothers Ḳaratay (see *Taʾrīkh-i Āl-i Selčūk*, facsimile of Paris, Bibl. Nat. MS supp. pers. 1553, publ. F. Uzluk, Ankara 1952, 52, 57, 66, 71). These *ghulāms* were used only for military duties; when Kaykāʾūs II granted important posts as *amīr* to various of his *ghulāms*, the other *amīrs* opposed him (*ibid.*, 52-3).

ʿOthmān Ghāzī appointed 'his *ḳul* Balabandjīḳ Bahādīr' to supervise the investment of Bursa (Neshrī, *Ğihānnümā*, ed. Fr. Taeschner, i, Leipzig 1951, 35). Baraḳ Baba, who was flourishing at this time (ca. 725/1325), advises in his *Kelimāt* that on the *ghazā* the leaders of the Christians should be flung into the sea and their '*ushaḳs*', *i.e.*, the young men following them, should be taken into the army. In documents surviving from the reign of Orkhān there are indications that the training of slaves as Palace and administrative officers existed under the first Ottoman rulers (*e.g.*, the names Evrenkush Khādim and Shahin b. ʿAbd Allāh, in Orkhān's *waḳfiyye* of Shaʿbān 761/June 1360, publ. I. H. Uzunçarşılı in *Belleten*, xxvii/107 (1963), 442, pl. 16; the name *ṭawāshī* Muḳbil, in a *temlīknāme* of Orkhān, *Belleten*, v/19 (1941), 280). Under Murād I the corps of *yeñi-čeri* [*q.v.*] was constituted from the prisoners of war who fell to the sultan as the fifth of the booty legally due to him (see ʿĀshıḳ Pasha-zāde, ed. Fr. Giese, Leipzig 1928, 50); this represents an extension of a *ghulām* system already in existence. The *devshirme*, [*q.v.*] a most important innovation which the Ottomans introduced into the *ghulām* system, may have developed from the practice of taking into Palace service or into the army the young sons of members of the local military class in newly-conquered regions. It is natural that in the Ottoman Empire and in Ottoman society, an *udj* state always in contact with the *dār al-ḥarb*, slaves gained a more important place than in other Muslim societies.

Under Bāyezīd I [*q.v.*], who endeavoured to found a centralized Empire, the *ghulām* system came to full development. Notes in *taḥrīr*-registers of the 9th/15th century which refer to conditions in his reign show that in all parts of the Empire he granted to *ḳul*s trained by the *ghulām* system not only important military and administrative posts but also *tīmār*s. Reactions to this radical innovation are to be detected in the anonymous *Tewārīkh-i Āl-i ʿOthmān* (ed. Fr. Giese, Breslau 1922, 31), which reflect the sentiments of *ghāzī* circles; and these reactions made a weighty contribution to his fall. Ducas (ed. Grecu, 87; Turkish tr. by V. Mirmiroğlu, Istanbul 1956, 34) speaks of the existence in Bāyezīd's palace of 'selected children' belonging to various nations; the *Chronique du Religieux de Saint-Denis*, of 1396, says (i, 427): 'Ils enlèvent les enfants pour les instruire dans leurs impures croyances'; Bāyezīd built a slave-market beside his *ʿimāret* at Edirne; in 836/1432 Bertrandon de la Broquière (*Voyage d'Outremer*, ed. Ch. Schefer, Paris 1892, 128) found that Messire Barnabo, who, like John Schiltberger (see *The bondage and travels* . . . , tr. J. B. Telfer, London 1879, 5-8), had been taken prisoner at the battle of Nicopolis (798/1396), was a highly-influential Ottoman officer.

For the reign of Murād II we possess abundant information about the system, not only from contemporary chronicles (*e.g.*, Ducas, ed. Grecu, 179, 187, 191, Turkish tr., 83, 88, 90; Chalcocondyles, book 5, Fr. tr. by Blaise de Vigenère, *Histoire de la décadence* . . . , Paris 1620, 108 f.), but also in official archive documents (*e.g.*, *Hicrî 835 tarihli Sûret-i defter-i sancak-i Arvanid*, ed. H. Inalcık, Ankara 1954; an *idjmāl defteri* for Sofia in the Sofia National Library belongs to the same year, 835/1431; a deed of manumission of Murād II, dated 848/1444, is also relevant to our subject, see H. Inalcik, *Fatih devri* . . . , i, Ankara 1954, 215 ff.). Mūsā Čelebi's *ḳapî oghlanî* numbered 7,000 (Neshrī, 135, 140), Murād II's 4-5,000 (B. de la Broquière, 182-3). The *defter* for Arvanid shows that in 835/1431, at every level of the military organization, most of the *tīmār*-holding *sipāhī*s there were *ḳul*s of the Sultan or of a *beg*. Among them are bearers of the titles: *shahindji-bashî, emīr-akhūr, silāḥdār, čāshnīgīr, ḳapîdjî, pashmaḳ-oghlanî, solaḳ, zaghardjî, ashdjî*; these had passed out from the Palace. Most of the *sandjaḳ-begi*s of Albania between the years 835/1431 and 859/1455 were of *ghulām* origin; some of them—Ḳavala Shahin, Zaghanuz, Ḳāsim—rose to be *beglerbegi* or vizier. The sons of the local nobility in regions occupied by the Ottomans during the 9th/15th century were by preference taken into the Palace, where they received privileged treatment, and on 'passing-out' (Turkish *čîḳma*, see KHARDJ, and below) were appointed, with the title of *beg*, to the most important posts. Thus at this period many members of the Greek, Bulgarian, Serbian and Albanian aristocracies served the Ottoman state in high posts. Nevertheless, as it had been under the Seldjūḳs of Rūm, only military posts were granted to these products of the *ghulām* system; the post of Grand Vizier and the posts of head of the financial department and of the chancery were usually reserved to Muslim-born Turks of the *ʿilmiyye* career. It is clear that the Muslim-born always felt jealousy and hostility for those of slave origin (cf. Ducas, 143; tr., 63); according to the Venetian M. Zane (987/1579), the Turks fretted at the power enjoyed by slaves (A. H. Lybyer, *The government of the Ottoman Empire* . . . , Cambridge Mass. 1913, 43). Although Ḥüseyn Ḥusām al-Dīn (*Amasya taʾrīkhi*, iii, Istanbul 1927, 191, 201-3, 210, 214) exaggerates the degree of rivalry between native-born Turkish statesmen and the converts, it is indisputable that such a rivalry was an important element in the early centuries (see H. Inalcık, *Fatih devri* . . . , 69-136).

In pursuit of his policy of establishing an absolutist and centralized empire, Meḥemmed II expanded the *ghulām* system (in 880/1475 the *ḳapî-ḳullarî* numbered 12,800) and entrusted nearly all influential posts, the Grand Vizierate included, to *ḳul*s (see H. Inalcık, art. *Mehmed II*, in *IA*, fasc. 75, 512): the *ʿulamāʾ* of the period regarded the vizierate as a post reserved to those of slave origin (see Tashköprüzāde, *al-Shaḳāʾiḳ al-nuʿmāniyya*, Arabic text, i, 144, Turkish version by Medjdī, Istanbul 1269, 104). According to Angiolello, most of the military commanders and other holders of important offices were, during the reign of Meḥemmed II, persons trained by the *ghulām* system. Literary sources and archive documents enable us to visualize in detail the system as it prevailed in this period (for Western descriptions, see Donado da Lezze [G.-M. Angiolello], *Historia Turchesca*, ed. J. Ursu, Bucharest 1909; Fr. Babinger, *Die Aufzeichnungen des Genuesen Iacopo de Promontorio-de Campis* . . . , *SBBayer. Ak.*, Jg. 1956, Heft 8, Munich 1957, 30-48; for Ottoman descriptions, Idrīs Bidlisī, *Hasht bihisht*, MS Nuruosmaniye 3209, fols. 359, 362; of the available archive material only a little has been published: A. Refīḳ, *Fātiḥ dewrine ʿāʾid wethīḳalar*, in *TOEM*, ix-x/49, 1-58; an important source for the *ḳānūn*s of Meḥemmed II is *Ḳānūnnāme-i Āl-i ʿOthmān*, ed. M. ʿĀrif, *TOEM*, supp., Istanbul 1330; R. Anhegger and H. Inalcık, *Ḳānūnnāme-i Sulṭānī ber mūceb-i ʿörf-i ʿOsmānī*, Ankara 1956; cf. N. Beldiceanu, *Les actes des premiers Sultans* . . , Paris-The Hague 1960). The generally accepted view (cautiously considered by B. Miller, *The Palace School of Muhammed the Conqueror*, Cambridge Mass. 1941, 10 ff) that the Palace training system and the organization of *oda*s was established by Meḥemmed II under the influence of Byzantine models after he had taken Constantinople is immediately disproved by the references given above for the reign of Murād II. Meḥemmed II did, it is true, build a 'New Palace' (the present Topkapı Sarayı) in Istanbul, but its organization was modelled on that of the Palace at Edirne (see R. Osman, *Edirne Sarayı*, Ankara 1957). In his *ḳānūn-nāme* he merely brought together, with a few additions and changes, the rules and principles in force before his time.

The explicit statements of contemporary Western and Ottoman writers show that this system was applied and expanded with a conscious appreciation of the advantages it offered. In the reign of Murād II Yazîdjî-oghlu ʿAlī wrote (*Selčūḳnāme*, Istanbul Topkapı Sarayı, MS Revan Köşkü 1390, fol. 566) that it was through the possession of slaves that a sultan could exercise power (cf. Machiavelli, *The Prince*, chap. iv); according to Kemāl Pasha-zāde (Istanbul, Millet Lib., MS 25, fols. 11-12), because all the *ghilmān* were equal at the Porte of the Sultan, none tried to rise above his fellows or dreamed of laying claim to the throne; in the 11th/17th century Paul Rycaut noted (*The present state* . . ., London 1686, chaps. iii-iv) that the system arose from the necessity that the Sultan should delegate his authority to persons inseparably bound to himself. It became a principle in the Ottoman state that the sultan's executive power, the *ʿörf-i sulṭānī* [see ʿURF], should be delegated only to his own slaves. In the 10th/16th century the term *ehl-i ʿörf* means slaves with the authority to carry out the Sultan's orders. The *ḳapî-ḳullarî* were a powerful factor in establishing the Sultan's central authority against the powerful *udj-begleri* of the early period; in the 11th/17th century, Ḳočî Beg stated (*Risāle*, ed. A. K. Aksüt, Istanbul 1939, 51) that the *ḳapî-ḳulu* provided a counterpoise to the provincial troops.

The *ghulām* system reached its fullest development under Süleymān I and his first two successors. The close interest which the Ottoman administrative system aroused in Europe in this period led to the writing of numerous detailed descriptions (for a fairly complete bibliography see K. Göllner, *Turcica*, i, Bucharest and Berlin 1961; for the Venetian *relazioni*, see Lybyer, 305-22). These descriptions, especially the memoirs of persons who, like G. A. Menavino (*Trattato de costumi et vita de Turchi*, Florence 1548), had served as *ič-oghlanî* in the Palace, are of great value for filling out the rich but bare data of the Ottoman archives (for the principal collections relating to the Palace see M. Sertoğlu, *Muhteva bakımından Başvekâlet Arşivi*, Ankara 1955, 31, 70, 73-4; these are still unexploited).

In the early days the principal source for *ghulāms* was the *pendjik* [*q.v.*], supplemented by prisoners presented to or bought for the Palace. Hostages too were raised as *ghulāms* in the *Enderūn*. In the chief cities, the Imperial superintendents (*khāṣṣa khardj emīnleri*) would buy the best slaves at the slave-market for the Sultan. As early as the reign of Bāyezīd I (see S. Vryonis, *Isidore Glabas and the Turkish Devshirme*, in *Speculum*, xxxi (1956), 433-43), these sources were supplemented by children recruited by the *devshirme*. B. Miller (*op. cit.*, 79) calculates that in the 10th/16th century the total of slaves collected annually from all sources was 7-8,000, some 3,000 of them, on an average, being from the *devshirme*. When the *devshirme* boys reached Istanbul, those whose physique and character were best were selected (the sultan sometimes assisting when the selection was made) and sent, as *ʿadjamī oghlan*s [*q.v.*], to the palaces of Ghalaṭa-sarāyî [*q.v.*] and of Ibrāhīm Pasha in Istanbul and to the palaces at Edirne and Manisa (I. H. Uzunçarsılı, *Osmanlı devletinin saray teşkilâtı*, Ankara 1945, 297-305). Most of the rest were sent, under the name *Türk oghlanlarî*, to stay with Turkish farmers in Anatolia, to be called up later into the ranks of the *yeñi čeri*; a few were made *bostandjî* [*q.v.*] and worked in the palace gardens. The children of noble families in the conquered regions were also sent to the palace (Critoboulos, ed. Grecu, 287, Eng. tr. C. Riggs, Princeton 1954, 175). At the beginning of the 10th/16th century, there were 300 *ič-oghlanlarî* in Ghalaṭa-sarāyî and 300 in the palace at Edirne (T. C. Spandugino, *Petit traicté de l'origine des Turcqz*, (1510), ed. C. Schefer, Paris 1896, 63; according to Ramberti (1534), *apud* Lybyer, 254, there were 400 in Ghalaṭa-sarāyî and 300 at Edirne). After being educated, under strict discipline, in these palaces for from two to eight years, they were put through a second process of selection (known as *čîḳma*), and the best were taken into two departments of the palace in which the Sultan actually resided (Yeñi-Sarāy, later Topkapı Sarayı), the *Büyük Oda* (or *Khāne-i kebīr* or *Eski Oda*) and the *Küčük Oda* (or *Khāne-i ṣaghīr* or *Yeñi Oda*) (Angiolello mentions only one *oda* as existing at the end of the reign of Meḥemmed II; the first to mention a *Küčük Oda*, in addition to the *Büyük Oda*, is Navagero, in 960/1553 (apud B. Miller, 41); ʿAṭā (*Taʾrīkh-i ʿAṭā*, i, 153) is probably mistaken in speaking of the *Küčük Oda* as existing in the time of Meḥemmed II). The *Büyük Oda* was to the right, and the *Küčük Oda* to the left of the *Bāb al-Saʿāda* (*Babüssaade*) (see Bobovi's plan of 1086/1675, apud B. Miller, 52-3). Those not selected for the Yeñi Sarāy were appointed to the *bölük*s of the *ʿUlūfedji*s [*q.v.*] and the *Gharīb*s see GHURABĀʾ], four of the six cavalry regiments of the Porte. According to I. de Promontorio (39-43) there were 400 *ič-oghlanlarî*, aged between 15 and 22, in all the *oda*s (80 of them were in the *Khazīne* (Treasury), the *Kilār* (Pantry) and the *Khāṣṣ-oda* (Privy Chamber), for which see below). According to Angiolello, there were 340 in the *Oda*. According to Yunis Beg (*apud* Lybyer, 263), in 944/1537 there were 700 *ič-oghlanlarî*, aged between 8 and 20, in the Sultan's palace (but Ramberti speaks of only 500 in 940/1534). An official account of expenditure, dated 900/1494, mentions 3 *agha*s of the *Enderūn* and only 178 *ghilmān-i enderūnī* (Ö. L. Barkan, in *Iktisat Fakültesi Mecmuası*, xv (1953-4), 308), but the numbers grew to about 400 in the *Büyük Oda* and 250 in the *Küčük Oda* (Miller, 129-30; Uzunçarşılı, 310-1); at the beginning of the 11th/17th century, ʿAyn-i ʿAlī notes 709 persons, *agha*s and *ghilmān* together (*Ḳawānīn-i Āl-i ʿOthmān*, Istanbul 1280, 97).

The lads in these two *Oda*s spent all their time at lessons and physical training. Their teachers were the Palace *muʿallim*s (*muʿallimān-i Enderūn*) and *ʿulamāʾ* and *dānishmend*s who visited the Palace at set times to give lessons; 12 of the lads were appointed *khalīfe*, 'tutor'. All had to begin by learning reading and writing, the principles of the Muslim faith, and the Ḳurʾān; after that each could 'specialize' according to his own capabilities and inclinations (ʿAṭā, i, 155). As they advanced, they learned the Muslim sciences, and the *ṣarf*, *naḥw* and literature of Arabic, Persian and Turkish. Bāyezīd II used to take a personal interest in the boys' education (Menavino, *apud* Miller, 83). Those who made great progress in the religious sciences were allowed to pursue the *ʿilmiyye* career (ʿAṭā, i, 75; Bobovi, *apud* Miller, 109). All kinds of skills were also taught in the *Oda*s: calligraphy, *inshāʾ*, arithmetic and *siyāḳat*, music; those who excelled at these would become *kātib*s. One point stressed both by Ottoman and European writers is the emphasis given to physical training, and to horsemanship and the management of arms (the *Hasht bihisht* dwells on this). The chief sports were weight-lifting and putting the weight, wrestling, archery, riding, throwing the lance, and the games of *tomaḳ* and *djerīd* [*q.v.*] (ʿAṭā, i, 177-82; Miller, 119); on feast-days competitions would be held in the Djerīd-Meydānî in the Palace garden and at the

Oḳ-Meydānî and the Sultan would award prizes. Literary works with such names as *Silāḥshor-nāme, Bāz-nāme, Ḳaws-nāme* were composed mainly for the use of these boys. Furthermore, each lad had to become skilled in one type of personal service or a craft; many masters of miniature-painting, drawing, book-binding and calligraphy were trained in the *Enderūn* (ʿĀlī, *Menāḳib-i hünerverān*, ed. Ibnülemīn M. Kemāl, Istanbul 1926). But over and above this practical education, the main aim of the Palace training was to inculcate absolute loyalty and obedience in the service of the Sultan. The lads were subjected to a very strict discipline, having no contact with the outside world or with their families and, so long as they remained in the palace, leading a monastic life completely cut off from women. Eunuchs watched over all their actions by day and night and slept among them in the dormitories. Menavino (*apud* B. Miller, *Beyond the Sublime Porte*, New Haven 1931, 63) describes the aim of this training as being to produce 'gentlemen', thoronghly islamized, who knew how to speak and behave politely, were conversant with literature, and were chaste and self-controlled. The overall supervision of the *oda*s was exercised by the *Ḳapî-oghlanî ketkhudāsî*, who had under him eunuchs (between 16 and 30 in number).

The White Eunuchs (*Aḳ Aghalar*) constituted the permanent staff of the palace; these were slaves who had been castrated to make them eligible for this service. It was they who maintained discipline and were responsible for the lads' behaviour. Under Meḥemmed II they were 20 in number (Angiolello), under Selīm I, 40 (ʿAṭā, i, 164). Their chief, and the general overseer of the palace, was the *Ḳapî-aghasî* or *Bāb al-saʿāda aghasî*. Beneath him were three *oda-bashî*, in the order of precedence: *Khāṣṣ-oda bashî, Khazînedār-bashî* (or *Ser-khāzinīn*), *Kilārdjî-bashî*. The *Khāṣṣ-oda bashî* might be an *ič-oghlanî*. These eunuchs were responsible for the protection of the sultan's person and personal attendance on him; they accompanied him wherever he went, and guarded him as he slept. Some of them enjoyed the right to make a submission (*ʿarḍ*) directly to the Sultan: according to the *Ḳānūnnāme* of Meḥemmed II (*TOEM*, supp., 13-4) those so privileged were the *Ḳapî-aghasî*, the *Oda-bashî*, the *Khazînedār-bashî*, the *Kilārdjî-bashî* and the *Sarāy-aghasî* (this last being the superintendent of the cleaning and repair of the palace). The number of these '*ʿarḍ-aghalarî*' was later increased (ʿAṭā, i, 162). The five next in rank after them were later known as *köshe-bashî* (ʿAṭā, i, 164). The *Ḳapî-aghasî* exercised absolute authority in the palace, in the name of the Sultan (see I. de Promontorio, 41; Spandugino, 63; Ramberti, 244; Uzunçarşılı, 354-7; *Sadrazam Kemankeş Kara Mustafa Paşa lâyihası*, in *Tarih Vesikaları*, i/6 (1942), 473; according to Angiolello he was chief over everyone in the palace except the Sultan); the Sultan consulted him not only on palace matters but on state affairs (the *ḳapî-aghasî* Ghaḍanfer Agha wielded enormous influence under Selīm II and Murād III). In 995/1587, however, Ḥabeshī Meḥmed Agha (a Black Eunuch) removed the harem from the control of the *Ḳapî-aghasî* (Uzunçarşılı, 354-5). The *Khazînedār-bashî* was eligible for promotion to *Ḳapî-aghasî*. After Aḥmed III appointed Silāḥdār ʿAlī (later Grand Vizier) as general supervisor of the palace, the *Ḳapî-aghasî* sank to second place. The *Ḳapî-aghasî* was by tradition eligible to pass out from the palace as *beglerbegi*, and later (in the 10th/16th century) as governor of Egypt with the rank of vizier.

The *Khāṣṣ-oda bashî*, the *Khazînedār-bashî* and the *Kilārdjî-bashî* were in charge of three higher *oda*s (or *ḳoghush*) which were responsible for the personal service of the Sultan. The *ič-oghlanlarî*, after completing the course of training (usually lasting four years) in the *Büyük Oda* and the *Küčük Oda*, were once more put through a process of selection. Those found most fitting at this *čîḳma* were taken into the *oda*s of the *Khazîne* and the *Kilār*; the rest were placed in the *bölük*s of the *Sipāhī-oghlanlarî* and the *Silāḥdārlar*, the other two of the six cavalry regiments of the Porte (*Kemankeş lâyihası*, in *Tarih Vesikaları*, i/6, 474). From the clothes which they wore, the *ič-oghlanlarî* in the *Büyük Oda* and the *Küčük Oda* were called *dolamalî*, those in the higher *oda*s *ḳaftanlî*. Of these higher *oda*s, the first in rank was the *Khāṣṣ-oda*; from the time of Selīm I onwards the chief duty of its members was to care for the *Khîrḳa-i sherīfe* room where the relics of the Prophet were kept (ʿAṭā, i, 189). According to the *Ḳānūnnāme* of Meḥemmed II (24), it comprised 32 *oda-oghlanî* and one *silāḥdār* (who looked after the Sultan's weapons), one *rikābdār* (in charge of his footwear), one *čoḳadār* (in charge of his outer clothing) and one *dülbend-oghlanî* (who looked after his turbans and under-clothes); to them was later added a *miftāḥ-* (or *anakhtar-*) *ghulāmî* (or *aghasî*). These five *agha*s were also called the *zülüflü aghalar*. The numbers in the *Khāṣṣ-oda* were increased to 40 under Selīm I. In 880/1475 these three higher *oda*s together numbered 80 pages (I. de Promontorio, 40). In 1090/1679 the *Khāṣṣ-oda* comprised, besides the *Oda-bashî*, 6 *agha*s, 12 *eski* (i.e. senior) pages and 22 *ʿadjemī*s (juniors). Later still, there was more specialization in the duties carried out and new ranks were introduced (for details, see ʿAṭā, i, 187-97).

Early in the 11th/17th century, a fourth *oda*, known as *Seferli odasî*, was created from among the attendants with various duties in the *Büyük Oda* (according to ʿAṭā, i, 153, it was created under Aḥmed I, cf. *Kemankeş lâyihası*, 472; according to Uzunçarşılı, 311, in 1045/1635). Its head was the *Sarāy aghasî*. It comprised first those who washed the Sultan's clothes, and included later the bath attendants, the clowns, the mutes, the teachers, the musicians and the singers; the total numbers were in 1090/1679 134 and in 1186/1772 149. The bandsmen (*Enderūn mehterkhānesi*) also belonged to this *oda*.

All matters relating to the pages—promotions, transfers, etc.—were settled by a *khaṭṭ-i humāyūn* of the Sultan in response to a proposal (*ʿarḍ*) made by the *Ḳapî-aghasî* or the *Khāṣṣ-oda bashî* (Uzunçarşılı, 304, 324). From time to time the Sultan would visit the *oda*s, attend competitions, and encourage the pages by awarding prizes. Each *oda* had a fixed complement, known as *gedik*. Appointments and promotions went usually by seniority (known as *odjaḳ yoliyle*); even the Sultan was obliged to respect this principle (*Kemankeş lâyihası*, 473), but exceptions were made in promotion to posts which required special aptitude, e.g. the position of *imām*, clerk (*yazîdjî*), bandmaster (*mehterbashî*). Each *oda* has its own bath, *imām* and *müʾedhdhin*. There were special libraries in the palace for the use of the pages (M. Refîḳ, in *TOEM*, vii/40, 236; I. Baykal, in *Tarih Vesikaları*, ii/9, 188). Messages were carried by *ḳolluḳčîlar*. Food for the pages and their clothes were provided by the Sultan. Each received, according to his rank, a stipend (*ʿulūfe*), an issue of clothes, and the occasional bonus (*Kemankeş lâyihası*, 472-4). All promotions and awards were made according to efficiency and seniority.

When the Sultan went out on campaign, the *Enderūn khalḳî* were provided with horses and weapons and accompanied him, only the *Sarāy aghasî* remaining behind to guard the palace.

Besides the 'Inner Service', the *Enderūn*, which we have considered above, there was a second complex of departments in the palace known as the *Bīrūn*, the 'Outer Service'. The *Enderūn* was the milieu in which the Sultan spent his private life, and at the same time a school where the *ghulām*s were educated and trained. The *Bīrūn* was the section composed of the services concerned with the Sultan's relations with the outside world. According to the *Ḳānūnnāme* of Meḥemmed II, the heads of departments of the *Bīrūn* were, in order of precedence: the *Yeñi-čeri aghasî*, the *Mīr-ʿalem*, the *Ḳapîdjî-bashî*, the *Mīr-akhūr*, the *Čaḳîrdjî-bashî*, the *Ḳapîdjîlar-ketkhudāsî*, the *Djebedji-bashî*, and the *Topčî-bashî* (in 933/1527 the order was: *Yeñi-čeri aghasî, Mīr-ʿalem, Ḳapîdjî-bashî, Mīr-akhūr, Čāshnīgīr-bashî, Süwārī bölükleri aghalarî, Čaḳîrdjî-bashî, Shahindji-bashî, Čawush-bashî, Čadîr mehterleri bashî, Ḳapîdjîlar-ketkhudāsî*, see Ö. L. Barkan, in *Iktisat Fak. Mecm.*, xv (1953-4), 308). Since (with the exception of the *Ḳapîdjîlar-ketkhudāsî* and the *Djebedji-bashî*) these officers were entitled to ride beside the Sultan, they were known as *özengi-aghalarî* or *rikāb-aghalarî* ('*Agha*s of the Stirrup'). In addition to the bodies of men under these officers, the *Bīrūn* included also the *müteferriḳalar* [see MUTAFARRIḲA] under the *Müteferriḳa-bashî*, the *Čawushes* [see ČAʾŪSH] under the Čawush-bashî, the *baltadjî*s [*q.v.*] under the *Dār al-saʿāda aghasi*, and the *bostandjî*s [*q.v.*] under the *Bostandjî-bashî* [*q.v.*] (for details on these and other groups belonging to the *Bīrūn* see Uzunçarşılı, 388-464). All these bodies belonged to the *ghulām* organization of the Ottoman Empire.

An idea of the relative importance of the various groups comprising the *Bīrūn* can be obtained by comparing the data of an official list of 933/1527 (published by Ö. L. Barkan, in *Iktisat Fakültesi Mecmuası*, xv (1953-4), 300) with the data for 1018/1609 given by ʿAyn-i ʿAlī (82-99): the table shows that in less than a century the number of the *ḳapî-ḳullarî* of *ghulām* origin increased well over three times.

	numbers in 933/1527	annual pay in *aḳče*s	numbers in 1018/1609
müshāhere-khōrān (*i.e.*, those with a monthly stipend, *čawushes*, *čāshnīgīr*s, poets, physicians, etc.)	424	4,381,458	1200-1300
Janissaries	7,886	15,423,426	37,627
*Sipāhī*s of the Porte (the *Altî Bölük*)	5,088	30,957,300	20,869
Ḳapîdjîlar, Teberdārlar	319	758,622	2,451
Djebedjiler	524	1,016,688	5,730
Topčîlar	695	975,624	1,552
Tailors	301	641,094	319
Cooks	277	654,900	1,129
ʿAlem mehterleri	185	466,570	228
Čadîr mehterleri and *Dīwān sāḳîleri*	277	562,860	871
Craftsmen (jewellers, swordmakers, etc.)	585	1,422,726	947
Top ʿarabadjîlarî	943	985,890	684
Falconers	259	509,760	592
Employed in the Imperial stables	2,830	5,133,000	4,322
Adjemī oghlanlar and *Bostāndjî*s in Istanbul	3,553	1,993,020	9,406
Totals	24,146	65,882,938	87,927

The institution which ensured that these *ghulām* groups and the provincial administration should function together as a harmonious whole was the *čiḳma*, that is, the promotions and transfers which were made at intervals (of from two to eight years) and at each accession (according to *Taʾrīkh-i Ghilmānī, TOEM*, supp., 99, every 7 or 8 years; according to Miller, 128, every 2 or 3 years in the *Büyük* and *Küčük Oda*s; cf. Uzunçarşılı, 336-9). At the *Čiḳma*, the most senior (*eski*) of the pages in the *Büyük* and *Küčük Oda*s were promoted to higher *oda*s, i.e. (in ascending order) the *Seferli*, the *Kilār* and the *Khazīne*; the rest were transferred to the *bölük*s of the *Sipāhī oghlanlarî* and the *Silāḥdārlar*, according to their pay. Satisfactory *eski*s in the three higher *oda*s were promoted to the *Khāṣṣ-oda* (for the ceremonies of transfer in the later period see ʿAṭā, i, 187-8). The satisfactory 'juniors' (*ʿadjemī*) in the four higher *oda*s became 'senior' (*eski*); the rest were transferred to the corps of *müteferriḳalar* or the *čāshnīgīr*s, in the *Bīrūn*. In each of the four higher *oda*s there were 12 *eski*s; as they were allowed to carry daggers, they were known as *bičaḳlî*. The 12 *khalīfe*s in the *Büyük* and *Küčük Oda*s used to teach the *ʿadjemī*s. The *agha*s of the three upper *oda*s were selected from members of the *Khāṣṣ-oda*, but the actual head of each *oda* was a White Eunuch (*Aḳ agha*). The *Khazīnedār-bashî*, if promoted, became *Ḳapî-aghasî* (there is documentary evidence, however, that in the time of Murād II the *Khazīnedār-bashî* was not a eunuch and that he was promoted to the post of *sandjaḳ-begi*, see *Defter-i Arvanid*, p. 1 and n. 5). According to the *Ḳānūnnāme* of Meḥemmed II (23), the *silāḥdār* and the *rikābdār* were promoted from the *Khāṣṣ-oda* to be *müteferriḳa* at 50 *aḳče*s or *agha* of one of the cavalry *bölük*s or *Čāshnīgīr-bashî*; as a special mark of favour he might be made *ḳapîdjî-bashî*. The *agha*s of the *oda*s were promoted to the post of *sandjaḳ-begi*. As time went on, the *agha*s of the *Enderūn* passed out to even more important posts: in the 10th/16th century it became the practice that the *Khāṣṣ-oda bashî* should pass out as *beglerbegi*. In general an *agha* of the *Enderūn* became *sandjaḳ-begi* or an *agha* in the *Bīrūn*; an ordinary member joined one of the *bölük*s or *djemāʿat*s of the *Bīrūn*.

At the time of a *čiḳma* each group in the *Enderūn* and in the *Bīrūn* was on the move. The *Özengi Aghalarî* of the *Bīrūn* moved to the command of a *sandjaḳ* or a *beglerbegilik*; ordinary members were granted *zeʿāmet*s in the provinces. But after the 10th/16th century they too, like the *agha*s of the *Enderūn*, began to receive appointments as *beglerbegi* and vizier; in fact an *Agha* of the Janissaries might be appointed directly Grand Vizier. *Čashnīgīr*s and *müteferriḳa*s and *sipāhī*s from the *bölük*s were given *zeʿāmet*s; *čawushes*, *ḳapîdjî*s and senior Janissaries were generally given *tīmār*s; thus they passed into the ranks of the 'feudal' *sipāhī*s in the provinces. The best of the *bostandjî*s and the *ashčî*s entered the cavalry *bölük*s or became *ḳapîdjî*s, the rest passed into the Janissaries. Thus the highest position which most of the *ḳapî-ḳullarî* in the *Enderūn* and the *Bīrūn* could reach was a *tīmār* in the provinces. We have seen that so early as the first half of the 9th/15th century *ḳul*s of the Sultan and of *beg*s were granted not only posts as *sandjaḳ-begi* and *beglerbegi*, but also *zeʿāmet*s and *tīmār*s; the view that the timariots were composed only of Turkish-born Muslim *gönüllü* [*q.v.*] or *aḳîndjî*s [*q.v.*] is erroneous.

In the classical period (up to the 11th/17th century), an important place in the ranks of the timariots—and thus in the basic military and administrative organization of the Empire—was occupied by the '*beg ḳullarî*' (or '*ghulāmlarî*'). Each *beglerbegi*, *sandjaḳ-begi* and *su-bashî* had to have his own force of *ḳapî-ḳullarî*, their numbers being regulated by *ḳānūn*. To own slaves was regarded as a necessary qualification for the exercise of executive power. Even the timariot had a small 'Porte', composed of *djebelü*s and *ghulām*s (*oghlan*s), its strength determined by the value of his *tīmār* (the proportions are given in the *Ḳānūnnāme* of Süleymān I, but the text published by M. ʿĀrif, *TOEM*, supp., contains many errors; cf. *Sûret-i Defter-i sancak-i Arvanid*); thus in 835/1431 the *ghulām-i mīr Yörgüč* held a *tīmār* of 6089 *aḳče*s, and hence had to put in the field one *djebelü* and one *ghulām* (*Arvanid*, 34). *Pasha*s and *beg*s endeavoured to support more *djebelü*s and *ghulām*s than the *ḳānūn* obliged them to (when Rüstem Pasha died he left 1700 slaves). *Djebelü*s, *ghulām*s and *nöker*s, in origin prisoners of war or purchased slaves, were, like their masters, subject to the regulations that applied to the *ʿaskerī* class (see H. İnalcık, *15. asır Türkiye iktisadî ve içtimaî tarihi kaynakları*, in *Iktisat Fak. Mecm.*, xv (1953-4), 53), and thus their status in society differed from that of the ordinary *ʿabd*; all the same, the *sharīʿa* rules relating to the *ʿabd*, to *ʿitḳ* and to *walāʾ* [*qq.v.*] applied to the relations between the *ghulām* of the military class and his master.

Some of the boys levied by the *devshirme* were placed in the mansions of prominent men. *Beg*s and *pasha*s, after training their *ghulām*s in various duties in their *ḳonaḳ*s, each a microcosm of the Sultan's palace, could procure that they passed directly into the military class; by presenting their meritorious *ghulām*s to the Sultan, they could obtain for them *tīmār*s, especially in newly-conquered territories. The *ḳānūnnāme*s provide for the allocation of *tīmār*s not only to the sons of *beg*s and *pasha*s but also to their *ghulām*s, in amounts proportionate to the *khāṣṣ* or *tīmār* of the holder [see TĪMĀR]. *Djebelü*s were slaves who rendered military service, while *ghulām*s (*oghlan*s) were in the personal service of the *sipāhī*. It was possible for a *ghulām* to become a *djebelü*, and a *djebelü* a timariot. In the first half of the 9th/15th century, the *udj begleri* were able to present *tīmār*s in their *sandjaḳ*s to their own *ghulām*s and *nöker*s (see H. İnalcık, *Fatih devri*..., i, 149-50) and thus maintain a quasi-independent status vis-à-vis the central authority. The *ghulām*s of executed *pasha*s, like their other possessions, became the property of the Sultan, and were sometimes taken straight into the palace (Ewliyā Čelebi, *Seyāḥatnāme*, ii, 472). Thus the *ghulām* system was in force at every level of the military-administrative organization.

In the classical period of the Empire, this system was not merely the source for recruitment to the administrative class; it was also, from the very beginning, of great importance in the social and economic structure of society, especially in the great cities. Examination of the registers kept by the *ḳāḍī*s of Ottoman cities in the 9th/15th and 10th/16th centuries (see H. İnalcık, *15. asır Türkiye iktisadî*..., in *Iktisat Fak. Mecm.*, xv (1953-4), 52-61) shows that one of the most profitable investments which a wealthy man could make was to buy slaves. Slave-merchants accompanied the armies, and at the end of a battle set up their markets (see for example C. D. Cobham, *Excerpta Cypria*, Cambridge 1908, 142). In the 11th/17th century the records of the Istanbul customs alone show an importation of 20,000 slaves (Miller, 81). In the second half of the 9th/15th century, the average price of a slave was 40-50 Venetian ducats. The use of slaves ensured various legal and economic advantages. The manufacturers of velvet and brocade at Bursa used slave-labour, usually on the *muḳāṭaba* [*q.v.*] system. It was profitable for merchants to use slaves and *ʿatīḳ*s (freedmen) as commercial agents (see H. İnalcık, *Bursa*, in *Belleten*, xxiv/93 (1960), 91-3). One factor encouraging this was the legal principle of *walāʾ* [*q.v.*]. The *sharīʿa* was supplemented by detailed *ʿurfī* regulations relating to slaves (see Ö. L. Barkan, *Kanunlar*, i, Istanbul 1943, index s.vv. *kul, esir*). The Ottomans did, in practice, extend the benefits which the *sharīʿa* ensured to the *ʿabd*. Slaves, whether in the service of the state or in private ownership, were not regarded as composing a base class in society: indeed in certain circumstances the name of *ḳul* procured influence and esteem. The *ḳāḍī*s' registers reveal that *ʿatīḳ*s, who had grown up in an active world of business and enriched themselves, without encountering any social obstacles, were surprisingly numerous in the upper classes of Ottoman society.

Right from the time of Orkhān Ghāzī, prisoners of war had also been used by the state as slave-labourers, being settled on agricultural land and in villages with the name *ortaḳčî-ḳul* [*q.v.*] (see Ö. L. Barkan, *Kulluklar ve Ortakçı kullar*, in *Iktisat Fak. Mecm.*, i (1939), 29-74, 198-245, 397-447). There is no resemblance at all between these and the *ghulām*s belonging to the military class.

The classical Ottoman administrative system, based on the use of *ghulām*s, developed greatly in the second half of the 10th/16th century, the number of the *ḳapî-ḳullarî* passing 80,000. With the decline in the authority of the Sultan at the end of this period, the *ḳapî-ḳullarî* acquired absolute control of the palace, the government and the provincial administration, and endeavoured to monopolize the military fiefs and the other sources of state-revenue. Their power became such that they could depose, appoint, and even murder (ʿOthmān II) the Sultan. Although the *ghulām*s of the palace sometimes made common cause with them, in general it was to their advantage to support the authority of the Sultan. Thus the palace attempted to pit the cavalry regiments against the Janissaries. Ottoman historians and writers on government in dealing with this period (Kātib Čelebi, Ḥasan Beg-zāde, Naʿīmā, Ḳočī Beg [*qq.v.*]) attribute the anarchy in the first place to the disruption of the *ghulām* system.

The revolt of Abaza Meḥmed Pasha (see ABAZA—i, and H. İnalcık, art. Husrev Paşa, in *IA*, fasc. 49, 606-9) is to be explained as a violent manifestation of the reaction which this domination of the *ḳul*s provoked in Anatolia. Later attempts on the part of the palace and the government to reduce the numbers of the *ḳapî-ḳulu* troops and bring them under discipline were fruitless; only when Köprülü Meḥmed Pasha [*q.v.*] assumed dictatorial powers was it possible to make some resistance to them. The lack of discipline among the *ḳapî-ḳullarî* was reflected in the *Enderūn*: when the *čîḳma* due at the accession of Meḥemmed IV was delayed, the *ič-*

ogh̲lanlarî mutinied (Naʿīmā, iv, 349-50); and finally in 1086/1675 the organizations of the *Büyük* and *Küčük Oda*s and of the palaces of G̲h̲alaṭa-sarāyî [*q.v.*] and of Ibrāhīm Pas̲h̲a were abolished (Uzunçarşılı, 304). After the wars which lasted from 1094/1683 until 1111/1699 the system of *ḳapî-ḳullarî* and *g̲h̲ulām*s lost its former significance and importance in the state and took on a new character.

As reasons for the collapse of the system, there come to mind, besides its losing its former function, such explanations as the reduction in the supply of slaves and the contraction of the financial resources of the state. But the basic reasons are to be sought among those which produced the decline of the Empire and compelled a change in its structure and institutions. In the provinces, individuals who had not passed through the system began to enter the service of the *pas̲h̲a*s and thus occupy an increasingly prominent place in the administration and in the army. The state was obliged to recognize these military groups who, under various names (*sarud̲j̲a sekbān, gönüllü, levend*), came into existence in the service of the various *pas̲h̲a*s. This meant the abandonment of the principle that the Sultan's executive authority was exercised only by the *ḳapî-ḳullarî*. Again, from the 11th/17th century onwards the application of the *devs̲h̲irme* among the Christian *d̲h̲immī*s became increasingly difficult, so that a *devs̲h̲irme* in this century could produce only 2000 boys (Miller, *Palace School*, 75). Finally, former members of the *Enderūn* and men of influence were able to introduce their own children, instead of *devs̲h̲irme* boys, into the schools of the palace and the *oda*s of the *Enderūn* (ʿAṭā, i, 113). When in the 12th/18th century persons trained in the Government offices began more and more to pass into executive positions and provincial posts (see H. İnalcık, art. Reîs-ül-Küttâb, in *IA*, fasc. 98, 671) and the *aʿyān* [*q.v.*] rose to control the provincial administration, the *g̲h̲ulām* system no longer had any significance or importance. The purge of the *Enderūn* under Aḥmed III and the changes introduced by Čorlulu ʿAlī Pas̲h̲a (ʿAṭā, i, 162-5) are, to some degree, the expression of new tendencies. In the *oda*s at this period greater stress was laid upon education. The *od̲j̲aḳ yolî* (*i.e.*, the principle that promotion was possible only after passing through a series of duties) was abolished, and the principle that a qualified person could take a short cut into the *K̲h̲āṣṣ-oda* was accepted. G̲h̲alaṭa-sarāyî was re-opened as a school training pages for introduction directly into the *oda*s of the *K̲h̲azīne* and the *Kilār* in the Topḳapî Sarāyî. The last great representative of the *g̲h̲ulām* system is K̲h̲usrew Pas̲h̲a [*q.v.*]. In his own *ḳonaḳ* he had many slaves, whom he had bought, educated and trained by private teachers, and appointed them to important posts in the services of the state; many of them rose to the rank of *pas̲h̲a* (M. T̲h̲üreyyā, *Nuk̲h̲bat al-waḳāʾiʿ*, Istanbul 1290, 269). Maḥmūd II, imitating the palace organization of Western courts, made fundamental changes in the Ottoman palace organization; the *Enderūn Naẓāreti* was established in 1831, the *Mābeyn Müs̲h̲īriyyeti* in 1832 (M. T̲h̲üreyyā, *Sid̲j̲ill-i ʿOt̲h̲mānī*, iv, 729), and in 1833 the *odalar* were completely abolished (Luṭfī, *Taʾrīk̲h̲*, iv, 112).

Bibliography: in the article. See also ḲAPÎ ḲULU, ḲUL, and SARĀY-I HÜMĀYŪN.

(HALIL İNALCIK)

G̲H̲ULĀM AḤMAD ḲĀDIYĀNĪ [see AḤMADIYYA].

G̲H̲ULĀM ʿALĪ [see ĀZĀD BILGRĀMĪ].

Sayyid **G̲H̲ULĀM ḤUSAYN K̲H̲ĀN ṬABĀṬABĀʾĪ** AL-ḤASANĪ b. Bak̲h̲s̲h̲ī al-Mulk Naṣīr al-Dawla S. HIDĀYAT ʿALĪ K̲H̲ĀN "Ḍamīr", *Bak̲h̲s̲h̲ī* to S̲h̲āh ʿĀlam (reigned 1173/1759-1221/1806), b. S. ʿAlīm Allāh b. S. Fayḍ Allāh Ṭabāṭabāʾī, was born at Delhi (S̲h̲āhd̲j̲ahānābād) in 1140/1727-8 in a poor family. When he was five years old the family migrated to Murs̲h̲idābād [*q.v.*], where Allāh Wirdī K̲h̲ān Mahābat D̲j̲ang, a kinsman of his mother, was then living in the service of S̲h̲ud̲j̲āʿ al-Dawla, the *Nāẓim* of Bengal. Soon afterwards, when Allāh Wirdī K̲h̲ān was appointed the *Nāẓim* of ʿAẓīmābād (Paṭna), S. Hidāyat ʿAlī K̲h̲ān went with him and settled there. Gradually he acquired extensive property and eventually became the *Nāʾib* of the province of ʿAẓīmābād under Zayn al-Dīn Aḥmad K̲h̲ān Haybat D̲j̲ang. In 1156/1743 his father lost his post and returned to Delhi with his family. Early in 1158/1745 G̲h̲ulām Ḥusayn K̲h̲ān went to ʿAẓīmābād, married a daughter of his maternal uncle ʿAbd al-ʿAlī K̲h̲ān, who was employed in the army of Haybat D̲j̲ang, and took part in the defence of the town against Muṣṭafā K̲h̲ān. In 1161/1748 G̲h̲ulām Ḥusayn entered the service of Saʿīd Aḥmad K̲h̲ān Ṣawlat D̲j̲ang, son-in-law of Allāh Wirdī K̲h̲ān, who was then at Monghyr. Soon afterwards he went to Pūrniya where Ṣawlat D̲j̲ang had been appointed *fawd̲j̲dār* [*q.v.*]. On the death of his patron in 1169/1754 G̲h̲ulām Ḥusayn refused to serve under his son and successor S̲h̲awkat D̲j̲ang, but was prevailed upon to change his mind. In 1170/1756, when S̲h̲awkat D̲j̲ang revolted against Sirād̲j̲ al-Dawla [*q.v.*], the independent ruler of Bengal, and was defeated and slain in battle, G̲h̲ulām Ḥusayn, fearing reprisals at the hands of the victor, fled to Benares and took refuge with his relations living there, who had earlier been banished by Sirād̲j̲ al-Dawla.

In 1170/1757, on Mīr D̲j̲aʿfar's assumption of power as the *de facto* governor of Bengal, G̲h̲ulām Ḥusayn returned to ʿAẓīmābād and through the intercession of Rād̲j̲ā Rām Narāyan, the local governor, recovered some of his family estates and was allowed to live in the town. He soon found favour with Rām Narāyan, but when prince ʿĀlī Guhar (S̲h̲āh ʿĀlam II) attacked Bengal in 1172/1759 he threw in his lot with the invaders. The attack having failed, he again went to Benares but soon sought the pardon of Rām Narāyan and returned to ʿAẓīmābād. Thereafter he involved himself in Bengal politics, siding now with Mīr Ḳāsim [*q.v.*] and now with the British, gaining favours from both sides. In 1176/1762 Mīr Ḳāsim gave him a cash present of Rs. 5000 and also ordered the payment of the arrears of his salary with a view to retaining his allegiance, for he was intimate with the British and Mīr Ḳāsim entertained strong suspicions of his loyalty (cf. *Siyar al-mutaʾak̲h̲k̲h̲irīn*, Eng. transl. 1926, ii, 436). His subsequent rôle as an intermediary between the various contending groups is a very dubious one (cf. *Siyar* . . ., Eng. transl. 1926, ii 458, 513, 517, 524-5, 532, 535-7, 553). It was through his efforts that the *ḳalʿa-dār* of Rōhtās arranged to surrender the fortress to the British. In 1187/1773-4 he was in Calcutta making preparations for a pilgrimage to Mecca but having been suddenly impoverished, gave up the intention. Some four years later he tried to ingratiate himself with Warren Hastings, the British Governor-General, but without success. In 1194/1780 he again approached the British but with the same negative results. The exact date of his death is not known, but according to the Bānkīpur MS. (No. 282) he was alive till 1230/1815. According to *Nuzhat al-khawāṭir* (vi, 200) he died at Ḥusaynābād, a village founded by his father near Monghyr. His descendants are still living in Patna.

An Iranian by extraction, he was thoroughly conversant with the art of Persian letter-writing. He was a *munshī* by profession and his letters and writings drew praise from, among others, Warren Hastings (*Mistar Hashting ... muḥarrarāt-i faḳīr-rā mī-sitāyad, Siyar ...*, ii, 674). Among all his activities as a *Mīr Munshī*, a political negotiator, a soldier and an intermediary, he found time for literary activities, undaunted by periods of penury and vicissitudes of fortune. His fame rests chiefly on the *Siyar al-mutaʾakhkhirīn*, his *magnum opus*, a detailed history of India from Awrangzīb's death in 1118/1707 to 1195/1781, begun in Ṣafar 1194/February 1780 and completed in Ramaḍān 1195/August 1781. An autograph copy of this work is preserved in the Oriental Public Library, Bānkīpur (vii, 582). Editions: Calcutta 1248/1836; Lucknow 1282-3/1866, 1314/1897; Eng. transl. by Ḥājjī Muṣṭafā, originally Raymond, Calcutta 1789 (most of this edition was lost at sea); reprint Calcutta 1902-3, another reprint with index, Calcutta 1926. Urdu translations: (i) *Iḳbāl-nāma* by S. Bakhshish ʿAlī, Delhi n.d.; (ii) *Mirʾāt al-salāṭīn* by Gōkul Praśād, Lucknow 1874. There are also several partial translations into English and one Persian abridgement: *Mulakhkhaṣ al-tawārīkh* (ed. Calcutta 1243/1827, Agra 1247/1831). His other works include (i) *Bishārat al-imāma*, a *mathnawī* on the lives of his ancestors, especially the miracles of his grandfather S. ʿAlīm Allāh Ṭabāṭabāʾī (d. 1156/1743) and his great-grandfather S. Fayḍ Allāh (MS. Bānkīpur Suppt., i, no. 1991); (ii) a theological work on the prerogatives of ʿAlī and his descendants, being a commentary of certain *ḥadīth*s quoted in the *Fawātiḥ* of Mīr Ḥusayn al-Maybudhī (defective MS. of unknown title, Bānkīpur, xiv, no. 1319); (iii) a *tafsīr* of the Ḳurʾān in 'idiomatic' Arabic (*tafsīr dar tāzī-i bā-muḥāwara*); (iv) a commentary on the *Mathnawī* of Djalāl al-Dīn Rūmī; (v) a *dīwān* of poems; and (vi) other theological works. No MSS. of nos. (iii) to (vi) are known to exist. A historical work of doubtful authenticity entitled *Sharaf-nāma*, written in 1221/1806-7 (MS. Āṣafiyya, iii, no. 1314), is also attributed to him.

Bibliography: *Siyar al-mutaʾakhkhirīn*, Lucknow 1866, ii (iii), 948-52; an abridged Eng. transl. of the above appeared in *The Asiatic Annual Register ... for the year 1801*, London 1802, *Characters*, 28-32; Dhu'l Faḳār ʿAlī Khān "Mast", *Riyāḍ al-wifāḳ* (MS.); Elliot and Dowson, *History of India as told by its own historians*, viii, 194-7; Buckland, *Dictionary of Indian biography*, 164; Storey, i/I, 625-640 (the most detailed account), 1027; ʿAbd al-Ḥayy Lakhnawī, *Nuzhat al-khawāṭir*, Ḥaydarābād 1376/1957, vi, 199-200.

(A. S. Bazmee Ansari)

GHULĀM ḤUSAYN "SALĪM" Zaydpurī, one of the earliest Muslim historians of Bengal, migrated from his home-town Zaydpur, near Bāra Bańkī in Awadh, to English Bāzār or New Mālda (Bengal), also called Ańgrēzābād, and became *Ḍāk Munshī*, or Postmaster, there under George Udny (Udney), the Commercial Resident of the East India Company's factory at that place. Apparently a well-educated man, he undertook to write, at the request of Udny, a history of Bengal, which he named *Riyāḍ al-salāṭīn* (chronogram of 1207/1787-8, the date of completion). This work is divided into a *muḳaddima* and four *rawḍās* (1) the viceroys of the Sultans of Delhi, (2) the independent kings, (3) the *Nāẓims* (governors) under the Tīmūrids and (4) the British. Edition: *The Riyázu-s-Salátin ... edited by Maulavi Abdul Hak Abid*, Calcutta 1890-1; Eng. transl., *The Riyazu-s-Salatin ... translated ... with notes* by Maulavi Abdus Salam, Calcutta 1902-4.

A man of considerable learning, he devoted his spare time to teaching. One of the pupils of a pupil of his, S. Ilāhī Bakhsh b. ʿAlī Bakhsh al-Ḥusaynī Ańgrēzābādī wrote *Khʷurshīd-i djahān-numā*, a general history of the world, which also contains a brief account of Ghulām Ḥusayn, his teacher's teacher (cf. H. Beveridge, *JASB*, lxiv/1 (1895), 196, 198). Other references are to be found in *Riyāḍ al-salāṭīn*, Engl. transl., 2-5; ʿAbd al-Ḥayy Lakhnawī, *Nuzhat al-khawāṭir*, Ḥaydarābād, 1378/1958, vii, 352. He died in 1233/1817. See also Storey, i, 178.

(A. S. Bazmee Ansari)

GHULĀM ĶĀDIR ROHILLA b. Ḍābiṭa Khān b. Amīr al-Umarāʾ Nadjīb al-Dawla [*q.v.*], founder of the town of Nadjībābād, remembered chiefly for his cruel treatment of the Mughal emperor Shāh ʿĀlam (*reg.* 1173-1221/1759-1806), and his family. While still young Ghulām Ķādir Khān was left at the Imperial court as his father's representative, most probably as a hostage. He escaped from custody, however, in 1190/1776 on the defeat of the imperial forces by Ḍābiṭa Khān, and joined his father at the fort of Ghawthgaŕh, the family headquarters near Thāna Bhawan, the birth place of Ashraf ʿAlī Thānawī [*q.v.*]. The very next year Ḍābiṭa Khān was defeated by the Marāthās and Ghulām Ķādir was taken prisoner and brought to Delhi. There he was lodged in the palace (Red Fort) and, to the amusement of the courtiers, was obliged to appear before the emperor clad in women's attire. All this seems to have been done to humiliate his father, the Rohilla chief Ḍābiṭa Khān. A handsome lad, he attracted the attention of the ladies of the harem, but was punished by castration. On the death of his father in 1199/1785 Ghulām Ķādir succeeded to the family estates but did not pay the customary succession fee to the emperor. In 1202/1787, the Marāthā leader, Sindhiyā (Scindia), entered into a pact with Ghulām Ķādir for controlling the Sikhs who were giving trouble in the Doāb. Instead of observing the pact Ghulām Ķādir began to drive out the Marāthā collectors of revenue and seize imperial territory, enjoying all the time the patronage of the eunuch Ḥāfiẓ Manẓūr ʿAlī Khān, who had a strong hold over the emperor and wanted to throw off Marāthā control. In August of the same year Ghulām Ķādir succeeded in defeating the Marātha forces at Shāhdara, near Delhi. He laid claim to the post of *Mīr Bakhshī* and the control of the imperial administration. The next month he occupied the capital and forced Shāh ʿĀlam to appoint him *Mīr Bakhshī* and *Amīr al-Umarāʾ*, offices once held by his father and grandfather. He then began his depredations in the Doāb and even usurped the crownlands reserved for the privy purse of the emperor (*ṣarf-i khāṣṣ maḥall*). In Shawwāl 1202/July 1788 he again appeared before Delhi and through the treachery and intrigue of his friend, the eunuch Manẓūr ʿAlī, superintendent of the royal household, was able to have an audience with the unwilling but helpless emperor. This audience proved to be the beginning of a period of great troubles for the imperial family—the House of Tīmūr. Shāh ʿĀlam was taken prisoner and deposed on 26 Shawwāl /30 July, and ten days later he was blinded. In a moving Persian poem S̲h̲āh ʿĀlam laments the loss of his eyes (cf. Ṣabāḥ al-Dīn ʿAbd al-Raḥmān, *Bazm-i Tīmūriyya*, Aʿẓamgaṟh 1367/1948, 317-8). Children and women of the harem were starved to death, princes flogged and the *bēgam*s dishonoured. For days together every conceivable cruelty was perpetrated on the royal family in vengeance for the act of castration to which the Rohilla chief had been subjected during his boyhood. Retribution, however, soon overtook him. In D̲j̲umādā I 1203/February 1789 he was captured by the Marāt̲h̲ā leader, Mahāddjī Sindhiyā, and after a short imprisonment was put to death; his body was dismembered and hung from a tree.

Bibliography: K̲h̲ayr al-Dīn Muḥammad Ilāhābādī, ʿ*Ibrat-nāma*, I.O. MS. 3908-10 (gives the fullest account of G̲h̲ulām Ḵādir's career); extracts in Elliot and Dowson, *History of India* ..., viii, 237-54; Amīn al-Dīn Ḥusayn Ḵh̲ān, *Pādās̲h̲-i Kirdār*, I.O. MS. 3979; ʿAlī Bak̲h̲t Gurgānī ʿAẓfarī, *Wāḳiʿāt-i Azfarī*, Urdu transl., Madras 1937; *Ferishta's History of Dekkan* ..., by Jonathan Scott, London 1794, ii, 285-306; W. Francklin, *The history of the reign of Shah-Aulum*, London 1798 (mostly based on G̲h̲ulām ʿAlī Ḵh̲ān's *S̲h̲āh ʿĀlam-nāma*, fasc. i, Calcutta 1912, fasc. ii, Calcutta 1914); *Nādirāt-i S̲h̲āhī*, ed. Imtiyāz ʿAlī Ḵh̲ān ʿArs̲h̲ī, Rampur 1944; Jadunath Sarkar, *Fall of the Mughal Empire*, Calcutta 1952, iii, 278, 280, 284, 287, 291 ff., 302-20 (where several other references are given); Durgā Pras̲h̲hād, *Waḳāʿi ʿĀlam S̲h̲āhī*, (ed.) Imtiyāz ʿAlī Ḵh̲ān ʿArs̲h̲ī, Rampur 1949; Naṣīr al-Dīn Barlās, *Nad̲j̲īb al-tawārīk̲h̲* (MS.); *A History of the Freedom Movement*, Karachi 1957, i, 129-35.

(A. S. Bazmee Ansari)

G̲h̲ULĀM AL-K̲H̲ALLĀL, usual appellative of Abū Bakr ʿAbd al-ʿAzīz b. D̲j̲aʿfar b. Aḥmad, a highly-esteemed Ḥanbalī traditionist and jurisconsult (d. 363/974). He owes his by-name to the fact that he was the principal disciple of Abū Bakr al-K̲h̲allāl (d. 311/923 [*q.v.*]). He transmitted his master's *Kitāb al-D̲j̲āmiʿ*, the first great *corpus juris* of Ḥanbalism; he completed it on a number of points by the *Zād al-musāfir* which, though of lesser importance than the first compilation, was also to become a much consulted work; the *Zād al-musāfir* was considered as presenting fairly numerous divergences not only from the *Kitāb al-D̲j̲āmiʿ* but also from the *Muk̲h̲taṣar* of al-K̲h̲iraḳī. Other works of *fiḳh* are also attributed to him, in particular a treatise on the differences of opinion between al-S̲h̲āfiʿī and Aḥmad b. Ḥanbal. Abū Bakr ʿAbd al-ʿAzīz also transmitted the *Kitāb al-Amr* of Ibn Ḥanbal; a manuscript of this work is preserved in the Ẓāhiriyya at Damascus; to the purely doctrinal interest of this treatise is added an interest of a social and political nature, for it contains a criticism of the life of luxury and pleasure which was led by the caliphs and their entourage, and one can detect in it the beginnings of a veiled hostility to the Turkish elements of the caliphate.

Bibliography: Abu 'l-Ḥusayn b. al-Farrāʾ, *Ṭabaḳāt al-Ḥanābila*, Cairo ed., ii, 75-127 (gives the list of the divergences from the *Muk̲h̲taṣar* of al-K̲h̲iraḳī); Ibn Kat̲h̲īr, *Bidāya*, xi, 278; Ibn al-ʿImād, *S̲h̲ad̲h̲arāt*, iii, 45-6; D̲j̲amīl al-S̲h̲aṭṭī, *Muk̲h̲taṣar ṭabaḳāt al-Ḥanābila*, Damascus n.d., 26; Brockelmann, S I, 311. (H. Laoust)

G̲h̲ULĀM THAʿLAB, nickname of an Arab philologist named Muḥammad b. ʿAbd al-Wāḥid b. Abī His̲h̲ām (Hās̲h̲im), Abū ʿUmar al-Zāhid al-Muṭar-

riz al-Bārūdī. A native of Abīward K̲h̲urāsān, he was born in 261/875 and died at Bag̲h̲dād on 13 D̲h̲u 'l-Ḳaʿda 345/16 February 957. He owes his nickname to his relations with T̲h̲aʿlab [*q.v.*] whose zealous disciple and successor he was; he himself had many pupils, and famous people did not scorn to attend his lectures. He made his living as an embroiderer (*muṭarriz*), but certainly received also subsidies from several patrons, as appears from an anecdote quoted by almost all his biographers.

Although he transmitted some *ḥadīt̲h̲*s and the traditionists regard him generally as reliable, his fame rests principally on his extraordinary erudition in matters of Arabic vocabulary; in this field he is considered as the most learned of all the philologists, and tradition has it that he dictated from memory 60,000 pages; the very extent of his learning caused him often to be accused of forgery and dishonesty, but, to judge from some anecdotes, his detractors seem to have been wasting their time; this was notably the case with Ibn Durayd [*q.v.*], who was one day shown up in public by G̲h̲ulām T̲h̲aʿlab and until his death never spoke to him again. He had an answer for everything and was even able to find a meaning, from the old Bedouin vocabulary, for words which mischievous pupils invented as a joke.

Politically, it is particularly interesting to note that he belonged to the party which, so late as the 4th/10th century, still revered the memory of Muʿāwiya (see Ch. Pellat, in *St. Isl.*, vi (1956), 56); he even wrote a little work (*d̲j̲uzʾ*) on the merits of the Umayyad caliph, which he insisted on his pupils reading before he allowed them to attend his lectures; al-ʿAsḳalānī himself (*Lisān al-mīzān*, v, 268) passes a rather severe judgement on this work because it contained apocryphal data, but he places the responsibility for these on other transmitters. It is precisely because of his hostility towards ʿAlī and the S̲h̲īʿa that Ibn al-Nadīm is by no means favourable towards him; all the same he devotes to him a long notice (*Fihrist*, Cairo ed., 113-4), which includes a page of exceptional interest on the way in which at that time a dictated text gradually acquired the form of a finished work, thanks to the care of the listeners and the final intervention of the master. Ibn al-Nadīm and the other biographers list a total of more than 25 works among which the *Kitāb al-Yāḳūt* (or *al-Yawāḳīt*) *fi 'l-lug̲h̲a* seems to be the most important. In this list he draws particular attention to a commentary (*s̲h̲arḥ*) and a supplement (*fāʾit*) to the *Faṣīḥ* of T̲h̲aʿlab, a "very good" *G̲h̲arīb al-ḥadīt̲h̲* based on the *Musnad* of Aḥmad b. Ḥanbal, a supplement to the *Kitāb al-ʿAyn* of al-K̲h̲alīl b. Aḥmad, a critism of Abū ʿUbayda (*mā ankarahu 'l-Aʿrāb ʿalā Abī ʿUbayda fīmā rawāh*) and a critical supplement to the *D̲j̲amhara* of Ibn Durayd.

Bibliography: apart from the works quoted: K̲h̲aṭīb Bag̲h̲dādī, *Taʾrīk̲h̲ Bag̲h̲dād*, ii, 356-9; Ibn al-Anbārī, *Nuzha*, 345; Yāḳūt, *Udabāʾ*, xviii, 226-34; Ibn K̲h̲allikān, s.v.; Suyūṭī, *Bug̲h̲ya*, s.v.; F. Bustānī, *Dāʾirat al-maʿārif*, iv, 477-9; for further bibliography and extant MSS see Brockelmann, S I, 183. (Ch. Pellat)

G̲h̲ULĀT (singular, G̲h̲ālī), "extremists", a term of disapproval for individuals accused of exaggeration (*g̲h̲ulū*) in religion. By heresiographers it was applied particularly to those S̲h̲īʿīs [*q.v.*] whose doctrines Ithnāʿas̲h̲arī Imāmī orthodoxy has regarded as exaggerated in reverence for the *imām*s or in other ways. In practice, the term has covered all early speculative S̲h̲īʿīs except those later accepted by Ithnāʿas̲h̲arī tradition, as well as all later S̲h̲īʿī groups except Zaydīs, orthodox Ithnaʿasharīs, and sometimes Ismāʿīlīs. During the early period, what are called the *Ghulāt* offered a distinctive speculative tendency within the general Shīʿī political orientation; their speculations continued to influence most later Shīʿī (and even some Sunnī) thought, and formed a reservoir of ideas from which many later Shīʿī movements drew their main inspiration. Accordingly, the term *Ghulāt*, if understood as a proper name without *parti pris*, may be made to serve for a heterogeneous but interconnected group of Shīʿī religious leaders and for the later tradition which went back to them.

Traditionally, the first of the *Ghulāt* was ʿAbd Allāh b. Sabaʾ [*q.v.*], whose *ghulū* may have consisted in denying that ʿAlī had died, and predicting his return (*radjʿa*), as the later Imāmīs did that of the Twelfth Imām. In any case, the notion of the absence (*ghayba*) of an *imām* who is due to return and establish justice as *mahdī* [*q.v.*] or *ḳāʾim* seems to have appeared first among the *Ghulāt*. Other positions which seem to have been labelled *ghulū* by early writers were the (public) condemnation (*sabb*) of Abū Bakr and ʿUmar as usurpers of ʿAlī's right, and the notion that the true *imāms* were divinely protected (*maʿṣūm*) against any sort of error. The *Ghulāt* were especially concerned to define the nature of the *imām*'s person and were ascribed varying positions on this: that the *imām* was the *waṣī*, executor, of the Prophet; that he possessed a prophetic authority (*nubuwwa*) himself, though one secondary to Muḥammad's; that he (as well as Muḥammad) possessed a spark of the divine light (*nūr ilāhī*) inherited from Adam through a line of prophets; or that he represented divinity itself, perhaps as a lesser god in the earth, or by infusion (*ḥulūl*) of the divine spirit in him.

They were almost equally concerned to define the nature of the true believer. Some seem to have expected all the truly faithful to receive some degree of prophetic inspiration. At least by the time of Djaʿfar al-Ṣādiḳ's friend Abu 'l-Khaṭṭāb [*q.v.*], a leading Ghālī, many thought of the soul in purely spiritual terms, essentially independent of any body; thus some expected a purely spiritual resurrection, and many seem to have adopted the principle of reincarnation (*tanāsukh*) and even that of transmigration (*maskh*) into sub-human bodies. In conformity with their depreciation of the body, many seem to have regarded the ritual law as not binding on those who had come to a deeper truth, that is, those who knew the *imām*. They were commonly accused of regarding all rules of conventional morality as inapplicable (*ibāḥa*); at the same time, some of them were blamed for introducing new rules, such as vegetarianism. Some of the *Ghulāt*, notably al-Mughīra b. Saʿīd and Abū Manṣūr al-ʿIdjlī, speculated on the nature of God himself, commonly in strongly anthropomorphic terms inspired by Ḳurʾānic passages, often with symbolic cosmological implications.

Much of this thought can be traced to the impulse of Islam itself and the experience of the Ḳurʾān. The expectation of continuing prophecy and the hope for a human leader who, under divine guidance, would order the world justly, represented an interpretation of Islam alternative to that of the leadership at Mecca and Medina. Some details, however, reflected pre-Islamic Arabian conceptions, for many of the early *Ghulāt* leaders seem to have been tribal Arabs. A form of divination used in the circle of Mukhtār and some conceptions of the *radjʿa* of heroes may have had old-Arabian origins. Finally, many of the later *Ghulāt* leaders were Mawālī, of Christian, Jewish, Gnostic, and Zoroastrian background, and they brought ancestral conceptions with them; probably the bulk of their speculations on the soul derive from such earlier Middle Eastern traditions (cf. I. Goldziher, *Neuplatonische und gnostische Elemente im Ḥadīt*, in *ZA*, xxii, 1909).

In the first generations, the *Ghulāt* seem to have been just especially intensely religious elements in the various Shīʿī movements. But by the second century, some of them probably initiated independent political activity against the régime (but in such "risings" as that of Bayān b. Samʿān [*q.v.*], it may have been the government which took the initiative in an attempt at suppression); while their ideas also helped justify the formation of certain inherited lines of imāmate, in which it was believed that a given claimant was *imām* whether he attempted to gain rule of the Islamic community or not. Both the lines of Muḥammad b. al-Ḥanafiyya and that of Muḥammad Bāḳir and Djaʿfar al-Ṣādiḳ were more or less willingly surrounded by *Ghulāt* thinkers (cf. Fr. Buhl, *Alidernes stilling til de Shiʿitiske Bevaegelser under Umajjaderne*, in *Kgl. Danske Viden. Selsk., Forhandling*, 1910, no. 5). Imāmī tradition automatically places all supporters of any claimants from Muḥammad b. al-Ḥanafiyya as *Ghulāt*, under the collective name of Kaysāniyya [*q.v.*]. Some of these Kaysānīs continued to support the ʿAbbāsids as *imāms* with supernatural authority for some generations. It seems that some of the *Ghulāt* allowed the imāmate to pass not only out of the ʿAlid but even out of the Hāshimid family, when some other man appeared to have the divine leading. *Ghulāt* Shīʿī ideas, finally, seem to have affected certain Zoroastrian sectarian movements, especially through reverence for Abū Muslim (cf. Gholam Hossein Sadighi, *Les Mouvements religieux iraniens*, Paris 1938).

By the 3rd/9th century, at latest, there developed, among the *Ghulāt*, *bāṭinī* [*q.v.*] systems of symbolical Ḳurʾān interpretation. These seem to have been influenced by philosophy of the Greek tradition. *Ghulāt* differed according as they asserted the supremacy of one or another principle, among those agreed to be embodied in certain religious offices and persons. The Mīmiyya exalted the *mīm*, or Muḥammad, embodying as prophet the principle of declared truth and outer reality; the ʿAyniyya exalted the *ʿayn*, or ʿAlī, embodying as *imām* the principle of inward meaning; a third principle was represented by the *sīn*, or Salmān Fārisī, the Gate through whom men came to the truth. Several of these groups played something of a rôle in the declining years of the ʿAbbāsid caliphate, when an enthusiast like Shalmaghānī held high political position.

Much of the *Ghulāt* heritage was absorbed into the Imāmī and Ismāʿīlī movements and disciplined by the exclusion especially of notions implying any compromise of the unity of God; thus the term *ḥulūl* seems to be rejected by surviving authors, along with the idea that the *imām* could be a god or a prophet. But even such ideas continued present within Imāmī and Ismāʿīlī circles and in sects like the Nuṣayriyya [*q.v.*]; in later centuries, numerous apocalyptic movements developed in which various of the ideas of the *Ghulāt* were used, and which often resulted in more or less long-lasting sects, those of the Nizārīs and Druzes from the Ismāʿīlī fold, and the ʿAlī-Ilāhīs or Ahl al-Ḥaḳḳ, who saw ʿAlī as God. The first Ṣafawīs likewise interpreted Shīʿism in a manner which orthodox Imāmism must term *ghulū*. Transformed into complex symbolic lore, as at the hands of the Ḥurūfīs, much entered the broad stream of Ṣūfism.

Bibliography: Julius Wellhausen, *Die religiös-politische Oppositionsparteien, Abh. G. W. Gött.*, phil.-hist. Kl., n.f. V, no. 2, 1901; Gerlof van Vloten, *Recherches sur la domination arabe, le chiitisme, et les croyances messianiques*, Amsterdam 1894; van Vloten, *Worgers in Iraq*, in *Feestbundel Veth*, 57 ff.; Sabatino Moscati, *Per una storia dell' antica šiʿa*, in *RSO*, xxx, 1955; Marshall G. S. Hodgson, *How did the early Shīʿa become sectarian?*, in *JAOS*, lxxv, 1955; Louis Massignon, *Les origines chiites des . . . Banū 'l-Furāt, Mélanges Gaudefroye-Demombynes*, Cairo 1935; idem, *Recherches sur les chiites extrémistes à Baghdad à la fin du troisième siècle*, in *ZDMG*, xcii (1938), 378 ff. See also the articles on sects and men above mentioned. Our chief sources of information on the early *Ghulāt* are of four types: (*a*) Chroniclers, when rebellion or violent suppression occurred; these were inimical and superficial; (*b*) Traces in later Shīʿī writings, both Imāmī and especially texts from various sorts of Ismāʿīlīs (*e.g.*, the *Umm al-Kitāb*, ed. W. Ivanow, *Isl.*, xxiii, 1936), Druze, Nuṣayrī, and also Ḥurūfī and Ahl al-Ḥaḳḳ; (*c*) Imāmī Shīʿī *ridjāl* books such as Kashshī, *Akhbār al-ridjāl*; (*d*) Heresiographers. These have been discussed by Helmuth Ritter, *Philologika III*, in *Isl.*, xviii, 1929, and R. Strothmann, *History of Islamic heresiography*, in *IC*, 1938; lists of heresiographers and of sect names are to be found in ʿAbbās Iḳbāl, *Khānadān-i Nawbakhtī*, Tehrān, 1311 s. The heresiographers are hostile; later writers tend to derive their lists of sects from the earlier, adding little on their own times. They commonly force their names into a traditional number of seventy-three, and use the term *firḳa* indiscriminately for an independent sect, for a school of thought, and for a minor doctrinal position perhaps shared among otherwise unrelated thinkers. Too often they attribute to a system supposed consequences of a given position alien to the system itself; perhaps many charges of immorality derive from this. Of the most prominent, al-Ashʿarī (*Maḳālāt al-Islāmiyyīn*, ed. H. Ritter, Istanbul 1929) takes up under *Imāmiyya* some of the same groups as he takes up under *Ghulāt*, but on different issues; Malaṭī (*K. al-Tanbīh wa 'l-radd*, ed. Sven Dedering, Istanbul 1936) has some very old material but can be grossly misinformed; Nawbakhtī (*Firaḳ al-Shīʿa*, ed. H. Ritter, Istanbul 1931) is relatively fair-minded, but sees all groups in Imāmī terms; Ibn Ḥazm is very thin on the Shīʿa, forcing the *Ghulāt* into a procrustean scheme, but the translation of him by Israel Friedländer (*Heterodoxies of the Shiites*, New Haven 1909, corrected from *JAOS*, xxviii and xxix) has useful notes; al-Baghdādī, *al-Farḳ bayn al-firaḳ*, is virulently unfair, but sometimes well-read in *Ghulāt* writings; al-Shahrastānī is late, relatively well-balanced, and has some early material from original sources.

(M. G. S. Hodgson)

GHUMĀRA (Gumera of Leo Africanus), Berber tribe of the western Maghrib. Ibn Khaldūn groups them among the Maṣmūda tribes and attributes to them as ancestor Ghumār son of Maṣmūd or, according to another tradition, son of Mesṭāf, son of Melīl, son of Maṣmūd. The Ghumāra were divided into a large number of clans—B. Ḥumayd, Mattīwa, Ighṣawa (= Ghẓāwa), Madjkasa, etc.—whose names are still borne by certain tribes of the Rīf. It is rather difficult to determine precisely the territory occupied by the Ghumāra. According to Ibn Khaldūn it was five days long, from the region of the "plains of the Maghrib" to Tangier, by as many broad, from Ḳaṣr Kutāma to the river Wargha. It was bounded by the Atlantic between Aṣīla and Anfā and was adjacent on this side to the territory of the Barghwāṭa. Al-Bakrī excludes the regions of Tangier and Ceuta from it and gives as its limits Nakūr on the east and Karūshat on the west.

The Ghumāra had been long established in this part of the Maghrib when Islam was introduced. When conquered by Mūsā b. Nuṣayr they became converted to the new religion but in the 2nd/8th century adopted Khāridjī doctrines and took part in the revolt of Maysara. Even after the defeat of the Khāridjīs they showed an inclination towards heresy: "Their countrified customs and rustic habits", says Ibn Khaldūn, "prevented them from recognizing the true principles of religion". Thus they gathered in multitudes around the false prophet Ḥā-Mīm [*q.v.*]. Later another prophet appeared, by name ʿĀṣim b. Djamīl al-Yazdadjūmī; in 625/1228 a revolt broke out at the instigation of one Abu 'l-Ṭawādjin, who claimed to be a prophet and magician. A taste for magic was also one of the characteristics of the Ghumāra. Al-Bakrī provides various items of information on this point and Ibn Khaldūn remarks that it was especially the young women who practised the art.

From the political point of view the Ghumāra suffered various vicissitudes. From the 2nd/8th to the 4th/10th century the eastern part of their clans was included in the kingdom of Nakūr. Sogguen, one of their chiefs, tried, it is true, to put himself in the place of the Banū Ṣāliḥ, the descendants of the founder of this state, but his attempt failed (144/761). At the partition of the Idrīsid empire the eastern clans fell to ʿUmar b. Idrīs and were governed by his descendants. They remained faithful to these princes even after the Idrīsids had been expelled from Fez by the Fāṭimids and supported them to the end in their struggles against the Umayyads of Spain. After the downfall of the Idrīsids (264/877) the Ghumāra recognized the authority of the Umayyads, then that of the Ḥammādids of Ceuta until the Almoravid invasion. On the approach of the Almohads the Ghumāra hastened to adopt the new doctrine and even helped ʿAbd al-Muʾmin to take Ceuta (541/1146). But this faithfulness, which had won them the caliph's favour, did not last long. Abū Yaʿḳūb was obliged to come in person to put down the revolt of a Ghumāran chief named Sabaʿ b. Managhfād (562/1166-7) and after the defeat of the rebel entrusted the government of Ceuta to his brother with the task of keeping a watch on the Rīf.

The Marīnids also had great difficulty in checking the turbulence of the Ghumāra and managed to subdue them only by taking advantage of the quarrels between *ṣaff*s which divided them. Even so their subjection was rather precarious. "In our days", writes Ibn Khaldūn, "the Ghumāra have become powerful and numerous, but recognize nevertheless the authority of the Marīnid government and pay taxes to it so long as it has the means to compel their respect. But if ever it shows weakness . . . it is forced to send troops from the capital to make them submit again. Protected by their inaccessible mountains, they do not fear to offer asylum to princes of the royal family and other rebels who ask for their protection". From the 9th/15th century onwards we lack exact information about the Ghumāra. Their name, still mentioned by Leo Africanus in the 10th/16th century, is borne today by a powerful tribe of the Djabāla.

Bibliography: Bakrī, *Description de l'Afrique septentrionale*, ed. de Slane, tr. 288 ff.; Ibn Khaldūn, *Berbères*, tr. de Slane, ii, 133, 144, 156 ff., 197 f.; Leo Africanus, tr. Épaulard, 12, 250, 256, 264, 268, 278, 544, 564; E. Fagnan, *L'Afrique septentrionale au XIIe siècle de notre ère (Kitāb al-Istibṣār)*, Constantine 1900, 45 ff., 144-7; Mouliéras, *Maroc inconnu*, ii, 291-355.

(G. Yver)

GHUMDĀN (epigr. ghndn, *CIH* 429), the castle of Ṣanʿāʾ (Azāl) in the Yaman, famous for its antiquity, its size, and its splendour. Arabian geographers give detailed descriptions of it (v. infra), esp. Hamdānī (in *Iklīl*, viii), who attributes its building to the king Ilsharaḥ Yaḥḍib (about 25 B.C.), probably correctly (cf. *CIH* 429). The castle was situated between the twin mountains Nuḳum and ʿAybān. It is said to have been destroyed by the Abyssinian conquerors in 525 A.D., but was rebuilt and served as the residence of Sayf b. Dhū Yazan after the Persian occupation in 570. It was finally demolished in connexion with the Muslim conquest of the Yaman, allegedly by Farwa b. Musayk or the Caliph ʿUthmān. Legend attributes the foundation of Ghumdān to Sām b. Nūḥ, more seldom to Solomon or al-Zabbāʾ. The castle is said to have had twenty storeys, each of them 10 cubits high; its lower part was made of freestone, its upper part, including the splendid terrace with four lions of bronze, was built of polished marble. Hamdānī locates its ruins opposite to the first and second doors of the chief mosque, which probably contains much material from the old castle. South Arabian poets, such as Umayya b. Abu 'l-Ṣalt and ʿAlḳama b. Dhū Djadan, celebrate Ghumdān as the residence of the Ḥimyarite kings. The poems quoted may, as Hamdānī remarks, partly refer to another castle, the homograph ʿUmdān in Mārib.

Bibliography: G. Ryckmans, *Les noms propres sud-sémitiques*, Louvain 1934, i, 360; H. v. Wissmann and M. Höfner, *Beiträge zur hist. Geographie des vorislam. Südarabien*, Wiesbaden 1952, 19 f., 27, 32; D. H. Müller, *Die Burgen u. Schlösser Südarabiens nach dem Iklîl des Hamdânî*, Wien 1879, 8-19, 45-48 (=*al-Iklīl*, viii, ed. Faris, 10-21; cf. Löfgren in *Orientalia*, N.S., xii, 141 f.); Hamdānī, *Ṣifa*, ed. Müller, 195, 202 f., 239 f. (trad. Forrer, 11, 276); *BGA*, i, 24; ii, 31; v, 35; vi, 136; vii, 110 f.; Bakrī, *Muʿdjam*, ed. Wüstenfeld, 299, 464, 698; Yāḳūt, *Muʿdjam al-buldān*, iii, 811 f.; Ibn al-Mudjāwir, *Taʾrīkh al-mustabṣir*, ed. Löfgren, 180 f.; Nashwān, *Shams al-ʿulūm*, ed. ʿAẓīmuddin Aḥmad (Gibb Mem. Series XXIV), 81; Masʿūdī, *Murūdj*, iv, 49; Dimishḳī, *Cosmographie*, tr. Mehren, 31.

(O. Löfgren)

GHUNDJĀR, a nickname given, allegedly because of his ruddy cheeks, to an early Persian *ḥadīth* scholar, Abū Aḥmad ʿĪsā b. Mūsā al-Taymī al-Bukhārī, who died at the end of the year 186/802. The Arabo-Persian word does mean "rouged", but it is, of course, highly doubtful whether this is the origin of the name.

The nickname was transferred to a later scholar who spent much effort upon collecting ʿĪsā's traditions and who is known as the author of a *History of Bukhārā*. His name was Abū ʿAbd Allāh Muḥammad b. Aḥmad b. Muḥammad b. Sulaymān al-Bukhārī, known as (al-)Ghundjār. He flourished in the second half of the 4th/10th century and worked in the book trade. Of the dates given for his death (410, 412, 422), 412/1021-22 is the most likely one; 422/1031 would seem too late, since he states himself that he said the funeral prayers for a scholar deceased in 350/961 (*Taʾrīkh Baghdād*, i, 296). Only brief citations from the *History of Bukhārā* have so far come to light. An abridgment of the work was made by al-Silafī, and additions were contributed by a certain Aḥmad al-Māmānī (b. Māmā?) (d. 436/1045). A certain Muḥammad b. Aḥmad b. Sulaymān al-Bukhārī, said to have died a hundred years earlier, in 312/924 (Ḥādjdjī Khalīfa, ii, 116 f.), and to have been the author of a *History of Bukhārā*, seems to be, in fact, identical with this Ghundjār.

Bibliography: For ʿĪsā b. Mūsā, cf., *e.g.*, Bukhārī, *Taʾrīkh*, iii/2, 394; Ibn Abī Ḥātim Rāzī, *Djarḥ*, iii/1, 285 f.; and, summing up the meagre data, Ibn Ḥadjar, *Tahdhīb*, vii, 732-4. For the historian of Bukhārā, cf. Samʿānī, *Ansāb*, fol. 411b; Yāḳūt, *Udabāʾ*, vi, 239; F. Rosenthal, *A history of Muslim historiography*, Leiden 1952, 386, 428; R. N. Frye, *The history of Bukhara*, Cambridge Mass. 1954, 103 f. For the alleged earlier historian of Bukhārā, cf. Wüstenfeld, *Geschichtsschreiber*, 98; Brockelmann (1st ed.), I, 138 (also I, 167, corrected in S I, 310); Frye, *op. cit.*, xvii.

(F. Rosenthal)

GHŪR, the mountainous territory in Afghanistan about the headwaters of the Farah Rud, Hari Rud, and Murghab, from which is named the mediaeval dynasty of the Ghūrids [*q.v.*]. The establishment of Islam came late in Ghūr, and raids by Arab generals continued until the 4th/10th century. A tradition of the existence of Jewish settlements finds confirmation in the discovery of a Judaeo-Persian inscription of A.D. 752-3 at Tang-i Azao, near Čisht. In 372/982 the *Ḥudūd al-ʿālam* claims that most of the inhabitants had accepted Islam. Originally the chief place was Mandaysh, in a district called Sanga near the mountain Zār-i Margh. These localities were placed by Maricq near Ahangarān—the name, still extant, of the fortress where Muḥammad b. Sūrī of Ghūr was besieged by Maḥmūd of Ghazna in 401/1010. The founding in the district of Warshāda of a new capital, Fīrūzkūh [*q.v.*], was the work of Ḳuṭb al-Dīn Muḥammad (killed by Bahrām Shāh of Ghazna ca. 544/1149). His successor, Bahāʾ al-Dīn Sām, established frontier fortresses at Kadjūrān, to the south, Shersang towards Herāt and Bindār and Fivār to the north-west. The rediscovery by Maricq in 1957 of the minaret and citadel of Fīrūzkūh was a triumph of modern exploration. Ghūr was noted for its export of armour, weapons, guard-dogs and slaves. Its historical role came to an end with the sack of Fīrūzkūh by the armies of Čingiz Khān.

Bibliography: A. Maricq and G. Wiet, *Le minaret de Djām*, 1959; W. B. Henning, *The inscriptions of Tang-i Azao*, in *BSOAS*, xx (1957), 335-42; C. E. Bosworth, *The early Islamic history of Ghūr*, in *Central Asiatic Journal*, vi/2 (1961), 116-33; *Ḥudūd al-ʿālam*, 342-4; Minhādj-i Sirādj, *Ṭabaḳāt-i Nāṣirī*.

(A. D. H. Bivar)

GHURĀB, (a.) "crow". In view of the diversity of their meanings the Arabic words formed from the three consonants *gh*, *r* and *b* cannot be traced to a single root, and it is probable that in the course of the history of the language there came about a convergence of terms with different origins; thus, *ghurāb* is too reminiscent of the Latin *corvus* for us to consider it a mere coincidence; moreover, early Arab philologists considered *ghurāb* to be independent, since they made to derive from it such words as *ghurba*, *ightirāb*, etc. which imply an idea of estrangement, of separation; later authors go so far as to regard the root *gh. r. b.* as being made up from the consonants *gh*, *r*, *b* which appear initially in words meaning a misfortune or something unpleasant.

Such theories are explained firstly by the place which the crow occupies in the literary tradition of the Arabs, secondly by its place in ornithomancy, where it is pre-eminently the bird of ill omen.

In poetry, although its black colour may symbolize the night (*ghurāb al-layl*) and be the object of favourable judgements, the crow is fundamentally synonymous with separation, with an unhappy event, and the poets make a sometimes immoderate use of the stereotyped expression *ghurāb al-bayn*, which strictly means the carrion crow, but which owes its origin to the fact that crows are led by instinct to encampments which their occupants are preparing to leave, and announce by their croaking the imminent departure (*bayn*) of the tribe—more particularly of the beloved—before swooping down on the deserted places, where the poet, arriving too late, is struck with grief on seeing them.

The mere sight of a crow is in itself unpleasant, and one can readily understand, without feeling the need to postulate a borrowing, that the early Arabs should have made it into a bird of ill omen and in addition applied themselves to observing and interpreting its flight and its croaking, in the context of what is called *ṭīra* [*q.v.*]. Examples from literature of these predictions, which were deduced more or less spontaneously, cannot be quoted here; but it is worth mentioning that they are the sign of a fairly rudimentary ornithomancy which only at a relatively late date was perfected and systematized, although the *Fihrist* (Cairo ed., 436) already refers to Arabic treatises of ornithomancy, one of which is the work of al-Madāʾinī. T. Fahd has studied a treatise attributed to al-Djāḥiẓ, comparing it in a very illuminating fashion with two Assyro-Babylonian texts; in spite of differences of detail, it does not seem that the Arabic text is the result of an enquiry carried out among the Bedouins: rather one has the impression that it is an attempt, made probably at a late date, to give some order to elements of diverse provenance. Nevertheless, it is strange that al-Djāḥiẓ, who is one of the few authors to have considered that the belief in the malicious influence of the crow and in the possibility of drawing omens from its flight and its cry is only a superstition based on verbal similarities (*Ḥayawān*, iii, 444), should have been later credited with two treatises of divination: the text studied by T. Fahd (found in al-Nuwayrī, *Nihāya*, iii, 130-2) and the *Bāb al-ʿIrāfa wa 'l-zadjr wa 'l-firāsa ʿalā madhhab al-Furs* (published and translated into Russian by K. Inostrantsev, in *Materials from Arabic sources for the history of the culture of Sassanid Persia*, St. Petersburg 1907, text, 3-27, tr. and comm., 28-120).

In the context of Islam the word *ghurāb* is used in the Ḳurʾān (v, 34/31) with reference to the crow sent by God to show Cain how to bury his brother Abel whom he had just killed; although rationalists see in this a manifestation of divine favour towards the bird considered to be of ill omen, they do not succeed in stifling the prejudices made still stronger by the legend of the crow (*ghurāb Nūḥ*) which Noah sent out to reconnoitre, but which, having found a carcass, did not return.

The malevolent character of this bird explains the considerable number of nicknames which it has in Arabic; but it is proverbial also for sharpness of vision, its suspicion, its pride and the blackness of its plumage, and the word *ghurāb* appears in a number of expressions such as "that will only happen when the crow turns white" (*ḥattā yashīb al-ghurāb*).

The Arabs knew several varieties of crow, including one which can learn to speak, and had observed their hostile relations with cattle, donkeys and owls; their habit of perching on camels to plunge their beaks into the pustules which form on their backs tended to increase the Bedouins' dislike for this bird, about which in any case they knew little, since some maintained that it reproduced itself by pecking the female with its beak.

The crow is among the animals that must be killed, and its flesh is forbidden; it possesses however certain medicinal properties, the dried blood in particular being a specific for haemorrhoids. A crow's beak carried on the person gives protection against the evil eye, but to see the bird in a dream is of course a sinister portent.

Bibliography: Djāḥiẓ, *Ḥayawān*, ii, 313 ff., iii, 409-64; Ibn Ḳutayba, *ʿUyūn*, *passim*; Damīrī, s.v.; Ḳazwīnī, s.v.; Bayhaḳī, *Maḥāsin*, *passim*; H. Pérès, *Poésie andalouse*, index; H. Massé, *Croyances et coutumes persanes*, Paris 1938, i, 195; T. Fahd, *Les présages par le corbeau. Étude d'un texte attribué a Ǧāḥiẓ*, in *Arabica*, viii/i (1961), 30-58.

(CH. PELLAT)

GHURĀB, type of boat [see SAFĪNA].

AL-**GHURĀB** [see NUDJŪM].

GHURABĀʾ (in Turkish *Ghurebā*), pl. of A. *gharīb*, Ottoman term for the two lowest of the six cavalry regiments (*Altî Bölük*) of the *Ḳapî-ḳullarî*. The regiment riding on the Sultan's right was known as *Ghurebāʾ-i yemīn* (*Sagh gharībler*, *Sagh gharīb-yigitler*), that riding on his left as *Ghurebāʾ-i yesār* (*Sol gharībler*, *Sol gharīb-yigitler*). The oldest terms used for them are *gharīb-yigitler* and *gharīb-oghlanlar* (see F. Babinger, *Die Aufzeichnungen des Genuesen Iacopo de Promontorio . . .*, *SBBayer. Ak.*, Jg. 1956, Heft 8, Munich 1957, 30; *Ordo Portae*, ed. Ş. Baştav, Budapest 1947, 7; Donado da Lezze [G.-M. Angiolello], *Historia Turchesca*, ed. J. Ursu, Bucharest 1909, 139); here *gharīb* means 'away from his native land', and *yigit* 'bold, impetuous man'. From the earliest days there were in the Ottoman principality Muslim warriors who had come from other principalities of Anatolia or other Muslim lands to take part in the *ghazā* under the banner of the Ottomans. An official document of 835/1431 (see *Sûret-i Defter-i sancak-i Arvanid*, ed. H. İnalcık, Ankara 1954, p. 42, *tīmār* no. 94) mentions a *gharīb-yigit* who had come from Karaman and received a *tīmār* on the Albanian *udj* (cf. also p. 81, *tīmār* no. 227, and p. 115, *tīmār* no. 320).

Of the six cavalry regiments of the *Ḳapı-ḳullarî*, the *Sagh ʿUlūfedjiler*, *Sol ʿUlūfedjiler*, *Sagh Gharībler* and *Sol Gharībler* were known collectively as the *Dört Bölük* (or *Bölükat-i Erbaʿa*, the 'Four Divisions'); they were regarded as *Ashaghî Bölükler* ('Inferior Divisions') in relation to the remaining two *Yuḳarî Bölükler* ('Superior Divisions'), namely the *Sipāhī Oghlanlarî* and the *Silāḥdārlar*. It has been suggested (Djewdet, *Taʾrīkh*, i, 35, 37; I. H. Uzunçarşılı, *Kapıkulu ocakları*, ii, Ankara 1947, 137) that the 'Inferior Divisions' were established in the first half of the 9th/15th century (whereas the 'Superior Divisions' date from the reign of Murād I). The *Sagh Gharībler* were regarded as slightly superior to the *Sol Gharībler*.

In the 10th/16th century, the men of these two regiments were recruited from three sources: (1) from *ʿadjemī oghlanlar* selected at a *čiḳma* at Ghalaṭa-sarāyi̊, the Palace of Ibrāhīm Pa<u>sh</u>a, or the palace at Edirne [see <u>gh</u>ulām]; (2) from suitable sons of members of the *Altı̊ Bölük*; (3) from young Muslims from other Muslim lands who had come to fight the *<u>gh</u>azā* in the Ottoman army and distinguished themselves (according to Idrīs Bidlisī, *Ha<u>sh</u>t bihi<u>sh</u>t*, MS Nuriosmaniye 3209, they were "ʿArab, ʿAdjem and Kurd'; according to Angiolello they came from Persia, the land of the Tatars, Cappadocia, the land of the Turcomans and Egypt). The name shows that the original source of recruits for these *bölüks* was the last (the only case where Muslims were taken into the ranks of the *Ḳapı̊-ḳullari̊* [see <u>gh</u>ulām]).

In about 880/1475 (I. de Promontorio, 30) the two *bölüks* numbered 1000 men (but *Ordo Portae*, of about the same date, mentions only 400; Angiolello speaks of 500-1000). In the 10th/16th century they numbered 1000 each, 2000 together (*Ha<u>sh</u>t bihi<u>sh</u>t*; Ramberti, *apud* A. H. Lybyer, *The government of the Ottoman Empire ...*, Cambridge 1913, 251: about 2000 together; in a document of 976/1568, see Uzunçarşılı, *op. cit.*, 196, the *Sagh <u>Gh</u>arībler* are recorded as 1000 men, the *Sol <u>Gh</u>arībler* as 1539); at the beginning of the 11th/17th century (ʿAyn-i ʿAlī, *Ḳawānīn*, Istanbul 1280, 9), the *<u>Dj</u>emāʿat-i <u>Gh</u>urebāʾ-i yemīn* numbered 928, the *<u>Dj</u>emāʿat-i <u>Gh</u>urebāʾ-i yesār* numbered 975.

Their organization was the same as that of the other *bölüks* of *ḳapı̊-ḳullari̊*. In each *bölük* there was an *a<u>gh</u>a* in command, a *ketk<u>h</u>udā* (*kahya*; according to Angiolello and Ramberti his pay was 30 *aḳčes* a day), a *kātib* or *<u>kh</u>alīfe* to attend to the paper work (with 20 *aḳčes*, according to Angiolello; according to Ramberti, half a century later, he received 25), and a *čawu<u>sh</u>* or *ba<u>sh</u>-čawu<u>sh</u>* responsible for discipline (for the organization see *Sadrazam Kemankeş Kara Mustafa Paşa lâyihası*, ed. F. R. Unat, in *Tarih Vesikaları*, i/6 (1942), 457). In the 10th/16th century the *a<u>gh</u>a* of the *Sol <u>Gh</u>arībler* was appointed from among the *čā<u>sh</u>nīgīrs*. At a *čiḳma*, the *a<u>gh</u>a* of the *Sol <u>Gh</u>arībler* was promoted *a<u>gh</u>a* of the *Sagh <u>Gh</u>arībler*, and the latter *a<u>gh</u>a* of the *Sol ʿUlūfe<u>dj</u>iler*. Sometimes by exception, and contrary to the *ḳānūn*, towards the end of this century the *a<u>gh</u>a* of the *Sagh <u>Gh</u>arībler* was promoted directly *a<u>gh</u>a* of the *Silāḥdārlar*, or *san<u>dj</u>aḳ-begi*, and even *beglerbegi* (see documents *apud* Uzunçarşılı, 172). Whereas each of the *a<u>gh</u>as* had in the times of Meḥemmed II and Süleymān I received an *ʿulūfe* of 80 *aḳčes* (see Angiolello and Ramberti), at the end of the 10th/16th century they received 100; in addition they held *zeʿāmets*.

The two divisions were sub-divided into 260 *bölüks*, each with its *bölük-ba<u>sh</u>i̊* (*Kemankeş lâyihası*, 457).

Since their horses needed grazing land, the majority of them were scattered in the outskirts of Istanbul, Edirne, Bursa, Kütahya and Konya; an officer appointed jointly by the *a<u>gh</u>as* of the six regiments, with the title *ketk<u>h</u>udā-yeri*, was in command of each of these scattered groups of members of the six regiments and maintained discipline. The *ʿulūfe* of the men varied between 6 and 20 *aḳčes* (*Ordo Portae*, p. 9; Angiolello: 10-20 *aḳčes*; I. de Promontorio: 12 *aḳčes*; Ramberti: 7-14 *aḳčes*). At each promotion the *ʿulūfe* was increased by 3 *aḳčes*. Their sons, if they showed themselves fit, could be appointed to the *<u>Gh</u>urebā* regiments. Their weapons were bow and arrow, shield, scimitar (*pala*), dagger, lance and axe. Though some carried muskets, firearms were not popular with them. They had assistants known as *o<u>gh</u>lan* (Ramberti, 251). Each of the two *bölüks* had a flag (*bayraḳ*) and a *tu<u>gh</u>*; the flag of the *Sagh <u>Gh</u>arībler* was white and that of the *Sol <u>Gh</u>arībler* of two colours, white and red or white and green.

Duties. Like all the *ḳapı̊-ḳullari̊*, at first they served in the field only when the Sultan himself went on campaign, but in the 10th/16th century it became the practice for them to serve also under a *serdār-i ekrem*, *i.e.*, a commander with the rank of vizier. The *<u>Gh</u>arīb-yigitler* had a reputation for valour, and so in the course of the fighting were sometimes entrusted with difficult tasks like penetrating the ranks of the enemy (*Ha<u>sh</u>t bihi<u>sh</u>t*). Their principal duty on campaign was to guard the Sultan's standards (*Ha<u>sh</u>t bihi<u>sh</u>t*) and later the *san<u>dj</u>aḳ-i <u>sh</u>erīf* [*q.v.*]; they took their station as the rearmost of the cavalry regiments guarding the Sultan's tent and protected the rear (*Ordo Portae*, 9). These two *bölüks* formed the rearguard of the *ḳapı̊-ḳullari̊*, stationed in the centre, and guarded the tents and baggage. From the end of the 10th/16th century onwards, when, during a siege, a battle developed it was their dangerous duty to guard the entrenchments.

With the general decay of the *<u>gh</u>ulām* system, the order and discipline of these *bölüks* too began to break up. Already in the 10th/16th century, the places of *ḳapı̊-ḳullari̊* in their ranks were in time of war increasingly filled by 'outsiders' known as *serdengečdi*; at the same time the principle was abandoned of enregistering *mülāzim*, candidates for future vacancies in the *bölüks*.

When in the 11th/17th century these *bölüks* began to take part in the mutinies and revolts, steps were taken to reduce the importance of the *bölükāt-i erbaʿa*. In 1071/1660, under Köprülü Meḥmed Pa<u>sh</u>a the numbers of the *Sagh <u>Gh</u>arībler* were reduced to 410, those of the *Sol <u>Gh</u>arībler* to 312. Later still, the *Sagh <u>Gh</u>arībler A<u>gh</u>asi̊* was made subordinate to the *Sipāhī o<u>gh</u>lanlari̊ A<u>gh</u>asi̊*, and the *Sol <u>Gh</u>arībler A<u>gh</u>asi̊* to the *Silāḥdārlar A<u>gh</u>asi̊*. In a list of 1123/1711, the *Sagh <u>Gh</u>arībler* are shown as numbering only 180 men and the *Sol <u>Gh</u>arībler* 162. On campaigns, however, these two *bölüks* maintained their entity as guardians of the *san<u>dj</u>aḳ-i <u>sh</u>erīf*. In Ṣafar 1242/September 1826, very shortly after the abolition of the Janissaries, all six of the *Altı̊ Bölük* were disbanded (for the text of the firman, see Uzunçarşılı, 210-2).

The so-called *<u>gh</u>urbet ṭāʾifesi*, groups of men who, from the 10th/16th century onwards, left their homes and sometime roamed the country as brigands, are quite unconnected with the *<u>Gh</u>urebā*.

Bibliography: in the article.

(Halil İnalcık)

<u>GH</u>URĀBIYYA, a branch of the <u>Sh</u>īʿī "exaggerators" (*<u>gh</u>ulāt* [*q.v.*]). Its adherents believed that ʿAlī and Muḥammad were so like in physical features as to be confused, as like "as one crow (*<u>gh</u>urāb*) is to another" (a proverbial expression for great similarity, cf. *Zeitschr. f. Assyr.*, xvii, 53), so that the Angel Gabriel when commissioned by God to bring the revelation to ʿAlī gave it in mistake to Muḥammad. ʿAlī was, they say, appointed by God to be a Prophet and Muḥammad only became one through a mistake. According to Ibn Ḥazm, some believed that Gabriel erred in good faith; others held he went astray deliberately, and cursed him as an apostate. According to al-Bag<u>h</u>dādī, the sectaries greeted one another by cursing Gabriel. According to the *Bayān al-adyān*, the <u>Gh</u>urābiyya were so called because they believed that ʿAlī was in heaven in the form of a crow. Ibn Ḳutayba (*Maʿārif*, ed. Wüstenfeld, 300) remarks that this is one of the few sects the origin of which is not attributed to an individual.

It is related that in the 4th/10th century the followers of this sect in Ḳumm raised a serious revolt against the decision of the judge Abū Saʿīd al-Iṣṭakhrī (died 328/940) when he divided an inheritance equally between two claimants, one of whom was the daughter and the other the uncle of the deceased. The Ghurābiyya demanded that the whole estate should go to the daughter and the uncle be quite excluded; as our source rightly observes, this was the result of their political creed, according to which the succession to Muḥammad was legitimate only in the line of his only daughter Fāṭima and not in that of his uncle (ʿAbbās) (Subkī, *Ṭabaḳāt al-Shāfiʿiyya*, ii, 194). Cf. the regulations made by the Caliph al-Muʿizz regarding the inheritance of daughters in Ibn Ḥadjar, *Rafʿ al-Iṣr*, ed. Guest (in the appendix to al-Kindi, *Governors and Judges of Egypt*, Gibb-Memorial, xix), 587, l. 3 from end. Ibn Djubayr, who visited Damascus in 580/1184, mentions the Ghurābiyya among the minor sects to be found in Syria.

Bibliography: Ibn Ḥazm, *Fiṣal*, Cairo, iv, 183-4 (Eng. tr. I. Friedländer, *The Heterodoxies of the Shiites according to Ibn Ḥazm* (New Haven 1909), i, 56-8, ii, 77 (= *JAOS*, xxviii, xxix)); Al-Baghdādī, *Al-Farḳ bayn al-firaḳ*, Cairo 1328, 237-8 (Eng. tr. A. S. Halkin, *Moslem schisms and sects*, Tel Aviv 1935, 67-8); al-Khʷārizmī, *Mafātīḥ al-ʿulūm*, Cairo 1342, 22; Abu 'l-Maʿālī, *Bayān al-adyān*, ed. C. Schefer in *Chrestomathie persane*, ii, Paris 1885, 158 (Fr. tr. H. Massé in *RHR* (1926)); al-Maḳrīzī, *Khiṭaṭ*, ii, 353; Ibn Rosteh in *BGA*, vii, 218 ff.; *The Travels of Ibn Jubayr*, ed. Wright-de Goeje, 280 (Italian transl. by C. Schiaparelli, Rome 1906, 272); ʿAbbās Iḳbāl, *Khānadān-i Nawbakhtī*, Tehrān 1311, 260; A. S. Tritton, *Muslim theology*, London 1947, 29.

(I. Goldziher*)

GHŪRĪ [see dilāwar khān and mālwā].

GHŪRIDS, the name of an eastern Iranian dynasty which flourished as an independent power in the 6th/12th century and the early years of the 7th/13th century and which was based on the region of Ghūr [*q.v.*] in what is now central Afghānistān with its capital at Fīrūzkūh [*q.v.*].

1. Origins and early history. The family name of the Ghūrid Sultans was Shanasb/Shansab (< MP Gushnasp; cf. Justi, *Iranisches Namenbuch*, 282, and Marquart, *Das Reich Zābul*, in *Festschrift E. Sachau*, 289, n. 3), and in the time of their florescence, attempts were made to attach their genealogy to the ancient Iranian epic past. The 7th/13th century historian of the Ghūrids, Djūzdjānī, quotes a metrical version of the genealogy of the family composed by Fakhr al-Dīn Mubārakshāh Marwarrūdhī and completed in the reign of Sultan Ghiyāth al-Dīn Muḥammad (*scil.* in the last third of the 6th/12th century). In this, the family is traced back to the tyrant of Iranian mythology, Azhd Dahāk, whose descendants were supposed to have settled in Ghūr after Farīdūn's overthrowing of Dahāk's thousand-year dominion. Within this genealogy, Shansab himself is placed in the first century of Islam, and the family now brought within the ambit of the new faith. Shansab is said to have been converted by the Caliph ʿAlī, who formally invested him with the rulership of Ghūr; his son Fūlād later espoused the cause of Abū Muslim in Khurāsān and in this way assisted the ʿAbbāsids. A further alleged episode can be directly connected with the political position in Ghūr in later times. According to this, the Caliph Hārūn al-Rashīd received at his court the Amīr Bandjī b. Nahārān Shansabānī and a rival chieftain from Ghūr, Shīth b. Bahrām. Bandjī was awarded the insignia of political sovereignty (*imārat*) over Ghūr, together with the title *Ḳasīm Amīr al-Muʾminīn*, whilst Shīth was awarded the military command (*pahlawānī*) of the forces of Ghūr, "an arrangement", says Djūzdjānī, "which has continued thus till the present time" (see further, below).

All these fabrications clearly aim at giving some lustre to a dynasty which had arisen from very obscure and localized origins, or as in the latter episode, they attempt to project into the past an explanation for the political situation of later times (cf. C. E. Bosworth, *The early Islamic history of Ghūr*, in *Central Asiatic Journal*, vi (1961), 125-7). Ethnically, we can only assume that the Shansabānīs were, like the rest of the Ghūrīs, of eastern Iranian Tādjīk stock. We are equally in the dark about the language which they spoke, except that in the early 5th/11th century it differed considerably from the Persian of the Ghaznavid court. It is possible that the earliest Ghūrids spoke some south-east Iranian language, one of the group which has been all but eliminated in modern times by the spread of Persian and Pashto (communication from G. Morgenstierne). There is nothing to confirm the recent surmise that the Ghūrids were Pashto-speaking.

We know nothing really definite about the Shansabānīs until Ghaznavid times, *i.e.*, the 5th/11th century; it was only in the early part of this century that Ghūr, and presumably the Shansabānīs, began to adopt Islam. The *Ḥudūd al-ʿālam* (372/982-3) mentions a Ghūr-Shāh who was tributary to the Farīghūnid Amīrs of Gūzgān to the north of Ghūr [*qq.v.*], but there is nothing to show that this ruler was necessarily a Shansabānī. Within the empire of Sultan Maḥmūd of Ghazna (338-421/998-1030), Ghūr remained an unabsorbed enclave; hence during his reign, at least three expeditions were sent by him to Ghūr. In 401/1011 a force attacked the Shansabānī chief Muḥammad b. Sūrī, capturing him at his stronghold of Āhangarān. He was now deposed, his pro-Ghaznavid son Abū ʿAlī set up as the Sultan's vassal and teachers left to instruct the people in the precepts of Islam (cf. ʿUtbī and Djūzdjānī in M. Nāẓim, *The life and times of Sulṭān Maḥmūd of Ghazna*, Cambridge 1931, 70-2, and Bosworth, *op. cit.*, 122-3, 127-8). From this, and from other information in Djūzdjānī, we can firmly identify the Shansabānīs as petty rulers of the region of Mandēsh on the south bank of the upper Herī Rūd, with its centre at Āhangarān, the place still known today by that name. According to Djūzdjānī, the stronghold of the Shansabānīs of Mandēsh lay at the foot of the Zar-i Margh, one of the five great mountain massifs of Ghūr, and believed by the Ghūrīs to be the mountain where the Sīmurgh nurtured Rustam's father Zāl. At this time, the term "Ghūr" seems to have had a restricted meaning and to have been synonymous with Mandēsh, *i.e.*, the north-eastern corner of the Ghūr of the early Islamic geographers.

The existence of several other chieftains of Ghūr (in the larger sense of the term) is known in the 5th/11th century. Of at least equal importance with the Shansabānīs were the lords of the region further down the Herī Rūd, around the later Ghūrid capital of Fīrūzkūh and the modern Khʷādja-Čisht; this district seems to have been distinguished from Ghūr (in the narrow sense) and called *Bilād al-Djibāl*. Bayhaḳī, ed. Ghanī and Fayyāḍ, 114-20, gives a detailed account of the Ghaznavid expedition of 411/1020 under Masʿūd b. Maḥmūd, which marched up the Herī Rūd from Herāt, captured the fortress of Djurwas and made the local chieftain Warmēsh-Pat submit. The occurrence at a later date of this name in the Shīthānī family (see above) points to the fact that this district of Djurwas in the north-western corner of Ghūr was the centre of the Shansabānīs' rivals, the Shīthānīs. Bayhaḳī mentions the names of other chieftains in Ghūr, and it is clear that, despite Djūzdjānī's attempts to inflate the early Shansabānīs' sphere of authority, these last were only one lot of petty chiefs amongst several in this inaccessible region. Moreover, it seems that the primacy of the Shansabānīs at a later date was only achieved after much jostling for power and local warfare, although explicit information on this process is meagre.

2. The period of vassalage to the Ghaznavids and Saldjūḳs. Maḥmūd of Ghazna's nominee Abū ʿAlī b. Muḥammad is praised for his beneficent rule and his encouragement of the newly-introduced Islamic religion; he built mosques and *madrasas* and endowed them with *awḳāf*. But during the reign of Masʿūd of Ghazna (421-32/1030-41) an internal revolution took place in Mandēsh, and Abū ʿAlī was deposed by his nephew ʿAbbās b. Shīth. ʿAbbās devoted his efforts to fortifying and rebuilding the castles and strongholds which were such a feature of the landscape of Ghūr, but his tyranny provoked an appeal of dissident Ghūrī chiefs to Sultan Ibrāhīm b. Masʿūd. Ibrāhīm therefore marched into Ghūr, deposed ʿAbbās and set up the latter's son Muḥammad. Muḥammad was succeeded by his own son Ḳuṭb al-Dīn Ḥasan (the first Shansabānī known to have a *laḳab* or honorific). Within this period, *scil.* the second half of the 5th/11th century, the Shansabānīs were trying to extend their authority beyond Mandēsh and over the lands of rival chieftains. Djūzdjānī speaks of the feuding and turbulence which went on within Ghūr both at this time and until much later; and it was during the suppression of a rebellion in Wadjīristān, the district to the west of Ghazna, that Ḳuṭb al-Dīn Ḥasan was killed.

With the accession of his son, ʿIzz al-Dīn Ḥusayn (493-540/1100-46), our knowledge of the dynasty becomes fuller. Since four of his many sons eventually became rulers, Djūzdjānī calls him *Abu 'l-Salāṭīn*, "Father of Sultans". By now, Ghūr had become a buffer region between the truncated Ghaznavid empire, reduced after the middle years of the 5th/11th century to southern and eastern Afghānistān and northern India, and the powerful empire of the Saldjūḳs. In particular, Saldjūḳ Khurāsān was after 490/1097 under the rule of the forceful Sandjar b. Malik Shāh. With the relative decline of the Ghaznavids after Ibrāhīm's death in 492/1099, Ghūr was drawn towards the Saldjūḳ sphere of influence. ʿIzz al-Dīn Ḥusayn was initially confirmed in power by Masʿūd III b. Ibrāhīm of Ghazna, but in 501/1107-8 Sandjar led a raid into Ghūr and captured ʿIzz al-Dīn, and thereafter the Ghūrid maintained close relations with the Saldjūḳ, sending him as tribute the specialities of Ghūr, including armour, coats of mail and the local breed of fierce dogs.

On ʿIzz al-Dīn's death, his son Sayf al-Dīn Sūrī succeeded as chief in Ghūr and overlord of the Shansabānī family. He now made a general division of territories amongst his brothers, an indication that political feeling amongst the Ghūrids was still tribal and patrimonial in nature, and unaffected by the administrative sophistication of their Ghaznavid neighbours, with their unitary state under one Sultan. Sayf al-Dīn retained the fortress of Istiya as his capital; Ḳuṭb al-Dīn Muḥammad was allotted Warshād or Warshār, where he now founded the town and fortress of Fīrūzkūh and assumed the title of *Malik al-Djibāl*; Nāṣir al-Dīn Muḥammad took Mādīn; ʿAlāʾ al-Dīn Ḥusayn took Wadjīristān; Bahāʾ al-Dīn Sām took Sanga, the chief place of Mandēsh; and Fakhr al-Dīn Masʿūd took Kashī on the headwaters of the Herī Rūd. It was soon apparent that the Shansabānīs' sense of family solidarity was not developed enough to allow this division to work, and fratricidal strife broke out. Ḳuṭb al-Dīn quarrelled with his brothers, fled to Bahrām Shāh's court at Ghazna, but was there poisoned. From this deed there arose, says Djūzdjānī, the deep hatred and enmity between the Ghūrid and Ghaznavid families. In retaliation, Sayf al-Dīn Sūrī marched on Ghazna and temporarily expelled the Sultan, but in the face of popular sympathy for the Ghaznavids was unable to hold the city; and in a battle which took place when Bahrām Shāh returned, Sayf al-Dīn was captured and ignominiously executed.

Bahāʾ al-Dīn succeeded in Ghūr in 544/1149, and after finishing the fortifying of Fīrūzkūh, set out with an army for Ghazna, but died en route in that same year. ʿAlāʾ al-Dīn Ḥusayn had been left behind by his brother to rule Ghūr, and he now took over supreme power there. His pressing tasks were to avenge his dead brothers and, if possible, to reduce Ghaznavid power in Afghānistān, for the hold which they had on the routes through eastern Afghānistān from Kābul to Ghazna and Bust blocked any potential Ghūrid expansion there. Bahrām Shāh massed his troops in the region of Tigīnābād (*i.e.*, the modern region of Ḳandahār). ʿAlāʾ al-Dīn moved into Zamīn-Dāwar and a great battle took place, in which the tactics of the Ghūrī infantry, with their walls of protective shields, overcame the Ghaznavids' elephants. Bahrām Shāh was pursued to Ghazna and again defeated, retiring now to India. ʿAlāʾ al-Dīn entered the city, and a frightful orgy of devastation and plundering followed, earning the Ghūrid his title of *Djihān-Sūz* "World Incendiary" (545/1150-1). The corpses of all but three of the Ghaznavid Sultans were exhumed and burnt, and on the way back to Ghūr, the other great Ghaznavid centre of Bust was sacked in an equally savage manner. ʿAlāʾ al-Dīn thus made no attempt at this moment permanently to annex the Ghaznavid territories in eastern Afghānistān, but he does seem to have aspired to a more ambitious position than that of a mere chieftain of Ghūr. According to Ibn al-Athīr, he now copied Saldjūḳ and Ghaznavid practice, calling himself *al-Sulṭān al-Muʿaẓẓam* and adopting the *čatr* or ceremonial parasol; previously, the Ghūrids had been content to style themselves *Malik* or *Amīr*. It was natural that his success at Ghazna should embolden ʿAlāʾ al-Dīn to throw off Saldjūḳ control. In 547/1152 he stopped paying tribute to Sandjar and endeavoured to support an anti-Saldjūḳ rising in Herāt. His army advanced from Fīrūzkūh down the Herī Rūd, but was met at Nāb by Sandjar's forces and crushingly defeated after the Turkish, Oghuz and Khaladj troops in the Ghūrid army had gone over to their co-nationals in Sandjar's army. ʿAlāʾ al-Dīn was personally captured and spent some time as a prisoner in Khurāsān. The last years of his life, until his death in 556/1161, were spent firstly in consolidating his throne in Ghūr against rival members of his family, and secondly in making conquests in Gharčistān and the upper

Murghāb valley, in the Bāmiyān and Ṭukhāristān regions and in the Zamīn-Dāwar and Bust regions.

3. The Ghūrids as an imperial power. The expansionist policy of ʿAlāʾ al-Dīn's last years meant that the Ghūrids were now breaking out beyond their mountain fastnesses in Ghūr and would soon become a major power in the eastern Islamic world. There was, indeed, something of a vacuum of power there at this time: the Ghaznavid empire was in decay, and Sandjar's capture by the Ghuzz and the consequent anarchy in Khurāsān facilitated Ghūrid expansion in the west. ʿAlāʾ al-Dīn's annexations gave the impetus towards a tripartite division of the Ghūrid empire, each under a separate branch of the Shansabānī family, and this division remained characteristic until the final fall of the Ghūrids.

The senior branch ruled over Ghūr from Fīrūzkūh and was concerned with expansion westwards into Khurāsān. When Ghazna was finally taken in 569/1173-4, another branch was established there and used Ghazna as a base for expansion into India. Finally, ʿAlāʾ al-Dīn installed in the newly-conquered town of Bāmiyān his brother Fakhr al-Dīn Masʿūd, and the latter ruled over Ṭukhāristān, Badakhshān and Shughnān, up to the Oxus bank. After Fakhr al-Dīn's death in 558/1163, he was followed by his son Shams al-Dīn Muḥammad. The latter is said to have extended his power over the Oxus into Čaghāniyān and Wakhsh; he also received from Ghiyāth al-Dīn Muḥammad in Fīrūzkūh the title of "Sulṭān" and the privilege of having a *čatr*.

ʿAlāʾ al-Dīn Ḥusayn was succeeded at Fīrūzkūh by his son Sayf al-Dīn Muḥammad, who took repressive measures against the Ismāʿīlīs who had infiltrated into Ghūr and had spread their propaganda there, but who only reigned for two years (556-8/1161-3). During his reign, there arose a feud between the Shansabānīs and their rivals in Ghūr, the Shīthānīs. The Sultan treacherously murdered his Commander-in-Chief Warmēsh b. Shīth, and in revenge, Warmēsh's brother, now succeeded to the office of *Sipah-Sālār*, murdered Sayf al-Dīn on the battlefield. It is to explain these tribal disputes that Djūzdjānī projects back the rivalry of the two families into ʿAbbāsid times (see above).

Under Shams al-Dīn (later Ghiyāth al-Dīn) Muḥammad of Ghūr (558-99/1163-1203) and Shihāb al-Dīn (later Muʿizz al-Dīn) Muḥammad of Ghazna (569-602/1173-1206), the Ghūrid empire reached its apogee. These two brothers maintained a partnership and amity rare for their age. Broadly speaking, the first was concerned with expansion westwards and the checking of the Khʷārizm-Shāhs' ambitions in Khurāsān, whilst the second carried on the *ghāzī*-tradition of the Ghaznavids in northern India. The Ghūrids thus challenged the Khʷārizm-Shāhs for supremacy in the eastern Islamic world, and initially seemed to have an advantage in that they were completely free agents, whereas the Shāhs were vassals of the Ḳarā-Khiṭāy. Moreover, the Ghūrids skilfully utilized the fears roused in the west by the Shāhs' imperialist ambitions. Ghiyāth al-Dīn kept up cordial relations with the ʿAbbāsid Caliphs, and embassies were frequently exchanged between Fīrūzkūh and Baghdād; Djūzdjānī's father took part in one of these. The Sultan was received into al-Nāṣir's *Futuwwa* order, and the Caliph more than once urged the Ghūrids to stem the advance of the Khāʷrizm-Shāhs in Persia.

Ghiyāth al-Dīn was joined at Fīrūzkūh by Muʿizz al-Dīn, who had been at Bāmiyān. The two of them then fought off a coalition of Fakhr al-Dīn of Bāmiyān, himself covetous of the power in Ghūr, and the Turkish governors of Herāt, Tādj al-Dīn Yïldïz, and of Balkh, ʿAlāʾ al-Dīn Ḳamāč, defeating them at Rāgh-i Zar in the Herī Rūd valley. After this, Ghiyāth al-Dīn campaigned in Zamīn-Dāwar, Bādghīs and Gharčistān, securing these regions for his empire. The Ṣaffārid *amīr* of Sīstān, Tādj al-Dīn Ḥarb, acknowledged him as suzerain, and even the Ghuzz in Kirmān, who had taken over the province after the overthrowing of the Saldjūḳs of Kirmān, sent envoys to Fīrūzkūh. After the last Ghaznavid, Khusraw Malik, had abandoned Ghazna for Lahore, his former capital was occupied for twelve years by Ghuzz adventurers, until in 569/1173-4 Ghiyāth al-Dīn ejected them and installed Muʿizz al-Dīn in Ghazna with the title of "Sulṭān". Herāt was captured in 571/1175-6 from its Turkish governor Bahāʾ al-Dīn Ṭoghrïl and held for a time.

Internal disputes within the dynasty of the Khʷārizm-Shāhs now favoured the Ghūrids. Ousted from Khʷārizm in 568/1172-3 by his brother ʿAlāʾ al-Dīn Tekish, Sulṭān Shāh had secured help from the Ḳarā Khiṭāy and had carved out for himself a principality in Khurāsān. He now clashed with the Ghūrids over possession of Herāt and Bādghīs, but Ghiyāth al-Dīn summoned troops from Bāmiyān and Sīstān and from Muʿizz al-Dīn in Ghazna, and in 586/1190 he defeated Sulṭān Shāh near Marw. Sulṭān Shāh was captured, and most of his Khurāsānian territories fell to the Ghūrids. In northern Afghānistān, the Bāmiyān Ghūrid Bahāʾ al-Dīn Sām occupied Balkh in 594/1198 after its Turkish governor, a vassal of the Ḳarā Khiṭāy, had died. In the same year, a general war broke out in Khurāsān between the Ghūrids on one side, urged on by the Baghdād Caliph, who was now threatened by the Khʷārizmian advance into western Persia, and on the other side the Khʷārizm-Shāh and his Ḳarā Khiṭāy suzerains. The Ḳarā Khiṭāy invaded Gūzgān and Tekish threatened Herāt, but both were decisively defeated by the Ghūrids. When in 596/1200 Tekish died, Ghiyāth al-Dīn took over most of the towns of Khurāsān, penetrating as far west as Bisṭām in Ḳūmis and installing in Nīshāpūr as governor of Khurāsān a Ghūrid prince, Ḍiyāʾ al-Dīn Muḥammad. Ghiyāth al-Dīn died at Herāt in 599/1202-3; latterly he had been ill and incapacitated, and Muʿizz al-Dīn had had to leave his Indian campaigns and attend to the west.

After his brother's death, Muʿizz al-Dīn followed the usual practice within the Shansābānī family of allocating the various provinces of the empire as appanages for Ghūrid Maliks; thus whilst retaining Ghazna as his own capital, he installed Ḍiyāʾ al-Dīn at Fīrūzkūh. Meanwhile, the new Khʷārizm-Shāh ʿAlāʾ al-Dīn Muḥammad was preparing to recover Khurāsān, where Ghūrid rule was proving unpopular; according to Djuwaynī, Muʿizz al-Dīn confiscated for his army grain which had been committed for protection to the *Imām* al-Riḍā's shrine at Ṭūs. In 601/1204 Muʿizz al-Dīn repulsed the Shāh from Herāt and pursued him back into Khʷārizm. However, the flooding of the Khʷārizmian countryside halted his troops, and the Khʷārizmians' allies, the Ḳarā Khiṭāy, routed Muʿizz al-Dīn's army at Andkhūy on the Oxus. The Sultan himself escaped, but all Khurāsān except Herāt was lost and in the next year he was assassinated in the Indus valley, allegedly by an Ismāʿīlī emissary, whilst returning from a punitive expedition against the Khōkars of the Pandjāb.

4. The end of the Ghūrids. Within a decade of

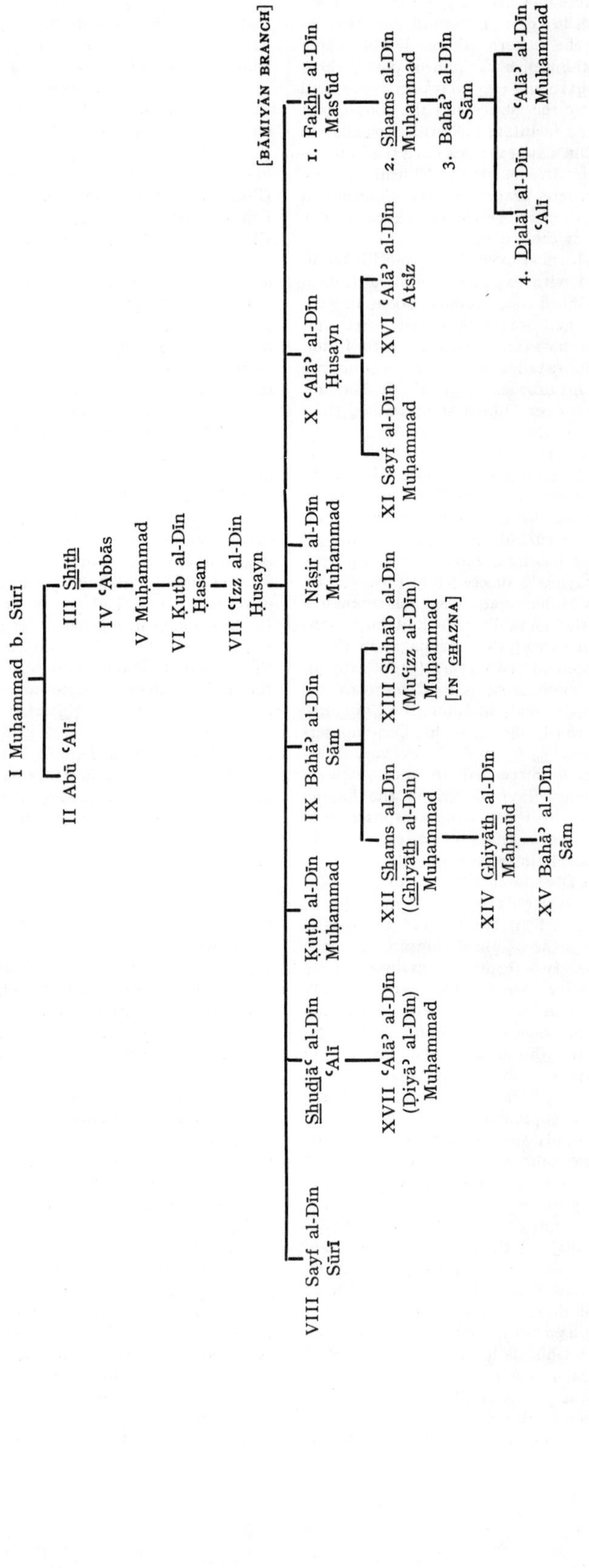
I Muḥammad b. Sūrī
II Abū ʿAlī
III Shīth
IV ʿAbbās
V Muḥammad
VI Ḳuṭb al-Dīn Ḥasan
VII ʿIzz al-Dīn Ḥusayn
VIII Sayf al-Dīn Sūrī
Shudjāʿ al-Dīn ʿAlī
Ḳuṭb al-Dīn Muḥammad
IX Bahāʾ al-Dīn Sām
Nāṣir al-Dīn Muḥammad
X ʿAlāʾ al-Dīn Ḥusayn
[BĀMIYĀN BRANCH]
1. Fakhr al-Dīn Masʿūd
XVII ʿAlāʾ al-Dīn (Ḍiyāʾ al-Dīn) Muḥammad
XII Shams al-Dīn (Ghiyāth al-Dīn) Muḥammad
XIII Shihāb al-Dīn (Muʿizz al-Dīn) Muḥammad
[IN GHAZNA]
XI Sayf al-Dīn Muḥammad
XVI ʿAlāʾ al-Dīn Atsïz
2. Shams al-Dīn Muḥammad
XIV Ghiyāth al-Dīn Maḥmūd
3. Bahāʾ al-Dīn Sām
XV Bahāʾ al-Dīn Sām
4. Djalāl al-Dīn ʿAlī
ʿAlāʾ al-Dīn Muḥammad

the later Ghaznavids (from 421/1030 to 583/1187), Hamburg thesis, 1956, 98 ff.; M. A. Ghafur, *The Ghurids*, Hamburg thesis 1959; C. E. Bosworth, *The early Islamic history of Ghūr*, in *Central Asiatic Journal*, vi (1961), 116-33; idem, in the forthcoming *Camb. Hist. of Iran*, v; Ch. Kieffer, *Les Ghorides, une grande dynastie nationale*, in *Afghanistan* (Kabul 1961-2, 3 parts). For chronology and numismatics, see Zambaur, *Manuel*, 280-1, 284; E. Thomas, in *JRAS* (1860), 190-208; Zambaur, in *Wiener Numismatische Zeitschr.*, xxxvii (1905), 185 ff.; D. Sourdel, *Inventaire des monnaies musulmanes du Musée de Caboul*, Damascus 1953, 114 ff.

(C. E. Bosworth)

GHURŪSH [see SIKKA].

GHUSL, general ablution, uninterrupted washing, in ritually pure water, of the whole of the human body, including the hair, performed after declaring the intention (*niyya*) so to do. For the living it is a fairly simple process, though it applies also to the washing of the corpse of a Muslim (see below). For the living, the essential *ghusl* is that which is obligatory before performing the ritual daily prayers; this *ghusl* becomes necessary as a purification following acts of a sexual nature which produce *djanāba* [*q.v.*]: intimate relations, normal or not, emission of sperm and of feminine *manī* (except in cases of illness when only the ordinary ablution, *wuḍūʾ* is required). *Ghusl* is also required after menstruation and lochia (other losses of blood do not demand the *ghusl* for purification). Whoever is thus in a state of major impurity is subject to the same taboos as those incurred by minor impurity (*ḥadath* [*q.v.*]); in addition, he may not recite the Ḳurʾān nor attend the mosque; women who are menstruating or who are in childbirth may recite the Ḳurʾān, but their fast and their ritual prayers are not recognized, and it is forbidden to have sexual relations with them before they have performed the *ghusl*. The general rules of the *ghusl* are more or less the same in the various schools, orthodox or not (with the Ḥanafīs, however, the intention is not an obligatory requirement), if we disregard any trifling casuistical details (*e.g.*, what if a person, after having sexual relations, proceeds with his *ghusl*, but does not ejaculate until afterwards?). Moreover, and this is much more important, the four orthodox schools agree in the fact that, if it is not possible to use water, the Believer may, for the *ghusl* as for the *wuḍūʾ*, have recourse to cleaning with dust (*tayammum* [*q.v.*]); however, there has been much discussion over this question.

Besides this obligatory *ghusl*, *fiḳh* recognizes others which are only *sunna* and the list and the number of which vary according to the schools (*e.g.*, 12 among the Shāfiʿīs); among the most important and the most generally recognized are the *ghusl* recommended for the Friday prayer and that of the Two Feasts, as well as that on the occasion of the *ḥadjdj*. Among the Shīʿīs, there are not less than 28, several of which are connected with the history of Shīʿism (as a curiosity of folklore, it is interesting to note that, according to certain Shīʿī doctors, the *ghusl* is obligatory if one has voluntarily looked at a hanged person or if one has touched a newly-born child).

The rules for the washing of the dead are of course different from those of the *ghusl* mentioned above. We give here a brief account of them. There is some disagreement (particularly among the Mālikīs) over whether this *ghusl* is obligatory or *sunna*; although in fact this washing is most often done by specialists, *fiḳh* gives detailed regulations concerning the principles of the devolution of this duty on the spouse of the deceased, then on his or her relatives; in all cases the legal nakedness of the dead person (*ʿawra*) must be covered during the operation; if the corpse of a man is washed by a woman who, being his wife, is not forbidden to see him, the point is disputed as to whether the corpse need be completely covered (and vice versa for the body of a woman). In the absence of water, here also recourse may be had to *tayammum*, as in some other hypothetical situations. The corpse of a martyr (*shahīd* [*q.v.*]) who has fallen in the Holy War is not washed.

As well as these legal dispositions, it is necessary, with this as with all other institutions, to examine what happens in practice in the Muslim world. In our view, the *ghusl* of the dead is generally practised, and the *ghusl*s which are only *sunna* are practised rather seldom. Concerning the *ghusl* for *djanāba*, it has not until now been sufficiently noticed that the existence of the *ḥammām* is connected with the purification from *djanāba*. As in other matters, the effective practice is sometimes much more lax than the theory: where the ritual prayer is neglected (this is very often the case for example in North Africa, particularly among women), the *ghusl* will naturally also be neglected; but sometimes the demands of practice are more rigorous than those of *fiḳh*. Thus, it has been noted that, in certain regions of Morocco, whoever has relations with a Jewess must wash seven times with water coming from seven different streams. Throughout Islam, however, for every minority very much preoccupied with observing the prescriptions of the law, we find a majority who often neglect them, although, in particular cases, they have a curiously inadequate idea of what they are: detailed systematic studies would thus show a discrepancy between the regulations of the *ghusl* and the practice.

Bibliography: For the sociological theory of the whole subject of purifications etc. in human societies, V. Pareto, *Trattato di sociologia generale*, i; Fr. tr., *Traité* ..., i, 649 ff.; Eng. tr. *The mind and society*, 1935, ii, 736 ff.; G.-H. Bousquet, *La pureté rituelle en Islam*, in *RHR*, cxxxviii (1950), 53-71 (with detailed references for what has been said above). The books of *fiḳh* begin with a chapter on ritual purity, where *ghusl* is dealt with, *e.g.*, Khalīl, *Mukhtaṣar*, excellent Italian tr. by Guidi, i, 28 ff., 141 ff., and Fr. tr. by Bousquet, i, 32 ff., 95 ff.; similarly the books of *ikhtilāf* (*e.g.*, the modern work of Muḥammad al-Djazīrī, *K. al-Fiḳh ʿala ʾl-madhāhib al-arbaʿa*, i, 78 ff., Cairo 1355: much detail and very lucid).

(G. H. Bousquet)

GHŪṬA, name given in Syria to abundantly irrigated areas of intense cultivation surrounded by arid land. A *ghūṭa* is produced by the co-operative activity of a rural community settled near to one or several perennial springs, whose water is used in a system of canalization to irrigate several dozen or several hundred acres. Each *ghūṭa* has its own particular system of irrigation based on cycles of varying length. The soil in a *ghūṭa* is usually laid out in platforms which form terraces of watered zones, the level sections of which are supported by stone walls two to six feet high. In them is carried out a closed agricultural economy, which provides an assured subsistence for men and animals. Near the source of the water there is an area in which vegetables and fruit are intensively grown, then the extent to which the land is exploited decreases in proportion to the time it takes for the water to reach

2. Detail of the minaret.

3. Surviving remains of the *madrasa* and mosque at Čis͟ht in the Harī-Rūd valley, also from the reign of G͟hiyāt͟h al-Dīn Muḥammad.

it. While birch-trees and poplars grow in the damp of the central area, as the distance from the spring increases, trees become sparser, unsheltered fields spread out and areas planted with vines or cereals are reached; beyond this there will be the region which is flooded in winter, and further still some temporary fields. This is a schematic picture of the *g͟hūṭa*s of D̲j̲arūd, Nabak, Yabrūd and Dimas̲h̲ḳ (see R. Thoumin, *Géographie humaine de la Syrie Centrale*, Tours 1936, 115-120; J. Weulersse, *Paysans de Syrie et du Proche Orient*, Paris 1946, 283-91).

The *G͟hūṭa* of Dimas̲h̲ḳ [*q.v.*] is the area of gardens and orchards which surrounds the former Umayyad capital below the gorges of Rabwa and which is made fertile by a close network of irrigation trenches fed by the Baradā [*q.v.*]. The *G͟hūṭa* extends from the eastern slopes of Mount Ḳāsiyūn [*q.v.*] as far as the streams and the water brought in from the Baradā allow bushes to be grown. Beyond this, to the east, is the *Mard̲j̲*, a region of pasture and wide stretches of arable land. These grass-lands, which are green from December to June and dried up from July onwards, end at the lagoon of ʿUtayba [*q.v.*], or "Lake of Damascus". Still further to the east is the scorched land of the steppe, which man's strenuous labour has pushed back to about 20 km/12 miles from Mount Ḳāsiyūn.

The charms of this place, which is considered by Muslim tradition to be one of the four earthly paradises, have been celebrated by many Arab poets (see Kurd ʿAlī, *G͟hūṭa*, 68-107) and described by more than one western traveller.

Consisting of a half of a basaltic basin filled with fertile limestone alluvions and facing eastwards, the *G͟hūṭa* is intersected by the Baradā, which flows down a slight natural slope split up into artificially constructed levels from Rabwa (699 metres/2,300 ft) to the point where it leaves Dimas̲h̲ḳ (650 metres/2,130 ft) and then to the *Mard̲j̲* (600 metres/1,970 ft). It is dominated by a screen of mountains 500 metres/1,640 ft. above the plain and is subject to the violent contrasts which are typical of a semi-desert climate. It has a rainfall of only about 250 mm/10 inches, most of which falls in December, January and February, with some autumn and spring rain. This is supplemented by the Baradā.

The structure of the *G͟hūṭa* is formed by six major diversions of the Baradā which fan out into the plain at Rabwa. The most important diversions, the Nahr T̲h̲awrā, which in fact forms the northern limit of the *G͟hūṭa*, has allowed the formation of an irrigation basin which includes the northern outskirts from Rabwa to D̲j̲awbar and is about 15 km/10 miles in width. The Nahr Yazīd, which runs alongside the district of al-Ṣāliḥiyya, swings round the basin of the Nahr T̲h̲awrā and turns towards Ḳābūn and Ḥarastā, driving mills and irrigating vegetable gardens and orchards. The Bānās and the Ḳanawāt supply the town of Dimas̲h̲ḳ with water, receive its drainage and sewage and go on to irrigate the southern section of the *G͟hūṭa*. In the western region the pure waters of the Nahr Mizzāwī and the Nahr Dārānī allow flowers and early vegetables to be grown. On leaving Damascus, the Baradā and the Nahr ʿAḳrabānī flow to the south-east, and supply an extensive network of channels (including the Daʿiyānī and the Mlīhī) which have allowed a wooded region, the *Zawr*, to be established in the lowest part of the *G͟hūṭa*. The absence of geographical features allows many channels to be drawn off and a series of basins without very precise limits to be formed, each one merging with the next. The Nahr Mnīn, coming down from Mount Ḳalamūn, comes in below Birza to complete the irrigation of the olive groves. Beyond Dūmā and ʿAd̲h̲rā, in the *Mard̲j̲*, use is made of the subterranean pools of water by installing hoists above the wells. In the south, a canal about 30 km/20 miles in length brings water from the Nahr al-Aʿwad̲j̲ to irrigate the sectors for which the Nahr Darānī cannot produce enough water.

The improvement and the exploitation of the land of the *G͟hūṭa* is dependent upon the harnessing and distribution of the water from the rivers. Skilful irrigation offsets the insufficient rainfall and permits regular agricultural work. This irrigation takes place at intervals, at fixed hours and days, and is effected without mechanical means of opening or closing. The distribution of the separate sections of water is carried out according to a conventional rotation which is called the *ʿaddān*. On the maintenance and supervision of the canals, on the measures which regulate the flow, and on the method of distribution of the water, see R. Tresse in *REI*, 1929, 473-90.

The crops grown in the *G͟hūṭa* are determined by the conditions created by the irrigation and the nature of the soil and the climate. Those that can be grown most intensely and are most remunerative are preferred. The agriculture of the *G͟hūṭa* can be divided into winter crops (*s̲h̲itī*): cereals, leguminous crops for food and for animal fodder, and summer crops (*ṣayfī*): market vegetables, mainly gourds, and industrial crops such as aniseed, hemp and sesame. Crops are grown in zones, some of which produce two crops, the most productive being the region between Mount Ḳāsiyūn and Dimas̲h̲ḳ with its great variety of fruit and vegetables, which already in the 10th/16th century consisted mainly of cucumbers, onions, aubergines, cauliflowers, carrots, *lūbiyāʾ*, melons and water-melons. The trees grown are those of temperate countries. Long before the arrival of the Ottomans the apricot had been the most important tree of the *G͟hūṭa* and from that time there are found also almond, cherry, fig, pomegranate, hazel-nut, walnut, peach, pear and plum trees. In the second zone, in the shade of the fruit trees, cereals (barley, wheat, maize) replace the vegetables. In the third zone, the cycle of irrigation becomes more widely spaced and olive trees take the place of the fruit trees. Finally there is a fourth zone of single cultivation, where vines replace the olive-trees, but where cereals still grow, though with a yield which decreases progressively until the steppe is reached.

There are crops peculiar to certain villages: thus the 14th century traveller Frescobaldi mentioned the flowers of Mizza and its rose-water industry, to which could be added that of violet oil. From Dārāyā and Dūmā raisins were exported to the West in the 10th/16th century. Olive trees are cultivated in two regions, one in the north including Birza, Ḳābūn, Ḥarastā and Dūmā, the other in the south including Mizza, Kafr Sūs, Babīlā, and Ḥūs̲h̲ Rīḥāniyya. Finally hemp (*ḳunnab*) is harvested in the autumn in the humid zone of the *Zawr*. This wooded district, which has no well-defined limits, includes the regions of D̲j̲isrīn, al-Aftarīs, Kafr Baṭnā, ʿAyn Tarmā, Zibdīn and D̲j̲aramānā, and in its many *g͟hayḍa* (pl. *g͟hiyāḍ*) many beech trees and black and white poplars flourish.

The *G͟hūṭa* has always been thickly populated, its inhabitants living in settlements built along the edges of the irrigated zones where groups of small-holdings tend to develop. Throughout the centuries, the number of villages has varied greatly; each writer gives a different list of them, and that of Ibn Ṭūlūn al-Ṣāliḥī (10th/16th century) has only a certain number of names and sites in common with that of the present-day writer Kurd ʿAlī (*Ghūṭa*, 218 ff.). To the names already given can be added those of some villages which have become places of pilgrimage by reason of legends connected with them, such as Birza in the north-east where, according to a legend which stems from the Samaritans, the birthplace of Abraham (the *Maḳām Ibrāhīm*) is to be found; Bayt Lahyā in the north, also connected with the legend of Abraham; the hill of Rabwa in the west, a legendary stopping place of ʿĪsā and his mother; and finally the village of al-Rāwiya, in the south-south-east, where there is the tomb of one Zaynab Umm Kulthūm (who has nothing in common with either the daughter of the Prophet or the daughter of ʿAlī and Fāṭima). There are also villages where the tomb of a Companion of the Prophet is revered; among these are Ḥadjīra, where Mudrik b. Ziyād is buried, al-Manīḥa, where Saʿd b. ʿUbāda is buried, and Mizza where Diḥya al-Kalbī is buried.

The history of the Ghūṭa is bound up with that of Dimashḳ [*q.v.*]. The excavations of Tell al-Ṣāliḥiyya provide evidence that the first human settlements in this oasis go back to the fourth millennium B.C. Greek and Roman remains are found at various places. In the Byzantine period there existed a great number of churches and monasteries such as Dayr Murrān, Dayr Bāwanna and Dayr Buṭrus of which the combined effects of time and man have removed every trace; others are perpetuated in present day place-names, such as Dayr Ṣalībā (now Dayr Khālid) and Dayr al-ʿAṣāfīr. It was in the *Ghūṭa*, at Mardj Rāhiṭ [*q.v.*], that Marwān, with his Yemenīs, gave battle to the Ḳaysīs in 64/683. Under the Umayyads, the *Ghūṭa* formed one of the districts of the province of Dimashḳ, and had an autonomous administration with a separate *dīwān* whose chief activity was the collecting of the *kharādj*. Many of the attacks on Dimashḳ were made less effective by having to get past the orchards with their network of paths edged by low walls on either side, and Crusaders and Zangids were able to appreciate their defensive value. At the end of the 6th/12th century, and even more in the 7th/13th century, under the Ayyūbid [*q.v.*] princes many monuments were built; *madrasas* and mausolea arose in peaceful surroundings among the orchards between the Nahr Thawrā and the Nahr Yazīd. From west to east could be seen the double cupola of the mausoleum of Kitbughā (8th/14th century), the Māridāniyya *madrasa* (7th/13th century) at Djisr al-Abyaḍ, the Shibliyya *madrasa* which formed part of a complex of buildings including the mausoleum of Shibl al-Dawla Kāfūr, a *khānḳāh* and a public fountain; the ribbed cupola of the Turbat al-Badrī, built in the time of Nūr al-Dīn [*q.v.*], rises not far from the *madrasa* of Sitti Ḥāfiẓa (7th/13th century). Finally, below al-Ṣāliḥiyya, the Rukniyya *madrasa* (7th/13th century) overlooked the gardens. Vegetable gardens and orchards survived to the north of Dimashḳ until about 1950, since when they have been gradually supplanted by new housing estates.

Bibliography: The essential work is Kurd ʿAlī, *Ghūṭat Dimashḳ*, in *MMIA* (2nd ed. 1952, 358 and map), which includes a good bibliography of the Arabic sources; Rubaʿī, *K. Faḍāʾil al-Shām wa-Dimashḳ*, ed. Ṣ. al-Munadjdjid, in *MMIA*, 1951, 60; Ibn ʿAsākir, *Taʾrīkh madīnat Dimashḳ*, in *MMIA*, 1954, 116-17, 145 f., 169; Ibn Shaddād, *al-Aʿlāḳ al-khaṭīra*, ed. S. Dahan, Damascus 1956, 13, 277 ff., 305 ff.; Harawī, *K. al-Ziyārāt*, Damascus 1953, 10-16 (tr. J. Sourdel-Thomine, *Guide des Lieux de Pèlerinage*, Damascus 1957, 24-40); Abu ʾl-Fidāʾ, *Géographie* (tr. Reinaud and Guyard), ii, 49, 135, ii², 9, 15; Ibn Djubayr, *Voyages*, tr. Gaudefroy-Demombynes, Paris 1953-6, 301 f.; Yāḳūt, iii, 825 (Beirut ed., iv, 219); Ibn Ṭūlūn al-Ṣāliḥī, *Darb al-Ḥūṭa ʿalā djamīʿ al-ghūṭa*, ed. A. Talass, in *MMIA*, xxi (1946), 149-61, 236-47, 338-51; Le Strange, *Palestine*, 33, 231, 237; H. Sauvaire, *Description de Damas*, in *JA*, 1894-96 (see *Index Général* by E. Ouéchek, Damascus 1954); R. Dussaud, *Topographie historique de la Syrie*, Paris 1927, 293-313; R. Mantran and J. Sauvaget, *Règlements fiscaux ottomans*, Damascus 1951, 16-18; J. Sauvaget, in *Monuments Ayyoubides de Damas*, ii, 65 ff., iii, 119 ff., 131 ff.; R. Tresse, *L'irrigation dans la Ghouta de Damas*, in *REI*, 1929, 459-570; R. Thoumin, *Notes sur l'aménagement et la distribution des eaux à Damas et dans sa Ghouta*, in *B. Et. Or.*, iv (1934), 1-26; idem, *Géographie humaine de la Syrie Centrale*, Tours 1936, 60-75, 120-25, 228 ff.; A. Latron, *La vie rurale en Syrie et au Liban*, Damascus 1936, 18, 21, 148, 207; J. Weulersse, *Paysans de Syrie*, Paris 1946, 283-99; Birot and Dresch, *La Méditerranée et le Moyen Orient*, vol. ii, Paris 1956, 441-42.

(N. Elisséeff)

AL-GHUZŪLĪ,, ʿAlāʾ al-Dīn ʿAlī b. ʿAbd Allāh al-Bahāʾī al-Dimashḳī, an Arabic writer of Berber origin (d. 815/1412) who composed, under the title *Maṭāliʿ al-budūr fī manāzil al-surūr*, an anthology on the model of the *adab* books but which, as the author justly boasts in the preface, is in its content favourably distinguished from the great mass of these writings. He deals with the house and its different sections, all the pleasures of life and sport and the accessories required for their realization; he illustrates these subjects with anecdotes and verses taken from later poetry but, at the same time he presents a very great wealth of material—still far from being exhausted—relating to the history of the civilization of the Muslim peoples. The book was printed in Cairo, in two volumes, in 1299-1300.

(C. Brockelmann)

GHUZZ, form generally used by Arabic authors for the name of the Turkish Oghuz people. The origin of the Oghuz, which for long was obscure because of the diversity of the transcriptions of the names of peoples in the Chinese, Arabic, Byzantine and other sources, seems to have been clarified by J. Hamilton, *Toguz Oghuz et On-Uyghur*, in *JA*, ccl/1 (1962), 23-64. At the beginning of the 7th century A.D. there was formed, among the eastern Turkish T'ie-lo tribes, a confederation of Nine Clans = Toḳuz Oghuz (a form known to the Arabic authors), who revolted against the empire of the western Turks and helped to form the empire of the most important tribe among them, whose name is the earliest attested, namely the Uyghurs. During the period of the extension of this empire (3rd/9th century) some groups of these peoples spread towards the west, losing their links with the structure of the Nine Clans and acquiring, in new countries and in their contacts with new peoples, distinctive characteristics: these are the people called by the western writers of that time, with no more reference to the "Nine", Oghuz (Arabic: Ghuzz; Byzantine: Ouzoi). The different deductions often drawn from the later legend of Oghuz-Khān (see below), or from rash linguistic assimilations, are to be rejected.

i.—Muslim East

We shall not deal at length here with the period of the history of the Oghuz/Ghuzz before they came in contact with Islam. It should however be mentioned briefly because, owing to their new habitat and the period during which they moved there, all that we know of them, admittedly very elementary and uncertain, is now based mainly on the Arabic (or Persian) authors. We shall ignore what these authors have said on the eastern Toḳuz-Oghuz (see V. Minorsky in his commentary and his translation of the *Ḥudūd al-ʿālam*, 1937, 268 f.) in order to concern ourselves here only with the western Oghuz/Ghuzz.

The earliest reference to the presence of Oghuz/Ghuzz (without the Toḳuz) in Central Asia is found in al-Balādhurī (431), writing of events belonging to the end of the reign of al-Maʾmūn, although Ibn al-Athīr, writing much later, reports the opinions of authors who consider those Turks who, under the caliphate of al-Mahdī, had supported the movement of al-Muḳannaʿ, as already then belonging to the Oghuz. In contrast to this, from the middle of the 3rd/9th century, nearly all the Arab geographers mention them. In the 4th/10th century they occupied a territory roughly bounded to the south by the Aral Sea and the lower course of the Sīr-Daryā, to the west by the River Ural or the lower Volga and the Caspian Sea, to the north-east by the upper course of the Irtysh. They then had other Turkish peoples as neighbours: to the north the Kīmāk, a branch of the Ḳīpčaḳ, to the east the Kharlukh (Ḳarluḳ), to the west the Pečeneg and above all the semi-Turkish state of the Khazar, and they were in constant communication with the Bulgars of the middle Volga who were also for the most part Turks; finally, to the south, and particularly along the Sīr-Daryā, they bordered on the Muslim world. For the most part they were nomads, herding camels (with one hump and resistant to cold though not to excessive heat), sheep, horses etc., and each tribe branded its animals with a special sign—a *tughra, tamgha* [*qq.v.*]. All the same, it should not be thought that they were exclusively nomadic, for both among the remains of the former populations and among the Oghuz themselves there were settled groups occupied with agriculture in the oases, and also, particularly on the boundaries of the Muslim world and along the routes leading to the Bulgars or the Khazars, markets which had often become small fortified towns where their chiefs and leading men came to barter, against the products of the civilized world to the south, animals, prisoners sold as slaves, and furs brought from the northern forests; and in the principal one of these little towns, Yänikänt, probably the ancient Nau-Kärdä of the pre-Turkish Indo-European inhabitants, the chief of the Oghuz/Ghuzz chose to live in the winter, though he may have stayed further upstream, at Djand (near to the modern Perovsk): the recent archaeological investigations which have located the sites and the ruins of these towns along the former course of the lower Sīr-Daryā confirm that they were certainly urban settlements and not the camps of nomads. It is difficult to state precisely what the Oghuz were ethnically, but, however important the Turkish element was (and the Russian chroniclers know the Oghuz only by the name of Turks/Torki), there is little doubt that there had been on the one hand inter-marriage with the remains of the earlier populations, and on the other hand an integration into the Oghuz/Ghuzz of non-Turkish groups, incorporated just as they were and later Turkicized: it has even been suggested that the name of the Oghuz/Ghuzz tribe of the Döger [*q.v.*] preserves the ancient name of the Tokharians; the result being that the Oghuz/Ghuzz of the west were no longer ethnically the same as the other Turks and particularly those of the east.

So far, then, as we can speak at all of a geopolitical configuration of Central Asia, it would seem possible to postulate, in the 4th/10th century, certain political and other interests in common between Khʷārizm, the semi-autonomous outpost of Muslim civilization to the south of the Caspian Sea, and the state of the Khazars, to the west of the Caspian Sea and the lower Volga, and that there was, in opposition to them, some form of alliance of the Oghuz/Ghuzz with the Bulgars (and at one time, with the "Russians" of Kiev). This is particularly the impression given by the account which has been preserved of the embassy to the Bulgars at the beginning of the century of the caliph's envoy, Ibn Faḍlān, who passed through Khʷārizm. Moreover, although the Oghuz/Ghuzz formed only a very loosely-joined confederation of tribes, they nevertheless recognized, within the framework of a western Turkish world which maintained a certain feeling of uniformity, the supremacy of a Yabghu [*q.v.*] of the left, to whom corresponded the Ḳarluḳ Yabghu of the right: a title and idea inherited from the ancient Turkish empire of the 6th century A.D. and from the early Central Asiatic states. The Yabghu of the Oghuz/Ghuzz normally lived at Yänikänt; he had a lieutenant (*Küdhärkin*) and a head of the tribal army (*subashî*).

Even if, as Ibn al-Athīr believes, the Turks (whoever they may have been) who had helped al-Muḳannaʿ had already embraced Islam, according to him Islam did not reach the western Turks, and in particular the Oghuz/Ghuzz, until the 4th/10th century and it was not until the end of that century that it became general among them. Before this the Oghuz/Ghuzz, like all the inhabitants of Central Asia, must have been influenced to some extent by Buddhism, Manichaeism, Nestorian Christianity and Khazar-Judaism, and the influence of the latter perhaps explains the later presence among the Saldjūḳs of characteristically Biblical names; but there are no grounds for believing that they abandoned completely their vague ancestral Shamanism. The Oghuz/Ghuzz came into contact with Islam in various ways: first through the raids and counter-raids which they exchanged on the southern frontiers of their territory with the Muslim *ghāzī*s of the state of the Sāmānids [*q.v.*], and the prisoners which were taken by both sides; then through some of the activities of the Ṣūfīs of the frontiers; and finally, and probably most of all, through the merchants whom they met in the markets, or "protected" as they travelled along the roads leading across Oghuz territory towards that of the Bulgars, the Khazars and the Chinese. Political or other reasons had caused Islam to spread among the Bulgars, and probably among the lower classes of the Khazar population, from the first half of the 4th/10th century. The Ḳarluḳ and the Oghuz/Ghuzz were not converted until the second half of the century, the former shortly after the middle and the latter at the end of the century, though it has of course still to be ascertained what form of Islam had been taught to them and how much of it they did in fact absorb at first. Moreover Islam did not reach all the Oghuz/Ghuzz, and those in the extreme west escaped the Muslim propaganda: the remnants of them were later, when incorporated in the Byzantine army, to receive Christian baptism.

The conversion to Islam, whatever form it may have taken, and the drive towards the south of those of the Oghuz/Ghuzz who were not already too much engaged in the west are related phenomena. The drive towards the territories of the Muslim Mā warāʾ al-Nahr, although these lands themselves were an attraction, may have been due also to pressure behind the Oghuz/Ghuzz from their other Turkish neighbours, for it is known that later the Ḳîpčaḳ were to occupy the territories left vacant by the migration of the Oghuz/Ghuzz. But another result of their conversion to Islam was that it prevented the *ghāzī*s from fighting against them as pagans and allowed the Muslim princes to enlist them under their banners; it could even make them into *ghāzī*s themselves to fight against the other Turks who were still pagan, and the part which the *ghāzī* formations were to play in the pattern of later Turkish history is indisputable even when, transferred to other fronts, they were directed against other adversaries. It is possible that there took place, between the supporters and the enemies of Islam, battles memories of which may be preserved in the (admittedly highly embellished) accounts concerning the origin of the Saldjūḳids; but Shāh-Malik, the Yabghu against whom the Saldjuks fought, was nevertheless himself a Muslim, and we should not exclude, merely for lack of evidence, the idea that the Oghuz/Ghuzz chiefs were attracted to Islam, as were those of the Ḳarluḳ (the Ḳarakhānids) and as has so often happened with peoples in a tribal stage of development, by the principle of authority which Islam conferred on them over the organization of the tribes, apart from the fact that they would soon be able to intervene in the conflicts of the traditional Muslim world itself.

As has just been said, the Oghuz/Ghuzz expansion towards the south took place mainly from the last years of the 4th/10th century, then especially in the fourth decade of the 5th/11th century, under the leadership of a family, the Saldjūḳids, which was to found a vast empire. This is discussed in other articles, so that we are not concerned to relate here the history of this expansion—contemporary with that of the "Ouzoi" towards southern Russia, the lower Danube and Byzantium—, but only to show its place in the history of the Oghuz/Ghuzz. The first migrations of the groups which followed the Saldjūḳids occurred as they took advantage of the appeals for help addressed to them in turn by the Sāmānids and various rival princes of the Ḳarakhānid family who had succeeded the Sāmānids in Mā warāʾ al-Nahr. In the official tradition of the dynasty, the ancestor Saldjūḳ is presented as having been the head of the army of a "Khazar" prince: presumably of a territory or a group recognizing Khazar suzerainty between the Aral Sea and the Volga. On the other hand, however, in the various political struggles of the first half of the 5th/11th century, the descendants of this Saldjūḳ were fighting against the Yabghu of the Oghuz, Shāh Malik, the ally of the Ghaznavids, and it is not impossible that they went so far as to lay claim to the position of Yabghu and that they were in fact recognized as such by a large section of their people. The details of the episodes of which little is known but which can lead to this conclusion have been the subject of a discussion between O. Pritsak and the present author which cannot be regarded as closed. (See O. Pritsak, *Der Untergang des Reiches des Oghusischen Reiches*, in *Mélanges Köprülü/Köprülü armağanı*, 1953; discussion by Cl. Cahen, in *JA*, 1954, 271-5 and Pritsak's reply in his communication to the Congress of Orientalists at Munich in 1957).

Thus the Saldjūḳid expansion drew into the old territories of Islam a substantial portion of the Oghuz/Ghuzz people; it is difficult to specify them more precisely, for the few names of tribes which are attested at that time do not distinguish them for us from the others, and also the fact that some elements of these tribes accompanied the Saldjūḳids does not preclude that others may have remained behind in their former habitat. Those who left it we find divided into two groups: one following Arslan-Isrāʾīl b. Saldjūḳ [*q.v.*] in the region of Bukhārā, and then established by Maḥmūd of Ghazna in 416/1025 in Khurāsān, the other, which was to take the place of the first group there in 426/1035, under the leadership of the nephews of Arslan, Toghrîl and Čaghrî [*qq.v.*]. The members of the first group, left without a leader by the disappearance of Arslan, proved themselves incapable of being assimilated to the administrative rules and the social structure of an old-established Iranian state: harried by the Ghaznavid troops, they succeeded, after detours across Iran, in reaching the frontiers of Armenia from which they returned when, on the death of Maḥmūd, the Ghaznavid family was split by quarrels, then, disturbed at the advance of the second Saldjūḳid group, escaped again towards the west, crossed the mountains of Kurdistan, and ended by being exterminated in Upper Mesopotamia in about 437/1045 by an alliance of Bedouins and Kurds. The Oghuz/Ghuzz of Toghrîl and Čaghrî, after several years of war, defeated Masʿūd of Ghazna at Dandānḳān in 431/1040, and conquered for their masters the greater part of Iran, and also ʿIrāḳ, etc.; most of them were concentrated in Ādharbaydjān, a country whose population is today still mainly Turkish; from there a section of them was to spread, in the second half of the 5th/11th century, into Byzantine Asia Minor, which they soon converted into what from then on was known as Turkey.

From the end of the 4th/10th century, however, there appears a new name (first attested in al-Muḳaddasī in about 375/985), that of Türkmen/Turcoman, applied to a large section of the Oghuz/Ghuzz peoples and sometimes also to the Ḳarluḳ, though it is impossible to state precisely in which contexts the term Oghuz/Ghuzz continued in use and in which Türkmen/Turcoman was preferred. Certainly it seems that at first the latter name was used exclusively of the Muslim Oghuz/Ghuzz in contrast to those who had not become Muslim and who continued to be called by their earlier name. But we find the name Oghuz/Ghuzz used later of those who had become Muslim. Broadly speaking it can be said that the name Türkmen/Turcoman is used by writers of the territories comprising the Saldjūḳid empire and its successor states to indicate those of the Oghuz/Ghuzz who were the descendants of the groups which followed the Saldjūḳids (even although they later abandoned them to go, for example, into Byzantine Asia Minor); these writers applied the name Oghuz/Ghuzz to all the others, even later, when some of them in their turn were to come and settle in the Saldjūḳid territory (but without really being incorporated in the state). Foreign writers, on the other hand, or those who were hostile to the Saldjūḳids and their successors, used the name Ghuzz universally, with pejorative intent, of all the Turks on whose military strength these régimes depended; this was the case with the writers of Fāṭimid Egypt, and even with those who, in the Yemen, wrote of the conquest (albeit half Kurdish) of the country by the Ayyūbids, or with those in the Maghrib writing of the Ayyūbid drive towards Tripoli and Ifrīḳiya. We cannot pursue all these branches here and for details of the later history of the Oghuz/Ghuzz who proceeded in the 11th century to Iran and beyond, the reader is referred to the articles SALDJŪḲIDS and TÜRKMEN.

There remained, however, in Central Asia a certain number of them who, from 538/1143, were driven back by the conquest of the Ḳarakhānid territories (including Mā warā᾽ al-Nahr) by the non-Muslim Ḳara-Khitay. The majority of them settled, with the more or less willing agreement of the Saldjūḳid authorities, in the eastern part of Khurāsān, in the region of Balkh. But, as was the case earlier when the first Turcomans settled in Ghaznavid territory, this new group of Oghuz/Ghuzz (thus called in contemporary sources) proved impossible to assimilate into an organized state. Sultan Sandjar tried to subdue them by force and, like the Ghaznavid Masʿūd, a century earlier, was himself heavily defeated by them (548/1153). But whereas the Turcomans, led by the Saldjūḳids, had founded an empire, the Oghuz/Ghuzz of this period merely helped to spread anarchy throughout Khurāsān. Finally they were decimated and subdued by the Khʷārizmshāhs, although one of them, Malik Dīnār [q.v.], ousting other Saldjūḳids, proceeded to make himself master for several years of their principality of Kirmān. The difference arises in part certainly from the fact that the Saldjūḳids had been able to lead their Turcomans on to other conquests, while the absence of a great leader and the general political conditions of the 6th/12th century allowed the Oghuz/Ghuzz of Khurāsān no prospect beyond that of converting Khurāsān into a region of grazing lands for their convenience.

The above episode is the last in which we find the Oghuz/Ghuzz in action under this name; beyond the frontiers of Islam their place had been taken by the Ḳïpčaḳ, many of whom moreover in their turn began to swell the army of the ruler of Khʷārizm. The foundation of the Mongol empire, in the 7th/13th century, led of course to the incorporation or to the expulsion of many Turcomans who were descended from the former Oghuz/Ghuzz, but henceforward the name is no longer found used of a group of people which still exists, whereas that of Türkmen has survived until the present day in Central Asia.

It was at this time, however, that among these descendants of the Oghuz/Ghuzz, confronted with the Mongols, there developed, in an atmosphere of veneration of the past and of their ancestors, the legend known as that of Oghuz-Khān, the vast spread and possibly also the relative antiquity of which are attested by versions extending from Central Asia (in Uyghur) to Asia Minor (in particular the popular Turkish story of Dede Ḳorḳut [q.v.], composed under the Aḳ-Ḳoyunlu in the 9th/15th century). It represents the descendants of Oghuz Khān as being divided into 24 tribes, and of these it is certain that 22 were already known, by name and by their tamghas, to Maḥmūd Kāshgharī, the Muslim Turk of the second half of the 5th/11th century whose dictionary provides such noteworthy information about his fellow-Turks; a certain number of these tribes are attested in historical events, but only the Ḳïnïḳ (and then solely as the tribe of the Saldjūḳids), the Yïva, Salghur, Avshar and the

Döger appear before the Mongol period. The Saldjūḳid conquest had taken place over their heads and broken them up. It was Rashīd al-Dīn, the great historian of the Mongols, who gave to the Muslim world the first written account of the legend, and it is from him that it was borrowed by the later authors who related it for educated Turks, writers such as Yazïdjï-oghlu, the 9th/15th century adapter of Ibn Bībī in Asia Minor, or the famous prince Abu ᾽l-Ghāzī in Central Asia in the following century. But although the legend reflects after its fashion the regions in which it grew up, there would seem to be no justification for using it as a basis for a reconstruction of the authentic history of the early Oghuz/Ghuzz, though a future scholar may find a way of making some use of it in this respect.

Bibliography: The Oghuz/Ghuzz are known in varying degree to nearly all the geographers from Ibn Khurradādhbih. The main information, much of which is collected in Russian translation in V. I. Belyaev, *Arabskie istočniki po istorii Turkmen i Turkmenii*, i, Moscow-Leningrad 1939, is found in the following: Iṣṭakhrī, 9 and 217-22, completed by Ibn Ḥawḳal, ed. Kramers, 389, 512 and Muḳaddasī, 274; works based on Djayhānī: Ḥudūd al-ʿālam, 100-1 and 122, Marwazī 29 (both ed. Minorsky), and Gardīzī; Ibn al-Faḳīh al-Hamadhānī in the Mashhad MS described by A. Zeki Velidi in *Izv. Ak. Nauk. SSSR*, 1924, 237-48; Masʿūdī, *Murūdj*, i, 212-3 and ii, 18-9 (pagination reproduced in Pellat's trans., in progress); Bīrūnī, and even, later still, Idrīsī and Yāḳūt. Of particular interest, at the beginning of the 4th/10th century, is the account of the journey of Ibn Faḍlān, ed. Zeki Velidi, 1939, A. P. Kovalevsky, 1956, and Sāmī Dahān, 1959, Fr. tr. M. Canard in *AIEO Alger*, xvi (1958). The principal historians to be considered are those of the Ghaznavids and the Saldjūḳids, especially Bayhaḳī and Ibn al-Athīr, but also the *Akhbār al-dawla al-Saldjūḳiyya*, ed. Moh. Iqbal, the *Saldjūḳnāma* of Ẓāhir al-Dīn Nīshāpūrī, ed. Gelāleh Khāvar (better than the adaptation of him by Rāwandī), the *Mudjmal al-tawārīkh*, ed. Bahār, 102-3 and 421, the anonymous *Taʾrīkh-i Sīstān*, Gardīzī already mentioned, ed. Moh. Iqbal, etc. See also Khʷārizmī, *Mafātīḥ al-ʿulūm*, 120. For the events of the 6th/12th century see the historians of the Saldjūḳids (reign of Sandjar); Ibn al-Athīr again; Djuwaynī, *Taʾrīkh-i Djahān-gushā*, ii. A special place is occupied by the *Dīwān lughāt al-Turk* of Maḥmūd Kāshgharī, a work not only of lexicography, but of remarkable and unique general information, ed. Kilisli Rifʿat (1917) and in facsimile with Turkish tr. by Besim Atalay (1939). For the legend of Oghuz Khān the principal texts have been cited in the article; the *Kitāb-i Dede Ḳorḳut* should be consulted in the ed. with a very full preface by E. Rossi. For the Chinese sources (on the Toḳuz-Oghuz only), see J. Hamilton, art. cited; for the Byzantine sources, J. Moravcsik, *Byzantino-Turcica²*, 1960, s.v. *Ouzoi*.

It is impossible to enumerate here all the studies which in one way or another refer to the Oghuz (a fair number of them are listed in Pearson's *Index Islamicus*); a good brief restatement of many of the questions has appeared in ch. vii of C. E. Bosworth, *The Ghaznevids ...*, Edinburgh 1963; and in spite of their date the contributions of Barthold to *EI¹* [GHUZZ and TURKS] remain generally useful, also his general survey in the *Histoire des Turcs d'Asie Centrale* (Fr. tr. of his

Zwölf Vorlesungen über die Geschichte der Türken Mittelasiens, lectures delivered in 1926), and his developments in his *Turkestan down to the Mongol Invasion*, Engl. tr. 1928; see also the commentaries of V. Minorsky in his editions of the *Ḥudūd al-ʿālam* and of Marwazī cited above, and the anonymous *Istoriya Turkmenii*, Tashkent 1940. Among the special works, for the origins we limit ourselves to referring to Hamilton cited above; for the history of the Oghuz/Ghuzz in Central Asia in the 4th/10th and the 5th/11th centuries, Houtsma, *Die Ghuzenstämme*, in *WZKM*, ii (1888); J. Marquart, *Ueber das Volkstum der Komanen*, *Abh. d. K. Ges. d. Wiss. Göttingen*, N.F. xiii (1914); M. F. Köprülü[zāde], *Oghuz etnolozhisine dāʾir taʾrīkhī notlar*, in *Türkiyāt Medjmūʿasi*, i (1925), 185-211; A. J. Yakubovskiy, *Seldjukskoe dviženie i Turkmenî v XI vekov*, in *Izv. Ak. Nauk SSSR*, 1936; S. P. Tolstov, *Goroda Guzov*, in *Sovetskaya Etnografiya*, 1947, and especially *Po sledam drevnekhorezmiyskoy tsivilizatsii* (German trans. *Auf den Spuren der altchoresmischen Kultur*), 1953, a basic synthesis of the results of the archaeological investigations carried out by the author and others up to that date, with significant historical implications; O. Pritsak, *Der Untergang des Ogusischen Jabgu* (see above in the art.); Cl. Cahen, *Les tribus turques d'Asie occidentale pendant la période seldjukide*, in *WZKM*, li (1948-52), and *Le Maliknameh et l'histoire des origines seldjukides*, in *Oriens*, ii (1949); Ibr. Kafesoğlu, *Türkmen adı, manası ve mahiyeti*, in *Jean Deny Armağanı*, 1958; Tahsin Banguoğlu, *Oguzlar ve Oguzeli üzerine*, in *Turk dili araştırmalar yıllığı Belleten*, 1959 (based on Maḥmūd Kāshgharī). For the events of the 6th/12th century, Barthold, *Sultan Sindjar i Guzy*, in *Zap. VO*, xx (1912); M. Köymen, *Büyük Selcuklular Imparatorluğunda Oğuz isyanı ve istilası*, in *Ankara Üniv. Dil. ve Tar-Coğr. Fak. Dergisi*, v/2 and 5 (1947), with German tr.; Ibr. Kafesoğlu, *Harezmşahlar devleti tarihi*, 1956. For the legend of Oghuz Khān, see W. Bang and G. R. Rahmati, *Die Legende von Oghuz Khan*, 1932; E. Rossi, preface to his ed. of *Dede Ḳorḳut* mentioned above; M. Kaplan, *Oğuz Kağan Destanı ile Dede Korkut kitabında eşya ve aletler*, in *Jean Deny Armağanı*, 1958. This article was prepared before the publication of the art. Oğuz in *IA*.

(Cl. Cahen)

ii.—Muslim West

In the Middle Ages al-Ghuzz (or al-Aghzāz, or al-Ghuzziyyūn) indicated the Turkish or Turcoman mercenaries who twice penetrated North Africa by way of Egypt. The first Aghzāz appeared, in the middle of the 6th/12th century, in the army which the Almohad ʿAbd al-Muʾmin sent to conquer Ifrīḳiya (553/1158). A group of them was introduced into Ifrīḳiya by Ḳarāḳūsh al-Ghuzzī [*q.v.*], an adventurer of Armenian descent, the freedman of a brother of Saladin, and Ibrāhīm b. Ḳarātakīn, who were sent by the ruler of Egypt and Syria to conquer the eastern Maghrib. Ḳarāḳūsh had appeared in 568/1172-3 in Tripoli. After several adventures, including imprisonment in Cairo, he was again in Tripolitania in 573/1177-8 to fight beside the Banū Ghāriya [*q.v.*]. But Ibn Ḳarātakīn was killed and the family of Ḳarāḳūsh, his sons, his possessions and some of his mercenaries fell into the power of the Almohad caliph Abū Yūsuf Yaʿḳūb al-Manṣūr, after the fall of Gabès (10 Shaʿbān 583/15 October 1187) and of Gafsa, three months later. These Ghuzz, of proved courage, having given proofs also of their submission, were then transferred to Marrākush and formed into a corps d'élite, regularly paid, which the caliph put at the service of the régime. Armed with a bow which was named after them (*al-ghuzzī*), they fought in all the battles and were very much in favour, but without being absorbed into the population (they had their own cemetery).

About 660/1261, there appeared in North Africa a new wave of Ghuzz, but the name this time refers to Kurds, fleeing before the conquests of Hūlāgū [*q.v.*]. When the Almohad dynasty fell, some took service with the ʿAbd al-Wādids of Tlemcen, others with the Ḥafṣids of Tunis, others finally settled at Marrākush where they passed into the service of the Marīnid dynasty who made much use of them in their expeditions of the Holy War in Spain where, with the archers of Ceuta, they formed the front line; they constituted also the personal bodyguard of the sultan. With time and with the appearance of portable fire-arms the Moroccan Ghuzz lost some of their importance. In the middle of the 16th century they are no longer referred to as Ghuzz but as Turks, whether they were mercenaries or not; in the 17th century their name, retained in Portuguese (*algoz*) with the meaning of hangman, is applied only to public executioners.

The Ghuzz used by the Almohads in their expeditions of the Holy War are mentioned by many of the mediaeval European historians.

Bibliography: A. Bel, *Les Benou Ghaniya*, Paris 1903; ʿAbd al-Wāḥid al-Marrākushī, *Muʿdjib*, ed. Dozy, 210-1 (ed. M. Elfassi, Salé 1938, 176-8; tr. Fagnan, *Hist. des Almohades*, 250-2; Sp. tr. Huici, 240-2); Ibn Khaldūn, *Hist. des Berbères*, tr. de Slane[2], ii, 91, iii, 43 and index, s.v. Caracoch and Ghuzz; Ibn al-Athīr, *Annales du Maghreb et de l'Espagne*, tr. Fagnan, in the index s.v. Turcs; Dozy, *Suppl.*, ii, 210; Gaudefroy-Demombynes, *Une lettre de Saladin au calife almohade*, in *Mélanges René Basset*, ii, Paris 1923; Ibn Faḍl Allāh al-ʿUmarī, *Masālik al-abṣār*, tr. G. Demombynes, Paris 1927; J. M. Solignac, *Trav. hydr. Ḥafṣides de Tunis*, 2ème congrès de la Féder. des Soc. Sav. de l'Afrique du Nord, Tlemcen 1936 (ii/1, 562-4); R. Brunschvig, *Ḥafṣides*, ii, 80; E. Lévi-Provençal, *Trente sept lettres almohades*, ar. Rabat 1941, tr. in *Hespéris*, 1941; A. Huici, *Historia politica del Imperio almohade*, 2 vols., Tetuan 1956-7; *Romania*, ccxliv (1935), 488; J. F. P. Hopkins, *Medieval Muslim government in Barbary*, London 1958, 79-82.

(G. Deverdun)

iii.—Sudan

In the Sudan the term Ghuzz was used of the hereditary *kāshifs* of Lower Nubia (between the First and Third Cataracts of the Nile) during the Ottoman period; more generally, the tribe formed by their kin. The name, as in Egyptian usage, was equivalent to *Mamlūks*, and the Ghuzz should therefore be distinguished from the hereditary garrison-troops (*ḳalʿedjis*) of Bosniak origin in Aswān, Ibrīm and Sāy, who were called *ʿOthmānlīs*. The founder of the tribe is called by Burckhardt, Ḥasan "Coosy" (probably *Ḳuzzī* for *Ghuzzī*), and his coming, as commander of the Bosniaks, is placed in the reign of Sultan Selīm I: this may be too early. The hereditary *kāshiflik*, which had its headquarters at al-Dirr, and was virtually autonomous, survived until the time of Muḥammad ʿAlī Pasha. At the time of the Turco-Egyptian invasion of the Sudan (1820-1), Ismāʿīl Kāmil Pasha appointed a member of the tribe, Ḥasan, to administer the territory between Aswān and Wādī Ḥalfā. The vestiges of the traditional authority of the G̲h̲uzz tribal chiefs vanished some sixty years later, when the area was placed under military government at the time of the Mahdia.

Bibliography: J. L. Burckhardt, *Travels in Nubia*, London 1819, 133-9; Naʿūm S̲h̲uḳayr, *Taʾrīk̲h̲ al-Sūdān*, Cairo [1903], ii, 108-10.

(P. M. Holt)

GIAOUR [see GABR and KĀFIR].

GIBRALTAR [see D̲J̲ABAL ṬĀRIḲ].

GĪLĀN, a historic region around the delta of the river Safīd-rūd [q.v.], was the homeland of the Gēl people (Gelae, Γῆλαι; = Καδούσιοι) in antiquity. The present Persian inhabitants, who speak a special dialect (cf. G. Melgunoff, *Essai sur les dialectes . . . du G̲h̲îlân . . .*, in *ZDMG*, xvii (1868), 195-224, and the article IRAN: Languages) bear the name Gīlak (at an earlier period also Gīl). The derivation of the name from *gil* "clay", in allusion to the marshes of the region, is a piece of folk etymology.

In the middle ages Gīlān first extended as far as the Čālūs in the south east; later it ran parallel on its eastern side with the Pulu-rūd and included Čābūksār. In the north east Gīlān verged on the region of Tālis̲h̲ [q.v.] which was sometimes counted as part of it. After Tālis̲h̲ was ceded to Russia by the Peace of Gulistan of 1813, this frontier was replaced by the river Astāra. For some 225 km. Gīlān is bounded by the Caspian Sea; towards the interior the frontier is the mountain-chain forming the northern limit of the high plateau of Iran, and in this direction Gīlān is between 25 and 105 km. wide. In the 10th-11th centuries the mountainous areas in the south of the region bore the name of Daylam [q.v.]; their inhabitants were often the enemies of the real natives of Gīlān. As the inhabitants see it, the area is divided by the Safīd-rud into two regions; "beyond the river and before the river"—Biya Pīs̲h̲ in the east (land of the early Amardoi) and Biya Pas in the west (land of the Gelae). In the 19th century the area was divided into first four and then five regions. In 1938 the population was estimated at 450,000, mostly S̲h̲īʿī Persians (Gīlak and Tālis̲h̲, particularly in the mountains) but also Jews, Armenians, and gypsies, who occupied an area of some 14,000 square km. In the middle ages the first capital was Dūlāb (= Gaskar (?) according to Muḳaddasī), then Fūman [q.v.] and Lāhīd̲j̲ān [q.v.] according to Mustawfī Ḳazwīnī, and finally, after Gīlān was incorporated in the Ṣafawī empire, Ras̲h̲t [q.v.], which remained the capital under Nādir [q.v.] and to the present day. Since 1938 Gīlān has formed the administrative district of Ras̲h̲t in the first canton (Ostān) of the empire of Īrān, linking the country with areas further south (see IRAN, with statistics and map).

Gīlān has a warm, damp, often tiring climate. Even in the middle ages, accordingly, its people were often to be seen dressed in only short trousers or "almost naked" (Ibn al-At̲h̲īr, Būlāḳ ed., viii, 77). The luxuriant forest provided (and still provides) the materials for the wooden houses with verandas (Iṣṭak̲h̲rī, 205, 211; Yāḳūt, i, 183) characteristic of Gīlān and Māzandarān [q.v.]. In the middle ages agriculture (which was a profitable pursuit) was left mainly to the women (*Ḥudūd*, 136 f.) and consisted chiefly of rice-growing and silkworm-breeding, which had been introduced by the Genoese; its products were exported to the Mediterranean area via Tana on the northern shores of the Black

Sea as early as the 14th century (W. Heyd in *Zeitschrift für Staatswissenschaften*, xviii (1862), 692). In modern times tobacco has come to be grown. Fishing made an important contribution to the inhabitants' food supplies; admittedly in the middle ages most journeys across the Caspian Sea began from Ābaskūn [q.v.] and not from Gīlān as in modern times (cf. B. N. Zak̲h̲oder, *Povolž'e i Yu. V. Kaspiya* [*The Volga Basin and the south-eastern part of the Caspian Sea*], in *Folia Orientalia*, i/2, Warsaw 1959, 231-50). As for mineral resources, Gīlān possesses a certain amount of copper and lead.

As with all the area along the southern shore of the Caspian Sea, the northern mountain-chain of the Iranian plateau and its climate have protected Gīlān from inland invaders (Arabs as well as Turks and Mongols) throughout the whole of its history. However, in 301/913-4 the Vikings (Rūs) made a successful attack from the sea (Masʿūdī, ii, 20-4; B. Dorn, *Caspia*, St. Petersburg 1875 (*Mem. Imp. Ac. of Sciences*, 7th Series, xxiii/1); idem, in *Quellen*, iv, p. IV f., 18) and in 1638 and 1667 the Cossacks followed their example in Ras̲h̲t. The inhabitants of the country, particularly the Daylamīs [see DAYLAM], had a great influence (above all in the 10th century) on the history of their neighbours and even on the Caliphate (cf. BUWAYHIDS/BŪYIDS). Since Gīlān with her clans and her local rulers was nearly always independent, from the period of the Achaemenids and the Sasanians, the Zoroastrian faith and some Nestorian colonies could survive there for a long time (Thomas of Marga, *Book of the governors*, ed. E. A. W. Budge, London 1893, ii, 480; Jean Dauvillier, in *Mélanges Cavallera*, Toulouse 1948, 279, with bibliography). The doctrines of the S̲h̲īʿī Zaydīs penetrated into Gīlān from the neighbouring countries of Ṭabaristān [q.v.] and Māzandarān [q.v.] and brought the Nāṣirwand dynasty into the country (on the literary productions of the Zaydīs there see R. Strothmann, in *Isl.*, ii (1911), 60-3). Little more is known as to the details of the history of Gīlān in these centuries. The country came under the nominal rule of the states of the Ziyārids [q.v.], the Būyids and the Kākūids [q.v.] as well as the Great Sald̲j̲ūḳs [q.v.]; on this see Ann K. S. Lambton, *Landlord and peasant in Persia*, London 1953, 60. Hence Gīlān paid tribute, at least for a time (for details see Spuler, *Iran*, 469). In connexion with this development Sunnī Islam found general favour and even occasional helpers in some of the many dynasties which shared the country until the end of the 16th century. Christianity and Zoroastrianism faded away. (L. Rabino di Borgomale, *Les dynasties locales du Gîlân et du Daylam* in *JA*, ccxxxvii (1949), 301-50, gives a full account of these dynasties, which is too detailed to be reproduced here). In 706/1307 the Ilk̲h̲ān Öld̲j̲eytü [q.v.] succeeded in forcing the country to acknowledge his overlordship, but its native dynasty remained. In the western part of the country at that time the *mad̲h̲hab*s of the Ḥanbalīs and the less numerous S̲h̲āfiʿīs preponderated as did the now extinct *mad̲h̲hab* of the historian and Ḳurʾān commentator al-Ṭabarī (who indeed came from this region). In the east the Zaydīs had remained (cf. Kās̲h̲ānī, *Taʾrīk̲h̲*, Paris, Bibl. Nat., supp. persan, ms. 1419, fol. 38r to 49v; this manuscript is to be published by Professor Horký of Prague). From 762/1361 the Kār-Kiyā dynasty managed to seize the dominant position in Lāhīd̲j̲ān and lost it only when S̲h̲āh ʿAbbās I incorporated Gīlān in the Ṣafawid state in 1000/1592. In 1060/1650 it was put under the direct rule of the central power (cf. Lambton, *op. cit.*, 108). Since then Gīlān has belonged to Persia, apart from the years between 1136/1724 and 1146/1734 when it was annexed by the Russians who, however, finally left it on account of its climate. From 1917 to 1921 the Bolsheviks tried to impose their rule on it; in the end they succeeded with the help of intermediaries in founding a Soviet republic of Gīlān (cf. Kurt Geyer, *Die Sowjetunion und Iran*, Tübingen 1955, 13-8, especially 14, note, sources and bibliography). All these attempts were finally brought to an end when Riḍa Shāh [*q.v.*] took over the government and, later on, the throne.

Bibliography: Apart from works named in the article: L. Rabino di Borgomale, *Les provinces caspiennes de la Perse*: *Le Guîlân*, Paris 1917 (condensed version of a special number of *RMM*, ix-x (1915-6); a detailed historical and geographical account with a list of the older and specialized literature on the subject, including descriptions of travels and consular accounts, and special maps). Geography: *Ḥudūd al-ʿālam*, 136 f., 388-91; Le Strange, 172-5 and Map V; Rabino, *Deux descriptions du Gîlân du temps des Mongols*, in *JA*, ccxxxviii, 325-34 (after Ḳāshānī and ʿUmarī); Brockhaus-Efron, *Entsiklopediya*, viii A (16), 1893, 688 f.; *BSE*², ii, 1952, 378 f. History: ʿAbbās Kadīvar, *Taʾrīkh-i Gīlān*, Tehran 1940 (inaccessible to me); Spuler, *Iran*, 545 and index; idem, *Mongolen*², 108 f., 165 f., index. Sources: Storey, i/2, 361-3 and 1298, no. 479, 481-3 (cf. with this no. ʿAbd al-Fattāḥ Fūmanī in i, 60). Maps (apart from those already named): Rabino, *Carte de la province du Guîlân*, Lyon 1914; *Ḥudūd*, 389. See also the Bibliographies of the articles on towns mentioned above and of DAYLAM, MĀZANDARĀN and ṬABARISTĀN.

(B. Spuler)

AL-**GILDAKĪ** [see Supplement, s.v. AL-DJILDAKĪ].

GILGIT [see Supplement; for the languages of the region, see DARDIC AND KĀFIR LANGUAGES, vi].

GIMBRI [see ḲONBUR].

GINUKH [see DIDO].

GIPSIES [see CINGĀNE, LŪRĪ, NŪRĪ, ZUṬṬ].

GIRAFFE [see ZARĀFA].

GIRĀY, cognomen borne by the members of the dynasty which ruled in the Crimea from the beginning of the 9th/15th century until 1197/1783. The family was descended from Togha Temür, a younger son of Čingiz Khān's son Djoči. Möngke Temür, the Khān of the Golden Horde (665/1267-679/1280), had granted the Crimea and Kafa as *nuntukh* (appanage) to his son Urang Temür (Öreng Timur) (Abu 'l-Ghāzī Bahādur Khān, *Shedjere-i Türk*, St. Petersburg 1871, 173). During the civil wars which from 760/1359 onwards convulsed the domains of the Golden Horde, the descendants of Togha Temür joined in the struggle and laid claim to the Khānate; they finally succeeded in establishing a state in the Crimea, independent of the other khāns ruling at Ulugh Yurt, the centre of the Golden Horde. There survives a coin of 796/1393-4 issued by Tash-Temür in the Crimea in his own name, and another of 797/1394-5 with Tash-Temür's name on one face and the name of Tokhtamīsh Khān [*q.v.*] on the other (A. K. Markov, *Inventarnīy Katalog musulmanskikh monetʾ Imperatorskago Ermitaža*, St. Petersburg 1896, p. 491, nos. 1239-40; Lane-Poole, *Cat.*, vi, p. 184, no. 558). In Tokhtamīsh's struggles against Tīmūr and later against Edigü, the descendants of Togha Temür were always on the side of Tokhtamīsh, and were from time to time forced to relinquish control of the Crimea to khāns supported by Edigü (for coins struck in the Crimea by Temür-Ḳutluḳ Khān between 802/1399 and 810/1407 and by Pūlād Khān in 811/1408 see Spuler, *Horde*, 140-1, notes 25, 32). Upon the death of Edigü in 822/1419, Tash-Temür's son Ghiyāth al-Dīn gained control of the Crimea, where we find his brother Dewlet-Birdi ruling in 830/1427 (when he sent an embassy to the Mamlūk sultan Bārsbāy: ʿAynī, *ʿIḳd al-djumān*, Bayazıd Public Lib., Istanbul, MS Veliyüddin 2369, *s.a.*). Henceforward the dynasty's efforts were concentrated on maintaining their hold on the Crimean peninsula and, when opportunity offered, on seizing Sarāy and thus acquiring the khānate of the Golden Horde.

According to local tradition in the Crimea (*al-Sabʿ al-sayyār* [see Bibl.], 72), Ghiyāth al-Dīn, in accordance with the customs of the Golden Horde (see *ʿUmdat al-tawārīkh*, 204), was brought up by his *atalīḳ* [*q.v.*], who belonged to the Kerey tribe, and later, out of respect for his *atalīḳ*, gave his first son the name Ḥādjdjī Kerey; thereafter the members of this family bore the cognomen (*laḳab*) Kerey/Girāy.

According to G. Németh (*A Honfoglaló Magyarság Kialakulása*, Budapest 1930, 265-8), the name is composed of *ker*, 'giant', with the diminutive suffix *-ey*. As a name borne by various sections of the tribe, it is found among the Ḳazaḳs, the Türkmen, the Bashdjirt, the Buriats and the Mongols, with various pronunciations: Kerey, Kirey, Kiray, plural: Kereit. When Čingiz Khān defeated the powerful Kereit ruler Ong Khān, some of the Kereit fled to the West, the rest being scattered among the Mongol tribes (*Secret history*, § 186; Turkish tr. by Ahmet Temir, Ankara 1948, 109; German tr. by E. Haenisch, Leipzig 1948, 74). Thus the Kereit, either fleeing before the Mongols or coming with them, were spread over a very wide area, as far west as the Crimea. Until recent times the Taraḳlī branch of the Uvak-Kirey led a nomad existence among the Ḳazaḳs in the valleys of the Irtish, the Sarı Su and the Chu (H. H. Howorth, *Hist. of the Mongols*, ii, London 1876, 6, 11). The *tamgha* of the Khāns of the Crimea (for its shape see the coins of Mengli Girāy in *Müze-i Hümāyūn*: *meskūkāt kataloghu*, 3rd section, Istanbul 1318/1900, 211, and *IA*, iv, 784b) was called *taraḳ tamgha*.

The Kerey were one of the four main tribes (*keshik*) upon which the Khānate of the Golden Horde depended. The Kerey, dwelling east of the Don and in the northern Caucasus, gave their support to Ḥādjdjī Girāy. Only one of his sons, Mengli, used the cognomen Girāy, but it was borne by all Mengli's sons and descendants, and was assumed also by some of the begs of the Shirin who married into the ruling family (*ʿUmdat al-tawārīkh*, 200).

Ḥādjdjī Girāy made an alliance with the Ottoman Sultan Meḥemmed II in 858/1454 [see ḤĀDJDJĪ GIRĀY], and this alliance was maintained by his successors. In 880/1475, called in by Eminek Mīrzā to assist him against the Genoese, who were stirring up internal troubles, the Ottomans responded immediately and occupied the Genoese fortresses in the southern Crimea; Mengli Girāy [*q.v.*], released from prison, was placed on the throne as a client of the Ottoman Sultan (H. İnalcık, *Yeni vesikalara göre Kırım Hanlığının Osmanlı tâbiliğine girmesi*, in *Belleten*, viii/30 (1944), 185-229).

At first, the Girāy rulers were in alliance with the Grand Dukes of Moscow, against the Khāns of the

Golden Horde (ruling at Sarāy and hoping to recover control of the Crimea), and against the Jagiellos of Poland. But after 926/1520, the k͟hāns of the Crimea laid claim, as being the rightful heirs, to the patrimony of the Golden Horde, and when the Russians began to threaten Ḳazan embarked on an unrelenting struggle against them, which bore the character of a religious enterprise (*g͟hazā*). In 927/1521 Ṣāḥib Girāy [*q.v.*] became K͟hān of Ḳazan; three years later he went to Istanbul, being succeeded, until spring 938/1532, by Ṣafā Girāy (Hādī Aṭlāsī, *Ḳazan K͟hānlig͟hī*, Kazan 1913, 125-35). When in Rabīʿ I 939/October 1532 Ṣāḥib Girāy returned as K͟hān of the Crimea, he attacked the Russians, and after a long struggle the Girāy house were obliged to cede the Volga basin and the old capital of the Golden Horde, Tak͟ht-ili (Ulug͟h Yurt); Ḳazan was lost in 959/1552, Astrak͟han in 961/1554. It is from this period onwards that the Girāy house, who had heretofore claimed to follow an independent policy, adopted Ottoman protection against the Russian threat, acting in ever closer cooperation with the Ottomans in the wars in Central Europe and against Persia [see ḲIRÎM]. The first joint military enterprise had been the Moldavian campaign of 881/1476, the second was Süleymān I's Moldavian campaign of 945/1538.

The Ottomans recognized the Girāy house as their intermediaries in their political relations with northern powers: ambassadors of Poland and Russia would first present themselves at the court of the K͟hān and then proceed to the Porte.

Domains. The capital is referred to in Ḥād͟jd͟jī Girāy's *yarlîḳ* of 857/1453 as "Orda-i muʿaẓẓam Ḳîrḳ-yirde Sarāy" (see A. N. Kurat, *Altınordu, Kırım ve Türkistan Hanlarına ait yarlık ve bitikler*, Istanbul 1940, 62-80, plate 173-84). His coin of 845/1441 was struck at "Beldet-i Ḳîrîm", that of 847/1443 at "Ḳîrḳ-yir" (for these towns see V. D. Smirnov, *Krimskoye k͟hanstvo pod verk͟hovenstvom ottomanskoy Porti do načala XVIII. veka*, Odessa 1887, 102-22). Under Mengli Girāy the palace was moved from the strong citadel at Ḳîrḳ-yir into the valley, to the site now called Bag͟hčesāray (Simferopol). In the *yarlîḳ* Ḥād͟jd͟jī Girāy claims sovereignty over Taman, the Ḳîpčaḳ and Kabartay. In their *yarlîḳ*s the Girāy rulers give themselves the title '*Ulug͟h orda we Ulug͟h yurtnîñ we Des͟ht-i Ḳîpčaḳnîñ ve Tak͟ht-i Ḳîrîmnîñ .... Čerkesnîñ ve Tat bile Tavg͟hačnîñ Ulug͟h Pādis͟hāhî we hem Ulug͟h K͟hānî*'. In the attempt to establish their sovereignty over the Des͟ht-i Ḳîpčaḳ (the steppeland to the north of the Black Sea) and Circassia the K͟hāns had to engage in long struggles, achieving partial success particularly under Ṣāḥib Girāy I [*q.v.*]. Sultans of the Girāy family, with the title *Ser-ʿasker Sulṭān*, were sent to govern the K͟hānate's territories in Ḳuban, Bud͟jaḳ and Yedisan. Like the k͟hāns of the Golden Horde before them, the K͟hāns exacted an annual tribute of money and furs (known as *tîyîs͟h* and *bölek*) from the rulers of Russia and Poland. Since the K͟hāns always claimed sovereignty over the ports on the southern coast of the Crimea (Tat-ili), from 889/1484 onwards the Ottomans made them a yearly grant (*sāliyāne*) from the customs revenues of Kefe [*q.v.*] (a million and a half *akče*s annually). Meḥemmed Girāy I, and some later K͟hāns, attempted to establish direct control over these ports.

The dynasty first openly acknowledged the sovereignty of the Ottoman Sultan in Mengli Girāy's letter of Rabīʿ I 880/July 1475 (see H. İnalcık, *op. cit.*). Although the new relationship resulting from the strengthening of this sovereignty was later presented as arising from a special agreement, the texts adduced are clearly fabrications.

From Mengli Girāy onwards, the K͟hāns each had a *ḳalg͟hay* [*q.v.*] (also *ḳag͟halg͟hay*) as *walī ʿahd*, 'heir apparent', and from 992/1584 also a second *walī ʿahd* known as *Nūr al-Dīn* (*Nuradin*). According to the *Ḳānūn-i D͟jengīzī* (*türe, yasa*), the *ḳalg͟hay* should be the Khan's brother; when the throne fell vacant, the *ḳalg͟hay* became K͟hān and the *Nūr al-Dīn* became *ḳalg͟hay*. The attempts of some k͟hāns to appoint their sons to these posts caused disturbances and civil war. When the tribal aristocracy of the Crimea [see ḲIRÎM], following the *türe* and without reference to the Porte, appointed a *ḳalg͟hay* as the new k͟hān (as in the cases of G͟hāzī Girāy I and Toḳtamîs͟h Girāy), the Ottoman Sultan withheld his recognition and fierce conflicts resulted, but in general the Porte was influenced in its choice by the claims of the existing *ḳalg͟hay*. Of the forty k͟hāns, 24 had been the *ḳalg͟hay*, and five the *Nūr al-Dīn*.

From the time of Saʿādet Girāy (930/1524-938/1532) onwards, it became customary that one of the K͟hān's brothers should be sent to Istanbul as a hostage (Ferīdūn Beg, *Muns͟haʾāt al-salāṭīn*[1], ii, 167; Müned͟jd͟jim-bas͟hî, *Ṣaḥāʾif al-ak͟hbār*, ii, 699). Two of these hostages (Islām Girāy II and Bahādîr Girāy I) were sent to the Crimea as K͟hān. The K͟hān chosen received his diploma direct from the hand of the Ottoman Sultan and was presented with the *k͟hānlîḳ tes͟hrīfātî* (a sword, a banner, a *ḳalpaḳ* with a jewelled *sorg͟huč* and a sable robe) (see *Silāḥdār taʾrīk͟hi*, ii, 131, 683). When there was a campaign, the Sultan sent the K͟hān a gift of 40,000 gold pieces, known as *čizme-bahā*, which was distributed to the K͟hān's household troops and to the *mîrzā*s. The Sultan could depose, imprison or exile the K͟hān; occasionally the K͟hān was executed. When a K͟hān had to be appointed, the Porte usually came to an agreement with the S͟hirin Begi, the leader of the Crimean tribal aristocracy. When a K͟hān succeeded to the throne, the hostage, together with other members of the dynasty who found themselves in danger, entered the Ottoman domains and were installed in *čiftlik*s in various parts of Rūmeli (Islimye, Yanbolu, Tekirdag͟hî, Čatald͟ja). When the succession to the Ottoman throne was threatened, the Girāy family was regarded as having a claim to it (*e.g.*, in the revolution of 1098/1687, see *Silāḥdār taʾrīk͟hi*, ii, 630).

The branch of the family known as Čoban Girāylar arose at the end of the 10th/16th century. The *ḳalg͟hay* Fetḥ Girāy, in return for ransom, sent back to her country the daughter of a Polish boyar who had been captured; on the way, the girl gave birth to a son, but Fetḥ Girāy refused to acknowledge the child as his and tried to have it killed. A certain Ḥād͟jd͟jī Aḥmed, who was travelling with the girl, hid the child in Moldavia and, when Fetḥ Girāy was killed in 1004/1596, brought him to the Crimea. He was appointed *Nūr al-Dīn*, with the name Dewlet Girāy; his descendants were called (pejoratively) 'Čoban Girāylar'. Although one of this line, ʿĀdil Girāy, was appointed K͟hān (1075/1665-1081/1670), the later K͟hāns denied that this branch was of royal blood and gave no further offices to its members.

By article 3 of the Ottoman-Russian treaty of Küčük Kaynard͟ja (8 D͟jumādā I 1188/17 July 1774), each signatory recognized the independence of the Girāy house, but on 20 S͟haʿbān 1197/21 July 1783 the Russians occupied and annexed the Crimea. In 1199/1785 the Ottomans considered appointing a member of the house as K͟hān over the Tatar tribes in Budjaḳ (Djewdet, *Taʾrīkh*, iii, 142); in 1201/1787, when war was declared on Russia, this plan was put into effect and Shahbāz Girāy, with the title of Khān, and later Bakht Girāy fought in the Ottoman ranks at the head of the Tatars of Budjaḳ. By article 6 of the treaty of Jassy (Yash), in 1206/1792, the Ottomans recognized the Russian annexation of the Crimea.

Bibliography: Further to references in the text: V. Velyaminov-Zernov, *Matériaux pour servir à l'histoire du Khanat de Crimée*, St. Petersburg 1864; A. Z. Soysal, *Jarlyki Krimskie z czasów Jana Kazimierza*, Warsaw 1939; K. V. Zettersteén, *Türkische, tatarische und persische Urkunden im Schwedischen Reichsarchiv*, Uppsala 1945, 78-128; B. Lewis, *Some Danish-Tatar exchanges in the 17th century*, in *Zeki Velidi Togan'a armağan*, Istanbul 1950-55, 137-46; O. Retowski, *Die Münzen der Girei*, Moscow 1905; Seyyid Meḥmed Riḍāʾ, *al-Sabʿ al-sayyār fī akhbār al-mulūk al-Tātār*, ed. Kāẓim Bik, Kazan 1832 (summary by Kazimirski, in *JA*, xii (1833)); Ḥalīm Girāy, *Gülbün-i khānān*, Istanbul 1287/1870, 2nd ed. Istanbul 1327/1909; ʿAbd al-Ghaffār, *ʿUmdat al-tawārīkh*, *TOEM* supplement, Istanbul 1324/1924; *Meḥmed Girāy taʾrīkhi*, Vienna National Lib., MS 1080. General accounts will be found in the works of Howarth and of Smirnov, cited above; also in J. v. Hammer-Purgstall, *Geschichte der Chane der Krim*, Vienna 1856, and H. İnalcık, article Giray, in *IA*, with a complete genealogical tree. (Halil Inalcik)

GIRESUN, a town on the Black Sea coast of Anatolia about 110 miles west of Trabzon, the principal town of a *vilayet*, with a population (1960) of 19,902. It is the Kerasos of antiquity (for the classical names and their possible permutations see A. D. Mordtmann, *Anatolien*, Hanover 1923, 405); threatened by the Turks from the 8th/14th century onwards, it came under Ottoman control with the Empire of Trebizond. The town has a favourable site on a peninsula of basaltic lava (tombolo) on which is built the acropolis, sheltering a small natural harbour, with an island nearby, the Ares of antiquity, now Giresun adası. The fortress was however of no great strength, and the town which spread out below it was exposed in the 17th century to the raids of the Cossacks (Ewliyā Čelebi, *Seyāḥatnāme*, ii, 70). Kerasos is said to have given its name to the cherry, introduced to Rome by Lucullus after his victory over Mithridates, but the cherry trees, which were still numerous in the region until the 19th century (W. J. Hamilton, *Researches in Asia Minor*, London 1842, i, 265) have been replaced by hazel-nut trees whose fruit is more easily stored and transported and for which Giresun is today the most important centre of preparation, trade and export, a position confirmed in 1961 by the completion of an artificial harbour enabling ships to come alongside the quay (trade about 1 million tons).

Bibliography: apart from the works cited, see *İA*, s.v. (B. Darkot); on the hazel-nut region of Giresun, X. de Planhol, *A travers les chaînes pontiques, plantations côtières et vie montagnarde*, in *Bulletin de l'Association de Géographes Français*, 1963, 2-11. (X. de Planhol)

GIRGĀ, (Djirdjā; an obsolete form Dadjirdjā is also found), a town and province of Upper Egypt. The name is said to be derived from a monastery of St. George (V. Denon, tr. A. Aikin, *Travels in Upper and Lower Egypt*, London 1803, ii, 25). The town originated in the late 8th/14th century as the tribal centre of Hawwāra [*q.v.*], who dominated Upper Egypt for the following two centuries. About 983/1576, the power of this tribe was broken, and Girgā became the seat of the governor of Upper Egypt, who was also *kāshif* of the Girgā district. The governors, who are variously referred to as *ḥākim al-Ṣaʿīd*, *amīr al-Ṣaʿīd*, and *bak Djirdjā*, belonged to the neo-Mamlūk élite, and frequently intervened in the factional struggles in Cairo. The *kāshiflik* of Girgā is represented today by the *mudīriyya* of the same name, although for some time after 1239/1823-4, in consequence of Muḥammad ʿAlī Pasha's administrative experiments, it was absorbed in a larger territorial unit. In 1859, Sōhāg (Sūhādj) took the place of Girgā as the provincial capital.

Bibliography: al-Maḳrīzī, *al-Bayān wa 'l-iʿrāb ʿammā bi-arḍ Miṣr min al-Aʿrāb*, ed. ʿAbd al-Madjīd ʿĀbidīn, Cairo 1961, 58; P. Vansleb, *Nouvelle relation ... d'un voyage fait en Egypte*, Paris 1677, 21-5; ʿAlī Mubārak, *al-Khiṭaṭ al-djadīda*, x, Cairo 1305, 53-5; H. A. B. Rivlin, *The agricultural policy of Muḥammad ʿAlī in Egypt*, Cambridge, Mass. 1961, 87-8, 323-4. (P. M. Holt)

GIRGENTI [see DJIRDJENT].

GIRISHK, a town of ca. 10,000 inhabitants, altitude 865 metres/2830 ft, on the Helmand River in present Afghanistan.

Girishk is not mentioned in sources before the time of Nādir Shāh, when he captured the citadel in 1737, but a fort probably had guarded the passage of the river at this site for a long time before this date. In the 19th century Girishk was the centre of the Barakzai Afghans, and as such assumed a new importance. The site was of strategic importance and Girishk played a role several times during the troubles of the 19th century.

At present the town is an important centre for the irrigation of the Helmand basin.

Bibliography: Le Strange, 346; S. K. Rishtiya, *Afganistan v XIX veke*, trans. into Russian, Moscow 1958, index; D. Wilber, *Afghanistan*, New Haven, Conn. 1954, index. (R. N. Frye)

GIRIT [see IḲRĪTISH].

GĪSŪ DARĀZ, Sayyid Muḥammad Gīsū Darāz, a celebrated Čishtī saint of the Deccan, was born at Delhi on 4 Radjab 721/30 July 1321. His ancestors originally came from Harāt, from where they migrated to India and settled at Delhi. His father, Sayyid Yūsuf Ḥusaynī *alias* Sayyid Rādjā, was a disciple of Shaykh Niẓām al-Dīn Awliyāʾ [*q.v.*]. Gīsū Darāz was a small child when Sultan Muḥammad b. Tughluḳ (725/1325-752/1351) embarked upon his Deccan experiment and forced the *ʿulamāʾ* and *mashāʾikh* of Delhi to migrate to Dawlatābād. Sayyid Rādjā left Delhi under duress and settled at Dawlatābād, where he died in 731/1330. In 735/1335-6 Gīsū Darāz left Dawlatābād with his widowed mother and returned to Delhi. He completed his study of the external sciences (*ʿulūm-i ẓāhir*) under Sayyid Sharaf al-Dīn Kaythalī, Mawlānā Tādj al-Dīn Bahādur and Ḳāḍī ʿAbd al-Muḳtadir. His search for a spiritual master brought him to Shaykh Naṣīr al-Dīn Čirāgh [*q.v.*], whom he served for years with single-minded devotion, and from whom he received the *khilāfa* and the title of Gīsū Darāz ('one possessing long locks of hair').

When Timur turned towards India (800/1398), Gīsū Darāz hastened to quit Delhi. He stayed for some time in Gwāliyār and then left for Gudjarāt where he was the guest of Khʷādja Rukn al-Dīn Kān-i Shakar. Later he migrated to Gulbargā and finally settled there. Fīrūz Shāh Bahmanī (800/1397-

825/1421) accorded him a warm welcome (no. 39 in the collection of his letters is addressed to the Sultan), but he could not enjoy the saint's confidence for long. According to Ghulām ʿAlī Āzād Bilgrāmī, it was his association with philosophers and the philosophic bent of his mind which alienated the saint from him. His successor, Sultan Aḥmad Shāh Bahmanī (825/1421-838/1435), however, succeeded in winning the golden opinion of Gīsū Darāz. According to the Burhān-i maʾāt̲h̲ir, the saint exercised a profound influence on his life. Gīsū Darāz died at Gulbargā on 16 D̲h̲u 'l-Ḳaʿda 825/1 November 1422. Aḥmad Shāh Bahmanī built a magnificent tomb over his grave. Hundreds of thousands of people gather there on the occasion of his ʿurs celebrations. The dargāh management now runs a publishing house, a monthly journal, a library and several schools and madrasas, including one for girls.

Gīsū Darāz was a profound scholar and a prolific writer. He was well-versed in the studies of the Ḳurʾān, ḥadīt̲h̲, fiḳh and taṣawwuf, and knew several languages, including Arabic, Persian, Sanskrit and Hindi. He was fully conversant with Hindū folklore and mythology and used to discuss religious problems with the Hindu yogīs and scholars (Dj̲awāmiʿ al-kalim, 118-9). He had correspondence and contact with eminent contemporary saints, such as Sayyid Muḥammad As̲h̲raf Dj̲ahāngīr Samnānī and Masʿūd Bakk. He expounded the Čis̲h̲tī mystic principles in the Deccan and produced a large number of works on different branches of the religious sciences. It is said that the number of his writings corresponds with the number of years he lived (i.e., 105). No Indo-Muslim Čis̲h̲tī saint has so many literary works to his credit.

Of the works produced by Gīsū Darāz, the following are particularly noteworthy: (A) Exegesis: (i) a mystical commentary on the Ḳurʾān (MS with Sayyid Muḥammad Ḥusaynī, sadjdjāda nas̲h̲īn, Gulbarga); (ii) another incomplete commentary on the lines of the Kas̲h̲s̲h̲āf. (B) Ḥadīt̲h̲: (iii) a commentary on the Mas̲h̲ārik al-anwār; (iv) Persian translation of the Mas̲h̲ārik. (C) Fiḳh: (v) S̲h̲arḥ al-Fiḳh al-akbar, edited by ʿAṭā Ḥusayn, Ḥaydarābād 1367. (D) Taṣawwuf: (vi) Maʿārif, an Arabic commentary on the ʿAwārif al-maʿārif of S̲h̲ayk̲h̲ S̲h̲ihāb al-Dīn Suhrawardī (MS in three volumes with the sadjdjāda nas̲h̲īn, Gulbarga); (vii) Commentary on ʿAwārif al-maʿārif in Persian (MS in two volumes with the sadjdjāda nas̲h̲īn, Gulbarga); (viii) S̲h̲arḥ Taʿarruf, commentary on the Taʿarruf of S̲h̲ayk̲h̲ Abū Bakr Muḥammad b. Ibrāhīm Buk̲h̲ārī; (ix) S̲h̲arḥ Ādāb al-murīdīn, Arabic commentary on the Ādāb al-murīdīn of S̲h̲ayk̲h̲ Ḍiyāʾ al-Dīn Abu 'l-Nadjīb ʿAbd al-Ḳāhir Suhrawardī; (x) Persian translation of Ādāb al-murīdīn; (xi) Commentary on the Fuṣūṣ al-ḥikam (this work is not extant, but from references to Ibn al-ʿArabī found in Maktūbāt (p. 22), K̲h̲ātima (pp. 18-9) and Dj̲awāmiʿ al-kalim (p. 99) it appears that he did not agree with his views); (xii) S̲h̲arḥ Tamhīdāt, a Persian commentary on the Tamhīdāt of ʿAyn al-Ḳuḍāt Hamadānī, edited by S. ʿAṭā Ḥusayn, Ḥaydarābād 1364; (xiii) S̲h̲arḥ Risāla-i Ḳus̲h̲ayriyya, Persian commentary on the Risāla of Ḳus̲h̲ayrī, ed. S. ʿAṭā Ḥusayn, Ḥaydarābād 1361; (xiv) S̲h̲arḥ Risāla-i Ḳus̲h̲ayriyya, in Arabic; (xv) Ḥazāʾir al-Ḳuds or ʿIs̲h̲k-nāma, edited by S. ʿAṭā Ḥusayn, Ḥaydarābād; (xvi) Asmār al-Asrār, edited by S. ʿAṭā Ḥusayn, Ḥaydarābād 1350 (commentary on a section of this work by S̲h̲āh Rafīʿ al-Dīn son of S̲h̲āh Walī Allāh Dihlawī in Madjmūʿ Tisʿ Rasāʾil, Delhi 1314); (xvii) K̲h̲ātima, edited by S. ʿAṭā Ḥusayn, Ḥaydarābād 1356; (xviii)

Maktūbāt, edited by ʿAṭā Ḥusayn, Ḥaydarābād 1362 (contains 66 letters; the As. Soc. of Bengal MS 1232 contains 61 only); (xix) Madjmūʿa-i Yāzda Rasāʾil, edited by S. ʿAṭā Ḥusayn, Ḥaydarābād 1360 (risāla 5 in this collection has been wrongly attributed to Gīsū Darāz; it was written by Imām Muẓaffar Balk̲h̲ī); (xx) Dj̲awāhir-i ʿus̲h̲s̲h̲āḳ, commentary on a risāla of S̲h̲ayk̲h̲ ʿAbd al-Ḳādir Gīlānī, edited by S. ʿAṭā Ḥusayn, Ḥaydarābād 1362; (xxi) Anīs al-ʿus̲h̲s̲h̲āḳ, collection of poems, ed. S. ʿAṭā Ḥusayn, Ḥaydarābād 1360.

Two early works—(I) Miʿrādj al-ʿas̲h̲iḳīn, (editions prepared by (i) Dr. M. ʿAbd al-Ḥaḳḳ, Delhi, (ii) Dr. Gopī Čand Nārang, Delhi, (iii) K̲h̲alīḳ Andjum, Delhi, (iv) Taḥsīn Sarwarī, (v) Dr. Nad̲h̲īr Aḥmad, ʿAlīgarh (typescript)) and (II) S̲h̲ikār nāma (editions: (i) Mubāriz al-Dīn Rafʿat, Ḥaydarābād, (ii) T̲h̲amīna S̲h̲awkat, Ḥaydarābād)—are also attributed to Gīsū Darāz but no convincing internal or external evidence has so far been put forward to establish the attribution.

Though these works are mostly in the nature of commentaries and summaries of earlier mystic classics, they are not wholly devoid of originality. Gīsū Darāz did not always conform to the traditional approach; in fact he had, as S̲h̲ayk̲h̲ ʿAbd al-Ḥaḳḳ Muḥaddit̲h̲ of Delhi has remarked, a peculiar mas̲h̲rab of his own. He was critical of both Ibn al-ʿArabī and ʿAyn al-Ḳuḍāt Hamadānī. He did not agree with the author of the Taʿarruf that a mystic cannot have the vision of God (ruʾyat) here in this world. He did not permit his disciples to adopt indiscriminately the practices of the yogīs. He was particularly fond of the Ādāb al-murīdīn and the ʿAwārif al-maʿārif, since they were of great value for one who wanted to organize k̲h̲ānḳāh life in lands without any deep mystic tradition. There is a desire in his works to bridge the gulf between s̲h̲arīʿa and ṭarīḳa, which he considered complementary rather than contradictory to each other. He explained some of the much-criticized practices of the Čis̲h̲tīs (e.g., prostration before the pīr and audition parties) in such a way that orthodox opposition to them was toned down. Great as an organizer, erudite as a scholar, Gīsū Darāz did not, however, succeed in maintaining the pan-Indian character of the Čis̲h̲tī sadjdjāda which he occupied. The era of the great Čis̲h̲tī S̲h̲ayk̲h̲s of the first cycle ended with his master, S̲h̲ayk̲h̲ Naṣīr al-Dīn Čirāg̲h̲ of Delhi.

Bibliography: ʿAbd al-ʿAzīz b. S̲h̲īr Malik Wāʿiẓī, Taʾrīk̲h̲ Ḥabībī wa-tad̲h̲kirat Murs̲h̲idī, a biography of Gīsū Darāz, completed in 849/1445-6 (MS As. Soc. of Bengal 246); Urdu translation of the above published from Rawḍatayn, Gulbargā; Sayyid Muḥammad Ḥusaynī, Dj̲awāmiʿ al-kalim, Kānpur 1356; Muḥammad ʿAlī Samānī, Siyar-i Muḥammadī, Allahabad; Niẓām Yamanī, Laṭāʾif-i As̲h̲rafī, Delhi 1295; S̲h̲ayk̲h̲ ʿAbd al-Ḥaḳḳ, Ak̲h̲bār al-ak̲h̲yār, Delhi 1309, 129-134; ʿAbd al-Raḥmān Čis̲h̲tī, Mirʾāt al-asrār, MS in personal collection, 734-42; Sayyid ʿAlī Ṭabāṭabā, Burhān-i maʾāt̲h̲ir, Ḥaydarābād 1355/1936, 43-4; Firis̲h̲ta, Taʾrīk̲h̲-i Firis̲h̲ta, Nawal Kishore, i, 316, ii, 399; Ghulām Muʿīn al-Dīn ʿAbd Allāh, Maʿāridj al-walāyat, MS in personal collection, i, 366-438; Āzād Bilgrāmī, Rawḍat al-awliyāʾ, Awrangābād 1892, 18-25; Muḥammad G̲h̲awt̲h̲ī S̲h̲aṭṭārī, Gulzār-i abrār, MS As. Soc. of Bengal, f. 45v; Min Allāh Ḥusaynī, K̲h̲awāriḳāt, an account of the life and spiritual attainments of Gīsū Darāz and his descendants, MSS: see Storey, 976; Gul Muḥammad Aḥmadpurī, Takmilat Siyar al-awliyāʾ, Delhi

1312, 20-3; Ghulām Sarwar, *Khazīnat al-aṣfiyā'*, Lucknow 1873, i, 381-2; Farīd al-Dīn, *Nawādir al-safar*, MS As. Soc. of Bengal 273, Safar 22; Ḥakīm Muḥammad ʿUmar, *Ḥālāt-i dil-gudāz maʿrūf ba Sawāniḥ Banda Nawaz* (Urdu), Delhi 1320; Abū Ṣāliḥ Muḥammad Čishtī, *Rasā'il-i Muḥammad Čishtī*, MS As. Soc. of Bengal 1265 f. 246v; anonymous, *Madḥ Gīsū Darāz*, a *mathnawī* in Dakhanī, MS As. Soc. of Bengal 1736; Bakhtāwar Khān, *Riyāḍ al-awliyā'*, MS Brit. Mus. Or. 1745, f. 162; Raḥmān ʿAlī, *Tadhkira ʿulamā'-i Hind*, Karachi 1961, 277; Mīrzā Muḥammad Akhtar, *Tadhkira awliyā'-i Hind*, Delhi 1928, i, 137-8; Sakhāwat Mīrzā, *Khwādja Gīsū Darāz ke Čand Hindī gīt*, in *Kawmī Zubān*, Karachi, July 1963, 21-4; Niẓāmī, *Ta'rīkh-i Mashāyikh-i Čisht*, Delhi 1953, 206-8. (K. A. Nizami)

GIZA, GIZEH [see AL-ḲĀHIRA].

GLASS [see ZUDJĀDJ].

GLĀWĀ, Arabicized form of the Berber Igliwa (sing. *glāwī*). Berber tribe of Morocco, belonging to the linguistic group of the *tashalḥit*. Population (1940) about 25,000 including 1600 Jews. Their territory, which straddles the centre of the High Atlas chain, is crossed by the ancient road which, at an altitude of 2260 metres/7400 feet, passes over the Tishka col, and which, from earliest antiquity, has provided communication between southern Morocco and the great palm-groves of the Wādī Darʿa. Although the tribe considers itself to be of Maṣmūdī origin, its native chiefs trace their origin to the marabout Abū Muḥammad Ṣāliḥ, the patron saint of the Moroccan town of Safi. With heads uncovered but with a black band round their foreheads, the Glāwā formerly wore the *akhnif*, a short burnous of black wool, woven in one piece, with a large red or orange medallion on the back. The Glāwā do not weave carpets; it is thus in error that their name has been given to the greatly prized products of the large neighbouring confederation of the Ayt-Wawzgit (Djabal Sirwā). The tribe achieved notoriety in the 19th century through the association of its chiefs with the penetration of the Sharīfī *makhzan* in the Atlas. Two personalities should be mentioned; the second of them became internationally known.

(1) Glāwī Madanī, born about 1863, was the son of the *amghar* [*q.v.*] Muḥammad Ibibat, whom he succeeded in 1886. The skilful way in which, in November 1893, he welcomed in his *ḳaṣaba* of Telwet (Tlwat) the old ruler Mawlāy al-Ḥasan, whose army was in difficulties in the Atlas because of cold, was the beginning of his success; he received as reward the title of *Khalīfa* for the Tafilalet and was given rifles and a cannon. He was to put these arms to good use for his policy of conquering the neighbouring tribes, and to become one of the great *ḳā'id*s of the Atlas. In 1902 he was nominated leader of the *djīsh* of Taza and was wounded and defeated by the agitator Bū Ḥmāra [*q.v.*]; he had to seek refuge in Algeria, whence the French procured his repatriation and that of his followers to Tangiers. His success was confirmed when, after having supported the claims of Mawlāy al-Ḥāfiẓ against his brother Mawlāy ʿAbd al-ʿAzīz, he succeeded, after his protégé had become sultan, in getting himself appointed as grand vizier of the Sharīfī government (14 June 1908). He used his power to impose his authority over vast territories, situated between Wādī Tensift and Wādī Darʿa. He fell from favour on 26 May 1911, played an active part during the temporary occupation of Marrākush by the "Blue Sultan" al-Hiba in 1912, and managed with difficulty to join the French. In 1913, with the accession of Mawlāy Yūsuf, he was restored to his high office and built an imposing palace at Marrākush where he died suddenly on 13 August 1918.

(2) Glāwī Tihāmī, the younger brother of Glāwī Madanī, who appointed him pasha of the town of Marrākush by a *ẓahīr* of 8 July 1909. He shared in his brother's disgrace in 1911 but was restored to office at the time of the French occupation of Marrākush, in September 1912. When his brother died he succeeded him in his high office and, with the help of his son, held the double appointment until his death. A courageous and experienced warrior and a devout Muslim (he twice performed the Pilgrimage), this harsh ruler kept the tribes and the town which he governed in fear and in poverty, but also in peace. Settled at Marrākush, in the triple palace which he had built for himself, he loved to offer extravagant hospitality to illustrious guests from all parts of the world, who would then proclaim afar his power, his generosity and his political acumen, thus contributing to the rise of tourism in Morocco. During the war of 1939-45 he was unshakeably faithful to the Allied cause and one of his sons, an officer in the French army, was killed in Italy. In 1953 he led a conspiracy of Berbers and Marabouts which resulted in the expulsion of the sultan Sayyidī Muḥammad. When the latter returned, in November 1956, he obtained *amān*, and died in his palace on Monday 23 January 1957.

Bibliography: See BERBERS and references given in R. Montagne, *Les Berbères et le Makhzen dans le Sud du Maroc*, Paris 1930 and in J. Berque, *Structures sociales du Haut-Atlas*, Paris 1955; also E. Vaffier, *Une grande famille marocaine, les Glawa*, in *France-Maroc*, 1917, no. 12 and 1918, no. 1; J. Célérier and A. Charton, *La position de Telouet et la politique glaoua*, in *B. Soc. de Géog. Maroc*, iv (1924); L. Voinot, *A travers l'Atlas, dans le commandement glaoua*, (with genealogical tree), in *Rev. géog. maroc.*, 1932, no. 1; M. Le Glay, *Chronique marocaine, Année 1911*, Paris 1933; P. Ricard, *Corpus des tapis marocains*, iii (*Haut-Atlas et Haouz de Marrakech*), Paris 1927; *Les Tapis Ouaouzguite*, special number of *Nord-Sud*, no. 20, Marrakech (1934); P. Chauveau, *Notes sur l'Ouarzazate, pays d'obédience du pacha*, in *Rév. Alg. Tun. et Mar. de légis. et de juris.*, Aug./Sept. 1937; A. Deverdun, *Inscriptions arabes de Marrakech*, Rabat 1956 (epitaph of Madanī, no. 251); Col. Justinard, *Le caïd Goundafi*, Casablanca 1951; Marquis de Segonzac, *Au cœur du Maroc*, Paris 1910; Ibn-Zaydān, *Itḥāf aʿlām al-nās bi-djamāl akhbār ḥāḍirat Miknās*, 5 vols. published, 1923-1933, indexes; ʿAbbās b. Ibrāhīm, *al-Iʿlām bi-man ḥalla Marrākush* . . ., 5 vols. so far (biographies not yet published); G. Babin, *Le Maroc sans masque*, "*Son Excellence*", Paris 1932; "Son Excellence", *En réponse à une campagne infâme, quelques documents*, Marrakech (n.d.); there is also an immense journalistic and polemical literature.

(G. Deverdun)

GOA [see HIND-iv and ṢINDĀBŪR].

GOD [see ALLĀH].

GODOBERI [see ANDI].

GOG AND MAGOG [see YĀDJŪDJ WA-MĀDJŪDJ].

GOGO [see GAO].

GÖK TEPE (Turkish "blue hill"), tianscribed in Russian "Geok Tepe", a fort in the oasis of the Akhal-Teke [*q.v.*] Turkmen, on the Sasïk su (Sasïk Āb), situated about 45 km. west of ʿAshkābād, today in the Soviet Republic of Turkmenistān. It consists of a series of isolated places, one of which, Dengil Tepe ($4^1/_2$ km. in circumference), was defended from 1 until 24 Jan. 1881 (new style) by about 12,000 Akhal-Teke Turkmen [see TEKE] against the Russians under General Mikhaïl Dmitrievič Skobelev (about 8,000 Caucasians and Turkestanis). Both sides suffered heavy losses, and after the capture of the fort, the majority of the Turkmen defenders were slain during four days of looting, or as they fled. Later, the Russians set up a new fort in a similar oasis, near Dengil Tepe; since 1883 the Trans-Caspian Railway has also reached this place in which a museum commemorates the battle.

Bibliography: M. Terent'ev, *Istoriya zavoevaniya sredney Azii* (History of the discovery of Central Asia), St. Petersburg 1906, iii, 157 ff.; Brockhaus-Efron, *Ėntsiklopedičeskiy Slovar'*, viii/1 (15; 1892), 403 ff.; *BSE*², x (1952), 499.

(B. SPULER)

GÖKALP, ZIYA, Turkish thinker, born Meḥmed Ḍiyā' (Ziya) at Diyārbakr in 1875 or 1876 and known by his pen name after 1911. Ziya became acquainted with the Young Ottoman ideas of patriotism and constitutionalism through his father, who died having entered him in the modern high school to learn modern sciences and French. From his uncle he learned Arabic, Persian, and the traditional Muslim sciences and became acquainted with the works of the Muslim theologians, philosophers, and mystics. The clash of orthodoxy, mysticism and modern science in his mind, heightened by the uncle's opposition to his aspirations for a higher education in Istanbul, led Ziya to attempt suicide from which he was saved by his elder fellow-townsman Dr. ʿAbd Allāh Djewdet [*q.v.*]. His subsequent career was an intellectual sublimation of his struggles between the three influences, and may be separated into three phases.

His liberal and revolutionary phase began with his coming to Istanbul to attend the school of veterinary medicine, and entrance into the secret Society of Union and Progress. He was arrested in 1897, sentenced to one year of imprisonment, and exiled back to Diyārbakr.

Following the Revolution of 1908, Ziya became the leading Ottomanist liberal writer and lecturer in Diyārbakr. His change into an idealist populist and nationalist, marking the second phase of his career, occurred in Salonika where he went in 1909 as a delegate to the convention of the Union and Progress and remained, having been elected to its central committee. He became associated with a group of young writers connected with the periodicals *Genč Ḳalemler* (Young Pens) and *Yeni Felsefe Medjmūʿasî* (New Philosophical Review) who were interested in the democratization of the language and literature, and in the development of a new ideology to serve as a guide in the social transformation believed to have been begun by the Revolution of 1908. The group crystallized two tendencies, one materialistic and socialistic and the other idealistic and nationalistic. Gökalp became the leader of the second while the first soon disappeared.

From 1912 to 1919, Gökalp lived in Istanbul, this being the most influential phase of his career. His acquaintance with émigré intellectiuals from Kazan, the Crimea, and Azerbaijan gave a more pan-Turkist colouring to his nationalism, though he did not subscribe to their racist tendencies. He remained primarily the nationalist ideologist of the Turks of the Ottoman Empire, who he believed had to cultivate national consciousness in face of the challenges of the non-Turkish nationalities of the dissolving empire. His key concept was that of "culture" as distinct from "civilization", and defined as the values and institutions distinguishing one nation from others comprised in a common civilization. The Turkish nation would emerge by a transference from the orbit of Eastern to that of Western civilization. In that transformation those elements of Islam that had become part and parcel of the Turkish culture would remain as a living spiritual force. The Turkish nation would be Westernized in so far as it succeeded in harmonizing modern civilization with its own culture and faith. In a series of articles and through his lectures as professor of sociology at the University of Istanbul he elaborated his approach, to demonstrate its application to the reforms needed in education, language, family, law, economy, and religion.

Following the end of World War I, Gökalp was exiled by the British to Malta together with several Turkish statesmen and intellectuals. Upon his release in 1921 he joined the national movement led by Mustafa Kemal. Though he fully supported the Kemalist reforms, he did not attain the position of foremost ideologist of the more radical Kemalist régime. He died in 1924, while a member of the Grand National Assembly.

Gökalp wrote poetry, but was primarily an essayist. His only book, *Türk medeniyeti taʾrīkhi* (The History of Turkish Civilization) which he began shortly before his death, remained unfinished; one volume, covering the pre-Islamic period, was published posthumously (Istanbul 1341). He attained nationwide fame as a thinker, but some of his ideas were overshadowed by the Kemalist reforms, some were distorted by the anti-Kemalist Pan-Turkists, while others were rejected after his death. The establishment of modern Turkey as a secular nation-state is greatly indebted to the orientation prepared by Gökalp's ideas. One of his inadvertent influences has been outside Turkey: Sāṭiʿ al-Huṣrī, who was one of his liberal opponents until he left Turkey in 1919 to join the Arab national movement, seems to have appropriated Gökalp's theory of nationalism, his social philosophy, his secularism, and his concept of national education.

Bibliography: Gökalp's published literary writings: *Ḳîzîl Elma*, Istanbul 1330, 1941; *Yeni Ḥayāt*, Istanbul 1918, 1941; *Altîn Ishîḳ*, Istanbul 1339, 1942; *Ziya Gökalp külliyatı*, i: *Şiirler ve halk masalları*, ed. F. A. Tansel, Ankara 1952. Collections of his essays: *Türkleshmek, Islāmlashmaḳ, muʿāṣîrlashmaḳ*, Istanbul 1918; *Türkčülüğün esāslarî*, Ankara 1339, Istanbul 1940; *Türk türesi*, Istanbul 1339; *Doğru yol*, Ankara 1939; *Malta mektupları*, ed. Ali Nüzhet Göksel, Istanbul 1931; *Ziya Gökalp ve Çinaraltı*, ed. Ali Nüzhet Göksel, Istanbul 1939; *Fırka nedir?*, ed. E. B. Şapolyo, Zonguldak 1947; *Ziya Gökalp: hayatı, sanatı, eseri*, ed. Ali Nüzhet Göksel, Istanbul 1952; *Yeni Türkiyenin hedefleri*, Ankara 1956; *Ziya Gökalpın ilk yazı hayatı, 1894-1909*, ed. Şevket Beysanoğlu, Istanbul 1956; *Turkish nationalism and Western civilization: selected essays of Ziya Gökalp*, trans. and ed. Niyazi Berkes, London and New York 1959.

Writings on his life and works: Niyazi Berkes, *Ziya Gökalp: his contribution to Turkish nationalism*, in *MEJ*, viii (1954), 375-390; J. Deny, *Ziya Goek Alp*, in *RMM*, lxi (1925), 1-41; Kâzım Nami Duru, *Ziya Gökalp*, Istanbul 1949; Emin Erişirgil, *Bir fikir adamının romanı*, Istanbul

1941; Ziyaeddin Fahri, *Ziya Gökalp, sa vie et sa sociologie*, Paris 1935; A. Fischer, *Aus der religiösen Reformbewegung in der Türkei*, Leipzig 1922; Richard Hartmann, *Ziya Gökalp's Grundlagen des türkischen Nationalismus*, in *OLZ*, xxviii (1925), cols. 578-610; Uriel Heyd, *Foundations of Turkish nationalism: the life and teachings of Ziya Gökalp*, London 1950 (see p. 173 for a list of Gökalp's lithographed university lectures and unpublished works); Ahmed Muhiddin, *Die Kulturbewegung im modernen Türkentum*, Leipzig 1921; Ali Nüzhet Göksel, *Ziya Gökalp: hayatı ve eserleri*, Istanbul 1949; Saffet Örfi, *Ziya Gökalp ve mefkûre*, Istanbul 1923; Ettore Rossi, *Uno scrittore turco contemporaneo; Ziya Gök Alp*, in *OM*, iv (1924), 574-95; Enver B. Şapolyo, *Ziya Gökalp, Ittihat ve Terakki ve Meşrutiyet*, Istanbul 1943; Osman Tolga, *Ziya Gökalp ve iktisadî fikirleri*, Istanbul 1949; Cavit O. Tütengil, *Ziya Gökalp hakkında bir bibliografya denemesi*, Istanbul 1949; Cavit O. Tütengil, *Ziya Gökalp'ın Diyarbekir gazetelerinde çıkan yazıları*, Istanbul 1954; *Türk Yurdu*, Ankara 1340, year 14, no. 3; H. Z. Ülken, *Ziya Gökalp*, Istanbul n.d.

(Niyazi Berkes)

GÖKČAY [see gökče].

GÖKČE-TENGIZ, Gökče-göl or Gökče-deniz; otherwise Sevan, from Armenian *Sew-vank*, 'Black monastery'; a great lake in the Armenian Soviet Socialist Republic, approx. 40° 20° N and 45′ 30′ E. Triangular in shape, Lake Gökče lies 6,000 feet/1830 metres above sea level and is surrounded by barren mountains; its area was formerly reckoned at 540 sq. miles and maximum depth 67 fathoms, but the level of the lake is being systematically lowered in connexion with the important system of hydro-electric stations on the river Zanga, which flows from the lake into the river Aras, and supplies a large part of the energy requirements of Soviet Armenia. A lava island (now peninsula) at the north-west corner is surmounted by two ancient Armenian monasteries, the monks of which were much persecuted following the Arab conquest in the 1st/7th century (cf. J. Muyldermans, *La domination arabe en Arménie*, Louvain 1927, 95). Lake Gökče is scarcely mentioned in Islamic sources prior to Ḥamd Allāh Mustawfī Ḳazwīnī [*q.v.*], but subsequently features in the accounts of Ottoman-Persian conflicts in this area, as well as during the Russian conquest of Transcaucasia early in the 19th century. The lake is famous for its succulent fish, particularly a trout called *is͟hk͟han*, which form the basis of an important industry. Lake Gökče is not to be confused with several rivers called Gökčay ('Blue stream'), *e.g.*, one in S͟hīrwān, another in Anatolia between Sivas and Kayseri.

Bibliography: H. F. B. Lynch, *Armenia. Travels and studies*, 2 vols., London 1901; Le Strange, 183; *BSE*, 2nd ed., tom 38, 294-95, art. 'Sevan'. (W. Barthold-[D. M. Lang])

GÖKLÄN, a Turkmen tribe mainly inhabiting the country round Bojnurd in northern Persia, but with some elements in the Turkmen SSR and the Kara-Kalpak ASSR of the Soviet Union. The number in Persia is difficult to determine but is probably about 60,000. Soviet sources now tend to avoid tribal distinctions, but according to the 1926 census there were 17,000 Göklän in the Kara-Kala district of the Turkmen SSR (South of Kizyl-Arvat) and some 38,000 in the area lying between Il'yaly (S. of Khodzheyli) and Turtkul' in the Kara-Kalpak SSR. The tribe was formerly divided into a number of clans (Čakur, Kirik, Bayandîr, Ḳayi, Yangak, Sag͟hrî, Ḳara-Balkan, Ay-Derwīs͟h, Erkekli, S͟heyk͟h K͟hodja) only traces of which now remain. The Göklän appear never to have been nomads, being occupied mainly with silk and more recently with cotton growing. Those in the Kara-Kala district are mostly market gardeners. They were in the past traditional enemies of the large Yomud and Teke tribes and were wont to side with the Russians during the latter's campaigns in the Turkmen country in the last quarter of the 19th century. They are nominally Muslim by religion.

Bibliography: R. Rahmeti Arat, article 'Göklen' in *IA*. For earlier details: E. Schuyler, *Turkistan*, ii, 382; Yate, *Khurasan and Sistan*, 212 f. For later information: Tokarev, *Ethnography of the peoples of the USSR* (in Russian), 356, and *Soviet Encyclopaedia*², ii, 587. (G. E. Wheeler)

GÖKSU, literally 'blue water', name given by the Turks to numerous rivers or streams, notably (1) one of the two small rivers flowing into the Bosphorus, by the confluence of which were the pleasure gardens between Kandilli and Anadolu hisarı called 'The Sweet Waters of Asia', a place particularly frequented in the 19th century by Ottoman and Levantine society; (2) the great river (168 miles/270 km long, drainage basin of 4000 square miles/10,350 sq. km) of Cilicia Trachea, the ancient Kalykadnos, the course of which occupies the axis of a large sedimentary marine miocene basin, corresponding to a saddle in the arc of the central Taurus. The regime, pluvio-nival, is that of Mediterranean regions, slightly modified by the retention of water in the Karst. In antiquity it was used for navigation (Ammianus Marcellinus, XIV, 2, 15; 8, 1); it has always been used for floating timber, and recently for the irrigation of the delta plain of Silifke (Saysulak barrage) and for hydro-electric power (two barrages on the upper left branch producing 18 million KW per hour).

Bibliography: in general see *İA*, s.v. (B. Darkot); for (1), *İA*, s.v. Boğaziçi, col. 690a; for (2) description of the course in H. Saraçoğlu, *Türkiye coğrafyası üzerine etüdler II: Bitki örtüsü, akarsular ve göller*, Istanbul 1962, 178-83; regime in I. H. Akyol, *Régime des cours d'eau méditerranéens de l'Asie Mineure, Congrès International de Géographie*, Lisbon 1949, ii, 330.

(X. de Planhol)

GÖKSUN, also göksün, a small town in south-eastern Turkey, the ancient Kokussos, W. Armenian Gogîson, now the chef-lieu of an *ilçe* of the *vilâyet* of Maraş, pop. (1960) 3697. It is the 'Cocson', 'Coxon', where the army of the First Crusade rested for three days in the autumn of 1097 (see *A History of the Crusades*, ed. K. M. Setton, i, Philadelphia 1955, 297-8).

Bibliography: *İA*, *s.v.* Göksun (by Besim Darkot), with full bibliography. (Ed.)

GOLD [see d͟hahab].

GOLD COAST [see ghana].

GOLDEN HORDE [see bātū'ids, ḳipčaḳ, sarāy].

al-**GOLEA** [see al-ḳulayʿa].

GOLETTA [see ḥalḳ al-wādī].

GOLIATH [see djālūt].

GOLKONḌĀ, renamed Muḥammadnagar by Sulṭān Ḳulī Ḳuṭb al-Mulk, the founder of the Ḳuṭb S͟hāhī [*q.v.*] dynasty, a hill fort about five miles west of Ḥaydarābād (Deccan) [*q.v.*], is situated in 17° 23′ N., 78° 24′ E. The hill rises majestically in a vast boulderstrewn plain. The site is a natural one for the construction of fortifications, as the summit, called Bālā Ḥiṣār or acropolis, is about four hundred feet above ground level and commands the whole countryside. The name, Golkonḍā, is derived from two Telugu words, *golla* (shepherd) and *konḍa* (hill). There is no doubt that part of the fortifications go back to pre-Muslim times, for certain constructions, such as a wall by the side of the Fatḥ Darwāza, are built of huge granite blocks piled one upon the other, which is characteristic of pre-Muslim citadels of Āndhra Pradesh such as parts of the historic fort of Konḍāpallī. Golkonḍā was ceded to Muḥammad Shāh Bahmanī by the Rādjā of Warangal in 764/1363, but did not become the capital of the *ṭaraf* or province (later, kingdom) of Tilang-Āndhra till the governorship of Sulṭān Ḳulī Ḳuṭb al-Mulk in 900/1494-5. Golkonḍā's glories were rivalled by the foundation of Ḥaydarābād [*q.v.*] in 1000/1591-2. In the heyday of its history Golkonḍā was the centre of trade and commerce where travellers, architects, calligraphers, learned men and men of the world thronged, and this inevitably resulted in a vast increase in the population of the walled city which led to the foundation of the new "City of Ḥaydar". Golkonḍā, however, remained the emporium and centre of the diamond trade of the Orient.

The fortifications of the city and the Bālā Ḥisār are threefold. The outermost circumvallation, which protects the whole city, is about 8,000 yards in circumference, enclosing a vast area, more or less oval in shape, with the rectangular *nayā-ḳilʿa*, "new fort", constructed in 1624, jutting out rather abruptly to the north-east. This wall, which is crenellated throughout, rises to an average of 55 feet, with 8 strong gates and 87 bastions, each with its own name. Four gates are still open: the Fatḥ Darwāza or "Victory gate" (through which the conquering army of Awrangzīb entered the city), the Makkī Darwāza, "Mecca gate", completed 967/1590, the Bandjāra Darwāza leading to the Ḳuṭb Shāhī tombs (which form a majestic sky-line in the neighbourhood), and the Mōtī Darwāza, "pearl gate". A very interesting bastion is the Naw Burdjī, "nine-lobed", which juts out of the defensive wall of the *nayā ḳilʿa* in a corrugated form, perhaps intended to provide a greater field for defence in all directions (but see Burton-Page in *BSOAS*, xxiii/3 (1960), 520). For other bastions see BURDJ, iii.

About 900 yds. above the Fatḥ Darwāza is the Bālā Ḥisār Darwāza, "acropolis gate", the entrance to the second line of defending walls. A short distance to the north of this gate is the Djāmiʿ Masdjid, erected by Sulṭān Ḳulī Ḳuṭb al-Mulk in 924/1518, in which he was assassinated some 25 years later. From this gate the road upwards is very steep, with hundreds of steps with recesses for resting. Half-way up the hill run the double walls which constitute the third line of defence. On the left are palaces, women's apartments, mosques, arsenals, offices, granaries, magazines, and on the right, open ground, parks and groves, wherever a space could be found for them. Before the Bālā Ḥiṣār proper is a well-preserved mosque reputedly erected by Ibrāhīm Ḳuṭb Shāh, and within a few yards of the Throne Room and the acropolis proper is an ancient Hindū temple which was renovated by the Brāhmin ministers of the last Ḳuṭb Shāhī king. There is another very steep path, also served by a number of irregular steps, connecting the lower palaces with the Bālā Ḥiṣār, and by the side of this can be seen the system of raising water from the ground level to the topmost citadel. There is a series of tanks, at different levels; the water was raised by teams of oxen at each level pulling huge leather buckets by rope and pulley and pouring it into the higher cistern. The waste water was brought down through earthen pipes which still exist.

The Bālā Ḥiṣār Darwāza is remarkable not merely for its mantlet but also for the figures and emblems of Hindū mythology which are worked in stucco between the arch and the lintel. Perhaps an even more remarkable structure is a small gateway piercing the penultimate fortification. It is a pillar and lintel gate surmounted by a fairly flat arch. In the centre of the broad stone lintel is a beautiful circular medallion with the lotus motif flanked by mythical figures of Yālī, half dog and half lion, and swans with snake-like worms in their beaks. Above the lintel is a simple pointed alcove surrounded by representations of lion-cubs, peacocks and parrots. The whole composition symbolizes the synthesized Indo-Muslim culture of the Ḳuṭb Shāhī period.

The Golkonḍā tombs, standing outside the fort to the north-west, are a group of some twenty buildings seven of which are tombs of the kings. Their appearance is uniform: typically a square building with an arcaded lower storey, supported on a massive plinth which may itself be arcaded; the lower storey bears a crenellated parapet with a small *mīnār* at each corner, and centrally a tall drum, which may be arcaded and balustraded, supporting a single dome arising from a band of petal-like foliations as in the Bīdjāpur [*q.v.*] domes. The grey granite is usually covered with stucco and with encaustic tiles. The projecting cornices are elaborately worked with plaster designs; this, and the addition of miniature decorative arcaded galleries encircling the *mīnār*s, are characteristic of the Ḳuṭb Shāhī buildings here and at Ḥaydarābād. An important early building in the group is the mortuary where the bodies were washed, the arches of which continue the Bahmanī [*q.v.*] style.

For illustrations of these buildings see HIND, Architecture.

The city of Golkonḍā was the most important mart for diamonds in Asia, as described by, *e.g.*, Marco Polo in 1292, Nicolo Conti in 1420, Tavernier in 1651, and it was here that diamonds were cut, polished and shaped and then exported to all parts of the world.

Bibliography: S. Toy, *The strongholds of India*, London 1957, detailed review and comment by J. Burton-Page in *BSOAS*, xxiii/3 (1960), 508-22; S. H. Bilgrami and Willmott, *Historical and descriptive sketches of His Highness the Nizam's dominions*; Ali Asgher Bilgrami, *Landmarks of the Deccan*, Hyderabad 1927; G. Yazdani, *Inscriptions in Golconda Fort*, in *EIM*, 1913-4, 47-59; idem, *Inscriptions in the Golconda tombs*, in *EIM*, 1915-6, 19-40; Sen, *The Indian travels of Thevenot and Carreri*; *Travels in India* by J. B. Tavernier, translated by V. Ball, Oxford 1925; Jadunath Sarkar, *History of Aurangzīb*, 5 vols., 1912-25; H. K. Sherwani, articles on the Ḳuṭb Shāhī dynasty in *JIH*, 1955, 1956, 1957, 1958, 1960, 1962; idem, in *IC*, 1957; idem, in *J.Pak.Hist.S.*, 1957, 1958, 1962. (H. K. SHERWANI)

GOMBROON, GOMBRUN [see BANDAR ʿABBĀS].

GONDAR [see HABASH].

GONDĒSHĀPŪR, (Arabic form Djundaysābūr) a town in Khūzistān founded by the Sāsānid Shāpūr I (whence the name *wandēw Shāpūr* "acquired by Shāpūr", cf. Nöldeke, *Geschichte der*

Perser, 41, n. 2), who settled it with Greek prisoners. It is the town known as Bēth-Lāpāt in Syriac, corrupted to Bēl-Ābādh, now almost unrecognizable in the form *nīlāb* and *nīlāṭ*; the site is marked at the present day by the ruins of Shāhābād (cf. Rawlinson in the *Journ. of the Royal Geogr. Soc.*, ix, 72; de Bode, *Travels in Luristan*, ii, 167). The town was taken by the Muslims in the caliphate of ʿUmar by Abū Mūsā al-Ashʿarī in 17/738, after the occupation of Tustar; it was surrendered on terms (Balādhurī, 328). Sayf b. ʿUmar's story in Ṭabarī, i, 2567, and Ibn al-Athīr, ii, 432, according to which the fall of the town was the result of a forgery made by the slave Mukthif, seems to be a romantic fiction. The skin of Mani [*q.v.*] was hung on a gate of the city. Gondēshāpūr was the capital of Yaʿḳūb b. Layth al-Ṣaffār (262-3/875-7), who died there in 265/878. In Yāḳūt's time only a few ruins marked the site of the town (ii, 130).

Bibliography: Al-Bīrūnī, *Chronology*, 191; Barbier de Meynard, *Diction. géogr. de la Perse*, Paris 1861, 169 f.; Nöldeke, *Gesch. d. Perser u. Araber*, 40-2; Brockelmann, I, 201; Ṭabarī, i, 2567; Ibn al-Athīr, vii, 201, 213, 231; Wüstenfeld, *Jacut's Reise*, in *ZDMG*, xviii, 425.

(CL. HUART)

Gondēshāpūr's main title to fame lies in its importance as a cultural centre which influenced the rise of scientific and intellectual activity in Islam. Its importance was enhanced by its having been closely associated with a secular field of learning, namely medicine, and by its having been the foremost representative of Greek medicine.

There was a hospital at Gondēshāpūr where, unlike the Greek *asclepieia* and the Byzantine *nosocomia*, treatment seems to have been based solely on scientific medicine. At any rate, this was a characteristic of the hospitals of Islam, for which the hospital at Gondēshāpūr may have served as model. The fourth Islamic hospital founded in Islam (by Hārūn al-Rashīd) was in fact built and run by Gondēshāpūr physicians.

There was a medical school at Gondēshāpūr which was probably in close association with the hospital there. There is also evidence of its ties with the Gondēshāpūr school for religious instruction. Systematic Gondēshāpūr influence on Islamic medicine seems to have started during the reign of Hārūn al-Rashīd, when Gondēshāpūr physicians began to take up their residence in Baghdād. Ḥārith b. Kalada, the Arab doctor contemporary with the Prophet, is said to have studied medicine at Gondēshāpūr. This story presents certain chronological difficulties in its details, however, and is, very likely, of a legendary character.

Arabic sources contain stories which trace back the medical interest of the district of Gondēshāpūr to a physician who had come from India. These stories imply that this initial Indian influence found a fertile ground for development in the Byzantine settlers of Gondēshāpūr which included a group of doctors and that this medical knowledge was further enriched in time through cumulative experience in treatment and through contact with local medical traditions. It is difficult to determine the factual value of such reports. The transformation of Gondēshāpūr into an important medical centre was undoubtedly the work of the Nestorians. But this may not have effectively taken place before the reign of Khusraw I Anūshīrawān (531-579 A.D.).

It is likely that the Gondēshāpūr medical teaching was modelled upon that of Alexandria and Antioch but that it became more specialized and efficient in its new Persian home. Apart from its influence as a medical centre, Gondēshāpūr may, more generally, be looked upon as a place through which the Nestorian heritage of Greek learning of Edessa and Nisibis passed to Baghdād.

Bibliography: *Fihrist*, i, 296; Ibn Abī Uṣaybiʿa, *Ṭabaḳāt al-aṭibbāʾ*, i, 109-26, 171-5, ii, 135; Ibn al-Ḳifṭī, 158-62, 383-4, 431; L. Leclerc, *Histoire de la médecine arabe*, i, 95-117, 557-9; B. Eberman, *Meditsinskaya shkola v Džundisapure*, in *Zapiski Kollegiy Vostokovedov pri Aziatskom Muzee Rossiiskoy Akademiy Nauk*, i (1925), 47-72 (résumé in W. Ebermann, *Bericht über die arabischen Studien in Russland während der Jahre 1921-1927*, *Islamica*, iv (1930), 147-9; E. G. Browne, *Arabian medicine*, 19-22; G. Sarton, *Introduction to the history of science*, i, 435 f,; M. Meyerhof, *Von Alexandrien nach Bagdad*, in *SBPr. Ak. W.*, *Phil.-hist.*, 1930, xxiii, 401 f.; A. A. Siassi, *L'Université de Gond-i Shâpûr et l'étendue de son rayonnement*, in *Mélanges H. Massé*, Teheran 1963, 366-74. (AYDIN SAYILI)

GÖNÜLLÜ, Turkish word meaning 'volunteer', in the Ottoman Empire used as a term (sometimes with the pseudo-Persian plural *gönüllüyān*, in Arabic sources usually rendered *djamulyān* or *kamulyān*) for three related institutions:

1. From the earliest times of the Ottoman state, volunteers coming to take part in the fighting were known as *gönüllü*; their connexion with the *mutaṭawwiʿa*, *ghāzī*s [*qq.v.*], of earlier Muslim states is evident (see M. F. Köprülü, *Les origines de l'Empire Ottoman*, Paris 1936, 102-3; İ. H. Uzunçarşılı, *Osmanlı devleti teşkilâtına medhal*, Istanbul 1942, 59). A high proportion of the *ghāzī*s and *aḳīndjī*s [*q.v.*] on the *udj* (the march-lands) of the Ottoman state were such *gönüllü*s. With the promise of the grant of *tīmār*s and *ʿulūfe* [*qq.v.*] the State encouraged men to join the army, especially when a major campaign was in prospect; the text of a firman, issued before the Moldavian campaign of 889/1484, by which the Sultan ordered such a proclamation to be cried in public, survives (in the registers of the *ḳāḍī*s of Bursa, A. 4/4), and it is recorded that a group of *gönüllü* came from Antalya to join the Ottoman army attacking Cyprus (978/1570). Such volunteers are found throughout Ottoman history, and this was the principal means by which native Muslims could become timariots or enter the ranks of the *Ḳapî-ḳullarî* [see GHULĀM], for volunteers who distinguished themselves were granted *tīmār*s or *zeʿāmet*s [*qq.v.*] or admitted to the *Ghurabāʾ* [*q.v.*] regiments; the rest were appointed to the bodies of *gönüllüyān* who performed garrison duties in the fortresses of the Empire, being supported by *ʿulūfe*. In the 11th/17th and 12th/18th centuries, with the ever-increasing need for men, the *gönüllü bayraghî* was unfurled and *gönüllü* troops, serving for pay, were recruited; this must have been a continuation of the old tradition.

2. In the 10th/16th century we find an organized body known as *gönüllüyān* in most of the fortresses of the Empire, in Europe, Asia and Egypt. It resembled the bodies of *müstaḥfîẓlar* and *beshlüyān*; its characteristics were that its members performed garrison duties, served for pay (*ʿulūfe*), and had for the most part begun as volunteers. It was organized, like the *Ḳapî-ḳullarî*, into *djemāʿat*s and *bölük*s. Reference is found to two main groups, the *Sagh Gönüllüler* (or *Gönüllüyān-i yemīn*, 'of the right') and the *Sol Gönüllüler* (or *Gönüllüyān-i yesār*, 'of the left'). In the main fortresses they formed two *djemāʿat*s, *süwārī* (cavalry) and *piyāde* (infantry). Each *djemāʿat*

was commanded by an *agha*, and each was divided into *bölük*s of 10-30 men each. The first *bölük* of the cavalry was called *Agha bölüğü*, and the second *Ketkhudā* (*Kahya*) *bölüğü*; the first *bölük* of the infantry was the *Ketkhudā bölüğü*. Every *bölük* had a *Bölük-bashî* (or *Ser-bölük*). In 1025/1616 the daily pay of the *Agha* was 50 *aķčes*, of the Clerk (*Kātib*) 20-25, and of the *Ketkhudā* 20-25; each *Ser-bölük* received 10-20 (for details see *Defter-i esāmī-i gönüllüyān-i süwārī we piyādegān we müstaḥfīzān-i ķalʿa-i Ḥaleb*, Istanbul, Başvekâlet Arşivi, maliye 2/6467). In 963/1556 the *gönüllüs* of Cairo received between 10 and 16 *aķčes*, in 1130/1718 those of the fortress of Nish received 14 *aķčes* a day. The establishment (known as *gedük* or *gedik*) of each *djemāʿat* was fixed. In the 10th/16th century, when there were vacancies, in response to a *tedhkire* [*q.v.*] from the *beg* or the *defterdār* of the *eyālet*, a *berāt* [*q.v.*] of the Sultan would be issued granting these vacancies to volunteers who had distinguished themselves on the frontiers, so-called *yarar yiğitler* and *yoldashlar*, the sons of *gönüllüs*, and Janissaries. There were in the fortresses separate *djemāʿat*s of pensioners (*müteķāʿid*) and *ķul-oghullarî* [see YEÑIČERI] connected with the *gönüllüyān*.

The *gönüllüs* in the fortresses might be called out to serve on a campaign or take part in frontier-fighting. Those that distinguished themselves might be granted *tīmār*s; in the 11th/17th century it could happen that distinguished *agha*s of the *gönüllüs* were appointed *sandjaķ-begi*.

3. In the 11th/17th century a body known as *gönüllüyān* is mentioned also among the paid auxiliaries who, under various names, were recruited in the provinces to serve on a campaign. In 1131/1718 a formation of auxiliaries called *sekbān* was abolished, and it was ordered that their place should be taken by the raising of *dīwānegān* (*deliler*), *fārisān*, *ʿazebān* and *gönüllüyān*; but the dismissed *sekbān*s re-enlisted in the new formations and continued their misdeeds. These groups, the *gönüllüyān* included, frequently cast off all obedience and discipline and plagued the provinces with their depredations.

Bibliography: in the article.

(HALIL İNALCIK)

GŌRĀN [see GŪRĀN].

GÖRDES, a small town in eastern Anatolia (38° 55′ N., 28° 17′ E.) at an altitude of about 1,500 ft on the banks of the Kum Çay. The town, with a small local market, has now lost all importance but it was famous until the beginning of the 19th century as an important centre for the making of prayer rugs. The population in 1960 was 5,071.

Bibliography: Ewliyā Čelebi, *Seyāḥatnāme*, ix, 55; *IA*, s.v. (B. Darkot); for the carpets of Gördes, see *IA*, s.v. *Halı* (M. A. Mehmedoğlu) and pl. 2 and 3. (X. DE PLANHOL)

GÖRIDJE [see MANASTÎR].

GÖRIDJELI ĶOČÎ BEG [see ĶOČÎ BEG].

GOSPEL(S) [see INDJĪL].

GOUM [see GUM].

GOVERNMENT [see DAWLA, ḤUKŪMA, SIYĀSA, SULṬĀN, etc.].

GOVERNOR [see AMĪR, WĀLĪ].

GRAMMAR [see FIʿL, NAḤW, TAṢRĪF].

GRAÑ [see AḤMAD GRAÑ].

GRANADA [see GHARNĀṬA].

GRÉECE, GREEKS [see, for ancient Greece, YŪNĀN; for the Byzantine Empire, RŪM; for Greece under Ottoman rule, MORA].

GREEK FIRE, GREGORIAN FIRE [see BĀRŪD, NAFṬ].

GROCER [see BAĶĶĀL].

GUADALAJARA [see WĀDI 'L-ḤIDJĀRA].

GUADALQUIVIR [see AL-WĀDI 'L-KABĪR].

GUADARRAMA [see AL-SHARRĀT].

GUADIANA [see WĀDĪ YĀNA].

GUADIX [see WĀDĪ ĀSH].

GUARANTEE [see AMĀN, ḌAMĀN, KAFĀLA].

GUARDAFUI, the cape at the north-east tip of the Horn of Africa, in Somalia, known also as Raʾs ʿAsīr, and, according to ʿAlī Čelebī, as Raʾs al-aḥmar. It was the Ἀρωμάτων ἀκρωτήριον of the *Periplus* and Ptolemy and the νότον κέρας of Strabo. The origin of the name is uncertain; the present form is one of several variants occurring in the Portuguese writers. It may be connected with Masʿūdī's Djafūnā and it appears as Dj.rd.fūn in the rutters of Ibn Mādjid and in ʿAlī Čelebī. Many absurd etymologies have been proposed. It may include the name Ḥafūn, given to a prominent cape further to the south. Guillain states that the local inhabitants gave the name Djardafūn not to Guardafui but to a small promontory a few miles away. It belongs to the area in which the Somali are first found and was once populated by Dir, later expelled by Dārod (Madjērtēn). There is a small group of Mahrī descent who have intermarried and speak Somali.

Bibliography: Yule & Burnell, *Hobson-Jobson*, s.v.; M. L. Dames, *The Book of Duarte Barbosa*, i, 32; M. Guillain, *Documents sur l'histoire, la géographie, et le commerce de l'Afrique Orientale*, ii, 402; G. Ferrand, *Relations de voyages*, Paris 1913-4; T. A. Shumovski, *Tri neizvestnie lotsii Ahmada ibn Madžida*, Moscow-Leningrad 1957; E. Cerulli, *Somalia*, i, Rome 1964, 109, 110.

(C. F. BECKINGHAM)

GUDĀLA, small Berber tribe belonging to the great ethnic group of the desert Ṣanhādja (the Berber phoneme *g* is usually rendered in Arabic script by a *djīm* but Ibn Khaldūn, in his system of transcription, writes it as a *kāf* which, in the original manuscript, presumably had a diacritical point placed above or below). They lived in the southern part of what is now Mauritania, to the north of the Senegal and in contact with the ocean. To the south their territory bordered the land of the Negroes; to the north, in the present Ādrār of Mauritania, lived their Ṣanhādja "brothers", the Lamtūna and the Massūfa.

Like the other desert Ṣanhādja, the Gudāla were essentially nomadic camel-drivers, and possessed fast dromedaries (*nadjīb*, pl. *nudjub*). Nevertheless they possessed a town, Naghīrā (reading uncertain), at a distance of about six stages from the river Senegal, and so probably in what is now Tāgānt.

Along the shores of the Atlantic they collected quantities of ambergris and caught enormous sea turtles the flesh of which they ate. There too they possessed, on the island of Āwlīl, not far from the mainland, a famous salt-pan. As al-Idrīsī places this island at about one *madjrā* (at most 150 kilometres/100 miles) from the mouth of the Senegal, it cannot have been, as was suggested, either Arguin or Tidra. With greater probability, it has been suggested that Āwlīl was the present Īn-Wolalan, between Nwākshōṭ and Saint-Louis.

At the beginning of the 5th/11th century the supremacy over the Ṣanhādja of the desert was held by the chiefs of the Lamtūna. Towards 425/1034 it was the Gudāla chief Yaḥyā b. Ibrāhīm who held it. On returning from a pilgrimage to Mecca he brought back with him from Sūs, to convert the Ṣanhādja to Islam, the famous ʿAbd Allāh b. Yā-Sīn al-Djazūlī, who was to launch the Almoravid movement. After the death of Yaḥyā b. Ibrāhīm the supremacy returned to the Lamtūna, in the person of Yaḥyā b. ʿUmar, and then of his brother Abū Bakr. From then on the Gudāla no longer made common cause with the Almoravid movement, in which mainly the Lamtūna and the Massūfa took part. After the expedition against Sidjilmāsa they retired to their territory in the Sahara, where they fought sometimes with the Negroes, sometimes with those of the Lamtūna who had remained on the spot.

They undoubtedly ended by wiping out the latter. In the second half of the 8th/14th century Ibn Khaldūn places them immediately to the south of al-Sāḳiya al-Ḥamrāʾ, in contact with the Dhawū-Ḥassān, nomadic Arabs of the Maʿḳil group. Later on the latter were to advance towards the south and occupy present-day Mauritania. At this point the Gudāla disappear from history. Their name is now attested only by two very small fractions of Gdāla, one in the north, in Tīrīs, the other in the south, among the Brākna.

Bibliography: Besides the classical historians and geographers, see: A. Huici Miranda, *Un fragmento inédito de Ibn ʿIdarī sobre los Almorávides*, in *Hespéris-Tamuda*, ii/1 (1961), 43; P. Marty, *L'émirat des Trarzas*. (G. S. Colin)

GŪDJAR (Gudjdjar, Gurdjdjar), name of an ancient tribe, wide-spread in many parts of the Indo-Pakistan subcontinent, akin to the Rādjpūts, the Djāṫs [*q.v.*], and the Ahīrs, who are claimed by Gudjdjar historians as off-shoots of the main stock. Both Western and native writers agree that the tribe migrated to the plains of Hindustan from Central Asia sometime in the middle of the 5th century A.D. Tall, handsome, wirily-built, and of a fair complexion, they are believed to be descendants of either the Scythians or the White Huns. The view of a minority of Gudjdjar historians, that they are of indigenous origin, finds little support. Largely agriculturalists, they also herd cattle and sell milk and other dairy products, but with the spread of education and a desire for bettering their economic condition they have taken to other occupations, mainly in the undivided Pandjāb and the Uttar Pradesh (India), and adopted a settled way of life.

The word Gurdjdjara first occurs in Bāna's *Harśačritra* where Harsha Vardhana's father Prabhākaravardhana is described as "the one who kept Gurdjdjara awake" (cf. K. M. Munshi, *Glory that was Gurjara-Deśa*, Bombay 1955, i, 3). Here Gurdjdjara stands for the "king of Gūdjars", the *malik al-djuzar* of the Arab historians (cf. al-Sīrāfī, *Silsilat al-tawārīkh*, Paris 1881, 126-7; al-Balādhurī, *Futūḥ*, 446; Ibn Rusta, *al-Aʿlāḳ al-nafīsa*, Leiden 1892, vii, 137; Ibn Khurradādhbih, 16, 66; al-Masʿūdī, *Murūdj*, i, 383-4), who ruled over Gudjarātra, whose boundaries it is difficult to fix precisely but which extended not only to the Narmda but also included parts of modern Saurāshṫhra and Rādjasthān, with its capital at Bhīlamāla or Bhinamāla (Bīlamān of the Arab historians, perhaps representing the colloquial pronunciation) near the present Mount Abu. This was a famous centre of swordmaking. Swords made here were highly prized, and there are several references in Arabic literature to the sword of Bīlamān (cf., *e.g.*, al-Kindī, *al-Suyūf wa adjnāsuhā*, ed. ʿAbd al-Raḥmān Zakī, Cairo 1952, 9-10, where it has been corrupted into *Sulaymāniyya*). In all probability this was the sword described by Arabic lexicographers as *al-muhannad* (cf. *Lisān*, s.v., *TA* under *HND*).

In course of time four ruling families of the Gurdjdjars emerged as empire-builders. These were: (1) The Paramāras or Paṅwāras, (2) the Pratīhāras or Parīhāras, (3) the Čāhamānas or Čawhānas and (4) the Solankīs or Čawlūkiyas known to the Arabs as the *Ṣalūḳiyya* (cf. Ibn Rusta, 135; al-Djāḥiẓ, *Ḥayawān*, Cairo 1945, i, 184, ii, 198, where *Ṣalūḳiyya* dogs are mentioned). Of these Mihir Bhodja the Great (836-890 A.D.), a Pratīhāra king, with his capital at Ḳannawdj, has been described as a mighty ruler. He had a well-equipped and strong army (Gurdjdjar-Bālā), and his military exploits made him a popular hero. Among the Čawhānas Prithvirādja of Delhi was the last notable ruler; he suffered defeat at the hands of Muʿizz al-Dīn Muḥammad b. Sām in 588/1192 at Tarāʾoṙi (Tarāʾin, near Karnāl). This victory paved the way for the foundation of a Muslim empire in India.

It has also been established that the Sultans of Gudjarāt, of whom Maḥmūd Begara (863/1458-917/1511) and Bahādur Shāh (932/1526-943/1536) (see gudjarāt) deserve mention, were of Gudjdjar origin, belonging to the Tāṅk branch of the Pramāras (cf. ʿAbd al-Mālik, *Shāhān-i Gūdjar*, Aʿẓamgaṙh, 1353/1934, 333 ff.); Ibn Khurradādhbih (16) also refers to the *malik al-Ṭāniḳ*, along with the *malik al-djuzar*. *Ṭāniḳ*, is obviously the Arabicized form of Tāṅk (variants Tāk, Tak, Taksh); this identification eluded both the historians of India and Arabists.

The Gudjdjars seem to have spread all over the country and founded many towns and places, some of them still bearing their name, as Gūdj(a)rānwāla, Gūdjarkhān, Gudjrāt, Godjara, and Gūdjargadh.

They were quite numerous in the Sahāranpur district of India and the neighbouring territory, which was known until 1857 as Gudjarātta or Gūdjara-deśa. A headstrong and prosperous tribe they were a source of great trouble to Bābur [*q.v.*] and Shēr Shāh Sūr [*q.v.*]. Notorious for their habit of plundering, they harried the British and the local people during the military uprising of 1857. Consequently they suffered heavily, losing their leaders and many of the *djāgīrs* that they had held during the Moghul period. The Gūdjars of Delhi and the neighbourhood harried and plundered refugees who fled from the city when it fell to the British in 1857. Even the members of the ex-royal family were not spared. (Cf. *Taʾrīkh-i Gurdjdjar*, ii, 415-6; Percival Spear, *Twilight of the Moghuls*, Cambridge 1951, 202, 207, 211; Ḥasan Niẓāmī, *Ghadr-i Dihlī ke Afsāney*: *Dihlī ki Biptā* (in Urdu), Delhi n.d., 34, 52, 59).

In Hazāra (Pakistan), Djammū, Kāṅgṙa (India) and some parts of Kashmīr there exist small pockets of Gūdjars who still lead a nomadic life. They move from place to place, in single families or in small groups, and pitch their tents or erect their ramshackle huts where they find grass and fodder for their animals. They speak a dialect known as Gūdjarī or Godjarī, which Grierson characterizes as a corrupt form of the Mēwātī dialect of eastern Rādjpūtāna.

It was the emperor Akbar [*q.v.*] who forced the Gūdjars to adopt a settled life. Thus many towns in the Pandjāb with the prefix Gūdjar, peopled mainly by this tribe, came into existence (Gudjrāt [*q.v.*], however, was founded by Alkhān, a Paṅwāra Gūdjar and commander-in-chief of the army of Mihir Bhodja). When they adopted Islam is not known; even to this day both Muslim and Hindu Gūdjars are found living as close neighbours. Many of the ceremonies and customs prevailing among them are of purely Hindu origin, for many of the Muslim Gūdjars take pride in being converts from Hinduism. They regard as their national heroes Djaypāla, the Hindu-Shāhiyya ruler of Lahore, whom Maḥmūd Ghaznawī defeated, Mihir Bhodja Pratīhāra, whose grandfather Nāga Bhaṭṭ II (792-825 A.D.) has been described as the inveterate enemy of the Arabs, Rādja Dāhir of Alōr, defeated and killed by Muḥammad b. Ḳāsim, Rāna Sāṅga and Rāna Pratāp of Mēwāṛ, and look upon their Muslim conquerors as despoilers and enemies of the Gurdjdjaras, because they destroyed their kingdoms, raided and looted their territories and subjected them to all sorts of indignities (cf. ʿAlī Ḥasan Čawhān Gurdjdjar, *Taʾrīkh-i Gurdjdjar*, Karachi 1960, iii, especially ch. iii and iv, which are full of the bitterest invective against the Muslim conquerors and invaders).

Bibliography: Ḥ. ʿAbd al-Ḥaḳḳ, *Tawārīkh-i Gūdjarāṅ maʿa ansāb-i Gūdjarāṅ*, Lahore 1931, wherein he refers to two Persian MSS on the history of the Gūdjars — (1) *Mirʾāt-i Gūdjarān* by Shaykh Djamāl Gūdjar and (2) *Muraḳḳaʿ-i Gūdjarān* by Čawdharī Fayḍ Muḥammad, but no copies of these works seem to be extant; Abu 'l-Barakāt Muḥammad ʿAbd al-Mālik, *Shāhān-i Gūdjar*, Aʿẓamgaṛh 1353/1934; Rāna Muḥammad Akbar Khān, *Gudjdjar-Gūṅdj*, Lahore 1955; K. M. Munshi, *Glory that was Gurjara-Deśa*, 2 vols., Bombay 1955; Rāna ʿAlī Ḥasan Čawhān Gurdjdjar, *Taʾrīkh-i Gurdjdjar*, 5 vols., Karachi 1960, a most uncritical account of the Gūdjars [full of historical untruths, halftruths and legends], to be used with care; *JASB*, iv/1 (1886), 181 ff.; D. Ibbetson, *Outlines of Panjab ethnography*, Calcutta 1883, 182-8, 481; A. H. Bangley, *Gujar, Jat, Ahir*; D. R. Bhandarkar, *Epigraphic notes and questions*, iii, Urdu transl. in *Shāhān-i Gūdjar*, *op. cit.*, 473-86; A. M. T. Jackson, *Bombay Gazetteer*, i/1 (1896), 526 ff.; *Imperial Gazetteer of India*, Oxford 1908, vol. 1 (Bombay Presidency); W. Crooke, *Tribes and castes of N.W. Provinces and Oudh*, Calcutta 1896, ii, 439 ff.; V. A. Smith, *Early history of India*, London 1913, 22, 303; idem, *The Gujaras of Rajputana and Kanauj*, in *JRAS*, 1909; *Gazetteer of Gujrat District*, Lahore 1892-3; Mirzā Muḥammad Aʿẓam Bēg, *Taʾrīkh-i Gudjrāt* (in Urdu), Lahore 1867; D. C. Ganguly, *History of the Paramar dynasty*; C. V. Vaidya, *History of medieval India*, 222-3, 236, 356; *Census Report of India* (1901), 498; M. R. Neville, *Gazetteer of the Saharanpur District*, ii, 198-205; see also the *Gazetteers* of Agra and Mathura districts; M. L. Nigam, *Some literary references to the history of the Gujara-Pratihāras Mahendrapāla and Mahipāla*, in *JRAS*, 1964, 14-7.

(A. S. Bazmee Ansari)

GUDJARĀT, a province of India on the north-west of its coastline, lying east of the Raṇ of Kaččh [*q.v.*] and broadly divided into Mainland Gudjarāt and Peninsular Gudjarāt (Kāṭhiāwāṛ, the ancient Sawrāshṭra, modern Sōraṭh). Mainland Gudjarāt is approximately the area of the plains in the lower reaches of the rivers Sābarmatī, Mahī, Narbadā and Tāptī, bounded north by the Mārwāṛ desert, east by the line of hills running south-east from Ābū to the Vindhyas. It takes its name (Sanskrit *Gurjarātra*) from the widespread Gūdjar (Skt. *Gurjara*) tribe, who, it has been suggested, entered India with the White Huns at the end of the 5th century A.D., and who in many ways closely resemble the Djāṭs [*q.v.*]; the name was even applied to the country north of Adjmēr in the 9th century A.D., but by the 11th-13th centuries, just before the coming of Islam, Gudjarāt referred particularly to the domains of the Solankī kings of Aṇahilwāḍā whose boundaries were much as described above.

(a) The ancient history of Gudjarāt covers a period of some 15 centuries before the advent of Islam at the end of the 7th/13th century: the Mawrya dominions extended to Sawrāshṭra in the 4th century B.C. (inscription of Aśoka at Djunāgaṛh [*q.v.*]); the region was under the Śaka satraps until the 4th century A.D. when it passed to the Guptas; after their overthrow by the Huns there followed the Valabhīs (perhaps overthrown by the Arabs from Manṣūra [*q.v.*] in Sindh, cf. the numismatic evidence adduced by G. P. Taylor in *Gujarat College Magazine*, January 1919), Čāwaḍās, and the Solankīs or Čawlukyas. The last-named dynasty were worshippers of the Hindū divinity Shiva, whose splendid temple at Somnāth in Sawrāshṭra was plundered by Maḥmūd of Ghaznī in Dhu 'l-Ḳaʿda 416/January 1026, in the reign of Bhīma I the fourth Čawlukya dynast (Ibn al-Athīr, ix, 242; so also al-Bīrūnī, ed. Sachau, ii, 9; Gardīzī, ed. Nazim, 86-7; Haig in *Cambridge history of India*, iii, 23 ff., gives an incorrect date, presumably following Firishta); gold and jewels worth two million *dīnār*s, the sandalwood gates of the temple, and the stone phallic emblem of the god were transported to Ghaznī. The rebuilding soon commenced, this time in the fine stone for which the reign of Bhīma I was distinguished—a genre which was to become very significant for the derivative architecture of the Gudjarāt sultanate. The sixth dynast, the great Siddharādja, who ruled for over 50 years in the 12th and 13th centuries A.D., extended the dominions and built the famous temple at Siddhpur later converted into a mosque by Aḥmad I; under his patronage the Djayn [*q.v.*] religion was firmly established in Gudjarāt. The ninth ruler, Mūlarādja II, sent a large army which in 574/1178 vanquished the army of Muʿizz al-Dīn Muḥammad b. Sām which was exhausted by its long march through Uččh, Multān and the Mārwāṛ desert (Muslim historians show Bhīma II as the victorious ruler; but the Sanskrit *Kīrtikaumudī* and *Sukṛtasaṅkīrtana*, and contemporary grants, leave no doubt that the invasion occurred in Mūlarādja's short reign). The defeat was avenged in 593/1197 when Muʿizz al-Dīn's general Ḳuṭb al-Dīn Aybak [*q.v.*] plundered Anahilwāḍa, the capital, forcing Bhīma II to take refuge in a remote part of Gudjarāt, and returned to Dihlī laden with booty. Mūlarādja and his brother Bhīma both came to the throne as minors; the central authority thereby became weak, and the kingdom was virtually divided among the nobles and provincial chiefs. The most powerful of these, the Vāghelās ruling at Dholkā, gradually usurped the royal power and transferred their capital to Anahilwāḍa; this was the regnant dynasty at the time of the Muslim conquest, and it continued to hold pockets of territory in north Gudjarāt for some time thereafter.

Pre-Muslim Gudjarāt seems to have been well known to the Muslim, particularly the Arab, world, for it is frequently referred to by travellers and geographers from the merchant Sulaymān onwards. Al-Balādhurī, 3rd/9th century, notices the pirates of the Sawrāshṭra coast, and mentions the great ports of Bharōč and Sindān [*qq.v.*]; al-Masʿūdī describes the strength of the kingdom and the power of its ruler, and mentions the gold and silver mines; Iṣṭakhrī, 4th/10th century, and Ibn Ḥawḳal, 4th/10th century, give itineraries and describe the topography; al-Bīrūnī, 5th/11th century, gives fuller details with greater exactness, as does Idrīsī at the end of that century; these two are the only geographers to describe the rivers of Gudjarāt. Most of these authors are especially interested in the ports of Gudjarāt, Bharōč, Khambāyat and Sindān, in the capital Anahilwāḍa (Āmhal, Nahlwāra, Nahrwāla, etc.), and in its trade and natural resources (gold, silver, pearls; horses and camels; teak, bamboos, aloewood, betelnut); they describe local Hindū and Djayn practices in some detail, and are impressed by the religious toleration shown in the region.

A most significant event in this period was the arrival of the Zoroastrian fugitives from Īrān. The 'traditional' date for their first landing, now challenged by many scholars, is 716 A.D.; but the exodus was spread over many generations, and refugees were still arriving at the Gudjarāt ports in the two succeeding centuries. They later became generally known in India as the Pārsīs, and while they are now to be found all over the Indian subcontinent their concentration has always been highest in Gudjarāt and the Marāṭhā country to its south, specially Bombay. For a general account of the Zoroastrians see MADJŪS; for this Indian branch see PĀRSĪ, in addition to later references in this article.

(b) Gudjarāt under the Dihlī sultanate. Gudjarāt fell to the Muslims in one decisive battle when Karṇa, the last Vāghela ruler, was defeated in 697/1298 (some textual confusion; cf. Hoḍīvālā, *Studies in Indo-Muslim history*, i, Bombay 1939, 248-9) by the aimies of the Dihlī sultan ʿAlāʾ al-Dīn Khaldjī under the generals Ulugh Khān and Nuṣrat Khān; Anahilwāḍa was sacked, the rebuilt Somnāth temple was despoiled, and local garrisons were established. Nuṣrat Khān moved on to the sack of Khambāyat, where in addition to enormous booty he secured the slave Kāfūr, nicknamed Hazārdīnārī "bought for a thousand dīnārs" [see KĀFŪR; DIHLĪ SULTANATE]. Asāwal, Dholkā, Randēr, Mahuwā, Dīw and Djunāgaṛh were also overrun, and the invaders extended even to Kaččh. Karṇa's queen Kawlādevī was sent to ʿAlāʾ al-Dīn, but Karṇa escaped with his daughter the celebrated Devaldevī to Devagiri [see ELURĀ, KHIḌR KHĀN].

In 700/1300 ʿAlāʾ al-Dīn appointed his brother-in-law Malik Sandjar, entitled Alp Khān, as *nāẓim* of Gudjarāt; the old Hindū capital Anahilwāḍa became the seat of the provincial governor, but was now more commonly known as Pāṭan. Alp Khān administered the province capably for sixteen years until he was recalled to Dihlī and murdered at the instigation of the now powerful Kāfūr. On his departure disturbances broke out in Gudjarāt; Kamāl al-Dīn Gurg, the victor of Djālor [*q.v.*], sent to restore order, was taken prisoner and put to death, and sedition spread. The lawlessness increased on the death of ʿAlāʾ al-Dīn. His successor Mubārak Shāh appointed the general ʿAyn al-Mulk to suppress the revolt, and sent his father-in-law Malik Dīnār, entitled Ẓafar Khān, as *nāẓim*. The latter, a competent administrator, restored order throughout the province, but was recalled and executed in 719/1319 when Ḥusām al-Dīn, the half-brother of the royal favourite Khusraw Khān, was appointed in his place. Ḥusām rebelled against the Dihlī authority and was replaced by Waḥīd al-Dīn Ḳurayshī, under whom Gudjarāt remained quiet.

Some twenty years later bands of Afghān and New Muslim adventurers, under disaffected *amīrān-i ṣada*, constituted a menace to the country; the massacre of *amīrān-i ṣada* at Dhār [*q.v.*] led to a general rising of the *amīrān-i ṣada* of Gudjarāt in 745/1344, who seized the state revenues as they were being taken to Dihlī. Accordingly, in Ramaḍān of that year/February 1345, the sultan Muḥammad b. Tughluḳ [*q.v.*] set out in person to bring the province to order. This he did with characteristic savagery, executing disaffected and loyal *amīrs* indiscriminately. He made his headquarters in Bharōč, and, discovering that its revenues and those of Khambāyat and other towns were several years in arrears, appointed agents who exacted an extortionate rate from the people. Many rebel *amīrān-i ṣada* fled to Dawlatābād [*q.v.*]; on being summoned back to Bharōč they suspected Muḥammad's treacherous intentions, killed the Dawlatābād officials, proclaimed Ismāʿīl Mukh as their king, and took control of much of the Marāṭhā country. The sultan therefore left Bharōč to quell the rebellion, and during his absence another revolt broke out in Gudjarāt under the leadership of a former slave named Ṭaghī, who was supported by many *amīrs*, some Hindū chieftains, and a large proportion of the population. Muḥammad b. Tughluḳ returned to suppress the main revolt, and spent much time and effort in pursuit of the brilliant Ṭaghī; during Muḥammad's preoccupation with Gudjarāt affairs the rebel king Ismāʿīl Mukh abdicated in favour of another *amīr-i ṣada*, Ḥasan entitled Ẓafar Khān, who was shortly afterwards (748/1347) proclaimed as ʿAlāʾ al-Dīn Ḥasan Bahman Shāh [see BAHMANĪS]. Ṭaghī withdrew to Soraṭh and thence to Ṭhaṭṭhā, but through Muḥammad b. Tughluḳ's energetic pursuit of him the whole of Gudjarāt was subdued as never before. The sultan pursued Ṭaghī to Ṭhaṭṭhā where he had taken refuge with the Djām, but died in camp there in 752/1351, his nephew Fīrūz Shāh Tughluḳ travelling to the camp for his enthronement. Fīrūz made a difficult retreat to Dihlī, and local events in Gudjarāt did not concern the historians until some fifteen years later when he marched against the Djām in 767/1366 (for the date see Hoḍīvālā, *op. cit.*, 322); the campaign was disastrous and he lost most of his army in the Ran of Kaččh. On finally gaining Gudjarāt he dismissed the governor for failing to send him supplies and guides, and spent much time there in recruiting a new army, appointing as governor Ẓafar Khān the son-in-law of Fakhr al-Dīn Mubārak [*q.v.*]. This efficient *nāẓim* was supplanted in 778/1376 by one Shams al-Dīn Dāmghānī, who had promised a greatly increased revenue from the province; in spite of severe extortion Dāmghānī was unable to fulfil his promise, and the oppressed population rose against him. The sultan then appointed Malik Mufarraḥ Sulṭānī entitled Farḥat al-Mulk, who remained governor for fifteen years.

The imperial control of the provinces slackened during the struggles for the Tughluḳ succession, and by early 793/1391 Farḥat al-Mulk was known to be supporting Hindū practices to gain the confidence of the Rādjpūts before attempting to establish his independence; the *ʿulamāʾ* protested to Dihlī, and Muḥammad II Tughluḳ sent Ẓafar Khān the son of Wadjīh al-Mulk as governor, with the title of Muẓaffar Khān. Farḥat al-Mulk defied the new governor, and the armies of both met in the decisive battle of Kamboī, 30 km. west of Pāṭan, on 7 Ṣafar 794/4 January 1392, when Farḥat al-Mulk was killed. Muẓaffar Khān proceeded to Pāṭan and diligently began restoring order and prosperity in the province, and quashed all tendencies to the toleration of Hindū idolatry. He several times besieged the fortress of the Rādjā of Īdar [*q.v.*] for withholding tribute, and destroyed the temple of

Somnāth in 797/1395 and 804/1402; on the latter occasion he followed the Somnāth Hindūs to Dīw where he established Islam.

When Muẓaffar Khān was appointed governor his son Tātār Khān had been retained in Dihlī by Muḥammad II Tughluḳ as his *wazīr*. On the death of the sultan, Tātār Khān was prominent in the intrigues for power, and in 800/1398 he came to Gudjarāt to raise an army in order to march on Dihlī. The invasion of Tīmūr prevented this immediately, and indeed Maḥmūd Shāh, the last Tughluḳ, took refuge for a time at Pāṭan with Muẓaffar Khān. In 805/1403 Tātār Khān endeavoured to persuade his father to march on Dihlī, but the latter, now aged over 60, refused and attempted to dissuade his son. Tātār Khān then imprisoned his father, proclaimed himself sultan of Gudjarāt in Rabīʿ II 806/November 1403 with the title of Muḥammad Shāh, and marched on Dihlī; but Muẓaffar Khān's brother Shams Khān caused Tātār Khān to be poisoned and released his brother from prison. Muẓaffar returned to Pāṭan and carried on the administration for several years before finally assuming the royal title.

(c) The sultanate of Gudjarāt. Muẓaffar Khān was persuaded by the nobles to assume the insignia of royalty in 810/1407, as the Tughluḳ dynasty was virtually extinguished, and no coin had been struck by the Dihlī sultan for six years; he thus acceded as Muẓaffar Shāh. Shortly after his accession he invaded Mālwa [*q.v.*] and imprisoned sultan Hūshang at Dhār on suspicion of his having murdered his father Dilāwar Khān [*q.v.*]; however, he restored him soon afterwards. Muẓaffar died in 813/1410 and was succeeded by his grandson Aḥmad the son of Tātār Khān—not without the suspicion of having been poisoned by him.

The reign of Aḥmad I, which did much to consolidate the new sultanate, lasted 33 years, much of which was occupied in warfare against neighbouring Rādjpūt princes and the contiguous Muslim rulers of Mālwa, Khāndesh [*q.v.*] and the Deccan: in 817/1414-5 against Djunāgaṙh, compelling the payment of tribute; and from this time the power of the sultanate was extended into the central regions of Soraṫh beyond the coastal towns already in its control; in 819/1416 a confederacy of Rādjpūts in the northwest, with the partial support of Hūshang of Mālwa, was defeated, and two years later Aḥmad marched against Čāmpāner and levied tribute; in 820/1417 the army of Naṣīr Khān of Khāndesh, supported by the Mālwa army, invaded the eastern border of Gudjarāt and invested the fort of Sulṭānpur, but was repulsed by Aḥmad Shāh who followed up and besieged Naṣīr Khān in his fort of Asīrgaṙh; Naṣīr swore fealty to Aḥmad Shāh and his claim to Khāndesh was in turn recognized by Aḥmad. The instigator of the Khāndesh attack having been found to be Hūshang of Mālwa, Aḥmad next attacked that kingdom in 822/1419 and 823/1420, effecting little but the plunder oṫ outlying districts; in 825/1422, during Hūshang's absence from Mālwa on his notorious expedition to Uṙīsā [*q.v.*], Aḥmad again attacked, besieging the capital Māndū [*q.v.*] for some months without effect; the Gudjarāt and Mālwa armies confronted each other later that year in Sārangpur without a major engagement, and Aḥmad returned to Aḥmadābād and undertook no further military action for two years.

From 829-31/1425-8 there were continued hostilities against Pundja the ruler of Īdar. Aḥmad built the walled city of Aḥmadnagar (renamed Himatnagar in the 20th century) some 30 km. from Īdar

as a base of operations. In 831/1428 Pundja was killed by a fall and his son sought peace and promised tribute; nevertheless he and his successors maintained intermittent warfare with the Gudjarāt sultanate for generations thereafter. In 832/1429 a Hindū prince of the house of Djālāwar (some doubt; his name does not occur in the dynastic lists), objecting to Aḥmad's discriminatory measures against the Hindūs, attacked Nandurbār with the help of a Bahmanī army, later reinforced by one from Khāndesh also; the attackers were utterly defeated by Aḥmad's superior skill. Two years later the Bahmanī ruler Aḥmad Shāh Walī sent an army to capture the island of Mahīm (now a part of Bombay), which was held under general Gudjarāt suzerainty by a semi-independent Muslim prince; but the generals of the Gudjarāt force first invested Thāna, the most important town of the northern Konkan coast and in Bahmanī territory, by land and sea, and after its capitulation drove the invader from Mahīm.

In 836/1432-3 Aḥmad in his last major campaign against his Hindū neighbours overcame the ruler of Pāwāgaṙh, sacked Nandōd, and forced tribute from the rulers of the distant Dungārpur, Koṫāh and Bundī; although Aḥmad had apparently been defeated on a previous occasion (see *Epigraphia Indica*, ii, 417; *ibid.*, xxiii, 239. The defeat is not recorded by the Muslim historians).

Aḥmad died in Rabīʿ II 846/August 1442 after a reign devoted to consolidating Islam in his dominions by relentless iconoclasm and oppression of the Hindūs. His justice was strict but impartial, and he was known for his piety and as a disciple of the great religious teachers Shaykh Aḥmad Khaṫṫū of Sarkhedj and Burhān al-Dīn Ḳuṭb al-ʿĀlam of Baṫwā. In 813/1411 he had founded his capital city of Aḥmadābād on the left bank of the Sābarmatī, with a citadel and spacious streets (Aḥmad Rāḍī, *Haft iḳlīm*, Bibl. Ind., 86-7), and struck coin there and at Aḥmadnagar. His soldiers were paid half in coin from the imperial treasury and half by grants of land (*djāgīr*); for the *wanta* system of land revenue applicable to Hindūs, originating in his reign, see TENURE OF LAND.

Aḥmad's eldest son succeeded him with the title Muḥammad Shāh, a mild and generous ruler. He followed his father's policy in a further attack on Īdar in 850/1446, the ruler buying peace by giving Muḥammad his daughter in marriage, and in 853/1449 against Čāmpāner, from which, however, he withdrew after the *rādjā* had invoked the aid of Maḥmūd I of Mālwa; on the return journey he fell ill and died at the capital in Muḥarram 855/February 1451. His eldest son Djalāl Khān succeeded him with the title Ḳuṭb al-Dīn Aḥmad Shāh II and reigned for less than nine years. He won an early victory in the battle of Kapadwandj against a Mālwa invading force; and in 861/1457 formed a Muslim alliance with Maḥmūd I of Mālwa against the Hindū *rānā* of Čitawr, who had earlier defeated his forces (Sanskrit inscription on *kīrtistambha* of Čitawr; the defeat is not recorded by the Muslim historians). Otherwise his reign was occupied in building, and in attempts to secure the person of his young half-brother Faṫḥ Khān who was under the protection of the Baṫwā shaykh Shāh ʿĀlam. Ḳuṭb al-Dīn Aḥmad died suddenly in Radjab 862/May 1458, and is said to have been poisoned by his wife in order that her father, Shams Khān of Nāgawr, might succeed to the Gudjarāt throne. The nobles first raised to the throne Dāwūd Khān, a younger son of Aḥmad I, but he was deposed after a reign of seven days of moronic

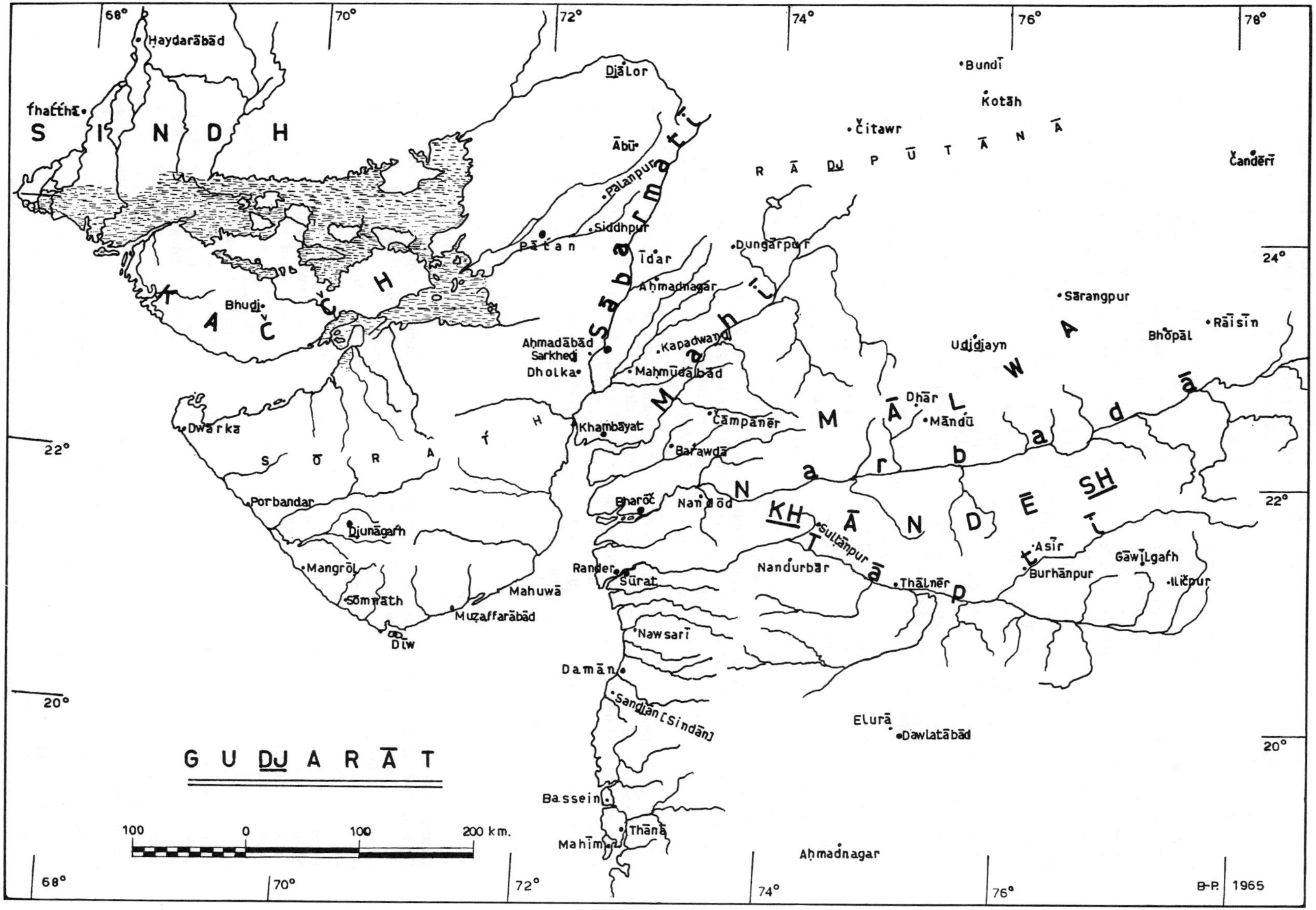

GUDJARĀT
SINDH
KAČH
SŌRAṬH
RĀDJPUTĀNĀ
MĀLWA
KHĀNDĒSH
Sābarmatī
Mahī
Narbadā
Tāpti
Haydarābād
Ṭhaṭṭhā
Djālor
Ābū
Pālanpur
Siddhpur
Pāṭan
Īdar
Aḥmadnagar
Aḥmadābād
Sarkhedj
Dholka
Kapadwandj
Maḥmūdābād
Khambāyat
Čampanēr
Barawdā
Bharōč
Nandōd
Bhudj
Dwarka
Porbandar
Djunāgaṛh
Mangrōl
Sōmnāth
Dīw
Mahuwā
Muẓaffarābād
Rānder
Sūrat
Nawsarī
Damān
Sandjān [Sindān]
Bassein
Thāna
Mahīm
Dungarpur
Čitawr
Bundī
Kotāh
Čanderī
Sārangpur
Rāīsīn
Bhōpāl
Udjdjayn
Dhār
Māndū
Sulṭānpur
Nandurbār
Thālnēr
Āsīr
Burhānpur
Gāwīlgaṛh
Iličpur
Elurā
Dawlatābād
Aḥmadnagar
68°
70°
72°
74°
76°
78°
24°
22°
20°
100
0
100
200 km.
B-P. 1965

incompetence, and Fatḥ Khān, then thirteen years old, succeeded as Maḥmūd Shāh. Within months he showed the courage and judgement that were to characterize the 54 years of his reign when he thwarted a conspiracy to remove him; and he was early involved in clashes with Mālwa when he intervened to prevent a Mālwa attempt on the dominions of the infant Bahmanī king Niẓām Shāh.

In 865/1461 Maḥmūd supported ʿUthmān Khān of Djālor in his struggle for the succession there, secured the extension of his domains—important for Gudjarāt as Islam was thereby securely established in south Rādjpūtānā—and conferred on him the title of Zubdat al-Mulk. The extension of Islam in the south of the Gudjarāt dominion was furthered in 869/1465 when an army was sent to take the hill forts of Bahrōt and Parnerā and the port of Damān from the hands of their Hindū *rādjā*s; and at this time the old Pārsī settlement of Sandjān was destroyed. The years 871-4/1467-70 saw Maḥmūd gradually overcoming the strong Rādjpūt power at Djunāgaṙh and its citadel-fort of Girnār. The defeated *rādjā* embraced Islam, and Maḥmūd remained some time at Djunāgaṙh, improving its beauty and its defences to make it a centre from which Islam could be propagated throughout the Soraṫh peninsula. He accordingly renamed it Muṣṭafābād and settled *sayyid*s and other divines there, and set it up as a mint town and as the headquarters of the *thānādār* or local administrator. To combat the laxity of the administration reported from Aḥmadābād while the sultan was on his Soraṫh campaign he appointed one Djamāl al-Dīn as *fawdjdār*, with the title of Muḥāfiẓ Khān. From his new headquarters of Muṣṭafābād Maḥmūd made expeditions in 875/1472 into Sindh and Kaččh, subduing the predatory tribes and sending their leaders to Muṣṭafābād for instruction in Islam; on his return he marched against the sacred Hindū town and temple of Dwārkā [*q.v.*] where pirates had been harassing Muslim pilgrims, and sacked the town and the neighbouring island of Beṫ (see J. Burton-Page, "*ʿAzīz" and the sack of Dwārkā* ..., in *BSOAS*, xx (1957), 145-57). He returned to Aḥmadābād in 878/1473 and undertook no major military operations for the next nine years; in this time he built the new city of Maḥmūdābād 30 km. south-east of Aḥmadābād.

In Ramaḍān 885/November 1480, when Maḥmūd was making his yearly visit to Muṣṭafābād, an attempt to dethrone him and place his eldest son Aḥmad on the throne was frustrated by the *wazīr* and Muḥāfiẓ Khān; Aḥmad seems to have been involved in the conspiracy, as he was passed over for the succession and Maḥmūd's youngest son Khalīl became heir-apparent. In Shawwāl 887/December 1482 Maḥmūd started his second great war against the Hindū princes, this time against the powerful *rādjā* of Čāmpānēr and his stronghold of Pāwāgaṙh, which fell after an investment of twenty months; for further details of this interesting siege see ḤIṢĀR. The *rādjā* publicly rejected Islam and was executed, but a son was brought up in the family of an Aḥmadābād noble and later attained distinction. Maḥmūd was captivated by the beauty and climate of Čāmpānēr, which he fortified and laid out as a new capital with the name Muḥammadābād; a mint was established (Shahr-i mukarram). Čāmpānēr remained the political capital, and the favourite residence of Maḥmūd, until the end of his reign.

In the years 896-9/1491-4 the activities of Bahādūr Gīlānī, a renegade from the Bahmanī court who committed repeated acts of piracy from Dābhōl in the south Konkan coast and had even ravaged Khambāyat and Mahīm, caused Maḥmūd to attack him by sea and call for Bahmanī cooperation by land; eventually Gīlānī was killed and full reparation was made to Gudjarāt.

In the early 10th/16th century Gudjarāt was one of the powers to intervene in the dynastic rivalries which arose in Khāndēsh on the death of ʿĀdil Khān II, finally resolved in 914/1509 with the acceptance of the Gudjarāt candidate, a kinsman of Maḥmūd's, as ʿĀdil Khān III (for a detailed account see FĀRŪḲIDS).

Since the arrival of Vasco da Gama in Calicut in 1498 the Portuguese had extended their maritime influence over much of the Indian ocean and the Red Sea, to the great detriment of the lucrative trade which passed through the Gudjarāt ports, especially Khambāyat, and depriving Egypt of the revenues of much of her Eastern trade. Their first opposition in these regions came from the joint force of the fleet despatched by the Egyptian Mamlūk sultan Ḳānṣawh al-Ghawrī, under the command of Amīr Ḥusayn, and that of Gudjarāt commanded by Malik Ayāz the governor of Djunāgaṙh, who won the first victory in Ramaḍān 913/January 1508 when Dom Lorenzo, son of Francisco d'Almeida the Portuguese viceroy, was killed in a battle off Čawl; but the combined Muslim fleets were defeated by d'Almeida in a battle outside Dīw harbour in Shawwāl 914/February 1509 (E. Denison Ross, *The Portuguese in India and Arabia between 1507-1517*, in *JRAS*, 1921, 545-62). Maḥmūd then attempted to establish diplomatic relations with the Portuguese (see W. de G. Birch (ed.), *The commentaries of the great Afonso Dalboquerque*, Hakluyt Socy., especially ii, 210 ff.); but after Albuquerque's capture and orgiastic sack and massacre of Ṣindābur (Goa), the port of the ʿĀdil Shāhī sultanate of Bīdjāpur, Maḥmūd realized the impracticability of maintaining any alliance with such an intransigent enemy of Islam and, to avoid provocation, broke the Egyptian alliance and liberated his Portuguese prisoners.

Maḥmūd died at Aḥmadābād on 2 Ramaḍān 917/23 November 1511 and was buried at Sarkhedj. In his reign the prosperity of the Gudjarāt reached perhaps its greatest height; certainly it knew its greatest internal security in the towns and in the ports. The army was efficient and well equipped, and Maḥmūd was solicitous for the welfare of his troops, including the families of those killed in battle, who were provided for by continuance to them of the assets of the late soldier's *djāgīr*, and consoled the next-of-kin of the dead in person after his battles. He was a great builder, and also laid out many gardens and orchards, and is credited with the introduction of many kinds of fruit trees into Gudjarāt. He was a tall man with a prodigious appetite and a moustache which he could tie behind his head, and was said to have been inoculated against poison by consuming it in gradually increasing doses "so that if a fly settled on his hand it fell dead". His sobriquet of "Begŕā" has given rise to some speculation as to its true meaning: one etymology seeks to derive it from the "two forts (*gaṙh*)" of Čāmpānēr and Djunāgaṙh which he captured; but the word is not written in Gudjarātī with *ṙh*; another derives it from Gudjarātī *vegaṙo*, a bullock with sweeping horns, in allusion to his moustaches; Dr. P. B. Pandit (personal communication) has suggested that it is the word

Beg with the Gudjarātī diminutive suffix *ŕā*, *-ḍā*, "the little Beg"; the form Bayḳarā, used in the article FĀRŪḲIDS, seems to be a false Mughalization. Valuable accounts of Maḥmūd and Gudjarāt in his reign are given in the works of the Portuguese traveller Duarte Barbosa and the Italian Varthema.

Khalīl Khān succeeded his father as Muẓaffar Shāh II, a mild and cultured ruler whose clemency bordered on weakness. Early in his reign he was involved in the affairs of the neighbouring state of Mālwa: in 916/1510 Maḥmūd II Khaldjī had usurped the Mālwa throne from his elder brother Ṣāḥib Khān, who had been proclaimed as Muḥammad II by the rebel *wazīr* and asked for Muẓaffar's assistance in coming to his throne. His claim was favourably reported on by the Gudjarāt agents in Mālwa, and Muẓaffar had agreed to attack Mālwa in his support after the rains. Muẓaffar was at the time entertaining an ambassador from Shāh Ismāʿīl I of Persia, whose mission was apparently to induce Gudjarāt to accept the Shīʿa faith, and who had become acquainted with Ṣāḥib Khān; one evening after a dinner party the ambassador in a moment of pederastic enthusiasm assaulted Ṣāḥib Khān, who fled in shame first to Khāndesh and then to Berār; the ambassador was sent back to Persia after a scarcely cordial reception. Ṣāḥib Khān's claim was quietly forgotten, and shortly afterwards Muẓaffar was called on to intervene on behalf of Maḥmūd II who found himself no more than a puppet in the hands of his minister Mēdinī Rāī and his Rādjpūt army. Muẓaffar accordingly marched on the capital Māndū with a strong Gudjarāt force which was joined by the Khāndesh army, hearing of which Mēdinī Rāī sought help from the powerful Mahārānā Sāngrām of Čitawr; the fort was taken by escalade in Ṣafar 924/February 1518, the Rādjpūt garrison massacred, and Maḥmūd restored to his throne. The text of a letter from Muẓaffar to the Ottoman Sultan Selīm I, congratulating the latter on his victory over Persia and announcing the capture of Māndū, is given by Ferīdūn (*Munshaʾāt*[1], i, 395-7).

Muẓaffar had been delayed in his actions in Mālwa by several skirmishes in and around Īdar, where a usurper had been established on the throne of this feudatory Hindū state by Sāngrām of Čitawr; this interference was ill received in Gudjarāt, and armies were sent to restore the rightful heir; the usurper continued, however, to harass the northern districts of Gudjarāt until Muẓaffar's return from Mālwa. Sāngrām, incensed by insults to his name offered by the Gudjarāt commander at Īdar, raided Īdar, Aḥmadnagar and other towns in 925/1519; Muẓaffar retaliated with a large force early in 927/1521, and compelled the Rānā to pay tribute and send a son to the Gudjarāt court as a hostage.

In Muẓaffar II's reign there was considerable diplomatic intercourse with the Portuguese at Goa, friendly at first. A mission sent to Gudjarāt in 918/1512-3 sought permission to build a fort at Dīw, which the sultan, on the advice of Malik Ayāz [*q.v.*], governor of Djunagárh and Dīw, did not grant. The Portuguese cause was pressed by one Malik Gōpī at the Gudjarāt court, but Malik Ayāz's wiser counsels prevailed and the defences of Dīw were strengthened. Two attempts by the Portuguese to take Dīw by force, in 926/1520 and 927/1521, were thwarted, and an attempt to take Muẓaffarābād, 30 km. east of Dīw, and establish a fort there, was foiled when some Muslim captives blew up a munitions ship in which they were travelling.

Muẓaffar II died in Djumādā II 932/April 1526. His eldest son Sikandar succeeded him but was murdered after six weeks and an infant son of Muẓaffar II was placed on the throne as Maḥmūd II; but the loyal nobles sent for Bahādur, the second son of Muẓaffar II, who was formally installed as sultan in the Ramaḍān/July following, the infant Maḥmūd II and other princes of the royal blood being quietly disposed of, except for his younger brother Čānd Khān who had taken refuge with Maḥmūd II of Mālwa.

The principal events of Bahādur's reign—the attack on the Niẓām Shāhīs of Aḥmadnagar in 935/1528 to settle a territorial dispute with Khāndesh, his conquest of Mālwa in 937/1531, the capture of the Rādjpūt strongholds Udjdjayn, Bhīlsā and Rāīsīn in 938/1532-3 and Čitawr in 941/1535, the defeat of the Portuguese at Dīw in 937/1531 but the loss to them of Bassein in 941/1534 and the grant of permission to build a fort at Dīw in 942/1535, the long war with the Mughal Humāyūn from 941/1534 in which Bahādur lost Mālwa and was dispossessed of most of his dominions until Humāyūn returned to face the threat of Sher Khān in 942/1536, and his death through Portuguese treachery—have been discussed above in the article BAHĀDUR SHĀH GUDJARĀTĪ: see also HUMĀYŪN, MĀLWA, MUGHALS; and add to the Bibliography of BAHĀDUR SHĀH GUDJARĀTĪ: Philip Baldaeus, *Description of the East India coasts* ... in Churchill's *Collection of voyages and travels*, London 1732, iii, 530 ff.

Bahādur's murder by the Portuguese took place at sea outside Dīw in Ramaḍān 943/February 1537, and with his death the greatness of the Gudjarāt sultanate ended. The Portuguese seized Dīw with the palace and treasury, and it thenceforth passed out of Muslim hands. Bahādur left no heir, and in the first confusion after his death Muḥammad Zamān Mīrzā, Humāyūn's brother-in-law whose refuge with Bahādur had provoked the war with the Mughals, aspired to the throne, entered into a treaty with the Portuguese whereby he granted them Mangrōḷ and Damān and a strip of coastal land in exchange for their support, and the *khuṭba* was read in his name in the mosque at Dīw; but the nobles of Bahādur's court sent an army against him, and he was defeated and fled to Dihlī. Bahādur had in his lifetime indicated that his sister's son Mīrān Muḥammad Shāh, who since 926/1520 had been the ruler of Khāndesh, should succeed him, and the nobles sent for him; but within weeks he died of grief for the uncle to whom he had been a constant and loyal companion for the previous ten years, and the eleven years old Maḥmūd Khān, son of Bahādur's renegade brother Laṭīf Khān, was then enthroned as Maḥmūd Shāh III.

Maḥmūd and his two successors were all minors, and the history of the sultanate after 943/1537 is mostly one of puppet monarchies and factious and suspicious nobles plotting for power against each other and against the best interests of the state. In 944/1538 the Ottoman sultan Süleymān I, apprehensive at the growing Portuguese threat because of Bahādur's death, sent a fleet from Suez to attack them at Dīw; the Gudjarāt land forces, fearing that the presence of the Turks at Dīw would be no more comfortable than that of the Portuguese, failed to give full cooperation, and on receipt of a fabricated letter announcing that the Portuguese main fleet was arriving from Goa, the Ottoman fleet raised the siege and sailed away; the Gudjarāt generals negotiated a peace treaty with the Portuguese, and built a wall separating the fort from the town of Dīw (see further KHĀDIM SÜLEYMĀN PASHA).

In 950/1543 Maḥmūd III escaped from his custody at the hands of the powerful regent Daryā K͟hān and fled to the protection of ʿĀlam K͟hān Lodī the fief-holder of Dhandūkā 100 km. south-west of Aḥmadābād; in the following battle Daryā K͟hān was defeated and fled to Māndū, but Maḥmūd found that he had exchanged one master for another, for ʿĀlam K͟hān placed him under guard in the citadel of Aḥmadābād and assumed direction of the kingdom. Two years later Maḥmūd persuaded a disaffected noble to attack ʿĀlam K͟hān, and assumed personal rule. He turned his attention first to the Portuguese, established a fort at Sūrat [*q.v.*], and in 953/1546 attacked Dīw with a large force; after a siege of eight months, in which the brilliant Gud̲j̲arātī commander K͟hʷād̲j̲a Safar was killed, the Portuguese received reinforcements from Goa, and on 17 Ramaḍān/11 November the governor João de Castro "conquered like a Christian and triumphed like a heathen": all Muslim prisoners and the inhabitants of the city were mercilessly butchered. A year later the Portuguese sacked and burnt Bharōč and massacred the inhabitants.

In 953/1546 Maḥmūd removed his residence to Maḥmūdābād where he laid out his famous deer-park. In 955/1548 he sent for Āṣaf K͟hān from Mecca where he had gone with the late sultan Bahādur's treasures and *ḥaram*; he was made absolute regent, and raised for the sultan a personal bodyguard of 12,000 foreign mercenaries. In Rabīʿ I 962/February 1554 Maḥmūd was murdered in his palace by a resentful attendant, and with him ten of the chief nobles including Āṣaf K͟hān. His assassin attempted to accede to the throne but was defeated in the first attack of the remaining nobles. Maḥmūd III left no heir, and the nobles sought out a boy called Raḍī al-Mulk, a great-great-grandson of Aḥmad I, whom they installed as Aḥmad S͟hāh III; the kingdom was virtually divided among the nobles, and the reign is a dreary chronicle of civil war, one Iʿtimād K͟hān, a converted Hindū, being prominent as regent. Almost the only event of external interest is the cession of the port of Damān to the Portuguese on condition that they drove out the Ḥabs͟hī governor who neither paid taxes nor acknowledged the central government; the Portuguese prepared to attack Damān in Rabīʿ II 966/February 1559, but the Ḥabs͟hī garrison abandoned the fort without a battle. Several members of the Ḥabs͟hī community rose to prominence at about this time and further weakened the power of the government. In 968/1561 Aḥmad III, who was beginning to resent his confinement, was murdered on Iʿtimād K͟hān's orders.

Again the problem of finding an heir presented itself. Iʿtimād K͟hān produced a child of unknown parentage as the child of Maḥmūd III by a concubine, who was duly proclaimed sultan as Muẓaffar III. The kingdom continued to be split up amongst the various nobles, who were now joined in their depredations by adventurers from the north of India. Prominent among these a little later were the so-called Mīrzās, descendants of Tīmūr and hence kinsmen of the Mug͟hal emperor Akbar. Eventually in desperation Iʿtimād K͟hān invited Akbar to invade Gud̲j̲arāt.

Akbar left Fatḥpur Sīkrī in Ṣafar 980/July 1572 and arrived at Pāťan early in Rad̲j̲ab/November of the same year, receiving the submission of the Gud̲j̲arāt nobles in what was more of a triumphal procession than a campaign at Pāťan and Aḥmadābād; he proceeded to Khambāyat, when there was some attempt at rebellion in Aḥmadābād on the part of some nobles who were having second thoughts but who were soon brought to submission. As he proceeded further south, however, he encountered some resistance: his kinsmen the Mīrzās [*q.v.*] had made themselves masters of Sūrat, Baŕōdā, Bharōč and Čāmpānēr, and together with the rebellious Ḥabs͟hīs formed a considerable opposition; they were defeated by the imperial forces at the battle of Sarnāl on 17 S͟haʿbān 980/23 December 1572, and after the long siege of Sūrat which ended on 23 S͟hawwāl 980/26 February 1573. Akbar returned to Fatḥpur Sīkrī in D̲h̲u 'l-Ḥid̲j̲d̲j̲a 980/April 1573, and Gud̲j̲arāt became a *sūba* of the Mug͟hal empire of sixteen *sarkārs*—there having been twenty-five *sarkārs* in the dominions of the Gud̲j̲arāt sultanate at its greatest extent. Within three months of Akbar's departure the Mīrzās again revolted and with the rebel Ḥabs͟hīs besieged the Mug͟hal governor in Aḥmadābād; Akbar returned to Gud̲j̲arāt in nine days by forced marches and finally suppressed the Mīrzās' revolt in the battle of Aḥmadābād in D̲j̲umādā I 981/September 1573. A minor outbreak of disturbances under one of the Mīrzās in 985/1577 was put down by the Mug͟hal expeditionary force from K͟hāndes͟h.

The last Gud̲j̲arāt sultan, Muẓaffar III, had been taken prisoner by Akbar's forces on his first invasion. In 986/1578 he escaped and made his way to Gud̲j̲arāt and rose in rebellion in 991/1583, actually assuming the sultanate for a period of about six months; he evaded capture by the Mug͟hal forces, and continued to offer resistance as a fugitive for the next ten years until his suicide after capture in 1001/1593 (for the final pursuit and capture of Muẓaffar see Burton-Page, *op. cit.*, 151 ff.).

For the largely peaceful history of Gud̲j̲arāt under the Mug͟hals see MUG͟HAL. The importance of the province to the Mug͟hals was largely commercial. The region was famous for its silk weaving and, especially at Aḥmadābād and Sūrat, the production of velvets (although sericulture never seems to have been practised in the region; the silk was imported from Bengal and from China); fine cotton cloth (*bafta*) was produced at the coastal towns, Bharōč in particular producing fine bleached calico; Sarkhed̲j̲ was the principal centre for indigo production in the Mug͟hal empire; saltpetre was refined at Aḥmadābād and Sūrat; and salt was prepared by evaporation from many districts bordering on the Raṇ of Kaččh. The conquest of Gud̲j̲arāt also gave ports to the Mug͟hal empire, where apart from the commercial traffic there was a busy pilgrim traffic to the Holy Cities. The trade suffered a great loss in the Satyāsiō Kāḷ, the "famine of eighty-seven" (the Vikram year 1687, 1040-1/1630-1), and took at least ten years to recover; an interesting account of Mug͟hal famine relief is given by ʿAbd al-Ḥamīd, *Bād͟s͟hāh-nāma* (text, Engl. trans., and comment in P. Saran, *Provincial government of the Mughals*, Allahabad 1941, 432-3).

The peace and prosperity of Gud̲j̲arāt under Mug͟hal rule gave way to disorder after the death of Awrangzīb at the beginning of the 12th/18th century. Previously there had been sporadic raids on Gud̲j̲arāt territory, especially Sūrat in 1074/1664 and 1081/1670, by the Marāṭhā chieftain S͟hivād̲j̲ī; now the Gāikwāŕ family rose to prominence in Gud̲j̲arāt affairs and wielded more power than the Mug͟hal *sūbadār*; by 1137/1725 they had started a reign of terror. Villages and towns were plundered, and in the next ten years the Marāṭhās had overrun almost all the province; eventually, with the fall of Aḥmadābād in 1171/1758, Mug͟hal rule was extinguished. For the history of the

Marāṫhà wars and their rule of Gudjarāt see MARĀṪHĀS. Some tracts of the province were not, however, under the Marāṫhā rule of the Gāikwāṙ or the Peshwa, but remained under the authority of independent Muslim nobles, the Nawwābs of Bharōč, Khambāyat, Rādhanpur, and Sūrat [qq.v.] among others, in addition to the large district of Djunāgaṙh [q.v.]. After the defeat of the Marāṫhās in the third battle of Pānīpat [q.v.] an imperial *farmān* was sent to Muʾmin Khān the Nawwāb of Khambāyat in 1174/1761 for the recovery of Gudjarāt. Muʾmin Khān prepared for battle but in the absence of imperial support was unable to take effective action, and Marāṫhā rule continued until Gudjarāt was ceded to the British by the Gāikwāṙ in 1817.

For the ethnology of Gudjarāt see HIND, Ethnology. For religious developments see DJAYN, PĀRSĪ; for Islamic sects see BOHORĀS, KHŌDJAS, IMĀM SHĀH, ISMĀʿĪLIYYA, MUʾMIN, SĀTPANTHĪ.

For the coinage of Gudjarāt see SIKKA. For the monuments, see HIND, also AḤMADĀBĀD, BHARŌČ, ČĀMPĀNĒR, DJŪNĀGAṘH, KHAMBĀYAT, MAḤMŪDĀBĀD, SŪRAT.

Bibliography: Sources for Gudjarāt history under the Dihlī sultanate have been given in the bibliography to DIHLĪ SULTANATE; especially important for Gudjarāt are Ḍiyāʾ al-Dīn Baranī, *Taʾrīkh-i Fīrūz Shāhī*; ʿIsāmī, *Futūḥ al-salāṭīn*; Amīr Khusraw, *Khazāʾin al-futūḥ*; ʿAbd al-Karīm Hamdānī, *Taʾrīkh-i Maḥmūd Shāhī*; ʿAlī b. Maḥmūd al-Mirmānī, *Maʾāthir-i Maḥmūd Shāhī*, Bodl. Elliot 237.

For the Gudjarāt sultanate: there is no purely local early work, but many lost histories are quoted in Shaykh Sikandar b. Muḥammad Mandjhū, *Mirʾāt-i Sikandarī*, a history from the Muslim conquest to 1020/1611, ed. S. C. Misra and M. L. Rahman, Baroda 1960, Eng. trans., incomplete and inaccurate, E. C. Bayley, as *Local Muhammadan dynasties: History of Gujarat*, London 1886; ʿAbd Allāh Muḥammad b. ʿUmar al-Makkī, known as Ḥādjdjī al-Dabīr, *Ẓafar al-wālih bi Muẓaffar wa-ālih*, ed. E. Denison Ross as *An Arabic history of Gujarat*, 3 vols, London 1921-8; Abū Turāb Walī, *Taʾrīkh-i Gudjarāt*, ed. E. Denison Ross, Bibl. Ind. Calcutta 1909; Muḥammad Ḳāsim Firishta, *Gulshan-i Ibrāhīmī*; ʿAlī b. ʿAzīz Allāh Ṭabāṭabā, *Burhān-i maʾāthir*; Niẓam al-Dīn Aḥmad, *Ṭabaḳāt-i Akbarī*, ed. Bibl. Ind. Calcutta 1927-35, Eng. tr. Bibl. Ind. 1913-40; especially for the Mughal conquest and subsequent Mughal administration: Abu ʾl-Faḍl ʿAllāmī, *Akbar-nāma*, Bibl. Ind. Calcutta 1873-87; idem, *Āʾīn-i Akbarī*, Bibl. Ind. 1867-77, Eng. tr. Bibl. Ind. 1894-1949. The foremost authority for the Mughal period is ʿAlī Muḥammad Khān, *Mirʾāt-i Aḥmadī*, 2 vols., with a very valuable *khātima* which is virtually a statistical gazetteer of Gudjarāt in the 10th/16th and 11th/17th centuries, ed. S. Nawab Ali, Baroda 1926-30; Eng. tr. as *The political and statistical history of Gujarat*, by J. Bird, London 1835; Eng. tr. of *khātima* only, by Nawab Ali and C. N. Seddon, Baroda 1928.

European travellers: especially M. L. Dames (ed. and tr.), *The book of Duarte Barbosa*, Hakluyt Society 1918; *The travels of Pietro della Valle in India 1623-6*, Hakluyt Society 1891; J. Albert de Mandelslo, *Voyages ... into the East Indies*, Eng. tr. J. Davies, London 1662; *The travels of Peter Mundy ...*, ed. Temple, Hakluyt Society 1907-36; J. Ovington, *A voyage to Suratt in the year 1689*, ed. Rawlinson, Oxford 1929; *The embassy of Sir Thomas Roe ...*, ed. Foster, Hakluyt Society 1899; *Travels of Ludovico de Varthema*, Hakluyt Society 1863; Albuquerque, *Commentaries*, Eng. tr. W. de G. Birch, Hakluyt Society 1875-84; Gaspar Correa, *Lendas da India*, Lisbon 1858-64; *Vida da Dom João de Castro*, Eng. tr. Wyche, London 1664.

Modern works: M.S. Commissariat, *History of Gujarat*, i, London 1938; ii, Bombay 1957; well documented with much cultural information. A research project of the history of Gudjarāt under the Muslims is currently being undertaken at the M.S. University of Baroda, from which there has appeared S. C. Misra, *The rise of Muslim power in Gujarat*, London 1963, which covers the years 697/1298 to 845/1442; idem, *Muslim Communities in Gujarat: preliminary studies in their history and social organization*, New York 1964; both these with extensive bibliography. Pearson, 20164-80. Much general information in *Bombay Gazetteer*, i-ix, xiii, xiv; *Baroda state gazetteer*, 2 vols., Bombay 1923. On the coins of the Gudjarāt sultanate, especially G. P. Taylor, *The coins of the Gujarāt salṭanat*, in *JBBRAS*, xxi (1903) 278-338; and Pearson, 10482-97. (J. BURTON-PAGE)

GUDJARĀTĪ, language spoken in the state of Gudjarāt (population 20,623,474) and in the communities of Gudjarātīs which have settled in various parts of India; it has always been the first language of the many Gudjarātī Muslims, in preference to Urdū, and shows some Muslim influence in its literary forms, notably in the introduction of the *ghazal*. Outside India, large communities of Gudjarātī speakers are settled in Asia and Africa.

Gudjarātī belongs to the Indo-Aryan branch of the Indo-Iranian subgroup of the Indo-European language family. The earliest inscriptional evidence of Aryan speech in Gudjarāt goes back to the Ashōkan edicts at Girnar (Sawrāshtra) of 250 B.C. Gudjarāt had a strong tradition of Sanskritic and Prākritic learning. A literary standard prevalent in the region bounded by Djaysalmēr to the north, Mālwa to the east and Sawrāshṫra and Gudjarāt to the west and south became a direct predecessor of modern Gudjarātī. Some of the dated documents of the 12th century and secondary copies of compositions of the 10th century mark the beginning of old Gudjarātī literature. Modern Gudjarātī literature is rich in belles-lettres as well as in serious prose. The Gudjarātī script is a cursive form of Devanāgarī; the syllabary is Sanskritic. The Perso-Arabic script has never been in regular use for Gudjarātī.

Southern, Central and Northern Gudjarāt and peninsular Sawrāshtra form the major dialect regions of Gudjarātī. The dialects of Sawrāshṫra are archaic and have preserved some older features. Notable among the occupational jargons are the speech of fishermen in Sawrāshṫra and along the southern Gudjarāt coast, the bardic and pastoral communities of Sawrāshṫra, the Ismāʿīlī Khodjas of Sawrāshṫra and the Pārsīs of South Gudjarāt. On the whole, central and northern Gudjarāt are innovating dialects, and modern standard Gudjarātī is based on the speech of the educated upper caste population.

Bibliography: G. A. Grierson, *Linguistic survey of India*, ix/2, Calcutta 1908, 323-477. (P. B. PANDIT)

GŪDJRĀŃWĀLA, an industrial town of West Pakistan and headquarters of the district of the same name, situated in 32° 9′ N. and 74° 11′ E., on the main railway line between Lahore and Peshawar [qq.v.]; population (1961) 196,154. The town, a mere village till the middle of the 19th century, owes its origin to a tribe of the Gūdjars [*q.v.*] who were expelled by Sāńsī Djāṭs from Amritsar [*q.v.*]. On changing hands the village was renamed Khānpur, after the head-man of the Sāńsīs. But this name never gained popularity.

It was of little importance during Mughal days and consequently finds no mention in the *Āʾīn-i Akbarī*. Early in the 19th century it was captured by Čarat Singh Djāṭ, grandfather of the Sikh ruler Randjīt Singh, who made it his headquarters. Randjīt Singh himself was born here and it continued to be the capital of the rising Sikh power until 1799, when the seat of government was shifted to Lahore. The Sikh general Harī Singh Nalwa, who led many punitive expeditions against the Afghāns of the Khyber, was also a native of this place. His house, in a narrow street of the town, is still preserved. The father and grandfather oi Randjīt Singh both have their *Samādhs*, last resting places, in this town. The former was cremated in a corner of the gardens named after him, but now called Jinnah Bagh, while the latter has his mausoleum in a quarter of the old city. A lofty cupola covering a portion of the ashes of Randjīt Singh, who has his tomb in Lahore and a *bāradarī*, a fine example of Sikh architecture, form a part of the complex. An old mosque, said to date from the times of Shēr Shāh Sūr [*q.v.*], with the typical onion-shaped dome, is also preserved.

The town remained quiet during the military uprising of 1857 but was badly disturbed during the Non-Cooperation and *Khilāfat* movements of 1921-22, when rioters uprooted the railroad track, burnt down the railway station and indulged in widespread arson and looting. By way of punishment the new railroad station was built at a considerable distance from the town. It is now used as a halting station for good trains while the passengers alight at the site of the destroyed station, which was rebuilt by the British Government. Politically unimportant, the town is a flourishing centre of iron, steel, copper and hand-loom industries and is rapidly expanding.

Bibliography: *Imperial Gazetteer of India*, Oxford 1908, xii, 355-6, 363; *District Census Report, Gujranwala*, Karachi 1961, 1.15, 4.1 - 4.12; Waḥīd Ḳurayshī (Waheed Qureshi), *Gujranwala: Past and Present*, in *OCM*, Lahore, February 1958.

(A. S. Bazmee Ansari)

GUDJRĀT, a town, *taḥṣīl* and district in the northern plains of the Pākistān Pandjāb lying between the rivers Djehlam and Čanāb. The district is thought to have once formed part of the ancient Gurdjara kingdom; but it is not specifically referred to in Islamic historical writing until the time of Bahlōl Lodī (855-94/1451-89) when the town of Bahlōlpur, 36 km. north-east of Gudjrāt town, was founded; the settlement of the district was continued by Shīr Shāh in the middle of the 10th/16th century, and completed by Akbar with the refounding of Gudjrāt town.

There seem to have been at least two succesive cities on the site of what is now Gudjrāt. One tradition gives the early name of the town as Udanāgarī and a foundation by Rādjpūt kings in the 5th century B.C.; a king Alākhāna is cited by the Sanskrit *Rājatarangini* as the defender of the town against Śankaravarman of Kashmīr between 883 and 902 A.D., and is perhaps the origir of the "ʿAlī Khān' reported as a re-founder in a popular local Muslim tradition; one city seems to have been destroyed c. 703/1303 by the Mongols. The modern foundation dates from Akbar, who in 995 or 997/1587 or 1589 persuaded some of the local Gūdjars to restore Gudjrāt and made it the headquarters of a large district; the local population is predominantly Djāṭ [*q.v.*], but the fort (Gudjrāt-Akbarābād) was garrisoned by Gūdjars.

The town and district remained under efficient Mughal control until the death of Awrangzēb, records of the period having been preserved by the hereditary *ḳānūngōs* of the region. In 1151/1738 it was ravaged by Nādir Shāh [*q.v.*]; the Gakkhars of Rāwalpindī, under Sultan Muḳarrab Khān, established themselves there in 1154/1741, but the country was an open prey from 1161/1748 to 1175/1761 to the marauding armies of Aḥmad Shāh Durrānī [*q.v.*] on whose route it lay. Muḳarrab Khān was confirmed in his possessions by the Durrānī ruler, and nominally administered them on his behalf; but "nothing was left to the people but the food and drink in their mouths; the rest was Aḥmad Shāh's". This nominal rule lasted until 1179/1765, when Gudjrāt fell to the Sikhs. The district came under British rule in 1846.

The district is largely agricultural, and produces some timber. Gudjrāt town has some reputation as a centre for fine furniture making, and had previously some renown as a centre of iron damascening. The shrine still exists of the *pīr* Shāh Dawla [b. 975/1567, d. 1125/1713 according to the local tradition], a saint whose intercessions were said to remove the curse of barrenness if the first-born were dedicated to his service. These children attached to the shrine are invariably freaks, of low intelligence and with absurdly pointed heads—deliberate distortion of the heads in infancy has been suspected; they are known as Čūhā-i Shāh Dawla, "Shāh Dawla's rats".

The name Gudjrāt used here reflects the conventional spelling Gujrat, adopted to distinguish this district and town from Gujarat (Gudjarāt [*q.v.*]); the two names are really identical. For the etymology see gudjarāt.

Bibliography: *Imperial Gazetteer of India*; *Punjab District Gazetteers, XXV-A, Gujrat District*, Lahore 1921. For Shāh Dawla's Rats see J. Wilson Johnston in *Indian Medical Gazette*, May 1866; abstract from settlement reports in *Indian Antiquary*, 1879, 176; letter in *JRAS*, 1896, 574-5, 793; M. Longworth Dames, *Shah Daulah's Rats*, in *Man*, xv (1915), 88-9. (J. Burton-Page)

GUERSIF [see garsīf].

GUILD(S) [see futuwwa, ṣinf].

GUINEA, an independent republic on the West coast of Africa (246,000 sq. km), bounded on the north by Portuguese Guinea, Senegal and Mali, on the east by the Ivory Coast, and on the south by Liberia and Sierra Leone. Within these limits, between 7° and 13° N., and between 7° and 17° E., every type of terrain and climate is to be found, starting with Lower Guinea which has a width of from 40 to 90 km, and where extensive deltas have been formed by the neighbouring rivers, often lined with mud-flats or strewn with islands; Central Guinea corresponds with the Fūta Djallon, dominated by residual high ground from 1200 to 1500 m. and distinguished by the *bowal*, a cap of laterite isolated by erosion, and where the introduction of cultivation has increased the sterility. Upper Guinea corresponds with the upper basin of the Niger, where the climate becomes continental; further south, in the Guinea forests, lies the mountain barrier containing Mount Nimba.

Guinea probably derives its name from the Berber *ignawən*, pl. of *agnaw*, which means "mute" and does not imply any notion of colour (see G. S.

Colin in *GLECS*, vii, 93-5), contrary to the view expressed by M. Delafosse (*Haut-Sénégal-Niger*, ii, 277).

The population of Guinea numbers about 3 million. There are still some centres of population that are either indigenous or were established in very early times, Coniagui and Bassari in the north, Kissi and Guerze in the south.

The Baga, Landuman, Mani or Mendenyi, and Nalu have been driven back from the Fūta towards the coast by Mande, Sarakole, Malinke and Sussu elements, and by the conquering Fulani. The history of these settlements corresponds in general outline with the history of Islamization.

This process was accomplished only slowly, under the pressure of political and military events in the Nigerian Sudan, first with Malinke elements, and then through the Fulani who, as soon as they believed themselves to be sufficiently strong, were to proclaim a holy war and to maintain their ascendancy over the Fūta until the French conquest.

It was in 422/1050 that Baramendana Keita, the sovereign of Mali, was converted to Islam. From the end of the 5th/11th century the first Diola to be Islamized by the Sarakole penetrated into Guinea and began to spread Islam into the Fūta and along the kola-nut routes leading to the coast. In the 6th/12th century, the Soninke Morikubala Dore introduced Islam into the Konian, Awrodugu and Kossadugu. In 658/1260 Amari Sonko, one of the commanders of Mansa Ule, king of Mali, conquered and converted the Kangaran. In the first half of the 10th/16th century came the Pouli from Macina and Tichitt, commanded by Bambi Diade. These first Fulani invaders were Ḳādiriyya Bakkāya (of the Kunta of Timbuctu). They set about converting or expelling the refractory elements. Koli Tenguela or Koli Pouli, great-grandson of Bambi Diade, created the first kingdom of Fūta.

Attracted by the mountain pasturages, the Fulani came in ever increasing numbers from Macina at the end of the 11th/17th century, and Islamization became more marked. However, the Muslim Mandingos, coming from Diafonu in particular, founded Kankan and the villages of Bate, Kuafodie and Tintiule. In 1105/1694 a powerful force of Fulani arrived from Macina, led by a certain Seri or Sidi. In about 1111/1700 leadership passed to Muhammadu Saïdi and then to Kikala, a man renowned for his piety. On the death of his son Sambigu, his grandsons Nuhu and Malik Si disputed the succession (1132-8/1720-6).

The Muslim penetration was, at that date, on so extensive a scale that it was tempting to make use of the religious pretext to evict the proprietors of the land. It was Ibrahima Mussu, still known as Karamoko Alfa, a man of immense piety, who was called on to fight against the pagans. He inaugurated the permanent state of holy war which was one of the constant and fundamental policies of Fūta. The first victories fell to the aggressive Fulani, but the pagans recovered and their chief, Pouli Garme, occupied Timbo when Karamoko became insane and died. In his place was chosen Ibrahima Sori ("the Wakeful"), known as *mawdo* (= the Great), who in practice was to be the great war leader of Fūta, defeating the Wassulonke and the Sulima in succession. He compelled the Fulani chief of Labe to recognize his authority over the Mandingo province of Niokolo in Upper Gambia, and forced Maka, king of Bundu, to become Muslim and take the title of *almami*. In face of these triumphs, the council of elders became perturbed and their head, the *Modi Maka*, with the support of the Alfaya had Abdullahi Ba Demba, a descendant of Karamoko Alfa, nominated as *almami*. But under the threat of perils from without, they recalled Ibrahima Sori who, in about 1194/1780, moved the capital of Fukumba to Timbo. On the death of Ibrahima Sori (in about 1784), the kingdom of Fūta, divided into two rival branches, the Alfaya and the Soria, was apportioned to each of the branches alternately every two years. During the reigns of Karamoko Alfa and Ibrahima Sori Mawdo, the Islamization of central Guinea (Kindia region) was continued. Some Kankan families broke away and founded Beyla (corruption of *billāh*).

These alternating reigns did not pass without serious difficulties. The Islamization of the Dialonke proceeded with increased momentum as a result of the founding in 1821 of the *madrasa* of Tuba, an important Ḳādirī centre, by al-Ḥādjdj Salimu, better known under the name Karamba. In 1830, Alfa Mamadu introduced Islam into the Rio Nuñez. The 19th century was dominated by the reign of the Almami ʿUmar (1837-72), who overcame his rival Ibrahima at Timbo (1851) and succeeded in conquering the fanatical Muslims who had revolted in the Fitaba at the instigation of a *marabout*, Mamadu Dj̲ue. These rebels were called Hubbu from the phrase *ḥubbu rasūl Allāh* (= the love of God's Messenger). Mamadu Dj̲ue having died, his son Abal ("the Wild") continued the struggle and contrived to kill the Almami Sori Dara at Boketto, the capital of the Fitaba, in 1872.

Treaties of friendship were signed in the reign of Ibrahima Sori Donhol Fella (1872-89) and Amadu Dara (1873-96) with representatives of England and France. In 1887-8, Aimé Olivier, Comte (?) de Sanderval, caused himself to be proclaimed a citizen of Fūta Dj̲allon by the Alamai, and to be given the highlands of Kahel and the right of coinage. Sanderval thereafter played a decisive part in the vassals' struggle against the Almami Bokar Biro, who was defeated at Bentiguel-Tokosere by the chief of Labe. Restored to the throne by the French administration, he agreed to sign a protectorate treaty, but in place of his name he wrote Bissimilaï (*bi-'smi 'llāh*). Captain Müller then marched on Timbo. Bokar Biro and his 1500 warriors were defeated at Poredaka. It was the end of the independence of the Fūta Dj̲allon.

The progress of Islamization was thus advanced notably; in 1850 al-Ḥādjdj ʿUmar had established the Dinguiraye (cattle-park) before carrying out his conquests in the north, and his adherents had penetrated the frontier zone of the present northern Guinea. From 1870 a former Mandingo pedlar, Samory Toure, set up the empire of Onassubu, the capital of which, Bissandugu, was his place of refuge after expeditions to what later became Ghana and the Ivory Coast.

Samory's invasions produced a renewed Islamic infiltration. By the treaties of Kenieba-Koura (March 1886) and Bissandugu (1887), Samory made himself secure from the direction of the French Sudan and, to protect himself from the British, he requested a French protectorate. Operations started again from 1891. In 1898 Samory, captured by the Gourand force, was deported to Gabon where he died two years later.

French Guinea was established by a decree of 17 December 1891, and its boundaries were fixed in 1899 with the neighbouring states, French Sudan (now Mali) and the Ivory Coast. Being included in 1904 in the Federation of West Africa, it became a

'Territoire d'Outre-Mer' and gained its independence on 28 September 1958 by voting *non* in the referendum under the guidance of the present President Sekou Touré.

The Islamization of Guinea was continued throughout the whole French period with the frequent help of the administration. On the other hand, since independence a strict neutrality has been imposed by the President, although himself a Muslim.

In conclusion, we may say that in Guinea as a whole, according to the judgement of the geographer J. R. Molard, "the Fulani are Muslim born, the Mandingos are adopting Islam, while the forest peoples (Kissi, Toma, Guerzé) have remained hostile."

Bibliography: Arcin, *Histoire de la Guinée Française*, Paris 1911; Demougeot, *Note sur l'organisation politique et administrative du Labé*, *Mémoire IFAN*, Larose 1944; idem, *Histoire du Rio Nunez*, in *BCHSAOF*, xxi (1938); Feral, *L'Islam en Guinée Française*, Doc. CHEAM Nr. 1022; Houis, *Guinée Française*, Paris, S.E.M.C.; Marty, *L'Islam en Guinée*, Paris 1921; R. Molard, *Essai sur la vie paysanne au Fouta-Djalon*, in *Revue de géographie alpine*, Grenoble 1944, republished in *Hommage à Jacques Richard Molard*, *Présence Africaine*, 155-251; Tauxier, *Moeurs et histoire des Peuls*, Paris 1937; Vieillard, *Notes sur les Peuls du Fouta Djalon*, in *FIBAN*, 1940, 85-210; see also the *Études Guinéennes* published by the Centrifan de Conakry before independence and the *Recherches Africaines* which have since replaced them. (R. CORNEVIN)

GUL (Pers., 'rose, flower'). In eastern Islamic literatures the (red) rose plays a very important part. The image of the rose (or the bud: *g͟hunča*) recurs in all manner of similes, metaphors and other figures of speech, in set phrases, idioms and puns. *Gul-āb* (rose-water) is considered one of the finest ingredients for sweets and drinks. With the nightingale (*bulbul* [*q.v.*]) the rose constitutes an old established pair of lovers, naturally not restricted to its actual meaning. The mention of either term of the binomial *gul - bulbul* evokes in the language of poetry the image of the other. *Gul* and its compounds are used as personal names (for example, *Gul-andām* and *Gul-s͟hāh*) as well as place names (*Gulk͟handān*, *Gulistān* and *Gulgas͟ht*). As rival claimant (*raḳīb* [*q.v.*]) for the rose, and occasionally its protector, the thorn is used. As symbol of the challenge to a match or contest the rose appears (similar to the glove in the West) in the expressions *gul-i d͟jang*, *gul-i hangāma* and *gul-i kus͟htī*, the last-named being also the title of a *mat͟hnawī* by ʿAbd al-ʿĀlī Nad͟jāt (d. ca. 1126/1714; see J. Rypka, *Iranische Literaturgeschichte*, Leipzig 1959, 286). The word, with separate derivations and numerous combinations, appears alone (even as a personal name) and combined (*gul-dasta*, *gulistān*, *guls͟han* and *gulzār*) with other personifications of things or with persons frequently in the titles of Persian, Turkish and Indian books. *Gul u bulbul* is the title of both Persian and Indian *mat͟hnawī*s (see H. Ethé, *Neupers. Lit.*, in *Gr. I. Ph.*, ii, 250 ff.). Well known is Faḍlī's Turkish *mat͟hnawī Gül ve bülbül* (*Gül ü Bülbül, Rose und Nachtigall von Fasli, ein romantisches Gedicht*, Turkish edition and German translation by Joseph von Hammer, Pest and Leipzig 1834; see Gibb, *Ottoman Poetry*, iii, 110 ff.), which is, next to that composed in Čag͟hatay by Luṭfī in 814/1411 (see A. Bombaci, *Storia della letteratura turca*, Milan 1956, 129), the best of all the epics of the same name (such as those of Baḳāʾī, G͟hāzī Girāy II and others) in the Turkish languages. But the rose was combined with yet other partners. See for example the indexes in *Gr. I. Ph.*; Gibb, *op. cit.*; Browne, ii, iv. Further material might be provided by catalogues of oriental and western manuscripts, further Edwards, *Cat. of the Printed Books in the British Museum*, London 1922; A. J. Arberry, *Persian Books* (*Cat. of the Library of the India Office*, ii/6), London 1937, and similar works. From Persian poetry might be mentioned *Gul u K͟husraw* or *K͟husraw u Gul* (usually *K͟husraw-nāma*) by Farīd al-Dīn Muḥammad ʿAṭṭār (d. 627/1230?) (see *EI*², i, 753; H. Ethé, *op. cit.*, 286; in more detail H. Ritter, *Philologika*, x, *Isl.*, xxv (1938), 160-72); *Gul u mul* ("Rose and Wine"; see *IA*, ii, 734); *Gul u Naw-rūz* by D͟jalāl al-Dīn Aḥmad Ṭabīb in 734/1334, and the same title by K͟hʷād͟jū Kirmānī in 742/1341-2 (see H. Ethé, *op. cit.*, 249); *Gul u Ṣanawbar* "Rose and Spruce", in prose and several times translated into Urdū (see H. Ethé, *op. cit.*, 321 and 323); Garcin de Tassy, *Histoire de la Littérature Hindouie et Hindoustanie*², Paris 1870, i, 157 ff.; and translated by him in *Revue orient. et amér.*, vii, 69-130). From Ottoman poetry, *Gül ü K͟husrev* by Āhī (d. 923/1517; Gibb, *op. cit.*, ii, 291); *Gül u Ṣabā*, "Rose and Zephyr", by Ned͟jātī (d. 914/1509; see Gibb, *op. cit.*, ii, 101); *Münāẓara-i Gül ü K͟husrev*, "Contest between (the) Rose and K͟husrev", also by Ned͟jātī (see Gibb, *op. cit.*, ii, 100), and *Gül ü Nev-rūz* by Muʿīdī (16th century; see Gibb, *op. cit.*, iii, 160).

Bibliography: In addition to that mentioned above, Charles Joret, *La Rose dans l'Antiquité et au Moyen-Age*, Paris 1892; S͟hiblī Nuʿmānī, *S͟hiʿr al-ʿAd͟jam*² (Pers. tr.), iv, Tehrān 1336 s., 165-9; Annemarie Schimmel, *Rose und Nachtigall*, in *Numen*, v/2 (1958), 85-109. (J. RYPKA)

GÜLBABA, a Turkish title, with the sense of head of a Muslim cloister (*tekke*) of the Bektās͟hī Order; the name of a *tekke* at Buda and of another *tekke* in the neighbourhood of Edirne; the name of a legendary personality.

The name Gülbaba, in connexion with the *tekke* and the *türbe* so designated at Buda, appears in Turkish documents of 974/1566 with the form كل بابا (Vienna, Flügel 1294); on a manuscript sketch-map of 1684 (E. Veres, *Marsigli jelentése és térképei Budavár 1684., 1686. évi ostromairól* [Report and maps of Marsigli on the sieges of the fortress of Buda in the years 1684 and 1686], in *Budapest régiségei* [Antiquities of Budapest], ix, 142) it occurs four times in the same form, though in each case without vocalization. Written in the same manner, it is found in several Turkish authors, *e.g.*, in Pečewī (ii, 141), Ewliyā Čelebi (vi, 244) and Naʿīmā (i, 289); and in Silāḥdār it occurs a number of times in the form كول بابا (ii, 401, 799, 801). In the writings of European authors the name is encountered as Julpapa in G. Wernher and E. Brown, as Gyulpapa in the superscription—from a European hand—on the above-mentioned manuscript sketch-map, and as Ghiul Baba in the text of L. Marsigli; about 1830, after the rendering of a dervish from India, it was written down as Tiulbaba. The forms given in the Latin script leave no doubt that the name, in its first syllable, has to be pronounced Gülbaba, with the vowel ü. A man with the name Gülbaba is known from the time of Meḥemmed II (Babinger, *GOW*, 213) and a locality near Edirne is also called Gülbaba. The word *gül*, as a component of personal names, is known, too, in other instances, *e.g.*, Gül Toḳmaḳ K͟hān, Gül Rüstem K͟hān.

The expression *gül*, in names of this kind, has not

the meaning of rose (*i.e.*, the flower), but a mystical sense, in that it alludes symbolically to fiery zeal on behalf of the (Muslim) faith. This meaning underlies, moreover, the compounds *gül-tesbīḥ*, *gül-benk*. In the life of the dervish, *gül* has the sense of "glowing iron rose", "particular ornament on the top of a dervish cap, especially in the case of the Ḳādirī order"; it is the mark which distinguishes the head of a house of the order and which is to be worn on the cap (*tādj*). M. d'Ohsson writes (*Tableau général de l'Empire Ottoman*, ii, 534) that the red-hot iron is called *gül*, which the Rifāʿī dervishes grasp, kiss and bite in the ecstasy of their religious dances. Th. Menzel observes (*Beiträge zur Kenntnis des Dervisch-tāğ*, in *Festschrift G. Jacob*, Leipzig 1932, 179 n.) that one of the objects in use amongst the dervishes is named "*zengīrli šiš = gül, charb* (Nadelspitze mit Kugel und Kettchen)", that part of the dervish cap is called *gül*, and this is regarded as the *damgha* of the *erens* (*ibid.*, 191); and that, furthermore, *gül* in various contexts is the badge of different dervish orders and of distinct grades within the orders.

In elucidating the name Gülbaba we have therefore to set out from this mystical sense of the word *gül*, with the result that *gülbaba* means "a zealous dervish, a rose on the branch of his order", *i.e.*, a man who, at the ceremonies held in common, leads and intones the prayers, one who knows how to take hold of the red-hot iron as of a rose breaking into bloom—the iron whose touch is as pleasing as the fragrance of roses, one who keeps and handles this iron, a man who bears the mark of a religious head (*gül*) on his cap fashioned from wedge-shaped pieces of cloth, etc. Ewliyā Čelebi (vi, 244) alludes to this sense of the word, when he addresses Gülbaba, in verses composed in his honour, as *güllü baba*, *i.e.*, as little father of the roses, as the *baba* recognizable by the rose. This meaning is also to be found in E. Brown, who notes that the head of the Buda *tekke* was "called *Julpapa*, or Father of the *Rose*" (Edward Brown, *A brief account* . . ., London 1673, 34, quoted in *Budapest régiségei* [Antiquities of Budapest], ix, 115), and in L. Marsigli, who remarks that the Turks, by Gülbaba, understand a "Padre Rosa", in much the same manner as the Christians use an expression like "Padre Giazinto".

Other explanations of the word are: that it comes from *Kel baba*, "bald father" (I. Kunos, in *Pallas Lexikon*, Budapest 1894, viii, 365); also that it derives from the verbal stem *gül-* (after the analogy of Gäl-bäri, see Gy. Németh, in *KCsA*, ii, 379).

Gülbaba is therefore a Turkish title. It is only on the evidence of Ewliyā Čelebi that Gülbaba would seem to be a personal name, referring to a historical personage. Ewliyā Čelebi remarks (vi, 225) that Gülbaba died at the Ottoman conquest of Buda and that Sultan Süleymān had his corpse laid to rest and commended the fortress of Buda to his protection. Of such an important event no trace is to be found in other sources. It is mentioned neither by Pečewī (the reference to Pečewī given by Cl. Huart in *EI*[1], s.v. Gül-Bābā, is the result of an error), nor by Djalāl-zāde, the official historian of the campaign. We have therefore to accept that there was never a person with the name Gülbaba in the time of the Turks, and in particular no historical personage of this name, but that on the other hand there existed at all times one or more *gülbaba* in charge of a *tekke*.

The *tekke* and *türbe* called Gülbaba at Buda were built by Meḥemmed Pasha before 958/1551. The *türbe* is still standing today. The hill on which these two buildings stood (it is now called Rózsadomb, *i.e.*, Hill of Roses) has been given the name Miḥnet tepesi in the historical literature as the result of an erroneous statement by von Hammer (*GOR*[2], iii, 706); it used in fact to be called Gülbaba bayrî, Tekke bayrî ("Gülbaba Hill, Tekke Hill").

Bibliography (further to works mentioned in the text): G. Wernher, *Moscouiter wunderbare Historien . . . Warhafftige Beschreibung . . . Der wunderbaren Wasseren in Ungaren Verzeichnuss*, Basel 1563; E. Brown, *A brief account of some travels in Hungaria, Servia, etc.*, London 1673, revised second ed. 1685, Fr. tr. Paris 1674; J. F. Miller, *Epitome vicissitudinum et rerum memorabilium de urbe Budensi*, Buda 1760; J. Podhradczky, *Eredeti két magyar krónika* (Two Original Hungarian Chronicles), Pest 1833; A. K. Fischer, *Gül-Baba*, Budapest 1898; *Vasárnapi Ujság* (Sunday Newspaper), 1855, 1862 and 1873; Rūm-beg-oghlu Fakhr al-Dīn, *Gül baba*, in *TOEM*, iii/15 (1328), 962-5; *Ün*, Isparta 1935; L. Fekete, *Gül-Baba et le bektāšī derk'āh de Buda*, in *Acta Orient. Hung.*, Budapest 1954 (the most recent review of the subject). (L. Fekete)

GULBADAN BĒGAM, the talented and accomplished daughter of the emperor Bābur [*q.v.*] by one of his wives, Dildār Bēgam, who was a lineal descendant of the Central Asian *ṣūfī* Aḥmadi-Djām *Zinda-Pīl*, was born c. 929/1523 in Khurāsān (Kabul?), two years before her father set out from Kabul on his last but historic expedition across the Indus in 932/1525, which won him the empire of India. That very year she was adopted by Māham Bēgam, mother of Humāyūn [*q.v.*] and the senior wife of Bābur, to rear and educate. In 936/1529 she left for Āgra [*q.v.*], the seat of Bābur's government, under the care of her foster-mother to join her father there. She remained in India till 947/1540 when Humāyūn suffered a crushing defeat at the hands of Shēr Shāh Sūr [*q.v.*]. She along with other royal ladies was sent back to Kabul where the fugitive emperor Humāyūn joined her in 952/1545. In about 946/1539 she married Khiḍr Khʷādja Čaghatāy, second son of Bābur's full sister Khānzāda Bēgam. An otherwise undistinguished man, he rose to the rank of *Amīr al-Umarāʾ* under Humāyūn (cf. *Āʾīn-i Akbarī*, Eng. transl. by Blochmann, 365 *n.*). She bore him many children but none attained greatness. In 982/1574 she left on a pilgrimage to Mecca, stayed in the Ḥidjāz for three and a half years and performed the *ḥadjdj* four times. She returned to India in 990/1582 after a perilous voyage involving a shipwreck off Aden, where she had to stay for a whole year. It was after her return home that she was asked by Akbar [*q.v.*] to write her personal memoirs, the *Humāyūn-nāma* or *Aḥwāl-i Humāyūn Pādshāh*, as material for Abu 'l Faḍl's *Akbar-nāma*. Only one incomplete copy, recording the events up to 960/1553, of this work survives; it is in the British Museum. It was published with a lengthy introduction and English translation by Annette S. Beveridge (London 1902). Another, but inferior edition containing only the Persian text, was published at Lucknow in 1925 under the title *Humāyūn-nāma-i Gulbadan Bēgam*. She died at Āgra on 6 Dhu 'l-Ḥidjdja, 1011/7 May, 1603 at the age of 82 lunar years. Akbar himself accompanied and shouldered her bier a little distance.

She was well-versed in both Turkī and Persian and was good at calligraphy and the art of *inshāʾ*. She used to compose in Persian and two lines of hers have been quoted by Mahdī Shīrāzī in the *Tadhkirat al-Khawātīn* (not seen by me).

Bibliography: Niẓām al-Dīn Aḥmad, *Ṭabaḳāt-i Akbarī*, Bibl. Ind., ii, 312; Abu 'l Faḍl, *Akbar-nāma*, Bibl. Ind., iii, 568, 815, 817; Muḥammad b. Muʿtamad Khān Badakhshī, *Taʾrīkh-i Muḥammadī* (MS.), *sub anno* 1011 A.H.; Rieu, i, 147*a*, iii, 1083*a*; Annette S. Beveridge, *The History of Humayun* (*Humāyūn-nāma*), London 1902, introduction 1-79; Storey, i/1, 538-9; Muʿtamad Khān, *Iḳbāl-nāma-i Djahāngīrī* (MS.); ʿAbd al-Ḥayy Lakhnawī, *Nuzhat al-khawāṭir*, Ḥaydarābād 1357/1955, v, 318-9 (the only notice in Arabic known to me). (A. S. Bazmee Ansari)

GULBĀNG, a Persian word meaning the song of the nightingale, and hence by extension fame, repute, and loud cries of various kinds. In Turkish usage it is applied more particularly to the call of the muezzin [see ADHĀN] and to the Muslim war-cry (*Allāhu Akbar* and *Allāh Allāh*). In the Ottoman Empire it was used of certain ceremonial and public prayers and acclamations, more specifically those of the corps of Janissaries [see YEÑI ČERI]. Such prayers were recited at pay parades and similar occasions, at the beginning of a campaign, when they were accompanied by three volleys of musketry fired in the air, and at the accession of a Sultan. They were led by an officer standing with crossed arms on the '*gülbāng* stone' which was to be found in Janissary barracks. The term *gülbāng* was also used in the rituals of the Bektāshī and Mewlewī orders.

Bibliography: Pakalın, i, 683-5; Ismail Hakkı Uzunçarşılı, *Osmanlı devleti teşkilâtından kapıkulu ocakları*, i, Ankara 1943, 249, 375, 421-2, 533-4. See further MEHTERKHĀNE and NAWBA. (Ed.)

GULBARGĀ, a town and district in the north of Mysore state in India on the western borders of what is known as "the Deccan" (Dakkhan [*q.v.*]); the town is situated at 17° 21′ N., 76° 51′ E. Of some antiquity in the Hindū period, it formed part of the domains of the Kākatīyas of Warangal before the Islamic conquest. It was annexed for the Dihlī sultanate by Ulugh Khān, the future Muḥammad b. Tughluḳ, early in the 8th/14th century, to pass first to the Bahmanī dynasty on its establishment in 848/1347, whose first capital it became under the name Aḥsanābād. It fell to the ʿĀdil Shāhīs of Bīdjāpur in 909/1504, and although it was recovered by Amīr Barīd ten years later it was soon retaken by the ʿĀdil Shāhīs; they held it until 1067/1657, when Mīr Djumla besieged it and captured it for the Mughals.

The majority of the monuments of Gulbargā belong to the period when it was the Bahmanī capital, and have already been described in the article BAHMANIDS. Of the monuments not mentioned there the following are of some importance: Ḳalandhar Khān's mosque (see *Report of Archaeological Department, Hyderabad, 1335F:/1925-6*, 7 ff., Plates IIa, Xb), built by a Bahmanī governor after the transfer of the capital to Bīdar; the mosque of Afḍal Khān, an ʿĀdil Shāhī general of the late 10th/16th century (Mīrzā Ibrāhīm, *Basātīn-i Salāṭīn*, 130 ff.), which stands in the court of the *dargāh* of Gēsū Darāz, in the later stone Bīdjāpur style [see BĪDJĀPUR, Monuments] similar to the mosque of Malika Djahān, with hanging stone chains below the cornice (*Report ... 1335F./1925-6*, 8, Plates IIb, XIa); the Langar mosque, early Bahmanī or possibly pre-Bahmanī, with a vaulted arch-shaped ceiling with wooden ribs recalling the style of the Buddhist cave-temples (*Report ... 1346F./1936-7*, 7 ff., Plate VIa); a group of 5 mausolea at Holkonḍa, once a suburb of Gulbargā on the Homnābād road, similar to those of the Haft Gunbadh (*Report ... 1344F./1934-5*, 1); the mosque and *dargāh* of Ḥaḍrat Kamāl Mudjarrad (*ibid.* 5-6 and Plates IIIa and b); the tomb of Čānd Bībī, of Niẓām Shāhī style (*ibid.*, 6, Plates IVa and b).

Bibliography: in the article; and see Bibliography to the article BAHMANIDS. (J. Burton-Page)

GÜLEK BOGHAZ, Turkish name for the Cilician Gates, for which see CILICIA, col. 35a.

GULISTĀN [see SAʿDĪ].

GULISTĀN, the name of a place in the Caucasus where, on 12 October 1813, a peace treaty was signed between Russia and Persia. In 1800 the Russians had annexed Georgia, and the Persians, in an effort to check their further advance southward, had suffered two defeats in 1812, at Aslandūz and Lankurān, and had been forced to sue for peace.

The terms of the Treaty of Gulistān, which was negotiated through the mediation of the British ambassador Sir Gore Ouseley, were disastrous for Persia. The regions of Georgia, Ḳarābāgh, Shakkī, Shīrwān, Darband, Bākū, Dāghistān, Gandja, Muḳān, and part of Ṭālish, were ceded to Russia, and Article 5 stipulated that only Russian naval vessels had the right to navigate on the Caspian Sea. The ambiguous nature of the Article relating to the territorial settlement led to disputes and to the renewed outbreak of war in 1826.

Bibliography: A. Waḥīd Māzandarānī, *Rāhnamā-yi ʿuhūd*, Tehran 1341s./1962, 294, 306. For an English translation of the Treaty, and additional bibliography, see J. C. Hurewitz, *Diplomacy in the Near and Middle East*, i, 1956, 84 ff. (R. M. Savory)

GÜLKHĀNE, (modern Turkish Gülhane) the "House of roses", or Gülkhāne Meydānî, is the name of a part of the gardens which lie along the Sea of Marmora on the east side of the Topkapî Sarāyî in Istanbul [*q.v.*]; the name is derived from the fact that in olden days the building, in which the rose sweetmeats for the use of the court were prepared, stood there. The place is famous in history because the celebrated firman of Sultan ʿAbd al-Madjīd, the so-called *Khaṭṭ-i sherīf* promulgating the reforms, was publicly proclaimed there on Sunday 26 Shaʿbān 1255/3 November 1839; cf. the description in G. Rosen, *Geschichte der Turkei*, ii, 14 ff.; Luṭfī, *Taʾrīkh*, vi, 59 ff.; B. Lewis, *The emergence of modern Turkey*³, London 1965, 104 ff., and article TANẒĪMĀT; on the place itself cf. White, *Three years in Constantinople*, i, 110, and *TOEM*, i, 291 ff.; it is now a park. (J. H. Mordtmann*)

GULPĀYAGĀN, district and town in the fifth *Ustān* (Luristān). The central chain of the Zagros range traverses the district; the highest peak is Ḥādjdjī Ḳārā (3650 m.). The district lies partly in the cold region and partly in the temperate one. The chief town, Gulpāyagān, which is situated in Long. 50° 18′ W. and Lat. 33° 26′ N., is 1924 m. above sea level and therefore has a cold climate in winter. It is an ancient town containing some buildings dating from the Saldjūḳ era. In 1951 the population of the town and the surrounding villages amounted to 22,000. The Arab geographers gave the name of the town as Djarbādhakān, *i.e.*, Gurbādhakān. It is only in comparatively recent times that frequent mention of the town occurs. The Arab geographers referred to it merely as a stage or station on the route uniting Iṣfahān with Hamadān. The chief industry of the town and its surroundings is agriculture.

Bibliography: Yāḳūt, ii, 40; Le Strange, 210; Ritter, *Erdkunde*, ix, 63; E. Stack, *Six months in Persia*, London 1882, ii, 114; Razmārā and Nawtāsh, *Farhang-i Djughrāfiyā-yi Īrān*, v, 316; for a discussion of the etymology of the name, see Aḥmad Kasravī, *Nāmhā-yi shahrhā u dihhā-yi Īrān*, Tehrān 1335/1956, 68. (L. Lockhart)

GULSHANĪ (Turkish: Gülshenī), Ibrāhīm b. Muḥammad b. Ibrāhīm b. Shihāb al-Dīn (?-940/1534), Turkish mystic, a successor of Djalāl al-Dīn Rūmī and a prolific poet. He came of a family settled in Diyārbakr, where his father Muḥammad al-Āmidī's *türbe* and a prayer-hall said to have been built by him still stand some 500 yards outside the Mardin gate (see ʿAlī Emīrī, *Diyārbekirli baʿḍ-i dhewātīn terdjeme-i ḥālleri*, 16; for the report that he came from Barda in Ādharbaydjān, see M. ʿAlī Tarbiyat, *Dānishmandān-i Ādharbaydjān*, 318). Muḥyī-i Gülshenī, whose *Menāḳib-i Ibrāhīm Gülshenī* [see *Bibl.*] is the richest source on Ibrāhīm Gulshanī's life and circle, continues the genealogy given above with four more names: b. Aydoghmush b. Gündoghmush b. Ḳutludoghmush b. Oghuz, thus making him a descendant of Oghuz Ata, but gives no information on his ancestors beyond his father and his grandfathers. His father Muḥammad al-Āmidī was the author of works on *fiḳh*, *kalām* and *manṭiḳ*; his paternal grandfather Ibrāhīm wrote a *sharḥ* on the *Farāʾiḍ*, completed the *Fakk al-mughlaḳ* (on the solution of various problems in *fiḳh*), composed much-esteemed works on *taṣawwuf*, and was for a time *ḳāḍī* of Diyārbakr (Muḥyī, *Menāḳib*, fol. 6r); his maternal grandfather Sharaf al-Dīn was descended from a certain Ḳāḍī ʿĪsā and was a *mudarris* at ʿAynṭāb (*Menāḳib*, fol. 6v).

The date of Gulshanī's birth is not exactly known. Muḥyī's statement (*Menāḳib*, 159v.) that when he died in 940/1534 he was 114 years old implies that he was born in 826/1422-3; but elsewhere he states that he was two years old when his father died and that his father had survived into the reign of the Aḳ-Ḳoyunlu sultan Ḥamza (838-48/1434-44), so that the date 826 must be advanced by at least ten years; another statement (see below) that he joined Uzun Ḥasan at Tabrīz at the age of 15 implies that he was born in 859 or 860/1455 or 1456, but for reasons which will appear this statement on his age is unacceptable. Most probably he was born between 838 and 840/1434-7. His father dying when he was two, he was brought up by his paternal uncle Sayyidī ʿAlī, who, according to the *Menāḳib* (7r.), had more than 200 *murīds*. While still a child, Gulshanī began to learn the Ḳurʾān and to read Turkish books of *tafsīr* and *ḥadīth*. Concerning his later education the *Menāḳib* gives only vague and confused information: it relates that he set out alone to study in Mā warāʾ al-nahr, but when he reached Tabrīz he was adopted by Uzun Ḥasan's *ḳāḍīʿaskar*, who told him that all the *ʿulamāʾ* of Uzun Ḥasan's realm would obey his guidance, and appointed him *tawḳīʿī*. The stipend he received enabled him to help his uncle at Diyārbakr and, probably at this time, to bring his sister to Tabrīz (*Menāḳib*, 9v., 73r.). (That he was given the post of *tawḳīʿī* and still more important posts and was recognized already as a famous *shaykh* shows that the statement, also in the *Menāḳib*, that he was only 15 when he went to Tabrīz must be rejected). Elsewhere (13r.-v.) it is stated that he travelled to Harāt to resolve a dispute between Uzun Ḥasan and Ḥusayn Bayḳara, and, on a similar mission, visited Shīrāz, where he met Djalāl al-Dīn Dawānī [see al-Dawānī]. He gives the impression to have been at this period a government official with an inclination to *taṣawwuf*, who enjoyed special inward experiences and was searching for a suitable *murshid*; soon afterwards at Ḳarabāgh, by the good offices of Uzun Ḥasan's brother Uways, he was introduced to and became the *murīd* of Dede ʿUmar Rūshanī ([*q.v.*], d. 892/1486) of Aydïn, who was the *khalīfa* of Sayyid Yaḥyā-i Shīrwānī, the *pīr-i thānī* ('second *pīr*, *i.e.*, founder') of the Khalwatī order [see khalwatiyya].

Thenceforth Gulshanī devoted himself to *dhikr* and to ascetic practices: he would walk in the streets with a wine-cup in his hand to demonstrate his attachment to *malāmī* doctrine and wore a sheepskin *tādj* (*Menāḳib*, 28r.). After Uzun Ḥasan's death (882/1478), his successor Khalīl had little esteem for Gulshanī, but the respect and fame which he enjoyed during the reign of Yaʿḳūb (883-96/1478-90) are demonstrated by a poem of Idrīs Bidlisī [see bidlisī], quoted in the *Menāḳib* (30v.-31r.); this respect was increased by the reverence in which Yaʿḳūb's *ḳāḍīʿaskar* ʿĪsā held him. Gulshanī assiduously attended the sermons of ʿUmar Rūshanī, who had come from Ḳarabāgh to settle at Tabrīz (*Menāḳib*, 26v.); he was present when Sultan Yaʿḳūb besieged Akhiska, settled various disputes within the royal family, and witnessed the rise of Shaykh Ḥaydar. When ʿUmar Rūshanī died (892/1486), he succeeded him (not without opposition) as *post-nishīn* [*q.v.*] and began to teach his disciples in the Muẓaffariyya mosque at Tabrīz. This period of *dhikr* and *samāʿ* did not last long: Yaʿḳūb's successors had little respect for him and even persecuted him. In 900/1495 he performed the Pilgrimage together with a numerous company of disciples and adherents. At Mecca he met some *ʿulamāʾ* of Egypt and wished to visit Egypt on his homeward journey, but gave up the plan out of consideration for his family waiting for him at Tabrīz (*Menāḳib*, 78v.-79r., 83r.). The Ṣafawī occupation of Tabrīz, consequent persecutions, and Alwand Beg's defeat by Shāh Ismāʿīl (907/1502) obliged him to hasten from Tabrīz with his family. He came to Diyārbakr, then governed by Ḳāsim Beg; but when, after Alwand's death (910/1504-5), Diyārbakr too fell to the Ṣafawīs (912/1507), he was obliged to flee again, first to Jerusalem (where he carried out a forty day retreat [see khalwa]) and then to Egypt, where he settled at Birkat al-ḥadjdj near Cairo. Timurtash, a Khalwatī *shaykh* who had earlier come from Shīrwān to settle there, procured for him the possession of Ḳubbat al-Muṣṭafā; while living there he met Sultan Ḳānṣawh al-Ghawrī while he was out hunting, and the Sultan granted him living-quarters at the Muʾayyadiyya mosque by Bāb Zuwayla. Though deprived by the Ottoman invasion under Selīm I of the patronage first of Ḳānṣawh al-Ghawrī and then of his successor Tuman Beg, Gulshanī was held in great honour by the Ottoman troops (Shaʿrānī, *Ṭabaḳat*, ii, 163), many of whom, encouraged perhaps by Gulshanī's old acquaintance Idrīs Bidlisī, became his *murīds*; indeed his quarters at the Muʾayyadiyya mosque could no longer accommodate his followers, which gave rise to complaints from Arab *shaykhs* also lodged there. This enormous popularity was the cause of anxiety to the successive Ottoman governors, who feared a rising; and indeed when Ibrāhīm Pasha came to Egypt to investigate the situation after the rebellion of Aḥmed Pasha (Khāʾin [*q.v.*]) his adverse report to Sultan Süleymān prompted the Sultan to summon Gulshanī in 934/

1527-8 to Istanbul (see ʿĀlī, *Kunh al-akhbār*, Istanbul Un. Lib. MS T 2359, ii, fol. 24v.). The Sultān interviewed him, and his work *Maʿnawī* was sent to Kemāl Pasha-zāde [*q.v.*] for a *fatwā* on whether it contained ideas contrary to the *sharīʿa*. The Sultan was impressed by *Gulshanī* and the *fatwā* (text in *Menāḳib*, 120v.) was favourable; so after staying six months (through the winter) in Istanbul, Gulshanī returned to Egypt. (This incident forms the subject of the first play in Turkish literature, see İ. H. Danişmend, *Türk tiyatrosunun ilk piyesi*, in *Türklük*, ii (1939), 73-91.) Five or six years after his return to Egypt, Gulshanī died during an epidemic of plague on 9 Shawwāl 940/24 April 1534; he was buried in a *türbe* at his convent, which still stands. Of his two sons Aḥmed Khayālī and Meḥmed, the former, a poet whose Turkish *Dīwān* contains many pleasing poems, succeeded him.

Works. Ibrāhīm Gulshanī was a poet so prolific that he is said to have dictated poems in three languages (Persian, Turkish and Arabic) to three scribes at once. A. His works in Persian are (i) *Maʿnawī*: written in imitation of the *Mathnawī* of Djalāl al-Dīn Rūmī, this work of 40,000 couplets was begun at Diyārbakr and finished in 10 months; like the *Mathnawī*, it contains many stories, and many couplets from the *Mathnawī* are quoted in it verbatim. There are many fine manuscripts with gold-inlaid bindings in the libraries of Istanbul (Ayasofya 2080 [copied in 927], Umumî 3588 [copied 928], Süleymaniye-Halet Ef. 272 [copied 927), Süleymaniye-Esad Ef. 2908 [copied 936]). A *sharḥ* of the first 500 couplets (which are written in a very complex style) was composed by Laʿlī Meḥmed Fenāʾī and has been printed (*Sharḥ-i Maʿnawī*, Istanbul 1289). (ii) *Dīwān*: in this collection of 17,000 couplets (almost as long as Djalāl al-Dīn's *Dīwān-i kabīr*) the influence of Djalāl al-Dīn, Ḥāfiẓ, and sometimes Yūnus Emre is to be detected; it has not been printed or thoroughly studied. MSS in Turkey: Istanbul, Fatih 3866 (copied 931); Millet, farsça manzum 418 (? 10th/16th century); Ankara, Dil ve Tarih-Coğrafya Fakültesi library (unnumbered, ? 19th century). (iii) *Kanz al-djawāhir*, a work of about 7,500 quatrains, some in *rubāʿī*, some in *tuyugh* form, written in fairly simple language, on the themes of Divine Love, *fanāʾ* and *baḳāʾ*, and the author's devotion to his *murshid*, ʿUmar Rūshanī. Only one MS is known: Istanbul Un. Lib. F 1233 (according to the *Menāḳib*, 167, Gulshanī's *rubāʿīs* in Turkish, Persian and Arabic, amounted to 12,000 couplets). (iv) *Sīmurg-nāma*, a work of 30,000 couplets, known only from references in the *Menāḳib* (83v., 167r.). B. His works in Turkish comprise only a *Dīwān* of about the same length (17,000 couplets) as his Persian *Dīwān*. In some of his Turkish poems, Gulshanī is clearly under the influence of Yūnus Emre and Nesīmī [*qq.v.*]. The work deserves study, both for its literary and for its linguistic interest. The best and fullest MS known is in the Library of the Dil ve Tarih-Coğ. Fak. (Üniversite kütüphanesi kitapları 982). Selected poems from the *Dīwān* are found in various libraries, *e.g.*: Dil ve Tarih-Coğ. Fak. (Mustafa Çon 289); Istanbul Millet (Carullah 1661 and manzum 379); Istanbul Un. Lib. (T 890). Some of his *ghazals* were translated into Persian with a commentary by Idrīs Bidlisī (*Menāḳib*, 30r.). C. The Arab *ʿulamāʾ* and poets of his day regarded Gulshanī as '*ummī*', and perhaps he did not speak Arabic well (Shaʿrānī, *Ṭabaḳāt*, ii, 163). His Arabic poems formed only a small *Dīwān* of 5,000 couplets (*Menāḳib*, 167r.). In form and content they are influenced by his Persian poems. The only known MS (of selections) is in the Library of the Dil ve Tarih-Coğ. Fak. (Üniversite kütüphanesi collection).

In his poetical works, especially in the final couplets of his *ghazals*, Gulshanī mentions, together with his own *makhlaṣ* or *nisba*, that of his *murshid* ʿUmar Rūshanī, whose thought so strongly influenced him. Gulshanī did not escape criticism, any more than his *murshid*, who, under the influence of the works of Muḥyī al-Dīn al-ʿArabī, adopted an extreme doctrine of *waḥdat-i wudjūd* and, for his efforts to spread in Ḳarabāgh and its neighbourhood the ideas of the *Fuṣūṣ al-ḥikam*, was condemned and persecuted as a 'Fuṣūṣī'. Condemnatory *fatwās* were issued concerning Gulshanī and his *murīds* and successors, who preached the same extreme *waḥdat-i wudjūd* (see *Fatāwā-yi Abū Suʿūd*, Istanbul, Millet Lib., MS şer'iye 80, fol. 267r.-v.).

Gulshanī's *ṭarīḳa*. The Gulshaniyya *ṭarīḳa*, which took its name from his *nisba*, was a branch of the Khalwatiyya. It assumed its characteristic form only after Gulshanī had settled in Egypt and built his famous convent there. It diverges from the Khalwatiyya, based on the principles of *khalwa* and *dhikr*, especially in its rules of behaviour (*ādāb*). The Gulshaniyya *ṭarīḳa*, which at first adopted *samāʿ* and other practices of the Mawlawiyya (Ṣāliḥ, *Manāḳib-i awliyā-yi Miṣr*, Būlāḳ 1262, 143), later absorbed practices from the Baktashiyya and other orders, and was thus regarded as having placed itself outside the *sharīʿa* (Ḳaraḳash-zāde ʿÖmer, *Nūr al-hudā li-man ihtadā*, Istanbul 1286, 7). The rules of daily life in Gulshanī's convent in Cairo, the weekly ceremonies held there and the practices of the *ṭarīḳa* as a whole present peculiarities which deserve study (see Shemleli-zāde, *Shīwe-i ṭarīḳat-i Gulshaniyye*, Millet Lib., MS şer'iye 888; for the convent and its buildings, see ʿAlī Bāshā Mubārak, *al-Khiṭaṭ al-djadīda*, *djuzʾ* vi, 54).

Bibliography: Muḥyī-i Gülshenī (d. 1026/1617), *Menāḳib-i Ibrāhīm-i Gülshenī* (references in the text are to the foliation of my own MS; for other MSS see *Istanbul Kitaplıkları Tarih-Coğ. yazmaları katalogları*, i/6, Istanbul 1946, no. 310); Ṣāliḥ, *Manāḳib-i awliyā-yi Miṣr*, Būlāḳ 1262 (details from Muḥyī's work, much abridged); Ḥulwī, *Lamaẓāt*, Istanbul Un. Lib. MS 1894; ʿAlī Emīrī, *Diyārbekirli baʿḍ-i dhewātīn terdjeme-i ḥālleri*, Millet Lib.; idem, *Tedhkire-i shuʿarāʾ-i Āmid*, Istanbul 1328; Laṭīfī, *Tedhkire*, Istanbul 1314, 52-4; ʿAṭāʾī, *Ḥadāʾiḳ al-Shaḳāʾiḳ*, i, 66; Ewliyā Čelebi, *Seyāḥatnāme*, i, 320, 335, 389, x, 243-6; Ṣādiḳ Widjdānī, *Silsile-nāme-i Khalwatiyye* (*Tomar-i ṭuruḳ-i ʿāliye*); M. Ṭāhir, *ʿOthmānlî müʾellifleri*, i, 19; M. ʿAlī Tarbiyat, *Dānishmandān-i Ādharbaydjān*, Tehran 1314; Shaʿrānī, *Ṭabaḳāt*, Cairo 1299, ii, 163; ʿAlī Bāshā Mubārak, *al-Khiṭaṭ al-djadīda*, Būlāḳ 1306, iv, 54; Mrs. R. L. Devonshire, *Rambles in Cairo*, 332.

(Tahsin Yazici)

GULSHANĪ (Gülshenī) Ṣarūkhānī, Ottoman poet who flourished in the reign of Meḥemmed II, was born in Ṣarūkhān, and lived a life of religious seclusion and devotion. His *Maḳālāt* (variously entitled in the MSS *Rāz-nāme*, *Pend-nāme*, *Esrār-nāme*) is written in seven chapters in the *mathnawī* form, containing 950 couplets; completed in 864/1459, it consists of homilies, stories and parables. After each homily or admonition, Gülshenī includes stories to illustrate his point.

He is the author of a Persian *dīwān*: the text of the *ḳāṣīdes* addressed to Meḥemmed II and Bāyezīd

II is reproduced from the unique MS (Istanbul, Bayezid Um. Küt. 5280) by Tahsin Yazıcı (see Bibl.). He wrote also a poem celebrating the Prophet's birthday (*mawlūd*).

Bibliography: Laṭīfī, *Te<u>dh</u>kere*, s.v.; Bursalī Ṭāhir, *ʿO<u>th</u>mānlī Müʾellifleri*, ii, 388; Gibb, *Ottoman Poetry*, ii, 378; Hammer-Purgstall, *Gesch. d. osm. Dichtkunst*, ii, 286; T. Yazıcı, *Gülşenî, eserleri ve Fâtih ve II. Bayezid hakkındaki kasideleri*, in *Fâtih ve İstanbul*, ii/7-12 (1954), 82-137.

(Günay Alpay)

GÜL<u>SH</u>EHRĪ, a Turkish poet of the beginning of the 8th/14th century. Hitherto, his personal name was taken to be Aḥmed, on the evidence of a single entry in a manuscript of his poem *Manṭiḳ al-ṭayr*. Recently, on the strength of several points in the same work, he has been identified with a certain <u>Sh</u>ey<u>kh</u> Süleymān, whose *türbe* is in Kïr<u>sh</u>ehir. It can be easily supposed that this town from which as a poet he took his name Gül<u>sh</u>ehrī was his home. The date of the poet's death is unknown, but it must have been after 717/1317, the year when his work *Manṭiḳ al-ṭayr* was completed.

Gül<u>sh</u>ehrī wrote two great didactic *ṣūfī* poems, *me<u>th</u>newī*s in *remel* metre, one in Persian entitled *Falak-nāma* (completed 701/1301-2), of about 4,000 distichs (*bayt*s), of which the so far unique manuscript is now in the Public Library (Genel Kitaplık), Ankara, as no. 817. The other work is written in Turkish and is entitled *Manṭiḳ al-ṭayr*; this likewise consists of about 4,000 distichs, and now exists in a facsimile edition with introduction by Agâh Sırrı Levend (Ankara 1957). A dissertation on this work, by Müjgan Cunbur, has not yet appeared in print. Gül<u>sh</u>ehrī's *Manṭiḳ al-ṭayr* ("Speech of the birds") is a free adaptation in verse of the poem of the same name also in the *remel* metre, by the Persian poet Farīd al-Dīn ʿAṭṭār [*q.v.*], and not really a translation. The ideas and construction of the work are the same as with ʿAṭṭār; it is an allegory of *ṣūfī* monism (*waḥdet-i wud<u>j</u>ūd*), in the form of a story of a journey by the birds under their leader, the hoopoe (*hüdhüd*), to their queen, the Sīmurg<u>h</u> [*q.v.*], whose eyrie was far off on Mount Ḳāf, and their arrival there, after the hardships of the journey only thirty of them attaining their goal, where they were finally compelled to recognize themselves to be the "Sī murg<u>h</u>"—"thirty birds". In matters of detail, however, Gül<u>sh</u>ehrī often goes his own way.

In one plaçe in his work *Manṭiḳ al-ṭayr* (text, ed. A. S. Levend, 297, l. 14), the poet names the *Gül<u>sh</u>annāme*, as a work written by himself; it is, however, probable that the *Manṭiḳ al-ṭayr* itself is meant. Another small *me<u>th</u>newī* is also in existence, probably by Gül<u>sh</u>ehrī, consisting of 167 distichs and also in *remel* metre, on A<u>kh</u>ī Ewrān/Evren (*Kerāmāt-i A<u>kh</u>ī Ewrān ṭāba <u>th</u>arāhu*), which is very closely linked with the *Manṭiḳ al-ṭayr* since they have whole verses in common. There is some difference of opinion as to whether this short *me<u>th</u>newī* on A<u>kh</u>ī Evren derives from Gül<u>sh</u>ehrī himself, or whether it was composed by another poet who may have been a follower of A<u>kh</u>ī Evren and who made use of lines from the *Manṭiḳ al-ṭayr* and misappropriated the then famous name of Gül<u>sh</u>ehrī. It is a striking fact both that in the *me<u>th</u>newī* on A<u>kh</u>ī Evren the *Falak-nāma* is in fact named (verse 159b), but not the *Manṭiḳ al-ṭayr*, and also that the name of A<u>kh</u>ī Evren does not figure in the latter work [see A<u>kh</u>ī Ewrān].— In another place in the *Manṭiḳ al-ṭayr* (text, A. S. Levend, 296 l. 12) Gül<u>sh</u>ehrī also speaks of a verse translation of a work by the poet Kudūrī in Turkish as his own work. A manuscript of a further work of Gül<u>sh</u>ehrī, *ʿArūḍ risālesi*, is in Istanbul (Millet Kitaplığı, Ali Emiri, Farsça yazmalar, no. 517).— Finally, from various manuscripts now dispersed there still survive some *g<u>h</u>azal*s by Gül<u>sh</u>ehrī. These have been collected together by Fr. Taeschner in his article *Zwei Gazels von Gülşehrī*, in *Fuad Köprülü Armağanı* (*Mélanges Fuad Köprülü*), Istanbul 1953, 479-85.

Bibliography: in the text; see also Fr. Taeschner, *Das Futuvvetkapitel in Gülšehrīs altosmanischer Bearbeitung von ʿAṭṭārs Manṭiq uṭ-ṭayr*, Berlin 1932; idem, *Gülschehrīs Mesnevi auf Achi Evran, den Heiligen von Kirschehir und Patron der türkischen Zünfte*, Wiesbaden 1955; idem, *Des altrumtürkischen Dichters Gülşehrī Werk Manṭiḳ uṭ-ṭayr und seine Vorlage, das gleichnamige Werk des persischen Dichters Farīduddīn ʿAṭṭār*, in *Németh Armağanı*, Ankara 1962, 359-371.

(Fr. Taeschner)

GUM, GUM ARABIC [see Ṣamg<u>h</u>].

GŪM (Arabic *ḳawm*; French *goum*), the usual form and pronunciation, in the Arab countries of North Africa, of the name given to a group of armed horsemen or fighting men from a tribe. The derivative *gūma* signifies "a levy of *gūm*s, troops, a plundering foray", "sedition", "revolt".

It was the Turks who, in the former Regencies of Algiers and Tunis, gave the *gūm*s an official existence by making them the basis of their system of occupation of the country. All the tribes had been divided by them into *ma<u>kh</u>zen* or auxiliaries, who were exempt from most taxes, and *raʿiyya*, who were liable to all taxes. The latter were the more numerous. When one or more of the latter tribes refused to pay a tax or revolted for some reason, the Turkish army rapidly advanced to the insurgents' territory. Though small in size, this army was reinforced by the exceedingly mobile cavalry groups of the *gūms*.

Soon after their occupation of the Algiers Regency, the French learnt how to make best use of the *gūm*s. But once the country had been pacified, the *ma<u>kh</u>zen* tribes disappeared. The system of *gūm*s was then extended to all tribes, without exception. Under the command of the chiefs, *ḳāʾid*s or *ag<u>h</u>a*s, appointed by the French authorities, the *gūm*s had to co-operate with the military police in the maintenance of peace in the country, and in protecting the migrations of the nomadic tribes and the safety of caravans.

In territory under military administration, the number of "goumiers", *i.e.*, members of the *gūm* of a tribe, varied according to regional needs. The goumiers received a monthly wage and encamped on certain State lands whose revenues went to them, but they were obliged to equip and mount themselves at their own expense. On active service they were also entitled to the *muʾna*, a special allowance for food.

In civil territory, the goumiers equipped and mounted themselves at their own expense. They did not draw any pay but, when called up, they received the special allowance for food. In civil territory *gūm*s were called up only in the event of insurrection or European war. They were, in fact, a territorial militia under the command of the tribal chiefs and subject to the orders of the administratuon. The *gūm* from each mixed commune consisted of 120 horsemen. The goumiers had the right to carry arms. Their distinctive badge was a green and red cord fixed round the turban. The goumiers' horses were not subject to any tax charges, and the goumier himself was exempt from the tax on livestock.

After the inauguration of the French Protectorate in Morocco, a similar organization was created, and the Moroccan goumiers particularly distinguished themselves during the second world war, in Italy and the south of France [see also MAKHZEN].

Bibliography: W. Esterhazy, *De la domination turque dans l'ancienne Régence d'Alger*, Paris 1840, 261 ff.; Soualah, *Cours moyen d'arabe parlé*, Algiers 1909, 100; Larcher, *Législation algérienne*, Paris 1903, i, no. 298, 147; Ménerville, *Dict. de Législation algérienne*, 20; *Circulaire du Gouverneur général de l'Algérie des 21-25 mars 1867*; Hugues and Lapra, *Code Algérien*, Paris 1878; *Arrêté du Gouvern. Général de l'Algérie du 11 Dec. 1872*, art. 4; *Circulaire du Gouvern. Général de l'Algérie* of 29 April 1910. (A. COUR)

GÜMRÜK [see MAKS].

GÜMÜLDJINA [see Supplement].

GÜMÜSH-KHĀNE (modern spelling Gümüşhane), literally "the house of silver, the town of silver", mining centre and town of Asia Minor, principal town of a *vilâyet*, on the road from Trabzon to Erzurum. The evolution of the town went through two distinct phases. (1) As a mining centre. It is probably Gümüsh-khane to which Marco Polo refers when he writes (xxii) of silver mines in the region of Bayburt. In any case the town was known by this name (Kumish) in the time of Ibn Baṭṭūṭa (tr. Gibb, Cambridge 1962, ii, 436). Situated at an altitude of about 5,000 ft., built in an amphitheatre on the steep slopes of the Musalla deresi (a left tributary of the Harşit çay), the ancient town, which during the whole of the Ottoman period was a busy centre for the mining of argentiferous lead, under a system of state encouragement and supervision (see N. Çağatay, in *AÜDTCD*, ii (1943), 124), was "important and lively" in the 17th century (Ḥādjdjī Khalīfa, *Djihānnümā*, 622, 623). But by the beginning of the 19th century the mines were in complete decline; in 1836, they employed no more than 50 or 60 workers and it was no longer profitable to work them. They were therefore closed, particularly because of the lack of fuel due to the deafforestation of the area, in the middle of the 19th century; then, after a last attempt to work them in 1883, closed finally a few years later. (2) As a town on a main route. The main centre of the town then gradually moved towards the Harşit valley $2^1/_2$ miles away, along which at first were scattered country houses surrounded by gardens and orchards, which provided at the end of the 19th century an important export of dried and preserved fruit (pears, plums, apricots, etc.). Gradually a commercial, and then an administrative, centre arose there along the main route from Trabzon to Erzurum. The decline of the old town was completed by the Russian occupation in 1916-18, which left it half in ruins, and by the exodus of the important Greek and Armenian minority (even so late as the beginning of the 20th century, the Greeks formed half of the 3,000 inhabitants). Today all the commerce and administration is concentrated in the new town. Pop., 1960, 5,312.

Bibliography: apart from the works cited and the articles of J. H. Mordtmann in *EI*[1] and of B. Darkot in *İA*, see Ewliyā Čelebi, *Seyāḥatnāme*, ii, 343. Gümüsh-khāne, situated on the main route from Trabzon to Iran, was visited and described in the 19th century by many European travellers; see especially W. J. Hamilton, *Researches in Asia Minor*, London 1842, i, 168-9, ii, 234-8 (detailed analysis of the position of the mines before they were closed); Th. Deyrolle, *Voyage dans le Lazistan et l'Arménie*, in *Le tour du monde*, Paris 1875 (xxix), 22-4 for the period of the growth of the new town and the trade in fruit in 1869.

(X. DE PLANHOL)

GÜMÜSHTEGIN, name of various Turkish chiefs, particularly the Dānishmendid prince known also as Amīr Ghāzī [see DĀNISHMENDIDS] and the atabeg of Aleppo [see ZANGIDS]. (ED.)

GUNBADH [see ḲUBBA].

GUNBADH-I ḲĀBŪS, the second town of Gurgān province, Iran, 110 km by road north-east of the provincial headquarters at Gurgān [*q.v.*], with an estimated population of 10,000 in 1956. Five km west of Gunbad (as it is popularly called) lie the ruins of the mediaeval city of Djurdjān, near the shrine said to be that of the ʿAlid Yaḥyā b. Zayd. The modern town is named from the mausoleum of the Ziyārid Ḳābūs b. Washmgīr, still standing at the northern end of the main street. It is a cylindrical brick tower 167 feet high, placed on an artificial mound 32 feet above the plain. Angular buttresses divide the sides into ten panels, the exterior diameter being 48 feet. Above the door a band of Arabic inscriptions in simple Kufic philosophically name the structure as the *ḳaṣr* ('palace') of Ḳābūs, ordered during his lifetime in 397/1006-7, or 375 by solar reckoning (*i.e.*, the Era of Yazdagird III commencing A.D. 632). The monument is nowadays much admired for its structural strength and simplicity.

Bibliography: A. Godard in A.U. Pope (ed.), *A survey of Persian art*, ii, 970-4; *RCEA*, vi, 62 (No. 2118); E. Diez, *Churasanische Baudenkmäler*, i, 39-43, 100-6; B. Dorn, *Caspia*, 91.

(A. D. H. BIVAR)

GUNS, GUNNERY [see BĀRŪD].

GÜNTEKIN, REŞAT NURI [see RESHĀD NŪRĪ GÜNTEKIN].

GŪRĀN, an Iranian people, now reduced to between 4,000 and 5,000 houses, inhabiting an area north of the main road from Kirmānshāh to the Persian frontier near Ḳaṣr-i Shīrīn and comprising the slopes of the Kūh-i Shāhān—Dālāhū mountain. The Gūrān 'capital' is Gahwāra, lying 60 km. due west of Kirmānshāh in the valley of the Zimkān, a southern tributary of the Sīrwān. An isolated community occupies the village of Kandūla, 40 km. north-east of Kirmānshāh, near the site of Dīnawar. Other, more numerous branches are formed by the Bādjalān and the tribes of the Hawrāmān [*qq.v.*].

An older form of the name was certainly Gōrān (< *Gāwrān-), as it is so preserved in Kurdish dialects, while Gūrānī itself has undergone the sound-change *ō*, *ū* > *ū*, *ǖ* respectively (*v. infra*). It is thus difficult to reconcile the name with that of the Γουράνιοι, mentioned by Strabo, xi, 14, 14, as neighbours of the Medes. The origin of the name is more probably to be sought in a form **gāw-bāra-kān* 'ox-riders' (*v.* Minorsky, *op. cit. infra*). This name is connected with the Caspian provinces, as also is the place-name Gīlān, which is of frequent occurrence among the Gūrān. The inference that their original home lay near the Caspian is further supported by the evidence of their language. Just as the closely related Zāzā [*q.v.*], or Dimlī, people moved west into classical Armenia, so the proto-Gūrān appear to have migrated south and peopled the whole southern Zagros area. Later they were largely submerged by an expansion of the Kurds, also from the north, but their language has left its mark on the ('Central') Kurdish of their conquerors.

Ibn Khurradādhbih, 14, preserves the older form

of the name as Djābārᵃḳa, and similar forms are used by Ibn Faḳīh and al-Masʿūdī, always in close connexion with Kurds. Ibn al-Athīr, ix, describing the rise of the Ḥasanōyid principality (ca. 350-420/960-1030), which stretched from northern Luristān to Shārazūr, frequently mentions the exploits of the *Djawraḳān, while for this name the author of the *Mudjmal al-tawārīkh* regularly substitutes Gūrānān. Shihāb al-Dīn al-ʿUmarī, *Masālik al-abṣār* (ca. 744/1343), mentions 'Kurds called al-Kūrāniya' in the mountains of Hamadān and Shārazūr, and Sharaf Khān, in the *Sharaf-nāma* (1005/1596), still uses the term Gūrān as if referring to the populace of Ardalān and Kirmānshāh as a whole, although he distinguishes their various rulers. The absorption of all but the surviving Gūrān population by Kurdish tribes thus appears to have proceeded slowly, the present equilibrium having been achieved little more than a century ago.

The Gūrān are mainly sedentary cultivators, yet they have long been renowned for their military qualities. In the last century they provided a standing regiment of between 1,000 and 2,000 men for the Persian army. Those subjected to Kurdish tribal overlordship, however, have completely surrendered their identity. The name Gōrān, synonymous with *miskēn*, is now used among the Kurds of Shārazūr as an appellation for the serf-like, Kurdish-speaking peasantry.

It is noteworthy that the name Gōrān is also borne by a small group of Kurds inhabiting the area north of the Great Zāb river above the confluence of the Khāzir. These 'Seven tribes', as they are also called, speak Kurdish dialects of the Southern group, unlike their neighbours, and have evidently been transported from the Kirmānshāh—Khānaḳīn region.

Language.

The Gūrānī dialects belong to the North-West Iranian group. Of those recorded Hawrāmī is consistently the most archaic. Characteristic of the phonology are (*a*) the preservation of initial *y-* and *w-*: H(awrāmī) *yáwa*, B(ādjalānī) *yaw*, K(andūlaī) *yaya* 'barley', H, B *wā*, K *vā* 'wind', H, K *winī* 'blood', (*b*) initial *w-* < *hw-*: all *wārd-* 'eat', H, K *war* 'sun', *warm* 'sleep', (*c*) initial *h-* < *x-*: H, K *har* 'donkey', *hāna* 'spring', (*d*) *-rd-* > *-l-*, in words unmistakably NWIr.: H *wilī* 'flower', K *zil* 'heart'. In general H and B have preserved the *madjhūl* vowels *ē*, *ō*, lost in the other Gūrānī dialects: H *hēla*, K *hīla* 'egg', H, B *gōsh*, K *gūsh* 'ear', where *ū* generally becomes *ü*: K *dür* 'far', *zü* 'quick'.

In the nominal system masculine and feminine gender, and direct and oblique case, are normally distinguished. Most dialects have a defining suffix *-aká*, F. *-aké* (*-akī*). The indefinite suffix, generally *-ī*, is *-ēw*, F. *-ēwa*, in Hawrāmī. H also preserves a genitive Iḍāfa form *ū*: *das-ū wēm* 'my own hand', beside the epithetic *ī*: *yānēw-ī kōn* 'an old house'.

The copula is characterized by the presence of an *-n-*, thus Sg. 1 *-anā(n)*, 2 *-anī*, 3 *-an*, etc. With the present tense the durative prefix is generally *m(a)-*: B *makarō*, K *makarū*, but H *karō* 'he does', B, K *māčān*, H *māčā* 'they say (*wāč-*)'. H has, in addition, a proper imperfect tense formed from the present stem: *karēnē* 'I was doing', *wāčē* 'he was saying'. The majority of dialects have preserved the inverse formation of the past tenses of transitive verbs: H, B *čēsh-it wāt* 'what did you say?', K *āwirdan-ish* 'he has brought it'. Passive stems are formed in *-ya-*: H *wāčyō* 'it is said', K *kiryān* 'it has been made'.

Gūrānī has attained literary status in the form of a κοινή which, besides being the vehicle of a number of Ahl-i Ḥaḳḳ writings, was cultivated at the court of the Wālīs of Ardalān. A sketch of the grammar of this literary language has been given by Rieu, *Cat. Pers. MSS.*, ii, 728 ff. Poets of name range from Yūsuf Yāska (fl. 1010/1600) to Mawlawī (d. 1300/1882). All Gūrānī verse, epic, lyric and religious alike, is in a simple decasyllabic metre. Its former popularity is reflected in the fact that *gōrānī* is the common word for 'song' in the neighbouring Kurdish.

Bibliography: V. Minorsky, *The Gūrān*, in *BSOAS*, xi (1943), 75-103; Benedictsen/Christensen, *Les dialectes d'Awromān et de Pāwä*, Copenhagen 1921; K. Hadank, *Mundarten der Gūrān*, (Oskar Mann) bearbeitet von . . ., Berlin 1930; M. Mokri, *Cinquante-deux versets . . . en dialecte Gūrānī*, in *JA*, 1956, 391-422. (D. N. MacKenzie)

GŪRĀNĪ, Sharaf (or Shihāb or Shams) al-Dīn Aḥmad b. Ismāʿīl b. ʿOthmān, known as Mollā Gūrānī, 9th/15th century Ottoman scholar and *shaykh al-islām*. [Sakhāwī sometimes found his name given as Aḥmad b. Yūsuf b. Ismāʿīl *etc.*; and in one place (ii, 1486) Ḥādjdjī Khalīfa mentions him with the *kunya* Abu 'l-ʿAbbās.] While noting that Maḳrīzī gives another date and place (the latter obviously a copyist's distortion), Sakhāwī has him born in 813/1410-11 in the Gūrān district of the Shahrizōr province of upper ʿIrāḳ, and it is probably only by inference from the ethnic character of this region that F. Babinger makes him a Kurd (*Mehmed der Eroberer und seine Zeit*, Munich 1953, 518). After having studied under local teachers, he pursued his further education in Ḥiṣn Kayfā, Baghdād, Damascus (where he arrived in 830/1426-27), Jerusalem and, finally, Cairo (835/1431-2). Here he studied under such famous scholars as Ibn Ḥadjar and Ḳalḳashandī, and he gained a reputation for learning which led to the patronage of important men and a teaching appointment at Barḳūḳiyya *madrasa*. Because of an unseemly quarrel with another scholar, he was dismissed his post and exiled to Syria in 844/1440-41 whence, in despair of his future in Mamlūk territories, he went over to the Ottomans and changed his *madhhab* from Shāfiʿī to Ḥanafī. His first appointment was to the Ḳaplīdja *madrasa* in Bursa, and in 854/1450-51 he succeeded Ḳaradja Aḥmad Efendi as professor at the Yïldïrïm in the same city (Belīgh, 283). Later he was made tutor to Prince Meḥemmed in Maghnīsa, and when the latter ascended the throne in 855/1451 he received the post of *ḳāḍi 'l-ʿaskar*. He was present at the conquest of Constantinople (ʿĀlī, *Kunh al-akhbār*, v, Istanbul 1277, 257) and composed in elegant Arabic a letter to the Sultan of Egypt announcing this great victory (Ferīdūn Beğ, *Munshaʾāt al-salāṭīn*, Istanbul 1274, 235). His intractable independence of attitude proving an annoyance to the new Sultan and his statesmen, he was removed from the centre of affairs by appointment to the *ḳāḍī*-ship of Bursa, but here, too, he acted in defiance of the royal will and was finally dismissed from office. He left Ottoman territory for a while, but returned in 861/1457 after having performed the Pilgrimage and was once again appointed *ḳāḍī* of Bursa with lavish monthly supplements to his salary from the Sultan. In 867/1462-63 he succeeded Mollā Khusraw as *ḳāḍī* of Istanbul (Belīgh, 260; but cf. Tashköprüzāde-Medjdī, 149 margin, where it is said that Khʷādja-zāde succeeded Mollā Khusraw in this office in 872/1467-68). In 885/1480-81 he was elevated to *shaykh al-islām*, and he remained in this office until his death in the latter part of Radjab 983/1488. He is buried in the mosque he built in the quarter of Istanbul which still bears his name.

The independence of mind which he exhibited in his public life is also to be found in his works. Thus, in his commentary on the Ḳurʾān entitled *Ghāyat al-amānī*, etc. (completed in 867/1463) he often takes issue with Zamakhsharī and Bayḍāwī (Brockelmann, II, 228, S II, 319; Ḥādjdjī Khalīfa, ii, 1190), and in his commentary on the *Ṣaḥīḥ* of Bukhārī entitled *al-Kawthar al-djārī*, etc. (completed in Edirne in 874/1469) he even refutes his former master Ibn Ḥadjar (Brockelmann, I, 159, S I, 262, S II, 319; Ḥādjdjī Khalīfa, i, 553). Several of his works are on Ḳurʾānic readings (*ḳirāʾa*): under the title of *al-ʿAbḳarī* he compiled his notes on the *Kanz al-maʿānī* of al-Djaʿbarī, the famous commentary on al-Shāṭibī's *Ḥirz al-amānī* (Brockelmann, S I, 725; Ḥādjdjī Khalīfa, i, 646); his *Kashf al-asrār*, etc. (not completed in 890/1485 as Ḥādjdjī Khalīfa, ii, 1487, says, for a ms. of it in the Süleymaniye, No. 47/2, is dated 874/1469-70) is a commentary on al-Djazarī's *al-Durra al-muḍīʾa*, etc. (Brockelmann, II, 202); the same Süleymaniye ms. also contains another work by him on this subject, the *Lawāmiʿ al-ghurar fī sharḥ fawāʾid al-Durar* which, from its title, may be a commentary on the *Durar al-afkār*, a work by al-Djaʿbarī not recorded in Brockelmann (Ḥādjdjī Khalīfa, ii, 1319). On *fiḳh* he wrote a commentary to al-Subkī's *Djamʿ al-djawāmiʿ* entitled *al-Durar* (or *al-Budūr*) *al-lawāmiʿ* which Ḥādjdjī Khalīfa (i, 596) implies is a spiteful attack on the *al-Badr al-ṭāliʿ*, also a commentary on the *Djamʿ* by al-Maḥallī, his successor at the Barḳūḳiyya (Brockelmann, S II, 106, 319). A few other minor works are also attributed to him.

Bibliography. The two basic sources for his biography are al-Sakhāwī, *al-Ḍawʾ al-lāmiʿ*, Cairo 1353, i, 241-3 and Ṭashköprüzāde, *al-Shaḳāʾiḳ al-nuʿmāniyya*, Arabic text in the margins of Ibn Khallikān, *Wafayāt al-aʿyān*, Būlāḳ 1299, i, 143-51; Turkish version by Medjdī, Istanbul 1269, 102-11; German translation from the Arabic by O. Rescher, Istanbul 1927, 48-53 (see also 114). Despite his fame and importance, he is scarcely mentioned in the historical works of the period: see the bibliography to the article by Ahmed Ateş in *IA*, viii, 406-8, and add: Belīgh Efendi, *Güldeste-i riyāḍ-i ʿirfān*, Bursa 1302. For his buildings in Istanbul and elsewhere, see Ḥusayn Aywānsarāyī, *Ḥadīḳat al-djawāmiʿ*, Istanbul 1281, i, 187, 207, and Ekrem Hakkı Ayverdi, *Fâtih devri mimarîsi*, Istanbul 1953, Nos. 73, 85, 90, 171, 199, 244, 384 and 486. He figures in a miniature among the illustrations to Sâmiha Ayverdi, *Edebî ve Manevî Dünyası içinde Fatih*, Istanbul 1953, 10.

(J. R. Walsh)

GURČĀNĪ [see Supplement]

GURDJISTĀN [see kurdj].

GURGĀN, Old Persian vrkāna, Arabic djurdjān, the ancient Hyrcania, at the South-east corner of the Caspian Sea.

The province, which was practically equivalent to the modern Persian province of Astarābādh [*q.v.*] (now part of *Ustān* II) forms both in physical features and climate a connecting link between sub-tropical Māzandarān with its damp heat and the steppes of Dihistān in the north. The rivers Atrak [*q.v.*] and Gurgān, to which the country owes its fertility and prosperity, are not an unmixed blessing on account of their inundations and the danger of fever which results.

Gurgān played an important part in the Sāsānid period, being the frontier province against the nomads pressing in from the north. The fortresses of Shahristān-i Yazdgird and Shahr-i Pērōz (see Marquart, *Ērānšahr*, 51, 56) were built as a defence against the nomads of the Dihistān steppes; a long wall was built along the northern frontier to defend the lands.

Saʿīd b. al-ʿĀṣ is said to have levied tribute from the "Malik" of Gurgān as early as the year 30/650-1; but the real conquest of the country was the work of Yazīd b. al-Muhallab (98/716-7). At that time the ruler of Gurgān was a Marzbān but the real power seems to have been in the hands of the Turkish chief Ṣūl.

After punishing the unruly population of the valley of the navigable Andarhāz, the modern Gurgān river, Yazīd founded the town of Gurgān, which henceforth was the capital of the province. It must have been a very prosperous place in the 3rd/9th and 4th/10th centuries. The gardens around it, irrigated by the waters of the river, were famous; its chief product was silk. Gurgān was also a station on the caravan route to Russia. The town was divided in two by the river, which was crossed by a bridge of boats; on the eastern side was the town proper or Shahristān, whose nine gates are detailed by Muḳaddasī, and on the western, the suburb of Bakrābādh (called after a settlement of the Arab tribe?). The prosperity of the town seems to have been early threatened by internal dissensions. ʿAlid propaganda had found a congenial soil in the lands along the Caspian, and the ʿAlid dynasty of Ṭabaristān included Gurgān in its sphere of influence. In Gurgān itself the tomb of Muḥammad b. Djaʿfar al-Ṣādiḳ, commonly known as Gūr-i Surkh (the Red Tomb) was an object of great reverence. The constant unrest in these lands enabled Mardāvīdj b. Ziyār in 316/928 to found a kingdom of his own in Gurgān with the help of the Daylamites: it survived for over a hundred years, although nominally dependent on the Sāmānids and later the Ghaznawids [see ziyārids]. The dome-shaped tomb (Gunbadh-i Ḳābūs [*q.v.*]) of the ruler Ḳābūs b. Washmgīr (366/976-7 - 403/1012-3) still exists as a memorial of this period.

The population was massacred at the time of the Mongol invasion and Mustawfī (transl. Le Strange, 156) writing in the 8th/14th century describes the town as a heap of ruins. Tīmūr is said to have built a palace in 795/1392-3 on the bank of the river, but Gurgān never again attained its former prosperity. Ḥādjdjī Khalīfa (*Djihān-numā*, Istanbul 1145/1732, 339), however, mentions Gurgān, which had been rebuilt since the Mongol period, as inhabited by fanatical Shīʿīs.

The position of Gurgān in the angle formed by the confluence of the Gurgān River and the Khurmā-rūd is marked only by extensive mounds, which have not yet been investigated. The very name of the town has recently been transferred to Astarābādh. Only the Gunbadh-i Ḳābūs, about 2 miles to the north-east and about a mile away from the river, has withstood the ravages of time.

Bibliography: As in the article astarābādh.

(R. Hartmann [- J. A. Boyle])

GURGANDJ, called by the Arabs Djurdjāniyya, and also in the period about 600/1200 described as Khwārizm (like the country round), the economic centre of the Khwārizm [*q.v.*] area and for a long period also the political capital of the territory, lay to the west of the lowest reaches of the Oxus (Āmū

Daryā). The town, whose age is unknown, was captured by the Arabs in 93/712. They attempted to deprive Gurgan<u>dj</u> of its importance by founding a city, Fīl (Fīr), on the further bank of the Oxus; but the new settlement was gradually inundated by the river (for details see KĀTH). In order to maintain their domination over Khwārizm, which was an area at that time on the outer fringe of the world of Islam, the Arabs divided the territory; the native dynasty, the Āfrīghids, who bore the title of Khwārizm-Shāh, were allowed to retain the northern part, with Kāth as their capital; Gurgandj became the residence of an Arab *amīr*, who had power over the south-west (*Ḥudūd al-ʿālam*, 122, § 25, and 371; Gardīzī, ed. M. Nāẓim, 1930, p. 57). This state of affairs lasted for over 250 years, until 385/995 (for details see KHWĀRIZM). Then the Arab *amīr* of the time, Maʾmūn b. Muḥammad, was able to expel the old dynasty and unite the whole of Khwārizm under his own rule. From that time he took over the ancient title of the rulers of that country, Khwārizm-Shāh. Thereafter Gurgandj ranked after Kāth as the second principal city, but after the overthrow of Maʾmūn's successors by the Saldjūḳs in 434/1043, it exceeded Kāth in importance and became once more the real centre of the territory as well as the intermediary for commerce with the Oghuz and other northern Turkish tribes (Gardīzī, 95; Iṣṭakhrī, 299 f., 341; Ibn Ḥawḳal, 350 f., 477 f.). At this time the town had four gates and a large palace near the Bāb al-Ḥudjdjādj, on the edge of a huge market place, and consisted of an outer and an inner city (*Ḥudūd*, 122). According to Muḳaddasī, 288, in the 4th/10th century the town grew rapidly; in 600/1204 it was besieged by the Ghūrids [*q.v.*] (Djuwaynī, ii, 55; Barthold, *Turkestan*[1], 349 f.) and at the beginning of the 7th/13th century it was included among the most prosperous cities of the Islamic Empire (an account dating from the period 613-6/1216-9 is given in Yāḳūt, ii, 54, 486; iii, 933; iv, 260 f.). Immediately thereafter, in 618/1221, Gurgandj was attacked by the Mongols and after a siege of many months was razed to the ground (there is a lengthy account in Djuwaynī, i, 98 f.; thorough discussion of details in Fritz Meier, *Die Fawāʾiḥ ... des ... Kubrā*, Wiesbaden 1957, 53-60, with presentation of all source material; cf. also Barthold, *Turkestan*[1], 433-7). The Mongols also flooded the town by diverting the Oxus; nevertheless a few remains of pre-Mongol buildings have been found (for instance an inscription of 401/1010-1: *Zapiski Vost. Otd. Imp. Russk. Arkheol. Obshčestva*, xiv, 015 f.; cf. also Djūzdjānī, *Ṭabaḳāt-i Nāṣirī*, ed. Raverty, 281, 1100). The question of how far the diversion of the Oxus at that time led to a displacement of the river bed is discussed in the article ĀMŪ DARYĀ. Gurgandj lay waste from that time forth. The new capital of the province, Urgenč, founded in 628/1231, was on a different site and presumably corresponds to the earlier so-called "Little Gurgandj", three parasangs from Gurgandj. For the history of this town see URGENČ.

Bibliography: Le Strange, 447-9; Barthold, *Turkestan*[1], index; idem, *12 Vorlesungen*, Berlin 1935, 65; Josef Markwart, *Wehrot und Arang*, Leiden 1938, 96, 102; Spuler, *Iran*, 31, 108, 115; idem, *Mongolen*[2], 28 (sources in note 7); idem, *Der Amu Darya*, in *Jean Deny Armağanı*, Ankara 1958, 231-48; A. Yu. Yakubovskiy, *Razvalinî Urgenča* (*The Ruins of Urgenč*), in *Izvestiya Akad. Material'noy kul'turî*, vi/2 (1930); S. P. Tolstov, *Drevniy Khorezm* (*Old Khwārizm*), Moscow 1948, index; idem, *Auf den Spuren der altchoresmischen Kultur*, German tr. by O. Mehlitz, Berlin 1953, 241-5 (with very ambiguous use of sources), 253 f., 263 f., 286-91, 313; idem, in *Vestnik Drevney Istorii*, 1953/I, 160-74 (with plans and illustrations); H. Desmond Martin in *JRAS*, 1943, 63 (plan of the campaign in Khwārizm in 1220-1); *Bol'shaya Sovetskaya Éntsiklopediya*[2], xliv (1956), 313 f. (illustrations). (B. SPULER)

GURGĀNĪ, FAKHR AL-DĪN ASʿAD, author of the first known courtly romance in Persian: *Wīs and Rāmīn*. In the opinion of Z. Safa (ii, 361) his achievement is to have introduced a literary genre which is now represented by a series of works, several of which are worthy of note. What is known of his life is limited to the little that he reveals in his poem. The accounts given by his biographers are negligible but agree in attributing to him the authorship of the poem (with the exception of Dawlat Shāh, who erroneously attributes it to one of the Niẓāmīs). ʿAwfī has preserved three of his lyrical poems (texts: Maḥdjūb, introd., 14), the others being lost. Shams-i Kays (*Muʿdjam*, ed. Mīrzā Muḥammad and E. G. Browne, 80) writes: "The poetic metre *baḥr-i hazadj-i musaddas-i mahdhūf* is that of Niẓāmī's *Khusraw and Shīrīn* and of Fakhrī Gurgānī's *Wīs and Rāmīn*"; later (140) he refers to him simply as Fakhrī, which was perhaps his *takhalluṣ*. In the last verse of his poem, Gurgānī refers to himself as young; in addition he inserts (ed. Minovi, 468, v. 72; ed. Maḥdjūb, 350, v. 72; tr. Massé, 431 bottom) this confidence (which partly explains his skill in depicting the passions of love): "How many days did I sample love! But it did not make me happy for one single day". He had certainly studied the Arab and Iranian philosophers (see the introd. to the poem, on the subject of a non-material God and His creation) and astronomy (description of the night: ed. Minovi, 80; ed. Maḥdjūb, 60; tr., 72). In this same introduction he sings the praises of Ṭoghrïl Beg, of his vizier and of ʿAmīd Abu 'l-Fatḥ Muẓaffar, who was appointed governor of Isfahan after the capture of this town by the sultan (441/1050); this governor was the patron of the poet and appointed him to various offices. In the course of conversation with him, as Gurgānī relates in detail (Minovi, 25-7; Maḥdjūb, 18-21; tr., 6-7), the subject arose of the love story of Wīs and Rāmīn, preserved in a Pahlavi manuscript: "a continuous narrative, but containing all manner of strange words", lacking in ideas and maxims—that is to say a prose narrative without any poetic ornament (perhaps like the Georgian translation of the poem). The governor having invited him to translate this story into Persian, "to embellish it as one adorns a flower-bed in April", Gurgānī set to work, and finished, in 447/1055 or shortly after, this verse romance which consists of 8905 *bayt* in *hazadj*, the metre most often adopted later by those who composed romances in the same genre.

The question arises whether Gurgānī knew Pahlavi. It is impossible summarily to deny this after having read his account, imprecise though it is, of the conversation with the governor, and it is possible to conclude from one of the verses of the poem that he had some, though not a complete, knowledge of the language ("For one who knows Pahlavi, Khurāsān signifies the place from which we receive light", ed. Minovi and Maḥdjūb, ch. 48, v. 4); in the course of this conversation, however, he refers to the prolixity and the strange (*i.e.*, archaic) words of the Pahlavi text. For the question whether he worked directly from it or through a Persian translation, see Maḥdjūb, introd., 20. The important thing is that he gave new life to an original which otherwise would no doubt have disappeared like so many other Pahlavi texts.

In his poem the influence of ancient Iran appears particularly in the frequent allusions to the divine or the evil powers, to the sacred fires (mentioned by their names) and to their maintenance, to the ancient months and feast days, and to legendary features; there is in it a case of trial by ordeal, and one of those consanguineous marriages which were characteristic of the royal families of ancient Iran. The subject of the poem is fatal love: from the time of the appearance of the first edition of the Persian text the similarities between the poem and the story of Tristan and Iseult were recognized—there is thus no need to give an analysis of it here (cf. Massé, 9 ff.). The romance may be based on a historical fact: V. Minorsky has sought to demonstrate that it probably relates the adventures of a descendant of the Arsacid family and of a princess of one of the seven noble families of the Parthian period.

In Gurgānī's poetry there are realistic features contributing to knowledge of customs and folklore. At times his style is affected and precious (tr., 20-1), especially when, like other Persian poets, he is describing feminine beauty in conventional terms (*e.g.*, ch. 37; tr., 90). Maḥdjūb has noted a series of images and of ancient proverbs (introd., 55-8), archaism sometimes used with a special meaning (*ibid.*, 34) and some words which are close to the Pahlavi forms (*ibid.*, 43). The poem had a lasting influence. Maḥdjūb points out similarities between some verses of Gurgānī and those of later poets, and even some borrowings (introd., 98 ff.). The ten passionate letters written by Wīs to Rāmīn (Minovi, 347-83; Maḥdjūb, 259-86; tr. 318-51) were imitated by the poets Awḥadī, Ibn ʿImād, ʿĀrifī, ʿImād Faḳīh (ten letters), Amīr Ḥusaynī, Kātibī and Salmān-i Sāwidjī (thirty letters). Of more significance is the similarity evident in the plan of Niẓāmī's verse romance *Khusraw u Shīrīn*, which was probably inspired by Gurgānī, though as regards style it may be suggested that Niẓāmī intended that his learned and highly artificial style should form a contrast to the generally simple and sober style of Gurgānī.

Bibliography: Editions: Nassau Lees and Munshi Ahmad Ali (Bibl. Ind.), Calcutta 1864, based on a manuscript in India; Minovi, Tehrān 1314/1935, based on three manuscripts including that of the Bibl. Nat., Paris, which is the best; Muḥammad Djaʿfar Maḥdjūb, Tehrān 1337/1959, which makes use of the two preceding editions. French translation with introduction, by H. Massé, Paris 1959; Georgian adaptation: *Visramiani*, tr. O. Wardrop (Oriental Translation Fund, new series, xxiii, London 1914). Studies: Z. Safa, *Taʾrīkh-i adabiyāt dar Īrān*, Tehrān 1336/1958, ii, index; *Gr.I.Ph.*, index; K. H. Graf, analysis and extracts translated into German verse, in *ZDMG*, xxiii (1869), 375-433; Fr. Gabrieli, *Note sul Wîs u Râmîn*, in *R. Acad. Naz. dei Lincei, rendiconti*, March-April 1939; V. Minorsky, *Wîs u Râmîn, a Parthian romance*, in *BSOAS*, xi/4 (1946); Ṣādiḳ Hidāyat, in *Payām-i naw*, Tehrān 1324/1946, nos. 1 and 2; M. Minovi, in *Sukhan*, Tehrān 1333-4/1956, nos. 1 and 2; A. Bausani, *Storia della letteratura persiana*, Milan 1960, 621-6; J. Rypka, *Iranische Literaturgeschichte*, Leipzig 1959, 176-8.

(H. Massé)

GURGĀNĪ [see DJURDJĀNĪ].

GŪRKHĀN, the title borne by the (non-Muslim) rulers of Ḳarakhitāy [*q.v.*] (Chinese Hsi Liao = Western Liao) who governed central Asia between 522-5/1128-31 and 608/1212 (or, with Güčlük, till 615/1218). The first ruler was Yeh-lü Ta-shih (d. 537/1143), a prince from the north Chinese dynasty of Liao, of the Kʿi-tan (Khitāy) people. He overthrew the regime of the Ḳarakhānids [*q.v.*] or Ilig-khāns and in 535/1141 defeated the Saldjūḳid sultan Sandjar [*q.v.*] decisively in the Ḳaṭwān plain, north of Samarḳand: the victory of a non-Muslim ruler from the East over one of the most powerful rulers of Islam probably provided the foundation for the legend of Prester John [*q.v.*] (Gūrkhān > Johannes).

The title Gūrkhān is probably taken from the Turkish words *kür/gür* (Mongol *kür*) ("broad", "wide", "general": cf. Maḥmūd al-Kāshgharī, *Dīwān*, ed. C. Brockelmann, Budapest 1928, 117; Radloff, *Versuch eines Wörterbuches* ...,[2] 1960, ii, 1447, 1637; *Mangḥol un Niuca Tobcaʾan* (*Geheime Geschichte der Mongolen*), ed. E. Haenisch, Leipzig 1937, 65 and ed. Kozin, Moscow/Leningrad 1941, 278); P. Doerfer in *OLZ*, 1960, col. 635 f. The Muslims also refer to Gūrkhān as "Khān-i Khānān".

Bibliography: K. A. Wittfogel and Fêng Chia-Shêng, *History of the Chinese Society Liao*, Philadelphia 1949, 431, 619-55 (History of the Gūrkhāns based on Eastern and Western sources, written in collaboration with K. H. Menges); K. Menges in *Byzantion*, xxi/1 (1951), 104-6; idem, in *RO*, xvii (1953), 71; Spuler, *Iran*, 360 n. 8. For the history of the Gūrkhāns see also the Bibl. to ḲARA KHITĀY and KIRMĀN (13th century).

(B. Spuler)

GUWĀKHARZ [see BĀKHARZ].

GÜZEL ḤIṢĀR [see AYDÎN].

GŪZGĀN [see DJUZDJĀN].

GWĀLIYĀR, formerly capital of the Sindhia state of Gwāliyār, now a town in Madhya Pradesh. "Tradition assigns the foundation of the city to one Sūradj Sen who was cured of leprosy by an ascetic named Gwālipa. The latter inhabited the hill on which the fort now stands, and this was called Gwāliyār after him". The early history of Gwāliyār is, however, shrouded in myth and romance. The Hūna adventurers, Toramana and his son Mihirkula, who partially overthrew the Gupta power in the 6th century A.D., are considered to be the first historical holders of this place. Later Rādjā Bhodj of Kanawdj, the Kačhwāha Rādjpūts and the Parīhars respectively held sway over it.

In 413/1022 when Sultan Maḥmūd of Ghazna marched against Ganda, the ruler of Kālindjar, he passed the fort of Gwāliyār. Since the Rādjā of Gwāliyār was a feudatory of Ganda, the Sultan stormed the fort. The Rādjā, despite his successful resistance, was so alarmed that he sued for peace (*Zayn al-akhbār*, 79). In 592/1196 Ḳuṭb al-Dīn Aybak took the fort from the Parīhars (*Ṭabaḳāt-i Nāṣirī*, 145; Eng. tr., Raverty, i, 545-6, with note on other versions). Iletmish's first territorial appointment was as the *amīr* of Gwāliyār (*Ṭabaḳāt-i Nāṣirī*, 169; Eng. tr. i, 604). It appears to have been lost to the Turks because in 629/1231 Iletmish is reported to have reconquered it and made appointments of the *amīr-i dād*, the *kotwāl* and the *ḳāḍī*. But the history of the Muslim occupation of Gwāliyār is a chequered one. Early in her reign Raḍiyya (634-7/1236-40) had to send an expedition towards Gwāliyār under Tamur Khān, but the position became untenable and the fort had to be abandoned to Čahardeva. In 649/1251 Balban led a full-scale expedition against Gwāliyār, but does not seem to have achieved any permanent success, for the numismatic evidence shows that

Gwāliyār was independent up to at least 657/1259.

In the disturbances caused by Timur's invasion (800/1398) it was seized by the Tonwar Rād͟jpūts. In 894/1488 Sultan Bahlūl Lōdī marched against Gwāliyār and forced the Rād͟jā, Mān Singh, to submit. When Sikandar Lōdī (894-923/1489-1517) shifted his capital to Āgra he considered the annexation of Gwāliyār necessary for the consolidation of his power, but he could not achieve his objective. Though subjected to frequent attacks by the rulers of Mālwa, D͟jawnpur and Delhi, the Tonwars managed to retain it till 924/1518, when the fort was surrendered to Ibrāhīm Lodī. When Bābur turned his attention to the Afg͟hān principalities after his victory at Pānīpat, he found Tātār K͟hān Sarang K͟hānī occupying the fort along with all its dependencies. It was through the help of Sayyid Muhammad G͟hawt͟h, a celebrated S͟hat̤t̤ārī saint, that he succeeded in establishing his hold over it. In 934/1528 Bābur visited Gwāliyār and spent some time examining the palaces of Mān Singh and Vikramāditya. He was impressed by their size and splendour although he grumbles a little at their want of taste and elegance. In 949/1542 Gwāliyār fell to S͟hīr S͟hāh Surī (945-52/1538-45) who forced Afg͟hān tribes to settle there in large numbers (Rukn al-Dīn, *Laṭāʾif-i Ḳuddūsī*, Delhi 1311, 85). This attempt at Afg͟hān colonization in Gwāliyār was closely linked up with his policy of consolidation in Rād͟jpūtānā. Besides, Gwāliyār was also important as one of the principal stages on the great route from the Deccan which passed by Sirond͟j, Narwar, Gwāliyār and Dholpur to Āgra. His descendants practically made it the capital of their dominions.

In 965/1558 Gwāliyār passed to Akbar. Abu 'l-Faḍl mentions it as a *sarkār* in the province of Āgra and refers to its 'exquisite singers', 'lovely women' and 'iron mine'. Gwāliyār was one of the 28 mint towns of Akbar for copper coins. *Dewriza* rice for Akbar's kitchen was brought from here. There was a quarry of red clay (*gil-i surk͟h*) in the hills of Gwāliyār.

It was due to Mubāriz K͟hān, the future Sultan ʿĀdil S͟hāh, that music received great encouragement in Gwāliyār, and musicians from Mālwa, the Deccan and other parts of the country gathered there. Out of 36 singers and players enumerated in the *Āʾīn-i Akbarī*, 15 had learned in the Gwāliyār school, including the famous Tānsen. The Mug͟hals used it also as a state prison (cf. Tavernier, *Travels*, Eng. tr. Crooke, London 1925, i, 51 ff.; F. Bernier, *Voyages*, Amsterdam 1724, 147 ff.; Eng. tr. Constable, London 1891, 106 ff.). Apart from the large number of political prisoners, princes and nobles, the great Naḳs͟hbandī saint, S͟hayk͟h Aḥmad of Sirhind, was interned here by D͟jahāngīr. It remained in Mug͟hal possession until the 12th/18th century. In the confusion that followed on the battle of Pānīpat in 1174/1761, Lokendra Singh, the D͟jāt chief of Gohad, obtained possession of the fort but was driven out by Sindhia soon after. There were many vicissitudes, and full Sindhia control could not be established before 1886. Gwāliyār lost its importance as the seat of Sindhia Government when a new town, Las͟hkar, developed near it.

"The old city of Gwāliyār is now a desolate-looking collection of half-empty, dilapidated, flat-roofed stone houses, deserted mosques and ruined tombs. As it stands, the town is entirely Muhammadan in character, no old Hindu remains being traceable" (*Imperial Gazetteer of India*, 1908 ed.). Of the monuments, besides the fort which is situated on a great table rock of Vindhyan sandstone and is considered to be one of the most impregnable forts of India, there are several mosques—particularly the D͟jāmiʿ Masd͟jid, commenced by D͟jahāngīr, and the mosque of Muʿtamid K͟hān—several tombs, wells, tanks (on the "never-failing" tanks see Tavernier, *op. cit.*, 51) and *bāʾolīs* etc. The tombs are noticeable for the excellent carved stone and splendid pierced screen work. The tomb of Sayyid Muḥammad G͟hawt͟h S͟hat̤t̤ārī (d. 970/1563), built in Mug͟hal times, perpetuates the structural traditions of the Lōdī period, but derives its decorative elements from Gud͟jarāt. The shrine of Bābā Kapūr (d. 979/1571), another popular saint of Gwāliyār, is situated in a cave, cut in the north-eastern face of the rock on which the Gwāliyār fort stands.

Bibliography: Bar Hebraeus, *alias* Gregory Abu 'l-Farad͟j b. Hārūn, *The Syriac Chronicle*, Paris 1890, 211-2; Gardīzī, *Zayn al-ak͟hbār*, ed. M. Nāẓim, 79; al-Bīrūnī, *Kitāb al-Hind*, tr. E. Sachau, London 1914, i, 202; Minhād͟j al-Sirād͟j, *Ṭabaḳāt-i Nāṣirī*, Bibl. Ind., 145, 169, 174-5, 247; Eng. tr. Raverty, London 1881, i, 546, 604, 619 ff., 743; Ibn Baṭṭūṭa, iii, index, Eng. tr. Gibb, London 1929, 224; *Bābur Nāma*, tr. Beveridge, ii, 539-40; Abu 'l-Faḍl, *Āʾīn-i Akbarī*, i, tr. Blochmann, Calcutta 1927, 32, 60, 235, 680-2; ii, Jarrett and Sarkar, Calcutta 1949, 192, 198; S͟h. D͟jalāl Ḥiṣārī, *Gwāliyār-nāma*, Brit. Mus. MS Add. 16,859; Hirāman Muns͟hī, *Gwāliyār-nāma*, Brit. Mus. MS Add. 16,709; Shrimant Balwant Row Bhayasahib Scindia, *History of the fortress of Gwaliyar*, Bombay 1892; Motī Rām and K͟hwus͟h Ḥāl, *Aḥwāl-i ḳilāʿ-i Gwāliyār*, Br. Mus. (Rieu, i, 304b), Ind. Office (Ethé 499); K͟hayr al-Dīn, *Gwāliyār-nāma* or *Kārnāma-i Gwāliyār*, Brit. Mus. (Rieu, iii, 1028a); J. de Laet, *De imperio magni Mogolis* . . ., Leiden 1631, 40 ff.; J. B. Tavernier, *Voyages*, Eng. tr. Crooke, London 1925, i, 51-2; F. Bernier, *Voyages*, Amsterdam 1724, 147 ff., Eng. tr. A. Constable, London 1891, 106 ff.; Tieffenthaler, *Description historique et géographique de l'Inde*, Berlin 1786, 184, 217 ff., 246; Ray, *The dynastic history of Northern India*, Calcutta 1936, ii, 822-9; *Gwalior State Gazetteer*, Calcutta 1908; *Imperial Gazetteer of India*, New edition, 1908, xii, 438-43; A. Cunningham, *Archaeological Survey of India*, ii, 330; *Epigraphia Indica*, i, 154-62; P. Brown, *Indian Architecture* (*Islamic period*), Bombay n.d., 30, 126 ff.; Nāẓim, *Sulṭān Maḥmūd of G͟hazna*, Cambridge 1931, 113, 207-8; Shamsuddin Ahmad, *Inscriptions from Gwalior State*, in *EIM*, 1939-40, 43-7; Ram Singh Saksena, *Moslem epigraphy in the Gwalior State*, in *EIM*, 1925-6, 14-19; *ibid.*, 1929-30, 7-9; *ibid.*, 1935-6, 52-7; idem, *Persian inscriptions in the Gwalior State*, in *IHQ*, i (1925), 653-6; iii (1927), 715-8; vii (1931), 55-6; xvi (1940), 592-5. (K. A. Nizami)

GWANDU. First mentioned in the *al-Infāḳ al-maysūr* of Muhammadu Bello (d. 1837) Gwandu was, at the beginning of the 19th century, a village in the prosperous little state of Kebbi (capital: Birnin Kebbi) in the western Sudan. In 1805, in the course of the Fulani *d͟jihād*, Shehu Usumanu dan Fodio (d. 1817) established a temporary headquarters at Kambaza, near Gwandu, but was attacked by a coalition of the Kebbawa, Gobirawa and Tawāriḳ. The Fulani army was defeated and the survivors fell back on Gwandu where they stood siege under daily attacks. Finally the Kebbawa and their allies withdrew but were courageously pursued and ambushed by the Fulani garrison. The Kebbawa force was

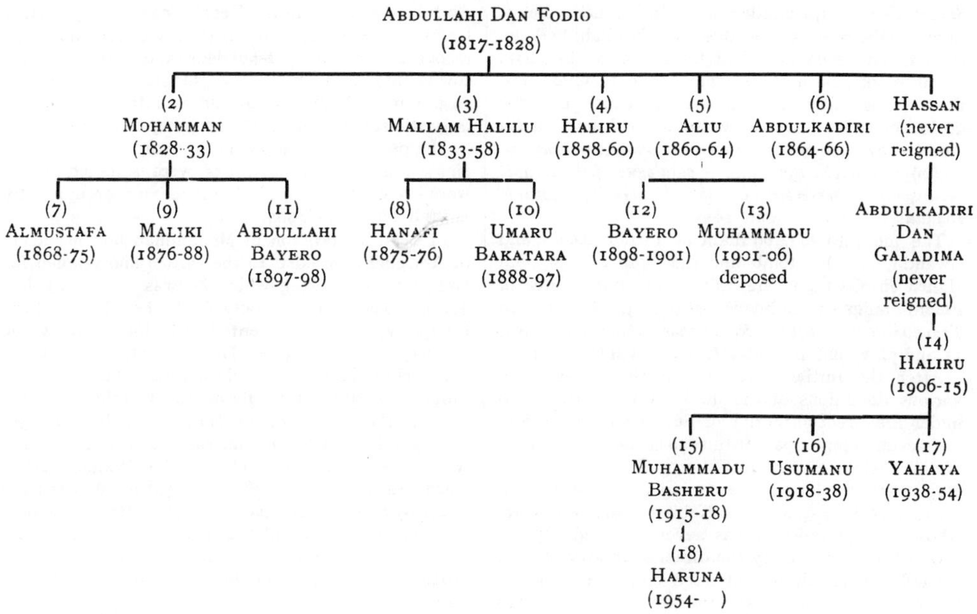

routed and put to flight at Gumbai and this was the turning point of the *djihād*. Shehu Usumanu was never again in serious danger and the Fulani forces, despite occasional reverses, proceeded to subdue most of an area in size approximate to (but not co-terminous with) that of the present state of Nigeria. Shehu Usumanu, the leader and inspiration of the *djihād*, fell sick in 1806 and remained in Gwandu, leaving the conduct of his campaigns to his Fulani commanders. His son, Muhammadu Bello, built a wall around the village to strengthen it and for the next two years it served as the capital of the incipient Fulani empire.

In 1808 Alkalawa, the capital of Gobir, was taken and Shehu Usumanu left Gwandu in favour of Sifawa. He then divided the administration of the conquered territories between his brother, Abdullahi dan Fodio, and his son, Muhammadu Bello. Abdullahi became responsible for the western dominions and Muhammadu Bello for the eastern. Gwandu was under Abdullahi's authority but he preferred to build the town of Bodinga, close to Sifawa, for his headquarters so that he might remain near his brother. From Bodinga, however, he led a series of victorious campaigns until, in 1810, he administered most of Kebbi (but which the Fulani were able to subdue entirely) and had exacted allegiance from Nupe, Ilorin, Yauri, Gurma, Arewa and Zabarma.

In 1809 Muhammadu Bello created a township of the hamlet Sokoto, and built a wall around it so that it might serve as the administrative headquarters of the eastern dominions, and it was there that Shehu Usumanu died in 1817. Abdullahi, on hearing of his brother's death, hastened the fourteen miles from Bodinga to Sokoto, but found that Bello had been proclaimed *Sarkin Musulmi* (Commander of the Faithful) and the gates of the town were closed against him. By Fulani custom succession passed to a brother rather than to a son and Abdullahi withdrew to Gwandu aggrieved. On his arrival he found that the nearby town of Kalembena was in revolt, hoping to profit from his weakness after his rejection by Sokoto. His position was desperate but Bello went to his aid. In a celebrated scene, the two met outside the walls of Kalembena; Bello, the warrior and chief architect of the Fulani empire, mounted on a charger, Abdullahi astride the mare which as a mallam (Arabic: *muʿallim*) he always rode. In accordance with Fulani custom, Bello, as the younger man, went to dismount but his uncle waved him back into his saddle, and himself bent forward to salute his nephew as Commander of the Faithful. Together they put down the revolt. Thereafter Abdullahi retained the administration of the western dominions subject to the recognised authority of the Sarkin Musulmi, Bello, of Sokoto. This situation established in effect a dual empire which they bequeathed to their heirs, and led to a close friendship between the *amīrs* of Gwandu and the Sultans of Sokoto which lasted unbroken until the British occupation of Nigeria and which still endures.

Abdullahi, who was born in 1766, was twelve years younger than his illustrious brother Shehu Usumanu and was instructed in the Ḳurʾān and the Mālikī rite by Mallam al-Ḥādjdjī Djibrilla, as was his brother. He was some thirty-eight years of age when, in 1804, he was the first to pay homage to Shehu Usumanu as Sarkin Musulmi. Deeply religious, he nevertheless played a prominent part in the Fulani wars of conquest; in the early campaigns he often served, as did Bello, in a subordinate capacity to other Fulani commanders but distinguished himself by bravery in hand-to-hand fighting. Always of a literary bent, he would celebrate his victories with an Arabic ode and may be said to have been the poet laureate of the *djihād*. After the submission of Kalembena in 1819 he left administrative matters in the hands of his son Mohamman (who was to succeed him) and his nephew Bohari and devoted his last years to study and writing. He did not himself adopt the title of *amīr* but preferred the simple style "mallam" (which he retained until his death in 1828).

All these principal figures of the Fulani *djihād*,

Shehu Usumanu, Abdullahi and Muhammadu Bello, were prolific writers in Arabic but Abdullahi had the most felicitous command of the language. For lists of his works, both those which have survived and those whose titles are known but which may be no longer extant, see the writer's ***Field notes on the Arabic literature of the western Sudan*** (*Abdullahi dan Fodio*), in *JRAS*, 1956, and *A catalogue of the Arabic manuscripts preserved in the University library, Ibadan, Nigeria*, Ibadan 1955-58.

The mosques of Abdullahi in Birnin Kebbi and Gwandu, and his tomb and the tomb of a S̲h̲ayk̲h̲ Haliru in Gwandu, are important monuments of Fulānī religious architecture (cf. J. Schacht, in *Travaux de l' Institut de Recherches Sahariennes*, 1954, 13 and pl. v, and in *Studia Islamica*, viii (1957), 136).

After the initial conquests of the Fulanis the various dominions of the dual empire were placed under the direct authority of Fulani *amīrs*; those of the western empire paid tribute to Gwandu, and those of the eastern empire to Sokoto. However, neither empire was for long at peace and revolts were constant, especially among the Kebbawa and Gobiwara, whose total submission was never obtained. By the end of the 19th century the direct authority of both Gwandu and Sokoto extended little beyond the boundaries of their own amīrates and when the British forces occupied the country in 1902 they found the Sarkin Kebbi sturdily maintaining the independence of Argungu, and the Gobirawa from Sabon Birni and Chibiri attacking the eastern and north-eastern districts of Sokoto itself. Argungu, the Kebbawa stronghold, was never occupied by the Fulani despite the fact that it lay between the twin capitals of Sokoto and Gwandu, being fifty miles from the former and less than thirty miles from the latter. The outlying dominions of both empires, however, still recognized the spiritual leadership of the descendents of Shehu Usumanu and a degree of temporal suzerainty pertaining to Sokoto and Gwandu.

The walled town of Gwandu remained the capital of the amīrate, until in 1860, the *amīr* Aliu, the fourth of Abdullahi's sons to succeed to the throne, transferred his headquarters to Ambursa in order to protect the towns along the south bank of the Gulbi against the attacks of the Kebbawa of Argungu. The other princes of the royal house continued to reside in Gwandu.

In 1864 Aliu died and was succeeded by his brother Abdulkadiri, the last of Abdullahi's sons to reign over Gwandu. By this time the power of the Kebbawa had so increased that Gwandu was obliged to seek an end to the constant hostilities and Sarkin Musulmi Ahmadu Rufai, in 1866, negotiated a peace treaty, known as the Lafiyar Toga, between Abdulkadiri and Sarkin Kebbi Toga. The principal terms of the treaty were (*a*) that Argungu should be recognized as an independent state, (*b*) that all towns then held by Argungu should be retained by Argungu, and (*c*) that all slaves hitherto captured in battle should remain the property of their captors.

The peace obtained by the Lafiyar Toga lasted for eight years, when hostilities were resumed which were to continue until Argungu was occupied by British troops in 1902.

In 1876 Maliki, son of Mohamman and grandson of Abdullahi, acceded to the throne and reigned for twelve years, during which he was visited by Mr. Joseph Thomson on behalf of the Royal Niger Company, and was presented with cloth to the value of forty million cowries. The Company's present to the Sarkin Musulmi was cloth to the value of sixty million cowries. After the death of Maliki in 1888, Umaru Bakatara, son of Mallam Halilu (1833-58) and grandson of Abdullahi, came to the throne and was visited by Sir G. Goldie and Mr. Wallace (afterwards Sir W. Wallace) who brought more gifts from the Royal Niger Company. In 1898 Bayero, son of Aliu (1860-64) and also a grandson of Abdullahi, came to the throne. He offered no resistance to the British occupation and died, two months later, in 1903.

To-day, Sokoto Province of the Northern Region of Nigeria is divided into three administrative divisions, Sokoto, Gwandu and Argungu. The headquarters of Gwandu Division is Birnin Kebbi (pop. 10,000) and the Division comprises the emirates of Gwandu itself (area 6,207 sq. miles, pop. 350,000) and Yauri (area 1,306 sq. miles, pop. 57,000). The present Emir of Gwandu, al-Ḥād̲j̲d̲j̲ī Haruna, is President of the House of Chiefs of the Northern Region.

Bibliography: E. J. Arnett, *The rise of the Sokoto Fulani, being a paraphrase and in some parts a translation of the Infaku 'l-Maisuri of Sultan Mohammed Bello*, Kano 1922; Muhammadu Bello, *al-Infāḳ al-maysūr*, ed. C. E. J. Whitting, etc., London 1951; E. J. Arnett, *Gazetteer of Sokoto province*, London 1920; O. Temple, *Notes on the tribes, provinces, emirates, and states of the Northern Province of Nigeria, compiled from official reports by O. Temple*, ed. C. L. Temple, Capetown 1919; S. J. Hogben, *The Muhammadan emirates of Nigeria*, London 1930; Sir B. E. Sharwood Smith, *Sokoto Survey, 1948*, Zaria 1948; E. W. Bovill, *The Golden Trade of the Moors*, London 1958; Adamu Abdullahi al-Iluri, *al-Islām fī Nīd̲j̲iryā wa-ʿUt̲h̲mān b. Fūdī*, Cairo 1370.

(W. E. N. Kensdale)

GYPSIES [see čingāne, lūrī, nūrī, zuṭṭ].

GYPSUM [see d̲j̲iṣṣ].